HOLLAND PARK SCHOOL

A place of scholarship; determinedly academic with outstanding A level and GCSE results.

A place of ambition, endeavour, drive and creativity, with outstanding success in placing students in top flight universities.

A place of self-effacing confidence.

A place to find oneself and hear the still small voice.

A place where the potency of academic prowess embraces the human beating heart.

A place which believes that lives and futures can be altered and that chance can be marginalised.

An Ofsted outstanding and DfE designated teaching school.

HEAD: Colin Hall | ACADEMY HEAD: David Chappell

www.hollandparkschool.co.uk
admissions@hollandparkschool.co.uk

AIRLIE GARDENS, LONDON W8 7AF

22nd EDITION

THE GOOD SCHOOLS GUIDE

www.goodschoolsguide.co.uk

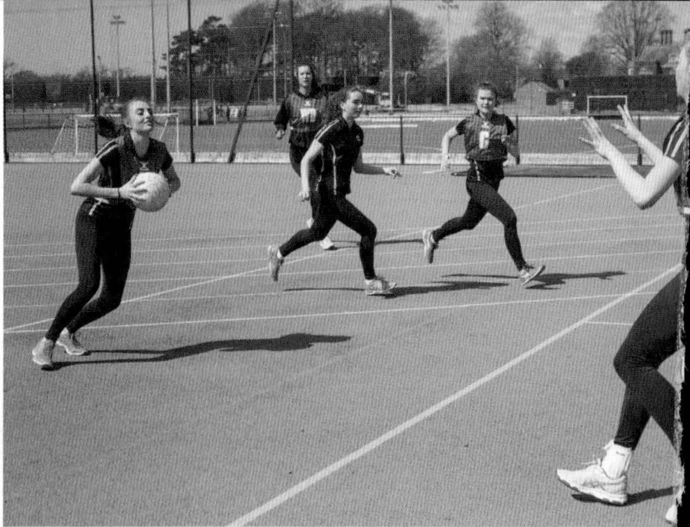

22nd Edition published 2019 by Lucas Publishing Ltd
4/4A Bloomsbury Square, London WC1A 2RP

ISBN 978-1-909963-19-1

A CIP catalogue record for this book is available from the British Library

Printed by www.beamreachuk.co.uk

Design: David Preston

Typeset by Theresa Hare, Optima Information Design

Editorial review by Beth Noakes and team: Janita Clamp, Charlotte Obolensky, Melanie Sanderson, Elsa Booth, Emma Lee-Potter, Kathryn Berger, Amanda Perkins, Claire Kingston

Advertising sales by Charlotte Hollingshead and Jo Dodds, Publishing Matters

Project management: Katja Lips

Everything held together by: Shari Lord

Writers
Ali Hutchinson
Alison Cooper
Amanda Lynch
Anne Hadley
Anne Prendergast
Ashley Cavers
Bernadette Henniker
Beth Noakes
Carolyn Murphy
Carolyn Thomas
Catriona Prest
Charles Cowling
Charlotte Obolensky
Charlotte Phillips
Charlotte Simpson
Clare Bore
Claire Kingston
David Hargreaves
Debbie Read
Denise Roberts
Elizabeth Coatman
Elizabeth Moody-Stuart
Elsa Booth
Emma Jones
Emma Lee-Potter
Emma Vickers
Faye Monserrat
Fenella Douglas-Miller
Godfrey Bishop
Grace Moody-Stuart
Guy Canning
Jackie Lixenberg
Jane Devoy
Janet Breeze
Janette Wallis
Janita Clamp
Jill Kastner
Judith French
Juliet Austin
Kalantha Brewis
Karen Fitzpatrick
Kate Hilpern
Kate Symington
Linda Tanner
Lisa Freedman
Lucy Heywood
Mary-Ann Smillie
Mary Bremner
Mary Langford
Mary Pegler
Melanie Bloxham
Melanie Sanderson
Nicky Adams
Patrea More Nisbett
Paul Nesbit
Phoebe Bentinck
Ralph Lucas
Reena Shaughnessy
Richard Field
Rosemary Taylor
Sandra Hutchinson
Sarah Evans
Sharon Cowling
Sophie Irwin
Stewart Binns
Susan Bailes
Susan Hamlyn
Suzanne Everest
William Bancroft
Zoe Bing

Contents

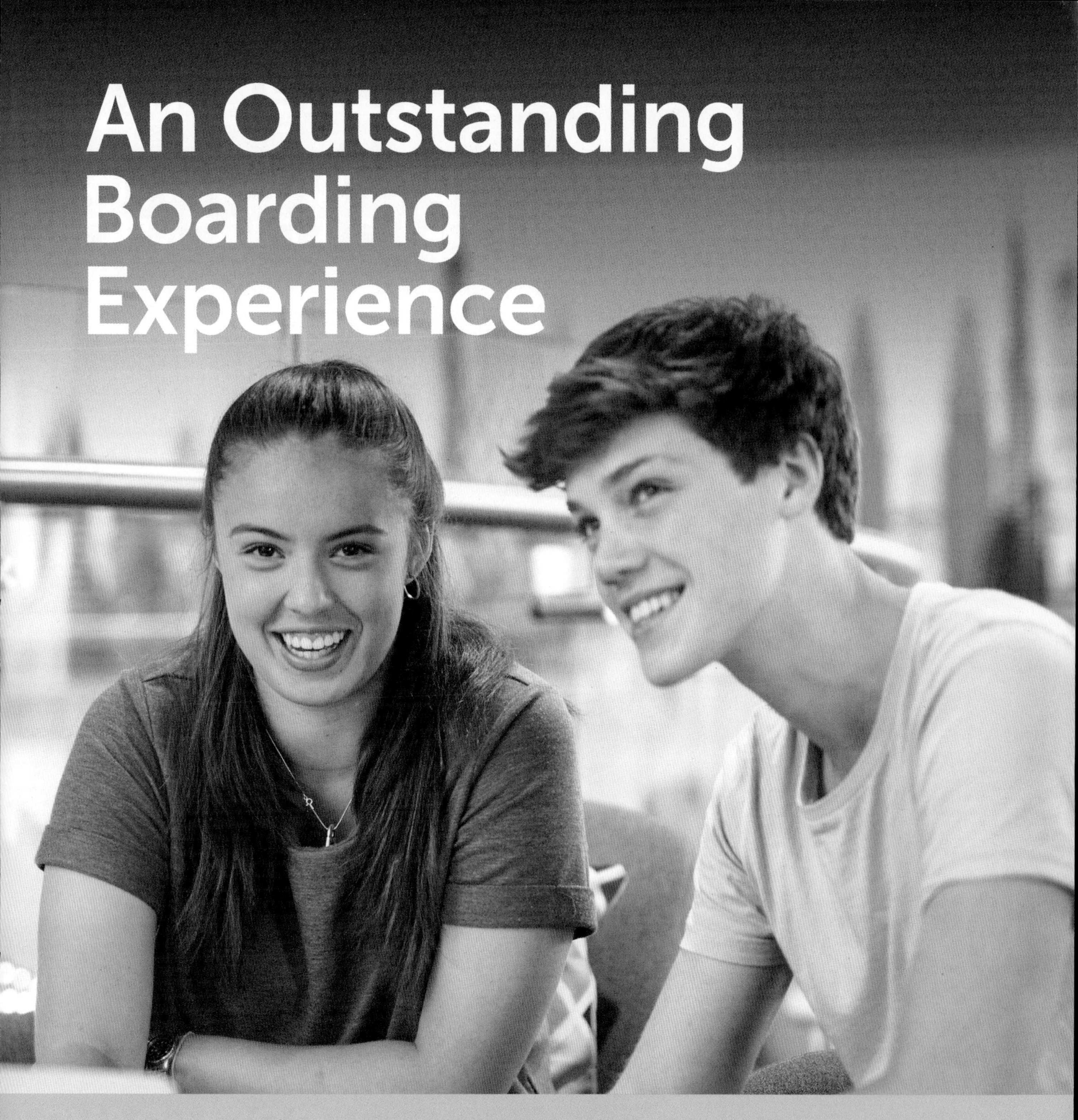
An Outstanding
Boarding
Experience

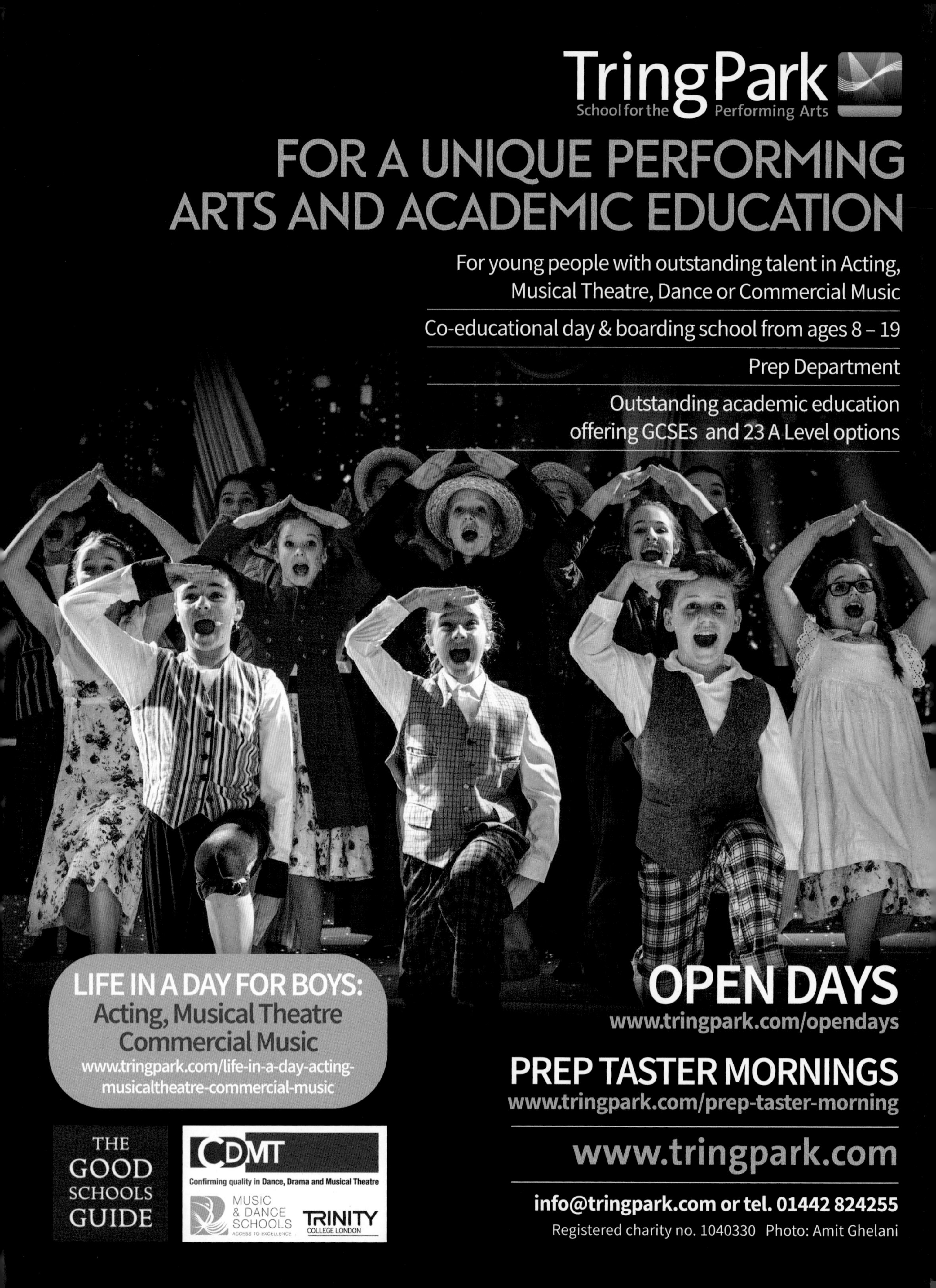

Key to symbols

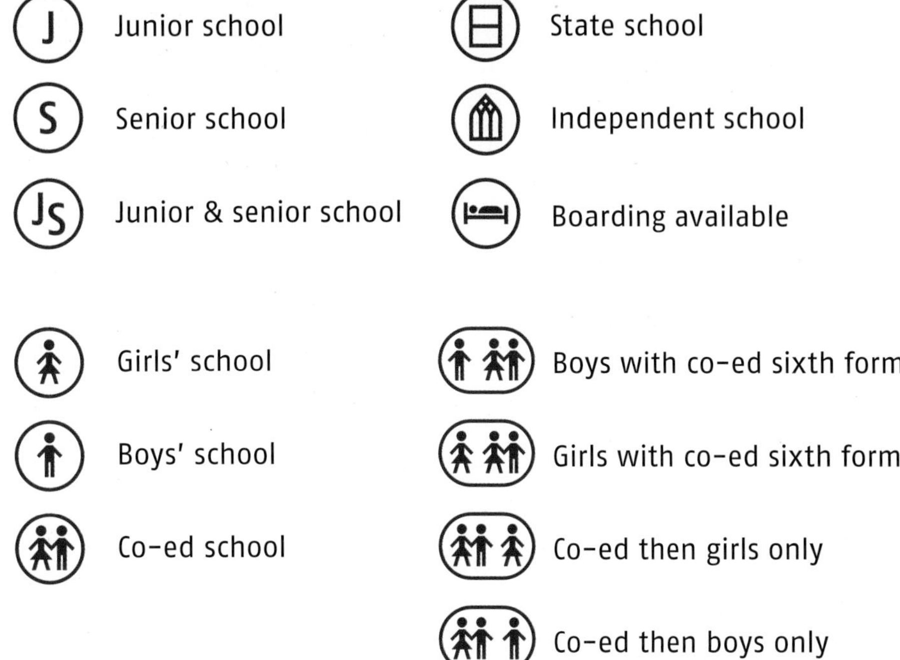

Map pin (reference number indicates school's position on the map at the front of the section)

Map of The Good Schools Guide regions

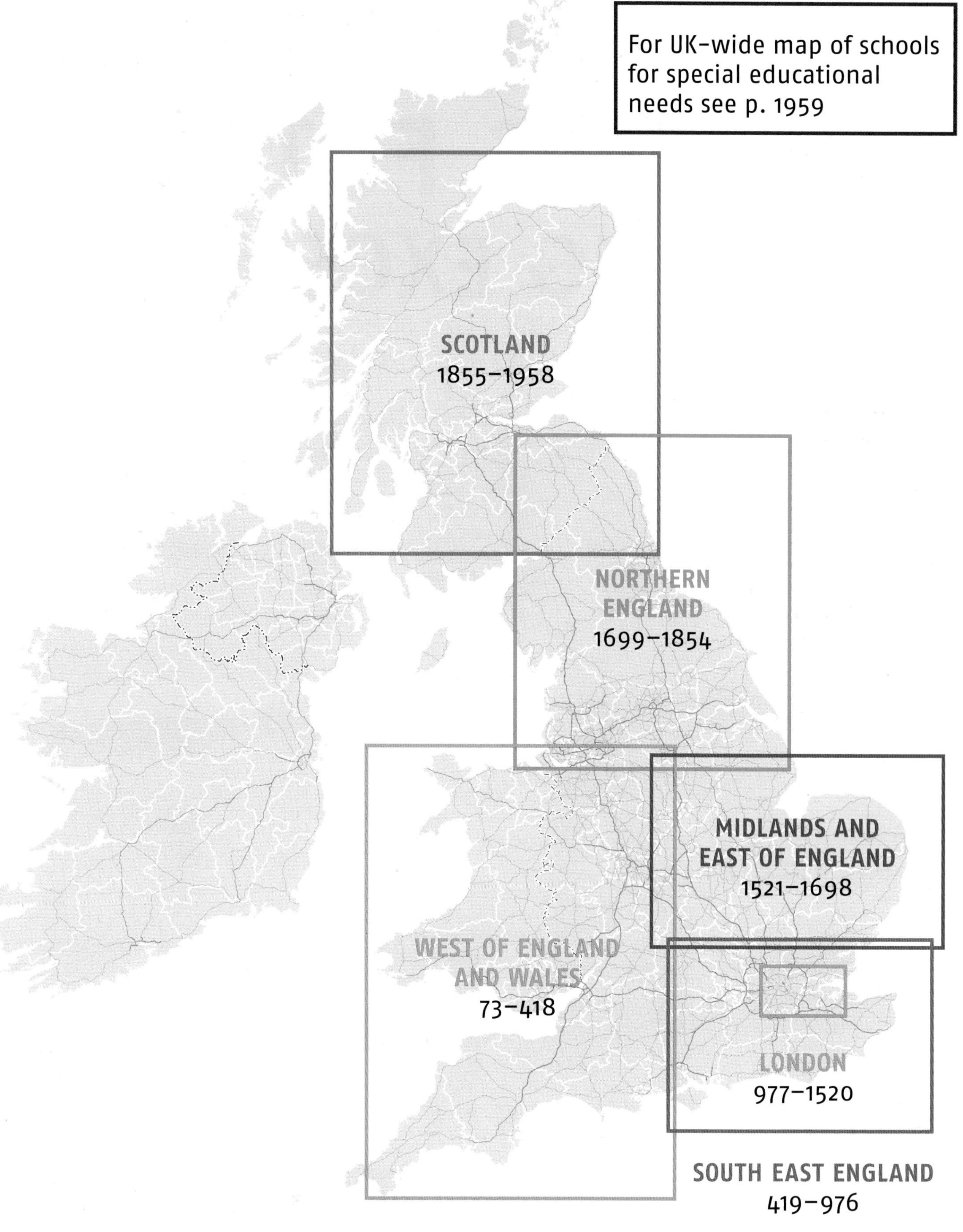

Introduction

Welcome to the 22nd edition of The Good Schools Guide. The world has changed enormously since the Guide was founded in 1986, but our uncompromising commitment to editorial integrity has never wavered. We remain as outspoken and independent-minded as ever.

In today's climate of intense educational competition and ever more glossy marketing we are proud that our reviews are trusted and valued by parents (and that they make quite a few schools cross). Now, as always, schools have no influence over what we write: they cannot pay to be included in the Guide and are not charged for reviews.

We are often asked how schools are selected for The Good Schools Guide. We choose which schools to review on the basis of, among other things, parental feedback and our writers' in-depth knowledge of the education scene where they live. This is how we get to cover lesser known local gems as well as world famous names. If you know a good school that we haven't visited yet, please get in touch.

We have a team of writers who spend happy hours talking to heads, pupils, staff and, most importantly, parents, in their local areas. They keep us up-to-date with school news and views from across Britain. We visit all the schools ourselves – most give us a warm welcome but very occasionally we have to resort to undercover tactics such as attending open days.

This is a good schools guide, but we know a school that is good for one child may be entirely unsuitable for another. It's the reason we make every effort to get under the skin of a school, to reveal its true character and to put across what kind of child would (or wouldn't) thrive there. We hope that in addition to shedding fresh light on well-known schools our reviews will introduce parents to wonderful schools they may never have considered.

GSG charter

In recent years we have helped to defray our costs by selling advertising space and licensing schools to reprint their own reviews for a fee. We make these offers only to schools that are already included in the Guide; whether or not they choose to advertise or take a licence has no bearing on their inclusion, nor on the content of their review.

The Good Schools Guide Education Consultancy is a fee-paying, personal consultancy service for parents.

We take our independence very seriously and the separation of commercial and editorial policy is absolute. If you have any questions or concerns please contact editor@goodschoolsguide.co.uk.

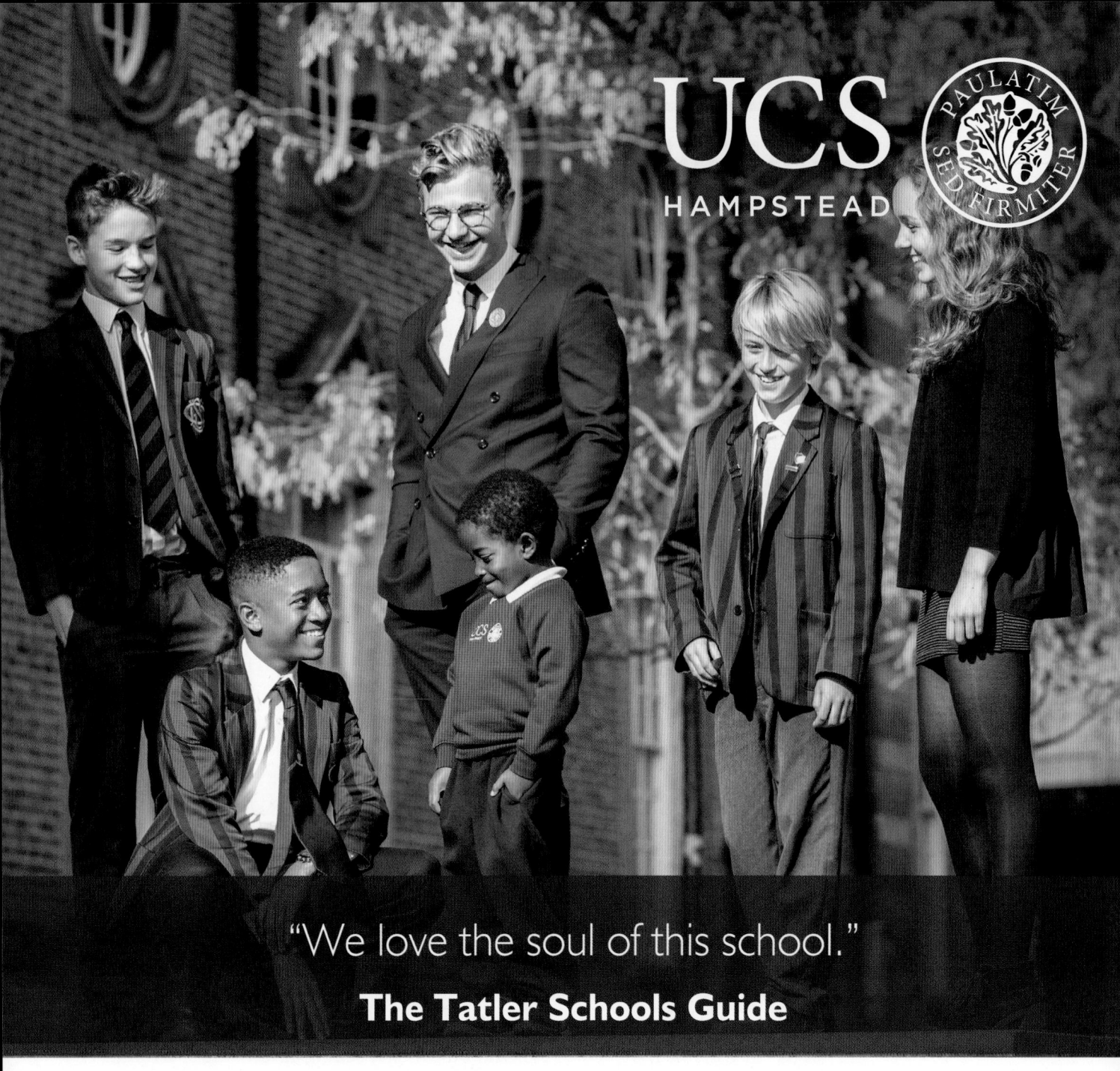

State and private schools

The vast majority of children in the UK attend their local state primary and secondary schools. Around seven per cent of children are educated privately, with some families mixing and matching state and private schools at different ages.

The state system

Primary schools

Primary schools start at 3 (if they have a nursery class) or 4 and most run through to 11, though there are some infants' schools (3-7) and junior schools (7-11), often but not always linked with automatic entry from one to the other. Increasing numbers of senior schools are opening linked primary schools, and will eventually become all-through schools.

The cut-off date by age is 31 August in both state and private schools in England (though some private schools may be more flexible). This means that if your child's birthday is on 31 August they will start in the reception class when just 4, whilst a child with a 1 September birthday will actually be just 5 when they start.

Only around seven per cent of children in the UK are educated at private schools

Virtually all British state primary schools are co-ed and non-selective academically, though faith schools mostly select by church attendance.

State primary schools may not have the specialist teachers, small class sizes or facilities enjoyed by private prep schools but the quality of teaching shouldn't be inferior. If you're lucky enough to live close to a good primary school and have a good state comprehensive down the road then your children's education is sorted. However, state primaries don't prepare children for 11+ entrance exams, so if you are aiming at a selective secondary school you will probably have to rope in a tutor in year 5 or so (see Tutors and Tutoring, page 51).

Secondary schools

There is a much greater variety of state secondary schools: single sex and co-ed, selective and non-selective, plus those that select a proportion of students on the basis of, for instance, academic, music or dance prowess.

The vast majority of secondary schools are non-selective. A few academically selective grammar schools remain in areas such as Buckinghamshire, Kent and Lincolnshire. The BRIT school in south London for 14-19 year olds is the only state performing arts school in the country with entry by audition. Some university technical colleges (UTCs) and studio schools, for children with a vocational bent, go from 14-18. Nearly all other secondary schools are for 11-16 or 11-18 year olds.

Some students move on after GCSEs to a sixth form colleges for 16-18 year olds. These tend to offer a wide range of subjects and to have an atmosphere more akin to a college than a school.

Academies and free schools

Increasing numbers of state schools – particularly secondary schools – are becoming academies. These are state funded but often run by multi-academy chains.

Free schools were originally intended to be set up by groups of parents and some of the early ones were, though many were set up by religious groups, and now most have academy chain backers. UTCs and studio schools are both types of free school.

Both academies and free schools are outside local authority control, can decide on their own admissions criteria (though they should abide by the national code), do not have to teach the national curriculum and may employ unqualified teachers.

Private schools

What's in a name?

Private school; independent school; public school. These three seemingly contradictory terms mean essentially the same thing: school fees.

Private schools charge for the education they provide. They do not have to follow the national curriculum, but senior pupils nearly all take GCSEs, plus A levels, Pre-Us or IB exams, so will follow roughly the same syllabi as those at state schools.

Pre-prep and prep schools

Pre-prep schools take children from 3 or 4 to 7 years, and are often linked to a prep school (7-11 or 13 years). They may go through from 3-13 without a break, and may be called junior schools. Preps/junior schools are likely to have small classes, specialist teachers and a relatively biddable intake. Don't assume the teaching will be better than at a state school – both sectors have great teachers (as well as a few individuals who would be better off in a different profession).

As the name suggests, prep schools prepare your child for entrance exams to secondary schools, and advise on which are likely to be most suitable. A prep school is judged at least partly by its leavers' destinations, so it will do its best to ensure your child moves on to a decent secondary school, even if the head has to dampen down your expectations.

Senior schools

Independent senior schools range from the ferociously selective to those that provide a gentle haven from hothousing or social integration – with admissions policies to match. A glance at the league tables will give a clue as to the degree of selection they operate.

Historically, girls' independent secondaries have started at 11 and boys' at 13, but increasing numbers – especially boys only schools that have turned co-ed – are switching their main intake to 11, with shrinking numbers of 13+ places. Thirteen plus schools with linked junior schools will often offer 11+ places in their junior schools with guaranteed transfer to the senior school, mostly aimed at state school pupils and those whose prep school finishes at 11.

Independent senior schools range from the ferociously selective to those that provide a gentle haven

Some independent schools go all the way through from 3 or 4 to 18, which can provide welcome continuity and freedom from 11+ or 13+ selection tests. However, few guarantee that a child who is struggling academically will be able to stay on with their peers, and teenagers may well decide at 16 (particularly if they have been in the same single-sex school since 4) that the grass looks greener elsewhere.

Independent sixth form colleges

Independent sixth form colleges, sometimes called crammers, were originally set up to prepare students for university entrance, particularly Oxbridge. They still specialise in this field, generally offering a variety of routes that include full two year A levels and shorter courses for those who need to improve on past grades. Classes are small, the focus is on exam practice and extracurricular options are limited.

Choosing a school

Put simply, a good school is a school that is right for your child; a place where they will be happy and enthused about learning. Unfortunately for prospective parents, battling through the whirlwind of information, hype and conflicting opinions that swirls around any school makes choice far from simple. Here are some factors to consider.

Results

Schools tend to be judged by their results – for a state primary, that will be key stage 2 Sats, the maths and English tests children take in year 6. Plus the Ofsted grade – with an Outstanding rating the Holy Grail. These two are often interlinked, with Ofsted caring more about data progression in maths and literacy than whether it is a happy school with an enriching curriculum. Or, for that matter, whether it is doing a fantastic job in difficult circumstances.

For a private prep school, the 'results' are the secondary school destinations, and these, of course, depend on how selective the entry is at 3+, 4+ or 7+. But just because a prep has good links with a top public school and sends a large proportion of pupils there it doesn't necessarily follow that your child will be amongst them – or that it would be an appropriate destination. A middle-of-the-road child is liable to lose confidence rapidly if they find themselves bumping along in the bottom sets of a highly academic school. If your child is showing signs of finding learning difficult, do talk to the SENCo about how and whether the school can help.

Unless you are prepared to be a long-term chauffeur, ensure that the school is easily accessible

At secondary level, there is a plethora of data to ponder, including GCSE and A level/IB/Pre-U results and university destinations. Again, these will depend to a large extent on the level of 11+ or 13+ selection – or, in a state comprehensive school, to the affluence of the intake. And again, other children's results won't tell you how well your child will do at a particular school.

Logistics

If you have boys and girls, how important is it that they all go to the same school(s)? Co-ed schools, and particular those with a sibling policy, will make life and logistics easier. State primary schools, of course, are more-or-less all co-ed and give siblings priority. The more competitive preps may look askance at a less academic younger sibling. All-through schools may offer a seamless transition from 4-18, but bear in mind that most will renegotiate at some stage if your child is really struggling to keep up.

Unless you are prepared to be a long-term chauffeur, ensure that the school is easily accessible – whether by walking, cycling, public transport or school bus. It will be much less stressful for all concerned, and it makes for a much easier and happier life if friends are nearby.

If you are choosing a boarding school, bear in mind that there will be school concerts and matches, parents' evenings and quiz nights. Experienced boarding parents advise that 90 minutes is probably the maximum realistic travelling time from home.

Environment

If your child is a gentle soul who needs lots of encouragement, will they flourish in an overtly competitive environment – particularly if they are amongst the less able cohort in a highly selective school? Alternatively, a child who likes to be top may get frustrated in a laid-back school that refrains from rankings or competition.

If you are a family with bohemian leanings, you may not feel at home with a boater-and-blazer type of school where everyone leaps to their feet when the head appears. Similarly, those with traditional leanings may find a no-uniform, first-names only environment too unstructured.

However good the results, your child is unlikely to thrive in a school where a blind eye is turned to bullying and they have no-one to turn to. All schools have pastoral care policies, but how confident are you that these are put into practice?

Enrichment

A town school is unlikely to have green acres of playing fields on the doorstep, but does the school make the best of what is available, perhaps going off to a nearby park or sports centre for regular games or playtimes? Are children encouraged to find their voice, to sing and play instruments, to act and dance? Is their artwork proudly displayed?

There may be plenty of extracurricular activities listed in the prospectus or on the website, but do they actually happen? If Japanese or polo or orienteering are important to your child, check that the relevant staff member hasn't just gone off on sabbatical to New Zealand. If your child loves sport but is athletically-challenged, are there teams for all? Are the grade 1 recorder players given a chance of the spotlight, or just the music scholars?

Staff

The head may not be a brilliant public speaker, but you should feel they are steering the ship in the right direction. Do the children shrink away as they pass, or run up to share news? When you have a problem – and there are bound to be some – do you feel you could approach the head without awkwardness and be confident of a fair hearing?

Do staff seem friendly – to you and to each other? Is there a good mix of ages?

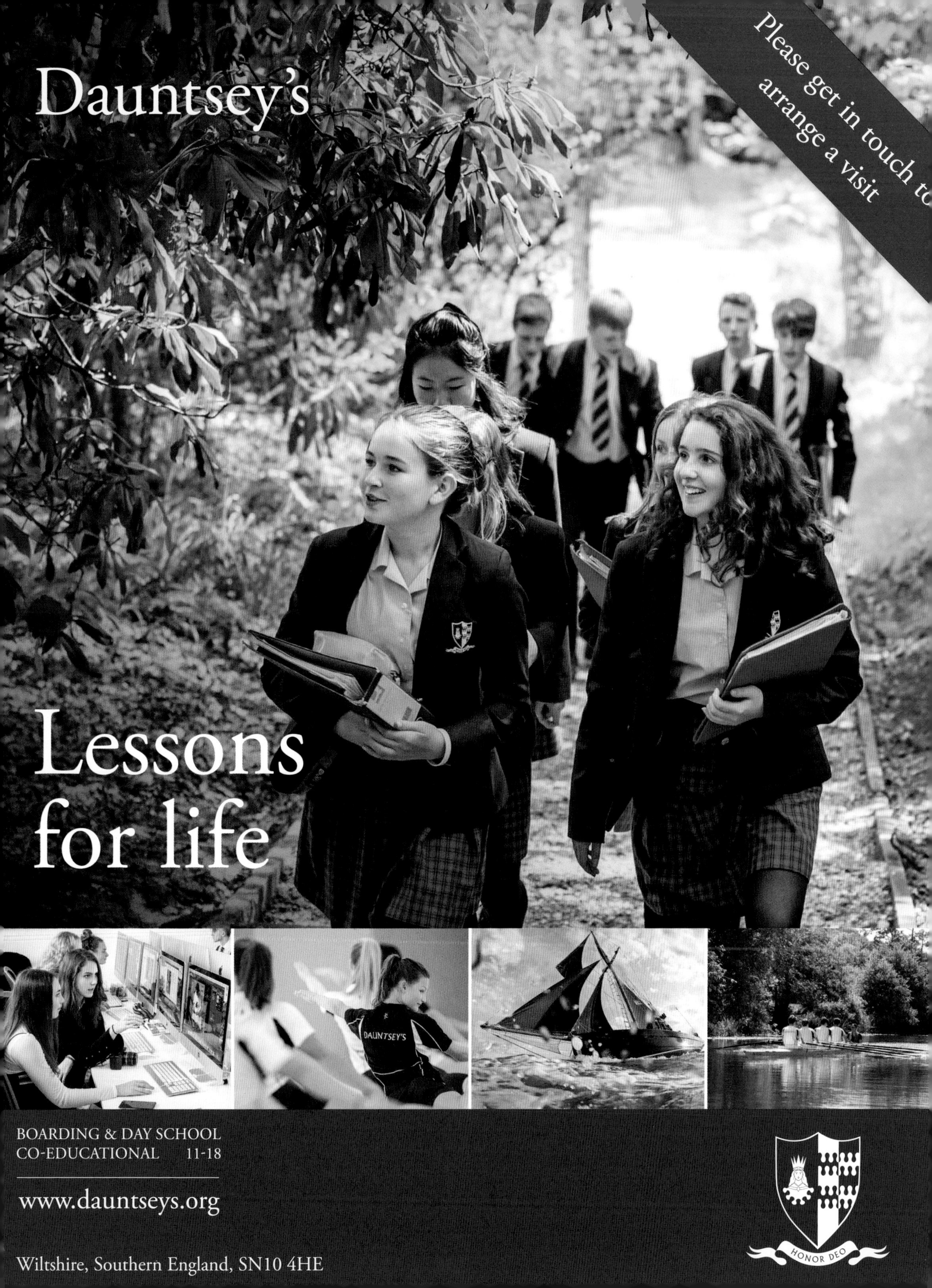
Dauntsey's
Please get in touch to arrange a visit
Lessons for life
DAUNTSEY'S
BOARDING & DAY SCHOOL
CO-EDUCATIONAL 11-18
www.dauntseys.org
Wiltshire, Southern England, SN10 4HE
HONOR DEO

A large proportion of very young staff can inject vigour and enthusiasm, but may signal that the school isn't willing to pay for experience and qualifications.

Feeling at home

It's vital to visit several schools, if only to compare and contrast. You'll know soon after walking in if the school is at least a possibility. Many independent schools have invested heavily in state-of-the-art facilities, but don't be swayed by glitz, unless this is particularly important to you. Does this feel like a place where you would happily drop off your child for years to come, confident not that it is the most fashionable local school, but the one where they are most likely to thrive?

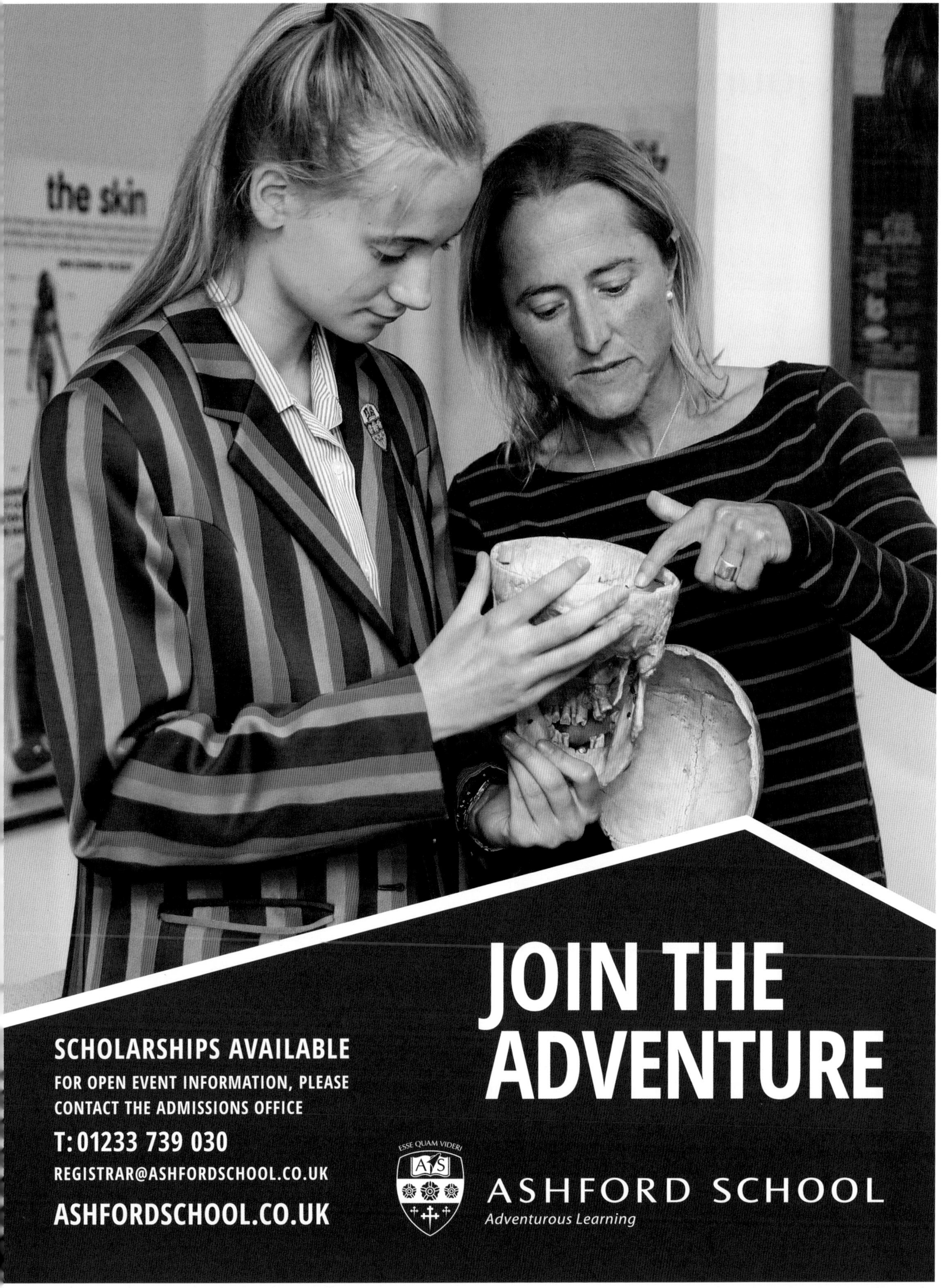
the skin
JOIN THE
ADVENTURE
SCHOLARSHIPS AVAILABLE
FOR OPEN EVENT INFORMATION, PLEASE
CONTACT THE ADMISSIONS OFFICE
T: 01233 739 030
REGISTRAR@ASHFORDSCHOOL.CO.UK
ASHFORDSCHOOL.CO.UK
ESSE QUAM VIDERI
AS
ASHFORD SCHOOL
Adventurous Learning

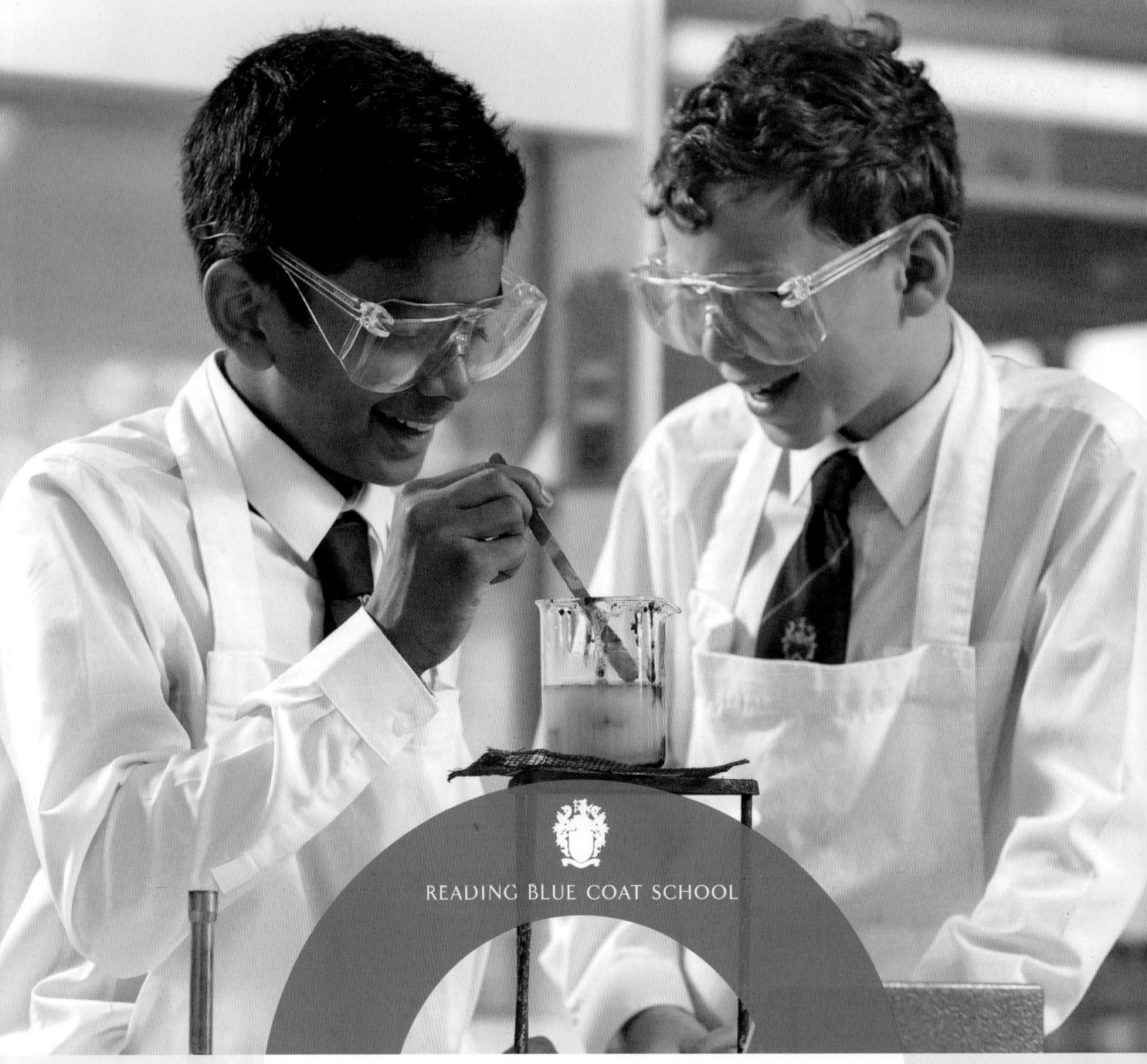

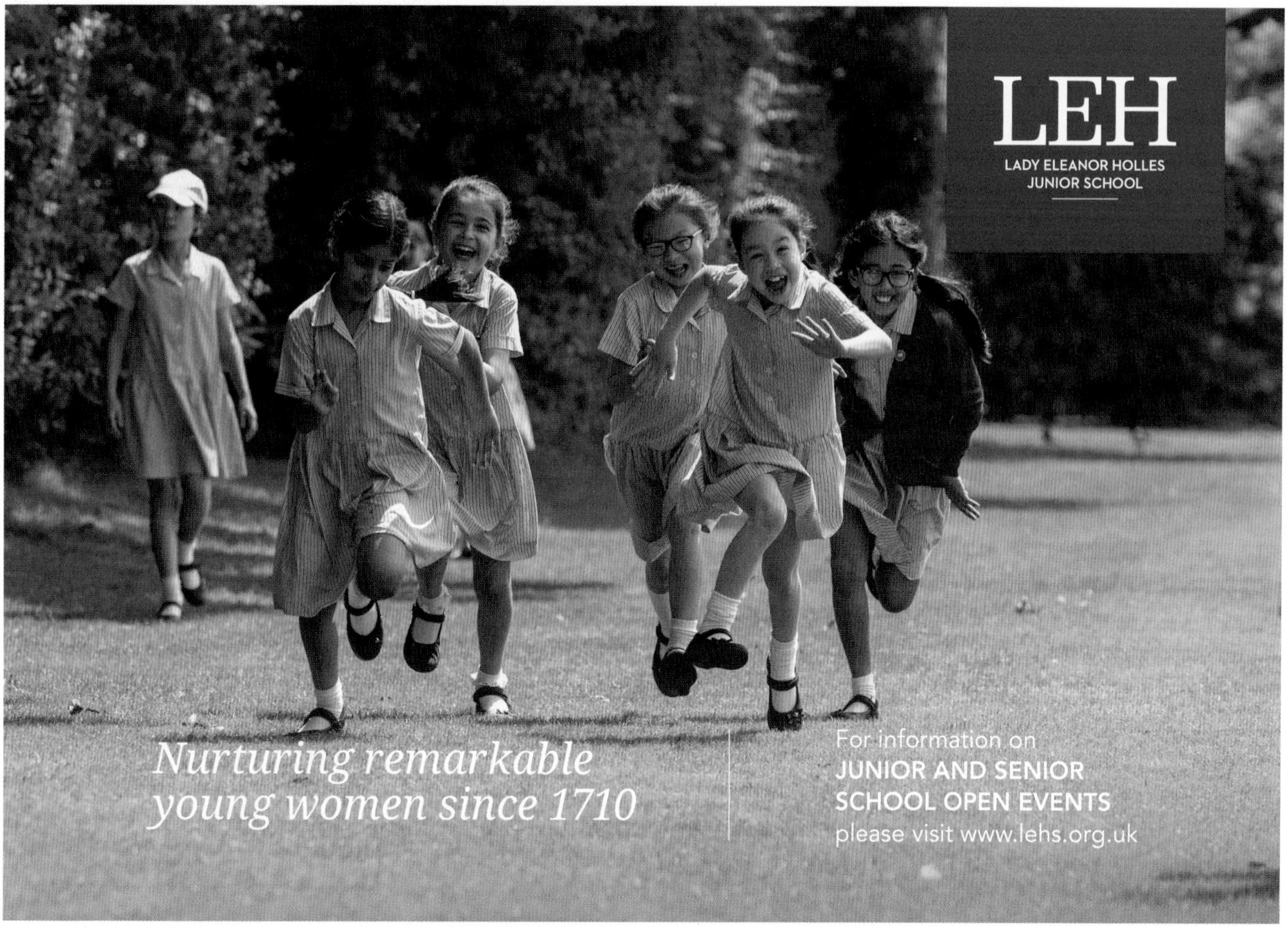

Applying to a state school

Choosing where you would like your child to take their first steps into school, or spend their teenage years, can be a nerve-wracking experience. For state schools, especially primary schools, where you live is likely to be a deciding factor.

Location, location

The primary schools you are considering are likely to be very local. The main admissions criteria for non-faith schools are generally siblings and then distance – which can be less than a few hundred metres for the popular ones.

Secondary schools are far more varied in their character and in their admissions criteria. These may also include academic selection and/or auditions for aptitude. You may be able to apply under more than one of these.

Timing

Applications are made through your local authority in the autumn of the year before your child starts school or moves on to secondary school. The cut-off date for secondary admissions is 31 October of year 6. For primary schools it is 15 January before the September start date.

If the primary school has a nursery class for 3 year olds you apply direct to the school when your child is 2; however, you will still need to reapply for a reception (4 year old) place via the local authority.

Academically selective grammar schools, and some that partially select by aptitude for eg music, now do their admissions tests/auditions in the summer term of year 5 or the September of year 6, so that they can give out initial results before the October closing date for applications. This will usually involve registering with the school during the year 5 summer term – so check dates carefully.

How do state schools offer places?

There are some general rules that most schools adhere to:

- Education, Health and Care Plan naming the school. These children come first in line and must be given a place.
- Looked after/previously looked after children. These generally come next.
- Siblings. These often, but not always, come third. Check carefully before you move miles away after your first-born has got a place.
- Exceptional medical or social need. This generally involves a letter from a doctor or social worker explaining why St Cake's is the only school that will cope with your child's needs. Very few children get a place by this route.

- Distance. Generally as the crow flies, but sometimes by the shortest walking route, Sometimes faith schools designate parishes, and other schools may designate particular areas as their catchment. Some secondaries have feeder primary schools. Grammar schools are increasingly limiting the distance applicants may travel to school. Your local authority should have information on how close you probably have to live to any individual school (except faith schools) to be in with a chance of a place.

Grammar schools

These are academically selective by entrance exam (usually some combination of maths, English and reasoning tests). Increasing numbers give preference to children who live relatively locally; some also prioritise students on pupil premium. You will be told if your child has reached the qualifying standard before the closing date for applications, but not if they will actually be offered a place.

Aptitude

Some schools select part of their intake by aptitude for eg music, dance, technology or languages.

Fair banding

An increasing number of non-selective schools use fair banding to divide applicants into ability bands, taking an equal number from each band.

Faith schools

These may demand that your child was baptised before they were 6 months old and that you have attended a specific church weekly for the past five years. They are no longer allowed to give points for eg brass polishing and flower arranging, such voluntary activities were felt to advantage middle class applicants.

Free schools and academies

These may set their own entrance criteria, though they should abide by the national admissions code. They, like most faith schools, also decide which applicants to accept (local authorities make that decision for community schools) and thus are vulnerable to accusations of cherry-picking easy-to-teach pupils.

Filling in the form

You can list between three and six choices of schools, depending on area, and it's vital to include at least one where you are more-or-less sure of getting a place – even if it isn't your first choice. If you don't, you may only be offered an undersubscribed school some distance away. For faith schools, you will probably have to fill in a supplementary application form and get it signed by your religious leader. If a new free school is opening in your area, you will quite likely in its first year be able to apply direct to the school in addition to your other choices.

NB Put your school choices in order of preference – if you qualify for places at more than one, you will only be offered the school highest on your list. The schools don't know where else you have applied, and don't know if you have put them first or last – only the local authority knows that.

Moving to the UK

As long as you have a right of abode in England, you can apply for a state school place here. However, you can't apply till you have an address in the country and are living here (except for Forces/diplomatic families and those applying to state boarding schools).

If you are applying for a school place not at normal admissions times – ie reception or year 7 – admissions will probably be handled by individual schools, though you will have to complete the in-year admissions form. Your local authority should be able to give you information on which schools have spaces, but it's worth contacting schools direct too.

Don't want the school you are offered?

You can appeal for a place at a school you prefer, but do it quickly. In the meantime, accept the school you have been offered (otherwise the local authority is under no obligation to find you a school at all). Ensure you are on the waiting list for any schools you would be happy with. And do visit the school you have been offered: you may find that contrary to local reputation, it is up and coming and will suit your child very well.

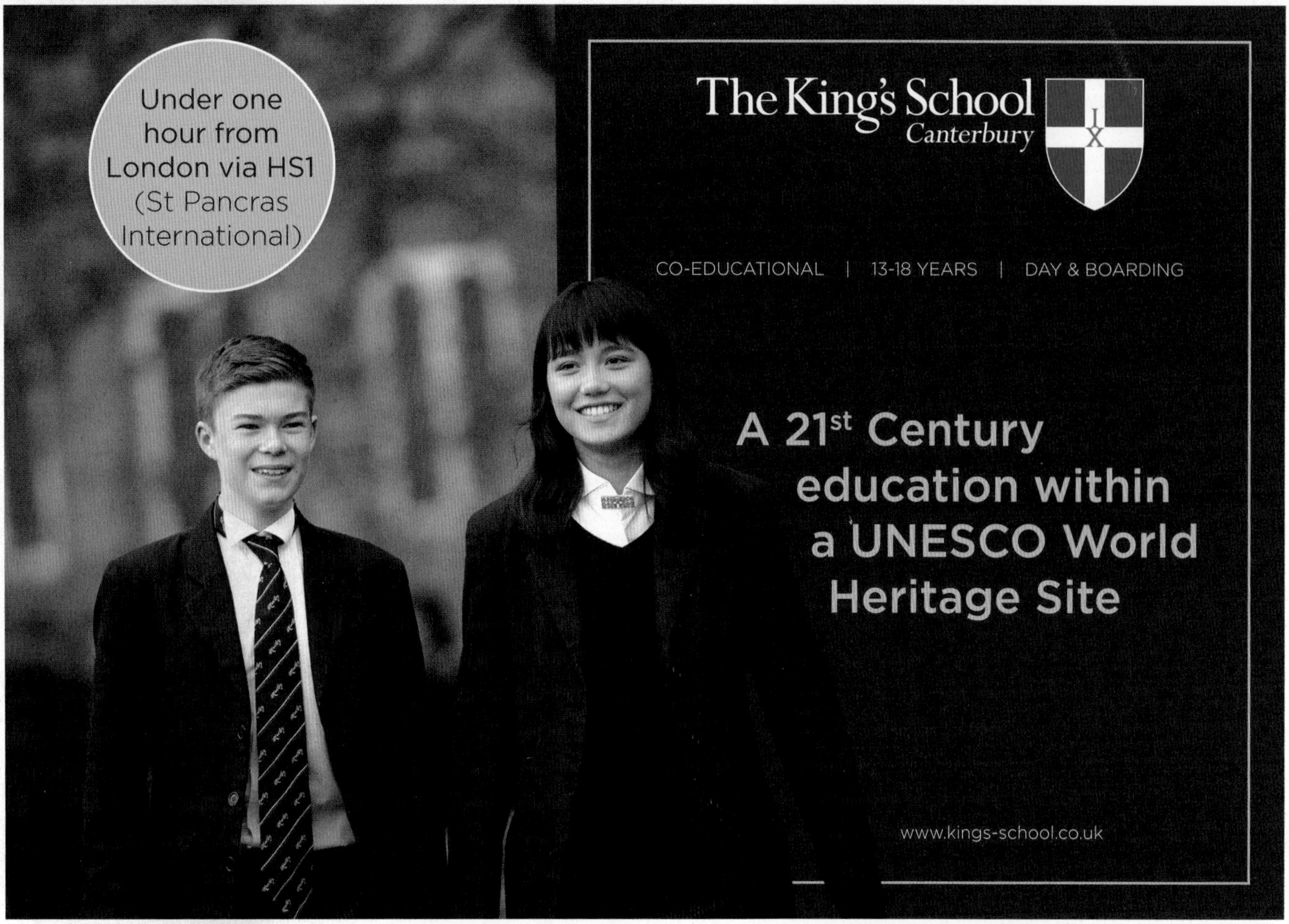

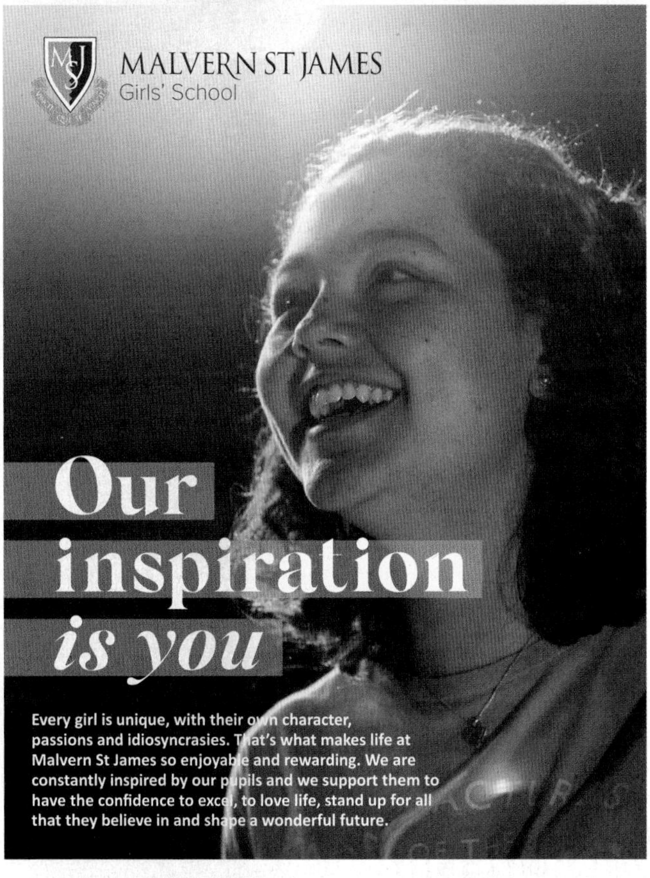

BE ANYTHING,
ACHIEVE EVERYTHING

GENEROUS SCHOLARSHIPS AND BURSARIES AVAILABLE

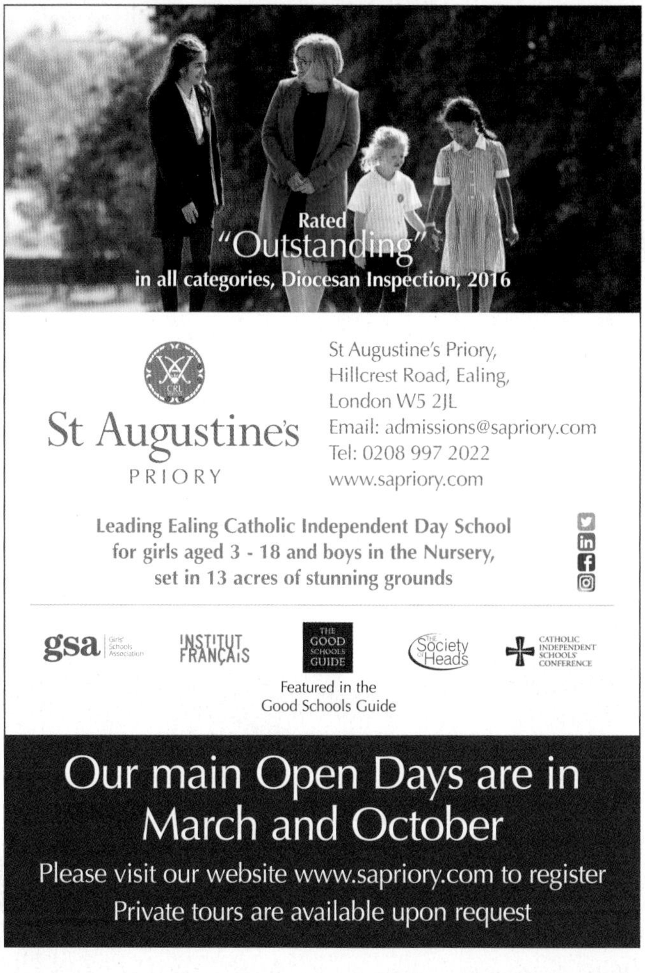

Lancing College
Senior School & Sixth Form
Be inspired
Be brilliant
Be you
OPEN MORNINGS IN MAY AND OCTOBER
FIND OUT MORE
LANCINGCOLLEGE.CO.UK
YOUR
INCREDIBLE
JOURNEY

Applying to a private school

If you think a school might be a good fit for your child, request a visit and make sure it includes time to see the head and watch the school at work. Each school will have its own entrance procedure but nearly all charge a non-refundable registration fee.

Preps and pre-preps

As their name suggests, the main aim of 'preparatory schools', or prep schools, is to prepare children for entry to fee-paying senior schools at 11 or 13. Traditionally, pre-preps take children from 3 or 4 and prepare them for moving on to preps at 7 or 8. There are fewer stand-alone pre-preps than there used to be as their main market, the boarding prep, has declined in numbers. Today, many pre-preps and preps are linked, with a more-or-less seamless transition between them and sometimes their senior school too. In London, with fierce competition for 7+ places at top prep schools, quite a few stand-alone pre-preps survive. Their raison d'être is preparing children for these competitive exams, which can mean the pressure starts in year 1 with regular practice papers.

Preps tend to stand or fall by their senior school destinations. Parents, whether they are aiming to get their 3 or 4 year old into the pre-prep of a chosen all-through school, or their 8 year old into a prep that sends many of its pupils to the top day or boarding schools, are generally looking ahead. Yet all-through selective schools rarely guarantee that children they take in at 3 or 4 or even 7 will have a seamless transfer upwards. If your child is felt to be struggling, you may well be advised to look elsewhere. Equally, a child who fails to gain a place at the pre-prep stage may well have developed sufficiently to sail in there or elsewhere later on. As ever, a school that helps your child to become a happy and confident learner is the best investment.

Fierce competition for places at top preps means London has quite a few stand-alone pre-preps

Try to get a balanced view of the school when you visit – chat to pupils, staff, other parents and don't allow the marketing manager to dominate your visit. Before (and after), browse the website, prospectus and marketing literature – they'll all be glossy with happy, smiley faces, but do you like the tone and the events they put centre stage? Same old faces, same old names or a good smattering of faces, across the ages? Some preps are very traditional – blazers and boaters are often a clue; others more relaxed – sweatshirts could be a signal. You can probably tell, even without visiting, whether or not your family ethos is likely to be a good fit.

Entry requirements at age 3 or 4 vary considerably from 'first-come, first-served' (this could in fact mean name down at birth, or depend on whether or not the head likes the look of you) to mini-assessment days complete with interview and observations to see just how well Harriet integrates with her peers and playmates. Few will expect children to read and write on entry but such is the pressure for places at favoured schools that, to the dismay of may heads, parents have been known to enlist the help of tutors for their 3-year-olds. In general the play and learning that goes on at home or nursery school should be adequate preparation. At age 7 or 8, nearly every prep school operates a formal assessment process.

Experienced heads can spot which children should be aiming for which senior schools fairly early on

Senior schools

If your child is already at a prep school then the process of selecting and applying to the 'right' senior school should mainly be taken care of – it's a large part of what you're paying them to do.

It used to be the case that parents rarely challenged a prep's advice about which senior school would best suit their son or daughter, but heads tell us that 'managing parental expectations' is now a significant part of their job. A prep school's reputation stands or falls on the destinations of its pupils at 11 and/or 13; prep school heads spend a large part of their time visiting senior schools and getting to know their pupil profiles. Experienced heads can spot which children should be aiming for which senior schools fairly early on and if this conflicts with parental ambitions then he or she will advise accordingly. No school will 'under sell' an able child, so if you disagree with the advice you have been given you should be able to have a frank discussion about the reasons behind it. The decision about which senior school to apply for should be at least as much about where a child would fit in and be happy as it is about academic ability.

State primary to independent senior

Plenty of children from state primary schools do move on to independent secondaries, often with scholarships or bursaries. It is not the state primary school's job to prepare children for independent school entrance exams, so most parents take on a tutor for a year or so to ensure their children are used to, say, writing a story in half an hour, and timing their answers. Neither can you expect a primary school head to advise on likely senior schools, so you will need to make your own judgement on which schools are likely to be suitable for your child.

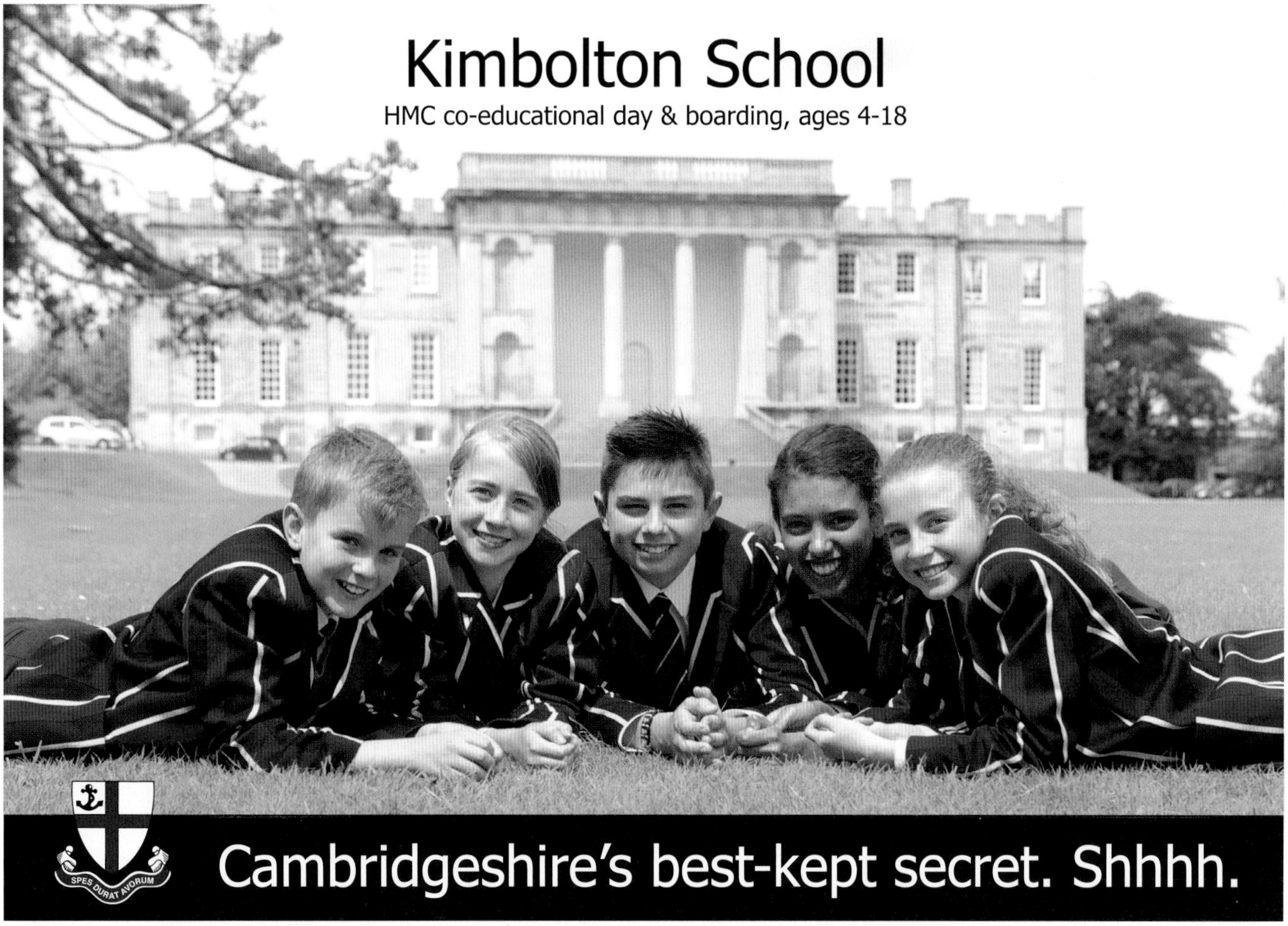
Kimbolton School
HMC co-educational day & boarding, ages 4-18
SPES DURAT AVORUM
Cambridgeshire's best-kept secret. Shhhh.

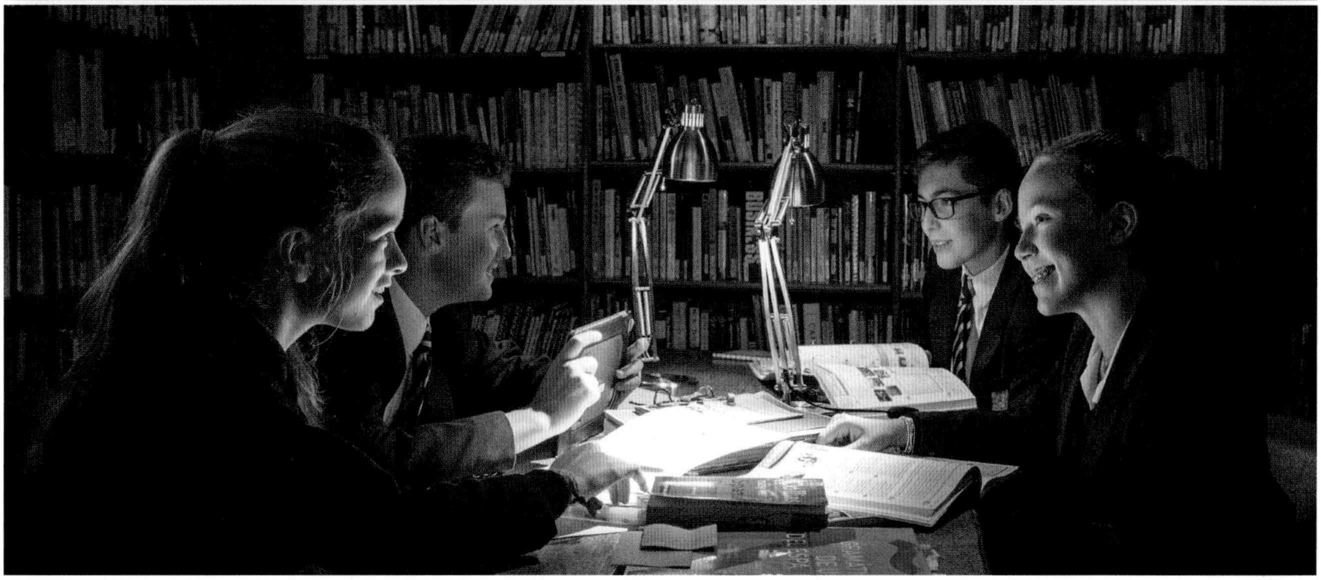

Applying from abroad

The first step is often an online UKiset test which measures academic English language skills. Most schools will also ask overseas applicants to sit their own entrance test and are generally happy to send tests abroad, though they may ask applicants to attend interviews in person.

Pre-tests

An increasing number of senior schools offer provisional places based on the results of 'pre-tests' taken in year 6 or 7 (age 10 or 11). Senior schools use these tests as a filter and to give an early indication of demand for places. Many prep school heads are concerned that pre-tests don't suit late developers (often boys) who may not come into their own academically this early.

Pre-tests are age-standardised and include multiple-choice tests in maths, English, verbal and non-verbal reasoning. If your son or daughter is offered a place after completing these tests, he or she will normally still be required to sit the common entrance examinations in year 8.

11+ and 13+ tests

The 11+ test is taken in year 6 and usually comprises papers in English, maths and sometimes reasoning. Some schools set their own papers, others are part of consortiums that set common exams and share results.

The 13+ common entrance is a test taken in year 8 for entry to many independent schools. Core subjects are English, maths and science and candidates may also sit papers in history, geography, modern foreign languages, ancient Greek and Latin. Tests are taken at the candidate's own school and are marked by the school to which they are applying.

Most independent girls' and co-ed day schools accept pupils from age 11. There are still some traditional boys' schools such as Westminster and St Paul's and boarding schools such as Eton and Harrow that start at 13+. Thirteen plus schools with linked junior schools will often offer 11+ places in their junior schools with guaranteed transfer to the senior school, mostly aimed at state school pupils and those whose prep school finishes at 11.

Interviews

While state schools are prohibited from interviewing any but potential sixth form (or boarding) students, the interview is an integral part of nearly every private school admissions process, and tends to send the applicant's parents, rather than the actual applicant, into a spin. Parents feel considerably more responsible for their child's social presentation than for his or her ability to do long division or conjugate French verbs. And, while a school may breezily describe the interview as 'just a chance to get to know the child better', this hardly quells fears about sending young Daniel or Daniella into the lion's den.

Oversubscribed selective schools will often only meet the child after a written exam (generally used as a first edit), and the interview itself will probably contain a significant component of maths, comprehension or reasoning. The aim here is to probe intellectual strengths and weaknesses in order to select from the central bulk of candidates or to pick scholarship material. Finding out a little about a child's character is only of secondary importance.

Even the most academic schools, however, are not necessarily just looking for those guaranteed to deliver a stream of A*s. Some use interviews as an opportunity to create as balanced a community as possible.

Personality, of course, will always be the most variable aspect of any interview and all interviewers have a personal bias. They may hate boastful children, or those who say their favourite leisure activity is computer games; they may prefer Arsenal fans to Tottenham supporters; but some schools do make a strenuous attempt to counteract the sense of one adult sitting in judgement on one child. One senior school sees candidates individually before sending them off to a lesson where they can be observed by another teacher as they work in a group.

The best interviewers can and do overcome the limitations both of the written examination and of the child. 'Children, even very shy ones, like to talk about themselves, their friends, their families and their pets. I get them to describe what they did on Sunday, or I turn my back and ask them to describe something in the room. Sometimes I even get a child to sing or dance. I am looking for sparkly eyes and interest. If a child just sits there like a pudding, you usually don't take them.' Some schools get over the 'what to talk about' dilemma by asking children to bring along a favourite object. If, however, the child pitches up with a copy of Proust or boasts a collection of Roman ceramics, parents shouldn't be surprised if the interviewer is somewhat sceptical.

'Children, even very shy ones, like to talk about their friends, families and pets'

Although most heads are honest in their report about a child – after all, their reputation depends on it – the interview can also benefit them. 'Occasionally, a prep school head knows perfectly well that a child is not suited to our school, but the parents just won't listen. Coming from us it doesn't sour the relationship with the school.'

Parents, stand back!

Concerned parents often do their best to control the outcome of the interview, but professional preparation is seen as a waste of time, both by those who interview and by teachers. 'I always tell parents if they're paying to coach 3-year-olds, they might as well burn £20 notes,' said a junior school head who has the daunting task of selecting 40 4-year-olds from 200 applicants in a two-tier interview. 'The only useful preparation is to talk to them, play with them and read them stories.'

The head of a west London pre-prep does her best to relax the 7-year-olds she sends to prep school interviews by providing them with as much factual information as she can beforehand. 'I try to prepare them for what they'll find. I usually describe the head — because I'm a smallish woman they might expect all heads to be like me — and I'll tell them what the school looks like. Beyond that I just say, "Look them in the eye, answer carefully and be honest." Children sell themselves.'

Some pre-preps and prep schools provide mock interviews, some will carefully guide children on what books or hobbies that might show to best advantage, but most interviewers say they always know when a child has been coached, and honesty – at least in theory – is the quality they're looking for. 'I tell children,' says one private tutor who prepares children for 11 plus, 'to say what's in their heart, not what their teacher told them to say.'

Parents, step forward

Although the school interview is nominally about the child, the school is also interviewing parents and it's they who may need a little preparation while their child can happily be him or herself. A balance between supportive, respectful (schools are ever keen to avoid the pushy parent from hell) and interesting (but nor do they like dull ones) is best.

THE
PORTSMOUTH
GRAMMAR
SCHOOL
EXPERIENCE
MORE

Applying to a boarding school from abroad

British boarding schools have never enjoyed a higher international standing; each year thousands of pupils from all over the world come to the UK for a taste of boarding life. The experience for all boarding pupils, including those from overseas is, much, much better than it was a generation ago.

Will it suit your family?

Pastoral care is now given as much prominence as academic standards. Newly refurbished accommodation is bordering on luxurious (but don't expect many en-suite bathrooms) and the transformation of school food is nothing short of miraculous, though fish and chips and custard – separately, of course – remain culinary fixtures.

But before completing the registration form and committing your sizeable deposit, it's worth double checking that you know exactly what you are buying and whether it will suit your family.

English language support

The vast majority of international pupils follow a mainstream curriculum and work towards standard 16 and 18 plus qualifications. For those whose English isn't yet quite good enough or whose previous education puts them behind others of the same age, extra support from teachers who specialise in EAL (English as an Additional Language) may be needed.

Some schools run separate classes in key subjects, structured to allow more time for the language component so that maths and science students, for example, have sufficient understanding to decode word-based problems. These classes may be charged as an extra cost, so check what's included in the fees.

A growing number of independent schools run international study centres aimed at preparing overseas pupils who are not yet fluent in English for mainstream schools. Alongside intensive English language tuition, many offer GCSEs or IGCSEs. If you are considering one, find out about their leavers' destinations. If most don't move into the mainstream school, where do they go, and how much help do they get? Others run a 'pre-IB' year for those coming into year 11, aiming to get them up to speed to join the school sixth form.

School food has undergone a miraculous transformation

Check how much interaction the study centre/pre-IB pupils have with their mainstream peers. Do they share sports, clubs, outings, accommodation? Who is around to socialise with during evenings and weekends?

Social life

While the academic side of boarding is undoubtedly important, the social dimension is just as vital. An isolated child is rarely a very successful one. Schools with substantial numbers of international pupils will invariably portray themselves as a glorious melting pot where nation speaks unto nation and pupils leave with their ideals intact, their horizons and tolerance vastly expanded and a lifetime of reunions all over the world to look forward to. In many cases, when a school selects a blend of nationalities, such as at UWC Atlantic College, this is exactly what happens. Good Schools Guide reviewers regularly hear of enduring friendships that span religious or cultural divides, or of lessons enriched by pupils on opposite sides of wars, sanctions or economic policy.

Many schools empty out seconds after the final whistle (or bell) sounds on Saturday mornings

It works less well when a school operates a monoculture policy. A large number of pupils from one nation in a single year group may help fend off homesickness but can also reduce the motivation for pupils to immerse themselves in their host country's language and way of life – an opportunity lost rather than gained. It's okay to ask admissions staff for numbers if you're at all concerned.

Similarly, a school where the number of overseas pupils is so small that they are swamped by the prevailing culture can also lead to a miserable experience – particularly if they are the only full boarders in the place at weekends while everyone else goes home. Immersion is one thing, invisibility quite another – so it's also essential to find out just how many pupils of your child's age are actually around over the weekend. Many schools start off with a packed house for Saturday morning lessons or matches but empty out seconds after the final whistle (or bell) sounds.

Exporting education – big names abroad

Finally, for those happy to ditch some of the trimmings, it's increasingly possible to get the ethos, results and teaching quality of a traditional British education without travelling anywhere near the UK. Over the past few years some of the most famous names in education have opened offshoots overseas. You can get a Harrow education in Bangkok, Beijing or Hong Kong, become a Haileybury pupil in Kazakhstan and or sign up for Cranleigh or Brighton College in Abu Dhabi. Ethos and teaching standards are recognisably the same even if the facilities (sport is often air-conditioned and inside, for example) aren't.

Be careful when employing agents

There are many agents, 'consultants' or educational firms who will offer to find your child a place in a UK school. If their service is free of charge to you, the agent may well be getting a commission from schools; this means that you will be guided to apply only to those schools the agent represents, whether or not they are right for your child. Similarly, firms or individuals charging a fee for securing your child a 'guaranteed' school place should also sound alarm bells. Reputable schools do not give agents (or anyone else) 'guaranteed' places. Speak to the schools yourself.

Worth knowing...

- Big names are attractive but famous isn't always best. A school may be trading on past glories rather than future brilliance, so check whether you're being sold the up to date version.
- Look past fabulous exam results. Top schools do well because they select top pupils. What it proves is that parents of the brightest children send them here. It doesn't necessarily tell you how well it teaches them.
- Do visit any school you are interested in, and bring your child if possible. No prospectus, however glossy, beats experiencing a school in the flesh.
- Check how EAL provision (if required) is organised. Ideally, ask to sit in on some lessons to give you an idea of the standards/commitment and enthusiasm you'll be getting – and try to talk to similar pupils.
- Consider applying for scholarships if your child is outstanding (academic, musical and sporting excellence are the norms) and ensure that your idea of excellence is the same as the school's but...
- Don't be won over by worthless scholarships, sometimes offered as an incentive by schools to seal the deal.
- The key entry points into UK schools are at age 11, 13 or 16. Many schools will look at potential pupils outside these times, but bear in mind that it's often on a one in, one out basis – places become available only if another family leaves.
- Check how often a child won't be boarding. Half terms, bank holidays and occasional weekend exeats all add up to a considerable chunk of time when pupils aren't in school and will need somewhere else to stay. A guardian – or local friends or relatives – is essential but you may also want to ensure family visits coincide with these dates.

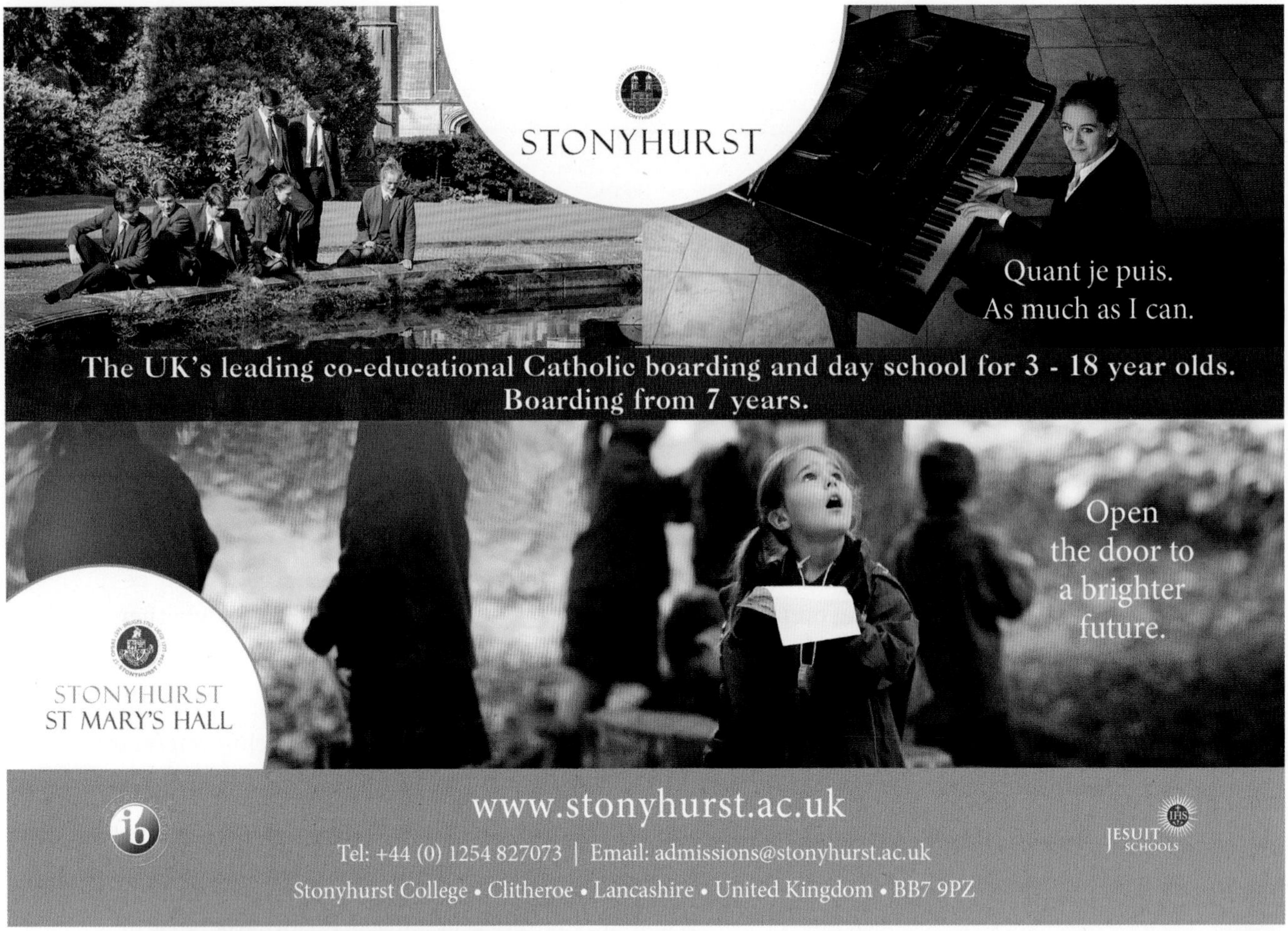
STONYHURST
Quant je puis.
As much as I can.
The UK's leading co-educational Catholic boarding and day school for 3 - 18 year olds.
Boarding from 7 years.
Open
the door to
a brighter
future.
STONYHURST
ST MARY'S HALL
www.stonyhurst.ac.uk
Tel: +44 (0) 1254 827073 | Email: admissions@stonyhurst.ac.uk
Stonyhurst College • Clitheroe • Lancashire • United Kingdom • BB7 9PZ
JESUIT SCHOOLS

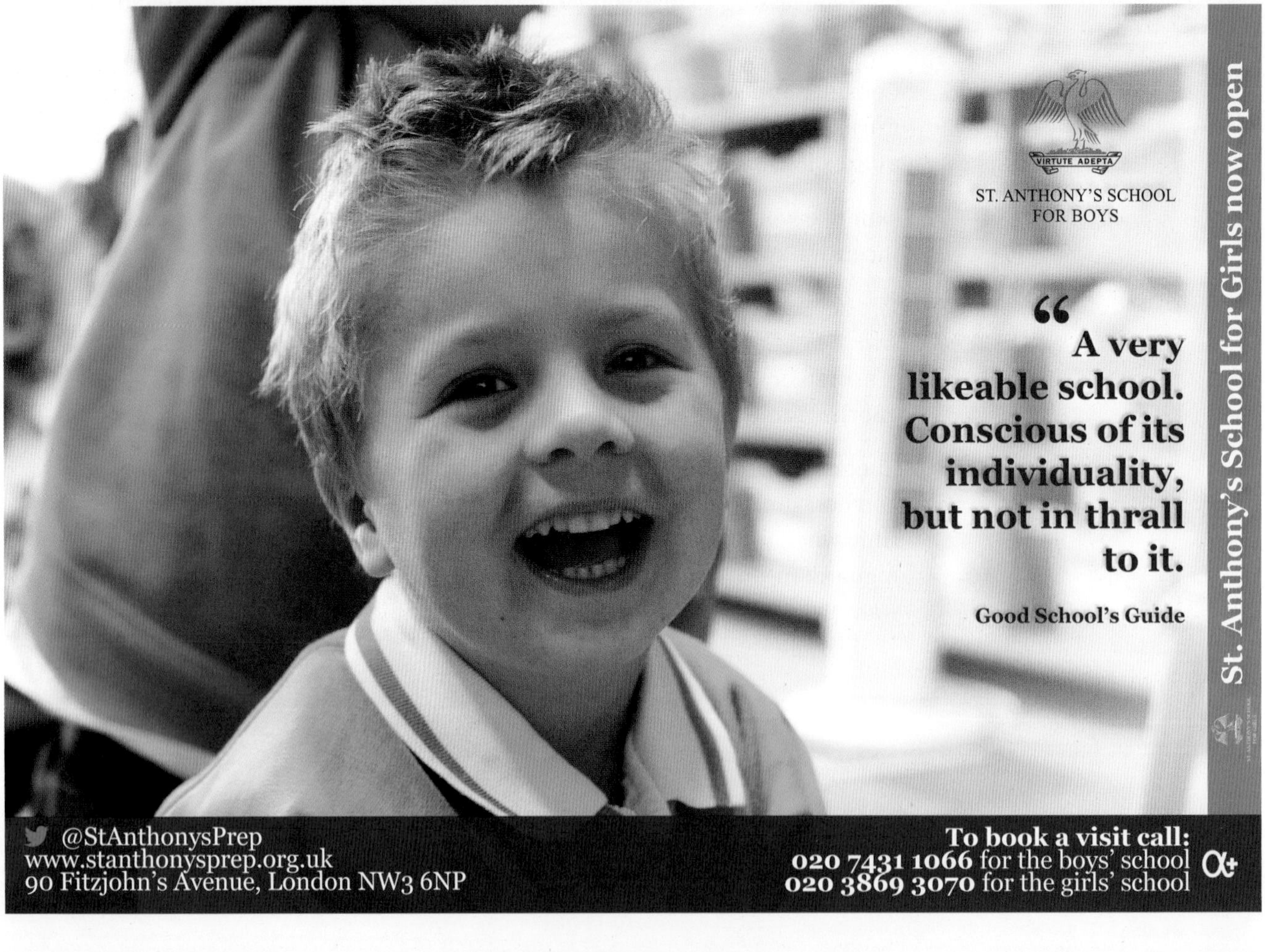
VIRTUTE ADEPTA
ST. ANTHONY'S SCHOOL
FOR BOYS
"A very
likeable school.
Conscious of its
individuality,
but not in thrall
to it.
Good School's Guide
St. Anthony's School for Girls now open
@StAnthonysPrep
www.stanthonysprep.org.uk
90 Fitzjohn's Avenue, London NW3 6NP
To book a visit call:
020 7431 1066 for the boys' school
020 3869 3070 for the girls' school

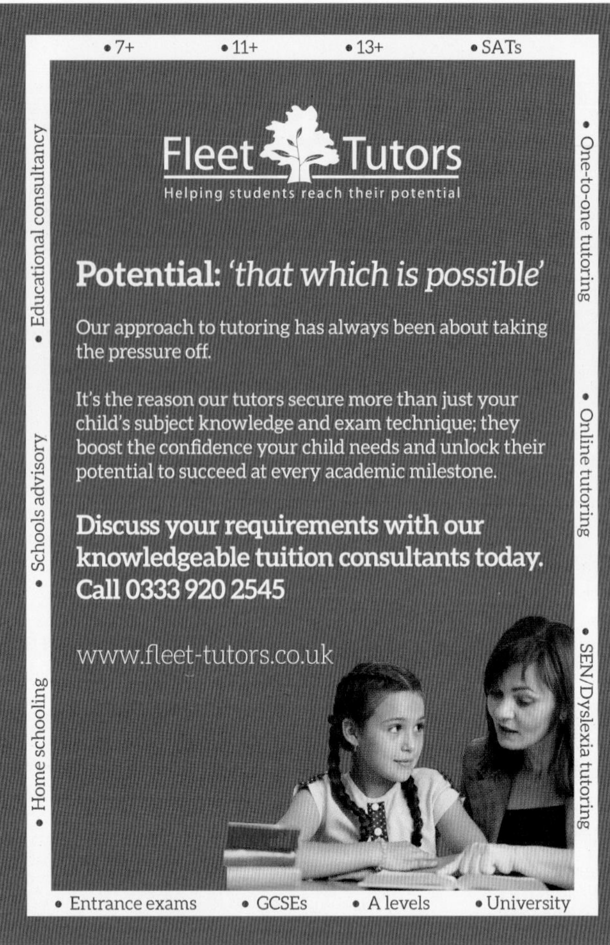

ST ALBANS SCHOOL

HMC Day School 860 pupils
Headmaster: Jonathan Gillespie MA

Entry for boys at 11+ and 13+
Entry for boys and girls at 16+

88% A*-B at A Level; 95% A*-B at GCSE
Excellence in and out of the classroom
Bursaries (up to 100%) and Scholarships available
Extensive Co-Curricular Activities

Email: admissions@st-albans.herts.sch.uk
St Albans School, Abbey Gateway, St Albans AL3 4HB
www.st-albans.herts.sch.uk

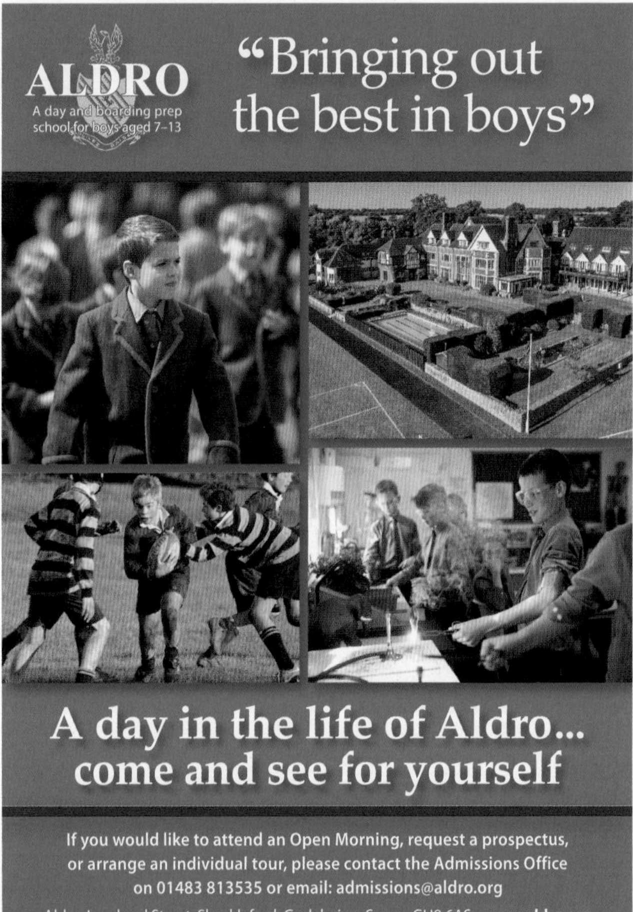

Tutors and tutoring

Tutoring is endemic in the UK these days; in London in particular the top agencies have parents queuing up to pay £80+ an hour to buy their child an advantage. They'd have you believe that without a tutor your toddler will miss the academic boat, but keep your head – there's still plenty of time.

Two is too early

Seriously, there *are* folks out there offering to tutor children as young as 2, but don't be taken in. Spend the money at a wonderful bookshop and read to your child instead. What pre-school-age children need is not tutoring and angst, but time and love from the grown-ups who care for them. If you're reading this article, you are by default an educated, thinking parent who wants the best for your child, so give her the treasures of your mind, your vocabulary, your tastes; they will far out-class anything a tutor can provide.

A clear reason

When do you need a tutor? Put simply, when there is a clear and specific reason for using one. Your child may need help with the 11+ or 13+ entry to an academically selective senior school. Or perhaps he's struggling with a particular GCSE/A level subject. Or she may be falling behind at school. Or he may have missed school through illness or some other crisis. Where there is a known goal to work towards, or a genuine problem to address, tutoring comes into its own.

For a shy child who's under-performing, a friendly tutor can be a godsend. Free from the distractions of the classroom and other pupils, he or she can sit quietly with your child and concentrate solely on whatever's confusing her, filling in gaps in her knowledge and building up her confidence. Grades start to improve, and the child becomes a happier learner, keener to put her hand up in class and more relaxed about going to school. For a teenager who's struggling with maths, demoralised by always coming last in his set and stressed about approaching exams, quality one-to-one teaching from someone with no preconceptions about him can make the difference between failure and success; between giving up and keeping on.

Pre-school children don't need expensive tutors, buy books and read to them instead

Or it could be that you're putting your child through the state system to begin with while you save up for the independent senior school you hope he'll attend. But an over-stretched primary school teacher, with 30 children to get ready for their Sats, will have no interest in helping Harry prepare for independent school entrance, and even mention of the local grammar school is unlikely to get a sympathetic response. After all, from her perspective, selective education isn't what school's about. No matter how bright your child is, he'll be up against other children who have been intensively coached, so tutoring is pretty much essential unless you are confident about your ability to fill in gaps.

A real need

Perhaps you feel your child needs a tutor even though he's already at a good preparatory school. Well, maybe. Be very sure, though, that the need is real. Parents of privately educated children are already paying for their child's education twice, once through their taxes and once through the school fees. Do you really want to make it three times? Depending on where he is, a year's tutoring in the run-up to common entrance may make sense, if only because it'll bring you peace of mind. But to have your tutored 7-year-old win a place at a high-achieving prep and then immediately start having him tutored some more just because everyone else is doing it will only exhaust him and your bank account. Wave him off to St Brainiac's with a proud smile, and let the school do its work.

Try asking a friend with an older child, who won't begrudge your using what they no longer need

On the other hand, if you've just relocated to the UK from overseas, using a tutor is an excellent way to get your kids up to speed with the English system and help them to feel more assured and comfortable in lessons. This in turn will help them to make friends, and the whole settling-in process will be smoother. For a child in a new country, confidence is key.

Where to look

If you want a tutor for your child, how do you find one? The best way should be word of mouth, of course. However, tutoring is one of those things parents usually do in secret, either because they don't choose to spread it around that their child struggles at school, or because they've no wish to increase the opposition's chances in the race for places. Try asking a friend with an older child, who won't begrudge your using what they no longer need. If this doesn't bring results, don't worry.

Tutor companies

The first of these is to approach a tutor company – we review many of the best of these on the Good Schools Guide website. A reputable agency will be skilled at matching your child to the right person, and will give you redress if you're not happy. The work of looking will be taken off your hands, and, since the tutors usually come to you, the whole process becomes very straightforward. Most are London based however, and this is the most expensive way of employing a tutor.

Almost all companies will charge you a registration fee, which can be anything from a few quid to a hair-raising £180, and the hourly rate for tuition will be high (be prepared for at least £45), because the company will take a cut before paying the teacher.

Some of the really big tutorial companies cover too wide a geographical area to interview all their tutors in person, but they will have interviewed them by phone, and checked their references and DBS record.

Online search

A cheaper option is finding a tutor online. Tutors often advertise their services via websites which usually charge around £20 to put you in touch with someone who seems suitable. The website companies run checks to ascertain whether the tutor advertising is who they claim to be, but otherwise it's down to you to judge people's suitability. Use your common sense. If a person's replies to your messages are semi-literate, don't engage them as an English tutor. Tuition rates vary from around £16 ph – probably an undergraduate trying to earn a bit of extra cash – to £45+ ph for an experienced and qualified teacher.

Sit in on the first lesson and afterwards ask your child what they thought about it

Do your homework

Whether you're paying top whack for Kensington's finest hand-picked Oxbridge scholars, or searching through the online jungle with only your five wits to guide you, there are some measures it's sensible to take. After all, this is your child. Self-employed individuals are unlikely to be DBS-checked, because the law prevents them from running a check on themselves, so ask to see references or to speak to previous clients. In fact, do this even if they are DBS-checked. Interview the tutor on the phone before fixing a first date, and don't feel pressured into accepting someone who doesn't sound right. Don't be afraid to sit in on the first lesson, and afterwards ask your child what she thought. If the tutor is travelling to you, check that they can get there easily. Lastly – and this wisdom comes from years of weary experience – insist on punctuality. A tutor who is routinely late will soon drive you up the wall.

In short, if you do your homework your child's tutoring experiences should be happy, productive and affordable. Good luck.

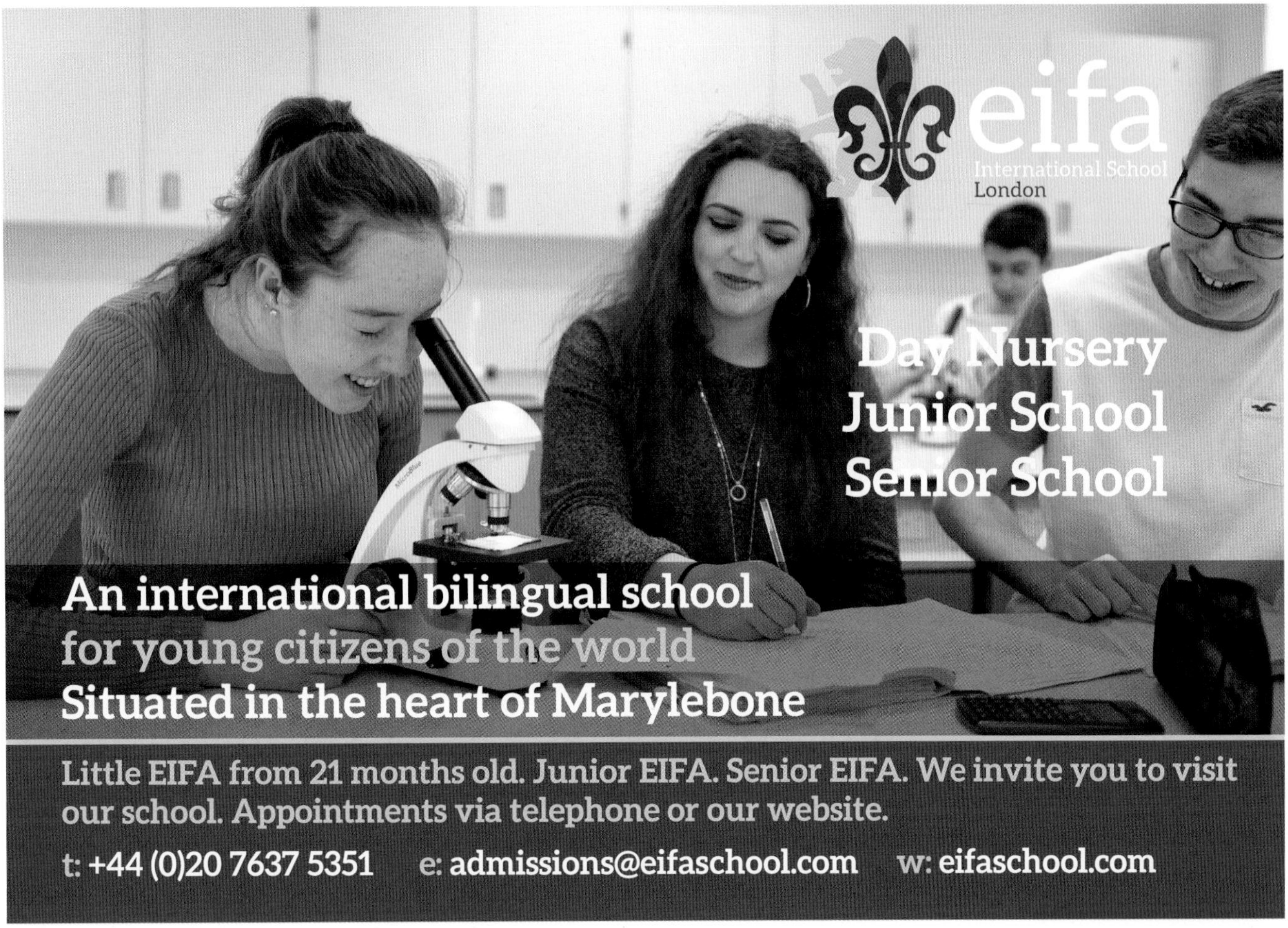

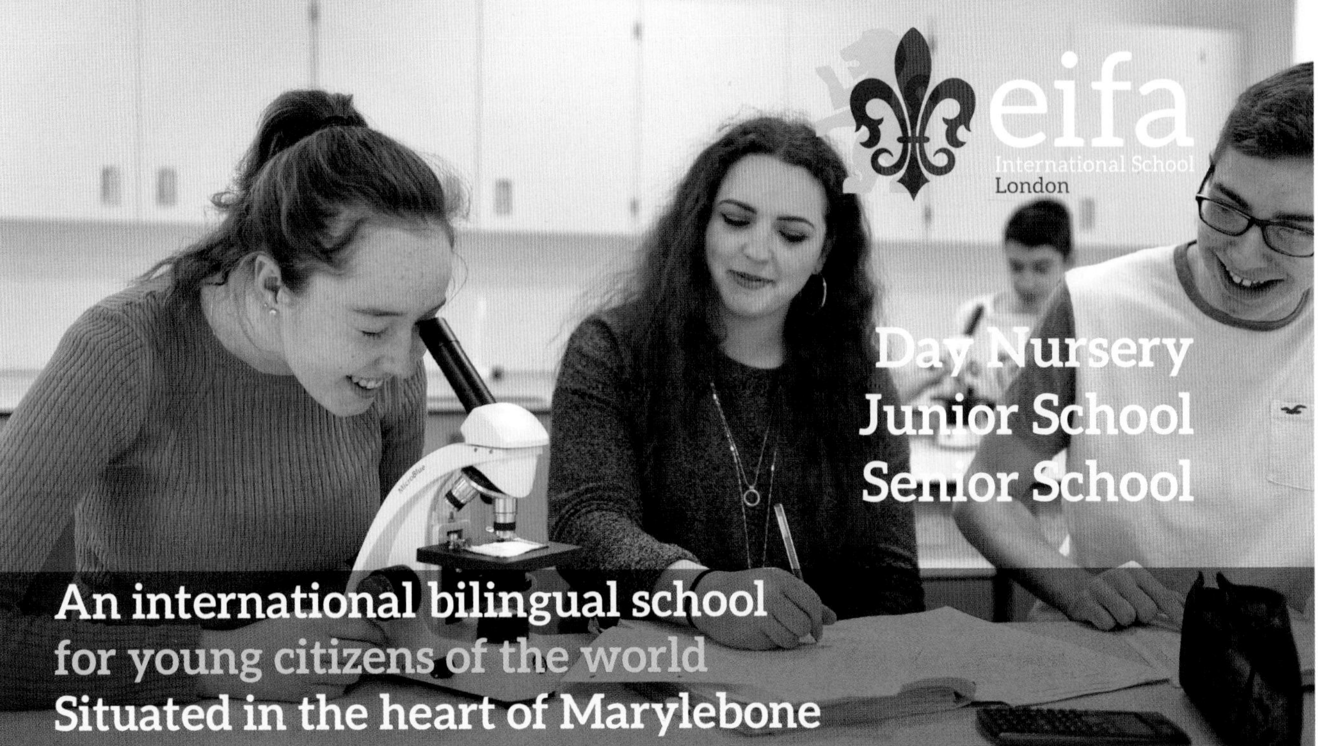

eifa
International School
London
Day Nursery
Junior School
Senior School
An international bilingual school
for young citizens of the world
Situated in the heart of Marylebone
Little EIFA from 21 months old. Junior EIFA. Senior EIFA. We invite you to visit our school. Appointments via telephone or our website.
t: +44 (0)20 7637 5351 e: admissions@eifaschool.com w: eifaschool.com

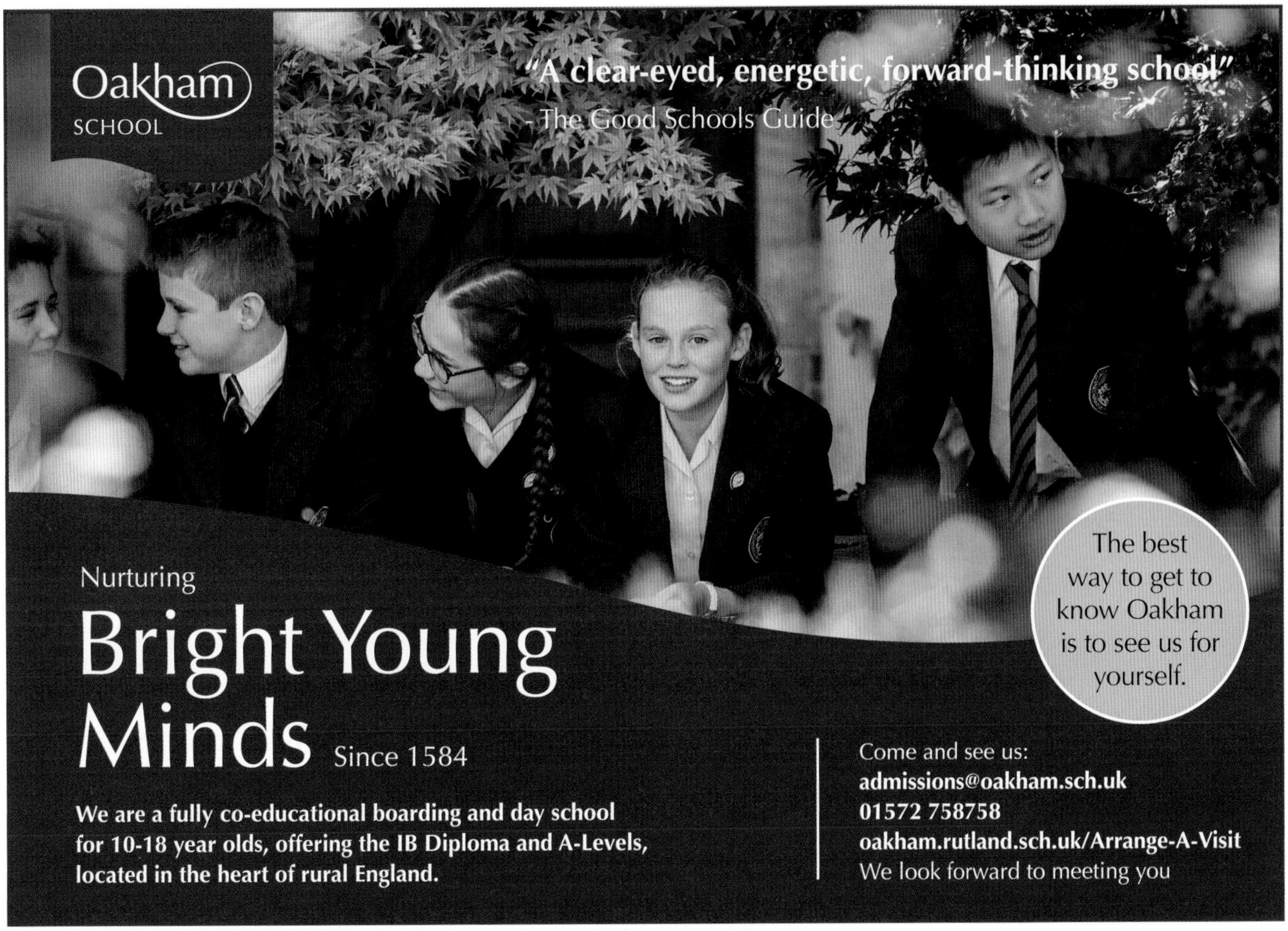

Oakham
SCHOOL
"A clear-eyed, energetic, forward-thinking school"
- The Good Schools Guide
Nurturing
Bright Young
Minds Since 1584
The best way to get to know Oakham is to see us for yourself.
We are a fully co-educational boarding and day school for 10-18 year olds, offering the IB Diploma and A-Levels, located in the heart of rural England.
Come and see us:
admissions@oakham.sch.uk
01572 758758
oakham.rutland.sch.uk/Arrange-A-Visit
We look forward to meeting you

Child protection

If you are preparing to entrust your child to a school – whether day or boarding – you will most likely assume that your child will be safe and that all members of the school's staff will take the greatest care to ensure that this is always the case.

The chances are that your expectations will be fulfilled. Unfortunately, in a sad minority of cases that is not what happens.

We have all read news reports of bullying and abuse and may have shuddered at the thought that those very people who smilingly welcome our children into their care may be the last people to whom we would entrust them, if we knew all.

A flood of historical allegations against schools, court cases, mobile phones, flexi-boarding, more parental involvement, the internet, sex education and heightened awareness have together helped usher in some sunlight and fresh air. Schools are now a less than perfect setting for paedophiles and bullies. Child protection policies, found on every school website, usefully make plain the possibility of abuse at schools – something rarely contemplated a generation ago.

Abuse can occur at any school, anywhere. Fame is no protection, and nor is obscurity. Some kinds of school, though, need to take particular care – and that they do should be obvious to you when you visit. International schools have transient pupil populations, and teachers whose histories may be overseas and hard to research. Specialist music teaching necessarily involves a good deal of physical contact with the teacher and the pupil alone in a closed room. Religious schools can have a system of authority that keeps abuse concealed. Boarding schools can become very closed worlds. Special schools may have to deal with a large range of communication and emotional difficulties.

Much can be gleaned from the head's attitude when questions about child protection are asked

What can you do?

Parents do well to warn their children – gently but seriously – of the dangers, however remote these may be, so they feel that it is easy to speak to you should they meet them. It is worth pointing out that abuse can come from anyone – including a teacher or an adult they know well, or from another child at the school.

Raise your own antennae at any school you may be considering. You can inquire about the steps taken to safeguard children in the same way you might ask about bullying or learning support. As always, much can be gleaned from the head's attitude when questions about child protection are asked. Is he or she ill at ease? Defensive? Or happy to engage, and proud of the steps their school has taken? Openness is what you're looking for.

How easy is it for a child, or a parent for that matter, to report an incident? Schools make this possible in a variety of ways; what matters is that passing on concerns is a routine thing (children and parents do it about lots of things all the time), and is welcomed by the school, and is low-stakes: the person registering the concern knows that they are not putting their relationships within the school at risk, let alone threatening someone's place in the school. That may seem an odd thing to say, but if you fear to report, say, careless management of a museum trip because it will harm an otherwise much-loved teacher, you probably choose to stay mum. Your concerns have to cross a high threshold before you communicate them, so you never pass on those troubling observations that may be the outward indication of serious problems. To be safe, schools need to hear the little voices, not just the shouting.

Do not think less of a school because a case of abuse has been brought to light there. Tabloid coverage can be the price the school has to pay for handling a case of abuse or bullying openly. It is inevitable that abuse will occur somewhere. What matters is how well the school deals with it, how well it performs in bringing the abuse to light and how open it is on the subject with current and future parents.

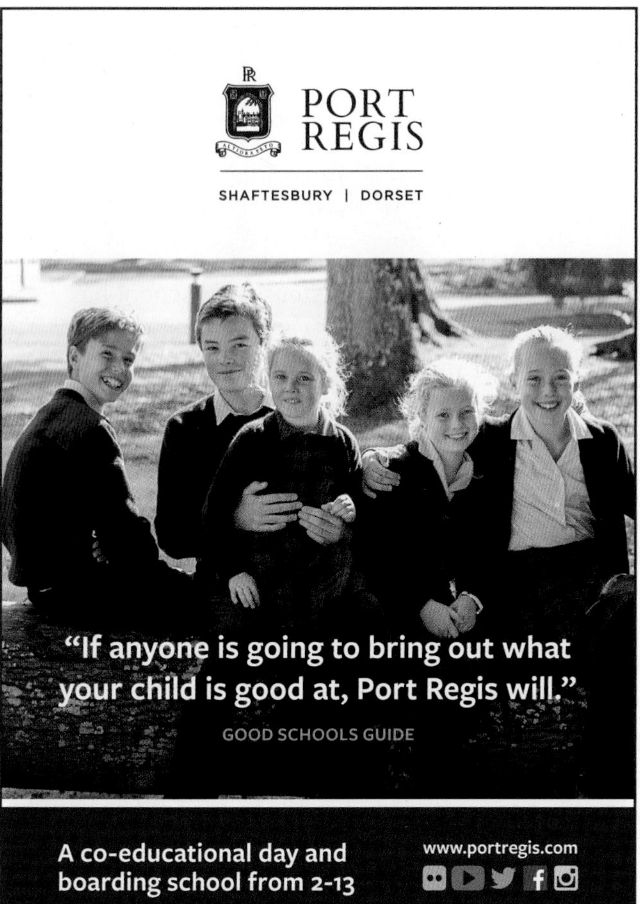

PORT REGIS
SHAFTESBURY | DORSET
"If anyone is going to bring out what your child is good at, Port Regis will."
GOOD SCHOOLS GUIDE
A co-educational day and boarding school from 2-13
www.portregis.com

SIR WILLIAM PERKINS'S SCHOOL
"Excellent results achieved with a big dollop of humour, humanity and freedom of thought"
The Good Schools Guide
A highly successful independent day school for girls aged 11-18 years, situated in Surrey greenbelt with easy road/rail access and school coach services.
• Outstanding academic results with excellent co-curricular opportunities
• State of the art facilities
• Scholarships – Academic, Music and Arts (Year 7 and Sixth Form), Sports (Sixth Form) and means-tested bursaries (up to 100%) available
• 34% GCSE grades at Grade 9 (national average 4.3%)
• Performance and Recreational Rowing Programmes
Please contact reg@swps.org.uk to reserve a place at our information events, for further details or a prospectus.
GUILDFORD ROAD | CHERTSEY | SURREY KT16 9BN
01932 574900
www.swps.org.uk
gsa Girls' Schools Association
HMC

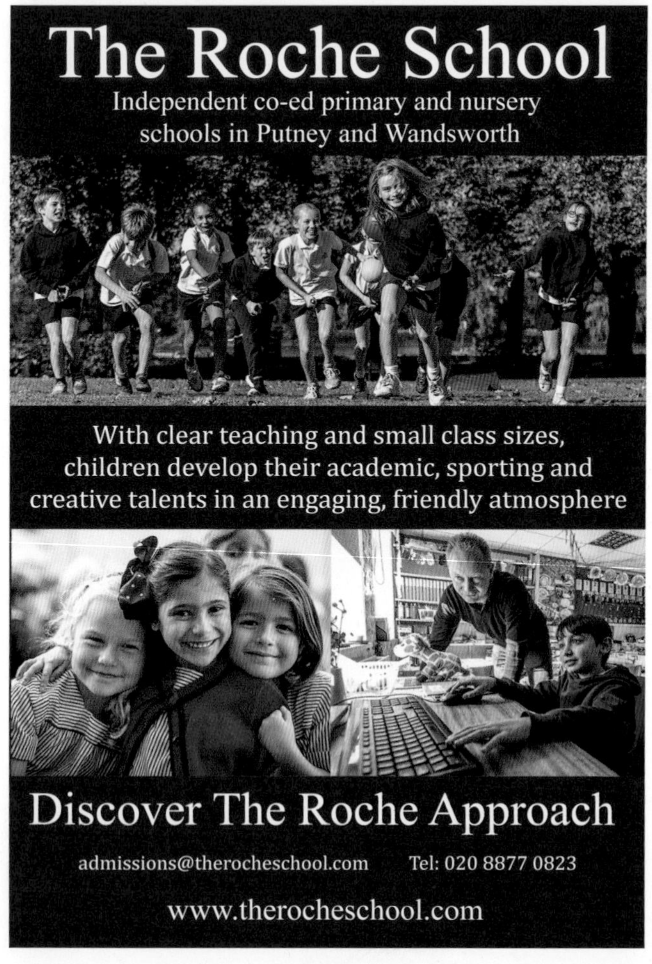

The Roche School
Independent co-ed primary and nursery schools in Putney and Wandsworth
With clear teaching and small class sizes, children develop their academic, sporting and creative talents in an engaging, friendly atmosphere
Discover The Roche Approach
admissions@therocheschool.com
Tel: 020 8877 0823
www.therocheschool.com

St Hilary's
Preparatory School Godalming 2—11 years
Also welcoming boys in Year 3 from Sept 2019 in a phased plan to be fully co-educational by Sept 2022
"Happy, charming and academically successful" The Good Schools Guide
Tel: 01483 416551 • @StHilarysSchool
Email: registrar@sthilarysschool.com
www.sthilarysschool.com

Offering an
ALL YEAR NURSERY

"An
all-round school
maintaining
high standards
& impressive results"
- Good Schools Guide

CRANMORE
CRANMORE
CRANMORE

Assisted places available

NEW
TRANSPORT
ROUTES

www.cranmoreprep.co.uk
01483 280340
admissions@cranmoreprep.co.uk

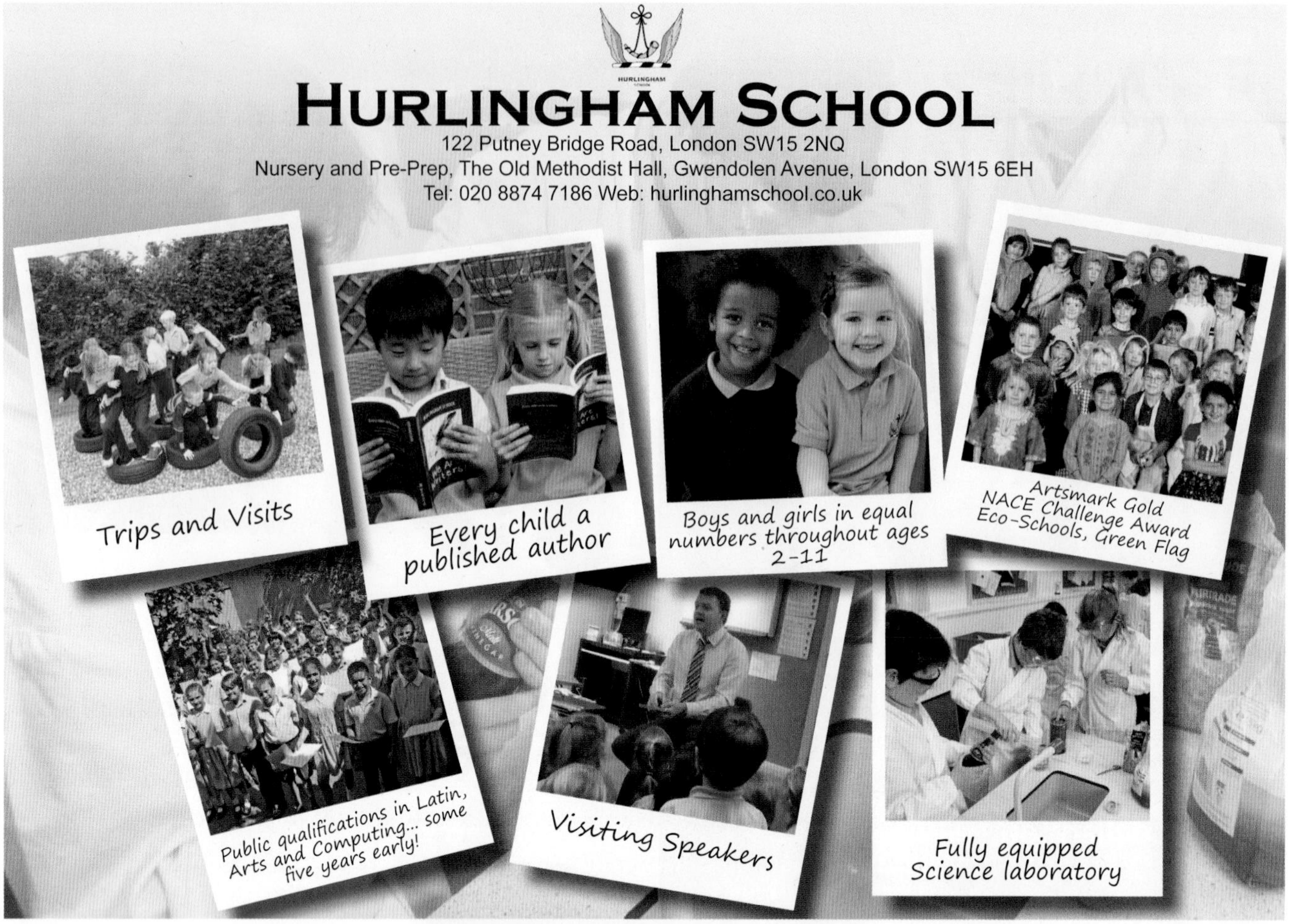
HURLINGHAM SCHOOL
122 Putney Bridge Road, London SW15 2NQ
Nursery and Pre-Prep, The Old Methodist Hall, Gwendolen Avenue, London SW15 6EH
Tel: 020 8874 7186 Web: hurlinghamschool.co.uk
Trips and Visits
Every child a published author
Boys and girls in equal numbers throughout ages 2-11
Artsmark Gold
NACE Challenge Award
Eco-Schools, Green Flag
Public qualifications in Latin, Arts and Computing... some five years early!
Visiting Speakers
Fully equipped Science laboratory

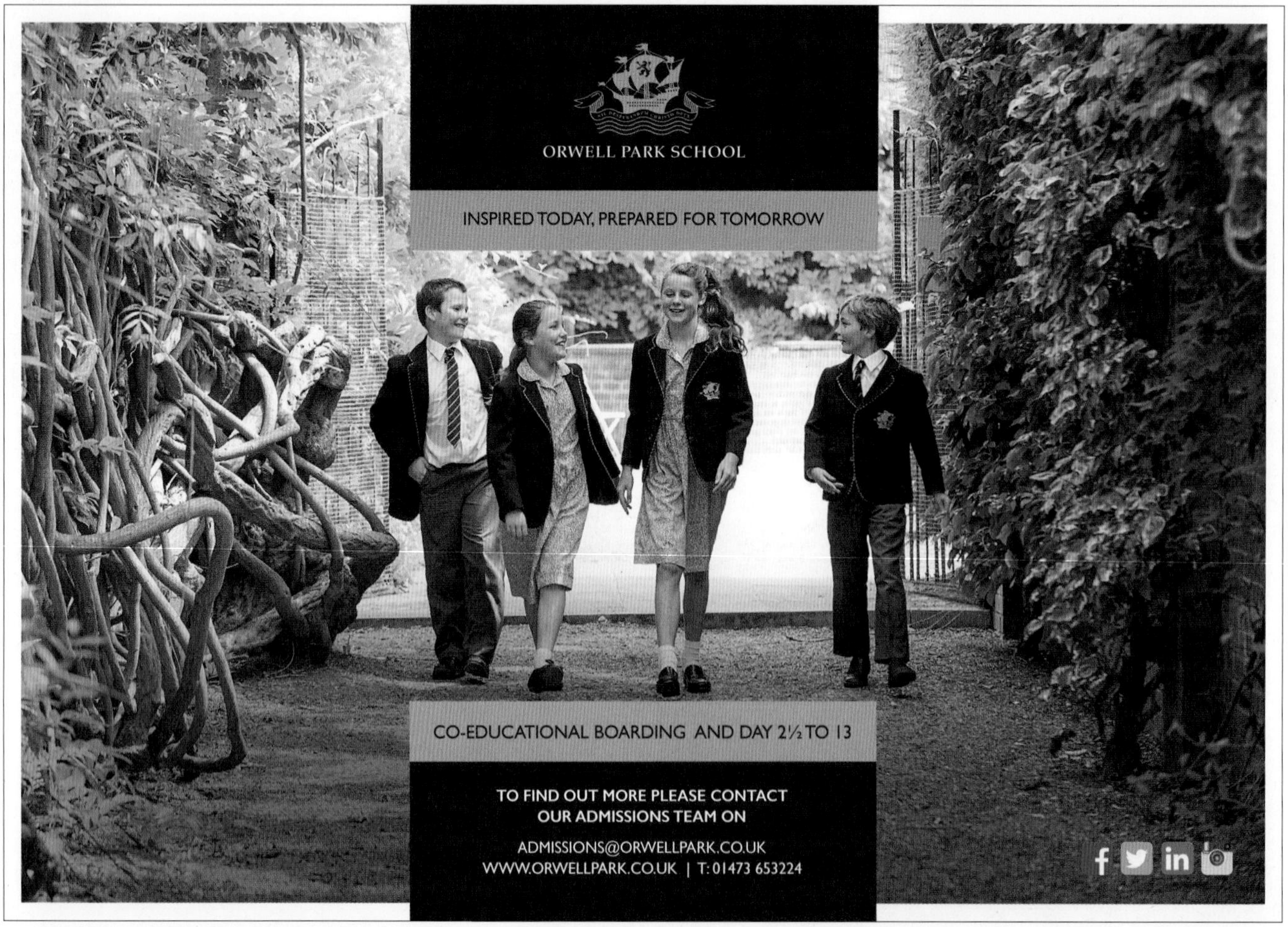
ORWELL PARK SCHOOL
INSPIRED TODAY, PREPARED FOR TOMORROW
CO-EDUCATIONAL BOARDING AND DAY 2½ TO 13
TO FIND OUT MORE PLEASE CONTACT OUR ADMISSIONS TEAM ON
ADMISSIONS@ORWELLPARK.CO.UK
WWW.ORWELLPARK.CO.UK | T: 01473 653224

Good Schools Guide Education Consultants

The Good Schools Guide has been trusted by generations of parents to provide expert, honest and unbiased information about schools. Our education consultancy provides the same high standards of expertise, independence and professional integrity to individual families.

We make our own decisions about which schools are worthy of inclusion in the Guide – no school can pay to appear. In the same way our consultants recommend schools to parents purely because we think they are the right school for your child – we take no commissions or incentives from schools.

Our highly-experienced consultants assist clients from all over the world to find the right schools for their children. We can help with state schools as well as independent schools, and special schools as well as mainstream schools. However urgent the deadline, however complex the circumstances, call 0203 286 6824 (UK) or +44 203 286 6824 (international) to find out how we can solve your educational dilemmas.

Our consultants

All of our consultants have personally visited and reviewed countless schools for our website and publications; many also have professional backgrounds or specialist qualifications in education or special needs. Between them they have direct experience of every aspect of both the British and international education systems, not to mention invaluable local knowledge about schools in London and all areas of the UK.

Our team includes experts in SEN, school appeals, scholarships and bursaries, grammar schools and relocation to the UK from abroad.

Consultancy built around your needs

Our consultancy packages range from a 30-minute telephone consultation to a fully bespoke service tailored to meet complex, urgent or other specific circumstances. Additional services include accompanied school visits, providing translators and educational assessments, and arranging specialist tuition. Our main consultancy services are outlined below; for full details please visit www. goodschoolsguide.co.uk.

London Service

Designed to meet the needs of families new to London who need guidance, not just on schools but on residential areas, commuting, family services, nurseries, playgroups, tutors and much more.

State School Service

This service is for parents who are interested in state schools only. It can give advice on admissions criteria, catchment areas, grammar schools, and understanding school performance data.

Special Educational Needs

Our team of SEN experts is unique. We have specialists in dyslexia, autism, learning difficulties, and speech and language difficulties, and we also help families dealing with rare conditions, physical disability, mental health problems, and so on. We know our way around assessments and the EHCP system, and we have extensive knowledge of both mainstream and special schools which cater for children with these difficulties.

Academic assessments

If you are not sure what academic level your child is at, particularly if you are coming from overseas, we can arrange academic assessments.

Scholarships and bursaries

We have a unique central resource, with information on the fee assistance available at more than 700 independent schools.

Contact us

Phone us on +44 (0)203 286 6824 or send a brief email to: consultants@goodschoolsguide.co.uk outlining what you need. Tell us the age of your child and where you live plus your contact details. We will contact you to discuss how best to help you and ensure we match you with the right consultant. Consultations can be by phone, email or face to face, and we can find a consultant to speak to you within an hour if necessary.

How much?

Ours is one of the most competitively priced tailor-made education consultancy services in the UK. Check our website for current fees.

Our guarantee

The Good Schools Guide has an international reputation for providing unbiased, independent advice on educational matters. We have no commercial links whatsoever with any school. This gives our education consultants the freedom to consider a huge range of schools in order to find the best one for you. You can have complete confidence that if our consultants recommend a school it is because, and only because, they consider it to be right for your child. You can also be assured that we maintain the highest possible standards of privacy and all dealings with clients are completely confidential.

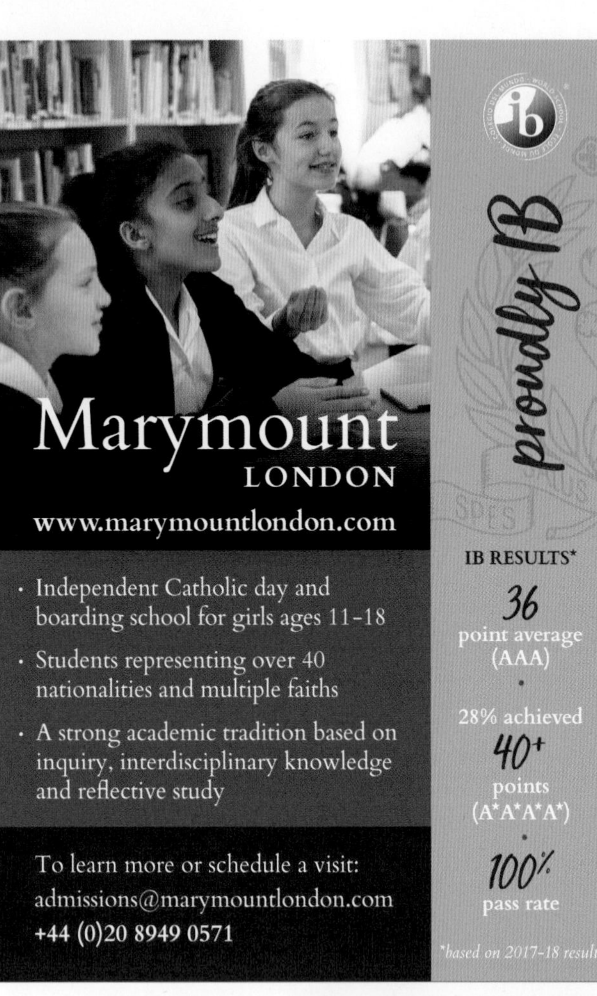
Marymount
LONDON
www.marymountlondon.com
proudly IB
• Independent Catholic day and boarding school for girls ages 11-18
• Students representing over 40 nationalities and multiple faiths
• A strong academic tradition based on inquiry, interdisciplinary knowledge and reflective study
To learn more or schedule a visit:
admissions@marymountlondon.com
+44 (0)20 8949 0571
IB RESULTS*
36
point average
(AAA)
28% achieved
40+
points
(A*A*A*A*)
100%
pass rate
*based on 2017-18 results

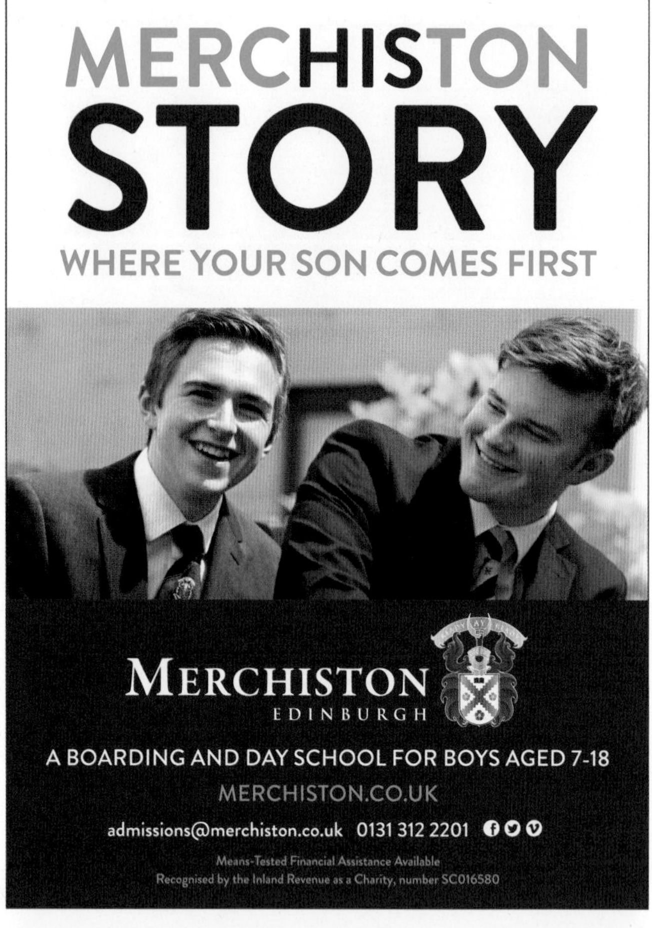
MERCHISTON
STORY
WHERE YOUR SON COMES FIRST
MERCHISTON
EDINBURGH
A BOARDING AND DAY SCHOOL FOR BOYS AGED 7-18
MERCHISTON.CO.UK
admissions@merchiston.co.uk 0131 312 2201
Means-Tested Financial Assistance Available
Recognised by the Inland Revenue as a Charity, number SC016580

EXETER CATHEDRAL SCHOOL
Nursery | Pre-Prep | Prep
What makes your heart sing?
School tours and visits welcome throughout the year.
01392 255298
@ECSprepschool
www.exetercathedralschool.co.uk

At Headington we offer:
Flexibility – Half-weekly, weekly and full boarding options available
Academic excellence and choice – at all levels, including IB or A Level in the Sixth Form
A balanced education – over 150 extra-curricular activities to choose from
WHAT COULD OUR FUTURES HOLD?
Book your visit at
www.headington.org/gsg
SIXTH FORM
SENIOR SCHOOL
NURSERY
PREP SCHOOL
HEADINGTON
SCHOOL · OXFORD

COFFEE
Show
your
education
questions
answered
SCHOOLSSHOW.CO.UK/TALKS
THE SUNDAY TIMES
EDUCATION THEATRE

The Good Schools Guide International

goodschoolsguide.co.uk/international

The Good Schools Guide International does for international schools what The Good Schools Guide does for UK schools ... visits and reviews the best ones for children 3-18, state or independent, wherever they are.

Written for parents, the GSGI covers top British, IB, American and international schools catering to English-speaking expats in over 55 cities worldwide. All schools reviewed have been visited by GSGI editors. Nobody can pay to be in the guide. We decide who goes in: schools are in (or out) whether they like it or not.

Reviews are completely independent, forthright and we stand behind every word. Overviews and articles give the inside scoop on everything from headmasters, sports, school runs and local traffic to life on the ground for expats.

For corporate or family rates or international school consultants, please call the Good Schools Guide office +44(0) 203 286 6824.

Uni in the USA

goodschoolsguide.co.uk/universities

The British guide to great universities from Harvard to Hong Kong. We tell you how to choose, how to apply and how to pay.

Q: How many Stanford students does it take to change a light bulb?
A: One, dude.

Written by funny, sharp-eyed British students and co-authored by Anthony Nemecek, former director of the Fulbright US Education Service, our popular British students' guide to US universities is available in paperback and online. The online version includes the contents of the US print edition plus reviews of selected universities worldwide.

The down-to-earth, often hilarious reviews of selected American colleges and international universities could only have been written by students interviewing students. One reviewer couch-surfed across the US by Greyhound bus, interviewing hundreds of students as he wrote his spot-on reviews, then legged it across Europe to start the process there. Still more intrepid souls — all students — took on universities in Asia and Australia.

All told, they reviewed over 100 universities in 12 countries and reported on getting in, money matters, fellow students, life on campus and life outside. In short, what it's really like to be there.

To subscribe online for all reviews, or buy the paperback for US uni reviews, go to goodschoolsguide.co.uk/universities for full details. For consultancies on schools abroad or UK universities, contact consultants@goodschoolsguide.co.uk or call us on +44(0) 203 286 6824.

Additional publications from The Good Schools Guide

The Good Schools Guide: Boarding Schools

Reviews 350+ boarding schools across Britain, independent and state, with advice on when to start boarding, applying from abroad, sex and drugs and homesickness, boarding for a child with SEN.

The Good Schools Guide: London North

Candid reviews of state and private schools north of the Thames. Packed with local north London knowledge. Also explains how the English school system works, state and independent school admissions and much more.

The Good Schools Guide: London South

Invaluable guide to state and private schools south of the Thames. Includes pen portraits all the boroughs, your guide to navigating the English schooling system, how admissions work and much more.

The Good Schools Guide online subscription

All the latest reviews plus details of every school in Britain, with exam data, catchment maps, university entrance information. Advice on choosing a school, SEN, tutors, talented children and much more.

Uni in the USA

Written by students who have been through the US system, features in-depth descriptions of 70 US universities, plus the inside track on getting in and preparing for life across the pond.

Uni in the USA...and Beyond online subscription

Includes student reviews of universities across Canada, Europe and the Far East, from Alberta to Abu Dhabi, and advice from SATs to visas.

The Good Schools Guide International online subscription

The one-stop educational shop for expats. Reviews of the best state and independent schools round the globe, plus insider knowledge on life overseas.

All available via goodschoolsguide.co.uk

West of England and Wales

City of Bristol
Cheshire
Clwyd
Cornwall
Devon
Dorset
Glamorgan
Gloucestershire
Herefordshire
Monmouthshire
Powys
Shropshire
Somerset
Staffordshire
Wiltshire
Worcestershire

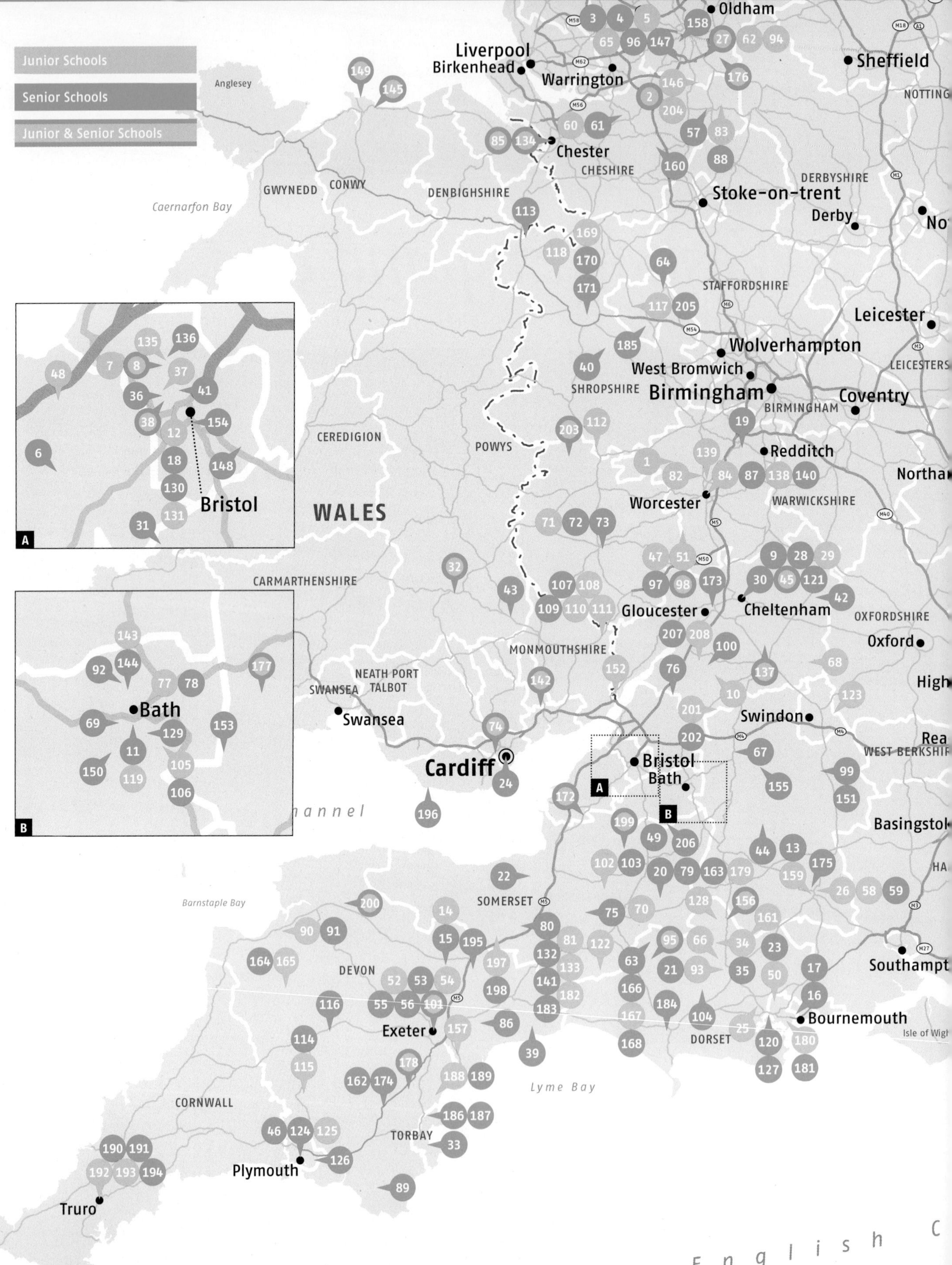

Junior Schools
Senior Schools
Junior & Senior Schools
Anglesey
Liverpool
Birkenhead
Warrington
Oldham
Sheffield
Chester
CHESHIRE
GWYNEDD
CONWY
DENBIGHSHIRE
Caernarfon Bay
Stoke-on-trent
DERBYSHIRE
Derby
STAFFORDSHIRE
Leicester
Wolverhampton
West Bromwich
SHROPSHIRE
Birmingham
BIRMINGHAM
Coventry
CEREDIGION
POWYS
Redditch
Worcester
WARWICKSHIRE
WALES
Bristol
Bath
CARMARTHENSHIRE
Gloucester
Cheltenham
OXFORDSHIRE
Oxford
MONMOUTHSHIRE
NEATH PORT TALBOT
SWANSEA
Swansea
Swindon
Cardiff
WEST BERKSHIRE
Basingstoke
SOMERSET
Barnstaple Bay
DEVON
Exeter
Southampton
Bournemouth
DORSET
Isle of Wight
Lyme Bay
CORNWALL
TORBAY
Plymouth
Truro
English Channel

WEST ENGLAND & WALES

Abberley Hall

1

Worcester WR6 6DD

Ages 2–13 **Pupils** 235 **Boarders** 84 full, 26 part (from year 3) **C of E**

Fees: Day £9,120 – £19,410; Boarding £24,375 pa

01299 896275
www.abberleyhall.co.uk

Headmaster: Since 2014, Will Lockett, previously classics teacher and housemaster at Bryanston. One of a small number of prep school heads who have moved from senior schools. In Will's case, the move was quite simply because he loves Abberley. An old boy of the school, he is reveling in the move to this age group. 'They are so refreshingly enthusiastic about everything', he says. He has a classics degree from Manchester, still teaches some and relishes it, no doubt contributing to the status the subject has with the children. A great believer in the value of routines, he says children respond to the structure of boarding and he has even introduced half an hour silent reading in bed before lights out. Everyone likes it. Will's style is brisk and vigorous. He knows exactly what is going on and children and staff are keen to keep it that way. 'He has respect without fear from the children,' a parent told us. His wife, Beth, is fully involved, overseeing junior boarding and doing some teaching. A headmaster's wife to die for is the verdict of parents, who say she is very maternal and nurturing in her approach to the children. There are three Lockett children, the youngest at Abberley and the older two at Shrewsbury. Will is spending his first few years at the school consolidating all the strengths and bringing new challenges in terms of independent learning and outdoor education.

Entrance: Non-selective. Children are assessed either before arrival or when they arrive to ensure there is clarity about educational needs and, with older children, to help determine which academic sets are appropriate.

Exit: The vast majority stay to the end of year 8. This is a school that is a serious player in the CE stakes and leavers depart with a significant number of scholarships/exhibitions each year (51 in 2018, 12 of these academic). The head says parents are keen to seek advice on senior schools, which they recognise as objective and in the child's best interests. They feed a large number of top co-ed and single sex senior schools including Marlborough, Oundle, Eton, Harrow, Cheltenham Ladies and St Mary's Ascot.

Remarks: Ninety acres of park and woodland surround Abberley Hall, a 19th century edifice of some significance. The bluebells were out along the drive on our visit to add to the idyllic rural setting in which the children grow up. Inside, the first impressions are of a grand but comfortable past. While we talk to the headmaster, a glorious peacock pecks at the window as if he wants to join us. Many of the original features of the old house remain – the headmaster's study is the old library, apparently untouched since an era of leisurely scholarship.

But there is nothing leisurely about the scholarship at Abberley today. It offers a traditional academic curriculum. The older children have 30 hours of lessons a week. 'It would be nice to have a few less lessons,' one or two year 8s said to us plaintively. Languages are a huge strength – Greek is taught from year 6, there are three hours of French a week and two and a half of Latin. It pays off in terms of scholarship examinations, the head tells us. From year 3, the children have twice yearly exams. It is low key to start with but it means the children are getting used to tests. Science, maths, design and manufacture have a practical, cross-curricular emphasis that is impressive.

The workshops are open at lunch time and after school for children to work on their own design projects – about a third of the school is engaged on one of these. Art is striking with a practising artist running workshops twice a week – 'It has been a huge help for the children preparing for scholarships', the head of art tells us. There are textiles, ceramics, print-making, painting onto canvas and use of different media. The head is keen to develop even further the profile and challenge of the creative arts.

The older children told us that the high academic standards were what made the school stand out. 'We can get help from teachers whenever we want,' they say, 'and we can sign up for extra academic coaching sessions'. The school is preparing the children for success in their future education. Parents are enthusiastic about the quality of the teaching. 'They go the extra mile'. Once year 8s have completed all their exams, there is a challenging leavers' programme of events for them. The head says that feedback from senior schools is that Abberley children are notably good at grasping opportunities.

As the school is non selective, learning support is taken seriously. Class size is kept to 15 maximum, allowing for much individual support within the classroom. There is dyslexia screening in years 1 and 2 and careful scrutiny of ongoing assessments. Where a need is identified, the head of learning support will step in. The school may do its own further assessment or advise an educational psychologist's report to help tailor future learning. What happens next depends on the level of need and is very much individually determined. Parents say that the children take needing extra help as a matter of course – there is absolutely no stigma attached.

The head says it is not what happens in lessons that distinguishes the outstanding boarding school, but what happens at weekends. Abberley Hall is committed to full boarding. There is no flexi-boarding but there is part boarding, where parents commit to specific days a week a term in advance. One weekend in three is full boarding, one is optional and the third is an exeat, so the most a child would be continuously at school is likely to be three weeks, which we think is right for children at this age and a good preparation for senior boarding schools. Many of the weekend activities, which the children tell us they adore and are keenly anticipated, are open to parents. Just before we visited there had been the annual fun run where everyone dressed up to complete various length runs around the grounds. The grounds are fully used. The children have built an outdoor pizza oven, there are outdoor classrooms and mini Duke of Edinburgh style award activities outdoors one afternoon a week. There are clear rules about where in the grounds children can explore but plenty of space for climbing trees and building dams.

Extracurricular life is teeming. Music is highly valued and a big part of the school. Not only lessons but practices are timetabled for the children which, with 200 instrumental lessons going on, must take some doing. There is a lunchtime concert series and, the emphasis is on everyone getting a chance to perform at some stage. Many take RSM exams and do very well. A group goes each week to the CBSO Children's Choir in Birmingham. There are lots of instrumental ensembles and choirs. The senior chapel choir is invited to sing around the area, regularly performing at Worcester Cathedral. Parents describe the music as 'sensational' and are delighted by the high expectations from staff. There is a 'phenomenally ambitious' annual musical. 'The staff are not just wanting performance but perfection', one parent told us approvingly.

The school is considered to punch well above its weight in sport, which happens every day with matches on Wednesdays and Saturdays and sports tours. Facilities are brilliant. Rugby coaching is exceptional even by standards outside the prep school world. Girls' cricket is taken as seriously as boys' cricket. Lots of the children said sport is a great thing about the school, but even those who admitted to not being particularly keen appreciate the choice they have and the chance to be outside.

There is drama and beekeeping, run by the headmaster, fishing and film making, spy club and electronics; the list goes on. Children can bring their horses from home and ride round the grounds on their bikes. It is a day packed full of intellectual and outdoor activities – 'Gumboots and Greek' is the school's current strapline and it is a good reflection of what life is like. Parents like the lack of hierarchy in school activities. There is no sense that the rugby players are any more valued or respected than the grade 1 flautist. The days are long and, particularly for parents considering boarding, it is important to ensure their child is ready for this degree of activity.

Abberley has its own chalet in the French Alps and all year 5s and 7s have a couple of weeks out there each year to immerse themselves in a different culture and pick up a bit more French, which they are learning alongside Spanish, Latin and Greek.

The children we spoke to enthused about boarding. The accommodation is very non institutional, using the variety of spaces in the old buildings. Pastoral support is strong and the turnover of staff small. Head has introduced a new tutor system for the older children so years 6, 7 and 8 have their own personal tutor for three years, who acts as a single point of contact for parents and with whom the children have a weekly individual meeting. We think this is an excellent model to ensure no one slips through the pastoral net.

'We are not big on punishment', says the head and indeed the discipline issues with which staff are dealing are low key. The focus is on getting children to think about their own behaviour and how it impacts on others. Parents say that the school's attitude to problems has always been to leave it to school and not encourage parents to be very much involved. The new head seems to be changing this a bit, but everyone we spoke to seemed very confident in the school's ability to sort things out quickly and humanely and follow through on issues. The school is keen on giving the children responsibilities and has created new roles in the last couple of years to ensure the opportunities are there to learn about leadership.

Family backgrounds range from landowners and farming families to professionals and business people, and they are highly supportive of the school, generally living close enough to attend matches, concerts, Sunday chapel and the many other events. There are some children whose family connections with Abberley go back several generations.

The children are strikingly open and unaffected, living witness to the head's belief that prep school children retain their innocence longer. They are unselfconscious, gutsy and ready to talk to adults appropriately. They are being prepared for a work hard, play hard culture. They love the outdoor freedom and they also know life is a serious and competitive business, which they are up for. The school is in its centenary year. It has much to be proud of in its past and everything to suggest the future is golden for the children lucky enough to come here.

Alderley Edge School for Girls

Wilmslow Road, Alderley Edge, Cheshire SK9 7QE

Ages 2–18 **Pupils** 501 **Sixth form** 65

Fees: £6,870 – £12,450 pa

01625 583028
www.aesg.co.uk

Headmistress: Since 2016, Helen Jeys BA (Durham), PGCE (Cambridge), previously deputy head at Manchester High for Girls. Visiting in the third term of her first academic year, we were blown away by the energising gusts of positive change sweeping through the school's corridors. Nothing to discompose existing pupils or parents, but nevertheless a deceptively strong current which looks set to take this school to a completely new level academically.

Her vision is not for any clichéd 'off the peg' hothouse, though. No, she wants something altogether more bespoke: a school which places well-being (about which she is passionate) at its centre, allowing girls to flourish and follow those ascendant academic pathways which she is laying down at remarkable speed.

How is she doing this? Well, she is looking afresh at the 'gifted and interested' (her words) programme, providing stretch work for pupils and introducing cross-curricular themes. So, for example, she might deliver a keynote speech on 'identity', which will then be explored, independently, across subject areas: DNA in science, body forms in art, Descartes in philosophy – the aim being to open young minds to new ways of seeing and being. She wants to nurture intellectual curiosity, so the whole school becomes 'an educational experience'. Her not unambitious aim is to make it the premier girls' school in Cheshire and buck the notion that to get to Oxbridge you need to attend one of the traditional, academic (some might say, three line whip pressured) schools in the area.

The school motto, 'Aspire not to have more but to be more', chimes here, as she wants girls to understand there is no area in life in which they cannot excel. A firm believer in girls-only schools, she seeks to unlock the potential of each girl, whether they want to study art at Central St Martins or biochemistry at Cambridge. 'STEM plus arts' is a principle she loves; why choose, she asks? Embrace it all.

Very aware of the world into which the girls are entering, she tackles modern topics in assemblies like avoiding fixed mindsets and how companies use setbacks to ensure success. All critical building blocks for resilience and reaching one's potential. It is hard to see where she gets time for her interests – playing the cello, running, and writing about education – but in doing so, she models what she teaches.

With year 7 entries increasing we would place good money on the presence of Helen Jeys being the key reason for this. As one parent said, 'They should put Helen on Brexit; she would crack it.'

Head of junior school: Since 2013, Bridget Howard BEd, who joined as deputy head in 2010 from Bolton Girls Junior School. Working in tandem with the senior school, she is placing a subtly increased emphasis on academic achievement and more vigorous tracking of pupils. She is also similarly passionate about opening up other opportunities for pupils and is keen on music, drama and art. Mindful of the numerous well-being and learning benefits of children being outdoors, she is investigating a small forest school aspect to the curriculum.

Seen every day welcoming pupils, an accessible daily presence in the playground, and parents enthuse about how terrific and quick she is at dealing with any problems presented to her. Out of term time, she loves travel and cooking.

Academic matters: The junior school tracks performance in maths and English by InCAS assessments every term. One teacher plus access to a teaching assistant per class (which can range in size from 10-23). In infants, the chief focus is on the core subjects – reading, writing, spelling, maths.

Reception class is delightful; play is integrated with learning, with an outside area for growing vegetables, a mud kitchen, a shed 'garden centre' and 'farm shop'. Year 1 was hearing about zebra stripes being unique like a fingerprint, when we visited. One older infant class was learning about oceans, another about fractions (by doling out marshmallows).

In juniors, a maths and English core are blended with an integrated curriculum of science, computing, languages (French from reception to year 5 and German in year 6). The juniors were learning about the earth's extremes or imagining plot lines for their own storybook. Music is part of the curriculum, aesthetically evidenced by rows of pink trombones and blue ukuleles. Art and drama are timetabled in year 6. As in the senior school, cross-curricular themes stimulate thought: on the topic of chocolate, science explored 'changing states', geography the origin of the cocoa bean. STEM week was centred around Heath Robinson, with pupils gathering junk and building fabulous contraptions.

Parents spoke glowingly about the familial atmosphere. True, there were a few (barely discernible through the wall of loyalty) murmurings about the 'really able' not being stretched, but they felt that change was in the air, with children being invited to participate in groups where they had chance to excel. Those needing extra support can receive additional tuition solo or in small groups. Parents of dyslexic children were effusive about their achievements.

The confident year 6 pupils we spoke to were brimming with happiness and keen to join the senior school; one wanted to be a zoologist, another a dentist, another a barrister. One bright spark said she wanted to create a small idea which made a big difference and alluded to the mobile phone revolution. Wonderful stuff.

So, to the senior school. It's fair to say that pre-Helen Jeys the local perception of the senior school was that while lovely, academic stretching was not necessarily a driving force. (Parents indicated tutoring tended to fill teaching gaps.) This is now all changed; she has introduced new rigorous systems tracking academic progress with targets for each pupil. Parents welcomed this and recognised the bar was carefully but firmly being raised academically. Everyone takes at least one language to GCSE, with French, Spanish, Latin and German available. iPads are used in lessons to enrich learning; the head sees technology as paving the way for increased interest in STEM subjects (in biology, for example, girls can see cells illuminated). In 2018 at GCSE, 41 per cent of grades were A*/A. At A level, 39 A*/A grades.

The staff we spoke to were eloquent and enthusiastic. Some in leadership roles were relatively new, suggesting the head is taking a tight, dynamic team forwards to help make this school take flight.

The learning enhancement department has lots of experience with dyslexia and dyspraxia. It carries out assessments in house and puts in place structured programmes for the 70+ pupils with SEN. The head was emphatic that providing the strategies are in place, issues like dyslexia should never be a barrier. Parents we spoke to with dyslexic children were more than happy. Extra support for all pupils is always available; one sixth former struggling with a challenging topic said she had received one-to-one sessions which had been transformative.

Games, options, the arts: Great emphasis is placed on the extracurricular; wisely, the head takes the view that a lot of problems can be eliminated if girls are kept occupied. Plenty of opportunities to listen to inspiring speakers, some of whom are alumnae, such as a lecturer in neuropharmacology at St George's, London. Building the alumnae association is a core project; the head hopes they will be able to give advice and mentoring. A mention of the great theatre director, Marianne Elliott (War Horse and The Curious Incident of the dog in the Night Time), leapt out of the school magazine as an inspiring example. Lauren Child and Beth Tweddle recently visited the school.

The head considers sport a confidence-building tool for girls to deal with setbacks and one million smackers has been sunk into new sporting facilities: a new fitness suite, a climbing wall and a new dance floor among others. The school was a recent finalist in the national netball tournament and parents mentioned a new dynamism had taken root: team tours and Saturday fixtures. Those not so keen on team sports can test themselves on the climbing walls or in the gym. The junior school shares the senior school facilities and they play the usual sports – tennis, hockey, netball, rounders, football – with some less usual options: a fencing course, trampolining, zumba.

Lots of great clubs: coding, drones, engineering, gardening, with Mandarin and French clubs too in the junior school. A panoply of musical possibilities in junior and senior schools: choirs, orchestras, a showband. Drama and dance opportunities are plentiful; The Bacchae was the senior school's recent and ambitious play, set in a modern day music festival, complete with wellies and sleeping bags. It's a nice balance: a serious play every other year, in between something more altogether more West End in flavour (2018: Beauty and the Beast). Year, 6, meanwhile, recently performed the Lion King.

The school enters pupils into an array of competitions to broaden horizons: Model United Nations; GCHQ on coding and cryptography; linguistics Olympiad; national biology challenge, bar mock trial competition and many more. Pupils recently got through to the regional finals of the UK Maths Challenge, with one pupil invited to the UKMT summer school. They were runners up in the National Big Bang Engineering Competition and recent winners of the Steve Nash Memorial Award for innovation in engineering (designing a huge playground clock for special needs education). One parent alluded to a fantastic careers evenings where lawyers, accountants, doctors gather and said girls are encouraged to think widely.

Pupils said they felt the school fostered leadership skills and saw perseverance as a crucial facet in this. (One girl, referring to her public speaking team's naively enthusiastic decision to do their competition speeches entirely in rhyme, proudly confessed the actuality required pure slog.) Juniors can enter the Youth Speaks competition and LAMDA exams; parents felt that reading aloud and learning speeches was great for building confidence.

Lots of trips on the horizon: Iceland, Madrid, Washington DC and New York.

Background and atmosphere: Founded in 1999 from the merging of Mount Carmel RC convent school on the present site and the Anglican St Hilary's run by the Woodard Corporation from the south end of the village. Now describes itself as an ecumenical unified Christian school.

The junior school is light, bright and vibrant. Celebration boards highlight achievements from creative writing to gymnastics. There is a lovely adventure playground and lots of Astroturf. A great cafeteria with healthy food and a grown up feel is a good touch. Apparently the children moan about it but parents were very happy.

Modernity and vibrancy are common denominators in the senior school. High up windows and a building flooded with light. Pupils said the school 'looked better' since Helen Jeys swept into town; a sense of community pulses through the corridors, a stronger connection with the school's heritage. The art on the walls, the photographs of trips are all aimed at reinforcing the spectrum of possibility on offer to the girls. Intelligent department displays; the English department's 'Who will I read next?', a web authors and novels, was terrific. The maths rooms had blackboards with calculations scrawled over them in different coloured chalk, illuminating the beauty of maths.

The library and IT rooms had a studious air and a quiet buzz. Pupils look smart; the navy blue uniform is strict and Helen Jeys is a stickler for skirt lengths (hurray for that!).

Pastoral care, well-being and discipline: Every parent spoke about the nurturing atmosphere at the junior school. Topics like friendship are discussed in assemblies and pupils seemed to have a very mature understanding about cyber-bullying. Teachers were there if you felt anxious, they said, and felt happy to approach them. A mindfulness programme consists of 'myHappymind' and 'Paws b' curriculum, and if playground politics runs amok, there's always the Orange Juice Club, a place to discuss worries.

The pastoral is at the centre of everything in the senior school too. With her experience in her previous role at Manchester High, Helen Jeys knows just how beneficial a nurturing environment can be in raising academic standards. Alderley Girls has always been strong pastorally – parents described it as exceptional – but her philosophy is proactivity before reactivity. She has introduced a SHARP system (student help advice reporting page), and a website where pupils can register concerns about themselves and other pupils (not eating or feeling low). The teachers can then keep a surreptitious eye out. The online mental health section gets lots of hits. Teachers can see what's being accessed and gear assembly topics around problematic issues.

The head recently went on local BBC radio to talk about measures the school is taking to prepare girls for life ahead, including mindfulness practice and learning about the neurology of the brain. Parents loved the pupils' wellness day, its focus on healthy eating and relaxation. One parent was very impressed that after her child had lost weight due to an innocent medical reason, the school had been immediately alert to the change. Parents said that since Helen, if they mentioned any areas of disquiet (one parent was concerned her daughter, with dyslexia, lacked confidence in one particular subject) it would immediately be actioned and sorted.

The sixth form pupils we met were confident, secure and talked openly about good teacher relationships and a sense of sisterhood. One girl discussed the counselling she had received for her shyness with no trace of self-consciousness.

A deputy head oversees pastoral care: there is a full pastoral team, peer mentors, a school nurse and the chaplain. Assemblies discuss bullying and mental health; Lenny, the chaplain, regularly tackles these topics. (The school embraces all faiths but in line with its Christian foundation, the chaplain supplies an extra layer of support.)

The school's phone policy is terrific: the girls hand them in each morning and receive them back at the end of the day. Wifi for all devices is turned off over lunch, so they have to talk, think, observe.

Pupils are listened to: student council meetings have importance and head sees smaller discussion groups of girls. At the time of our visit, new online work planners were being tested by a pupil focus group. The process for voting in a new head girl is rigorous and taken very seriously. At the last Celebration Evening, the girls did the presenting; a subtle way of introducing them to leadership, one parent felt.

Pupils and parents: Pupils come from local Wilmslow, Altrincham, Prestbury, Knutsford, Hale, Bowdon, Macclesfield and further afield. There is a broad highway of communication between staff and parents; an open door policy, half termly reports, parents' evenings, 'consultations' and coffee mornings.

Entrance: Most enter the junior school as early years pupils without assessment. Those entering from year 3 have a short assessment in maths and English.

Virtually all junior school pupils move up to the senior school; teachers say they 'take it in their stride'. One parent felt – and she perceived this as a positive – that there was now a sense of uncertainty around the 11+ exam as to whether all pupils would 'get through', which she thought was indicative of greater emphasis on the academic. Nearly half of year 7 comes from outside, the rest from the junior school; 11+ papers in English and maths.

Exit: Around 40 per cent leaves post-GCSE. Majority to northern universities to study eg medical biochemistry at Leeds or design engineering at Manchester Met, with other courses in 2018 including professional dance and musical theatre at Greenwich, real estate management at Oxford Brookes and international relations at Nottingham.

Money matters: Usual reductions for siblings. Scholarships available in the senior school for girls who excel academically and/or in music, performing arts, art and sport.

Remarks: Whatever you think you know about this school, think again. Its fusion of increased emphasis on the academic combined with a stellar pastoral system is going to make it a winner. If you want your daughter to be intellectually curious and fulfil her academic potential but without any attendant hothouse pressures, this is just the place.

Altrincham Grammar School for Boys

Marlborough Road, Bowdon, Altrincham, Cheshire WA14 2RS

Ages 11–18 **Pupils** 1,298 **Sixth form** 346

01619 280858
www.agsb.co.uk

Headmaster: Since September 2018, Graeme Wright, previously senior deputy headmaster at Victoria College, Jersey. Degree in history from Liverpool and qualified as a teacher at Manchester. Before taking up teaching, he served in the Royal Marines for seven years, where he took part in operational tours of Northern Ireland and the former Yugoslavia. He has also taught at Liverpool College, King's School, Macclesfield and Trent College, Nottingham.

Previous head Tim Gartside is now executive head of the multi-academy trust.

Academic matters: Highly selective, it's no surprise that results are excellent but it's also outstanding for value-added at A level, clear evidence of some very good work going on. Most boys take 12 GCSEs; it's a heavy load but the thinking behind it is to deter boys from dropping subjects too early, thereby allowing them then to consider the widest possible range of options for A level. The head hints that the downside of this approach is that they probably lose out on a percentage of As and A*s as a result of extending the GCSE workload, but with 78 per cent A*-A/9-7s in 2018, it's probably a moot point. The system clearly works because at A level in 2018 an impressive 59 per cent of grades were A*/A. The range of options at A level is narrower, with a keen focus on trad subjects.

There are five dedicated IT suites with additional help on hand from undergraduates from Manchester University. Maths seems to dominate thinking, it's a third of the entrance exam and there are even maths prefects here – the wiz kids willing and able to assist with any tough assignments ('or even long division,' chipped in a younger boy) as and when necessary; strong in science, as evidenced by exam results with triple science for all the norm; history, geography and geology are also very popular. No shortage of linguists either, beginning with two languages in year 7, choosing from French, German and Spanish; these then continue into year 8 though one can be dropped in favour of either Latin or Chinese. MFL exchanges take place annually with partner schools in France, Germany and Spain; immersion courses in China, Russia and the Middle East have taken intrepid boys and staff to far flung destinations, as have the school's links with the Apeejay schools in Delhi, India. For boys who are super-keen or super-able when it comes to languages there are after school classes in Mandarin Chinese, Spanish, Italian, Japanese and Arabic, and if you're a parent or simply someone who lives locally, then you too can join these classes. The school's own prospectus offers up a masterclass in persuading boys to take up languages: 'If have you've ever scoffed at Ronaldo's grasp of English, Joey Barton's French or felt puzzled over Messi's Spanish..' Brilliant.

Heartfelt praise from the boys for the school SENCo who works alongside enthusiastic and knowledgeable teaching assistants. Boys tell us they are supported not only in their learning but also in managing and supporting the occasional health issue such as diabetes.

Games, options, the arts: Sporting facilities are superb, and couple that with some of the most enthusiastic PE teachers we've ever met. Numerous pitches (Astro and grass), a large multi-functional sports hall, well equipped fitness suite. There's even a coffee shop. It's very refreshing to hear staff elucidating on their healthy sport-for-all approach: it's all about breadth and finding something that works for everyone and they can proudly boast of top results in minority sports such as table tennis and badminton – you don't have to play for the first XV rugby team to be a hero here. The boys are proud of their sporting prowess; when asked who are the toughest schools to play against they claim: 'We can pretty much take on anyone in football and rugby; the only ones who might threaten us are a few random, obscure private schools where the players are all steak-heads...' – a veiled hint for more protein in school lunches, perhaps? The extracurricular sport, including yoga, widens the range even further, and if ultimate frisbee is your thing, then this may just be the school for you. A fiercely contested rowing competition – that's rowing machines, we're not on the Thames here – brought out the heroes amongst staff and pupils alike.

It's cool to be good at music here; everyone in years 7/8 learns a musical instrument and many continue throughout their school career. A dedicated music IT suite contains 19 iMacs with professional sequencing and publishing software; there's also a well-equipped keyboard suite; six practice rooms each with a piano and amplifier with MP3 connectivity and a large rehearsal area containing enough percussion instruments to make a serious amount of noise. A range of ensembles include choirs, orchestras, wind, jazz and swing bands and it would be a challenge to find an instrument not taught by visiting peripatetic teachers. There's even a barber shop choir and a staff choir. One of the pupils runs a guitar club and there are music mentors for those who are serious about the subject.

Superb artwork on display around the school, much talent in evidence; design technology is impressive with all the necessary kit, including laser cutters, to boost jeopardy and excite and challenge the boys with some real hands-on skills and learning.

There's not much drama on offer in lower school, much to the chagrin of some of the younger boys who have happy memories of their primary school productions, but staff are aware and it may happen, though they might struggle to fit it in to their extremely busy timetable. A number of the older boys are working on LAMDA qualifications and they take the lead roles in the school's annual drama production, with expert training from a TV and film actress in aspects of voice and movement.

Societies and clubs are plentiful; take your pick from Amnesty International, Christian society, Duke of Edinburgh Award, Hindu society, ICT, Islamic society, public speaking & debating, robotic club, scheme film club, science club, website design and Young Enterprise. The school chess club dates back to 1912.

Background and atmosphere: The Altrincham County High School for Boys, as it was originally known, was founded in 1912. The original distinctively decorated red-brick building still forms the central block of the school; numerous additions over the years have culminated in an imposing physics centre opened by Professor Brian Cox in 2014.

Located just outside the town centre, the school is bang on the railway line with Hale station just 400 metres away and half a mile to the Altrincham tram stop. No need for school buses here, public transport is excellent and, helpfully, comes from all directions. Too many boarded up shops in the town centre, which seems at odds with the large expensive properties on the school's doorstep; what a difference a mile makes. Bags of history telling the story of this long-established school, and the Old Altrinchamanians Society meets annually to regale success stories. Parts of the old building feel a little austere with its wood panelling and tiled walls, but the boys genuinely don't notice or feel it and the younger ones remark on the 'friendly feel' and seem to thrive in this competitive, rigorous environment.

The cover of a recent annual school review depicts a striking cartoon of a schoolboy ripping open his shirt to reveal a superhero vest bearing the school logo, and inside the cover are the names of the heroes of the year, both in and out of school. Definitely a school for boys, it's written right through the place like Blackpool through a stick of rock, exuding masculinity from every pore..there's lots of wood and tiling in the original building alongside portraits of war heroes – old boys and former masters are decorated with poppies for remembrance. It's a place that recognises and remembers its heroes..

Pastoral care, well-being and discipline: 'I've always been a friendly, outgoing chap,' said the head boy who, along with his fellow prefects, plays a central role in the day-to-day running of the school. They, along with staff, are visible around the school site at breaktimes and lunchtimes, keeping an eye on the well-being of pupils. 'Bullying is rare,' they tell us, as is fighting, the older boys appearing supportive of the younger ones and keen to keep the peace. Pupil mentors from year 10 upwards work with younger pupils advising on academic or pastoral matters. Pupils whose attainment or effort is not up to expectations will be monitored closely – 'there's a big difference in the level of support for those who are struggling with their work and those who simply can't be bothered,' the boys tell us.

A

A yellow card system keeps everyone in check and sanctions are tangible, with litter-picking being one option for those who fail to toe the line. Plenty of recognition and commendations for excellent work and/or effort with praise through postcards home to parents. Usual rules re phones – you can carry it but it has to be off, and disrespecting teachers is, say the boys, 'a big no-no'. They acknowledge the presence of a small number of smokers amongst the older boys who disappear from the premises at lunchtime to head for a nearby alley (the teachers are apparently in a different alley); they know they're there but they keep an eye. Typically very conscious of sticking to the rule book, for the boys it's all about fairness and a sense of justice; they know where they stand and they prefer it that way.

Food, they tell us, is 'authentic, nutritious and ethically sourced', just a shame about the small portions.. 'bring your own if you have a big appetite,' say the boys. They would also like 'more space in the dining hall please', though year 10 and 11s have their own space in the sports hall coffee shop and sixth formers have the option of eating in the sixth form centre, which has a coffee bar with leather sofas and the lingering aroma of toast.

Pupils and parents: The school has undoubtedly changed over the years, particularly in respect of its ethnic mix, reflective of a wider area demographic. A third come from beyond the local area, bringing a good school mix from Cheshire and central Manchester. 'Don't use tutors to help your son pass the entrance exam,' say parents, adding, 'if they are able they will pass, if not, it could be a miserable experience for them.' One parent of a clearly bright boy chose this school because 'he needed to be pushed' and commented on the fact that the school is especially 'well-organised when it comes to supporting/preparing for exams'.

Pupils are a bright, articulate and enormously likeable bunch – no arrogance but plenty of ambition. Very happy to chat and they clearly feel lucky to be here, countering our suggestion that 'the perfect school doesn't exist' with a polite but firm 'I beg to differ – this school is perfect for me'. They are well turned-out too, no long hair, no facial hair, no piercings, shirts in, ties tied, all they need is a smidgen of shoe polish and they'd rival Sandhurst. For sixth formers it's a business wear dress code; most wear suits.

Entrance: Up to 70 feeder schools, Altrincham Prep probably the largest. Priority for catchment is WA13, 14 and 15, then Trafford LA addresses in M33. Entrance exam on the second Saturday in September for places in year 7, with application made directly to the school by late July of year 5. There are a small number of places available for sixth form applicants each year; entrance requires 48 GCSE points including three grade 7s or better.

Exit: A very small number leave post GCSE to join co-ed or sixth forms offering less trad subjects; by far the majority stay put. Good number to Oxbridge each year, 17 in 2018, plus 16 medics/dentists; most to Russell Group universities, a few with gap years and/or work placements. Former pupils include Graham Brady MP, two members of the Stone Roses band, cricketer Paul Allot and educationalist Dylan Wiliam.

Remarks: An article in the Sunday Times on the best places to live in Britain described Altrincham as the number one place for schools – and AGSB is one of the reasons why. The school motto translates as Work Conquers All and it's as though these boys are on a mission to prove that. They seem super-competitive in all things, yet it appears friendly and good-humoured with plenty of banter. They've got the message, they're here to work and play hard, and they do.

Altrincham Grammar School for Girls

Cavendish Road, Bowdon, Altrincham, Cheshire WA14 2NL

Ages 11–18 **Pupils** 1,352 **Sixth form** 353

01619 125912
www.aggs.trafford.sch.uk

Executive headteacher: Since 2014, Stephanie Gill (40s), born here in the north west, has two daughters. Formerly deputy head at West Kirby Grammar on the Wirral (previous pupil); has experience of both state and independent school sectors. Read natural sciences at Cambridge, though describes herself as a mathematician. Had a spell working in the civil service 'just to check' before moving into education. Relaxes with Argentinean tango and salsa dancing. Bright, blonde and bold, she exudes a quiet yet determined ambition for the girls in her care; she has a lot of high expectations to manage here, but seems unfazed by the challenge. Describing her staff as 'able and committed' – there is nowhere to hide with plenty of school-led high quality professional development going on in this dynamic school.

Academic matters: Some 1,000 apply for 174 places each year so yes, it is very selective, having a large pond in which to fish. The expectation is nine GCSEs, which is the 'right' number they tell us, followed by a choice of 20 A levels from which most will choose four in year 12. In 2018, at GCSE, 83 per cent A*-A/7-9 grades. Equally impressive at A level; 90 per cent A*/B grades and 66 per cent A*/A grades. Plenty of rigour here. The girls drive themselves and each other quite hard, foot to the floor most of the time. There is no setting in any subject anywhere. Maths is important, as is science, with half taking separate sciences at GCSE and biology, chemistry and maths leading the field at A level. While independent study is encouraged and supported, school also acknowledges many girls prefer a cooperative learning style – hence plenty of group work.

A choice of two languages from French, German and Spanish at key stage 3 before choosing one language as core and one other as optional in key stage 4. The school was awarded the British Council's prestigious International School Award for 2015-18 and they are proud of their links with other schools and institutions across five continents. There is a busy and flourishing English department with a year 7 and 8 creative café writing club, literary film club, KS3 blog, mentoring clubs, the sixth form reading group, English Society and Oxbridge preparation. Regular visits to the theatre also encouraged and there's a stimulating programme of visits from outside speakers including young fiction writers and lecturers from prestigious universities to deliver workshops for sixth formers. The range of subjects is very traditional with the possible exception of psychology, a popular choice at A level. The EPQ is optional in year 13 but most see it as useful preparation for university or even a valid add-on if entering straight into a career.

Few with learning difficulties/disabilities – mostly mild dyslexia. In-class support for statemented pupils; mild physical disabilities can be accommodated. The gifted and talented blog is fascinating for those who wish to take their thinking a little further and deeper – consider maths, Japanese fashion: 'Do you realise you are wearing a MATHS equation at this very moment in time....?' is the opener, or try rapping and learning numbers in Japanese, apparently a great way to get tired muscles moving on cold, frosty mornings. Then when the music died down, the girls got to work putting their new-found knowledge to work on a Japanese book marker (with a bit of macramé thrown in); or even combining science and Japanese in the building of bee-houses (yes, we were intrigued as well...). If Elizabethan English is more your thing, try the mouth-watering Shakespeare takeaway: 'I'll have a stuffed pig's bladder with onions and a side order of...gooseberry foole please, and make it snappy!' And all this before the school day even starts...

Games, options, the arts: While there are heaps of sport on offer, a new sports hall remains high on the wish list for both girls and parents. PE specialists lead national innovation pilots and the school (Youth Sports Trust member) believes that 'health and exercise go hand in hand with academic achievement'. Netball and hockey seem to dominate: there are six netball courts and two Astroturf hockey pitches with matches for A and B teams on Saturdays. The range on offer is wide, on and off curriculum, and includes badminton (at Altrincham Leisure Centre), dance, athletics, tennis, rounders, cross-country running, cricket, rugby, taekwondo and football, so hopefully something for (almost) everyone. Plenty of sporting success locally, regionally and nationally.

Music is strong and plays a very powerful role here with numerous concerts each term. On alternate years there is a music tour at the end of the summer term; destinations have ranged from Durham cathedral to China. Eighteen ensembles and choirs meet weekly and include a number of student-led groups – try Quakapella for something different... Art, design and textiles are all evident around school, hugely impressive work; standards are very high with some inspirational teaching going on. There is lots to inspire aspiring drama queens, both on and off curriculum, with ample theatre visits.

The extracurricular range on offer is vast; some of the more unusual activities to tempt you include the youth action group, politics society, street dance crew, Indian dance club, worldwide quiz, Japanese, Chinese, Italian, Latin, jewellery club, medical society, LGBT alliance, pro-share investor challenge and, for Harry Potter aficionados, Quidditch. Add to those DofE and all the usual clubs and societies you might expect and it's a wonder they ever make it home.

Trips and excursions are many and varied, but no lightweight jollies; it's all about learning and 'opportunities to develop'. Take, for example, the keen scientists who went to CERN in Geneva and the Florida Space Centre and linguists actively involved in Comenius projects. We spoke to one parent whose daughter spent a month in Ecuador helping in a local village project – including a spell in the jungle. For sporty types there are netball and hockey trips to Barcelona and ski trips to California.

Background and atmosphere: You'll find the impressive gateway to the school in the upmarket, leafy residential area of Bowdon. Don't even bother trying to park on site; no spaces and possible dressing down if you risk illicit parking. The school reception is very smart, light and bright with chrome fittings giving it an almost corporate feel, echoed in the conference and training facility. But it's a smorgasbord of buildings that are now home to the biggest girls' grammar school in England. As it is a split site, one parent hankered after a footbridge until her daughter pointed out that crossing this road afforded the girls the opportunity to become safer road-users. The daughter was quite right, of course, and it's not an especially busy road; there is a crossing, and the girls (and staff) all look out for one another.

It all began in the late 19th century when Cheshire County Education Authority acquired Bowdon Lodge, a substantial but derelict local landmark. Much vociferous opposition because the potential school might lower the 'tone' of the neighbourhood. In 1910 the building finally opened its doors to 60 boys and girls under the care of eight members of staff. The Education Act of 1944 saw the school become selective and 30 years later it became Altrincham Grammar School for Girls. In 2011, AGGS was one of the first schools to be awarded national teaching school status and during that year the new Breeze Hill facility was opened. The building incorporates an ICT suite, more classrooms and a teacher training facility. Also in 2011 AGGS became the lead sponsor school within The Bright Futures Educational Trust, a multi-academy educational trust. However, the troubled trust has since been served financial notices to improve or face closure.

Pastoral care, well-being and discipline: They take their anti-bullying policy seriously with anti-bullying ambassadors (who have their own blog and Twitter account). 'It's not a major problem,' say the girls, whilst admitting that kids in general 'can be cruel to each other sometimes'. Detentions serve as effective sanctions for those who don't play the game but most do and they wear their much-decorated school blazers with pride – lots of lapel badges in evidence for academic and sporting success as well as additional leadership roles in school. The head tells us that 'it's fine to be different here – ok, in fact, to be geeky'. The school has adopted mindfulness as an approach to managing stress and pressure and there are clear targets based around resilience. Plenty of discussion around school on pastoral care, support and well-being, acknowledging the 'ups and downs of teenage girls'.

Pupils and parents: There are a good few appeals each year, unsurprising considering the competition for places and school expects an increase in the number of pupil premium students. Technically it is an eight mile catchment area, but realistically probably more like 5.5 miles most years. School reflects the ethnically diverse population of this very popular local authority with around 39 per cent ethnic minority on roll. The academic success of the school is well-documented but the 'cultural diversity and spirit of tolerance' are also high on parents' priorities here, as is the 'mutual respect between staff and pupils'. Parents mostly live locally and feel the pressure at entrance exam time: 'it was nerve-wracking for parents'. They also advise that prospective parents: 'think carefully about their child's ability to thrive in a strongly academic school'. Most parents are delighted with the level and frequency of communication from school, for a small few it's a little heavy on the inbox.

Pupils are polite, articulate and hardworking; there's always a target to hit, a challenge to take on. Displaying a gritty northern determination to succeed, they are aware of high expectations, from both home and school, and the need to manage and keep up with the rigour. They are quite a political bunch, encouraged to share their views with mock referendums and a presence on the youth parliament. Uniform is navy, green and yellow, short skirts, long jumpers and blazers, with business attire for sixth form. Former pupils include Helen Czerski, physicist, oceanographer and broadcaster.

Entrance: Entrance exam (verbal and non-verbal reasoning plus maths) held in September each year; apply to the school between April and June of year 5 for a place in year 7. Now offers 10 priority places for students on pupil premium. Up to 50 feeder schools including Bowdon Prep, Withington and Manchester High plus a large number of maintained primaries. High entry requirements for sixth form: at least four 7s and two 6s, with 6+ for English and maths.

Exit: Nearly all stay on for sixth form – 80 per cent in 2018. Vast majority (95 per cent) straight to university, mainly Russell Group (northern universities particularly popular). Good Oxbridge numbers most years (five in 2018; down on previous

A

year's 11) and good number of medics (17) plus seven dentists and one vet. Handful to high level apprenticeships (eg IBM) or art foundation courses.

Remarks: The Latin motto translates as 'bravely, faithfully, cheerfully'. It may not be the most accurate description of your average teenage girl but at least AGGS students know what their school motto is and try their best to go with it. It's no walk in the park here but it certainly appears to be a happy and busy place, with bright, ambitious girls challenged and supported in equal measure by a very strong team of staff.

Altrincham Preparatory School

Marlborough Road, Bowdon, Altrincham, Cheshire WA14 2RR

Ages 2–11 **Pupils** 330

Fees: £6,615 – £8,640 pa

01619 283366
www.altprep.co.uk

Head master: Since September 2018, Andrew Whittaker BEd FCTT.

Entrance: Not selective at 3+ and 4+; higher up, prospective candidates spend a day at the school.

Exit: The majority to Altrincham Grammar School for Boys, a representative sample to other local state or independent grammars, most notably The Manchester Grammar School, plus Sale Grammar, Cheadle Hulme, King's School Macclesfield and Stockport Grammar.

Remarks: Although the school isn't selective, it is carefully and deliberately selected by parents who put their sons here for a reason. Yes, they buy into the ethos but they are also here, crucially, as a major and proven entry point to the school right across the road – Altrincham Grammar School for Boys. The big brother over the road, although no direct relation (they are very distinct and separate entities), offers what parents consider to be a welcome fee break in the sandwich between prep and uni. It is a credit to this school that, despite not being selective on entry, they still manage to get these boys through the rigour of the 11+ exam into an excellent and highly oversubscribed state grammar school.

The school is a limited company; governors are both shareholders and directors, with strong family links back to the 1936 founders. Split between two sites – one for the younger boys (nursery to year 2) set in two older refurbished buildings, and one for the older boys (years 3 to 6) in an open, spacious site in very impressive brick-built modern buildings. Both sites offer attractive, well-managed areas for learning and playing in an upmarket residential area of Altrincham, a short drive from the town centre, the wealthy, leafy suburbs of Bowdon and Hale close by. The younger ones enjoy a delightful spacious play area, mainly grassed plus soft surface play space, and the continuous provision across indoor and outdoor space means that good use is made of the whole setting.

Pre-schoolers, at the time of our visit, were enjoying the toys and bikes in the sunny gardens. 'Lots of nurturing,' say parents, with a teaching assistant 'never too far away to offer a few words of encouragement and a little hug if needed'. Maroon and grey uniforms for all with slight age-appropriate variations in style and oodles of sports kit for the older ones.

This boy-centric school exudes energy and enthusiasm – plenty of competition in everything from sport to reading and times tables. The youngest learn phonics with actions (no sitting still here), and whilst admittedly the boys gravitate to non-fiction as their default choice for reading books, fiction choices are carefully selected to include dungeons and dragons, the macabre and ghost stories a-plenty. An engagement with fiction is a must according to the school as a tool in 'promoting civilised behaviour' from which they can learn a great deal about self and others. Yes, your writing can be about sport if you so wish, but no gender excuses for bad handwriting – some fabulous examples on display and from an early age too. Maths is very strong here, the boys are super-keen, but in maths, as in all other subjects, there is no setting, no streaming, no pigeonholing and likewise no limited expectations. Desks for the older boys, tables for the younger ones and plenty of interaction between the boys and their teachers. Currently two parallel classes per year group; form teachers have a pastoral role alongside teaching the core curriculum; specialist staff for French, music, art, design technology and sport. School houses (names after World War II heroes) add extra fizz and competition to school events, house points are gained and guarded by the boys with real fervour. Minus points, far less popular and, to be fair, far less prevalent, are doled out for bad behaviour, shouting out in class and for 'failing to put your name on your homework or test papers,' according to the boys. The boys, typically, have a keen sense of fairness; they value their role on the school council, assessing areas of school life from school rules to the improvement of school lunches ('we're currently working on the chicken nuggets'). The school has its own chef and the food is good; 'chips could be better,' say the boys, presumably noting that they aren't yet triple-cooked here. They bring their own healthy snacks for break time.

Classrooms are bright, well-equipped and attractive. Generous specialist teaching areas for non-core subjects and terrific sports facilities include all-weather hockey pitches (off-site) and football, rugby, cricket and tennis on-site. It would be hard to find a primary or even prep school that could match their sporting facilities, so no surprise that they are leading the IAPS field nationally at hockey and reaching the finals in a range of other sports. Of course this high sporting achievement may come at a slight cost, with one or two mutters from parents about those with plenty of enthusiasm but less ability 'frequently being left out', though this appears to contradict the school's philosophy that all boys will represent the school at some point during their time at APS. There are adventure playgrounds on both school sites for fun and games during breaks. Music is very strong here; everyone plays the recorder, there are senior and junior choirs, an orchestra, guitar, brass and string groups and peripatetics working alongside to offer individual tuition in a wide range of other instruments. There are various plays, musicals and concerts throughout the year for proud parents. As a non-denominational school with an ethnic mix (as befits the local demographic), there is no proselytising but the school is comfortable enough in its own skin to mix the singing of hymns in assembly with the teaching and appreciation of all other faiths. SEN support is offered where necessary, though school shies away from diagnoses and labelling, adopting an approach of teaching strategies to cope rather than 'allowing labels to become excuses'. School trips, home and away, are popular, the Lake District and France being favourites.

Apart from the occasional grumble about homework, the boys are a happy bunch. They describe the teachers as 'friendly' and whilst they are undoubtedly kept very busy, that's exactly the way they like it. They know the rules and mostly play by them, proud of their blazer lapel badges in recognition of sporting and academic achievements. They also note that working hard and 'even holding doors open for people' is noticed and appreciated, which gives everyone, regardless of ability, a shot at public praise and appreciation. They are well-mannered, happy to chat (about anything) and yet businesslike in their approach to getting the job done in terms of working towards the next step on their educational ladder. No phones allowed, though if you walk to and from school you can bring a phone, but it's left in the school office for the day.

Parents describe 'an amazingly calm and welcoming atmosphere; it was a bit like house-hunting when you walk into a property and you know it's "the one" – we walked down the school drive..turned to each other and said "yes, this is the school for our son".' The advice from current parents is to join in with Parent Society activities – they are 'great fun and a fantastic way to meet other parents.'

Staff are a mix of long-standing individuals and newer blood. Much praise for staff from parents, including admin, support staff and the 'great PTA'. The school is very much serving the local population: parents are predominantly professionals; medics, accountants, company directors and lawyers much in evidence and, as ever, the school gate committee is strong. They like this suburban school that 'feels as though it is in a village', and whilst parking at the site for younger children can be a little problematic, they value the improved space, systems and facilities offered by the newer site as their sons grow, literally, into the bigger school. Staggered start and finish times and before and after-school care mean that parents can easily manage the drop-off and pick-up for younger and older sons at both sites.

'I could write a whole essay on why APS is a fantastic school,' said one parent. 'We have watched our son develop into a fine, confident, caring and intelligent young man from being a shy and timid 3 year old. He has always been happy at APS and they have prepared him well for the next big step to grammar school.'

Backwell School

Station Road, Backwell, Bristol BS48 3BX

Ages 11–18 **Pupils** 1,754 **Sixth form** 365

01275 463371
www.backwellschool.net

Headteacher: Since 2017, Jon Nunes (early 50s), having held the fort as interim head for 18 months and before that, deputy head and a member of staff in the history department for over 25 years. A graduate of Oxford, where he represented that august university at darts, and with a PGCE from Bristol, Mr Nunes has spent his entire career at Backwell, taking on increasing responsibilities along the way. A proper selection process preceded his appointment, which was greeted with enthusiasm.

Urbane and sharply dressed in suit and tie, Mr Nunes appeared confident and assured (but friendly) when he addressed the assembled group of nervous-looking year 6 children and their parents at the tour morning we attended. Backwell School joined the Lighthouse Schools MAT in 2018, and Mr Nunes is keen to 'maintain what is excellent about Backwell, while sharing good practice with [its] other schools'. Obviously Mr Nunes is well known to parents, but they are pleased to report that, in his new job, he is innovative, approachable and interested in parental opinion. He also keeps his ear to the ground with students by teaching a few hours each week, with the added benefit of keeping him 'relatively safe from the intervention of the urgent email, phone-call or knock on the office door'. Backwell is quite the family affair: Mr Nunes' wife teaches at the school, and his eldest daughter attends it. Any free time might find him reading for enjoyment or following sport, especially baseball, in memory of his late father, who was American.

B

Academic matters: Longstanding local reputation for excellence is borne out in latest results. At A level in 2018, 54 per cent of entries were graded A*/B, with a particularly good showing in French, creative writing, media, photography and further maths. At GCSE, 83 per cent of students gained grade 4 or above in English and maths, with over half achieving the English baccalaureate. Science results outstanding, with food tech and maths not far behind. Teaching struck us as traditional, with a French class not spared the rigour of good old-fashioned grammar, and history students undeterred by an IT malfunction as they looked at the political causes of the second world war. Maths is setted from the start, and all new students start either French and Spanish, good linguists being able to take up a second language in year 8. One parent felt her child had been 'forced into languages' in pursuit of the EBacc 'and spent three years doing something she did not want to do'.

Curriculum booklets contain hints and links to resources for homework and further study, setting a tone of academic endeavour. Key skills such as independence, creativity and team work are taught off-timetable in the first year on 'break-out days', an initiative popular with students, parents and teachers alike. A huge library includes a sixth form study area, where students worked quietly on laptops when we visited. At sixth form, the emphasis is on A levels (28 subjects available), but the Cambridge Technical Diploma and level 3 extended certificates in more vocational subjects are also offered for those preferring applied learning. Maths and English GCSE retakes, if necessary. The EPQ is expected to be done by all those doing three A levels.

Students with special needs are looked after by the educational support department. All newcomers are screened on entry into year 7, and anyone with a reading/spelling age of less than 10 is given extra help, either in tutor time or in targeted withdrawal from class; maths boosters also laid on. A 'return to learning' base helps youngsters who find managing mainstream school and lessons difficult. The emphasis is very much on inclusion and positive reinforcement for good behaviour.

Games, options, the arts: Sport/PE is compulsory right up to GCSE, whether a GCSE option or not, and is given five sessions per fortnight. Plenty on offer and not just ball sports, but there are firm lines of demarcation between girls' and boys' games: rugby for boys, netball for girls. Backwell has a fine sporting tradition and boys' rugby is particularly successful, locally (winners of North Somerset Rugby Cup in 2018) and on occasion nationally. Plenty of green space, some of which is set aside for younger students, includes a 1500m running track, but no Astro or all weather pitches, nor plans for any in the present financial climate. Students are lucky enough to be able to use neighbouring Backwell Leisure Centre for swimming and fitness.

Masses of clubs both at lunchtime and after school tempt joiners and surely provide something for everyone – from the physical (running) to the fun (Bang! The junk orchestra) and philosophical (mindfulness). School also lays on an enrichment week each June, part of which entails residential trips both here and abroad for certain year groups, and where there is no escaping the 'world famous Backwell fishing trip', where

B

sea/lake/river fishing are all laid on. Historians visit Berlin and linguists benefit from exchange programmes in France and Spain. Lots of music (gospel choir, ukulele for example) and musical theatre; Legally Blonde a recent and popular choice. Art and DT both strong too: we liked the examples of dystopian and fantasy art we saw on display. Keen student designers recently made a replica cockpit of the Bloodhound Supersonic Car, a project rescued from bankruptcy around the time we visited. A coveted Arkwright Scholarship was awarded to a Backwell girl in 2017.

Background and atmosphere: Tucked away down a lane in the pleasant village of Backwell, a few miles south west of Bristol, the school sits in the centre of its community, yet its size (over 1,700 strong) and reputation means it attracts families from miles around. Its original buildings date from its founding as a secondary modern in 1954 – and look like it: the excellent science results emerge despite their facilities, not because of them (school tells us two new labs are to be built in 2019). Later additions vary in aesthetic appeal: the newish maths block with its corrugated steel exterior and coloured glass roof is eye-catching, others less spectacular and utilitarian, scruffy in places, but in line for new windows. Open space between buildings mean a chance to oxygenate the brain – or get wet. The cashless canteen is strictly functional and puts through a huge number of students on staggered lunch breaks in as short a time as possible, offering bacon rolls and pizza on a 'grab & go' basis, among other fare. Outside tables take the strain off indoor space when the weather permits.

The atmosphere feels traditional but not stifling, purposeful but not pressured. Initiatives and info on mental health appreciated by parents, doubtless students too. Sixth formers are refreshingly involved in life lower down the school: some clubs eg Christian Union run by senior students, who also help and mentor younger ones with their studies, such as French. Students are placed in one of four houses with fine local names: Sedgemoor, Quantock, Mendip and Cotswold, with physical bases around the 'quad' including somewhere to assemble as a house, as well as providing a focus for friendly competition on the sports field and other arenas, and distinguished by coloured tabs on the ubiquitous polo shirt.

Pastoral care, well-being and discipline: The first port of call for any pastoral concerns is the student's tutor, who has links to the pastoral team. School places significant emphasis on mental health and well-being; a trained counsellor is in school two days per week and runs drop-in sessions. An active equalities group enjoys a high profile at school, where it's OK to discuss matters of faith/lack of it, sexuality/gender and so on with respect and openness. Parents report that any bullying is dealt with 'well and firmly', but one thought the school focused 'too much on results and too little on the interests of the child', on occasion. The need to crack the whip does not appear to raise its ugly head very often among the biddable flock at Backwell and the school takes pains to make its expectations clear in the home-school agreement. Mobile phone use during the day is forbidden.

Pupils and parents: Predominantly white, but school works hard to counter any lack of diversity by maintaining strong links with a school in Ethiopia and the Za Foundation from South Africa. Local families are content to have a school of this quality on the doorstep. The youngsters we met were open, candid and funny, and appeared to enjoy good relationships with other year groups, and to toe the line in terms of uniform (usual fare of black trousers/plaid skirts, sweaters, polo shirts) and flights of personal fancy with hair, piercings etc. Sixth formers are expected to 'dress in a way suitable for the working day'.

Entrance: At year 7, 270 sought-after places up for grabs, mainly available to children living within the designated long, narrow and rural 'first geographical area' with the village of Backwell at its centre. Applications go through the local authority of North Somerset, though the school handles admissions admin. At sixth form, 50 places for external candidates, who must satisfy the entrance requirements of five GCSEs at a grade 4 or above, to include English language. Ideally, hopefuls should have a grade 5 or 6 for any proposed A level choice.

Exit: Good retention rates into the thriving sixth form. More emphasis now placed on broader options than straight degree courses, eg apprenticeships, and specific information and guidance available for Russell Group applications and gap years. In 2018, five got Oxbridge places, plus three medics and a dentist; universities in the south west and Wales seem most popular. A modest roll-call of famous former students comprises a decent crop of young people making a success of careers in sport (notably cricket) and performing arts.

Money matters: Parents are asked for a voluntary contribution of £12 per year to prop up the school's budget. 'The number and scope of school trips make it expensive', claimed one mother, who then conceded that there exists a fair system of subsidising hardship cases. Active PTA – Backwell School Association – lays on social events and fundraising.

Remarks: Fortunate indeed are families with this school on their doorstep, combining academic endeavour with a rich extracurricular offering, both on and off site. The kind of place parents move to get their children into, and a credible counterweight to the independent schools of nearby Bristol.

Badminton Junior School

Linked with Badminton School

Westbury Road, Westbury-on-Trym, Bristol BS9 3BA

Ages 3–11 **Pupils** 137 **Boarders** From 9 years

Fees: Day £9,750 – £11,235; Boarding £21,840 – £24,945 pa

01179 055271
www.badmintonschool.co.uk

Head of Junior School: Since 2010, Emma Davies BA PGCE (40s). Brought up and educated in Wales (where she still lives) and maintaining her Welsh lilt to this day, Mrs Davies has taught in a variety of prep schools including one in Malaysia, most recently as deputy head at the junior part of Bristol Grammar. Her first degree is in English, but she admits to a love of history and runs the history club at school. Ms Davies exemplifies the lifelong learning the school aims to instil: she is doing a distance MEd in educational leadership and writing a children's book 'very slowly'. Interests outside work centre mainly on her family – she has two daughters at the school – and include indulging her love of history at museums and National Trust properties. Warm, very approachable, and has at last acted on parental concerns about SEND provision, now vastly improved.

Entrance: Non selective until year 3, though all are informally assessed during a taster day, partly to judge social skills and 'readiness to learn'. From year 3, more formal assessments in English, maths and non verbal reasoning

Exit: Ninety per cent to the senior school via exactly the same entrance exams as external candidates will sit. These appear to hold no terrors, as girls have been well prepared throughout their time at the school; end of year assessments (aka exams) take place from year 3.

Remarks: Nestling on the edge of the Badminton site, the junior school is certainly the senior school's little sister and firmly under its wing. Whilst it is non-selective before year 3, academic expectations are set out early: '..some misspelt words will inevitably occur in written work. Great store is however set by accurate spelling which does not come naturally to many,' says the handbook. As well as high rates of entry to the senior school, Sats results at the end of year 6 tell a remarkable story: against a nationally expected level 4, these girls are all achieving high level 5s and some level 6s in maths, partly as a result of very small classes, and perhaps partly from learning their times tables to the funkiest rap we have ever heard. French is taught from the off, and from years 3-6 girls also try out Spanish, German and Latin in rotation.

Younger girls are taught by their class teachers and expected to practice reading at home, but from year 3, subject teachers take over and there is formal prep every night. Moving between classes and having the right books and equipment demands much of these 7-8 year olds, and some parents we spoke to were very critical of the lack of support given to the less organised or mature. In fact we picked up considerable dissatisfaction from some about SEN provision generally, and the school's website is curiously evasive on the matter.

School offers the broad curriculum and facilities which parents opting for an independent education expect, with some kind of sport, PE or swimming every day, and timetabled drama and music. Girls try out a range of three musical instruments early on; bizarrely, the cello is the most popular choice for private lessons – about a third of girls take these – which take place in the school day at the senior school. (We heard a heartrending account of one little girl in tears because she could not remember the door code to the music school, so missed half her lesson and was in trouble all round.) Self-confidence is built by performing in concerts, plays and by the English Speaking Board exams, where poetry is learnt, delivered and discussed. Sport and exercise loom large – hurrah – but apparently only the best players are selected for teams, which tends to demotivate less skilled players.

We loved the way the bigger girls supported the littler ones: at the end of our visit, they were snuggled up on beanbags looking at books with year 6s. One little dot could not stop yawning at the end of her busy day; another could hardly be torn away from her riveting story to talk to us. Vertical tutor groups lie at the heart of these close relationships and are a feature of the school. A handful of boarders in the top two years.

Badminton Junior is a great choice for bright, organised and confident girls, where they will receive excellent opportunities in the classroom, on the pitch and on the platform. The diffident, disorganised, dyslexic, dyspraxic or ditsy should look elsewhere.

Badminton School

Linked with Badminton Junior School

Westbury Road, Westbury-on-Trym, Bristol BS9 3BA

Ages 11–18 **Pupils** 472 **Sixth form** 105 **Boarders** 172 full

Fees: Day £9,750 – £16,425; Boarding £21,840 – £37,575 pa

01179 055271
www.badmintonschool.co.uk

Headmistress: Since 2012, Rebecca Tear (40s) BSc MA PGCE. Her degree in chemistry from Exeter preceded a career in teaching science almost exclusively to girls, and which included other significant responsibilities eg head of sixth form and deputy head at Wycombe Abbey, taking in a masters in leadership in education along the way. An unequivocal believer in single sex education from her early teaching practice, where she saw how the less confident girls needed bringing out in lessons, she says, 'Teaching girls by themselves breaks down any preconceptions, barriers or stereotyping; when subjects don't acquire masculine or feminine connotations, girls tend to make more realistic personal choices.'

Somewhat jolly hockey sticks in manner – she strode across the drawing room, extending a hand and introducing herself as 'Bex' – we warmed to her no-nonsense and open personality; staff describe her as a real hit with the girls. For her part, Mrs Tear has made strenuous efforts to bring parents and guardians into school more: new ventures like the summer fair and fireworks night have been welcomed. 'I don't want the first time I meet a parent to be in a bad news situation', she says.

Married to another chemistry teacher, she has two young sons who doubtless counterbalance all those girls. Passions include outdoorsy things like running, ski-ing and cycling with her family, and she is a keen cook – though at home she regrets the lack of a lab technician to wash up for her.

Academic matters: Selective entry, rigorous exam preparation and small classes (averaging 14 until GCSE) all the way through the school make for stunning results, and a reputation as Bristol's most academic school. A level results in 2018 saw 56 per cent A*/A, with the majority of girls taking four subjects. At GCSE, 87 per cent A*-A/9-7 grades in 2018. Options are (unusually) not blocked, so virtually any subject combination is possible. SAT training also provided for those hoping to go to American universities.

Girls greatly encouraged to take on all manner of academic challenges outside school; one recently came in the top 50 of the intermediate maths Olympiad, and a few presented by invitation of CERN and the Institute of Physics at WOMAD in 2018. Everyone does English Speaking Board exams, which, for the year 8 class we visited, involved learning, reciting and discussing chunks of poetry – a Shakespeare sonnet in one case. Years 8 and 9 are also offered a 10 week STEM experience with engineering or manufacturing companies with Go4SET. Global Thinking Skills course for year 9 'which combines enhancing the girls' knowledge of the world they live in alongside developing their ability to think critically'. 'They push them, but not in any way too much,' said one mother, who also appreciated the way teachers go over work with individuals when they find it difficult.

SEN provision is modest – not much call for it here – and mostly delivered by 'flexible in-house support'. Weekly sessions at Bristol Dyslexia Centre to improve skills in English and maths are laid on for more severe cases: whilst some parents accept this, others resent the extra time expended, and the stigma associated with leaving the school by taxi, and feel that daily intervention would be a darn sight more use. More emphasis is given to extending the gifted and talented – a term the school avoids. EAL is also offered in school to support overseas girls.

Games, options, the arts: Games and sports are now exceedingly well catered for (Astro, tennis courts, netball courts, 25m pool, and since 2018 an eye-catching new sports hall incorporating cricket nets and climbing wall) on the school's site, unlike so many of Bristol's schools, whose playing fields are a bus ride away across the suspension bridge. Hockey, netball, tennis and swimming are the main sports, but an innovative range of activities including kickboxing and water polo means that no-one has an excuse to be idle. Badminton's riders have enjoyed past success too. Hockey and netball players are regularly selected for the county. One parent was unhappy that only top players were ever picked for teams, and that mediocre participants barely got a game; also that the (beautiful) pool was used very little by the girls 'because it was always being hired out'. The absence of swimming teams or even a swimming club is an oddity.

Artistic life flourishes too, with top notch music, drama and art. Much is rightly made of high calibre musicians (one to the Royal College on Saturdays, two to the National Children's Orchestra, several playing in city orchestras, a recent leaver in training for The Sixteen) and school is fortunate to perform in St George's Bristol, a national concert venue. Most girls learn one instrument if not two, and school is proud of the number and scope of ensembles it lays on for musicians of all standards and persuasions. New music building has enabled school to bring all of its music teaching and practice activities to a single location and created a new focus for the department. The building includes teaching and practice rooms, a new music library and a generous classroom for curricular music lessons. Drama reasonably prominent too, with six productions a year plus a staff pantomime, as well as collaborations with outside initiatives at local innovative theatre the Tobacco Factory and Garden Opera, recently as a chorus of urchins in Carmen. Several notable actresses are OBs: Clare Bloom, Phyllida Law and Rosamunde Pike.

Art is housed in a most appealing setting, where mannequins dressed in creations fit for a Milan catwalk grace the entrance. Textiles, ceramics, painting, digital media (aka photography) and all types of artistic endeavour go on here. Badminton girls gain places at prestigious colleges such as Central St Martins.

Boarding: From age 9 although there's only a handful of junior boarders. Boarders accommodated in three houses grouped by age – Bartlett houses girls from years 5-8, spanning both junior and senior schools. Sanderson is the newest build for the middle girls; sixth formers are separate. One parent reported a tendency to cliques among the girls, which she felt the school did little to address, and that it 'feels like a boarding school which day girls attend'; another felt that integration was fine.

Weekends fairly relaxed for those who stay in school: girls might be involved in sports or drama, off on a surfing trip, going out for a meal or to the theatre. As elsewhere boarders from abroad are required to have a guardian, but here they do so much more than that rather dry word suggests and are more like surrogate mums – we applaud this.

Background and atmosphere: Founded over 160 years ago, Badminton is older than most girls' schools of its type and was set up to provide the same educational opportunities for girls as their brothers enjoyed. That sense of academic seriousness, courage, confidence and an international outlook still prevail – girls here tackle any academic challenge head-on. Originally sited in Badminton House in nearby Clifton, it moved to its present premises on the edge of the downs in Bristol, arguably the greenest and most desirable part of the city. Main building is Georgian and gracious (we were ushered in to a warm and luxuriously carpeted drawing room, where Classic FM played discreetly); over the years the site has been filled in with all sorts of additions of varying degrees of beauty, making the school compact, rather than crowded. Nestling on the edge of the Badminton site, the junior school is certainly the senior school's little sister and firmly under its wing.

Groups of girls scurry purposefully about the place in their practical uniform of blue shirts, sweaters and checked skirts. 'Why no trousers?' asked one mum. Sixth form dress is much less restricted than in some schools: torn jeans and strappy tops are out, otherwise more or less anything goes.

Male company is provided mostly by QEH, Bristol's only remaining boys' school (which now admits sixth form girls) – academic and social interactions, we gather, which include a shared minibus from Chepstow.

Pastoral care, well-being and discipline: Discipline, in as much as it is needed in this high-achieving environment, works on girls' general desire to please, and dislike of letting people down, so the head might well say, 'I am rather disappointed that I have to speak to you, Jemima', on the rare occasions that girls come before her. Smoking, alcohol and drugs will lead sinners straight to her study. Achievement of all kinds is recognised, but interestingly there is no honours board, and school's annual open day is as much about displays, demonstrations, music, drama and food than interminable speechifying; the only prize awarded is the Iris Murdoch (another OB) prize for creative writing.

Pastoral care reads as well as one would expect for a school like this, with a tutor assigned to each girl, a vertical house system and peer mentoring, but one mother told us her daughter's confidence had been undermined by too great an emphasis on academics, and too little on making supportive friendships.

Pupils and parents: Quite mixed socially and ethnically, but united by high academic expectations and aspirations. We found the girls friendly, unpretentious and open-minded – and were pleased to see some tucking into the sponge pudding we are probably no longer allowed to call spotted dick. 'The school does not turn out a mass product,' said one mother with several years' knowledge.

Overseas girls are welcome here and come in droves, mostly from Hong Kong but a good few from Russia and Nigeria; a sprinkling from the rest of the world. Bristol's own ethnic and religious mix well represented and catered for too: any dish containing pork was firmly labelled at lunch. Old Badmintonians include Indira Ghandi and Princess Haya Bint Al Hussein of Jordan.

Entrance: Most arrive in year 7, but everyone below sixth form is required to sit papers in English (English as a foreign language for those who have been at school in the UK for less than two years) and maths and to do an online reasoning test. The transition from the junior school is not automatic and girls do exactly the same assessments as those coming from elsewhere (in practice, the vast majority are accepted). Sixth form hopefuls must sit papers in two of the subjects they intend studying at A level, plus a general paper. All applicants are interviewed, via Skype when necessary. School prefers overseas girls to do UKiset.

Exit: Some fall-out after GCSEs (around 20 per cent) from day girls wanting pastures new, and perhaps boys in particular. Those who stay go not only to our most prestigious universities, but also to top notch international ones in Asia, Europe and the US eg New York, Arizona, Washington and Hong Kong. London is the most popular destination, followed by Durham, and a good handful to Oxbridge each year (four in 2018). Wide choice of degree courses, more sciences than arts; five medics and a vet in 2018.

Money matters: Fees are much in line with comparable schools, though boarders from outside the EU pay over £2,000 more per year to cover the cost of escorted journeys to UK international airports – and of the boarding travel co-ordinator. Scholarships are awarded to a maximum of 20 per cent of fees; bursaries are means tested. New-ish regional award for girls 'who will bring something special to Badminton'; the school intends this as a way to recognise wider achievement and potential than the range of scholarships currently on offer.

Remarks: Undoubtedly a distinguished Bristol institution, yet its size, compact site, high proportion of boarders and fearsome academic reputation (which frightens some off) mean it enjoys a lower profile than it should in the city. The head describes it as a hidden gem, so her mission, should she choose to accept it, is perhaps to polish up all its facets so it shines a brighter local light.

Balcarras School

East End Road, Charlton Kings, Cheltenham, Gloucestershire GL53 8QF

Ages 11–18 **Pupils** 1,391 **Sixth form** 376

01242 515881
www.balcarras.gloucs.sch.uk

Headteacher: Since 2016, Dominic Burke MA PGCE (40s). Born in Wakefield and educated entirely in Yorkshire at the universities of York, Sheffield and Leeds, he moved south to Evesham to take up his first teaching post, thence to Balcarras in 2007, climbing steadily through the ranks to be appointed head. 'At least there were no horrible surprises when I was appointed!' he said wryly. Teaching is in the family; both his parents taught children with special needs, but he did look fleetingly at publishing and journalism before opting for a successful career teaching history. The students we spoke to gave him the thumbs up as a teacher, and indeed as a head: 'He knows everyone and is seen around' they told us. One parent felt he has yet to make major waves, but all are glad to see him attend concerts, matches and productions. We were thrilled to catch him tickling the ivories of a brand new boudoir grand in the splendid new music block, and to be invited to the lunchtime rehearsal of the staff choir, making a fantastic job of a Beatles medley. Mr Burke is totally committed to comprehensive education and he is determined to ensure that Balcarras stays at the top of its game, not just academically, but also as a place where all are welcome and where they will do as well in all respects as they possibly can. 'I'd like to banish elitism in the arts' he told us: 'In this school, everyone's on the stage'. Smiley and youthful (perhaps because he has two young sons of his own), Mr Burke is not the kind of head for whom his students flatten themselves against the wall as he marches by, but that is more indicative of the school than of the man. Apart from his family, any spare time he has might be spent on the golf course or pounding the roads/piano keys, and keeping an eye on the fortunes of Leeds United.

Academic matters: Completely non-selective at entry, yet achieves the kind of results at A level and GCSE which might lead the unwary to suppose otherwise and which mean it was voted the best comprehensive in the south west, out-performing all but two of the Gloucestershire grammar schools. In 2018, A level results were the best ever, with 69 per cent graded A*/B. Stand-out subjects tend toward the artistic (art and photography) but strong showings in modern languages, food science & nutrition, maths and applied science also. Twenty-four subjects on offer: religion, philosophy & ethics alongside more usual fare. Four BTECs in creative media and health & social care among others. Students are still expected to sit four AS levels, taking three on to A level, but the school does not throw them out if their results are not up to snuff at the end of year 12. Mr Burke added as a note of caution, 'Sometimes we have to have conversations with them about what might be in their best interests,' EPQ is big here too, with nearly half of all sixth formers doing it.

In 2018, 33 per cent of GCSE grades were A-A*/7-9, and 84 per cent of students achieved English and maths above a grade 4. School concentrates on ensuring that as many students as possible get that crucial passport to sixth form, college or employment; retakes laid on in sixth form for those who don't quite nail them. School also cites discredited and disliked EBacc, with over half of students achieving it. Separate sciences are not offered; instead, it's combined science comprising a mix of physics, chemistry and biology worth two GCSEs. Options include Russian – maybe the proximity of GCHQ has something to do with it! Among students, top subjects appear to be maths, languages and sciences but 'sometimes there's too much emphasis on grades and not enough on skills and enjoyment' they told us, but in the next breath the 'commitment and passion of the staff like coming in at half term' was remarked upon with approval. This enthusiasm for learning is passed on by the teaching staff to the students, and conveyed to the parents: 'My daughter loves every single subject' one mother enthused 'and the teachers accommodate different children's needs'. Lessons we witnessed included conjugation of French verbs taught by a native speaker (who also teaches Spanish), the filming of a devised drama piece and a fascinating debate in an ethics class on the fate of whistle-blowers vis-à-vis Edward Snowden – oh and the most mouth-watering cheese soufflés beautifully presented on slate, restaurant style.

Balcarras is big on inclusion and 'welcomes students with a wide range of abilities and learning needs', according to its website: its Individual Learning Department is the biggest in the school. Support is literacy-based and personalised to each student, just over 10 per cent of the school's population; its reputation attracts those with EHCPs and other needs. Liaison is close between ILD staff and heads of houses, providing academic and pastoral support. We rarely hear such high praise as that coming from parents whose children had been in receipt of their attentions. 'Absolutely amazing – they could not do any more than they do', a mother told us; 'The flexibility the school gave us makes a huge difference in our ability to organise our ASD son's life'.

Games, options, the arts: The school's compact rectangular site means space for sport is not unlimited, but good use is made of it to provide pitches for rugby and football, courts for netball and tennis, cricket nets and an Astro, plus a decent-sized sports hall. Interestingly, a cycle speedway track here too and an active cycling club. Younger students have 4-5 hours' timetabled PE per week, added to by an extensive extracurricular programme making use of the time before school for badminton, at which the school is rather good. Fixture lists include matches against all the Cheltenham schools. Some student grumbles about too little variety in girls' games – just netball and hockey, coaching efforts concentrated on top teams 'with everyone else somewhat neglected' and a frustrating lack of commitment to training on the part of students and staff.

Music has been the lucky beneficiary of superb new facilities, funded by local founder and former boss of hip clothing brand Superdry. Even before its new home, there was always masses going on, with enough choirs and ensembles to satisfy those with tastes both ancient and modern, plus the opportunity to take grades in several instruments and singing. House music hotly contested and greatly enjoyed, as in most schools. An annual collaboration with the drama department is a highlight in the school's calendar: 2017's whole school production was It's a Wonderful Life, not performed very often. Recently, plays in modern languages have been introduced. Visits from theatre companies and trips to local productions complete the drama offer. Dance thriving too; it too has its own house competition.

Lots else to do apart from the academic, athletic and artistic: the school lays on D of E, a trip to New York, a ski trip to Norway and an ambitious expedition for older students to more challenging parts of the world – most recently Malawi, Thailand and Laos. Participants are expected to sign up for training in the UK for that trip – it is far from being a jolly.

Young Enterprise also strong as a sixth form option; school has enjoyed considerable success at this in past years. Recent ventures include VeganKind, tapping into the zeitgeist.

Background and atmosphere: The school's work-a-day buildings (new sixth form block with space for teaching, study and lounging should not be damned with such faint praise – it's terrific) occupy a long thin site on the eastern side of Cheltenham with pretty countryside views. Although it sounds like a Scottish estate or a villain from Poldark, Balcarras takes its name from the tiny lane which borders it, and is in fact the product of a reorganisation of secondary education in Cheltenham in the 1980s, taking the place of the former secondary modern, Charlton Kings. Greatly sought after, as an ideologically palatable alternative to the highly selective Pates Grammar on the west side of the town, and exceedingly proud of its comprehensive offer to local children (whose parents pay inflated house prices to live in its catchment), it has a palpable sense of purpose and aspiration for all. The growth in selective education is 'dangerous territory' in Mr Burke's opinion, so we are curious as to why he works with Dean Close and Cheltenham Ladies, though such cross-fertilisation is, in our view, a good thing. Students told us 'It's much better than Pates – far more inclusive', appreciate the prevailing work ethic and expressed their irritation at the behaviour of some children disrupting the class. An insistence on high standards of behaviour is certainly one of the head's priorities. Inside, Balcarras looks and feels traditional, with uniform for everyone including sixth formers – they get to trade in their ties (mandatory for all till then) for coloured polo shirts. Blazers for all, with coloured tabs denoting one of four houses named for local notables. Fountain pens are required and 'pupils are asked not to use ballpoint pens for neat work': a stricture not often heard in the 21st century. We overheard Mr Burke chide one student for not having a tie, but everyone seemed oblivious to the very short skirts barely covering sixth form girls. Both parents and children appreciate the relationship and mutual respect between staff and students, and the length of time that some members of staff stay at the school suggests it's a decent place to work.

Pastoral care, well-being and discipline: First port of call for students and indeed parents is the head of house for matters pastoral, but the school lays on an impressive amount of resources and links on its website: specific advice on popular social media sites, sexting, LGBT support and how to access the school counsellor, both in and outside school hours, being just a sample. Students and parents more than satisfied with the way in which the school looks after the whole person, including 'coping with me crying in the office' from one mother's moving account of an exceptionally difficult period of illness. Issues like bullying are 'nipped in the bud and dealt with quickly' another parent told us. Expectations of behaviour inside and outside the classroom are clearly listed – we liked the classroom covenant. Sanctions for poor work or behaviour also clear, but the emphasis is very much on praise and reward, rather than nit-picking and blame.

Pupils and parents: School is not what could be described as a maelstrom of diversity; just two per cent of students have English as an additional language. Efforts are made to address this by the range of speakers the school asks in, such the local imam. Cheltenham is an affluent town, but not without pockets of deprivation, so there is perhaps a wider socio-economic profile among Balcarras families than its address might suggest; the school certainly gets about seven times as much in Pupil Premium than Pates, the grammar school the other side of the town. Students we met seemed pretty happy with their lot, but not blind to things the school could do better.

Entrance: Massively oversubscribed at year 7 by a factor of 3. The school's catchment area appears on its website; we heard of families moving to live within it. Children arrive from about five local primary schools and their parents appreciate the transition arrangements made for them. At sixth form, about 50 new youngsters arrive from neighbouring schools; minimum requirements for entry are five GCSEs, two at grade 6 and three at grade 5, to include maths and English. Most subjects demand a 6 to study them at A level, but maths a 7.

Exit: Around a third leave after GCSE for sixth form colleges and a handful to apprenticeships or training. Those who stay on in sixth form benefit from the Futures programme, mainly aimed at UCAS but not letting those not intending to go straight to university off the hook either. 'The rising cost of university means we concentrate on alternatives such as employment and apprenticeships too' the newly appointed and very enthusiastic head of sixth form told us. 'We really care about the destinations of all our students, and don't want any of them to leave without a sense of where they're going. We certainly don't have any 'neets'!' he affirmed. Seventy per cent go to university, and a third of those to Russell group; 15 per cent take a gap year; a sprinkling to art foundation courses or into employment or apprenticeships. Three to Oxbridge and two medics in 2018.

Money matters: School does not beat about the bush in asking parents to contribute to the school's Gift Aid scheme, which brings in about £60k per year, spent on school resources including IT.

Remarks: Super, unpretentious yet ambitious school providing a truly comprehensive education for all in a town where the independent and selective options colour the landscape.

Beaudesert Park School

Minchinhampton, Gloucestershire GL6 9AF

Ages 4–13 **Pupils** 450 **Boarders** 1 weekly, 132 flexi (from year 4)

Fees: Day £9,195 – £17,661; Boarding £22,677 pa

01453 832072
www.beaudesert.gloucs.sch.uk

Headmaster: Since September 2018, Chris Searson, previously deputy head at Highfield School in Hampshire, where he had also been head of English and boarding houseparent. Married to Harriet; two young children.

Entrance: While not fiercely selective, school says it attracts a 'generally high level' and 'families with bright children'. Pupils come from local nurseries or the school's own. Transfer from pre-prep generally straightforward.

Exit: Most to Cheltenham College, then Cheltenham Ladies' College, Radley, Winchester and Bradfield. Good spread of scholarships every year. In 2018, 11 scholarships were taken up.

Remarks: Beaudesert Park School was founded in Warwickshire in 1908, moving to its mock Tudor Cotswold folly 10 years later. That folly has been joined over the years by buildings in a variety of architectural styles, the latest being a superb performing arts centre. Any deficit in architectural coherence is more than made up for by character – round every corner is a different view, whether it's terraced lawns and playing fields or the free-range cattle on Minchinhampton Common, who look as though they could wander into the car park (they can't, thanks to a grid). Towers, curved walls, covered outside staircases and walkways – it all looks rather like an animated Escher drawing as pupils go busily up and down between lessons.

As several parents told us, at Beaudesert the balance between academic work and the myriad of other activities on offer is skilfully maintained. Those who have moved their children from London preps really notice the difference and value the unpressurised environment – even more so when their children go on to gain places at top senior schools. 'They challenge the children academically by keeping them engaged,' said one. Homework is sensible too, certainly not hours every night. Nursery and pre-prep have their own mini-school with all the facilities including a hall and stage.

Pupils setted for maths, English and languages (French, Latin from year 6, optional Greek for scholars). No separate scholarship stream. Well-equipped labs where legendary 'screaming jelly baby' and other spectacular experiments are staged – obviously science is not impervious to school's performing arts campaign. Old-fashioned values do not extend to technology and there's a full complement of whiteboards, iPads and the like. Delightful, bright art studios with separate ceramics room and proper kiln.

SEN provision received mixed reviews. Pupils told us the help they'd received was 'brilliant', but parents raised concerns. Several thought that a school with a relatively non-selective intake should have wider in-house experience to identify specific learning needs early on.

Part of the charm of Beaudesert, according to parents, is that it's a proper 'outdoors' school: 'It's a real country school', 'a proper all-round education', 'the children are connected to their surroundings.' Several made the distinction between country preps that are 'sporty' and Beaudesert, where, in addition to plenty of sport, there's free range tree climbing, den building, night camps, forest school for the little ones and bushcraft ('It's mainly about knives', a Just William character told us).

Main sports arranged along pretty traditional lines, rugby, football and cricket for the chaps, netball and rounders for the girls. Both do hockey (girls very successfully) and there's some overlap with cricket coaching. Athletics for all in the summer, plus tennis and cross-country. We didn't hear any grumbles about teams and matches, most parents thought the arrangements were fair enough and that pupils in the B and C teams enjoyed their games just as much as those in the As. Swimming is a real strength – all Beaudesert pupils learn to swim and indoor and outdoor pools mean year round training. The school regularly qualifies for IAPS national finals and swimmers compete in local and national teams. This being Gloucestershire, there's a fair amount of equestrian activity – school team recently won national junior polo championships. Golf, fly fishing and mountain biking also on offer. Pupils can bring their own bikes and learn cycle safety and maintenance.

In defiance of Noel Coward's advice, school believes that everybody's daughter or son benefits from taking to the stage. Even before the opening of the recent performing arts centre, music and drama were enthusiastically pursued by the majority. Minutes after the builders left preparations were under way for the inaugural concert, featuring school choirs, orchestra, ensembles and soloists. This glass and Cotswold stone building sits, appropriately enough, at the centre of the school and hosts plays, concerts, assemblies, parents' evenings, music and drama lessons and exhibitions. The exterior features distinctive cedar planks, rather like xylophone keys, positioned to deflect the light.

Pupils can board from year 4 and most will have some experience of boarding by the time they leave. Options are flexi or weekly – everyone goes home after Saturday school (lessons until 12.30) or matches. Boarders up to year 6 can work towards bronze, silver and gold Beaudesert Badges – activities include first aid, cookery, gardening, outdoor skills and charity work.

One boarding house with boys' and girls' sections up different staircases. Jolly kitchens and comfortable shared areas for 'TV and talking'. Brightly decorated boys' dorms run into each other (no doors), girls have separate (shared) rooms. Everything clean and homely. 'I love boarding, you get to sleep over with all your friends,' said one of our guides. Houseparents plus matrons, nurses and gappies oversee proceedings. 'There's always someone to talk to,' we were told. Food gets a big thumbs up, especially pulled pork buns and good old treacle sponge.

Year 8 girls informed us proudly of the small privileges of seniority – white shirts in winter, benches in assembly, 'senior snacks' (cereal and squash at 8pm on a Friday) – none typical 12 year olds' aspirations. Advocates of the 'real world' undoubtedly educate their children elsewhere and even its biggest fans concede that there is a Beaudesert bubble, but how many parents would wish their children to grow up more quickly?

Houses, we were told, are 'no big deal', thus rather suiting their prosaic names: A, B, C and D. No head boys and girls, instead all year 8s have duties and responsibilities. School council has achieved victories including modifications to the year 8 uniform. 'Boys can choose their own socks, but they mustn't be luminous or white.' What else would improve their school, we asked? Modest proposals included golf buggies to transport pupils to games fields over the common, flattening the bump in the Astro, compelling teachers to sit their own exams, and 'unlimited ice cream'.

These days both parents are probably working, often weekly commuting to London. School welcomes the fact that parents are 'in a lot more' and encourages their involvement. Families

B

all fairly local – few alternatives in the immediate area see to that. No PTA but active Friends of Beaudesert who organise fundraisers and socials. No class reps either – they don't really feature in the boarding model – but most parents happy with home-school communications, prompt replies to enquiries and general delightfulness of front of house staff. High praise, too, for pastoral care and teachers' 'genuine concern' for pupils, 'Nothing's too much trouble. You can't fault it', we were told.

Happiness isn't a subject to be taught; it should be the founding principle of any school – it certainly is at Beaudesert.

Beechen Cliff School

11

Alexandra Park, Bath, Somerset BA2 4RE

Ages 11–18 **Pupils** 1,332 **Sixth form** 410 (133 girls) **Boarders** 33 full (boys only)

Fees: Day free; Boarding: £10,500 pa.

01225 480466
www.beechencliff.org.uk

Headmaster: Since 2005, Andrew Davies (50s), history graduate of University of Sussex, married to Anne, an assistant head. Both of his children have been through Beechen Cliff, his daughter having now left the sixth form. Previously principal of Kings International College in Surrey, having risen on the well trodden career path of head of department, head of humanities, deputy head in five local authorities and a private school, ranging from deprived inner-city Bristol to the leafy heights of Bath.

No pretentions to anything other than a sound, old-fashioned, well run school, as academic as possible for each pupil's capacities. 'Our thing', he claims, 'is a comprehensive ability range, outdoor pursuits and real leadership training.' The mixed sixth form is being beefed up academically with new stricter entry requirements 'because the academic bit is what we do best at this level'. No more one-year non-academic courses and only a few AASE rugby players (a scheme for potential top players) scraping in with anything but top GCSE grades.

This rosy picture of a school at the top of its game and possibly a little complacent was rudely shattered by an unannounced visit from Ofsted in 2018, whose damning report is likely to preoccupy the head for some time to come. He has been quick to acknowledge that rapid improvements need to be made in crucial areas (steps are already in place, to include a close eye from a neighbouring school which has kept its own eye on the ball rather more successfully) while reassuring parents of the school's future and traditional strengths, of which there are many.

Open, humorous, warm and seemingly informal, despite addressing his pupils as 'gentlemen' with an ironic twinkle that encourages them to enjoy living up to the epithet, he is obviously trusted rather than feared. Pupils tuck in shirts without rancour, ask him to sort out small problems for them and confidently pop into his office when necessary. Passionate about encouraging his flock to extend and test themselves, and to take carefully guided responsibility for their own learning, he is realistically aware that boys generally need pushing to work hard.

Still teaching a GCSE history group and involved in cricket coaching and lots of shooting activities (one of his passions, so almost everyone has a go), Mr Davies also champions the Centurion march. He describes this incredibly tough 100 mile walk, done in 48 hours from the school front door to Hungerford Church door and back along the canal path, as a defining feature of the school which everyone wants to do once – and some do every year, getting the dates embroidered on their house ties. The inevitable Bath/Roman association is also celebrated by a life-size centurion model greeting visitors to the reception area. Immensely proud of his school, Mr Davies wants all pupils to leaving feeling they have had opportunities to match the most exclusive of independent educations. Parents we spoke to agreed that he achieves this.

Academic matters: Completely non-selective on entry except that it reflects the population of Bath and tends to get more able boys. Cognitive ability tests on all year 7s after entry gives a good basis for value added measurement, especially as a number of boys come from prep schools, which do not do Sats. Results at GCSE and A level have crept up over last few years and academic aspiration encouraged. In 2018, 78 per cent got 9-4 in both maths and English GCSE, which is pretty good considering the school is open entry for 11 year olds. Far more than national average achieve the English Bacc. At A level 56 per cent A*/B grades, 30 per cent A*/A.

Competitive sixth form getting a few into Oxbridge and medicine every year, and aiming even higher now the sixth entry qualifications have been tightened up. A good take-up for EPQ. Twenty-seven subjects offered at A level, plus the possibility of more at Hayesfield or Bath College, though no drama, textiles or classical languages, Four or five groups in some subjects with sciences, history and geography most popular but prepared to put on minority subjects for very small groups eg two for German and Italian. Apparently a good record in getting candidates into medicine and vet school is attracting even more able girls. 'Truly an academic sixth form now!' one parent commented. In the light of recent bad rap by Ofsted, however, school will no doubt be looking at progress sixth form girls and the intellectually and/or economically disadvantaged make.

Virtually everyone takes French from year 7 and all but a few add German, Spanish or Italian in year 8. Year 7 is streamed in four groups but after that pupils are in ability based sets for English, maths, science and humanities. DT choices are particularly wide and include food tech and product design. Though some parts of the buildings are what the head calls 'decrepit', their equipment is bang up to date and there is a shiny new humanities centre and really inviting new sixth form teaching block.

Plenty of homework but not on sports days, and the chance to do it supervised after school three days a week, sometimes made compulsory for those who need help getting organised. Most of the school library was in boxes on the floor on our visit as it was being reorganised to give better access and encourage the love of 'having a book in one's hands'. A parent was delighted that reading is really encouraged by, for instance, having books written by boys' sporting heroes, and commented that the literacy lady is brilliant.

Full time SENCo with a flock of four teaching assistants, necessary in a school that takes some EHCP pupils. In the past the pupil premium payments, which disadvantaged children attract, have been used effectively to provide extra help in literacy. Pupils with special needs invariably achieve some GCSEs, though not necessarily at top grades.

Class sizes are commonly about 28 except in minority exam subjects, though smaller groups for less able pupils. Work ethic seems to be pretty well automatically assumed.

Games, options, the arts: Illustrious sports record, as one would expect from a school which offers places to rugby players in the AASE (Academic and Sporting Excellence) scheme in conjunction with Bath Rugby. Both sixth form admission standards and year 7 entry criteria adjusted for outstanding players. The enormous sports honours board in the entrance says it all, starting with Roger Bannister and including rugby players Freddie Burns and John Hall, football manager Paul Tisdale and Olympic gold medal sprinter Jason Gardner and skeleton bob champion Amy Williams (GB's only gold medallist in the 2010 Winter Olympics). Enough choice for sixth form girls, including rugby (Ailis Egan of Ireland Ladies is an old girl), but they say they are not compelled to do anything in the sporting line.

Beautifully kept pitches with masses of Astroturf for all sports; as well as the staples of rugby, football, tennis and hockey, rowing and other minority sports all get a look in. This is one of the few state schools offering a full sporting programme on Saturday. Super sports hall has exterior climbing wall on one end, funded through parental gift aid. Uses top notch facilities (such as a 50m pool) and expertise at nearby Bath University too. School's philosophy is that everyone should have a go, so masses of opportunities for less skilled enthusiasts.

The new music centre brimming with exciting technology means that the department realistically offers both straight music A level and music technology, with alumni at music college. Plenty of choirs, orchestras and small groups. Art, on the other hand, is jumbled into an unreconstructed collection of buildings, but is none the worse for it. Outstanding photography equipment and a light-filled studio plus full printing workshop mean the department can offer pretty well anything, and certainly some very fine work in all media was on display.

Challenge is a key word and boys, plus sixth form girls, respond to it in CCF, DofE, Ten Tors, Three Peaks, the Centurion walk and a cross-Cornwall bike ride. Other clubs and activities abound, allowing young Warhammer and Lego enthusiasts, for instance, to retain their small boy passions, while a prominent notice in the humanities block advertised a philosophy film club. All year 7 boys have a bonding stay in a remote and primitive Welsh cottage, which teaches them to value such luxuries as running and hot water and electric light. The usual foreign trips with some financial help if needed.

Boarding: A small part of the school, boarding is for boys whose family circumstances mean they would benefit from the stability of boarding, or those from further afield participating in Bath Uni's specialist sports training. Lucky boarders get one of the best views in Bath from the terrace regularly used for outside dining in the summer, which opens from their spacious common/dining room. Good, clean, new-looking single rooms, all ensuite and with Wifi facilities, spacious and almost luxurious. With only about 30 boarders, the rule is that most stay in at weekends to provide a group for activities. This does not seem to be controversial. Housemaster lives in a house in grounds and several staff sleep in overnight. Head says he is seeking to expand boarding – the facilities are certainly good enough, though the school needs to keep a closer eye on comings and goings within them, Ofsted states.

Background and atmosphere: Looks like an independent school despite the lack of plush reception areas and the odd dilapidated corner and shabby classroom. Superb site with panoramic views and lush greenness all round. Bath stone softens the distinguished 1930s main buildings and the view does the rest. Occasional tarmacked spaces are left unadorned so boys can just kick about in them. Originally the Bath City School, founded in the Guildhall in 1896, it moved to Beechen Cliff in 1932 as the City of Bath Boys' School. Its present name dates from 1970s when the City of Bath school amalgamated it with Oldfield Boys' School, a local secondary modern, to form a comprehensive school. A huge campaign saved it from being axed in the 1990s. A founder member of Bath Educational Trust, set up in 2009, a collaboration between 10 local secondary schools, both universities in Bath and City of Bath College.

Steadily improving facilities to match the academic and sporting prowess of its pupils. The atmosphere is friendly but definitely traditional with short hair, smartly tied ties, natty striped shirts and smart black blazers. ('Really good value,' said an enthusiastic parent, 'considering it looks smart and gets twice the wear at half the cost of weekend casuals'.) Good second hand shop run by PTA. Discipline, courtesy, academic confidence and pride in the school are encouraged by the high standards and the gentle courtesy with which staff and pupils treat each other. Lots of past pupils on the staff vouch for how highly they value the school. Old boys/girls (Old Sulians) and former members of staff come in to teach extra sessions – for love.

Pastoral care, well-being and discipline: Pastoral care is vertical and based on houses named after the literary figures which have given their names to the roads in this residential area of Bath, known as Poets' Corner. With no year heads, housemasters manage pastoral care and sixth formers are part of the houses. Mixed age tutor groups meet every day, providing an excellent means of integrating older and younger pupils.

Head of sixth form pastoral care gives more specialist help to sixth formers, who 'massively trust' the staff and regard them as 'expert godparents'. One parent commented that the staff all work amazingly hard, taking on anything they think will benefit pupils, and all subject staff are passionate about their subjects, while another 'would love to work under such inspiring leadership'.

Sixth form girls have to wear suits and 'soon find that a couple of work suits is a better option than daily competitive dressing'. Good take-up for school meals indicates food is pretty ok, and staff say only top quality locally sourced ingredients used. It was acceptable rather than brilliant on our visit, but the dining room is pleasant and practical with pleasingly solid furniture and calm friendly feel.

The reward culture for all achievement (exemplified by the head's limitless supply of Mars bars freely handed out to boys who have 'gone the extra mile') is balanced by traditional sanctions for both academic and social misdemeanours. Uniform breaches get 250 lines on the vice of scruffiness; slackers get academic detentions on Saturdays and have to attend supervised prep. 'Parents have to go along with this.' Parents told us there was minimal bullying and, when they had heard of it, it had been well and promptly dealt with. Also minimal drugs, 'just not tolerated but rarely a problem anyway'. 'Boys know the line and take the consequence if they step over it'. Well, mostly: a recent distasteful racial prank attracted international censure – and from Ofsted, whose unambiguous criticism meant a regrading from 'outstanding' to 'inadequate' overnight. Expectations laid out in the code pupils sign before entry; they just need to abide by them, and to expect trouble if they don't.

Pupils and parents: Bath's middle class aspiring parents obviously love Beechen Cliff: recent fierce criticism from Ofsted was not borne out by parental survey, and sparked public expressions of support for the school, both from parents and current students. Its wide entry from a strictly drawn and very local catchment, including some much less affluent areas, is also appreciated. Some 20 per cent of boarders from overseas or sports scholars from a wider area. Great rapport between parents and school through constant online info available about progress, but friendly staff like to drop the odd handwritten note or send a photo of a son achieving something amazing, and parents love this personal touch. Supportive PTA runs a gift aid scheme, providing extra equipment that the independent sector takes for granted – rugby balls, for example.

B

Old Sulians include Arnold Ridley (Private Godfrey in Dad's Army), Andrew Lincoln (Drop the Dead Donkey, This Life, Love Actually), Curt Smith (Tears for Fears), Sir Richard Roberts (Nobel Prize winning biochemist – mechanism of gene-splicing – and generous benefactor), Dan Rivers (ITN News correspondent) and the ex-head of MI6, Sir John Sawers.

Entrance: There are 162 day places on offer at 11. Precedence to looked after boys, followed by siblings, staff children and then 12 sporting aptitude places. Eighty per cent of remaining places to those living within Bath City boundary, divided between those living north and south of the River Avon (split reviewed annually). Boys come from nearly 20 different primary schools – and the odd prep. Sixth form entry – boys and girls – by interview, but requires 5+ 9-6 GCSE grades with at least 4 in English and maths and 6+ in subjects to be taken at A level (7+ in maths). Competition is really fierce here with 250 or more applicants for the 20+ external day places.

Up to seven boarding places at 11+ and four at 16+, with similar criteria to day places but principally a 'significant degree of boarding need' with priority to Forces children.

Exit: Up to half leave after GCSEs, some failing to meet sixth form entry requirements. Some 80-90 per cent of upper sixth leavers to universities all over the country to pursue a diversity of courses. Two to Oxford and three medics in 2018; Cardiff, Exeter, Birmingham, Bristol, Manchester, Swansea and Cardiff Metropolitan all popular. Plaudits from work experience placements indicate that those who start work straight from school are well equipped to do so.

Remarks: An exceptional, thriving, go-ahead school but with a traditional feel and traditional manners, but now needing to stop resting on traditional laurels, Beechen Cliff is the best of both worlds, offering free education that is comparable to any in the independent sector but has the advantage of being open to pupils from all walks of life. Hence the most academically or politically ambitious respect the aspirations of others to enter trades or practical careers. The head hopes no pupils will leave without having had opportunities as good as anywhere in the country.

BGS Infant and Juniors

Linked with Bristol Grammar School

Elton Road, Bristol BS8 1SR

Ages 4–11 **Pupils** 333

Fees: £8,475 – £9,960 pa

01179 736109
www.bristolgrammarschool.co.uk

Head of junior school: Since 2011, Peter Huckle BA, MEd, PGCE. Educated at Monks Park School, Bristol; Birmingham and Bristol Universities. Taught geography at Patchway High School for two years before joining BGS in 1980. Has held various teaching roles in 35 years here including head of house, head of years 7 and 8 and deputy head but describes current role as 'the best job in the school'. Soft-spoken and smiling, his passion for education is clearly as strong as ever. Believes the introduction of the infant school in 2010 has brought fresh energy to the school as a whole. A rugby referee, reader and theatre goer.

Retiring in July 2019. His successor will be Heidi Hughes, currently head of the Royal High Junior School in Bath. Has also been deputy head of Royal Russell Junior School in Surrey and a member of management teams at British schools in Singapore and the Philippines. A PE specialist who can turn her hand to teaching most subjects.

Entrance: Infants usually join in reception at age 4 following an informal assessment and a report from the child's current nursery. Entrants to junior school, mostly at year 3, sit tests in English and verbal and non-verbal reasoning. Expanded entry at start of year 5. Some financial assistance for highly academic pupils from low-income families through the Peloquin Award scholarships.

Exit: Children transfer to the senior school on PH's recommendation – no entrance exam if here since year 5 or before. Around 98 per cent go through.

Remarks: Children start at age 4 in two reception classes in one of the school's several houses on Elton Road. Free-flow over two floors including three play spaces and an outdoor area with Astroturf, ride on toys and a covered area for outdoor learning. The school may be anything but purpose-built but it makes imaginative use of its restricted space. Wipe-clean parent information boards outside classrooms at pick-up times outlining 'What we did today' are a nice touch. Electronic communication with parents via a secure log-in, parent portal will be next step. 'Partnership with parents very important right from the outset.' Comprehensive weekly newsletters too. 'There's almost too much communication – it can be overwhelming.'

Vibrant learning on show in the year 1 and 2 classrooms. Teachers make good use of the city's historical and cultural assets such as Brunel's SS Great Britain, Clifton Suspension Bridge, Bristol Central Library and the aquarium – to plan exciting lessons in a topic-based curriculum. Volunteer parent help in school is valued and encouraged. Infant children have regular forest school sessions in the school's own woodland at its sports centre at Failand. It's magical. On our visit, year 2 children gathered in a purpose-built 'Hobbit hut' to be given their challenge: to capture spring by taking a photograph of a raindrop on a leaf using an iPad. Reception go one full day every fortnight and years 1/2 for a morning a week. Years 3/4 alternate forest school with PE and swimming.

Failand has a superb newish pavilion, overlooking the impressive sports fields, which is used for talks, events and junior leavers' assemblies. PE takes place in BGS sports hall; swimming lessons at Henbury and Bristol University pools. Junior boys play rugby, hockey, tennis and cricket; girls do hockey, netball, tennis and rounders. One parent complained that there was less emphasis on girls' sport than boys – fewer matches. Currently, boy: girl split at this level is about 60:40.

A gentle transition from infants to juniors in year 3; cosy areas, a reading corner, and a teaching assistant in each class. Children are set for maths from year 3. English curriculum includes Talk for Writing and Shakespeare in Schools. Teachers supported by specialist teaching assistants for maths, English, arts and PE. Older children make use of senior school sports, science, languages and DT facilities. In-class support for individual pupils with specific learning needs, overseen by assistant head. Whole school approach, supported by two specialist TA and a part-time literacy teacher for one-to-one. Additional support for pupils with exceptional ability and EAL.

Junior pupils have two outdoor play areas and have access to facilities in the senior school. All infant and junior children dine in the main school. Glass-lined passages link some of the old buildings, with an effective history timeline running around the campus. Creative use is made of space, for example, yoga classes are held on one of the infant outdoor all-weather areas. 'A variety of learning experiences – in different places doing things in different ways – helps keep the school vibrant and exciting,' says the head.

Amount of homework builds from one short task a week in year 1 to half an hour a night by year 6. Accepted by all. 'It develops robust character,' a parent noted. High standards and expectations from staff and, especially, parents, but school makes sure pupils don't feel under pressure and parental comments include 'There is a certain drive but the children are not aware of it;' 'Everyone has a chance to shine;' 'Verbal praise, rewards, lots to strive for;' 'The school has been life changing for my child, an absolutely amazing experience.'

Very strong emphasis on building confidence through opportunities for performance: a MADD (Music, Art, Dance and Drama) evening, teatime concerts and a performing arts day. Also creativity – participating in Arts Award scheme and developing skills. Individual musical instrument tuition (everyone learns violin from age 5), and speech and drama classes. Every Friday afternoon, there's a wide-ranging activities programme for juniors, some with professional instructors. Staff – including some from senior school – run clubs, often following their own passions, whether for Irish dancing or chess. BGS hosted semi-finals of English primary schools' chess championships, with 500 entrants. Children love the activities and trips – dry ski slope a particular favourite. Ukulele, blogging, coding and Mandarin just some of what's on offer. 'Children could do something every five minutes of the day if they wanted to,' said one teacher. 'My kids love it; they come out buzzing,' said a parent.

House system – four houses, not linked to those in the senior school – supports pastoral care and personal development giving children contact with different peer groups and providing opportunities for competition and rewards, such as star of the day and house captaincy. It's also important for charity activities, a priority for the head. Fairy cake Friday is just one popular example.

'Bucket filling' is a principle introduced in year 1. The idea is that if we are kind and help others we make them feel good, i.e. 'fill up their bucket', while the opposite also applies. A side effect of being considerate is that we make ourselves feel good too. 'Year 1 children regularly note examples of filling each other's buckets and have gone into house assemblies in the senior school to explain the concept to 11-18 year-olds. Senior pupils love the concept and are amazed by how articulate and confident 5 and 6 year-olds can be,' head explains.

Nurturing and supportive culture extends to staff and peer observations between the infant, junior and senior school are seen as beneficial to all. One long-serving staff member observed that the increase in support staff and the feeling that everyone is part of one team was very different to the more regimented style of decades past. Parents praise easy access to staff and swift action on any concerns. Some staff are perhaps a touch too accommodating – answering emails from demanding mums and dads at 7am.

Paradoxically, since the introduction of infant school classes in 2010, a stronger 'whole school' ethos has developed across BGS, staff, students and parents value the all-through, 4-18 mix. All ages share the same breakfast club; sixth formers help infants with reading; year 2s sing in the BGS assembly. The head, who has been around long enough to remember the introduction of girls to the senior school in 1980, says it's great. 'Everyone is valued equally.'

He concludes: 'High academic standards remain at the heart of what we do but there are so many other things – sport, charity and adventure activities – that we think provide a really rich education for the children.'

Bishop Wordsworth's Grammar School

11 The Close, Salisbury, Wiltshire SP1 2ED

Ages 11–18 **Pupils** 956 **Sixth form** 258 **C of E**

01722 333851
www.bws-school.org.uk

Headmaster: Since 2002, Dr Stuart Smallwood BSc PhD PGCE NPQH (50s), formerly deputy head. Brought up in Kent and a product of a grammar school like the one he now heads, Dr Smallwood graduated in geology from Leeds and got his doctorate from Cambridge. A brush with the civil service preceded his move into teaching; he has taught in only two schools, though his career followed a conventional path to his current post as head of one of the best state schools in the country. As such, he can press on in pursuit of even greater academic glory without the burden of having to fill fee-paying places; Bishop's offers places only to one in three applicants. 'I only ever wanted to work in this type of school', he told us from his modest, darkly panelled office, where a sheaf of commendations awaited signing on his desk, 'and my aim is to build on this school's particular character and location to create a regional entity'. Somewhat uncompromising in manner, Dr Smallwood is respected by the boys, who describe him variously as 'authoritative', 'dedicated' and 'ambitious for the school'. Married to Charlotte, who teaches English at the girls' equivalent, South Wilts, with a daughter at university and two sons in the school, Dr Smallwood might be found bird-watching, star-gazing or tinkering with his model railway in his spare time; sadly, his failing knees mean no more running

Academic matters: The raison d'être of this top performing school: it's not all that matters here, but nearly. 'Academic excellence for starters,' said the head, when asked about his priorities for the school. Results reflect the high academic bar at entry: in 2018, 70 per cent A*-A/9-7 grades at GCSE, with particular strengths in maths and all three sciences. Oddly, for a specialist language college, language results lag a little behind, despite the requirement to study two languages to the end of year 9, then to take at least one at GCSE. We liked the quadrilingual notices around the school – bon effort! Many GCSE courses start in year 9, and some (languages mostly) are taken a year or 2 early.

At A level, 27 subjects are offered, half of which are taught in collaboration with South Wilts. Again, stunning results, with 43 per cent A*/A and 71 per cent A*/B in 2018. Star subjects at A level are maths, sciences, geography and geology both in take-up and results, again fewer languages including English. EPQ now offered and increased take up. Boys talked about the calibre of teaching staff and academic respect, working both ways between them and their teachers: 'They beg you to take their subject for A level,' said one, whilst others praised the amount of support given. 'They fall over themselves to help you,' said another, hot from a one-to-one session on mechanics. We were struck by the keen attention paid to rainfall graphs by a large geography class we dropped in on, but a group of younger boys in a German class were fidgety. One mother reckoned the language teaching is too dry, and inclined to miss the point that language is primarily a means for communication. Some reservations about the science teaching also reached us – a bit old-fashioned and not always right for boys who find it hard.

Standards are kept up by close and supportive relationships between teachers and the boys, and 'by just the right amount of homework, though it might be sacrilege to say it', opined one year 7 lad. The transfer to sixth form is 'an achievement, not a given'; as well as a minimum of six GCSEs at 6 or above, including 6s for English and maths, there is also a chat with each hopeful about subject choices and possible careers. The head is not above booting boys out if their year 12 results are not up to snuff but he would do so only if a boy was clearly not suited to post-16 study – 'very rare,' said he – and despite the best efforts of the mentor each boy is assigned. SEN provision caters for the usual range of dyslexia, dyspraxia and Asperger's, and helps boys with difficulties in getting organised, having liaised with feeder primary schools – but it's pretty low profile at this school, we sense.

Games, options, the arts: There is life beyond rugby and cross-country, if you look hard, but both these sports are taken with incredible seriousness: 'loyalty verging on the psychopathic and the coach is terrifying', said one mother whose son was proud to play in the 1st XV. The fixture list includes the gamut of schools more closely associated with the game: Sherborne, Bryanston, Millfield, Marlborough and other local titans, and top teams get to play at prestigious venues such as Rosslyn Park. Passions run exceedingly high on the touchline, say parents. Cross-country also has a massive following and produces successes at county level.

All the playing fields are a brisk trot away – the school is truly shoehorned into a confined space behind the cathedral close – but the boys grumble less about this than they do about the lack of space in the yard to play football at lunchtime. Some parents think the school is 'myopic about other sports' and bemoan the lack of tennis courts, for example, but basketball enjoys a strong following. At least sport-phobes are allowed to hate it in peace and, in sixth form, to spend their Wednesday afternoons in other profitable ways like hospital volunteering; everyone we spoke to confirmed that there will be a group of like-minded boys to hang out with, whether that be geeks, nerds, jocks or eccentrics, which we found reassuring and refreshing. Slackers and rebels won't find too many kindred spirits, however.

Music also very strong at Bishops, as befits a school overlooked by Salisbury Cathedral, with its distinguished choral tradition. Choir sings at school functions in the cathedral and tours regularly, as well as the odd national event like the schools' prom in the Albert Hall, and accompanying the LSO. About 10 per cent learn a musical instrument, taught by a small army of peripatetics. Two orchestras, string groups, wind bands and other ensembles cater for players of all abilities (and possibly none).

Art and drama less important at this somewhat two-dimensional school: many more creative pursuits take place outside the timetable as part of the 40 clubs on offer, but it would not be the right choice for an artistic and delicate flower, reckon parents.

An ambitious range of trips is laid on – as well as destinations one might expect for the linguists, classicists, musicians and (art) historians, rugby teams travel the world. Two ski trips, junior mountain-biking in Croatia or Morocco and a biennial trip to the developing world (Himalayas, Vietnam) add to the offer.

Background and atmosphere: Named after its founder in 1890, who set it up entirely out of his own pocket, and true to its founding principles, the school still delivers an education 'within the context of Christian belief and practice', but this perhaps plays out more in the relationships forged in school than in overt religious observance. It looks and feels like the city grammar school it is proud to be, occupying a very central site accessed through two unmarked entrances. Reception is housed in an ancient coach-house, whose cobbles still deter anyone unwise enough to wear heels. Just as well it's a boys' school, though it was co-ed till 1928. Inside its confines, a remarkable amount of ancient and modern has been crammed, including the chapel, sports hall, a gorgeous new teaching block and – amazingly – some green space. Everyone mentioned the lack of space as the school's only real limitation (new block houses the increased year 7 intake and there's also a new maths block); we visited on a Wednesday when the place was eerily empty, the boys being occupied on the rugby pitches. But we did spot the lines painted in the yard, presumably to control lunch queues.

A discernible air of academic seriousness pervades – 'the boys have to work,' said one mother approvingly – and do substantial amounts at home, particularly in the case of keen sportsmen. Expectations are pitched high – top universities come to school's careers evenings. The boys we spoke to unquestionably feel lucky to be there. Parents also appreciate the efforts the school makes to turn them into good citizens, and are generally happy with the quality of reports and parents' evenings. It all feels jolly conventional – and no bad thing, in our view. The boys looked much tidier than many we meet and we did not see any adventurous hair, tattoos or piercings. When asked about drink, drugs and other extracurricular pursuits, one brave soul cited one incidence of drugs he knew about, which he felt had been dealt with the right degree of severity. Not cool in this school, evidently.

Pastoral care, well-being and discipline: Boys rate pastoral care highly and reckon there is always someone to talk to when times are hard; heads of lower and middle school came in for particular praise, as did sixth form mentors. The view from parents was mixed: 'I think it's good, but not all of us would agree,' said one. When we brought up the dreaded subject of bullying, the boys looked a bit blank, and confirmed they felt school was 'a safe place to be'. Academic discipline is tight, and a falling off in performance will swiftly be gripped; parents and boys both felt that such rigour would not suit everyone. Commendations for absolute and relative achievement provide a good balance, especially when incentivised with chocolate.

Pupils and parents: Almost exclusively white and middle class, very few pupils in receipt of free school meals: something the head wants to address. Everyone involved in Bishops appears to share a palpable sense of aspiration, whether in academic, musical or sporting pursuits; 'It suits those who come from families with traditional values,' said a parent. The edgy or unconventional might not feel Bishops was a natural home. Most parents are in professional occupations of some kind.

Entrance: Tough, tough, tough. Huge competition for 160 places in year 7 (reflects increase to five form entry) from about 50 local primary schools and some independents. Eleven plus (school's own test in English, maths and verbal reasoning) is taken with utmost seriousness: 'I've been crammed since I was 4', said one boy with a wink. The formal process starts in year 5 when the prospectus is sent out to all primary schools within the 'designated area', roughly a five mile radius around the city. Applications are made via Wiltshire council, and the exam is taken in September of year 6. Priority, amongst those who have passed the exam, to looked after children and those on free school meals. School runs coaching sessions as part of its commercial activity (free for those on state benefits), and we imagine that local tutors make a mint. Over 50 arrive at sixth form, with a clutch of good GCSEs at grade 6 or (mostly) above.

Exit: University applications receive top priority, with the school hosting a university fair attracting all the top names. Also very clued up on summer schools, chances to study abroad and all sorts of ways to enhance applications. One aspiring medic told us his personal statement had gone through 10 drafts before submission. Most jump through the UCAS hoops in their last year, but we were assured that the school continues to support boys who opt to apply post A level (around 20 per cent take gap years). In 2018, eight to Oxbridge, four medics and some 65 per cent overall to Russell Group universities. Bishops is now a SAT centre for entry to American universities: in 2017, one boy gained a place at Harvard (liberal arts and sciences), one at William Penn (football scholarship) and one at Southern Charleston (athletics scholarship). A few boys thin out after GCSE (around 10 per cent) and those that do are generally seeking more freedom and possibly girls eg at sixth form college. Distinguished old boys include Ralph Fiennes, Lord MacDonald (ex DPP), Hamish Milne (concert pianist), international rugby players Richard Hill and David Egerton, hockey international John Shaw. William Golding taught at Bishops for 17 years.

Money matters: School asks parents for a termly voluntary contribution to fund extras, gift-aided where possible, and supplements its income with commercial activities such as adult non-examined language and art classes and lettings to a non-residential summer school. Interestingly, the boys we spoke to alluded to the careful use of school resources – 'the school does well with what it has' said one.

Remarks: Bishops occupies some interesting territory between the independent and state sectors, and is a member of HMC. As its founder said, 'I should like to found a school which shall be equal to the greatest and best of our public schools' – it seems in many ways he has done exactly that. 'We're so grateful to escape the burden of school fees!' admitted one parent. 'Even if I had had the money for an independent school, I would still have sent my son to Bishops,' stated another – sums it up, really.

Blundell's Preparatory School

Linked with Blundell's School

14

Milestones House, Blundells Road, Tiverton, Devon EX16 4NA

Ages 2–11 **Pupils** 207

Fees: £6,900 – £12,195 pa

01884 252393
www.blundells.org

Head: Since 2011, Andrew Southgate BA Ed (30s). Raised in Maidstone, but ventured westwards for his degree in physical education and history at St Luke's, Exeter. He spent the first 13 years of his career at Moulsford Prep, ending up as deputy head. Impossibly youthful, he came bounding out of his office to meet us, and his enthusiasm for Blundell's, Devon, prep schools, children and life in general is infectious. Though he denies it – 'I talk quite a good game of rugby,' he says – he looks pretty fit: there is talk of introducing a veterans' rugby team for keen dads, and he still coaches and referees. Married to Sarah, with two children in the school, Mr Southgate has gone down very well with parents, who appreciate the aspirations and pride he has injected into 'what was a somewhat complacent offering', according to one. We also heard 'passion, energy and buzz, yet willing to take criticism'. Praise indeed.

Entrance: Prospective pupils spend a taster day in school, during which an assessment in English and maths is carried out.

Exit: Vast majority move on to the senior school at 11+ by means of entrance tests in English, maths and non-verbal reasoning. In 2018, there were 20 scholarships to it, 15 of which were academic.

'No-one is looking anywhere else now,' remarked one mother, but those who might are equally well prepared for entrance tests elsewhere.

Remarks: Sited next to Blundell's itself, so able to use some of its facilities, but separately run and administered. Attractive semi-rural setting in 12 acres on the edge of Tiverton, where outdoor learning is top of the pops, complete with pond and wetland area. Old red-brick house has been beautifully extended and adapted to create light and airy spaces, where art is effectively displayed. We particularly liked the science lab and the fabulous and well-equipped food technology room, where sessions for everyone are timetabled and keen young Blumenthals knock up delicious fare for parents and any other lucky diners. School lunch looked and smelled pretty good too.

'The children who come here are a broad church,' says the head, 'and our challenge is to accommodate them all; we're not an academic hothouse'. The last few years have seen significant changes to SEN provision (not least its renaming as Learning Success), increased hours for the SEN specialist, targeted reading groups every morning of the week (no extra charge) as well as handwriting club and a TA in all lower sets.

Lots of sport on offer, but everyone gets a game and the chance to represent the school: sport for all rather than winning at all costs. Valuing the individual child is top priority, as is the nurturing environment: 'After all they are still little at that age', say parents.

School's location in Devon means all its glories are there for the taking – hearty stuff on Exmoor, derring-do on the coast, culture in Exeter or Taunton and so on; parents report far more trips and visitors, such as a circus school for a day, which has gone down extremely well. Much loved by local community – one commentator said faintly dismissively that Blundell's is the school for those who will never leave Devon – and refugees from the urban rat race. A beguiling proposition for all takers.

Blundell's School

Linked with Blundell's Preparatory School

Blundell's Road, Tiverton, Devon EX16 4DN

Ages 11–18 **Pupils** 598 **Sixth form** 205 **Boarders** 213 full, 187 flexi
C of E

Fees: Day £14,130 – £22,410; Boarding £16,350 – £35,205 pa

01884 252543
www.blundells.org

Head: Since September 2018, Bart Wielenga, previously senior deputy head here. Degree in economics from the University of Natal in South Africa and postgrad qualification in human resource development from the Rand Afrikaans University in Johannesburg. Also taught at Michaelhouse in KwaZulu-Natal and was a housemaster and head of economics at Wellington College before joining Blundell's in 2012.

Academic matters: In the past, not the brightest star in the firmament of south west schools, but a determination to make the school as academic as it is sporty is paying off. Key appointments include a head of learning support, who is an ed psych, and a switched-on academic deputy from Wycombe Abbey, and there's now a proper tutor system, which has gone down well with parents. A level results are climbing, with 71 per cent graded A*/B and 46 per cent A*/A in 2018; sciences, business studies, geography and maths – good take-up of further maths too – are most popular, languages lamentably not, though it is impressive to note that the school has run Spanish, Japanese and Latin for sole takers. Parents reckon that student aspirations are being raised; many already take EPQ in sixth form alongside A levels. The brightest sparks are invited to join the scholars' club, which 'offers stimulation for rapid progress' in the dry language beloved of inspectors.

At GCSE, 46 per cent graded A*-A/9-7 in 2018, slightly down on the previous year. DT enjoys stunning results and a big take-up: we would have been happy to give house-room to many of the items of small wooden furniture we saw. Students with a wide range of intellectual gifts are catered for: at GCSE science, for example, school offers choice between IGCSE or less demanding boards. Everyone does French and Latin from the start with the choice of German and Spanish in year 9. Just over a fifth of students receive SEN support, including plenty of help for those whose first language is not English.

Games, options, the arts: Make no mistake, this is a very sporty school, and might not be the place for a pale aesthete. That said, there is masses on offer for those with little or no eye for a ball, as well as the usual fare of rugby, hockey (both huge here), netball and cricket (for girls too, plus football, tennis, squash and fives): CCF, DofE, Ten Tors and the Devizes to Westminster canoe race keenly pursued. In the spring, the whole school participates in the (frankly bonkers) Russell (named for the eponymous Jack of terrier fame and an OB): a hotly contested cross-country race for which local landowners open their land. We had never seen quite such cheerfully muddy girls as the ones we met just back from a practice. General heartiness extends to an outdoor pool only – 'reassuringly heated,' says school – though an indoor one is on everyone's wish list, and keen swimmers can use the indoor facilities in Tiverton. Riding strong here too – Blundell's riders regularly compete at events in the south west and recently won the National Schools Jumping-with-style contest – but it's not the kind of school where turning up with a horsebox is de rigueur; no equines on site.

Activities range from aerobics to yoga; everyone is expected to sign up for a minimum of two. Boarders are offered an adventure and leadership programme over eight weekends comprising gorge-walking and survival training along with other feats of derring-do. But Blundell's isn't just good at the strenuous stuff: a long tradition of debating both in school and beyond was crowned by winning the ESU national final recently. Artists in all media compete and show their work far beyond the school, with success at the Tate, in the Saatchi Art Prize for Schools (online but also, more excitingly, in the Kings Road) and more locally in Tiverton and Exeter. We were gutted that an art scholar's rendition of the Mona Lisa in peanut butter and chocolate spread had (presumably) been eaten before our visit. Music facilities have just been brought bang up to date with an editing suite and composition/technology studio, but there has long been masses of music both sung and played: concerts and recitals, plus recently Grease, Cabaret and open mic night on the lighter side. In the last couple of years groups have been to Prague, Brittany and Venice, as well as prestigious venues nearer home. Drama takes places in the Ondaatje Hall, named for its generous donor, the notable philanthropist, brother of the author and an OB; plenty of backstage and technical experience on offer as well as acting, plus visits and workshops from French and Spanish theatre groups – a great initiative which other schools would do well to emulate. A long tradition of house and year group plays means there are opportunities for all budding thespians.

Boarding: Relationships between staff and students seem extremely good, with house staff coming in for particular praise – some email parents with photos of boarders' activities and high jinks just about the moment they happen. The seven houses accommodate a mix of all kinds of boarders (full, weekly, flexi) and day pupils, divided into two co-ed at the beginning and end of a student's time at Blundell's, two girls' and three boys'; all are known by their initials – NC, SH etc. Twice as many boys as girls are full boarders and parents of full boarders rather wish more kids stayed in at weekends, and that the food was, on occasion, more girl-friendly. Some of their accommodation could do with a bit of tlc too. The crowning glory of boarding has to be Westlake, the co-ed sixth form house where students get as close a feeling of university life as possible before they get there, yet where girls and boys respectively can retreat from the hurly-burly to their own part of the house

Background and atmosphere: Four-square Victorian red-brick buildings face more modern additions across Blundells Road in Tiverton – such is the importance of the school to the town that it has a road named after it – set off by gracious green spaces and a distinctive clock tower; though the school was founded by the generous legacy of one of England's wealthiest cloth merchants, Peter Blundell, over 200 hundred years earlier, it moved to its permanent home only in the 1880s. The values of that time persist in some measure today with the school's emphasis on 'distinguished performance in those games which the Victorians [had] developed to replace the rude sports of earlier centuries'. No more cock-fighting then.

Definitely a traditional feel about the place, with a bewildering number of ties, though certainly not fuddy-duddy, with boys below sixth form wearing tawny tweed jackets, the colour of autumn bracken on Dartmoor, and girls red ones. Even the sixth form wear uniform; their jackets are navy blue, striped for those who have been awarded full colours – given not only for sports, but all manner of accomplishment.

What in other schools might be called assembly takes place in Big School and is called Latin Prayer, concluding as it does with the Lord's prayer in Latin; chapel on other mornings in the school's own beautiful chapel.

The first girls arrived in 1975 and the school went fully co-ed in 1992. We are delighted that a recent head girl exercised her right to keep a pig at school for her final term, something conferred on the head boy from the start.

Parents love the friendly and inclusive feel of the place, the lack of arrogance among the students and the resilience the school instils in them. 'Absolutely non-stop programme of extracurricular activities means my children are absolutely exhausted by the time they come home – perhaps they need more soothing down-time at weekends to recover,' observed one mother of boarders. Great affection and loyalty for the school from past and present students and staff – one finally took retirement after 30 years' service; terrific and longstanding network of events for OBs, not just the 'winter lunches' in Devon, but all over the world.

Pastoral care, well-being and discipline: Discipline appears to be kept with a lightish touch – parents of drinkers and smokers can expect 'to be invited in to discuss a way forward'. Drugs weren't even mentioned, and bullying gets zero tolerance.

'There's a sexting issue every year in year 9,' said one mother phlegmatically, 'but the school just deals with it'.

Pupils and parents: Mostly local but a good handful (about 15 per cent) from abroad, giving the school a more cosmopolitan feel than mid Devon might otherwise manage. Among the farmers, local professionals and the military, there are boarders from Cornwall, where there is little on offer, and of course refugees from London in search of a better life; some first time buyers of independent schooling too, one of whom said, 'My son is having the kind of education that I work for and dream of him having'. Pupils are as grounded and unpretentious as any you will find at a UK boarding school, the kind who will have a go and take a risk; we suspect that the rebellious, the precious and the show-off would not thrive here.

Entrance: Mostly at 11, by means of papers in English, maths and non-verbal reasoning in the January preceding entry; at 13+ via common entrance or the school's own entrance test in English and maths in June. At sixth form, hopefuls have to satisfy relatively undemanding entrance requirements of a minimum of five GCSEs at a 5 or above with at least a 6 in subjects to be taken to A level, plus interview

Exit: Up to 20 per cent leave after GCSEs. The vast majority to university and traditional ones at that, up and down the country. 'No-one goes to Exeter – too close to home,' sixth formers informed us. Recent Oxbridge successes (three in 2018, five the year before, plus five medics) may well boost applications in that direction. Popular universities include Durham, Imperial College, Warwick, Reading, Bristol, Leeds and Manchester. Degree choices again tend towards the conventional and/or vocational, such as medicine, geography, economics, biochemistry, law and business management. Very loyal links to the old school tie all over the world. Famous OBs include RD Blackmore, (whose Lorna Doone was a fictional pupil), 40s actor Gerald Hamer and his director son Robert (Kind Hearts and Coronets), defence correspondent and author Robert Fox, organist Peter Hurford, TV journalist Claire Marshall and the drummer of The Vamps, Tristan Evans.

Money matters: For the first 300 years of its existence, Blundell's was maintained by the profits from its properties in Tiverton and estate in south Devon, but these days fees charged are in line with comparable schools. Decent range of scholarships for sport, music, art, drama, all-round as well as academic; only music and academic at 11+. Peter Blundell Foundation bursaries are awarded in cases of financial need where 'Governors wish to reflect the spirit of Peter Blundell's vision'. The school is innovative in attracting an array of corporate sponsors to fund events.

Remarks: Ancient and distinguished Devon institution preserving traditional values and feel, yet turning out considerate and balanced young people all set for careers across the globe. Not perhaps for those seeking exclusively to scale the heights of academia or social cachet, but deserves far higher prominence than the lowish profile ('Not in the west country!' protests school) it currently assumes.

Bournemouth School

B

East Way, Bournemouth BH8 9PY

Ages 11–18 **Pupils** 1,039 **Sixth form** 285 (33 girls)

01202 512609
www.bournemouth-school.org

Headmaster: Since 2009, Dr Dorian Lewis CChem MRSC (early 50s), previously deputy head of Queen Elizabeth's School, Wimborne. Educated at Jones' West Monmouth Grammar School for Boys (now West Monmouth School), then read chemistry at the University of Southampton. While he was doing his PhD at Southampton he taught undergraduates practical organic chemistry and found it 'the most enjoyable part of the week' so decided on a teaching career. After a PGCE at Nottingham he taught at The Thomas Hardye School in Dorchester for four years before moving to Queen Elizabeth's as head of science.

He knew Bournemouth School was the place for him the moment he walked in, partly because it reminded him of his own grammar school. He says 'the mantra of hard work, discipline, smart appearance and respect echoes the traditional values that had been instilled in me as a boy'. As he writes on the school website: 'We have not sought to be trendy, have resisted the temptation to jump on educational bandwagons and have not manipulated examination statistics to rise up the league tables. We have simply focused upon the basics and the needs of our students.' He's adamant that the school shouldn't be 'an ivory tower' and has worked hard to widen access for all pupils. He chairs the local Pupil Placement Panel and is also an Ofsted inspector, which 'keeps me current and is my best professional development'.

Still teaches chemistry – year 7 pupils this year, year 13s next year – and says teaching is still the best part of his day. 'It's very difficult to make demands of your teaching staff unless you are prepared to teach yourself. As a head you have to deal with a lot of admin, policy and political shenanigans and that can be quite draining. But when you spend time with your students it's all worthwhile.' He's clearly a polymath; over the years he's taught everything from chemistry and maths to ethics and philosophy, even art (he did art A level). The school is active on Twitter and the head's tweets are often chemistry-related. We visited during the World Cup and he shared the following nuggets of information: 'Here's some of the chemistry you can look out for over the next month; polymers make up the ball and the shirts and chemistry has a part to play in the vanishing spray that referees will be using during the games.'

Energetic, driven and ultra-focused, he is very disciplined, working hard during term-time and taking time 'to stand back and reflect' during the holidays. His wife Denise is an exam invigilator at the school (she's also stepped in as a teaching assistant and midday supervisor) and they have two sons, both pupils at the school, and a daughter, who hopes to join the sixth form in due course. In his spare time he enjoys spending time with his family, 'being outdoors' and walking along the Dorset coast.

Academic matters: School was judged to be outstanding at the last Ofsted inspection in 2011. In 2018, 41 per cent A*/A at A level and 67 per cent A*-B, with maths the most popular subject. At GCSE, 65 per cent A*-A/7-9 in 2018.

A total of 22 subjects on offer at A level, including business studies, further maths, RS, PE, politics and psychology. Up until now most have taken four A levels but students can now opt to do three A levels, plus a Pre-U, core maths or CREST gold award. 'We are giving them a degree of flexibility,' says the head. The school is known for its strength in STEM (science, technology, engineering and maths) subjects but pupils and parents say it's good across the board. Most pupils take 11 subjects at GCSE, including maths, English language, English literature, biology, chemistry, physics, RS, a language (French, Spanish, German), history or geography and two other subjects.

A number have learning support and the school does everything it can to help. Individual Learning Needs department staff tell pupils: 'If you have an issue with anything, raise it.' One boy praised his English teacher for flagging up an issue with his handwriting and enabling him to use a laptop for written work.

Games, options, the arts: School is very sporty, with notable successes in rugby, football, cricket and tennis. Lots of other sports on offer too, including surfing (the beach at Boscombe is four miles away), climbing, table tennis, dance, martial arts, basketball and badminton. The Sir David English Sports Centre (named after the famous Daily Mail editor, a former pupil at the school) is a three-minute walk away, with a vast sports hall, gym, four floodlit tennis courts and an Astroturf. School playing fields comprise three rugby and two football pitches, a 400m running track and two cricket squares. Music is an integral part of school life, with choirs (singing is popular here), orchestras, bands, assorted ensembles and concerts galore. Art is stunning – six students doing A level art at the time of our visit and the department is developing strong links with Arts University Bournemouth.

Very active CCF. The school is one of the few state schools in the country to offer CCF and pupils can join their chosen section, Army, Navy or RAF, from year 9 and up. Cadets and band members play a prominent role in Bournemouth's annual Remembrance Day parade. There's also a Royal Navy Sea Scout troop, which is inspected by a Royal Navy flag officer every 18 months.

A vast range of extracurricular activities, everything from science club and theatre club, D of E and young engineers. Many are student-led and pupils are encouraged to launch new ones each year. Students do work experience in year 10 and the sixth form, often at nearby JP Morgan Chase and Bournemouth Hospital.

Background and atmosphere: The school came into being on January 22, 1901, the day Queen Victoria died. Moved to its current site just as the Second World War erupted. During the war years the school buildings were used by pupils from Taunton School in Southampton as well as by Bournemouth School boys. Only staff and sixth formers can use the echoing front hall and staircase, with walls lined with awards and achievements. Wooden boards commemorate pupils who died in the First and Second World Wars and our sixth-form guide told us he always stops and reflects as he passes them. 'It's nice to be in a school that has a real legacy,' he told us. 'It's hard to walk by and not look at the names of those who died. Some of them were our age.' The school became an academy in 2011 and admitted girls to the sixth form from 2012. Almost half the school's 68-strong teaching staff are women.

Main school building is impressively long, with an outsize clock tower. The school library has 17,500 catalogued resources and is well-used by all. 'The pupils here are prolific readers,' the librarian told us, adding that current favourites are Robert Muchamore's CHERUB series and The Hate U Give by Angie Thomas. Library is open from 8am to 5pm, with an after-school homework club where pupils can work, read or play board games. Extensive wooded grounds, included the much-loved copse which pupils are allowed to visit at break and lunchtime. School atmosphere is busy and purposeful, with pupils chatting amiably as they scurry between classes. Year 7 to 11 boys look smart in grey blazers and trousers and bright blue ties. Student voice is regarded as important, with pupils airing their opinions and suggestions at year group councils and a whole school council.

Pastoral care, well-being and discipline: A house system (five houses, plus a sixth on the way) and form tutor groups provide a forum for informal monitoring of progress and social issues. 'We see our form tutors twice a day,' one boy told us. 'They have a pastoral role too so they are our first port of call if we have a problem with anything.' Few discipline issues. 'Most of the boys are very biddable,' says the head.

Sixth formers get privileges to denote their seniority, including wearing business suits rather than school uniform, having the option to work at school or at home during study periods, being allowed to walk down the front staircase and driving to school. Leadership and responsibility are prevailing themes. Some pupils become prefects in year 10 and more are added in year 12. The 30 school prefects take their responsibilities very seriously, mindful of their role in the school community and keen to support younger pupils. There's a school captain, deputy school captain and house captains too. The current school captain told us he had been inspired by 'brilliant role models' when he was in year 7 and he wanted to follow in their footsteps.

Pupils and parents: Most pupils come from around Bournemouth and the surrounding area, with a handful from places like Lymington and Salisbury. A star-spangled and eclectic list of alumni, including the afore-mentioned Sir David English, Blur guitarist turned cheesemaker Alex James, educationalist Sir Mike Tomlinson, choirmaster Gareth Malone and TV journalist Mark Austin.

Entrance: Admissions policy has changed in recent years to prioritise eligible students from Bournemouth and parts of Christchurch (93 per cent who joined the school in 2018 come from Bournemouth). School is expanding from current 150 year 7 intake to 180. Since 2016 the school has prioritised admitting disadvantaged pupils (around six per cent of pupils are currently eligible for the pupil premium grant) and hopes to improve access for pupils from the most deprived local areas in the coming years.

Competition for places is tough. Around 229 boys applied for 150 places for September 2018 – most from primary schools, a few from local preps. There's one set of tests for Bournemouth School, Bournemouth School for Girls, Parkstone Grammar and Poole Grammar, with students taking tests in maths, English and verbal reasoning a year preceding entry. Pass mark for Bournemouth School is currently 300. Asked who will thrive at the school, the head says: 'We are looking for those who will best accept the whole ethos of the school – hard work, discipline, smart appearance and respect. If they are able to buy into that they will succeed here.' As a rule of thumb, if boys are in the top three or four of their primary school class they stand a good chance of gaining places. The head isn't keen on tutoring. 'I don't want them to have extensive tutoring,' he says. 'We want bright, able children who are interested in learning.'

Pupils admitted into years 8 to 11 by assessment if a vacancy arises, but not within 12 months of a previous assessment. A number of students (girls as well as boys) join in the sixth form. All sixth formers (from inside and outside) need a 'best eight' GCSE points score of at least 50 points, at least grade 5s in both English language and maths and at least grade 6s in the subjects they want to study at A level.

Exit: Fewer than 25 per cent of boys leave after GCSEs – some because the school only offers 'traditional' A level courses and doesn't do subjects like media studies, sociology and drama, others who head to local sixth form colleges.

Almost 80 per cent of year 13 leavers go to university. The school's 2018 leavers included three to Oxbridge and eight medics. Half to Russell Group universities, with Cardiff one of the most popular destinations. Two or three to universities abroad (at the time of our visit a student had just been offered a place at the world-class MIT), some to apprenticeships.

Remarks: An impressive mix of traditional and modern, with bright, enthusiastic, motivated pupils who are keen to learn and play their part in the school community. Definitely a school to be reckoned with.

Bournemouth School for Girls

Castle Gate Close, Castle Lane West, Bournemouth BH8 9UJ

Ages 11–18 **Pupils** 1,150 **Sixth form** 300

01202 526289
www.bsg.bournemouth.sch.uk

Headteacher: Since 2004, Alistair Brien, married with three children. Deputy at BSG from 1998, and previously director of sixth form studies at Arnewood School, housemaster at Keswick School and teacher at Aylesbury Grammar. Degree in German from Exeter, author of several German textbooks, and Ofsted inspector.

Most likely to say 'this is not an exam factory' (once you've passed the one to get in); and 'he is true to his word', said a parent. 'Warm and approachable', said another. 'He is very involved with the school', she added, and came to her daughter's final presentation for her EPQ at lunchtime to be supportive.

Pupils like him and clearly think he's game – 'he drinks all the cocktails in the cocktail challenge' (20+ concoctions – a challenge in itself). Does magic tricks in assembly – much appreciated by pupils.

Academic matters: Pupils at BSG, the highest best state school in the area, are selected for their high ability and aptitude, and 'it is a pressurised environment', says the head, 'but from the girls and their parents, not me'. The head's view is: 'Do your best: your best is good enough'. There are some very competitive groups, say pupils, who always ask each other their grades, but equally some that are less so: girls cleave towards their natural community. Pupils generally take work seriously – one saying, 'being amongst your intellectual equals makes you work harder'. ['Pupils] all had to work hard to get in', said a parent, 'so both they and their parents are quite motivated. I'm not saying there're not any shenanigans', she added. Thank goodness for that.

Good exam results are expected by both girls and parents, and excellence is generally achieved – 66 per cent A*-A/9-7 at GCSE, 40 per cent A*/A, 73 per cent A*-B at A level in 2018. Most take 11 GCSEs. There's plenty of one-to-one support from form tutors and heads of house, and many sixth formers become study buddies to help younger pupils. Attainment and progress are regularly monitored, so any problems are picked up early. Pupils say that teachers are very supportive of problems, There's also the head's secret weapon: his learning centre, staffed by TAs, where those with SEN or anyone in the need of a bit of extra help can benefit from one-to-one support; someone who has been off sick long term might come here to catch up.

There are not many pupils with SEN (currently 35), who need to excel in the entrance exam to get here, just like everyone else (although special provision made as necessary to sit the test). But once you're in, the support is 'amazing,' said a parent. It is provided both in and out of lessons, a parent of an autistic child saying assistance had been designed to cater specifically for her daughter's needs: 'Going to BSG has transformed her life. She wouldn't be in the same place without it...it has really levelled the playing field for her, and helped her perform to the best of her capabilities'. A pupil with Asperger's went to Cambridge recently, as did another with special needs.

At GCSE there are seven teaching groups with 24 per class, with bigger classes lower down the school (not currently exceeding 29). The school will try to run A level courses however small the number of interested pupils, so some classes have just two pupils (they will have one fewer lessons a week than better populated subjects).

'Teachers range from good to inspirational', said a parent, who also appreciated the good mix of female and male teachers. Psychology is consistently amongst the most popular A levels – the teachers 'capture and ignite imaginations', said a parent, this class also benefiting from regular visits from a tortoiseshell cat, curled up asleep on a chair when we visited. Biology, history, maths, English literature and maths are also popular A levels. Sixth formers are expected to be proactive in their learning, with teachers happily marking any extra work done. 'Lessons go at a fast and furious pace', said a parent, often surprising those joining the school in the sixth form.

The careers department has recently been transformed – 'it's very outward looking now', say the girls. There's no longer an assumption that all pupils will be going to university, and it offers advice about work, colleges and apprenticeships. The head described the advantages of a year in industry for a pupil who was initially rejected by Cambridge, but accepted after a year out: there's no lack of enterprise here, and understanding the world of work is quite a focus. There's plenty of enterprise, not least the famous cocktail challenge competition, which has whiffs of The Apprentice in the challenge to construct a (non-alcoholic) cocktail, design the packing and do a marketing presentation.

Games, options, the arts: The head says 'academic excellence is important but so is being a well-rounded person who makes a difference – and finding an area where you can shine'. And this could be anything – recently a pupil achieved dog obedience champion at Crufts. 'Finding a passion gives a child that all-important self confidence', claims the head.

Sport is one of many activities here, and despite the limited and rather tired facilities (a new sports hall is a priority when funds are available), they do very well. All the usual teams, excelling at national or county level. The school finished second in the National Schools Badminton Championships – 'even though they're just playing in the hall or the gym, where all the markings have worn away', said a bemused but happy parent.

Public speaking, debating and quizzes are extremely popular here, and must partly account for the great articulacy of the pupils. Plenty of clubs: Amnesty is well attended, as are knitting and jewellery making; many clubs are run by sixth formers for younger pupils, and most take place at lunchtime (school buses mean the after-school slot is tricky). CCF is very popular: they join and outnumber the grammar boys next door for this, and enthuse about the super trips: the RAF to Gibraltar, the navy section 'on actual boats'. Lots do DofE, with a growing number gaining gold.

A splendid new art block, art also being displayed neatly around the school, and some lovely textiles including a gorgeous

Swan Lake dress, and light up ball dress (the batteries are stored in a pack on a strap underneath – not perhaps for vigorous dancers). Art and textiles are not as popular as more academic subjects here, but the work is exciting and imaginative, and nearly all those taking these subjects excel in exams.

The music room was full of year 7s and a cheerful cacophony of noise – flute, keyboards, other instruments and chatter. In a side room, some girls were trying to add chords to their compositions. 'It's difficult', said one, 'but easier if...' she gestured at the keyboard, note names scrawled on keys. Most girls learn an instrument, and if their parents can't afford lessons, the school will help. Pupils audition for the chamber choir (performing with the Bournemouth Symphony Orchestra as part of its concert season); all comers to the Big Heart and Soul choir. Drama also very popular, most of the school playing some part in the annual production, usually with the boys' grammar, with whom they take it in turns to host.

Background and atmosphere: Considering the ferocious competition to get into this school, the atmosphere is surprisingly relaxed and friendly. One parent chose BSG because of this, adding that they were 'shocked' by the confidence of the girls who showed them around, compared to other grammar schools.

A parent whose daughters had both come from a local private school said the atmosphere of the grammar is more 'real'. The overwhelming impression is of an efficient and focused school. Girls here know they are fortunate (having battled in through the 11+) and are generally studious and concentrate in lessons.

Girls are delighted to be without boys: 'disruptive and loud,' said one, evidently remembering with some horror her primary school; though pupils hastened to add that they have plenty to do with boys, joining the boys' grammar next door in a political society, debating (they regularly flatten the boys) and CCF. Boys from the Bishop Winchester Academy (which the school sponsors), also come in for economic and finance lessons.

Communication is good, parents being kept put to date by email, and the parent portal, where parents can pay for lunches and trips. Tutors and head of house respond promptly to emails, and the head is available to parents on a drop in basis every morning.

Smart blue and white uniform with a snowdrop badge (the only flower out when the school opened in 1918, and chosen as a symbol of hope). 'It's nice when it's not rolled up at the waist', said a parent, who chuckles at the head's annual reminder to parents that 'skirts grown out of need replacing'. Casual dress for sixth formers, required to be 'modest' but actually they wear pretty much what they want to. No blue jeans allowed, but no shortage of short skirts – modest apparently draws the line at bare tummies.

Buildings were state of the art in the early 1960s. They're not beautiful, but largely well kept, and the two new centres were built in complementary style. Peaceful, well-stocked library.

A school with a social conscience which has been recognised nationally by Prince Charles's Step Up to Serve campaign. All the usual charity work, but it's not just buying donuts from Asda and flogging them at exorbitant prices. Pupils are strongly encouraged to get involved with the local community, and many take part in the National Citizen Service programme and the Lions Club service awards.

School council, two reps from each class, whose purpose is to take school forward, not whinge. Pupils report back on new staff, who have to teach a trial lesson, and may even be involved in the interview process.

Delicious food, with a good array of options. Sixth formers also have Heidi and her food bar constantly available in their common room (a lovely sixth form perk – their common room is a very happy place).

A house system was introduced a few years ago to encourage a sense of community across age groups, charity fundraising and friendly competition – and the girls are keen participants in house events. 'They're all involved', says the head, 'not just the crack squad'.

Pastoral care, well-being and discipline: Parents praise the support offered, one citing extra care during a family illness and another the concern shown when a child had lost lots of weight. The school works hard on promoting healthy friendships amongst new year 7s as the best way of preventing bullying – 'I give you permission to make lots of friends', says the head, trying to dilute small established cliques. A parent described how one her daughters experienced name calling in year 7: the whole class was told in no uncertain terms it must stop now, and that made a big impression. Her shy daughter also found lunchtime clubs a salvation, enabling her to avoid braving the playground.

School nurse has a direct link to local authority services, and we were told how she had helped a child suffering from anxiety before a school residential trip. Upper school can self-refer, and stressed or anxious pupils may well end up in her care, though it is usual to go through the tutor and head of house first.

School policies contain a detailed code of conduct for misbehaviour, which rather belies the enlightened approach to discipline here. Rules on jewellery and make up are flexibly enforced, one parent describing her daughter receiving a 'polite reminder' when discreet make-up got a bit much, and ruminating that 'a certain amount of tolerance means less abuse'. Girls are dealt with gently, on the basis that harsh rules are more likely to lead to rebellion; head encourages staff to praise good behaviour and let the others conform in response.

Pupils and parents: All walks of life, said a parent. Parents are often 'very focused,' said one carefully, some of them anticipating their child's grades, university and career trajectory with extraordinary certainty.

Entrance: Some 450 going for 180 places. Of those who pass the exams in English, maths and verbal reasoning, places allocated firstly to those with an EHC plan, then looked after children, next to the 130 who scored highest in the test, then to those on pupil premium who are resident in one of the designated Bournemouth postcodes, then local residents not on pupil premium.

'Prepare (as you would for any exam) but don't coach', says the head. Seventy places for pupils from other schools in the sixth form, allocated on the basis of GCSE results.

Exit: About a quarter leave after GCSEs, with equal numbers joining from elsewhere. Most sixth formers to university, around half to Russell Group; three to Oxbridge in 2018, plus nine medics; Exeter particularly popular with Cardiff, Warwick and Durham close behind. A scattering to foundation art, employment, apprenticeships and gap years.

Money matters: Bursary fund available for sixth formers.

Remarks: The head says it wouldn't suit someone who failed to take advantages of all the opportunities the girls have here, and they agree: competitive entry perhaps results in pupils who are particularly aware of their good fortune and determined to take advantage of it. Not for those who aren't academic, say parents; the value added to those who just scrape in is excellent, but they may find the competitive atmosphere hard on their self-esteem.

A fast paced academic school, which manages to offer the girls a wealth of opportunities on a limited budget, and which has more of a lively social conscience than many wealthier schools. Produces relaxed and confident girls who feel well set up for life.

B

Bristol Grammar School

Linked with BGS Infant and Juniors

University Road, Bristol BS8 1SR

Ages 11–18 **Pupils** 1,015 **Sixth form** 310

Fees: £14,610 pa

01179 736006
www.bristolgrammarschool.co.uk

Headmaster: Since September 2018, Jaideep Barot MA MSc, previously deputy head (academic) at Marlborough College. A particle physicist with a fine academic pedigree (Manchester Grammar, Cambridge and Durham), he previously held leadership roles at Westminster School and Godolphin & Latymer. He worked in international banking for Goldman Sachs before he saw the light and went into education.

Academic matters: Proportion of students achieving highest grades in GCSE, IGCSE and A level holding up well. In 2018, 54 per cent of grades were A*/A at A level, 65 per cent A*-A/7-9 at GCSE. Excellent outcomes are result of improved teaching, according to previous head. IB offered since 2018.

Broad curriculum is reviewed regularly to ensure it meets changing needs and demands. Sciences taught separately from year 8. French and Spanish taught in year 7; option to drop one MFL in favour of German or Russian in year 9. 'Personalised curriculum' in year 9 is proving popular: students choose nine subjects from a range of 20 to study alongside English, maths, biology, chemistry and physics. Students usually reduce to five options plus core subjects in years 10 and 11, with most sitting 11 GCSEs. Classes are split into two groups of 12 in year 11.

Large sixth form means excellent range of A level subjects on offer. Maths very strong – about half year group doing A level, with 30 studying further maths too. English literature follows Cambridge Pre-U course. English language and creative writing are A level options. One parent praised 'phenomenal support for girls in engineering and science'. Science labs have been refurbished to a high standard – some parents may lament the loss of the old wooden benches, but there's no such sentiment from the students. Being close to University of Bristol and its ChemLabS state of the art facilities is a big plus. Lots of opportunities for fieldwork and work outside the classroom. EPQ on offer to all, plus a scholars' programme for the most talented students; also a BGS Leadership Diploma.

Level of homework gradually increases from year 7 and end-of-term exams are held for all. Students and parents see them as positive – 'it helps to keep things in your brain' – and they praise the interactive lessons and the standards of teaching. 'This school prepares you to deal with the wider world,' said one student. One parent who has seen three students through the school said the process was well managed. 'Exams every year makes them feel comfortable with it by the time they come to GCSE and A level. There is plenty of time for exam practice and revision. My sons were pushed without feeling they were under too much pressure or fear of failure.'

Parents also generally happy with the standard of information and reports on achievement and progress. Much sharing of data and tracking online. 'The traditional school report is often six weeks out of date by the time it has been written, collated, checked and posted,' says school. 'Nowadays it is about "working with" children and families, not "doing to" children and families. Young staff are very comfortable with this.'

Prolific use of iPads by children in year 8 and year 9, especially for languages teaching. 'We won't have textbooks in 10 years' time.' Teachers all have iPads and laptops and make use of interactive whiteboards. Timetable has been altered to give longer lessons and travel time between classes, and an unusually long lunch break – 90 minutes. This allows time to eat and 50 minutes to attend one of the many clubs. One parent said her son had found this difficult at first, struggling to concentrate for four one-hour lessons, but overall staff and students like the arrangement.

A pivotal change, according to staff, is in being open to learning from one another and sharing good practice. 'There's been a real push to let people in to classrooms, hold learning walks, get everyone involved. Teachers are approaching lessons more like artisan makers.'

Significant number of pupils with dyslexia and a few with dyspraxia, ADD, hearing impairment, physical disabilities. Whole school support for SEN overseen by an assistant head, supported by a part-time SENco and part-time dyslexia teacher. Additional support for pupils with exceptional ability and EAL too.

Games, options, the arts: Staff, students and parents are unanimous: BGS is a very busy school. 'There's no end to the variety of opportunities for students in and out of school hours,' said one parent. 'It's almost impossible to keep track of all the stuff that's going on,' said another. A teacher acknowledged: 'Students can be challenging – they are always looking to extend their knowledge. They want us to provide as much as possible – fixtures, activities, trips.'

School has a long and proud sporting history, especially for hockey and rugby. Recent tours to South Africa and New Zealand were 'brilliantly run,' one dad reported. More than 20 sports on offer, including track cycling, yoga, street dance and fencing. Synchronised swimming star Anastasija Bates is a recent alumna. Fabulous on-site sports centre includes a gym and a climbing wall as well as sports hall and squash courts. Facilities at the sports ground at Failand include impressive pitches overlooked from a superb pavilion. There's also a low ropes course and woodland for forest school activities.

BGS has a director of outdoor learning and three staff trained as outdoor leaders. Many staff, not just PE teachers, involved in sports and other extracurricular provision. It's accepted by them that taking part in activities after school and on Saturday morning is all part of what makes BGS work. 'Engagement and commitment is more than just what happens 9-4 on weekdays.' Being taught geography by the person who took cricket practice 'creates a definite dynamic', building relationships that benefit all. Also, allowing teachers to follow their passions inspires and encourages students. 'You can't salami-slice children – you have to care for the whole child, building their confidence and making them feel safe and secure,' as the previous head put it. Parents agree that these informal conversations on the touchline – and, equally, after rehearsals and performances – help reinforce shared values and bonding.

'About a third of students and staff are involved on any one Saturday, and not always the same third,' we were told.

Very strong emphasis on music, arts, dance and drama. New performing arts centre in 2016, incorporating a 240-seat theatre, 180-seat auditorium, music classrooms and a dance studio. Last head was passionate about maximising opportunities for performing and creative arts both in and outside the curriculum, believing it to be crucial in helping prepare for adult life in 21st century by fostering skills in communication, collaboration and presentation.

Definite move away from 'macho' image in recent years: for example, all boys do dance in senior school. 'Softer' activities are encouraged for boys and girls, with clubs such as textiles, beekeeping and Bake Off. This adds to a quirky feel around the school site, with yarnbombing in the trees, beehives on the science block roof and kayaks parked under the cherry blossom.

Facilities for creative arts – housed in one of Elton Road houses, complete with garden studios – and design technology, in a superb underground workshop, are outstanding. BGS regularly excels in the Greenpower build-a-car competition. The school stages its own annual Wildlife Photographer of the Year competition and the stunning winning entries are on display around the campus.

Music is currently taught in the performing arts centre, and many students also learn instruments – you'll find up to 40 having lessons at any one time, in the multiple individual or group practice spaces. Lots of opportunities to perform in choirs, bands and choirs, in prestigious venues and on tour as well as for school events. House singing competition a highlight of the year. New centre will means music technology courses can be introduced. Food and nutrition is an increasingly popular subject, taught in well-equipped kitchens. Pupils split into smaller classes – maximum 14 – for DT, art and music.

Trips and expeditions are on offer for all age groups. The year 9 expedition, which gives pupils the choice of sand, sea or snow, epitomises BGS's aims – life-changing, learning, friendships and adventure. Wild camping in the Atlas Mountains, or under the stars in Finland 'creates the magic and allows time for proper conversations', according to staff. 'It is is quite nice not having to worry "where's my phone?"' a student commented. DofE scheme also popular.

Sixth formers value their wide-ranging lecture programme – from hypnotism to James Bond. They also follow a Back Yourself programme to develop confidence in social situations.

Appropriately for a school that has Allen Lane, founder of Penguin Books, among its alumni, BGS is famed for its literary events – more than 200 author visits in 15 years – and for its library, which houses more than 34,000 titles and has a generous budget for replenishment.

The wood-panelled Great Hall is used for all manner of activities, from daily lunch for 1,500 to grand occasions. One memorable event in 2015 was a 15-hour whole-school reading of Homer's Odyssey (in English) involving students of all ages, teachers, ex-students, support staff, parents, university staff and undergraduates.

Guidance on future choices is provided by two careers staff, who are supported well by returning alumni.

Background and atmosphere: Friendly and welcoming. Location alongside the University of Bristol is a great advantage, providing a harmonious academic setting. BGS was founded in 1532 and has been at Tyndall's Park site since 1879. Whole school population now takes part in Charter Day procession down Park Street to Bristol Cathedral. 'We celebrate our identity as a school at the heart of the city, where we began. We are reminded of our legacy and the achievements of our predecessors.'

Staff, students and parents speak of 'tremendous ethos of achievement in the school' and are glad that 'achievement in any field is celebrated'. Teachers seen as cheerful, positive, busy, enthusiastic, with some described as 'extraordinary,' 'fabulous' and 'inspiring'. Parents in awe of way school is organised. 'I've not heard of anything poorly run or poorly delivered.'

One said: 'The last head dragged the school into the 21st century. He made it highly competitive with other schools in Bristol – less stuffy.'

Paradoxically, since the introduction of infant school classes in 2010, a stronger 'whole school' ethos has developed across BGS. Staff, students and parents value the all-through, 4-18 mix. All ages share the same breakfast club; sixth formers help infants with reading; year 2s sing in the BGS assembly.

Pastoral care, well-being and discipline: Senior house system has been strengthened in recent years, with head of house as pastoral leader. Six houses, each with its own colour. Trips, parties, social and competitive activities as well as personal support and a family atmosphere. 'Classic boarding school model. House is like a school within a school,' says a staff member. Peer mentoring is a strong feature of pastoral care too.

A student help desk is staffed all day to answer any enquiries. There's also a full-time nurse and two part-time counsellors. One parent praised 'immediate and appropriate response after a family bereavement – it was nice to know the school knew and understood'.

Strong investment in transition, as children come into year 7 from many different primary schools. One mum said: 'Coming from a small primary, I was worried my daughter would struggle in a big secondary, but she is relishing the different characters, has made friends and is enjoying lessons. She has discovered climbing and is absolutely obsessed with it.'

Emphasis on positive reinforcement and encouragement of expected behaviour. Parents appreciate the many cards, postcards, and letters commending their children. Some are less keen on the necessary communications about infringements; one parent said being texted because his son was late for school was 'a bit nanny state-ish'.

Pupils and parents: BGS became independent in 1979 following abolition of direct grant system and went co-ed a year later. Steady increase in proportion of girls. One long-serving staff member said there was 'no doubt this had benefited the school enormously; it has created a more amiable atmosphere'. Males still in majority but most students, staff and parents agree 'it has never felt an overly boys' school'. Nature of the school changed again with the move to bursaries from assisted places scheme. Majority of students come from north west Bristol. Not many from excessively wealthy backgrounds; bias towards professionals. Phenomenal number of staff send their own children to BGS because 'it offers so many opportunities. Something for everyone to fit into'. Several recent leavers have returned as teachers.

Entrance: Most students join senior school in year 7, about half from the juniors and the rest from up to 40 primaries in Bristol and beyond. External candidates sit January entrance exam tests in verbal reasoning, problem solving and English and also attend a meeting with a member of staff. Reference from the primary school and Sats predictions where applicable also required. Additional tests for entrants to years 8, 9 and 10.

More than 90 per cent of year 11s stay on for sixth form. Admission to lower sixth from elsewhere is dependent on interviews in proposed subjects and reference from head of current school. Offers usually conditional on good grades at GCSE or equivalent.

Exit: Small percentage leaves at 16 to go to state or other sixth forms. Most leavers at 18 go to higher education: seven students made it to Oxbridge in 2018, half the number of the year before, but chuck in six medics, one to Yale and many more to our finest universities pursuing a huge range of courses and the leavers' onward destinations surely impress.

Money matters: Some financial assistance for highly academic junior school pupils from low-income families through the Peloquin Award scholarships. Academic scholarships, creative and performing arts scholarships, and sport scholarships, available in years 7 and 9. Two Pople Trust Awards (for outstanding maths, physics, chemistry and biology students) on offer in year 10. Means-tested School Assisted Places Scheme available to excellent candidates from low-income backgrounds.

Remarks: Mutual respect goes a long way in ensuring that the shared commitment to enabling young people to leave BGS as well-rounded individuals, equipped for life in the fast-changing world of the 21st century, is fulfilled.

Bromsgrove School

Worcester Road, Bromsgrove, Worcestershire B61 7DU

Ages 13–18 **Pupils** 950 **Sixth form** 429 **Boarders** 386 full, 48 weekly
C of E

Fees: Day £16,665; Boarding: £24,720 – £37,290 pa

01527 579679
www.bromsgrove-school.co.uk

Headmaster: Since 2014, Peter Clague, following a glittering career in New Zealand that embraced the state and independent sectors. Attracted by the school's sense of heritage and purpose, Peter says it was Bromsgrove's challenge to the traditional public school image that clinched the deal for him. He is a huge supporter of IB and believes that its genuinely international spirit suffuses the whole school, bringing with it a progressive liberalism and excitement about modern educational developments. He has introduced more flexibility in the timetable, with longer lunch breaks for pupils to pursue co-curricular interests, and aligned the prep and senior school more closely, but perhaps the biggest changes are in the importance he is giving to the arts. There is more music and drama than ever before and a huge investment into the building of a new theatre at the prep school and concert hall at the senior school.

'He is not as scary as he looks', said one girl to us, which is more a comment on his height and presence than anything else because he is universally seen as charming and warm. The school is proud of its international leader and feel he mirrors the increasingly global outlook of the school. They like also the way in which he respects the traditions of the school but helps them all to look critically at what works and change what could be better. He is described as a visionary and also praised for being in touch with reality. 'He's not all idealism – he has his finger on the business pulse and is very data focused', one senior member of staff told us. He is a skilled wood turner and works beside staff and students building stage sets. He is an 'awesome' public speaker, pupils told us: 'we never know where his metaphors are taking us'.

His litmus test for everything is 'Is it good for the pupils?'

Academic matters: This is a school that really does embrace and value the vocational and the academic. A Level, IB and BTec are all on offer in the sixth form and each has its strong supporters. The IB group loves the small, but growing, tightly knit IB community and tells us that they get all the very best teachers – but the other groups said the same, so we assume there are just a splendid lot of wonderful teachers. A level students assured us they get the breadth through all taking the EPQ. Geography is 'amazing', politics is 'brilliant' and both attract large A level groups. Science and maths flourish. There are usually some nine sets taking single maths and three further maths groups. Results are strong. At the end of the sixth form, virtually all BTec results are double distinctions, the average IB diploma score was 38 in 2018 and at A level or equivalent 75 per cent of grades were A*-B and 46 per cent A*/A. At GCSE, 41 per cent A*-A/9-7.

The only criticism on curriculum breadth came from parents who wanted the school to be offering much more on the home economics and cookery side of things, but apparently the school is taking this on, and other than that there is an impressive range of opportunities.

Saturday mornings are not compulsory but a large proportion of pupils are likely to be there, not least because that is when some of the additional academic classes take place – whether in the form of catch-up and support 'surgeries' or Oxbridge preparation. There are plenty of other academic interest groups running too for anyone not falling into those categories. For those who miss a Saturday, there are departmental tweets that keep you interested.

Learning support is highly rated, though one parent gave a word of caution that moderate learning difficulties were beyond the scope of the school. There is a very attractive and well-used learning resources centre on three levels and we were delighted to hear it is open till 10.00 in the evening and at weekends. This is the sort of opportunity that makes boarding so attractive to the serious student as well as those who want one long sleepover.

Games, options, the arts: Everyone was at pains to tell us that this is not just a rugby school. Well it certainly brings home the rugby silverware, winning the last two national finals, but then the girls' netball team are national champions too. There is genuinely a big variety of sport on offer with D teams that inspire just as much enthusiasm as the A teams. The school was ranked fourth in the country recently in School Sports Magazine. The elite senior rugby players do have to make the sort of serious commitment you would expect at national level, so it is not really an option to be in the U18 squad and play the lead in the school play. Sports facilities are excellent as you would expect, with a particularly impressive new indoor arena with pull-out seating for 400 where the national indoor hockey finals take place. The pool and gym are open at weekends for boarders.

There is an exciting variety of clubs and societies and the school has invested heavily in staff on the co-curricular side to make a strong offering for all. Everyone was rightly proud of a girl who had entered an international competition to build an electric car and had ended up racing it at Rockingham. Drama is big and lots of departments – including art and DT – contribute to productions. Music is getting stronger all the time with smaller lunchtime concerts as well as the big school showpieces. New performing arts centre (opened in November 2017 by Julian Lloyd Webber) features a Vienna concert grand piano. There is Model United Nations and the school sends pupils to the European Youth Parliament. Pupils and parents were keen to tell us that the school looks for what every individual is good at and helps them find their niche and passion.

All year 10s do CCF. Some continue and others take up DofE awards separately. There are service projects running so everyone makes a community contribution at some stage.

Boarding: At first the size may be a little intimidating but it is that which ensures the wide opportunities and it is ameliorated by the house system. Each house has its own internal family structure with older pupils acting as mothers and fathers and the younger ones as children. At the end of year 11, students can move to a sixth form house, but some can't bear to leave their first boarding house, home from home, at that stage. Apart from those in the sixth form house, everyone eats in a central dining room. There are separate day houses and one with day pupils and boarders.

House tutors have about eight in a group and, with a 50 minute weekly session timetabled, get to know their tutees well. Sixth formers say that if you act like an adult, tutors treat you like an adult. Houses are good at communicating with parents and pupils – there are house newsletters and blogs as well as balls that help create a strong house identity. House competitions are seen as big bonding experiences and we were urged to get onto the school website to enjoy the full splendour of house music competitions.

The medical centre is highly praised. The nurses visit each boarding house every night to check all is fine and the focus on well-being, which includes bringing in outside speakers, is welcomed. Boarders say it is a 'full on' school. If you want to spend your weekends and evenings on a couch, the Bromsgrove experience would be wasted on you.

Background and atmosphere: Teaching staff come from a range of educational backgrounds – Oxbridge as well as the old polys – and this gives a sense that the school is grounded in the realities of life outside. There is a drive to ensure an authentic connection with the local community, who use the sports facilities and will be enjoying the new performing arts additions. Senior pupils have links with local state schools through CCF, DofE and university preparation. There's a sense of energy and hard work. The days are long for boarders and day pupils but they are full of purposeful activities.

It is a large campus, 100 acres, in the middle of Bromsgrove, a medium sized Midlands town. Buildings vary in age and the overall impression is of a site loved, cherished and very well maintained. Teaching blocks are attractive with wide corridors and big classrooms, all well lit. There is a delightful little school museum in the old chapel which is just one of a number of reminders of the school's heritage. There are 11 houses, all but one single sex, some in modern buildings, some in charming older ones; the only co-ed house, in a converted hotel a few minutes from the main campus that was once the home of A E Housman, is a real stunner. The 'new' chapel is very prominent on the school site and there are assemblies three times a week for everyone.

There is a popular café, open all day, for older pupils – but we were assured by sixth earnest formers 'it is never a substitute for a proper lunch'.

We were impressed by the careers department where there has been a serious investment in staffing. Year 11 and sixth form pupils have a number of one-to-one interviews and these are supplemented by a Bromsgrove Futures programme of weekly visiting speakers. The contact with ex-pupils is also strong, so current pupils can get advice on careers and university choices and the chance to practise interview technique. There is a diverse intake and the careers department is well aware it is catering for wide range of needs – another example of how, despite its size, the school is interested in individuals.

Pupils clearly feel the school is good at listening. The head boy and girl lead regular school forums with no member of staff present and they told us the very positive results from these meetings. Pupil voice is increasingly bedded into all aspects and creates an atmosphere that pupils really are at the centre of this school.

Pastoral care, well-being and discipline: The pupils do need a degree of self-discipline to flourish, parents told us. They need to manage themselves to some extent especially as they get older – which is seen as excellent preparation for life beyond Bromsgrove for those who succeed, but some parents knew pupils who had struggled with it. Discipline is seen as being robust and fair and pupils need to be prepared to accept it without arguing the toss. Uniform regulations are enforced strictly. Punishments for serious breaches of school rules ('but it's very rare,' pupils assured us) are consistent and take sensible account of the culprit's previous history, but there is very little debate round drugs or sex – you are out. The underpinning rule is that you must not stop others from learning.

Pupils and parents spoke very warmly and appreciatively about members of staff both on the academic and pastoral side. The overriding sense is that well-being and the whole person really do matter to staff.

Pupils and parents: The school sits somewhere between highly competitive Birmingham and posh boarding school clientele. Families typically have both parents working and are fairly diverse, but probably not a lot of old money and a quite a number of military families. It attracts English families who want an international community – there are boarders from all over the world – and a choice of routes post-16. Bucking national trends, there has been an increase in British boarders and prep boarding in recent years. The pupils we met were delightful and genuine. They were articulate and thoughtful and all quite different from each other, which was refreshing. The situation of the school is an asset – it is in a good central England location, easy to reach from all corners of the country.

Entrance: At 13+ tests in English, maths, verbal and non-verbal reasoning and essay writing. The largest cohort from the school's own prep. No automatic entry, but parents seem to feel that plenty of warning and advice is given if a child is unlikely to be accepted to move through. At sixth form level, entry depends on GCSE results and an interview for UK candidates.

Exit: There is a seriously impressive range of courses, universities and countries in terms of pupil destination that reflects the wide sixth form clientele. In recent years, pupils have gone on to do catering, boat building, digital games study as well as maths at Cambridge, PPE at Oxford and mainstream academic subjects at strong UK and global universities, including lots of future doctors and engineers. Two to Cambridge in 2018 and three medics; UCL, Exeter, Birmingham, Bristol, Liverpool, Durham, Nottingham Trent, Loughborough, LSE and Nottingham all popular. Others to universities in several European countries, the US, Canada and Australia.

Money matters: You are paying for the excellent facilities and opportunities as a boarder or a day pupil. Learning support is included in the fees as is ESL tuition. The head is very conscious of the need to widen access and play a part in promoting social mobility. He is actively building a bursary fund and currently there are 98 children on significant fee reduction. He tells us that past pupils are very receptive to raising funds for bursary support. Scholarships are on offer for academic, sporting, artistic and musical talents.

Remarks: Bromsgrove manages to combine the feel of a local family day school with an international boarding school, attracting pupils both for its sporting reputation and also its academic offer and results. It is a carefully crafted hybrid that works. There is a culture of hard work and hard play and an earnestness about the pupils that is beguiling, far from the arrogant outcome some parents fear in independent schools. The arts side of the school is definitely in ascendency, both in terms of the huge financial investment and in the mindset of the community. We want to be invited back for performances in the new theatre and concert hall – we expect them to be world class.

Bruton School for Girls

Linked with Sunny Hill Preparatory School

Sunny Hill, Bruton, Somerset BA10 0NT

Ages 11–18 **Pupils** 201 **Sixth form** 45 **Boarders** 55 full, 2 flexi

Fees: Day £17,805; Boarding £30,330 pa

01749 814400
www.brutonschool.co.uk

Headmistress: Since 2012, Nicola (Nicky) Botterill BSc MA NPQH FRGS FRSA (late 40s). A geographer with a first degree from Middlesex Poly and a masters from the Institute of Education, she has taught in girls' schools for her entire career, except for one stint in a mixed state school, ascending through the hierarchy as far as the deputy headship of St Mary's Calne, from where she was appointed head of BSG.

'I felt immediately at home here and found the girls grounded and unstuffy', she says. Early exposure to travel and living abroad as a child imbued her with a love of adventure and foreign climes; the fact that she took a mid-career gap year has done it no harm at all.

Bruton is small girls' school in a part of south west England that is richly populated with good schools. Mrs Botterill was brought in to increase numbers but has achieved rather more than that – her work supporting newly qualified teachers within the Girls' Schools Association was recognised by their award for 'an outstanding contribution from a recently appointed head' in 2014 – and has garnered approval from all quarters. 'You know she's in charge,' say parents. In her trademark fuchsia jacket and pashmina, we found her engagingly warm, frank, chatty, approachable – all reiterated by parents and girls. Any free time she might have could be spent doing arts and crafts, such as pottery and stained glass, even DIY on occasion.

Academic matters: School scores highly on value-added. Nearly 60 per cent of GCSEs were graded A*-A/9-7 in 2018; 45 per cent A*/A and 57 per cent A*-B at A level. Before GCSE, the curriculum includes compulsory classics (including Greek and Latin), DT and 'home technology'. In sixth form, Leiths certificate in food and wine is popular – we would happily have stayed in any ski chalet catered by BSG students, judging by what was being made in the kitchen. Typically, girls take nine or 10 subjects at GCSE, to include separate sciences, but no language, ancient or modern, is compulsory; a choice of French, German, Spanish or Latin is offered. Flexible and enlightened enough to allow girls to take certain GCSEs (eg French and maths) two or three years early, in exceptional cases. Twenty-one subjects to choose from in sixth form.

Small class sizes, averaging under 10, hard work and the 'enthusiastic, effective teachers – the kind you get in a grammar school,' according to one parent, contribute to the school's academic success and high praise is given to SEN diagnosis and support: 'My daughter's in-house plan is tailored to her', said another, whose daughter had fled the local comprehensive. The wide ability range 'has meant my girls have learnt to tolerate all levels of ability, which is much more like real life,' commented one thoughtful mother of clearly bright girls. Stand-out subjects are English, drama, art and biology; some report that maths is currently in flux. Our impression was of interesting subject matter (West Side Story being used to demonstrate the realities of immigration for Hispanics, capital punishment v the safety and protection of prisoners) being delivered with IT as support rather than as a substitute for honest-to-goodness teaching, to a very compliant, quiescent flock – just for our benefit?

Games, options, the arts: Hockey and netball the main games here, with no fewer than 17 netball teams. An impressive fixture list where BSG looks more like David up against local Goliaths Sherborne Girls and King Edward's Bath. Several netball courts doubling up for tennis, a delightfully sunny Astro where strenuous hockey practice was taking place when we visited, plus an athletics track behind the main group of buildings. At present the swimming pool is an outdoors, solar-heated, summer only affair; the five swimming teams use opponents' indoor facilities for matches at less clement times of year. An indoor pool is top of the parental wish list. Although there is a riding team, this is not the kind of place where girls bring their own steeds, and the ability to pilot a horsebox is not a requirement for entry. Sporty activities include quidditch and tchoukball (truly – we wished we'd seen either).

Music comes in for high praise – deservedly so, judging by the singing practice for the director of music's own composition that we heard, the recital at assembly and admissions to national and county youth choir and orchestra. A school orchestra, smaller ensembles for brass and strings inter alia, a Baroque group, theory classes for those taking grades and plenty of opportunities to play beyond the school gates make for a rich musical offering: we enjoyed the CD (and cookies) we were given on departure very much.

Drama takes place in the Hobhouse theatre: although it is a popular option, outside the devised and scripted requirements of public exams – when we witnessed genuine belly laughs and dramatic talent in the GCSE piece we saw – the scope seems limited to one musical per year, but 'Please please don't make us play boys again,' beg the girls. The art department is truly vibrant – a crammed creative space where girls seem to be able to pursue any artistic fancy: the series of photographs resulting from one girl persuading an obliging friend to immerse herself in milk in a variety of poses was memorable. Good links with the arty town of Bruton enrich the life of the school – the installation by a local artist of felt poppies suspended on threads to commemorate the First World War was innovative and moving. Plenty of trips to local and not so local theatre, concerts and galleries complement the lively arts scene within school.

Boarding: Boarding (officially from year 4 in Sunny Hill Prep, but occasionally younger in the case of one small girl we met whose elder sisters all board and who was determined not to miss out) takes place in the cosy old vicarage where all junior boarders (just a handful from the prep) up to year 9 are housed. Day girls are free to join in with weekend activities and intermittent sleep-overs. Two other boarding houses for senior school boarders. Accommodation is homely and not obsessively tidy: a couple of sixth form girls had transformed their room into a Christmas grotto, complete with glitter and a snow scene, without attracting the wrath of the domestic staff. Intra-school allegiance, which might attach to houses with full vertical boarding in a bigger school, is created by assigning each girl (day and boarding) to one of four halls named for local stately homes.

Background and atmosphere: One of a disproportionate number of schools in Bruton (owing to the beneficence of Hugh Sexey, an auditor of the exchequer in the early 1600s), a small charming Somerset market town of golden stone, BSG sits on Sunny Hill, certainly so the day we visited, with distant hazy views of Glastonbury Tor. Established in 1900 and known originally

B

as Sunny Hill School (the name retained by the prep), it has mostly been independent but spent 30 years in the maintained sector early in the last century. It is possibly this which gives the school a delightful lack of pretension and snobbery, 'a place where the teachers don't parade like cockerels, but where they get a remarkable amount out of the girls,' in the words of one mother. 'It's slightly Enid Blyton with cocoa and biscuits at break,' said another. We liked the fresh air and heartiness about the place – the gaps between buildings necessarily mean a breather between lessons, through the beautifully tended grounds and eccentric pop-up garden, with its giant chessmen.

Proud and unapologetic to be a girls' school, where both the girls and their parents choose to be: 'My daughter was offered the chance to move at sixth form and declined,' one parent told us, another recounted a story of her daughter taking refuge from the local state offering and finding sanctuary at BSG. 'We landed on our feet here', said yet another satisfied customer. The school's size means that girls form friendships across year groups, and we felt a genuine sense of community over a delicious lunch of steak pie and fresh veg. 'Friendly' kept popping up as the most common adjective used to describe the school: 'My daughter took all of two days to settle in,' reported one happy mother.

Pastoral care, well-being and discipline: The pastoral side and the immense care the school takes over every girl in it are hugely appreciated by parents. Hot on friendship issues, a perennial subtext in girls' schools. 'Bruton stood out over other local schools,' in one parent's view, 'and the school is not afraid to tackle issues head on, yet sensitively'. Tutor groups are mixed age until sixth form (these meet daily), and between tutors and heads of halls, no-one appears to fall through the net. Relationships between staff and students and between the students themselves are sound and supportive, 'but we do teach them resilience and that things going wrong isn't necessarily a problem,' adds the head. 'Honourables' are awarded for exceptional work, 'hallmarks' for acts of courtesy and community-mindedness, colours for sporting prowess. Discipline is not a matter which seems to rear its ugly head very often: rudeness, lateness and wilder interpretations of uniform do not go unremarked; smokers and drinkers can expect a sliding scale of punishment, whilst druggies and persistent offenders face exclusion. 'Fluffy and lenient we are not,' states the head.

Pupils and parents: 'Confident without being arrogant' – that overworked phrase to which every school aspires – is echoed by parents. We found the girls, who arrive in anything from helicopters to old bangers, cheerful, unpretentious and very happy to be at this school. 'This isn't the place for hair-flicking city types, but for well-grounded families, wanting the best for their girls. Our parents aren't flashy but aren't without aspiration either.' A welcoming parent community helps to reassure first time buyers that they have made a wise choice. About one fifth of girls from overseas.

Famous old girls include Clarissa Farr, ex-high mistress of St Paul's Girls' School and journalists Viv Groskop, Imogen Sellars and Catherine Davies.

Entrance: Via online verbal and non-verbal reasoning tests to assess potential, plus interview. At sixth form the bar is higher, at five GCSEs at grade 5 or above, with 6s at subjects to be taken at A level. Termly open days and visits by arrangement. Main feeders at year 7 are the prep and local primary schools, at year 9 local preps. Several buses serve surrounding area within 20 mile radius.

Exit: Around half leaves after GCSEs. Sixth formers to a wide range of universities and an equal variety of courses. Most girls get to their first choice: everything from astrophysics to creative events management. Two medics in 2018.

Money matters: As independent education goes, good value for money, at about 25 per cent cheaper than its most expensive competitors. 'Bruton offers everything academic and holistic a parent could ask from a 21st century girls' school, without charging the ridiculous fees that most other schools charge', so said one mother. Scholarships, awarded for the usual range of talents, are nominal, but governors' exhibitions are awarded in cases of means-tested need to a maximum value of 40 per cent of fees.

Remarks: 'It's just not very BSG to promote itself,' one father remarked, but if we were expecting an apologetic little school lurking in rural Somerset, we did not find it. Hidden gem is more like it – a place of unpretentious endeavour where girls can be girls and achieve as much as they are capable of. 'Follow the gleam,' may be the school motto, but in our view it could be time for a spotlight.

Bryanston School

Bryanston, Blandford Forum, Dorset DT11 0PX

Ages 13–18 **Pupils** 694 **Sixth form** 298 **Boarders** 592 full **C of E**

Fees: Day £31,311; Boarding £38,184 pa

01258 452411
www.bryanston.co.uk

Head: Since 2005, Sarah Thomas. She is an Oxford-educated classicist who before coming here did time at Sevenoaks and Uppingham. The kind of head who listens, thinks, questions and fixes. Very much embodies Bryanston values. 'She knows us all,' one parent told us, 'and she's always approachable.' Another added 'and funny.' Ms Thomas likes to switch off by losing herself in a good book. When we visited her in the blissful rural idyll that is Bryanston she was relishing John Emsley's Molecules of Murder.

Fourteen years on since she took the reins, Ms Thomas will soon be free to reflect on, inter alia, a legacy of astute management, some excellent staff appointments and the oversight of the creation of some fine buildings, viz, a Riba award-winning science and maths block, a stunning music school and a splendid sports centre. Not bad for someone who, after writing cheques for millions, can still claim, 'I'm a northerner, I don't like spending money.' The money has been notably well spent: these haven't been vainglorious oligarch-bait projects, every pound has been targeted on giving students the best.

Retires at the end of the summer term, 2019. She'll bid farewell to a future-proofed school in excellent heart, its DNA intact. All Bryanston's heads have left big shoes to fill. Ms Thomas is no exception. Many of them are still quoted. Her predecessor is celebrated in the collective memory for describing the school's best teachers as 'lunatic enthusiasts' (so true, so true). Too early to say what words of Ms Thomas will echo down the years. 'We don't mould people here' has to be a contender.

Her successor will be Mark Mortimer, currently head of Warminster School. History degrees from Loughborough and

London; PGCE from Oxford, MBA from Henley Business School. Also spent time at the Royal Military Academy, Sandhurst. Has worked, inter alia, at Hampton and Giggleswick, and been deputy head at St John's School, Leatherhead. Interested in the arts, especially ballet, and a keen sportsman, particularly rugby, cricket and cycling. His other interests include cooking, leadership development and military history. He has twice rowed across the Atlantic Ocean and in 2017 he successfully completed the Marathon des Sables race across the Sahara.

Academic matters: Academically they do things differently at Bryanston. It's a DNA thing. It derives from an educational theory adopted by the school's founders favouring self-reliance – the Dalton System, they used to call it. Assignments aren't bite-size, set to be tested tomorrow, they're bigger and they're completed over a week. Instead of a central library there are departmental ones with specialist teachers on hand to help out. You get more 'free' periods than you would at most schools. To support you there's your tutor, who you meet at least once a week to review how things are going. This enables you learn from what's going well and what isn't, and incrementally apply the lessons of experience. From year 12 you also have one-to-one meetings with your subject teacher to iron out bugs. Keeping on top of the workload requires rigorous time management. Progress is assessed weekly by grade and comment, recorded electronically and shared with student, teachers and parents. The eChart, they call it. The objective is to develop a spirit of self-motivation and independent enquiry, and any independent-minded child is going to love it.

If you're a fired-up self-starter, great. But if the classroom doesn't play to your best strengths and your appetite for intellectual enquiry isn't your defining characteristic, there's a danger of daydreaming and dawdling. Which is why, over the years, the system has become more interventionist. A parent told us admiringly that if you start goofing off 'they're on your case immediately'. Another savoured the irony that though the school is often mistakenly perceived as progressive and a bit laissez faire, 'I can't imagine a school more tightly controlled'. Is it nevertheless the case that a child who is not especially self-reliant and/or academic could find this tough, and may therefore be better suited to smaller assignments with a faster turnaround? The school is aware of this lingering anxiety and any apprehensive parent would do well to take it up with them.

As for the eChart, a parent advises, 'Read it, but my advice: don't discuss it with your child, it works best as an internal document'. Which goes to show how much faith parents (rightly) place in Bryanston's teachers and testifies to the amount of time teachers give to their students. It is exceptionally rare for a student to spend as much structured time on their own with a teacher as they do here. As one teacher expressed it, 'It's all about relationships – we're all in it together'.

Stats matter, though, and for better or worse exam stats matter most, here as anywhere. There's an increasing focus on results, and the personification of increased rigour is the deputy head academic, who won instant adulation among the students by banning headphones in prep. Yep, no messing. He's not one to post a full breakdown of results on the website, but we got them in the end. They are entirely respectable bearing in mind that the students' academic range here is pretty broad. In 2018 at GCSE/IGCSE (they do a mix), 51 per cent A*-A/9-7 grades. Noteworthy that a quarter do Latin.

At A level, students opt for the full range and there's something for all abilities. As many do Eng lit as maths. Sciences are strong, design and tech very much so. Art is a longstanding strength. Most popular of all? Economics. In 2018, 35 per cent A*/A grades and 62 per cent A*-B. Value added score places the school in the top 15 per cent nationally. Average IB points score 33.

Special needs are assessed at the pre-test stage and tracked from there on. Specialist one-one lessons for those who need it in English and maths. Dyslexia and dyspraxia mostly, and some ASD. The school has a good name for bringing on late developers.

Games, options, the arts: In keeping with the head's definition of Bryanston as a place where you can 'discover who you are and what you want to be', there's high-level coaching for those who love their sport and, they claim, healthy fun for those averse to being buried alive under a scrum. We met the head of sport, who expresses his philosophy in a strikingly humane, even poetic, way. He wants, he says, Bryanston boys and girls to develop 'an affectionate connection with sport'. Everyone can have a go at everything, see how they get on and settle for their level. He adds, 'If we get the process right, the results will follow.' And they do. All the usual sports on offer and there's a full fixture programme featuring up to three teams per year group, so anyone wanting to play for the school gets a good shot at it. The new sports centre is an amazing resource, shared with the local community. Highlight for those who like to let off steam after prep is the new climbing wall with super-cushioned base.

To know anything about Bryanston is to know that it is famously creative. It's one reason why it is often mistakenly typecast as progressive. It remains as creative as ever in art, design, drama and music. Standards in all three remain outstanding. But you don't have to be arty to get in; in the head's words, 'people respect all achievements', a sentiment fervently echoed by the students, who are adamant that there is no hierarchy of achievement here. Having said which, a creative, artistic child can only soar. Facilities are first class. The new music school is a thing of great loveliness – it even has a professional-standard recording studio and masses of scope for aspiring techies, too. Much of the music and drama here is student devised and directed. One parent whose daughter wanted to do design technology at university found that 'the facilities are just as good, if not better, at school'.

Best testament of all, perhaps, is the number of outstanding arty alumni the school has produced, many of whom remain committed to the place. Very few schools can boast quite so many. In art: Lucian Freud and Howard Hodgkin. In music: Sir John Eliot Gardiner, Sir Mark Elder and Mark Wigglesworth. In stage and film: Ben Fogle and Emilia Fox. In architecture and design: Quinlan Terry, Terence, Jasper and Sebastian Conran. These are just the eminent creatives; there are heaps more in other fields.

There are masses of after-school activities to choose from and they're not just for fun. The schools sets great store by its co-curriculum, regarding it as a vital part of a student's voyage of self-discovery. The students we spoke to buy in to this. Extracurricular activities abound plus charity outreach – visits to care homes, working with SEN pupils in local schools, hosting riding for the disabled and fortnightly meetings of senior citizens. Lots of outdoor ed, no CCF. No excuse ever for time hanging heavy.

Boarding: Full-time boarding being, now, not so much normative as a matter of circumstance (eg, parents abroad), many families like to get together of a weekend. Roughly every other weekend they can and you can leave for Salisbury station at 12.30pm on a Saturday, commitments permitting, and be at Clapham Junction by 2.30pm. On other weekends everyone stays in school and works towards a community event. Students who mostly board full time told us they feel anything but left behind and the school always lays on something fun and different. One parent who lives abroad told us, 'The children are kept very busy. Many times we had to encourage them to go and visit their grandparents!'

Background and atmosphere: The school was founded in 1928, a time when you could buy a secondhand country house for a

B

song, start a school in your own image and do things differently from the sclerotic Victorian public schools with their fagging, flogging and character-building subordination of individuality. The Bryanston estate is a whopping 400 acres and the school is centred on a handsome 'château' designed by Norman Shaw.

The founders' manifesto centred on 'putting right everything that was wrong with their own [school]'. Out went fagging and flogging, in came 'freedom, self-development and self-discipline'. And short trousers and bags of fresh air. The founders weren't revolutionaries, mind, they were pragmatists; they embedded the school's genetic code in, of all places, the deceptively simple motto: 'Et nova et vetera' – 'both new and old', the best of both. This was a stroke of genius because it has informed the continuous evolution of the school.

To this day Bryanston remains, in the words of one of the teachers, 'a school that thinks about itself differently.' In the head's words, 'Bryanston likes change, new ideas, we like to challenge convention' while at the same time remaining, in this Guide's view, in many ways thoroughly conventional. It's the near-paradox of 'et nova et vetera' that explains why the school eludes lazy stereotyping. Progressive? Sure, there's no school uniform but there are also no first names for teachers. Creative? Yes – in the broadest sense. Liberal? Absolutely. Easygoing? This conjures up another paradox. One parent told us, 'I've never seen anything so monitored – yet they feel so free'. No ambiguity whatever attaches to what everyone agrees is the salient characteristic of the school: its happiness. 'My children adore the school,' one parent told us, speaking for all. 'Twas ever thus. Of the school's 18 governors, 10 are former pupils. They have, in the head's words, 'a fierce focus on who we are'.

Pastoral care, well-being and discipline: Given the highly personal nature of the school, responsibility for the emotional health of pupils is the responsibility of everyone. For teachers this is indeed a lifestyle job. We were struck by the warmth, humanity, commitment and sheer calibre of every teacher we met. The school depends on 'lunatic enthusiasts' as much as, if not more than, ever. It is typical of the values of the school that it acknowledges also the pastoral importance of non-teaching staff, indicative of the 'we're all in it together' mindset here. Another example was supplied by a student who told us, 'Everyone turns up to school events' and illustrated it by telling us of the student who was giving an after-prep piano recital. He didn't expect more than a handful – he was playing Schubert. As he connected with his mum on Skype so she could watch him, his whole year group rocked up to support. One parent told us, 'All of the key people who surrounded all of my [three] children had their fingers on all pulses at all times. In a short time they figured out my children's various characteristics and embraced them'.

Formal responsibility for well-being lies with the houseparent together with the academic tutor, handpicked for compatibility. Such is the bond that, if a pupil gets into hot water, their tutor will act as advocate of last resort and defend them to the death. Rigorous vigilance is the best way to nip bad stuff in the bud, but even so, it occasionally happens, and if it's something like drugs you're likely to find yourself packing. The school used to be reckoned absorbent of a little bit of offbeat recreational malarkey. If it ever was, that's history.

Teachers are trained in mental health. The school has Stonewall silver school champion status and is on the way to gold. All staff have received training in LGBTQ+ issues. The lead teacher told us, 'The school is very accepting so the training fell on fertile ground'.

The chaplain is something of a one-man pastoral powerhouse. He sees all new students alone to explore what religion they identify with, if any, and arranges for Muslim and Jewish students to attend mosque and synagogue. He agreed that his role is similar to that of a Forces padre. On Sundays students must either go to a lecture in the theatre or walk a mile to the little estate church. An impressive 200 opt for the latter and 40-50 are confirmed every year. He observed, 'Christian values blend well with Bryanston values'.

There are houses, three of them in the big house, which helps to reduce tribalism, which is further diluted not just by the emphasis the school places on being yourself but also by the fact that the big house is big enough to be the school's social hub. Top tip: if you want to plug in to the vibe, spend some time on the basement corridor. Boys go into a junior house for their first year to acclimatise; girls don't because older girls are reckoned better at looking after little ones. There are prefects, whose role is more pastoral than disciplinary. They support the younger boys and girls, for which they get minor rewards but no privileges; the job is its own reward.

The dress code – polo shirt, black trousers/skirt – is, they say, 'hard to subvert', and enables students to 'blend in with the local community'. The sixth form code is more relaxed. We saw no evidence of competitiveness or self-consciousness. Everyone looks natural and businesslike – unremarkable. The look is deceptively tightly regulated. Food is exceptional, the best we've eaten anywhere, and the dining hall was designed by former pupil Terence Conran.

Pupils and parents: Most from up to an hour or so away but a good chunk from west London and further afield. Coaches from London, Oxford, Exeter and Lewes. Especially popular with the arty/liberal elite. Small international contingent. Around 12 per cent day students; their day ends at 9pm.

Entrance: Online ISEB pre-test in year 7 to determine if your child is in the zone academically. Common entrance used as a 'profiling tool', pass mark 50 per cent – not a high bar – though the average score is 60-70 per cent. Parents really like the way the school suits brothers and sisters of differing personalities and talents. Sixth form takes on 25-30 new students per year, 40 points needed at GCSE – as for current students – plus tests and interview.

Exit: Some 15 per cent leaves after GCSEs. University applications guidance recently beefed up by adoption of the BridgeU platform. Almost half apply after A level. Terrific after-sales service, no problem if you don't make up your mind for even a year or two, just get in touch for, as they say, 'Bryanston is not just a five year experience'. Most to university in the UK or abroad and most do conventional courses. Some join the Forces. Army liaison officer visits.

Five to Oxbridge in 2018, two vets and one medic. Popular destinations: Bristol, Edinburgh, Leeds, Manchester, Bath and Oxford Brookes. Others off to Washington, British Columbia and Melbourne.

Money matters: Fees nudging the upper end of the scale. Scholarships up to 25 per cent. Top-up or standalone bursaries from 5-100 per cent; around 100 beneficiaries and 20+ students in receipt of 90+ per cent support. Two significant measures of value: the amount of personal attention here and the excellent use made of the educational opportunity offered by the long boarding school day.

Remarks: Secure in its identity, superbly staffed, safe, kind, rigorous and highly likeable, a school in buoyant form that celebrates all sorts and all achievements.

Brymore Academy

Cannington, Bridgwater, Somerset TA5 2NB

Ages 11–17 **Pupils** 318 **Boarders** 150 full

Fees: Day free; Boarding £10,500 pa

01278 652369
www.brymoreacademy.co.uk

Head: Since 2011, Mr Mark Thomas (acting head since September 2010). Originally from Cornwall, Mr Thomas came to Brymore from Courtfields School, Wellington where he had been deputy and acting head. Previously deputy head at Brittons Academy in Rainham, his early teaching career was mainly in London. Down to earth, no-nonsense and determined, he is married with one young son – 'too young to think about Brymore yet!' – and his wife teaches locally. He spends several nights each week in his school house in the grounds. Sport is both his subject and his hobby though he says, cheerfully, that he hasn't had time for anything except Brymore since his appointment. Determined to 'keep the unique identity and nature of Brymore but create a truly secure atmosphere while raising academic expectations and achievement'. The pride of boys and teachers in their achievements, their interest in academic as well as practical work, as well as the national 'Raise Online' statistics, give strong witness to how much he has achieved in four years. Parents were a little apprehensive about changes, particularly the number of new staff and higher academic expectations, but now feel 'it has all come together'.

Academic matters: Since Mr Thomas' appointment there have been huge changes, with nearly three-quarters of current teaching staff appointed since 2011. Five of these are Brymore alumni, so tradition has certainly not gone out with the bathwater.

The farm and gardens are the heart of learning at Brymore. Practical hands-on farm work: tractor driving (from 13), milking, winter and summer feeding of cattle, pigs and poultry, calving and lambing, cultivation of vegetables and maintenance of the grounds. Getting up at 6am, come rain, come shine, come snow and ice, for seven days a week, making and maintaining heavy equipment, means learning to keep yourself fit and disciplined enough to do it all. If, in the past, the academic curriculum has taken second place, this balance is being altered in a major curriculum overhaul.

From year 10 up boys are now in sets (so a boy may be in a fast set for one subject and a more supportive group for another according to individual need) and years 7 to 9 are three streamed groups. A six day timetable gives 30 one hour lessons (doubles for practical subjects). Much more flexible options now with horticulture and agriculture compulsory for first three years but for not for exam years (10 and 11). This makes room for choice such as art, modern foreign languages, history and geography, though there is still huge and successful take up in practical land-based subjects. Sadly for Brymore, these subject results won't register in the new league tables, though Mr Thomas is fighting the cause! Modern foreign languages haven't worked though to results yet, but there is a big take up of French in the lower school. Engineering can be taken to 'Industry standard' and DT is a core subject. Academic expectations are high. One boy aiming at an engineering career told us he hoped to go on to grammar school to study maths, higher maths and economics A Level, while another, readily admitting to struggling with English, relished his reading and was an exceptionally articulate living proof of success. In 2018, 48 per cent got 9-4 in maths and English at GCSE; 5 per cent A*-A/9-7.

Classes average 16, though there are much smaller groups for boys needing more help and every boy has an individual learning plan. Mentors regularly discuss progress, both academic and personal, and help boys to set and achieve appropriate targets. Very comprehensive learning support is managed by a SENCo with a team of 10 full time, qualified learning support assistants. Most are subject specialists working in their subject area, and the others plug gaps. Resourceful staff are dedicated to improving achievement, and initiatives such as reading nights – just being read to – for younger boys, house points for reading journals, triple input marking, which encourages boys to correct and learn from their own and others' work, are clearly having an impact. Statistics for improvement in maths are not quite as impressive as in English, where the school is in the top three per cent in national stats for improvement, but are OK, and the maths department is still developing new strategies.

Games, options, the arts: Brymore is a sporty school with good rugby, doing respectably at district level – no mean achievement with year groups of under 30 in competition with year groups bigger than the whole Brymore population. Hockey, mountain biking, with an exciting new track and bikes sponsored by Sport England, daily training on the MUGA (multi usage games area), a small Astroturf area, and above all, the Chad Hill daily run: three and a half miles of cross-country which is all but compulsory ('expected' is official terminology) keep everyone fit.

Sport and activities are partly in curriculum, partly after school, but central to everything is the agricultural and horticultural practice and theory. Taught elements are in the teaching day but in addition every boy has to take his turn in the routine of the farm, boarding for a seven day week in order to be up 6am and be permanently on hand for emergencies. DT and engineering centres round farming. One boy explained that a few days fencing showed him the need for an efficient trailer for fencing materials. Brymore's metal and wood workshops, including smithy and foundry, enable really professional work, from handy little metal hammers made by beginners to roadworthy trailers and specialist tractor accessories – things with real practical value on the farm.

There is a farm manager and a head groundsman, but all the work on the farm and maintaining the grounds and gardens is done by boys. There is nothing to make you understand better why people shouldn't trample across a perfect lawn than mowing it yourself! Horticultural minded boys can have personal plots in the walled garden and use of the potting and tool sheds to grow their own crops – Brymore's kitchens happily buy salad, potatoes and veg from them. Art and music are newly available as options. Languages and other options may be taught outside the main school day.

Boarding: Since a major refurbish, boarding is comfortable and clean, the slightly institutional layout softened by posters of giant tractors, 'great big combine harvesters', animals and sport and no institutional smell. Bins outside the doors of the two newish boarding houses take muddy farm clothes and sports gear. Dorms sleep four, except in the main house, where it's up to six. Very tidy – a few unwashed coffee mugs in the boys' kitchen sink confirmed that it is actually lived in. Each house has its own houseparents and relief team for continuity.

Background and atmosphere: Brymore was founded as a School of Rural Technology in 1952 for sons of Somerset farmers on an impressive 60-acre farm on the edge of Cannington, between the Quantocks and Bristol Channel. Half a mile of tree-lined drive ends in a cluster of farm buildings which surround the original 13th century house, once owned by the Cromwell's financier John Pym, and much augmented over the centuries, the latest addition being a new farm building 'to keep agricultural studies fresh'. Exceptionally loyal ex-pupils meet and encourage the current generation at the annual, misleadingly named, Pym's Night. Boys really seem to value the traditional standards of Brymore and are proud of taking part in the local church festivals – harvest especially – and of their reputation among local farmers: Brymore boys are useful on the farm. Shoes are miraculously clean despite farmyard mud, smart black uniform sports the Brymore spur and motto Diligentia et Labore on the pocket. It is also emblazoned on the walls in each boarding house, as the boys' chosen decoration. Parents and staff praise Brymore as 'feeling more like an independent school'. 'The noise of 180 boys singing out at full volume nearly knocks you out,' a proud parent commented after her first carol service.

Pastoral care, well-being and discipline: Brymore had a reputation as a pretty tough place in the past, but its toughness now focuses on the personal resilience and responsibility of the boys rather than rough and tumble rivalries. 'Resilience, Responsibility and Resourcefulness' is used as a strap-line by staff and pupils alike and there is no doubt constant reference to it has rubbed off on the boys' approach to academic and farm work. Day and boarding pupils mix in the three houses (not to be confused with the boarding houses), with house masters and tutors, who meet them weekly. Vertical tutor groups means the oldest mentor the year 7s and get to know all age groups. Year 11 boys take the usual prefect duties (hotly contested) and supervise younger ones for milking and feeding duties. Currently, they are very keen on creating an anti-bullying atmosphere, and are super-watchful over the newly-admitted first years. Down to earth matron on duty all day and liked by boys. Food said to be 'better than it was' but still a cause of some contention.

Pupils and parents: The farming community both local and much further flung (boarders from Hong Kong, France, Norway and midlands) definitely dominates, but boys and parents are beginning to demand a wider outlook and academic curriculum. Past pupils visit frequently and are still part of school life. One, teaching blacksmithing at Brymore alongside his own small business, makes an excellent role model. Others include MEP Neil Parish, Mark Irish, England U21 rugby player, Alex Wright, British race walking champion, and Robert Watts, Brymore's head of boarding. Both alumni and parents fundraise enthusiastically.

Entrance: About 50 pupils, 28 boarders and 22 day boys, admitted to year 7. Currently there is a similar intake to year 9, though this will inevitably diminish once the early years are full. Now oversubscribed. Day places on the usual Somerset criteria, a combination of first come first served and distance from the school. Boarding places also now oversubscribed, open to any boy qualifying for UK schooling and 'suitability for boarding'. Brymore is good with boys who haven't thrived in mainstream, but increased demand has meant that the academic profile of the school is now higher that previously.

Exit: A few boarders stay on to year 12 but attend all courses at Bridgewater College. A large contingent to agricultural colleges, Kingston Maurward, Duchy College Cornwall, Bridgwater College (Cannington Centre) and all over the country. 'Brymore boys often get fast tracked at college,' said one farmer dad. A significant interest in engineering, and some boys go on to do A levels with a view to uni places. Lack of modern foreign language teaching has been a bit of a barrier with local sixth form college, so it's as well it's now on offer. Good number join the armed forces or work within local government, the medical profession or vet sciences; others to apprenticeships and a significant number end up running their own businesses.

Money matters: Fees only for boarding, not tuition, so miles cheaper than the independent sector, despite recent fee rises. Some pupils obtain educational grants from home LAs. All day boys, known as 'out boarders', have to board and pay for the weeks they are on farm duties, though some have found educational grants for this.

Remarks: There are still too few schools like Brymore and, though more are being established, it will be hard to rival its atmosphere and achievement. Articulate, friendly boys are not afraid of the pressures and daily grind of farm work. If this is what hands on experience and responsibility gives to children, schools could do with more of it. No hayseeds at Brymore – more business aware agriculturalists who understand the need to supply food and respect the land that grows it. Parents appreciate that every member of staff is there to give the very best possible education to their children.

Canford School

Wimborne, Dorset BH21 3AD

Ages 13–18 **Pupils** 656 **Sixth form** 285 **Boarders** 419 full **C of E**

Fees: Day £27,723; Boarding £36,420 pa

01202 847207
www.canford.com

Headmaster: Since 2013, Ben Vessey BA MA MBA (40s). Educated at Magdalen College School, Oxford, then read history at Southampton. Intended to join the army but after tearing both knee ligaments playing rugby worked as an oil and gas broker for five years in the City and on placement in Texas. 'But when I came back from the US I realised that it wasn't what I wanted to do,' he says. Applied to Dauntsey's, who snapped him up to teach history. Became head of history and housemaster there, followed by four and a half years as head of history, politics and law at Millfield. Spent six years as senior deputy head at Christ's Hospital – 'it was a great apprenticeship for headship,' he says. Along the way he did an MA in history, a PGCE and an MBA in education management.

Loves teaching and teaches five periods a fortnight to a year 9 history set. 'I write reports and do parents' meetings and it keeps me in touch with the rhythms of teachers' busy routines,' he says. Much in evidence around the school and makes a point of dropping in on lessons to see colleagues in action in the classroom. Has lunch with pupils and staff as often as possible and supper with them twice a week. 'I leave them alone at breakfast,' he jokes.

Energetic, enthusiastic and impressively focused, he lives and breathes the school. He loves Sounds of Canford (the school's informal concert series), watches as many concerts, plays and sports matches as he can and catches up with Year of Genius, an innovative enrichment project launched by the school, as he cycles on his spin bike. Lives in a house on-site with his wife Harriet, their three sons (the eldest of whom started as a day boy at Canford at the same time as his dad) and two black labradors.

In his spare time he plays golf, cycles and reads (he's a fan of Bernard Cornwell's Sharpe novels and other historical fiction). Winston Churchill is his hero and a bronze miniature of the legendary PM left to the school by old boy Terrence Cobden Pike has pride of place in his study. Churchill was a relation of the Guest family who owned Canford before it became a school and apparently he spent many summer holidays there.

Academic matters: Results are easily as good as other co-ed schools with illustrious names. In 2018, nearly 20 per cent of all grades at A level were A*, 53 per cent per cent A*/A and 78 per cent A*-B (figures include Pre-U for art and languages). Considering the breadth of intake this speaks volumes for the first-rate teaching. Maths and chemistry are the most popular A level subjects but many pupils do a mix of sciences, arts and humanities subjects. EPQ on offer too, with over 75 per cent of 2018 entries awarded A*/A grades. Sixth formers we spoke to were full of praise for the support in the run-up to A levels and the study skills workshops on offer. Study leave is awarded on an individual basis but most sixth formers opt to stay in school, keen to make the most of timetabled lessons, past papers and one-to-one help. 'Everyone works hard here,' a sixth former told us while another said: 'The teachers want you to do well and they really support you.'

All year 9s do French and Latin, as well as German or Spanish. Most take 10 subjects at GCSE, including at least one language and two sciences. In 2018, 70 per cent of grades were A*-A/9-7. Pupils are set for maths and languages from the word go. Computer science has been introduced throughout the school and is increasingly popular – 16 taking it at GCSE when we visited, 11 at AS and three at A2. 'Prep schools should be trying to embed computer science in the curriculum, rather than just IT,' we were told. Year 9s curriculum focuses on developing 'habits, skills and literacy' with plenty of cross-curricular projects.

Good provision for those with learning difficulties, mostly dyslexia, mild dyspraxia and language attention difficulties. Learning support housed in the Lovell Building, along with the humanities department. Year 9 pupils who need additional support can take extra English instead of Latin, while in years 10 and 11 learning skills are offered for a number of pupils instead of one GCSE subject, with focus on developing study skills. One-to-one tuition available when the need arises. Average class size is 15 in years 9 to 11, nine in the lower sixth and eight in the upper sixth.

Facilities throughout the school are second to none. New library under construction, with current facility offering 18,000 books, DVDs and audio CDs, plus thousands of virtual resources. Excellent science labs. We liked the fact that every classroom and office has an inspiring and appropriate moniker – Roddick (after Body Shop founder Anita Roddick) for economics and business and Olympus for classics are just two examples. Even the book cupboard in the classics department gets its own name – Hades, of course.

Proactive careers department organises advice on GCSE and A level subjects, annual careers symposium and interview experience. Work experience isn't compulsory but a growing number of students are applying for internships and work placements. In 2018, sixth formers gained places on two of the UK's top corporate career programmes.

Games, options, the arts: Sport is a big deal here and Canford teams score notable successes at every level. Main sports are rugby, hockey and cricket for boys, hockey, netball and tennis for girls and athletics and rowing for both. Rowing VIII were Henley finalists recently. Acres of pitches, floodlit Astroturf, Real tennis court (there aren't many of those around), fitness suite and a 25m indoor swimming pool. In years 9 to 11, four teams regularly fielded per year group so everyone gets the chance to represent the school. Other options include cross-country, sailing, dance, basketball, golf, squash, badminton, canoeing and fitness. Sports facilities and pool are used by local community at allotted times. When we visited a keep fit class for the elderly was in full swing in the sports hall.

Art is stunning – and in many cases highly original and ambitious. We were particularly taken with a vast oil painting (3.5m x 1.5m) of a turtle family. Canford pupils achieved the highest Pre-U grades for art for two years running and up to eight students a year go on to do art foundation courses. Music is terrific, with a large number of choirs, orchestras, strings groups and jazz band. Around half of pupils take individual music lessons. Two major concerts a year, one at Canford, the other at the Lighthouse in Poole, home of the Bournemouth Symphony Orchestra. Lots of drama, with opportunities on stage, backstage and in technical roles. Several pupils have won National Youth Theatre places in recent years. Productions, house plays and an annual school musical take place in the Layard Theatre, opened by film and theatre director Sir Richard Eyre in 1999. Theatre used by professional companies too.

CCF isn't compulsory but is very popular. A few years ago nine cadets from the Royal Marine section beat the likes of Harrow, Winchester and Shrewsbury to win the Pringle Trophy, the premier inter-schools' cadet competition. Others opt for DofE, adventure training and/or community service programme. Seniors work in local primary schools and with disabled groups, run drama workshops and coach sport while juniors work as conservation volunteers. School is the lead sponsor of The Bourne Academy, a secondary school in Bournemouth. Canford pupils act as teaching assistants for languages, computing and science and sign up for book clubs and quizzes.

School is full of bright ideas – everything from Radio Canford to Connections, a general studies programme that challenges pupils to think beyond the curriculum and links different academic disciplines. Another innovation that caught our eye was Yellow Hour, an hour set aside twice a term for pupils and staff to perform in front of an informal audience. Recent highlights included the director of studies performing a maths equation and the head reading a short story he'd written. Year 9s do a carousel of activities every Wednesday – sculling, mixed lacrosse, bell ringing, even etiquette. A plethora of academic, sporting and cultural trips abroad as well as community projects in Argentina, Ghana and India. The Canford Partnership was set up following the discovery (and sale) of a £7 million Assyrian Frieze in the school tuck shop in 1994 and supports worthwhile community projects in the UK and Third World.

Boarding: Full boarding only, no weekly boarding. Flexible exeat system means pupils can spend several Saturday nights a term at home if they want but some 70 per cent of boarders stay in school at weekends. Seven boarding houses – four for boys and three for girls (plus three mixed day houses). Each house has a married houseparent, three tutors and at least one matron (described by one teacher as 'the heart and soul of the boarding house'). Houses are modern and well equipped. In Beaufort, one of the girls' houses, youngest girls are in dorms of four, year 10s and 11s in twos and sixth formers get singles. When pupils arrive at 13 they are assigned a mentor from the year above and are so busy that they settle in quickly – weekend activities programme includes an assault course, pizza nights and trips to the beach. Beaufort housemistress has two cats and two dogs – 'they're brilliant therapy for anyone who feels homesick,' she says.

Most boarding houses are close to the main school buildings but Court and Franklin, two of the boys' houses, are a scenic seven-minute walk from the main school. Boys told us they enjoy the stroll and some bike or skateboard back and forth. Youngest pupils hand their mobile phones in at night but a housemaster we spoke to says pupils are so busy that electronic

C

devices aren't generally a problem. Boys in his house prefer to play Connect Four and chess than stare at screens in their spare time. Very refreshing to hear.

Background and atmosphere: Canford is one of the most beautiful schools in the country. Located in 250 acres of parkland beside the River Stour, it even has its own Victorian arboretum, complete with 350 tree species and one of the largest sweet chestnut trees in the UK. A building of some sort has stood on the Canford site since the Domesday Book. The oldest parts are a pretty Norman church, used for services but too small to take the whole school, and the early 15th century John O'Gaunt's kitchen, used for debates, meetings and receptions. The stunning 19th century main building, originally known as Canford Manor and designed by Edward Blore and later Sir Charles Barry (architect of the Houses of Parliament), is grade I listed. Lord Wimborne sold the manor in 1923 and the school was founded the same year. It first admitted girls into the sixth form in 1969, went fully co-ed in 1995 and is now 60 per cent boys, 40 per cent girls.

School is a mix of grand, historic buildings and ultra-modern, but stylish additions. Dining hall, known as the Great Hall, where Edward, Prince of Wales danced in 1890 following a ritual slaughter of birds at a shooting party, is particularly magnificent. These days a modern cafeteria system is in place. Food is cooked in-house and gets the firm thumbs-up from pupils. All meals eaten in the Great Hall but there are kitchens with tea and toast-making facilities in every house, plus a tuck shop known as the Grubber.

The whole place fizzes with activity from dawn till dusk. Youngsters we spoke to said there's so much going on that it can be 'a bit overwhelming' at first but they quickly learn time management skills. Day pupils must be in school by 8.15am and leave at 6pm, although many stay on later. All look smart – blue jumpers and tartan skirts for girls up to year 11, tweed jackets and ties for boys, sixth form girls in navy. Everyone has to be presentable, we were told. No heavy eyeliner for girls – the look is 'healthy and glowing.'

Pastoral care, well-being and discipline: Parents told us that there's plenty of support via the tutor system. Doctors' surgeries held every weekday and confidential counselling services available on site. Pupils describe the chaplain, known as Rev Jack, as 'really charismatic' and praise him for the way 'he involves everyone.' Midweek chapel for all, plus compulsory service for boarders on Sundays.

Zero tolerance on drugs. If pupils are caught smoking outdoors they get detention and parents are informed. If caught smoking indoors they are suspended. School aims to educate pupils about 'sensible, social drinking under controlled conditions' and sixth formers are allowed to have maximum of two drinks (wine and beer) with food at Saturday evening socials in the sixth form centre. 'It is very closely monitored,' we were told by a group of upper sixths.

Pupils and parents: Most pupils live within a 90-minute drive of the school. A sizeable chunk come from Dorset, Hampshire, Sussex, Surrey and Wiltshire and a smattering from London and further afield. Around three per cent of boarders are international students – from places like Hong Kong, Poland and Bulgaria. Quite a few sons and daughters of Old Canfordians and lots of siblings and cousins. Day pupils come from all directions. School puts on 50-seater coach from Bournemouth and Poole, plus minibuses from Dorchester, Blandford and Wool to the west and Christchurch, Ringwood and Fordingbridge to the east.

The pupils we met said personalities of all types thrive at Canford. 'If you are a quiet sort of person the teachers will help you gain confidence,' one girl told us. Those we met were enthusiastic, full of appreciation for the quality of teaching and delightfully unpretentious. Parents (who include lots of medics) praised the place for its academic results, good communication and down-to-earth atmosphere. 'It's not stuffy at all,' one said. Their only criticism was that no building is big enough to hold the whole school for the Remembrance Day service.

Entrance: ISEB common pre-test is the first sift. Pre-assessment in years 6 and 7 (literacy, numeracy and reasoning, plus interview, group activities and prep head's report), with offers made to more than 60 per cent for conditional 13+ places. Registrar says school is looking to identify 'attitude and a have a go mentality as much as raw ability.' If you don't register early, 'the door isn't closed'; a few places usually come up in year 8. CE benchmark is 55 per cent, although vast majority achieve higher. Candidates who haven't attended prep schools take entrance exam in year 8 (this aims to spot academic potential rather than test knowledge). Around 125 places for year 9 cohort (known as Shells), including 30 to 35 scholarships. Pupils come from around 100 prep schools. Large numbers of boarders from Twyford, Port Regis, Highfield, Chafyn Grove, Walhampton, Westbourne House and Forres Sandle Manor. Day pupils often from nearby Castle Court and Dumpton.

Twenty-five to 30 join in the sixth form – assessment test in November the year before plus minimum of 42 points on students' best seven GCSEs. Grade 7s expected in subjects to be studied at A level and at least 6s in English and maths. Highly competitive at this stage – around four applicants (slightly more girls than boys) for every place.

Exit: Around 10 to 15 a year leave after GCSE – for academic or personal reasons or for a change of scene. After A level, more than 95 per cent to university. Seven to Oxbridge in 2018, and nine medics; Bristol, Cardiff, Durham, Exeter and Manchester perennially popular, with courses ranging from biochemical sciences and medicine to history and business. Interest in US universities is growing and school has its own international university adviser and is an official SAT testing centre. Four to the USA in 2018 including two scholarships.

Money matters: A range of 13+ and 16+ scholarships, plus means-tested bursaries worth up to 100 per cent of fees.

Remarks: As we said last time, a very special school and one that can easily hold its own with the most popular in the country. With its first-rate teaching, stunning setting and innovative ideas, Canford is definitely at the top of its game.

Cardiff Sixth Form College

1-3 Trinity Court, 21-27 Newport Road, Cardiff CF24 0AA

Ages 16-18 **Pupils** 320 **Boarders** 280

Fees: Day £16,600; Boarding; £42,750 – £44,450 pa

02920 493121
www.ccoex.com/

Principal: Since October 2016 Gareth Collier, previously head of business development here. Georgraphy degree from Dundee and PGCE from Leeds in geography and PE (outdoor activities). Has taught at schools in Tanzania and Kenya as well as being a houseparent at Gordonstoun, director of sport at Moreton Hall and international registrar at Taunton School.

Academic matters: The recent BBC programme entitled Britain's Brainiest School did not encourage everyone. Although we were sent a CD of the programme we did not watch it before we visited, but people who had watched it insisted on telling us what they thought. Some were impressed by the professionalism of the approach, the overall success of the pupils and the astonishing A level results 'that would help pupils get into any university.' For those who like statistics, 89 per cent of A levels were A*/A and 96 per cent A*-B in 2018. That's one side of it. 'But they must get an awful grinding,' others said. By the time we arrived we had been dragooned into expecting a hothouse atmosphere of gritted teeth, furrowed brow and clenched fists.

In fact from the moment we set off on our tour, during break, we met with something else. We came across pupils and staff lolling around in passageways, talking and laughing with all the ease of natural friendship. The leading actors in The Lion King were effortlessly discussing the play with the producer, who happened to be head of maths. We were generously drawn into the animated and entertaining conversation and invited to watch the extracts being performed during the Evening of Culture later in the week. We met a student who was reading Milton for English A level and who discussed it with zest and perception; other students were involved in critical thinking, politics, business studies, economics et al. Of course maths, further maths, chemistry, physics, biology – the usual suspects – were there. Best of all we were almost literally locked into a small room with about five mathematicians. The conversation was lively, witty and enjoyable. These were highly experienced and committed maths teachers who were blissfully happy because they no longer taught in schools where they had distracting responsibilities. Instead they were teaching/sharing the subject they loved, and to such bright and enthusiastic pupils. Later, during our visit to the Cultural Evening, we saw those Einsteins appear in a song and dance routine. The chorus went something like 'the more Maths you do, the better looking you become'. These teachers were a wonderful demonstration of scholarship and fun.

Games, options, the arts: Pupils looking to play competitive rugby or football, cricket or golf will find it difficult, though it is possible. 'Physical well-being,' as the school calls it, is more practical and utilitarian: health and leisure facilities are the centre of physical activities and 'students will be provided with custom-made fitness plans based on their individual needs......' It's all there in the prospectus: a balance to the more cerebral side of their time studying. All carefully and sensibly worked out and supported by a professional medical team who come on a regular basis. There are numerous sports clubs including football, netball, swimming and tennis. But not in the school's grounds.

Boarding: The term 'boarding' is not quite what people familiar with boarding schools in the UK might expect. Boarding here means literally sleeping in rooms which offer modern furniture and excellent facilities for working in – as good if not better than many universities. There are specific houseparents dealing exclusively with boys or girls in their houses, as well as other staff around checking the students in and out and qualified counsellors who lend an expert ear to anyone who needs some TLC. The delightful person who showed us round seemed to know everyone's names. The atmosphere is calm, friendly and inviting and the building, which is over a coffee shop, is just over the road from the teaching block. Clean, comfortable and safe.

Background and atmosphere: This is a multi-cultural atmosphere with students from 40 different nationalities. One of the students told us, 'Internationals, while mixing with other nationalities, of course, keep their nationality. There's no compulsion but we appreciate the freedom to express ourselves. We are different and we rejoice in that. One of the obvious expressions lies in the different costume worn with pride and dignity on special occasions.' We witnessed this during the Cultural Evening and very exciting it was. The atmosphere was one of open friendliness between pupils and staff, a friendliness which was most generously extended to this ancient interloper. Overall it seemed a happy place. We met some Welsh students, all of whom were obviously clever – they'd been given very generous scholarships – but they are very much in the minority. One of them, in particular, is a very promising rugby player, who replied in response to our questions, 'I love the opportunity of meeting so many people from around the world.' He's global as they all are. It was very good to see so many alumni coming back for the evening and being cheered in.

Recently bought by Dukes Education; an investigation by the Charity Commission into suspected financial irregularities relates to former trustees, not current management.

Pastoral care, well-being and discipline: Students have tutors to support and advise and told us that staff overall were very friendly and understanding. Certainly the atmosphere is cheerful as well as purposeful. There is a tremendous amount of preparation for entry into universities including much interview practice and many tutor-led societies exploring eg critical thinking, extended learning, various competitions such as senior maths, debating, Model United Nations, study skills – on and on it goes. No wonder the entrance level into universities is so high. As for discipline there are groups, called houses and given classical names. Apparently they are looked after by individual masters but there was no mention of that during our visit. Perhaps it's all done so well that it's taken for granted. Certainly the students were courteous and well behaved in a natural, friendly manner.

Pupils and parents: Parents mostly come from far away, but we met one delightful, happy parent who had made the journey from the far East especially to discuss the possibility of another of her children joining the school. 'They all keep us in touch,' she said, and, 'Skype is wonderful, though when my daughter first left home I was very sad.' At the Culture Evening we met many, many parents who were thrilled to be there and part of the whole occasion, enjoying the food and the dancing. We heard nothing but praise and appreciation, including from those (few) parents who live in Wales.

Entrance: Everyone takes entrance tests and are interviewed (by Skype if necessary). International students may be accepted purely on these results, as long as they have a high level of English fluency (IELTS 6.5), or if they already have at least six 7s at GCSE including their proposed A level subjects. Day students must obtain at least six 7s grades at GCSE (those applying for scholarships must get at least nine 7s, or numerical equivalents), plus passing the entrance test and interview.

Exit: In 2018, 19 to Oxbridge, with 54 off to the London colleges, plus many to top universities round the country to study courses including law, engineering, economics and PPE. Large numbers of medics (44 in 2018); 16 to university in Hong Kong.

Money matters: There are generous scholarships for locals – up 100 per cent for those with all A*s/9s at GCSE – and those we met seemed very happy. Scholarships of up to 50 per cent for overseas applicants.

Remarks: People who spoke to us before we visited expressed suspicion. 'It must be very tough, very restrictive, utterly humourless. Think force-feeding: the embodiment of Brave New World; robotic machines.' Such were the comments we heard from people who had not visited. This ageing GSG scribbler came away impressed by what was being achieved. There is, of course, a difference between education and the achievement of excellent grades. One might be seen as infusion for life; the other might be seen as stamp collecting. But what we saw was youth working hard to achieve results worthy of their talents and for which they deserved credit. The teaching is excellent and, most important, morale seems high with delightful relationships between staff and pupils.

That wonderful evening of music and dance, energy and liveliness with bags of skill, humour and well-tuned banter revealed the synthesis of this society. National dress, a variety of hats and music. What a colourful evening of creativity, happiness, joy and delight. One member of staff sitting next to us leaned over and whispered, 'and this is the collection of young who are described by critics as ground down, overworked and harassed. Remember!' We will remember, and with much pleasure.

Castle Court

Knoll Lane, Corfe Mullen, Wimborne, Dorset BH21 3RF

Ages 2–13 **Pupils** 325 **C of E**

Fees: £8,790 – £15,825 pa

01202 694438
www.castlecourt.com

Head: Since November 2018, Luke Gollings, previously deputy and acting head. He worked as a gap student here in his early 20s, and later teaching roles included housemaster at the Old Malt House School and at Monkton Prep. After a year as sales director in Central and South America, he returned to teaching as deputy head here. His wife, Kate, is an Old Castellan.

Entrance: Children visit with their parents prior to starting but no interviews or formal testing. The most common entry points are nursery, reception and year 3 (where there's a three-form entry) but it's worth trying in other years too. Some year groups are full so places further up the school may be harder to come by. Scholarships offered, plus some means-tested bursaries.

Exit: At 13, around a third head to Canford (just down the road), 20 per cent to Clayesmore and the rest to Bryanston, Millfield, Sherborne, Sherborne Girls, Winchester and the like. Most to co-ed schools and a third choose boarding. An impressive array of scholarships and exhibitions (21 in 2018). Up to 10 pupils a year leave at 11 for the four local grammars. School runs grammar school preparation sessions for boys applying to Poole Grammar and Bournemouth School and for girls applying to Parkstone Grammar and Bournemouth School for Girls.

Remarks: Delightfully rural, yet accessible too, just a few miles from the coastal towns of Bournemouth and Poole. Founded in 1948 and moved to its present site in 1968. The rambling country house at the heart of the school is tucked away in 50 acres on the outskirts of Corfe Mullen and the site boasts everything a child could wish for – 17 acres of woodland to play in, two adventure playgrounds, a 17-ft tepee and a menagerie of guinea pigs, chickens and four pigs. The place has a Famous Five feel to it (indeed Enid Blyton's famous novels were inspired by her holidays at nearby Studland), with children encouraged to enjoy the great outdoors, pond-dipping, badger watching and making camps in the woods. Girls were admitted for the first time in the 1970s and a female teacher is 'head of girls'.

Children seem to have a whale of a time here, while achieving impressive results. Older pupils taught by subject specialists. Maths set by ability from year 1, English from year 3 and Latin, languages and science from year 6. French taught from reception, Spanish from year 3 and most do Latin from year 5. Teaching is exciting and forward thinking. Maximum class sizes of 16 in reception and 18 after that. Each child has a form tutor (who may or may not teach them) and tutor groups meet every morning. 'The children know that their form tutor is the first person they go to if they've got a problem. We believe that if they are happy they will learn.' Pupils' progress carefully tracked, although director of studies points out that while data is important, it's simply 'a tool'. 'We don't reduce the children to a number,' she says. Year 3 pupils and up are given iPads (no 3G though). Children take them to every lesson but aren't allowed to use them at break-times or on the bus. Year 3 and 4 pupils leave them in smart red lockers at the end of the day but older children are allowed to take them home (not at half-term or in the holidays).

All pupils screened for dyslexia from year 2 onwards. Learning development department is housed in three rooms – 10 per cent of pupils receive support for dyslexia, dyspraxia and mild or moderate communication, emotional or behavioural needs, either one to one or in small groups. A healthy mix of experienced and more recently qualified teachers (during our visit we met a geography teacher who was about to celebrate his 100th term at the school). 'We want people with experience and longevity and people with fresh ideas,' says the school.

School is very sporty. Boys play football, rugby, cricket, tennis and athletics and girls do hockey, netball, rounders, cricket, tennis and athletics. Facilities are excellent, including a full-size Astroturf, eight games pitches, five tennis courts and a 22-metre swimming pool. New sports hall. Old-fashioned virtues of shaking hands after matches and entertaining away teams are held in high regard (the school's homemade Battenberg is much admired too). Tennis and swimming academies are popular and older children get the chance to try other sports, like rowing, sailing and golf. 'It's about getting to know what suits them.' Year 3 children camp in the woods each summer, year 4 camps off-site, year 5 goes to Normandy and year 6 heads to the Dorset coast, where they try their hands at kayaking and coasteering.

Music is excellent, with 70 per cent taking instrument lessons, mostly from year 3. A plethora of music groups to join, including junior and senior orchestras, rock bands ('an Ed Sheeran number had all the mums in tears,' says the head), a guitar group, string ensemble, clarinet ensemble, even a samba group. Art and DT are impressive. The first thing visitors see when they walk into the school is a stunning sculpture of multicoloured birds in a papier-mâché tree. We admired the pop art skateboards created by year 8 pupils too. New design centre includes a pottery studio. Drama galore – 'we get them up on stage as much as possible,' say staff. Every pupil gets their moment in the spotlight – a year 3 performance of Alice in Wonderland featured 13 Alices. In the same vein, every child is invited on to the stage on speech day to receive a book.

Nursery and pre-prep children are housed in the main school so they're very much part of things. Bright, welcoming classrooms buzzing with activity, plus a forest school. Nursery and pre-prep head says 'small children like to be active and busy' – and they certainly are here. They venture outside in all weathers, kitted out in wellies and jazzy red and blue splash-suits. When we visited we saw a reception class enjoying a 'Smartie maths' lesson, where the children were enthusiastically counting different coloured Smarties and recording them on a graph. No eating allowed – but teachers promised they could take the sweets home for half-term.

Food is cooked on-site and the whole school sits down to lunch together, younger children with their year groups, older ones with their houses. No cafeteria system – teachers sit at each table and serve out the lunch. Pupils stay on the same table for a term, then move round. Grace said at the start. When we visited the pupils happily tucked into homemade pizza, potatoes and salad, followed by Rice Krispie cakes and chocolate sauce. 'The food's good here,' said one boy appreciatively. 'Especially the Eton mess.' They take it in turns to stack the plates and clear away.

Breakfast club opens from 7.45am for children from year 1 (younger ones by special arrangement) – a boon for working parents. School day finishes at 4.15pm but there's a host of after-school activities, everything from film making and 'pig patrol' to cross-country and mountain biking. Children can do their homework at school but the school prefers them to take it home – so they learn to be organised and parents get an idea of what they are doing.

Year 7s and 8s get the opportunity to be prefects – 'everyone has a chance' – but there's no head boy or head girl. Pupils' uniform looks very smart. Ties for boys and girls and chic stripy blazers that fashion-conscious parents reckon bear a distinct resemblance to a recent Mulberry collection. We heard a few quibbles about the price but apart from that everyone seems to love them.

Pupils are sparky and enthusiastic but ultra-polite, standing up when visitors enter the classroom. Good communication between school and parents – teachers' email addresses available to all, plus parents' evenings in the autumn and spring terms and a written report in the summer. Pre-prep children's red diaries go back and forth between school and home each day, keeping parents up to date with pupils' progress. School also provides a very civilised sitting room, where parents can sit and have a coffee. Pupils come from all over – lots from Poole, Bournemouth and Wimborne and others from Ringwood, Blandford, Swanage, Wareham, Dorchester and Weymouth. Fourteen minibuses ferry children to and from school in the mornings and afternoons. Parents include quite a few old Castellans and some who have relocated from London. No open days: 'Every day is an open day here.'

Chafyn Grove School

26

Bourne Avenue, Salisbury, Wiltshire SP1 1LR

Ages 3–13 **Pupils** 263 **Boarders** 28 full, 15 casual (from 8 years) **C of E**

Fees: Day £7,170 – £17,295; Boarding +£6,000 – £7,365 pa

01722 333423
www.chafyngrove.co.uk

Headmaster: Since September 2016, Simon Head, previously headmaster of Moreton Hall School in Suffolk. He held a short service limited commission with the Royal Green Jackets before studying classics at Cambridge, where he also acquired his PGCE. He has taught at Dulwich College Prep and Pembroke House in Kenya, and was then deputy head at St John's Beaumont in Windsor before becoming head of Moreton Hall. He is married to Sarah, also a teacher and they have two young sons.

Entrance: Children join at all ages and stages and from all over the area. Entry is non-selective. All are invited to spend a day at the school the term before they begin. Scholarships of up to 15 per cent are available in year 6 (academic, sport, music, art and drama). Forces discounts (normally 10 per cent day and minimum 15 per cent boarding) and sibling discounts from five to 15 per cent available. Means-tested bursaries typically range between 10 and 40 per cent of the combined tuition and boarding fee.

Exit: Dauntsey's, Sherborne and Warminster top the list of 'next schools'. Sixteen scholarships offered in 2018, eight of them for sport. Around 10 leave at 11 each year for the Salisbury grammar schools and independents.

Remarks: A 1914 school photograph shows just 17 boys and three members of staff sitting in the grounds of a large Victorian building. Today, that solemn handful of Edwardian scholars would be very surprised to find nearly 300 pupils at Chafyn Grove, including over 100 girls. Founded in 1876 as Salisbury School and changed its name in 1916 following an endowment by Lady Chafyn Grove.

They have taken the unusual step of dropping history, geography and RS from the CE syllabus to focus on maths, English, science, French and Latin. The subjects still feature but lessons can be more flexible: early history topics such as the Crusades and geography lessons on South America. French is taught from year 1, Spanish in years 4 and 5 and Latin from year 6. Latin is strong and some pupils get to near GCSE standard. The odd truly hopeless linguist is allowed to drop languages rather than self-destruct in CE. Maths is set for everyone from year 3, top sets are streamed for all subjects from year 5 and lower sets in the last two years. Scholars aiming for the likes of Eton are educated separately with extra lessons and lots of practice papers. This is certainly a change from times past, when 'Eton, Winchester and Harrow were not Chafyn's remit'.

Sessions in thinking, presentation, research and current affairs freshen up the timetable. Year 8 also studies business skills, involving Dragon's Den-style pitches and advertising campaigns. Teaching body is very stable, with several married couples and long-standing staff members. 'You only realise how well they're being taught when they get to the next school.' At the time of our visit, there were 42 pupils on the SEN register. Taught by five members of staff in two dedicated rooms, there is a broad sphere of activity which includes study skills, spelling and learning support alongside help for dyslexia, dyspraxia, EAL etc. One-to-one sessions once or twice a week are free and the school is honest about which conditions it can support.

School has the strongest sport in Salisbury, inducing fear in opponents. Everyone plays in a team and with so many – up to 20 on match days – school can send its top teams further afield to other seriously sporty schools. All the usual sports on offer plus archery, riding, sailing, cross-country and steeplechase. There is an equestrian and a sailing team, both of which compete successfully. Outdoor swimming pool used in summer. All four first hockey teams reached the national final recently, which school promptly won. Lots of individual success in athletics, eg U13 Hurdles National Prep Schools Champion. A team of coaches fosters everyone's talent (not just the superstars) on school's pitches and Astroturf which spread out behind the school up to the (distant) railway embankment. There's enough space for a gym and squash and tennis courts. Phone app keeps parents abreast of sports fixtures. 'I try to tone down sport a bit as the children do win a lot – they have to get used to the fact

C

that it isn't all about winning,' said a parent. Saturday school (from year 4) is often taken up with matches.

Art department is roomy and light, with plenty of quality work on display including some excellent papier-mâché creations. We noticed a good reference library for art and DT. Drama has long been of a high standard and parents rave about the quality of the annual spring production. Years 3 and 4 put on their own play in the summer term. For music, we'd award a merit. One third of pupils learn an instrument and school teaches up to grade 6. Some parents feel this isn't enough but we consider that, given the excellent sport and academics, school does a pretty decent job since many serious musicians are more likely to head for the Cathedral School. Singing is very popular and there are three choirs, as well as a school orchestra, training orchestra and jazz band. Large performance hall has good acoustics, a grand piano and an organ. Practice rooms are small but masses of space for storing instruments and music.

Lots of trips, including the usual, eg Normandy, London, the theatre and skiing, and the less usual – a visit to a Sikh temple. Activities during the last two periods on Monday and Thursday are intended to 'give children room to breathe' and include gardening, cookery, golf and Mandarin. In a nod to childhoods of yesteryear, year 4s go on annual Pioneer Camp and learn to put up tents, tie knots and stalk. Bushcraft weekends for seniors involve building shelters and campfires, as well as catching, gutting and cooking their own fish. Chafyn Challenges for all age groups range from 'make a paper boat' to 'climb a mountain' to 'be good company at table' to 'deliver a lamb'.

Boarding accommodation is comfortable and homely; parents speak very highly of houseparents and matrons. 'They are totally on top of who, where, what and why.' Rooms are shared (6-8 per room) and boarding life is well organised. Year 8 girls have an ensuite shower room which, though clean, is crying out for new tiles. Boarders have a sitting room and green room where they can Skype parents. Mobiles are allowed in free time but must be handed in at night. At the time of our visit, there were 26 full boarders and 40 to 50 part-time per night. One third stay in on weekends and there is a full programme of activities, eg bowling, shopping, cycle rides in the woods and trips to London and the beach.

The original Victorian building is still home for the boarders, but most of the teaching takes place in modern buildings which seem to flow into one another on school's compact site. Children were engaged and interested in academic lessons; traditional classroom seating with everyone facing forwards. 'Children like their teachers and don't want to disappoint them.' However, atmosphere is neither old fashioned nor very strict (no standing for visitors). Our two student guides were polite, confident and very honest in their answers to our questions. 'It's a great school if your child is confident and outgoing and knows who they are,' said a parent.

Pupils feel comfortable about reporting any problems to teachers, who do their best to resolve unkind behaviour. 'They name names and know exactly who is doing what.' Likewise parents feel that they can turn to the staff. 'They are very likeable and approachable and they're always in the playground at pick-up times.' School will summon parents and children and rap heads together if a situation appears to be escalating. There is a seven-point system to discourage bullying and extra mentoring sessions in place for girls in years 5 and 6. Every pupil belongs to an Eight (house) with appealing names – Wasps, Frogs, Birds and Knights. Food is prepared in-house by the chef and served cafeteria style; meal times are informal and children sit where they like. We enjoyed our lunch with plenty of fruit and veg. Day children can arrive at 8am if parents work and stay on for supervised prep until 7pm.

Lovely modern pre-prep with bright, spacious classrooms, own hall and play area. Reception starts small, after which numbers gradually increase. Children in pre-prep can stay until 5:30pm and have their own after-school club and activities including paper craft, football, netball and hockey.

Like most Salisbury schools, there is a mix of local professionals, Forces, business and London commuters. Only a handful from abroad, mostly Spanish and a few English with parents working overseas. 'We can't distinguish parents' wealth and professions.' Parents confirm that atmosphere is 'not snooty or overpowering'. A quick snoop along Bourne Avenue at pick-up time confirms that cars are mostly common or garden.

A busy, happy and academically sound school which still retains a friendly, family atmosphere. Will suit confident children who are happy in their own skin. Needless to say, sporty children are in their element here, although parents of the very talented might need to keep small feet firmly planted on the ground. Is, without a doubt, the go-to school for sport in Salisbury.

Cheadle Hulme School

Claremont Road, Cheadle Hulme, Cheadle, Cheshire SK8 6EF

Ages 4–18 **Pupils** 1,456 **Sixth form** 273

Fees: £8,950 – £11,880 pa

0161 488 3345
www.cheadlehulmeschool.co.uk

Head: Since September 2018, Neil Smith, previously deputy head (academic) at Manchester Grammar. History and politics degree plus PGCE from Keele; taught at The Grammar School at Leeds (history and politics teacher) and at Cheadle Hulme (head of politics) before joining Manchester Grammar in 2002, where he was head of history before becoming deputy head. He has written several educational and history books, served as an educational consultant for the BBC, and is a senior examiner for history A level. His daughter attends Cheadle Hulme.

Head of junior school: Since 2009, Barbara Bottoms BSc (50s). Married with two grown up children. Educated at Liverpool University, where she studied chemistry and maths. Previously head at Bury Grammar School for Girls' junior department. Overjoyed to have returned to co-education. 'When I look into the playground I see a normal society where we are all learning about each other,' she told us. 'It's been like coming home.'

Parents praise the positive changes she's made. 'She's not the sort of head who has huge presence,' said one. 'She's not there at the school gates, but all the teachers are being made to teach new year groups and she's brought in specialist teachers. She is accessible if you need her but she likes to get on with things quietly. No big fanfare.'

Head is a keen theatre-goer in her spare time, and loves watching any sport.

Academic matters: Class sizes in the junior school are bigger than other independent schools in the area and this causes some parents to grumble. Two form entry throughout, with 20 in a class in the infants, 24 in years 3 and 4 and 26 in years 5 and 6. However, classes are split for many lessons. Netbooks are used in years 4 and 5 and there are plans to introduce them throughout school. French is taught all the way through the infants and then rotated with Spanish and German in the juniors.

Children we spoke to were delighted that Wednesday is 'no homework night.' Some parents complained, however, that a lot of homework has to be done on a computer via the school's virtual online environment. This seems to cause problems for families with multiple children all trying to use the home computer at once.

Continues to have good exam results – 68 per cent A*-A/9-7 grades at GCSE in 2018 and 46 per cent A*/A at A level (80 per cent A*/B). However, although exam results are ultimately the paymaster, the school says that 'there must be fun in education. Hard work must be balanced with support'. Pupils appreciate the wide range of teaching styles the school employs and comment that teachers are very approachable. All subject areas hold weekly clinics – pupils can drop in if they need assistance and regular revision classes are held for those taking exams.

Regular effort grades have been introduced to ensure no child slips through the net. All pupils in the upper sixth take extension classes to gain depth in subjects unrelated to their A level work. IGCSEs and Extended Project Qualification (EPQ) available in some subjects and the Pre-U offered in philosophy, business studies and economics.

The school has seen a rise in popularity recently and prep schools are reporting more pupils turning down places at other prestigious independents to take up places here. As a result, an extra form introduced to cope with increased demand. Although school denies any desire to keep climbing the league tables or to become more selective (it currently has a broader intake than some of its competitors), does seem to be a move to broaden and enrich academic opportunities.

Full-time head of learning support can cope with mild to moderate SEN, as long as pupils can access the curriculum. Pupils assessed on an individual basis.

Games, options, the arts: Drama is very popular and has its own studios. Many performances take place in the atmospheric, but slightly cramped, Holden Hall. Music is outstanding, with many orchestras, choirs, a cappella group, concert band, ensembles, samba and rock bands, to name but a few.

Lots of sport in the juniors, including cricket, hockey, football, cross-country and netball. Plenty of extracurricular activities, from bird watching to string ball. 'Every child can find something they love,' one dad told us, 'whether it's music, drama, sport or a hobby. This place does it all. My daughter loves the fact that the head takes tennis after school every week.' Successful sporting teams in the seniors, but still plenty of opportunity to get involved if you don't make the teams. Many pupils represent their sport at club, county and country levels.

Vast array of extracurricular activities on offer, including school's own radio station, film club, table tennis and a charities committee.

Background and atmosphere: Established in 1855 as a co-educational school for 'orphans and necessitous children of warehouse men and clerks'. Expansive, leafy grounds have a collegiate feel. Pupils look very at home but seem purposefully busy. The main stately Victorian building sits comfortably next to the modern counterparts with their spacious, airy classrooms. Year 7 has own block to ease the transition from little to big school. Sixth formers have their own common rooms and butty bar, but the few we spoke to grumbled that their facilities could do with a revamp. Smart bottle green and black uniform, changing to navy blue in the sixth form.

Food gets a big thumbs-up. Plenty of good quality options to choose from in the canteen (which boasts stained glass windows and high tech finger print recognition system). 'Grab and go' lunch bags available for pupils too busy to queue.

Light, modern junior school buildings with music, art, IT and science rooms. Ovens for baking are regularly used and we saw a group of little ones making cookies, or 'yummies,' as one boy called them. Big TV screen in the entrance runs a good news feed celebrating pupils' achievements and keeping everyone up to date with what's going on in school.

Pastoral care, well-being and discipline: Junior school a lively place that manages to have a relaxed feel and where children seem genuinely happy. 'When they leave here,' says the head, 'they are confident, responsible children who have learned from failure and experienced success.'

Parents can't praise the pastoral system highly enough. One mother, whose son found adjusting to senior school life very difficult, said that staff were fantastic, often taking the time to ring her in the evening.

Sixth formers act as peer mentors to new year 7s, to help them settle and give them someone to talk to. 'It was brilliant,' one boy told us. 'I could ask him lots of questions that I felt silly asking a teacher.'

Pupils and parents: Mainly from south Manchester, Cheshire and Derbyshire. Parents are mostly professional and from a cross-section of backgrounds. Now starting to pick up more Asian families, who have in the past tended to choose the Manchester independents. Extensive bus routes, plus a pick up and drop off service from the local station.

Notable former pupils include MEP Chris Davies, BBC political editor Nick Robinson, political correspondent Lucy Ward, BBC broadcaster Katie Derham, political correspondent Stephen Day, soprano Susan Bullock, Labour peer Lord Dubs and actor Daniel Rigby.

Entrance: Assessment for reception takes place in the autumn term of the year prior to entry. Places are offered in December, earlier than other schools. 'It's play-based in small groups,' the head told us. 'We want children we can engage and interest – they need to be excited to learn.' The school take another four to six children in year 3, and then four more in year 5. Assessment at this stage is formal, in English, maths and reasoning.

Competitive entrance exam at 11 in English, maths and verbal reasoning, followed by separate interviews with pupils and parents.

Exit: Most (around 90 per cent) of juniors progress to the senior school after sitting entrance exam along with external candidates, although a few are lost to the single sex schools in Manchester. Head meets all year 4 parents individually to discuss progress, so there is plenty of time to look at other possibilities if your child won't make it. 'We'd feel like we'd let them down if they didn't go up,' says the head.

Some 20-30 per cent leaves after GCSEs. Nine to Oxbridge in 2018, plus six medics; others to eg Liverpool, Leeds, Nottingham, Manchester, Newcastle, UCL. And three off to the US in 2018 (UCLA, NYU and Northwestern).

Money matters: Substantial bursary fund makes a Cheadle Hulme education a reality for many families. No academic scholarships, but sports and music scholarships offered for year 7 entry, plus music scholarship also offered for sixth form.

Remarks: A vibrant, action-packed school that is rapidly increasing in popularity. Pupils are bright, well supported and gently cared for to achieve their best.

Cheltenham College

Linked with Cheltenham College Preparatory School

C

Bath Road, Cheltenham, Gloucestershire GL53 7LD

Ages 13–18 **Pupils** 708 **Sixth form** 282 **Boarders** 461 full, 118 weekly
C of E

Fees: Day £27,585 – £28,575; Boarding £36,780 – £37,770 pa

01242 265600
www.cheltenhamcollege.org

Head: Since September 2018, Nicola Huggett (40s) MA PGCE (Oxon), previously head of Blundell's School in Devon. Educated at St Gabriel's and Marlborough, she read PPE at Oxford (where she was captain of her college boat club and president of the university riding club) before embarking on a brief career in advertising with J Walter Thompson – brief because she soon realised it was not for her. 'Why did no-one tell me about teaching before?' she says of her experience shadowing a teacher in a comprehensive near her home. Since then her career has taken her via Haileybury, ultimately as head of boarding, during a time when the school went fully co-ed and introduced IB, and Downe House as deputy head, before being made the first female head of Blundell's since its inception in 1604: and, indeed, she is the first female head at Cheltenham since it was founded in 1841. Clearly a superwoman, she also runs marathons, rides – she has competed in several international three day events – and raises four children. Husband Spencer works for an automotive software development business.

Academic matters: In 2018, 59 per cent A*/A at GCSE. IGCSEs are offered in maths, English literature and science and were recently introduced for history and geography. Maths, English, DT, music, history and science results are particularly impressive. At A level in 2018, 47 per cent A*/A grades and 76 per cent A*/B. School has no time for the excuse 'you can't do all things well', and while there are no plans to become more selective or chase league table rankings, there is a strong drive to enrich the academic opportunities for all students via a broader approach to the curriculum and programmes that enable pupils to learn more effectively.

Lessons are 35 minutes long and the new two-week timetable is, apparently, much less confusing than its eight-day predecessor. We saw thoughtful group work (boys and girls at separate tables) in Latin and a biology class where all but one were learning to love leaf mould and get to know its inhabitants.

The sixth form has received considerable attention with the introduction of an independent learning project for the lower sixth designed to extend and deepen subject knowledge (offered in addition to the EPQ). Also runs an innovative accredited leadership and life skills course in the sixth form based on Sean Covey's book 'The 7 Habits of Highly Effective Teenagers'. Pupils can choose from 24 A level subjects including textiles, theatre studies, history of art and Latin and Greek. Critical thinking can be taken as an AS.

One of the assurances staff give is that no pupil is allowed to 'slip under the radar'; academic problems are tackled promptly via an 'academic support plan' drawn up with the pupil, parents, housemaster, tutor and subject teachers. The school is also very keen for pupils to learn from each other: disorganised pupils are assigned a buddy to help them on the path to order; older and wiser pupils give talks along the lines of 'Things we wished we'd known ...'

EAL pupils attend an induction programme prior to the start of the academic year and are supported by two EAL specialists. Learning support department caters not only for those with mild dyslexia, dyspraxia, ADHD etc but also ensures the gifted and talented are suitably challenged. The role of this department extends to the whole school, overseeing initiatives to develop the learning potential of all pupils.

Main school library has been completely revamped, its wonderful tiers of gothic windows pour light onto new shelves and lounging readers. Banished with the old furniture is conversation; a kind of un-modernisation which, according to our guides, has been welcomed by all. Even more enticing than golden silence are the iPads mounted on black metal plinths that pupils can use to search the library catalogue which does not, we are told, extend to Angry Birds.

Games, options, the arts: Dr Edward Wilson the Antarctic explorer was educated here and no fewer than three intrepid members of staff (one of whom is director of activities) have climbed Everest – surely some kind of a record. The first ever inter-school rugby match was played on the school's splendid pitch in 1844, overlooked no doubt by the confection of a pavilion that resembles a miniature Brunel railway station. In the summer this perfect pitch plays host to the venerable Cheltenham cricket festival.

County and national triumphs in rugby, hockey, cricket, tennis, rowing and polo; coaching for all abilities is now 'much more professional' and even third and fourth team matches are keenly contested and enthusiastically supported. Rackets (a forerunner of squash) is one of the more arcane sports on offer and the college has won the national championships three times and is consistently in the top four. Golf, swimming, water polo, dance and fitness are part of the exhaustive (and exhausting) sports programme as is yoga, a surprising hit with the boys; apparently it is very effective for rugby injuries.

CCF, Young Enterprise and DofE are all enthusiastically tackled, the latter being offered in its less common cycling, horseback and ski-touring options in addition to the usual walking challenge. Service activities take place every Wednesday and volunteers give their time locally at schools and residential homes. Longstanding links with Kenya see college pupils working on projects there, often carrying this on into gap years.

Art, music and modern language teaching takes place in the rather grand neo-classical surroundings of Thirlestaine House, a former gentleman's residence. Its original features – huge mirrors, chandeliers, ornate cornices and radiator covers – have survived generations of school children (just) and create a suitably bohemian home for the creative chaos of art and pottery studios. The long gallery is venue for exhibitions, lectures and public events. Two students have gained places at RADA for costume design and backstage training courtesy of the outstanding DT department while another gained a place for acting.

Nearly half of pupils learn a musical instrument, a lower uptake than comparable schools but the figure is increasing. Chapel and chamber choirs plus orchestras, bands and ensembles must keep that 40 per cent pretty busy. Performing arts centre complete with dance studio, green room and, less predictably, a plaster frieze of the Parthenon uncovered during refurbishment. School and house plays and reviews are hugely popular, everyone is encouraged to get involved either performing or backstage.

The college also plays its part in Cheltenham's cultural life, participating in the annual festival fest. The combined choirs of the college and Dean Close opened a recent music festival. Harmony with nearby Dean Close and the Ladies' College is described as 'cooperative' with pragmatic sharing of visiting speakers, careers events and collaboration between international students' societies. Pupils are more forthright, acknowledging and enjoying the rivalry.

Boarding: Houses are in residential roads just outside the campus perimeter – separating 'home' and school is considered very important: the staff encourage pupils to adopt a professional attitude to school, 'it's a place of work', whereas houses are a home from home, informal and a place for relaxation. Parents are encouraged to join in with weekend or social events and are pretty much in agreement with Ofsted's conclusion that boarding provision at the college is 'outstanding.'

In addition to a matron, each house has a resident tutor who hosts academic 'clinics' outside school hours. Christowe, one of the original Victorian boys' boarding houses, has been beautifully decorated by the current housemaster and his wife (an interior designer) and there's not a whiff of the institutional in the first floor family rooms. As with all the boys' houses, 60 or so boys live here, sharing for the younger and single rooms for sixth formers. The common room and library are full of house memorabilia (house names a constant in the college); fascinating archive photos and a mini museum all foster a sense of continuity and house identity. Wonderful cushions decorated with the piratical house insignia of skull and crossbones were a gift from a parent. Clubby red-painted snooker and games room much admired. Ashmead, one of the girls' houses, was built round a garden quad with lovely light bedrooms and civilised socialising areas. New girls' day and boarding house, College Lawn, in two beautiful Regency buildings, overlooking the college field and 19th century chapel. Boys are allowed to visit for film evenings and the like – apparently rom-coms are rather favoured. The housemistress heads off cliques by splitting up prep school groups and changing room-mates each year. All residents meet twice a day – a practical system that also enables staff to observe shifting dynamics. House staff and prefects alert to meal skipping and similar warning signs when 'faddy could tip into eating disorder.'

Background and atmosphere: Beautiful mellow Victorian gothic buildings along Cheltenham's busy Bath Road, having undergone a major re-vamp – grade 1 listed status an expensive headache but good news for Gloucestershire's stonemasons and other master craftspeople. Public areas certainly getting the five star treatment though classrooms remain workaday and well used (all have requisite IT and smart boards). Students and parents tell us that much has changed for the better, not change's sake. Singled out for mention were improved home school communication and relations between teachers and pupils. Interestingly, members of staff said that they thought this had always been one of the strengths of the college but our sixth form guides were very certain that things were different and teachers were 'much more involved and friendly'. The staff we met lived up to their billing and were indeed friendly, funny, charmingly young fogeyish in a few cases, and clearly enjoying both the teaching and strong sense of community at the college.

Pastoral care, well-being and discipline: Pupils start each day in the glorious chapel, no doubt energised for study by the famously enthusiastic hymn singing. This is such a feature of college life that a recent group of upper sixth leavers asked if they could record themselves in the chapel singing favourite hymns as a parting memento. The house system is everything here, for boarders and day pupils alike; each is a community within a community and fiercely competitive. Every house has its own character and distinguishing traditions such as prefect blazers and boaters (worn with pride, apparently).

Houseparents first in line for problems whether academic or social, and liaise very closely with teaching staff to ensure 'joined up' care. Older pupils train for peer mentoring responsibilities and can often pick up on wobbles before they become serious. Mobile phones (aka 'the biggest headache') only allowed in houses and, along with laptops, must be handed in before bed. If a houseparent overhears parents being berated or harangued – not uncommon in a school population that is totally teenage – they will challenge (hooray!). The writing of proper thank you letters (to former prep schools, weekend hosts and the like) is another courtesy expected of pupils. While most pupils come from similar backgrounds, staff are alert to potentially insensitive displays of conspicuous consumerism – affording one the unexpected chance to ask a parent to 'take back the mink'.

Some pupils disgruntled about tightening up on trips into Cheltenham town centre – now only Sundays unless there's a legitimate need. School has responded to parents' view that since it offers so many activities, 'hanging around in town' need not be a supplementary option. Bath Road still in bounds for banks, supermarkets and cafés, not that the last should be necessary – food is plentiful with lots of choice: salad bar, curries, carvery and good puds served in the former chapel and 'legendary' bacon rolls and snacks dispensed by the very friendly ladies in the tuck shop. This is a town school and necessarily takes firm line on drugs, drink and similar misdemeanours. Sixth form privileges are realistic – at 17 pupils can go out for a meal at an 'approved' restaurant; at 18 they may visit a similarly endorsed pub. The sixth form social room in the main school has a café/bar; 'we have to prepare them for life beyond school', one housemaster told us.

Pupils and parents: Good mix of first time buyers, second generation Cheltonians, Forces and international. Around 18 per cent from outside UK – 30 countries represented. Not snobby or excessively label conscious. Many boarders are from local area or within a few hours of Cheltenham. Children don't have to grow up too fast here; they're down-to-earth, polite and confident without being arrogant. 'It's not a London school', one parent said approvingly. Uniform of navy and cerise plus usual complexity of ties generally adhered to, all pupils wear own choice of pastel shirts; boys' individuality expressed mainly via hair. Boy:girl ratio now nearly equal.

OCs include Rageh Omar, journalist; Tim Bevan, film producer; General Sir Michael Rose; Nigel and Jack Davenport, actors; James Whitaker, royal correspondent; James Stout, world rackets champion; Sir Alan Haselhurst MP, The Right Hon Lord Anthony Colwyn CB and the Norfolk coroner, William Morris.

Entrance: Increasingly competitive. Most via common entrance, 40 per cent from own prep school, others from plethora of localish preps including Beaudesert Park, Abberley Hall, Pinewood, St Hugh's, Hatherop Castle, The Dragon, Bilton Grange, Moor Park and St John's on the Hill. Entrants from state schools take exam (papers in English, maths and, where appropriate, French); sixth form candidates require at least five grade 6s at GCSE and must sit papers in subjects to be studied.

Exit: Around 10-20 per cent leaves after GCSEs. Almost all sixth formers to higher education. Handful to Oxbridge (four in 2018, plus one vet), most to top universities, huge range with Manchester, Exeter, Edinburgh, Cardiff, Bath, Leeds, UCL and Bristol amongst those currently favoured. Some to overseas universities, including New York, Virginia, Madrid, Hong Kong and Dublin. Most popular subject choices: biological sciences, psychology, economics and management, history, engineering.

Money matters: Scholarships (up to 15 per cent) and exhibitions (10 per cent) offered at 13+ and 16+ in academic, art, drama, music and sport. All-round award may be made at college's discretion. Additional means-tested bursaries also available.

Remarks: Radical modernisation does not always fit easily with old traditions, whether architecturally or educationally, but

C

Cheltenham College has emerged refreshed and ready for a new era. This school is a happy, spirited community inspiring real affection and loyalty in its members.

C

Cheltenham College Preparatory School

Linked with Cheltenham College

29

Thirlestaine Road, Cheltenham GL53 7AB

Ages 3–13 **Pupils** 372 **Boarders** 39 full/flexi (from year 3) **C of E**

Fees: Day £8,175 – £18,315; Boarding £18,255 – £23,790 pa

01242 522697
www.cheltenhamcollege.org

Headmaster: Since September 2018, Tom O'Sullivan, previously head of Old Buckenham Hall. Educated at Pate's Grammar School in Cheltenham and Durham University where he read law; people always said that he would become a teacher but, for a while, he resisted, spending an extra year at Durham as JCR president before deciding that a career spent in a quest for silk was not for him. Work began in a variety of roles: as a graduate trainee for WH Smith, for a recruitment firm in Singapore, and in drug education for a pharmaceutical company. He then followed his destiny, taking a PGCE, specialising in science, at Homerton College, Cambridge. Here he discovered in the first 10 seconds of his first lesson that 'the buzz from teaching' was better than anything he had previously experienced in his working life. Appointments at Beaudesert Park and a deputy headship at Mowden Hall followed, before he assumed command of Old Buckenham Hall.

Entrance: Taster day for entrance to nursery and up to year 3. For years 4-6 it's a taster day and entry assessments in maths, English and non-verbal reasoning. More choosy later on to ensure pupils are up to CE at 13. Discount available for third and subsequent siblings. Generous discounts for Forces families; means-tested bursaries available. A further 20 or so children arrive at 11+ and at this age some means-tested bursaries are available.

Exit: 'Four or five' leave at age 11 for local grammars or girls' schools. Majority stay on until 13 and then move over the road to senior school. Those who don't stay go on to (recently) Eton, Harrow, Marlborough, Radley, Wellington and Cheltenham Ladies'.

Remarks: School has been on present site – friendly jumble of Edwardian red-brick and newer additions in extensive grounds just across the road from senior school – since 1908. It was founded in 1863 as the College Juvenile Department and spent a couple of years squashed into a corner of the big school. Parents might be interested to learn that boarding fees in 1865 were 50 guineas (£52.50) a year and it was an extra £1 for a seat in the chapel. Smart rebranding has seen the name change from Cheltenham College Junior School to Preparatory School, with typography emphasising the Preparatory School part of the name. 'It's about trust; parents must be confident that we will do the same job as a stand-alone prep. If Cheltenham College is not the right senior school for your child then we'll say so.' Understandably, school would prefer pupils to remain until age 13, but the local education market is a competitive one and realpolitik extends to 'help' for children applying to grammar schools.

This has always been a popular prep but parents' loyalty has been tested in recent times by the drift that inevitably results from a rapid turnover of leadership. Previous head, in consultation with parents, reinstated French classes for the youngest children, brought back 'proper' prize-giving (we saw the new trophies in head's study), revived the very popular school musical which had 'got lost' and appointed a director of co-curricular activities to beef up this aspect of provision.

High-ceilinged classrooms, old wooden desks and iPads – teaching and learning at Cheltenham College Prep is a creative mix of the best of traditional methods and the latest technology. Small classes, subject specialist teaching and plenty of individual attention enable pupils to progress at their own rate – something parents really appreciate. 'The teachers are very encouraging, it's made such a difference to my child's confidence' and, 'they make time to follow a child's interest in a subject and take teaching beyond the curriculum.'

Pupils learn French as soon as they start in the Kingfishers and between years 6 and 8 pupils can opt for French or Spanish. Most are expected to take Latin – the class we saw looked like so much fun we wanted to stay and decline a verb or two – and there's also the option of 'off timetable' Greek. There are currently lessons on a Saturday morning but school says that this is 'under discussion.'

Learning support has its cheerful offices in the Coach House; there are two full-time members of staff plus a team of part-time assistants. All children are screened and extra support is mostly given in small groups or parent funded one-to-one sessions. EAL is also based here; Cheltenham may not strike the observer as excessively multicultural but the headquarters of ARRC (NATO Allied Rapid Reaction Corps) is close by.

Pre-prep, known as Kingfishers, occupies low-rise chalet, not an architectural gem but more than compensated for by the fresh air facilities, including forest school. Information boards outside let parents know what their children have been doing each day – great for conversations on the way home. During our visit head reduced a class of 3-year-olds, their elegant ballet mistress and this reviewer to hysterical laughter by his attempts at 'naughty toes' and 'good toes'.

Whether it's sport, music or drama, 'inclusion' is the starting point – there are teams from A to E and bands and choirs 'for all'. Every child has the opportunity to play in a competitive sports team from year 3. Lively house competitions – not just the usual sport but creative stuff too such as poetry, photography and music. Plenty of matches; pupils claimed that the win/lose rate with nearest rivals is pretty even. National winners in schools' rugby recently; finalists in national comps for hockey, netball and also skiing.

Everyone is enjoying the extended range of after-school clubs – 30 or so options including polo, equestrian, archery, chess, street dance and the enticingly named 'Grow your own money.' In addition to termly calendars the school now produces a what's on of events for the whole year – much appreciated by busy parents – with dates for everything from school photos to 'try boarding' nights and theatre visits.

As we walked through the grounds in golden autumnal sunshine, we stop at a muddy pen to scratch the backs of the Gloucester Old Spots, two of which would be attending bonfire night in sausage form. Plans to extend the forest school provision to include more animals: lambs are next and also chickens who will take up residence on an island in the lake – we hope Gloucestershire foxes can't swim.

Improvements to the school's rather convoluted layout are next on the to do list – to consolidate teaching into departments. A consequence of this has been a sad farewell to the atmospheric

DT room with its parquet floor, wooden cupboards and historic sawdust from thousands of bird boxes in favour of a new DT block. Outside in the corridor are glass cases displaying beautiful model boats made by a former teacher (they used to be sailed on the lake) and a drop-down model railway track. Art room similarly characterful but will be spared the same fate, not being located in the path of progress. The music department has a rather grand home, Lake House, with baronial fire places and wood-panelled walls. Nearly all pupils learn at least once instrument and there are plenty of opportunities to play or sing – whether it's chapel choir, jazz band, guitar group or, as on our visit, to compose and perform at a polyphone (surprisingly tuneful blue plastic tubes) workshop.

Fortunately this prep occupies a large site and any sharing of facilities with senior school is by choice rather than necessity. A new senior science block, full size rugby pitches, Astros and a sports hall with a £7m makeover are all at the disposal of the juniors.

One parent told us that 'children are encouraged to express their own opinions,' so we put this to the test and asked a few what they thought about their school. 'There are loads of new activities', 'We have a proper roast on Sunday, everyone sits down and is served at the table.' Yes, yes, but how about some constructive criticism? 'I wish they hadn't stopped us playing football in the car park. There's not enough time at lunch to change into a tracksuit and go out on to the field.'

One central boarding house on two floors (girls below, boys above, shared common room) and dorms divided into rather charming old style curtained cubicles with notice boards and cabin beds – those we saw were not over tidy, just comfortable, with soft toys, photos and the ubiquitous bunting. All freshly painted and carpeted, new bathrooms too. Lots of staff on hand – house parents, a matron and five gappies. After activities in the evening there's 'properly supervised' prep – overseen by the head or deputy head. School is aware that even very young children are under increased pressure these days and the head and teachers are vigilant to ensure that pupils keep things in perspective. 'School can be pretty full on, we need to be sure there's a good balance.'

Boarding reasonably flexible but school can no longer accommodate 'drop of the hat' requests, especially at the end of the week. At around £35 a night we're not surprised it's so popular – the majority of prep parents are both working (medics, GCHQ, Forces, not so many farming families these days) and this certainly helps.

A few unsteady years would dent the confidence of any school so it's testament to staff and parents' faith in Cheltenham Prep that they've come out of the experience bigger, brighter and bolder. It's heartening to see this historic school facing the future with energy and optimism.

Cheltenham Ladies' College

Bayshill Road, Cheltenham, Gloucestershire GL50 3EP

Ages 11–18 **Pupils** 850 **Sixth form** 300 **Boarders** 680

Fees: Day £24,810– £28,230; Boarding £36,945 – £41,610 pa

01242 520691
www.cheltladiescollege.org

Principal: Since 2011, Eve Jardine-Young MA (40s). Educated in Malawi, won a sixth form scholarship to the school she now leads, a place she credits with 'changing her life profoundly.' After graduating in engineering from Cambridge she worked for Ove Arup (structural engineers) before moving into teaching. Taught economics at Radley, moved to Epsom College where she was housemistress and head of sixth form, thence to Blundell's as director of studies. Married, her husband also works in education. Hobbies include reading, music (she is, apparently, rather a good pianist) and gardening.

Her appointment surprised some, but the CLC Council has a record of selecting left field candidates although they've only had to choose 11 since the school was founded in 1853. Ms Jardine-Young described the protracted recruitment process as: 'Extraordinary, the Council is very involved and take their responsibility extremely seriously.' Ms Jardine-Young lives up to her name and looks scarcely old enough for such a heavy mantle. When first asked if she felt the weight of history on her shoulders she said she saw her responsibility as 'stewardship, not of buildings but of tradition and future potential.'

So far Ms Jardine-Young has kept her head down and only turned up in the press a few times, including hitting the headlines for suggesting schools need to tackle mental health issues head on and that wellbeing should be put on an equal footing with academic achievement. She is, however, a keen blogger for the Huffington Post UK, taking on subjects such as whether single-sex or co-education offer the best preparation for 'real life' and girls' participation in sport and engineering, two areas of the curriculum that have been reformed during her headship. The words most often used by parents and girls to describe the principal are 'friendly,' 'approachable' and 'sincere,' and indeed she is; talkative she may be but she is not a loose cannon, so we wondered why a marketing person sat in on our interview. Apparently it was for 'training purposes.'

Ms Jardine-Young is her own woman and, in the best possible way, has not developed a headish persona. She isn't fixed, she likes exploring ideas and thinking aloud, but don't be fooled, she brings a formidable intellect to her alma mater. Nostalgic talk of a Proustian flashback courtesy of the smell of varnish is followed by discussion of the school's institutional 'meta language'...'while we rightly praise girls who achieve, do we give enough thought to what it means to be a winner? Do we articulate other values frequently enough?' She brims with excitement and vigour and her commitment to and passion for the school shine through.

Academic matters: League tables may come and go but CLC's academic record remains mostly mighty. In 2018, 92 per cent A*-A/9-7 at GCSE. At A level 66 per cent A* -A, 92 per cent A*-B. Sciences, maths, economics, history and English by far the most favoured subjects but there are plenty of options and small numbers take Japanese, physical education, theatre studies, classical Greek and history of art. IB was introduced in 2008 and results are extremely strong: points average of 38.4 (out of 45) in 2018. Regular national achievements and awards for science, maths and the arts and now also engineering, thanks to new engineering, enterprise and technology department. It must be said that, as in similar schools, pupils from the Far East raise the bar considerably in subjects such as maths and music. We have also heard from several sources that for some a popular summer holiday activity is subject extension classes in Hong Kong. The principal says, 'We're not producing clones, the model of exam grades at any cost leads to mental brittleness.' Try telling that to the tiger mothers.

The year 7 music lesson we observed was pretty serious, girls working at a high level, keen to answer questions, otherwise quiet and diligent. IB French – a debate on the uses of philosophy – was a bit livelier. The science labs looked like those in a university, girls in white coats utterly engrossed in their experiments. Parents tell us that while the prevailing mood is indeed serious there are 'inspirational' teachers and the girls enjoy their lessons. Average class size is 16 (seven in the sixth form), progress is monitored closely and girls move up or down through sets as necessary. The brightest may take one or two subjects early but most do 10 or so GCSEs at the normal time and in their stride. Parents impressed by proactive way in which teachers identify any problems and put solutions (extra lessons etc) in place swiftly. Pupils must learn to manage their time from day one – not only do they have to get to and from house to school promptly but they also have free periods for music lessons/practice and homework.

Small numbers with EAL or SpLD, mainly dyslexia. Specialist support for girls who need help with study skills, literacy and mathematics, but clearly CLC is not the place for those with significant problems and the school is frank about this. Most areas of school fully accessible by wheelchair but distance of houses could preclude all but a day pupil in these circumstances.

Games, options, the arts: Full programme of music and drama – size of school means there are opportunities for all who wish to perform; impressive results in LAMDA and music exams. Up to 50 music scholars must delight the ears at concerts and lunchtime recitals. College's jewel in the crown is its arts centre, the Parabola (it's in Parabola Road). Just across from main school, it has a 300-seat theatre, dance rehearsal rooms and small gallery primarily for school use but also hosts public shows and exhibitions. Cheltenham's many festivals also provide plenty of opportunities for cultural enrichment and school is 'strategic sponsor' for four: literature, music, science and jazz.

Impressive plate glass and metal arts building, school often has artists and writers in residence too, most but not all, women. Super art dept (school produced designers Katharine Hamnett and Amanda Wakeley) and a cornucopia of extracurricular options as one would expect, but school is explicit in warning girls that academics must come first. Strong tradition of charitable volunteering and fundraising – each year pupils nominate and then vote on which four charities to support, these are in addition to St Hilda's East, the charity established in 1889 by the 'Guild' (alumnae association, now 10,000 strong) in London's East End. 'Of what,' we asked naively, 'is Hilda patron saint?' Answer came there none but a few red faces and a Google later we discovered that she is saint in charge of learning. Old girls who work at City law firms also do pro bono work for the charity. We doubt Miss Beale would recognise today's East Enders but the area served by the charity is still very deprived and there remains much for the Cheltenham Ladies to do. Closer to home there is a well established community links programme and girls from year 11 upwards are to be found all over the locality helping out at homeless shelters, animal sanctuaries, primary schools and retirement homes.

Sports acreage and facilities (partly open to public) are pretty good and about to get even better when the brand new health and fitness centre opens. This will enable sports such as hockey, tennis and lacrosse to be played all year round. Notable individual achievements in athletics, tennis, skiing, riding, netball; team sport triumphs more frequently at county level although recently CLC has got through to national finals in hockey, cross country, swimming and riding. Most agree that sport not in premier league with few opportunities for the C,D,E team players to turn out (given size of school there must be a fair number of these). Physical activity compulsory all the way through with zumba and pilates for the less sporty, but the sixth formers we saw were hardly rushing to the gymnasium. On the other hand we hear of considerable efforts made to find something for the keen but not so able to participate in. The school is most successful at national level in hockey, netball and equestrian sports, with a girl in the GB under 16 team and talented riders competing internationally. Not sure the school can take direct credit for this – Gloucestershire with its links to the European riding scene may have been a deciding factor. No stabling at the school but girls may keep their mounts at a stables nearby. Polo is played at Birdlip.

Boarding: Younger girls' dorms spacious and very jolly with home duvets, under-bed storage and lots of photos and personalisation. At the foot of every bed was a brightly coloured tuck box. Single rooms for older girls are small but characterful, many with inspiring views. A place in one of the old-fashioned 'cubs,' dorms where beds have a curtain around them, highly coveted.

Parents full of praise for pastoral care whether for boarders or day girls – house mistresses in particular singled out for responding to email/telephone calls by return. Incidents – friendship issues or bullying – nipped in bud equally promptly, we hear. Girls bring their own laptops but internet use is heavily monitored. Boarders may use social networking sites from year 9 up out of school hours. The sixth form house we visited was originally the indefatigable Miss Beale's teacher training college. With its elegant library (plus wireless of course), it is intended to be a 'halfway house to university.' Girls may come and go with more freedom but the academic tutors and house mistresses liaise to minimise girls pushing themselves too hard and staff on each floor listen out for late night working.

Background and atmosphere: Miss Dorothea Beale led the school (including a nursery and a teacher training college) from 1858. She was a suffragette who pioneered women's education at a time when biology had to be code-named 'human geography' to stop irate fathers taking their girls home, because to learn about such things would make them unmarriageable. Not content with revolutionising women's school education, the astonishing Miss Beale also founded St Hilda's College, Oxford. What would she make of today's Cheltenham Ladies as they sweep all before them, outperforming most boys and becoming leaders in their chosen careers? Ms Jardine-Young says that the college has become 'more open, less introspective,' since she was a pupil there. Her aim is to take that forward and enable girls to 'become more adventurous learners, prepared to succeed but resilient enough to cope with failure.'

The main entrance to the college is on one of Cheltenham's wide boulevards. If it weren't for girls in PE kit massing on the steps it could be mistaken for a corporate HQ and, with 800+ pupils and over 600 employees, in one sense that's what it is. Behind lies a glorious quad, three parts Victorian gothic creeper-clad grandeur, one part grim 1970s concrete modernism. Miss Beale wanted her girls to learn in surroundings as beautiful as those boys had been favoured with for hundreds of years. The original fabric of the college, with its wonderful chequerboard marble corridor, grand library, mullion windows and arts and crafts frescoes, was thus as much a political statement as a seat of learning. The teaching rooms we saw were in the main functional and surprisingly anonymous. You couldn't tell you were at such a legendary school unless you happened to be daydreaming and looked out of the window (and we're sure that never happens).

On the day of our visit there had been something of a non-story in the national press about 'draconian guidelines' issued to ensure that 'mufti' (or home clothes) were sufficiently modest. Parents say they resented the tone of the letter rather than its content (some outraged by both). Uniform is pretty dreary though – the most enthusiasm we could elicit from parents was that 'it does the job.' The good people of Cheltenham may have nicknamed the girls 'greenflies' but something a little less evolved, 'algae', perhaps, would more precisely describe the shade of the green skirts and jumpers. Sixth formers may wear navy pin-stripe trousers although to this reviewer the effect of these with regulation shirt and jumper is a curious half-bank worker, half-schoolgirl centaur. But away with such frivolous concerns; we feel the disapproving shade of Miss Beale urging us to look at the bigger picture. She's right, of course.

Pastoral care, well-being and discipline: This is a big school and the house system works well by breaking it down into manageable units – roughly 60 girls per house. In 2015, CLC introduced a whole-school wellbeing programme, complete with sessions in healthy lifestyles, coping with stress, study skills, self-defence and mindfulness. School meets every day in the Princess Hall for prayers, notices etc. Houses, most substantial and Victorian, but pleasingly not too unsympathetically subdivided, are scattered in nearby leafy residential roads and strings of Ladies' College girls walking to and fro are one of Cheltenham's perennial sights. Some houses are quite a hike away, conveniently making sensible footwear a must. Fair bit of road crossing necessary and this concerns new parents as girls travel in unaccompanied groups. Girls eat all meals in their house, a buffet lunch is available in the main school for those taking exams or with commitments that use up travelling time. Each house has its own chefs but meals are planned centrally – economies of scale no doubt, also cuts down on lunch envy – girls get to choose favourite menus. Eating environment and food seemed pleasant enough in the houses we visited. A significant boarding refurbishment is underway and to enable this a new junior boarding house has been built into which each house will 'decant' in turn.

Pupils and parents: So sorry to undermine a popular cliché but we encountered no braying Henriettas or snooty aristos, just normal girls – friendly, unaffected and full of fun. Our year 9 lunch companions were sweetly excited about how much they 'loved going to Waitrose' (store has wisely established itself as the nearest supermarket) and triumphant that they had persuaded the local ice cream van to call at their house. Some observe (as did we) that nationalities tend to stick together both in and out of lessons – inevitable perhaps – and a look at the results lists in the excellent school magazine tells its own, by now familiar, story of the formidable Chinese work ethic.

We hear whispers on the GSG grapevine that the school is not quite as fashionable with metropolitan parents as once it was, but London is still the home city of boarding majority. In the main, parents are the usual spectrum of by no means rich professionals who choose the college because of the opportunities it offers their bright daughters. Several mentioned that they valued the school's relative conservatism and high expectations in a world of declining standards. All said that the pace is fast; too fast for a few.

Entrance: Entrance exam at 11+ (English, maths, VR). 'Please don't coach,' the school begs parents. 'We can spot the child who has been coached.' We imagine most parents have their hands over their ears and are singing loudly. At 13+ exams in maths, English, science, VR and French (if previously studied). For entry to the sixth form girls must sit exams in the subjects they wish to study.

So what exactly, we quizzed the head of admissions, does CLC look for? All girls take the same exam, thus candidates from outside the UK must have a very high standard of English. Every admission is considered on an individual basis; a girl's extracurricular interests are an important factor. The message from parents is, if you think it will suit your daughter, have a go. One told us, 'my daughter wasn't top in her prep school but she got a place and is loving it.' CLC wants girls who 'accept that they are joining a community.' Families are strongly encouraged to visit several times so that they know 'what they are getting.' Indeed families are under nearly as much scrutiny as girls themselves. Great importance is attached to what the school calls 'generosity of spirit' – interpret that as you wish. Roughly 25 per cent from outside the UK (expats as well as foreign nationals), many from the Far East, and the IB programme attracts strong candidates from Europe. The 200 day girls keep school's Gloucestershire roots strong.

Exit: A few leave post-GCSE but most stay on and benefit hugely from the higher education and careers advice provided by the school's Professional Guidance Centre. Support includes subject mentors to aid with further reading and personal statements, interview training and the opportunity to talk with Guild members about university and career choices.

In 2018, 20 Oxbridge places and 18 medics. Rest to top universities at home (eg Edinburgh, Durham, UCL, Bristol, St Andrews) or abroad. US increasingly popular with offers in 2018 from eg Yale, Brown and Stanford, and others off to Italy, Hong Kong and Switzerland. Careers of old girls give a flavour of what Cheltenham ladies do next: heaps of lawyers, MPs, medics and scientists. They include Nicola Horlick (financier), Cheryl Gillan (Conservative MP), Rachel Lomax (first woman deputy governor of the Bank of England), Dame Mary Archer (scientist), Lisa Jardine (historian), Rosie Boycott (journalist) and Amber Rudd (Home Secretary).

Money matters: Plenty of 'merit based awards' and scholarships for eg academics, art, sport and music. 'Limited amount' of funding for means-tested bursaries and some help for families of current pupils in financial difficulties. Bursaries intended to widen access to college are 'carefully awarded' to girls who would benefit from a college education. Principal very keen to extend opportunities in this area.

Remarks: A top flight school with strong traditional values and a clear sense of purpose. For the bright and energetic all rounder this school offers an exceptional education that is both broad and deep, with endless opportunities for fun and enrichment along the way.

Chew Valley School

Chew Lane, Chew Magna, Bristol BS40 8QB

Ages 11–18 **Pupils** 1,108 **Sixth form** 162

01275 332272
www.chewvalleyschool.co.uk

Head: Since 2016, Gareth Beynon (40s). Originally from Wimbledon, Gareth studied geography at Manchester and a masters in education management at the Institute of Education. Previously head of school at Clevedon School.

His enthusiasm is infectious; he is proud of the school he has inherited and impressed by the community spirit and support that makes it what it is today. Regularly teaches geography and passionate about sport, he is a regular supporter of the school teams. A rugby man, but no longer a player, he now runs (still aching from the Oxford half marathon when we met).

Lives in Bristol with his wife and daughter. Parents told us, 'Headteacher is great, on the ball, approachable, experienced, really trying to make a difference and thinking of the future.' Another added, 'He is very visible at school attending every event we go to and attends local events occasionally. He seems to fully support and really value his staff, and is enthusiastic about the students and all they can achieve.'

Academic matters: Solid results. In 2018, at A level, 37 per cent of grades A*-B, 18 per cent A*-A, down on previous year. At GCSE, 71 per cent achieved 9-4 in English and maths; 24 per cent of grades were A*-A/9-7.

Twenty-six A levels offered plus seven vocational courses. The popularity of extracurricular activities have led to the addition of a Cambridge Technical Extended Certificate in engineering (equivalent to A level), and a BTec in sport (PE A level also available). One parent said they chose Chew Valley because of this: '[It is a] good school in a great setting and offers options for less academic students.' Academics are taken seriously too, and Oxbridge hopefuls are assigned external mentors chosen from the governors or local businesses. Maths setted from year 7 and science from year 9. French, Spanish and German taught. English is strong along with maths, sciences, sociology, psychology and drama.

The learning support department works closely with parents and pupils are supported by TAs in classes. Two qualified specialist dyslexia teachers plus several staff are trained and experienced in working with pupils with ASD or Asperger's Syndrome. For more complex difficulties, external agencies may be used. Not fully wheelchair accessible but ramps and lifts in place where possible. Work with the Sensory Support Services have led to improvements in the auditory and visual environment, such as greater use of ICT and the use of a radio aid for hearing impaired students. Lower than average number of pupils with SEND for a school of this size, but very supportive of those who do have needs.

Low staff turnover; many are settled in the local community. Parents are generally happy with the standard of teaching but some feel a little more encouragement would help. One told us, 'My son is fairly middle of the road and well behaved; sometimes I think he can get a bit lost in class and doesn't receive the push that he needs to fulfil himself.' Another agreed, saying, 'More engagement [is needed] to push those kids that are not working at their full potential.' However, it is widely agreed that most teachers go the extra mile for pupils and really get to know them, particularly through the extracurricular activities. At the last D of E weekend there were no less than 15 staff on hand.

Games, options, the arts: Top reputation for sport. Site is surrounded by playing fields, plus there are hard pitches, floodlit Astros, a sports hall, squash courts, a gym and dance studio. Plenty of success too. Teams in almost every sport were crowned BANES District Champions recently. Regular fixtures and tournaments are complemented by annual sports festivals that include local primary schools.

Fantastic reputation for performing arts too. Annual dance festival consists of six sell-out shows showcasing the talents of Chew Valley School, local primary schools and local dance clubs. Dance, music technology, drama and theatre studies all offered at A level. One main whole school production each year, most recently Bugsy Malone, Jesus Christ Superstar and Twelfth Night. Smaller productions each term plus concerts, cabarets and musical extravaganzas. Chew Valley is an Artsmark Gold school, running more than 30 lunchtime and after-school arts clubs every week with over half the pupils regularly taking part.

Music is popular, and again, the community links are strong. As well as the local festivals that the school gets involved with, there are a number of former pupils who come back to perform regularly. There is a definite band culture at Chew Valley. There really is something for everyone here; there's a joint staff and pupil choir, chamber choir, production band, resound choir, engineer and recording club, guitar ensemble, wind ensemble, soul band, percussion band, concert choir and swing band (to name but a few).

Art and photography offered at A level, as well as textiles and product design. Good studio and standard of work on display but the performing arts really do seem to be 'the big thing' here. However, we were impressed with the design technology department. Sponsored by Dyson, the facilities are top notch. It feels like a working workshop with a reception sofa area at the front and open-plan classrooms and work areas. Pupils are lucky to have three 3D printers, a CNC router and two laser cutters, all industry standard and size. This department is popular and you can see why: there is an annual Dyson Challenge, a reward system (from guru to apprentice) that wins pupils privileges like access at break times, and an engineering club. The club now has three teams who design and make 4x4s and compete at Silverstone.

Clubs are mostly during the long lunch hour instead of after school. The list of extracurricular activities is long and offers more than just the usual suspects. Pupils can try climbing, circus skills, cheerleading, taekwondo, Frisbee Friday and choreography. Parents told us the activities are 'a great opportunity' and 'there is a fantastic range, really something for everyone,' but some struggle to get their children to attend – more encouragement, please! Sixth formers take part in enrichment activities once a week and these include sailing on the lake, Ten Tors, D of E, community sports leadership award, basic expedition leadership award, Young Enterprise, mentoring and arts award.

What impressed us most was the leadership opportunities on offer. The Chew Valley School Community Council encourages pupils to get involved in their school community. To date there are 14 project teams, led and managed by the pupils. The teams plan projects that are then fed into the school development plan and supported by staff. There is a reptile team, a poly (tunnel) team, a film team, a chicken team, a politics team – the list goes on. The teams have been so successful that Chew Valley was awarded the Learning to Lead gold award.

The equalities team deserves a special mention as they have achieved national recognition for their campaigning work, addressing a Stonewall Conference in London and being made Stonewall Champions. Sir Ian McKellen, a founder member of Stonewall, even paid them a visit to talk about their work and his experiences. They have been raising awareness on transgender issues and one parent told us, 'The school has successfully eradicated homophobia and hopefully can do the same on racism.' They went on to tell us that the school dealt with a recent incident appropriately and swiftly.

Plenty of trips offered. We saw photos from a recent Pompeii trip, plus there are annual French and German exchanges. Older pupils have been to Borneo, Tanzania, Zambia, Malawi and Honduras. The school also has links to Kenya and there is an annual trip for years 11 and 12.

Background and atmosphere: Founded in 1958, Chew Valley School sits on an impressive 30-acre site between the villages of Chew Magna and Chew Stoke. Just eight miles south of Bristol, the school feels pretty rural, surrounded by extensive playing fields and overlooking Chew Valley Lake. Part of a multi-academy trust, Lighthouse Schools Partnership.

'The school feels like a real community,' parents agreed, and it really does serve the Chew Valley well. The leisure centre on site is open to the community and there are plans for a community performing arts centre. Fundraising is currently underway for a 250-seat auditorium, a dance studio, rehearsal and meeting rooms, cinema facilities and exhibition space. Also on site is a children's centre.

Site is made up of several one or two storey blocks that neither offend nor inspire but are practical and in reasonable condition. Blocks are based around courtyards and walkways, surrounded by field upon field. Pupils here are lucky to have so much green space, enough to grow veg, keep chickens, and spend their days outside (weather permitting) chilling on the grass or kicking a ball about. A new wooden shelter in the middle of the buildings has become a focal point to catch up with friends; it was erected in memory of a staff member who passed away.

Inside, the classrooms are a little tired, but spaces are good and walls are filled with work. Inspiring quotes from famous people are dotted around the corridors and walkways. The sixth form block was the latest development (in 2008), and is a great space; feels just like a college and is separate from the rest of the school. Downstairs is a canteen that was packed with students on our visit, and suitably lively. Upstairs there are flexible study spaces and seminar rooms with beautiful views of the lake, plus art and photography and a gallery space. Also new-ish is the music centre with an Apple Mac suite, recording studio and practice rooms.

This is a fairly traditional school. Old-fashioned values like opening the door for each other, being polite, and mutual respect are held in high regard. No mobiles allowed, except for sixth formers.

Fundraising is big at Chew Valley and a couple of events that caught our eye were the Chew Valley Santa Scramble (5K or a mini 1K for under 11s) and the Mind Over Mile Challenge. The Santa Scramble is an annual event and involves not just the school but also the local community; Santa suits provided. The Mind Over Mile Challenge is a whole school event that not only raises awareness and money for mental heath charities but is something that the head actively encourages: using sports as a release.

Pastoral care, well-being and discipline: Good pastoral care. Pupils are assigned a tutor for the duration of their school days, plus there is a head of year and a non-teaching assistant head of year. Registration is twice a day to keep everybody in check, but also to allow pupils an opportunity to raise any issues or worries. Pastoral care is managed by the deputy head and supported by pastoral support workers. They support pupils who are showing signs of mental health issues, or those struggling to make friends, or who are generally worried or anxious. A full-time home school welfare manager is on call for students or parents so that matters can be raised immediately instead of waiting until a teacher is free. Two counsellors also available and a school nurse visits once a week. One parent whose child has received a great deal of counselling said '[It's the support that] makes Chew Valley stand out as well as the high academic achievers and extracurricular activities.'

On our visit there was the usual break time rabble but nothing worrying to report. In class, pupils were attentive, responsive and engaged. The school deals with issues appropriately, we were told. One parent told us, 'In general the teaching standard is high and teachers seem to support the students in their learning,' even calling parents when homework isn't completed. Another suggested there should be 'more consequences for poor homework (or no homework).' Some disruption in classes reported – that 'some teachers just ignored or were unable to control' – but the general consensus was that 'teachers are of the highest calibre. They know their subject matter and the exam syllabus and teach in an interesting way.'

Pupils and parents: Some families have moved to Chew Valley for the school. Parents and, in some cases, grandparents have been pupils here; large majority are incredibly supportive. Close-knit community with Chew Valley School at the centre. Not particularly ethnically diverse, we were told, with some 70 per cent local white middle class families. Free buses cover the whole valley. Bristol residents pay £500 each year.

Good communication. 'They communicate in a variety of ways including letters home, text messages and via the Portal.... they are very approachable,' parents reported. However, one parent grumbled: 'As a late joiner to the school I have had no way to meet or communicate with other parents. The school society does a great job of hosting several evenings of events each year but it is almost impossible to meet other parents from my children's classes as we don't know who they are!' One for the PTA, maybe.

Years 7 to 9 wear green jumpers, years 10 to 11 wear black jumpers, and no uniform for sixth formers. One parent suggested, 'The uniform seems to be a fashion show for many of them ie extremely tight, skinny trousers and excessive makeup. I would therefore suggest a clamp down on uniform expectations and limit the use of makeup.'

Entrance: Large catchment area covering 120 square miles of the Chew Valley with some pupils trekking in from as far as south Bristol. Over 40 feeder primary schools. School works closely with the primaries throughout the year to ensure the transition is as seamless as possible. A number of activities and festivals, like the dance festival and sports tournaments, familiarise primary school pupils with the site. Plus teachers from Chew Valley teach languages, music and PE at the primary schools and there are visits and an induction day before the start of term. If a child is particularly anxious or has special needs, extra support and additional visits are offered. Applications through the Bath and North East Somerset admissions.

At sixth form, a minimum of 5 GCSEs including English and maths at grade 4 or above is required; individual subjects set their own grade requirements.

Exit: Less than half stayed on for sixth form in 2018, but a handful of externals join each year. Leavers go to Bristol colleges or local ones offering more vocational qualifications.

On average two-thirds go on to university. Popular destinations in 2018 included Cardiff (and Met), Plymouth, UWE, Leeds and Liverpool. One to Cambridge, others to colleges for foundation courses. Good links with local industries; a large network of supportive, well-connected parents helps some pupils into apprenticeships with a focus on engineering and law. A sprinkling go straight into employment or training: royal naval officer and pilot training in 2018.

Famous alumni include Josh Eggleton, Michelin star chef, Louis Carey, ex-Bristol City Footballer, John Garden, keyboards in The Scissor Sisters, recording flautist Nicola Woodward and professional percussionist Justin Woodward.

Remarks: A successful comprehensive that serves a large and supportive local community. Extensive grounds in a rural setting not far from Bristol. Renowned for performing arts and sport as well as a fantastic range of extracurricular activities.

Christ College, Brecon

Brecon, Powys LD3 8AF

Ages 7–18 **Pupils** 383 **Sixth form** 114 **Boarders** 165 full, 41 flexi (from year 5)

Fees: Day £9,165 – £18,546; Boarding £17,544 – £29,043 pa

01874 615440
www.christcollegebrecon.com

Head: Since September 2017, Gareth Pearson (40s), previously senior deputy head at Lord Wandsworth College in Hampshire. Has also been a housemaster at Wellington College and maths teacher at Millfield, as well as a captain in the Royal

Marines for eight years. Mechanical engineering degree from Loughborough, teaching qualifications from Plymouth and Bath. He is married to Rhian and they have two children.

Academic matters: Christ College, Brecon does not go in for pictures of A level students jumping in excitement at their results, though, naturally, they are happy to share their delight. They have always had their bright pupils moving on to Oxbridge and top medical schools but overall results have improved. In 2018, 46 per cent A*/A grades at A level. This school is less about numbers, it's about human beings and their deserved achievements. A recent publication contains a wonderful account of two boys, great friends, and the academic rivalry which they shared for most of their time in the school.

Having said all that, the overall statistics are impressive and not to be ignored. We witnessed some absolutely tremendous teaching. Pupils spoke to us about the exciting quality of the teachers, the energy and fun they injected and the extra time they offered for catch up and clarification. We saw sparky language teaching, lively music and drama, history, sciences, maths, biology: all demanding subjects and all warmly appreciated by pupils. It pays dividends. Medicine, science and engineering degree courses are the most popular. GCSE results are excellent, demonstrating the popularity and success of technical and creative subjects. In 2018, 52 per cent A*-A/9-7 grades.

And what about those people with SEN? Those few who do were described as 'moderate, mostly'. But it's almost worth cultivating some SEN in order to be closeted with the highly qualified, approachable teacher ever ready to help anyone who drops in. She perceives her visitors as engaged in learning to overcome weaknesses, developing a sense of belonging and togetherness, of readiness and enhanced expectations. Let them stop by when they want to. She is full of wisdom and compassion. Every Thursday afternoon is tea party time: often, we were told, pretty lively. The parents we spoke to about her 'couldn't find the words to do her justice.' One final joy: most schools charge for help with SEN. At CCB pupils and parents pay with heartfelt gratitude and affection.

Games, options, the arts: Rugby is regarded by many as the number one sport at CCB, with coaching from a former professional, but it is by no means the only game. There is some football played, a lot of hockey – the school has a number of international hockey players, past and present, boys and girls. Both sexes have been recent Welsh champions at U18s, U14s and U12s and there are outstanding netball teams. Lots of cricket, including a 20:20 Festival involving players from the UK and abroad. Previously outdoor swimming pool now has a roof. There's masses to do and much to be admired. Most pupils enjoy getting involved with a variety of sports and activities. Just as well. One pupil told us that he had been selected for five different sports 'and I'm not much good at any of them. But it was terrific fun and we didn't lose them all.'

Brecon is the HQ of the army in Wales; CCF, compulsory in years 9 and 10, is enormously popular, and when you've met the man who runs it you're half way towards understanding why.

Drama is driven by a dynamic head of department who enthuses not just the pupils but local amateur thespians to join in. There's an annual community project as well as an ambitious school production for the different age groups. Their Les Mis was 'jaw-dropping', according to one West End fan we met who had seen the Christ College version.

Music is terrific. We met some delightful and talented pupils practising and returned to listen to a thrilling concert full of energy and skill, sensitivity and passion. Choral singing that might have been written for Polly Garter, multi-age orchestras, a delightful pupil making an excellent debut on the drum – the evening was moving and exciting.

Sixth form curriculum includes speaker sessions on topics ranging from financial literacy to politics and society, plus encouragement to get involved in extracurricular options.

We met a lot of parents at the school concert and they all agreed that it was 'cool to work' here. One parent volunteered that the pupils worked hard 'out of inspired interest and loyalty.' Another phrase that remains is about the school, overall: 'Whatever they do, they do well.'

Boarding: Boarding is convenient, of course, that's part of it all, and fun. There are four boarding houses for pupils in year 9-13. One or two of the students with older siblings recognised that these rooms were much nicer than those at most universities. Snooker tables, luxurious, comfortable sofas, large screen televisions, efficient showers and always friends to talk to. Many also talked of their satisfaction at being given positions of authority. All staff are involved in boarding.

Alway House is a day and boarding house where year 5 and 6 pupils from St Nicholas House junior school can weekly board with the year 7 and 8s and which is, unbelievably, over 50 years old. A joyous building and full of intelligently conceived fittings and decorations, an area for sleeping, playing inside and out, ICT for researching particular topics, challenging climbing frames and always kind, creative helpers from all walks of the school and not just walks, because on Fridays they go for a country run.

Background and atmosphere: Founded in 1541 by Henry VIII on the site of the sacked and wracked Black Friars' church, victim of the Dissolution. Students are touchingly proud of this ancientness, as of the crowned 'h' tag, which is the school's logo, and of the fact that the chapel where they meet every morning has been worshipped in since around 1250. Wonderful newish junior school: the St Nicholas House, for pupils aged 7-11 (opened in 2014). Newly refurbished St David's is the house for day pupils in years 9-13.

This small school is amongst the happiest we have ever visited. From the genuinely warm welcome at reception, throughout the whole tour (with a thoughtful and entertaining mixture of guides) and during lunch in the wonderful, ancient refectory with delightful sixth formers, we were treated with courtesy and spontaneous good will.

Pastoral care, well-being and discipline: The happiness is palpable and high spirited and that says much about the discipline. Pupils and staff walk around greeting, smiling and chatting and, when they see visitors approaching, focus the eyes and smile inclusively. Staff and pupils clearly get on well with each other. Discipline is based on common sense and mutual consideration. We were told of incidents in which anxieties and problems were spotted and addressed by teachers, class assistants, senior pupils and ground staff. In reply to our question about the school's tangible happiness, one sixth form girl told us: 'It's like a jigsaw: everyone seems to fit in.'

The head of school and deputy (one boy and one girl) are selected by the head following nominations from staff and pupils, and there are 15 prefects. Duties? 'Not arduous,' said one. 'People are pretty reasonable.' 'Cowed?' Certainly not. 'Comfortably co-ed' – no difference of opportunities.

Pupils and parents: Most pupils come from a radius of some 50 miles, the sons and daughters of army officers, farmers, businesspeople. 'Fewer demanding expectations,' we were told by parents who also had experience of the home counties. You do not get the impression that the overseas students have been imported in lorry loads simply to boost grades. In the nicest possible way, those 17 per cent or so of pupils from Germany, China, Hong Kong, Japan and Nepal – there's a strong contingent of Gurkhas in Brecon – in the sixth form are almost invisible at first visit. The school seems much better than some at fully integrating pupils from abroad so that many get stuck in to rugby, cricket and choir singing. The overseas pupils we met were genuinely happy and involved.

Entrance: Into year 3 for St Nicholas House via an entry morning with 'a range of academic and creative activities', plus small group meetings with the college head and the head of St Nicholas House. Into years 7 and 9 by English and maths assessments and IQ test, plus interview and school reports. Sixth form entry by GCSE predictions, IQ test, school report and interview.

Exit: About 15 per cent leave after GCSEs. Of those who stay, most go on to university and to a wide range of subjects. Three to Oxbridge in 2018 and around a third on total to Russell Group. One off to study maths at the University of Waterloo, Canada.

Money matters: There are scholarships and bursaries available for the able and needy. Incidentally there are no inescapable extras – in fact The Good Schools Guide recently voted CCB in the Top Ten Value for Money Boarding Schools in the UK. We do not have shares in the school.

Remarks: When you step back from GCSEs and A level grades; from rugby results and hockey triumphs; from CCF marches and medals; when you pause to marvel at the hills around, enfolding the school and beckoning; when you listen to the wonderful singing in the chapel founded nearly 800 years ago and restored by Gilbert Scott about 600 years later; when you consider that at the time the English Bible was being hammered out by that group of scholars and fanatics presided over by James 1, the Scottish King, Christ College Brecon had already been in existence for nearly 100 years, it is not difficult to feel that much has been absorbed from history and the world around. Perhaps it is not too fanciful to think that the extraordinary atmosphere of friendship, mutual loyalty and academic endeavour has emanated from the variety and insistence of the past. Like many schools of ancient foundation CCB hasn't always been in a good place, but it certainly is now. What's more there is history in the making. Ask about the expansion into the Far East. Great things are being delivered, even more is promised and this is a school that warrants admiration, loyalty and, above all, trust. Go and see for yourselves.

Churston Ferrers Grammar School

Greenway Road, Churston Ferrers, Brixham, Devon TQ5 0LN

Ages 11–18 **Pupils** 1,034 **Sixth form** 281

01803 842289
www.churstongrammar.com

Headteacher: Since 2007, Robert Owers BA PGCE CFES NPQH. Educated at Warwick University, Owers taught at two large co-ed comprehensives in Essex before becoming deputy head at Chelmsford County High School for Girls.

A family man, the school is home from home. His wife teaches drama and both his children are pupils. Chatty and approachable, he's a keen sportsman, particularly football and cricket, but jokes that any spare time is spent as the 'dad taxi'.

Keen to emphasise that although the school is a grammar school, it's not elitist and does not 'aspire to the single-sex public school ethos'. No blazers, no Latin, no old school traditions. Sensitive to the different social backgrounds of the children and families, he tries to ensure everyone is comfortable and not intimidated – Churston is a school 'for the most able local students irrespective of social background.'

Parents say, 'The school is clearly very well led by a charismatic and outstanding head and team; the general feeling is that whilst the academic aspects and outcome are key, they also want their students to experience many different things, be brave and join clubs, try sports they might never have thought about, fundraise, help out, be open to new things and the school will support them.'

Leaving in July 2019.

Academic matters: Grades fluctuate. In 2018, a greatly improved 38 per cent A*/A and 70 per cent A*-B at A level. Top results in biology, history, maths and psychology. Interestingly, these subjects also have the highest number of pupils taking them. Few takers for languages. At GCSE, 57 per cent A*-A/9-7 in 2018; GCSE curriculum now begins in year 9.

Churston takes great pride in its links to other schools around the world. One such project is Comenius, a European Union educational project which has helped them set up partnerships with schools in Hungary, Italy (Sicily), Norway, France and Germany. Not only do the students get the opportunity to learn about other European cultures, but it also helps their personal development.

There's an impressive DT lab with food technology and textiles to GCSE. After GCSE, there is a strong split between girls taking textiles, and boys taking design. This is a real shame and was disappointedly written off as stereotypical. Around 600 computers across the school but these are gradually being replaced by Chromebooks.

Learning support is looked after by the student services team and SENCo along with a LSA, a full-time counsellor and literacy support co-ordinator. Action plans for individual or group work are set up according to needs, and screening is ongoing. Literacy groups available for any pupils not reaching their full potential, in place of second language lessons.

One parent commented, 'Given that the school is a grammar school in an area of low wealth and low expectations, it is disappointing that the school does not do more to lift the ambitions and aspirations of its leavers. Given the academic potential of its students, it perhaps should be sending more students each year to Russell Group or equivalent universities. However, that is as much a reflection of the geographical area and the families here as it is of the school.'

Games, options, the arts: Great sports facilities. The playing fields outside the new sports hall are pretty inspiring, with a view down the valley to the sea. The old sports hall is still in use, plus there's a gym for older pupils, Astroturf and cage for basketball and netball, four tennis courts, three football pitches and a heated outdoor swimming pool for summer use only. The school has had some outstanding successes: the basketball team, led by two ex-England coaches, is renowned Devon champion, and has been national champion twice in the last 15 years. Several pupils play at county or national level in a variety of sports, with full support from Churston. One parent said, 'Our request for our son to tour South Africa with Devon cricket board was well received and supported.'

'The academic emphasis can mean the arts are under-invested,' said one parent, but there's now a new music and art block. A recent production, The Lion, the Witch and the Wardrobe, involved 80 students of all ages. Others have included Blue Remembered Hills and Born to Dance. 'Over the last five years, music in the school has improved dramatically, with some great school concerts,' say parents. Around 25 per cent of pupils learn an instrument.

Impressive artwork on display in the art rooms and corridors. One project that caught our attention involved a group of year 11 pupils and ex-students. They decorated an old Mercedes in a day then drove it to Croatia to raise money for Rowcroft Hospice. A great project on many levels.

There's the usual array of lunchtime and after-school clubs in sport, music, drama, science and debating, plus Sustainable Futures and Food For Life groups. A recent addition is a Quidditch Club that pupils set up themselves. Other extracurrricular activities include DofE, for which Churston has the largest commitment in the area. Parents enthuse, 'The extracurricular trips abroad that the school organises are superb, with trips to visit WW1 battlefields, to sing in Italy, language exchange trips, adventure trips to France, as well as opportunities to travel to China, South Africa and Peru. The commitment from staff to organise these and commit their own time is outstanding.'

The school helps families plan these trips with a programme called Seven years at Churston. It kicks off with a residential trip in year 7, foreign exchanges in years 8 and 9 plus the battlefields trip. From year 10 up the most talked about is the social enterprise trip to Peru. One parent commented, 'He relished the month spent in Peru this summer, where a group of 20 students and three teachers undertook a mixture of helping local primary schools [build shade canopies from old sails] and exploring the culture and history of Peru. He matured a great deal in that month.' There are also cultural trips, recently to China and South Africa, and sports tours, which recently saw netball, football and basketball teams touring Holland.

Background and atmosphere: Originally Dartmouth Grammar School, Churston Ferrers is one of 42 co-educational grammar schools in the country. Set amongst the rolling hills of Devon in a picturesque seaside location, the school gives an impression of calm and tranquility. Extensively modernised since 1957; the modern entrance with sliding doors and reception is more like a business building. However, the displayed trophies, wooden plaques for heads of houses and photo galleries make this very much a school. A particularly nice touch is the screen at the entrance that gives live updates.

Modern with wide corridors and windows looking onto adjoining classrooms, Churston doesn't feel like a traditional grammar or public school; no signs of old school traditions here. It feels and looks much more like a modern comprehensive. A small beep indicates the end and start of lessons but there's no mad rush to get to the next class. Lessons average 75 minutes, and are followed by a 10/15 minute break for drink, snack or breather. This is all rather civilised and pupils seem relaxed.

The Cube was built in 2008 as a learning and resources centre, open from 8am to 5pm with both reference books and Chromebooks available. There's also a teacher on hand.

The recently built sixth form centre is across a large courtyard scattered with seating and table tennis tables and surrounded by allotments. Approximately 300 students are catered for here; they have their own snack kitchen and a large, comfy common room. Upstairs are classrooms and a large computer room with 60 computers. Part of the computer room is sectioned off as a supervised study area – that's detention room to you and me. Unsurprisingly, this is mainly frequented by boys.

Most of the staff have been here for less than 10 years. A third are under 30 years old and around two-thirds are female. The head has recently appointed two female physics teachers in the hope that they can encourage more girls to take the subject and start putting these stereotypes to bed. They still have a long way to go with persuading any boys to take textiles or join a dance group, but the girls are taking note and getting involved in maths as well as physics.

Five houses are led by year 11 students. Regular house assemblies, inter-house competitions, charity fundraising, growing and selling allotment produce, recycling and drama productions bring pupils of all ages together and encourage them to work as a community. A mentor website enables younger pupils to ask sixth form ambassadors for help – usually maths homework, we hear.

Pastoral care, well-being and discipline: All parents agreed the school's pastoral care is outstanding. 'We feel the school is very well run with a truly human hand'. A large student services team ensures there's always someone available. Pupils are from all walks of life and the school is keen to make sure they are supported in any way needed. Head considers this to be the most important part of the school: 'happiness is more important than grades,' he told us. Quirkiness and individuality allowed. Kindness promoted. Relationships respected.

'The school manages the balance between approachability and discipline in a careful manner, resulting in a positive culture and ethos in the school,' say parents. 'We have seen very little evidence of bullying.' Incidents seem to be 'handled appropriately and sensitively, and resolved in a timely manner. Was very impressed with the skill of the team involved.' One parent said of their experience: 'Our son did not lose his confidence as a result of this incident but retained his self-esteem...He felt safe and supported...and there have not been any problems since. He also received a huge amount of support from all years in the wider school community.'

Lunchtime detentions for failure to complete work usually apply to around 10 students. Five detentions leads to an after-school detention. Friday night detentions are for repeated detentions or more serious issues like smoking or bad behaviour. Second offences lead to suspension. Zero tolerance of drugs, immediate expulsion.

Pupils and parents: Most families are local, from Torbay, Brixham or Paignton, but some from as far as Totnes. As with all grammar schools, there are pupils from varied backgrounds; parents are solicitors, directors, nurses, PAs. One said, 'Churston was all our first choice, for its academic achievement, positive attitudes towards learning and family friendliness. Churston is a comparatively small secondary school, so the staff and students (and parents too if they join the PTA) get to know each other well.'

Communication is good. Parents and pupils are invited to complete surveys. A recent request for more drama led to the construction of the new drama studio. Cardigans can now be worn instead of the unflattering sweatshirts, and boys (and girls) can wear earrings from year 10 onwards. Another request, undoubtedly from parents, was the installation of a salad bar. And a change championed by parents and pupils alike was the reduction of homework to one hour a night for years 7 and 8, increasing to two hours higher up. A voluntary homework scheme has also been set up, one parent explained. 'He has been given appropriate extension work in subjects he is particularly good at and encouraged to reach his potential.'

Any famous leavers? Andy Parsons, the comedian.

Entrance: The three grammar schools in Torbay operate a co-ordinated joint entrance exam in English, maths and verbal, numerical and non-verbal reasoning. No practice material but familiarisation booklets provided. Approximately 140 out of 300 applicants are successful, usually split as 75 girls and 65 boys.

Plenty of induction days and events. Parents said, 'All of them settled very quickly – the transition was handled very smoothly with meetings and events in the summer term before they started and lots of information. One added, 'There were several events organised to help integrate us as families and these were extremely helpful.... we did a Lego exercise to show team-building and how they work with the children to help them come out of their shells, or stand back for a while if they are natural leaders. This was fascinating, and incredibly exciting to think that they were considering the whole child in this way.'

Around 40-55 pupils join the sixth form from elsewhere, mainly Brixham and Dartmouth Community Colleges. Students must have at least a 5 at GCSE in English and maths and 6 in four other subjects, plus individual subject requirements.

Exit: Around 80 per cent stay on for sixth form, and most go on to university. About 40 per cent to Russell Group universities, including two to Oxbridge in 2018, plus two medics. Exeter, Cardiff, Plymouth, Bath, Bristol and Swansea all popular. One off to study journalism in France, one to Italy and one to the Netherlands (liberal arts) in 2018.

Money matters: Bursary fund 16-19 for sixth formers.

Remarks: If you live in Torbay, there are three grammar schools to choose from, one for girls, one for boys and Churston for those in favour of a co-ed school life. Churston is a family-orientated school that is academic, but not exceptional. The biggest difference is that it's more relaxed than your average grammar school, maybe because it's co-ed or maybe because it's less traditional. The head and his team work hard to keep the school open to new challenges, fully adaptable for change and in tune with the rest of the world, not just the rolling hills of Devon.

Clayesmore Preparatory School

Linked with Clayesmore School

34

Iwerne Minster, Blandford Forum, Dorset DT11 8PH

Ages 2–13 **Pupils** 235 **Boarders** 70 full (from year 3) **C of E**

Fees: Day £7,710 – £18,750; Boarding £17,670 – £25,110 pa

01747 812122
www.clayesmore.com

Head: Since 2014, Will Dunlop (40s). Previously at Kingston Grammar School after 10 years in the army. Enjoyed teaching map reading to other CCF recruits at school, interest in education consolidated as an army trainer with realisation that so many school leavers – particularly with undiagnosed learning needs – were being failed by the system.

His move into teaching in 2006 was 'a step into the dark – had to put papers in before I had a job to go to,' though serendipity helped. Was on night duty when saw ad for ideal job – CCF contingent commander and 'any subject' teacher at Kingston Grammar School – deadline 9am the following morning. Hit the fax machine with minutes to spare and got the job. Two years on, head of prep form and year 7- won over by curiosity and creativity of younger pupils along the way.

A former pupil here, then a prospective parent, was bowled over by the school – SEN strengths the clincher – before the job came along.

Noted for enthusiasm. 'Gets really excited,' reckoned a parent. 'You get this impression that he's the most amazing teacher first and foremost.' 'Mr Dunlop has tons of energy and made our time there very enjoyable,' said senior pupil. Thoughtful and erudite (peppers conversation with literary quotes), he's well-liked, as is his wife. 'One of the genuinely nicest people I have ever met,' said parent.

'Kids absolutely adore him,' said one mother. 'My son came back very excited to say he'd had lunch with Mr Dunlop and couldn't quite believe it,' said mother. It's a similar high spot for Mr D – 'shows me how far they've come.'

Gives staff the credit for own initiatives (not always the case) and delegates. No killer questions for prospective staff (unless he wasn't letting on) – he's looking for creative people who understand difference 'between being a teacher and doing teaching.'

Bar slight boarding blip (2016 inspection found flaws in vetting of prospective staff, now corrected), it's all been – largely – plain sailing.

Happiest in the classroom, boarding houses or on the pitch, there's not much he doesn't love about the job. Sees sense of pastoral care as vital aspect of his role, 'If you don't understand where the children are coming from and what affects their feelings then you really have to ask if you're doing the right thing.'

Moving on in July 2019.

Entrance: Pre-prep numbers now growing again after slight fall, helped by free come and play toddler and parent sessions. Plenty of well-connected locals, but don't expect huge amounts of socialising as many work full time. 'Some parents...think they'll get into a niche little coffee club but it doesn't happen,' said mother.

Further up, healthy levels of prep applications in top years, but not a school for all comers. While take from wider ability range than competition, pupils must be able to access curriculum. Ask for reports and may observe child at current school (avoids shattering expectations if attend taster day here and aren't offered a place). Will only accept in top junior years if child will make transition to senior school and 'at least get some GCSEs'.

Wide range of scholarships awarded to year 7 pupils, though fee reduction – between 2.5 and 10 per cent – doesn't shave much off that chunky termly invoice.

Best to recover equilibrium by reciting routes of the school buses – who wouldn't be drawn to Compton Acres, Sturminster Marshall and Spetisbury.

Exit: Currently, 95 per cent plus move up to senior school but not prescribed. Happily accommodate those preparing for entrance exams elsewhere, including grammars and other independents (Canford inevitably takes a few) though fewer as 'our reputation moves away from SEN focus,' says school.

Once here, families tend to stay on, decision reinforced during compare and contrast open day visits elsewhere. 'I suddenly thought "I love it but need to look around," so did all the local ones and came back,' says mother. 'Has just got the most amazing feel to it.'

Only time pupils have been asked to leave (single figures, says Mr Dunlop) is down to bullying. 'We do everything we possibly can but there comes a point where it's not viable,' he says.

Remarks: Set in a generous corner of school's 62 acres with a comfortable, home-like feel. Operationally run as a separate school with own uniform including much loved long tartan skirt. 'It keeps your legs warm and the stains don't show – had food all over mine,' said nostalgic senior pupil.

While resources are shared with senior school, they're clearly delineated. Path from main building to music block

C

divides the play areas. 'Like Mexican wall though more porous,' says Mr Dunlop. Pupils go to main hall for lunch and use e.g. swimming pool and forest school. Memories of original prep school site, in nearby Charlton Marshall, are summoned by impressive Cedar of Lebanon which tower over the turning circle – decision sentiment rather than species-led. ('One of my successors will have difficult decision to take,' says Mr Dunlop).

Tales of year 8 pupils still enjoying school's adventure playground, the perk of ringing large, wall-mounted bell at supper time and links with the community – Brownie pack, run by staff, is the only one 'in the valley' and includes local children and pupils – reinforce sense of a compact and reassuring world.

Low rise buildings house the youngest pupils- nursery and reception/year 1 in big, bright and open plan classrooms, amid plentiful greenery and the odd unexpected touch (sixth former's 'spaceman' sculpture.)

Given push on standards filtering down from the senior school, no surprise that Mr Dunlop is also felt to be giving teaching a gentle shove. Nothing that will cause resettlement of its axis, mind you – and not that most teachers (bar the odd one who 'should be moving on,' said one parent) need it. A recent prospectus may state firmly that 'every child achieves academic success', but is more specifically about recognising individual potential.

Plenty to enjoy including path that winds round the back, taking in glasshouse (once used to grow melons, now used for ceramics). Out front there's the Everett Building (2008) – very attractive – and 70s teaching and boarding block building that isn't, though disguised by greenery. 'A well-functioning machine if not a beautiful one,' says Mr Dunlop, diplomatically.

Boarders mainly year 4 upwards, though one pupil in year 3 having a great time courtesy of year 6 mentor – 'very kind and does French plaits for me.' All happens above the shop, in large, generally bright and very clean rooms, if a tad low on ambiance. Loads of clothes storage (often empty thanks to almost non-stop, highly efficient laundry system).

Gentle approach to rewards and sanctions keeps things home-like. Spickest, spannest dorm gets surprise 'muck' (jargon for afternoon break treat). Individual winners get slap up meal at head of boarding's house. For older boarders, perks include moving closer to the bathroom. Saturday school keeping bustle going well into the weekend.

Focus is on encouragement and thoughtful planning, from visual timetables in boarding houses – sun for wake up, 'good for reluctant readers' – to description of mini adventure playground as 'confidence equipment' (Mr D's words). Seems to work (two boys tearing around on crutches during our visit).

Keep work pressure to a minimum (no prep until year 5, for example) – sensible given range of activities done by some pupils and timetable recently rejigged so tutor time happens at end of day ('more effective learning time').

Specialist teaching in all subjects from year 5, and in art, music and DT from year 2. (Latin added in year 7). Much setting and streaming (English and maths from year 3, most other subjects by year 6) so can cater for broad ability range.

Emphasis throughout on sensible learning habits. Youngest 'plan, do and review' while new Clayesmore Compass emphasises collaboration (contribution award has replaced man or woman of the match), plus risk taking, challenge and (from year 6) creativity.

Not that pupils need much telling. Macbeth-inspired poems were enjoyably big on yuck factor – 'sprinkle in fly vomit so grim...'; an autumn dragon with '...hurricane breath.' Librarian encourages ambitious reading with initiatives like book spine poetry (pile up the titles and see how they sound): 'The railway children/bowl like the devil/into battle/a wrinkle in time.'

Plenty of high tech resources as well, courtesy of Google Classroom – now in use across the school – 'helps children become responsible for own learning'. While not everyone was convinced ('I don't like reading, it's boring – have to sound out the letters and do it at home,' thought one little lad in reception) we couldn't see much in the way of deprivation, judging by universal enthusiasm for recent task – delights of windmills they'd just created. 'Had to make the sails turn.'

Learning support praised by all and accredited by CReSTeD (specific learning difficulties) and NACE (gifted children) though felt to be poorly understood in wider world. 'There is a misconception that school specialises in SEN. It doesn't specialise, it just does it amazingly well,' said mother.

Currently around 90 pupils with SEN – most SpLD but also ASD and ADHD, support courtesy of learning resource centre in middle of school, staff able to do just about anything, one working with pupil to pick out describing words for teeth – 'mysterious, tiny, heavy...' In class, gap year students are not so hidden weapon – one looks gangling next to the pupil he's supporting (though doesn't look so very much older) – a particular asset with behaviour management.

Upwards pressure on ambition translates into other areas – such as sports – though not excessively so. Mr Dunlop reckons that rival teams who used to be drawn primarily by the location and the quality of match teas now come because 'they'll get a good game as well as all the trimmings.'

Main sports rugby, hockey plus soupcon of football though most successful tend to be cricket (U13 county champions) and cross-country – school organises major inter-school event for 20 schools or so. Most pitches grass plus Astro shared with senior school.

Bar desire for slight pepping up of sports generally (less rounders, more football), few mega grumbles from parents who feel that there's a decent number of matches. 'There is an A, B and C team and they do ensure that they have fixtures,' said parent. 'Quite a variety – and can do horse riding,' agreed another.

Arts generally very highly rated. Music team ('the noise department,' says Mr Dunlop) housed in what was once the trophy room with must-have zebra heads would be all the better for purpose built performance spaces – chapel, currently main venue, just too small.

Otherwise, impressively successful, with over 130 pupils learning at least one instrument, numerous ensembles and assorted competitions across the school.

Clayesmore School

Linked with Clayesmore Preparatory School

Iwerne Minster, Blandford Forum, Dorset DT11 8LL

Ages 13–18 **Pupils** 450 **Sixth form** 164 **Boarders** 206 full **C of E**

Fees: Day £26,220; Boarding £35,730 pa

01747 812122
www.clayesmore.com

Head: Since 2016, Joanne Thomson BA MBA 940s). First headship. Previously joint deputy head for eight years at Christ's Hospital School, preceded by 13 years at Aiglon College. First post was at Repton Prep as English teacher, assistant houseparent and sports coach.

Model of modern marriage offers cheering example of give and take. Husband Frank, another senior teacher, is head of PSHE here, has worked at most of same schools and is happy to let Mrs T take the lead. 'There's never a power struggle,' she stresses. Two children, both at young adult stage.

Parents at Christ's praised her 'industriousness and conviviality'. We were struck by her calm, understated kindness (the only head this reviewer has ever met who physically booked us a cab back to the station – though possibly to ensure we actually left ...).

Never envisaged being a head and, 'it's not about the power but making a difference.' She's succeeding, said a parent, by effective delegation. 'Doesn't have a finger in every pie but lets the school get on with it which is better for the staff.' Senior pupil praised her 'interaction' with pupils. 'Clear to see philosophy,' said year 10 guide. Particular strength is 'thought for the day' speeches. 'I was like "How is she able to be so relatable?"' How, indeed?

Spent first year desk-bound, sorting systems and structures that under pressure from rise in pupil numbers. Time-consuming but necessary which meant that some parents felt they didn't see enough of her. That's now being rectified. Also – somehow – completed an MBA over the school holidays. Sent out questionnaire and is implementing suggestions – including extending autumn half term to two weeks.

This school (like others she's worked in) is notable for exceptional pastoral care – it's a must-have, she says. Isn't planning drastic change but sensible rethinking so school can do its best by all pupils throughout the ability spectrum. Inclusiveness will be helped along with greater focus on tailored learning and monitoring, supported by extensive, joined up digital technology. Small but beautifully designed booklet serves up changes with strong dose of reassurance.

Her younger (state educated) self woul balk at independent school career – hence desire to share resources as widely as possible. Community-related activity includes pupils working at local special school, local elderly regularly invited in for events, while pipe band – goes with school's name, rather than location – 'is out and about' (not as threatening as it sounds).

Best part of the job? No surprises that it's the pupils. 'They keep you grounded, especially ours, they're very open and tell it like it is, they're great.'

Academic matters: Everyone – not just teachers and pupils but their parents and our taxi driver (a past parent, daughter now on the way to being something massive in the City) stress that families don't need to divide and rule, sending most academically able child elsewhere. School will do wonders with them all. In 2018, 33 per cent A*/A at A level; 29 per cent A*-A/9-7 at GCSE.

Particular strength is whole-school commitment to SEN. Around 130 pupils have needs such as SpLD, mild ASD and ADHD/ADD and school ensures that training and regular insets extend to all staff, including rugby coaches. Differentiation is 'staggering,' says head. 'I've never been in a place where teacher are so united and committed to the cause.'

All pupils have CAT test in year 9 designed as 'stress free screening' to establish 'range of possibilities.' Those needing extra support can attend informal drop in maths sessions or may swap languages for extra classes in teaching and learning centre – (TLC, geddit?) which is located slap bang in middle of school – 'no wooden hut in the grounds,' says head – and universally rated as phenomenal. Separate classrooms for those needing EAL support.

Specialist staff, some full, some part time, many with teaching responsibilities, all with post-grad qualifications, are regularly consulted by other teachers wanting to know eg how to support the very able. Accreditation from NACE (gifted children) and CReSTeD (specific learning difficulties) reflects school's strengths in both areas.

'Still marked as being a school where they do a fabulous job with learning support but they're brilliant with everybody else as well,' said parent. Not everyone will get A*s and As but 'what you will see is people who nobody ever expected it doing well.' Even inspectors could only pick on the consistency of marking as needing improvement.

Teachers hold frequent meetings about pupils. 'Try get beyond the label,' agrees deputy head – and are equally good at winkling out hidden staff talent. One, outed as successful novelist, now runs creative writing workshops.

Class sizes drop steadily down the years, average 16 in year 9 (maximum 17), 11 in years 10 and 11 (max 19) and just eight in sixth form (13) with a pupil/teacher ratio of eight to one. Teachers 'young and dynamic,' says school – average age is 41, so perhaps young-ish, but definitely committed (16 at the school for more than a decade).

Does the range, from facilitating A levels plus others – economics to psychology, photography to textiles as well as (very unusually) six BTecs (IT – most popular – plus sport, music technology, hospitality, travel and tourism and performing and production arts). Were sniffed at by Russell Group unis but things are changing, says school – though pupils are encouraged to mix with A levels.

Mega A level subjects are business (most popular) followed by geography, maths and photography – an eclectic mix that reflects the diverse enthusiasms of pupils though a fair few D and E grades in tough subjects at GCSE and A level.

Not much that's outré, unless offer of computer science and ICT IGCSE counts. Large take up for DT, no surprise given rave reviews from teacher and range of goodies produced – papaya chess board a highlight mentioned by parents. Surprisingly low numbers for drama – single figures, just ahead of Latin.

Teaching is fun and animated. We watched year 10 maths where teams worked on probability problems, chains of different coloured arrows climbing up the whiteboards. Maths teacher is 'best I've ever had,' testified pupil. 'Understands how to have the class gripped as well as learning.'

Sensible use of technology, so joined up it must have created a virtuous circle, is now a feature of all subjects. Former head of drama, heavy Twitter user who's 'really into pedagogy,' says head, is clearly loving new role as digital learning supremo – runs regular insets on the wonders of podcasting (many staff do their own).

Other fresh ideas include the new Clayesmore Courses, covering areas like history of art. No assessment pressure. Instead, 'we're starting to show kids that school can be quite fun.'

For those in need of reassurance, you'll hear (lots) about school's most successful pupils. The bottom line is that this is learning without tears – an exceptionally happy and successful school that does well by all its pupils.

Games, options, the arts: 'Don't have to be good at activities to have fun,' said pupil. 'I'm not specially good – I just like to get involved.'

If the grounds and activities weren't enticement enough (CCF so popular that one year 11 pupil joined them for major chunk of summer holidays), school also invites pupils to complete 100 activities in 10 categories including sport and arts – as well as academics. Must demonstrate leadership, participation and passive involvement (watching stuff – our favourite). (One year 10 winner of – external – debating competition even watched inauguration of President Trump).

Award for completion (including chunky cash prize) currently being rethought. 'I want pupils to participate for intrinsic reasons rather than monetary reward,' says head.

Strongest sports tennis, athletics and, especially, cricket (school makes Wisden's top 100), played three times a week, with year 10s upwards adding individual favourites including dressage (Jemima and Buttons the stars here). The head, sporty herself, is keen to boost excitement levels for girls with more staff and own cricket team (if worthy opponents can be found) – girls' rugby and football already offered.

Parents positive but realistic. 'We go to win but it's a numbers game. It's a very different culture.' Consolation provided by exceptional match teas, renowned in the area – scones, cheese straws, sandwiches and 'massive cakes,' said pupil.

School's small size leads to variable results (not necessarily ideal for families fixated on winning at all cost) – but has benefits, too, when younger and older pupils work in same space in art and drama, for example. 'Gives positive role models,' says art teacher.

Bar school-wide desire for bigger and better performance space (delightful but bijou chapel with electric – though not, sadly, solar-powered – organ is currently a major venue for whole school), music and drama both highly praised and on everyone's radar, including parents whose children aren't performers. Dedicated head of music felt to be upping standards across the board – particularly for choral music, though range of opportunities for instrumentalists (to grade 8, a few at diploma level) – concert band, jazz and brass ensembles, for example – also highly rated.

'Might not have the sportiest or the most academic reputation but it does all of them to a very good level and includes everyone in that,' said parent.

Boarding: Five boarding houses – three for boys, two for girls, each housing up to 50 pupils and strictly segregated (sight of boy boarder briefly wandering, shirtless, down corridor, reduces female tour guide to helpless giggles).

Appearance ranges from the grand (Wolverton – girls – approached up impressive staircase in the main house) to the homely (Gate – boys – prettily set around former stable yard). Devine, the most distant, village-based house, has been revamped and pupils given day room at school.

Varying dorm sizes, some sleeping of six or more in junior years, though a couple of spares kept unoccupied for emergencies. Otherwise boarding full with waiting lists in most year groups. Nicest (girls' rooms) are elevated with wardrobes at the end. 'We lean up on the wardrobes and chat,' said girl. Single rooms for some lower and all upper sixth, who also get more advanced cooking privileges and own meeting areas. Only downside can be lack of space for day pupils.

No official weekly boarding but locals are allowed to go home after Saturday school. Some overseas Brits – FO, MoD, expats – though fewer than you might think (currently less than 20) given substantial presence of army bases in the area. Others from all over including Germany, China and Russia, with a few others from USA, Italy, Japan and Sweden.

Strong sense of community. Boarders and day pupils 'all mix and match,' said a parent. 'School is really lovely if you want to have a boarder for the weekend.' Pain of staying in eased by dogs (owned by staff in three out of five boarding houses), hot chocolate and plenty of talking therapy for homesickness, plus luxurious lie in to 10.45am on Sunday morning with potato cubes (baby chips) and bacon and egg sandwiches the star attractions on the brunch menu.

'Suits people who like to be busy,' said pupil. 'You'll be joining in without realising it.' What with regular off-site outings – shopping bus, cinema, spectacular coastline – and onside delights of, among others, squash, archery and kayaking, pupils reckon 'there's just not enough time to fit everything in' (no doubt the reason for untouched copy of The Times in boarding house reception).

Background and atmosphere: Founded in 1896 in Enfield, school led peripatetic existence, settling in Pangbourne, then Winchester, before final landing here in 1933. House, Iwerne Manor, was rebuilt in peak Victorian perpendicular gothic style by local squires (whose goodness to villagers extended to equipping each house with red blinds).

Main house floats like an island in a sea of grass in the centre of 62 acres, commanding splendid views of land and sky, represented in the blue and green crescents on girls' blazer crests. (Traditionalists may prefer double headed dragon – still sported by boys – over corporate minimalism.)

Many attractive original buildings survive, though with substantial additions and rebuilds, ranging from striking new DT extension to three classroom blocks. Large sports hall, swimming pool, multi-surface pitch don't detract from lake, fountain and scenery and with exception of grimly functional 70s prep block, new builds generally fit into place rather than attempting to dominate it, a tribute to good architect ego management.

Doing bit for the environment, too, with biomass boiler plus big solar panels on three of the roofs (now produce almost 10 per cent of energy – as well as pepping up temperature and pressure to delightful levels in boarding house showers).

Pupils – some here with considerable sacrifice from parents – do count their blessings. 'Everyone feels very lucky to be here – it says something that you realise it now,' said thoughtful guide.

Pastoral care, well-being and discipline: Fabulous and A-Z. Starting point is (relatively) small size of school – 'can spot quickly if things aren't quite right and get in early,' says head.

Strong tutor system, supplemented with pupil mentoring and low levels of cynicism – house loyalty, we were told, stays at fever pitch levels even at the top of the school. Lots of house competitions – organised by upper sixth who 'choreograph dances, pick song, arrange music, lower key if pitch too high.'

Occasional departure for drugs but more humane than most: instant expulsion for dealing and hard drugs, potential for discussion at least for cannabis, though 'only if it's a first offence and then followed up with regular testing to ensure no repeat,' says school.

Fully aware of how issues (such as eating disorders) can escalate and potentially shattering consequences if not spotted in time. 'So far, no transgender pupils but would go all out to make sure needs met,' says school. Approach geared to individual needs – haven created for one pupil, for example, who found classroom environment overwhelming and went on to achieve top exam grades.

Currently developing digital journal where pupils record, in images or writing, their emotional journey through school. 'Will help them think about times in their lives where they've made real leaps forward or had setbacks....could be so powerful when they look back,' says Mrs Thomson. Aim is to help them see social media as tool for future reflection – no just for mass transmission of selfies.

Pupils and parents: When it comes to socialising, spirit is willing but, with both parents working in many families, flesh and timetables are weak and coffee morning slots often elusive. When they do meet up, mood is correspondingly jolly. 'Gifted chaps' and 'all-round splendid fellows' pop up at intervals in annals of Clayesmore Society (open to all), and retiring nurse is a 'vision in waterproofs and wellies.' Translates into mixed bag of alumni from artist Edward Ardizzone to Beatles manager Brian Epstein and top surgeon Sir Rodney Sweetnam.

Locals and neighbouring counties (Dorset, Hants and Wiltshire) dominate – inevitable army contingent – though London is also on its patch (have had some families fleeing terrorism as well as its hothouse atmosphere). Low sterling value has upped interest from overseas, though long term Brexit impact yet to be seen.

Though a fair few parents arrive from state sector, there's plenty of dosh about, with school events ranging from clay shoot (a tenner a head) to a reunion with lavish canapés and fizz (free, but you have to get yourself to Guernsey).

Entrance: The normal battle over semantics. School says 'non-selective' when what it means is 'as non-selective as you can be,' says head. Bottom line is that all prospective pupils must be able to access the curriculum and be capable of achieving 'some' GCSEs (numbers will vary fairly widely but will include core subjects).

Around half of senior entry comes from junior school plus local preps (Forres Sandle Manor, Castle Court, Dumpton, Walhampton, Durlston Court, Salisbury Cathedral). Increasingly fed by families from London and the south east. Boy heavy – 100 or so more than girls. Evenly split day and boarding.

Take around 90 in year 9; handful in year 10 and around 20 into the sixth form (with at least five grade 4 passes at GCSE).

Exit: The 20 per cent fall out after GCSEs includes several short stay Germans returning home. Others relocate or move to state sector. Others leave (after extensive discussion) if demands of curriculum would simply be too much. Most to uni or apprenticeships – vast range of courses and destinations: arts and acting foundation to business studies and engineering everywhere from Loughborough to Southampton. A few on gap years. One to Cambridge in 2018 and one medic, with another to RADA and one to Bristol Old Vic (stage management).

Money matters: Generous sibling discounts – ask as not easily discoverable online. About a quarter of senior school pupils receive means-tested bursaries (some substantial) and though generous, head would like to extend 'for talented but needy.'

Scholarship are available (10 per cent off fees) but head isn't a big fan. Feels labelling the talented can impose unnecessary pressure at an early age and ignores late developers, who very often go on to scoop the glittering prizes. Children 'should just be enjoying time at school for the right reasons.'

Remarks: Lovely location; warm, inclusive ethos. Ignore dinner party chit chat about SEN focus and do all your children a favour by seeing it for yourself.

Clifton College

Linked with Clifton College Preparatory School

32 College Road, Clifton, Bristol BS8 3JH

Ages 13–18 **Pupils** 938 **Sixth form** 207 **Boarders** 320 **C of E**

Fees: Day £24,300 – £24,690; Boarding £36,060 – £37,170 pa

0117 315 7000
www.cliftoncollege.com

Head of College: Since 2016, Dr Tim Greene MA DPhil (early 50s), an inorganic chemist by academic discipline and indeed by occupation in his earlier life, as a senior research fellow at Oxford (his alma mater), before moving on to Exeter. During his time there he involved himself in outreach to schools, widening access to higher education in particular, and grabbed an opportunity to fill in for a member of Queen's Taunton's chemistry department on a year's sabbatical – 'and that was that', as he put it. Teaching seemed upbeat and positive, and Dr Greene still loves to do it, putting A level chemists through their paces and wanting to extend his reach to lower years, time permitting. 'It's a huge mistake for heads not to teach,' he avers. He also does duties in boarding houses, as it connects him to students, and 'gives them a hotline to the top,' he added with a wink. Judging by the jolly but purposeful meeting with the senior prefects ('praeps' in the school's vernacular) we sat in on, he enjoys excellent relations with the students, boundaries into excessive familiarity never seemingly crossed either way.

Raised and educated in Northern Ireland – still discernible if you listen carefully. He came to Clifton in 2006, rising to the post of deputy head before being appointed to head it in 2016, after a difficult chapter in the school's history. We are told that a three minute standing ovation greeted news of his appointment when it was announced in the school's (magnificent) chapel. 'Friendly, welcoming, approachable and very visible: he makes an effort to come and watch things, and he knows people's names,' students said of him, approvingly. Parents we spoke to are also fans: 'He knows who I am, and I know I could knock on his door,' said one mother, while another liked the fact that he 'doesn't waste time with fancy sales speeches'. 'A very good thing' and 'doing a good job', we also heard.

Married to Lydia, whom he met at Oxford; they have three sons, the youngest still at the college. Holidays are likely to be spent walking with the family, but term time has become too busy for him to pursue any singing: 'I miss it,' he said regretfully. 'It would be good really to exercise the diaphragm occasionally'.

Academic matters: Right up there with the other Bristol independents (but not top) in terms of results in 2018 36 per cent A*/9-8s at GCSE and 75 per cent A*/B, 45 per cent A*/A at A level. Ancient and modern languages results at GCSE and A level particularly impressive, probably related to their early emphasis (two is normal, one for weaker linguists or non-native speakers); Latin and/or Greek available as a third language.

In the sixth form, 34 subjects, including history of art, and some BTec options are on offer; no IB though. Sixth formers are expected to embark on four subjects, usually dropping one half way through lower sixth. They are also encouraged to lift their eyes from the purely academic and allow them to fall on the interesting possibilities in soi-disant Sector E: BTecs in IT and teamwork and personal development, a performance certificate from LAMDA and a non-examined photography course, inter alia. Favourite subjects? 'Maths, biology – in fact science in general and humanities,' replied our delightful lunching companions when asked.

Parents note the calibre and collective intellect of the teaching staff, one describing the academic offering as 'fantastic' and expressing her appreciation that her son got to try out 'a load of different stuff' intellectually, even though for him, the point of going to school is to play with a ball. Plenty of opportunity for that too. Teaching spaces, light and functional rather than fancy for the most part, eclipsed by two of the most sumptuous school libraries we have ever seen: the Percival, with a splendidly ornate wooden ceiling, and the Stone, a dedicated science library boasting some 5,000 volumes, including a first edition of Isaac Newton's Principia Mathematica. Book learning is brought to life by a range of trips of which classics, most recently to Crete, garners particular praise. Clifton has produced a good crop of academic heavyweights, such as Sir Henry Newbolt, pioneering computer designer John Pinkerton, LP Hartley, three scientific Nobel prize winners, mathematicians, philosophers and engineers, of whom WO Bentley is the most eminent.

Learning support is housed in a small building down a side street, but is not sidelined in importance. The department and in-house educational psychologist look at issues lying behind barriers to learning, such as ADHD or high levels of anxiety. 'You can lay on all the reading programmes you like, but if that child is unhappy, they probably won't be very effective,' staff told us. The holistic approach involves pastoral staff as well as academic, and includes the management of poor behaviour – 'It's less punitive,' the ed psych (on maternity leave at the time of writing but who phoned in to speak to us) affirmed. Students with more complex needs get longer term interventions and the department works closely with parents. We did not pick up any sense of stigma or discrimination towards those who get extra help. EAL shares the building: it's a busy place as 38 per cent of Clifton students use a language other than English at home. These may take EAL as a language option, with IGCSE English as a second language.

Games, options, the arts: No entry would be complete without the celebrated lines of Sir Henry Newbolt: 'There's a breathless hush in the Close tonight, Ten to win and the match to make', and the later exhortation to 'Play up! play up! and play the game!' Cricket in summer and rugby in winter are played by girls and boys on this hallowed turf, overlooked by the school's fine Victorian buildings, but most ball sport takes places on the expanse of pitches at Beggar's Bush, a short minibus ride away across Brunel's iconic suspension bridge. Here, 90 acres encompass several all-weather and grass pitches, indoor tennis courts housed in a bubble, plus facilities to welcome visiting teams and host other events. A swimming pool and indoor sports complex, including courts for the rarefied games of rackets, fives and real tennis, are within the school site.

Sport is massive at Clifton, but we did not detect a jock culture – thankfully. Rugby has long been a success story, but recently girls' hockey has burst through the tape, producing several international players in the last 10 years and the super-talented Lily Owsley, who captained the England team while still at the school and nabbed an Olympic gold at Rio in 2016. The head told us he is keen that the school should 'take the top sportspeople through, as we do the top academics', but that he believes sport is for all and that everyone will find something which will suit them, as well as being given the chance to play for the school. There is certainly plenty on offer for those not mad about ball games, some provided on site (eg aerobics, fencing), others in the surprisingly dramatic environs of Bristol, such as climbing in nearby gorges – Avon or Cheddar – and water sports eg water polo, sailing and kayaking. The trackless expanses of Wales and surprisingly wild Mendip and Quantock hills provide an easily accessible setting for DofE practice, CCF and an eight week survival course, where participants learn to make string and rope from animal sinew, amongst other life-skills. Post-Brexit, this could be handy. Clifton in the Community caters for those of more pacifist ideals, who do good altruistic stuff locally.

Terrific music, too. At the top end, the school produces a commendable crop of Oxbridge choral, instrumental and organ scholars (six in the last eight years) and at least one recent musician of the calibre to play with the Royal Philharmonic while still at school, Julia Hwang, who attributed part of her success to the fact that the school tweaked her timetable to accommodate all that practice. Joseph Cooper, an Old Cliftonian, gave his name to the music school which boasts a gorgeous recital hall and high tech recording and mixing facilities alongside normal practice rooms. Truly some sort of music for everyone (orchestra and chamber groups to blues and swing), and it was touching to hear the enthusiasm, nay love, expressed by our guides for congers, the compulsory hymn practice in chapel each Saturday morning for Sunday services, to which day students are encouraged to go about twice a term. Sir David Willcocks, another notable OC, would be proud.

Clifton was one of the first schools to have a theatre, named for Sir Michael Redgrave (yet another OC) which opens to the public, both audience and players, and hosts 40 productions a year; recent shows include School of Rock, the technical challenges of The Railway Children and Miss Saigon and plenty of Shakespeare. A junior play and hotly contested house drama also: last year's winner staged Posh, where characterisation ranged from 'arrogance to unease' – qualities we absolutely did not find in any of the students we met. Dance also strong, and enjoying a revamped studio.

Art, strangely, gets less exposure in the school's glossy literature, but the provision is wide: we like the fact that the compulsory course in the first year moves away from Europe to study Islamic, Asian and Aboriginal art, inter alia. A sculpture specialist and ceramicist on site. At A level, students choose either drawing/painting or sculpture/ceramics. Plenty of other artistic pursuits available as activities. Museum and gallery trips for all. Bloomsbury art critic and artist Roger Fry, Peter Lanyon of the St Ives school and impossibly romantic painter Robbie Duff-Scott are distinguished OCs.

Boarding: School runs on a boarding model, but manages the integration of and equality of the experience for day students better than many. Boarders are allocated to one of seven single sex houses scattered about the gracious roads surrounding the main school. Staffing is generous and ensures plenty of support with matters academic and pastoral, including a cuddle with the resident dog or cat, where necessary. We found the girls' houses notably cheerier than the boys', some of whose bathrooms could definitely do with a facelift. Communal space divided by age: some of the spaces for younger boys struck us as subterranean and drear. Leather sofas, a huge TV and a dartboard surrounded by holes in the wall from near misses seem to be the only décor deemed necessary for the boys; the girls tend towards cosier sofas, colourful rugs and bean bags. Younger ones housed in small dorms, some with study facilities, integrating a bed and desk. Modern purpose-built furniture in pale wood makes the best of available space. Some houses could use an upgrade, in the view of students. Parents we spoke to had varying views. 'My daughter's housemistress really listens to the kids and gives them mummy-love. She is easy to contact and quick to respond,' one parent told us. Another, though, expressed his son's view that the boarding experience is not so good for a full British boarder whose parents live abroad and who therefore doesn't go home at weekends. The majority do after Saturday commitments; overseas students tend to stick together and relax into their native tongues after a week of speaking English, and apparently there isn't always enough to do at weekends eg when matches are cancelled.

Background and atmosphere: Founded by local businessman Sir John Percival in the 1860s and, at his insistence, placing an equal emphasis on science and humanities. This progressive thinking extended to racial and religious tolerance, influenced by having a close friend who happened to be a practising Jew, and a belief in the education of women, though it took well over 100 years for the school to admit girls, who did not arrive until 1987. There is no longer a Jewish boarding house, but the synagogue is still there and still used: one parent told us that the reason his father had chosen the school for him was so that he could maintain his Jewish heritage; this holds true today.

The impression given by outstanding high Victorian gothic buildings, built of warm red stone and surrounding the manicured green velvet of the close, is of a very traditional public school, but we were amused to find out that the head was put straight by a young hopeful at interview, who informed him that the school was not covered by the original Public

Schools Act. Whatever – one would be hard put to spot the difference: glossary, different ties for everything etc. Eleven day and boarding houses are dotted about the surrounding roads – all quiet and residential – and all within earshot, if not sight, of Bristol Zoo in the smartest part of the city next to the glorious expanse of the downs. Students seem genuinely appreciative of their privileged setting, and abide by the rule of silence when walking through the memorial arch, where the names of the school's war dead are inscribed.

House identity and friendly rivalry flourish: masses of ways in which to compete such as house matches and music, and to bond over trips, dinners and so on, but this does not descend into tribalism, perhaps helped by the fact that most meals are taken in the fabulous lofty two storey dining hall (Big School), adroitly serving the entire school, upper and lower. Extra rations can be bought from Grubber (tuck shop) and each house has a kitchen for each age group for the preparation of that vital school fuel: toast.

Despite the highly traditional setting and undoubted Anglican principles preached every day in chapel, an atmosphere of acceptance prevails towards those of different faiths, races and sexuality: it seems a safe place to be different. 'Pupils are permitted to wear the uniform which best corresponds to their gender identity, with permission from the headmaster' according to the policy, but it is only recently that girls have been allowed to wear trousers in school routinely. The LGBTQ+ group meets on a Tuesday like any other club.

Pastoral care, well-being and discipline: Pastoral care appears to be wraparound. First point of contact for any concerns or questions is the housemaster/mistress (HoMs) both for students and parents, but all teachers are members of the pastoral team in individual houses, and all do duties there. The well-staffed medical department keeps its eyes and ears out for problems which extend beyond the physical. Mental health is prominent on the school's agenda: the chaplain is an accredited mental health first aid trainer, each house has its own mental health first aider and some sixth formers act as voluntary mental health peer mentors. Students told us there was no taboo surrounding it, and that they could 'tell my houseparent anything. There are loads of people to go to when things go wrong and someone would notice, anyway'. The emphasis the school places on the growing problem of our youngsters' mental health may or may not be one response to the horrific discovery in 2014 of a housemaster spying on and videoing students without their knowledge, which knocked the school community sideways and shattered confidence in it in some quarters. Since then, the school has tightened up its practices and a climate of unobtrusive vigilance prevails. It is the only school where this editor was asked to read and sign a leaflet outlining the school's safeguarding guide before proceeding beyond reception.

Rewards for all kinds of endeavour and contributions to the school community are abundant, and the climate is undoubtedly one of positive reinforcement. A 'good egg' prize is awarded in each house for – well, being a good egg. Punishments on a sliding scale are meted out for all the misdemeanours one might expect. Poor work might attract detention to improve or finish it, frequent poor behaviour or the breaking of rules 'gating' – ie being confined to the house or school grounds. Suspension is reserved for the most serious (such as drugs) or persistent breaches of school rules; the purpose is to give the student a chance for 'reflection and [doubtless full and frank] discussions with parents and guardians'. We were most disappointed not to meet the Marshal, the distributor of lighter sanctions and upholder and recorder of weightier ones; students try not to catch his beady eye as he looks for uniform infringements. On balance, the students we spoke to reckoned punishments were fair, though one described some as petty.

Pupils and parents: Hearteningly down to earth and aware of how very fortunate they are – and not, we hope, just because they are instructed to 'check their privilege' in PHSE lessons. They appreciate the importance the school places on the whole person, the care they receive in all aspects of their school lives, and the fact that they can get everything done at school. This is certainly Bristol's smartest school, but those we met did not behave like that. Students arriving from state schools speak well of welcome and integration.

Parents seem extremely happy with the school, and enjoy an active social scene on the touchline or at house events. 'The least judgmental set of parents I have ever met' in the opinion of one mother. Like all but a tiny minority of boarding schools, Clifton families tend not to live more than an hour or so away, apart from the 25 per cent overseas students, most of whom come either from Russia or China, including Hong Kong.

Entrance: At 13+, the 130 students arrive not only from Clifton's own prep school but several others. The process starts early, with visiting suggested at least three years before (regular open days) and a pre-assessment in year 7 by means of interviews and references. Academic testing – either common entrance, scholarships or the school's own tests in English, maths and science – does not take place until year 8. Application dates vary: beware. At sixth form, three GCSEs at grade 7 or above and three at grade 6 are expected, as well as tests and interviews in two subjects to be taken at A level for the 45 or so external candidates.

Exit: Few – 15-20 per cent – after GCSEs. The vast majority of sixth form leavers go on to university – about 85 per cent to their first choice; fewer than a fifth of them take a gap year. A good handful to Oxbridge most years (six in 2018); other popular choices include Cardiff, Edinburgh, Exeter and the London universities. A sprinkling of art foundation and overseas universities, and one to the Central School of Speech and Drama in 2018. The sixth formers we encountered were full of praise for the help and guidance received, from the careers fair and the weekly bulletin to the outside speakers and the nitty gritty of the personal statement. And it doesn't stop there: 'Clifton's not just for when you're there,' the head told us. 'There's support at university and the whole of the OC network'. Judging by the list of reunions both around the country and across the Atlantic, it's thriving and has some pretty distinguished members such as Simon Russell-Beale and John Cleese.

Money matters: Fees much in line with comparable schools both for boarding and day students; it's the most expensive day provision in Bristol, however. 'I want to ensure we offer more bangs for the parental buck,' the head told us in justification. Scholarships for art, music, sport and drama as well as academics at 13+, to a maximum of 25 per cent of fees. Sixth form scholarships available as above, but include an organ scholarship – good fodder for collegiate universities. Bursary provision subject to normal means-testing, including one worth 20 per cent for a Forces child and some for Jewish applicants who 'demonstrate an interest in Judaism and take part in Jewish activities in the school'.

Remarks: Clifton, with its fancy buildings, gorgeous situation, sparkling alumni and own vernacular, is arguably the city's poshest school and the subject of dinner party gossip; the one the Daily Mail might most like to take a pop at. But that would be to ignore or skate over its other, less visible achievements. These include some significant advances in and resources directed towards child protection, mental health and ironing out the differences between the haves and the have-nots, albeit in a privileged environment. 'We've made considerable sacrifices to send our daughter here,' one mother told us, 'but it's worth every working moment and every night of worry'.

Clifton College Preparatory School

Linked with Clifton College

C

The Avenue, Bristol BS8 3HE

Ages 3–13 **Pupils** 515 **Boarders** 45 full, 10–12 flexi (from year 6) **C of E**

Fees: Day £13,230- £17,460; Boarding £16,305- £28,650 pa

0117 315 7503
www.cliftoncollege.com/prep

Headmaster: Since January 2018, Jim Walton, previously head of Elizabeth College Junior School on Guernsey. He was educated at Warwick School before going on to Sheffield to read business studies. Has taught in both prep and senior schools, including Clifton High School and Cheltenham College Prep, where he was a housemaster, and part of the senior leadership team, for 11 years. He is married to his wife Melanie, also a teacher, and they have two young sons.

Jo Newman is head of the nursery and pre-prep.

Entrance: Informal assessment in literacy and maths for Y1, Y2, Y3 (none in EYFS). Entrance tests in English, maths and general ability for Y4-8, Minimum requirement usually appropriate national curriculum Sats level for age group.

Exit: Majority (between 90 and 95 per cent) take scholarship exam and move on to Upper School. Some sit common entrance for other major public schools such as Winchester, Marlborough and Cheltenham.

Remarks: Restructured from three separate schools – nursery, pre-prep and prep school (popularly known as the Pre) – to an all-through school, aligned with Clifton College upper school, allows for a more seamless curriculum and learning experience for children and for families. School admits it has been hard for staff – 'not without its issues' – but everyone realised it was being done for the right reasons. 'Some were initially territorial but are now seeing tangible benefits.' In the transition, seven staff with a total of 198 years' experience left. Those who remain are 'reinvigorated', enjoying the challenge of being responsible for curriculum progression from Y1-Y8.

Children benefit from being taught by specialists for music, science, technology, languages, and from access to improved facilities for art and IT. 'There can't be many pre-prep schools that have these kind of facilities at their disposal. We have found subtle ways to keep the best bits and give each part of the school its distinct identity. We were braced for a reaction but parents have embraced it. They were confident the merger would work. They now feel part of one college, not a piece of a big jigsaw. They buy into the Clifton lifestyle and ethos.' Term dates and exeats aligned too. One parent confirmed: 'There was a lot of difference academically between Butcombe (the pre-prep) and the Pre – that's not the case now.' Parents are impressed that the school has sought their views and acted upon them. 'There has been a real willingness to listen.' 'It's a sign of a school that wants to move forward.'

Very strong EYFS provision with nursery and reception in own building, fabulously equipped for child-led learning. Messy room was a beach when we visited – one child had insisted on bringing her swimsuit. Children love the smart table, with age-appropriate games and apps, which encourage collaboration. Wonderful early years library. Lovely outdoor area with willow tunnel, fake grass, sandpits, spider frame. Three reception classes. Forest school – every week – an integral part of the curriculum. Lots of feedback for parents – interactive learning diaries, including video and audio, with mums and dads encouraged to add photos and information from home.

Y1 and Y2 follow a topic-based curriculum, with plenty of innovative and imaginative activities to suit all types of learners. Children use iPads increasingly. More specialist teaching in various subjects as children move up the school. Scholarship class for high fliers in Y8. Standards and expectations high, but parents and staff adamant that school is not a hothouse. One parent said she specifically chose the school because she felt it would not 'push them to hard too quickly academically' and would develop the whole child. One-to-one support from specialist teachers where needed for children in pre-prep found to have dyslexia, dyscalculia or dyspraxia or other specific learning needs. Prep school has its own specialist learning centre, the Coach House, where short and long term needs are addressed 'as part of the school, not an added extra.' Parents feel that communication has improved. 'Previously reports were a bit vague. A really positive change is that we can access achievement points online through the parent portal. It means I can give my children immediate praise and feedback.'

Music very strong from the start. Every child in Y2 learns violin and in Y3 recorder. Singing, composing, choirs, individual instrumental tuition encouraged. Art is of exceptional quality. Dance and drama are very popular; children relish the opportunity to stage shows in the school hall and in the Redgrave Theatre. DT facilities are better than many a secondary school.

Swimming lessons in the college pool from reception onwards. A host of other sports both on site and at the college's sports ground at Beggar's Bush, including rugby, hockey and football. 'My boys absolutely love the sport, even though they are not A-team kids,' said one mum. Saturday school for years 4-6 now sports activities only, no lessons. Years 7 and 8 have two lessons followed by matches.

'It's not every school that has a zoo in its back garden.' A firm link has now been established with Bristol Zoo education centre. Positive relationships with state primaries too, and not just in the middle-class area near the school. Music projects and teacher exchanges have been set up with inner-city schools and those on deprived estates and there are aspirations for more local schools to be able to make use of the Beggar's Bush facilities.

'There is a perception of Clifton as "the toffs on the hill" and I think we have softened that image,' says school. They are determined to continue to break down barriers and ensure pupils realise how fortunate they are and how important it is to care for others. 'We are very much changed, more engaging and more accessible. We can't afford to follow what we did 50 or 70 years ago. The thing we are most proud of is the way social impact has taken off in the prep school. We have always been charity minded but we are taking a step further than cake sales.' As well as working with organisations such as Fairbridge and Prince's Trust, the school runs a unique project called Colour My Life in which staff, parents and some children redecorate and refurbish a home for an underprivileged family, Changing Rooms-style. 'It is one of the most meaningful things we have done. It changes children's outlooks dramatically.'

Another factor that helps pupils realise 'that Britain is not the centre of the universe' is the international nature of the school. Contrary to popular perception, it's not full of rich Russians. Biggest growth area is western Europeans, some of whom attend for a few years while their parents are working in aerospace or energy industries in the west country. Because they arrive speaking Spanish, French or German, their English is not always good enough to hit higher level Sats, meaning Clifton misses out in league tables, but that's a small price to pay. And, as one pupil said, having native MFL speakers is a great help when it comes to homework and practising for oral exams. 'We have friends from all over the world,' one pupil observed. This is seen as an asset by many Bristol parents, including doctors, lawyers and other professionals. Proportion of girls in the school continues to increase – now around 40 per cent.

There's a day house and a combined day/boarding house each for girls and boys. Children join the houses from Y4; Y3s have a common room where they can start to feel more independent. Families value the pastoral support from matrons, houseparents and their teams. 'I feel like they are surrounded by people who care. There is always someone to talk to.' 'It is a very nurturing environment.' 'So many people get to know your child, each from a different perspective.' Houses, mostly in Victorian buildings, are well maintained and continually upgraded.

Most full boarders are Y7 and Y8, although some are younger. British boarders largely from Forces families. 'School is 24/7 even for day pupils.' Weekly boarding and flexi-boarding options popular with busy local families, as are early start and late pick-up wraparound care. Sleepovers for day pupils popular. 'Still a critical mass of boarders around at weekends.' Recognition that children (and adults) get tired and possibly tearful from busy school day and need TLC. Emphasis on supporting families – 'one stop shop, we take care of everything'.

Incredible range of clubs and activities for children from dawn until beyond dusk, seven days a week. 'We want everyone to find their niche; discover their passion.' Older children also encouraged to take on responsibilities and to celebrate the achievements of their peers. 'Everybody has a chance to shine here,' one said.

Clifton High School

College Road, Bristol BS8 3JD

Ages 3–18 **Pupils** 596 **Sixth form** 67

Fees: £10,365 – £14,580 pa

01179 730201
www.cliftonhigh.bristol.sch.uk

Head of school: Since 2008, Dr Alison Neill (50s) PhD BSc PGCE. At Clifton High School for 30 years, progressing from biology teacher to head of sixth form, deputy head, then head of school. Universally (and deservedly) admired by students, staff and parents for not only securing the school's future after what its own literature understates as 'a period of uncertainty at the start of the 21st century' but transforming it. Excellent ratings across the board in 2016 ISI report validate her action in developing a genuine all-through school and turning it co-ed throughout, with a diamond model where boys and girls are taught separately for some subjects in years 7-9. 'It was the right thing to do,' she says. 'We have found our niche.'

Her trademark red hair and colourful clothes mirror Dr Neill's undiminished passion and enthusiasm for inspiring and supporting young people. She delights in seeing old girls return with their own children and takes a keen interest in all current pupils, reading every report from nursery through to sixth form and spending one-to-one time with university applicants as they prepare personal statements.

'Honest' and 'truthful' crop up often in her description of the school's recent history – and its future. Flash new facilities aren't an option. Careful research underpins any changes; astute recruitment of younger staff has added dynamism and a sharper edge. Very outward-looking.

C

Academic matters: Realising Individual Brilliance is the school's tagline and this emphasis on bringing out the best in every child is valued by parents. Some pupils achieve straight As, but the achievement of everyone who achieves better than expected results is celebrated. Small sixth form cohort causes fluctuating A level headline figures with 2018 – 40 per cent A*/A grades, with 69 per cent A*-B – an improvement on the previous year, as were GCSEs with 38 per cent A*-A/9-7 grades. Culture of high expectations and attention to detail. Some parents think brightest pupils used not to be pushed enough but say this has changed recently.

Diamond model and all-through might be the USPs but principal reasons cited by parents for choosing the school were the 'safe and friendly environment'. This starts in nursery and reception, where there is emphasis on learning through play, led by trained teachers and following the early years foundation stage framework, with perhaps a stronger leaning towards mark-making and introducing letters and words than in some settings. Cursive writing taught from reception. Tapestry online communication system used to share learning journeys with parents. Syllabus based on national curriculum but 'we handpick what suits our children'. On-site weekly forest school for early years children; off-site for years 1 and 2.

A feature of the all-through school is the use of specialist teachers right from nursery for music and reading. By the time they reach year 6, children have lessons from specialists in eight subjects in the senior school building. 'It gives them a new view of the world,' a parent said. Aim is for seamless progression, avoiding dips at transition points.

Science and modern languages are strengths. Separate sciences are taught from year 7. Children study a rotation of French, German and Spanish in year 7, dropping to two languages in year 8. Latin taught in years 7 and 8 and optional thereafter. Tech rotation in years 7 and 8 too, encompassing music tech, design and innovation, food, creative technology and textiles. Boys and girls are taught separately in years 7-9 for English, maths, sciences, computing and sport and in mixed classes for everything else. From year 10, all classes are mixed. Staff say diamond model system is now embedded and enables stretch and challenge. ISI endorsed it, saying 'pupils benefit greatly from the way teaching is adapted to meet the differing needs of boys and girls'. Parents generally happy with it, although one wondered whether putting brightest students of both genders together would be more beneficial. Another said her son liked diamond as it meant he was with more of his friends for more lessons. Students barely seem to notice; they are split into groups for various activities anyway, so this is just one more.

Nineteen subjects on offer at A level as well as EPQ. HLPQ recently introduced for younger students. Clifton High is also only school in Bristol to offer French speaking children specialist teaching of the French curriculum set up by CNED (Centre National d'Enseignement à Distance), so they can return to schooling in France at any stage.

Children with SEN are looked after by the enhanced learning department, which also provides for the most able pupils and those with EAL. Additional learning needs include dyslexia, dyspraxia, dyscalculia and ADHD. One-to-one, small group and in-class support by five specialist teachers as needed. Two-week induction for EAL students, followed by individual support. Bespoke provision for pupils with exceptional ability, for example, a maths prodigy in year 4 is already doing GCSE course.

Games, options, the arts: Remarkable number of clubs in proportion to number of pupils – more than 90 across juniors and seniors. Before and after school and at lunchtimes, with senior sports fixtures on Saturdays. One parent suggested pruning for 'quality rather than quantity' but others, and children, value the range. 'More clubs than anyone can fit in a day. Suits my rather quirky boys,' said a mum. Everything from water polo to dissection; circus skills to robotics; debating to singing. Serious about enriching experience for children. Scores of trips too, at least two a week – geography field trips, foreign language visits, World Challenge, ski-ing, sports tours, theatre outings, a volunteering venture in The Gambia. Curriculum trips included in fees, which is appreciated by families.

Swimming pool on site; lessons from year 1, supported by sixth formers. Synchronised swimming club and partnership with Bristol Henleaze Swimming Club and University of Bristol swim coaches to train elite squad swimmers from years 4 to 13.

PE lessons and some games at on-site school gymnasium and MUGA but most team games at the school's pitches at Coombe Dingle, shared with the university. Traditional options – rugby, football and cricket for boys and hockey and netball for girls. Tennis and badminton popular with those less keen on team games. Parents insist that rugby and football are strong and smaller numbers of boys can be an advantage: 'if you want to be in the team, you're in!' High number of fixtures also welcomed. Students would like a fitness gym on site.

Music, art and drama all have many outlets too – school production during annual Marquee Week is a highlight. Large scale art installation in stairwell planned to mark 140th anniversary. Private speech and drama lessons and instrumental lessons on offer.

Strong commitment to eco issues, with Eco Schools Green Flag. Grounds, used as extension to classrooms, include a pond, an insect hotel known as Bugingham Palace, beehives, bird boxes, compost areas and a wildflower meadow.

Background and atmosphere: 'It's more like a community than a school,' said a student. All-through ethos much more than lip service. Deputy heads have cross-phase responsibilities; one for up to year 2 and KS3 and the other for KS2 and KS4. Lots of opportunities for pupils of different ages to work together. One mum told how her son was so impressed in reception by his head boy buddy, a historian, that eight years on he still aspires to emulate him. Years 3 to 13 have joint assemblies – or 'squashy prayers' as the younger children call them. It's becoming a bit crowded as pupil numbers grow. Maximum class size is 20, with two forms a year up to year 6, moving to three forms from year 7. Girl/boy numbers now nearly equal.

Students hugely appreciative of teachers' efforts on their behalf. 'Great support, both in their subjects and pastorally. They actually care.' Staff know pupils extremely well and delight in celebrating their talents. Parents, pupils and staff say everyone wants to do well and top academic performers are not considered geeks or nerds – nor are boys who like cooking or singing.

'Culture of safety' is central to the strategic plan for Clifton High, which is explicit in its expectations of children, staff, parents and visitors – a sensible child protection and safeguarding leaflet is issued to the latter on arrival. There's even a 'no photography' notice in the staff loo.

Communication is another priority. Website and printed marketing information is very clear and of a high standard. Parents happy with levels of information they receive about children's progress and find staff very approachable, face to face or on the phone for younger pupils and email for older. 'We have an email address for every teacher and if there are any issues they are dealt with quickly.' Dr Neill is adamant, though, that staff will not answer emails after 6pm, to protect teachers' well-being. Pupils say internal communication could be better – often short notice of events and activities.

Gradual programme of refurbishment; a new food room had been added before our visit as well as a welcome room for prospective parents. Science next on list for an update, but leaders won't rush into change for sake of it. Wifi being installed and upgraded – not an easy task in Victorian buildings – so school can consider options for using technology to aid teaching and learning. No rush for iPads. Aim is for future-proofing. Continued use of lovely grounds as an asset – an outdoor classroom is latest addition. Parents are realistic: 'They don't have the facilities that other schools have. It's the quality of the teaching staff that keeps us here, their passion and enthusiasm, and also the pastoral care.'

Pastoral care, well-being and discipline: Pastoral matters are top of the agenda at every staff meeting at Clifton High. Dr Neill is acutely aware of increasing pressures on young people, especially from social media, and potential effects on mental health and emotional well-being. She believes becoming co-ed throughout has helped the atmosphere in the school: 'Even a handful of boys dissipates the angst among women and girls.' Male head of pastoral care insists all staff have a pastoral commitment, as well as pupils and parents, and must develop emotional intelligence. 'We're all in it together.'

Two tutors for every class of 20. Where possible, one man and one woman per class. Timetabled fortnightly one-to-one tutorials, covering personal issues and life outside school as well as academic matters. All backed up with extensive online records. There's a school nurse and two school counsellors. Sensitive handling – their offices are deliberately sited so that children can visit without anyone knowing where they are going and why and there's a text appointment system – though ultimate aim is to remove stigma over asking for help. Strong peer support programme, with appropriate training, valued by pupils and parents. Year 7 bonding trip also highly successful.

Emphasis on developing pupils' sense of responsibility, rather than too many strict rules. For example, no ban on mobile phones, just expectation that they will be used sensibly. Clear 'what to do if' information in pupil planners. Broad PSHCE programme. 'Respect other people's decisions, opinions, individuality and differences,' says pupil charter.

Very big on rewards at all key stages: house points, brilliance points, emerald envelopes, merit certificates etc etc. Positive reinforcement. Clear ladder of consequences for misdemeanours.

Oddly restrictive on sixth formers, who are expected to remain on site all day and work in the library during all free periods. Extensive Futures and Skills programme to prepare them for adult life.

Early birds club, after-school activities club and a homework room accommodate the need for children to be at school out of hours.

Boarding with host families is offered to some sixth form international students. ISI described this provision as 'exceptional'. No boarders at the time of our visit, but facility to use host families when necessary is viewed as invaluable.

Pupils and parents: The school's vision is to 'develop and attract pupils of above average ability'. There's a recognition that children have talents other than passing exams. Dr Neill also keen to honour loyalty of parents. Most pupils come from professional and business families in Bristol. More than 50 children are French – a reflection of international local employers including Airbus and EDF – with quotas per year group to ensure balance.

Entrance: Nursery, non-selective; reception to year 2, informal assessment by class teacher; years 3-6, formal assessment in English, maths and reading, school report. Year 7, entrance exams in English, maths, verbal and non-verbal reasoning for external candidates, meeting for child and parents with head or deputy; similar for years 8 and 9 plus school report. Sixth form, school report, actual or predicted exam results, interview, possible subject-specific exams. International students must sit English and maths exams and achieve IELTS score of more than 5.5.

Exit: Typically between a fifth and a third leaves after year 6, usually for bigger schools rather than for single sex. Similar proportion leaves after year 11 for bigger independents or state sixth forms that offer wider range of subjects. Popular university destinations include Manchester, LSE, Oxford Brookes, Birmingham, Edinburgh and Bath.

Money matters: Scholarships, including for music and sport, and school assisted places bring reductions of up to 50 per cent. Foundation aims eventually to offer 100 per cent scholarships for academically able from disadvantaged backgrounds.

Remarks: 'Everybody knows everybody else.' This was the remarkably consistent message we received during our visits, with parents, children, staff, leaders and governors all agreeing that it was what made Clifton High special. Although the school is growing, it remains small enough for each individual to matter. 'It's very nurturing,' said one parent. 'The atmosphere is quite lovely. It makes me feel I've come home.'

Colyton Grammar School

Whitwell Lane, Colyford, Colyton, Devon EX24 6HN

Ages 11–18 **Pupils** 911 **Sixth form** 225

01297 552327
www.colytongrammar.com/

Head teacher: Since 2016, Tim Harris. Previously deputy head, Reading School. By no means the progeny of privilege but, rather, a one-parent family in Cardiff where he was educated at his local comprehensive. History degree from Newcastle, PGCE from Sussex. Taught in a range of non-selective schools in the Berkshire area. Keeps his hand in in the classroom. Married with a young son. Relaxation notional, mostly; likes in theory to curl up with a work of sanguinary crime fiction but in practice finds himself most evenings held spellbound by the DfE's latest bloodless policy doc. Yes, bit of a workaholic. Owns a labrador racily named Jasper.

Interesting appointment. A change agent for sure. ''Agree,' said a parent; 'he's taking the school into the 21st century'. Comes with a track record of achievement at Reading. Acknowledges that he is 'less posh than previous heads'. You could rephrase that as 'possesses impeccable working class credentials'. Not the urbane, debonair sort of crowd-pleasing charmer that some parents expected and even wanted but, rather, a serious-minded and notably earnest head who is also, in the words of one parent, 'open and approachable'. We endorse that. Has a strong – some might say puritanical – sense of mission informed by a clear set of values. Everything we do,' he told us, 'must be about the students: the school must be designed exclusively around them.' Has definitely made waves.

Clear about what the school is for: 'We specialise in the able'. Keen to dispel the idea, prevalent in some local primaries, that the school is not for the likes of them, so he's taking the good news about Colyton out to them and staging 'familiarisation events' designed to show children and parents that 'there's something exciting going on here' and 'it's all right to be bright'. Wants the school to be more outward-looking, more tuned into social mobility and more focussed on precisely what steps might be verifiably effective in promoting it. Determined to recruit more bright children who don't come from comfy homes. Resists the charge that the model of the grammar school is inherently 'more socially and economically exclusive than some comprehensives' and notes that the number of students at Colyton eligible for Pupil Premium is already double the national average for grammar schools.

Academic matters: Mr Harris has designs on the school's ways of working in the classroom, summed up in the battle cry 'high challenge, high support'. His methodology is evidence-based pragmatism. He wants his students to 'feel comfortable with being challenged appropriately' and learn that 'getting it wrong is a step to getting it right.' Won't this, we asked, just add to already high stress? 'No, they only get stressed by challenge if they're not used to it.' Colyton teachers, he claims, 'get to know their students quickly and excite them with subject knowledge', so lessons are 'exciting and fun as well as challenging'. Mr Harris wants to encourage more of a 'research culture' among the staff so that 'their teaching is based on an understanding of what works'. If the lessons we attended are a guide we can testify to incredibly attentive students engaging in complex tasks that made them think hard and independently. A parent agreed: 'they are certainly not spoon-fed; they are regularly challenged to come up with their own thoughts and ideas'. It's not all work and no play, mind. Out of class, Mr Harris told us, 'They may be able kids but they are still kids and need to have space to be children together.'

Parents we spoke to were unanimous in assuring us that 'the students are certainly not simply data fodder and the school is not just an exam factory'. It's not all unremitting syllabus-bashing. In the words of a parent, 'There is also room for expansion of the subject beyond the requirements of the exam; students also do extension projects, researching and presenting subjects of their choice.' There's a Devon myth that Colyton students stagger home under a backbreaking burden of homework (how otherwise would they get those amazing results?). We found no takers for this theory among either students or parents. One parent told us, 'We have found the homework reasonable, and the large majority of teachers respect the limits on it.' Another parent said gratefully, 'There is not a lot of homework requiring computer or internet use'.

The school now follows a conventional two-year A level programme. In a highly competitive local sixth form market with some very distinctive and attractive players Colyton has expanded its provision. This will mitigate the present funding shortfall. Like all Devon schools, Colyton's funding is grievously below the national average.

Curriculum unyieldingly academic, geared wholly appropriately to top university entrance. At GCSE nine core EBacc subjects plus a choice of two others and Latin coming on stream. Eighteen subjects at A level. STEM subjects and humanities all dependably excellent. No DT: there are 'more effective ways of providing the same experiences'. Very good to see art, drama and music thriving both results-wise and outside the classroom. Splendid library, excellent librarian, lots of flopped boys (and girls of course) reading after lunch. All in all, the achievement of Colyton's students may be said to owe as much to innate braininess as to superb teaching if what we saw was any guide (it was). These students feel incredibly lucky to be here and work their socks off, both in thanksgiving and because they're good at this stuff. Every class we passed or popped into was lit up and purposefully going places.

At GCSE in 2018, 41 per cent of all GCSE grades were grade 9 and 87 per cent 9-7. Progress 8 score was a very commendable 1.01.

At A level in 2018, nearly 66 per cent of grades were A*/A and 85 per cent A*-B. Over 30 per cent of all grades were A*, the highest percentage for any state school in the south west. In art and French everyone got either an A* or and A. Value added score of 0.78 tells us that students are officially achieving well above expectation.

Special educational needs support covers all the usual suspects from ASD to complex medical issues. One proviso: the pace here is brisk and you do need to be able to survive in the mainstream.

Games, options, the arts: A good mix of activities outside the classroom, many on the swotty side, clubs for computer buffs, engineers, historians and mathematicians. There's a creative writing group and, delightfully, a junior reporters' club whose uniform, we solemnly hope, is trench coat and trilby. All ages can join the staff of the school mag, Seven Stripes, winner of the Shine School Media Awards 2017. There's VEX robotics, various Olympiads, maths challenge, debating, mock trials. Real writers (eg Patrick Gale) come in and run workshops. Most of these activities happen in the generous lunch break. Students we spoke to were very happy with what's on offer and told us that when one of them wants to start a club the school gets right behind them. It's that kind of place.

Given the school's enigmatic geographical location, most students have long commutes, so numbers involved in after-school clubs, sport in particular, are thinner, but the school enjoys commendable success regionally and beyond in all mainstream sports. Decent sports hall, popular tennis courts. You can't fault provision or participation, only the lack of any sports info on the website. You'd hardly know they do any.

A crowning glory of the school (again, you wouldn't know it from its website) is its cultural life. In so many schools the creative arts have been a casualty of reduced funding and Goveian curricular malarkey, but absolutely not here. Drama thrives. The art is so good we hunted down the head of dept and demanded to know how she does it. Turns out there's no accounting for alchemy. And then there's music. Instrumental lessons, some 60 per cent sign up. Notably strong choral tradition and an annual choir tour which alternates between European and UK cathedrals. They sing ancient and modern, all of it hard. Students notably shiny-eyed when telling us about this and a parent soared into superlatives, describing the head of music as 'AMAZING' (the caps were clearly audible down the phone). Well-equipped performance hall for music and drama panelled in shouty red, the colour of one of the houses, to the high dudgeon of members of the other four.

There's DofE – the school claims to be the largest provider in the south west. There are foreign exchanges. And Ten Tors of course. Students for whom these and other trips would be unaffordable go at a subsidised rate. The same goes for students from low income homes wanting to learn a musical instrument. One-night residential for year 7-8s in very basic accommodation: 'You have to dig a hole for a toilet'. Glowing accounts by students. Sounds like a great bonding exercise.

Background and atmosphere: Satnav a must for first-time visitors as you thread your way through narrowing country lanes wondering how on earth a school as big and important as this got to be built in the remote and unremarkable village of Colyford. Surely not up here, you splutter, as you turn into a single track road. And then suddenly: ta-da! Why this place? The answer is that what began in 1546 as a tiny local grammar school for a handful of 'goodly and virtuous' local children acquired a reputation that made it attractive to families for miles around. That this remains the case in an area where the market for education is mostly working well speaks for its pulling power.

Began life in the nearby village of Colyton. Moved to Colyford in 1927, the only recorded example of a day school moving from a small place to an even smaller place. Ceremonial facade which looks as if the quantity surveyor glanced at the architect's drawing and said 'Shrink it'. It's a charming period piece with a porticoed entrance and, behind it, a quadrangle (just about). Parents praise its 'university campus feel', which is stretching it a bit, but you can see what they mean. Newer buildings are small blocks, mostly, none more than two storeys, giving the school an agreeably unimposing feel, unterrifying to fresh-faced 11 year-olds. That it's all done well, the facilities up to date, speaks of the successful application of thrift and money well spent. Hats off to those who tend the beds of shrubs and flowers, impressively unflattened, indeed a source of pride to the students and emblematic of the civilised values that prevail here.

A notably calm school when lessons are on. When the students are out and about it's the interactions between them that speak volumes about the social climate here. They're a jolly, nice, unaffected lot. They rub along, they enjoy each other, the sporty, the geeky, the quirky, the normal as rice pudding. We agree with the parent who told us that the school 'seems to have evolved a culture of mutual respect and tolerance which embraces all types'. We encountered a truly rich and richly enjoyable range. Because students are encouraged to think for themselves there's no premium on dutiful conformity. A parent told us, 'We think our children have a lot more freedom to be themselves than they might have had elsewhere'. Another said, 'I like the fact that the school encourages the children to be self-starters and take responsibility for themselves'. The head told us he wants students to 'learn to think and come up with their own viewpoints'. Because questioning things is good, rebelliousness isn't really an issue. There's a widespread if unsubstantiated view that the school is terribly middle class. A parent conceded, 'well, quite middle class but not too middle class,' and stressed: 'All the children are treated equally, all are given the same opportunities.' They seem not to be mollycoddled. A parent said, 'Things are not served up for them on a plate, they are not over-privileged, they have to make the effort to take advantage of what is on offer.'

Pastoral care, well-being and discipline: We asked the students if they felt cared for and supported and they said they did, all of them. We could elicit no reservations. 'Tutors,' they told us firmly but kindly, 'are very supportive.' Nevertheless, the head intends to reinforce the pastoral system in response to increased pressures on young people. A meeting with the head of PSHE brought home to us just how hard they are thinking and how urgently they want to get it right. Impressive. Much talk about mindfulness. The PSHE syllabus includes an element of cognitive behavioural therapy. Issues around gender identity addressed in partnership with the Proud Trust. A non-binary student has produced materials for a lesson on gender. One delightful initiative: last class of the day ends five minutes early and the time used to decompress by listening to music or doing a spot of colouring – a much valued lacuna, especially after high-energy classes. Pastoral care is house based. There are five, and they are hotbeds, too, of inter-house rivalry in competitions ranging from strenuous to sedentary, so everyone can pitch in.

Mutual respect and a strong sense of shared purpose pervasive account for rapid reporting of, eg, teasing. The social climate is one of good order, discipline and looking out for each other. There's respect for classroom furnishings and facilities. There are warm relationships between students, teachers and support staff. A parent told us that Colyton is 'a welcoming and happy school, its students confident and capable'. So it is and so they are.

Pupils and parents: Parents a mix of indigenes and incomers as this area becomes increasingly attractive to DFLs (down from Londoners). A boon to parents looking to save themselves the expense of going private, so a number are happy to shell out in the early years to give their child the best possible chance in the 'tutor-proof' entrance test. A grammar school-educated parent who described himself as a 'classic example of social mobility' told us, 'I have been less than enamoured with having to pay for [my child's] education up to year 6 as a result of the poor quality of local state primary education; but it was the only way to improve their chance of getting into Colyton'. Middle-class colonisation of grammar schools is a hot potato just now, so has that happened here? Judge for yourself. Roughly 14 per cent of students come from independent schools – bang on the national average for grammars. Recruiting a higher number of students from less well-off homes is currently top of the agenda, seen as both a social duty and an urgent political and ideological imperative.

No circumscribed catchment area, so the school recruits from all points within a manageable commuting distance, roughly Chard to the north, Exeter to the west and Bridport to the east. Colyton is very much the go-to school in this area ahead of some excellent competitors. Parents who reckon an unalloyed collection of very bright children to be somewhat rarefied may want to consider, also, The King's School, Ottery, a high-achieving comprehensive which opposes selection on principle.

Entrance: Standard grammar school 11+ test papers set by CEM (Centre for Evaluation & Monitoring). Test in Sept of year 6. We asked students how it felt. 'Not too traumatic,' they told us; 'there were sixth formers to support us and they got us to relax.' Stressful all the same, don't doubt it. Slim familiarisation booklet downloadable from the school's website, all you need, they say, to get you ready for the big day. Priority for students qualifying for Pupil Premium: eligibility score significantly below the usual entry point for rank order entry.

Entry also at years 8 and 9. Places like hen's teeth of course. Twelve plus and 13+ tests in maths, Eng and science.

Sixth form entry requirements as for serving students: at least 50 points from eight GCSEs, incl 5s in English and maths. If you want to do maths and sciences at A level you'll need 7s in your chosen subjects. If further maths, an 8. For all other subjects 6s.

School's website when we visited deficient to the extent that this Guide, a representative newbie to the school, had little clue what to expect before it got there. It's a work in progress, they tell us. Hurry up, we say.

Exit: A smattering leaves after GCSE, choice of A level subjects normally the reason. Of the vast majority who stay, pretty much all to good universities, some to higher apprenticeships (eg accountancy). Always plenty of medics and engineers. Students we spoke to praise the advice they get on courses, gap years and the dreaded UCAS form. Ten to Oxbridge in 2018 and 10 medics/vets. Colyton was the top co-ed state school for Oxbridge entries in 2017, and second for Russell Group entries according to the Sunday Times Parent Power destinations data.

Money matters: Statutory support for students qualifying for Pupil Premium, who are also the beneficiaries of two sixth form bursaries. Bequest by former teacher enables trustees to make discretionary payments for, eg, books, trips, art materials.

Parents' Association raises £30,000 plus for special projects and bits and bobs, most recently new science labs and, inter alia, the school Christmas tree. It's a respectable sum but straitened times urge each according to their ability to dig a little deeper.

Remarks: Longstanding track record of success in all areas – lots to like. The school that most parents locally would cheerily saw off an arm and a leg to get their child in to but, tellingly, not all – a grammar school by its nature is somewhat set apart. Engagingly humane and well-intentioned. Eccentric location paradoxically enables it to serve a remarkably wide area.

C

Concord College

Acton Burnell Hall, Shrewsbury, Shropshire SY5 7PF

Ages 13–18 **Pupils** 593 **Sixth form** 390 **Boarders** 489 full

Fees: Day £14,280; Boarding £39,900 pa

01694 731631
www.concordcollegeuk.com

Principal: Since 2005, Neil Hawkins MA (50s), a Cambridge historian whose previous posts include director of studies at The Leys and head of history at Sevenoaks. Has built on splendid work of his visionary predecessors – and how! As we visited, a new science block with 22 laboratories including a research laboratory was going up, and boarding houses were being extended and kitted out with ensuite rooms. But it is the underlying ethos of the school, its commitment to internationalism, to excellence, to a global, harmonious meritocracy that has kept Neil and his wife here, though he admits the gorgeous views of the Shropshire countryside from his spacious study have helped.

Parents, staff and students clearly respect him hugely. They say he listens and empowers, that he is liberal and takes everyone with him in the drive for excellence. He comes across as approachable and incredibly enthusiastic, with a vision not just for the school but for the world. He models the warm, unpretentious, positive and driven behaviours that he wants in the students. 'I have in my mind whenever I speak to groups of students, what values will these young people be passing on to their grandchildren. I want those values to be the core Concord ones of decency, trust, responsibility and service'.

Warm and welcoming, Mr Hawkins clearly delights in being at Concord, 'As a historian, it is wonderful. Look out there. Over to the right the castle and to the left the Parliamentary Barn'. He talks with infectious enthusiasm about the students, the staff and the whole set up, cheerfully and convincingly dealing with common misconceptions of the college. His wife Vanessa runs marketing, and does some teaching and pastoral leadership. They met at Cambridge where their son now studies after five years at Concord.

'He really cares about us,' said a student. 'He knows our names, comes into lunch every day and asks us how we're getting on and listens to our answers. That is why so many student-led initiatives are implemented.' 'He certainly has his finger on the pulse,' said one parent. The right man for the job, and during his reign the college has gone from strength to strength. No school will stand still under Neil's leadership.

Moving on in September 2020 to become global principal of Concord International and oversee the development of schools overseas.

C

Academic matters: Whichever league table you choose to consult, you'll find Concord among the top selective schools in the country. Exam results are consistently impressive. In 2018, 81 per cent A*/A at A level and 87 per cent A*-A/9-7 at I/GCSE. Huge numbers take maths, further maths, economics and the sciences. Other disciplines are smaller but achieve equally stellar results. Class sizes are small and the whole emphasis is on individual attention. We visited as A levels were kicking off; teachers had provided a list of all their non-contact time each week so students knew when each teacher was available for individual support.

Results reflect not only the high calibre of teaching staff but also the fact that students come from backgrounds that are very goal orientated and where education is highly valued. Expectations are stratospheric. After regular Saturday tests teachers are bombarded by students wanting to know how to move their 98 per cent to 100 per cent. Many are aware that this is a very different style of education compared to that offered in the top schools in their own country and they relish the relative liberalism. The pace is fast and teachers find they get through twice the material in a Concord A level lesson that they would expect to in other schools. While English language support is available, a student with weak English would undoubtedly struggle because of the pace of lessons.

Students and teachers were at pains to explain that although the atmosphere is competitive – there are notice boards with the top students from last year's external results featured – it's also highly supportive. The students want everyone to achieve and helping each other is seen as part of the principles of a Concord education. This may be true, but parents did raise questions about how it must feel to be a student who doesn't get all A*s and a place at a top university.

Student after student to whom we spoke was high octane; ideas came pouring out of them. They want a school with a brilliant reputation and results so that they can go on and be significant players on the global scene. They know that it is not just about their sharp intellect, but also about wider awareness and they are just as keen to grab that too with both hands.

A level choices confined to what might be considered the safe traditional subjects and one student commented that there was a limit to the possible combinations. Music is offered as a Btec rather than GCSE and as an EPQ (extended project qualification) in the sixth form, rather than as an A level subject. Rather like sport, music is seen as high quality recreation rather than purely academic study and both the Btec and EPQ focus on a practical approach.

Games, options, the arts: 'Sport', one teacher told us, 'is not God here. It is a recreation for everyone and something you are expected to manage as part of your daily life.' That said, PE is timetabled for everyone including final year students during the week. In addition to the usual suspects there are probably more minority sports on offer here than at other schools – badminton, table tennis, basket ball, volley ball. Facilities are marvellous and going to be further extended with the recent purchase of a large field adjacent to the main school site. Links with local and regional clubs support the elite sports people and the college boasts the occasional national champion. On the other hand, one father told us his son disliked sport and coming to Concord had been a huge relief to him.

There are wonderful performance opportunities for the musically gifted and a lot relish these, unsurprisingly given the number taking individual music lessons. But again the emphasis, particularly in the house competitions and international society cultural events, is on everyone having a go. The day we visited, everyone was talking about a concert the night before that featured student ensembles playing students' own compositions. Like a number of other performances, it was also a fundraising event for a local social enterprise charity. It had been professionally recorded by a music producer – the school has its own recording studio – and CDs were being sold to raise funds.

Performing arts opportunities consciously draw on Concord's international demographic, offering ample opportunities for creative expression within a culture that is familiar but also exposing students to ones that are less so. House arts competition is hugely popular and includes songs, poetry, dance and ensembles.

Myriad of clubs and societies including the important international ones. 'It is good preparation for university where international societies are a valuable anchor for some of our students', a member of the SMT told us. Many are student led and intellectually based – behavioural economics, CED (Create, Engage, Discover – the Concord answer to Ted talks)

There is a real awareness of social issues in a college where firsthand experience of Third World problems is common. A committee coordinates charity outreach and there is a lot going on which requires a level of business acumen.

Boarding: Boarding has undergone reorganisation to reflect the needs of a larger college. All boarding houses are single sex. Some students are housed outside the main school campus around the village, but all lower school boys and girls are now accommodated on site (not all parents completely comfortable with this arrangement, so getting the younger ones on site has been a popular move).

High quality accommodation with an increasing number of single en-suite rooms; security is unobtrusive but rigorous. Food was praised – lots of variety and not surprisingly, an international or fusion flavour.

After academic lessons finish, boarders' time is carefully structured for younger pupils, becoming less so as they move up through the school. Weekends are pretty packed with the school facilities being well used and plenty of day trips organised. Students spoke warmly of the relationship between staff and students.

One group of boarders commented that it was a very trusting community and speculated on how prepared they would be for the more edgy outside world.

Background and atmosphere: Concord stands in 80 acres of Shropshire countryside, its sympathetically designed modern buildings blending with the 18th century and medieval. The school was founded after the Second World War as an attempt to foster healing between nationalities through language teaching and personal warmth. The word 'Concord' means harmony, a value which remains at the heart of what the college is today. It may be an intellectual power house, but it's a calm and gentle one where community and service are held in as much esteem as individual success.

Not being bogged down in sacred past traditions, the school responds quickly to new ideas and will run with whatever students' passion of the day might be. Recent initiatives include bee keeping and an outdoor movie event as well as a buggy competition.

Parents felt there was a difference between the atmosphere in the lower and upper parts of the school, observing that while lower school had a genuine family feel, the big annual influx of new sixth form students caused a change in atmosphere. One or two felt that the new students saw Concord purely as a means to an end – top universities – and the environment was more hard edged as a result. 'But that's what their lives are going to be like', commented one parent philosophically.

Pastoral care, well-being and discipline: These students want to please. They hold teachers in high regard and behavioural problems, even the low level class disruption that you often find in Year 9 and 10, simply do not occur at Concord. 'The students self regulate,' staff told us. Occasionally, if a new student is not focussing in class, it is his class mates who get him in line. Students wear their own clothes, proving that uniform has nothing to do with inner discipline and motivation. But everyone knows there are boundaries and if drugs were brought into the College, the perpetrator would be heading out.

Impressive, all embracing pastoral structure includes outside counsellors, a psychotherapist, student counsellors and lots of staff training, as well as tutors, house staff and those in the leadership team with pastoral responsibility.

Pupils and parents: Parents are largely from the international business community. They are not families who want or need the social cachet of a traditional English public school. Local Shropshire parents of day students are particularly keen on the cultural, racial and religious mix. Lack of uniform lends an informal air, but underlying ethos of rigorous endeavour is palpable.

Students clearly love the place and can't speak highly enough of what they have gained from it. About 80 of the 550 pupils are from the UK, the rest come from many countries, predominantly Asian. The ones to whom we spoke were articulate, confident but unassuming. Most were very natural and charming, but you could also spy the next mandarins, carefully considering our questions and weighing up their responses!

Entrance: Highly selective and getting more so, particularly at sixth form level. For entry to year 12 spoken and written English has to be competent. Those coming in at 13+ have more time to get it up to standard.

Exit: The influence of family background can be seen in pupils' higher education choices. Parents have done well themselves in business and they value degrees in economics, finance, medicine, law, maths and the sciences. Having said that, quite a few go on to study architecture and the art department has considerable success with the London art schools. Twenty Oxbridge places in 2018 with a further 35 heading for Imperial and LSE. Impressive numbers to medical/dental/vet courses (25 in 2018).

Money matters: Fees are high but you get the impression no expense is spared when it comes to the goal of academic excellence. Facilities are superb and always improving. School is working on developing its own bursaries and scholarships and some students attend on scholarships from their home governments. Fees include being able to stay at half terms and, for sixth formers, during the Easter holidays. Some bursarial support for day pupils.

Remarks: Concord isn't for everyone. It won't suit a child who doesn't want to work or who is made uneasy by a fierce academic pace. It may also not be right for a child who is solely interested in the arts – not because they wouldn't find high quality and wide ranging arts teaching, but because they might not find enough like minded students.

Concord is, however, as near perfect a place as you could want for the student who is academic. This is where the next generation of global high fliers is being nurtured. If you want your offspring to have a chance in this stratosphere, want them to engage with issues beyond the shores of the UK or just want them to make life-long international friendships, then do look at Concord. It is in a league of its own and one that is increasingly in high world demand.

Cotham School

C

Cotham Lawn Road, Cotham, Bristol BS6 6DT

Ages 11–18 **Pupils** 1,478 **Sixth form** 405

01179 198000
www.cotham.bristol.sch.uk

Head: Since 2015 Ms Jo Butler (late 40s) MA PGCE NPQH. We learnt that this head's early educational experiences have informed her career in an emphatic and unconventional way (when we finally got to hear about them – after six months of trying. We have to congratulate her PA on being the best gatekeeper of any head we'd ever eventually managed to meet). Starting from unpromising beginnings at a girls' secondary modern in Essex, she was rescued by a couple of teachers at the tertiary college she went to. 'For the first time I found myself in a truly comprehensive environment full of grammar school rejects and middle class people,' she revealed, 'and it was a very powerful influence on me'. A levels, a degree in fine art from Hull, PGCE at Goldsmiths, a masters from the Institute of Education and stints in three London schools, the last as head of secondary at Preston Manor School in Wembley, brought her finally to Cotham. She was lured by its great diversity: ethnic, economic and social, and her mission is to make the school truly representative of the city of Bristol and to narrow, if not close, the gap in prior attainment of the children who arrive there. 'I want this school to improve the life chances of deprived children, but not at the expense of high ability ones who should be flying and getting top grades, irrespective of circumstance,' she explains.

Her draconian enforcement of school uniform and what she wryly referred to as 'lanyard-gate' (cue massive resentment from many parents and students alike initially, but now accepted) are at odds with the slight, quietly spoken woman she turns out to be. Married to a teacher of computing, she and her family live outside Bristol with their Bedlington terrier. Free time might take in running, cycling and, of course, the odd art gallery. Parents appreciate her passion for getting the best for the least advantaged, eg children in receipt of free school meals and/or pupil premium, and her strenuous efforts to integrate the BME families. 'She has tried her level best to involve the Somali community,' one father told us. The school has had a cultural diversity group for many years, which comes up with practical solutions such as EAL training for parents, rather than confining itself to lofty ideals. Her insistence on meaningful consultation with parents also goes down well: shortly before we visited, discussions about being absorbed into a multi academy trust had been seen off by adverse parental opinion. Most parents we spoke to felt Ms Butler could be more visible in school ('But I'm here every day, walk the school and do lunch and break duties along with the other staff!' she protests) and a stronger public speaker. 'A bit stern,' say students – not a bad thing in our book.

Academic matters: School prides itself on doing the best it can for every one of its students, irrespective of ability or starting point. All are screened on entry using CAT, and parents are promised 'robust measures' for tracking progress. In their first year, students appear to do a carousel of humanities subjects and 'skills' (making coleslaw inter alia). Somewhat contentiously, new students are also randomly assigned to study French or German – and never the twain shall meet. Some parental concern came our way about the school's intransigence over changing languages, and many students regret that they do not learn or mix with their peers studying the other tongue, except at break for the first two years. A modern language is a core subject running up to GCSE, whether taken as far as the exam or not, and there's a long list of other options including child development, psychology and a couple of BTecs, so something for everybody. The food tech looked and smelt jolly good: the GCSE set in monogrammed aprons were making ravioli from scratch with two different fillings the day we were there. Parents also praise the process of choosing options.

Results are sound, given the wide ability range: in 2018, 74 per cent of students got 4-9 in both English and maths at GCSE; 26 per cent A*-A/9-7. Nearly all students do well enough to progress to the North Bristol Post 16 Centre, the joint sixth form Cotham shares with Redland Green School, with centres on both sites. This last offers Pre-U in English literature and global perspectives, as well as five BTecs, alongside A levels. North Bristol Post 16 Centre has 37 A level options, one of the widest ranges we know of, and it is heartening to see that courses will be run even for just a handful of students. Results at A level tend to be particularly strong in further maths, economics and performing arts, with biology, chemistry, maths and psychology being the most popular subjects. In 2018, 54 per cent A*-B grades. BTec results also commendable, with three quarters of students receiving distinctions.

Teaching and classrooms seem traditional (desks in rows, students facing the front for the most part) but lively: we dropped into a French class engagingly taught by a native speaker: 'Top guy,' remarked our guide, unprompted. We liked the wet/dry labs too, keeping scientific theory and practicals apart. Parents rate the teachers: 'Inspirational,' said one mother, adding that her children could have 'good conversations with them' and thrived on the research they were asked to carry out. We also heard 'enthusiastic' and 'caring'. The fact that teaching staff and heads of year are generally quick to respond to parental concerns also appreciated, as are the short reports issued six times a year and an annual consultation with each child's tutor.

Special educational needs are described in detail in the school's documentation, which lists both EAL and ethnic minority achievement co-ordinators on the staff. Support for identified gaps in learning is provided either in class, in small withdrawal groups or one-to-one. Children who might struggle in unstructured times, such as lunch breaks, are offered lunch time clubs where 'social interaction with other children is encouraged'.

Games, options, the arts: Not premier league in terms of sports, partly because of a chronic lack of space at school, apart from an airy sports hall. Within its boundaries there are three hard courts with lines for tennis and netball, an Astro and enough grass perhaps to kick a ball about, but not much for a school with nearly 1,500 students. That said, in common with many Bristol schools, Cotham students travel by minibus to football/rugby/hockey pitches elsewhere in the city, but school has reclaimed its former playing fields at Stoke Lodge and plans to build a new pavilion, following a protracted legal process with the city council.

Some fixtures against other schools, but the focus is as much on inter-house matches. Individual successes outside school with one athlete tipped for the top, football and rugby players for the city's academies and county cricket players – Gloucestershire, interestingly!

Where Cotham excels is performing arts, dance in particular. Numbers hold up at GCSE and A level, but such is its popularity that a group for younger students taught by GCSE students has just been set up. School wins at regional level of the Great Big Dance-off. We were impressed by being completely ignored by the dance students who were engrossed in their self-directed session in the studio when we dropped in. Recent whole school drama productions include Macbeth and Guys and Dolls, participation in the Schools Shakespeare Festival and hosting Cue Bristol, a drama company open to all secondary age children in the city. Music reflects the diversity of the student body and seems hearteningly inclusive. The steel pan band is famous within school and the world music room is a sight to behold with its collection of instruments including a gamelan, sitar and gourds. Cotham Rookies is the beginners' orchestra and Cotham Chorus is for all singers. Musical prowess evidently goes back some time: three members of the original National Youth Orchestra in 1948 were Cotham boys. Several options at GCSE for those of an artistic or creative bent, but we would love to have seen more art and DT on display; the art rooms seemed suspiciously tidy. Innovative things going on with textiles though – Bristol Cathedral exhibited 'parcels of comfort', replicas of letters and parcels sent to the soldiers at the front, rendered in fabric and mixed media by Cotham students as part of its WW1 commemorations.

Trips and activities a-plenty at Cotham, to include DofE bronze and gold and a long list of visits to theatres, galleries and sites to enhance the curriculum for historians and geographers. Forays abroad include the ubiquitous battlefields tour and language exchanges.

Background and atmosphere: A long, varied and interesting history precedes Cotham's present manifestation. Able to trace its roots back to diocesan origins in 1812, it soon acquired a scientific bias, becoming variously a trade and mines school and a technical college before moving into its present 1930s buildings with their endless blue-tiled corridors and being renamed Cotham School. A brief period as a grammar school followed the Education Act 1944 when fees were abolished. All this was just for boys of course: the school would not become fully co-educational until 1977. Since then, it has opened its doors to admit a far wider cross-section of society than just girls, and added considerably to the buildings. Squeaking in under the wire of Building Schools for the Future finance meant an innovative suite of labs with a roofed walkway could be built at the back, though bits of it had blown down the week we visited. Lunch can be bought and/or consumed in the dining hall or in a covered area outside in clement weather. Food is good, according to students, but queues can be long at lunchtime 'so I buy my baguette at break, then eat it later – in class if it's boring!' our guide confessed.

Changes to the catchment area and the opening and popularity of nearby Redland Green School in 2006 have meant that Cotham admits children from parts of Bristol considerably less affluent and white than the one it inhabits. This variety in economic advantage, ethnic origin, cultural experience and religious affiliation makes it a hugely diverse community and one to which all constituents seem to sign up with enthusiasm. Diversity was the first thing everyone we spoke to brought up as a reason for choosing the school – yet we picked up the feeling that integration between students from different communities was not quite as seamless as it could be. Students tend to form their own groups in areas of the playground, 'though the children are completely colour-blind,' one mother told us. One father, though he was glad of the CCTV used to provide evidence of playground incidents, felt that the finger of blame was not always pointed in the right direction. That said, we heard no stories of bullying of any kind, and we were impressed by the school's lack of squeamishness at addressing culturally sensitive issues such as FGM, about which there were posters all over the place.

The atmosphere is one of achievement and recognition for all – not just in the heartfelt wishes of the head, who talked of aspirational choices and her view that all children need a decent set of grades and social confidence, but appreciated by parents and students too. In the opinion of one mother, 'The school raises the expectations of all communities'; another said of the head that 'her thing is to get everyone to achieve – equality and attainment for all'. One youngster liked his one-to-one sessions tailored to his higher ability, the fact that extension classes are offered at the University of the West of England, and wished that more subjects, eg languages and English, were set for ability. Weekly vocab tests go down well, but a detention for getting less than half marks is academic rigour taken a bit far, in the view of one mother. Achievement of all kinds inside and outside school is nonetheless celebrated.

Cotham has been a co-operative academy since 2012, espousing global co-operative values and introducing a thread of democracy in the form of elected representatives to the co-operative forum, who advise the senior leadership team and governors. Pupils, staff, parents/carers, the local community and former students are all involved.

Pastoral care, well-being and discipline: The welfare of individual students is overseen by their tutor, who is responsible for both academic and pastoral matters; parents generally think this works well. The school expects high standards of behaviour, and mostly gets them: we saw posters about Basic 8, a statement of positive actions to promote good manners and good habits, all over the place. The culture is one of praise over blame, where postcards bearing commendation are sent home and Amazon vouchers awarded for attendance, attitude and achievement. That said, the school is draconian on the subject of uniform and mobile phones: zero tolerance on deviation from uniform and any use of a mobile during the school day; neither does it shrink from excluding persistent offenders such as smokers, of whatever persuasion. Students are allocated to one of four houses, named for the Greek alphabet and each with its own colour which will adorn the collar of all regulation white polo shirts – an embellishment which, along with the lanyards, has not gone down well.

Pupils and parents: Extremely diverse in every way, with students from quite deprived areas of Bristol mixing with those hailing from the most privileged – and all the differences which that encompasses. Parents range from the pushy and articulate to the ones who struggle with English; we were told with pride that Cotham lists 37 different native tongues among its population. More language classes for the latter would be widely welcomed, or more services from an interpreter, but these initiatives appear to have fallen prey to funding cuts. 'It's two schools, really,' opined one parent, which we took to mean a model of peaceful co-existence. 'I would not send my children anywhere else,' she added. 'Confident personable kids, but not arrogant,' we were told, borne out by the ones we met.

Entrance: Via the Bristol local authority website against a hard deadline of 31 October for admission into year 7. School currently consulting stakeholders about increasing entry from eight forms to nine, 'making it even bigger and more overwhelming,' said a mother. Transition from primary schools comes in for praise. Admission to the North Bristol Post 16 Centre – 60 places on offer for Cotham students – requires 5-7 GCSEs (depending on the number of A levels/BTecs chosen) at grade 4 or above including English and maths for the more academic pathway. Lower entry requirements for BTec level 2 courses.

Exit: 'The overall aim of the school is to have no NEETS' says the careers policy, and the school hasn't for years. Younger students receive careers education from their tutors; further up the school, a range of speakers, activities and pathways are laid out to reflect the diversity of the student body, including employability. A handful leave for local alternatives eg Cathedral or independents such as Bristol Grammar, a few more for college after GCSE. Four medics, Five to Oxbridge in 2018, and 55 per cent of university places Russell Group. Distinguished alumni reflect the school's pre-eminence in science: Paul Dirac, a Nobel prize winner who established the principles of quantum mechanics, the medical officer on the first Antarctic expedition and Peter Higgs, of Higgs boson/God particle fame and another Nobel prize winner. Names from the media and performing arts also feature, such as local TV news anchor David Garmston and Edgar Harrison, who played Dan Archer from the eponymous radio soap.

Remarks: A Bristol institution, which continues to evolve to meet the changing needs of this vibrant city, and which still, in the dry prose of a 1959 report, 'can be justly proud of its reputation and achievements over a number of years'. A diverse, busy, happy place.

The Cotswold Academy

The Avenue, Bourton-on-the-Water, Cheltenham, Gloucestershire GL54 2BD

Ages 11–18 **Pupils** 1,072 **Sixth form** 250

01451 820554
www.cotswold.gloucs.sch.uk

Principal: Since 2011, Will Morgan BSc (Econ) NPQH and Ofsted inspector. Born in Wales, the lilt lingers. Born to teach, too, something that strikes you at once, in his case vocation being not so much innate as congenital, for his father was a teacher also. Has been at The Cotswold since 1997. Promoted from the ranks to head of sixth form in 2002, from thence to the top, quite an achievement since fortune rarely favours the internal candidate and everyone was after this job. Fizzing with physical energy, the possessor of a mind 100 per cent present in the moment, he gives you his complete attention. He's the sort – you can see this at first sight – who gets things done and makes things happen, but he's not one of these kickass super-heads drafted in to turn a school around – because The Cotswold has been riding high for years; the way they do things now is deep in the school's DNA. His job, perhaps rather more invidious, is to keep it where it is. At the top. That's not a recipe for resting on laurels, of course; schools are like sharks: stop swimming and you die.

He evidently loves this place and, though charismatic (and engaging and funny), is not in any way a 'l'ecole c'est moi' sort of head. On the contrary, he is quick to spread the credit: 'I'm only the captain of the side, I am very well supported.' He is, too, by staff and parents, and also by his governors. He has a strong sense of humour and he does a disarming line in self-deprecation: 'My successor as head of sixth form is doing a much better job than I ever did.' So he is comfortable in his position and unquestionably in charge. He's not the ruthless sort but he's resolute – 'unrelenting,' says Ofsted – because he is filled with a sense of mission. School represents the best start a child can get; nothing must stand in the way of that. By all accounts Mr Morgan is an effective manager, but he's not the type who blathers stats slathered with jargon. Okay, 'we're very tight on the data,' not so that the school can look good on paper but so that any student on the blink can be rapidly and precisely supported – as also any underperforming teacher. Underpinning all this is the school's bottom-line belief that the model of a comprehensive school is capable of serving all the needs of every single one of its students, regardless of ability or background: 'Ours is the ethos of a comprehensive school translated to the new environment of competition.' A string of rave inspection reports would seem to endorse this idealistic, egalitarian vision. As, also, the number of students beating a path from local independent schools, something Mr Morgan relishes. 'Cobwebby' is his word for them.

The regulatory architecture and administrative systems of the school are state of the art, but how does it all actually work at the human level? Here is perhaps Mr Morgan's strongest suit. He's a great believer in relationships – interconnectedness. His understanding of the students is impressively insightful. We watched the rapport. He knows them. They all know him. 'He really does care about them,' said a parent. He has a very good students'-eye view of his school as also, we discovered, do the teachers.

Initial first-hand accounts of the school we received were so glowing that we felt impelled to dig deep to uncover the discrepancies between amplification and actuality. Toil as we might, we unearthed nothing but golden nuggets. Truly, there is something special going on here.

Academic matters: Subjects studied are exclusively mainstream, traditional and academic. The school set this course when it started, resisted fads and fashions along the way and finds itself, rightly and happily, on the right side of educational history with nothing to learn from the present government's reform agenda, and nothing to jettison. Results over recent years have been consistent with only minor, inevitable fluctuations.

In 2018 the percentage getting 9-4 in both maths and English was 84, way above the national average. Thirty-three per cent of all GCSE entries were at the top A*-A/9-7 grades. Value-added scores were excellent at all ability levels, especially – this is the really significant bit – among the lower attainers. What's more, progress made by disadvantaged students was at a very similar rate to that of all the others. So the school is unquestionably bringing out the best in all of its students, not just those who are going to look good in the shop window. Around 70 per cent of students proceed to the sixth form; the rest go on to vocational courses at FE colleges or begin apprenticeships.

At A level in 2018 two-thirds of grades were A*-B; a third were A* or A. Maths and sciences especially strong, as are business studies, geography and history. French, Italian and Spanish on the menu. The school does not cull less able students in order to protect its statistical bottom line. Value-added scores respectable, reflective of the distance covered up to GCSE. In the aftermath of cuts in the post-16 budget, it is encouraging to see the sixth form expanding to 250, which ought to enable the school to fund a good range of subjects.

The sprinters are exceptionally well catered for, no doubt about it: 'I don't believe any other school could have helped my daughter get such good results,' said one parent. But what about the strugglers? Most schools are good at one or the other, not both. We found that students with special needs are exceptionally carefully provided for, as evidenced by the school's Pupil Premium Award in 2016. Support specialists address the full span, from a little light dyslexia to significant learning difficulties and physical disabilities. Provision does not happen in therapeutic isolation but, instead, blurs imperceptibly into pastoral care because all the teachers here spend a good deal of time talking and thinking about the well-being of all their students and constantly share insights with each other and the SEN team. Yes, the aspiration of a 'level playing field for every single student' is not just wishful thinking in a policy document or a bit of eyewash in a vision statement, it really is borne out and made real at the front line. Any prudent scepticism we might have had was blown away by the testimony of parents: 'This school really does have a very big heart'. There was the Asperger's lad with 4s in his Sats on entry who left with straight As in his A levels. He was the recipient of an impressively multi-agency regime which included gap year students hired in to help him with his social skills. 'This was the only school that was positive,' said his mother. 'We still can't believe how well he did. They even picked his classes around him, teachers and students.' Her daughter won a place at a local grammar school but unhesitatingly opted for The Cotswold instead. The mother of a boy with learning difficulties said, 'I can't praise them enough' and is still marvelling that he left with a GCSE in art. 'He made lots of friends – we never had any problems with him being picked on.'

The school is able to attract excellent teachers not only because of its reputation as a great place to work but also because they can find affordable housing in Cheltenham and Gloucester before rising up the pay scale and moving into one of the villages.

Games, options, the arts: With ample grounds and plenty of outdoorsy students, sport thrives here. Weekly fixtures with local schools for rugby, football, cricket, netball, hockey. Inter-house competitions. Other sports on offer range from cross-country to horsemanship. Yes, there is an equestrian team, for this is racehorse country and at Festival time, in the classroom, minds must be lured back from the Gold Cup. There's a temptingly rich range of extracurricular clubs on offer at lunchtime and after school – 'something for absolutely everyone, indoors and out,' a parent told us. There's Duke of Edinburgh, there's an annual fashion show. There's plenty of music, which is on the up – choir to Gloucester cathedral annually, jazz group to Cheltenham Jazz Festival, tours abroad, inter-house comp, concerts by professional players. Drama is really going places with a brilliant new head of dept. Art is longstandingly stunning.

The school has British Council International status and sponsors trips to faraway places – big point of pride and some big name destinations: Nicaragua, New York, Iceland. There are language exchanges, sports, art and IT trips to Europe. When we visited, the physicists were very fired up about their upcoming trip to CERN. These students certainly get to discover that there's life outside Bourton.

Background and atmosphere: The present school is the offspring of the forced marriage in 1988 of the local secondary mod and Westwood's Grammar School (founded 1589). Wouldn't be where it is today without 16 years' outstanding leadership until 2011 by the redoubtable Mrs Holland, for she it was who set the course – core subjects for all until age 16 – so there's been no frantic pulling up of socks post EBacc. The Cotswold remains a school that very much looks to itself and whose inspiration comes from the values it has set itself, making it not a 'better than' but, rather, a 'best we can be' sort of place. Accolades when they have come have come unlooked for – to their slightly surprised gratification.

Technically The Cotswold is an academy (one of the first wave in 2010) but in Mr Morgan's analysis it is 'a grammar school within a comprehensive'. True up to a point, but no grammar school vanities here and the sixth formers are in any case more reminiscent of sixth form college students in their general grown-upness and pre-university demeanour. When we burst into their common room unannounced... sssh, everyone was beavering away in an amazingly purposeful way. You don't often see that.

Set in all of 32 green acres on the outer fringes of Bourton. Some handsome new buildings. Good new maths block (2014). Overall, better than yer average. Classy sports hall with swimming pool, gym and steam room spa used by the whole community. Bright displays in the classrooms. Lively, cheerful, roomy. Panoramic views of the glorious Gloucestershire landscape from classroom windows – the students sit with their backs to them – so, a country feel. Expansion is constrained by an archaeological preservation order on most of the grounds and also by self-denying ordinance: they feel that to grow is to risk losing something so they do so only circumspectly.

The school is upping its presence in the community and beyond. There's a marketing and development manager – an uncommon appointment – whose role is to improve links with local schools and businesses. There's one-to-one careers guidance, as you would expect, plus a programme of guest speakers from universities and vocational colleges. Local employers come in to talk about apprenticeships. Strong links with the Rotary and a strong showing in Rotary competitions.

They're a charitable lot. They've sent coats to Syria, and every year at Christmas time the year 11 students lay on an afternoon of festivities for local senior citizens.

Former students include jockeys Sam and Willy Twiston-Davies, motor racing ace Alice Powell and stammerer Richard Whincup (Google him) whose speech day adventures say so much about this place.

Pastoral care, well-being and discipline: The first thing that strikes you when you arrive, along with the cheery greeting from the receptionist (makes such a difference) is the marvellous calm of the place. It's an impression confirmed when you tour the school – purposeful students, fired-up teachers, all of them going places. Too good to be true? Sure, occasional evidence of fleeting teenage world-weariness behind some desks, but on the whole exactly as you'd like it. Significantly, teachers don't break stride when the principal walks in, neither do the students.

Parents rate the pastoral care highly. Support systems are actively interventionist – and some of these students need a lot of support. All feeder schools are visited in the year before a child comes so that strategies can be created for those with issues of any kind, from special needs to chaotic home life, where efforts are made also to get parents onside. The school wants, said a parent, 'everyone to be busy, to try new things, never to miss out', especially the less confident and those from deprived homes, who are equipped with refurbed laptops so they don't feel different. Teachers play an active part in monitoring the morale of all their students. They really are an impressively extra-mile lot. There are even 'invisible tutors' unknown to their charges, making sure they're happy having a go. How good is that?

Pastoral care systems reactively pick up on and address discipline issues, nipping bad things in the bud at the talk-it-through stage if possible. Everyone agrees that good conduct is an expectation exerted with rigour – 'they can come down hard,' said one parent, 'but they're fair' – and the code has plenty of student buy-in. One parent whose Asperger's son lashed out on the school bus feared the worst, but the head sat the two lads down, they talked it through and now they're great friends. Mr Morgan says that young people are kinder today. Has human nature really changed that much? We think he should credit himself and his team for a culture in which diversity of personality is celebrated. Is this a safe space for the bookish, the nerdy and the eccentric? One mother was reassured when her daughters were about to start here: 'There is a friend for everyone at The Cotswold.' Sounds a bit cheesy? Well, the best schools are. Exclusion is rare. One capital crime is affecting the work and happiness of other students. Another is a one-off act of violence. They're hot on bullying and actively discourage Facebook. School uniform is worn exactly as prescribed, shirts adrift instantly denounced. Dress code for sixth formers smart casual, with the scales tipping towards casual. Parents praise response times when problems arise: 'They really do care if something's not right'. There is a thriving PTA.

Pupils and parents: The complete Cotswold spectrum, socially, from the landed to the dispossessed. Bourton, self-styled Venice of the Cotswolds, is a never-never land English idyll – the old part, that is, twee as can be, frozen in time, mossed cottages, babbling brook, golden stone, the full monty – the sort of place where tourists daily overwhelm the inhabitants and possibly trample them underfoot. All this make believe quickly dissipates at the periphery of the village, where mundane contemporary realities and associated dowdy domestic architecture reassert themselves. The same is true of surrounding villages where well-heeled prosperity and rural deprivation live cheek by jowl. Does this lead to stratification at school? Cliques? No, say the students, but we didn't take no for an answer and drilled down. And, d'you know, they're right. It turns out that the school really is what it sets out to be: socially, a level playing field. One student said 'It's funny, you get invited to someone's house and when you arrive it's, like, really big and you think wow, I never knew'. One prominently posh student assured us she'd had 'no problems at all' transferring from an independent school. The experience had certainly not impaired her vowels. The mix here is majority white and 'working class'.

The recent decline in rating of another local school has left The Cotswold pre-eminent. It was Sunday Times Comprehensive of the Year 2015-16 and is listed by Tatler. Its resultant popularity means that the area from which it recruits outside its catchment area is shrinking year on year, but not significantly on account of middle-class colonisation.

Entrance: Priority to looked after children, siblings, those living in the catchment area then by distance. Five A*-C/9-4s at GCSE for sixth form, mostly with top grades for chosen A levels. Accepts new students at all ages if there's room.

Exit: Some 40 per cent leave after GCSEs. Those with a vocational bent urged to stay to the end of year 11 and get some decent GCSEs under their belts. Big focus presently on post-16 education pathways. In 2018, three to Oxbridge, plus one medic, and around half to Russell Group universities.

Remarks: Difficult to land a glove on, try as we might. Here is a school which has been marching to the beat of its own drum for decades, propelled by its idea of an education and making good on its commitment to providing a level playing for all, regardless of ability, disability or social background. For parents who can afford an independent education it offers a compelling alternative; for those who can't it offers a best-chance saloon.

C

Crickhowell High School

New Road, Crickhowell, Powys NP8 1AW

Ages 11–18 **Pupils** 923 **Sixth form** 203

01873 813500
www.crickhowell-hs.powys.sch.uk

Headteacher: Since 2010, Jackie Parker, originally from the South Wales valleys, studied English at Birmingham University before deciding to become a teacher. Once qualified, she taught in Walsall and at some 'tough' Birmingham secondary schools, picking up promotions on the way including head of English and assistant head. In 2006, she joined Crickhowell as deputy head, becoming acting head in 2007 and, finally, head in 2010. Since then, the school has grown from 600 to 900+ pupils.

One parent said, 'I hugely admire [the school's] desire to constantly develop and progress in a wide variety of areas.' Another added, 'I think Mrs Parker has an incredibly difficult job as a head teacher of a diverse and large school. She is keen for parents to come in should they have issues to discuss. [She] stands by their open door policy.'

Academic matters: In 2018, at A level 40 per cent of grades were A*/A, and 61 per cent were A* to B. At GCSE, 77 per cent of students achieved 4-9 in both English and maths, and 27 per cent of all grades were A*-A/9-7, down on last year. Still one of the top performing schools in Wales, classed as a 'Green Category/Band One' school by the Welsh Government since 2012, Crickhowell has a strong reputation for achieving good academic results.

27 A levels offered including business studies, computer science, law, Welsh and health & social care. A BTec in sport and a Cambridge Technical in ICT are also available. Options can be combined with vocational courses at local colleges. Maths is particularly popular at A level and the school has been awarded the Tribal Award for Excellence in maths.

A pioneer curriculum school, Crickhowell is part of the Pioneer Schools Network, a group of 120 schools across Wales responsible for the design and development of a new curriculum planned for September 2021. At Crickhowell pupils get the opportunity to answer the 'big questions,' and focus on skills-based independent learning in years 7 and 8. As part of this, they run regular cross-curricular events and activities. On our visit the sports hall had been taken over by a year 7 activity day. An external leader was helping groups build F1 cars to be raced later. Students had been appointed roles like project manager and design lead. These activities not only inspire students, but allow them to learn new skills outside the classroom, giving everyone a chance to shine. Other events include an annual science day and Lab-on-the-Lorry; a chance for pupils to get involved in experiments not usually carried out in school.

GCSE study starts in year 9. This gives pupils more time to study and carry out practical experiments, as well as can developing a passion for their subjects. This not only helps those with additional learning needs, it gives all students a better idea of what they would like to do in the future. A supportive and helpful careers department steers students to courses best suited to individuals – even if that means choosing a local college rather than Crickhowell sixth form, parents told us. As part of the MAT (more able and talented) Wales scheme, pupils are tested in year 7 and anyone identified is given more challenging opportunities. Maths and English are taught in ability sets in all years and older pupils are encouraged and supported to apply to universities including Oxbridge.

French, German, Mandarin and Welsh are taught from year 7. On average half of students choose one language or more at GCSE. Latin is offered as an extracurricular subject and at GCSE. Crickhowell has an official Confucius classroom and its own dedicated Chinese teacher, teaching not just language skills and calligraphy but also insight into China, its people and culture. After year 7, Mandarin is taught as an extracurricular subject and offered at GCSE. Exchanges with schools in China are next on the agenda. Crickhowell has a strong global focus: as well as links with schools in China, South Africa and Uganda, they have an International Award from the British Council and have two ongoing Erasmus + projects, one of which is a year 12-led project working with students in schools in Finland and Austria. Never forgetting its roots, Crickhowell celebrates all things Welsh, offering Welsh at GCSE and A level as well as teaching Welsh heritage as part of the curriculum.

With around 23 per cent of pupils with additional learning needs (ALN), the school takes great pride in being inclusive and was awarded the Inclusion Quality Mark and Centre of Excellence status in 2016. The site is fully wheelchair accessible and the ALN department caters for a whole range of needs from moderate to complex, including medical needs. Pupils here make good progress academically. Based in a specialist wooden cabin, called The Success Centre (students have re-named it The Department of Awesome), there are spaces for small group classes and one-to-one teaching. There is also a quiet area and a room to reflect on behaviour. The department operates a card system so that students can ask for some time out, or teachers can refer them if necessary. The overall supportive ethos of the school means that there is no stigma attached. One parent whose child needed support told us, 'The support, care and encouragement [our child] and ourselves received from this department was tremendous. We will be eternally grateful... The quiet area/space was essential... and it became a home from home [for them].' Counselling services are also offered.

Homework club runs every lunchtime and the learning resource centre is open for quiet study before and after school. Sixth formers run a buddy system to support younger pupils in science, literacy and numeracy.

Games, options, the arts: Parents are impressed by the sport and drama departments. Sports facilities were improved in 2016 with a new 3G all-weather pitch and a refurbished fitness suite and dance studio, also open to the local community. Good professional sports links include a full-time Welsh Rugby Union officer, a Sport Wales development officer, as well as an established link with the Cardiff Blues rugby club that runs the BTec in sport.

Success across the years in basketball (girls and boys), cricket, tennis and netball, with several pupils now competing at county, regional and national level. An annual awards ceremony celebrates every success as well as crowning the sportsmen and sportswomen of the year and recognising good leadership. Annual overseas sports tours, most recently to Canada. Duke of Edinburgh award scheme is popular.

'The drama department is excellent and the teachers demonstrate great passion for their subject,' parents enthused. There is a main production each year, most recently Beauty and the Beast, plus plenty of smaller productions and competitions to get involved with. As part of the Shakespeare Schools Festival 2017, Crickhowell performed A Midsummer Night's Dream, and each year they take part in the UK Rock Challenge, a national inter-school performing arts competition.

Decent art studio with a good range of art on display including masks, sculptures, paintings and photography. Art and design is offered at both levels. Plenty of music performances and concerts throughout the year as well as the opportunity to take part in the annual Young Musician competition. Extracurricular clubs include orchestra, choir, jazz band, string group and various rock and chamber music groups. Individual music lessons are available.

A good range of extracurricular clubs at lunchtime and after school. Apart from the usual offering, there is golf, rock climbing, caving and horse-riding.

A skiing and snowboarding trip is offered every year. Year 7s have an annual outdoor adventure residential plus various Welsh heritage trips. Other trips include going down a mine, language exchanges, and trips to Auschwitz, Iceland, Normandy and New York for the older students. Sixth formers can opt for a World Challenge trip, the last to Uganda and Ethiopia. Plenty of local day trips to theatre and museums as well as further afield to London. Parents are impressed: 'The recent trip to Italy was exceptional! Our daughter said it was one of her best experiences yet: it really left her with a taste for Italy. She also felt very safe and well looked after.'

Background and atmosphere: Founded in 1983, this English medium co-educational secondary school was purpose built for the growing local community, and community is very much at its heart. Situated in the small town of Crickhowell, between Brecon and Abergavenny, it is part of the beautiful Brecon Beacons National Park.

Built into a hill, the school's entrance is deceiving: the site is far bigger than it first seems. The back of the school opens out onto playing fields. Just over 30 years old, the buildings and classrooms are all fairly modern. The leisure centre is open to the community out of hours and recently the school saved the local community library, which is now the school's main library. The original library on-site has been turned into an extra study room for sixth formers. They also have their own workroom and common room, but no separate sixth form block.

Crickhowell is a Platinum Eco School and was the first secondary school in Powys and the third in Wales achieve a third Green Flag award. Riverside Rescue helped win this accolade: every half term pupils and staff don their wellies and clear debris from the stream that flows through the school and off through the Bull Pit Meadow to join the River Usk. There are also community litter picking activities at lunchtimes and a popular eco committee. Student voice is powerful: they are 'empowered' and truly listened to, we were told. The student council campaigns for practicalities like more benches and a covered picnic area, but also chooses charities to support (and track their impact), interviews new staff, and even sits on the senior management board meetings with the governors.

Not just community-focused, Crickhowell has a keen eye on the rest of the world and has close links with St Peter's School in Uganda. The head is determined that pupils have a good understanding of the world and of the impact they have or could have on it. To add to the long list of awards, the school is a Global Lead School and has been awarded a British Council International School Award and the Fair Achiever Award for fair trade.

The ethos of the school is based on the Olympic and Paralympic values of respect, excellence, friendship, determination, inspiration, courage and equality. These values are clearly instilled across the school, on the sports fields, in the classroom and in the school grounds. The house system gives pupils more opportunities to work together and the five houses compete in a multitude of events throughout the year.

Inclusion is important and the school achieved the Inclusion Quality Mark and Centre of Excellence status in 2016. Differences are accepted and idiosyncrasies are embraced, we were told. Diversity and issues are talked about openly and are built into curriculum. Recent discussions on transgender equality have been led by students in a bid to support their peers.

Pastoral care, well-being and discipline: Strong pastoral care; well-being is central to the school's ethos. As well as tutors, students can turn to their heads of year, progress leaders, well-being leaders or student support officer for guidance or support. Parents praised the heads of year for being supportive over friendship and health issues, one saying, 'I feel incredibly thankful that my child has an adult that she feels comfortable to go to, to discuss sensitive issues.'

Pastoral care covers the canteen too. Not only have they won a National Healthy Schools Award, the head of the team regularly joins ALN medical plan meetings to keep up-to-date with any allergies or dietary requirements. The team apparently does a great job steering children away from certain foods and generally keeping a good eye on them. An emergency action plan is in place for those with complex medical needs, and staff discreetly observe pupils at break times.

Crickhowell actively encourages mutual respect. There is an ethos of openness; students are not afraid to knock on doors, ask questions and talk to staff. This extends to the head and her senior team, as we saw for ourselves when students popped into the head's office during our meeting. This is not a school run on fear, it is a school that nurtures relationships, encourages individuality and gives children the confidence to grow. There were mixed reports on behaviour: some parents feel that 'tougher sanctions' are needed for misbehaviour. Others feel that the caring ethos of the school has resulted in good morale among pupils, which in turn has led to good behaviour.

In line with the Olympic and Paralympic values, students are hugely supportive of each other, respecting differences and encouraging and cheering each other on at sports day, regardless of ability. Finishing is as much of an achievement as winning, particularly for those with special needs. With around 15 mid-year entries each year, this supportive ethos, along with a successful system of buddies and mentors, helps newcomers settle easily. An anti-bullying box for anonymous messages and a dedicated email box are regularly empty, proving Crickhowell is on the right track.

Pupils and parents: Some travel from as far as Brecon, but most are local. Several teachers have children in the school and many parents were once pupils. On our visit, it was Children In Need day so we can't comment on uniforms, but parents are impressed with Crickhowell students; they are 'smartly dressed and confident.'

Communication from the school is 'excellent' via the SCHOOP social media system. Twitter and Facebook are used for announcements and achievements. 'Personally I feel that I can approach the school with any concerns,' said one parent. 'Reports are regular and thorough,' said another.

Entrance: Five feeder primary schools but the large catchment area covers 26 schools. Open days followed by induction days help with transition from small village schools to secondary school. Regular inter-school sports tournaments help younger ones get to know the site.

For sixth form entry, minimum of five GCSE grade 4s and at least a 6 in chosen subjects is preferred.

Exit: Some 80 per cent complete sixth form. Others leave to go to local colleges, join the Forces or go onto employment and training. Just under 70 per cent of sixth formers go on to university. None to Oxbridge in 2018, but one medic, one dentist, and one geographer to New Zealand.

Money matters: The school runs a hardship fund to help with costs of school trips.

Remarks: A community comprehensive school that is proud of its Welsh roots, but at the same time has a global-focus, teaching Mandarin and exploring other cultures. Diversity is embraced and students are supportive of each other. Regardless of ability, students progress well academically, emotionally and socially, helping them to grow in confidence ready for the world beyond Crickhowell.

Dauntsey's School

West Lavington, Devizes, Wiltshire SN10 4HE

Ages 11–18 **Pupils** 820 **Sixth form** 270 **Boarders** 300 full

Fees: Day £18,990; Boarding £31,440 – £36,300 pa

01380 814500
www.dauntseys.org

Head master: Since 2012, Mark Lascelles (40s), previously lower master, and temporary acting head of King's School Canterbury

– something of a rough ride. Educated at Shrewsbury School and Durham (geography) where he was keen and proficient in cricket and football, reaching county level and beyond. Now he only plays social cricket – frustrating, as he is very competitive. Back at Shrewsbury for a further 17 years, becoming housemaster, before joining King's School in 2009. Married to Amber, a teacher and Durham graduate, who was a national level canoeist. They have three young daughters.

D

Parents like him and say he is accessible, listens and takes a personal interest in all pupils, meeting the school bus every morning and being a friendly presence at most activities. He 'has finally mastered the art of feeding biscuits to paddling canoeists as they pass in the Devizes to Westminster race!' Out of school he enjoys travel, skiing, reading and theatre – and is rapidly developing a taste for musicals, which is just as well as, at the time of our visit, the school was about to put on Sondheim's Into the Woods followed by Mamma Mia.

Says he is so impressed by 'the quality of pupils' here, not just their academic level but their genuine niceness and the energy injected by having an intake at 11+, something he had 'missed out on before'. Sees Dauntsey's as a collegiate school for families who understand about good education and are not blinded by fashionable pretension.

Academic matters: Dauntsey's has moved up several pegs in the academic stakes (local rivals take note) and shows a pretty impressive record for a 'not overly selective' school – though of course success breeds demand which ups the ante. In 2018, 48 per cent A*/A at A level and 71 per cent A*/A-9-7 at GCSE – mostly IGCSEs which, pupils say, 'prepare better for A level'. Both the curriculum and the classrooms are quite traditional but the stunningly high level of pupil satisfaction registered in the recent ISI inspection bears witness to the excellence of the teaching.

Curriculum includes a four language carousel of French, German, Latin, and Spanish for the first year. Other languages – Mandarin, Russian, Japanese, Greek, Arabic etc – are done in extracurricular time. Native speakers are encouraged to take exams in their own languages. Three science IGCSEs for two-thirds of the year group; the rest do dual award. Science labs feature spectacular full-size skeleton monoplane in the hall and charming courtyard with super bosky pond and raised beds crammed with Japanese anemones.

No limits on choices at A level. Pupils can now take three the EPQ, sport or the school's own leadership qualification. DT (resistant materials), in a whizzy new class room, with new courses in psychology, history of art and English language starting. Outstanding in maths and further maths and more than sound across a very wide board including theatre studies, music technology and class civ as well as the mainstream stuff.

Class size around 16 in GCSE years. Busy SEN department with three full-time staff providing help, within the timetable but at extra cost. Mainly helps mild dyslexia and offers a safety net for the organisationally challenged but, 'If pupils pass the entrance exam' says the head 'it is rare for us to say we can't cope with their special needs'. Impressively wheelchair friendly (even disabled wet-room showers) for a school with no current need for it. Thirty or so receive EFL tuition, included in the special enhanced international fees. Efficient IT taken for granted, though pupils are impressed by free-standing printers at convenient points that access and print from their personal files, activated by thumbprint. Pupils register by thumbprint too for afternoon school, but house staff like to lay eyes on everyone in the morning.

Games, options, the arts: Sport is definitely big and timetabled three times a week. Boys' and girls' hockey, rugby and cricket doing pretty well at county and regional level. Football played in senior years, tennis, for all and netball for girls, all tackled competitively. Girls regularly send a hockey team to South Africa to match the triennial rugby tour of Australia. Recently acquired Mercers' field has extensive pitches, 'levelled by computer,' pupils say. A huge range of 'strenuous pursuits' available in the 'long break'.

Bracing, whole school cross-country race was underway when we visited. Our delightful lower school guides, when asked what happened to non-sporty people, didn't think there were any. Some parents feel that less talented enthusiasts need more chances to play in teams, even against each other. Masses of expeditions like the Brecons Challenge and a long distance canoe race from Devizes to Westminster. Moonrakers, a third year programme, offers all sorts of outdoor adventure challenges (at no extra cost), and the more ambitious Mountaineering and Expedition Society travels to the orphanage they have adopted in Romania or visits their contacts in Bhutan. Lots do DofE, though they skip silver because of exam pressure.

Solid rather than spectacular facilities – indoor swimming pool, two handsome Astros, sports hall, new dance studio, athletics track a hike away – source of a few grumbles. Macho fitness area with scary weights and levers has been given a facelift and a bit more space. Too unusual to omit is the sailing club: no Optimists or Picos on a pond for this school – instead everyone gets the chance to crew a century old tall ship, the Jolie Brise (winner of the first Fastnet Race in 1925). Parents are envious.

What the music department lacks in size it makes up for in enthusiasm – groups of every genre happily play away – choirs, orchestras, ensembles, bands. It could still do with a bit more space. Good take up of instrumental tuition on every instrument ever invented makes for plentiful concerts and accomplished performances.

There is serious drama (King Lear, for example), but the star attractions are the many enormous musicals and 'extraordinary performances' which sometimes even make it to London theatres. Smashing A level results in theatre studies too. The multi-function 'memorial' school hall has really good lighting and equipment thanks to links with the West End. Plans are afoot to refurbish, though it would be a pity to end such bizarre juxtapositions as the stately school altar, sanctuary and organ at one end and a stunning, life-size puppet cow at the other. Annabel's, the well-equipped drama studio, has everything needed to launch careers via the Edinburgh fringe and similar venues. Good and popular dance studios too – it's in the curriculum – with a few boys taking part.

The chimneyed art block may look arts and crafts, but it's full of all the requisite IT and pottery kit. Bags of school trips – modern languages to Spain and France, geography to Iceland, RS to India, Adventurers to Bhutan, skiing in Italy. There's not much you can't do, which is probably just as well for 300 or so boarders residing in a leafy backwater

Boarding: Boarders in particular enjoy the benefits of lots of space. Manor House (co-ed junior) comes with its own seven-hole golf course and pupils can ramble to and from their Victorian mock Tudor mansion along a woodland path. It's a spick and span version of Hogwarts, with galleried hall, long oak tables and panelled common rooms smelling of furniture polish rather than 60 small boys and girls. Dormitories are functional but sizeable and have lovely views. In winter, tea and delicious-looking scones and cake are laid out in front of a blazing fire. Weekends are full of well planned, child friendly activity, mostly on the spot.

Senior boarding houses (single sex), both old and new, are also much larger than average. All well equipped, with kitchens and work spaces – although a picky sixth former quibbled 'certainly better than adequate but not quite luxury'. Day houses get everything the boarders have, except the bedrooms, and juniors have their own similar on-site day centre.

Background and atmosphere: Founded in West Lavington in 1542 on the deathbed largesse of William Dauntsey, master of the Worshipful Company of Mercers, the present school opened in 1895. Mercers' Company still provides six governors, occasional generous financial help and annual knees-up for its associated schools – an unlikely spread from St Paul's Schools in London (both boys' and girls' versions), to Peter Symonds College (state sixth form in Winchester), two new academies and The Royal Ballet School.

Lawns and trees enhance the setting of the handsome main school building. Reception area is reminiscent of a five star hotel with glass topped tables, comfortable furniture and well-lit pictures changed regularly by the art department – nice to see the artist's names. Other facilities are more functional, but very well maintained. Could be a bit too rustic for some hardened Londoners (until 1930 it was known as Dauntsey's Agricultural School).

What impresses is that Dautsey's has absolutely every facility a school should have, but nothing extravagant. The most spectacular feature is a superb, bright and airy new library. Exposed desks/computers down the centre of the building may not be everyone's cup of tea (where do they hide the sweet packet?), but more sheltered study space is available upstairs, plus round tables and comfy chairs for a good read. Socialising happens in the cyber-café or the tuck shop. Lessons finish at 4pm and it is technically possible for day pupils to creep off then but most stay on for prep or take part in clubs or sports until the mass bus exodus at 5.30pm. Boarders have two hours of prep in the evenings, one before supper and one after.

Girls' uniform is a rather limp blue check skirt, blue blouse and pullover; boys wear blue shirts and grey-blue jackets. No uniform in sixth form but smart-ish dress required – quite widely interpreted. Busy school shop has an endless supply to lend to those who forget games things. The san is modern and inviting with quiet places to sit and suffer and comfortable looking bedrooms. Pupils definitely value the care given there, including counselling.

Pastoral care, well-being and discipline: Much less privilege orientated than many schools, so apart from the 17 Club, which is the hub of sixth form social life and morning break, sixth form and prefects live and work alongside the upper school and take a full part in house life. Relationships between year groups are definitely flexible. The pastoral system functions through the houses, in which the house staff and at least four assistants act as tutors to about 60 pupils. Parents say problems are handled successfully and with great sensitivity.

Responsibilities taken seriously by prefects and captains of houses. Pupils say rules are, 'a matter of common sense' – though a new rule book is issued each year. The comments they made about 'how far into the opposite sex house' they are allowed to go showed they had a pretty shrewd idea of what is and is not acceptable.

Pupils and parents: Not toffs on the whole, more local families, farmers and small business owners with quite a number from state primaries or first time buyers. Lots of professional families with two parents working to earn the fees. Being just over an hour from London, Bristol and Southampton makes boarding pretty accessible from UK or abroad. International intake widening from Hong Kong and Russia to a spread of other countries. Fifteen bus routes from Salisbury, Swindon, Frome, Hungerford and Andover, which puts them into competition with a number of good grammar schools as well as some big name independents.

Entrance: At 11+, from state schools and a few preps, by Dauntsey's own exam (maths, English, VR and optional music auditions). Selective in that they accept about the same standard of candidates as Salisbury Grammar, according to the head. At 13+ (two extra forms) they take mainly boarders from prep school and some from abroad via 13+ CE or scholarship exams. Very few day places at this stage. Feeders include Chafyn Grove, St Francis (Pewsey) and St Margaret's (Calne), All Hallows and Thorngrove plus many local state primaries. Everyone sitting an exam at 11+ is automatically considered for a scholarship and awards are granted to around 15 pupils out of 80. Fifty or so join the sixth form, around a third from abroad. Minimum of three 7s and three 6s at GCSE required from UK pupils, plus an interview.

Exit: A few leave after GCSEs, mainly for local sixth form colleges. Large proportion to solid courses with Cardiff, Exeter, Bristol and Birmingham currently popular. Eight medics in 2018.

Money matters: Much more aware than many schools that parents' resources are finite. The parental vibe is that day fees here are particularly good value for money. A few nice touches: music lessons cost the full whack for first instrument but less for second and subsequent ones; a 10 per cent reduction for siblings (a very sibling-friendly school). Mercers' connection is a help when it comes to funding building projects but not a bottomless pit.

Remarks: Parents and pupils value Dauntsey's special atmosphere, rooted in being reasonably non-selective, both academically and socially. With steadily improving results and facilities it is now firmly established among the educational front-runners in this part of the world. Friendliness, fresh air, activity and academic focus – Dauntsey's is fab!

Dean Close School

Shelburne Road, Cheltenham, Gloucestershire GL51 6HE

Ages 3–18 **Pupils** 929: senior 475, junior 454 **Sixth form** 196 **Boarders** 278 full, 34 flexi (from year 7)

Fees: Day £8,241 – £24,600; Boarding £19,260 – £37,413 pa

01242 258044
www.deanclose.org.uk

Headmaster: Since 2015, Bradley Salisbury MEd PGCE (40s), previously acting headmaster, deputy head since 2009. Son of a vicar, he was educated at Monkton Combe school. First degree (theology) from Leeds, and then on to Bristol where he completed his PGCE and later a masters in educational leadership. It was while training for his PGCE that he met his wife, Claire. Taught religious studies at Gordano School before moving to Bristol Cathedral School as head of RS and head of years 10 and 11; thence to Wells Cathedral School where he was head of RS and a housemaster.

Friendly, full of energy and clearly enjoying his headship. Parents approve: 'Holistic, open-minded, very approachable', 'definitely listening'. Pupils lost for sufficiently eulogistic words when asked to describe him and settled for, 'Just so, so good.' His assemblies are 'amazing', and he 'gives everyone targets for the year ahead and writes pupils personal letters if they do well'. Oh, and, 'He's always walking round the school and he knows everyone's names.'

Mr Salisbury acknowledges that boarding has changed hugely since he was at school but believes that one of its enduring strengths is that it teaches young people how 'to work through relationships. You can't just go home at the end of the day and sweep problems aside, you have to figure out ways of getting on with everybody ... it's great for social agility.'

A fair bit has changed since The Good Schools Guide last visited Dean Close, not least its acquisition in 2015 of Monmouthshire prep, St John's-on-the-Hill, plus five nurseries. It's a rather canny way of 'growing the brand' by ensuring a good flow of pupils into the on-site prep as well as the senior school, but Mr S has no plans for significant expansion. 'Our size is just right for us to be a real community – we have lots of events where the whole school can come together in one place, and that's really important.' Ambitious five-year building and refurbishment programme well underway – yes there will be new stuff, but emphasis seems to be on 'ergonomics', improving classrooms and streamlining departments to form academic 'hubs' (eg maths/science; business).

Unlike many schools, Dean Close has not consigned the robust Christianity of its founders to history and an obscure corner of its website, nor is this likely to happen on theologian Mr Salisbury's watch. He sees it as central to the school's educational ethos. 'We value each pupil and will always put an individual's best interests first, even if they may be at odds with those of the school. For instance, we don't just push everyone to go to Russell Group universities, even though that would be advantageous for our profile.

Mr Salisbury's wife works in the prep as head of religious studies and the couple have three daughters at the school. Relaxation takes the form of kite flying – he used to be in a kite team – and cooking, 'I don't have a signature dish, I never cook the same thing twice!' Favourite read? True Blue (captain facing down a mutiny and sticking to his guns in the heat of competition in the Oxford and Cambridge boat race).

Head of prep: Since 2015, Paddy Moss, BA in geography and economics from SOAS (40s). Joined after nine years teaching in a prep school in Kenya and has 'lived all over the world.' Though Cheltenham may be less exotic, he describes the move as 'a wonderful fit.' That's pretty much exactly what parents say about him and Mr Salisbury too. School's recent acquisition of a Monmouthshire prep and several local nurseries, in addition to own pre-prep on site, mean no shortage of 'feeders'. Apparently they 'don't lose many to the local grammars' but prep now 'guarantees' all its 11-year-olds a place at the senior school. Thinks the prep's size (around 300) 'ensures close pupil, parent and staff relationships.' Families must agree, there's now a waiting list for places.

Mr Moss is a big fan of the year 7-9 curriculum (all 13+ prep school heads are ...) and says school is developing its own syllabus, 'uniquely designed to promote love of learning' and a 'seamless transition' to senior school across the way.

Has brought his love of the outdoors with him from Africa and enjoys bushcraft, camping and walking the Cotswold Way. Like Mr Salisbury he also has three daughters at the school. A good fit indeed.

Academic matters: Twenty-two subjects offered at I/GCSE most take 10 or 11, smallish numbers for classics, Latin and Greek. In 2018, 51 per cent A*-A/9-7 – maths, separate sciences, English and religious studies fare particularly well. At A level in 2018, 80 per cent A*-B, 52 per cent A*/A. Maths, further maths, art and design, history and modern foreign languages lead the A* pack, but there's a healthy spread of marks in all subjects.

In addition to three A levels, sixth formers take timetabled 'enrichment courses', each of which leads to a qualification. One-year options include an EPQ plus a music diploma, computer software or sports leader qualifications. Two-year options include GCSE German, AS philosophy, maths or ancient history. Sounds pretty full-on so it's no surprise that even some local sixth formers opt to board.

Parents incredibly positive about how teachers bring out the very best in each child, whatever their ability. 'They are so generous with their time, nobody minds asking for help.' Praise too for careers guidance – school has good links with local businesses and supports pupils applying for apprenticeships and degree apprenticeships.

Teaching in the prep school was described to us as, 'progressive, but with old fashioned values.' Half the teachers are male and school thinks this 'makes a positive difference.' Latin introduced in year 6 (some drop this in year 7); Spanish starts at age 3 in the pre-prep. 'Moving away from common entrance.' Big focus on making year 9 transition as smooth as possible.

Learning support came in for much praise. Short or long-term specialist tuition offered for literacy, numeracy or 'curriculum' (for pupils who need help with organisation/study skills). The most able are stretched via extension societies and participation in school and national competitions (maths and physics Olympiads; Latin and Greek reading; European Youth Parliament). Top set mathematicians take IGCSE maths a year early and then do IGCSE additional maths in year 11; triple science and the charmingly named 'Gratin' (Greek and Latin) can be taken as accelerated double and single GCSE options respectively.

Games, options, the arts: All of the above pursued with gusto and considerable success. Year 9 do a carousel of 'creatives' (product design and manufacture, art, music, drama and cookery). Product design is one of the school's particular strengths and we saw some very impressive work – fabulous wooden standard lamps that wouldn't have looked out of place in an interior design showroom. Product design teacher says she's 'in heaven' and couldn't stop smiling proudly as she showed us her domain – full of traditional and high-tech kit. 'Our focus is on teaching skills, but we don't spoon feed, they have to work things out independently – it's what the industry is looking for.'

Lots of excitement about new cookery school – home to GCSE food and nutrition, cookery clubs and (fanfare) the Leiths Introductory Food and Wine Certificate. Sixth formers can do this either as part of their timetabled extension programme, or off-timetable in the evening. In return, not only will they get UCAS points, they also join the 'Leiths List', passport to a gap year cooking in ski chalets and private dining rooms.

Long tradition of choral excellence starts in the prep with the exquisitely trained voices of the Tewkesbury Abbey Schola Cantorum choristers (boys only). Both prep and senior school attract serious musical talents (regular choral/organ scholarships to Oxford and Cambridge). Prep has two orchestras and four choirs of its own.

Members of the school's quartet in residence, the Carducci Quartet, teach string players of all ages alongside their professional commitments. They also give performance classes, coach chamber music groups and run orchestra sectionals. All this excellence doesn't mean exclusivity, each pupil is encouraged to find their own voice/instrument. One of our guides said, 'I came to Dean Close on a sports scholarship, but now I'm singing.' Parents agree: 'music is incredible, but it's really inclusive – everyone's encouraged. Drama comes in for similar praise but some felt that it could take a leaf out of music's book, 'it can be a bit cliquey', said one. Another said, 'anyone can have a part, but not everyone gets to speak and that puts some off'. 'Twas ever thus.

Bacon Theatre (named after former pupil, Francis Bacon) seats 550 and apparently has 'the largest stage in Gloucestershire'. More than 50 concerts and 10 major drama productions (including regular sell-out slot at Edinburgh Fringe) a year, plus lots of ad-hoc performance opportunities. School sponsors events and takes an active part in Cheltenham's literary, science and music festivals.

School says that 'participation and team spirit are the real values of sport' and it used to be that in rugby at least Dean Close were plucky underdogs, rather than top dogs. That's no longer true, school has partnered with Gloucester Rugby Club and pupils told us proudly about how 'our rugby's so much better, we got through to the last 16 of the Nat West Cup.' Hockey is excellent and boys' and girls' teams have played in 19 national finals in the last five years. Riders are galloping ahead and it's rosettes all the way in team and individual show jumping, eventing and dressage. No on-site equestrian facilities, lessons take place at nearby stables; polo training is offered at Birdlip and school regularly fields tournament teams.

In addition to wide range of extracurricular options including CCF and DofE, parents praised the school's community action programme, 'all pupils do voluntary work every week, they don't make a big thing of it, it's just expected.' Energetic fundraising supports school for poor and orphaned children in Uganda.

Boarding: Just over half of pupils are full boarders and school has also rather smartly addressed local demand for something a little less full: 'day boarders' are attached to a boarding house and have the option of staying two nights a week. Shelburne, a senior girls' house, is school's flagship boarding accommodation and very nice it is too. Year group to a floor, three or four to a dorm, sixth formers have single rooms with connecting bathrooms. Apparently boys' accommodation is somewhat plainer fare – as is often the case. Meals are eaten together in the dining hall; boarding and day houses also provide fruit, tea and toast. Saturday morning lessons, followed by afternoon matches, mean a six-day school week for most pupils whether they're boarders or not.

Around a third of prep school pupils board and nearly all are full boarders. Accommodation is in three Regency houses with live-in house parents who run things on an 'extended family' model. Up to three nights a week flexi boarding option also proving popular. Being on the same site as the senior school means access to facilities such as the swimming pool and cricket nets on summer evenings and there's a full programme of weekend activities.

Background and atmosphere: Founded in 1886 as a memorial to the Very Reverend Francis Close, Dean of Carlisle Cathedral and well known for his robust sermons decrying the evils of tobacco, alcohol, horseracing and the theatre. What would he make of Cheltenham today now that racing and the creative arts are two of its biggest attractions?

In 2015 the school became a foundation when it acquired St John's-on-the-Hill, a prep school in Monmouthshire, and five nearby nurseries. Another addition to the DC stable has been Mrs Emma Taylor, the warden. She's hugely experienced and delightful company and it's her job to ensure that the foundation is run in a 'businesslike way' but that the individual schools themselves remain 'personal'.

Site and buildings are familiar mix of old, newish and very new – the latter thoughtfully designed. Nothing grand or ostentatious, that's not the Dean Close vernacular. Currently under construction are a sixth form common room, a 'village' of four new day houses and a separate 'hub' for socialising between houses.

Pastoral care, well-being and discipline: 'Safe, happy, comfortable' was how one parent summed up the Dean Close experience. Others said it was a school where pupils are 'expected to be kind', that it was 'good for square pegs' and there was 'no one type, no cool crowd.' Parents say tutors, house parents and teachers all respond promptly to calls and emails, 'they're on the case and really get to know the pupils.' Head puts big emphasis on school as a 'community' and says 'our size means we can have whole school dining and come together for chapel or theatrical performances.' He's also directing attention to things like pupil induction, improvements to changing room facilities (more privacy) and mobile phone use. Parents are positively encouraged to get involved if they can and there's now a parent society that hosts social events as well as talks on issues such as drugs and mental health (pupils get these too).

Pupils and parents: Mostly local. 'It's not a posh school' thought one parent, 'pupils aren't spoilt or precious, they're aware how fortunate they are.' Longstanding links with Forces, diplomatic and clergy families. Smallish international contingent, includes Spanish and German children who come over for one year ('can make it hard to develop friendships,' thought one parent). Nearby GCHQ and Hitachi add Americans and Japanese to the mix. Former pupils (Old Decanians) include lots of eminent members of the clergy and military plus rugby players, cricketers, artist Francis Bacon, actors Will Merrick and Hugh Quarshie, and writers George Adamson (Born Free), George Wilson Knight (Shakespeare scholar) and Jon Foster (TV comedy).

Entrance: Admission to pre-prep by taster day. For year 3 upwards it's cognitive ability and English papers, interview and school report. Around a third more pupils enter prep at year 7 and all are 'guaranteed' a place in the senior school. External candidates for senior school need 50 per cent or more in CE; entrants from state schools sit verbal reasoning, English and maths tests. Six I/GCSEs minimum grade 4-5 (grade 7-9 for subjects to be studied at A level) required for entry to sixth form, plus verbal reasoning test and papers on three A level subjects.

Exit: A few leave prep at 11 or 13 for grammars or single sex boarding schools. Loses some (around 15 per cent) post-GCSE to FE colleges and also apprenticeships. Over 60 per cent to Russell Group, seven to Oxbridge in 2018, and five off overseas (US and Australia). Engineering and business courses particularly popular. One or two to degree apprenticeships; four to art foundation courses and one to drama school in 2018.

Money matters: Comparatively good value for money. Scholarships and exhibitions at 13+ and sixth form. Some full bursaries available, including some specifically for children from Forces or church families.

Remarks: We sensed renewed verve and confidence when we visited Dean Close. Energetic and forward-thinking leadership has resulted in nimble moves to accommodate changing work and family patterns. Yes, the school is looking to the future, but its founding moral and social values are as secure as ever.

D

Devonport High School for Boys

46

Paradise Road, Stoke, Plymouth PL1 5QP

Ages 11–18 **Pupils** 1,233 **Sixth form** 337 (77 girls)

01752 208787
www.dhsb.org

Headmaster: Since 2015, Dan Roberts (30s). Originally from Manchester, studied a degree in marine biology at Plymouth University before completing his PGCE at University of St

Mark and St John. His first teaching jobs, as science teacher, were at Tamarside Community College, now Marine Academy Plymouth, and later at saltash.net school, as head of science. For a complete change of scene he then jetted off to the Seychelles to be head of an international school for two years before returning to Plymouth as deputy at DHSB (moving up to the role of head two years later). Dan has not only won national and international teaching awards, most recently the TES ICT Visionary in Education, he also has a worldwide reputation for IT and consultancy. He still teaches IT and is able to pull on his extensive network to share knowledge and provide pupils with unique insights into the world of technology. Recently a class studying future homes and smart technology were treated to a personal workshop via Skype with the inventor of Smart Rings.

Father of two young boys, he's made a good impression on parents; 'I find the head teacher extremely amiable and approachable,' we were told. After our visit, we agree. Popular with pupils, too; 'a lot of the boys were very pleased when Dan Roberts was selected for the job.' With his passion and expertise for technology (he even runs his own blog posting on learning, technology and leadership), he is guiding the school to the next level, making it more than just a traditional boys' grammar school. Parents are pleased with this new direction. 'The school is constantly evolving and embraces technology which I see as extremely positive, leaving the boys both socially and academically ready to move on to the next stage of their lives.'

Academic matters: In 2018, at A level, 55 per cent A*-B, 29 per cent A*/A grades. At GCSE, 51 per cent A*-A/9-7 grades. Consistently in top 200 schools for A level total point score. Some girls join the sixth form and 26 A level subjects are offered, with more available from local schools in the consortium (Notre Dame, St Boniface and Eggbuckland). One language is compulsory at GCSE after an opportunity to try them all (French, Spanish, German, Mandarin and Latin) in year 7. All three science subjects are also compulsory at GCSE. Everyone takes non-exam courses in RS and PSHE.

Science and maths are the strongest subjects and the school's reputation for this is well known locally. And nationally, they have been in the finals of the Big Bang science and engineering competition for the last two years. Prospective sixth form pupils hoping to specialise in these subjects make a beeline for DHSB. Other popular subjects with equally impressive results are engineering and business studies. Psychology also growing in popularity.

The learning support department is housed in a small cottage on the school campus that provides a suitably calm environment for anyone needing extra help. The school can support pupils with dyslexia and dyscalculia plus those diagnosed with autism spectrum disorders. All teaching staff are given ongoing training plus there is a SENCo, a counsellor and six teaching assistants in the learning support department. Also available at the school but provided by the LA is a communication interaction team, an educational psychology service and a sensory service for children with visual or hearing needs. The school has a SEND webpage with a whole range of resources and information for parents and pupils, and one parent told us, 'I particularly like the openness of the school to support different areas of children's development. The transparency of available sources ensures that there is no stigma in asking for help.'

Games, options, the arts: Good reputation for sport and plenty of options so there really is something for everyone. Football, rugby, athletics, cricket, fencing, rowing, cross-country, badminton, swimming. table-tennis, gymnastics and even American football. Basketball is particularly popular and successful; some pupils play for the Plymouth Raiders. Ultimate frisbee is another top sport and they are currently the national champions. Successes at rugby and football and some pupils have gone on to play at national levels. Other recent success stories include a European U17 hurdles champion and a 2012 Olympic swimmer. For a city school there's plenty of space and facilities; rugby fields, a cricket pitch, a cross-country route, hard courts, Astroturf, a new sports hall and a fully equipped gym.

For the arty types, there's a newly decorated drama studio, brighter now; apparently the old blackened version was 'scary'. Regular productions are performed in the excellent theatre with tiered seating for 300. In the last few years the school has produced Macbeth and Romeo and Juliet plus musical performances of Joseph and the Amazing Technicolour Dreamcoat, The Wizard of Oz, Bugsy Malone and Guys and Dolls. These large productions are often run in collaboration with girls from partner schools. There are also three termly musical concerts and plenty of after-school activities including school orchestra, swing band, choir and rock club. Music is based in a small cottage on site, which includes a classroom with Apple Macs, a recording studio and individual practice rooms. Art is in the main building and standards on display were good; interesting collages of local landmarks as well as some portraits. Good DT facilities, 3D printer, lathes, CAD, plus engineering software and product design equipment.

Extracurricular clubs are run during lunchtimes as many have long bus journeys home. A great variety of activities including table tennis, circus skills, philosophy, photography, bands, investor challenge, trampolining, street surfing, Chinese and Young Enterprise club. Lots of engineering activities including one dedicated to remote controlled 4x4 vehicles. The Ten Tors challenge and DofE awards are increasingly popular and the school has strong links with the local air training corps.

Plenty of trips too. Year 7s get started straight away with a week of bushcraft, camping and survival, plus every year has an enrichment week in the summer and a challenge week in the winter. Boys can go surfing and camping in Cornwall, on residentials in France or paddle boarding, caving, canoeing; the list is endless and adventurous. There's also an annual ski trip, sports tours and language exchanges (the Mandarin class was off to China). One parent commented, 'DHSB offers many opportunities so that different subject areas and outside interests can be explored. In year 7 my son took part in the Christmas show and the band performance. This year he is going on a school trip to Italy to visit, amongst other things, the Lamborghini museum.'

Background and atmosphere: Founded in 1896, DHSB moved to its present site in 1945. The main building is a huge grey stone grade 2 listed building, which served as a prison during the Napoleonic wars and as a hospital during WW2. At the back of the school runs the colonnade (46 archways in total, we were told) overlooking the Astroturf, hard courts and playing fields below. On the second floor, classrooms open out onto a wide walkway balcony above the colonnade. Inside, it's spacious; high ceilings and wide corridors. And grey with a hefty amount of blue paint everywhere else. Basic and functional, no soft touches, very much a boys' school.

However, the new library (the learning commons) was a pleasant surprise, colourful and modern. There are workstations and study benches made of whiteboard wipeable tops ('the best bit', boys told us). All have orange USB ports or Mac chromebooks. The reading area is sectioned off with bookshelves and covered in fake grass and beanbags. Upstairs is a quiet study area, all fitted out in same modern style, with a small canteen on hand next door.

Sixth formers have their own area, renovated in the same style and design as the library, and their own canteen. All the canteens on site are called Refuel and the pupils we spoke to were very happy with the food. Parents are not so pleased: they believe the long queues for the popular food is steering their boys towards the more unhealthy fast-food options. Possibly.

Pastoral care, well-being and discipline: 'The pupils' polite and courteous behaviour is very impressive,' parents said. The boys we met were well mannered and proud of their school. The head has had a recent overhaul of the rules and has made things a little stricter. The focus has been on very low level disruption, which had never been monitored before, and after three offences, it's detention. Although this has seemed a little harsh or unfair to some, it has cut the number of higher-level incidents to almost zero. However, one parent suggested, 'I wonder if better communication about discipline might help parents and boys so the perceived disparity is minimised?' Good idea.

The head is keen to give pupils plenty of leadership opportunities. Sixth form girls are encouraged to challenge boys and give the younger boys female role models too. There are peer mentors from year 9, subject ambassadors, prefects, house leaders, digital leaders and eco-leaders, to name but a few. One parent told us, 'I can see both my boys developing into more confident young men with each day that passes.'

Pastoral care is good and pupils have access to a counsellor in the learning support department plus the school nurse. As well as tutors, teachers, mentors and peers for support, pupils have information, advice and guidance lessons led by tutors and external speakers. There is also a dedicated family support adviser and a support link page on the website for families and pupils.

Pupils and parents: Pupils travel from within a 750 square mile catchment area. A local bus company is used by all three Plymouth grammars. Some pupils come from as far as Okehampton, Truro or Beesands, others are local city boys. Parents told us, 'I find the communication at the school excellent. We are constantly kept in the loop with text, email and Twitter.' To improve the communication further, the school has recently added educational workshops for parents. Recent topics have been 'How a teenage brain works' and 'How the boys use Google apps.' Parents have also been offered training on the new homework platform, designed and built by the head.

Entrance: Admission tests include multiple choice English and maths papers plus an internally set DHSB English paper (testing composition skills).

Once accepted, pupils are given transition projects to work on at home and then in groups on the induction days. One parent told us, 'The boys thoroughly enjoyed the induction days and came home extremely excited at the prospect of joining the school.' Another added, 'The year 7 bushcraft week away is also a great way for the boys to bond.'

Sixth form entry requires a minimum average of six points in each of their best eight GCSE subjects, and at least a 5 grade in both English language and maths. Approximately 20 students from other schools join at sixth form, around 15 per cent of the intake. Girls are recommended to apply in the first instance to DHSB partner girls' or coeducational schools.

Exit: The majority – around two-thirds – stays on for A levels. Around 85 per cent of sixth formers go straight on to university, with four Oxbridge places in 2018 and four medics. DHSB continues to support gap year students in their applications the year after they leave. South west universities are popular – Exeter, Plymouth, Bristol, UWE, Bath. Generous sponsorship from Engineers' Employers' Federation and BAE Systems results in large number heading into engineering and science courses.

Remarks: Built on traditional foundations, this boys' city grammar school has a great reputation for science and engineering. With his own passion for science, and expertise in IT, the head has been building on this. There are now so many more opportunities for the boys; by the time they leave they are not just academically wise, but worldly too.

The Downs Malvern

Linked with Malvern College

D

Brockhill Road, Colwall, Malvern, Worcestershire WR13 6EY

Ages 2–13 **Pupils** 260 (two-thirds boys) **Boarders** 51 full, 10 flexi (from year 3) **C of E**

Fees: Day £7,107 – £17,076; Boarding £12,882 – £22,602 pa

01684 544104
www.thedownsmalvern.org.uk

Head: Since 2009, Alastair (known to everyone as Sam) Cook. Previously head of Pembroke House in Gilgil, Kenya, he is a graduate from Westminster College, Oxford. There is something of the gentleman's club about his study. The comfortable chairs, old school photos and stirring mountain landscapes speak of a man and school at ease with the world. Alastair Cook certainly is that and much more. He has energetically meshed three schools (The Downs merged with Malvern College Prep in 2008) together into a now seamless unit, worked on relationships with Malvern College to mutual benefit and made himself much respected and loved by parents and the children whom he places firmly at the centre of everything. He teaches, does sport with the pre-preps and runs a swimming club. 'He is always around when the children arrive, there with his dog, at matches, just all the time', said one parent. He knows all the children, even those who have just arrived. 'You would never worry about approaching him over anything', said a mother.

Entrance: Non-selective – can support all but those with serious learning difficulties. Informal observations and interviews on taster days, combined with discussions with parents, lead to offers. Depending on the age of the child, may also request information from the current school.

Exit: More or less all take the common entrance and most go on to Malvern College – there is a strong flow through in curriculum terms. A smattering goes to other local schools or further flung public schools. If there is a problem academically, parents are told at an early stage and alternative plans discussed.

Remarks: The Downs has the feel of a much loved school with bucketloads of unspoilt charm that you find in the very best rural preps. It spreads over the Malvern Hills and the only downside we could see were the narrow roads and precipitous bends on the way there. There is a flexibility and breadth about everything. Pick up times are to suit parents not the school, boarding can be when families need it – it is all about individuals growing up in a community that cares, and for which families too care and show respect. The curriculum has all the academic rigour combined with creativity that you would hope for – strong science in suitably equipped labs ('We get to use proper chemicals,' one 10 year old was bursting to tell us), French is all the way through with Spanish or German in years 7 and 8, Latin from year 6, art has its own kiln and there is masses of music.

All of this spills out of the classroom into the rich extracurricular programme that runs at lunchtimes, after school and on Saturday mornings (not compulsory but much loved by parents). There is sport galore (including girls' soccer), gardening, chess, Chinese, pottery, cookery, world history, computer coding, current affairs, science in the news, touch typing, debating, Scrabble, endless drama and music and so it goes on. Perhaps what best sums up the timeless charm is the little steam train that runs through the school grounds. The oldest miniature light railway in the world, this is a serious educational tool. The children learn to drive and maintain it. The wholesome environment too is fully utilised – the children are outside as much as possible, soaking in subliminally, we would like to think, the awe-inspiring rolling landscape, but also using it for serious geographical and scientific measurements and as inspiration for their artwork, which is of a seriously high standard.

There are plenty of links with the world outside the school. Its own first rate facilities are supplemented by some use of Malvern College – its theatre, chapel, swimming pool, for instance. The choir sings locally and the school hosts national music and art events for other schools. About three-quarters of the boarders are from overseas (11 different countries when we visited) and parents commented on how well the school integrates the day pupils and the boarders. The school offers excellent preparation to overseas boarders wanting to brush up their English and understand British values ready for senior school. There are fun and cosily low key events organised at weekends for boarders – a visit to the circus, theme parks, ice skating, Christmas shopping. The flexi-boarding is popular with parents who want to give their children a taste of boarding before the full immersion as they move on to Malvern College. The boarding accommodation is in The Warren – rightly named as it rambles round the centre of the original school buildings, not smart but very homely.

Parents say the teachers are very quick to pick up on any individual needs and that they take huge pride in the children's small achievements. 'Go to Friday assemblies', parents urged us. 'Everyone is invited and we really get a sense of how much the school praises the children, how the discipline works in practice, the clear moral message the school is getting across, and we can see the opportunities all the children get for developing confidence through public speaking.'

The head told us, 'care comes first and then education'. Parents and children praised the flexibility and common sense – no rigid rules that stunt children. Fairness is the basis of the approach to discipline. Teachers want to find out what the situation actually is by spending time talking to children involved in any difficulties – and then it is a quiet word and a real attempt to equip the children with the skills to move forward.

'So what do you give school out of 10?', we asked one boy. 'Ten+++', he said with a big grin.

The Downs Preparatory School

Charlton House, Wraxall, Bristol BS48 1PF

Ages 6m–13 **Pupils** 282

Fees: £10,845 – £16,425 pa

01275 852008
www.thedownsschool.co.uk

Headmaster: Since 2001, Marcus Gunn MA (Ed) PGCE BA IAPS. Originally from Yorkshire, Gunn studied history at Liverpool before qualifying as a teacher. A keen windsurfer, he taught history and games for several years and went on to study a masters in education and leadership. Lives in the school grounds with wife Valerie, the 'glue that holds it all together.'

Parents have nothing but praise. One told us, 'he clearly likes children...He wants them to do well and he certainly wants them all to be happy.' Another added, '[He is] not afraid to get his hands dirty and to reach the children on their level'.

Working closely with Gunn is head of pre-prep, Heather Fulton. Originally from New Zealand, her previous post was head of kindergarten at DUCKS, Dulwich College. Like Marcus, she is an independent schools inspector.

Entrance: The only independent prep school in the area. Now has its own nursery and pre-school from 6 months.

Admission by application and informal assessment. Inclusive, but restricted by numbers, and at least one or two children per year won't be accepted if needs cannot be met by learning support. Scholarships available at year 4 entry, mainly for academic potential, and can equate up to 25 per cent of the day pupil fee. Means-tested bursaries also available.

On entry, each child is allocated a guide to help them settle. Parents told us, 'The settling in process is smooth and anxiety free. Cleverly the school invites new mums to coffee on the first morning straight after drop off...the children are quickly distracted by cheerful classrooms, pet guinea pigs and smiley teachers.'

Exit: Almost all stay on until 13; at most one pupil a year leaves at 11. 'They are prepared for the rigours of year 9 both academically and emotionally,' parents told us. There are also privileges; on our visit, our year 8 guides showed us a 'secret' door under the oak panelled stairs. Stone steps lead down to a cellar and their very own common room equipped with sofas, TV, music system, mini pool table and a toaster.

Only school in the area that follows the common entrance syllabus. Families are supported in choosing the right school, so it is rare that pupils do not get accepted by their first choice. Many gain scholarships. In 2018, over half of leavers went on to Clifton College. The majority of the remainder went to Bristol Grammar School, Marlborough and Sherborne.

Remarks: The long drive to the school, the stunning setting, the grand entrance with huge fireplace and oak panelled walls (even more amazing with Christmas decorations); it's easy to see why parents are bowled over immediately. This is a family run prep school that makes the most of the outdoors – overalls and wellies for outside play, and lessons in the forest school. 'Our children are happy there, and safe, and cared for, and challenged,' parents enthused. 'It is a haven in which all of my very different children are thriving and learning and playing in a culture of freedom and inclusivity that we as a family are delighted to be a part of.'

Situated in Charlton House, a magnificent Victorian mansion surrounded by 60 acres of idyllic parkland, it's just five miles from Bristol. 'Traditional' but 'progressive,' claims the head. Old fashioned-expectations are the norm; standing when an adult enters the room, shaking teachers' hands at the end of the day, good eye contact. Old fashioned play too; building dens, playing with skipping ropes, making daisy chains. One parent confided, 'Mr Gunn once told me that if the year 8 children didn't still want to go outside and build dens then he wasn't doing his job properly. Children are encouraged to be children.' The school is progressive because they are 'brave enough to be independent and go off curriculum,' the head told us. In addition to the curriculum, they teach theory of music, history of art, etiquette and even accountancy. Life and leadership skills are taught on camping trips.

Recently, well-being has been top priority and the very full curriculum has been reviewed. Up until 2004 The Downs was a boarding school and in some ways it is still run like one – long days and sports every Saturday. Breakfast is from 7.30am and the day finishes at 5pm (clubs until 6pm). Supper is available until 7pm. To ease the pressure and allow pupils to enjoy home life, sports fixtures on Wednesdays have been reduced as well as homework for younger pupils. And. One parent told us, 'The Downs is a lifestyle choice...from year 3 they will be joining in Saturday sports, which can be at any time of day...If you are a family that likes to go away at weekends, it will not fit that lifestyle. '

Academically, pupils do very well. Two classes in each year group and class sizes average 15. Science is popular and practical. Other subjects like history also use this tack – each year group has a history day, Vikings or Normans, for example. Pupils dress up, make weapons, re-enact battles. French is taught from reception, Spanish from year 6, and Latin is available to those hoping to go to Winchester College. Parents say, 'Some of the teaching is excellent (biology and chemistry, humanities, English, in particular), some is not so excellent but none of it is poor. All the teachers are very approachable, and as it is such a small school all teachers know all of the children... it's like a big family.'

Classrooms are in Charlton House, and also in the recently built new block. 'Much warmer!' pupils told us. Interactive whiteboards in all classrooms, and two ICT suites with touchscreen computers. IT is taught from reception. There is a strict no mobile phone policy. One parent felt that technology could be improved, 'The school has been slow in embracing new technology that can help children with learning differences... it's getting better.'

Around 22 children need extra support from the learning support team, mainly for dyslexia, dyscalculia and dyspraxia. 'The learning support department is lovely, very kind and supportive. Help with maths is superb,' one parent told us. Head of the department used to be head of learning support at Clifton College. Team members are all specialist trained; there is an in-house speech therapist and an occupational therapist. As well as one-to-one therapy, they also provide informal group therapy in the form of social interaction role-play sessions, aimed at pupils with behavioural management issues. One parent told us their story: '[My son] is a very intelligent child with very complex learning difficulties who felt he was useless....Within one term [he] had transformed into a confident child who began to love school.' The school also challenges talented children (scholars) – they do well here; results are impressive all round.

Sport is a big part of life. Great facilities. Two Astroturf pitches, rugby and cricket pitches, sports hall with cricket nets, an outdoor heated swimming pool, two netball courts and nine tennis courts. Remarkable success for such a small school. One parent explained, '[My daughter] had only seven girls [in her year] but made it to the netball nationals in years 6 and 8, and hockey nationals in year 6, an amazing achievement.' Rugby and hockey are the main players and there was a recent tour to Edinburgh. Many of the sports are played at national level, including athletics. All pupils from year 3 play in a team. Girls can play rugby and cricket. For non-sporty children there is The Downs Award Scheme, offering alternatives like caving, climbing or orienteering.

Good art facilities including a pottery and textiles room. The parents' association sponsors an annual arts week, inviting artists in for workshops. The Christmas pre-prep production of the Nutcracker Nativity was in full flight on our visit, and year 8s were busy preparing for the talent show auditions (the school now has a new drama studio). Other recent productions include Bugsy Malone and Porridge, a 'nursery-noir' by year 6, 'Goldie Lox and friends do organised crime.' Every year group performs a production annually. All productions take place in the school's theatre. Dance is on offer: jazz, tap and ballet tuition, plus Bollywood and street dance after school clubs. Some 85 per cent play a musical instrument. In year 3, pupils learn the violin, ukhele and clarinet. In year 4, trumpet, violin and fife. Years 4 and 6 study the theory of music, taking Associated Board exams. Choir is compulsory. There are four choirs plus a soul band. Formal and informal concerts allow everybody to 'have their moment of glory.'

As expected of any traditional school, there is a house system, and each regularly raises money for charity. The eco-committee has made a big impact with its 'switch off fortnight' and is planning a 'waste week' and a 'water week.' The school council is busy 'making small changes that make a big difference'; pre-prep would like mangos and strawberries in fruit snacks, and the preps would like a pot in each classroom with spare ink cartridges. Parents told us the school allows 'them to explore within and without their comfort zones, always encouraging adventurous decisions and offering praise when due.' Annual exchange trips to France and Spain, geography trips, camping trips and the usual local visits to museums and galleries.

Definitely no complaints about the pastoral care. Matrons, led by a qualified nurse, 'are absolutely fantastic. [The nurse] knows all the children well and is happy to give plenty of hugs and TLC whenever required.' Another told us, 'Our eldest son has a severe nut allergy...The school was brilliant; it wasn't a problem for them at all.' Pastoral care is stretched to give parents support too. Head of pre-prep regularly sets up coffee mornings and organises seminars, most recently on the teenage brain and e-safety. The school has an open door policy for parents and pupils alike.

There is so much on offer at The Downs School it's hard to see how they fit it all in. But they do, and the children thrive on it; 'They love the longer days, the more varied education, eg match teas and socialising with opposition after sports matches, the vast music opportunities, informal and formal concerts, and the clubs available.' The Downs is a school where tradition is important, but not to the point where outdated thinking holds back development. It's a school that challenges academically, but never loses sight of the fact that children need to play, and enjoy to learn. And where the parents love school life as much as the pupils.

Downside School

Stratton-on-the-Fosse, Bath, Somerset BA3 4RJ

Ages 11-18 **Pupils** 342 **Sixth form** 138 **Boarders** 268 full, 3 flexi **RC**

Fees: Fees: Day £16,242 – £19,251; Boarding £25,236 – £33,861 pa

01761 235103
www.downside.co.uk

Head: Since September 2018, Andrew Hobbs, previously acting head. Read classics at Magdalene College, Cambridge, where he also gained a rugby blue. Taught classics at Hurstpierpoint; head of classics and then housemaster at Canford; joined Downside as deputy head in 2008, becoming acting head in January 2018.

Academic matters: Results have come on leaps and bounds in recent years. In 2018, 35 per cent A*/A and 64 per cent A*/B at A level and 48 per cent A*-A/9-7 at GCSE. Usual subjects at A level, plus business studies, economics, history of art, PE, photography and psychology. History department offers the Pre-U – head of history says the qualification involves 'good, old-fashioned essay writing' and enables youngsters to study topics such as monasticism in the 9th century and the Gregorian reforms of the 11th century as well as more recent fare.

Most pupils take 11 GCSEs. English, maths and RS are compulsory and all are encouraged to take at least one language, a humanity and a creative subject. French, German and Spanish are the main languages, but Italian, Mandarin, Russian, Polish, Chinese, Portuguese and Arabic can be arranged. Most pupils do three separate sciences. Computer science on offer too. Director of studies says the school believes in setting 'ambitious realistic targets' and tracks and monitors pupils' progress throughout. School's intake is 'selective, but broadly mixed ability' and its value added scores are particularly impressive. Maximum class sizes of 20 up to GCSE and 16 in the sixth form but classes are often smaller than this. Pupils are set in maths and science up to GCSE. A variety of academic societies, including the Knowles, where Oxbridge candidates present their own research papers.

Learning support department now in the heart of the school (it used to be housed in a separate block). Support given to 30 pupils, either one-to-one or in small groups, but department also offers drop-in sessions for anyone needing additional help. EAL is also available.

Games, options, the arts: With 500 acres of grounds to run around in, fresh air and exercise are an integral part of Downside life. As well as rugby, hockey, football and cricket for the boys and hockey, netball, tennis and rounders for the girls, there's a wealth of other sports on offer, including aerobics, athletics, badminton, cross-country, fencing, squash and swimming. Pupils have three games sessions during the week, plus matches on Saturday afternoons, but many do far more than this. Sixth formers get just as much sport as their younger counterparts – everything from boxercise to circuit training. When we visited, a group of older girls were in the middle of an energetic zumba class, music blasting across the courtyard. Sports facilities include an indoor pool (donated by a family whose son tragically died in a Naples swimming accident in 1925), rugby pitches galore, football pitches, cricket squares, Astroturf, a glorious 1930s sports pavilion and a sports centre with a weights room and fitness suite.

Parents report that the music is outstanding. Half the pupils have instrumental lessons and there's a multitude of orchestras, chamber ensembles and choirs (the Schola Cantorum is the oldest Roman Catholic school choir in the UK), along with jazz ensembles, a barbershop ensemble, pipe band, brass band, even an open-mic night. Art department has been refurbished and is equipped with Macs, photographic studio, 3D printers and glass making facilities. Printmaking, textiles, oil painting, landscapes, portraits, graphic illustration, photography, fused glass – you name it, Downside does it. 'I'm a firm believer that everybody is creative in some shape or form,' the dynamic head of art told us. School has strong links with Hauser & Wirth Somerset, the contemporary art gallery in nearby Bruton. Busy drama department. School puts on a whole school play and musical every year, plus a host of other performances in refurbished 500-seat theatre. Refurbished performing arts centre with recording studio, editing suite and 18 practice rooms circling around a 500-seat performance space is inspiring musicians, dancers and thespians.

All year 9s are expected to do CCF for at least part of the year. Many carry on while others opt for D of E and Ten Tors expeditions across Dartmoor. Action-packed co-curricular programme includes chess, astronomy, Model United Nations, Young Enterprise, sewing, contemporary dance and fly fishing.

Boarding: Most pupils board – boarding is 'part of our USP'. Four boys' houses and two girls' houses. All junior boys (years 7, 8 and 9) start in Powell, a boarding house located in the main school, with open plan dorms and bunk beds for the youngest and a homely kitchen where boys get to cook (and eat) cookies, crumbles and pizza. A parent said some of the boys' dorms could do with a bit of updating but her children think they are fine as they are. Junior girls go straight into Isabella or Caverel, the two girls' boarding houses.

House staff are adept at helping children to settle in. 'No one gets lost here,' we were told. A housemother reckons that Ovaltine, warm wheat bags (the modern answer to hot water bottles) and talking helps to stave off homesickness. Pupils are kept occupied at weekends with lots of trips and inter-house competitions. Up until the sixth form pupils hand in their mobile phones at night so they get a good night's sleep and aren't distracted by Facebook, Snapchat and the like. Parents thoroughly approve.

Although technically doesn't offer weekly boarding, boarders can go home on any bar four of the weekends each term. These are 'closed' weekends, the ones immediately after or just before holidays or half terms. Otherwise, pupils are welcome to go home after they have completed their sports involvement on a Saturday afternoon, which is some time between 3:30pm and 5:30pm, on other weekends. They then return to school for the Sunday evening.

Background and atmosphere: The magnificent Downside Abbey adjoins the school and is visible for miles across the rolling Somerset landscape. The school has been on its present site in the village of Stratton-on-the-Fosse since 1814 but dates back more than 400 years. The Benedictine community of St Gregory the Great was founded in France in 1606 by English and Welsh monks living in exile because of the penal laws in England against Catholics. By 1617 English Catholics were sending their boys across the Channel to be educated there. When it became safe in the early 19th century for Catholics to provide education once more the school moved to England. Downside's monastic community (currently 12 monks, some of whom teach) has been in residence for 200 years. Members of an apostolic community from Chile – the Manquehue Apostolic Movement – have a base at Downside too. The school went co-ed in 2005 and the boy/girl ratio is now 60:40.

Downside has a rich cultural heritage. The abbey's Monastic Library, housed in a 1970s building, is one of the largest private libraries in the UK and has a collection of more than 400,000 books and papers, many of them very rare. 'It's like having an Oxford college library on the campus.' The school's atmosphere and setting are traditional, with historic corridors (the science corridor is lined with pictures of old boys who died in the First and Second World Wars), parquet floors and pupils hurrying to classes in their eye-catching uniform. Worn by all (including the sixth form), the uniform comprises mid-length kilts and red or black jumpers for the girls and black jackets and pinstriped trousers for the boys. The pupils' maroon and gold game kit is particularly jazzy – good for spotting players on the games pitch.

School food much improved following the appointment of new caterers (manager formerly worked for River Cottage Canteen Bristol, part of Hugh Fearnley-Whittingstall's culinary empire). A stylish café serves cappuccinos, cookies and toasties during breaks and evenings. Fifty per cent of teaching staff live on site or in Stratton-on-the-Fosse.

Pastoral care, well-being and discipline: A strong sense of spirituality pervades the school. Around 80 per cent of pupils are Catholic but children from other Christian denominations are welcome. School has a distinctively Catholic and Benedictine character and incorporates the eight aspects of a Benedictine education – welcome, listening, reverence and humility, teaching and learning, personal discipline, concern for the individual, building communion and stewardship of gifts.

School's most recent inspection report commented that 'pupils of all faiths and none possess an inner confidence, and a strong sense of their own identity.' Everyone is expected to participate in the school's spiritual life. Sunday mass in the abbey is compulsory, as is hymn practice on Friday afternoon. While Downside's monastic community prays formally six times a day, each boarding house has prayers in the morning and evening. School chaplains visit each house at least once a week and the school chapel is always open for those who want to go and pray. A third of the school takes part in voluntary prayer groups but it's very much up to individuals. A father with two children at Downside emphasised that religion isn't forced on the pupils – 'it's a gentle, subtle part of what is there,' he said. A mother we spoke to praised the school's ethos. 'There's an emphasis on the whole person,' she said. 'Everyone is made to feel welcome.'

Excellent pastoral care and tolerance for the individual produces happy children. Each pupil has a tutor to oversee academic matters and there's a raft of people to talk to if they encounter problems – tutors, housemasters and housemistresses, housemothers, the chaplaincy team, health centre staff and a school counsellor who visits twice a week. Pupils generally well behaved. Policies on smoking, alcohol and drugs are very clearly spelled out. Smokers are enrolled on a smoking cessation programme in the health centre. 'Responsible' drinking permitted at the sixth form bar.

Sixth form has its own study centre (very quiet and studious when we visited). UCAS coordinator guides pupils through their university entrance. Pupils are prepared well for life after school via spiritual, moral, social and cultural education (SMSC) – topics covered include how to set up a bank account, relationships, even mortgages. School also runs themed weeks on issues like e-safety, alcohol and drugs.

The Independent Inquiry into Child Sexual Abuse, which looked closely into historical, and relatively recent, cases of abuse by monks at Downside, and at the Benedictine practices which appear to have made them more likely, came to the damning conclusion: 'the evidence that we have seen and heard during the course of our Inquiry, outlined above, indicates that a number of systemic child protection and safeguarding challenges remain at Downside to this day'. It mentioned in particular that the school has still not become separate and independent from the monastery, 10 years after this was recommended. If/when you visit, it might be worth asking questions because, at the very least, whilst pupils may well remain unaffected, these will almost certainly have proved a distraction internally.

Downside have been admirably open on their website about the difficulties that they have faced with safeguarding, and have had an encouraging ISI inspection report on the improvements that they have made. We await a substantial reform of the governing body, to introduce the strong independent voices that it lacks at the time of writing.

Pupils and parents: Boarders (28 per cent international students) come from all over. At the beginning and end of term school buses ferry pupils to London, airports and local stations. Day pupils tend to live within a 30-minure drive – places like Shepton Mallet, Frome, Bruton and the Chew Valley.

School says that while some of the pupils are from very privileged backgrounds no one is materialistic or showy. A parent with three boys at the school concurred. 'A lot of schools are quite flash these days,' she said. 'Downside isn't like that at all. The pupils are very well mannered and the school gives them really good values. They know what is right and what is wrong.' An old boy with two children at the school told us that while his daughter was 'almost surgically attached' to her mobile phone before moving to Downside she hardly uses it these days. 'The school is very good at keeping them busy,' he says. 'In my day Sunday was a quiet day but now there are coaches going off all over the place.'

Alumni (known as Old Gregorians) include writer and journalist Auberon Waugh, hotelier Rocco Forte, scriptwriter Peter Morgan and interior designer David Mlinaric. You can spot an Old Gregorian at a dinner party, we were told, because they will always offer to do the washing up afterwards. 'It's that blend of good manners and service,' explained the director of pastoral care.

Entrance: Pupils must be able to cope with the school's 'traditional academic curriculum.' At 11+ and 12+ entrance is via the Downside Junior Assessment Test (English and maths), plus reports and references from pupil's current school. At 13+ most applicants take CE (required mark of 50 per cent but the average is 65 per cent). At 16+ pupils sit tests in subjects they are planning to take at A level. B/6 grades at GCSE required (A/7s for maths and the sciences if they are planning to study these at A level).

Quite exceptionally helpful and welcoming admissions staff. A real sense – not found everywhere – that they will take the time and care each applicant deserves.

Exit: Some leave after GCSE (a quarter in 2018), usually for day schools or to study vocational subjects. At 18 the vast majority head to university (gap years not so popular these days). Cardiff, Cardiff Met, Edinburgh, Exeter, Manchester and Oxford Brookes are favourite destinations. Two to Oxbridge in 2018 and three to do medicine.

Money matters: A 'substantial number' of scholarships and exhibitions are available (the number and size are at the discretion of the head). Means-tested bursaries, discounts of 2.5 per cent for children of Old Gregorians and 10 per cent for siblings.

Remarks: A boarding school with a strong moral compass. Downside is a great choice for Catholics and those seeking strong spiritual direction in a school. Its unpretentiousness, happy atmosphere and keen academic focus give pupils the chance to concentrate on acquiring their own intellectual and spiritual toolkit and to grow up in their own time. However, as the IICAS report concluded, there remain safeguarding challenges here.

Dumpton School

Deans Grove House, Deans Grove, Wimborne, Dorset BH21 7AF

Ages 2–13 **Pupils** 320

Fees: £8,844 – £15,849 pa

01202 883818
www.dumpton.com

Headmaster: Since 2005, Andrew Browning BSc PGCE MA CChem MRSC (50s). Educated at Farnborough Grammar, read chemistry at Southampton University, followed by PGCE and masters in education at the Open University, the latter whilst teaching at Canford. He spent 22 years there, progressing to head of chemistry, housemaster and finally registrar – 'useful experience in advising parents on choice of secondary,' he says. Along the way he won the prestigious Salter's Prize for the teaching of chemistry. He still relishes teaching the subject at Dumpton (he spends about a third of the week teaching), as well as coaching CE and scholarship pupils and running the school's beekeeping club.

He lives and breathes Dumpton. He and his family live in the school's main building. His wife Jo, an experienced teacher with eight years at Castle Court under her belt, runs the mothers' and toddlers' group, acts as child protection officer, sorts out pastoral niggles and sometimes steps in as a supply teacher. They have two children.

Retiring in July 2019. His successor will be Christian Saenger, currently deputy head (academic) at York House School in Herts. He is married to Hattie and they have a young daughter.

Entrance: Most join Dumpton nursery, often via toddlers' group, but pupils can come at any time, provided space – though usually not much. No test, but academic criteria apply after pre-prep and a good record is expected. Pupils are mainly local, but such is the school's reputation that local can mean as far as Hampshire or north Dorset and Wiltshire.

Exit: Canford is currently top of the pops, followed by Clayesmore and Bryanston, then Talbot Health and Poole grammars, plus a smattering of the big names. A minority opt for boarding or single sex schools. Many parents are reluctant to let children miss 'that special last year' at 13 and the dazzling record of scholarships (academic, sport, art and music) to top independent schools. Annual scholarships often reach 20 (25 in 2018).

Remarks: School moved from Kent (where they were at Dumpton House) to Dorset during the Second World War, and then had a peripatetic trip round local stately homes, arriving at Dean's Grove (previously the headquarters of the Dalgety piggery) from Gaunt's House in 1986. Red-brick classrooms, labs, barn-like art room (at the top of a spectacular outdoor spiral staircase), DT and food tech dept and sports hall (not in its first youth) cluster round the pleasant and spacious main house in a series of courtyards.

A parent of three told us that the teaching staff are 'brilliant, really committed and inspiring', and the curriculum is demanding enough for plenty of pupils to sweep up spectacular scholarships. French is taught from the beginning of the pre-prep – by fully qualified native speakers; Latin but no Greek, proper science – taken for granted in a school run by a chemist – and plenty of technology, music and art, all backed up with theory as well as practice. Everywhere bristling with technology – several computer rooms now and interactive whiteboards et al everywhere. Some streaming, especially in scholarship years. Lessons are evidently enjoyed as well as taken seriously. Pupils have traffic light coloured pages in their homework diaries and leaving a red page open on the desk indicates to the teacher that you have not understood – a system which seems to work. No Sats but masses of careful tracking and assessment pick up anyone struggling. Lots of unobtrusive help for special needs, with a team of three to provide it.

No boarders now – every scrap of former boarding space is in use for teaching. The long school day (from 8.20am to 5.45pm for the prep section, though the younger ones do less) means that no one needs to take work home apart from some reading or at scholarship time. Prep is done after tea, except on Wednesdays, which are games afternoons – so comparatively little games at weekends. Loads of activities packed in as well as prep after tea and at lunchtime. Head is an eco enthusiast, so an enchanting eco trail, complete with dipping ponds, pontoons, plentiful but tasteful information points and a BBQ and camping site for summer sleepovers. Lots of awards for this project mean real scientists work with pupils, encouraged by input from the Ecology and Hydrology Centre at Winfrith. Splendid all weather pitches, fantastic play areas with tempting climbing structures, a real small boat, a run for the family/school dog and multiple seating and shelter areas (enjoyed in summer outdoor classes and by waiting mums). The newly covered pool is not quite so ecological but justified by a footprint less than that of frequent bus trips to Wimborne.

The bursar plays an unusually pivotal role in this family orientated community. He followed head from Canford, where he had run the catering, and has since become not only a planner and designer of facilities but also a sports coach.

One of only three negative school rules forbids crossing the road without an adult – the others forbid swearing and making others unhappy. The attraction over the road is a huge cricket pitch and athletics track with a stunningly picturesque oak in the centre; has recently bought two more acres of adjoining land which will become another sports area. Sports facilities are so good that Dumpton hosts festivals in netball, rugby etc, thus upping its impressive sporty record. Every child from year 3 up was in a match somewhere the day after our visit and the pupils sweep the board in most sports locally and beyond. As one parent commented: 'Dumpton's the perfect size, small enough to have a real family atmosphere and big enough to have proper teams, plays and music.'

Music is now vibrant, since the recent restructuring of the music department. Masses of instrumental and choral work emanate from the music school and a separate hut takes the steel band (so popular that staff have one too). The comfy school hall – 'just big enough to take the prep or pre-prep all together, so we can't get any bigger' – has a seriously well-equipped stage lighting system, courtesy of the Friends of Dumpton. An extension has created a multi-purpose performing arts venue with Arts Courtyard. With all this going for it, Dumpton is generous with its support of the local community schools and clubs. Parents are welcomed into school and given chances to sample the delicious nut-free lunches and watch the children in the revamped dining area. Free choice of meals for older children and staff sit with pupils.

Tinies progress from Ducklings to Robins and Woodpeckers in the nursery (phonics from year dot) and thence to pre-prep. Boys in shorts for summer until 11 and grey trousers for winter. Girls in blue tartan skirts and all older pupils in snazzy gingham shirts or white blouses with dark blue edging. Buses to major surrounding towns. It feels like a traditional prep school but everything is bang up to date. We can't fault it.

The Elms School

Colwall, Malvern, Worcestershire WR13 6EF

Ages 3–13 **Pupils** 166 **Boarders** 27 full, 45 flexi (from 8 years) **C of E**

Fees: Day £9,270 – £19,500; Boarding £21,120 – £24,480 pa

01684 540344
www.elmsschool.co.uk

Head: Since January 2018, Chris Hattam, previously a senior housemaster at Sedbergh School, where he also taught philosophy and RE and coached rugby, cricket and hockey. Degrees from Edinburgh and Manchester; worked as a probation officer with young offenders before turning to teaching. He is married to Jess, with three children (and three spaniels).

Certainly enjoys life, throwing himself into anything he does, believing that he can't ask others in his community to do what he isn't willing to. He sees that value in giving every child the opportunity to explore their potential and be excited by what lies ahead of them. The outdoor elements of the school and giving children the chance are both close to his heart, whilst ensuring that the academic potential of each and every one is unlocked. Deep understanding of the all-encompassing remit of a boarding school for all pupils whether they board or not and how to prepare boys and girls for the next stage.

Jess, a paediatric nurse, is fully involved in all aspects of school life. Enjoys hosting the 'Tuesday lunches' with Chris for the pupils, ensuring that all the children get to enjoy lunch and social time in the headmaster's family home.

Entrance: Entrance into Montessori early years at 3, regular intake at 7 and 8. Most children from Herefordshire, Gloucestershire, Worcestershire, Monmouthshire and Powys. A few Forces families and a handful from overseas. Entry is by assessment rather than selection, and children who are intending to board can stay the night to test the waters. No scholarships but means-tested bursaries of up to 100 per cent for those 'who could benefit from what we offer'. 'We can and do get our children into leading public schools but we also support children who struggle'.

Exit: To a variety of schools eg Malvern College, Cheltenham College, Cheltenham Ladies', Radley, Marlborough, Eton, Rugby, Winchester, Wellington, Harrow, Millfield, Oundle, Shrewsbury, nearly half with scholarships.

Remarks: The oldest prep school in England, founded by Humphry Walwyn in 1614. Facing away from what passes for the main road in the village of Colwall, near Malvern, it opens out onto a site of 150 acres full of lovely green spaces and beautiful gardens. The school itself has rather the feeling of a collection of period houses that have grown together, sometimes in a slightly idiosyncratic manner. However, it is much more than its academic buildings. For a start it has enviable sports facilities – including Astroturf, games field, swimming pool, a large sports hall, stables for about 15-20 ponies (boarders can also bring their own) and a new outdoor riding arena. Sport obviously important – riding and shooting particularly so; the school has its own pistol and rifle shooting clubs. Then there is the school farm – rural studies compulsory up to and including year 7 – which boasts a prize Hereford bull as well as Gloucester Old Spots, walked by the children round the grounds, a large flock of hens and a rather lovely vegetable garden. Each year group has a plot in which it is expected to grow its own vegetables. The children clearly love their involvement in the farm and take pleasure and pride in it. And they all speak very highly of the food – beef, pork and eggs come from the farm when available.

Boarding and teaching accommodation require some modernisation. The boarding facilities are a little overcrowded, although homely and tidy. Every child in the prep school (not pre-prep) has a designated bed; there are rest periods after lunch every day. This means that day children can board when they want.

The children are genuinely charming – friendly, respectful but responsive, confident and very happy indeed; well motivated and thoroughly self disciplined – we saw groups working on their art, music and sports during break, all purposeful, focused and notably unsupervised, teachers within range if needed but leaving them to their own devices if not. There is an impressive auditorium/theatre with some good music practice spaces, a beautiful new grand piano, and good sized music classroom attached at the back. A good art room too – full of innovative, varied and careful work. Parents say their children are very happy.They appreciate the variety of activities offered and the freedom of each child to 'be a little bit eccentric' if they want to.

Relatively high fees fund a staff:pupil ratio of about 1:7. Academically sound with many long-serving staff who say relationships with children are excellent, respectful but friendly and that parents are extremely supportive. Two ICT rooms, a new teaching block including state of the art science labs, a pleasant library, not much prep as Saturday school is compulsory, and most reinforcement/prep style work is done within the classroom. Traditional curriculum includes a strong classics department. Follows a policy of moving children through classes as the need appears – the school calls this the ladder system – which can mean that the brighter sparks might spend the last two years in the top class. However, it is clear that the school is sensitive to parental concerns and in reality the majority of pupils are taught within a cohort of their own age. Groups are very small and no class is larger than 15; the smallest we saw was seven. The teaching model seems to work well and certainly destinations on exit don't point to any major hiccups.

On the whole a very traditional feel – there is something of the flavour of the Famous Five about the place – which may raise the hackles of some potential parents. Boys wear cord shorts and tweed blazers, girls wear kilts and jumpers, the children go out for a walk before breakfast and have outdoor activities every afternoon. There are no mobile phones, no cash, no sweets and no straying out of the school grounds. Chapel four times a week with visits from the local vicar and Catholic pupils taken to mass once a week. There are proper napkins at mealtimes, and grace is said. Some staff keep dogs in their classrooms and there is a 'pet palace' for the children's own rabbits and other small animals. Some parents may think it too sheltered by far, others will breathe a sigh of relief when they find it.

Weekend activities range from The Elms Tetrathlon to bugboarding to Nerf Gun War. Children might also go off geocaching in the Malvern Hills, paintballing or ice skating, or on a shopping trip to Cheltenham.

A school which wears its differences from the mainstream with pride. With its farm, fields and outdoor ethos this is a glorious place to get muddy while you learn – and somehow it manages to preserve childhood while fostering independence.

E

Exeter Cathedral School

The Chantry, Palace Gate, Exeter EX1 1HX

Ages 3–13 **Pupils** 256 **Boarders** 6 full/weekly, 54 flexi (from 8 years)

Fees: Day £7,125 – £11,877; Boarding + £7,410 (£8,985 overseas)

01392 255298
www.exetercathedralschool.co.uk

Headmaster: Since 2016, James Featherstone (30s). Previously head of lower school at Perse School, Cambridge. Studied French and Spanish at Durham, followed by a PGCE. He was a choral scholar at Durham Cathedral and later joined the choir of Jesus College, Cambridge and became part of the professional quintet at St-John-at-Hampstead, London.

Lives with his family in Hall House, the pre-prep school. Julia, his wife, teaches music part-time at ECS. Both are well-suited to this lifestyle; James is son of a headmaster so grew up in boarding schools, and Julia spent her childhood in vicarages.

To date, he has made significant improvements at ECS. Parents are impressed. 'I think he has exactly the right attitude for ECS,' one parent reported. 'A breath of fresh air,' said another. 'He is dynamic, accessible, enthusiastic and ambitious for the school with a passion for nurturing the best in all his pupils and ensuring that they understand that success is not just based on grades but being a good person too.'

Entrance: Taster days with informal assessment, plus interview with headmaster. Voice trials for choristers (boys and girls). Children may be turned away if behaviour is not up to scratch on taster day (most are given a second chance). If academic standards are not met, a place may be offered as long as a learning support plan is agreed. Mild special needs can be supported. One parent reported, 'It was very much what the school could offer them, rather than whether the [children] would assist their results. Very refreshing compared to some of the other schools!' Choristers must be above the baseline academically. Choristerships are worth 25 per cent off tuition fee; there are currently 36 choristers.

As well as taster days there are 'come and be a chorister for a day' and 'taste of boarding' sleepovers. For transition there is a tea party for new pupils and teachers. Parents said, 'We were impressed with the staff, and the general warmth of the place.' Most choose ECS as it is a natural step on from a small village primary school.

Exit: Majority stay on to 13. A head of scholarships guides families through the process. Destinations include Sherborne, King's College Taunton, Taunton School, Exeter School, Maynard, Torquay Boys Grammar and Blundells.

Former pupils include 14th century theologian Boniface; more recently, bass player Orlando le Fleming; Chris Martin, lead singer of Coldplay (who apparently once said, 'ECS is where it all began'); Hampshire CCC manager, Giles White and Dave Webb, ENO.

Remarks: Founded in the 12th century as a choir school, ECS is one of 35 choral schools in the UK, and the only independent boarding school in Exeter. As one parent put it, 'ECS is a rare kind of school,' and we agree. The Chantry, the prep school, and Hall House, the pre-prep, are on either side of the magnificent Exeter cathedral; an impressive backdrop to learning by anyone's standards. Although the multiple sites mean there is a lot of to-ing and fro-ing, it also means that the school feels very much part of the city. In fact one of the opening clips on the local news shows a line of happy children in royal blue tartans and sunny sweatshirts snaking across Cathedral Green.

Hall House is a former canonry and houses reception up to year 2. Securely enclosed by ancient Roman walls (and keypads), it is welcoming, bright and playful. A new 'spongey' all-weather playground separates the main building from the nursery, which was purpose-built in 2015. This is a fantastic area, free-flowing from inside to out. From the cosy keyworker areas and rooms, little ones (all in uniform) can play under awning in an area that leads to the shared playground one end, and the Woodland Garden at the other. This is a child's dream. Centred around a huge hawthorn oak tree, there's a mud kitchen, a bug hotel and The Hide, their very own shed to bird watch, play games or make dens. Beyond this there are allotments for each class and the gardening club. Worried about noise from the city's neighbours? Next door is the bishop's garden.

Classes are small, between 11-18 pupils. And the classrooms are imaginatively set up; we saw one with a zoo area, another with a bakery café. The creativity continues into The Bookwormy, the library, which has a car for a bookshelf and bug beanbags. On our visit, pupils were just back from swimming and were settling down in comfy tracksuits, devouring healthy snacks, ready for storytime. The balance feels just right here; 'there is an expectation for children to do their best and give their all at any task, and there is an academic push, but it is a gentle, perfectly pitched push,' parents said. 'My son has only been at ECS for a year but the school has made him more inquisitive and he has learned so much already,' said one. 'Even this morning, at the age of just 4, he was explaining to me why he could hear building work echoing as he walked across Cathedral Green.'

Pupils walk to the Chantry for lunch or to the cathedral for worship. For sport they are minibussed around the city; there never seems to be a dull moment here and it adds to the charm of this inner-city school. School begins with daily morning worship in the vast cathedral chapter house. This includes spiritual readings, hymn practice and a chance to 'just be'. The Chantry houses the offices, plus years 3 and 4. Other buildings including Evans for years 6, 7, and 8 are dotted around nearby. It feels like a maze but it's not; it's full of character. Walks between buildings are across pedestrianized walkways, and glimpses of the cathedral, pretty cobbled courtyards, small peaceful gardens and cleverly planned playgrounds areas make it all feel really rather special.

The boarding accommodation is made up of three Georgian houses with 22 boys' beds and 18 girls' beds for 7-13 year olds. All boarders are from the UK, most live within an hour's drive, and around half are choristers. Girl and boy choristers sing on alternate evenings so pupils do get downtime, but this adds to the irregularity of the boarding numbers throughout the week. One parent said, '[They] are at home there and I know they are happy.' The large dorms have three bunkbeds each and a piano, or in some cases, a harp. Older pupils can have a double room with two single beds. Decent showers and toilets. Efficient laundry system; even flexi-boarders get their own laundry basket. There's a comfy common room, a TV room, a prep room, and the Cosy Club in the basement with sofas, DVDs, a games table and a crafts area. One parent admitted, 'parts of the boarding house could do with a lick of paint!' and this is true, but the housemistress is gradually upgrading it. After supper, prep, choir practice and Mrs Jolly's Hot Choccie Trolley, there's not much time for activities during the week. At weekends there can be anything from a handful of pupils to 25, and activities include trips to Haven Banks, Dartmoor or beaches. Spanish tapas evenings, Irish evenings and making sushi are also popular.

As expected, music plays a big part. One parent told us, 'Her music has gone from strength to strength and she has gone from a child who never stopped singing to a violinist, pianist and a member of Devon County Junior Choir with a place as a cathedral chorister. Yet the music hasn't taken over and she is developing a real love of hockey and netball.'

Mornings are for core lessons with form teachers and afternoons are for specialist lessons and sports. 'The English department in particular has exceeded our expectations – my son has studied TS Eliot, Roald Dahl, Ted Hughes, Seamus Heaney, Shakespeare, Michael Morpurgo and Michelle Paver in the past three years,' we were told. Specialists teach science as separate subjects. French, from reception, is popular. As is the teacher's dog. We met Ted, a floppy puppy who was thrilled to have tickles as pupils made their way between lessons. Latin is taught from year 6. The arts are just as impressive; we saw some fantastic (and huge) decorative masks on display. Pupils are encouraged to think big and express themselves. For drama, year 4 recently performed Splash, a musical based on Noah's Ark. And year 8s perform a leaving review each year.

Learning support caters for mild needs including dyslexia and dyscalculia, at extra cost. Small classes are beneficial and a big draw for parents. One explained, 'We were amazed at how quickly and accurately the teachers understood what made each of our boys tick and used the knowledge to help them both move forward.' Parents are impressed with the 'all-round education.' One told us, 'her love of reading, spelling, maths

E

and sport have all been developed at the school but I have also seen her become a kinder and more considerate child.'

No sports facilities on site, but ECS makes good use of facilities in a traditionally sporty city. There's some 60+ fixtures per term plus an U7s festival for netball, soccer and athletics. Other sports include judo, squash, swimming, cross-country and athletics plus outdoor pursuits like climbing, kayaking and Dartmoor walks. Some pupils play county-level hockey and take part in the National Prep Schools Athletics Championships; there are also talented sailors and netball players.

Sports clubs take place after school and musical activities throughout the day. Judo is particularly popular. Other clubs include fencing, ukulele, cricket, maths, poetry, bell ringing, tennis and cooking. Equestrian club at weekends. Parents are delighted, 'After-school clubs cover an incredible variety (and are inexpensive) – but if you're running late for pick-up ECS happily keeps them for prep and supper...As working parents this has been perfect.' Trips make the most of the local area including Roman walks. Years 5, 6 and 7 go to France for a week every two years, year 8 goes camping on Dartmoor, plus there's a Buckfast Abbey choir camp.

The only grumble we heard from parents was that 'The food is not great,' and 'the school dinners are very unappetising.' We have no doubt that the head and his team will be onto this with a fix straight away. This city prep school isn't perfect but it's definitely doing it's best to head that way. It's full of charm, balances academia and childhood brilliantly, and most importantly, it gives pupils and their parents exactly what they want and need.

Exeter College

53

Hele Road, Exeter, Devon EX4 4JS

Ages 16–19 **Pupils** 5,600

01392 205222
www.exe-coll.ac.uk/

Principal: Since 2016, John Laramy, previously vice-principal. After a career in the construction industry, John decided it was time for a change. So in 1996 he sold his sports car and studied for a PGCE at the University of Greenwich. He also holds an MSc in educational leadership and a BSc in construction management. Once qualified, John became a lecturer at what was then North Devon College (now Petroc), and moved up to the senior management team in 2005, before joining Exeter College in 2009.

A proper Devonian, John grew up on a family farm in the north of the county. Married with two young boys, he loves to play sport if he has the time, but is just as happy to watch the local teams at Exeter City Football Club, or Exeter Chiefs Rugby.

Not well known amongst parents; in fact one told us, 'To be honest I've got no idea who the head teacher is, but my son says he's a very nice chap!' This is a college, not a school, and the way it is run reflects this. When John took the reins, the college was already in a strong position and he is determined to keep it that way. His approach is best described as 'evolution not revolution', currently focusing on strengthening relationships with local schools, and 'supporting the skills and educational ambition of Exeter and the south west.'

Academic matters: Huge range of courses on offer. Around 60 per cent of students opt for vocational courses and 40 per cent for academic subjects. As well as over 40 A level choices and the International Baccalaureate, there are over 90 vocational and industry-led courses (from entry level to level 3), plus the largest choice of apprenticeship frameworks in Devon. The college also offers some adult learning and university level courses.

In 2018, 28 per cent A*/A and 61 per cent A*-B grades at A level, the best results for the college to date were echoed in the average IB point score of 35. Vocational/BTec success rates at all levels are consistently well above the national average. Recent apprenticeship success rates placed Exeter College as the number one college provider in the south west and number nine across the country. Graded outstanding by Ofsted at its most recent visit and since then has won the TES Apprenticeship Programme of the Year Award, as well as the City & Guilds UK Centre of the Year Award for technical and vocational training.

With such a great deal on offer it's no wonder that new students and parents can sometimes feel a little overwhelmed. However, the college is committed to finding the 'right learner for the right course,' and the variety of subjects and levels to choose from means that they can find a course for anybody, whatever their interest or ability. Course information, guidance and support are all provided by the college advice team.

For those studying three A levels, the college offers an 'extend' course including subjects like criminology and gaming. For the most academically gifted students there is the Reach Academy where students commit to an extra 60 hours a year to extracurricular activities and experiences that develop skills and knowledge to benefit university and job applications.

Students of vocational courses are not neglected either: the college has excellent links with local businesses including Exeter Chiefs (rugby), Flybe, John Lewis, Exeter Phoenix and Michael Caines MBE. Extensive local employer contacts for the apprenticeship team too. Vocational courses are run in the (mostly) corporate academies that are scattered across the city centre and beyond.

Students speak highly of teachers, saying they are 'friendly, very open and approachable.' They feel they can chat to them about anything and there is 'no sense of hierarchy.' Parents agreed saying, '[I'm] very impressed by their commitment to both high academic standards and student welfare; and their generosity in supporting students.'

Students with learning difficulties are given good support including individual one-to-one additional tuition or support from an enabler during lessons. This is an inclusive college and each individual is assessed and accommodated if possible. One parent told us, 'Some teachers have been very skilled and informed about offering dyslexia-friendly teaching options.' If the needs are high, the Foundation Studies Centre can provide specialist teaching plus care facilities such as hoists and specially adapted furniture and equipment. Some faculty areas are wheelchair accessible. The college also offers courses to help students with confidence, self-esteem, or for those unsure of which course or training to choose.

Games, options, the arts: Sporty types will be more than happy here. Outstanding sports facilities at the new Exwick Sports Hub including playing fields, rugby and football pitches, tennis courts and a state of the art sports hall and fitness centre. A new 3G pitch is on the cards next. The college also uses the Haven Banks Outdoor Education Centre for sailing, canoeing, kayaking, windsurfing, climbing, caving and orienteering. Along with the Exeter Chiefs Rugby Academy, a women's rugby academy has just been launched. Hugely successful sports teams: the mixed hockey team won a national title and the athletics team were crowned champions of the south west recently.

As well as the Centre for Music and Performance, the college has opened a new Performing Arts Academy. The current facilities include the latest recording and sound equipment and studios, a theatre, an amphitheatre, plus dance and rehearsal rooms. Recent performances include Alice in Wonderland and The Diary of Anne Frank. Annually there are carols in Exeter cathedral and a Music Academy Showcase. Weekly there is the very popular Wednesday Live Lunch, an open mic performance event run by the students.

The Centre for Creative Industries is a fantastic place to be inspired. The building not only houses all the equipment a media student could dream of, but there is plenty of artwork, photography, textiles and design work on display in The Yard Gallery. The standards are high and parents told us, 'its reputation for visual arts is very good.' For anyone with an interest in radio presenting or production, the college has its own Spark Radio, open to all.

Huge variety of enrichment activities on offer. There are music activities such as student choir, big band and drama, or recreational activities such as introduction to Italian, radio production and debating (Exeter College students were recently crowned winners of the west and south Wales). Sport and fitness activities including fitness training, basketball, skiing, football and jiu jitsu, plus the Duke of Edinburgh Award Scheme, the Ten Tors Challenge, British sign language qualifications and volunteer programmes.

Each department or academy runs trips: to Berlin for history students, New York or San Francisco for film studies students, and the Cheltenham races and holiday parks for travel and tourism students. There are also cross-college trips like the annual ski trip, and enrichment club trips eg the recent surf trip to Portugal.

Background and atmosphere: In 1970 Exeter Technical College became the UK's first tertiary college: the former grammar schools' sixth forms joined Exeter Technical College to provide all post-16 education and training in Exeter. The college has now almost doubled in size, educating and training over 11,000 young people and adults. There are over 5,600 full time 16-18 year olds.

The college is spread across the city. Most centres or academies are within walking distance from stations, and as Exeter is a relatively small city it is fairly easy to navigate from one to the other. Some cities are safer than others, and Exeter definitely falls into the safer category; it's pretty low-key and doesn't have a huge pub/club/party scene, a big tick for parents of teenagers. For rural kids living outside the city, it is exciting enough and it's easy to see why so many want to go here instead of other more rural colleges or school sixth forms.

The Technology Centre, the Construction Centre and the Flybe Training Academy are on the outskirts of the city and are very much separate entities. Due to location, students at these sites have fewer opportunities to get involved in the city centre life and facilities, but most students don't let a bus trip get in their way. On the whole the facilities at the college are fantastic. The new Maths and Science Centre has 11 high spec science laboratories, a full size lecture theatre and a forensic science suite. At the Flybe Academy, students learn in replica air hangers and most go onto to jobs at Flybe, or are snapped up by BA or Lufthansa. There are new developments happening continually. The Technology Centre now includes robotic technology (the only facility in the UK), virtual and conventional welding, electro-pneumatic equipment, 3D printers, industrial automation and two new fully equipped machining workshops.

There are seven learning resource centres where students can study and access books, PCs, journals, DVDs and equipment. For downtime, there are plenty of cafés and relaxing sofa areas. It's here that students are given the opportunity to mix with others outside their courses. Enrichment activities, tutor groups, induction sessions and student union events also help students to get to know each other.

For those that want to get involved, the SRS, the student union, is very active. It plays a huge part in Learner Voice, as does the principal, who is prepared to listen to student feedback regularly. A recent result of this has been new water fountains along with free, refillable bottles. SRS also runs free tea/coffee mornings and a free soup pop-up during health and well-being month. Plenty of fundraising activities too: particular favourites are 'jailbreak', sponsored abseiling and battle of the bands. The college raised an impressive £13K for the Teenage Cancer Trust recently.

Pastoral care, well-being and discipline: As well as a personal tutor to support academic progress, and an employability and progression team for guidance and advice, there is a student services team and a welfare and well-being team to help with any other areas of concern in life. For apprentices, there are training and recruitment advisors for support, plus skills officers who act as a link between students and employers.

Pupils and parents: Students travel from all over the south west. Exeter is easily accessible and college sites are within walking distances of train stations. Most parents and students we spoke to said they were drawn to the college because the city centre has so much to offer. Students told us they love the size of the college, the social scene and the fact that it is in the city centre. Another bonus is being able to access the university facilities like The Northcott Theatre. Parents told us, 'My teenager has developed academically and socially in a very positive way'; '[My child] has done a lot of growing up during the last few years and Exeter college has provided real opportunities for this development.'

Parents are kept up to date through reports twice a year, progress evenings and termly newsletters. Drops in attendance are flagged immediately.

Entrance: There are five main secondary schools in Exeter; none has a sixth form so Exeter College is the main destination. Having said that, 66 per cent of students come from outside the city.

For A levels (level 3), entry requirement is eight GCSEs to include at least six at grade 4 or above including English and maths. For level 3 vocational courses, it's five grade 4s at GCSE including English language or a good pass with a full level 2 qualification. Lower entry requirements for levels 1 and 2, and no formal qualifications needed for entry level courses. In 2016, the college opened applications to international students and there are currently around 50. This is set to increase with recruiters taking 360 promotional video boxes to schools worldwide recently. There is a dedicated international team to support students and families.

Plenty of open events. Interviews after application, then enrolment starts at the end of August with induction/team-building sessions and the freshers' fair. Mixed views on settling in. One parent told us, 'As a trans teenager [they] found the college very supportive during the initial registration process and in ensuring sufficient initial support was available.' Another parent said their son found the first year 'quite hard... He floundered and it took him some time to find his feet.' However, they went on to say that 'he has done a lot of growing up during the last few years and Exeter College has provided real opportunities for this development.'

Exit: Some 40-50 per cent to university, with 24 to Oxbridge in 2018, including five medics. Some 30 per cent went into employment, training or an apprenticeship. A few stayed on for a university-level course at Exeter College.

College alumni include Michael Caines MBE, chef and entrepreneur, Jo Pavey MBE, British long-distance runner,

Conrad Humphreys, long distance sailor and Spencer Dale, group chief economist, BP.

Money matters: Bursary fund available for those in care, in receipt of benefits or with a household income of less than £23K. This can help with the costs of transport, meals, books, resource fees and equipment. Army bursary scheme for anyone looking to join up after college. All students can apply to Devon County Council transport scheme to receive a contribution towards an annual travel pass. For those with children, there is a nursery on site and students can apply to the government's Care to Learn Fund for help with costs.

Remarks: Great city college, one of a kind in rural Devon. Fantastic range of courses available for all levels – something for everyone with the right guidance and support. Multiple sites across the city could take some getting used to, but most seem to embrace and thrive on the city life offered here. Worth a visit and worth spending the time researching the courses to make it work.

Exeter Junior School

Linked with Exeter School

Victoria Park Road, Exeter EX2 4NS

Ages 7–11 **Pupils** 194

Fees: £11,925 pa

01392 273679
www.exeterschool.org.uk

Headmistress: Since 2015, Sue Marks. Educated at Palmers, Essex, when it was a girls' grammar school. A degree in biochemistry set her up for an early career as a clinical biochemist. Saw the light and retrained as a teacher in the mid-1990s. Taught in a series of state schools until appointed head of the junior school at St Joseph's, Launceston.

She brings to her job an array of attributes which, taken together, make her an impressively capable administrator. She's a jolly good teacher, too – in 2012 she won the Astra Zeneca Primary Science Teacher Award. One parent said, 'She's serious, driven to get it right for every child in the school'. She's also an advocate of female empowerment. At the time of our visit, girl power was trending big time. The school she leads is in an especially good place just now, something that particularly struck us as we had first visited almost exactly a year before – when, be it noted, we very much liked what we saw. In the interim, things had only got better.

Ms Marks has a hinterland and it's mostly about physical exertion on a mission-impossible scale. When we met first she was in the throes of training for the Brighton marathon. More recently, together with other staff at the school, she had successfully completed a charity bike ride from John O'Groats to Land's End. So, to her soft skills, add grit and stamina, qualities no head should be without.

Retiring in July 2019. Her successor will be Saskia van Schalkwyk BA (Roehampton), currently deputy head of The Granville School in Sevenoaks, where she is also head of maths and of PSCHE. Has teaching experience in both state and independent co-ed schools. A trained ISI inspector, her interests include umpiring netball, running and cycling. She is married to a teacher and has two children.

Entrance: Boys and girls come from a wide range of feeders, both local primaries and also The New School, an independent pre-prep in Exminster. There's a small contingent of relocators – from London, mostly – who are pleased to discover that their child can start any time so long as there's room. The school is exceedingly popular with medics and you see why when you gaze over to the south east side of the campus and there, in all its vastness, perfectly positioned for picking up and dropping off, looms the Royal Devon and Exeter Hospital. Fees are pegged at a level that makes them as affordable as possible and among the most competitive in the country.

There's an entrance test in literacy and numeracy to assess potential and determine whether your child will thrive not just here and now, but also later, in the senior school. Anything to be said for staving off disappointment by calling in the tutors beforehand? Some parents do. But the selection process is canny and thorough, and who would want to squeeze their child in at the bottom? Don't. There's no set number of children admitted every year so there's no cold cut-off and no calculating the success rate. The school declares its ability range to be 'national average and above'. Typical of the thoughtful care that percolates all areas of the school, if your child doesn't reach the pass mark you'll get formative feedback on all papers. They'll point out areas for improvement and offer another go the following year.

The school takes great care to familiarise newbie pupils with their new environment – their parents, too. Every new pupil gets a buddy. In addition to an induction designed to give children a feel for who's who and what's where, there's a tea party a few days before the start of term where parents, also, can get to know each other and, if the spirit takes them, keep in constant touch thereafter (as some do) by forming their own WhatsApp group.

Exit: Pretty much everyone moves on aged 11 to the senior school. A smattering – some 5-10 per cent – leave for the free grammars, Torquay and Colyton, fewer than the number who had initially set out with that intention. Why's that? The combined income of some of the parents we spoke to made moving on to a free grammar a very sensible choice and yet, they told us, their children were so happy at Exeter Junior, and doing so well, they'd decided to go without holidays for the foreseeable future and counted it a sacrifice worth every penny. Parents express a lot of love for this school: it's that kind of place.

No entrance exam to the senior school for junior school pupils; screening for entry to the junior school is so effective that it is rare for anyone not to move up. If there's a chance a child will bump along the bottom of the senior school (it hardly ever happens), parents are made aware and other options explored in good time. Because juniors have already been to classes in the senior school and done sport, science and music there, the school's claim that 'the transition is near-seamless' stands up: 'They already feel they're members of both'. Parents agree. Not having to break your stride and start over is not without its obvious attractions.

Remarks: Occupies a much-altered Georgian villa on the edge of the main campus, separate but not severed, very much its own place and right in the centre of Exeter but with lots of grass and romping room. Some recent redesign and refurbishment, all of it well done, has brightened it and brought it up to date. Parents with an eye to value for money will note with shrewd approval that the quality of the fabric and furnishings may best be described as 'good ordinary', not bells and whistles. The focus here always is on optimising the pupil experience, never fluttering eyelashes at the plutocracy.

Junior and senior school are closely aligned in all things – they call it their 'whole school ethos'. The head and her deputy are members of the joint schools' senior management team and both schools share the same governors. Juniors have access to the facilities of the whole site – dining hall, pool, labs, sports pitches, chapel, etc. Speech day is a joint event. There is some crossover of teachers. The effect is that a pupil at the junior school feels like a mainstream member of the whole institution. It's not hard to see what an advantage this offers over a standalone junior school.

The curriculum is what you'd expect of a school almost all of whose pupils, aged 18, go on to top universities. Academic. The pace is sprightly but, parents reassure us, never excruciating. A parent said, 'No, honestly, the children really don't seem to find it pressured'. It's easy enough to see how it's done: the school employs seriously outstanding, some of them amazingly outstanding teachers, all of them life's enthusiasts, the sort who fire the imagination, set high expectations and make it masses of fun, too. There's Latin on offer. And of course there's the currently voguish emphasis on STEM subjects (science, technology, engineering, maths) only here they call it STEAM (A is for art). Think Leonardo da Vinci and it immediately makes sense. There's learning support for those who need it. Everyone is screened for dyslexia on entry. There are personalised learning strategies for those with special needs, shared with their teachers. There are clubs open to all which support maths, literacy and handwriting. The head of learning support goes on working with her pupils for the first two years of the senior school, providing valuable continuity. Nice touch: as a parent you get a leaflet every term setting out exactly what your child will be studying in class.

Ambition is unquestionably a good thing, but when you hear that a recent drama production was Hamlet you wonder if we aren't getting just a little ahead of ourselves here... until you meet the drama teacher, a former West End actor and dancer. Yep, she knows exactly what she's doing. Shakespeare plays are cut to 30 mins and the pupils prepare by improvising analagous scenarios, a process devised by the Shakespeare Schools Foundation. Weenier ones do age-appropriate stuff like The Gruffalo. There are several productions a year and a thriving lunchtime club. The purpose is very much to instil confidence and teamworking, not breed Oscar winners. This is a school with its feet on the ground.

Music is another great strength, very much the beneficiary of shared resources with the senior school. Most children learn an instrument and in addition to opportunities to play in an ensemble and an orchestra there are two, yes two, choirs.

Sport is big. It is also inclusive, which means you don't have to be brilliant to play for your school – it's not all about just the A team, there are teams for all levels. Fact is, PE teachers everywhere are so much more humane than PE teachers used to be and those at Exeter are some of the kindest. They don't just pay lip service to the 'sport for all mantra', they really mean it; they really want everyone to find what they like doing and not mind in the least being only half decent at it. The parent of a dreamy girl who had never shown the remotest interest in sport told us how her daughter now loves her hockey and is proud as punch to be in a team. They haven't gone soft, mind. At the top level sport is expertly coached and red in tooth and claw.

The extracurricular offering – clubs and activities – is perhaps best summed up by the parent who said to us, 'Have you ever heard of a school that does so much?' And with lunch time opportunities ranging from climbing to Lego robotics to African drumming, we can see what she means.

The feature of the school that elicits the most clamorous unanimity is the way it looks after the children. The head told us that the overriding value here is kindness – 'everyone matters'. Aspiration or reality? Unquestionably reality because, we find, this is a place where all sorts really do mix and make friends. A parent told us 'they are incredibly accepting of difference', and went on to relate how her child, after distressing experiences in several schools, now at last feels 'safe and happy'. Other parents related comparable experiences. There is amazement at rapid responses to emails and no inhibitions about flagging up problems – 'Feedback is second to none'. Children are 'respected, and if they need to speak out they are given the confidence to do so'. We very much like the way that pupils in the senior school, in testament to their affection for the place, come back under supervision and help out with reading, science, orchestra, games and in the playground. Teaching assistants and gap year students also play a strong pastoral role. In short, this is a school which excites both admiration and strong affection. One mum told us that in the distant future when her daughter has finally sat her A levels she's going to start her again in year 3 and send her through all over again.

Exeter Junior is not a school with a highly distinctive identity. It doesn't go out of its way to catch the eye by doing things differently or pelting you with thrilling marketing messages. It's not a branch of the luxury goods market. As one mum expressed it: 'There are no independent school airs and graces, it's a very grounded place', and went on to compare it with John Lewis: an excellent product and 'a real partnership between children, teachers and parents'. What's more, she might have added: never knowingly undersold.

Exeter Junior does what it says on its tin. It's a school. It endeavours, in the words of the head, 'to enable all the children to find their thing and be the best person they can be'. It keeps things simple and does them superbly well, with high professionalism: it is very well led and staffed by some blisteringly good teachers. Which doesn't make it a 'good ordinary' school, it makes it a darn fine one.

Exeter Mathematics School

Rougemont House, Exeter, Devon EX4 3PU

Ages 16-18 **Pupils** 125: 31 girls, 94 boys **Boarders** 32 weekly: 7 girls, 25 boys

Fees: Weekly boarding up to £9,800 pa

01392 429020
www.exetermathematicsschool.ac.uk

Headteacher: Since 2014, Kerry Burnham, founding headteacher. West Country through and through, educated at Plymstock School and Exeter university, BSc in maths and education. Accredited advanced skills teacher. Since 1998 maths teacher and gifted & talented coordinator at Torquay Boys' Grammar. Not imbued in the least with a sense of manifest destiny and had never considered going for a headship until the Exeter Mathematics School (EMS) job came up. It's the maths that got her blowing the moths off her CV; she just can't get enough of it. Like any maths teacher anywhere she is perfectly certain that hers is the most important subject of them all.

A big step up, starting a new school from scratch. She's at ease with the responsibilities and conspicuously good at people. Warm, cordial, intuitive, fun to be with. No side to her at all; indeed, her candour may be her most refreshing and appealing attribute. Has presided over, inter alia, an Ofsted inspection just two and a bit years post-launch. It rated EMS outstanding across the board. So: Ms Burnham makes things happen. What's more, she pays heed to students and parents. One parent told us, 'She takes our suggestions seriously and if they're any good acts on them'.

Married with children, Ms Burnham has fond if distant memories of biking, badminton, modern jive and walking on Dartmoor. All have been more or less sidelined by her workload. But, now that her school has developed beyond baby steps, she is beginning to win back lost recreational territory.

Academic matters: As you may suppose, the curriculum goes way beyond A levels – in the head's words, 'We're not thinking about exams, we're thinking about maths'. What you must be in no two minds about is that the diet is basically maths enriched with more maths. So everyone does A level maths and further maths plus either physics or computer science. If you don't want to do one of the latter two, you can choose a fourth option over at the Exeter (tertiary) College campus 10 mins walk away. But EMS is not a school for renaissance students, it's a specialist school: it's for students and teachers who can't get enough of pursuing and assigning value to that tantalising shapeshifter they call x. Adding the option of philosophy to the A level mix could arguably work rather well for pure mathematicians, but there are no plans to do so.

On top of A levels you take your Exeter Mathematics Certificate, a unique qualification co-designed with Exeter university's maths department. The idea is to pique curiosity, inspire self-directed study and encourage you to play to your particular mathematical strengths and – head's words – 'personal passions'. Lots of stress on problem solving. In the first year, a variety of activities including working on a task set by one of the school's industry partners, which include ATASS Sports, QuinetiQ, the Met Office, the Hydrographic Office, Apple and Dyson. In the second year you undertake your own research project and present your findings on a poster and in a formal presentation to your fellow students (scary, obvs) and members of the public (scarier still). Students are mentored by maths undergrads from the university and work with peers across the south west. They enjoy fortnightly Inspire lectures, an academia sans frontières programme designed to join up all knowledge about everything. The guiding idea is to enable you to segue effortlessly into your chosen university. The aptness of the process is self-evident.

So, a hothouse-cum-sweatshop characterised by fiendish pressure and fevered stress, then? Anything but. Quite the contrary. First impressions are that EMS closely resembles, in tone and structure, one of those progressive schools. Or Google. The ambience is notably relaxed-seeming. And collaborative. Mutually supportive. Convivial. A student told us, 'No one's trying to prove they're better than anyone else'. There's a very popular ping pong table. We encountered a group of students playing cards... until we realised that what they were actually doing was maths. We didn't encounter a single serried rank in any of the classrooms and the observable status gap between teachers and students is close to zero. But make no mistake, there's masses of maths going on – in the head's words, 'There are no dutiful learners here'. And given that much of a mathematician's work is at the level of the subconscious, everything we saw came across as wholly appropriate. A student told us that 'the focus is on enjoying maths, not being driven'. Another said, 'There's a good level of intensity – keeps you focussed, not stressed.' Other quotes from students: 'The big emphasis here is on formulating and researching a problem'; 'The teaching is amazing'; and 'Such a shame it's only two years'. A teacher told us, 'I feel lucky to teach here; you can cherish every student'. The head told us, 'We tell them it's okay to be wrong, you learn so much from your mistakes. It's all right to say "I don't know".' A parent said, 'The school teaches in such a way that subjects are relatable to the real world, and the level of enthusiasm in the teaching is transmitted from teachers to the students.'

As EMS establishes itself, competition for places is hotting up and (head's words), 'we are taking additional care with the selection process to ensure the students that will most benefit attend'. Expect exam results to improve in line with this. In 2018 they harvested their third crop of results. Sixty-three per cent of grades were A* or A and 83 per cent A*-B. Very high value-added. Not surprising that a student told us, 'I feel a long way from where I was. I'm ready now for university'. Students rate the guidance they get in this respect. We spoke to a former student who'd had a last-minute change of heart about the university she'd chosen. Much praise for the guidance she got and the invitation to come into school in her 'lost' year and keep maths-fit.

More than 25 per cent have a learning difficulty and/or disability, a significant minority on the autistic spectrum, the remainder the customary range, eg, dyslexia. The school is fully geared to this. For students on the spectrum EMS's size is an important factor in the socialisation process. With only 60-odd students per year group you 'soon get to know everyone and it's easy to make friends'. Whole-school approach to learning support includes specialists, one of whom observed, 'Outstanding teaching is the best way of helping those with special needs'.

Games, options, the arts: You'd think the small number of students here would restrict the scope for extracurricular activities, but in this context EMS students join up with their fellows at Exeter College, which supports a wide enough range to engage almost 6,000 students. In short, there's heaps to choose from. Do EMS students tend to get stuck in their mathsy bubble and not get out enough? Well, there's a strong and insistent requirement to commit to recreation and there's also respect for those who, whether by disposition or because of undeveloped social skills, find it hard to do so. Insistence is firm but gentle, yet some parents aren't quite yet altogether happy with the school's extracurricular provision. It's a work in progress. Worth pointing out that one parent told us her daughter, who has autism and is physically disabled, was perfectly comfortable doing an AS level up at the college. Lots use the gym. Important to sign up for courses and activities before all the places are gone. A parent told us, 'the option is there and the school encourage students to take advantage of it, but ultimately it comes down to the student'.

Boarding: Supervised accommodation for those who live more than an hour away – around 30 of them. Families in financial need can access a bursary to cover the cost. Some live in flats on the campus – en suite bedroom and living room, six per flat, grouped by age. Two staff members on duty overnight. Boarders do a food and hygiene qualification, cook for each other (supported by staff) and are coached in keeping clean and tidy and living with others. A tutor told us, 'It's a great way to learn life skills'. Agreed. No access during the day. Popping into town for an alcoholic drink in the evening flatly, utterly and remorselessly banned. Ever.

Background and atmosphere: EMS occupies Rougemont House in the heart of Exeter next door to the castle – a pretty enough spot and a great location. No grounds to speak of. Sort of Tuscan-style building of negligible architectural value protected by a flattering grade II listing. Regrettable. Has a rambling quality which imparts something of an MC Escher vibe. Perhaps. Point is, it serves.

The idea of specialist maths schools is new to the UK. They make sense inasmuch as mathematicians constitute a distinct clan (just as ballet dancers, musicians and performing artists do and, say, geographers on the whole don't). STEM subjects (science, technology, engineering and maths) are trending bigtime right now and prime minister May wants a maths school in every town in Britain to enable the country to 'stand tall in the world after Brexit'. She won't get all she wants because a number of universities have mulled it over and for various reasons (terror of accusations of elitism, mostly) said no. Politics and local feasibility apart, the business case is entirely sound. EMS is sponsored by the University of Exeter. This relationship makes for a fast track and ensures students already have a foot in university before they leave school. The school's co-sponsor, Exeter College, complements what EMS can offer in terms of fourth-choice A levels and what they call enrichment. So EMS is deficient in nothing. Critics of specialist maths schools claim that their existence will open a gulf between good and poor standards in maths education and deprive non-elite mathematicians of great teaching but in fact the reverse is the truth: EMS works with teachers throughout the south west to improve maths education for all – eg year 10 residentials, enhancement courses, maths student community.

E

The social climate is relaxed, with an egalitarian flavour. It's easily possible that some prospective parents looking round could find themselves stifling a harrumph and coming to the conclusion that it's all a bit free and easy and unstructured. Let's address that. We visited on a warm spring day when most of the male teachers were wearing shorts. Students are schooled not to address their teachers as Sir or Miss but by their first names. So yes, informal. But according to serving parents and students there's plenty of respect for teachers: respect based in esteem. Yes, there's rigour. Teachers here don't sweat the small stuff but, in the words of a parent, 'they come down hard on what really matters'. We are in no doubt about that. The ethos here is college, not school so, in the words of a parent, 'The school rightly expects students to be proactive and engaged in order to maximise their potential.'

Clan values mean that students here really enjoy being around, and sparking off, each other. For some this is the first time at school that they have discovered fellow spirits. They flourish in an environment where, a parent told us, 'everyone can be themselves'.

Pastoral care, well-being and discipline: Pastoral care is shared among teachers and a specialist team who spoke to us with full-strength seriousness and much fervour about their role and its importance, because 'these students spend a long time outside their comfort zone'. We heard about an autistic student who had outstripped predictions and developed a capability for independent living. The philosophy is that when a student has a problem it is acknowledged as being of equal perceived gravity by staff. Nothing is ever trivialised. Given the complexity of needs presented by some students, pastoral care here has to be the best it can. We are in no doubt that it is. The highly personal approach is of course aided by the school's small size. Everyone knows everyone so there's no slipping under the radar. A former student told us, 'When I needed them they really were there for me'. A parent told us, 'I've been impressed with how well the teachers seem to know my son, and how encouraging they are, with specific advice for improvements. They are happy to talk to parents about any concerns or questions at any time'.

Pupils and parents: Catchment area is Devon, Dorset, Somerset and Cornwall. Currently, most from Exeter and environs, but furthest flung student from Penzance. Open to students at independent schools, keen that they are not disproportionately favoured but by no means anti either. Prospective students from schools with a sixth form likely to come in for persuasion to stay on. We spoke to a head who had 'lost' a brilliant mathematician to EMS. He said bravely, 'We would have loved him to have stayed but it's important that the right student finds the right course'. Only natural he was wistful because a star student is a feather in the cap.

Mission to recruit students from low income homes and currently 20 per cent are. Proportion of female students has increased from a fifth to a third, below the school's current target of 40 per cent, the national average for female learners taking maths A level. However, well above the national average for girls doing physics and further maths. Year groups 64 strong and no plans to expand. Currently, four out of 120 transgender.

Entrance: At year 12 only – none at year 13. Maths and science GCSEs at grade 8-9 plus six others at 5 and above, a 6 at Eng lang preferred. Some intelligent flexibility. References, interview and school's own entry exam in maths. Head spelt out paramount criterion: 'We want no dutiful learners here: you must love maths and be prepared to be challenged'.

Exit: Almost all to universities everywhere to study STEM subjects overwhelmingly. A few to degree apprenticeships and accounting. In 2018, six to Oxbridge; others off to Bath, Bristol, Oxford, Cardiff, Durham, Manchester, Surrey and West of England.

Money matters: EMS enjoys £350,000 a year on top of its statutory funding to enable the school to deliver its outreach programme. Additional funding to support, and give accommodation bursaries to, students from lower income families.

Remarks: A birds-of-a-feather school which owes its existence to the theory that elite maths ability is best turbocharged in a specialist environment but never to the exclusion of other educational and cultural experiences. EMS is a young school now hitting its stride. Students are well looked after and, far from dematerialising into a mathsy parallel reality, are closely in touch with all the day to day stuff that animates young people everywhere. Great teaching a given. Attention to life skills especially impressive.

Exeter School

Linked with Exeter Junior School

Victoria Park Road, Exeter EX2 4NS

Ages 11–18 **Pupils** 728 **Sixth form** 209

Fees: £13,230 pa

01392 273679
www.exeterschool.org.uk

Headmaster: Since 2003, Bob Griffin MA. Educated at Wallington High School for Boys, then Oxford – first in modern languages (French and Spanish). Taught at Markham College in Lima before becoming head of modern languages at Haileybury. Came to Exeter from RGS Guildford, where he was second master for five years. Son and daughter both went through the school. Enjoys all things Hispanic, walking on Dartmoor and choral singing. Unique distinction among UK headteachers, he's a member of the Incorporation of Weavers, Fullers and Shearmen.

Unusually long tenure for this day and age – must be one of the longest serving heads in the country. Gives no impression whatever of age having wearied him. Students, parents and teachers give no impression of having wearied of him, either. Quite the contrary, they all want him to stay for, if possible, ever. Warm, bright, open-minded. All-important good sense of humour. Teaches Spanish. May be said to embody his school, which he has raised to the level of Sunday Times South West Independent Secondary School of the Year 2018. Sees his role as sustainer of standards – 'high standards, not punishingly high'. He speaks of 'maintenance rather than revolution'. This is after all an evolved school in no need of a revolution. It continues to evolve, especially the senior management. A parent told us, 'he is aware of the need to keep moving forward'.

Straightforward, talks plainly (never gruffly). 'We're like an old-fashioned grammar school,' he tells us. He's proud of the range of extracurricular activity on offer: 'The school emphasises the whole person.' Why does the school teach Latin? Because 'education isn't all about utility.' Why do sixth formers wear business suits? 'Because this is a certain kind of business.' Does the school put a premium on conformity and obedience in the interest of good exam results? 'We cherish a little bit of eccentricity in the ranks.' It wasn't long before we glimpsed a student wearing the loudest suit you've ever seen. Music to our ears, don't know about yours; the head told us, 'I don't believe in marketing for marketing's sake.' To be able to return to our car unburdened by one of those eco bags bulging with narcissistic brochures, key rings, fridge magnets etc was a joy. And the school does make a very good fist of its communications: there's a Twitter feed which 'develops a sense of community', as does its Instagram feed and weekly newsletter, which celebrates students' in-school and out-of-school achievements.

Academic matters: Results terrific – which you may think you're entitled to expect from such a selective school, but note this: the school's value added (Progress 8) score is above average, an exceptionally difficult feat to accomplish with conventionally bright boys and girls who have been achieving at a high level relative to their ability all their schooldays. Proper grammar school curriculum. English language and psychology recent additions. Maths and science formidable; humanities impressive, notably history, geography and English; modern languages stunning, boosted by assistants, native speakers, in French and Spanish. Around 85 per cent move up from GCSE to A level, a notably high figure, the more so in a city with a very good tertiary college. Sixth formers start with four subjects and most go down to three at the end of year 12. Max class size 24. Results in 2018: at A level 58 per cent A*/A; at GCSE 75 per cent A*-A/9-7.

If you're academically robust and emotionally self-reliant this is a school where you can really fly. We attended a maths class. First up, warm-up exercises beginning with times tables at breakneck speed (this Guide got 96 per cent and was inordinately proud of it). Hard on its heels, a spot of code-breaking (Guide: waah!). Brains whirred, hands flew up all round us exultantly – it was high octane stuff, the sort that bright boys and girls thrive on. So, perhaps, not the most comfortable environment for a child given to self-doubt or dreaminess. A parent who reluctantly decided not to send their daughter to the school did so on the grounds that she needed 'a more nurturing environment'. Not that this is a harsh, Darwinian sort of school by any means, and passing the entry test is your assurance that you're definitely good enough to be here. But a degree of inner confidence does help you go a long way. A student we spoke to described their school as 'accepting and challenging'. Another said, 'It encourages pupils to do their very best but always puts pupils' well-being first'. A parent said, 'There is plenty of guidance and support, with explanations and helpful staff always willing to listen if there are problems'.

Effective but not trendy use of tech, eg smartphones being used in a biology class to create animations of enzyme activity. No smartboards but they're leapfrogging them and moving on to tablets instead. Classrooms well-appointed, functional rather than glamorous, entirely fit for purpose, dressed with intelligent displays. Excellent library and a reading programme that encourages students to read six books from a selection in the course of a year. As we toured the school we surveyed well-behaved, lit-up students and purposeful teaching. Teachers run their own teaching and learning committee where they keep up to date and share good practice (ie, stuff that works). Healthy turnover of staff achieves a good balance between continuity and renewal. We got the impression that those who don't fit move on fast.

Learning support co-ordinator draws up a learning plans for students with special needs, which tend to be on the mild side here. Needs addressed have included dyslexia, a registered blind pupil, hearing impaired, cystic fibrosis and mild autism. Dyscalculia mostly handled within maths department.

A large number of out of school clubs are spun off from academic departments. In addition to subject workshops there's a Medsoc for aspiring doctors, a film and literary society and three clubs that stage one-off events across the intellectual spectrum.

Games, options, the arts: Historically a sporty school and it still is, all of it done well to judge by results. The trad three seasonal sports for each sex (rugby, not football, for boys, but you can play football in the sixth form). By year 11 you get to choose from 14 sports and for those who can't get enough there are out of school clubs which raise the total to 25. First-year sixth formers can take a course which yields a recognised sports coaching qualification. We took to the PE teachers we quizzed and satisfied ourselves that they really do try to find something for everyone and don't compel non-gamesy types to shiver and endure. A parent said, 'it's good to see the school focus on providing for those who do not aspire to be in the A team'.

Music formidable, choirs, orchestras, ensembles galore. Good concert hall and gigs at other top venues, eg the cathedral. Drama is run by an ex-actor and playwright (makes such a difference). Nice studio theatre and dance studio, big productions in the assembly hall. Ambitious programme: back-to-back Julius Caesar and Henry V, Guys and Dolls recently. Art vibrant. Very good exam results. Work on display all through the school. Competitions, staff art show, annual summer exhibition with catalogue, and a joint show with a local school for young people with disabilities. Annual residential GCSE trip to St Ives.

Wide-ranging programme of after-school clubs, some run by students, ranging from Model United Nations to sewing and science, taking in masterclasses of all kinds. Plenty of outdoor pursuits – DofE, Ten Tors. Popular CCF. And in term time and holidays a multiplicity of field trips, departmental outings, sports tours, expeditions abroad. This is a busy campus right through the weekend, and it's a tribute to the teachers that they give up so much of their time to make it all happen.

Background and atmosphere: Founded in 1633 as the Exeter Free Grammar School for 'tradesmen and the better class of working men'. First intake 25 street boys selected at random to be educated and taught a trade. Allegedly. Moved to its present site in the Heavitree area in 1877 where, though surrounded by houses, it enjoys the luxury of acres of greensward. Post-war the school became direct grant. Independent since 1976. Girls throughout since 1997. Unquestionably handsome thanks to its flagship buildings and chapel, designed by the High Victorian architect William Butterfield in characteristic polychrome style – brick and banded stone, irreverently termed 'streaky bacon'. Pevsner sniffily censures 'insensitive C20 additions' but most people would reckon they blend in rather well. Highlight is the old dining hall – stained glass, sombre portraits – used now as a meeting room. All in all, every facility a school needs and plenty of room for sport together with a new swimming pool (2017). Covers 25 acres in all, and just a mile from the city centre.

Handsome it may be, but not in the least snooty. The ethos is grammar school, the mood music meritocratic and it does its best to make itself available to those who would otherwise be unable to afford an independent education. Manners are pleasing. Students are common sensical, they know what they're here to do and they get on and do it. Efficient. Level-headed. Together. No drama. We spent some time in the sixth form common room. There was a fair amount of lounging and good-natured banter which, give them a break, is what a common room is for. There was also a fair amount of work being done in the quiet part. Overall impression: a cohesive, purposeful community. A parent said, 'Academically children do need the right attitude but the school seems to manage to instil this'. Perhaps the social climate is best exemplified in a recent school magazine where, in the farewell-to-staff bit, the lead 'obit' is for the retiring groundsman. No 'them' and 'us' here.

F

Pastoral care, well-being and discipline: Discipline not a big issue given the common sense levels – skiving and larking not cool. Expectations are clear and firmly laid down. Uniform worn properly. At the school gate of a morning the school marshal, aka CCF instructor, with peremptory good humour, alerts students to any inadvertent or poorly concealed sartorial faux pas.

Pastoral system: form tutor and house staff. We were struck by the dedication of those we met and their concern to monitor for any signs of distress or overstretch. A parent told us that the pastoral staff she talks to are 'always thoughtful, personal and kind'. House system provides an effective support system. Sixty teachers have completed a course of Youth Mental Health First Aid training. A measure of emotional health here is the exam results: students wouldn't do so well if they weren't so happy. Parents can contact pastoral staff and teachers direct by email. Inspired choice of chaplain, loved, admired and available to all (faith status irrelevant), the best of good eggs. It's not just students who beat a path to him; teachers do too.

What do the students particularly like? Responses included 'the range and quality of facilities'; 'the range of games'; 'the range of extracurricular activities'; 'the way the school keeps us busy'; 'the fact that we can initiate new clubs and activities'; 'that we are listened to'; 'the head meets with every new student'; 'the head and deputy head of house take good care of us and talk to us individually'; and 'the way the school sets you up for later life'. Sixth formers spoke approvingly of their life skills course in helping them prepare for life after school.

Pupils and parents: All from within an hour or so of the school. Around 100 per year group. Just over 40 per cent are girls, a stable ratio influenced by the presence of a competitor girls' school in the town. Year 7 joiners enjoy a weekend of outdoor pursuits bonding at Dartmeet.

Parents a mix of business and professional, some academics, popular with doctors. Parents' association enjoys social events and fundraising for school facilities and activities. Weekends here have a big family feel.

Entrance: Main entry points at ages 11, 13 and 16, but any time if there's room. At age 11, papers in Eng, maths plus a tutor-proof computer component which tests non-verbal reasoning, Eng and maths. At age 13, papers in Eng, maths, a modern language and science. Post-GCSE, reference, interviews, appraisal of extracurricular achievements and interests plus three GCSEs at 7-9 and three at grade 6 including Eng and maths.

Exit: Nine to Oxbridge in 2018 and 11 medics. Rest to a range of destinations – Durham, Sussex, Glasgow, Bath, Nottingham, Southampton, Edinburgh, Sheffield, UWE and York all popular, with one off to Yale in 2018.

Money matters: The head told us, 'The governors find every excuse they can not to put the fees up'. Accessibility is all. Notably astute financial management, seriously good value for money, the best exam grades in the area per pound spent (we checked). Eight free places a year for deserving external candidates whose families would otherwise be unable to afford it; in the same spirit, bursaries for those whose child meets the entry criteria and need a financial top-up. Music scholarships up to 10 per cent of fees. Academic scholarships in the form of prizes at speech day.

Remarks: Everything you'd expect of a good grammar school, both in the classroom and out. Lets its achievements speak for it. An admirable school. A humane school. A very agreeable sc hool.

The Fallibroome Academy

Priory Lane, Upton, Macclesfield, Cheshire SK10 4AF

Ages 11–18 **Pupils** 1,531 **Sixth form** 336

01625 827898
www.fallibroome.academy/

CEO for the Trust: Since 2002, Peter Rubery BEd (MMU) MEd (Liverpool) MBA (Lincoln) FRSA, previously headmaster of Ercall Wood Technology College, Wellington; joined as headmaster, a role which evolved into principal and finally into the grandly titled executive principal and CEO of the multi-academy trust of which Fallibroome is part.

Although understated in his chat, it is clear Peter Rubery is one of life's quiet innovators. Pseudo-corporate lingo about 'continuous improvement' might roll off his tongue (he did an MBA in international educational leadership), but there is nothing empty about his rhetoric; under his visionary leadership, the school has clocked up a number of trailblazing firsts. It was one of the first schools to convert to an academy; one of the first to become a college of performing arts, one of the first to be designated an outstanding teaching school, and latterly, one of the first to create a multi-academy trust. So what is the significance of all this? Well, it's huge; the associated fiscal incentives for early adoption of all these initiatives has created a mighty lot of funds which has resulted in Fallibroome being able to boast the sort of jaw-dropping, high calibre facilities (theatres, recording studios, enormous sport pitches and flootlit tennis courts) which, frankly, the more beleaguered pockets of the independent sector could only dream about.

Just idly chewing the cud – because he is very easy to talk to – it is clear his eyes are always scanning the horizon for new opportunities for pupils. In passing, he refers to having attended a couple of TED conferences (the world-famous event around Technology, Entertainment and Design), after which he 'happened to meet' TED's founder, Chris Anderson, only to discover that TED was looking to replicate its formula to a youth audience via a franchised version, TedX. Blink your eyes and bob's your uncle and Fallibroome has been hosting TedX conferences (since 2009) with around 450 of its own over-16 students attending and 150 students from other schools. The live streaming of all its talks are held in archived recordings on the TedX website and a couple – a fairly huge honour, this – of the Fallibroome youth TEDX speakers have made it onto the main TED website. (An achievement you won't see every day on a university application form, that's for sure.)

And this is by no means a one off example of serendipity and force of will happily colliding; having learnt about the world famous Venezuela Youth Orchestra (a community project which cascaded music teaching down to underprivileged children resulting in a world class orchestra), he decided to model it at Fallibroome (as you do), likewise cascading musical knowledge down to the primary schools via peer tuition. So what next for Fallibroome – a world class orchestra, perhaps? Watch this space.

At the time of our visit, the school had just released an extraordinary video, First day at Fallibroome. No empty marketing exercise, it was a carefully choreographed theatrical extravaganza with every pupil and teacher taking part; five days after its release, it had clocked up 37,000 hits globally and shortly after made it onto regional BBC news. What a joyous 11 minutes; a single tracking shot inside the school, pupils singing, dancing, showcasing what the school offers: scientists doing experiments with fire, orchestras playing, actors reciting, linguists dancing flamingo, woodworkers sawing away, sporty types dribbling footballs. A more inclusive, dazzling display we have rarely seen.

An obvious team player, Rubery refers frequently to Francis Power – now headmaster, previously deputy head – and to whom he attributes much of the school's success, as well as his dedicated team of teachers.

Not surprisingly, having started out as PE teacher, he is keen on team sport and used to play in the national volleyball squad. And showing a little of that cultural diversity he so wants pupils to foster, he loves music, the blues in particular. But there ain't no Muddy Waters about this visionary man or his splendid school.

Francis Power BEd (Limerick), MEd (Dublin) was appointed headteacher in 2016, having been head of school, deputy head and assistant principal.

Academic matters: At GCSE in 2018, 29 per cent of entries got A*-A/9-7. At A level 36 per cent A*/A and 66 per cent A*-Bs. The school does particularly well in maths at A level. Generally, across A levels over the last few years in core subjects (sciences, maths, languages, English) between 45-50 per cent of the entries have got A or A*. Also offers BTecs and other vocational qualifications. Both genders fare about the same and subjects tend to have an even split, possibly with more boys opting for science but only marginally.

From year 8, students are taught in ability groups in English, maths and languages but no pupil should ever rest on their laurels or feel trapped; there are termly reviews and mobility between groups. All start with French plus either Spanish or German, about half take one or more to GCSE and about 14 continue to A level.

To adopt the corporate language which is scattered through Fallibroome's prospectus, its key USP is breadth of curriculum. So beyond the more traditional core A level subjects, pupils can opt for psychology, sociology, dance, music technology or media studies.

Average class size is 30. It's a national teaching school so there is a strong focus on improving teaching quality. The parents we spoke to grumbled a little about high staff turnover over the last 12 months and the inconsistency in teaching styles which resulted, as well as the detrimental impact on pupils when teachers left at a crucial time. One parent said her child had had four changes across four GSCE subjects at crucial times.

So it's not all golden; one parent felt her child had clashed with a teacher in a core subject and that pupil, along with a few others, had resorted to private tuition to fill the gaps where he had 'come into his own' in the subject. Conversely, the same parent praised the school's flexibility; when her child wanted to swap a subject at GCSE, a successful transition was made. Likewise another parent said he felt the 'individualised care and attention for students' was staggeringly good; the staff were 'very supportive in helping pupils reach their potential'.

The school facilities certainly help back up the teaching – nine science labs and every teaching room has e-learning facilities. One parent commented on her child's 'fantastic' IT knowledge, saying the school was 'always one step ahead'. The IT suites had, Peter Rubery said, the highest quality of equipment, the best kit being crucial for high achievement in computing or electronics.

SEN students are well catered for under the school's Quality First Teaching initiative. Different strategies are adopted for different subjects and inclusivity is a driver. Where the student has a EHC plan – there were 23 in place at the time of our visit – they receive the specified help which may include one-to-one. Those without a statement may receive specialist support outside lessons. According to Peter Rubery – and their vast database of metrics can no doubt back this up – SEN students make faster progress than their non-SEN peers.

Games, options, the arts: Fallibroome's status as a college of performing arts has resulted in an embarrassment of riches. The glossy What's On programme was worthy of a West End theatre: spanning all types of concerts, and theatrical offerings, including a play out of the National Theatre Connections Programme. Pupils don't just perform, either; they refine their craft in workshops with the professionals and go on arts trips all over. The impressive performance photos all around the school reinforce a sense of vibrancy, slick production values and widespread participation. Parents spoke with awe about ambitious musical productions like Les Misérables. One parent said such evenings were a 'parade of brilliance' and was quick to add that those who tried hard, but who weren't necessarily the most talented, got recognised at the school's awards evenings for effort. The same parent also said the creative culture meant, refreshingly, boys plunged into music and dance without any self-consciousness. The extracurricular music similarly runs the gamut; orchestras, choirs and ensembles. If you want to compose, do folk or rock guitar, play in a string quartet or a samba band, you can.

With sport, there is a decent spread and good facilities, such as an all-weather pitch. Recently the school's netball team won the National Netball Champions (the first comprehensive school to win the title). Parents of boys who were keen footballers seemed a tad peeved, saying a greater emphasis was placed on rugby (Peter Rubery didn't necessarily accept this). One parent of a talented footballing son said he didn't get the opportunities he would like to play competitively. That said, the school boasts a former Manchester United player (not to mention an ex-Olympic gymnast). The school doesn't have its own pool but the leisure centre is, quite literally, next door.

There are all the usual clubs and societies – not quite as plentiful an array as one might find in pockets of the independent sector, but there are still some unusual ones, such as training in TV (camera work and editing), and when we visited we noted the school had won the British Orienteering Championships recently (again unique for a comprehensive school). One parent said, 'whatever they're interested in, it's happening in the school'.

At sixth form stage, there is an enrichment programme; one inspection report said 'it sets a benchmark for sixth form extracurricular'. So pupils might form part of management teams, debating teams, gain work experience in South Africa (the school's commitment to raising funds for charity means it supports two schools in the rural western Cape) ....or if they fancied it, take up Mandarin. When it comes to writing their personal statement at university application time, these pupils are not going to be scraping that barrel for something arresting to say.

Background and atmosphere: The buildings are mostly modern red brick and, over the school's 36 year history, the many additions have evolved in an organic way. The modernity has a clean Scandi-feel, sunk as it is into woodland lined grounds, vast playing green fields always in sight.

Every wall carries something inspiring to prise open the most closed of adolescent minds. Dazzling art displays, attractively framed photos of school trips from Iceland to the Isle of Man, alongside beautiful photo stills from dance, theatre and music performances. The school's ethos – Trust, Respect, Optimism – hangs in a banner in one of the entrances and, even to sceptical corporate-averse minds such as ours, manages to sound full of gusto. This school really does seem to do what it says on the tin.

The facilities – from the relatively new sixth form centre, described by one parent as 'like being at university', to the recording booths – are extraordinary.

Pastoral care, well-being and discipline: Peter Rubery is keen to reinforce the big investment in this area; a pastoral support centre has a student counsellor and a behaviour support coordinator for more troubled students. Plus, all the usual courses are run in the RESPECT module on drugs, use of online, social media.

Learning managers (heads of year to you and me) monitor the welfare of their group of pupils and are the first point of contact. The pastoral system is overseen by two assistant principals. One parent, whose child had had a few integration difficulties when he started school, referred to the high levels of teacher support, spurring him on to become involved in music; he was quickly assimilated into broader friendship groups. Another parent stressed the pastoral system was not 'cut and paste' but reflected the caring culture; when his child encountered difficulties in sixth form, massive efforts were made to make him feel valued.

None of the parents we spoke to had encountered bullying, but of course with a school of this magnitude, it exists. Peter's Rubery's response, when asked, was to imply to zero tolerance. And we were inclined to believe that.

Peter Rubery is hot on uniform; the pupils wander in herds of bottle green blazers, while sixth formers wear business clothes. A recent inspection report found behaviour to be 'exemplary'. Pupils are motivated into good behaviour with carrots not sticks (house points, letters of commendation – but also attempts to channel a pupil in a more positive way via interests). If this doesn't work, the metaphorical stick kicks in; the usual panoply of detention-type punishments. One parent referred to the 'spectrum of behaviour issues' which existed but felt there was a 'very well designed system of escalating sanctions'; all pupils knew where they stood, it was very effective. Another parent felt it was a respect, not fear-based system.

Pupils and parents: Pupils are drawn from a number of areas; from Cheshire 'wealth spots' like Prestbury to less affluent areas like Upton Priory, so it's a diverse bag. The parents we spoke to found the web portal, The Parental Gateway, helpful in updating them. One parent, a working single mother, found being able to book appointments online helpful. All were complimentary about the school – emailing a teacher was, one said, 'an efficient business'. The only grumble from one was that registering a child's absence was troublesome (having notified the school her child was ill, she would invariably get a follow up later asking why her child was not at school). An irritant rather than a complaint.

Another parent felt that while the children were given heaps of information on universities, parents needed more to help guide them (adolescent monosyllables not always being the best conduit). Conversely, another parent waxed lyrical about the very detailed reporting on each child – postcards, texts, emails – to flag up progress or even if a pupil seemed a bit off colour.

The parents at this school are busy working people; they admire the school, shout from the touchlines at matches and give rousing applause at concerts, but they don't have the time to be caught in a quagmire of pushy parental competitiveness.

Entrance: Applications from pupils from the seven feeder primary schools are prioritised, along with other criteria, such as siblings. All new joiners are invited to spend a day during the summer term to acclimatise.

Exit: Some 60 per cent stay on into sixth form. Every pupil must have 5+ 9-4 grades at GCSE and 6s in A level subjects. In 2018, five to Oxbridge, plus five medics, with about 40 per cent to Russell Group unis: eg Southampton, Bristol, Durham, Warwick, Edinburgh, Newcastle, Leeds, alongside the very popular Manchester and Liverpool. Spread of courses from sciences and social sciences to business and engineering. The spotlight on performing arts means that many go off to drama or music school. Recent destinations have included LIPA, Bird College of Dance, Music and Theatre Performance and Leeds College of Music.

Remarks: This large, wonderful school offers an educational smorgasbord which is as rich and as plentiful as you will find anywhere. It is a place where your child will firm up their identity as a young adult, discover intellectual passions and open their mind to reach academic heights. If you want this for your child, then keep your fingers crossed for a place. If you are wavering between state and independent education for your child, visit this school as a priority.

Godolphin Preparatory School

Linked with Godolphin, Salisbury

Laverstock Road, Salisbury, Wiltshire SP1 2RB

Ages 3–11 **Pupils** 99

Fees: Day £7,125 – £13,905; Boarding £18,720 – £25,230 pa

01722 430652
www.godolphin.org

Head: Since 2014, Julia Miller BA MEd (50s). Having studied history at Queen's University Belfast, followed by a PGCE, she taught at Banbridge Academy, Victoria College and Cheltenham Ladies' College (where she ran DofE and was a deputy housemistress). Head of history and head of house at Godolphin, she was appointed head of the prep after 22 years at the school. She clearly loves it and puts huge enthusiasm and kindness into her dealings with children. Her interests include 16th-20th century history (she still keeps her hand in in the senior school A level course), 20th century historical novels, travel and gardening. Godolphin Prep girls are encouraged to support the local Chalke Valley History Festival.

Entrance: Entry at all stages following an assessment day in the school and satisfactory report from current school head. Ten per cent discount is offered to girls from Forces' families, five per cent for sisters.

Exit: Vast majority (some 75 per cent) choose to remain at Godolphin but can also be prepared for CE. Good record of academic scholarships – some gain music and sporting awards too. Some to popular state secondary South Wilts Grammar School (prep runs 11+ practice sessions for girls' grammar entry) and St Edmund's.

Remarks: Founded in 1993 and nestling in a modern building on the edge of the Godolphin School campus, just by the railway line, the school is a delight. Access is easy with no public parking on site, but masses of space on the road in front of school entrance so dropping off in the morning is a breeze.

The school prides itself on good, solid traditional teaching all round, 'the national curriculum plus a bit more'. Maths is solid, reinforced by clubs in lunch breaks and 'mathletics' programmes on school computers in ICT room. 'Girls have to write every day and put their skills into practice'. French begins in the nursery at 3 and continues throughout; Spanish and German introduced in year 6. Latin, Greek and science after-school clubs; reasoning group provides extra practice for those aiming for 11+. Nice light library perches on a mezzanine floor above main hall in which, on the day we visited, the evening's exciting art exhibition was going up competing with some extremely sophisticated rhythmic clapping from a music class. Small class sizes (12 on average), with some really enterprising teaching and a few new teachers including some men. Our allocated guides were, not surprisingly, slightly reluctant to leave a science class in which they were planning sports events, taking account of the conditions of planets other than the earth. However they waxed lyrical over the pets' corner, were warmly welcomed by Sister Gill and clearly loved every bit of the school.

One pretty expert parent commented that school's learning support teacher is 'wonderful', championing girls' needs, liaising with staff (even the slightly wary ones) and exceptionally well qualified with an impressive array of degrees in psychology and special needs education. This is a school that fits the style of teaching to the child.

Three double games lessons each week, using the senior school's grass pitches and hard courts. Gymnastics for all, lacrosse is introduced in year 5. Until then the main team sports are hockey and netball. Swimming excels with a terrific programme in which all girls swim amazing distances winning handfuls of ASA awards. Everyone swims each week (including for nursery-age children) in fabulous 25-metre swimming pool; the best swimmers are invited to join a competitive swimming squad after school. Extracurricular clubs include kick boxing and yoga; in summer, girls can choose tennis and rounders at break and after school and riders can join senior school equestrian teams.

Recently introduced Elizabeth Godolphin Award is based on the sixth form scheme. Amongst the opportunities available are first aid and life saving courses, robotics, leadership and responsibility roles, mock interviews, debating, independent projects, meetings with senior school leadership team, budgeting and event management.

Instrumental music flourishes, especially now there is a joint senior/junior orchestra. One parent was delighted that her daughter suddenly stopped complaining about orchestra practice. Music is even scheduled for tinies in the nursery. All instrumentalists perform in their own annual concert. Occasional workshops take place with visiting musicians. Lots of obviously enjoyable music – enthusiastic rhythmic clapping happening during our visit. Choir has performed at the Bath Festival and Barbican Centre and regularly joins the senior choir to sing in Salisbury Cathedral. Unusual music theory club open to years 1 to 6; girls regularly pass ABRSM theory of music exams up to grade 2.

Lucky prep girls also have lessons in the amazing senior art block, where the staff are passionate about encouraging art from the beginning, teaching painting, drawing, ceramics and textiles. Drama productions take place every other year in the Blackledge Theatre (impressive performance space). Plenty of lunch time and after-school activities, well timetabled so that children are not too torn between them. Residential trips to Normandy for years 5 and 6 every other year.

Prep school feels quite separate from the main site; older pupils, however, appear very much at home in the senior school buildings. Girls play happily in the small outside playground to the front of the school which features the 'friendship bench'. Anyone sitting there is immediately given care and encouragement by other pupils under the wary eye of Miss Miller, whose room overlooks the playground. The nursery has the lion's share of the grounds at the rear with plenty of safely enclosed spaces. The prep has a lovely light atmosphere enhanced by good use of colour and a spacious feel. Not a revolutionary design, but everything done with children in mind, like the whiteboards that pull down to eye level for the youngest children.

Eagle-eyed staff ensure that everyone chooses sensibly at lunchtimes, when girls walk up to senior dining room. Girls may arrive for breakfast at 7.30am and stay on for prep until 5.40pm. School uniform mirrors senior school kit, with red pinnies (worn over full school uniform), straw boaters (known as boards) and blazers. The nursery children look enchanting in their gingham version of the 'pinny'. Student food council meets once every half term to provide direct feedback to school chef, whilst year 6 leads school council and year 5 selects school charities. Friday assemblies (musicians and public speakers have informal opportunities to perform here) close the school week and parents are welcome.

The very few boarders (6 full, 3 flexi from age 7) are housed in the junior boarding house with 11-13 year olds from the senior school, with wide age ranges within dorms. Weekend activities tailor made though small numbers must limit variety.

The older girls gave the impression that life is fun in the prep school, and the interaction between staff and pupils indicated a real kindness and affection. Gentle and girly though its pupils may look, the priority undoubtedly is education, and parents report that children gain in confidence. Its close proximity to the senior school gives it some outstanding facilities, but none the less this feels and behaves like an autonomous, friendly community.

G

Godolphin, Salisbury

Linked with Godolphin Preparatory School

Milford Hill, Salisbury, Wiltshire SP1 2RA

Ages 11–18 **Pupils** 380 **Sixth form** 95 **Boarders** 60 full, 58 weekly/flexi

Fees: Day £18,975 – £21,090; Boarding £25,530 – £36,225 pa

01722 430509
www.godolphin.org

Headmistress: Since 2014, Emma Hattersley, previously deputy head, pastoral, at Sherborne Girls, before which she was a housemistress at Canford School. Mrs Hattersley trained as an opera singer at the Royal Academy of Music and has a music degree from Durham. Married with three children, she says she took her career break early so that now, in her early 50s, with her children pursuing their own careers, she is able to devote her time entirely to Godolphin. Her actor husband is immensely supportive, to the extent of running 'speakeasy' communications and other workshops in school.

Her calm, unthreatening exterior deceptively understates the determination beneath. Since arriving at Godolphin she says she has identified needs for brightening up areas of the fabric, developing staff and increasing opportunities for charitable activities. In fact she has already started on a programme of new showers, 'nice enough to make the girls feel good', surveyed parents of all leavers, consulted girls and produced her vision document for the future. She has also initiated the Elizabeth Godolphin Award for sixth formers, which gives focus to a programme of self-development and preparedness for work/life demands.

She says she believes in the Godolphin ethos: happiness, warmth, development which is aspirational but 'absolutely not at the expense of well-being'. 'We are not a hothouse' she says, but aim at 'the best we can possibly be in each girl's own style, celebrating diverse talent' and encouraging everyone to 'succeed at the level right for them'. Having taken on a school a little stunned by losing its new head to 'higher things' after three years, she has restored confidence and won parents' and girls' respect with her ability to perceive and develop what is best at Godolphin. A parent commented that 'under Mrs Hattersley staff can really develop their own teaching and pastoral skills.'

G

Academic matters: Definitely academic, with Latin up to A level and Greek on offer, though not taken up much for exams. Spanish, German and French also on offer though with a few following through to A level. Spectacular results in maths and art at both A level and GCSE. In 2018, results were the highest overall for many years, with over 50 per cent A*/A at A level and 83 per cent A*-B. At GCSE, 50 per cent of grades were A*-A/9-7.

French, German, Spanish and Latin taught from first year with Mandarin via a club. All available up to A level except currently Latin, and classical Greek done at GCSE via an 'Academic Society', Girls do either double award science or three individual subjects. The usual subjects are offered plus PE, design and food technology, economics, business studies and drama. Godolphin will put on an A level course for one or two students if necessary, so there's not much you can't do, and options are designed round each girl's requests every year. There is a real buzz of enthusiasm from girls and teachers with excitement that geology is now on-stream as an A level. Parents are enthusiastic about the level of encouragement and individual attention given by teachers. One commented that teachers support girls' particular interests by finding articles and information for them even if it is outside the curriculum. Able girls enjoy events put on by the scholars and Alpinists (Accelerated Learning Programme) activities, though sometimes the compulsory ones are 'a bit groan-worthy'. Girls say most are really interesting and attract lots of non-scholars too. The REBEL (Recreational Enhancement for Bright Energetic Learners) scheme provides appreciated stimulus for year 9.

The few SEN students have plenty of help organised by SENCo/ed psych much praised by parents. Help is one-to-one, in groups, or takes the form of advice to teachers about learning styles of individuals. EAL is managed by SEN department – up to three lessons a week if necessary. Not many pupils need support, but advice to teachers is available from occupational therapist and maths specialist. Godolphin can cope with mild Asperger's. Healthy, friendly respect and affection between teachers and girls abundantly evident.

Games, options, the arts: Art has a huge and impressive building bursting with stunning work in every medium and hugely talented and enthusiastic staff. Very professional looking fabric design work on display as well as fascinating mixed media landscape work and spectacular studies based on work done in the cathedral. Two spacious studios for drawing/painting, with separate rooms dedicated to textiles, ceramics, photography and 3D; another smaller room full of iMacs for graphic design. This a truly brilliant department, making creative use of visits to and by local artists, who regularly initiate GCSE projects, and welcoming parents and visitors to view two floors of really breathtakingly exciting work – smashing results too. DT is no less impressive, with lots of colourful and innovative constructions in wood and plastic on display. It's not surprising academically gifted girls take up art or history of art here and a record number go on to art related courses at uni.

An attractive rotunda houses the performing arts centre with lovely in-the-round theatre, plenty of entertaining space and good practice rooms. Music is very well served, with the head running a popular junior orchestra of girls from prep and senior schools, a head of music who is as encouraging as he is talented, and the meticulous Mrs Sparkhall, who inspires the girls in a choral tradition that wins them the Barnardo's School Choir of the Year and other accolades. Individual lessons still in the unprepossessing and unreconstructed Rose Villa, but pupils and parents don't seem to mind and there's plenty of chamber music, though not much evidence of pop..

All the creative forces come together in drama, typified by recent Oklahoma – spectacular and full of home-grown music and dance. Girls also perform with Portal Theatre, a small, professionally run theatre group. Masses of LAMDA exams and smaller performances.

Lacrosse dominates amongst a total of 90 different teams covering all the usual girls' winter and summer sports. Netball actually fields 23 teams and tennis 14, as well as teams in all the major girls' school sports – quite a feat for a smallish school. All sports reach a pretty high level considering the school's size, swimming aided by a sleek 25 metre indoor pool. Highly competitive equestrian stars, and lacrosse and netball high fliers get to county and regional teams. Achievements include U13 netball team winning county championships and one girl selected for England U18 lacrosse squad and one for Wales. One hockey lover's parent commented that perhaps it came second best to lacrosse, but acknowledged that there is plenty of opportunity, even so. No lack of outdoor and other related activities. One girl reported enthusiastically on taking part in the Dartmoor Ten Tors expedition after thorough training through CCF (quite unusual in a girls' school).

Boarding: Girls can start boarding from 7 or 8 in the prep, when they join the junior house, Cooper. Boarding is about as flexi as it goes, with everything from full time to weekly to flexi (one or more nights per week). One parent commented that though full boarding had been ideal for her daughter because they were not too far away, it tends to focus a bit much on activities for foreign students. Current flexibility is dependent on there being some beds available.

Accommodation is simple, modern and not unnaturally tidy, with Walter House now home to girls aged between 11 and 16 and School House dedicated accommodation for sixth formers. Complete refurbishment of boarding is still in progress; study bedrooms are comfortably spacious with plenty of storage and common areas.

Shared dining hall adjoins junior and senior houses. Sixth form house has its own dining room, kitchen, study areas, often with staff at hand, careers advice and leisure space with a proper Café Aroma serving the obligatory coffee shop range of expresso etc. Health provision is supervised by the indomitable Sister Gill, who creates an aura of calm, unfussy friendliness much appreciated by all.

Background and atmosphere: Unusually for a girls' school Godolphin has a long history, dating from a bequest made in 1726 by Elizabeth Godolphin, eventually resulting in the establishment in the cathedral close of a school for 'eight orphaned gentlewomen' who followed a remarkably enlightened curriculum for their day. It moved to its present 16 acre site in Milford Hill in 1891, retaining its links with the cathedral, with the bishop and chapter still represented on the governing body. Skilful use of space and the site still has a gracious feel, generated by the mellow red brick of the original building and the lovely open grass pitches with views of the downs enhanced by banks of lavender at the time of our visit. One has to look quite hard to find the few scruffy corners that Mrs Hattersley is determined to clear. The huge gothic school hall has the dusty feel (it certainly isn't, as the school is exceptionally clean and fresh) which old wood, high ceilings and portraits of ex-heads inevitably evoke. Road access is made awkward by several right-angled bends in the road, but efficient planning of parking helps, though parents report it can still be a bit of a maelstrom at pick up time.

Uniform is unremarkable: pale blue shirt, plaid skirt and navy blazer enhanced by stylish boater with crested red ribbons, known as a 'board'. All, however, is concealed by coverall old fashioned pinafores in royal blue for seniors (except sixth who wear own clothes, plus suits for going to the cathedral), red for preps and gingham for nursery. Oddly, girls seem to like this antiquated touch, while one parent attributed the school's exceptionally friendly and unthreatening atmosphere to the fact that no ultra-trendy girl would be seen dead wearing one. This is certainly a school where those who have been bullied elsewhere find general acceptance and support. An exceptionally happy place with few exclusive 'in groups', where the occasional 'falling out' is sympathetically dealt with by friendly staff, evidently liked and trusted by pupils. With its historic cathedral links, this is an overtly Christian school with a chaplain, using the cathedral for services and confirmation, though one parent regretted that it had to be on a Thursday to ensure parent availability.

Pastoral care, well-being and discipline: Pastoral care is delivered to day girls – known as 'Sarums' – and boarders together through the residential houses, which all have provision for day girls and welcome them to work and relax with the boarders. Lessons end at 4pm, but the myriad of school activities and prep run in three sessions after tea. School houses involve all ages from nursery to sixth form for competitions, fundraising and social events. Personal development is delivered in the PERSIL programme (another quirky Godolphin acronym representing Personal, Ethical, Religious and Social Issues in Life). In the sixth form the Elizabeth Godolphin Award encourages activities aimed at preparation for life after school. Truly all-embracing, it includes Prue Leith cookery (expensive), banking and finance, with car maintenance, emotional literacy, women's boot camp and dawn visits to Stonehenge all part of the bigger picture.

Firm, friendly, no-nonsense discipline leads to an atmosphere in which girls and teachers are at home with each other. The best is expected of everyone. Rules are few but clearly stated, and parents say problems such as drugs, smoking or alcohol are 'simply not part of the culture'. Girls rarely abuse the freedom they have to go into Salisbury attend socials with other schools, or entertain guests in the sixth form. 'Staff seem to care as much as I do', one parent commented.

Pupils and parents: Mostly middle class with a total of about 14 per cent international students, mainly from the Far East. Not a 'toff' school, though pupils are not averse to joining up with Eton and Winchester for social events. Huge day catchment area has bus routes from every direction. In an area with ambitious state schools, art and music still attract pupils, as does the excellent pastoral care. Parents are pleased at how open pupils seem, speaking easily to adults and confident in public, but also that younger ones still behave like children.

Past pupils (with houses named after them) include the full spectrum of women writers, Jilly Cooper, Minette Walters and Dorothy Sayers as well as prolific novelist Amanda Brookfield. TV personalities include Dragon's Den businesswoman Deborah Meaden, Katie Knapman of Countryfile, presenters Helen Bishop and Louise Beale, sportswoman Ruby Smith, yachtswomen Hannah White and Nicola Rodriguez as well actress Charlotte Longfield.

Entrance: At 11+, 12+, 13+ and sixth form, with 'snapshot' mornings running throughout the year. Registered 11+ pupils invited for a preview day in the autumn term, before taking entrance exams in the spring term. Uses its own 11+ entrance test – maths, English and verbal reasoning, plus interview and team building exercises. Organises its own 13+ assessments 18 months prior to entry (13+ CE only used for setting purposes).

Exit: In 2018, 35 per cent left after GCSE, to local state schools and sixth form colleges. Most sixth formers go on to higher education, plenty art related, and a good proportion of Russell Group universities, with top destinations Exeter, Cardiff, Durham, Edinburgh and Bristol. One to Oxbridge, one medic and one to Parsons School of Design in New York in 2018; lots of bright hopes for the future.

Money matters: Scholarships at 11+ and 13+ for outstanding merit or promise in academic work, music, sport or art. Awards are worth 15 per cent of boarding or day fees. In sixth form, scholarships awarded for all of the above plus drama. Additional bursaries may be awarded to scholars in case of financial hardship. Six Foundation Bursaries (worth 70 per cent) are offered to orphans in need of financial support, when one parent has died or whose parents are separated or divorced. An Old Godolphin Association Bursary (25 per cent) is occasionally available to the daughter or granddaughter of a former pupil at the school. Entrance bursaries are available to all eligible candidates (including at 14+) in order of registration – so it may pay to get in early.

Remarks: It seems an idyllic school, almost too good to be true, and there is no doubt that it offers the very best of single sex education. For all its gentleness and Railway Children look, teaching is tip-top, especially now a real effort has gone into IT. Art and music are about as good as you can get and drama and games exceptional for a small school. Girls can really be themselves and the eccentric and the sociable are equally accepted. A very special place to grow up in.

The Grange Junior School

Linked with The Grange School

Beechwood Avenue, Hartford, Northwich, Cheshire CW8 3AU

Ages 4–11 **Pupils** 423

Fees: £8,340 – £9,045 pa

01606 77447
www.grange.org.uk

Headmaster: Since 2014, Guy Rands (40s). Previously academic deputy head of the Grange Senior School. Studied molecular biology at Manchester University. He began his career working for a pharmaceutical company in Switzerland and moved into teaching after a stint volunteering in a special school and time working in residential childcare. His first teaching job was at a grammar school in the Wirral and he had always worked in secondary schools – teaching science and in leadership roles – until, as academic deputy head at the Grange, he became interested in 'the formative stage' and decided to spend half a day a week at the junior school, focusing his thoughts on 'how to get that stage spot on' and 'embed the values that will set the children up for life'. When the previous head of the juniors decided to move on, Mr Rand surprised everyone – maybe even himself – by applying for the job.

He seems delighted to have made the move and comes across as a people-person, equally loved by colleagues, parents and pupils alike. 'I really enjoy the interaction with parents,' he says; '90 per cent of what I do is talking to people – actually mainly listening.' He's certainly won the parents over. Not only is he at the school gate every morning to greet families as they arrive but, parents told us, 'he makes a point of talking to people he hasn't spoken to before – you don't just go and talk to him if you've got a problem, he'll come up and start a conversation'. We haven't got room to list all the examples parents gave us of Mr Rands going the extra mile for them and their children but our favourite story is that he phoned a little girl at home on her birthday because he hadn't been able to get a card to her – as he normally does for all pupils – and didn't want her to think he'd forgotten.

Mr Rands has the charm and confidence you'd associate with an ex public-schoolboy (he went to Abingdon) but he's also unassuming and quick to talk about the successes of others. He seems to lead by bringing the community together and developing people. He said the leadership structure was 'top heavy' when he arrived and one of his first acts was to make several internal appointments – giving staff more responsibility and building a bigger leadership team.

He continues to teach science – weekly to one year 6 class – and he also brings his passion for outdoor activities to the school. There are 'empty classroom days' when all the learning happens outside and Mr Rands himself often leads 'headteacher's walks' through Delamere Forest – inviting all the children in a year group to join him and other staff members for a hearty Saturday hike. He also plays the piano (his wife is a piano teacher) and involves himself in the local community – having made a conscious choice to live in the village. He is married, with three sons.

Entrance: At 4+ by a play-based assessment group session. Not hugely selective – they take in a fairly mixed ability cohort, just a little above average ability, so most applicants get a 'definite yes'. The 'definite nos' are usually the children who 'aren't listening to anyone' in the assessment. For entry to later years assessment is a little more formal. If the response is a 'not yet', parents get detailed feedback on what progress their child needs to make to be accepted and, the school says, up to 80 per cent of applicants are successful on a second try.

Exit: There's an expectation that all will go to the senior school and they've recently stopped making all junior school children sit the entrance exam. However, if by about the end of year 4 a child is slipping behind, the school will talk to the parents about senior school options. They will be supported to find a suitable other school or, if they really want their child to stay on, the school will work to life the child's progress sufficiently. If there are still concerns by the autumn term of year 5, the child may be told they have to sit the entrance exam – though this proviso may be lifted if they buckle down. One or two children a year do end up going to other secondary schools.

Remarks: We don't come away from every school visit sighing that we wish we could send our own children here, but the Grange Junior School did have that effect on this particular reviewer. We've never yet found a school that says 'the only thing that's important is the academic side. We have no interest in developing the whole person or making children happy,' but the level of pastoral care we witnessed on this visit was out of the ordinary. The senior leadership team meets every morning to plan the day ahead and go through every incident – every worried parent, unwell child, friendship issue or confidence crisis – that has made it onto their radar. The school's response to any pastoral issue – from bereavements, family traumas or serious illnesses through to the most seemingly low-level upsets – is joined-up, empathetic and proactive. Once the senior leaders have talked, they head out into the playground – come rain or shine – to greet the children and parents as they arrive and make themselves as available as possible to anyone who might need to speak to them.

The parents we met absolutely concurred that the pastoral care here is second to none. One mum gave the example of some friendship issues her daughter went through in year 4. After the parents had got together and tried, unsuccessfully, to sort things out, they approached the school. Staff were already aware of the issue and intervened with a number of sessions with the girls involved – mediating their conversations to help them work through their problems and running sessions with them on how to be a good friend. 'They're all really good friends now,' said the mum, 'and now whenever anyone around her is going through any sort of conflict, I can see my daughter putting what she learned into practice and trying to be a mediator herself!'

A couple of parents talked to us about how well they felt the school takes care of children with serious medical issues. A child with type 1 diabetes has been included in all sorts of activities, trips and residential visits that, according to her mum, 'I know she wouldn't have been enabled to do at some other schools'. Another child, who was hospitalised for a few days with shingles, was inundated with visits from the school staff. The ethos of taking care of each other seems to have permeated everyone in the community from reception-age children to parents and ancillary staff. It's not uncommon for parents to go to the school with concerns about someone else's child; but it is uncommon for them to be met with a response other than 'Yes – we know about that issue. We're already on it.'

There's a wide range of enrichment activities on offer to junior children – outdoor pursuits are a big thing here and there are plenty of outdoorsy trips and activities. 'I don't think I've ever seen my son so animated and happy as when he got off the bus after the visit to Coniston,' one mum told us. There's also an emphasis on fundraising – both for local and international charities (the school is partnered with a school in Gambia); the junior school raised nearly £5,000 in just a few months. The main sports are rugby, football, netball and hockey – with regular opportunities for boys and girls to play against other local schools. Clubs – held both at lunchtime and after school – include textiles, philosophy, rowing (a big thing at the senior school), Lego and debating. There are nativity plays for the infants and years 4 and 6 have a chance to take part in a lavish performance in the senior school's professionally-equipped theatre. Parents can also pay for their children to have private drama tuition as well as music tuition – and there are plenty of opportunities for young musicians, in the junior school orchestra, its choir or playing their instruments solo, to perform in informal school concerts and to larger audiences at venues like Manchester's Bridgewater Hall.

The facilities are better than you'd find in some secondary schools. There's a lot of specialist teaching and the resources to go with it. From year 5 the children are allowed to use the Bunsen burners in the beautifully equipped science lab and they also get specialist languages (French and Spanish), music, PE, DT and art teaching. Now that pupils in year 6 don't have to sit the senior school's entrance exam, they work towards a Junior School Curriculum Award instead.

Parents felt the school would equally suit a very bright child and one that was just above average. 'They work to find out what your child is good at and take it from there,' said one parent. 'I feel my daughter is getting a bespoke education,' said another.

We couldn't coax the parents into any sustained grumbling. The only minor point a few agreed on was that the school could do more to instil good table manners. In fact one mum said her child's manners had actually worsened since he started school. 'They're in such a rush to go out and play,' said another, 'they just stuff their food down and run.' Another mum was not impressed when she suggested to her children that they should say grace one evening. 'Who's Grace?' they replied. But beyond the Grange's abject failure to function as a Swiss finishing school, parents say the children are proud of their school and respect the facilities: 'After a sports match I watched my son telling a child from another school, "you can't wear your muddy boots in here".' They also feel the school's values shine through every aspect of life at The Grange. 'They do compete but most of all they want to be the best they can be,' said one mum. 'And they celebrate each other's successes,' added another. 'When I praised my son for being a good friend to someone, he said "it wasn't just me," and he went on to list all the other children who'd been kind.' Parents say they feel the school is nurturing children to grow up 'feeling they can change the world'.

The Grange School

Linked with The Grange Junior School

Bradburns Lane, Hartford, Northwich, Cheshire CW8 1LU

Ages 11–18 **Pupils** 727 **Sixth form** 166

Fees: £11,160 pa

01606 539039
www.grange.org.uk

Head: Since 2016, Debbie Leonard MEd BEd (early 50s), previously head of Croydon High School for Girls. She comes across as warm, straightforward and practical. Brought up in Cumbria, her family background is a world away from privileged life of an average Grange pupil. She was raised in a town where 'the boys went to the shipyard and the girls went to the slipper factory' and she was the only one of her four siblings to go to university. She did her BEd – in PE with maths – at Leeds Metropolitan University and continued to teach maths as well as PE throughout her teaching career, alongside being a high level hockey coach. Although she doesn't play hockey any more, she's still active and outdoorsy and as committed to sport as ever. With a masters in management and learning, she had senior management and leadership roles at Thetford Grammar and Nottingham Girls' School before becoming head of Croydon High.

She has introduced an online progress tracker and communications tool called Firefly (which the parents and pupils seem to love. 'It really helps us to know what's going on,' said a mum; and sixth formers raved about the range of academic resources and articles it gives them access to.

Parents we met were universally positive about her – saying they 'like her style' and find her 'warm' and 'approachable'. Pupils told us she's 'really nice', turns up at 'every school event' and she's 'really interested in knowing all about you'. 'She's really open,' said a sixth former; 'you can ask her anything and she'll tell you the truth straight out.'

Academic matters: Pupils do very well here academically and they're encouraged to follow their passion. In 2018, 56 per cent of A levels were A*/A; at GCSE, 72 per cent A*-A/9-7. The school offers a wide range of A level subjects – with art, graphics and textiles each available as a separate choice as well as Spanish, German, drama, business, philosophy and computing. Many of these subjects run with very small classes – low down into single figures – but sixth formers told us they'd felt no pressure from the school as to which subjects to choose, regardless of class numbers or the perceived academic status of the subject (they said they couldn't say the same for their parents).

The school is selective but the bar is not as high as people think and Mrs Leonard says it does well at GCSE by going for quality over quantity. 'If a child's got a lot going on with sport or another passion, we're not going to force them to give it all up just to put everything into the academic side,' she says. 'It's about making sure they've got options. Helping them to get a good core set of GCSEs – but they don't need 11 9-8s. Nine 7s is still great.'

G

The school supports pupils with mild special educational needs such as dyslexia – generally at no extra cost to parents. One mum told us her daughter's dyslexia was only discovered when she joined the senior school (the school screens all children in year 7 for SEN issues) but that the support she's had with it since has been 'phenomenal'. The head says 'quite a lot' of children have some kind of processing difficulty like dyslexia and the school finds ways to give each child the individual support they need. It is also accessible to pupils with physical disabilities and has had several wheelchair-using pupils in recent years.

Pupils tell us they get a lot of support from teachers and have strong and respectful relationships with them. 'The teachers try to understand what you're good at,' said one. 'If you're struggling you can ask for help and you'll get it,' added another pupil. 'So long as you're trying and you're not just doing the bare minimum, it'll be OK.' 'And there's stretch if you need it,' chipped in a third; 'you can always do extra work but they don't force it on you.' One sixth former told us she went from a B in her year 10 chemistry mock to an A* in the GCSE because she did the school's Boosting Bs programme. Another girl told us she had always found maths hard but she was never made to feel that she was at the bottom of the class. 'The teacher found a way to bring us all together as a class,' she said, 'so I always felt part of things and supported.'

Games, options, the arts: We met a well-travelled group of pupils on our visit. Between them they'd visited the Galapagos Islands, Mexico, the Hague (for the Model United Nations), Thailand and various cities across the USA. Only the depth of parental pockets limits the travel opportunities. But the Grange community doesn't just feather its own nest. The school supports countless charities – both locally and internationally – and sends generous amounts of funding to a school in The Gambia. It also celebrates the individual children who go to great lengths to help a good cause – like the little girl who donated her hair to a charity that makes wigs for children or the boy who raised over £20,000 for Alder Hey Children's Hospital. The Grange's Community Action Group sends pupils out volunteering to local primary schools, care homes or to help with riding for the disabled.

There's a spirit of joining in, the pupils tell us: 'you don't have to be the best at something to have a go.' Drama is big here – doubtless helped by the lavishly equipped theatre in the round. There are a lot of musical opportunities too – with orchestras, a big band, choirs and smaller singing ensembles and countless informal opportunities for pupils to gather together and make music.

We walked through inspiring and well-equipped textiles, art and graphics studio spaces, staffed by specialist practitioners, where pupils could put in the hours to experiment and develop their own creative practice.

If there's demand for a club that doesn't yet exist – they'll set it up. Different year groups mix and make friends in the clubs, and not many schools we've visited have been so wholehearted in their commitment to the arts.

The rowing club has a fleet of over 50 boats, housed in two boathouses on the river Weaver, with opportunities to compete at high level. New sports centre. Traditional sports divide: we met a couple of girls who said they'd like to have exactly the same sports on offer to them as boys have (although the school says a recent pupil survey showed this isn't a priority to most).

Background and atmosphere: The Grange begin its existence in 1933 as a prep school but, in the 1970s, the parent body didn't want their children to one of the new comprehensives and so the school made the unusual progression to teaching children right up to 18.

So it's not steeped in centuries of tradition; you won't get a tour of a resplendent chapel with stained glass windows by Burne-Jones and you don't need a jargon-busting phrase book to understand what the pupils are saying.

The lack of a long history seems to run alongside a relaxed attitude to some of the sacred cows of the independent sector. 'We do encourage Oxbridge,' says Mrs Leonard. 'If a pupil's got the ambition to go, we say: "go for it," and we'll prepare them. But it's not the be all and end all. And university isn't right for some children at all. We're really open to apprenticeships.'

The school is nominally Christian but welcoming to all faiths. Mrs Leonard has just updated the school values: 'they were lovely but a bit comfortable'. She's big on building resilience and encouraging a growth mindset: 'I don't want children who just crumple because they've failed,' she says. 'They need to understand that you learn through failure'.

Pastoral care, well-being and discipline: Parents say pastoral care here is second to none. They gave countless examples of the lengths the school has gone to to support their children and get on top of problems early. Pupils say they feel well known by the staff and that there are lots of people they could turn to if they are in trouble. There's a full-time trained counsellor on site and sixth formers run a peer support scheme. 'It's nice to speak to someone who's been there,' said a year 11 pupil, talking about the stresses of GCSEs. 'The school is really on top of mental health,' added another pupil; 'there's a culture of talking about feelings and supporting each other.'

Teachers seem to know what's going on with individuals and friendship groups but they don't always barge in to resolve a problem. 'My head of year noticed my best friend was struggling with her workload before I did,' one sixth former told us. 'He asked me if I could look out for her. I thought that was really impressive. Somehow they always know what's going on.'

Everyone we spoke to – staff, pupils and parents – said misbehaviour is low level and uncommon. On our visit we found all the children to be friendly, polite and well-behaved. Though we did walk past some sort of play-scuffle outside a classroom, which culminated in a resounding slap, that echoed down the corridor. it seemed good-humoured enough. We mention it only because we were amused by the horror-stricken whispers of 'that was the Good Schools Guide!' 'Did she see?' 'She didn't see.' She did. But she was impressed that the perpetrators didn't want to let their school down.

When it comes to more serious infringements of the rules, Mrs Leonard is inclined to support and protect a child – so long as they're not putting other pupils at risk. She says she believes in second chances and that 'it's not always black and white', but there certainly are instances where she would have no hesitation but to remove a pupil.

Pupils and parents: We met pupils who travel up to an hour to get to school. About a quarter of Grange pupils are very local – a good number walk to school – and the rest travel in from other parts of Cheshire. School buses come in from as far away as Chester, Crewe, Nantwich and Knutsford. Most pupils are white, although we've seen less diverse schools.

Parents we met were fiercely supportive of the school. Some got quite emotional telling us how much it means to them. They evidently have enough money to afford the fees but several hadn't expected to send their children to independent schools and had been state educated themselves. The small group of parents we met came across as nurturing rather than competitive.

Entrance: The Grange is academically selective but not hugely so. If your child is in the top third of their class in primary school they'll probably get in. 'It's about making sure they can access the curriculum and thrive here,' says Mrs Leonard. 'We won't fill up just for the sake of it.' The school sets its own English, maths, verbal and non-verbal reasoning tests. 'Parents ask me "where's the line?"' says Mrs Leonard, 'but the reality is there isn't a line. We look at the whole child and try to make sure we can meet their needs. We don't want a child to be bottom of the form at everything – that's no good for them.'

Sixth for applicants have an interview and need a reference from their current school. They also need 7+ at GCSE in every subject to be studied at A level – or related subjects if they didn't do them at GCSE – and at least a 6 in all their other GCSEs.

Exit: Up to 15 per cent leave the school after GCSEs. Almost all sixth formers go to university – some take a gap year first. Lots go to Russell Group universities; four to Oxbridge in 2018 and four medics.

Pupils told us they get good careers education. There are fortnightly breakfast talks with former students, careers evenings and careers interviews. Professional parents also help – we met a physiotherapist who worked with a group of sixth formers interested in this as a career.

Money matters: Fees are a touch lower than other independent schools in the north west, but parents do pay extra for school dinners, trips and exam fees. There's a 10 per cent siblings discount and a very small bursary fund – based on academic merit and means-testing. Also music and sixth form scholarships.

Remarks: A nurturing, buzzing and unpretentious school. Pupils are happy, inspired and purposeful. They get great results and seem to be having a lovely time.

Greenbank Preparatory School

Heathbank Road, Cheadle Hulme, Cheadle, Cheshire SK8 6HU

Ages 3–11 **Pupils** 138

Fees: £8,400 pa

0161 485 3724
www.greenbankschool.co.uk

Headmistress: Since 2007, Janet Lowe, Cert Ed (50s). Previously head of infants at Stockport Grammar School. Married to a chartered surveyor, with two grown up children. Enjoys book club and attending performances by the Hallé Orchestra, also an honorary member of the Cheadle and District Rotary. Has a hands-on approach to her headship, taking a weekly story time in reception class, running year 2 and 3 recorder club and teaching RE to years 1 to 6. 'I want to be involved with the children', she tells us. 'I really get to know them and their families'. Parents describe her as 'strong, approachable and forward thinking'.

Retiring in July 2019. Her successor will be Malcolm Johnson, currently deputy head of Cheadle Hulme Junior School.

Entrance: At age 3 into pre-school with some places held back for those who want reception entry. Entry is non-selective, on a first come, first served basis, with the only preference given to siblings. Places can and do become available later so always worth trying. There is also a day nursery on site and many children come from here.

Exit: Top choices in 2018, Cheadle Hulme School and Manchester Grammar. Also Withington Girls, Stockport Grammar School, Alderley Edge School for Girls.

Remarks: Founded in 1951 in the house that is now the day nursery, now in modern, light and airy buildings on a spacious, green plot. Not much parking on site, but enough space on Heathbank Road for dropping off and picking up.

Mixed ability classes, but school believes strongly in differentiating work so that each child is treated according to their ability. Small groups receive extra support in all the different areas of the curriculum so that no child slips through the net. One mum told us, 'Never once have I felt that my children have been left to struggle. Support is always there'. 'Every pupil is set individual targets and it is up to us to make sure they achieve them', the head tells us.

French is taught throughout the school, with German and Spanish introduced in the juniors. Additionally, year 6s have a French conversation club and are also taught Latin and Mandarin. A part-time SENCo dyslexia specialist and teaching assistants work with small groups and one-to-one. Gifted and talented programme stretches bright pupils and offers a range of educational experiences. Recently children have attended workshops on space, art geometry and poetry.

Good sport including football, rounders, water polo, netball and swimming. Thriving and impressive range of extracurricular activities for a small school, including drama, gymnastics, cheerleading, art, football, cross-country and cookery. There's even a mums' keep fit club.

Excellent music department. Nearly half the pupils have individual instrumental tuition, school holds regular music and drama productions and there are infant and junior choirs. We saw a rehearsal for an assembly on Bollywood dancing and both the staff and children looked as if they were having great fun.

Specialist art teacher with her own large, bright room. Art is taken seriously here with pupils regularly winning inter-school competitions, and there is some amazing work hung throughout the school. We were very taken by the Gaudi lizards created by year 6.

Library and computer room staffed by a librarian who also runs popular lunch-time touch typing club. Truly wonderful eco garden, complete with herb and vegetable patch, bird hide and pond. Regularly used for lessons, but also by the science and gardening clubs.

Lots of trips and residentials, including Lake District, London and France. Smart grey and yellow uniform. Before and after-school care offered at extra cost. Children told us that school dinners were 'yummy' and the dinner ladies were 'very kind'.

Small, friendly school that does fantastically well for its pupils. Head tells us, 'it's a combination of fabulous teaching and our commitment that all our children should have very high self-esteem. Then they'll learn and achieve'.

The Gryphon School

Bristol Road, Sherborne, Dorset DT9 4EQ

Ages 11–18 **Pupils** 1,572 **Sixth form** 374 **C of E**

01935 813122
www.gryphon.dorset.sch.uk

G

Headteacher: Since June 2017, Nicki Edwards, previously deputy head since 2002. A graduate of Imperial College (biology), she went on to complete her PGCE at Oxford. Ofsted has praised Mrs Edwards in their latest inspection (November 2017), saying she has 'brought renewed focus and energy to the school's drive to ensure the quality of teaching, learning and assessment is as strong as it can be'.

She is a mother of twins, both Gryphon alumni and living in London, one of whom is a teacher and the other works in finance. Active in the local community, as church warden of Milborne Port Church and Bishops' Advisor, she also enjoys travelling, reading and when time allows, needlepoint.

Former headteacher Steve Hillier has taken on the role of executive head of the Sherborne Area Schools' Trust (SAST) of which The Gryphon is a founding member.

Academic matters: Commendable results by any standards and particularly for a non-selective school. Vibrant, ambitious sixth form with significant influx from other schools offers vocational options alongside A levels, such as level 3 BTec courses. At A level, 32 per cent A*/A in 2018. GCSE results also impressive: in 2018, 25 per cent A*/A/7-9 grades at GCSE and 70 per cent got 9-4 in both maths and English, well above the national average. Good showing in vocational choices too. Academic commitment is expected from the off; some parents feel that too much homework is given in year 7.

Pupils speak very highly of their teachers: 'approachable, passionate about their subject, willing to give up their time'. Maths, economics and art were singled out for particular praise – we were less sure about the guillotine in one history class room. Library and computer provision modern and well-resourced and the school places great emphasis on e-learning through its BYOD policy.

The proportion of students with SEN is higher than average; we suspect because of the school's excellent provision, which includes a 35-strong SEN team all of whom have their own particular expertise, plus a dedicated space 'the blue room' where the troubled and overwhelmed can withdraw when it all gets a bit much. Here, sessions on self-esteem and anger management are run alongside more conventional catch-up sessions in literacy and numeracy. All new arrivals are screened on entry and school maintains close links with local services such as CAMHS; efforts are made to intervene early and to investigate causes behind disruptive behaviour, rather than merely dealing with it.

Games, options, the arts: The breadth and enthusiasm for sport and the arts make The Gryphon an all-encompassing school and the recipient of the Artsmark gold award. Its site on the edge of Sherborne means ample space for pitches, courts, Astroturf and a leisure centre with fitness suite, dance studio and sports hall (which could do with updating, say parents), also available to the community at certain times. Swimmers use the indoor facilities of the two independents in the town. Usual offering of rugby, hockey and netball (where some teams are coached by local club coaches) branches out into golf, basketball, karate, shooting and solo star-dance up to national standard. School also has a show-jumping team in this horsey part of the world, though set up and run by parents.

Participation rates are high – two hours PE per week are timetabled up to year 11 with options changing every six weeks, 'and there's a team for everyone', according to our small guide, a keen netball player. At the weekly enrichment afternoon for sixth form, sport is the most popular choice at whatever level; members of staff and some sixth formers took part in a 10K Christmas Pudding run for charity. School an undoubted presence in the local sporting scene – 'nakedly competitive,' said one sixth former, grimly – which takes on all comers with relish, particularly the local independents, and with considerable success. The Sports Award evening is a highlight in the school calendar.

Music a real strength here too, in this most musical of towns; school benefits from close relationships with the abbey and the other Sherborne schools, all of whom contribute to the Sherborne Symphonia, a joint orchestra, and lots of other collaborations. Success on the national stage too, with high rankings in the BBC Songs of Praise Choir of the Year and students gaining places in the National Youth Choir and Orchestra. But the school celebrates its own music too, with two full concerts, a carol service in the abbey and a European music tour every year, for both singers and players, and numerous opportunities inside and outside its gates.

Drama and film-making also prominent: musical theatre the runaway favourite with recent productions of Les Misérables, Oliver! and West Side Story, but more adventurously, a version of Dr Faustus updated to 80s London and a feature film of Far from the Madding Crowd in recent years.

Art and design of similarly high standard; some stunning furniture made by recent A level students would grace any avant-garde shop window. 'We're not spoon-fed – we're encouraged to develop our own ideas', said one A level artist. Younger ones work with textiles, food and resistant materials in rotation; school boasts a professional catering kitchen alongside its art and design studios. Photography also popular, and much work is exhibited locally.

Background and atmosphere: Founded in 1992 out of an amalgam of local schools, the Gryphon's undistinguished buildings were purpose built for 800 or so, and now house double that number. The gripe we heard from everyone was lack of space: considerable congestion in corridors at peak times and no room for lockers, but addition of two new classrooms helps. Outdoor sitting space with nice wooden tables and benches a precious overflow, but surely bleak in midwinter.

Not yet 30 years old, the school nonetheless feels agreeably traditional in terms of its expectations, aspirations and values, reflected in its naming after an ancient and noble mythical beast. The gryphon appears on the uniform navy blue sweatshirt and all published material. School rightly makes the most of its position as Sherborne's secondary school by holding prize-givings and carol services in the abbey.

Relationships between students and staff, which are collaborative and supportive without crossing the boundary into familiarity, are universally praised: 'We want this to be an island of civility, not a shouty school.' Even the newest/youngest/shyest students feel as though they are recognised as individuals. School appears to cater for all comers: 'I've got one very bright one, one really naughty and one not very bright and it's suited them all,' said one frank mother.

Parents report mostly good communication from teachers via email (it could be sharpened up when a child is absent, for example), but that parents' evenings are a scrum. A local church which has outgrown its premises meets every Sunday in the conference room, and one of its clergy has been appointed chaplain three days a week, but the school does not feel overtly Christian. That said, we did not spot much religious or ethnic diversity, but significantly a few years ago one student felt moved to start a campaign called 'I am Me', celebrating difference and amounting to a powerful statement against bullying – an initiative which gained her a national award.

Pastoral care, well-being and discipline: Exceptional. School has UN Rights Respecting School status and expectations of behaviour are laid down with positive reinforcement under the guidelines which grace every classroom – 'catch them being good' is a policy statement, and the prevailing culture is one of reward and recognition. 'Teachers are good at making us feel our age and giving us the right amount of responsibility, but they don't nag', said one older boy. Everyone we talked to commented on the close eye the school keeps on healthy relationships between students, and a sixth former remarked on the sense of community between the staff. Sanctions, which are not applied in haste, take the form of detentions of increasing length and seriousness.

Pupils and parents: Mostly white and relatively to very prosperous – school has a lower than average percentage of free school meals – and with a genuine commitment to education and a sense that they are fortunate indeed to be at The Gryphon. Masses bussed in from anything up to 20 miles away; 'I was determined to go to The Gryphon, even though we live out of catchment,' said one new girl. Several teachers from local independent schools send their children; yet more blurring of the lines between the Sherborne schools. The students we met were jolly, chatty yet thoughtful – and pleased with their lot.

Past students of note from this young school include two actors (Sam Dorsey and Ben Hardy), one rising star in film production and another at Bath Rugby.

Entrance: Officially 240 places for year 7, which are almost always oversubscribed by 30 or so – no wonder the place is such a squash. Most come from nine partner primary schools but a quarter of the intake from outside the (largely rural) catchment area; this is a highly regarded school locally. Though transition arrangements appear to be good once the kids arrive at school, at least one parent felt more effort could be made to reach children coming from outlying schools.

At sixth form, nearly 40 per cent arrive from local state and independent schools; entry requirements are five GCSEs at grade 4 or above to include maths and English, preceded by an interview in the spring. A level choices in maths, the sciences and languages require a 6 at GCSE. Some 95 per cent of sixth form students stay on to complete year 13. 'They're knocking at the door to get in at sixth form', remarked one mother.

Exit: Some leave after GCSE to pursue less academic courses at Yeovil College. UCAS guidance gets top marks from students: almost everyone to their first choice universities in 2018, including two to Oxbridge and one medic. Bristol, Edinburgh, Exeter, Manchester, Newcastle and UCL popular; one off to do French studies at the University of London Instutute in Paris and one to study architecture at Georgia Tech in Atlanta (on a full scholarship) in 2018. Some apprenticeships and a few gap years.

Remarks: Super, much sought-after school at the very centre of its community and taking on the Sherborne independents. Truly a model of comprehensive education at its best – a place for all comers, which children and parents set their heart on, so it bulges at the seams.

Haberdashers' Adams

High Street, Newport, Shropshire TF10 7BD

Ages 11–18 **Pupils** 926 **Sixth form** 334 (94 girls) **Boarders** 93 full, all boys

Fees: Day free; Boarding: £11,550 – £13,000 pa

01952 953810
www.adamsgs.uk

Headmaster: Since 2015, Gary Hickey BA (music, Manchester Metropolitan University) MA in education (Birmingham) and Fellow of the Royal Society of Arts. Previously deputy head at Ercall Wood Technology College in Wellington, became deputy head at Haberdashers' Adams in 2009, head in 2015. Since then, he has set about transforming the outlook and ethos of this boys' state grammar (also offers boys' boarding and open to day girls at sixth form) with great vigour and a clear social focus.

Ten years ago, he tells us, Adams was perceived as a closed shop to locals. One parent described it as 'the Willy Wonka' factory, iron gates firmly shut. 'Elitist and inward looking' is how he himself sums up the ghost of Adams past, a school turning out hearty medics with a penchant for rugby. A lingering perception he has set about dismantling. For starters, he has strengthened school's links with the diverse community it serves, actively seeking to attract as broad base of pupils as possible. One of his three deputy heads has a specific outreach remit and spends a lot of time in local primary schools. Mentoring is offered and pupils on free school meals have priority entrance, as do local pupils. He has also done his best (he concedes this is a WIP) to make its entrance exam tutor-proof. Open events see parents, whose children are in local state primaries, flooding in. Oiling the wheels for social mobility in this way, it's no wonder he was invited to 10 Downing Street to discuss the role grammars might play in society.

Another key change has been a greater emphasis on the arts. Mr Hickey alludes to the 46 after-school clubs on offer; you put opportunity on the table, he says, and then it is up to every pupil to take advantage. As a serious professional musician himself, who also directs plays and films (as you do), he feels the arts are crucial in creating well rounded personalities. So if the Adams pupil of today likes rugby (and plenty do), it will be rugby plus Chekov.

We imagine all these changes have caused a ruffled feather or two among the hearty old Novaportans who thought things were just fine the way they were, so it's only right to stress that these changes are not in any way about eroding Adams' enriched 400 year heritage. On the contrary, Mr Hickey is, in fact, incredibly proud of the school's heritage, so much so that in 2018 the school's name was changed to Haberdashers' Adams (which – surprise, surprise – also proved a tad controversial with a certain segment of parents). It is a change that reinforces the school's links with its founder, Alderman William Adams, a haberdasher. The backing and support from the Habs' brand, he says, runs through the school like a stick of rock. It is part of the Haberdashers' Adams Federation Trust, which also includes Haberdashers' Abraham Darby.

Married to Rhian, a teacher, they have three children. A quietly spoken innovator, he is mightily high profile as well as being something of a polymath; invited to give lectures at international 'Inspiring Leaders' conferences, garnering a special commendation in the National Teaching Awards and gaining a fellowship from Cambridge University. In his beautiful wooden panelled office, there is a notice on the wall: 'Follow your heart but take your brain with you'. This sums up both the man and the reinvigorated spirit of the school over which he presides.

Academic matters: Mr Hickey believes in breadth of curriculum; an overview of the results, however, suggests that while results in GCSE English language/ literature and modern languages are strong, the school still really excels in maths and the three sciences, with GCSEs and A levels boasting a swag bag full of A*s (and 8s and 9s) across those subjects year on year. That said, the humanities do pretty well too. At A level in 2018, 38 per cent A*/A and at GCSE 67 per cent of entries were A*-A/9-7.

The sixth form pupil who showed us round was a poster for the well-rounded Adams' student; studying double maths and physics at A level, he had a place at a top university to read music. Music A level had not been on offer but a few pupils had been keen to take it and so hey presto, it had been sorted. This is not necessarily the norm, however, one parent mentioned her son had not been able to take the (fairly standard) combo of arts subjects he wanted. Yet things are transitioning, the curriculum is being broadened, geology is a recent addition as an A level and drama GCSE is next in line. All pupils have to take two languages from year 7. At present, 98 per cent of pupils take one language at GCSE but only around three per cent go on to study a language at A level. All pupils sit EPQ in sixth form.

One parent grumbled a little about the recent emphasis on languages, his son not having a flair for them, but he was impressed by the support plan offered in the form of booster lessons and mentoring. Performance is tracked carefully at Adams and monitored every six weeks. Every pupil sits down with a mentor-tutor twice a year to discuss progress. Parents say the school works on small weaknesses and although class size is around 30, the teachers are tuned in to nuance. They describe the teaching as outstanding across the board.

Another key change in the school is a greater emphasis on helping pupils with barriers to learning. Mr Hickey is keen on this. One to one is available and there is every effort to identify issues at an early stage. The school uses information from previous schools, listens to the concerns of our pupils and parents, and undertakes its own observations and assessments.

One parent queried the value-add to Adams' pupils, suggesting a tough entrance exam meant only the academic cream got through and so the crop of stellar results was not surprising. Conversely, another parent said her son failed to get in at 11, got in at 13 as a boarder, didn't necessarily fit the academic mould but had been catapulted into straight As. Go figure.

Games, options, the arts: Every school says they are about the well-rounded child but, here, this is no empty cliché. Yes, the school excels at science and maths but parents say the drive is about cross fertilising interests, getting students to find other passions.

Alongside the usual character-building DoE and CCF, there is an astounding array of clubs: astronomy, debating, creative writing, raspberry pi robot building, engineering, sculpting, taiko drumming. Clubs start up if a pupil wants it, Mr Hickey says, referring to bridge club with its handful of members.

Sport figures highly – playing fields are down the road – boys can choose from rugby, hockey, football, cricket, athletics,

H

badminton and cross-country. A swimming pool (now with roof) is an added bonus. Sixth form girls have hockey, netball, rounders and athletics. Athletics and cross country are strong, as is the recently introduced dance option.

Lots of trips; recently Washington, charity trips to Africa and sport tours to South Africa, not to mention a music tour of Australia. Likewise, heaps of competitions, such as the Royal Society of Chemistry's Schools Analyst Competition, Young Enterprise, Maths Feast...it goes on. Mr Hickey has also kick started a rich array of speakers on world affairs, topics like, 'what's the difference between a refugee and a migrant?', all presented like university lectures.

The house system means lots of competitions, small to large scale. Parents enthused about the house music, where participation levels were very high and the full spectrum of opportunity available, including choirs, swing bands, saxophone group, and guitar groups.

A greater emphasis on drama now within the school. One or two school productions happen per year, most recently Cabaret and Guys and Dolls.

Responsibility in the final year comes in fairly traditional form – team captains, house captains and head boy and head girl. Lots of opportunity to experiment, too, the lower sixth had developed an AGS radio station.

Boarding: The school is one of nine state boarding grammars in the country. There are around 100 boarders, of whom 25 per cent are international students. Boarders can go home at weekends but some choose not to, to take advantage of trips to Alton Towers, treasure hunts or archery competitions. There are themed events, such as the circus when magicians and jugglers came. A wilderness weekend saw them camping out and skinning rabbits. Two houses, Longford Hall for years 7 to 10 and Beaumaris for years 11 to 13.

Diving down an off-track road and seeing a Georgian mansion at the end (Longford Hall) seemed more Mr Darcy than state grammar. Overlooking vast playing fields, it took our breath away. It has a welcoming entrance (likewise the house master was warm and cheery) very decent rooms, charming sash windows, many with great views. Boys are bussed in and out each day (five minute journey). Dorms are 3-5 boys, bunk beds until years 9 and 10. The configuration of pupils tends to stay the same but boys can request a move if they feel the dynamic isn't working. Lovely TV room which, with its long billowy curtains and high ceiling, reinforced the stately home air. Mobile phones are allowed till 9pm. In the spring/ summer evenings, the boys play outside on the vast playing fields after school, with chance to let off steam, then tea and prep. Parents very happy with the communication and the way in which school deals with any issues. One mother said she felt listened to and spoke glowingly how the school had eased her child's initial home sickness.

Senior boys board a couple of minutes away from the school and while Beaumaris is a modern building, it is also a wonder to behold. Chairs, beanbags, cushions in vibrant jewel colours, a huge graffiti mural on entering saying 'senior'. The kitchen – hold the dogs – is a replica of an American diner with all the Juke Box 1950 trimmings, great attention to detail. The house mother exuded warmth and a realistic understanding of what makes teenage boys tick. (Put it this way, those boys know not to leave mess in the kitchen and understand how to use a washing machine.) Rooms are single, double or triple, all en suite and very roomy. Great games room and every effort made to integrate the new arrivals. Paint balling is a typical ice breaker. Lots of theme nights, sushi nights, Halloween party (even a Valentines' night – clearly just a crafty excuse for a jolly but the boys looked mortified when it was mentioned).

Mentoring system in place and everything seemed super organised. Older pupils can go out into Newport which, boasting agricultural University Harper Adams, has a student feel.

Background and atmosphere: The school was founded in 1656 by Alderman William Adams. Within, it has a traditional vibe, corridor displays were varied, some departments opting for huge glossy photos, others for more modest subject-related poster displays. It is a mish mash of the new (the sixth form centre was completed in 2013) and the historical. While there are some aspects in need of funding – the sports pavilion – others are laden with charm. The main library, where the school was started originally, is dripping with heritage, vast black and white photos of previous heads on the back wall.

Science labs are nice and dapper, music department newly minted. Performance spaces adequate. A general sense of focused industriousness as we walked about. Lots of quiet study places for students. It's a team-driven school, the huge poster showing all the staff is in alphabetical, not hierarchical, order and in a nice quirky touch has mug shots of the school dogs.

Ex Dragon's Den Judge Nick Jenkins is an old boy, so too the current leader of the labour party, Jeremy Corbyn. The latter, not being a fan of selective education nor his school days, was invited by Mr Hickey to see the many changes to the school. The invite was never taken up but the story made it onto national TV news. Mr Hickey says pupils especially love listening to old boy, Radzi Chinyanganya (ex-Blue Peter and Winter Olympics' presenter), talk about his time at school.

Pastoral care, well-being and discipline: Pastoral care is centred round the house system (Clive, Darwin, Talbot or Webb). Parents said this fostered a great sense of belonging and was a buffer zone between the leadership team and the pupils. The pupil showing us round was a tad more low key about it, saying that like anything else the blend of people in your house was a matter of chance.

One parent, whose son took a while to settle into the school, spoke enthusiastically of the 'bespoke pastoral programme' the school had assembled, structuring it around ex-curricular activities. His son went from not wanting to go to school to absolutely loving every day. It wasn't so much the immediate success of the plan, the parent told us, more the fact that they all worked together and would have carried on working together until a good solution had been forged.

Alongside all this, there is a respecting and valuing diversity programme. Or as Mr Hickey niftily puts the latter 'challenging the rugby ethos'.

Disciplinary matters or a perceived whiff of bullying are dealt with quickly. One parent told how her son had been sent home after a misdemeanour for an afternoon of cooling off and had been dealt with brilliantly.

In the sixth form the ratio of boys to girls is roughly 2:1. This would not suit every girl and in the past – perhaps when the school had a different vibe – some girls apparently found it was not for them. It is worth re-emphasising that Mr Hickey is laying down a very different sort of culture within the school now. One parent told us their daughter loved it, felt the teaching was better than her previous (very good) all-girls school and her confidence had grown enormously, so much that she was now able to do public performances in music where previously she had felt inhibited.

Pupils and parents: Social mix is broadening and 60 per cent of pupils, the head estimates, have two working parents. Mr Hickey's initiatives have only been going since 2015 so it will take a little while for parents to feel there is a true cross section of society but it is getting there. All parents enthused about how much their sons loved it, some children making the voyage from initial uncertainty to a life-defining loyalty by GSCE stage.

The boys we spoke to – across all years at school – seemed down to earth, friendly, enthusiastic and without arrogance.

Entrance: Priority is given to those on a pupil premium. The school has introduced an 'attendance area' (catchment area) and priority is now given to boys who live locally – although there is a possibility that this may expand to whole of Telford and Wrekin Borough from September 2020 – watch this space. In 2017, pupils actually came from around 40 different schools.

Hugely over-subscribed; 1000 sit the exam for a 100 places. One of those state grammars where parents might be tempted to fake ID or pretend a distant cousin is really a younger brother to get a place. Beware. Stringent scrutiny is applied. No one makes it through the Adams ID-detector, even with a cunning plan and a fake moustache.

The entrance exam, according to a pupil, has a science/ maths bias and Mr Hickey agrees with this but says the test is being reviewed to make it more creative.

External candidates, including girls, may enter at sixth form (application form and reference from previous school). (Five GCSEs at grade 7 required and at least a grade 7 in their chosen A level subject).

Exit: Most stay on to sixth form (12 per cent left after GCSEs in 2018). In 2018, nine to Oxbridge and 13 medics. Leavers go to universities all over the UK, though Newcastle is very popular, followed by Birmingham, Leicester and Manchester. A smattering go on to study arts and humanities, but most opt for science or business: biology, bio-chemistry, engineering courses, economics, maths.

Money matters: Boarding is a fraction of the cost of the independent sector and the accommodation great.

Remarks: A wonderful state grammar with stellar academic standards and a multitude of enrichment activities on offer to create real depth of character. Boarding is incredible for the pr ice.

Hale Preparatory School

Broomfield Lane, Hale, Altrincham, Cheshire WA15 9AS

Ages 4–11 **Pupils** 201

Fees: £7,860 pa

01619 282386
www.haleprepschool.com

Headmaster: Since 1980, John Connor (head and proprietor; he set up the school), who exudes twinkly-eyed warmth and northern good humour. He says he and his staff share a sense of humour and it really shows, laughter reverberates around the building and, by osmosis, seems to pass to the children, who were all impeccably behaved and irrepressibly cheerful.

Beneath John Connor's good humour, however, lies a very serious educational vision which he grittily pursued back in 1980 when he bought a Victorian house and opened his own school (no governors or accountants breathing down his neck). His was one of the first schools to adopt the Durham InCAS assessments (used to monitor pupil development), has authored numerous education books, been a chief examiner and quoted in parliamentary reports. He doesn't much like the term educationalist (we imagine it is too pompous for his tastes), but in the best possible sense he struck us as just that.

The intake for Hale is non-selective so we were curious to learn how he manages to get so many children through to the fiercely competitive Altrincham grammars or the uber-academic independent Manchester schools. The answer seems to be careful tracking; each child's current level of intellectual development is assessed every year and every effort is made to ensure academic progress is aligned to that. Recent papers submitted to CEM (Centre for Evaluation and Monitoring) for Hale Prep showed 97 per cent of pupils were in line with their intellectual levels of development, 30 per cent exceeding them. The school is concentrating on the three per cent outside of those stats, he says.

In this way, he audits the school's performance; they identify very early on pupils who need extra support, and take them out of maths or English for one-to-one tuition to bring them up to speed. A practice so embedded that the children see it as the norm. You need a lot of staff to provide this support and Hale has that; he jokingly describes them as over-staffed and sees this as a fundamental tenet of the school. The rest of the budget goes on books, glorious books and lots of expensive IT. Hale is bang up to date.

He has, ahem, been running the school for quite a while now and is probably in his 70s; one parent affectionately described him as Gandalf-like, another the Pied Piper. He is clearly an important figurehead, one who turns up at every school event. That said, the Connor touch is perpetuated by his son and daughter, both deputy heads with the same lovely manner and humour. The dynasty rocks on.

Entrance: Roughly equal balance of genders (22 places at reception.) John Connor is testament to the Field of Dreams' refrain, 'built it and they will come' and they did, and do, in their droves. Always oversubscribed with a hefty waiting list so it's the old adage: put your child's name down in utero. This is pretty astounding when you think that other prep schools in some pockets of the north west are fighting for pupils, but the reasons are understandable, the clamour justifiable.

At year 3 up to an extra 14 places (this allows for two classes, with a maximum size of 18 pupils, in years 3-6).

Exit: The freebie local Altrincham grammars are a huge pull (kill your grandmother to get a place? You bet). Recently, Hale got 22 through. Others went to Manchester Grammar, Manchester High, Withington Girls and Cheadle Hulme School (along with the other usual suspects in the independent sector like King's Macclesfield for which there are usually a clutch of scholarships, recently two sports and one academic).

Remarks: Parents speak of a nurturing environment very much in tune with the ambiance of this cosy Victorian residential house with its thick pile carpets.

Every infant class has a teacher plus assistant; every child has one-to-one reading every day. The incredibly wide curriculum runs from infants onwards; whilst 50 per cent of the curriculum is devoted to maths, English and science, there are weekly lessons – brace yourselves – in drama, music, dance, art and design, ethics, computing, history, geography, French, Spanish, ethics, physical education/games and Latin in year 6. John Connor sees this broad curriculum as a cornerstone to creating a happy environment; you need to keep children interested, he says.

No streaming in the juniors; each group is taught by the same specialist teachers, covering the same curriculum with the same homework. Year 4 was learning about myths during our visit, with some very impressive essays displayed on King Aegon. Having separate teachers for different subjects, as one parent pointed out, creates variety if you don't happen to gel with your form teacher.

The learning support system gathered lavish praise from just about every parent for its effectiveness, discreet way it is handled and its acceptance by pupils as the norm. The support system also operates at a high level to stretch pupils. During the long summer hols, children can go in and do booster work for entrance exams and there is a maths 'drop in' on a Friday. The term 'magical' kept being used by parents; it's magical what they do with them, they repeated.

For more specific learning issues, like dyslexia, there is a SEN specialist to assess and help children. If the teacher feels they would benefit from a more detailed screening then a referral is made.

The staff are a blend of genders, seasoned experience and young blood. Communication seems spot on; all test results are shared with parents (and expectations managed). Parents vouched for being involved in discussions and said chats were frank.

The building, while small, has everything. Subject-specific classrooms – like geography, science – seemed good preparation for senior school. There is a small but wonderful library and a very well equipped IT room. A music room choc full of school-owned instruments and a lovely adventure playground for outdoors play.

H

Pastoral is overseen by two members of staff. Behaviour seems excellent. A small but significant point is that the playground is covered by CCTV (as well as having three supervisors present), so any bullying would soon be rooted out were it to start. John Connor said bullying was simply not an issue; as a small school, you could easily see any issues arising. He suggested that children might have other problems instead; while materially most were in clover, emotional problems from the break ups of marriages were not uncommon and the children needed a bit of extra care then. One parent spoke candidly about 'a fall out' between a bunch of girls which she said was immediately picked up on and 'get togethers' organised where they were all encouraged to be open about their feelings.

The grounds aren't big enough for sport so they are ferried around for fixtures and games lessons. All usual sports are offered; cross-country meetings are at local athletics clubs. The girls' team recently won the Altrincham Schools Football League.

Extracurricular activities include dance club, theatre club, ukele, judo, cookery, fencing, chess, sewing, gardening (a sweet little area for this), maypole, choir and orchestra.

There is an annual performance by the infants in the Christmas concert, the juniors do a more sophisticated production, such as A Christmas Carol. Lots of opportunity to perform in the Bowden Festival and ISA dance competitions. School choirs also get to sing in Manchester cathedral. Small school, big canvas.

Lots of trips sorted, such as Tudor day, Wimbledon, Bridgewater Hall, Jodrell Bank. Interesting speakers, with children's writers and a couple of magistrates thrown in the mix.

School meals are compulsory and extra. A salad bar every day, sandwiches, baked potatoes, and the day we went the hot meal was roast turkey. Yum.

This is a wealthy pocket of Trafford and the parents are very involved. The school doesn't advertise and the pupils come from round about Hale and Altrincham, with the odd one from Knutsford or Wilmslow. The final great thing about this school, and this will not have been wasted on wealthy Hale (because we northerners like value for money), the fees are very reasonable.

Try as we might during this review to extract some criticism from parents (and on the Guide, believe us, we really do try) we could find none. So we resorted instead to the parents' survey and got something of the flavour of critique which prevails there. Not enough choices in the canteen, one person said. To which it was pointed out with impeccable politeness that the café catered for 49 special dietary requirements. One parent disagreed that the school promoted values of respect and tolerance, and again with the greatest deference the response was: 'I can only assume there is no knowledge of the ethics curriculum....the range of visits to temples, churches and synagogues and, most crucially, the atmosphere in the school itself.' Nuff said. Westminster politicians could learn a thing or two from John Connor.

A fabulous, nurturing, high-achieving, non-selective small prep which deserves its excellent reputation.

Hanford School

Child Okeford, Blandford Forum, Dorset DT11 8HN

Ages 7–13 **Pupils** 100 **Boarders** 80 full **C of E**

Fees: Day £18,750; Boarding £22,500 pa

01258 860219
www.hanfordschool.co.uk

Headmaster: Since 2014, Rory Johnston BA (Cantab), Mr J to the girls. He's a classicist, a good fit for a school which has always excelled at classics. He's also a chartered accountant, a good fit for a school whose finances needed some grip – he's already upped the numbers and restored balance. Parted company with the City after 20 years and followed the hunch of a friend who reckoned he'd make a good teacher. Previously head of classics and boarding housemaster at Horris Hill. Wife Georgina, Mrs J to the girls, George to parents, works alongside him and heads up pastoral care. Very highly rated. Rory and George have two children.

Sarah Canning, daughter of the founders, head and owner since 1959, handed over to a charitable trust in 2003. She died in 2017. Her legacy lives on: Hanford remains very much the school she made.

Entrance: Informal, non-selective, girls can come at any time if there's room (lately a big if). Some at 7, most as 8 or 9 year olds, a few at 10 or 11. Locals, Wessex girls, Londoners (regular coach to Battersea) and numerous families posted or working abroad (especially popular with Forces and FCO families). A smattering of Europeans from Spain, France, Poland, Belgium and Germany. Parents as ever unshowy and unsnobby, new money prefers anywhere blingier. Some bursaries and a good deal for Forces families.

Exit: All over, most to boarding seniors – Bryanston, Sherborne Girls, Marlborough, St Mary's Calne, Shaftesbury and Ascot, Downe House, Benenden, St Swithun's, Clayesmore.

Remarks: Ask any former parent or pupil about Hanford and you'll be bombarded by passionate paeans in celebration of its glories: its quirkiness, its changelessness, its quintessential Englishness. Evocations of Malory Towers and Hogwarts will ensue, together with a reverent inventory of the school's more bonkers traditions – the manners system which grades girls from Piglet to Royal Guest and the nutty names of the branches on a cedar tree that girls are encouraged to climb. You'll get the sense of a school that has somehow lain undisturbed for aeons, a time capsule, a girly Neverland; a place of butter-coloured sunlight, blissful children, long shadows, honey for tea, the whole timeless-idyll schtick. And to be sure, all of this grabs you when you go and see for yourself. The school's location is paradisal, the manor house beyond beguiling. Stand and be captivated by the genius loci. Blandings Castle must surely be on the other side of the hill.

The cold reality, back in the days before overarching regulatory frameworks, didn't fall far short of this arcadia. This was the school where the late Tara Palmer-Tompkinson remembered, 'After swimming we used to run naked round the gardens because it saved the bother of tumble-drying the towels.' But Hanford needs to keep moving somewhat with the times; you can't do that sort of drying-off thing any more. Your typical Hanford parent is change averse, though. They expect a head to be a worthy guardian of the Sacred Flame, bringing as much of the past with them as possible while at the same time enabling the school to earn its keep, propitiate inspectors and prepare girls for the world of things as they are. It's a darn difficult trick to pull off.

The problem is not aims, it's means. It always is. Mr J's mission statement contains nothing that Sarah Canning didn't also sign up for, which, actually, every school in the country signs up for – fulfilling potential, nurturing talent, all that caboodle. But here's the rub: in a changing demographic where parents' needs, expectations and above all values are moving on, how can Hanford go on being Hanford?

Hanford has always had a free-radical feel to it. When the Rev Clifford Canning, newly retired headmaster of Canford, founded it with his wife in 1947, they decreed no uniforms and no prefects – which raised eyebrows back then. But the thing that's especially made the school brilliantly different is the spirit in which it's done things, with idealism, creativity and joy, wholly unselfconsciousnessly. The name for this spirit is eccentricity, and eccentricity is hard to perpetuate in process-driven times. Well, Hanford's heritage behaviours are underscored by strong seriousness, they're integral. They're loveable but they're not cutesy. Any head who fails to understand this must answer to those who feel exceedingly strongly about this school, ie, every single person who's ever known it. Mr J is winning high approval ratings.

His fans like the way he has committed to ensuring that girls enjoy rich, low-tech childhood in the core heritage Hanford way, out in the fresh air, playing, riding their ponies, making up games, tending the chickens, climbing trees, looking after their gardens (they get around a square yard each). They like the way this builds self-reliance and develops friendships; the way it instils, as one parent put it, 'gumption' – these are decidedly not snowflake children. Hanford parents like the adventurousness and muddy knees. They want their daughters to enjoy what they call 'a traditional upbringing' and that's exactly what they get, watched over at an unobtrusive distance, never fussily superintended. A notably horsey school from way back, pretty much everybody rides, but no worries if you don't. In the summer you can enjoy a gallop before breakfast. Ancient, lovely stables, grade II listed – 'more listed than the manor', a groom told us.

Hard to say the same about the sports hall complex, performing arts centre, design tech centre or indoor swimming pool, all of which the school has not got. But it gets by very well with what it does have – a perfectly serviceable outdoor pool, for instance, a halfway decent gym and some terrifically nice grounds. Okay, so a couple of the classrooms have been temporary for the last 30 years; what matters most is who's standing in front of the girls. Hanford's triumphant lack of state-of-the-art facilities does not, mostly, denote a lack of anything indispensable to the raising of 21st century children; indeed, it very much reflects the unmaterialistic mood music here and effectively – to be brutal – deselects the wrong sort of parent. Mr J does entertain architectural daydreams, mind, but wants to build beautifully.

In the meantime, it's amazing what the girls achieve without benefit of stuff. By dint of excellent coaching and that indefinable Hanford spirit the girls are at the very least a match for the schools they play against with their fancy floodlights and their electronic scoreboards. All the usual sports here plus pistol shooting. Yes, pistol shooting. The time, though, has finally come to lay some Astroturf because other schools are reluctant to come and play any longer on Hanford's grass. So that's very much towards the top of Mr J's shopping list.

Masses of music, instrumental and choral – especially choral. Almost everyone plays an instrument. Dedicated music block. Drama very strong as you'd expect of a school which sets such store by play and imagination. Annual homemade production every summer performed outdoors, everyone has a part, natch. Art another heritage strength, seriously good, very well taught. The teacher told us 'The girls are amazing, they just get stuck in to whatever I give them'. Well, uninhibited spontaneity is very much a Hanford hallmark.

Academically tip-top – 'excellent,' as the inspectors express it. Recent influx of new teachers reckoned to be a shot in the arm. ICT now on course and high time too; next stop, please, DT and some engines to play with. The school bangs on an awful lot about scholarships won, around half a dozen a year, and hats off to that, fair dos, but what if your wee lassie isn't a likely Nobel shortlister? Our judgement: what the school is doing for the brightest it's doing for the rest. Just as the brightest are beneficiaries of extra attention (not special sets), so are the strugglers, because this is a very personal school. One parent who had switched her daughter here from somewhere glitzier described her learning as 'transformed'. Good library, newly beefed up. Around 10 per cent of the girls have a SEN and are attended to by specialists. Interventionist support given to anyone needing it as and when. Physical disability not easily accommodated here owing to the insurmountable architecture, wheelchair sadly a no-no. Not the right school for 'substantial' SENs.

If you want the full seclusive, immersive experience of Hanford – because shared experience and the joyous intensity of living together with your friends are what the school is all about – then you board, and that's what four-fifths do. But boarding doesn't suit everyone, nor the fees, so some don't. They have a bed all the same and can stay overnight more or less at the drop of a hat for free up to 20 days a year. Day girls go home after prep at 6.35pm. Dormitories are upstairs in the manor house, hugger-mugger, in rooms that adapt remarkably congenially to the purpose. They were once famous for their super-spartan furnishings and absence of lavatory doors, so we braced ourselves for a spot of memory lane and were almost disappointed to discover that they are cheery, snug and utterly unobjectionable even if, here and there, yes all right, a dab of paint wouldn't go absolutely amiss. Okay, so one prospective parent said she wouldn't expect her pig to live up here, but that only goes to show how much she just didn't get it. Perhaps she had a very fastidious pig. Whatever, we pictured only happy faces having heaps of fun – and reflected on how self-selecting Hanford parents are. What did concern us were the perils of pressure-cooker factors – girls getting on each others' nerves and being beastly to each other. But the quality of supervision by Mrs J, the matrons, including gap year students, is, we find, up to the mark and quickly onto this. One girl (her dad's in the Forces) protested under strong questioning, 'I've been to several schools and this one's easily the kindest.' So there. Mr J is keen to integrate the boarding and teaching staff more closely. Yes, all for that. In year 8 you graduate to a separate house, Fan's, where you get TV and feel more grown-up. A recent visitor reckoned the showers there resembled 'a 1970s campsite block, complete with soggy towels left on the floor. The tack room in the stable is tidier.' It happens.

A lot of people think that Hanford is an alternative sort of school. Couldn't be wider of the mark. Kindness matters most here. Close on its heels comes old-fashioned courtesy, hence the quaint manners league where you begin as a Boa Constrictor and earn your way up through Squirrel, Primrose etc, but risk plummeting to Piglet. It's aspirational, so there's very little Piglet-shaming. By all accounts it works. The same goes for the committee system, which takes the place of prefects. It's designed to bring out the helpfulness in girls, not the bossiness. Mr J, having watched its workings in his first year, finds it works extremely effectively. Both systems contribute to what one parent described as the school's climate of 'support, positivity and warmth' – a place where 'no one thinks they're better than anybody else'. All agree on this but no one can give you the full formula. One teacher said 'We just don't know how it works'. Being single sex has got to be a factor. That and the ban on mobile phones (but not email). Testimony to the extraordinary happiness of the place comes from the same parent: 'I'm sometimes mortified by how keen they are to get back to school'. None of the potential competition issues you might expect from a school without uniform. Why not? A girl explained 'If you wear something nice, it's probably just going to get dirty.'

If Hanford merely recreated a (mythical) 1930s childhood it would be no more authentic than one of those living history TV programmes in the mould of Wakey-Wakey Campers. It's nothing like that. It has judiciously preserved all those abiding elements which nurture the wonder of childhood at the same time as giving girls a good academic grounding and teaching them how to behave. Sounds simple, but who else does it this well? In a market where schools are increasingly differentiated by nothing more than geography, Hanford retains its measurable quality and its elusive magic. The Sacred Flame is alight and well.

Hardenhuish School

Hardenhuish Lane, Chippenham, Wiltshire SN14 6RJ

Ages 11–18 **Pupils** 1,523 **Sixth form** 285

01249 650693
www.hardenhuish.wilts.sch.uk

Headteacher: Since 2015, Lisa Percy. Previously deputy head for seven years, including a one-year handover period. Originally from Bradford on Avon, Lisa studied geography and French at Wolverhampton Polytechnic (now part of Wolverhampton University), followed by a PGCE at Bristol University. Still teaches geography (had just rushed from a lesson on our arrival) to stay 'grounded and in touch' with the pupils and teachers. Married with two girls, she is friendly and down-to-earth, capable of wearing many hats; she's a teacher, a mum, and 'an exceptional leader,' according to parents. Probably one of the nicest heads we've met. One mother told us, 'Mrs Percy is very approachable and is very well respected by parents and children alike. My son is taught by [her] for geography and this is now his favourite subject.'

Academic matters: Consistently good results for a non-selective comprehensive. In 2018, at A level, 55 per cent A*-B grades (29 per cent A*/A). At GCSE, 79 per cent achieved 9-4 in both English and maths and 28 per cent of grades were A*-A/9-7.

Currently only A levels offered in the sixth form, but Hardenhuish is looking to introduce some subjects for those who would like to opt for a combination of vocational and academic qualifications. Sciences and maths are the most popular subjects at A level year on year. French is taught from year 7 and Spanish from year 8, but a language is not compulsory at GCSE. Everyone up to year 11 takes RE but the emphasis is on lifestyle for the last two years, with discussions on marriage, parenting and different religious backgrounds. It is also a popular option at A level.

Hardenhuish is a Microsoft Showcase School so every PC has the latest software and all teachers have tablets and ongoing training. Pupils with special needs use tablets in class, and sixth formers can bring their own to school. There are ICT suites in every department, plus trollies of laptops. Apple Mac suites in the music and photography departments. Microsoft is planning to host events here with other local pupils also invited to learn about the latest technology.

'Teachers are fantastic and we have come across so many over the years that are just "born" to be teachers,' one parent told us. Another added, 'The staff are all very kind, caring, positive and encouraging.' Average turnover and a good mix of ages; the head likes to balance 'experience and new fresh ideas.'

Learning support department is based in the manor house (along with Rupert the school dog). Led by the SENCo, there are three SEN teachers specialising in ASD, MLD and SpLD, plus 20 teaching assistants. One parent of a child with Asperger's syndrome told us, 'We struggled to get [our child] into school in the mornings and now [s/he] goes willingly.' High praise for the teachers: 'This term the ASD teacher allowed [our child] to go into school a day early to look at new teacher's photos and go over the timetable. This one hour has meant so much to [our child], who is now feeling much calmer,' she continued. 'She even arranges coffee gatherings for us parents to help support us too. '

Hardenhuish is Lead School for Gifted and Talented learners in North Wiltshire. Provision and support for AGAT (Able, Gifted and Talented) pupils includes challenging learning activities in lessons, enrichment opportunities beyond the timetable, and close tracking of pupils' progress and achievement. Parents agreed higher achievers 'appear to be pushed and challenged a lot more in [their] studies,' but one parent expressed concern that those who are 'middle of the road' academically are not always 'stretched and encouraged to strive to move up.'

Games, options, the arts: Hardenhuish is first choice for many families, not just for the academic opportunities but also for the sport and the pastoral care. The sports facilities are fantastic. Playing fields are shared with neighbouring secondary school, Sheldon, plus there are netball/tennis courts, a gym, a sports hall with a very impressive climbing wall, and use of a large dome in the winter if it's wet. No swimming pool but the school has recently entered for several galas as there are now so many talented swimmers. Rugby and football teams do well, with successes at county level, and there are national rugby and athletics competitors.

Other sports include badminton, netball and cricket for both boys and girls, hockey and rounders. Extracurricular activities include the equestrian club, cross-fit, climbing, trampolining and table tennis. Sports tours have taken teams to Barbados to play netball and cricket, to the USA for an east coast rugby tour, and Barcelona to compete in football, netball and hockey. Annually there are trips to eg Newport Velodrome, Wimbledon, and outdoor pursuits in the Brecon Beacons for year 9s. Visiting speakers include Sarah Ayton, Olympic sailing gold medallist, Robert Mitchell, Great Britain high jumper, Katy Curd, European women's downhill mountain bike champion and Stephanie Millward, Paralympic swimmer.

'The concerts are always amazing, and the Christmas one particularly so,' one parent enthused. 'Even children with little or no musical background are able to participate in some form, and those with musical experience never cease to amaze both in ability and diversity of instruments played. One concert we attended had over 200 students involved.' There are three large concerts per year, plus smaller performances including band night for the gig crowd. Music groups range from flute to African drumming. There's a biannual musical, recently Anything Goes and Singing In The Rain, an annual trip to perform at the Fringe festival and with local performing arts centres in Chippenham.

Art has recently been moved into the new C centre (Creative). Three new art classrooms all boast high ceilings and are flooded with light. Displays are changed weekly so everything is current; on our visit we saw paintings of skulls and shells, plus portraits, and an interesting take on the history of graffiti by sixth formers. Textiles room and the photography studio are fully equipped with Macs and Apple laptops. There are three resistant materials classrooms (including industry standard laser cutters used for product design) and two well-equipped food technology rooms. Both catering and food technology options are offered.

Lunchtime and after-school clubs include science, chess, creative writing, animation, horrible histories, sheep, sci-fi and fantasy and knitting. Activities days enable pupils can try out new experiences.

Plenty of local trips to art galleries, the theatre or local interests. Also language exchanges, ski trips to Austria, trips to the Battlefields and to Berlin. For sixth formers there is the opportunity to go to Kenya to Camps International.

Background and atmosphere: Founded in 1975 amidst the extensive parkland of the former Hardenhuish Manor and Chippenham Grammar School. The three schools in the area, the secondary boys' school, the secondary girls' and Chippenham grammar were merged into two comprehensives. One became Hardenhuish and the other became Sheldon, based just next door, and separated by the shared playing fields.

Despite its size it feels spacious, welcoming and safe. The manor house and grounds must be the envy of every independent in the area. One parent told us, 'The sense of green space at Hardenhuish and the atmosphere when looking around were the deal clinchers for us and our children..along with the sheep!'

However, the downside of inheriting a grade II listed house and extensive grounds is the maintenance expense. The school has earned a Green Flag for sustainability: there are solar panels, a biomass boiler, a wind turbine, and pupils are heavily involved in the environmental projects like tree planting and pond clearance. There's even a flock of rare breed Jacob sheep on site helping to keep the lawns respectable.

All buildings are named by letter; there's a C Centre (Creative), A Centre (Advanced for sixth formers), M Centre (maths), E Centre (English and performing arts), L Centre (Languages and humanities); you get the idea.

The sixth form study room is large, bright and airy. Sixth formers helped with the design and at their request there are modular tables, a separate quiet study room, and of course, good Wifi. The next door meeting room is used by The Syndicate, the school council, which chooses the school charity every year, runs fundraising events and regularly makes teaching or learning suggestions. The Raising Awareness and Mental Health groups also use it regularly.

The resources centre, designed with a teenage bedroom in mind (without the mess), is bright and funky with a beanbag mezzanine area, group tables below and PCs for private study. Open every break and lunchtime, plus an extra hour after school as after-school care.

One parent said, 'The school has a nice feel to it,' and we completely agree. Perhaps this is because the clever layout makes it easy to navigate. Perhaps it's the short strolls between centres that allow a minute to breathe in that lush green space and wave at the sheep. Perhaps it's because everything is so well maintained and the facilities are so good. It's hard to fault it... except that it is very green. Everywhere. In every shade you can think of...and more.

Pastoral care, well-being and discipline: 'The pastoral care provisions, which the school is renowned for, are second to none,' one mother confirmed. Pupils have a pastoral manager as well as a tutor. Both stay with them all through school. Pastoral managers are non-teaching staff and are on hand every day for pupils or parents to contact. 'They really do get to know the students well as they grow up through school and can identify any issues early on,' parents told us.

'Supportive' and 'caring' were words we heard over and over again. There is a school counsellor available three times a week. There is also a 'nurture room' based in the learning support centre, run by two full-time staff. This is a safe haven, somewhere to calm down or just be alone.

Pupils and parents: Families are mainly local. Many have moved just to be near the school. One confided, 'If we had to choose again, we would still choose Hardenhuish.'

School uniform is green but thankfully rather tasteful. Pupils are a well-behaved bunch. We saw boys and girls playing netball as we drove in and plenty on our tour; all seemed engrossed in their day and happy about it. One parent told us that her child 'comes back from school always with a smile on her face and a story to tell.' Another added, 'Hardenhuish has certainly helped them to develop into polite, respectful and educated young [adults].'

Open door policy and 'transparent communication process' praised by all parents we contacted. Issues are dealt with 'in a sensitive and timely manner', we were assured.

Entrance: Oversubscribed. All applications through local authority. Large catchment area including 40 feeder primary schools. Families living in the villages surrounding Chippenham are given priority so the nearer you can get the better.

'Seamless' transition, according to parents, helped by induction days and visits to feeder schools. Once started, all year 7s are packed off on a residential to Swindon to get to know each other properly. One parent, whose child struggled to settle at first, told us, 'The school was proactive and employed several strategies to help her with forming friendship groups, and while it's not perfect, she is a lot more settled now.'

Entry to sixth form is minimum of five GCSEs at grade 4 or above (including maths and English), with 6+s for specific subjects.

Exit: Around 60 per cent stay on for the sixth form. Hardenhuish has the second highest percentage of students going off to HE in Wiltshire (beaten only by South Wilts Grammar). In 2018, one to Oxbridge and one medic. Consistently popular: Bristol, Cardiff, Exeter, Nottingham, Plymouth, Reading, Southampton and Swansea.

Fairly young school to have a long list of famous alumni, but a couple worth noting are Jordan Smith, professional golfer, and one unnamed leaver who recently became the first female to win an engineering scholarship at BMW.

Remarks: An extremely successful and caring school. Hardenhuish has it all: good results, fantastic facilities on an impressive site, a huge range of extracurricular activities, and a top reputation for pastoral care. Some schools are worth moving for; this is one of them.

Hatherop Castle School

Hatherop, Cirencester, Gloucestershire GL7 3NB

Ages 3–13 **Pupils** 220 **Boarders** 20 weekly/flexi (from 7 years)

Fees: Day £8,385 – £14,250; Boarding + £7,050 pa

01285 750206
www.hatheropcastle.co.uk/

Headmaster: Since September 2017, Nigel Reed MEd BSc PGCE (30s). Formerly deputy head of Wallhampton School, Hampshire. Educated at Trinity School and Kelly College, both in Devon, and boarded from the age of 10 ('I loved it'). His father and grandfather were both in the navy and so, nearly, was he, but a taste of sports coaching while studying for his degree precipitated a sharp about turn into teaching. He started at Dulwich Prep in Kent where he taught PE and was a boarding house tutor, thence to Wallhampton where he was director of sport and, ultimately, deputy head.

Mr Reed met his wife, Jo, at Wallhampton – she's a forest school leader and a qualified teacher of mindfulness and meditation to children. She is also trained as an emotional literacy support teacher and has introduced emotional literacy to the school's pastoral care team, 'We already do a huge amount to promote physical well-being so we're keen to give the same attention to emotional literacy – offering support to parents, as well as children.' The couple have two boys at the school; 'It's a great adventure for us all.' We think they make a great team – relaxed, cheerful and full of energy.

Mr Reed is only the second head since the school started in its present guise as a prep in 1992 (before that it was a girls' school). We imagine that stepping into the shoes of Mr Easterbrook, who ran the show for 26 years, must have been a little daunting, but all seems to have gone very smoothly. Mr Easterbrook himself continues to work for the Wishford Group, who have owned Hatherop since 2014. Parents seem to agree, 'The transition was managed really well; we saw him (Mr Reed) quite a few times before he started and knew he was just the right fit.' The rapport was mutual; Mr R told us, 'I loved the feel of the place at once.'

He favours a collaborative style of headship and has appointed two new deputies, one academic, one pastoral. Of course, he has other plans – what new head doesn't – but parents who adore Hatherop because, not in spite of, its faded grandeur and old-fashioned courtesies have nothing to worry about on that score. 'Good manners are so important. We sit together at meals and all pupils from reception to year 8 shake a member of staff's hand at the end of the day.' Building up the boarding has been one of the school's priorities and London parents keen to 'educate their children out of the rat race' are catching on.

Mr Reed teaches computing and coaches rugby and girls' hockey. Since knee problems forced him to give up football, golf and cycling have become his recreational sports. He likes the fact that golf 'turns frustration into a positive' and that you can 'have a game at any age.' When he's not outside, Mr R enjoys reading crime novels and autobiographies – Douglas Bader's Reach for the Skies 'inspired him as a child'. And if all this sounds a bit hearty, he's also a huge fan of musical theatre and loves a good, old fashioned panto. He says he 'always wanted run his own school' and now finds himself doing just that – and king of a castle to boot. 'It's fabulous, I'm loving every minute.'

Entrance: No formal entrance tests; prospective pupils are assessed during the course of a taster day and on the basis of reports from previous schools. Exams and assessments for academic, art and music scholarships take place during the lent term. Some means-tested bursarial support available.

Little Owls Nursery takes from age 2 and there's a toddler group on Friday mornings where parents can bring their children (6m upwards) to familiarise them with nursery life.

Exit: At 11+ to Gloucestershire state schools and grammars. At 13+ mainly to local-ish day and boarding schools including Marlborough College, Dean Close, Rendcomb, Cheltenham College, Cheltenham Ladies' and Abingdon School. Five scholarships in 2018 – mostly drama, plus one music and one all-rounder.

Remarks: Hatherop is recorded in the Domesday Book as 'Etherope', which means 'high outlying farmstead', and 900 years have not diminished the name's descriptive accuracy. To reach village and school requires a delightful meander through the lush meadows of the River Coln, followed by a steep ascent of its eponymous valley. At the height of summer this is a vision of quintessential English pastoral; what it's like on a dark winter's evening may be another story (imagine less romantic, more slippery); we hope it's on the council's gritting lorry route. The approach through classic estate parkland is hardly likely to disappoint, but the building that rises to meet you is definitely more stately home than fortified residence. If you happen to have any back-seat passengers who demand crenellations and a moat of their castles you may need to manage expectations (but only until you get inside).

For the youngest pupils at Little Owls nursery, the emphasis is on creativity, outdoor learning and imaginative play, embodied by the delightfully sticky 'mud kitchen' and wooden pirate ship outside. Pirates and mud chefs were having 40 winks when we crept round but we spied nothing amiss. Like much at Hatherop, nursery facilities are spick and span, if somewhat make-do and mend. Friendly, dedicated staff and nurturing atmosphere more than make up any lack of superficial glitz and parents we spoke to were verging on evangelical; 'It was the nursery that sold the school to us,' said one. Several said that for them, the fact that the nursery is run along 'traditional' lines was a deciding factor. 'There's a caring, family ethos and they're brilliant at slow, but sure, nurturing.' Specialist teaching from 'transition' (age 3-and-a-half) onwards in French, music, and gym. Little Owls is open for 50 weeks a year. From the nursery buildings in their walled garden just off the yew walk, pupils move to the stable yard for reception and pre-prep. A serious game of Castle Vet was under way when we dropped in here (we very much hope the blue snake has recovered). Reception pupils may not yet be 5, but it's never too early to have a taste of work experience and they enjoy the chance to 'help' school maintenance or kitchen staff.

This is a small, inclusive school and parents love the fact that every child is known as an individual, 'teachers work with parents on developing each child's strengths – each child finds their place and all progress is celebrated.' The learning support department says school can accommodate children with 'mild to moderate SEN.' Staff will work with pupils who may just need a 'couple of terms' catch-up' and longer term one-to-one help is also available at extra cost. Study skills sessions are provided for pupils in years 7-8 to help them prepare for entrance exams. Our pupil guides took us in and out of lots of lessons and we saw quiet individual study, energetic teamwork, eager questions and answers, role play and great pupil teacher rapport. One parent told us, 'I've yet to meet a teacher here who regards their work as "just a job"; they all give so much time and energy.' School has won the Lego robotics regional finals for the past two years and last year came eighth nationally.

An Astro was high on everyone's wish list and one is now destined for the newly acquired market garden site. It will make a huge difference to the sports fixture programme, enabling school to host home matches. Head wants to build up girls' sport – not just hockey but also football, with girls' rugby 'a possibility.' Other sporting ambitions include developing school's own equestrian team – riders currently put through their paces at the local riding stables – and introducing golf. Fencing is one of Hatherop's strengths – the high-ceilinged ground floor reception rooms must make excellent salles. Also on offer as clubs are judo, gymnastics, cross-country, ballet, Scottish dancing and yoga. The new performing arts centre is a well-designed modern venue that sits comfortably in the grounds. Drama and music programme is busy and ambitious, pupils of all ages and abilities are encouraged to take part in plays and concerts.

School offers full, weekly and flexi boarding; numbers aren't huge, but they're growing as parents from further afield 'discover' Hatherop. There are currently about 30 beds but scope for expansion in this area if necessary. Small regular contingent of short-term boarders from Spain and other, mainly European countries, dilute the Anglo-Saxon mix just a little. No Saturday school means everyone gets a proper weekend and weekly boarders from London can return home by train, accompanied all the way to Paddington on the Friday Cotswold Flyer (Kemble/Swindon stations are both close by), homework done and with a packed supper provided. A member of staff will meet them at Paddington on Sunday evening for the return journey. There's a programme of castle fun and excursions for boarders who stay at school for the weekend and weekly boarders can join in at no extra cost. Things are flexible enough that pupils can be scooped up in a crisis and one-off bed and breakfast option is very reasonable £35 per night – better value and more convenient than a babysitter. Working parents love the 8am-6.30pm wrap-around care option too.

Head describes the Hatherop boarding vibe as 'homely' and we'd agree. Boarders sleep in large, comfortable rooms up in the eaves – apparently the children 'prefer to be together in a big dorm' together rather than smaller rooms. We were impressed by the decoration of both boys' and girls' rooms – there was a competition to redesign them and parents judged the entries. Home duvets and lots of quirky touches, not to mention stunning views over trees and honey coloured Costwold stone cottages, more than make up for paintwork and carpets in the corridors that are showing inevitable wear and tear. A recent ISI inspection declared the boarding provision (and pretty much everything else at Hatherop) to be 'excellent' and we concur. Apart from the library, that is. Girls who studied here in the 1940s had the use of the house's original grand ground floor library. Today Hatherop's pupils make do with a fairly dreary kind of box-room cum book store – let's hope that new library comes after new Astro Mr R's to-do list.

Parents told us it was the pupils who made the biggest impact when they visited, 'I saw the year 8s and just thought how much I wanted my own child to turn out like that.' Another said how impressed she'd been with pupils' good manners and confidence: 'that's what sold the school to me.' Our guides were charming, thoughtful and very proud of their school, telling us with some nostalgia about 'cross-country runs through the woods', 'wonderful' Christmas activities and the disco in the front hall; 'Pupils from all the Wishford schools come here for that.' The tradition of year 8 leavers jumping into the outdoor pool in uniform on their last day was being eagerly anticipated.

Food got the thumbs up, particularly fish and chips, roast chicken and brownies. Parents say it's much improved over the last few years with increased use of local produce and sensible efforts to reduce sugar. We certainly enjoyed a delicious roast when we visited.

Like many stately homes, Hatherop (and its charming adjacent church) has been owned, sold, built and rebuilt over the centuries. In the 1860s it was leased by a Maharajah – there are tales of elephants on the lawn – but he didn't stay long because the railway authorities refused to give the estate its own station. It first became a school (of sorts) in the 1920s when the owner's wife, Mrs Francis Cadogan, offered to educate a handful of her friends' daughters alongside her own. One of those girls was Nancy Mitford, who recalls enjoying her time at Hatherop apart from the cold – morning wash with an icy sponge, anyone? When Mrs Cadogan's children had all flown the nest the school was moved to Cambridge where it became known as Owlstone Croft (hence Little Owls Nursery and school owl mascot), under the governance of a Mrs Theodora Fyfe. By 1946 the school had outgrown its Cambridge premises and returned to Hatherop where Mrs Fyfe was known for producing girls who 'finished very well and debbed beautifully.' Mrs Fyfe and her successor, Dr Pandora Moorhead, sound like redoubtable characters; apparently Dr Moorhead installed a carousel on the lawn to provide relaxation for the girls. Her idea of discipline was 'come to the drawing room for a sherry darling and we'll talk about it.' Those were the days.

Hatherop was acquired by Wishford Schools in 2014, joining a group of seven preps located in Kent and along the M4 corridor. Prior to this the school was suffering as a result of changes to Forces school subsidies (RAF Fairford and Brize Norton are nearby), not to mention the financial burden of upkeep to a historic building. Let's be frank, if it's flash you're after then Hatherop isn't the place for you, but parents say that investment from Wishford has made a real difference, citing improvements to everything from food to communications.

Venerable trees, an Italian garden, rumours of secret passages, mullion windows and acres of green space – Hatherop feels like the setting for the kind of storybook childhood most parents, above all urban parents, want their children to have. It's an idea the school has taken and run with – their interactive prospectus is even called 'The adventure of childhood' and references Narnia, Enid Blyton and, of course, Harry Potter. Cynics may scoff, but if your school happens to be a castle in glorious rural surroundings, conjuring such visions is hardly a liberty. Any resident dragons and fairies must have made themselves invisible when they heard The Good Schools Guide was visiting, but we still caught a whiff of magic in the air.

H

Hayesfield Girls' School and Mixed Sixth Form

Upper Oldfield Park, Bath BA2 3LA

Ages 11–18 **Pupils** 1,340 **Sixth form** 281 (60 boys)

01225 426151
www.hayesfield.com

Headteacher: Since 2014, Emma Yates (early 40s) BEng (Sheffield). She came to Hayesfield by means of unswerving resolve – 'I knew from the age of 7 that I wanted to be a teacher' – and a swift ascent up the rungs of science teaching and preparatory stages of headship, her last post being at highly regarded Backwell School. Now a staunch advocate of single sex education, her views are reinforced by previous spells at mixed schools, where she experimented with single sex science sets –

and watched results rocket. 'I wanted science to become a more equitable experience, where the girls can't just sit back and let the boys get on with it'. This empowering of girls spills over into the rest of life at Hayesfield, where the calm, collaborative, academically serious atmosphere is appreciated by students. 'My science-minded daughter thought she would do better at Hayesfield than anywhere else,' one father volunteered.

Small, neat, blonde in her neutral bouclé suit (with its nod to Chanel) and nude suede heels, Miss Yates sets the tone for the professionalism she expects of her school; her students describe her as 'fair, firm, inclusive, driven'. This last attribute perhaps makes her the keen and competent skier she has become in the last few years; she tries to spend 5-6 weeks a year on snow – 'There's always some somewhere!' she says. Presumably her Yorkshire terrier, Sugar, stays home on those trips, but she accompanies her on some school occasions, such as the induction camp-out at the start of year 7.

H

Academic matters: All comers are catered for, yet results sit comfortably above national averages for all sorts of measures including the English Baccalaureate at GCSE (one of top state schools in the Bath area), where in 2018 41 per cent of all entries were graded A*-A/9-7 and 86 per cent got 4-9 in both English and maths. At A level, 30 per cent A*/A and 54 per cent A*/B. To what can this success be attributed? Well, it could have something to do with the Hayesfield Teacher Mind Set, which enshrines in print the non-negotiables of teaching and learning to 'ensure an outstanding learning experience for every student'. Add some committed, well-behaved girls (who can do without boys in the classroom till sixth form), the importance they and their parents place on education, the prevailing, though not ubiquitous, affluence of Bath, some super new teaching space – et voilà. All the parents we spoke to praised the commitment of teaching staff, which extends to running pre-exam sessions on Saturdays and in the holidays, as well as more mundane matters, such as being readily contactable and not letting GCSEs 'come rumbling at them like a snowball'.

The lessons we saw tended more towards traditional pedagogy, with students sitting in sometimes somewhat crowded rows facing the front – and not reliant on IT. Rules on the use of personal devices in class are strict; everyone seems perfectly happy with laptops which travel around school on trolleys as required, and reckon there is enough computer provision in school. We enjoyed the rigour of a year 7 English class where girls were conducting a textual analysis of a passage from HG Wells, but felt it was a pity that so little of the French class we went to was done in the desired language, unlike the Spanish class, which was. Hayesfield acknowledges that not all its students will be high achievers, and strives to support them equally to achieve their goals: all subjects are setted except for the creative ones, which is thought to foster a culture of aspiration rather than demotivation. In the mixed sixth form, the pastoral manager oversees those who won't necessarily get to university by encouraging them to apply for and be accepted onto foundation degree courses with less demanding grades – a welcome change from previous years where weaker brethren (and they were brethren) were encouraged to take their poor AS results elsewhere for their final year. School defends current record on keeping students till the bitter end.

Games, options, the arts: For an urban school on two sites, a remarkable number of facilities and outdoor space is shoehorned onto its premises: an Astro, outdoor netball courts and plenty of grass with tables and chairs for relaxation in clement weather. Main games are hockey and netball, but a wider range of physical activities are on offer as part of the comprehensive array of extracurricular pursuits known as Period 6; these take place after school every day and girls are expected to sign up for at least two sessions per week. Lacrosse, cricket, rowing and fencing all feature, and like all the Bath schools, Hayesfield makes use of the top-notch sports facilities at Bath University, a short drive up the hill. Several fixtures a week against local schools of all persuasions and competitions at county level, but one parent voiced her regret that there aren't often enough staff to coach B, C and D teams so that everyone gets a game and a chance to represent the school. D of E is run with Beechen Cliff, the corresponding boys' school about half a mile away, and CCF with best-in-Bath King Edwards.

Art of all kinds prominent: super studios and exhibition space, plus outstanding pieces on display in the atrium of the fabulous new building. The black dress with feather trim incited our envy, and A Gormley would, we are sure, be delighted with the installation of tiny clay figurines inspired by his work. Performing arts given a tremendous boost by the recent opening of the splendid Roper Theatre, named for a local philanthropic family trust which subsidised it in return for its supporting community events. Beauty and the Beast in rehearsal at the time of writing. Music vibrant, too: the timetabling of music lessons and practice time within the school day shows it isn't just an add-on. Two auditioned choirs, Hush and Host, both win awards in the city, but other ensembles provide opportunity to play and sing at any or all of the three main events in the musical calendar, the carol service in Bath Abbey and winter and summer concerts. If the intellectual life appeals, Period 6 offers basic Russian, a polyglots' club, computing, the Hayesfield newspaper – or manifold opportunities to catch up on weaker subjects.

Background and atmosphere: The current school on its split site (divided by function, rather than by student age, in an effort to integrate year groups) provides an insight into education policy changes enacted in Bath, what with previous manifestations as City of Bath Girls' School, Somerset Industrial School for Boys, West Twerton Secondary Modern – we could go on. In 1973 Hayesfield was born, the child of the local girls' grammar and secondary modern, and still makes use of both sites: Brougham (pronounced Broom, for the uninitiated) Hayes and Upper Oldfield Park, some seven minutes' walk apart (hour long lessons allow for the trot between sites). The latter is all Bath stone, high ceilings, lots of glass, stunning modern additions and stonking views, including a new refectory where delicious chicken and leek pie was on the menu, along with equally tasty home-cooked choices. Brougham Hayes is, well, tired and in widely acknowledged need of a facelift, but it boasts a new design studio, equipped with help from Dyson, which provided industry-quality machinery usually beyond a school's budget. But it is the simply fabulous Nucleus, a new science centre, which must be the envy of schools up and down the land. Eye-catching design which includes student contributions, serious green credentials and extreme functionality (we loved the write-on walls, also in the refurbished maths rooms, with their formulae-in-progress as well as more permanent aperçus, and the witty and efficacious use of hay as an insulating material in the walls) mean it is far more than a pretty face.

This sense of modish practicality extends to the uniform, which is amongst the most smartly worn (read rigorously enforced) we have seen anywhere: themed colours of black and purple, with a braided blazer, open collared white blouse and choice of a skirt or trousers. That said, Hayesfield sixth formers are attired with marked degrees of quirkiness, liberated from the deadening (and generally wildly off the mark) expectation of 'office wear' laid down by so many schools. The prevailing atmosphere is one of opportunity – it's all there for the taking. 'Special talents will be developed and supported in this school,' says the head, adding that 'Opportunities should not have to be bought. Parents choose Hayesfield as a social decision – girls come from all kinds of backgrounds, reflecting Britain as a whole'. Subject-specific homework clubs abound, and there's an outreach initiative to support girls from a less advantaged part of the city. We also picked up a spirit of enterprise: the vision and amount of private funding bid for and secured for the sensational new buildings on the upper site, the strong links with China through the Bath-Suzhou Education Partnership, and the ski trip to Canada being just three examples. Market forces too: 'You're going to have to develop yourselves as a desirable commodity,' the head instructs her sixth formers

Pastoral care, well-being and discipline: Very highly rated: 'in our experience, second to none,' some enthusiastic parents told us; 'a safe, nurturing and happy environment,' said one; 'staff and pupils are attuned to each other,' remarked another. As for the girls: 'We can go to anyone when things go wrong – the school nurse, the counsellor – anyone!' It was heartening to see the deputy head greeting everyone (and many by name) at the start of the day when we visited. Effective buddy system in place for year 7 intake from the year above. But a clear system of sanctions is also applied rarely and fairly, according to students, starting with detentions for sins of academic omission and commission. As to behaviour: 'No-one has the right to disrupt the learning of other people,' states the head, who does not shrink from sending the persistently disruptive to Beechen Cliff for their lessons, as a step short of excluding them completely.

Pupils and parents: The girls we met were pleased and proud to be at Hayesfield – 'The school encourages them to be confident from the start,' say parents, while the head's view is that everyone should be encouraged to take risks and to 'colour outside the lines. Coping with failure builds resilience', she says. We certainly found students forthcoming, articulate and go-getting: school lists founder member of the Women's Equality Party among its students. Families come from grade 1 listed Georgian piles and from rather humbler dwellings across the socio-economic spectrum. Brothers tend to go to Beechen Cliff; the two schools share an admissions policy, term dates and inset days. Mary Berry is indisputably its most famous alumna, but sports fans will know of Amy Williams, GB's skeleton bob gold medallist and Anya Shrubsole, cricketer.

Entrance: About 180 girls join in year 7 from a variety of local primary and prep schools, mostly in Bath but 20 per cent coming from outside the Greater Bath Consortium; all applications done via the local authority, whose edicts merit careful study. Those with brothers at Beechen, as well as those with sisters here, get priority under the siblings policy. Open days in September and October. School is currently full but not oversubscribed – some parents hedge their bets with abundant Bath independents. At sixth form, 65 new students can join; no more than a quarter of the total sixth form may be boys, although teaching is joint with Beechen. Some parents think that 60/40 would make for a more viable offer, particularly in terms of boys' sports teams and activities. Entry requirements are six GCSEs at grade 4 or above including English and maths (the unsuccessful are expected to retake) to enrol on A level courses; some subjects require a 6 for further study. Lower or fewer GCSEs might mean entry to BTec courses.

Exit: Hardly any leavers before the end of sixth form. After A levels or BTec, 81 per cent go on to higher or further education, a sprinkling of gap years, very few straight to work; school is proud to have Employability Chartermark – not many have. A goodly percentage goes to top universities, helped by school's own Oxbridge and élite course programme (one to Oxbridge, two medics, in 2018). More information on destinations for the less exalted would be helpful.

Money matters: Striving to be a cashless school, but parents report frustrations with Tucasi, the system chosen, which fails to flag up low or empty balances. Otherwise, a sensible and egalitarian attitude to money and costs in particular, in common with most maintained schools. We applaud the accounts of wise and compassionate use of pupil premium and bursary funds in cases of financial nightmare that came to our ears.

Remarks: Defiantly, proudly, pre-eminently a girls' school, freshened up by a mixed sixth form. A particular hooray for the school's emphasis on STEM subjects for girls – this is a place where they can literally reach for the stars.

Hazlegrove School

Linked with King's Bruton

H

Hazlegrove, Sparkford, Yeovil, Somerset BA22 7JA

Ages 2–13 **Pupils** 355 **Boarders** 95 full, 20 flexi (from 7 years)

Fees: Day £8,787 – £17,811; Boarding £20,658 – £26,361 pa

01963 442606
www.hazlegrove.co.uk

Headmaster: Since September 2017, Mark White, previously deputy head (academic) at the Dragon School in Oxford. Educated at Eton and read politics and modern history at Edinburgh. Worked in retail for five years before turning to teaching and a PGCE in history from Bristol; taught in a 1,800 pupil comprehensive school in Cheltenham for 10 years, becoming assistant head, before moving to the Dragon School. Married to Serena.

Entrance: Broadly non-selective. All hopefuls are invited for a trial day at which reading/spelling ages and mathematical ability are assessed, plus any need for additional learning support identified.

Exit: To a panoply of greater and lesser public schools at 13+, majority in south west England. Between 40 and 50 per cent to the Sherborne schools, Marlborough, Bryanston, Millfield, Winchester, Eton, Oundle and Wells. Around half to its own senior school, Kings Bruton. The array of awards year after year impresses – 18 in 2018, six of these to Kings Bruton. A recent parent was delighted by the school's efforts in researching a senior school where Hazlegrove pupils do not usually go. Former pupils include Peter Wilson (Olympic gold medallist in shooting), Maddie Hinch (GB hockey goalie), sculptor Will Newton and author Tobias Jones.

Remarks: A long drive through glorious parkland – we narrowly avoided cows and 4x4s en route – leads to a fine example of 18th century domestic architecture, enhanced by formal gardens. Less sightly parts of what is undoubtedly a well-resourced and purposeful school are mostly hidden away, but facilities and space abound: super indoor pool, two Astros, tennis courts and acres of pitches satisfy the most sporty. Recent additions include new girls' changing rooms and upgrades to swimming pool including new viewing area and additional entrance. Pigs and chickens enthusiastically looked after by pupils, and there's no ducking their eventual fate either. Full use appears to be made of this bucolic setting (faintly marred by the services visible on the A303), recently enhanced by the planting of a five acre Jubilee Wood.

We were enthralled and impressed by a scholarship English class of 13-year-olds who were getting to grips with the complex themes in William Blake's poetry. Parents recognise and greatly appreciate the fine teaching that goes on at Hazlegrove, and acknowledge the school's insistence in recruiting staff only of the highest calibre: 'The quality of the discussions at parents' evenings is phenomenal,' said one mother. But Hazlegrove is no hothouse, though the children are 'pushed enough,' say parents, and does very well by the breadth of ability it admits. About 15 per cent of pupils receive learning support. All these lucky children benefit from exciting and innovative ways to learn, such as a Skype call with astronaut Nicholas Patrick in which the whole prep school participated, and the millionaires' club which encourages children to read 1,000,000 words in the course of a term. The latter is part of the Accelerated Reader programme, where books are carefully graded to eliminate unsuitable choices. The librarian gets rave reviews.

Sport, music and drama ditto. There's an extensive fixture list with other schools and plenty of silverware in the trophy cabinet. One parent articulated the common tension between winning at all costs/sport for all, and wondered if there could be more chances for less skilled players to represent the school at matches. (School defends its record on this.) As for the music, well, our socks were knocked off by the impromptu marimba recital (we had not met one before either) the head asked a boy to perform when we happened upon him jamming with a couple of other pupils in the music department. Masses going on of all standards, from absolute beginners to one already at grade 8, and a clutch taking grade 5 theory – plus giant outdoor chimes in pre prep playground. Conventional choices for drama, such as Wind in the Willows and The Wizard of Oz put on in purpose-built theatre and much enjoyed by performers and audience alike; pupils also take LAMDA exams. Mandarin club has proved hugely successful and Mandarin introduced for year 5 pupils.

About a third of pupils board routinely (around 10 per cent of these are international pupils), and there is scope for occasional boarders too. Accommodation is fine (quite big dorms with a strong smell of disinfectant in the boys' quarters) with a bit of recent pepping up (includes a new common room) though rules are quaintly old-fashioned: no mobiles, letter-writing on Sundays and proper shoe-cleaning once a week. That said, activities are myriad and sometimes rather trendy: we were shown the film the boarders had devised, scripted and made the previous weekend. The feel of an extended family is palpable, enhanced by the fact that half the staff live on site. In the evenings, seating for meals is rearranged into family-style groups so boarders get to know everyone; a black tie dinner with five sets of cutlery enlivens proceedings from time to time.

Hazlegrove is quite smart and not a typical country prep school. A broad cross-section (says school) of local and not-so-local families drive or bus their kids in from all over the place up and down the A303, and it's the school of choice for many families making the big move out of London. The school defined parents, when asked, as the 'sort of people who don't look in the mirror before they come to pick up'; their occupations include farmer, lawyer, doctor, plumber, cheese-maker, helicopter pilot, entrepreneur, designer, author and chef. There is an active and welcoming social scene and parents, mums in particular, take up the exercise classes and tennis coaching with enthusiasm. Try as we might, we could not find anything to fault about this super one-off school.

Hereford Cathedral Junior School

Linked with Hereford Cathedral School

28 Castle Street, Hereford HR1 2NW

Ages 3–11 **Pupils** 201

Fees: £8,028 – £10,320 pa

01432 363511
www.herefordcs.com

Head: Since September 2014, Christopher Wright, previously assistant head at Exeter Cathedral School. Degree from Warwick in industrial economics, and masters in economics. Has taught at Winchester House School, St Edward's Oxford, The Banda School in Nairobi and Moor Park. Married to Jo; their youngest child has joined the school. Likes squash, tennis, scuba diving and surfing.

Entrance: Not selective in its lower years and accepts children into the nursery from age 3. There is also an intake in reception and at age 7, although entrance is possible at other ages, subject to space and suitability. As children get older there are interviews and entrance tests and a requirement for reports from their current school. Substantial scholarships are available for boys who join the school as cathedral choristers (from age 7).

Exit: The vast majority of pupils, 92 per cent, go on to the senior school on the head's recommendation and without taking the entrance exam. The remaining pupils usually go to other Herefordshire schools or overseas.

Those whom it is felt would not thrive there are generally counseled in year 2 or 3 to consider alternatives, so there should be no nasty surprises in year 6, and it is rare for the school not to be able to get a child up to the right level by then.

Remarks: Like the senior school, a mixture of old and new. Three schools in one – a nursery, pre-prep and junior school. Also like the senior school, the junior school is almost in the shadow of Hereford Cathedral, and shares very similar links. It is a charming place, with a very embedded sense of nurture and encouragement.

The junior and senior school combined offer what they hope will be a one stop solution for Herefordshire parents, for children from 3 to 18. As the school also offers a breakfast club from 8am and after-school care until 5.30pm (and has a policy of never shutting, whatever the weather) there is much to attract parents who need a few additional hours around the edges of the day. The catchment area runs all around the county and into Wales, with school buses from Bromyard, Ludlow, Ross-on-Wye and Presteigne (all supervised, and shared with the senior school).

The principal junior school building – a mixture of medieval and Georgian splendours – has more than its fair share of paneled walls and ornately plastered ceilings, although it also has the feel of a slightly overgrown country house in which a school happens to have landed. Brightened by lots and lots of children's work on the walls and attractive displays.

In complete contrast, the purpose-built moat, tucked into what would have been a terrace in the old school garden, houses the pre-prep. This really is a great environment for children to learn. It is airy and child friendly, with small classrooms for an intimate learning space and good areas for play, lots of natural light too. The reception class has its own little garden to play in – well-resourced but not overcrowded.

The art room, complete with kiln, is well kitted out and full of exuberant work – willow structures and ceramics as well as the usual paintings and drawings. There is also a small but well put together DT room where the slightly older children begin learning about resistant materials. The creative arts are plainly very important here – a lovely feature is the Olympic wall in the main garden – a tiled mural which incorporates designs by every child in the school, reflecting on the themes of 2012, coordinated by local artist Clare Woods (whose works were commissioned for display in the Olympic park).

There are separate gardens for different age groups to play in – one for the reception class, one for years 1 and 2 (with a recent adventure play area), and one for the older children, as well as a lovely wild garden with a pond, lots of homes for masonry bees and ladybirds, wild flowers and so on. The children in year 5 are responsible for the gardening and there is a pond club too.

The nursery (in a recently new building) has high staff ratios (we saw a group of 15 being looked after by four staff). In the pre-prep and junior classes, groups tend to be no larger than 13 or 14. Setting for maths and English in year 6. The school 'doesn't do' a gifted and talented programme as feels it is counterproductive to label children as either in or out of such a category, says 'it's all about hard work' and emphasizes the importance of respecting the different learning pathways and intellectual growth spurts of different children. There is instead a detailed programme for what the school refers to as high achievers.

No children with EAL when we visited. Learning support is available and carefully tailored. There are two learning development specialists working across the year groups so that any learning support issues can be identified early. A specialist SEN teacher assists those in years 5/6 who require support.

French and music from reception upwards, and all pupils are also involved in drama and performance – starting with poetry recital and working up to debating, improvisation and puppetry by years 4/5.

Lots of extracurricular options – about half the children take instrumental lessons in the senior school music block in the adjacent building – as well as pottery, ballet, first aid and various other clubs. And, of course, there are some 14 choristers, who have rehearsals and cathedral services six days a week.

Sport, teamwork and having a go are considered very important parts of the school experience, with regular matches against schools from Shropshire, Worcestershire, Gloucestershire and Wales. Hockey, netball and rounders for girls; rugby, football and cricket for boys. The children have use of the senior school playing fields and sports hall – and, unusually, says the school, get a completely fair share.

The children, from the nursery class eagerly talking about their book choices in the school library, to the reception children, busy with puzzles and problem solving, to year 4s enthusiastically reciting poetry, are the best possible advertisement for the school. Each child with whom we spent time was friendly, relaxed, happy and engaged. Bouncing about full of things to talk about. You can pretty much hear their little brains fizzing. A delightful place to start exploring life's possibilities.

Hereford Cathedral School

Linked with Hereford Cathedral Junior School

Old Deanery, The Cathedral Close, Hereford HR1 2NG

Ages 11-19 **Pupils** 505 **Sixth form** 116

Fees: £13,881 pa

01432 363522
www.herefordcs.com

H

Headmaster: Since 2005, Paul Smith BSc. Originally a zoologist (undergraduate at Manchester, postgraduate at KCL), his first teaching post was at Rugby, followed by stints at King Edward's School Birmingham and as head of science at Haileybury, then second master and acting head at Portsmouth Grammar School. A softly spoken, friendly, but determined character. Married with two daughters.

Works hard at getting to know every child and speaks of teaching as a 'humbling experience'. Insists on the importance of staff respecting pupils and not becoming 'myopic' about children who don't fit a particular mould. Emphatic about the importance of strengthening relationships through extracurricular activities. Pupils say he is 'nice, funny, witty and approachable'. Staff say he is 'calm and considered – you can ask him anything'.

Very keen that the school should be 'all round' – not, for example, a music academy or languages specialist. Looking to broaden the horizons of the school and has introduced a small number of international homestay boarding students in the sixth form.

Academic matters: Strong academically, with 50 per cent A*/A and 71 per cent A*-B at A level in 2018 and 54 per cent A*-A/9-7 at GCSE. At A level, English, modern languages, history, art, music and RS all do very well. Good results in sciences too – no really weak areas. Nice range of A levels – the usual suspects plus Latin, history of art, philosophy and ethics.

As well as receiving half termly grade reports for effort and achievement, with target grades included from year 10, pupils have to fill in a self-assessment form every term that is issued alongside their reports – something parents value highly. Staff say this is not a crammer and that the range of abilities is reasonably wide. Nonetheless, expectations are high.

All students take maths (top sets take two AS modules in year 11), two English, and short course RS as compulsory GCSEs. Some 60 per cent take triple award science and the remainder dual award. The vast majority take French or Spanish, although a handful use the curriculum time for learning support. An additional three subjects are chosen from a range of options, GCSE Japanese is offered as an extracurricular addition, and the school is about to introduce Mandarin.

Interactive whiteboards in most classrooms, school email used to set and receive work – although traditional means are also used, and there is good access to PCs within school, including a dedicated area in the sixth form centre. A well-stocked library with its own small IT suite and a galleried, silent study area. Welcoming and evidently well used, also the venue for the school's book clubs, debating club and film club.

Learning support is well organized with all children MIDYIS tested on entry and supported as necessary, either within class or small group withdrawal. A sense of 'open door' for any wanting assistance. Pupils say they can go into the learning support unit for 'anything and everything'. A handful of international students in the sixth form, all of whom are tested on entry, have EAL timetabled into their week.

Games, options, the arts: Art, music and design are simply outstanding here. The A level art results speak for themselves, and the quality of work on display is excellent, varied and innovative, complemented by a small but very well-resourced history of art department. Beautiful, naturally lit studio for the use of sixth formers and large, light rooms for the lower years. Textile work is also beautiful.

At the other end of the design spectrum, the DT workshops (for both resistant materials and electronics) are well kitted out with and well organized. Some interesting project work, and DT seems to have been fairly successfully sold to the girls, who make up around 25 per cent of the GCSE cohort.

Music is a central part of school life. The school remains the choristers' school for the cathedral but aside from that there are masses of choirs, chamber ensembles, jazz bands and piano trios as well as a music technology club. About half of all pupils take instrumental lessons, and the school is a choral power to be reckoned with. The senior girls' choir (Cantabile) has won the senior children's choir section of the Llangollen International Musical Eisteddfod.

Sporting success is seen as important but participation is also perceived as a means of increasing pupils' confidence and strengthening relationships. Successful teams fielded in rugby (two Welsh U18 players in recent years), cricket (a number of county players – the girls' cricket team have played at Lords several times in the last few years, reaching the finals of Lady Taverners indoor cricket competition), hockey (boys and girls – county and regional players), netball, rounders (two England players) and tennis. Football has also now been introduced for boys and rowing is popular too. Large and well-equipped sports hall. Fencing and swimming also available as options. Spacious, well-maintained sports fields are a 15 minute walk from the cathedral green (slight moan from pupils who have to walk there and back); netball courts are close, though not actually on site.

Unusually, CCF is compulsory in year 10, and many stay with it into the sixth form. It runs a huge range of courses including leadership, sailing, gliding and diving. There is a regimental dinner, summer camps, annual field days. The school also runs an annual trek for year 12 students to the Annapurna range in Nepal where it supports a local school. D of E also well supported.

Extracurricular clubs in just about everything – including mycology, Japanese, New Testament Greek and (reassuringly) board games. Definitely a school where all interests are catered for.

Background and atmosphere: Herefordshire is a deeply rural county, and Hereford itself has something of the quiet county town about it. It is impossible not to feel slightly removed from the cut and thrust of the 21st century here. The school, originally for choristers in the 12th century, is set around the stunning cathedral green, and the splendours of the cathedral lend a special flavour to the place. That connection (the chaplain is a minor canon of the cathedral, as well as teaching full time) gives the school an implicitly Christian flavour and pupils clearly appreciate the depth and beauty of the place.

Quite traditional in feel. Monitors (prefects) wear gowns to chapel, as do academic staff. Services are held four times a week in the nave, and much of the musical and artistic excellence of the school seems to feed off the cathedral tradition of creative and artistic expression. Good spaces between the buildings, which are a combination of listed glories and more modern blocks (such as the sports and dining halls). But for all the leafy tranquility, the school is a very busy place, with lots to do, lots going on, and great enthusiasm from top to bottom about the possibilities 'out there'. One of very few schools whose pupils can claim to have founded a charity with a national ambit (The Little Princess Trust). And there is another under construction. Pupils evidently feel that not only do they have a responsibility to do the right thing, but also that they have the capacity to make a difference.

Pastoral care, well-being and discipline: Pastoral care is evidently a very integrated part of school life – four school houses, each with eight tutors, so tutor groups are small. Academic staff are positively encouraged to run extracurricular activities and to strengthen relationships and pastoral links through them. Parents are encouraged to email academic and house staff with any queries, and say that any concerns are dealt with 'instantly', and 'children are kept too busy to have time for cyber bullying'.

Pupils say there is no problem with reporting bullying and getting it sorted out if it arises, but that it is rare. They also say that the school system of detentions is applied consistently, but that need of it is infrequent. Staff say they have very little to deal with on the disciplinary front.

Pupils and parents: Pupils are an absolute delight – very supportive of one another, articulate and appreciative. Comfortable in their own skin, but not full of themselves. Extremely positive about the school and proud of their achievements, but no trace of entitlement or arrogance – if they are a little on the quiet side one gets the impression that this is a result of not having to shout in order to be heard. Parents are a combination of local farmers, businesspeople and professionals. Many attended the school themselves. Busy, supportive PTA. Parents say, 'All children have something special – and here the teachers help them find it'; 'The school builds self confidence' and 'identifies needs quickly', both academically and pastorally.

Entrance: School is selective, but with Herefordshire school numbers in a demographic dip, cannot afford to be hugely so. Most of the junior school pupils end up here, and unless there is a particular cause for uncertainty, are offered a place without taking the entrance tests. All external candidates at 11 examined in English, maths and VR. There is also an interview for every candidate. Successful candidates at 11 can defer their place to 13+ if happy in a prep school elsewhere, and there is also a separate entry procedure at 13 (not CE). For the sixth form at least six B/6s at GCSE and at least C/4s in English and maths GCSE are required plus references, interviews etc.

Exit: About 80 per cent stay past GCSE and into the sixth form though others go to the local, and very well thought of, sixth form college. Five to Oxbridge in 2018, one to New York University, with over half to Russell Group – especially Bristol, Cardiff, Swansea, Birmingham, Leeds, KCL etc. A good mix of subjects – including medicine (five places in 2018), dentistry, physics, veterinary science, law, history, business and economics. A number, too, taking art or music – including one recently to Parsons Fashion, Art and Design School, New York. Not many into electronics or ICT.

Money matters: Academic scholarships worth 15 per cent of fees available at 11+, 13+ and 16+. Other scholarships worth 10 per cent of fees for music, sports and all rounders (also for art at 13+). A number of bursary awards and some Ogden Trust bursaries for science students joining the sixth form. Previously a direct grant school and actively fundraising to broaden access.

Remarks: Justifiably growing more self-assured, a school with a great deal to offer and an ethos of careful, thoughtful, nurture. Much to impress, with truly outstanding arts and music, a wide curriculum, a great sense of community service and genuine commitment to developing courage, confidence and a sense of adventure in even the quietest child.

Hereford Sixth Form College

Folly Lane, Hereford, Herefordshire HR1 1LU

Ages 16–18 **Pupils** 2,013

01432 355166
www.hereford.ac.uk

Principal: Since September 2017, Peter Cooper, who had already been deputy principal at the college for 18 years. Chemistry degree from Nottingham; has also worked at Kenilworth High School and Priestley College, Warrington. He is deeply committed to the college and to the sector, being a member of the national Sixth Form College Association's Curriculum and Quality Board since 2011. Enthusiastic in his advocacy of the sector, he runs a well-oiled large institution which focuses on the student experience and support. No money wasted here on layers of management. It is a lean machine and a personal one. Peter likes to be seen out and about in the college but always tries to make time for bridge club and his weekly staff football.

Academic matters: This is no sleepy rural backwater. The college consistently comes out as one of the top institutions nationally for value-added exam results and it was awarded outstanding in every area at its last Ofsted inspection. In 2018, 54 per cent A*/B and 26 per cent A*/A grades. There is an impressive range of A levels on offer including subjects difficult to find in smaller institutions such as archaeology and geology. Offers French, Spanish and German. At least two-thirds take one science, and numbers for maths are huge too. There are also BTecs in IT and performing arts, the BTec extended diploma in sport and exercise science, and technical certificates in engineering and cyber security as well as a one-year GCSE programme. Everyone follows a general education programme where general studies A level sits along side a progression studies course that includes careers education, personal finance, healthy living and environmental sustainability.

About 10 per cent of students have identified learning difficulties and support is tailored to individual need. Students rated the learning support very highly and said the college was particularly strong on sorting out dyslexic issues. They were very conscious that teaching was aimed at the top end, but described very effective lunchtime surgeries in all subjects to sort out individual difficulties. Set size is around 20.

Wednesday afternoons are when students engage in enrichment activities in a strikingly wide range of high quality areas. There are some lectures preparing those who are thinking Oxbridge – Cambridge regularly brings a coachful of academics to run talks and masterclasses. The highly structured approach to this extension work is unusual even in high performing selective independent schools.

The college attributes its high performance to an insistence on the highest standards and rigorous, effective use of data. Each student regularly receives three grades – a minimum A level grade expectation based on prior achievement at GCSE, a grade which reflects the current level of performance, and then a grade that tutors feel a student is capable of achieving. These are closely analysed by the college and tutors, who talk through concerns and patterns with each student throughout their programme. Not much can slip through the net here, and parents commented on how successful the college is in keeping students on track. 'It has turned my son's attitude to education round', said one parent whose son had had something of an 'attitude' in his secondary school.

The close-knit Association of Sixth Form Colleges allows regular benchmarking of academic progress against other similar institutions and the college makes effective use of this, which is another way of quickly highlighting any areas of weakness that need addressing.

Games, options, the arts: The college runs an enrichment programme with the motto 'something for everyone' – and there is. Most activities take place outside lesson time, but some are directly linked to subjects and are actually part of the timetable. The most innovative and structured areas are sport and performing arts, particularly music. Some two-thirds of students take part in at least one activity.

There are Sports Academies for basketball, football, hockey, netball and rugby. These have links with local sports clubs and top quality sports coaches – with consistently impressive successes. Each sports player has an individual fitness programme.

The college is the biggest centre for music in the Three Counties. There are masses of ensembles and groups and an elite programme for top musicians which, rather like the sport, gives students opportunities to perform alongside and learn from professionals. A music scholarship programme offers the best performers training on a par with a music college and is not confined to those taking A level music; many gain choral or instrumental university scholarships. The Academia Musica choir, comprising music scholars and musicians in residence, has a performing contract with a record company, performs weekly in British cathedrals and has a substantial calendar of engagements around the UK and abroad. We are talking serious professional quality here. Instrumental scholars form the basis of the Academia Musica Orchestra that manages its own weekly recital series and has played with the English Symphony Orchestra.

The college theatre company, Upstage Productions, recently performed Romeo and Juliet in Hereford Cathedral, with voice coaching from professionals.

Background and atmosphere: The college started 40 years ago at a time when Herefordshire was moving away from 11 to 18 schools. The majority of the county schools are now 11 to 16, though some have small sixth forms. The strength and challenge of HSFC is its size. You get the brilliant academic and extracurricular option choices and the college works hard to overcome the impersonality that such a large institution could mean. Students say that some do find the size off-putting, particularly at first if they have moved from a small school. However the ones we talked to made it clear they had chosen the college partly because they wanted the stimulus and interaction of large classes.

The site is undoubtedly small for such a huge number of students. Student social spaces and the library can be crowded during the common break and lunch hour, although these and the dining area have been extended recently. There are new classroom blocks and everything has been refurbished in the last few years. It looks modern, fresh and cared for, and there is a real studenty buzz about the place. It is very different in feel to a traditional school, particularly an all-through school, and some young people are more than ready for this at 16.

Pastoral care, well-being and discipline: This is a genuine half way house between school and university. All students have a tutor who stays with them for the two years and teaches them for one of their subjects. The tutor meets with each tutee for a 'settling-in' interview in the first term and uses this information to build a nuanced picture of each individual, understanding their lives outside of the college as well as their academic needs. Students are also allocated a director of studies, who is another port of call for any difficulties; students told us they rated their director highly.

Parents are still very much kept in the loop. They are invited in for an information session as soon as the student starts at the college, there are parents' evenings with the student and tutors, and they are encouraged to email tutors. However, the college expects to provide support directly to students. There is a well-being centre offering a range of confidential services. The college chaplain, college counsellor and independent well-being adviser are all based there, offering advice and help when needed on issues ranging from emotional and family problems to housing and legal rights. One parent whose son had had health problems couldn't praise the college highly enough for its flexibility and understanding, which ensured the boy could get back to college at the earliest possible opportunity.

Students say that one of the advantages of the college is that everything is geared to a very small age group with very specific needs. That is true of the pastoral care and extends to the comprehensive careers department, which is held in very high esteem by students and parents. One parent commented on the patience of the careers adviser whilst their daughter was agonising over which pathway to choose – a common dilemma for many at this age.

We asked about discipline issues, but no one felt there were any. 'Everyone wants to be here,' said a student, and the college felt that any disruptive influences were diluted compared with a school by the sheer scale of the place.

Pupils and parents: Some 75 to 80 per cent of Herefordshire sixth formers attend the college, with others from surrounding counties and Wales, from state and independent schools. Many come from low income families, but there are also parents well able to support the strong careers department by offering top quality work experience and interview practice. Two places for parents on high calibre governing body.

Entrance: Open access, though the college considers five 4s at GCSE sensible for those wanting to start on A levels.

Exit: Despite the fact that entry is open, there are significant numbers going on to top universities, including Oxbridge (19 places in 2018, plus 15 medics) – and reading a wide range of subjects. Cardiff, Birmingham, Swansea and London universities very popular, plus Bristol and UWE. Others to eg sound engineering apprenticeship at the BBC, intelligence analyst in the RAF, quantity surveying and mechanical engineering apprenticeships. A number of parents were lavish in their praise of the way the college prepared students both intellectually and socially for higher education.

Money matters: It is free! There are a few costs associated with certain areas such as foreign travel, but the college has set up a bursary fund for financial hardship. Parents are invited to pay £50 a year into this, which most are able to do. The county council subsidises daily travel for those living over three miles away.

Remarks: HSFC is as good as it gets in the state sector for sixth form education, and it gives independent schools a terrific run for their money. Families who live near enough are very lucky to have this seriously good option on their doorstep.

H

Howell's School, Llandaff,

Cardiff Road, Llandaff, Cardiff CF5 2YD

Ages 3–18 **Pupils** 745 **Sixth form** 175 (35 boys)

Fees: £8,371– £13,999 pa

029 2056 2019
www.howells-cardiff.gdst.net

Principal: Since 2007, Sally Davis BSc PGCE NPQH (50s). Born and schooled in Wales, she left to read geology at Bedford College and spent several years teaching in London; her last post was director of studies at Harris City Technology College, before a wish to return to Wales and the post of deputy head at Howells coincided in 1992, a point at which she was the second youngest member of staff. Totally steeped in state education as both pupil and teacher, she had never considered working in an independent school, 'but this place changes lives, and I wanted to be a part of that'. She is held in great affection and respect by everyone we spoke to. She cites cementing the community between the teaching/support staff and senior and junior schools as her greatest achievement in her tenure, but we would also highlight excellent results and the highest retention rates post-GCSE of all GDST schools, possibly as a consequence of the exceedingly successful co-ed sixth form college.

Not all heads would have the nerve to dress as flamboyantly as Mrs D – a diaphanous black fur-trimmed wrap and sparkly shoes added a touch of exuberance to a sleeveless black dress the day we met her, and she is known for her statement jewellery, some of which she makes herself. A neon sign in the sixth form café designates it Sally D's, but not at the expense of her authority in school, which is unquestioned: 'She's strict when she needs to be' said one young lady. Mrs Davis is married with two grown children; she is a keen traveller with a penchant for house-swapping, so she can be part of a community whether in Europe, Canada or the US.

Head of junior school: Since 2006, Judith Ashill BEd. Born in Cyprus, but definitely Welsh. She trained originally as a nurse, yet wanted very much to go to university, hence her degree from Swansea. In those days, Welsh was compulsory in Welsh state schools and Mrs Ashill did not speak it, so she spent 14 years at Redland High, before 'this job came up, and I could be this side of the bridge'. Her priority for the junior school, other than getting the academic best out of the girls, is its pastoral care, wrap-around in both senses of encompassing the whole child, and topping and tailing the school day. Hard-working teachers, a palette of opportunities and great expectations are the watchwords of Howell's Junior. Her young charges and their parents find Mrs Ashill 'kind, helpful, calm and open-minded'. She is married with two talented hockey-playing daughters, and likes to take one good holiday a year to distant climes.

Academic matters: Junior school teaching is based on the national curriculum and is topic-based and multi-sensory for all subjects. Science teaching obviously effective: Tesco had written to a year 6 science class asking for tips on growing cress. Welsh is compulsory from the start, French, German, Spanish and Mandarin also on offer as chargeable clubs. Girls evidently enjoy their learning: maths, art and swimming come top of the charts, but 'even spelling tests are fun,' and 'teachers explain in more and more detail to us if we find it tricky', said our interlocutors. Any girls with 'additional learning needs', as SEN is known here, receive Read Write Inc teaching where applicable; no stigma attached. The grounds are used as an outdoor classroom, as far as a city site permits; elements of the forest school programme are incorporated.

In 2018 A level results came in at 49 per cent A*/A and 74 per cent A*/B; mathematicians and musicians were particularly successful. At GCSE, 75 per cent were graded A*-A/7-9, and school is definitely (and correctly) seen as the academic option in Cardiff. 'It is very academic, but then I'm really geeky,' remarked one student, disarmingly. Take-up is greatest for maths, biology and chemistry; stand-out subjects in terms of enjoyment and effective teaching are thought to be maths and physics, all giving ammunition to the apologists for girls-only education. Surprisingly small numbers choose English or modern languages at A level, including Welsh, despite having to do two languages in year 7; modern about equal to ancient, where it is heartening to see a smattering of Greek. All four of the sixth form interviewees we met were doing A level maths, and reported a 'healthy perspective' on Oxbridge and support for those applying for medicine. The teaching we saw struck us as taking the best of old and new: during a physics class, teaching was divided between interactive whiteboard and the good old-fashioned kind with pens – no dazzling with technical wizardry. An eye is kept on the world beyond school by academic competitions and challenges within GDST and beyond – Salters for science, maths Olympiads and so on; EPQ and MOOCs are encouraged at sixth form.

SEN is known here as ALN – additional learning needs – and includes the gifted and talented and those with emotional issues alongside generally accepted definitions of special needs. All are screened on entry in year 7, but liaison with the junior school SENCo is close, 'so we know what we're getting'. School provides much SEN expertise in-house, such as its dyslexia unit, run by Dyslexia Action Cymru; other measures include a modified timetable with fewer languages. 'The learning support room is seen as a place of safety – it's sometimes rather hard to get rid of people!' said one member of staff. Support is not restricted to those with identified needs, but, for ordinary mortals, is provided by the pastoral team.

Games, options, the arts: Hockey, netball and athletics are the main compulsory sports on offer in the two winter terms, tennis and rounders in the summer. Sixth form boys play rugby, football and hockey. Existing swimming pool, tennis courts and sports hall now joined by spanking new Astro and pavilion as part of a revamp of all sports facilities. School competes locally in the Cardiff and Vale Schools fixtures, within GDST and individuals on occasion for Wales; somewhat improbably, it enjoys considerable success at ski slalom. DofE numbers are highest in Wales; riding much more recent with a small, keen and successful following.

Art is taught thematically exploring various media for the first three senior years; at GCSE and A level, it is coupled with design as a joint course. Art and photography can also be done as clubs. We cast covetous eyes on a marvellous swimsuit made of shells... Performing arts, whether song, dance, theatre or poetry, come together in the fine tradition of the school's annual Eisteddfod, hotly contested and enthusiastically embraced by all, but there is plenty else going on all year. Foundations for music laid early here, with the help of a specialist music room – quite right for daughters of the land of song, who have lifted their voices in St David's Hall Cardiff, Wales' premier concert hall. Musicians of all standards and talents will probably find an ensemble, and if not, are encouraged to start one. The senior four-part female auditioned choir has been as far as Beijing on tour. Theatre tends towards lighter tastes – Beauty and the Beast, The Sound of Music; willing staff with (or without) dramatic leanings are co-opted into the house pantomime competition; serious plays also staged, school assures us. Debating and public speaking also strong here, inside and outside school. Masses of clubs on offer, from the cerebral (philosophy) to the physical (tag rugby), by way of the environmental.

Background and atmosphere: Howell's particularly interesting back story is amply explored and illustrated in the best school history we had ever seen, the salient points being that its founding in 1860 was the eventual result of the legacy of a wealthy Tudor merchant, Thomas Howell (a member of the Drapers Livery Company, which still funds the school to some extent), one of whose clauses provided for the dowries of four orphan maidens, of his kin if they could be found; if not to 'four other maidens of good name'. After protracted difficulties in tracing descendant maidens and staving off claims from girls who were neither maidens nor orphans, an Act of 1852 was passed to set up two boarding schools in Wales for the 'education and advancement of deserving maiden orphans'. Job done: splendid new buildings (a mix of medieval, ecclesiastical, Tudor, gothic, Rhineland schloss and French château – truly) were erected in the (then 'primitive and unsanitary') village of Llandaff, now subsumed into Cardiff.

H

Housed in a couple of sunny brick houses (one once lived in by Roald Dahl) with an eye-catching curved extension on a corner of the main campus, the junior school has the advantage of its own site and super well-equipped playground, yet shares the senior school facilities just a walk away.

In 1980, Howell's joined the GDST, benefitting from its voice for girls' education, and opportunities for all manner of competitions while at school, and networking beyond – but it manages to keep its Welshness, a vital part of its identity. 2005 saw the admission of boys into the newly constituted college, the renamed sixth form; unlike a similar initiative at its sister school in Bath, this has been a huge success, and numbers of boys remain steady at about one third, and enough (crucially) to muster a rugby team. The girls appreciate doing male-dominated subjects like engineering, little pressure to wear make-up and 'the chance to get my weird phase out of the way' before chaps arrive in year 12. ('We do "odd" well', says Mrs Davis). The atmosphere is one of fun and great affection for the school from its pupils past and present, but certainly not at the expense of hard work and scholarly ambition. Much of this appears to be fuelled by cake: nowhere have we been offered so much so regularly, on top of a tasty lunch where choices were two kinds of pasta, baked potatoes, a salad bar and sandwiches in extremis.

Pastoral care, well-being and discipline: Parents greatly appreciate that 'the [junior] school works with all their pupils to ensure they find their own individual niche or specialism where they can succeed and be recognised for their achievements'; that it isn't just a proving ground for the rigours of the senior school. The academic standards are beyond reproach but 'it's also good at manners, music and making sure no-one is mean'.

Senior school pastoral side also highly praised by students and parents alike. One mother summed it up: 'The teachers really are interested and care for their pupils. The school responds swiftly to problems that may turn into something bigger – like bullying – and has a network in place to help any student who is overwhelmed or feeling nervous'. Another spoke movingly of the care the school had taken of her and her children during a particularly difficult time. 'I believe in the concept of mental wealth, which I extend to my staff,' says the principal. Students reckon the balance between reward and sanction is about right: they appreciate the freedom and latitude given them at sixth form and celebrations of all manner of school life, as well as the good cop/bad cop apparently played out between the principal and her deputy. The evils of city life do not appear to impinge greatly on Howell's: we heard no tales of drink, drugs or inappropriate goings-on

Pupils and parents: 'Courageous, creative, caring and willing to have a go,' according to the principal, from families with widely differing economic backgrounds, and whose belief in the importance of education means, in some cases, sending their children considerable distances to be there. Extensive bus routes from a 40 mile radius include Newport and Merthyr Tydfil.

Entrance: Main points of entry to junior school are at year 3 and year 5, but encouraged at other times by arrangement. Girls are assessed over the course of a day, using NFER and non-verbal reasoning; if the latter shows potential, they are likely to be accepted. Nursery and reception hopefuls are informally assessed.

Senior school entrants arrive from the junior school in year 7, but also from over 20 local primary schools, by means of exams held each January in maths (no calculators permitted) and English; rubrics can be in Welsh for native speakers, but written answers must be in English. Questions are on topics covered at school; girls should be working at Sats level 4, but school 'looks for evidence of level 5 work'. All hopefuls are interviewed and spend a day at school. For the college (sixth form), a minimum of six GCSEs are required, with at least a 6 in subjects taken for A level. Scholarships give typically a five per cent reduction in fees and are awarded for academic excellence (separate exam for sixth form but not at year 7), sport, music, art/DT, drama.

Exit: Juniors mostly to the senior school by means of its entrance tests; parents are told in year 5 if there is likely to be a problem. Limited tutoring goes on outside school; we heard of one small person being 'tutored for stress' but we suspect this is unusual and probably unrelated to school. 'We take well-being very seriously,' we were told – and we don't doubt it.

Around a quarter leaves after GCSE, but vast majority to a range of university courses up and down the land; a bias towards Welsh universities (particularly Cardiff) and some across the bridge in south west England. Lots of medics (three in 2018), a smattering to Oxbridge (two in 2018), plus one off to the Juilliard School in New York. Careers and UCAS guidance comes in for particular praise. Close and fond links with previous pupils mean a strong Hywelian Guild. Alumni are represented across the professions, academia, arts and sports; the most famous are Ann Cotton, founder of Camfed, Hannah Mills, an Olympic sailor who won gold in 2016, and Charlotte Church, of whom no more need be said.

Money matters: Very good value for money, like all GDST schools. Deserving cases for financial help in the form of bursaries are considered centrally by GDST; a couple supported by HSBC each year. Additional support for sixth form studies provided by Welsh government in the form of an allowance paid to lower income households, an initiative phased out some years ago in England....

Remarks: Howell's looks and feels like a good old-fashioned girls' grammar, but is so much more than that. Masses of fun, laughter and cake make the task of scholarly slog so much more palatable; everyone appears to come up with the goods without buckling under the pressure. 'Every inch of Howell's seems to exude care,' observed a parent. Expect Welshcakes and pink branded lip salve in your goody bag – and hulking lads in the sixth form. 'I'm disappointed we have had to wait this long to be able to get my son there,' said a happy parent of three Hywelians. Any sooner, though, and it would alter the unique character of this Cardiff institution.

H

Huish Episcopi Academy

Wincanton Road, Huish Episcopi, Langport, Somerset TA10 9SS

Ages 11–18 **Pupils** 1,530 **Sixth form** 194

01458 250501
www.huishepiscopi.net

Principal: Since September 2017, Christopher Wade, previously executive lead at Inspirational Futures Trust (2016 –2017). Degree is sports and PE from the University of Wales Institute Cardiff; posts include head of year and PE teacher at St Katherine's School, various leadership roles at Bridgwater College Academy, and headteacher at Nailsea School.

Academic matters: In 2018, 43 per cent A*/A grades, 66 per cent A*-C at A level. At GCSE, 22 per cent A*-A/7-9 grades and 70 per cent got 9-4 in both English and maths. Strong subjects at all levels are expressive arts, science and maths. Twenty-seven options offered at sixth form including A levels and vocational courses such as BTecs in IT, sport, music technology, public services and health and social care, but the main emphasis is on A levels rather than the vocational courses available at the local sixth form colleges. At GCSE, a language is not compulsory but is strongly advised – everyone studies French from year 7 and can take up German or Spanish in year 8. More able students are offered more taxing subjects like statistics, further maths, Latin or triple sciences. World studies (RS) is compulsory, as is PE. Pupils are assessed a few weeks after starting in year 7 and are put in ability sets for the core subjects.

Teachers, many of whom have their own children at the school, rated highly by parents. One told us, 'The majority of teachers bend over backwards to respond to any concerns from parents and to help the kids achieve their target grades.' However, one parent did express concern that sometimes the quieter pupils could do with a little more encouragement, 'at least to try to see if they like something.'

The Student Guidance and Learning Centre (SGLC) supports needs including dyslexia, dyspraxia, autism, ADHD, visual impairment, hearing impairment, language difficulties, mental health difficulties and physical difficulties. They provide individual learning programmes and run clubs such as homework club and a Forces club for service children. There are also vertical tutor groups, an 'aspire to inspire' group, forest school activities, land-based activities and esteem-building clubs; 'go girls' and boys' clubs. A new programme, 'achieve for all,' engages and involves parents too. One parent said, 'The SENCo, Mrs Hills, was absolutely fantastic with my son.' The school will go the extra mile to accommodate all the needs of every pupil and prospective pupil. If pupils need extra help, this is given in class wherever possible so they don't miss anything or feel different. This, in turn, has helped other pupils to become more accepting of differences.

Games, options, the arts: Fantastic reputation for sport and outstanding facilities to match. Huish Leisure Centre is on campus and houses a sports hall, fitness and dance studios, tennis courts, squash courts and a swimming pool. The leisure centre is run by the school and serves the local community too. Sixth formers get free use even out of school hours. There are also playing fields, floodlit courts and a new Astroturf. Considerable success at county, area and even national level for many sports teams from football to basketball to netball to girls' rugby, with several individuals selected for high performance squad training. One year 10 boy, winner of SW Open Water 5K, led an U16 relay team across the Channel.

Also renowned for art, design and textiles, Huish has produced stars like Alice Temperley MBE. Fantastic displays of work around the school are impressive and no doubt inspiring to younger pupils. There is a biannual fashion show and art is very popular at both GCSE and A level. For budding musicians, there are clubs aplenty: Huish strings, junior jazz band, a capella, choir, orchestra, taiko drumming, Huish jazz, rock band, plus tours locally, nationally and internationally. There has been a music and drama tour of Belgium with the academy orchestra and regular visits to The Lighthouse in Poole. The music and drama departments work closely together to perform the annual musical, recently We Will Rock You, Les Misérables, West Side Story and Guys and Dolls; coming soon, Arabian Nights. On our visit we saw two very enthusiastic drama classes so we have no doubt the performances are sell-out. KS3 also recently performed Maria Marten.

Great variety of extracurricular activities run during break, lunch times and after school. Not just sports, arts and languages, but National Cipher Challenge Club, sewing, product design, JAM (Christian union), film club, plus a debating club which has just won a competition for post-16 students in Youth Speaks, led by the Rotary Club. Boards games are available in the library. Year 10s have a work experience week and one pupil recently spent a week in the House of Lords. The school also runs a Results Plus programme to learn skills in communication, teamwork, presentation skills, problem-solving and independent thinking.

Plenty of trips. Duke of Edinburgh is popular and there are regular science and humanities field trips, arts trips, language exchanges, sports tours, music tours and drama tours. Most recently there was a visit to Cologne, a Auschwitz visit, a trip to New York, Iceland and a ski trip, plus residentials for years 7/8 to Barcelona, Normandy and Berlin.

Background and atmosphere: The name Huish derives from the lands or household, and Episcopi means belonging to the Bishop of Wells. The bishops held the manor area of Langport and its environs from Saxon times until 1859. The origins of the academy can be traced back to 1675 when the original grammar school foundation was created. Today, as an academy, numbers have increased to over 1,500 pupils. No further plans to expand. Set in the heart of the Somerset levels, this rural school is made up of three main sections: Huish Academy, Huish Sixth and Huish Leisure.

The academy centres around the quad, which was originally constructed in the 1930s. Over the years a modern languages block, a science block and a brand new geography block have been added. The science block is made up of older traditional wooden labs plus more modern facilities. The design technology department is well equipped with 3D printers, CADCAM and a laser cutter. Great work on display: definitely some budding designers here. The older students run a club where pupils make gliders to enter in a local competition. Other projects have included a 'quadcopter.' There are four ICT suites, tablets available and plenty of PCs throughout the school. The music technology department in Huish Sixth has an Apple Mac suite and a recording studio. All in all, great resources.

Huish Sixth opened in 2010. It's the most prominent building as you drive into the school, and it's impressive: bright, open and colourful. As well as classrooms, study areas and a common room, there's a performance theatre space, a café and a balcony looking out over the Astro pitch and the playing fields. With some 140 students, it's large enough to offer a good range of options but small enough for everybody to get to know each other well and for teachers to provide good support. Huish Sixth is self-contained and sixth formers don't need to go to the academy unless they need to use the facilities: for design technology, for example. However, some students do opt to help younger pupils with their work, as we saw in the library where a sixth former was taking a maths session with three younger pupils.

The campus is fully wheelchair accessible and a new disabled area for physiotherapy, with hoists, has just been granted funding. The campus and buildings are easy to navigate and even when we crossed the playground as pupils emerged from lessons to their break time, there was a sense of calm. Three catering venues on campus, the latest one to be updated 'striving to be be a bit more like M&S.' Daily assemblies, one year per day. No house system but inter-form events by year group range from year 7 benchball to whole school cross-country. Like all traditional schools, there is a head boy and girl and a prefect system. There are 120 positions to apply for with the senior prefects in charge.

Pastoral care, well-being and discipline: 'I was impressed by the academic results, the facilities, the behaviour of the children and the feedback of parents with children already at the school,' a parent told us. Well-behaved and noticeably polite children; plenty of doors held open (willingly) on our visit.

H

The school is large, and bullying can happen, but it is dealt with well. One parent told us how their child had a difficult time after an incident, but 'The school have been great. [They] helped by giving [my child] a pass to leave lesson two minutes earlier to miss the rush of children in corridors. I also had the head of year in contact with me and can say we felt the process of [my child] regaining confidence and settling in was supported 100 per cent.' After four warnings pupils get a red card and detentions. Any misbehaving pupils will be sat outside the principal's office instead of being locked away.

Pastoral care is good. As well as a staff of almost 200 teachers and support staff, the school has progress leaders who are supported by student support workers. The Student Services Hub is the heart of the pastoral system; there are two student support workers, one parent family support worker, one attendance officer and a director.

Pupils and parents: Huge catchment area spanning some 200 square miles. Great reputation: several parents told us they had moved house 'specifically to get our children into the school.' Buses reach most areas. The library stays open until 4.30pm to help working parents or those travelling long distances. Due to the wide catchment, evening and weekend events are tricky, but the school does it best to be as inclusive as possible. After a recent evening prize-giving event, it was noted some of the more disadvantaged prize winners didn't turn up; the school – commendably – now pays for taxis.

A simple, plain black uniform is worn by all, but apparently this can be interpreted in a variety of ways and parents feel pupils need 'a set uniform, as this would allow them to concentrate more fully on their work.' On our visit most pupils looked presentable: there was the odd scruff or short skirt, but nothing alarming at all.

Communication is good. The school apparently deals with any type of problem promptly, and staff are happy to communicate via email. The website and online payment, and especially the new parent system where parents can monitor things from homework to payments for school trips or lunch, is 'fantastic,' according to parents. The Parents' Forum works well and parents are happy that suggestions are being taken on board and results are seen.

Entrance: School accepts children from in and outside the catchment area, and to date has not turned anyone away. Works with 11 feeder primary schools and there are visits to and from these schools throughout the year to help with the transition. Many of the pupils come from very small primary schools so

Huish makes a big effort to get to know everyone and help ease any worries, talking to them individually and asking them to complete a booklet about their hopes and fears. Children can get to know the school by using the leisure centre facilities or getting involved in some of the sports events or galas. There is also a treasure hunt event and an induction day. One parent said the settling in process was 'fantastic. The treasure hunts were a great success, The children both settled and made friends quickly.' Once they start, pupils join a tutor group which is mixed ability and based on primary school friendships, and meet up every morning and afternoon.

Sixth form entry requires five 9-4 GCSE grades with grade 6 required for A level subjects where there is a GCSE qualification, plus interviews and an induction programme. Those without a grade 4 in English and/or maths are invited to retake, for which the school provides specialist teachers.

Exit: Two-thirds leave after GCSEs to go to local colleges, Yeovil, Bridgwater or Taunton, often for vocational courses. About half of sixth formers go to university; popular destinations include Bath, Exeter, Loughborough, Aberdeen, Plymouth, St Andrews, Southampton, Warwick, Cardiff and Keele. One parent told us, 'Careers support has been fantastic for [my child], to keep her on track.'

Impressive alumni; Sarah Ball, creator of Bob The Builder, Alice Temperley MBE and Gavin Echlin Patterson, CEO of BT.

Money matters: Pupil premium fund available, plus school has its own fund to help families pay for trips etc. Financial support available for eligible sixth formers.

Remarks: Fantastic school. Very rural, so pupils come from far and wide, but the facilities and resources here make it more than worthwhile. The head is driven and dedicated to making it the best it can be. Quite a traditional community school in many ways, but very modern too.

K

Katharine Lady Berkeley's School

Kingswood Road, Wotton-under-Edge, Gloucestershire GL12 8RB

Ages 11-18 **Pupils** 1,468 **Sixth form** 214

01453 842227
www.klbschool.org.uk

Headteacher: Since April 2019, Timothy Rand, previously deputy head at Sheldon School in Chippenham. Has also been head of sixth form and assistant head at Farmor's School and deputy head at Archway School in Stroud.

Academic matters: Although totally non-selective, the principle is one of grouping by ability 'with a reasonable degree of refinement – another advantage of a large school. Particularly good for maths'. Students are set in maths after the first month, with setting in most subjects from January of their first year; languages and sciences follow in year 8 and 9 respectively. For GCSE, students are set by ability for all subjects. Everyone does French; Spanish, Japanese and Chinese are offered as second languages. Weaker linguists do NVQ level 2 in French, rather than GCSE. We saw students engaged and focused in their language classes: French (and Chinese) taught by a native speaker and a small intense A level Japanese set. Such concentration on setting is intended that everyone achieves all of which they are capable; vocational options such as BTecs and the Certificate in Personal Effectiveness are also there for the taking.

Results at GCSE in 2018 were, by the school's admission, disappointing: normally the percentage of A*-A/9-7 runs at over 30 per cent, but the latest figure was 25 per cent; 72 per cent got 9-4 in both maths and English. There was a happier story at A level, with 67 per cent entries getting A*/B and 37 per cent A*/A from the 25 subjects offered. We liked the vibe and look of the teaching spaces we saw, particularly the refurbished laboratories and the fabulously welcoming library, whose alluring display on the open evening made us want to go back to school on the spot, as did the history lesson where students were looking at the ways in which a portrait of Elizabeth 1 demonstrated her power and wealth. Students and parents equally content with the academic offering: from the amount of homework to the way in which further maths teaching helps with engineering, to the provision of computers (not having a laptop does not a second class citizen make) and the three monthly tests giving the flexibility to change sets. But 'I wish there were more languages,' said one young lady plaintively; 'we used to be a language academy, after all'.

About 13 per cent of students have an identified SEN and they are well looked after by the highly experienced, no-nonsense SENCo and her team. Those needing extra support in English tend not to do a second language and all benefit from the programme specially devised to consolidate pre-GCSE work in close consultation with subject staff. Some lessons are put on during sports sessions. We heard reports that children with social difficulties and exam anxiety are well supported, as are dyslexics, one of whom did so well that he was offered the chance to pursue a second language. SEN provision is tailored to the school's above average academic profile, which led one parent to remark that KLB might not be the place for a child with severe learning difficulties. Physical disability needs well catered for, with the whole place wheelchair accessible at ground level.

Games, options, the arts: A huge green site with masses of room for grass and access to Astro and 3G surfaces must contribute to KLB's strong sporting tradition and success in hockey, rugby and football in particular. This is a sporty place – make no mistake – with an extensive fixture list against the many state and independent schools in the area. Minority sports such as table tennis and badminton also appear to nail the competition locally, but it is heartening to see that the less sportingly inclined are also encouraged to be active, with initiatives such as the girls only running club, which tripled its membership in just a few months. Sports centre (includes dance hall and fitness suite) on site also made available to the public outside school hours; some wish the gym in particular was more available. No swimming pool, but talented swimmers compete against schools with pools such as Westonbirt. Outside school, the keen equestrian team does well in this horsey part of the country.

Music also a serious feature of the school and there's an ensemble for almost everyone: string players, singers, percussionists and a training orchestra to equip players for the senior orchestra. Recently a student was offered an organ scholarship at Queen's College Cambridge. The music department, despite being stuck away at the back of the site, is evidently thriving, putting on a concert for the newest students in their first few weeks, inviting solo contributions. A rock band's heroic playing took everyone's minds off the rain in the dash between buildings on the wet open evening.

KLB contains a small drama hall where a musical is staged each spring, recently Chicago. Other productions include a show put on by the drama club (recently The Snow Queen), which older students direct and produce with a cast of younger ones.

Art also prominent, with fine and graphic art both on offer at A level. The portraits of famous people were especially accomplished. But it is perhaps DT where the school really shines with the support of local engineering firm Renishaw, who generously funds the place in various ways, such as recently providing the very latest in 3D printers and CAD/CAM wizardry. Lots of work on display all over the considerable acreage of corridor walls.

The lucky youngsters at KLB certainly get out and about. Linguists visit Japan and China – trips to the former have been running for more than 20 years – artists Venice and everyone else to myriad theatres and galleries and, in the case of RE students, a cathedral and a mosque. DofE and World Challenge also feature.

Background and atmosphere: Very ancient, dating as it does from 20 October 1384 when its eponymous founder, 'daily defeated and frustrated by poverty' (not her own, you understand), brought about the purchase of a school house in Wotton-under-Edge 'for the habitation [...and] maintenance of a master and two poor scholars of the art of grammar, which is the foundation of all liberal arts'. It's been going ever since without a break, never moving far, but since the early 1960s in its present spacious setting just outside the town. This school remains hearteningly true to its founding principles, in that it is open to all, regardless of need, ability or indeed gender. Its history may be long, but its location and buildings have kept pace with its transformation into the all-embracing school for Wotton it has become: no architectural marvels here, but space between buildings (if not always quite enough inside them – there is no one place where the whole school can assemble, and lunch time can be a bit of a scrum in the cheery canteen) reoxygenates brain cells between classes.

The atmosphere is one of endeavour and acceptance of all kinds of achievement, from the Oxbridge shoo-ins to the girl who said candidly that she had struggled at primary school but that the support at KLB had been fantastic 'and now I'm off to university!' 'The school's ambitious: it always wants the best of you and for you', added one boy. Everyone we spoke to remarked on the sense of community, where all students, even in this large school of 1,500, are known and treated the same regardless of background, race, sexuality and so on. 'We know each other as people before anything else,' as one boy put it.

Pastoral care, well-being and discipline: Widely praised by students and parents alike; school employs an education welfare officer which sets the tone. Sixth formers are trained to act as TICs (Talk in Confidence) and mentor younger ones, and we were assured that there was always someone to talk in case of difficulty. Bullying is pounced on and well handled, according to parents: both victim and perpetrator are mentored and encouraged to find skills and sources of fulfilment in order to spend time productively.

Good behaviour and work and generally being a good egg are rewarded by PACE points: punctuality and attendance, attainment and achievement, contribution, effort. Students find the balance between sanction and reward about right, and are pleased that bad behaviour is picked up and dealt with. 'We work with children who are truculent and dismissive, and we have had the occasional permanent exclusion: sometimes the result of unhelpful outside influences. We can't tolerate physical aggression or drug-dealing, for example'.

Pupils and parents: KLB sits in quite an affluent and predominantly white rural area, but one with pockets of deprivation. Rather than taking pains to point out the vast range of the students' economic circumstance, the school described the majority of parents as 'very positive about their child's experience of school: pleased that their child is here'. A typical KLB student 'enjoys school life, understands its expectations, and has good friends whom he/she cares about'. We found both students and their parents most appreciative of all the school provides: 'It's been the best choice for our family – and worth travelling from Bristol every day,' one mother with three children of differing skills assured us. Swift close communication with staff and the kind of IT which enables anxious mothers to see what their child had for lunch and 'Show my homework' also go down well. Students we met were polite but open, thoughtful but articulate, frank but not racy, clearly supportive of each other but not soppy.

Entrance: Around 250 arrive into year 7 from local and not-so-local primary schools and a handful from independent prep schools, which recommend KLB. School's reputation goes before it, and it is oversubscribed. At sixth form, a minimum of 50 places are offered to external candidates, who must meet the same entry criteria as those staying on after GCSEs: three passes at grade 5 and two at grade 4; grade 4 in English also required. Certain subjects eg languages and maths demand higher GCSE grades to access A level courses.

Exit: About half to two-thirds stay on into the sixth form. The majority of those who leave after GCSE do so for FE colleges, a good few to Hartpury, known for its equine and agriculture courses. Just a handful into employment, some via apprenticeships. Post A level, well over half go to Russell Group universities (one to Cambridge in 2018), Bristol, Exeter, Leeds and Cardiff currently popular; tiny numbers take art foundation courses, gap years or go straight into employment. Senior students rave about UCAS support and timetabling; praise also for careers advice. Most famous former pupil? Edward Jenner of smallpox vaccine fame.

Money matters: No monetary contributions requested from parents, despite the lamentable state of school funding, and the school still purchases text books for sixth formers: not the case in many schools. Friends of KLB raises funds for the school and runs social events, but could lean more heavily on parents to donate regularly, in the opinion of one mother.

Remarks: 'Just fantastic: can't fault it – the school or its teachers,' is the verdict of the parents we spoke to. Plenty of options locally: selective and single sex choices in the maintained sector and fee-paying options, 'but parents understand the difference between KLB and the independent sector and choose this'. All a comprehensive school should be, and more.

King Edward's Junior & Pre-Prep (Bath)

Linked with King Edward's School (Bath)

North Road, Bath, Somerset BA2 6JA

Ages 3–11 **Pupils** 327

Fees: £8,370 – £11,250 pa

01225 463218
www.kesbath.com

Head teacher: Since 2008, Greg Taylor, BA (education, Exeter), who joined King Edward's from the George Ward Secondary

K

School in Allington with experience of 'special' education. He progressed from head of PE, then maths to deputy and eventually to head of junior school. He is also a serious sportsman, especially about football, which he played professionally from 14, and has four children.

Head of the pre-prep: Since 2008 is Jayne Gilbert, whose teaching career before King Edward's was initially in the state sector before moving to a British International School in Penang, then returning to be deputy at Bedales pre-prep from which she was appointed to King Edward's.

Mr Taylor and Ms Gilbert share a refreshing accessibility. On our arrival, Mr Taylor was busy arranging tables in the sun so that the parents coming in later could enjoy an informal meeting with tea and cakes, while Ms Gilbert was about to join a group of parents for coffee and feedback in the pre-prep dining room.

Entrance: Though it is possible to start in the nursery and go all the way through to sixth form, there is also entry at pre-prep level and into the junior school at 7. Both take about half from other local schools. Good to get in early, as entry to senior school is competitive, but the vast majority pass the entrance exam, having flourished in the junior system

Exit: Nearly all progress to the senior school, whether they join at 3, 4 or 7. There is an entry exam to pass, but anyone who is really unlikely to cope will have been forewarned and advised about alternatives. There is lots of competition in Bath, so a few move elsewhere locally or away to boarding school.

K

Remarks: The junior school nestles at the far end of the KES site surrounded by gardens and wildflower meadows, giving masses of opportunity for ecological study. It is cunningly designed so that the class units, each with its storage, display and cloakroom area, feel rather like a little houses in their own right, built in a staggered line to get the best of the sun and view. The school remained in the original King Edward's building in Broad Street until 1991, when a benefactor sponsored the construction of the new buildings. Behind the little street of classrooms is a unifying hall and library space on two levels, essentially a gallery running round an attractive school library. A few extra wings house the school hall, music department, labs and dining area.

The feel is definitely more like a very good state primary school rather than a traditional prep school. Masses of artwork and displays everywhere – the school is constructed to encourage this, and the whole environment is both absolutely child friendly and encourages ecological awareness. Divided from the main school by a band of trees, the site, overlooking Bath's panorama, has a wildlife meadow, delightful wild pond, two new dipping ponds and lots of wonderful stone blocks and trees for climbing. Adventure is encouraged, though carefully supervised. The latest project is the greenhouse, where children are growing their own veg – tomatoes from last year were still going when we visited – and doing wonderful experiments involving breeding and releasing butterflies into the wild. Specialist subject teachers, for languages (French from year 3, with German and Spanish from year 5), science (with a smashing, well-equipped lab), maths etc.

Parents comment that the key to education here is inclusion and encouragement rather than educational pushiness. 'Effort is rewarded as much as achievement and the school does not feel the need to get children to peak at junior level'. As in the senior school, the integration of pastoral care and academia is taken very seriously. New children are encouraged to support each other in a scheme which allocates different 'talk partners' each week. 'Working with everyone in turn, not just friends, creates cohesion,' one parent commented. 'They really value citizenship and social awareness. Friendships extend across year groups and classes and pupils won't stand for bullying or turn a blind eye to it'. SEN is integrated with the senior school department. Tests at appropriate levels and plenty of help available.

Sport is competitive (new Astro pitch) but, according to parents, very inclusive – everyone encouraged to participate. Boys do a short rugby tour and girls a hockey tour, playing matches all over the country. The same applies to music, with lots of singing, a yearly young musicians' challenge and an inclusive scheme in which a different instrument is taught to all pupils in each year group. We enjoyed the first session of the ukelele band, but other years do gamelan etc and in year 6 steel drums, which are said to be 'just incredible!' The art programme is enhanced by taking part in a National Gallery competition, which has culminated in pupils' sculpture and painting being on show there several years running. Drama, dance etc all included, with an impressive filmmaking project on the year 6 French trip.

Pre-school breakfast club from 8am in the new Wessex Building is open to juniors as well as seniors and there are after-school activities and supervision until 6pm in the junior school.

The pre-prep is separate from the senior and junior schools in a 'leafy suburb' on the other side of Bath, but there is a staffed minibus between them which means parents with children in both can make one drop-off and know children will be supervised from there on. It provides an ideal environment for little children, with cleverly planned outside areas equipped with every kind of equipment and divided into age-related areas, including an outdoor story telling corner and outdoor classroom. On our visit there was a lovely activity, involving walking around the shapes of letters, going on in one place, while the real tinies were enjoying their miniature tricycles – good for directional skills.

All year groups have weekly forest school visits. More conventional classes are in large double areas with two classes in each year group, semi-divided so they can work separately or together. SEN experts are brought in at an early stage to do specific tests where necessary, so emerging problems can picked up and special help given if expected progress is not being made. Lots of music and PE both indoor and out. Art specialist works in all three schools.

Sensible simple navy blue uniform with white shirts, but masses of tough-looking coveralls for outdoor stuff and also for art and craft. Spacious dining room where staff like to eat with children and healthy eating is promoted. Parent contact seems to be high priority and a parent group was enjoying coffee and discussion with Ms Gilbert on the day of our visit.

Before and after-school care provided in Teddy's Lodge, a small house on the edge of what once must have been the front lawn to the main Edwardian House, but is now convenient car park. This is a cosy space that has become something of a community centre for the area, offering parentcraft and similar workshops, such as craft, music and dance for babies and toddlers during the daytime. A calm and gentle environment with children everywhere just happily getting on with things.

KES feels like a happy school. Pupils are friendly but not over-sophisticated. Parents feel included, have well-organised channels for feedback and suggestions, and say there are 'no serious gripes'. The synchronisation of information through careful co-operation between teaching and pastoral staff and the heads in the senior, junior and pre-prep sectors is truly impressive, and everything is directed towards the well-being of pupils. No wonder they enjoy their education and do so well in it.

King Edward's School (Bath)

Linked with King Edward's Junior & Pre-Prep (Bath)

North Road, Bath, Somerset BA2 6HU

Ages 11–18 **Pupils** 816 **Sixth form** 237

Fees: £14,235 – £14,475 pa

01225 464313
www.kesbath.com

Headmaster: Since 2008, Martin Boden MA (40s), a French and German Cambridge graduate. After his PGCE he was invited back to teach at his old school, Bolton School, progressing from there to head of German at Cheadle Hulme School, then head of modern languages at Bradford Grammar, from which he came to King Edward's as director of studies. Appointed as an exceptionally young head, he has brought the school a stability and capacity for development with his clear vision and strong sense of ethos. Academic standards have become even stronger due, according to Mr Boden and to the ISI inspectorate, to unrivalled outstanding pastoral care underpinning really good teaching. Parents definitely agree. Meanwhile, the sporting reputation of the school remains undiminished, whilst art, drama and music have flourished under his regime.

Dedicated to the grammar school tradition of accessibility, he has kept the fees unusually low 'by lots of good housekeeping' and encouraged bright pupils from less advantaged families through bursary provision. He is insistent that though the school is selective, it is not super-selective, despite the fact that its results put it in the super-selective league. As director of studies, he masterminded the now well-established two-week timetable with hour long lessons, giving an 80 minute lunch break for an overwhelming number of activities and staggered access to the fantastic new dining facilities. Next on his wish list is a proper performing arts centre. He cites concert and cinema going as the only recreational activity he still manages to fit into a life as headmaster and father of two small children currently entrusted pre-prep at King Edward's. Married to head of geography, Jane.

Academic matters: This is a seriously academic school. In 2018, 63 per cent A*/A and 86 per cent A*/B grades at A level, with astronomical results in maths, further maths and English literature. All three sciences, Latin and photography are pretty distinguished as well – so they certainly excel in humanities as well as science.

At GCSE in 2018, the A*-A/9-7 percentage was 79. Normally some stunning results in subjects including maths, sciences, both Englishes and languages with Greek and Latin surpassing the excellent French, German and Spanish.

As well as the strong, sympathetic pastoral back-up to stimulating teaching, there is an all-embracing and friendly SEN department picking up quickly on children needing support. A three-strong team covers the senior and junior schools with a part-timer in the pre-prep. Lots of monitoring done via standardised tests, at crucial stages and when problems crop up, so potential issues are picked up early. Appropriate supportive help, either one-to-one or in small groups. They are expert in most common areas of difficulty and have good liaison with staff and exam officers as well as providing encouragement and sympathetic back-up.

Parents comment that lessons seem to be really enjoyable and pupils are not overburdened with homework. Plenty of tests in class, but they take them in their stride. The prevailing atmosphere is that while academic study is interesting, serious and needs effort, it is also exciting and even fun.

Games, options, the arts: Sport as strong as ever. Oodles of teams, particularly in rugby, netball and girls' and boys' hockey, in fact, in just about everything except lacrosse. Sport is taken seriously with teams doing a pre-season sports training sessions before the autumn term to get off to a good start and a sports physio set up in the school medical centre, but the team practices in progress on our visit still looked a lot of fun. It seems to work, as teams in just about all sports reach national school final level, and there are individuals at national and international competition level.

Rugby and netball, which are outstanding, do regular overseas tours, recently to South Africa. Smashing sports hall with teaching area, cricket nets, all weather ECB-accredited cricket lanes and the usual indecipherable tube map of sports markings on the floor. Extensive playing fields at Bathampton, a very short minibus-ride away, and cricket practices get the benefit of Bath Cricket Club. (Everyone has a two-hour weekly games slot, so plenty of time for travel etc.) Huge all-purpose Astroturf with viewing area and lots of tennis and netball courts on site. Using the University of Bath Olympic training swimming pool and athletics track seem a better option than building their own.

K

Arts and music excellent and getting stronger. Drama has smashing GCSE results and thriving theatre groups, one of which took Jackie Kay's Takeaway to Edinburgh, and were thrilled that the writer came to see it. Orchestra has a link up with the Bath Philharmonia, doing joint concerts and workshops, and choirs have similar musical links with the abbey, since the original school was just up the road from it. The music we heard was of a high standard with bags of enthusiasm from pupils and staff. The calendar shows a swathe of workshops, masterclasses and concerts. Contemporary music is encouraged by the school's resident composer and there's plenty of scope for enjoying film scores and more popular stuff. Sadly, take up of academic music at exam levels is very small, but drama and art are much bigger and super-successful. Drama currently has use of a large well-equipped theatre in mid school and a smaller studio in the sixth form area. Music has lots of soundproof teaching and practice rooms, some curiously lined with what looks like sea blue formica, but which is actually proper efficient soundproofing. There is plenty of space, but the proper performing arts centre – building set to start in early 2019 – will be a bonus.

Art and masses of heavy duty DT equipment occupy a separate building. Art is up above with a Swiss-looking balcony giving panoramic views of Bath's sweeping terraces. A Level classes we visited were just getting down to some really thorough but fascinating drawing technique. DT looks very suitably industrial and up to date.

On the day of our visit the Socrates Club was absolutely packed with 50 or more pupils and staff eagerly debating the problems of migrants in Europe with real concern and some discernment. The knitting club, however, had no takers, though it had done well the previous year. The range of options is impressive, including the academic, such as the Battle of the Books club, as well as music, drama and masses of sports. CCF, DofE. Outdoor pursuits such as Ten Tors can be taken for granted, and there are both curricular and extracurricular opportunities for trips local and further afield, including prestigious ones like the South Africa tour.

Background and atmosphere: This was one of boy King Edward VI's many original grammar schools, as the lovely little roundel coloured glass window in the junior school proclaims. It was originally in a small neo-classical building in Broad Street just up from the abbey, and moved up to this rural-feeling site in the 1960s. The elegant Nethersole House on which the school is centred still gives rather old-fashioned room to RE, philosophy, history and classics, plus SEN and the headmaster's office with accompanying meeting and admin space. Flowing along the hillside, the hotch-potch of undistinguished purpose-built facilities benefit from the sweeping grassy slopes and mature trees. B Block, a new stylish and high tech building, includes separate labs for practicals and ordinary teaching.

The site has been transformed into an organic whole by the brilliant addition of the new Wessex building, opened by the Earl of Wessex in 2015. The attractive dining suite with café-style verandas overlooking the central all weather pitch links the sporting and academic areas. The dining room overlooks a sunny (on our visit) terrace with fountains, and milling-about and sitting areas including a miniature Greek theatre. The top floor has flexible lecture cum co-curricular and entertainment facilities, while the basement, cunningly dug out of the hillside, houses one of the very best school libraries.

Manned as long as the school is open, it offers cleverly placed reading, discussion and research areas, even a corner with whiteboard walls for teaching/conferencing. It was hearteningly full of older pupils busy working, reading or having serious-looking discussions – though this may have been partly due to the sixth form being temporarily out of its quarters while last minute refurbishments were completed. Even so, it seemed a good demonstration of genuinely independent work, with help at hand when necessary. The stray new boy, clearly confused about where he should be, was sympathetically directed to the right class.

The refurbished sixth form centre has spacious study and IT areas as well as a modern, spruced up social area complete with coffee shop. Breakfast club from 8.00am and the library is open for study etc until 6.00pm. Definitely a day school feel, with main activities at lunchtime, though there are masses of clubs and team practices after school and matches on Saturday, with major performances and rehearsals in the evening.

Neat uniform with navy blazers, grey trousers/skirts (or Lindsey Tartan for younger girls) and a particularly smart V-necked jumper with the KES Tudor rose on it. Girls, in particular, like to wear the stylish games uniform (navy with dark red and white) in the afternoons if they can get away with it (only worn for sport not for classes, say the staff). Sixth form boys in smart suits (like young estate agents), though the girls' interpretation of suit-equivalent clothes seems rather more casual, and parents would support tightening up here. The complete uniform list is formidable, but there is a good secondhand shop, now with a plentiful supply of games items (rather expensive new) after a short hiatus when suppliers changed.

Pastoral care, well-being and discipline: The school rightly prides itself on its pastoral care. Bonding trips and activities for new groups in year 7 start a process of building a cohesive and supportive community in which pupils feel confident enough to take any concerns for themselves or others to staff. Exceptionally good collaboration between academic and pastoral staff ensures that needs are identified and supported. In lower school this is delivered via heads of years who coordinate with the form teachers, who 'lay eyes on' pupils twice daily at morning and afternoon registration. Both get to know them really well as they stay with them as they move up through the years. In sixth form tutors supervise groups of about 15 pupils. Pupils were enthusiastic about the trust, sympathy and expertise of their teachers.

Part-time school chaplain doesn't push religion but is exceptionally supportive to church-going families and runs a prayer group. The school recognises the mix of faiths among pupils, describing itself as non-denominational. Parents comment that though some may have a healthy disrespect for formal religion, they still sing very enthusiastically in the abbey. Throughout the lunch hour we came across teachers chatting or in serious conference with pupils. Special care taken with university preparation, including a special Oxbridge and medicine applications help forum.

The atmosphere seems to be a happy combination of academic and personal rigour underpinned by care and respect. Pastoral care was particularly commended by the ISI and the head's belief that care for pupils is absolutely key to academic achievement is central to the exceptionally close working relationship between head pastoral and academic staff – no slipping through the net here.

Sixth formers are expected to be rôle models and mentors to the lower school: in the lower sixth they can try out being deputy prefect for three weeks before standing for election. Forty per cent of upper sixth then become prefects, with 10 or so senior prefects, from whom a head girl and boy are appointed. There is also a mentoring system targeting less confident pupils, including those in the junior and pre-prep, which both mentored and mentors value highly.

Pupils and parents: Pupils seemed relaxed and pretty well organised. Some more open than others, but all appeared to have a sense of purpose and were polite and natural. The head likes to remind them that having all those opportunities does not make them better people. Parents, from all walks of life, include the very well-heeled but also lots who have to work hard to afford what one described as 'unbelievably good value'. Academically ambitious for their children 'but not at the expense of all the extras,' they support the school in all it does, by active fundraising for extras. In common with most co-ed schools, about 60 per cent boys.

Famous Old Edwardians range from Thomas de Quincy, the English Opium Eater, to comedian and TV presenter Bill Bailey, with more recent additions of actor Tom Payne, author Lawrence Norfolk and quite a panoply of distinguished academics and military men.

Entrance: At 11, by passing an entrance exam in maths, English and verbal reasoning. Some 100 or so places up for grabs. Half come from junior school and take the same exam, though parents can be confident that the school would have been in discussion with them if a child were unlikely to pass it. Head says that the few children who 'would not cope' are gently steered elsewhere, and though thorough, the entry test is not unreasonably stringent. Most of the other half come from local-ish primaries.

Some 25-30 external sixth form places offered, on strength of good GCSE passes (9-7 desirable for A level subjects), interview and references from previous school. Sixth form entry tends to attract girls from local single sex schools.

Exit: They lose up to a fifth after GCSEs, odd one at end of year 12. Of those who stay, nearly all to university, with six to Oxbridge in 2018, and other popular destinations Bristol, UCL, Cardiff, Birmingham, Durham and Exeter. School is exceptionally helpful to those few with unexpected results, helping to ensure they have a suitable offer by the end of the day.

Money matters: Exceptionally good value, according to parents. Lots of trips, most pretty inexpensive, but no pressure to take part in the more expensive ones and lots of pupils fundraise for these themselves. Approximately 15 per cent of pupils receive means-tested bursaries, total fees in exceptional cases; the head very keen to encourage able but less affluent candidates to apply.

Remarks: This is a school which achieves its exceptionally high standards by support and inspiration. 'Teachers are exceptional', one parent said, 'a real inspiration to our children'. The atmosphere is relaxed and constructive, which is probably why the results are so impressive. Parents say teachers have the knack of identifying an area where a pupil can shine and the confidence gained infuses everything else. Pupils accept that, in the few subjects they may not enjoy, effort is worthwhile. High standards are expected and achieved, but the achievement is grounded in confidence, trust and support rather than academic pressure. Though highly academic, certainly not an 'academic hothouse', but a school where even the process of getting into Oxford can be happy and relaxed. The synchronisation of information through careful co-operation between teaching and pastoral staff with the heads in the senior, junior and pre-prep sectors is truly impressive. Everything is directed towards the well-being of pupils. No wonder they enjoy their education and do so well in it.

King's Bruton

Linked with Hazlegrove School

Plox, Bruton, Somerset BA10 0ED

Ages 13–18 **Pupils** 356 **Sixth form** 147 **Boarders** 222 full

Fees: Day £22,626; Boarding £32,553 pa

01749 814200
www.kingsbruton.com

Headmaster: Since 2009, Ian Wilmshurst MA PGCE (early 50s). A Scotsman by birth and, in his own words, born into and schooled in the Edinburgh educational mafia (his father taught at the Edinburgh Academy, even now his sister is deputy head at Fettes), the last thing he was going to do was teach. But wind the clock forward a few years, after reading geography at Cambridge and the briefest of flirtations with the army, he returned to his old college for his PGCE, after two terms' trying teaching out at the Dragon School. The roll call of schools where Mr Wilmshurst has taught since then is impressive: Highgate, Merchiston Castle and Royal Hospital where, as the sole deputy head, he had terrific exposure to the top job.

On arrival at King's Bruton, he had cause to call on that invaluable experience: at several years' safe distance, he candidly admits that he had plenty of work to do on appointment. Seven years on, he has increased numbers (it's now full for girls) so setting it on a secure financial footing, without sacrificing the welcoming and cosy feel of the place, revitalised the sport and brought the alumni on board. A very different place indeed – and one whose merits he was determined to show us, after spending some time rubbishing what he considered our previous lukewarm and out of date write-up.

Though initial impressions are of unremitting seriousness and focus (no lazy national stereotyping here), we uncovered a compassionate and reflective side, not afraid to discuss the seamier side of education. Not only easy to chat to on the touchline, according to parents, but also 'approachable and kind,' according to one mother whose family had been through a very rough patch. 'Not pretentious – what you see is what you get,' opined another. By his own admission, Mr Wilmshurst is not at all musical (though he certainly appreciates it): his hobbies revolve round sport – a sometime rugby player and cricketer, he now enjoys golf and cycling in particular. Married to Helen, who is a tutor here, he has two daughters, both in the school.

Academic matters: Not very selective, King's prides itself on accommodating all academic abilities: 'One of my priorities is to keep the balance between SEN and Oxbridge,' says the head. No room for slackers, though: everyone is expected to achieve all they are capable of and the whole sixth form does the EPQ. 'We reckon our top 30 per cent is comparable to academically selective schools,' he told us. All assessed for SEN on arrival, then setted in maths and, interestingly, French; classes are then compiled on ability.

Twenty-four subjects on offer at (I)GCSE with particularly strong languages, in scope and in grades, though this may well reflect the numbers of overseas students wanting an almost effortless GCSE. In 2018, 45 per cent A*-A/9-7 grades at GCSE.

At A level, 51 per cent A*-B and 28 per cent A*/A grades, down on 2017; maths, further maths and history consistently good performers. Small numbers can make results fluctuate considerably, and mean that classes are all mixed ability except for maths. Sixth form timetable allows for the odd maths and English GCSE retake, and it is extremely rare that anyone would be thrown out for poor grades either then or at AS – not unknown, sadly, in other schools. BTec – 'after A levels reverted to a linear format, we felt we wanted alternatives for our less academic students,' the head told us – also offered in health & social studies, sport, enterprise & entrepreneurship and hospitality (now boasting a commercial kitchen). We were lucky enough to sample the (delicious) edible submissions at tea time the day we visited, complete with immaculate napery and serving staff. Initiative generally reckoned to be a success, providing access to good universities: Exeter, Bath, Portsmouth inter alia.

SEN was described to us (in a wonderfully mixed metaphor) as the engine room where difficulties are unravelled. The staff of three, plus other prominent teaching staff with SEN qualifications, address a range of special needs: mainly dyslexia and dyspraxia, but also processing difficulties. Speech therapist and ed. psych visit routinely. Two dedicated EAL staff to support the 40 students for whom English is not their mother tongue.

Games, options, the arts: 'Everything we touch turns to gold,' we were told, with not a little chutzpah – but it is true that the hockey in particular (girls' and boys') scales heights which would be remarkable for a much bigger school, such as reaching national finals eight times in the last four years and the U16 girls third in the national schools final. But, joyously, everyone gets a game and to represent the school, and are coached from the start by the hockey pro and director of sport to identify any burgeoning talent – 'but we manage expectations in the minds of pupils and parents', we were sagely assured. Rugby, netball and athletics also prominent and successful. No pool, but school makes use of the 25m pool at Hazlegrove; two élite swimmers currently train in Yeovil. Sport phobes accommodated with a range of recreational options, including volleyball and frisbee. Facilities fine (eg floodlit Astro) but not extensive, owing to the limitations of the school site, but massive recent redevelopment.

Music, likewise, is of a scope and standard befitting a much bigger school, and the complementary talents of voice and instrumental heads of music mean a fruitful cross-fertilisation of choral, jazz and orchestral music. From the military band, whose stirring strains and precise marching we were witness to on the most impeccably diagonally striped lawn we had ever seen, to the intense practice of a self-directed trio of violin, cello and piano, there truly is something ancient or modern for everyone. Music tech offered at A level: a handful of students have gone on to study the highly specialised Tonmeister degree course at Surrey. Fifty concerts a year give even beginners a chance to conquer performance nerves. Music scholars receive Kodaly and Alexander technique lessons. The splendid new music school completed in time for King's 500th anniversary in 2019 now provides a fitting home for it all.

Drama well provided for in Fitzjames theatre, where everyone – not just those studying GCSE or A level theatre studies – is encouraged to get involved, whether treading the boards or backstage in lighting, sound or set design. Two house plays per year on rotation, alongside whole school, sixth form and junior productions, in close collaboration with the music dept. Recent shows include Twelfth Night and Oliver! (yawn) but we were impressed that current theatre manager also writes new material. Annual trip to London takes in workshops as well as several shows.

'Not everyone is going to be a painter,' says the head of art, whose department – housed in a stunning former mill, complete with new gallery opened in 2016 – offers an exceptional range of media (3D design, sculpture and digital media, for example) to students who might go on to take a GCSE in art, craft and design. New students experience the whole enchilada, and enjoy the annual team video competition. Unusually, history of art is laid on as an A level – with outstanding results. Of course it does no harm at all to have the internationally renowned Hauser and Wirth gallery just down the road, with its education director keen to be involved. Former students have made waves in innovative artistic careers all over the world, to include a commission to beam multi-coloured images onto the Sydney Opera House.

Trips (historians to Poland, linguists and musicians all over Europe, adventurers to Costa Rica) and all manner of physical and artistic exploration abound, with strong showings at CCF, D of E (where expeditions can now be done on bicycles) and that perennial west country ordeal, Ten Tors.

Boarding: Two-thirds of students (13 per cent from overseas) board in seven single sex houses where day students are fully integrated. The school's long history – all 500 years of it – means no homogeneity in houses: Old House is where it all began, whereas the girls of Wellesley House occupy an elegant Georgian mansion of cream stucco several minutes' walk from the main school. Dorms of up to four to start with; most have single rooms at sixth form. Parents rate the care given to their children, both pastorally and health-wise, and appreciate the option of flexi-boarding. 'There's a good critical mass staying in at weekends and my children like Saturday nights and the chance to chill on a Sunday at school,' one mother reported, in tones of faint regret. More space in the girls' houses would be welcome, but school tells us that places for girls have all been filled. One local pub will deliver late night cheesy chips to boarding houses on request.

Background and atmosphere: Very ancient (sits on the site of a Benedictine monastery dissolved in 1537; one wall survives), but doesn't shout about it; much will be made of the 500th anniversary in 2019, with an upgrade to sixth form facilities for study and socialising. One of several distinguished schools in Bruton, where three generous benefactors born in this small Somerset town built of golden stone decided to found the first of them. Varying fortunes meant it was down to just one boy in 1812, but the first half of the 20th century saw it increase in numbers approximating the ones it has today, and take over buildings the other side of the busy road to Castle Cary and elsewhere in Bruton. Charming and quaint but not posh, the school works with its venerable buildings, not against them, using the parish church for whole school services, but its own simple beautiful memorial hall for assemblies.

Parents and students love its size, praising the friendliness and the fact that no-one appears to slip, drift or hide. 'Everyone is valued,' one mother told us; 'even if they aren't especially good at anything, they can just jog along'; another liked the fact that fewer students meant that her children would have to get involved in everything. The school cites its strong Christian ethos and celebrates major festivals and rites such as confirmation, but we did not get the sense that religious belief is imposed upon the unconvinced or the agnostic (respect is non-negotiable, that said): the exuberant chaplain is so down with the kids that his weekly and legendary TGI (Friday) sessions attract many comers and make the deeper exploration of faith voluntary and fun. 'It's not your belief in science that holds you together when tragedy strikes', as he puts it. A handful of Catholics and Muslims fit in comfortably and lend diversity.

Pastoral care, well-being and discipline: No adverse remarks about pastoral care whatsoever, and the tutor system, with its overview of the whole child, came in for high praise from parents; likewise health care and communications with houseparents, meaning that many problems are nipped in the bud. Though King's students might seem a biddable lot, transgressions are treated seriously – and publicly: drinkers can expect to wear uniform at the weekend, for example. We liked the sound of the relationship policy, which cleverly omits any assumption of gender in these more enlightened times.

Pupils and parents: 'Not arrogant, good company and unassuming,' says the head – and we could not disagree. Most day pupils arrive from immediate vicinity; boarders from southern England, Europe, SE Asia and Kenya. All integrate so well that day pupils often come or stay in at weekends to join in with whatever is going on; we picked up some discontent from day parents at the long days and six day week which is more suited to boarders than their daily counterparts. More likely that one would find a child of a (successful) cheese farmer here than of a merchant banker, though the head claims to attract the same day pupil market as Millfield.

Entrance: For 13+, places offered in year 7 based on standardised test scores, school reports and interview with head. Sets in year 9 allocated from this and from common entrance results. Scholarships are awarded on the basis of papers in six subjects, plus a cognitive ability test. About 40 per cent come from Hazlegrove, the rather smarter prep school linked to King's; others from anything up to 15 other prep schools and secondaries. At sixth form, the bar is lowish at five GCSEs with a B/6 at subjects to be taken at A level, plus interview and references. Places in other year groups occasionally come up. The welcome extended to all new pupils was praised.

Exit: A handful go elsewhere after GCSE on economic grounds. Of those who stay for sixth form, only about three-quarters get to their first choice university. One to Cambridge in 2018, and one vet. Some criticism was voiced about support for UCAS preparation, specifically that the school cut up rough on occasion about Saturday commitments clashing with university open days. Famous alumni include some heroes (Hugh Sexey, auditor to Elizabeth I, RS Blackmore, author of Lorna Doone), one villain (William Dampier, 17th century buccaneer) and one comedian (Marcus Brigstocke). The affection between the school and its former pupils is mutual: a higher than normal proportion of OBs come back to work at there – in proper jobs, after the school got rid of gappies. Since 2006, 150+ leavers have been to work in their gap years at the Indian orphanage where the school has established strong links.

Money matters: Not a wealthy school in terms of its own assets or the families who come there, but restored to sound financial foundations under current head. Scholarships available to a maximum value of 20 per cent of fees; bursarial help available on application.

Remarks: A down to earth, unpretentious, happy school for virtually all comers in increasingly trendy Bruton (one might run into Mariella Frostrup or other celebs down from London) 'where no-one is ever made to feel second class,' according to one mother, but achieving remarkable success in the sporting arena. 'You get all the big names – then there's li'l ole us!' marvelled a proud hockey player.

King's College (Taunton)

Linked with King's Hall School

South Road, Taunton, Somerset TA1 3LA

Ages 13–18 **Pupils** 470 **Sixth form** 180 **Boarders** 292 full **C of E**

Fees: Day £22,380; Boarding £33,165 pa

01823 328204
www.kings-taunton.co.uk

Headmaster: Since 2007, Mr Richard Biggs (early 50s) BSc MA, a product both of the UK's and South Africa's finest: his first degree (physics) from University of Cape Town, his masters (maths and philosophy) from Oxford as a Rhodes scholar. Some barely discernible vowels hint at his upbringing in South Africa; his subsequent career has been entirely in the UK, at Magdalen College School as teacher of maths and physics then director of studies, from where he was promoted to deputy head at Lancing, thence to King's. Now into his eighth year of headship, he can look back with justifiable satisfaction at his achievements since he started, mainly an increase in numbers and improvements to facilities. 'We can really concentrate on academics now, without being over-selective – the market in this part of the world wouldn't stand for it', he says.

Much liked by parents and students alike, who find him 'very bright, approachable and friendly', but we imagine he fixes miscreants with the eye of a basilisk when required. 'Runs a good ship,' remarked one mother succinctly, and writes a jolly good blog. A musical challenge to pass grade 1 on an unfamiliar musical instrument spurred him on to grade 8 proficiency on that most recalcitrant of instruments, the French horn ('a bit of a devil to play') and a seat in the school's wind band. He is married to Sarah, who edits the school magazine and oversees boarding house design, and has two sons in the school. When term ends, he escapes to his cottage on the north Cornish coast with his family for some rugged maritime r'n'r.

Academic matters: Academically inclusive, as attested by recent A level results, 31 per cent A*/A in 2018 (59 per cent A*/B) and yet do not quite achieve 100 per cent pass rates in all subjects. A sprinkling of U grades perhaps indicates that students are permitted to pursue their dream subjects, even if they are unlikely to get top marks; several popular and rigorous subjects (eg chemistry, physics, maths) receive grades from superb to dire, via mediocre. At GCSE, it is a similar story. In 2018,40 per cent of grades at A*-A/9-7. A modern language is expected at GCSE; many study two, and minority languages (German, Japanese, Latin, Russian, inevitably Chinese) laid on for just one taker on occasion. Sciences can either be taken separately or as a dual award. Good range of SEN catered for, and 70 pupils currently receiving extra support; highly praised by a mother of four very different children whom we spoke to: 'My dyslexic child did as well here as anywhere; he received massive support, which meant he exceeded his predictions'. A BTec in sport in collaboration with Exeter City FC and Exeter Chiefs Rugby Club recently introduced.

Games, options, the arts: Make no mistake, this is a sporty school. Masses going on, and no exeat weekends mean a full programme of fixtures against other titans of the west country: Millfield is the one to beat. Football and rugby top sports in the winter terms, cricket the undoubted Queen of the May in the summer; school is a centre for cricketing excellence as befits its location in Taunton, home of Somerset county cricket with which the school has close links. Year round facilities: beautiful pitches in the heart of the school and brand new Sports Performance and Cricket Centre with appropriate hi-tech wizardry mean this is truly a top school for cricket. Hockey and netball also popular with plenty of opportunities for matches). We thoroughly applaud girls' football, cricket and hockey being promoted and resourced as well as the boys' games.

Minority sports include tennis, swimming, golf and athletics, whilst riders' lives transformed by new King's Schools Equestrian Centre: a private yard close by with stables, two outdoor arenas, a small cross-country course and off-road hacking, where horse owners can bring their own mounts. Again, chances to compete and bring home the silverware are legion. Usual range of outdoor roughy-toughy stuff like D of E, Ten Tors, CCF and its precursor, the Chindit programme for year 9.

About half the school learns a musical instrument, brass especially popular and school has notable jazz band. Some grade 8 and diploma level players among senior students. Singers abound, their repertoire from the popular to the highbrow, from rock bands to the chapel and chamber choirs, via the barbershop quartet, Quartones. Performance of whatever standard is encouraged.

Musical talents useful for annual school musical too: recently Guys and Dolls, Les Mis and The Wizard of Oz. One significant play per year, sometimes Shakespeare, many other less elaborate productions in school's own theatre, black box drama studio, recently built amphitheatre – or, memorably, in a pod of the London Eye.

Four floors of art school, including new art studio with doors onto the terrace, mean there is room enough for a gallery as well as studio space, where visiting artists can exhibit; one created a willow sculpture of the school's emblem, a pelican. Fine art is the basis of work here but digital media such as film and photography also laid on, and textiles GCSE is a new addition. We were especially taken by the newspaper tutu. King's has stand-out DT, which has won Arkwright scholarships and GSG awards on several occasions. A car in varying states of (dis)repair lurks in the DT studio for budding mechanics and designers to get their hands on, but the range of objects emerging from this studio combine beauty and functionality in equal measure: the tree-hung beehive is definitely on our wish list.

Despite the wealth of extracurricular activities on offer, 'the school does not push the kids into doing things, but once they sign up, they are expected to commit', according to one parent. 'Some parents don't like this, but the kids can then take credit for the activities they do, which makes them into secure self-starters'.

Boarding: Nearly two-thirds of students board, and it's the real deal: no flexi or weekly, they either board, or they don't. Busy and obligatory Saturdays mean a short weekend, during which a good range of activities is devised and offered by a designated co-ordinator; some of the students seize the advantage of being near-ish to the coast to surf and sail, some might choose to relax, swot or pop home instead. However, pupils may sign out on certain weekends as long as they don't have prior commitments. Around 12 per cent of boarders come from abroad: Chinese and Germans predominate, but the head actively explores different markets and will cap the overseas quota at 15 per cent. Military families now have their own liaison officer. Boarders stay in touch with home by email, Skype or Facetime. Devices belonging to younger students get handed in at night but enforcement varies from house to house, we were told. Boarding houses were, in our view, so-so: the girls' house we saw had a bitty lay-out separating year groups, but at least some baths still remain for muddy hockey players to soak it all off. Boys' boarding appears to be more integrated between year groups and definitely fewer frills – communal space boasted but some grubby leather sofas ('Eek!' said school. 'Not typical') and a huge TV. Day students get one night a week boarding included in the day fee.

Background and atmosphere: A Woodard School, one of about 30 founded by a visionary Victorian cleric, where, these days, Christian values of understanding, diversity and tolerance – 'religious literacy' in the words of the resident chaplain – are inculcated without a whiff of evangelism. The chapel (white, light, beautiful with a decent organ and great acoustic) and collective worship are big parts of school life; all faiths and none are made welcome. But the roots of the school go back to an ancient boys' grammar, founded in the 16th century, but relocated to its current Victorian gothic pile in the 1860s.

K

It's fair to say that it still feels and looks quite traditional, with conventional uniform with designer tweed jackets and blue shirts, and neatness being identified as a virtue. The dining hall boasts not ancestral coats of arms, but sporting achievements painted on shields all over the walls. We did not have the chance to sample its wares, as we were instead treated to quite the grandest lunch we had ever been offered in the headmaster's dining room: curried monkfish followed by fig beignets washed down with pink bubbly – reader, we succumbed. Not surprising to read that 'the art of tying a bow tie has been revived' at King's: its reputation as being Taunton's smartest school seems entirely deserved, and its parents are disparaging about the others, their attitude on the sports fields in particular. Whilst the façade is impressive, some of the other buildings hit low points of British school architecture – with the exception of the library whose modern touches integrate wonderfully with the warm reddish Somerset stone.

Pastoral care, well-being and discipline: Highly rated, particularly in the person of the deputy head pastoral, and a sine qua non of Woodard schools. 'Pastoral scaffolding,' as the school explained it, includes tutors, house staff and the school chaplain, who doubles as an additional school counsellor (as well as coaching several sports); parents can raise any concerns they have through the parent portal. Considerate touches include a Facebook page for Chinese non-English speaking parents. 'Any breach of good manners and good sense' will attract censure; punishments range from detention to more community-minded activities like litter-picking, but not in orange jumpsuits. The ultimate sanctions of suspension or exclusion are rarely, if ever, necessary. Commendations are given for all manner of good works and we liked the sound of the Ferrett Prize for 'all round unobtrusive contribution by a member of the 4th form' – if you can spot it.

Pupils and parents: Unpretentious, happy to be there and grateful for all the opportunities the school offers. A boy from Hong Kong told us that he and his family had 'looked at every school in the country and chosen this one'. Families come from a wider geographical area both in the UK and abroad than the other Taunton schools, and inevitably some parents use the fast railway line to London to commute; the professions, the military, agriculture and the county set are all represented. The school welcomes parents new and existing (but perhaps not vegetarian) with a hog roast at the start of every year.

Entrance: Ninety arrive in year 9 by means of common entrance (passes expected in all subjects but school a bit coy about revealing pass mark), or by school's own papers in maths, English and verbal reasoning. Many, but not all, come from King's Hall, the school's associated prep school; others from prep schools in the south west or from overseas. A handful come into year 10 to start GCSE courses, where space permits, and a few international students join the school in year 11 for an intense one year GCSE programme comprising core subjects, a language and economics. Twenty-five new into the sixth form after 'satisfactory performance at GCSE' or school's own papers for those without GCSEs.

Exit: About a dozen peel off after GCSE, some to the very good and free sixth form college across the road, Richard Huish. Leavers' destinations in recent years include a sprinkling to Oxbridge (just one in 2018, plus a medic) and a bunch of conventional destinations up and down the land, a third to Russell Group, notably Exeter, Newcastle and Cardiff; and a couple off to the US. Some less orthodox choices like the Philip Green Academy for retail and the Academy of Contemporary Music in recent years. Several students apply post A level. All become Old Aluredians in any event – surely in the running for the most arcane alumni title. OAs of note include sportsmen/women (cricketers Jos Buttler and Roger Twose, hockey player Maddie Hinch, rugby player Tom Voyce), broadcasters Jonathan Meades and Dominic Wood and actress Juno Temple.

Money matters: The difference between day and boarding fees is closer than at the other Taunton schools but broadly in line. Scholarships for academic, sporting and artistic prowess plus DT, to a maximum value of 20 per cent of the day fee, are awarded at 13+ and sixth form. Academic scholars are expected to contribute to the intellectual life of the school, not just pulling in stonking exam results, but also attending weekly meetings at which papers are presented.

Remarks: Look no further for a traditional public school with distinctly sporty leanings sited in a county town. A Somerset institution housed in a suitably imposing stone monolith and serving its environs.

King's Hall School

Linked with King's College (Taunton)

Kingston Road, Taunton, Somerset TA2 8AA

Ages 2–13 **Pupils** 331 **Boarders** 32 full, 12 weekly/flexi **C of E**

Fees: Day £7,725 – £16,500; Boarding £18,450 – £23,985 pa

01823 285920
www.kingshalltaunton.co.uk

Headmaster: Since 2009, Justin Chippendale BSc (late 40s). His education and subsequent career have caused him to shuttle between Oxford and Taunton, starting at the Dragon, thence to King's Taunton, back to Oxford Brookes for a degree in biology, exercise and health, a stint as housemaster at the Dragon, a detour to Chafyn Grove as deputy head, then back to Taunton. Affectionately and inevitably known as Mr Chips, he works hard to put the child's experience (of personal development, academic stimulus, physical challenge, artistic exploration and so on) as top priority at King's Hall, closely followed by the quality of relationships: between staff and pupils/parents/each other. 'I work on the invisibles and immeasurables', says he. But that's not to endanger academic expectations: 'It has to be cool to work, and ok to talk about work here,' he adds, and makes it his business to ensure that his charges (and their parents) make well-informed suitable choices for their next schools, even when the majority go on to King's Taunton.

Mr Chips is a keen sportsman and retains the physique of a rugby player, still occasionally coaching. Married with three children at the school, he enjoys entertaining parents 'in order to understand each family's own context' (though a few grumble about not being on the head's dinner list), and he is generally well-liked by both pupils and parents. 'He knows everyone, takes a real interest in us, and we love the Chips Challenge,' opined pupils, who might be asked to research an arcane matter, solve a puzzle or achieve a physical feat.

Entrance: Many join the pre-prep (school also comprises a nursery from 2), but some come from local primary schools and London at 7+. From years 1-4, new children are informally assessed during a welcome day; from years 5-8 they are tested in maths, English and verbal reasoning for which special preparation is not required, says school. Quite an intake also welcomed into year 7 for the final two years before moving on at 13+.

Exit: The majority (74 per cent) to King's College at 13+, but a good sprinkling to the Sherborne schools; also the likes of Wellington College, Blundell's, Millfield and Canford. Every child gets into the school of his/her first choice, apparently; 'We didn't get the hard sell for King's', said one mother with a sigh of relief. Famous ex-pupils include actress Juno Temple, founder of Everyday Sexism project Laura Bates, and mad adventurers Ross and Hugo Turner.

Remarks: Sited in the mellow golden former home of the Yea baronetcy Pyrland Hall, dating from 1760, and surrounded by 50 acres of parkland and woods, this is an idyllic setting just minutes from Taunton. But it's not precious – pupils here make the most of the space, freedom and mud to pursue a terrific range of activities and outdoor pursuits beyond the school day which finishes at 4.30pm, mountain biking and archery being just two. Some 15 acres of pitches, an Astroturf and a sports hall mean all major sports are well catered for and fulfil all expectations, but an indoor pool is undoubtedly on the parental wish list; as it is, swimming is an extracurricular activity until the school's outdoor pool is opened in the summer term. But it all amounts to a slice of gracious enough living for the young.

King's Hall is reckoned to be Taunton's smartest and most academic prep school, partly because it's the only place which prepares children for common entrance (and scholarships) at 13+, still the measure and starting point for the most prestigious public schools. From year 3, children are taught in classes of about 15 by specialist teachers. All begin French in year 1 but there's the opportunity to pick up Spanish from year 5 or Latin from year 6. Science and geography get thumbs up from pupils, but 'We don't go to any lessons and think 'Oh no!', said one. Prep amounts to two half hour subjects per night for the oldest: 'It's OK to make mistakes and they will be explained to you again,' said another. One mother observed that some children are held back until they have learnt some basics by rote, and wondered if there should be more 'aspiration and challenge before they have everything right'. Both prep and pre-prep have own library. Some 49 children are currently on the learning support register; school has policy of not withdrawing children from vital lessons to have their two half hour individual sessions per week.

Pastoral care for the children highly rated; class teachers assume pastoral responsibilities in year 3, tutors with mixed horizontal tutor groups thereafter. The newly formed Friends of King's Hall provides purely social events for parents, and is working on extending its reach to everyone. We liked the enshrining of the school rules into six positive exhortations, such as 'do work hard, and do be honest'.

About 50 children board (four per cent of boarders from overseas) in a variety of arrangements; school entices children with regular year group boarding nights and film nights for the whole prep school. One busy mum told us her youngest had boarded just for a night at the age of 5 – and loved it. The sole boarding house has separate areas for senior boys, junior boys and girls, each with its own common room and quiet areas. 'It's fun and as homely as possible – I board to relax!' one boy told us, and all reckoned that boarders of all persuasions are well integrated. Parents tell us that facilities have improved, but the school 'doesn't have that horrible bling-tastic feel that the other Taunton schools have'. Well, thank goodness! Day pupils are welcome to join in the weekend activities with boarders, which might include dry ski-ing or making the most of the beautiful Quantock Hills nearby for a 16 mile orienteering exercise; facilities at King's College are also on offer at weekends.

The arts are well catered for too. Pupils' art was displayed everywhere we went and the design side has facilities for 2D and 3D design. Three major productions a year for years 4, 6 and 8 put on in the school's theatre or outside in the rose garden are complemented by prizes for acting and poetry recital at local festivals. About half the children learn a musical instrument, achieving grade 6 or 7 in rare cases, and the newish director of music has gone down well.

So what's it really like? A question probably best answered by the pupils: 'I look forward to going back'. 'The weeks pass really quickly'. And to sum up? 'I don't instantly feel like the walking dead when I arrive'.

Job done, Mr Chips.

K

King's Hawford School

Linked with The King's School (Worcester), King's St Alban's School

Hawford Lock Lane, Worcester WR3 7SD

Ages 2–11 **Pupils** 322 **C of E**

Fees: £6,680 – £13,221 pa

01905 451292
www.ksw.org.uk

Principal: Since 2006, Jim Turner (early 50s), who is not in the flashy CEO-style head mould. He is comfortable feeding the chickens that are on site and breeding the birds that the children delight in watching. But alongside the gentleman farmer image, there is a man who cares passionately about the sort of education that is right for young children. The children are learning from doing – and a lot of the doing goes on outside. Jim Turner's first headship was in Sunderland and the children tell us that the trials and tribulations of the football team there are a running theme at assembly time. To say it is just a place of work for him would be travesty – he lives and breathes the whole school. Parents say that he is more comfortable around the children than around them but that is the way everyone likes it. The children want to tell him about all their successes and they want his approval and praise. People often say a good head knows all the children – at King's Hawford that means a lot more than just knowing everyone's name.

Entrance: The school pretty well fills up at kindergarten and only occasional places become available later on, if someone moves out of the area. Certainly at kindergarten level it is fairly non-selective. Children visit the school and are informally observed.

Exit: Most (over 90 per cent most years) go on to the senior school King's in the centre of Worcester. A number win scholarships there each year (11 in 2018). Parents are given plenty of warning if their child might not pass the exam.

Remarks: When we arrived the whole school was outside engaged in a cross-country run around the 23 acre site. The school is just to the north of Worcester and has all the open-air feel of a rural paradise. As well as the extensive grounds, the children are encouraged to make full use of the adjacent river, canal and farm. They embrace the full forest school curriculum, working on real tasks with real tools. They start using the school's own swimming pool from the age of 3 and from 7 they paddle canoes on the canal. They learn to be confident around water and this relevant life skills approach characterises everything about the school.

The head and parents described the site as 'a children's village'. Apart from the deliciously quirky, original Georgian house where there are now some classrooms and a dining hall, the buildings are all low level and spread out, giving plenty of space for chickens and children to run around. It is a school where children climb trees (' I often wonder what a health and safety official would say,' said one parent wryly) and get muddy ('You have to expect to have the washing machine on every evening,' another told us.) You feel the children are not confined in a way that many schools have to restrict movement. 'The children never stop moving,' one parent told us, and we saw no child who looked even a tiny bit overweight. There is a brand new sports hall/performance space where the architects have taken the concept of a barn to enhance the village feel of the site.

Drama, music and dance are all prominent for everyone. The children can read music by the time they leave, they all learn an instrument and over 80 sing in the choir that takes part in local festivals as well as school events. There are about 60 in the school orchestra with masses of formal and informal opportunities to perform. Sport is also hugely popular with two sports afternoons a week and the children have had national successes – the U11 netball team had just competed in the national finals when we visited. The head believes in giving children lots of opportunities – he wants them to be open, eager and wanting to try out the new, so the extracurricular programme is extensive – construction and sewing, story tellers and IT, cartoon/comic drawing and bridge to name just some of the startling range.

Somewhere in the midst of all this, the children have the normal school lessons – though even here it is in fact quite unusual. The 3 year olds learn German. Years 5 and 6 take three modern languages. They are taught old-fashioned loop handwriting and the forgotten arts of carpentry and cookery. There is no IT room but the school is dripping with technology that the children can take outside the classroom and use. There is a school radio that you can access from the website which the children run. After the cross-country that we watched, the current radio team did interviews with the runners for next week's radio show. The head says there is a bit less time for traditional English and maths than some other schools give, but he points out that the children nevertheless achieve highly, the vast majority getting places at the King's senior school. Class sizes are small – 16-20 – and in year 3 and above, the two classes are split three ways for English and maths. There are tracking systems in place to pick up any progress problems and support teachers are used from year 1 onwards if a need is identified. Additional support is not charged to parents. Nor is the wrap-around care offered from 7.45am to 6.00pm, except at kindergarten level. The after-school provision has recently been restructured so there is a supervised prep time before activities, allowing the children to go home with no school work to complete – totally in keeping with the school ethos of letting children be children and not tiny undergraduates.

The children are happy, healthy, open and engaged – far more interested in getting on with their next activities that making polite conversation to visitors. This is not a school for children who want to sit in front of a PlayStation all day. Parents say King's Hawford has a warm, close community, village school atmosphere with all the opportunities of a much bigger school. 'It is no hothouse but it gets the results,' we were told. The discipline seems to work on the basis that highly motivated and challenged children behave well, and parents love the fact the school doesn't have to be disciplinarian in any way. The parent body is pretty mixed – lots of doctors from the local hospitals, established farming families and business people.

'No one gives up at King's Hawford', said parents, watching the cross-country races. 'Everyone is encouraged and they all believe they can do anything.' This is a 21st century Swallows and Amazons school. We want to ship Department for Education officials out here to see what can be done away from the deadening performance table approach to education.

King's Infants and Juniors (Macclesfield)

Linked with The King's School in Macclesfield

Cumberland Street, Macclesfield, Cheshire SK10 1DA

Ages 3–11 **Pupils** 315 **C of E**

Fees: £4,935 – £10,500 pa

01625 260000
www.kingsmac.co.uk

Principal: Since September 2018, Rachel Cookson, previously head of lower school at Queen's Chester. Degree in modern languages from Southbank University and a PGCE in primary and early years education. Taught at state primary schools in Bristol and Macclesfield, then joined the original infant team here, where she helped to set up the new division and stayed for 13 years. Moved to Terra Nova Prep as head of EYFS then head of pre-prep and nursery before joining Queen's.

Effervescent and dynamic, Mrs Cookson is raring to go with the school move, in September 2020, to the new whizz bang, state of the art school site near the village of Prestbury. It is at this point that infants, juniors and seniors (the latter becoming officially co-ed at that point, abandoning its current diamond structure) will move lock stock and barrel to the new 80-acre site.

Mrs Cookson relishes the prospect of a purpose-built school (right now they share a science lab with the senior girls) which comes with age-appropriate spaces and kit. She is keen to tap into the senior school expertise across areas like philosophy and expand the languages offering, adding Japanese in the current mix of French, German and Spanish. She is also planning to ramp up the drama offering, starting LAMDA and using the senior school theatre.

Entrance: Infants' (3-7 years) places offered by date of application (registration from birth). Juniors: full day at school in January – assessment in literacy, numeracy and VR in morning (looking for above average ability), afternoon activities with a regular class. Before this, report on academic progress, interests and potential requested from current head. Numbers rise in years 3-6 – some influx from state schools, often in year 5. External candidates who join King's Juniors before or at the start of year 5 no longer need to sit the 11plus entrance exam for transfer to senior school.

Exit: Virtually all to senior school – external candidates (including those starting at the junior school after the October half-term of year 5) need to sit entrance exam.

Remarks: Achieves well above national average in reading, writing and maths at key stages 1 and 2 (covers national curriculum with extras); sets for maths all years; more specialist teaching in juniors – French, music and and sport; homework from year 3. Infants do EYFS curriculum plus French and music – all achieve expected level for age and many achieve higher. Emphasis on developing learning and independent thinking skills. No noticeable gender gap, though girls tend to do better at writing, boys at maths – lots of extra reading and writing activities for boys to develop skills, more boys at level 6 in literacy recently. Max class size 20-24 – may split into smaller groups for focus work. Happy, lively children wearing version of senior school uniform.

Spacious, well resourced classrooms with colourful displays throughout. Extensive grounds overlooking hills; uses main site facilities – assembly hall, IT suite, library. Outdoor classroom – a wildlife study area, the Gingko meadow. Charming play area for EYFS with little willow beehives (for children, not bees). Several activity days and trips. Infant and junior division learning support co-ordinators overseen by foundation head of learning support – planning to screen all for dyslexia at 7 years and provide EAL support for all years.

Strong sport – the usuals plus cross-country, trampolining, swimming and athletics, much success in local and regional competitions, national success at trampolining, plenty of chances to represent school. Christmas single made to raise funds for school in Kenya (video on YouTube); various ensembles, including guitar; summer music festival; jazz dance group. Years 5-6 production of Guys and Dolls (ambitious). Art and DT in darkish Portakabin (school says light on a sunny day), plus well stocked junior library and separate infant library area.

Wide choice of lunchtime clubs, eg chess, Latin, science, golf. Junior clubs in school day run by teachers – eg puzzle,drama, construction. After-school sports practices run by staff plus some after-school clubs run by external agencies (with charge), eg golf, Spanish, drama. Optional activity holidays in France, Shrewsbury and Derbyshire; biennial ski trip.

Breakfast club from 8am, after-school service 3.45-6pm (at extra cost). Flexible pre-school for 3 year olds – half/whole day, holidays too: happy little tots in mini versions of school uniform.

We were pleased to see the 'every child matters' values displayed in the cheerful entrance hall – be healthy, make a positive contribution, enjoy and achieve, economic wellbeing, staying safe. Weekly award for children who have shown especially positive qualities in memory of former deputy head boy who died at 12 years. School council. Older pupils do reading work with juniors, helps transition to senior school. Infants have playtime buddy system – year 2 helpers in red caps, plus 'buddy bench'.

Mostly white British, some Europeans (business families working for locally based AstraZeneka, also commuter belt for airline companies at Manchester Airport) – very happy parents. Thriving lowest segment of King's diamond structure.

King's St Alban's School

Linked with The King's School (Worcester), King's Hawford School

Mill Street, Worcester WR1 2NJ

Ages 4–11 **Pupils** 195 **C of E**

Fees: £7,008 – £13,989 pa

01905 354906
www.ksw.org.uk

Headmaster: Since January 2016, Richard Chapman (early 40s). He was educated in the Midlands (Solihull School, where he was head boy) and read economics at Bristol. He worked briefly as a trainee manager at Marks and Spencer, then balanced his early teaching posts with a stint as a semi-professional rugby player. He was head of sixth form and coach of the 1st XV at Warwick School before joining the King's Foundation in Worcester as second deputy in 2007. He went on to become senior deputy at King's before being appointed head of King's St Alban's. He knows the school and the area very well and brought considerable experience to his latest role.

He still enjoys sport and continues to play cricket. He is determined to grow sport at King's St Alban's, having recently appointed a new head of boys' games. His favourite time of the week is celebratory assembly on Fridays when a huge range of the children's achievements at all sorts of different levels are applauded. He revels in the youthful exuberance all around him. 'What I love to see is the children outside having fun playing tag one minute, then the next coming into the classroom and settling down calmly and purposefully to a challenging academic lesson'. Father of two children, both in the Kings' Foundation, Richard is clearly relishing the opportunities to grow the reputation of the foundation at the bottom end. He has plans to move IT forward, away from being a discrete subject to an integrated teaching and learning resource, while boosting the status of the library to encourage a love of reading. He is having considerable success with the growth mindset work that he has introduced to build confidence and resilience. Parents who already knew Richard from his senior school days were delighted when he took on King's St Alban's. They see him as being outward facing, very determined and with a competitive edge to him that can only be good for the school. They like the fact that he drops in on clubs and activities as well as lessons.

Entrance: Reception up to year 3 involves spending some time in the school with the appropriate class, being observed. From year 3, there are entrance tests in verbal reasoning, English and maths, which normally take place in the spring term for September entry, but the school will arrange for individual testing at other times of the year. Typically, there are three forms in years 5 and 6 and two in the younger years. Class sizes are usually between 15 and 20.

Exit: The vast majority of children go on to King's senior school. In 2018, 10 won scholarships. A few go into the state sector or to boarding schools. Parents felt the children were very well prepared to move on to King's. For example from year 4 the school starts to build homework steadily so the children are ready for the amount of work they will be expected to do in year 7.

Remarks: King's St Albans was originally a traditional prep school starting at 7 years old. In 2008, it expanded to take children from age 4 by buying an adjacent house and converting it into bright, light, children-friendly spaces. Partly because of this, the buildings have an attractive, non-institutional feel about them and the resources in the pre-prep reflect the best modern educational practice; it is a purpose built pre-prep department. Every bit of space is imaginatively used to provide outdoor play and activity spaces.

K

Teaching in the pre-prep is topic based and becomes more subject focused as the children get older. The teachers describe it as traditional but creative and rigorous. Parents tell us that teaching is both nurturing and challenging. 'Teachers show them that they can do more than just well enough.' The small class sizes, enhanced with the use of teaching assistants, ensure that informal assessment is a daily feature and any learning concerns are picked up very quickly. Generally these will be supported in the class room but the senior school SEN specialist can assess and support if necessary. A few children have additional lessons outside normal class time, at no extra charge. Also in the main fee package is wrap-around 8am-6pm care if parents need it, and quite a number do. Lots of families have both parents working. The after-school structured prep and activities are run by teachers.

The children are enthusiastic and serious. Everyone loves sport and the aim to have everyone involved clearly works. The older children we saw were very much enjoying their PSE discussions on a range of social issues. The head has introduced debating to stimulate new intellectual channels for the children. The choristers, who are from year 3 upwards in particular, have a highly structured timetable with long days. Music features prominently for everyone whether a chorister or not. All year 1s have a 'violin experience', lots play instruments and there are a number of different music groups. The head is keen to present aspirational experiences to the children, and choirs from the cathedral and senior school regularly come to perform. The creative arts are a very strong feature generally. Children spoke enthusiastically about Creative ConneXions, an annual occasion that is the culmination of various arts events that go on through the year. There is dance, poetry and singing. The nearness of the senior school is a resource the head is keen to exploit even more. He is encouraging sixth formers to support clubs in order to get a real buzz to the already extensive extracurricular side of the school.

The facilities, as you would expect, are excellent. There is a fully equipped science lab, brilliant for the year 6 annual science week, art room, a swimming pool and sports hall. The school has its own chapel and a lovely light library. King's has an outdoor education space in Wales which the pupils utilise at various stages – a much-anticipated adventure. There are plenty of trips out of school, a particular favourite being year 6's visit to Normandy.

The school is very positive about relations with parents. In the lower years, reading records go home daily. There are assemblies to which parents are invited two or three times a year, and at the start of every academic year there is a curriculum evening for each year group where teachers share the school's methods of teaching as well as the actual material. Parents appreciate the school's conscious work on developing character. The key words that provided the focus for everyone on the week we visited were concentration, enthusiasm and curiosity. These themes are shared with parents, who like the way the school uses moral scenarios to help the children with their own daily decision making. Discipline is described by parents as very understated. 'When a bell rings in the playground, everyone stops and goes in – no teacher has to raise their voice'. Parents told us any concerns are picked up quickly and dealt with discreetly as far as the children are concerned.

A number of teachers told us that children at the school do not have to fit a particular mould and that all can thrive. Parents say it is a 'really happy school' and the children we met bore this out. 'They care about celebrating children's individuality', one parent told us. The head is very ambitious for the school and has made some timely innovations to this already very nurturing and successful school.

The King's School (Chester)

Wrexham Road, Chester, Cheshire CH4 7QL

Ages 4-19 **Pupils** 1,101: 395 girls, 706 boys **Sixth form** 204 **C of E**

Fees: £9,150- £13,515 pa

01244 689500
www.kingschester.co.uk

Headmaster: Since 2017, George Hartley MA Cantab (geography), MSc (environmental science, Imperial College, London). Previously principal at Elizabeth College, Guernsey and prior to that head of sixth form at Berkhamstead School, having taught at Highgate School, Queen's College, Taunton and Eton.

As well as academic strength, thinks 'it is really important that the school has life and soul and fun'. Parents say that before his arrival King's lacked personality, but now 'he is bringing warmth back into the school'. One said, 'it's like he has lifted the lid off the school and shone a light inside'.

Mindful of the huge mental health issues plaguing teenagers everywhere, 'a constant striving for perfectionism', he wants to mix academic excellence with outstanding pastoral care. It's an educational elixir he hopes to deliver by helping students 'learn in a way that is sustainable': to take the undue pressure out of exams and introduce appropriately paced studying. He has started by scrapping end of year exams for years 7 and 8; to sit 17 exams over two weeks at the end of the first two years in secondary school, he suggests, is not beneficial to any student. No kidding. Put in that Gradgrind kind of way, you wonder why they weren't scrapped earlier. Instead, he wants to use those crucial two years to help students revise more effectively, all the while being continually assessed behind the scenes to ensure everyone is on track academically. Assessments, he says, allow students to learn from setbacks in a 'more humane way' and 'fail forwards'. By year 9, 'they should each have a clear revision strategy and be able to handle the intensity of end of year exams'.

Perceiving student feedback as a very powerful tool, he has injected some oomph into the open forum and sought to foster a 'have a go' culture. 'When pupils remember this school, I want them to have a smile on their face', he says. The school is no bubble, either; although on the outskirts of Chester, it is now collaborating with other key Chester institutions to put King's at the heart of the community. One initiative is Saturday masterclasses (shared with a couple of state schools), offering a range of opportunities such as sculpting.

Parents say Mr Hartley attends every school performance (so that's three helpings of Beauty and the Beast) and is always on the touchlines, ready to chat. What most impressed them, though, is his frequent presence in the junior school; the fact that he makes himself approachable, even doing reading sessions with the children. 'He has the best interests of the child at heart,' said one parent, 'and the "new" [which we took to mean the Hartley effect] is permeating through the whole school'.

Head of the junior school: Since 2016 is Margaret Ainsworth LLB (Leeds) PGCE MEd, previously at Queen's, Chester, who joined King's in 2015 to head up Willow Lodge infant school before assuming overall responsibility for the juniors.

The move to Willow Lodge, she says, meant she got to set 'the tone and ethos of the school'. By the time she became overall head, she knew exactly what needed doing, immediately increasing the extracurricular offering and opening up opportunities in sport so every child could represent their school at some level. They play, she says, 'in a very supportive environment'. Parents love this. 'They never get the door slammed on them', one parent said.

A strong advocate for the forest school dimension – Willow Lodge recently received the gold award from the Woodland Trust – Mrs Ainsworth is a fan of children learning without boundaries, learning about team building and risk taking. She exudes warmth, care, accomplishment and efficiency. 'A well run ship' one parent said. Another described her as 'phenomenal'.

According to parents, both heads are out there greeting students each day, come rain or shine.

Academic matters: While literacy and maths take centre stage from day one, this is soon expanded to include French, Spanish, PE and swimming and forest school sessions. Later, science, humanities, art and design and technology, music and drama are integrated. Specialist teachers are a blend of genders and age groups. The forest school, open to both infants and juniors, is a hugely popular part of the curriculum, allowing children to make dens, go tracking and, under supervision, light fires. Older pupils also get to go off site for this. Parents were fans: 'they get to do amazing things'. Class sizes 22 max in infants, 24 in juniors.

Each term has a theme, picked up across the curriculum; at the time of our visit it was space, with the Mars landing a focus. Another was rain forests, where they studied use of palm oil and wrote a David Attenborough-style commentary. Rather wonderfully, the activities programme stitched into the curriculum also means that for one afternoon each week pupils try a new experience, from baking to cycling to archery.

There is a learning support teacher and parents are kept informed at every stage where issues are identified. Mrs Ainsworth says each child will get the support they need to thrive. One parent whose child had struggled in maths said the school had worked with him at lunchtimes, even pulling in a maths teacher who was also his football coach because they communicated well. They work on little weaknesses, was the parental echo; they see the whole child, and don't label them.

In the senior school, a broad curriculum prevails through years 7-9. Around 90 per cent of students study at least one language to GCSE but only some eight per cent take one at A level. Academic standards are very high but one parent suggested that since Mr Hartley had 'lifted the mood', students were more motivated to work hard (less adolescent grumbles). Head is keen for teachers to incorporate different ways of learning into each lesson, perhaps an element of kinaesthetic or tactile learning. Interestingly, a pupil later told us that she had started to find biology 'really interesting' since they had started being asked 'to do practical things'.

Girls are currently outnumbered in some year groups, but the school says there is no consistent trend between subject choices and gender. However, it may be worth checking on the situation in particular year groups.

In 2018, at GCSE, 72 per cent A*-A/9-7 grades (17 per cent of these the top grade 9). At A level, 64 per cent A*/A, with sciences, maths and economics the most popular and successful subjects. Far fewer takers for humanities and very few linguists.

SEN seems very well catered for and all students go through a screening process. Mr Hartley says in 95 per cent of cases, the diagnosis is already identified when they start in the seniors. Describing the SEND department as 'superb', he adds, 'they will use whatever strategies work, whether one-to-one or in groups'. He is clear the school does not see issues like dyslexia as 'either a difficulty or a deficit'.

Games, options, the arts: All the usual sports in the junior school, plus more offbeat sports including fencing and dodgeball. Clubs run the gamut from The Blazer newspaper (recently scooped a best school newspaper award), mindfulness, chess, world explorers to gardening (the infant school alone has 20 clubs). One parent described the music as 'amazing'. Choirs (of all descriptions), orchestras and many performance opportunities including a summer concert and a winter one in Chester Cathedral. LAMDA on offer; two drama productions per year with opportunities to perform at Chester Festival as well as Shakespeare workshops. Guys and Dolls and Singing in the Rain recent productions which, from the photos, looked astoundingly professional. Every school year is involved in a production so even the shyest child adjusts, Mrs Ainsworth says. One visiting speaker, workshop or trip per term for everyone; these may include outdoor pursuits, museums or overseas to eg Barcelona.

We asked the junior school children about all these great activities on offer. Each had a story of triumph to relay: dropping a cello on stage and getting back up, a scary football trial, playing the tiger in Jungle Book. Each grinned madly after relaying their satisfaction at having mastered the skill or faced down their fear. 'The school gives them wings,' a member of staff said; 'they will have a go at anything'. 'I love the Improvisation club,' said one, 'cross-country,' another, 'the cool science experiments,' piped up his neighbour....the list went on. These are interesting, interested (and well-mannered) children.

Senior sport is strong for both sexes; all the usual suspects on offer (netball, football, hockey, track and field, cricket et al) plus taikwando, water polo, lacrosse. Mr Hartley is keen to ensure everyone gets chance to represent the school, at whatever level. Parents welcome this, one saying that previously there had not been 'enough sport for all'. Around 170 in the rowing club, some of whom go to achieve great things at Oxbridge or nationally.

Some 25 music clubs, and every type of choir and band from madrigals to jazz cats, with around of a third of pupils throughout the school involved. Heaps of drama clubs, with glossy productions from Shakespeare to Nicolas Nickleby; a few take drama to A level.

In the senior school, enrichment sessions are part of curriculum and range from academic (philosophy, debating) to skills (life-saving) to creative (animation). One pupil relished thinking skills where they had been asked 'what is a point?' Others enthused about costume design or debating. A mass of clubs from to Polyglots to Random Acts of Kindness. Numerous competitions, such as science Olympiads and TEdX. Trips to eg CERN, Iceland, the UN, battlefields. Pupils particularly liked the adventure trip to Aberdovey, having enjoyed the challenges. DofE and CCF popular.

Of course opportunities come at a cost; one parent mentioned that some of these great trips – in particular a rather fabulous football tour – cost a mighty amount of money. To be borne in mind in these cash-strapped, uneven times.

Background and atmosphere: Spacious 33 acre site.

Willow Lodge, the purpose-built, self-contained infant school, is all wood-cladding and eco touches. The library had terrific displays dotted around, a life-sized igloo and a large papier mâché version of War Horse when we visited. Classrooms were a riot of colour with an outside play area, complete with friendship bench, a stage and a fantastic forest area with mud kitchen, veg growing and willow caves.

The bright, modern junior school boasts the swanky 'learning centre', opened in 2015, which houses the library, science labs, ICT room, art studio (wonderful displays of African forms and birds caught our eye). Overall, it gives off a vibe of a well-equipped, stimulating environment. It has its own playing fields, playground and little cricket pavilion. It shares many senior school facilities, including the theatre and swimming pool.

K

The corridors of the senior school, also stimulating, are lined with displays from book covers to thought-provoking questions: 'Is it possible for a person to be entirely fulfilled by technology?' Top notch facilities, great theatre and, like the junior, the excellent library at the centre. The DT room displayed various prestigious design prizes and wonderful gadgets, from iPad chargers to ingenious lighting. The sixth form centre has a nicely grown up feel with a little café and lots of study rooms.

A flash new sports centre is due to open in 2019. Students seemed very excited about pools, cafes, dance studio, ergo room.... just a little desperate for it to open.

Pastoral care, well-being and discipline: This has assumed much greater importance under the new regime. Juniors have assemblies on friendship issues and pastoral concerns are monitored at weekly staff meetings. Plenty of staff around at break times. Parents say the emphasis is on 'kindness, warmth and care'. The classes are mixed up each year, which 'felt quite hard at first but we soon realised they really knew what they were doing,' said a parent. The result? Less dependency on one group of friends. Another parent said, 'The junior school breeds self-esteem and independence, all very carefully planned'.

Mobile phones are not allowed in school. Increasing responsibilities such as election to the school council (posters, badges, campaigns, it's all taken very seriously). The senior school house system was recently overhauled; pupils keep the same house tutor throughout, and groups have been halved in size to 12.

There is a school counsellor and 18 members of staff have so far completed the 'mental health first' training; other teachers and older students sport the turquoise badge of anti-bullying mentors. Sixth form prefects act as 'aunt' or 'uncle' to year 7s.

We spoke to mature senior school pupils; one described mental health issues 'as common as any other injury you see'. Another talked about addressing friendship issues she had encountered a few years previously. They were aware of the online facility where they could share any concerns and, in these gender-sensitive times, conscious that 'banter' was not always a good thing. Parents, too, seemed very aware of the increased pastoral emphasis; one suggested the school suffered locally from the perception that it was concerned only about academic results. 'And it's not, it's all genuinely about looking after the child,' he said.

Parents praised the phased-in smooth transition from junior to senior school.

Pupils and parents: Parents a mix; some privileged, most hard working two-income families who prioritise education. One junior parent described the parent body as 'very warm and doting on their children'. As any school, one hinted, there will always be competitive parents and those who sign their child up for anything that moves. Senior pupils' career aspirations included becoming a vet, a doctor, working in aviation, 'something with sport'.

Communication good: weekly junior school newsletter; Firefly app allows senior school parents to override adolescent monosyllables and see what's really going on.

Entrance: Into the Willow Lodge by play-based assessment. Junior assessments in small groups. Automatic entry from junior to senior school for those making sufficient academic progress, otherwise sensitive conversations with parents. The tracking is so good, Mrs Ainsworth says, that this rarely happens. External senior school applicants sit verbal and non-verbal reasoning, maths and English tests. Sixth form admissions by interview and GCSE results.

Exit: Almost all junior pupils move up to the senior school. Around three-quarters of sixth formers to Russell Group universities, including Bath, Birmingham, Durham, Leeds, Liverpool and Newcastle; eight to Oxbridge in 2018. Nine medics/dentists/vets; engineering, business and economics also popular courses.

Money matters: Currently around seven per cent receive a bursary; school fundraising to increase this to around 20 per cent.

Remarks: A fantastic, vibrant and friendly environment in which your child can attain high academic goals while nurturing their interests and passions, whatever they may be.

The King's School

Cadhay Lane, Ottery St Mary, Devon EX11 1RA

Ages 11 –18 **Pupils** 1,094 **Sixth form** 181

01404 812982
www.thekings.devon.sch.uk

Headteacher: Since 2016, Rob Gammon BSc PGCE. Educated at Enfield Grammar and Loughborough University: physical education, sports science and physics. Began teaching in 1997 in Lincs. Came first to King's in 2006 as deputy head responsible for the school's specialist sports college status. Left in 2013 to head up Robert Blake Science College, a struggling comprehensive in Bridgwater, which he raised in short order to Ofsted good status. Second coming to King's, this time as head, 2016. Widely acclaimed, popular choice. Here is where he absolutely wants to be. Remains a keen sportsperson – a onetime pole vaulter, he now swims, runs, cycles and occasionally strings all three together in triathlons. Other interests outdoorsy. Keeps chickens. Lives in the catchment area. Three children, all at King's.

When the Ofsted inspectors investigated Mr Gammon's work in Bridgwater they fearlessly exposed 'clear vision and relentless drive for further improvement'. They also noted that 'all teachers are held firmly to account for the impact their teaching has on the progress pupils make.' Which makes him sound, if effective, a bit like one of these martinet superheads we read about, the sort who carry with them a little cloud of fear. For sure, Mr Gammon ensures the classes run on time and students wear exactly the right uniform, exactly the right way, but his style is not command and control from behind a distant desk. He likes to get out and about and hear what teachers and students think. Affiliative is the buzzword he applies to his leadership style. Team building. Head coach. Approachable. He told us: 'I take a great deal of time to talk to students, staff and parents in order to try and get to know them personally'. We can attest to this, having toured the school with him, and can also vouch for his stated aspiration to make his school 'a community where students feel loved and cared for – in a professional manner: you've got to make sure the rigour is there and at the same time promote warmth and relationships.' He added, 'There is a culture of high expectations for all and I hope that I model this in my own professional and personal attitude and behaviour.' We very much think he does. We like the way Mr Gammon feels about his school. We like his cheery openness and admin super-efficiency, for he seems to manage to do it all without the help of a PA. We queried him about below-par exam results in one subject and he didn't blink or blind us with blather but in plain English described the staffing difficulty responsible – temporary, as it turned out. Candour in a head is a marvellous thing.

Academic matters: King's is a comprehensive school. Actually, it's an academy but retains the heart and mind of a comprehensive: it exists to provide a good education for every single boy and girl locally, regardless of gifts or calibre. This is as much about ideology as pragmatism. It's the right thing to do, they believe. And it works. There is huge pride in the school's 'diversity'. A student told us flatly, 'You don't need to go to a grammar school to succeed'. There is unapologetic mixed ability teaching throughout except in maths: 'You'll find no bottom-set culture here,' said the head. We cast about for evidence that some students as a result feel held back. Overwhelmingly no. 'Well yes, once in a while,' conceded the parent of very bright children. 'Tough' she tells them, 'life's like this'. Didn't hold her eldest back from going to Oxbridge. Parents who fancy a more rarefied atmosphere where their brilliant child can spark off like-minded other children can check out the highly selective Colyton Grammar nearby. It's an alternative. We wouldn't say it's any better.

Given the exam results they achieve you'd have to say that the comprehensive formula is holding up rather well at King's – calls for a market offering greater choice of schools are decidedly muted hereabouts. Exceptionally good value-added score places King's in the top 17 per cent of schools nationally for those achieving grade 4+ in English and mathematics at GCSE. They do well by their disadvantaged students. And there's a 'challenge programme' for the gifted and talented which hosts visiting speakers.

Up to GCSE the curriculum has something for everyone. Foundational academic subjects, English and maths in particular, especially well taught: 79 per cent got 9-4 in English and maths in 2018. Sciences notably strong, as are French and Spanish, all of them significantly above the national average. No weak areas. A leavening of hands-on subjects include food prep and nutrition. They like to talk about 'achievement for all' and they mean it with fervour. Head especially proud of 'doing well by our boys'. He told us, 'We encourage all students to believe that there is no ceiling for them'. In their GCSEs overall 23 per cent of entries got A*-A/9-7 in 2018.

Sixth form more academic. Head said, 'It's not right for everyone but we know what we do well'. Twenty-six subjects including BTec IT. Set sizes vary from low single figures to high teens. An ingeniously designed setup, attractive to those who don't fancy the hugeness of Exeter College but want a pre-adult experience which also enables them to practise the school's communitarian values. We like the sixth form centre a lot with its snazzy café, study room, IT suite and specialist classrooms – almost a school within a school. We also think highly of the head of sixth form.

He told us: 'This is not just an exam factory', which in many schools is a self-incriminating denial, but actually sixth formers here do plenty in the wider school community, organise a number of house events, eg music competition, and apply to be prefects – workplace-style interview for head girl and head boy. They labour and ask not for any reward save that of knowing that they done good because a spirit of above-and-beyond is pervasive here. Careers guidance happens in PSHE classes, highly rated by students. Individual support for the 30 per cent or so of students who want to sidestep university and crack on with an apprenticeship or the world of work.

Bottom line shows strength in all areas, from maths (attracting record numbers) and sciences, to English and history, and languages. In addition to main subjects you choose one other from a tasty range which includes extended project qualification – EPQ, silver DofE and a life skills course which includes cooking on a budget. In 2018 20 per cent of all entries achieved A*-A and 47 per cent achieved A*-B.

Special needs provision famous, making the school attractive to students outside the catchment area who have an Education, Health and Care plan (EHCP). These students can name the school they want to go to, adding somewhat to pressure on places. Individual programmes for each student. Life skills room – a safe space for students with additional needs. Full range of SENs addressed. Focus on nurturing independence: the head of dept, also the school's deputy head, told u, 'We have no velcro teaching assistants or key workers here'. Exceptional dedication from these, who reeled off with pride marvellous successes, including a student now at university whose parents had been told would probably never speak. Parents very happy with level of communication with school.

Games, options, the arts: King's was a specialist sports college in the days when specialisms were à la mode and, with a sporty headteacher, remains a sporty kind of place. The head told us, 'Sport is right at the heart of what we do; it develops skills for leadership'. In addition to PE classes there's a range to suit all sorts from keep-fit for those who aren't much turned on by the team stuff. Girls' hockey and boys' cricket very strong. Other strengths: girls' cricket, football, athletics and cross-country. For students with disabilities there's boccia.

By no means a superabundance of lunchtime and after-school clubs compared with some schools but what there is is well chosen and ample, said parents and students. Plenty of sport. Some exam support. General interest activities include writers' group, coding club and school band. Daily mindfulness session. Sports leadership. Crochet. Some art to complement what goes on in the classroom, where results are commendable. Performing arts a bit thin – there are lessons in years 7-9 and a big biennial production. If a student wants to start a club the teachers will get behind them.

Lots of departmental field trips. Sixth formers can apply to go to India and work in a children's home. Biennial trip to New York. Ten Tors. DofE. Your best insight: read the buzzy weekly newsletters archived on the school's website and check out their Twitter and Facebook.

Background and atmosphere: This is a venerable school. Founded 1335 as a choir school, became a grammar in 1545, a comprehensive in 1982 and an academy in 2011. Of its former days not a wrack survives, not a ruinous oratory, not yet so much as a fragment of stained glass. Its best side is its early and very ordinary C19 bit. Survey the school as you emerge from your car and your first impression is of a common-or-garden comprehensive.

Second impressions tell you everything you need to know in microcosm. As you approach the school you observe students criss-crossing the playground on their way to their next lesson and think, Gosh, what extraordinarily nice, happy-looking young people. Then the welcome you get in reception is warm and genuine. Within three mins max you feel perfectly certain that you are in an exceptionally good school. You're right. What's the secret?

Partly, longstanding culture. Mr Gammon must fill big shoes because the school's established corporate personality is his inheritance from his highly successful predecessor and ex-boss, head for 12 years and flag bearer for the school's comprehensive values: 'I do not like selection in any way whatsoever. We are totally inclusive here and that is something we are proud of. A school has a responsibility to its community and should be the hub of it.' Because it comes so close to this ideal, the school has been able to attract really good teachers and support staff. Nice touch: on its website the school lists teaching staff and support staff by department alphabetically, so between careers staff and cover teachers you find cleaning team. None of the usual us and them. We asked around why the school is so darn nice. Everyone told us, 'It's always been like this'.

Not that it sits now in a state of self-satisfied stasis, because a school rapidly rots (from the head down) if there's any slacking. As Mr Gammon observed, 'even "nice kids" can be hard work if they are not on board'. Not that they are all preternaturally nice, they're normal and they number a few of the usual suspects – lead swingers, refuseniks – about whom Mr Gammon spoke with affection and humour. A student told us, 'The teachers push us to achieve the most we can rather than trying to make us into different people.' Mr Gammon added, 'They know the students well enough to be able to guide them when they go off track'. So let's hear it for a really strong team of teachers; we enjoyed and were impressed by every one we met. A parent told us, 'They try to find everyone's talent and help them to achieve in that'. Academic students here learn to take a rounded view of achievement. A parent told us what a great learning experience it was for her daughter when an unprepossessing lad suddenly emerged as a great chef. Mr Gammon's principal criterion when appointing new teachers is to identify 'a passion for young people'. Parents, we learnt, respond to how much the teachers care for their child and, in few cases, 'get their act together'.

Mr Gammon has focused on how his students feel about being at school. So the campus has been secured and a pedestrian cut-through cut off. Benches have been installed in the playground to impede hurtling and enable calm conversation. There are tubs of shrubs and flowers. This is not cosmetic, it is very clever. In these days of shrinking budgets and clamouring priorities it is money well spent. There are some tired-looking buildings and some fine new ones, latest being the dining hall, which fits Mr Gammon's feelgood brief to a T, new sixth form café and IT suite. Sports centre shared with the community.

A crown jewel of the school is its parliament – its student voice. Each house elects reps to this consultative body from all year groups, who then elect leaders. On behalf of the school community the parliament addresses staff and governors on matters of concern. They're effective: one of them told us, 'Our needs become their priority'. They interview all candidates for teaching posts. They advise on development projects. They've even addressed a secretary of state for education. They're very proud of their school and its values. They impressed upon us that 'if we weren't as diverse we wouldn't have such a great school community'.

Samuel Taylor Coleridge's father was headmaster of King's. His precocious son attended and, in his own estimation, 'soon outstripped all of my age'. Sir Walter Raleigh may or may not have come here, it's hard to pin down. More recently, Jo Pavey, long-distance runner, definitely did.

Pastoral care, well-being and discipline: There are four houses (all named after men) and your house is where pastoral care is based in a tutor group which is vertical by age. Aside from the formal pastoral structure care is, in Mr Gammon's words, 'all about depth', meaning that everyone plays a part in how a student feels when they're at school. PSHE is passionately taught. 'Well-being,' we were told, 'is at the heart of the school; students must feel good about themselves in order to learn'. We saw that borne out. Student members of the school's national award-winning Respect group train the staff on issues of diversity. There is rigour: a system of strikes and incremental intervention including partnership with parents – 'our relationship with parents is central'. Low level disruption is not tolerated. Exclusion is rare but every student knows that there is a clear boundary. There are rewards, eg the Fab Fifty students with the most house points who win a non-uniform day. Those involved in, eg, health or anti-bullying wear coloured lanyards so that others can approach them. Phones? 'We don't want to see them.' Elegant. Uniform? Rules for wearing it are so ingeniously thorough that there's no room for 'misunderstanding'.

The house system incubates all the values the school holds dear: healthy competition, leadership, throwing yourself into everything and being a community-minded good egg. There are lots of inter-house competitions from silly to serious, and students abundantly relish the rivalry. Everyone wanted to tell us about the house dance, 15 mins of choreographed knees-up created and directed by sixth formers. Huge fun of exactly the right sort.

Pupils and parents: Nice place to live, Ottery, twixt moor and sea, where incomers aren't given the silent treatment as can happen further west. People move here for the community spirit and, in droves, the school, which has added a good 10 per cent to house prices. Some parents move here for the brilliant SEN provision. A parent whose child has autism described it as 'a fantastic experience'. Pupils mostly from five local feeder primaries.

Exactly the sort of 'nice' area where you expect higher standards, but some 10 per cent come from backgrounds of rural poverty and are eligible for pupil premium funding. At the high end are parents who could easily afford to go private but see no need and not one of these could explain to us why those who do, do. Makes no sense to us. Some well-off parents, in gratitude, make financial donations for specific purposes. The school has strong communitarian values and plays a leading part in the life of this area. Livewire PTFA (the F stands for Friends).

Entrance: The school is oversubscribed, so you need to live in the catchment area. Admissions criteria as per customary local authority procedure. Brilliant induction process – a whole week in school at the end of the summer term so you feel you belong when you arrive.

For sixth form, looser geographical constraint. You need five 4s at GCSE and a proven 'capacity to achieve on your chosen courses'. Open evening or tour. Report and interview. 'We do the homework.' A tad less stringent than Colyton. Competes also with Exeter College and Exeter Maths School. Distinctive culture and lifestyle, more personal, you're less on your own.

Exit: After GCSE a wodge – around half – departs to pursue vocational courses at Exeter College. After sixth form, 70 per cent to university; 30 per cent to apprenticeships or work. One to Cambridge in 2018.

Money matters: All Devon schools have for years suffered from below average funding and King's receives less even than the average for Devon. If King's were in Birmingham the school's income would be boosted by a million pounds a year. Impressive therefore to see how far they make a little money go. School has its own charitable fund (Foundation and Jubilee Trust) to support less well-off students and worthy enterprises. Gifts amount to less than £1,000 a year so there's probably scope to encourage more philanthropy.

Remarks: Does exactly what all parents wish their local school would do: provide a first-class education for everybody. All good schools inspire strong admiration. King's is a good school. Of these, a small fraction inspire strong affection. King's is one of these precious few.

The King's School (Worcester)

Linked with King's Hawford School, King's St Alban's School

5 College Green, Worcester WR1 2LL

Ages 11–18 **Pupils** 890 **Sixth form** 265 **C of E**

Fees: £13,989 pa

01905 721700
www.ksw.org.uk

Headmaster: Since 2014, Mathew Armstrong MA PGCE: from Oxford in modern and medieval languages and from Birkbeck College, London in Renaissance studies and English literature. He taught at Winchester and spent 11 years at Charterhouse, where he was assistant head. He had previously been a business analyst for McKinsey and Co, where his wife still works.

Pupils find him friendly and accessible as well as impressively intellectual. He is concerned to widen the diversity of the intake and wants King's to be at the very centre of the Worcester community, and has managed to build a terrific leadership team around him who share his vision. Together, they want to put King's firmly on the national map, so that it moves beyond being the local go-to school and leads the way in innovative teaching and learning approaches across the country.

Academic matters: The school produces consistently strong exam results year on year. In 2018, 46 per cent A*/A grades at A level (77 per cent A*/B) and 70 per cent A*/A/7-9 at GCSE. Maths, biology, art and DT all popular. Latin and classical civilisation are offered at A level and GCSE as part of a rich choice that also includes three modern languages, politics, computing and drama/theatre studies. Good value-added scores.

There is currently a huge drive in teaching and learning – 'persistent innovation shared across subjects' is how one senior leader described the growing aspirational culture. The leadership team encourages teachers to engage with other outstanding schools and to model the excitement of the intellectual life. This is a dynamic place to work and it is out to attract the top teachers nationally.

Reporting has recently changed to reflect effort as much as achievement. Everyone is monitored carefully through regular formal and informal assessments and there is a particular drive to ensure that the scholars are strong academic role models for the rest of the school. House tutors, year group tutors and the pastoral team discuss the effort grades with students and implement swift action plans if they are not exceeding expectations. Reports no longer have target grades – everyone can aspire to top grades. There is an innovative academic enrichment programme before lessons start, aimed at introducing students to new ideas. The scholars must attend but it is also open to all senior pupils.

An experienced learning skills department offers a range of support, in small groups or one-to-one. Some find that half a dozen lessons – typically cover studying and revision skills and exam technique – is all they need. Others may require a longer period of lessons covering language skills and problem-solving. A few may need additional support from external agencies. There is no charge for internal support. One parent with a bright but underachieving boy who had hated his previous school described the learning skills department as 'amazing'. It had turned her son around completely – he now loves school and is doing very well. Perhaps more importantly, he no longer needs the additional support.

Games, options, the arts: Everyone we spoke to said there is something for everyone. The games facilities are wonderful: a state of the art, national standard sports hall, indoor climbing wall and a gym to die for. The architecturally exciting Michael Baker boathouse (also in demand of small concerts and other events) juts out over the river which edges the school and, across the river next to the Worcestershire County Cricket Ground, there are extensive playing fields. Keen sportspeople represent the county and there have also been national successes. Dance is taken seriously by both boys and girls and is benefiting from a new dance studio with sprung floor.

Music, as you would expect in a school with close links to a cathedral, is strong. A large number of students learn instruments and there are lots of ensembles, choirs and orchestras. The school has a variety of venues for concerts including the wonderful College Hall, the old monastic refectory dating in part from the 12th century.

There is lots of drama – a big annual production and smaller ones, in the 300 seater theatre or the new drama studio, which boasts top quality up-to-the-minute technology. Art is very popular and there are excellent examples around the school. A level artists have their own studio space.

A few of the other highlights, according to some pupils, are the CCF, DofE, Model UN, dance club and an annual Jaguar Landrover activity to build a 4x4. Lots of trips, both domestically – the school has its own outdoor education centre in Wales – and overseas.

Background and atmosphere: A 16th century foundation, originally the choir school, today's school nestles behind Worcester Cathedral and the heart of the community is College Green. For such a city centre site, it is extraordinarily well hidden from view, and that may partly explain why it feels like a world of its own that cocoons students and adults alike. Buildings range from 12th century to 2016, but it is by no means the hotch-potch that it sounds. Each century has produced its own architectural gems and the overall effect is one of great charm; tradition shoulder to shoulder with the contemporary. The classics and Latin departments are housed in the medieval Edgar Tower, accessed via a romantically precipitous spiral staircase. The ascent is worth it just for the views over Worcester. It is possibly not a site for a permanently physically disabled child.

K

The sense of a British cathedral tradition is in the air, but there is also the feeling of a school gathering itself for a leap forward from this wonderfully secure and comforting position into a more high-octane stratosphere. Parents repeatedly told us it was the feel of the school that attracted them, and that the close links with the cathedral create more than just a religious heritage but also a deep sense of respect that comes from tradition. A small but increasing number of Muslim families choose the school because they believe it enhances the values they foster at home.

The historic boarding aspect of the school has left its mark both in the strong house system and in the rich extracurricular life. King's feels more like a seven day a week school than most city day schools. Pupils have always been encouraged to develop a sense of service to the wider community. This is now both global and local; there are links to the Himalayas, providing educational and medical resources, and close connections are fostered with local businesses.

Parents, teachers and students speak of the exceptionally warm relationships that the school generates. 'There is a place for everyone,' one parent told us. 'My children couldn't be more different but they both feel a close part of the school community and so do I'. 'This is a school with a heart and soul', one relatively newly arrived teacher observed. There is a strong sense of community and inclusivity.

Pastoral care, well-being and discipline: The school has used its past boarding structure to excellent effect. Years 7 and 8 operate as a slightly separate group with a form structure; then, when pupils enter year 9, the full house system kicks in. This means that the school can use the early years to build a sense of belonging and identity amongst all the children, who enter not only from the two junior schools but also from a lot of other feeder primaries. Parents confirm that younger pupils are very happy to share concerns with sixth formers as well as staff and we witnessed the huge excitement and affection generated when our senior guide bumped into a group of year 8s that he mentored. Pupils all spoke about how much they appreciated really getting to know well students in other year groups. While many schools use the house system to stimulate competition, the heart of the system at King's seems to beat around the importance of relationships – though of course the competitions are there too.

Parents feel that house staff handle any pastoral concerns very discreetly and also promptly. There is also a school counsellor. Discipline is along fairly conventional lines – 'we are tough when we have to be,' one member of the senior leadership team told us. Parents feel there are few discipline problems and when there are, parents are fully involved and generally supportive of the school's line.

Pupils and parents: The school has been co-ed for a number of years. Pupils are unpretentious and charming, very aware of how fortunate they are to be at such a distinctive school. A number of parents told us that it was the demeanour of the senior pupils that had clinched their decision to send their offspring to King's. There is a very attractive air of relaxed confidence about them – you feel they are comfortable with themselves and the world. Former pupils flock back to the school, sharing all sorts of experiences and expertise with present pupils. Pupils travel considerable distances to attend and there are signs, which the head intends to fuel, of families moving out of the home counties for the school. Family backgrounds are mixed – some old Worcestershire moneyed families, professionals, business people and those who need the bursary support to keep children there. It is not particularly mixed ethnically, reflecting the Worcester population rather than that of the wider West Midlands, but the Muslim families that are there say there is no hint of racial prejudices.

Entrance: About two-thirds join from the two junior schools, King's St Alban's and King's Hawford. Parents say the transition is very easy for them. The school goes out of its way through the pastoral structure to ensure everyone quickly feels part of the community.

Entry is primarily at 11+ but there are places at 13+ and 16+. At 11, entry is by examination in maths, English and verbal reasoning. In the sixth form, it is dependent on GCSE results, a cognitive abilities test and an interview.

Exit: Some 15 per cent leaves after GCSEs. Nearly all sixth formers go on to university and many get into the top ones. Currently the most popular destinations are Exeter, Birmingham, Bristol and Loughborough and a growing number are getting Oxbridge places – eight in 2018. Students off to a range of courses from interior design at Falmouth to design engineering at Imperial to medicine at Nottingham.

Money matters: Academic and music scholarships at 11+ and 13+, with academic scholarships and leadership awards at 16+. Both new entrant and hardship bursaries are available up to 100 per cent of fees, with up to 90 pupils generally getting bursary funding. The head's aim to wider access includes a drive to increase bursaries.

Remarks: This is definitely a school on a journey. It has taken the head a bit of time to get everyone on board, but now they are. He wants to make it the school that people move out of the south east for and we think he will do it. The environment and pupils can't help but charm, and there is a sense of revving up to take on the national big names in independent education. It is becoming the go-to school for ambitious teachers, which can only make it that much more attractive to parents and their children.

The King's School in Macclesfield

Linked with King's Infants and Juniors (Macclesfield)

Cumberland Street, Macclesfield, Cheshire SK10 1DA

Ages 11–18 **Pupils** 1,120 **Sixth form** 319 **C of E**

Fees: £10,500 – £12,990 pa

01625 260000
www.kingsmac.co.uk

Headmaster: Since 2011, Dr Simon Hyde MA DPhil. Born in Macclesfield and an old boy, degree in modern history at Oxford, doctorate there and at the University of Bonn plus a bit of teaching, history master at Loughborough Grammar for three years, swift ascent to senior teacher and head of humanities at Oakham, deputy head at Haberdashers' Aske's Boys, Herts, for seven years, where he was responsible for school development and strategic planning.

Approachable, balanced, financially shrewd, good sense of humour, ambitious in a realistic way for the school, appreciative of staff. High approval rating from all the parents we spoke to, who praised his communication skills – 'a breath of fresh air', 'very impressive and dedicated', 'terrific..not a strutter..makes the parents chuckle in the first five minutes'. Has seized the opportunity to make a number of new senior appointments (enjoys full backing of governors). In his first year taught a year 10 history and lower sixth politics group to establish his teaching credentials to staff and pupils – clearly loves teaching.

He is very enthusiastic about King's move, in September 2020, to an entirely new site near the well-off village of Prestbury. There is no doubt about it, the 80-acre campus will offer everything whizz bang, state-of-the art that there is to be had. It will also mean the school will officially go co-ed and leave behind the current diamond structure, operating out of two sites (where boys and girls are educated separately at senior school until sixth form stage) to embrace co-ed on one site.

Co-ed can't have been an easy to sell to current parents but it seems they have now embraced it wholeheartedly, since only two families have opted out since the consultation process began. There are real educational benefits, Dr Hyde stresses, in diversity of opinion in class which you get from mixing genders; he is clear there is no convincing evidence that there is any benefit to the separate education of boys and girls.

Judges national and international debating competitions (ran the regional ESU Mace and judges at world schools comps). Interested in German culture and likes reading historical and detective fiction (the classy Swedish kind, Henning Mankell's Wallender series, so definitely on the side of the angels).

Academic matters: Until September 2020 when it goes fully co-ed, there is a diamond structure – co-ed infant and junior school, single sex years 7-11, co-ed sixth.

Very consistent at A level – 2018: 74 per cent A*-B, 42 per cent A*/A. Wide range of academic subjects (no IB nor vocational options) including economics, business studies, government and politics, geology, psychology, philosophy, sport and PE, computer science, Latin and classical civilisation (small but steady numbers). History and psychology very popular, then biology, economics, maths, chemistry; no drama, but can do theatre studies in year 13 extended studies programme, which allows a fifth AS in, eg, critical thinking, or LAMDA, public speaking, Japanese, sports leadership qual; all complete ECDL then too. Max class size 15, but year 13 sets can be as small as five. Much proficient use of electronic whiteboards throughout, but we enjoyed the English language class demonstrating that low tech skilful questioning can also engage students successfully.

GCSE very consistent too – 2018: 47 per cent A*-A/9-7; all do at least nine, with a modern lang (Spanish most popular); can do separate sciences; options include drama, religion & philosophy (excellent results); all work on ECDL. Gender divide closing here (but not at A level).

Very broad curriculum in year 7 – 17 subjects, including three modern langs (French, German, Spanish – several native speakers on staff), choose two in year 8, two or three in year 9; setting in maths from year 7; max class size 25; children encouraged to go beyond homework. Separate sciences in year 9 and have to choose two from art, music, technology and drama. Praise for teachers from a disconcertingly poised and articulate, very new year 7 boy – 'They're fun and good at what they do'; 'They're firm but help you understand,' added a voice from year 9; 'You're encouraged to learn independently, not just rely on the teacher,' from a year 13. According to parents, the teachers know their pupils well as individuals, expect them to work hard, do the best they can, but recognise not all will excel. Various kinds of commendations for especially good work or effort – certificates, letters and postcards to parents, assembly presentations. Several computer suites, huge language lab in girls' division with masses of PCs.

All departments impressively active outside the classroom – workshops, trips, lecture visits, science shows, exchanges; success in a wide range of external competitions; psychology department has 'adopted' a female Bonobo at Twycross Zoo. Lively English – strong creative writing, eg slam poetry workshop, literature quizzes, play trips, videoed performances of book reviews for World Book Day by year 7-9 classes, participation in BBC News School Report Day; trip to BBC at Salford for boys to work with film-making equipment.

Scholars have extensive enrichment programme – eg extra modern language in year 9 or Latin; some activities run by sixth formers, who create and deliver workshops at feeder junior schools; residentials on very stimulating topics going well beyond the curriculum for years 8-11.

SENCo confident school can accommodate mild versions of dys-strata, Asperger's, ADD/ADHD, visual and hearing impaired plus physical disability (but boys would find the last more problematic, owing to the geography of their part of the site). She is a qualified dyslexia and literacy specialist, with two p/t dyslexia specialists and TAs for class support, in and outside class. Extra charge for individual dyslexia session (pairs possible); all departments have a member of staff who links with learning support department. Infant and junior division learning support co-ordinators overseen by foundation head of learning support. All year 7s and later entries screened for dyslexia. Well resourced generally – school 'happy to provide what's needed'. Homework club at lunchtime provides refuge for less secure pupils.

Games, options, the arts: Very strong sports – right now, on the existing site, there are 25 acres of playing fields (main ones for matches, Derby Fields, one mile away); Astros with floodlighting; four new netball courts for girls; boys' and girls' divisions have large gyms but no modern sports hall (yet). Wide range – the usuals plus golf, sailing, orienteering, fencing, skiing: caters for the keen and those who just want enjoyment. Very successful rugby (boys and girls), hockey, trampolining, netball and cheerleading: witness a cabinet crammed with elaborate, glittering red, blue and silver trophies (no English modesty here) – a shelf literally collapsed beneath their weight; riding, swimming (despite having to use the town's leisure centre). An Olympic gymnast, two British biathlon champions (all female); several pupils represent their county or region.

Music huge and very impressive – full and string orchestras, various bands, including jazz – Big Band highly regarded locally; various choirs; lots of concerts at school and in the community; participation in youth orchestras (Hallé, Wigan jazz, Stockport symphony, guitar ensemble). Some in Cheshire and national youth choir; recent tour to Budapest. Wide range of music including film, blues and barbershop.

Unusually ambitious plays produced – next one planned is Blood Brothers (girls taking lead role); biannual musical; art department creates excellent sets and props. Whole school productions plus separate boys' and girls' ones; years 8-10 panto.

Tremendous multimedia art (we saw more 3D than 2D), displayed throughout the school – we were struck by some interesting glass work (own kiln, gets remnants from local window company), very realistic cakes made of coloured felt on a stand and expressive year 8 ceramic masks. A level students have produced video and sound installation exam pieces. Annual residential in North Wales; 12 students selected for Cheshire GCSE gifted and talented residential. Busy DT – talks, trips, competitions, eg Lego League.

Heaps of (mixed) societies and activities – DofE, sixth form community action, sound technology, arts and philosophy soc, European youth parliament, Amnesty International, debating, fair trade, Arabic. Vigorous financial arm – Young Enterprise, investors club – 30 teams across the three divisions competed in student challenge, sixth form economics department honoured by Bank of England for 10 years' outstanding contribution to their National Target 2.0 competition. Sixth form council; charities and social committee raises thousands of pounds; sixth formers help run clubs for younger pupils. Good careers programme – work experience week for all in year 10, more possible in sixth form, one full-time careers officer.

Fab trips – Cerne, skiing in Colorado (pricy), château study week in Normandy for sixth form linguists (tasty), also (mixed) chateau trip at end of year 7 (memorable); year 13s can do work experience in France with a company, returning just before their oral exam. Rugby tour to Canada, hockey to South Africa, history trip to China, diving in Egypt, World Challenge to India. Very testing outdoor activities trips – coasteering, canoeing, surfing; mixed ages for these leading to friendships across years. The pupils we met all very appreciative of this wealth of opportunities – the only downside was finding enough time to fit in all they wanted to do.

Background and atmosphere: Founded by Sir John Percyvale, Lord Mayor of London, in 1502, as a grammar school. Moved to present site in 1854; in 1946 became independent fee-paying school. Girls were introduced into the sixth form in 1986 and in 1992 new girls' and (by now) co-ed junior divisions established in refurbished ex-Macclesfield High School in Fence Avenue, about a mile away, followed by infant department in 2007. Lovely views of the Peak District. C of E with ecumenical ethos.

The boys' and sixth form campus is very large, mostly pleasant red-brick or sandstone and harmonious modern additions around a central green fringed with trees. A bridge over a street leads to sixth form block and practice pitches. Colourful, attractively cluttered Alan Cooper library with masses of magazines and DVDs as well as books, wooden beamed sixth form study area on upper floor, honours board for First World War war dead on wall, with an OB's medals beneath it. Separate junior library with lots of fiction. 'The school will get you any magazines, newspapers and books you need,' according to a sixth former. Sixth have common room, study area and café in own centre.

Separate girls' division (370 girls, three forms of 25 per year) and boys' (500 boys, four forms of 25) reduces gender stereotyping re subject choices – several boys choose art and girls maths and science at A level – and allows flexibility of teaching approaches; year 11 house captains and prefects allow more and earlier opportunities to develop leadership skills, eg mentoring younger pupils, supplemented by plenty of co-ed activities and trips.

Academics well balanced by the extracurricular – head of boys' division observed that the introduction of music at start and end of assemblies encouraged respect for more than just sporting prowess: all achievements celebrated. School council meets every three weeks, issues frequent questionnaires to canvass views, proposals heeded. Parents and pupils feel it has a friendly atmosphere. Food praised for quality and choice (smart cards used); sixth allowed into town in lunch hour.

Almost all the pupils smart-ish – indeed we wondered whether one very elegantly turned out sixth former in suit with waistcoat was a member of staff (but were relieved to see more than one boy with a tie veering towards half mast).

School moving to a completely new campus, costing 60 million smackers, in 2020.

Pastoral care, well-being and discipline: Older pupils do reading work with juniors, helps transition to senior school. Year 6 taster day (our year 11 tour guides still remembered their fish, chips and chocolate cake lunch); year 7s said older pupils very helpful if you get lost; bonding form residential trip early in first term. Sixth formers train as peer supporters for years 7-9. We were assured bullying not a problem – the school would stop it immediately: 'It's something King's wouldn't tolerate because it just shouldn't happen'. Mixed age activities encourage general friendliness and there's 'always a teacher you can talk to about problems', as well as the nurse or heads of year. Sixth in tutor groups of 12; induction morning and welcome evening organised by year 13s for new year 12s.

Pupils and parents: From various backgrounds (majority professional, some farming families and a sizeable minority of blue-collar workers) – 'very rounded parents,' one told us; AstraZeneca based locally, also commuter belt for airline companies at Manchester Airport. Praise for speed of response to queries – 'totally fabulous lady in the office, who will put you in touch with everyone you need to communicate with'; 'Teachers get back to you soon if you phone'; email alerts, regular letters with email addresses of people to contact.

Extensive catchment area, about 20 mile radius – lots of bus routes, 10 minute walk from train station to both sites. Three-quarters white British. Lively, confident, happy and energetic pupils. According to head of girls' division, 'Quirkiness and slight eccentricities are liked', girls of different types 'rub along well' – but they need to want to learn, to be happy.

Entrance: For external candidates, eleven plus exam mid January. King's junior children are continually assessed and provided there are no issues (which, in any event, are picked up in plenty of time) transfer to the senior school, making up 50 per cent of the intake in year 7. Roughly 10-15 per cent entry to sixth from outside – need at least four 7s and two 6s at GCSE, plus interview (parents as well) and reference from current school.

Exit: Some 20-30 per cent leave post GCSE – mainly to take vocational courses at FE colleges; some may want a more relaxed, less structured atmosphere.

After A level students depart to a wide range of universities – Nottingham most popular, then Nottingham Trent, Manchester, Newcastle and Birmingham; one Cambridge 2018 and six medics/dentists; two musicians off to conservatoires. Broad mix of subjects including biomedical sciences, veterinary sciences, geography and law. Three off to apprenticeships (Astra Zeneca, Ernst & Young and Rolls Royce).

Money matters: Means-tested bursaries – strong performance in entrance exam needed; scholarships for outstanding performance – worth £1,200pa; both music scholarships worth £1,200pa and music exhibitions worth £600pa toward cost of musical tuition awarded at time of entrance exam – minimum of grade 3 required. Quincentenary bursaries for new sixth formers. Sibling discount.

Remarks: Interesting marriage of traditional values with progressive educational approaches. Dedicated, astute head continues to augur well for King's next phase in 2020 with the big move.

K

Kingsbridge Community College

Balkwill Road, Kingsbridge, Devon TQ7 1PL

Ages 11-18 **Pupils** 1,399 **Sixth form** 331

01548 852641
www.kingsbridgecollege.org.uk

Principal: Since 2016, Kenny Duncan. Qualified at Moray House, Edinburgh University (also has an MA in education from Bath) before moving south to teach in England. Has taught in schools across the south west and also supported schools as a consultant and a subject adviser. Assistant principal at John

Cabot Academy (Bath) and deputy head at Ralph Allen (Bath) before taking up his first headship at Sidmouth College in 2012. Totally committed to comprehensive, inclusive education. Highly visible about the college, greeting pupils at the entrance in the mornings, seeing them onto buses in the afternoons.

KCC was one of the first schools to be designated as a teaching school, and over the last few years over 600 people have been trained here. It is now part of a multi-academy trust that includes Dartmouth College and four primary schools.

Academic matters: Excellent results: in 2018, 52 per cent A*-B grades at A level and 20 per cent A*/A. At GCSE, 70 per cent achieved 9-4 in both maths and English, and 23 per cent of grades were A*-A/9-7. Most subjects are taught in ability sets. A language, either French or Spanish, is compulsory, as is RE and a GCSE in IT business and communication systems. In 2018, 41 per cent passed the EBacc. Twenty-five options at A level plus BTecs in science, sports, music, media and design. The college also offers work-based learning programmes, with local placements in childcare, customer service, business administration and retail.

Maths and science are very popular at A level – there are two or three sets for each subject. There are currently 90 students taking chemistry – that's one in four sixth formers. This may have something to do with the new science block, opened in 2015. There are 12 practical labs that are designed to encourage working together in groups, pairs or as a class. To celebrate the opening of the building, there was a Science Week. Students made rockets, got involved in dissections and ate insects from Paignton Zoo. The week ended with the annual Saturday Science event when families came along too. Two of the younger KCC students (aged just 12 and 13) recently won the Faraday Challenge for building the best rocket – their launch vehicle, equipped with LED warning lights and brakes, sent their rocket more than 4m into the air.

A recent project, the Learning Café for year 11 students, has been a huge success. The staff here obviously know that the way to a teenager's heart is through their stomach. So in exchange for some decent grub, pupils turn up regularly, and in their droves, for their revision classes. One parent explained to us, 'I have been extraordinarily impressed by the support his year group has received throughout the GCSE period. This has included (a) an evening explaining revision techniques and approaches to parents (invaluable); (b) after-school Learning Café for all subjects; (c) continual revision sessions throughout the exam period itself; (d) additional exam/revision sessions including on a Sunday which I thought was well beyond the call of duty; (e) Facebook updates and reminders for students.' Another said, 'I know that the school has excellent GCSE results and is constantly striving to improve them, but this year, as a parent of a GCSE child, I really saw the commitment, time and investment that all the teachers put in – not just for the students but for the parents as well.'

The learning support department is in the student support centre. There are 18 TAs and specialist teachers providing one-to-one, group or in-class support. There is a lower than average number of pupils with SENs at KCC. However, that doesn't mean that the facilities and teaching are not of a high standard. In the English centre there are small rooms used solely for one-to-one literacy sessions. Ofsted said, 'Very effective and targeted support for students with learning difficulties and/ or disabilities, particularly in literacy and numeracy skills, allows them to make outstanding progress.' One parent, whose child has recently been diagnosed with dyspraxia, said, 'KCC staff have faith in his abilities and understand how to manage and motivate him to do his best.... In fact many of the subject teachers have gone above and beyond to provide [him] with extra support and mentoring.'

All sixth formers take part in leadership and enrichment activities. The choices include mentoring, supporting teachers, working for a charity, doing work experience, taking a sports leader award, and practising mock interviews. The college constantly strives to raise aspirations and parents told us, 'Study, support and advice on careers has been very good, and guidance through the UCAS medicine application was superb.' There are also regular guest speakers and visits, most recently the army medical services, the RAF cadets and the royal marines. One parent told us, 'Our studious daughter is thriving. She wants to be a midwife and is being given every encouragement.'

Games, options, the arts: Great sports facilities on site and lots of success all round. One parent told us, 'Football has always been the poor relation in terms of sports at the school – rugby is king here.' Great success for rugby, netball and badminton teams recently. However, one parent said, 'Most team sport clubs tend to end up just being populated by the kids who are best at that sport. Another team for the less able would be good and may encourage others to take up things they thought they weren't good at.' Surfing is unsurprisingly big and KCC was crowned champion again at the South Devon Inter Schools Surf Competition. It also includes the taekwondo world champion and the judo national champion, plus two brothers who have recently taken part in a GB ski camp. Outdoor pursuits like Ten Tors and DofE are very popular, and the annual gym and dance show brings sport, music and dance together.

Incredibly high standard of artwork displayed around the school. On our visit we saw scary clay pieces entitled Man and Machine, contemporary dresses by the textiles students, kitchen designs by the graphic designers and superimposed photos of trees by the budding photographers. They have exhibited locally and at the Centre for Creative Industries at Exeter College, and collaborated with students from the Exeter Royal Deaf Academy to learn more about art and British sign language, and how each other learn.

Well-equipped art, photography and technology departments – there are lathes, welding machines, a forge, a 3D printer and a laser cutter. We saw an up-cycled chair made from car doors, art deco iPod docking stations, lamps, boat storage and a POS display made for local company South Devon Chilli Farm. Students are encouraged to go on design residentials, and local companies run design and manufacturing workshops.

Drama productions take place in the main hall where, at the push of a button, tiered seating for 200 people appears from the walls. Plus there's a professional lighting rig and sound booth. Past productions have included Jesus Christ Superstar, Miss Saigon and The Sound of Music. A collaboration between drama and business studies departments resulted in a prize winning marketing campaign to promote their 'fantastic' production of Richard III for the Shakespeare Schools Festival.

Light and airy music building hosts numerous bands and choirs in year round concerts – recently an evening of musical theatre and jazz pieces from the 30s and 40s, entitled Puttin' on The Ritz.

As well as the usual sports, drama and music clubs, there's trampolining, busking, animation club, a radio station and science clinics. Students gain house points by taking part, which gives them an extra incentive. Annually there's Challenge Week for years 7 to 10, that could be anything from a week surfing to a cultural trip to Iceland. During this week, year 12 goes on work experience. All Year 9s do half a term of citizenship, where they work once a week in a setting such as a charity shop or an old peoples' home.

Regular visits to theatres and galleries, annual language exchanges and ski trips plus expeditions biannually to places like Ecuador, Kenya, Argentina and Peru.

Background and atmosphere: Founded in the 16th century as Kingsbridge Grammar School, it moved to the current site in the 1930s with just 200 boys. Became a comprehensive on two sites in 1976. It's been on one site since 2002, and has had more than £14 million invested in new buildings and facilities. Major recent developments include the new English centre, the sixth form centre (including the media department with Apple Macs and the latest editing software) and a science block. It is a fantastic learning environment, thoughtfully designed inside and out.

There are multiple cafés, so no queues at lunchtime. One specialises in pasta and curry, another in paninis and wraps. Plus there's a salad bar and a free piece of fruit with every meal. The whole site is very well maintained and has unexpected additions like a climbing wall on one side of a building, and a totem pole, made on site by local stonemasons with KCC pupils.

Students are well presented and polite; they seem happy, relaxed and calm. And they all look noticeably healthy – all that surfing and country air is obviously working wonders on these teenagers.

Pastoral care, well-being and discipline: We spoke to one parent who told us, 'While working briefly as a governor at the school, I had the chance to work with the pastoral care team, which left me in awe at the amount of effort they put in to help the development of children less fortunate than my own.' Another said, 'KCC is in a relatively well off area, but of course there are pockets of deprivation – not uncommon in rural areas – and I think it's very important to note that KCC doesn't just work with "nice middle class kids" – they constantly strive to get every child to achieve to the very best of their ability.'

Lower than average number of pupils have been excluded; the last was four years ago. 'We can't guarantee bullying won't happen, but we can guarantee we will deal with it.' They will invest as much time as necessary to try to change attitudes and behaviour at a deeper level. Recently, staff decided to mentor one troublesome lad rather than exclude him – when he left (with qualifications under his belt) he sent a card that said, 'Thank you, you changed my life.'

Pupils and parents: KCC is at the centre of the community here. The majority of the staff have or have had children at the school. The catchment area is small, and so people tend to know each other. A fair number of families have relocated here; one mother told us, 'We chose to come to Kingsbridge because of the quality of the school. We considered private schools after GCSEs but decided to stay with KCC, and it has totally lived up to our expectations.' What could be improved? 'Sixth form transport for rural areas. A big cost for parents living outside Kingsbridge.'

Entrance: Designated catchment area. Good induction and settling in period, one parent told us: 'This was seamless and well managed with transition days and sporting events. [My children] were very proud to have started and to "belong" to KCC.' Another added, 'Fantastic. Made our shy daughter feel very secure.'

Entry to the sixth form requires 4+ grades at GCSE. Entry onto NVQ level 2 courses are by interview with no prior qualifications required. Attendance and attitude are the main criteria.

Exit: On average 70 per cent of pupils stay on for sixth form. Around 70 per cent of sixth formers go onto university. One to Cambridge in 2018 (computer science) and two medics. Other popular university choices include Falmouth and Plymouth.

Money matters: There is a trust fund to help with trips.

Remarks: A large but friendly community school. Fantastic facilities and so many opportunities for all types. KCC works on traditional values like respect and good behaviour, but provides cutting edge opportunities – not just equipment, but also their approach to learning. If you live in Kingsbridge, you are very lucky indeed.

K

Kingsley Junior School

Linked with Kingsley School

Northdown Road, Bideford, Devon EX39 3LY

Ages 4–11 **Pupils** 268 **Boarders** 1–2 (from year 5)

Fees: Day £5,940 – £10,035; Boarding £16,740 – £25,920 pa

01237 426200
www.kingsleyschoolbideford.co.uk/junior-school/

Head: Since September 2017, Andrew Trythall, previously head of junior school and head of music, as well as boarding parent, at Hebron School in South India. He was educated at Kingsley School's next door neighbour, Shebbear College, before going onto the University of East Anglia to study music, where he specialised in recording engineering and electro-acoustic music, and later did his PGCE. As a teenager, he met his wife Joy in Bideford, and they now have four children. Before teaching in India, Mr Trythall taught in Suffolk at Gislingham Primary and Sir Robert Hitcham's Primary as an ICT specialist, running ICT courses for primary schools in Suffolk, and speaking at conferences around the UK and in Europe. He is the author of three books about teaching ICT, as well as writing a monthly column in Nursery World.

Entrance: Non-selective entry to junior school. There is also a nursery that offers dedicated year-round 8am-6pm care for children from three months. One family who relocated looked at several schools in the area, and said 'in the end it was decided upon Kingsley as the final say was what the children themselves wanted.' Another told us, 'When school started, the children seemed to settle in quite quickly and find their way around the school easily.'

Boarding available though very few takers. Junior boarders are looked after in the senior school younger boys' house by a very friendly houseparent/mum and her husband. One of the best 'family homes' we've seen.

Exit: Some 80-90 per cent go on to the senior school. Assessment is for awards and scholarships. Parents told us, 'It was a very smooth transition from Kingsley Junior School to the secondary school.' In their final year at the junior school, pupils and parents are invited to the senior school to meet teachers and have a tour, including the year 7-9 centre; a dedicated area for younger senior pupils which includes their own common room.

Remarks: Situated on the same campus as the senior school, the junior school has use of all facilities including a purpose-built theatre, a multi-sport gym, 25 acres of playing fields, woodland, an adventure playground and a forest school. They have their own very decent-sized hall that opens out onto their own playing field. As part of the Methodist group of schools, there are two all-school assemblies each week, to share and celebrate achievements and birthdays. Senior pupils often pop over to perform too. One recently treated the little ones to his own rendition of Postman Pat, and another, an aspiring rock star from the upper sixth, took the time out to sing for his younger friends.

For such a small junior school, great sports success. They have reached the U10 football finals, the indoor athletics final, plus three year 4 girls represented the south west in the national Milano gymnastic finals. There's also the very popular and successful Kingsley School judo club plus netball, hockey, cross-country and rugby. A new football coaching programme has recently been introduced for boys, girls and teachers too. The school regularly invites other local schools in for things like 'handball activity day'. A popular sport in the senior school, the day gave everyone a chance to try it for the first time. Good links with local primary schools for tournaments, and annually there is a cross-country event at Kingsley that involves around 1,000 runners from 35 schools.

Throughout the school, teaching is based around the national curriculum, 'but not as a be-all and end-all in itself.' For example, 4-6 year-olds enjoy swimming, forest schools, arts and crafts and French. Afternoon performances of French songs are sell-outs, apparently. The 7-11 year-olds have classes in food technology, personal, social, health and moral education, Spanish and DT. The school has a specialist dyslexia centre on site for senior school pupils, but junior pupils do have access to specialist teachers if needed. Other SENs catered for include dyspraxia, Asperger's and issues like behavioural problems that are often associated with dyslexia. Classes are not streamed in the junior school.

Music, singing, dancing and drama are a big part of life here. The junior choir practices during the lunch break for concerts and regular performances at local nursing homes or festivals. Most pupils learn an instrument, and as well as extra singing and drama lessons, ballet, tap and modern dance are also available. Plenty of opportunities to perform with productions like Peace Child, Charlie and the Chocolate Factory and Joseph. Productions are led by years 5 and 6, but everybody gets involved making props in forest school or painting sets in art classes.

Art is important at Kingsley and we were pleased to hear how much they make the most of their beautiful surroundings. For year 1 a typical class on natural art may involve a walk around the grounds followed by a session creating their art pieces, inspired by recent lessons on certain artists. Another class, who were inspired by a trip to a local art gallery, have been making ice sculptures.

After-school clubs from 4-4.50pm. After-care can be arranged until 6pm. Good range of activities, from Mandarin Chinese to gymnastics, from science to Lego. Trips include the local lifeboat station, Ilfracombe tunnels, the Roman Baths, Exmoor Zoo and local farms. In year 6 there is a residential trip; last one was to Somerset for abseiling, grass sledging and circus skills.

This small, friendly school offers a bit more than just a standard education, whether it's planting trees, or singing French songs, or introducing a new sport. They extend this invitation to other schools regularly through sports, and also the annual children's festival, packed with bands, street dances, cakes, bouncy castles, welly throwing, face painting and candy floss. And last year, they even managed to sneak a chocolate-themed week onto the curriculum. This approach to learning particularly helps children that may need some encouragement, or are struggling to learn. As one parent put it, 'Kingsley School takes the child, and has in place lots of systems and strategies to help with the development of confidence and self-esteem.'

Kingsley School

Linked with Kingsley Junior School

Northdown Road, Bideford, Devon EX39 3LY

Ages 11–18 **Pupils** 151 **Sixth form** 56 **Boarders** 63 full, 3 weekly/flexi

Fees: Day £12,660 – £16,665; Boarding £20,985 – £30,720 pa

01237 426200
www.kingsleyschoolbideford.co.uk

Headmaster: Since January 2017, Pete Last, previously deputy head pastoral, senior housemaster, head of boarding and housemaster of a boys' house at Stowe School. Read geography at Cambridge and has a masters in educational leadership from Buckingham. Married to Debs, an art specialist. Both from Kent but met in India while working at Hebron International School in Ooty. Returned after six years to teaching posts at Lord Wandsworth College in Hampshire, also running a boarding house, moving to Stowe nine years later. Passionate about education (and Arsenal).

Academic matters: In 2018, at GCSE, 12 per cent A*-A/7-9 grades. At A level, 61 per cent A*/B and 45 per cent A*/A grades. Fourteen A levels on offer, plus BTecs in business, outdoor education and performing arts, a Cambridge Technical in sport, a diploma in food, and the EPQ. French, Spanish and theatre studies offered if sufficient demand. Maths is strong and around 60 per cent opt for it at A level. Other top performing subjects include English and geography. A language is compulsory up to Year 9. BTec in engineering is available at GCSE level, replacing DT.

Admits 25 per cent dyslexic pupils. Other SENs are catered for, mainly those associated with dyslexia, like behavourial issues, but nothing too complex. In the Grenville Dyslexia Centre on the campus, pupils are taught English and maths in small (5-10) dyslexia-only classes, by qualified SEN teachers. One-to-one tuition and support in after-school prep sessions also available. One parent commented, 'My younger child who is dyslexic has been given strong support from the dyslexic centre staff and enjoys attending it. It is a friendly and inviting place to be and recently had extras added to entice the pupils, such as tea and toast! We (both parent and pupil) have been asked how the centre could improve and so I can see that they are striving to keep up with expectations.'

There are now regular and formal meetings where mainstream and Grenville staff exchange information on individual pupils, and discuss how best to teach them. Teachers use visual aids for all lessons, and reminders of current topic or homework tasks are clearly displayed on the wall. One teacher told us this is all done in a subtle, unobtrusive way 'without anyone blinking an eye.' One parent said, 'It is a friendly school and the staff seem to work well together for the good of the pupils.'

The value added is impressive; SEN pupils are given good support in class and in exams and do well. One recent leaver with A level grades A*, A and B had been told by his previous school he would never amount to anything. With hard work and the specialist support of the dyslexia centre he has more than proved them wrong. Some take fewer subjects, often dropping a language, if it helps them to focus. There is 'no stigma' at Kingsley and children are given the confidence to learn. One parent said, 'Kingsley School has positively changed our profoundly dyslexic son. He was very passive and feared failure, he felt that he was not an achiever and his contribution was of little value, but in the six years that he has attended Kingsley School, we have seen him grow into a very confident and happy young man.' We heard similar stories from several parents. One parent of an overseas boarder said, 'He identifies completely with the school and we are very happy to see his progress in developing self-confidence and regaining fun in learning.'

The centre's mantra is 'Don't make dyslexia an excuse.' This approach relies upon a nurturing, safe-to-learn classroom environment, and interactive, hands-on, multisensory and memorable teaching methods. In year 7 they focus on spelling and touch-typing. In years 8 and 9, the focus is reading, using a scribe and learning to use software like Dragon Dictate and Read and Write gold. And in years 10 and 11, it's speed-reading, exam strategies and dealing with exam stress. One parent confided, 'Before he started at Kingsley School at the age of 9 we had very low expectations, but now our son is a year away from taking his GCSEs and we are approaching them with a confidence for his future and that is solely down to the school.'

Games, options, the arts: In line with the school's 'quirkiness', the main sports are judo, handball and surfing. Judo is up to Olympic standard, one pupil plays handball in the U19 England team, and another is a member of the GB surfing squad. Surfers and windsurfers do well in local, regional and national competitions and pupils regularly win national titles in gymnastics, netball, judo and biathlon. The U15 girls' football team is very successful, and there are regular weekend fixtures for rugby, cricket, hockey, athletics, table tennis, swimming and cross-country. Golf has just recently been introduced.

K

There's a choir and a small orchestra – numbers are limited, so quartets and ensembles are more common. Regular performances like An evening of ...The Bare Necessities... Pie Jesus...My Favourite Things to Guns and Roses... Annual collaborations with the drama department have included A Midsummer Night's Dream and Alice in Wonderland, in the 400 seat theatre. Pupils take part in the National Theatre's Connections programme and haved perform at the Theatre Royal, Plymouth and the Bristol Old Vic.

Art department commands the whole of the top floor of the main building, School House. Two huge studios, plus photographic facilities. Some great, and very large pieces on display, with plenty more space to fill. Annual exhibition at the local Burton Art Gallery.

After-school activities include choirs, Mandarin Chinese, judo, trampolining, debating, surfing, yoga, gardening and DofE. The local scouts and cubs are based on the school campus and are very popular. Plenty of trips locally to places like the Eden Project, Cheddar Gorge and Exmoor and further afield to eg London, Paris and Iceland.

Boarding: Currently a 70:30 boy:girl split amongst boarders, 65 per cent from overseas (two-thirds Asian and a third European). Majority board full time, but some short-term boarders from Spain and Germany, usually to brush up on their language skills for a term or two. Three large, well looked after boarding houses on the school campus: Belvoir for girls, Carisbrooke for junior boys and Longfield for senior boys.

Most houseparents have children attending the school. Gap students and house prefects add big brother or sister role models to the mix. Brilliant pastoral care. One parent said, 'He felt immediately at home and still appreciates the warm-hearted atmosphere of the school and the boarding complex.' The houseparent we met in the younger boys' house really does run the house like a mum: she was friendly, welcoming and has created one of the best family homes we've seen. The fairy lights are always on when the kids come home, there's bowls of fruit and plants in the lounge, two dogs and even a boyfriend/girlfriend sofa. Next to the huge lounge there's a pool table and table tennis table. Decent kitchen; they would like to upgrade it but the boys don't want this: they love it the way it is, apparently. Rooms are doubles or triples, the odd single for older pupils and a six-bedder for flexi-boarders.

Plenty of activities, but pupils are also given downtime, just like home. No Saturday lessons but there are sports fixtures or shopping trips in the afternoons, and activities like quad biking, combat zone, cinema, bowling, climbing, theatre, zoo, theme parks and local city trips on Sundays. As soon as the weather brightens up, surf's up, and as much time as possible is spent making the most of north Devon's beach life. Awesome. One parent told us, 'He enjoys it very much. He likes living in this big family.'

No set exeat weekend, a real plus for Forces families. Kingsley also runs its own guardianship scheme so overseas boarders can now stay at school, in their own rooms, during half-terms. Around 50 boarders currently take advantage of this scheme.

Background and atmosphere: Formed in 2009 by the amalgamation of Edgehill College and Grenville College. School House is the main building, an inviting white building with a 'Kiss and Drop ends here' sign cheekily sending parents on their way.

The sixth form centre is separate, in another spacious building. Well-equipped with a modern café area, social area with pool table, table football, piano and large dining table. Several study rooms for small groups, all being well-used on our visit. No uniform but there is a dress code, loosely described as 'business dress'. Sixth form social events take place throughout the year culminating in the summer ball. Leadership opportunities and positions of responsibility are available as prefects, sports captains, competitive house captains and within the boarding houses. Students are also encouraged to act as mentors to younger students and can do work experience in the junior school.

Pastoral care, well-being and discipline: Not formally rigid, 'but clear red lines.' Parents said, 'We welcome very much the straight rules concerning, for example, smoking, leaving the school ground and so on.' This is a small school community and along with good pastoral care including form tutors, heads of years, house parents, school sister and the chaplain, pupils are given the 'confidence that they will be heard' and 'can have their say,' even if the school doesn't always necessarily agree. As a Methodist school, Christian ethos and values are embedded into life here in a subtle way. One parent believed, 'Pastoral care and academic encouragement are key points to the school and are their strengths, I feel.' Device free in years 7-9.

Pupils and parents: Day pupils come from a wide local area and school buses go as far as Croyde, North Molton, Torrington and Holsworthy. Termly airport buses for overseas boarders.

The school communicates well with parents with the usual channels of emails, letters and reports. Queries or concerns are responded to quickly, 'usually within a matter of a couple of hours,' one parent told us. 'We also have phone calls from the form tutors to make sure that there are no concerns.' Another said, 'We have regular contact with the dyslexic centre, and in fact any teacher is readily available either personally or via email.' Another: 'The teachers all seem professional and friendly and I feel that they care for the well-being of my children.'

Entrance: Open days, plus taster days and nights. Entry by entrance test and interview. Entry at sixth form is a decent set of GCSE results, school reports and the right attitude.

No problems with settling in: 'From day one he absolutely loved it! We have never heard him say he doesn't want to attend.'

Exit: Some 40-50 per cent of day pupils leave after GSCEs, many to go the local free colleges. Most boarders stay on to the sixth form. Nearly all go to university, with a wide range – from Cambridge (one in 2018 – natural sciences) to Cardiff Met, Imperial and the Royal School of Speech and Drama – to do subjects varying from creative writing to neuroscience to business management. Some take a gap year, go into employment, or return to their home country to continue their studies.

Money matters: Academic, performing arts or sports scholarships available at 11 and 13. Sixth form scholarships are based on GCSE performance, or excellence in music, drama, art and sport. Means-tested bursaries offered, plus bursaries to Forces families, and sibling discounts. In the senior school, the fees for the dyslexia department and EAL are additional.

Remarks: What teenager wouldn't want to combine school life with beaches, surfing and friends from around the world? That may all sound too much like fun rather than education, but Kingsley has got the balance right; a great campus, an open, caring approach, and specialist teachers. The dyslexic children at Kingsley progress further than anyone's expectations and so it's not surprising that one parent told us, 'We can honestly say it was and will remain the best decision we have made for his education.'

Kingswood School

    92

Lansdown Road, Bath BA1 5RG

Ages 11–18 **Pupils** 772 **Sixth form** 228 **Boarders** 156 full, 32 weekly

Fees: Day £15,183; Boarding £23,868 – £32,727 pa

01225 734200
www.kingswood.bath.sch.uk

Headmaster: Since 2008, Simon Morris MA PGCE NPQH (early 50s). Educated at Ipswich School (he is one of three current HMC heads – the others are Mark Bailey, high master of St Paul's, and Nick Gregory, head of Wycliffe College – to have attended the school). Read modern and medieval languages at Cambridge, then went into the City, where he qualified as a chartered accountant with Arthur Andersen. He grew up in a boarding school (his father was deputy headmaster of The Royal Hospital School) and admits that 'the call of teaching was pretty strong'. PGCE at Canterbury Christ Church University, followed by first job at Warwick School (he became head of German after a year). Head of modern foreign languages, then housemaster at The Leys. Deputy head at St John's, Leatherhead for seven years prior to Kingswood headship. 'I'm not saying that every day is easy but I have never regretted my change of career,' he says.

First-ever non-Methodist head of Kingswood. Intensely proud of the school – particularly its sense of community and breadth of opportunity. Passionate about instilling high but attainable standards in every individual and results have risen under his leadership. School isn't highly selective but head says pupils have to be 'academically able' – or as he puts it, 'doers who want to get stuck in and have a go at things'. Supported by two deputies (one academic, one pastoral). Taught languages when he first arrived but now teaches PSHCE to year 7 pupils. 'It's a brilliant way to get to know them,' he says. Visible around the school, approachable and easy to talk to – 'a round peg in a round hole,' as we said last time.

Wife Caroline teaches modern languages at Kingswood (she has lots of state school experience too) and they have three children. Elder two were pupils at Kingswood and are now at university (one doing medicine at King's College London, the other reading geography at Sheffield) and the youngest is still at the school. A keen sportsman (cricket and golf), he also enjoys travel and reading. Lives in a house on-site but family (plus labrador) decamps to their house near Axmouth in the holidays.

Leaving in July 2020.

Academic matters: Results are as good as some other co-ed schools with illustrious names. In 2018, 46 per cent A*/A at A level. At GCSE, 68 per cent A*-A/9-7. School says it does brilliantly on value-added – apparently in the top 20 nationally. Masses of subject choice, with 24 subjects on offer at A level and more than 20 at GCSE. Most students take three A levels (some add the EPQ) and a few, particularly mathematicians, do four. Impressive deputy head (academic) has focused on academic development and says the school does everything it can to give students 'total free choice' of A level subjects. 'We don't pigeonhole anyone here,' she says – a claim borne out by a talented artist who at the time of our visit had just won a place to study medicine yet had managed to do A level art too.

At GCSE the majority take 11 subjects, with all doing English, English literature, maths, three separate sciences (a few do double award) and religious studies. Most take at least one language (French, Spanish or German) although some requiring study support may not. Study support department has three full-time staff and runs an informal drop-in centre for students needing help with anything from managing their time to learning how to revise. Independent support programmes in place for those with specific learning difficulties such as dyslexia and dyscalculia. One mother told us: 'The school isn't just interested in the kids who are going to get three A*s at A level. They mean it when they say they are interested in children with all kinds of talents and skills.'

Games, options, the arts: Sport is a big deal here and there are lots of unbeaten teams. Main sports for boys are rugby, hockey, cricket, tennis, athletics and swimming while girls do hockey, netball, tennis, athletics, rounders, cricket and swimming. School fields at least two teams per year group, with 30 fixtures against other schools each week. Up until year 10 all pupils do a double period of PE every week, plus games. From year 11 some opt for social sports, including aerobics (80 pupils doing this when we visited), cycling, cross-country, multi-gym, orienteering, equestrian sports and more. 'We try and give them more options as they go up the school,' explains the director of sports and PE.

Great facilities, including eight rugby pitches, three cricket squares, two Astroturfs, sports hall and new pavilion. Some pitches are a half-mile walk up the hill but it keeps everyone healthy. School a tad defensive about its 100-year-old swimming pool but says it is 'a great pool to teach in'. Strong links with Bath Rugby Club and the University of Bath.

The arts are outstanding and there is an annual award ceremony for artistically talented pupils in art, drama, DT and music. A third of pupils learn a musical instrument and there's something for performers of all styles and standards. Recent highlights include a performance of Fauré's Requiem, the jazz orchestra playing at the opening event of the Bath International Music Festival and the annual Kingswood Voices Festival, which celebrates the contribution that singers make to the school life.

Drama department has two spaces – a 366-seat theatre and a drama studio. Up to 30 students take drama GCSE each year and between six and 12 do drama and theatre at A level. Three major productions a year and pupils are encouraged to get involved in lighting, sound, stage management and scriptwriting. Unusually, there's a comedy improvisation event for budding comics called Exit Stage Right, loosely based on Whose Line is it Anyway? Art is glorious. Housed in a three-storey arts and crafts style building, it boasts top-notch facilities for drawing, painting, printmaking, sculpture, ceramics and photography. Annual summer art and DT exhibition is a highlight and we saw some breathtaking work, including a vast wire sculpture of a birds' nest by year 8s, a portrait made from tights and pins and a 12-ft long drawing of hands. Sadly, the pupils' monogrammed smocks of old have given away to smart grey aprons embroidered with the Kingswood logo – 'the smocks were too hot,' says the head of art.

Boarding: Even though day pupils outnumber boarders, Kingswood feels like a co-ed boarding school with day pupils. Seven day/boarding houses, some of which are in the process of being updated. The first to be completed, Hall House (for 42 year 9 to 13 boys), is one of the most stylish boarding houses we've seen in a long time, complete with outdoor decking area, wholesome bedrooms (12 en-suite), the housemaster's prized vinyl collection in the common room and views across Bath to the Mendips. We particularly liked the kitchen rules painted on the boys' kitchen wall: 'If it smells, throw it away. If it's dirty, wash it. If you get it out, put it away. If it's on, turn it off.'

Westwood, for year 7 and 8 pupils (some 170 day pupils and 30 boarders), provides a gentle introduction to the big school. Homely and sprawling, the four-storey building is a hive of activity, with the housemaster's friendly border collie running around with the children after school. Girl boarders live on the second floor, boy boarders on the third, all in dormitories of six to eight and out of bounds to day pupils. The Westwood pupils are allowed to grow up in their own time and, rather sweetly we thought, are read a weekly bedtime story – Ted Hughes's The Iron Man has been a particular favourite. Boarders love the place. 'I'm an only child,' one boy told us, 'so being here is like having lots of brothers'. No Saturday school for anyone these days but a vast array of weekend activities. Sports matches on Saturdays and trips to places like Drayton Manor and Legoland on Sundays.

K

Background and atmosphere: The only school founded by John Wesley, who believed that education should engage the heart as well as the head, and the first Methodist one. School opened in 1748 for the sons and daughters of Wesley's friends but was soon restricted to the sons of Methodist preachers and leaders. Went co-ed again in 1974.

School moved from Bristol to its current site (just across the road from the Royal High School) in 1852 and has occupied an imposing collection of purpose-built Victorian gothic buildings on the steep northern slopes above Bath ('Satan's throne', according to Wesley) ever since. Even on a grey day, the views from the school are magnificent. Pupils from all denominations and faiths.

School is ideally placed – a 20-minute walk down the hill into the city, but with a country feel about it. Other buildings of varying age and beauty are dotted around the school's 214 acres of manicured grounds, including the chapel (too small these days to house the whole school, which gathers for religious and secular assemblies in the theatre).

Central dining in splendid gothic hall, with pupils allowed to sit where they like. Food is good, with plenty of choice. We much enjoyed the Moroccan potato salad and lemon couscous with pumpkin seeds on offer when we visited. Uniform is tidy and businesslike, with girls in black blazers, white blouses and tartan skirts and boys in black blazers, charcoal trousers and school ties. Sixth formers wear dark suits – girls in years 12 and 13 are allowed to wear natural make-up, nail varnish and modest jewellery. Sixth form housed in The Dixon, slightly scruffy but much loved sixth form block, completely with cabin-like studies, kitchen and chill-out space.

Pastoral care, well-being and discipline: Head says school is 'non-confrontational' and that discipline structures are clear. 'We are quite prescriptive in terms of what is acceptable and what isn't,' he adds. 'I refuse to be complacent but we don't have a huge discipline issue. We educate pupils to make sensible choices.' Pupils and parents agree. Parents describe pastoral care as 'outstanding' and say communication between school and home is excellent – high praise for the head's regular drop-in sessions and the school's weekly newsletter.

Impressive support structure from year 7 up. Pupils are in house-based tutor groups of around 10 (tutors change in years 8,10 and sixth form). Tutors have day-to-day responsibility for pupils but there's a raft of people to help if issues arise. These include housemasters and housemistresses, head of boarding, medical centre (open 24/7) and chaplain. PSHCE for all, often linked to assemblies. Clear system of sanctions, with emphasis on support and redirection rather than chastisement.

Prefect body is known as PR, with head boy and head girl, deputies (one deputy head boy and two deputy head girls recently) and senior prefects. School council meets once a week – recent topics of discussion range from school menu suggestions to exam timetabling issues. 'We want them to air their views,' says the deputy head (pastoral). Very comprehensive pupil and parent handbook details everything from the school's philosophy and aims to behaviour, health and dress.

Pupils and parents: Moderately to exceedingly affluent families, but not particularly posh. Lots of medics, lawyers, business people and an increasing number who have relocated to Bath from London. Around 10 per cent of pupils from overseas (more than 20 different nationalities represented).

Pupils are polite, friendly, unpretentious and confident. A mother whose two children are weekly boarders told us: 'What I love about Kingswood is that the pupils are an eclectic lot – you've got the city children, the country children and the overseas boarders. I wanted my children to grow up kindly and nicely and they really have here, while at the same time being stretched academically.' Most day pupils come from the north side of Bath (crossing the city during rush hour is horrendous and there are plenty of schools south of the river). Pupils come from as far afield as Calne, Chew Valley, Wiltshire, south Gloucestershire and north-east Bristol. Famous alumni include actor Tim Curry, director and writer Jonathan Lynn, the historian and writer EP Thompson and Reggie Tsiboe, one of the lead singers of pop band Boney M.

Entrance: Increasingly competitive, although year 7 recently expanded from four form entry to five form entry. 'More are applying but we are taking more,' says the head. Main intake is in year 7. Around 50 per cent join from own prep school (they share the same site). Others from 20 preps and primary schools (St Stephen's down the road is a major feeder). Maths, English and non-verbal reasoning tested, plus report from current school and interview. Coaching discouraged. Up to 20 pupils start in year 9, with applicants taking exams in English, maths, non-verbal reasoning, science and a foreign language, plus report from current school and interview. At sixth form stage (20 to 30 newcomers arrive in year 12) students need a minimum of four 6s and two 5s at GCSE.

Exit: Virtually all stay for sixth form. A handful leave, usually due to financial reasons. Almost all to university (three to Oxbridge in 2018 and two to do medicine). Cardiff, Exeter, Oxford Brookes, Leeds and Warwick popular. A few to US universities. A high achieving pupil recently opted to do an apprenticeship with Barclaycard.

Money matters: Academic and special talent (art, DT, drama, music and sport) scholarships offered at years 7, 9 and lower sixth. John Wesley awards available to boarders in year 9 and sixth form – for 'candidates who show the potential to offer a significant all-round contribution to the life of the school'. Head is keen to increase bursary provision throughout.

Remarks: A terrific school, with a culture of creativity, kindness and academic hard work. Kingswood has a strong sense of community, achieves fine results and is definitely on the up.

Knighton House School

Durweston, Blandford Forum, Dorset DT11 0PY

Ages Girls 3-13, boys 3-7 **Pupils** 105 **Boarders** 42 full/weekly/flexi (from 7 years)

Fees: Day £8,100 – £14,850; Boarding £17,400 – £22,800 pa

01258 452065
www.knightonhouse.co.uk

Head: Since September 2017, Robin Gainher BSc. Educated at King's Bruton and the LSE, he's a historian who also teaches some maths. He's sporty, too. A lifelong teacher, he rose to be deputy head at Cranleigh, then head for seven years of Beeston Hall. Left to found an international school in Casablanca. Returned to England when he became concerned about the project's backers. Married to Ali, three daughters. Chair of governors promises 'a raft of new ideas and initiatives'. We grilled Mr Gainher about this. He's not a firebrand, neither does he have a manifesto – 'I'll take it as it comes', he says. So he's a pragmatist. His values? 'Giving children confidence is key. Schools are for children; everything we do should be to make their experience more enriching.' He also believes in 'working closely with parents to share the same philosophy and values'. What may raise eyebrows is that, shock horror, he has never in his life sat astride a horse, nor has Ali. The good news is that they are both devotees of lifelong learning and faithfully undertake to leap into a saddle soonest and embark on their new chapter at a rising trot.

Entrance: Non-selective. Come any time so long as there's room. Invariably an ongoing swelling of numbers by children unhappy at their present school. Taster days. Scholarships. Bursaries (Greenwood Awards) for families who wouldn't otherwise be able to afford it. Parents local, Forces and expats. Not much of an ethnic mix, this being Dorset, but it wouldn't be an issue in the slightest. Always a horizon-broadening contingent from Spain, France, Italy, Belgium.

In 2018, school announced it had 'rebased' fees, and fixed them for two years, effectively reducing day fees by about 15 per cent. Year 4 and 5 boarding fees have also been reduced.

Exit: Most to independent seniors, some to state schools. Experts at matching children to the right one. Dorset offers a full range of choice from highly academic to those offering learning support. Bryanston especially popular, plus Canford, Clayesmore, Lewiston, Milton Abbey, Sherborne Girls, St Mary's Calne and The Thomas Hardye School. Trickier if you're looking for a boyish doppelganger post-pre-prep. Sandroyd, Clayesmore, Port Regis popular.

Remarks: Standing on rising ground above the floodplain of the river Stour in the hushed and tiny village of Durweston (very pretty church), Knighton stands apart from busy world yet is well connected by road to all parts Dorset – and beyond. Once a dower house on the estate of the viscounts Portman, the building is domestic in scale, not a bit stately, a wisteria-clad hodge-podge. The toffs (back in the day) lived a mile away up in the Norman Shaw chateau that is now Bryanston school.

A still-young school founded in 1950 by Peggy and John Booker (parents of controversialist Christopher) as an antidote to their own character-building schooldays which had been defined by all the miseries, chilblains, iron bedsteads, splintery floors and random acts of discipline reckoned indispensable to the raising of young persons in those days. Knighton was instead to be a home from home where girls could be girls, play in the fresh air to their hearts' content, learn kindness, love learning and develop what a present parent identifies as 'bedrock confidence'. Romantic and gently revolutionary in its time, this is mainstream stuff nowadays; everyone else has played catch-up. There's quite a lot of retro-country boarding around just now, done somewhat self-consciously via artful marketing – prospectuses read like fashion shoots for Boden, and look, there's the head in the just the right country casuals, accessorised by a dog. Knighton, a governor told us, is forward-looking, 'we're not seeking to return to the 1960s'. At the same time, it remains recognisably the Knighton everyone remembers. A parent who was a pupil there in the 80s told us the school 'remains exactly what it's always been'. Not a lot of schools could have pulled that off.

The Bookers' greatest legacy was that, unlike so many schools created by reformers in their own image, Knighton never developed the sort of captivating idiosyncrasy (cultishness, if you like) that makes the job of successors so difficult. Captivating, yes, idiosyncratic, no; progressive yes, offbeat never. So the school has enjoyed a remarkably steady and howl-free evolution. This played to its advantage in 2013 when some of the school's governors almost made a strategic misstep of existential proportions. A proposal to merge with a nearby school was swiftly strangled by a coalition of parents and there have been no aftershocks, but it was a crisis that wasn't allowed to go to waste – indeed, one parent described it as 'the best thing that ever happened to us'. The episode focused minds on the intrinsic qualities that make Knighton so distinctive and precious. It awakened awareness of the school's uniqueness and value and reinvigorated the parent body. Other happy outcomes include the purchase of the school's freehold and the appointment of a very bright, eclectic board of governors.

Parent power is one of those things that can go either way. Knighton parents have not by any means taken to throwing their weight around; on the contrary, they're a supportive lot. Notably unpretentious and dressed down, they range from what one parent described as 'heavy duty aristocracy' to members of the armed forces, expats, local professionals and farmers, businesspeople, creatives and other members of the digital diaspora. In the words of one parent, 'They're not remotely flashy, they're cheery, low-key and I have no idea who's rich and who isn't'. They find the school 'brilliantly supportive of working parents', 'wonderfully accommodating of late-to-collect crises'. Significantly, Knighton is very much the school of choice for teachers (who know a thing or two about schools) at local independents; there's always a tranche from Bryanston. Nice touch: grandparents' days.

Single sex important for some, not so much for others. What chance the school will accede to some parents' preference for one school for all their children? Don't rule it out. But standalone girls-only boarding preps in the UK are up there with the snow leopard and the black rhino on the endangered species list; they're down to the last three. Quite a USP.

Academically hearty. Until the merger-most-foul episode the school had been falling off the pace. Now, gaps have been plugged, below-par staff eased out and there's a continuing focus on the quality of teaching. Rising numbers of scholarships testify to this, and they'll let you know about it. It's not all about getting the best out of just the brightest, though, and non-schol girls don't feel at all like also-rans. Small classes play their part, and teachers who really know the children. No danger of Gradgrind values; the mother of a very bright 8-year-old told us, 'They are definitely stretching her, but not in ways she's really aware of.' The overall philosophy remains 'in your own way, in your own time' – but definitely not 'when you feel like it', or as one mum put it another way, they're 'challenged and encouraged'. A parent who moved down from London reckons his daughter got to the same place academically that she would have reached in her mirthless pressure-cooker; another said, 'People are once again sending their bright girls to Knighton'. Senior schools confirm this.

Conventional curriculum, maths 'brilliant', Latin from year 6, art superb and there's a fine personal enrichment programme that goes off-piste into history of art, public speaking, you name it. In common with many other preps, school now moving away from Common Entrance (will be completely phased out by 2020) and creating own KED (Knowledge Enlightenment Discovery) Curriculum.

Surprisingly well-resourced across the board, classrooms in converted farm buildings. Careers talks for years 7 and 8 because 'there are no limits to what girls can achieve'. Special needs a strength as you've every right to expect of a non-selective school. Learning support spans short-term interventions – everything from reinforcement to gifted and talented – to long term SENDs: dyslexia, ADHD, ASD, etc. No wheelchairs when we called but, says the school, 'We'd do what we needed to do'. Something you don't notice til it's pointed out: no ungainly school bags being lugged, swinging, from class to class. They're banned. Take just what you need from your locker. Amazingly civilising.

L

Knighton girls are mostly outdoorsy types so it's no surprise they're a sporty lot. There's been a focus on quality of coaching in the last few years and the best go on to county and national levels. If you're bookish or not sporty that's fine but you'll be expected to join in. Riding is huge and maybe why you're reading this. Knighton is one of Horse & Hound's 'Six dream schools for horsey children' and ponies have been at the centre of school life forever. Around half the children ride. They're good, too, up there with the best.

A lot at Knighton happens in fresh air. They play outside in their dens, make up games with bits of sticks, climb trees and converse with ponies, goats, hamsters etc. We watched them at it. A delight. What they (arguably) do best indoors is sing. The music-making tradition here is as old as the ponies. Instrumental practice begins before breakfast (yes, seriously) and most girls play something. Lots of ensembles and an orchestra. Singing compulsory for years 3-5 and if you're top-drawer you can audition for the super-elite chapel choir which sings at, no less, professional standard in some really nice venues. Music is a big part of Knighton's identity; it's a bigger deal to be head chorister than head girl.

Around 25 full-time boarders plus all the flexi options. Overnighting and weekending joyously popular because the boarding staff are lovely and make it such fun, and the head of boarding is a force of nature who lives and breathes her job and is amazing, and has to be marched off the premises on her days off otherwise she'd never have one. It took the school a while to find her and on the way it parted company with a few who didn't make the grade – a reminder that extraordinary kindness in any regime is achieved only by rigour and, yes, steel.

Universal praise for pastoral care. Teachers are 'very accessible and always give you time'; 'they really understand the children'. Knighton has long been noted for this; in the words of a former pupil it's 'deeply ingrained'. Wherever we questioned we got the same responses: 'nurturing', 'loving', 'home from home'.

Unanimous and, dare we say, fervent praise for the pre-prep, the Orchard – 'exceptional,' in the words of a mother you wouldn't want to get on the wrong side of. Girls and boys 3-7 plus babies and toddlers every Thursday.

Knighton judiciously makes sure its pupils outgrow the school by setting them slightly above and apart in their final year in the Alpha flat. They swap dungarees for a grey skirt, get some more independence and turn their eyes to what comes next. It's well done.

By their bright red dungarees ye shall know them, for this is the school uniform. They're not about aah-factor, though they are certainly not deficient in that; they're just the job for playing out and doing horses. They can be spotted by teachers if the occupant strays too far or climbs too high. Above all, they're democratising. Red dungarees are just one of the elements that create the rare social atmosphere you find at Knighton, the unaffected friendliness, the way the girls look out for each other, older ones for tiny ones. Single sex may be a factor; the school's small size definitely is: girls feel they belong here, this isn't just a school they go to. Another factor is the example set by the staff, because nothing good happens in a school that does not derive from role modelling by adults who care deeply about their work.

While we were in the head's office we scanned the books on the coffee table. One was by Christine Pullein-Thompson, author of wildly popular pony books for girls. For us it provided the vital clue to what Knighton is all about. The PTs (there were three of them) created a world whose values are wholeheartedness, pluck, resourcefulness and good humour. They invented a genre which has been described as 'feminist way before its time': in their own words, 'we convinced girls they were as good as chaps'. Their spirit lives on here not as creed nor affectation but in an internalised way – eg, in the annual award for Gumption. Triers are rewarded, exemplifying a culture of 'you can do anything' which is borne out by the estimation of senior schools, one of which told us that their Knighton girls 'are amongst the most rounded academically and socially'.

Knighton has never blown its own trumpet other than understatedly and is free of the sort of marketing machine that blights so many other schools. Hurrah. The school is clad in values and practices that make it very current, unencumbered by trad baggage, financially strong and blessed by a once-and-future ethos which makes it, in the words of a parent, 'very happy in its own skin'. Is there magic in the air? Yes.

Lady Barn House School

Schools Hill, Cheadle, Cheshire SK8 1JE

Ages 3–11 **Pupils** 482

Fees: £1,675 – £8,640 pa

0161 428 2912
www.ladybarnhouse.org

Head: Since 2016, Mark Turner BA PGCE NPQH (early 50s). He has a first class classics degree from Exeter University and did his teacher training at Cambridge University. Before coming to Lady Barn House, he spent seven years as head of Warwick Prep and before that he worked in the state sector in Gloucestershire.

He says he was attracted to the caring ethos and tradition at Lady Barn House. He also particularly wanted to lead a school that sends children to a variety of secondaries rather than heading the junior division of an all-through 3-18 school; a child's future, he says, shouldn't be set at the age of 3 or 4.

Pupils told us he's 'really amazing' and has 'made good changes'. They love the school mascot he's brought in – a school uniform-clad barn owl called Barney, who was based on a year 5 pupil's design. Parents find him 'supportive and responsive' and 'proactive'. 'Mr Turner is very much one to put children at the centre,' said one mum. Another told us how much the school's offering to children with special educational needs has improved since his arrival. 'He really listens,' added another mum; 'we told him the summer dresses were too expensive – £40 a dress, which really adds up – and he spoke to lots of suppliers and he's got the price down.'

We found Mr Turner relaxed, friendly and open-minded. While he clearly does things properly and takes his responsibilities seriously (we noticed shiny new gates outside the school, brought in to improve the children's security), he also relishes the freedom that the independent sector gives him to downplay those aspects of the national curriculum that he finds wrongheaded – like drilling 7-year-olds in reams of grammar. So yes, parents can expect their children to have homework most evenings, but at least they should be spared the pleasure of desperately Googling 'what is a fronted adverbial?'

Entrance: Roughly two-thirds of the children at Lady Barn House have not been selected by ability. There are 44 places for the nursery (for entry at 3+). 'It's difficult to select at that age,' says Mr Turner. These places are currently allocated first to siblings of children already at the school and then on a first come, first served basis. A year later, for entry to reception at 4+, a further 22 places are made available. Applicants for these places are invited in and informally assessed – mainly on their social and communication skills. For entry to later years children are invited in for an assessment day, to experience a typical working day at the school.

From years 3 to 6 a few means-tested bursary places are available. 'We aim to have 10 to 12 children with bursaries in the school at any one time,' says the head. These are given to children judged as most likely to 'gain the most' from being at the school – whether that's because of their academic strength or because of their potential in another area such as music or sport.

Fees are fairly low, compared to the local competition. They come in at just under £9,000 a year when you add in the cost of compulsory school dinners. There's a five per cent discount for a first sibling, 20 per cent for a second sibling and additional discounts for subsequent siblings in school.

Exit: The most popular destinations in 2018 were two of the region's most selective schools: Manchester Grammar School and Withington Girls' School. Other independent secondaries popular with Lady Barn House leavers are Manchester High School for Girls, Stockport Grammar and Cheadle Hulme School. A good number of children also secure places at local state grammar schools – especially Altrincham Grammar.

Most children sit between three and five entrance exams to ensure they have a back-up and staff try to guide families towards the most suitable school for their child. Not all will get into MGS or Withington but, given the largely non-selective intake, an impressive number do.

Remarks: Lady Barn House is quite a big school – its numbers edging towards 500 pupils – but staff and parents say it doesn't feel big and class sizes never go above 22. One of its strengths is the number of specialist teachers. With expert subject leaders in science, art and technology, music, languages, computing and PE, classroom teachers have a generous amount of time to plan excellent lessons in the core subjects, to manage their pastoral responsibilities and to put their energies into the thriving extracurricular life of the school (all teachers run at least one club). The fact that scientists deliver science lessons and linguists teach languages (French, Spanish and Mandarin) means that the curriculum is relatively traditional; pupils learn subject by subject rather than through the cross-curricular, project-based approach that some schools take.

Academic standards are very high and the pupils make excellent progress from their starting points – with average standardised progress scores of 117 to 118 in maths, English and reading (on a scale where 100 shows the expected level). But Mr Turner says the school's reputation in some quarters as a hothouse is undeserved. Pupils' progress is measured and monitored on an individual basis – so teachers are watching how each child matches up to their own potential rather than how well they keep up with their classmates. However, the school concedes that the 'pacy' lessons at Lady Barn House wouldn't be right for all children.

Parents we met seemed happy with the amount and type of homework their children are given, but it is set every night – and expected to be handed in the next day; so disorganised children – or parents – beware. 'There's the odd bit of homework when you think: "what are they actually getting from this?"' said a parent, 'but in general I approve and I don't have trouble getting my children to do it.'

Parents told us the provision for children with special educational needs is much improved. 'If you'd asked me what the school could do better a couple of years ago, I'd have said special needs support,' said one mum, 'but under Mr Turner and with a new SENCo it's so much better and my dyslexic child is making really good progress.' She told us there's now more small group work for children who need extra support in maths or English and communication between staff about children's individual needs has improved.

Class teachers are at the centre of the pastoral care system, with help from support staff as well as the heads of the four departments (EYFS, infants, lower juniors and upper juniors) and a deputy head for pastoral care. The anti-bullying policy is regularly reviewed and children are encouraged to speak up if they are either a victim of or a witness to bullying. Older children are taught assertive strategies to deal with unpleasant behaviour before they go to a teacher. Parents told us the school deals with friendship problems really effectively, although none we met had experience of anything more serious than that.

Large numbers of pupils learn instruments (at an extra cost) and they have opportunities to perform in all sorts of settings. In the past, membership of the school choir was by audition only but the school is moving in a more inclusive direction and now, while only the most talented singers can join the chamber choir, anyone who wants to sing can join the main school choir. We were pretty awed during our visit when we popped in to watch all 60-odd year 6 children rehearsing for their forthcoming production of Oliver! (Once the year 6 children have got through their entrance exams, the last couple of terms are fun, fun, fun.)

The school has fantastic facilities and spaces to rehearse music, drama and dance but, the head admits, opportunities for dramatic performance have in the past tended to dry up in the years between the infants' nativity plays and the year 6 leavers' play. This is set to change with the appointment of a new head of drama. Many pupils also receive private speech and drama tuition at the school in preparation for LAMDA exams.

We loved looking at the students' artwork during our visit, in the beautifully equipped and specialist-teacher-led art room; and we were even more impressed by the science room – where small scientists dressed in white lab coats test, measure and record their observations of the world, watched impassively from various glass tanks by a pair of tortoises, Buzz and Tim the gerbils and Aristotle the axolotl.

We were also impressed with the school library – which had a wide and inspiring range of children's fiction. Tucked away in a converted attic, it feels warm and inviting – a cosy nook where pupils can retreat for a bit of escapism.

Pupils do a lot of sport with great success. Children from Lady Barn House perform at a high level in the main sports of football, cricket, netball and hockey, but also achieve high standards in cross-country and swimming, and excel in gymnastics. 'It's not a pink and fluffy sort of school,' said one mum; 'they're out in the rain, running around. It's all about creating a robust child.' There are countless opportunities for children to take part in all sorts of physical activities, from judo to ballet – and generally everything is open equally to boys and girls. From year 3 pupils walk in convoy down the road to Cheadle pool for swimming lessons.

There are lots of school trips on offer – typically educational and/or outdoorsy. Year 6 pupils we met had just come back from France. 'At the market we split into three groups and had to go and ask for bread – in French: I was the one in my group who got to order for everyone!' There's also an annual year 5 and 6 trip to the south coast – which is currently included in the school fees. While many of the residential visits encourage the children's independence, there's also a strong family focus to what's on offer: the school runs family outdoor activity weekends in the Lake District and even a family skiing holiday, where parents can go away with their children but hand them over to teachers from time to time. Sounds magnificent...

Pupils we met were charming. The older children were affectionate and protective towards the younger ones and keen to set a good example. They told us they love the school, the teachers, the lessons... We had to prod to uncover any complaints. 'Our classroom's really hot,' said one girl. We did notice that in one or two rooms that once formed part of a rather grand old house, there appear to be two heating settings: tropical or arctic. A couple of children also grumbled about school dinners: 'They're definitely not terrible. It's just that some are nicer than others.' But their objections were hardly damning: 'So there's always a meat option and a vegetarian option. And if you don't like either of them you can have a jacket potato. Oh and there's a salad bar. But, if you don't like any of those, you don't really have anything to eat. Except pudding. Puddings are really nice.' Furthermore, we ate the same food as the children on our visit and thought it was great.

Almost all children at the school are involved in some sort of extracurricular activity – either at lunchtimes or before or after school. Clubs run by school staff are free, but parents pay extra if their child attends a club led by an external teacher. At the end of our chat, the pupils we met spelled out 'good bye' to us in British sign language. 'We go to sign language club. It's really fun.'

Leweston School

Sherborne, Dorset DT9 6EN

Ages Girls 2–18, boys 2–13 and in sixth form (becoming fully co-ed) **Pupils** 298 (37 boys) **Sixth form** 60 (1 boy) **Boarders** 50 full, 25 weekly, 20 flexi, all girls (from year 3) **RC**

Fees: Day £5,925 – £14,420; Boarding £17,265 – £27,780

01963 211010
www.leweston.co.uk

Head: Since 2015, Kate Reynolds MEd LLB PGCE (early 50s). Educated at St Mary's Ascot and Wellington College (where she met her husband). Read law at Bristol, followed by two years at a top London law firm. She then did 'the best thing I ever did' and decided to become an English teacher. After a PGCE at Bath Spa University she taught English and drama at Gillingham School, then Sherborne School. Joined Leweston in 2002, became head of EAL in 2013 and was appointed as head two years later. 'It was one of those serendipitous things,' she says. 'Leweston is so much part of me, as is the local area.'

The head is very proud of the girls. 'There is no homogenous product,' she says. 'They are very individual, with a real "can-do" attitude, and they smile all the time. We never pigeonhole them.' She cites the example of a shy girl who wanted to clarify a theological question so emailed every bishop in the country on her own initiative to ask their views. Armed with her findings, she then led assemblies at both the prep and senior school. Asked who the school is right for, the head says: 'It's a decision parents make with their hearts. We are not shiny – some call us shabby chic – but what you get is a fantastic, supportive environment.'

Warm and approachable, she loves teaching and still teaches six periods of English a fortnight. Married to Giles, head of history at nearby Sherborne School, with four sons (one studying materials science and engineering at Imperial College, two at Sherborne School and one at Sherborne Prep). They live in a house on site with their collie-labrador cross. In her spare time she plays the piano and cello, runs and swims. She's often in the pool at lunchtime with other staff but wisely leaves the 6.30am swim training to the pupils.

Head of the junior department: Alanda Phillips BA PGCE MEd, former head of the school's early years foundation stage.

Academic matters: Results are good, particularly so since the school is non-selective. In 2018, 44 per cent A*-A/9-7 at GCSE, 42 per cent A*/A at A level or Pre-U equivalent. The school currently holds Good Schools Guide subject awards in English and LAMDA. Most pupils take 10 subjects at GCSE, including English, English literature, at least one language (French, Spanish or German), maths, RS, history or geography and either combined science or three separate sciences. The school regularly excels in STEM Olympiads, with one pupil representing Team GB recently.

When it comes to value-added, performance at GCSE consistently ranks Leweston in the top 10 per cent of schools nationally. Pupils are able to choose almost any combination of 21 A level subjects. Also offers BTecs in health and social care, hospitality and sports and exercise science. Small A level classes (often three or four for less popular subjects so lots of individual attention) appreciated by the pupils, who also have the option to do the EPQ. Around 16 to 20 in year 7 (including 11 who move up from the prep school) and 35 to 40 in year 9 and up (but classes are far smaller than this). EAL is compulsory and included in the international fees; learning support available to those who need one-to-one help. A sixth former praised the support she'd received when she struggled to memorise poetry for her English literature GCSE.

Co-ed prep school is housed in a separate building and fizzes with activity. Pupils are proud to show off their badges – awarded for everything from picking up litter to taking part in the school's eco day. Fidget spinners all the rage at break-times but they aren't allowed in class. When we visited, the year 6 teacher was showing the first edit of an impressive 20-minute film of A Midsummer Night's Dream made by his pupils. Most move seamlessly from the prep to the senior school. When we visited the prep our sixth form tour guide told us nostalgically: 'It still has the same familiar smell.' Separate nursery takes children aged 3 months to 4 years.

Games, options, the arts: Leweston is a very sporty school, with a 25-metre covered pool, eight netball courts, 15 tennis courts, sports hall, fitness suite and Astroturf. Besides the conventional hockey, netball and tennis the school is also one of only eight pentathlon academies in the country, offering opportunities in the triathlon, biathlon, tetrathlon and modern pentathlon. Ten pupils qualified to represent Team GB at the European Triathle Championships in 2017 and a year 6 girl holds four national titles in her age group – for pistol shooting, biathle and the triathlon. 'We have got some gutsy pupils,' says the director of sport. 'Despite our size, we really punch above our weight.' Ballet, zumba, kickboxing, fencing, shooting and sailing (at nearby Portland Olympic Sailing Academy) on offer too. It's possible for boarders to stable their horses at a livery yard nearby.

Around a third of pupils play a musical instrument and there are choirs, orchestras and bands galore to join. Seniors also take part in the Sherborne Schools' Sinfonia and Symphony Orchestra. Up to four pupils take GCSE and A level music each year. Art is very popular, giving pupills the chance to try their hand at everything from portraiture to graphic design. The school also offers A level textile design (including a fashion component). Year 12s are encouraged to do work placements and in recent years pupils have worked at Boden and Cath Kidston. Lots of drama, from Aladdin at the prep school to The Ash Girl, 'a darker version of Cinderella', performed by the seniors.

All pupils do practical cookery and many opt to take home economics (cookery and nutrition) GCSE. A group was busy making sweet potato and shallot quesadillas and Viennese tartlets when we visited. One young pupil, completely unprompted, sweetly gave us one to take home. School is one of only 12 in the country to offer Leith's basic certificate in food and wine, a professional qualification designed to run alongside the school timetable at A Level. Around 10 a year do this – not surprisingly, they are far better equipped than most to cook for themselves at university.

A plethora of clubs and activities on offer, including den building in the woods for year 2s and up, with a new accredited forest school. Lots of opportunities for community work, including mentoring younger pupils and visiting the elderly and young mums. One of our sixth form guides was just off to teach Spanish in a local primary school, a voluntary activity she'd fixed up off her own bat. Sixth formers also have a programme of enrichment activities, including public speaking, art appreciation and politics and debating.

Boarding: Girls can board from year 3 onwards. Very few at this young age but the boarding numbers increase as the girls progress up the school. By the sixth form most girls board, on a weekly or full basis. Flexi-boarding available too. Four boarding houses, all within the main school – three for girls of different age groups and a new one for boys of all ages. Pretty dorms with views across the lush green countryside – eight in the youngest dorms, four in year 9 dorms and single rooms for older girls.

Head of boarding is a registered nurse with a background in school nursing and interest in adolescent mental health (as well as being the school's lay chaplain) so is well equipped to deal with any problems. Sixth formers act as peer mentors and the head girl told us that as Leweston is a small school and everyone knows each other so well they are often the first to spot anything amiss.

Background and atmosphere: The school is set in 48 acres of beautiful parkland, at the end of a long drive and three miles outside Sherborne. Founded in Sherborne in 1891 by the Religious of Christian Instruction, a group of nuns from Ghent. Moved to its present site, a Palladian manor house, in 1948 (the house was bought from the Rose family, of lime cordial fame). Lots of later additions to the sprawling site, some visually pleasing, others less so. No nuns these days but the chapel is central to school life. Daily prayers, masses and other school services are held there and pupils, staff and parents can visit when they wish. The tiny 17th century Trinity Chapel, one of the first post-Reformation Catholic churches in the country, seats 50 and is used for smaller services. A palpable sense of Catholicism still prevails but girls of any faith and none are welcomed.

The school day starts at 8.15am and ends at 4.20pm, followed by clubs, activities and after-school care for the youngest. Uniform is distinctive – tartan skirts and blazers for girls up to year 11, plus sailor dresses for juniors in the summer. Boys wear grey trousers, navy jumpers and blazers. No uniform for sixth formers but they are encouraged to look smart – definitely no denim. We didn't spot anyone flouting the rules although a girl once turned up in slippers as a joke. Older pupils are allowed to go into Sherborne several afternoons a week, to meet friends and have coffee. There are socials with Sherborne School too. Sixth formers also have their own sixth form area, complete with comfy Chesterfield sofas, outdoor courtyard and dedicated study centre.

Atmosphere everywhere is friendly, yet purposeful. As one parent put it: 'We wanted somewhere that would stretch our girls, whilst giving them the confidence to be themselves. We didn't want a product.' Pupils eat all their meals in the dining room but spill out onto the outside picnic tables in good weather Plenty of choice, with vegetarian and gluten-free options.

Pastoral care, well-being and discipline: Pupils say the school is warm and welcoming and like the fact that they are encouraged to achieve their potential. 'Everyone is kind to you here,' a year 6 girl told us. When pupils arrive they are each given a peer mentor to help them settle in and everyone knows everyone.

Head girl, two deputies, heads of the four houses and other prefects in place. They all keep a weather eye out for each other and for the younger girls. Pupils can turn to tutors, houseparents, chaplain, counsellor and the two health centre nurses for help if they need it. The head of boarding, mindful of the pressures on today's young people, says: 'One of the things that Leweston does very well is helping the pupils to develop a sense of balance.' PSHE covers everything from e-safety to tolerance.

Pupils and parents: Day pupils come from within an hour's drive away. School minibuses ferry pupils in from as far afield as Wincanton, Beaminster and Dorchester. Boarders mostly from the south west but a sprinkling from London. Around 17 per cent of pupils are from overseas – including mainland China, Hong Kong, Mexico and Europe – and the head says they integrate well. No Saturday school but around 80 pupils stay at school every weekend so there's plenty going on. A third of the pupils are Catholic and everyone is expected to attend church, whatever their faith.

The pupils we met were enthusiastic, unpretentious and charming, with a sense of fun. 'They're comfortable in their own skin,' agrees the head of boarding. Unlike peers elsewhere they aren't alarmingly sophisticated – the head loved it when the head girl gave a speech on open day about the sixth formers playing hide and seek in the corridors at night. Former pupils are known as Old Antonians and include Dame Kristin Scott Thomas, Erin Pizzey, founder of the UK's first women's refuge, former TalkTalk CEO Dido Harding, entrepreneur Sarah McVittie and sculptor Serena de la Hey among their number.

Entrance: Non-selective. Pupils join at multiple points so it's always worth contacting the school. Leweston accepts all-year-round applications and when we visited after the summer half-term, two girls had just started in year 9 and one in year 10. Pupils join the senior school from state primaries and preps like Perrott Hill and Hazlegrove. Prospective pupils take part in a taster day – juniors have an informal assessment while seniors take academic, numerical and perceptual reasoning tests. Prospective year 9 entrance can attend an Early Promise Assessment Day in year 7. New sixth formers require six good GCSE passes.

Becoming fully co-ed, with boys in years 7 and 8, and in year 9 from September 2019. Will then introduce a diamond model, with boys and girls in year 9-11 having separate maths and science lessons but joining together for all other lessons and activities.

Exit: Around 20-30 per cent pupils leave at 16, sometimes for financial reasons. Some head to local state schools like The Gryphon School in Sherborne and The Thomas Hardye School in Dorchester while others go to independents like Hurtwood House. The head says that a few miss Leweston so much they 'boomerang back' after a few weeks. At 18, most progress to university. A vast array of destinations, with one or two to Oxbridge most years (one medic to Cambridge in 2018, plus another to Exeter). Others to eg UCL, York, Newcastle, Bristol, Warwick and Leeds. 'They aim high,' smiles the head.

Money matters: Mindful of the tough economic climate, the whole school recently took the decision to reduce its fees substantially. 'Our parents are very down-to-earth and many make sacrifices to send their children here,' says the head. The school has done this by a raft of measures, including getting some senior teachers to teach subjects like Latin in the prep school too.

Prep school offers scholarships for entry into year 5 – academic, music and sports. At senior school level there are scholarships for academic attainment, art and design (13+ and sixth form only), drama, music and sports, including equestrian and pentathlon.

L

Remarks: Leweston is a hidden gem in a stunning setting, definitely worth a look by parents looking for a small, friendly school that achieves good results. The pupils work hard, make lifelong friends and absolutely love the place.

Loreto Grammar School

96

Dunham Road, Altrincham, Cheshire WA14 4AH

Ages 11–18 **Pupils** 1,046 **Sixth form** 257 **RC**

0161 928 3703
www.loretogrammar.co.uk

Head teacher: Since 2006, Jane Beever (40s). Mrs Beever came to the school as deputy head in 2002. Three years later she took over from Sister Patricia as the school's first lay head teacher. Previously she taught modern languages at Impington Village College in Cambridge. She studied French and Italian at Liverpool University, did a PGSE in York and a masters in Leeds. She comes from a family of teachers and always wanted to teach.

She's a leading head teacher – sharing her knowledge with other local schools (and executive head teacher of another school that's on a 'journey of improvement'). She's a National Leader in Education and a member a network of leaders in Catholic education. Comes across as collaborative and quick to credit colleagues and pupils with the school's success.

A committed Catholic, Mrs Beever also comes across as modern, open-minded and outward looking. On the day of our visit she was wearing an anti-human-trafficking badge – made by pupils. Under her leadership it's clear that spirituality at Loreto Grammar goes hand in hand with an active commitment to Catholic social teaching.

Almost every pupil we met used the word 'lovely' to describe Mrs Beever. 'Fair and just,' added another girl. They say she's warm and approachable and they wonder how she knows all their names. Her office – a comfortable mix of stylish Mid-century Modern chairs ('they were not expensive!' she assures us), pupils' artwork and religious inspiration – welcomes a steady stream of visitors, staff and students. Pupils say she's 'always around' and she still sometimes teaches when colleagues need cover.

Parents spoke about Mrs Beever's warmth and kindness. One parent, whose family was going through a very traumatic experience at the time his daughter joined the school, told us: 'I visited a number of schools but the warmth, understanding and support offered to us by Mrs Beever was nothing short of outstanding. She went out of her way to try and help us...'

When she's not working Mrs Beever sings in a choir, she enjoys travelling – especially to France and Italy – and she still has the languages bug. She told us with excitement that a colleague has secured funding to send 25 members of staff abroad for language training and she herself will be spending a week in Santander, Spain learning Spanish.

Academic matters: Although the school doesn't push academic excellence above all else, its results are stunning. In 2018, 75 per cent of A levels awarded A*-B with 42 per cent A*/A grade. The most popular A level subjects psychology and history, followed by sociology, then maths, philosophy and ethics, biology and then English literature. Although the school specialises in STEM subjects, parents we spoke to all singled out how well it does in the arts and creative subjects. ('But STEM subjects are creative too,' points out Mrs Beever, who isn't keen on categorising pupils in a way that might limit their potential to one or other side of the arts v science divide.)

At GCSE 65 per cent A*-A/9-7 grades in 2018. Latin, French, Spanish and German offered; some of the other options include food technology, textiles, expressive arts, classical civilisation and both ICT and computer science. The school's success isn't just down to the above average intake; Loreto topped the league tables of schools in Trafford for pupil progress with a 'well above average' Progress 8 score recently.

A significant number of pupils do have some kind of specific learning disability, a sensory processing disability or a physical disability. A full time SENCo is available to talk to parents about their daughters' specific needs and to address them – liaising with outside agencies if necessary. Full details of the SEND offering are on the school website.

The head teacher puts the academic success down to excellent teachers and to the attitude of the girls themselves. The school is also extremely proactive in terms of monitoring its pupils term by term. Each girl is tracked according to her own potential and so a bright girl who's near the top of her class could still be given a targeted intervention if the monitoring system shows that she's not doing quite as well as she could. Pupils also have the opportunity to sit down with subject teachers in small groups – usually at lunchtime – to go over subjects they might have missed or need extra support with.

Parents we spoke to all told us they were very happy with their children's progress and that they felt the teachers understood their academic potential well. Pupils said they loved their lessons and their teachers and felt the academic atmosphere was supportive rather than competitive. That old fear of being called 'teacher's pet' isn't entirely absent though, according to one mother. She told us that since joining the school her daughter 'has become more confident in her views and academic ability,' but that she has also 'perhaps been tempered by comments from her peers about her eagerness to answer questions and she has found this feedback, which has not always been done kindly, difficult to swallow'.

Games, options, the arts: A busy programme of extracurricular activities includes a wide selection of musical groups and plenty of sporting clubs (mostly held after school). Other societies that caught our eye include engineering and robotics, literary film club, Christian mindfulness, chess and several art clubs for different year groups. There are also regular lunchtime debating competitions and school council meetings.

Mrs Beever is proud that the school continues to offer a wide selection of arts subjects despite funding pressures, including music, drama and art at both GCSE and A level. We saw a striking display of bold and confident abstract sculptures and, in the student-produced school magazine, stunning examples of A level art and textiles work and powerful examples of poetry and prose writing.

Several parents singled out the school's musical and dramatic activities for particular praise: 'both [of my daughters] have gained immense satisfaction from the musical activities. The performing arts department is nothing short of phenomenal and the standard of performance they encourage from the girls is truly outstanding... My younger daughter has gone from a nervous, shy, though musically talented girl to a confident performer.' Parents and pupils talked about the many opportunities girls have to speak, sing or play instruments in front of large audiences – at school events such as speech night or Loreto's Young Musician of the Year and at external venues such as the Bridgewater Hall.

'My eldest daughter loved the art experiences and opportunities, said a mum. 'My middle daughter thoroughly enjoyed the range of music and performance activities on offer and my youngest daughter has had the opportunity to take part in sporting activities.'

There's a particularly wide range of charitable, volunteering and spiritual opportunities. Students have campaigned about issues such as child labour, Fair Trade food ethics and animal rights and they raise serious amounts of money for various charities. The head girl has been running a project that gets pupils to knit blankets for the homeless. The chaplaincy offers an annual religious retreat for each year group and there are many opportunities to travel to spiritual events in the UK and abroad. Pupils have visited Loreto-run schools for street children in India and attended World Youth Day in Poland. There are also language exchange trips and several pupils and parents talked to us about a particularly memorable visit to World War 1 sites in Belgium.

Sports teams regularly compete in netball, football, cross-country and athletics, and there's hockey, rounders, tennis, badminton, basketball, tag-rugby and lacrosse opportunities. Many different kinds of dance taught; one year 7 pupil described how learning Indian dance was a highlight for her.

Sixth formers were less positive about PE at Loreto, and glad that they had been able to give it up, saying that 'PE teachers have their favourites and they're not interested in you if you're not going to be on a team.' Some younger pupils said PE was really inclusive and that they got a lot of help and encouragement from teachers. One year 11 girl told us, 'lower down in the school the PE teachers did have their favourites but I think it's different now. They're really trying to get us all engaged.' One parent told us she had requested a club for girls who enjoy sport but don't make the teams, but was told the school didn't have the resources.

Background and atmosphere: The Sisters of Loreto founded the school in 1909 and it's always been at its current site, originally a convent. The building is neat and tidy, a little worn in places, but feels well cared for. There's nothing showy about it, but there are some lovely features: original parquet floors, heavy wood-panelled doors and a particularly beautiful and peaceful chapel (of which the girls are evidently proud). Crucifixes adorn many a woodchip wall, alongside displays of pupils' work, and photographs – old and new – of life here.

There's also a strong sense of internationalism. It is part of a worldwide network of over 120 Loreto schools and has particularly strong links with sister schools in India, Australia, Germany and Spain.

The atmosphere is quiet and purposeful. Traditions – of the church, the school, and the Loreto Sisterhood – are clearly important, but the school community looks outwards on the modern world, its problems and the girls' own role in making things better. Pupils and staff talk a lot about Mary Ward – the trailblazing nun, born over 400 years ago, who founded the Loreto sisterhood. 'My friends at other schools haven't got someone so inspirational to look up to,' said one girl when we asked what makes this school special; indeed a standard question in the school magazine's interview section is 'What's your favourite Mary Ward quote?' Everyone seems to have one.

The Catholic ethos really is central to every aspect of school life. Virtually all the pupils are Catholics and while, as the head acknowledges, 'some may reject it,' the girls we met really enjoyed the religious life of the school. Several said they felt that it helped pupils maintain a supportive and loving community. 'Women in time will do much,' said Mary Ward, and Loreto Grammar is here to ensure that that time is now. 'We have strong girls, with strong opinions,' says Mrs Beever. Loreto was one of the first schools in the country to offer the Student Leadership Accreditation. 'I cannot think of anything more powerful than young women living out the values of Mary Ward in positions of influence in which ever field they choose,' enthuses a teacher promoting the award on the school website.

Pastoral care, well-being and discipline: Parents say pastoral care is 'excellent.' 'Loreto has a warm, caring, supportive, all-inclusive atmosphere. Each girl is celebrated for who and what she is,' said one mum. 'The chaplaincy provision is very supportive and the needs of the students as individuals are central to how the school operates,' added a father, who told us all about how the school had gone 'the extra mile' for his daughters during a terrible time and concluded: 'All I can say is thank you to the staff'.

Girls we met agreed that they felt supported and known. 'There are so many people we can talk to,' said one. Year 7 pupils told us the transition from primary school had been positive: 'I didn't really know anyone because I travel in for over an hour to come here but they were all so welcoming and my form teacher really seemed to understand how it feels.'

Pupil well-being is deeply embedded in the ethos of Loreto. The school 'focuses on the holistic development of pupils,' said one mum. 'It's about finding a balance,' says Mrs Beever. 'Our curriculum is built to consider the girls' needs. We want them to be "fully human, fully alive",' – another Mary Ward quote. The school offers parents 'well-being evenings', where they don't just share information about how to support their children's mental health or protect them online, they also offer workshops to help parents improve their own well-being.

Pupils told us discipline was 'firm but fair'. They described the teachers as 'understanding' and 'helpful' rather than strict. The issue of skirt length divides opinion. 'I think they do obsess about it a bit,' said one pupil. 'It's hard because we're growing. You can only just buy a new skirt that fits and then suddenly they're telling you it's too short and you have to buy another one.' A mum had a more positive view: 'There is a great emphasis on skirt length and maintaining dignity which gives young women a strong counterbalance to the growing pressures they are under through social media etc.' Mobile phone usage is also strictly policed and girls in years 7 to 11 found to have brought their phones into school have to surrender them to the head mistress.

Our sense is that, with the calm and purposeful atmosphere and its strong emphasis on self-discipline, incidents of bad behaviour are few and far between but we don't doubt that the school is quite ready to intervene quickly, effectively but thoughtfully when problems occur.

Pupils and parents: The catchment area is wide and some pupils travel significant distances. There are significantly fewer pupils from deprived backgrounds than in the local area. Majority of pupils are white; a significant number speak English as an additional language.

The girls we met were all polite, confident and engaged. Some also came across as a little innocent – in the sense that they didn't seem hugely touched by a culture that expects teenage girls to care about their appearance above all else. 'It's really nice not having boys here,' one sixth former told us, 'because it means we don't feel like we have to spend ages doing our hair and getting ready before we come in to school.'

Old girls often come back – particularly to help with careers education. Notable alumnae include former BBC weather presenter, Suzanne Charlton and film columnist, Antonia Quirke.

Parents are pleased with home-school communications and say they feel 'appropriately involved'. There's one parents' evening and two written reports a year. the active parents' association recently bought the school a minibus and has raised money for outdoor seating and play equipment for the linked prep. It runs barbecues, a Christmas fair and a charity ball. (The Mary Ward Ball – obviously – we're told you could not get Mary Ward off the dance floor...)

M

Entrance: Entrance exam in verbal reasoning, English and maths. Beyond passing the exam, the first four of the seven entry criteria prioritise baptised Roman Catholic girls (who must provide a baptism certificate) and are fairly standard – putting looked after girls and then those with siblings at the school at the top of the list. Pupils who live in a nominated pastoral area or who attended an associated Catholic primary school, even if it's some distance away, are in as good as a position as those who live next door to the school.

The entry criteria for the sixth form are similar, but subject to GCSE results. It is unusual for an existing pupil not to be allowed to go on to the sixth form even if her GCSEs didn't go as well as expected – although these results would determine which A level subjects she could pick.

Exit: Around a quarter leaves after GCSEs. Degree subjects and universities are varied and the school celebrates whatever path a girl chooses, not just the most academic destinations. One to Oxbridge in 2018, plus two dentists, two vets and six medics (one of those off to Kiev). The figures fluctuate significantly from year to year.

Remarks: An oasis of calm, purposeful and sisterly endeavour that celebrates the individuality of its bright, outward-looking pupils.

Malvern College

Linked with The Downs Malvern

College Road, Malvern, Worcestershire WR14 3DF

Ages 13–18 **Pupils** 650 **Sixth form** 290 **Boarders** 480 full

Fees: Day £25,455; Boarding £38,127 – £39,459 pa

01684 581500
www.malverncollege.org.uk

Headmaster: Since April 2019, Keith Metcalfe, previously deputy head at Harrow. Geography degree from Cambridge; after working for Christians in Sport and completing his PGCE in Oxford, he joined the geography department at Harrow in 2000. He is married to Clare, a photographer and primary school teacher, and they have three young children.

Academic matters: The school offers an interesting academic dynamic. On the one hand, there are super bright European students who are there for the IB and do very well indeed. Then there are the home grown pupils who are much more mixed ability. The common entrance pass mark is a relatively modest 50, and about 20 per cent of those coming in at year 9 receive some level of learning support. A levels at 35 per cent A*/A in 2018, and 60 per cent A*-A/9-7 at GCSE, but school is coy about giving IB results, though nearly a third got 40+ points and two achieved full marks. School says that it wants to be open to as wide an ability range as it can, partly because it is interested in a broad range of talents and partly because it wants all the family to come, not just the bright one of the clan.

Parents rave about the level of academic support. There are carefully tailored individual programmes, and whatever their level, pupils say their teachers really know their strengths and weaknesses. Some parents feel there is rather too much pressure and the school is expecting pupils to spin an awful lot of plates, but others recognise that this is what gets the results. Parents are full of praise for the availability of teachers and the tight level of communication between staff that ensures each pupil is getting the academic support and challenge they need.

Academic profile upped by very visible encouragement of intellectual societies, with a range of top quality outside speakers as well as opportunities for sixth formers to present papers reflecting their own intellectual interests. Here is the stretch and challenge that the bright sixth formers need.

The subject range is much what you would expect in a well-resourced school catering for a mixed ability range where the sixth form is split more or less exactly in half between IB and A level. Parents talk about how strong history, economics, English, maths, classics and modern languages are. Sixth formers also enthuse about politics and business studies. Science had a real boost with the opening of a modern science centre named after a past pupil, the current prime minister of Malaysia, Najib Razak. Teachers and parents told us that there is a lot of effort put into constructing sixth form timetables that will really play to the strengths of the pupils, resulting in some strong results and a thoroughly valuable sixth form experience for those of fairly modest academic ability as well as the high flyers.

Academic facilities are strikingly good across the board. Not every department has the spanking new facilities of the sciences, but music, which is housed in one of the older buildings, shows that energy, enthusiasm and high achievement are certainly not dependent on buildings alone. The library has all the aura of an ancient seat of learning with the buzz of a 21st century learning resource centre. Pupils commented on the helpful library opening hours.

Games, options, the arts: Sport is outstanding – and there is a lot of it. The sports facilities are excellent, with a splendid new sports centre and a new water based professional surface hockey pitch. We were pleased to hear of the girls' football teams' successes. There are special programmes for the elite sports players with high quality coaches and professional contacts, but everyone is expected to join in at some level. Outdoor pursuits are a large part of life, and during summer 2019 12 pupils aim to reach Paris by trekking, biking, canoeing, sea-kayaking and stand-up paddle boarding. We spoke to parents who had specifically chosen the college for its sporting excellence and were delighted with how it had delivered, but also to one or two with unsporty children who resented the amount of time they had to spend on games, especially if they had really strong other passions – such as music – that required a big time commitment. We would recommend a parent whose 13 year old is clearly not sporty to think hard about whether the other considerable attractions outweigh all that compulsory games.

The art is phenomenal and the whole school is enhanced with a great deal of the pupils' artwork in a brilliant variety of media. It was wonderful to see pupils encouraged to work on a large scale, with great big canvases giving the senior art areas the feel of an art school. DT is another strength, and both boys and girls spoke passionately about projects they were undertaking. Drama is housed in the redeveloped Rogers Theatre, and again there is masses going on, both within the houses and at school level. Thespians benefit from the very close proximity of Malvern Theatre, which has a number of pre-West End runs, and there are house trips to see various productions. Music is very strong too, particularly choral and chapel singing, but there is a huge range of ensembles and orchestras. Every year 9 learns a musical instrument. Those looking for choral scholarships at Oxbridge are well prepared. The music offers welcome links with the local community – the brass band played at the switching on of the Malvern town Christmas lights, and the choir were doing three carol services in the town during the week we visited.

Most of the school is involved in CCF at some stage. The school makes the most of the wonderful Malvern Hills, with various hill runs being an important part of the annual school calendar. Community service involves IB and DofE candidates, and the school has links with a local school for blind children.

'It offers all a great school should – and more', one parent told us.

Boarding: Eighty per cent of the school are full boarders. There is no flexi-boarding (though day pupils can stay the occasional night for official school events) but there are two compulsory weekends out of school each half term. Day pupils are incorporated into the boarding houses and have the same study space as the boarders. Pupils eat in the houses and house staff make the most of this opportunity to understand exactly what is going on in the daily life of their charges. Non-house staff and other visitors eat with the pupils at lunchtimes too, and the atmosphere is warm, stimulating and highly conducive to developing the best social manners. Pupils and parents say they know the house staff are there for them and will give unstintingly of their time to offer support.

The school suits high energy all rounders and there is a tremendous amount on offer round the clock. One or two parents felt the demands on the pupils were almost too great, with very little down time, but the pupils we met absolutely thrived on the high octane atmosphere and recognised the diversity of gifts that make up a flourishing and healthy community.

Background and atmosphere: The school is very cosmopolitan in feel and outlook – about 35 per cent are from overseas, and there are about 40 different nationalities represented at the moment. This global feel is grounded in the quintessentially British landscape of the Malvern Hills. The site is stunning, set on the side of the Malverns with spectacular views. There are 11 houses (six boys' and five girls') around the 250 acre site – many in huge 19th century villas that could well have been the houses of the successful financiers of the Empire who made their home in this health resort for the Victorian rich. Malvern is a delightful and slightly quirky town to wander around – staff and parents can feel as relaxed as they could anywhere in permitting pupils to go out to do a bit of shopping or have a coffee.

The Victorian foundation of the school, 1865, with that glorious mid 19th century architecture that exudes confidence in Church and Country, is an essential part of the school's feel today. Everyone goes to the chapel four times a week for a broadly CofE service, where hymns are still sung and prayers said although the emphasis is on wise words that will speak to those of all persuasions. There are non-Christians in the school – dietary and other religious observations are happily accommodated – but this is a Church of England foundation and you do feel that is a living reality. We hear that past pupils really value the regular worship as they move out into the wider world.

Pastoral care, well-being and discipline: Everyone said valued the pastoral care highly, even parents who had other grumbles. The emphasis is on the individual needs – there is no one-size-fits-all here. One parent told us how accommodating everyone was when her daughter suffered a bad sports injury, and pupils spoke about the staff with genuine warmth. Staff, too, showed a strong sense of loyalty to pupils, wanting to ensure they had the smoothest possibly transition to the next stage and making it clear each was valued for themselves not just for their A* exam results. The atmosphere felt well-disciplined without being too formal. The rules are clear and everyone recognises a no-nonsense approach to any transgressions, but it is rewards rather than punishments that reinforce the school's strong moral values.

Pupils and parents: Among the alumni of the college are at least two Commonwealth prime ministers, two Nobel prize winners, an Olympic gold medallist and many other notables from the worlds of science, law, the military, business, politics, sports and literature – including CS Lewis. The school produces an eclectic range that bears out its claims to suit the all rounders.

There are a lot of wealthy families forming the backbone of the school. Bursary help is available and we heard of families who were pooling generational resources to send children to the college, but one or two parents speculated that this might not be a comfortable school for a child whose parents were really having to push the boat out financially to pay the fees. The international clientele rubs shoulders with the children of successful Hereford farming families, of London commuters, and of the technological elite who can choose to live in such a delightful part of the country.

The school has been co-educational for about 20 years and there are now more-or-less half boys and girls. Some said that the families put children under some pressure to look good as well as do well, and we certainly saw none of the much publicised childhood obesity here. Housemistresses are aware of teenage girls' desire to look slim and beautiful and on the alert for any obsession, but the girls we met relished the outdoorsy, sporty opportunities of the school and didn't appear to be under pressure to present as cover girls. Both boys and girls appeared pleasingly extrovert and outward-looking. Perhaps not a school for the very quiet and reflective who need a lot of time to themselves.

Entrance: Register three years before 13+ entry; some houses fill up faster than others. New system of online entrance tests based on verbal and non-verbal reasoning. There's also entries into year 10, and to year 11 for a one-year pre-A level/IB course. About 50 join the sixth form each year and they normally do tests in the subjects they want to study at A level or IB, including an English and maths paper as appropriate. The interviews are important too, as are school reports and GCSE results.

Exit: Almost all the sixth form go on to higher education. Those staying in the UK are attracted to campus and collegiate universities like Durham and Exeter or big names such as Bristol, UCL and Imperial. About a quarter go on to US, Canada and mainland Europe top institutions. High flyers in 2018 off to study eg law at Oxford, medicine at Liverpool, accounting at LSE, to Luiss Business School in Italy and to Princeton. Some go on to apprenticeship programmes with companies such as Jaguar Land Rover and Ernst and Young.

Money matters: This sort of education, staffing level, facilities, opportunities and general ambiance does not come cheap. There are means-tested bursaries and scholarships for a wide range of talents. Pupils can accumulate these but learning support and EAL tuition come as extras.

Remarks: This is a school for the international set, and those who come from the local area, or even 'over the hill' – as the other side of the Malverns is described – undoubtedly benefit by having their horizons expanded beyond the comfortable values of the English shires. There are huge opportunities for pupils to learn from different cultures here and the college does well to work on its links with the local community, so it is not just the moneyed international culture that pupils assimilate, delightfully appealing though that is. There is a wholesomeness about Malvern for those who lift their eyes to the hills that can balance the daily busyness. The offshoots in China and Egypt will add to the global dimension and set everyone looking to the far horizons – not just at the opportunities but also, we hope, at the challenges. This is a school deeply bedded in the British public school tradition but with its sights now set across the globe to prepare the pupils for world citizenship.

Malvern St James Girls' School

15 Avenue Road, Great Malvern, Worcestershire WR14 3BA

Ages 4–18 **Pupils** 403 **Sixth form** 110 **Boarders** 142 full, 25 weekly/flexi (from 7 years)

Fees: Day £8,445 – £19,380; Boarding £21,915 – £36,720 pa

01684 584624
www.malvernstjames.co.uk

Headmistress: Since 2016, Olivera Raraty, a historian (Leeds) with impeccable girls' school credentials. Senior deputy at Notting Hill and Ealing High, assistant director of studies and head of history and politics at Wycombe Abbey, history specialist at Francis Holland NW1. With a warmth that has captivated the whole community, Olivera has brought the academic clout of her former roles with her, and while she loves the breadth of the ability range at MSJ, she is determined to build on the intellectual force blossoming in the school.

The girls say there has been a bit of general tightening up since Olivera's arrival but no worrying dramatic changes. 'She is there at everything', they note. She has got the staff on board because they can see she puts in the hours, loves the school already, has masses of exciting ideas for focussing the academic life of the school and the confidence to move things forward. 'She is just great to work with', we heard over and over again from her colleagues. Parents are pleased to have a mother of two daughters with whom to share the ups and downs of adolescence (both Olivera's daughters are now safely through the teenage years).

Marina Stentiford (history degree from Worcester) set up and has run the prep school since 2008. She is regarded as 'lovely' by parents and totally committed to the development of the whole child. Staff see her as collegiate and keen to support career development in her staff. She is enthusiastic and revels in the advantages for her girls of the all-through school.

Academic matters: GCSE results have been improving steadily with 61 per cent at A*-A/9-7 in 2018 – impressive for a school that is by no means highly selective. At A level in 2018, 57 per cent A*-A (80 per cent A*-B). Nearly 90 per cent of sixth formers are studying one or more STEM subjects (60 per cent are doing maths A level) and an unusually high number go on to study some form of engineering. An MSJ team got into the finals of the UK Maths Challenge in 2016. There is computer science on offer at GCSE and A level as well as DT product design. In fact the sixth form offer is unusually broad and undoubtedly one of the strengths of the school.

School is proud of its tailored approach to the individual in all areas of academic and personal development and is working on building an active learning approach where girls take responsibility for their own attitude to school work. In the classes we watched there was a sense of real engagement in learning and teachers were enthusiastically promoting creativity and challenge. Prep also fosters independent learning, so the girls who move up already have a strong basis which is then developed through a new year 7 curriculum that includes a Philosophy for Learning course.

The offer for the most able pupils is being refined, there are academic enrichment opportunities for everyone who wants them and some who may need a bit of initial prodding. The extension programmes include exciting outside lecturers, the prestigious Somerville suppers and various debates. New mentoring and coaching programmes have also been established.

Staff report it is an exciting place to teach and they feel free to try out innovations. The impressive senior team is keen to take the school's enthusiasm and expertise outside its grand walls and is busy plugging gaps in the local area by providing all sorts of opportunities for local primary schools – modern languages days, maths challenges, technology workshops – that get out the message that academic rigour can be fun and creative.

Careers education is far reaching, including an increasing input from alumnae. With various old girls in the Debretts/Sunday Times 500 Most Influential Britons list, the girls can connect with women who are at the top of their careers and wanting to give back to their alma mater. 'My friends at co-ed schools always have to sit through talks from lots of old boys,' one of the sixth formers told us. 'Our alumnae are all important women'.

Stunning library, well stocked and with long opening hours. The librarians are enthusiastic and fully involved with curriculum innovation across the school, in particular critical literacy – vital for independent learning, and understanding and interpreting information sources.

Learning support operates at various levels. There is a drop in session for juniors during prep. All staff have training on learning difficulties and there are two full-time SENCos in addition to literacy and numeracy specialists. Support is provided within a graduated framework after a problem is identified. This may include short term focused group work as well as one-to-one lessons (extra charge) – all designed round the needs of the individual.

The prep department is at the heart of the school, not just physically but also in its ability to access high quality facilities and specialist staffing. Not that the movement is all one way. A recent Toy Story theme allowed the girls to get to grips with mechanics while the woodland school lets them get messy and use serious tools to make tree dens. We spoke to a number of parents who had moved girls from state primaries for the range of opportunities the prep department offers.

At the other end, the sixth form is going from strength to strength. Tutors and tutees are matched as far as possible by interests and support is coherent – enough to ensure they learn how to maximise their potential without floundering when they leave. The size (about 60 in each year) means the school can be fleet footed when change and innovation are needed. EPQs are increasingly popular and topics reflect the diversity of interests – How to Organise a Tough Schools Day, Training a Racehorse, The Drawbacks of Volunteering Abroad.'

Games, options, the arts: Given the size of the school its sporting success is remarkable, and the head is determined to take it still further in line with some parents' views that there could be even more wins. There are a number of elite national athletes – at hockey, lacrosse, rounders, golf, cricket, fencing, athletics, eventing – and the school receives lots of accolades for its willingness to support individuals when they are off competing. The excitement around sport is reflected in the girls' very small wish list where bigger sports facilities came pretty near the top. We thought they were very generous already.

Interest groups abound. Quest, a liberal religious literacy group, got a special mention. Model United Nations is popular and MSJ works with state secondary schools to help them get involved. Year 9s ran a mock election for the whole school and the staff are keen to develop the girls' confidence in public speaking. There is a STEM club where much of the enthusiasm for all forms of engineering is born. MSJ is really doing its bit to redress the gender imbalances. 'Coding is boring until you see the application', one enthusiastic teacher told us, 'Hence the STEM club'.

Drama is flourishing and much loved. Some girls and parents say music is the strongest department in the school – there are lots of performance opportunities including choirs, orchestras and ensembles. Visual arts are vibrant, we saw lots of evidence of ambitious, high quality pieces. Textiles is also strong.

Boarding: One junior boarding house for years 3-8, two for years 9-11 and two sixth form houses, one of which is in the main school building. The latter is much coveted by those who want to stay in bed a bit later and those who want to burn the midnight oil in the library. Other houses are in nearby Malvern, lovely properties with large country gardens, high ceilings with light and fresh air flowing through.

Weekend activities are highly rated and compulsory up to year 9. Girls are very positive about relationships between day girls and boarders.

There is a strong and experienced pastoral team. Pastoral care plans are put in place quickly and unobtrusively when necessary to provide additional support to girls. Parents say that considerable work has been done on improving home school communications.

All pupils eat together in the newly designed dining hall and the food is fresh and diverse, catering for a cosmopolitan set. There was a healthy eating week when we visited that certainly sold the concept to us.

Background and atmosphere: Malvern St James is the result of the 2006 merger of Malvern Girls' College (founded in 1893) and St James's School (founded in 1896). The school is located opposite the railway station (good links to Birmingham and London) in buildings that were formerly the Imperial Hotel and which lend a certain grandeur and spaciousness to the bustle of school life.

Having the prep department in the centre of the school gives a light and fun atmosphere – this is certainly not a school that feels dominated by teenage angst. The younger girls dart around a glorious copper beech, reminding everyone in the summer term when we visited that there is a life outside GCSEs and away from computer screens. 'They look up to the seniors who they see around all day – it gives them something to aspire to,' the prep head told us. While it is clearly a whole school and everyone loves that, each phase has its own distinctive features. 'We dress up a lot in the junior department and parents are in and out all the time.' Senior girls get involved with the juniors in lots of ways: prefects from the senior school are attached to the pre-prep, there are house links and junior girls sit on the school anti-bullying and food committees.

Although it's not a school weighed down by its past, several much loved traditions endure. These include the exchanging of prefects' gowns ceremony, the annual staff pantomime and ships' events (the competitive houses – as distinct from the boarding houses – are called 'ships' here and run from the junior department right through the school). It is a place with the imagination to go with the creative ideas that the girls come up with, celebrating the quirky as well as the more mainstream.

'It's warm but not fluffy,' says the head and we think that just about sums it up.

Pastoral care, well-being and discipline: The school prides itself on its tailored, personal, family feel. There is a lot of careful, professional attention given to defining and meeting individual needs and the decision to offer an unusually broad range of options, particularly at sixth form level, supports this principle. Girls tells us that they stay at the school because its size means everyone looks out for everyone else.

The growth mindset philosophy is being well bedded in for both girls and staff and builds on the can-do mentality the school has historically cultivated. A new year 10 course looks at negative and positive coping strategies and the school intends to encourage parents to get to grips with current mental health theories, recognising that in such matters school and home need to be giving the same message.

Mental health issues are discussed very openly. There is a 'brilliant' health and well-being centre, the girls tell us, and staff are complimentary about how well the centre communicates with the rest of the school. Girls have access to an external counsellor.

Behaviour is exemplary, as you find in so many girls' schools. Staff and girls scratch their heads to think of naughty actions, but if they find something, there is a range of the usual sanctions – detentions, withdrawal of privileges. Staff say an awful lot of listening and talking works as prevention.

The management team has been looking at extending leadership opportunities for everyone. This is just as true at year 6 as at year 13. The girls appreciate this and relish the chance to try new roles in a fairly small and safe environment.

Pupils and parents: Pupils here have that unique quality you can find in non-city girls' schools – a gentleness combined with a sassy competitiveness. These are girls who know what is trending globally on social media, but who also love a hike in the rolling Malvern Hills. These are girls who are comfortable in their own skins, they are accepted for who they are and give others the same respect and kindness. It is not nerdy to like science, we were told, and even if you are no good at sport you can still have fun on the games field.

While families are in the main pretty well-heeled, bursaries and scholarship dilute this a little. There are old farming families, those working in the new Worcestershire high-tech areas, businesspeople and professionals from the local vicinity and overseas.

Entrance: There is an element of selection but it is not ferocious. Up to year 3, the girls are invited in for a day to see how they get on. After that there is some assessment through tests. The juniors sit the same 11+ tests as external candidates but if teachers think they won't cope with the step up, there are early discussions about where would be more suitable. Nearly all of the juniors do move up, forming about half of the new year 7. Eleven plus and 13+ entrants are often moving from co-ed preps. Sixth form entrants take papers in their three A level subjects, plus an EAL paper if English isn't their first language.

Exit: Some 60 per cent to top 10 UK universities. Two to Oxbridge and one medic in 2018; others to study eg bioengineering at Sheffield, veterinary science at Liverpool, criminology at Cardiff and music at Trinity Laban.

Money matters: Range of scholarships (academic, sports, music, art drama etc) of up to 10 per cent of fees offered in years 7, 9 and 12. Some means-tested bursaries up to a total of 40 per cent. The prestigious Founders' Awards Scholarships are for top-notch scholars and all-round ambassadors, there are additional assessments and interviews for these. Wrap around care is available at no extra cost.

Remarks: While MSJ may not be smart and shiny, there is something of a Bloomsbury feel about it, but a Bloomsbury fit for the 21st century. Operating in a competitive area, MSJ continues to carve out a niche for itself as being at the forefront of thinking on girls' education. The fact the new head has come from the GDST stable is helping this still further. The school feels driven and full of girls who are going to change the world, but keeps a sense of a small, close knit community. Undoubtedly brilliant for the all-rounder, but increasingly meeting the aspirations of the high flying academics.

Marlborough College

Marlborough, Wiltshire SN8 1PA

Ages 13–18 **Pupils** 969 **Sixth form** 412 **Boarders** 936 full **C of E**

Fees: Day £32,145; Boarding £37,815 pa

01672 892300
www.marlboroughcollege.org

Master: Since September 2018, Louise Moelwyn-Hughes (40s), previously head of St Edmund's School in Canterbury. Was senior deputy head of The Perse in Cambridge, and has already spent 13 years in various roles from year head to housemistress at Marlborough. Educated at Methodist College, Belfast and read classics at Magdalene College, Cambridge. Now immediately dismiss the picture you've formed, because she's far from the Cambridge to public school head you're imagining. Still has the accent from her humble but bookish Belfast background, and says she didn't really know what Cambridge was when a teacher suggested that her schoolgirl love of ancient Greek could be a ticket there. Two young children are currently curbing her hobbies of squash, running, walking and reading.

Academic matters: College motto is Deus dat Incrementum ('God gives the increase') but steady advance of exam results may have less divine origin. Admissions criteria are now somewhat more academically demanding (although prep school head's reference is still crucial). CE result mainly used to 'keep them on the boil and help us with setting'. In 2018, 55 per cent A*/A grades at A level; 72 per cent A*-A/9-7 grades at I/GCSE. Stand out results in A level art, drama, sciences, geography and maths but good tail of non-vowel grades as well. Astronomers fare well, but then they do have the famous Blackett Observatory to aid their stargazing – local schools also get their turn to view the cosmos from a field in Wiltshire. Parents singled out teaching in philosophy as 'inspirational', and its popularity at Pre-U, not to mention the results, endorse this. We know, we know, it's not all about exams and comparisons are invidious, but just out of interest that puts Marlborough some way ahead of many co-ed rivals.

Exam syllabi excepted there seems to be an (admirable) ideological aversion to the churning out of standard curriculum fare at Marlborough. Shell (first year)'s first taste of their new school's academic approach is Form, a multi-disciplinary enquiry into the 'origins of human civilisation', no less. These lessons take the place of separate English, history and RS lessons. Run in parallel with this is the Artemis PHSE course: new pupils take part in guided discussions within their boarding houses. All do two modern languages and Latin, some may also take ancient Greek. Sixth formers can choose from around 35 'electives', mini courses that teachers – including the master – devise to impart specialist knowledge on subjects from cryptic crosswords (now that's a life skill) to special relativity or conducting – the baton, not electrical, kind. These must be as much fun for the staff who run them as they are for pupils.

Average class size is 15, eight in the sixth form. Approximately 100 students have learning difficulties such as moderate dyslexia, dypraxia and ADHD. School says a great deal of thought goes into assessing pupils with SEN to ensure Marlborough is the 'right learning environment' before places are offered. Learning support department works one-to-one and provides a programme of support appropriate to the individual's needs. School also helps a number of students with planning and organisation.

Games, options, the arts: It's no surprise that we filled an entire notebook and ran out of ink during our visit to Marlborough; there's so much on offer beyond the academic timetable. Lest we also deplete our stock of superlatives, suffice it to say that art, drama, sport and music are all very, very good. Generous facilities and 'inspirational' specialist teaching help every pupil, from the most talented to the least coordinated, play, sing, throw or create something to be proud of.

The college may have been co-ed for nearly 50 years, but on the sports field rugby is still king. Four England captains and 38 internationals is indeed a noble heritage. 'The first X1 get clapped onto the pitch at the start of the season,' one parent told us. 'They are the undisputed heroes,' said another. These were observations rather than criticisms and everyone agreed that there are so many fixtures everyone gets the chance of a good match. Besides, the girls are doing just as well: the U14 hockey team recently retained the Wiltshire County Championship and several girls have been picked to represent their county and country in sports such as netball, sailing, lacrosse and athletics. Long tradition of excellence in shooting. Most sports including fly fishing and clay pigeon shooting take place within the college grounds, but there's also a off-site programme that offers beagling, canoeing, caving, coasteering, mountain biking, mountaineering and sub-aqua.

Seemingly universal admiration for 'amazing' drama and music, although the former gets more takers at A level than the latter. Performances and teaching take place in the Bradleian studio theatre and on the flexible stage of the Ellis Theatre that seats up to 400. There are three ambitious audition-only main school productions a year, a musical every two years and a house play festival each summer. Nearly half of pupils take individual music lessons and house music competitions get everyone doing something tuneful. There's a symphony orchestra, choirs, loads of ensembles and plenty of opportunities to perform in the college as well as nationally and internationally. Chapel choir has made several recordings and recently returned from a tour of France. Organ scholars get to learn on the beautiful and recently restored Van Beckwith teaching organ. The department also has an impressive concert programme of visiting professionals and partnerships with the Southbank Sinfonia and individual musicians including Julian Lloyd Webber and Ioan Davies, head of chamber music at the Yehudi Menuhin School.

The college is a founder member of the CCF and has 300 cadets and a 25m indoor range. Those who choose not to join the CCF take part in a variety of service activities, working at primary schools, with younger children in the homes of local families or at a school for children with learning difficulties in Swindon; another group helps at a local riding for the disabled group. There are also opportunities to work with the elderly or on conservation projects.

There's a real energy and buzz at Marlborough; you can feel it. Pupils are busy, busy, busy. Maybe too busy, sometimes. Sensible advice comes from several parents: don't try and do it all, especially in the sixth form. You can't star in the play, play in the firsts and come first in the tests. 'You can do your academic work and one other thing well,' we were told. School says most do more than one thing well but they are vigilant about possible overload. Girls especially can feel the strain: 'The boys are more laid back but girls put themselves under tremendous pressure,' said one mother.

Boarding: Sixteen boarding houses (six boys', six girls' – with another under construction, four mixed ie boys plus sixth form girls) are run by housemasters or housemistresses who live there with their families; they are supported by resident tutors, dames and other members of the pastoral and support staff. Vertical (mixed age) boarding promotes cohesion between year groups and house loyalty is fierce. 'It's really competitive,' several parents told us. Plenty of opportunities to do battle – house shouts (singing), plays, matches and so on.

Every house has its own character, dictated as much by its position and architecture as the team running it. In Hermitage, one of the older houses, we admired a wonderful ground floor bedroom with huge marble fireplace. This prize billet is given to the chap (it's a boys' house) the housemaster thinks is the hardest working, and its occupant looked very proud to have been chosen.

While we did spy some distinctly less than fancy corners as we ran behind a very long-legged housemaster, most boarders at Marlborough seem to get a pretty good deal. Some of the recently refurbished accommodation we visited looked fit for an interiors magazine – walls painted in the sort of modish shade that might be called Vole's Whisper – and, in one, a spectacular glass wall in the kitchen/dining area that overlooked playing fields.

Shells (first years) sleep in four or five bed dorms, graduating to twin and then single rooms from Hundreds (fifth year) up. Occupants are moved around every half term or so. Shell have supervised prep (no gappies, house prefects do this job), Removes (second year) have separate shared studies, after that pupils work in their own rooms. Pupils may Skype their parents (or vice versa) any time apart from during prep; 'we are flexible because of time zones'. Sensible rules re mobiles etc. Meals are taken centrally but continental breakfast, snacks and drinks available in houses.

Although we didn't inspect all 15 houses, we very much liked those we saw. Considerable thought and expense is going into boarders' surroundings and we're sure the refurbishment programme will eventually transform even the ugliest corners. We often say that boarding school accommodation is of a higher standard than university rooms, but at Marlborough some would surely outclass many homes.

So we asked, how can parents ensure their son or daughter is in the 'right' house? Short answer is, you can't. 'There is no 'best' or 'right' house', we were told firmly. What, no sporty house? No musical house? No. 'Parents must come to house open days and visit as many as they can – at least four; some end up seeing six or seven.' Applications are then made to three but school is in charge of mix and has final say. And parents, while you are inspecting the houses you can be sure members of staff are giving you a surreptitious once over.

Background and atmosphere: Marlborough has both in spades. Surely there is no other school on earth where one can walk out of a glorious Victorian gothic revival chapel (stained glass by Burne Jones and former pupil William Morris, sculpture by Eric Gill) and come face to face with a neolithic mound. Merlin's Mound, as it was dubbed by the 12th century tourist board (complete with 17th poetic grotto at its foot), is the second largest man-made mound in Europe. 'Mound,' though alliteratively effective, doesn't really describe its stepped shape: it looks more like a fancy Victorian pudding mould. In the 10th century the mound was recycled into the motte of a motte-and-bailey castle – its moat flows beneath the performing arts centre.

Take a few paces more and you will see the Memorial Hall, a neoclassical theatre and assembly hall built in 1925 to honour the 749 men who fell in 1914-1918. Constructed upon a floating 'raft' over the water meadows, the 'Mem' no longer holds the whole school (actually it could, but not if school wants to stay on the right side of health and safety legislation). Apparently the acoustics are excellent and the beautifully preserved interior remains very evocative. The hall has been restored in time for the centenary of the end of the Great War in 2018. Peeping out from behind the Mem is the 'most architecturally important building in the school', a white painted 1930s concrete science block with ocean liner style aluminium windows and topped with a gourd (head of science at the time was Mr Gourd). It is hoped that this building can be converted into a new design centre.

Forgive all this talk of bricks and mortar – we know schools are about people – but somehow the eclectic mix of ancient and modern across the school estate embodies the breadth and quality of a Marlborough education. We were fortunate enough to be shown around by the head of admissions, an architectural historian. He describes the college site as both 'its greatest asset and a glorious problem' and knows the provenance of every wall and window. If ever a chap was in his happy place...

Marlborough College was established in 1851, the Church of England's response to a shortage of vicars. It wanted to provide a good, affordable education for clergymen's sons from the south west of England on the assumption that these young men would go on to take the cloth. List of clerical OMs testament to success of this operation. School was established in an 18th century mansion and former coaching inn which was gradually joined by Georgian, Victorian and Jacobethan buildings including the former town gaol (now converted into a gym). The master's garden looks down to the River Kennet but alas, the Tennyson tree, a glorious copper beech planted by the poet laureate (his son, Hallam, was a pupil), is no more. Its huge canopy of leaves proved too heavy to bear and crashed down during a summer storm.

Marlborough claims to be the first public school to go co-ed (sixth form only, 1968). Surely Bedales, founded in 1893 and fully co-ed in 1898, should get that prize. But let's not quibble, it'll be 50 years in 2018 and even if boys still outnumber girls in the lower years it definitely doesn't feel like a boys' school. Marlborough College Malaysia was established in 2012 and has already doubled in size. This is not a franchise but a 'genuine expansion of the home school', with linked management and governance.

It's impossible to cover everything that goes on at Marlborough in this review. The school is a 24 hour educational, creative and cultural challenge to teenage apathy and we can only stand back in admiration. 'We ask a great deal of our staff. During term time there's no such thing as working hours.'

Pastoral care, well-being and discipline: All food is prepared in house and eaten in the large communal dining hall. Lunch is staggered between 12 and 1pm, an arrangement that we hope has improved the lot of Shells who we hear sometimes used to go hungry, elbowed out of the way by older children. Pupils eat with their friends at long wooden tables, there's plenty of choice and what we tried was delicious. Breakfasts and lunches get full marks but (and we heard this from several quarters) supper could do better – not an uncommon complaint at boarding schools, must be something to do with leftovers. Former pupil John Betjeman wasn't a fan of this meal either, although we're sure it's much nicer than what he got in the 1920s.

So what about discipline? It hasn't always had a robust reputation at Marlborough, although our impression is that it is now an extremely well run school. A rummage through the college's many 'policies' leads somewhat circuitously to chapter and verse. Suffice it to say that 'explicit or intimate sexual relations' will get you suspended or excluded. Likewise drugs, alcohol, bullying, theft, use of weapons and a whole load of other nasties. Prefects can go to some of the town pubs but on the whole partying is an in-school affair (there's a policy about it on the website) or – and this sounds like more fun – takes place at friends' houses during the holidays or on exeats.

Relations between boys and girls seemed friendly and relaxed, more best mates than Romeo and Juliet. 'There's great banter between the girls and boys,' a father told us. 'There's the odd bit of snogging in the bushes but nothing serious,' said another parent. While we can't comment on the activity we can confirm that the school grounds are well supplied with shrubs of all kinds.

Great praise for houseparents, tutors, dames and all others directly involved in pastoral care. Parents like the 'clear' chain of command and felt that anxieties or problems were dealt with swiftly. Good medical care, plenty of joined up thinking and sharing of information (where appropriate) in cases of illness, stress etc. Medical centre or 'Sanny' looked rather forbidding and was described by one parent as 'grim' (building, not people).

House identity is great for bonding but there are still a few grumbles about pupil hierarchy and the lot of the youngest. Efforts are being made, there's a mentoring system and older children write to new pupils before they start, but maybe there's still room for improvement here.

Pupils and parents: Traditional full boarding families broadly sums up the type you will meet here but school doesn't (and doesn't want to) feel like the 'default outcome of a dinner party conversation.' Yawn. It's sparkier and quirkier than that – fish pie and a decent Muscadet at the kitchen table with slightly naughty friends perhaps, rather than 'faine daining', competitive parenting and house prices. Less country than schools further south but 'not too London' either. Some very local day pupils, six per cent international students.

Pupils are a great advert for co-education – self-assured, good company, the sort you could see fitting in anywhere. Many parents get to know their children's friends socially at weekends (exeats, privis) or during holidays. 'They're a great bunch', we heard, 'the sort who always help clear up after a party.'

In addition to ranks of clerical and military worthies, notable former pupils include artists: William Morris, Graham Shepard, Lauren Child; writers: John Betjeman, Louis MacNeice, Siegfried Sassoon, Bruce Chatwin, Frances Osborne; actors: Wilfrid Hyde White, James Robertson Justice, Michael Pennington, Jack Whitehall; politicians (and their spouses): Hallam Tennyson, Rab Butler, Christopher Chope, Mark Reckless, Sally Bercow, Samantha Cameron; plus Sir Francis Chichester, Mark Phillips, Simon Fanshawe, Mark Tully, Frank Gardner, HRH Princess Eugenie of York and HRH Duchess of Cambridge (she was a prefect). Quite some school reunion that would be.

Entrance: Parents are advised to start the process (visiting boarding houses etc) at least three years in advance. According to the director of admissions, 50 per cent of the decision to admit a child rests with the prep school head's reference, 10 per cent on the ISEB test (to check the academic part of the head's reference) and two interviews in a boarding house by HM and a tutor to verify other aspects of the reference. CE's biggest use, he maintains, is to help with setting once a child joins. Important part of the interview is to discover whether a child will be boarding by consent or 'compulsion'. No one wants the latter. Nor do they want children who have been tutored, 'we're looking for potential for happiness.' Someone will be offering to coach children in that soon.

Consensus from many parents that Marlborough is a great family school. School says it does its best to accommodate siblings, but warns it's not automatic. 'We can't be a closed shop and sometimes this isn't the right place.' Pupils come from over 100 preps but main suppliers are Beaudesert, Cheam, Cothill, The Dragon, Farleigh, Highfield, Lambrook, Ludgrove, Pinewood, Twyford and Windlesham.

We have in the past heard from parents somewhat bruised by Marlborough's 'brusque' response to admissions enquiries. School horrified to learn this: 'we go out of our way to be welcoming and give people time'. Certainly all the front of house staff we met could not have been more charming and less intimidating.

Exit: Very few leave post-GCSE; certainly no kicking out for under par results. Influx of girls in sixth form swells numbers. Big improvements in careers advice; we loved the huge signposts showing all the directions OMs can take. As previously, Edinburgh, Manchester, Bristol, Exeter, Durham and Leeds popular destinations; much the most popular courses are in history, art history, modern languages. Ten Oxbridge places in 2018, six medics, several off to the US (one to Harvard, one to Duke), Canada and Europe.

Money matters: Fees on a par with other similar schools. Still lots of scholarships (more honour than hard cash) but before you bask in the warm glow do check small print and talk to your child about the expectations that go with these.

Means-tested bursaries of up to 100 per cent available and school may assist in individual cases of hardship. Marlborough is one of 'very few schools' who have followed the Charity Commission's advice and transferred all scholarship funds into bursaries. College is currently raising an appeal for substantial additional bursary provision.

Remarks: The college defines its 'triple foundation' as 'rigour, respect and responsibility', an ethos that is at once modern and yet in keeping with its Anglican traditions. Pupils at Marlborough are part of a diverse, creative and academic community – 21st century co-ed boarding at its very best. To paraphrase lines John Betjeman wrote after revisiting his old school in the 1960s, Marlburians 'Live in a world as rich as is a king's. How sweet are tastes to them, how deep their dreams. How hopeful and how possible their schemes.'

Marling School

Cainscross Road, Stroud, Gloucestershire GL5 4HE

Ages 11–18 **Pupils** 967 **Sixth form** 249

01453 762251
www.marling.gloucs.sch.uk

Headteacher: Since 2010, Dr Stuart Wilson PhD (50s). A first in geology from Bristol, staying on to do a PhD, then worked as an engineering geologist for a few years before coming to the realisation that 'nothing I had worked on had ever been built' and being inspired by spending a day shadowing teacher friends. He loved GCSE science teaching but his move to Cleeve School in Cheltenham provided A level experience and the requisite senior management roles before his appointment to Marling. That time fell in a low point in the school's fortunes, and part of the appeal of the job was to drag it out of the stagnant waters. 'He has reinvigorated and reshaped the school,' said one father.

Outwardly relaxed (though setting a high sartorial standard in suit and tie), Dr Wilson's undoubted ambitions for the school extend beyond its boys and buildings to its staff. Marling is now a national teaching school and the lead in a teaching alliance of some 10 local schools; it provides opportunities for career advancement for teachers and leaders, and trains those wishing to learn on the job via Schools Direct. Growing its own talent is part of the culture of aspiration and advancement alive and well at Marling.

Dr Wilson is married to the bursar at a local school, and his son attends yet another. Out-of-hours pursuits include walking, skiing, the allotment, travel to further flung parts of the world and, recently, fly-fishing. When asked to describe him in three words, the group of boys we talked to decided that 'inspiring, positive, helpful' summed him up; one bravely elaborated, telling us he was 'superficially stern, but warm personally'. Parents find him visible and approachable; his presence at parents' evenings is especially valued.

Academic matters: Proud to be a boys' grammar in a world where these are increasingly rare. Selective entry, followed by screening for all, thrice yearly tracking, setting of potential grades and 'constructive specific comments' in marking (HTIs – how to improve) keep most noses to the grindstone most of the time. Results are generally good, but then they jolly well should be: GCSE A*-A/9-7 grades at 56 per cent in 2018; A level A*/B grades at 64 per cent, with 33 per cent A*/A. Top subjects in the boys' view are the sciences, Latin, psychology, philosophy'n'ethics, RE – so we were not surprised to learn that debating is also popular. At A level, maths, the sciences and history are far and away the most popular subjects; modern languages barely get a look in, though three are offered. STEM was happening here almost before the term was coined: this is the school that once built a plane – which flew and landed safely with students on board. And there's a cosmic ray detector on the roof as part of a research project with Birmingham University. Parents appreciate that it is not a hothouse and that 'there is not a stupid amount of homework', but we found some who thought the boys could be pushed harder. The sixth form is run jointly with Stroud High School.

SEND boys are overseen by a SENCo with a place in the senior leadership team, and three specialist members of staff. The focus is on literacy rather than numeracy, which is catered for within the maths department. Liaison between teaching staff is close, and those needing extra help – but not deemed to have SEN – get it. Awareness of boys on the autism spectrum is good; the school has also recently trained its first mental health first aider.

Games, options, the arts: Yes, lots of games here, principally rugby, football, cricket and athletics, but other sports catered for in the sports hall (and fitness suite) across the road, such as basketball, indoor tennis and fencing. All taken quite seriously and Marling first teams set out to crush local and not-so-local opposition. Recent success at county level in running, table tennis, handball and badminton. We heard widespread criticism from parents that only the first teams mattered, that no-one else got an external game or a match, and from one boy that he 'wouldn't put himself forward – the school is only interested in Team GB'. Head counters that there are B and sometimes C teams in younger year groups. DofE strong here and trips (skiing, New York, Pompeii inter alia) sometimes run with Stroud High girls, get thumbs up.

A similar taint of élitism lingers about the drama and music too, according to parents – commendably high standards and plenty of it for those who arrive accomplished or who quickly become so, but not many crumbs for the less gifted. House competitions go some way to address concerns and at the time of writing, recruitment was underway from years 7-11 for a Christmas production of Elf. But there's a limit to what one drama teacher and 1.2 music teachers can achieve in a school this size. Some joint ventures (eg orchestra) with Stroud High, just next door.

A brighter picture emerges with clubs, some which cross age boundaries: we loved the sound of the 'greedy reader' and the Greenpower car team; enthusiasts are also rebuilding a Jaguar with help from company engineers.

Background and atmosphere: Founded in 1887 and named after local benefactor Sir Samuel Marling, it was fortunate enough to inherit endowments from far older defunct schools and educational charities, and has stuck resolutely to its grammar school foundations. These days, it's a somewhat divisive topic locally, some parents reckoning that it and Stroud High (the girls' equivalent across the playground) cream off the academic crème de la crème – especially since they both increased their intakes recently – leaving the town's comprehensive schools the poorer in several respects. That said, the boys are happy and feel lucky to be there: 'It's an aspirational environment', said one and 'we're intellectual rather than privileged,' added another with a wink. Rest assured that the work gets done: Marling boys have a serious attitude and the prevailing winds are ones of solid academic graft.

It certainly looks and feels like a good old-fashioned grammar school with its beautiful darkly panelled, vaulted school hall, portraits and parquet as standard. The cloister – the quaintest and most charming example of redundant school architecture we had ever seen (useful when it rains) – links the two original buildings, good solid Victorian monoliths. Elsewhere some stunning modern buildings, including the new West Block and creative arts block, add contemporary counterpoint – and luckily the functional green tin sports complex is safely out of shot across the road. IT is not overwhelming; this is not a place where everyone has a laptop or iPad tucked under one arm. 'The return of linear A levels mean manifold three hour papers – which need handwriting!' as the head expressed it. The boys appear to toe the line as far as uniform and hairstyle go, and to keep banter within limits, in class at any rate. 'It's not a laddish culture,' opined one mother, but others demurred: 'You can be bright, but it's harder to be a nerd'. 'Non-conformists can be bullied', said another.

Pastoral care, well-being and discipline: Reservations about isolated bullying apart, pastoral care is highly rated by all we talked to. Response to parental concerns is quick and effective, and the school will contact parents over any unease it may have. Heads of year come in for particular praise. The boys reckon the balance struck between sanction and reward is about right, and that the reasons behind any punishments are fully explained. 'Clarity and consistency,' says the head confidently. Sixth formers appreciate being treated like the adults they will soon become. Plenty of accessible and sympathetic members of staff to talk to when things go wrong in whatever sphere of school life.

Pupils and parents: No catchment area, but most students arrive from within a 10 mile radius of Stroud by a web of buses, public and private. The furthest flung might come from Swindon, an educational desert, or Cheltenham, which isn't. It need hardly be said that families whose sons are at Marling set much store by schooling and might be glad to have many of the advantages of independent education without the price tag. 'We're proud that parents see us as an alternative', concludes the head, with a refreshing lack of chippiness. His boys are lively, funny, thoughtful – delightful, in fact, but not too burdened by the weight of academic expectation the school and their parents place on them. Parents enjoy an active association with staff involvement which raises considerable funds for the school and a good sideline in second hand uniform.

Entrance: Quite selective, aiming at the top 25 per cent of the ability range for its 150 year 7 intake. The seven Gloucestershire grammar schools share the same CEM 11+ entrance test (verbal ability, numerical reasoning and non-verbal reasoning) devised by Durham University, for which tutoring is very common; some parents disapprove massively, however, on the grounds that such selectivity is local government policy and that the playing field should therefore be level. Those who don't make it can have another crack in subsequent years for entry in year 8, 9 or 10. Fortunately, Stroud's other comprehensive schools are well regarded, as is Deer Park in Cirencester. At sixth form, another 25 per cent arrive with the requisite number of GCSE grades (at least five, with a 5 or above in English and maths and no lower than a 6 in A level subjects).

Exit: Few after GCSE (max 25 per cent) – why would they, with the scope and lure provided the combined sixth form offer with Stroud High, and from 2019, girls in its own sixth form? School will pick out likely candidates for Oxbridge and Russell Group (three to Oxbridge in 2018) – though they can also 'self-identify'. Requirements exacted by medicine (one in 2018), veterinary or overseas universities (2018 saw one boy to a Finland to study engineering) also catered for. 'Local options, perhaps less prominent but given no less support,' the head confirms, as are apprenticeships and other non-university destinations. Strong leaning towards maths, engineering and science courses, but English, humanities and politics also prominent. The sixth formers we met were extravagant in their praise for UCAS support and for Futures Day, where speakers from universities, employers and gap year volunteering providers set out all conceivable (acceptable) options. The Old Marlingtonians' Association another useful resource for careers advice.

Remarks: Stroud can be proud of this school, which maintains a high academic profile and traditions for boys without any risk of their becoming arrogant, stuffy or sexist. Bringing home the silverware, literal and metaphorical, matters – but please could everyone have a game? Or a part?

The Maynard School

Denmark Road, Exeter EX1 1SJ

Ages 4–18 Pupils 415 Sixth form 103

Fees: £6,285 – 13,248 pa

01392 273417
www.maynard.co.uk

Headmistress: Since 2016, Sarah Dunn BSc NPQH. Educated at St Andrew's International School, Bahamas, Exeter University (biology); trained to be a teacher at Oxford. First job at Torquay Boys' Grammar, biology teacher, deputy head of sixth form, head of pastoral care and careers. Never one to be daunted by a gender headwind, she opened up her next school, Plymouth College, to girls. As deputy head there for 21 years she was instrumental in developing the school's sports partnerships to Olympic standards.

Fizzes with energy, openminded, wholly unfazed by our more penetrating questions. Competitive, as you'd expect, dead set on bringing out the best in this, one of the oldest girls' schools in the country. She plays to win and retains her 'real passion for sport' – she runs, cycles and rows. If this sets you thinking, 'Ah, the jolly hockey sticks sort', think again. Divides her working day into two parts: daylight for people, darkness for paperwork. Impeccable sou'westerly pedigree, 'all my friends' network is down here', so she has a sound knowledge of the school's place in the local market. She's pragmatic: she understands that life's greatest joys are attained through self-belief and hard work, making her a good modern role model for her girls. Sound a bit austere? At heart hers is a romantic conception of what school is all about: 'School,' says Miss Dunn, 'should be as much fun as possible'. Then you walk round and see for yourself and discover that, by jingo, that's exactly what The Maynard is. In the words of a parent, 'If I didn't know it, and someone described the Maynard School to me, I would probably feel it sounded too good to be true.'

The school's minibuses proclaim the school to be 'the leading independent girls' school in the South West'. To a faint-heart this may look like a hostage to fortune, while a sceptic might observe that it all depends on what you feed into your calculation. Without going there, we can attest to the school's longstanding excellence on any number of measures from academic to the arts to sport. So it's not as if Miss Dunn inherited a fixer-upper. Far from it; in the year she took over the school inspectors marked it 'excellent' in most categories. Her focus is on marginal gains (incremental improvements that add up to an overall improvement – think Sky cycling team) while at the same time safeguarding the unique and precious happiness of the school community, which is its most conspicuous attribute. At the heart of that is the single-sex nature of the school, and it is on the perceived value of this that parents choose between The Maynard and equally high-achieving competitors.

Head of junior school: Since 2006, Steven Smerdon, originally from Bath, educated at Exeter University. His career has taken him to Edinburgh, Australia and back to Exeter again. Friendly, welcoming and enthusiastic. Teaches RE and drama and is child protection officer for the whole school. In his 40s, he enjoys the great outdoors and is a keen cyclist. Maynard Junior is above average academically, but he says, 'the most important thing we teach is how to get on with people.' Parents say, 'Mr Smerdon clearly loves his job and the girls love him'.

Academic matters: Solid academic curriculum plus food & nutrition and psychology. STEM strong and evident in university choices. Humanities strong too. Three modern languages + Latin, popular and successful at GCSE but less uptake at A level. Twenty-two subjects on offer at A level including fashion and textiles, introduced 2017 by student request. Notably small set sizes in the sixth form. Good library with, commendably, the Booker shortlist in a prominent row when we visited.

A very high standard of work on display in the junior school and we saw some impressive written work. There is a teaching assistant for one-to-one reading sessions and the end results have been remarkable. A breadth of reading is encouraged and the library provides a cosy reading area.

These are bright girls you'd expect to do well, but they and their parents are unstinting in their praise of the teachers. In the words of one, 'they always deliver on their promises'. It's the warmth of the relationship that makes all the difference. And the laughter. One girl told us, 'We all work hard because we don't want to upset them'. Teachers go out of their way to support the girls in their own time; we were told about one who came in during the holidays to help a young woman prepare for an audition. They are creative in finding time outside lessons for a bit of extra tuition. Relationships between students and staff are supportive, humorous yet entirely professional. Students see their teachers as human beings and work all the harder because if it. And if you're not the brightest girl in the class? A student told us, 'It's cool to be the nicest girl in the class'. Another told us, 'Teachers here tend to get to you before you know you've got a problem'. A parent told us there is a 'definite sense of purpose and drive, yes, but with equal measures of warmth and respect' between students and staff. All agree that this is definitely not a sweatshop and no one is left behind. Girls are 'both competitive with, and completely supportive of, each other.' We spoke to any number of girls and were struck that none of them talked about stress. About being as busy as can be, yes, but not stressed.

As you would expect of a selective school, numbers of students with (mild) special educational needs (SEND) are low – around 20. Specialist support is reinforced by the close understanding of the pupils by their teachers. All girls are closely monitored so that any who are overstretched can also be supported. All new junior schoolgirls are screened for dyslexia. Some have one-to-one specialist teaching outside the classroom, including use of a structured spelling and reading scheme, study skills, support for sequencing and memory difficulties. The teaching assistant also covers one-to-one sessions for numeracy. This is all overseen by SENCo. The head is keen to emphasise that 'self-esteem is the most important aid to learning and the whole school works to improve this in all our girls.'

A level results 2018: 81 per cent A*/B, 52 per cent A*/A. GCSE results: 60 per cent A*-A/7-9. Value added score at the top of the 'average' range, perfectly respectable but arguably susceptible to marginal gains yielding more Oxbridge places.

Games, options, the arts: Not blessed by a patrimony of green acres, like many another city school. But the nearby university has plenty, and there's the local swimming pool, so there's a rich provision of sports on offer including nascent football together with some high-level coaching. We watched a bunch of girls larking happily until galvanised by a single whistle-blast into mightily impressive netball players. The school has long been noted for its sport at all levels from inter-school to international. Under the impetus of Miss Dunn, with her background in elite provision, this is set to improve further; indeed one of her intended building projects is to provide a fitness suite in the present sports hall. Impressed as we were by the athletic prowess of the team players, our favourite Maynard activity remains junior running club. It's a lunchtime thing for the younger girls. They jog and skip around a tennis court, pink and giggling, and stand and do exercises under the guidance of a PE teacher and some senior girls. It epitomised for us everything that makes the school so admirable and so charming.

Art thrives at a high level. Lots going on, all of it eyeworthy. Here's a measure: recently all three three A level candidates (not an especially small group by Maynard standards) got A*. In the spring the school hosts a public art exhibition featuring top local and national artists. New performing arts theatre. Much needed. Big annual whole-school production and biennial musical in cahoots with the art and music departments. Performances normally at the Barnfield theatre a few streets away. Music a longstanding crown jewel, all the ensembles you can think of. Very strong choral tradition; the choir is invited to participate in projects by such organisations as the British Council and the Royal Opera House. Yes, they're that good. A few years ago they were selected to sing at the welcome ceremony for the Australia World Cup rugby team.

For outdoorsy girls there is DofE and Ten Tors – with Dartmoor and the seaside a stone's throw away. Decent range of out of school clubs: lots of sport and music, Model United Nations, chess, eco-warriors, maths Olympiad, Young Enterprise. Mostly curriculum linked. Senior girls play a big part in leading clubs. Exchange visits and trips, of course, masses of trips, cultural, musical and recreational.

M

Background and atmosphere: Founded in 1656 as the Blue Maids Hospital School, renamed after its founder Sir Henry Maynard in 1912. Moved in 1882 to the leafy suburb of St Leonards where it resembles nothing so much as, in the head's words, 'a walled island'. Buildings mostly late C19 and later. The sort of site that necessitates the most ingenious use of space. It feels hugger-mugger but it works. Interiors cheered by artwork, displays and the like, not to mention the school dog, Nula. When we met her she was being read to along with a class of little girls.

The prevailing atmosphere is, of course, girly. This is what girls can be like when there are no boys around. Unselfconscious. Natural. Growing up in their own way, in their own time. The small size of the school plays a supporting part: everyone is known to everybody; there's a strong sense of community promoted by events like the annual staff play, and the annual sixth form review when students gently (or not so gently) pull the legs of their teachers. All agree that everyone knows where to draw the line. Nobody takes themselves terribly seriously while at the same time taking education very seriously. Year groups mix and senior girls give back in a big-sisterly way that's magical to behold – yes, magical. Little girls told us they see sixth formers as role models and admire not just their talents but their caring attitude to other students. One girl said, 'Girls are naturally kinder to each other when there aren't boys around'. Another said, 'This is a place of strong, lifelong friendships', a place where, in the words of a parent, 'You're allowed to be quirky, you can be who you want to be'. Another parent said, 'Girls are engaged with their learning, full of infectious enthusiasm for life, keen to reach their potential in everything they do, but are not highly strung, pushed or that dreaded, much-used accusation "hothoused" in any way.'

We asked girls if they'd like to have boys around, even in small quantities – for things like plays (where they're quite useful for, say, male roles). The response was 'No need for them'. Not having them certainly makes available a far wider range of interesting and challenging parts. Not that they're anti-boy; some of them have brothers, some live next door to one, they like boys, they mix with them after school. And they like their school as it is. They are encouraged to identify with eminent women role models. This is a feminist environment characterised by strong confidence. Is it all just a bit too cosy and sheltered? Some may think so, though every parent we spoke to evinced no reservations; they want their child to be nurtured. When it's time to leave, are these girls ready and prepared to take on the world as it is? Again, no parental misgivings. Our observation is that the senior girls we met and were looked after by were completely at ease with, and uninhibited by, strange adults. We were especially struck by one parent, a local business person who'd had no intention whatever of sending his daughter to the school... until he took a Maynard girl on for a summer holiday job. Industrious, commonsensical and personable, she had him ringing for a prospectus.

The benefits of a single-sex education are all out there in the form of statistics and studies and theories. Regarding statistics, there is evidence that the so-called reformed GCSEs and A levels are narrowing the gender attainment gap. Regarding theories, every argument has its counter-argument.

Pastoral care, well-being and discipline: Discipline not a big deal here. There's a widely held sense that 'we're all in it together' so instead of rules there's a culture of trust between students and staff together with a widely held feeling that the school genuinely values every child. Mental health issues rare, lots of meetings deal with it. An essentially practical approach to social media develops students' understanding of it so that their approach can be self-regulating. Students noted that staff keep a watchful eye on what they're eating, particularly lower down the school. Parents report that teachers are very responsive to email contact by parents and girls out of hours and really like the way the head welcomes students and parents at the school gates every morning. It was clear from discussions with students that the school provides excellent careers advice from year 10 onwards. We pressed both parents and students by means of the most ingenious questioning to tell us what they think the school could do better. They thought and they thought and collectively came up with two interesting ideas. One mum said, 'A bit more interaction with boys.' One girl said it would be 'nice to have ham more often at lunch'.

Trad uniform: Black Watch-y kilt, navy jumper, white blouse. In the sixth form you get to go smart casual. A parent told us: 'There's nothing buttoned up about it,' adding, with feeling, 'no sixth formers dressed like office workers'.

Pupils and parents: Parents and their daughters from up to an hour or so away, most from business and professional backgrounds plus a sprinkling from the university, which brings smartness and dash to the city, making it appealing for DFLs – down from Londoners.

Hugely supportive parents with their own charitable trust, the Maynard Parents Association. Lots of jolly socials and a lot of fundraising. Especially popular: the annual new parents' supper.

Entrance: Assessment for reception to year 2 in new pre-prep by 'a series of informal and play-based activities'. Assessments for junior school (7+) – in English, maths, reasoning and reading – are taken seriously as girls are not expected to re-sit for entry to the senior school (although places are not guaranteed, some 90 per cent move on there). School encourages sending your daughter for a taster day before you commit.

Online tests in January in English, maths and reasoning for years 7 and 8 with a science paper thrown in for years 9 and 10. Papers pretty much tuition-resistant. Apply whenever in the school year if there are places available. For sixth form entry, interview + reference from current school together with the academic requirement of level 6 in all GCSEs and level 7 in proposed A level subjects.

Exit: Some 80+ per cent stay on after GCSEs, Exeter (tertiary) College being a popular alternative destination. Post-A level, Bristol, Birmingham, Oxford Brooks, Warwick and UWE all popular. One to Oxford in 2018, plus two medics, two vets and two dentists.

Money matters: There's a culture of low fees at the top academic schools in Exeter so expect to pay up to £1500 a term less than at other schools in the commutable hinterland. Usual range of scholarships – academic, sport, the arts. Means-tested bursaries up to 45 per cent of full fees for girls whose parents who can't afford full whack. Special Maynard Awards – 'because we have a moral obligation to open the school gates a little wider' – offering a bursary plus scholarship, so potentially a huge discount. Three free places for sixth formers. Sibling discounts. The school is open from 8.00am til 5.30pm including free wraparound care.

Remarks: Parents of a bright girl in Exeter are spoiled for choice: co-ed or single sex. Take a spreadsheet approach and you'll end up having a statistical breakdown. Take the line that the goal of education is the attainment of selfhood and you'll start getting somewhere. This Guide doesn't take sides, obviously. We simply note that The Maynard is a heartstealer.

Millfield Prep School

Linked with Millfield School

Edgarley Hall, Glastonbury, Somerset BA6 8LD

Ages 2–13 **Pupils** 473 **Boarders** 130, 12 flexi (from 7 years)

Fees: Day £8,505 – £18,705; Boarding £28,380 pa

01458 832446
www.millfieldschool.com/

Headmistress: Since 2010, Shirley Shayler MEd BSc PGCE (early 50s). Born and raised in Northern Ireland and grammar school educated. Degree in biology (Stirling), returning to Northern Ireland for her PGCE. Spent all her career in England, though she has never quite lost the cadences of her upbringing. A spell at Millfield Senior, teaching biology, coaching hockey and being a houseparent, a deputy headship at Taunton School, a headship of Stonar and then back where she started. There was much dismay when she left the senior school, testimony to the respect and affection in which she is evidently held at Millfield Prep; everyone we spoke to remarked upon her approachability and her visibility. However, she's no soft touch, 'strict' and 'professional' we were told, and her speeches were described as inspirational.

M

Her experience was evident and reassuring, as was her warmth, her perceptiveness, and her sense of style: there's generally a place for a discreet split in a pencil skirt and an elegant up-do. She is something of a visionary – she designed the unusual and beautiful pavilion housing an imaginative space for theatre in the round – and still has a long list of improvements. She is pleased to have already joined up the pastoral care with academic and sporting matters: 'they can be disjointed,' she says, 'but the pastoral tutor groups ensure that no child is over-committed [something which would be easy at Millfield].' Married to Gary, a biology teacher at the senior school, she has one daughter plus her horse and four dogs. 'I just about have time to cook a Sunday roast in term time.'

Entrance: Essentially non-selective, though 'we do have an academic and behavioural benchmark,' the head points out. The school professes to be looking for 'well-motivated boys and girls with [...] interests that stretch beyond the academic curriculum'. Hopefuls are interviewed and assessed – the latter a computer-based verbal and non-verbal reasoning test. Children needing or likely to need extra help meet the head of learning support for their assessment. Admissions into the pre-prep from 2 and the prep from 7, but the largest intake is into year 7; applications are considered into any year group at any time, space permitting. One mother was full of praise for the welcome her son had received in year 6. Scholarships to 15 per cent of fees (but often honorary) for academic, sporting and musical prowess and, unusually, in chess, plus all rounders, and headmistress' scholarships to a generous 50 per cent for outstanding ability or talent.

Exit: Mostly to the senior school (85 per cent), where transfer is automatic barring the blotting of any copy books, but quite open to children going elsewhere at year 9. In 2018, this included Bryanston, Stowe and King's Bruton.

Remarks: This a school that has pretty well everything for pretty well everybody with the means to pay for it. Academically, the range is very broad indeed: we loved the Latin class for better linguists who were busy bringing a dead language back to life by speaking it, but the sensitive and encouraging teaching in the tiny physics class of just five – to whom this subject evidently didn't come easily – was inspiring too. From the off, pupils are set for maths and English; languages follow in year 7. Most subjects are taught by a group tutor until year 6, then all by specialists. Classes are small, and the curriculum extensive, enquiry-based and global in outlook. Parents feel that the 'lingering reputation of the school as being not very academic,' as one put it, and so not suitable for a very bright child, is misconceived.

Chess lessons with the resident grandmaster are compulsory in years 3 and 4, and students are encouraged to take part in national competitions, such as Salters Festival of Chemistry (winners in 2017). Thoughtful Learner programme aims to set its adherents up for life. Technology is not quite as embedded as in the senior school, but students are expected to have their own iPad from year 7. Millfield generally is known for its SEN provision, notably specialist dyslexia support, and is the reason why some parents choose the school. A busy learning development centre staffed by one part-time and five full-time members of staff delivers multi-sensory programmes to address many, if not all, aspects of dyslexia, such as processing and organisational difficulties. The centre is so integral to the school that students attend extra lessons with no stigma attached to it whatsoever. 'He just goes – he doesn't care,' said one mother of her son.

Outside the classroom, there's everything a young person could possibly want to do – and then some. The facilities, coaching and degree to which timetables can be tweaked for the sporting elite are exceptional for a prep school and some choose it for that reason. All are, however, encouraged to try a variety, and all represent the school at some point in something. Particular recent successes include girls' hockey (at the time of writing, the girls U13 were IAPS champions), golf, fencing and triathle, in which the school boasts a junior world champion. Pitches, courts, nets abound, plus a 25m pool, nine hole golf course, stables and an outdoor arena, where a solitary rider on a palomino cantered circles in the dusk as we concluded our visit. The school's wonderful setting, nestled under Glastonbury Tor, means a limit on artificial lighting.

Artistic achievement limited only by talent: from the artist in residence, to the 3D laser cutter, to the area dedicated to the sculpting of stone – it's all here for the taking. Clubs thrive alongside timetabled art, plenty of space to show it all off and a prominent place for Picture of the Week in the dining room. Imaginative collaborations take place with the music department on occasion, such as Painting Sound and Woven Sound.

No shortage of ambition on the drama front, either. Everyone is encouraged to get involved and there are productions for individual year groups; recent shows include Beauty and the Beast (where three of the principle male roles were played by girls) and The Highwayman. Music is outstanding. The number and scope of ensembles would not disgrace a senior school, with opportunities in school (we liked the sound of brunch masterclasses in piano and strings) and out (such as workshops with eminent vocal performers such as the Gesualdo Six). Every child is encouraged to perform, producing a varied crop of confident and accomplished singers, fiddlers, trumpeters and so on, plus those who just do it for fun. The highlight of our visit was the tea and music concert, in which children of all ages played and sang short pieces. From breathy flutes to hesitant pianists to a talented young singer who could make Adele look to her laurels – all were brave enough to strut their stuff in front of parents and staff and receive warm applause. And we haven't even mentioned the array of cakes...

We found more than satisfied customers and very few gripes. 'Unlike the senior school, everyone knows each other at the prep,' one mother told us. 'My son's friends are lovely, grounded, thoroughly good people,' added another. The global friendships formed and the school's skill in dealing with friendships gone wrong get the thumbs up. The nurturing environment – not so cosy that children are not gently pushed beyond familiar pastimes – also meets with parental approval: 'He's tried cookery and public speaking, and has grown in confidence so much that now he volunteers for things at school,' one happy parent reported.

The group tutor is the go-to person for day students and has the overview of their lives at school; for boarders, it's houseparents. Very little boarding until year 6, then numbers pick up in years 7 and 8, until about 60 per cent finish their prep school careers as boarders. High praise for boarding, including some rather rueful in tone: 'You don't need to board – we live five miles away!' one mother told her children, but board they do, 'because they love it'. Another told us that her child was hard to get hold of, as he was so busy and 'within five minutes, he's saying Bye!' International parents kept fully in the picture; in fact everyone we encountered spoke highly of communication in general, and the full page email from each subject teacher for those parents unable to make parents' evenings is much appreciated.

Boys' houses tend to be older and more scattered; recently one girls' house was relocated to be next to the other, both purpose built. We found them warm, homely and welcoming, with cosy dorms and kitchens for those all-important snacks. All mobile devices have to be handed in at night. It would be hard to find a child who would not enjoy Millfield Prep, though the head did concede that they have to be organised – it's a huge site with a lot on. 'Might not suit an agoraphobic either,' she added wryly. At the request of students, the uniform has recently been rejigged to include culottes for anyone who wishes to wear them. Checked shirts for every day, white for best, ties for all; sports kit in Millfield colours of navy, scarlet and green branded within in an inch of its life.

Millfield Prep is less daunting and more nurturing than its size might suggest, and previous (mis)conceptions of it being somewhere for sporty, rich children with a bit of schooling thrown in are inaccurate. But there's no ducking the immensely privileged environment – it's all there for the taking.

Millfield School

Linked with Millfield Prep School

Butleigh Road, Street, Somerset BA16 0YD

Ages 13–18 **Pupils** 1,240 **Sixth form** 595 **Boarders** 936 full

Fees: Day £25,605; Boarding £38,610 pa

01458 444296
www.millfieldschool.com/

M

Head master: Since September 2018, Gavin Horgan, previously head of Worksop College. Classics degree from Oxford; worked in schools in Sri Lanka and Argentina before returning to the UK as deputy rector of Glasgow Academy. He gathered headlines for organising a Worksop school trip to climb mountains in Greenland, believing that risk is essential to children's development – and more for his somewhat woolly response to the account of initiation rites in the national press just days after he arrived. He is married to Alison and they have a young family.

Academic matters: Our previous review said that 'academics will never be the point of Millfield' and that remains true, but school has devoted considerable efforts to beefing up the intellectual offer with, amongst other initiatives, an enviable programme of academic enrichment, including a lecture series and subject conferences with such scientific colossi as Robert Winston, Maggie Aderin-Pocock and Jim Al-Khalili on the same platform. Brainboxes are invited to join Eureka! or Think Tank, mixed aged groups which meet fortnightly. 2018 GCSEs 46 per cent A*-A/9-7; depending on ability and aptitude, students might do any number between six and 12, including core subjects but not necessarily a foreign language. A level results in 2018 were 55 per cent A*/B, 27 per cent A*/A, with a staggering 33 subjects to choose from, including world development and classical Greek.

One parent was critical of Oxbridge preparation – or lack of it, feeling that the school was much more interested in and geared up for applications to American universities; the school is a SAT centre. But it is heartening to see the range of qualifications on offer at Millfield: for the less academically inclined, BTecs attract growing numbers, along with the British Horse Society's Preliminary Instructor's certificate and the ever popular Leiths food and wine course – just the thing for running that chalet in Verbier. Judging by the longevity of some teachers' careers there, teaching at Millfield can be a job for life; we picked up a feeling that some could usefully be moved on. The last head addressed effective recruitment at least by providing the kind of accommodation designed to attract top notch staff. Class sizes noticeably small here, max 14; the staff pupil ratio is very low at just 1:6.5. Students are generally grouped into ability bands via literacy tests, then into sets within those bands, but some A level language and science classes are taught across the ability range.

School's website cites 'sophisticated use of digital technology for learning' but this greatly understates the almost total integration of iPads throughout the school. Every student must have one, and through it, almost everything flows, in and out of the classroom. That said, it does not replace live teaching, but aids it: we were privileged, if not faintly repelled, to witness the dissection of a horse's lung, where the lesson went on to explore human lung capacity at rest and after exertion via an iPad app, one boy gamely leaping up and down outside as a live experiment. Unhelpful chatter from Facebook, Instagram and Twitter is blocked in lesson time, and there's a tracking system which monitors any reprehensible activity. 'But what about old-fashioned skills like note-taking?' we asked – and received a somewhat prickly assurance that these were also taught. 'We're about adapting, not adopting.'

SEN provision underpins much of Millfield's successes and its appeal. When we asked about Millfield's being viewed as a haven or magnet for SEN, the response was unequivocal: 'Well it is! We make strong assessments of SEN which we normalise here, and occasionally have to say no to those whose learning we cannot support'. Just over a third of students have an identified need, addressed and supported by a team of SpLD experts in the exceptionally well-resourced learning support centre (no fewer than four educational psychologists on the staff), sited right at this rambling school's heart. Support is based on literacy, the key to the entire curriculum, but help is available for all manners of barriers to learning including dyscalculia (sometimes delivered to milder cases among younger students by sixth formers alongside the maths tutor), dyspraxia and organisation skills. Just about everyone gets GCSE English and maths at grade 4 – hurrah – but retake classes are run in year 12 for anyone just missing that important hurdle. The sheer numbers receiving support means a total lack of stigma: our delightful young guide came straight to the point: 'I am very dyslexic and here I get all the help I need'. Close liaison between teachers, house staff, tutors and SEN staff provides continuity and reassurance.

Games, options, the arts: Genuinely exceedingly difficult to know where to start. This is unquestionably the place for your budding Olympian, and the fact that it has produced so many top flight athletes and sportspeople is no accident. Both provision and facilities abound, from the famous 50m Olympic swimming pool with all the wizardry and coaches associated with training future national champions to the recent acquisition of a stretch of the Huntspill river (a world class water facility, apparently) and Swingulator which trains oarsmen/women on dry land. It is typical of the Millfield seriousness of purpose that, having only introduced rowing a few years ago, investment in a year-round programme including nutrition, video analysis and diverse training has resulted in this Jonny-come-lately beating many established rowing schools and even universities. But whatever Millfield does – and it does almost everything – it does exceptionally well, devoting considerable sums, land and care in recruiting top coaches to its unequalled sporting offer. We could wax rapturous about the provision for riders, comprising a polo ground, cross-country course and gallops, or about the fencing salle, but the more usual school sports are outstandingly provided for also. The school's level of commitment has to be matched by that of the students': a daily 5.40am reveille is quite common for élite swimmers, for example. Parental opinion about the school's attitude to sporting élitism varies: clearly some send their offspring here exactly for that, others feel that the push for excellence has rather meant other kids being 'left to get on with it', according to one father. At junior levels, by contrast, we found some frustration that previous top prep school players (rugby, but maybe other games too) were regularly substituted, meaning that they played less often/for less long than they were used to, demotivating them at times.

Art and DT all happen in the same gorgeous spacious block; needless to say, all equipment is bang up to the mark and, claims school, equals some university facilities. The nationally known Atkinson Gallery hosts four major exhibitions a year; when we visited, the most innovative work coming out of the UK's top art schools was on show. New work for the sculpture trail is regularly commissioned or purchased. Music facilities marvellous – lots of it, very high spec too – and the exposure to the musical life a part of every Millfieldian's first year, when learning an orchestral instrument is compulsory. Major concerts often take place in the sublime contrast of Wells Cathedral, where the choir sings also regular services. It was an unexpected delight to happen across a member of the music staff practising Poulenc for his own pleasure. Drama is popular and very well-resourced, with several studios as well as the Meyer Theatre. Just one whole school production a year but a ton of other things, such as a sketch show and a Spanish play, and opportunities to get involved in all goings-on back stage. Applications to drama school are exceptionally well supported here, and success rates high in this competitive area.

The Millfield Activities Programme (MAP to its friends) offers 100 different pursuits for all students up until year 12, and is intended to offer breadth – alongside élite sport, for example. French cinema, German card games, skiing race training, silversmithing – it's all there for the taking. Local volunteering opportunities with a range of charities provide an outlet for altruism and perhaps a chance to reflect on all that privilege.

Boarding: Three-quarters of students board in 19 boarding houses scattered across the 240 acre campus. We were whisked around a selection of them in a golf buggy, on account of the sheer scale of the place (not because we had visited unsuitably shod in stilettos). Year 9s have their own houses for that vital first year, to ensure solid friendships across the year group and to integrate the large numbers who arrive from Millfield Prep. After year 9, students have a say in their final house, but staff are careful to try to avoid the forming of cliques. Most rooms are twins, singles further up the school, some with ensuite shower rooms; all was clean and functional rather than luxurious, and we noted the congenial common room space with pool tables and ping pong, rather than more screens; all i-anything is handed in at night to a named charging compartment. Pleasant outside space specially designed for barbecues and summer socialising. House staff come in for praise: one housemaster was described as a 'cracking bloke', and parents like the high staff:student ratio and the 15 bed medical centre, with physio clinic. We did, though, pick up a sense of social divide between the day students and boarders, and one father said bluntly that the former are 'disproportionately bright'. Boarders and day students alike eat in the magnificent cafeteria, where the range of choice is almost bewildering; menus embrace all sporting diets. The tortilla and salads we chose from the Spanish counter as part of the world food bar was delicious, and it was made even more authentic by the Spanish staff jabbering away on the next table. Further flung boarding houses have the occasional dinner in their own dining rooms on special occasions.

Background and atmosphere: For one of the UK's most successful boarding schools, Millfield is really quite a new kid on the block. Just over 80 years ago Jack Meyer, a bright young civil servant and accomplished cricketer, went out to work with the Indian Civil Service. Attracting the notice of a passing maharajah as a jolly good chap, 'Boss' Meyer, as he became known, returned to the UK in the mid 1930s at his request with seven Indian boys, six of them princes, to found a school – Millfield, initially set up in a private house of that name rented from the nearby Clark family (of shoe fame). Innovation was the name of the game from then on: co-ed from 1939, as much emphasis on excellence and opportunity in sport and the arts as on academic success, and from 1942, an interest in and commitment to overcoming dyslexia and other barriers to learning, following the arrival of the 'word blind' son of the then deputy PM, Martin Attlee, who (most unusually for dyslexics of the time) went on to higher education.

These three markers have defined the school ever since, sometimes unfairly, but the feel and look of the place is fresh and contemporary – no hallowed portals here. Instead, buildings of all materials, types and function ('No great architectural merit,' said one father, drily) are scattered across the huge site, more akin to a small university campus, whose grassed areas were strewn with crocuses when we visited. A culture of entrepreneurship still prevails: on the school's part, ambitious plans for a new enterprise centre, on the part of one new sixth former, encouragement and plaudits for setting up his own charity club to raise funds for less fortunate youngsters. No overwhelming sense of entitlement, privilege or history among the students either; all the ones we spoke to expressing in forthright terms their good fortune at being there. Uniform unexceptional – standard issue navy suits with the finest of pinstripes and v-necked jumpers for the girls below sixth form, but boys get to buy their own suits: we saw one dandy clad in immaculate Prince of Wales check. 'Not fair,' opined one mother of a girl...

Pastoral care, well-being and discipline: Concerned that no-one gets lost, overlooked or away with too much in this big school, house staffing levels increased considerably to try to ensure none slip through the net, though initiation rituals still persist and featured in the national press recently. The general levels of affluence and huge geographical catchment might cause some to suspect illicit contraband like drink and drugs, but this passed unmentioned by all those we spoke to. Parents are mostly happy with the way in which their concerns are dealt with, and students feel that punishments are fair and appropriate; sixth form gating is a particular deterrent to wrong-doing. The fact that academic work is commended both for achievement and effort goes down well also. What most schools call PHSE has been redesigned as Positive Education – a through-going programme covering, inter alia, resilience and emotional intelligence; this is reinforced in day/boarding houses as well as in class. A dedicated email address exists to report any incidents of bullying.

Pupils and parents: Everyone, nay everyone, talked of the diversity of families – the much-vaunted Millfield Mix – and given the range of bursaries on offer, this is not as fanciful as it might appear (OK, OK, a few children arrive by helicopter, but others in much humbler hatchbacks). 'We work on the Robin Hood principle.' Maybe its sporting prowess, international clientele (20 per cent come from overseas but no one nationality predominates) and openness to a wide intellectual spectrum create the 'egalitarian feel of a southern hemisphere school' that the last head was keen on, but there's certainly 'a lot less tweed on the touchline than there is at Radley,' as one dad put it. The students we met looked us in the eye and shook us firmly by the hand – 'confident in the qualities that make them wonderful,' in the words of the previous head. Worth noting that there are roughly 60 per cent boys.

Entrance: Mainly into year 9, many from its own large prep school, but from 120 other prep schools all over the world. Thirty-five places are available in year 10. Places are offered on the basis of an interview with a senior member of staff and a computerised verbal and non-verbal reasoning assessment for which it is not possible to prepare. Overseas applicants sit the UKiset test. Sixth form entry for the 130 who join at this point depends on a minimum of six passes at GCSE including English and maths for those doing A levels; just four for those doing BTecs.

Exit: A handful seem to leave in the first couple of years, about 20-25 per cent after GCSE and, unusually, a scattering at the end of year 12. Those who stay for the duration praise the quality and administration of the support given university admissions, whether in the UK or abroad. Three to Oxbridge and four medics in 2018; Cardiff and Oxford Brookes currently top of the pops in the UK, and American universities leading the field by miles for study abroad (22 in 2018, plus three to Europe), some awarding sports scholarships, particularly in hockey and tennis. Surprisingly few gap years. Famous alumni, especially sporting ones, too numerous to list, but stand-outs are Gareth Edwards and Chris Robshaw (rugby), Duncan Goodhew, Joanne Atkinson and James Guy (swimming). Eight Old Millfieldians competed at Rio 2016 and won four medals between them (swimming, rowing and rugby). But Old Millfieldians are also to be found at the top of their game in journalism, finance and even one medieval history don among the dreaming spires.

Money matters: In the past it enjoyed the reputation of being the most expensive school in the UK, but at the moment it comes in at less than Eton. It would, however, be easy to go large on the extras (endless racks of monogrammed house team kit etc) in the school shop, where items can be bought and bunged on the bill with the houseparent's permission. Some activities are chargeable where outside staff are brought in (eg polo); specialist therapy such as speech and language and vision, EAL, individual learning support also. Scholarships (including for design & innovation and chess) awarded to a maximum of 15 per cent of fees, but a generous 50 per cent for exceptional all-rounders into year 9. Extensive bursary provision which goes to 100 per cent in cases of phenomenal hardship

M

Remarks: A big open-hearted school welcoming all talents but not, we think, none. Only the best will do, in terms of facilities and IT and its ambition seems boundless, with its new centre for enterprise. Besides, where else would you meet princes and paupers?

Milton Abbey School

104

Milton Abbas, Blandford Forum, Dorset DT11 0BZ

Ages 13–18 **Pupils** 211 (144 boys, 67 girls) **Sixth form** 109
Boarders 173 full **C of E**

Fees: Day £20,250 – £21,750; Boarding: £38,550 – £40,050 pa

01258 880484
www.miltonabbey.co.uk

Head: Since September 2018, Judith Fremont-Barnes, previously head of Duke of Kent School in Surrey. English degree from Oxford, where she became an Oxford Union debater, and toured the US as a debating scholar during a gap year. First post at JAGS, where she fell in love with teaching, then spent five years in Japan where she lectured at Kobe Kaisei College for Women and Kobe University, as well as bringing up two sons and taking a masters degree in inclusive education at the OU. On her return to the UK, joined King Edward VI School and then Radley College, where she became head of English, was involved in boarding and a member of the school's academic planning group. Next post was deputy head at More House School in Surrey; she moved to Duke of Kent in 2011. Leisure interests include long walks with her border terrier Ruby, theatre and gallery visits, and time spent with her family: her husband Gregory, a military historian and lecturer at Sandhurst, and their two grown up sons.

Academic matters: Milton Abbey's strengths lie in its value-added. School doesn't publish its exam results (though 69 per cent A*-C at A level or BTec equivalent in 2018, and 70 per cent of pupils got 5+ GCSEs at 9-7 or equivalent grade level 2 BTecs), taking the view that students have such a broad range of ability that their achievements wouldn't be accurately represented by what the school calls the 'crude mechanism' of league tables. Students range from a boy who got three A*s at A level and headed to Oxford to read archaeology and anthropology to those who find formal academic learning 'really difficult' and opt for a more vocational route. The school talks a lot about 'parallel learning pathways' and prides itself on tailoring an academic programme to suit individual students. At sixth form, a third of pupils take A levels, a third take a combination of A levels and BTecs and a third take BTecs. Pupils' GCSE profiles are taken into account and subject combinations are based on advice from tutors and teachers (no chance of doing physics A level and a BTec in hospitality). Pupils are encouraged to pursue their passions and interests and all the usual A levels are on offer, plus economics, politics, history of art and music technology.

The school is ahead of the curve when it comes to vocational learning, saying it offers the broadest range of BTecs in the independent sector and is one of the few schools to offer BTecs at extended diploma level – equivalent to three A levels. BTecs (available in countryside management, performing arts, enterprise and entrepreneurship, equine management, hospitality, creative media production and sport) aren't an easy option, though. They are made up of continued assessment, with a small percentage of the course assessed by exam at the end of two years. The school's 2015 ISI report commended its approach, saying that 'pupils, who come with widely different educational backgrounds and needs, often suffering a negative experience of education elsewhere, are enabled to rebuild the foundation of their knowledge and skills, as well as the self-confidence needed to progress.' The assistant head (academic) concurs with this. 'We're all about getting the best out of our pupils,' she says.

Pupils take between seven and nine GCSEs, with everyone doing English, maths and a science. Class sizes are small – average of 12 up to GCSE and six at A level. 'The small class sizes mean that we have much better outcomes for learners.' Pupils are streamed by ability for the core subjects. Lessons are now one hour long – school says this helps pupils to concentrate better.

Milton Abbey is resolutely mainstream but learning support, with four teachers and six teaching assistants, is the biggest department. Some pupils are screened before they start and around two-thirds access learning support in some way – for a wide range of difficulties, including dyslexia, dyspraxia, dyscalculia, mild Asperger's. Learning support assistants provide additional help in lessons and there's one-to-one or group support too (charged on top of the fees), sometimes instead of languages. EAL and study skills help on offer. The department is very welcoming, with its door permanently open to help anyone who wants to drop in for revision tips, essay planning and time management. 'Quite often their self-esteem and confidence is low and it's our job to raise that,' says the head of learning support.

School library has 9,000 resources and pupils are encouraged to read books for pleasure as well as for study. Robert Muchamore and Meg Rosoff are two current favourites – 'we like to get the pupils in the habit of reading,' the school librarian told us.

Games, options, the arts: Sport taken seriously but the emphasis is on enjoyment and there's loads on offer. Rugby, hockey, cricket and football predominate but golf (there's a course in the grounds and a full-time pro on staff), sailing and polo have a strong take-up too. The fixtures list and results show the school punches above its weight on the sports field. Relatively small number of girls means they all get the chance to represent the school at hockey, netball, lacrosse, tennis and rounders. Mountain biking and road cycling increasingly important (regularly enters two teams for road racing events). Facilities include a 25-metre swimming pool, two gyms, squash court, all-weather pitch, sports hall and outdoor pitches galore. Everyone does games on Tuesdays, Thursdays and Saturdays but the sportiest do far more. Wednesdays are given over to CCF or community service (including visiting the elderly, taking dogs for walks and cleaning the local church). There's all manner of country pursuits, like fishing, ferreting (you can bring your own ferret, although none were in residence when we visited), clay pigeon shooting and beagling.

It's possible to combine a burgeoning equestrian career with school life. Pupils can bring their own steeds – many of the keenest riders take a BTec in equine management and keep their horses at the school stables. They manage the day-to-day care of their horses and can choose to ride instead of playing other sports.

Art is a popular subject and a year 12 boy showed us an astonishing oil painting inspired by renaissance art that he'd worked on over the summer. School puts on a big drama production in its theatre every year and there's a vast array of music. Hymn practice is held in the abbey every Friday, when the whole school gathers to sing at the tops of their voices. 'The volume creeps up bit by bit and it sounds wonderful,' a sixth form boy told us.

Entrepreneurship in Residence competition aims to inspire pupils with ambitions to launch their own business. Top-notch designers like Anya Hindmarch, Johnnie Boden and Cath Kidston and Carphone Warehouse founder David Ross have all fronted the scheme. Unlike some boarding schools, students do work experience – usually with school alumni (an Inner Temple barrister and a Coutts banker were among those who volunteered recently). Other activities include DofE, farm club and the Ten Tors expedition across Dartmoor. School is a member of Round Square, a worldwide organisation that encourages young people to broaden their horizons and gain greater understanding of the wider world through exchange trips, community work and themed activities within school.

Boarding: Offers full boarding or day places – 'we don't have anything in between'. Two three-day exeats a term to allow for longer journeys home. Five boarding houses – four for boys and one for girls. We visited the two newest houses, both wholesome and welcoming, with disabled access and underfloor heating. Each has a housemaster or housemistress, resident tutors and two matrons, who take charge of laundry and cleaning, offer support to pupils and help them to prepare for life beyond school. One matron told us she'd just taught a boy how to iron his shirt – 'it was important he learned how to do it himself'.

Common rooms in the boarding houses are equipped with TVs, out of bounds during the day. There's no mobile phone signal on much of the site so phones are less of a problem here than at other schools. Most use the old-fashioned landlines in the boarding houses to phone home.

Background and atmosphere: With 76 acres of rolling countryside, it is one of the prettiest schools in the country. You can't fail to be enchanted by the ancient abbey nestling in a wooded Dorset valley, one of the finest Capability Brown landscapes, 15 minutes' drive from Blandford. 'It's deeply rural, but not remote.' We visited on a sunny day but were assured that it looks lovely in the rain and mist too. Founded in 1954, it occupies the converted monastery buildings. The vast abbey belongs to the Diocese of Salisbury but the school has full use of it, with services four times a week. It also has its own farm (with pigs, sheep, goats, turkeys and chickens), makes its own honey and grows flowers, fruit and vegetables.

Pupils eat all their meals in the Abbot's Hall, a grand dining room complete with stags' heads and a huge mural of the school painted by a parent to commemorate the school's 50th anniversary. Pasta, salads, wraps and paninis on offer at lunchtime, as well as hot meals, plus snacks at break, fresh fruit and cake in the afternoons. 'No one goes hungry,' grinned one boy. Younger girls wear tartan skirts and blazers while sixth form girls are clad in grey skirts and tweed jackets of their choice. Boys wear tweed jackets, grey trousers and ties.

Pastoral care, well-being and discipline: Pupils keep the same tutor from years 9 to 11, and see them two or three times a week. In the sixth form students get a say in their choice of tutor – often someone who teaches them or whom they have a good relationship with. School operates a system of rewards and sanctions when it comes to behaviour – awards given for good work, sporting achievements and acts of kindness.

Good communication with parents – there's a parent portal where parents have access to weekly notes on everything from a missed prep to an academic triumph. Pupils told us that 'there aren't hundreds of rules. They give you a degree of trust.' Student voice is considered important. Head boy and head girl (who meet the head every morning), heads of houses and a raft of prefects – called 'pilots' here.

Pupils and parents: Quite a few from London and from as far afield as Northumberland. International students from France, Italy, Germany, Italy, Kenya and the US. Day pupils ('our day fees are really competitive') tend to live within a 30-minute drive. School minibus service covers Blandford, Wimborne, Poole, Dorchester, Shaftesbury and Salisbury. Day pupils leave at 6pm but there's the option to stay on for activities and prep.

Despite such privileged surroundings, the pupils we met were outgoing, enthusiastic and delightfully unsnobby. Sixth formers summed the school's appeal up in a nutshell. 'For the people it's right for, this is the best school in the country,' one boy declared. 'I love it. My sister's at Millfield and her year group is as big as this whole school. Here, everybody knows everybody and the support you get is second to none.' A girl said she liked being 'a big fish in a small pond' while parents told us they love the family atmosphere, plus the fact that their children get loads of country air and aren't glued to their phones, tablets and laptops (though Wifi now upgraded).

Former pupils include Professor Jonathan Freeman-Attwood, the principal of the Royal Academy of Music, photographer, screenwriter and TV director Harry Hook, restaurateur Oliver Gladwin, sculptor Robert Rattray, documentary maker Anthony Geffen and Professor Alastair Bruce, royal, religious and constitutional affairs commentator for Sky News.

Entrance: School is 'inclusive and non-selective.' Around 70 per cent of pupils do CE – pass mark is around 50 per cent but school is flexible on this and says 'there's no hard and fast rule.'

Applicants attend a taster day to see if the school suits them. Usual entry points are 13 and 16 but a handful of pupils start in year 10, often because they didn't settle at their original choice of school. It doesn't chuck pupils out if they don't make their GCSE grades either. Head believes that when a school accepts a youngster at 13 it should stick with them for the duration.

Exit: School loses around 10 per cent of pupils after GCSEs – largely due to relocation or for financial reasons – but larger numbers choose to join from other schools. At 18 or 19 pupils choose a plethora of routes, ranging from agriculture to film and creative media courses. Has forged a close relationship with The Arts University Bournemouth, which specialises in art, design, media and performance across the creative industries. School also has strong links with international catering colleges, such as Glion and Les Roches in Switzerland, and several pupils have headed to these in the past. Others off to take up apprenticeships, military training or set up their own companies.

Money matters: A range of scholarships at 13+ and 16+ – academic, all-rounder, art, DT, drama, music and increasing numbers for sport. All worth 10 per cent of the fees, although these may be increased 'where financial need is demonstrated.' School also offers means-tested bursaries, plus scholarships for day pupils living in Dorset.

Remarks: Milton Abbey's setting, countryside expertise and innovative mix of qualifications give pupils, some of whom may not have thrived elsewhere, a host of opportunities to shine – both inside and outside the classroom.

M

Monkton Prep School

Linked with Monkton Combe School

Combe Down, Bath, Somerset BA2 7ET

Ages 2–13 **Pupils** 217 **Boarders** 40 full, 4 weekly, 25 flexi (from year 3)

Fees: Day £9,735 – £17,130; Boarding £22,890 – £24,690 pa

01225 831202
www.monktonprep.com

Head: Since 2017, Martin Davis BEd (late 40s), a Monkton old boy and graduate of what is now the University of Gloucestershire. Born to missionary parents, Mr Davis spent his early life in Thailand (and indeed his gap year), although he was sent back to the UK to Monkton as a boarder – aged 5. 'They looked after a small boy only used to wearing shorts and flip-flops very well', he adds, slightly misty-eyed. Between starting out at Monkton and ending up there, Mr Davis' career has taken him to St Andrew's Turi (a well-trodden path to or from Monkton) and a long stint at Hazlegrove as deputy head. That long experience of prep schools gives him a delightfully relaxed yet assured demeanour, but it would be underselling this man of quiet resolve and his vision for the school to say that Mr Davis is a safe pair of hands. That said, stability is exactly what Monkton Prep needs, after a period of uncertainty at the helm. 'I believe passionately in childhood' he told us, 'and I want to create an environment where children thrive, a place where they can achieve whatever they want to achieve.' To that end, he has introduced the thematic international primary curriculum, hour-long lessons and slowed the 'frenetic' pace of the day to include half an hour's reading in the middle of the day with tutors. Married to the lovely Nicky with twins at the senior school and a son in the prep, Mr Davis enjoys all sport and a spot of wood-turning and guitar-playing to relax.

The pre-prep has been headed by Catherine Winchcombe (40s) since 2016, with a first degree from Cambridge, a masters in educational leadership from Nottingham and a career which encompasses the state sector and posts in the Middle East. Dynamic, stylish and warm, she fizzes with enthusiasm for all things Monkton, not least the fantastic new building which opened as she arrived. 'Exciting!' was the word she uttered most often during our visit. A consummate professional, whose way of leading the school is tacitly underpinned by her Christian faith, Catherine is married to Simon and has 2 daughters, one at university, one about to go.

Entrance: Non-selective to the pre-prep, though there's an informal interview, and an automatic pass to the prep school at year 3 in almost all cases. For the prep, children are assessed in English, maths and, 'if appropriate', reasoning. Joiners in year 7 are asked for CAT scores and invited to one of 3 assessment days in the year

Exit: The only prep school in the area which prepares children for common entrance or scholarships at 13+. A few leave at 11 to join local day schools, state and independent; a significant majority of the rest to Monkton Senior School, others mostly to day and boarding schools in Bath and the south west, including Millfield, Canford and the Sherborne schools. Generally a good clutch of various scholarships, especially to Monkton.

Remarks: Founded in 1888 and beautifully positioned on top of a hill in Combe Down (a desirable villagey part of Bath) with stunning views over rolling countryside from the back of the site, Monkton's buildings range from handsome to utilitarian – but the acres of green space surrounding them (mostly turned over to rugby or cricket pitches or an athletics track in the summer, plus Astro) make up for any aesthetic failings. The pre-prep and nursery was purpose-built in 2016, with safe enclosed play areas and delightful light classrooms where lots of phonics are dinned into happy children by means of Read, Write, Inc, and where they are praised for what they can do, and encouraged to adopt the growth mind-set philosophy of 'I can't do this – yet'. Cross-curricular learning here too, and a healthy attitude to risk: tiny children were chopping up apples with sharp knives and close supervision when we visited in late summer. Average class size 16, and children benefit from specialist teachers from the prep school for sport, French and music.

For the first years in the prep, children are taught mostly in their own classrooms, but subject teachers feature from year 6; a mixture of streaming and setting is used for differentiation. Common entrance (scholarship for the most academic) syllabus proper starts in year 6: those exams are set in English, maths, the sciences and languages (French and Latin; Greek for the brightest sparks) with extended projects in the humanities. Parents generally reckon that just enough pressure – 'but not to the point of freaking them out', as one mother put it – is applied to ensure entry to the senior school of choice, but some felt children could be stretched more, with greater focus on getting them into better known public schools outside the south west. Monkton is the only Bath school to retain Saturday school from year 5; this time is now used for the study of themes beyond the narrow CE syllabus, such as migration and the concept of a just war. Masterclass Saturdays laid on three times a year: the principal of the senior school might teach Chaucer, or kids might learn to play the ukulele in a morning.

Children with SEN are looked after by the learning support team, and four categories of need are clearly set out in the school's policy, including social and emotional aspects alongside mild to moderate SpLD. The behaviour management policy acknowledges that 'some pupils on our SEN register find [shouting out, fiddling, making silly noises for example] very difficult not to do' and offers ideas to help manage them in the classroom. Some children arrive with identified needs, others are diagnosed while at the school. Parents greatly value the inclusive approach taken by the school as a result of its overt Christian ethos: 'we believe each individual is uniquely created by God and has a distinct contribution to make to our community'. One mother told us how the family had moved 200 miles to go to Monkton and that the school had been 'unequivocally welcoming' to her child with a complex chronic long term health condition. A few children are turned away at the enquiry stage if the school genuinely feels it cannot meet their needs.

Masses on offer outside the classroom too, for 'the guiding principle of a Monkton education – the development of character'. Extensive outdoor space – not just for sport, but also for play – is complemented by a super indoor pool, dance studio and rather tired sports hall, in line for a facelift. Usual sports on offer but these days, boys can (and do) opt out of rugby. Sports teaching widely praised and even the tiniest in the pre-prep benefit. Minor grumbles from competitive parents about small schools having to field the sporting talent available to them – and being (on occasion) thrashed by bigger ones. Cross-country running a Monkton perennial, and it was wonderful to see any stumbling stragglers cheered home as warmly as the loping long distance runners. Monkton runners is open to anyone, and enthusiastically led by the joint head of boarding. Drama traditionally a strength too, with several productions grouped by age in a year: recent offerings include A Midsummer Night's Dream – not watered down, either – and Joseph and the Amazing Technicolour Dreamcoat. Much enjoyment and silverware gained at LAMDA and the Mid Somerset Festival. Music has had a shot in the arm with the arrival of a new head of music, teaching 'Oats and beans and barley grow' to the youngest children to the accompaniment of her guitar when we saw her in the pre-prep's charming assembly hall with its glass lantern. Over a third of pupils learn an instrument individually, but class music and singing are timetabled. Musical highpoints of the year include hotly contested house music, a joint concert with the senior school and the carol service in Bath Abbey. Art has a proper messy room, where work of considerable talent is produced, and then hung around the walls of the school. DT is taught by an infectious dynamo, whose projects include a Greenpower car – which has been round the famed race track at nearby Castle Combe.

Although boarders are in a minority, Monkton is run as a boarding community with its long days, Saturday school and spare beds. Hatton House occupies the two upper floors (one for girls, the other for boys) of the main building, all presided over by the delightful and flamboyantly clad houseparents and team, not forgetting Spotto the whippet. Light dorms with homely touches and plenty of space to pin up photos and posters alongside clean, functional bathrooms and cosy communal spaces make it comfortable rather than luxurious, but there's a tangible warmth coming from all the staff: it's a very happy and united ship. Children are kept busy with activities in the evening and a weekly pancake night in the houseparents' kitchen. Mobile phone use kept to a minimum and as a means of keeping in touch rather than mindless YouTubing or Instagram; all devices are handed in to charge overnight.

Unapologetically Christian in its foundation and prevailing ethos with all chapel Bible-led, Monkton's faith is a living one, according to the head, who explained it in terms of 'doing what we talk about in chapel. You can't inflict faith on people'. Whether believers, church-goers or not, everyone we spoke to profoundly appreciated the school's values, and often chose the school for them. 'Christian values are not just a strapline,' said one mother. 'Every child really is a unique blessing'. And looked after as such: two parents told us how their child 'walked taller since coming to Monkton and was the best version of [him/herself]'. Had they been primed? We suspect not. Even when things go wrong, the school seems to handle it well, with the emphasis on remedy and explanation rather than punishment, though detentions are given for repeated offences.

Monkton has particular appeal in Bath and beyond to those seeking an education based as much on Christian values and opportunities as on academics, but also to those wanting an 'old school' prep school, to take their offspring through common entrance to the public school of their choice, likely as not Monkton Senior. Many families make great sacrifices to send their children, and fortunately find little to complain about. 'If I had beef, I'd tell you,' affirmed one mother; we didn't doubt it.

Monkton Combe School

Linked with Monkton Prep School

Church Lane, Monkton Combe, Bath, Somerset BA2 7HG

Ages 13–18 **Pupils** 375 **Sixth form** 159 **Boarders** 261

Fees: Day £19,890– £20,910; Boarding £29,490– £33,345 pa

01225 721133
www.monktoncombeschool.com

M

Principal: Since 2016, Christopher Wheeler BA PGCE (early 40s). The son of a general and educated at the thoroughly pukka institutions of Winchester, Durham (where he read English and philosophy) and Bristol (PGCE), Mr Wheeler started his teaching career at St John's Leatherhead, where he left as head of English to take up several roles (head of English and drama, registrar, deputy head – where did he find the time??) at Peponi School in Kenya. Since then, his working life has ping-ponged between the UK and Kenya, never staying anywhere very long and combining teaching with the usual climb up the managerial ladder with spells as a housemaster at Brighton College, head of its prep St Christopher's Hove and, latterly, principal and CEO of Hillcrest International School in Nairobi. 'Africa gets under your skin' he says – something he discovered during his gap year in Zimbabwe – but now as a father of three young children, he is conscious of security concerns in Kenya, prompting a move back to the UK.

Very different from his cerebral predecessor, Mr Wheeler has something of the showman about him: one might even say show-off, with the remarkable breaking into a rendition of One Day More (that stirring number from Les Mis) in the middle of his address at Speech Day 2017. (It went viral and the school has been shortlisted for a social media award.) But he has taken the place by the horns since his arrival with the introduction of the notion that Emotional Quotient (EQ) is a more helpful measure than IQ, and of the growth mind-set, developed by Carol Dweck, where students are encouraged to believe that intelligence is not fixed but malleable, and that improvement and achievement are therefore very much in their own hands. More controversially, he has brought in peer review of staff; several key members of long standing have left.

Improbably boyish for such a senior role, he bowled us over with a flood of exuberant verbiage: future plans include repositioning the entrance to befit 'a proper public school' and creating an equestrian centre on site in a redundant part of the extensive grounds. 'After all, riding, rowing and reeling are life skills, aren't they?' says he (reely??). Students find him approachable and charismatic: he has made a point of weekly lunches with different groups and take-up of his morning dog walks was so popular that he was begged to reinstate them after discontinuing them in the winter. He reckons they provide a brilliant opportunity to chat to teenagers without discomforting eye contact. Parents broadly positive, staff possibly less so. Married to Georgie, who teaches sport and is a keen horsewoman, Mr Wheeler doubles as action man during the holidays, enjoying paragliding and snowboarding in the Alps.

Academic matters: Not particularly selective, though the previous principal upped the academic ante. The 2018 results (66 per cent A*-A/9-7 at GCSE; 81 per cent A*/B and 52 per cent A*/A at A level) are more than respectable, especially at sixth form. Two languages taken in year 9, which can include Mandarin and Latin – why no German? – and pupils are strongly encouraged to take a modern language but not obligatory at GCSE. Extra English or maths takes the place of languages for those needing it. Twenty-seven subjects on offer at A level, of which maths is the most popular and DT (3D Design) and Latin the least – but good that the choices of the minority are still honoured. Monkton sixth formers are expected to start and complete three A levels and an EPQ. No IB nor plans to offer it.

Our visit fell during exam season, so much of what we saw was rigorous preparation and revision classes; of the teachers' commitment and dedication including at weekends there can be no doubt whatsoever: 'My daughter's ambition to get to Oxbridge was fully supported by her teachers,' one mother told us, adding that the school had also suited her dyslexic sibling. Small class sizes averaging at 15 or so below sixth form and around nine at A level must help. 'Inspiring academic ambition is a key priority,' intones the website, an aspiration underpinned by the importance placed on growth mind-set (see above) and the instilling of a good work ethic by one-to-one tutoring; students have some discretion to change if the allocated tutor does not work out. Well-stocked library for all ages with limited computer facilities: the vast majority of students doubtless have their own laptops. Though the bright and modernised classrooms and labs we saw were all suitably equipped with interactive whiteboards etc, we did not sense that this was a school where technology was, refreshingly, the be-all and end-all.

Monkton used to be something of a refuge for SEN students, but it no longer has CReSTed status, catering only for minor difficulties these days. The learning support department is right at the centre of the school and staffed by two SpLD teachers. Difficulties in organisation and processing as well as exam technique are also addressed, and all students are assessed on entry. Most of the site has been made accessible for wheelchairs.

Games, options, the arts: Surely something for everyone here, with acres of pitches including, according to Wisden, one of the most beautiful cricket grounds in the country, with its views of the perfect honey-coloured viaduct carrying the busy A36 out of Bath. Rugby, hockey, netball and tennis (hard and grass courts, plus Astro) all onsite, though swimming takes place in the delightful indoor pool at the prep school just up the hill, since Mr Wheeler had the old outdoor pool filled in. Rowing is a big deal here: with a good stretch of river just yards from school and Olympian oarsmen Steve Williams and Rowley Douglas, plus GB single sculler Olivia Caesar among former pupils. Senior rowers benefit from a splendid new boathouse and a (better) stretch of the Avon at Saltford (about 20 minutes away), used also by the university crews of Bath and Bristol. Lots else to do too, though, such as fencing, dance, riding – and yes, CCF, D of E and Ten Tors of course. More sedate extracurricular choices include baking, knitting and chess.

It's the upgrade to the arts facilities, though, which is astonishing. Both art/DT and music have had sensational new (or hugely enhanced) buildings, creating pleasing contemporary touches to quite a traditional campus. Visitors to the art school go straight into the gallery, filled when we saw it with enormous textile print hangings using beetroot juice. Textiles a particular strength and the specialism of the current artist in residence. The art dept is proud of the numbers getting places at Central St Martins. Huge dark room and industrial printing facilities (busy with a school promotional banner when we were there) complete a superb set-up. As for music – it's just 'Wow!' Jewel in the crown must be the concert hall, quite an intimate space with acoustic design and its requisite mosaic (non-technical term for technical necessity) ceiling, but the more hi-tech musicians are thrilled with the recording facilities all linked to a central studio. It's not just the surroundings though: the head of music is widely lauded for his 'desperate enthusiasm', and his innovations like the choir who can't sing (mostly boys) and the choir who won't sing (mostly girls). The vast majority who can and do play and sing, however, gain merits and distinctions in their music exams; accomplishment a rigorous counterpoint to enjoyment. Monkton has had a long tradition of jazz and the Longmead jazz festival attracts the general public, who can enjoy a smart picnic in a spectacular setting. Drama facilities fall behind those for art and music (on the list for improvement), but commendably less usual fare produced, such as Arabian Nights, Swallows and Amazons and After Mrs Rochester recently. Informal drama evenings give aspiring writers as well as actors a chance to participate.

Boarding: First and foremost a boarding school, with the late evenings (10pm pick-ups not uncommon for day students and their long-suffering parents) and the only compulsory Saturday morning school in Bath. All age single sex houses are presided over by married houseparents, who go out of their way to create a homely and welcoming feel, with their own families and pets. Just as well really, as the boys' accommodation we saw was, shall we say, functional rather than luxurious 'but being refurbished! says the school. Girls are reckoned to need more 'talking time' – to house staff, rather than each other – so school has policy of making girls' houses smaller by around 10 students. A new girls' house opened in 2017. Each year group has a kitchen for making snacks, toast and hot drinks; pizza, curry and Chinese food can be ordered in no more than three times a week. What with and a good supply of fruit and tuck, no-one appeared to miss nipping into Bath for comestibles. School food ok (not the most inspiring menu we've seen), but 'definitely improved and breakfast is the best meal of the day,' say students. Everyone eats in the beautiful light dining hall, with its huge windows and high ceilings. Five and four night boarding options exist alongside full boarding, and day students get 10 nights' free boarding thrown in each year.

Background and atmosphere: In the lusciously green Midford Valley just outside the golden city of Bath snakes a narrow lane lined with the honey-coloured buildings of Monkton Combe. The school, founded by the evangelical Revd Pocock in the 1860s, takes up much of this idyllic village, and still attracts many families wanting an overtly Christian setting for their children's education. Although it's definitely not a faith school, the Christian underpinnings exert a palpable influence: 'It's a very kind place,' we kept hearing. 'Even if you're not a fervent Christian, you're not made to feel bad for that, and it teaches you a way to behave,' one mother told us. Mutual respect for personal faith (of whatever kind – a few Muslims also attend Monkton) or a lack of it seems to be the (commendable) watchword. 'There is rigorous questioning in RE lessons, and we're taught all about comparative religions,' students told us, alongside a very active student-led Christian Union.

It struck us as a tolerant place – tolerant of difference and celebrating all kinds of achievement, not just academic. Its relative isolation outside Bath and general feel suggest somewhere where children don't have to conform quite as rigidly, or grow up quite as fast – fondly referred to as the Monkton bubble at the school, disparagingly so by other Bath institutions. School held in great affection by students and parents alike, and much made of the Monkton family, something that persists long beyond school days with a very strong alumni network: the school was way ahead of the game in developing links with former students (and doubtless tapping them up for funds).

Pastoral care, well-being and discipline: Traditionally a great strength and the reason many families choose the school – and an aspect much touted by the principal and registrar. Transition arrangements and welcome praised by parents, and the efforts houseparents and academic staff go to to get acquainted with each new student. 'Pastoral care is integral to creating academic success stories,' we were told; parents describe it as 'stand-out' and 'unparalleled'. This school goes one step further with its recent introduction of Affective Social Tracking: a twice yearly online questionnaire taken by all students as a gauge of their emotional well-being and 'areas for development'. No outright opposition to this from the biddable flock of Monkton students; we heard some cynical mutterings about it being a ridiculous waste of time, but none about what struck us as the slightly sinister intrusion into the adolescent mind with its growing need for independence and privacy. Discipline is not a concept that looms large here: the emphasis is much more on celebrating achievement and intrinsic rewards. Bullying is tackled through the lens of restorative justice, where appropriate. 'The kids feel safe here,' we kept hearing, one mother adding that 'as the students have no fear of cruel ridicule, they are not afraid to make fools of themselves'. Our last review talked of 'unfailing support for the troubled' – and we see no change. But we sense that the principal would not hesitate to get tough with miscreants if required, even if he thought very hard before throwing them out.

Pupils and parents: Kind, thoughtful and nice to each other (we liked the easy way in which students from different year groups interacted over our shared lunch). Some might say unworldly, but that would be to undersell the extent to which these kids think about the profound problems of the world such as hunger and poverty, albeit from a largely Christian perspective. Parents 'do all they can to send their children here,' according to the principal, 'and the car park is full of Land Rovers and Audis, not Maseratis.' Many drive considerable distances to get to school; boarders, unless from overseas tend, to be no more than an hour and a half away. Monkton family dynasties still exist.

Entrance: At year 9, half come from the prep school by means of common entrance, provided hopefuls have come through broad assessment, taken in year 6 and 7. Overseas students are required to sit UKiset and, if English is not their first language, an English Placement Test. A few students come straight into year 10 by means of the CAT 4 test. For sixth form entry, at least five GCSEs above a C (new grade 4/5) with an average of a B/6 across them all is required from the 30 or so new students who come. Maths and sciences require an A and languages a B. Monkton reserves the right to restrict entry to year 13, if AS results are not up to what the school considers snuff.

Exit: About a dozen leave after GCSEs, possibly for greater freedom and post-16 choices, possibly for financial reasons. After A levels, the vast majority go to university – a range of degree courses at institutions old and new up and down the land, and abroad. We picked up some dissatisfaction about guidance on university choices from one parent, however. Two to Oxbridge and three medics in 2018.

Notable alumni include Antarctic explorer Eric Marshall (school has his sledge from Shackleton's expedition of 1909), author Bernard Cornwell, musical funny man Richard Stilgoe, former head of MI6 Sir Richard Dearlove and Olympic oarsmen Stephen Williams and Rowley Douglas.

Money matters: Fees are comparable with similar schools and the full boarding makes this arguably better value than those schools with a shorter week. Scholarships amount to a maximum of 25 per cent of fees but bursaries go as far as full fees in exceptional cases; special consideration is given to the offspring of clergy or missionaries. For many years the school has cultivated a highly effective development office, so its financial health is, we are sure, rude.

Remarks: An appealing option in an idyllic location for those wanting a truly Christian education for their children, or at least one that embraces its values and where they do not have to grow up too fast. Atheists, agnostics, humanists with inquisitive and open minds also welcome. New principal pushing the exceptional pastoral care, while buffing up its boarding houses, social cachet and media profile too.

Monmouth School for Boys

Linked with Monmouth School Boys' Prep, Monmouth School for Girls, Monmouth Schools Pre-Prep & Nursery, Monmouth School Girls' Prep

M

Almshouse Street, Monmouth NP25 3XP

Ages 11–18 **Pupils** 644 **Sixth form** 140 **Boarders** 154 full

Fees: Day £15,816; Boarding £29,982 – £32,061 pa

01600 713143
www.habsmonmouth.org

Headmaster: Since 2015, Dr Andrew Daniel, who has a breadth of educational experience from the liberal, global atmosphere of his own student days at UWC Atlantic College, the University of East Anglia and Washington, Seattle, to the established British independent schools where he has forged his career – including head of maths at Taunton and senior deputy at Wellington School, Somerset. His PhD was on mathematical modelling of plate tectonics in Patagonia, though we refrained from questioning him on this.

Andrew comes across as wise and experienced, a man you would seek out for educational advice. He has looked at the Monmouth site with a fresh pair of eyes and is focused on new buildings and refurbishments. His attention has been on the science facilities, now completely refurbished, plus upgraded boarding house and sixth form centre. He is keen to exploit further the strengths of collaboration between the five schools that make up the Monmouth Haberdashers' family – it is in their combining strengths that he sees the huge potential for growth. He has the unbeatable mixture of people skills ('He really gets on well with grown ups as well as us,' we were told, with some awe, by the boys), a sharp, analytic approach to the business side of running a school and an academic's passion for educational research. He is very clear on the school's priorities. It is academic work first for everyone, then sport and enjoying all the wonderful range of extracurricular activities.

Academic matters: Selective but not frantically so, which makes the results even more impressive. At A level, 44 per cent at A*-A in 2018 and 65 per cent A*-B. At GCSE, 72 per cent A*-A/9-7 grades. Value-added scores are impressive. Maths is very successful and popular, as are the sciences. Economics, history and classics all get much appreciation from the boys. Computer science is a big growth area. The sixth form is now a joint one with the girls' school up to hill. Minority subjects may be taught at one or another school and combinations that might not work at one school can often work across both. Everyone we spoke to saw this as a real strength. The school also collaborates with Monmouth state schools on the Monmouth Science Initiative, which brings young people together regularly to work with specialists in the science world, who come and speak at the schools, plus twice yearly visits to Cardiff University. The school believes that single sex academic classes up to GCSE mean the boys flourish in the creative arts and languages as well as maths and sciences, unperturbed by narrow gender stereotypes. Parents say the teaching staff 'get boys', know how their brains work and can get them inspired academically. There is much praise from both boys and parents for the high quality of the teaching. The learning support department works with boys with mild learning needs, either for a few sessions to help with such difficulties as time management and organisation or by offering a longer term programme for ongoing difficulties such as dyslexia.

M

Games, options, the arts: There is a phenomenal sports programme. Although the jewels in the crown continue to be rugby and rowing, other sports are getting a look in and gaining considerable success. Some, such as swimming, are now putting out mixed teams. Although the first teams do very well regionally and nationally, everyone agrees the coaches show the same respect and commitment to the 3rds, who in fact also do very well – the 3rd XI football team being the most successful in the school last season. There is an impressive fixture list with up to four teams per year group out most weeks. The sports centre is open day and night for senior and junior school boys and incorporates a private members' sports club for the public and parents. It is home to a canoeing club, pilates studio, fitness suite, huge all purpose sports hall and gym. An impressive sports pavilion with a terrace cum large social space overlooks the playing fields that fall away to the Wye river. The quality of the pitches is professional – including new all-weather pitches – the wicket county standard, with the grounds staff to support this.

But that is only a part of what is on offer outside lessons. There is lots of quality music and drama. Drama, often jointly with the girls' school, includes musical theatre as well as the big drama classics. Large scale as well as smaller music performances take place throughout the year. There is a wide range of ensembles including choirs, who sing at various church and cathedral venues as well as in school. The list is extensive. There is a CCF, literary and debating societies, DT workshops, reading groups, science clubs. Many sixth form clubs are combined with the girls. Lots of the residential and overseas trips are also for both boys and girls.

Boarding: Monmouth is a delightful small town and it is very safe, so the boys walk out of the school gates into the life of the town, avoiding the isolation bubble that can sometimes be a boarding experience. The school is very committed to its boarding and the boarding houses feel very much part of the whole school. About 60 per cent of boarders are British and there are pupils from a range of countries. Houseparents, who are also teachers – something parents value – are totally devoted to the school and boys. There is a boarding house for juniors in years 5-8, three for years 9-12, and then year 13s all come together in a house designed as a stepping stone to fully independent university life. Here the boys learn how to cook on a budget and how to operate a washing machine. They also all have their own en-suites – a luxury they might not experience at university. The houses are all different physically, ranging from Georgian town houses to a recently done up 60s block. Older houses have a quirky feel adapted creatively to the needs of today – no boring regimentation here. 'Relaxed and purposeful' is how staff describe the atmosphere in the houses. Staffs regularly tour overseas to meet international parents. There are activities with the girl boarders some evenings and at weekends.

Background and atmosphere: The school was founded in 1614 by William Jones, a member of the Haberdashers' Company, as a local school. It expanded its boarding throughout the 19th century. The 400th anniversary was commemorated by, among other things, the creation of a new building with classrooms, offices and meeting spaces, all ecologically high quality. There had been a major rebuild in the 1880s in magnificent Jacobean style, so the campus embraces a mix of architectures from the almshouses, now offices, to the highly modern builds, to the sensitively refurbished chapel, now a library. This is a school that inspires a lot of loyalty, both from parents, old boys and the wider Monmouth community. The head noticed on his arrival a marked lack of 'town and gown' division and the crowd at the big rugby matches is swelled by locals. The school theatre, The Blake, is a brilliant resource for the town as well as the schools, showing NT Live streams and hosting a number of touring companies as well as local arts groups. The school runs computer programming classes for the local community. There is a much-loved tradition where the school parades through the town to church for the annual commemoration service, and all the key local dignitaries are invited to events such as the carol service. The school feels friendly and purposeful, with a wholesome sense of balance about the whole place.

Pastoral care, well-being and discipline: Mental health issues do not dominate the pastoral agenda here as they seem to be increasingly doing elsewhere. Some staff say this is down to very strong and flexible support systems so everyone has someone to go to if anything starts to fall apart. The head says it is also the consequence of sport for all, quoting research which shows how good physical exercise is for warding off serious mental health problems. The boys themselves are serious about the emotional problems that can occur, happy to talk openly about them, and agree staff are hugely supportive. Staff say discipline problems are largely pre-empted. Behaviour expectations are made very clear and it unusual for boys to overstep the line. Usually, one of the house staff tells us, there is just a lot of trust and respect on both sides. Parents comment on how responsive staff are to queries or concerns, getting back swiftly by email or phone.

Pupils and parents: Families come mainly from the south west, the Bristol/Cheltenham area and south Wales. A lot of parents buy into the Habs' Monmouth suite of schools, which have an increasingly family-friendly approach as seen in the school bus policy, with routes adjusted each September accordingly to where the children in all the schools live. We thoroughly approve, though some parents comment on how expensive the service is and, like so many other schools, it is not possible to take into account everyone's after-school commitments. Parents are a cross-section both professionally and financially. Teachers and parents comment on the easy social mix. The boys seem very comfortable in their own skins, welcoming to newcomers, completely unpretentious and conscious of how fortunate they are to be at such a wonderful school in such a wonderful location.

Entrance: Most of the boys at the prep move up to the senior school and they are joined by about as many again from outside. At 11+, assessment has a three pronged approach – exams in English, maths and verbal reasoning, an interview and a report from the present school. At 13+, by common entrance or the school's own exams in maths, English and French with interviews. Sixth form entry depends on GCSE results, an interview and report from existing school. Non-nationals must speak reasonable English, although the school does offer EAL support.

Exit: Some 10 per cent leave post-GCSE. After A levels, the school is proud of the range of universities and courses to which the boys move on. Three medics in 2018. One off to Hong Kong, others to Germany and Paris. The majority choose science based-subjects, but there is a fair smattering of languages, humanities and the arts.

Money matters: For escapees from the south east, the comparatively low level of fees brings tears of joy to the eyes. This school offers excellent value for money. There is bursary support and scholarships at each level: academic, music and sport.

Remarks: An excellent school for the all rounder who wants to work and play hard. It is a place of high aspiration in the most idyllic setting, far away from the city scramble but not isolated socially or intellectually. It would probably not be ideal for those who detest sport or who want to be hothoused for a scholarship to Harvard. The family of schools work closely together and undoubtedly gain strength not just from having the Haberdashers behind them but also from the collegiate approach at leadership level. Perhaps the fact that leadership is not the usual lonely business is one reason for the tension-free atmosphere of palpable enjoyment that cascades down from the senior levels.

Monmouth School Boys' Prep

Linked with Monmouth School for Boys, Monmouth School Girls' Prep, Monmouth School for Girls, Monmouth Schools Pre-Prep & Nursery

Hadnock Road, Monmouth NP25 3NG

Ages 7–11 **Pupils** 131 **Boarders** 10 full (from 9 years) **C of E**

Fees: Day £11,091; Boarding £20,280 pa

01600 715930
www.habs-monmouth.org

Head: Since 2016, Neil Shaw, who exudes the calmness that comes from vast leadership experience combined with a passion for all the educational opportunities that a school like this offers. A geography graduate from Exeter, with an MA from Nottingham, and previous posts as head at Westonbirt Prep and before that at Kingswood School in Solihull, he is clearly a powerful addition to the Haberdashers' Monmouth leadership team. He finds meeting with the other heads stimulating and supportive. 'We are all focused on the benefits of cooperation and we are all fairly new and up for change', he tells us. 'I really value the camaraderie of the leadership group and also the financial stability and backing of the Habs' foundation.'

Having two children at two of the other Habs' schools, Neil knows firsthand the huge convenience factor for parents of the five linked foundation schools over such practicalities as coordinated timings, dates and shared buses. He sees the key to the success as being single sex. 'We do boys' things very well and the boys find having their own space truly liberating in terms of creativity.'

Entrance: About two-thirds come from Monmouth Schools Pre-Prep and Nursery, and a third join from outside. It is selective and the school is looking for boys who have a good chance of getting into the senior school at 11.

Exit: Most go on to Monmouth School for Boys (90 per cent in 2018), some with scholarships. A few leave for the state sector. If there is likely to be a problem getting into the senior school, this is flagged up with parents early on and advice given about other options.

Remarks: Housed in a modern purpose built school, The Grange, it does not have the physical charm of other Habs' Monmouth schools but it does have masses of space, a light, airy feel and is super convenient for the much-used sports facilities next door. What it lacks in prettiness it makes up for in the sort of practicalities that matter to small children – a climbing wall and fort in the playground. It has its own vegetable garden and the lettuces were nearly ready to be cut for lunch when we visited.

Academically, in some ways it offers a traditional curriculum with a focus on preparing the boys for the senior school. But the head is interested in more continuity from the pre-prep so is developing a creative, topic-based approach in the first two years. French from year 3. There is also a lot on offer that is not standard KS2 fare: they had just completed an impressive bridge-building project. A visit from GCHQ staff had resulted in a day of code breaking. There are maths and science competitions going on but also a walk in the local bluebell woods to inspire watercolour painting and sketching.

There are four year groups with two forms in each year – varying in size from 16-22 – and the classrooms peel off from the central space, opening out onto a huge enclosed play area. The library, crammed with the series boys love, is at the heart of the school and overseen by its own librarian. The teachers are all specialists so the boys get used to moving around the site in preparation for senior school. There are music, art (with pottery wheel and kiln), science and computer specialist areas. Because of its location, the school can draw on a wide area when looking for high quality staff: for example the art is taught by a Bristol university teacher who relished the freshness and creativity of the boys.

There is one-to-one learning support available with a policy of early intervention. School expects that difficulties can be addressed with a short term intervention programme for which there is no extra charge. Anything more long term will be charged in discussion with parents. Parents tell us the key to the school's success if that it instils an expectation of focused academic work. They report there is no disruption in classes, the teachers respect the boys and are able to challenge and stretch even the most academic. The boys clearly like and respect their teachers and relish talking to them.

The opportunities for the boys out of class are impressive for any school, never mind one this size. 'Yes, we have got the sport, but the quality of the music is a great joy too,' the head told us. Last year saw a highly successful production of Noye's Fludde with endless creative opportunities: the exciting headdresses were made by the boys, they had the opportunity to perform beside professional musicians. 'It was awesome', one of the boys told us. Music is taught through the Hungarian Kodály method and there are plenty of performance opportunities for the many groups and choirs, not just at the school but also in the senior school's Blake Theatre, plus outside venues – St David's Hall in Cardiff and St John Smith Square in London.

The boys say the best thing about the school is the sport but parents were keen to say that the school is keen to recognise boys' talents in all directions and unsporty boys have plenty of opportunities to shine and enjoy their interests.

There are joint activities with the girls' prep and the pre-prep schools. The day before our visit the boys and girls had put on a joint science fair at the senior school's Blake Theatre. There are joint teams for general knowledge quizzes and maths challenges.

The head told us that as a newcomer he has found the parents and the whole community very welcoming and supportive. Parents clearly have high expectations, but this is not the tiger mum set. Some are professionals, perhaps working in Bristol or even commuting some days to London. Some run local businesses and farms. The school offers wrap-around care and stay overs in the boarding house.

There is a resurgence of interest in junior boarding in school's own delightful Georgian house, Chapel House, off site, with transport by minibus. Flexi-boarding and weekly boarding is available but there are plenty of weekend activities on offer too. The boarders love the large walled garden that allows masses of outside space for playing in at the end of the day.

The school has that energy and bustle that many boys' junior schools exude, but you are also reminded all the time that this is part of a larger family. Whether it is seeing older boys and girls in the Blake Theatre, when they come visiting or on the sports fields, the boys have role models to look up to and aspirations to follow. The school applauds individual achievements, but without doubt encourages community values and sense of belonging.

M

Monmouth School for Girls

Linked with Monmouth School for Boys, Monmouth Schools Pre-Prep & Nursery, Monmouth School Boys' Prep, Monmouth School Girls' Prep

Hereford Road, Monmouth NP25 5XT

Ages 11–18 **Pupils** 614 **Sixth form** 125 **Boarders** 133

Fees: Day £14,778 – £15,816; Boarding £28,932 – £32,061 pa

01600 711100
www.habsmonmouth.org

Headmistress: Since April 2019, Jessica Miles MA PGCE (late 40s), previously head of Queen Margaret's School in York. Educated at girls' boarding school Farnborough Hill in Hampshire and a scholarship student at Oxford graduating with a degree in modern languages. Worked for short time in arts administration, then did PGCE at King's College, London. First teaching post at Dulwich College, where over 11 years she became head of Spanish, deputy head of upper school, head of sixth form and director of rowing. After a move to Dorset in 2007 and a year teaching Spanish and French at Sherborne School, she moved to Leweston School as deputy head. She joined Queen Margaret's in 2015.

At Oxford was a member of the university drama society touring in Japan and Russia; she also rowed for her college. Fluent Spanish speaker, who once wanted to be a flamenco dancer. Married to Paul, a former teacher who now works in cricket development for Help the Heroes; two young sons.

Academic matters: The results at GCSE and A level are very good and the school says it achieves this without putting the girls under too much pressure. In 2018, 69 per cent 9-7 grades at GCSE and 46 per cent A*/A, 76 per cent A*-B at A level. Art, modern languages, maths and science are popular choices. Now has a joint sixth form with Monmouth School for Boys, allowing 25+ subjects to be on offer across both schools, which ensures virtually everyone gets the combination of subjects they want. It means some girls are taught in some subjects at the boys' school and boys at the girls'. This works well. The girls say they like the different perspective the boys bring to subjects and comment on an often-repeated observation that it is noticeably that the girls think before they speak, unlike the boys.

Parents say that the school doesn't heap unreasonable amounts of pressure on the girls, but that doesn't mean that HMSG has any lower expectations that the big London day schools, with which parents were often comparing it. Learning support is available on an individual/shared basis from suitably qualified staff. The girls say teachers will always make time for them if they need a bit of extra help on a less formal basis. Most departments run surgeries for individual help, too.

Links with outside organisations enhance the academic work. Renishaw plc sponsored a STEM competition recently that led to further work supported by the school staff, which led in turn to two girls exhibiting their invention at the NEC, pitching it on Dragons' Den and selling to national retailers.

Games, options, the arts: The school has a deserved reputation for being very sporty, and clearly even the girls who aren't games mad are very proud of the reputation. There is a tennis academy across all the Habs Monmouth schools, and they compete at softball, rowing, show jumping and eventing as well as the more traditional sports. Girls regularly play for the region and Wales, and there are sports and dance scholarships. One parent told us that her daughters had asked the PE staff if they could start a gym club. Within a few months they had it – well resourced and competing nationally.

Drama and dance are popular, music is strong with 50 per cent taking some additional music lessons, all housed in the new performing arts centre which includes a recital hall, dance and drama studio and a rock room. The annual inter-house Eisteddfod gives an extra frisson to these activities. The glass atrium is hung with house flags on such occasions. Art is popular and high quality – lots is displayed around the school. Parents praise the standard of the drama productions.

At senior level, most of the extracurricular performing arts are done with the boys' school along with CCF, shared visiting speakers and a number of societies. It would be nice to have even more, the girls tell us. DofE and other local community service opportunities as well as fundraising for overseas projects. Girls are committed to these ventures both for their own personal development and also, we felt, out of a genuine desire to serve others.

Boarding: The boarding houses are on the school site and are purpose built. They are strikingly attractive and friendly in feel. From year 11 up, girls have rooms of their own. Below that they share in twos or threes. There is a lot organised for the boarders outside lesson time, some trips including the boys' school. Much sport goes on at weekends and in the evenings. There is shopping, cinema trips, salsa evenings, BBQs and generally a purposeful but relaxed atmosphere, which is very appealing and might account for the very low incidence of illness, despite the attractions of the medical facilities – there are soft toys on every bed. It might also account for the equally low level of law breaking. The girls really struggled to think of naughty things that anyone did. The worst seems to be not doing your kitchen duty or being late to breakfast (punishment – go in early the next day).

Boarding is flexible but that hasn't meant the school opts out of providing after-school and weekend activities. This is an active school with high energy pursuits on offer throughout the days and weekends. The meal menu is wide and quality good with meals served in an attractive extended dining room.

Background and atmosphere: Founded in 1892, to offer girls the opportunities that Monmouth School had provided since 1614, the Girls' School was funded by the original bequest of a local man, William Jones, a member of the Haberdashers' Company who made his fortune in Russian. The livery company is responsible for the school and provides financial support and stability, which reassures staff and has allowed for continual development of facilities. Although the boys' school is not far away, the girls' school has its own extracurricular facilities such as an Astroturf and swimming pool. The original Victorian buildings have been enhanced by imaginative, modern expansions such as a glass atrium and sixth form centre.

The school works hard at being a part of the Monmouth community and seems liked and respected. We arrived in the middle of the Monmouth Literary Festival – Carol Ann Duffy had been speaking the night before – which is organised entirely by the sixth forms of the three Monmouth secondary schools, the two Habs schools and Monmouth comprehensive. A remarkable achievement involving contacting agents, organising programmes, ticket sales and so on. There is another serious collaboration through the Monmouth Science Initiative, where state and independent schools work together with Cardiff University to bridge the gap between A level science and university science.

There is a lovely sixth form centre with study areas and a cool common room café – 'The boys love it', the girls tell us. 'We have to remind them that they are here for lessons not to drink hot chocolate all day.' Sixth formers still wear a uniform, suits, and tell us that they like it as they don't want to feel separate from the rest of the school. The dropout rate between year 11 and the sixth form is quite small – girls can't wait to wear suits and go to the café, we are told.

Pastoral care, well-being and discipline: The atmosphere is one of calm and sunny good manners. The relationships between the girls and staff are universally praised and we saw lots of warm and relaxed exchanges. 'They are interested in you and what you want to make of your life', sixth formers say. We heard about the much-anticipated annual satirical review put on by staff as part of the sixth form Christmas entertainments, a good indication of strong relationships. There are anti-bullying ambassadors and a buddy scheme working between year 7 and year 13. The girls tell us they would like even more integration between year groups. Prefects apply for their role and are eager for an opportunity to give back to the school. 'It is the school empowering us to experience responsibility', we were told by a successful applicant. The school covers the effects and dangers of social media and bullying. It is less focused on punishment and more concerned that the girls understand the ramifications.

A coloured card system operates for minor disciplinary infringements throughout the school – three yellow cards for something like late homeworks leads to a detention. 'It is really to help us get caught up,' the girls say. There are orange cards for uniform matters – zero tolerance for nail varnish: it gets that naughty. Parents say problems are nipped in the bud early and the staff are open and honest in their communications on pastoral issues. Pastoral care is outstanding, we were told.

Pupils and parents: Pupils come from a wide local area. There are buses from Cardiff, the north Bristol area, the Monmouthshire border, Hereford, Newport and the Ledbury area. The calendars for both day and boarding pupils are coordinated across the five Haberdashers' Monmouth schools, which is clearly a huge advantage for parents.

The bursary scheme ensures a good social mix. There are émigrés from the home counties, old Monmouth families, families with very little in the way of income and lots with both parents working hard to afford the fees. Staff commented to us that you find none of the sense of entitlement that some schools engender – pupils seem grateful to be here.

The school takes parents' surveys very seriously and we were impressed by the positivity about parental criticisms to help with raising the game. School council is valued by staff as well as by the girls: it pays more than lip service to parent and pupil voices. Parents complimented the school on its proactive approach to keeping them aware of current problem issues such as e-safety. 'They are taking care of my education as a parent,' one mother told us. Parents' view of the HMSG 'product' is one of engaging, confident, interesting girls who are keen to try new things, unaffected and enthusiastic. We would agree.

Former pupils include Lisa Rogers, Sandra Huggett and Jackie Ballard MP.

Entrance: About a third from their own prep school, Monmouth School Girls' Prep, a third from other independent schools and a third from state schools. Entry is by entrance exam, interview and junior school report. At 13+ by own exam or common entrance. Some join at sixth form following an interview and good GCSE results.

Exit: There is less of the problem than some girls' schools face with large numbers of year 11 leaving for mixed schools. A few go for financial reasons or because A levels really aren't for them, but most (some 85 per cent) stay on for the final two years. Sixth formers and parents say the school prepares girls very well for university and beyond. There are lots of links with old girls – staff meet up semi-formally with those who are London-based very regularly. There are plenty of opportunities to visit universities and the girls are starting to think about apprenticeships. At the moment virtually everyone goes to university – two to Oxbridge in 2018, the majority to Russell Group universities and others to do niche high quality courses such as stage management and technical theatre, agri-food marketing, anthropology and media. A number study science, including medicine (two in 2018) and engineering. A few go overseas – one to an art and design course in Los Angeles in 2018.

Money matters: One in five receive financial assistance through a means-tested scheme that reassesses every year from endowment income.

Remarks: Habs has been in Monmouth for 400 years and reinvented itself over that time. The current structure is a selling point, parents tell us. They like the all through concept with co-ed for the little ones in Agincourt and at sixth form level. Parents frequently used the word 'honest' when describing the school. You feel the fresh, clear air from the Welsh hills permeates the whole ethos. The location is very inspiring. From the sports fields you look out along the Wye

Valley and from anywhere in the school you have views down to the rest of Monmouth and beyond. It is a lovely place to live.

We wondered if it was all a rather awful shock when girls had to move outside the Monmouth bubble, but we were assured that the school was anything but parochial. There are lots of visits to far-flung parts of the globe. Having said that, there is no doubt that Monmouth feels a very long way from Cardiff or Bristol, where a number of day girls live – no doubt part of its appeal for many families. It has the ambitious feel of a big city school without any of the traffic jams and tower blocks.

One parent summed up the feel of the school well: 'HMGS may lack a little of the pomp, ceremony and glitz of some public schools, but what you get is genuine care and a commitment to help your child reach her potential, whatever that may be.'

Monmouth School Girls' Prep

Linked with Monmouth School Boys' Prep, Monmouth School for Girls, Monmouth School for Boys, Monmouth Schools Pre-Prep & Nursery

Hereford Road, Monmouth NP25 5XT

Ages 7–11 **Pupils** 139 **Boarders** 21 full (from 7 years)

Fees: Day £11,091; Boarding £20,280 pa

01600 711100
www.habs-monmouth.org

Head: Since 2013, Hilary Phillips, mid 40s, who came from a London prep school where she had been director of pastoral care, head of French and PSHE and classics teacher. She has the professional appearance of a stylish London head who is used to the competitive south east prep school bear pit. She arrived to a caring and nurturing school, and she wanted to maintain these qualities but bring to it a bit more of the south east edginess. She has widened the scope, opened the school out more to the wider community and brought in what she describes as a 'healthy competitiveness'. She has sharpened up the academic side of the school, introducing rigorous monitoring, and is hot on differentiated activities in every class. She has also introduced the St Cuthbert Diploma, which is a sort of Monmouth School Girls' Prep baccalaureate. This is awarded by careful tracking of each girl's progress – not just academic, but extracurricular contributions and the development of social skills too. It is personal to each girl and reflects Mrs Phillips' genuine commitment to valuing the whole person.

Parents have welcomed her openness. She has got them contributing to the school by helping with and running clubs. 'Mrs Phillips has encouraged us to come to her with ideas and any concerns. She doesn't want us standing round the car park gossiping and moaning', a parent told us approvingly.

Leaving to head Ashdown House in September 2019.

Entrance: Applicants come in for a Saturday morning. It is supposed to be a fun time, and the school puts on sports activities, but they also do a maths assessment, a piece of writing and a non-verbal reasoning test. Almost all the girls from Monmouth Schools Pre-Prep and Nursery (the mixed 3 to 7 Habs Monmouth school) come into Monmouth School Girls' Prep and the head tells us that there should be no surprises for those parents, who have been given a very good idea by this stage if they will make the grade.

Exit: Virtually all the girls go on to the senior school – 95 per cent in 2018. The head says it is not an 'old fashioned' selection process to get there. Neither school is interested in girls who fit neatly into a traditional academic mould, although the senior school is obviously offering an academic curriculum. 'We want every girl who leaves us being able to say "I can do this well",' the head tells us.

Remarks: Monmouth School Girls' Prep (then known as Inglefield) was opened as a distinct school in 1990 – before that it was just a department of the senior school. Now there are two classes in each year with a maximum of 20 girls. There is a real variety of parental backgrounds – local farmers, those who have moved out of London for a more outdoor life with their family, those where one or both parents commute into London on a weekly basis.

The school uses standardised tests to benchmark the girls on arrival and identify each one's needs. Interim grades ensure early intervention throughout the year, and parents receive these along with two parents' evenings a year for each year group. We liked the head's obvious preference for face-to-face conversations rather than impersonal reports and emails. There is one-to-one learning support from a dedicated teacher if necessary, for which parents pay extra, but the head tells us that there is not a great deal of need. There is no setting, but girls sit with others at the same level for maths and lesson plans include at least three levels of activity. The girls we spoke to loved maths and said the teachers wanted them to 'find our own ways of getting the answer'. Strong science is seen all around the school. It was good to find the girls well informed about geology, a science much needed but slightly undervalued in schools these days. PSHE, called 'confidence for life', is wide ranging and includes Apprentice-style activities where the girls give a presentation with a business plan for a new product.

The importance of the extracurricular life reflects the school's active aim of ensuring everyone discovers what they are good at and love. The head is keen that girls of this age find something physical that they enjoy to take with them through life. Sport is pleasingly inclusive. There are a lot of matches and the girls say that everyone gets a chance to play. The head herself is a keen sportswoman. They use senior school sports facilities and theatre. The Eisteddfod is major annual fixture, watched by everyone, which includes academic as well as artistic competitions. There is poetry, music, dance and song-writing. The title of the competition poem this year was 'If the moon could talk'. The winner sits on grand chair and is crowned. Then everyone sings the Welsh national anthem – our guides sang it confidently to us – peace is declared and competitive rivalries forgotten.

We were interested in what the girls, who had mainly been taught with boys before coming to Monmouth School Girls' Prep, thought about their single sex experience. Apparently they still go on trips with the boys but were pleased they could play all the parts in the school plays and throw themselves into a recent re-enactment of the Battle of Bosworth – no boring learning about domestic life in the Middle Ages here.

The girls are very proud of their school council – there is none of the cynicism that you can get in senior school with criticisms of pseudo democracy. 'We bring our ideas to make the school even better,' the girls assured us, and said that the gardening and sewing clubs came about because the need was raised through the council.

We got a real sense of community from talking to the girls. They look out for each other and know that the staff are doing just the same. When it comes to Charity Day and making their own stalls, the girls assure us that teachers are checking no one is left out. The dinner ladies keep an eye on what everyone is eating – not too many carbohydrates, one girl told us seriously. They are very proud of their school, not so much because of great success stories but more because of what adults would see as the balance and creativity of what is on offer. The art is all around, with some wonderful collages. There is evidence of lots of focused day and residential trips. There is a practical emphasis with projects like the geography scheme to make the playground more eco-friendly.

Boarders share School House on the senior school site with girls from years 7 and 8 in rooms of three or four.

Parents confirmed the excellent liaison between Monmouth Schools Pre-Prep and Nursery on one hand and the senior school on the other. The heads from each school regularly visit Monmouth School Girls' Prep, taking assemblies and talking to the girls. Senior girls help with junior clubs, coach music and academic subjects as well as taking the lead in the technical side of school productions, and run some linked assemblies. They also run the hugely important and popular annual Eisteddfod. Parents tell us that while each school has a very distinctive feel about it, progression really works, and you can see the girls flourish and develop at each stage.

Monmouth Schools Pre-Prep & Nursery

Linked with Monmouth School for Boys, Monmouth School for Girls, Monmouth School Girls' Prep, Monmouth School Boys' Prep

Dixton Lane, Monmouth NP25 3SY

Ages 3–7 **Pupils** 89

Fees: £4,518 – £7,572 pa

01600 713970
www.habs-monmouth.org

Head: Since 2014, Jennie Phillips (40s), who burst upon Monmouth Schools Pre-prep and Nursery from Badminton School and no one's feet have touched the ground since. Passionate and enthusiastic about the key role of these early years, Mrs Phillips has been building on a highly successful enterprise to make the school something very wonderful indeed. Like lots of her staff, she looks and sounds more like an escapee from Hampstead than you might reasonably expect to find in rural Wales. Polished and poised, she is a whirlwind of imaginative energy and clearly adores the children and the whole environment of the school. On the one hand, she has upgraded the IT so it has the all singing, all dancing facilities of a much bigger school, on the other hand she has encouraged the children to build their own chicken house and run. She doesn't believe in wet break times – the children go outside in their heavy duty waterproofs and wellies and make mud slides. Not surprisingly, she has also got rid of carpets in the vicinity of any outside doors. Parents credit her with introducing a modern approach to special educational needs. 'Mrs Phillips recognises that everyone has special needs and the children are given individual input that they wouldn't get elsewhere,' said one delighted mother of twins who attend the nursery.

A maths specialist, Jennie Phillips has firm views on how to encourage children to love maths and insists on at least three differentiated activities going on at one time in a class. 'The children all come to it from different places and I want them all to find activities that they can do and that stretch their understanding at the same time'. She is introducing a new creative curriculum that is school-wide and themed based – it is Turrets and Tiaras next term.

'I want the children to learn how to work together and be inquisitive learners', Mrs Phillips tells us. She has introduced a range of development opportunities for staff and everyone is buying into her vision of 'succeeding together'.

Entrance: Non-selective entry and children come for an induction day. Parents select the school for its size, its surroundings and the sense of a can-do, loving community. The school offers before and after-care as many parents both work.

Exit: More-or-less everyone moves on to the single sex 7-11 girls' and boys' schools within the Haberdashers' Monmouth Foundation, Monmouth School Girls' Prep and The Grange. However, they are not guaranteed to move right through the school and a few are offered a place on the understanding that they will need support. There are lots of links with the prep schools for the year 2s as the children get ready to move on, and Mrs Phillips regularly takes assemblies in the next schools so the children continue to see her even when they have moved 'up'. Similarly, the heads of the prep schools are frequent visitors to the pre-prep.

Remarks: A short distance from the senior school, Agincourt was taken on by the Haberdashers 16 years ago. The listed rectory nestles in a tiny valley with the church on its doorstep. ('The vicar wants us to use it as another classroom', says the head.) As the setting for a nursery and infant school, it is many parents', and our, idea of idyllic. As we arrived, one class was working outside on a gently sloping grassy bank, intently measuring and timing objects, while blossom from the cherry trees floated down in the breeze around them.

With non-selective entry, early intervention to support any learning difficulties is seen as automatic and is free at this stage, either on a one-to-one basis or in small groups. There are regular workshops for the most able and talented. Up to 18 children in each class, and each teacher has a teaching assistant. Children work towards the national early learning goals and there is testing in years 1 and 2, all of which is tightly tracked to ensure appropriate and speedy intervention and keep a check on value-added scores. A new whole school assessment and achievement programme is being introduced.

The school abounds with evidence of the range of activities. There are decorated tiles fired in their own kiln, scary masks, paper mâché lighthouses, some more convincing than others. All the children can read simple music by the end of year 2. In PSHE lessons with Mrs Phillips, they were writing survival plans for a desert island stint and learning how to apply for jobs and be interviewed. 'We have to always remember to knock on the door and not just walk in', a serious year 2 told us. Reading is a high priority and the school gets both parents and children committed to rapid progress here. There have been curriculum changes this year with a new approach to phonics and a stress on a skills-based curriculum with lots of outdoor learning going on, including a forest school, where the children make ladders and houses with proper saws and axes. We saw the chicken house and run that the children had planned and helped the deputy head to build. They had themselves petitioned to keep chickens and given a presentation to governors, with a full risk assessment including flood risks and what to do with the hens during the school holidays. Not bad at age 6. The extracurricular side of the school is evidenced wherever you look, and the children talk enthusiastically about the sport, chess, music, sewing and the construction/deconstruction club where they engage in activities such as taking apart a Dyson and putting it back together again.

Parents talk about the school being a home from home, with lots of hugs and kisses. The children are gently persuaded into the structure of school and this approach to progression works. Particularly commended was the very individual pace at which each child is taken forward. 'When I read the Agincourt reports, it is as though a member of the family has written them,' we were told.

It is possible that a child that liked to be indoors and was very fastidious about getting dirty might be unsuited to this school. Otherwise the only downside we could find was that the chicken run has had to be given a mesh roof as the buzzards circle overhead in chick season.

Moor Park School

Moor Park, Richards Castle, Ludlow, Shropshire SY8 4DZ

Ages 3m–13 **Pupils** 172 **Boarders** 11 full, 30–60 weekly/flexi (from year 3) RC

Fees: Day £6,180 – £17,235; Boarding £21,360 – £25,590 pa

01584 876061
www.moorpark.org.uk

M

Headmaster: Since 2015, Charlie Minogue. It is never easy taking over from a popular longstanding head, but the word among parents is that Charlie is different and brilliant. He has won their hearts by singing Can't Stop Me Now with the parents' band at a school ball, wearing his kilt. He previously worked at Aldwickbury School (deputy head), Harpenden and St Paul's Cathedral School, having started his career in a secondary state school, an experience that has shaped his educational values. 'That first school taught me to never give up on a child and always be aware of what else is going on in their life. No-one is only a school pupil.' He is not a practising Catholic but very drawn to the moral framework that the Catholic foundation provides and subtly underpins everything.

There is a gravitas about Charlie that is balanced by boyish good looks and a twinkle in his eye. He knows all the children by name and what they are up to. The children are clearly keen to win his approval and attention. While we visited, one boy came up to him to arrange to be his partner in a golf match on the school's nine hole golf course that evening and it was clearly the highlight of the boy's week.

Charlie, his wife and two children are loving the open air life that the Shropshire 85 acre estate allows after the restrictions of the south east. Both children are at the school and Charlie says that when they went back to Harpenden to meet up with friends, his son commented, 'It was nice seeing them, Dad, but we can be outside so much more now and never seem to use our mobiles much'. Smartphones are not a feature for the family at Moor Park – there is far too much climbing trees for that. Charlie's wife is totally involved in the school, entertaining visitors, teaching the double bass, running the marketing. 'She's fantastic,' one parent told us. She exudes charm and common sense and is a very reassuring presence for parents of boarders. Parents like the fact Charlie has an open door policy for them. 'Don't moan in the car park', he says. 'Come and tell me'.

Entrance: Non-selective, with assessments (before or after entry) to establish educational needs. Joiners at all stages, with some spending a few years here to prepare for full boarding at senior school.

Exit: The UK's best known senior schools figure as destinations including Eton, Winchester, Rugby, Cheltenham, Harrow, Moreton Hall, Christ College Brecon, Malvern College, Hereford Cathedral School and Downe House.

Remarks: In physical terms, this is the site to die for. Parents talk of the delight of seeing distant deer appear through the early morning mist as they drop their children off. The original house is Queen Anne, much developed in the late 19th century and includes arts and crafts features such as Morris stained glass. The entrance hall is inviting, with a big fireplace and imposing staircase that boasts remarkable tooled leather wallpaper and leads up to the boarding area. Just off the entrance hall is the chapel, the old ballroom with a wonderful ceiling. The 85 acres include a deer park, lake, terrace, lots of woodland and lawns.

But this is no sterile stately home. The delight of the grounds and buildings is that all are used both formally and informally for the children to have a full outdoor life and rich childhood. The dormitories in the old house are in the quirky top rooms with slanting ceilings and irregular lines. The old coach house has made a spacious pottery and art space. Full use is made of the stream as part of an assault course – mud runs are the fun activity of the moment. There is an outdoor classroom in the woodland where the children have poetry lessons and an Astroturf. The night before we visited, there had been a bonfire in the woods where the children had baked their own bread. 'Awesome', said the year 8s. Around the main house are lots of small outdoor areas and as you turn a corner, you find a swing with a group of girls playing, then round the next a small grass area with half a dozen boys playing cricket, then you see individual raised beds for vegetable growing for the incipient gardeners. You couldn't get further from the typical urban fenced-in school playground. There is a big sports hall, a swimming pool, excellent outdoor sports facilities as well as a large multi-purpose space with banked seating for performances and whole school assemblies.

The school is non-selective and caters for the full ability range. There are two children on formal EHC plans and also a lot of academic scholarships to highly regarded senior schools. When children join their needs are assessed and if necessary a plan is put in place with the SENCo ('She's a brilliant asset,' says the head). The school works successfully with children who have dyslexia or dyspraxia or are on the autism spectrum. One parent told us how quickly the teachers picked up on her son's dyslexia, despite it having been undiagnosed for years at another school. There are two forms most years with up to 16 children in each form, so class sizes are small enough for a lot of one-to-one support as a matter of routine, which the children are quick to point out and appreciate.

School has recently reviewed the curriculum and teaching methods to encourage everyone to develop curiosity, confidence, creativity, independence. No more formal homework for years 3 and 4: instead they are taught how to learn eg spellings and times tables, with the aim of making revision easier.

Art is undoubtedly one of the outstanding strengths of the school – the standard of work is way above what you would expect for children of that age. The DT workshop is home to an enormous crocodile made by the children that hangs from the ceiling and the emphasis is on teaching crafts using the professional-looking array of tools and equipment. The children have made a compost loo for the woods and a hovercraft as well as tables and chairs that can actually be used.

The children say there is always lots to do and that the best thing about the school is the freedom. Sport is huge and very successful – the girls' U12 hockey team had just been in the national finals when we visited. New performing arts centre, Many are involved in out-of-class musical activities. We were impressed by a flautists' group that arrived in the school chapel for their lunchtime rehearsal and just got on with it before any teacher appeared. Those involved in speech and drama – now on the curriculum for year 3 upwards – regularly take part in local festivals and competitions and again do very well. There are school plays and concerts. No compulsory Saturday morning lessons for years 3-5 now: instead there are optional activities ranging from kayaking to cookery to musical theatre, open to other local children. Other weekend activities are wildly anticipated. These are often themed – a Bake-Off weekend, a Camo weekend, with the highlight being Capture the Flag at night.

The emphasis is on flexi-boarding. There are full boarders, some of whom are foreign nationals coming over for perhaps a year or even a term, mainly from Europe. A lot of children dip in and out of boarding on a weekly basis and that works well both for the children and families. Everyone is welcomed for special boarding weekends. It all feels very relaxed. There is a separate purpose-built boarding house for younger children, The Tree House, a wooden building that has impeccable eco-credentials. This allows for 10 girls and 10 boys to board at any one time and children typically stay for two or three nights a week.

Pastoral care is regarded as outstanding. The children say that staff sort out any problems very quickly and the head tells us that he was very struck when he arrived by how very positive the weekly staff pastoral meetings are, with is a sense that everyone is supportive of the holistic approach to pastoral care. The children and staff comment on how the children all look after each other, particularly boarders, where the older and younger children play together all the time. Parents describe how the staff are very good at dealing with relationship upsets sensitively, getting everyone to sit round and have a general discussion about being kind and thoughtful.

Daily mid-morning assemblies give the children a sense of calm and something outside their busy daily lives. Mass is held each week and although now most children and staff are not Catholic, that tradition is very visible and very much a part of the school's fabric. The children said that one of their most memorable events in the school calendar was the Benedictus at the end of the Michaelmas term. 'They trust us to hold the candles and the sheet of paper with the mass on', we were told. The school is concerned to ensure that those who board have some time just to be quiet by themselves, and the small bedrooms help this. Having said that, children who were very introspective or fixated on their play technology might not settle here. The head said that staff have to like the outdoor life, and we would say the same for children. If your child really doesn't enjoy getting muddy, Moor Park would be a bit wasted on them.

About half the children are fairly local – school minibuses bring children in from the rural areas. Traditionally it has been a school for established farming/landowning families and those wanting a preparation for the big Catholic boarding schools. Nowadays there are increasing numbers of escapees from the home countries. Families tend to share a belief in a holistic education and want their children to enjoy every minute of their childhood. 'Moor Park is unflashy', one parent said. 'Everyone's car is dirty'.

Moor Park is the most magical bubble. Children have a childhood experience that will never be forgotten and will shape them whatever life brings. They leave with the ability to interact positively with others of all ages, with a striking degree of self-reliance, and a sense of knowing themselves and knowing the delights of our natural world – things which can never be taken away. Parents can't bear to think their children will ever have to leave. 'It is a blessed place,' one said to us.

Moreton Hall School

Weston Rhyn, Oswestry, Shropshire SY11 3EW

Ages 11–18 **Pupils** 309 **Sixth form** 107 **Boarders** 232 full

Fees: Day: £26,550– £28,725; Boarding: £33,015 – £34,875 pa

01691 773671
www.moretonhallschool.com

Principal: Since 1992, Jonathan Forster BA PGCE (50s), who still 'just loves every day at Moreton Hall'. His daughters have been through the school and he and his wife, who's heavily involved in school life, can testify as parents to what a wonderful place it is bring up children. Jonathan – who has a degree from Leeds and was previously housemaster and English teacher at Strathallan – rescued the school from imminent closure, and he has continued to drive it at a pace that speaks of a life-long mission and endless creative energy. He is always ahead of the game, ensuring the school leads not follows market demands. He has kept true to the liberal educational vision of its founders and provided that liberalism with a modern twist, to give Moreton Hall girls the edge when they enter the adult world of work. Jonathan says he has been empowered by the environment, and it must be mutual, because his entrepreneurial spirit, his thinking outside the box, shows in the girls and in the whole ethos of the place. He has done remarkable things and when he eventually does leave, it will take someone very special to take his place. Indeed, retiring in July 2019.

His successor will be George Budd, currently deputy head at Godolphin School. Geography degree from Durham; began his teaching career in the state sector before moving to Lady Eleanor Holles in 2007 as geography teacher and later assistant senior teacher. Then to Sir William Perkins's School as head of geography and then head of sixth form before joining Godolphin in 2016.

A keen mountain biker, he is married to Nicky, currently director of sport at Lady Eleanor Holles and head coach for the U19 England lacrosse team.

Academic matters: Academic results are strong; A level to 51 per cent A*/A grades in 2018; GCSE 60 per cent A*-A/9-7, and the value-added scores at both GCSE and A level are usually huge. Its increasing success draws in star teachers and bright girls, so it's mostly on an upward trajectory. With lots of living accommodation on site, the job becomes a lifestyle choice for teachers as well as families. There is no deadening insistence on the latest Department for Education pedagogy here. The principal is far more interested in bringing in people who have done things – the English department boasts a writer, the art department has practising artists and the girls told us that their chemistry teacher had been testing perfumes before joining Moreton Hall. There is a strong science drive in the school (innovative science centre includes medical science facility – the first for any UK school) and well over half are taking at least one science A level. Close links to Keele University and the orthopaedic hospital at nearby Gobowen.

Though edging up all the time, the ability is quite wide on entry, which makes the results particularly encouraging. It's down to excellent teachers as well as small class sizes. The girls describe their teachers as 'passionate and enthusiastic' and are very aware that they are there literally all the time. 'They give you as much extra as you need,' said one sixth former who told us that when she was working late on a piece of work, she had emailed her teacher with a query at 11pm and had a reply that night.

There is no extra charge for learning support, whether it is Oxbridge preparation or getting through GCSE maths. Teachers are there for the girls whatever their needs – no sense of children having to fit into rigid school systems here. One parent commented on the flexibility the school offered in terms of curriculum – girls can study more or less any combination of subjects they want at GCSE and A level.

Games, options, the arts: It's in this side of school life where its radical and constantly progressing nature really shines. In sport it embraces that most traditional of girls' sports, lacrosse, where the Moreton Hall teams win everything this side of London and a fair bit nationally as well, but there are masses of other successes and opportunities with the fabulous sports facilities on site – a nine hole golf course and grounds that mean cross-country really is cross country. Cricket popular summer sport – now has indoor nets. Elite sports scholarship programme gives access to top quality coaching.

Lots of music goes on, classical and popular, with girls performing regularly to both large and small audiences. Drama is hugely popular and professional. 'Musical theatre can consume everything', said one non-thespian parent, worrying about exam results, but the girls are queuing up to take part.

All this is nothing like enough for Moreton Hall. The school is strong on connections and is extraordinarily well linked with a network of influential men and women whom Jonathan brings into the school for inspirational talks. Outside London this is not easy, and you would never guess this school was in the depth of gorgeous Shropshire. Dame Jocelyn Bell Burnett, world famous astrophysicist, had just been when we visited, and strong links with Keele University produce a steady flow of high-powered visitors. These not only enhance academic lessons but often come to speak at one of the many societies to which parents also drop in. There is wine-tasting, a feminist society, a medical science group, share dealing and so it goes on, reflecting the scope of opportunities for young women in the 21st century world.

All the girls get involved in the English Speaking Board to enhance confidence, presentation skills and the ability to think on their feet. One parent said, 'Everyone gets a 2.1 from Bristol or wherever these days, but Jonathan Forster really understands that the girls will need a lot more than that – he is giving them the life skills to succeed.'

Moreton Enterprises is part of this – a unique business venture consisting of a shopping mall run entirely by the girls. There is a branch of Ryman's stationery, Barclays Bank and home grown shops. The girls have business mentors, but basically the lower sixth operates as a small business turning over £50,000 a year. It is seriously impressive. Moreton Connect aims to create a network of OM and parent contacts for careers advice and work experience opportunities.

Boarding: About 90 per cent are boarders, and there is Saturday morning school, but apart from that, it is pretty flexible. One parent felt that girls new to boarding could be unsettled by friends coming and going, but we didn't find any girls who worried about this. The school wants girls to love boarding there and they do, partly because of the very special staff and partly because there is so much going on. 'It's like a long sleep-over but with loads to do as well,' said an enamoured 13 year old who had started as a day girl and then converted to boarding after a few taster nights.

We asked the sixth formers whether they felt a long way from all the city lights and boys, but were assured they saw quite as much as they wanted to of Shrewsbury School boys and often stayed Saturday night with friends in Manchester or Birmingham if they could fit it in between rehearsals, choir, talks. 'But it is just so lovely to come back,' they said with heartfelt sincerity.

Senior boarding accommodation is single or double (very popular in holidays with overseas adults as well as children), adding to the home from home feel. Junior girls and boys, often boarding one or two nights a week, have their own cheerful dormitories.

Background and atmosphere: As you would expect from girls who run a business at the age of 16, they are confident and at ease with themselves. They work and play hard, but there is something in the rural Shropshire surroundings (the school is set in 100 acres of parkland) that takes any unattractive edge off the ambition and drive. We felt that every girl in England should have at least a term in this environment.

The school was started by women educationalists 100 years ago, and Jonathan holds firm to their liberal view of education. He has used the school's centenary year to ensure the girls know about the strong female role models in the school's past. 'It was never meant to be like other schools,' he tells us. 'The Lloyd Williams family wanted a school where girls could enjoy the country and experience a rounded education that would set them up for life and all the different people they would meet'.

The very English country landscape and original school building, a moated Tudor house with the current façade dating from William and Mary, are balanced by new state-of-the-art purpose built areas. There is a stunning new science block, planned in a collaboration with Keele University and local state schools. The facilities are used by the university to run science taster session for local students with a particular emphasis on medical careers. The library is both welcoming and very modern. One girl talked about working in the library before her GCSEs and being able to take her kettle, mug and biscuits in there for a real go at her revision – good for the librarian.

Pastoral care, well-being and discipline: The principal wants the girls to love Moreton Hall as they would love their home, and to care for the school and each other in the same way. From what we saw, they do. There was a genuine warmth between the older and younger girls and a sincere appreciation for their surroundings and the attention they receive from teachers and boarding staff. Given the entrepreneurial energy about the place, the girls are amazingly relaxed. One member of staff said, 'They have time and space here so you don't get a frenetic atmosphere building up where no one has room for anyone except themselves'. These are not privileged princesses who think the world owes them. They are self-disciplined young women who have learnt in school that you can make a difference and live happily together. The centenary pageant included everyone who is a part of the school – not just teachers and girls. It's an inclusive place. Discipline was not a word we heard mentioned, and for a school that can happily host tribute bands in the outdoor amphitheatre on the last night of the summer term without a qualm – who needs lots of rules and punishment?

Pupils and parents: Some 80 per cent of the boarders are from the UK, a deliberate policy, and about 90 per cent of those girls are from within one to two hours travel. The school caters for business, diplomatic and professional families where often both parents are working and see the boarding option as a lifestyle choice, with the girls having endless activities and friends on tap. Communication, both formal and informal, works very effectively. Overseas parents tell us the school makes brilliant use of modern technology and emails are responded to very quickly by both the head and staff. Parents are supportive both in terms of social events and also by acting as mentors for the business enterprises. They can drop in to more or less any event

M

going on, and the division between home and school seems very fluid compared with many schools. One parent said, 'There are very traditional families who find it all rather liberal, but the principal soon shows them it works'. The principal and staff are well known for their assiduous attendance at school events and their detailed knowledge of the girls and their families.

Alumni include Zanny Minton Beddoes, editor of The Economist, Thea Musgrave, composer and musician, and Dame Linda Dobbs, high court judge.

There is a separate study centre for overseas students and multi-activity holidays for children and their parents.

Entrance: Many of 11+ entrants from co-ed junior school, Moreton First, with further entry points at 12 and 13, by common entrance or school's own exam, designed 'to test potential ability rather than factual recall'. Sixth form entry by current school report and interview. Number from overseas capped at 10 per cent. Once girls are there, the school sticks with them and very few leave.

Exit: Up to a quarter leave after GCSEs. Almost all sixth form leavers to university. Leeds very popular (including for physics and biology), then Bath, Exeter, Liverpool, Bristol, UCL and University of the Arts, London. In 2018, four to Oxbridge, plus a three medics, and one off to Melbourne to study economics. Not surprisingly, given their experience in school, a remarkable number of Old Moretonians are running successful businesses.

Money matters: The school has worked hard to increase means-tested bursaries, particularly to allow local girls from state schools to join the sixth form. Everyone pays something, but the aim is to give girls who would otherwise not have the opportunity a chance to experience the high-powered, aspirational world of Moreton Hall.

Remarks: It is outside the radar of parents who don't look beyond the home counties but more fool them – they are the ones missing out here. When asked why he had chosen Moreton Hall for his daughters, one parent looked vaguely bemused and said, 'Well, why wouldn't you?' We agree. This is a school with a difference, rigour in everything but going about it in a way that shows girls they can lead the world in a new way. And they will.

Mount Kelly

Linked with Mount Kelly Prep

Parkwood Road, Tavistock, Devon PL19 0HZ

Ages 13–18 **Pupils** 331 **Sixth form** 125 **Boarders** 178 full, 10 weekly
C of E

Fees: Day £17,520; Boarding £30,570 pa

01822 813193
www.mountkelly.com

Head master and principal of Mount Kelly Foundation: Since April 2019, Guy Ayling, previously head of Llandovery College in Wales. Degree in medieval history from St Andrews; spent 15 years at Sedbergh, where he was housemaster and senior deputy head. A keen rugby and hockey player, he captained the St Andrews 1st XV and played for Scottish Universities. He and his wife, Heather, have three sons.

Academic matters: A level results commendable, especially for a school which is not academically selective, with maths definitely impressive at all levels. In 2018, 37 per cent of grades were A*/A and 64 per cent A*-B; at GCSE 37 per cent A*-A/9-7 grades.

Class sizes are small – sometimes very small at A level. Currently the school will put on a course for one pupil – sadly necessary since the take up in modern foreign languages, art and music is select but able. Pupils we spoke to were full of praise for the extra help offered by their teachers when necessary. A good range of solid academic subjects on offer, with excellent language and IT areas. Parents spoke of the expert and sensitive advice they had had from staff when trying to help their children choose the most suitable subjects for them. Perhaps fewer now feel the urge to go further afield for a 'real academic education'. Parents and pupils speak very highly of the help given to those with special needs.

Games, options, the arts: Mount Kelly is rapidly becoming synonymous with swimming. Its reputation, built up over 30 years, is currently growing under a team of coaches running a comprehensive coaching programme for swimmers with competitive ambitions. The programme is built round the academic day and so is considerably less stressful and probably less expensive than the constant travel, early mornings and compromises with school that many young swimmers have to make. A parent commented that only one or two British schools have anything like comparable swimming and coaching facilities, including an Olympic standard 50m pool, and that Mount Kelly's pastoral care for such pupils is leagues ahead. No wonder the school boasts that, on average, a Mount Kelly swimmer a year has represented the UK either nationally or internationally.

M

Non-swimmers, however, are far from sidelined. Pupils spoke with enthusiasm of music, debates and outdoor activities, and there are myriads of curriculum supporting events. It's a lively place but also cheerful, friendly and definitely not frenetic, even at exam time. It is old fashioned enough to insist on school blazers with ribbons and badges festooned all over athletic gods and goddesses, but musicians, artists, thespians and prefects can be equally decorated – the school is just good at celebrating and acknowledging. The pitches and grounds in both prep and college areas are superbly managed and the acquisition of the Mount House School site has brought the one missing element, a fantastic sports hall. Sport plentiful but traditional – rugby and cricket for boys and hockey and netball for girls. Both girls and boys play hockey and compete in a mixed summer league.

A splendid and most interestingly designed performing arts centre with superb facilities for music, drama and debate – to say nothing of interval entertainment – is close by, as is the art building with evidence of creative painting and pottery. Since the college snuggles into a valley on the edge of Dartmoor, it's hardly surprising that outdoor education, DofE, CCF and all those sort of things are available and popular. Huge numbers of girls and boys complete the 125 mile canoe marathon from Devizes to Westminster and the Ten Tors expedition, as well as training as divers, rifle shots and mountaineers.

Boarding: Despite its monastic appearance, the renovated sections of boarding are exceptionally well done. Clever planning means that day pupils and boarders can socialise on the lower floors with plenty of well-equipped work and milling about space, while the bedroom floors above remain private. The four houses are divided into girls' sixth form, boys' sixth form and two co-ed houses for years 9-11, each managed by housemasters with a team of tutors drawn from academic staff as well as non-teaching matrons. Full medical service on hand. Boarders spoke enthusiastically of the sixth form centre and the activities arranged at weekends. Flexi boarding is very flexi.

Background and atmosphere: The buildings, tucked under the edge of Dartmoor just outside the pretty little town of Tavistock, have historical connections with the Duke of Bedford, who donated the land for the college, founded in 1877 by an Admiral Kelly. Despite its gentle lawns and lush green pitches, it's a craggy looking place, all gothic arches, dark wood and stone staircases, echoing corridors and lots of pointy bits. Academic mustiness, however, is banished by skilfully placed features of interest, pictures, honours and information about the school's past and the pupils' futures. Handsome library presided over by enthusiastic librarian and dusty looking (actually it isn't) chapel still exuding an odour of past sanctity, used four times a week.

Attractive new buildings higher up the hill behind the Victoriana, one of them the delightful Conway House, where the younger boys and girls live in comfortable harmony before joining the senior houses. Co-ed has been going here for nearly 40 years, so it all feels very relaxed and natural.

Pastoral care, well-being and discipline: Lunch in the dining room (masses of choice – cooked meals, salads and faster-looking stuff – particularly delicious lemon posset) was a good insight into the relationships between staff and pupils. Enough mutual respect and genuine affection to allow friendly banter on occasions. The pupils were forthcoming, friendly and honest in their conversation with us, though we were not shielded from meeting the odd awkward customer – treated with helpful sympathy and understanding. While accepting that bullying was always a possibility, they felt that the tutorial system in place was a good safety net and protection – always someone to talk to; above all they said they genuinely like the staff. Pretty common sense school rules result in very little indiscipline. Pupils all looked smartish, though lots dressed in mufti or sportswear towards the end of the day.

M

Pupils and parents: Parents come from a broad spectrum. Mount Kelly is trying to bridge the gap between being a good local option for the West Country and an upmarket public school. Boarding is boosted by swimmers from England and abroad (around 25 per cent of boarders are from overseas). One parent commented: 'My son can swim but hates it. But he gets stuck into lots of other things and that's the point. I take the view that excellence breeds excellence.' Others praise the community feel among parents, stressing how welcoming they are to families who move to Tavistock for schooling. The pupils we met and observed were open, friendly and trusting, and we noticed how much family-like interaction existed between the different age groups. Though there is definitely a sense that Mount Kelly is on its way to joining the league of 'top schools', it still feels a friendly, relaxed place where children can be children as much as is possible in this day and age.

Entrance: At 13+, about 75 per cent of entries come from the prep. Academically, the emphasis is on literacy and numeracy, with as much attention paid to potential as to knowledge. Entrance at sixth form is based on GCSE results (or equivalent) – normally about 20 new sixth formers joining each year. The important thing is to be alert, bright-eyed and willing to be taught. That applies as much to rugby players as potential Nobel Prize winners.

Exit: Three-quarters go on to the sixth form. Nearly all of these to university. A sensible number to well established ones all over the UK (and occasionally USA) to do old fashioned academic subjects, with the occasional one or two to Oxbridge, proves they can do it. Two medics in 2018.

Money matters: Scholarships and bursaries are available. Forces families may receive 10 per cent discount – don't be afraid to ask.

Remarks: Definitely worth watching. The signs are that it may succeed in providing an excellent environment for girls and boys set on local schooling as well as building up a boarding clientèle based on academic success enhanced by the lure of swimming. A sound, progressive place, where effort is rewarded and friendships flourish, unhampered by snobbery or over-sophistication, and on its way to giving the West Country a really fantastic school. Numbers up in the college with more boarders, so the signs are positive.

Mount Kelly Prep

Linked with Mount Kelly

Mount Tavy Road, Tavistock, Devon PL19 9JL

Ages 3–13 **Pupils** 274 **Boarders** 29 full, 13 weekly, 1 flexi (from year 3)
C of E

Fees: Day £7,230 – £14,070; Boarding £18,120 – £23,970 pa

01822 813193
www.mountkelly.com

Head of prep: Since 2016, Dominic Floyd, previously assistant head at Hazlegrove. Geography degree and PGCE from London University; taught geography at Cothill House and Westminster Under School; director of studies and deputy head at Polwhele House; head of Ashdown House. He and his wife Maria have three young children and his interests include micro-adventure, hiking, tennis and golf.

Entrance: Wide ability range – tests in English and maths 'more for benchmarking than selection,' says head. Most entrants attend a taster day in February prior to admission. Majority join the pre-prep at start of year 3, but growing numbers delay start until year 7, transferring automatically to the college at 13.

A few means-tested bursaries available.

Exit: Pupils prepared for 13+ transfer to the College at Mount Kelly or elsewhere. Presumably any pupil wanting to 11+ transfer elsewhere is prepared for this. The hope is for the majority of prep children to move into the main college at 13 and about 80 per cent do so.

Remarks: In the merger which established the Mount Kelly Foundation in 2014, Kelly Prep children moved into the sumptuous Mount House facilities, which are conveniently adjacent to the main Mount Kelly College buildings. The prep benefits from the college's Olympic size pool and college pupils gain access to the prep's sports hall, extensive grounds and other impressive facilities.

Stunning grounds include a trout stream (ideal for fly fishing) and a beautiful lake (great for science) bordering on Dartmoor National Park. A recent team of inspectors dubbed it 'an inspirational learning environment'. The prep is based in and around an elegantly proportioned, stone-built Georgian manor house with an assortment of additions, some historic and some ultra-modern purpose built. The attractive hall, accessed rather curiously through an office rather than its lovely glass doors, fulfils a variety of functions including regular assemblies and church services. The head's oak-panelled study leads off on one side and the school dining hall on the other. Upstairs are all the boys' and girls' dormitories in separate areas plus the sick bay. Dormitories of between four and eight are extremely well designed, with bathrooms between each pair of dorms. Boys' rooms are clean, fresh and pretty tidy, while the girls obviously like to express themselves more freely via plenty of pictures, and personal touches.

A plethora of buildings cluster behind the main house, some old and definitely unusual – the original stables have been converted in a variety of ways, including the 'giraffe house', which features a climbing wall, plus some really impressive purpose built facilities: the modern sports hall (with two squash courts), two large science laboratories and impressive music school. Music had a bit of a hiatus after the merger but seems to have recovered to 'even better than before', partly thanks to the 'best singing teacher in the universe'. 'Proper' church choir contributes to festivals and music is definitely 'in'. Full orchestra, jazz band, woodwind, choir, rock band all perform regularly. The school has a record of music and art scholarships, and the inviting art department had work on display which more than explained this.

Prep schools with such an array of enterprising ventures are few and far between, especially in deepest Devon. Recycling motivates the highly organised CDT department, where self-sufficiency and sustainable technology become second nature, and everything from day-old chicks to bicycle wheels finds a use. It is masterminded by an enthusiast who also runs a small farm in the school grounds. All ages contribute and 'truly love it'. Amongst animal and other agricultural activities, pupils are building a sustainable hut which even provides it own electricity (solar micro generators) while the tractor runs on the kitchen's recycled vegetables and the water supply comes from a borehole.

Most of the classrooms are an extension of the main building: attractive internally – some with stunning displays – and all with high level of equipment (smartboard in every classroom). Eighteen PCs in IT suite and staff are mostly IT savvy. 'Some fantastic teachers with a wide variety of styles from formal and well organised to lots of fun' – but all of them kind and good at building confidence. The recurring theme from parents, however, is that teachers are kind while children enjoy lessons and are happy. 'Mix of old timers and new blood on staff works well,' commented one father. Average class size is about 16. Curriculum is designed to allow pupils to go off piste and generate individual enthusiasms. High quality of written work wherever you look; motivational French lessons was another strong point noted.

Director of studies acts as SENCo with some 35 pupils on special needs register. Pupils are screened for dyslexia and a dedicated education psychologist will develop an IEP if required. Two part-time SpLD staff give one-to-one help where required.

Pre-prep in purpose-built, low level accommodation for 60 children up to end of year 2 with discrete outside area. High level of care and individual attention – most pre-preps transfer seamlessly aged 7. Lots of fun and outdoor experience for this end of the school, as well as developing strong foundations in the classroom basics.

Boarding ethos is all-important, especially to day pupils. One who begged to do a term's boarding loved it and found it problem free. No cliques or bullying and the occasional loner supported and encouraged. The new régime has relaxed some of the compulsory weekend elements but includes Saturday evening pick up after activities, then low key, on site Sunday programme. Ten couples/families live on site and rotate weekend duties. All staff stay here until 6pm every day; prep finishes at 7pm for older pupils (younger ones have clubs) and duty team of staff remains until dorm staff take over at 8.30pm. Most pupils spill out into grounds after prep but there are also lovely hidey-holes in the subterranean library for dedicated bookworms, and a lovely decked space for quiet relaxation complete with multi-lingual telephone box.

Five days a week sport here – facilities include fine pitches, heated outdoor pool (very popular) and full size Astroturf; national/regional successes principally in rugby, cricket and girls' hockey. Boarders love to play in the nets or swim after prep in the summer. Pony mad pupils get a look in with the local hunt and inter-school equestrian events. The Shackleton Award scheme (junior D of E award type project aimed at building confidence) was in full swing doing splashy things down by the enchantingly beautiful lake during our visit. The exceptionally beautiful grounds with waterfall and sloping lawns are meticulously managed by a groundsman who is endlessly kind to pupils, and even to parents with engine trouble or no petrol.

Pupils are well turned out – variety of dress according to age and season; they come mainly from Devon and Cornwall, professional, farming and Forces' families plus a few from London or elsewhere (very few overseas). Twice-termly lectures, alternating between the prep and the college, for parents and pupils across the Foundation, tap parental know-how: recent outside speakers have included explorer Pen Hadow and yachtswoman Tracy Edwards. Lots of local visits for all ages, annual trips to Northern France for the older pupils and regular ski trip to Alps. Former pupils include Phil de Glanville (England rugby captain), Adrian Lukis (actor in Pride and Prejudice), former foreign secretary and SDP co-founder, Lord David Owen, and explorer, long-distance swimmer and environmentalist, Lewis Pugh, to name but a few.

This combination of traditional prep and local junior schooling has given the far west a potentially remarkable school. One parent commented that the last few days of summer term are a triumph and say it all. Pupils leave, some to take up academic, sporting or artistic scholarships at the college itself, or other schools, able to 'catch a fish, thread a sewing machine and bake a cake', full of the confidence to face the next step eagerly.

Okehampton College

Mill Road, Okehampton, Devon EX20 1PW

Ages 11–18 **Pupils** 1,451 **Sixth form** 209

01837 650910
www.okehamptoncollege.devon.sch.uk

CEO: Daryll Chapman, executive principal since 2005 and since January 2018 CEO of the Dartmoor MAT, grew up in Derbyshire. Started his career playing professional football for Derby before training to become a PE teacher at a specialist college for physical education in Bedfordshire. After four years teaching at Cavendish School in Hemel Hempstead, he became head of PE at Misbourne School, Bucks, later becoming deputy head at a school in Aylesbury. Joined Okehampton College in 2001 as vice principal, taking on the role of principal four years later.

Married with three children; his youngest is at OC and his eldest daughter also went here, so he knows how valuable insight from children can be. No longer teaches PE, but he does teach maths to some of the more challenging students. Still playing football? No, he smiles, more of a spectator these days, and too busy ferrying his children around various athletics events across the county.

Daryll's adamant that the school isn't run like a business; it's a community. 'It's important to give the local children the opportunity to work and grow together,' he says. It's a big school, but he is more than happy to continue to grow, fully confident of their ability to cope with this. He also strongly feels that they haven't lost their personal touch at all. We agree – the school didn't feel huge. He believes in traditional values, meaning 'old school' values like being 'firm but fair', but not traditional in the sense of heritage and customs. Positive comments all round from parents, one saying, 'very impressed with Mr Chapman, he is part of the reason we didn't look around elsewhere.'

Head teacher of Okehampton College is Derrick Brett. Zoology degree from Durham and MEd from Cambridge; has also been assistant principal at Ilfracombe Community College and vice principal at Oakhampton.

Academic matters: In 2018, 52 per cent A*-B grades and 27 per cent A*/A grades at A level. At GCSE, 67 per cent got 9-4 in both English and maths; 19 per cent A*-A/9-7 grades. Ofsted said, 'All students make excellent progress from their generally below-average starting points.' Maths is a strong subject, and results have been in the top five per cent value added over the last few years. In science, another popular subject, students have recently won bronze awards and commendations in the National Physics Challenge.

Twenty-five A levels offered, plus BTecs in business, sport and dance. Vocational options cover catering, childcare and customer service. French is compulsory at key stage 3; German and Spanish are also offered. The school supports EAL students who wish to take a GCSE in their mother tongue. Recent examples include Polish, Dutch, Russian, Portuguese, Japanese and Spanish, but only in small numbers. Parents all agreed they were 'very pleased with the quality of teaching'. One teacher even called the college a 'career stopper,' happily refusing promotions elsewhere to stay there.

Large learning support department that recently won a Devon Dyslexia-Friendly Award. Twenty-five TAs, three special needs teachers, two literacy tutors, two numeracy TAs, all headed up by their SENCo. More than a quarter of students at OC have a recognised need. This includes the gifted and talented high achievers, as well as those needing support with reading or writing. One parent told us their child is 'studious and anxious and [we are] very pleased with the level of emotional support offered.' The site has been specially adapted for those with physical disabilities. There are wheelchair ramps, automatic access doors and yellow lines for partially sighted students. SEND is considered a priority and there's an ongoing teacher-training programme. Support is tailored to meet individual needs. Small groups for literacy and numeracy, a social skills group, a buddy system for reading and socialising, plus in-class support. There's also a number of clubs – breakfast club, break-time club and after-school homework club – when learning support staff are on hand to help.

Games, options, the arts: Excellent sports facilities. Astroturf, four floodlit tennis courts, extensive playing fields and a sports hall. The town's leisure centre is attached to the campus so although they don't have sole use, they have access to the dance studio, sports hall, fitness suite and swimming pool. Offers all the major games, plus gymnastics, trampolining, dance aerobics, athletics, cross-country and fitness courses. Outdoor pursuits are very popular: orienteering, canoeing, sailing, windsurfing, and moor walking. Notable success in table tennis – they are currently the national U13 table tennis champions, having county champions in their midst. One girl plays cricket for Devon county, one boy was recently crowned national judo champion and three students have represented England schools in athletics.

Good drama faculty (faculties, not departments here), popular and a good exam pass rate. There are regular trips to the theatre, plus opportunities to take part in dance and drama workshops with visiting theatre companies. Recent productions include Les Misérables with over 100 actors and West Side Story. The school has its own 200 seat theatre with a professional lighting rig and a sound booth. Sixth formers regularly visit London for plays or to take part in National Theatre acting workshops with professional West End actors and directors.

Art and textiles are offered at GCSE and at A level. Plenty of opportunities to visit galleries locally, plus in London and Paris. Textiles popular and the classroom has spectacular views of the sports fields and the moors beyond. Very good art on display, landscapes no doubt inspired by the surrounding area, and a huge number of papier-mâché shoes, no doubt inspired by, well, the love of shoes.

Music in its own well resourced area, each classroom with a piano/keyboard, drum kit, amps and guitars. We saw students recording their individual exam pieces on the drums in one room, and practising as a band (teacher on drums), in another room. The whole building was alive with activity and ad hoc practice sessions. The school encourages individual lessons and although parents contribute, there is a charity set up to help keep costs down. Wide range of ensemble activities, including orchestra, big band, little band, junior and senior choirs. Big Band has travelled to New York, Hong Kong, Paris and recently Barcelona. Major concerts each year at Christmas and Easter.

There's a well-resourced and modern building for technology and ICT. Six large suites dedicated to ICT, plus a sixth form suite, and Wifi covering the whole school. For technology, there's professional standard catering equipment, two labs for resistant materials, two labs for electronics, a CADCAM suite and workbenches. All hand and computer skills are covered here.

The school offers a good range of extracurricular activities and even provides late buses to ensure that everyone can take part. However, the head did say, 'my only disappointment is that more of them do not take advantage of these opportunities.' Annually there's a curriculum extension week and recently students have gone sea fishing, cycled along the Devon coastline, travelled to France and Germany, and taken part in cooking, drama and even magic courses. Other trips include regular French exchanges with a school in Brittany and recently, cultural trips to Germany and Poland.

Background and atmosphere: Founded in 1910 as a grammar school, the college is set in a large park, surrounded by woodland and Dartmoor. A good mix of old and new – there's the original Victorian building with its large arched windows, a modern three-storey block, plus 70s buildings, all linked by covered walkways. It's easy to find your way round. The site feels open and friendly and has courtyards, picnic tables and even its own trickling leat.

The most recent development added a second floor to the lunch hall, creating an upstairs dining area. It feels more like an airport café than a school dining hall and we could see why the pupils love it. Sixth formers have their own café (year 11 can get passes as rewards). Lunch is cashless for everyone and nobody is allowed off site.

The student council is busy at OC. To date they've created a 'peace garden', improved the toilets, sorted the bus shelters and are even allowed to get involved in the interview process for senior staff members. They take the lead in raising money for charity and run events like the annual school sponsored walk across the moors. The school also has its own weekly 'memory café' for local people and their loved ones who are affected by dementia. Students work at the café as 'dementia ambassadors.'

Okehampton College is seriously green. It has won several sustainable energy awards. There are solar panels aplenty, a biomass boiler, on-site waste composting, allotments, polytunnels and a heap of activities and clubs that students can get involved in.

Now part of Dartmoor Multi Academy Trust with a group of other local secondary and primary schools.

Pastoral care, well-being and discipline: No 'rules' boards. 'Respect' is the big word here. The head believes that pupils should be treated with empathy and sensitivity within a culture of high expectations. He calls it 'the sensible approach – work with them, but be firm but fair'. OC is a big school and there are children from all walks of life here. There's a low rate of exclusions; the school is prepared to support them rather than isolate them. There is a good student support department here, plus vertical tutor groups and clubs or drop-ins where pupils can ask for help. Ofsted was very impressed and said OC is 'an outstandingly caring and supportive community where students flourish and develop as individuals.'

Pupils and parents: The catchment area is huge – over 400 square miles – so there are school buses to ferry pupils around. This part of Devon is very rural and so the college is central to the social lives of everyone as a community. Pupils are 'enthusiastic and happy to go to school', but a number of parents 'would like to see a smarter uniform, shirt, tie and blazer.'

Entrance: Eleven feeder primary schools and lots of opportunities for prospective pupils and parents to get to know the school. One parent confirmed they were 'very pleased with how the transition is handled.' When we were there, we bumped into two primary school pupils on a tour; they were really excited about the upcoming science and sports tournament day as part of their induction.

Entry to the sixth form requires five GCSEs, usually including a grade 6 in the chosen subject.

Exit: On average, 40-50 per cent stay on for sixth form. The majority who leave go to Exeter College or specialist colleges for land-based studies or art. The sixth form here, graded as 'outstanding' by Ofsted, isn't separate from the rest of the school and can't provide the lifestyle offered by Exeter College.

The college offers plenty of careers advice and support, with trips to universities and careers lessons to raise aspirations. Most students go on to university: two to Oxford in 2018 and one medic. Popular destinations Cardiff, Bristol UWE, Liverpool, Nottingham Trent, Southampton and Sussex.

Famous leavers include Steve Holliday, CEO of the National Grid, and Matt Woodley, Radio Devon's breakfast DJ (now a parent here).

Remarks: Good rural comprehensive. Good results, friendly atmosphere and, as one local business put it, 'confident kids.'

The Old Hall School

Linked with Wrekin College

Stanley Road, Wellington, Telford, Shropshire TF1 3LB

Ages 4–11 **Pupils** 232

Fees: £8,310 – £13,065 pa

01952 223117
www.oldhall.co.uk

Headmaster: Since 2007, Martin Stott BEd, previously deputy head at Laxton Junior School, Oundle. Says he seeks to nurture intellectual curiosity in his pupils, posing philosophical questions to older years, such as: if you read a newspaper in a newsagent, put it back and leave without paying, is it stealing? He wants to prepare children for the modern world they are facing; for them to try new things so they don't pigeonhole themselves. He comes across as very tuned in to modernity generally, whether it be the use of technology or the sober sense that children may have to pursue several different careers over their life span.

This is a head who really listens and refines his thinking in line with the evolving needs of the school. Any changes should be about benefiting the children, he says emphatically, not the staff. He refers to the fact they now set older children only for maths, not English, having found those who scored lower in the English assessments often turned out to be more creative. All pupils benefit from seeing each other work in different ways, he says. The children listen, they question each other.

The school is a family team; his wife is a teacher here and his children at the senior school, Wrekin College. Parents say he is at the gate every morning, shouting out cheery questions to pupils, all of whom he knows well.

Entrance: Non selective, so at 4+, a visit to meet the head; a first come, first served, two form entry. Entry to year 1 and above is dependent on availability; children attend an assessment day to see how they would fit in. Two class entry is split; classes balanced by gender, ability – the latter gleaned on assessment day – and personality.

Exit: Around 65 per cent go to its partner senior school, Wrekin College. For others, the local selective state grammars are a big pull (Newport Girls' High or Adams' Grammar School), as well as Thomas Telford School (where there is an assessment on entrance). The pupils clock up a healthy number of scholarships, especially for Wrekin.

Remarks: Work is differentiated and pupils tracked to align work with ability. In house academic assessments in maths, spelling, reading and non-core subjects. CATS (cognitive ability tests) are used as a strong indicator of academic potential and shared openly with the parents.

For those needing extra help, perhaps a child with an underlying issue like dyslexia, there is a learning support unit (high resource levels: one full time, three part time staff) which Martin Stott describes as one of the jewels in their crown. The school pays attention to the data; so a child with higher non-verbal reasoning (fluid intelligence) than verbal reasoning scores might have a learning difficulty and need extra support.

Roughly 20 per cent receive extra support, some just needing a confidence boost, head says.

In lower school (reception to year 2), the focus is on literacy and maths. Head is aware that phrases like 'I'm rubbish at maths' all too easily trip off the tongue and wants to eliminate this negativity. Maths teaching seeks to 'break down complicated calculations by chunking'; explaining to children how each stage of a sum works and why (little rote learning then – 'death by worksheet' – but intelligent understanding). In years 1 and 2 they make the teaching as practical as possible; at playtime, when children 'buy' their snack (grapes, French bread and butter), they take some money out of a pot and work out what they need. Problem solving on practical lines is interwoven everywhere. During these early stages, rather than stacks of homework there are exercises to reinforce what is going on at school. Rote learning only kicks in across spellings, times tables and phonics.

In year 3, about 60 per cent of time is spent with the class teachers with an element of specialist teaching. From year 4, the children have specialist teaching in DT, IT, PE, games, swimming, French, art, music and drama. In year 6, the curriculum also includes German, Spanish and philosophy.

DT projects looked impressive, such as the school hovercraft (invitation-only to year 6). All upper school children work in wood, plastics and electronics, making robots, rockets, go karts. The school recently designed an entry system to count vehicles to a new hospital's construction site.

Parents say that building confidence and a 'having a go' mentality within every child are achieved through nurturing. One parent said the school had been open with them about encouraging effort over pure results. Another said her son, who had initially shied away from activities which didn't interest him, was now 'gung ho' about trying most things and had developed a love of learning for its own sake. Another parent said lessons were made fun (geography was jolly-ography) and cross-curricular themes inspired (ancient Egyptian history became hieroglyphics in art, time pieces in IT). There was a slight question around whether really able children were stretched but parents were quick to say that any whiff a child was becoming complacent, the school responded swiftly.

Extracurricular activities are abundant or, as a recent ISI said: 'pupils attain conspicuously high standards in sport, choral music, art, speech and drama'.

P

Sport is important; the fabulous sports facilities at Wrekin College (they share the same site) must help. All the usual sports are played: football, rugby, cricket, hockey, netball, rounders and athletics, and a range of teams play competitively. Every child in years 5 and 6, says head, has played for the school at some level. Swimming, weekly from reception age, is a strength.

Music is part of the curriculum; concerts every term and informal lunchtime ones. Drama is also on the curriculum with many opportunities to perform (reading in assemblies, poetry competitions, LAMDA). Every year group does a play, the older children more ambitious productions like Annie, the lower school The Wizard of Oz. Wonderful big hall which doubles as a drama space.

Wide range of frequent trips to museums, galleries, theatre. A nice range of clubs like archery and coding, chess, scrabble, cookery and clubs by invitation to stretch, like maths.

School encourages work outside; younger children sow fruit and veg. Each year group does an outdoor course; upper school a residential for a few nights: when they hit year 6, France for five days with visits to a snail farm. Also a trip to World War I sites, as well as outdoor pursuits, kayaking and canoeing.

Numerous confidence building initiatives; the end of year celebration now thanks every pupil for their contribution with a personalised certificate (prizes only for academic achievements). Selected pupils speak in front of an audience of 600.

A merit card system for rewards and a 'golden' table in the dining room (every child gets to sit on it at some point) where a child's achievement is recognised (instead of water, there's fruit juice and the head comes along to chat to each pupil).

Behaviour is generally good but to help focus, days have themes: manners Monday, thoughtful Thursday etc. The head says bullying is rooted out before it takes off and parents involved; he recognises there is often an underlying reason for the bully's behaviour. The school knows its pupils well; one parent said her daughter was demoralised not to be selected for a school team but the teachers picked up on it and found fantastic solutions to build her confidence.

A matron provides an extra layer of pupil welfare.

Founded in 1845, the school moved to its present site on the same campus as Wrekin College in 2006. A modern, open plan building flooded with light; completely uplifting. The first thing you see, through a glass wall, is the library, then through another glass wall the snazzy IT room, on to the art room. It cheers the heart. Two-tiered building, so you can see pupils scurrying about on the gallery above. Great wall displays everywhere which danced with vibrancy, pictures of costumes from school plays, a huge model of a Harry Potter book. Fantastic science lab, too.

Huge grounds with imaginative adventure playgrounds, a small climbing wall, cricket pitch (sweet pavilion looking onto both netball courts and cricket pitch for fairness). A real outdoorsy vibe, a wooded area with bug hotel. A giant chess set in one place, a huge world map pinned to the wall in another, a wooden storyteller's chair like a throne. Great stuff.

Parents are a blend of business backgrounds, farmers and professionals; usually both parents working. Great comms with parents; calendars given well in advance, including what head calls the Christmas comic (a nod to the bonkers nature of the school pre-Christmas period, letting parents know exactly what they will need, from panto costumes to school fair items).

If parents have any issue, the school sees it as an opportunity to improve: 'weakness in a member of staff is a weakness in the system'. This is backed-up by parents themselves: one requested more non-verbal and verbal reasoning practice for pupils – it was followed through.

Children smile, are polite and confident. Frankly, they all had a sparky look about them.

Fees are somewhat lower than similar schools further south. In a nod to today's economic climate, school offers means-tested bursaries and interest free monthly payment plans.

A delightful, vibrant, forward thinking prep which nurtures intellectual curiosity and gives the right level of support to help all children achieve their academic potential.

Packwood Haugh School

Ruyton XI Towns, Shrewsbury, Shropshire SY4 1HX

Ages 4–13 **Pupils** 198 (136 boys, 62 girls) **Boarders** 73 full, 53 flexi (from 7 years) **C of E**

Fees: Day £8,805 – £18,330; Boarding £23,430 – £26,430 pa

01939 260217
www.packwood-haugh.co.uk

Headmaster: Since April 2019, Robert Fox, previously assistant head (pastoral care and boarding) at Harrow International

School, Hong Kong. Geography degree from Bristol and PGCE from Nottingham. After the post of head of boarding, with his wife Kate, at Foremarke Hall, they moved to Hong Kong, where she was admissions officer.

Entrance: Co-ed (some two-thirds boys), non-selective. Informal assessment for prep – Eng and maths. No assessment for pre-prep, Packwood Acorns. Range of scholarships. Bursaries for Forces families and local children, one of whom is off to Eton. Children come from all adjoining counties and north Wales. Some, sons and daughters of devoted former pupils, journey from afar. Less than 10 per cent from overseas – Spain, Japan, China.

Exit: Packwood has long furnished some of the top public schools. About half to Shrewsbury, others to usual suspects, including Sedbergh, Malvern, Moreton Hall, Rugby, Oundle, Wrekin, Cheltenham. Eminent one-time pupils include Mark Rylands, Bishop of Shrewsbury; Tom Salt, head chef at Manicomio; Tom James MBE, double gold medal winning Olympic rower; and Rhys Bevan, Toby Fairbrother in the Archers. There were 30 scholarships in 2018, including four to Shrewsbury.

Remarks: A time honoured top tier prep school which celebrates its headmasters by inscribing their names in gold on the panelled ceiling of the entrance hall. Co-ed since 1968; we still await the first headmistress. Former pupils celebrate glorious character-building idiosyncrasies, all now superannuated (Molesworth, where art thou?). Packwood is fully C21-compatible with heritage values: country prep school, 'proper boarding', traditional values, old-fashioned manners, fresh air, friendship, give it a go, play out of your skin. The food's great – official. So nothing here evokes St Custard's. But there is a skool dog, the head's border terrier Belle, never more cheerful than when egging on the troops from the touchline on match days.

There's none of your oligarch-magnet hotel quality accommodation and associated blingy 'facilities' here. We're not talking spartan, we're talking quite comfy enough – in the case of the girls' dorms, very nice indeed (the difference perhaps being boys here tend to call each other by surnames, girls by first names). What else do you want? Purpose built theatre? Tick. Sports hall? Tick. Swimming pool? Tick. All weather surface? Tick. Er, golf course? Yep. Lamasery? Oh yes, got one of those (it's a quiet room set aside for contemplation.) Spinney? Yes, that's where we go to make dens and Packwood Acorns have their outdoor school. Everywhere you go you don't see children staring moodily into the middle distance of their smartphone screens. None, we asked? None, said the head (a non-negotiable no). Don't need them. They can skype home from their dorm in the evening. All good.

Packwood is a classic country house prep school set in a mere 66 acres of lark-filled Shropshire. It is not set haughtily apart, though; you happen on it off a side road, you don't motor up an avenue to get to it. It adjoins the splendidly named Ruyton-XI-Towns (always XI) with which the Smith-Langridges have forged friendly relations on several fronts. There are collaborative links with local schools; many who work in the school live in the village and Packwood boys and girls sing in the church choir. There are activity days to which all and sundry are invited. Some prep schools orbit real life. Not Packwood.

Honours boards, honours boards everywhere. There's no mistaking what's expected of you. Oppressively so? Not so far as our inquisitorial investigations revealed. Aspirational, more like. In any case, pupils know perfectly well who their brainy peers are and where they stand in relation to them. More to the point, how does it feel to be in the wake of them? For one dyslexic pupil, no problem, the learning support is great, some of the brightest have it too and anyway your friends don't measure you by how many marks you get. Hats off to the teachers, though: for an open access school all these scholarships represent an extraordinary achievement. Hurrah for the SENCo, too. Parents praise the way their children are 'pushed and stretched'. Mr Smith-Langridge has upped the game in terms of monitoring individual progress and thereby also the effectiveness of the teaching. He likes his data and he wants more of it. But he doesn't want to run a hothouse or a sweat shop. For him it's all about making the best of all the opportunities of the long, boarding day – and not just academic opportunities, either. He and his colleagues delight in the richness of achievement of all their charges according to their lights, not just their 'honours board worthiness'. Art is good, drama on the up, music ubiquitous and top notch.

If boarding isn't done well, 'twere well it were not done at all'. Packwood has intelligently reinvented it and, just as important, made it a specialism, because no one wants to board at a school where most children go home at night. Boarding is phased in, there's a range of flexi-options and the majority graduate to full-time in preparation for their senior school. Weekends are busy with numbers boosted by those returning late on Saturdays from sports fixtures in faraway schools. Boys are in the big house, hugger-mugger, as they like it. Girls have their own residence. A number of teachers live in school, there are houseparents and there are lovely matrons. There's masses of care and oversight from warm, watchful adults who know these children and mind about them. There are bright posters bearing improving/banal quotes on the walls (we'd have preferred quotes by the children). Beds are cosy and teddy comes too. But take a look at the boys' washbasins, tidy as can be, and you'll see there's rigour here. This is no sleepover city, it is home from work; talking after lights out is a big no-no.

A happy school is a deceptively rigorous place and all the happier for it. All parents praise Packwood's code of conduct and the way the children buy into it. Said one parent: 'They know when they've done wrong and genuinely feel contrition'. Another indicator of emotional health: Packwood children are no respecters of age and happily chat to those below and those above. There are boarding captains, older children to whom the younger ones can turn for counsel. And here's the point; we were accompanied by a viscerally antipathetic visitor to whose mind boarding is a bad, weird thing to do to a child. She visibly melted, the more she saw and heard, and ended up easily envisaging her grandson here, happy as a sandboy. One recent parent wistfully said she wished she'd known about Packwood for her other two girls.

Yes, the children really are terrifically nice and lit up, their manners are excellent, they're very at ease among adults, they're great company. It's easy enough to see how an outdoorsy, sporty child will thrive here, and the school aims to enable every single child to represent the school at something. There's a big games playing tradition at Packwood, another heritage touch, and not just in main sports. To survey the offering all round is to find yourself muttering clichés about punching above their weight. Like all knackered clichés, it exactly pinpoints the truth.

So what of the ones who are indoorsy, solitary, geeky? They're the ones you worry about, so we pried. Unlikely as it may seem, more than you'd think take to fencing; indeed, Packwood is nationally famed for its swordsmanship. And for its horsemanship. Some take to cross-country running (very strong here). We learned of one child who managed deftly to schedule guitar lessons in games time. All the parents we spoke to assured us that eccentricity in all its guises is simply not an issue. And then Mr Smith-Langridge recalled the boy who loved knitting.. and no one gave him a second glance. It helps to be gregarious, though, obviously, it's in the nature of the place. And at least a bit fresh-airy. Outside, after all, is where it happens every afternoon.

Packwood has a devoted fanbase of parents. Former pupils keep in close touch and their feats serve as an inspiration to the present generation. The school has shrewdly and effectively remodelled itself to align with the needs of today's working parents and carried with it the best of the old values. Our view: you get the best of both.

The Paragon School

Linked with Prior Park College

Lyncombe House, Lyncombe Vale, Bath, Somerset BA2 4LT

Ages 3–11 **Pupils** 270

Fees: £9,255 – £10,500 pa

01225 310837
www.paragonschool.co.uk

Headmaster: Since 2012, Andrew Harvey BA PGCE (late 30s). Brought up and educated in Dorset (Milton Abbey) with a degree in history and theology from the University of Derby, he taught briefly before joining the Royal Dragoon Guards for three years 'mainly for the rugby – but also the leadership values', though he always intended to return to teaching; 'I'd conk out if I did it for 40 years, though'. Mr Harvey's career has been forged in prep schools (most recently Lambrook), except for a stint as head of pastoral care at Sherfield School, and it is here that he appears to feel most at home. The unstuffy atmosphere and Bath location of The Paragon appealed to him, but it was the fact that he and his wife Anna thought it would be the ideal school for their two small daughters that swung it. Parents find him visible, very approachable and hands-on – he pops into every class every day. The children find him 'funny', 'jolly' and 'religious' by turns and 'he doesn't like spending time in the office', said one perceptive little chap. Hobbies include rugby, cricket and squash, and reading up on matters educational.

P

Entrance: Main entry points are at nursery, reception and year 3, though children are welcomed at any stage; most come from Bath and the villages south of the city. An individual visit and interview with the head will generally secure a place; he is, however, not afraid to turn away children whose behaviour or academic delay would stretch the teachers' resources and disadvantage the class. Trial day provides opportunity for informal assessment.

Exit: Around 60 per cent at year 6 to Prior Park College, up the hill from the Paragon and part of the same foundation (Anglican rather than Catholic though), but some to other schools around Bath, state and independent (King Edwards School Bath, Beechen Cliff School, Kingswood, Royal High School and Monkton Combe School).

Anyone wanting traditional common entrance at 13+ would need to go elsewhere for years 7 and 8, and a few do. In some years, nearly half the children gain an award of some kind into their next school – more given for sport than anything else. Any doubtful runners for Prior Park are given the nod in year 5; that said, the schools' learning support departments work closely together.

Remarks: Tucked away in a wooded dell surprisingly close to the centre of Bath, The Paragon now occupies what was a private Georgian house with a mineral spring still in its grounds, but it owes its name to its century old origins as an educational gymnasium in the street of the same name in the city. Its seven and a half secluded acres comprise pitches, both astro and grass, a conventional playground for younger children but – gloriously – masses of wooded slopes too, complete with a yurt and a tepee. Head, parents and children all very keen on outdoor learning; the school really lives it (eg acting out scenes from the Bayeux Tapestry) with help from Swainswick Explorers, instead of merely taking children outside to read on sunny days, as some do.

Classrooms are split between the main building and the charming stable block a minute's walk away. Not a school which bowled us over with technological wizardry; rather we liked what we saw and heard going on in classrooms, where one lucky English class was rewriting Cinderella in the style of Roald Dahl. Year 6 reading books lying about on desks impressive for children of that age. Head determined to extract more academic juice than has sometimes been the case before – to that end, he lured the director of studies from his previous school and introduced philosophy to the curriculum – yet remains a school where children can continue to be children until they leave. One parent felt that it's not a moment too soon to raise academic standards, and that attainments in maths in particular could be higher, given the small class sizes and biddable children. The head is certainly conscious of local competition in the form of KES Junior and excellent Widcombe Primary.

Sport is a serious matter, and even the tiniest children are taught the basic skills of the major sports. 'Rounders is a silly game,' says head, so introduced cricket to the girls, and appointed a head of girls' games to beef them up; high quality coaches also take regular sessions. School performs amazingly well in competition, especially considering its size; rugby, hockey and swimming stand out. Though its own facilities are limited, the pitches and swimming pool at Prior Park are but a short ride in a liveried minibus up the hill.

Music gets thumbs up from parents too, and the majority of prep school children learn an instrument, many achieving grade 3 or 4 by the time they leave. Local successes and two accepted into Young National Schools Symphony Orchestra. New music centre, The Lodge, apparently looks like a Swiss chalet.

We loved the expansive displays of art on the walls: a mixture of work based on established artists and the purely creative, but most of all we loved the craft room, up a mysterious staircase, and pervaded by the scent of lavender, where dear little bags were being made for charity. Paragon children emerge being able to sew on a lot more than a button. Drama is performed in the hall which doubles as a gym and the dining hall (older years in the theatre of the senior school).

Everyone raves about the family feel of The Paragon, further enhanced by teachers now lunching with the children at the same tables. 'It's done wonders for their manners,' said one mother approvingly. Indeed: one boy we lunched with (pasta, pasta or pasta the day we visited) nearly choked rather than speak with his mouth full. Definitely time to get rid of the garish 'prison trays' the children eat off, though – staff get plastic plates. Active PTA raises funds but also has a strong social agenda and an impressive newsletter, The Bulletin.

The Paragon is unquestionably taking on a higher profile in Bath's competitive educational market place, but there remains an interesting contrast between its flamboyant rebranding (surely the most pukka uniforms locally, with red stripes in abundance for all) and its quirky relaxed feel, for which many parents choose it.

Parkstone Grammar School

Sopers Lane, Poole, Dorset BH17 7EP

Ages 11–18 **Pupils** 1,222 **Sixth form** 368 (67 boys)

01202 605605
www.parkstone.poole.sch.uk

Headteacher: Since 2013, Tracy Harris. Was previously deputy headteacher at South Wilts Grammar School for Girls and has a strong track record in selective single sex education. Educated in the south west and studied history at Exeter University. Her husband Ian is also a teacher and she plays in a brass band in her spare time.

Currently on parental leave; David Hallsworth is holding the fort. Advertising for a new head for September 2019.

Academic matters: Results at GCSE and A level generally live up to its local reputation for excellence. Almost all do three sciences at GCSE, with pretty spectacular results; in 2018, 51 per cent A*-A/9-7 grades across all subjects. At A level, maths, English, biology and chemistry have a high take up rate and pretty impressive results. In 2018, 71 per cent A*/B grades and 38 per cent A*/A overall.

This is a maths, science and modern languages academy with a wide choice of other subjects: drama, electronics, textiles in addition to usual GCSEs; plus computing, food, media studies, graphics, geology and politics in the sixth form.

Girls learn French, German and Spanish in year 8 and choose between German and Spanish on year 9. Most (85-90 per cent) continue with at least one language to GCSE, and girls can do up to three. No Latin, Greek or eastern languages at present, though Italian is now on stream. Girls are absolutely confident that the school would support anything they really wanted to do. Astrology currently on offer.

Sixth forms are sufficiently coordinated for girls to be able to slot into all-boys Poole Grammar School courses if Parkstone can't offer the combination they want and vice versa. Further maths, computing, geology and graphics A level courses available at Poole Grammar; the boys come to Parkstone for sociology, theatre studies and politics.

Large classes of up to 30 plus in lower school but very good monitoring. Subject prefects are good at providing help schemes and revision clubs with lots of encouragement from staff. Exceptionally good staff-pupil relationships with girls declaring, 'at risk of sounding cheesy, our staff are amazing, inspiring, working really hard to give us good lessons and ready to do anything to help.' SEN help available and an atmosphere of trust makes emotional, organisational etc support easily available. A small percentage with SENs including physical/medical and emotional difficulties and school can support those with mobility problems. Almost no EFL needed.

Homely library, evidently much used for borrowing, as well as study in the sixth form computer section. Help on hand and girls encouraged to read anything they fancy.

Games, options, the arts: Well-known in Poole for their lavish joint musical productions with Poole Grammar, but these are led by Parkstone. Lots of smaller drama things going on, often with Poole via theatre studies; art gets a smaller take up. Music is important and has the most attractive building on site, purpose-built and homely in brick complex shared by sixth formers who use it as a class base. Orchestras and groups (string, saxophone, choir etc) abound.

All girls do PE to the end of year 13, and rugby, cricket and football are popular. Netball and cricket strong – national finalists in recently; but sport cannot be underestimated in a school boasting three Olympic athletes (sailing, volleyball and beach volleyball) amongst its recent past pupils. There's a fantastic sports hall with stunning beechwood sprung floor, masses of tennis courts and room for everything else, but sixth formers can do their own thing off-site in local clubs etc.

Extracurricular options extensive and adventurous; some shared with Poole Grammar. Twenty or so clubs include, of course, debating, books, films and drama etc but also some further educational opportunities: Japanese at several levels, Mandarin Chinese, Russian plus engineering and robotics. Parkstone girls have built three racing cars from scratch – as opposed to one from a kit at Poole – and raced them nationally, winning commendations for their exceptional teamwork. As a team, the school has been totally behind a member of staff walking 630 miles of the South West Coast Path to raise funds for several charities, plus a bit for the school's technology department. Parkstone has a British Council award for its links and work with other countries – Zambia and Kenya particularly. Trips on offer for languages, skiing etc, with Poole Grammar providing geology and other exciting options. Concert band and choirs recently did open air concerts in Rome and performed in Barcelona. Girls say that financial help is available and they can spread the cost – and regard trips as unprecedented opportunities.

Background and atmosphere: The school started as co-educational in Parkstone and has been at its current site since 1961. Its 20 acres abut residential lanes of bungalows and industrial areas – the derelict Poole pottery is just up the road. The nearby sewage works, which occasionally make their presence felt, were not detectable on the GSG visit. The buildings reflect their surroundings and even the bandbox-new £6 million technology, maths and art block could be mistaken for a factory, though the long wide interior corridor with its distant glass wall opening on to silver birches is a felicitous piece of design. This was funded to provide the extra facilities needed when the Poole schools, hitherto starting in year 8, began to admit year 7 pupils in 2013.

New £1.8m sixth form hub, and sixth formers have also had access to the spacious and welcoming dining area at all times, and find it a good place to work. Early risers can use its café at 8am. Food, say the girls, is really good, with plenty of choice and cheap too. 'You can order an omelette and have it made in front of your eyes!'

The language block, dating from 1995 but looking curiously like a 70s product, is well-equipped, and a deceptively large new lecture theatre, full of girls being given some gruesomely graphic anti-drugs education on our visit, has been squeezed in between buildings.

Pastoral care, well-being and discipline: Big tutor groups, with the same tutor for the first four years, get an hour's tutor time/PSHE each fortnight. Mentoring schemes help new girls fit in and are continued for those who need it. All staff take a positive role in pastoral care – the school stresses, and the girls confirm, that any member of staff can help any girl, not just their allocated charges. Uniform quite stylish and, surprisingly, girls like pale yellow shirts, grey v necks with striped edges and crested and multi-pocketed black blazers. Expensive-ish, 'but cheaper than us having to provide constant fashion updates.' Sixth formers value an own-clothes-but-suitable-for-work dress code.

School has a few rules about jewellery etc and girls do not take advantage of this. Few problems, but girls say they make their own pressures and find the staff are good at recognising the signs and helping them to cope with stress. Girls' trust in staff and respect for the amount of trouble they take to support them is impressive.

Pupils and parents: Poole has a largely white Anglo-Saxon population with both some very affluent and some very underprivileged areas, and families come from all over. Parkstone's reputation is good enough to attract those who could afford independent education and the school is keen to make sure those who most need Parkstone find it accessible. Sixty-five per cent come from Poole, the rest from up to an hour away. Around 40 per cent of girls come to school by bus – local bus company, city bus or via private arrangements made by parents. One of the nicest things about the girls is their awareness that not all their primary school friends get the opportunities that they do – which both motivates them to make best use of their chances and to want to make things better. Parent-staff association raises lots of funds for extras like minibuses and special equipment.

Entrance: There are between two and three applicants for each of the 180 places in year 7. Multiple choice English, maths and verbal reasoning tests in late September. Pupils are told their test score and whether or not this meets the required standard (but not whether they have got a place) before the deadline for applications. Preference to those living within the borough of Poole or in specific local postcode areas. Girls come from a mix of state and independent junior schools.

Can take up to 50 girls at sixth form – currently, the school requires a bare minimum of six GCSEs at 5+, with at least a 6 in subjects to be studied at A level.

Exit: A few – some 15 per cent – go after GCSE – either to good local sixth forms or occasionally to independents; others join from elsewhere. At 18, nearly all to uni. Surrey, Bath, Exeter and Birmingham currently popular, though a sprinkling everywhere, with some 40 per cent to the older, well-established universities, including Oxbridge (six in 2018, and four medics). Law popular, masses of scientific courses and a very wide spread of other subjects.

Remarks: A hive of clever, purposeful girls, who nevertheless have wide interests. Unpretentious but high powered, Parkstone gives girls an exceptional level of support and a rich experience. The enthusiasm of the girls speaks for itself.

P

Pate's Grammar School

Princess Elizabeth Way, Cheltenham, Gloucestershire GL51 0HG

Ages 11–18 **Pupils** 1,105 **Sixth form** 407

01242 523169
www.pates.gloucs.sch.uk

Headmaster: Since 2012, Russel Ellicott BA, previously deputy head. Originally from East Anglia, Ellicott studied history at Royal Holloway before completing teacher training in Hull. Taught history and PE at local grammar schools, The Crypt and Marling, then moved onto Pate's in 2008. Chair of the Grammar Schools Heads Association, he loves sport and will play or watch anything with a ball. With little time to teach, he serves in the refectory as much as possible because 'being with pupils is what I signed up for when I went into teaching.' Married with two children.

High praise from parents: 'The headteacher is quietly strong, an innovator, not frightened to break the education mould, a great leader and communicator.' He knows his pupils and their families well and is proud of his school, striving for the best in all areas. Pupils find him approachable, friendly and fair, 'You feel like he really knows you,' they told us. Always at school events ('I dread to think what hours he works,' said parents), 'he gets involved and leads from the front,' a great role model, parents agreed.

Academic matters: Results are consistently strong and improving year on year. In 2018, at GCSE, 87 per cent A*-A/7-9 grades. All take single sciences, maths, English language and literature. The majority also take a modern language, French, German or Spanish. Budget cuts have meant that Latin has been dropped from the curriculum but the head is determined to maintain a broad range of subjects. Other options include DT, PE, RS, business and economics and drama.

Particularly impressive are the A level results in 2018: 92 per cent A*/B grades and 72 per cent A*/A grades. Exceptional grades in the most popular subjects – maths, physics, chemistry and biology. 21 subjects offered including politics, psychology, theatre studies and EPQ. Pre-U also offered.

Learning at Pate's is based on pupils taking personal responsibility for their learning and becoming independent. They are encouraged to explore ideas, to take risks and to try new things. Teachers 'get pupils really thinking about things rather than just jumping through the hoops of a syllabus,' parents told us. Pupils we spoke to were thrilled with this approach; they are keen to learn and are naturally curious. The result is self-motivated independent learners who are willing to give things a go and who understand that failure is part of the learning journey.

'Teachers give everything 110 per cent and the standard of teaching is outstanding,' say parents. One added, teachers are 'kind and caring, passing on their passion for whatever they teach with ease, always approachable if a student needs help, full of praise when they do well and supportive when they struggle.'

Homework 'is not pointless,' say pupils. Pate's values family life and with long commutes and so much extracurricular activity, homework is relevant and manageable. Pupils assured us that the work balance is good and parents are fiercely adamant that Pate's is not an exam factory: 'Our children are nicely kept on their toes and challenged but without any undue pressure.' Annual internal exams are welcomed by older pupils who are pleased that they have been so well-prepared for GCSE's and A levels.

The SEN department is small but highly effective according to parents. Needs include ASD, Asperger's or mental health issues. The Hub, opened in 2015 and managed by two full-time staff, is a space where pupils can go for quiet time or to do work alone. For some this is a regular outlet, others not, but whatever the issue, the SEN team will go 'above and beyond to help the kids achieve their potential in spite of all the hurdles,' say parents.

Games, options, the arts: Pate's is a selective school so pupils are unsurprisingly capable. However, instead of focusing exclusively on their strengths, pupils are encouraged to diversify their talents and try new things. This is what sets this school apart. We spoke to one sixth former who explained that Pate's had taken him out of his comfort zone at 11 years old; he didn't like drama, music or sport, and he was shy. School changed everything and he has been singing and dancing on stage throughout the years and goes rugby training four times a week.

All the usual sports; rugby, hockey, netball cricket, athletics and basketball. Fantastic range of extracurricular activities and clubs including climbing, shooting, an on-site Combined Cadets Force and D of E. Good facilities too; an impressive climbing wall, sports hall with weights and fitness rooms and playing fields. A separate website dedicated to fixtures and announcements keeps everybody reliably informed. PE offered at GCSE and A level.

Sport is strong. Music equally so. Four big concerts a year plus plenty of opportunities to perform in orchestras, ensembles, choirs, charity concerts and recitals. A good range of school instruments available to those wishing to learn and good practice rooms. One parent of musical children told us, 'Head of music, who is the lifeblood of the vibrant music throughout the entire school, is absolutely fantastic. What is extraordinary is the dedication you hear about from other parents across art, sport, drama and many other subjects as well.'

Music is strongly linked with drama and dance, which are also very popular. Latest production was Chicago and the annual staff panto is a highlight according to pupils. All ages are encouraged to get involved in the house music and drama events each year. The theme of the house drama event was Roald Dahl so productions included Witches, Fantastic Mr Fox, Charlie and the Chocolate Factory and James and the Giant Peach. The emphasis is on taking part and having fun, no talent required.

Art is everywhere. Canvases are displayed on walls, paper-mache sculptures dangle from ceilings and ceramics are carefully placed on windowsills. For a school that excels in the sciences, art is by no means forgotten and the standards are high.

Education is a priority at Pate's, but this is not limited by the curriculum. To broaden pupils' horizons, lessons on Tuesday afternoons are replaced with an exceptional range of enrichment activities. These include first aid courses, courses on disabilities, how to budget, or even driving lessons (year 11s). Community work is also an option and older pupils visit local primary schools to read and run masterclasses. As well as this, there are flexible learning days when pupils can find out about things like the new degree apprenticeships for example. Then, after the summer exams, years 7 -10 have 'activities fortnight,' where they go on trips or try out archery, shooting, climbing or cookery.

Many pupils have a long commute so the majority of extracurricular activities, clubs and societies are scheduled for lunchtimes. All the usual sports, music, arts and drama clubs are offered. Then there are the student-run societies. Sixth formers run, manage and facilitate some 20 – 30 societies. At the beginning of each year they set up a fair, very much like a fresher's fair, and sign up members for literature, art, music, philosophy, history, politics, science, computer programming and debating. If they have an idea for a society, they can go ahead and make it happen. Pupils at Pate's have a voice and are listened to. In fact, according to the pupils themselves, the best thing about the school is the way they are treated as equals and adults by the teachers. The active school council, responsible for social campaigns and helping to choose new staff, is just another example of this.

If you accept a place at Pate's, you must buy into the ethos of 'work hard and play hard.' Although most clubs run at lunchtimes, there are often events after school, including fixtures, practices, rehearsals and productions, and CCF. There are plenty of trips too. This year, as well as the annual ski trip, there has been a music trip to Prague, a politics and history trip to Berlin, a canoeing trip in Canada and a rugby tour of South Africa. Strong links with schools in Europe and China means there are also opportunities for exchanges.

Background and atmosphere: Founded in 1574 by Richard Pate, Pate's was a free grammar school for boys until 1904 when a girl's school was added, the two merging about 20 years ago. Located just outside Cheltenham, surrounded by housing estates, Pate's is not in the posh part of town. Numbers have increased from four to five forms per year and although the head is sure it's not crammed, parents are not so convinced. Thankfully this is a short-lived issue as a new sixth form block (with science labs, performing arts area and ICT) is due to open in January 2019, freeing up areas to give them the much-needed space.

On campus, modern buildings are based around a large quad making it easy to navigate. Playing fields are at the back and newer builds include the business, psychology and economics block, the refectory and the IT suite. Inside, corridors are lined with lockers and classrooms and labs are a mix of old and new.

The head is determined to make education as much fun as can be. 'They are only children once,' he told us. And one way they do this is through the house system and the hugely popular house events. Each event, drama, singing, dancing or sport is organised by sixth formers and ends with several evening performances. They are given six days to produce each performance – writing scripts, directing, managing, choreographing, and most daunting of all, organising hundreds of pupils. House music rehearsals were underway on our visit. It's 'music carnage,' one sixth former chuckled. This whole school event is scheduled at the end of September each year – a fantastic way for year 7's and new year 12's to get to know their peers and be involved in something fun. Six days of fun, then it's back to hard work. Next up is the house dance event before Christmas.

At Pate's, pupils are encouraged to try new things and get out of their comfort zone. When they get to sixth form they are challenged in a different way – they are encouraged to get involved in setting up societies and take on leadership roles in the house events. They are encouraged to think for themselves and many ideas come from the pupils themselves. Staff are more than willing to let them 'give it a go'. Sixth formers told us about a recent debating competition they wanted to take part in; the teachers supported them and they are now off to the finals in Moscow in November.

'Pate's was the only school that we felt had a buzz about it and that we came away from feeling genuinely excited,' one parent explained. The pupils that we met seemed happy, self-assured and engaging. One parent summed them up saying, 'Pate's is full of pretty bright and talented kids and they learn that they can't be top at everything, but they also learn to admire others and see that different people have different qualities.'

P

Pastoral care, well-being and discipline: Outstanding pastoral care. Parents that have been faced with unexpected health issues told us, 'We know first hand they really care about their pupils and put their health and well-being above everything else.' This a school that supports families 'as if they were our extended family' and 'champions children' whatever the difficulties.

As well as The Hub, there is a school counsellor and a nurse onsite. Encouragingly, Pate's is pro-active in letting students know that 'it's ok not to be ok,' and one pupil reassured us, 'It's easy to get help here'. Pupils are also encouraged to be individuals, to 'be the me I choose to be'. Parents are impressed: 'Pupils are respected as individuals and not moulded into a certain type. My children and their friends all comment that at Pate's you can 'be yourself'.'

No rules or sanctions, just classroom codes and a clear set of boundaries. Teachers are not rigid disciplinarians: Pate's is run on high expectations. One parent explained: 'Pate's doesn't sweat the small stuff and hands over responsibility for behaviour to the pupils from the moment they arrive aged 11 with a quiet and firm, but not draconian, set of expectations that continues throughout their time in school.' For the few cases that this doesn't work, there is a strong pastoral system of heads of year, houses, tutors and counsellor to find out why.

Well-being is a priority for pupils and the well-being committee often bring in mental health speakers to destigmatise mental health. Working closely with the student mental health society, they have organised a well-being week which includes a competition for year 8s to present their ideas on spreading kindness. The winning presentation will be adopted by the committee and used to spread kindness around school. There are committees for everything and after the summer exams, there is a charity day when all the committees do fundraising activities for their chosen charities.

Pupils and parents: Some live a short bike ride away, others an hour-long bus or train ride. 45 per cent live in Cheltenham or the surrounding areas. Some trek in from as far as Bristol, the further corners of Gloucestershire, and even Worcestershire, west Oxfordshire and Herefordshire. Parents are mainly professionals but there is 'a healthy range of backgrounds', parents assured us. Some have re-located to be near the school.

Communication with parents is 'outstanding,' parents report, helped by the ever-improving technology. A weekly newsletter from the head and regular email updates from heads of year keep parents up-to-date. With little school gate action, parents rely on events to meet up, and to help this, the PTA has been recently re-invigorated and is proving to be popular with lots more getting involved.

Uniform is black blazer and tie. Sixth formers must be smart and business-like. Ties are mandatory.

Entrance: Highly oversubscribed – about 10 candidates per place for year 7. Selection is via the LA but using Durham University CEM test (register in June for test in September) and places are offered strictly to the 150 top scorers. Parents agree this is 'tough,' but worth it. How did they get through it we asked: 'On exam day we got them to eat 24 blueberries because we had heard that that helped with memory,' one family confided.

At sixth form entry, over 100 additional places are available to external students. Internal and external candidates need to meet the same requirements: A/7s, preferably A*/8-9s, predicted in the subjects chosen for A level study, and strong results across the board.

Open evenings are held throughout the year. Pupils are available for tours and current parents are on hand for a chat. Once accepted, 'the school is fantastic at welcoming the children and helping them settle,' parents agreed. With around 90 feeder schools the head of year 7 has her work cut out – she visits every child in their primary school to get to know them. As well as summer transition days, every newbie will receive a letter from a current year 7 pupil who will be their buddy. Once they start, fun activity days such as archery, climbing and bush-craft help them bond with their peers. And just to make them feel even more welcome, the head sends every year 7 a birthday card and invites year 8s to his office for cake.

Exit: Just 10 per cent leave after GCSEs. All go onto university – an impressive 31 to Oxbridge in 2018, plus 23 medics, four vets and four dentists. A few go abroad each year, although just one to Harvard this year. Sixth formers report there is lots of 'brilliant' support and help in choosing courses and putting UCAS forms together, the coordinator often sending them information to read or work experience opportunities to explore.

Most famous leaver is the composer, Gustav Holst. These days leavers tend to go into creative jobs, (the arts, music, design, engineering) or the civil service, particularly health and education. Several leavers have come back to teach through Pate's own teaching school.

Money matters: Discretionary fund helps with trips, travel and anything extracurricular. This is not just for pupils on free meals, it's for anyone who is struggling to make ends meet.

Remarks: Pate's is so much more than outstanding results. Yes, they work hard but they play hard too. Pupils are given so many opportunities to broaden their horizons and to try new things. The result is self-motivated, independent learners. A fantastic house system and student-run societies gives sixth formers opportunities to learn leadership skills and explore their own ideas. As well as this, Pate's really cares about its pupils and their well-being. One parent said, 'I wish I could have gone to this school!' Us too.

Perrott Hill School

122

North Perrott, Crewkerne, Somerset TA18 7SL

Ages 3–13 **Pupils** 167 **Boarders** 10 full, 24 weekly, 63 flexi (from year 3) **C of E**

Fees: Day £6,675 – £16,305; Boarding £19,875 – £24,690 pa

01460 72051
www.perrotthill.com

Headmaster: Since September 2018, Alexander McCullough, previously head of Polwhele House prep near Truro. Music degree from Durham; after his PGCE, he became a primary school deputy head whilst still in his 20s, moving on to Foremarke Hall as academic director. His wife, Helen, is a pre-prep teacher and head of early years and they have two children, who have joined the school.

Entrance: Via an interview with the parents, consideration of previous school reports and short academic assessment on test day. 'These are seamlessly arranged for the new little person to snuggle into the class: the experience is homely, smiley, personal and fun,' said a parent. Means-tested bursaries available, and scholarships awarded for academic, sport, music, drama and art/DT excellence.

Exit: Nearly all stay until 13. To a wide range of destinations: King's Bruton currently much the most popular, with others to Blundell's and Queen's College Taunton; 17 scholarships offered in 2018.

Remarks: Founded in 1946, Perrott Hill is situated in 28 acres of beautiful grounds and woodland close to the Somerset-Dorset border. It is a traditional prep that embraces its surroundings and promotes good country living, a big selling point for many parents. One told us, 'They love the outdoor opportunities; double woods sessions, golf before lunch, farming in the afternoon – they didn't get to do that in London!'

An average of 12 in a class. Years 6 and 7 are streamed in preparation for common entrance. Excellent learning support department, highly praised by parents. One told us, 'My child, having received learning support for a few years, is now leaving with scholarships, has been made a prefect, his confidence has increased and his academic ability has improved enormously.' Another told us, 'He had lost his confidence; with the individualised teaching and fantastic learning support it is like Pandora's box has been opened, it is so wonderful to see.' The head of SEN is a literary specialist and there is an in-house team of five assistants plus an external team who provide speech and language therapy and educational psychology. The school provides good support for dyslexia and dyscalculia and extra tuition can take place instead of Latin or French, at an extra cost. Overseas students with at least basic English can come for a term or more; the EAL specialist offers two weeks intensive tuition to bring them up to speed.

The long school day – 8.20am-5.45pm – includes a variety of activities: ballet, karate, fencing, riding and gymnastics at extra cost, and free activities such as art, sports, eco-club or playing in the woods. Year 5s upward have is Saturday school until 4pm with lessons, sports fixtures and – the highlight of the day – French lunch. Not all pupils and parents are enthusiastic about the extra day but they all agreed 'you soon get used to it.'

We saw plenty of projects in the small but very productive art studio. One pupil, inspired by his recent travels, had created a collage of a world map showing flight paths. A class trip to Lulworth Cove was another inspiration. The teacher sets up still life projects and even life drawing sessions – recently a geisha. One parent who used to work for John Galliano ran a 'punk' workshop recently, another ran a photography session. One parent said, 'The art department is fantastic at school and with the resources it has bats way above other schools, but we would love there to be a bigger art room and facilities as it is such an amazing department.' We would definitely second that.

A similarly creative environment for science in the old changing rooms, with movable benches and storage to allow room for experiments of all kinds and flexible teaching. There is also a Tinker Lab full of Lego, Meccano, BBC microbits and anything else that can be taken apart and rebuilt, plus the chance to try out new technology such as drones and 3D printing.

The new music centre sits in the natural slope of the hill, clad in cedar. Concertina doors open out onto the decking looking across the Somerset hills. Fantastically inspirational. The department is run by 'excellent' teacher who has set up a good-sized string orchestra for such a small school (all year 2s learn violin for a year), and a choir that has been to Venice, Prague, Rome and London. There are plenty of drama productions, too, in the well-equipped theatre. Recently year 6 performed Why the Whales Came, and the leavers' production was Beowulf.

The library opens out on to a terrace, a rose garden, the monkey woods (a maze) and fields as far as the eye can see. Alongside playing fields and courts, including an Astro, there's a sports hall, swimming pool, climbing wall and pitch and putt course. Nestled under the trees is the forest school with a newly built roundhouse and large fire-pit. When we visited, it was alive with activity: one group was rubbing flints to make fire, another was learning to saw and a third group was making doughnuts – normal and gluten-free, of course. Other culinary delights have included wild garlic bread and nettle soup, all foraged and picked themselves.

Full (from year 5), weekly and flexi-boarding (from year 3), with a few pupils from Spain and France, but most from the UK, a large number fairly local. One parent said, 'They love it! We live only 15 minutes away and the older boys choose to weekly board and flexi board. Sometimes they don't want to come home – they have a lot of fun!' Flexi boarders must book regular days; the school is keen not to be used as a hotel. Parents said, 'The boarding house is very family orientated and they have a lovely time in the evenings.' Activities include a variety of games as well as more sedentary pursuits. There are 'family weekends' spent with the houseparents and 'activity weekends' when day pupils can join in too – themes have included Inspector Gadget, Indiana Jones (with an assault course), Harry Potter and Making a Musical. 'The boarding staff are fantastic; my children have always been very happy to board, although we tend to build it up over a few years as they get older, and have more stamina,' parents told us.

The pupils love the school. One parent said, 'She will not hear a bad word against it or anything to do with it and cannot under any circumstances be persuaded to stay at home if she is under the weather.' The academic results are undeniably impressive, but not the most important thing for many parents. One parent told us, 'My eldest was very shy and within a year was in the final of the school poetry recital performing in front of the whole school and parents – in less than one year!' With confidence and self-belief you can go far.

Pinewood

Bourton, Shrivenham, Wiltshire SN6 8HZ

Ages 3–13 **Pupils** 403 **Boarders** 27 weekly, 86 flexi (from year 5) **C of E**

Fees: Day £9,300- £17,895; weekly boarding +£4,365 pa

01793 782205
www.pinewoodschool.co.uk

Head: Since 2002, Philip Hoyland BEd (60s), educated at The Downs, Malvern, followed by Cheltenham College. Read English and education at Exeter; previously housemaster, then deputy head, at The Dragon. Married to the warm, compassionate Henrietta; they met at Ludgrove when she was under-matron and he a rookie teacher (they have three grown-up children). Very much a partnership – she is head of girls' boarding and central to much of school life, particularly the pastoral side.

Eloquent, charming, a gentleman, he has a great sense of humour and even greater sense of adventure, wanting education to be both explored and enjoyed and for children to learn through taking risks. 'Let them be children, I say – there's plenty of time for stress in adulthood.' Old-school in demeanour, but thoroughly modern in outlook, he embodies exactly what he seeks for the school: 'old-fashioned values, coupled with innovative learning.' More than a sense that his Quaker heritage (his great grandfather was businessman and philanthropist George Cadbury) shapes his views. Says, 'I'm more detached from daily school life than I used to be – more of a CEO these days, with much of my time taken up with compliance, strategy, recruitment, staff and showing parents round.'

But a remote figure in a suit he is not, still eating with the pupils and giving assemblies (wearing jumper not jacket). A kind of grandfatherly dignitary, he circuits the school to a flurry of waves and excitement from animated youngsters, eager to tell of their day, show off work, badges, awards – and while older children stand to attention, communication is well peppered with humour. His office, a relaxed, homely first floor room with stunning views, is regularly inhabited by pupils showing off their work, 'and checking if they're due their packet of Skittles, which they get once they've shown me three outstanding pieces.' Parents call him 'kind', 'a strategist' and 'fantastic with the children,' who in turn describe him as 'lively', 'funny' and 'really nice.' All that's missing is the obligatory labrador – he has one, of course, but keeps it at home 'as you never know if children will take to dogs.' Retiring in July 2020.

Entrance: Mainly via nursery and pre-prep; register early (many do so at birth). Unselective, but prospective pupils come in for a taster day. Deliberately takes broad-ish ability range, 'deal with what we get,' with very rare exceptions. Assessment for entry into prep. Most years full with waiting lists, though movement, especially of day children, and flexibility for additional groups, means places materialise.

Exit: Primarily Cheltenham College, and Marlborough, then Badfield, Dean Close, Rendcomb and Dauntsey's in 2018. A clutch of scholarships (art, music, sport, academic and all-rounder) to a range of schools is the norm most years.

Remarks: Founded in 1875, moved to current pretty Victorian Cotswold stone house in 1946. Noughties, and the arrival of the Hoylands, saw shift from a school languishing in the doldrums ('bad headships,' say parents) to one riding a wave, albeit with a few choppy interludes.

Expect a home-from-home welcome as soon as you enter the oak panelled hall, complete with squidgy sofas and open fire – in full use (to our delight) by the children at break times; definitely not just a showpiece for prospective parents. The main house is also home to other recreational rooms, dining hall, dorms for borders, admin and head's office, as well as some year 5 and 6 classrooms (although there are plans to move them to a swanky new building). Nursery and pre-prep in former stable block with fantastic play area in old walled garden. Super performing arts centre, modern sports hall, outside swimming pool, library rehoused in the Orangery and newish science labs packed with test tubes, microscopes, Bunsen burners etc ('We dissected an eyeball last week,' one boy told us, elatedly) – a real world of discovery and experimentation.

Be sure to pack your children's wellies as outdoors is as important as in, with 86 acres of land for the children to enjoy – and enjoy it they do. Pinewood is one of the country's leading outdoor schools, so besides the Astro and sports pitches you'd probably expect, there's a treetops adventure playground, outdoor classroom, fairy garden, super sensory gardens, polytunnel and lawn after lawn. 'I have a tonne of conkers in here,' one excitable young boy with a heavy tub called out to us. The children couldn't wait to tell us how they 'break the ice' at the start of every summer term in the outdoor pool – not literally, but an annual event that usually sees the head dive in first, followed by a posse of pupils. They also enthused about spotlight, a unanimously favourite (don't panic – it's risk assessed) pastime in which children try to get from one point to another outside in the dark without being caught in the teacher's torchlight. And don't even get them started on the list of Thursday afternoon outdoor activities (indoor ones also available) unless you've got a spare half-hour on your hands. In fact, the only thing stopping us from saying this school is all about getting outside and climbing trees is pupils' claim that this where the limit is drawn – 'health and safety means no tree climbing,' one told us disappointedly, with other grumbles of some out-of-bounds woods that 'we keep being promised access to, but it never happens.'

Most teachers are head's own appointments; admits he has taken a few risks, going for the fizzy or alternative to encourage excitement and develop a joy of learning. Big on teaching the children the learning process, a strategy that hasn't been lost on the youngsters, with pupils eager to talk us through how they got from A to B when showing us their work – and there wasn't a single classroom we saw that wasn't ablaze with gusto. 'Why do the French only ever eat one egg at a time?' the headmaster called out to a year 8 French class who were just about to embark on role-play of a French restaurant. 'Because one egg is un oeuf!' responded a boy, reflective of the humour and laid-back vibe that defines this school.

Between 42-48 pupils per year group, split into three forms of 16, until year 5 when pupils are taught in three sets, with an extra scholarship set added from year 7. French from age 4, Latin or classics from 10, enrichment for anyone who will benefit. History, geography and RE recently dropped at common entrance 'to free the children from the treadmill of exams and subjects that just require children regurgitating facts'. RE replaced with theology, philosophy and ethics. Clear focus on teaching collaboration, problem solving, independent learning, presentation skills, linking ideas etc. Lessons recently lengthened to 45 minutes – 'It's made us all a bit less frantic,' says head. Computer science important for all, even wee ones are encouraged to Google. Saturday school unpopular with pupils and parents alike, but head has 'no plans to stop it.'

Solid learning support is well integrated, not an add-on. A genuinely multi-sensory approach mean those with mild dyslexia, dyspraxia, ADD (Bluetac et al for fiddlers), high functioning ASD are well served. OT, speech and language therapy, play therapy, plus one-to-one or small groups if required (most incur additional fee) but not the place for those with moderate or severe needs.

Usual plaudits for art; DT replaced with graphic design for older ones; lots of applause for drama (year group performances, not whole school, with plenty of Shakespeare) and music thrives (includes ensembles, jazz band, a chorus of choirs and inclusive performing opportunities, with around three-quarters of the children learning an instrument). Daily sport for all, plus Thursday activities which include touch rugby, girls' football, ballet, clay pigeon shooting, archery, sketch and paint, yoga, mindfulness, drama, mountain biking, model making, camp building and more. Main school sports are rugby, football, hockey, cricket and tennis (girls' hockey and boys' cricket the strongest performers). A hardy bunch who practise in all weathers and of course play to win (which they often do) in weekly fixtures but, as one parent said, 'It's not the kind of school that gets in the best rugby coaches to help them win the most matches – it's more a case of making sure every child gets a chance to represent the school and have fun doing it.' Trips generally within the UK ('so everyone can go'), the highlight of which (to the pupils anyway) is the annual PGL-style Pinewood Adventure Weekend for year 4s upwards.

Think greenhouse not hothouse; tender plants (and tough weeds) will be nurtured, watered but not pruned, though delicate darlings might flounder: 'You need a have-a-go attitude,' pupils insist. Concentrates on extending childhood, Enid Blyton-style – the pre-pubescent 'make-up and manicure' brigade would either roll up their sleeves and regain their innocence – or, likely as not, hate it. But for those happy to don a boiler suit, roll down a hill, play hide and seek or chase through a meadow, it's a blast. 'I don't get hung up about untucked shirts – a smiley face is much more important,' says head. Small-scale transgressions are dealt with swiftly and discreetly, although pupils told us 'some teachers are a lot stricter than others.' Bullying not seen by anyone as an issue; school is a mobile phone free zone ('none of us minds,' a pupil told us); recent appointment of head of well-being and mental health.

Parents consider this a local school, majority live within an hour's drive. Boarding (from year 5) popular, though, and on the wish list for most pupils. Opt for either regular boarding (sticking to set nights per week, often increasing as children go up the school) or weekly boarding (particularly popular for year 8s). Comfortable, homely accommodation ('the girls' accommodation has recently given the Hotel du Vin uplift,' jokes head about the new carpets, door frames etc; boys' equally as shiny but a little cramped under the eaves), with between four to nine beds in a dorm and great food – 'better than the lunches,' say pupils. Prep finishes at 5.30pm, after which 'there's plenty of activities and free time – it's like a huge sleepover every night,' say pupils. Squabbles usually sorted over a mug of hot chocolate in Mrs Hoyland's kitchen.

Pre-prep suits the worms, germs and stones brigade; aims for children to fall in love with learning, which extends well beyond the regular primary diet. Parents genuinely welcome to spend time with their child at beginning and end of the day; no classroom barriers here.

This is a true country prep, with more mud-splattered four-by-fours than flashy Ferraris. Expect relaxed rigour, not blazers and caps; cobwebs on windowsills, not spic and span. If you could recreate The Secret Garden you'd probably do it here; active children fizz with enthusiasm, happily maintaining the innocence of a bygone era but with the benefits of modern technology and teaching. A genuinely wholesome school that emphasises cooperation rather than competitiveness, confidence not arrogance and team before me. Especially good for the creative boy or girl with boundless energy, sporty or not, and limitless curiosity.

Plymouth College

Linked with Plymouth College Preparatory School

Ford Park, Plymouth PL4 6RN

Ages 11–18 **Pupils** 480 **Sixth form** 143 **Boarders** 110 full, 9 weekly, 2 flexi **C of E**

Fees: Day £7,680 – £16,290; Boarding £27,435 – £31,440 pa

01752 505100
www.plymouthcollege.com

Headmaster: Since April 2019, Jonathan Cohen, previously deputy head at Brentwood School. Masters in educational leadership and doctorate in education. Investment banker at Lehman Brothers and UBS before becoming a teacher. Has also worked at Haileybury and King's Bruton. Keen interest in sport, particularly rugby, football, hockey and cricket, as player and coach. Married to Claire, also a teacher; three children.

Academic matters: In 2018, at A level, 49 per cent A*-B and 29 per cent A*/A grades. At GCSE, 34 per cent A*-A/9-7 grades. Twenty-two options at A level offered. Top performing subjects are maths, science, economics and business studies. Most do three A levels plus one elective subject eg EPQ or a BTec in sports leadership, ICT, performing arts. A one year IGCSE course is available in year 11, popular with international students. Also offers the sport baccalaureate, which is based round the BTec level 3 extended diploma in sport (outdoor adventure), and includes topics such as fitness, nutrition, coaching and leadership.

Class sizes are small, around 13. Setting or streaming in maths, science, and English from year 8. As well as the standard GCSE options, the school offers some that can be studied as an after-school activity, including philosophy, Greek, computing and film studies. Most pupils study two of French, Spanish or German. Extra support in maths and English can be provided for those that only take one language.

The head of the learning support department is a qualified educational psychologist. In-class support and individual tuition is provided for mild needs including dyslexia, dysgraphia, dyscalculia, and dyspraxia, though some parents felt that 'earlier identification and intervention' would be helpful. One parent, who had eventually organised her own child's assessment, commented: 'The SEN department has improved hugely since then, but integration in teaching and lessons as well as regular SEN feedback still needs improving.' All comments on teachers, including SEN, were positive; 'supportive and communicate well' and 'very committed and enthusiastic.'

Games, options, the arts: Well known for producing top athletes including swimmers, modern pentathletes, fencers and divers, all supported through their rigorous training programmes as well as their academic studies. As expected, top sports facilities here. There's a large sports centre, a cardiovascular gym, two squash courts, a weights room, a climbing wall, Astroturf, playing fields and cricket nets. Plus a fantastic 25 metre indoor pool (the elite swimmers use the Life Centre facilities in Plymouth). Has produced Olympic swimmers and divers and international rugby players, with national pentathletes, pupils playing football for Plymouth Argyll and cricket for the Surrey county professional team; one girl was selected for the U15 south west England rugby team. No problem if you're not a top sportsperson: 'He has not felt out of place among elite sports people even though he is an amateur,' a parent told us. Basketball, badminton, hockey, netball, gymnastics, cross-country running, golf and equestrian also available.

For the more arty types, there's plenty of productions to get involved with, Beauty and the Beast. And a recent house drama was Scrooge – each house had to adapt the original story giving it a modern twist or unexpected makeover. Most pupils learn a musical instrument; even the harp is offered. Lots of formal music concerts but informal guitar and piano evenings are popular too. There's a chamber choir, rock school, flute group, orchestra and string orchestra.

There is a small sixth form classroom adjoined by a computer suite for photography and graphics. The Art Haus, a two-storey cottage hidden by trees, is appropriately decorated with a graffiti-type mural. Sixth form art, photography and graphics room with adjoining computer suite.

Sailing in Plymouth Sound, and adventures on the moors including the Ten Tors and DofE. Also caving, climbing, mountain biking, sea kayaking, scuba diving, hill walking etc. Then there's eg CCF, archery, snooker, school of rock, samba club, model railway club and a Young Enterprise group – around 40 activities on offer.

Sixth formers have their own enrichment programme which also includes financial studies, politics, cookery, journalism, photography and volunteering placements. Pre-med course heavily supported by parents and ex-pupils, many of whom are GPs and consultants.

Regular trips range from Dartmoor (geography) to Berlin (German), Switzerland (physics), Sri Lanka (cricket). Annual charity expedition to Malawi.

Boarding: Six boarding houses, a row of large villas dating from the mid-19th century. On the main school site is a boys' house, a girls' house and three smaller houses/annexes for sixth formers. The Captain's House, specialist accommodation for the elite swimmers, is on the prep school site, 10 minutes away, housing around one third of boarders. One parent told us, 'The boarding facilities have improved dramatically....A tremendous amount of work has been done to improve the accommodation.'

Around 50 per cent of boarders are from the UK, the rest from over 40 countries. A few weekly boarders, but we were told the majority are resident at weekends these days. If your child is going to be a full boarder, do check how many of their age group will be around at weekends, particularly in the lower years, to ensure they have plenty of company.

About half the boarders in the girls' house are athletes – swimmers, divers, pentathletes etc. Friendly, approachable housemistress who lives here with her husband and three young children. Parents told us, 'The current boarding staff are exceptional in creating an environment in which both our girls are currently thriving.' Rooms are mostly doubles and a few triples; common areas include arts and crafts room, games room and lounge. This is a busy house; some athletes start training from 4am and others are training until 9pm. There are a lot of comings and goings and the housemistress does a great job staggering food times. She says it keeps the house alive and interesting, buzzing. Boys and girls are free to socialise between the houses, cooking food in the kitchen, playing games, chatting or watching TV.

Head of boarding runs the boys' house with a good balance of discipline and fun and is a father figure for many. If he finds a bed unmade, he will hide the duvet as punishment, so beware. Plenty of common areas including rooms for table tennis, pool, table football and music room. The annexe, or the Boat House, provides sixth formers with very small but private single rooms. Great for the transition to university life.

The co-ed Captain's House supports over 40 elite swimmers with high levels of pastoral care, specialist nutritional needs and complicated logistics. There is a regular minibus service between the boarding house, the pool and school. One parent whose child swims for GB said, 'The boarding house dedicated to swimmers is ideal....The only problem [my child] sometimes has is the transport arrangements from school to the boarding house.'

Most evenings there is a game of football or dodgeball in the sports hall or on the Astroturf. The swimming pool is open at weekends, and there are trips to the beach for surfing or paddle boarding, days out to Adrenaline Quarry or the Eden Project, outings to the cinema, 10-pin bowling, ice-skating, paintballing, dry-slope skiing. No exeat weekends but the school closes at half term.

Background and atmosphere: Founded in 1877 as Plymouth High School for Boys, the school moved to its current site at Ford Park in 1880, changing its name to Plymouth College three years later. A number of mergers with girls' schools (the school became fully co-ed in 1995), most recently with St Dunstan's Abbey School for Girls in 2005. It was then that the prep school moved to its current site in The Millfields, the old naval hospital, three miles away.

The site is tucked behind the hustle and bustle of Mutley Plain in Plymouth. The main buildings are grand Victorian villas with high ceilings, stone steps and beautiful ornate windows: stunning, but cold in places. The library is grandiose and the classrooms are traditional; original wooden benches in the science laboratories, everything you'd expect in a school as old as this.

Decent sixth form centre with bistro and lounge area to socialise or work. Very small and uninspiring quiet study area upstairs. Sixth form social life is thankfully much more vibrant and fun with a freshers' ball to kick it all off, followed by a Halloween ball, quiz nights, DVD and pizza nights, and an end of year ball.

P

The active school council 'gets things done.' Members planned and created the outdoor classroom, set up and now keep a flock of rare chickens at the school, have installed a wildlife pond, and successfully campaigned for a salad bar and pasta bar. Their latest project is the Gutter Grow system for cultivating fresh herbs, vegetables and fruit on the roof of the school canteen.

Pastoral care, well-being and discipline: Very good pastoral care. Parents told us, 'Staff work hard to integrate the different nationalities and the welfare and medical support is outstanding. Both our [children] have had medical issues that have been dealt with comprehensively and with compassion.' There is a school nurse plus a day matron in each boarding house, also in charge of physio for the athletes. Out of hours, responsibility lies with the boarding staff, all first aid trained. For athletes there's a 'playground to podium' ethic, which involves regular communication between boarding and pastoral staff, parents, coaches and the athletes themselves. Sixth form course includes coping with stress and mindfulness as well as eg money management.

At a small school with a strong and very competitive house system, pupils have opportunities to make friends across the years. Boarders, athletes and day pupils live, study and train together well; pupils seem to make good lasting friendships that continue beyond their school years. Plymouth College has a Christian ethos but it is 'understated,' the head told us.

Pupils and parents: UK parents are doctors, surgeons, teachers, business owners, engineers, members of the Forces. One said, 'Communication has always been superb with easy access to teaching, boarding and support staff with prompt responses to issues. This has been tremendously important in living at some distance from the school'.

Past pupils include Tom Daley, Olympic diver and Cassie Patten, Olympic swimmer, plus Henry Slade and Paul Ackford, both England rugby internationals.

Entrance: Non-selective, but entrance exams in maths and English 'to maintain minimum standards,' and for scholarships. Around 50 per cent of intake is from the prep school. One parent told us their child 'settled well into year 7, with a great head of year leading the team and a weekend away in Whiteworks, Dartmoor. It's a good thing to do in the first few weeks of term.'

For sixth form entry, at least six GCSE passes at grade 5, including English and maths, and three passes at grade 6+ or higher. International students are assessed for English speaking and writing skills.

Exit: On average, 50 per cent leave after GCSEs to go to local colleges or grammar schools. The same number join the sixth form. Some sixth form boarders are particularly attracted by the sports programmes on offer; several have gained sports scholarships at American universities in recent years. One to Oxbridge in 2018; popular UK destinations include UWE, Cardiff, Coventry, Plymouth, Bath and Bristol. Others off to Melbourne, Lausanne, Colorado, North Carolina and Rotterdam.

Money matters: Scholarships include all-round, academic, art, drama, music, performing arts and sport. Means-tested bursaries also available, as well as discounts for siblings and military families.

Remarks: Elite athletes plus day pupils and boarders of all abilities and nationalities study, train and live together harmoniously. Pupils are able to develop at their own pace, and most importantly gain confidence. One parent confirmed, saying, 'She is now oozing self-esteem, loves going to school'.

Plymouth College Preparatory School

Linked with Plymouth College

Saint Dunstan's Abbey, The Millfields, Plymouth PL1 3JL

Ages 3–11 **Pupils** 189 **Boarders** 2 full **C of E**

Fees: £7,995 – £10,605 pa

01752 201352
www.plymouthcollege.com

Headmaster: Since 2007, Christopher Gatherer BA Cert Ed. Originally from the north west, studied English at Keele. Taught at Sherborne, then joined Plymouth College senior school in 1982 as head of year 7. Teaches drama and PSHE to years 5 and 6 and takes storytelling sessions in reception once a week. 'The head teacher has a wonderful rapport with the children which he establishes early on by telling stories about his Wolfie character.' Popular with parents too: 'He takes pride in the successes (big and small) of each individual and is quick to praise good or discipline unacceptable behaviour. A remarkably energetic and motivated man whom the children look up to.' 'He clearly loves his job and is very good at it.'

Entrance: Taster days include an informal assessment to ensure children are ready for school. One parent whose child started half way through a term said, 'On her trial day, she was chaperoned by two lovely girls.' Settling in was good too: 'The other boys and girls in her year were kind and considerate and we were amazed at how quickly she found a genuine sense of belonging.'

Exit: Some 75 per cent go on to the senior school, with parents appreciative of 'the promise of an excellent next step education without the risk of rejection', the rest to local grammars. The transition starts in year 5 with activity days, plus the prep school DT teacher is also the head of year 7. The senior school is on a different site, Ford Park, three miles away, and apart from swimming lessons, prep pupils rarely go there. However, the schools do share the same ethos and pupils seem to look forward to moving up to 'the big school.'

Remarks: Founded in 1877; the prep school moved to its current site in 2005. It is the old naval hospital building on a gated development, and for a city prep it is surprisingly spacious with several green areas, an adventure playground, an outdoor classroom and even its own chapel. Some original naval hospital facilities and memorabilia are still in place; even the disco ball is still hanging in the old dance hall, now the school theatre.

A large walled field, 'our very own Lost Gardens of Heligan,' says the head, is a real pocket of calm. It is used for athletics, cricket, rugby and football. There is also a long jump pit and a netball/tennis court. There is also a sports hall, used for a multitude of activities especially on rainy days, the norm in the south west.

The lovely little chapel is used for daily assemblies, all including some religious content, with parents welcomed to the weekly awards assembly. These can be for earning house points, reading books, helping others, being polite, thoughtful, kind, cheerful or just generally positive. One parent told us, 'They are very clever at ensuring every child feels valued.'

The early years outdoor classroom includes a wooden castle, trees and a sunken-decked mini-amphitheatre. Reception's 'messy Monday' involves a great deal of puddle jumping, as well as collecting leaves and sticks to analyse (and paint) later. The indoor classrooms are full of creative displays – pirates, farm shops, ladybirds. There are infant and junior libraries, a better than average science lab, an art classroom for painting and pottery and, nearby, a well equipped food tech room. The building is wheelchair accessible with a lift.

The senior school has a good reputation for sport, swimming in particular, and there are plenty of opportunities for prep pupils too. There's athletics, rugby, cricket (some pupils have reached county level), hockey, netball, football (one girl plays for Devon), gymnastics and cross-country. One pupil became a national biathlon finalist and has now gone on to represent GB. There are also plenty of inter-house competitions that carry on into the senior school. Parents told us, 'We really like the sports teacher as he is getting the training and clubs all sorted.' Don't be put off if your child isn't sporty, though; parents report that there is plenty of encouragement from staff and other pupils.

Children are taught 'not to fear failure.' Pupils we saw and spoke to were confident, articulate and very keen to answer questions. Parents say, 'The school is adept at identifying strengths and encouraging individuality, whilst gently exposing them to new ideas and challenges within their capability.' Specialist teaching increases higher up the school, with all year 5 and 6 classes taught by specialists. French from year 3 and Spanish from year 5.

The learning support department can help children with mild needs including dyslexia or dyscalculia. According to parents, the support is good but 'the extra resources are very limited.' One parent told us they are paying for home tuition to fill the gaps. However, others told us how the learning support has helped improve their child's confidence dramatically. 'The school has instigated appropriate support and tailored lessons and homework to meet her ability and needs and, importantly, helped her understand why she finds learning so difficult, and provided her with strategies to cope whilst integrating her with the rest of her year so she doesn't feel different.'

Drama productions for each year group have recently seen Snow White by year 4, Midsummer Night's Dream by year 6, Ballooning Round The World by year 2, and Rapunzel, starring reception and kindergarten. Some take LAMDA exams and a few perform at Plymouth's Theatre Royal. Everyone learns recorder in year 2, violin in years 3 and 4, and playing and composing on keyboards in years 5 and 6. Some set up their own bands. There are regular concerts and recitals plus 'first steps concerts,' just for beginners.

Wrap-around care is from 8am – 6pm, at no extra charge. A wide range of clubs runs until 5pm. Year 6 goes to France for a week and year 5 goes to an eco-camp in Cornwall for a night. One parent said their child 'is now oozing self-esteem, loves going to school.'

Plymstock School

Church Road, Plymstock, Plymouth PL9 9AZ

Ages 11–18 **Pupils** 1,570 **Sixth form** 230

01752 402679
www.plymstockschool.org.uk

P

Headteacher: Since 2016, Robert Diment BSc PGCE NPQH. A local, went to school at Ivybridge Community College and studied environmental biology at Plymouth University. First teaching job took him to Hampshire, but then in 2001 he joined Plymstock School. He has never left, gradually moving up the ranks to deputy head and now headteacher. He proudly claims to be a 'product of the school,' evolving and developing together over the years.

Parents agree 'he has made a really good impression.' He is 'visible and approachable...a dynamic individual.' Lots of praise for his weekly blog and also the improved communication between parents and school. We got the impression he lives and breathes the school.

Academic matters: In 2018, 45 per cent A*-B grades at A level (21 per cent A*/A). At GCSE, 70 per cent got 9-4 in both maths and English (19 per cent of these grades were A*-A/9-7). Over 30 A levels offered and some vocational courses but these are mainly covered by the local colleges. Maths, English and the humanities are popular with an increasing number opting for psychology, sociology or criminology.

Sets from year 7 for English and maths. This is a huge school, currently 260 in a year group, split into 10 classes. There are 12 sets per year which gives some flexibility in numbers and enables the school to create smaller classes for the lower sets. Enhanced specialist provision – centre for communication difficulties and intensive numeracy and literacy programme for SEN in years 7 and 8.

Renowned for reading enrichment and other schools are now replicating the model. Years 7 to 9 have 30 minutes set aside for reading every day. We followed the yellow brick road to the library and saw pupils curled up on beanbags nose in book, or sitting at tables with older pupils (literacy readers) to read together. The library is central to life at Plymstock and as well as regular guest visits (recently Marcus Sedgewick), they run the Hogwards – similar to the Carnegie shortlist where pupils write recommendations for others. One parent described how her very quiet younger son was allowed to visit the library whilst still at primary school. 'The library became his support when he joined in year 7...He is now a reading mentor and helps out too – this has given him a real sense of belonging.'

Very low staff turnover, unusual for a (near) city school. Parents were quick to praise, saying teachers are 'positive and enthusiastic' and they are 'prepared to go the extra mile.' One parent commented that her son, during an open day, had enjoyed the 'hands-on activities that made maths interesting'.

Games, options, the arts: No longer a specialist sports college, but lucky enough still to be reaping the benefits with the outstanding facilities. There are two sports halls, a fully equipped gym, dance studios, two new 3G artificial playing surfaces, a rugby pitch, tennis/netball courts and a running track. All major sports catered for: rugby, football (girls and boys), netball, rowing, swimming, badminton, athletics etc. Older pupils can try alternative health/fitness options including zumba. 'One of the major reasons we chose Plymstock over other local schools was due to the superb range of sports facilities available to pupils,' a parent told us. We particularly liked hearing that local primary schools also get to join in – year 13 students recently put on a successful (and to be repeated) sports event for a local primary school. Year 5s were invited to Plymstock to take part in fun football, basketball and rollerball sessions.

Art is popular with around four full classes at GCSE level. Regular visits to galleries in London and St Ives. Printmaking, photography, ceramics and 3D. We saw some high standard work, in particular some stunning photography. Pupils' work is exhibited annually in the university's Cube3 gallery. Recent drama productions have included The Little Shop of Horrors, Beauty and the Beast, and We Will Rock You. The music department has been on a roll since the appointment of new head of music; A level is now offered, plus there is a violin ensemble, a blues guitar jam club and a 70-strong Plymstock Singers group.

Over 80 extracurricular options from film, to building a race car or sports, DofE and Ten Tors. Plenty of trips for sixth formers: a trip to Berlin for German students and an expedition to Peru. For younger years there is an annual ski trip and language exchanges.

Background and atmosphere: Founded in 1911 as a boys' school on the same large site, Plymstock is one of the oldest schools in Plymouth. Feels miles away from the city, but the electronic entrance gate is a harsh reminder that it is in fact very close. Once inside, the central roundabout with its blossoming trees is far more inviting and by all accounts a lasting memory for many pupils. Buildings are one and two storey, all clad in electric blue. Tired and in need of attention in several areas, but the sixth form building, music department and lecture theatre were all renovated recently. The head feels that it is always the arts that get overlooked when it comes to funding, so it's great to hear that a new 450-seat arts centre with dedicated professional performance space and art gallery will be ready by September 2019.

Over £2 million has been spent recently on sports facilities, the new art café called The Galley and an environmentally sustainable social sciences building. There is an ICT room per department and trollies of iPads. The English block is the only original building, built round a pretty garden courtyard. Pupils we saw were calm, well-behaved, and obviously mindful of the head as we walked by. Wheelchair friendly.

Plenty of leadership opportunities including head boy/girl plus deputies and the school council. Sixth formers have (some) control over their own affairs through the Senate – an elected forum that organises social events, fundraising activities and sports activities and represents students' views to the head of sixth form.

Pastoral care, well-being and discipline: The odd misdemeanour that we saw, eating en-route to class, walking too slowly between lessons, playing ball in the corridor, all rectified immediately with a short, sharp bark from the head. Bad behaviour is always punished but the school will also talk it through with pupils and parents. Strict, traditional school: stand when an adult enters the room; swear at a teacher and you will be suspended immediately.

Heads of year and assistants are based in the student support hub so there is always someone on hand to talk to. Every day starts at 8.45am with tutor groups.

One parent told us, 'The tutor system – of having the same tutor throughout KS3 and 4 – has been excellent, as their tutors have been able to understand and support at each stage of their school life.' Another added, 'My child is happy at the school, he has settled in and made new friends; the school seems a very positive place to learn.' Mindfulness sessions available for both pupils and teachers.

Pupils and parents: Families are local. Parents are pleased with the improvements in communication, though a few mentioned that the 'progress reports would benefit from a little more detail if the student is below target.' The school has also set up a parents' forum to discuss ways in which the school and parents can work more closely together.

Uniform is navy blazer and shirt and tie. Ties correspond to houses, all named after National Trust properties. Pupils we saw looked presentable, a large number decorated in badges denoting mentor status and sports achievements.

Former pupils include Steve Bartlett, CEO Social Change, Heather Knight, captain England women's cricket team and Sharron Davies, Olympic swimmer.

Entrance: Five feeder primaries but other pupils also accepted; usual criteria with distance as a tie-break. Now increased to 300 year 7 places to accommodate families from the housing development next door. There is space on the campus but no doubt some green will disappear.

Lots of open days. Plymstock works closely with the five feeder schools with plenty of transition opportunities. Parents told us, 'It gave the boys the chance to meet the teachers and other pupils that were thinking of joining the school.' Another said, 'They were also lucky to have students from Plymstock come to their school to help out.' More transition events in the summer term and then an overnight camping trip in the first few weeks of year 7. Team activities with their tutor and tutor group gives them real opportunities to make new friends.

Exit: Around half leaves after GCSEs for apprenticeships and vocational courses at the local college. One medic in 2018; popular destinations include Plymouth, Cardiff, Marions, Exeter and Swansea.

Remarks: Popular community comprehensive. The sheer size may be daunting for some, but for sporty types it's a no-brainer, the facilities are superb. New arts centre will be a fantastic addition for arty types. Good all-round education serving a large local community.

Poole Grammar School

Gravel Hill, Poole, Dorset BH17 9JU

Ages 11–18 **Pupils** 1,199 **Sixth form** 359

01202 692132
www.poolegrammar.com

Headteacher: Since 2014, Andy Baker, previously deputy head. BA from Lancaster (politics and economic history), PGCE from Keele and MA from Middlesex (social and industrial history). Taught at schools in Essex before joining Poole as deputy head in 1993. Likes pottery, skiing, period property restoration, music (listener and performer). Married with two grown up children.

Academic matters: Specialises in maths, computing and cognition, so it's no surprise that maths is top of the pops at A level, closely followed by the three separate sciences, which everyone does at IGCSE. All students take French, Spanish or German to GCSE, though no classics or eastern languages. Fantastic results in maths and chemistry but also, impressively, in English, RE, geography and history. In 2018, 56 per cent of GCSE grades A*/A or 7-9.

At A level about 30 subjects to choose from. Joint sixth form teaching in many subjects with Parkstone Grammar School (girls) means almost any combination of subjects can be timetabled. Lots of enrichment choices in AS levels and a few unexpected AS subjects, including archaeology and ancient history. English language is a popular A level, plus computing, the inevitable sciences and above all maths, while most boys take general studies. At A level, 70 per cent A*-B grades in 2018. Masses of add-ons: boys can take the AQA Baccalaureate virtually in their stride if they do the right mixture of subjects. Accelerated courses in maths etc supplemented by school extension courses, mainly in form of IGCSE in preparation for A level. Poole has Cisco and Microsoft Academy status and students can earn the CCNA networking qualification in the sixth form.

Setting only in maths, from year 9. All pupils do two weeks' work experience in year 11. Class sizes not more than 30 and some much smaller groups in sixth form.

Less of an academic sausage machine than you might expect. Surprisingly for a grammar, SEN is one of school's specialisms – head sees it as truly cross-curricular and serving the needs of the most able, gifted and talented, as well as those with identified academic difficulties. Excellent results for disabled pupils and those coping with profound deafness and other personal challenges. A five-strong department recognises that almost everyone has some sort of need, hand-in-hand with the belief that supporting pupils through any kind difficulty will be beneficial to their academic performance.

Games, options, the arts: Boys are adamant that music, art and the humanities are important to the school. Exam take-up in art and music belies this, but the life-like and often enormous paintings and drawings in the art department and the impressive music department, with its record of concerts, musical and drama productions (often with Parkstone Grammar), all justify their pride. A completely pupil-led play – written, performed, produced, managed by pupils – is on the bill. Popular orchestra and huge year 8 choir etc.

This is a pretty sporty school. Head believes the largely Poole-based population makes for a sense of identity and commitment to teams. Football is the most popular sport, but rugby, cricket (on 'the best cricket square in Poole') and athletics are probably more successful. Sports hall rather outmoded now, ditto the fitness room, but good new outdoor facilities. No pool but pupils use nearby Dolphin pool, which currently occupies the school's original site. Distinguished past and current athletes have trained through local clubs as well as in school. Inevitably there is sailing (at Hamworthy), plus squash, outdoor education etc off the premises. Parents say sport is good but that school also encourages pupils to use excellent local facilities and clubs, where specialists can (and do) excel in minority pursuits like trampolining.

Bags of clubs at lunchtime and after school. These include philosophy, debating, classics... and lots of subject-specific extras. Enterprise and languages well catered for as well as Formula 24 Greenpower car club, aero modelling et al. Big theatrical productions on alternate years, with smaller studio plays in between and some boys opt into Parkstone Grammar's big musicals. Terrific range of DT rooms, including a new food lab complete with rhubarb growing by the front door. Masses of trips – language visits, expeditions to Second World War sites and popular geography beano to Iceland post-GCSE.

Background and atmosphere: Poole bucked the usual trend and the school started as a co-ed in downtown Poole in 1904, before splitting into boys' and girls' grammars in the 30s. Present site in Gravel Hill, a nondescript wooded artery into Poole famed for its speed traps, has acres of well-groomed space, including good pitches and athletics space. The original red-brick 60s blocks marry well with the square glass and brick modern extensions, giving a pleasant though unremarkable whole. Inside the new bit, with libraries (always manned), state-of-the-art music and drama and some pretty smart classrooms, is bright, light and user friendly. Boys keen on the little work carrels tucked in at the top of the stairs. Reception area bristles with achievement certificates (over 40 of them) and trophies, plus huge historical photos of the school. Main dining hall serves locally sourced largely organic food ('delicious,' according to one pupil we spoke to) and certainly a majority of pupils and staff vote with their stomachs. A Gold Food for Life award earned partly for the supply of fresh fruit and vegetables planted in the school grounds and partly for the school spreading its culinary largess to a swathe of Poole primary schools using their catering – a nice income for the school. Chef recently presented with catering worker of the year award at 10 Downing Street.

School has academy status so has more freedom in what and how it offers. Part of the South West Academic Trust (consisting of several grammar schools and Exeter University), it takes a lead in local academic matters and is formally linked with several primary and special schools. Proud of its lead in staff training – all in-house by own staff – and of the links forged with schools in Europe and further afield. There are nearly as many female as male staff – possibly why the atmosphere is so normal – though heads of department are mostly men.

School has now expanded to include year 7 and has a remarkably calm feel for what is essentially a hothouse for more than 1,200 teenage boys. Humanities and enterprise flourish, lessons evidently absorb attention and boys are enthusiastic about all aspects of school. Adding 'cognition' to the potentially 'nerdy' specialisms of maths and computing allows the staff to boost their care of individual boys, whatever their needs.

Pastoral care, well-being and discipline: Heads of year take responsibility for all boys in the year. Head of year 7 makes sure the little lambs settle and takes them into year 8. There's a remixing of forms in year 9 which then remain static through to year 11. Uniform requirement relaxes over the years – from blazer and tie for years 7 and 8 to jumper and tie for years 9,10 and 11, to ties only (not literally) in sixth form. Out (either temporarily or permanently) for bringing drugs on site. Bullying could result in exclusion – either entirely for a time or in school's exclusion room, though there are few reported incidents. Strong mentoring of year 7 and 8s by senior boys is valued by both. Prefects are a very select few elected by senior boys and staff. Parents praise the discipline here and the rapt and concentrating faces in lessons certainly bore this out. Social events arranged with Parkstone Grammar for all year groups and older boys take lessons in both schools.

Pupils and parents: Head says has a particularly wide social mix because it positively seeks to provide first and foremost for the bright boys of Poole – so is less open to 'advantaged' children from further afield. Small but varied ethnic minorities – 19 languages spoken other than English and bilingual boys increasingly encouraged to do GCSE in their mother tongue. Ability range broader than you might expect, perhaps because of Bournemouth School just down the road, some very good local comprehensives and also because entrance policy favours local pupils above potentially brighter but more distant applicants.

Entrance: Complex and intensely controversial. Priority to those who live in Poole, are on pupil premium and/or sons of staff members. Applications by early September; tests in maths, English and verbal and non-verbal reasoning – common to Poole schools consortium – in late September. Results (whether or not the boy has met the required standard – not a guarantee of a place) sent out in mid-October, in time for local authority school applications. Main feeder schools include Broadstone, Oakdale and Canford Heath Middle Schools and Dumpton Prep.

Sixth form entry is much less competitive – surprising that more people haven't caught on. Applications depend on 'satisfactory achievement' at GCSE.

P

Exit: Occasionally boys defect after year 8, in search of small classes at local independent schools. Some 10-15 per cent leave after GCSEs for vocational courses, apprenticeships or sixth form college. Several a year to Oxbridge.

Remarks: A high achieving school for the bright boys of Poole.

Port Regis

Motcombe Park, Shaftesbury, Dorset SP7 9QA

Ages 3–13 **Pupils** 320 **Boarders** 80 full, 110 part (from year 3) **C of E**

Fees: Day £8,970 – £19,350 pa; Boarding £26,850 pa

01747 857914
www.portregis.com

Headmaster: Since 2016, Stephen Ilett (50s). Educated at Rossall School in Lancashire, where his father was a housemaster, and Oxford, where he read history and played rugby for the university's first XV. Spent 18 years working in the City (for Lloyd's of London) before moving into education. Reckons his early career equipped him well for headship. 'I held positions of responsibility in the City and ran teams of people so I'm used to keeping all the balls in the air,' he says.

First post was teaching French and coaching rugby at Caldicott. He was promoted to director of studies within two years. After eight years at Caldicott he became head of Milbourne Lodge, the Surrey co-ed prep. Five years later he took the reins at Port Regis. 'Port Regis has the reputation of being one of the best schools in the country,' he says, 'and when the headship came up it was too tempting to turn down.'

A keen linguist, he taught modern foreign languages at Milbourne Lodge – 'I love teaching French,' he says. He believes Port Regis' stand-out qualities are its facilities ('which are genuinely acknowledged to be second to none') and the high calibre staff.

Married to Amanda, who is the Port Regis marketing manager, and they have five grown-up children between them. They are passionate believers in the benefits of boarding and are keen to show that Port Regis is 'very friendly, very caring and very nurturing'. In his spare time the head likes cricket, golf, travel, reading and walking his two dogs. They live in a house on site.

Entrance: Main entry points are nursery and year 3 but children join all the way through the school. Pre-prep is first come first served, while entry to the prep is via an interview with the head, assessment (verbal and non-verbal reasoning) and report from previous school. Children join from a raft of preps and from local state primaries. Virtually all pre-prep children move up to the main school (no assessment required).

Exit: Port Regians go on to a wide range of co-ed, single sex, boarding and day schools. Most popular destinations in 2018 were Bryanston, Marlborough and Sherborne.

Senior schools tell Port Regis that Port Regians are children who are 'resilient, self-reliant and know how to get on with things'. Most pupils stay until 13 (one or two girls leave at 11 for schools like Wycombe Abbey but school doesn't encourage this).

Remarks: Located in 150 acres of sweeping Dorset parkland, yet only a couple of miles from the hilltop town of Shaftesbury. Visitors gasp at the setting – it could easily be mistaken for a senior school, with its long drive, stunning architecture, modern classrooms, central lake, huge treehouse and extensive playing fields and grounds. Main school building is a Victorian mansion built in 1894 by Baron Stalbridge but it is surrounded by a collection of stylish, purpose-built additions. School was founded in London in 1881. It moved to Motcombe House in 1947 (via stints at Folkestone, Broadstairs, Bryanston and St Albans). First admitted girls in 1972.

Mildly selective – head says the school is 'a broad church' – but academic results are very good. Setting from year 5, with scholarship sets introduced in the last two years. Maximum class size of 15 throughout. French taught from the start and Latin from year 6. Spanish on offer from year 6 and there are opportunities to study Italian, Russian and Mandarin outside the main curriculum. Ancient Greek is taught as an after-lunch club in years 6-8. Staff give it a try too; when we visited the director of studies had just signed up.

Pupils have a form teacher till the end of year 6, then get the chance to choose their own tutor for years 7 and 8. Excellent learning support department led by dynamic head (who used to be head of science and also teaches mindfulness). A fifth of pupils access learning support, mainly for dyslexia, dyspraxia, ASD, mild ADD and speech and language therapy. School has produced a senior school guide to help parents choose the next schools for their children and head meets parents to discuss choices when children are in year 5.

Well-known far and wide for its sporting prowess, school offers a plethora of sport. Boys play rugby, football, hockey and cricket while girls do hockey, netball, rounders and tennis. As well as acres of playing fields there's an Astroturf, nine-hole golf course, rifle range, heated swimming pool and impressive indoor sports complex that serves as a national centre for junior gymnastics. School does particularly well at hockey, rugby and athletics (11 pupils qualified for 15 different events at a recent IAPS national athletics championships).

Art, DT and pottery (there can't be many prep schools with a whole room devoted to ceramics) are amazing. We were particularly taken with a vast sculpture of a pear core created by a 13-year-old. The year 8 guide who showed us round the DT department told us: 'This is a place where ideas can be formed.' Many senior schools would give their eyeteeth for facilities like these – everything from a 3D printer to a laser-cutting machine (great for making stickers). The children really let their imaginations run riot here. We saw an iPod speaker inspired by an old-fashioned toaster, a hanging chair and a lamp that projected a bat-shaped shadow on the wall. 'They surprise me all the time with their designs,' beams the head of DT. Annual summer exhibition gives pupils a chance to show off their creative flair.

Music is top notch too. Every 7-year-old learns the recorder and how to read music and every 8-year-old learns the violin. Music is taught in the striking Farrington Music School, an octagonal-shaped building overlooking a small lake known as Bob's Pond. It boasts a 132-seat recital hall, music technology room and 17 teaching rooms. Wind, brass and string ensembles, school orchestra, senior and junior choirs, samba band, swing band and lots of other groups, all of which put on regular concerts. Plenty of drama. Each year group puts on a play and there's a leavers' show at the end of the summer term. More than 70 activities and hobbies (we'd love to do them all), including aerobics, backgammon, beekeeping, film animation, computer coding, friendship bracelets and trampolining. Debating, or 'persuasive talks', are very popular, with children encouraged to discuss the issues of the day.

School is firmly committed to boarding. 'It feels like a second home really,' one boy told us. Around 60 per cent of children board in some way, whether it's full boarding, flexi-boarding or the odd night here and there (via an efficient online booking system). 'We have tried to listen to what our parents want,' says the head, who introduced flexi-boarding on his arrival. Apart from half term and holidays, the school never shuts. While some boarders go home at weekends, 70 to 80 children (around a third of the main school) stay at school. Around 35 per cent of boarders are from overseas (17 per cent of the school community). Lots on offer for the boarders – staff and 12 gap students put on activities like face painting, cooking, weekend walks and trips galore. Most staff live on site.

Boarding facilities are top notch – way better than some senior schools we've seen. Junior boarders (years 3 to 6) are housed in the main school building – girls on one side, boys on another. Dorms of four or six, each with a dorm captain. Older boys and girls have separate boarding houses in the grounds. The girls' boarding house is stunning, complete with disco lights on the hall ceiling, a double tier sofa to snuggle up and watch movies at weekends and breakfast bar stools made from riding saddles. Each girl has her own 'cubie', with a bed, desk and wash basin – separated with a stylish bead curtain at the door. There's even a retro caravan in the garden (the enterprising bursar snapped it up on eBay). The senior boys' house is pretty nifty too – the games room ceiling is decorated with real surfboards. A lot of thought has been given to helping new children settle in. New pupils get a shadow to guide them through the early weeks.

Year 8s given responsibility – there's a head boy and head girl, plus dorm captains for boarders. No prefects. 'We don't think it's good to single out children at this age,' says the head. Children encouraged to be children for as long as possible. No electronic devices or mobile phones (apart from pupils whose parents live abroad). Boarders can Skype their parents on the boarding house computers. Pastoral care is very much at the forefront, with form tutors and houseparents the first port of call when problems arise. Very few behaviour issues here. Indeed, Port Regis is hot on manners, pleases and thank yous and holding doors open for visitors. Boarders write letters home every Tuesday. School is also planning a kindness day – 'we want children to understand that it's cool to be kind,' says the head. 'It's not to be derided. It's a real strength.' Slightly more boys than girls but school has appointed a head of girls' games and a senior tutor, who is effectively head of girls (she is also head of classics, has a PhD from Cambridge and has written two critically acclaimed books).

School food is among the very best we've tasted. Head chef (whose family runs a local restaurant) and his five-strong team cook up to 1,000 meals a day – breakfast, lunch and supper, using fresh locally sourced ingredients as much as possible. We happily tucked into a lunch of fillet of sea bass (freshly caught off the coast of Brixham) topped with caper and lemon sauce, spinach and roasted new potatoes. Salads and vegetarian options always on offer – avocado and chargrilled peppers, quorn wraps and lentil soup when we visited.

Pre-prep (with 52 pupils) is housed in a stable block, just a few minutes walk from the main school. Idyllic setting, complete with forest school, enclosed playground, rose garden for imaginary play, loads of outdoor space and plenty of scooters and helmets. When we visited children had been picking apples and were about to cook their own apple crumble. Head of pre-prep is a former Team GB underwater hockey player and is passionate about outdoor learning.

Pupils are chirpy, enthusiastic and refreshingly down-to-earth. We saw a group of year 4s, all dressed up as chimney sweeps, street children and lords and ladies of the manor, throw themselves with relish into a Victorian Day workshop led by a guest speaker. Parents say there's 'a buzz about the school' and like the way it treats every child as an individual. A mix of local families and those who have moved to the country in search of a healthier, less pressurised lifestyle. Some from London – school is only two hours from the capital and Heathrow by train. Day pupils come from as far afield as Sherborne, Salisbury, Bruton and Warminster, mostly places within a 40-minute drive. School is building up a network of minibuses for day pupils. Parents are very involved in the school, attending quiz nights, balls, the Christmas fair, debates and lectures.

Illustrious alumni include the abstract painter Adrian Heath, former Press Council chairman Sir Louis Blom-Cooper, fashion designer Jasper Conran, singer/songwriter Bo Brudenell-Bruce, Olympic medallist horsewoman Zara Phillips and historian Jonathan Gathorne-Hardy.

As we've said before, it's difficult to find fault with Port Regis. It has sometimes been seen as the preserve of the very rich but in reality children come from a wide variety of backgrounds. Scholarships and means-tested bursaries on offer too. The pupils we met clearly love the place and as a parent told us: 'If anyone is going to bring out what your child is good at, Port Regis will.'

Prior Park College

Linked with The Paragon School

    129

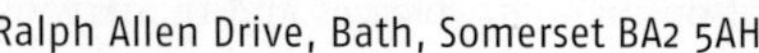

Ralph Allen Drive, Bath, Somerset BA2 5AH

Ages 11–18 **Pupils** 617 **Sixth form** 189 **Boarders** 108 full, 33 weekly, 7 flexi boarders **RC**

Fees: Day £15,000 – £16,995; Boarding £20,745 – £30,945 pa

01225 831000
www.priorparkcollege.com/

Head master: Since 2009, James Murphy-O'Connor MA (Oxon) PGCE (40s). Historian, married to Ali with whom he has four children, all former or current students. Educated at St Benedict's, Ealing. Degree at Greyfriars Hall, Oxford, PGCE at Peterhouse, Cambridge. Thence to Stamford followed by Sherborne, where he was a housemaster. First headship was the brand new Sherfield. Says 'Prior Park is in my DNA' and justly so, his father, Jim, was educated here along with all four uncles. Jim's younger brother Cardinal Cormac is the retired Archbishop of Westminster and still engages with the religious life of the school. JMO'C is a fan of F Scott Fitzgerald and Thomas Hardy, plus Picasso's 1920s art. Passionate Tottenham Hotspur and Ireland rugby fan. Enjoys retreating to the mountains and wild Atlantic beaches of his beloved County Mayo with his dalmador (dalmatian x labrador) Holly.

Students note admiringly that 'he knows your name and things about you from day one'. Score-lines both sporting and academic have risen measurably on his watch, but his legacy will be the emotional health of the school community. Nor is this a bandwagon response to recent alarm bells about teenage mental health issues. Perfect examples are a fledgling peer mentoring scheme and a give-something-back enterprise originated by sixth formers and empowered by JMO'C. All the parents we spoke to said it was the pastoral care and evident happiness of the community that got them reaching for their registration form.

P

Prior Park delivers, says the head, a rounded education. Lots of heads say this. When they do, raise an eyebrow as we did, for this is an inexact term. The way to find out what it really means is to investigate whether, down on the shop floor, teachers and students are walking the talk. What we found by dint of interrogation is that they most emphatically do. Yes, they echo and act out what their head says, but never parrot fashion – they like what their head wants, they really do. Work matters most, but everything else matters too. One parent told us that your typical Prior Park student is 'accomplished, compassionate and humble'. Of the head, another said, "Each student, honestly, matters to him,' and 'He's passionate about encouraging pupils to become rounded'.

Leaving in July 2019 to become principal of Haberdashers' Monmouth Schools.

Academic matters: No point in looking at government performance tables for raw data and comparison because this school, along with others, is boycotting them. Why? Because in the head's book there's more to education than exam results and performance tables take no account of 'creativity and inspiration', the only true measure is how far a school raises its students. He'd happily sign up for value-added league tables.

Headline figures vary little from year to year. In 2018 at GCSE, 53 per cent A*-A/9-7 grades; at A level 33 per cent A*/A, 65 per cent A*-B. So: the school does consistently well by its fairly broad intake. This is not an exam factory because there is no relenting in the commitment to all-round personal development. Neither is roundedness achieved at the expense of best-possible exam results – a neat trick which the school pulls off adroitly. There's pressure all right, but it's judiciously applied and it works because – this is the culture of the place – teachers know their students very well as people, they pick up on stress, lethargy and waywardness just like that and make time to give support. One student said, 'They always help when you're finding it difficult and get you back for a bit of tuition to help you through.' Another said, 'No teacher here would ever turn down a request for help'. The PHSCE programme is substantial and delivered with purpose.

Prep (homework) is supervised up to sixth form and the relatively long day (no Saturday school) means that you can break the back of it before you get home. Parents like this: 'There's usually not all that much to do at home so we can relax together as a family'. As you age it increasingly spills over, of course. There's currently a curriculum review in progress which aims to fine tune already estimable value-added scores. Having rejected the International Baccalaureate, they aim now to offer a bespoke version. The outcome the head seeks is 'an educational framework that enshrines our values.'

No statemented students accepted, but SEND provision supports milder SENs and intervenes when disparity emerges between a student's potential and ongoing achievement, or a student needs, say, organisational strategies or exam-stress support. Extends to students who develop mental health issues. Parents speak well of the expert sensitivity of the support given to their children. Mobility impaired students accepted where possible, but the school's architecture is a constraint.

Games, options, the arts: Sport, says the head, is 'one of the things we do'. Puts it in its place nicely, neither bigging it up nor doing it down. Parents like the way the school 'encourages everyone to give it all a go regardless of ability.' Hockey's what they do best in shop-window terms (national champions 2016). Netball is strong, rugby has an ex-England international coach, the rest competitively respectable given the size of each year's intake. Spacious playing fields, plentiful Astroturf. Sport for all, they say, greatest involvement by the greatest number, borne out by number of teams per sport sent forth to battle for their school every Saturday – around 10 on a good day. Individuals regularly play at regional and international level. One of the lessons we learn from sport, they say, is humility. That's so Prior Park. No, it's emphatically not a philosophy of loser takes all – they love to win. Sports centre, source of great pride, includes multi-sport gym, fitness suite, you name it. It's been a boon for the less sporty types.

Art and design happen in and around a refurbed dorm. Fine art good, photography especially strong just now as is textiles. Healthy numbers, decent results. Design technology in a good place, partnerships with local industries, lots of energy input from staff. A bit boy heavy but efforts being made to bring in the girls.

Music universally praised. Inspirational head of music also performs with singing group Opus Anglicanum. No elitism here when it comes to genre: anything goes from Gabrieli to grime. In cases of indie genres his smart ploy is to offer 'hands-off facilitation' thus enabling students to retain ownership of their sounds. High-end choral tradition longstanding and outstanding, biennial opera, multiplicity of ensembles, concerts formal and informal, for they love to go live and give others 'an experience of the sublime'. Two, yes two, musicals every year, all singing, all dancing – one parent said, 'Never a duty date, I simply can't believe the standard they reach'. Music here reaches all parts and catches up those who never knew they could. There's an inter-house music competition including student-rehearsed house song in which everyone sings and thereafter dwells on, marvelling fondly, for the rest of the year. A level numbers small, but of these a good number go on to top music colleges. Chapel choir is 90 per cent day students who come in every Sunday to sing at mass. What does that tell you?

Drama's right up there with music (let's call it a dead heat). Up to 14 productions of all sorts a year, much of it high-end stuff. Staff (superb) all come from professional theatre, that's what makes the difference. Fabulous Julian Slade theatre (1993) largely funded by Cameron Mackintosh's Foundation – he's a former student – palpably redolent of the magic created in it down the years by dint of passion, sweat, discipline, creativity and self-discovery. It's the real thing all right. Mackintosh also funded the excellent dance studio.

You get to do your after-school activities in school here. Recreational options, both lunchtime and after lessons, are multifarious and eclectic, embracing a diversity of endeavours from tricky physics to knit-and-natter – more than 60 to choose from. Saturday (morning) Active programme spans street dance and cookery. There's a CCF – voluntary sign-up from year 8 upwards – and DofE. There's even an equestrian team.

Sixth formers have their own after-school (ad)ventures. They concoct a social programme – film nights, music nights, BBQs etc. The charities committee coordinates competitive fundraising for good causes and the best house wins a cup. Then there's Prior Concern, which sends forth students to do their bit for the homeless, nursery-age children and the elderly. Catholic values in action.

Boarding: Some 160 students board from age 11, around a third of them girls. Of these, around 50 are weekly and flexi boarders. Compulsory residential course early in year 7 and team building day for year 8 students underpin community values. Roughly 60 full time boarders are international students. Stopover beds for day pupils. We had initial reservations about the boys' accommodation in St Paul's – gorgeous as the building may be on the outside, its bigness seemed inimical to snugness on the inside. This is an adult perception; the students reckon it does very nicely. Boys live alongside residential staff and their families.

Girls occupy the unarguably cosier Priory nearby. Prep is supervised by a teacher. Weekend activities, the bugbear of any boarding regime, continually addressed. Mass on Sundays compulsory. To be honest we wondered about the head of boys' boarding being an ex-Marine – until we met him. Bit of a martinet? No way. He's a man who understands the vital importance of addressing individuality in all its manifestations.

Background and atmosphere: The stunning grade 1 listed Palladian mansion, set on a hill overlooking Bath, was built by quarry owner Ralph Allen to advertise the golden glories of Bath stone. The estate was purchased by Bishop Baines in 1829 and first opened as a school in 1830. Run by the Christian Brothers until the 1980s, it's now under lay management. Inside, 17th century architectural grandeur doesn't always adapt readily to the needs of a 21st century school and can play the part of an awkward host. 'Don't agree,' say the students as you fight for breath up an endless spiral staircase; 'it's quirky, it's part of the charm'. A parent concurred: 'Yes, all right, it's a bit shabby in places but in the nicest way – a bit basic but kids love it.' Lovely chapel, lovely name, Our Lady of the Snows, used also for weekly assemblies – all get in, just. Science block purpose built.

Refined architecture notwithstanding, the social climate here isn't the least snooty; this is a down to earth place where ordinary people go to school, a place whose unpretentious personality answers the values of the sort of parent who celebrates 'a school that doesn't set itself apart from the city but participates in local events'.

Pastoral care, well-being and discipline: In a Catholic school with 65 per cent non-Catholics, Mr Murphy O'Connor unabashedly decrees Catholic values of kindness, service and 'being the person God wants you to be'. None of these values is objectionable to parents of a broadly secular disposition. Discussion of topics like abortion and homosexuality hears out and respects all points of view.

There's a culture here of looking out for each other, teachers for students, older students for younger ones – one parent said, 'they got to know my daughter very quickly and genuinely appreciated her as a person'. Intervention is prompt. One parent said, 'It is a fantastic strength of the school that they are so diligent with the students' well-being. This doesn't all come about by wishing it so or generating policy docs, it derives from expectations, watchfulness, example-setting and buy-in. It works because it's hard work.'

Boundaries are set and are the same for everyone, 'There is no room for anyone to bend the rules,' said one parent. This has created a school of pupils who take pride in how they are being perceived by everyone.' Another said: 'We are constantly amazed by the school's ability to encourage and maintain an exquisite level of behaviour and compliance without the need to instil enormous amounts of discipline.' Major concern over any issues raised by social media; sexting, by way of example, is a regular assembly topic and parents join in the discussion. One parent commented '... it's a constant conversation.'

Pupils and parents: Co-ed since 1982, almost 50:50, boys slightly more numerous. Common rooms are same-sex; lessons and dining mixed. Roughly a third of pupils are from Catholic families. Sizeable contingent of parents are dahn-from-Londoners, who have colonised Bath in recent years – yes, even raggle-taggle Walcot Street has capitulated to the hipsters. Monocultural tendency is mitigated by international students, never more than 10 per cent of the roll. To cope with demand from overseas the school has just launched Prior Park Gibraltar. With two outstanding (Ofsted) state schools and four rival independents in Bath alone, the education market locally is working well, with competitive pressures driving up standards and heightening distinctiveness.

For day students, buses from all corners up to 30 miles away. Parental involvement welcomed: twice-monthly coffee mornings hosted by Parents Of Prior, which even has its own private Facebook page. Regular parent forums with the head so he can hear what you think. Weekly newsletter from the head. Listings of parent phone numbers by year group (voluntary) a nice touch. Business-like, highly functional website. Parents really like the 'wonderful feeling of community'.

Entrance: Selective. Don't miss the application deadline – details on the website. Tests for 11+ entrants; CE and scholarship at 13. At any other time, report and interview. Year 7 entrants from, equally, local state schools and Paragon Junior. At year 9 a wodge from the prep school in Cricklade plus a smattering from other preps and international schools. Around 20 join post-GCSE from other schools, telling you something about the strength of the sixth form, whose entrants need a minimum six GCSEs with As in A level subjects preferred.

Exit: Small exodus post-GCSE, most to vocational courses. Sixth form leavers are Russell groupies, most of them, Exeter, Manchester and Cardiff especially popular. Good and varied balance of arts and sciences. In 2018, four to Oxbridge, two medics and two to US universities on tennis scholarships.

Money matters: Customary range of scholarships up to a value of around 25 per cent, more in deserving cases. Bursaries can be standalone or added to a scholarship. Head says he likes to help where he can, and in another clear-cut case of walking the talk an examination of the accounts reveals that the school awards roughly half as much again in bursaries (as a percentage of income) as other Bath independents. Some carry-over scholarships from prep school. Discounts for siblings. Lunch bundled with fees but not transport. Taking account of the long school day and the 4-6pm activities programme, good value for money. The head says, 'We recognise that we have a lot of working parents who stretch themselves to afford the fees. We don't want to let them down.'

Remarks: Confident in its Catholic values, happy in its own skin and distinctive in its commitment to a genuinely all-round education, this is a school which inspires esteem and affection in equal measure.

Queen Elizabeth's Hospital

Linked with Queen Elizabeth's Hospital Junior School

130

Berkeley Place, Clifton, Bristol BS8 1JX

Ages 11–18 **Pupils** 640 **Sixth form** 196 (43 girls)

Fees: £14,406 pa

01179 303040
www.qehbristol.co.uk

Headmaster: Since 2000, Stephen Holliday MA (early 50s). Educated at Batley Grammar School and Jesus College, Cambridge, where he read history. Worked for British Rail as an operations manager in Dundee and Glasgow before hearing call to return to school life. Six years at Dean Close in Cheltenham, where he became a boarding housemaster, then joined Giggleswick School as head of history. Ventured across the border to become deputy head (pastoral) at Queen Elizabeth's Grammar School in Blackburn before moving to current role. Since 2013, he has been treasurer of HMC, which represents the heads of many independent schools.

At QEH, he has overseen closing of boarding and opening of junior school in the same premises, developed a new sixth form centre and a new science/arts block. He is a Methodist preacher, and parents describe him as 'honest' and 'forthright'. Married to Gail, a teacher, and they have two sons.

Mr Holliday loves watching all sport, especially cricket, and is a keen fan of Leeds Utd. He has presided over a change from the previous rugby-dominated culture at the school to one that gives equal weight to rugby and football. 'Market forces,' he says. 'Boys just want to play football.' Admits he does not remember all boys' names, although he still teaches year 7 at the start and end of their first year to help get to know them. He has recently started teaching A level history, 'a complete indulgence', he admits.

Leaving in July 2020.

Academic matters: Boys sit 10 GCSEs; school has moved to IGCSEs in sciences and languages as well as English and maths, for rigour, better preparation for A level, and more consistent marking scheme. 'Boys enjoy them more and they are more fun to teach,' says head. Maths and French setted from year 7, English from year 10. Class sizes 22-25 until year 9 then much smaller. In 2018, 68 per cent A*-A/9-7 at I/GCSE; 48 per cent A*/A (75 per cent A*-B) at A level. High proportion of gifted and talented pupils; enrichment programmes for all abilities.

Maths is strong throughout school and is most popular A level subject – boys are 'proud of being maths geeks'. Those who take maths and further maths dub them 'hard maths and double hard maths'. Separate sciences from year 7. More than half of sixth form studying one or more science subjects. New science block increases number of science labs and there will be more space for the art department, music and design tech. Spanish most popular language choice, Latin on offer at GCSE and A level and some study ancient Greek A level in their lunch hours. Small numbers enable QEH to tailor curriculum to individuals in response to occasional demand for a subject such as photography or music tech. Thinking skills important too, with several completing the EPQ. QEH is pioneer of Future Problem-Solving, a six-step project to solve a global issue.

School says recession has affected A level choices, with many having a sharper focus on career prospects and aiming for medicine, science, engineering. Rise in business studies and economics and fall in arts, music, drama, languages. Head 'hopes they bounce back' and notes that some students 'still delightfully go with the flow'. Concern too about changing university landscape, with worries that unconditional offers are unhelpful to boys. Detailed Oxbridge preparation valued highly.

Good library, with boy-friendly titles and a wide range of periodicals. Regular reading weeks, where homework is replaced by sharing of books. Otherwise, homework goes from an hour a night in year 7 to two hours in year 11. Parents rate 'high standard of teachers across the board'. 'Staff are inspirational, and aspirational for the boys,' said one.

Games, options, the arts: Aim is for students to be not only well qualified, but well educated, hence phenomenal range of activities. Sport has always been a strength, but these days is now just one element in a wide-ranging offer. One term rugby, one term football in winter; athletics, cricket and tennis in summer (sports ground at Failand currently being upgraded to include 3G pitch). Almost half of boys opt for bronze DofE and up to 30 a year achieve gold. School teams highly successful in Ten Tors. Boys encouraged to take risks, 'They do allow them to do quite crazy things sometimes,' a parent said. Extreme example is Lewis Clarke, who was permitted to abandon his GCSE studies for two months to become, at 16, the youngest person to walk to the South Pole.

Has long been known as a musical school. At least half a dozen boys in National Youth Orchestra, one student won a place at the Yehudi Menuhin School. Lessons offered in almost every instrument – even bagpipes. Annual Battle of Bands and Unplugged events. Choirs are of high standard and boys are proud to be involved, even up to sixth form. Choir is only occasion when traditional bluecoat uniform is worn. Old boys recall this with pride but some sons less keen on 'all that old stuff'. Debating also popular and successful.

Many opportunities to perform in school's 220-seat, purpose-built theatre. New £3.5m development has increased space for art and music, including new ensemble rehearsal space, practice room and a ceramic studio.

Many trips, both those related to curriculum and extracurricular activities – WW1 battlefields, Iceland, Pyrenees, Slovenia, Morocco, China, Himalayas etc. Links with Bristol girls' schools for social and learning activities including cookery, quizzes, salsa dancing and philosophy.

Background and atmosphere: Imposing grade 2 listed Victorian building on Brandon Hill. 'Looks intimidating from the outside,' one pupil observed. Hogwarts-style features inside too, with stone staircase leading to 'headmaster's landing'. Atmosphere is overwhelmingly friendly and respectful. Total of 60-70 staff, including several who've been there more than two decades and some recent former pupils who have returned as teachers. Parents value the stability, but head also likes to see young teachers move on and further their careers. Long-serving staff note there are many more female staff now, and boys are no longer addressed by their surnames.

Wifi everywhere (not an easy task in such a building), laptops, whiteboards, projectors where needed. Head is considering more use of iPads and students' own devices, but says he will 'only move in that direction when I am sure it will improve teaching and learning'. As he points out, exam system is still paper-based. One good example of using technology is where dyslexic boys photograph the board with their iPhones so they can have more time to study it.

Food is good. Meals prepared in £400,000 new kitchen and eaten in the hall, where a hand-sanitiser adds a somewhat incongruous though probably necessary note. School believes strongly in a healthy diet and 'boy-sized portions' to fuel learning in and out of lessons. The Yard, one of the biggest tiled areas in Europe, provides an excellent space for running around.

Pupils belong to one of four houses – Bird's, Carr's, Hartnell's and Ramsey's – named after benefactors, and are intensely loyal. School's motto is 'While we have time, let us do good' (dum tempus habemus, operemur bonum), and charity fundraising and help for others are major focuses. Pupils listen to reading at a state primary as well as helping out at QEH Juniors.

Pastoral care, well-being and discipline: Prides itself on 'strong but unobtrusive pastoral care' and parents and boys confirm that this is very much the case. School unashamedly promotes 'boys being boys', but at the same time seeks to develop pupils' emotional intelligence. 'They embrace each child and what he has got to offer. The school has met both my boys' very different needs in a superb way. I only wish my daughter could go there – though that would mean the school changing, and I don't want that,' said a parent (school sixth form now co-ed). Boys are trained well to participate in peer mentoring, peer support and 'ebuddies' schemes, which are highly valued by all. 'It is not a monoculture. There is not an unpleasantly masculine atmosphere,' said a mum, who admitted she had previously been against single sex schooling.

The philosophy that boys should be 'stretched not stressed' also appears to work well. 'They have got tabs on them but in a very subtle way. They seem to know when to push the buttons to get them to perform well – in time but not too soon,' a parent observed.

School rules are short, simple and sensible – from time-honoured 'all roofs out of bounds' to the 21st century 'no social networking posting that affects well-being of another boy or brings school into disrepute'. Not to mention the classic 'facial hair must not be grown unless specific permission has been obtained from the headmaster'.

One parent praised help for son's dyslexia; another said support used to be patchy – but unanimous plaudits for the way the school prepares boys for the outside world. Sixth form offers sessions on cooking, sewing, budgeting, car and bike maintenance and healthy eating.

Pupils and parents: More robust academic profile makes QEH a serious option for the sons (and sixth form daughters) of Bristol's professionals, academics and medics. Demographic has changed somewhat and 85 per cent pay full fees; ending Saturday lessons also attracted a wider range of families. School aims for a wide social mix, and there are more pupils from modest backgrounds than might be imagined. Some boys with mild Asperger's, ADHD, dyslexia. Former pupils, known as 'Old Elizabethans', include inventor and motion picture pioneer William Freise-Greene, screenwriter Ashley Pharoah, sports commentators Simon Mann and Jonathan Pearce and racing driver Dino Zamparelli.

Entrance: About 150 applications a year for 75-100 places at 11. Entrance exams in verbal and non-verbal reasoning, maths and English. There's also an interview. A handful of pupils also admitted at 13+. Entrants to the sixth form (including girls) need minimum of six B/6s at GCSE (higher for external applicants).

Exit: Almost all (some 90 per cent) stay for sixth form. School will discuss with parents and pupil well in advance if this is unlikely to be the best option. At 18, most progress to leading universities, sometimes after a gap year. Four to Oxbridge and seven medics in 2018; other popular universities include London, Cardiff, Exeter and Edinburgh.

Money matters: When it first opened in 1590 with a Charter from Queen Elizabeth 1, the school was specifically charged with the education of poor children and orphans. Nowadays, only 15 per cent of pupils receive some financial help. No bursaries in junior school but two academic scholarships offered in year 3. Scholarships for music, sport and academic ability are worth 10-50 per cent of senior school fees. Some bursaries are awarded, with old boys increasingly supporting the school, in some cases funding 100 per cent of a needy pupil's education. Head would like to offer all bursaries, rather than scholarships, but says he is prevented from doing so by the 'Bristol market'.

Remarks: It is rare to find a school that so accurately reflects all the claims in its impressive literature. QEH has adapted to meet the needs of each age but remains true to its history.

Queen Elizabeth's Hospital Junior School

Linked with Queen Elizabeth's Hospital

Q

Berkeley Place, Clifton, Bristol BS8 1JX

Ages 7–11 **Pupils** 100

Fees: £9,654 pa

0117 930 3068
www.qehbristol.co.uk

Headmaster: Since September 2017, David Kendall, previously deputy head at Newton Prep in London. History degree from St David's University College, Lampeter, PGCE afrom Roehampton Institute and studying for a masters in educational leadership. He has taught at a variety of preps in London and the south east, including the role of head of upper section at Westminster Under School. Married with three children and two stepchildren, and has a wide variety of sporting and other interests.

Entrance: Main intakes are years 3 and 5, but increasing demand to join in year 6. Some children come from independent schools but most from local state primaries. During assessment days, boys work with head on maths, reading, writing and verbal reasoning. 'We hate the idea of a formal exam for children of that age. We're looking for potential – a spark of inquisitiveness and imagination.' No bursaries but two academic scholarships offered in year 3. No SEN statemented children on roll; a few with mild dyslexia. A joint venture co-ed pre-prep school at Redland High Junior School now takes 3-7 year olds.

Exit: Almost all progress to senior school via entrance exam. Parents warned well in advance if this does not look like the best route for their son.

Remarks: Boys will be boys – that's the starting point for the school's entire approach. Curriculum geared to capturing interests. 'We have tried to develop a prep school feel, with an emphasis on preparing them for senior school,' says the school, adding that the style and teaching are 'very practical.'

Year 3 pupils mainly learn with class teacher. From year 4 upwards, subject specialist teachers for maths, English and science. French taught by senior school staff and some senior staff help out with coaching games. Years 3 and 4 have cross-curricular topics, incorporating history, geography, RE and ICT and integrating it with literacy, numeracy, and creative subjects. Years 5 and 6 have some of these subjects taught discretely, but also follow topic themes, including Azerbaijan and China as well as the Romans and Second World War.

ICT is up-to-date but unobtrusive. Maths lessons largely follow national curriculum. English too, though teachers say 'we are not confined by it'. Shakespeare and poetry feature strongly. Lots of creative writing, again based on active experiences, using Pie Corbett's Talk for Writing. Reading is regarded as key. Regular reading weeks, when homework is dropped in favour of half an hour's reading every night. Pupils participate enthusiastically in in-house reading competitions, involving reading and reviewing books. Boys praise the library for being well stocked with titles of interest, including 'speedy reads' and 'riveting reads'. Years 3 and 4 generally get 20 minutes' homework a night, while years 5 and 6 get 30 minutes. SENCo shared with senior school.

Great atmosphere of creativity throughout the school, with excellent use made of the split-level classrooms. Music and drama are strong – lively rehearsals for the house singing competition were taking place during our visit. Boys learn a host of instruments including piano, flute, clarinet, saxophone, trombone, cello and drums and have the chance to play in groups and an orchestra. There's a mind-boggling range of clubs, which take place before school, at lunchtimes and after school and include problem-solving, brain-boosting, Lego, debating, general knowledge, chess, Italian and robotics as well as arts, music and sports.

Boys use the sports ground at Failand (a 10-minute coach ride away) twice a week for rugby, football and cricket, for which major developments are in the pipeline. Facilities shared with Bristol City Football Academy.

Competition is encouraged 'but is not the be-all and end-all.' Outdoor space includes a climbing wall. Boys have access to the huge senior school yard at break-times to run around and let off steam, but any who prefer to stay indoors and read can do so. One parent said the confined site and lack of green space was 'not great – though none of my boys has ever complained.' There is a garden where year 3 boys grow vegetables, a grassed area and brand new outdoor classroom for forest school, inter alia.

The school opens on to Brandon Hill, a Civil War battle site, and is within walking distance of the SS Great Britain, Bristol Museum and Art Gallery, the Royal West of England Academy, We the Curious science centre and the M Shed museum. Trips further afield include an Easter ski visit. Outdoor pursuits popular, with year 5 and 6 boys taking part in the school's own QE Award, similar to D of E, but tailored to their age group.

To help working parents, a free breakfast club operates from 7.45am each day. No charge for after-school care until 5pm, though there is from 5 to 6pm. The school has a deal with the multi-storey car park, so parents can drop off and collect children easily and safely.

Junior pupils eat their meals in the senior school dining hall. 'We say grace every day,' a pupil told us. The school says it has a Christian foundation and welcomes boys of any or no religious faith.

Staff, parents and pupils value the family atmosphere and careful pastoral approach, which helps develop confident, well-rounded boys. 'The staff are sensitive and they really know the boys,' a parent told us. 'They help them, but in a subtle way.' School has links with girls' schools like Redmaids' High and Badminton but it is the single-sex education that is the big draw for parents. 'It means they can have a go at anything without any constraints or worries – they don't have to feel embarrassed,' we were told.

One mother added: 'I had never intended my sons to go to a boys' school. They don't have a sister. But QEH has worked for them so well and I have no regrets. Most of all, it's really good fun.'

Q

Queen's College (Taunton)

Linked with Queen's College Junior School

Trull Road, Taunton, Somerset TA1 4QS

Ages 11–18 **Pupils** 495 **Sixth form** 132 **Boarders** 203 full

Fees: Day £15,300– £18,450; Boarding £25,965 – £31,980 pa

01823 340830
www.queenscollege.org.uk

Head Teacher: Since September 2016, Dr Lorraine Earps, previously deputy and then acting head here (following the sudden departure of previous head Chris Alcock in May 2016). Degree in chemistry and biochemistry from Southampton, plus a doctorate in protein chemistry; taught in the state sector for six years; has also been head of chemistry at Stockport Grammar and director of studies at Withington Girls. Married with a son.

Academic matters: Not particularly academically selective, and latest exam results dropped off somewhat in 2018, possibly a function of more rigorous GCSE and A level demands. At GCSE, 43 per cent of grades were A*-A/9-7; at A level 56 per cent were B or above, with 33 per cent A*/A. Pressure to achieve top grades is not the way Queen's goes about things. Class sizes average 17, and there's a choice of 24 subjects for GCSE and A level. A modern foreign language is compulsory at GCSE; business studies and ethics & philosophy more unusual options. Students are grouped by ability for core subjects but mixed for options. At A level, option blocks are changed yearly in an effort to accommodate individual subject choices and the school's flexibility at the start of sixth form while A level choices bed down is appreciated. Critical thinking, EPQ and TUG (top universities group) offered alongside these. One parent we spoke to chose Queen's specifically for its academics, another because her child 'did not shine academically, but has not been made to feel inferior by staff or pupils'. Stand-out subjects for the students are geography, chemistry and maths – 'but the sport and music are also amazing', our guides reported.

SEN support is provided through an integrated approach with the learning development unit (sic), where an electronic register shared with teaching staff records and tracks the needs of the high-ish proportion of SEN students. 'We haven't and don't wish to acquire dyslexia-friendly status,' says school, but it appears to serve its SEN population well, maths support in particular provided by the same teacher throughout the school, using traditional methods. Active EAL programme for the 100 or so overseas students.

Games, options, the arts: Sport is important – more a question of a game for all than winning at all costs. Just the place for sportsmen and women, but 'equally OK for incredibly anti-sports daughter,' according to one mother, who added that it is 'much more geared towards music, drama and the arts than the other Taunton schools'. Nonetheless, Queen's excels at sports and now has academies for both hockey and cricket (for which Taunton is famed), not just for its own promising players, but also for high flyers locally. Thirty acres of pitches, two Astros, an indoor pool – swimming is a strength here – and well-equipped sports hall make for a comprehensive offering. 'Rugby and hockey have been fundamental to my son's time here,' stated one mother. Off site, riding, sailing, canoeing, climbing and caving in nearby Mendips suits those with less of an eye for a ball, but everyone is encouraged to explore the great outdoors: almost all do at least bronze D of E, and a high number complete gold.

Performing arts shine too – school boasts largest performing space(s) of any school in the south west: two theatres and a studio big/smart enough for more intimate productions, and uses expertise of Somerset College's specialist film and TV make-up course. Recent shows include Seussical, Coram Boy, Macbeth and Storm Boy, adapted from the book by the head of drama, a published playwright. A massively ambitious arts festival, Quartz, takes place at school each October, which brings in actors, musicians, dancers and artists of all persuasions for performances and workshops. Dancers extremely well looked after in terms of facilities and the school's own academy of performing arts, which attracts the likes of Birmingham City Ballet to give classes; strong on contemporary dance too, such as street jazz. Musicians jolly fortunate, too, to have a dedicated concert hall as part of the music school, complete with Steinway and 30 stop organ, plus music tech facilities. Choirs and ensembles abound – we were intrigued by the 'exuberant arrangements' apparently played by Sound School, a sax ensemble. Trips for local and international (recently Germany and Italy) performance and trophies from Taunton Festival round off an extensive, if traditional, musical offering.

Art of all kinds is housed in a gorgeous art school overlooking the cricket pitches; students are exposed to all media, techniques and materials so that they are well prepared for GCSE art and design. Painting, ceramics and textiles are areas of particular expertise, but all benefit from trips here and abroad (Barcelona and New York, inter alia) as well as the influx of visiting practitioners at the annual Quartz Festival. But despite the range of diversions to choose from, some parents still feel it's too narrow, and that a shove could usefully be applied to the idler students to sign up to more of them.

Boarding: More than a third of students board, and some parents, at least, appreciate the finishing time of 4pm, which suits those who come daily. The absence of Saturday school does not mean a fallow day, however: au contraire, there's a full programme of activities or rehearsals in the morning, with sports fixtures and expeditions in the afternoon.

We felt some of the senior boarding accommodation was on the cheerless side of acceptable; doubtless legally compliant, but the bare walls and lack of personal touches in some of the dorms was a bit bleak – and a bath list a relic from an earlier age. The continuing refurbishment cannot progress fast enough. That said, the evident warmth of the staff and close friendships between year groups compensate for any dreary living quarters awaiting tarting up. Food generally reckoned to be good: a tasty choice of stew with Yorkshire pudding, cheese and onion pie, breaded chicken or salad bar the day we visited is not, though, perhaps enough to satisfy every palate, witness the group of Asian girls we saw tucking into noodles in one of the house kitchens... The boarding community enjoys eating together in the evenings and the tweaking of boarders' teas with extra carbs and meat to suit sportsmen/women is appreciated.

Background and atmosphere: Originally and fabulously named the West of England Wesleyan Proprietary Grammar School and founded in 1843 by local Methodists dissatisfied by the kind of schooling accessible to nonconformists, Queen's was renamed for Queen Victoria's golden jubilee in 1887. A run of imposing Victorian gothic buildings redolent of the timeline along a stretch of road leading out of Taunton to the village of Trull; modern additions are concentrated behind the original buildings, leaving a view across the extensive sports facilities to the distant Quantocks. A super sixth form centre has been created from a former rather ugly civil service club, now greatly appreciated by its new occupants who enjoy areas for silent study, as well as space to chill, chat and rustle up those staples of British education – toast and coffee. In the view of one parent, it gives students 'independence, self-respect and responsibility'. Sharing the same stretch of road and major facilities as Queen's College, if not its architectural merits, is the junior school.

Founding Methodist values still prop the place up today: tolerance, friendliness and a lack of pretension underpinned by Christian principles and practice define it; a full time chaplain is on the staff. Individuals are valued, quirks and diversity welcomed: 'We looked at several schools,' one mother told us 'but this one had a good feel and was right for both my very different children. My son was initially shy but has really grown into himself'. Other parents praise the school's 'gentle approach' which builds confidence in the diffident, as well as 'the lack of social/wealth/class issues'. Hurrah for that.

Pastoral care, well-being and discipline: Pastoral care highly rated by students and parents alike, from the tutors to the house staff. Close attention is paid to every child – 'We notice if anyone is off-colour'. No in-school counsellor, as staff feel that students would be 'naturally suspicious of anyone from inside school'; the view from one girl we spoke to was that she wouldn't know who to talk to if she had a problem – 'there are just so many options'. An extensive reward system recognises not only achievement but also students who have triumphed over adversity in some form. Discipline was not a word we heard much – we suspect that it doesn't rear its head that often – but 'to incur the disappointment of the head is a crushing blow,' one mother told us. Prefects have the power to administer 'fatigues' for minor infringements of rules or poor behaviour.

Pupils and parents: Mostly pretty local (Somerset, Devon and Dorset), augmented by a contingent of overseas boarders such as Forces' children and an array of nationalities, with Russian and SE Asian predominating. 'Queen's wouldn't suit very competitive sporty, hearty, Sloaney families,' we were reliably informed. Parents tend to be loyal and to involve themselves in the life of the school, but some think school communications need a kick in the posterior: poor grammar, six copies of the same email just two examples.

Entrance: About 60 per cent of senior school entrants come from the junior school without let or hindrance, unless they are trying for a scholarship or have specific learning difficulties. Others arrive from local primaries at 11, yet more from the odd prep school at 13+ and all sit tests in English, maths and verbal reasoning. At sixth form, the bar looks quite low at five GCSEs above a C/5 with 'preferably A*-B/9-6' for subjects chosen for A level, but hopefuls are also required to take two papers in their likely A level subject choices. Children from overseas take a paper in English as an additional language.

Exit: Some leave after GCSE but almost all sixth form leavers go on to their chosen degree courses up and down the land – Warwick, UCL, UWE, Essex and Harper Adams popular. Two to Oxbridge in 2018 and three medics, with five off overseas. Some gap years. Notable alumni include Sir Nick Harvey (long-standing MP for N Devon), Lord Widgery (former Lord Chief Justice of England and Wales), and clutch of other luminaries across the professions, armed forces and arts, including a prime minister of Newfoundland and Elephant Bill, an army officer known for his work in Burma in World War 2.

Money matters: Fees about 10 per cent lower than comparable schools for UK students, but work out about the same for those from overseas. Lunch is charged separately for day students; learning support, EAL and any kind of extra tuition cost extra. 'Singing lessons are a bit steep,' remarked one parent. Usual range of scholarships on offer, more bountiful than many at a maximum of 25 per cent for a major academic award. Sibling discounts more generous than some we have seen, too.

Remarks: A Taunton institution which distinguishes itself from the local competition by its family feel, yet continues to cut the academic, sporting and artistic mustard year after year, Queen's is a welcoming, inclusive, unpretentious place which could sell itself better. A lick of paint here and there wouldn't go amiss either.

Queen's College Junior School

Q

Linked with Queen's College (Taunton)

Trull Rd, Taunton, Somerset TA1 4QP

Ages 0–11 **Pupils** 175 **Boarders** 31 (from year 3)

Fees: Day £6,450 – £12,990; Boarding £14,655 – £26,670 pa

01823 278928
www.queenscollege.org.uk

Headmistress: Since 2010, Tracey Khodabandehloo BEd MEd PGDip (50s). The name must be the most exotic in all the GSG canon, but it soon comes rolling off the tongues of all but perhaps the tiniest children. Brought up and educated locally, Mrs Khodabandehloo was a parent at the school when the headship came up; she was pursuing a successful career as a state school head of 15 years' standing, looking not to join the independent sector, but 'when a job came up in the school I passionately believed in, I had to take it'.

She has enjoyed breaking free from narrowness in the maintained sector: of the curriculum and measures of success, most of which seem to be data-driven, and has revelled in resetting the curricular bounds. That said, there are, in her view, benefits which could usefully be employed by independent schools, such as pitting their academic data against national norms and developing formal professional links with teacher training institutions.

Warm, motherly and compassionate, Mrs Khodabandehloo believes in, embodies and inculcates the family atmosphere and strong relationships for which all different parts of Queen's is famous, whilst prioritising an environment where learners are motivated and learning flourishes. Her three children are now grown and in fruitful careers of their own – one setting up a business using the skills learnt at Queen's business department. Spare time might see her riding in the Quantocks or perfecting her craft as a barista in a local church coffee shop; holidays are spent travelling, especially to Barbados.

Entrance: Essentially non-selective at all points of entry into the nursery and junior school, but low-key assessments are carried out in the classroom setting during taster and assessment days.

Exit: Mostly and automatically to the senior school at the end of year 6 (currently 95 per cent); standardised scores in English and maths are passed on for setting purposes. In very rare cases, doubtful candidates are identified in year 5 and gently encouraged (and indeed supported) to look elsewhere.

Remarks: Sharing the same stretch of road and major facilities as Queen's College, if not its architectural merits, is the junior school. The fact that most of its pupils go on to the senior school at 11 means that air of fevered preparation for entrance exams to premier league independent schools is absent, and consequently that they can enjoy a more relaxed pace. But that doesn't mean lack of rigour (eg knowing up to 12x12 by the end of year 4) or breadth – they learn French from the off and the school prides itself on its specialist teachers. Younger pupils are taught largely by form teachers, but from year 5, subject teachers take over.

While Christian foundations underpin much of the religious and PHSE syllabi, we were impressed by the airtime given to other significant religions and their deities, prophets and manifestations. Independent and interlinked learning definitely encouraged, with topics spread across traditional subject boundaries. Classrooms are bright and busy with plenty to draw the eye – children's work included; good to see a science lab and art studio too. All pupils are screened for SEN on arrival and provision for the milder end of the spectrum is woven into the life of the school; we were told that even when the need for intervention had passed, pupils still revisited the learning development department. Key SEN personnel at each stage of a Queen's education liaise closely.

Sport is important – more a question of a game for all than winning at all costs. The junior school shares the Astro and pitches with the senior school, timetabled so that younger players are not trampled by the first XV, along with the gorgeous swimming pool adorned with its mosaic dragon. Plays and concerts take place in its own hall – performed with similar panache and enthusiasm as those at the senior school.

Boarders are accommodated in charming Cotlake House, a home for 8-13 year olds with a delightful family feel which crosses the transition between junior and senior parts of Queen's. We liked the handbook greatly, with its dedicated section on cultural differences for overseas boarders, stating an insistence on eating with a knife, fork and spoon, rather than (in some cases) more habitual chopsticks. Importance placed on emotional welfare comes cross very strongly, with regular liaison between staff and parents, particularly crucial when boarders below year 7 are not permitted a mobile or iPad; other methods of communication, such as good old-fashioned email, are made clear and there are communal in-house computers. Day pupils tend to be local, from families where education is prioritised, often taking two incomes to support it.

'Our parents expect the academic offering', the head confirmed, 'but much more than that: they want their children to be confident, effective, willing to have a go and to have a social conscience'. Queen's Junior is not, thankfully, an academic proving ground for the next pressured stage, but a place where 'We're really good at the individual – any parent wanting their child's passions, skills and talents unlocked should look no further,' as the head says – and we'd be inclined to agree. And don't lose sight of the fact that the senior school is no slouch academically either.

The Queen's School

City Walls Road, Chester CH1 2NN

Ages 4–19 Pupils 580 Sixth form 95

Fees: £9,351 – £13,341 pa

01244 312078
www.thequeensschool.co.uk

Headmistress: Since September 2018, Sue Wallace-Woodroffe, previously head of Princess Helena College in Hertfordshire. Degree from Edinburgh in biological sciences and genetics, then studied genetics at Cambridge and a masters in educational leadership and management at UCL. She has previously taught at Eltham College and been deputy head of Sedbergh School. She is a Cambridge double blue in athletics, ran for Britain and for Scotland and has represented her county in swimming and cross-country. She is married with two sons.

Head of lower school: Since September 2018, Iona Carmody MSc, previously head of pre-prep at the Prebendal School in Sussex.

Academic matters: One form entry with maximum 20 per class in infants, rising to 22 in juniors. Gentle, fluid setting from year 3 in maths and English, then more formal setting from year 5. Mandarin, French and Spanish are taught on a language carousel from reception to year 6. The enquiry-based Learning Challenge Curriculum used throughout the lower school to teach history, geography, art, design and religious studies. Curriculum is thematic in infants, with outdoor space used as much as possible. Specialist teachers for languages, music, PE, art, drama, ICT and ceramics. SEN children given help by three members of staff but head says they need to be 'bright children who can keep the pace.'

An academic school; 61 per cent A*/A grades at A level (85 per cent A*/B) and 67 per cent A*-A/9-7 at GCSE in 2018. Language provision is worth noting. All year 7 girls study Mandarin, with the option of continuing it in year 8 right up to A level if they wish. A trip to China is run every other year, subsidised by the Chinese Government's department of education. Main European language is Spanish, with Latin also taught.

Critical thinking in year 12 for everyone. One girl we spoke to felt exam results could feel 'like the be all and end all at times here,' but others felt that the pressure was manageable. Part time SENCo can offer one-to-one support if needed to a broad spectrum of SEN, although girls must be able to keep up with the fast pace of work. Own sixth form baccalaureate – A-levels, additional units of academic study, enrichment activities and the EPQ. Widely stocked library, spanning many rooms, with plenty of workspace, but some girls say its relatively early closing time of 4.15pm can be inconvenient.

Games, options, the arts: New sports pavilion with changing rooms, spectator space and kitchen opened by Olympic bronze medallist gymnast and old girl Beth Tweddle. Girls complain about the lack of sporting space but the school achieves success in both team and individual events. New fitness suite, tennis courts and Astroturf have been resurfaced and the school has recently introduced rowing and sailing.

Music and drama both popular. All year 7 girls encouraged to try different instruments and around two-thirds take individual tuition. Wide range of extracurricular clubs and activities, including podcasting and riding, with young journalists' club, St John Ambulance Badgers (programme for 5 to 10-year-olds), skipping and fencing for lower school.

School has introduced the Pre-U in art after teachers became frustrated with the subjectivity of examiners at A level. We saw some breathtaking artwork in the bright, airy studios in the school eaves.

Background and atmosphere: Founded in 1878 by the Dean of Chester to educate 'the daughters of the middle class.' Moved to its present location (once the site of the city gaol and house of correction) in 1882, a short distance from Chester racecourse. The school has expanded over the years as neighbouring houses and a hotel were bought. However, space is limited and any changes are encumbered by the need for archaeologists to hunt down Roman remains. Sixth form areas could do with a makeover.

Lower school is housed in two Victorian buildings with modern extensions. New reception building, Honeybee House, has increased facilities for play and learning. Large grounds enable the school to boast fantastic facilities, including a swimming pool (shared with senior girls), sports fields, netball court, science, art and cookery rooms. Our guides were extremely excited to show us the pet chickens they had incubated themselves. One mum told us: 'My daughter's experience is so broad here, but in a real practical sense. They do everything.'

Pastoral care, well-being and discipline: All new girls teamed with a peer buddy. Older pupils mentor younger ones. Sixth formers have the liberty of being able to pop into town for lunch. Pupils told us they feel comfortable talking to their tutor or head of year about any problems. A number of pupils we spoke to reported incidents of bullying via Facebook, mobiles and emails and some felt that the school didn't do enough to combat this. The school, however, feels it deals with such episodes firmly and this is backed up by the ISI inspection.

Pupils and parents: Mostly white and middle class, with a small percentage of British born minorities. Some foreign families brought to the UK by work. Most pupils live in Chester, but a good bus network brings pupils in from other parts of Cheshire, Warrington and the Wirral and 20 per cent from North Wales. Notable old girls include Vivienne Faull, the first woman to become Dean of an English cathedral, and Olympic gymnast Beth Tweddle.

Entrance: By informal assessment for entry into reception and formal assessment in English, maths and verbal reasoning for later entry. Head or her deputy visit all prospective reception class parents at home and the school has links with nurseries within a 40 mile radius to raise awareness of the school.

Around 50 per cent of senior school entrants from lower school, the rest from other preps and state primaries. Girls take 11+ exam in English, maths and verbal reasoning. Written reports from current schools are important and all candidates are interviewed.

Exit: No stressful exams for these lower school girls at 11 as they are virtually guaranteed a place at the senior school (any problems flagged up in year 5). A few leave to enter the state grammar school system. Transition is made as seamless as possible by getting the girls used to moving around for lessons, subject specialist teachers and mirroring senior school routines.

Queen's girls are very successful academically, with most making it to redbrick universities – almost all to first choice. Handful to Oxbridge most years (three in 2018, plus four medics, three dentists and a vet). Durham, Leeds, Newcastle, Manchester and Birmingham very popular. Steady trickle (around 20 per cent) at 16 to sixth form colleges or boarding.

Money matters: Small number of honorary scholarships are awarded to girls who perform exceptionally well in school's entrance exam. One Hastings bursary awarded every year and one Owen Jones bursary, with preference given to freemen of the City of Chester. New sixth form bursary.

Remarks: Elegant campus within the city walls for girls who aspire both academically and personally. Those who might struggle with the high expectations may be happier elsewhere. One girl told us: 'It's not good here to be able to spell anything with your exam results.'

Redmaids' High Infant and Junior School

Linked with Redmaids' High School

Grange Court Road, Westbury-on-Trym, Bristol BS9 4DP

Ages 4–11 **Pupils** 150

Fees: £9,810 pa

0117 962 9451
www.redmaidshigh.co.uk

Headteacher: Since 2015, Lisa Brown. She has a BSc in psychology from Leicester and a PGCE from Oxford Brookes. She joined the school in 1995 and was previously year 3 class teacher, also overseeing science, DT, pastoral care for new girls, and links with QEH.

Entrance: Girls aged between 4-5 are invited to spend a morning in the classroom, which can be either with or without a parent, depending upon the needs of the individual child.

For year 1, pupils are invited to spend half a day in the classroom where teachers review their literacy and numeracy skills. For year 2, girls spend a whole day in school and are assessed in maths, writing and reading but in a relaxed way.

Year 3 pupils are assessed by the head through one-to-one assessment while year 5s take part in a small group assessment. Up to two classes in each year group. Girls come from a wide range of local state and independent schools. Recruitment is influenced by positive word of mouth and assessment begins in the autumn term.

Exit: Most to senior school. Normally automatic entry (including scholarships via entrance examination) except where head indicates child will not cope. This would be flagged by the start of year 6 and parents given advice about alternatives. Parents of averagely bright girls can be pretty certain they will get in but shouldn't take it for granted. A tiny trickle go to state education or scholarships to other Bristol independent schools, not seriously increased by hard times financially or the current advent of academies and free schools in Bristol.

Remarks: Wonderfully welcoming, homely feel despite impressive facilities. A wet indoor break time buzzed with happy children using every inch of the school for play. Girls are lively and friendly, neatly dressed in red kilts and jerseys with white blouses in winter. Summer uniform is red and white striped dresses with red cardigans.

The curriculum allows for some 'proper' subjects. 'Girls get on with learning rather than spending all their time getting ready to learn as in some state schools' (a parent). 'Homework is about consolidating what's been done not just endless projects' (another parent). Good academic standards with written work on display but plenty of IT, art (smashing little art room staffed from senior school and an after-school club), PE, weekly swimming, with every facility except a pool on hand. All girls now learn French (replacing Mandarin). Entrants are screened for dyslexia and given specialist support on site where necessary.

Play area has both natural and artificial grassed areas for games, wooden climbing frames, a pirate ship, pagoda, tepees and a mini climbing wall, all surrounded by protective surfaces.

Everything is pristinely well maintained but there's no restriction on putting a nail in the wall to hold up a circus tent or covering classroom with brightly coloured work. Some classrooms have their own cloakrooms and loos, with décor of swimming fishes imaginatively designed by the class, and some share between two. The drama room is full of Shakespeare – literally a life-size collage figure – and girls get to know his plots early as well as winning drama awards themselves. The music room bursts with keyboards and other instruments including the various parts of a gamelan. Lots of singing and masses of music generally, with orchestra, brass band and choir. Computer technology etc taken for granted.

Wide choice of clubs and activities. Robotics with Lego is popular, as are fencing and caving. You only pay extra for things done by outside organisations, and even the residential week at Skern Lodge outdoor education centre is included in the fees, as is after-school supervision – though breakfast club has to be paid for. Loads of visits including a ski trip with QEH boys.

Parents feel this a friendly, nurturing place able to draw out the best from the most reticent child and harness the most ebullient. Difficulties such as unkindness happen but they are not allowed to grow into problems. Their greatest fear is that success in games may mean that the A team get all the attention, but there's no sign that anyone is left out at present. Not a snooty school where the car you drive matters, but one where parents are prepared to make financial sacrifices to access it for their daughters.

Redmaids' High School

Linked with Redmaids' High Infant and Junior School

Westbury Road, Westbury-on-Trym, Bristol BS9 3AW

Ages 11–18 **Pupils** 650 **Sixth form** 140

Fees: £14,430 pa

0117 962 2641
www.redmaidshigh.co.uk

Headmistress: Since 2001 (at Red Maids' School), Isabel Tobias BA PGCE (50s). Read English at New Hall, Cambridge and started work in publishing. Began teaching at Henrietta Barnett, London from where she moved to Royal High School, Bath as head of English then deputy head before taking up headship at Red Maids'. She maintained the headship when Red Maids' merged with Redland High in 2016 to form Redmaids' High.

Keen to be forward-looking and modernise, she nevertheless really listens to her girls and respects their sense of tradition. Kept the school's original red capes and bonnets for a coveted few to wear in the annual founder's day procession through Bristol.

Terrific new sixth form house has materialised under her management as well as numerous exciting projects, such as a joint observation of cosmic rays with Bristol Uni using equipment on the school roof, funded jointly by school and parents, with year 12 physicists processing and interpreting data. She was also responsible for introducing the IB, which now has a take up of about a quarter of sixth formers.

Her own children being largely off her hands, she has a bit more time to enjoy Bristol's theatre and do more walking and reading. Deeply involved in all that goes on in school, she is obviously proud of the girls' achievements in all fields.

Academic matters: The only Bristol school offering A levels and IB; some A level girls also enter for the EPQ with distinguished results. Choice of languages includes French, German, Spanish and Russian with everyone doing at least one to GCSE. Psychology, English and history consistently popular A level subjects alongside maths, biology and chemistry, with a proportion of girls moving on to medical school every year. Latin but no Greek.

Some pretty impressive GCSE results recently with 68 per cent A*-A/9-7 in 2018. English, maths and science all done as IGSCEs. Splitting the sixth form between IB and A level means groups are really too small to identify trends, but results have gone steadily upwards over the last few years. Average 38 points in IB in 2018; 47 per cent A*/A, 76 per cent A*-B grades at A level.

Choices at both are wide enough for most needs with lots of creative stuff. Shiny new food technology kitchen. Resistant materials (the tough stereotypically male bit of technology, harder for schools to do as it's expensive) is incorporated into textiles, which may look more girly but is certainly not sidelined. Surprisingly for a 'not religious' school, a goodish take up of philosophy and ethics. Spirituality and 'thoughtfulness' definitely encouraged. Even its small group of IB students earn it a 'top IB school' status.

A small proportion of SEN but the school is 'accessible' and has one partially sighted pupil, supplying every required facility, and the few dyslexics are well and considerately catered for. Almost no need for EAL but there is a Talented and Gifted programme targeted to stretch the brightest. The weekly sixth form Academic Symposium is part of this, presented alternately by girls and academic outsiders on topics such as stem cell issues. Similar initiatives in place for younger groups too.

Games, options, the arts: Enormous sports hall with dance studio as well as acres of Astroturf. There is an additional sports facility at Golden Hill and the school has just bought a 16 acre plot which includes four full size grass football pitches, four tennis courts, a 3G all-weather Astroturf pitch and extensive changing and social facilities. Endless teams for hockey, netball, etc plus football and some high flying tennis stars. Options include fencing, judo, dance (to GCSE and A level), and athletics. Staff are very hot on encouraging girls to join local sports clubs as well.

Strong music department includes iMacs (Sibelius and recently Logik, ie music writing and multitrack recording programmes) for composition. Over half the girls learn a musical instrument (including singing at a very high standard with choir, chamber choir and barber shop group). Three orchestras, ensembles etc and frequent musical productions on stage, though girls looked a little surprised when asked about pop groups. Absolutely fabulous art department, and that's saying something in Bristol, where the competition at school level is strong. Some delectable fashion design too; dresses made from sweet wrappers are popular, say sweet-toothed girls.

It was interesting to see several girls sporting neat black moustaches in preparation for the evening performance of Twelfth Night at the new Bristol Tobacco Factory Theatre. Big adaptable performance space in the 300 building (named for school's 300th birthday) with an energetic American head of drama who is galvanising the school's already enthusiastic performances. Whizzy new performing arts centre. A well-tried programme of annual concerts, joint productions with QEH and an annual whole school festival alternating between drama and dance and drama.

Masses of clubs – a whole wall full of club posters in the dining room and trips of every sort both educational (exchanges or China with QEH boys) and philanthropic, and some impressive international links: Emma Willard School in USA and Pymble Ladies' College in Melbourne, Australia. They really did build a small school in Cambodia and start a charity for Moldovan children. They do pretty well in all the school speaking, debating and the like competitions and have all sorts of whizzy projects such as a link with local GKN Aerospace where there's an ex-Red Maid 'young engineering ambassador'. Career advice includes the gamut of conferences and top local speakers from all disciplines. Special conference on medical and engineering careers open to all SW schools now and annual event.

R

Background and atmosphere: The original 'Red Maids' benefited in 1634 from the generosity of Bristol mayor and MP, John Whitson, who having been widowed thee times and lost a daughter from each marriage, died, leaving no heirs but bequeathed £90 per year to provide a dwelling house for 'one grave, painful woman and modest woman' and 'forty poor women children' who would be taught to support themselves. As, amongst other things, he imported red dye, they were to 'go apparelled in red cloth.' It is the oldest surviving girls' school in the country (albeit now merged) and moved from inner Bristol at beginning of the 20th century to its present 12 acre site. Wide lawns and green Astroturf shaded by a winding avenue of lime trees are edged by an array of purpose-built school buildings centring on the pillared mansion bought with the site.

An impressive array including the huge 1930s '300' building housing much of the teaching areas, and airy 2011 sixth form centre complete with teaching and recreation areas, cafeteria, 'film theatre', as the girls call a resources room, and careers library. Latest development, Redland Hall, a replacement for the former 1970s-built Denmark Hall, includes auditorium/ performance space as well as classrooms and music rooms. WW2 air raid shelter is hidden under a bank in the grounds, complete with anti-Nazi graffiti – a popular attraction for local primary schools.

Girls were quite enthusiastic about the food: much healthier than it used to be and things like Caesar salad made specially for you as well as masses of pasta etc. Breakfast club runs from 7.45am.

Redmaids' High merged with Redland High to form Redmaids' High School in 2016, and the joint school now operates from the Redmaids' High site.

Pastoral care, well-being and discipline: Houses are named after John Whitson's merchant ships but main pastoral care is through form teachers who meet girls twice daily. Excellent 'big girl/little girl' buddying system – Mrs Tobias was persuaded to let them keep the name – for new arrivals. 'Big girls' meet their new girls on induction day and write to them in the summer holidays as well as shepherding them through their first term. It's all part of the culture of respect for each other's feelings that she sees as instrumental with dealing with bullying. 'Of course girls are sometimes unkind and sometimes upset,' but staff talk to all concerned as long as they know about it and it's tackled along with other life skills in PHSE. The girls we met say bullying doesn't happen.

Head of year 7 oversees transition from wide range of state and independent feeder schools; pastoral evenings in autumn term for years 7, 8, 9 and 10. The senior tutor is in charge of pastoral for whole senior school including sixth form. Plenty of chances to 'develop leadership potential' as girls can be appointed to positions in houses, school clubs and tutor groups as well as head girls, head almoners, games captains and house captains. Sanctions include detentions or at worst suspension or expulsion, but the school favours a positive behaviour code and encouragement. A clear list of policies and appeals procedure on the website means it's easy to know where you are with things.

Pupils and parents: Friendly, open girls from a wide social and ethnic background, though the majority look distinctly English. Though sounding quite sophisticated and some very academic, girls on the whole look natural and not artificially grown up. They look neat, wear simple red jumpers over a white blouse with red and green tartan skirts for ages 4-16. Sensibly interpreted dress code for sixth formers. Parental discussion group meets regularly with head.

R

Former pupils include novelists Susan Lewis and Kate Sedley, TV anthropologist and presenter of Coast Dr Alice Roberts, Helen Marsden, winner of a WISE (Women into Science and Engineering) excellence award, and Daily Express journalist Tina Moran.

Entrance: The school now has four form entry at year 7, allowing a maximum of 24 per class. Candidates (including those at junior school) sit entrance exams in January in English, maths, verbal and non-verbal reasoning. Brief interview with headmistress for all including short presentation on subject of girls' choosing. For sixth form entry, minimum six grade 6s GCSEs with 9-6s in chosen IB or A level subjects plus interview with headmistress/ sixth form leadership team.

Exit: Some 20 per cent leaves after year 11 for colleges or co-ed and/or state sixth forms, but majority stay despite the advent of academies and free schools in Bristol. All sixth formers go to uni; two to Oxbridge and eight medics in 2018.

Money matters: One of the very few girls' school with a good scholarship and bursary programme, thanks to the founder; all development is paid for, not funded by loans, so it's really financially stable. Two major awards of up to 100 per cent, plus two music and two sports scholarships awarded at 11+. Entrance scholarships at year 9 (13+) and sixth form (year 12) for external candidates. A number of bursaries available.

Remarks: Far from a stuffy school, despite its historical cachet and strong academic record. 'Staff care hugely' and 'girls are genuinely proud of their school,' say parents. It feels like a school on the up. Head definitely has her eye on the future of her girls. We will watch with interest how the newly merged school develops.

Rendcomb College

Rendcomb, Cirencester, Gloucestershire GL7 7HA

Ages 3–18 **Pupils** 380 **Sixth form** 80 **Boarders** approx 190 full/ weekly (from year 7)

Fees: Day £6,030 – £23,325; Boarding £22,410 – £32,445 pa

01285 831213
www.rendcombcollege.org.uk

Headmaster: Since 2015, Rob Jones, previously deputy head at Shiplake College. Educated at Swansea (economics), Worcester (PGCE) and Buckingham (MEd). After a brief period mixing banking with elite rowing, he became a teacher and has taught economics and business at Canford, Clifton College, King's Worcester and Dauntsey's, as well as coaching rugby and rowing and running boarding houses. Teaches business economics to sixth formers at Rendcomb.

A keen sportsman, parents say he is an excellent head teacher. One explained, 'When we first met he told us that if there wasn't a lot of noise and laughter in the corridors there was something wrong...[He] runs a caring, happy, pupil-focused school.' Another added, 'He has a compelling vision for the future of the school, with the interests of the students at its heart, and isn't scared to innovate and modernise.' Lives in the college grounds with his family.

Head of junior school: Since 2017 is Gavin Roberts, previously deputy head. Before that he was senior tutor (academic) at Cathedral School, Llandaff, for 11 years. Teaches year 5 English and is 'warm, down to earth and approachable,' parents told us. 'The children absolutely love him to bits; he allows them to be who they are.... There is always a lot of fun when Mr Roberts is around.' A rugby man, he is a qualified WRU referee. Lives in the village with his wife.

There is a One College approach at Rendcomb, one ethos and one vision for juniors and seniors. The two heads are very much united on this and we get the feeling that this fairly new team are steering Rendcomb College towards a bright future.

Academic matters: In 2018, at A level, a disappointing 56 per cent A*-B and 27 per cent A*/A grades. At GCSE, 51 per cent A*-A/9-7 grades.

Twenty-three A levels offered including a new design and technology option and a travel and tourism BTec. EPQ optional. Consistently strong subjects are the sciences and maths.

Oxbridge applicants are supported well with external business experts conducting mock interviews and providing feedback. Bespoke courses for overseas pupils available.

French is taught from nursery along with some Latin and German in the later junior years. French, Spanish and German are the main languages in the senior school. Specialist teachers teach art, music, drama, PE, English and maths from year 3. Talented junior pupils are encouraged to take part in senior school activities. One parent told us, 'Our son has gone from struggling/being somewhat disenchanted with school to really finding himself. His academic side has picked back up extremely well and he has taken up new hobbies (rock band, film club) and the school has been great at helping him open up and grow.'

Technology is taken seriously. Computers are upgraded every three years, the latest have facial recognition and touch screens. There is a maker-space full of bits and bobs – we saw game consoles under construction and 3D printed prosthetic limbs have been created in the past. There is also a computing laboratory, 3D printer and Oculus Virtual Reality headsets. This forward-thinking department won the ICT Facility Award at the Education Business Awards in 2017 and were shortlisted for the ICT Innovation category for the use of technology across the school's 230-acre campus. Even the juniors have been crowned Gloucestershire's Coding Champions and are ranked first place in the Discover Education Coding League Table.

SEND department caters for the whole school. Provides one-to-one support as well as catch up programmes in small groups. Needs include dyslexia, dyscalculia and dyspraxia. Specialist dyslexia teachers teach pupils from 4 to 18. The department has a quiet room. More complex needs are considered on an individual basis.

Games, options, the arts: Not the sportiest of schools. As it is small, teams are mixed ability and often mixed year groups. However, the school ethos is that everyone tries their best and gets the opportunity to represent the school. Outdoor facilities, including the 10-acre sports park known as Top Pitch, are excellent, but parents would like to see indoor facilities to match.

'Rendcomb is probably not going to be first choice for the highly competitive, sports-mad child,' we were told, but parents would still like to see more than just the traditional sports on offer. Badminton and basketball fixtures are arranged throughout the year but these are minor sports, offered as clubs. Equestrian club and clay pigeon shooting are offered from year 5. Shooting teams 'hold their own' against larger and more experienced schools like Harrow and Eton. An athlete development programme supports pupils competing at county and national levels. Junior pupils have swimming lessons from reception. From year 5, in the summer, the outdoor swimming pool is used.

Forest school is one of the stars of the show at Rendcomb (the other is The Griffin Theatre). The site has been in the grounds for 10 years, run by four fully trained staff and used by everyone. Every week nursery pupils have two sessions and juniors have one afternoon up to year 4. After that it's an extracurricular option. Nestled amongst the trees they have a fire pit, several dens, rope swings and an eco toilet. Senior pupils have their own dedicated space as part of the outdoor education curriculum.

Art, music and DT are in one building with art studios, textiles and a design technology studio. A small exhibition area at the entrance confirms the standard is high. Upstairs is the music department; plenty of practice rooms and pupils told us they can practice whenever they like. Four concerts a year include both staff and pupils. Around 50 per cent learn an instrument. Plenty of music clubs and particularly talented juniors are welcome to join senior groups.

In 2017, the £3.3m Griffin Theatre opened, the first development in almost 30 years (Godman boarding house in 1989 was the last). An impressive building, it has a 350-seat auditorium plus a dance studio and drama classroom, it will undoubtedly inspire pupils to take part in performing arts. First production was Agatha Christie's And Then There Were None, next will be Les Misérables. Past senior productions include Macbeth, Jerusalem and Footloose, whilst the latest junior production was Porridge. All juniors get a part, (even the head), and all year 6s get a speaking part. Next up is Pirates of the Curry Bean.

Classical ballet is offered from 3 years and contemporary dance from 11 years. Royal Academy of Dance and Contemporary Dance Association exams and grading. Stretch and tone classes offered to grade 3 pupils and above. Performance group club encourages pupils to choreograph pieces and enter dance competitions such as the great big British Dance Off and Cheltenham Festival of Performing Arts.

Good range of extracurricular clubs including debating, sailing, dissection, martial arts and gardening. Juniors can opt for mixed year and ability sports or music clubs, knit and stitch, scrabble, or clay pigeon shooting (ammunition is extra). Sixth formers can choose an in-house leadership programme, a buddy scheme or DofE.

Funds for expeditions to places like Patagonia must be fundraised by pupils. Other trips are kept affordable, including a trip to Norway for hiking and trekking, a sports tour to Netherlands, language exchanges and outdoor challenges in the UK. Junior trips include a year 6 outdoor challenge residential, and a biennial French trip for years 5/6. Day trips include Bristol and Cheltenham Literature Festival.

Boarding: From year 7. Around 45 per cent board either on a full, weekly or flexi (up to three nights a week) basis. Only about 10 per cent of years 7 to 9 board, meaning numbers at weekends are low (four to 12 in each house). However, numbers increase in the older years with around 55 per cent of years 10 and 11 boarding and 70 per cent of sixth formers. At weekends there are around 30 to 40 pupils in these houses. Some 75 per cent of boarders are from overseas covering some 14 nationalities. Year 11 students from Germany do short stays.

There are five houses, all on campus. House system is horizontal rather than the traditional vertical. All have common rooms with pianos, table football, projectors, TVs, X-Boxs, private Skype rooms and kitchens (used for cooking as a family at the weekends). We were impressed with the homeliness of the houses; rooms are well looked after and the houseparents are friendly and caring. Gap students help out in the younger boarding houses.

The Old Rectory is a grade II listed building with plenty of character and has been housing year 7-9 boys since 1966. The girls are in Godman. Dorms are a good size, for threes or fours. Phones and such are removed at lights out. Both houses have gardens.

Years 10 and 11 boys are in Lawn House, and the girls are in Stable House. Here, boarders have individual bedrooms with a study space. In the boys' house there is a large media room for quiet study, and in the girls' there is a library, a hobbies room and a gym. Plus two house dogs.

Park House is the mixed sixth form house. Again, all rooms are individual. A short stroll away is Garden House, a cottage in the village. All sixth formers spend two separate weeks here; they budget, shop, cook, wash and get to school on their own as an introduction to university life. Some fare better than others, we were told, but the excitement around this was ubiquitous.

A boarders' committee decides on evening and weekend activities. These include dance or yoga, craft nights, laser tag or climbing on the grounds, shopping and cinema trips, roller discos or canoeing down the River Wye.

Plenty of socialising between boys and girls, and across year groups. Years 10 and 11 have The Barn and sixth formers have a bar, open twice weekly. This is tucked away in a basement with sofa snugs, a snooker room, poolroom and a dance room. Think, no windows, flashing lights, graffiti walls – every teenager's dream; they absolutely love it. No place for parents, but rest assured this is a fully supervised, responsible zone.

Background and atmosphere: Founded in 1920 by Frederick Noel Hamilton Wills as a boys' school with just 12 pupils; girls were introduced into the sixth form in 1972 and the school became fully co-ed in 1992. The junior school was added in 2000 and the nursery five years later. There are now some 280 seniors and 90 juniors, with around 30 per cent from overseas.

Set within 230 acres of parkland in the Gloucestershire Cotswolds, the school is in, and very much part of, the small village of Rendcomb. Cheltenham and Cirencester are nearby. Within the beautiful grounds lies a deer park, home to over 70 fallow deer and classified as an 'ancient tree hotspot' by the Woodland Trust. This is an 'outdoor' school that makes the most of its setting, with regular events like treasure hunts for the juniors and laser tag days for the boarders. 'Our children come home with pink cheeks and muddy trainers and yet still excel in the classroom,' parents told us.

A traditional school steeped in history, it takes great pride in the 'Rendcomb family'. Not just a marketing strapline, we were told by parents; 'Rendcomb has an amazing community spirit...an all-round, family inclusive, friendly feel.' Pupils are often seen chatting sociably with teachers over lunch, and 'the children all mix and play together regardless of age.'

The main house is stunning inside and out. The staircase has stained glass windows that beautifully illustrate the Aesop's fables. The school recently held a concert here (yes, this is no ordinary stairwell), taking full advantage of the acoustics and backdrop. Heating and maintaining a building like this with its huge windows and stone corridors must be challenging and the school reflects this; it is practical and far from flashy.

The grand dining hall is used solely for dining. Huge floor to ceiling windows and ornate ceilings give a sense of tradition and old-fashioned splendour. Next door is a large reading room and beyond that is a library with a 150 year history; it doesn't get more authentic than that.

Juniors have the luxury of sharing the senior facilities. Junior school is attached to the main building and classrooms are based around a quad with the nursery ('excellent,' reported parents) tucked snugly in the middle. Rooms are large, overlooking the outdoor swimming pool or gardens, and class sizes are small (16 max). Large art, design and technology classroom is upstairs next to a modern and rather grown up science lab. Daily assemblies are run by 'the very funny' head of juniors. Achievements are celebrated and parents happily join too. 'When they have been awarded a distinction they go up and tell the school and the parents why they were awarded it.. a clever way to get used to public speaking at a very young age!'

Boarders and day pupils share the same boarding houses. All pupils register at their houses to 8am daily. Most day pupils are still on-site at 4pm and, for a small fee, can stay on for evening activities or supper. No lessons on Saturdays just sports fixtures.

Pastoral care, well-being and discipline: Excellent pastoral care. 'During some challenging health issues...the children now view the school as a part of their extended family,' one mother told us. Another added that the nurturing environment 'brings out the best in each pupil regardless of their abilities or likes/dislikes. It instils confidence, encourages and builds an all round sense of respect for fellow pupils and staff.'

Pastoral care is further reinforced by the family ethos, including big sister and big brother events when younger pupils are shown around the houses. This sense of 'looking after each other' is not exclusive to these events, we were told. 'I am really impressed with how many students across all years know each other and support one another,' parents said.

Services once a week in the listed St Peter's Church on site are conducted by the school chaplain, Reverend Bob Edy, an old Rendcombian with many a story to tell.

Pupils and parents: Day pupils commute from Gloucester, Swindon, Stroud, and as far as Oxford. 'The parent community is really friendly, refreshingly unpretentious and richly diverse,' one new parent confirmed. Another added, 'The teachers and students have very strong relationships and the parents are welcomed into the community as well.' Communication with parents has improved under the current head.

Inclusive too. 'With its Noel Wills ethos of offering an inclusive education – even to a child who would not otherwise be able of afford it – we felt much less intimidated and genuinely welcomed and valued in the Rendcomb family,' one parent confided. In 2015, the school reduced sixth form day pupil fees and numbers have since doubled.

'We love the way the school not only provides the children with academics but teaches them manners, confidence and to be all round great children.' Based on the pupils we met, this is definitely true. Interests and passions are encouraged rather than stifled, resulting in a real mix of children here. Rules are of course in place, but this isn't a strict school in the traditional sense. More of a place where pupils will be 'steered by conversation' as a parent would at home.

Smart blue uniform with a touch of red. Sixth formers wear business dress.

Entrance: Nursery from 3. For junior school entry, taster days plus assessments in English, maths and verbal/non verbal reasoning, plus school reports.

For senior school entry, entrance exam and interview with the head. Automatic entrance for juniors, but all pupils must sit the exam for assessment purposes. Entrance day tests include exam in the morning followed by an outdoor education session so children can be observed working in teams in a relaxed, fun environment. Overnight stays available.

Transition is seamless from junior to senior school. 'New pupils settle in quickly and are not judged by whether they are good at maths, music or throwing a ball,' parents told us.

Sixth form entry is based on GCSE results, an interview with the head and school reports.

Exit: Majority of juniors go on to senior school, others to Pate's Grammar, Marling School, Cotswold School and Stroud High.

Around 75 per cent stay on to sixth form with 90 per cent then going onto university. Destinations include Exeter, Bath, London and Nottingham. One to medical school in 2018.

Notable Old Rendcombians include Issy Bailey, Paralympian (shooting); Jonathan Suffolk, technical director at the National Theatre; Richard Dunwoody, jockey; David Tyler, chairman of Sainsbury's.

Money matters: Scholarships are awarded at 7+, 11+, 13+ and 16+. Noel Wills Scholarship and the Rendcomb Scholarship are offered at 11+.

Remarks: A small family-focused school where everyone knows everyone. One parent summed it by saying, 'When it comes to kids, nothing top trumps the development of character, and on this metric I haven't seen a school in the area that comes close to Rendcomb.' Set in amazing grounds, this outdoorsy school is traditional with some modern twists – an impressive performing arts centre and a forward-thinking ICT department. Not for competitively sporty types, but Rendcomb is a bit of find if you're looking for a school that nurtures individuals.

RGS Springfield

Linked with RGS The Grange, RGS Worcester

138

Britannia Square, Worcester WR1 3DL

Ages 2-11 **Pupils** 130

Fees: £8,160 – £12,546 pa

01905 24999
www.rgsw.org.uk

Headmistress: Since 2012, Laura Brown (40s). Displays all the dynamism necessary to be a successful leader. 'I love my job,' she says – and clearly means it. Educated in London day schools, then boarder at Kent College followed by spell in retail management before taking philosophy degree at the University of Kent. Part of her course involved working in schools, which sparked her ambition to become a teacher. Took a PGCE in primary education, then combined bringing up her three children with prep teaching posts in Berkshire and Gloucestershire, followed by six years as director of studies and deputy head at Dean Close in Cheltenham, which involved 'Lots of forward-facing stuff' – invaluable for her present role.

Style is hands on. Knows every child, which is 'a privilege and just lovely,' she says, teaches year science to years 5 and 6 and exudes command of her happy ship. Unusual enjoyment of piles of paperwork no doubt explains why she describes role as a compliance inspector as 'really entertaining' (takes all sorts). For relaxation, rides – owns highland pony named Creagy, just the ticket for skimming the hurdles at nearby Worcester racecourse.

Entrance: For early years, informal assessment of a child's readiness for schooling; most children at this stage attend for mornings or afternoons only. More formal from year 3 onwards, with papers in English, maths, VR and NVR. Academic and musical scholarships (10 per cent fee reduction) available for year 5 entry. No separate scholarship exam; at least two instruments (voice can be one) at grade 3 or above, for music.

Exit: Overwhelming majority at 11+ to RGS Worcester situated a quarter of a mile away. School's introductory literature stresses the 2-18 journey which it hopes RGS pupils will experience.

Remarks: Part of the RGS triumvirate consisting of RGS Worcester and another prep, RGS The Grange. People, 'just don't know we're here,' says head, though satnav had been fully briefed. Small scale, with single forms in years 3-6 feels like a throwback to earlier age, combining intimacy and modern outlook. Cross-curricular learning a feature of academic life, spanning (among other subjects) history, geography, science and ICT. Early years pupils might study Fire and Ice and Splish, Splash, Splosh. For older children it could be an analysis of Food of The Gods and Delightfully Dazzling Dahl. Not flimsy 'project' style explorations: clear learning objectives are stuck into each of the pupils' theme books.

Digital learning programme lets all pupils in years 3-6 bring in own iPads. It 'shows you that there is not just one way of learning,' says one (a view slightly counterbalanced by another who pointed out how much iPads cost). Equally, the old ways have not been sacrificed. It is, for example, the school's ambition that at least 95 per cent of pupils should leave with a reading age of two years beyond than their chronological one, helped by 15-minute period of compulsory solo-reading after lunch. And hurrah for the traditional desks in every classroom, giving sense of ownership and self-organisation.

For those who need additional academic support (around 10 per cent of pupils), individual programmes are designed by the school's learning development co-ordinator, with her team of four teaching assistants. Individual, small group and class-based guidance is provided at no extra charge.

The school is the central building on a six-acre site at the heart of Britannia Square and was described to us as 'a green oasis.' Though the building is listed, some shrewd amendments have been made including a hall, constructed in the mid-90s with specialist rooms for art and design, science, ICT and music.

Pre prep (divided into Ducklings, Tadpoles and Dragonflies) is full of fizz – two boys sitting in a box, taking their teddies to the moon in a cardboard rocket. Meanwhile, year 1 pupils were rehearsing for an assembly about the seaside where we learned that 'women didn't wear bikinis back then'. All senior classrooms are on the top floor of the building so transition from one year to another holds no mysteries. Indeed, the mingling of senior and junior children is something of a feature. At lunchtimes, the oldest take care of the youngest, cutting up food and clearing away. Good manners abound, regardless of age group. We were struck on our tour that, as we entered each classroom, we were welcomed with a handshake and a brief explanation of what was going on by a class ambassador.

Good selection of sports: boys play rugby, football and cricket; girls hockey, netball and rounders; swimming is taught at the nearby Perdiswell pool. As you'd hope, given small size, there is sporting inclusivity. Each child will represent the school and some year groups have to combine at times in order to form teams. With a maximum of 17 pupils in each year-group, sporting standards are, understandably, not always as high as in larger schools.

Choir sings regularly at Worcester Cathedral. There's an orchestra plus ensemble groups – brass band, strings and flooters and tooters. Recent whole-school spectaculars include Alice in Wonderland, The Jungle Book and a WW2 play, The Vackees. Nativity plays, one recently performed by candlelight and overseen by a donkey, are also produced. House system, made up of Panthers, Jaguars, Lions and Tigers, provides competition in music, sports as well as house Easter egg hunt. Plenty of activities – highlight for year 5 and 6 pupils a residential trip to Normandy. Extracurricular clubs include riding, pottery, creative arts, cooking and animation, though other suggestions from the school council (massage and party clubs) have been rejected.

Over an impressive toad-in-the-hole lunch, pupils showed unforced enthusiasm for school. Thinking back to their early days, they recalled that 'everyone was jolly.' Now, due to the small class sizes, I know everybody,' and 'I learn more because I get more attention.' One observed that 'the teachers are quite strict but kind as well – that's what makes a good teacher.' The only real drawback, for one boy, was that the breaks were too short, only apparently giving him brief respite from what he had calculated as 'my five hours of learning.'

Staff – who clearly work much harder than that – praised their colleagues who were described as 'warm, welcoming and supportive,' and see head as 'a first amongst equals' who, with senior management team, is quick to communicate good news. When dealing with parents, open-door strategies operate; an ideal given added punch by the fact that the early years team conducts around 30 home visits each year to meet parents and introduce themselves to their children. Two-way communication is enhanced, not just by an impressive series of newsletters, but also by Seesaw – an app that enables staff to zap best of moments to parents' mobiles.

The Springfield Parents Association (SPA) runs The Secret Garden Summer Ball, family quizzes and pamper evenings, among other events. They also raise money for the school: recent purchases including buggies for early years children and adventure trail equipment. Also much involved in the school's charitable giving which supports medical assistance dog-training and aid for communities in Cambodia, Nepal and Malawi.

Parents we met repeatedly stressed how pleased they were with the school's communication. 'Makes you feel that you are all a part of it,' says one. Staff 'go the extra mile.' Weekend replies to email enquiries are not unusual. No weak links, bar the high cost of uniform and the small car park, luxurious by London standards but still a potential bumper-cruncher. The final verdict came from a mother who described the school as 'like a whole lifestyle.'

Most schools trot out clichés such as 'happy family atmosphere' and 'home from home,' but we found a genuine sense of intimacy and belonging here. The secret in the square is well worth discovering.

RGS The Grange

Linked with RGS Worcester, RGS Springfield

Grange Lane, Claines, Worcester WR3 7RR

Ages 2–11 **Pupils** 342

Fees: £8,160 – £12,546 pa

01905 451205
www.rgsw.org.uk

Headmaster: Since 2009, Gareth Hughes (50s). Previously assistant head here for two years, though association with RGS family of schools goes back to 1996, when he was appointed head of rugby at the senior school, subsequently becoming director of sport, then head of lower school. A West Walian, he was educated at Llandysul Grammar School where he was head boy and captained the 1st XV. His first teaching post, after completing sports science degree at Greenwich University, was as a PE teacher at a state secondary school in Kent.

Knows the RGS ethos and structure inside out as a teacher and parent – son and daughter both attend the senior school. Presides over contented staff, who praise 'pathway of excitement' on offer (primrose or otherwise) as well as dedication and sensitivity of senior leadership.

Sport an abiding interest. He was a fly half for a range of clubs including London Welsh, Saracens and Llanelli and rugby continues to feature – he currently coaches the U17s at Worcester Wanderers.

Periodically zips on the lycra to pedal the Malvern Hills and also enoys the theatre. Practical as well as polished, he prides himself on redesign of the car park, though pupils will no doubt have been more impressed by the double handstand he performed at recent speech day, teaming up with deputy. It was 'like something from Ant and Dec,' reported a member of staff.

Entrance: Taster day for places in year 2 and below. At year 3 and above, assessments in English, maths, and reasoning. Academic and music scholarships available at year 5 for internal and external candidates.

Exit: Almost all year 6 leavers (95 per cent or so) progress to senior school. Unlike external candidates, only have to sit papers in VR and NVR with school record also taken into account, though scholarship hopefuls (academic, music, drama, art and sport) can opt to take additional papers in English and maths – pupils normally scoop a dozen or so awards each year. A few switch to the grammar school system in Cheltenham or Birmingham or to other local schools.

Remarks: Though 50-acre site with a late Victorian farm and farmhouse has a rural feel, it's just three miles from the centre of Worcester. Drive notable for well-tended playing fields on either side of the broad roadway and ferocious speed bumps that would wake even the sleepiest policeman.

May evoke centuries-old tradition, but school was founded only in 1996, starting with just six pupils. Academic standards are high, helped by small classes (about 12 in reception rising to just over 20 at year 6) and an imaginative timetable featuring discovery afternoons with sessions on science, DT, art and creative media. Pupils enjoy their lessons, say parents. '[They're so] happy and enthusiastic to learn,' says one. Evident on visit, with a boy in a reception class rushing up to exclaim that 'I'm working really hard on my numbers.' Matched by staff energy, one teacher almost as excited by pupils' handwriting progress as the pupils.

Head of learning development coordinates a team of nine teaching assistants who provide small group, individual and class-based support for around 15 per cent of pupils. A recent external audit of this department's effectiveness was extravagant in its praise.

Bar desire to broaden language provision – currently only French is offered – parents happy with curriculum and say school communicates well, from online weekly newsletters (with retro-pop titles such as Love is in The Air and Great Balls of Fire) to information evenings to talk through approach to maths, phonics and reading.

Technology is much in evidence but not allowed to dominate. 'Just as the calculator replaced the slide rule and became another tool in the pencil case, so has the iPad,' reassures the website. They (iPads rather than slide rules) are provided to all year 5 and 6 pupils and used for what school terms blended learning where tech adds an extra layer eg in art lesson where coats of arms, reflecting an individual's personality, were being designed on screen. School is Worcestershire hub for computing, hosting sessions in ultra-impressive ICT suite for county's teachers to share best practice. It's all coordinated by school's digital leaders who also film concerts and design and present internet-based assemblies.

Parental resistance to this digital form of education, says school, 'has dissolved' while pupils, clearly a committed bunch, describe iPad-related study as 'like a fun way of learning ... the more fun you have, the more you will learn.'

One of the school's charms is that it remains a single entity, with generously sized classrooms, reception area, library and multi-purpose hall all incorporated into the original farmhouse and new extension. Consequently, the youngest children – known as Ladybirds, Caterpillars and Butterflies in the early years – are a part of it all (even if the Ladybirds had temporarily opted out on day of visit in favour of a darkened room and a siesta after lunch).

Top floor of the extension houses specialist rooms for science, ICT, French, food technology and music (which lacked, we thought, some of the sparkle of the others).

Outside, pitches, a pavilion, a traverse wall – funded by the PTA – a major range of playground equipment and a twin-pitched Astroturf. The only facilities that the school lacks are a separate sports centre and – high up on pupils' wish list – a swimming-pool.

R

Rugby, football and cricket for boys while girls have hockey (U11s recent national champions) netball and athletics. For years 3-6, match day squads frequently run down to E team level. Judo, fencing, and sailing also on offer, with enrichment programme including jewellery, cooking and Lego.

Singers and instrumentalists well catered for with orchestras and ensembles. Chamber choir performs and has won at the Cheltenham Festival. Recent drama productions include Annie, Bugsy Malone and Alice In Wonderland.

Competition is encouraged via the house system, where the four houses (Cash, Cornwall, Goodrich and Perowne – all former Bishops of Worcester) contest for supremacy in music, sport, English, art and even in pancake races.

School notably good at confidence boosting – one parent who hadn't previously considered independent education was converted after her 'shy girl' started at pre-school and 'really came out of herself.'

Polite and articulate children, who routinely stand aside for adults to pass them on the stairs, praise life here. One, who thought starting here would be 'really scary' was instantly put at easy by teachers who were 'friendly, young, entertaining and (reassuringly) clever.' Another felt that her school was so good because 'it feels like a family.' Their only criticism was of match teas which are apparently 'always the same with pasta and that cheesy stuff.'

Good for working parents – no extra charge for before and after school care (7.45am-6.00pm). Active PTA run a series of events ranging from fireworks spectacular to a festival with music and crafts and, of course, the summer fete featuring year 6 pupils with their Smoothie Challenge, bouncy castles, pony rides and stalls run by local businesses.

When even the knitting club is so alluring that one parent, who had chosen the school as 'an upgrade', experienced great difficulty in dragging her daughter away from its excitements, clearly a school which has got the balance right.

RGS Worcester

Linked with RGS The Grange, RGS Springfield

Upper Tything, Worcester WR1 1HP

Ages 11–18 **Pupils** 762 **Sixth form** 190

Fees: £13,080 pa

01905 613391
www.rgsw.org.uk

Headmaster: Since 2014, John Pitt, an individual in the prime of his middle years. Educated Dulwich College, he studied history at Cambridge and remained in Fenland in order to gain his teaching qualification. He started his career at Whitgift where he became head of sixth form, before moving to Portsmouth Grammar as deputy head (academic). He then returned to Whitgift for eight years as second master – posts which quite clearly have prepared him comprehensively for leadership. Conspicuously devoid of the ego and the swagger that is demonstrated by some of the boorish beasts in the headmaster jungle, he has in his demeanour something of a top-ranking surgeon about him as he dissects our questions, steepling his fingers in thought.

Astute, crisp and quietly proud of all that his school is, and promises to be. Ask him about the advances that RGS has made post-2015 and he describes a pattern of progress that is highlighted by a more focused academic and pastoral approach in which pupils are given far more individual support. He has instigated 'lots of work' across the estate so that everything looks well cared for, being of the view that this has a positive impact on both atmosphere and performance.

More personally he cites the major difference between his first term and his ninth as being the growth of trust, so that staff, parents and pupils know that the school and he 'can make things happen'. As time passes and more sixth formers leave he can savour July days in the knowledge that 'they have been a part of me and I a part of them'. This could all sound rather schmaltzy and redolent of a gravelly-voiced film trailer, but the depth of his conviction is clear.

Any notion of achieving any sort of work/life balance in the swirls of term time is swept away as he insists that he has 'to live the life of a head.' And so, along with teaching history to year 8 he blends, for example, weekend time on the touchline with taking his three young children to their activities. Being married to Anna, a prep school teacher who understands the breadth of school life, is undoubtedly a great help. In the holidays, he likes sailing and exploring the Malvern Hills, whilst favourite authors are CJ Sansom and Graham Swift. One of Swift's later novels is titled, rather aptly for prospective parents, Wish You Were Here. He would like to be thought of as a head who is known to be 'committed and friendly'. Parents describe him as 'inspirational, approachable and respected' – an enviable adjectival triangle that sums him up so well.

Academic matters: To find a summary of the school's recent academic record do ask for a copy of the Academic Highlights document which, in admirably lucid fashion, details all the subject-by-subject statistics that parents and their children could wish to know. At A level in 2018, 35 per cent A*/A grades and 72 per cent A*-B. At GCSE, 53 per cent A*-A/9-7.

Offers 24 A level subjects plus the EPQ. As in any school there is a quest for refinements to produce still better results (even running to an 'in your face' notice in the chemistry department that details recent top grade attainments). The school has clearly explained the mystifying changes to the GCSE grading system and A level reforms. Consequently, despite one member of staff's observation that 'exam boards have been barren in their guidance', the school is confident that it will manage this period of change successfully. It is revisiting post-16 provision and is now accredited to offer a BTec level 3 diploma in sport, with the possibility of adding on engineering in the near future.

Both the head and senior staff lay equal stress on assisting those who find aspects of study difficult. The head of learning support leads a team of five teachers, support being given via small group and individual tuition. Some 15 per cent of students benefit from this over varying periods of time. School runs exam clinics from December onwards for both GCSE and A level students.

Active careers department organises the Annual Careers and Higher Education Expo (with 110 exhibitors the largest in Worcestershire), 30 careers lectures and numerous work placements. A 'significant sea-change' in careers provision targets pupils from year 7 upwards, with initiatives such as the Enterprise and Employment scheme, which runs in conjunction with Worcester University's Business School.

Games, options, the arts: Girls' and boys' sport both of a high calibre, underpinned by school's Charter for Sport with its expectation that players are 'resolute, gracious, selfless and willing.' Main sports are hockey, netball and rounders for girls and rugby, football and cricket for boys. The focus is clearly not just on first teams. Rowing is conspicuously strong as are cross-country and fencing; a year 7 girl recently finished as Great Britain's top-ranked U17 épéeist cadet and was also ranked second in the under 20 listings. On a wider scale, much sporting interest develops through the rivalry between the school and King's Worcester that has as its twin showdowns The Superball, with netball played at Worcester University's indoor arena, and a rugby clash at Worcester Warriors' Sixways Stadium. Wonderfully, these local contests attract up to 5,000 spectators.

The chamber choir recently sang evensong at Christ Church Oxford whilst the annual choral concert, featuring all three RGS Worcester schools in Worcester Cathedral, is a centre-piece of the year. There is a big band, a senior jazz ensemble, any number of instrumentalists at tea-time recitals and a senior piano concert. The music department also provided the band for last year's big show, Guys and Dolls. Drama clearly benefits from the GCSE and A level programmes of study; recent spectaculars have also included Romeo and Juliet and Alice's Adventures in Grammarland. The department recently visited New York to take part in a series of stage workshops, observe auditions and to see a Broadway production of The Color Purple'.

Competition in a wealth of activities, including debating, creative writing, the Christmas card contest and golf, is spurred on by the house system. This comprises Elgar (after the composer), Ottley (to mark the school's 2007 merger with Alice Ottley School), Wylde (after a 16th-century benefactor) and the exotically named Whiteladies (named after a building that used to house a nunnery, complete with its secret tunnel to the cathedral). There is a CCF and an equally flourishing debating society whose year culminates with a black-tie dinner (presumably with some discussion over which course should be eaten first) and the Billingham Society for academic enrichment. This is named after a former pupil who became NASA's chief of the extra-terrestrial research division. It is open to everyone but scholars must attend. Last year, twilight discussions included Lovenomics: Can the Head Rule the Heart?' (yes) and Science or Religion? (both).

Background and atmosphere: In busarland some scroogey financiers are of the opinion that lawns and flowers, hedges and fresh scrunch on the drive are 'vanity projects' that matter little when compared to the 'core business'. However if the school cares about everything then it is likely that students will follow its lead, and parents on tour will feel that they are on some kind of National Trust trail. The highlights here consist of a number of Georgian and Victorian buildings (school dates back to the seventh century and will celebrate its 150th anniversary on its present site in 2018) such as Britannia House, where head has initial meetings with parents.

R

Conversely, there are the odd post-war architectural examples that can be classified as carbuncley. An extension to the art department, for instance, resembles an ugly UFO or a giant lunar capsule from a moon landing and adjoins some tennis courts, with their park-like surfaces and saggy nets, that took us back to the age of wooden rackets and green flash plimsolls. Pleasingly plans, are afoot for their refurbishment. Elsewhere, however, things are far more impressive. We especially enjoyed our visit to a year 9 art class which had been given the task of interpreting Vivaldi's most famous concerto in painted form, using colour to depict the mood and shape of the four seasons in a target-time of 53 minutes. In the language lab year 8s were testing year 7s. The fitness suite, which the sixth form can access during non-contact time, is packed with modern muscle-building machinery.

Ask, too, to see the library, situated in the early Victorian Eld Hall. Most school libraries are just full of volume-filled shelves and workstations but here, in central position, is a giant, gold- lettered honours board in gratitude to those staff who have served the school for 25 years or more. RGS Worcester inspires loyalty, as demonstrated recently when four members of staff retired with a combined teaching tally of 130 years. And on this board current staff who have reached their quarter-centuries are also named.... a typical touch of style. Then there is Joe's Café for sixth form coffee and snacks – a spacious L-shaped facility, well in advance of normal Starbucks décor, that features Chesterfield sofas and framed prints on the walls and is mercifully free of the table-football and pool tables that some schools seem to think are necessary to create a 'relaxed atmosphere'.

Pastoral care, well-being and discipline: Pupils, looking back, told us first day nervousness had quickly disappeared because the teachers were 'really supportive' and, in modern management-speak, 'always ready to go the extra mile'. This had made them 'way more organised'. They admitted to a degree of pressure, sparked by the school wanting to 'push our potential', but said that much of it was caused by trying to balance their academic and extracurricular lives. Apparently, though, staff are quite understanding if requests are occasionally made to miss clubs so that academic deadlines can be met. No doubt the splendid pastoral team that comprises a deputy head, section heads, heads of year and the school counsellor will in future be put under more strain as the pressures of teenage life sharpen. More progress can be made in the development of student-mentoring and personalised records of achievement. There will always be the heavy expectation that every year will result in higher league table positions.

Pupils and parents: The actress Lauren Bacall was of the opinion that 'character, character is all that matters', and although that is momentarily irrelevant when examination result envelopes are torn open each August, it is in the personalities of its pupils that the heart of a school can be found. We were toured by the head girl and boy (both of whom were sitting on Oxbridge offers) who demonstrated the sort of easy affability, wit and willingness to talk that eludes many adults. Equally at lunch, representatives of different years waited to be given permission to start their meal and were the best of company, speaking with a sustained enthusiasm about their school and the multiplicity of opportunity that it offers.

Ideally, they would like a swimming pool on site (although it's only a few minutes away) but spoke enthusiastically about the influence of the school council that has led to a more varied menu and ended the monotony of cod goujons and chips each Friday. In response to our question for some nouns to summarise what the school has given them they answered 'guidance', 'confidence' and 'independence'. The most impressive statement, from a lower sixth girl, was 'school is about who you become'.

Parents were enthusiastic in their praise, citing the school's flair for communication, with teachers trusted to reply to emails rapidly, and the efficiency of the parent portal. The reception is fantastic'; 'Learning support has been amazing'; and 'Teenagers can be themselves... the little things get noticed'. The only negatives that they were aware of came from families who didn't 'get involved'. The Parents' Association runs a Summer Ball and Octoberfest' – a Germanic event with beer, sausages and an oompah band.

Entrance: At 11+, English, mathematics and verbal reasoning exams. Around 70 to 80 pupils transfer from the two prep schools – RGS The Grange and RGS Springfield – who, along with their senior partner, constitute the RGS family of schools. A further 40 to 50 pupils join from other schools.

For sixth form entry, six grade 6s at GCSE.

Exit: Around 20 per cent leave after GCSEs. Five to Oxbridge in 2018, plus three medics. Russell Group institutions are predictably popular, but for the future, the school predicts that there will be a somewhat wider destination list as the reality of student debt bites. Already, for example, some are exploring options at foreign universities – one off to study in the USA in 2018.

Money matters: A range of scholarships (academic, music, sport, art and DT and textiles) are available at 11+, 13+ and 16+. Means-tested bursaries of up to 100 per cent.

Remarks: Our dominant feeling is that RGSW does what it does with a vision and a panache that not many can match. There is a Swedish word – 'lagom'- which translates as 'just right – a state of perfect balance'. This school is nearly there.

Richard Huish College

South Road, Taunton, Somerset TA1 3DZ

Ages 16–99 **Pupils** 1,800 **Boarders** 47 full, 6 flexi

Fees: Boarding £9,900 pa (EU or UK) – £17,700 pa (international)

01823 320 800
www.richuish.ac.uk

Principal: Since 2013, John Abbott, originally from Blackburn, studied sport and exercise science at Manchester Metropolitan University, then completed a masters in sports psychology and exercise physiology. Previously assistant principal, Abbott joined RHC in 2003 as faculty director for maths and sciences, before being promoted in 2009. Prior to that, he was section leader at Bridgwater College. Father of two girls, he is a keen sportsman, particularly passionate about squash and basketball. He ensures all 1,500+ students know him, through tutoring and recording video messages for college induction tutorials and other messages. Plus his office is in a prominent position at the front of the college, and he does his fair share of bus duty. One parent told us, 'He is a calm, inspirational leader who wants the best for every student in his care. John, and all the teachers we met, are committed teachers with the best interests of their students at heart'.

RHC differs from the average school sixth form. Head told us there are three reasons for this. Firstly, RHC has an 'adult approach.' Secondly, students that were 'top dog' at school find themselves amongst other 'top dogs'. This in turn creates a collective energy and competitiveness, and raises the aspirations of all students – they thrive on it and achieve so much more. Thirdly, there is greater freedom of choice at the college. Due to the high numbers, they can offer a wider range of courses and provide greater flexibility around subject and enrichment choices.

Academic matters: In 2018, 52 per cent A*-B and 25 per cent A*/A grades at A level. One of the best sixth form colleges in England, in the top 10 for A level results for the last eight years. Consistently good results at BTec too. RHC is a Beacon college designated 'outstanding' by Ofsted.

Over 35 subjects offered at A level. As well as traditional subjects, options include archaeology, critical thinking, environmental studies, law and philosophy. Plus BTecs in applied science, business, media, health and social care, popular music, music production, IT, public services and sport. Most popular courses are psychology, biology and maths. Best value-added results are in science and maths. Statistics recently revealed by the A Level Performance System (ALPS) show that Huish ranks in the top 100 out of 1,164 for the value it adds to students. Value added is measured by comparing students' predicted achievement based on their GCSE results with their actual achievement at A level.

Students follow a study programme of of three core A Levels, an extended diploma, or a combination of A levels and subsidiary diploma. Any combination is possible. As long as students achieve the grades for entry, all are accepted. Fully wheelchair accessible. If needed, specialist one-to-one study support, specialist equipment and software, support during exams and links to external specialists can be provided. One student, with sensory integration dysfunction commented, 'all my exam scribes have been excellent.' Another with visual impairment said, 'I am thoroughly enjoying it, all the subjects have been able to adapt resources and I feel that I am keeping pace with the class.'

Games, options, the arts: Sport is huge here. Participation is nearly double the national average of other colleges, and many compete at a national level in a whole range of sports. Academies for cricket, tennis, football, golf and recently rugby union. One student recently chose to come to the college solely because of the excellent reputation of the cricket academy, even though it meant a daily three-hour commute. Hockey men's and women's 1st teams are reigning South West League Champions. There are regular fixtures for 1st, 2nd and 3rd teams for most sports so all abilities can get involved. And the Active Huish scheme, part of enrichment activities, encourages students to take part less competitively in sports like ultimate frisbee and dodgeball.

New two-storey state-of-the-art sports hall, including a full sized multi sports arena, a viewing gallery, changing rooms, a gym and a classroom, next to the sports fields. Most sports activities take place on campus, but some facilities are used at Taunton Vale Sports Club, The Wyvern Sports Club and Kings College.

Along with sport, music is hugely popular. There are concerts and gigs including performances from the choirs, orchestra, jazz bands, big bands, and ensembles. To date there are 35 pop bands, and they all do gigs. Teachers regularly set up tours in local pubs and venues; this is a big hit with the budding musicians, their friends, and of course the parents and teachers. Annually the college hires a venue for two nights to showcase their greatest hits. RHC even has links with the organisers of the John Peel stage at Glastonbury, giving bands the chance to perform, and media students the chance to work with the BBC crew. On campus there's a recording studio, four rehearsal rooms, and Apple Macs galore in the music technology room. The standards here are very high, and just this year two guitarists were accepted at the Royal Northern College of Music – a highly competitive university where only musicians who have passed grade 8 music exams are considered. Another success story is the student who wrote and conducted his own rock opera featuring a full orchestra, choir and soloists.

The drama department puts on three big productions a year. When we were there, we saw Sweeney Todd in rehearsal in both the dance and drama studios. There must have been at least 50 students involved in just that one part.

The art department is split into three large studios. Wide range of creative media including painting, drawing (weekly life drawing classes), mixed media, installation, print making, 3D, textile arts and contextual studies. Plus facilities for dyeing and constructed textiles, a dedicated print room, a large scale printing press, a studio and a dark room. For Apple Mac enthusiasts, top software is available in the media and film studies departments. Recently students have produced a film called Hitting the Road, aimed at giving bikers practical advice to stay safe. Somerset Road Safety has commissioned it.

Enrichment activities take place during the school day as most students are restricted by bus timetables. For this reason, the college day finishes at 4.35pm. Subject enrichment activities include politics, debating and public speaking. There's Active Huish for sports, a wide range of musical activities, the Duke of Edinburgh Award Scheme, BELA, and drama and dance productions. Plus trips – volunteering in Sri Lanka, trips to Iceland, ski and snowboarding in France and archaeology trips to Rome.

Boarding: Oak House, a 53 bed boarding house, opened in 2017 to house international students (who have the alternative of staying with local families), plus some flexi boarding for home students.

Background and atmosphere: Originally founded as a grammar school for boys in the 18th century by Richard Huish, RHC has recently celebrated its 400th birthday. It became a sixth form college in 1993 and since then has grown from 660 full-time students to nearly 2,000. It has expanded again to include Huish Business School for adults (adult students make up less than five per cent of the college's full-time equivalent students), International Huish, and even a driving school.

The 20-acre campus, in the south of Taunton, is predominantly sports fields. The college itself is alleged to be on the site of an old Arboretum and each building has been named after trees. Most buildings are new and have been designed with the same footprint. Each department has its own study centre, which is more informal than the learning centre (library); students can work in groups or chat while working. Learning resource centre is at the heart of the campus. There are two silent zones, PCs, and a careers area with two staff on hand. Over the last three years, there has been an impressive programme of improvement and new building. The Juniper building with its state-of-the-art editing suites, is a purpose-built centre for a range of media studies. The newish Cedar Building accommodates a range of teaching in 10 classrooms, and all laboratory facilities have been upgraded. The new Maple building houses an art studio and graphic design Mac suites as well as state-of-the-art computing and computer science teaching rooms. Finally, there is the new two-storey café, complete with Costa restaurant.

RHC has long-been Wifi enabled. A remote desktop service is available as well as a free laptop loan system. Simply scan the lockers with an ID card, take a laptop, return when finished. No printers on campus; all have been replaced by multi-function devices; more convenient, greener and cheaper. Students can log on to any device and print their work. No regular bins on campus either: after rigorous campaigning by the environmental group, they have all been replaced by more eco-friendly recycling bins.

Pastoral care, well-being and discipline: There are three clear and simple expectations of students at Huish: be on time, do the work given (if you can't, ask for help), and be nice. No strict policies or statutory rules – one of the differences between a sixth form college and a school. One family told us, 'We did consider other colleges, but chose Richard Huish mainly due to the respect the teachers gave the young people and how they treated them as adults.' They went on to say, 'At this stage parents obviously need to be involved/kept in touch but I found that trusting [my son] and his teachers to work together as a team resolved most issues.'

Students have their own tutor and all tutorials are one-to-one. There are group tutorials initially when the term starts, but these are the exception. Tutors assess students individually and set out plans based on individual needs. For example, a tutor may decide to see one pupil weekly and another less frequently. Students are encouraged to speak to their tutors and ask questions whenever needed. They are also made aware, through tutorials and signposting throughout the college, of the help and counselling on offer.

Parents praised, 'the support and caring nature of the staff at the college.' One parent whose child had had some difficulties said the 'tutor is amazing and has been a real rock for our [child] through a very difficult time, going over and above to [help].' Another family told us that when their child had to extend their studies due to unforeseen medical issues, the college was more than accommodating and supportive. The college provides 'fantastic out of lesson support,' they said.

Pupils and parents: This is a college for the students. The website makes this clear: student case studies and videos, student quotes and stories; it is aimed at students, not parents. Of course parents are involved, but it is obvious they are not the main customer. Parents are happy with this approach. 'Communication has been fantastic and staff are very approachable,' said one. Another confirmed, saying, 'Newsletters kept coming, informing us of the college's activities, and termly reports were very informative, covering the areas which parents like to know: attendance and level of work quality. Contact details were available if we needed to contact the college and when we used them we had prompt, honest responses.'

The students we saw looked presentable and happy. Green hair after Halloween is standard. There's bound to be a real mix of people here due to high volumes, and individuality is encouraged. The college isn't producing clones as some schools tend to do; they are encouraging the students to develop with confidence, and providing them with the best tools and environment to do so. One parent explained 'He had loads of potential, but was headstrong. We hoped RHC would channel all that enthusiasm in a positive way and help him to mature and fulfil his potential; they did exactly that. I feel this was achieved by working with him almost as mentors, not teachers, and by treating him as an adult. I think if he had stayed at a school sixth form he would still have felt like a school boy, not a young adult.' Another parent gave a similar view, '[...] has benefited more than he would at a school sixth form. We can see he has become more independent and self-driven and studies hard to a high standard, which has all been encouraged by the college.' Students come from all over Somerset, and some from as far as Devon and Dorset.

Entrance: Requires five GCSEs at grade 4 or above including maths and English language. Offers a 12-month GCSE resit programme – around 60-65 students are currently on this.

Prospective students can join taster sessions and days. Students can choose a combination of A levels and BTecs and there is a two-week period at the beginning of term when changes can be made. Good parent feedback on this. 'Starting at college is always daunting, however RHC made it a controllable process, offering flexibility, points of contact for concerns with a sensible amount of time allowed for it. Plus I feel it was the start of a process where students took responsibility for their future and started to stand on their own feet by seeking answers to any concerns.'

Exit: Around 75 per cent go on to university, with a third gaining Russell Group places. The most consistently popular subjects are psychology and law, with nursing, sport, history and English always in the top 10. In 2018, nine to Oxbridge, plus six medics (one in Malta and another in Bulgaria), three vets and two dentists. Others off to the Netherlands, US and Hong Kong.

Former pupils include science fiction writer and inventor Arthur C Clarke, a former pupil of Huish's Grammar School, Andrew Castle, former British number one tennis player and television presenter, William Gibson, professor of history,

Rebecca Huxtable, former co-presenter on Radio 1, Keith Parsons, cricketer and Andy Robinson, former head coach of the England national rugby union team.

Money matters: RHC can help with travel costs, and college discretionary bursaries are available. Eligibility depends on household income or benefits received. There is also a Care to Learn scheme to help young parents, and a 19+ means-tested bursary. The Heathcoat Trust Bursary is for students from the partner schools of Uffculme, Cullompton and Tiverton High Schools who apply to university; it is worth £3,000 over three years.

Remarks: The results are impressive year on year. The facilities are enough to make any teenager (or young adult) want to learn. The opportunities are endless due to economies of scale. College life here is far more exciting than at many a school sixth form, and the adult approach to learning is a positive step towards university and work. Some parents may find it hard to take that leap of faith, but from everything we saw and heard, we think it's worth it.

Rougemont School

142

Llantarnam Hall, Malpas Road, Newport NP20 6QB

Ages 3–18 **Pupils** 550 **Sixth form** 100

Fees: £7,245 – £13,536 pa

01633 820800
www.rougemontschool.co.uk

Head: Since 2014, Robert Carnevale BSc Med PGCE (late 50s). A proud Welshman and nuclear physicist, Mr Carnevale has spent his whole teaching career in Wales, venturing to spend time over the bridge only as an undergraduate at Bath University. 'I did have options!' said he, in tones of mild protest: 'It's the family that kept me here'. Since then, he has taught in both local state and independent schools, rising through the hierarchy to his current position, one he had had a taste of when covering the previous head's sabbatical.

Mr Carnevale's appointment was an inside job after many years at Rougemont, following the retirement of several key members of the senior leadership team; his offer to throw his hat in the ring was gladly accepted, and he duly spent his first year bedding in the new SLT. Since then, he has increased teaching time for GCSE and A level classes, changed the uniform and is now embarking on an ambitious building programme to include a 650 seat performance space, new refectory and sixth form centre. Other priorities include beefing up the status of the sixth form, doing something about its interpretation of 'business wear' (loose, in our view) and turning out young people who can handle the future, whatever it holds.

Reassuring and compassionate but much more than a safe pair of hands, Mr Carnevale is reckoned to rule by fear of disappointing him, rather than fear itself, 'though he can be stern on occasion, say students. 'Not quite often enough!' in the view of one mother. We also heard 'bubbly, crazy, enthusiastic (especially about physics)' and they love the fact that he knows everyone. Married with three grown up sons, all of whom he taught in sixth form, his free time might be spent playing tennis or golf, or enjoying the fabulous walking in the Welsh countryside, sometimes even in Devon.

Head of prep school: Lisa Pritchard. Parents think she runs a tight ship and communicates well with them, including tackling any problems which arise.

Academic matters: Not an overtly academic school, but one which 'admits pupils who will be happy in the school, and who will thrive here, academically and socially'. Small mixed ability classes of between 10-18 pupils, where setting is not introduced until year 7, and then only in maths and French; English in year 9. A school which welcomes pretty well all comers must be doing something right with added value, then, with results well above national averages, with 74 per cent A^*-B at A level, 50 per cent A^*/A in 2018, and 63 per cent A^*-A/9-7 at GCSE, all up on last year. Subjects garnering the best results are maths, physics and chemistry, somewhat surprising when just one science is compulsory at GCSE. We were impressed by the differentiation between a top set putting quadratic equations on a graph and the bottom set having them explained using an analogy of a café and prices of tea and coffee. As for the sight of conjugations of verbs and the ablative absolute on the board in a Latin class – joy unconfined. Bright sparks can take GCSEs early in certain subjects. Some students want greater choice at A level, eg business studies and vocational options, though now offers film studies as an AS, and more teaching time. Extensive displays of student work throughout.

In the prep school, children love the small classes 'where everyone's your friend'. The love of maths and science starts early: we too loved the maths activity where a cake stall was the setting for an exercise in pricing. The 'broad and balanced curriculum' so many schools boast about is apparent here: younger children learn coding, about wildlife and eco-matters in the outdoor classroom and enjoy deep discussions and meditation alongside the three Rs.

A wider range of special needs are catered for here than in many schools, to include autism spectrum, ADHD ('Many of our pupils are neurodiverse,' says school) and visual impairment. Nearly a third of students have some kind of additional need, addressed in or by the learning development centre with three members of staff. Support is provided either individually or 2:1 and lessons are charged separately, although TAs will work with small groups in or outside the classroom. We like the fact that centre cites itself as 'a place for parents to come for advice and any problems related to learning'. Despite what appears to us as wider provision than many schools address, the head told us firmly that the school is 'not an SEN magnet'.

R

Games, options, the arts: Rougemont's 55 acre grounds means games and sports can be on site (floodlit Astro, tennis courts, rugby pitches and cricket nets), with the exception of swimming: prep school children do a two week intensive course at a local pool. Swimmers do well notwithstanding, with several girls in the junior Welsh national squad and one promising water polo player. Usual array of sport, with an impressive list of players in local and national development squads, enlivened by sprint kayaking (one student on Olympic watch list), climbing and sailing. Wide fixture list taking in local state and independent schools, though one parent told us she did not think the schools was as competitive as it could be. 'Parents with outstandingly sporty kids might make a different choice,' she added. Sporting achievement recognised at annual presentation evening. Fresh air and exercise prioritised, with the prep school children enthusing about the Astro and their regular one mile run.

Performing arts get similar thumbs up: recent productions include Honk! and Oliver! at the prep school, Sweeney Todd at the senior school, with a blood-curdling gaping mouth framing the former stage: a spanking new auditorium (with added refectory and sixth form centre) now provides contemporary performance setting. All kinds of music on offer too, though only a fifth of students learn an instrument. At the top end, musicians have been accepted by Welsh National Youth Orchestras and National Children's Orchestra of Great Britain; all players and singers, however, appear to enjoy the range of opportunities on offer such as string, percussion and brass groups – and what school in the land of song would be complete without its own eisteddfod?

Objects of beauty and/or functionality emanate from art and DT, the former benefiting from a new kiln, the latter with separate rooms for wood and metals/plastics. Results at both GCSE and A level are slightly better for art than for DT. Life-drawing a new activity. D of E increasingly popular at all levels, much encouraged by school. Plenty of clubs laid on at lunchtimes and after school, a mix of academic clinics, the cerebral (chess, defying gravity academy) and the contemporary (mindfulness, Minecraft). The littlest ones can take part in Rougemont Rangers, addressing matters such as in-school democracy and eco-matters.

Background and atmosphere: Named for the house in Newport in which it was originally founded as a junior school in the 1920s and which prepared children for grammar school, Rougemont moved to its present site only in 1995. Growing from the bottom up to become the all-through school it is today (A levels were offered for the first time in 1983), its junior pupils occupy the moderately imposing Victorian Llantarnam Hall with its magnificent staircase and sloping parkland, just outside Newport on the Cwmbran road. Other, less imposing, buildings have since been added and form the senior school and offices, but all enjoy the views of distant hills and doubtless its easy access from inside and outside Newport. The town has lost much of its industry, but as road links improve, the school attracts students from a wide catchment.

Its origins as a tiny school live on in the family feel it still retains, where everyone knows each other: 'Relationships between staff and students are not at all stuffy, and forms and year groups are like families,' older students told us, while a younger one remarked cheerfully that 'We always get through our ups and downs'. Despite being the sole independent school in the area, we heard no reports of town v gown animosity, even if its students are viewed as posh in their natty uniform; local clubs use its facilities after hours. It certainly feels very inclusive and welcoming to all comers, and not at all insular: much pride is taken in entering prestigious competitions such as Arkwright scholarships, Young Enterprise and the Engineering Education Scheme in Wales, as well as taking full advantage of the cultural and academic lure of Cardiff. Neither is it as overtly nationalistic as some schools in Wales we have been to, though the three houses have – quite rightly – fine Welsh names: Dyfrig, Caradog and Gwynog. Many staff members have been at the school for some time and remain greatly committed to it; impressive that the library is open for five hours a day at summer half term in exam season.

We sense that this is a school where the murkier and more confusing sides of teenage lives are expressed and explored: 'We talk about stuff like sexual exploitation,' one sixth former told us; another that the school works with Stonewall to work out a best etiquette for teachers over LGBT matters.

Pastoral care, well-being and discipline: Praise indeed for this aspect of school life, where support for anxiety and the close collaboration between teaching and pastoral staff is seen and appreciated by older students. As for the littler ones, they love the 'worry-eater', where teachers recover slips of paper with anonymous worries written on them, and act on them. School counsellor, and 'plenty of people to talk to,' students confirm. When things go wrong, teachers 'work with you and don't just punish you,' one boy said, his friends adding, 'We get warnings and time to improve'. Parents greatly value the support given to students by their peers: 'The school has created an environment where it's OK to ask each other for help,' said one. Try as we might, we couldn't find a mention of drink or drugs, so we must assume school deals with any transgressions with the same calm good sense with which it appears to tackle everything, but a more specific steer on absolute no-nos would help students and indeed parents. On the flip side, however, remarks from a few parents suggest that a tougher stance on poor behaviour in class would not go amiss, and that the school does not always react fast enough to any dissatisfaction raised about teaching staff – 'and there's not enough turnover,' remarked one mother.

Pupils and parents: 'Wide-ranging but mostly from professional families,' says the head, 'and some make considerable sacrifices to send their children here.' Some had been completely won over by Rougemont, even though they started out ideologically opposed to independent education. We found the students we met thoughtful and appreciative of all Rougemont has to offer, particularly in terms of opportunity and support. Most come from Newport or Cwmbran but a sprinkling from further afield, including the eastern fringes of Cardiff, many using one of eight bus routes the school lays on. A wider proportion of BME than might be expected for Wales, at just under 20 per cent.

Entrance: Hopefuls for the prep school spend two days here and are interviewed by its head. For the senior school at year 7, students from other schools sit assessments held in January each year, where there is no pass mark as such, but which are used to screen out those 'who will find the level of work at Rougemont unduly difficult', to cite the admissions policy. At sixth form, the school expects five GCSEs at a 6 or above from its own students, as well as incomers. New scholarships at years 5, 7 and 9. Rougemont is obviously getting its open days absolutely right: we were told by several parents that they had been 'blown away' when they attended one.

Exit: Up to 20 per cent leave after GCSEs for greater subject choice in sixth form or because of financial constraints. Advice on university choices and work experience gets the thumbs up from sixth formers and includes visiting speakers. Almost everyone gains a place at their first choice university: four to Oxbridge in 2018, many to the Welsh universities or not too far away to Bath, Bristol or Exeter. A sprinkling of medics vets and dentists most years. Very few gap years, and just a handful of leavers go straight to work.

Famous former students include chef Matt Tebbutt, children's poet Susan Richardson and retired Welsh rugby international Richard Parks.

Money matters: Not a rich school and one charging much less than the going rate, but able to offer academic and non-academic scholarships to a maximum of 25 per cent of fees. Limited number of means-tested bursaries on offer from year 7 upwards, but sixth form applicants must have five GCSEs at grade 7 to be considered. Relaunched PTA raises funds, sells second hand uniform and has fun.

Remarks: The only independent game in town, as far as Newport goes, providing a useful alternative to its state schools for those wanting smaller classes, lots of tlc and more space and/or sport. 'It's as near to a comprehensive school as I could get – with small classes,' said one parent. The fact that it isn't full is more of a comment on the prevailing local economy rather than the school, which appears to be loved by everyone connected with it. 'The best decision I ever made,' according to one happy customer. Reckoned to live up to its motto or aspiration as a school for life – a strapline devised by a parent.

Royal High Prep School Bath

Linked with Royal High School Bath

Cranwell House, Weston Park East, Bath, Somerset BA1 2UZ

Ages 3–11 **Pupils** 130

Fees: £9,945 – £10,479 pa

01225 422931
www.royalhighbath.gdst.net

Head: Since 2013, Heidi Hughes BSc PGCE MA. Previously deputy head of Royal Russell Junior School in Surrey. Before that she was a member of management teams at British schools in Singapore and the Philippines. A PE specialist who can turn her hand to teaching most subjects, she's a strong advocate of linking learning in and beyond the classroom. Outside school, her interests are sport, travel and family. She often volunteers at local sporting events (including the London 2012 Olympics).

Moving on in July 2019 to head BGS Infant and Junior School in Bristol.

Entrance: Prospective pupils are invited to a taster day, where their English and maths skills are assessed, followed by a chat with the head.

Exit: Virtually all progress to the senior school – via the transfer exam in year 6.

Remarks: The junior school is housed in a beautiful Grade II listed building, Cranwell House, set in 11 acres of landscaped grounds on the north side of Bath, one and a half miles from the city centre. Once the Mayor of Bath's house and later an art school, it boasts a wealth of period features and has been converted into a junior school with great sensitivity and flair. The Royal High's junior girls moved to the site in 2014.

The school is rightfully proud of its creative curriculum (it was shortlisted for the TES's Creative School of the Year award in 2017). Introduced six years ago and known as the Cranwell Curriculum, it draws on the Reggio Emilia approach to education, where children are encouraged to use words, movement, art, building, sculpture, drama and music to express themselves, discover new things and communicate what they know and understand. Girls have discrete maths and English lessons every day but other subjects are taught thematically. Themes are 'fluid and adaptable' and change every year (recent examples include The Victorians, the Second World War and Historical Heroes). The head says that taking a creative approach like this enables girls to develop independent thinking and fosters an understanding of the world, citizenship and collective responsibility. It clearly works – junior girls transferring to the senior school are regularly awarded scholarships. When we visited, we watched a spirited year 2 class discussing (with animated actions) the British suffragette Emmeline Pankhurst. 'The academic standards we achieve and the levels of attainment are amazing,' says the head. 'It's wonderful to see the girls' enjoyment and love of learning.'

Classes are small – nine in reception. Maximum is 24 so 31-strong year 6 group is split into two. Teachers incorporate the five Rs (not three) into lessons – relationships, resilient, reflective, resourceful and risk-taking. Resilience is a major theme and like other GDST schools girls at the Royal High Junior learn to take risks and persevere. They learn from their mistakes and realise it's important not to fear failure. In 2016 ISI inspectors commented: 'Pupils in years 1 to 6 gain self-esteem through the opportunities that they are provided to recognise their own and one another's strengths. They are not afraid to admit mistakes, due to the encouragement and praise they receive when using initiative and the resilience they display when things go wrong, embracing fully the junior school initiative: "Dare to fail. Bounce back."'

Big emphasis on science, discovery and the great outdoors – hardly surprising in such a stunning location. Girls grow vegetables, watch badgers, deer and foxes in the garden (cameras have been set up to observe the animals) and played a major role in the construction of an impressive Celtic round house in the grounds. Pupils chose the site, marked out the circle and helped to create the wattle walls. An eagle-eyed teacher spotted a local thatcher getting rid of some thatch and asked if the school could have it instead.

Lessons end at 3.30pm but mindful of parents' busy working lives, the school runs a breakfast club between 7.30 and 8am every day and after-school care till 6pm. Girls do their homework first and then take part in a host of activities. Like the senior school, the junior school is ultra-keen on music. Around 80 per cent of junior girls have instrument or singing lessons. Girls learn modern languages from an early age – French taught by subject specialists from nursery, Spanish in years 3 and 4, Mandarin in year 5 and Latin in year 6. They also have strong links with other schools – with The Crane Academy in Kenya and Howell's School, Llandaff, another GDST school (year 1 and 2 pupils have pen pals from corresponding year groups at Howell's). Lots of sport, including inter-school fixtures, festivals and tournaments and a whole-school sports day held at the University of Bath.

Hope Hall is used for assemblies, PE, drama and music productions and lunch. The school places huge emphasis on extracurricular pursuits. Year 3 to 6 girls have a weekly 'inspire' session, choosing activities like coding, animation, upcycling and navigation, where they learn to use maps and compasses. Pupils are encouraged to articulate their ideas and views confidently – with lots of opportunities to take part in the school council. Every year 6 is a prefect. They apply for their jobs and learn to take responsibility, helping with library duties, younger classes and even the head's office. Pupils also belong to one of four houses – Charlcombe, Grosvenor, Lansdown and Northfields. Keen to earn house points, they represent their houses in events throughout the school year.

The school is small, family-orientated and friendly. Most pupils come from Bath, many living within walking distance of school. For those with daughters at the senior school, there's a shuttle minibus that runs from Lansdown Road to the junior school in the mornings and back in the afternoons.

A lovely, nurturing school in an exceptional location. Girls learn to have a go at all manner of academic and extracurricular pursuits and achieve fine results.

Royal High School Bath

Linked with Royal High Prep School Bath

Lansdown Road, Bath, Somerset BA1 5SZ

Ages 11–18 **Pupils** 500 **Sixth form** 150 **Boarders** 122 full, 5 weekly, 3 flexi

Fees: Day £13,509 – £14,100 pa; Boarding £26,280 – £30,894 pa

01225 313877
www.royalhighbath.gdst.net

Head: Since 2015, Jo Duncan MA PGCE (40s). Previously head of Princess Helena College in Hertfordshire. Grew up in Northern Ireland, where she attended a girls' grammar school. Studied English and theology at St Andrews, with the intention of working as a lawyer or teacher. After stints working in schools in Hungary and Romania during her university years she realised she felt 'very at home in the classroom' so opted to do a PGCE at Homerton College, Cambridge. First teaching post was at The Latymer School, a high performing state school in north London, where she taught RS for four years. Then moved to Benenden, where she spent seven years and 'fell in love with boarding and its community feel'. Encouraged by the then Benenden head Claire Oulton to apply for the Princess Helena headship – and was appointed at the relatively young age of 33. Spent seven years at Princess Helena – 'a nice length of time' – but was attracted to the Royal High by its bigger size, boarding (it's the only Girls' Day School Trust school with boarders) and the fact that it offers the IB as well as A levels. 'The quality of the teaching really struck me,' she says, 'and being part of the GDST is exciting. It's the most fabulous network for heads, teachers and pupils and the opportunities are amazing.' Parents are impressed by her energy and drive. 'She has very good ideas,' one told us, 'and she has really improved the boarding facilities.'

Asked to describe Royal High girls, the head stresses that the school is 'not a hothouse', with pupils ranging from the highly academic to those with a 'much broader academic profile'. As you'd expect, she's a firm advocate of single-sex schools and says the Royal High 'focuses on how girls learn' and helps them achieve in all aspects of life, from lessons to leadership. Coincidentally, on the day of our visit, the papers featured apposite comments from Ofsted chief Amanda Spielman, saying that single-sex schools help to cut gender stereotyping and encourage girls to explore 'typically male subjects'.

Married to Murray, a London lawyer. They have two children – their son is a pupil at Kingswood, just over the road from the Royal High, and their daughter is a pupil at the Royal High's junior school – and live in a house on the school site. In her spare time she enjoys travel, skiing, theatre, ballet and reading.

Off to head Wycombe Abbey in July 2019.

Academic matters: Excellent teaching and very good results. One parent praised the Royal High's teaching as 'the very highest calibre' while another told us that girls achieve their potential without the element of pressure sometimes found in girls' schools. 'They are expected to do well but they don't seem to be stressed about doing well,' she said. In 2018, 69 per cent 9-7 at GCSE and 53 per cent A*/A at A level. School has offered the IB since 2008 and girls achieved average score of 39 in 2018. Lots of help and guidance about the respective merits of the IB and A levels, including an IB/A levels-themed Any Questions event. Sixth formers are encouraged to take the EPQ too. Most girls do 10 or 11 subjects at GCSE, including two or three sciences and at least one language.

Strong focus on STEM (science, technology, engineering and maths) subjects, with impressive numbers choosing sciences at A level (when we visited, a quarter of the sixth form were taking chemistry). 'We do lots of experiments and practicals,' a year 10 girl told us. 'My favourite lesson was when we made toy helicopters and flew them off the balcony. Science is so much fun.' Maths is the most popular A level subject, with year 13 girls giving extra help to younger pupils during their lunch break. Languages are particularly strong – French, German, Italian, Spanish and Mandarin on offer, plus Latin from year 7. Head girl told us she did four languages at GCSE, as well as Mandarin AS. Pupils are keen on Vocab Express, an online vocab learning challenge, and at the time of our visit a group of year 10 and 11 girls had been placed eighth nationally. Lots of language and exchange trips. A sixth former waxed lyrical about a recent trip to China, where she'd taught English in a primary school.

School is broadly selective, but probably not the place for girls with extensive learning needs. Learning support ranges from in-class support to one-to-one help (girls are never withdrawn from core curriculum subjects). As the school says: 'The majority of girls we currently support are those with specific learning difficulties such as dyslexia. We also have some girls with ADHD, autism and a few girls with sensory impairments such as hearing difficulties.'

Games, options, the arts: Pupils are proud of the school's sporting successes, notably in hockey, netball, athletics, swimming, fencing and taekwondo. 'We hold our own,' says the head. At the time of our visit a year 13 had just been selected for Bath Rugby Ladies team after a year of playing the sport. Sports facilities include sports hall, outdoor swimming pool, fitness suite, hockey pitches, netball courts and new Astro opened by Olympic gold-medal winning hockey player Kate Richardson-Walsh. The school also uses the University of Bath's sports pitches.

Performing arts are big at the Royal High. Dynamic director of music (a composer who previously worked for EMI and the BBC) encourages musicians of all standards and abilities to have a go. All-inclusive music programme features 35+ events a year, performed by five choirs, orchestra, swing band, strings group, woodwind ensemble, rock bands and more. Carol service at Bath Abbey is the highlight of the year for many parents. All year 7, 8 and 9 pupils get an hour's classroom music a week, learning about different styles of music, performance and composition, plus taster lessons to help them decide the instruments most suited to them. Around 300 instrumental lessons per week, with 14 girls a year taking GCSE music and up to eight doing A level. We met a talented sixth form singer who has already released two EPs of her own.

Wonderful art produced in the light, airy art school, with four studios and panoramic views to inspire girls' creativity. We particularly admired a sculpture made of wire, tights and teapots representing pattern and rhythm and a remarkably accomplished series of countryside paintings by a sixth former who brought in bags of twigs, sticks and leaves for inspiration. Up to 40 girls a year take art GCSE, 20 take A level and four or five take art as part of the IB. Well-equipped DT department has an ultra-sophisticated 3D printer and a four-axis router. Head of DT says he's 'constantly surprised' by the girls' ideas, showing us a student's stunning faux-leather backpack inspired by an armadillo. Drama and dance in the Sophie Cameron Performing Arts Centre and school's dance studio. Loads of successes in the Mid-Somerset Festival and LAMDA exams. Year 13 girls run a drama club for year 7s and there's a plethora of school and house productions throughout the year. Recent shows include The Tempest, The Wizard of Oz and The Crucible, with rehearsals for Oliver! taking place when we visited.

School has a strong international focus and links with schools as far afield as New York, Kenya and Sydney. Year 9 girls get the chance to do a five-week exchange with Australian girls – 'the most fantastic experience,' a parent told us. An enterprising sixth former set up a charity project, designing and producing cards and gifts to raise money for a school in Kenya. Year 8s take part in an enterprise day with nearby boys' state school Beechen Cliff and older girls do Model United Nations debates with Kingswood and King Edward's School, Bath. There's also the Aspire programme, an academic enrichment programme featuring after-school lectures, activities and debates.

Boarding: Boarding numbers are growing steadily. New head of boarding joined from Benenden in 2016 and is responsible for the development of boarding at the Royal High. Around two-thirds of boarders are from overseas – from China, Hong Kong, Spain, Germany, Brazil, Kenya (30 nationalities in all). Boarding from year 7 (also available to year 5 and 6 girls from the junior school). Two boarding houses – School House for younger girls and Gloucester House for sixth formers. Full and weekly boarding only. Flexi boarding is available subject to availability of beds. Lots of weekend activities, including pottery painting, baking, zumba, spa days, expeditions to places like Harry Potter World and theatre and cultural trips. Girls are allowed to walk the mile down the hill into Bath – year 7s are escorted while year 8s go in groups of four.

Boarding houses are comfortable, homely and chic, so much so that day girls jump at the chance to do the occasional sleepover. Youngest girls are in wholesome dorms of four or five while sixth formers get doubles or singles. Sixth form boarding house is 'a stepping stone to university', with girls able to cook and do their own washing if they wish. Sixth form café attached, where day girls and boarders can relax and chill.

Background and atmosphere: Bath is a Unesco World Heritage Site and the first glimpse of the school is an impressive Victorian stone monolith at the top of a steep drive off the city's picturesque Lansdown Road. Extensive refurbishment programme in progress when we visited on a blustery October day but the school's listed Grade II buildings are stunning, especially when viewed under a glowing orange sun. Many of the classrooms, dorms and the head's office boast panoramic views across the school's 11-acre site to the city and beyond. The Royal High has blazed a trail as the only GDST school to offer boarding – a legacy from the amalgamation between Bath High School and the Royal School back in 1998. It admitted boys for a brief period but has been all-girls since 2010.

Sixth formers wear business suits rather than uniform. Younger girls are very happy with their new navy blazers and tartan skirts. Unlike some schools, no over-the-top make-up – 'we don't do contouring here,' grinned a year 9 pupil at lunch, to the merriment of her friends. Food, provided by catering company Holroyd Howe, is very good. Lots of choice, including vegetarian and gluten-free options, all carefully labelled, pasta, salads, sandwiches and hot meals.

Pastoral care, well-being and discipline: Girls are well looked after and look after each other well. No behaviour problems – just the occasional social media or friendship issue typical of girls of this age. Parents like the school's size ('not too big, and not too small so everyone knows everyone') and say that if an issue arises the school 'is on it very quickly'. 'We talk to the girls all the time about who they are and what they want to achieve,' says the head. 'As a girls' school we want to be a positive place where girls can flourish and grow.' All pupils have a one-hour PSHEE (personal, social, health and economic education) session per fortnight and school also runs Your Daughter, a programme of talks for parents on topics like developing resilience and happiness, surviving social media and the dangers of illegal drugs and legal highs. When suitable, girls attend these talks with their parents or hear their own version in school.

One of the most popular members of the school community is Spitfire, an 18-month-old black lurcher, who belongs to the student welfare co-ordinator (she also teaches biology and is known as 'Spitfire's mum'). A well-being dog, Spitfire is a comforting presence when girls feel stressed, worried or tired. When the registrar announced to a group of year 9s that Spitfire had just become a father to seven puppies, a unanimous 'aaaaah' went round the room. He even got a round of applause on a recent open day.

School is keen on encouraging leadership and responsibility. It hosts the annual GDST Young Leaders' Conference, where year 13 student leaders from all 25 GDST sixth forms get the chance to network, take part in teamwork challenges and hear a host of inspiring speakers. The sixth formers then feed back to the rest of the school in assemblies. Head girl, boarding deputy, day deputy and four additional prefects – all voted in by staff and pupils (year 10s and up). Year 13s mentor younger girls and everyone takes pride in belonging to one of four houses named after impressive women – Austen, Bronte, Wollstonecraft and Du Pré.

Pupils and parents: The pupils are sparky girls who throw themselves into lessons, music, sport and extracurricular activities with enthusiasm and panache. We particularly enjoyed lunch with a group of chatty year 9s, who, with the amused registrar in attendance, talked about everything from the 'great' integration of boarders and day pupils to the 'reasonable' amount of homework they get. They were funny, charming and keen to extol the virtues of their school. 'We feel like we can be ourselves here,' said one girl. Another said that that everyone was 'so accepting' and she didn't feel any peer pressure.

All agreed that the Royal High is not a snobby school. Parents come from all backgrounds, including business people, medics, media types and ex-Londoners. Sixty per cent of day pupils live in Bath, others are from Somerset and Gloucestershire – some walk to school, some commute by bus and train. Famous alumnae include baking supremo Mary Berry, Baroness Elspeth Howe and entrepreneur Emily Brooke, who designed a pioneering laser bike light.

Entrance: Competition for year 7 places is less intense than you might think. Around 100 girls a year apply and the school offers 80 places. The entrance assessment takes place in January – an interview first, then English, maths, verbal reasoning and non-reasoning tests a few days later. Around 95 per cent from the junior school progress to the senior school via a transfer test.

Up to 15 girls join in year 9 and 35 or so in year 12. Sixth formers need six 6s at GCSE including 7s in subjects they want to study at A level or the IB.

Exit: Around a quarter leave after GCSEs, either for a change of scene or to do other subjects. At 18 almost all to university with a healthy smattering of medics and engineers, plus a few to art foundation courses and drama school. Three to Oxbridge and two medics in 2018.

Leavers join the GDST's Alumnae Network, which offers mentoring for GDST alumnae and sixth formers, university advice, career development and networking opportunities. The Royal High encourages former pupils to inspire and mentor their younger counterparts – old girls return to talk about their careers and many offer work experience.

Money matters: Good value for money, especially as textbooks, stationery, most extracurricular activities and sixth-form laptops are included. Boarding fees are cheaper than many other boarding schools due to GDST economies of scale. A raft of scholarships and bursaries available, including academic, art, dance, drama, music and sport. STEM scholarships offered in year 9 and year 12. Means-tested bursaries (up to 100 per cent of the fees) for students demonstrating 'outstanding all-round academic ability'.

Remarks: A happy, high achieving, very go-ahead school with a distinctive ethos, sense of community and impressive results. For parents looking for a single sex-school (day and/or boarding) we can't think of any girl who wouldn't thrive here.

Rydal Penrhos

Pwllycrochan Avenue, Colwyn Bay LL29 7BT

Ages 2–18 **Pupils** 472 **Sixth form** 121 **Boarders** 71 full, 23 weekly, 8 flexi (from year 7)

Fees: Day £7,452 – £16,785 Boarding £20,901 – £33,450 pa

01492 530155
www.rydalpenrhos.com/

Interim head: We heard as we went to press that Simon Smith, head since January 2017, left in January 2018. John Waszek is holding the fort.

Simon graduated in history from York. Has worked extensively in the boarding sector, and was a senior leader at Worth and deputy head at Haileybury before coming to Rydal Penrhos. His interests look beyond the walls of the school – he writes for the educational press, runs half marathons, joins in the Saturday park runs and is restoring a 19th century barn. Wife Karen has had a successful career first in publishing and then marketing, now a highly knowledgeable and effective registrar here, where she can speak as a parent as well as a professional, having her son and daughter both in the senior school.

While a strong supporter of the warm atmosphere of the school (he joins the lunch queue with the pupils so he can chat to them), Simon is working on driving up academic achievements, developing his teachers through first rate professional development opportunities and research-based pedagogy, and emphasising the vision of a learning community. He is focused on the strengths of the all through school – the best practice of both the prep and the senior are shared. Determined to listen to all the constituent groups and draw on their experience and wisdom, he has used feedback from teachers, parents and pupils to good effect, for example the school now uses Show My Homework app. Pupils love his passion for the school. 'He really wants to understand student issues', they told us.

Head of prep: Alison Hind; BEd from Goldsmiths and a NPQH. Before coming to Rydal Penrhos in 2009, she was deputy head at Uplands School, Poole. Longstanding parents say it has been lovely to see how she has grown into her present role and really flourished. Her own two children are in the senior school. Parents find her highly approachable and they, too, see the prep school as a lifestyle choice. As well as being committed to a broad school curriculum, Alison is constantly moving it beyond the school gates to offer the children as wide an experience as possible.

R

Academic matters: A level results reflect the quite wide ability range. In 2018, 45 per cent were at A*-A, with 63 per cent A*-B. At GCSE in 2018, 51 per cent A*-A/9-7 grades.

The school has run the IB – average points 32 in 2018 – but the last cohort finishes in 2019. Instead, it is introducing more vocational courses by popular demand – BTecs in applied science, sports and business, A level psychology and a Leiths course – plus new personal development courses that focus on leadership and challenge. The sixth form curriculum can be tailormade, with modern languages courses running with just few – Italian and Chinese offered recently.

The prep school teaches French from reception and there is a Welsh lesson each week. We watched a year 3 science lesson where the topic was rocks and the pupils were making fossil casts. Huge fun. ICT has moved away from word processing – every department can do that, the ICT specialist told us – to teaching coding, programming and animation. In the younger years, there is topic-based work, the topic changing every half term. It was space when we visited. Parents were getting involved, going out at night to observe stars and the moon with their children.

Wonderful play areas which are used for forest school studies. The children in their waterproofs are out in all weathers. The prep is also making use of its location to develop a very popular coastal school. The outdoor curriculum is all about problem solving in its widest sense.

Class sizes are typically 20 or so from reception to year 4, then two forms of around 12/13 in years 5 and 6, from where nearly all move on to the senior school.

Learning support may be within lessons or one-to-one, at extra charge if intense help needed. Parents say how effective it is and genuinely tailored to each individual. Pupils tell us teachers are always willing to give extra help and the lunchtime surgeries are very useful for small concerns.

High ability and potential is spotted early and teachers are constantly working to take children to the next level. In the senior school, there is a programme for the academic scholars to promote breadth of learning and stimulate intellectual curiosity.

Games, options, the arts: This is a sporty and an outdoorsy school, well known for its traditional sports prowess, with other options ranging from skiing to sailing – the school has its own boathouse. There is a golf academy and pupils represent Wales in various international competitions. We liked the golf bags lined up in the boarding houses – ready for pupils to make a dash to the onsite short game golf course. Sports scholars benefit from individualised fitness programmes and a competitive fixture list.

The music department is 'genius,' we were told by various pupils. There is a real diversity with an emphasis on getting everyone involved. We heard a harmonics group sing very professionally in chapel. There is a community choir that includes parents and staff. Regular senior and junior concerts. One mother spoke enthusiastically of how her prep school son, who wasn't passionate about sport, had taken to harp playing and how it had hugely increased his confidence. The school runs successful music and drama workshops for local primary schools. There are popular drama and musical theatre performances throughout the school and pupils can't speak highly enough of the passion of their performing arts teachers.

Art is a great strength with lots of opportunities that the department fits around the special talents of the pupils. Everything you could want is there – kiln, potters' wheel, textiles room, a vintage printing machine and etching press, photographic studio for wet photography and also Apple Mac for film making, graphics and Photoshop. Artwork around the school is stunning. We saw displays in the style of African, Aboriginal and Mexican art as well as felt work and Batik. Art workshops in the prep department encourage parents and grandparents to get involved.

DT is also very popular and has a well used and resourced space with 3D printers and facilities for CAD and CAM. Large scale A level projects were in the process of construction – one to improve rugby fitness. Year 9 and 10s are involved in the Greenpower car building competition.

Lots of clubs and societies. The eco committee recently organised a meat free day – and everyone survived, even the rugby players. The prep eco club has built a greenhouse out of plastic bottles. 'It wasn't easy,' one 10 year old told us, eyeing it critically. Other prep clubs include gardening, cooking, bug hunting, soap making, Welsh, robotics, coding as well as lots of sport, dance, music and drama.

Some prep school members had spent a couple of days at Ironbridge, making bricks, candles and buggies and visiting the Science and Technology Centre and Tile Museum. Others had a week at an outdoor centre gorge walking, mountain climbing and washing their own dishes. All year 9s start Dof bronze award and many go on to complete silver and gold. A recent Japanese rugby tour was a great success. There are strong links with a school in Uganda which pupils visit once every two years and support with funds.

Sixth formers have set a vibrant school newspaper, by the pupils for the pupils – The RePorter – an example of the entrepreneurial spirit that the head is encouraging.

Boarding: The school has bought up large Victorian and Edwardian villas in the streets around the main site and this means the boarding houses have the feel of large family homes, with quirky original features and lovely gardens. The vertical organisation of the houses enhances the family feel, with year 7s living alongside year 13s. The girls' boarding is in the top three floors of the prep school, a simply amazing building that has previously been a palatial family home and a hotel, with breathtaking sea views.

No academic lessons on Saturdays but plenty of sports fixtures, training sessions and a parkrun. The art department and sports facilities are open at weekends. Trips for boarding and day pupils to see Manchester City play, ice skating, trampolining, indoor climbing, shopping.

Many of the house staff are longstanding, experienced with teenagers, proactive in relation to mental health and relationship issues. Sanctions are clear but individual, and pupils described then as fair. Academic staff spend time in the houses in the evenings which mean help is on hand for any prep problems. The school will cease boarding become a fully day school from September 2021.

Background and atmosphere: Many of the buildings date back to the founding of Rydal in 1885. The school merged with the all girls Penrhos College in 1995. Some of the distinctive Penrhos features, such as wonderful stained glass, were incorporated into the Rydal buildings and enhance the slightly clerical feel of some parts. The old mock-gothic dining room is now the library, with a modern mezzanine floor for sixth formers with a careers centre. The Memorial Hall was added in the 50s, a serviceable if somewhat traditional performance space. A new building houses the current dining hall, sixth form centre and indoor sports facilities with fitness suite and dance studio. Pupils can use the gym from 6.30am – and plenty do. The prep school is in an amazing white mansion on the hillside just above the main campus. Early years pupils have their own entrance and lovely small play areas.

Pupil voice is a strong feature. Recently year 13s requested a refurbishment of their sixth form centre. They did the research, decided on the plans and worked with the staff to mount a fundraising programme, and the refurbishment – including a new café for sixth form and parents – is now complete. There is a compellingly positive, can-do attitude about the school and the pupils.

Pupils comment on the warmth of the relationships at all levels in the school community.

Pastoral care, well-being and discipline: There is an atmosphere of tolerance, respect and openness that underpins pastoral care and discipline. The school's values are reinforced through a well structured and developing PSHE programme. The prep pupils do sessions on working together and older pupils take leadership modules. Six formers trained in peer mentoring can support younger pupils.

When something goes wrong, pupils report that staffs' first response is, 'Let's fix this together. What can I do to help you stop this happening again?' Beyond that, there is the usual range of warnings, detentions, on report, gating for boarders and the occasional more serious exclusion for offences like bringing illicit alcohol into school.

Pupils and parents: It is quite a varied school body. Scholarships and bursaries ensure a greater diversity than in some other boarding schools. A few of the day pupils have never been on an aeroplane before their first school overseas trip.

There are seven minibus routes bringing in pupils from all over north Wales and Cheshire. Most UK boarders live within an hour or two of the school and flexi-boarding encourages families who are not typical boarding families to give it a try. Overseas boarders – about half of the total – come from some 20 different countries. Many parents went to school here and parents we spoke to had a strong sense of loyalty to the school.

The prep school is keen to involve parents. There are drop in sessions and open classroom times. A reminder app lets everyone know what is happening the next day. Art workshops, family reading sessions and weekly celebratory assemblies all engage the parents in the life of the school – and they love it.

Entrance: Entrance to the prep school is non-selective; entrance exams from the prep to the senior school are for setting purposes. Prep pupils regularly take national standardised assessments and if a child wouldn't flourish at the senior school, discussions begin early with parents.

For outside senior school applicants, there are tests in literacy, numeracy and non-verbal reasoning and for year 10/11 applicants in English and maths. Sixth form requirements are GCSEs at 5 or above with 6 in the subjects to be studied at A level.

Exit: University destinations and subjects are diverse. Two to Oxbridge in 2018 and one medic. Others off to Canada (conservation and forest management, and maths and economics), Santa Barbara and Amsterdam (economics).

Money matters: Fees are middle of the range. Ten per cent scholarships – academic, art, drama, music and sport – plus means-tested bursaries and two funded day sixth form places for students coming from a state school in north Wales.

Remarks: This is a school where continuous improvement is part of the culture. Both parents and pupils say their views are actively sought and the school wants to listen in order to keep getting better and better. The head is upping the academic stakes and one or two pupils did mention lots of homework, but overall there is general agreement that the school wants pupils to have a rich balance in their lives. It is not a school for the pushy parent, or if they do find themselves there, they will be encouraged to move from a highly competitive approach to one where the emphasis is on each pupil flourishing to the best of their ability.

'Our whole family is just in love with the school', one mother told us,and we can see why.

The Ryleys School

Ryleys Lane, Alderley Edge, Cheshire SK9 7UY

Ages 21m–11 **Pupils** 204 (145 boys, 59 girls)

Fees: £10,260 – £11,538 pa

01625 583241
www.theryleys.com

Headteacher: Since September 2016, Julia Langford, BEd (Chester), previously deputy head. Arrived here in 2011 from Hale Prep as head of English.

Since taking up the reins, Mrs Langford has instigated some bold changes but stresses that she has sought to fuse the school's traditional values with a more forward-thinking education. One new element has been introducing global perspectives into the curriculum; children now study countries from all angles: historical, geographical and cultural. She has also created a rather splendid outdoor classroom. 'Learning about rivers', she says, 'means the children can now get out and build one with dams'. A passionate advocate for practical engagement and children being hands-on when learning, she believes outdoor activities bring a fresh perspective and improved concentration.

As we walk around the school, pupils call out to her with a big grin and she replies, knowing each of their names. One parent summed up her style as 'all-encompassing'; 'she is able to relate to children of all ages while retaining gravitas'. Mrs Langford is especially keen on pupils developing independence because she knows that parents can fall into the trap of micro-managing. She wants to provide a nurturing environment where children build resilience, so those who persevere or take a risk with learning are rewarded with a much-coveted merit.

Her ultimate quest is for the school to be 'hitting top marks' in every area and 'be recognised as a 'centre of excellence'. It seems she is well on her way or, as one parent put it: 'she has made instrumental changes and been amazing'.

When she is not striving to hit top marks at school, she has her head in a book, fiction or perhaps cookery, and is currently learning to play golf.

Entrance: Non-selective with a 'huge spread of ability'. Two class intake.

R

Exit: Conversations about senior schools start in year 5; head says 'anything is still possible' early in year 6 so is careful not to rule out options prematurely. All the usual destination schools: Alderley Edge School for Girls, Cheadle Hulme, Kings' Macclesfield, Manchester Grammar, Withington Girls, Manchester High School for Girls.

Remarks: A broad curriculum kicks off at nursery stage, with specialist French and music teachers. Nursery is in a delightful space with a little sleep area for afternoon naps. Parents love it. Pre-reception has its own lovely classroom – some super displays, including some rather good self-portraits – which heralds a slight shift to more formalised learning. We did come across a couple of parents who queried the organisation in a class the previous year but new staff have been appointed since then. The previous year had been 'all about change', head said to us and now she wanted a period of consolidation while changes bedded down.

At pre-prep (reception to year 2) the emphasis is on literacy, maths, learning about the world but also music, French, PE, science and art. Pre-prep has its own play area complete with story-telling chair and a texture kitchen. We stopped by a reception class, where the French teacher was reading We're Going on a Bear Hunt in French: 'Marche lentement,' she ordered, as they leapt to their feet. For year 1, it was newspaper publishing and dabbling in coding within two very well stocked IT rooms, while year 2 were learning about the Victorian age. We noted an impressive display of year 2 essays in cursive handwriting: 'we put a great emphasis on introducing cursive in year 1,' head says, noticing our gaze.

The school adopts Singapore maths, which aims to eschew rote learning in favour of understanding concepts and practical applications of problems. 'There is no such thing as being either good or bad at maths and Singapore maths is proof of that', head says. 'It helps children find their own methods and develop an innate understanding in the process'.

At the prep (years 3-6), the curriculum is extended with DT added, then in years 5 and 6, Italian. A super library showed a reading tree wall display with pupils' post-it notes of their fave books. Pleasingly, head is a fan of integrating Shakespeare in little ways so that by year 6 they can maybe tackle some Macbeth or Romeo and Juliet. A global perspectives lesson was focusing on Australia; 'lessons are child-led', teacher says. (So anything from boomerangs to kangaroos kick-start the chat.) Rooms for science (lab due to be refurbed) and DT woodwork room looked reasonably well-equipped. The Greenpower kit car was laid out in one, a year 6 project after entrance exams.

Historically, Ryleys has always been known as a lovely school but not always, perhaps unfairly, for its academic prowess. This is all changing; while it has a non-selective intake, the head has introduced more focused data tracking so a true measure is taken of a pupil abilities and potential. She has also rolled out booster sessions. Parents of children aiming for the very academic schools in Manchester say their children are stretched. The differentiated teaching is less about setting (though parents we spoke to seem to perceive them that way), more about fluid groups peeling off for separate teaching.

Learning difficulties seem very well catered for; the school has a SENCo and assistants and a dyslexia specialist comes in to do assessments and devise programmes. Extra lessons for all those who find reading and writing difficult. Small interventions make a big difference, head says.

She has instigated greater communication with parents, including an app, Seesaw, giving daily feedback. Parents receive termly written reports, along with end of term assessment results and a personal development report. Three parents' evenings per year. One parent said: 'the education has always been good but now there is more visibility and accountability'.

Music is popular with choirs and a summer concert. In one music lesson, children were tiptoeing with great delight across a floor piano mat, the cushioned sections sounding out the notes. Drama is also big; LAMDA is on offer and parents praised productions like Charlie and the Chocolate Factory. The art teacher told us pupils were 'all eco-warriors', very keen on upcycling (many art projects tie in with global perspectives: totem poles, South American weaving). Arts awards are also on offer.

Great sports facilities: pitches, Astroturf, courts, playgrounds galore. Visiting on a gloriously sunny autumn day, we witnessed pupils' fun in the outdoor swimming pool. As the gender ratio varies, sports teams are mixed: 'Sport is for everyone,' head says breezily. 'It's all about equality of opportunity, pupils collaborating'. One parent said her son 'absolutely loved' netball and was very enthusiastic that they also got chance to play hockey: 'it would be great if more girls arrive, though,' she added wistfully.

Clubs number around 30 from computer programming to jewellery making to Mandarin. Scholars' club (an enhancement programme) membership by assessment (delicacy and tact required from the head if a child might not be suited and alternative avenues are found). The Study Skills club enables children to do supervised homework (a winner with parents).

Heaps of trips from making pizzas in Pizza Express to Cadbury's World to going to hear Lauren Child reading. Competitions such as Maths Challenge. One parent said the residential trip to Menai had been a stand-out for her child.

Behaviour doesn't seem to be an issue: 'We say keep your hands and feet to yourself,' says head, 'and only say something if it is kind'. Girls, a minority in many years, all go to lunch together so friendships across year groups flourish. Each year group has a reward system which runs alongside the house system and there are the usual celebration assemblies. A recent initiative, a Friday afternoon tea party with the head (popcorn, squash and cakes), has been a huge hit. An invitation is sent by post to a child whose behaviour or achievement, personally or academically, has been outstanding. One parent said, 'has the post arrived yet? ' was a constant refrain from her child.

The school was founded in 1877, moved to its present site a few years later and went co-ed in 2009. It is a truly cheery place, not just because of the smiling faces and wonderful displays of pupil work (we particularly liked the Egyptian Selfies) but also because the fabulous art teacher has cheered the most functional of spaces with fantastic murals of sea worlds and rainbows. The facilities are great (although one parent felt they could do with a facelift here and there).

The outdoor classroom (previously a wasteland transformed by staff and children) is a field where children can explore, build dens, observe bugs in their hotel and grow vegetables. One parent said it was 'making a big impact'. A hobbit door leads to a small secret garden for younger children and a fenced off area displays a gaggle of adored guinea pigs. All children have waterproofs and wellies in school.

Parents talk of a familial and relaxed atmosphere. Most come from wealthy Alderley Edge but plenty from Wilmslow, Congleton or Macclesfield. Traditionally attracts parents who aren't short of a bob or two. Head is quick to point out that five per cent of pupils receive a bursary: 'it's more of a cross-section than people might think'. Lots of dual income families. There seemed to be a good blend of nationalities and cultures and children seemed bubbly and spirited.

Fees aren't the lowest nor the highest in the area. A hefty sibling discount of 10 per cent, 20 and 30 per cent for consecutive children, which is worth having. School lunch, which looked healthy, is a compulsory extra.

Altogether, a vibrant, happy school with great facilities and a key emphasis on individualised learning and personal development allowing each child to excel.

St Ambrose College

Hale Road, Halebarns, Altrincham, Cheshire WA15 0HE

Ages 11–18 **Pupils** 1,018 **Sixth form** 201 **RC**

01619 802711
www.st-ambrosecollege.org.uk

Acting Principal: Since 2018, Dermot Rainey. Degree in RS and history from St Mary's University College, Belfast. Taught at all boys Edmund Rice secondary school in Mayo before moving to Manchester, where he took on leadership roles at All Saints Catholic College and Cardinal Langley RCHS before being appointed vice principal at St Ambrose College in September 2017. He cites his experiences as a cathedral chorister and numerous pilgrimages to Lourdes as being of particular influence in shaping his views on the importance of the church in the 21st century.

He continues his love of choral singing when family commitments allow. Having been a member of the Hallé he now prioritises opportunities to perform with Codetta, an internationally acclaimed choir based in Derry (particularly targeting weekends when Derry City FC have a home fixture).

Academic matters: There is a very strong sense of personal and academic motivation supported by extracurricular clubs, clinics and one-to-one tuition sessions. The emphasis is on achieving as well as you can. A great camaraderie was on display with boys actively encouraging and helping each other. In 2018, 66 per cent of GCSE grades were A*-A/9-7; at A level, 70 per cent A*-B and 40 per cent A*/A.

Trips to France and Spain are available throughout the school years giving the opportunity to experience the respective cultures as well as learn the languages. From the fourth year on, pupils get the chance to live with Spanish or French families and sixth formers are offered work experience in Málaga or Caen – muchas gracias and merci beaucoup frequently heard in response.

While the school genuinely believes all of its boys are talented, it offers more challenging work to high flyers. Sixth formers have an Oxbridge recruitment programme, which includes visiting speakers, mock interviews and advice from former pupils now studying there. There is also additional support for prospective medics and dentists including work experience placements in local hospitals and GP practices.

The college has also introduced online mentoring for sixth formers to communicate directly with undergraduates about revision techniques and university life and to make the transition from school to university as seamless and stress free as possible. The common room and study areas provide pockets of sanctuary for private study and detailed subject research.

The school has a detailed SEN policy with a dedicated SENCo supported by senior tutors, sixth form mentors and the pastoral team as well as close liaison with outside agencies and specialists. They provide a wide range of interventions such as differentiated teaching and learning strategies. Some are offered at lunch time or after school to ensure that pupils don't miss out on the curriculum or extracurricular opportunities.

Games, options, the arts: Over many years St Ambrose has earned an enviable record in competitions, especially in rugby. It also excels at cricket and athletics in local, divisional and national competitions.

The new sports hall boasts some very impressive facilities, including badminton courts, a fully equipped fitness suite and, the jewel in the sporting crown, a 25 metre swimming pool. Outside facilities include three rugby pitches, an all-weather 4G pitch, two artificial wickets, a 7-a-side all weather football pitch and three full sized tennis courts. Many Old Ambrosians have gone on to play rugby for England or Scotland, and as professional footballers.

Senior sports students have visited Barbados, South America, South Africa, Australasia, USA and Canada. Juniors have enjoyed visits to Ireland, France, Italy and the Netherlands.

On the school walls are displayed some high calibre artistic exhibits, a testament to the encouragement the college gives its more creative pupils and those who aren't really interested in being 'roughty, toughty rugby players,' as one mother observed.

Music is on the curriculum at both GSCE and A level and enjoys extracurricular life in a thriving orchestra, School of Rock and various choirs – all with busy and rewarding schedules. Instrument tuition is offered one-to-one from specialised teachers.

Each year, pupils perform in the school musical – 'an extremely rewarding experience for all involved'. The highlight of the school diary, however, is the annual presentation evening that includes a comprehensive musical programme.

Background and atmosphere: Founded in 1946, it became an academy and was completely rebuilt in 2012 – as relevant to the members of its active and vibrant old boys' association (SAOBA), some of whom remember those early days, as it does to the boys currently using its leading edge technology and top class facilities.

The college is part of the global network of Edmund Rice Schools Trust, which has schools on every continent, and closely follows the Eight Essentials of its Christian Brother philosophy. Recent Ofsted and Catholic diocesan reports rate it Outstanding and the school places as much emphasis on 'compassion for those in need' as it does to 'striving for excellence'.

There is no official catchment area and boys come in from areas across Cheshire and Greater Manchester including Warrington, Wilmslow, Knutsford and Didsbury. However, the emphasis is on ability and active participation, irrespective of background or how affluent your parents might be.

Boys start in 1st year, a nod to the original form numbering system rather than year 7 as used in most other schools. The uniform for senior school is unashamedly traditional, although this doesn't mean boaters and gowns. Black blazers with badge and plain black shoes are the standard with school tie denoting their year group or prefect status. Sixth formers wear business suits, white/pale blue shirt with dark shoes/socks and a sixth form tie.

There is a vigorous policy of encouraging pupils to take a full and active interest in wider society and boys engage in the Youth Parliament, debate current affairs, discuss issues of the day and everyone gets the opportunity to join a retreat during their school years. The Catholic faith is both a spiritual and literal presence in the daily life of the school, and amidst the bustle of break and meal times boys can take time for refuge for prayer and quiet reflection in the chapel built in the school atrium and the very heart of the school. 'I've never known it to be locked during all my time here,' said the head boy.

The college is twinned with its namesake in Sierra Leone, for which pupils raise funds and resources and make regular trips to this academy. Recently, pupils and their families raised £10,000 through a sponsored walk for the Sierra Leone school and are hoping to reach this figure again. The school is perhaps proudest of the help it provides for those on its own doorstep by helping out at Cornerstone, a service for homeless people, and Revive in Salford, a refuge for asylum seekers.

Pastoral care, well-being and discipline: The college prides itself on being a well-ordered, caring environment where high standards and good manners are expected. Boys are rewarded with house points for behaviour, effort, sporting, musical and dramatic activities.

Responses to poor behaviour include a quiet word, written work or a task commensurate to the offence. More serious or persistent misbehaviour can lead to involving the parents, detention and in rare instances, temporary or permanent exclusion. A behaviour support mentor is employed at the college to intervene when necessary but such occasions are rare, and commitment to the school's ethos is reflected in the very low rate of unauthorised absence.

The layout of the school also makes it easy for pupils to approach teachers and mentors to discuss any issues or problems. Teachers are visible even when working in office spaces. An achievement mentor works with pupils to help them overcome difficulties and support is also available from a sixth form mentor who very often is able to offer practical advice gained from similar experiences. The school house system encourages wider friendship networks as boys mix with other year groups for half an hour each day.

Pupils and parents: Most boys need little encouragement to learn and are provided with a wide range of resources and support throughout their time at school. Parents value the Catholic moral standards as much as they do the academic achievements. 'It's not the building that attracted me but the ethos and pastoral care,' said the mother of a 1st year pupil. 'The school's helped make my son become a "nice young man".' One dad liked how 'keen the college is' in keeping him on board at all stages of his son's progress through school. A robust and enthusiastic parents' association (SAPA) supports the school and parents are involved through regular online updates and emails.

The social mix of boys does seem to facilitate a greater understanding of the complexities of society. Generally, the boys are level headed and fully aware they occupy a privileged academic position but don't exhibit any sense of self-entitlement, and it was gratifying to hear them speak with gratitude and appreciation of their time in school – 'teachers know what they're doing and give you the time and tools to succeed'.

The school is well settled into its newish home and has become accustomed and comfortable in its surroundings but still appreciative of the facilities it provides. Built as a Celtic cross with classrooms and study areas located around the head of the cross, the building is stunning not just architecturally but also in how it manages free movement around its floors, corridors and staircases. It is 'very cool and inclusive,' said one boy. 'The old place felt like it was every man for himself but here, not just the facilities and technology but the natural light actually helps me study. Wow, I'm going to miss this place for being so student friendly,' said one sixth former, a little wistfully.

St Ambrose's most famous old boy is probably Lonnie Donegan, the inspiration behind the Beatles and Rolling Stones, who was a pupil in 1945. Others include graphic designers Malcolm Garrett and Peter Saville, portraitist Keith Breeden and Sir John Pethica, professor of material science at Trinity College, Dublin. A number of old boys went on to ply their trade as men of the cloth while a handful of others have been elected to another, more temporal House as MPs, such as Damien Hinds MP, education secretary.

Entrance: Entrance tests at 11+ in English, maths and verbal reasoning. Oversubscription criteria prioritise several categories of baptised Catholic boys, with other baptised Christians lower down the pecking order. The current school roll is not exclusively Roman Catholic, although all pupils are strongly encouraged to practise their faith both in and outside school.

The sixth form usually has between 180 and 200 pupils with a high percentage having come up through the school, although places are only guaranteed for those with at least five GCSEs at 9-6 with at least a grade 6 in the subjects to be studied at A level and at least a 5 in maths and English. Progression from lower to upper sixth is dependent on appropriate progress in all subjects, high levels of attendance and a positive attitude to learning. New entrants generally settle in quickly, made friends and become integral and active contributors to school life. There are leadership opportunities for sixth formers and all are encouraged to be excellent role models and to mentor younger pupils.

Exit: About two-thirds stay on for the sixth form and many go on to Russell Group universities; two to Oxbridge in 2018, plus one medic; other subjects include astrophysics, engineering and maths.

Remarks: This school consistently attains higher levels than the national average in all official measures but it is far more than the sum of these figures and its appeal to parents is also in how it develops its pupils towards becoming outstanding adults. There was a real sense of support and camaraderie in the school, with no-one left on the sidelines, and boys are clearly helped to become active members of society with a social conscience.

St Brendan's Sixth Form College

Broomhill Road, Brislington, Bristol BS4 5RQ

Ages 16–19+ **Pupils** 1,725 **Sixth form** 1,725 **RC**

01179 777766
www.stbrn.ac.uk

Principal: Since 2012, Michael Jaffrain. Originally from France and briefly worked as a bank cashier at the Bank National of Paris, before moving to England to become a language assistant at South Cheshire College. Thence to Shrewsbury Sixth Form College, from where he was appointed assistant principal at St Brendan's in 2010. Approachable, bouncily enthusiastic and easy to talk to, Mr Jaffrain likes to have contact with and personal knowledge of his students, despite the size of the college, and to be at the centre of activity. He has repositioned the college's academic status by terminating level 1 (sub GCSE) entry, which was very small and 'which other more specialist institutions can do better', and 'concentrated on raising the aspirations of students at level 2 (GCSE etc) and level 3 (A level etc)'. Amongst all this he still finds time to be an enthusiastic rugby fan.

Academic matters: College offers two main levels of post-16 study: level 3 (over 70 different A levels and BTecs), and level 2 (GCSE retakes for those who have not passed English and maths at school plus a number of BTec courses providing the equivalent of four GCSEs at grades 9-4). The City and Guilds CAD course provides a back-up for A level design students, whilst other level 2 and 3 courses include BTecs in applied biology, business, IT, law, media, music technology, performing arts, public services and sport.

A cohort of over 1,700 students means that there is an exceptionally wide choice of courses and students can pick freely without timetabling restrictions. Results for those who enter the Advanced Graduate Programme, for the most academic students, compare favourably with the best in the school league tables, though college is cagey about releasing A level results. Advanced Graduates also get specialist options including extra help for Oxbridge and other high demand applications, and are encouraged to take the EPQ, which develops research skills, time management and a whole host of other skills.

A suite of learning development provision allows students to drop in if needing help and about half do at some stage. Some 200 of these students have regular support or exam entitlements and are helped, either one-to-one, or in small groups, with special arrangements for them such as a relaxation of age limits. A high percentage of pupils receiving learning development support achieve better grades than predicted, and do at least as well both in terms of results and value added as other students. ESOL candidates from abroad have to complete GCSE or an equivalent in English before embarking on A level. All areas of the college are accessible to wheelchair users.

Students seem happy to take the RPE (religion, philosophy and ethics) course, one of the few compulsory aspects of the college, commenting that 'the philosophy bits are really interesting,' though the ones we met were non-committal about the religious content.

Games, options, the arts: While absence of compulsion is highly valued by students keen to get away from schooliness, most acknowledged that there are great opportunities and even the least sporty could enjoy yoga, using the comprehensive fitness gym or popular sprung floor dance studios. Enthusiastic dancers, including some boys, were energetically rehearsing for a production during our visit. Lots of spectators for the netball match in progress, and more queuing up to watch impending basketball. Exceptional facilities for most sports, though no pool (but there is an Olympic one just up the road) and programmes such as Total Pro Soccer (TPS) for boys and girls allow students to include sport in their portfolio of qualifications. Several students have gained US sports scholarships, and the success for students applying to sports-related HE courses and apprenticeships has tripled. Lots of dynamic overlap with arts, especially for theatre productions.

The arts equally well served. BTec performing arts courses incorporating musical theatre, dance and acting are especially popular. Film students very innovative and even have their own Oscars evening. Trad music A level is limited, as is the chance of orchestral experience in college – no hoards of up-and-coming younger pupils to swell the second violins and half the cohort leaving every year makes this difficult – but lots of singing, with a popular choir doing public things like welcoming the Georgian rugby team ahead of the Rugby World Cup, and singing at Bristol matches. Production and studio engineering also on offer. Parents speak warmly of the support given to students in entertainment studies, facilitated by fantastic links with Bristol Old Vic, BBC and ITV for internships and career opportunities.

Exceptional art, with some magical work going on in both graphic communications and straight art A levels. Students benefit from highly sophisticated printing and IT facilities, encouraged by an ex-professional design teacher who inspires such stunning work as the variations on an underwater theme. Art is as impressive. One fine art A level student, working on expressing emotion through physical disease and malformation, eschewed the 'pretty', while others were using entrancing flower and seaweed images with a really professional-looking finish. Some spectacular results in graphic communications and sound all round.

Background and atmosphere: Originating from a boys' independent school founded by the Christian Brothers in 1890, St Brendan's finally evolved into a co-educational, Catholic sixth form college in 1979. Masses of recent building work has produced a harmonious, if brightly coloured, modern-looking campus, into which the few surviving but updated original buildings fit comfortably. While the access is unprepossessing and the security impressive (but friendly), the grounds themselves feel spacious, informal and park-like. Plenty of inviting-looking areas for outdoor relaxation in summer. Students look informal but not, on the whole, scruffy.

Lots of work-friendly places in the spacious library where a quiet and studious atmosphere seems taken for granted. It remains open until 5.30pm and has extensive computer facilities. Computer 'break out' areas (20-30 computers for general use) nestling in handy corners all over the college including one internet café/IT work area adjacent to student canteen where a staff member is on hand to help.

Flexible auditorium with raked seating for about 250 provides performance and lecture space. Assemblies held here to celebrate Christian festivals. The tiny rotunda chapel, the central feature of the original school, is still central. The chaplain offers an informal welcome to all with masses etc for Catholic students, who are very much in the minority of only about 12 per cent, but college is the favoured choice of a number of other Christian churches in Bristol. A parent commented that the Catholic ethos gives the college a calm and caring feeling, nurturing 'bright young people keen to make difference but not afraid to be different'.

Activities, visits and sports rely heavily on input from a strong students' union, committed to providing social life and doing charity fundraising, which also has a student rep on the college governing board. It definitely feels more like a college than a school.

Pastoral care, well-being and discipline: Unlike uni, however, the pastoral care is exceptional, and valued by parents and students. Problems are identified and action taken effectively. One parent reported that her daughter's exam nerves were effectively tackled by teachers and tutors. Qualified counsellors/psychologist on hand.

Masses of feedback to parents and lots of encouragement to students to undertake revision programmes, catch up sessions and such. Since there are several groups studying each subject it is usually possible to find a repeat lesson for something scantily understood. A tight rein is kept on attendance and progress. Role of student support managers is pivotal: each has 10 tutorial groups for 45 minute periods a week in groups of 25 or individually. In cases of poor work or behaviour students can be placed 'on contract'. Rolling programme of fairs, visits, speakers tutorials and careers advisors ensure that course choices lead to ongoing opportunities.

Very strict guidelines on alcohol and drugs, with surprisingly few incidents. For the few problems that do occur rehabilitation is aimed for and often achieved, but no quarter given to those who do not respond to help.

Attractive canteen with plenty of choice, though what sells seems to be mostly breakfast type fast food.

Pupils and parents: Huge catchment area from Gloucestershire, the borders of Somerset, Dorset and Wiltshire. Fifteen per cent ethnic minorities. Being part of Bristol's south east area partnership alongside City of Bristol (FE) College has opened the doors to many more non-Catholics. Usual choice for Catholics from Bristol and Bath Catholic Collegiate for whom it is the only denominational post-16 option. Increasing uptake from ex-independent school pupils.

Entrance: All students are admitted to the college rather than to a specific course or level. Choices are confirmed or made post-GCSE or equivalent results via extensive interview and discussion. Disappointing GCSE results can be rescued with a year consolidating GCSE before starting A level or its equivalent. As the college manages to offer the third year post-16 without any fees, this is an excellent option for someone needing to sort out disastrous GCSEs.

Exit: Academic ambition definitely on the up. Majority proceed to wide range of degree courses including Oxbridge. Many to vocational and arts-related courses. Some into employment or to 'elite apprenticeships' – such as Deloittes – encouraged by the college's strong links with industry around Bristol.

Remarks: Fantastic environment post-GCSE for both high flyers and those needing to salvage something from weak GCSEs. Ideal transition from school to uni or work. All the support and expert guidance of a good sixth form developed by staff with sustained concentrated experience in sixth form teaching and pastoral care. St Brendan's offers opportunities that many schools cannot provide. Atmosphere deceptively like uni but underpinned by stringent but informal academic supervision and genuine generous care for students. A very special place.

St David's College

Gloddaeth Hall, Llandudno, Conwy LL30 1RD

Ages 9–19 **Pupils** 218 (150 boys, 68 girls) **Sixth form** 67 **Boarders** 81 full

Fees: Day £11,250 – £17,850; Boarding £23,250 – £33,300 pa

01492 875974
www.stdavidscollege.co.uk

Headmaster: Since 2017, Andrew Russell, previously acting head. Degree in accounting and economics from Southampton and PGCE in maths from Bangor. He has taught at St David's for his entire career of over 25 years (maths, business studies and IT) and risen through the ranks as head of year, head of department, housemaster, assistant head and deputy head.

Academic matters: What a joy it was not to have examination results and league tables thrust under our noses. There is a belief in some quarters that education is dead and has been replaced by a slavish seeking after grade levels and that dreaded, often misused, word 'targets'. At St David's there are individual goals for each pupil but they are personal rather than political. Education at its best is very much alive and shining here. The reticence they have in not trumpeting their grade results is for no reason other than the firmly held conviction that grades are not the most important aspect of life at this school. They offer a combination of GCSEs, A levels and BTecs; in 2018, 33 per cent A*/A grades and 67 per cent A*-C grades at combined A levels and level 3 BTecs, with 24 per cent A*-A/9-7 and 81 per cent A*-C/9-4 at combined GCSEs and level 2 BTecs.

Average class sizes are 10 and every teacher is a qualified dyslexia teacher. An infinitely better system than that where a pupil is given one session of help a week and then goes back to a class where the teacher is making no allowances at all. That happens in a number of schools. This school was one of the first to adopt a multi-sensory teaching policy and we witnessed some marvellously lively, creative and stimulating teaching from a staff who seem universally dedicated and fun. None more so than those we met in the Cadogen Centre, a specialised building where each pupil enjoys one-on-one teaching with a programme individually planned for them after careful discussion with their class teachers.

The facilities for IT are excellent and we had a wonderful time with some very bright sixth form pupils who were about to go off for an exhibition. Not only was the work they were doing as part of NVQs in CAD outstandingly good, but so were the fluent and perceptive comments which accompanied the work. 'Dyslexics often think out of the box,' a teacher told us. Recently a young man from St David's, who while there had attended one-on-one lessons, graduated in architecture at Manchester University. Another is reading nuclear physics. There are so many success stories.

Games, options, the arts: To gaze down from the beautiful terrace in front of the house is to marvel at the immaculate state of the games pitches, the superb Astroturf and the lure of mountains beyond. Virtually every game you can think of is on offer, and other schools talk of the verve and energy with which St David's teams perform. In addition there is a shooting range, an indoor climbing hall and vast amounts of equipment for outdoor activities, one of the distinctive features of the school. The excellent prospectus and online introduction to the school reveal the depth and breadth of the activities on offer. There is an activity, an expedition, a challenging outing once a week, but lest anyone think this is an attractive offer replacing academic pursuits, think again. The school academic day continues until 5pm Monday to Friday and there are additional lessons, activities and games sessions timetabled on Saturday mornings. When questioned about Saturday morning lessons, 'Fair enough,' said the boy we asked. Sixth formers can take a BTec in sports (traditional or outdoor ed).

A particularly popular activity is 4x4 off road driving in a spectacularly battered and mud caked old Land Rover. The school really is a paradise of activity, challenge, determination, broadening horizons and going beyond the syllabus.

Very lively art in an old building where budding artists can express themselves without worrying about spilling paint. Those are often the best buildings for producing the exciting art work. There was plenty here and in the photographic section adjoining. Such creativity and such joy, delight and encouragement.

Boarding: The boarding houses (three for boys and one for girls) are bright, airy and friendly; the house teams dedicated and involved. Boarding seems to work well, which is probably one reason why pupils come from so far afield from throughout the UK. Huge variety of indoor and especially outdoor activities available at weekends.

Background and atmosphere: In 1965 a deputy head from Cheshire, John Mayor, upset by the way boys and girls with learning difficulties were smothered, if not dismissed, because they were seen as lazy or stupid, decided to found a school where their needs were addressed. It was founded on three main principals: a determination to respect, understand and help the pupils; adventurous outdoor activities where the young could experience freedom and excitement; and all this within a gentle Christian ethos. Over 50 years later the school largely continues to follow those guidelines. And it shows. We met happy pupils who spoke confidently and unselfconsciously about how miserable they had been on arrival, with a bleak and cheerless outlook on life and no self-esteem at all. For some, St David's was last chance saloon, and some of them were far from home. They spoke of the warmth of the welcome they received from the whole community.

'Community' is a word which sits easily on the lips of pupils eager to talk about their school. And that's not a cliché either: they really do feel as if the school belongs to them and they to the school. There's a very real closeness. They talk of the increasing delight they derived from their lessons; the love and interest shown by the teachers; the friendliness of their contemporaries. 'It's just everything,' said a young boy, struggling to articulate the indefinable. 'Surely there must be some things you don't like?' we pressed. 'Of course,' came the reply, 'but there's far less to worry about than there was at my previous school. It could be very depressing there and a bit scary on occasions.' What they all agreed on was the 'overall atmosphere'. They looked surprised when we suggested that that came from them. These young have not been stuffed with cheesy old clichés raked off that useful pile plundered by professional prospectus writers or that irritating band of media trained heads. These are real people making real discoveries about themselves.

Pastoral care, well-being and discipline: Within the academic, as well as the sporting and sporty side of life at the school, there are practical and generous ways in which pupils help each other. This is manifest by the way in which older pupils help younger pupils with academic subjects as well as more personal, private anxieties. The people we spoke with were unanimous in the feeling that there was always someone there to help. A word they were fond of evoking is 'banter.' Affectionate teasing. One of the most moving moments of our tour was when our guides pointed out the Prayer Garden, 'or whatever you like to call it. You can approach it in any way you like, but it's essentially a place for reflection. You can take it or leave it.' It's a lovely touch, and the statue in front, created by Nick Elphick, an old boy of the school, is a thought-provoking addition. This is not a threatening environment. Discipline is sensible, thoughtful, considerate. It seemed as natural as breathing.

Pupils and parents: From a wide range of primary and prep schools. Day pupils from across the whole of North Wales. Boarders from all over the UK, a small number from overseas. Inclusive entry helped by quite a number of pupils being funded by their local education authorities. Apart from those with special educational needs, many parents choose the school because of its broad all-round education and its small class sizes. Recent extension to boarding provision due to increase in pupil numbers.

Entrance: The majority enter aged at about 10 after an interview and a report from their school (although some join age 9 into year 5). A large number come from local primary schools, but others come from far afield. We heard how sensitively the business of arrivals is handled. Always a sign of a happy school. A few leave and a number come into the sixth form, attracted by the reputation of the teaching and the breadth of subjects on offer. The sixth form handbook says that the most important qualities for entry into the school are commitment and enthusiasm. That handbook is, incidentally, one of the best of its kind we have ever seen.

Exit: Around 15-25 per cent leave at 16. The school goes to tremendous lengths to help the students choose the courses that match interests and abilities. The vast majority do go on to further or higher education eg industrial design and technology at Loughbourough, marketing management at Manchester Met and psychology and neuropsychology at Bangor. Technical subjects seem the most popular, but not exclusively so.

Money matters: The school works hard to keep the costs down. The wonderful expeditions are very carefully budgeted. No swanky hotels. Parents we spoke to said that they felt the school was very thoughtful about money matters and we got the impression that those who ran into severe financial difficulties would be carefully listened to.

Remarks: This is a very special school, almost a magical place. Pupils develop in an unsentimental atmosphere of love and generosity. The staff are almost as amazing as the pupils and, yes, there is plenty of banter along with the seriousness. Over the years a strong bond has matured with Kampala. Pupils and gap year students are deeply and genuinely involved. 'The projects we are involved in come from the dreams of our own pupils,' says that handbook. The same could be said about the school as a whole.

Saint Gregory's, Bath

150

Combe Hay Lane, Odd Down, Bath, Somerset BA2 8PA

Ages 11–18 **Pupils** 1,064 **Sixth form** 146 **RC**

01225 832873
www.st-gregorys.bathnes.sch.uk

Headmistress: Since 2016, Ann Cusack, previously deputy head at St Augustine's Catholic College in Trowbridge, and before that assistant head at Sacred Heart in Camberwell, London. Originally from Ireland, Ann grew up in Cheltenham, studying history at North London Polytechnic (now part of London Metropolitan University) and later a PGCE at University of East Anglia. Married with three children.

Parents told us, 'She's making her mark with innovation and she is a force to be reckoned with!' Another added, 'I think the head has found her feet extremely well and the school has done remarkably to maintain its happy core.' She has made a number of changes and, 'the future looks bright for St Greg's,' a happy father confided.

Academic matters: In 2018, at A level, 45 per cent A*-B grades, 25 per cent A*-A. At GCSE, 82 per cent of students achieved 9-4 in both English and maths and 33 per cent of grades were A*-A or 9-7. School is rated outstanding by Ofsted and by Clifton Diocese. Head recently introduced a balance of mixed-ability classes plus setting, rather than streaming.

Twenty-four A levels offered; no vocational courses. Sixth formers told us the teachers are 'enthusiastic and supportive' and the smaller classes of 10 to 15 pupils are 'a huge bonus.' Strong on languages. In 2017, the school was successful in its bid to become one of only a handful of schools regionally to offer the British Council's Mandarin in Excellence Programme, enabling students in year 7 to study Mandarin alongside French, German and Spanish.

Geography department recently been awarded the Quality Mark. RE compulsory at GCSE; curriculum also covers other faiths and the diversity of religion. Sixth formers can do enrichment RE rather than A level. This involves open discussion on relevant issues such as human rights or philosophy. One parent told us, 'They help open the kids' eyes to the simple core values that, once embedded, will no doubt help them later in life ... honesty and respect for yourself and others, always doing your best while promoting dignity for all; being sensitive and caring, and looking outwards with tolerance before rushing to anger.'

It was great to see a young team of teachers with plenty of good rapport between them and the pupils. One parent commented, 'they're more on their wavelength than we are!' Average class size is 25/26 below A level. Parents seem happy with the standard of teaching, telling us, 'as it's a small school the teachers know all the students individually ...[and] they do not take a 'one size fits all approach'.'

New learning support centre block (Emmaus Centre) along with a garden area and outdoor classroom. Tuition is provided in small groups, in classes with support from teaching assistants, or on a one-to-one basis. One parent of two children with dyslexia explained, 'With dyslexia, you want them to enjoy learning. Our oldest son was already at boarding school mid-GCSE when we moved. He got one GCSE! Daughter has just got 10 at Saint Gregory's..It speaks for itself.'

A technology development group has been set up, consisting of students, teachers and ICT professionals, to regularly review the ICT provision and to keep up with the latest changes and developments. Currently, there are three ICT suites and an Apple Mac suite for music technology. iPads are regularly used in PE and performing arts.

Games, options, the arts: Decent sports facilities include a new outdoor gym and two Astros. For a small school, they more than hold their own, with success in football (boys and girls), rugby, netball, basketball and table tennis. Athletics is the one to watch here; it's gaining in popularity and success every year, we were told. Both the KS3 boys' and girls' teams won the recent local athletics competition. Lunchtime clubs change seasonally, but on our visit in September we saw posters for clubs including trampolining, orienteering and cross-fit. D of E is popular and Ten Tors has just been introduced.

In line with the school's strong reputation for the arts (particularly performing arts) pupils are involved in the Bath Literary Festival annually. 2017-18 saw the school's first writer in residence.

Two drama productions each year. The main production involves the whole school – most recently, Miss Saigon. Younger ones also get the chance to cut their teeth in a summer production: over 150 pupils took part in Beauty and the Beast recently. Pupils enthused about the productions, 'It's like a mini-community, and a great way to make friends across the years', they told us.

Music performances are also highlights, with three main concerts a year plus regular performances, masses, liturgies with local primary schools and the annual Mid-Somerset Music Festival. Groups and ensembles include orchestra, choirs, big band, flute group, brass group, ukelele group and string group.

Photography A level is offered alongside art. The work we saw on our visit was fantastic. Some can be seen in the sixth form centre where the annual art exhibition takes place in the summer – quite an event by all accounts, with bands performing amongst the exhibits.

As well as the usual clubs, the head is keen on extracurricular activities that can enhance knowledge and life skills. One club that does just that is an investment club where pupils can try their hand at virtual stocks and shares and learn financial literacy. Pupils are encouraged to take any of their own club ideas to the senate (student council) and if they can make a strong case they will be supported to set it up. The head boy did, and recently set up the cycling club. Sixth formers have one afternoon a week of enrichment activities including revision sessions for younger pupils, volunteering, sports leadership awards, D of E, first aid courses or working with the chaplaincy team.

Plenty of trips locally to Bath and Bristol, or further afield to London. Travel abroad includes science trips to CERN, to the battlefields for Year 9, ski trip to Canada, trips to Washington DC and China, plus Spanish, German and French exchanges. The latest charity expedition for years 9 to 11 was to Borneo where they spent three weeks in the jungle helping to build a kindergarten. St Greg's international connections include links to schools in China through the Bath-Sino Educational Partnership. They are also part of the Erasmus+ programme that develops links with European schools. Pupils have the opportunity to meet and work alongside visiting students, as well as the chance to travel abro ad.

Background and atmosphere: Saint Gregory's was founded and built in the late 70s by Clifton Diocese so that the eight (local-ish) Catholic primary schools that make up the South Clifton Catholic Federation had a secondary school to feed into. This small school sits just inside the city boundary on top of one of Bath's seven hills.

Catholic and proud of it. However, everyone is welcome and a surprising 40 per cent of pupils are not Catholic. Parents we spoke to (Catholics and non) all agreed that there is a 'good balance' of religious activity. For practising Catholics, St Greg's is the obvious local choice, but others said it was the 'very caring together feeling' that won them over. One parent explained that their decision was based on 'the happiness factor that is so evident at St Greg's. Plain and simple, the kids are genuinely happy and self-motivated in what I can only call a close family community.'

The day starts with a prayer, either in assembly or in tutor groups. This is a time to reflect, a moment of calm. The staff lead by example and start their day with a morning prayer too. The day ends in the same way with 'a moment of thoughtfulness. The whole school gathers for weekly assembly with scripture readings, hymns, prayers and reflections. They also cover topics such as promoting peace, our vast universe and leadership. Weekly mass in the chapel is voluntary. Whole school mass takes place three times a year

Over the access road from the main site is the Gateway Building, built in 2013, and home to the sixth formers. The New Sixth (St Greg's used not to go beyond GCSE) is a collaboration with St Mark's, a C of E school on the other side of Bath. At the moment it is small, with some 140 students. The aim is to grow it to a maximum of 250. Currently, most students are from St Greg's with less than a third from St Mark's. This bright and friendly modern building with a definite green theme (especially in the learning resource centre) also houses the English department, two labs for whole school use and, now, a café and chaplaincy area, exclusive to sixth formers. This a spiritual space, managed by the chaplains that doubles up as a common room with X-box, Wii and table football. Students can chill out here as well as seek support and guidance.

St Greg's has a traditional feel with a house system (houses named after popes), a head boy and girl, and prefects. All pupils stand when an adult enters the room. The school day has recently been changed, much to the approval of pupils: six lessons have been reduced to five slightly longer ones to deal with any flagging in the afternoon. Pupils did have a grumble about homework though: 'There's far too much and sometimes it's not even relevant to the lesson', they moaned.

The school council, the Senate, is popular (biccies at every meeting, apparently) and successful. They recently campaigned for hot drinks to be sold before school to warm them up on arrival, and have been on a mission to report all the 'broken bits' including picnic tables, benches, loo doors and water fountains, and have campaigned for girls to be allowed to wear trousers. Pupils agreed that food is good, but the healthy options run out too quickly and there are far too many 'tempting' cakes and slushies on offer.

As to be expected of a Catholic school, there is plenty of charity work and fundraising activities. Each year group chooses their own charity annually, plus the whole school supports a local homeless hostel. Every year around 20 staff and sixth formers sleep rough in aid of the Big Sleep Out, plus the whole school takes part in a sponsored 10k walk around the local area.

Pastoral care, well-being and discipline: The whole ethos is based on Christian values, supported by the chaplain. The chaplaincy group meets regularly in the chapel – which is used for a variety of activities – and organises meditations, morning prayers and fundraising activities. The chaplain also provides mentoring. The pastoral care is headed up by the director of pastoral studies and supported by a pastoral team as well as a house and tutor system.

Teachers are supportive, according to parents. One explained how her son struggled when he started school; he kept forgetting everything, so the school arranged for a teacher to act as his mentor and meet him at the school gates every morning to discuss the coming day. Another parent told us how their child had been helped during bereavement. One family summed it all up by saying that the school had encouraged their child 'to find and grow a healthy sense of self' that 'aligns nicely with our beliefs and values.'

Pupils describe discipline as 'firm but fair.'

Pupils and parents: The catchment is huge. Clifton Diocese extends all the way to Wells, Bristol, Chippenham, Wiltshire and south Gloucestershire. The school runs buses from Chippenham and Kingswood. Good communication on all matters according to parents.

Familes are a mix of Catholic and non-Catholics, around a 60/40 split. Some parents went to the school themselves, others have moved to Bath specifically for St Greg's. One told us, 'We were privately educating our children in London and couldn't afford it any more. I cannot get over this amazing free education. We were mad not to have done it earlier.'

Pupils we met were a good bunch; they were polite and chatty. Best bit about St Greg's? 'The opportunities', they told us – 'so many clubs and activities to get involved in'. In our opinion pupils looked neat and tidy (it was the beginning of term), but one parent grumbled that 'the school sometimes looks scruffy... uniform all over the place.'

Very active PTFA is keen to get everyone involved and provide a 'sense of belonging.' Head goes to every meeting. Plenty of coffee mornings, discos and community fundraising events. They regularly raise funds to ensure the annual prize-giving is fully inclusive, and contributed to the garden space outside the new learning support centre.

Entrance: Open evenings and mornings offered. Governing body responsible for admissions, but applications are made through normal LA channels. Baptised Catholic children first in line, with priority to those living in the designated area, and those attending any of eight partner Catholic primary schools. Up to 16 performing arts places for those in designated area. Seamless transition for year 7's: 'Very smooth and welcoming with excellent tutors and kids being buddies,' parents told us.

For sixth form entry, GCSE passes at 5+ for maths and English plus recommended minimum grades for chosen A level subjects. Few join from outside.

Exit: Around 50 per cent of year 11s move up to the sixth form. Popular destinations include Bristol, Leeds, Exeter and Plymouth to study a range of subjects including medicine (one in 2018), aerospace engineering, sports science and music.

Remarks: The Catholic secondary school of choice in this area. And just as popular with non-Catholics who are happy to embrace a spiritually-led education. Small enough to be personal, but large enough to be able to provide a good range of extracurricular opportunities and plenty of chances to perform.

St John's Marlborough

Granham Hill, Marlborough, Wiltshire SN8 4AX

Ages 11–18 **Pupils** 1,700 **Sixth form** 400

01672 516156
www.stjohns.wilts.sch.uk

Principal: Since January 2019, Ian Tucker, previously head of Abbeyfield School in Chippenham. Has also been associate principal at Rushden Academy in Nothampton and before that head of several primary schools in Wiltshire. Originally form Yorkshire, he studied theology and philosophy at Gloucestershire and Durham. Began his teaching career in Bradford before moving down to Wiltshire in 1996. Teaches RE, philosophy and ethics right through to A level keeping him in touch with both students and teachers. Musical, he plays the cornet and used to play in brass bands. Currently training for an Iron Man triathlon. Married with three teenage children.

Academic matters: In 2018, at A level, 48 per cent A*-B, 21 per cent A*-A grades. At GCSE in 2018, 74 per cent of students achieved 9-4 in both English and maths, nearly 30 per cent of grades were A*-A/9-7.

Twenty-five A levels offered including classical civilisation, Latin and government & politics. Maths, sciences and psychology are popular at A level, as is English. All produce consistently solid results. Vocational courses were added in 2016 to give more students the opportunity to stay for sixth form; some 40 per cent currently choose to study at local colleges. BTecs and Cambridge Technicals are offered in art, music, performing arts, sport, IT and forensics.

Parents told us, 'The school has quite an academic focus and it seems keen and good at developing the brightest pupils to fulfil their potential.' Sets for English and maths from year 7 and sciences from year 9. School is researching whether it's better to have one top set plus mixed ability lower sets, because they have noticed that children in the lower sets tend to make less progress. Pupils choose French or German in year 7 and have the option of picking a second language such as Spanish in year 8. A language is not compulsory at GCSE but some take two. Careers education lessons start in year 7 and individual careers guidance is offered a year later.

Parents have a high opinion of teachers and 'our children are generally happy with them', one told us. Another said, '[My child's] confidence has grown in the short time he has been at school and he is keen to take on new challenges. He has benefited in subjects areas which I didn't expect – such as art – and to me that shows that the teachers are teaching (rather than just nurturing natural talent) and allowing children to grow and develop.' Posters for revision sessions and clubs were unmissable, plastered on every classroom and door, and the school also runs 'walking-talking' mocks where the teacher takes the class through old papers in the exam hall.

Additional educational needs include gifted and talented as well as SEND and EAL. Some 13 per cent of pupils have SENDs, ranging from dyslexia to complex needs and medical problems. They may have in-class support, teaching in small groups, specialist teaching or specialist support from external agencies. There are three dedicated SEN classrooms and specialist staff are all in house. The Hub is a new learning area that can be used for small groups or one-to-one teaching. It caters for pupils who have behavioural issues, like outbursts, or those suffering from emotional issues or anxiety. Some pupils may have all their lessons here for a term; others may just come once a week. The whole school site is fully wheelchair accessible.

S

Games, options, the arts: Plenty of opportunities for the sports-mad child. Lots of success, too: St John's boys' cricket teams are unbeaten in every age group and several pupils play at national level in basketball or compete internationally in athletics, figure skating or water-skiing. Sports pitches and courts, a sports hall and dance studio on site; a multi-use games area (MUGA) was under construction when we visited. Swimming lessons and galas take place at the local pool. Recent sports tour to Barcelona for the football and hockey teams. Lunchtime clubs and after-school fixtures for rugby, football, netball, tennis, cricket, athletics, rounders, hockey and basketball. PE GCSE and sports studies and PE A level are popular.

Art is also popular with around 20 pupils opting for A level each year. On average, 50 per cent of these go on to do foundation courses. The fantastic studios, with floor to ceiling windows overlooking the playing fields, are open every break and lunchtime. There is a kiln and a dark room for photography.

Theatre On The Hill is the school's 350-seat auditorium, also open to the public. Annie rehearsals were underway on our visit and the last production was The Tempest; one musical and one Shakespeare each year is the norm. Plus X Factor of course. The drama and music department work closely together and recently took pupils to NYC to see School of Rock on Broadway. Budding musicians regularly enter for competitions including the Savernake and Stedman Music Cups and perform at termly concerts and music evenings. Parents are impressed; they told us, 'The standard of musicianship amongst pupils and the school plays are particularly high.'

Another strength of St John's is the extracurricular activity; 'the opportunities are excellent', parents agreed, with lots on offer. All are encouraged to take part in clubs for at least two hours a week. There are lunchtime and after-school clubs, anything from debating to equestrian club. The core club subjects, sports, music and performing arts, are free. These may be rugby, netball, choir, jazz band or homework club. Other clubs like squash, basketball, rock club or CAD modelling may cost. St John's Opportunity Fund provides money to subsidise costs and ensure all pupils can take part. Other options include falconry and animal workshops for year 7s, a six-week fishing course for year 9s and DofE from year 9 upwards. Sixth formers can get involved in community service or an enterprise scheme.

In addition to visits to theatres or museums, many subjects include residential visits such as a classical civilisation and Latin trip to Pompei and Rome, a physics trip to CERN, a science trip to Gambia, German and French exchanges, and a battlefields trip to France and Belgium. There also annual ski trips and watersports trips to France. St John's is a host school and regularly invites Chinese pupils; a return visit is being pl anned.

Background and atmosphere: Founded in 1975, St John's Marlborough (formerly St John's School and Community College) took over the site of the recently closed Marlborough Royal Free Grammar School (founded in 1550) and the Marlborough Secondary Modern School. In 1998 the school was awarded its first specialism in technology, and in 2005 a second languages. In 2010 it moved to its current site on Granham Hill. It is now run by Excalibur Academies Trust.

Situated in an area of outstanding natural beauty above the historic and well-heeled market town of Marlborough, St John's is just a stone's throw from the prestigious Marlborough College. The high street reflects this, with an array of top boutiques and a flagship Rick Stein restaurant. The whole area is rather affluent and this is reflected in the families and pupils at St John's.

Pupils here are lucky; the buildings date from 2008. Facilities are modern, fresh and bright. Not a large site, but the main building is a bit of a maze. However, the generous layout and clear signage help. Classrooms are on two floors connected by bridges and set around an amphitheatre (The Tempest was performed here last summer). Just next door you can see Marlborough College's playing fields and, beyond, beautiful Wiltshire.

The huge atrium at the entrance is a multifunctional space used for break times as well as a dining area at lunchtime ('it's supposed to serve "healthy" food, but this could definitely be improved,' one parent commented). Windows everywhere, internal and external. From the atrium you can look up and see into the library, or you can look down and see into the sports hall. Beyond the sports hall is the dance studio and theatre. Further along are the music rooms, equipped with an Apple

Mac and keyboard per pupil, recital rooms, practice rooms and a recording studio.

The library is inspiring to visit and is certainly doing a great job, according to parents. 'I have been surprised to learn how enthusiastic he and his peers are about visiting the library – sounds like it has real soul, which is brilliant,' one told us. On our visit the theme was Egypt and there was even a mummy in a tomb. The display was fantastic. Another theme was WW1 and the library became a trench scene and field hospital. Next, in time for Christmas, it will display the history of theatre, including pantomimes. No surprise that there is a queue outside every lunchtime.

Upstairs is a sixth form area and the Hub, the learning area for small groups. Sixth formers have their own dedicated library for silent study, as well as a common room and café. There is also the sixth form block, built in 2015, which has six classrooms and a large open study area.

There are wide corridors, windows looking into every classroom and modern curved desks. Top notch labs and technology classrooms. As well as five ICT suites there is also a large enterprise centre with 60 computers and plenty of room for meetings and presentations.

Pastoral care, well-being and discipline: A senior medical coordinator, qualified first aiders and a visiting school health nurse look after the general health of all at St John's. There are also two counsellors as well as key workers, non-teaching staff members who can be contacted by parents or pupils at any time of day. The tutor system has recently been changed to a horizontal system, so pupils can be better supported in their year groups though the new GCSE process.

The Hub is for pupils who are struggling emotionally or have behavioural issues. They may be overwhelmed by school or suffering from a grievance or problem at home; this new space gives them the opportunity to take some time out and work at their own pace.

Discipline at St John's means high standards and clear expectations. Not draconian, we were told.

Pupils and parents: Catchment covers over 250 square miles of north east Wiltshire and beyond. Pupils come from as far as Avebury and Oxfordshire, with some sixth formers travelling further.

We arrived at break-time as the atrium filled up with 1,700 pupils. As we picked our way through bags and wrap-eating pupils we were pleasantly surprised by the behaviour. Yes, it was noisy, yes it was busy, but it was by no means raucous or unruly. Uniform is navy blazer and sweater. No uniform for sixth formers and no business dress required. There's a relaxed, college vibe rather than a school sixth form.

For most families, St John's is first choice; it has 'an amazing reputation,' we were told, and parents are won over by the 'great facilities, very good teaching and high standards.' Communication is good for such a large school, we were assured. Not necessarily a 'community' school, as families are scattered across a large catchment area with many living in small villages. However, the local community does use the facilities for adult education courses in the evenings.

Entrance: Oversubscribed. At least 12 feeder primary schools in a large catchment area. Many pupils come from small primary schools, so arriving at St John's with its 1,700 pupils can be a little overwhelming for some. However, parents agree that the process of open days, visits and induction days, as well as maths masterclasses and language events, give newbies plenty of introduction.

Entry requirement for most A level courses is four 6 grades and two grade 4s. For BTecs and Cambridge Technicals it's six 4 grades or equivalent.

Exit: Some 60 per cent of students stay on to sixth form. The rest tend to go to New College or Swindon College. Around five per cent go on to apprenticeships. On average 35 external students join the sixth form.

Around 80 per cent go to university, 40 per cent going to Russell Group universities. In 2018, four to Oxbridge. Other popular destinations include local ones such as Exeter, Bristol, Reading and Bournemouth, and further afield eg Nottingham, London universities and Manchester. Popular courses include English, maths, history, environmental studies, business, medicine, psychology and engineering.

Famous alumni include Andy Devonshire, director and producer (The Great British Bake Off), Lauren Child, author of Charlie & Lola, and William Golding, author (former grammar school pupil).

Money matters: Pupil premium plus an opportunities fund to help with cost of trips or clubs. 16-19 bursary fund available.

Remarks: A modern comprehensive with fantastic (almost new) facilities. Great reputation for sports and performing arts, and an impressive range of extracurricular opportunities. Good at developing the brightest as well as those that may struggle either academically or emotionally.

St John's-on-the-Hill School

Castleford Hill, Tutshill, Chepstow, Monmouthshire NP16 7LE

Ages 4–13 **Pupils** 183 **Boarders** 10 full, 20 flexi

Fees: Day £8,280 – £13,632; Boarding £19,362 pa

01291 622045
www.stjohnsonthehill.co.uk

Head: Since 2016, Ruth Frett, previously housemistress at Cranleigh School. After reading English at St Andrews, she studied music at Trinity College then performed all over Europe as a professional singer. Enjoying giving school masterclasses led her into teaching in London primary schools after having four children, eventually becoming head of RS and middle school and chaplain at Cranleigh Prep. Married to American Dan, who is curate in the local parish church as well as working for a software company. Her four children are now past school age but her fifth, a foster child, is at St John's.

Dean Close, the owners of St John's, are wisely leaving her a free hand to put St John's back on the map. Filled with enthusiasm and energy, she has transformed the look of the school with new paint and much-needed refurbishment of boarding and other areas – new art, DT and geography block. The curriculum now includes reading time as well as a renewed emphasis on IT, with keyboard skills for everyone. Though staff turnover has not been huge, Mrs Frett appointed has a new director of studies – 'impressive,' say parents – who is overhauling curriculum content and delivery, plus new heads of music and boarding. She has also taken on a fully qualified nurse, who not only looks after boarders' health and everyone's minor accidents and ailments but also coordinates monitoring of day pupils.

Endlessly enthusiastic, Mrs Frett clearly loves her school and her pupils visibly blossom in response. She evidently relishes the challenges of St John's, and numbers, which had dipped, have started to rise.

Entrance: Entry is by gentle taster day assessment. Children come from Newport, the Wye Valley, Cardiff, Monmouth and Forest of Dean, both sides of the border. Lots of minibuses make this work. St John's runs two nurseries off-site in Newport and Chepstow as well as the on-site Hedgehogs, which provide about half the reception intake.

Exit: St John's has maintained its long-established reputation for scholarships and common entrance to secondary schools. Clifton College, Dean Close, Monmouth School, Monmouth Girls and King's Gloucester are popular, with a dribble to a huge range of others including Wycliffe College, Talbot Heath in Bournemouth and Millfield.

Mrs Frett says that she does not believe in cramming for secondary school entrance because the senior schools know and value the results of a St John's education. A few leave at 11 but Mrs Frett, who is exceptionally good at maintaining links with senior schools, says that most schools value the extra confidence the last two years at St John's give their 13+ intake.

Remarks: Perched on an idyllic site above the River Wye, St John's is jumbled into a pretty little Georgian manor with a scatter of other houses and purpose built school facilities. The overall impression fluctuates from the gracious Embassy Room and black and white flagged passage through a few darkish corners brightened with child-created murals to some really up to date buildings like the pre-prep. School has been in situ since 1923, under a number of guises, and as a co-ed educational trust since the 60s. The Dean Close Foundation took over when the school got into financial difficulties in 2015. Under Mrs Frett, it is recovering from a stormy interlude of acute money shortages and anxious parents, leaving a few year groups with uneven numbers of boys and girls. Bustling and friendly with confident children, there's masses going on. A full court hearing with real judge and magistrate advising the pupil barristers and officials was in progress on the day of our visit.

Lovely pre-prep department with private gardens for each class, delightfully muddy and enjoyable forest school and exceptionally attractive and well-planned modern buildings. Classes were quietly enjoying reading time in our visit but there was evidence of academic progress all around, with joined up writing from the very beginning. Oodles of work on display and really up-to-date IT.

Prep years are in less luxurious but cheerful classrooms with small classes (16 maximum) with good science areas and recently updated IT. One parent said staff had been a little slow to 'get behind' a reluctant learner but everything is now tightening up. The curriculum, currently offering French, Spanish and Latin, is being overhauled for 'modern needs' which may include another language in future replacing Latin. After pre-prep there is a gradual transition to specialist teaching in all subjects and gifted children get the chance, for instance, to tackle GCSE maths. Learning support is for high flyers as well as strugglers. The non-selective intake means some need quite a lot of help, mainly in class but occasionally one-to-one. All pupils are tested with a battery of CATs etc. Regular reports are now electronic. Plenty of inspiring trips and in-school one-offs to enhance learning like the visit to St Fagan's iron age farm, or entering the competitive maths challenge, with some pretty impressive results. A particularly enjoyable English department inspired bout of typoglycemia (being able to read a word with the letters wrongly ordered) spawned some cunningly misspelt notices around school – which believe it or not is a great way to reinforce spelling and reading because pupils have to think.

Plenty of sport, in keeping with school's distinguished past record, and they had already notched up several rugby wins in September when we visited. Enthusiastic girls were practising hockey and clearly delighted with Mrs Frett's knowledgeable support. One mother was thrilled that children were getting extra coaching and games skills from Dean Close specialists. Good sports hall and lovely covered pool with doors opening in summer to outside viewing areas which also give a view of Astroturf. Acres of grassy grounds with a lovely treehouse project under way for year 8s to learn practical skills on. The music department has some ambitious musical projects: audition processes and organisation being licked into shape by head of music. All children are encouraged to take up instruments (at the time of our visit, 97 pupils were learning an instrument). Encouraged by Mrs Frett, choirs are beginning to take off. Year 7s have and love a three week trip to South Africa including time on safari and a day in a township school, and there is an annual sports trip. Those we spoke to really appreciated the opportunities they get here and the kindness of the staff.

Boarding accommodation, in a rambling town house on site, has been freshened up and is spruce and welcoming. Currently it is very flexi, though some children with distant, military or expat parents stay for weekends with matron or go to guardians. Separate boys' and girls' dorms but everyone mixes in together, and like everywhere at St John's a family feel is the key. Regular influxes of groups from China and Spain each year bring an international flavour as well as taking up current spare places, though boarding has already expanded a little. Wraparound care possible for day pupils with supervised after-school homework and masses of activities and sport, sustained by biscuits and fruit. No charge for any activity run by the school though some – such as dance – requiring outside tuition have to cover their costs. Parents can drop off children early for breakfast though few do. Mrs Frett says her staff are exceptionally dedicated and all take on after-school or weekend duties and activities.

Parents say that the smallness of the school means that it has a truly family atmosphere and that staff know children exceptionally well, though the downside of this is that one or two year groups are have very small groups of either boys or girls. Friendliness and a happy atmosphere seem to extend to all parents and visitors as well. Poor behaviour is sensibly dealt with and bullying picked up quickly and effectively, though it seems to be rare. Food is pretty good and children like it. The house system is largely social, since the main pastoral care for all pupils is via the form. Lots of responsibility for year 8 pupils with head boy and girl as well as house and sports captains, who speak confidently of their duties and ambitions.

Supportive parents' association provides activities like fireworks parties for school and raises funds. Parents from all backgrounds, mostly within the large catchment both sides of the border, and they hope for more from Bristol now the toll on the Severn Bridge has been removed. A few military families. Past pupils include Richard Mead, Olympic show jumper, and Welsh rugby player Marc Batten.

Much loved by parents, pupils and staff for its exceptionally friendly and supportive atmosphere, and for the sporting and academic traditions it strives to maintain. The school is part of the Dean Close Foundation and plans to increase numbers to about 250, which should mean it is financially viable in the future. Certainly a school well into recovery and worth watching for the future.

St Laurence School

Ashley Road, Bradford-on-Avon, Wiltshire BA15 1DZ

Ages 11–18 **Pupils** 1,413 **Sixth form** 275

01225 309500
www.st-laurence.com

Headteacher: Since 2013, Fergus Stewart (early 50s), a chemist by academic discipline, with an MA from Oxford and a PGCE from Nottingham. Despite the Scots name, upbringing and colouring, Mr Stewart has spent most of his career in Wiltshire, latterly as deputy head of Nova Hreod (no, it's not a misprint) school in Swindon, before moving to 'that good school that I'd always been aware of in the corner of the county'.

An unequivocal believer in comprehensive education, Mr Stewart expresses his two key aims for his school to be academic excellence for all and the development of well-rounded young people – and holding those in tension. So does he achieve it? Ask parents, and you will find a pretty satisfied lot: 'Thrilled, blown away by it', said one mother with sons with very different needs. 'It shames the private schools'. Everyone we spoke to had chosen the school over local independents and state options. Mr Stewart has gone down well with these same parents, who find him approachable, receptive to suggestions and, crucially, quick to respond to concerns raised with him. We found him very much on-message, but we did uncover a fisherman, a runner and a walker not averse to enlivening his peregrinations with a pub lunch. Mr Stewart is married with cats, two children at university and one at school.

Academic matters: Curriculum is predominantly broad and academic, offering GCSEs and more than 20 subjects at A level, but there are vocational options such as BTecs in a few subjects and ESPE (employability skills and personal effectiveness) which helps the less academic with pre-16 education and training. 'We teach the classes in front of us,' says Mr Stewart, though the raw material at entry is more promising than at many comprehensives. Results at A level variable with 54 per cent A*/B and 28 per cent A*/As in 2018 – quite a bit down on the year before. But 'My boy was very happy at the school and came out with his three As', said one delighted mum of an undergraduate. At GCSE, 82 per cent of pupils got 4-9 in both English and maths; 33 per cent of grades were A*-A/9-7.

Teaching staff come in for high praise: 'encouraging, supportive, they clearly enjoy what they do, committed – volunteering to help strugglers in their own time, very good at understanding individual children, particularly the problematic ones' were some of the comments made to us by parents; 'they are incredibly proud of the school,' adds the head. Their commitment is evident by the long list of revision and catch-up sessions laid on in the 3-2-5 sessions after school. Clear expectations are set, and individual targets recorded in possibly the best student diary we have ever seen, equipped with the periodic table, a world map and a trigonometry crib sheet. Only irregular verbs and musical notation were missing.

Sixth formers have their own new centre with common room, IT facilities and study areas.

For the first year, teaching is done in mixed ability sets, but maths and languages are set from year 8. SEN provision and care is highly rated, where the balance between those needs and other students' progress is finely struck.

Games, options, the arts: St Laurence is known locally for its music, as the Wiltshire Music Centre is built in its grounds and the school has day time use of its excellent facilities: 'the finest acoustics outside London', apparently. Some musicians achieve diplomas before they leave; music is timetabled. When we visited, two St Laurence girls had just won the Amnesty Young Songwriter competition – sadly, technical difficulties and time constraints meant we did not see it performed, but we were treated to the wonderful GCSE dance display which was that day's house assembly. Productions range from Hamlet to Joseph, via Les Mis, and include less formal and highbrow events, such as the 70s gig night.

Sport also prominent: rugby, netball, hockey, football and athletics the main ones, but also HRE (health-related exercise), for the ball-phobes, presumably. National swimmer and skier among current students. Advantage also taken of nearby river Avon for rowing, and as training ground (water?) for Olympic and European kayaking champions. Staff also don their whites on occasion, taking on Prior Park at cricket – and winning.

Art comes as part of a rolling programme with design and technology; parents like the range of opportunities younger pupils experience, such as cookery and textiles, 'where boys are free to explore things which might be considered a female preserve', as one mother put it. There was certainly a selection of smelly boys' shoes outside the dance studio. The new Mac suite is also 'as good as anything you would find at a private school,' opined the same lady. Extracurricular activities are many and varied, much taking place off site and at weekends, such as D of E, Ten Tors, a ski trip (where staff have gone to considerable lengths to include at least one pupil with SEN), French and German exchanges every year, plus a practical building trip to Romania with a local charity, a spiritual trip to India and World Challenge to Nepal.

Background and atmosphere: Very much the town school of the charming, historic and prosperous town of Bradford-on-Avon, with its honey-coloured buildings tumbling down to the river (we could get quite carried away), and determined to remain at the centre of the community: sixth form students volunteer for a number of organisations as part of their community service. Built in the 70s from an amalgam of previous schools on a site at the top of the town, where there is still a fine Roman mosaic floor buried under the sports pitches – seems a pity. As the town's only secondary school, there is a very inclusive feel about the place, appreciated by parents and students alike. A heartening initiative is the pairing of children with special needs with abler companions on an away-day, all of whom can miss a day in the classroom without detriment, or (better) to their mutual benefit. 'The staff have really stuck with my daughter who has ADHD,' said one mum. The Christian ethos of the school is apparent – it is a Church of England school – and the head's personal faith is clearly important to him, but regular church-going plays no part in the admissions process. Neither is it touchy-feely to the exclusion of real endeavour and winning, whether places at Oxbridge/Russell group, on the rugby pitch or eventing at nearby Stonar – but all achievement is celebrated. Despite its ancient setting, the buildings are largely unremarkable, with the exception of the Moulton maths block, named for its benefactor, local cycle manufacturer Moulton Bicycle Company, which boasts such eco-wizardry as a turf roof. 4 lab extension to science building due to open in 2019.

Pastoral care, well-being and discipline: Very much a place where achievement is talked up, and positive reinforcement rules. Vivos (sic) – an electronic points system – are awarded for good work, mannerly behaviour and everything one would wish to encourage, then totted up and go towards house totals for ceremonies at the end of term. We heard very little about discipline from anyone. The vertical tutor groups were universally praised – as well as offering support to younger students, one parent suggested that they also reduce bullying, as bullies would not want to be known as such by their tutor group and risk consequent disapproval. Tutors appear to play a more meaningful role here than many who bear that overused title, and teachers praised for knowing children as individuals.

Pupils and parents: Representative of the town and surrounding (affluent) villages. A lower than average percentage of children on free school meals and predominantly white, but, as the head points out, the absence of notorious estates in Bradford-on-Avon does not mean an absence of pupils with difficult home circumstances. 'We try to reach less confident parents who find negotiating herds of middle class parents very daunting', says he. When asked to describe a typical St Laurence student, he replied, 'Terrific, in terms of sociability, openness and enthusiasm.' We will have to take his word for it, as we met but two of them when we visited.

Entrance: At 11, 232 places applicants mostly from five local primary schools, but a significant number from outside the catchment area, including some from local prep schools; oversubscribed. As an academy, the admissions policy is set by the governors but applications are made through Wiltshire LA. Transition arrangements highly praised. At sixth form, applications are made direct to the school: five GCSEs at grade C/4 or above including English and maths are required, with C/5s in A level subjects, four for BTec courses. All hopefuls are interviewed at the school.

Exit: Negligible, if any, fall-out at year 8 when children could go to local independents at 13+. 'We didn't even consider it,' said one mother who might perhaps have wavered at year 7. About 40 per cent leave after GCSEs, the majority of those to further education. Vast majority of sixth formers go to university: 51 per cent to Russell group in 2018 including two to Oxford and one medic. Famous former students are mostly sportsmen and women, in rugby and water sports.

Money matters: Lots of extras on offer, such as trips, for which parents pay, but amounts seem very reasonable, payment terms are long and gradual and anyone likely to experience difficulty is encouraged to say so at the earliest opportunity. Very active parents' association, which, as a registered charity, maximises its revenues by tapping the CSR resources of parents' employers, as well as dealing with second-hand uniform and holding fundraising events to provide extras, such as special effects for drama and data-logging equipment for the science labs.

Remarks: Comprehensive education does not get much better than this. Parents in a position to choose from the entire range of education on offer in the UK choose St Laurence. If you live locally, why look anywhere else?

S

St Mary Redcliffe and Temple School

Somerset Square, Redcliffe, Bristol BS1 6RT

Ages 11–18 **Pupils** 1,707 **Sixth form** 625 **C of E**

01173 772100
www.smrt.bristol.sch.uk

Headteacher: Since 2005, Elisabeth Gilpin MA, formerly head of St Augustine of Canterbury Joint Roman Catholic and Church of England school in Oxford. A science teacher by background, she has also taught in schools in Bath and West Sussex. As a state-educated Oxford graduate, she is keen to encourage the most able students at her comprehensive to aim for Oxbridge. She is a National Leader of Education and vice chair of Anglican Academy and Secondary School Heads Association.

Small in stature, she is big on enthusiasm for young people and hopes for their future. Her joy at her students' successes means that on results day she is as likely as they are to be leaping into the air for the photographers. She embodies the school's belief that 'the glory of God is a human being fully alive'.

She is married with a teenage son and loves salsa dancing.

Academic matters: SMRT is consistently one of the highest achieving state schools in the west of England, with 34 per cent of GCSE grades A*-A/9-7 in 2018. In the large sixth form, 64 per cent of grades were A*-B. The school was one of the first to be rated outstanding by Ofsted under the new, tougher framework, and it was also judged outstanding in its latest diocesan inspection.

The curriculum is mainly an academic one, although some BTec level 2 courses are offered. Humanities have always been a strength; SMRT became one of the first humanities specialist schools in the country in 2004 and has worked with other secondaries to support them in these subjects, leading to the development of a successful revision website called Take Five. Unsurprisingly, there is a strong emphasis on RE and 'values-based' learning.

The school says it will be flexible with how and what it teaches 'where that is useful', but resists changing to meet every new idea. Mrs Gilpin says: 'We keep the best of the traditional approach and combine it with up to date teaching methods.'

The KS4 and KS5 timetable is built each year to take account of student choices and, because of the size of the cohort, can accommodate some unusual combinations. The sixth form offers about 40 A level courses. 'We want students to go where their strengths are. What makes us distinctive is the balance we can provide,' says the head.

Parents seem generally happy with what is on offer, although one expressed a disappointment with modern foreign languages in KS3. 'I don't like the system of alternate years being taught French and German – in my opinion it would be much better to either do both or give pupils a choice from year 7.' The amount of homework is quite high, which is welcomed by some parents and is a slight concern to others.

It has been designated a school of excellence for gifted and talented as a result of its position as a high performing specialist school and also has teaching school status. Learning support is an integral part. 'We generally intervene early to sort things out before they become a problem,' says Mrs Gilpin.

It has an unusually large leadership team of nine, including the head, which Mrs Gilpin says helps enable it to be outward-facing, sharing its successes and learning from others.

Games, options, the arts: A recent £23 million modernisation enhanced the sporting offer. The swimming pool was retained so swimming lessons continue – not to the delight of all students – and the gym was also kept, to be used for dance lessons. A huge new sports hall, the width of four badminton courts, provides a full-sized basketball court that is used by a professional side, Bristol Storm, as well as students. Volleyball is also a popular option. Outside, there are more facilities than might be expected on a cramped inner-city site, including tennis and netball courts and a long-jump pit. Moves to floodlight the new all-weather pitch are progressing. For field sports, students have to travel to grounds at Brislington and, from this year, some slightly nearer in Knowle.

Music is a strength, both within lessons and in extracurricular activities. The staff have a range of talents and are supported by visiting teachers, and the facilities for practice and performance are first rate. The gospel choir is a particular highlight, as are the annual musical theatre productions. In recent years, shows have included Little Shop of Horrors, West Side Story, Hairspray and Les Misérables.

The public art aspect of the redevelopment of SMRT involved the Bristol-based photographer, Martin Parr, making a pictorial record of a year at the school. It began with students wearing the former grey uniform and ended with them in their new raspberry sweaters. Eight of his shots are displayed in huge format around the building.

Students take part in DofE and there are regular World Challenge expeditions to eg Ecuador. The school has a long-established partnership with Ikoba School in Uganda as part of links between the Bristol diocese and the church in Uganda and the Bristol-Masindi Schools Partnership, with staff and student exchanges.

There's also an emphasis on green issues and on what Elizabeth Gilpin describes as 'creative, confidence-building opportunities'. A student won the television The Speaker competition a few years ago and every year students enter the citywide Gabblers public speaking contest. Young Enterprise, Envision, Christian Union and voluntary community service are among other activities.

Background and atmosphere: It is hard to believe this is such a big school – it is so quiet. The atmosphere is calm and the building is modern, functional and well-ordered. Facilities such as breakfast provision and the learning resource centre are available off the covered 'street', which works well for those who arrive early from outlying areas of Bristol. The school says the standard of behaviour was always good but has improved thanks to the well-designed wide corridors and social spaces. Students are proud of the new building and look after it well. Memorabilia from the school's 430-year history is on display.

SMRT is clear about its high expectations for creating a school community of hope based on Christian principles and featuring good relationships, safe boundaries and empowered learning. What this boils down to, it says, is that it wants every student to be able to say: 'I feel safe; I belong here; I enjoy learning and achieve well; this school helps me to make my hopes for the future come true.'

A parent commented: 'There is a compassionate ethos which seems to be shared by staff and pupils. Teaching in most subjects is excellent and expectations are high, which leads to great results. Communication between the school and parents is open and supportive.'

Worship is an important part of school life and one of SMRT's most distinctive features. Services take place in the historic and beautiful St Mary Redcliffe Church at the start and end of each term and for the annual Colston Day. These are supplemented by regular clergy visits and house assemblies.

Pastoral care, well-being and discipline: SMRT has clear systems in place for behaviour. Students are given levels from A* to E. The highest grades are not merely for complying with rules but must include behaviour that supports and enhances learning for others. Anyone who needs help gets it in the appropriate way and liaison with parents is strong. There has been only one permanent exclusion in the past three years. Attendance levels are good too – close to 96 per cent.

The school is proud of its pastoral care. Children come into year 7 from schools in every Bristol postcode and some will not know anyone else when they arrive. Year 7s register in a separate place, the Temple Colston building, and have their own house.

A parent whose child started recently said: 'The school was excellent during the induction day in showing the children where the bus stops were, so that this was never a difficulty for her. Since starting, the school has carried out several assessments across all subjects and found work at exactly the right level for our child. She has made friends very easily and the children were given time to adjust to the new school before homework was set. Everything has been paced very well. We are delighted and are full of confidence that she is being very well taught and cared for.'

Vertical tutoring has become trendy in recent years but at SMRT years 8 to 11 have been organised in mixed age tutor groups since 1966 as part of the school's Christian family ethos. Students are allocated to one of four houses – Canynges, Cartwright, Colston and Francombe (moves to modernise the traditional names were resisted). 'It is a way of creating smaller units of belonging within a large organisation,' says Mrs Gilpin.

The sixth form is in a separate building, the Redcliffe Sixth Form Centre, about five minutes away from the main site. Students come to the school to run clubs and mentor younger children. Some feel they would like to integrate more with the rest of the school while others value the independence and the more college-like atmosphere. Parents value the supportive atmosphere of the sixth form, which takes in external students as well as those from SMRT.

'The sixth form is excellent – support for learning and for the university application process is very strong and there is a very good rapport between students and teachers,' said one.

Pupils and parents: Pupils come from a range of communities across greater Bristol. Elizabeth Gilpin describes the school population as 'uniquely socially diverse' and says, 'We are passionately committed to social inclusion and want everybody from every background to achieve their best'. A comparatively high number of looked after children among the pupils. Mrs Gilpin says the admissions policy is deliberately structured to create a rich ethnic mix. The school has a higher than average number of students from black and minority ethnic backgrounds – over a third. Some parents from predominantly white areas have made positive choice to send their children to SMRT because of this diversity.

The school takes pride in students of all backgrounds who overcome challenges. One lad with Asperger's and sensory neuropathy gained four A*s at A level and won a place at Cambridge recently. The experienced sixth form team helps support a number of students into Oxbridge and medical school every year.

Communication with parents via monthly newsletters and a comprehensive website is good. One parent of a sixth-former who joined SMRT from another school said: 'She has had a great start in all her classes where the staff have made high expectations very clear from the outset and been supportive where needed. Our daughter was able to take all the A level subjects she wanted to study and has already been on art and physics trips. There are so many extracurricular activities in the large sixth form that there is bound to be something to suit the vast majority of children. Thanks to the excellent online school calendar and sixth form newsletter, we already know the key dates that our daughter and we need to be aware of this year in terms of mock exams, university applications, parents' evenings and more. There are plenty of opportunities to develop leadership and communication skills too.'

The school runs regular training and briefing sessions for parents, which are much appreciated.

Entrance: SMRT is an Anglican voluntary-aided school and admits children from all Christian communities in the Bristol area. More than 80 places of worship are represented, including mosques. The school offers 216 places each year. Sixteen are reserved for children of any faith living in immediate vicinity of the school and four are allocated to children of other faiths. Priority is given to those who attend church most regularly.

SMRT has come under fire from the Fair Admissions campaigners, who accuse it of selecting wealthy pupils by the back door because it has a low proportion of students on free school meals compared with the numbers living in its immediate locality. But the school says this is a misrepresentation, as few teenagers live in the tower blocks close by and the number of places it has available is sufficient to meet demand.

Exit: The majority of year 11 leavers (about two-thirds) go into Redcliffe sixth form. A high proportion of year 13 leavers (around 70 per cent) go to university. Degree subject choices include maths, physics, geography, history, English, film, journalism and psychology. In 2018, five Oxbridge places.

Money matters: Children in care, care leavers and students in receipt of income support are guaranteed a non-discretionary bursary. Beyond this all awards are discretionary and depend on the availability of adequate funds and the volume of eligible applications.

Remarks: A school so firmly based on a second century line from St Irenaeus might seem incongruous in the 21st century. The words 'The Glory of God is a human being fully alive' could even be a tad embarrassing to some believers (and to some teenagers) – yet at SMRT they are embraced without apology and feel totally natural and right. They provide the roots on which a happy and thriving school has been built.

St Mary's Calne

Linked with St Margaret's Prep School

S

Curzon Street, Calne, Wiltshire SN11 0DF

Ages 11–18 **Pupils** 365 **Sixth form** 120 **Boarders** 290 full **C of E**

Fees: Day £29,025; Boarding £38,925 pa

01249 857200
www.stmaryscalne.org

Headmistress: Since 2013, Dr Felicia Kirk MA PhD (early 40s). Born and raised in Maryland, USA, Dr Kirk's distinguished academic career in languages, both ancient and modern, took her to the École Normale Supérieure in Paris, where she met the Brit she would later follow to England and marry, leaving the groves of academe for the real world of teaching children. Her first job was at the Royal Hospital School in Suffolk, followed by a move into girls' education as director of higher education at Wycombe Abbey, then latterly as head of sixth form at Ipswich High School. Of her move to Calne, she says, 'I missed the boarding, and I liked the fact that the school is small, yet ambitious'.

Totally committed to girls' education, she intends to build on breadth of opportunity at Calne 'unencumbered by gender stereotyping'; building both literally and figuratively, that is, with an ambitious 10 year development plan to squeeze every last square inch (OK, centimetre, then) out of this school's compact site, with increased provision for arts, sports, a new library and more science labs. Any faint question marks about an American leading this very British institution are utterly dispelled on meeting her – she's hardly even mid-Atlantic in accent, and elegantly clad in a tweed jacket with velvet collar the day we visited. Parents appreciate the richness brought by experience from elsewhere, as well as her plans for the place: 'The school needs more than academia to keep it at the top table,' said one mother. Try as we might, it was impossible to break through her professional, though charming, veneer. Her girls describe her as enthusiastic and easy to talk to, are pleased to see her walking her dog in trackies and to receive a birthday card in their first year. 'Plus she's innovative,' said one. What does that mean again? 'It's new stuff like introducing company jumpers,' said a helpful friend.

Dr Kirk is married to an accountant. Her home is in Suffolk, where she also keeps her retired eventer.

Academic matters: Undoubtedly what the school is about, but not all it's about. At A level, 57 per cent A*/A grades, 84 per cent A*/B in 2018. Stand-out subjects are maths, history, Spanish and Latin; sports science and computer science new additions.

At GCSE, results down a bit in 2018 at 80 per cent A*/A. Geography, Latin, art and music excel here. Results are more exciting than the classrooms which produce them, and teaching does not appear to be as reliant on IT as is the case in many schools we see; that said, refurbishing the labs cannot come a moment too soon. Library provision too is good but scattered; a new one planned for 2019.

Enrichment week – inter alia, gung ho girls in camouflage crawling enthusiastically under netting taking orders from an army officer – was in full swing when we visited, but we were pleased to note an A level history class of about six discussing Mary Tudor's relationship with the clergy, rather than the apparently ceaseless rehashing of the two world wars. Ditto Northanger Abbey read in its entirety in year 9 – none of these bite-sized chunks beloved of modern exam setters. Recent success enjoyed in prestigious maths and German Olympiad competitions too.

SEN provision is as expected at a school of this calibre – definitely the mild end of dys- spectra – though everyone is tested on entry. About eight per cent of girls have an identifiable educational need catered for; provision equally is made for EAL and the very brightest sparks too.

Games, options, the arts: An astonishing amount of sporting facilities is crammed into this compact site, with more planned. A full-sized floodlit Astro and netball/tennis courts now joined by brand new sports complex, including dance studio. Lacrosse is the winter sport on offer, alongside netball, which is played against schools not offering lax; hockey is played in the spring term. The youngest girls all represent the school early on; later, team practice becomes optional and from year 10, girls can drop ball sports altogether, as long as they do something to get them off the couch and away from the toaster. Tennis, swimming, fencing happen all year round, rowing and sailing in summer. Though no horses reside at school, show-jumping and eventing are a successful part of the sporting calendar. Skiing is prominent too: as well as the usual ski-trip, school also takes part in the quaintly named but deadly serious British Schoolgirls Races in Flaine each year, to some acclaim.

The arts take centre stage. Huge portraits adorn the entrance (colloquially known as the goldfish bowl), and paintings most of the walls. Sculpture is big here too – long before art becomes a GCSE option, junior girls experiment with life-sized figures. A full size war horse and cavalry officer in the early stages of construction out of wood and chicken wire has to be built in a gazebo outside the art school: 'I can't wait for the new studios,' remarked one member of staff with feeling. Drama a high point too: an inspirational head of drama who retired a few years ago left a legacy of adventurous excellence, which is not limited to an annual musical, Shakespeare (recently an all-female Hamlet), performances at the egg theatre in Bath and at the Edinburgh Fringe. Tess of the d'Urbervilles was on the week we visited – we were charmed by the hay and ancient agricultural machinery strewn throughout the foyer of a somewhat tired theatre. Quite the glossiest programmes we had ever seen.

Much of the singing harks back to its roots in the English choral tradition, to be expected in a school where chapel is still central to its life, but its reach extends to the charitable, profitable and glittery: a concert at Chelsea Old Church with a sideshow of celebrities raised £19,000. A symphony orchestra, jazz band, opera, string and flute groups complete the offering, which both brings top performers into school, takes musicians out of school (not only in the UK but abroad to Paris and so on) and music to local venues and primary schools as part of its community outreach. Generously resourced and imaginative in scope, the music department commissioned an opera to commemorate the centenary of the start of WW1.

Boarding: The majority board, housed in year groups and moved into accommodation of increasing luxury each year as they progress up the school; day girls belong to houses along with their boarding counterparts and integration seems seamless. The new lower sixth house with its en-suite bathrooms and groovy décor (not sure about the bilious green chairs, however) will surpass anything likely to be encountered in most freshers' lodging, or even at home. House unity, as generally understood, is generated through 'companies', five groups of girls of all ages named after former bishops of Salisbury; a coloured band on the regulation navy jumper denotes it, and the company shout (known elsewhere as house music) loudly affirms it.

Background and atmosphere: An astonishing amount of sporting facilities is crammed into this compact site, with more planned. A full-sized floodlit Astro and netball/tennis courts now joined by brand new sports complex, including dance studio. Lacrosse is the winter sport on offer, alongside netball, which is played against schools not offering lax; hockey is played in the spring term. The youngest girls all represent the school early on; later, team practice becomes optional and from year 10, girls can drop ball sports altogether, as long as they do something to get them off the couch and away from the toaster.

Tennis, swimming, fencing happen all year round, rowing and sailing in summer. Though no horses reside at school, show-jumping and eventing are a successful part of the sporting calendar. Skiing is prominent too: as well as the usual ski-trip, school also takes part in the quaintly named but deadly serious British Schoolgirls Races in Flaine each year, to some acclaim.

The arts take centre stage. Huge portraits adorn the entrance (colloquially known as the goldfish bowl), and paintings most of the walls. Sculpture is big here too – long before art becomes a GCSE option, junior girls experiment with life-sized figures. A full size war horse and cavalry officer in the early stages of construction out of wood and chicken wire has to be built in a gazebo outside the art school: 'I can't wait for the new studios,' remarked one member of staff with feeling. Drama a high point too: an inspirational head of drama who retired a few years ago left a legacy of adventurous excellence, which is not limited to an annual musical, Shakespeare (recently an all-female Hamlet), performances at the egg theatre in Bath and at the Edinburgh Fringe. Tess of the d'Urbervilles was on the week we visited – we were charmed by the hay and ancient agricultural machinery strewn throughout the foyer of a somewhat tired theatre. Quite the glossiest programmes we had ever seen.

Much of the singing harks back to its roots in the English choral tradition, to be expected in a school where chapel is still central to its life, but its reach extends to the charitable, profitable and glittery: a concert at Chelsea Old Church with a sideshow of celebrities raised £19,000. A symphony orchestra, jazz band, opera, string and flute groups complete the offering, which both brings top performers into school, takes musicians out of school (not only in the UK but abroad to Paris and so on) and music to local venues and primary schools as part of its community outreach. Generously resourced and imaginative in scope: the music department commissioned an opera to commemorate the centenary of the start of WW1.

Pastoral care, well-being and discipline: Highly rated by both girls and parents. Each girl is allocated a tutor (who can be changed in the unusual event of it not working out) and has a weekly individual meeting. Between the housemistress and tutor, 'it's like having a mum and dad at school,' said one. Plenty of avenues to seek help if ever things go wrong, and generous provision for anyone needing medical attention, with a fully equipped, permanently manned medical centre. Not only is good work (both absolute and relative) rewarded by 'blues', but so are other virtues such as kindness, punctuality and tidiness. A 'good egg' prize is awarded each year for the sort of qualities which make a community run joyously. Miscreants who talk after lights might be made to do the house washing up the following day; major sins attract an escalating scale of punishment. Smokers' fines are donated to cancer charities.

Pupils and parents: Well-mannered and forthright with plenty of get-up-and-go. 'If you want something started, ask a Calne girl,' said the head. The ones we met were certainly privileged but not in the slightest bit tiresome. One mother said she chose the school because she wanted confidence not arrogance instilled in her daughters; something the girls in Grosstete company might be particularly mindful of. The school appears to run on old money, rather than new – 'The car park is full of Audis, Volvos and battered old Fords,' one parent observed – with a tangible affection from its former pupils, some of whom send their daughters. Considerable camaraderie on the lacrosse touchline too.

Entrance: Registration is advised three or four years ahead of proposed entry at year 7 (LIV in school parlance). Places conditional on entrance exams (either CE or school's own 11+ exam) are offered after an assessment day held in the September one year before entry. Process for 13+ (year 9, UIV) starts at the end of year 6. Bright sparks are invited to apply for scholarships. Girls come from the smarter prep schools in the south and south west, some from London, some from school's own prep, St Margaret's, and a few from local primaries.

Around 15 new into sixth form with good GCSEs, sparkling in subjects to be taken to A level.

Exit: About 15 per cent leave after GCSE in search of (in no particular order) boys, brighter lights, wider subject choices, more freedom; the rest to top notch universities up and down the land or art foundation. A handful to Oxbridge every year (eight in 2018, plus one medic and one to drama school), the majority of the rest to Russell Group. School takes great care over the next stage: hosting a higher education conference for GSA, Oxbridge aptitude testing in school and Futures, a new half termly publication covering exclusively university applications, developments and more adventurous overseas options, plus alumnae experience. Increasing number of gap years. Famous OGs include Laura Bechtolsheimer, Olympic dressage medallist, and writer Lucy Hughes-Hallett (plus former PM David Cameron's sister).

Money matters: Not a rich school, but one husbanding and developing its resources to ensure its place amongst the UK's top girls' schools. Usual range of scholarships offered, including a choral scholarship at 13+. A nominal five per cent fee reduction is given, but up to 40 per cent depending on means-testing. Two sixth form scholarships to internal candidates and one to external on offer too. A foundation scholarship of up to 100 per cent of day fees at both year 7 and sixth form is aimed exclusively at state school pupils for whom 'reasons of financial restriction' would otherwise preclude going there.

Remarks: A school for clever girls? Certainly, though 'it doesn't matter if they're not – they're usually good at something else.' Quintessential English girls' boarding? Absolutely. Social cachet? Unquestionably.

St Mary's School (Shaftesbury)

Donhead St. Mary, Shaftesbury, Dorset SP7 9LP

Ages 9–18 **Pupils** 203 **Sixth form** 52 **Boarders** 104 full **RC**

Fees: Day £16,200 – £20,850; Boarding £20,085 – £31,470 pa

01747 852416
www.stmarys.eu

Headmistress: Since September 2018, Maria Young, previously deputy head pastoral and head of boarding at Worth School. Music degree from Durham and a PGCE in music from Cambridge; she has taught music at a variety of schools including Bryanston, and was director of music at Simon Langton Girls' Grammar School before joining Worth, where she was also lay chaplain. She has spent 30 years as a director of music, writing and directing musicals and opera, as well as directing school choirs and taking them on tours around the world.

S

Academic matters: Popular A level subjects include English literature, history and history of art, geography, fine art and photography. Steady uptake of science, economics, business studies, maths and modern languages. For a small school with pupils of mixed ability, results are usually good. In 2018, 52 per cent of A levels graded A*-B and a disappointing 18 per cent A*/A.

GCSE results also good with 60 per cent A*-A/9-7 in 2018. Girls do well in English literature, modern languages, science, the humanities and art. Languages department has introduced IGCSE exams throughout. French and Spanish exchanges for those interested.

Parents praise 'very experienced teaching staff' for their dedication, openness and lack of pretension. Some have been there for years, but school says the average age is beginning to come down. General consensus is that self-motivated girls are very well supported. 'If you do want to be bothered [with work], the teachers will bend over backwards.' One commented that the school 'hides its academic light under a bushel', although all agreed that 'the teaching shines'.

Three dedicated SEN rooms at the top of humanities block helps those with mild learning difficulties (dyslexia, dyspraxia) as well as running revision sessions and helping girls to improve their grades in maths and English. At the time of our visit, 46 pupils (up to three at a time) were receiving EAL coaching.

Games, options, the arts: 'Sport for all' is school's aim and girls play all the usual sports up to GCSE plus a few less common, eg yoga, pilates and zumba. School will lay on an activity if there is sufficient interest, eg scuba diving. Year 10s upwards have access to the school's fitness suite and can begin the sports leaders programme which continues in sixth form for those taking A level PE. Circuit training and conditioning machines used for school's elite athlete training programme. Large sports hall and 25m pool sit side by side, surrounded by Astroturf pitch, netball and tennis courts. Swimming and tennis available year round. A few girls play hockey at county level and train at the county netball academy, with some year 10 girls put forward for LTA tennis league each year. Regular match fixtures and swimming galas; teams hold their own and win against much larger schools. Dance tuition from professionals.

Stunning, spacious art block opened in 2014; the creative arts are a real strength here and evidence of this hangs in corridors throughout the main school building. 'Art is outstanding and all visual arts are very good.' Busy textiles room with lots of sewing machines humming; textiles and design taught in six-month blocks, fine art all year. Photography offered at GCSE and A level and textiles at GCSE. Trips abroad to exhibitions in Paris, Florence and Barcelona for sixth formers.

Excellent music block, with 25 individual practice rooms, small concert space, music technology room and dedicated classroom, plus a well-stocked music library with archive material and CD recordings. Some 60 per cent learn an instrument, 15 per cent study two and some learn two instruments and singing; practice is timetabled. Ensembles include school orchestra, percussion and wind bands plus a rock band; others are formed depending on instruments and girls are encouraged to take the initiative. Everyone sings each week, either in class or as a form. 'The school needs a bit more singing outside the chapel choir.' Two school choirs, one of which is the 'awesome' chapel choir which rehearses three mornings a week for chapel assemblies, Saturday mass and tours abroad. St Cecilia's pupils' concert takes place each year. Regular outreach to primary schools and local choirs, including annual Choral Day.

Extensive range of extracurricular activities, clubs and societies on offer; these include fencing, forest school and beekeeping. French society is very popular and includes a literary circle. Sixth formers can qualify for Leiths Basic Certificate in Food and Wine in well-appointed cookery school. Several drama productions across the age range each year and LAMDA exams are popular. DofE awards are a big part of school life, with two-thirds completing these every year. In keeping with school's Catholic ethos, girls fund raise and lead charitable expeditions to countries such as Rwanda, Chile and Zambia to work with schools and orphanages. The Mary Ward Lecture Series encourages girls to think through listening to speakers on topics such as war theory, bioethics and religious pluralism.

Boarding: Boarding arrangements work well; years 5, 6, 7 and 8 board in a junior boarding house which day girls are welcome to visit. After this, girls move into one of the main houses where they sleep in single, double or four-person bedrooms. Some bedrooms are small, but each house has a spacious common room and a kitchen. Rooms rotate regularly and day-to-day housekeeping is efficient. 'A brilliant woman runs the laundry and the shift system for washing clothes works.' Parents full of praise for sixth form housemistress. 'She's seen everything and can deal with anything.' Girls in sixth form move into a stand-alone house similar to halls of residence which gives them greater independence, eg preparing their own breakfast and entertaining outside friends to dinner parties.

Half are full boarders, so school doesn't empty out on weekends, though flexi-boarding is available. Day girls can go home after lessons, but many choose to stay on for clubs, homework and supper. Enrichment programme on Saturday mornings and plenty to do on weekends.

Boarders are taken to and from various airport terminals by school minibus on exeat weekends, at half-term and at the beginning and end of term; those going to London on exeats can travel by escorted coach to Richmond. Parents confirm that school is very aware of girls' whereabouts.

Background and atmosphere: St Mary's was founded in 1945 and can trace its origins back to Mary Ward, an English Catholic nun who championed the rights of girls to receive an education, despite living in hostile Tudor times. Imprisoned for her beliefs, she succeeded in establishing a school for girls in York before her death in 1645.

With the school set in 55 acres of parkland and approached down a winding, tree-lined drive, there is a sense of leaving the outside world behind as one arrives at an imposing early Victorian mansion. Sensitive efforts have been made to modernise the interior, with glass screens to let in light. Spread around the main house is a collection of buildings ranging from ultra-modern to slightly frayed labs and other older classrooms. New and old nestle side by side and somehow manage not to look incongruous, but the impression is of much brown and green.

In contrast to the school's cooler colours is its warm, family atmosphere. Teachers, parents and girls alike champion it as safe and nurturing. 'It's a very caring school which fosters life-long friendships.' Walking round, we were struck by the genuinely supportive relationships between girls of all ages. 'If you could bottle the atmosphere at St Mary's, it would be invaluable.'

School has reinstated years 5 and 6.

Pastoral care, well-being and discipline: Strongly underpinned by school's Catholic faith, pastoral care is 'brilliant' and 'house assistants are excellent'. 'Somehow the school makes the girls very caring and respectful.' School's own priest in residence from Thursday to Saturday. The school operates more on praise than sanction,' said one parent. Any misdemeanour earns the culprit a lavender ticket, 'lavvies' to the girls. Punishments range from parental meeting to suspension. 'The girls want their community to work – we have to deal with so few sanctions.' Strict on smoking and alcohol, the odd suspension has happened for having one too many at socials with boys' schools.

Despite being 'in the sticks', parents insist their daughters don't feel cut off as school allows enough freedom. Thirteen-year-olds don wellies and stride off in small groups over the fields for Saturday afternoon shopping in Shaftesbury; older girls catch the train to Salisbury.

School meals served in cafeteria with staff on hand to supervise; good food with several choices including a vegetarian option, plenty of fresh fruit, cheese and puddings.

Girls are allowed mobile phones, but no Skype or Facebook until year 11. School Wifi switched off at night. School says that trust between staff and pupils forms the basis of school community; 'older staff are very good at dealing with any minor teasing or bullying'.

Pupils and parents: Girls joining in years 5 to 7 come from local primaries, London day schools and boarding preps. Intake doubles at 13+ from prep schools such as Farleigh, Sandroyd and Port Regis. Some foreign nationals join the school later. Average year group numbers 35, with 70 per cent of families within an hour's drive. Some 15 per cent from abroad, mostly Mexico, Spain and China, with a few from Nigeria, Japan, Germany and the rest of Europe. There are some 20 military families and a 10 per cent discount is offered. Parents are a mixed bunch, some wealthy, some not, whilst girls are natural, unspoilt, polite and articulate. 'The girls like themselves, know themselves and are very confident in their own skins.'

Entrance: Main entry points are at 9, 11 and 13, although girls can join in any year. Entrance examination day takes place in January and includes tests in maths, English and verbal reasoning plus an interview. At 16, girls need a minimum of eight GCSE grade 4s. The school welcomes children of all faiths, but families must be 'sympathetic to the Catholic ethos' of the school.

Exit: Up to half leave after GCSEs. Most sixth formers to Russell Group universities throughout the country, eg Bristol, Exeter, UCL, Manchester, Newcastle and Edinburgh. Oxford Brookes also popular. A couple off overseas in 2018: to Prague and to Georgia Institute of Technology, USA. A good handful to art college each year, eg Bournemouth, Falmouth and Plymouth. Most choose arts degrees; good to see that a sprinkling of girls opts for the sciences, eg anatomy, biomedical sciences, physics and nuclear astrophysics. A small number pursues practical courses such as agriculture, publishing and events management.

Money matters: Usual range of 9+, 11+, 13+ and 16+ music, academic, sports and art scholarships on offer together with one 11+ Catholic Local Primary Scholarship. All-round scholarship 'for excellence' plus means-tested bursaries available at school's discretion.

Remarks: In the past we have described St Mary's as 'a jolly nice girls' Catholic boarding school' but this belies its true character. A reasonably pacey school, St Mary's is performing pretty well on all fronts, albeit with great modesty. 'They don't blow their own trumpet enough,' remarked a parent. With lower fees than many independent schools, this school is quietly delivering excellent value. Girls wanting to be educated with boys and/or dolled up to the nines should look elsewhere, but those looking for a warm and caring environment where they can achieve and be themselves will be right at home.

St Peter's Preparatory School

S

Harefield, Lympstone, Exmouth, Devon EX8 5AU

Ages 3–13 **Pupils** 250 **Boarders** 114 flexi (from 7 years)

Fees: Day £7,650 – £13,065; Boarding £19,935 pa

01395 272148
www.stpetersprep.co.uk

Head: Since September 2016, Charlotte Johnston, previously deputy head (academic) at Edge Grove School in Herts. Schooled at St Albans High School for Girls and Uppingham, studied

English and history of art at Birmingham; PGCE primary from University of Herts; MEd from Buckingham. Worked as a change management consultant for PwC; after starting a family she retrained as a teacher and joined Edge Grove in 2002. She and Oliver (a police officer) have two children. Charlotte enjoys tennis, skiing and yoga, music in all its forms and walking the school dog Monty on the Devon cliffs.

Brims with energy and exudes capability. The latest in a line of excellent heads, she's had no Augean stable to muck out, but Mrs Johnston is not here to hold steady and consolidate. No, she's forward-looking, full of plans to make an already very good school even better. Her prescription is straightforward enough: 'Put the opportunities and support in place and everyone will shine'. Well capable of audacity and not afraid of making waves. Excellent recent appointment of deputy head of teaching and learning. Has revamped the PTA. This is a school in very safe hands.

Entrance: Parents a mix of west country businesspeople and professionals plus an increasing number of lifestyle migrants from London. Academically non-selective, come one, come all from rising 3s upwards. No terrifying tests. All children do a taster day so that teachers can stand back, observe and evaluate. Academically painless, greatly appreciated by parents who want no winnowing ordeals for their child at this age. One parent of three children said, 'It's just such a relief to know they'll take all of them'. Note: the appraisal process includes a behavioural audit. A child must be able to fit in socially. Developmentally delayed social skills (eg Asperger's) taken into account but disruptiveness an adamant no-no. Join at any time of the year if there's room. Because this is a popular school there is often a waiting list in one or more year groups. For tinies, childcare vouchers accepted and, if places oversubscribed, priority given to those who commit to moving on to the prep. Bursaries on discretionary basis; some scholarships awarded for years 7 and 8 up to 30 per cent of fees.

Exit: Year groups here number about 30. Around five pupils a year, some of them the brightest, leave at 11 for state grammars eg Colyton. Entrants for the highly selective independents in Exeter leave at the end of year 8. Expert advice given about which independent senior to go on to, sensitively handled. The head has visited and got to know every one of them. Although there's a dearth of decent stand-alone preps in Devon, there's a senior school for everyone down here, all of them keen to recruit St Peter's boys and girls, whom they rate. Lots to Exeter School and The Maynard, others to the Tauntons, Blundells, Sherborne, Wellington (popular just now). Some to Truro, some to Stover, some to Millfield. Lots get scholarships of all sorts, far more than you'd expect of a non-selective school, up to 70+ per cent of year 8 leavers. Credit the breadth of the curriculum for this. Starting to send further afield.

S

Remarks: Founded in 1882. Centred on a modest stuccoed mansion house built on high ground in the 1820s in an architecturally indeterminate style with classical features. Could almost pass for 1920s, the more so since it is now painted a striking seaside cream. Prime location, lovely rural setting, ravishing view – it'll stop you in your tracks – across the fields down to the estuary of the Exe and the high seas beyond.

Present owner is Jon Middleton, former bursar. Knows the workings of the school inside out, meets the head once a week in the role of strategic sounding board, financial guru and guardian of the ethos. Loves this place and is invested for the long term. Governance notably lean, agile and responsive, embodied in a 'board of reference' numbering around eight.

Ample grounds, 28 acres, timeless cricket pitch, generous playing fields, outside heated pool. Sports hall that'll never win any beauty contests but fit for purpose and versatile: comprises a basketball court and squash court, is readily adaptable for assemblies and plays, and houses up-to-date science labs.

Early years classrooms fit the bill: purpose built, we liked the air of calm. Forest school and, highlight of the week, yay, beach school. Many classrooms for years 5+ are timber buildings of uncertain age and WW2 appearance. Characterful for sure – in the words of a parent, 'They have their charm, a classroom is a classroom'. Indeed. Our view: eligible for updating. Some classrooms in the main house plus the library, handsomely accommodated.

Academically, this is a school with a shining USP: it profiles children holistically and awards them the St Peter's School Baccalaureate (SPB). So good they registered the trade mark, the SPB has influenced the way a number of other prep schools now assess their pupils. The brainchild of the deputy head of teaching and learning, a teacher of remarkable good sense and bottomless dedication, it both tracks and measures all of a child's skills throughout their time here. Takes account not just of knowledge but also skills, citizenship, sporting prowess, effort and personal qualities – including things a child does out of school. Appropriate in itself for a mixed-ability school, it challenges children at their own level and is tailor-made for each pupil – what the school calls a 'personalised learning journey'. Greatly appreciated by senior schools as a detailed cross-curricular gauge of abilities and disposition, where it's usually preferred to common entrance, now increasingly rarely sat by St Peter's pupils. Two happy side effects of the Bacc: first, it enables teachers to keep parents comprehensively informed and keep them real; second, it unshackles teachers from the narrow range of the common entrance curriculum, allowing them to range more widely and in a cross-curricular way. It also enables them to take their classes out of doors, investigate and use the landscape, a distinctive feature of the St Peter's curriculum.

Many are the merits of the St P Bacc, but it's the teachers here who are the stars of the show. We were astonished by the quality of those we met in this tucked-away corner of Devon, buried in greenery – fired up, very bright, very able. It is they, more than anything else, that make this school remarkable and explain why the children are working up to a year, some of them two years, above their level. They're not slave-drivers, you can't be one of those in a mixed-ability school; they're just very good at bringing out the best in a broad spectrum of pupils. They monitor the progress of their pupils closely and, in the words of a parent, 'step in quickly if there's a blip'. Parents also praise frequent reporting and quick response to concerns. Streaming in maths and English from year 1. Subject specialists from year 5. Scholarship sets in year 8. Two modern languages, Latin club and Italian club. Centre of excellence status in science – 'Children here do experiments, they don't watch teachers do them'. Optional GCSE in critical thinking for 12 year-olds.

Special needs under the umbrella of 'learning success', so includes gifted and talented. Broad range of SpLDs here, individual needs expertly mapped. Yes to mild Asperger's. No children with EHC plans.

Outdoor pursuits a major feature of the curriculum, the career achievement of one of the deputy heads. Opportunities start in year 5 and the programme kicks in big time in the last two years when all work towards their Cross Keys award. Think D of E. It's all about initiative, self-reliance, team working and leadership and constitutes a persuasive argument in terms of personal development for going the distance to year 8. We wondered whether everyone is suited to this sort of thing. The head said, 'We're looking at addressing that by adding more performing arts and other areas of certification to validate different achievements.'

Customary seasonal fare of sports, impressive results, plenty of scholarships to senior schools and if your team is unbeaten you get to win a bacon butty. Head keen to promote sport for all and get more girls playing in mixed cricket and hockey teams. Rugby and squash especially strong, and sailing, of course. Selection for county and national teams routine. A highlight of the sporting year: the cricket match vs the Lympstone village team. A good neighbour, the school opens its facilities to the local community.

Art good, comprises also craft and textiles. Take your easel outside and paint away sur l'herbe. House competition. Full marks to the head for reviving the annual show where every pupil hangs their own masterpiece. After-school sketching club. Regular annual plays. Drama itself a relative newcomer to the classroom curriculum and coming on vigorously. Looks like being a legacy issue for the head, this; she's already installed music tech kit in the music room and converted it into a performing arts room suitable also for dance. Music a longstanding strength, and boy is it good. Distinguished choral tradition with away fixtures at, eg, Exeter cathedral and Eton College. Lots of ensembles plus rock choir and community band for kids, staff and anyone local. A parent whose children had been at a cathedral choir school told us how pleasantly amazed she was that 'there was no let-down at all, musically' when she switched schools. Well chosen range of after-school activities from martial arts to Trinity College Arts Awards, maths clinics to mindfulness and tons of music. One parent said, 'There are opportunities to do whatever you're good at'. Heaps of trips home and abroad including annual immersion week for year 7s in a French château.

Pastoral care rated by parents. Most frequently used word to describe the social climate is 'kind', with 'warm' coming in a close second and 'nurturing' third. One parent observed, 'There's a fantastic energy here'. This is a small and diverse school where everyone knows everybody so there are just three rules: courtesy, consideration and common sense.

Boarding is weekdays only. There are regular stayers but no weekly boarders. Plenty of sleepover boarding, Friday night babysitter-boarding a speciality. Last minute boarding available if mum or dad gets held up. It's all great fun, activities are fab and as a result more than three-quarters give it a go.

School day runs from 8am to 5pm but for super-busy parents there's the option of drop off at 7.30am for breakfast, pick up early evening after supper. Supervised homework session after school. Lessons run from 8:30am to 3:30pm/4:15pm depending on the year with childcare from 8am – 6pm included in the fees. Minibuses driven by cheery ex-coppers gather children from as far as Newton Abbot, Exeter and Honiton. When term time is over there's a holiday club here.

There's nothing wacky about St Peter's, it's very trad. Good manners are prized, hard work rewarded. Seriously nice children. Some facilities less than ritzy. Amazing teachers. Exceeds expectations.

Sale Grammar School

Marsland Road, Sale, Cheshire M33 3NH

Ages 11–18 **Pupils** 1,200 **Sixth form** 350

01619 733217
www.salegrammar.co.uk/

Headteacher: Since 2010, Mark Smallwood (physics, Manchester and Lancaster), BEd, MA, PGDP, NPQH, previously head of Fearns Community High in Bacup, Lancashire, and before that at Failsworth School, Oldham. Open, down to earth and exuding warmth (with not one whiff of academy-style jargon), he is an immensely likeable man who is very clear that Sale's main mission is to maintain its academic excellence while ensuring students also pursue other creative or technological areas of study (the latter, a goal he achieves through limiting the subjects in the GCSE option blocks). In essence, he wants students to appreciate that life is a rounded business and not just about notching up the 9s and A*s (though they do that anyway, of course, in abundance) so the maths and art departments are side by side in the same area of the school to underline the breadth of choice open to everyone.

School became an academy in 2011 and continues to be an Ofsted 'outstanding', boasting specialist status in the 'visual arts' – which is evident in every corner of the building with arresting and intriguing displays of work – and in 'science with maths', which Mr Smallwood says is a 'big strength'. A third of students opt for these latter subjects at sixth form. Yet unlike some grammars which may have a science or arts bias, he feels there is great strength 'across the whole curriculum'. This is born out by the results, with a glut of top grades in a spectrum of subjects from maths to textiles. He points out that in 2018, the school came first in the Manchester Evening News Guide to Greater Manchester state secondary schools, toppling other prestigious local grammar schools from the top spot for the first time.

Mr Smallwood describes the students' progress scores (the 'value added' by the school to a student's ability) as 'outstanding' and suggests the secret, aside from having a baseline of very clever students, is 'very strong teachers' who tend to stick around 'because they like it here'. We suggest, tentatively, that sometimes longevity can lead to staleness but he tells us the school invests a lot in continuous training to avoid this, so that 'innovation and tradition co-exist happily'. Innovation, he later stresses, not fads. A parent later tells us pupils are sometimes invited on teaching training days to tell them how they might do their job better. Courageous stuff which is sure to keep teachers on their toes.

In true northern style, Mr Smallwood sums up his and the school ethos as this: 'we are not big on accolades, we just like doing what we do really well and we are constantly tweaking and improving what we do.' Parents enthuse about his accessibility, loving the fact that he stands by the gate as the children leave each evening and his down to earth attitude.

Academic matters: In 2018, Sale had its best GCSE results ever, with 62 per cent of the results being 9-7. Sciences, business studies, maths and history fared very well for the very top grades but so too did textiles, art, music and graphic products. So, there's that roundedness, which the school seeks, right there in the stats.

At A level, 68 per cent of all entries got A*-B; and 35 per cent A*-A. As Mr Smallwood succinctly puts it: 'on results days, there are very few tears'. Again, a range of subjects pulled in the A*/As with further maths, art and business studies faring well. English literature fared less well for those top grades which was not the case a couple of years ago, although each subject generally is prone to fluctuation in grades year on year.

Girls outperform boys marginally overall. Numbers are generally equal and there's no gender splits in subject choices.

A broad curriculum operates from year 7, although languages are limited to French and Spanish (no Latin or German). Pupils are helped with revision in 'learning to learn' sessions. Years 7-9 also benefit from splendid active learning weeks outdoors – learning in a more practical way, such as a rainforest roadshow with some rather nasty-looking spiders or a doing a Shakespeare workshop with an actor.

At GCSE options stage, all pupils must take one creative or technological subject. Mr Smallwood says this is 'to ensure balance'. He firmly believes it is beneficial in helping a child be rounded and adds that many of these subjects 'teach skills which are important to industry'. As AI nips at all our professional heels, this is a very good point, and subjects like electronic products will no doubt be very useful. Even so, this might not suit a child who is keen to take 9 or 10 traditionally academic subjects. However, one parent tells us that this option block now includes computer science, so a more academic dimension might have sneaked in through the back door.

There is a broad base of subjects on offer at for A level, including sociology, psychology, product design, two different history courses, government & politics.

The school has deployed IT to introduce greater transparency with parents via systems like 'show my homework'. Parents love it: no longer having to reply on patchy adolescent communication, they now know when their child has won an award or when there is a test looming.

The SEN department is very well staffed. Sale has about 50 students on the register, four with an EHC plan. Most areas catered for tend to be dyslexia and autism, although a couple of students are physically disabled. Teachers keep an eye out for students who may not have had a dyslexia diagnosis but start to display the subtle signs in later years when the work gets harder – and ensure they are tested. Bottom line, Mr Smallwood says, is 'if a student needs support, they get it'.

Games, options, the arts: Students are not pressured but they do put pressure on themselves, head says, so they are encouraged to 'think beyond' with extracurricular activities. One parent echoed this, saying 'here children are given a more rounded approach to life'. The house system, here halls not houses, has heaps of fun competitions from bake-offs to Halloween pumpkin competitions.

Sport is strong with the usual spectrum on offer (hockey, football, netball, rugby, cricket, tennis, athletics) but also basketball and handball. Loads of fixtures too. Girls' football is a strength and U15 girls recently won the national handball championships, while the year 8 and 10 boys' football teams are Trafford League Champions. One parent, when pressed by us, hinted (almost whispered) she might have liked more competitive fixtures for those not on the sports A teams.

There are all kinds of dance, including Bollywood. Music includes orchestras, swing bands, jazz (the Duke Ellington Project saw students working with a jazz quartet) and choirs. Much emphasis is placed on performance, with recitals and waterside summer concerts and competitions like Battle of the Bands. Rather touchingly, Mr Smallwood picks up his tuba and plays alongside students on many such occasions. Productions are very professional, usually with full orchestra, we are told. Recently Oklahoma, and rehearsals in play for Sister Act. Parents say it's also a great opportunity for pupils to get know other students from younger or older years. LAMDA is also on offer.

Loads of clubs from creative writing to astronomy and frequent creative annual school events, such as the visual arts extravaganza (students getting stuck into art and design with collages and printing techniques).

Trips range from the local Lowry theatre, Manchester art galleries to Westminster and standard language trips. Lots of mind-expanding opportunities too; a digital surgery with local MP, a trip to BBC studios to do news report, author visits, Science Crest Awards.

The sixth form personal enrichment programme sounded truly terrific with an array of options in sport, a fantastic current affairs programme; horticulture, community arts, ethics, bar mock trial. The works. Mr Smallwood sees competitions like the mock trial as a great conduit to building resilience and helping students understand that there can only be one winner, no matter how great your performance.

Background and atmosphere: Initially girls only, it became a mixed grammar after amalgamating with Sale Boys. In its current form it is under 30 years old and something of the new kid on the block, when set against Altrincham Girls and Boys, but its popularity as a mixed grammar and waiting list grow ever stronger and longer.

With its special status in visual arts, the overall vibe across the school is one of intelligent and vibrant creativity. Not a single corridor flags; everywhere we saw arresting subject-based displays which were, frankly, fascinating. And not just that, many posed enticing questions: 'Can social media have a positive impact on young people?'

Although the red-brick building is a mishmash of ages, from 1900s to the present day, it has a uniform feel of light, bright modernity with flashes of the school's colour purple dotted around. Facilities looked great – not flashy, just clean, modern and up to date from smart labs, to well-equipped music rooms and recording studios to an airy kitchen for food tech. A smart gym. The overall vibe is one of a well-equipped and very well maintained school. It's also a big site with a load of pitches, Astro and courts and a pond area with allotments.

The sixth form area is separate but all students have to file through it to go to the English department. Cunning. From year 7 upwards, they walk past studious-looking sixth formers, hunched over laptops. In another smart move, sixth formers don't have a common room (which is generally more of a loaf room) but a modern white open plan study area. If they want some downtime, they get a coffee in the refectory. Although even here they were all going over notes, checking things out on their laptops (and it wasn't images of amusing cats on Youtube either).

We swallowed back minor disappointment with the library, which had a fair selection of fiction but was chiefly filled with IT work stations. Times change, we get it. But even so, where were the books, glorious books?

Pastoral care, well-being and discipline: The parents we spoke to felt the co-ed aspect had been a significant factor in choosing Sale (many of the other local grammars in Trafford being single sex). There is a strong pastoral team and a 'confide' online network where students may share issues or suspected issues regarding other students confidentially (head says it is used respectfully).

Very aware that academically-driven students may sometimes be emotionally brittle when dealing with setbacks or confronting difficulties in subjects they might previously have found easy, head is keen to develop 'resilience in learning' and various programmes are bedding down in the school to achieve just that.

One parent said her children 'are happy to go and come home happy'. They do a 'phenomenal job of the overall care'. Another, whose daughter had experienced (sadly, fairly common in every school) excluding behaviour via social media from other girls, confessed to being 'blown away' by the school's speedy, supportive and transparent handling of the matter. This was echoed by another parent whose son had been on the receiving end of a spot of unpleasantness: 'it was fixed, sorted and handled professionally and really well.'

Mobile phones not allowed in school until sixth form and only then in certain areas where there is Wifi.

A lot of emphasis is placed on leadership with students taking on roles (which are advertised with job descriptions and for which they apply) as leaders in science or maths or perhaps helping with clubs or revision sessions lower down the school. 'They are given responsibility and expected to deliver on that,' one parent said.

There is a strong diversity group and Mr Smallwood thinks one positive thing to emerge from the ceaseless flow of 'sharing' on social media is that students, generally, tend to be accepting of differences, 'very inclusive'. The code of conduct is straightforward and punchy: 'sensible, responsible, respectful'. Three words, says Mr Smallwood, but 'it's the way we operate'.

Pupils and parents: Pupils seemed a vibrant bunch and if the displays are anything to go by, astute and interested in the world around them. Teachers, Mr Smallwood says, 'like taking them out on trips because they behave very well' – and that says a lot.

Reflecting the district of Trafford itself, parents are a hotchpotch of professions and different ethnic backgrounds. Many not overly affluent. PTA very supportive. Parents say comms are superb with great praise for the information evenings and the clarity around expectations. As one parent put it: 'the only fault is there aren't more Sale Grammars'.

Entrance: Entrance test is from the University of Durham (verbal, non-verbal and maths). Around 2,800 pupils sit the common exam for the Trafford grammar schools consortium. There are 180 places. Priority is given based on a tightly-defined postcode area and after that, on rank order based on test performance (many still get in on the latter who are out of postcode). Robust procedures in place so fake addresses won't cut it. A great many appeals each year. Expect a house price premium to be within the postcode.

Pupils come from around 50 schools, a blend of primaries and preps. There is no sibling policy.

Most stay on till sixth form but there are an extra 50 places available to pupils from other schools (entry requires Attainment 8 score of 60 or above, including grade 5 in English and maths. Minimum of grade 6 in desired A level subjects).

Exit: Currently, there is a trend for north west universities like Manchester, Keele, Liverpool, Leeds, Sheffield. Sciences, maths, engineering, economics tend to pop up a great deal as popular subjects, though pretty much everything is covered from psychology to architecture to politics. A couple every year go to drama or music school and handfuls go on to do medicine and law, along with the odd one for dentistry. It is usual for a few to go to Oxbridge, but not necessarily every year.

Remarks: A truly wonderful co-ed grammar which delivers academic excellence while nurturing creativity, resilience and a balanced approach to life.

Salisbury Cathedral School

The Old Bishop's Palace, 1 The Close, Salisbury, Wiltshire SP1 2EQ

Ages 3–13 **Pupils** 193 **Boarders** 24 full, 19 weekly/flexi (from 7 years) C of E

Fees: Day £8,700 – £15,690; Boarding + £7,365 – £8,250 pa

01722 555300
www.salisburycathedralschool.com

Head Master: Since 2013, Clive Marriott MA BEd. Single. Raised and schooled in Crediton (Haywards and Queen Elizabeth's), finished at Winchester (geography). Just the one string to his vocational bow from earliest consciousness: to be a primary teacher. After eight years in a state primary at Landscore, Crediton he was for 14 years deputy head at St Paul's Cathedral School where he made a name for himself for, especially, pastoral care. Work-life balance seesaws between total immersion in school during term times and full-on recreation in his holidays at his home in Devon. Loves walking and sailing, French culture and cuisine and urban design. Keen musician, interests span church music and musical theatre.

First impression: tremendously nice. With him, children come first, they're his primary avowed motivation. (Next in order of precedence, fyi, come 'parents, then faith, then teachers'.) Children first, that's the key, each and every one. When in their midst he either sinks to his knees or adopts a sort of walking crouch that brings him level – 'Hello Isobel, having fun? Bless you!' They are drawn to him. Bubbling with bonhomie, he scatters greetings and benedictions wherever he goes.

Subsequent impressions reinforce a sense of grip and capability. A parent warned us: 'He doesn't stand for any messing'; another said he's 'both soft and tough'. Consensus parent view: 'We all adore him ... simply the most wonderful headmaster'. Not the sort of head you ever have to hunt down if you've something on your mind; you'll find him out and proud every morning at drop-off time, an easy catch. Some parents have questioned whether this is a good use of his time. If the sort of head you like is one who puts himself about, prioritises people over paper, gives it to you straight and fixes stuff, Mr Marriott's your man.

Putting children first has equipped him with the resolution to do what he's needed to do. Of that, to understate it massively, there has been a lot. He's now well on his way to overhauling teaching by restructuring, raising professionalism and increasing accountability – there you are, he's good at paperwork and back-office stuff, too. There have been astute new key staff appointments and overdue departures. Oversight of pupils' well-being has been beefed up. Sports coaches have raised their game. Never a man to harden his heart, Mr Marriott's simple, implacable focus – and probably the saviour of his sanity – has been: children first. So academic attainment is very much on the up here, but never, never at the expense of general and individual happiness.

Entrance: Non-choristers – a term Mr Marriott greatly dislikes; he prefers scholars – come at any age. Academically non-selective. Informal test from year 3 on to ensure your child can keep up. Parents mostly local and include, says one, 'an awful lot of doctors'. Boarding numbers swelled by Forces children, an occasional Spanish or Swedish pupil and two or three South African exchange students. Gender balance: roughly 60 per cent boys. Scholarships discretionary, currently under review.

For those in pursuit of a cherished choristership, highly selective. Consider an informal pre-audition and get a steer on whether your child is in with a chance. Consider also the open taster day. White-knuckle voice trials for boys in years 2, 3 and 4 and girls in years 3 and 4. Places awarded 'regardless of financial circumstances'. A choristership is worth 30 per cent of day fees. Around a half of all choristers receive additional means-tested top-up bursaries. Boarding is not obligatory.

Exit: Most stay to 13 and go on to eg Sherborne, Wells, Canford, Clayesmore, Millfield, Lancing, Christ Hospital, Marlborough, Dauntseys, Warminster, Godolphin. Up to a third leave at 11 and go on to South Wilts or Bishop Wordsworth's grammars.

Much pride in scholarships won, most of which are for music. Other scholarships growing in number, academic still a bit thin on the ground and impacted by bright children leaving at 11, but decidedly on the up.

Remarks: Abounds in kerb appeal, tucked away as it is in the privacy of the close against the backdrop of the cathedral and chapter house. Masses of green space – 27 acres – for sport and play. When you learn that cricket teas here are renowned, you get the vibe (the scones really are excellent). Founded by an actual saint, St Osmund, in 1091 up the road in Old Sarum, origins traceable back to a druidical henge school established in the early Iron Age. We made that last bit up. The bishop's palace wasn't of course built with classrooms in mind, hence the (genuinely) Hogwartsian aura – origins 1220s, lovely creaky staircase, portraits of po-faced divines gazing down with worldly piety. Fit for purpose? Very much so in the eyes those of the right sensibility. We quoted to a parent the words of the (now ex-) dean: 'many of the rooms within the Bishop's Palace are unsuitable for modern teaching methods'. The testy response was 'They're children, for heaven's sake!' Quite so. They're fine. However, the dean was unquestionably less wide of the mark in observing: 'the external classrooms are in temporary or dated buildings ... the need for the school to have modern facilities ... is as true today as it was in 2008 – perhaps more so'. She's right. Shabby chic is good, shabby ad-hoc ain't.

Here's how it all works. The school's short name is SCS. There are 190-odd pupils. Of these just 16 boys and 16 girls are choristers. Their fees are subsidised by an endowment fund established as recently as 1314. When they're at the palace the choristers are schoolchildren just like anyone else, no difference. The school does not swirl around the choristers, the choristers are part of the swirl. When called upon to sing, gowned and ruffed, they form up two by two and enter under the auspices of the cathedral. School, cathedral: two separate but conjoined entities. Mr Marriott links them by attending evensong in the cathedral pretty much every day – his PA says 'it's his Zen'. Non-CofE parents should note that other denominations and religions are indulged (but not accommodated) because the charitable object of the school is to 'promote and provide for.. the advancement of religion in accordance with the practices of the Church of England'. The girls' choir was established 900 years after the school's foundation to quite a bit of bah-ing, now abated.

Academically improving under the head's push for professionalisation. Enhanced progress tracking in development overseen by deputy head. We saw some really good teaching. Regard for what Mr Marriott is trying to accomplish is a motivator; one teacher said: 'He trusts us and we trust him'. We happened upon some superbly marked English essays, full of advice and encouragement together with a full audit of grammatical errors. DT not all that well endowed with T, but ('They're children, for heaven's sake!') we admired a freshly made array of really excellent wooden automata whose construction called for sophisticated 3D conceptualisation plus craft skills requiring a hands-on understanding of the properties of wood. Art is well taught but in too small a space, with the curious result that all the finished work is small, too. Recent investment in IT well spent. No scholarship class, but extra challenge from teachers who know you inside out. Humane touch: no institutional bells at the end of lessons. Learning support brilliant, marvellously led. Includes gifted and talented. Focus very much on the whole child, not just the administration of remedial tweaks – big crossover with pastoral care. Around one child in five in receipt of support and 10 per cent of pupils at any time are being monitored closely with an eye to intervention. Some dyslexia, some ADHD, some Asperger's, some mental health issues.

Never had much of a name for sport, SCS. At a schools' jazz festival, which SCS creamed, a parent was told: 'Well of course, the Cathedral School is a music school'. But things are changing. At a hockey tournament, where her daughter's team ran out winners, the same parent was informed: 'Well of course, the Cathedral School is a hockey school'. This is new and testifies to improved standards of coaching. Good artificial pitches. Girls and boys play cricket on equal terms up to 1st XI. On match days, so many teams do they field, it's all hands to the pump. That's the spirit. Well chosen selection of after-school activities including, how civilised, calligraphy.

Around 95 per cent learn an instrument. No pressure to be a musical genius, there's just a very wide ability span. Full range of ensembles and every genre of music. Jazz band just one much admired public face of the school's music. Informal concerts, where your friends drop in to support you, very much part of the mutually affirmative ethos here. One parent told us her son 'struggles to find a quiet place to practice'. Performance happens in what was the bishops' 18th C drawing room. It's splendid, it's roomy but it's not, we wistfully think, a patch on a purpose-built auditorium. Parents agree: 'it would be good to have a dedicated hall'. Annual festival features ensembles involving pupils, staff, parents and grandparents. Drama ambitious, sometimes way outside the children's cultural experience, teacher passionate. All good, but would benefit from a dedicated performance space. Yup, that auditorium would be just the job.

Pastoral care simply superb. There are systems and frameworks but let's cut to the chase: people here – children, teachers, support staff – really care about, and look out for, each other. Over and above formal structures, children tend to identify their preferred adult; for one or two that's the head's PA. Choristers especially closely monitored for upcoming crunch points. They learn to be, ahem, 'very organised'. When they cross over to the cathedral they are accompanied and watched over by – new appointment – the chorister tutor. No wonder parents tell us that years 7 and 8 here promote 'huge levels of growth' and personal development. Around 30 board in their own house in the close. Lovely houseparents, walled garden, homely. Best place to take the social temperature of the school is the undercroft at lunchtime. See how they chatter. The food's great, too, all cooked fresh including sauces, meat from a local butcher. The catering manager – he loves his job – and his staff keep an eye on eating patterns and report concerns.

School inspectors haven't the instruments to measure anything as soft as a school's loveability factor but we can because we trust our intuition. On our scale, SCS scores a max 10. There's a naturalness about the children here that gives the school a timeless feel. This is not a workplace school, it's a fellowship school, a little band of friends. It's an admirable school, too, and it's on a roll.

Sandbach High School and Sixth Form College

Middlewich Road, Sandbach, Cheshire CW11 3NT

Ages 11–18 **Pupils** 1,463 **Sixth form** 284 (21 boys)

01270 765031
www.sandbachhigh.co.uk

Headmaster: Since 1993, John Leigh, BA economics (Nottingham Trent) Adv Dip MA. At the school since 1990. He has been the driving force behind its dizzying ascendancy to becoming one of the best state schools in the country with results well above the national average. In particular, Ofsted selected it a few years ago as a good practice example of a school encouraging girls into STEM-related careers.

Intellectual humility is arguably the rocket fuel for this trajectory: 'Be prepared to learn from mistakes and continually reinvent,' head says, referring in passing to his additional role as a school inspector where he sees the best and worst other schools have to offer. This evolutionary approach seems to lie at the school's core, summed up by its impressive electric car

S

club where pupils are forever refining car prototypes. This refinement process, he thinks, is a wonderful metaphor for life and learning.

No wonder, then, that the school recently won the accolade of Young Engineers' School of the Year in the Big Bang Competition and one of its pupils secured an unprecedented work placement with Formula 1. However, it is not just about STEM activities: its overriding aim is to give girls a chance to experience as wide a variety of learning opportunities as possible, nurture existing passions and develop new ones. So if their natural curiosity tends towards science, then great. (Frankly, if you want to become an engineer, doctor or rocket scientist, there is no whiff of bluestocking here. It's commonplace.) Likewise, if you tend towards the arts or love languages, that is viewed as equally great. What this school seeks to give its girls, head emphasises, is a limitless platform to experiment academically, free from artificial gender restraints or social pigeonholes.

John Leigh exudes warmth, accessibility and calm – when parents speak of him words like decency, integrity, inspirational keep cropping up. There is also an impressive transparency about the way he conducts himself; he made a point of not telling staff nor the pupils in advance about our visit. He wanted us to see how it really was.

And how it is, is this: each year has been incrementally better than the one before and opportunities for pupils bubble over everywhere you look. For him, this labour of love has been a family affair; his wife (now sadly passed away) used to teach at the school and his two grown-up daughters are both alumni. Keeping this school at this level must be a gargantuan all-absorbing effort by him and his staff but they have created something really quite special.

Academic matters: Work to generate interest in STEM begins in year 7. Innovative examples include year 9s making models of microbes; one pupil made a cake model of chicken pox pathogen (Mary Berry eat your heart out). In the same year group, students were participating in the Engineers' EEP Robotics Challenge. During our visit, a glance in the product design workshop showed lamps worthy of Ikea and complicated revolving multi-photo stands. Likewise, during a recent celebration of British Science Week, entries to a product design competition included research into improved methods of eradicating bedbugs, along with drone robots to help the police (no Blue Peter style sticky backed plastic, then). To give you a taster: a typical engineering-type project might involve redesigning a Smartie tube; how to get a certain weight into the right size of container, minimizing the material used? Go figure.

However, STEM is only the start of it. As broad a curriculum as possible operates; at GCSE, along with the sciences, core subjects and languages (French, Spanish, German), there are more diverse subjects on offer like travel and tourism, Arabic, dance, statistics, catering, politics. One parent was thrilled her daughter, who loved science and engineering, had also developed a love for the arts. Her daughter's eyes had been opened to all doorways onto the world, she said.

Head is keen on innovation in classrooms, for pupils to work in groups and explore. Lots of after-school support is also on offer for those who want to challenge themselves further or consolidate. Feedback at parent's evenings is very detailed, not just pupil academic strengths but also individual personality traits. One parent said that while her daughter had a very obvious outer confidence, her teachers sought to nurture her self-belief, which flagged. An astute observation, she felt.

Another parent said her daughter had been chosen to be creative director of her dance team not because she was the greatest dancer but because the school identified her innate leadership skills. This resulted in some very mature conversations between them about what leadership required, such as addressing conflict.

So, to the nitty gritty: at GCSE 2018, 31 per cent of entries achieved A*-A/9-7 (with 82 per cent getting 9-4 in both English and maths). Nearly everyone takes one language at GCSE, under 10 per cent take two.

At A level in 2018, nearly 52 per cent A*-B and 25 per cent A*/A grades. The numbers taking languages are small but increasing: head feels they are battling the perception that language A levels are made harder by native speakers entering.

SEN pupils are well supported with an additional needs team that offers a wide range of interventions (in lessons and outside, such as the morning challenge club). Currently 44 students on the SEN register plus six students in receipt of EHCPs. One parent whose daughter has global leaning difficulties (along with some health issues) spoke rather movingly about a 'life-changing' educational programme that had been put in place for her daughter and another pupil, with a view to them emerging more independent and able to care for themselves better. They also took part in some mainstream lessons, albeit with different work, to foster social inclusion.

Games, options, the arts: The Complete and Utter Chaos Club (CAUC, or Electric Car Club, as it is known) is fantastic: girls get to design, build and race electric cars in the F1 in Schools Technology Challenge competition. The current prototype, Dylan (all are named after characters in the Magic Roundabout), has been particularly successful. The team is, in fact, international champion in the Green Power F24 Championships.

There is also a STEM club. In the Team Tech competition for product designs, pupils were required to generate an idea which makes life easier. The school had two finalists; one pupil won her category by creating a Bluetooth speaker.

The student body – unlike a lot of student rep bodies – has teeth. Pupils proudly told us that the canteen has been less crowded since they had implemented styrofoam boxes for takeaway: 'We can't take problems to teachers, we have to take solutions and also present the positives and think through the consequences of what we ask for', they said. (Manna to multi-national companies looking for resourceful recruits.)

The school has been a specialist sports college for a decade; it has a huge gym, synthetic track and swimming pool. Options abound: trampolining, hockey, netball, volleyball, badminton. The cupboard was full of south Cheshire champion trophies. The school also boasts many national and international student athletes in gymnastics, karate, taekwando, even bowling. The football, cricket and rugby teams benefit from a vibrant intra-school sports programme where forms play each other. As pupils told us, your form members are also your team mates. Mixed gender posters of inspirational sports figures are scattered about, women like Laura Trott and Katherine Grainger.

Drama runs the gamut from Shakespeare to Grease. Each year a very professional production is put on, recently Hairspray. There is a regular programme of performances, often linked to GCSEs, of drama and dance, as well as clubs like musical theatre. There are various showcasing performances put on all over too, such as the Crewe Lyceum.

Music is fairly popular with 150 students taking instrumental lessons. There are jazz bands, brass bands, choirs, soul bands. The school's concert band and chamber choir both made it through to the final of the Cheshire East Music Competition, the choir scooping up first in its category for the second year running.

Art A level tends to garner lots of A*/As. The art department was a dazzling blend of WIPs. One of the very eloquent pupils we spoke to was studying photography, taking derelict buildings as her point of inspiration.

There are also many other clubs, from beginners and advanced Latin, to creative writing, to What the Papers Say. Sixth form has started its own publication, for students by students – The Scoop.

School trips are plentiful. Skiing, yes, but also Poland, Pompeii, Johnson Space Centre Houston. A Tudor trail in London, mining museum, castles, Edinburgh Mary Queen of Scots trips, Brontë land.

Further on, girls might also choose to attend the 'So you want to be a doctor' day at Keele where they hear short lectures and mix with students. They also work with businesses.

Background and atmosphere: There is a scathing saying in the north: 'all fur coat and no underwear' – fancy façade and no substance. This school, though, is all substance. Sure, it has very good facilities for sport and academia, with eight science labs, DT suites and a new sixth form building which smells of freshly minted carpet with IT facilities, music studios etc. But we don't think you would choose this school for these. Nor indeed for its well-worn 60s style build (the brickwork is ordinary and, if one were being picky, one might say the building lacked charm). You would choose it because of what happens within it, for the electric pulse of intellectual curiosity which runs through the corridors and brings those faded carpet tiles to life. And in case you are in any doubt of this, posters and displays along all corridors, evidencing the multiplicity of projects and clubs, remind you of what this school is all about.

Pastoral care, well-being and discipline: There is a nurse and a counsellor; their photos are everywhere, including the loos. The head has created an open environment where dialogue about mental health issues is no big deal. So there is no stigma about having counselling. Only when problems are hidden away, head says, do pupils feel they can't ask for help. The school magazine carried a feature on self-harm, another on Mindful Mondays, highlighting the importance of concentrating on the moment.

The head feels the quality of the relationships between staff and pupils means teachers identify troubling issues at an early stage. Parents agreed; one said there were pre-emptive conversations about hormones and friendship groups. The culture also means pupils are open in sharing concerns about friends – perhaps a failure to eat – in a compassionate way. Bullying, of course, exists. Some 80 per cent of fall outs, head estimates, often have social media as a trigger. Some of the fall outs may tip over into subtle forms of bullying. When this happens, girls can go to a 'safe space', a room where there are people to talk to so they will never feel alone. In the first instance, they may talk to a bully mentor, a pupil who has been trained by the school (any pupil mentor has to go on the school's training programme). The contents of the chat will be passed on to a designated teacher (part of the overall formal pastoral structure) who will monitor the situation.

A recent glowing Ofsted report attests the school is extremely successful in promoting students' self-esteem, confidence and raised aspirations. This would undoubtedly seem to be the case and, as ever, courses are run around internet safety for pupils and, crucially, for parents, who are often less savvy than their children.

At sixth form the PPD programme has recently been re-branded Life Choices. This, commendably, involves a 45 minute session each week on diverse topics, including an alternative learning week on practical topics like car maintenance.

Pupils and parents: Like Dickens' Pip, the parents here have, quite rightly, Great Expectations. Although the school is non-selective with a broad demographic, their ambitions for their children are well honed. Communication channels between school and parents perhaps caters for this, with newsletters, termly mags, headmaster surgeries, open door policies. Parents can also track pupils' progress via Gateway 3 to check grades, attendance etc.

The parents' and friends' association provides evenings on maths and science to help parents help their children. One parent did say she felt more frequent use of social media in highlighting the achievements of the school as a whole – eg victories in sports matches – would foster a greater sense of connection.

As for the pupils, well the ones we met seemed very much aware of their good fortune, saying it was only when they met pupils from other schools that they realised that they were attending somewhere really quite unique. Behaviour was excellent but not overly formal. The exception to this informality is school uniform which head says evidences respect for community, and uniformity also being a way (a pupil told us) of eliminating an avenue for potential bullying. The girls we met were confident and articulate.

Entrance: Priority, after looked after children and those with medical/social needs, to girls living in the catchment area. Siblings come next, then children of staff, then those at a partner primary school.

Has recently been admitting more than the set 210 pupils into year 7. Head insists on parents and potential pupils visiting the school, suggesting that if a parent sees that spark of anticipation in their child's eyes to attend his school, then they should have a place. The number of classes has therefore increased so there are 10 teaching groups in the year, with an average group size of 27 students. The pupils we spoke to grumbled about the corridors and canteen being jammed. It is definitely a victim of its own success.

Entrance to sixth form requires at least four GCSEs at grade 4. Boys may apply; some five per cent of sixth formers are boys. Head says boys apply because of the genuine diversity of subjects on offer (for example, classical civilization, triple maths) and perhaps also the culture of staff accessibility which shines out on open days.

Exit: About 70 per cent stay on for the sixth form and around 70 per cent of these go on to high education, a third or so to Russell group universities across the UK: Durham, Leeds, Manchester, Cardiff, Nottingham. Two to Oxbridge in 2018. They opt for a broad spectrum of subjects: mathematics, English, history, law, Spanish, architecture, accountancy, as well as other more creative areas like fashion design and journalism. Some 10 per cent straight to employment and 5-10 per cent to apprenticeships.

Remarks: This marvellous, forward-looking and caring school is an empowering place for girls to be taught which delivers great academic results and opens up all life avenues to them. And since the one thing Steve Jobs, Larry Page and Bill Gates have in common is a Y chromosome, it's via schools like this, leading the way on STEM, that the tide will be reversed. The X factor – which this school has in every sense – is dominant.

Sandroyd School

Rushmore, Tollard Royal, Salisbury, Wiltshire SP5 5QD

Ages 2–13 **Pupils** 180 **Boarders** 110 full, 30 weekly/flexi (from 7 years)
C of E

Fees: Day £8,760 – £21,000; Boarding £20,100 – £25,410 pa

01725 516264
www.sandroyd.org

Headmaster: Since 2016, Alastair Speers BSc MEd PGCE (40s). Educated at Elstree and Sherborne. Read building engineering

S

at Loughborough and UWE, followed by seven years as a consultant engineer (during which he worked in London, Boston, Mexico and Athens). Inspired by his role as a mentor to new graduate engineers, he started to think about a career in education and decided to do a PGCE at Cambridge. His first job was as a design technology teacher at Oakham – he stayed for 10 years, becoming a housemaster, then senior housemaster and completing an MEd in educational leadership at the University of Buckingham.

He grew up in Dorset so when the headship at Sandroyd came up he jumped at the chance to return, drawn by 'the beautiful setting, wonderful facilities and fantastic staff'. He sees preparing pupils for their senior schools as a key part of his role and his experience as a housemaster at Oakham gives him a unique perspective. 'We want them to make their mistakes here so when they get to the next stage they hit the ground running,' he says. Keen for children to reach their potential academically while developing traits like resilience and organisational skills along the way, so they're well equipped to deal with life's challenges. 'I feel very strongly that being successful and happy in your life is not directly related with academic success,' he says. 'It's to do with your social and emotional resilience and how you deal with being dropped from a sports team or having a difficult day.'

Positive, energetic and approachable, he still teaches maths and design technology and knows all the prep children by name. 'I look forward to the teaching more than anything,' he says. 'This age group has such energy and enthusiasm.' If pupils have a particular hobby or enthusiasm they're encouraged to pursue it – one boy was an avid coin collector and produced a regular magazine about his coins. 'That's what Sandroyd is about,' says the head. 'Our pupils are the ones who say: "I'll give it a go." Our two mantras are "challenge yourself and try different things" and "respect everything that everyone does".' Parents like his dynamic approach, particularly his unstuffiness and ability to blend the school's traditional values with new ideas, such as a dance studio and cricket for all (not just the boys). 'Sandroyd is a traditional prep school with traditional core values but it's very forward-looking too,' one parent told us.

Lives in a house on the school site with his wife Alice, whose two brothers were pupils at Sandroyd. She teaches English here and is very involved in school life. They have two young daughters, both pupils at The Walled Garden, Sandroyd's pre-prep. Outside term time the head's interests include cricket, sailing and 'renovating a cottage in Ireland'.

The head of The Walled Garden is Kate Blomfield BA QTS (30s). She joined as a teacher 12 years ago, was a houseparent at the prep for five years and has been head of The Walled Garden for four years. She still does some boarding duties at the prep.

Entrance: The Walled Garden takes children from the age of 2 and most progress to the prep. Many children join the main school in year 3 from local primaries or pre-preps, while others relocate from London with their families. Waiting lists in some years but it's always worth checking. Families looking to join Sandroyd are invited to an activity morning or taster session and also take part in an assessment (creative writing, verbal reasoning and maths for prospective prep pupils). The school 'isn't hugely selective,' says the head. 'It's just to make sure they will be able to access the curriculum here.'

Exit: Virtually all stay till 13, when the vast majority head to boarding schools. The head is ultra-knowledgeable about senior schools – he and his wife did 12,000 miles in the car before they started at Sandroyd, visiting as many senior schools as possible. Most popular current choices are Sherborne followed by Marlborough, Bryanston and Radley. Most of the girls go to co-ed schools but a few head to St Mary's Shaftesbury, St Mary's Calne, Sherborne Girls and Downe House.

Remarks: Delightfully rural, the school is off the beaten track – situated up a long, winding drive, surrounded by playing fields, woods and parkland. The entire school (except the pre-prep) is based in the original house, although there have been significant additions and alterations over the years. Beautiful entrance hall, with open fireplace, cosy sofas and impressive wood panelling. The head's study is vast, with stunning views of open countryside.

The school was founded in 1888 by the Rev Wellesley Wesley as a 'small coaching establishment' for aspiring Etonians and quickly flourished. It moved first to Surrey and then in 1939 to Rushmore House (the Pitt-Rivers' family home) on the Wiltshire/Dorset borders (film director Guy Ritchie owns a country estate nearby). School purchased the house and 60 acres within the 500-acre Rushmore estate in 1966. It went co-ed in 2005 and there are equal numbers of boys and girls in most year groups.

Average class size is 12 (no bigger than 16) and staff know the children well. Parents particularly like the fact that pupils achieve great things on the academic front while 'being allowed to be children'. 'They've got the balance absolutely right,' a mother told us. 'It's a happy, family-run place where my children have really flourished.' Languages are taught from nursery and most do Latin from year 5. We saw a sparky year 7 French class, with children learning vocab by role playing characters in a French café. They fizzed with excitement about the impending annual year 7 trip to Burgundy, where they are totally immersed in the language. General science up to year 5 and then chemistry, physics and biology taught separately from year 6. Science labs are smart and modern and the philosophy is to get children interested by making science fun (activities include a science club, where children make their own slime and watch teachers exploding film canisters). We liked the sign on one of the lab doors – 'Before you come in you need a pen, pencil and ruler, lots of enthusiasm and a big smiley face.' Around a fifth of children have learning support (school caters for pupils with dyslexia, mild dyspraxia, slow processing speeds and visual issues). One-to-one learning support available, plus in small groups too.

Sport is a big deal here. Children play sport virtually every day and everyone gets the chance to represent the school at some point – riding, girls' hockey and boys' rugby are particularly strong. When we visited, the U12 girls' hockey team had just come third in a national tournament. Swish sports hall, opened by Olympic gold medallist yachtsman Sir Ben Ainslie in 2015, has an indoor swimming pool, gym, squash courts and badminton courts.

All children have class music once a week and 90 per cent have instrumental lessons (they get a term's free tuition at any point between year 2 and year 8 to help them decide what to play). There's a host of groups, ensembles, choirs and clubs to join. Drama and dance take place in the impressive Sandroyd Theatre, opened by Zoe Wanamaker in 2008 – recent shows include Macbeth and Joseph and the Amazing Technicolour Dreamcoat. Dance is increasingly popular with girls and boys, whether it's street dance, ballet or jive. Director of the performing arts is keen to give as many children as possible the chance to appear on stage – 'we try and make sure there is something for everybody,' she says. Art is housed in a converted cart shed and all age groups have at least 50 minutes of art a week. Design technology is impressive too – we watched year 6 children designing and making their own ping pong bats, to be used later, of course. Around 50 extracurricular activities on offer – everything from martial arts to film appreciation to bridge.

Pupils make the most of the grounds, whether they're playing sport, climbing trees (yes, they're allowed to here) or riding (the school has its own riding department, complete with an outdoor ménage, show-jumping paddock and cross-country course, and children are allowed to bring their own ponies).

The children appreciate the school's beautiful setting. A year 4 pupil we met enthused about the red kites he could see from his classroom window. Pupils aren't allowed to have mobile phones or tablets in school (a popular move with parents) and teachers highlight the importance of good manners, holding doors open and saying sorry if you're in the wrong.

Children are encouraged to read as much as possible. They have 40 minutes of reading during the day and boarders read for at least 20 minutes in the evening. School is very proud of Strive, a new programme that promotes 'intellectual curiosity and a love of wisdom' (the name comes from the school motto, Niti est Nitere, meaning 'to strive is to shine'). Year 3 pupils and up have four 40-minute Strive sessions a week, with tasks designed to build their self-confidence, questioning skills, teamwork and resilience.

School food is wholesome and nourishing. Everything is cooked in-house and pupils and staff eat together on long, convivial tables. We sat with a charming group of year 7s – one boy told us he'd recently had a practice interview with the headmaster in German. 'In German?' we queried. 'How impressive.' The boy dissolved into giggles. 'No, for Sherborne,' he clarified.

Boarding is an integral part of the school. Children are expected to board in years 7 and 8 – it's not compulsory but virtually all do. At least 50 boarders stay in school every weekend and day pupils opt in when there's something exciting going on (such as laser tag or bouldering). Instead of staring at screens in the evenings the boarders play board games and table tennis, build creations out of Lego and Hama beads and take part in quiz nights. Junior boarding house for boys in years 3 to 5 and girls in years 3 to 6, middle boys' house for year 6 and 7 boys and senior house for girls in years 7 and 8 and boys in year 8. Girls and boys housed in separate wings. Around 50 per cent of the staff live on the school site, many with young families.

Dorms mostly of four, with bunk beds and lots of posters and family photographs. Health centre is staffed 24/7. Homely touches in the junior boarding house include a tree for pupils to hang 'happy thoughts' on, hot chocolate evenings and the chance to win dorm stars for the best decorated dorm (the winners get a dinner party hosted by houseparents at the end of term). Pupils can either Skype or phone home from landlines in each boarding wing. Letter writing is encouraged too. Communication with parents is excellent. We particularly liked the weekly Sandroyd Times, a lively amalgam of news, views and even the local weather forecast. A recent edition explained why the grass on Sandroyd's sports pitches is cut to 75mm (as opposed to Twickenham's 35mm).

Seventy per cent of boarders live within an hour's drive (some as close as Sixpenny Handley, four miles up the road), others come from Devon, Cornwall and London. Ten children from overseas, including Russia, China and a Spanish contingent who spend a year at the school. Day pupils tend to live within a 30-minute drive – the school runs minibuses to Sherborne, Warminster, Blandford and Salisbury. Distinguished former pupils include Sir Terence Rattigan, Randolph Churchill, Sir Ranulph Fiennes, Lords Carrington, Gladwyn and Wilberforce, Lord Ramsey (the former Archbishop of Canterbury), Ian Gow and ex-soldier and novelist Harry Parker.

Nursery and pre-prep children are based in The Walled Garden – the building is thus named because it's built on the site of an old walled garden and retains one of the original walls. Children are taught in small classes, often by specialist teachers, with a strong focus on numeracy and literacy. The pre-prep is very much 'part of the Sandroyd family' – children walk up to the main dining room for lunch, often sitting with older siblings, and use the main school's facilities, including the swimming pool, library, games pitches, theatre, gym and IT room. Children get a taste of French, German and Spanish from a young age and make the most of the school's stunning location, from team building and survival skills to literacy and numeracy in the great outdoors. Parents pop in for a host of events – nativity plays, class assemblies and social activities. 'We welcome parents who come and chat to staff in the mornings,' says the head of The Walled Garden, who as well as leading the pre-prep spends half her time teaching all year groups. Some pre-prep children travel in on the school minibuses, others live very locally.

Sandroyd is a small and nurturing school that offers a well-balanced education in an exceptional location. The pupils we met bubbled with happiness and enthusiasm for the school, while achieving impressive academic results and having fun (and lots of fresh air) along the way.

S

Sands School

48 East Street, Ashburton, Newton Abbot, Devon TQ13 7AX

Ages 11–17 **Pupils** 60

Fees: £10,395 pa

01364 653666
www.sands-school.co.uk

Head: No-one. Everybody. Sands is a democratic school, a co-op, so there's no hierarchy. All decisions are taken collectively by teachers and students at the weekly, student-chaired school meeting, one person, one vote. This applies both to day-to-day decision making and strategic planning, which you'd expect to be the job of governors but at Sands the governors don't govern in the usual sense, they don't even get to vote. Nor do parents, by the way.

So Sands has a rationale. But it is not in thrall to a Big Idea. There's no guru calling the shots here – no Neill, no Steiner, no Hahn, though they do own up to a dash of Tagore. The point is, Sands is not the keeper of anyone's flame and this frees it up to respond to the here and now and reinvent itself as it sees fit. It makes it up as it goes along? Yes, that's exactly what it does, it's in a state of continuous evolution under the influence of the democratic process. And if that makes Sands sound like some sort of counter-cultural cloud cuckoo land blithely defying societal norms, inspired by a school motto of 'If it feels good, do it', sorry, it's all much more down to earth than that. When you visit, Sands feels at first little like a school what with students sprawled on the grass chatting when surely they should be in class, dammit. Go deeper and you discover both the strong seriousness that drives the school and a reassuring mundanity in, for example, the way it pairs rights with responsibilities: 'Everyone in the school has the right to eat school lunches, but if you choose to do so, you then have the responsibility to do your fair share of washing up.' This essential pragmatism is testament to the school's trust in the common sense and goodwill of its teachers and students and expresses itself in the down-to-earth simplicity of its core value: 'We believe that everyone should be treated equally, be happy, and have access to a good education.'

Mark Twain said: 'If voting made any difference they wouldn't let us do it', a sentiment with which students in some democratic schools would agree. The perils of kidology are obvious here. Teachers, by virtue of an accumulation of life experience and the accretion of wisdom, could use the force-field this creates to dominate debate in school meetings – even to spin off into something cultish. They acknowledge the perils of dominant personality syndrome: 'We carry great authority as the owners of the knowledge and skills that children want to access. With the best will in the world, this does create huge inequalities between the possessors of learning, the teachers, and the consumers, the students.' They guard against undue influence, in our observation, by exercising respectful self-restraint. The best decisions, they say, are made when everyone decides together – an empirical appraisal. In the school meeting we attended you could see the adults swap glances at one point as a motion approached a vote. They seemed to be sharing something like, 'We'll possibly need to come back to this and debate it some more – that's okay.' Because of this, students engage full-bloodedly and amazingly articulately in debate, justly confident that their voices count equally. They do. And they do get to decide everything – from humdrum practicalities and discipline issues to admissions and staff appointments. One parent told us, laughing, 'all this democracy isn't always welcome at home – they're forever questioning things'.

When, say, Ofsted comes calling, Sands' public-facing spokesperson is Sean Bellamy, one of the school's founders. He rejoices in the title of administrator. He didn't put himself forward when we visited, a student took charge of us; we only got to speak to him by hunting him down at lunch.

In addition to the customary legal duties of charity trustees, the responsibility of the governors is to defend the school against corruption of its foundational values – eg, by dominant personalities or entryism. Both they and parents can lobby the school meeting and have their views debated, but the autonomy of the student-teacher body is everything, hence the school's arm's-length position on parental interference. Budget setting remains with the governors.

Academic matters: Some seriously bright and thinkerly teachers here inspire a reverence for learning, no question. Sands teaches up to GCSE, 'flawed' as it is. Students sit exams when they're ready; the school is more interested in promoting self-discovery and personal development as essential factors in awakening innate talent and promoting self-directed learning. No teaching to the test, no fact-cramming, no coercion, no competition. Osbert Sitwell once said, 'My education takes place during the holidays from Eton'. Chances are he could have fitted it into term times at Sands. There's hardheadedness to this approach. Sands believes that the emphasis in mainstream schools on factual recall and the application of ordered methodologies prepares children for the very jobs that computers will soon do better. The future, they reckon, lies with soft skills: creativity, collaboration, communication and lateral thinking.

Classes – average 12 – comprise a mix of ages. The school acknowledges that 'kids increasingly feel like they have to do exams more than they ever did'. Some students go for it big time, bag all the GCSEs they can and go on to soar; others go for no more than they need for whatever's next, regarding GCSEs as negotiable currency – necessary 'bits of paper' – 'You do what you need do'. One arty student had settled for just four, three for art school and one for fun, and felt 'in no need whatever of any more' – her time was better spent painting. She's not typical. No one's typical. Unsurprisingly, the school isn't remotely interested in looking good in league tables and the record shows that it doesn't. Don't read that as blasé; they take aspiration seriously (in 2018, 24 per cent of GCSE grades were A*-A/9-7, and four of the nine students got 5+ 9-4 grades including maths and English). Ofsted, never knowingly effusive, said in 2013: 'Pupils' achievements are good, as a result of good teaching, an effective curriculum and the excellent learning environment.' Market forces determine what makes a good teacher: students empty-classroom those they reckon aren't up to it. All staff – 50:50 male and female – are appraised by students, who are also integral to the selection process. All are qualified, most have worked at mainstream schools. No shortage of recruits: the recently advertised post of art teacher lured more than 100 applicants.

Going off-topic in classes in pursuit of fruitful and fascinating digressions is normal. One student said, 'I still remember the arguments I had with Nathan, my maths teacher, about philosophy and climbing'. If you want to pursue an interest in astrophysics or circus skills, they'll fix it for you. If it snows, they drop everything and go up to the moors. If you're in the middle of a great painting, you can go at it three days straight. The last week of the summer term is devoted to camping beside the sea.

If a mainstream school is a place of decrees and proclamations, Sands is a school of delicate balances, sensitive negotiations and unrelenting tensions. Sure, you don't have to go to lessons if you don't want to... 'but we only offer places to students who want to learn'. If you opt to attend, make sure you get to class on time or you'll face a sanction. You don't have to do subjects you dislike... 'but we'd like you to give them a second chance'. There's a criticism made of schools like Sands that freedom to bunk off when you feel like it can be lethargy inducing, and they work hard to demonstrate the link between hard work and joy in achievement. Most students do go through a phase (or two) of skiving and larking in a spirit of, say, Hey, party! or adolescent angst. One mother described her initial feelings of 'Oh my God, what have I done?' but had learnt that all's well that ends well. You won't be surprised to learn that this is no place to stand and watch students, like heroes of Soviet labour, march in shining-eyed cohorts past developmental milestones bang on time. They breeze on by when they're good and ready.

Special needs are addressed by all teachers and three specialists. Everyone chooses their academic tutor, with whom they devise their timetable. Tutors liaise with parents and also have a pastoral role, acting as advocate of last resort for any tutee in especially hot water. There is no staff room at Sands, no uniform, no us, no them and no bells, obviously. Imagine.

Games, options, the arts: You've sussed there's not a lot of snarling, tribal rugby going on here, what with the lack of numbers and the absence of playing fields, not to mention a general disinclination. Not that they're against competitive team sports. Students who want to play at a decent level join local clubs. The school promotes, on a broad front, in line with demand, anything that's hilarious and physically active, including tree climbing, swimming in the river, hockey, football, weight training, kung fu, skateboarding, surfing and cycling. Music making tends to be similarly ad hoc but of a higher order of accomplishment – instrumental specialists brought in according to need. Concerts happen as and when. The performing arts BTec serves as a focus for musicians as also for dance, drama and art students. The tenor of Sands is markedly arty – 'we're known for our art'. And crafty. Woodwork thrives under the auspices of the well-loved Peach. The art room is heaven on earth.

Background and atmosphere: Arose from the ashes of Dartington Hall in 1987, but not as a reinvention. The radical difference is that Sands was co-designed by students and teachers, it's not the offspring of a single seer, and it's fuelled by dreams and intuitions, not certainties, in a spirit of 'We'll know what we think when we see what we do'. Call it creatively muddling through if you like – creativity implies ferment. The school's name derives from the salutation used by David Gribble, a founder, in letters to the other two founders, Sean Bellamy and Sybilla Higgs – 'Dear S and S'. Geddit? The school has evolved under continuous and, it has to be said, unsparing self-examination – what you see is where we are. It reckons it's in better shape now than ever, but it's still light years away from complacency – 'Oh no, we're not perfect'. Admin is, though. Bursar Peta runs a tight ship.

The school occupies an early Victorian townhouse with a nice garden in the middle of Ashburton. Expect no hush (so fashionable just now) for hush there is none, not ever, there being masses going on in all directions. This an infectiously friendly, happy place where everyone meets your eye – they are the only young persons we have ever met who don't talk up to you or down to you but treat you exactly as if you were one of them. Scuffed but comfy – the building, that is. Lived in. Fit for purpose. Zero prestige facilities but everything perfectly serviceable. Classrooms roomy. New science block coming soon. Toilets are marked male and female but actually they're inter-gender. Skateboarding is mostly outside. They all know each other, of course, and mostly rub along together just fine (lots of high fives and hugs) – 'We're one big happy dysfunctional family!' Most impressive, we thought, was the spirit in which they equably received probing, challenging questions – they never bridled. Parents do their bit with, say, an occasional paintbrush. The school likes having them around as long as they don't start backseat driving. Food is excellent, plentiful and vegetarian – to get around H & S concerns. Despite the high student-teacher ratio and small numbers, finances are sound and there's a good reserve.

Pastoral care, well-being and discipline: There are complex and ever-present tensions to be addressed here, strenuously and unendingly – free expression vs foul language, exam results vs self-directed learning, the individual vs the community, spending time vs wasting time, parental input vs student autonomy... It all calls for courage, care and steadfastness and must be nerve-racking. A do-as-I-say regime would be – you see it so clearly here – oh, so much easier.

In the words of one student, 'everyone here has their own backstory'. Actually, not everyone here has a backstory, though there's an easygoing perception locally that they're all a bit bonkers. We spoke to parents whose children had no prior hangups, one whose son is quite interested in becoming a policeman. Backstories involve unhappy experiences of mainstream schools because of bullying or a cast of mind that will not surrender to demands for conformity and obedience. Sands is a happy landing for characters, daydreamers, dyslexics, eccentrics, refusers and mavericks, some statemented, others not, some angry, some muddled, some howling. 'People come here to be saved,' a student told us, and when they arrive – some of them funded by the local authority – it can take time for their sails to fill, and during this phase they may bunk off big time until they feel calm and validated, ready to come in and do some work. For such, Sands is a therapeutic environment. Teachers reconnect them with their best interests by talking, listening and above all respecting. Parents whose daughter who had become impossibly wild and furious told us how amazing the school had been. At a crisis, one of the teachers sat with her on the floor of toilet for three hours. It was a turning point and now she's 'as lovely as we always knew she was – lovelier.'

Liberal regimes that work require everyone to go the extra hour. We watched the school meeting debate sanctions for two students who had been making others unhappy. They were present, there were adversarial episodes – it's quite something when your peers hold up a mirror to your conduct. As a student told us, 'You get big life experience here, but it doesn't work for everyone.' Another said, 'Actually, there's not much here to rebel against.' And although the school clings to the conviction that 'there are no bad kids – difficult kids but no bad ones', some, rarely, don't go the distance and are excluded.

There are rules. Not many, most of ancient heritage, a bit like common law, not written down. You have to take your shoes off before you go upstairs so as not to ruin the carpets. Everyone has to play their part in washing up and cleaning the school at the end of the day. It's quite something to see a teacher doing the pot wash. If you want to smoke, a student told us, 'Go and do it alone, not somewhere idiotic and public like a bus stop'. These are longstanding conventions rooted in common sense. And the greatest of these is: 'you have to want to be here'.

First stop for infringements, disputes, etc is the school council – sic students and a teacher – who arbitrate and make recommendations to the weekly school meeting, which is the ultimate arbiter and ratifier of everything.

Pupils and parents: Just 15 mins by road from Totnes, epicenter of a region famously populated by counter-cultural, freethinking folk of all hues. A good demographic for Sands, you might think. Yes, some parents are principled objectors to 'factory schooling' but others are just like parents everywhere, swayed not by ideology but what works for their children. It's all about size, teaching to students' needs and personal and intellectual development – 'Our friends just can't believe the difference in them'. Many parents scrattle about somewhat to find the fees – one mum cooks lunch to help pay hers. It's not for the social cachet they go short in a good cause, but because they reckon the school brings out the most in their kids. Others, whose children the school has restored to emotional health, echo the words of one such: 'Sands is a lifesaver.' There's an early-stage PTA.

Students span the spectrum from exotic to withdrawn; all are incredibly easy around adults, they're supportive of each other and most radiate purpose. Not all, some are getting there. They're not chauvinistic, they're not inward-looking, they don't think Sands is the only school in the world. Any number told us 'This school isn't for everybody'.

Entrance: Come and do a taster week, get to know everyone, decide if you like it. Interview at the end of the week, after which your application goes to the school meeting. They won't have you if they feel they can't meet your needs or you have been a serious pain. Roughly 20 per cent from home education, 10 per cent each from Park, Totnes, S Devon Steiner and local primaries; 20 per cent from local secondaries in yrs 7 & 8 – 'some last less than a week before they are on the phone to us'. School website very informative.

Exit: A range of further ed choices, sixth form or FE vocational mostly – Exeter College, Kennicott sixth form and Plymouth Art College – thence to uni, some even unto Oxbridge. Is the school is a good springboard? Transition may be difficult but, having taken ownership of their education, these students know themselves and what they want, making them, arguably, high-value applicants.

Money matters: Fees on the low-ish side for an independent day school. Expect to shell out a bit extra for the odd school trip and over-the-odds special needs. A few bursaries, income based, offering up to a third off.

Remarks: The decline of difference in all mainstream schools has left Sands looking decidedly far out, incapable of appraisal by prevailing quantifiable outcomes. If you reckon it might well be the right school for your child the only way you'll know is by going to see, whereupon your guts will tell you just like that whether these kids are on an incredible journey or the high road to havoc. If you are persuaded of the former, you may need to move house.

Sexey's School

Cole Road, Bruton, Somerset BA10 0DF

Ages 11–18 **Pupils** 606 **Sixth form** 120 **Boarders** 170 full **C of E**

Fees: Day free; Boarding £10,695 pa

01749 813393
www.sexeys.somerset.sch.uk

Headteacher: Since September 2018, Helen Cullen, previously vice principal at Preston School in Yeovil. Educated at Leweston School with a degree in Sports and Exercise Science with Human Biology and a PGCE from Exeter, Ms Cullen started her career teaching PE, and has worked entirely in the south west.

Academic matters: Results are consistently good, though slightly down in 2018. At GCSE, 70 per cent got 9-4 in both maths and English, with 24 per cent of grades 9-7 and at A level, 34 per cent A*/A grades, 66 per cent A*-B. The DfE recently named Sexey's as the best performing state school in Somerset and Dorset for GCSE. Most pupils take 10 subjects at GCSE, with around 38 per cent doing triple science.

Newish deputy head (academic) has launched major focus on teaching and 'supporting students to be successful' and school continually looks at how pupils can improve. Strategy has paid dividends – school recently won two national awards for being in the top 10 per cent of schools for progress made by pupils between key stage 2 results and GCSE and in the top 10 per cent nationally for high attainment. Year 7 to 9 pupils are set for maths, science and languages (French and German). Average class sizes are 22 at key stage 3, fewer at key stage 4 and 10 to 12 in the sixth form. Good SEN provision – SENCo and her five-strong team offer literacy and numeracy support in small groups to pupils who meet county criteria. One boy increased his spelling age by 22 months after 10 weeks of specialist literacy classes.

At A level, all the usual subjects, plus business, government and politics, media studies, photography, psychology and sociology. Sport and exercise science is the only BTec available. School is continuing with AS levels and pupils must achieve three Ds in year 12 to continue into year 13. One or two opt to retake their AS exams each year. Impressive head of sixth form keeps a weather eye on all and advises on higher education and career choices. A third of sixth formers do the EPQ and all year 12s do work experience.

School is forward thinking when it comes to technology. Prep diaries have been dispensed with and students use the Show My Homework app – so pupils and parents alike can see the prep that has been set and when it's due in. School has introduced philosophy as a discrete lesson for year 7 to 9 pupils and Mandarin as an after-school enrichment subject. Younger pupils do food technology for three years (everything from nutrition and healthy eating to cooking and food safety) and the subject is offered at GCSE and A level too.

Games, options, the arts: Sport has progressed in leaps and bounds in recent years. School now plays loads of matches against independent and state schools (including two Saturday fixtures a term, one for boys, one for girls) and holds its own against the likes of Millfield and Dauntsey's. Parents contribute to a voluntary sports subs fund to help cover transport costs to matches – but there's no compulsion. When we visited, the under-15 girls' cricket team had just beaten their rivals at Millfield and King Edward's. All age groups do at least two hours of sport each week. Rugby, hockey, netball, cricket, football, equestrian pursuits, sailing – you name it, they do it. Sports hall with weights room and gym, 18m heated indoor pool, good pitches and five hard tennis courts that double up for netball and five-a-side football. Emphasis is on healthy, active lifestyles and sixth formers can also choose activities like yoga, keep fit and pilates. Dynamic director of sport says her aim is to broaden the PE curriculum for all – 'the girls want to do football and rugby and the boys want to do basketball and hockey,' she says.

Loads of music, drama and dance on offer. Around 130 pupils play instruments (lessons are rotated so pupils don't miss the same lessons each week). Music department is housed in former head's house and includes large classroom, recording studio and practice rooms. Reasonable numbers take music at GCSE but the subject isn't offered at A level. Performance groups include choir, wind band and folk group. Yearly drama production (Little Shop of Horrors recently) – studio space for smaller productions and traditional hall for major performances. Drama and theatre studies available at GCSE and A level. Art is breathtaking. We were particularly impressed by a montage of year 10 kaleidoscope paintings inspired by artist Brian Moss. The school has wisely formed close links with Hauser & Wirth Somerset, the stunning contemporary art gallery just a mile up the road.

A plethora of extracurricular activities – including circuit training, creative writing, radio club and Warhammer. Two boys who are gardening enthusiasts are developing the school's centenary garden. D of E, plus Army Cadet Force and Air Training Corps (at nearby Castle Cary). Pupils produce their own termly school magazine – recent issue included an insightful advice column on coping with exams.

Boarding: Boarders (weekly and full boarding available) account for nearly half of the school roll. They occupy three vertical, mixed boarding houses – Coombe, Lisbury and the newest, Macmillan. Boarders' dorms are mainly for two or three pupils. All well-kept and wholesome. Each house has its own houseparents, most of whom have teaching or support roles too. After-school activities between 3.40pm and 5pm every day, then boarding team takes over. Two hours of prep a night for most – year 7 to 9 boarders are supervised, older pupils can work in their rooms.

Loads of weekend activities – everything from foraging to theatre trips. Younger pupils are allowed (with permission) to visit Bruton once a week, older pupils twice a week. The mother of a year 7 boarder told us that she likes being able to drop her son off on Monday morning and pick him up on Friday afternoon. 'I feel we get the best of both worlds,' she said. 'There is no Saturday school so we get a proper family weekend.'

Background and atmosphere: School is named after Hugh Sexey, the son of poor parents who rose to become royal auditor to Elizabeth I and James I. After his death in 1619 the trustees of his will established Sexey's Hospital, which still provides care for the elderly today. The trustees later established a school for apprentices within the school grounds but it closed 200 years later. The current school was founded in 1891 and was the inspiration of East Somerset MP Hugh Hobhouse, who drafted the 1902 Education Act (his great, great grandson is a boarder at Sexey's). School later became a grammar school and then metamorphosed through voluntary controlled, grant maintained to voluntary aided. Went co-ed in 1977 and expanded its boarding provision in the 1980s to become one of the largest state boarding schools in the country, with boarding fees but free tuition.

The school's expansion over the years has resulted in a hotchpotch of architectural styles (some new, some old) squeezed into a narrow, 30-acre site, with a main road on one side and a picturesque valley on the other. Some areas of the school are slightly tired-looking but the glorious countryside that bounds it on three sides more than makes up for it. In recent years Bruton, with its ancient streets of stone and stucco houses, has become one of the most sought-after places to live in the country. So many showbiz and fashion names have houses in the area – Cameron Mackintosh, Dominic West, Rhys Ifans, Sam Taylor-Wood and Mariella Frostrup to name but a few – that it's been dubbed 'the new Notting Hill' and the opening of Hauser & Wirth has added to the cachet. Mariella Frostrup was the guest of honour at a recent school speech day, cautioning students about the power of social media.

Year 7 to 11 pupils wear blazer and tie uniform (burgundy polo shirts in summer). Head recently changed dress code for sixth formers – they now wear business suits. Most like this, a few don't. 'I'd been waiting for five years to wear my own clothes,' a year 12 girl told us. Sixth form has its own common room with views over the Somerset landscape and a pervading air of studiousness when we visited at exam time. Sixth formers who have passed their driving tests are allowed to drive to school. We asked a year 12 group what they'd miss about the school when they left and they unanimously said 'Squares' – a playground game invented by Sexey's pupils. Parents praise the school's sense of community and family atmosphere and say that its size means that teachers know every child. 'Children feel proud to say they are at Sexey's,' the mother of a year 11 told us.

Food is excellent. Most have school dinners, with only a tiny handful bringing packed lunches. Everything is cooked in-house by talented chef (a former chef de partie at Heathrow) and his 20-strong team. Six hundred lunches served every day. Food is locally sourced where possible and halal, vegetarian and gluten-free options are available. Bustling canteen, with pupils allowed to sit where they want.

Pastoral care, well-being and discipline: Every pupil (day and boarding) belongs to one of four houses, each of which has a head of house and team of tutors. Lots of healthy inter-house rivalry – houses compete in sport, music, drama, enterprise, poetry and more to win the annual Bint Shield. Vertical tutor groups, with 15 minutes of tutor time every morning. School takes a huge amount of care in helping pupils' transition from primary school. Pupils due to board in year 7 come and stay for a boarding weekend in the July before they start. 'It means they're not sitting at home worrying over the summer holidays,' explained the previous head.

School is very keen on creating a culture of well-being and happiness. The key words at Sexey's are tolerance, respect and kindness and with that in mind the school has created The Sanctuary, a quiet place for children to go and reflect or chat about anything that's bothering them. 'The pastoral care is second to none,' a mother told us. 'The communication between teachers and parents is good too. They seem to take pride in going that extra mile.' As a C of E school, it prides itself on its close links with Diocese of Bath and Wells and St Mary's Church in Bruton (boarders regularly attend Sunday services there). School san, staffed by rotating team of three nurses, is open 24/7 for boarders. Active school council, plus head boy, head girl and raft of prefects.

Pupils and parents: A real mix. School prides itself on its diversity and pupils come from a wide variety of backgrounds – from horsey types who compete in the school equestrian team to youngsters with 'chaotic' home lives. Boarders come from all over (from Spain to Hong Kong) but must be UK nationals, hold an EU passport or be domiciled in the UK. Quite a few boarders are from army families, others from RNAS base at Yeovilton. The students we met were friendly, enthusiastic, down to earth and unpretentious. A sixth former reckoned she might have been a 'bit of a brat' if she'd gone to an independent school but said no one was like that at Sexey's.

Parents are very involved – thriving parent and staff association, with spring ball hosted in the school hall every year. Former pupils include the late Ned Sherrin, Million Dollar website creator Alex Tew and BBC wildlife film-maker James Brickell.

Entrance: Demand for day places is intense. Day admissions are handled by Somerset County Council but there's virtually no chance of a day place in years 7 to 10 unless you live within two kilometres of the school. Boarding numbers are increasing so boarding places are easier to come by. Main intakes are year 7, year 9 and sixth form. Head and head of boarding interview prospective boarders and reference from previous school required.

No new pupils admitted in year 11 and no catchment area rules for day pupils in the sixth form. Around 60 new pupils join the sixth form each year. Minimum of five GCSEs at 9-4 needed, plus some subject-specific requirements.

Exit: Up to 60 per cent leave after GCSE, mainly to take vocational courses at FE colleges in Street and Yeovil; some to do apprenticeships.

After A level 96 per cent go to university. A wide variety of courses – from physics and biomedical science to law and history. Universities in the south west are perennially popular: Exeter, Bath, Falmouth and Plymouth. An increasing number are going further afield, to places like Durham, Leeds, Manchester and Southampton – and two to Cambridge in 2018. A few do art foundation courses.

Remarks: If you want your child to be a day pupil and you're lucky enough to live in the (tiny) catchment area then applying here is a no-brainer. If you want your child to board then Sexey's offers all the advantages of boarding in a small school – but without the enormous price tag or social pretentiousness.

Shebbear College

Linked with Shebbear College Preparatory School

Shebbear, Beaworthy, Devon EX21 5HJ

Ages 11-19 **Pupils** 287 **Sixth form** 77 **Boarders** 98 full, 21 weekly/flexi

Fees: Day £12,975; Boarding £14,250 – £26,325 pa

01409 282000
www.shebbearcollege.co.uk

Headmaster: Since 2013, Simon Weale MA (Oxon). Previously deputy head at Brentwood School and before that, head of sixth form at Reigate Grammar School, head of year at Latymer Upper School, London, and history teacher at Judd School, Tonbridge. A keen sportsman, he has played rugby for London Cornish RFC, hockey for the London Schools Hockey Association, cricket for Oxford University and was captain of Teddington Cricket Club. Still plays cricket. In fact, from the headmaster's house at Shebbear he can step straight onto the cricket field, something he can't wait to do again this summer. Married with three children ranging from tot to teens.

One parent commented, 'I like the headmaster enormously. He has a great sense of humour and is happy to listen to issues and pass them on appropriately.' Another added, 'I feel he has a good long term strategy for the school but at times does not sell himself or the school as well as he might.' What do the pupils think we asked? 'I know my daughters have the utmost respect for him while having no qualms if they needed to speak to him. That is just as it should be,' we were told.

Leaving in July 2019.

Academic matters: In 2018 at A level, 36 per cent of grades were A*/A and 61 per cent were A*/B. At GCSE, 30 per cent 9-7/A*-A grades. Parents are happy with the teaching, saying, 'Academically, I feel the teachers understand [my] children's strengths and weaknesses and work with them so they achieve their best.' Another agreed, '[My children] may not be grade A students, but they are encouraged to give it their all.'

Seventeen subjects offered at A level. Maths and science are strong with at least half of sixth formers opting for these at A level. One pupil was recently ranked number one in the Maths Challenge UK, and another is now studying at Cambridge. Art and music have produced top marks at both levels. Now offers BTECs in creative digital media and sport. Religious studies and a language are compulsory at GCSE. Spanish is taught from year 7 and French from year 8. As an international school, some pupils take qualifications in Italian, German, Russian and Cantonese. EAL also offered.

Pupils are annually assessed for reading comprehension, spelling and writing skills. Learning support is provided at an extra cost. A foreign language can be dropped if extra tuition is needed. One parent told us, 'She needed some additional help, but wasn't bad enough to get any at the state primary school. Shebbear offered, gave, and are still giving her the additional support she needs.' The learning support department produce Individual Teaching Plans (ITPs) twice a year and Individual Education Plans (IEPs) for all pupils with a EHC plan. The department uses a number of tried and tested methods to help pupils, including a handwriting scheme using music, coloured reading rulers and overlays to help dyslexics. For pupils that find it difficult to retain information and to concentrate, they motivate them using multi-sensory techniques, educational puzzles and computer programmes. This provides structured learning, in a playful, fun way. Assistance during exams is available; reading, scribing, word processing, prompters, transcriptions and extra time. Nurses assess pupils too, and any seen to be showing signs of fine motor skill difficulties can take part in exercise classes designed for neuro-developmental delay.

Games, options, the arts: All the traditional sports are played here. For boys, the major games are rugby, hockey and cricket, and for the girls there's hockey, netball and rounders. Other sports on offer include basketball, football, surfing, horse riding, hiking, table tennis, badminton and trampolining. There are several playing fields, an all-weather floodlit pitch, cricket nets, a dance studio, a gym overlooking the sports hall, and a weights room. For a small school the teams do pretty well; the U15 and U14 rugby teams are strong (an ex-head-girl now plays in the England women's rugby team), and the U14 cricket team recently won the Devon Cup. Latest sports tour travelled to Barbados and St Lucia where the boys and girls played football, netball and cricket. Next tour is a trip up to London for matches and tournaments. Swimming lessons start in year 3.

On our visit, preparations were underway for the upcoming performance of Oliver! Two casts performing over four nights. The art teacher was busily working on an impressive set in the main hall; he definitely has a great eye for design, and a passion to match. Past performances include Sweeney Todd and The Rocky Monster Show, plus An Evening of Music Drama and Readings from the First World War. Senior pupils have been lucky enough to take part in a drama workshop with actor Joseph Fiennes. Prep school productions have included Joseph and His Amazing Techicoloured Dream Coat, Panto Pandemonium and Pirates of the Currybean.

Strong musical reputation. Brand new music centre with recording studio and Steinway concert hall. The department is run by a husband and wife team, and several budding musicians have gone on to top music colleges, some with scholarships. Plenty of musical activities and groups – choirs, orchestra, flute group, saxophone group, brass ensemble and a string group. Plus regular performances such as informal chamber concerts, gig nights, and more formal concerts for ensembles, choirs and orchestras. Recent visits by professional musicians have included Voces8 and Festive Flutes.

Art department is on two levels in the main building, with separate pottery, woodworking and food and technology areas on the ground floor. The top level has a large studio for sixth form use, as well as an ICT suite (for all pupils). The downstairs level has another large studio. There is screen-printing equipment as well as a cylinder and roller press, plus a kiln room. Artwork is displayed everywhere, no wall is left uncovered, and good use is made of the ceiling, too, with plenty of pieces dangling overhead. The art teacher is keen on pupils being able to compare and contrast their work, learn from each other, and be able to go back to pieces and give them more attention. We felt this approach gave the space a real creative edge, a great way to motivate and improve. Standards of work were in some cases very high. Regular visits to art galleries, local cathedrals and museums for all, plus A level students can visit London, Barcelona and Paris. Weekend workshops and some evening classes are on also offer, including life drawing.

Extracurricular activities include the usual array of sports, science, drama and arts clubs, plus a few more unusual offerings such as archery, shooting, Minecraft, wildlife studies and gardening. Outdoor pursuits like Ten Tors, Duke of Edinburgh and army cadets are very popular. Other projects like World Aims and Eco-Schools allow pupils to get involved in events like the Global Student Forum and Model United Nations, campaigning for War Child, Amnesty International and Christian Aid. There are also Fairtrade fashion shows, plus a daily Fairtrade tuck shop. Recent trips abroad include a trip to Poland visiting Auschwitz, and a sixth form charity expedition to Uganda.

Boarding: Just over a third of boarders are from Hong Kong and China, a third are from the UK and the rest are from Europe. A large number of the UK boarders – including four 7-year-olds – are from Forces families. One parent told us, 'We chose Shebbear because it had such a homely feel and the head of boarding made a lasting impression on both of us. The location was and still is stunning, and the facilities for the boarders are very good. I also felt that the school really understood the needs of military children and in this I haven't been mistaken.' They went on to say, 'When asking for time off in special circumstances eg bereavement and holiday when dad was back from Afghanistan, the school have been understanding and always honoured my request.'

The older boys' boarding accommodation, Pollard, is in the main school building and currently houses the majority of boarders. Pyke House, which has recently been reopened, is for the 11 to 13 year old boys, and is above the prep school kindergarten and lower years classroom. There are currently 12 boys there. The girls' house, Ruddle, is across the campus and has around 25 boarders. Most rooms are doubles or triples; sixth formers are offered singles. All rooms have internet connection. Common rooms vary – power hockey and snooker tables in the boys' houses and a decent kitchen in the girls'. The girls often invite the boys over for meals and cooking evenings. Parents said, 'I have always been completely happy with the rooms, the pastoral care and the general facilities. My girls have been properly cared for and helped if feeling homesick or angry or just plain miserable. I have been able to ring the houseparents if I've been worried and within minutes they have been with my child and then calling me back with an update.' Majority are full-time boarders but families do make use of the flexi arrangements. Weekly boarding is becoming more popular, particularly during the summer term to aid revision.

Sports hall and library are open to boarders in the evenings and at weekends. Swimming is on Mondays. Plenty to do at weekends; shopping trips, National Trust visits, theme parks, cinemas, theatres, paintballing, surfing, cycling, and horse riding by arrangement. No school on Saturdays, just sports fixtures. Annual social events include the summer ball, discos, themed parties and talent contests. Summer is when the school really comes into its own, lovely light evenings and sprawling countryside, perfect for barbeques, picnics or evening sports.

Background and atmosphere: Founded in 1841, Shebbear College is one of the oldest schools in Devon. Originally set up as Prospect College by Bible Christians in 1829, it was re-founded by the Bible Christian Church as Shebbear College over a decade later, and eventually became part of the Methodist Church, becoming co-ed in 1992. Set in 85 acres of the North Devon countryside, this is as rural as it gets. In fact it's surprisingly rural, so be prepared. Nearest cities are Exeter and Plymouth, both about an hour away, nearest big town is Barnstaple, half an hour or so away. The school rents out 65 acres of the land to local farmers but has plenty of room left for the main campus, playing fields and a decent cross-country course. The campus itself is very flat, open to the elements, ensuring any cobwebs are blown away as pupils make their way between buildings. The main building used to be an old printworks and some of the original 100-year-old tables are still used in the dining area.

Great science block; all laboratories have been updated in the last 18 months. Lovely, modern, bright classrooms; we particularly liked the biology lab, equipped with a hamster colony and tubes for them to run across the ceiling. A python is also in residence.

Sixth formers have exclusive use of the upper floor of a new block. With views of the Devon countryside on all sides, there's a modern kitchen, sofas, a study room and a quiet area, all divided by glass windows rather than walls. Plus separate tutor rooms, a small classroom, and a viewing balcony looking over the cricket field. Downstairs, the building opens out onto the cricket pitch, perfect for match teas in the summer. There are also changing rooms and a kitchen as well as toilets with underfloor heating, much to the delight of girls who happily take their shoes off.

S

Sustainability is a priority at Shebbear. As an Eco School they have been awarded a Green Flag award. They have two biomass plants that provide heat and hot water to the main buildings, and solar panels that provide around five per cent of the electricity. A wind turbine was opposed by locals, but Shebbear is undeterred; they are now planning electric car charging points. Even the minibuses are eco-friendly: all run on biodiesel made from oil from a local pasty company.

Pastoral care, well-being and discipline: Polite, well-behaved children. Standing when an adult enters the room and opening doors is the norm. One parent said, 'It is very important that our children should be kind and have good manners and these values are constantly reinforced through example.' Good pastoral care, as well as tutors (each pupil has a designated tutor who is responsible for overseeing both academic and social progress), houseparents and nurses, there is also a full-time resident chaplain. Chapel is every day except Wednesday, and although the school's Methodist roots are central to the school's ethos, students of all faiths and none make up the community – less than 10 per cent of pupils are Methodists. One parent commented, 'Both of my daughters are excelling themselves academically and I have to put this down to the quality of the teaching staff and the environment they live in. They are happy, cared for and have a fantastic group of friends around them.'

Pupils and parents: No school gate life; pupils come from far and wide. Free buses are provided to Tavistock, Bude, Holsworthy, Launceston, Okehampton, Bideford, Dolton, Bridestowe, Hartland, Merton, Petrockstowe and Torrington at 5pm so everybody gets the chance to participate in after-school clubs. One parent told us, 'Our daughter was not getting on very well at the local school, always came home very tired, grumpy... Despite a longer day at Shebbear she still comes home tired, but is happy and achieving lots.'

Parents are kept up-to-date with regular newsletters. 'The school is good at communicating to parents. We have email addresses for all the teachers, who are very approachable and are good at coming back with answers to any queries,' parents told us. The only grumble from parents was around sports fixtures – 'Organisation at times could be better – particularly with regard to matches where the children don't know until the day before whether or not they are playing.' And the only grumble from pupils, 'The food is the only thing which our children occasionally complain about!'

Entrance: Non-selective. Entrance exam to the senior school is for assessment purposes and scholarships. Open days and taster days, including boarding, plus induction days once accepted. Smooth transition from the junior school, which makes up nearly 50 per cent of the senior intake. Others come from local primary schools including Bradworthy, and St Petroc's in Bude.

On settling in, one family told us, 'Our elder son is not particularly confident. It took him a whole year to settle but we had a lot of help from the pastoral team who went to great lengths to try and make him feel comfortable; they even established a new club based on his main interest.' A parent of a boarder told us: 'The entrance process was simple and straightforward. The settling in time was awful for me as I felt like I had lost a child. The boarding mistress and staff were incredible and made my daughter feel immediately at home. They also gave me regular updates as to how she was doing which made me feel a million times better.'

Exit: Just over two thirds stay on for sixth form. Many pupils come from farming families so some leave for vocational colleges to study land-based courses. Most sixth formers go on to university. Popular destinations include Exeter, Plymouth, Bath, Falmouth, Durham and York. One to Oxford to read medicine in 2018. Some boarders return to their home country to study.

Money matters: A range of scholarships are offered at year 7, year 9, and sixth form entry. Bursaries available for service families, plus there are means-tested bursaries, a college bursary scheme, a Methodist church bursary scheme, siblings discounts and allowances for old Shebearians, families in the parish of Shebbear and Methodist ministers.

Remarks: Shebbear is a traditional, historic school set in rural countryside. Parents choose it 'because of its excellent reputation for pastoral care, the very good relationship between the teachers and children based on mutual respect, and the lovely family atmosphere.' The new buildings are great assets; hopefully this is just the beginning and Shebbear will continue to develop and move forward.

Shebbear College Preparatory School

Linked with Shebbear College

    165

Shebbear, Beaworthy, Devon EX21 5HJ

Ages 3–11 **Pupils** 70 **Boarders** From year 4

Fees: Day £5,235 – £9,486; Boarding £14,250 – £18,750 pa

01409 282000
www.shebbearcollege.co.uk

Head of prep school: Since April 2017, Matthew Foale, previously head of Mount Kelly Prep for six years; other posts have included deputy head of Orley Farm School in Harrow and director of sport at the Hall School in Hampstead. Gained his teaching degree at the College of St Paul and St Mary in Cheltenham and then a masters degree at Bristol University.

Married to Marie-Claire (a manager in an end of life care home in Plymouth), they have three children, Jude, Bella and Mia, as well as an Irish setter, Arthur.

Entrance: Non-selective. Open days and taster days available, including overnight stays for prospective boarders. Entry by application and fee. Parents commented, 'We did look at other schools but chose Shebbear because of its excellent reputation for pastoral care, the very good relationship between the teachers and children based on mutual respect, and the lovely family atmosphere that we felt existed there.' Another parent added, 'Lots of help from the staff and support staff to ensure they settled in well.'

Exit: Smooth transition to the senior school. By year 6, pupils are taught specialist subjects by senior school teachers in senior classrooms and laboratories; they are well-prepared for the next step. Nearly all go on to the senior school.

Remarks: Small prep school in very rural Devon. Pupils come from far and wide but a free bus service runs daily. Recently renamed preparatory school to reflect the education offered here. Pupils benefit from senior school specialist teachers in French, ICT, music, PE and gymnastics. French is taught from year 1, Spanish in year 6. Everybody learns a musical instrument. Swimming lessons start in year 3, as does a little homework each week, increasing to daily homework tasks by year 5. The school takes full advantage of all the senior school facilities including the sports hall, fitness studio, all-weather pitch, tennis courts, indoor and outdoor cricket nets, dance studio, playing fields and cross-country course. Plus they have their very own adventure playground fully equipped with wooden pirate ship and climbing ropes and frames. Traditional sports are played competitively, rugby, football, hockey, netball, cricket and rounders. Some older pupils play for senior school teams. Basketball, gymnastics, badminton and tennis and athletics are also offered. On Mondays to Thursdays the school day ends at 3.45pm and buses leave at 5pm, so everybody can take part in extracurricular activities and clubs; science, sports, chess, ceramics, watercolours, most interests are covered. Wrap around care is available from 7.30am-6pm on request.

One parent told us, 'I wanted my children to be safe, happy and to achieve the best that they were capable of achieving in their studies. I can honestly say that the school has provided all of these things.' The prep school is small and friendly. Kindergarten and years 1 and 2 are on the ground floor below Pyke House, the boarding house for younger boys. Years 1 and 2 are taught together, a challenging task carried out by their class teacher with the support of a full-time teaching assistant. The class of around 15 is split for group work to accommodate and cater for the varying abilities and needs. Extra support from the learning support department comes at an extra cost. This generally covers help with reading, writing and maths. One parent told us, 'Our daughter was not getting on very well at the local primary school, always came home very tired, grumpy. She needed some additional help, but wasn't bad enough to get any there. Shebbear is giving her the support she needs. Despite a longer day here – she still comes home tired – she is happy and achieving lots.'

Shebbear has a good musical reputation and the prep pupils can now make use of the new music block, with recording studio and Steinway concert hall. In year 1 everybody learns the Irish whistle, year 2 the violin, years 3 and 4 the recorder and years 5 and 6 the keyboard. Individual tuition is also available. Specialist singing teachers train and coach pupils who perform at events throughout the year in the college chapel. Other groups include a string ensemble, wind ensemble, orchestra and choir. An annual production in the summer term includes the whole school and past productions have been Joseph and His Amazing Techicoloured Dream Coat, Panto Pandemonium and Pirates of the Currybean.

Makes good use of its rural location. They have a forest school and are often out on walks on campus, learning about birds, pond dipping or naming plants and trees. Pupils plant potatoes to grow, harvest and then make their very own potato wedges. They also get out and about to local farms, collecting eggs to bake in cakes the next day. Regular trips to the seaside to learn about sea creatures and rock pools. Other recent trips include Tiverton Museum, Dingles Heritage Centre where they learnt about the life of a travelling fairground family, and a whole school trip to Paignton Zoo. Year 6 went further afield to Dorset for their annual PGL residential. Lots of fundraising events too, one being for South West Children's Hospice when pupils did sponsored cycling, skipping marathons, gym challenges, and of course sold lots of cakes.

Boarding is available but currently there are no boarders (other than occasional flexi-boarding). These children are often from Forces families and Shebbear is particularly good at looking after such families. One told us, 'I would highly recommend this school to anyone, particularly military families. The location is stunning and the facilities for the boarders are very good. I also felt that the school really understood the needs of military children and in this I haven't been mistaken.' Another said, 'The boarding mistress and staff were incredible and made my daughter feel immediately at home.'

'The teachers are all lovely and the children like them too,' said parents. Several mentioned the fact that they are 'Very friendly, open and honest about children's abilities, they give honest feedback, such as child needs to concentrate, slow down.' One parent told us, 'My son had been badly bullied at the local state school so we moved him to Shebbear where he flourished.' Due to its rural location, this school is not for everyone, the days are long and the lack of a 'school gate life' may make some parents feel disconnected. However, its small size, the use of the senior school facilities and resources, and the way the school embraces its rural location – making it a part of learning – will sway many parents. Worth a visit to decide.

Sherborne Girls School

166

Bradford Road, Sherborne, Dorset DT9 3QN

Ages 11–18 **Pupils** 488 **Sixth form** 183 **Boarders** 451 full **C of E**

Fees: Day £21,285; Boarding £28,920 – £35,880pa

01935 812245
www.sherborne.com

Headmistress: Since September 2018, Dr Ruth SullivanBSc PhD PGCE, previously deputy master (sic) at Haileybury. Educated at City of London Girls and Sherborne Girls, she has a geography degree from Edinburgh and a PGCE from Moray House (Edinburgh), a masters in population and health and a PhD in non-communicable epidemiology, both from the London School of Hygiene and Tropical Medicine. Her first teaching job was at St John's Leatherhead, where she was head of outdoor pursuits and a housemistress as well as teaching geography; she moved to Glenalmond (head of geography) then queen's School Chester (head of sixth form) before joining Haileybury as acting head of geography.

Ruth coaches netball, is a qualified MLTB mountain leader, a computer software trainer and has taken numerous Duke of Edinburgh gold award expeditions to such places as the USA, Morocco, Scotland, Iceland and Norway. She also trained the first-ever all-girls Scottish Islands Peaks team (a 72-hour sailing and fell running event), has run several marathons for charity, taken part in ironman competitions, climbed Mount Kenya and Mount Kilimanjaro and trekked in the Vietnamese Highlands, Argentinean Andes and around Bolivia.

Academic matters: The number of girls taking IB has grown. Sherborne Girls now offers it as the boys' school dropped it from their curriculum. School says girls thrive on its rigour and staff return from IB training courses full of enthusiasm which filters down to everyone. Evidently it's horses for courses, as one girl said she had started it but found she preferred A levels. A disappointing 32 point average in 2018.

At A level greatest uptake is art history and maths. Wide range, including Russian, Japanese, theatre studies and DT reflects broad curriculum. In 2018, 47 per cent of A level entries were graded A*/A. IGCSE now used for sciences, maths, and English. Mandarin recently introduced. Sciences amongst strongest results. In 2017, 65 per cent of GCSE papers were graded 9-7. One parent commended the school for being hot on picking up and remedying any weakness in the curriculum.

New labs, each with practical and teaching areas, don't even smell of chemicals and announce their purpose to the world via curious sundial on the squat turret. Adjoining is the bright, refurbished language department with lots of lovely language IT. When Sherborne refurbishes it's root and branch, not just a lick of paint. French, German, Spanish (plus Latin) on offer and native speakers of other languages can study them to GCSE. Coding and robotics introduced to year 9; aim is to add it to the digital curriculum from 2019.

There is flexibility to take subjects jointly with Sherborne Boys' at A level. Theatre studies is genuinely a joint enterprise but has quite a small take-up.

Much setting and streaming from age 13. No form tutors; girls meet individually with personal tutors moving to a new one approximately every two years. The Junior Diploma is an initiative to keep girls consciously reflecting on their own competencies in the foundation areas of knowledge, learning skills, personal attributes and contribution to the curriculum. About 20 per cent of pupils have mild special needs; they may get extra lessons outside hours.

Games, options, the arts: Sport has a high-ish profile now at Sherborne and girls' teams are definitely up with the best in Dorset. They are old hands at the increasingly popular lacrosse and have hosted ELA lacrosse finals for 1st and U15 teams throughout UK. The girls are proud of their record and Sherborne holds pop lacrosse tournaments for prep and primary schools. Even the less sporty get encouragement.

Hockey (county champions and have provided England team members) and netball seriously competitive. All levels of players have access to good coaching. The Oxley Sports Centre, with indoor pool, fitness suite, gym, dance studio plus floodlit Astro is getting a facelift, and offers first class facilities to girls and to the town in a smooth-running shared arrangement. Plenty of grass pitches and 27 tennis courts (eight floodlit), mostly artificial.

Bags of other sporty things. Riding team does well in National Schools' Show Jumping at Hickstead, ski trips, various martial arts, dance etc and opportunities via Sherborne Boys for things like rifle shooting as well as everything (almost) put on for the town in the Oxley Centre.

Art block with libraries, photography and printmaking has cunning wooden bars across the wide stairwell and entry, allowing for effective display of textiles etc, about to be linked with the new peforming arts centre. Masses of accomplished architectural studies all over the school as well as a few landscapes that might be mistaken for one of the modern masters. Head of art is an inspirational teacher. Good studio space for A level candidates who appear virtually to live here. Weekend workshops offered on juicy topics eg book-binding, stained glass, paper or jewellery making. Overseas trips made jointly with history of art dept. Computer-aided design and manufacture suite.

The lovely singing from above when we arrived was Friday choir practice. Several choirs sing in the abbey and even Salisbury Cathedral and benefit from having accessible boys' choirs. Sherborne Choral Society runs jointly with boys' school, one area in which their proximity really enables girls to keep up in an area notoriously hard for girls' schools to build a good tradition. Sherborne Schools' Symphony Orchestra skims off the cream of musicians from Sherborne Girls, Sherborne Boys and nearby Leweston to produce two joint orchestras. Singing, chamber orchestra, jazz band, senior choir, elite madrigal choir etc etc. Girls enjoy music and even take up instruments when previous experience has been off-putting. Current music building bursting out of its breezeblocks into huts alongside, so the new performing arts centre (due in spring 2019) is eagerly awaited. Joint musical theatrical productions with Sherborne School and some separate drama.

'A plethora' of societies and clubs for intellectuals (from astronomy to current affairs), the arty crafty (life class – gardening), domestic goddesses (cookery – all sorts) or sporty types (ballet – yoga). D of E gets about 150 and 40+ go on to gold.

Lots of charitable activities including a lovely project for the juniors in the New Aldhelmsted West (just say West) with past pupil Camila Batmanghelidjh CBE, who opened the house. Trip to Nepal exploring and helping in an orphanage – plus all the usual exchanges and field trips such as sea kayaking and trekking in the Spanish Picos. School exchange links with Toronto and Tasmania.

Boarding: Sherborne is one of the few true boarding schools remaining with only about 40 day girls. Day girls are allocated to boarding houses and given their own space (some even their own bed) there. They can stay for the occasional night. No flexi-boarding and there is Saturday school. The majority want to be in on the weekend activities. Ideal for expat parents. Day girls allowed home at 6pm but some stay to do prep until 8pm.

Massive refurbishment of boarding houses means all have pleasant meeting, working, library and dining areas plus 'drawing rooms', for entertaining or watching Downton Abbey. Some girls sleep in cubicles (partitioned compartments in a dormitory – they claim not to make a habit of vaulting the partitions) but most in double or single rooms. Upper sixth girls move into Mulliner with individual study bedrooms and bit of independence. After February of their final year they are allowed into Sherborne pubs.

Background and atmosphere: Founded in 1899 by the Wingfield Digby family – local bigwigs owning Sherborne Castle – the main building is a rambling Victorian warren in the pretty local hamstone. Meticulous planting makes an attractive site with the main boarding houses and teaching facilities forming a crescent round a green expanse of playing fields and lawn on the edge of the town. Still a few 'huts' for drama and music but the five year development plan is nearing completion.

Recently completed Aldhelmsted West is a fabulous environment for the first two years with sunny dining room, laid out for birthday tea on our visit, work rooms for homework, lots of comfortable play space and room for music practice. Parents get involved in sports as West positively encourages them to get to know one another. Several live-in staff and a housemistress' house attached with openings onto all three floors. Good big bedrooms, mostly for four, with loo and shower en suite.

The undoubted advantage of an all boys' school in the same small market town (the two schools have launched a Separate Yet Together campaign) means the girls can share entertainment and have sensible and reasonably safe access to town life, a situation envied by similar girls-only schools in the area. Younger girls can go into town at weekends. Lower sixth can go as far as Yeovil, Exeter, Salisbury. Upper sixth girls allowed into the sixth form bar at Sherborne Boys. Common features include coordinated term dates, some A level courses, social events, two joint plays, the Academic society and Epicurean society as well as music.

Pastoral care, well-being and discipline: School rules are straightforward, based on 'keep safe and consider others'. Exclusion for dealing drugs; experimenters can 'expect' to go but 'touch wood no issues' and smoking not really a problem. 'Robust' attitude to alcohol, shared by boys' school, includes possibility of breathalysing. Daily living still done the old school way with all meals in houses with their own separate kitchens and dining rooms. Formal lunches (sixth form do table plans, staff at each table), but cafeteria-style suppers. Hot drinks machines for girls to entertain friends, male and female, in the downstairs areas. Afternoon tea at 5pm and supper at 7.30pm means sensible pre- and post-supper time for supervised prep and activities. Girls say food's pretty ok.

Resident housemistresses, some with families and pets (one house is pet free for allergy sufferers), run the houses like homes with minor medical help and a friendly ear available during the day. Proper school san. The popular school chaplain teaches, offers confirmation etc and keeps an eye that all denominations get spiritual support. Has the right balance of welcome and warmth with respect for girls' views, say parents. Teams of house tutors give personal and academic support on an individual basis. Issues (homesickness, cliques, etc) do crop up but they are very well resolved, said one parent.

Pupils and parents: Still lots of old west country families but also Forces families, diplomats, Londoners with south west connections (Sherborne is on the main line to Waterloo). About 10 per cent come from Hong Kong and elsewhere: Dubai, Nigeria etc plus Europe since IB was introduced. Around 25 need EAL support of one lesson per week. Recently awarded the DfE International School Award in recognition of the international dimension being a key part of school ethos. Sixth form are let out of uniform but have regulation black tailored suit (with a quite skimpy skirt) worn with their own accessories.

Old girls – Camila Batmanghelidjh, soprano Dame Emma Kirkby, violinist Ruth Rogers, writers Sophie Kinsella, Santa Sebag Montefiore, Dames Deirdre Hutton of the Trading Standards Institute and Juliet Wheldon, who was legal advisor to the Bank of England. Sherborne old girls are exceptionally efficient: organised into regional circles, they support all sorts of school initiatives, their own charitable causes and a careers information network. Such benevolent networking may lie behind the remarkable collections of speakers who visit Sherborne – AC Grayling on the day of our visit, Germaine Greer, recently, Becky Anderson of CNN, Matthew Pinsent, Simon Weston, Ann Widdecombe, Griff Rhys Jones.

Entrance: Visit, registration, 'at work days', taster weekends, deposit paid, then scholarship exams, common entrance papers or own entrance exams in maths, English and reasoning plus an interview. One form enters at 11, a few girls join at 12 but the majority (three forms) enter at 13. Mainly from Hanford, Port Regis, Hazlegrove, Knighton House, Sherborne Prep, Leaden Hall, Perrott Hill, Cheam, Bute House, Newland, Thomas's, Mount House Farleigh, Forres Sandle Manor, Twyford and Sunninghill. About 20 join for sixth form – at least five grade 6 or above GCSEs required for A level or IB.

Exit: A few leave after GCSEs, mainly to sixth form colleges. After A levels, practically all go on to university to read a wide variety of courses (modern languages, theology, lots of sciency things including medicine). Bristol, Edinburgh, Oxford Brookes, Exeter, UCL, Manchester, Newcastle, Durham, Cardiff and Bath currently leading the pack. Two medics in 2018; usually several to art schools or to study academic art history.

Money matters: Boarding fees about what you would expect, on a par with co-ed fees for boarders though less than the boys. New fee structure for day students with two options: day boarder (with the option for overnight stays) or day girl (no overnight stays, but her own space for storage and study in a boarding house). The school hopes the new cost structure will offer a competitive day fee to local families whilst still ensuring that day girls feel fully involved in the busy life of a boarding school.

Scholarships generous for a girls' school. Academic, art and music awards pay up to quarter of fees, plus bursaries based on need. Music scholars get up to three lessons per week – more than at most schools. Nearly 100 girls are receiving some sort of award or bursary. Currently appealing for bursary fund. School has also introduced elite swimming programme for which scholarships are offered.

Remarks: No longer the stuffy warhorse of girls' education, though its academic standards are undiminished. Parents appreciate that its good teaching avoids hothousing and encourages a balance of activities. A real gem amongst the girls' only full-boarding schools with all the advantages of its symbiotic proximity to Sherborne School.

Sherborne Preparatory School

    167

Acreman Street, Sherborne, Dorset DT9 3NY

Ages 3–13 **Pupils** 270 **Boarders** 45 full (from year 3) **C of E**

Fees: Day £9,060 – £17,130 pa; Boarding £23,445 – £24,540 pa

01935 812097
www.sherborneprep.org

Headmaster: Since 2015, Nick Folland (50s). Educated at Exmouth Community College, one of the largest comprehensives in the country, and Loughborough University, where he read PE, sports science and geography. Worked with deaf children for three years, did a PGCE at Loughborough and then moved to Blundell's. Played professional cricket for Somerset for three years before taking a housemaster's post at Blundell's. Appointed as inaugural head of Blundell's Prep and after a decade there took on the headship of St John's on-the-Hill prep in Chepstow, where he spent four years.

Married to Di, a charming Australian speech and language specialist who is immersed in school life. They live in a house owned by the school, a five-minute walk away, and have two children. Head is go-ahead, energetic (his wife describes him as a 'can-do person'), refreshingly down-to-earth and popular with parents. 'I'm a pretty open book,' he says, 'and if there are things to improve then I get on and improve them.' Very proud of the fact that the school is not selective yet gets excellent results. 'I'm really enjoying the job,' he says. 'The children are what it's all about and they are wonderfully positive and really want to achieve.' His hectic schedule means he doesn't teach these days but he's very visible around the school, lunching in the dining hall, chatting to children in the corridors and coaching the under 9s rugby team. Plans are afoot for him to coach netball in the coming year. He isn't in the least fazed by taking on a new sport – 'I'm a gamesy person,' he says. Enjoys sport, film and travel in his spare time.

Entrance: School is non-selective and unpretentious. Entrance is by interview with the head and previous school report, plus informal assessment when pupils come in for a taster day before joining, to ensure that the school is the right fit and can meet child's needs. Most pupils start in the pre-prep or year 3 but there is a steady trickle joining from years 3 to 7 and at least 10 new starters arrive in year 7. School is happy to consider new pupils all year round, not just those starting in the autumn term. Academic, music, sport, art, DT and all-rounder scholarships available – school says 'talent and enthusiasm are especially sought'.

Exit: Sherborne Prep is independent of Sherborne School and Sherborne Girls but has strong links with both, and around half of the pupils head to one of these. Others go to Bryanston, Canford, Kings Bruton, Winchester, plus a few to Eton, Harrow, Cheltenham Ladies, Marlborough, Blundell's, Dauntsey's, Radley, Rugby, Downside, Milton Abbey, more than a third with scholarships. Some to local state schools The Gryphon or Thomas Hardye at 13+.

Remarks: Founded in 1858, the school moved to its present location, just off a quiet Sherborne side street, in 1885. Went co-ed in the 1970s. The school site combines the best of both worlds – it's five minutes' walk from the centre of town but has 12 acres of grounds (including five acres of sports fields) for children to play in.

Teaching is excellent throughout. Teachers are a dedicated bunch, full of ideas and enthusiasm. A parent described them as 'outstanding, with a diversity of styles and approaches'. Exam results are first rate but a member of staff emphasised that the school isn't an exam factory. 'Exams aren't the be all and end all,' she said. 'They are part of the journey. People get so focused on exams and it's important to realise that they are just a stepping stone.' As well as their form tutors, who they see every day, the children get to choose their own independent tutors – anyone from the teachers to the head of maintenance.

Classes are mixed ability, apart from scholarship sets at the top of the school. Maximum class sizes of 18, but rarely more than 16. Three classes per year group in years 6, 7 and 8 and two per year group for younger pupils in the prep. Learning support (accessed by 13 per cent) is provided by the Learning Hub. Children receive one-to-one help or work in small groups.

Debating and public speaking are notable. When we visited a year 8 boy had just won the local round of the Youth Speaks competition, speaking without notes about finding strength through adversity. No lessons on Saturdays. School runs an optional programme of activities – children come into school in their home clothes and take part in three-hour clubs (everything from forest school and pond club to circus skills, cartoon character drawing, LAMDA and sport). Saturday lectures for year 7 and 8 children and parents tackle a raft of unusual subjects – the history of salt to 'is levitation possible?'

Head of sport (previously at Glenalmond) is keen for every pupil to get the chance to wear a team shirt during their time at the school. Main sports for boys are rugby, hockey and cricket and hockey, netball and cricket for girls (rounders less popular these days). Hockey is particularly strong, with the U13 girls reaching the 2018 IAPS hockey final. Sportiest pupils get pro cricket and hockey training but school also has a 'team of the week' award, where individual children are commended for their efforts in promoting school values on the games pitch. School mainly uses its own playing fields but also has access to the facilities at Sherborne School, just over the road, and the swimming pools there and at nearby Sherborne Girls. The children get loads of fresh air, running off steam in the grounds at break and lunchtimes. Pupils enjoy playing conkers (a previous head thoughtfully planted a row of chestnut trees for precisely that purpose).

Parents are full of praise for the school's music, drama, art and DT. A father with two older children and two at Sherborne Prep said a year 7 play he'd recently seen was 'creatively delivered and outstanding', far better than productions he'd seen at senior schools. Music is integral to the prep and the school provides 14 choristers (boys only) for the choir at Sherborne Abbey. More than half of the children play a musical instrument and the new director of music reckons numbers will rise to 75 per cent before long. A host of opportunities for budding young musicians, including full orchestra, senior choir, junior choir, chamber choir, brass ensemble, jazz ensemble and piano trio. The art room is a vision to behold – light and airy, with views of Sherborne Abbey and the children's work proudly displayed everywhere. Head of art is a acclaimed artist who encourages the children to explore different art forms, including drawing, painting, sculpture, film and experimental media. 'They never have the same lesson,' he says. The art room is always open and he encourages pupils to go in at break times and in the evenings.

The pupils are spirited, chatty and well mannered. They stand up when visitors enter the room and are keen to talk about their school. Asked what they like best one said: 'The teachers. They understand you as a person.' Another told us that the teachers have 'a fun way of teaching' while a third described the school as 'small and cosy'. A boarder waxed lyrical too. 'It's easy to make friends here,' he said. 'It's more like a family.' They all gave the Sherborne Prep uniform the thumbs up (especially the navy blazers with jaunty green trim and assorted badges) though said sweet and sour chicken wasn't so popular. Senior schools say Sherborne Preppers are mature, independent and like 'having a go'.

School has 45 full boarders but offers flexi and occasional boarding too. Boarding from year 3 upwards but few board before year 5. Seventeen international pupils when we visited, from France, Japan, Thailand, Korea, China, Russia and Spain. The boarding facility is now co-ed with girls and boys sharing joint common rooms, and there is a plethora of weekend activities to sign up for. Day pupils come from Sherborne itself and from as far afield as Dorchester, Shaftesbury, Shillingstone, Langport and East Coker. Five minibus routes at present. Parents range from architects and business people to writers and directors, many of whom have swapped London for the wilds of the West Country. A mother told us she 'couldn't sing the school's praises highly enough.' She added: 'It's a very warm, unsnobbish, lovely place.'

Pre-prep (completely refurbished) and nursery housed in a separate building on the main site. Head of the pre-prep says there's an outdoor ethos, with children spending lots of time outside (clad in wet weather gear on rainy days). 'You don't know until you try' is her motto and there's a plethora of after-school activities, including recorder club, ballet, golf and cross-stitch.

Sherborne Prep is an exciting school. Full of character and great ideas, it's friendly, unsnooty and fun – and achieves top-notch results.

Sherborne School

Abbey Road, Sherborne, Dorset DT9 3AP

Ages 13–18 **Pupils** 543 **Sixth form** 218 **Boarders** 503 **C of E**

Fees: Day £30,375; Boarding £37,500 pa

01935 812249
www.sherborne.org

Headmaster: Since 2016, Dr Dominic Luckett (early 50s), previously head of Mill Hill School. Educated at King Edward VII Grammar School (now King Edward VII Academy) in King's Lynn, the University of Leicester, where he gained a first in history, and Oxford, where he did his DPhil in early Tudor history. Encouraged by an inspirational history teacher, he was the first of his family to go to university. 'I suspect that if it hadn't been for him I would have ended up working in Sainsbury's,' he says. Taught for 11 years at Harrow School, where he was head of history and an assistant housemaster; subsequently moved to Worth School as deputy head. In 2007 he became head of Mill Hill School and chief executive of the Mill Hill School Foundation. He is an ISI inspector and a member of the University of Leicester's governing body.

His wife Cara is a barrister and they live in a school house with their two young daughters. Head loves the fact that Sherborne is 'a proper boarding school' and 'doesn't empty out at weekends'. When he first visited he was delighted to see boys in their early teens playing tag in the school grounds. 'You don't get boys in north London playing tag,' he says wryly, adding that boys at Sherborne get 'a year to 18 months more childhood' than their London counterparts.

Parents and boys talk about him in glowing terms. They say he has upped the academic ante, put an emphasis on kindness and smartened up the uniform. In turn, the head is full of praise for the pupils. 'The boys are interesting, engaging and decent,' he says. 'They know their own minds but there is a reservoir of kindness there. People say that you never meet an unpleasant old Shirburnian and it's true.' He often mentions acts of kindness in assemblies. 'It's very easy to celebrate a first XV victory or a university place but if you aren't kind you're not a proper Shirburnian, however much you achieve.'

A thoughtful, likeable man, he clearly loves his job and is delighted by Sherborne's sense of community. He is determined to raise Sherborne's profile and is proud of the fact that the school is in the top one per cent in the country for value added scores at GCSE and A level. 'We haven't been very good at banging our drum but it's an extraordinary school,' he says. In his spare time he enjoys paragliding, music ('the music here is incredible') and collecting clocks. He points out his 'third favourite clock' in his drawing room – a late 18th century long case clock.

Academic matters: Results are good. In 2018 at GCSE, 56 per cent A*-A/9-7 grades; at A level, 43 per cent A*/A grades (75 per cent A*-B). Art, further maths, geography and physics are the best performing subjects. Most boys take 10 subjects (a mix of GCSEs and IGCSEs). French, German, Spanish, Latin and Greek are taught across all year groups. Boys can learn additional languages, including Arabic, Italian, Japanese, Mandarin and Russian. Reviewed lower school curriculum will see the option of a creative subject rather than classics from 2019, with computer science introduced at GCSE and A level. All the usual A levels on offer. The school also pools its teaching expertise with nearby Sherborne Girls to extend A level subject choices and overcome timetable clashes. So Sherborne gives girls the chance to study A levels in PE and music technology while Sherborne Girls takes boys for photography and history of art. EPQ on offer to sixth formers.

Teaching is praised by boys and parents alike, many commenting that lessons are stimulating and inspiring and teachers go the extra mile to help. School takes a forward-thinking approach to technology. When we visited a lower sixth English class some boys were writing notes by hand, others were tapping away at their laptops and phones. Learning support is housed in its own building (West Lodge). All boys are screened on arrival and sessions on learning styles and study skills are timetabled. One of our guides told us he had suffered anxiety during exams and the school had organised for him to take his exams in a separate invigilation room. 'They are so helpful,' he said.

Games, options, the arts: Sport is a big deal here and there are lots of unbeaten teams. Acres of playing fields (a 10 minute walk away), including two Astros, plus courts and sports hall with squash and fives courts, swimming pool and an indoor shooting range. Traditional main sports but the school offers 26 in total. All new boys play rugby but they can switch to another sport later on if they prefer – choices include sailing, swimming, equestrian sports, fives, cross-country, squash, water polo and cycling. A sixth former relished the fact that he could spend two afternoons a week on his road bike rather than on the rugby pitch. County champions in rugby, hockey and cricket, and ski team won gold in team and individual competitions at the British Schoolboys Ski Racing Championships recently. Other notable successes in judo and Sherborne boys have represented GB in the modern tetrathlon, pentathlon and sailing.

Music is astounding, up with the very best. The music school with recital hall is in the middle of the campus. The choir sings in Sherborne Abbey twice a week, boys give free lunchtime recitals at Cheap Street Church (lucky locals) and there's a host of orchestras and bands. When we visited a lively swing band rehearsal was in, yes, full swing, led by the exuberant director of music. Two-thirds of pupils play instruments, some at grade 8 and diploma level. The school sets aside an hour after lunch each day for rehearsals, known as Q Time. The result is that boys don't have to choose between music and sport. It's quite usual for at least half the first rugby XV to be in the choir. The school has also produced a number of rock musicians, including Chris Martin of Coldplay and more recently, New Carnival, an indie dance band.

Sherborne counts a plethora of top actors among its alumni, including the late John le Mesurier, Jeremy Irons, Hugh Bonneville, James Purefoy, Charlie Cox and Charles Collingwood (Brian Aldridge in The Archers), as well as the director Sir Richard Eyre. School hosts two major productions each year, plus four house plays and a junior school play, most of these in the school's 220-seat Powell Theatre (has planning permission for new performing arts centre). Some joint productions with girls from nearby Sherborne Girls and Leweston.

Art studio, designed by the architect Sir Reginald Blomfield, is open seven days a week and offers painting, life drawing, sculpture, printmaking and digital media. Around 30 boys take art GCSE each year (doing the course in one year rather than two) and 16 to 18 take the subject at A level. We particularly admired a huge golden eagle with a three-metre wingspan, made entirely of cardboard and hanging from the art studio ceiling. An art teacher, an old Shirburnian himself, had given his year 10 group a pile of cardboard and a hot glue gun, challenged them to make something 'life-size' and this was the result. 'It was an opportunity for them to be creative and have a bit of fun,' he told us. DT is popular too, with the emphasis on coming up with ideas, making prototypes and considering whether they have the potential to be commercially successful.

Vast co-curricular programme, including DofE, CCF, Amnesty International, the Ten Tors expedition and Young Enterprise. Academic societies include classics, debating and philosophy, as well as scholars' societies for each year group.

Boarding: The overwhelming majority of boys board, joining one of eight boarding houses. Around 70 boys per house (13 or so in each year group). The houses are dotted around the campus and are wholesome and comfortable rather than luxurious. We visited The Green, a homely house with a large garden that's perfect for kicking a ball around in. Youngest boys in dorms of four or five. Sixth formers get their own rooms. Oldest boys act as mentors to younger ones. We liked the subject guru system, whereby pupils flummoxed by their physics or maths prep (or any other subject for that matter) can consult a sixth former for help. 'And we do,' said an appreciative year 9 boy.

Background and atmosphere: A beautiful school in the heart of a charming, well-heeled Dorset market town. Sir John Betjeman once described the town as looking 'like a junior university city, with every other house an old college'. Some school buildings date back to the 12th century but the school itself was refounded in the mid-16th century under the auspices of the monastery at Sherborne. It survived the Reformation to become a free grammar school during the 17th and 18th centuries and has been a boys' boarding school since the 19th century. At the heart of the school are The Courts, a vast quad surrounded by ancient golden stone buildings – 'our beauty spot,' said a sixth former. The Courts boast two cloistered walls and share one with Sherborne Abbey. Later additions to the school, such as the Pilkington science labs, are sensitively designed and blend in well.

S

When boys pass a wall bearing the names of Old Shirburnians killed in the First and Second World Wars on the steps up to the chapel they fall silent as a mark of respect. It's very moving to witness. School chapel plays a key role in the boys' lives. Every morning starts with an assembly or a chapel service and the whole school attends services at Sherborne Abbey on Wednesdays and Sundays. There's also a candlelit service in the school chapel on Fridays. 'It isn't excessive,' a sixth former told us. 'Some come for the prayers, some come for the peace and quiet.' As the school puts it: 'While we welcome boys of other faiths, and no faith, to the school, we hope these moments of calm will bring structure to their routine, and nurture their spirituality.'

The pupils we met loved living in the heart of town and being able to pop into shops and cafés during their free time. 'It's nice to have a bit of freedom,' one said. 'Some schools are in the middle of nowhere but I prefer being in the middle of things.' Sixth formers wear smart suits and ties, while younger boys are kitted out in practical navy shirts and trousers, known as 'blues'. Breakfast, lunch and supper are eaten in the central dining room. Food gets the thumbs up, especially the breakfasts, and the boys say there is plenty of it.

Pastoral care, well-being and discipline: Sherborne prides itself on being 'boy-focused' and is quick to respond if and when problems arise. Tutors keep a close eye on pupils, meeting them at least once a week. 'They've always got your back,' a boy told us. A sixth former whose tutor had moved to another school said his former teacher still emailed to see how he was getting on. Youngest boys are allocated a tutor from their houses but sixth formers can choose their own.

The boys have plenty of people to talk to, including housemasters, tutors, a counsellor and the (female) chaplain, known as Rev. Two head boys appointed each year, plus deputies and a raft of prefects. Sixth formers also act as peer mentors. PSHE is taught by housemasters to year 9 boys and by specialist teachers after that. A broad range of topics covered, from coping with bereavement and divorce to the stress of exams. School has a sensible attitude to mobile phones. The youngest boys all hand their phones in before bed while some houses organise device-free weekends.

Pupils and parents: All the boys we met were down-to-earth, full of fun and clearly enjoying their busy lives at Sherborne. Pupils come from more than 40 prep schools. Around 10 per cent from overseas (including sons of expats and Forces families). Many come from the south west, plus a smaller proportion from London. Sherborne is only 140 minutes by train and South West Trains lays on trains for pupils from Sherborne, Sherborne Girls and Leweston at exeats and half-term.

Parents from a mix of professions, the Forces and local gentry. Some boys from long-established Shirburnian families (one of our guides was a third-generation Shirburnian and proudly showed us the names of his forebears on his house board). Other famous old boys include Enigma codebreaker Alan Turing, John le Carré, Major General Patrick Cordingley DSO and ITV News journalist Tom Bradby.

Entrance: Boys looking to start in year 9 (third form at Sherborne) are tested at an assessment day in January of year 7 (register at any time but preferably by the end of year 6). They sit verbal and non-verbal reasoning tests, take part in a group task, complete a piece of creative writing and have an interview with a senior member of the academic staff. The head then offers guaranteed places for entry in year 9 although boys still take CE for setting purposes. Impressive induction system in place. Deputy head (pastoral) writes to parents of new boys asking how the school can help their sons settle in and 'hit the ground running'. Around 20 new boys join in the sixth form each year. At 16, entry requirements into the sixth form are the same internally and externally – an average of at least grade 4 across all GCSE subjects, plus grades 8 or 9 in subjects boys wish to study at A level.

Exit: Almost all stay on after GCSEs and most head to university at 18. The majority go to Russell Group universities, including Durham, Bristol, Exeter, Imperial College and the LSE. Growing interest in US universities. One boy recently won a highly prized Rolls-Royce apprenticeship.

Money matters: A range of scholarships. Academic scholarships and exhibitions with a maximum fee remission of 20 per cent. Closed awards available to sons of serving or former officers in the armed services or for sons of Royal Navy officers. All-rounder awards, plus art, drama, DT, music and sport awards. Means-tested bursaries, some worth 100 per cent of the fees. A third of boys receive some financial assistance.

Remarks: A terrific boys' boarding school in a breathtaking golden setting. Sherborne, with its strong sense of community, good academic results and opportunities galore on all fronts, succeeds in combining the best of ancient and modern without diminishing either. For parents debating the merits of single sex versus co-ed schools for their sons, it offers the best of both worlds.

Shrewsbury High Prep School

Linked with Shrewsbury High School

Old Roman Road, Kingsland Grange, Shrewsbury, Shropshire SY3 9AH

Ages 3–13 **Pupils** 180

Fees: £9,825 – £14,178 pa

01743 494200
www.shrewsburyhigh.gdst.net

Head of prep school: Since 2015, Kate Millichamp, previously assistant head of Wolverhampton Grammar Junior School, which she helped set up with the head. Before that was at Brewood Middle School for seven years, teaching maths and art to years 5-8.

Entrance: Entry into the nursery from age 3 'with no formal testing.' Places in reception by means of formal assessments during a day spent at the school with the class that the pupil might eventually join. Parents are advised of any areas which might need special attention from a tutor. So it isn't just in London that the young are being specially prepared, though parents assured us it wasn't as grueling as that extract from the prospectus might suggest. In truth, children would probably be accepted at any stage if they were up to it and space was available. Music, academic, sports and all-rounder scholarships for boys entering year 7.

Exit: Most girls move on to Shrewsbury High School at 11 – indeed, that is really the reason for the existence of the prep, though acceptance is not automatic. Boys mostly remain at the prep until 13, though a few leave at 11 to local grammars. Boys are prepared for CE or scholarship and most (about three-quarters) progress to Shrewsbury School, with some to Concord College, Wrekin College, Repton, Purcell School of Music. Shrewsbury is no longer the automatic first choice for parents of talented boys, 'perhaps because of the fees in this difficult (financial) climate,' the head told us. One parent suggested another reason. Lots of really good scholarships have been won recently.

Remarks: For over 100 years the impressive black and white house, which is the first house you see after you've been let in through the electric gates, was the main building of a boys' only prep school called Kingsland Grange. From 1964 for about 30 years the wonderful Groves brothers, Alan and Dick, both Old Salopians, ran the school with marked success, particularly on the sports field. But there was always scholarship and some music. Boarding, in common with many schools, became less popular and eventually the school, while remaining strong, became a day school. In 2007, it merged with Shrewsbury High and the wealth and vision of the GDST began to kick in.

It wasn't just the railings outside the school being painted blue which signalled to the world a new ownership; the 13 acres of land were skilfully, sensibly and attractively landscaped so that the view from the outside of the house is even more delightful. We met children who actually pointed out their favourite views. In amongst the trees and valleys a cross-country course has been laid out as well as cricket pitches and other games fields. William Kent, it is famously said, 'jumped the fence and found all nature was a garden.' He'd have been pleased with what has been done in this campus, and amazed that apparently some of nature has jumped onto the roof. There has been some marvellous recent building: a wonderful dining room with, it is said, delicious food; bright classrooms kitted out with modern gizmos; a superb sports hall; a science lab; and a design and technology workshop. A ICT facility has also recently been created, along with the redevelopment of an art studio. This building boasts its own solar power generation unit, sun-pipes for illumination, and a green roof planted with sedum to keep the building cool in summer and warm in winter.

Meanwhile, back in the old house with the wonderful main staircase, the higgledy piggledy back stairs and the late Victorian stained glass windows, with dance music filling the hall (not the head practising), that venerable old house has been fully refurbished and modernised with state of the art technology and the music department. Music is particularly strong, and a number of excellent music scholarships have been won to top schools. In fact, if you want to know if the teachers are making the most of these facilities, read the prospectus and visit. Good academic results, good drama, art, music and sport; good out of school activities. The adventure all begins in a wonderfully imaginative nursery with magic grass, a Once Upon a Time chair in the trees, and bright, glorious teachers. It feels like a very cheery school. One parent told us, 'it's almost too good to be true.' There are several ways of looking at that but we recommend you visit and see for yourselves.

Shrewsbury High School

Linked with Shrewsbury High Prep School

32 Town Walls, Shrewsbury, Shropshire SY1 1TN

Ages 11–18 **Pupils** 371 **Sixth form** 107

Fees: £14,178 – £14,481 pa

01743 494000
www.shrewsburyhigh.gdst.net

Head: Since September 2018, Jo Sharrock, previously deputy head pastoral at Queen Elizabeth's Hospital School in Bristol. History degree from Leeds; worked in the finance industry for HSBC, ABN AMRO, NatWest Stockbrokers and Goldman Sachs, before deciding to pursue a teaching career. She spent

14 years at QEH, teaching history and politics and taking on various leadership roles, including becoming the school's first female deputy head. She likes outdoor pursuits and adventure, hiking, climbing, swimming and skiing with her husband. She has travelled extensively in Africa, Australasia, Europe and the Americas and is a qualified mountain leader and a DofE assessor.

Academic matters: In 2018, 55 per cent A*-A/9-7 at GCSE and 27 per cent A*/A, 58 per cent A*-B at A level. Two houses have recently been bought backing on to the secret garden of the school and complementing the delightful collection of buildings clustered around. One for the Business School, the place for business studies, economics, for manufacturing and selling, for enterprise. The other an amazingly swish sixth form centre with an eye on university-style living.

'Here, through technology linking up with the outside world and the main school network, girls can research, explore, experiment. This is a great symbol of how we are trying to combine an awareness of the girls' lifestyles with a forward-looking take on independent study in preparation for college.'

Well, not many universities have computer rooms hung with chandeliers, cooking facilities with granite work surfaces, common rooms with chandeliers (encore), leather sofas, arm chairs and side tables, a patio for elegant luncheons overlooking the gardens and a gym next door. Despite this new sixth form centre representing a preparation for university and life beyond, some may gasp at a charitable institution spending £1m so luxuriously.

The school is alert to the fact that the sciences are becoming increasingly popular in girls' only schools. So how can the school increase the momentum and raise the interest in physics? Enter them for the competition to design an electric car in the national Greenpower electric racing car competition involving 400 schools. Rumour has it that the girls have been drawn to race Shrewsbury boys at Brands Hatch next year. Watch this space. Buy a crash helmet.

All this is trendy, ground-churning stuff, but what of the old fashioned virtues? Well, there's a delightful library with decent books. We saw some inspirational teaching in the arts, in the superbly equipped IT facilities and science labs, and in the magical cottage which houses the very lively and successful music department.

Games, options, the arts: Fabulous sports centre provides wide variety of activities. Tennis courts, lacrosse, hockey, they're all available – no doubt helped by new floodlit Astroturf. Rowing (on nearby river) also on offer. Recently the school enjoyed county championship successes in athletics, netball, rounders, hockey and cross-country, all this achieved without seeming at all hearty. Optional activities abound and the range of possibilities listed in the enrichment programme is endless, from jazz ensemble to DofE, from helping in primary schools to yoga.

S

We saw an excellent art exhibition and met talented, enthusiastic and happy artists. Drama is extremely active and popular with a recent performance of Noye's Fludde taking Shrewsbury by storm and involving a number of schools around the town. There's no doubt there's a lot of lively creativity abo ut.

Background and atmosphere: A GDST school which, since its foundation in 1885, has been a distinguished feature of Shropshire education. The bridge which separated it from Shrewsbury school for boys – the Santa Trinità Bridge of the West Midlands – witnessed much to-ing and fro-ing, both in terms of shared activities and social encounters. When Shrewsbury School decided to take girls, following a brief period of girls only in the sixth form, shock waves permeated throughout the county, in particular, the High School. However, calmness prevails.

Wandering around the school, lost in the warren of buildings – some old and institutional; others plate glassed and modern – the visitor must be struck by the open friendliness of the girls, the smiling faces, the courteous offers of help. This feels like happiness and those to whom we spoke did not deny it. 'It's good fun here. The days are packed.'

Pastoral care, well-being and discipline: There seems to be a happy relationship between staff and pupils, and the provision for pastoral care, support and help over academic matters and guidance over more personal issues is well in place, and much appreciated by those we spoke to. Rules are clearly delineated, all girls have personal tutors and form teachers, and parents are invited to discuss worries and concerns. One of the most appreciated aspects of care is the help and advice given not only with choice of GSCEs/A levels but with university and what to read there. We spoke to a mother whose daughter had benefited enormously from the various layers of academic support. She was delighted with the outcome. It feels like a very cheery school. One parent told us, 'it's almost too good to be true.'

Pupils and parents: Yes, SHS students appear confident, outgoing, friendly and stylish. Not really a school exclusively for toffs. Most parents come from the professional classes, with some farmers and a hint of county. A good Shropshire mix. The catchment area is large and the head has introduced an extraordinary bus service from Church Stretton, Ludlow, Oswestry, Bridgnorth, Ellesmere, Welshpool. SHS is no shrinking violet, any more than the students themselves, let alone the marketing department. Alumnae include Mary Beard, Hilda Murrell and Lois Baxter.

Entrance: Entrance at 11+ is by examination in verbal reasoning, non-verbal reasoning and quantitative skills. Intake is not overly selective and staff are good at helping those with learning difficulties, including dyslexia. Sixth form applicants are expected to achieve a minimum of six grade 6s at GCSE with at least 6s in A level subjects.

Exit: Up to a third leave for sixth form elsewhere – for co-education, boarding, a change – but on the whole the majority stay. Popular destinations include Cardiff, Newcastle, Sheffield, Bristol and Durham. Wide range of subjects – classics, dentistry, anthropology, management, psychology, medicine and engineering.

Money matters: Academic, sport, music, art and drama scholarships available at 11+, 13+ and sixth form.

Remarks: The school is not in the middle of town as has been suggested: it is actually on the site of the old medieval town walls overlooking the river and Kingsland. The school has recently taken out an 80-year lease on the only remaining wall tower. Close to the sixth form centre, it will be used as a museum, curated by interested girls. It's another example of the zany, the original, the questing way in which the school is seeking to extend horizons, to encourage research and inquisitiveness: to enliven. There's a fresh approach and much excitement and buzz. What lies behind all this is new stuff is how the years ahead are perceived. Will it be chandeliers? The main theme seems to be preparation. That, after all, is what schools are for. This is a school well worth visiting if you live within an hour's drive. Do check it out.

Shrewsbury School

The Schools, Shrewsbury, Shropshire SY3 7BA

Ages 13–18 **Pupils** 789 **Sixth form** 376 **Boarders** 618 full **C of E**

Fees: Day £24,885; Boarding £36,270 pa

01743 280552
www.shrewsbury.org.uk

Headmaster: Since September 2018, Leo Winkley, previously head of St Peter's School, York. Read theology at Lady Margaret Hall, Oxford. Taught at Ardingly College and The Cheltenham Ladies' College as head of religious studies; has also been managing head at Bedales. A keen runner and follower of sport, he also enjoys watercolour painting, supports Arsenal Football Club (more recently Shrewsbury Town) and, apparently, has 'an obsessional love of anteaters.' Married to medical oncologist Jules; they have three young children.

Leo Winkley was born into a teaching family and grew up as a staff child at Cranleigh School in Surrey. When his father was appointed Second Master of Winchester College, Leo and his brother remained at Cranleigh School as boarders. After school, Leo studied Theology at the University of Oxford (Lady Margaret Hall) where he played hockey and was involved in drama productions. After university, he qualified as a teacher of English as a Foreign Language and lived in Paris and the Loire Valley for two years, teaching and helping to restore a run-down château.

Leo then began his teaching career as Head of Religious Studies at Ardingly College (1994-99) where he also looked after a Lower Sixth boarding house. From there, he moved to The Cheltenham Ladies' College as Head of Religious Studies (1999-2004) where the subject became the most popular A Level choice. In 2004, he was appointed Deputy Head of Bedales School (2004-10) where he was responsible for boarding and pastoral care. He then spent eight years as Head Master of St Peter's School in York. The school was rated 'excellent' in all areas by the Independent Schools Inspectorate in 2017. Leo was thrilled to be appointed 28th Headmaster of Shrewsbury School, taking up the post in September 2018.

A passionate advocate of boarding, Leo was Chairman of the Boarding Schools' Association (2016-17) which represents over 500 state and independent boarding schools. He believes strongly in community engagement and partnership work, chairing the City of York Independent State Schools Partnership (2017-18) and sitting on the Independent Schools' Council expert group 'Schools Together'.

Leo is married to Jules, a medical oncologist. They have two daughters and a son, who share the family house with two cats and two pet rats. The Winkleys love spending time outdoors together enjoying the beautiful Shropshire countryside. Leo is also a keen runner, having completed a number of marathons in what he describes as "solid and unremarkable times".

Academic matters: In 2018, 80 per cent A*-B at A level/Pre-U and 57 per cent A*/A. Particularly good showing at maths and further maths. Sixty-six per cent A*-A/9-7 in IGCSE (most subjects) and GCSE in 2018. Wide choice at A level/Pre-U – usual academic subjects plus ceramics, photography, computing, design, theatre studies, PE and most combinations can be accommodated. 'Clinics' offer support for anyone who is struggling. Vibrant academic life outside main curriculum – voluntary complementary study programme in sixth form, some examined and some not eg global perspectives Pre-U, BTec in public services, extended project, sports leadership programme, Russian, Arabic, law and book-keeping for beginners as well as debating societies and Model United Nations. Range of academic societies with presentations by pupils and visitors. School hosted the International Young Physicists tournament and received a gold medal in the British Biology Olympiad.

About 130 pupils with SEN – mainly mild dyslexia. One full- and five part-time members of staff provide support. EAL offered but pupils must be able to follow the curriculum. Plenty of careers and university advice includes help finding work experience and talks on what employers are looking for. The school offers tuition for SATs (American university entrance exams) and is a registered SAT centre. Lectures from universities, agricultural and art colleges and the world of work plus lower sixth talks on interview technique and an interview coaching course (charged for).

Low turnover of staff – loyal band, some were at Shrewsbury themselves. Increasing number of NQTs but most changes come from retirements. Hugely supportive staff who 'bring out the best in everyone and take children as far as they want to go academically'. One parent told us, 'The school has brought out things in my son that none of us knew he had'.

Games, options, the arts: Sport taken seriously here both at house and school level but still with an emphasis on 'fun, friendship and fitness', as the school puts it. Wide range of sports; big on rowing, girls are now also afloat in numbers – lots of national competitions, significant presence at Henley and many Shrewsbury boys have represented their country on the water. Newish Yale boathouse with training room and indoor rowing tank. Newish head of rowing is from Abingdon – so interesting times ahead on the river. The elite can take it as a major sport for all three terms, the rest compete at house level. A leading fives school (Eton variety) with 14 courts – a recent pupil was one of the first girls to be awarded a half blue at Oxford.

Venerable cross-country running club known as The Hunt is prominent on national circuit. Stunning cricket pitches described by Sir Neville Cardus as 'the most beautiful playing fields in the world'. Top class indoor cricket centre also used by local and regional clubs, funded by the Foundation. Recent winners of the national boys' cricket 20:20 championships.

Masses of non-team sports including canoeing, kayaking, climbing, mountain biking, and sub-aqua club. Outdoor pursuits and hill walking weekends to Tally, the school's own cottage in Snowdonia, with the aim of having 'serious fun'. Thriving CCF and Duke of Edinburgh up to gold.

Rich and impressive musical tradition with numerous ensembles and choirs (places in the chapel choir particularly sought after), annual house singing competition. Pupils often take productions to the Edinburgh Fringe and perform concerts in London and Birmingham. All new pupils offered a free lesson on an instrument of their choice and there are several Steinways and an organ to practice on. Two major drama productions a year a well as house plays.

Buzzing art department with mezzanine art gallery where upper sixth students can hold solo art exhibitions – particularly strong ceramics. A number go on to art school each year.

Dozens of societies, both academic and not so academic, from millinery and wine tasting to beekeeping and the green power electric car racing team. Witty and irreverent school magazine follows in the satirical tradition of the Old Salopian founders of Private Eye.

Community service popular, but not compulsory; involves work in old people's homes, schools, charity shops etc – oh, and a trip to Malawi. School has close links with Shrewsbury House community centre in Liverpool, known as The Shewsy; sixth formers can spend a week there and see another side of life and children come back for a return match to Shrewsbury.

Boarding: Now seven boys' boarding houses, of about 60 beds, plus two boys' day houses; the four girls' houses are mixed day and boarding. Houseparent, matron and team of four or five tutors in each house. Boys' houses scruffy and comfortable – girls' houses newly built or refurbished with en suite bathrooms – some harrumphing from the boys about this but their houses next on the list for refurbishment. Boys start off in dorms and then graduate to study bedrooms as they move up the school.

Background and atmosphere: Founded in 1552 by Edward VI, the school throve, faltered and then revived in 1882 when it moved across the river into the old workhouse-cum-lunatic-asylum. It was named as one of the 'great' public schools by the Clarendon Commission in 1886 along with Eton, Harrow et al. Set in 100 acres high above the river Severn with distant views to the Malvern hills. Sir Arthur Blomfield's chapel was one of the first buildings to be built and is very much the centre of the community, with its vibrant red and blue interior, striking modern ceramics and pew runners representing the River Severn. Not everyone can fit in the chapel so houses take it in turns to have a Sunday lie-in.

Elegant Edwardian houses cluster round the cricket pitch connected by immaculate lawns and fine avenues of trees. Programme of refurbishment under way and new buildings (more to come) blend into the landscape overseen by imposing statues of famous old boys Charles Darwin and the warrior poet Sir Philip Sydney.

The ancient Chained Library, open on Sunday mornings, contains some remarkable books including John Gower's Confessio Amantis, printed by Caxton in 1483, and Newton's Principia, which the school bought on publication in 1687, as well as books, manuscripts and letters of Charles Darwin.

The first girls joined sixth form in 2008 and school started taking in girls at 13+ and 14+ in 2014, aiming for 65:35 ratio with scope for numbers to increase to 780. Parents divided on this change between the huffers and puffers and those who felt it was a bit of a pity but probably inevitable. The blow softened by the evident high quality of the current sixth form girls, and the long lead time that means that all who joined for a boys' school with girls in the sixth got just that. In our view Shrewsbury boys will adapt well to co-ed – a civilised and courteous lot.

Pastoral care, well-being and discipline: Strong sense of community and a family atmosphere with many staff living on site. 'Staff totally committed and often find it difficult to leave' but still a healthy number of young teachers. Comfortable relationships between staff and pupils who are still expected to call teachers 'Sir'.

S

The house system 'preserves the innocence of school days but makes sure children are ready for the next stage,' said one happy mother. Children not allowed out on Saturday night without good reason (granny's birthday dinner likely to be as exciting as it gets) and they mostly keep to their side of the river anyway. It is too far away to 'bunk off to the King's Road on a Saturday night', said another. Strong house loyalty with lots of inter-house competitions in music, drama and sport. Enormous dining room where everyone can eat together – pupils sit in house groups with tutors. Food much improved in recent years – lots of choice, praised by children.

Sixth form common room, known as Quod (no one knows why) with separate social and study areas and a shop, is run by a committee of sixth formers who organise talks, lectures, film nights and socials. Sixth formers choose their own tutor and anyone who wants to be a prefect, known as a praeposter, has to write a letter of application to the headmaster.

The chapel is central to school life but Catholics can attend services at the cathedral across the river and other faiths are accommodated. Whole school policy on bullying is underpinned by extreme vigilance from housemasters (a comfortable and friendly crew): none of the parents we talked to mentioned bullying as a concern, and we heard no grisly stories from the boys either. If there is clear evidence of drug taking a pupil will be asked to leave, if it is unclear they have to comply with a testing regime. When asked about drinking, children said there was 'no point as you would only get caught', and there is no doubt in their minds as to how staff would react.

Pupils and parents: An eclectic mix of landed gentry, City money, local farmers and intellectuals, all happy to keep their children away from the rat race of the south east. From all over the country including London but most live within a couple of hours of the school. About 10 per cent from overseas. Fleet of coaches ferries children home for exeats – as one father said, 'the school has something special and it is worth the long journey'. Lots of children of Old Salopians, sometimes fourth or fifth generation.

A school with a genuine sense of individuality, 'where you can really be yourself and where everyone's personality has a place,' according to one sixth form girl. Described by a parent as 'interesting, interested and able to get on with people from all backgrounds'. Lovely quirky Salopian sense of humour can be seen in the Blue Chair Charity set up some years ago to raise money for leukaemia research. Old Salopians take two blue chairs with them on their gap year and photograph them in unusual places – they have been spotted outside the Blue Mosque in Istanbul, and at the Taj Mahal; one fell down a ravine and had to be rescued and another was being held hostage on the Somali border and an £8,000 ransom had been demanded. The 8,000 members of the old Salopian Club have a great bond and sense of community. Most famous old Salopian of all is Charles Darwin, who was at the school from 1818-1825. Others include Sir Martin Rees, cosmologist and astrophysicist, Richard Ingrams, Willie Rushton and Christopher Booker, who cut their satirical teeth on the school magazine The Public Nose and went on to found Private Eye, and Paul Foot, who was a major contributor; also Michaels Palin and Heseltine.

Entrance: Fairly broad church and also looking for potential. Most come from about 12 preps within about two hours of the school. Entry mainly via CE (55 per cent required) or academic scholarship (held in the May before entry). School's own tests in English and maths for those at non-CE schools. A few join in the fourth form (year 10) if things have not worked out elsewhere but must be able to 'hit the ground running'. Some 25 boys and 50 girls join for sixth form – a number of boys come from local state schools.

At sixth form entry they are looking for candidates who will make a contribution to school life – sport, music academic, drama. Assessment weekend in Nov prior to entry – candidates can choose three or four subjects in which to be assessed, plus a reference from current school, interview and personal statement.

Exit: About 30 per cent take a gap year – Shrewsbury International School in Bangkok useful source of employment for gappies; travel scholarships available for interesting and challenging gap years. Nearly all to university, mainly Russell Group – Bristol, Newcastle, Leeds, Edinburgh. Twelve to Oxbridge and 20 medics in 2018. Anyone who does not achieve at least five 6s at GCSE will be asked to leave – parents get plenty of warning if this is likely to happen.

Money matters: Scholarships and bursaries a tradition since the school was founded. Not a rich school but very supportive

Old Salopians and parents put their hands in their pockets for the annual Foundation appeal, a telephone campaign staffed by sixth formers and recent leavers. Range of Foundation awards and scholarships worth up to 50 per cent can be topped up with a bursary – testing, interviews and consultation with prep schools (and some primary schools) for talented children who can't afford fees. Academic, sports, all-rounder, drama, music, DT and arts awards offered. Sixth form Margaret Cassidy Sports Scholarship worth up to full fees for talented footballer, cricketer or oarsman, and Alex Wilson day boy scholarship also worth up to full fees, for academic and sporting excellence (we assume girls not eligible for these).

Remarks: A school where individuals and individual talent are truly celebrated and where there is a 'breadth of opportunity without pressure cooker atmosphere'. Produces people with a wonderful and quirky sense of humour who are not afraid to be different.

Sidcot School

172

Oakridge Lane, Winscombe, North Somerset BS25 1PD

Ages 3–18 **Pupils** 597 **Sixth form** 118 **Boarders** 133 full, 4 weekly (from year 7)

Fees: Day £7,860 – £17,640; Boarding £26,610 – £33,570 pa

01934 843102
www.sidcot.org.uk

Head: Since 2012, Iain Kilpatrick BA Med FRSA PGCE, a former RBS banker who saw the light and turned to schoolmastering in the mid-90s, by way of a degree in English from Stirling and a PGCE from Edinburgh. Though English-born, Mr Kilpatrick's upbringing, education and career until Sidcot was north of the border, but 'Much as I love Scotland, there's not a huge diversity of schools. IB was quite a draw, plus the mix of day and boarding, the area and the size and atmosphere at Sidcot'. Having thrown himself wholeheartedly into the holistic life of Strathallan and during his first headship of Beaconhurst, an all-through day school, he has shown himself ready to do the same at Sidcot, and is often to be seen around school, at its performances and indeed away matches.

Parents reckon he has smartened up the place and the people in it, made it 'more corporate' (for good or ill), and on occasion let technology obfuscate the message – some parents would be perfectly happy with good old-fashioned letters or emails, rather than having to download an app to check what's going on. Some also suspect that he is eyeing the academic performance of the Bristol independents with which Sidcot competes for Bristol families – with a view to upping Sidcot's game. Personally, he is dapper and articulate – 'Not to be messed with,' said one mother – and possessed of a good firm handshake. His students find him 'Scottish, smiley, interested in everything you do, with the power to make things happen'. Married to Katrina (a pharmacist), he has a son and a daughter in the school, and is very family-minded: 'children are an endless source of optimism, humour and entertainment'. Though he admits to being that kind of annoying person who always enjoys their job, he takes much pleasure in the countryside (walking and golf), as well as theatre.

Head of junior school: Since 2012, Claire Lilley (early 40s). Educated at Tunbridge Wells Grammar and Homerton College, Cambridge, where she did a BEd in music. She worked at Sidcot as a year 5 teacher and after a foray down a different career path realised that teaching was what she truly wanted to do: 'I felt as though I had come home when I came back to Sidcot in 2009,' she says. A rapid ascent through the hierarchy culminated, after a proper selection process, in her appointment to the headship.

Tall and blonde, with an infectious laugh – 'you can always hear Ms Lilley,' said one boy – she is described by pupils as friendly, cheery and 'really in control but does not have to shout to get her point across.' Has a young daughter.

Academic matters: Non-selective at junior and senior level – 'we think labelling children according to their intellectual ability is counterproductive,' says the junior school head. But that is not to say that the teaching lacks rigour or focus. 'We follow the national curriculum, but are not slaves to it, and we certainly don't expect children to come in and conform to the way we teach. We look for a learning style that suits each child.'

Closer tracking to monitor progress in the junior school. Languages are strong: there is even a competition to recite a poem in a foreign tongue. Forest school from the nursery onwards, with benefits including managing risk, getting up close and personal with nature, teamwork, cross-curricular learning and making an Iron Age round house. Phew! Alongside the three Rs, children here also learn emotional intelligence, to have a voice and to learn independently: each pupil has to research a topic to present on a double page spread in any way which appeals – writing, pictures, photographs, diagrams. Anything goes and is peer-reviewed. Work is often marked by two stars and a wish – the stars for things done well, a wish for something to be done better next time. The friendliness of the school is noted and appreciated by the children and SEN support is extensive and totally without stigma.

Results are solid if not stellar, with 21 per cent of GCSEs graded A*-A/9-7 and 34 per cent A*/A at A level in 2018. That said, maths is acknowledged as being exceptionally well taught. Year 11 Pathway (up to seven GCSEs taken in a year) scoops up students who need GCSEs, and fast – perhaps because they have bombed elsewhere, perhaps because they plan to do A levels or IB and need the groundwork, or because their English requires a shot in the arm. IB (taken up by about one in five) average score was 30 in 2018. Resolutely not an academic hothouse, which is a large part of its appeal – 'Being force-fed academically just because she is bright would not suit my daughter,' remarked one mother – yet parents are confident that bright children will be inspired and well enough taught.

Mr Kilpatrick is keen on breadth, and has introduced the Sixth Form Passport, comprising the CAS elements (creativity, action and service) of the IB syllabus for all sixth formers, plus 'post-school survival skills'; EPQ is also encouraged. SEN students with mild to moderate learning difficulties, as well as social and emotional issues like anxiety and (a lack of) social skills, are well provided for by qualified staff in a light and colourful room; school has CReSTeD status, and staff work closely with English and maths depts. Integration and acceptance are total here – everyone is screened on entry, and periodic assemblies on dyslexia to raise awareness mean it's just part of school life. The undiagnosed are also welcome to ask for support, for example at exam time, and 'Everyone who needs support, gets it,' according to one parent. 'The teachers will help you hundreds of times till you get it right,' affirmed one child.

Games, options, the arts: Twenty acres of pitches, including new all-weather pitch, and a multi-purpose sports hall with the nicest school pool we have ever seen – base for lifeguarding and kayak tuition – mean there is plenty on offer at Sidcot. The size of the school causes some parents to bemoan the strength and depth of rugby talent – but naked aggression is not the Quaker way. Sidcot is not, perhaps, the place for an élite sportsperson – more serious players often belong to local clubs. The equestrian centre open to the public for livery, Pony Club and equestrian studies. All benefit from an indoor and outdoor school (floodlit) and 160 acres of glorious country to hack in. Plenty else for those unmoved by ball games or horses, such as trampolining, archery, TV production, debating and so on.

Visual arts, drama and music are housed in a new light, airy centre. We witnessed the most controversial A level art exhibit we had ever seen, depicting the conflicting duality of Muslim women, the siren beneath the burqa. Ceramics and textiles also noteworthy. All manner of artistic media are on offer, and those not studying art are welcome to scratch any creative itches at a club or society. DT and product design stand out too: from a man-powered bushfire extinguisher to an iPhone-powered record player – a range of practical, aesthetic and downright eccentric projects are realised.

Seven drama productions a year; recent ones include Into the Woods and A Midsummer Night's Dream (directed by students) performed in the grounds; facilities exist to make film and radio also. International students are encouraged to take part, partly to improve their English – but Struwwelpeter in Chinese was surely not to be missed. School takes a show to Edinburgh every other year. Sidcot's music, the school readily admits, would appeal more to fans of One Direction than the Endellion Quartet, resulting in some of the school's most talented classical musicians choosing to take their lessons in Bristol, rather than at school – but they don't half sound impressive at concerts. The auditioned choir (all girls, necessarily limiting the repertoire) tends towards 'the Gareth Malone end of the spectrum', quite possibly because there has never been a tradition of church music. Facilities and tuition designed rather for music tech, creativity and composition.

Outdoor stuff on offer such as DofE, and good use is made of the extensive grounds for gardening, beekeeping and the construction of a nature trail, inter alia. Trips include a French exchange, Tanzania, Vienna for culture/art/language. PASS – Programme of Activities for Sidcot School – 'a co-curricular initiative based on our key values of integrity, stewardship, self-reflection, adventure and community'.

Sports and music are junior school favourites: everyone adored composing music for Tom and Jerry on the computer and the pop choir is – well, popular. Separate PE for girls and boys from year 3. Trips, laid on every year for each year group, also get thumbs up: a camp-out in the grounds for the littlest, progressing all the way to outdoor pursuits camp in Okehampton for year 6.

Boarding: Majority full but a few flexi boarders; around half from overseas. The five boarding houses are sprinkled through the grounds, facilities are clean, tidy yet homely; we were struck by the warmth and knowledge of each boarder the house staff displayed. Three or four share a room in the younger years; sixth formers in ones or twos. Usual range of sporting and artistic activities after school and at weekends, plus trips to eg cinema, ice skating rink, local festivals.

S

Background and atmosphere: Everyone, nay everyone, we spoke to singled out the atmosphere at the school as being the reason for being there. The school's proud Quaker origins (dating from its founding in 1699), history and traditions are lived out every day, giving it a curiously contemporary feel which is so much more than lip service. The school's first ever founding director of peace and global studies has recently been appointed, with a brief to 'bring 21st century Quakerism to life' right through the curriculum, weaving in themes such as social justice, conflict resolution and global responsibility. Sidcot is now a 'change-maker school', as a member of the Ashoka movement, which aims to 'empower the next generation to lead social, environmental and economic development'. Specifically, the atmosphere is one of respect and tolerance – for those of all faiths and none, for different nationalities, for different gifts, skills or shortcomings, for each individual. Quaker half hour is held every week and presided over by sixth form elders, at which teachers and students have equal rights to speak and to be listened to.

We had never met a more thoughtful bunch of young people. 'The children look out for each other, and the school does its best to bring out well-rounded young adults'; 'a home from home for your child, with similar principles as the ones we have brought them up with at home'; 'the teachers are accountable to the children' were just some of the views we heard. One mother described her daughter as a 'bruised and tender plant when she arrived at Sidcot', but who 'had turned into a strong, forthright and confident young woman, which is moving to see'. We heard of several parents choosing Sidcot for its ethos (dread word) over other schools whose academic, sporting or musical prowess was more notable. Learning is conducted in a calm and conducive environment, where 'punishment is not a word we use,' said one member of staff; some parents though feel on occasion that the benign Quaker view of children needs to be tempered with a dose of realism when it comes to high jinks in class.

The Quaker foundations and conventions are not lost on the juniors, either. 'The elders are year 6 and we sit silently in a circle with our teachers at our Wednesday assemblies. We think about stuff like keeping secrets.' Perhaps because the children and their achievements in every field are fêted, there is no need for anyone to feel undervalued, 'We absolutely do not brag at this school,' said one perceptive year 6

Conveniently situated just beside the A38 running south from Bristol, the school's main façade is a pleasing white stucco building, with the inevitable less sightly additions behind it. Some charming gardens, covered in brightly coloured gazebos on the scorching summer day we visited, to represent each of four virtual houses. We were enchanted by the ponies grazing beyond the fence bordering the garden to one of the girls' (physical) boarding houses, with a tantalising glimpse of the Mendips behind.

Pastoral care, well-being and discipline: Respectively, exceptionally good and deploying the lightest of touches. We did not uncover any rebels, tearaways, lads or ladettes, and when quizzed, students listed acts likely to attract reproof as 'not listening, disobedience, laziness, doing what you want'. Hardly hanging offences. Censure from one's peers would be a greater deterrent, we sense. According to parents, the head is adamant about drink and drugs in school – one strike and you're out. Sidcot has no bar, unlike most boarding schools with a vibrant sixth form.

Pupils and parents: An intriguing mix of individuals conforming to shared expectations and outlook, but card-carrying Quakers a small minority. Though the students look conventional enough, with uniform on the posh side (striped shirts, blazers), we suspect that Sidcot families conform to fewer than usual independent school stereotypes. When asked what sort of parent would send a child to Sidcot, the head replied, 'Guardian readers indifferent to sipping sherry on the lawn on speech day, whose children see diversity as a strength, who are prepared to stand up for what they believe in'. A few locals, refugees from Bristol schools and nearly 20 per cent from overseas thrown into the mix. Notable alumni include Sir George Trevelyan (dubbed the hippies' champion), geologist Robert Shackleton, founder of Macmillan Cancer Support, Douglas Macmillan, Zoe Wanamaker, Justin Webb and Deborah Warner.

Entrance: All junior school hopefuls attend a two-day taster session, including assessments in maths, reading and spelling, non-verbal reasoning plus an informal interview with the head – but the policy is non-selective. Children are welcomed in at all stages; quite a few arrive in year 5. Scholarships on offer from year 1, 'both talent and academic.'

Academically non-selective so transfer is automatic (and highly praised) from the junior to the senior school; otherwise applications are taken at any stage except into years 11 and 13, and places offered on the basis of previous school reports and interviews at the school.

Exit: The majority of juniors automatically to the senior school (around 80 per cent). Baseline assessments for setting and monitoring purposes. Some 40 per cent move on after GCSEs for a change if they have been there since nursery, some to a greater range of courses and subjects post 16, and quite possibly the brighter lights of Bristol. Destinations comprise old and new universities up and down the land to do an array of courses, with a leaning towards art and design; some gap years. Popular current destinations include UCL and Manchester with a few off to eg Berlin, Slovenia, Italy and France; one to Oxford in 2018.

Money matters: Fees are stepped according to year group, and a loyalty discount (about 12 per cent for boarders, seven per cent for day) applies to anyone staying on to sixth form. In general, fees are noticeably lower than local boarding competition in Bristol, but more expensive than the Bristol day schools. Ten per cent sibling discount. Quaker families on occasion receive 100 per cent remission of fees. Scholarships awarded for academics or talent; level of funding is discretionary.

Remarks: A school more likely to produce the head of an NGO than a merchant bank. For those untroubled by notions of social pretension or academic snobbery, yet for whom a considerate altruistic atmosphere really matters, this is just the place

Sir Thomas Rich's School

Oakleaze, Gloucester, Gloucestershire GL2 0LF

Ages 11–18 **Pupils** 1,056 **Sixth form** 398 (150 girls)

01452 338400
www.strschool.co.uk

Headmaster: Since 2013, Matthew Morgan (early 40s), studied geography at Royal Holloway and Bedford University of London. Originally from Buckinghamshire, he completed his PGCE in Cambridge. First teaching role at Royal Latin Grammar School in Bucks, where he stayed for 10 years, progressing to head of sixth form. Joined STRS as deputy in 2007.

Trained as a geography teacher but also teaches chemistry. Not a rugby man but enjoys sport so he regularly trains the U12 C team. Likes to lead by example – 'you don't need to be the best at something to enjoy it and get involved'. His true passion lies in the world of music and he leads the brass band.

Parents are very supportive and full of praise: 'Mr Morgan is, quite simply, the best'; 'He is likeable, friendly, authoritative, a good leader and also runs the school with a good business brain'. He also clearly has a great rapport with the boys and gets to know them all individually. One mother told us, 'Mr Morgan also went on the [settling-in trip to the Lake District] and seemed to take the opportunity to get to know the boys and set the ground rules of what is expected: respect, discipline, etc. He earned a lot of respect from our son on that trip'.

Academic matters: Impressive results. In 2018, at A level, 72 per cent A*-B grades, and 40 per cent A*/A grades. At GCSE, 66 per cent A*-A/9-7 grades. The school has received national recognition for the value it adds at GCSE; this puts them in the top 10 per cent of schools nationally for progress made at this level.

Parents told us, 'There is a strong work ethic.' And one commented, 'What I have learnt from hindsight and something I wish I could pass on to other parents is the fact that Tommies is a very academic school. If your child is not academic then it really is not the school for them.' However, it is far from being a hothouse. 'There was very little pressure on the boys in the first two or three years although the teachers were very clear about what they expected. Homework was regular but not too excessive,' a parent said. Boys seem to respond well to praise from teachers and one parent commented how 'it really boosted his confidence and the belief of the teachers in him meant he started to believe in himself.'

With four classes in a year group this is a fairly large school. In the younger years, boys have one period a week of reading, do separate sciences from year 8, and are setted in maths from year 9. French and either Spanish or German are taught, as well as a term each of food tech, woodwork and technology. RE is compulsory to GCSE. Computer science is a new A level option.

According to parents, STRS seems to really understand what boys need. There are eight short lesson periods in a day to keep their focus and attention, plus there is a reasonable amount of sport timetabled in. And apparently there is not much of a focus on messy handwriting and spelling – the emphasis is more on the underlying intellectual thought processes. Progress is monitored closely: one father said, 'It is fairly rigorous and there is frequent testing but it seems to work.' There is plenty of support for the boys here, but the bottom line is, 'expect to put in the work.'

Head is also the school's SENCo. Once a boy passes the entrance test, the school will speak to him and his family and make an individual plan if there are any special needs. All teachers are informed of any needs and adapt appropriately: enlarged type for a pupil with a visual impairment, for example. Teachers are all aware of any dyslexic pupils and any on the autistic spectrum. No individual tuition or help available. There is one learning support assistant and outside agencies are used as necessary to help in specific areas. One parent of a child diagnosed with ADHD told us, 'After seeing the formality of a STRS assembly and the air of respect and authority, surprisingly to us, our son preferred STRS. He said that he was sure he would be able to focus better in the calmer, more disciplined STRS environment than at other schools.' They went on to tell us that the close liaison with the school and good communication had been a great help. The teachers were very understanding, allowing him to take sometimes work alone, suggesting noise-cancelling headphones to help him focus, and even driving him home when he became very upset one day.

Games, options, the arts: Rugby is king here and plays a major part in the sporting curriculum, one of the reasons for many boys choosing STRS. The rugby club is one of the strongest in the county and it's taken seriously. Year 8 boys told us they regularly play five times a week in practices and fixtures, including Saturdays. One parent commented, 'Rugby has been great for his confidence and he's definitely maturing all around'; another added, 'Our boys enjoy the rugby and get a lot from it, but we wonder if it holds back some children's creativity and exploration of other talents.' Parents did criticise the fact that

S

boys are taken out of lessons for matches. However, the benefits of rugby and sport in general at STRS are positive: 'The sporting side of the school has been great in developing his team work abilities and building his self-confidence,' we were told.

Other major sports include cross-country, football, cricket, swimming (small pool on site), basketball, netball, badminton, hockey, athletics and table tennis. There are two multi-purpose sports halls and playing fields, all on site.

'The school doesn't excel in everything – music has probably improved but isn't really a strong suit, and drama is a bit under-represented,' we were told, though theatre studies A level is a new addition. However, there does seem to be plenty going on; perhaps it is just a little overshadowed by the sports. There's a jazz band, brass band, choir, an orchestra, and as well as assembly and community performances, they regularly perform at the Cheltenham Jazz Festival. In drama, there's plenty of trips to Stratford and even a Shakespeare society. The drama department boasts its very own published playwright so as well as the major productions, there are plenty of smaller, more bespoke ones to get involved with. Latest productions include Oliver!, A Midsummer Night's Dream and The Little Shop of Horrors. One mother of a year 7 boy said, 'The school has exceeded our expectations and our son is completely immersed in everything about school life. He has developed in areas such as music and art, which have only come to the fore since September.' Impressive standards of art seen in the classrooms and displayed around the school.

Extracurricular clubs are mainly at lunchtimes, except for sports. Everything from bridge to Warhammer, DofE, karting, taekwondo, kitchen club and Young Entreprise. Plenty of trips. Local field trips for geography, and further afield to Iceland for older pupils. The Shakespeare society runs trips to the RSC in Stratford-upon-Avon four times a year. Plus there's an annual ski trip, language exchanges to Berlin, Madrid and Dordogne, history trips to Belgium, sports tours (rugby to Australia) and sixth form expeditions to Uganda to visit their link school. However, the main event according to our year 8 guides was of course the trip to Thorpe Park to mark the end of exams.

Background and atmosphere: Affectionately known as Tommies, the school has a very long history, founded in 1666 after Sir Thomas Rich left money and a house in his will to set up a school for 20 poor boys. Blue Coat Hospital, as it was then called, ensured all boys went onto apprenticeships once they left school. Became Sir Thomas Rich's School in 1882. One mother commented, 'We particularly liked the masculine feel of STRS, the politeness of the boys, the sense of history and the warmth and personable manner of the teachers.'

The first thing that strikes you is that everything is very blue. The second thing is the relaxed, calm atmosphere. The school's strong reputation for rugby can lead you to assume that this is a boisterous, masculine place, but it does have another side. The head confided that he was one of the quieter boys as a child, and STRS caters for everyone. They are proud of their sports teams but equally proud to be amongst the top six schools nationally at chess. They promote and teach kindness and tolerance. It's these softer skills that keep the boys younger for longer, and has created a rather more gentle school than the rugby façade may suggest.

S

All on one campus, no major mod cons, but it's functional. Large, bright classrooms, traditional wooden science labs (some recently upgraded with funds from local charities), fully equipped technology and food tech classrooms, music practice rooms (no music tech), and three computer rooms equipped with PCs (no iPads or laptops). The general feeling is that of an independent school, but with the added of bonus of no fees. Latest development is the sixth form centre. It houses a large library with a spiral staircase to a mezzanine study area, not for those with vertigo. There's also a large common room and canteen. Girls have been accepted in the sixth form since 1987. Parents all agree STRS 'is an excellent school for boys,' but one did comment, 'I think more needs to be done to make the school better suited to the needs of the girls and to integrate them more quickly into the sixth form.'

Pastoral care, well-being and discipline: Great induction, a parent told us: 'The summer science camp definitely helped with settling in – our son made some friends there who are still close friends.' Once the year starts, there is a form trip to Stratford and an adventure activity residential in Lake District later in year, 'as a bonding exercise.'

One parent said, 'The boys are fun-loving and the atmosphere is energetic but contained. They are courteous and confident with the staff. I think high spirits are accepted but the boys know where the line is drawn.' On our visit the behaviour was impeccable, and our guides were polite, chatty and totally unfazed by being pulled out of a class unexpectedly. There is an air of no-nonsense, but the general consensus is that 'Most of the teachers strike a very good balance between being warm, caring and interested in each boy while demanding respect and discipline. They set very clear boundaries but at the same time there is a lot of witty humour going on, which the boys enjoy.'

Form tutors first port of call with any problems. The school approaches any issues by talking with pupils and involving parents if necessary. One mother, concerned that the school had 'had enough' of her son (diagnosed with ADHD) and that he may be expelled, said the head assured her that 'Tommies would have failed, were that ever necessary.' On bullying, one parent confided, 'Our son had an issue with the unrequited attention of another boy; the situation was dealt with with respect and at an appropriate level. It was managed commendably.' For bad behaviour or slacking there's the usual detention system leading up to Saturday detention for regular offenders. One parent summed it up, 'I believe he is at a school where there is far smaller chance of pupils going off the rails, due to the discipline, great sporting ethos and respect shown throughout the school to adults and students alike.'

Pupils and parents: Some come from as far as Bristol, Birmingham and Swindon. Lots from Cheltenham and of course Gloucester. Parents very supportive of the school and nothing but praise for the communication with teachers and staff. 'They are all very approachable and respond immediately' says it all. Very popular. 'He was extremely keen to attend STRS because of the academic challenge and the sporting reputation. He is a very capable sportsman, and keen on activity and adventure.'

Well-presented boys in blue blazers and black trousers.

Entrance: Selective grammar school taking 150 boys into year 7. Entrance by the Gloucestershire Grammar Schools' Test, with preference to those on pupil premium and looked after children. Registration deadline is the end of June. Once accepted, STRS visits most pupils at their primary school.

Sixth form entry requirements (girls and boys) are five grade 7s at GCSE.

Exit: Over 80 per cent stay on to sixth form. Majority of sixth formers go to university. Around 75 per cent go to Russell group universities; three to Oxbridge and three medics in 2018. Cardiff, Loughborough, Swansea, Nottingham, Birmingham and Exeter currently popular.

Money matters: A 16-19 bursary fund available.

Remarks: Traditional boys' grammar school that 'gets' boys. Highly academic but without the pressure. Best for bright boys who are willing to work hard. Those with a passion for rugby, apply now!

South Dartmoor Community College

Balland Lane, Ashburton, Newton Abbot, Devon TQ13 7EW

Ages 11–18 **Pupils** 1,600 **Sixth form** 300

01364 652230
www.southdartmoor.devon.sch.uk

Head teacher: Since 2010, Hugh Bellamy. Originally from Taunton, Bellamy studied history and education at Homerton College, Cambridge. He spent the early part of his career as deputy head at a specialist dyslexic school and then special needs co-ordinator at schools in Somerset and Wiltshire. During this time he was also a course tutor for the RSA teacher training diploma. He went on to become deputy head at West Somerset Community College for six years, before taking on 'missionary work' at George Pindar Community College in Scarborough. In seven years the school went from 'failing' to being crowned 'the most improved school in the country.' Bellamy is a firm believer in 'building learning power', a principle based around six key approaches to learning, and it is this tried and tested strategy that he has introduced at SDCC.

Married to a primary school head teacher, and father to two daughters, one a teacher and one an ecologist, Bellamy says they are all very pleased to be back in the southwest. As busy as he is, running has become a major part of life and he's even got his colleagues hooked. Recently, 36 teachers ran the London marathon with him – the school raised a whopping £60k. Last year he did it again, and is now in training for the Florence marathon and the London-Brighton race.

Still teaches English, he is also the executive principal of The Atrium Studio. Opened in September 2015, this school for 13 to 18 year-olds specialises in the built environment. It will eventually take 375 students and reduce the numbers at SDCC – Bellamy knows the school has become too big; it's much larger than the average secondary school.

Academic matters: In 2018, 36 per cent of students got 5+ in both maths and English at GCSE, with an average grade of C at A level. Post 16, SDCC offers 40 courses ranging from vocational NVQs through to A levels and AQA Baccalaureate. A level results have been rated in the top 10 per cent of colleges for value added progress. Vocational options with on-site facilities include catering, land-based studies, vehicle maintenance and hair and beauty.

Strong subjects across the board include art, photography, history, music and dance. Maths has improved so much that one of the teaching staff is now supporting schools across the country and advising the DfE. One language, either French or Spanish, is compulsory at GCSE. Science is popular, there are regular science café events, and students recently reached the finals of the National Science & Engineering Competition, representing the south west in Parliament. Parents say they'd like to see more; 'Our son took part in the Big Bang competition ...This was a fantastic experience for him and he loved every minute of it..I think it would be great if there were more opportunities like this. When young people are excited and enthusiastic about things they learn so much more.'

Special needs are looked after by a large team of TAs. There is a specialist resource base for students who display autistic spectrum disorders. Ofsted said, 'Disabled students and those with special educational needs make good progress.' Student support operates at a number of levels, helping with exam stress, anxiety and problems at home. For younger pupils not ready for secondary school there's a Learning Enrichment Centre. The focus is on support with literacy, numeracy and thinking. The classroom is bright, colourful and uses fun primary school-type learning displays. When we were there students were getting ready for a pizza night, all to be cooked in the oven they had worked hard to make and decorate with individually painted stones. They cheekily told the head he would get a free pizza – it looked as if it was going to be a fun night!

Games, options, the arts: SDCC specialises in sport and it shows. The hockey team was the first state school team to be national indoor hockey champions, and the girls' cricket team has been a national finalist for the last two years. There's an annual football tour to Sweden for the Gothia World Youth Cup, and links with Chelsea Football Club. Plus there's a golf academy on site. One parent told us, 'Since joining SDCC my oldest daughter has become more confident and is willing to take part in anything; she has also excelled in sport, taking part in hockey at county level and cross-country at national level.' Another student was recently crowned National Juvenile Mountain-biking Champion, and there's been success in life-saving, horse-riding and even go-karting. D of E and Ten Tors are popular; a part of life at SDCC.

Brilliant sports facilities. Astroturf, all-weather cricket nets, football pitch, hockey field, netball, basketball and tennis courts, golf facility including a driving range, sports hall, dance studio, and a sports centre equipped with spinning bikes and a full gym.

Music is popular. Plenty of bands, some even play gigs outside school. Facilities are good too, huge classrooms with practice rooms set to one side, and lots of opportunities to get involved, whether it's in the choir, orchestra (one pupil is a harpist in the National Youth Orchestra) the annual Live Sessions performances, or the recent production of Carmen. Dance is also a big hit, and Body Language was apparently a sell-out. Drama productions include Bugsy Malone, Oliver! and Aladdin.

Not a great deal of art displayed around the school, except in the sixth form house, but the exam pieces we saw were of a high standard. One particular piece, a stone and shell formation, was impressive but unfortunately students were at a loss as to how they were ever going to move it. Decent photography department including an Apple Mac suite, a studio and a dark room.

Good selection of lunchtime clubs and activities including skateboarding and a boys' dance project (street dancing or break dancing). The annual enrichment week for years 7 to 9 provides the opportunity to do something different – gardening, surfing, water-sports, sea-fishing, climbing – the list is endless. Trips abroad include annual football tours, ski trips, language exchanges, classics trips to Pompeii, and for sixth formers there's World Challenge trips and cultural excursions to France, New York and Italy. There are annual visits to Thailand, as the school has links there through a project run by the British Council and Youth Sport Trust. Teachers also get the chance to do exchanges in Australia, Spain, France, Thailand and India. SDCC is a training school, so there's a regular turnover of younger staff.

Background and atmosphere: South Dartmoor Community College has existed in a range of guises and under a number of names since 1314, making it one of the oldest schools in the country. Initially founded by the church, it became a grammar school in the 16th century and managed to survive the interventions of Henry VIII and Edward VI. In 1845 the school started taking boarders, and it became co-ed in 1912. It then fell on hard times and closed in 1938. It re-opened 20 years later as Ashburton School, and has grown ever since.

A large site, it's more like a higher education campus than a school, with a mix of one and two-storey concrete blocks, temporary prefabs, and tented areas. The entrance and car parks have been developed as part of Atrium Studio project. Due to its location, the school covers a large catchment area, and apparently there's an eye-watering £1.3m spent every year on coaches. This results in a mass coach exodus at 4pm.

When we were there the spring concert was being set up in the dining room. The line-up included pieces from the choir, orchestra, and jazz and folk bands – plus the house band that's been around for 20 years, of course with new members.

The on-site vocational facilities include a restaurant where students cater for staff once a week. Outside the DT rooms there is a vehicle maintenance garage with an old banger and motorbike to tinker with. The hair and beauty salon is run by a local professional company and Bright Beginnings is the social care department. We saw a class of girls who were blowing eggs with the challenge of 'caring' for them for the next 24 hours. Some had exploded, much to their amusement, and ours.

Maths and English are in the in same block as the library. High ceilings and lots of light create a modern learning environment equipped with pods of PCs and an additional media suite. English classrooms have been given names like Duffy's Den, Tolkien Tower. There's one large ICT suite with 60 PCs plus six smaller suites. The science block is the newest addition to site, built in 2002.

Food is catered for by the on-site café, Scoffers. It's well-liked and nutritional. Outside, the covered eating area is decorated with large colourful graffiti letters, much more appealing than the huge one-way and no-entry signs on the school corridors. Admittedly it's a bit of a maze, and there are a lot of pupils to herd, but the signs are far from friendly or welcoming. Very few creative displays either. Maybe this is one of the negatives of being such a big school: practicalities come first. One parent told us younger students sometimes struggle, 'I think the way they organise the timetables seems very complicated and could be improved...the pupils get mixed up for every single lesson... and it did make it more difficult for him to make friends in the first few months at school.'

The sixth form is in Place House, a large impressive Georgian building (gifted by Glendinnings) set in its own grounds. On the way (it's all uphill, you need to be fit), we passed the a bunch of students taking a break from building a dry stonewall, and toasting marshmallows on a fire. This is Devon, after all. Dilapidated barns at the back of the sixth form building have been tagged for a future renovation project. This grand building sits pretty at the top of the hill overlooking the Glendinnings quarry below. The surrounding land is going to be used for farm studies. Inside, the building continues to impress with original cornices and huge marble fireplaces. The modern extension has been designed thoughtfully and the two buildings blend well to create a fantastic place to study – the sixth formers seemed suitably happy as a result.

S

Sixth formers are given the chance to show off their leadership skills by acting as learning mentors for younger pupils. They also organise social events such as ice-skating, meals out and an annual leavers' party. There's a sixth form magazine and a very active Young Enterprise club, plus they can gain an Employability Award (supported and accredited by the Devon and Cornwall Business Council) that officially recognises extracurricular activities and achievements.

The school council has played a part in improving the canteen and the recycling as well as running regular mufti days for charity. As a school, they have fundraised for Whizz-kidz through marathons and events. The house system, named after local tors, also raises money for good causes. One group recently designed t-shirts for the YMCA. This is a community school and its carnival float sits proudly in the car park waiting for its next outing – apparently Star Wars is the theme.

Pastoral care, well-being and discipline: It's all about taking personal responsibility at SDCC. And it seems to work a treat. Ofsted noted, 'Students' behaviour is outstanding.' The general consensus from parents and pupils alike is that they 'feel safe.' Apparently any bullying, including cyber bullying, is rare and is dealt with swiftly. There's a students' support group that has been specially trained to help any of their peers. Plus there are tutor groups and heads of houses. The large support department is on hand to help at all times. The number of exclusions is below average. The head says they take a hard line on issues like bullying, drugs or behaviour, but they use a restorative approach, and he believes that the pupils look out for each other. Parents confirmed to us that their children are happy at school.

Pupils and parents: Families come from far and wide due to the large catchment area. Some live beyond it. Parents are nurses, builders, teachers, fitness instructors, computer programmers. A Parents' Forum is used as a sounding board for ideas and feedback. One parent said, 'We have always been happy with the way they have dealt with any concerns or issues that arise.' Communication is good. 'At parents evenings, the staff have been very easy to talk to and helpful, and clear about the next steps in order to progress. One teacher who was not able to attend one parents evening even phoned all the parents later that week with an update on progress. Regular progress reports are also very helpful.' Parent support advisors are available to support families as well as regular parenting courses.

Entrance: Large catchment area due to its location on the edge of the moors. Children from outside the catchment area will also be considered. 'There are lots of opportunities for children in year 5 and 6 to go to workshops at SDCC and they spend a week there in the year 6 summer term as well. By the time they get there at the start of year 7 it is quite familiar and not too overwhelming,' parents told us. Sixth form entry is dependent on grades.

Exit: Around 50 per cent go to university, 30 per cent to Russell Groups. Popular choices are Falmouth, Plymouth, Bristol, Cardiff and Exeter. Two medics in 2018. Around 15 per cent of leavers take a gap year, 25 per cent into employment, apprenticeship or training, and 15 per cent to local FE colleges.

Famous leavers include jockey Bryony Frost, the comedian Josh Widdicombe, Julian and Chris – the plasterers from DIY SOS, CBeebies presenter Ben Cajee, and singer Jo Harman, hailed by the press as 'the finest female soul and blues vocalist in the UK'.

Money matters: Pupil premium funds available to help with trips, uniform, equipment, school meals etc. Plus a learner support bursary for sixth formers.

Remarks: Great if you're sporty or musical. Fantastic range of extracurricular activities and an impressive sixth form centre, but we felt the site lacked colour and stimulation, and it's just too big. It has, however, been undergoing major changes – the building improvements are making a positive difference, and the new Atrium school will help to reduce numbers. One parent told us, 'I could not have hoped for a more rounded education for our children...They did have to work hard to achieve their grades, but they have learnt to take responsibility for themselves and knuckle down.'

South Wilts Grammar School for Girls

Stratford Road, Salisbury, Wiltshire SP1 3JJ

Ages 11–18 **Pupils** 1,066 **Sixth form** 319

01722 323326
www.swgs.wilts.sch.uk

Headteacher: Since 2011, Michele Chilcott BSc PGCE NPQH (40s). An environmental geographer with a degree from Wye College (now Imperial) and a PGCE from Oxford, Mrs Chilcott taught in a range of secondary schools in southern England before coming to South Wilts as assistant head in 2004. Clearly still enthusiastic about her subject, she teaches all of year 7, partly as a means to get to know them all, lives on the coast (well away from school) and is a keen and adventurous traveller: 'I don't want to visit the same place twice', she says. She's also very pro single sex education: 'Coming here means girls can still be girls at 11', she says, 'before going on to excel in traditionally male subjects like maths and sciences'. Highly regarded by her girls and their parents, if not terribly visible ('Superb', said one father simply, and 'She knows where she's going and is really hot on recognition – and not just for academics', according to one girl), we found her understandably keen to talk about the school, but somewhat guarded as a person.

Academic matters: An outstandingly academic school and makes no bones about it. Highly selective at entry, with three bright girls trying for every place at 11+, its results jolly well ought to be good – and they are. In 2018, 68 per cent A*-A/9-7 grades at GCSE and 47 per cent A*/A at A level, results which place South Wilts among the top 100 schools in the country. Preparation for such stellar performance starts early: these girls work hard from day 1, with an amount of homework which is sometimes baulked at, even by parents, but 'when my daughter said she was jealous of the little homework her friends at the local comprehensive got, I just said that's the deal at South Wilts', said one.

Teaching appears traditional; everyone was sitting at desks facing the front in the lessons we saw. Subject choices are wide – most girls take 11 or 12 at GCSE (some at IGCSE) and 33 subjects are offered at A level in conjunction with neighbouring and similarly excellent boys' grammar Bishop Wordsworth. A level Latin now on offer, but there is no media studies – though communication studies is included. The top five per cent of this exceedingly bright bunch are tracked and encouraged to enter national competitions, such as maths Olympiads etc, though this is open to all, and specific support is laid on for any girl considering Oxbridge, medical or veterinary school. Progress is closely monitored: parents appreciate the frequency (three per year) and quality of reports, but one mother described parents' evenings as 'a time-wasting scrum', which would be better replaced with exception reporting if things go awry.

All girls are CAT tested on entry, and school employs a dyslexia expert. Extra time can be given for 11+ exams, where girls come with a recommendation from primary school; South Wilts is keen to open access to very able girls with SEN. Once in situ, there is help available for spelling, handwriting and organisation, such as scheduling work and completing exams. An assembly at the start of sixth form deals expressly with barriers to learning and where to seek help for them.

Games, options, the arts: Plenty of all these on offer – this school is not just about what goes on in the classroom. Extensive grounds (for a city school) include tennis and netball courts, hockey pitches and – jewel in the crown – an all-weather athletics track. Sport of some kind is compulsory up to the end of year 11; school has Healthy School award. For a school which has neither a pool nor horses, its success at swimming and riding is commendable, and it brings back quite a bit of silverware from local-ish state and independent schools and from regional contests; national badminton player a current pupil too. Minority choices include trampolining and tap-dancing – plus some alternative sports (ultimate frisbee and American football inter alia) laid on by a sixth former as part of the Sky Sports Living Programme.

Arts scene also strong, as befits a school which holds the gold Artsmark award. Masses of music (a third of girls take individual music lessons) for all standards: three orchestras, wind band and guitar group, plus three choirs, one of which is good enough to sing at weddings and at evensong at Queen's College Oxford, where several of the choral scholars are ex-South Wilts. School takes full part in the musical life of this cathedral city. Recent drama productions include Grease, A Midsummer Night's Dream and Animal Farm, the latter in collaboration with Bishop Wordsworth; there's also an annual Oscars ceremony. Visual arts are clearly a strength too and on display all over school. Recently the Arts Award was run for the first time; two lower sixth girls gained their gold straight off.

Packed schedule of clubs at lunchtime, some for just for fun, some with more serious intent, such as the pond club, which helped the school gain its green Eco Flag; good take-up for DofE too. A wide range of trips and jaunts – most are educational, for linguists, historians and geographers – but also ski-ing just for fun. School proud of its international links with schools in France, Germany, India and China and has sent staff and pupils on exchanges to all those countries.

Background and atmosphere: Four-square brick buildings in a leafy suburban street, dating from 1927 when the school was founded, convey the impression of no-nonsense academic seriousness we imagine the school would wish for. The usual collection of 'temporary' buildings providing extra space do not encroach too much on to the grassy grounds, where girls were relaxing at lunchtime in sizzling sunshine the day we visited. Bits of the school could do with a coat of paint, but we loved the new learning resources centre (aka library) with its sofas and beanbags, and super new sixth form block, complete with lounging Bishops' boys, sofas, toasters and kettles. Canteen kitted out with garish chairs seems small for the number of girls passing through it at lunchtime; much of the sixth form prefer nearby Waitrose. Practical and good value uniform (kilts, polo shirts, sweaters in navy and bottle green) in keeping, and sixth formers tidier than many we have seen. Fearsome reputation for academic rigour borne out by a sense of intellectual endeavour we could almost smell: 'I was bullied for being clever at my last school,' one girl admitted, 'so I wanted to come to South Wilts because everyone would be a boffin'. All this is not at the expense of fun, however: 'The girls have rather a jolly time while learning really quite a lot,' as one mother put it. Local opinion that the school might be 'boring' is stoutly denied by the girls, who appear to enjoy the fact that they can pursue whatever subject takes their fancy without fear of ridicule, 'though having boys here would mean fewer arguments', said one. It seems a happy place for staff too: one father commented on the positive relationships between staff, their commitment to the place and the rapport between them and the girls.

Pastoral care, well-being and discipline: Gets the thumbs up from parents, as does the school counsellor from the girls, though this is not a touchy-feely school. Parental concerns are dealt with swiftly and effectively; the only real gripe we heard, and which is common to most state schools, was the lack of medical facilities (eg sick room) and trained staff. Sanctions mostly handed out for poor behaviour, and certainly for late work, and take the form of detentions at break, lunchtime or in the most serious cases, Friday afternoon. 'We're generally pretty well-behaved,' said our sixth form guide, 'but the school would certainly act if something outside school like drink or drugs was affecting academic performance' – we did not feel anyone was much troubled by this

Pupils and parents: Girls unpretentious, bright and not afraid to admit it. Refreshing lack of preoccupation with personal appearance: hardly any make-up, micro-minis, body art or piercing – no boys to impress, see. Parents clearly relieved their daughters got in and grateful for all the school offers; there's an active PTA, raising about £10k per year, which has a 'symbiotic relationship' with the school, said one dad. All seem remarkably content with their lot; the only things on the wish list might be a proper sports hall and better lights at the entrance. 'Not a hotbed of ethnic diversity' our last write-up noted, and little has changed.

Entrance: By way of the 11+ exam in VR, maths and English in the previous September; passing the exam does not guarantee a place at the school, to which applications are made through the LA once results are known. Coaching for the exam is endemic – 'You play the game, because everyone does it,' according to one parent, 'but it's not the place for someone who has been coached to the max just to get in'. Girls come from 58(!) local primary schools and several prep schools; those who don't make it often to go to independent schools. Now has 160 year 7 places.

At sixth form, about 80 girls arrive with a minimum of six GCSEs at 5 or above (including English and maths or a science), with at least a 6 in any subject to be taken at A level. In our view, this is quite a low hurdle for a school of this calibre, and a few newcomers find the academic pace daunting initially, though the school does its best to integrate them on arrival. At time of writing, consulting on a possible move to a co-ed sixth form from September 2020.

Exit: About 10-20 per cent leave after GCSE, mostly to local sixth form college – more choice and greater freedom. Those who stay get into top universities – a good handful to Oxbridge (10 in 2018), the rest to worthy runners-up, such as Bristol, Cardiff and Birmingham universities. Broad range of subjects; six medics and a vet in 2018, geography, politics and philosophy also popular recently. Careers revealed at a recent reunion included an architect, doctor, opera singer and controlled risk consultant. Thirty-three reapplying over a gap year.

Remarks: Unapologetically academic no-nonsense girls' education. Certainly not no-frills, though: this school has a range of activities to nurture all talents – and none. When we put it to the head that her school was so good it could be independent, her face gave her away: 'We're a state school and the only form of élitism we go in for is academic. We're here to serve the community'. Sums it up, really.

S

Stockport Grammar School

Buxton Road, Stockport, Cheshire SK2 7AF

Ages 3–18 **Pupils** 1,423 (409 juniors) **Sixth form** 196

Fees: £8,766 – £11,700 pa

01614 569000
www.stockportgrammar.co.uk

Headmaster: Since September 2018, Dr Paul Owen, previously head of Birkdale School. Degree and PhD in physics from Cambridge; after a spell in industry he discovered that he enjoyed teaching and joined Wellington School in Somerset, where he taught physics, was a day housemaster and latterly deputy head. He joined Birkdale as head in 2010. He is married to Gail and they have three children, the youngest of whom have joined the school. He is keen on outdoor pursuits, trumpet playing, and watching sport.

Head of junior school: Since 2014, Tim Wheeler (BA MA PGCE FRSA, Sheffield, Cambridge and Bath). 'Respect without awe' his preferred style; during our visit, smiley children wander up to him to enthuse about various charitable projects and he, with perfect recall of their last conversation, is able to give them next steps. Previously headmaster of Hereford Cathedral Junior School, before that director of studies at Bilton Grange, he worked for several years as an educational consultant specialising in strategic school improvement. Widespread changes have been introduced since his arrival but subtle change by stealth seems to be his method, tweaks which people can embrace at their own pace but which result over time in innovation. All the parents to whom we spoke effervesced about their children's happiness and progress. They felt he had implemented lots of positives and was actively 'shaping the future of the school'.

'It should be plastered across the wall,' he says, 'that "They are just children"', adding that we must, however, never limit them on this basis. Very balanced, very human. School, he maintains, is a place to make mistakes, to learn, to navigate social groupings. One parent said that the children were encouraged to be 'independent, empowered; fully prepared for the senior stage'.

He's a keen long distance runner, usually marathons in daft costumes for charity; it is clearly important for him to dig deep, have grit, with the belief that inspiration can follow. Music is a great love; he tells us he isn't the best bass player in the world but raises his game when playing with gifted musicians. This seems intrinsic to his attitude to learning, which is all about perseverance, hard work and inspiration. He cites Andrew Murray and Mo Farrah as inspirations for children – not just raw talent but the capacity to work very hard at honing that talent to make it into something great.

Academic matters: At infant stage, subjects include modern languages, computing and music. Science and the arts integrated at junior level. Work is differentiated with a bespoke plan for each child, the watchword at this school. Individual progress more important than grades. Tim Wheeler says each child's individual 'upward trajectory' is the important aspect. Parents tell us that their children have fantastic form teachers who 'won't allow mediocrity' but drive them to achieve in a positive way.

Children move between iPads, Chromebooks and exercise books with fluidity, although one parent felt it was quite a traditional way of learning. Are the more able children stretched? One parent told us that she had to pursue extra work for her child; another parent said one of her children, who was a little slower than his siblings, had been given excellent support and made huge strides forward. 'It's not about A grades, effort is rewarded and recognised'.

Around one quarter of pupils in the junior school receive some kind of learning support. The recently expanded team aims to identify issues early on; additional help may be extra classroom work or time in a booster group. A few receive a small amount of one-to-one support for issues such dyslexia.

The senior curriculum is traditional with extracurricular options including further maths, Greek and astronomy. School flagged up maths and single science subjects as being particularly strong (and with five female physics teachers, gender across these subjects 'not an issue').

Languages also figure highly; French from the first year, German and Latin introduced in the second year, and from the third year students choose two of French, German, Spanish and Latin. The take-up at A level, though, is modest.

Overall, in 2018, 52 per cent of A level grades A or A*, and 58 per cent A*-A/9-7 at GCSE. So the results are strong and solid; and the teaching likewise.

The faint grumble in a school's last inspectorate report was that teaching gave insufficient scope for pupils to explore. We encountered a few grumbles ourselves; one parent said her children took the jaded view that the quality of the teacher you got was the 'luck of the draw'. 'If your child is motivated and driven,' she said, 'they will do well, they will go seek', implying it was not necessarily great news if they did not 'go seek'. However, another parent said that when she had not been happy about a teacher, the school had immediately swung into action to rectify the matter. This latter parent found the academic environment very nurturing, with her less academic child being supported as much as her academically high flying older sibling. 'She's encouraged to do as well as she possibly can.'

The school can also accommodate a range of SEND requirements (these may include physical disabilities, sensory problems, English as an additional language and specific learning difficulties). A learning support department works with pupils, parents and teaching staff to ensure pupils make progress in line with their ability. Specialist timetabled teaching – no additional charge – in small groups.

Games, options, the arts: All parents commented on the 'amazing' range of activities in the junior school; alongside the usual sports, more unusual options include archery, puppet making and fencing. New activities are evolving all the time. Lacrosse, fondly remembered by old Stopfordians, has recently been resuscitated and had a huge take up. Tim Wheeler supports the 'have a go' culture, so many sport clubs do not select just by talent but are also for children who want to see what they might be able to achieve if given the chance. Children can use the sports centre in the senior school grounds (alongside its cheery all-weather turf).

Everything is gender-inclusive; one parent liked her boys being encouraged to sing in choirs. The drama productions – a recent one being Beauty and the Beast – are wide ranging.

In the senior school, the core sports fare very well; at the time of our visit, the girls' hockey team had excelled, so too the boys' rugby. For the more specialist pursuits, such as for climbing and golf, there are specialist teachers.

A wide range of clubs eg Big Band, Japanese, philosophy. Some fun challenges; a MasterChef competition, judged by a Bake-Off celeb, had clearly gripped the school's imagination. Participation is an important driver; one parent summed it up: 'If you turn up to practice, you will get a go'. So there is swimming training for the gala and swimming for fun. There didn't seem to be a gender divide about activities; a noticeboard showed photos of boys and girls involved in a dance show (a parent told us a male dance teacher had been hired to encourage boys to join in).

Extensive concert programme (more than 400 pupils learn instruments). Pupils have been selected for the National Youth Orchestra and the National Youth Music Theatre. Diverse plays and shows run the thespie gamut, from modern drama to the classics; one play had a cast of 86, with 50 people involved in the production side. For aspiring politicos, there is lots of opportunity for public speaking; the school team at the Model United Nations conference fared well, with lots of 'outstandings' awarded.

If your child's tastes run more to the more quietly cerebral, however, there are other temptations; lower sixth historians had produced SGS Historian, a super little magazine looking at figures who shaped history.

Background and atmosphere: Stockport Grammar was established in 1487 by Sir Edmond Shaa, who became the 200th Mayor of London. The move to its current site took place in 1915 and this, the old part of the senior school, is charming and cloistered. Since then, the school has added numerous attractive, modern, buildings (the library placed at the heart of the school to feed intellectual watercooler moments). It is spread out over a large site with flashes of green everywhere. While it makes for a slightly fragmented feel akin to a campus-based university, it is nonetheless impressive in its sweep and facilities.

The junior school opened in 1944 but moved to its current building in 1975 and has expanded considerably since then. The moment you step through the door into the entrance hall flooded with light – a collaborative space where a community of animated children gather in throngs of chat – there is an overwhelming sense of vibrancy, warmth and happiness. This is reinforced by corridors and classrooms, which are an explosion of colour with innovative art displays everywhere you look.

Pastoral care, well-being and discipline: Pastoral care in the junior school seems strong. A parent whose child had specific health needs was glowing about the emotional and practical support she had received, the delicacy and tact with which it had been handled. A sports fan, Tim Wheeler has introduced a card system akin to football rules to maintain good behaviour. One or two breaches of school rules – such as eating in the classroom – might result in a yellow card. Three yellow cards = a red card – no dramatic football send-off ensues, but the parents are called. It is not, he says, enforced with excessive rigidity. One parent we spoke to felt it embedded basic manners within the children. Certainly all the children we saw were happy, bubbly and deported themselves admirably.

The children are gradually given responsibilities: first in their form, later via opportunities like the school council. All year 6 children are prefects with responsibilities which, says the head, 'won't eat into their time'. He is very respectful of the latter, always bearing in mind that children need their downtime.

At senior school, form tutors are first port of call and they in turn liaise with heads of year and upwards with the deputy head pastoral. The school has expanded the pastoral staff in recent years and school counselling facility in order to provide the care perceived to be 'essential if children are to navigate the den of adolescence and flourish in and out of the classroom'. The school seems pretty clued up and there are heaps of talks for pupils on the dangers of misusing social media and the internet.

One parent we spoke to, however, while acknowledging the good work done by the school, had experienced the trauma of her child being bullied. She felt the whole matter had been brushed under the carpet, with the bullying policy being enforced weakly. She also felt the remedies offered– counselling – were so conspicuous (pupils having to leave lessons to attend) as to intensify the problem rather than aid the recovery. She summed up the school community in this respect as having 'lots of grit. It is a tough environment'.

One person's grit is, of course, another's pearl; other parents spoke glowingly of their children's happiness, saying the teachers seemed genuinely interested in what made each child tick. One parent felt her three, very different, children had flourished: 'every achievement is really valued; you are no better just because you are A* pupil.' Lots of the parents we spoke to really reinforced how happy their child was and how well rounded they had become with all the diverse activities on offer.

Another parent paid tribute to the pastoral care, saying she had been 'bowled over' by staff who had 'bent over backwards' when her high-achieving academic child hit tricky times in sixth form for personal reasons. Teachers had rearranged their diaries to help her; sought her out at lunchtimes to chat and provided her with support to rally again at a critical time.

Pupils and parents: The school's locational name – Stockport – is a tag which usually precludes starry footballer parents, often seen prospecting for schools in the north west. Parents may not necessarily have reams of spare cash, but what they do have, they want to channel into education. It tends to be very much a local school. Where parents in other high profile schools in the area might be termed 'driven', the junior head says parents are 'grounded, solid and loyal'. The senior school described parents as 'proactive and representative of its broad social intake'. So not of the sharp elbowed variety.

The usual comms channels prevail – newsletters, parent portal, parents' evenings. Most said you could speak to a teacher on that same day. One parent said: 'if you work in conjunction with the school, you get the best out of them'. So all very fluid, relaxed and not too competitive.

Entrance: At junior level, most come from the nursery. At reception – two classes of around 20 children – entry is a matter of observation; how a child interacts and responds to simple instructions. In years 1 or 2; they attend a taster day which includes tests – English, maths, reading and non-verbal reasoning. It is all done with a light touch. Head stresses It's not about judging them, but about working out whether this is the right school.

At senior, around 370-400 children from local schools take the entrance exam (comprehension, essay, maths and verbal reasoning papers), competing for 90 or so places (60 of the 150 total places are generally taken by Stockport Junior pupils). There are informal interviews for parents and pupil and a school report. Those who apply for entry later on, up to year 10, sit maths and English papers.

Sixth form admissions by interview with generally 6+ 9-7 grades required at GCSE.

S

Exit: Almost all children move across from the junior to senior school – a few go elsewhere, to local high schools or relocate. Junior head says he has 'downgraded' the status of the entrance exam so that it is part of what the school does, rather than 'everything'. Children who would not thrive at the senior school are nicely eased out. By year 2, the school has a sense which children need an alternative environment, and an extended conversation begins with the parents, often lasting a couple of years, and parents and children supported towards a decision around year 4 or 5. When children leave the junior it is usually related to a special needs issue.

At the senior school, a fair number leave after GCSEs, usually for a fee-related issue or occasionally because sixth form is not for them. Ten to Oxbridge in 2018, plus seven medics. Others go off to study eg anthropology at Durham, maths and philosophy at Edinburgh, engineering at Nottingham, fashion marketing at Nottingham Trent and French and international management at Bath.

Money matters: School is committed to keeping fees as low as possible and feels it is reasonable compared to others in the area. School bursary scheme available. Bursaries based on family income and a child's performance in the entrance exam. Music scholarships also available and Ogden Trust Bursaries in the sixth form. In addition, Shaa Scholarships offered to children based on 'outstanding performance' in the entrance exam.

Remarks: Your child will receive an excellent 360 degree education in a relatively diverse environment, where achievement at every level is celebrated, allowing all pupils to thrive.

Stonar

177

Cottles Park, Atworth, Wiltshire SN12 8NT

Ages 2–18 **Pupils** 325 **Sixth form** 42 (33 girls, 9 boys) **Boarders** 72 girls, 17 boys full (from 8 years)

Fees: Day £8,496 – £16,500; Boarding £21,954 – £33,195 pa

01225 701741
www.stonarschool.com

Head: Since 2015, Dr Sally Divall MA PhD PGCE, previously deputy head academic. Originally from London, Sally gained a PhD in natural sciences at Cambridge before working at BP, the Bristol Exploratory, UWE and Bath University. As a scientist she was inspired by the 'hands-on approach to learning' and teaching seemed to be a natural progression. Sally joined Stonar as head of physics in 1999. Leaving in July 2019. Her successor will be Matthew Wray, currently deputy head of Milton Abbey School.

Head of prep: Since 2008, Mark Brain BA (Ed), formerly deputy head of Kelly College Prep (now Mount Kelly Prep). Also an independent schools inspector, he lives on site with his young family. Originally from the Cotswolds, Mark studied education at Exeter University. Previously director of sport at Repton, sport will always be his 'first love,' he told us. Still teaches PE and coaches local teams. Parents told us, 'He has a calm and gentle manner with the children and has introduced a sound ethos having implemented 'growth mindset' across the school.' Moving on in July 2019. His successor will be Rob Cunningham, currently deputy head of The Mead School in Trowbridge.

Since 2013, Stonar has been part of the NACE schools group, an international educational group with 21 schools across five countries. Stonar is the only English school; others are in Spain, France, Italy and India.

Academic matters: Head prefers 'broad academic intake' rather than 'non-selective'. Value-added scores are more important than grades alone and the school uses the Yellis system from Durham University to keep track, helping pupils to reach their full potential.

In 2018, at A level, 49 per cent A*-B grades, 22 per cent A*-A. At GCSE, 49 per cent A*-A/9-7 grades. Pupils are encouraged to take three A levels; vocational courses are 'add-ons.' Sciences are popular at A level with most opting for at least one science or maths or psychology. The arts are also strong, particularly photography and art. Vocational courses include British Horse Society qualifications and a Leiths Toolbox Cookery Course which help to develop 'personal attributes' as 'academic qualifications are just not enough these days', says head.

With a staff to pupil ratio of 1:6, classes are small, usually around 15 or 16, and no more than 20. Girls we spoke to all agreed this is one of the advantages of Stonar, especially at A level when some subjects are one-to-one. Parents told us the teaching staff are 'incredibly supportive and inspiring,' and 'understanding and encouraging.' One mother added, 'Both my husband and I are educators and we are delighted with the standard of teaching and the sheer quality that Stonar offers.' High praise too for the careers advice; one aspiring doctor told us it's 'amazing'.

At the prep school, 'Getting the children out of their seats, out of their class and indeed out of the school makes learning more memorable and this is a driving force,' the head told us. Lessons are often linked to trips and activities. The curriculum focuses on learning as well as understanding what learning means. Parents are invited into the school at the end of each topic and pupils 'teach' parents what they have learnt. The head has introduced a culture of 'growth mindset' across the school. A large part of this is rewards, which are celebrated in assemblies and the weekly newsletter. Pupils are taught in mixed ability classes and not streamed. 'We want to nurture a love of learning, not turn them off and create reserved, demoralised children,' the head told us. Senior school specialists languages and music.

Prep pupils receive learning support in the form of extra maths and English lessons and/or a TA in class. In the senior school, around a fifth of pupils have TA support, though one-to-one not currently offered. Needs catered for include ADD, ADHD, ASD, Asperger's, dyspraxia, dyslexia and speech and communication difficulties. More complex needs are considered on an individual basis. One parent told us, 'they treat each [pupil] as an individual.' However, learning support is not just about special needs; one pupil told us she was having extra maths lessons to support her through her physics A level.

Games, options, the arts: For horse-lovers this is a dream come true. The new equestrian centre (British Horse Society approved) is impressive. There are stables for 65 horses, BSJA jumps, a floodlit, outdoor all weather manège, a cross-country schooling field with a wide variety of different fences, a large indoor school with viewing gallery and a lecture room. The Olympic-sized outdoor arena with seats is used for jumping and dressage as well as seasonal shows. Competition squads regularly compete on and off site including National Schools Equestrian Association competitions and Stonar's own inter-schools one-day event championships.

Parents told us, 'The equestrian staff are highly knowledgeable.' Pupils with horses are up at 7am to muck out. Horses can be loaned or pupils can earn a riding lesson by working as a stable help. Around 50 per cent of pupils ride, but at various levels; some may own a horse, take qualifications and compete, others may just have a weekly riding lesson. And it's not just about the riding; stable management skills are taught too. However, the main priority at Stonar is academic studies and pupils told us that however passionate they are about horses, schoolwork cannot suffer.

Other activities include all the traditional sports, but one parent did suggest that other options would be welcome. Good sports facilities including a swimming pool; lessons from pre-prep up to year 12. The annual NACE Sports Olympics was hosted at Stonar recently.

In the prep there's a progressive sports programme: pupils have lessons up to four times a week in basketball, tennis, rugby, athletics, swimming and gymnastics. Plus there's a sports performance programme (football, hockey and cricket) for older talented pupils.

Main art studio is above the sixth form centre, kitted out with kiln and adjoining photography studio and dark room. Separate sixth form studio. High standard of art and photography on display. Latest addition is a DT suite (will become a curriculum subject in 2019).

The newish head of drama is shaking things up a little; one excited girl told us that he used to run a London theatre company and has 'contemporary' ideas. Traditionally, the school has alternated the main annual production between musicals (Guys and Dolls, Oklahoma) and Shakespeare plays. This year something different may be on the cards. Speech and drama available as well as LAMDA and RADA qualifications. The prep school has a classic nativity play every year as well as a large summer production for all of years 3-6; recently, Scheherazade.

Plenty of music groups including choir, chamber choir, wind band and orchestra and plenty of opportunities to perform. The annual NACE music festival is a highlight, bringing pupils from around the world together to perform. A fantastic opportunity and great fun, by all accounts. In the prep school there are termly musical assemblies and larger theatre performances twice a year. Formal carol concerts take place in Bath Abbey, plus musical concerts in the Wiltshire Music School.

Extracurricular activities aplenty. Sixth formers must do at least one club, younger years two. There's everything from sports to debating. DofE popular. Sixth formers run lunchtime clubs (Science Base and Maths Base) to help younger pupils.

Plenty of trips including ski trips and exchanges. One parent said, 'My two daughters have had opportunities to visit other NACE schools with sports, academic and choir groups.' There's a biannual trip to a sister school in Barcelona for years 5 to 8. Pupils stay in a 'very posh' hotel and go to the partner school every day, immersing themselves in Catalan life and studying Gaudi. Other trips include outdoor challenge residentials for years 3 and 4. Sixth formers take part in charity expeditions to Romania, Borneo or Kenya. Fundraising events are innovative – baths of jelly was one.

Boarding: Stonar offers full or flexi boarding, no weekly. Mainly full boarders with few below year 7.

Some 65 per cent are from overseas including Europe, America, Australia, China, Holland, Nigeria, Russia and South Africa. Around a third of these (mostly those from France, Germany and Spain) are short stay boarders, usually for one term. Parents and pupils are positive about this; 'My younger daughter spent a half term holiday in Madrid at the invitation of a boarder from Spain. It really is one big happy family!'

Three boarding houses, all of which have had a makeover (thanks to NACE). Ganbrook is above reception and houses younger pupils. York is the sixth form girls' house and is very much part of the school campus. Hart, a grade II listed farmhouse with a new boys' boarding wing, is a short stroll away, set amongst the teachers' houses. All houses have decent sized rooms in doubles or singles for sixth formers, and dorms of four for younger pupils. Common rooms are large with plenty of sofas and a TV but lacked decoration or homely touches on our visit. Perhaps this was because it was the beginning of the year? Hopefully the boarders will be able to put their stamp on it now (absolutely, yes, the school confirmed). Good kitchens for snacks. Latest exciting addition is the new social area fitted with a bar (older pupils are allowed two ciders over a week), a projector and a Wii.

Parents spoke highly of houseparents and 'the caring environment'. Plus, they told us, there's a great deal of fun; 'baking cakes, playing games, talent shows, movie and pizza nights...Even when we relocated to be closer to the school, they still wish to board as they love school life so much!' Day pupils often stay for the evening activities (mocktails, canapes and science nights are favourites) and everybody gets two free sleepovers per term.

No exeats; pupils are free to go home any weekend. School weekends are filled with trips to Bath, Laser Quest or Cotswolds Water Park. Younger pupils have to join in but older pupils have more freedom. Sixth formers can go out for up to five hours alone, and from year 10 groups of four can go to Bath for the day.

Background and atmosphere: Stonar was originally established at Stour House in Sandwich in 1895. It relocated to its current location in Wiltshire at the beginning of the Second World War. Cottles Park is a grade II listed mansion set in rural countryside about eight miles from Bath. Riding was firmly established back in 1934.

Since 2013, NACE has been funding Stonar as its flagship English school; new buildings and refurbishments have transformed it, giving it a modern edge and an international feel. Pupils now have an exciting programme of cultural and academic exchanges and events with schools in the NACE group.

As the number of boys grows, more upgrades and developments are inevitable. But the head aims to keep the school 'family-sized,' remaining flexible and providing individual support. One pupil may be passionate about riding, another an aspiring musician, another may need learning support; all can be looked after well at Stonar, the head told us. The addition of boys to the senior school (since 2016) is undoubtedly changing the dynamics of what has always been 'a traditional girls' school.' On our visit we felt the change was being fully embraced by pupils and teachers alike.

Parents say, 'The school is a good mix and has a nice feel to it. The size of the school and community gives it a family feel and it's not too overwhelming.' Prep school and nursery are very much part of the school. Facilities are shared and little ones can be seen playing out on the front lawn of the main house every lunchtime. Inside, the main hall, used for assemblies, performances and drama, is central, with classrooms adjoining. Upstairs on a mezzanine level is the library, fitted out with cosy beanbag areas under the wooden rafters. Outside there are playgrounds, a play area with sandpit, a nursery sensory garden and a forest school for the younger years. The whole school comes together for celebrations, carols at Bath Abbey and the summer fete.

'The grounds are amazing and my girls go for lovely hacks around the school parkland,' one parent enthused. The actual campus is a mix of old and new. It's easy to navigate and compact. Traditional wooden-style chemistry labs contrast with the modern physics laboratories. Library is a good size, equipped with PCs. Sarum, a cedar-clad classroom block opened in 2017, houses humanities and languages, along with an ICT suite. The sixth form area has also been upgraded with a plush café and outside decking area.

S

Technology has improved dramatically in recent years. Wifi works well across the site and mobile signal has improved (not that phones are allowed). Several ICT suites with 3D printers, plus iPads available in language and science lessons. Recent addition of Show My Homework App is 'brilliant' according to sixth formers. In the prep, the ICT suite is used for a computer science curriculum that involves programming and robotics – 'the children love it,' the head told us.

There are hymns and prayers in assembly but pupils told us this is 'not a particularly religious school'. It is, however, a traditional school, and a strong house system carries pupils from prep to senior school. Prefect system too – our guides all wore cloaks for the tour. Plus there's a school council and 'committees for everything,' we were told.

Stonar is a 'no-nuts' school; pupils reported, 'Veggie options are always tasty; never an afterthought.'

Pastoral care, well-being and discipline: 'Nurturing environment,' parents told us. And pupils agreed; teachers are approachable and helpful and 'everybody knows each other,' we were told. One mother told us that her daughter, who had been bullied at a previous school, felt reassured by teachers who not only worked her hard but let her 'play hard and, most importantly, be herself.'

Discipline is based around asking pupils to question their actions and consequences. One parent told us, 'I really like it that there aren't reams of ill-thought-through rules; rather, the children are really encouraged to think about values instead.'

Nurses (very popular for chats, according to our guides) hold daily drop-in sessions at the health and well-being centre. Counsellor available once a week.

Pupils and parents: The prep school is co-ed throughout and the senior school is expected to be fully co-ed by September 2019.

Pupils we met were happy to be back at school after the summer holidays. They were enthusiastic about Stonar, well-spoken, and confident. One girl told us, 'it really isn't a case of just going to school and then going home at the end of the day; it's a whole community thing – there's much more going on than just school.' Another girl said she was sold on Stonar after reading Mallory Towers books.

Good communication. One parent said, 'I have even had same day responses sent at the weekend!' Another added, 'Be it from the head to the tutor and everyone in between, we feel we have had all matters dealt with quickly, professionally but in a friendly, supportive and helpful manner.' There is a weekly newsletter plus the head holds informal weekly drop-in breakfast sessions for parents.

Entrance: Open days and taster events available. For entry to the prep school, literacy and numeracy are assessed as well as social interactions and approaches to learning. The learning support team will assess on a second visit if necessary. Nursery from 3, open all year round.

For entry to the senior school, entrance exam to assess strengths and weaknesses – Stonar is a non-academically selective school. For sixth form entry, school reports and an interview with the head. If English is a second language pupils must take an EAL exam and a maths paper.

Parents told us, 'The site makes transition much less stressful between prep and senior...it is not daunting.' One parent whose child started mid-year said they were 'happy from day one.'

Exit: Around 80 per cent of pupils move from the prep to senior, and 60 per cent stay on for sixth form. Some 80 per cent of sixth formers go to university. One medic in 2018; destinations included Loughborough, Queen's Belfast, York, UCL, St Andrews, Liverpool, Kent and Plymouth. Old girls include big names in riding such as junior and young rider gold medallist Georgie Spence, and twice Olympic short-lister Lucy Weigersma; actor Romola Garai and controversial author Gitta Sereny. Boys soon to be added.

Money matters: Scholarships offered for entry into years 7, 9 and 12 for academia plus art, drama, music, sport and riding. Sixth form scholarships also available.

Remarks: Stonar is transforming itself from a traditional girls' school into a modern co-ed with a strong international influence. New buildings keep popping up and makeovers have been swift; this school is definitely embracing change. However, it isn't losing sight of what makes it special: it's a small school that treats pupils as individuals. You don't need to be horsey to go here, but with facilities like this you will probably end up having the odd lesson – why wouldn't you?

Stover School

Stover, Newton Abbot, Devon TQ12 6QG

Ages 3–18 **Pupils** 400 **Sixth form** 35 **Boarders** 33 full; 7 weekly/flexi

Fees: Day £8,220 – £12,780; Boarding £18,450 – £26,190 pa

01626 354505
www.stover.co.uk

Head: Since 2014, Richard Notman BSc. Studied finance and stats at Birmingham University but soon discovered he was not made to be an auditor. After taking his PGCE in Manchester, he spent the next eight years in inner-city comps before teaching maths at Withington Girls School and becoming head of maths at Alderley Edge School for Girls. From there he went to Longridge Towers, Northumberland as deputy head, and finally Cundall Manor School, Yorkshire as head teacher.

'A breath of fresh air', said one parent. Some major changes are under way and parents have been impressed so far. 'He has focused the staff on the bigger picture and has given a renewed energy across the school.' Pupils are 'very inspired by his assemblies and messages he is getting across.' Lives on site with his wife and two children who attend the prep school.

Head of prep school: Since 2016, David Burt, previously head of primary at Compass International School, Madinat Khalif, Qatar. He has a degree in geography and sociology and a PGCE in primary education. Originally from the Isle of Wight, he is a keen fisherman, sportsman and avid gym-goer. Married with two young children.

Academic matters: At GCSE in 2018, 31 per cent A*-A/9-7 grades. At A level, 20 per cent A*/A and 39 per cent A*-B. BTecs offered in home economics, sport, ICT and performing arts. Maths is a strong subject with top grades at both levels. Stover has performed well in recent Regional Maths Challenges. Chemistry another strong subject with three students recently winning places at the prestigious Salters Chemistry camps. Photography very popular at A level. Spanish is taught from reception and French from year 3.

Stover welcomes pupils of all abilities. One parent said, 'It's a non-selective school and does very well in terms of exam results given its mixed ability (and after the grammar schools cream the top academics off).' A boarding school with 15 per cent of overseas students, and English is not everyone's first language; this is sometimes reflected in the grades. Parents speak highly of the learning support department, 'When extra help is required they have the staff to support your child and our daughter was given her own "adult" in maths to sit with her and help her on a one-to-one basis, which helped hugely.' One-to-one specialist support for autism or Asperger's is available.

Stover is setting up 'bring-your-own-device' and is planning to invest heavily in a new (and safe) server instead of upgrading equipment. The ISI inspectors reported that 'teaching was excellent,' but we heard some concerns from parents about its quality. One said, 'I think there should be a review of the current teaching staff to ensure any weaker members of the team receive up-to-date training to help them improve their methods.'

Games, options, the arts: Extensive grounds and good sports facilities. Pupils 'relish the 60+ acres at Stover.' There are six all-weather floodlit tennis courts (some recently resurfaced), netball courts, a gym, plus football, rugby, hockey and cricket pitches. The only drawback is that Stover is a small school and there aren't always enough players of the same standard to make winning teams. One parent said, 'They seem to punch above their weight and have won hockey and netball leagues recently against much bigger schools.' However, other parents agreed that there's room for improvement: they would like to see 'a bit more sport and a few more fixtures in the senior school,' as well as 'investment in a school swimming pool.' Extracurricular activities include table tennis (big here), judo, fencing, clay shooting and more recently a Stover riding team. With the school on the edge of the moors, D of E and Ten Tors are popular. Links with the Devon Schools Sports Partnership enables other local schools to make use of the grounds, and they recently hosted the Devon Schools' Area Athletics Cross-Country Championships.

Good music department. One parent said her daughter 'has been inspired by the head of music....they have nurtured her talent; she was very disengaged with it when she first joined.' Most pupils learn an instrument – the ukulele is popular in the prep school – and there are plenty of concerts and groups to join: the orchestra, brass and jazz bands and choirs. Another parent explained, 'Stover has several choirs and is very good at singing and music. They win almost everything in local and regional competitions. My son's year even went to Bruges Cathedral after winning one competition.' Productions, assemblies and concerts all take place in the dome-shaped Jubilee Hall, which also houses a recording studio and practice rooms (more rooms recently added).

As well as music, performing arts and public speaking are strong themes throughout the prep and senior school. Regular productions and plays, including one each year for the prep and pre-prep. 'The ones I have seen are very well produced. I went to Bugsy Malone the other year and the Match Girls last year. So, very different ones,' said one parent. Stover also offers LAMDA speech and drama lessons with Stagecentre plus performance exams.

The art department is in separate building with art downstairs (sixth form area at the back) and photography upstairs. Art studio the latest add on. Pupils 'love being able to go outdoors to learn – in science and art they will often make use of the natural world around them.' Great displays and some impressive work including a John Lennon mural, and large fish sculptures inspired by a recent trip to the aquarium. We were particularly impressed by the photography upstairs, including some portraits taken on a trip to Brick Lane. Good take up for A level art.

Clubs take place at lunchtime, with a late-ish school finishing time of 4.30pm. Mixed messages from parents on this. It suits some, but not all. When we were there we saw the Ukulele Club doing karaoke, and the Ready Steady Fry club had just finished making dough in the well-designed home economics room. Other activities, apart from the usual offerings, include bush-craft, astronomy, Dragons' Den, the Raving Reporters, Knitting Club and Man Choir.

Day trips from reception, residential trips from year 4, with a night away, then a three-day trip to Cornwall in year 5, three days in Mount Batten for year 6. As well as language trips abroad, there are regular theatre trips, art trips to galleries locally and in London, field trips to Dartmoor, history trips to Flanders, and a recent sixth form expedition to Tanzania.

Boarding: Stover is not as 'regimented' as other boarding schools, head told us. Admissions criteria now focuses more on language (interviews by Skype). There is a mix of nationalities (currently 17), with pupils coming from Bulgaria, Serbia, Russia as well as China, Vietnam, Spain, Germany and Cuba, though Brits are now in the majority in both houses. The plan is to recruit mainly full boarders and offer the flexi option in a limited and controlled fashion – they don't want it to 'feel like a motel.' Short stays will still be offered during the summer as these serve as good tasters, and day pupils will still be able to take advantage of the wrap-around care.

Girls board on the opposite side of the main school building to the boys. Both areas have been recently refurbished. The boys are lucky to be in the original part of the building with high ceilings, ornate cornices, huge bay windows with shutters, original fireplaces, domed ceilings, arched hallways and great views. It's very tidy; the military background of the houseparent keeps them in check, apparently. He's also known for getting the boys together for regular evening chats round the dining table. Cheerful rules boards dotted around – live, laugh, love etc – make it feel homely. The large dorms feel light and spacious.

The girls' side, without the original features, is less impressive. The common room felt stuffy, and although it was equipped with PCs, a Wii, a drinks area and dining table, it didn't have the same inviting feel as the boys' room. On the plus side, the girls do have single, double and treble rooms as well as dorms. When we were there the girls were obviously getting ready for the prom, dresses proudly displayed on most wardrobes. Good-sized showers and bath facilities. In fact all the facilities are good – kitchen areas, drinks area and laundry facilities all promote independent living as much as possible.

Usual rules for mobile phones and such, but all seemed pretty relaxed. The boarders here really get to know each other, and the staff, well. Parents say it has a 'friendly, family atmosphere.' Some students even come back for more. Gap year students help out with admin duties, evening activities like football or tennis, and weekend trips to the cinema, the beach, shopping and just recently Stonehenge and Thorpe Park.

Background and atmosphere: Stover School is set in beautiful grounds, 64 acres of parkland located between Dartmoor and the sea. Founded in 1932 by two sisters on the Stover Estate, the object was to help pupils lead independent lives. Boys and girls have been in the prep school since it started in 1996, and boys in the senior school since 2005. The Clock House, built in 1843 and housing the prep, was originally stables and is set around a charming cobbled courtyard. Several of the classrooms have interconnecting doors and are linked by very narrow hallways and stairs. It's small, some would say it feels cramped; others would say it's full of character.

The main house, built of granite ashlar, is an impressive sight as you drive in. With its double flight of portico steps it wouldn't look out of place on a film set. Inside, the grand entrance hall continues to impress with high ceilings, beautiful plasterwork and ornate fireplaces. The school is proud of its heritage and cups, plaques and photos adorn the corridors. The rest of the school is housed in various well-designed buildings and wooden outbuildings in the perfectly manicured grounds.

S

The Millennium building is modern and bright with science labs downstairs, and maths upstairs. Floor to ceiling windows, new equipment and colourful murals by a teacher make the labs cheerful and inviting. Small class sizes also mean that there is always enough equipment. Fish, gerbils and even an adopted stray ginger cat add to the happy vibe here. Recent trips include The Big Bang and the Eden Project. Upstairs are two bright and sunny maths rooms, linked by a large balcony, also used as form rooms.

Separate wooden buildings or cabins are used for English, humanities and modern languages. All freshly painted; we could still smell it.

Amongst the acres of land, there's a large playground with a sandpit, a wooden pirate ship, a football pitch and even an outdoor chess board. The new outdoor classroom has replaced the forest school that was destroyed by bad weather. There's a pond, a fire pit and parents have recently planted fruit trees. They are keen to make as much use of the grounds as possible with activities like bushcraft and gardening club. The nursery is next to the playground and is a homely space for toddlers.

All pupils agree full-heartedly on two things at Stover. Firstly, it's friendly. And secondly, the food is excellent. We saw long queues of hungry pupils looking forward to the curry of the day. One said, 'I love Roastie Wednesday and Fishy Friday!' and apparently lots of pupils happily get dropped off early in time for the boarders' breakfast.

Parents like 'the friendly, family atmosphere.' One told us, 'We chose Stover for a number of reasons – yes, the grounds are lovely and the buildings beautiful but a school needs to give more than that. We were inspired by the ethos of the school as a whole. You don't have to get the highest scores in maths and they aren't going to force your child into a shape they don't naturally fit. [Stover] helps them to excel in the areas they have a passion for.'

Pastoral care, well-being and discipline: Well-behaved, well spoken and polite. Good behaviour is part of life here and is instilled at a young age – walk into any prep class and they will all stand. The pupils we spoke to seemed happy and proud of their school. Due to its small size, problems are spotted quickly and dealt with swiftly. Everybody knows everybody, but there is a solid support network of house parents, tutors, the school nurse, the school counsellor and the school chaplain if needed. The chaplain takes an active role in school life as well as regular collective worship and running the Christian Union Group.

The house system runs throughout the prep and senior school and gives pupils a sense of belonging. There are three houses, but strangely they are then split into boys and girls, making it six houses in all. The pupils we spoke to had no idea why it was like this as the only aspect they are separated for is sport. Presumably this is just a hangover from days gone by when boys and girls didn't mix. Strange that it hasn't changed with the times.

Pupils and parents: Day pupils from Newton Abbot, Exeter, South Hams, Torbay, Bovey Tracey, Plymouth. Boarders mainly from overseas. Parents mostly in professional occupations. Good bus service. Wrap-around care offered from 7.30am to 6.30pm for 6 year olds and above. Former pupil Debra Newbury awarded the MBE for her services to transatlantic rowing.

Communication is good, there's even a parents' app for news, events and photos. Plus Soundcloud to access all the latest music. Friends of Stover are always busy fundraising, and the upcoming Summer Ball was causing a bit of a buzz. 'There is also a monthly Friend's of Stover coffee morning where parents meet with the headmaster and his wife, and can exchange information, chat and generally catch up, which is lovely,' said one mother.

Entrance: Main entry points at 4, 7 and 11. By interview, school reports, and a taster day where academic ability and attitude to learning are assessed in an informal manner.

One parent told us, 'New pupils are embraced.' Another agreed, saying, 'We all found the entrance process very good. The older two started half way through the year but they didn't seem to have any problems fitting in and finding their feet. The staff were welcoming, helpful and informative and communication with us was good. Since starting we have not had one single morning that they haven't wanted to go to school.'

A system of parent class reps helps new parents settle in too – 'one parent per class keeps a database of details so that round-emails can be distributed with details of coffee mornings, birthday parties and play-dates – you soon feel like part of the furniture even when you've only been at the school for a matter of months!'

Exit: Most prep school pupils move up to the senior school, with a few peeling off to local grammars. Around 60 per cent leave after GCSEs, mostly to non-fee-paying alternatives. Popular university choices are London, Plymouth, Exeter, Bristol, Cardiff and Falmouth.

Money matters: Academic, music, art and sport scholarships available at most ages, up to 20 per cent of day fees. Two means-tested scholarships at year 10 and sixth form, the Maurice Key and Laurus scholarships offering up to 100 per cent of day fees. A maths scholarship is available to international sixth form students covering 25 per cent of fees at Stover and 10 per cent of fees at Plymouth University. Armed forces and police force are offered a 10 per cent discount.

Remarks: Stover is a small, friendly school. It's for mixed abilities, and for those that wouldn't suit a larger mainstream setting. It's undergoing some major changes. For the better. Everyone agrees there are 'exciting times ahead'. As one parent put it, 'It was a good school in many ways, but now I think it has the chance to be really outstanding.' And having met the heads, we think this is just the beginning. One to watch.

Sunny Hill Preparatory School

Linked with Bruton School for Girls

179

Bruton School for Girls, Sunny Hill, Bruton, Somerset BA10 0NT

Ages Girls 3-11, boys 3-7 **Pupils** 50 **Boarders** Up to 10 (from year 4)

Fees: Day £8,505 – £13,116; Boarding £21,300 – £23,880 pa

01749 814427
www.brutonschool.co.uk

Head of prep: Since 2010, Helen Snow BEd (50s), previously deputy head. A breadth of teaching experience preceding her arrival at Sunny Hill (elementary teaching in the US, secondary in the UK, a stint in Berlin – some occasioned by her husband's job moves) means she truly knows that primary is where her heart lies. 'I've taken the best bits of the national curriculum and left the rubbish', she says: outdoor learning and bushcraft are big here and the school is a forest school (there's a nature reserve on site in a former railway cutting), leading on naturally to the rigours of DofE in the senior school.

Warm and cuddly (we imagine), one father described her as 'everything you would want in a prep school headmistress', with the sort of compassion and vision which led her to set up an office in the school for a father whose child had broken her leg, but who wanted to be in school. A lover of the outdoors, Mrs Snow has two black labradors (and a teenage daughter); she is currently learning to ski – 'It reminds me of how it feels to learn something from scratch,' she says. She also enjoys less hearty delights such as gastronomy and theatre and possibly (though not necessarily) her current training to be an ISI inspector.

Entrance: Non selective from nursery upwards; meeting with head and maths and English assessments for entry into prep. Scholarships (academic, music, art, all-round) are on offer.

Exit: Boys leave after year 2; the majority of girls to the senior school by means of verbal and non-verbal reasoning tests, for diagnostic purposes only.

Remarks: Sunny by name and sunny by nature, the prep school sits at the top of the Bruton School site, a short walk from the senior school. Though very small, it benefits from the facilities and specialist languages and games staff of its big sister, whilst retaining its own cosy atmosphere. 'In and of itself, the prep school is none too impressive, but its alliance with the senior school makes up for a lot,' was the cool appraisal of one father – but even he would surely have been impressed with the dissection of a cow's heart (from an obliging local butcher) we saw in a year 6 biology lesson. (The squeamish were taught from a 3D model by a kindly TA.)

Non-selective it may be – very strong value added – but there is no shortage of scope or range (or fun) in the academic offering, which caters equally well for the brightest little sparks. We loved the wall frieze of This Little Piggy captioned by the Latin club – 'Vii vii vii usque domum'. 'Whatever the ability of the girl, we'll do jolly well by her', as the head says.

Plenty on offer after school too: 'My daughter would stay until 5.30pm every day in some club or other,' said one mother: 'folk club, netball, judo, viola...' Wrap around care from 7.45am-6pm. The pastoral side and the immense care the school takes over every girl in it are hugely appreciated by parents, too. 'The staff really get to know the children and don't just tell you the things you want to hear, they tell it how it is', added the same mother, who had no notes of criticism whatsoever. Sports provision is good, though small year groups inevitably mean mixed aged teams.

Boarding (officially from year 4, but occasionally younger in the case of one small girl we met whose elder sisters all board and who was determined not to miss out) takes place in the cosy old vicarage where all junior boarders (just a handful from the prep) up to year 9 are housed. Day girls are free to join in with weekend activities and intermittent sleepovers. In short, Sunny Hill can be summed up in the words of one exacting father, not given to hyperbole: 'The school can cope with the whole dynamic range academically, but it will get your girl where she wants to go. My daughter is just blissfully happy there'.

Talbot Heath Junior School

Linked with Talbot Heath School

180

Rothesay Road, Bournemouth BH4 9NJ

Ages 3-11 **Pupils** 250 **C of E**

Fees: £6,603 – £11,754 pa

01202 763360
www.talbotheath.org

Head: Since September 2018, Liz Pugh, previously deputy head. Degree in law and history from Oxford Brookes; joined the school in 2010 as year 2 teacher, becoming year 5 teacher and SEN coordinator, then promoted to deputy head in January 2017. Her daughter, now grown up, attended the school.

Entrance: Not selective until year 2, from when girls are tested in English, maths and verbal reasoning, with a head teacher's report.

Exit: Nearly all to the senior school. The rest to local or other state schools.

Remarks: A lovely environment, surrounded by woods (although the pines do gloom a little). Woodland area with tents and wigwams for the early years – used under supervision, of course. Flocks are watched closely here – few trips to A&E from this school. Hard surface play areas to use when the woods are muddy. The juniors have a special area of woodland, carefully fenced off, complete with log cabin. And no, they can't climb trees.

Rather forbidding architecture, daunting on approach, though windows attractive 30s fare. Lovely modern hall with glorious wooden roof, and craft area upstairs. Juniors and pre-prep occupy separate wings, with a courtyard eco-garden separating them – it looked a bit sparse, but it was carefully explained that this is a working garden of useful plants – a description that could aptly apply to this school.

Inside the school a feeling of order and purpose dominates – displays are as likely to be of written work, as of art – and goodness, the handwriting is good. Clearly something emphasised here. Girls were keen to show off their work, and very proud of their efforts. There was much enthusiasm in the classrooms, hands reaching to the ceiling and girls practically leaving their seats in an effort to answer questions.

A well stocked and popular library: as well as the usual books, topic bags also contain toys and games relating to the book's subject. Three computer rooms; just a couple of iPads, though.

Academically rigorous – girls in year 2 are doing mixed tables tests each week, though it was emphasised that they are trying to beat their own score and time, and the ability level will vary immensely between the girls. English and science particularly strong, said one parent. Class sizes no more than 20. Despite the focus on academic work here, a lot of girls get tutored for entrance to the (ferociously competitive) grammar schools.

Girls were friendly and articulate, with ready smiles. Leapt to their feet as we toured the school and were very prompt with their 'good morning' chant. School is strong on discipline; or 'strict in a nice way,' as one parent put it. 'Old fashioned values [and] a lot of respect,' said another. Praise for exceptional performance, but also exceptional behaviour of any sort. Harold the toy hare goes home each week with someone who has been especially kind.

Community and the high level of pastoral support greatly praised by parents: 'they always find time for the girls'. Very strong on anti-bullying – anything dealt with very efficiently, agree parents. All girls 'feel slights' and the school says it manages them carefully. They will sit down with someone who is upset; but it often just comes down to thoughtless comments.

Transition (at 11) between junior and senior schools is easy, say parents. Year 6s go to the senior school daily for lunch to help them find their feet. Own school exam to gain entry to senior school. Girls are well prepared and most, but not all, pass. For those who don't make it, every assistance will be given to help find a new school.

Communication with parents through learning journals for the early years, then link books, and homework diaries for juniors. These books are more than just a reading record, and contain in some cases a significant dialogue between parents and school. Targets appropriate to child – so those in reception varied from writing own name, to finding someone to sit next to on the mat.

Learning support available for those with mild learning disorders. One-to-one support available for no extra charge, and support can be given to those who need a bit of extra help in the run up to the senior school entrance exam.There are also maths and literacy clinics available for those who need a bit of an extra shove – always in assembly time. 'It's important that they don't miss out on social time.'

Not a posh school. A school where many parents make sacrifices to pay the (reasonable) fees. Typically both parents work, and they don't have elaborate holidays.

T

Talbot Heath School

Linked with Talbot Heath Junior School

Rothesay Road, Bournemouth BH4 9NJ

Ages 11–18 **Pupils** 579 **Sixth form** 74 **Boarders** 24 full, 4 weekly, 12 flexi **C of E**

Fees: Day £14,403; Boarding £25,515 pa

01202 761881
www.talbotheath.org

Head: Since 2010, Angharad Holloway, previously head of MFL and IB at The Royal High School, Bath. Married, with two girls at the junior school. Mrs Holloway has made some 'fantastic changes,' said a parent, who described the the previous head as somewhat old fashioned. Not so Mrs Holloway, who is gently updating school, curriculum and thinking with a largely conservative constituency of parents. Lively energy – 'enthusiastic all the time,' said one mum. Not goaded by Jeremy Paxman on his visit, so unlikely to be shaken by much.

Keen her girls should have coping strategies for life, and teaches women and leadership to her 12 year olds, who end the course understanding not just about leadership, but also work/life balance and the right to flexible working. Teaches international politics to 11 year olds to broaden their horizons. Most desired quality for her girls on leaving school – resilience. Quite.

Academic matters: 'A first class education for girls,' say parents, who expect results – '[the] priority's always academic,' said one. And they generally achieve them. In 2018, 78 per cent of A levels were A*-B (49 per cent A*/A). GCSEs – 42 per cent A*-A/7-9 grades. 'We do it well,' says the head. 'We are not a hothouse, but [we] do wish each girl to give of her best.' It's not a school where it is cool to muck around. Girls are very aware of why they are there and the importance of exams – 'all the girls want to achieve,' said a parent – but there are light touches. One mum described how her daughter had the school webcam – situated in a nesting box in the woods – on while she revised, so she could keep an eye on the babies.

A great school for value added. Entry requirements not stringent, so the high standards are all the more remarkable. At least in part due (says the head) to being an all-girl environment where girls can flourish – there is not that 'second's hesitation' before a hand goes up. Attracts a number who didn't make the grammars, who do very well – 'I think it's because...the staff genuinely care that the girls do well. Parents' evenings are very businesslike – this is what we need to do for your daughter, and this is how we will do it.'

'Subjects are traditional,' said a parent, 'nothing weird.' It is a conventional and fairly short list (classical civilisation finds a natural home here), but with Mrs Holloway at the helm parents can be confident the girls are not being limited. Good take up (around 40 per cent) for A level chemistry and biology – the girls say the teaching of biology is outstanding. Physics is not so popular (just 10 per cent), and the results are less stellar. The head has set up a number of projects with local universities: music, drama – even forensic science; and of course there are her own pet subjects – international politics and women and leadership. EPQ also available. Languages are limited to French, Spanish and Latin, but they added extracurricular Italian to assist a girl who wanted to study modern languages at university, and attracted a number of other takers, all enthusiastic about achieving GCSE Italian in a year. 'They provide extra if they can,' said a parent.

Sixth formers spoke with great enthusiasm of coming into school with extracurricular questions about favourite subjects and discussing them with teachers during lunchtime – 'It's like we're exploring and learning about it together.' Lunchtime lectures are very popular with sixth formers – one spoke eagerly about listening to Professor Frances Ashcroft talking about ion channels: 'they suddenly fitted in to life.'

Learning support (free of charge) gets a thumbs up from the girls – apparently no stigma here. 'They help a friend with her spelling every week,' said one matter of factly. Around 10 per cent have support for a range of mild learning disabilities, and they can drop a subject to make life easier. Girls have the highest opinion of teachers, who apparently go out of their way to help those who are struggling. One pupil, who had what she described as a 'maths crisis', spoke with enormous praise and affection about the maths teacher who devoted so much time to helping her regain skills and confidence. Lunchtime maths and science clinics available for those who are struggling.

Girls who speak English as a second language are welcome, providing they pass the entrance exam. Specialist in-house EAL lessons, and will be supported by staff in class. Children from many countries, including Russia, Spain, Germany and Jordan.

Lots of change in the staff – around 50 per cent in the last four years (but largely due to retirement). Small class sizes (maximum of 20) please parents, who believe they promote good relationships between staff and pupils – and of course get those results.

Games, options, the arts: Dedication to sporting excellence described by parents as 'second to none'. Special tennis programme designed with the nearby West Hants tennis club. About 10 girls are enrolled on the programme, and it is sought after and pricey, though scholarships are available for talented players.

Some 20 girls at play at national level in sports including tennis, netball, rowing and badminton, and there are Youth Olympians among the pupils. School is small enough to tailor-make timetables, and flexible teaching accommodates those with training and competing commitments – or indeed musical talent. But genuine efforts are made to encourage all: some 56 rowers and 70 netball players of all abilities turn up to training sessions. One parent said they are always coming up with weird and wonderful sports to keep the girls engaged.

'[Sporting] facilities are not as good as at more expensive schools,' said a parent, 'things need to be bigger and better.' However, an indoor swimming pool is part of a brand new STEAM hub building that also includes a 600 seat auditorium with sound and lighting facilities, plus drama, art and design studios. Although facilities are not 'as fantastic as they could be...it doesn't really matter,' said one. 'The staff are the thing, and they're amazing, and they work really long hours.'

There are members of the National Youth Ballet, the National Youth Choir, the National Children's Orchestra, the National Youth Orchestra and Wessex Youth Orchestra. Many win classes at the Bournemouth Music Festival, and there are monthly informal concerts for parents and friends, as well as more formal affairs.

Drama is popular, likely to become more so with fantastic new facilities. There are five productions a year, using the black box or the decent sized stage in the school hall. Girls often write their own adaptions – The Lion, The Witch and The Wardrobe was in dress rehearsal when we visited, written by 14 GCSE drama pupils. Productions may be less than slick but the parents we spoke to appreciated the team spirit and the 'all hands on deck' feel, and pupils certainly have a wonderful time.

There's a well-attended debating society, very popular with girls after their stint with the head in international politics. Art is a strong department, say parents (and did we mention the new studios?).

Boarding: Glossy newish facilities in St Mary's boarding house (after a mediocre report from Ofsted). Spacious shared dormitories for years 6, 7, 8 and 9, with semi privacy created by desks and cupboards, all in crisp new pale wood. Own rooms from year 10.

Bathroom facilities clean and new – 'the shower's better than home,' said one girl feelingly. Food varies from average to good, depending on the chef that day, say boarders. Practice room with a piano, and comfy lounges with TV and Wifi. Boarders can have laptops, Kindles and phones – although latter removed at night.

The 40 or so boarders mix across age groups – which creates a family feel, says the housemistress. Boarders seem very happy and well cared for. Most stay at school for the weekend, and are kept busy with a variety of activities, from ice cream making and adventure days to archery and shooting, even a pamper afternoon with homemade facial scrubs (inspired by a trip to Lush).

Background and atmosphere: School formed in 1886 by Mary Broad to provide a first class liberal education for girls. She shocked the locals by exercising her girls on the local common and taking them on trips around Europe.

'Traditional' is a word which comes up a lot when speaking to parents (although the current head is certainly blowing away any remaining dusty elements). One parent liked it for being 'organised and friendly, [with a] structured discipline.' It is a disciplined environment – but although it didn't feel stifling, rebellious and disruptive girls would certainly stand out.

Rather foreboding buildings in the pine woods (but what a lovely smell). Some 30s charm, particularly a gorgeous gym (there's a modern sports hall too). Even has original WW2 bunker classroom, complete with toilet buckets bearing TH emblems. And of course there's the new STEAM hub.

One parent moved to the area for the selective grammars but fell for Talbot Heath. She 'loved the calmness...the silence during lessons, and the sense of purpose'. One pupil chose the school because it was the most welcoming, and they 'focused on me as an individual.' A sixth former said she felt she had learnt that you need to spend time doing things just because you enjoy them.

Navy uniform, with a super blue cloak for the juniors (or coat alternative for the self-conscious). No uniform for sixth formers; more comfortable than smart, these friendly and articulate girls have a tremendous sense of purpose. They like their sixth form common room with kitchen facilities, and they appreciate being treated more like adults, the tutorial feel of some of the lessons – cosy further maths lessons for two at the moment.

Communication good – school does take notice of feedback, said a parent who had protested about the large amount of homework in year 9. Another said 'food...is the biggest moan,' but she thought the school was trying to address the issue (on the day of our visit it varied from average pasta to excellent sticky toffee pudding). Parent Staff Society (PSS) meets every three months and responds to every point raised. Parent portal has got better recently, and the school is proud of its newish website.

Pastoral care, well-being and discipline: This is a strong community, and there is a great feeling of vigilance here. Teachers go out of their way to support pupils; parents had high praise for their efforts, and for the girls' tendency to encourage and care for each other – 'they positively want each other to succeed'.

Head says there is a strong ethos of respect and care, so those who don't follow this stand out a mile. School motto is 'honour before honours' (one does feel a hint of Malory Towers here). The school aims to resolve any issues rapidly, and through discussion: 'this is a talking school,' says the head. One parent described how a personality clash between her daughter and another child was sorted out amicably and quickly. Staff are very approachable, say parents, and it's easy to come in and talk.

Usual system of sanctions for unsatisfactory work or behaviour. No one we spoke to had come across drug taking of any sort – of course they experiment at some point, said one parent, but the strong school culture militates against it, at least on school premises.

Pupils and parents: Pupils arrive by bike, train and school buses. Most full boarders from overseas, plus Forces parents – also the tennis whizz kids, who work long days and find it helpful to be on site.

Some comfortably affluent parents, but most feel it's a big decision to pay for education, and those who fork out have academic results as their main priority. Typically both parents work, and they don't have elaborate holidays. Not a posh school.

Former pupils include Judge Cosgrave, Lady Faithful (social worker and reformer), Charlie Lee-Potter (journalist), Pat Smythe (show jumper), Natalie Clein (cellist), Dame Shirley Williams (politician), Kate Royal (opera singer), Nicole Faraday (actress), Caroline Gledhill (engineer) and Frances Ashcroft (geneticist).

Entrance: Own exam at 11+ – maths, English and verbal reasoning. Waiting lists for some years, currently 10-12. Most juniors pass the exam to progress to the senior school.

Exit: Loses some to the grammar, mostly for financial reasons, although around 25 per cent depart before sixth form to study something more unusual. After sixth form to universities all over eg Winchester, Exeter, Plymouth, Sheffield, Cardiff. Four medics and one vet in 2018.

Money matters: Parents say the school is cheaper than many independent schools in the area, and very good value for money. 'Prices could go up, and we would still go,' said one parent with enthusiasm. 'Bargain,' said another. Around a quarter of pupils are on scholarships or bursaries of around 10-20 per cent.

Remarks: Does what it says on the packet: a first class education for girls, provided with a great sense of purpose and vigour. Though academic, sport also strong, and excels in accommodating sporting and other extracurricular specialists. Feels like a very safe and caring environment. Better introduce boys yourself along the way though, suggested one parent, or some girls could go a bit crazy at university.

T

Taunton Prep and Pre-Prep School

Linked with Taunton School

Staplegrove Road, Taunton, Somerset TA2 6AE

Ages 0-13 **Pupils** 457 **Boarders** 22 full, 2 weekly (from 7 years)

Fees: Day £7,350 – £15,375; Boarding £14,685 – £25,500 pa

01823 703307
www.tauntonschool.co.uk

Headmaster: Since September 2017, Andrew Edwards BA PGCE. Early 50s. Also an all-rounder: degree in French and German, coaching qualifications in football, tennis and cricket, cellist to diploma standard, school inspector – and solicitor. Two years of lawyering in the City just didn't do it for him so he pluckily bundled sports kit, French text books and a cello into the boot of his disreputable Nissan Cherry and went peripatetic until snapped up by Cottesmore. Here he is 20+ years later having done time at Port Regis, Dumpton and Castle Court. Previously head of Park School, Bournemouth for the last six years.

He likes things just the way they are here, so no major engine rebuild planned, fine tuning only. Not a believer that an eye-catching USP is everything – 'There's nothing wrong with doing what other schools do, the important thing is to do them extremely well' – so no hey-look-at-us joy-riding, either. Not so much a continuity candidate, more a continuous improver. Parents feel that following recent restructuring and staff departures – for the best, all agree – a period of calm is in order. Mr Edwards is a believer in rigour, challenge and respect, but his educational philosophy has it its heart the s-factor. Smiles. The more the merrier. Sound a tad, we don't know, mawkish? Okay, so what better way to measure a school? Our view: Mr Edwards is a Good Thing, a good fit. As an all-rounder, he's exactly what his new school is. Following two relatively quickfire headships here parents will be pleased to know that he has his eye on a decent innings. Married to Robyn, also a teacher. Two boys.

Entrance: Non-selective. Start at 0 in the nursery or come any time from a local school or other prep schools if (big if) there's room. Overseas students join when they're ready from Taunton International Middle School. Taster days on request. Range of scholarships at 11+ for entry to year 7.

Exit: Pretty much everyone to the senior school, a natural progression and for most parents the whole point. No one is de-selected; this is a cradle-to-adulthood school.

Remarks: Taunton isn't one of those towns that tops any tables for loveliness, well-being or up-and-comingness. Closer inspection reveals that it's no-one's best kept secret, either. When you discover that the town is the beneficiary of a regeneration scheme your expectancy levels may droop some more, leading you to suppose that its schools aren't necessarily going to be anything to write home about. And there you'd be bang wrong. Just as we were. The town is home to a couple of blisteringly good state schools ('outstanding' in Ofstedspeak) and three independents. When it comes to education, the good people of Taunton and environs are spoiled for choice. So how do you choose? One parent we spoke to chose Taunton Prep

School – TPS they call it in everydayspeak – because 'We liked the way it made us feel.' Much to be said for that.

TPS occupies its own self-contained campus bang next door to the senior school in the leafy northern outskirts of the town, bounded by the railway to the south and the A358 to the north. It has none of the huddledness of so many town schools, while the spacious playing fields further mitigate any urban vibe. It feels like its own place. Buildings a mix of Victorian and later, nicely maintained. That's not all: we have never seen a cleaner school nor have we met cleaners who so much enjoyed their work. Shares its chapel with the senior school. Established to educate the sons of dissenters but not Methodists. In place of foundational sectarianism we found only indulgent broad church values. An international contingent, around 10 of them, feed through from the international middle school – TSIMS (tee-sims) – when their English is up to it.

Demographically there's no pinning TPS down. It's popular with hardworking local entrepreneurs and businesspeople wanting the best for their children and for whom this is their first experience of private education. They told us that the school didn't talk down to them like others they looked round, it's not 'grand and intimidating'. TPS is also attractive to parents for whom private is second nature and who like the (relatively) wide social spectrum here. TPS has long been attractive to Forces families, for whom the school very much sets out its stall – to officers and other ranks equally. The draw for them, as for other nomadic families, is that TPS, together with the pre-prep and the senior school, gives them a fixed point from 0-18. So: not a muddy-wellie school, nor a set apart school, but a modern school very much part of, and involved in, the local community. To use a word du jour, inclusive.

Academically a very safe pair of hands across the board – just the right blend of extra-mile dedication and judicious professionalism. Every subject is well resourced. Parents of bright children tell us their child is stretched but not to snapping point; parents whose children need support tell us that's what they get, and never in such a way as to make them feel like dawdlers. Lots of praise for the teachers. One parent said, 'You fire off an email last thing at night and get an almost instant reply – it can be embarrassing'. Plenty of celebration of achievement according to your lights – a word oft-repeated by parents is 'nurturing'. One pupil told us she'd really taken off at the school and showed us written work which demonstrated sound understanding of the parenthetical comma. You don't see them very often these days. Maths exceedingly strong – terrific showings in Maths Challenge and an inspirational head of department who left one of your profoundly innumerate reviewers feeling there may still be hope. DT especially strong. Thinking skills a new addition to the academic mix. The head speaks of the children being on a 'GCSE continuum' which makes sense when pretty much everyone goes on the senior school. Lots of dialogue with the senior school and, big strength, some teacher sharing, especially in languages, classics and sport. Currently working on a joint IT strategy with senior school, a bring-your-own-device scheme 'the intention for the future'. IT has just enjoyed a £600,000 investment. Good blend of male:female teachers, roughly a third male. Saturday school til lunchtime for years 7 and 8. Special educational needs addressed by a team headed up by a head of learning success (neatly standing a downside on its head). The full spectrum of SENs, mostly, note, on the mild side – 10 per cent on the register. Architecturally wheelchair-unfriendly but they're willing to put themselves out for visually and hearing impaired children and wobbly walkers – head expresses a willingness to 'address the needs of any prospective pupil and see what reasonable adjustments could be made'.

Former England batsman Marcus Trescothick coaches cricket here and former England netball team manager Lisa Manley coaches netball so yes, this is a school that takes its sport seriously, generates good stats and crowns a sportsperson of the week at every Monday morning assembly. A very few parents feel sport is taken a bit too seriously, worry that it distracts from the academics and don't relish traipsing in of a Saturday evening and collecting their child from a bus. But maxing out every daylight hour in the week is what a good prep school does; it's all bang for your buck, and busy children who do lots, studies show, get the best results. Around a dozen of the best children rise to county level. No also-rans if they can help it: they try to give everyone the chance to play for their school at least once. It doesn't matter a bit if you're not sporty, if a thing's worth doing, it's worth doing inexpertly, it's meant to be fun. Decent mix of other sports on offer. Facilities are on the amazing side, many their own, some shared with the senior school.

Not many prep schools have their own performing arts centre but TPS does. Not many prep schools have quite such a passionate head of performing arts, either. We were particularly beguiled by five little French hornists parping away pluckily. The French horn is a frightfully difficult instrument at any age and to see so many seemed to set an aspirational benchmark. One mum we spoke to was taken by surprise when her son, having previously evinced neither interest nor aptitude, suddenly took to the trumpet, and this after a daughter had been identified as having an unsuspectedly good voice – 'They spot talents you never knew they had'. Here's a thing: in years 4, 6 and 8 everyone plays a part in a musical for which a whole week of all-day rehearsals is set aside. Everyone. The whole week. Don't parents march on the school demanding proper lessons? No they don't, they reckon the benefit outweighs any academic impact, they trust the school completely. Given that this is not a school whose parents are the sort to allow it to play fast and loose with scholastic attainment, what does that tell you? Lots of performance opportunities, formal and informal, at some of which parents join in. Senior choir sings in churches abroad. All in all, a rich and very classy mix. Heaps of lunchtime and after-school activities on offer. Go home at 4pm or stay to 5.30pm for clubs and prep (homework) periods.

Parents praise pastoral support and rapid response to glitches arising. First port of call is the form tutor. Head's door is ever open – stride on in. No prefect system; it was abolished by the previous head to universal crossness and dismay – a parent told us, 'It's the only time I went to the school and complained' – and replaced by year 8 councillors. Senior pupils apply for a role in writing then stand for election by everyone, including teachers. All are trained in peer mentoring. And it has all come good, making for a kinder environment with higher mutual respect levels and without saying goodbye to leadership opportunities. Parents praise the way the school celebrates kindness and 'is quick to support self-esteem'. You quickly pick up on the social atmosphere here because everyone is so naturally nice and courteous, welcoming of strangers, and that's not something you find everywhere by any means. Try this: flip through the photos in the school magazine – the unstaged ones. Don't all parents want their children to look like these?

Some 20+ children are full boarders, around 10 per cent of the roll, a number small enough to make you justly jittery. Aren't these simply left-behind children? Lots of schools couldn't make this work, not with so few. But TPS does. The accommodation is clean and snug. There's access to senior school facilities. The staff are brilliant, that's key, and the children are clearly well looked after and happy. Our misgivings evaporated. In the course of the year around a third of all pupils board. All flexi options available down to sleepover, and if you're caught late at work the boarding staff will look after your child till you come to collect.

The nursery and pre-prep is self-contained on the prep school site. None of the higgledy-piggledness that characterises some pre-preps, no sense of being an architectural afterthought.

Described by one parent as 'the jewel in the crown'. Lovely atmosphere, really good staff, brilliantly led. Intelligent use of teaching materials, the best of the new plus golden-oldie classics. Huge pride in their forest school – outdoor areas where the children can play, hunt for bugs and bumble about. Aftercare til 5.45pm at no extra cost.

Marmite schools are schools with a highly distinctive personality and probably a stand-out specialism. These are schools that some children love and others don't. TPS is not a Marmite school. So, a very good ordinary school, then? Well, if you want to put it that way, yes, this is a school for every child, a place where values of humanity come first, where happy children find out who they are and what they can do and then go on and play out of their socks. Ordinariness at its best, then. Extremely personable. A terrific all-rounder.

Taunton School

Linked with Taunton Prep and Pre-Prep School

Staplegrove Road, Taunton, Somerset TA2 6AD

Ages 13–18 **Pupils** 555 **Sixth form** 243 **Boarders** 266 full, 24 weekly, 59 flexi

Fees: Day £19,395; Boarding £33,225 pa

01823 703703
www.tauntonschool.co.uk

Headmaster: Since 2015, Lee Glaser MA BSc PGCE, deputy head since 2009. Educated at his local comp in Blackpool and Liverpool University (maths). Qualified as a chartered accountant with Coopers & Lybrand, then turned his back on bean-counting and trained to be a teacher. Millfield for 14 years, maths teacher, senior master and director of sport; he's a diehard sports enthusiast rather than a dead good player. By general agreement he has made a very decent fist of taking over from a bouncy, charismatic head with a silver tongue and a penchant for continuous change. There's been enough of that; Mr Glaser's here to get the trains running on time and bed things down. Doesn't mean innovation is off the cards by any means, mind. Spent his first year appointing a new senior management team and agreeing vision and strategy which is expressed graphically by five pillars – see website – and is, we find, very definitely not a confection of buzz words and blah. If 'challenge, inspire, nurture' is what you want to hear, Mr Glaser is right behind them. A realist (as well as an accountant) he's a big believer in sound finances. Everyone likes him – he's 'approachable', a wysiwyg kind of a guy, 'good sense of humour', 'accessible, a good listener', 'right person at the right time', 'a nuts and bolts person', 'sticking to the knitting'. Very visible, his door is open to students first thing every morning. Oratorical skills reckoned to be improving. When he eventually steps down he hopes the consensus view of his bottom line will be that he 'improved everything'.

Wife Liz is a practising accountant. Two girls, both at the school. Chocolate lab, Lola. Mr Glaser enjoys music and drama. Faced with shipwreck on a desert island he would lunge for Sympathy for the Devil (Stones) and Sebastian Faulkes' Engleby.

T

Academic matters: Results are sound considering the non-selective intake: 46 per cent A*/A at A level or equivalent in 2018 (a massive jump from 2017), 43 per cent A*-A/9-7 at GCSE. IB diploma average score down a little at 34. GCSE results broadly strengthening. Good range of subjects offered in the sixth form resulting in some very small class sizes. In terms of national averages strong in maths, history, biology, geography. Fewer top grades in physics, economics, business studies and psychology but signs of recent improvement. Curriculum well judged to accommodate a relatively wide range of abilities. Subject range embraces the usual suspects and includes, classy touch, Latin to A level. Open-minded about adding vocational subjects (eg BTecs in business as well as sport and exercise science) to the mix if sufficiently broad-based to act as a springboard to a spectrum of career choices equivalent to three A levels, and laying the ground for a variety of employment sectors. Just under half of the first cohort achieved three triple starred distinctions. Performance table data shows expected progress at A level and BTec while IB students do rather better. Saturday school popular with working parents.

Classrooms bright and well equipped, students engaged even as lunchtime became imminent, teachers giving it plenty. A good number of teachers here did something else first. Lovely library – the new name for a learning resource centre – staffed by specialists and open til 9 every evening. Design technology blinking brilliant, masses of kit – oscillating spindle sander, inverted trend router, plasma cutter, you name it.

Huge efforts to retain students post-GCSE, some of which redound to their benefit – ah, the joys of a highly competitive market. Outstanding guidance in opting between A levels, IB and BTec, choosing the right subjects and thereafter making university and careers choices.

Learning support – 'educational progress', they call it – delivered by a staff of five who also support children in the prep school, offering continuity for long-haul students. The customary range of interventions spanning long-term SLDs to short-term study support. SLDs on the mild side – you've got to be able to keep up. Typically professional, all learning assistants are graduates. Head of department told us it's all about 'celebrating the differently gifted'.

Games, options, the arts: 'This is a school that really values breadth,' a parent told us. Another: 'Taunton students have absolutely no understanding of boredom'. All parents agree that when lessons are over there's masses to do. Sport, for example. This is a sporting hotspot that takes a characteristically professional approach to maxing out the talents of all students. Cop these coaches: Pete Sanderson, ex-Somerset CCC first team coach; Marcus Trescothick, ex-England opening batsman; Nic Sestaret, ex-France, Exeter Chiefs and Toulouse rugby player; and Lisa Manley, ex-England netball development squad manager. Yes, blimey. If you're any good you'll go all the way. That's not all. For students whose enthusiasm outruns their innate gifts there are B and some C teams where you can do your bit. Famous victories and lean spells alike are recorded in the Courier, the excellent weekly e-mag that records dash and enterprise in all areas of school life. Exhaustive coverage allows for the greatest number of students to be namechecked, a source of pride and joy to doting parents. As well as progressing to regional and national levels, students also play for local clubs, with some of whom the school shares facilities. All in all, impressive.

Some parents say the focus on sport has got a bit much, others disagree. One said, 'If your child is not in one of the top two teams [As or Bs] you don't get value for money'; others disagree. One said that there's a danger that a sporty child will do nothing but sport and miss out on everything else on offer; others point to manifold achievements on a broad and eclectic front by their own child. Given the strength of the sporting culture here, what is the fate of the non-sporty? Do they shiver on the wing only to be hooted at on the rare occasions the ball reaches them? We spoke to the parent of a resolutely non-sporty child. After popping in for a constructive talk with the right people, a personal fitness programme was agreed. Very civilised, all happy, no stigma. Putting this in context, another parent remarked: 'This is a school which is far more interested in the welfare of every one of its children than it is in looking good to the outside world'.

The school's minibuses carry the strapline 'Offering more'. There may be something in it. The music offer is multifarious, everything from chamber music ensembles to big musicals – in recent years Phantom, Evita, Cats. There are choirs, overseas tours – in short, around 40 public performances a year. The busy drama department offers courses at GCSE and A level in addition to productions for which anyone can audition. The art studio is similarly open-house and evidence of the quality of work made here surrounds you. Students spoke glowingly of working relationships with their teachers as we gazed.

Outside the classroom there are heaps of clubs and activities on offer, many of them student-generated. There's a fully fledged rationale behind the co-curricular programme – Horizons, they call it. It's all about reaching out beyond the confines of the classroom, it's self-directed and it embraces all abilities. There's a CCF, compulsory for years 10 and 11. And for fresh air fans there's a thriving D of E scheme. Is there enough range? Students told us unanimously yes; parents told us that their children are operating at the outer extremes of busyness, and cited by way of verification the way they sleep for much of the first week of every holiday. One parent said, 'They are trained to cope with lots to do'. Lots of cultural, sporting and exchange trips worldwide reflecting the school's global outlook.

Boarding: Around 45 per cent board, of which roughly the same percentage are girls. House system in discrete houses, visitors need permission, so privacy (which tends to be in short supply in boarding schools) is safeguarded. Not a hotel school awash with pampering and fine fittings (though refurb ongoing) but students perfectly content with comfort levels, girls' dorms softer and tidier than boys', it goes without saying, for most chaps are strikingly insouciant in matters of interior decor at this age. Zero sock odour in the boys' houses, testimony to regulated lifestyles and the care of terrific support staff whose pastoral role is crucial and, well done Mr Glaser, officially recognised. Happy campers, all. 'One big family,' say the teachers, as they do; 'home from home'. When you hear the children say this too you give it credence. Eventide hunger pangs, long the bane of boarding, sated by after-prep snacks – we liked that. Busy weekend activities programme. Big boys look after little ones. Young people these days really are so much kinder to each other (sigh), the more so when vigilantly and benignly overseen as these are.

Background and atmosphere: Began life in 1847 as the West of England Dissenters' Proprietary School supported by the Wills family, Bristol ciggie kings, who built the chapel. Original neo-gothic flagship building imparts an image of tradition at modest cost. Target market was nonconformists – manufacturers, industrialists, tradespeople. Within 40 years the sectarian rationale had largely evaporated, denominational differences not being what they were, and the school moved into the public school mainstream, competing directly with, eg, the two other Taunton indies, Queen's and King's. Never a supertanker sort of school, the sort that can sail serenely through economic bad weather, it has looked disaster in the face a few times, most recently the late 1990s. Existential peril has arguably been the school's greatest friend, compelling it to look repeatedly to its wits and jolly well deserve to exist, denying it the doubtful luxury of complacency. Ever-adept at identifying new markets it went co-ed in 1976 – one of the first – and has offered IB since 2007. Business savvy – in the holidays there's a thriving venue hire business including weddings.

A legacy of this adaptive mindset is the global outlook of the school today built on an admirably enterprising business model. Two separate international schools between them take overseas students aged 8-17, bring them up to speed and feed them into either the prep or senior school – somewhere around 45 different nationalities. This makes Taunton fundamentally different in spirit from schools that look abroad opportunistically to top up ad hoc. There's a fully developed rationale behind this in tune with that of other international schools, yet Taunton remains essentially British because that's what its overseas parents want. Another stand-out feature of the school is that it will take your children and educate them from 0-18. Their market research tells them this is what parents want, and parents we spoke to concur – 'I didn't want my son to lose all his friends at 13'. One parent, new to town, was only looking for a nursery. One thing led to another; her third child has just started as the eldest gets ready to leave. Taken together, the cradle-to-adulthood model and the international model account for the fact that the head girl who showed us round had been at the school for 16 years, the head boy for just two (he's Russian). Striking for us, perhaps, not a big deal for them. Point is, it works. 'The friendships my daughter has made,' said one parent, 'have made the world a smaller place.' How chill a wind Brexit is going to be is yet to be seen. Taunton students emerge as global citizens, definitely not citizens of nowhere.

The campus, on the northern outskirts of Taunton, embraces also the prep and the pre-prep. The 15-17 year-old international students are semi-detached, just over the A358; the 8-14s are 10 mins to the north in Kingston St Mary. None of the crammedness you get in many town schools, the spacious playing fields and unnecessarily blue artificial pitches of the 50-acre site give way to agriculture. Architecturally there's nothing here to take your breath away, though the Loveday building may elicit a low whistle. At the same time, there's absolutely nothing to make your heart sink. No, there's one of everything and everything's eminently fit for purpose – deceptively so in the case of the theatre which, as performing arts spaces go, is a piece of work. It's all at one with the down-to-earth nature of this place, a school that has no truck with servicing bank loans or wowing have-yachts. One parent said, 'The facilities meet its needs. In real life most people don't have pots of money to spend.' Another said 'One of the best things about the school: it's not in the least up itself.' Our observation: this is a school you quickly feel at home in.

Very much a part of its local community, the school issues invites to university fairs, talks, etc. There's a community choir. The head enjoys good relationships with local state schools and sixth form college. Townsfolk come in and use the fitness suite. Taunton parents highly approve; they definitely don't want their children growing up aloof and apart. Confident in its identity and values, very much its own place, wholly free of minor public school hangups.

Pastoral care, well-being and discipline: Of all the school's greatest hits, pastoral care stands at number 1. However hard we tried (and we did, we did) we could lure no one into uttering a bad word. First up, this is, in the words of one parent, 'a school where teachers really like kids' – which, interestingly enough, is exactly what the teachers told us when we asked them why they love working here. There is praise for rapidity of response times and sensitive, effective nipping in the bud of problems as they arise. One parent, worried about an unsupervised party planned for a weekend, went to share her misgivings with the deputy head. Sorted. Discipline is reckoned judicious and firm; a parent praised the way the school 'doesn't pander to parents' in this respect. Another parent observed, 'Family values are important to Taunton parents'. A new parent was rung by a teacher in the first fortnight to tell her how well her son was doing, point being this teacher didn't even teach him. We fielded countless 'extra mile' plaudits and enjoyed 'this is the biggest family ever'.

If the school looks big, 'it's not when you're there; the house system divides it into manageable chunks'. There's praise for the way year groups mix, look out for each other and integrate the newbies. There's peer mentoring. Year 9s share their space with year 11s. One parent told us they reckoned the house groups socially too small. All parents see this as an open door school, they'll always make themselves available and listen to you. You can drop in and taste the food anytime – to be dished out from a 'spectacular new facility' from 2019, the school tells us. It's an inclusive sort of place; a parent told us 'You'd struggle not to fit in'. Another said 'There's never been a day when my children have not wanted to go to school'. It's an open-hearted sort of a place, too: there's a pupil-led feminist society open to the full spectrum of LGBT students.

Pupils and parents: Especially popular with hardworking local entrepreneurs, business people and professionals for a number of whom this is their first experience of private education – a higher proportion than you'll find at many independent schools. Not so different, then, in terms of values, from the school's original nonconformist parents – attributes of enterprise, thrift and social responsibility score high with them. They're looking for a return on investment, they like the school's groundedness and professionalism – and they bust a gut to pay the fees. We also encountered a number of seasoned veterans of private education who'd always seen themselves sending their child to a major-brand flagship school but, having found Taunton – in one case because their child was unhappy at a big-name school – count their blessings and have become passionate, even fierce, advocates of the school's virtues. Worth noting the relatively high proportion of state educated teachers here, too, including the three most senior managers. Most children come up from the prep school, some from local preps, some from state schools. Longstandingly popular with Forces families. Buses bring day students from a 30-mile radius from all parts of the compass – Yeovil, Exeter, Weston-super-Mare.

Entrance: Essentially non-selective. Assessment test and interview. Years 9 and 12 the customary boarding points but any other time if they've got room. Go to an open day or schedule a personal visit.

Exit: As many as 30 per cent leave after GCSE in some years, lured by the excellent local (free) sixth form college. A number of these, missing the nurturing, find their way back to the mothership, postponing installation of the new dream kitchen back home for another two years.

Pretty much every sixth form leaver to university, half of them Russell Group. Given the international intake, there's expert advice available for all students looking abroad. Some British students go on to Harvard, UCLA, etc and the school is a national SATS centre. Plenty of support for anyone opting for vocational training or apprenticeship – eg, hospitality, design at NABA Milan. School prides itself on parity of support for all routes from academic to apprenticeship. Four to Oxbridge in 2018, plus two medics. Others to Australia, Canada, Germany, Italy, Netherlands, Spain and the USA.

Money matters: The usual range of scholarships for year 9 entrants. Same for sixth form entrants plus IB scholarships up to 100 per cent of fees. Extras include books, food, daily bus and some trips. Big ongoing investment in bursaries. Application process as far as possible businesslike, never an ordeal. Help for students at all ages who exhibit 'talent and determination'.

Remarks: Most of Taunton's hard-headed, analytical parents choose the school because it 'feels right', something that leaps out at them. It does. You quickly pick up on the professionalism – the admin systems are superfast. Never a school to fall in love with its own reflection, the new senior team, with its 'improve everything' agenda, is tweaking underperforming areas with precision. What makes the school so likeable, so agreeable, is its individuality: kind, hardworking, ambitious, terrific fun, very much its own person – a great fit for everyboy and everygirl.

The Thomas Hardye School

Queen's Avenue, Dorchester, Dorset DT1 2ET

Ages 13–18 **Pupils** 2,115 **Sixth form** 727

01305 266064
www.thomas-hardye.net

Headteacher: Since 2011, Mike Foley BA MEd (50s). Educated at The John Fisher School in Purley, Surrey, then St Mary's University, Twickenham, where he read history. He originally planned a career in law but decided to do a PGCE first – 'someone said it would stand me in good stead' – and found that he loved teaching. More than 30 years on, he still loves it. When we met him he was looking forward to teaching an A level history class on his favourite subject, the English Civil War. First job was at Kesgrove High School in Ipswich, where he had 'an inspirational' head of department. 'He still inspires me to this day,' he says. 'One simple thing I took on board was that when students walk into the classroom you should have the room set out for the lesson. They immediately know you mean business.' Worked at a range of schools before becoming head of Great Cornard Upper School in Sudbury, Suffolk (now Thomas Gainsborough School) for nine years. Along the way he did an MEd at Cambridge.

The Thomas Hardye School was already an outstanding school when he arrived and friends joked that becoming head would be like taking over at Manchester United. 'But I always have this philosophy that no matter how good something is it can always be better,' he says. Sure enough, the school has gone from strength to strength under his leadership. One of his key aims from the start was to ensure that even though the school is huge 'we make sure that every youngster is monitored, looked after and cared for.' He brought in a new college system, dividing the school into four mixed-age colleges. Each college is led by a teacher but also has a guidance leader – a non-teaching member of staff who is responsible for pastoral care and day-to-day issues. Rather than staying at their desks, the school's leadership team is out and about throughout the day, including breaks and lunchtimes, ensuring that problems are picked up quickly and dealt with.

Head firmly believes that it's crucial for pupils to get off to a good start the moment they arrive in year 9. 'People establish patterns of behaviour from day one,' he says. 'When the year 9s come in all the staff are available and we make sure that no one leaves school that day with a worry – or if they have a worry we make sure we know about it.' At the start of the autumn term he emphasises to year 11, 12 and 13 students that they have 32 weeks at school before study leave and by half term almost a quarter of the year's teaching time will have gone. 'We tell them that every lesson and every day has to count,' he says. Wise words indeed.

Wife Teresa is a secondary teacher and they have four children. He's a season ticket holder at Crystal Palace and enjoys sport, skiing, reading and travel.

Academic matters: In 2018 at GCSE, 62 per cent got 9-5 in both English and maths. A third of grades A*/A at A level. All the usual subjects on offer at A level (maths the strongest subject), plus accounts, business studies, economics, electronics, food tech, media studies, performance studies, sociology and travel and tourism. IB average score of 33 points in 2018. Also offers the EPQ (extended project qualification) and CACHE diploma in childcare and education.

Good value added. Assistant head attributes this to 'high expectations, purposeful atmosphere, focus on learning and the dedication of the staff.' Although year groups are big (between 400 and 450 pupils), class sizes are relatively small. GCSE classes, for example, tend to be between 10 and 22. Pupils are set for maths while English is taught in mixed ability classes. Most do a language (French or German) at GCSE. Science is strong here – 18 labs, enrichment activities and community lectures ranging from 'what are black holes and how can we study them?' to 'the story of the aurora.' School has appointed an industry partnership development manager who forges links with local companies. School is above average when it comes to numbers of girls taking STEM subjects but is determined to improve further. Also working hard to close gap in attainment of pupil premium students (a total of 120 in the school).

School has a physical disability base and a speech and language base, each with 15 pupils. Six per cent of pupils on SEN register – support given one-to-one, in small groups and before start of school. Head takes the view that 'everyone is a learner, no one is the finished article' and teachers are encouraged to do their own research projects too. School operates on a two-week timetable but pupils say they soon get used to it. Impressive library, opened by novelist Tracy Chevalier in 2010, with 22,000 resources, 32 laptops and 14 computers. Librarians encourage reading for pleasure and popular choices include John Green, Robert Muchamore and Manga.

Games, options, the arts: Sports facilities are excellent – floodlit Astroturf, sports hall with climbing wall, fitness suite and dance studios and acres of playing fields, plus use of neighbouring leisure centre (with two swimming pools, no less). School concentrates on traditional sports – rugby, football (boys and girls), netball, cross-country, athletics, cricket and swimming. 'We're a very sporty school,' the dynamic deputy of PE told us. Outdoor education is part of the curriculum, with activities like sailing (the Jurassic coast isn't far), kayaking, water polo and the Basic Expedition Leaders Award.

Art, music, drama and dance departments buzz with activity. Art department has six staff, all with different specialisms – from painting and sculpture to printmaking and animation. More than 180 individual instrument lessons every week and loads of ensembles to join – orchestras, concert band, wind band, jazz orchestra, rock groups, chapel choir, the list goes on and on. Music popular at GCSE and A level. Music and dance tour abroad every two years to eg Rhineland. Drama in school's own theatre and two performing arts studios. Regular student productions, with frequent visits by professional performers and companies too.

Loads of extracurricular clubs at lunchtime and after school – electronics, Raspberry Pi, murder mystery, fossils to name but a few. CCF, D of E, Model United, plus a host of charity events and trips. Sixth form pupils visit the US and Russia in alternate years.

Background and atmosphere: Thomas Hardye founded the first free school in Dorchester in 1569, with five pupils on the school roll. The school has nothing to do with renowned Dorset novelist Thomas Hardy, who somewhat confusingly attended Mr Last's Academy for Young Gentlemen in Dorchester in the 1850s. School doubled in size in 1993 when it amalgamated with a girls' school. Today it's even bigger, with more than 2,000 pupils and 780 in the sixth form alone. 'I think we're the biggest school-based sixth form in the country,' says the assistant head. Belongs to Dorchester Area Schools Partnership (comprising 15 first schools, three middle schools and Thomas Hardye itself), which means there's masses of collaboration, especially when it comes to staff training and development. School is situated at the end of a long, tree-lined avenue on the edge of Dorchester. Swish office and reception area in central redbrick building, plus lots of modern additions, including £2.7 million English and modern languages block with glass atrium.

School has a real 'can-do' approach. Younger pupils look up to sixth formers and sixth formers mentor the younger ones. 'There is nowhere else like this place on terms of the atmosphere and ethos,' the assistant head told us and as we walked round the school with two keen as mustard year 10s we had to agree. Despite its size the atmosphere is calm and purposeful, no rushing about or chaotic corridors. 'It's quite a grown-up sort of place,' agreed one of our young guides. 'We don't have a lot of rules,' the head told us. 'We give pupils a degree of responsibility and they respond to that. Behaviour here is outstanding. That's not to say we don't have some difficult youngsters but the vast majority are a delight.' No permanent exclusions in recent years and fixed term exclusions 'very low.'

Smart uniform – blazers, white shirts and college ties, plus grey skirts or trousers for girls and grey trousers for boys. Sixth formers can wear what they like, within reason. School says (very sensibly): 'We do not think that denim shorts, very short skirts, skintight leggings or clothing with inappropriate slogans are suitable for school.' Sixth formers have their own centre, with a huge common room, study area and mini-canteen. Main school canteen opens for breakfast at 8.15am.

Pastoral care, well-being and discipline: Prospective parents often worry about the sheer size of the place but it doesn't seem to be an issue once pupils start. Children are divided into manageable-sized year groups and colleges and say it works well. Good induction – thanks to Thomas Hardye's partnership with local primary and middle schools most pupils know the school reasonably well by the time they arrive in year 9. 'And we get maps to help us find our way round,' said a year 10 girl appreciatively.

Pupils join one of four colleges, all named after the original signatories of the school's 16th century foundation deed – Henning, Napier, Stratford and Trenchard. Each college has a college leader, deputy college leader and guidance leader (one of whom is an ex-police officer). All four colleges are further divided into five year 9 tutor groups, five year 10 tutor groups and five year 11 tutor groups and pupils see their tutor before lessons and after lunch every day. School's 2015 Ofsted report described its pastoral leadership as 'remarkable' and noted that the college system meant that all pupils 'are known as individuals.'

Pupils and parents: Pupils come from a vast range of backgrounds, from very disadvantaged families to the incredibly privileged. Head says that one of the things he's most proud of is the school's 'inclusivity.' Before he arrived a parental quibble was that they'd like to be more involved. School has addressed this by running a parents' focus group to share ideas and trial new initiatives.

Entrance: At 13, most pupils come from three middle schools, two in Dorchester and one in nearby Puddletown, plus a few from Weymouth and a handful from Sunninghill, a Dorchester prep. At 16 the catchment area widens considerably, with pupils travelling from as far afield as Bridport, Lyme Regis, Axminster, Sherborne, Poole and Bournemouth. Most arrive by bus (there's a 16-19 bursary fund for students who struggle with the cost of transport, trips and equipment) but a few drive (there's plenty of parking). School asks for at least five 6s at GCSE but says 'everything is case specific.'

Exit: Around 10 per cent leave after GCSEs, for apprenticeships, employment or to do vocational courses at Weymouth College or Kingston Maurward College. At 18, 90 per cent to higher education, including half to Russell Group and an average of 10 to Oxbridge each year (11 in 2018, plus six medics). Popular destinations include Exeter, Cardiff, Bath, Southampton, Bournemouth and London.

Remarks: A well-run, purposeful comprehensive. Its impressive results, value added scores, high expectations and excellent leadership show a school at the top of its game. Rather than resting on its laurels though, Thomas Hardye is determined to get even better.

Thomas Telford School

Old Park, Telford, Shropshire TF3 4NW

Ages 11–18 **Pupils** 1,374 **Sixth form** 510

01952 200000
www.ttsonline.net

Headmaster: Since 1991, Sir Kevin Satchwell, who has been head here since its inception and rightly takes pride in the huge success story of his tenure. OU degree plus educational management diploma, Sir Kevin's background is PE and he worked through head of department positions and deputy head role to his first headship at Moseley Park, Wolverhampton. Appointed to the new Thomas Telford with a brief to raise educational standards in Telford and Wolverhampton, Sir Kevin did just that and has sustained the upward trajectory. Many of the innovative ideas from the early days of the school are still in place and some have become educational mainstream eg smartboards and learning online.

Super confident and assertive, this is a head you would not want to get on the wrong side of. The students are thrilled when they see him supporting football matches or joining them in the dining room for a brief word, and staff appreciate him picking up the occasional piece of litter. Parents can't praise him enough. His address to new parents was quoted to us a number of times. It clearly impresses. They love his national profile and seeing him pop up on the television from time to time.

His legacy will not just be about establishing a strong brand for this school as a flagship for technological innovation, but spreading the model that has been seen as so successful there to other schools. A Thomas Telford Multi Academy Trust has been established, with Thomas Telford School currently supporting three schools in disadvantaged areas of the West Midlands. Money formally generated through educational business initiatives at the school has been ploughed into these disadvantaged schools.

Academic matters: GCSE results are consistently well above the national average. In 2018, 31 per cent A*-A/9-7 grades. Ninety-four per cent of pupils got 9-4 in both English and maths.

The school offers 25 A levels (sixth form is selective by GCSE results) as well as BTecs in business, performing arts triple and sport single, double and triple. Results in 2018 were 43 per cent A*/A, 64 per cent A*-B grades. Maths is consistently the most popular subject at A level, as you might expect in a school which aims to promote sciences, technology and business. As well as the sciences and business studies, English literature is popular and successful as are psychology, history and geography.

The school pioneered lessons lasting half a day and these have stood the test of time, though a few departments split sessions and year 7s have shorter stretches. Teachers say the long slots allow them to innovate and that there is more variety in teaching styles here than you will find in other schools. Trainees tell us it is a very exciting place to learn to teach.

The layout of the school combines separate classrooms and labs with some learning bases where a number of lessons in the same subject go on at one time, separated only by dividers, as well as open plan teaching spaces, all of which allows for a range of teaching approaches. The curriculum is online and teachers all teach the same lesson at the same time to a year group, planned centrally in advance. GCSE courses are spread over three years rather than the more usual two.

Setting starts in core subjects early and those with special educational learning needs have learning plans and specialist support. Nurturing groups offer bespoke programmes to motivate SEN pupils and equip them with social as well as learning skills.

Games, options, the arts: Formal academic lessons now finish at 3.15pm with the final session of the day voluntary and co-curricular. Staff report that most children stay at least one day a week for this. During this time, some academic support is on offer – subject specific catch-up sessions or enrichment classes. Med Soc, a law group that takes part in mock trial competitions, debating etc seen as a good preparation for university selection tests. Also drama and robotics clubs and lots of sport.

Sport is very strong throughout the school with many regional and national success stories. More than 200 students (including more than 100 girl and boy footballers) play at levels ranging from district to national in sports including hockey, golf, roller hockey, kickboxing, swimming, athletics and biathlon. Facilities include an Astroturf, playing fields, outdoor courts, a big indoor sports hall and fitness suite.

Musical theatre is very popular and performing arts groups showcase their work regularly. There is a theatre used for assemblies as well as performances. Music includes various bands and choirs. Those wanting to play in classical symphony orchestras are likely to join regional groups.

There are lots of visits out of school, often linked with understanding the world of business, industry and higher education as well as curriculum interests.

Background and atmosphere: The school continues to be supported by the Mercers' Company and it has significant partnership arrangements with a number of businesses and industries. There is very much a Midlands business feel about the buildings – lots of glass, professional and motivational wall displays celebrating the many achievements of teams and individuals. The school is very well maintained and the pupils clearly treat it with respect. It has been at the forefront of technology, both in terms of teaching and finance.

Twice yearly achievement assemblies highlight special aspects of the school's work, for example its charity work, and past pupils are invited to share their experiences. Two year 8s told us one of the best things about the school was hearing about the achievements of senior pupils. The first thing you see as you enter the very corporate entrance hall is a big trophy cabinet, bursting with silver cups. The boards around the school all celebrate those aspects of school life that have measurable successful outcomes.

Pastoral care, well-being and discipline: Tutor groups are vertical and younger students speak positively of the advice offered by older ones, both on quite formal matters such as applying for university and less formally, such as discussing the latest fitness regime for footballers. The aim is that personal tutors will stay with the same children throughout their time at the school and that older pupils are given responsibility and leadership opportunities.

Another way the school tries to create identity is through the weekly Broadcast, put out every Monday with a magazine format, complete with theme tune, curriculum news, sports reports, star pupil celebration, messages and a thought for the week. Year groups also have weekly assemblies.

The atmosphere is calm and because of the long lesson slots, there less movement between classrooms than in most schools. The lack of bells, other than for emergencies, adds to the calm. Most discipline problems are dealt with through personal tutors but parents are pulled in very quickly if anything looks as though it might escalate, and solutions are very much a partnership between home and school. For example, if a pupil breaks rules about mobile phones use, the phone is confiscated and parents have to come into school to retrieve it. The head says he has only permanently excluded one pupil in the last 10 years. Tight security with CCTV cameras, and staff are visible around the corridors and in the large dining room.

Pupils and parents: The pupils are very smart. Business wear is the order of the day for sixth form and staff. Most of the girls wear trousers – the regulatory knee length skirts not being popular. Pupils are slightly reserved in the company of visitors but willing to answer questions thoughtfully. As we walked round, a female student looked disapproving when it took a group of boys a little time to notice we were waiting to go through a door. She went out of her way to ask if she could help us with directions.

Rather than waiting to raise concerns at traditional parents' evenings, the school sends out progress reports seven times a year and parents are expected to respond. The school acts immediately on these parental comments, inviting parents into school if necessary. The head says the vast majority of parents are very supportive. They know what the school's expectations are and all have signed up to a parents' charter – in the knowledge that the school is heavily oversubscribed. Parents say communication is very quick and very personalised, with academic concerns acted on quickly and parents kept informed.

The parents choose the school because of its high profile and sustained reputation for delivering on exam results as well as attracting motivated, well-behaved children. The school is proud of its aspirational ethos and values of hard work and respect for others.

Entrance: An NFER non-verbal reasoning assessment divides applicants into nine ability bands. The school asks for year 5 reports and attendance records, and gives priority within the bands to those who score well for attainment and effort in technology, science and maths, and are deemed 'most likely to benefit from the education on offer at the school and who have the strongest motivation to succeed'. Wildly oversubscribed. Most children come from Telford or Wolverhampton. School buses currently free.

Sixth form entry dependent on GCSE results, and most A level subjects now need grade 6 or 7 for their subject and at least a 5 in supporting subjects.

Exit: About 80 per cent of year 11 stay on and the sixth form offers BTecs as well as A levels. There is school leavers' programme with visitors from the world of business and technology as well as academia, some being past pupils.

In 2018, nearly three-quarters of leavers went on to higher education, with two Oxbridge places, plus six medics and two vets. A lot of pupils pick vocational rather than purely academic courses and a noticeable number opt for Midlands universities. Several move on to high quality apprenticeships, a course promoted by the school.

Remarks: The school has had a superb reputation in the Midlands and beyond for many years. While the exam focus is not for all families, many find the purposeful pressure just what is needed to get the strong results. The reputation means the school continues to attract good teachers who find it a strong launching pad for their careers. Families and pupils know they are very fortunate to have a place here and this, in its turn, minimises any conflict between staff, pupils and families. Commendable partnership with and outreach to the business community and, increasingly, to its successful alumni, and the school is constantly on the alert for any opportunities that will give pupils an advantage in the future.

Torquay Boys' Grammar School

Shiphay Manor Drive, Torquay, Devon TQ2 7EL

Ages 11–18 **Pupils** 1,078 **Sixth form** 252 (27 girls)

01803 615501
www.tbgs.co.uk

Head: Since 2014, Peter Lawrence BSc. In his 40s, originally from the Midlands, he studied maths at Exeter University and taught at TBGS for five years in early part of his career. Left to become a head of department and taught in three comprehensives in Devon before moving to teach in Jersey. Returned to TBGS in 2001, taking roles as head of house, assistant head and then pastoral deputy head.

Now firmly settled in south west (Exeter Chiefs season ticket holder), with his wife (she teaches maths at TBGS), he is the sixth head, and modestly proud. He says, 'it's a privilege', something he's reminded of every morning as he drives into school. His predecessors had long careers. Pete is definitely in for the long haul, but laughed at the thought of being head in 30 years. Well, you never know.

He's friendly and open, and made us feel relaxed on our wander round the school, a school he is more than happy to show off. A keen sportsman, he plays five-a-side football every Sunday (regrets it every Monday morning). He says, 'Our school mantra has long been to maintain the best of the old and combine it with the best of the new'. Parents rate him as excellent.

Academic matters: In 2018, 36 per cent A*/A at A level (66 per cent A*-B), and 69 per cent A*-A/9-7 at GCSE. Top scores in maths (regular national Maths Challenge successes), English and science. Twenty-two subjects on offer at A level. The school works with neighbouring Torquay Girls Grammar School to ensure that all options are available. One parent said, 'The school went out of its way to try and find a solution rather than asking [my son] to change his fourth option.' Choice of A level or

IB in the sixth form (average IB score 38 in 2018); girls can join the sixth form, but must study IB. The school also offers a range of BTecs such a health and social care and travel and tourism, in conjunction with Torquay Academy, though in reality all TBGS boys opt for A levels or IB.

TBGS has sponsored Torquay Academy (formerly Torquay Community College) and set up the Torquay Boys' Grammar School Multi-Academy Trust. The aim is to help raise standards and provide all students in Torbay, regardless of ability, the same opportunities and access to a top rate education.

Good range of MFLs on offer: Spanish, French, German, Japanese and Chinese. Now a Confucius school promoting Chinese; around 75 year 9 pupils are currently studying it, and the annual trip to China is in great demand though A level not currently offered. Every subject department has access to a dedicated IT suite; no shortage of computers, with around 800 in total. There's also a boardroom with 25 computers, dual flat screens and Reuters links, all thanks to a previous business and enterprise sponsorship. A good insight into the real thing, and high numbers of students are choosing economics at university.

SEND panel for pupils who are dyslexic or have problems with numeracy; two are currently statemented. SEND panel also deals with all emotional support and counselling for the pupils. Ofsted report says, 'This drive for academic achievement is balanced by a deep commitment to students' wider personal and social development.' Achievements, academic or otherwise, are all commended regularly. Pupils are given 'effort grades' for each subject on a termly basis, and screens around the school announce the latest Student of the Week award. One parent said, 'It really does encourage the students to do well.'

Games, options, the arts: National football champions three times in recent years; one recent ex-student has been selected for the U20 England rugby team this year; cross-country, hockey, athletics, cricket and tennis also on offer. Strong tradition in swimming and water-polo. Ex-pupil, teacher and swimming champion from the 1940s now coaches the very successful teams.

As expected, facilities are impressive. Sports hall large enough for four badminton courts, with viewing gallery (also kitted out for seminar-type lessons for A level PE students). Astroturf shared with TGGS next door, plus a half-size one. Five hours of PE a fortnight. Matches on Wednesday afternoons or after school. Outdoor education classes for years 7, 8, 9 include lifesaving (beach and pool), potholing, canoeing, rock-climbing, orienteering and sailing. Large numbers of students take on Ten Tors (school holds 45 mile record time), D of E and occasionally Three Peaks Challenge.

Parents say, 'The school has a very strong music department, which encourages musicians and puts on numerous concerts, including a musical, every year.' New block with light and spacious rooms. All year 7 students are given the opportunity to learn a brass or woodwind instrument for a year and take part in the annual concert. Many continue with private lessons. Jazz band recently played at Montreux Jazz Festival; trip to Grenoble for the orchestra and choir. Full scale musical each year at end of spring term; tickets on sale for The Sound Of Music when we visited.

Recent improvements to the drama facilities include a new theatre and a well-equipped studio. Media studies also popular, students heavily involved with film-making, local radio and podcasts.

Brilliant art department in the newly refurbished Manor House. The art on display was of extremely high standard, with a huge variety of styles and techniques: aboriginal paintings, cartoons, pop-art, portraits, masks, sculpture and digital design. Average of 30 students in each sixth form year study art.

DT also has well-designed space, with workshops set around a central foyer and spiral staircase. This is a good example of the old working well with the new. As well as the traditional workshops, there are CADCAM suites, laser-cutters and the latest production software. Good displays showing the history of product design – The Mini Story and The Story of the Portable Music Player. Cabinets full of clocks by year 7 plus impressive A level assessment pieces on display.

Huge choice of clubs and activities at lunchtimes and after school; they even offer mountain-biking, fencing and golf. The orienteering club recently won the national championship, so they're now off to Turkey to compete in the World Schools competition. Chess is also prominent, and top players have gone on to win at national and international level. Local Air Training Corps has HQ on site, and the school has its own scout troop. Astronomy club is lucky enough to have a refurbished observatory with a brand new Celestron C1400 telescope on site. The school's patron was famous astronomer, Sir Patrick Moore, and is now Chris Lintott, Sky at Night presenter, a past pupil.

Trips aplenty. All the usual foreign exchanges plus departmental trips – art to Barcelona, philosophy and applied ethics to India, biology to Costa Rica, geography to Snowdonia and Iceland.

Background and atmosphere: Founded in 1904 as the Pupil Teacher Centre, it relocated in 1915 and became Torquay Secondary School with just 170 boys. In 1983 the school moved to its current site, a stone's throw from Torquay town and the English Riviera. From 750 boys in four houses, they now have nearly 1,120 boys and girls in six houses. Extensive building programmes have taken place on the 40 acres through grants and investments, and the result is a well-presented and well-planned campus. A good example of this is the Cavanna Centenary Hall, which houses assemblies and theatrical productions.

Past glories and present day achievements are on display in the entrance foyer, along with uniforms of days gone by and rows and rows of school photos. Past pupils (many are parents of current pupils) love roaming the corridors studying these at school events.

Each subject area has its own IT room and each area corridor is filled with subject-led designs and artwork by pupils, or latest achievements and competitions. This immerses you in each subject, sparking interest in a fun and colourful way. The Ofsted inspectors wrote: 'The school is enthused with a lively and open atmosphere which encourages innovation and underpins a relentless drive to provide the very best education for the student'.

The Manor House is by far the oldest building on site. It has been a home, a hotel, a nightclub and a sixth form for the neighbouring girls' school. It now belongs to TBGS and was refurbished in 2013 into an impressive space for art. The old character remains with a grand, winding staircase and tall windows overlooking the grounds. Perfect gallery spaces. New sixth form common room and café. One parent said, 'The environment is excellent – one that encourages the students to study – which is great, particularly if they're not very studious!'

Refurbishment of the Manor as an art centre meant the school could upgrade and expand the science laboratories. The school's annual science fair is a real crowd-pleaser and gives pupils and parents alike the opportunity to experiment and to learn – think rocket launchers and explosions.

There is a strong house system at TBGS. One parent said, 'Belonging to one of the six houses gives the students a sense of identity, and works very well for inter-house competitions. Each house [Blake, Davys, Frobisher, Gilbert, Hawkins, Ralegh – named after British seafarers] also organises events to raise money for a nominated charity each year, which builds friendships and team-building skills.' Pancakes for Malawi was one of the latest events.

Pastoral care, well-being and discipline: Parents agree that 'the school is very good with its pastoral care, which ensures that any problems are sorted out smoothly and efficiently.' Key words are 'respect' and 'responsibility' and the school hopes to develop 'well-rounded students who have a strong moral compass and compassion for others'. One parent said, 'Teachers are excellent at resolving any difficulties', and bullying is dealt with immediately and sensitively. Bullying tends to be 'boys' banter that goes too far' and is dealt with accordingly. No recent exclusions to speak of and only a few suspensions for behavioural problems. Zero tolerance on drugs.

The school employs a full-time counsellor and there is a pastoral support team. The house system also helps, by breaking the school down into smaller groups and giving the students more individual attention from heads of houses. Seniors are encouraged to take leadership roles. Year 13 students mentor years 7 to 9. Active school council – recently acquired a new recreational Astroturf as pupils complained they had nowhere to go when it was muddy. The power of a council.

Pupils and parents: Mainly local, but some live as far as Plymouth or Exeter, and many have relocated to be near the school. Parents' association changed some time ago from being a fundraising machine to running social events (no pressure to contribute). Wine & Wisdom night particularly praised. The charitable trust takes care of fundraising now.

The list of famous leavers is long. One recent addition is Olympic rower, Bill Lucas. CEO of Rated People, Chris Havemann, is the next ex-pupil booked in for speech day. Others include Chris Read (Nottinghamshire captain and former England wicket keeper); former Wimbledon tennis player Mike Sangster; newspaper mogul Sir Ray Tindle; Marcus Bateman (world champion rower); six times British swimming champion Malcolm Windeatt; Professors Simon Whittaker (St John's, Oxford), Ian Diamond (vice chancellor, Aberdeen University) and David Southwood, president of the Royal Astronomical Society. One former languages graduate, Marcus Richardson, now fluent in Serbo-Croat, became interpreter at the War Crimes Tribunal at The Hague, and Tom Ewing is one of the UK's top fund managers.

Entrance: Takes top 25 per cent. Same entrance test as two other local grammar schools. Recently changed to two CEM 11+ tests. Some 270 try for 156 places. Around 70 primary schools feed in. 'The entrance process was very well organised and the school made them feel at ease,' one parent told us. 'Current sixth formers were there on the test days to assist the teachers and to look after the boys. The sixth formers were mature, courteous and excellent role models for the school. Between tests there were impromptu games of football, which helped to make the day more relaxed.' Another said, 'On the first day at TBGS there are only year 7 and year 12 pupils at school, which gives new pupils a chance to settle in and get their bearings.'

Three 7s and three 6s or above for entry to sixth form. Of around 360 pupils in sixth form, around 80 are newcomers – many of them girls, who must take the IB.

Exit: Some 15-20 per cent leave after GCSEs. More than 95 per cent to university, vast majority to Russell Group universities including Oxbridge (11 places in 2018, plus nine medics). Other favourites are Cardiff, Bristol, Bath, Southampton, Exeter, Warwick, London. Most popular courses, engineering, science and maths.

Money matters: Families can apply for help with costs through pupil premium. All trips can be paid for in instalments. Bursaries available for sixth formers

Remarks: One of the top 20 boys' schools in the country. Deservedly so. Fantastic facilities and teaching that produces top results and very successful young men and women. Every area is given the same attention and passion, whether it's sport, maths, languages or arts. All types will find their niche here. As one parent put it, 'TBGS has been extremely supportive to all of my sons and has nurtured their individual talents. We couldn't have asked for any more. TBGS gives every child the opportunity to achieve their full potential.' Brilliant.

Torquay Girls' Grammar School

30 Shiphay Lane, Torquay, Devon TQ2 7DY

Ages 11–18 **Pupils** 980 **Sixth form** 250

01803 613215
www.tggsacademy.org

Headteacher: Since 2007, Dr Nick Smith MB BS PGCE NPQH, a pragmatic, determined man in his late 40s. A qualified scientist who practised medicine for a couple of years – and yes, he did work at London Zoo looking after the penguins – he has brought the clear thinking of a trained empiricist to his task at TGGS.

Dapper, self-effacing and charming, he has brought vision and vigour to an old-fashioned grammar school. 'He knows what he wants and is relentless in achieving it' was typical of the comments we heard from parents. But we got the distinct impression within the school that the culture was not just geared towards better and better results. 'Caring for others' and 'working in a happy and caring environment' were the kind of phrases mentioned often and there was much evidence that these were not just platitudes.

Universally admired by pupils, parents and teachers alike, Dr Smith could deservedly rest on his laurels at his home on Bodmin Moor, where he lives with his wife (and fellow teacher) and two children, and from where he yomps across the Cornish wilderness (he's a former marathon runner), but he is not finished yet.

Although his justifiable claim that TGGS is very successful in 'adding value' to his incoming cohort, he wants to do much more, especially in terms of enhancing the aspirations and ambitions of his female pupils. Of course, phrases like these are often spoken by headteachers, but this man has a gleam in his eye when he uses them that is very convincing.

Academic matters: The girls are encouraged to work hard and aim high. There is an aura of quiet industry about the place, with an absence of the more typical mayhem of narrow corridors channelling too many youngsters to the next lesson and of doors being slammed with teachers bellowing orders over the din.

But the girls do not learn by rote, nor do they learn just to pass examinations. Here are the school's Four Common Teaching Elements: Are the girls told why they are doing this work? Are the girls made to think? Does the lesson maintain the girls' focus? Are the girls shown how to improve?

Results generally continue to progress in a steady climb and the school has the graphs to prove it. In 2018, 82 per cent A*-B and 52 per cent A*/A grades at A level (including a few subjects shared with Torquay Boys' Grammar School), with GCSE at 70 per cent A*-A/9-7.

Geography is particularly strong, but there are strengths across the curriculum, including good biology, maths and art departments. It also offers the AQA Baccalaureate.

There is an admirable procedure to support those girls who find the rarefied intellectual atmosphere difficult. The incoming intake is assessed by the MidYIS cognitive test and all the girls are then colour-coded on a huge display board in the staffroom. This then becomes the touchstone for the girls' progress throughout their school careers. Significantly, there are clear strategies for girls who are at the bottom of the league and those who start to slip downwards. In some years it can be as many as 15 (slightly more than 10 per cent of the intake), in other years it can be as few as five.

Underperforming girls are supported by a study programme in the hallowed silence in the school's study centre, run by two full-time members of staff. Girls can be taken off timetable, or subjects dropped, to create more time to concentrate on other priorities. Each of the senior staff, including the head, 'adopts' up to five girls in this category and becomes their mentor through this remedial programme. All the while the objective, in a telling phrase, is the desire 'to get them through', a worthy sentiment that is mirrored in the school's approach to any girls who may be having emotional or behavioural problems, or issues at home. At examination time they can engage in a study programme which provides breakfast, keynote sessions and revision in the library.

Games, options, the arts: Wide range of sports include aerobics, cricket, fitball, boxercise, badminton, outdoor pursuits, athletics and football, plus scuba diving, mountain biking, dry-slope skiing, squash, horse riding, sailing and windsurfing further afield. Frequent fixtures at all levels.

Sport appeared to us to be more about 'rounding' the girls, and an opportunity for them to let off steam, than central to school life. Facilities are good and improving, including an Astroturf, plus a second one shared with their neighbours (Torquay Boys'), and a sports hall replacing the antiquated, yet evocative, previous hall, which had the wooden wall bars and climbing ropes many of us remember from our own school days – ah, happy memories!

There is a very strong art department with commendable results and its impressive work on display. The music, media and drama suites are modern and there is a range of drama productions and performances from the orchestra, choir, flute group and jazz band. New amphitheatre for performing arts built to celebrate the school's centenary in 2015.

There is a somewhat whimsical House Culture Calendar, which includes several Dr Smith 'traditions' designed to bring the school its own idiosyncratic identity. They include the House Shout, where the girls and the staff in each house sing a song of their choice at the end of term assembly, and the formal handover ceremony of the head girl's jacket – as at the Augusta Masters' golf tournament.

Not surprisingly, given the school's proximity to the marvels of Dartmoor, DofE is prominent, as is the Ten Tors Challenge. The school owns a residence in Brittany, to which all pupils go twice in their school career, while the current rota of trips includes China, Cuba, Iceland, Mongolia, Nicaragua, Croatia (to study Adriatic dolphins) and Kenya, where TGGS supports a local school.

T

Background and atmosphere: 'Never judge a book by its cover'; this aphorism sits well with TGGS. Its central building is a 1939 structure with an unconvincing claim to be art deco; it is better described as pre-war drab. It is the school's least endearing feature, although new buildings, including a new dining hall and sixth form centre, help alleviate the dour central block.

Not surprisingly in this jaunty institution, nobody within the school seems to bemoan their dreary abode. In fact, they tend to nurture it like an aging relative: 'Yes, it's a bit cold in the corridors and some of the rooms are cramped, but we love it; it's our home.'

The central reception area is a motif of the school in miniature. Compact and brightly decorated, four black and white portraits of former headmistresses hark back to the old days. But everything else reflects the new TGGS. No photographs of the staff in their austere academic robes here, rather a collection of pen pictures of smiling faces, including all the non-academic staff. A new archive corridor includes a 100 year time line to help mark the 2015 centenary.

The school is proud of its membership of the South West Academic Trust, an elite 'Russell Group' of nine Wessex schools in association with the University of Exeter, which brings shared values and commitment to excellence.

Pastoral care, well-being and discipline: The school boasts, legitimately, much pastoral care and little need for discipline, with a strong pastoral care regime led by the heads of year. Inevitably, there are 'problem' pupils as at any other school, but a strong emphasis on human relationships and core values.

There is strict code on bullying; a phenomenon that pupils and parents are unanimous in reporting is almost non-existent. They are equally adamant that ill-discipline is a rarity. The school promotes an ethos of support and mutual care and the girls we spoke to were at pains to explain that they felt it is their responsibility to deal with most issues and that they hope members of staff would only need to become involved on rare occasions.

Further bulwarks are the class tutors, year heads (who follow their year group up through the school), the school's own dedicated personal counsellor, a part-share of careers adviser and a visiting nurse. Finally, Dr Smith's three deputies oversee the heads of year.

Wholesome food is a top priority and a recent innovation is a cashless service (operated biometrically by thumbprint) which allows parents to monitor exactly what their daughters are eating. Indeed, the entire school is cashless and every parent has an online account. The new kitchen and servery gleam and are staffed by a very cheerful group of dinner ladies.

Pupils and parents: There is a strong consensus in this focused and happy school between parents and pupils about its ambitions and ethos. 'The school punches well above its weight'; 'There is a strong emphasis on decency and human values'; 'The rapport between the girls and their teachers is remarkable' were a few of the positive comments from parents.

Pupils were equally voluble with their positive comments: 'It's like nowhere else', 'The staff are always there to help', 'We want to do well for them'. The word 'pride' came up repeatedly. They also stressed that the pejorative terms 'nerd' or 'boffin', sadly so common in the adolescent vocabulary, are not in the lexicon at TGGS. 'We are admired for being clever here'; 'it is easier to succeed here than at schools our friends go to'.

School uniform is an uncomplicated navy blue for the main school and a black and white ensemble for sixth formers. However, the current vogue of pulling skirts up as high as they will go is a blight at TGGS, just as it is in so many schools.

Alumnae include leading academics, people in the media, lawyers and doctors. But Dr Smith is very committed to new employment opportunities for his girls. Because women remain underrepresented at the highest levels in many areas of employment, he feels his continuing mission is to expand the personal development of his charges. 'Encouraging future leaders in industry, finance and commerce' is his avowed cause.

Entrance: Selection at 11+ for 150 places is determined by verbal reasoning, maths and English examinations in two sessions and the intake represents the top 25 per cent of ability.

About 60 girls join the sixth form from other state schools. The entry requirements are seven GCSEs at 6+, plus some subject-specific requirements set out in the school's sixth form prospectus.

Exit: Some 80 per cent of girls stay on for the sixth form. Some 90 per cent to their first-choice university, around three-quarters to Russell Group institutions; two to Oxbridge in 2018, plus eight medics and a vet. There is a broad range of future careers for TGGS girls. A recent cohort included a typical spread of lawyers, teachers and jobs in other public sectors.

Remarks: 'Definitely one to watch' was a key phrase in our previous report. We also proffered the thought that it was time for the school to claim a 'bigger share of the limelight'. Sharp eyes would now readily attest that TGGS has indeed moved directly into the bright glare of the academic elite of the South West.

Not for nothing has the school been awarded an 'outstanding' accolade by Ofsted. If you are looking for a single-sex haven for your daughter, which places great emphasis on intellectual gifts and the future employment prospects of its girls, this is the school for you.

It does not disregard those towards the lower end of its academic intake, indeed it offers them great support and encouragement, however, it is unashamedly about nurturing excellence for as many girls as possible.

It firmly believes in creating a cheerful and caring environment and in producing rounded individuals, but is candid in stating that its primary concern is academic success.

Trinity Preparatory School

Linked with Trinity School

Buckeridge Road, Teignmouth TQ14 8LY

Ages 3 -11 **Pupils** 165 **Boarders** From year 4

Fees: Day £7,755 – £10,650: Boarding £18,945 – £22,425 pa

01626 774138
www.trinityschool.co.uk/

Acting Head: Since September 2018, Michael Burdett BEd (Oxford), previously deputy head and year 6 teacher.

Entrance: Entry is by registration fee, recent reports, and a taster day including a verbal assessment for KS1 entrance, and a written for KS2 entrance. Assessments are to ensure the school has the appropriate provision is in place, not as a selection process. They rarely turn anyone away, unless special needs are too complex. For entry to reception, several trial mornings in the summer term to ease transition. One parent told us, 'Taster days worked well and he clearly enjoyed them. When being shown around the school, the sixth former showing us around was open and honest, which provided a credible experience.'

Exit: Around 60 per cent go onto the senior school, 20/30 per cent go local grammars and 10 per cent to other schools in the area – Exeter School, Maynards School and Millfield.

Remarks: A small school, one of the main attractions for some parents: 'I wanted to find a school that provided real care for my children as we relocated. The class sizes were right – not too small and not too large – and a good balance.'

The day starts with a 'wake and shake' exercise to music. Assemblies with the senior school twice a week. The day finishes with a 20 minute PSHE session to talk about any issues or problems. The school provides good wraparound care; breakfast club from 7.45am, plus after-school clubs for all year groups and supervised prep for years 3 to 6. Supper club also available.

The prep school is set apart from the senior school but shares its facilities; outdoor heated swimming pool, playing fields and tennis and cricket academies. In addition, they have their own tipi, a forest school (busily sawing up Christmas trees when we visited), and a film studio in their ICT suite that uses green screen technology. Classrooms are bright and cheerful.

The SEN team for the whole school looks after special needs. Experience with dyslexia, ADHD, pragmatic and semantic disorders, autism spectrum disorder, non-verbal language difficulties, dyspraxia and general learning difficulties. Complex needs and some behavioural issues may not be catered for. One-to-one specialist tuition with qualified SEN teachers is charged by the hour. All staff are giving on-going training in-house and updated on individual pupils' IEPs. One parent told us, 'My boy has language delay and needed educational support...His prep teachers have been excellent in supporting him. They have adjusted the teaching materials according to his abilities.' Some staff are trained Thrive practitioners. They can assess the pupils' personal, social and emotional development, and help to ensure the right support is in place.

For such a small school, impressive sporting success and achievements. U11 ISA SW football champions, U9 rugby winners of local tag rugby festival, U9 South Devon badminton champions, mixed hockey Devon U11 champions, third year in a row, two pupils have been selected for the Devon U10 cricket squad, and another is the Devon U8 county tennis champion.

Plenty of opportunities for budding performing artists. The choir involves all children from years 3 to 6, plus there is a chamber choir, entry by audition. They have performed at the Devon County Show and Powderham Castle. Most pupils learn an instrument, plus there's a string ensemble, a recorder club and a ukulele orchestra after school. An inter-house music festival is held annually as well as a summer concert, and regular 'tea-time concerts' to give everyone a chance to perform. Trinity Prep has been awarded Best Primary School at the Torbay and South West of England Performing Arts Festival for five out of the last six years. Recent joint productions between the drama club and music department include the musicals Doo-Wop Wed Riding Hood and The Rocky Monster Show.

Every half term, there is a 'life skills day' when everybody takes part in a round robin of three activities in house teams, so year groups are mixed. Activities include building shelters, survival skills, internet safety exercises, storytelling in the tipi, and more recently creating pizza toppings and meeting a police officer. After-school activities include sports, music and drama clubs plus dance, lawn bowls, chess, debating, puzzles, Lego and film-making, to name but a few. Class trips include local attractions like Pennywell Farm, Kents Caverns and Dartmoor. Residential trips start in Prep 2 with an overnight stay at the school. Older pupils go to Heatree activities centre or Manaton on Dartmoor. Year 6 go up to London for museums and West End shows.

Boarding available. Some families of older pupils make use of the flexi boarding options. Have had some full-time boarders – none currently. A parent of one told us, 'He was homesick the first night, but the houseparents kept him busy so that he didn't have time to think too much. He settled down very quickly, much quicker than I expected. The houseparents are simply the best. They looked after him so well. He loved them.

They would send me emails to tell me how he is doing without me asking.'

Lots of happy parents. Communication is good, 'The weekly newsletter is invaluable and the use of Twitter is really helpful as a working parent. I can always email the school and the office is very responsive.' Not many improvements needed at all, although a roof on the swimming pool would be 'nice to have rather than required.' One parent made a suggestion to help pupils with dietary requirements or allergies; 'The school should as a matter of course provide menus with [ingredients] on it, so children can make an informed choice without feeling like the odd one out.'

On the whole this is a good prep school, one parent told us. 'There is no one size fits all approach, each child is given the right opportunity for them to develop their own strengths.' Another summed it up for the majority: 'It has been the perfect start in school life for my children.'

Trinity School

Linked with Trinity Preparatory School

Buckeridge Road, Teignmouth, Devon TQ14 8LY

Ages 11–19 **Pupils** 167 **Sixth form** 50 **Boarders** 58 full

Fees: Day £12,300; Boarding £25,590 – £27,750 pa

01626 774138
www.trinityschool.co.uk

Headmaster: Since September 2016, Lawrence Coen BSc Hons (Aberystwyth), PGCE (St Lukes, Exeter), NPQH. A science teacher, specialising in biology, Mr Coen was previously senior deputy head and spent time as a residential boarding master, as well as being involved in sport and co-curricular activities at the school.

Academic matters: In 2018, 31 per cent A*/A grades and 57 per cent A*-B at A level. At GCSE, 11 per cent A*/A grades. Trinity is a non-selective school, catering for a wide range of academic ability so results vary considerably from year to year.

Nineteen options at GCSE, 18 A level subjects offered, plus BTecs in performing arts, music, sport and travel & tourism. BTecs were introduced in 2014 and are becoming popular; around half of grades generally D*. Strong subjects across the board include maths, business studies, economics, art and psychology. A language is not compulsory at GCSE; psychology can be taken instead. RS is compulsory; everyone takes ICT at KS3 but can drop it at KS4 if taking single sciences.

T

Some 22 per cent of pupils, mainly boys, have special educational needs, double the national average. Experience with dyslexia, ADHD, pragmatic and semantic disorders, autism spectrum disorder, non-verbal language difficulties, dyspraxia and general learning difficulties. Complex needs and some behavioural issues may not be catered for. One-to-one specialist tuition with qualified SEN teachers is charged by the hour. All staff are given on-going training in-house and updated on individual pupils' IEPs. When we were there a deaf scriber and BSL signer were supporting a profoundly deaf student in a biology class.

Providing a supportive learning environment for children that lack confidence, or have had a bad experience of learning, seems to be what Trinity does best. A parent of an oversea boarder told us, 'He had shut himself off from learning; he just lost interest in school totally. Confidence completely drained away from him.' Now, he is 'happy' and 'interested' in school again; 'teachers have been excellent at supporting him.'

Classes are small, rarely reaching double figures. For some, Trinity's size is a definite plus, but some parents feel it can sometimes be limiting: 'For its size I think it does an excellent job but I think a larger year group, particularly in [my child's] year would be beneficial. This is not the fault of the school.' Most teachers have been there a while, several more than a decade. 'The teachers are extremely dynamic, passionate and enthusiastic about their topics and are always available to communicate with parents,' we were told.

Games, options, the arts: Great opportunities for sporty types and successful for such a small school. Medals aplenty in recent years in national ISA swimming and athletics championships. Tennis is a major sport and several play at county and national level, one even at international. The U13s are Devon county champions. Trinity came second in the SW schools climbing championship, and U16 runners up in the netball ISA SW finals. One family commented, '[Our children] are both extremely sporty and have represented both Trinity and the south west in the ISA championships (daughter – netball, cross-country, athletics and swimming; son – cross-country, athletics and aquathon). My daughter also embraced all extracurricular activities available and was a member of the CCF and took the D of E Award.'

Facilities on site include an outdoor pool and indoor and floodlit tennis courts; they use local sports hall, swimming pool and Astro. There is a tennis academy on site, run by former junior international player Mark Syms, plus an indoor cricket academy. Pupils can sign up for individual, group or squad training in both. Trinity takes full advantage of its coastal location and pupils can take part in surf lifesaving, rowing, sailing and other watersports. At the national surf lifesaving championships, Trinity won two golds, one silver, and one bronze. One pupil has been selected for a GB sailing squad. However, table tennis is not on offer competitively and one parent from the Far East said, 'it is a real pity that this sport is left out.'

Combined Cadet Force is compulsory in year 9. Very popular. Activities on the cards the week we visited were sailing, a powerboat course, and helicopter rides over Teignmouth. CCF meets once a week, and there are also weekend activities and holiday camps. Cadets take part in Ten Tors and the Duke of Edinburgh's Award scheme. Plus they can play in the National CCF Band, and last year the CCF team raced in the Tall Ships' Race from Falmouth to Greenwich, coming in second out of 50 ships. Cadets can also take a level 2 vocational award called BTec Public Services First Diploma. This equates to four GCSEs.

Good art facilities including a kiln and a printing press. Fantastic studio – the star of the show for us. Unlike much of the school, it is large and spacious. A huge diamond shaped window almost fills one end of the room. The art teacher says the mix of nationalities creates an 'international flavour.' Some of the sixth form pieces on display were particularly abstract and demonstrated thinking beyond their years. No surprise that Trinity won two golds, two silvers and two bronzes at the recent ISA national art competition. One recent leaver has had her first exhibition of artwork open at Living Coasts in Torquay.

Music department is well-equipped with the latest Apple computers, a grand piano, drum set, keyboards and electric guitars. The senior school choir has been named South West choir of the year – again, they've won three out of the last four years at Torbay Festival. Individual music lessons available, plus clubs including Big Band and a recorder club.

Recent major senior drama production was Les Misérables. Rehearsals were underway for Joseph and the Technicolour Dreamcoat in the drama studio. Plenty of after-school clubs for aspiring thespians, including theatre workshops and public speaking. Recently four pupils won at the poetry recitals at Paignton Festival. Other options include anything from chess to salsa dancing to public speaking or judo, fencing or even cross-stitch.

Regular trips to Normandy for French and history classes. Geography students to Iceland. Plus cultural trips to Berlin, and skiing in the Alps. In the UK, there's an adventure and challenge week in Wales. For sixth formers there are volunteer opportunities on the Grass Roots Project in South Africa where students work in township schools, develop sports fields or build vegetable gardens. There's now a second project choice, an orphanage in Johannesburg.

Boarding: 'The boarding staff provide excellent pastoral care in a safe, loving and caring environment. They also encourage each individual with both their school studies and extracurricular activities,' said one parent. Boarders currently range from 10 to 19 years. The majority are full time, there are occasional flexi-boarders and some European short-termers. Some 75 per cent are from overseas, a third from the Far East, a third from Europe and a third from elsewhere. Around 50 per cent are sixth formers. A parent of one told us, 'He was homesick the first night, but the houseparents kept him busy so that he didn't have time to think too much. He settled down very quickly, much quicker than I expected.'

Two mixed gender houses – one for year 11 and below, one for sixth formers, with university-style accommodation. Parents told us, 'We looked at a few schools and liked the homely atmosphere at Trinity.' The boarding accommodation is part of the school building and as such pupils don't leave school 'to go home'. For some this may make a difference. Rooms are nearly all doubles. Only sixth formers are allowed to study in their room, but all boarders are allowed back to their rooms at lunchtime. We saw quite a few taking advantage of this rather than socialising with fellow pupils over lunch.

Activities in the evenings and weekends can be 5-a-side football, cinema, climbing, go-karting, paintball, or anything the pupils request. Each house votes for their house captains who then assist the boarding staff in the running of the house. All activities are compulsory for the younger ones. From year 9, pupils can go into Teignmouth, and from year 11 they can go to Exeter, back in time for supper. Occasional evenings out are allowed if arranged in advance with set home times. Church on most Sundays in Teignmouth for everyone.

Regular Skype calls to parents, plus updates from houseparents. One parent said, 'Houseparents are simply the best. They looked after [him] so well. [He] loved them. They would send me emails to tell me how [he] is doing without me asking. They are really excellent.' Other parents told us, 'Very safe environment with a lot of activities.' Exeats in the middle of each half term, one being compulsory in the autumn and spring terms.

Background and atmosphere: Founded in 1979, Trinity used to be a girls' convent school. Set in a stunning location in Teignmouth, it has views over Lyme Bay and the English Channel. Not far from the rugged moors of Dartmoor and the surf beaches of South Devon, Teignmouth is a traditional English seaside town. It is a quiet town, not known for nightly rowdiness like other nearby hotspots. This is part of the attraction for parents; it's safe. 'The smaller size of the boarding school in a safe area was attractive given [he] was travelling on his own,' said a parent of a boarder.

The main building is old; narrow corridors, even narrower wooden winding stairs, and panelled wood. The red library on the red corridor is in the oldest part of the building. It's set on two levels, with a reading room to one side and a large teddy in residence in the middle. The reading room is also used for lunchtime films plus the girls' and the boys' (separate) 'brew clubs'.

Up the stairs are the chapel and the boarding accommodation. At the very top of the building, aptly named The Attic, is the sixth form area. Here, there is a (very warm) study room, a quiet zone and a common room. Basic and functional, but ideally located at the top of the school away from everybody else. The new building links into the original building with a courtyard in middle. In the new part is a DT lab with laser cutter and CNC cutter, four science labs and three ICT suites.

The school's motto is 'Optimism, Confidence, Charity.' Recently they have raised over £4,500 for local, national (mainly British Heart Foundation) and international charities like the one in South Africa. Annually there is a Giving Nations' Day when pupils set up stalls and sell their wares for charities around the world. Students are also encouraged to volunteer to help in the prep school or work in a local elderly home. Trinity has won the school float contest in the Teignmouth Carnival for the last two years.

For sixth formers, there's quite a social calendar to keep up with. They kick off the year with a disco or gig night, followed by quiz nights, a fancy dress party and a film festival. That only takes them up to the Christmas festivities. Then it's the Valentine's ball, a prefect dinner, a summer barbeque, a beach barbeque, and finally the sixth form summer ball.

Pastoral care, well-being and discipline: 'The head teacher and all of the staff involved in pastoral care have been excellent,' said a parent. Another told us that they chose Trinity because 'I wanted a caring supportive environment which I felt was important as I am a single parent.' Form tutors, key stage heads, boarding staff, two qualified nurses, the school chaplain, and a school counsellor are all available to support the pupils. The school also runs pastoral review meetings every half term to share information amongst staff, and discuss any potential issues or support needed.

The prefect system, including the pastoral prefects and the mentors, provides peer support and ultimately friendships across the years. The house system also gives pupils the chance to make more friends throughout the school – and it is taken very seriously; pupils love the competitiveness. There are regular sports competitions, talent shows, science and maths challenges.

Trinity is a Christian school built on a joint Anglican and Roman Catholic foundation. The school chapel is central to the spiritual life of the whole school community. Mixed year chapel services throughout the week plus hymn practice every other week. Employs a full-time chaplain, a C of E priest. As well as formal celebrations, chapel and assemblies, his role includes the pastoral care of pupils and staff. He also teaches PE and looks after the boarders a few nights a week; he is keen to get to know everyone. He is also keen that the school becomes a part of the local community and that pupils 'don't live in a bubble.' He encourages them to 'look outward' and participate in local charitable events. Pupils we spoke to were happy with the school's approach to religion and said 'it's not pushed, it's a way of life' at Trinity.

Zero tolerance on drinking, smoking and drugs. Persistent smaller offences lead to detentions. Further persistence leads to suspension and expulsion. Trinity works with pupils and parents as much as possible to prevent this.

Pupils and parents: Parents of day pupils are mainly local professionals. Recently many more people are relocating to

Devon and commuting into London. Some pupils come from as far as Totnes, Paignton, Ivybridge and Honiton. This is the advantage of having a train station on the doorstep; pupils can catch the train to school and jump on the school shuttle. The Dartmouth bypass should also help bring more pupils from that part of Devon. Escorted airport bus service for boarders. Parents all agreed, 'Communication is good, proactive and responsive. No complaints.'

Entrance: Entrance test and interview. Copies of school reports if applicable. For sixth form entry five GCSE passes at grade C/5 or above. Overseas students must complete a personal statement and English skills assessment. Parents commented, 'The school was very helpful in helping the children settle in. I could not have asked for more.' Another confirmed, 'The children now feel at home at the school.'

Exit: Around 40-45 per cent leave after GCSEs to go to the local grammar schools or vocational colleges. Around the same number of new pupils join the sixth form. Around 65 per cent to university. A good number of pupils go to Russell Group universities; some overseas students return to their home countries.

Money matters: Scholarships available, mostly at 11+, offering up to 50 per cent off fees. Plus means-tested bursaries, armed forces discounts and sibling allowances.

Remarks: Trinity School is a small school that provides a safe and supportive environment for pupils of all abilities – particularly those who may have struggled to learn in the past, or lacked the confidence or support to reach their potential. Trinity ticks all the boxes, but it doesn't push any boundaries, it just does what it does well.

Truro and Penwith College

College Road, Truro, Cornwall TR1 3XX

Ages 16+ **Pupils** 5,300

01872 267000
www.truro-penwith.ac.uk

Principal: Since 2010, David Walrond MA MBA PGCE (50s). Read English at Exeter University (followed by MA in 20th century religious verse), PGCE at Oxford and an MBA in education management at Leicester University. Previously director of curriculum, quality and planning at Truro and Penwith College for seven years. Has worked in post-16 colleges in London, Hampshire and Cheshire and was an associate Ofsted inspector for five years. Early in his career he lived in Italy for four years, doing everything from driving a forklift truck to lecturing in English at Padua University – 'a real life education,' he says.

Although his PGCE was in secondary education he has always worked with post-16 students. He believes that '11 to 18 is too big a phase to teach under one roof,' whereas a post-16 college can specialise and teach a vast number of subjects (50 here) in any combination. 'We understand this age group and its challenges very well,' he says. Still gives the occasional English literature lecture. Hugely proud of the college's myriad achievements: it was the first FE college to be awarded outstanding status by Ofsted, is the best performing state A level provider in Cornwall and is in the top two per cent nationally for progress made from GCSE exam results. As he says: 'We add value.' Unlike some heads he doesn't denigrate subjects like media. 'Media can be a fantastic career,' he says. 'We have a hugely successful media and creative industry in this country and it can be a very profitable thing to get into.'

Principal is based at Truro campus but drives down to the Penwith campus in Penzance once or twice a week (his Penwith office has the best outlook we've seen in a long time – a stunning view of St Michael's Mount). Married to Carol and has three children. In his spare time he enjoys music (Bach in particular), cricket, literature and languages.

Academic matters: Results are truly impressive – even more so given the number of students (some 2,200 currently doing A levels or IB) and the range of ability. In 2018, 37 per cent of A levels were A*/A and 69 per cent A*-B. College also offers IB – average scores (36 points in 2018) make it a consistent high performer compared with other non-selective state providers. Teachers are post-16 specialists 'who love their subject.' A girl hoping to study forensic science at university said her tutor 'had made maths enjoyable' for the first time in her life. Recently designated as a maths hub and 300 students take maths A level every year.

The college is big but classes are small – 15 on average, although the sciences are sometimes larger. College monitors students' attendance and tracks their progress throughout their time here. A budding medic described the college as 'a stepping stone to adulthood, from calling your teacher "Sir" to being friends with your tutor,' but added: 'We all know that if we want our grades we have to work.' Parents' evenings once a term – students attend with their parents.

Revision sessions and extra classes on offer in the run-up to exams and students can email their tutors for help. 'This place helps students to be the best we can be,' said a teenage boy, while a girl told us: 'Coming here has made me grow as a person.' College runs a range of academies to support gifted and talented students and promote excellence – these include an academic academy, medics academy, STEM academy, music academy and 11 sporting academies (from cricket and rugby to sports leadership and, not surprisingly given the location, surfing).

A host of vocational options are given the same parity of esteem as more traditional academic routes. Total of 1,400 students on two-year level 3 vocational programmes – anything from bricklaying and carpentry to hospitality and catering. Hair and beauty students are based in a very professional looking salon called FACE (staff and students get discounts) and a nail technician student recently scooped silver in advanced nail art at the World Skills UK competition. Another won gold in the computer games development section of the same event. Apprenticeships are growing in popularity – everything from art and design to computing and IT. College has close links with Rick Stein and is the training provider for the chef's apprenticeship programme.

College offers diagnostic testing when students start. Learning support tutors work with students on literacy, numeracy, revision skills, exam technique, essay writing and more – one-to-one, in small groups or in workshops. Broad range of students includes those with profound and multiple learning difficulties and university undergraduates (college launched higher education provision in 1998).

Games, options, the arts: College offers Study Plus – an enrichment programme of activities like drama, driving theory, IT, languages, music, photography, skateboarding and work experience. DofE is popular, plus fundraising for charity and trips abroad (either as part of students' studies or for enrichment). 'There are far more opportunities here than there were at school,' a student said approvingly. College has its fair share of sporting successes – 'you'll find the most able sports people in Cornwall here,' we were told. England rugby player Jack Nowell is a former student and college wins scores of sporting honours every year.

Art, music and drama, as we said last time, are seriously top notch. Even if the arts aren't for you there are plenty of other pursuits. A teenager heading for university told us that while she'd been at the college she'd trained as a barista, learned Makaton and volunteered with a local food bank.

Background and atmosphere: When the college opened in 1993 it expected to take 500 students from Truro and the surrounding area, but more than 700 turned up on the first day. Its reputation is so impressive that some travel up to 90 minutes to attend, with others from further afield lodging with host families during the week. The college merged with Penwith College in Penzance in 2008.

The Truro campus, three miles west of the city centre, is purpose built, architecturally striking and wonderfully resourced. It is the sort of place that tempts fee-paying parents to chuck their chequebooks aside – and the list of students' previous schools shows that many do just that. Breathtaking facilities, ranging from the White building, an art and design department filled with gleaming Macs and light, airy studios, to the Mylor building, which houses science, music, dance and the performing arts. The buildings all have their own libraries and IT suites and are bright, well equipped and immaculately kept – no litter or graffiti here.

The college has a university campus feel – bells don't ring, there's no uniform and students address lecturers by their first names. The principal reckons that in today's society, where teenagers are 'protected and often infantalised' by their parents, the college prepares youngsters well for university. He says that students learn to be self sufficient and independent here, while being supported through their studies. The size and bustling atmosphere can be bewildering at first but it's not a place where students feel lost in any sense of the word. Plasma screens in each building give news about what's going on and, as we discovered ourselves, students are happy to stop and point newcomers in the right direction.

Pastoral care, well-being and discipline: Students spend their working lives in 15-strong tutor groups. Every student has a tutor (usually a lecturer who teaches them) who is the first port of call for advice and guidance. Very effective student services department offers help on everything from careers to a lost bus pass and from money worries to problems at home. Student counsellor for graver problems. College runs a series of induction days for new students before term starts in September.

Staff told us that students know what is expected of them and discipline isn't an issue. No drink or drugs – college tries to educate youngsters about drugs and alcohol issues and provides help for those who ask for it. Designated smoking areas. A plethora of canteens and snack bars throughout the college, even a mobile burger bar – all cashless and paid for by card.

Pupils and parents: Cornwall is the poorest county in the country and students come from a cross-section of backgrounds and from state and independent schools.

None of the students we met were intimidated by the size of the place. One boy told us: 'If school had been more like this college I would have liked it more' while a 17-year-old girl in her second year said the college had exceeded her expectations. 'I wanted to be more independent and this seemed like an amazing place to study,' she said. 'Before I came here I was at a school with only 300 pupils but everyone is so friendly here that I knew straight away that I was in the right place. It's more grown-up and more informal than school, but you are expected to work hard.'

Entrance: Students applying to do A levels need at least five 4s at GCSE, preferably 6s in the subjects they want to study at A level. However the principal stresses that the entry requirements aren't set in stone. 'If we had a very rigid entry it would be selection by school,' he says. 'Not all schools perform equally well.'

'Interviews are very friendly,' said a member of staff. 'We ask students why they want to come here and what their goals are.' Those who don't get their grades are invited in to discuss their options and some retake English and maths GCSE here. 'The college doesn't give up on people,' we were told.

Exit: 'We understand higher education very well here,' says the principal, adding that the college processes a staggering 1,500 UCAS forms a year. Between a dozen and 20 to Oxbridge every year (18 in 2018, plus 21 medics/vets) and around a quarter to Russell Group universities.

Money matters: Subsidised travel available to full-time students under 19 who live further than three miles from the college. Bursary fund assists students with travel, essential equipment and trips – all means tested.

Remarks: Exciting and forward thinking. Truro and Penwith College is at the top of its game and thoroughly deserves the accolades heaped upon it. Offers a broad range of qualifications for all and provides the perfect bridge between school and higher education. Despite its size, it is nurturing, inclusive and achieves glittering results.

Truro High School

Linked with Truro High School Preparatory Department

Falmouth Road, Truro, Cornwall TR1 2HU

Ages 11–19 **Pupils** 195 **Sixth form** 35 **Boarders** 28 full, 2 weekly, 10 flexi

Fees: Day £13,896; Boarding £26,040 – £28,182 pa

01872 272830
www.trurohigh.co.uk

Head: Since September 2018, Sarah Matthews, previously acting head of St Mary's Shaftesbury. Degree in philosophy and RS from Lancaster and PGCE from St Martin's College. Spent 12 years at Stamford Endowed Schools before moving to Harrow International School Hong Kong as housemistress and teacher of philosophy and RS. Joined St Mary's Shaftesbury in 2017 as senior deputy and then acting head. She is an avid reader, with a particular interest in anthropology, and also enjoys baking and hiking in her spare time. She is married to Richard, and they have two young children.

Academic matters: In 2018, 59 per cent A*/A grades and 83 per cent A*-B at A level; 55 per cent 9-7 at GCSE. The school is regularly top of the county league for A level and GCSE.

T

Twenty-one subjects on offer at A level. Maths and physics are strong, and all girls take separate sciences at GCSE. English is consistently good at both A level and GCSE. Latin holds up very well at GCSE and is still there at A level. MFLs include Spanish, French and German, as well as EAL and a Japanese club. Religious philosophy is compulsory. Has opened the first solar observatory on mainland UK. New Aspiring Medics programme has already produced a Cambridge medic and a Nottingham vet, and there are programmes for lawyers and engineers too, plus a brand new engineering workshop. The school has its own racing car team with five cars and the girls are raring to compete in national events.

With so few pupils, all classes are small, and at A level some are even one-to-one. Very low turnover of staff but a few recent retirements have made way for some welcome new blood. Parents told us, 'We are impressed by and have every confidence in the teachers who have been involved in our child's education.' One was a bit more critical: 'I think the teachers are pretty good, but listening to the girls talk about them, I think covering illness etc could be better handled. I still feel there is a lot of stuff which goes unchecked, spelling errors in work displayed on the wall etc, errors in reports.'

All staff are trained in assessment techniques and the school provides extra study support for pupils in the prep and the senior school with dyslexia or dyspraxia. The small class sizes enable regular monitoring and support.

Games, options, the arts: Facilities are pretty good. There's a 25 metre heated indoor swimming pool, full sized Astroturf, a playing field, two netball/tennis courts, and an athletics area for long/high jump, javelin, discus etc. There's also a separate dance studio building, historically only used for ballet, now packed with yoga classes, and street and lyrical dance ensembles.

Weekly netball and hockey fixtures and the school has won many county titles, with girls representing the West of England too. Football and tag rugby are now on the curriculum and the new rugby club on Mondays was hot news of the day. Proper rugby, not tag, we were informed. They even had the Cornish Pirates in for a session. Swimming is popular, as is horse riding; they have their own team. Outdoor pursuits such as DofE and Ten Tors are a part of life here.

Most girls learn an instrument and there's a 120-strong choir and a 60-strong orchestra, plus a jazz band, samba band, flute choir, chamber choir and a ukulele club. Recent choir trips and tours include Belgium and Hong Kong.

Rehearsals were under way for Into The Woods when we visited; the year before it was The Importance of Being Earnest. Girls are keen on debating and taking part on public speaking competitions, with large numbers doing LAMDA qualifications. One parent told us, 'I think Truro Hugh ultimately gave my daughters self belief. My youngest became the member of the youth parliament for mid Cornwall; she had been taking speech and drama lessons, and joined the debating society. These little extras can make a huge difference to one's future.'

Art rooms are a good size and sixth formers have their own area. Plenty of girls go on to do the prestigious Falmouth foundation course. Textiles also popular and former pupils have gone on to land jobs at Mulberry or Karen Millen. Head of department once worked for Laura Ashley and knows not just the creative side but also the logistics of production and manufacture. On our visit there was a lot of excitement about the fashion show that night, with part of the proceeds going towards buying a laser cutter for the department.

Boarding: 'The fact that both girls loved weekly boarding had a huge bearing on their success at school.' Majority of full boarders are from abroad, though the school also promotes its flexi facilities, and they provide some welcome cultural diversity. The German students tend to come just for a term to improve their English, but other boarders from Russia, China and Australia and the Scillies stay longer.

Two boarding houses – Dalvenie (up to year 10) and Rashleigh (years 11-13). Trips for all boarders on Saturdays and Sundays. Treasure hunts in town for the new girls, beach trips, horse-riding, shopping in Exeter and visits to the Tate in St Ives and the Eden Project. For nights in, there's pool parties with inflatables, barbeques, baking and movie nights. The older girls are allowed into town in pairs after school – back for supper at 6pm.

The younger girls are four to a room with communal showers and toilets. The older girls can opt for either two in room, or individual rooms, all with ensuites – very much like university rooms (actually a little better). In Dalvenie the common room has a TV, Wii, a pool table, piano, PCs, a dining table and a comfy sofa area. Rashleigh was refurbished a few years ago and the lounge is really rather grown up, set out like a large apartment with sofa/TV area and a fully fitted kitchen. Next door is a quiet room with pianos, a room for the girls to be able 'to get away from it all'. Girls do their own laundry and have a council and regular meetings. Houseparents live on site with their families (and cat). Their daughters also attend the school, so it really is a family affair here.

Background and atmosphere: Founded in 1880 by Bishop (later Archbishop) Benson (first Master of Wellington College) who built Truro cathedral and gave Henry James the idea for The Turn of the Screw. Situated close to the centre of Truro, the school has been on the same site since 1896, retaining its founding links with the cathedral and Christian ethos but welcomes girls of all faiths or none.

The main building is partly castellated and made of Cornish granite, not a grand entrance but a welcoming one. Inside, narrow corridors, wooden staircases, plaques dating back to 1800s, fairly antique toilet facilities, in need of a lick of paint here and there. Well maintained site with lovely gardens, though outbuildings and extensions feel a bit ad hoc. Shining stars are the most recently built language centre, music block and performing arts building.

The library seems well-used and well-resourced, with a separate sixth form area. School is definitely not overrun with computers; best IT resources appeared to be suite of iMacs in the music room. All social media is blocked until 4pm, when the boarders can log on.

'The sixth form building is fantastic,' say parents. Both floors have workstation rooms with individual carrels – the girls call these 'caroles' and personalise them as much as possible. Kitchen with dishwasher, toaster and coffee machine. Girls seemed happy and relaxed, chatting away over a mountain of toast.

Pastoral care, well-being and discipline: Discipline problems are rare and pastoral care is led by the form tutors and houseparents. There is also a nurse on site. Good mentoring and prefect system means that girls of all ages get to know each other – lots of impromptu hugging on our tour as our guide saw her younger friends. This is a small, friendly and unintimidating school. One girl told us she was bullied in her last school and that she couldn't have felt more welcome when she started Truro High. She made friends easily and says she has never looked back: 'Coming to Truro High was the best thing I've ever done.'

One parent of a boarder told us, 'Only last week my youngest, now in upper sixth, was not feeling very well, but a quick call to the boarding house reassured me. One of the senior members of staff has been there many years and I have formed a good relationship with her. Boarding at Truro High really worked for my girls, it's fun, friendly, relaxed.'

Pupils and parents: Parents are professionals, company directors and the like; many have relocated and now commute by plane or train to London. One told us, 'We were looking for a "third way" of excellent schooling without some of the arrogance, stress levels etc found elsewhere. We wouldn't have moved to Cornwall if it wasn't for Truro High.'

Others said, 'We were delighted by the atmosphere of the place. The wit and dynamism between children and teachers, the warmth between the girls – the spark was exactly what we were looking for.' Communication from the school to parents is good, with teachers viewed as 'approachable and helpful'.

Uniform up to year 11 is a Balmoral tartan skirt and green pullover. Sixth formers could easily be mistaken for staff – very mature, not a rebel in sight. Parents enthused, 'Can't speak highly enough of the culture of Truro High. Our girls come home at the end of the day with a smile on their faces. They look forward during the holidays to going back to school.'

The school has recently had a publicity makeover thanks to the director of marketing, a former ITV Cornwall news presenter. Smart promo packs, new-look magazines, local news articles, radio plugs and a Facebook page that is updated several times a day. An old girl herself, she has two daughters at the school and continues to fly its flag by setting up events like the fashion show in conjunction with local businesses, and letting parents use the grounds – one recently put on a refugee in crisis event.

The school is also strengthening its relationship with local community and parents with events such as 'family swim days' at weekends. Anyone is welcome for a small token that is then used to pay the (qualified) sixth formers to lifeguard.

Old girls include Dame Lynne Brindley (master of Pembroke College, Oxford), TV presenter Hannah Sandling, comedien and writer Morwenna Banks and mezzo soprano Anna Burford.

Entrance: Entrants mainly from own prep plus Polwhele House, Roselyon, St Piran's, Bolitho and Truro prep. A decent number are from local state primaries. Biggest overseas market currently is Hong Kong; others from Russia, Germany, Spain and Australia.

Applicants for the senior school are invited to a taster day (boarders have a trial night), then sit an exam and interview before admission. For sixth form entry, GCSE grade 9-7 in proposed A level choices, plus interviews for UK candidates and test papers/school assessments for overseas students.

Exit: On average half leave at 16 to go to (free) Truro College up the road, Truro School or co-ed boarding elsewhere. One to Oxbridge in 2018, others to eg York, Warwick, London College of Fashion and Falmouth.

Money matters: Academic, music, drama, sports and art scholarships available, plus means-tested bursaries at year 7 entry, and into sixth form.

Remarks: Truro High School is unique in Cornwall. It's a small, all-girls school that delivers on qualifications, but nurtures and cares. One parent said, 'We wanted all girls, so it was a no-brainer.' But most have been overwhelmed by the 'spark' and 'atmosphere' of the school. A few minor grumbles about teachers' spelling and communication, but all we saw were happy, well-behaved girls. One parent said, 'I thoroughly recommend Truro High, for sciences and humanities, for quieter children and more vocal – I have one of each!' It's the type of school that needs to be visited; parents will know immediately if it's right for them or not.

Truro High School Preparatory Department

Linked with Truro High School

Falmouth Road, Truro, Cornwall TR1 2HU

Ages 4–11 **Pupils** 82 **Boarders** 5 flexi (from year 5) **C of E**

Fees: Day £8,001 – £13,032; Boarding £25,185 – £27,261 pa

01872 272830
www.trurohigh.co.uk/our-school/prep

Headmistress: Since 2016, Annabel Ramsey, previously a class teacher here for two years. Brought up in Falmouth, she has a BEd from University College Chester, and began teaching at a junior school in Wootton Bassett, moving to Porthleven School and then Archbishop Benson CofE primary as deputy head. She joined Truro Prep after a year's sabbatical touring south east Asia and Australia. Loves to explore the world – whether it be close to home on the Cornish coastline and surrounding villages or far flung places in other continents. She is a great fan of the theatre, visiting at every opportunity, with a particular passion for Les Misérables.

Entrance: Application process followed by a taster day and informal assessment. Once accepted, there is a 'buddy system' to help all the girls settle in and feel at home. Boarding is available from year 3 upwards.

The nursery has recently been taken over by a company called Naturally Learning Nursery. They are able to provide all-year nursery care, plus aftercare for the primary school. Although they have strong links with the prep school (sharing facilities and combining forces for trips), applications are separate.

Exit: Almost all go on to senior school. No further assessments to transfer, but girls do sit the entrance exam to determine setting. For academic reasons some may be asked to look elsewhere, but these situations are reasonably rare and are handled early on with parents. From year 6 some lessons are in the senior school, and girls are allowed to use the senior school library. Since it is such a small school with shared facilities, a joint weekly assembly and an all-through house system, girls are already familiar with senior school life when they start..

Remarks: Truro High Prep is a happy school. Academic progress is important here, but so is fun, and well-being is key. There are opportunities galore to express and be creative, and the girls can do so in a safe and nurturing environment. The results are obvious, and one parent enthused, 'we were delighted by the atmosphere of the place. The wit and dynamism between children and teachers, the warmth between the girls – the spark was exactly what we were looking for (and what was lacking at the other schools).'

With under 100 girls, the prep school is in a small, unmodernised building next to the boarding houses. The playground is pretty standard, quite bland, but the inside of the school is a different story. Photo collages fill the stairway, and classrooms and corridors are brimming with artwork and displays. We particularly liked the paper mâché tree in the library, adorned with butterflies, and even a fluffy squirrel.

Uniform is tunics for the pre-prep girls and kilts for the prep. Classes are very small throughout the school and often the younger ones have lessons like RE together. On our visit we were treated to an impromptu demonstration on how to use an abacus (made by the girls), plus a poetry reading. The poem had been written in the last 20 minutes and the subject was anything to do with National Maths Day. The young poet had chosen shapes as a theme and the result was most impressive. Another treat was hearing about the Egyptian Extravaganza, 'Tomb Time.' Girls showed us their mummified Barbies in shoe box tombs and explained how they had mummified tomatoes. The girls were polite and confident, but not overly precocious. They were enthusiastic and excited to show us their work, but it's clear they know their boundaries. The study support department supports both prep and senior schools, and staff are trained in assessment techniques. The school provides extra study support for those pupils with dyslexia or dyspraxia.

At the end of our tour, the head teacher was off to help with the singing auditions for the upcoming production, Cinderella Rockefeller. On our way out we were lucky enough to sneak a peek at the reception class rehearsing Noah's Ark. The school is passionate about putting on plays and musicals, and of course the annual nativity. They even put on an open-air production of The Princess and the Frog by the school pond last summer. Music is a big part of life here too, with many taking part in the junior choir, and the majority learning instruments.

The prep school has use of the senior school facilities including a heated indoor swimming pool, netball/tennis courts and playing fields. There's an annual sports day and a swimming gala. There's also a dance studio and due to popular demand, street and lyrical dance has now been introduced to the curriculum. Ballet is still available as an extracurricular activity.

As you would expect in this part of the country, plenty of outdoor learning. This could be anything from bird watching to taking care of the bug hotel and studying worms. Gardening club is popular; recently they have been very busy planting trees in a local park for a community project. There are regular trips to local art galleries and museums, and the older girls have been enjoying enrichment activities based on the theme 'When I grow up I want to be....' This has led to trips to a local wedding dress designer and an artist, so far. Who knows what will come up next, a fireman, a pilot, an astronaut? Let's hope so. There's annual residential trips for years 3 to 6, most to Barton Hall, and plenty of other fun days out for the whole school. There's the Royal Cornwall Show trip where the choir sings and girls enter pieces for Best In Show. There's Ladies' Day when girls design and create their own hats and race on hobbyhorses. There's even an Annual Pet Show. Don't panic if you don't have a pet, get creative and make one – pineapples make great turtles, apparently.

The school is keen to keep in touch with its Cornish roots and proudly celebrates St Piran's Day, but other cultures are not forgotten, with a Chinese New Year parade and Japanese Children's Day. The girls are encouraged to fundraise and support charities, including the School in a Bag fund to help children in Nepal affected by the earthquakes, Comic Relief and Race For Life.

This is a school where little girls are allowed and encouraged to be just that, little girls. If a single-sex prep is your preference then, as one parent put it, 'The Truro High School experience is unique. It has a wonderful atmosphere and feel to it. Speaking as a parent in the prep school, all the children seem to be happy. What more could you ask for?'

T

Truro Prep School

Linked with Truro School

Highertown, Truro, Cornwall TR1 3QN

Ages 3–11 **Pupils** 259

Fees: £8,895 – £12,990 pa

01872 272616
www.truroschool.com/prep

Head of Prep: Since September 2016 Sarah Patterson BEd, previously deputy head at The Junior King's School, Canterbury since 2012. Degree from Birmingham; has taught in a variety of schools including prep schools in Kenya and Chile. She has been head of English and director of studies as well as class teacher and deputy head.

Entrance: Children are admitted to the nursery at the beginning of the term following their third birthday (previously children were only admitted if they had turned three before the 1st September). Entry to nursery is first come, first served but school emphasizes from the start that it is 'education, not childcare,' with children encouraged to do two full days and gradually build up to four or five. School likes parents and children to visit first. 'We don't like to offer places to people who have not been to see us.'

For entry into reception, year 1 and year 2, admission is based on a taster day and informal assessment. For prep (years 3 to 6), entry is selective, with English, maths and non verbal reasoning tests, informal chat with the head and taster day with their year group. Children joining in year 6 and aiming for the senior school have to take the Truro School entrance exam along with external applicants.

Exit: Vast majority – 95 per cent – head to senior school at 11 (in 2018, eight scholarships awarded to year 6 leavers). Progression to senior school is by head's recommendation – parents get a letter when their children are in year 5 to say whether they've got a place or not, although they still take the entrance exam 'as an assessment exercise.' A handful of pupils go elsewhere, including Truro High (girls), Mount Kelly and the occasional scholarship to Millfield.

Remarks: An idyllic, 10-acre setting at the end of a winding, rhododendron-bordered drive, surrounded on all sides by the local golf course, extensive woods and sports grounds. Originally known as Treliske School, it was founded as Truro School's prep in 1936. Victorian main school building is grade II listed manor house and boasts a wealth of period detail and stunning art collection (we particularly admired the Terry Frost painting in the hall). A new building (completed at the end of 2017) includes six classrooms, a music/drama studio and an assembly hall.

Academic standards are good (excellent, said latest ISI inspection), with teachers praised for their ability to bring out the best in everyone. All pupils have a form tutor whom they see for registration, reading period and 10 minutes at the end of the school day. Specialist teaching from years 4 to 6. Pupils set for English and maths from year 4. On the languages front, pupils have taster year of German in year 3, taster year of

Spanish in year 4 and start French in year 5. No Latin on offer – 'there's no time.' SEN department offers individual and in class support. School has pupils with mild dyslexia, hypermobility needs and some with autistic spectrum behaviours. Maximum class size is 20 from years 3 to 6, 16 from reception to year 2 and 30 in the nursery. A good blend of male and female teachers.

Year 6 'is a fantastic year,' with all year 6s taking the Truro Prep diploma, a mix of core academic subjects (English, maths and science), humanities, performing arts, creative arts, sports and outdoor activity and life skills (including IT, languages, first aid and cooking). It's 'good, solid preparation' for life in the senior school. We reckon that with its research project and cookery lessons (everyone has to cook a two course meal) it'll set them up well for the university years too.

School is hot on reading and staff urge parents to read with their children – not just idly listen while they concentrate on doing something else. 'We want them to sit down together and share a book.' More than a third of pupils play musical instruments – year 3s learn curriculum music and year 4s learn strings, brass, woodwind or percussion for a year in small groups.

Nursery and pre-prep housed in spacious, modern building, separate from main school and with own gated grounds. Built in 1991, it was extended in 2009 and has a forest school, Enchanted Garden and Magic Tree – all wonderfully Enid Blyton. Nursery staff give parents a video record of their children's early years – saved on a memory stick at the end of each term.

As you'd expect, children spend lots of time outdoors here – playing in the woods, working in an outdoor classroom designed and built by the DT teacher and growing fruit and vegetables at the gardening club. School brims with imaginative and creative ideas – a group of pupils recently made a racing car and raced it at Newquay Airport while others started a company called Cornish Jammers, making and selling strawberry jam. In typical forward thinking fashion, prep has also applied to set up a partnership with local state and independent schools to make their own apps. All pupils do ICT, including coding and animation. Sport is hugely important too – particularly rugby, football, cricket, netball, athletics, tennis, swimming, sailing and kayaking. Everyone learns to swim by the age of 7. Like the senior school, which runs a fencing elite academy programme, the prep is excellent at fencing. A pupil who started fencing sabre at the prep has been ranked second in Europe at under-17 level and current pupils won gold and silver medals at recent IAPS fencing championships.

Around half the pupils are Truro based while a fifth live near the A39 corridor to Falmouth. Others travel long distances to the school, from the likes of Wadebridge, Fowey, Padstow, St Ives and Helston. School runs a very popular early birds breakfast club for pupils, parents and siblings from 7.45 to 8.15am, offering bacon butties, croissants, cooked breakfasts etc. For pre-prep children there's a tea club from 3.45 to 5.30pm (at a small cost), while prep pupils can stay till 5.30pm for homework club (free), clubs and activities (everything from sailing and kayaking to chess and dance). There is a supper club that runs from 5.30pm until 6.15pm. Mindful of some children's long journeys, school offers a packed tea for them to munch on the way home – parents order in advance and it goes on the bill. Lunch said to be excellent – everything cooked in house, organic and local food where possible and served up café style. Navy uniform is smart and practical and everyone keeps a pair of wellies in school for rainy days (there are quite a lot of them in this part of the world).

A happy school, where children get the chance to learn, have fun and grow up in their own time – as well as make the most of the glorious countryside and coastline. Parents (many of whom are recent arrivals to Cornwall) are hugely supportive and appreciate the prep's distinctive Cornish vibe. 'It has a very friendly, laid back atmosphere,' one mother told us, 'but it gets very good results too.' Another said: 'It reflects the area. It's not a hothouse and it offers exactly the right balance of work and play.'

Truro School

Linked with Truro Prep School

Trennick Lane, Truro, Cornwall TR1 1TH

Ages 11–18 **Pupils** 768 **Sixth form** 164 **Boarders** 62 full, 15 weekly

Fees: Day £14,070; Boarding £24,120 – £28, 065 pa

01872 272763
www.truroschool.com

Headmaster: Since 2013, Andrew Gordon-Brown BCom MSc QTS (40s). Educated at Hyde Park High School in Johannesburg, read commerce at University of Cape Town and then qualified as a chartered accountant. He rowed for South Africa in the 1992 Olympic Games (team came a creditable eighth) and set his heart on rowing for Oxford or Cambridge. He achieved his dream when he completed an MSc in agricultural economics at Keble College, Oxford and picked up a rowing blue along the way (he rowed for Oxford in the 1994 Boat Race). After 12 years in banking and financial services, working for blue chip companies such as Deloitte, UBS and JPMorgan Chase, he had a 'Damascene conversion' and decided to become a teacher. 'I turned my back on the big bucks,' he told us with a smile. Achieved his QTS via the University of Gloucestershire, taught economics and rowing at Radley for four years and then spent five years as deputy head at Stonyhurst College in Lancashire.

Dedicated, energetic and charming, he has always loved Cornwall (his family owns an old farmhouse on The Lizard) so jumped at the chance to take the reins at Truro School. Keen to use his business background to help pupils, he teaches careers guidance to year 11s and runs financial literacy classes as part of the sixth form's enrichment programme. Has a very global outlook and tells students they should see the world 'as their labour market.' He holds regular lunches for year groups and describes pupils as 'wonderfully unpretentious.' 'Unlike in bigger conurbations, they don't have an edge to them,' he says. Discipline isn't a problem either. As he puts it: 'The teachers teach, the pupils learn and the parents are very supportive.'

His wife Harriet (who was on the same MSc course as him at Oxford) is very involved in school life and they have three children, the eldest at the senior school, the younger two at the prep. They live in a house on the school site.

Still a keen sportsman, he enjoys running, cycling and going to the gym. His family has recently bought a boat – 'but I'm a novice sailor' – and he sings whenever he can (most recently in the Truro School Choral Society performance of Faure's Requiem at Truro Cathedral).

Academic matters: It's cool to work hard here – and the pupils do. Fifty-seven per cent of GCSEs were A*-A/9-7 in 2018. At A level, 36 per cent A*/A. The sciences and maths are particularly strong and many go on to be medics, dentists, engineers and, perhaps not surprisingly given the location, geologists. The school is one of only 230 in the country to offer geology – 'we've got a department that isn't far off a small university department.' School runs more than 20 subjects at A level, including business studies, economics, PE and psychology. Thanks to a bit of timetabling wizardry, students can take any combination (for options submitted in the preceding spring term). EPQ on offer too.

Everyone does at least one language at GCSE and some take up to three (students can study a third language from year 9 in extra twilight sessions first thing, at lunchtime and after school). Mainly French, German and Spanish but the school will do its best to accommodate requests for others (students have taken Chinese, Dutch and Russian in recent years). Exchange trips for younger pupils and work experience in France and Germany for older ones, with CVs written in French and German of course. Music is offered to talented musicians off-timetable as an extra GCSE.

Learning support department with full-time head and two part-time staff. School caters for students with moderate learning difficulties – dyslexia, dyspraxia, dyscalculia, dysgraphia and Asperger's. All students are tested during their first year at the school – extra support given individually or in small groups (no extra cost).

All pupils are encouraged to be the best they can (school motto is 'To be rather than to seem to be') and they get regular progress reviews, on attitude in lessons, ability to study independently and organisation skills, as well as academic achievement.

Games, options, the arts: A very sporty school, with county champions in rugby, hockey and netball. First XV regularly gets into the last 16 of the NatWest Schools Cup and a sixth former was recently selected for the England U18 XV. Teams often have to travel long distances to compete but pupils don't seem to mind. The school has 40 acres of playing fields, Astroturf, eight tennis courts, cricket pavilion and grounds, climbing wall and a 25m pool, but the jewel in the crown is the new Sir Ben Ainslie Sports Centre, opened by the man himself, which boasts an eight-court sports hall, two squash courts, fitness suite and dance studio. It's used by the local community too – 400 members signed up in a flash when it opened. The days of the school being regarded as 'the rich kids on the hill' have long gone. The school also excels at fencing and runs an elite academy programme. Several youngsters are aiming for the 2020 Olympics. As the head reminded us, 80 per cent of Cornwall's county border is sea, so the school makes the most of the plethora of water pursuits on the doorstep – like sailing, surfing and snorkelling.

The music department buzzes with activity from dawn till dusk. A third of pupils takes instrumental lessons and there are orchestras, choirs, bands and jazz bands to join. Pupils frequently selected for National Youth Orchestra and National Youth Choirs. Around three or four a year take music at A level. School has a strong relationship with Truro Cathedral – girl choristers aged 13 to 18 can now join the cathedral choir and get a 25 per cent scholarship from the school.

Drama is top notch. When we visited, the school was gearing up for a production of Sweeney Todd, complete with an ambitious two-storey revolving stage. Theatre was opened by Sir Tim Rice, and as well as school productions, it opens its doors to touring companies. Art is superb – everything from oil paintings and life drawing to sculpture and ceramics line the head's study, corridors, boarding houses and art department. School has strong links with nearby Falmouth University and with local artists (work exhibited at school's new Heseltine Gallery). We loved the graffiti-style mural painted up the side of the gallery steps – pupils came up with ideas and street artist Cosmic spent five days on a cherry picker creating it. Theatre studies and art are popular at A level. So is DT, which is taught in a proper workshop. Pupils' work is often inspired by the sea – we spotted model yachts, a gadget for cleaning boat chains and a rocking hammock.

Wednesday afternoons are given over to extracurricular activities – everything from sport and music to surfing and war games. Truro pupils certainly don't lack fresh air, that's for sure. DofE is huge here (over 100 take part each year) and there are always school teams in the gruelling Ten Tors Challenge across the wilds of Dartmoor. World Challenge on offer, plus a raft of expeditions at home and abroad.

Boarding: Small number of boarders but head says that he has 'given boarding a bit of a push', and recently opened an additional boarding house for girls. There are now four boarding houses (two for girls, two for boys), all small and homely and each with a resident housemistress or housemaster. Boarders do 90 minutes prep a night in the library, overseen by staff and sixth formers. Lots of activities organised at weekends, particularly for the youngest – kayaking, coasteering, surfing, barbecues etc. Older pupils get time to socialise with their friends – 'it's important not to timetable every part of their day,' said a housemistress. Some flexi-boarding available.

Background and atmosphere: Gloriously situated on a hill overlooking the River Truro and the cathedral (tantalising glimpses as you walk between the buildings). A Methodist school founded in 1880, it opened with 35 boys and two teachers in a schoolroom in the centre of the city and moved to its current site in 1882. Original gothic building in local stone has been much added to – it's 'a bit of a warren,' said a parent – but it adds to the charm. School went co-ed in 1990 and these days 40 per cent of pupils are girls. Buildings include a lovely 1920s chapel and library with 18,000 resources. Whole school assembly every Tuesday. Library staff are dynamic – they produce a reading for pleasure guide and invite the likes of Meg Rosoff and Patrick Gale to do author events.

Food gets the thumbs-up – 800 lunches served up every day, payment by lunch cards and lots of choice. Boarders eat in the main school, although they can make toast, pasta, hot drinks etc in boarding house kitchens. Sixth formers have to be in school every morning but if they haven't got lessons, they are allowed out after 12 noon. They also have their own café and sixth form centre, complete with common room, study area and thumping music at break time.

Pastoral care, well-being and discipline: School has clear expectations of pupils but everyone we spoke to reckoned it's a fair, equitable place. Prefects are trained to play a big brother/sister role to younger counterparts. Most lower sixth pupils do a 16-week peer counselling programme led by the chaplain (who's known as the Rev). When we asked if the school is strict, a year 7 pupil told us: 'There are lots of rules but they are reasonable ones.' Homework is pretty sensible too – starting at 20 minutes a night per subject (up to three subjects a night) and rising as youngsters get older. Good support for new pupils – sixth form prefects look after younger pupils and maps doled out to help them navigate their way round the site. The only improvements year 7s and 8s could think of would be a mini-buggy or ski lift to transport them around the campus. Unlikely to happen any time soon.

Deputy head is responsible for pupil progress and welfare. Tutor groups organised by year and tutors are pupils' first port of call if there are any problems (they can also go to their head of year, chaplain, medical centre, school counsellor and sixth form peer counsellors). Head boy and head girl, plus deputies and a raft of senior prefects, and a house system in place. Current head is said to be stricter on uniform than his predecessor and pupils are well turned out. Sixth formers wear business dress – 'we have our own fashion sense but we have to look smart,' said one. No jeans and trousers must have a crease.

Pupils and parents: The youngsters we met were down-to-earth, motivated and refreshingly modest about their individual achievements. Our guides included a talented 800m England schools champion and a jazz singer who's in the National Youth Choir, but we had to drag the information out of them.

T

'Anyone can fit in here – even if they are quite shy,' we were told. Pupils come from all over Cornwall – around half from Truro itself, but others from up to an hour away and as far afield as St Austell, Bodmin, St Ives and Penzance. Many travel long distances by train (a fleet of double-decker buses ferry them from the station) and parents have organised minibuses from places like Helston.

The boarders include weekly boarders who live in the Scilly Isles, children of expats and a small number of international students from countries like Germany, Spain, Italy, Hong Kong, China, Nigeria, Georgia and Ukraine (around 40 with EAL requirements). Everyone mixes in together – 'it's a really friendly place,' a sixth former told us.

Parents are an eclectic group – lots of doctors, accountants and lawyers plus farmers, holiday park owners and entrepreneurs. Just like their children, they are genial, unpushy and appreciative of the school. As we said last time, there's 'nothing flash or lah-di-dah here.' A mother who'd moved from Surrey told us: 'The teachers are incredibly supportive and down-to-earth – questions and queries always get dealt with, and unlike my son's old school, I never come home grumbling.' Parents also said they approve of the way the school treats youngsters as individuals and seeks to discover everyone's talents.

Former pupils include former M&S chairman Lord Myners, actors Robert Shaw, John Rhys Davies and Nigel Terry, baritones Benjamin Luxon and Alan Opie, sopranos Lynette Carveth and Saffron Jones, quadruple Olympic gold medallist sailor Ben Ainslie, chess grandmaster Michael Adams and Queen drummer Roger Taylor.

Entrance: Around 40 per cent of the pupils come from the school's own prep, the rest from a host of state and prep schools. School is moderately selective (around 110 applications for 85 year 7 places) and main entry points are at 11+, 13+ and 16+. Admission before sixth form is by entrance exam, school report and interview. For pupils joining sixth form, predicted GCSE grades, school report and interview.

Exit: Around a third leave after GCSEs, either because they want a change or to do subjects not offered by Truro School (many head off to the mighty Truro and Penwith College four miles away, although new head says he is determined to increase retention). After the sixth form most go to university (80 per cent straight from school), including a handful to Oxbridge – one in 2018, plus one medic. Maths, sciences and geology are the most popular subjects and Cardiff, Exeter and Bristol the most popular destinations over the last five years, with a few off to Europe or the US. The school offers a specialised careers programme for budding medics, dentists and vets.

Money matters: Academic, art, music, drama, fencing and sport scholarships worth five to 10 per cent of the fees offered. Not a rich school – no endowments – so relies on prudent husbandry and strives to be as inclusive as it can afford to be. Some means-tested bursaries and headmaster's boarding awards (fee discount of 25 per cent) for boarders.

Remarks: A friendly, high achieving school with a real sense of purpose. It combines the best of old and new, makes the most of the bracing Cornish sea air and encourages pupils to find their own niche, whatever it may be.

Uffculme School

Chapel Hill, Uffculme, Cullompton, Devon EX15 3AG

Ages 11–16 **Pupils** 1,032

01884 840458
www.uffculmeschool.net

Head teacher: Since 2007, Lorraine Heath, grew up in Yeovil and studied at Exeter University. Never straying far, she taught English at several schools in Somerset before working as an English advisor for the local authority for a year. After five years as deputy head at Ladymead (now Taunton Academy), she joined Uffculme. Already a very good school, she was determined to make it better.

Lorraine met her husband, also originally a teacher, at Exeter University. He now runs his own business. Her eldest is at university studying philosophy and her youngest is still at school. Any hobbies, we asked? Her friends would say 'shopping and champagne,' she laughed, but in reality it's the gym and time with her family. Definitely 'doesn't do camping'. When invited on a trip by her staff (very outdoorsy, here), she politely declined – 'nowhere to plug in her hair straighteners'. Fair point, we agreed.

Lorraine still teaches – currently GCSE media studies. She likes to be part of the team and wants to get to know the students. One parent said, 'She has the right blend of professionalism and friendly approach. Students respect her, trust her and like her...The teachers all follow her example too. They are friendly and approachable and all teach with amazing diligence.' She says of the school's success, 'The trick is not to overcomplicate – keep it simple – do the right things well.'

Academic matters: In 2018, at GCSE, 84 per cent got 9-4 in both maths and English, with 31 per cent A*-A/9-7 grades. Results are consistently far above national averages and make Uffculme one of the top performing comprehensive schools in the country; rated outstanding by Ofsted at last inspection. One parent told us, 'We chose Uffculme because of its great reputation. The reputation continues to be good in the area as the academic results have been so impressive.'

Alongside core subjects, all students must take PE, ICT and RE. The majority here take all three sciences separately – when we were there almost an entire class put up their hands when asked if they had chosen separate sciences. Parents would, however, like to see them 'push languages more and offer Spanish and Latin.' For most subjects pupils are taught in ability sets; one parent told us, 'Teachers deal with the mixed abilities well, pushing and challenging in good measure.' Another said, 'The teachers are inspirational, lessons are fun, motivating and engaging.' Some students – around 15 a year – combine fewer GCSEs with vocational qualifications at local colleges. This involves a day a week at either Exeter, Petroc or Bicton Colleges studying mechanics, land based studies or hairdressing, for example.

'Students who receive the pupil premium, disabled students and those with special educational needs all make very good progress', says Ofsted. Good learning support department, with specialist teachers. Students are supported in lessons, in small groups or one-to-one. All pupils take screening tests on entry to the school and there is plenty of literacy and numeracy support for year 7s. One parent we spoke to whose child has significant learning difficulties said, 'We firmly believe that a good quality education should be available locally, within our community. This is sadly more difficult to achieve when your child has significant learning difficulties; however, Uffculme school gets it right, expecting the best from all its students whilst supporting, coaching and nurturing their whole development.' Another parent told us, 'We chose Uffculme because it seemed the only place that seemed able or willing to cater for a child with extreme academic intelligence but also intense special needs. Our decision was based on the learning support team with its clear expertise, understanding and experience of similar children. In particular the HLTA with a specialism in autism gave us confidence.' They added, 'Certain special teachers have genuinely touched and transformed my child's experience of school with a shared enthusiasm for learning.'

The Aspire programme is a way of supporting student aspirations to gain entry to highly competitive universities. Any year 10 students predicted top grades can attend a regular mentoring session to keep up to date with their academic and emotional progress. There are college and university visits, plus guest speakers and lessons on how the process works. However, it's not just about university and careers; the programme challenges the brighter kids with tasks that they might fail, and teaches them to cope with that failure.

Games, options, the arts: Lots of sports success with some pupils competing at a national level in women's rugby, golf, sprinting and cross-country. The U13 and U15 girls' rugby teams are county champions, as are the U12 boys' team. In basketball, it's the girls winning again – both the U14 and U16 teams are regional winners, and are through to the last eight in the country. Past pupils include an Exeter Chiefs player, a national BMX champion and those playing hockey, rugby, wheelchair badminton and golf for England, plus sailing and horse riding for GB.

Good facilities. Playing fields, plus tennis, netball, basketball courts and a large sports hall. Health and fitness is in a separate building, run as a separate business by the school, with pupils given full and exclusive use during school hours from 7am. There's an impressive fully equipped gym, spinning bikes, weights and a huge dance studio with double-height ceiling (for trampolining). The only thing missing here is an all-weather pitch, but there's one in nearby Cullompton. Uffculme is also very big on outdoor pursuits: canoeing, kayaking, surfing, sailing, climbing, caving, mountain walking, skiing, and of course the Duke of Edinburgh and Ten Tors.

Drama is very popular. As well as drama clubs at lunchtimes there's a major production every other year. Last time it was Les Misérables, and now they're working on The Lion King. With over 100 in the cast and many more involved in costumes, props and music, the drama teacher was suitably excited. He was particularly keen to make use of the music department's African drums and drummers. The new theatre, The Venue, has flexible seating for 400 and is used for drama teaching, assemblies and lectures and well as plays and concerts.

Good music department, another popular subject. Concerts are held every term and there are various groups such as the jazz band, choir, singing groups, samba band and other band ensembles. There's a large recording studio, plus the main classroom, and a separate tech room. Individual music lessons are available and if music is chosen at GCSE, the school pays for the lessons to support pupils who are in need of financial assistance.

The school has a good reputation in art and some impressive work is displayed around the school. The art department is in a recently refurbished building, and it's brilliant. In the entrance there's a large papier-mâché tree, huge canvas pieces, murals and 3D pieces. Upstairs are two fantastic studios overlooking the playing fields. Very high standards of artwork; some could easily be mistaken for sixth form work. Students annually exhibit their exam pieces at the local Coldharbour Mill exhibition, and some even sell them there. There are regular visits to art galleries, as well as theatres and concerts.

Extracurricular clubs take place mainly at lunchtime, with sports and revision classes taking place after school. Clubs include chess, computers, Scrabble, film, religious groups, book clubs, plus the usual array of music, drama and sporting activities – however, surf club in Croyde on Friday afternoons sounds particularly appealing. There's an annual summer activities week for years 7, 8 and 9 (most popular is the cycling and camping trip to France) and a work experience week for year 10. On average there's six opportunities a year to go camping or on residentials on Dartmoor, Exmoor, Wales or on the coast. There are regular exchanges with France and Germany, as well as skiing trips and an opportunity to travel to China.

Background and atmosphere: Uffculme School was founded in 1954 as a secondary modern with around 200 pupils, turning comprehensive in the 70s. Situated in mid-Devon, Exeter and Taunton are equidistant, Exmoor and Dartmoor are within easy reach, and the north and south coasts are just a short drive away (surfboards and kayaks optional).

It feels a lot smaller than it actually is. It's a small site but it's not cramped. New blocks have been added as and when funding has allowed. The latest addition is the history block with light, airy classrooms all fitted with large screens. Most impressive is the science block. Seven brand new labs, walls of windows and large open hallways decorated with creative scientific abstracts. The art building (built way back in 2013!) used to be the science block but the head won funding to refurbish. She seems particularly good at this; the key, she says, is to 'never give up.' Below the art studios, there's the Art Café. This is year 11's own dedicated space, designed by and run by them. It is far better than most sixth form areas we've seen. There are PCs, an outside picnic table area and barbecue, a radio blaring, café style drinks and snacks, comfy seating. It's the perfect introduction to sixth form life. Parents say, 'The Art Café has helped them to feel more independent and to grow into being year 11 students so that they are ready to move on.'

Uffculme is wireless enabled, and along with the use of laptops and tablets, there are three dedicated ICT suites, each with 30 PCs. In the library, as well as books, there are laptops, digital cameras, video cameras and microphones. There are regular authors' workshops, most recently children's writer David Almond (Kit's Wilderness).

The school feels calm, well managed, and most definitely well maintained. Traditional values like good behavior are a priority, but this doesn't go as far as standing to attention in class. And there are no bells between lessons; it's fairly informal and relaxed here. The head has done a great job in ensuring that the interiors are 'vibrant and attractive', and even 'pretty'. The school feels welcoming; there are photos to make you smile, artwork to inspire, and the stunning views are an added bonus.

Pastoral care, well-being and discipline: 'Pupils are treated with respect at Uffculme and as a result they are very mature,' said one parent. Ofsted agreed, saying, 'Behaviour is exemplary.' The pupils here are provided with fantastic facilities and in return they look after the school and are proud to be part of it. However, it's not just about the material environment; one parent told us, 'I don't know whether [they] would have faired so well in a different school. I put this down to the pastoral component of the school and the supportive style the teaching staff have for each other and the children.'

There's a student nurse, welfare officers, parental support advisors and weekly lunchtime drop-ins with a youth worker. There are tutor groups and a flexible learning centre for those that need to study away from others for one reason or another. Low rate of exclusions. One parent told us, 'They deal with issues without the involvement of parents as much as they can; however, they do call in the parents if things go up to a more serious level.' Another said, 'Issues are dealt with very professionally and personally. The teachers really care about the pupils.'

Pupils and parents: Real mix of families. 'Economically diverse,' we're told. Some are local, some have relocated. 'We were looking around the Exeter area but we heard about Uffculme's great reputation through estate agents and we refocused our house search on villages in the catchment area for the school.' Parents are directors of companies, nurses, estate agents, farmers, doctors; the list is endless. There's a large and active PTA; the last annual craft fair raised almost £6k.

Most parents say they based their decision on local reputation. 'We didn't look at other schools as Uffculme had such a good reputation.' Parents feel involved in the school; one told us, 'The school is great at communicating with parents. The thing they do incredibly well is celebrate the successes of the students. Not just academic but sports activities too.' The school promotes participation and the head and her teachers are frequently seen at local, regional and national events supporting their students. The badge system encourages participation and celebrates success and achievements too. One parent said, 'Uffculme has helped her to think, to aspire to succeed and to see the bigger picture.'

Entrance: Based on catchment area. Seven feeder primary schools, and Uffculme Primary School recently became part of the Uffculme Academy Trust. One parent said, 'it was either Uffculme or Blundell's.'

Good transition. Uffculme's teachers visit the primary schools and set up plenty of opportunities for children and parents to visit the school. 'The process was great; they used to come to Uffculme for sports from primary school which really helped them to settle in. The sports teachers were familiar and friendly, having worked with them before. They also had a wonderful teacher who came to their year 6 lessons and talked about life at Uffculme.' Once started, pupils are split into tutor groups, and in the first few weeks they take part in a variety of team-building activities to give them all a chance to make friends and settle in. Children with special needs are given an 18-month transition phase, and one parent told us, 'This meant that when September came she was absolutely ready to start and coped exceptionally well with the change.'

Exit: Most choose to take advanced academic or vocational courses at Petroc in Tiverton, Richard Huish College, Somerset College of Arts and Technology in Taunton, Exeter College, Bicton College or the sixth forms of independent schools and other colleges. Any famous leavers? Joss Stone, of course!

There are mixed feelings on the lack of a sixth form. Historically there's never been a sixth form and there probably never will be. On funding issues alone, the local colleges are very good so it would be hard to compete. 'My son is definitely ready to leave as he is in a hurry to grow up. I think the year 11 Art Café helps the children adjust towards becoming more independent.' 'The addition of a sixth form would be an excellent improvement to the school. [My child] will be very sad to leave the school and wishes there was a sixth form there.' The jury is out on this one.

Money matters: South West Regional Winner at the Pupil Premium Awards 2015, receiving £100k. This funding is mainly being used for the year 7 Catch Up programme to help improve literacy and numeracy. It will also be used to provide free meals and breakfasts, uniforms, books and emotional support. The school has its own charity trust to help with additional costs like music lessons, extracurricular activities and trips.

Remarks: Great. Stimulating and creative learning environment; fantastic place to go to school. Strong head teacher with a good team – the results speak for themselves. The general consensus is that 'Uffculme offers pretty much what the local private schools offer.' Children of all abilities fare well here. We might just have to look up a few estate agents ourselves.

UWC Atlantic College

St Donat's Castle, St Donat's, Llantwit Major, Vale of Glamorgan CF61 1WF

Ages 15–19 **Pupils** 378 **Boarders** All full

Fees: Boarding £33,000 pa

01446 799000
www.atlanticcollege.org

Principal: Since April 2017, Peter Howe, previously head of college at UWC Maastricht in the Netherlands. Degree in accounting, finance and economics from Queen's University in Ontario and PhD in art and architectural history from University of Toronto. Had a brief stint in sales and marketing at Procter and Gamble before switching to teaching, and spent 13 years at Canadian universities. His UWC career began in 2005, as the IB coordinator and head of economics at the Italy-based UWC Adriatic. Later, he became the school's deputy head and director of studies and ultimately, its rettore (head of school), before moving to Maastricht in 2012.

Academic matters: Education starts with the IB but, like the battery-powered toy bunnies in those long ago TV ads, keeps on going long after other schools have ground to a halt, courtesy of the Diploma Programme, the compulsory, wrap-around co-curricular programme introduced in 2012.

Diploma extras take up a good 30 per cent of pupils' time, 'and probably more,' requiring the academic component of the IB (no picnic at the best of times) to be breezed through in just five mornings plus an afternoon in the classroom each week. Pupils choose one of four 'experiential' faculties, each big on the redemptive powers of active, selfless participation (very Kurt Hahn), that add to the IB's magnificent seven and tick off its creativity, action and service component en route.

There's outdoor (focus on those in peril on the seas – best-selling RIB boat developed by past pupils and teacher then, combining brilliance and philanthropy in equal measure, selflessly donated patent to the RNLI); social justice (first hand encounters of a robust kind, including work with refugees and prisoners' families); global (everything from organising peace events to sharing a dorm with traditional enemies); and environmental, where commitment to sustainability is no light matter (students, who recycle everything, deeply miffed by college's failure to consult over green disposal of fittings following boarding house refurb).

It's education the immersive way, students picking a theme that interests them and following its thread through their studies – real world, practical applications dovetailing with academic side. Someone with an interest in Middle East might study Arabic, prepare an extended essay in world studies, help set up a project week in Jordan and, through this, 'understand the UWC mission in the way they choose to develop their strengths,' says head of curriculum.

At its best (which is much of the time) diploma activities feed back into lessons, making for a buzzy classroom atmosphere where passionate debate is a way of life. There's nothing like hearing about refugees' experiences then discussing them back at base to add bite to economics or geography lessons. 'Makes it much more interesting and stimulating. I think it affects their exam grades, too.' Worked wonders on inspectors too, who assumed students leading lessons (spreading the word to peers in other diploma facilities is part of the syllabus) were teachers and had graded them outstanding before misunderstanding pointed out.

Structure won't be for everyone, particularly those with league-leaping performance as sole aspiration. College holds trenchant views on results, which are 'meaningless after a few years. It's the outcome that is important. We measure the success in the effect our students have on the world'. Hasn't published IB results for several years, though average of 35 points in 2016.

Hot spots include spectacular languages (nine mother tongue or foreign options and a further 21, including Khmer, Mongolian and Welsh, as self-taught subjects). Maths and science are also very strong, say students – big clue to expectations the vast university physics textbook toted with pride by first year student.

With run of the mill IB students elsewhere already reckoned to be worked more intensively than A level counterparts, it's useful to arrive with work ethic fully formed and be good with stress, say students, who rapidly acquire super-efficient learning techniques.

In the main, it's attitude of mind that determines student suitability. 'Not for the weak-hearted,' thought one. Just as true for teachers, many with similar international background. Total conversion to college philosophy the norm and few move back to conventional posts afterwards. Once recruited, becomes a forever post, others paling into comparison. 'You're spoiled for life', thought one, while college newsletter praised students' freedom to 'chase academic hares into the undergrowth of learning [...] keeping an eye on the syllabus and sometimes even a blind eye'.

Generous with their time (lots of impromptu one-to-one sessions were under way in final run up to IB exams), teachers praised for effective problem-spotting system that kicks in early, tutors the first point of call, subject specialists alerted and involved as necessary.

Other areas (notably EAL, learning needs, gifted and talented), formerly a bit piecemeal but are having policies written and in some cases coordinators, including SENCo, appointed. Essential, given some pupils' patchy educational history and/or imperfect grasp of English (no minimum language requirement for EU students). Lack of screening during committee-based recruitment system also means learning needs (mostly mild Asperger's, SpLD and ADHD) will only be picked up on arrival, though good to see real commitment to disabled access. Wheelchair access determinedly provided wherever possible, whole classes relocated if necessary when it isn't.

Overall, exceptionally demanding curriculum covers emotional, intellectual and practical terrain that many adults would find hard going. Though something you'd hesitate to impose elsewhere, impressively mature bunch here take it in their stride. Only student doubt was perception that college is putting greater focus on IB scores. College is adamant this isn't the case.

U

Games, options, the arts: Whichever diploma faculty they choose, students are unlikely to spend much time sitting on their hands, all areas being long on activity. Derring-do comes with the territory no matter what the gradient, acquisition of skills in graceful failure as important as trappings of success (fallibility reckoned by Kurt Hahn to be essential part of the learning process). As a result, there isn't much pupils here would say no to, from consorting with top scientists and politicians at climate change summit in Fiji to qualifying as a music therapist.

Outdoor faculty is the most obviously action-packed of the bunch. Students join either aquatic water activities team (kayaking and surfing on offer but highlight lifeboat training at college's own RNLI station) or sign up to Terra Firma, which features mountain walking, navigation, emergency first aid and climbing (Brecon Beacons, a few miles inland, the venue for unlimited yomping).

While physical activity is compulsory, organised sport isn't. Stems from character building the Kurt Hahn way, which almost heretically relegates organised games to an 'important but not predominant' position in the hierarchy. The newly built Moondance gym and sports hall is a 'purpose-built and fully equipped facility with a student social centre to complement a student well-being agenda.'

What happens and whether it happens at all is largely down to pupils. Though specialist coaches visit (pupils seemed slightly hazy about the details), there's no head of sport and activities vary from year to year depending on each cohort's enthusiasms. As a result, vast games field is intermittently used. Only sound on a fine spring afternoon was the bleating of newborn lambs from on-site farm. Anyone expecting pitches groaning with glory-seeking team endeavours may well be in for a bit of a shock.

Similarly, though IB studies are efficiently catered for with public showcases including drama reviews and weekly music recitals, there's not much in the way of large scale musical or dramatic endeavours.

Boarding: Seven boarding houses. Their distinctive characters, reflected in not always flattering secret student nicknames (we know what they are, too, but had to promise not to tell), are home to just under 50 pupils each. Pastoral care efficiently provided by brace of well-liked houseparents. Facilities are 'simple', says college, and they're not wrong. Perfectly acceptable though, with extensive communal drying rooms and welly racks (essential given climate) and enough single showers to ensure sufficient privacy for those who find communal versions problematic. Pre-diploma pupils have their own house.

There's the odd idiosyncrasy when it comes to equipment – irons are allowed in dorms, kettles are not (one boarding house has recently been rebuilt following a fire). But this is outweighed by impressive, all-round sensitivity, subtle pooling of kitchen equipment in mixed common rooms avoiding distinctions between haves and have-nots, daily deliveries of communal food essentials.

Background and atmosphere: For mood and idealism, think educational version of Star Trek, the crew's goal less about finding 'strange new worlds' than improving the one they're in, one dilithium crystal at a time. While hippies might give peace a chance by putting flowers in gun barrels, Hahn's solution to unify Cold War ridden world of the 1960s and ward off what he saw as the physical and moral decline of the young was to found a school (two, if you count Gordonstoun, many more if you allow Round Square schools).

Here, the aim was to create a harmonious blend of nations and cultures, pairing opposites of every sort, oppressors and oppressed, poor and rich, who by living and studying together would develop shared outlook and common purpose (though took until 1967 before they got round to adding girls).

College remains a one-off in the UK and was the first of what is now 17-strong United World Colleges international movement. Its niche status and relatively low profile (even amongst heads, let alone the average parent) is, however, in inverse proportion to behind the scenes clout. Former students are embedded in some of the most powerful organisations and political administrations in the world, from the Chinese and US governments to top banks, providing under the radar alternative to conventional old boys' (and girls') network and one with huge clout.

Setting – in 800-year-old castle by the sea – is out of this world and much appreciated by production companies (has featured in Dr Who). In addition to as many corkscrewing staircases as you can shake a medieval flail at, castle interior features terrific library, galleried and home to municipal quantities of books including Harry Potter (a college favourite) in assorted translations.

Lessons in many cases a perfect match for surroundings. History lessons compete with hard to improve vistas through arrow slits to wooded hill beyond, art and music located in nicely converted stable block. Other subjects are taught in three 1970s teaching blocks (science and maths, perhaps appropriately, in crumbliest and flakiest), all apparently constructed, together with admin centre, by embittered town planner having a bad day and featuring urban-style mini-underpass. Recent developments as described (in somewhat corporate language) by the school include The Agatha Christie Library, a 'modern resource and IT centre, fit for purpose for the 21st century', the Great Hall, a 'fully-resourced meeting and conference facility in the heart of St Donat's Castle to support our education programme' and The Seafront, 'refurbished accommodation and teaching areas to provide a centre for outdoor activity courses, and for schools and community groups.'

With just one communal TV to its name, a climate that's far from tropical and the nearest cinema nine miles away by land (or 13 if teamed with a bracing swim across the Bristol Channel), this is a place that needs decent social events more than most. Until recently, though, it wasn't getting them, felt pupil. Far better now, with weekly disco (noise levels bravely borne by principal, who lives opposite), boarding houses charged with weekend event organisation, and much more to do.

The sense of being a body apart is reinforced by two-term structure that follows the beat of the IB drum – with the result that pupils only have four days off between January and May and are then off on holiday until early August when second year pupils arrive back for a week's bonding before new intake turns up.

Physical apartness makes it something of unknown quantity within the local community. 'Out of my league,' thought one local. 'Feels exclusive – if you can afford for your kids to go there, you're doing well'. No wonder the college is contemplating a hearts, minds and meters job to get locals, starting with taxi drivers, who are probably the college's most frequent visitors, on side.

Pastoral care, well-being and discipline: New arrivals are paired with 'excellent' buddies, big on tea and sympathy (favour returned when it comes to exam time). Their first task is probably to settle nerves after meeting and greeting ceremony, where they're drummed in with chorus of pots and pans pillaged from common rooms by second years ('it leaves terrible dents', said one pupil, who as kitchen monitor was charged with subsequent search and rescue mission).

With full boarding the only option (though parents can come and stay nearby at beginning and ends of term), inner core of steel probably helps, given policy of picking room-mates for differences, the more apparently irreconcilable the better. 'We would always put Israelis and Palestinians together'; college is spearheading drive to recruit Syrians from both sides of current conflict.

Pupils aren't just in favour of approach but drawn to college because of it. Beliefs that elsewhere would be on collision course (there's a strong LGBT movement, for example) spark enduring friendships and sometimes more, with potential for heartache when relationships breach cultural barriers.

Whether deliberately or by chance, student bonds are well and truly cemented by decision to involve them in the nuts and bolts of college operations. Open book policy on everything from finances to rebuilding ensures that student voice isn't merely heard but is a force to be reckoned with, from spontaneous orations in assembly on whatever issues take their fancy, college-related or otherwise (polemic following death of Mrs Thatcher made for edgy listening) to indignation over any perceived high-handedness. 'If they give us a voice, that's what they have to expect', said one.

Impressive maturity means that nobody sweats the small stuff. Courtesy on both sides is a given, teachers generally liked (only one got thumbs down) and while big issues go to the wire, there are minimal rules elsewhere, nous and good sense taken as read. 'We don't need a rule about using phones in lessons when it would clearly be rude', a pupil told us.

Pupils and parents: Easy to gush over pupils' self-assurance and intelligence which carries all before it (just one non-show in recent memory, pupil so overcome with nerves that unable to board the plane). A sassy bunch, it's no surprise that many have persuaded their parents that this is the place to be and in one case at least secured the sponsorship to pay the fees.

Though fees are 'low compared to other top boarding schools', says college, they are still high enough to skew social mix towards luxury ingredients rather than salt of the earth. Or in UWC words, 'similar people simply born in different places'. A pupil said that this 'isn't the place for the materialistic or those who believe the world can get better with money alone'. Parent philanthropy is a way of life, one family funding not only their own child but three others, too. Similar acts of generosity both widespread and long term. Some 55 per cent of students have means-tested assistance with fees.

Five-strong development department works with alumni who include King of the Netherlands, chairman of Shell and vice-president of European Bank to get that giving feeling early. And give they do. Vocal and passionate espousal of college and ideals often continues for life, endorsements from everyone from Nelson Mandela to Queen Noor of Jordan setting the tone. It's resulting in growing numbers from the poorest and most war-torn regions of earth.

Some local recruitment, extending to deprived Liverpool, Birmingham and Valleys schools, requires a bit of careful eggshell treading to avoid Orphan Annie connotations, college raising grateful poor to a life of privilege. So far so good.

Entrance: 'The world is our catchment area', says college (90 nationalities currently). Makes a refreshing change from same old distance from home criteria, but downside is labyrinthine admissions process requiring minotaur-seeking levels of persistence (though no string). Think Oxbridge inter-college pupil swapsies at admissions time, add international dimension requiring agreement between parents, students and UWC staff who may all be on different continents, and it's not surprising that entrance process is officially badged as 'extremely complicated'. On the surface it's highly competitive, too, with nearly 100 nations jostling for places, just 20 available for UK nationals and a further 17 places in other UWC colleges.

Would-be pupils submit applications either to one of 150+ UWC national committees (in countries ranging from Afghanistan to Colombia), often staffed by alumni, or direct to colleges – specific requirements as individual as they are. Though they can express college preferences, they're assumed to be signing up to UWC aims rather than a location, and so could end up being offered a place somewhere completely different. Loving care is advised to ensure that focus on community work and support for UWC ideals shine through. Also useful to ensure academic endorsement (no GCSE minimum grades specified, every application considered on merit) is from teacher '... who supports the idea of you going to a UWC'. (Our tip: use the word 'mission' at least once.)

Shortlisted UK candidates have an overnight stay at the castle, followed by informal 20-minute interview with committee members, alumni and, unusually, former rather than current teachers. Final decision communicated around three weeks later (though can take longer). Whole process is an excellent Kurt Hahn-style challenge and, if you meet the age criteria (students normally start aged 16 or 17, though there's some flexibility), there's the chance to do it all over again the following year.

Exit: It's off to better things not just for pupils, but with 70 per cent ultimately ending up in humanitarian-linked careers, for the world as a whole. While US admissions tutors zoom in early, like dealers at a jumble sale before the doors open to the general punters, other top unis aren't far behind.

US is the most popular university destination overall with close to 40 per cent of places (college doesn't train students to take SATs, but is a test centre), followed by UK (some 30 per cent – vast majority to Russell Group members) then Canada and Europe, with a few to Asia. Recent destinations include Harvard, Cambridge, Brown, MIT, Yale, Princeton, UCL, Sherbrooke and Cornell.

Around 18 per cent take a gap year or go off to complete national service. Courses many and various. A pupil we spoke to hoped to major in physics with laudable aim of investigating travel across vacuums in outer space.

Money matters: Admissions process supported by large fundraising and development department working overtime to bring in the dosh. Latest initiative themed to college's 50th anniversary (think of a number, any number, with a 50 in it and hand it over) is generating over £2 million a year, almost all used to fund scholarships. Other countries chip in, too (Norwegian government funds 10 of its own students, for example). In all, over 55 per cent of students have some sort of financial support.

Remarks: Once a glorious experiment, still out on a limb (and, we suspect, in no hurry to shed iconoclastic status), Atlantic College provides an education as remarkable as the feisty, impassioned students it attracts. The ticking of admin boxes may annoy, but it's a necessary evil that parents will welcome. Its location may be isolated but its perspective, genuinely global, is anything but. Just don't expect a picnic by the sea.

Wellington Prep School

Linked with Wellington School

197

South Street, Wellington, Somerset TA21 8NT

Ages 3–11 **Pupils** 240 **C of E**

Fees: £6,330 – £11,820 pa

01823 668700
www.wellington-school.org.uk

Headmaster: Since 2010, Adam Gibson. Took him a while to stumble on his vocation. He started as an info systems manager for the NHS. Struck by the realisation that he's not a back office kind of guy, he was on the point of switching to frontline medicine when, by chance, he spent a day in a school. That's when the lightbulb above his head lit up and that's where it blazes undimmed today. Taught for 10 years in state schools in the Midlands, then headed a prep school in Devon before returning to his alma mater. Has a more than ordinarily strong affection for Wellington, a characteristic, we discovered, of all its alumni. 'When I appoint new colleagues, I look for them to have the capacity to love the school.' Teaches some ICT and maths. Married, two children in the senior school.

Personable, approachable, terrifically good fun. Attracts the attention of children by clapping a rhythm which they keenly join in. Clearly in his element when he's around them, you can see it in his face: very kind eyes. He's accountable, too. He or his deputy are in the playground every morning to field the concerns of parents, who say he's 'definitely a go-to person'. Lean, athletic, can-do. So you're not surprised to discover that he accommodated the arrival of his own children by giving up team sports and taking up the triathlon instead, at which he has represented GB. 'Every child,' he says, 'should be inspired every day.' Lots of heads say this sort of thing but few so fervently. His aspiration is borne out as much by the shining eyes of the children as those of the teachers. 'I don't do boredom,' he told us. We'd got that. Believes in 'looking at life from the children's point of view' and is wide open to 'doing something different' as a result. He's a detail man. And a values man. Robust, for sure, a bit full on for some parents, possibly. We very much like the strong and serious sense of purpose and spirit of adventure. His is an exceptionally buzzy, questing school where nothing is left to chance. Mr Gibson is supported by a conspicuously able senior leadership team.

Entrance: Gently non-selective. Main criterion is that your child will be able to move up comfortably to the senior school. A few parents buy into just the prep school to give their child a really good grounding in the basics; they say it sees them through from 11 to 18. The school is more affordable than its local competitors. Excellent nursery in a converted chapel takes children from 3.

Exit: Nine in 10 go on to the senior school – many with academic, sport, music, drama or art scholarships. Transition to senior school reckoned by parents to be 'exceptionally well handled'. There's an entry test – the same one external applicants sit; a parent told us, 'my daughter was entirely relaxed and at ease'.

Remarks: Opened in 1999 in the heart of the market town of Wellington, bang next door to the senior school with which it shares facilities, including acres of playing fields. There's a forest school too, not a scrubby little patch off the playground but a decent swathe of woodland in the Blackdown Hills. As well as getting to grips with the ins and outs of the natural world, children light fires and whittle wood with sharp knives – eg, make beads and whistles. Supervision is anything but laissez faire, of course, and the school is justly proud of what goes on here.

Academically, parents are happy across the board – 'best start possible', said one. Another parent told us, 'All the teachers are good, some are inspirational'. We encountered some really high-octane teaching right up to the lesson before lunch and very much wanted wanted to sit out a particularly gripping history class. IT is taught by a teacher with industry experience. Maths is taught by the Singapore method (Google it). They like to think big here, in the belief that if a thing is worth doing there's nothing to be said for holding back, and are now a Beacon School. There is much praise for the support given by the Learning Success team to children who need it – the gifted, those with special needs and those whose performance (tightly monitored) calls for intervention. They create pupil passports, a partnership approach involving child, parents and teachers, and work collaboratively to fix glitches or handle special needs – dyslexia through to ADHD (light to moderate).

W

Sport is paired with well-being, and, they claim, 'we're the first school in the world' to do this. By well-being they don't mean touchy-feely happiness remedies so much as PE+, the + being teaching children to make good, lifelong lifestyle choices. The brightest and best are coached, do team sports and play to win. Those for whom this would be wretched tyranny learn to keep fit (Fitbits all round), to play for fun, to eat well, to say no to bad stuff and generally look after their minds and bodies. The programme was spelled out to us with a passion that is entirely normal here. The head of PE is a former county cricketer who also played professional rugby, no less.

Music especially strong. Opportunities to try out different instruments and once you've mastered a few notes you're eligible for the orchestra. Drama not so big. Nativities for the weenies and one biggish annual production.

An attraction of the school to all parents, regardless of means, is that the social climate is more diverse than most indies, more grounded, 'not at all precious or snobby'. Parents like the way the school plays its part in the town's economy and they approve of the way it spends their fees – 'They're very good with money'. To our eyes it feels easily as well-resourced as other independents. Several parents we spoke to even praise the marketing – 'What they say about themselves is genuine'.

Parents also like the values the school imbues: 'respect', 'politeness', 'have a go, try your best, it's okay if you make mistakes'. They like the way the school involves all of the children – 'It's not just all about the high-flyers' – and how the head finds ways to 'reward those who don't stand out from the crowd'. They like the early morning clubs, 'great for boys who can't sit still'. They like the way that children develop an awareness of the wider world – 'preparing without scaring'. They couldn't wax more lyrical about pastoral care. And they feel they can play their part in the school although, as one pointed out, 'that's hard for many parents because lots of them work'. For them, in particular, the school is open from 8.00am to 6.00pm.

It's rare that we come away from a school feeling quite so lit up. Wellington Prep is proud of itself but not in the least pleased with itself. It vibrates both with the thrum of new ideas (the bigger the better) and, vitally important this, the fine detail of their execution – what the head animatedly calls 'the detail of what makes things work'. This is a striving, happy, human school which is also very much its own place.

Wellington School

Linked with Wellington Prep School

198

South Street, Wellington, Somerset TA21 8NT

Ages 11–18 **Pupils** 572 **Sixth form** 151 **Boarders** 127 full, 9 weekly, 10 flexi (boys from 11, girls from 13) **C of E**

Fees: Day £13,545 – £15,225; Boarding £23,130 – £30,810 pa

01823 668803
www.wellington-school.org.uk

Headmaster: Since 2014, Henry Price MA. Eton and Oxford (classics). A career teacher, first post at Sydney Grammar, Australia, next Sherborne then Rugby for 13 years where, in addition to being head of classics and a housemaster, he was involved in all manner of extracurricular activities. Married, four young children. Circumscribed cultural and recreational hinterland just now, given the demands of his large family. In holiday time enjoys the beaches and mountains of Wales from his base in Anglesey.

Mr Price was guarded in his responses to our questions, leaving us with a lot to find out for ourselves. We did learn that he is fiercely proud of his school, its values and attributes. If it has a USP, he said, it is that it is 'grounded'. And he gave us a valuable insight into his philosophy of education. Our ears pricked up when he spoke of Wellington's teachers as 'schoolmasters' and 'schoolmistresses'. You don't hear those heritage words very often these days. What does he mean by them? Is his ideal of the teacher as all-rounder massively behind the curve? Or is the richness of the school's pastoral and co-curricular provision a testament to his, and his predecessors', vocational, holistic approach? We suspect the latter. And we applaud his focus on supporting the development of his teachers both in and out of the classroom. A parent told us, 'He has refocussed on work and sport without losing the essential decency of the school'.

The overwhelming majority of parents we spoke to like their headmaster. Even after correcting for choice-supportive bias, he gets good chitty – and that's after taking into account those who say 'I wish he had more presence' and 'more sense of humour'. His fans are vigorously protective and speak with strong affection, for they have got to know him and acknowledge that yes, he can come over as reserved, and no, 'he's not an in-yer-face head'; he's the sort who 'quietly sees what's going on and takes it all in'. 'He's shy and may have felt burdened by the step up to headship, but he's growing in confidence'. 'Heads at Wellington learn on the job.' 'He's the softly-softly sort.' 'He's a thoroughly humane, decent man with a strong sense of justice'. Also clearly bright and scholarly, his interests span philosophy, modern lit fic and medieval history. His speeches on formal occasions are highly esteemed and contain a lot of heart – together with some rather good jokes. Plainly a man who enjoys honing a sentence.

Hosts a sticky bun club for students every Friday break where he gets to hear what they think. Teaches Latin – 'I'm still a schoolmaster'. Sends all students a birthday card. One of his students, we learned from their mum, really likes his warmer, funnier classroom persona.

Moving on in July 2019 to head Oakham School. His successor will be Eugene Du Toit, currently senior deputy head at Trinity School, Croydon. Degree from the University of the Witwatersrand, Johannesburg and an MA in educational leadership from the Institute of Education. Began his teaching career at King Edward VII School in Johannesburg before moving to England and taking up a position at St Paul's School, London as a teacher of economics and mathematics, undermaster (assistant head), and head of house. A keen sportsman who has coached rugby, water polo and athletics. He is married to Angela and they have two young daughters.

Academic matters: Typical grammar school curriculum, all the subjects you need for a top university and the right ones to suit the full range of students here – 24 of them. Actually, more than enough, uptake varying from 40+ to, in one or two subjects, 0, so some very small class sizes. Four modern languages including Chinese and two ancient ones (Latin and Greek). No vocational courses eg BTecs. Maths and sciences an enduring strength. Results in 2018 commendable by any standards, and that's without factoring in the ongoing lurch to 'reformed' A levels. Seventy per cent A*-B and 40 per cent A*/A grades at A level. Value added score admirable. Best of the best: geography, maths (historically strong), Eng lit and classics. Less strong: business studies, economics and physics (improving). Notable: the number of B grades attained by students who

W

might otherwise have got Cs. At GCSE the 2018 harvest was 50 per cent A*-A/9-7 grades. Broadly, strong on all fronts, physics especially so. Sixth form foundation course for international students.

Exceptional special needs provision addresses everything from classic special needs (dyslexia et al) to support for students who have hit a wobbly patch, to a few with mild behavioural problems. Some of these (120 when we visited) have an eye kept on them remotely (they don't know), monitoring mechanisms having registered a blip. Hugely impressive SENCo, masses of experience, wise and thoughtful. He told us: 'Our relationship with our students is key; there's a pastoral element to this. Our department is a good place for a time out, especially for those struggling with sociability'. Big believer in empathy exercises for teachers to give them some idea what dyslexia feels like.

Careers counselling and course guidance highly rated. You see the evidence for that in the well-chosen universities students go on to, from the highly academic to the best of the rather more doable. As a flagship achievement this is as impressive us as Oxbridge triumphs: they're bringing out the best in all their students. Head of sixth form much admired and strongly liked by students and parents.

Games, options, the arts: Novel approach to physical exercise – may even be trend-setting. Well-being, they call it. Potentially confusing, too, when you're told, in the school's words, that 'The well-being programme ... replaces the subject that schools have traditionally called physical education'. Acting on a perhaps understandable misunderstanding, The Sunday Times shouted 'zumba puts team games on the bench at top school ... Wellington School in Somerset has abandoned traditional PE lessons ... and replaced them with "well-being" classes'. But it's simply not true. The new and pioneering look for PE here is, in the head's words, 'evolved'. He explains: 'There is plenty of physical activity but also classroom sessions based around nutrition, mindfulness and leadership, which links into our PSHE programme. Our aim is not only to increase fitness and confidence at school, but also teach pupils how to look after themselves long after they leave school.' In other words, there's as much traditional team sport here as there ever was (heaps), but also a recognition that 'it is.. important that an increasingly sedentary generation understands the importance of physical fitness in their working lives'. We can testify that the splendid sports hall was not reverberating to a chant of ohm when we visited, and while some might regard the way the school addresses mindfulness as a tad narrow, we were struck by the benevolence of the PE staff, their borderline-messianic dedication and their concern to find something for everyone. One mum told us that her daughter had become sporty for the first time in her life. Strong girls' cricket and rugby. Head of sport is an ex-pro rugby player and ex-county cricketer. Team sports are compulsory to year 10; thereafter you get to choose. The one thing you can't choose is nothing. To the gratification of many parents, mainstream sports have been boosted by Mr Price: 'Wellington needed to up its game'.

Music exceptionally strong, much raved about by the mother of a scholar: 'The head of department is inspirational'. Rich range of ensembles and styles and a choral tradition that spans all-girl a capella group and a chapel choir that sings choral compline in local churches. Drama 'could be bigger,' said one parent. Happens in the converted old school hall, ideal for big musicals; also in the South Side studio theatre opened by alumnus David Suchet. Director in residence, thesp background, aims to drum up numbers for GCSE and A level, presently on the low side. Club for techies under the watchful eye of a BBC-trained overseer. Art department buzzy as can be, lots of big ambitious work in progress, everything from paint through ceramics to digital. Well impressive.

Heaps of extracurricular activities likely to render students paralysed for choice. On offer Saturday mornings too, but only compulsory for boarders. Head very keen on outdoor ed, so DofE has enjoyed a recent shot in the arm. CCF hugely popular – very Wellington, this; it's an esprit de corps sort of school. Attractive adventurous activities on offer including arduous Ten Tors trekking event. CCF comes with enhanced outcomes here: you can put your service towards a BTec level 2 diploma in uniformed public services or an Institute of Leadership and Management qualification. Lots of holiday expeditions home and abroad, some educational, some recreational and some downright gruelling. Brilliant initiative, student generated, enables boys and girls to get their Amateur FA basic refereeing badge. Absolutely not the sort of school that lets anyone skive off but, as a student told us, 'They try really hard to cater for what you want to do'.

Boarding: Around 150 board, roughly 50 per cent of them international students from all over, mainly Russia, China and Europe – 25 nationalities when we called in – numbers of any one nationality limited in order to spur integration. Good systems for boarders to make their views heard. Weekend activities, always a bugbear in boarding schools, have been beefed up under the impetus of the head. A parent we spoke to who'd sent her son elsewhere entertained a lasting sense of regret that she had not opted what she described as 'Wellington's smelly-socks boarding'. She may have been misinformed. No odour of hosiery when we dived in, everything clean and gleaming. Doesn't score five stars for luxury, more like a solid three, though we hear five star things about new girls' boarding house. The point is the students like it, enjoy their relationships with house staff and express contentment.

Background and atmosphere: Founded in 1837 as Wellington Academy, offering a commercial, mathematical and classical education. That 'commercial' tells you something about the target clientele, still a sector today. In 1879 it rebranded as the West Somerset County School. During WW1 the pupils grew vegetables on the playing fields and made munitions for the front line in the school engineering shop – and the name was changed to Wellington School. In 1945 it became a direct grant grammar school. On the abolition of that scheme in 1976 the school's application to join the state sector was refused, so it went independent. As it has grown it has spilled over into a hodge-podge of handsome buildings bisected by a traffic-calmed road. The main campus is altogether more unified, blessed for space and recognisably public-schooly with its chapel and commodious playing fields. Well resourced throughout, money carefully spent. Never the sort of school to be seduced by the spirit of the present age and blow cash on fancy-pants prestige buildings. Opened its doors to international students in 1904 and girls in 1979.

The school sits squarely in the midst of the architecturally handsome market town of Wellington, once a wool town, now more of a dormitory for Taunton. Nice Georgian town houses, a branch of Waitrose and a Wetherspoon pub named in honour of the Iron Duke whose link to the town is in fact notional. He visited just once. His brother chose his territorial title for him when he got his dukedom – the great man was tied up with the Peninsular war at the time – and plumped for the name Wellington for no better reason that that he thought it sounded a bit like Wellesley. A lofty if decayed obelisk celebrating Waterloo stands just outside the town. The town itself nestles on the banks of the M5, enjoying excellent transport links, so much so that some parents to the east of Taunton find it easier to get to Wellington than its competitor schools in Taunton itself. Not to be confused with the namesake college in Berkshire, obviously, except that a surprising number do. The realisation dawns at some point when they're looking round, by which time they have lost their hearts and signed up.

The social climate of the school is influenced by the level at which it sets its fees – some 20 per cent or so lower for day students than local competitors (the difference for boarders is less than 10 per cent). This broadens its social base, opening it up to local families who would otherwise be unable to afford an independent education. It also opens it to sneery jibes, eg 'the state school you have to pay fees for', precisely the sort of remark that makes it attractive to affluent folk who don't want their children to be infected by hauteur. We spoke to a number of such parents who had chosen Wellington rather than the sort of school they had been to themselves, who spoke of their pride in the down-to-earth, unpretentious nature of a school whose students go out into the world with an ability to relate to people of all sorts with absolutely no sense of entitlement. We spoke to a working mum for whom finding the fees is a heroic struggle. She told us, 'I never feel intimidated when I go up there', and rejoices that when her daughter leaves 'she will be sure of herself, not full of herself'. One parent talked of a 'school happy to be itself' and there's no doubting its strong sense of identity; we've rarely encountered such ardent loyalty from both students and parents.

Parents also like what one described as 'a thoroughly traditional ethos' and 'Christian values unashamedly proclaimed'. Another said, 'It's the sort of school where it's cool to work hard and make something of yourself'. This is widely endorsed: 'Wellington is good at finding out what your child is good at'. Yes, this is a meritocratic environment whose grammar school inheritance lives on.

Pastoral care, well-being and discipline: Sound and recently reinforced systems for pastoral care. Principal guarantor of well-being is good relationships among students and between them and staff, whether 'teachers, who really care' or support staff. Some intermingling of year groups; sixth formers pretty good at looking out for the youngest. Parents report rapid response to problems and feel their views count. Though this is a school notable for its camaraderie it is, in the words of a parent, 'not overly conformist'. A student told us 'character is valued; some need more leeway'. For all that the climate is notably orderly. A problem with good schools is that there's so little to rebel against.

Pupils and parents: Most day students come in by bus from Exeter and Chard to the south, Minehead and Dulverton to the north west and beyond Bridgwater to the east. Good social spread of down to earth parents. 'Not a posh school by any stretch of the imagination', one told us. Another: 'No one judges you by what car you drive, only by how nice you are'. And another: 'A good solid cohort of decent parents. Lots of doctors.'

Entrance: Main entry at year 7, everyone sits school's entry test in January. At year 9, tests in Eng, maths + paper of own choice. Post-GCSE they'll have you as long as you got three 6s and three 5s. So, not fiendishly selective. International students from year 7.

Exit: Varying numbers – around 30 per cent – leave at the GCSE watershed. Of these, most to vocational courses, especially Taunton's Richard Huish College. Some parents make a strategic decision to fund just years 7–11. Majority of leavers go on to uni. Two to Oxbridge in 2018, both to study classics; two medics and a vet. Popular destinations Cardiff, UCL, Reading, Nottingham and York.

Money matters: High value, especially for day students. Fees what they say on the tin, none of the mum's-the-word discounts you can haggle at other schools and no sibling discounts either. Scholarships up to 20 per cent. Top-up bursaries to 40 per cent subject to means test. The school is committed, according to its means, to educating local boys and girls. Notably astute money management.

Remarks: Down to earth. Punches above its weight. No sense of entitlement. Good value for money. Not our words, those of a parent. Says it for us, too.

Wells Cathedral School

The Liberty, Wells, Somerset BA5 2ST

Ages 3–18 **Pupils** 716 **Sixth form** 186 **Boarders** 273 full, 8 weekly, 8 flexi (from year 5) **C of E**

Fees: Day £7,641 – £18,801; Boarding £20,322 – £31,464 pa

01749 834200
www.wells.cathedral.school

Head: Since 2018 Alastair Tighe MA (Cantab). An Old Wellensian and chorister himself, he read English but was also organ scholar at Magdalene. His career encompasses the teaching of music, assistant house-mastering and latterly deputy head (academic) at Bedford School.

Head of junior school: Since 2014 is Julie Barrow, a longstanding member of the junior school staff, whose appointment delighted parents. 'The school is thriving under her care,' wrote one parent, 'she is down to earth, has a great sense of humour and clear leadership skills. She also has a truly professional and committed team around her.' Another grateful mother added, 'Mrs Barrow is the most wonderful, kind and caring head teacher. She is always approachable, and in every instance the child comes first.'

Academic matters: Wells's unique selling point is flexibility. The school goes out of its way to address individual needs and preferences, and the results are highly creditable. In 2018, 56 per cent of GCSEs A*-A/9-7 and 40 per cent of A levels were graded at A*/A, down on last year. Compared with the other specialist music schools, offers a broad and challenging curriculum, with a good range of languages on offer: French, German, Spanish, Italian, Mandarin and Latin. Really excellent maths provision, owing to the innovative Specialist Maths Scheme, which allows able students an extra three hours of maths per week and aims to turn out creative mathematicians who can think beyond the syllabus. Why maths in particular? School says, 'It grew out of the music – we already knew how to specialise and be flexible.' Science labs endearingly shabby, but science teaching is 'very good, one of the strengths of the school,' according to a parent, and the pupils we spoke to – one of whom was off to Edinburgh to read medicine – agreed. Humanities also popular: one mother wrote, 'The school is now providing some really exciting and interesting history, philosophy, etc.' No IB – previous head disliked the amount of assessment involved, and preferred the depth of A levels (Cambridge Pre-U also offered in history). Everyone praised the teaching staff's willingness to give students the support they needed and to work constructively with all pupils, including those for whom music came first. Small class sizes and kind, knowledgeable staff, many of whom have been here for years and have a huge loyalty to the school.

SEN well catered for, with specialists in both the junior and senior schools ('second to none,' according to the mother of a dyslexic pupil), and school excels at adapting its provision to the individual student, an approach the previous head clearly relished. One mother ran out of superlatives when describing the way the staff had worked with her to draw up a care plan for managing her child's epilepsy. At the other end of the scale, parents rated the way their bright children had been stretched and challenged: 'The teaching is really good for an able child, and the maths has been wonderful.'

Given that Wells isn't overly selective in terms of academic ability, we were much struck with the school's achievements in this area and asked how it was done. 'By tailoring, by playing to people's strengths, by being can-do, and by having staff prepared to put the grounding in place,' was the answer. Parents agree: 'The children do incredibly well there, but it comes without the hothousing stress that other nearby schools create,' said one. 'They're really, really good at getting the best out of their pupils, no matter what their level is,' wrote another.

Games, options, the arts: Wells is one of five UK schools accorded specialist music school status by the government's Music and Dance Scheme and, as you'd expect, the music here is very special indeed. We heard a stunning young violinist rehearsing Korngold's violin concerto with the school's equally stunning symphony orchestra, which pretty much set us up for the day. For those who love music, there's a pulse-racingly good range of ensembles and other opportunities offered by the nine performance faculties: brass, composition, choristers, jazz, keyboard, percussion, strings, vocals and woodwind. The new Cedars Hall offers a world class concert venue within the school grounds, adding to the school's already-top-notch music facilities. Quirkier aspects of music also catered for: the percussion suite includes a World Percussion room, complete with its own Indonesian gamelan – other specialist music schools, please take note. All children in year 1 are offered free violin lessons, and the lovely end-of-year performance we heard testified to their impressive progress in this area. Fantastic and inclusive junior choir performs in concerts and all children aged 3 to 11 are involved in the school shows. For the specialists, there are two highly-regarded sets of junior choristers, one for boys and one for girls.

Parents and students alike praised the inclusivity of the music provision at Wells, saying that all pupils had the opportunity to take part and to excel if they wished, and many felt that the music benefited pupils in ways beyond the music itself: 'I think that being in a place where musical excellence is encouraged has inspired excellence in other areas,' wrote one mother, and others made similar comments. May not suit young musicians seeking the hardcore, all-or-nothing ethos of the other specialist music schools, but the parents we spoke to felt this was a strength: 'That's the real and very special feature of Wells,' wrote a father. 'It makes highly skilled musicians feel normal and grounds them in real life.'

Better sports than at any of the other specialist music schools, and pretty good for any school. Lovely new sports pavilion, all blond wood and glass, fronts the tree-dotted cricket pitch that boasts 'one of the best wickets in Somerset,' according to proud students. Teams are fielded in cricket, rugby, hockey (boys and girls), netball, rounders, tennis, swimming, soccer and basketball, and everyone who wants to participate will get the chance. Again, inclusivity is the watchword. 'I love that the emphasis is not on winning at all costs,' wrote one parent. 'Sometimes the order will be changed to ensure that the lower order players get to play the key positions, even if that means we are likely to lose the match. I think this is brilliant, although not all parents agree!' It's not all losses, either: remembering a recent victory against Millfield clearly raised our tour guides' testosterone levels. Excellent covered swimming pool used all the year round. Dance studio is home to compulsory dance for both boys and girls up to year 9.

Flourishing drama with at least two productions per year, and remarkably good art and photography, reflecting the very creative ethos. A huge programme of clubs and societies, everything from jewellery making to CCF. School embraces the forest schools initiative – children in years 1 and 2 learn to eg build shelters and cook on open fires.

Boarding: The boarding provision was given the thumbs up by everyone we spoke to, with all boarders confirming that they enjoyed their time here ('It's really nice! Lots of activities at the weekends,' said a sixth former who joined in year 12). Very small numbers of boarders in junior school (currently nine), all of them housed with the older pupils – didn't sound ideal to us, but no complaints of any kind reached us. Boarding houses are frankly dilapidated – the ones we saw, at any rate – and numbers to a room rather high for this modern age, with four or five being fairly normal. Living in one of the country's prettiest and oldest towns has its flipside, perhaps. But the students seemed cheerful enough about it, and although we dug hard, we couldn't unearth any complaints. Appraisals of the food were mixed. 'Like the food I had to endure when I boarded 25 years ago!' said one parent, while another countered loyally, 'I'm told it's amazing!' But again the students, all of whom seem to radiate good health, seemed happy with it. We ourselves were served a pleasant and wholesome lunch, so can't comment on this further.

Background and atmosphere: Tracing its roots back to 909, Wells is one of the world's oldest schools, and wears its age beautifully; there surely can't be a lovelier place of learning anywhere. Whether picking our way down the cobbled Vicar's Close, where we heard mellifluous treble recorder playing drifting out of the mullioned windows, or wandering about the many elegant Georgian buildings cocooned in greenery, we thought that growing up here must be a gift. 'I am not sure our children yet realise just how lucky they are,' agreed one parent, 'and when I visit I do have to pinch myself sometimes.'

Co-educational since 1969, and a specialist music school since 1970, and remains the only such within the setting of a normal school, something which parents clearly value. Music department housed in gorgeous – if rather cluttered – medieval building directly opposite the cathedral. We liked the library with its stock of 2,000 vinyl records plus turntable, although it did seem too small for quiet study, and one parent said that this was a problem throughout the school, describing the boarding houses as noisy. Junior school on a cloistered, lovely, leafy, tree-dotted site with a very nice games courtyard and a delightful early years play area. All rooms made attractive and colourful, and when we visited on a blisteringly hot day, they were refreshingly cool.

This is undoubtedly a very happy community; everywhere we looked we saw a kind of upbeat tranquility blended with lively creativity. One mother spoke for everyone when she wrote, 'What I love about Wells is the happy and welcoming atmosphere. Everyone has a smile – and it is really infectious!'

Pastoral care, well-being and discipline: Highly praised by everyone. The school motto is 'Be what you are' ('Esto quod es'), and all parents commented how confident and happy their children had become since starting at the school, and on the good friends they'd made there. Indeed, we spoke to parents whose children had previously been miserable – in one case at a top academic school, in another at a different specialist music school – but were now simply loving life after transferring to Wells. School communications on pastoral issues rated by parents as prompt, efficient and helpful. (Exception to this appeared to be some of the music teaching staff, who, some said, were reluctant to keep parents in the loop and clung to an outdated 'what goes on in my lessons is my business' attitude.) One parent wrote, 'We love this school. It expects high standards of behaviour and achievement but allows children good levels of independence and autonomy in reaching these. The children learn to motivate themselves. They are supported and nurtured and helped with strategies and tools, but they are not micro-managed.'

Focus is on 'mutual consideration, respect and courtesy,' and discipline problems are few. Children are charmingly polite, but very much themselves: 'Hullo, Mrs Cairncross!' exclaimed a 6-year-old lad with grave propriety as we walked by, 'I looked away and when I looked back again you'd popped up!' Older students showed the same style of courteous assurance, duly matured.

One parent, whose child had moved to the junior school after an unhappy time at another school, commented, 'My daughter is now the happiest child you could ever meet. She goes into school smiling and comes out so excited about her day.'

Pupils and parents: Day pupils drawn from large local radius – school operates bus routes to bring children in from Bristol, Bath, Taunton, Yeovil and comparable. Boarders come from all over, but a significant proportion still from the south west, perhaps because Wells remains off the beaten track: the nearest train station is Castle Cary, some 13 miles away. International students bring cultural diversity: they are welcomed into the purpose-built International Centre and offered very good EAL support. Parents mostly hardworking professionals, keen for their children to turn out right on all fronts – many families choose to send all their children to Wells for their entire education. Pupils are well-mannered, well-spoken, well-adjusted, well-turned-out, and very likeable.

Entrance: A broad church academically and, as always with Wells, flexibility is key. Informal assessment for the pre-prep plus meeting with its head, Janet Bennett. At junior level, more formal tests but still 'friendly'. Chorister auditions held in January each year.

Children can join the school at any point in their school career, even year 13 – the school works to make it a success. At the usual senior entry points of age 11 and 13, however, a formal entrance assessment is held in maths and reasoning, and satisfactory report from previous school is required. Entry to sixth form is subject to interview and at least six grade C/5 passes at GCSE, with grade B/6 or above in subjects to be taken for A level. Auditions for music places currently held in November (sixth form) and January (all age groups) after a pre-audition meeting.

Exit: Almost all juniors move up to the senior school, after sitting an entrance test to gauge academic levels. Some 20 per cent after GCSEs. At 18, almost all to higher education, with a high proportion to Russell group universities; Bath also popular. In 2018, no fewer than 27 went to music conservatoires in the UK or abroad, including the Juilliard in New York, many with scholarships. Two to Oxford and three medics.

Money matters: Historically, not a wealthy school, but Wells has made what it's got go a very long way. An unusually wide variety of scholarships on offer: maths, music, sports, creative arts, academic and all-round. Most of these worth no more than 10 per cent, but a sliding scale of means-tested bursary assistance is also available, and school is working overtime to build up its endowment and reach a 'needs-blind' point of admissions. Funding of up to 100 per cent available for some 'elite' specialist musicians via the government's Music and Dance Scheme. Special provision pupils – children who are musically gifted but want to follow the full academic curriculum and keep their options open – often receive financial support for their music tuition.

Remarks: As one parent summed it up, 'We really love this school, and believe that by sending our children here we are giving them the best possible start in life.' A magical place, where children grow into kind, confident and accomplished young adults.

West Buckland School

West Buckland, Barnstaple, Devon EX32 0SX

Ages 3–18 **Pupils** 611 **Sixth form** 131 **Boarders** 100 full, 21 weekly

Fees: Day £8,070 – £15,060; Boarding £24,345 – £33,660 pa

01598 760000
www.westbuckland.com

Headmaster: Since 2016, Mr Phillip Stapleton BSc MA Ed MBA (40s). Educated at Bishop Stopford School in Kettering, followed by Durham University, where he read biochemistry and immersed himself in music, drama and sport. Several university friends became actors (including Alex Macqueen of Peep Show and The Inbetweeners fame), but he modestly says: 'I wasn't good enough'. Initially set on a career in molecular genetics, he stayed on at Durham to take part in a show, embarked on a PGCE and discovered he loved teaching. 'It brought everything together – working with inquisitive minds, a passion for my subject and the chance to perform,' he says. First teaching post was at Stonyhurst, followed by Charterhouse, where he taught chemistry and became a housemaster. Then moved to Ardingly, where he was deputy head for five years. He is also an ISI inspector.

Head was struck by West Buckland's friendly atmosphere and beautiful location the instant he arrived for his interview. 'The sun was shining and a group of students were setting off for a run,' he says. 'It was a breath of fresh air to see their sense of enjoyment. There was a real buzz of opportunity and potential.' The school is selective but he's determined that the school should cater for children from all backgrounds. He's very proud of West Buckland's decision to offer 100 per cent bursaries to local youngsters whose families don't have the financial means to send them to the school (there are currently 17 children benefiting from this programme). During his first year at the school he focused on teaching and learning, observing every teacher in the classroom and broadening the extracurricular opportunities on offer. He's determined to raise the school's profile, citing its academic results, musical prowess and emphasis on character development.

Energetic and approachable, he still teaches (many heads don't). This year he's got a year 12 A level chemistry set. Married to Jules, who teaches maths at West Buckland. They live in a house on-site and have three children, all pupils at the prep. Keen on sport (he once ran four ultra-marathons in a year – respect) and has recently taken up the double bass.

Prep school head: Since April 2018 is Nick Robinson MSc PGCE, previously deputy head of Dunhurst, Bedales's prep school. PGCE at the University of Portsmouth in 2002 and a masters in leadership and management in 2013. Before this, he pursued his passion in swimming as a high performance coach and was head coach for the 1996 Zimbabwe Olympic team and placed three swimmers on the 2000 Great Britain Olympic team. Has also been assistant head at Castle Court. The younger two of his four children will join the senior school.

Academic matters: Results are good. In 2018, 53 per cent A*-A/9-7 at GCSE and 48 per cent A*/A at A level. Most pupils take 10 subjects at GCSE, including at least one language (French or Spanish) and two or three sciences (the majority take three). School is the highest performing sixth form in north Devon, with around 20 subjects on offer at A level. Chemistry, maths and biology are the most popular A level choices, followed by geography and economics. A small number took the EPQ in the past but now AS exams have been ditched all pupils will do it. Other options available to sixth formers include a BTec in applied science and core maths (a new level 3 qualification). No Saturday school.

Unusually, the school doesn't charge extra for learning support (now called personalised learning and development). Around 100 children have help in some shape or form and the dynamic new head of department has brought in a wealth of ideas and strategies, including coloured reading rulers to reduce visual stress, pencil grips, spell checkers, prep diaries and a quiet room for children who might be having a difficult day and want a bit of peace and quiet. Reading for pleasure is encouraged throughout the school. Imposing new library has 14,000 resources and pupils can use it whenever they like, whether they're studying or curled up with a good book. Favourite authors at the time of our visit included Sarah Crossan and Kim Slater for younger pupils, Emma Cline, Deborah Levy and Ta-Nehisi Coates for sixth formers.

Prep school is housed in a separate building. The head boy, one of our tour guides, reminisced nostalgically about his days at the prep and said he'd be very sad to leave the school. Prep teachers work closely with the senior school – children learn French from nursery and get the chance to use the senior school's art department and science labs (the prep has its own lab too). Ninety-five per cent of prep school pupils progress to the senior school. Pre-prep has its own building, with views across fields full of grazing sheep – no wonder parents race to get their children's names down. It's not all splashing paint and building sandcastles though. When we visited, a group of year 2 children had just learned the meaning of 'onomatopoeia' and were excitedly coming up with their own examples.

Games, options, the arts: West Buckland is a sporty, outdoorsy place, with acres of playing fields and excellent facilities. The sports centre (named after distinguished old boy and Olympic triple jumper Jonathan Edwards) boasts a vast sports hall, fitness suite and 25m indoor pool. Boys' main sports are rugby, hockey and cricket and girls' main sports are hockey, netball and tennis. Lots of pupils play for local and county teams. The school also offers specialist performance and development programmes in tennis and dance. Sport is compulsory till year 11 and optional after that ¬ but around 98 per cent continue with it, whether it's mainstream sports or activities like squash, swimming or dance.

Pupils are encouraged to get out into the fresh air as much as possible. The school has its own forest school, where pre-prep pupils – under strict supervision – play in the woods, build bivouacs, make fires and learn to tie knots. The older ones take on challenges like the gruelling Ten Tors hike across Dartmoor and the school's annual Exmoor run, once described by school archivist Berwick Coates as 'the oldest, longest, roughest, toughest, regular scheduled, compulsory school cross-country run in the length and breadth of England'. Around two-thirds of pupils do the run each year (the length of the run varies according to age), while others mark the course, administer the race and cheer their pals as they run across Exmoor's hilly terrain, through muddy streams and over rugged moorland. Staff, parents and old boys and girls take part too and as one of our young tour guides told us: 'The Exmoor run defines the school.'

Music is an integral part of the school, led by dynamic director of music Emma Kent, who's also musical director of the award-winning North Devon Sinfonia. Pupils and staff queue along the corridor to join her lunchtime choir rehearsals – we watched the junior girls' choir singing their hearts out before heading off to afternoon lessons. Music department comprises a recital room, teaching room, computer suite, recording studio and eight practice rooms. Everyone does music till year 9. Up to 25 pupils take the subject at GCSE and around six a year do A level music. Musicians get plenty of opportunities to perform in public – everything from Verdi's Requiem at Exeter Cathedral to Guys and Dolls in the Queen's Theatre, Barnstaple.

School is rightfully proud of its stunning timber-clad 150 Building, built in collaboration with former West Buckland parent Damien Hirst and opened in 2010. As well as the school theatre it houses the art and DT departments. Sixth formers have their own art studio – and their own individual space within it. 'If you treat someone as an artist, they'll work as an artist,' says the head of art. The standard of artwork is inspiring – we were particularly taken with a vast painting of the Exmoor run being painted by a sixth form art scholar as a gift to the school.

Lots of extracurricular options, everything from astronomy to jazz. Enterprising head of sixth form is keen to develop 'academic enrichment' and youngsters are encouraged to take part in the STEM Club, Phoenix Society (debating) and Aldiss Society (guest lectures). Outdoor learning is the jewel in the school's crown. Many youngsters do D of E (bronze, silver and gold) while CCF is compulsory for year 9 pupils (optional after that). New head of outdoor learning encourages pupils to challenge themselves. 'We've got enough tents to put 100 people under canvas,' he told us with a note of pride in his voice. Outdoor activities are voluntary but most take part, whether they surf after school or try their hands at coasteering. There's also the aptly named Adventure Society, which gives pupils the chance to experience new outdoor pursuits. Pupils excel at climbing, with two brothers gaining places in the GB bouldering team in recent years.

Boarding: Pupils can board from year 7, and occasionally younger ('we are always open to discussion,' a member of staff told us). Three boarding houses – one for year 7 to 11 girls, one for year 7 to 11 boys and a brand new sixth form boarding house, with separate wings for girls and boys. Sixth form house (Parker's) is very civilised. All sixth form boarders have their own en-suite rooms – far more salubrious than many university rooms we've seen. They're encouraged to do their own laundry and learn to cook. Stylish common room on ground floor is open to all sixth formers. Lots of activities for boarders at weekends, including cultural visits, shopping in Bath and Bristol, cinema trips, surfing, running, kayaking and paintballing.

Background and atmosphere: The school is set in 100 acres of idyllic countryside on the edge of Exmoor, 220 metres above sea level and eight miles from Barnstaple. Initially known as the Devon County School, it was founded as a boys' boarding school in 1858. The school's enterprising founder, the Rev JL Brereton, thought that the boys could do lessons in the schoolhouse in the morning and work on the school farm in the afternoon. They would then sell the produce and the income would pay for the school's upkeep. The school was renamed West Buckland School in 1912.

Imposing main building dates back to the 19th century but in recent years there have been many new additions, including the Michael Morpurgo Library (the celebrated War Horse author has a farm 20 miles away), the 150 Building and the sixth form boarding house.

Pastoral care, well-being and discipline: Universal praise for the school's friendly and welcoming ambience, with just the 'right balance of formality and friendliness'. One parent describes it as 'a hidden gem' while others say it produces 'grounded, socially aware and respectful individuals with a positive self-assurance'. Pupils particularly like the house system (everyone belongs to one of four houses and there are lots of inter-house competitions).

Plenty of people to talk to if problems arise, including personal tutors, housemasters and housemistresses, the school nurse and a school counsellor who comes in twice a week. School has its own chaplaincy team – a school assembly with a spiritual dimension takes place once a week and the carol service at South Molton Church, six miles away, is a highlight of the autumn term. Christian values are part of school life but students of all faiths or none are welcomed and encouraged.

Most day pupils travel to school by bus so they are allowed to bring phones to school but must put them away during lesson time, unless asked otherwise. Pupils' behaviour is excellent – murmurings about the occasional minor misdemeanour but that's all.

Pupils and parents: Day pupils come from within an hour's drive away, mostly from Barnstaple and North Devon villages. Some choose weekly or flexi boarding (parents can book online up to 24 hours in advance). A fleet of school buses ferry pupils (and sometimes staff) in from areas as far afield as Chawleigh, Tiverton and Winkleigh. Buses start as early as 7.30am to allow for the winding country lanes. Senior school day fees include travel costs but prep school fees don't. Around 20 per cent of pupils are boarders – a third of the boarders are from the Far East, a third from Europe and a third from the UK, mostly the south west.

The pupils we met were enthusiastic, unpretentious and refreshingly down-to-earth. No quibbles about the smart navy school uniform (sixth formers wear business suits) or the food, served in the newly refurbished dining hall. Parents range from families who've lived in the area for generations to those who've moved out of London in search of a better work-life balance – plus the chance to surf at nearby Putsborough Sands after work. Notable alumni include novelist RF Delderfield of To Serve Them All My Days fame, former Whitbread boss Alan Parker, science fiction author Brian Aldiss, triple jumper Jonathan Edwards, former England rugby players Steve Ojomoh and Victor Ubogu, and Somerset and England cricketers Craig and Jamie Overton.

Entrance: Entry into reception isn't selective. After that, those joining the prep higher up spend a taster day at the school and meet the prep school head. Entry into the senior school is selective, but not dauntingly so. Pupils joining year 7 from other schools take English, maths and verbal reasoning tests in the preceding January (but pupils in the prep don't need to take entrance tests for the senior school). Children can start at multiple points so it's always worth talking to the school.

Some new pupils join in the sixth form (27 in 2017), many from local secondary schools finishing at 16. A minimum of five grade Cs/5s required by all, although it's not set in stone. Those aiming to do maths A level need at least a grade 7 in maths and a minimum grade B/6 is required for A level biology, chemistry, physics and modern languages.

Exit: Up to a quarter of pupils leave at 16, for a change of scene, to take the IB (not offered by West Buckland) or to do vocational subjects. At 18, around 90 per cent head to university, including one or two to Oxbridge most years. One to do medicine in 2018. Most popular universities are Bristol, Cardiff, Bath and Southampton, with subjects like engineering, geography, business, English and biology leading the pack. A few opt for apprenticeships and the world of work. Pupils get plenty of guidance about university and careers. Youngsters are encouraged to get some work experience from year 10 onwards – everything from working at local law, marketing and architecture firms to volunteering at a children's hospice in Barnstaple.

Money matters: Mindful of the tough economic climate, the school has kept its fees as low as possible, with learning support, travel, exams and books all included in the senior school fee. Academic scholarships available to year 7, 9 and 12 pupils, plus music, art and sport.

Remarks: A gem of a school in an exceptional location. West Buckland is an impressive all-rounder school with excellent facilities, great teaching and a real sense of community. Children work hard, get lots of fresh air and don't grow up too fast. Best of all, they seem to have a whale of a time while they're at it.

Westonbirt Prep School

Linked with Westonbirt School

Westonbirt, Tetbury, Gloucestershire GL8 8QG

Ages 3–11 **Pupils** 155 **C of E**

Fees: Day £8,400 – £11,595; Boarding £19,470 pa

01666 881400
www.westonbirt.org

Headmaster: Since 2016, Mr Sean Price, previously deputy head and year 5 teacher. He joined the school in 2013.

Entrance: Visit then taster day when child is informally assessed in classroom setting.

Exit: Between 40-70 per cent of girls move on to the senior school; from 2019, so can boys. Boys and some girls to local grammars or other independents eg Kingswood, Royal High Bath.

Remarks: Prep shares the beautiful grounds, if not the breathtaking architecture, of senior school, occupying a former boarding house and san. Classrooms are light and spacious with fantastic views over woods and meadows. Over a third of the pupils are boys and there are three full-time male members of staff. Specialist teaching from nursery upwards for music, French, swimming, ICT, art, science and DT. Parents describe teaching as 'really good' and 'thorough'; several told us that they particularly liked the attention paid to public speaking. Everyone is encouraged to find their voice, both in lessons and by contributing to class assemblies: 'When she started my daughter was very shy, but she's flourished and has so much more confidence now.'

In a year 2 class we saw boys and girls writing first person descriptions of life as a WW1 soldier. Children had brought in family photos and memorabilia and were using these along with poems and other resources for inspiration. Pupils were fascinated by the topic and their imaginations were up and running; mini whiteboards were covered with words and the room was buzzing as children discussed their ideas. The class teacher and teaching assistant were on hand to guide but this lesson was pretty much running itself.

Numbers are rising and as the school starts to attract more families the range of potential secondary destinations becomes wider. While the majority of girls generally go up to the main school some feel that advice about, and links with, other senior independents could be improved. Parents told us that they welcomed what they see as a 'rebalancing' from previous 'overemphasis' on 11+ grammar school preparation and hope this balance can be maintained for the benefit of the boys and girls who are headed elsewhere.

Forest school is just a few minutes away in The Spinney – huge old trees make it a magical place, ideal for dowsing, worm charming and cook ups over the fire pit. Wellies and waterproofs, not to mention a canopy slung between trees, mean that outdoor learning can take place whatever the weather. 'It's an open challenge to create, do and be resourceful,' we were told. Muddy fun for the youngest and the older children love it too; their activities are linked to classwork – whether it's science, nature, poetry or drama. 'It's great for self-esteem. It can bring out unexpected talents from a child who may not shine in the classroom.'

Swimming, gymnastics and dance taught from early years then rugby, football, hockey, netball, cross-country, tennis and cricket. Very popular is the new all weather wicket; 'now we can invite other schools to play at home.' All weather facilities for other sports still on school's, and parents' wish lists. Parents tell us that there are plenty of fixtures and the school is more than able to take on and win against other, often larger, opponents.

Swimming is big here with lessons for all in the 25m pool in nearby school sports centre. Twice weekly for the nursery water babies (the aim is that all should be able to swim by the time they leave reception) and an hour a week for the rest. Schol very appreciative of the parent volunteers who bravely don their costumes to help out. It's paying off: Westonbirt Prep recently won silver in the national IAPS finals – the smallest school ever to make it through. Music is equally starry – the school's recorder ensemble won 'everything in every age range' at a recent Cheltenham Performing Arts Festival. Verse speakers also came away with gold and silver medals. LAMDA preparation offered.

School day runs from 8am until 4pm and there's wrap-around care until 6pm. This, plus holiday clubs, has made the prep increasingly popular with working parents. Minibus service brings children in from Cirencester, Chippenham and Malmesbury.

Westonbirt Prep is a caring, friendly school with a 'real local, family feel'. Several parents also described it to us as 'unstuffy' and we agree. First rate teaching and big school facilities in a beautiful setting mean a great start for girls and boys alike.

Westonbirt School

Linked with Westonbirt Prep School

Westonbirt, Tetbury, Gloucestershire GL8 8QG

Ages 11–18 **Pupils** 200 **Sixth form** 52 **Boarders** 72 full, 15–20 weekly, 15–20 flexi **C of E**

Fees: Day £14,985; Boarding £29,250 pa

01666 881301
www.westonbirt.org

Head: Since 2013, Natasha Dangerfield BA (40s), previously deputy head and head of boarding at Harrogate Ladies' College. Also taught at North Foreland Lodge and Downe House and was director of pastoral care at Gordonstoun School. She studied physical education and English at the University of Brighton and thought she wanted to be a physiotherapist, but while working in sports camps she met teachers who inspired her to change direction. Parents describe her as 'dynamic', and 'approachable' and a great role model, 'she speaks their language.'

Westonbirt inspires fierce loyalty and we got the impression that any head who messed with the school's fundamental character would do so at their peril. Most agree that her changes so far have been the right ones – modernisation of some material aspects, gentle 're-booting' in other areas. The fact that she is a parent herself (she has three young children, two boys and a girl, who attend the prep) must be a good ice-breaker. Her husband works in the fire service.

The combination of over 200 lively pupils and a grade 1 listed building must be a little worrying, we suggested to Mrs Dangerfield. 'This house is built so well that everything is in pretty good order,' she told us. Fortunately, the Westonbirt Trust takes care of historic preservation; 'To put Venetian silk back on the walls is not our responsibility.'

Lacrosse is Mrs Dangerfield's sport (back in the day she played for England) and she continues to coach – even taking pre-season training for her school team. 'I'm not very good at standing on the sidelines,' she confessed.

Academic matters: In 2018, a upswing to 31 per cent A*/A (57 per cent A*-B) at A level. At GCSE, 46 per cent A*-A/9-7 grades. Highs and lows in all subjects reflect the relatively non-selective intake. While there has certainly been a tightening up of standards and a review of the subjects on offer, head has no plans to change entrance requirements. Focus here is on helping girls reach their potential, whether that's 10 9/8s at GCSE, or three 'good' A levels.

Parents have told us how well their daughters are doing and the University of Durham has put a number on it: Westonbirt is in the top five per cent of schools in the UK for value added. This objectively assessed measure calculates pupils' academic improvement between the ages of 11 and 16. Analysis by the University of Durham shows that girls here achieve almost a grade higher in each subject at GCSE than expected.

All learn French in year 7, Spanish, Mandarin and Latin 'tasters' in year 8 and all learn touch typing. In addition to academic subjects, girls in all years follow a 'skills for life' programme that focuses on practical (communication and study skills) as well as personal and social development. With an average class size of 10 (maximum 15), girls here receive what is practically customised teaching; the parents of several girls who had joined from large preps were astonished at their daughters' progress. 'She thought she was bad at maths and science but now she's so confident and doing really well.' Subject teachers set targets and academic progress is closely monitored by tutors. In a year 7 maths class the atmosphere was collaborative rather than competitive, girls attempting questions confidently, undaunted if they were wrong. Even we wouldn't have been scared to hazard an answer.

Choice of 25 A level subjects – all the usuals plus history of art, classical civilisation and business studies. School says that it is able to accommodate most combinations. Now offers a range of BTecs from performing arts to equine management to creative digital media production. Enrichment for sixth formers includes a lecture programme and weekly personal finance lessons.

Technology was somewhat prehistoric but is now much improved and used in lessons 'appropriately and with relevance,' although Mrs Dangerfield's announcement of the 'death of the handout' might be a bit previous. iPads now on kit list although school will lend if necessary. Great boon for dyslexic girls who can use the speech facility for essays. Apps etc stored in the 'Westonbirt cloud' and controlled by school. As we were visiting the science, art, design and technology block, we spied a classroom of very overgrown schoolgirls and boys, concentrating hard. 'Oh, that's the teachers,' our guide said. 'They're having an IT lesson.'

'Outstanding' learning support department caters for wide range of SpLDs including dyslexia, dyspraxia, dyscalculia and mild speech and language impairments. Gifted and talented programme also in place.

Games, options, the arts: 'There's so much drama at Westonbirt!' we heard. Ditto singing, dancing and playing of instruments. Emphasis is on enabling everyone to perform, whether it's in the intimate setting of the Camellia House – a charming venue, used for recitals, 'little plays' and socials – or in the 450 seat Orangery Theatre. Fresh air fiends can also tread the grass of the amphitheatre in the grounds. Music practice block suffers somewhat by comparison with the smart Marriott Centre, home to brand new recording and music tech kit. Three choirs and weekly whole school hymn practice keep everyone in good voice. Huge art studios looking out onto peaceful pastures, DT workshops with laser cutters and CAD equipment.

Mrs Dangerfield is applying her expertise to sport. Local opposition is formidable, and while no one expects Westonbirt to carry home the silverware at every match, there was room for improvement. Sensible trend in this and other girls' schools is a shift from privileging team sports to an equal emphasis on health and fitness – that way you can keep everyone doing something.

No shortage of running around space here and opportunities to play for the school abound, whether it's lacrosse, netball, tennis, golf (there's a nine hole course), riding or polo. In the £3m sports centre, opened by near neighbours the Prince of Wales and Duchess of Cornwall, there's a dance studio and fitness suite. Very popular is the new all weather wicket; 'now we can invite other schools to play at home.' All weather facilities for other sports still on school's and parents' wish lists. Parents tell us that there are plenty of fixtures and the school is more than able to take on and win against other, often larger, opponents. Or you could just take a book and find a secluded spot in the gardens.

As befits the alma mater of Baden Powell's daughter, the school has a girl guide troop – 1st Westonbirt Guides, although members tend to be from local villages rather than the school itself. DofE to gold level offered plus clubs and activities from app design, through gardening and poultry, to zumba.

Sixth formers have the opportunity to enrol on the very popular Leiths certificate in food and wine. Westonbirt was one of the first two schools to run this course, and to have Leiths on your CV is great for holiday and gap year jobs such as a spot of chalet girling. For those whose ambitions go beyond holiday jobs, there's the Young Enterprise scheme and a separate business school with office space and classrooms – A level business studies is taught here.

Boarding: Years 5-8, day girls and boarders, live together in Beaufort House. This junior house is a stepping stone between prep and senior school. There are three senior houses for years 9, 10 and 11 – Badminton, Dorchester and Holford – plus the sixth form. Girls in Holford sleep in what were the family state rooms on the first floor, little beds dwarfed by grand proportions (grade 1 listing is not at home to subdivision). Priceless silk wallpaper, preserved under Perspex, rubbing shoulders with One Direction posters. Beautiful painted panels on the wardrobes and tall wooden shutters instead of curtains. All day girls get one free night of boarding per term and sleepovers are very popular. Wonderful views over the park from common room 'perfect for moon watching'. We asked girls what they thought of the food and the general consensus was breakfast fab, lunch pretty good (we can vouch for that) but catering seemed to run out of steam by supper time. We hope this is on Mrs Dangerfield's to do list.

In the sixth form house every girl has her own study bedroom so day girls can decide at the last minute to stay overnight. There's a dining room, kitchen, laundry facilities, yoga room and bar/café. Not surprisingly, over three-quarters of sixth formers board. Many like to remain in school over the weekend, because it 'helps them stay focused on their studies'. An international student (around 20+ girls are from abroad) told us how much she appreciated learning in such 'serene and calm surroundings.' We loved the spacious common room, newly decorated in a modish putty colour ('seagull'), a simple vase of marguerites on the coffee table.

Background and atmosphere: Formerly one of the Allied Schools, an umbrella body for eight Martyrs' Memorial Trust schools including Canford, Stowe and Harrogate Ladies' College. In June 2018 Westonbirt announced it was joining Wishford Schools, a family-run group of preps and senior schools in Gloucestershire, Berkshire, Wiltshire and Kent. Shortly afterwards came the announcement that the senior school would start taking boys into year 7 from Sept 2019. 'With sufficient demand transition to co-ed may be accelerated, with year 9 entry in 2020 and year 12 in 2021'.

The move to co-ed was, according to the head, not a 'sudden' consequence of joining Wishford but something the school had been considering for several years: 'I think because today, in this climate, the change is not radical. The question I am now asked by parents all the time is not, "Why aren't you co-ed?" but "Why are you single sex?" '. The move seems to have been widely welcomed, not least by prep school parents.

Westonbirt was founded in 1927, acquiring Westonbirt House and 210 acres of park and garden from the Holford family who had lived on the estate since the 17th century. The house itself, built in Jacobethan style (later than, though not dissimilar to, Highclere Castle), was completed in 1871 and used by Lord Holford as a country retreat (his main residence was Dorchester House, Park Lane, now site of The Dorchester Hotel). Just over the road is the world famous Westonbirt Arboretum, another of Lord Holford's enduring projects. When the head told us the house was 'well built' she meant it – constructed around a steel frame, it had all the mod cons of its day (gas lighting, central heating), not to mention fire-proof cavities between each wall and floor. Interior décor was in the distinctly un-modern classical style, with splendid marble halls and corridors on the ground floor, richly gilded wood and plasterwork and intriguing architectural details wherever you look. Friday notices and vespers are held in the galleried great hall, and year 11s dine under a ceiling festooned with plasterwork goat skulls.

As we sighed over the refurbished Gentleman's Library, enjoying the irony while we still could, we wondered what the girls thought about studying in such sumptuous surroundings. 'It is a bit like Downton Abbey', one confided, and we would not have been surprised to see Hugh Bonneville and his arthritic labrador taking a constitutional in the Italianate garden. What a place.

Pastoral care, well-being and discipline: Pastoral care has always been one of Westonbirt's strengths. In a small community with a high staff to student ratio, problems become visible sooner. Parents say that friendship troubles and the like are dealt with fairly and swiftly. 'Everybody has to get along,' we were told, and 'the older girls look out for you.' Not really the place for 'tricky' personalities, observed one mother. We agree; Westonbirt girls are more likely to ride the horses than frighten them.

Girls are encouraged to take responsibilities such as organising social events – planning for a charity ball was under way when we visited. There's a 'much improved' programme of socials with boys from Abingdon, Radley and even co-ed Cheltenham College. A less welcome visitor is the school's lone peacock, Westy, who frequently has to be escorted off the premises. We hear that the class of 2014 bought him a friend, christened (you guessed it) Birty.

Pupils and parents: From all over the UK, although majority of families live relatively locally. Easy to reach from Bristol and Bath and handy for M4, Heathrow and London. Parents tell us it's 'not posh.' Hmmm. It is, but in a quiet way. Nearest places to spend pocket money are Cheltenham and Bath, although you could do some damage in Tetbury. Smallish cohort (some 25 per cent) of international students from all corners of the globe – as elsewhere, more attention being paid to the mix.

Former pupils include the Hon Mrs Betty Clay (Lord Baden-Powell's youngest daughter); Mercia MacDermott (historian); Anna Hornby (painter); Salma Sobhan (academic and human rights activist); Patsy Toh (pianist); Georgia Byng (author of the Molly Moon series of children's books); Lady Natasha Rufus-Isaacs (designer, founder of Beulah London); TV presenter Ruth Watson; TV producer Patricia Llewellyn; Lady Jenny Bland; Jenefer Greenwood, OBE.

Entrance: Entry includes many from the prep, rest from wide range of preps and local primaries. Non-CE candidates sit school's own entrance exams in maths and English plus an online adaptive test. Head likes to interview everyone in person (or via Skype). For entry to the sixth form girls need at least five 9-4 grades at GCSE (including maths and English), with at least 6 in subjects to be taken at A level.

First intake of boys into year 7 in September 2019.

Exit: A few girls leave for pastures new after GCSEs but are replaced by others from elsewhere doing the same thing. Occasional one or two to medical school, likewise Oxbridge (though none recently); destinations range from Edinburgh (sustainable development) to Coventry (international finance and accounting) to the Condé Nast School of Fashion Design.

Money matters: Fees restructured since 2017, with flat rate boarding fees and day fees reduced by some 25 per cent. Academic, art, drama, music, sport, performing arts, organ and choral scholarships up to a maximum of 50 per cent of day fees. Means-tested bursaries may be available – applications considered on an individual basis. Fee reductions for siblings, Forces and clergy families. Girls transferring from prep also get a five per cent discount throughout their senior career. Sixth form bursaries offered to girls from local state schools.

Remarks: Westonbirt has always been highly regarded for inclusivity and exemplary pastoral care, but perhaps its other strengths have been overlooked. Until now. Parents told us that 'there's a new energy, a real buzz' about the place; one described it as 'added sparkle', and they're right. Inside this solid Victorian stately home we found a vibrant and forward thinking community of young women, hugely appreciative of their beautiful surroundings but very well prepared to take on the world beyond Gloucestershire.

Wigmore School

Ford Street, Wigmore, Leominster, Herefordshire HR6 9UW

Ages 3-16 **Pupils** 608

01568 770323
www.wigmoreschool.org.uk

Headteacher: Since 2014, Dean Curtis, previously senior deputy head. Originally from south Wales, Dean studied modern languages (French and German) and marketing at Salford University before a spell in the corporate world in Hamburg and France. After teaching colleagues in France he decided to become a teacher, qualifying at Keele University and then studying a masters in education and leadership at Gloucester University. Before joining Wigmore in 2007, he taught at schools in Staffordshire, Gloucestershire, Herefordfordshire and Worcestershire.

Curtis is a busy man. Wigmore is a National Support School, supporting and training newly recruited teachers, and when we met he was just off to run a course. Since becoming head, the school has also set up an ICT business that supports seven local schools, and he has been appointed executive head of Leintwardine Primary.

Married with three children under 10, Curtis is well liked; he is 'very approachable,' 'dedicated' and 'works incredibly hard,' parents reported

Academic matters: At GCSE in 2018, 82 per cent of students achieved 9-4 in both English and maths, and 29 per cent of grades were 9-7. Core subjects aside, there are 15 GCSE options. There is something for everyone and design technology, business studies and drama are particularly popular. One parent explained, 'Our two children are very different...[Wigmore] suits them both in very different ways; one is academic and has been encouraged and challenged in order to stay motivated, the other requires more help and support to do well.'

Chemistry, physics and biology are taught separately from year 7. In year 8, one class is accelerated and the other three remain mixed ability. Pupils are in sets for maths all through high school. French is taught from primary school and Spanish from year 8. Smaller groups for DT and food technology so there's enough equipment for everyone. All years have life skills classes.

Specialist teachers from the high school teach French, science (in high school labs), PE, computing and cooking in the junior school. One parent told us, 'I am impressed with how often we get to see how the children are doing during the term, with opportunities like the maths café and phonics evenings which are very useful.'

As a teaching school you would expect the teachers to be good, and they don't disappoint, according to parents; they 'strive for academic excellence for all their students' and, importantly, 'children are constantly singing their praises!' Another parent added, 'Staff are readily available to listen to concerns and make time whenever necessary, before or after school.' The teaching school leads training and network meetings for local Hereford schools and has been asked to be involved in the set up of the new Hereford University Centre.

Learning support is based in the student support centre along with careers guidance, student support and EAL. There are three rooms for small group and one-to-one teaching, plus a larger classroom for up to 16 pupils. The department covers the whole school from 3 to 16 years. Moderate to complex difficulties are

W

catered for and the school will modify facilities for usability or access as necessary. The SENCo regularly travels to prospective pupils' annual reviews, wherever they may be. Laptops are used for voice recognition to prepare pupils for exams.

Games, options, the arts: Sport is particularly strong. Successful, too, for such a small school. The U16 1st XV are currently runners up in the county rugby union leagues and the U14 and U16 netballers are county netball champions. As well as traditional sports, they offer athletics, badminton and cross-country. Several pupils play at county and regional level and several have gone on to win sporting scholarships at sixth forms.

Wigmore has solid links with the local community and surrounding sports teams including Luctonians Sports Club, which is renowned for rugby union, cricket, netball and rounders. Their 1st XV rugby union team plays in the fourth tier of a national league. The club supports the extracurricular activities at Wigmore and helps with coaching, encouraging and inspiring pupils to take sport seriously. One parent told us, 'Both my children are extremely happy at the school...They are sporty and creative and enjoy the after school clubs that are on offer.' Primary pupils play traditional sports including tag rugby and hockey, as well as handball, orienteering, gym and dance.

Great reputation for performing arts. Major productions are biennial; the next will be Oliver! Pupils regularly take part in the Performing Shakespeare Competition; they reached the finals in 2016. Plus there is the annual design technology and creative arts showcase, musical evenings (the latest was a 'music from the movies' evening), the annual Christmas concert and various awards evening performances. Parents and staff get involved too and there's a jazz band, a string band and Wigmore Voices, the school choir. In the primary school, recent productions include Alice in Wonderland and Cinderella Rockerfella, plus of course the annual nativity. All Year 5 and 6s learn the violin or ukulele, and lots take part in the annual inter-school Young Voices competition.

Wigmore has been awarded the Artsmark gold. Arts projects range from studying graffiti to Picasso to Henry Moore. There is an art and design after-school club as well as trips to London to the Tate Modern and National Gallery for older pupils, and creative art trips to Cardiff for the younger years. Student ambassadors from Herefordshire College of Arts also run workshops in the high school.

All subjects offer extracurricular activities including extra revision clubs and catch up sessions. Other clubs include drama, sport and music as well as a writing society, debating society (recent regional finalists of a mock trials competition), science club, juggling club and a weekly feeding and animal handling session – very popular at lunchtime, we heard. Parents are particularly impressed with the range of activities on offer as well as the 'dedication of the staff who give up their own time.' Duke of Edinburgh award scheme has been recently introduced.

Every summer term, years 7 to 9 have an activities week while year 10 have work experience placements. There are a good number of residential trips too. In fact there's one for each year group every year. Year 6 go to York for a week, Year 7 have a week of survival and bushcraft, Year 8 visit Normandy, Year 9 take in the London sights, and the older pupils can opt for a Slovakia expedition, a skiing trip or a trip to CERN. Plus there are language trips to Paris and Valencia. Pupils 'love' the trips, and parents feel they benefit hugely from the residentials by learning to take responsibility for themselves. Day trips include theatres, art galleries, museums, geography field trips and life skills trips; when we visited pupils were off to the NEC's The Skills Show. There are also RE trips to Christian churches and the National Buddist Centre, as well as a regular exchange with a Muslim school in Birmingham.

Background and atmosphere: Originally founded in 1963, Wigmore Primary and Wigmore Secondary became one all-through school in 2007, governed and led by one senior team with one headteacher for both schools. Became an academy in 2011 and a teaching school in 2013.

Set in the pretty village of Wigmore in a remote and very rural part of Herefordshire, Wigmore School is 15 miles north of Hereford and five miles from Ludlow. A small site; the primary and secondary school are within seconds of each other. The nursery, opened in 2011, is based in the primary school and although privately run, it is very much part of the school, managed by the headteacher and his team. Nursery children have their own classroom and playground, but also have access to all primary and high school facilities. Fantastic for transition.

Almost 170 pupils in the primary school, a small one storey building. Pupils have access to all high school sports facilities as well as some specialist classrooms. Everyone eats in the high school canteen but at different times. Inside, a small library opens out onto a large hall used for daily assemblies, sing-songs and music. Classrooms, named after trees, are based around the hall. Each opens out onto the playground and some look across the playing fields to the high school. Reception has its own playground with a reading den shed, an eco garden and occasionally, sheep next door. What struck us most were the fantastic displays on every wall; this school truly celebrates pupils' work and encourages them to be creative. In the hall, year 6 had created a 'trip advisor' display for their recent residential trip to York, full of photos, drawings and their own written reviews. Year 2s had been busy with a Great Fire of London display, year 3 had worked on a Stone Age display, year 4 on the Vikings and year 5 on WW2. Teaching follows Bloom's taxonomy, a principle based on the theory that in order to learn something properly, you must understand it and analyse it first.

None of the buildings here are new, with the latest the student support centre, built in 2011. The high school in particular could do with some updating. We were assured that plans are underway and it will be updated gradually. Portable cabins were added in years gone by and a replacement block is well overdue. Funding issues, as always. Inside, the school is a little drab and feels rather dark. The classrooms are spread across three floors and conditions vary. There are good-sized laboratories overlooking the playing fields and three ICT suites. Permission has been granted to start a sixth form at Wigmore. With funding, a new block could replace the portable cabins with classrooms and a sixth form centre. The high school has 460 pupils so sixth form numbers would be fairly low. However, some parents would welcome it; one said, 'I'm just sad they don't have a sixth form so they can stay out in the sticks for longer!' A makeover of some kind would, in our view, complement the level of education that is provided here. Having said that, the pupils and parents don't seem to mind: 'My children enjoy all of their subjects and feel safe and happy at Wigmore,' parents assured us.

As an all-thru school, staff and families really get to know each other well, growing together from an early age. Its small size means the school can focus on developing individuals and nurturing relationships with families; there is a strong sense of community spirit. The Great Wigmore Bake Off, business enterprise competitions and sports day are hugely popular. Parents love the fact that Wigmore is focused on academic standards but 'retains a caring family perspective.' The whole school comes together each week for assembly and the house system is a fundamental part of the school.

Pastoral care, well-being and discipline: Traditional school with traditional expectations; 'the school instils positive values and insists on good behaviour so the children know what is expected of them,' one parent told us. Strict in some ways, we were told: no make up, no room for creativity with uniform, and KS3 must line up in silence before entering school each day. The pupils we met were well-behaved and polite, even the youngest primary pupils held open doors. Any bullying is addressed immediately and appropriately, parents confirmed.

Pastoral care is good. One parent told us how the school appointed a mentor to help their struggling child. The result has been 'fantastic,' their child is happier, keeping up with the work and, as parents, they are kept up-to-date. Another parent told us her child had had a very difficult time at a previous school, 'but from the first day they supported [him] to integrate and build new friendships....[He] continues to make good progress and has many friends.' Pupils stay in the same mixed ability tutor groups throughout the school and parents agree they have benefited from the positive relationships built over the years.

The student support centre supports all pupils. A counsellor is available once a week, a family support worker three days a week and a nurse once a week. One parent who has needed support told us that they feel they can turn to the school whenever they need to.

Pupils and parents: Catchment area covers predominantly agricultural land so lots of pupils have farming backgrounds. Wigmore has a great reputation locally and parents are drawn by the 'consistently good results and good morals.' Many parents attended the school themselves and several staff have children there. Extremely supportive parents regularly drive miles across country to pick up after extracurricular activities. Wrap-around care is available. Parents are kept well informed and Wigmore actively encourages them to contact them with any queries or problems. Regular communication is via newsletters, emails, texts and class blogs on Twitter and Facebook.

Entrance: Nursery from 3 years. Pupils are well prepared for full time school and 'take this huge step in their stride,' parents told us. Those starting primary school have a home visit plus several class sessions before September.

Primary classes are small in the lower years but grow in the older years as parents are keen to secure places for the high school (entry is not guaranteed, but primary school pupils are always accepted). Families tend to join the school when children are old enough to travel independently.

Entry to the high school is oversubscribed. Based on catchment area, which runs north to Ludlow and west towards Presteigne. Primary school pupils make up one third of the cohort of 90. Others come from local schools in Bucknell, Kingsland, Leintwardine, Luston, Orleton, Shobdon and Wigmore. There are transition days in year 5 and 6, plus an induction day. Additional visits for children with special needs or those who are particularly vulnerable or anxious. Bushcraft activities, taster days and a team-building trip early in year 7 help pupils to settle quickly. Pupils also receive a 'Quest book' to help them find their way around and get to know everyone.

Exit: All primary school pupils tend to move on to the secondary school.

At 16, around half of pupils go to Hereford Sixth Form College, a fifth go to Ludlow College, another fifth to Hereford & Ludlow College, and the remainder go to Hereford College of Arts or do apprenticeships. Around 75 per cent opt for A level courses, the rest choose vocational qualifications. Farming and rural studies are popular.

Remarks: Small, rural, friendly community school. Could do with a makeover in parts, but pupils and parents are happy here. Staff are caring and passionate about learning. An impressive array of trips and extracurricular activities prepare pupils well for life after Wigmore.

Wilmslow Preparatory School

Grove Avenue, Wilmslow, Cheshire SK9 5EG

Ages 3–11 **Pupils** 119

Fees: £9,315 – £10,785 pa

01625 524246
www.wilmslowprep.co.uk

Headteacher: Since 2014, Helen Rigby BEd NPQH, previously of Offley Infant School. Has a natural empathy with parents whose children attend her small but perfectly formed co-educational, non-selective prep school. And so she should, having started out as one. It fact, so impressed was she as a parent with this warm and welcoming school that she made a successful application to join the teaching staff in 2001.

Fast forward several years and she's headteacher. It is seemingly impossible for parents to describe her or her school without using words like nurturing or caring because that's what this little school – which the head says (and with good cause) punches well above its weight – is all about. That and really top notch academic achievement which means all pupils consistently achieve entry into the secondary school of their first choice (with several offers under their belt).

Yet while the academic bar is set high, what Helen Rigby most wants for her pupils is for them simply to have a go, keep persevering. An approach which she hopes will imbue them with the spirit of the Olympians (a theme picked up in a recent school play). A keen horse riding fan, she cheered loudly when, during the 2016 London Olympics, veteran rider Nick Skelton finally achieved individual gold in his seventh Olympics. It's that spirit of determination she wants to foster in her pupils. Always try, never give up, you will succeed.

Entrance: Most children join the kindergarten at 3; the rest enter the school between 3-5 with a taster day and an informal assessment with literacy and numeracy.

Exit: Parents tend to choose small preps to give their children options at 11. Here, they sit exams for all the usual suspects: Cheadle Hulme, Manchester High School for Girls, Withington Girls, Stockport Grammar, Alderley Edge Girls, Kings' Macclesfield. Two academic scholarships in 2018.

Remarks: The school used to be girls-only; boys joined the kindergarten in 2013. Currently, every year up to and including year 4 is mixed and broadly 50:50 between genders. Both infant and junior years have a teaching assistant assigned so individual attention is available at every age level. Class sizes around 15.

The school boasts excellent facilities: up-to-date IT room, art room (and specialist art teacher), music room, science lab (age-appropriate). A lovely junior library, along with a sports hall (secured via inspired fundraising) and a small playing field with long jump pit, big enough for a decent game of rounders and infant sports day. It also has some imaginative play areas with Astroturf and an outdoor 'learning environment' worthy of the National Trust. Head is keen that children learn to manage risks in safe spaces.

Small classes mean individual attention; as one parent put it, every task and challenge is tailored to a child's individual needs. Along with the core subjects, languages, computer work and science are integrated at a basic level from day one in infants. French for the infants, Spanish for the juniors. A broad curriculum really matters to the head; while she appreciates year 6 exams are crucial, she also considers arts, science and sport to be essential for development. At junior level, there is a shift in emphasis to specialist science, maths and English, along with verbal and non-verbal reasoning. Collaboration across the curriculum means a particular reading book, for example, might also be picked up in drama or art. The latter, a recent initiative – the Power of Reading – is an open sesame for minds.

About five per cent of pupils are on the SEN register but a larger number receive extra support to ensure they are on target to reach high academic goals (often booster activities in English or maths with a teaching assistant). One parent said her child had been performing below the expected level at a state primary but following a move to WPS is now above expectations. Pupils who want to leap ahead are likewise stretched. A parent whose child happened to have an EHC plan spoke glowingly about this (he had a reading ability well beyond his years), and about his increased confidence (he was encouraged to take lead roles in school plays). One parent, however, struck a note of caution, saying she thought that whilst children who were struggling or excelling fared incredibly well in the school, those in the middle of the class were overlooked.

Even so, a recent inspection report asserted that 'children's achievements and progress exceed age-related expectations in all areas of learning'. The same report also alluded to imaginative learning: Welly Wednesdays, where children did mini-beast hunts and Thinking Thursdays for problem solving.

Head asserts that children in year 6 take exams in their stride. Yet while one parent said that year 6 pupils were incredibly confident, another said she had expected the children in year 6 to be in a 'better place' and felt it was all a bit stressful for them.

Generally, though, the tone and register in the school is one of bursting, bubbling happiness. Dazzling wall displays suggest it is a crucible for creativity. The entire school is crammed with wonderful art displays: Egyptian masks, self-portraits (by year group showing evolution in maturity) and impressive pieces 'in the style of' an artist, such as Henry Moore. Unsurprisingly, in a recent ISA Art Competition, the school scooped six first prizes. (On the flip side, one parent thought there was too much art. You say Tomaito, I say Tomarto.)

The school has choirs, junior and chamber orchestras. A large proportion of pupils also takes individual lessons at an extra cost. In the Alderley Edge Music Festival, the school recently won first prize for both the chamber choir and year 2-3 choir. All pupils are encouraged to enter and thrive on the buzz, parents say.

All children take the ESB (Communication with Drama) Awards where distinctions are vacuumed up. Parents felt this was terrific for confidence. In addition, school productions are bold and imaginative – they recently staged Go for Gold, the history of the Olympics, starting with Zeus.

All the usual sports – football, hockey, athletics, netball, cross-country, badminton – are played locally and nationally. There are also offbeat extras, like judo and fencing. When bigger playing fields are required, they jump on the WPS minibus to a local sports club. One parent said the sports teacher was quick to identify potential talent; her daughter had done so well at cross-country she was now a member of Stockport Harriers. Another parent felt the school was not as well equipped sports-wise for boys as it might be. A sentiment echoed by others. Here, perhaps, the school is transitioning.

Heaps of extracurricular trips: infant favourites like farms; juniors to more cerebral or outdoorsy destinations like York or the coast. Lots of wonderful clubs like mad science and book clubs.

Behaviour seems exemplary; pupils stand when an adult enters the room, the teachers shake each pupil's hand at the end of each day. (These children will not be looking at their feet, mumbling, if a secondary school interviewer wishes to converse.) School rules consist of lovely directions to be kind, give a helpful hand. A merit and courtesy system is applied which is celebrated weekly in assemblies. Children love it. Well, who wouldn't – fame for being the best version of yourself. A winner.

A team ethos is encouraged via the house system and its various charming competitions (never underestimate the power of a conker on a string to galvanize) and charitable initiatives organised by the school council. Each child in year 6 is an 'ambassador' for a discrete area, such as learning or sport, with a 'job description'. A nice touch to prepare them for that giant lunar step to secondary education.

Though small and cosy, this school is no bubble: interactive assemblies cover important issues like festivals across faiths and crucially, with iPads more ubiquitous than colouring books, internet safety.

The school, established in 1909, moved to these premises in 1912. Buildings cluster round the play area and banks of windows and skylights give it a real sense of lightness and zip. Rooms are large and colourful, evidencing projects simmering away, an explosion of nascent knowledge. From around 11am each day, the smell of cooking permeates from the school kitchen. All children have to eat school meals – it looked good and healthy nosh to us (it also clocks in as an extra payment per term).

Communication with parents is via three parents' evenings per year, reports and regular emails. Parents are local (Hale, Prestbury, Wilmslow, Alderley Edge), professional – grounded – many of whom had to do the maths before committing to school fees. The size of the school necessarily lends it a familial feel. The parents' committee seems something of a tour de force.

We agree with the headteacher: this terrific little school does indeed punch above its weight. You remember the Andrew Murray fist punch? The victorious, happy air punch when he knows he's done well? Well, it's that.

Wrekin College

Linked with The Old Hall School

Sutherland Road, Wellington, Telford, Shropshire TF1 3BH

Ages 11–18 **Pupils** 470 **Sixth form** 130 **Boarders** 76 full, 26 weekly/flexi

Fees: Day £14,820 – £17,925; Boarding £27,360 – £32,040 pa

01952 265603
www.wrekincollege.com

Head: Since September 2016, Tim Firth, BA English Literature, Sheffield University, PGCE Oxford University. Previously deputy head and then acting head at Hurstpierpoint College, West Sussex; came to the school after Wrekin's unfortunate run of heads (three in quick succession). Nothing Lady Bracknell-ish about losing all these heads, just a quirk of fate. And possibly one that has benefited Wrekin since it resulted in the arrival of Mr Firth, who is, according to parents, a 'great fit', a 'dynamo who is very energising' and brings 'solid leadership'. Parents like him; children like him. They say he is approachable and chatty and after the first few weeks of him arriving, 'everyone relaxed'. Being the warm, funny, open sort of chap that he is, we imagine that he will be very adept at taking people with him on what he plans will be an 'enlightened evolution' of the school. We hope everyone's ready: his development plan, outlining numerous aims including targets for value added to pupil grades and a reformed appraisal system for teaching staff, suggests the evolution will be pacey.

In the past parents may have selected Wrekin for its happy vibe and reputation for pastoral care, rather than its academics. Mr Firth has set about addressing this. A big change has been to introduce Challenge Grade Review cards; parents tell us that they finally know where their child stands academically. Clear targets are given to each pupil based on his or her ability, regarding where pupils could be if they successfully carried out measurable tasks. They are given clearly defined 'stretch' work to enable them to meet these challenge grades (head describes the process as a coaching manual) and teachers are able to see which pupils might need a bit of extra support (one on one, for example). Having recruited new heads of lower and middle school to work alongside the tutor system, he says there is now a whole team around each child academically. Greater coordination. Greater tracking. The head says they want to harness the excellent pastoral care that allows frank but supportive conversations about academic achievements

So far so (very) good; GCSE and A level results solid and improving and we predict this uplift will settle into a trend. Number of students has also increased – an extra 50 have been lured in by the Firth factor over the last 12 months.

While raising the school's academic profile is a clear goal, head is also acutely aware that young people are entering a competitive job market and their employability needs to be equally strong. To that end a new Business School opened in 2016, which focuses not just on CV and interview preparation, but also offers a wide programme of career talks on practical topics like 'what an office is like' and industry-focused subjects, such as engineering. Pupils are introduced to apprenticeship schemes and discover what could work best for them as individuals post school. The centre's curriculum is designed to include pupils of all ages. While Mr Firth has far too much humility (and realism) to claim these aims are unique, the dedicated nature of the centre perhaps is. He describes it as a 'standalone temple to employability' – not a phrase you hear very often. It's certainly shaping up into a significant USP and is especially popular with those parents who are in business and want their children to be better prepared for the world of work.

Mr Firth recognises that the straight A student, who may have been a bit spoon fed along the way, does not always make the most agile, creative, resourceful presence in the workplace. The centre is dedicated to resolving that conundrum. His ambition is for Wrekin students to be more stalagmite, less snowflake. He refers in passing to the high number of golds in the Duke of Edinburgh awards clocked up by Wrekin students, testament to their sturdy, resourceful characters.

Above all, Mr Firth is keen for Wrekin to continue to be an inclusive environment, one which reflects a broad spectrum of children. Or as one impressed parent put it, quoting the head's words in his first communication with them, 'no one under the radar, no one on the bench'. That phrase went down like manna with parents. He says he relishes the diverse intake because it reflects the real world and this mix 'breeds thoughtful teachers'.

Mr Firth is a keen sportsman, particularly interested in cricket (he was a cricket blue), loves reading, particularly poetry, and Bob Dylan (he has 60 albums). He and his wife, Jane, have three children: two at university, the third, a daughter, is at Wrekin.

Academic matters: Wrekin offers a broad curriculum to suit its diverse intake, including BTecs and A levels in subjects like accounting and psychology. Languages are fairly healthy: 52 per cent of students take one or more language at GCSE; 12 per cent continue to A level. School is very supportive of apprenticeships and does not automatically assume that university is the right path for everyone. Classes are small: typically no more than 20 for the younger pupils and 8-15 at A level.

In 2018, 24 per cent A*-A/9-7 at GCSE and 21 per cent A*/A (47 per cent A*-B) at A level. Most of the A*s at A level were in maths and further maths with a sprinkling across languages.

Tutoring system means each pupil has personalised academic support. Pupils' academic progress is closely monitored with twice weekly meetings. The mix of pupils means teaching, as Mr Firth explains, is all inclusive but differentiated, depending on stage and ability (this might manifest itself in slightly different homework).

The Franklin Society is in place to challenge the most academically gifted pupils. It is aimed at developing logic, science and the arts (game theory, science projects, study of the classics, architecture). After a rebranding, there are now timetabled weekly lessons. Pupils are chosen from second form upwards based on their performance in non-verbal reasoning and/or exams (pooling all the academic data). About 10 out of 60 students in a year get the nod.

There are also the usual subject-related extension activities, mind-expanding lectures and academic challenges in national and inter-house competitions. Parents say head has added polish to the teaching and upped ambition in pupils. (Although one parent wondered if staff might be a bit stretched, master of a lot of roles.)

Good learning support team for mild to moderate difficulties. A learning profile is drawn up for all pupils, identifying strengths/areas for development, as well as strategies to help teachers. All have agreed termly targets. Progress is measured against these targets and reassessed each term. Support also available on a temporary or permanent basis for pupils experiencing difficulty with a particular area of the curriculum. No extra cost.

Games, options, the arts: House system provides a healthy platform for competitiveness, team playing and support. Parents say it results in every child wanting to participate in a range of activities and have a go; it 'puts fire in their bellies', as one parent said.

All the usual sport is on offer (vast grounds, lots of playing fields), netball, rugby, football, rounders, cricket, cross-country, tennis, athletics. Also fives and fencing. Large sports halls, gym and tip top swimming pool. Very good to see the girls have a strong six-a-side football team. Netball teams seem to excel, frequently ending up county champions.

Very vibrant art department with an annual exhibition and trips to back it up, like a recent Photoshop workshop with a local artist. Around 200 pupils have music lessons every week and there is the usual array of orchestras, bands of all types (rock and jazz) and choirs. A regular programme of school soirées ('soirees at six') recitals and concerts means heaps of opportunities to perform for all, including house singing competitions and house concerts. Also, Wrekin Musician of the Year competition, concerts off site at eg Shrewsbury Abbey and overseas tours. Recent very ambitious production planning of Carmina Burana involved 200 singers. Music is a clear strength of the school. At least one whole school play per year and lots of house productions, from Macbeth, to Shadowlands. House drama competitions allow senior students to manage younger ones.

Around 130 pupils each year are involved in CCF. Duke of Edinburgh popular – remember that healthy stash of gold awards.

Lots of trips, including annual house camping; cultural visits to Hampton Court, Tate Modern, design and business trip to Jaguar Land Rover.

Boarding: One girls' boarding house and two boys'. Rooms are fine, not huge – pretty standard boarding fare. Younger years share four or five to a dorm, older students have their own study bedrooms, some with ensuites. Communal facilities are okay, some have had a refurb so are a tad smarter. All houses have common rooms with decent sofas, cushions, relaxed vibe, kitchens (fridge, toaster, microwave) and games rooms (pool tables). Boys can visit the girls' common rooms for a short time after prep; one girl called their common room a 'social hub'.

All well supervised, houseparents on hand along with matron and prefects, who have a duty roster. Phones are allowed but wireless turned off at 10.30pm. Day pupils don't go into the boarding areas but common rooms for day students, within the houses, are open to boarders so there is a fair bit of downtime mingling. On site medical centre staffed throughout the day and a nurse is always on call overnight.

Lots of trips into nearby Shrewsbury, Ironbridge, Chester, Birmingham and London. Also, there are a great many clubs on a Saturday morning from squash to jewellery making, horse riding, archery, rowing, maths.

Background and atmosphere: Founded in 1880 by Sir John Bayley on a large and lush site above Wellington, a market town in Shropshire, Wrekin is a combination of old and new buildings (no eyesores), on a large campus with plenty of green space. It became co-ed in the 70s and in 2006 merged with The Old Hall School, which moved on to the same site.

Cheerful studiousness might best capture the atmosphere, students going about their business with a smile. Classrooms have an old style charm, some with the smell of refurbs, like the chemistry labs. In the corridors displays don't jump out at you, but it all feels very friendly and 'community-led' with all the information and updates pupils need.

Inevitably, lots of hoofing required to cover distance between boarding houses and buildings – our legs could tell we had walked a fair distance by the end of our visit.

Pastoral care, well-being and discipline: By all accounts, a massive strength of the school. As one parent said, every day their son 'had gone to school with a smile on his face and come home with a smile on his face'. Others spoke of a happy and secure environment where children are social, look people in the eye and are making the best of who they are.

While every school says there is a caring environment, the students we saw and spoke to – who really did smile and make eye contact without knowing who we were – looked cheery. We also noted the impeccable manners – door opening, standing aside. They didn't seem formulaic, just natural consideration, true courtesy.

A very inclusive environment; most parents seemed to think the house system was instrumental here – the spectrum of inter-house competitions (a house play, a house singing competition etc) all offering a sense of identity. The children relish being part of a group, not wanting to let the group down. First and second form (years 7-8) are all in Lancaster House, which parents said was an excellent stepping stone and a good way of introducing them to the whole school. From the third year, they join one of three boys' or two girls' houses. Parents say pupils all look after each other and being part of the house is viewed as an honour.

Experienced counsellor on site and all the usual assemblies on pastoral matters. Pupils can train as mentors, identified by a distinct badge to encourage others to approach them. Every new pupil is issued with a school handbook and it is genuinely useful, packed full of all the information necessary (mobile phone use, security, map, routines, who does what on the staff).

Wrekin is a Christian foundation and worship – four times per week – is very much part of the makeup. Services are also an opportunity for pupils to perfect their public speaking – prefects often give 'thought for the day' talks on topics such as 'determination to achieve goals'

Our House is a week's compulsory boarding for sixth formers who have to cook and clean for themselves – good preparation for university

Pupils and parents: Pupils are friendly, social, polite and without a whiff of arrogance or entitlement. As the head says, Wrekin's broad mix ensures its leavers are rounded and prepared for the world beyond school.

Parent demographic is similarly broad; many have business backgrounds (this is a part of the country where manufacturing still thrives); others are professions or from the farming and county set. Head welcomes parents' support – and their high expectations. Those we spoke to said home-school communication is good and they appreciate the open door policy. Head has also started discussion forums where parents can contribute ideas and give feedback about the school.

Entrance: Around half come from the on-site prep, Old Hall. Rest from local primaries and preps including Packwood Haugh and Prestfelde. All candidates sit 11+ exam, papers in maths, English and non-verbal reasoning, but bar is not set too high for entry. Entry at 13 + by Wrekin entrance exam.

Exit: Nearly all sixth form leavers head for university and the spread is typically broad for both subjects and locations. Parents praised the UCAS support. Most choose northern, Midlands or Welsh universities: Leicester Bangor, Cardiff, Keele, Leeds, Manchester, Hull, Sheffield, York. Economics, engineering, business management and sports courses (sport science, sport and health education) seem popular. Not many takers for arts degrees, just a few for English lit and languages. Two to Oxbridge and one medic in 2018.

Money matters: Boarding and day fees are somewhat lower than similar schools further south. In a nod to today's economic climate interest free monthly payment plans are offered, as well as a reduction loyalty scheme for those who attend its associated Old Hall prep.

Remarks: A wonderfully nurturing and inclusive school which is on the up academically but also offers something rare: the chance for pupils, in this tough old world, to hone their employability factor.

Writhlington School

Knobsbury Lane, Writhlington, Radstock, Somerset BA3 3NQ

Ages 11–18 **Pupils** 1,500 **Sixth form** 316

01761 433581
www.writhlington.org.uk

Head teacher: Since 2011 Mark Everett BSc MA PGCE NPQH (early 40s). By his own admission, an Army brat from 'mostly around Manchester'. He read physics at Nottingham as an officer cadet, but had a crisis of conscience at the end of the first Gulf War, at which point he turned his back on officer training and worked in a cheese factory after graduation. His patience with other cheese-makers indicated that he might make a good teacher, so he enrolled on a PGCE course at Hull, going on to forge a successful teaching career in some pretty rough inner city schools in London and Southampton. 'I've seen it all', he says, and this gives

W

him an unshakeable belief in the value of truly comprehensive education: 'No school should isolate less advantaged kids when the social profile of the school changes; our job is to ensure that everyone, irrespective of background, goes on to achieve more than his/her entry assessment would suggest'. His military background still obvious 20 years on in terms of his physique, energy and confidence – we were amused that he turned out of his office for us to chat to pupils, one of whom dared to swivel around in his big black chair. Generally respected by parents and pupils alike for his local and global ambitions for the school; an 'excellent front man – who should not lose sight of standards closer to home such as behaviour and uniform,' according to one mother. Married to another teacher with a small son, and admits to a love of surfing when time permits.

Academic matters: For a completely non-selective school in a socially mixed, if not ethnically diverse area, 39 per cent A*-B grades at A level in 2018 is impressive. At GCSE 59 per cent of pupils achieved 9-4 in English and maths. Academic superstars can sparkle here.

This was the first school which has handed us an academic paper as a going-home present. A few years ago, a year 11 pupil carried out research in Sikkim (India) comparing historical records of altitudes where orchid species grew with present data, as a means of recording climate change: He was awarded Young Biologist of the Year for his pains.

Parents have noticed a greater emphasis on top universities, not merely local ones. 'I didn't know what Russell Group meant till I heard the head go on about it', admitted one dad. We were put in our place by one brain-box, who, when we asked if he was aiming for Oxbridge, said, 'No, MIT actually'.

However, the school appears to look after everyone by assigning each student to a pathway according to his/her intellectual lights – academic, applied learning, sport or STEM. This assumes particular significance in year 10 at the point where choices made will affect sixth form courses of study. It's a meticulous and collaborative process, resulting in an agreement signed by parents. One parent felt, however, that his child had been written off academically and that the school could do better at recognising his other achievements and attributes; another was disgruntled that her child had changed GCSE subjects without the school telling them; yet another said that her bright son was frustrated and bored in mixed ability sets.

The design of the building and emphasis (plus funding) given over to technology, results in teaching innovations: every child has an iPad to be used as a learning resource and means of communication – 'makes life a lot easier for my dyspraxic son too', said a father. The school has learning zones, where a whole year group can be accommodated: we were impressed by the purposeful way in which 90 children were getting on with their differentiated work with just one teacher and a couple of TAs overseeing them. Traditional methods still employed where effective: one class was studying graphs of rainfall, sitting in rows, facing the front and paying attention.

SEN, and in fact any intervention for all abilities, has been brought right into the centre of the school: small groups brought out of class into the atrium to work on literacy and numeracy under the watchful eye of a staff member. We wondered if it would be distracting or stigmatising but were assured not – quite the reverse, in fact. Some parents do report a lack of communication between SEN and subject teachers.

W

Games, options, the arts: School is fortunate to have a community sports centre on site; with its sports hall, gym and squash courts, although it lacks a pool. Rugby pitches, an Astroturf (used by the FA), indoor nets and an outdoor pitch for cricketers. A tennis centre run in conjunction with the Lawn Tennis Association – also used by local clubs and members of the public. Recently launched outdoor education programme means students will be able to take up DofE and Ten Tors. School has been selected for training by Bath Rugby. A smattering of outstanding sportsmen/women (Commonwealth Games hopeful for target shooting; one year 7 boy chosen to play football for Welsh National side; another for the World Trampoline Championships; a sixth former offered 13 (!) tennis scholarships to American universities) mean Writhlington keeps in the news.

Musical life also abounds, with all year 7s offered free instrument tuition for their first term. A Musical Association has been in existence for 20 years; its primary aim to raise funds to support the school's many musicians with instruments, transport and more recently, snazzy waistcoats for band members. Happy collaboration and perhaps rivalry with nearby Downside, particularly at annual Battle of the Bands. Individuals excel too: recently two girls got grade 8 singing, one with distinction. Facilities top notch, with high tech recording studio particularly praised – and let out to local groups seeking low-cost recording facilities. Productions of all kinds staged in 400 seat theatre where recent drama productions include Little Women – the Musical – and The Tempest. Students can choose a performing arts option from years 10-13, which covers not just acting but also production, direction and technical support. Art occupies four specialist rooms on the first floor, and from year 10 students can choose either art or art and design; their work is exhibited on occasion in Bath and Bristol's most prestigious venues.

Extensive enrichment programme with plenty of clubs in school time; enterprising parents and staff offer ventures outside school such as the equestrian team, run by the head's PA.

Background and atmosphere: Fifteen years ago, 'Writhlington was a dump, and no child of mine will ever go there,' declared one mother, recalling with a shudder its depressing concrete buildings, windswept site and low aspirations. Historically, it had served the mining community in and around Radstock but it is now federated with the town's other schools, so relations are greatly improved. Enter a dynamic and visionary head and an exceptional business and finance manager. They succeeded in pulling the place up by its bootstraps and securing some of the last funding available under the Building Schools for the Future programme resulting in £42m worth of brand new buildings of truly innovative design – a recipient of an award from the British Council for School Environments ('but looks like a prison,' say locals).

'However, it is what goes on behind its doors that I believe makes this school simply remarkable,' says the current head, an opinion largely shared by the parents we spoke to, including the mother cited above. Now very much the comprehensive of choice for the area, where students are given myriad opportunities to shine, and where success of all kinds is recognised. The new buildings, insistence on higher standards of turn-out than many schools we know and the weekly appearance of the CCF in their uniform make for a smart, clean, rather businesslike school. Thriving sixth form retains many of school's own students and attracts others from the area, including from local independents.

School belongs to Career Academies UK, so that students taking that curricular pathway have access to a mentor, paid internships and contact with leading businesses. Because of the school's non-selective intake and inclusive philosophy, university is (refreshingly) not regarded as the be-all-and-end-all of sixth form achievement. One father, however, commented wryly that the students needed to see more of, and be ready for, the realities of the working world.

Parents and their offspring recognise that the school successfully brings the world to the school, with its offer of

Mandarin, the China exchange and the increasingly famous orchid project. They have recently ventured to Rwanda to teach schools laboratory and conservation techniques and to promote science education. The trip was funded by orchid sales from the school, which now has a new hybrid 'Oncidium School Days' named in its honour.

Has recently opened the Mendip Studio School, offering STEM courses to 14-19 year olds.

Pastoral care, well-being and discipline: Appears to be a school where concerns are acted upon, and where students have places to go when things go wrong. 'The support and guidance staff sort you out and cheer you up,' was the consensus from the group we spoke to. Parents generally approve of the discipline, but one felt that those meting out punishment should be answerable for their actions; the students' view was that it was 'quick, effective and tailor-made'. The fact that achievement of all kinds is celebrated was universally praised, but part of the reward system consists of a trip for the class, for which the parents pay – to the outrage of some, who consider that to be socially divisive. 'And what about recognition for the kids who are good all the time across the board?' said a mother plaintively: 'The system specifically aims to reward those whose work ethic is consistently high,' says the school in response

Pupils and parents: Very mixed, as befits a truly comprehensive school. Catchment is economically varied (though a lower proportion of free schools meals than the national average) with dreary Norton Radstock at its heart, yet prosperous little villages and madly arty Frome close by. Two university academics we met chose it over other local options. Building purpose-built for kids with limited mobility, which gives it a lovely inclusive feel.

Entrance: An open day in September and subsequent open mornings helps decision-making, thence applications are made through the local authority, BANES. Year 7 intake is over 250 from several local primary schools, and other years are already oversubscribed. Sixth form numbers are lower: entry requirements are five GCSEs at 4+ including English and maths; some A level choices will require specific grades. Open day in November each year. Great care taken over information available for new students on the website, such as several student video clips.

Exit: Post-GCSE, some leave for college and a few to apprenticeships or work. Some 70 per cent of sixth formers go to university, and most of those to their first choice, including Edinburgh, London School of Economics, Imperial College London, King's College London, Exeter, Cardiff, The Royal Veterinary College London, Manchester, Southampton, Bath, Bristol, and Nottingham. Subjects include medicine, law and veterinary science.

Remarks: This school is a phoenix rising from some pretty unpromising ashes. The process of bringing it back from the moribund, if not dead, started long before the dramatic new build of 2010, and now it has the setting to reflect its considerable aspirations. The school aims to make these attainable for everyone. 'The whole place makes me feel as though I wanted to go back to school', said one father, a little wistfully

Wycliffe College

Linked with Wycliffe Preparatory School

Bath Road, Stonehouse, Gloucestershire GL10 2JQ

Ages 13–19 **Pupils** 417 **Sixth form** 166 **Boarders** 230

Fees: Day £19,935 – £20,985; Boarding £21,660 – £36,570 pa

01453 822432
www.wycliffe.co.uk

Head: Since 2015, Nick Gregory (40s), previously pastoral deputy head at Mill Hill School in London. He graduated in French and Spanish at Nottingham, then spent eight years at Barclays, including time in Madrid, before teaching modern languages, first at Barnard Castle School, County Durham, then at Merchant Taylors' School, Northwood. He then became boarding housemaster at Old Swinford Hospital. He and his wife, Helen, have three sons, two of them at Wycliffe. He believes school needs to be more than a teaching machine, somewhere that gives a lived and valued experience which will lay a foundation for life.

He is 'nurturing boys' sport from the bottom up' to ensure that there are promising signs of success (girls are doing pretty well at present). He aims to support 'the gifted and talented pupils the school attracts, while maintaining access to all academic levels, and supporting bringing out the best in those with difficulties'. He expressed his approach very simply as enabling his pupils 'to be good people'. His pastorally orientated philosophy works on the premise that young people learn and are motivated when they are confident secure and feel valued. If the these sound like 'soft' skills, he is also determined that the school will be supported by the best in teaching and technology, and have well structured opportunities from tutors, careers advice, business links and university access. Exceptionally accessible and easy to talk to, Mr Gregory is also someone who works fast and gets things done quickly. 'A force of nature,' said one parent. He and his family live on the premises, and when he actually gets some time away he likes to spend it giving full time attention to his family life in their house in southern Spain.

Academic matters: Considering that the school has an open access policy with exams only used for purposes of setting or scholarships, GCSE and A level results are usually very respectable. There is no doubt that gifted pupils do really well, with the relatively few high flyers, including those who have been right through the Wycliffe experience and some more recently arrived from abroad, getting straight A*/A grades. In 2018, 30 per cent A*/A and 58 per cent A*-B at A level. Mr Gregory says the long-term aim is least a third of A levels A*/As and two-thirds at B or above and he is getting there. Choice is impressive with over 30 A level subjects including BTec equivalents in travel & tourism, digital production and sport, which have impressive results. Languages (French, Spanish, German, Russian and Japanese) have good take up as does maths, with a consistently sound record, though whilst economics and business studies are also much in demand, As and Bs are thin on the ground.

2018 GCSE results 33 per cent A*-A/9-7. Often some spectacular results here in maths, further maths, German, Russian and Chinese – the latter possibly accounted for by some native speakers.

Value-added is key to the school's approach and all the statistics indicate that this is impressive. Masses of help available when needed – with teachers exceptionally ready to go the extra mile with one-to-one and special help. Lots of careful supervision and expert help on subject choice. Teachers always keen to help even after exams have started. Boarding and day pupils have study space in their houses and the library, which is also a fabulous multimedia resource centre. Very popular, spacious and well planned, with plenty of help on hand; it was very full and had an extremely studious feel on the day of our visit. All this is underpinned by a careful tutorial programme and rigorous tracking of pupil progress which stops pupils slipping through the net. PHSEE provides life and study skills and every year group has courses such as teamwork, problem solving etc, aiming to develop skills as useful in life as they are in academic approach.

Newish labs, biology sporting a fish tank that wows prep school visitors. Classrooms jigsawed into every part of the buildings with plenty of the relevant IT etc, and without exception those we passed looked busy and purposeful.

Extensive remedial and special needs programme with lively, sensitive and fully qualified teachers who help and support. Pupils are automatically assessed on entry to the school, as much to identify gifted and talented as those with learning difficulties. Wycliffe has received accreditation and plaudits from both CResTeD (for SEN) and NAGC (for specially talented), which endorses the quality of teachers' work with pupils. Emphasis is on differentiated teaching as well as individual help. EAL support is on hand.

The 'development year' is a pre-A level course designed to give pupils from abroad both basic English and some GCSEs or equivalent on which to ground A level study. Some 30 or so pupils each year from all over the world benefit from this, with 15-20 staying on into the sixth form and contributing a range of sporting and other skills. Mr Gregory, parents agree, has certainly 'turned up the gas' a bit on the academic side but not, they also agree, at the expense of Wycliffe's happy and supportive community feel.

Games, options, the arts: Sport is a vital aspect at Wycliffe and a number of parents cite it as their deciding factor in choosing the school. Facilities are excellent, with smashing new Astroturf and smart multipurpose sports hall (full of aspiring small cricketers avoiding the rain on our visit) with professional standard squash courts, fitness gym and viewing areas. The pool is on the prep site. Massive pitches and lawns surround the school. Teams in hockey, netball, rugby and tennis reach county level at least on a regular basis, while individuals perform at national level in a huge range of sports including rowing, biathlon and an abundance of all branches of athletics. Girls' teams have acquitted themselves particularly well recently, with recent district and county successes at netball, hockey, rounders and tennis. Squash is truly exceptional, with boys' and girls' teams winning national events, and the school has an internationally-renowned programme that pupils from across the world come to join as boarders, producing recent British and European champions.

Choral singing – with a 75-strong chapel choir and the upmarket Vox chamber choir for the real elite – is the heart of performance music, but a vast swathe learn instruments with a few getting to grade 8, and National Youth Orchestra or Choir standard. No full orchestra, but lots of thriving ensembles and an emphasis on music technology. Several take A levels in music and music technology each year, with some progressing to uni on the technology side. Fantastic support and inspiration from the two exciting musicians who head the department.

Strong drama boasts established theatre studies and emerging film studies, with pupils carrying both of these on to post-school study and ambitious school productions. The Sibly Theatre, named for the founder, now looks a little dated, so not quite as slick as the junior theatre, but bigger and very well equipped with studio spaces behind the stage.

Art inhabits its own building with a chaotic barn-like upper art room and pottery, classrooms and other media below producing some striking work, which reflects the team of professional artists. Sadly we missed the A level work, which had been packed up for dispatch, but there was some exciting painting and in most years the results are A* studded.

Not surprisingly for a school offering a whole life experience, the range of co-curricular activities is wide and diverse. Up to GCSE pupils have to opt into two activities weekly. Since the alphabet of activities starts with astrology, beekeeping and cryptology, continuing in the same vein, this is no hardship. Opportunities to take up fencing or yoga, the staples of CCF and DofE, and academic extensions such as robotics, studying newts or serious debate are an integral part of what Wycliffe is about, and a chance for every pupil to excel – and they do.

Beyond this there is serious programme of exchanges, visits and expeditions: cricket to Barbados, squash to Canada, hockey and netball to Sri Lanka. Language visits include Japan and there are careers and education trips to theatres and museums etc, and year 12 is launching a charitable project in Costa Rica.

Boarding: Having pupils from all over the world, plus Brits who live some distance away, means there is a solid core in school at weekends. Some locals choose to stay as there seems to be a thriving social scene, so boarding really is a good bet for Forces families or expats.

Boarding houses with full and flexi boarders plus attached day pupils form the core of the social life. The system is a real mixture with a designated sixth form house but some sixth formers in the main school houses, and a day pupils' house, as well as some day pupils in the main boarding houses. Co-ed Loosley (named after the third and most illustrious Wycliffe head) houses some of the sixth form, with spacious common rooms, small kitchens and laundry areas for washing casual clothes and a campus feel for milling about. The mixed day house, with generously broad corridors, brightly painted studies and common rooms with balconies overlooking the green sward, is clearly much appreciated.

Rooms (for two to four and the odd single for prefects or heads of houses) are fairly basic and include work space. Most boarding accommodation is utilitarian rather than palatial, though some houses are being upgraded in a multi-million pound project – new boarding house has all ensuite rooms and a sauna. Pupils with study periods can use their rooms – so the houses are certainly not unnaturally tidy. Houses looked after by friendly and very approachable non-teaching staff, who seem to be available throughout the day as well as in the evenings, plus a teaching houseparent in charge of each house.

Sixth form boarders are allowed a pint or glass of wine at weekends and the occasional early evening visit to the pub in the neighbouring Cotswold town of Stonehouse, which despite its quiet atmosphere is conveniently on the main line from Paddington.

Background and atmosphere: The parkland feel of the huge grassy campus is created by wide, well-maintained pitches (cricket/rugby and some Astroturf) sited amid trees and well-kept garden. A succession of buildings, some inspired and some less, has divided the whole into a series of campus 'rooms', each with its lawns and distinctive buildings, ranging from the elegant Georgian Haywardsend House, though the bizarre exterior of the Sibly Theatre (really good facility inside) and the workmanlike labs to the inspired modern wood and glass of the huge curved dining area, serving delicious food with a tantalising variety. Sunday brunches 'are to die for'. The last looks out on a massive expanse of new, green Astro used for hockey etc in the winter and tennis in summer. It is spectacularly edged in dark purple, which echoes the head's penchant for this colour – which, conveniently, is the school colour, emphasized by the pale mauve of the large Wycliffe sign boards and, more attractively, by the wisteria which swarms over several of the buildings.

Founded by the Sibly family in 1882 and named for the pioneering Christian spirit of John Wycliffe, the school now goes out of its way to make this spirit accessible to all denominations and races. Pupils and parents set immense store by the Wycliffe ethos, friendly, nurturing and pupil centred. A busy campus with friendly staff and well-mannered but unaffected pupils strolling purposefully around. The school has been fully co-educational for more than 30 years and it feels absolutely right. The happy purposefulness of the place is most evident in the exceptionally user-friendly library, full of pupils working quietly and calmly (it was almost exam time) with help on hand. It is designed to divide into areas for quiet study, computer research, reading and even discussion and is clearly a real centre of academic life.

Pastoral care, well-being and discipline: The house system is the pastoral structure for both boarders and day pupils. The houseparent, matron, house staff and a team of house tutors are supported by prefects and responsible sixth formers, who provide the essential links between staff and pupils. Both pupils and staff give the impression that the relationship between them is free and easy. Students say there is little or no bullying, certainly nothing serious. 'It's just not what we do and absolutely not tolerated'. One parent reported that he was informed of a minor incident which his son had not mentioned because 'it was not a real problem'. It had clearly been nipped in the bud before it became serious. Communications are excellent and parents who want frequent updates are well satisfied. Pupils from abroad seem to mix in well – a table of very all-inclusive chatterers in the dining room proved on our enquiries to consist of a real mix of recent and new pupils, from both the locality and as far away as Latvia and the Ukraine. Awkward moments, like the transition from prep school, are extremely well handled, according to parents.

All faiths catered for and the chaplain is very open and inclusive. Pupils evidently felt real affection for the beautiful chapel, and recounted its history with pride: rebuilt post war by pupils and staff incorporating wood from a pier on the Isle of Wight and stone from a bombed church.

Houses do lots of social, competitive and charitable events, which give creative opportunities involving everyone in mixed age groups in cultural and aesthetic activities: singing, drama, film quizzes etc. Usual structure of prefects etc clearly relishing their responsibilities.

Pupils and parents: Plenty of army families but also lots of locals as well as a high proportion from abroad (30 per cent, which means about 60 per cent of boarders): Europe, ex-USSR countries and the Far East. The chair of the PA says parents who want to take a large part in their offsprings' education are given real support, but those with a less hands on approach seem equally satisfied. Head finds pupils refreshingly unaffected in comparison with the London set. Parents here are exceptionally supportive of each other, and those from further away say they get invitations to stay and offers to entertain their offspring.

Entrance: The majority of pupils joining in year 9 come from the school's own prep school, though recently increasing numbers come from other prep schools as well. Entrants sit exams but only for setting purposes. The school really prides itself on value added, which is one of its key aims, and only turns down those with learning difficulties too severe to be managed well. Entry into the sixth form usually requires at least five GCSEs at grade 5 or above, but they do consider, more carefully than many, the question of potential, and the variety of academic pathways post-16 allows pretty much anyone to be accommodated appropriately.

Exit: Just over one-third leaves post-GCSEs to vocational courses and sixth form colleges. Over 97 per cent of the sixth form go on to university with a few Oxbridge places on occasion (one in 2018). Royal Holloway and Manchester popular destinations recently. A number apply successfully to USA and other unis all over the world, and when the specialist adviser on US places moved on, the replacement was expert in international university entrance. Some art foundation courses and drama school, otherwise business-related careers very popular, as are law and digital/creative courses.

Money matters: In terms of endowments, the school is not particularly wealthy, though it stresses that it is 'strong financially.' Scholarships are available at 13 and 16 for academic excellence, art, music, DT, ICT, drama and sport (10-20 per cent). This seems to be a particular draw in sixth form and there are a few pupils with exceptional circumstances who get pretty full financial support from the school, dependent on school reports and financial circumstances.

Remarks: A school which offers a way of life as much as an education. That the Wycliffe experience clearly breeds the confidence and openness is evident in its pupils. Definitely hotting up academically under the current head, but still faithful to its broad academic ability range. If success increases demand, will it be able to maintain an open admission policy? At present it is doing a remarkable job of being 'all thing to all men' – and women. A real gem of a school.

Wycliffe Preparatory School

Linked with Wycliffe College

Ryeford Hall, Stonehouse, Gloucestershire GL10 2LD

Ages 2-13 **Pupils** 247 **Boarders** 61 (from 7 years)

Fees: Day £9,675 – £15,795; Boarding £13,380 – £26,655 pa

01453 820470
www.wycliffe.co.uk

Headmaster: Since 2003, Adrian Palmer BA (rapidly approaching 60 but with no intention of retiring). An ex-maths and PE teacher, he had a spell as head at Warminster Prep then moved to Rendcomb, where he started the junior school and built up numbers rapidly before moving to Wycliffe. Works closely with the senior school head but has complete control of development in the prep. Married to Julie, a lynchpin in the school, managing SEN and, as author of The Write Path, assisting everyone to develop legible handwriting; they have son and a daughter who both went through the prep and the college.

Exceptionally talented at inspiring children and setting them at their ease; they positively bubble with delight at his arrival. His office boasts masses of impressive artwork including a stunning pencil portrait of him done by a pupil. His lurid collection of over 200 ties are the source of endless discussion and delight to pupils. Though he does not teach, he is very much in evidence around the school, showing round every prospective parent and aware of the individual needs of every child. His efforts grading system, based on skills like persistence, cooperation, organisation etc, may account for the confidence with which one pupil told me that coming top was less important than fulfilling potential and achieving a personal target grade. End of year exams for the top three years are intentionally tough with 'opportunities provided' for revision, so that children can learn to deal with this situation.

Utterly pupil-centred, Mr Palmer – and hence the school – believes in pupils enjoying their education. Responsibility appointments, prefects etc are made 'when children are ready for it' throughout the final year, and head boys and girls hold the post for part of the year only so that leadership is shared out. He runs the school with a light and humorous touch; the hanging model of a bee in the dining room was left after a food info project 'because it was fun'. While his approachability is clearly appreciated by pupils, staff and parents, his professionalism is evident everywhere. Everything runs like clockwork.

Entrance: Many join the nursery across the road, and move up seamlessly; pupils applying other schools take a cognitive ability test and attend a taster day (or skype interview for international pupils). Moderate learning difficulties can be given appropriate help. An increasing number comes in at 11+, when scholarships and awards in music, drama, dance, sport and art are available. Fleets of buses from all over the place.

Exit: Most pupils (some 85 per cent) move up to the senior school, with exams for setting purposes only and early warning of any problems. Pupils heading elsewhere are prepared for CE etc. Destination schools include Cheltenham College, Marlborough and Wynstones.

Remarks: The campus is divided by a main-ish road with the nursery, boarding and massive playing fields over a bridge to the north, the rest nestled tightly but comfortably on the smaller southern area. Teaching facilities include bang up to date Etheridge Hall, an attractive modern and spacious class and subject room centre with latest high-tech facilities, and large common room for year 8 pupils (tea and toast making facilities). In contrast the largely unreconstructed original house, with its high ceilings and steep stairs, houses the library and lower forms. It's not very accessible, though the school will switch what's taught where to accommodate anyone's needs. The main campus is an amazing hotch-potch, attractively united by some remarkably well-designed gardens and wonderful views. Little sheltering pagodas with blue roofs harmonise the haphazard older buildings, which include a hugely impressive art room, full of deconstructed cubist guitar paintings and occupied on our visit by a class learning to make Egyptian cartouches.

The nursery is next to the boarding houses, surrounded by little secure areas for digging, outdoor play and exploration. More log-clad portacabins make a light-filled flexible space with all the nursery equipment imaginable. It is filled with small children absorbed in play activities or books, dressed in cheerful red tops or cardies with bright gingham dresses for girls, quite different to the smart jerseys and girls' kilts of the older pupils. Good library – 'the nursery eats books,' said one teacher. It all feels happy and purposeful, provides after-school care and has terms which are much longer than school ones to provide a consistent service. There are even beds available for occasional rest time.

Gym and good sized indoor pool are serviceable but undistinguished, and there's a really state of art modern theatre building, much used for really exciting performances – Hairspray, The Lion King etc. Stunning sensory garden with open-air pavilion for either teaching or just sitting and thinking.

Sport is really important, with the usual rugby/soccer/cricket for boys and netball/hockey/tennis and rounders for girls, and there are some distinguished athletes – one girl reached national biathlete standard, and other talented children are taken to local clubs in the evenings and get top coaching, with some spectacular results. Masses of other activities after school, and day pupils can go home at 4.45pm or stay later for prep and activities.

Everywhere is well equipped. Two IT lessons a week in the prep. Good labs, French taught from tinies on and German and Spanish from year 8. The school accommodates a wide range of abilities, demonstrated by its affiliation to both CResTed, which confirms its good SEN provision, and NAGC, which accredits work for gifted and talented pupils.

Pupils genuinely believe that there is no bullying and that any potential problems can and will be sorted out by sympathetic but firm pastoral staff. Parents confirm that the merest sniff of trouble is dealt with well. A zero tolerance of bullying and a real sense in older pupils of their responsibility to take care of younger ones make it 'a bit like a family,' one said. A boarder explained that there was no need to be homesick because some members of staff were really like another mother.

Lots of Forces' boarders and a few from abroad – occasionally short term visitors like it enough to want to stay on for the rest of their prep years. Weekends great fun and, though boarders are allowed out, there tends to be an inflow of day pupils staying for special activities rather than a general exodus. The boarding houses (one each for boys and boys and girls of all ages, with a connecting lobby) are at the top of the site and have splendid views. The large dormitories have been split into rooms taking two to four pupils with loos very near and showers – some definitely catering for privacy and some less so – and baths downstairs. Boys and girls are allowed to visit each other's common rooms under supervision. Lovely touches abound, like the heart-shaped 'memories' collage of photographs. All prep is done in school so work doesn't come home, but mobiles and computers are allowed during waking hours in the boarding houses – handed in at night and during lesson hours. It's all feels very secure, homely and not too tidy, with the inevitable bunk beds which children seem to like.

Food is 'pretty good now', especially breakfast with croissants and pain au chocolate. Dining is informal with a separate round table area for little ones. Early bird day children welcomed into boarding houses and taken down to breakfast by helpful prefects. At weekends boarders go up to the college for Sunday lunch – one parent said this was the only feature of the school she had reservations about, but not a serious one. Noticeably kind and motherly kitchen staff. Saturday morning school (for years 6, 7 and 8) was one of the few things pupils could think of that they didn't like – but then they decided that actually it's fun 'on the whole'.

Parents get a chance for input via parent forum groups, and one noted that several suggestions had been taken up and were working well. Those stationed abroad are particularly grateful for a parent community prone to scooping up boarding children with absent parents and ensuring they get to birthday parties etc, and being on hand to offer visiting parents a bed for the night.

The key feature of Wycliffe Prep is its happy atmosphere. Children and parents enjoy their experience of the school as well as getting second to none opportunities in sport, music and drama, combined with some exceptional teaching. Its atmosphere, creativity and endearing quirkiness are typified by an extraordinary portrait of Mr Palmer, done in string on the wire-netting fence to the tennis courts – smiling, as usual.

South East England

Berkshire
Buckinghamshire
East Sussex
Essex
Hampshire
Hertfordshire
Isle of Wight
Kent
Oxfordshire
Surrey
West Sussex

Northampton
Cambridge
Bedford
WARWICKSHIRE
BEDFORDSHIRE
Milton Keynes
Stevenage
Luton
OXFORDSHIRE
BUCKINGHAMSHIRE
Harlow
Oxford
Enfield
Ilford
Harrow
GREATER LONDON
Swindon
London
Reading
Croydon
SURREY
Guildford
Basingstoke
HAMPSHIRE
Winchester
WEST SUSSEX
Southampton
Brighton
Worthing
Portsmouth
Bournemouth
Isle of Wight
M1
M4
M3
M11
M25
M23
M27
M40
A1
A
B
C

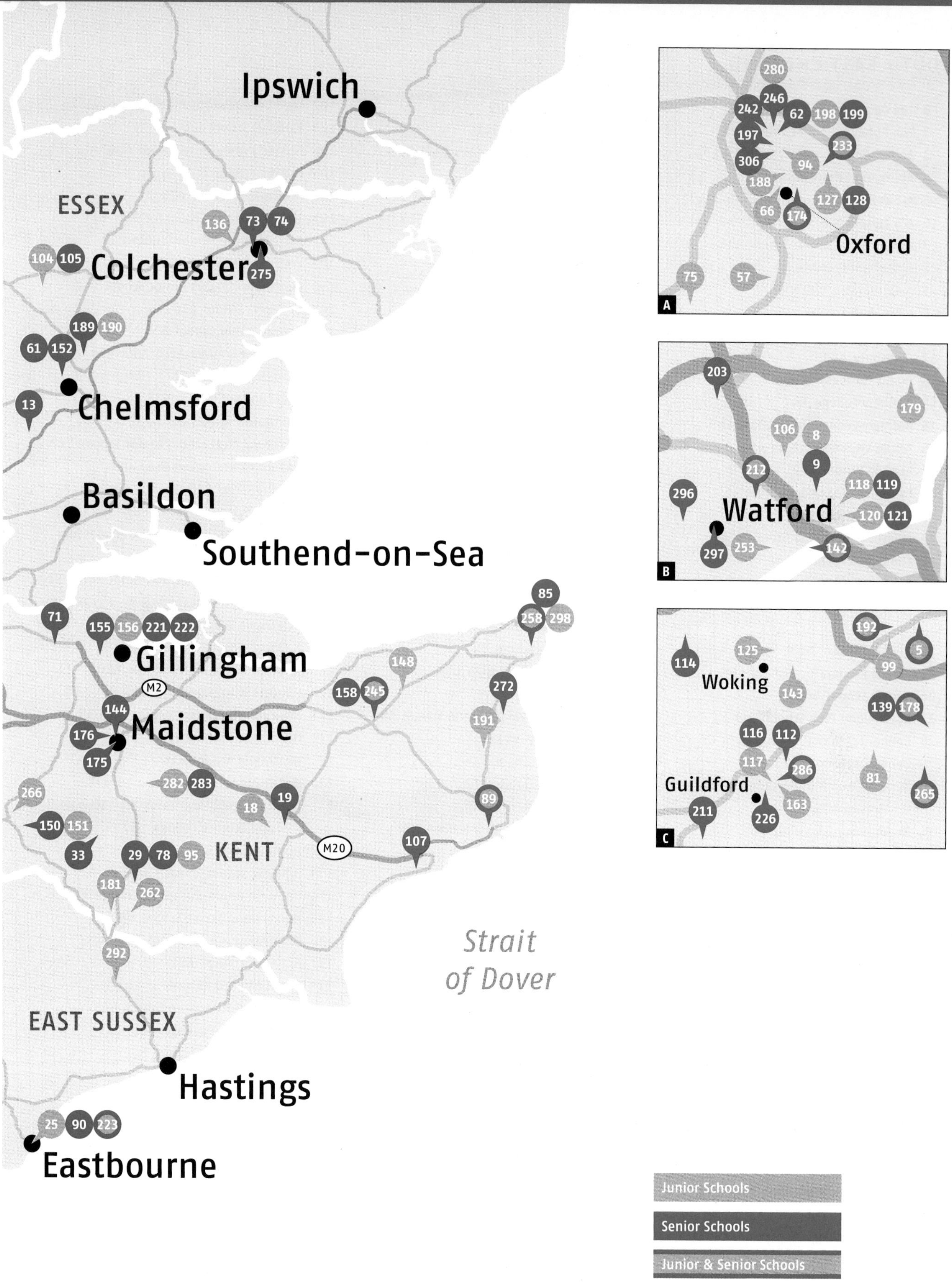

Ipswich

ESSEX

136 73 74

104 105 Colchester 275

189 190

61 152

Chelmsford

13

Basildon

Southend-on-Sea

85

258 298

71

155 156 221 222

Gillingham

M2

148

158 245

272

144

Maidstone

176

175

191

266

282 283

19

18

89

150 151

33

29 78 95 KENT

M20

107

181 262

Strait of Dover

292

EAST SUSSEX

Hastings

25 90 223

Eastbourne

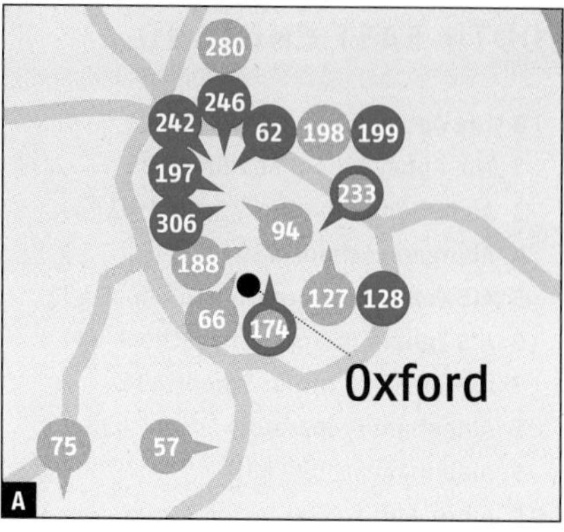

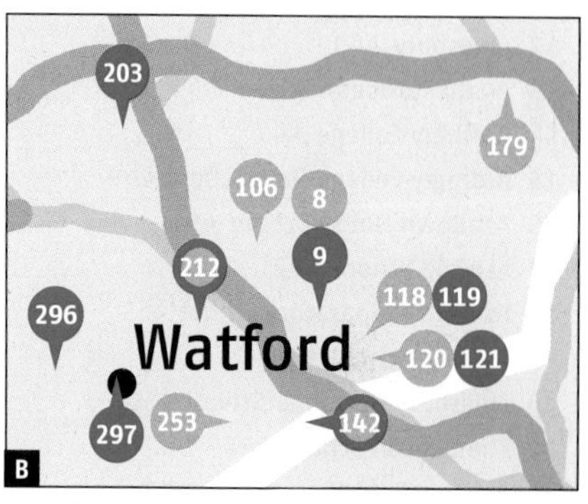

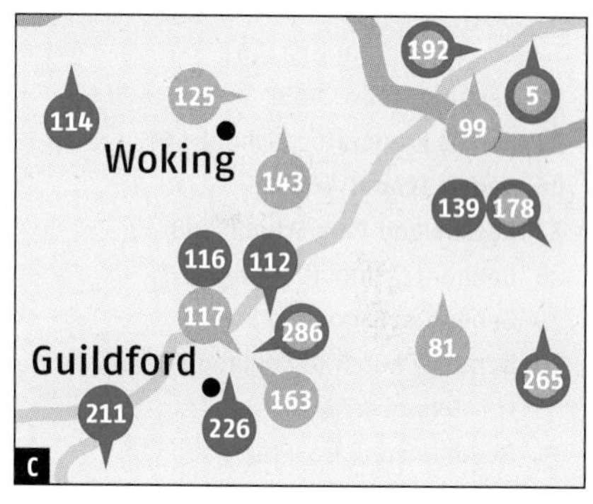

Junior Schools

Senior Schools

Junior & Senior Schools

SOUTH EAST ENGLAND

A

The Abbey Junior School

Linked with The Abbey School Reading

30 Christchurch Road, Reading RG2 7AR

Ages 3–11 **Pupils** 334

Fees: £10,410 – £14,850 pa

01189 872256
www.theabbey.co.uk

Head: Since 2015, Nicola Dick-Cleland MA Oxon QTS (50s), previously deputy and then acting head. She joined the school in 2011 and was rapidly promoted to deputy. Has a degree in experimental psychology from Oxford and a teaching qualification from Reading. Was a senior manager at BT (the second most senior woman in BT at the time) before turning to a career in psychotherapy and, later, music teaching before embarking on formal teacher training. 'For me, being a head brings together everything I know – leadership, psychology and education – perfect,' she says.

Refreshing to hear a head talk enthusiastically about working with adults (many primary heads complain that they miss working with children), she nevertheless has a wonderful rapport with the kids here, whose faces light up when she bounces informally into classrooms. This is a warm and cuddly head, but with an underlying authority. We were surprised, then, that our pupil guides had absolutely no clue at all where her office was; she later explained she purposefully keeps her office a largely child free zone: 'I go out to them – an office isn't really an environment for children.' Parents also keen on her.

Lives locally with her husband, with whom she has two grown up children. Her daughter was a pupil at The Abbey. An outdoorsy type, she loves walking.

Entrance: Nursery, reception and year 3 are the main points of entry, with some spaces elsewhere. A short morning of informal play and assessment for youngest; tests plus interview for older girls. 'We're not looking for rocket scientists, but a good average,' says the head, who adds that conversations with prospective parents are taken into consideration. 'In the end, it's all about whether the family has a fit with a school that has quite an academic pace and depth.' Some parents apply from their child's birth; others call mid-academic year when their partner has been relocated to the area; increasingly, girls move from state primaries. Class sizes generally 22 maximum, with many much smaller.

Exit: Around two thirds move up to the senior school. Big feeder for nearby Kendrick Grammar, although girls who gain places at both often choose to stay on. Others to the good local comprehensives, such as Maiden Erlegh. A handful to other independent day schools. Those who leave before the end of year 6 generally do so for relocation reasons.

Remarks: Open the magnificent door to this charming primary school in the university area of Reading and the tone is immediately set by the welcoming, down to earth staff and the seemingly endless displays of photographs, artwork, booklets, written work and more that decorates every single room and corridor. 'That's my work!' come the squeals of delight from the girls, making it immediately obvious how much pride they take in their work, and the boards are colourful, bold and tasteful too – a joy to see.

Nursery is based in Knell House, a converted Alfred Waterhouse villa, which boasts light and airy classrooms for these 20 children (plus those displays again). One downstairs classroom we visited had a straw based area that looked so much like a mini farm that we half expected a live animal to appear. In fact, teachers had set it up to prepare the children for a school trip to a local farm. Good outdoor space, with astroturf and adventure climbing equipment, overlooked by the church (with which the school is closely linked). Emphasis on learning through play – no writing until reception.

Things get slightly confusing when it comes to reception and year 1 as these classes have been relocated just down the road to Abbey Gardens, which was opened in 2014. Originally a judge's lodgings, the school bought it for its large garden, which has been converted into an impressive all-weather sports pitch surrounded by a 'Willow walkway,' utilised by the whole junior school. But the house itself, built in the late 1800s, also makes for a delightful learning space, with a purpose-built gym added on. Specialist teachers for PE, music, drama and languages (then sciences and computing from year 3); remaining subjects taught by form teachers. We saw spirited girls having a whale of a time with paper, glue and plenty of glitter, as well as engaging in more advanced activities.

Back in the main junior school, a mix of Victorian and later additions are home to years 2 to 6. Impressive facilities include a great science lab, where year 6 were busy purifying salt, a large dedicated dining room (no packed lunches here and nobody minds) and computer suite.

Good facilities for drama (which is timetabled across many of the year groups) and dance (which is taught as part of the PE curriculum and via clubs); every year group does some kind of annual production, with girls enthusing about how they get involved in everything from choreography to set design. 'By year 5, we are allowed a microphone,' one girl told us, practically jumping with excitement.

Music outstanding and very much part of the life blood of the school. We met the head of music – a delightful woman who teaches, oversees 15 peripatetic teachers and heads up the orchestra and four school choirs. Lots of public performances, some award winning (finalists in Barnardo's Choir of the Year was the most recent when we visited). Plenty of visiting workshops from the likes of composers specialising in children's songs to those teaching world music. Art, although mainly done in classrooms, also notable, with a particularly impressive series of charcoal drawings from year 6s on display.

Sport almost daily. 'We want it to become part of who they are,' says the head, and although it's more about inclusivity than competition, there are fixtures for those who want them. Netball, hockey, athletics, biathlon, swimming (at the senior school), football, frisbee, gym and dance all on offer, among others. 'My daughter's not naturally sporty, but they get her having a go and she enjoys that,' said one parent.

Conversational French in reception and year 1; conversational Spanish in year 2; conversational German in year 3; then back to French, which is taught more formally, in years 4, 5 and 6. No setting – 'We don't need to as all the girls are relatively able and whilst they might need help in fractions one week, they might be a whizzy-whiz at 2D shapes the next week,' says head. Homework only if seen to be genuinely aiding learning.

Lively and engaging teaching was palpable in every classroom we visited. Teachers given plenty autonomy, plus lots of complementary visiting workshops – Roman workshops; maths puzzle; zoo lab, to name a few. A lively house science quiz was in full swing in the main hall when we visited.

Specialist small group and individual support for mild SEN available, although most extra help is in the classroom via teaching assistants, many highly qualified. 'We don't want children to become dependent or resentful of having set extra help every week. We want a learning support model that anyone can use anytime – for instance if they're struggling with a particular maths concept,' says head.

No school rules here (none needed, says head) – only values and a class contract, written by the girls and teacher at the beginning of each academic year. Lots of praise for good behaviour, with special merits in assembly, particularly for effort (more likely for 'Jemima really persisted in her fractions' than 'Jemima got an excellent maths score').

When we asked the girls about bullying, we got a blank look. 'We know what it is,' explained one, 'but we haven't come across it.' Head believes this is down to keeping conversations alive about what bullying is and how you are just as culpable if you stand by and watch it – and this, together with a form tutor-led pastoral system, seems to keep them on the straight and narrow. The head's psychotherapy background must surely come in useful pastorally. 'Children don't come to school to behave badly – and if they do, you need to look at the root of the issue,' she says, as if reading our minds. Happy relationships aided by the classes being regularly muddled to promote group bonding, and year 5 girls are trained to be 'playground buddies.'

Residential trips build up from one night away in year 3 up to 6 nights in year 5 (then back down to 5 in year 6). Day trips start from nursery (remember that farm) to the likes of Windsor Castle, Legoland etc.

School day from 8.30am to 3.45pm, with an optional breakfast club from 7.30am and after school care until 6pm (costs extra). Full club programme, mainly at lunchtimes, including Lego club, nature detectives, archaeology club, chess and judo, among others.

Parents range from the very wealthy to the struggling-but-determined to afford the fees and everything in between. Lots of dual income families. Not a school to consider unless you're prepared to get involved, say parents. Catchment area quite wide, generally within a 15-mile radius. School bus and kiss-and-drop service seen as godsend by parents. Healthy ethnic mix, with around half traditional white British and the rest as mixed as you can imagine – so for every yummy family from Henley, there's a Russian, Indian, Chinese etc family. Active PA and lots of socialising among parents.

Girls are cheery, jovial and excitable, although parents assured us there's room for quiet ones too, 'but the academically challenged might struggle here,' said one.

A confident and well-run school that knows exactly where it's going, with happy girls who are stretched and challenged but not pressurised. While many girls will attend The Abbey from 3 to 18, the junior school provides opportunities to help the girls reinvent themselves at different stages along the way. In fact, a word you'll hear a lot here is 'refresh,' which neatly sums up the school's attitude to constantly keeping things fresh and ahead of the game.

The Abbey School Reading

Linked with The Abbey Junior School

Kendrick Road, Reading RG1 5DZ

Ages 11–18 **Pupils** 730 **Sixth form** 167

Fees: £17,040 pa

01189 872256
www.theabbey.co.uk

Head: Since 2014, Rachel Dent BA QTS (40s), previously deputy head. Grew up in the Midlands and read English at Southampton University, then embarked on a career in journalism in 1992, although she quickly realised it wasn't for her, quitting her first job at Time Out magazine after just two weeks. Travelled to Egypt to 'find herself' and when she realised she needed some money, she 'blagged her way into teaching English GCSE' and 'never looked back'. Did her formal teacher training back in the UK via fast track QTS at Reading University, then worked at Wisbech Grammar and Cokethorpe School. Joined The Abbey in 2007 as director of sixth form. Her office is plush, swanky and large – think Farrow and Ball grey and white tones, stone fireplace and fresh flowers.

Whilst she's done odd bits of teaching since becoming head and leads Wednesday assemblies, the general consensus is that she's more of a CEO-type head than a hands-on teaching type (in fact, she'd recently been on a Henley Business School course with CEOs when we visited). A working mum, she is adamant that overworking isn't good for anyone and keenly leads by example to both staff and pupils when it comes to achieving work/life balance. 'There will always be tomorrow' is her mantra. Described as 'modern', 'dynamic', 'energetic' and 'visionary', we found her all these things, as well as warm and relaxed. Particularly keen to make the school's spaces more user-friendly and fit for modern teaching methods. 'I want to move away from traditional wooden desks,' she explains.

Lives locally with her husband and daughter. Regularly spotted walking her two dogs across Berkshire and Oxfordshire in her spare time.

As head of the senior school since 2015, Jan Cresswell – who has a degree in English lit from Durham and has taught English, drama and RE – is second-in-command and most likely 'go-to' person for parents and pupils. Previously head of sixth form at Portsmouth High School, she also served on the senior leadership team of a large co-educational HMC school. She is famed around the school for her fondness for literary references and her warm and persuasive leadership style. Since joining, she has overseen a restructuring of the pastoral support system.

Academic matters: Impressive results across the board. In 2018, 88 per cent A*-A/9-7 grades at GCSE. Refreshing to find students encouraged to take average of 10 GCSEs (previously it was 11 or 12), with most popular options being geography, history, food tech, textiles and drama (in that order). Choice of double and triple science. Computer science on the up.

At A level, girls can choose from 24 subjects, with the school priding itself on its ability to support some unusual combinations. In 2018, 65 per cent A* or A grades (92 per cent A*-B). IB results also impressive with an average of 39 points in 2018. In fact, it seems incredible that its introduction to the school in 2009 was seen as a brave and controversial move, with IB now as embedded into sixth form life as A levels, with a sports science module recently added. Teachers enthuse about how it has opened up the school's global community, made the school much more outward looking, as well as being energising for all sixth form teaching staff.

French and Latin from year 7, with the addition of Spanish or German in year 8. Some setting in year 7 in maths and French, but there's plenty of movement and no more setting until year 9. Sciences split from year 7, making students with strong preferences very happy. No homework for homework's sake here (back to that work/life balance ethos) and no homework at all during certain weeks, such as Intellectual Curiosity Week, Festival of Performing Arts Week.

Much praise from pupils and parents for teachers, who are described as 'committed' and 'enthusiastic', with high attendance at the non-compulsory monthly teacher-led learning innovation group meeting, which focuses on sharing good practice. No single style of teaching, with much autonomy given to individual teachers. Whiteboards, computers etc are all present in lessons, but no overdependence on them, as at some schools. 'I always say that if we lost the buildings, we could carry on,' says the head. Informal teacher-student relationships, backed up with a huge mutual respect that was palpable during our visit. 'Teachers are never patronising here, even when you're in year 7,' girls told us.

Around 30 with mild SEN receive one-to-one sessions either before school or in lunchtime (no lessons to be missed); small number (and often none at all) have EAL support from qualified teacher. 'SEN here is more a case of students using pink paper in exams than anyone being statemented,' says head.

Sixth form provides a better transition between school and university than it used to, say parents. Itchy feet cured by no uniform, even less hierarchical teacher/pupil relations, tutorial style lessons where students can bring coffee along, superlative careers support and magic timetabling to enable endless permutations of A level and IB choices. The common room, with its own kitchenette, is fabulous – spacious, yet cosy and highly sociable, with music played during breaktimes and plenty of computers in the corner for those who don't mind studying with the low-level noise. Surrounding this space are 12 sixth-form teaching classrooms, along with an open study area with communal tables for quieter working. Many pupils told us their classes can have as few as two or three students in.

Outstanding careers advice, but there's an emphasis on keeping your options open, rather than pigeonholing yourself. 'We are constantly encouraged to explore what kind of a person we are – not just what subjects we're good at,' explained one girl. Lots of showcasing of work around the school. Tests and quizzes all part of daily life, but 'they're surprisingly relaxed,' say pupils.

Games, options, the arts: If you tour the school, don't make the mistake (many do) of singing the praises of the large, well-kept playing fields that much of the school overlooks – sadly, they belong to the adjacent Reading Boys'. It's the one thing the pupils and parents we spoke to would change, although most agree sports facilities still have a wow factor, including a large Astroturf sports pitch, indoor pool with bespoke competition level diving boards (early morning swim fit a popular class) and large sports hall. Main sports are hockey, netball, swimming and athletics, with rugby, football, volleyball, cricket, rounders and biathlons also popular. Fitness options range from belly dancing to zumba. Very much a case of 'sport for all here,' with an emphasis on inclusivity over competitiveness, although there are plenty of opportunities for girls who do want to compete, with county and national triumphs for teams and individuals. When we visited, the school had an U19 England netball player, five U19 England rowers and several regional winners in netball, swimming and ice hockey. 'Even if you don't like sport, they make it fun,' one girl told us. 'I should know – I'm not keen. But this morning, for instance, we did long jump and shot put and they helped me with technique in such an engaging way that I actually found I'd quite enjoyed it.'

Over a third of pupils learn a musical instrument at school and girls make a big noise in both grade examinations and numerous bands, choirs, ensembles and orchestras. There is a major musical production every two years and an annual overseas tour. Drama is popular and girls we spoke to love the fact that the absence of boys (no shipping in for male roles) means that they get a chance to play all the star parts. Art is a dazzling department, with lovely big art studios and plenty of striking examples of everything from textiles to furniture on show throughout the school.

The Abbey Edge is an exhaustive (and quite possibly exhausting) programme of clubs and activities (mainly lunchtimes) from crossword club to film society. It includes Chinese club, book clubs and news quizzes in the library, drop-in clinics for academic subjects (an excellent alternative to an evening's bad tempered homework trauma), DofE (this is one of the biggest DofE schools in the south east, for which the school has a gold award from Buckingham Palace), public speaking, gymnastics, drama, choirs, orchestras, ensembles, West Wing Club, altruistic society and golf. And that's just the start. 'It was the sheer breadth of extracurricular activity that made us choose the school, and the opportunities our girls have had as a result means we've never regretted our decision,' said one parent. How on earth girls find time to do all this and get great results is an Abbey mystery, all the more astounding when you take into consideration that many girls are also involved in sports and clubs where they live. 'I did swimming training for 18 hours a week during my GCSEs and never once did the school suggest I should give it up, because they recognised that swimming is part of what makes me who I am – classic stuff for The Abbey,' one girl told us.

School trips plentiful – about 10 a week across the school, ranging from theatres to museums. Residentials include outdoor pursuits courses (home and abroad), battlefields (history), Iceland, Grand Canyon (both geography), France (water sports), Austria (skiing) and much more besides. Vietnam, Uganda and Equador were also mentioned during our visit. Fundraising and volunteer work is seen as important, with 70 girls involved in the Reading Refugee Programme when we visited.

Background and atmosphere: Based in the 'nice bit' of Reading, about half a mile from the university and a quarter of a mile from the town centre, the school was founded in 1887 as Reading High School. In 1914, it departed from the Church Schools Company and took its present name. Located in a leafy street with Victorian villas, it feels far, but not too far, from the madding crowd and is practically next door to both of Reading's massively oversubscribed state anomalies, Kendrick Girls' and Reading Boys' grammars. But while there is some cooperation (careers talks, university presentations), neighbourly relations remain at the polite nod rather than 'come in without knocking' level.

Old girls apparently horrified when they saw plans to demolish much of the Victorian frontage, but less so when the work was completed. The gothic entrance has been retained and old and new blend together pretty well, although – like many schools that have been added onto over the years – some of the buildings 'lack flow' and some areas are less lovely than others. Notable facilities include great science labs (well-equipped but not soulless); large and airy school hall (including balcony) which was all set up for exams when we visited; and library, which – whilst not the most hi-tech or modern – is roomy, well-stocked and welcoming. Lots of break-out areas, many with sofas ('You never feel you're bound to your classroom here,' said one pupil) and a terrific conference room, which is used for girls' presentations, IB exams and board meetings for the Young Enterprise club, and wouldn't look out of place in the likes of Silicon Valley.

Atmosphere is active, busy and buzzy – never silent. 'I don't like it when the school is too quiet,' laughs the head. It's about learning through doing here, she explains, with girls expected to try new things throughout their time here. 'This is not a school for girls who don't like trying new activities. It's fine if you don't like them, but there is an ethos of having to give things a go,' one girl told us. Other girls told us that highly competitive girls might also struggle, such is the atmosphere of collaboration and support.

Food, which all girls eat (no packed lunches here), widely praised.

Pastoral care, well-being and discipline: Form teachers are at the heart of pastoral care, supported by heads of year. These staff members meet every week for a detailed pastoral meeting, so any problems are picked up quickly. 'The teachers seem to know exactly know when to step in and when not to – the pastoral care is simply amazing,' said one parent. Disappointing to find no school counsellor, although head assured us there are links to external provision and girls seem clued up on where to go for support. Our guides also pointed to sixth form buddies, whom you can email if you're shy.

All the usual leadership opportunities – form captains, school council reps, house captains etc – and you get the feeling they're much more than just labels here, with library prefects, for example, running assembles. 'Our leaders are do-ers and they love it,' says head, and pupils concur.

Discipline? Not needed, says the head. 'I can't remember the last time someone had a detention.' Rules? Nope, she says, unless you count those relating to respect. Girls told us that rules do exist and year 7 girls told us you get a black mark (you're not supposed to call it that, but they do) in your planner for crimes against uniform, homework etc. 'I got one yesterday for forgetting my apron for food tech,' one told us. But they all agreed the ethos is more about setting the standards in the early years, rather than focusing on punishment. Plenty of recognition and merits, including for those who are quietly good and often overlooked by other systems.

Bullying not problematic. When girls fall out, there are good strong tactics to sorting it out quickly and not letting it develop. Friendship groups, in the main, very wide-reaching. 'If we're trying to organise a night out, we soon find there are 40 people on the list,' a sixth former laughed.

Pupils and parents: Hardworking and unsnobby, definitely no princesses here. Many from Reading's business community (Sage, Microsoft and Pepsi nearby), with many also in public sector, including academia (university and hospital also nearby). Others from Henley, Windsor and Basingstoke. Ethnic mix much as you'd expect in Reading – that is, mainly white British, but plenty more besides, with a plethora of languages spoken by students. Good transport links: school and public bus network and new Reading train station. Old girls include Baroness Brigstocke, Elizabeth Taylor, Helen Ganley, artist and social reformer, and a trio of BBC reporters, Miranda Krestovnikoff, Kate Humble and Sally Taylor. Alumni seen as increasingly important, with the school having introduced a 'school version of LinkedIn,' as one girl put it.

Entrance: Main entry point is 11, with around half coming from The Abbey Junior School. Others from independents (Highfield, Dolphin, Eton End, St Pirans) and local state primaries; small intake at 13. Girls sit exams in maths, English and reasoning. Interview with member of staff on their taster day and reference from their current school also taken into account. Sixth form candidates come in for a taster day of lessons in the subjects they want to study at IB or A level. They are expected to gain 9-6 in these subjects at GCSE. Same grades required of existing pupils.

Exit: Around 20 per cent leave after GCSEs (often when parents' purses dry up), mostly to attend local grammars and a few to local comps and colleges. Almost exclusively Russell Group universities, with popular destinations including Nottingham, Durham, Royal Holloway, Southampton, Exeter and Birmingham. Four to Oxbridge in 2018, plus nine medics and one off to Berkeley on a full scholarship. Heavy duty science subjects popular but also psychology, languages and English. 'Humanities hold their own,' says head, who adds that combined courses are increasingly popular – no doubt largely thanks to the Abbey ethos of staying open-minded about your future.

Money matters: Fees pretty competitive – they have to be and, unusually, they include exam fees, all text books and lunches. Means-tested bursaries of up to 100 per cent available; academic scholarships (10 per cent) at key entry points. Special awards for music (instrumental tuition paid) and talents in sport, art and drama – all with an accompanying enrichment programme.

Remarks: Yes, of course the girls work hard (and joy of joys, it's not seen as nerdy to do so here), but Abbey girls take things in their stride and manage to do plenty more besides. Indeed, for a high-achieving girls' schools, we found a reassuring lack of pressure, although we suspect some legs are paddling furiously below the surface. We also found it pleasantly down-to-earth and grounded. For bright girls, this is a fun, supportive and motivating place to be, providing excellent preparation for the modern world.

Abingdon Preparatory School

Linked with Abingdon School

Josca's House, Kingston Road, Abingdon, Oxfordshire OX13 5NX

Ages 4–13 **Pupils** 250

Fees: £12,090 – £16,620 pa

01865 391570
www.abingdon.org.uk/prep

Headmaster: Since September 2017, Craig Williams MA (Oxon) PGCE (40s). Educated at Bradfield College and studied geography at Oxford. Previously at Taunton Prep (head of geography and cricket) and then senior deputy head at Thorngrove School. Mr Williams is an accomplished sportsman – played hockey, football and was in the university second team for cricket while at Oxford. Still enjoys turning out for the Thames Valley league and Bradfield Old Boys, 'I have a very forgiving wife who also loves cricket'.

Grew up in Surrey, not Sydney, but if you catch a hint of antipodean in his voice it's because his father is Australian. Claims he 'desperately tried not be a teacher' despite coming from something of a teaching dynasty (both parents were teachers and his brother is head of Lord Wandsworth School), but after a couple of years working in recruitment post-university he succumbed to the inevitable and signed up for a PGCE. Chose to teach in preps because 'you can make the most difference'. Loves his subject, 'geography is great because it's got an element of everything' but now confines his teaching to games and some 'other half' activities. He also gets to know the younger boys by reading with reception, year 1 and 2 classes. While maintaining professional diplomatic neutrality on the question of single sex versus co-ed education ('a good school is a good school'), he says he admires boys' 'lack of self-consciousness' and enthusiasm to embrace all the school's musical, dramatic and sporting opportunities.

In common with increasing numbers of preps Abingdon has waved farewell to CE. 'Abingdon Prep Plus' (AP+), the new curriculum for years 7 and 8, focuses on skills as well as knowledge and has been devised in conjunction with the senior school. According to Mr Williams this 'allows us to stop teaching to the test and frees up the timetable.' Apart from this significant change, what else has he up his sleeve? New quarters for music and DT and another science lab are on the cards but there's no plan to expand pupil numbers, he believes the prep is 'just the right size'. Parents agree.

Mr Williams lives close to the school with his wife Hannah (also a teacher, they met while working at Taunton Prep), young son and ... you guessed it, a black labrador. As a child his favourite book was Tarka the Otter so he was quite excited to tell us he thought he'd seen 'otter evidence' (as he put it rather delicately) when out dog walking by the river.

A cursory glance at his biog might lead one to imagine Mr Williams is one of those rather trad, sports mad, alpha male types. Having met him we're happy to report that this is absolutely not the case – he seems to have nailed being modest, humorous and confidence inspiring all at the same time. His advice to his charges is 'work hard, get involved, be kind', with emphasis on 'be kind.' Parents seem charmed by his 'relaxed' and 'informal' style – 'he's very visible and really knows the boys as individuals.' One told us, 'he comes across as quite laid back, but don't be fooled – he's on top of everything.' Boys we spoke to settled for 'awesome'.

Entrance: No formal academic testing for pre-prep, but boys should be sufficiently mature to settle into a class. Thereafter testing in English, non-verbal reasoning and maths, but school says that it also looks for 'that spark', boys who 'would thrive', rather than relying wholly on test scores. Population is fairly stable, but if there's space and 'if we're sure they'll cope', boys can enter after year 5, for example from primary schools.

Exit: Prep pupils for whom Abingdon School is appropriate, receive an offer of a place for year 9 at the end of year 5. There's 'an early dialogue with parents' if it's felt that senior school is not the best option. The offer is based on continuous assessment and conditional on the pupil maintaining his profile of achievement in years 6 to 8. In most years, around 80 per cent go on to Abingdon; others to Magdalen College, Radley, St Edward's, or at age 11 to Our Lady's, The Oratory, Bloxham, Cokethorpe.

Remarks: Our visit started at the very beginning, in a reception class kinaesthetic phonics lesson. Oblivious to visitors, boys sat cross-legged on the floor making signs with their fists, shouting sounds, using their 'sad and happy' voices and writing with their elbows. School has a single form intake from reception up until year 3 when it expands to two classes. Parents really appreciate the school being small at this early stage – boys get 'all the individual support and attention they need.' Thereafter it's two classes per year group until year 8 when a scholarship class is added.

Then it was on to the science labs to see a year 8 scholarship set investigating light intensity with silhouettes they'd made. Boys were conducting their own experiments, using trial and error to work out the relationship between a shadow's size and distance from the light and recording the findings in a graph. The lab is used from year 4 upwards and there are regular trips to events at the senior school's fantastic science facilities.

We were told that since our last visit much work has been done to enhance academic 'partnerships' between the senior school and the prep, including 'masterclasses' in English, maths and science at for year 8s. The two schools are about a 15-minute drive away from each other (depending on traffic), so these things have to be planned and timetabled – it's not a case of pupils just popping over to the senior school for activities. Fortunately, the prep lacks nothing in terms of academic or sporting facilities so trips to the senior school are an additional bonus, not a necessity. And, of course, they are a motivator, keeping the younger boys' eyes on the prize.

The year 5 English lesson was such great fun we could have stayed for the duration. Had we done so our ability to identify the features of a Victorian detective story would have been much improved. After asking the boys whether he had 'hit the success criteria' in his effort (read aloud in a virtuoso performance of comedy voices), boys had to write their own chapters, the only caveats being 'nothing too rude or silly'.

CDT (craft, design and technology) room was buzzing with boys working on colourful Christmas projects in acrylic and wood – decorating them with jewels and sequins. We admired the display of rather chic tree decorations – angels made from folded recycled paper. The teacher told us that one of her classes had designed and made their own mini-golf game for the Christmas bazaar and another had come up 'Billy's Bones' (dog biscuits) for a Dragon's Den competition. All boys have one double CDT lesson a week and there are extracurricular (known at both prep and senior school as 'other half') arts clubs including textiles (apparently very popular), clay club and oil painting.

Learning support dept has a new sensory area and 'calm space'. All boys are assessed on entrance and small group and one to one support is on hand (former is not charged, latter is). Mostly caters for mild to moderate dyslexia and high functioning autism, 'we want to know they will thrive in this environment'. Library is a delight, huge range of books – from old favourites such as Enid Blyton or the Willard Price adventure series to Captain Underpants and the latest graphic novels. Emphasis very much on getting boys to find a type of book they like, whatever it is, and building on that.

Our year 8 guides were a hoot – quite unlike the preternaturally mature mini-me PR execs we sometimes get. Living proof that there's no 'typical' Abingdon boy. They were particularly proud of the new wooden fort – designed in consultation with the school council and emblazoned with a school logo (a rather fierce unicorn) and we were patiently taken through the highly complex rules of the games it has inspired. Our notes are somewhat rain-blotched but we can make out 'angel of death' and 'bulldog take-down' – 21st century iterations of 'I'm the king of the castle' we think.

Masses of outside space – including quiet areas for those not wishing to play 'bulldog take down' plus acres of pitches and a new Astro. All the major games tackled with gusto and great results – notably so in rugby and hockey. Other sports on offer as 'other half' clubs include fencing, golf, karate, volleyball and water polo – school has a heated indoor pool and swimming lessons are on the curriculum for all year groups. Anything they'd like to add to the sports facilities we asked our guides? Basketball nets and a putting green, one thought.

Unsurprisingly, given the senior school's stellar reputation for music, there are many and varied ways to get even the youngest boys involved in singing and playing, with 17 other half music activities in addition to what's on the curriculum. Facilities and practice rooms all in place, but they do look a bit tired – good to hear from the head that they're due for a move and an upgrade. One boy thought there ought to be 'more singing tours' but there's certainly no shortage of chances to perform music or drama, with at least seven productions every year.

Founded in Oxford in 1956, school occupies a large Victorian country house three miles outside Abingdon with extensive grounds that merge into woods and meadows. Nice rural feel despite adjacent main road which gets a bit gnarly at peak times even without school run traffic. At just over 250 boys in total, parents we spoke to reckoned the prep's size was just right, 'definitely not too small' – 'everybody knows everybody and no one gets overlooked.' School also offers wraparound care from 8am to 6pm, greatly appreciated by families where both parents are working (the majority). No lessons but some matches and other activities take place on Saturdays. School bus service covers Oxford, Abingdon and surrounding area – families are fairly local.

Most send their sons here in the hope, if not expectation, of a smooth progression to the senior school at age. The introduction of AP+ for years 7 and 8 certainly indicates 'all-through' thinking – the curriculum was designed in collaboration with the senior school – so what about boys who are not going to follow this route? Parents are assured that CE/other entrance exam preparation is available for any boy who needs it.

It may be a boys' school but there's a great mix of staff and definitely no narrow 'boys will be boys' ethos here. Down to earth, fun, lots of challenge, lots of nurture – Abingdon Prep is a great place to start.

Abingdon School

Linked with Abingdon Preparatory School

Park Road, Abingdon, Oxfordshire OX14 1DE

Ages 11–18 **Pupils** 1,018 **Sixth form** 317 **Boarders** 109 full, 29 weekly
C of E

Fees: Day £19,950; Boarding £33,210 – £39,750 pa

01235 849041
www.abingdon.org.uk

Head: Since 2016, Michael Windsor, previously head of Reading Blue Coat School. The son of two linguists (his father was a lecturer at the University of Bristol and his mother taught French and German at Badminton School), he was a chorister at Bristol Cathedral School. Thence to Durham University and first-class honours in French and German. Worked briefly in publishing before heading to Bologna where he 'toyed with the idea of becoming a professional musician' and making a living from his double bass. That lasted until he got hungry, at which point although he 'knew he definitely didn't want to be a teacher', he gave up jazz for teaching English as a foreign language – and met his future wife. On his return he did a PGCE at the Institute of Education and then joined King's College Wimbledon to teach foreign languages and become the first director of its IB programme. He describes his work introducing the IB as 'an amazing project' but has no such plans for Abingdon (we checked). Moved to RGS Guildford where he was deputy head (pastoral) and after five years there took up the headship at Reading Blue Coat. Has coached rugby, hockey and athletics and was involved in CCF and World Challenge expeditions. That's three academic boys' schools (okay, two have co-ed sixth forms) and Abingdon makes it four. Must be habit forming.

Mr Windsor also has an MA in modern German studies from Birkbeck and is an ISI inspector. He's a keen musician, plays the double bass in classical and jazz ensembles and recently surprised (and delighted) boys and parents with a guest appearance playing bass guitar in the school's Big Band (jazz). Married to Shanti, who works at Reading University; they have two daughters.

He says he 'felt drawn' to Abingdon, especially the culture of 'exceptionally high expectations' that pervades all aspects of school life. He's also enjoying working with the prep school. Even without the prep, Abingdon is much larger than his former school and he concedes his new role is 'less hands on' and he doesn't have time to do any teaching, although he says he would like to.

Abingdon has been through a period of significant growth – both in terms of pupil numbers and building projects – and Mr W feels that the school is now 'as big as it will get.' He does have plans; he's keen to 'develop more areas of collaboration' (academic, pastoral and extracurricular) with St Helen and St Katharine, the neighbouring independent girls' school (where his daughters are pupils). We wish him good fortune. There have been attempts in the past to take things beyond sharing actors, musicians and school buses, but as one boy put it, 'timetables never seem to match up.'

Academic, musical and sporty – Mr Windsor is such a good fit for Abingdon, embodying three of the school's great strengths. He's also down-to-earth, good humoured and at ease with himself – very much a head, rather than a figurehead. The boys think he's 'great' and love the way he seems to turn up and enjoy everything – quite an accolade considering just how much goes on at the school. We felt a genuine groundswell of goodwill and support for Mr Windsor – boys, staff and parents, even those parents we spoke to who have yet only 'seen him in the distance,' are right behind him.

Academic matters: Academics matter hugely, but not exclusively. I/GCSE headliners are English, maths and sciences, but A*/9-8 by far the most common mark in all subjects apart from art, RS and drama (where the A/7s have it). In addition to IGCSE maths, boys in the top sets also sit the freestanding OCR additional maths qualification – and take it in their stride with the vast majority gaining top marks. French, Spanish and German are the core language options with Russian and Chinese offered as additional subjects. Healthy numbers and outstanding results for Latin, ancient Greek and ancient history (Latin is compulsory in years 7 and 8). I/GCSE results in 2018: 84 per cent A*-A/9-7. Only a very few marks at grade C/4 or below, but the boy who gets a grade 6 in one or two subjects won't feel alone. Not a school that kicks unexpected underperformers out post-GCSE either

A level results in 2018: 62 per cent A*/A (87 per cent A*-B). Most popular A level by far is maths (followed by chemistry and physics); over half of sixth form boys take maths and the vast majority get A*/A, further maths is an option. Parents generally very pleased with A level maths teaching, but one or two felt that boys in lower sets didn't always get sufficient support. Word on the local tutor grapevine confirms that some feel the need to buy in external help.

Large take up and excellent results too for history, economics and geography. Pre-U exams only for French, German and Spanish (results outstanding), but as elsewhere, modern foreign languages are a minority interest – there are more takers for Latin. Indeed, classics department is thriving (described to us as 'inspirational'), sending annual small, but perfectly formed contingent of brightest and best to Oxbridge. High praise also received for history teaching. Psychology has been a fairly recent introduction to previously 'ology' allergic A level menu. Jury is still out – as yet the subject's popularity and exam record are on a par.

Lessons are fast paced and challenging – setting for maths and science from year 9, but selective intake means all are working above and beyond. Good staff mix of male and female, old timers and recent graduates; sensible creative latitude given to non-standard teaching styles – much appreciated by boys, parents and (we assume) the teachers in question. Great engagement and rapport between boys and teachers in lessons we saw – lots of fun and sparky ideas in year 9 English where boys were coming up with literary foods: apple pie for Paradise Lost, Pina Colada for Robinson Crusoe and our favourite, a 'saucy stir-fry' for Chaucer's Canterbury Tales.

Abingdon is an academically selective school, but it's a broad enough church to accommodate bright boys with mild to moderate SEND (mostly dyslexia and dyspraxia). In-class, small group and one-to-one help provided by well-regarded learning support department. Pupils who are identified as needing short-term help with, for instance, study skills, receive six one-to-one sessions free of charge. Parents tell us that the department is 'on the ball' and that staff are extra vigilant at high pressure times such as school and public exams.

Games, options, the arts: Abingdon's sporting alphabet runs from athletics to water polo, taking in a wide range of team and individual pursuits along the way. The letter 'r' gets more than its fair share of kudos, with rugby and rowing being two of the school's chief glories, along with hockey. Full-on fixture list for these and other sports – regular opponents include Marlborough, Radley, Bradfield, Wellington and Eton. Fine sports centre with swimming pool, several grass pitches and popular climbing wall on site; more extensive facilities including athletics tracks and a 4G pitch just down the road at Tilsley Park. Much success too in less mainstream sports such as fencing, cross-country, sailing and shooting.

Abingdon's pupils have been rowing on the town's stretch of the Thames for nearly 200 years and boys in their pink and black kit jogging down to the beautiful wooden boathouse are a familiar sight on summer afternoons. Rowing laurels have suffered a few soggy seasons lately, but boys told us excitedly that the coach was 'making huge changes.'

All boys, including sixth formers, must do at least two sessions of sport a week, but most do many more, including Saturday training and matches. Lots of tours and specialist development camps (some abroad). Boys who duck when they see a ball coming (yes, such boys do exist) are expected to have a go at different options and find something they enjoy – karate and canoe polo have proved popular recent additions to the sports mix.

Music, art and DT don't attract huge numbers at A level, but are well resourced and get good results. Dynamic music department will seek out and nurture every kind of musical talent – from pipers, choristers and counter tenors to, famously, all five members of Radiohead. Every boy is encouraged to take up an instrument when they join the school if they don't already play one. Unsuspecting parents may find their son coming home drooping under the weight of a French horn or bassoon in an ever-optimistic effort by the school's director of music to uncover a virtuoso in these vital, but less popular, orchestral instruments. A plethora of choirs, bands, orchestras and chamber groups, plus an ambitious programme of concerts for all abilities, equals quite a few nights out for supportive parents. Regular organ and choral scholarships to Oxbridge and music colleges.

Annual drama productions for lower, middle and senior school boys plus house drama and joint ventures – and theatre studies A level – with girls from St Helen and St Katharine. Theatre design workshops, modern foreign language plays and a podcasting club add to the repertoire. Newly refurbished Amey Theatre is the main venue for concerts, plays and other whole school events. The addition of a projection screen and surround sound has made it a popular local venue for films, live theatre and opera screenings.

All the above and much, much more is included in the school's famous Other Half programme. You won't hear music, art, DofE, CCF, community service or the 120+ clubs and societies referred to as 'extracurricular activities' here. At Abingdon such things are not optional extras, but essential parts of a well-rounded education. Close harmony singing? Lego architecture? Ceramics? Entomology? Code-breaking? Take a look at the school's (excellent) website and you'll wish you could sign up for one or two options. Worthy of note are debating – the debating society is believed to be the school's oldest non-sporting society and the dinner debates with local girls' schools are a big draw – and Abingdon Film Unit (AFU). The AFU is quite possibly unique, a semi-autonomous organisation run by professional film makers to enable secondary school pupils to make short films – mostly documentaries and stop-motion animations. Since it was set up in 2003 over 120 films have been produced, a number of which have been screened at national and international festivals and won awards.

Boarding: Majority of international boarders are from Hong Kong and China. Small weekly contingent from local families. The three boarding houses (School House, Crescent and Austin) are home to roughly equal numbers of boarders and day boys – ensures good integration. Communal areas we saw were well cared for and rather clubby (pool table, stags' head on the wall); bedrooms are, well, just like those in all the other boys' boarding houses we've visited: two or three beds, floor garnished with huge trainers, lots of Lynx and stashes of snacks. Not overly tidy – always a plus point. Each house has a resident housemaster and his family, at least one resident tutor, and a matron. Other house tutors live nearby. School has its own health centre with a nurse on call overnight and an on-site counselling service. Four meals a day, plus a school cafe; sixth formers can cook their own lunch in the house kitchen or forage in Abingdon's shops and takeaways.

Excellent range of joint and individual house activities and trips, making full use of Abingdon's proximity to Oxford and London. Socials and sixth form dinners with girls' boarding schools such as Westonbirt, St Mary's Calne and Headington. Boarding 'enrichment programme' aims to equip boys with vital life skills such as cooking, cleaning and ironing plus information about English law, taxes and applying for student loans. Attendance at boarders' chapel services is compulsory and we heard one or two polite grumbles about this ('a bit boring'). School says it has listened to boys' comments about this and services are now less frequent.

Background and atmosphere: One of England's oldest schools, Abingdon was 'officially' founded in 1256 when the Abbot of Abingdon, John de Blosneville, left money for the support of 13 poor scholars. Earliest references date back to 1100 when a school was likely to have been established alongside Abingdon Abbey. Having survived the dissolution of the monasteries its fortunes waxed and waned over the ensuing centuries, according to the generosity of benefactors and the quality of headmasters. School moved to its present site, adjacent to an elegant crescent around a park, in 1870 and proceeded to buy up more land and some of the crescent's houses. Architecture is sturdy Victorian red brick and running up and down stone staircases between lessons keeps boys and staff pretty fit, but could present a challenge to those on crutches (most of the school except Big School, the oldest part, is wheelchair accessible). Original library in Big School is a bibliophile's delight and the 21st century additions such as the arts centre, sports centre and the new Yang Science Centre have been thoughtfully designed and well executed. Brand new Beech Court houses sixth form centre plus a library, UCAS resources and careers office.

The Yang Science Centre is a superb addition to the school – three floors of labs and work rooms with an extraordinary metal tree-like sculpture, the Fusion Tower, that fills the stairwell, ascending and morphing into a representation of the science pursued on each level. Apparently, the only drawback of this is that 'physicists have nowhere to drop things from.' (Surely they've got gravity sorted out by now?) At the sculpture's base are 1,256 discs, one for every boy in the Abingdon foundation at the time of the piece's creation.

On the ground floor is a large, dedicated 'outreach' laboratory where pupils of all ages from local schools and organisations such as Scouts and Guides can come for science clubs, projects and subject extension activities. The work tables and seats are designed so that they can be adjusted to fit proto-scientists and there are mini-lab coats and goggles too. Abingdon boys also go out into local primary schools to run science clubs as part of their service activities. This exciting and generously resourced venture has really taken off and the Abingdon Science Partnership (ASP) co-ordinator told us that the school is now a centre of expertise for science continuing professional development, running teacher training workshops for Oxfordshire and neighbouring counties. School has a burgeoning partnership with Fitzharrys, a local maintained secondary, and the classics department has a long-standing tradition of teaching pupils from other local secondaries too.

With three other independent schools in the immediate vicinity and several others very close by, this corner of South Oxfordshire is rather a hotspot for educational privilege. That being said, Abingdon School isn't regarded as snobby and despite impressive facilities seems to retain the faintest, pleasingly meritocratic whiff of an old-style grammar. Uniform is fairly standard (grey trousers, blue blazer) and most components can be bought from M&S; there's also a second hand uniform shop, run by the parents' association. Ties are another matter, almost 50 possibilities at the last count: house ties, half and full colours, scholars, societies, prizes, and so on. Boys know what they all mean, but parents usually lose track after the first few.

Pastoral care, well-being and discipline: Parents tell us that the house and tutor system works well to ensure all boys receive individual academic and pastoral attention – vitally important in such a big school; staff are 'very observant', a parent told us. Boys who arrive at age 11, many from local primaries, join Lower School, which gives them two years to ease in to things before another influx at age 13 from preps, including Abingdon's own. In common with other schools, much more attention is now paid to pupils' mental as well as physical health. Boys can book directly or through the health centre to see a counsellor (on site, four days a week). PHSCE sessions – in class or during tutor time – cover a multitude of age-appropriate topics including healthy eating and body image, bullying, drugs, alcohol and relationships.

High expectations, both from the school and parents, and long, busy days, generally ensure good behaviour. Rules are sensible and consistently enforced. There's a lot of 'banter', but boys tell us that most know 'how far they can go.' There's no stereotypical Abingdon boy and school has enough alternative milieux for the unusual or eccentric to find their tribe.

Pupils and parents: School buses (all morning and some evening routes shared with the St Helen's girls) bring pupils in from as far as Reading, Newbury, Fairford and Bicester. Parents are fairly typical Oxfordshire mix of medics, academics, IT professionals and business people – not conspicuously wealthy, probably because they're paying school fees. Active parents' association organises socials and fundraisers, runs a popular second hand uniform shop and a car share scheme. Boys themselves are the most persuasive advert for their school – prospective parents attending open days are allocated a current pupil as a guide and most are ready to sign on the dotted line by the end of their tour. Old Abingdonians include Francis Maude, former MP and cabinet minister, Sir Kim Darroch, British ambassador to the US, Tom Kempinski, playwright, Thomas Dolby, musician and producer, actors Tom Hollander, Toby Jones and David Mitchell, all five members of Radiohead, lots of rowers and rugby players and centuries of churchmen, soldiers, academics, lawyers and all round good chaps.

Entrance: At 11 candidates from local primary schools and some preps, such as Chandlings, are tested in English, maths and reasoning. On the basis of performance in the test boys are then selected for a 'friendly' interview. Year 7 pre-tests for 13+ entry. For entry to sixth form a minimum of 6 in all I/GCSEs, and 7 in the subjects to be studied at A level (8 for further maths) required.

Exit: Nearly all sixth formers head for mainly Russell group universities to study serious subjects. Lots of engineers, chemists, economists and theoretical physicists as one would expect, but also historians, classicists and philosophers – it's that kind of school. In 2018, 21 to Oxbridge and six medics. Others to eg Bath, Birmingham, Bristol, Cardiff, Durham, Edinburgh, Exeter, Leeds, UCL; and to Boston, Columbia, Pennsylvania, Yale and Hong Kong.

Money matters: Range of scholarships which confer more prestige (and ties) than dosh. Means-tested bursaries available for part or all of day fees.

Remarks: Bigger, yes, and even better. We were delighted to revisit Abingdon and see how it has skilfully managed significant growth and development without compromise to its traditions, ethos and humanity. An outstanding school for bright all-rounders.

ACS Cobham International School

Portsmouth Road, Cobham, Surrey KT11 1BL

Ages 2–18 **Pupils** 1,360 **Sixth form** 316 **Boarders** 114 full, 37 weekly, approx 20 flexi (from 12 years)

Fees: Day £7,750 – £27,110; Boarding £38,810 – £46,930 pa

01932 867251
www.acs-schools.com

Interim Headmaster: Simon Leyshon is holding the reins until a new head is appointed. He joined the school in 2017 as deputy head. His degrees include a masters in education and a postgrad certificate in management. His senior leadership posts over 16 years have included two headships and he is an ISI inspector. A keen sportsman who can coach a variety of sports. In his spare time he enjoys cooking, walking, the theatre and painting.

Academic matters: Non-selective so a real mix of ability throughout. A truly international school – 72 different nationalities represented and a multitude of different languages spoken.

In the early childhood years pre-schoolers are prepared gently for the future. They build their social skills and interact with each other, developing their language and communication abilities through play. With such a large range of backgrounds, we were delighted to see them chattering away together and enjoying participating in group discussion and activity.

The lower school contains grades 1-4 and the majority of core lessons are classroom-based. They largely follow the American curriculum, but elements of the International Primary Years programme are also included. These are the preparatory years, when teachers discover strengths and weaknesses and begin to unearth any particular talents. All classes are mixed-ability. No formal exams or tests at this stage, though parents say general testing is continuous – presumably because MAP (Measure of Academic Progress) begins in grade 2.

At around 10 they move into the middle school for four years. This is when their futures begin to be mapped out. Timetables are based on the individual needs of the children, who are grouped by ability within their own age groups. Each child begins to follow a curriculum based on his known strengths and weaknesses. Classrooms are now subject-based, and it's the pupils not the teachers that move. The school is determined to provide a solid grounding and ensure that pupils can work together in teams, sharing their ideas and listening to each other. Exceptionally able children will sometimes be transferred to work with older pupils for particular subjects, thus assuring that they are being properly stimulated and working at their correct levels. Middle school children can be found studying their native language several grades higher than their ages.

At 14 it's high school, still in the same building as the middle school. They are separated by a large marble hall where these older pupils have Wifi access and the use of computers. The curriculum is wide and mixed, with 17 languages currently available. Timetables are based on each child's needs, exams are coming into the picture – decisions will soon have to be made. Some opt to study IGCSEs for a year, though they don't sit external exams in all subjects. For their final program(me), some decide to follow the International Baccalaureate, others take a variety of AP courses (18 available), and the rest work for the American High School diploma and SATs. Much depends on whether they are heading for university in the UK, the USA or continental Europe. This school prepares them for all, thus really meriting the international label. IB average 32 points in 2018; average AP grade 2.99 per exam. Not bad for a non-selective school.

Games, options, the arts: At a school sitting in 128 acres of country, with plenty of playing fields and its own a six-hole golf course, you'd expect the sports to be good. And they are. Not only outdoors, but in the all-singing, all-dancing sports centre as well. We were fascinated by the swimming pool with its computerised touch pads, enabling the raising of the pool bottom or adjustment of water temperature, at will, depending on activities of users. And with the dance studio/gym with a professional sound system and sprung wood flooring; the fitness suite for older exercisers where the equipment is card controlled; the international-sized basket/volleyball show court and the café for spectators and participators alike – these children have no excuse for being unfit. PE is compulsory for all the whole way through the school.

From middle school up, all take part in a good mix of indoor and outdoor sports, competing against other schools and, once in high school, in the ISST (International Schools Sports Tournaments) programme Europe-wide. A varied selection of different sports each season, something for everybody. A parent said, 'Sport is a big deal. Even the less sporty children find something they enjoy doing.'

Theatre, drama and music are also 'a big deal'. The amazing new performing arts centre provides everything budding thespians and musicians need. Several drama studios and music practice rooms; a music technology suite and an amazing high tech theatre which some drama schools would die for – even has an automated fly-tower. Instrumental and choral groups to suit all tastes. For those who want it, it's all there. No wonder the middle school singers have won their category in the Godalming Music Festival at least twice and drama students have been selected to participate in the National Theatre Connections project. Plenty of opportunities for students studying theatre for the IB. And for the musicians, it's all there for them as well – there is even a large lift so that a grand piano can take its place on the stage for a special recital. Good artist in residence programme when, for instance, a visiting band spends time with all instrumentalists, working with them and introducing them to new concepts.

Art on display all round, certainly appears to be plenty of talent. Imaginations run riot. Well-equipped studios enable experimentation, self-expression and developing talents to thrive.

Plenty of expeditions and field trips within UK, Europe or worldwide – exploratory, educational or languages involved. Around 100 working for the DofE, at all levels. Recently two current students got their golds – a significant achievement given that most don't complete this till university.

Boarding: More than 100 boarders aged 12-18, most full, with equal numbers of boys and girls. About 80 per cent from overseas. Boys and girls in separate wings, but plenty of chance for social mixing. A banner in the entrance hall reads: 'Because we are all different, we are all the same'. Jolly, caring, head of boarding says, 'We are a home from home and, with children representing so many nationalities, this is a great opportunity to understand and embrace different cultures. All are well integrated, no cliques.' New boarding house with single rooms for grade 12 (year 13) students plus twin rooms for grade 11s.

Trips organised every Saturday. Supervised prep every evening between 7.00pm and 9.00pm; the younger ones in a study room, the older ones in their rooms with the door open. Rooms look clean and comfortable. Seniors given personal privacy and do their own washing.

Background and atmosphere: Originally built in the 13th century, the main house at Cobham went through a variety of owners, from the aristocracy to businessmen, until it was acquired by ACS in 1975 in order to create their first American school in England. They now have two others in Surrey and Middlesex, and one overseas in Doha. Originally aiming to provide an American education for families living and working here, they have now become 'international' and the curriculum has been broadened to include the IB programme and enable pupils to attend universities worldwide. Looking round at the huge mix of nationalities represented, 72 at present, the change is merited. And you certainly notice it as you walk round this ultra-modern, high tech school where classroom and studios are fully equipped with every possible learning aid. This is the 21st century.

No uniform, but a code, for both pupils and staff, and those not sticking to it are in trouble. Some parents told us they would prefer to have one, and felt staff should perhaps be stricter on the boundaries, but they also agreed that their children are perfectly happy with the way it is. We noticed no extremes: most pupils we saw looked neat, tidy and relaxed. The school says having no uniform 'means focusing on the child'.

A closed campus, surrounded by its own land, no entry without a pass; this is a safe place for children of all ages. The early childhood village cossets the very young, giving them a sense of security before they move on to the lower school building. Here floors and classrooms are colour coded, all mixed ability, light, bright and welcoming; they only move for specialist classes. Great library, where language books are plentiful and some are colour coded to lend variety to different reading levels. For the first two years children are each lent an iPad for class use; from grade 3 onwards, they are given their own to take home. Both lower school and early childhood have their own playgrounds, while the middle school has its own playing fields, and the high school pupils have their own designated areas during break times.

The technology is blinding in the middle/high school building. From the interactive learning centre in the basement where they appear to be able to reach out all over the world, to the science labs where they can work together with their iPads, to huge divisional libraries again filled with books in a multitude of different languages, you could say the atmosphere buzzes.

And as for fuelling the inner child – the new dining area is high tech. Canteen style, children collect their food from a range of options, in coded containers, which are then scanned and a thumb scan identifies the child – no money changes hands, and parents are digitally informed what their children are eating. Or, at least, what they are taking to their tables. Big Brother is definitely watching over these children. Selections are such that no-one can get away with eating unhealthy food, and staff are watching carefully for any secret non-eaters.

Pastoral care, well-being and discipline: With such a large range of nationalities, there is a huge need for EAL support, particularly in the lower and middle schools. So EAL numbers are capped. Children are initially assessed by EAL teachers and given as much support as they feel necessary. Depending on need, this can be in class or out of class, either in small groups or individually. iPads are used for translation and general help.

About 250 pupils have some form of mild to moderate learning difficulty or EAL need. Each one is looked at individually, 'one-to-one case management', and a programme devised for them. Learning support numbers are capped each year and children are only accepted if the school feels it can support their particular needs.

Parents report some communication problems over learning support, as teachers are not always ready to listen but, on the whole, happy with the situation. The holistic approach adds extra dimension, treating the whole child. Excellent occupational therapy room, and imaginative ways of helping. Enthusiastic, sympathetic teachers with specialists at even the youngest age groups.

School says substance abuse problems rare and dealt with quickly and efficiently on a case by case basis. Can't realistically control what happens outside the school grounds, but does not believe anything serious. As school is in own guarded grounds, cases of bringing forbidden items rare. No toleration of antisocial or unkind behaviour. Rules are there to be obeyed.

Pupils and parents: A multi-national, multi-cultural school. Around a third are American and about a third of the rest are from the UK and other English speaking countries – the remainder cover Europe and the rest of the world. Inevitably, turnover quite large in the early years. Lots of expats from various different walks of life, some in transit, some who have decided to settle here – at least while their children are at school. Truly representative of today's mobile world. Excellent bus service, covering a huge area from Godalming to Hyde Park Corner, before and after school, means that quite a few travel from London. Beware the fleet of buses at arrival and departure times.

Parental involvement huge, as you would expect from a largely American school. Also makes relocation and transition easier. Plenty of charity support, organised social gatherings and careers advice.

Students appeared relaxed and happy. We asked one what he would change about the school: 'Nothing, really but maybe lessons could be shorter?'

Entrance: Inevitably, because of the transitory national side of the school, places can crop up at different stages. So it is always worth trying. Academic records examined and references required, but no testing until 13+, when English is assessed. However, school adds the caveat: 'We will take any child at any stage providing we have space and can meet their needs academically and socially'. In the last two years, they will only take IB pupils if they are already following the programme and their courses can be matched. Any child can join the American Programme, even, occasionally, for their last year. But they do have to stay for at least one semester.

Exit: Typically 40 per cent of students to UK universities, 40 per cent to American universities and the remaining 20 per cent worldwide. Every student assigned a college counsellor at high school level. A huge and varied exit list, with Exeter, King's College London and Bath the most popular UK universities in 2018; around 40 off to the US, favouring Miami, New York and Northeastern. Others to McGill in Canada, Spain, Netherlands, France and Belgium.

Money matters: Well, it's certainly not the cheapest. But just a look around will tell you why. That said, fees cover pretty well everything, including curriculum related field trips, all books and those iPads. Private corporate owners of all four ACS schools. Means-tested bursaries available, and has introduced 16+ all-rounder scholarships with a 10 per cent fee discount.

Remarks: If you are looking for a large, lively, international school with a multitude of opportunities and facilities to die for, or if you are in transition round the world, then this could be perfect for your child. Shy, retiring children might just get a bit lost, but then again the holistic approach could also help them. Anyone looking for a traditional, structured, English establishment, however, should probably look elsewhere. That said, this school has a huge amount to offer any child prepared to think outside the box.

ACS Egham International School

Woodlee, London Road, Egham, Surrey TW20 0HS

Ages 3–19 **Pupils** 605 **Sixth form** 107

Fees: £10,870 – £25,360 pa

01784 430611
www.acs-schools.com

Head of school: Since 2010, Jeremy Lewis MA PGCE. He has been at ACS Egham for longer than most heads of international schools, perhaps because in many ways it feels like a local school. He was brought up in South Africa during apartheid, which made him more politically aware than most young men, and he 'came to London as soon as he could, at 15 years of age' to finish his education and to go on to study English at Portsmouth, then history at Nottingham, followed by a masters in educational administration from Bath. He travelled and taught at a range of international schools, including Kuwait, Hungary and Japan, and his last post was as head of Istanbul International Community School. ACS Egham has been good for his family: his wife works at the school, his daughter graduated and has gone to study at Exeter University and his son left the school for a sixth form college where he could attend football academy.

A calm, self-effacing man who seems good at delegating and sharing, not a dictatorial head. 'He doesn't rest on his laurels but pushes the school to reach for more'; 'a dynamic head,' according to parents. Known to all pupils (partly because he is at school gates each Monday on bus duty), and parents say he is 'well respected'; 'approachable and knows all the children by name'; and that he 'explains and communicates'. Perhaps more communicating and persuading than listening and acting, and so despite the fact that he is a 'responsible leader', there is an intimation amongst parents of a possible need for new energy after nearly eight years of headship. Clearly very committed to the school, but also interested in theatre and politics and mad about football – 'sadly only watching, not playing any longer'.

Academic matters: IB philosophy permeates all learning – pupils aware of the 'pupil profile', which involves being inquiring, knowledgeable, thinking, communicating, principled, open-minded, risk-taking, balanced, caring and reflective. These attributes are key to all learning and so teaching is enquiry-based and very open ended, allowing each child to develop at their own pace. This can be felt throughout the classrooms with pupil-led project based work and a coherent curriculum.

Early years have separate, modern classes with plenty of outdoor space and large windows, making it a bright and cheerful introduction to school. Lower classes have themes for study that follow the primary years project, and much practical and outside learning (plenty of tables and fake grass in outdoor classrooms) as well as integration of forest school classes (from the tiniest pupils, 'scramblers', to year 5) with their science learning in particular.

The lower school head seems popular – a British teacher who has taught abroad as well. 'She has a good balance between running a tight ship and being nurturing and inspiriting'. 'My child is challenged and stimulated every day and there is no hint of boredom or restlessness'. 'We have never had a poor teacher in the whole time we were in the lower school,' according to one parent.

Middle years programme in upper school, with pupils feeling they 'have control and choice about what and how we learn'. Parents seem committed to the IB system – several saying that is specifically why they chose the school or why they are now staying on. 'It creates acrobatic thinkers and learners who will be fit for future employment,' said one parent.

All classrooms have interactive whiteboards and most classes we saw involved in work on iPads or laptops, with students often working in groups. Six serious science labs with a technician in a separate block. Maths and IT successful despite difficulty recruiting maths teachers. French and Spanish taught from the earliest years, with mother tongue classes for all pupils (if less than three pupils, parents pay for individual language lessons). This Native Language Enrichment is not only a matter of teaching but evident in numbers of foreign language library books being bought and used. Class sizes never more than 20, so several classes in some years.

We like the fact that teachers' performance is also graded, linked to the success of pupils. This monitoring and emphasis on teaching is achieving results with a record number of 60 pupils achieving an average of 35 IB points in 2018.

Bright, well resourced, junior and senior school libraries. We liked the fact that there were books on stands all around the school, with one stand next to the sports hall café – reading is widely encouraged, and not only inside classrooms.

SEN staff in both lower and upper school (4.5 teachers) as well as four EAL teachers give support both inside and outside classrooms. Pupils get assessments outside school which are fed into their support and learning in class. The active use of technology and project based, more open ended style of studying is helpful for pupils' different learning styles. The school has pupils with mild to moderate needs including mild Tourette's, ASD, dyslexia and ADD. It is wheelchair friendly though there are currently no pupils in the school who use wheelchair permanently. One past pupil to be accepted but asked to leave when the school considered their minor physical disability too great to accommodate – so make sure that you disclose all special needs fully.

Parents get emailed reports and can see progress online; however, some have found it hard to adjust to the lack of grades with PYP and MYP, although MAP tests (Measures of Academic Progress) are also used to help students set goals. 'First time you get grades is at IB diploma, by which time it is too late,' mused one parent, but all agreed that it made their children 'independent learners, responsible for themselves and their learning'. 'Parents are not doing their kids' homework, and so projects are not a matter of looking at other parents' work,' was one astute observation. 'Kids resolve problems themselves and speak directly to teachers without parental intervention.'

Games, options, the arts: One term music, one term art and one term of design technology each year. Large and well used drama studio with full lighting and annual productions. Art rooms for both lower and upper schools, with impressive IB displays. Interesting to see the collaborative aspect of IB present in art too, with particularly wonderful class Guernica collage. Multimedia with clay kilns and sculpture, mosaics, plaster masks and printing. Textiles possible for older pupils doing IB art. Design technology with 3D and laser printers for wood, plastic and jewellery design. Plenty of computers for designing. And a first for us to see architectural design taken so seriously, with plenty of mapping, designing and planning in evidence.

Music starts with instruments: each pupil learns an instrument and goes on to composition work higher up the school. Parents liked the fact that their children are given a new instrument to learn each year, exposing them to plenty of musical opportunity, and spoke of excellent music teachers. Certainly music teaching active with plenty of clubs, groups and bands; individual music lessons take place after school. African drumming, ukulele, guitar ensembles as well as rock bands and the upper school band called the Wall of Sound.

Sport hall quite the largest we have seen – fitness rooms, smaller soft areas for younger children, dance studio, courts and seating for competitions and for when the gym is used for whole school assemblies. Climbing walls, both at lower level and for advanced climbers. As well as ball sports – foot, volley, basket and base – there are track and field sports, dance, cross-country running. Sadly, not only is there no swimming pool at the school (planning restrictions very tight on Crown land), but parents disappointed by lack of any swimming programme, even at a nearby pool.

Outdoor pursuits trips in upper school start with bushcraft and move on to a stay at Skern Lodge in north Devon, with trips for the oldest pupils to Nepal after they have raised the funds and to a Kenyan school with which they have a long term partnership. DofE an option – there's endless countryside at the doorstep of the school.

Plenty of clubs for those whose parents who don't mind collecting later – cookery, judo, crafts, pottery, yoga, chess, climbing. Clubs are an added cost, however, and some families choose to join local clubs rather than stay at school, where the sport is not super competitive.

Background and atmosphere: An elegant main building with very high ceilings and an gorgeous staircase was built in 1880s for a family with 12 children. Its original walled gardens, ancient yew trees and areas of surrounding green parkland are truly splendid. The school uses 21 acres for school buildings and playgrounds, but has a further 80 acres which it rents from the Crown (well, they are next door to Windsor Great Park) and uses for orienteering and to ensure that it has no near neighbours. Space and trees – what luxury for a school so very near to London. The old buildings lend character and style, but the new buildings provide fabulous facilities – state of the art low build science blocks, maths and IT blocks, DT rooms and the enormous gym complex. New IB diploma centre with teaching spaces works as a common room and study centre for oldest pupils, next to IB coordinator and university counsellors. The lower school doesn't get lost in all the space, as it is grouped closely together with the bright early years buildings and enclosed outside learning areas near the dining hall. All very manageable for the younger children.

Pastoral care, well-being and discipline: 'Good behaviour policy' sets the positive tone of the school, with well travelled children who support each other and few behavioural issues, according to both staff and pupils. Not to say there aren't problems, but plenty of workshops, particularly around cyber-bullying, drugs and self-protection in its widest sense. The head has only had to expel one child so far. All else is dealt with by bringing in parents and a report system.

Lunches in a dining hall with impressive emphasis on healthy eating: 'if we finish our vegetables we can go for seconds,' say younger pupils, whilst older pupils enjoy the choice and generous portions. Menu involves a different country's cuisine each day, with the American choice of organic beefburgers very popular.

Pupils and parents: The usual wide range of countries represented, but this is the most English of the three ACS schools in the UK because it only does IB, rather than the American curriculum, and so has a stable core of students who are wedded to this. Staff, too, are surprisingly stable for an international school, with many teachers who have taught here for years and clearly love their subjects, and pupils say they love them for it. Needless to say, there are still teachers and pupils who stay for shorter periods (20 per cent turnover each year, mostly at 11 years old) and staff retention and recruitment is a priority in the school strategic planning. Usual difficulties finding maths and science teachers and losing teachers to other schools following their good training at ACS. The head feels it is the price to pay for having a school with a good reputation. A recent marketing push has increased proportion of British pupils to 25 per cent, with Americans the next largest population, and thereafter a sprinkling from a huge range of countries. Parents in oil, IT, finance – many commuting into London on the fast Woking train.

As is usual with international schools, parents tend to be very involved as it is often the basis of social life for them as well as their children. Active parent teacher organisation, plenty of open houses, fun runs, fairs, coffee and cookie mornings, celebrations and supportive orientation for new parents. And while some parents might choose to come in to collect children and so they can use the sports facilities (open until 9pm), half of students come in by school bus. Wide catchment area reaching from Hammersmith to Reading. About a quarter of pupils come from nearby Virginia Water.

Entrance: Families may arrive from abroad at any time and are welcomed by an experienced admissions registrar who recognises that the need to accommodate visits and admissions as and when. This transience means occasional places do come up. Non-selective and welcoming to a range of abilities. Parents liked this as it 'gives an understanding of difference and other perspectives'. Application form and current school reports considered along with school reference and family questionnaire ('so we can ensure a match of expectations'). English testing (can be done at current school) from year 9 onwards to ensure pupil can manage the academic requirements of middle years programme and IB diploma, so those requiring EAL really only accepted lower down the school.

Exit: International families often transferred with work, but the increasing percentage of local British students means a more solid core of long term students than is usual in an international school. Those that stay to complete the diploma programme are welcomed by universities, who recognise IB diploma students as having independent study skills ideal for higher education. Around half go on to British universities: two to Oxford in 2018, plus one medic,others to eg Exeter, Imperial, Durham Edinburgh, Queen's Belfast, Kent, Leicester. Others to the US, the Netherlands, Italy, Denmark. Two college counsellors help with advice on open days, references and choices of college; US university applicants can do PSAT in school and get SAT support.

Money matters: Most unusually for an international school, it is in the process of applying for charitable status, which requires an element of benefit to the community – opening access to facilities, local community projects, and particularly much involvement by sixth formers as they complete the community aspect of their IB. Full bursaries for two sixth form students each year from local state schools as well as mean-tested bursaries for bright pupils at 11 and 13. A new set of carefully recruited charity trustees join a few of the existing directors and give new direction as a charity. The school is part of a group of four ACS schools (Cobham, Hillingdon and Doha), and previously parents have been concerned that Egham was the poorer relative, but recent building projects have reassured them.

Remarks: Glorious grounds with enhance the independence that is a key feature of the IB programme. Students are 'taught to think' and parents are pleased that children are 'independent, organised, and it is up to the child to get their work done'. Not the school, necessarily, for a competitively sporty child, but ideal for those who want to learn to think for themselves, set their own goals and work at their own pace to achieve it. Great skills for life.

Akeley Wood Junior School

Wicken Park, Wicken, Milton Keynes, Buckinghamshire MK19 6DA

Ages 1–11 **Pupils** 305

Fees: £10,245 – £12,630 pa

01908 571231
www.akeleywoodschool.co.uk

Headmistress: Since 2008, Clare Page BEd (50s). Educated at Ancaster House in Bexhill and Chelsea College, Eastbourne where she read PE and science. Cut teeth at Haberdashers' Aske's School for Girls in Elstree, joining Akeley Wood in the senior school as head of girls' games before defecting to Beachborough School, a competing local prep. Happily returned to Akeley in

2001 as year 6 teacher and head of year 5 before being promoted into current job. Has made changes aplenty during her tenure – 'we've really been on a journey of getting everything in the right place, and every gap is plugged now'. Proud of school's 'vast curriculum' but mainly of the contented brood of children we watch frolicking on the lawns (again, vast) as we chat. 'Happy children learn', she beams. Motherly and approachable – parents say 'her door is always open'.

Entrance: After nursery, not oversubscribed – 'competition from good village schools is fierce', says head. Prospective reception children spend a morning with their peer group in the pre-school, with a visit to the reception class, and are observed in play. Older applicants come for a taster day (two if either party isn't sure) and are assessed in reading and maths, spending time with the SENCo if necessary. 'The idea is that they have a nice day', says head. 'We always try to offer.' Stresses that she likes parents to be honest about any difficulties their child may have and that only those who it is felt genuinely won't thrive or whose needs can't be met that would not be accepted.

Exit: At 11, vast majority (around 75 per cent) make the seamless move to Akeley Wood Secondary School with places guaranteed subject to head's recommendation. Almost unheard of for a child not to be accepted. At time of writing many changes afoot at senior school so worth asking how new staff, curriculum and integration of pupils with SEN is working out. About one fifth – generally the more academic cohort – leave for selective grammars such as The Royal Latin, Aylesbury Grammar or Sir Henry Floyd, with one or two each year going to Bedford either for transport reasons or boarding and some parents feeling simply that their children need to grow beyond 'the Akeley bubble'.

Remarks: Who knew that just out of earshot of the M1 lay this gem of a setting, approached by winding drive (complete with lambs grazing by its side), leading to idyllic Georgian mansion and a dozen or so acres of dreamy fields and gardens? Two form entry reception class, growing to three in year 3, with lessons for classes up to year 4 taking place almost exclusively in the well converted mansion ('we've extended into every available space', says head.) Years 5 and 6 housed in a separate (although equally beauteous) house just across the garden, although visit main school building for some lessons – 'they love the feeling of being away from the little ones'. School well equipped across the board, thanks to massive investment by owners, Cognita. From the gleaming IT suite (new computing curriculum taught by 'really vibrant' specialist) to the immaculate cricket pitch, adventure playground equipment and multi-purpose sports hall, it feels like there's nothing that a child couldn't do here. Stunning artwork adorns almost every millimetre of wall space and there's even a food tech room with child-sized units – the only one we've ever seen.

Pupils mainly class taught to year 6 with specialist teaching for science, French, IT, music and games. French from year 1 with Spanish or German added in year 6 and clubs on offer along the way for any budding linguists. Setting for maths and English from year 3, with as few as seven children in the lower maths sets.

School boasts 'the most amazing' SENCo, winner of a global award by Cognita. This just one factor in securing Akeley's reputation as a natural destination for children needing extra help, particularly with dyslexia, although also well equipped to work with dyspraxia, dyscalculia and children on the autistic spectrum. Early intervention is part of school culture with SEN programmes including a mix of support either one to one or in small groups, plus initiatives such as touch typing club. 'Children have one chance and we have to get it right', says head. TAs used flexibly across school to enable them to support both those with SEN and the top five per cent of all year groups identified as gifted and able. Do parents worry that their bright child will be held back by such an inclusive culture? Apparently not. Pupils at the top of the academic tree 'continuously stretched', say parents, with extension activities such as maths trips to try coding at Bletchley Park and workshops with published authors, from which 'they come back buzzing'. Also extension work in school and at home. EAL also all in a day's work here, with occasional new joiners (mainly German speakers with parents relocated to nearby Mercedes or VW) arriving with very little or no English quickly up and running.

'Loads' of drama and music, both on curriculum throughout. Four choirs – one for boys only (launched with the promise of biscuits for attendees and now buzzing with a capella performances of Beach Boys medleys in four parts) – perform and compete in local and national shows and competitions such as Young Voices and the Northampton Festival. Around one third of pupils take peripatetic music lessons. Head says parents are 'blown away' by performances, often scripted by pupils themselves. Inclusivity is the name of the game in the drama department, with main parts cast multiple times in major productions to ensure everyone gets a chance to shine. School awarded Artsmark in 2014 and now working towards its gold award.

Sport specialist taught from nursery. It's a traditional menu of rugby, football and cricket for boys with netball (coached by Welsh national player), hockey and rounders for the girls. With A-D teams fielded for Wednesday afternoon fixtures most weeks, everyone gets a go at representing the school. Super results too. No on-site pool but swimming takes place at nearby Wolverton Pool for all year groups – again with plenty of trophies in the cabinet.

House system runs through whole junior and senior school with house captains elected termly, a weekly house trophy and competitions galore for everything from sports to music and art. Copious reporting keeps parents well up to date with two parents' evenings and three full reports a year plus half termly gradings. 'They're continually assessed', reported one parent, 'but not in a stressy way – and they all know what targets they're working towards.'

With just the occasional grumble about school dinners, Akeley parents gush with enthusiasm about the start their children are getting: 'thriving' was used almost uniformly by all we spoke to. Perhaps not an obvious choice if you're looking for an academic hothouse, but an idyllic school where juniors can flourish whatever their ability.

Aldenham Preparatory School

Linked with Aldenham School

Elstree, Borehamwood, Hertfordshire WD6 3AJ

Ages 3–11 **Pupils** 187 **C of E**

Fees: £9,750 – £13,971 pa

01923 851664
www.aldenhamprep.com

Head: Since 2011, Vicky Gocher BA BEd MA (late 40s). Educated to A level at Gwernyfed High School in Powys, Wales followed by Hull University (English) and a PGCE at Roehampton. A vocational teacher ('I knew when I was 16 exactly what I wanted to do'), and always focused on teaching younger children: 'I want to share everything with them,' she says. Completed masters in educational leadership and innovation at Warwick in 2011. Formerly deputy head at Caterham Prep School, having previously taught at Downsend School, Leatherhead.

Purposeful and businesslike in manner, head inherited a young prep school 'riding the coat-tails of the senior school,' and set to work to cement school's reputation and smarten up discipline and behaviour. Consistent with the Aldenham ethos, enthuses about school's nurturing atmosphere – a refreshing approach (some might say USP) in comparison with local pressure cooker rivals. 'A wide range of abilities mirrors life,' she says. Parents approve – she's front of house every morning and 'never says no to a quick word.'

Lives on site with husband and has two adult daughters, both of whom are in the teaching profession.

Entrance: Broad selection criteria – not just academic; school is oversubscribed with around four applicants for each place. Entry at 3+ and 4+ by gentle 'playgroup style' assessment to ascertain readiness and sociability. Applicants for occasional places thereafter assessed in maths, English and reasoning.

Exit: Between 50 and 65 per cent to Aldenham School. Entry not guaranteed but 'we won't allow a child to take the exam if they're not going to thrive there,' says head. And all efforts made to help find suitable pastures new for those who won't. Conversations regarding next steps carefully timetabled 18 months in advance, kicking off with a session with head of senior school. School fully supports and prepares for entry to other destinations, with pupils heading off in small numbers to a range of schools including Haberdashers' Aske's, Merchant Taylors', John Lyon, North London Collegiate, St Albans, Emanuel, St Margaret's and the Watford Grammar Schools. Happy to support Herts 11+ hopefuls but limited in ability to offered tailored tuition.

Remarks: Nestled in a picture perfect postcard village, yet just a stone's throw from the M25 in the grounds of Aldenham School, location is clearly a big draw for urban families who describe the setting as 'fantastic'. Pupils housed in two low rise structures, the first catering for the pre-prep's two nursery classes, reception class and years 1 and 2. Lovely bright and airy classrooms, decked with cheery displays, which for the younger years lead directly onto wonderful outdoor play zones and gardens, keeping each age group separate while they settle into school life. These segue into woodland where little ones can play on adventure equipment, looking onto further endless idyllic grounds and playing fields. Nursery and reception classes benefit from their own kitchen with hot lunches prepared on site – and picnics in the grounds once a week when weather allows. Parents rave about atmosphere – 'caring from day one.'

Years 3 to 6 are in a functional, purpose-built dwelling with a large multi-use entrance hall with classrooms leading off. Artwork, accolades and information on school initiatives neatly displayed in corridors and in the atrium, ranging from information on how school is working towards eco school status to pupils' impressive achievements outside school (our guide was UK's youngest ever taekwondo black belt) including regional gymnasts and a national team figure skater.

Prep benefits from sharing some of the senior school's facilities (sports hall, theatre and dining room, where years 1 to 6 take lunch) which is not to say that it lacks a few of its own. Super ICT suite boasts a gleaming fleet of computers and year 6 pupils all have a Kindle on which to follow the class reader. A stand-alone drama studio was host to initial rehearsals of upcoming year 5 and 6 show, Bugsy Malone, on our visit. Stunning sports field, Astroturf and well organised library, packed with immaculate sets of books. The small, suspiciously tidy art room was sadly bereft of display work on its walls, although some super 3D work in display cabinets compensated somewhat and head assures that art is 'on the up,' with work recently accepted into the prep schools art competition.

School has a gentle, friendly feel, almost like a village school, with a quietly confident mixed ability cohort who, parents say, 'flourish, whatever their academic ability' in this environment which, despite its bijoux headcount, is abundant in space both inside and out. Pupils, mainly hailing from nearby London suburbs (Edgware, Stanmore) and neighbouring towns (Radlett, St Albans) chat with enthusiasm and pride about their school, struggling to choose one thing they think is best.

Unlike senior school where number of boys dominates, here it's exactly 50/50. Excellent cultural mix reflects the local community with every main religion represented. Plenty of London commuters in the parent community, helped with their long days by before- and after-school care on offer, starting at 8am and ending at 5.30pm, with pupils in years 3 and up able to commute on one of eight school coaches. A nine week holiday over the summer is parents' main grumble.

Reception room, to which nursery children transfer 'without batting an eyelid' according to parents, has teacher and two TAs with all other year groups of maximum 22 children having one full time TA. All year groups are class taught with specialist teachers for music, drama, French, art and sport. Head still keeps hand in with the troops, teaching PSHCE. Setting in maths and English almost from the start enables teaching staff to stretch the brightest and support those who need more help. A 'very talented' SENCo assists a handful of children across the school (mainly mild dyslexia or dyspraxia, occasionally mild ASD) with one-to-one sessions held in the aptly named Launch Pad, and joins classrooms to provide booster maths groups where required. EAL well catered for. Despite an atmosphere which parents describe as 'a bit more laid back' than other schools in the vicinity, they say the standard of work is 'amazing...but without pressure'. Dynamic young music and drama teachers enthuse pupils, with a large proportion taking LAMDA examinations and all learning recorder in year 2 and violin in year 3 (but don't let that put you off).

Sport three times a week, comprising games, PE and swimming, which takes place at a nearby leisure centre. The usual culprits of football, hockey, cricket, netball and athletics take centre stage with a wholly inclusive ethos that ensures all those who want to have a chance to represent their house and school. Head admits that with such small numbers of children, the talented ones can feel stifled, as it's not always easy to put out an A and a B team for fixtures, so those looking for a ride on the school minibus to battle it out at fixtures on a weekly basis may need to look elsewhere – or pursue their chosen sports outside of school.

An impressive list of extracurricular activities to broaden horizons at lunch times and after school ranges from Lego robotics and animation to fencing, gardening and choir. Lots of accolades and rewards for achievements from badges for house point excellence to commitment to sports. Head boy and girl are chosen by staff, with opportunities for others to pitch themselves to the masses as prefects or school counsellors.

For parents looking for balance, roundedness and a school where their child will have the space – physically and mentally – to grow, look no further. Unashamedly kind without compromising on quality teaching, this is a school that allows its charges a childhood whilst keeping plenty of options open for the future if the call of the north London academic hothouses proves too loud to ignore.

A

Aldenham School

Linked with Aldenham Preparatory School

Elstree, Borehamwood, Hertfordshire WD6 3AJ

Ages 11–18 **Pupils** 608 (459 boys, 149 girls) **Sixth form** 181
Boarders 33 full, 137 flexi **C of E**

Fees: Day: £16,491 – £22,614; Boarding: £22,791 – £33,234 pa

01923 858122
www.aldenham.com

Headmaster: Since 2006, Mr James Fowler MA PGCE (50s). Educated at Merchant Taylors' School, Northwood and New College, Oxford where he was a choral scholar. Previously head of sixth form at Brentwood School and deputy head at Highgate. Permeates every facet of school with his relaxed charisma and understanding of what makes parents and pupils tick. Unusually, interviews every candidate with their parents before admission. Is he interviewing the parents as well as the child, we asked? 'Of course,' he says. 'I spend a lot of time helping people understand what we are and are not.' And it's to this level of mutual soul searching that he attributes the happy, enthusiastic nature of his cohort in evidence all over the school, almost all of whom he knows by name and who claim that their voice is 'genuinely heard' by him. It's not just the children who are happy with their leader, either. Parents describe head as 'always available', and 'very good at resolving issues in the right way,' adding that 'his attitude filters down to all the staff.'

Definitely not a head chasing glory in the league tables – and one totally at ease with this status; a breath of fresh air in the ferociously competitive north London landscape. Keen to provide a totally different experience to his urban competitors as applications from London families increase, and determined that his charges feel 'secure and safe'. Single-mindedly focused on school providing 'the best possible pathways' for each student, regardless of academic prowess. 'We celebrate successful entry to art school in the same way as entry to Oxbridge,' he says.

Lives on site with wife and two sons.

Academic matters: Situated in the heart of UK's spiritual home of secondary academia (Habs, Merchant Taylors', North London Collegiate et al), Aldenham stands apart with its unpressurised vibe and mixed ability cohort. Perhaps not a destination for the single minded scholar, although pupils say they are strongly encouraged to hit their own personal best; 'the natural spread of ability makes for breadth and roundedness,' according to head. Although those bright enough to get to Russell Group universities – and occasionally Oxbridge – will do, it's immediately evident that it's the journey that defines Aldenham rather than the destination.

In 2018, 45 per cent of A*-B grades at A level (17 per cent A*/A) and 32 per cent A*-A/9-7 at I/GCSE. Many subjects have now moved to IGCSE to stretch brighter students, who are also recruited into small study and discussion groups such as Les Philosophes with visiting speakers, including Anthony Grayling, enabling them to exchange ideas and broaden horizons. 'Parents trust us with children of all abilities,' says head.

Small class sizes of maximum 22 and often down to 10 in sixth form, with setting from year 7 in maths and science. Eleven GCSEs the norm with a broad range of subjects available, from the traditional ('the brighter students tend to gravitate towards sciences,' says head) to dance, textiles and DT. French, Spanish and Latin on offer in the languages department. Non-traditional subjects on offer at A level include psychology, media studies, government and politics and computing. Parents and pupils appreciate extra revision lessons at lunch times, after school and even on Saturdays laid on in the run up to public exams. University conversations start in year 12, with a series of events including visiting professionals brought in to 'give insights' into the world of work. Pupils feel well supported and guided through uni application process, although one or two parents felt that school could secure more top level places for the brightest if things were slightly slicker.

Good provision for SEN run in dedicated area by full time SENCo, with around 10 per cent on the register – mainly catering for mild dyslexia or dyscalculia although can deal with mild Asperger's and recently sent one such child to Cambridge. One-to-one teaching rooms well used by overseas pupils requiring EAL support.

Games, options, the arts: In a setting that needs to be seen to be believed – over 110 acres encompassing woodland, playing fields plus full-sized Astro hockey pitch, tennis courts, dance studio, well-utilised weights room and an enormous sports hall (recently resurfaced) plus manicured cricket pitch that lies literally at the heart of the school ('the pavilion is one of my favourite spots,' says head) – sport is integral to life at Aldenham and thrives at all levels, from the most elite to the 'just for fun'. It's football, hockey and cricket for the boys, no rugby, while girls focus on netball, hockey and rounders. School known for its footie prowess, with a handful of boys training with top academies, and also embryonic links with Southgate Hockey Club, but parents say it suits students less inclined towards team pursuits well too. Options include zumba, archery, sailing, tennis, athletics, Eton fives, judo and climbing on its climbing wall – in the words of one parent: 'all that's missing is a swimming pool.'

Two compulsory activities a week, ranging from bell ringing, horse riding and film club to a very popular CCF, make for a long school day which for most ends at 5.30pm. This gives school a unique boarding atmosphere, even for those who do not take advantage of the marvellously flexible boarding on offer. Aldenham is 'synonymous with trips,' according to pupils, who enthuse about the 'amazing experiences' they have had on CCF trips to Holland, language trips including a Spanish trip to Cuba, cricket tour to Barbados, geography to Iceland, choir to Rome and a three week charity volunteering trip to Malawi.

Outstanding art department, unanimously acclaimed by everyone from head to parents and pupils, and so popular that school recently built a superb new art cabin to accommodate the large numbers electing to pursue art A level. Fabulous work on display: huge canvasses, three dimensional installations and sculpture with as much rigorous preparation and development of concepts on show as final works. Pupils say that head of art won't accept anything less than excellence and parents report offspring joining school 'unable to draw' and emerging with A grades. Dedicated textiles room also displays high quality fashion design and DT labs are hives of industry, complete with 3D printers in motion.

Music thrives, with bands, orchestras and choirs galore, run by 'fantastic' and 'passionate' musicians, according to pupils. As with sport, there are opportunities for musicians of all levels to participate, with pupils enthusing that the fiercely competitive annual house music event (compulsory participation for all) is one of the highlights of the year. All year 7s offered opportunity of one term's free music lessons on the orchestral instrument of their choice, leading to many taking it up more seriously. Futuristic music technology equipment puts department very much in the 21st century.

'Really strong' drama on and off curriculum, headed by 'inspirational' head of department who clearly drives excellence and pushes boundaries. 'We're into serious drama,' she says – school refreshingly veers away from the usual hackneyed shows and rarely produces musicals, mainly delivering productions of the Sophocles and Brechtian variety, oft performed in the purpose built 150 seat theatre, but sometimes out in the grounds or as a promenade, which are 'just fantastic,' according to parents. A handful of students are members of the National Youth Theatre, some take part in the Edinburgh Fringe and it's not unusual for one or two each year to head off to destinations including Central School of Speech and Drama or LAMDA, and these applications are taken seriously – head says that in the year school sent three students off to drama school and three to med school, both were supported and celebrated in equal measure.

Boarding: Around 30 per cent of the school community (some two-thirds boys) participates in boarding life at some level – enough to lend it a 'proper' boarding ethos without any trace of 'them and us' between boarders and day pupils. Boarding starts in year 7 in a small co-educational junior boarding house with 25 beds. No full boarding at this stage, meaning that cohort tends to be exclusively UK based with vast majority never having boarded before. Pupils enjoy a 'home from home' environment here – but still relish having a 'lot more freedom' when they move into one of the four main single sex boarding houses (three for boys and one for girls), each with its own strong identity, that shape the school.

Head keen that students 'experience boarding as part of their overall education,' hence provides excellent flexibility with boarders able to stay from just one night to, for a minority of mainly older, overseas students (some 25 per cent of boarders), full time. Up to sixth form, majority are reasonably local though, with boarders heading home at weekends to homes in north London, Herts and Bucks. 'Terrific' live-in houseparents supervise their charges in spacious houses – not the most luxurious we've seen, but functional (well-equipped kitchens and study spaces) and welcoming with plenty of nooks and crannies for down time and socialising. Boys dorm in fours until year 11 when they double up, with girls mostly in twos and threes then single rooms in sixth form. An ongoing programme of renovations is brightening things up.

Evenings see boarders participate in the clubs or activities of their choice, or gather in the art block, library, media suite or gym. Most popular nights to board in sixth form are Tuesdays and Thursdays when the bar opens and pizza is served in the wonderful sixth form centre. Sunday brunch is 'the best meal of the week', attended by most staff who live on site, plus their families as well as weekend boarders, and whilst there are weekend outings, trips and activities on offer, quite often students, having had a long week and sports fixtures on Saturdays, just 'want to chill.'

Background and atmosphere: Founded by brewer, Richard Platt, in 1597 after Queen Elizabeth I granted him letters patent to build 'the Free Grammar School and Almshouses' at Aldenham for elementary children. The Brewers' Company then had a controlling interest in the school and links remain strong. Original Tudor buildings demolished in the 19th century to make place for two new schools – one providing an elementary education for the local population, the second a grammar school for fee-paying boarders. School now occupies a prime position in protected green belt, attracting pupils from affluent local villages like Radlett and Sarratt, London suburbs such as Edgware and Stanmore and increasingly north London, with parents attracted by the fabulous country campus, handy coach services and inclusive ethos.

Main school building is Hogwarts-esque Victorian gothic with gables, tower and turrets, with additions – some more appealing than others – from subsequent decades. Most notable new facility is fabulous sixth form centre – all white walls, squidgy sofas and sliding glass doors offering panoramic view of cricket pitch – complete with its own coffee shop and bar where years 12 and 13 can socialise, study and generally commune outside of school hours. A few tatty corners in other areas, but plenty of up to date Mac technology and a luxurious feeling of abundant space.

An extraordinary chapel (the largest consecrated building in Hertfordshire after St Albans Abbey) which can host entire school – and frequently does – lies across the road that bisects the school. Surprisingly welcoming, the Stanley Spencer altar pieces of yesteryear are but a part of school history now (sold to raise funds during the desperate 1990s) and an attractive ironwork cross and dove now dominates the altar. Despite the diverse religions of the school community (about 60 per cent Christian, 20 per cent Jewish and all other main religions represented) all attend chapel twice weekly to underscore the 'feeling of one community' that's so integral to the school. Beautiful panelled library complete with mezzanine level, spiral staircase and view of cricket pitch and miniature replica statue of old boy Alfred Gilbert's Eros. There's an annual run on the last day of term for those brave enough, from Eros in Piccadilly to the school's statue, just one of the many traditions that pupils say are 'a huge part of the school'.

Break times see pupils congregate en masse on the field with cross year group socialising in evidence everywhere ('we're like a family – everyone knows everyone,' said one happy pupil). Although not the most polished cohort we've ever seen, pupils without exception seem totally at ease with the school and are arguably one of the most sociable and understatedly confident bunches we've met. Quite possibly one of the happiest too. Girls now make up around one-third of the school – many join in sixth form – and school is content with this balance – 'we'd ideally like 35 to 40 per cent,' says head.

Pastoral care, well-being and discipline: Parents report excellent pastoral care, thanks mainly to the system that places all children in a boarding house, even if they don't board, so staff have a close eye on everyone's well-being. Good sign that many boarders we spoke to live locally and board 'because we love it.' Food has been a small bone of contention although pupils say it is 'getting better'.

The usual disciplinary issues but in the main very few incidents. Suspensions for major breaches of rules (eg boarders driving off campus) but in the main little need to transgress as students given sufficient freedom to spread their wings.

Pupils and parents: Majority of pupils from a 20 mile radius. Lots of busy, professional commuters and London parents attracted by the flexible boarding uniquely on offer here – as well as the atmosphere that they say gives their children 'space to breathe', both literally and metaphorically. Mixed financial demographic – plenty of first time buyers and parents stretching themselves to afford Aldenham – with these children fitting comfortably in with those who can easily cover the fees.

Overseas boarders tend to be in higher year groups. Of these, around 30 per cent from Germany, then handfuls from China, Hong Kong and ones and twos from elsewhere. All are well respected and well integrated – boarding pupils embrace and relish the diversity of their peers. Around 40 boarders stay in school at weekends.

Entrance: Around 60 places in year 7 with between 15 and 20 of these taken by children coming up from on-site prep school

A

and the rest made up of children joining from the state sector (40 per cent) and local 11+ preps. About 30 per cent of year 7 are girls. Another 25 to 30 join in year 9 from a vast array of preps, notably Lochinver House, Orley Farm, Northwood Prep, St Martin's and St John's and further afield The Beacon, The Hall and Davenies. Applicants at 11+ take papers in maths, English and reasoning with the addition of science and a language at 13+. Scholars are interviewed away from their parents.

Late arrivals come from other, more pressured, local schools – not always because they can't cut the mustard but mainly because they are looking for a school that's about more than exam results. And that, here, is what they find. Around 30 places available in sixth form.

Exit: Approximately 30 per cent leave after GCSE to follow vocational courses or A levels elsewhere (mainly state schools or colleges) or to employment. A broad spectrum of destination universities reflects mixed academic intake, with about 20 per cent to Russell Group, a couple each year to art schools (often Central St Martins) and regular success with applications to top drama schools. Other degree courses tend to veer towards the vocational, many with a business/management focus. Two medics in 2018.

Money matters: Scholarships at 11+ and 13+ in music, art, sport, DT as well as academic, with a maximum of 15 per cent off fees awarded. Means-tested bursaries available.

Remarks: Head describes Aldenham as 'an extraordinary school for ordinary children' and we concur. An unpressurised environment such as this makes for some of the most contented pupils we have met, and self-motivated children can fare well academically too. Tread carefully if scholarly accolades are top of your wish list or if your offspring need stick rather than carrot, but if it's a rounded and happy child you're after, then Aldenham's definitely one to consider.

Aldro

Lombard Street, Shackleford, Godalming, Surrey GU8 6AS

Ages 7–13 **Pupils** 222 **Boarders** 12 full, 90 weekly/flexi **C of E**

Fees: Day £17,544 – £19,479; Boarding £23,346 – £25,281 pa

01483 810266
www.aldro.org

Acting headmaster: Deputy Chris Rose is holding the reins.

The new head from September 2019 will be Chris Carlier, currently a senior housemaster at Bradfield, where he has spent his entire teaching career of over 20 years. Degree in modern languages from Oxford, PGCE from Cambridge, masters in educational leadership from Buckingham. Joined Bradfield as assistant head of the new first year boarding house, and was head of French before taking on the senior housemaster role in 2005. He also teaches French and German and has coached several sports, including squash and canoeing.

He is married to Nicky and they have three children.

Entrance: One form entry in year 3, rising to three parallel forms by the middle of the school. Parents either join an open morning or have a bespoke tour with headmaster. Once registered, boys attend an assessment day. For those entering year 3 or 4, this involves online tests in spelling, writing and maths. Boys also given a taste of school life with music, drama and sport. Older pupils sit online reasoning tests and written assessments in English and maths. Some participation in academic lessons and sport in the afternoon. School asserts that 'no preparation is necessary for the entrance tests'.

A report from pupil's current school is viewed as an important safety net in case the boy significantly underperforms on the assessment day itself, 'which can be an issue with younger candidates'. If a boy does have a wobble, then a member of staff from Aldro will often visit the boy's school and watch him in action. 'We want to get a full picture and want to create opportunities,' says school.

About a dozen families turned down each year 'if the fit is not right'. School will not take overseas boys if their English is too weak to fully access the curriculum. Would also not accept a boy if he had a learning or behavioural challenge that could not be fully supported. School explains, 'If we think the length of the day and length of the week will be too much for a child emotionally, then we won't take them. It is not fair on the child'. No sibling policy but school does what it can to take brothers.

Exit: Leavers' destinations include Charterhouse, Eton, Wellington, Harrow and Winchester. Some head for Royal Grammar School, Guildford at end of year 6. One mother we spoke to felt that 'some parents feel that more advice on a greater range of senior schools would be welcome.' Scholarships thick on the ground.

Remarks: School's 20-acre grounds in prime Surrey countryside include an adventure island, complete with wooden fort, only reachable by rope bridge or rowing boat. Aldro boys have fun, whether den-making in the woods or playing with the model railway. As one pupil explained, 'The thing I love about Aldro is that there is always something to do.'

Average class size is 14 and maximum is 18. Lessons now one hour long, extended from 35 minutes, to avoid time being wasted as boys move from place to place. Compulsory Saturday morning school from year 4. Boys need stamina and resilience to cope with mega long day, stretching to 10 hours for older boys. Once home, however, they can totally chill as all homework is completed at school from year 5 upwards.

Inspiring lessons in full swing when we visited. Pupils fully engaged, whether racing through timed Latin quizzes on the interactive whiteboard or dissecting poetry by Thomas Hardy. Soothing music and soft candles created serenity in chemistry lesson, as boys worked at full capacity on the reactivity of metals.

Setting in year 4 for maths, year 5 for English and maths, and year 6 for English, maths, science, French and Latin. No separate scholarship class until final year – 'if this happens too early then you risk dividing the whole year group, including parents. Also, some boys are slow developers'. Three criteria for selecting for boys for scholarship class: initiative, self-motivation and natural flair. 'We recognise their potential and we feel that the additional burden placed on them is something they can take.'

'Reading is the centre of our world,' and the light library is well used. Now offers a third language – French, Spanish and Latin (from year 5). A smattering of Greek at the top end: 'Just a drip feed. We can't give everything in a prep school. We don't want to spoil all their senior school joys!'

School prepares boys well for pre-tests, including copious amounts of online reasoning. No manic tutoring going on here, unlike the London scene, but if a boy needs a top-up then school pushes for clear dialogue with external tutor. Numerous parents emphasised 'Aldro is not a hothouse.'

Currently 46 on SEN register. School can support pupils with mild levels of difficulty – mostly dyslexia, dyspraxia, processing and working memory. Some individual learning support lessons with three on-site teachers.

A newish cohort of lively, younger teachers to replace some of veteran members of staff. 'We're not interested in an 'old school' master who teaches history and cricket – we want someone who is going to be brilliant in the classroom.' Would rather have excellent part-timers than a full-time jack of all trades. Through lesson observations, teachers share good practice so are constantly learning from each other. Roughly half teachers are female. Student masters from Harrow and Shore College in Sydney stay for a year and are put on a pedestal by boys.

'We are a day school with a boarding house'. Boarding is racing ahead at full throttle with supremely dedicated housemaster. Boarding grows organically as boys move on up the school. 'We don't push it and the parents don't push it. It tends to come from the boys themselves,' comments housemaster. 'We are preparatory in every sense of the word and want to prepare them for boarding if that is the route they are going down at their next school.' Big boarding weekends regularly laid on, with day boys welcome. Paintballing and laser quest activities prove quite a pull. Out of the 200 boys in the school, 150 experience boarding in some form during the year. 'It really is like a second home,' chirped one happy boarder. Housemaster explains, 'I prefer the term "family friendly boarding" rather than "flexi-boarding", as we are not a hotel nor a babysitting service'. Full boarding possible from the start, but a minimum of one night per week, and has become a hit with juniors.

Around 10 per cent of boarders are overseas. Not much homesickness but dealt with sensitively when it does occur. Numbers are going up – 'it's popular and it's working, as the statistics show. Boys feel they get so much more done when boarding. Thankfully, it is very different now to what it was 30 years ago,' says housemaster. Evening routine for boarders involves dinner, then activities such as Swedish longball or Capture the Flag. This is followed by Mars time: work (on prep or revision), rest (reading) and play (musical instrument).

Daily sport. Extraordinary facilities: rowing lake, sports centre complete with climbing wall, all-weather tennis courts, swimming pool, croquet lawn, rifle and pistol ranges. School hosts annual regatta. Impressive range of sports offered including polo. Boys we spoke to felt the school excelled at cricket and rugby. Pupils perform at a very high level, frequently winning tournaments, cups and swimming galas. 'We're quite a competitive school,' explained one boy. Every child plays in a team; no one excluded for lack of ability. The rule is that everybody who is fit plays sport.

Breadth of education seen as important, though some parents bemoan the fact that there are not enough school trips. 'We need to devote time to music, drama and art to let children fully develop.' Music is certainly flourishing, with over 90 per cent taking individual music lessons. Thirteen different ensembles, including 50-strong brass ensemble. String quartet recently won the Ensemble Rose Bowl at the Godalming Festival. Choir of 40-50 described as an 'all singing, all dancing club,' which is cleverly timetabled, so boys do not have to skip break. Outstanding chess, which is part of the curriculum, pupils winning over 20 national titles.

One boy we spoke to said 'the drama productions are the things I will remember most once I have left here.' Every child takes part in plays (such as Lion King and HMS Pinafore) and form assemblies; some 50 boys take LAMDA exams. Informal showcases allow boys to gain confidence before performing on the big stage. Art described by one mother as 'definitely not as high profile as sport and drama,' though some impressive work displayed around the school, including meticulously executed wooden chessboards complete with glazed pottery pieces.

'We have a strong Christian heart,' says school. Boys of all religious backgrounds or none, though all are expected to attend morning chapel most days of the week. 'Chapel needs to be fun – it is hugely participative. When you ask for a volunteer, 195 hands go up!'

School says it wants boys who will throw themselves into everything, though insists there is room for the quiet, retiring types. 'Parents need to buy into the ethos of our school. Everyone needs to take part'. Will not take girls because 'in our area we want to stand out, to be unique. We are the only school for miles around that does what we do' ie all boys, full boarding, family-friendly boarding or day, not attached to a senior school.

School now boasts a six-strong pastoral care team, all of whom have been through mental health training. 'It's an all-boy world at Aldro and because we have sport every day, there is always competition there. We need to manage that.' Parents mentioned occasional bullying but say it is dealt with effectively. 'They clamp down on bullying very quickly,' one boy reassured us.

School celebrates achievement. Badges for drama, art and cookery sewn on boys' sleeves, like cub scouts, when they have done well. Pupils also rewarded with golden tickets for 'collective amounts of really good behaviour'. Can be used to get to the front of lunch queue, double rations of break or a handful of sweets from head's study.

Mainly professional and business families from Surrey, 'but we have the complete spectrum'. Mixture of single and dual income families. About 10 from ethnic minorities. School welcomes diversity as it teaches the boys to respect different cultures. Thriving parents' association. Great sense of community.

Ten to 12 full bursaries a year. Some set aside for candidates who approach the school via the Royal National Children's Foundation; and in line with the school's Christian foundation, some are earmarked for the sons of people in full-time Christian work. School is keen on social mobility and is delighted to be able support a boy who could not otherwise afford to come here.

The pupils take huge pride in their school and in each other and the ones we met were happy, courteous and articulate. One member of staff described Aldro as 'a 100 mile an hour, Boys' Own paradise.' An outstanding prep, perfect for an energetic all-rounder.

Aldwickbury School

Wheathampstead Road, Harpenden, Hertfordshire AL5 1AD

Ages 4–13 **Pupils** 370 **Boarders** 50 flexi (from 10 years) **C of E**

Fees: Day £13,110 – £16,209 pa; Boarding + £31.50 – £38.50 per night

01582 713022
www.aldwickbury.org.uk

Headmaster: Since 2003, Vernon Hales BEd (50s). Educated at Langley Park Grammar School and Exeter University, where his education degree majored in PE. After a year in the state system, he started his prep school career at Papplewick before heading off to New Zealand, becoming deputy head in its then largest boarding prep school. Returned as deputy head and boarding housemaster at Elstree School, then joined Aldwickbury as the school's fourth head. Partnered through entire professional journey by wife Claire, also a trained teacher and now the school's head of marketing. Two sons educated at Aldwickbury, then The Leys.

Personable and relaxed; pleasingly jovial manner with the boys. When asked what he has improved during his tenure so far, he has trouble answering – 'I don't want to sound arrogant' – but parents are quick to praise his instant insistence on boys being called by their first names and snacks being offered at break-times – 'made me instantly popular,' he quips, but more importantly shows he knows how boys operate. 'I am a big fan,' one parent corroborated. 'I enjoy the sheer enthusiasm and care that the school shows.' Doesn't teach but supervises years 7 and 8 prep and is in the car park to welcome every morning. 'We try to be as available to parents as we can – it's important that we know the little things that matter to the boys in case they need support'. Parents appreciative: 'He clearly guides the ethos of the school with his calmly confident and very human approach, which percolates the whole place,' said one. 'The values and morals of the school definitely hark back to a bygone age, but they are delivered in a way that is relevant to today's world.'

Entrance: Boys join from a range of local nurseries in St Albans, Harpenden, Wheathampsted – staff go out and visit before joining to smooth the process. Twins are generally separated, following discussion with parents – Aldwickbury's reception classrooms are inter-connected so twins can peek at each other for reassurance. Three-form entry, no more than 16 to a class. Head is happy with the roll of around 380 – 'we fit well on the site'. A few spaces at the bottom of the school but otherwise full. Non-selective at 4+ but boys joining higher up the school are invited in for an informal assessment (English, maths, reading – not a test) with relevant year group staff to ensure they can cope with the curriculum. Means-tested bursaries available; no scholarships. Boys' sisters often at Wheathampsted House, St Albans High School for Girls Prep, St Hilda's.

Exit: A handful of boys leave for state system at end of year 6 but – unlike many other preps – the intention is to reduce in numbers slightly for years 7 and 8 to allow for more individual focus and positions of responsibility; 'more elbow room,' says head. St Albans is a key year 9 destination – 'good local school which ticks lots of boxes for our pupils' – Haileybury and Bedford also popular. St Columba's, Brighton, Stowe, Shrewsbury, Berkhamsted also considerations. Most want day or the opportunity to grow into boarding. Majority of academic scholarship candidates aim for St Albans; music, art, drama and all-rounders an even spread. Head invites in parents to discuss next steps; 'alternatives are politely suggested' to those aiming unrealistically high. Noted a parent, 'He believes that if your son needs excessive coaching to get into a particular secondary school, then that probably isn't the right school for him – not a message that every parent in Harpenden wants to hear.'

Remarks: Aldwickbury Mansion, a character Victorian house just a stone's throw up the hill from Harpenden's second high street in Southdown, became the school's home in 1948. Now surrounded by a collection of sympathetically designed more modern buildings as well as playing fields, an Astro and 25-metre indoor pool, this leafy 20-acre site makes for a friendly and well-functioning school campus of the ideal scale for prep school age children – big enough to stretch your legs in but small enough to know your way around. Planning application in for a new-build sports hall on-site.

Pre-prep has its own little world – a self-contained, purpose-built base secured with a large, squeaky gate. Three classes of 12 to 14 per year in reception, years 1 and 2. Pre-prep day is 8.30am-3.15pm, though 3pm finish for reception. Wraparound care morning and afternoon. Head of pre-prep welcomes all in the morning and answers questions to nip any misunderstandings in the bud, and reception parents have their own parents' evenings. Exempt from early years curriculum, children go at their own pace, some on a play-based regime. Each class has a teacher and dedicated teaching assistant. Large classrooms well suited to the age of the children and with plenty of storage (teachers' delight). Much recent investment in the pre-prep outdoor learning environment and adventure playground with outdoor areas differentiated by age stuffed with bikes, trikes etc for engaged play and fewer incidents. Little distinction in reception between learning time and playtime. Swimming from reception, all year round, plus drama and music taught by specialists. Instrumentalists on the rise from year 1, particularly piano and violin, though some take on cellos, guitars, drums; later woodwind and brass. French from year 1 with popular annual Languages Day, focusing on pupils' mother tongues. Year 2s use school art room, DT studio and library and have clubs for choir, recorders, drama, football, tennis, eco. Regular Celebrations of Learning showcase children's work for the admiration of parents and family.

Junior department for years 3 and 4 has a year per floor in three classrooms. Class teacher for all subjects, bar specialist ICT, art, DT, music and drama in dedicated rooms. 'They're taught to walk sensibly between lessons by the teacher,' explains head. 'Then in years 5 and 6 they know how to do it on their own and take all the relevant equipment with them.' Fifteen to 18 per class, which our guides judged just right – 'You don't want too many but enough that you can choose your friends'. Good point.

Subject classrooms for seniors (years 5 to 8). Tasters in Spanish and German added to the mix in year 5 and Latin from year 6. Individual needs met in mixed ability classes until end of year 5 and plenty of small group work; teaching assistants dotted around the timetable and gappers help with reading, as do year 8 boys who support year 5s and 6s through the Reading Lab programme (those who have benefited from help are often keenest to repay later). Setting and streaming introduced from year 6, with two or three classes and a scholarship class in year 8. SEN all in a day's work – full provision within the classroom and also one-to-one, ranging from a few weeks to constant. 'The right support helps them to flourish but we might find a passion as a trumpeter, or an artist, to give them self-esteem,' says head. Early discussions with parents of strugglers.

Clocktower clock recently stopped ticking and needed repair, so head seized the moment to refurb the upper floor of main school building to create a new music room, now hanging with computers for Mixcraft and traditional instruments. Whole of year 3 learn the violin and all in year 4 and 5 may try out a brass instrument with the aim of keeping up the flow of trumpeters and euphonium (really) players. Practice rooms well used for individual lessons with visiting peris. Ambitions of dynamic music teacher with choral background being realised – 14 music ensembles, from choir and orchestra to school rock and samba bands, some for all-comers, some auditioned. 'I don't expect them to be able to play a Mozart piano concerto when they leave here,' he says rationally, 'but I do want them to be able to tell me why they do or don't like it.'

DT studio well-equipped – strict rules re which year groups are entrusted with which tools (hacksaws from year 3). Art department on two floors – year 5s intently recreating Gaudi's mosaics when we visited – concentration etched on young faces. At least an hour of art on the timetable every week and popular art club. New kiln.

Hall named for a former headmaster with raked seating, the venue for assemblies for years 3 to 8 and chapel on Friday afternoons, school plays – this year the Wizard of Oz. Auditions open to all, and also opportunities for essential behind-the-scenes involvement. Well-used library stocked with 'every book you could possibly think of,' confirmed our guide sagely. Large dining hall – pre-prep eat lunch first, followed by years 3 and 4, and 5 to 8. Rotating menu, now with the popular introduction of soup in the winter. 'Breakfast and supper are the best' – unlimited eggs, bacon, sausages, toast for the largest of appetites.

'Sport' was the quick reply when our guides were asked the best thing about school. Football, rugby, hockey, basketball in winter; cricket, athletics, volleyball, tennis, swimming in summer. Specialist teaching twice weekly from year 1 and boys from year 3 up have a daily games lesson (what a lot of boys crave – clever). School ski teams and squads compete in English Schools events and around 90 boys involved in the school's ski programme. Fencing now major with 70 or 80 boys regularly en garde (old boy in national team). Some 12 to 15 teams from years 5 to 8 regularly represent the school in Wednesday fixtures. Everybody in years 3 and 4 plays for the school; more selective higher up but by the end of term all who want to have played. Boys not in teams may opt for photography, climbing or sailing. Cyclo-cross added recently. Two nights a week after supper in summer boys may play on the nine-hole par 3 course which surrounds the school.

Colours system recently overhauled – boys awarded Half, Full or Headmaster's Colours when they have earned enough Wheatsheafs, which are awarded for notable deeds in any areas of school life including sports, arts, academics and citizenship. Prize-giving in a marquee at the end of term kept under the hour – 'it's important that every boy in the school is there and that's as long as it is reasonable to expect the youngest to engage,' says head.

Huge choice of clubs and activities – 'busy boys are happy boys,' says head. Chess, tech club, general knowledge, debating, skiing and fencing top the bill. School makes full use of being on the capital's doorstep, with trips to art galleries and theatres. Curriculum-related trips all year round with the more fun visits saved until the end. Annual ski trip run by head of maths, year 7 to France, year 8 football tour to (exotic) Eastbourne, year 4 camping on-site. Year 7s throw themselves into a two-day on-site camp as part of their leadership programme which also comprises team events such as crossing the river blindfold and talks from professionals about leadership in later life. 'In seven years I've never had any of my three boys not wanting to go to school,' declared a parent. 'I put that down to the stimulating environment they find themselves in. That can be in the academic work or in the extracurricular activities, that are legion and legendary – there is something for everyone to grab and enjoy and the breadth is quite remarkable. In sports, the desire to win is always finely balanced with the Corinthian spirit of gentlemanliness and amateurism.'

World of Work talks for years 7 and 8 – doctors, airline pilots etc – and informative parent talks throughout the year too, recently 'why 13+ is better than 11+' for those with children in years 5 and 6. Great loyalty to 'sections' (houses) – Highlands, Midlands, Uplands, Lowlands. Competitions ranging from the sporty (eg football) to the silly (eg foam rocket launching and 'tunnelball' – passing the ball through a tunnel of everyone's legs). Plus points for good work and behaviour. Sanctions not really a thing here. 'Boys want to please,' says head; 'you tell them off and you move on.'

A day school run along boarding school lines, but no full boarders currently or recently. Flexi boarding best suits local families – a good chance for boys heading off to senior day schools to experience boarding, or a run-in for those boarding full-time from year 9. Boarding starts at year 5, with taster nights beforehand. Thirty beds with 50 boys currently booked in to board once a week. 'Boarding is really fun – you can stay when you want,' grinning boarders told us. Popularity of the boarding week night tends to be dictated by the activity laid on after supper – Superhero Night and Nerf Night fully booked. A fun sleepover in reality. Matron is on hand in the bright and welcoming boarders' house, along with two New World gappers. Lounge has TV and Wii; several large and comfy four- to seven-bed rooms – bring your own own duvet or sleeping bag. Boarders usually sleep in the same bed whenever they stay. Large windows with lovely views across the school fields and woods, to which boarders have privileged access.

Day boys may join boarders for breakfast and supper for a small cost – handy for commuting parents. All boys from year 5 up may stay after school for prep and there is an after-school club for pupils of any age which runs until supper time at 5.50pm. Post-supper activity until 7.30pm.

A local school – half the boys in the school have the same home postcode, within a 20-minute drive. School buses not needed – mum or dad's taxi does the job; carpools are common. Parents 'invested in and engaged with their children's education,' says head. Accountants and other professionals, many with offices in London thanks to easy commuting and family-friendly semi-rural environs. School recently moved breakfast forward 10 minutes to 7.30am to help parents make the 7.50 to St Pancras. A sociable bunch, by all accounts, many are committed members of the Aldwickbury Friends Association – 'a real force for good,' says head – committee meetings 'fun'; parties 'late and loud'. Money raised through events and social occasions split between charity and school wish list purchases, eg adventure playground equipment – school presents ideas but AFA also suggests in line with its remit to 'raise friends and make memories'.

Certainly, those lucky enough to be educated here will look back on a golden childhood few today experience. A warm, well thought-out school, genuinely for and about boys, producing good eggs of the modern variety.

Amesbury

Hazel Grove, Hindhead, Surrey GU26 6BL

Ages 2–13 **Pupils** 359 **Boarders** Taster boarding years 5–8 **C of E**

Fees: £10,395 – £15,915 pa

01428 604322
www.amesburyschool.co.uk

Head: Since September 2018, Sheina Wright, previously deputy head at Guildford High Junior School. English QTS degree from UWE Bristol; taught history at St Albans High junior before joining Guildford High Junior in 2003 where she has been head of year, head of English and director of studies. She and her partner, Adrian, have a son, Benji. The family enjoy travelling (most recently to Japan, Vietnam and Cambodia) and keeping active – running (with Benji as coach) and yoga are important pursuits, she is a sports fan and an 'avid' Spurs supporter.

Entrance: Through registration plus visit – not a formal assessment but the opportunity for child and school to get acquainted, pupils accepted until spaces filled. Scholarships (academic, tennis and expressive arts) available years 3 to 7 for those 'head and shoulders above other very talented children'; worth applying for, with awards worth up to 50 per cent of the fees.

Nursery flexibility a given, with full days for those who need them (complete with freshly cooked hot meals, served in

A

nursery classrooms; reception eat in dining hall, served like year 1 and 2 pupils at the table) and though school will suggest at least two consecutive sessions a week, there's no minimum nursery stay, with staff on hand to plug gaps at relatively short notice if there's a sudden bulge in numbers, now recovering after a lean patch. Will not adopt government suggestions to ease staffing ratios but up entry qualifications by way of compensation. 'Stupid,' says nursery head. 'It doesn't matter how well qualified you are, you're still only one person.'

Exit: Fall out after year 6 no longer an issue, says school, with more girls staying on. Pupils, in no doubt as to the benefits, all happily cited kudos-factor of being top in the pecking order. Seaford College most popular destination in 2018 followed by Cranleigh, Charterhouse, Canford, Lord Wandsworth and Bryanston.

Remarks: One of a cluster of preps in this well-to-do area of Surrey, now more primrose path than rat run following opening of Hindhead tunnel – 'Other schools build a new sports hall, we spend millions on an underpass' – school is considered a breath of fresh air by its supporters, who extol approach as trad with a twist.

On the surface, it oozes convention, second occupants of Lutyens' only purpose-built school, having moved here in 1917 from Bickley in Kent (was originally founded in 1870 in Redhill) to swap air raids for fresh air. Designed like a scaled down Hollywood set, main building features windows at two-thirds height, with a baby grand entrance and chapel, added 1938, which potentially reduces a wrath-filled God to a Wendy house-sized deity – a much more comforting notion to the young. Even the reception signs, so tiny that this reviewer walked past them twice, may have been boil-washed one too many times.

Some areas, a bit factory second here and there on date of visit, have been improved with considerable smartening up: blue-canopied entrances on more modern buildings, including super new visual and performing arts centre, an attractive and well-equipped example of the genre, as well as impressive giant, echoing sports hall – a yodeller's dream – a new dance studio, refurbished science department and general pepping up of floor surfaces and corridors.

Also notable for exceptional cleanliness. Wherever we went, a mop or broom was sure to be in attendance close by. Much appreciated cleaning team was particularly busy in recently (and handsomely) refurbished separate nursery/reception building – all whiteness and brightness, with space for big, pristine, set piece indoor toys, recently enhanced with modish free flow into secure outside area (complete with inevitable free flow mud), all presided over by caring, multi-tasking staff (capable of spotting child in need of TLC while extolling multiple uses of home-made Play-doh).

While parents appreciate surroundings, heading praise list (which is extensive) is school's philosophy – 'holistic,' said one. 'They balance the academic side with lots of other things so that all the children can find a way of expressing themselves.' Approach can manifest itself in an absence of surface polish: hair that little bit longer than the norm; uniform (traditional skirts for girls, boys in viyella shirts with dress down brown guernseys for all – 'only itchy with short sleeves,' said plucky pupil) occasionally lacking in parade gloss finish; productions and matches feature all comers.

We'd written originally that these were in consequence 'a tad rougher round the edges' based on parent feedback. 'Inaccurate' says school. 'We are rougher round the edges on a day to day basis, hair is sometimes longer. However, we are neurotic about getting it absolutely right on match days.' Ditto chapel choir and school plays, which are 'super professional.' The trick 'is to be more relaxed until the moment when it matters and then we are absolutely spot on.'

There's also convention where it matters – 'very strict on how they speak to the teachers, so not liberal in that respect,' said a parent and no shortage of competition. But while two houses, carefully matched for ability, are expected to slug it out for supremacy during the year, what shines through is wrap-round encouragement for everyone, not just the most able, with the slightest flicker of talent breathed into a living flame.

Upbeat approach embraces learning needs, catering for rather more than advertised. One parent who packed tissues before meeting teachers, expecting to discuss behaviour issues, ended up being overwhelmed by praise. Dyslexia, official speciality, had own separate centre until a few years ago. A new head of learning support, also qualified to carry out assessments, has now been appointed and most support is now provided in class. Considerable flexibility, however. 'If pupils need somebody physically sitting alongside them in the lesson to support them, that's what we'll do – focus is not on one size fits all: it's the right programme for the right child,' says head of English.

Sets the tone for excellent pastoral care, in and out of lesson time, from twinkly matron, popular with the walking wounded and others – 'we have our regulars' – to staff mingling with pupils for 'usually good and never awful' lunches in delightful blue-painted dining hall, dominated by bison's head (which lends its name to major house trophy, though history and significance remain an apparent mystery to all).

Register ensures that everyone eats (older pupils can choose when) though latecomers have to negotiate bottlenecks either side of diddy double doors as two-way queues of well-nourished, 21st century children jostle for supremacy, accompanied by fairly vigorous shoving by all.

It's the only sign of anything other than cordial pupil relationships, with friendships, seen as a huge strength, crossing between year groups, welcome sense of 'freedom to talk,' said pupil and little in the way of conflict. One pupil who had experienced bullying in previous school felt 'there's just not the space for bullies. If you did it, you'd find yourself on your own.' Bonds strengthened by taster boarding week for everyone in years 5 to 8, groups of 10 boys or girls at a time – Mallory Towers lite, big on the hot chocolate with marshmallows element.

Academically, it's emphatically not a hothouse, though parents feel that standards are rising across the board, helped by emphasis on focus group teaching and calm but engaging class lessons notable for levels of discussion (lots of confident participation through the age ranges, reception children working on 'ay' sounds as a group; year 3 children engaged in quick fire mental maths and a school-wide absence of furrowed brows).

English and maths are excellent, remaining subjects being brought into line, recent staff additions generally reckoned to be plugging previous gaps (Latin and French now much improved, felt one mother). Humanities, headed by hugely popular teacher (has starring role in whole school charity remake of Pixie Lott hit, worth three minutes of anyone's time on Youtube) who is also very dashing, notable for dynamic text book light, tech-heavy approach to geography (we enjoyed contrast with low tech lunchtime message system – communicated in chalk, on a blackboard). Years 7 and 8 now do the Prep School Baccalaureate rather than common entrance.

Plenty of extras on offer in the form of clubs, too, and if more pupils hadn't taken up Mandarin, it was only, they said, because there was so much else going on, with many ecstatic about performing arts, much open to all and sweeping plentiful numbers of boys as well as girls into their orbit.

Music embraces everything from formal chapel choir to semi-secret bands formed each year, strutting stuff at annual concert. There's plentiful dance and drama including ambitious takes on Shakespeare (a swinging 60s Comedy of Errors and

1920s gangland style Hamlet amongst them) while inaugural action-packed arts week successful but so energy and resource sapping, hoovering up just about everyone, staff and pupils, into its maw, that likely to become every other year wonder.

While arts feature large in pupils' career horizons, sports almost as popular. Aspirations and confidence stem, think pupils, from school's desire to 'want you to like sport.' Taken seriously ('steely' is description of sports teams in prospectus), as so it should be, with four grass pitches, one Astroturf and 'very fancy' sports hall, foyer decorated with motivational images of assorted sports, to do them in. No swimming pool and wouldn't be on pupils' wish list in any case. 'It would get cold and crowded and you'd want to get out,' said one, sensibly. Tennis, a big thing (with full time professional), is now offered from nursery, two ping pong tables installed primarily for year 7s and 8s 'and other years when they're away or not using them' also hitting the spot. But, just as school prizes aren't just awarded to 'the obvious people but the ones with the right attitude,' say pupils, team selection favours the also rans as well as the stars. It's a brave strategy, given level of local opposition, main rival prompting something close to pupil bloodlust when you quiz them.

All in all, adds up to an atmosphere that substantiates the blurb. Many a school may claim to be 'academically rigorous'. Not all would also make such a virtue out of also being 'relaxed' (prospectus wording). This one does. Parents in search of an education which will deliver confident children who see their futures in terms of unlimited options rather than curtailed ambitions – 'I'd like to be an international sportsman, I just don't know which sport yet,' said one – would be well advised to pay a visit.

Anglo European School

Willow Green, Ingatestone, Essex CM4 0DJ

Ages 11–18 **Pupils** 1,461 **Sixth form** 332

01277 354018
www.aesessex.co.uk

Co-headteachers: Since 2005, David Barrs MA BEd Cert Ed NPQH (60s); educated at London and Bristol Universities and St Paul's College, Cheltenham. Taught in Basildon and Saffron Walden; deputy head for over 12 years before he became co-head in 2005. He says co-headship is a good role model for students – reaching compromise, having two people collaborating at high levels of leadership towards a common goal to create better solutions, and having someone with whom to consult. He is passionate about the United Nations and politics generally and is committed to making students 'good world citizens', believing that the IB delivers an ideal breadth of education.

Joined as co-head in 2015 by Jody Gee BA, PGCE, NPQH (40s) previously deputy (since 2007). Educated at Shenfield High then taught at Newport Free Grammar School, Eirias High School in Gwynedd and the Plume School in Maldon, where she was head of English, then assistant head teacher. She has a particular interest in teaching and learning, bringing new pedagogy to improve learning experience for students.

Both heads continue to do some teaching (Mr Barrs teaches geography and citizenship, Mrs Gee teaches English). Parents can, and do, speak to either head, and are expected to consult whichever is available.

Academic matters: The first state school to take up the IB in 1977 when Essex saw itself as 'a European facing county' and was keen to build up European links and develop language teaching; now one of only 40 IB state schools. By the 1990s this European ethos had extended to include students from all over the world, and it was one of the first state schools to offer the Mandarin Excellence Programme. It was also the first school in the UK to offer the IB career-related programme, with more vocational applied courses. An international education is the bedrock of Anglo European with the European flag on the school logo, signs in several languages, all students learning languages right through to the sixth form. There are annual study visits abroad and exchanges available for all students, school partnership programmes with overseas schools, and school places offered to students with an international background or a second language.

Two languages compulsory up to GCSE (and eight Mandarin lessons a week for those opting for MEP). Setting in maths from January of year 7 based on KS2 Sats results, CATS and internal testing, and in other subjects from year 8, but also differentiation in class with higher targets set for academically more able pupils. All six official UN languages taught (Arabic, Chinese, English, French, Spanish, Russian) as well German, Italian and Japanese. Possibility to take mother tongue language GCSE early. Generous range of GCSEs on top of core subjects includes textiles, citizenship, drama, food technology, music – creative subjects valued. One parent said that 'the difference in lesson quality is stunning' from her child's previous school.

Classrooms have interactive whiteboards, and some suites of computers. No iPads, and library airy but old fashioned (though the school points out that they have 14,000 books and 30 computers). Evidence of good marking and evaluation schemes to ensure pupils learn from each other and from their own mistakes; they are encouraged to respond to teachers' comments. Emphasis on improvement rather than grade as seen in 0.25 value added Progress 8 score, meaning students from Anglo European achieve a quarter of a grade better than expected in GCSE. In 2018, 85 per cent of students got 9-4 in both English and maths GCSE, and 78 per cent got 9-4 in a language GCSE, bucking the national trend of diminishing numbers taking languages.

The sixth form is a school highlight. Nearly 30 per cent of students take IB diploma, some seven per cent the IB career-related programme, and around 60 per cent choose A levels (some add on IB courses to get more UCAS points). The fundamental principle, according to co-heads, is the resulting breadth of study. Parents and students praised director of sixth form (a city trader in his previous life) who makes sure that students match the courses they are taking with their aspirations and interests. The flexibility and diverse range of subjects offered is extraordinary given that, as a state school, cash is in short supply. On top of solid core of subjects, there is a wide range of languages, psychology, drama, politics, travel and tourism, business studies, textiles, music, sciences. They all study citizenship (voting, opening a bank account, politics, drug education, how to change a car tyre – everything to help meet adulthood well prepared); some take the challenge of the EPQ; and all do the IBs creativity, activity and service (CAS) programme, whether they are doing A levels or IB, plus work experience. In 2018, IB points averaged of 34 out of 45 (two pupils achieved 43), and average pass rate of C for A levels, with 17 per cent A*/A grades and 42 per cent A*-B.

Parents and pupils are particularly grateful to be given the option, in some cases, of completing their sixth form study in three years rather than usual two. Ideal if students come from abroad into year 11 not ready to take GCSEs but not wanting to go back to year 10 for the whole two year GCSE curriculum. One parent was very grateful that her child could change from sciences to English after predicted results. Parents spoke of children 'taking their books on holiday' and 'wanting to go to school', and said 'independent learning encouraged'.

The breadth of learning and international emphasis is seen also in the educational visits – whole of year 7 goes to an activity centre in France, year 8-10 students go on language exchanges to France, Germany, China, Italy, Japan or Spain, depending on the language they are learning, and year 11s have a geography field trip. Exchanges and work experience abroad in sixth form (France, China, Germany, Spain) in addition to optional visits to Geneva and Lesotho. Whilst not compulsory, more than half pupils go on a school visit.

More able students given extra challenges and leadership roles. Learning support overseen by SENCo and six teaching assistants (no special needs teacher and interestingly only two per cent on the SEN register). EAL very much part of the school teaching since this applies to nearly half the pupils, and these are given extra lessons by specialist EAL teacher and assistants until they have caught up. After-school study club in the library provides quiet and supervision in a 'structured environment not always possible at home'. It also allows students access to resources for projects.

Parents said that 'teachers have classes under control'. One parent specifically mentioned that 'lesson cover works so all lessons happen', and 'teachers seem to stay on so there is continuity for our kids'. We were also told that 'homework gets set regularly and appropriately' and students said that it was 'about right', too.

Games, options, the arts: Plenty of playing fields, and two gyms. Rugby, football, cricket, tennis, netball, rounders etc, with fixtures against other Essex schools. Inside – trampoline, weights, table tennis, dance, self-defence. Swimming at local centre (school pool out of action). Not the most sporty of schools but runs clubs during break times, since many have long journeys home. Students said that girls' teams treated just as seriously as boys' teams; netball particularly strong. Sixth formers who are encouraged to take leadership roles, initiating activities and organising clubs (anime, signing, coding, art history, sports). Elite Performer Programme supports a handful of students who are exceptional in their chosen activities (dance, football, acting etc). Around 50 students doing DofE.

Drama popular, LAMDA exams taken at school as well as drama GCSE and A level. Big annual production with students also involved in lighting, set design and costumes and we saw some rather wonderful yellow paper wigs created for the production of Hairspray. Pupils excited about the Battle of the Bands and with concert band, sixth form band, staff band and several rock groups, we can imagine it is a lively event. Students see Eisteddfod festival of literature, music and drama as an in-house talent show. Summer Arts Festival a chance for students to display work done in the year. Music lab for composing (Mac books for music editing); all pupils encouraged to learn an instrument when they first join, such as guitar, ukulele, piano.

Art rooms open to all, textile room, technology room, design studio, 3D laser printer, computer aided design. We saw 'items of clothing based on a musical instrument' and photography exhibits.

World Challenge, Model UN (organised by sixth formers as part of their service requirement), visits to Downing Street and UN in Geneva. Students encouraged to take an interest in national and international politics. Work experience compulsory in year 10, and possible in the sixth form – some abroad. Enterprise Day a big event for year 9 – make an ethical business in a day and present it, Dragons' Den style.

Background and atmosphere: Set on the outskirts of a pretty village surrounded by fields and bordered by the A12. Established in 1973, it still feels very much like a 1970s school – same dark wood floors, metal framed windows, two portacabins, low ceilinged dining hall. Newer extensions include the maths and science block. A well used old building with patches at the elbows, but not unloved or unkempt in the least. There is art all over the walls – 'the school is our canvas,' according to sixth form art students. Sixth form block includes study areas and canteen. Generally a really tidy school with lockers all over and no coats strewn around the day we visited. No graffiti, no mess, no muddle. Orderly school with good systems that mean there is no pushing or shoving for lunch or down the corridors. Though the lunch menu certainly gave no reason for rushing – and whilst the school has recently acquired Healthy School status, baked beans were the only vegetable we saw, together with carbs – pasta, bacon baps, baked potato, panini. Plenty of pupils bring their own lunch.

Unexciting playgrounds, highlight being a new hillock for kids to lie out on (and a new science garden). Mostly flat and open, and when we asked about smoking and bullying, pupils said there was none and that anyway there was nowhere to hide or be hidden.

Pastoral care, well-being and discipline: Student services office very central, open and well used – 'it is where we go if we have lost property, need help, want to see a counsellor or are worried about anything'. Mental well-being including 'social anxiety' awareness, and pupils spoke about being able to email any teacher at any time or 'go to any teacher to be heard'.

Students told us that 'difference is celebrated here' and parents spoke about the sense of acceptance and even welcoming of difference at AES. Pupils said there was 'teasing but no bullying' and that 'everyone feels safe here – we look out for each other'. They explained the mentoring system between year groups, called 'helping hands'. System of prefects also helpful – we saw one new pupils rush up to a prefect to ask where the nearest toilets were. 'If tensions arise, other students step in to quell it,' according to pupils. Heads said that they rarely if ever have to exclude, but work hard to find the right way to teach individuals. Teaching aimed to be 'personal and personable', with sharing, conversing and making sure students 'have the right to a voice and to be heard'. Parents said students 'are encouraged to be responsible – for their work and for themselves'.

Students treated as individuals and parents said, 'the school is respectful to the kids and the kids are respectful in return'. They said that issues raised by parents were 'tackled immediately by staff'.

Pupils and parents: Nearly half of students currently EAL, from 35 different nationalities; comprehensive intake, covering the whole of Essex, Suffolk and Herts and also from London boroughs of Hackney, Islington, Newham and Redbridge (30 minute train journey from Liverpool Street).

A wide socio-economic mix as parents chose to send their children to a school where 'they will meet and get to feel comfortable with a whole swathe of humanity'. Parents said that their children were welcomed even if they joined mid-year (as many do if from abroad). 'They are not judgemental but interested in different nationalities and welcoming.' Parents involved in Anglo European School Association, mostly fundraising at the moment, but also a mouthpiece for parents' ideas or concerns.

Students come on foot, by bicycle, car, bus or train, the latter the school's 'life-blood'.

Entrance: Priority to pupils from three local feeder (CofE) primary schools (usually some 50-60 pupils), then siblings. Remaining pupils with an international aspect to their family life – having lived or come from abroad, mixed nationality parents, with ability to communicate in another language and a degree of 'cultural engagement' as well as a willingness to become involved with what the school offers.

Two very interesting aspects for students applying from overseas is that they do not need an address in the UK before applying for a place at Anglo European, and the very rare three year sixth form course for those joining in year 11 from abroad.

Places come up mid-year as families move abroad and often at short notice, though students felt that they needed better induction systems for those not joining in year 7. School says that new students meet with the pastoral manager every day and given a 'buddy' to shadow for the first two weeks.

Exit: Around 40 per cent leaves after GCSEs for local colleges and other sixth forms (more vocational courses, agricultural colleges and in order to attend courses not available at AES). Some 85 per cent of sixth formers to university, around 35 per cent Russell Group. One to Oxford in 2018, two medics and two vets. Other destinations included civil engineering at Coventry, English at Warwick, architecture at UCL and musical theatre at Guildford School of Acting. One each to Segovia, Helsinki and Amsterdam.

Careers advice also for students not going to university (worryingly not enough of this at some schools we visit) with enterprise education lead who helps find work experience placements and jobs.

Money matters: Some fundraising by Anglo European School Association and money raised by students for charity and the school's benefit. Otherwise, all parents frustrated by the need for more state funding for basic needs.

Remarks: Really dedicated teachers go beyond the call of duty to extend and provide a broad education. Parents and pupils aware that the school is accommodating all their various needs – 'my child was hospitalised for a while, so the school sent her work and gave her extra support when she returned', 'my child needed to change her courses completely and the school allowed that'. If you can look beyond some of the older buildings, you will find a kind environment, caring teachers and an education in how to be an independent, internationally minded adult.

Ardingly College

Linked with Ardingly College Prep School

College Road, Ardingly, Haywards Heath, West Sussex RH17 6SQ

Ages 13–18 **Pupils** 586 **Sixth form** 261 **Boarders** 295 full or flexi
C of E

Fees: Day £22,995 – £23,610; Boarding £33,405 – £34,410 pa

01444 893000
www.ardingly.com

Headmaster: Since 2014, Ben Figgis MA (Cantab), married to Joanna. Previously deputy head at Oakham, and was history teacher, housemaster and head of boarding at Abingdon. Before taking up teaching had a life in media, which he left after concerns about the ethical compromises involved in newsgathering. Keen to provide pupils with a modern education, and a world view. Enrichment is a word which comes up a lot – an interest and excitement in subjects is as important as achieving a particular grade.

Pupils are very enthusiastic about the head and say he's 'balanced'. Described by a parent as 'approachable'; she said her children all really like him.

Academic matters: Record-breaking GCSE results in 2018 with 75 per cent A*-A/9-7 grades. Subjects are almost uniformly excellent, with sciences and maths being popular high performers, and humanities also doing very well.

IB points a very good 38 per pupil. A levels: 46 per cent A*/A, 80 per cent A*-B in 2018. The international nature of the sixth form means a good showing in MFLs such as Chinese, Russian and German; but performance is less strong in other areas. A reasonable list of subjects on offer, although one parent said she would like to see the inclusion of some less purely academic subjects, such as sociology.

High take up of IB in this internationally minded school (40 per cent): they're in the top 10 IB schools in the UK, and very enthusiastic about it. The IB way of learning and thinking is here viewed as so beneficial that it has been adopted for A level pupils, who also study the IB core of extended essay, theory of knowledge, and action and service. A parent described her daughter as 'a bit miffed' at the extra written work, but can see the benefits of the community service and mindfulness elements.

There are plans to develop science and technology to enhance pupils' preparation for undergraduate study – computer science is now on the timetable, and the head is particularly keen to make sure science options, usually dominated by boys, are appealing to girls.

Ardingly is keen to promote independent learning and one of the parents we spoke to said this was one of her favourite things about the school: she praised their promotion of independent research, thinking outside the box and examining information with a critical eye. 'It sparks their interest', she said. The skills for independent learning start in year 9 with iMind which includes a personal project on any chosen subject – one group of pupils built a solar car which was entered for 3,000 km World Solar Challenge across Australia. Didn't complete the course but was a first for a school in Europe.

Pupils here are lively and interested in what they're doing. We joined an English lesson on The Importance of Being Earnest, and were impressed by an energetic teacher, and pupils' interested and thoughtful approach. A parent commented that she loved the 'relaxed open relationship with teachers', and this was evidently the case.

Learning support good for those with mild disorders. We spoke to a parent whose daughter has mild dyslexia, and whose LS with maths and English helped her get the grades she needed at GCSE. Pupils need to be able to cope on their own at A level.

Games, options, the arts: Grounds are extensive and gorgeous – it is succulently green all around. One of our guides glanced with familiar affection across the fields: one of them, the scene of a recent victory, had become his favourite place at school.

Strong sports department with county and national winners. Pupils were keen to point out that the glory is not exclusively for high performers: pupils in first XI all the way down to the sixth XI go on school tours, and receive school awards, although a parent said she felt that the greatest focus was on the senior A and B teams. A bit boy-heavy in emphasis, said a mum, with the girls only really excelling in hockey; but the head points out the same resources are put into girls' and boys' sports and girls are excelling in football as well as hockey, with national representation in both sports.

Monday activities include minor sports such as horse riding, and sailing and an ever-changing variety of other activities, from beekeeping and book binding to the interestingly named

Ardinglay (it's a chicken club). DofE: lots do silver, and a few gold. It's not cliquey – the head relishes the fact that footballers about to play in the Boodles cup opted to spend the morning at the Ardingly national Shakespeare conference. You can choose to be very busy indeed; but pupils assured us that not everyone does, and that's fine too.

CCF is not popular here, to the chagrin of one of our guides, who clearly has a wonderful time. 'I think the parades put people off,' she said wistfully, 'but it's so much fun. There's a section attack on the headmaster's field this afternoon,' she added enthusiastically, as a cannon was wheeled into the quad.

Large number of instrumental lessons and ensembles; in particular the 70-strong flourishing chapel choir which sings at cathedrals at home and abroad – and is a good outlet for exam stress. A vocal ensemble and the London Philharmonic visit to coach and inspire, and Ardingly hosts a concert series which stars national and international musicians.

Drama is popular, particularly with boys, to the delight of the head, who feels that creative art is too often the preserve of girls. Pupils perform at the Edinburgh fringe and home grown ArtsFest each year (a post-exam joy here), fun even for those not into drama, who do half day workshops on anything from making short films to mask mimes.

Superb art department with a gallery packed with amazing work – we could happily have spent hours here appreciating the extraordinary creative work on view, showing that art students at Ardingly see life from all sorts of interesting angles, from butterfly dresses to a view inside a body which almost seemed to pulsate. There's a free range element to the GCSE, A level and IB art curricula, with students choosing which areas they wish to pursue; and you can see how much this freedom is appreciated by the quality of the work. Pupils can even have lessons from the sculptor in residence.

Boarding: Feels a bit like a university campus, with boarding houses reached by a path through a tranquil bluebell-lined woodland glade. Boarding houses are modern purpose-built blocks, decorated in house colours. Corridor walls covered in photos chosen by boarders, organised by year, up to lower sixth on the top floor. Very strong house feeling – all must compete in cross-country run, and apparently even reluctant runners are happy to compete for their house. A map of the world decorated with flags and photos shows where each boarder comes from in this truly cosmopolitan school; and there's a list of names of older students from whom youngsters can seek academic help. There's a teacher on duty every night too, but one boy said that older pupils can often help better – they explain things in a different way.

Parents of boarders were full of praise: one said all her children wanted to board, and really enjoy it. The boarding master responds promptly to emails, and she likes the easy mix between boarders and day pupils.

Rooms for two to four younger boarders, with singles for older pupils. A housemaster admitted rooms are on the spartan side, being limited to bunks, desks and wardrobes; but said he doesn't want pupils lingering in bedrooms: they are for sleeping and studying, and the rest of time should be spent in the common room: spacious, squashy leather sofas, TV, pool, table football, the Times and Telegraph. Girls' houses recently refurbished. Brew rooms (kitchens) on each corridor, and one equipped with oven for more serious culinary matters (used under supervision). Lower sixth supervise youngsters' studying and bedtime rituals, studying supervision being much preferable, said one of our guides, with small shudder at the thought of bedtime duty (they are given advice about how to manage this).

Activities and sports on Saturday – recently a night of cowboy fun complete with hired rodeo bull; the head of boarding was moving with due care for bruises. Sundays for relaxation (gym and pool are open), with a trip out every three weeks. There's a tremendously popular Sunday shuttle to Sainsbury's, with each year group getting £50 for ingredients: serious cooking follows. No making their own breakfast, though: kitchens are locked to ensure pupils go to the dining hall for a proper breakfast – 'no surviving on just toast until lunchtime.' Each floor has a disabled loo and lift access.

Around half of boarders are overseas students, including expats, so there's no dominant country and no general exodus at weekends. Every Wednesday the blog is updated to communicate boarders' latest doings to parents.

Upper sixth have their own boarding house – like Premier Inn, suggested a member of staff; there is some similarity, though we've never seen a Premier Inn in such a lovely setting; or with such a nice gym. Super en suite study bedrooms, kitchens, huge common room, which is divided at 10pm between boys and girls, and opens at 7am. There's even a bar (two beers or two wines limit) but not many choose to drink. Encouraged to do own laundry – some actually do.

Background and atmosphere: One parent chose the school because the children who go there seem so 'normal', and for the strong sense of community. There's no held breath tension in the corridors here: pupils are relaxed and happy, with an outward looking politeness (pupils enquired after reviewer's journey etc – it doesn't often happen). It's not a leap to your feet school, but there was a genuine friendliness in the courtesy and smiles we encountered on our tour.

Charming red-brick buildings form the older parts of the school. Modern and rather nondescript buildings house the music and boarding houses, but the green surrounds offer ample distracting beauty. One of the favourite places of our guides was the terrace, with its stunning views over the Sussex countryside; just below lies the head's garden, viewed longingly by both pupils and the head of prep – it's clearly Eden here.

This Woodard school was originally for the children of clergy; and it is no surprise that there is a clear religious structure here, with a weekly communion service in the chapel for all (including non-believers and other faiths). High church with bells and smells, and what one parent called 'some obscure hymns'. The parents we spoke to liked the weekly service, one saying she felt it was important for children to develop the ability to sit still, be silent and respectful: 'you can hear a pin drop,' she said approvingly. The head believes there's a value in exposing pupils to chapel, but there is no expectation of them adopting Christianity – 'pupils need to feel comfortable and welcome.' Notably, divinity is joined by philosophy in the curriculum, and in the latest edition of Logos, the school magazine, there are articles on the Bible and feminism, and whether the Christian tradition ever treated women with respect. The Sophos philosophical debating club regularly debates pupil chosen topics such as life after death. This is not a school for unquestioning acceptance, and this critical eye extends to its founding Christian ethos.

Pastoral care, well-being and discipline: Pastoral care is 'outstanding,' said one parent; 'paramount,' said another, who said the ability to cater well for each child's individual needs is the best thing about the school. What's more, 'they take on difficult kids from other schools and bring them into line.'

Eudaimonia, not a rare disease, but 'human flourishing' à la Aristotle (PHSE to the rest of us) is part of the curriculum throughout senior school. Encompasses the usual sex, drugs and internet warnings; but also friendship, positive thinking and the wonder of every individual.

Firm line on bullying: pupils are encouraged to whistleblow, and expulsions will follow if the situation's unresolvable, say pupils, who also commented on some expulsions a few years ago for smoking dope, which they completely supported – 'we wouldn't have wanted them here,' they said in shocked voices.

The head has expelled a pupil for being rude and disrespectful to a member of the catering staff. But he seems likely to understand that children experiment and less likely to damn them for doing so: those who come clean about offences and promise not to reoffend are likely to have a second chance.

Pupils meet their personal tutor fortnightly to ensure individual needs are being met – for example in timetables or teaching methods. However, the head also has a strong belief in the values of service and community, and is wary of growing expectations from customer parents to have school life flexed to suit their children. Some requests are reasonable, but there is some danger that children who always having things adjusted to their needs feel everything will always revolve around them: the values of living in and adapting to a community need to be understood.

The community here is very strong, say parents, which is reflected in the reward structure: the usual system for effort and attainment, but with extra emphasis on becoming a good citizen: ACES (Ardingly Citizenship Exemplary Student award) is given to pupils whose good behaviour models the justice and compassion desired for all pupils at Ardingly.

Pupils and parents: Thirty different nationalities in the school, with some 30 per cent of pupils coming from overseas. The head deliberately manages the numbers of overseas students, from around 18 per cent in Shell (year 9), up to a third in upper sixth, increasing diversity and international thought as students get stuck into the IB.

Parents include many London professionals, expats and foreign office. 'There is wealth in the school, but it has a down to earth quality.'

Entrance: ISEB pre-test in summer of year 6, with common entrance used for setting purposes only. For those not in a prep school, written assessments in English, maths and verbal reasoning. Overseas students need to have fluent English, and pass the same assessments as English counterparts.

Entrance to the sixth requires six or more grade 6 passes at GCSE, including at least a 5 in English and maths.

Exit: Some 30 per cent leave after GCSEs, mostly for local sixth form colleges. Lots of sixth form leavers to top universities eg KCL, UCL, Warwick, Exeter, Liverpool, Bath. Four to Oxbridge in 2018, plus one medic, and others to the US (three), Canada, Brussels and Bayreuth.

Money matters: Over a third of pupils on some sort of support or bursary. Once a prospective pupil gets a scholarship, the level of support depends on need, and is not restricted by the numbers already in receipt of scholarships.

Remarks: A strong and caring community which finds a balance between excellent pastoral care and academic achievement. This modern school with its focus on independent thought would suit those with a broad outlook and interests.

Ardingly College Prep School

Linked with Ardingly College

Haywards Heath, West Sussex RH17 6SQ

Ages 2–13 **Pupils** 397 **Boarders** 35 weekly, 28 flexi boarders (from 7 years) **C of E**

Fees: Day £13,110 – £15,750 pa; Weekly boarding + £3,300 pa

01444 893200
www.ardingly.com

Headmaster: Since January 2018, Harry Hastings, previously head of Brighton College Prep. His introduction to teaching was through gapping at his old prep and his path to this second headship has led him through Exeter and Oxford Universities, a prep in Devon, Peponi House in Kenya, the Dragon School and eight years as assistant head at Cumnor House, Sussex.

Entrance: Most join in nursery (pre-nursery from age 2), year 3 and year 7, with a scattering across the other year groups. Taster day with assessment of reading, spelling, vocab and maths. Doesn't accept those performing below their age in all tests, and below the standardised performance in maths. For year 7 and 8, entrance exams in English, maths, verbal reasoning and reading, and an interview with the head.

Exit: Majority (90 per cent) move on to Ardingly College (pass in core subjects needed), a few off to Bede's, Eastbourne, Brighton College and Hurst or state secondary schools. Common entrance in all subjects except humanities. Need to pass core subjects to move up.

Remarks: The all-round ethos appealed, said a mum. '[Ardingly] don't expect everyone to get straight As...they cater for the super bright and the not too bright at all ...[they] find out what you're good at and celebrate it, which gives the children huge self-confidence.'

Independent learning and thought is the great strength here. Children get as much choice as possible, younger children deciding the term's topic – year 2 chose circuses, and all subjects were taught through the circus medium, children learning their tables through juggling; year 3 chose chocolate and for their stunning starter a parcel from Willy Wonka arrived during assembly.

Older children are more constrained by the CE, but year 8s choose the books to study in English – and read many more books when they've made the choice, says the school. Parents like the removal of history, geography and RS from the CE – fewer exams mean less stress and hoop jumping for kids, who instead choose a topic which encompasses these subjects – one child chose the Mafia, another picked Vietnam, and parents are delighted as their children become absorbed and fascinated by their chosen topics.

They're always thinking and arguing, said one mum, not just downloading information off the net: the weekly thunk, on the school website, is often a moral question, such as would you like always to be happy? Pupils are encouraged to write a response, the emphasis on there being no right answer, but forming arguments to support your view.

The mindfulness teaching which is prevalent in the senior school is also present here: in year 3 the children learn to massage each other. It's a moment to pause and respect each other; and you can see how most people's day could be improved by the cat grip or ice skater moves. 'Would now be a good time for a massage, mummy?' one child asked mum after a stressful phone conversation. Older prep children also learn Paws b mindfulness – about breathing, pausing, and making calm choices in moments of stress.

Teaching here can be really exciting, and one parent described her un-history minded child coming home enthusing about Thomas Becket and keen for a trip to Canterbury Cathedral, after dressing up as a monk and acting the 'will no-one rid me of this troublesome priest?' part out on the playing fields.

There's a large new computer suite (year 4s are already programming apps),and iPads are in regular use. A grateful parent commented on the help at parents' evening from sixth formers, who were available to help parents with the foreign lands of privacy settings and Instagram. iPad use is carefully policed – a 'poor comment' made by a boy about a girl in a class email chatroom was down within two hours, and she received a written apology from the boy.

Not much prep lower down in the school: years 3 and 4 just have reading, spelling and tables (much emphasis on reading here – the children write reviews of children's books for the local Waterstones, and have a super new library with colourful lava lamp style bubbly water containers alongside the books – to underline the joy of being there). Year 6 has two prep sessions a week; years 7 and 8 have three, which are completed at school, to parents' delight.

One shell-shocked London prep parent glowed about the balanced curriculum and pastoral care at Ardingly: 'I could see them blossom before my eyes'. She admitted it was a jolt for her children, who were used to being spoon-fed in London, but commended the dedication shown by the staff in providing extra classes for her daughter to catch up. Children are set from year 5, and class sizes usually around 16.

Learning support is available for mild special needs. A child may have two half hour support sessions in English and maths each week; more than that is not really do-able, says the school. A couple of children depart each year to find a school capable of providing more specialist support.

'They're huge on sport,' said a pleased parent: there are all the usual ones, and sailing, water polo and riding as well. Second all weather Astro pitch recently added. The prep has use of the superb college facilities for games. Three games lessons a week and a PE lesson, which might be swimming, dance, or gym. Ardingly achieves excellence in football, hockey, cricket and swimming, but rugby is not perhaps their most prominent sport: one parent commented on the brutality in matches against 'rugby schools'.

Lots of clubs, including Lego, knitting, massage, Ardingly adventurers (own version of scouts for boys and girls) and tag rugby for the girls.

Drama is super, said a mum. Annual big production in a professional theatre, Oliver! the last one; anyone and everyone gets involved. Lots of singing at this school, with trips in the UK, and abroad; last year to Paris, next year to Rome. New art studio.

Weekly boarding from year 3. Boarding accommodation is immediately above the prep school, rooms varying in size: there's a huge barn-like bedroom for 10 – very popular – to smaller rooms for two or four. Houseparents (who are 'lovely', said a parent) are situated in between the boys and girls. Girls' rooms are rather pinker, and (whimsically) named by the girls: Narnia, Pandora and Fantasia (the boys inherited their rather more feisty dormitory names – Hogsmeade, Camelot and Helmsdeep). Showers and basins are all modern and spotless – the kids take good care of them.

Comfy common rooms with squashy sofas and bean bags, and more upright rooms with tables and chairs for working. The girls and boys run their own small tuckshop with mini versions of sweets. The strong community is evident – parents say older pupils look out for the younger ones, and some volunteer for community service, which involves getting up an hour early to help make breakfast or pick up litter. Children generally keep in touch with home by email. They can phone (from the school phone), but there's no point in taking mobiles because there's no reception anyway, said a mum diplomatically.

Celebration assembly every Friday – the entire prep and the least 100 parents assemble to watch those who had received an HMI describe their achievement – 'my handwriting used to be like a spider on the page.'

Bullying is taken seriously, and may result in exclusion. A mum whose son was bullied confirmed that the school resolved the matter thoroughly and quickly, and there was no recurrence. Her son received a written apology from the perpetrators by morning break on the day she complained. Children may also be excluded for continuously naughty and disruptive behaviour, but the school tries to avoid using the label – 'these children just need more support than we can give them,' says the head.

One parent, who loves the feeling of community at the school, said her favourite memory was of the taking of the school photo, 700 children, squeezing onto a stand. Nursery children were last up, crying and upset by the whole exercise. The older children spontaneously started singing nursery rhythms, and within a few rhymes the little ones were laughing and clapping along.

A religious school with weekly chapel – 'my son hates it, but it's good training to sit still and be taught respect', and it's not 'shoved down your throat.'

A variety of parents, but mostly professionals living locally and working in London. Not a posh school, said a parent, although some are incredibly wealthy. The Russian pupil who required an armed guard was refused a place.

Communication is excellent – if anything they over-communicate, said a parent. Easy access to teacher or head with problems. Parents receive reports five times a year which detail effort and attainment. Reports issued in the middle of terms please parents, who can then talk about the contents with teachers –'it makes such a difference.'

Pre-prep, headed by Hilary Nawrocka since 2010, is down the lane in the old Ardingly farmhouse. Low-slung farm buildings with beamed ceilings on three sides of the farmyard, a long broad corridor library running the length of one building, so children are always moving past books. Reception dozed peacefully to music at rest time, a lively year 2 were in a circle on the floor: huge excitement as they took it in turns to pull an item from the bag to identify a story. Nursery class occupies the old pigsty, and takes pre-nursery tinies who have just turned 2. Free flow inside and out for nursery and reception. Lots of outside equipment, and a magical place to sit in the felled tree carved into seats and badgers. Weekly forest school lessons for nursery to year 3; forest club for the rest of prep.

Ashdown House School

Forest Row, East Sussex RH18 5JY

Ages 4–13 **Pupils** 154 **Boarders** 80 full, 31 flexi (from 7 years) **C of E**

Fees: Day £8,850 – £20,100; Boarding £27,450 pa

01342 822574
www.ashdownhouse.co.uk

Interim Headmaster: Since 2018, Mike Davies. Mike and Isabelle Davies took on the headship (sadly, only he gets the title of head; hers, we are told, is 'headmaster's wife') having been long-term friends of the school. After seven years as deputy head here in the 90s, they ran three other prep schools – Perrott Hill, Edge Grove and Chesham Prep.

The new head from September 2019 will be Hilary Phillips, currently head of Monmouth School Girls' Prep. She has also been director of pastoral care and head of languages at Edgeborough School in Surrey and taught at Arnold House School in London.

Entrance: Entrance by interview with head and ed psychologist report if necessary. Not selective. Steady intake all the way through, many coming from local big preps where they are unhappy and 'not flourishing', and others who are relocating from London. Foreign nationals only if English is up to scratch.

Exit: Benenden, King's Canterbury, Millfield and Ardingly popular in 2018. Parents want a 'named' school. Some feeling of an expert matchmaking service in the way in which the school matches up pupils with senior schools: 'the biggest and best thing we do'. A subtle art.

Remarks: 'Slow – free range children and animals', says a sign on the drive, and this is quickly proved by wellied children noisily playing amongst the rhododendrons, Charles and Camilla (turkeys) strolling amongst them. 'There's a lovely feeling of coming home', said a parent.

The rather splendid main house, with its elegant columns, was designed by the Yorkshireman who went on to design the White House; but here the oval office is a lobby full of wellies and ceramics. 'If they're a long way from home', said a parent in the Cayman Islands, 'you want small school with nice homey feel about it', and this school certainly has that.

'Not a school who focus on petty things', said a parent, 'like top buttons, ties and shiny shoes. It concentrates on the important things, like kindness and being able to talk to grown ups and hold open doors'. Another parent told us that when they were shown around the school, their pupil guides disappeared. The head came out to look for them, and pointed up a tree, where the guides' legs dangled, finished in scuffed shoes. 'Perfect'.

'It is structured – but doesn't look like it. When you walk in, kids are running around everywhere', a parent commented, and the kids say the best thing about school is the freedom. 'In your free time you can go anywhere', said one, including the woods: they're not allowed near the pond or the pit of death (a muddy sink hole), but can climb trees, 'even if you break your arm'. Pupils hone their skills in the Larva Tree and the Spaghetti Tree, progressing to the Love Tree (pupils scratch name of their beloved into the top of the trunk). Not the Welly (Wellingtonia), 100ft+, out of bounds since a pupil, aptly named Everest, made it to the top a few years ago. 'Not cotton wool and cosset', said a parent approvingly. 'They let children take risks and explore their environment'.

Freedom extends to access: there are keypads everywhere, but all the doors are left open during the working day – 'we trust the children', says school. 'You can wander in, but I don't think anyone ever does', said a parent.

'Academically strong – all sorts of different types thrive there', said a parent. Pupils are streamed from year 6 upwards. Not a frenzied approach to work, and homework pressure is not excessive – year 8, an hour a day, year 7, 45 minutes. And with this calm measured approach, Ashdown feeds top public schools.

Lessons are generally fun, say pupils: not Latin, but DT is extremely popular, and geography and science also got a mention as really enjoyable subjects. Pupils enjoy a half a term at Château Sauveterre to improve their French, and science, geography and outdoor pursuits trips to the Old Malthouse in Dorset.

There's not the usual emphasis on IT – 'not the driving force'; though iPads are available as an enabling tool in lessons. Only year 3 has an interactive board – the rest of the school does very well with whiteboards and projectors. 'Get lost in a book, not a computer game'. For pupils who like playing computer games, they can – but only if have programmed it themselves first.

Class sizes 10, max 15. If numbers reach 18, a class will be split in two. Saturday school is optional for year 3, and compulsory thereafter: lessons until 11, then clubs and matches. The weekend is just a couple more working days for staff, which parents feel is fantastic – 'staff are the school's biggest asset'; 'they're dedicated, like spending time with the kids'; 'they make lessons exciting and interesting'.

Learning support – learning enhancement here – is accessible to all. Wouldn't suit those with severe special needs, but prides itself on helping those with mild dyslexia extremely well, and has successfully helped a profoundly deaf pupil. Learning support is charged as an extra.

Classrooms vary from modern, light and smart in the Jungle block to old and bit shabby, but perfectly functional. Pre-prep (14 pupils) has recently moved into a refurbished bungalow – light and colourful, with trainers in a scruffy tumble on the floor and laminated poppy handprints in flower bed.

Drama is described by a parent as 'an absolute dream', explaining that they don't take it too seriously: lines are handed out the week before, so if you fluff up, no one minds – but it's very good. Everyone's involved – backstage and lighting, if not performing. Farce is popular, as is the annual Mock Trial.

Clubs for evenings and weekends include gardening, cookery, poker and a gentlemen's club for the first XV (they learn how to iron a shirt). Strolling through the dance studio (also used for discos and exams), we saw something that resembled a mangled skateboard – apparently the head was rip sticking with kids the evening before.

Art is everywhere – not just the best stuff – with the artist's name dangling on a luggage label from the picture. One pupil said her favourite place in school is the art room: 'cosy... you're not forced to be hard working...it feels free'.

Several pupils said they were attracted to school for the sports; it's odd when you consider this is a small school which is rarely able to field winning teams against big schools. '[You're] not allowed to be a bad loser', said a parent. They play sport every afternoon here, seriously and with much enthusiasm, polo and golf featuring amongst the usual, with the girls also playing football, and cricket (as a club). 'As long as enough pupils to put together a netball team, it doesn't matter there aren't ABC teams – purpose and dedication are installed...', said a parent.

A parent described the 'extraordinary care' of their son while his brother had heart surgery, and the school's amazing care of both boys subsequently: 'they were willing to take our son... who was a walking time bomb. Ashdown goes out of its way to keep children safe'.

Both pupils and parents told us how good Ashdown is at helping problem children: 'Children who have had a terrible time at other places and been bullied or expelled are turned around by Ashdown', said a parent; 'They don't give up on anyone', confirmed a pupil.

They're very supportive of mental health here, particularly aware of the anxiety that kids can suffer near CE. Children are divided into groups with a supportive mentor and learning support will provide extra help to anyone who needs it, with extra tutoring available in maths and English – 'fantastic', said a grateful parent. For those who are really worried, there is an art therapist and a baking counsellor – 'because no child wants to just sit and talk to someone about their problems', said the head. A CBT counsellor helps pupils by Skype, giving them practical exercises to help them cope with exam stress.

Parents told us incidences of bullying are dealt with by the school 'quickly and efficiently'. 'They don't put up with any nonsense at all'. Punishment is a 'pause for thought' (detention). Parents said children could go to anyone with a problem – teacher, form tutor, matron – would get immediate responses from all.

Communication is good, and parents appreciate the school office being open on Saturday, though views vary on school administration, from 'brilliant' to 'a bit dodgy', and another thought that a greater use of social media could make a more efficient school – 'if matches are cancelled, I would like to know'.

'A true boarding school', said one parent, 'with a seven days a week presence'. Some 80 full time boarders, flexi-boarders on regular nights, with designated beds. Boarding is a 'way of life'; the boarding community takes priority here, and half the staff live on site. A parent thought that it would have been a shock to go directly to boarding senior school, and Ashdown is a 'cosy [first] experience of boarding...' Two fixed exeats a term, and two floating, 'but the children never want to take them', said a parent; 'there are so many things on at the weekend'.

'No rules for rules sake', says the school, which accommodates parents who want irregular contact with their children; for instance, when Foreign Office parents are on tour, Ashdown will care for their kids full time, but when parents are home they can pop in and take the kids out for pizza.

Rules do have their place in the day-to-day mechanics of boarding, which is very structured – much like having strict but kind parents who know the importance of a good night's sleep. 'Not a sleepover atmosphere...'. Homesickness is addressed with a mixture of comforting and keeping you busy.

Boarding accommodation is comfortable, though not plush: dorms for 6-12 in bunks and singles with duvets from home, decent bathrooms and friendly common rooms with TV, water cooler, ample supply of fruit and books. Matron can make toast for those who ask. Photos all over corridors – 'I adore this', enthused one parent.

Pupils write a proper letter home every week – 'quite sweet,' said a parent – and parents can phone in to the landings between 7-8pm. All devices kept in head's study, but pupils can ask for their mobiles to call parents or use the phone room. Contact home for overseas pupils is arranged taking into account time differences – one pupil leaves morning lessons to Skype her parents each week.

Everyone agrees that the food is delicious and it is no surprise that the chef also runs a restaurant. He has reduced the salt and sugar in food, and bottles of ketchup, used to happy excess by pupils, have been replaced by a one sachet policy. Pupils would like a tuck shop: it's just one chocolate bar on Sundays at this health conscious school. 'There are no fat children here', said a parent bluntly.

Would suit pretty much anyone, think parents, from the over-assertive (whom the school will mellow) to the quiet and shy ('If you can play one note on the oboe, you'll still be in the concert'). 'A sadistic bully would probably be asked to leave though', said one parent, on further consideration. Pupils thought this school would not suit someone who doesn't try hard. But it's not, they say, a school which expels people – 'they give people a chance'.

Ashdown families are generally traditional, wealthy and established. Not many new Porches here. Some 30 per cent from overseas. No scholarships, but can support families if things go wrong.

Ashfold School

Dorton House, Dorton, Aylesbury, Buckinghamshire HP18 9NG

Ages 3–13 **Pupils** 281 **Boarders** 45 flexi (from 9)

Fees: Day £9,525 – £16,845; Weekly boarding £20,190 pa

01844 238237
www.ashfoldschool.co.uk

Headmaster: Since September 2018, Colin MacIntosh, previously deputy head of Beaudesert Park School. English degree from St Andrews; started his teaching career at Shrewsbury School, then spent 15 years in various prep schools before joining Beaudesert. He is a keen sportsman, playing football, cricket and golf. He is married to Anna and they have two children.

Entrance: Non-selective, with the majority joining reception from the nursery. Prospective pupils for all year groups invited to spend a day in school for assessment only. School likes children from state primaries to join by year 2 and will hold places for them to this point. From year 3, places are harder to come by, with waiting lists for most year groups.

Exit: Leavers to a wide variety of schools, with about 50 per cent heading off to board most years. Popular choices include Stowe, Bloxham, Harrow, Rugby, Wellington College, Headington and St Edward's. Impressive scholarship record – on average, more than 40 per cent of leavers have won scholarships or awards to their senior schools over the last few years. School takes care to place less academic children in schools where they can shine. Very few to state maintained grammars (just a couple each year), with head discouraging 11 plus unless for financial reasons.

Remarks: The cross country drive through rolling hills and farmland and rising fear that the satnav is playing tricks on you is well worth it for the first sight of Ashfold's stunning Jacobean mansion set in 33 acres of fields and woodland. Rugby pitches in the foreground give the impression of a traditional boys' prep but behind the magnificent building are three hard tennis courts, a well maintained, heated outdoor pool, full size Astroturf, netball courts and a lovely adventure playground, proving that that the girls who make up roughly 40 per cent of the school population are well catered for and now integral to the culture of the school.

Wood paneling, winding staircases and cobbled stable blocks bring Hogwarts to mind, and rosy cheeked, windswept and slightly disheveled children litter the grassy play areas, giving an overall impression of an idyllic country school – worlds apart from the urban London schools many of its commuter families have left behind. Lacks some of the dazzling showcase facilities boasted by many preps, but every part of the campus is put to excellent use (and in the words of one parent: 'you're a bit restricted with a grade I listing') and the overall effect is of an inspiring, functional and nurturing environment, which 'celebrates children.'

Purpose-built pre-prep building houses nursery to year 2 in a light, spacious and colourful setting with its own well-equipped playground and large field, complete with bug hotel. Pre-prep children well integrated into the main school, sharing its assembly space (often the village church, situated on site), sports hall and playing fields. Junior department housed in main wing of house, while most senior lessons take place in recently renovated courtyard classrooms.

Largely rural catchment from surrounding villages, with majority of children from hard-working middle class families ('hardly any old money,' said one parent), who travel up to 30 minutes to school. Very few from non-Caucasian families. School keen to prove its country credentials with a flourishing veg patch tended by pupils and weekend challenges set for families, resulting in the presentation of the school's 'countryside certificate' on completion of all 30. Small number of scholarships, with the Stowe-Ashfold scholarship and the Tudor Hall-Ashfold scholarship covering 100 per cent of fees and other awards up to 30 per cent, available for pupils 'who show outstanding academic, artistic, sporting, musical or all-round ability' for the last two years at the school.

Girls have been part of the furniture at Ashfold since the 1980s and make up 40+ per cent of the total cohort. Parents say that all children get the same opportunities, regardless of gender.

Whether arty, sporty, or musical, there's something for every child here ('they look at the child as an individual,' say parents) and academics are solid all round too. Class sizes are small. French with a specialist teacher from year 1 and Latin from age 9. Setting has been introduced in the core subjects. Pupils entirely specialist taught from year 4 and move around the school for different subjects from thereon. All children screened for dyslexia aged 7 or whenever they join the school. Currently around 12 per cent of pupils under the SENCo for mild needs (SpLD, dyslexia or dyspraxia). In class support and small group work with a learning support assistant covered by fees. One-to-one lessons with the school's SEN specialist charged as extra.

Parents find channels of communication excellent and are able to email class teachers – who they describe as 'a really talented bunch' – directly with queries or issues. Recent introduction of e-learning online assessments for all children from year 3 up have 'really freed up teachers to focus on creative lesson planning,' says school.

High standard of art on show in and around a lovely bright art room; 'you can't usually see the ceiling for work,' said the head of department when we visited (it was the first week in September), although it would be nice to see a bit more of the pupils' work festooning the walls around the rest of the school. A swanky art and design centre opened recently with facilities for DT, cookery, art, ceramics and textiles.

Almost 60 per cent of pupils learn a musical instrument. The head of music introduced Music Masterclasses and lots of workshops with senior schools, as well internal events such as an instrument fair to introduce the children to all the instruments on offer at Ashfold. Collaborates with drama teacher to produce fantastic musical theatre – recent productions include the musical Honk! (performed outside in the walled garden) and The Canada Years (the true story of Ashfold's evacuation to Canada during WWII) as well as A Midsummer Night's Dream. Waiting lists for all choirs underscore the school's renewed collective passion in this area and all pre-prep children learn the violin and recorder from year 1. Lots going on in the drama department too, with productions including Sherlock Holmes and The Secret of Immortality and The Wind in the Willows.

Once children reach the prep school they have an extended day, ending at either 5 or 6pm, depending on age. This enables the curriculum to include daily sport for all, which although adored by most is 'a struggle' for some of the less sporty ones, according to parents. All the usual suspects played to a good level but school exceptionally proud of the U13 girls' hockey team which won the IAPS championship recently and the clay shooting team, also IAPs U12 and U13 champions and runners up at the British Schools and Young Shots Clay Shooting Championships recently. This and other sporting successes put down to a 'real focus on coaching' with specialist talent brought in to coach rugby, hockey, netball and football (with an ex-Oxford United coach). Gymnastics and indoor games take place in a good sized sports hall incorporating wonderful changing facilities – 'with hot showers'. From year 6, those demonstrating talent in other areas are selected to join scholars' groups (academic, art, drama et al) in place of time allocated to games.

Boarding allowed from year 5, where children can stay for supper after games, then take part in one of a multitude of activities on offer (from rifle shooting or fishing to chess and cookery). Given that this takes them up to 8pm it's a bit of a no brainer for parents of children keen to sample boarding life, and up to 30 children board on any given night (up to three nights a week in year 5 and four nights in year 6). Dorms of up to seven beds have been recently revamped and provide spacious, comfortable accommodation in the mansion, girls at one end of the building, boys at the other. 'It's proper boarding, not a sleepover,' and boarders sleep in the same bed on their chosen boarding nights. Refurbed boarders' common rooms, complete with pool table, two flat screen TVs and comfy sofas, provide a home from home feel and open onto the houseparents' accommodation. No mobile phones, iPods or other gadgets allowed with the exception of Kindles – a very popular move with parents. Lights out at 9.30pm and cooked breakfasts are a hit.

School has a Christian ethos but accepts other denominations. Rightfully proud of its pastoral care with parents reporting 'very clear lines of escalation' should things ever go wrong. Three houses (Gryphons, Lions and Dragons) compete in lots of eagerly contested competitions (parents describe the standard of work in the inter-house art competition as 'unbelievable') with the each term culminating in a house cup. Pre-prep pupils presented with star of the week awards for effort and attainment in weekly assemblies. Head boy and girl chosen at the beginning of year 8 amid great excitement; rest of year 8 are all prefects. School clear that 'leadership is about serving others,' and won't have any arrogance, on occasion passing over obvious macho choices for head boy for 'a lovely gentleman with outstanding manners.'

No school buses so that parents bring children into school to keep lines of communication open: 'If a child has had a sleepless night, for example, we want to know about it'.

Ashford Preparatory School

Linked with Ashford School

Great Chart, Ashford, Kent TN23 3DJ

Ages 3–11 **Pupils** 392

Fees: Day: £10,500 – £15,000; Boarding £24,000 – £37,500 pa

01233 620493
www.ashfordschool.co.uk

Headmaster: Since September 2017, Penny Willetts. Educated at Benenden, she trained as a PE teacher in Sydney, and was head of games at Falkner House in the mid 90s. She travelled the world as an expat, did a PGCE and had two children, arriving at Ashford in 2005. Both her children were educated at the prep school. She was acting head from 2015. A keen golfer, she enjoys holidaying in new places.

Entrance: Not overly selective. Majority join in the nursery and reception and there is also an entry point in year 3 but children can join at any time if there are spaces. At nursery stage children (and parents) meet headmaster and have a taster session. Older children have a taster day and literacy and numeracy tests. The latter are for setting purposes and a child will not be accepted only if it is felt that they would not cope with the curriculum.

Exit: About two-thirds go on to the senior school, many with scholarships, others mainly to grammars including Judd and Skinners. Some to Benenden and occasionally to Wellesley House and other preps for last two years before common entrance. Will familiarise children with the Kent Test but no intensive coaching. Children's progress tracked via CAT tests so school aware of any weakness and can advise on appropriate next step. Close liaison with parents and school is expert at managing expectations.

Remarks: There has been so much development since our last visit that the school is hardly recognisable. The Georgian house with arts and crafts additions remains the heart of the place, but now there is a fabulous glass atrium and classroom block with wide bright corridors, all sensitively blended with the original buildings.

Pupils set in maths and English from year 3 but plenty of movement between sets and scholarship children are taught within the class. Lessons seem to be enjoyable and interesting; our guide remarked, 'I have never been a fan of science but they make it such good fun'. Accelerated reading programme known as the Millionaire Club has been a great success for keen and reluctant readers alike. Children have to choose a book and do a quiz, and then their name is put on a board. Anyone who reads a million words gets a hoodie. Soundswrite, a first phonics programme, is used to teach reading and writing in the pre-prep. About 20 children have significant learning difficulties, one or two with mild Asperger's or dyslexia, and some who need help with organisational skills. There is one full-time SEN teacher plus several teaching assistants and a specialist dyslexia teacher. School very supportive of those who do not find academic work easy, so long as they are ultimately likely to be able to take GCSEs.

School sits in 25 acres of grounds and playing fields and offers the usual sports including lacrosse and Kwik cricket for the girls. Good results in biathlon, triathlon, cross-country and swimming and a number of children play hockey and rugby at county level. Strong cricketing tradition – England cricketer Richard Ellison is an old boy; there is a pitch on site plus school has use of Ashford Cricket Club for matches and borrows floodlit Astroturf from the senior school.

Plenty of concerts and musical events, about 65 per cent learn an instrument (school has recently become proud owner of a harp) and there is specialist music teaching from reception upwards. Year 3 pupils have free music lessons for two terms and the school is always on the look out for hidden talent. Good drama with something for everyone leads to blossoming self-confidence; most children are comfortable standing up in public and a 'have a go' mentality pervades. Two plays a year for years 6 and 2 and every class does annual mini production and entertainment.

Lots of healthy inter-house competition with weekly house points keenly contested – academic, sporting and fundraising events, plus points also awarded for effort and progress. Over 30 clubs and activities to choose from including sports, music, chess and even dry slope skiing. Saturday mornings are also for sports and activities but attendance is not compulsory. Cooking offered from nursery upwards and by the time they leave some pupils are quite proficient – we watched the construction of some beautiful gingerbread houses. Vibrant art department celebrating different styles: self-portraits, Venetian masks, pop art, funky landscapes and interpretations of Guernica. DT very popular and children often put in extra work on their projects in the lunch break. Numerous trips and visits all covered by fees, including the residential adventure training camp for leavers.

No boarding on the Ashford Prep site but children in year 6 can board on the main school campus and come over on the shuttle bus. Attracts children from a wide range of cultural and social backgrounds – lots of locals plus a number of European, Asian and Nigerian families who have relocated from London. Seven thousand houses are being built around Ashford and the high-speed rail link is changing the population of the area – it is now only 37 minutes into St Pancras. Some parents make huge sacrifices to send their children here and like to be actively involved. Flourishing PTA raises about £25,000-£30,000 a year and organises lots of social events. Generally a pretty happy bunch who 'like the way the teaching is adapted to suit the way the kids learn' and value the fact that their children are allowed 'the freedom to make mistakes'. Working parents appreciate the option of wrap-around care from 7.30 in the morning until 6.30pm, not to mention holiday clubs.

Ashford Prep is a happy, caring school with a strong moral purpose. Appetite and enthusiasm for learning much in evidence but we detected no whiff of a pressurised atmosphere.

Ashford School

Linked with Ashford Preparatory School

East Hill, Ashford, Kent TN24 8PB

Ages 11-18 **Pupils** 475 **Sixth form** 157 **Boarders** 150 full, 4 weekly (from year 6)

Fees: Day £16,800; Boarding £24,000 – £36,000 pa

01233 625171
www.ashfordschool.co.uk

Headmaster: Since September 2018, Michael Hall, previously CEO and principal of GEMS Wellington Academy in Dubai (possibly the largest British school in the world, with 4,100 pupils). Economics degree from Liverpool and has a masters in education management. Started as a boarding master and economics, geography and sport teacher at AKS Lytham, ending up as head of sixth form; deputy head at Kingston Grammar, then eight years as head of Bedford Modern. A keen adventurer, he has trekked in the Pyrenees and the Alps and also enjoys cycling, rugby, swimming and many different forms of music.

Academic matters: Broad intake, results improving year on year. In 2018, at GCSE, 45 per cent A*-A/7-9 grades. At A level, 76 per cent A*/B grades and 53 per cent A*/A grades. Particularly good results in science and maths. All learn two languages from Spanish, German and French; German most popular. Pupils from abroad also encouraged to take GCSE in their first language eg Chinese or Dutch. Good range of subjects at A level including Chinese, business studies, psychology, textiles, sports studies and drama. In sixth form Russian, German and Spanish offered as a business language (basic language skills, mostly conversation). Very accommodating timetable and school willing to offer a subject to only a handful of students. Digital literacy programme for year 7. A very tech savvy school – radio voting handsets have proved popular and effective: children text answers to the screen anonymously, useful for shy children but also means there is no chance of a snooze at the back of the class as everyone has to participate. Pupils set by ability in core subjects but there is plenty of flexibility and children can be moved up or down mid-term if appropriate.

Loyal team of teachers who love the challenge and freedom to innovate and are encouraged to use their initiative. Good mix of old hands and NQTs – school runs a leading and innovative graduate teacher training programme. Biology teacher won a UK top teacher award and also organises the school's rock festival, AshBash. A new higher education adviser has recently joined the team to help with UCAS forms and beyond – he was previously a university admissions tutor. The Oxbridge Club provides extra coaching in problem solving and analytical and critical thinking. Lots of language exchanges and trips that help bring learning to life and 'take school work into the real world,' according to one happy father. A level physicists visit CERN.

Adventurous Learning programme is all about taking people – staff and children alike – out of their comfort zone and challenging in all areas, personal as well as academic. It might be trying something new like speaking in front of the whole class and then the whole school.

Some 35 pupils with SEN ranging from organisation skills to severe dyslexia, dyspraxia, dyscalculia and school can support children with physical disabilities. 'The teachers really go the extra mile for a child who struggles – nothing is too much trouble'.

International Centre for 11-16 year olds offers a one-year intensive English language course.

Games, options, the arts: Good sports facilities also include new sports centre, two gyms as well as a fitness centre and dance suite, indoor swimming pool and all weather basketball court. Cricket played at the local club a few minutes' walk away. Boys' sport now fully developed and there are senior first teams in rugby, hockey and cricket, but fixtures still a bit sparse as other schools are a 'bit slow to twig that Ashford boys are actually rather good at games'. Teams maintained into sixth form and everyone has to take part in a physical activity at least once a week. Yoga and exercise classes popular, especially with the senior girls, along with street and jazz dance and personal survival. Strong house loyalty and everyone expected to take part in house events.

Lots going on in the drama department from house plays and speech and drama recitals, lower school productions and the spectacular whole school summer musical. Active junior drama club as well as technical drama club for those who prefer to keep out of the spotlight. Drama a popular option at GCSE and also offered at A level and school prepares pupils for speech and drama and LAMDA exams. Vibrant music and art departments: head of music is a colourful character who has transformed the musical life of the school; numbers participating have shot up, as has the standard. Tuition on most instruments available from the bassoon to the organ and school has two Steinway pianos as part of the Steinway schools programme. Lots going on: concert band, chamber music groups, string quartet, rock bands, string ensembles, community orchestra. Concerts every three to four weeks. School wants music to be 'about performance and enjoyment' with plenty of opportunities for showmanship from 'teatime tootles' in the atrium to singing in Westminster Abbey.

Fabulous textiles and 'big and bold' approach to art; several go on to art foundation courses each year. A group of pupils recently designed a stained glass window for a church in the Holy Land and were then invited to install their work in situ. Another group made some wall hangings for the local hospice. 'We do random and different things and let it all come out', said one pupil.

Huge range of clubs and activities, from Lego robotics to cooking and debating – something for everyone and all have to take part until sixth form. Strong debating team has represented the school at the Oxford and Cambridge Unions' competitions and taken part in the European Youth Parliament at the Foreign Office. Amnesty group won an award for Best Fundraising Event in UK Schools with their Dare to be Different Day. CCF popular and each year about 12 pupils complete their DofE gold.

Boarding: Boarding from year 6 (bussed over from junior school) but very few in this age group. Boarders well supported and cared for; they are also allocated a house and are not allowed back into their boarding houses during the day, which means plenty of interaction with day children. Lots of boarders' activities and birthdays always celebrated. Houses recently refurbished; sixth formers have en suite bathrooms. Six houses, each led by a head of house, a teacher who oversees academic progress and personal development of each child. Children from abroad spend the first weekend of term with a day pupil – helps integration. Close liaison with parents and tutor and regular progress reviews. Lots of leadership opportunities running house events and activities, from community work to the house play. No lessons on Saturday mornings but time devoted to sport, rehearsals and activities – day children always happy to come in and it means the boarders are kept busy.

Background and atmosphere: Founded in 1898 with the aim that the pupils should play an active role in the life of the town and with an emphasis on 'training and development of character', the school moved to its present site in 1913 and became part of United Learning in 1999 (a group of state primary and secondary as well as independent schools). This brought a welcome injection of cash resulting in new buildings springing up all over the place. Senior school is at the foot of the High Street, approached by a narrow lane and enclosed by high red-brick walls with lawns and greenery stretching down the hill. It's a green oasis in the middle of busy Ashford and quite difficult to find if you don't know where to look. Extensive rugby and cricket pitches are a short walk away. It's an international and friendly community – pupils are expected to engage with school life, and head says he 'does not want passengers on board and expects everyone to take part'. Good food, cafeteria style, lots of choice and healthy salad options. Brightly painted Atrium café a popular meeting place, also open to parents at pick up and drop off time.

Pastoral care, well-being and discipline: Strong pastoral care via house system; everyone is allocated a house on arrival as well as a specialist tutor; new joiners in year 7 also have a sixth form mentor.

Pupils and parents: About 70 per cent day children from as far afield as Maidstone, Sittingbourne and Cranbrook (minibus service). Very few weekly boarders so room for growth here. Families from a broad social spectrum; parents have high expectations and are encouraged to get involved and be part of the community. Twenty per cent foreign nationals, over 24 nationalities and particularly popular with Chinese, Eastern Europeans and Nigerians – school takes care that no nationality dominates. 'Ashford is very good at taking kids of any type and getting the best out of them', says a parent, 'and I like the way the school takes trouble to develop the kids' characters as well as the academic side.'

Entrance: About 60 per cent come up from the prep school, others from local primaries and prep schools eg Sutton Valence, Dulwich and Spring Grove. Wide ability range – some very bright,

A

others who struggle, but all must have the ability to pass at least six GCSEs. Almost automatic entry from prep school but must be within the academic range. Children joining from other schools sit assessment tests in English, maths, science and non-verbal reasoning and take part in a team building exercise. Preference given to siblings where possible. A further 15 or so join at 13+ via school's own tests. Sixth form entry tested in proposed A level subjects and must have six GCSEs at 6+, plus English proficiency test if appropriate. Lots of foreign nationals come for sixth form as well as several each year from local state schools.

Exit: A few leave at 13+ – no coaching for CE but good relationships with other local schools; a few depart after GCSEs. Sixth formers to a huge range of different institutions: two to Oxbridge and one medic in 2018; others to eg Edinburgh, Exeter, Leeds, Liverpool, UCL, Bristol, Warwick and York. Three off overseas: Hong Kong, Tokyo and Victoria, Australia. Broad minded higher education and careers adviser takes huge trouble to guide right student to right course.

Money matters: Academic, music, art, drama and sports scholarships offered – usually 10-30 per cent of day fee. Means-tested bursaries for children of clergy, mostly Anglican but will consider other Christian denominations. Twenty per cent discount for Forces families, discounts for siblings. Church Schools Foundation Assisted Places assessed on a combination of academic ability and financial need, worth up to 85 per cent of fees – offered to those entering in year 7, 9 or sixth form. Short-term emergency bursaries available.

Remarks: A forward-looking school with a strong international contingent which is going from strength to strength, benefiting in part from the huge growth of Ashford town. The school has 'changed beyond belief in the last eight years' and appeals to a wide range of families with its strong pastoral care and adventurous learning programme.

Aylesbury Grammar School

Walton Road, Aylesbury, Buckinghamshire HP21 7RP

Ages 11–18 **Pupils** 1,299 **Sixth form** 388

01296 484545
www.ags.bucks.sch.uk

Headmaster: Since 2014, Mark Sturgeon (40s). Educated at Dr Challoner's Grammar School, University of Liverpool (geography) and the Institute of Education, University of London (PGCE). A qualification as an FA football coach took him to the USA (unpaid) and the decision to embark on a teaching career. Returned to qualify in the UK before landing his first job at Burnham Upper School. Openly ambitious, he made head of department at Aylesbury Grammar School aged 26. A local boy through and through, he returned to his alma mater (DCGS) becoming deputy headmaster four years later.

Describes AGS as 'pastorally driven – high performing but caring and happy. We don't want the students to feel extreme pressure. The focus now is to take a closer look at learning and what makes a good learner'. Clear that talent is not just innate and that it's school's job to offer opportunities: 'exam results will open the door but the boy has to walk through it and we have to give him the tools to do that.'

Retired from first XV rugby (which he took up aged 30) a couple of years ago but keeps competitive playing squash and golf. Still teaches year 8 geography ('I'm the same teacher I always was') and modestly sees himself as the school's custodian – respectful to those who came before but keen to keep improving and defining the future. Married to Angie, a primary school teacher, with three young sons.

Academic matters: Respectably placed in the league tables and climbing steadily – now challenging the big guns in South Bucks' leafier suburbs. Broad, traditional-ish curriculum with options including economics, business and Latin as well as all the usual suspects. Head's pick of top departments are maths (all do at least one module of further maths in addition to GCSE), sciences, history and geography – adding that languages are 'unbelievably good'. In the languages department all study French from year 7 plus either German or Spanish (allocated by teachers). Latin from year 7 and plenty take two languages at GCSE. All take three separate sciences at GCSE. Top notch value added – features in top 10 per cent nationally. GCSE options (most take 11) chosen with help from teachers – degree choices already in mind. Sixty-nine per cent graded A*-A/9-7 in 2018. Strong support wherever needed with drop-in sessions offered for almost all subjects, whether to iron out creases or stretch the most able.

Setting for maths from year 8. Surprisingly small class sizes across the board from year 10 up – maximum of 25 for most GCSE classes, some subjects with as few as 12 students. Individual target setting enables boys to take ownership of their progress – one of school's key cornerstones. They set their own academic goals and, reportedly, mostly exceed them. Teaching we observed was mainly of the traditional genre with formally laid out classrooms – but notably boys were attentive and engaged. In the words of one who joined in year 12, 'we all want to do well here – there's no messing about'. That said, a pressure cooker it's not. Boys were clear to point out that there was equal support for those wanting to chase Oxbridge and Russell Group places and those aiming for vocational destinations.

Over 20 A level subjects on curriculum, with strong performance across the board. In 2018, with 49 per cent A*/A and 72 per cent A*-B; boys, proud of their achievements, told us 'the academic high scorers are the leaders in this school'. Teachers praised for their expertise and boys appreciate the outside knowledge of those who have had previous careers. Sixth form lecture series recently introduced.

Super SEN provision – known as Student Support – described by head as a 'phenomenal department'. Over seven per cent of the cohort have identified needs (mainly dyslexia and dyspraxia but also several on the ASD spectrum) and are watched over by one full-time SENCo and two assistants. All screened for learning difficulties on entry and supported in small groups. In addition, boys benefit from department's creative approach to managing their needs. Tuesday lunch times, for example, see a social club for students, receiving help from the SEN team, to talk over their challenges and triumphs: some told us it was the best part of their week. Absolutely no sign of stigma attached to department – in fact used by many 'for a bit of peace and quiet'. Parents included too, with regular 'autism coffee mornings'.

Games, options, the arts: Rugby rules ('massive', say boys) – national and county level players and strong links forged with Wasps. Glory also achieved in footie (finalists and sometime winners in county cup for several years), tennis, squash, basketball, cricket and handball. Not bad for a school where students' only wish is for more sports pitches. Games compulsory to sixth form, so there's also fencing, hockey, swimming, table tennis and badminton to cater for all tastes, as well as one of the best equipped gyms we've seen in any state school – well used by boys both as part of PE curriculum and in own time. PE available as option at GCSE and A level.

Facilities more than adequate and ranging from gleaming (newly refurbed squash courts) to shabby (the old sports hall), as well as a functional newer sports hall and indoor swimming pool. Is there sport for all? To a degree: 'it's not as cliquey as you might think', boys assured us. Most year groups field A and B teams for major sporting fixtures with wannabes able to attend school training as an extracurricular activity. Minor sports such as badminton or squash also well attended with occasional fixtures. Importantly, less starry sportsmen have a host of other activities from chess to creative writing or debating to flex their intellectual muscles.

Music definitely not just a poor relation compared to sport: one elite rugby playing year 13 boy wistfully told us he wished he had joined the choir; 'It would have been cool to have played for the first XV and have been a chorister.' Music, DT, art and drama all popular options at GCSE and A level. DT covers woodwork and textiles in years 7 to 9 and school boasts four spacious DT labs, complete with laser cutters and all manner of equipment to enable boys to spread their practical wings. Art room not the most inspirational we've seen but quality of work high – and boys' work on show at every turn. Productions often in conjunction with conveniently positioned Aylesbury High and there are colours awards for music as well as sport, underscoring school's ethos of roundedness. Plenty of opportunities for boys to showcase their talents – from a cabaret evening at the Aylesbury Waterside Theatre to intimate solo evenings with musicians performing to a handful of parents.

'Amazing' array of trips and tours both curriculum linked and just for fun, from the ever popular year 7 residential outing to rugby tours to Australia, ski trips to USA, language exchanges and history excursions to Auschwitz or Washington DC. DofE well run according to parents and 'encouraged'.

Background and atmosphere: Founded in 1598 by Sir Henry Lee, a champion of Elizabeth I. Situated in centre of Aylesbury until 1907, now in a residential area on the edge, with its sister school, Aylesbury High, just a few yards away across the Walton Road. Buildings, although all highly effective in their functionality, range in their aesthetic appeal. The main school building has definite shades of Alan Bennett's History Boys with its gleaming parquet floors and half tiled walls, complete with large, airy, sash-windowed classrooms. A solid showing from the recently refurbed music labs, complete with Macs, rock equipment and lighting for performances, plus studio theatre, recording suite and large multi-purpose sports hall with enviable gym and weights room – used by all.

Other outbuildings – mainly erected in the 1960s, the decade that architecture forgot – serve their purpose well and the only complaints from boys is that they wish they had more fields. Science labs recently refurbished, ditto library, funded mainly by alumni and dedicated parents' committee. Large sixth form area includes snack bar, common room and new area for private study. Others take lunch (typical school dinner fare – pizza and chips anyone?) in a canteen setting.

Thriving house system with fierce (but friendly) competition in every area. Two coveted trophies presented to winning houses each year for sporting triumphs and cultural and artistic excellence. House athletics and house quiz competitions are held on the same day so that jocks and brainboxes can bask in equal glory.

Pastoral care, well-being and discipline: The boys we met glowed with pride when talking about their school and were aware of their privileged situation in a way that many grammar students from more affluent catchments fail to be. They praised 'diversity', teachers that 'always try to bring out our best' and 'the confidence the school gives us'. The result of this is very few major transgressions and scant need for a hefty rule book as self-discipline tends to come naturally to most, although parents describe school as 'quite strict'. Pastoral care in strong evidence from head (who sends handwritten notes home to boys for outstanding learning or behaviour) all the way down to the year 8 buddies who are on tap to help (using their own experiences) newbies with any problems or questions. School motto Respect and Aspire is most befitting – we felt that the sixth form boys electing to continue wearing school uniform rather than business suits spoke volumes.

Pupils and parents: With less than 10 per cent of cohort joining from the independent sector, school has a genuine grammar feel to it (couldn't be mistaken for a private school), but matches and, in some ways, exceeds its slicker south Bucks counterparts in purposefulness, drive and ambition. With one mother commenting 'there's no money in the school' and around 15 pupils in most year groups eligible for free school meals, this surely is what selective state education is all about. Entitlement not part of the AGS vocabulary – parents say boys 'all want to work' and the sample we met were likeable, articulate, diverse and thoroughly grounded. School not filled from catchment so boys come from as far afield as Milton Keynes – around an hour each way by bus. Tiring for the youngest, but one such traveller of almost seven years told us 'it's totally worth it'.

Entrance: Via secondary transfer test administered by Bucks County Council in September of year 6. Admission purely on qualifying score (121). Further opportunities for admission at 12+, 13+ and 14+ by Late Transfer Testing, if places available. Around 30 places open up in sixth form with boys needing 368 points from best eight GCSEs and at least a 6 in potential A level subjects.

Exit: Around 15 per cent leaves post GCSE, sometimes a small number at end of year 12. Excellent guidance takes boys to a broad array of universities. Eight to Oxbridge in 2018, and one off to Pennsylvania. Significant numbers to Southampton, Nottingham, Exeter, Warwick, Bath and Birmingham. Loughborough a top choice for those interested in pursuing careers around sport. Sixteen medics in 2018. History, maths and chemistry also popular.

Money matters: Like most state grammars, rather strapped for cash, but dynamic parents, staff and alumni enable school to fund improvements and new equipment. Bursaries available for trips abroad.

Remarks: A grammar school in its purest form: purposeful, determined and socially diverse. In the words of one mother: 'I'd more than happily pay for this school.'

The Beacon School

Chesham Bois, Amersham, Buckinghamshire HP6 5PF

Ages 4–13 Pupils 530

Fees: £11,850 – £17,250 pa

01494 433654
www.beaconschool.co.uk

Headmaster: Since 2015, Will Phelps MA (40s), joined after five years as headmaster of British International School of New York. His first teaching job was at Aldenham School, followed by

12 years at Abingdon School where he taught religious studies, was senior housemaster and head of boarding. He's relaxed, friendly, full of ideas and has seemingly boundless energy – to talk with him was like being bundled on to the non-stop charm express, one arrives at one's destination slightly dazed, but feeling positive. No doubt some of this ebullience is a result of the years he spent in New York – after dealing with Manhattan mummies and daddies, home counties parents probably aren't a tough crowd – but it's also his natural mien.

Comes from a large 'clan' and something of a teaching dynasty. He was brought up in Oxford where his father was a maths don, attended the Dragon School (where his brother is now deputy head) and Clifton College, Bristol where one of the boarding houses had been run by his great grandfather. Studied theology at King's College London, takes all the school assemblies and teaches his subject when he can, 'but not as much as I'd like to.' The shelves in his study hold not just books, but also clocks and wands, providing an insight into his enthusiasm for Tolkein and JK Rowling: 'I wish I could be Dumbledore!' His hobbies are walking, cooking (Sunday roasts and barbeques a speciality) and watching cricket and rugby, 'I support, I don't play. I was never any good.' He's married with three children, two at Marlborough and the youngest at Godstowe. Latest additions are two puppies, Merlin and Luna.

On taking the reins of the largest boys' day prep in the country he had some remedial work to do, 'reasserting leadership' and being 'genuinely present and accountable to over 1,000 parents'. The school's demographic is a complex one: some families are pinning everything on the 11+ Bucks grammar school tests, others are aiming for big name day and boarding schools at 13+. 'We must have equal commitment to both,' says Mr P, but adds, 'I truly believe that the last two years of prep school are golden.' Likewise, while the school's website isn't averse to mentioning the number of boys who get into Dr Challoner's Grammar, it's clear that 13+ is the preferred route.

We found Mr P's views on prep schools, and education more widely, to be both robust and compassionate. He believes that single sex education, ideally to age 13, gives boys a 'sense of belonging' and the freedom to 'relax and grow into who they want to be. By 13, most know who they are.' He is also alert to the pressures his pupils face, including 'massive parental anxiety' about the 11+, 'We don't want to overheat these kids.' Believes school's pastoral care should extend to parents, especially interested in how to encourage 'resilience' in parenting: 'School is about letting go, allowing children to fall, but to fall forward. Children learn by making mistakes, they have to do this.' Shakes his head when we ask about tutoring, 'We resist it as much as possible, but it still goes on.'

The Phelps mantra is thus: 'I run on three things. Be kind, be kind, be kind.' He makes a point of 'shaking hands with every boy in the morning' and promises, 'no grey suits', no pupils 'passing through unknown.' Parents are impressed, 'He's always there, at the school gate.' 'Lovely, very approachable and so knowledgeable about senior schools.' Optimistic? Definitely. But not idealistic, 'Of course I don't run a perfect school. How could I? It's full of boys.' We like his style.

Entrance: Early registration advisable – places fill very quickly. Informal assessment for boys joining at age 4. Entry points also at year 3, when an additional class is added, and year 7. Places occasionally available in other years.

Exit: Around half leave for grammars at end of year 6, most to Dr Challoner's. Most of those who stay until 13 head for Berkhamsted, with a few to Merchant Taylor's and most others to a range of boarding schools – Eton, Harrow, Wellington, Winchester, Haileybury etc. Ten scholarships in 2018, many for sports, DT or drama.

Remarks: School was founded in 1933 by Mr Stanley Fieldhouse and started with just five boys (hence the five-pointed star of the logo). It moved to its current site, Bois Farm, in the 1950s. Of the farm's 17th century buildings only the timbered barns remain and prior to becoming a school they accommodated a variety of non-agricultural ventures including a repertory theatre and a dance hall in the 1930s (Chesham Bois must have been quite the destination village) and a billet for soldiers during WW2. So, not much burdened by history, 'no quirks', as Mr Phelps puts it, but nevertheless a classic boys' prep in the traditional mould.

If arriving by road for the first time be prepared for a sharp turn into an unprepossessing frontage that looks more like a cottage hospital than a school, but never fear, it all gets better from here on in. Main school is arranged round a delightful courtyard with a tree at the centre and the low-rise wooden barns and brick buildings make for a rustic, friendly aspect. Inside there's evidence of skilful design that maximises light and space, notably in the double height foyer hung with papier-mâché dinosaur heads and other large artistic endeavours.

Pre-prep is on a domestic scale with its own building and artificial grass playground; the latter used to be full of the usual climbing equipment but this has now been replaced with a selection of bikes, scooters and go-karts. 'What the boys wanted was space to let off steam and things they could zoom around on,' we were told, as we watched them do just that.

Throughout our visit we got a very strong sense that education in its widest sense is pursued here, with all activities, not just core academic subjects, being valued and properly resourced. Parents agree – we heard practically everything on the timetable singled out for praise. Maths is set from year 3 and five sets ensure all abilities get the attention they need. No setting for English until years 7 and 8. Library staff oversee a structured reading programme with online tests to ensure boys are properly ready to move on; an accelerated reading scheme enables them to keep an eye on free readers 'who sometimes lose their way' when they come to the end of guided reading. Research skills are also taught: 'Yes to books and Google, but no to copy and paste.' Huge praise for learning support: 'They really understand,' and also school's attitude to the same, 'If a pupil needs learning support it's never viewed as a negative.' It's a big school but they 'never lose sight of the individual child' and 'the teachers really make an effort to develop boys' talents, whatever they are.'

The Beacon has been at the forefront of developing alternatives to the 'narrow' common entrance system, first designing its own Beacon Certificate of Achievement and subsequently becoming an early adopter of the not dissimilar Prep School Baccalaureate (PSB). Take-up of the PSB is gradually increasing and it is recognised by many senior schools as a broader and more balanced modern alternative to CE. Preparation is given for pre-tests and there are extra classes in year 8 for boys applying to schools who still require them to sit CE. Mr P is a great fan, both of the PSB's value-added (it fosters independent learning and recognises achievement in such areas as teamwork and leadership), and the benefits of presenting senior schools with a portfolio of a candidate's achievements. 'The CE exam is very high stakes, it's only a snapshot of a child's ability,' he comments. He also believes that the PSB allows teachers to flourish, 'the finest teachers should be allowed the most freedom.' School now also runs a middle years PSB.

Head believes that 'eye to eye' will always be the most effective way of teaching and the school library is bursting with books, but there's a sensible balance between old and new tech. Classrooms are well equipped with appropriate kit and there are specialist-taught ICT lessons from reception onwards. Lots of e-safety work, with parents as well as pupils. Boys use email to contact teachers and all homework is set and sent electronically (paper free, no planners). Older pupils learn how to shoot and edit digital video and make films. Perhaps some of these skills could be applied to the school's rather uninspiring website?

International studies, a cross-curricular programme that introduces pupils to a wide range of different cultures, is taught from year 2 to year 4 – parents are encouraged to get involved (over 16 different languages are spoken by Beacon parents). All learn French and Spanish from year 5 and Latin from year 6.

Art and DT enthusiastically pursued and boys' work is exhibited around the school. Bright, paint-spattered art room and very well-equipped DT room where boys start by learning traditional skills using hand tools before moving on to CAD, laser cutters and 3D printers. Beacon boys also leave school with a thorough grounding in nutrition and culinary skills. By year 8 they can all knock up a loaf of bread, and the school's own Masterchef competition is keenly fought. School lunches are beautifully presented and taste delicious: puddings such as lemon meringue sponge served in rustic boxes or watermelon pizza; 'adventurous' salads, curries and different breads – all made on site. Masses of after-school activities including sport, Lego, gardening, creative writing and 'extreme reading' clubs. Lots of opportunities for boys to get involved in charity fundraising, head also keenly developing partnerships with community and local charities eg making theatre and other facilities available.

Pre-prep assemblies, small plays and drama lessons take place in the Old Barn which is, well, just that. It's not, however, big enough to showcase the theatrical talents of all Beacon boys, nor the ambitious programme of productions, from class playlets, to musicals, Shakespeare and light opera. Cue the splendid new Spinney Theatre whose completion was overseen by Mr Phelps while he was still in New York – it was obviously a hot summer over there because he agreed to the installation of air conditioning! There's even an annual 'community' play for which staff, pupils, parents and even the chair of governors audition (recently Oliver!). Senior boys take a play to the Edinburgh Fringe every two years. All year 3 and 4 pupils do a LAMDA exam and school prepares boys for 13+ drama scholarships.

Masses of opportunities for boys of all abilities to participate in music and over 300 individual lessons take place each week. Music is timetabled from reception and in year 2 'bow or blow' trials to help boys chose which instrument to learn. There are five choirs, starting with Little Voices and culminating in Beacon Voices (auditioned). There's even a parents' choir, Vintage Voices. School's size means that in addition to the various choirs it can support a full orchestra, instrumental ensembles, wind bands, rock bands and music technology and theory clubs. Parents think the standard of music is 'incredible', one told us that the school's approach is 'what instrument are you playing?', and another commented that music is so much part of normal school life that boys don't view it as an extra commitment and are thus less inclined to give up.

Unsurprisingly, sport is a big deal, with masses of teams and a full fixture list. Head told us: 'For major sports we field up to five teams to maximise participation; players' performances are assessed post-match and movement between the teams is genuinely flexible.' On the whole parents agreed that there was more than enough glory to go around: 'The cricket B team and the rugby C team still get kudos.' One or two comments to the effect that the Beacon spotlight might not linger on a non-sporty boy, but others disagreed, saying there were plenty of other ways to shine. Standard issue sports hall and lots of space to run about on site, but school's stand-out sporting asset is its playing fields. A few minutes' walk via a quiet suburban cul-de-sac and down a leafy footpath leads to a truly breath-taking vista of pristine pitches rolling away to the Chilterns. Glorious it may be in summer, but apparently it's at least a couple of degrees colder than down town Chesham Bois in the winter. School regularly gets through to the IAPS national finals in rugby and hockey and has an admirable track record in cross-country, tennis and swimming (the latter in spite of an outdoor pool). Matches are played throughout the week and occasionally on Saturday.

Pastoral care is right at the centre of school's three-part management structure (pastoral, academic, executive) and along with well-being and 'lifestyle' is a key component of the Beacon Vision, a statement of how the school sees its future development. Parents we spoke to felt that the school's size was not a barrier to children receiving individual attention and monitoring; they said that home-school communication was much improved and that any problems were handled promptly and with sensitivity.

Catchment is from within a 25-mile radius: surrounding small villages, Rickmansworth, Chorleywood, Gerrards Cross and Aylesbury. Head describes parent body as 'Very aspirational, very grounded. We have plumbers, members of the police force, doctors, London escapees and families where grandparents are paying the fees.' Parents' society organises all kinds social and fundraising activities, it's a 'very active, sociable group', we were told.

The Beacon is a dynamic, busy and above all, happy place. It's a big school that thinks big and while the head and governors have ambitious plans for the future, these are firmly founded upon the school's existing core strengths and values. All aboard for interesting (in a good way) times ahead.

B

Beaconsfield High School

Wattleton Road, Beaconsfield, Buckinghamshire HP9 1RR

Ages 11–18 **Pupils** 1,455 **Sixth form** 288

01494 673043
www.beaconsfieldhigh.bucks.sch.uk

Headmistress: Since 2015, Rachel Smith BA MA NPQH, previously deputy head at Langley Grammar. English degree from Sheffield and masters in educational leadership from Roehampton. Has also been head of English at Robert May's School in Hampshire and acting principal of Kings College for the Arts and Technology in Surrey.

We found her welcoming, gregarious and informal and while she's overflowing with enthusiasm, she's also sincere. And it is this dynamic yet candid approach to discussions about all things educational that gives her both a refreshing sense of authenticity and the 'this-school-might-be-excellent-but-there's-always-more-we-can-do' mindset that she's admired for. 'I love her,' more than one dreamy-eyed girl told us. 'You can literally go and see her anytime about anything.' 'My background is in challenging schools and so I'm very aware of the power of the relationship,' the head told us. 'I'm always saying to the girls, "Come and knock on my door, I'm lonely!"' Big on mantras – 'dare to be remarkable', 'look for happiness', 'we are creative thinkers, not memory sticks' etc – although some go a bit far, one student felt. 'Smile and strive is illogical – you really can't do both at the same time!'

Most parents we spoke to said they had little, if anything, to do with her (and saw that as a good thing), but all seem impressed. 'She's really shaken things up.' 'It was a good school, now it's a great one.' 'She's set the teaching standards much higher and isn't willing to let any department fall behind.'

Lives in Surrey with her husband and two of her five children. Enjoys spending time with her six grandchildren, scuba diving and travelling with her husband in their caravan.

Academic matters: School sits very comfortably in the league tables, currently in top 30 best performing state schools in the country and now quietly outperforming all local competitors without the hothouse reputation, or bookish atmosphere, of some. Also strong on value-added which, say parents, is very much reflected in the teaching approach. 'It used to be all about what grade you get, with no room for dreaded Bs, but now the emphasis is on progress, so the praise comes for getting from X to X, whatever that is,' said one. Girls encouraged not to compare grades to others, although some say it's 'inevitable.'

In 2018, at GCSE, 73 per cent A*-A/7-9 grades. At A level, 76 per cent A*/B grades and 46 per cent A*/A grades. Among the top performing subjects at GSCE are sciences, geography, dance (part of core curriculum), Latin, RS, music and drama, highlighting the academic/creative mix that girls are steered towards. Computing (the only Bucks girls' school to offer it now) is a popular subject, and interest is growing in government and politics too. 'We are desperately trying to hang onto minority subjects,' says head. At A level, sciences, humanities and performing arts get the strongest results.

Spanish, French and Latin from year 7, which girls then choose two from in year 8. Setting in maths and science from year 7, although school tries to call it anything but ('we want to avoid talk of "bottom sets",' explains head). Sciences popular and thriving, although some feel there's still room for improvement in physics department. Girls take 10 GCSEs plus further maths for top set ('the natural mathematicians') and three A levels + EPQ. 'Nobody needs four A levels, so we advise three to show depth of learning and the EPQ to show their passion for subjects – an approach universities tell us they like,' says head.

Teaching generally interactive – in fact, we didn't see one classroom with students sitting, glazed over, in uniform rows. No complaints about homework levels, with most assignments used to prepare girls for future lessons 'as we just don't have the time to present and analyse the knowledge in one lesson.' Teachers deemed to be approachable in relation to homework as well as being 'prepared to give up their time' at breaks and lunchtimes, according to girls, to offer pointers. Peer mentoring and homework clubs also available and a close eye kept on any potential lost sheep. From year 11 up, independent study periods help aid the transition to more independent learning.

Praise for support given during the university application period, especially the all-important personal statement preparation. Career speed-dating goes down well, as do guest speakers (including by high-flying parents) and the school is increasingly teaming up with businesses such as Hitachi so girls get valuable work experience.

Parents and pupils enthuse about the learning resource centre and support and understanding from SENCo in relation to help with anything from autism to visual impairment and dyslexia to dyspraxia. 'They embrace the challenge of SEN here – it's never talked about as a problem and they fight for your daughter to reach her potential, no matter what it takes,' one parent told us; others concur. 'Our centre is all about reducing the tail, and there are very few girls with SEN who don't do as well or better than the main cohort,' says head.

Games, options, the arts: Netball and hockey are the two biggies when it comes to sport, with plenty of gleaming trophies to prove the girls' prowess (netball team regularly wins at national level and they've beaten the likes of Stowe in hockey). But PE (which is compulsory from years 7 to 11) is not just about the elite, with something for everyone including zumba, self-defence and trampolining for those less competitively inclined. A love of dance, which takes place in a dedicated studio, pervades the school – the annual dance show manages to include around 300 girls (and some of the more game teachers) in some capacity across all year groups. Some exceptional gymnasts, swimmers, sailors and rowers, although head admits, 'it's because the girls are really talented, not because we are amazing at teaching these subjects.' Better playing fields than many local counterparts, plus a good sized Astro (although it needs updating), add to the sporty feel of the place.

No shortage of opportunities for budding thespians to showcase their talents in biannual whole-school productions, plus smaller ones. 'The drama department having moved forward leaps and bounds in recent years,' one girl told us.

Art also strong, with some stunning examples of dressmaking and silver sculptures around the front of the school. Whole class projects also presented in and around the two roomy art studios and girls regularly show their work at local art exhibitions. No surprise that art is a popular option at both GCSE and A level. But while the two abstract paintings by a local artist that adorn the reception area are magnificent, you can't help wondering why they didn't hang their own students' work.

Music historically weak, but very much on the up, with orchestras, choirs, jazz band and rock bands, plus around 12 peripatetic teachers. 'The top end performances are jaw droppingly good,' one parent told us.

Tours and trips galore, both curriculum and enrichment-based, with girls heading off near and far to locations such as Iceland (geography), France, Spain and Italy (language trips) and Australia (hockey tour). Super selection of extracurricular activities – mostly free and often led by the girls themselves. These range from chess, coding and knit-and-natter to lyrical, contemporary and hip hop dance.

Background and atmosphere: Like most South Bucks grammars, the bulk of the school is made up of low rise 1960s buildings, but they look noticeably less tatty – and the girls here are far less cramped than their Challoner's equivalents. Subject to the restrictions of local authority funding, the majority of improvements are funded by parents of the steadfastly middle-class cohort. 'We need an update to the Astro, so we'll pay for it,' one parent told us. Good facilities, for the most part, with a revamped, bright and airy reception area and main hall, while the modern canteen brightens up the feel of the school's fabric, with a buzzy adjoining sixth form common room. Also of note are the three new science labs and new sixth form study areas. Library disappointing, with a few measly rows of books, but school says books are mainly fiction now 'as we use the librarian for help in non-fiction research.' School also admits to 'playing catch-up' where technology is concerned, although they have put in a new server, improved Wifi and got some new computers in their computing suite.

Atmosphere is, as one parent put it, 'home counties twee – a conveyor belt turning out well-mannered polished girls.' But make no mistake, these are confident young women, with strong views and razor sharp minds. As such, a purposeful buzz pervades, with chattering girls move noisily around the school and communication with teachers refreshingly non-hierarchical.

Pastoral care, well-being and discipline: 'Everyone has a narrative – be it divorce or death or something else,' says the head, who is determined any difficulties outside school doesn't hold the girls back. As such, pastoral care is top-notch, with girls reeling off a list of people they can talk to from tutors to heads of year and matron to the four-day-a-week counsellor. There's a lot of prevention work too. 'Well-being is a big buzzword here,' one girl said. 'How you make yourself strong, how you deal with failure – there's a lot of talk around that.' Parents note the flexibility of pastoral care. 'My daughter had difficulties in year 10/11 and they really thought outside the box to help her. It's always "how can we help you?" not "this is how we do things,"' a parent told us. But despite the school's best efforts, parents told us the girls can feel pressurised academically.

A tightly-run ship with a no-nonsense approach to keeping the girls in check, but pupils say 'there are no random rules' and there's plenty of allowance for student voice and time for letting off steam during breaks. Detentions (which are for the likes of forgetting homework) are rare and there is no obsession with uniform and length of skirts here.

Lots of chances for older girls to notch up CV-worthy responsibilities, with a head girl elected by students, teachers and governors in a process that would give some job applications a run for their money, plus over 30 senior prefectures and numerous subject prefectures up for grabs. Student council extremely active.

Bullying low level and rare, according to school, which prefers to call it 'friendship issues.' Girls told us it can be particularly cliquey in year 7, but less so from year 8 as girls mature.

Pupils and parents: With grammar schools being the holy grail of the south Bucks education scene and hardly an academic competitor from the private sector in sight, it's no surprise that the vast majority of pupils live in catchment. One third of the cohort join from independent prep schools, with main feeders including High March and Maltman's Green.

Unlike DCHS, neither social nor ethnic diversity are in huge evidence here, reflective of the immediate – but not the broader – catchment, although numbers of Asian girls is on the rise. Parents say school suits girls who like to take on a challenge and can pick themselves up and carry on after a setback, as well as those ready to develop collaborative and leadership skills. Parents a sociable bunch, but most complain communications from the school aren't as efficient as it could be. Bus service covers surrounding areas.

Entrance: Selective. The mysterious business of catchment waxes and wanes on an almost annual basis according to how many are successful in the much hyped Bucks 11 plus. Preference currently given to looked after children and, in rare cases in this super-affluent demographic, those qualifying for free school meals, then siblings. Vast majority, say parents, are tutored, despite school's disapproval.

The competition for places means many girls join in ones or twos from their junior schools, with even the largest (mainly private) feeders sending just 15 to 20 girls. BBQ in the summer holidays means that when asked if any parent hasn't met another one at the start of term, generally not a single hand goes up, while the 'yummy mummies' (as they're known locally) also meet up throughout the year.

Around 22 additional girls join at sixth form, mainly from local private schools such as Piper's Corner, or high achievers from local comprehensives looking for a more academic environment. These girls need to average a high B (or numerical equivalent) overall and usually an A in the subjects they want to study – around a third of applicants get accepted. These girls integrate well into this friendly, supportive school, but are expected to hit the ground running and be able to keep up from day one.

Exit: A number (26 in 2018) leave after GCSES, mainly to private schools; a few to Dr Challoner's Boys, which is now open to girls; and one or two to sixth-form college for a wider syllabus or a change. After A levels, everyone onto higher education or high-level apprenticeships. Of those that choose uni, around 80 per cent to a broad mix of Russell Group universities with popular destinations including Exeter, Birmingham, Durham, Nottingham, Warwick, Bath and Newcastle and a handful each year to Oxbridge (five in 2018). Strong numbers to study medicine and veterinary science each year, and one or two to international universities. The rest are a broad mix of subjects ranging from history and Latin to art.

Money matters: State maintained, although the extremely active Friends' association and highly supportive parent body take fundraising very seriously (this is Beaconsfield, after all), occasionally securing one-off parental donations of up to £10,000. Small hardship fund for those who need it for extras like school trips.

Remarks: 'Becky High' soars above the competition in the league tables, but somehow keeps hold of its relaxed, friendly vibe. Parents and girls fortunate enough to have the choice will find a totally different culture to nearby Dr Challoner's High School and girls will typically fit one mould or the other, with this school offering a gentler transition into senior school and a somewhat more nurturing – some would argue rounded – approach throughout. 'They let you be who you are here' was a common phrase among parents and pupils. Despite repeated changes in leadership, current head looks set to stay. All that's missing is a brother school.

Bedales Pre-prep, Dunannie and Bedales Prep, Dunhurst

Linked with Bedales School

Alton Road, Steep, Petersfield, Hampshire GU32 2DR

Ages Dunannie 3–8; Dunhurst 8–13 **Pupils** 285 **Boarders** 45 full, 36 flexi (from year 4)

Fees: £9,525 – £24,930 pa

01730 711733
www.bedales.org.uk

Head: At Dunhurst since September 2017, Colin Baty, who had previously taught at the prep, and his wife, Debbie, at the pre-prep. Degree in education from Waikato (New Zealand). His 21 years' teaching experience across primary and senior age range includes posts as deputy head (of Moreton Hall) and headmaster of Great Walstead Prep.

At Dunannie since September 2018, Victoria Homewood, previously head of pre-prep at Westbourne House School near Chichester. Degree in English with education from Goldsmiths; her 22 years of experience teaching across the primary age range has included posts as head of pre-prep at Cumnor House Sussex and director of studies at Kew Green Prep. She has also been a literacy consultant and a school inspector.

Entrance: They are looking for children and families who like and understand the Bedales ethos, and this, plus an intention to progress through the school, is all that is necessary for entrance into nursery and reception. For entrance to years 1-3, informal assessment of reading, writing and maths. For Dunhurst, English and maths assessments, reasoning papers and interview. Prospective pupils are considered in the round. Prospective pupils spend time with their peers to see how well they cooperate: three day assessments for 10+ and 11+ applicants. No waiting lists, but a new class in the Groups (years 4-6) due to demand, other classes very close to full. Eight plus and 11+ are natural points of entry.

Exit: Nearly all progress on to Bedales, after sitting a maths and English test. A small number to other senior schools, including Canford, Marlborough, Gordonstoun, ICS, St Swithun's, Cranleigh and Bryanston in recent years.

Remarks: Pupils sitting on chairs, tables, leaning against radiators. Excited laughter, witty chat between teacher and pupils, the energy almost tangible. Were they perhaps discussing a forthcoming party? No: it was a lesson on longshore drift. Rare indeed that longshore drift generates such excitement; but this exchange of energy between teacher and pupils was replicated in other classrooms again and again. Pupils didn't leap to silent feet when we appeared – they were engrossed in learning. The point here is not neat quiet rows, but the work you are doing; and the pupils were fully and busily engaged.

No carrot or stick approach to learning here: it's not an awards assembly sort of place. Time is not wasted on the common entrance – years 7, 8 and 9 do a three year pre-GCSE curriculum. A parent commented that 'children are expected to raise questions which require discussion and debate'; another that 'lessons are rigorous and stretching'. Although one parent commented that a greater insistence on accurate spelling would be nice, most felt that high standards were expected, particularly of those with potential.

Parents agree that English, dance, music and art are outstanding, and that there has been a significant effort to raise the game in sciences and maths, which are now also strong – 'pupils do now routinely learn things by rote, such as tables'. One parent commented happily on the cross fertilisation between subjects, giving the example of a school trip where everyone had to make a snack for everyone else: a happy blend of maths, domestic science and altruism.

Class size is a maximum of 18. Years 4, 5 and 6 have a double in intake, with three or four classes a year in years 7 and 8. Children are only set for maths – they're keen to avoid any labelling here. Saturday morning school starts at age 12 (year 7). Parents aren't terribly keen on it, but the kids don't seem to mind.

Homework is integrated into the day, pupils having a number of free periods called Greens for homework, and any LAMDA or music commitments. Parents say it's great for those who are self-motivated and can organise themselves, and love the fact that prep gets done at school, so kids are free when they get home.

No competitive parenting here; one mum told us if people were heard talking about their child's levels of achievement, other parents would raise eyebrows of horror: they were certainly at the wrong school.

Learning support both in and out of lessons – we spoke to a pupil who chose Dunhurst particularly for its SEN support, and to the happy parents of a dyslexic pupil who had regained lost confidence here.

The whole idea of jaw (a weekly lively discussion forum with a speaker) seems made for the self-assured to fly, reflected in a parent's comment that this is a school which would best suit those who know their own minds, are self-motivated, and not easily influenced by their peers. But this caring environment could also suit those who are more tentative. Development of individual rather than the mass is a focus which pleases parents, and shy children can find their feet and their confidence at Dunhurst.

Those seeking a traditional prep school education might be disconcerted here. 'If a parent has pigeonholed a child as just academic then it won't suit them,' says school. As a parent told us, 'It's not so much which child the school wouldn't suit, as which parents...'.

The pastoral care here is highly praised by parents – the clincher for this school. There's much emphasis on well-being; down time, such as meditation, is incorporated into the school day. The Friday custom of staff shaking hands with pupils stems from the idea that knowing the nature of each pupil's handshake means you can tell if something's wrong; it connects you with every child and gets rid of any bad blood before the weekend. 'It's totally unique', said a parent, describing his son's happiness, and his development of social skills, self-confidence and worldliness at Dunhurst.

Bullying not tolerated here, confirmed a parent, who said that older children have a responsibility to look out for the younger ones, and blow the whistle on any bad behaviour. This is mentioned frequently, as is the Raktivators (new version of peer listening network) and the school counsellor. '[The children are] all very tuned in and look out for each other', said a parent. The school says the approach will depend on the severity: if year 4s are getting a bit tetchy with each other, being a good friend might suddenly become a topic in PHSE.

In disciplinary terms, it's not so much which punishment fits the crime, as what can you give back to the community. Offenders might be put on beauty duty cleaning out the greenhouses; but bring your friends along, some other teachers might join in, and someone brings a radio.

First names between teachers and pupils, and the lack of uniform, might seem strange to newcomers, but there is plenty of respect here – 'when kids talk to adults, they're not frightened', said a parent. Most kids chose to dress very casually – jeans, leggings and hoodies are the norm.

Head, heart and hand are the guiding principles here, and the head part is not just academic; there needs to be something for the soul too: time for stillness and thinking; opportunities to appreciate beauty and contemplate life. So there's lots of art, drama, and music; the divine smell of a room devoted to woodwork – 'Dunhurst pupils wouldn't go to B&Q to buy a shed'. An art room with views over the countryside; a colourful paper model village, with circuits underneath for night time lighting; a table of cupped pottery hands which look as though they are awaiting communion. All do outdoor work – a hand-painted gypsy caravan will become a small classroom. There's an outdoor hut with pizza oven, rows of wellies on pegs, mud and clucking hens; tasks range from building to planting to clearing bracken. There was schoolwide participation in RSPB Birdwatch.

Wednesday afternoon is activity time, which includes outreach for years 7 and 8 (visiting the elderly or helping at local primary schools), outside work, shopping in Petersfield, cooking in Scoffs (the pupil run café) or sports. Sport is not something which is overemphasised, and you can opt out of matches. There is plenty of sport available, with excellent tennis provision, and access to all the Bedales facilities, including the lovely swimming pool, but 'if you're not strong at sports, it's not a big deal', said a parent.

Communication is good, with a Friday report reviewing the week's events. Staff will contact parents by phone or by email if something is going wrong, and one parent described thorough and regular reporting of his child's medical condition.

There are some 80 full and flexi boarders, the latter staying from one night a week. Most boarders are from years 7 and 8. Beds are singles, two to six per room. Comfortable clean facilities, showers and baths – the girls protested at the suggestion of segregating the triple bathrooms – apparently simultaneous bathing is a happy community activity (curtains can be drawn if the girls choose). Kitchen facilities are available at certain times, with cereal, toast and fruit on offer (but boarders must go to the dining hall for proper breakfast and supper). Very few overseas boarders, but pupils can stay at weekends, and trips are organised for those who do.

Dunhurst connects to Dunannie, the pre-prep, but the nursery is separately situated in an old barn, full of light and sunshine, a safe magical world. All the usual tiny person activities, with the addition of an area devoted to planting vegetables, which they subsequently enjoy making into soup.

Dunannie children take learning outside for around a quarter of each day – 'it's not just an add on here'; all-in-one rain gear and wellies hang neatly in a boot room – the children learn how to change very quickly so they can maximise their outside time.

Relaxed classrooms, children sitting happily on the floor, chatting with teachers. Lessons are practically based: year 3 are studying birds, and there are home-made willow bird feeders hung outside the large windows so the class can appreciate visitors.

Individualised learning plans for each pupil, with no expectation that they will all progress at the same rate. A child can do a year again if seems advisable for their happiness and development. Class sizes up to 18, split into two at year 3, where class sizes are up to 15.

Dunannie can cope with quite a profound level of special needs, but those with severe needs are unlikely to be able to progress to Dunhurst. Pastoral care is very strong. The golden rules at Dunannie are to listen and be respectful, and they talk about these rules a lot.

Bedales School

Linked with Bedales Pre-prep, Dunannie and Bedales Prep, Dunhurst

24

Church Road, Steep, Petersfield, Hampshire GU32 2DG

Ages 13–18 **Pupils** 466 **Sixth form** 196 **Boarders** 310 full

Fees: Day £28,515; Boarding £36,285 pa

01730 300100
www.bedales.org.uk

Headmaster: Since September 2018, Magnus Bashaarat MA PGCE (early 50s), previously head of Milton Abbey School and before that deputy head of Stowe. Educated at The King's School, Canterbury (he and Stowe head Anthony Wallersteiner were contemporaries there), followed by University of Edinburgh, where he read English. After work experience at the York Evening Press he decided to become a journalist and worked for the Observer and Evening Standard for a while. He changed direction after taking a course in teaching English as a foreign language – found he loved 'standing up in front of a class and helping people to learn.' PGCE at King's College London, followed by two years at Sherborne and a 15-year stint at Eton, where he taught English and drama and was a housemaster for seven years. He also did a year at Sydney Grammar as part of a teaching exchange with Eton. Moved to Stowe in 2009 and spent five years as deputy head.

His wife Camilla used to work in communications for the NHS and they have three children. In his spare time, he cycles, rows and goes to the theatre as much as he can. He likes 'serious drama'.

Academic matters: Education is different here, its value much more in itself than the end qualifications – the qualification hoops to be jumped to get to the university to reach the gold-plated job. It's not that Bedales ignores these reasonable parental desires – most students end up at the same universities – but it tries as far as possible to make education of the individual the thing: 'to develop inquisitive thinkers with a love of learning who cherish independent thought'.

Qualifications look different here too, to fit this more holistic vision of learning: 'the wonderful BACs' (as described by a parent) are a living alternative to GCSEs. They focus on cross-curricular, independent thought, with a range of assessment methods from written assignments to presentations and performances: an organic process of learning over time, with few make or break final day assessments. And universities are happy with them too, though Bedales retains a compulsory core of five IGCSEs in English, maths, modern languages and sciences. Parents and pupils like the mixture of assessment methods in the BACs, and they're done and dusted in time to leave a clear month to revise for IGCSEs.

At BACs/IGCSEs in 2018, 62 per cent A*-A/9-7. It's a classical looking curriculum, but global awareness and sports science BACs are new. Philosophy, religion and ethics (PRE) is one of the most popular BACs, with nearly half of the students taking this option. 'It really makes pupils think, and they carry those skills and that knowledge with them. It's evident in their thinking at A level...a really impressive linking of ideas', said a parent. Classics was also particularly highlighted by parents, who said the quality of teaching is 'superb'. '[students are] really stimulated and pushed to the limit'.

Uniquely at Bedales, there is no dead time after IGCSEs and BACs. Pupils start their A level courses immediately, so they have a two week A level taster before the summer holidays. If pupils don't like what they have opted for, they can change courses before starting A levels properly in September.

At A level, 42 per cent A*-A, 69 per cent A*-B in 2018. Maximum class size is 14 but often significantly smaller. Enrichment, compulsory for those not taking four A levels, safeguards time to learn something just for the joy of it; it could include beginners' Russian, oak framed building, dance or astronomy. 'Education at its best', said a parent, another describing her child's delight at doing art again, having given this up to concentrate on academic subjects.

The counter-side of all this educational roaming is a strong and structured guidance system: there's a six weekly review by teachers of each student's effort and attainment, and students have a fortnightly one-to-one tutorial. The tutor's job is to get students to self-motivate and organise, and help them realise that what they put in to learning is what they get out. This 'got it' moment should happen earlier at Bedales because of the innate value placed on learning, but in the rare case that it hasn't clicked by the sixth form, they will put a military structure in place to try and help.

In this strong community, students are encouraged to help others academically: year 13s can be Badley seniors (from founder John Badley) and help year 9s with their work; others become dons – English dons, physics dons etc – and champion a subject to help others.

Homework is generally fitted into free periods during the day, one parent commenting on the different homework culture at traditional schools: her non-Bedales child swots all evening. A parent commented that his daughter feels the pressure a bit, but the Bedalian atmosphere helps: 'If she was surrounded by little Miss Perfects it would be much worse'.

Students at Bedales are generally highly motivated, owing, a Harvard study suggests, to a love of learning, and the level of autonomy and choice enjoyed by students here. But 'some don't bother at all', said a parent, who wondered whether a more pushy environment might galvanise the lazy. Here, the approach is to try to find out why children are not performing, and help them develop their full potential. And generally this works much better than an order from above: parents refer to the unusual mutual respect between teachers and pupils – 'a powerful developmental thing'. '[They're a] really gifted staff', said another.

Learning support (LS) is staffed by one full-timer and six part-timers, two of whom are maths specialists, and is charged as an extra. A speech and language therapist comes in as necessary. Up to two sessions of support a week during free periods.

Around a third of students use LS at some point: the department is happy to provide spasmodic support for particular difficulties. LS generally supports mild learning difficulties (but can cope with severe dyslexia). Progress rates of dyslexic students are the same as others, with some doing exceptionally well.

Several parents described dyslexic children who suffered from self-esteem issues while attending high achieving, pressurised schools, and the difference in their children once they started at Bedales: 'Bedales is outstanding in the support it offers pupils'; 'they draw out the best in children'.

Games, options, the arts: This must be the only school in the country which has 'appreciation of the beautiful' as one of its aims. 'There is an intense delight in seeing your work grow under your hand...It is the delight of creation, of shaping something that shall have use and beauty, the delight of an artist' (John Badley, founder). Outdoor work is a key part of the curriculum: from planting, to building a posh pig sty, to putting a new engine in an ancient Land Rover.

Parents eulogise about the music, arts and drama here – 'art is very, very good – they're really pushed and well prepared for A level'. Music receives similar accolades: the BAC is much more demanding than GCSE, dismissed by the head of music as a 'pub quiz': students go from the BAC to music Pre-U. Performances take place in the lovely timber-framed Olivier Theatre and there is an award-winning new art and design building with arching roofs and skylights. Bedales arts feels a thoroughly professional affair, from a display of Matisse, visiting theatre, music and dance, to in-house productions.

'Sport doesn't dominate the extracurricular', though Bedales competes in the usual rounds of county, regional and national competitions. But sport is just one option in the compulsory activities programme, allowing pupils to choose from a range of cerebral, social and physical activities (heads up for the boys – this is not a big rugby school).

Plenty of charity initiatives, D of E, no CCF. No noticeable community service either, which parents feel is an omission, and surprising since one of the school's aims is engaging with the local community.

Boarding: Pastoral care for boarders is excellent, agree parents, one saying that the housemistress 'did a better job than we would have done' with his anxious daughter: she 'knew instinctively' what would work.

Comfortable, well-kept single sex boarding houses, with mixed aged dorms, which are a big plus, parents feel. Year 12 pupils take the responsibility of running dormitories and caring for younger pupils, although one parent said her daughter opted out of boarding to avoid being dorm mentor, which is a time-consuming post. No flexi-boarding, so those who aren't interested in boarding full time may revert to day pupil status. Year 13 pupils live in a separate, co-ed boarding house as preparation for university. Dorm size varies from two to six beds. Dorms have a comfortable, homely feel even during the day, students returning during breaks to lounge happily on beds and chat or work. To clamp down on overuse of technology, school Wifi is switched off at 10.30pm and the Block 3s (year 9s) hand in their phones at night.

Laundry is done for younger children; year 13s learn to do their own. Kitchens in boarding houses are open 8.30-9.30pm, with pasta, bread and butter, and fruit available. Students do kitchen duty twice a week – 'a bit grim' said a boarder.

Most students return home on Saturday afternoon until Sunday evening. Those left at school – overseas boarders (some eight per cent), or those who live further afield in the UK – can enjoy much-needed downtime. Non-compulsory Sunday activities range from bake-off and pizza making using the school's pizza oven in the barnyard ('anything to do with food is a winner,' says head of boarding), to visiting a steam fair, cinema or bowling. Some walk into town; 'some just slump', said a student.

'It's the ethos of boarding school with day pupils', said one parent, who feels this is a boon – even day students have to do activities in the evening, so can be at school until around 9.30pm.

Background and atmosphere: Nonconformist. No Sir or Miss, no uniform – unless the prevalence of hoodies could be described as such. Emphasis on development of the individual, and collaboration between individuals.

This school is in many ways quite extraordinarily lovely: you can feel the life and energy in the wood when you enter the oak-framed arts and crafts memorial library. There is an integrity about the buildings, their construction and materials: a clear coherence with the school's ethos. Bedales sits comfortably in the surrounding gentle countryside: a world apart in many ways – a 'Bedales bubble,' said a parent.

The school wants this to be a protected part of life, but says there 'needs a breeze to come through from beyond'. This evident in the fortnightly Jaw, a more inclusive version of other schools' assemblies, with student or visitor led debate on matters of moral or spiritual engagement. 'It opens their horizons', said a parent; 'makes them feel they can do anything'. The breeze is also evident in careers advice, which aims to develop ambition and show horizons, old Bedalians playing their part by mentoring and networking.

'Not pressurised', said a parent, whose academic children benefit from being big fish in a small pond. 'Work is not carried out in a competitive fashion'. She sometimes asks herself whether more pressure might make them do better (her son just failed to get into Oxford) – '[but] the ethos of the school is very attractive, and of more benefit than attending a school which would have helped achieve Oxford. And socially Bedales is the best', the parent concluded. Another parent commented on this positive atmosphere: her daughter was lazy at her old school, but now never wants to be late, is really trying hard and working her best.

'Bedales doesn't do prizes', said a parent, 'it just doesn't believe in them'. An egalitarian, no marks on the wall sort of establishment. This means if you're not very good at something, no-one need know. Achievement is celebrated via a handwritten card, or email, with those doing really well being invited to a head's feast.

Pastoral care, well-being and discipline: Pastoral care is the real strength of the school, said a parent – 'if you're vulnerable, if you've had a terrible time, it's lovely'. Another said that 'people are understanding, friendly, kind, and very open'. 'They will find something good about you'. Understandably, in the light of this, Bedales does sometimes find itself receiving serial offenders from other schools. Sometimes it works; sometimes parents are not happy that these kids convince peers to follow them into 'naughty projects'; worth perhaps bearing in mind the comment from a parent that this school suits best children who know their own minds.

'Before we went to the school, we had the impression it was all about sex and drugs', said a parent, who was very pleased to find it was zero tolerance in many areas. 'There are a fair number of pupils who smoke', she added, but the school firmly tries and stop this amongst Block 3s (year 9); it is harder to control amongst sixth formers. 'They try to keep an eye out, but the kids need some freedom', she added. Parents are pleased that the school talks to them about its approach to drugs, taking into account their views. There are occasional incidents of bullying, said a parent, but they are dealt with appropriately

– 'it's harder to get away with here because of the strong integration between the years'.

Many parents spoke of the strong relationships at this school: between pupils, and pupils and teachers – '[it's] as close to family as possible to get'. 'Pupils good at celebrating each other', said another, describing the time when her child had to wear sunglasses for an eye problem, and was teased by a couple of classmates. The housemistress sent out a carefully crafted light email: some kids sent apologies, and the next day all the kids in class turned up in sunglasses in support. The day mistress called the parents and kept them informed. Several parents commented on the unusual level of involvement: at other schools, the doors are closed, school knows best. Not at Bedales. Parents are very involved here. 'It's almost like being at primary school', said one, who said school is very welcoming to parents and 'very, very patient'.

Food was delicious on the day of our visit, though no meat Thursdays, the brainchild of the vegan head boy a couple of years ago, is controversial with committed meat eaters, who don't see why they should be forced to abstain.

Pupils and parents: Parents include media, actors, business, celebrities, professionals, scientists, a few bankers ('with exceptional educational views', said a parent), trust fund kids, and a few from overseas. A broader range than there used to be, says school, with more traditional parents reassured by good behaviour and academic records. 'Good alumni', said one parent practically – 'you're buying a network'.

Communication with parents is generally good, though there are occasional blips on the school website.

Entrance: Maths, English and general ability test for 13+ entry in the January 18 months before entry. Just over half from Dunhurst, and most of the rest from preps in London and the south east, in particular Westbourne House, Highfield and Amesbury. For sixth form entry, minimum average of grade 5 at GCSE.

Exit: Around 15-30 per cent leave after GCSEs, but these are more than replaced by a large sixth form intake which forms 30-40 per cent of the new year 12. Pupils depart for a variety of universities, music conservatoires and art colleges, a small number of Oxbridge (four in 2018), and many to Russell group (eg Edinburgh, Bristol, LSE), plus some overseas: three off to do liberal arts (at Yale, Washington and San Diego) and one to Amsterdam for European studies. Ten per cent of 2018 cohort are studying science-based degrees, including two medics and one nurse.

Money matters: Innovative approach to scholarships gives scholars access to an individual research fund. The school funds around 70 bursaries at a cost of over £1 million per annum, and offers fully funded bursaries through its John Badley Foundation from age 11 upwards.

Remarks: Most children would thrive at this lovely school. Parents described the very clever, the quirky, the academic and those in the middle, all of whom are happy. Not perhaps for a child who needs lots of boundaries, or a large degree of privacy; and it wouldn't, perhaps, suit all parents, who need to be broad-minded about the purpose of education. But for most children, this would be a wonderful place to grow a rooted sense of self, and joy in life and learning.

Bede's Preparatory School

Linked with Bede's School

B

Duke's Drive, Eastbourne, East Sussex BN20 7XL

Ages 3 months–13 years **Pupils** 388 **Boarders** 14 full, 11 weekly, 3 flexi (from year 4)

Fees: Day: £10,230– £17,400; Boarding Supplement: £8,250 pa

01323 734222
www.bedes.org

Headmaster: Since 2013, Giles Entwisle (BA, Loughborough). Previously deputy head at Highfield; has also been head of year, housemaster and head of MFL at Holmewood House, near Tunbridge Wells.

'All the parents love him', said one, 'he's fabulous'. Pupils love him too – 'really kind'; 'can talk to him and feel like you're having a conversation'. This is not a school where they'll brush you off with 'not on the syllabus': if you're interested, it's relevant. Bede's prides itself on encouraging individuals in their passions whatever they may be, and this head is keen for a challenge. What could they do for an astronomer, your reviewer asked at random: the junior galactic challenge, to create a habitat for humans on Mars... 'Give me another one...' said the head with relish.

Entrance: Not academically selective. Entry by interview and screening for SEN.

Exit: A small number leave to return home overseas, or to attend a more traditional academic school such as Brighton College. The rest progress to the senior school.

Remarks: You can't beat it for location. At the upmarket end of the grassy Eastbourne seafront where the land curves and rises to the great cliff of Beachy Head, perches an attractive five storey, mock-Tudorbethan pile, its long windows facing the sea. Surrounded by fields on all but its southern aspect, with a cluster of smaller buildings round about, it sits like a benign hen comfortably supervising its offspring, assured that all can run about safely in a healthy, beautiful, open space.

Space is a key asset and to anyone used to, for example, an urban prep or primary, Bede's is a revelation. There are more fields five minutes up the hill and another five minutes inland – all facilitate the range of sports available to these lucky children, who have the look of relaxed freedom that inhabiting such openness gives. Space also in, for example, the dining hall, one wall of which is just large windows fully open on warm, sunny days, so that the outside and the inside blend.

Two main buildings. Holywell Mount – a large Edwardian house to the right of the main building if you face the sea – houses the pre-prep and nursery. We visited at the end of a long day and were astonished by the bright-eyed vitality of the teachers. They told us of the new topic with which each term is launched in each classroom: 'It's so exciting – they can't wait to come in and see what we're going to do!' And on offer in just some rooms were: Under the Sea World, Ice World, Out of the Egg (and you should have seen the egg!) and Knock Knock – imaginative stuff, inviting exploration and discovery of all kinds.

Sports are exceptional – and not just because of facilities – at both ends of the spectrum. Says Mr Entwisle: 'We're the best

B

cricketing prep in the country' and, as parents told us, 'even the non sporty get enthused – and they have elite schemes for the really talented'. 'They do wonderful trips, especially for sports and languages.' Children concur: 'We went to Portugal and got trained by Benfica.' They have a cliff top walk to reach their playing fields – a walk many remember with great affection years later – but many sports are now played up at the senior school. They do, though, have their own swimming pool on site. Several teams in most sports for all years so that all but the child with thumbs glued to his iPad get a look-in, though some sense that more could be done for the less than athletic. Dance is serious – remember that Bede's is home to The Legat Dance School – so all do dance up to year 5 and many continue. Teachers seen as 'brill!'. Music has a relatively new director and is set to sparkle; art and drama well on the way.

An overhaul of maths has effected learning and results, and is starting to influence other subjects, as the effectiveness of the new method becomes evident: before studying in the abstract, a subject is examined form every angle and thoroughly embedded – no racing from topic to topic to tick the boxes of rapid progress. 'Maths lessons are now noisy', said the head; in fact one was quiet, but the next was, indeed, noisy – 'that's better...', said the head. Parents enthuse: 'The teachers are wonderful – so imaginative and approachable!' – and especially about individual needs and pastoral care: 'superb – any problems or hint of bullying are dealt with at speed' and 'they answer emails practically before you've sent them'. Weekly staff meeting to discuss and act on academic or pastoral concerns with head of learning support on hand if needed. Pupil praise too – 'They push you to your potential and we are only 10 in some groups so they can really help you'. Small group specialist work in eg fine motor skills, writing, reading, phonics for tots who seem to be falling behind. All lower classes have a TA to support individuals but some feel this should continue into upper years, 'where they need it just as much if they are struggling with a subject'. As a pupil told us, 'When I'm stuck, if they take time to explain it to me, I really get it!' Individual support – and around 25 per cent on the SEND register here – described as 'good but pricey'.

All staff are being trained in first aid mental health. The head says anxiety is sometimes a problem for pupils coming in from hothouse schools – pupils can be school phobic and need to be reintegrated into school. For pupils feeling pressured, the school counsellor runs 'chill and chat' drop in sessions at break time. 'Health and safety are taken very seriously,' parents tell us, as are efforts to integrate newcomers, especially into year 7 when there is a fairly substantial intake.

And there is masses to do. 'My daughter was very shy but there are so many performances and so on – her confidence has grown unbelievably.' No shortage of facilities, inside and out – big sports hall, 18m pool, climbing walls, decent library – 'they'll get books you want if you ask' – good theatre and lovely, light rooms with the downside that 'if I'm facing the sea I just go into a daydream,' as one youngster confessed.

Most are local, though word is spreading and pupils now bus or car in from a wider range of villages. School runs its own bus service on eight routes. There are a small numbers of boarders, in a family house over the road from the school. Lovely warm houseparents and Molly the dog, of bounding, bouncing love, a garden big enough for football, and blankets to snuggle down under to watch TV. Rooms allocated sensitively, the quiet girls who like their sleep separate from their noisier peers.

Bede's prep and senior are increasingly one school, the heads busy building strategies to ensure smooth academic and co-curricular progression through the schools. Service is a mantra senior school head returns to again and again, and he's determined to make it school wide – 'year 1 can be collecting for the food bank and the sixth form can volunteer there'.

A happy school – 'It's good at turning out all-rounders,' said several. 'It's pretty unsophisticated and relaxed – you don't get awful pushy parents there – they trust the school to know what it's doing.' And, in the words of a pupil, 'My parents wish they could have come here.'

Bede's School

Linked with Bede's Preparatory School

The Dicker, Upper Dicker, Hailsham, East Sussex BN27 3QH

Ages 13–19 **Pupils** 449 **Sixth form** 316 **Boarders** 186 full, 101 weekly

Fees: Day £22,110; Boarding £33,060 – £35,160 pa

01323 843252
www.bedes.org/

Headmaster: Since 2016, Peter Goodyer (Rhodes, BA, Keele, MBA), previously deputy then acting head at Colston's school, Bristol. First came to this country from his native South Africa as a teacher of history and geography to a school in Leatherhead, and never went home. Dad was a vicar, and there is something of the pastor with flock about Mr Goodyer: he wants his pupils to make a difference in their community and the world, and understand what it means to give of themselves.

Pupils are very enthusiastic about him: 'easy to talk to'; 'knows us all'; 'down to earth'; 'his priority is our well-being... and the teachers' well-being...and the bus drivers' and the cleaners'...'. Pupils find Mr Goodyer 'accessible', in what he says and how he says it, and although some parents might miss the smooth charm of his predecessor's oratory, pupils prefer Mr Goodyer's straightforward approach. They believe him, and think he believes in them.

Parents like Mr Goodyer too: 'Extremely friendly, always smiling, easy to talk to, good sense of humour. Good psychology – about finding the talent in your child and helping them to grow'.

Academic matters: A pupil who left Bede's returned a term later – 'the difference was in the teaching – at the other school things were just presented, with no engagement...[here] they care'. Both pupils and parents praise the dedication of teachers, one describing chatting to her German teacher during the holidays over My Bede's (a sort of firefly); another saying her son emailed a teacher at 11.45pm, and he answered at midnight.

'Bede's has a reputation as not terribly academic, but from what we've seen, he's not held back at all', said a parent. Results are good, sometimes exceptional (maths is a consistently strong subject), and a parent said that both the prep and senior school have become more academic, 'but not scarily so'. In 2018, 40 per cent A*-A/9-7 at GCSE; at A level, nearly 42 per cent A*-A. There are some extremely academically bright pupils here, but they're not all like that, and Bede's wouldn't want it so. The best mainstream independent school in Sussex for value added; evidence of the strong culture of growth mindset here for the pupils.

A good range of subjects on offer, and seven BTecs, including animal management. No feeling that they are a second class option – a pupil who wanted to study marine biology at university, but struggled with A levels, got to the same place by doing a double BTec in animal management. As the head says, 'BTecs can get you where you want to go'.

Class sizes 15-20, eight or nine classes per year, with pupils from the prep making up a third of the first year.

The first year creative carousel is very popular, and, says the head, very important – 'Once a child understands by what it is they are fulfilled, motivation will follow...You don't have to be successful to be happy – you need to be fulfilled'. Carousel subjects range from graphic design to sculpture. First years also take 21st century studies, which teaches important skills like personal finance, psychology (taught by the head) and cooking – 'my child can make a Mexican breakfast and an omelette', said a parent.

The Bede's diploma is for sixth form pupils, and includes the EPQ; a lecture series, much approved of by parents – 'from Oxbridge to the New York school of dance'; leadership and teamwork competencies; and community service, options ranging from Meow Mondays at the Cats Protection League to assisting at a local primary school. A junior version of the diploma is in the pipeline.

Learning enhancement is much praised by parents for its 'really really good support...he was not achieving in other schools'; another said that his bright dyslexic daughter has done better academically here than in her academic prep. Individual, small group and in class support available. Parents report good liaison between LE and class teachers.

Games, options, the arts: 'Co-curricular is extraordinary', said a parent. Activities take place three times a week, chosen from a vast range, from the BEden project (creating a sustainable, organic healing garden using recycling and freecycling), making a homebrew in wine-making (sixth formers only) and UK space design. Pupils say that strong community groups which span ages develop in different activity areas, and that trying new things is one of the best things about the school; but those who want something calm and low key are also catered for: in reading for pleasure, pupils sit peacefully in the library with thermoses of tea and coffee and a plate of digestives – no feeling that this is a choice for second class citizens. In animal management, pupils look after a range of zoo animals, and help with the dormouse breeding programme to increase numbers in the wild. One activity must be something physical, but determined games haters could choose walking, along the sea front or across the downs.

Many pupils are attracted by the choice of sport – others by not having to play it. The main sports are hockey, cricket and football because both sexes can and do play, in mixed and single sex teams. One family was attracted to Bede's by the tennis academy, which is excellent. (Not a school for rugby devotees, but rugby 7s available for those who like a taste.) Sports facilities which could serve a small town – 'second to none', said a parent – and the sports coaching is outstanding, say parents and pupils. BTec sport is popular.

Art and DT are superb here, some of the most popular subjects in the school, from fine art, to weird and wonderful photography, to furniture that would not look out of place in Heals. Pupils consistently attain top grades in art and photography, and serious art lovers will receive the encouragement and help to take their studies further.

Drama is another strength popular – 'productions are fantastic – if you close your eyes...on a par with X Factor', said a parent. The theatre on site is small, but the school uses Devonshire Park Theatre in Eastbourne for big productions, such as the recent Oliver!, described by a parent as 'simply fabulous. Evidence of fantastic teaching and mentoring...Such team work and commitment demonstrated...'.

Not many take music as an examination subject, but there are plenty of choirs, orchestras and bands, and for those keen to dance, Bede's is home to the Legat dance school – the head boy of the prep dances every day.

Boarding: 'A real atmosphere of family...brotherhood', said a pupil. In large boarding houses of around 80, pupils are organised into family groups of 10, spanning the year groups, who look out for each other. It works, one pupil saying, 'I've got really good friends who are older than me'. A parent commented that the houses are run in a very inclusive way, with all sorts of events to bring them together; there is certainly a vigorous house system, with fierce competition ranging from cross-country (most run, but one pupil strolls, reading a book) to pumpkin carving.

Some 40 per cent of senior pupils board, weekly and full time only (for the same cost – pupils can choose whether to stay weekends). Day pupils can join in boarding activities at weekends if they book in advance, and there's always plenty going on, from target rifle shooting to South Downs photography, with Sundays for lie-ins and shopping trips.

Boarding houses range from converted houses to modern and purpose built. The girls' house decorated in pink and bunting, the boys' with flags of all the different nationalities in the house. The houses we saw were in excellent condition – a pupil said some of the others are bit tireder, but good in essentials.

Younger pupils are four or five in a room, lower and upper sixth one or two. Kitchens with toast and fruit freely available. Kids have to hand in tech at 9.30pm, recently tightened up to ensure compliance, and Wifi is turned off at night. Sixth formers can keep phones.

Day boarders also belong to boarding houses, with a place there to stay and study at school in the evening – 'quiet and comfortable,' said parent. 'More support, a belonging feeling...'.

'Good communication from tutor and housemaster', said a parent who lives abroad. 'They really look after my son...he's very secure in the boarding environment'. If parents have a concern, they need to be proactive – 'you need to be a partner, don't sit back', said a parent.

Such a variety of views about food it is difficult to believe they are talking about the same meals. Delicious on the day of our visit, with a good range of choice. Breakfast is 'the best meal of the day,' said a boarder – full English is available, plus fruit, cereals, and homemade yogurt and bread. There is the usual boarding takeaway pizza community, and boarders are keen supporters of the village shop, but the pupils' food committee talks directly to caterers, and suggestions are implemented.

Background and atmosphere: 'Its location is a real plus... beautiful, surrounded by green...got a bit of a wow factor', said a parent. A first impression of the school is one of great size, with school buildings a mish-mash of styles – some old and charming, some modern and splendid, and a few huts.

Plenty of international students – 'it's exciting to hear the variety...makes you tolerant of everyone...you can be yourself in that', said a pupil, and a similar variety of religions.

School buses cover a 35 mile radius, and you may well see their philosophy quotes darting past on their way in to Bede's. There is some real effort to be true to these sayings; pupils saying, 'you don't have to fit the mould'. The appreciation of individuals is clear, not just in their choice of activity, but also their choice of appearance, with no attachment to traditions empty of meaning: boys can have long hair, providing it's kept neat (though the head doesn't particularly like 'those top knots'); boys can put their earrings in once they get back to the boarding houses in the evening; and with clear-sighted ease, the head put uniform changes to the vote: girls voted to wear trousers, then chose the design, and a tie in house colours, loosely tied (in truth, slightly BA style). But, most importantly: the head asked the pupils, and they decided.

B

Bede's prep and senior are increasingly one school, the heads busy building strategies to ensure smooth academic and co-curricular progression through the schools. Service is a mantra Mr Goodyer returns to again and again, and he's determined to make it school wide – 'year 1 can be collecting for the food bank and the sixth form can volunteer there'.

Pastoral care, well-being and discipline: '[They] make the kids feel good about themselves...[with] emotional support as well as academic support', said a parent, another adding she has noticed a real difference in her child since going to Bede's – body image, clothes and make up matter less, and her daughter told her to 'embrace who you are – don't worry about how you look'.

Another parent told us they chose Bede's in the hope their introverted son would gain social skills; he's now 'coming out of his shell, more confident, speaking up.... Bede's is the right place', she went on; 'it identifies the weakness of a child, and finds ways of taking them out of their comfort zone' (her sports-loving son is encouraged to organise competitions).

A pupil transferring from another school said she couldn't believe how well behaved everyone was, and pupils agreed it might not suit someone with really challenging behaviour – 'but lots of chances are given', said one earnestly. Misbehaviour is not generally a problem here: 'Pupils are really happy, so they don't need to misbehave', suggested one.

There is less bullying than at many schools due to diversity and increased tolerance, thought one pupil – 'from year 9 you have to accept difference'. The online Whisper programme allows pupils to report concerns anonymously; pupils are encouraged to blow the whistle, and have done in an incidence of sexting, which was dealt with thoroughly.

Mental health is 'quite forensically managed,' said the head, with an online system of recording anything of concern, from behaviour which is slightly out of character upwards, with regular reviews. A parent told us that when her daughter had anxiety problems, the head of house was 'straight on to it', and she praised the good relationships with tutors – 'very supportive, know the children really well'. There are two school counsellors, and a mental health nurse.

Pupils also mention getting support from the chaplain, and from attendance at chapel – a message, or moral or a reflective piece of music. 'We try and touch on all religions', said the head.

At prep school, all staff are being trained in first aid mental health. The head says anxiety is sometimes a problem for pupils coming in from hothouse schools – pupils can be school phobic and need to be reintegrated into school. For pupils feeling pressured, the school counsellor runs 'chill and chat' drop in sessions at break time.

Pupils and parents: Social all sorts. 'Not typical public school... as you imagine them to be', said parent. 'Bede's has more variety...it has the diversity that a modern school needs'.

'Caters for all sorts', said a parent of three very different children who are all happily accommodated at Bede's.

Entrance: Not academically selective. Entry to prep by interview and screening for SEN. Those applying to senior school must attend the Bede's experience day: MIDYIS test, discussion and problem-solving tasks with prefects, then choice of activity. The head seeks diversity and balance – a year group will not consist solely of the loudest voices with best academic scores.

Exit: Some 25 per cent leave after GCSEs, mostly for sixth form colleges. After sixth form, students head out in every direction: two to Oxbridge in 2018, others to a range including Bath, Oxford Brookes, Exeter, Leeds, Liverpool, Nottingham, Sussex, UCL and Warwick. Plus: maths in Lausanne, business admin at Syracuse and Ontario, physics at NYU, engineering at Dartmouth, media in Paris, Rome and San Francisco.

Money matters: Scholarships of up to 25 per cent and a good and growing bursary fund.

Remarks: Bede's fosters individual strengths and helps individuals with weaknesses. As a parent said, 'You don't have to be good at everything...if they thrive at something it spills over into the rest of life'.

Beechwood Park School

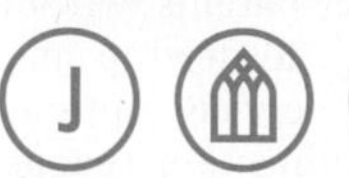

Pickford Road, Markyate, St Albans, Hertfordshire AL3 8AW

Ages 3–13 **Pupils** 540 **Boarders** 60 flexi (from year 5)

Fees: Day £9,735 to £16,530; Flexi boarding plus £3,930 pa

01582 840333
www.beechwoodpark.com/

Headmaster: Since 2015, Edward Balfour (40s), Winchester born and educated at Pilgrim's Prep and King Edward VI School Southampton, followed by Cardiff University where he read English literature. Started career at the Royal Grammar School, Worcester, then gained a PGCE at Homerton College Cambridge. English teacher at Uppingham, followed by Whitgift, then 13 years at Bradfield ('where I was educated most'), taking over as head of drama aged just 27, before turning around an 'unruly' boarding house, transforming it into school's 'most successful and desirable'. Entered prep school stratosphere with first headship at Northbourne Park School in east Kent.

A skilled marketer with soundbites to rival top politicos (but don't let that put you off), says 'fluidity and progressiveness' are key strengths of school. Self-proclaimed 'evangelist' on the modernisation of prep school education. Asks 'what does preparatory actually mean? It certainly doesn't mean pushing children.' Wants to remove 'useless formality'. We approve. As does the parent cohort who, in the main, are big fans and say he's 'exactly what the school needed.'

Married to Emma, a Cambridge linguist, who teaches at Beechwood, with three children, the youngest of whom attends Beechwood, the others at school in Canterbury and St Albans.

Entrance: Only 'slightly' selective, according to head. Now oversubscribed at 3+ thanks to the on site Woodlands Nursery, which has 40 children, all of whom typically move up to the reception class. Nursery places given on first come, first served basis. A further 20 places in reception, with a gentle assessment during the year prior to entry. Small intake each year into year 7.

Exit: Around a third of total cohort (the majority of girls plus a handful of boys) leave at the end of year 6, heading to a broad mix of private and state schools (including some of Harpenden's excellent comprehensives, eg Sir John Lawes, St George's and Roundwood). Girls also to St Albans High and Berkhamsted in numbers and ones and twos to Queenswood, Haileybury, Abbot's Hill and Habs' Girls most years.

At 13+ boys move to St Albans School in droves plus small numbers to eg Bedford, Berkhamsted, Haileybury and Merchant Taylors' – parents report extremely favourably on preparation at this stage (a few grumbles that it could be better at 11+, although school says it has been tackling this): each child is given a study plan and, for potential scholars, extra classes are put on – sometimes even at weekends. Not an obvious choice if Eton, Harrow et al are top of your wish list (you'd be in the minority – parental aspirations tend to err on the side of quality day schools) but small numbers of pupils do head off to board at eg Millfield, Oundle, Uppingham and, occasionally, Harrow – so school can deliver the goodies for these destinations if it needs to. Decent clutch of scholarships most years.

Remarks: Approached down a seemingly endless winding driveway, the main school building is an immaculately restored Tudor manor house nestled amongst fields and woodland as far as the eye can see. Walled gardens and wrought iron gates surround the main building as constant reminder of the grand history of the house as, most notably, the family seat of the aristocratic Sebright family.

At 3, pupils enter the Woodlands Nursery, a wood-clad, purpose built structure on the edge of the school's woodland. Vast space, with super indoor and outdoor play areas. A true haven to introduce littlies to the school world without the rough and tumble of their older peers, and parents love the almost daily online feedback on their child's progress. From there, pupils progress to the less picturesque but heartily practical junior block where they join one of four reception classes of 15 pupils, changing to three classes of 20 in years 1 and 2. Compact and colourful with its own gardens, although mobile library in makeshift area not the most inspiring for young readers. This, however, is more than compensated for by the stunning senior school library in the main school building. We were assured by the head before our visit that we would be 'blown away' by the wealth of space and facilities – we certainly couldn't fail to be.

French taught from the get-go by a specialist teacher; reception were playing French fruit bingo when we visited and at the top of the school pupils write and perform their own French play. History equally engaging: what's not to love about a year 2 class setting fire in the playground to paper houses they have made to bring the Great Fire of London to life? Pupils split into four sets for maths in year 4 and for English in year 5. From year 6 onwards, all are split into tutor groups of around 10, with whom they stay for the remainder of their time at school, and are specialist taught for all subjects. Staff mature enough to be experienced but not over the hill, and across the board seem to ooze passion for their subject; science (despite the somewhat rickety appearance of the labs) impressed on the basis of the departmental head's enthusiastic description of a recent 'dunkability of biscuits' experiment alone ('we keep it very practical; it has to be') as did the year 6 pupils rehearsing for the Latin play, Cinderella. Beats reciting verbs, that's for sure, and parents describe the Latin teaching as 'phenomenal'.

All children screened for mild specific learning difficulties and around 60 on register. Three full-time staff offer one-to-one sessions in a dedicated space (mainly either before school in the morning or during library lessons to avoid withdrawal) as well as in-class support to those that need it. Whole school monitored for progress in reading and spelling and children referred for a booster if they need it. Touch typing offered as early morning club and those who satisfy the criteria are allowed to use laptops in class and in exams from year 6. Support is very much dyslexia focused. School says it provides outstanding care for a number of high functioning children with mild ASD although we felt that those classed as moderate would be better placed elsewhere.

All the usual sports – the newish director of sport has 'transformed' the offering at Beechwood, say parents, and happily now year 3s get to play fixtures against other schools, with a match for everyone regardless of ability in years 3 and 4. Things get a bit more selective from year 5 upwards but those who don't make it onto the match day minibus can choose from a plethora of activities under the new 'sport for all' banner. And there are always those all-important house matches where everyone can get stuck in.

The super performance hall with its flexible seating plays host to productions such as Around the World in 80 Days and The Lion King – often cross-curricular productions – and we are assured that everyone who auditions gets a role. A whopping 80 to 90 per cent of pupils take peripatetic music lessons, with groups and ensembles galore playing everything from percussion and harp groups to rock and big band at the weekly lunch time recitals. Choirs are non-selective to year 5, when the elite are creamed off to join the chamber choir and taken on tour to perform in European countries, recently Belgium. Minor parental grumbles that they should jazz up the formal repertoire a little. New music technology suite, ensemble room and recording studio.

And there's no need for multi-talented pupils to have to choose between music and sport – the two departments make a point of working harmoniously together to ensure that 'there's no tussle' when it comes to commitments. Art and DT equally well resourced and a high standard of work on show. The latter is taught in a charming former stable block – and we genuinely cannot think of a better use for the former wine cellar of the main house than a pottery studio. Pupils in years 7 and 8 can claim their own space in the mezzanine area of the art block. No surprise that there is a good handful of art scholars most years.

With almost all pupils living within 10 miles of school, boarding for most is all about enhancing their overall prep school experience rather than necessity or rigid preparation for a future at public school. Pupils can choose to board for two nights from year 5 under the watchful eye of the popular houseparent couple, building up to a maximum of four nights – no remainers at weekends – and around 60 boarders take advantage of this flexible arrangement. Despite that, it is very much representative of any full boarding school, with absolutely no 'hot bedding' and all the warmth and character of any boarding prep.

A warren of spacious boys' rooms takes over the upper floor of the main school building, with between seven and 17 pupils in a room. The girls are up in the eaves in a haven of pinkness and unicorns and have their own areas to chill out away from their raucous male counterparts. Communal areas, like all things Beechwood, are spacious and well resourced – we can't imagine an 11 year old who wouldn't want to give boarding a try with such a heady mix of pool, table hockey, table tennis and a tuck shop on offer – and that's on top of a full schedule of boarders' after-school activities with intriguingly named games including Colditz and Murder in the Dark. What's more, they are 'fed every hour' with fruit and veg on offer after school, tuck, tea and sandwiches and milk before bed. Special events such as the Harry Potter evening, complete with dry ice, and parent and child golf competitions and barbecues, are the icing on the boarding cake.

On the pastoral side, head says, 'we try to catch and reward good behaviour' and school definitely has an overall feel of carrot rather than stick. Pupils say they feel 'safe and at home' and can be given a house credit simply for making a staff member smile, with parents glowingly describing 'a very caring community'. Badges galore are sported proudly on lapels by a cohort of smiley, individual and thoroughly charming children. Parents optimistic that bullying will be dealt with more effectively under current head than previously. With many pupils from dual income families, a fleet of coaches brings pupils from Harpenden, St Albans, Dunstable and Redbourn.

Going places. With its dynamic head and, in the words of one happy parent, 'feel good factor', Beechwood should definitely be on the list of parents who want the certainty of a quality end destination for their child without compromising the joy of the journey.

B

Belmont School (Dorking)

Feldemore, Holmbury St Mary, Dorking, Surrey RH5 6LQ

Ages 2–13 (gradually expanding to 16+ from 2020) **Pupils** 212
Boarders 5 weekly, 35 flexi (from 7 years) **C of E**

Fees: Day £9,390 – £15,930; Boarding + £1,635 – £6,765 pa

01306 730852
www.belmont-school.org

Headmistress: Since 2006, Helen Skrine BA. Following a music degree at Exeter, she took up posts teaching music, English and Latin at Wrekin College, Greenacre School and Chinthurst Prep and was deputy head at Highfield School, Liphook.

A sound business head comes across when she describes how she has steered the school through the challenges of the recession, but there's also a strong maternal streak. On our tour we came across a boy with a bloodied knee being helped in by his friends. 'Oh my darling boy,' she exclaimed. 'Let's get that knee up. Matron is coming with her blue light on.'

Described by parents as 'very hands on and responsive' and 'a strong but caring leader.' Much praised for pastoral care. 'She has even offered support to our son whilst he struggles to adjust to secondary school,' said one mother. Another said: 'She is completely honest and open when it comes to issues with bullying. We were approached by her regarding our daughter being upset in school, something we found most refreshing.'

Her home is next door to the school building, not even a stone's throw away. She's not remotely tempted to move off site for a more private off duty life, as some heads are. 'Last evening the children were all outside here playing,' she said. 'Some boys came to borrow the dog. I love it. It's a life, not a job.'

Entrance: 'First and foremost I look at the parents,' says the head. Yikes. No need to brush up on algebra though – she means she wants to be sure that they are buying into the school's ethos, which is not of the all-stations-to-Oxbridge variety. 'We want parents who understand what the ethos of this school is,' she says. 'We do a really good job academically but we are also interested in developing the co-curriculum areas and developing the children as people. I really believe school should be fun, not weighed down in endless testing, stress and strain.'

Who wouldn't it suit? 'Some of the tiger mums I met in my daughter's previous school,' says one mother. Another parent concurs, telling us: 'I haven't met any overly pushy parents at Belmont but I imagine that they would struggle to fit in.'

Next on the head's selection list is: 'Does the child have a spring in his/her step, will they throw themselves into everything and will they fit academically in the range of the year group?' Assessment is through reasoning tests and classroom observation. 'We won't take children outside the average range, but we will take low average pupils – sometimes it's just that they're not thriving in their current school,' the head says. Once in, school says the children are now guaranteed a place until 16, unless any serious learning difficulties arise. However we've heard from one or two disgruntled ex-parents who felt the school was unhelpful when their child proved to have additional needs, and they had to move them elsewhere.

Key points of entry are at 2, reception, year 3 – and some come from other preps at 11. Entrance mid-school is well catered for. A mother told us: 'The parents in my daughter's year have been extremely welcoming. A barbecue and trip to Legoland were organised by the class rep before the start of the academic year so the new children could meet everyone before their first day. Mothers were quick to give me tips and advice about matters such as games kit.'

There's a two form entry per year, and that's the limit. 'I won't go to more than 32 to a year group,' says the head. 'I don't believe big is beautiful.'

Exit: Most parents are buying into private education for the duration – it's rare for a child to leave at 11 for local state secondaries. The head is a big fan of boarding and so far children have spread their wings far and wide. St John's, Hurstpierpoint College, Lancing, Manor House all popular recently. From 2020, though, they will be able to stay on as school expands gradually to 16+.

Remarks: The campus is a glorious 65 acres, with children's playtime roaming through nooks and glades – only constrained by dots on the trees, which indicate when they are out of hearing range of the bell. The main school building is based around the one time home of Edwin Waterhouse (of the Price Waterhouse Cooper accountancy firm), and although the original 1880 house was rebuilt after a fire, it retains its grandeur, with high corniced ceilings, lots of wood paneling and deep window seats. Classrooms for the older children are based here, while younger children have their own buildings and the foundation stage pupils have The Mews arranged around a courtyard, patrolled by three cats.

Specialists for French, music, drama, art and sport are involved from the early years onwards and from year 5 pupils are split into two sets for all CE or scholarship subjects in years 5 to 8. This is flexible, with lots of movement between the sets, and pupils feel it's no big deal to be in a lower set. 'It's exactly the same work – they just slow it down to your speed,' they explained to us.

Parents are overjoyed by the fact there is little homework until year 7. Up until then most prep is timetabled in a daytime session. 'This is where Belmont differs from most prep schools,' a parent told us. 'They actively keep the pressure off the children and parents right up until year 7. The work handed in is theirs alone, and not the parents'. In addition, the school never sets time consuming projects for the children where the parents end up spending endless hours making models of Egyptian vases or the like. 'It's such a relief, as a working parent.'

Feedback to parents comes in the form of half termly grades, full written reports twice a year and parents' evenings. There's lots of informal reporting. 'Every parent has the email address of every teacher,' says the head. 'I encourage email and we have a policy of getting back within 24 hours.' There's also afternoon tea with the head on a Friday afternoon, which parents say is a great way to meet other parents and have an informal chat with the head and teachers.

The head is passionate about ensuring that it's not just academic achievement that carries kudos here. 'We get lots of awards for things such as work of the week, good manners, boarder of the week,' said the children. During our visit the head's table was strewn with rosettes and certificates – all being sorted ready for prize giving at the weekly assembly. 'Winning a commendation certificate from the headmistress is a most sought after prize,' said one parent.

An array of clubs. These can be mixed and matched, most having no requirement to commit for a term – no battles then to haul a recalcitrant child along to a club which he didn't like by week two. Invitation clubs for the most talented run alongside general access clubs.

Sport is very much an all-inclusive affair. The commitment to involve everyone may mean that if a prestigious A team is high on your list, it may not be the place for you. 'Some may feel it does not have enough children to pick teams of excellence,' said one parent. 'We feel our daughter plays major sports at county level, so for us she is learning to be a team player, to lose sometimes and enjoy sport.' That said, the school is keen to point out it has an excellent record of success on the small schools' circuit, with a number of invicti seasons in recent years.

Head also points out that the school fields U13, U11 and U9 teams that are selected on ability, and says they 'win many more games than they lose.' Parents praise the school's willingness to embrace individual needs – timetabling cricket and tennis sessions with the boys' teams for a very sporty girl, for example.

On the arts side, the head says 'every child is on stage in front of the parents at least once a year.' Bands, choirs and string groups, with teaching from a professional opera singer and a director of drama. The school has its own biannual festival, Bel Artis, where visiting professionals lead workshops for children, culminating with an evening of performance.

The school shares the site with Moon Hall, a specialist school for dyslexia. The two have separate governing bodies and are separate companies running separate academic programmes for their pupils, but there's much crossover outside academic lessons. The Moon Hall children wear Belmont uniform and join Belmont for playtime, assembly, lunches and extracurricular activities. They can be in a school play and board alongside the Belmont pupils. Superb option if you have a dyslexic in the family.

Children can be dropped for breakfast from 7.30am and parents have a broad range of pick up times to choose from – at the end of the school day at 3.30pm or 4.30pm, after clubs at 5.45pm, after supper or extended day care at 6.30pm, after prep at 7.45pm, or children can board for an occasional night or any number up to five nights per week. All of this can be done on an ad hoc basis, so there is great flexibility for the working parent. 'Our daughter begs to board as often as we will let her,' a mother told us. 'It is a wonderfully warm and friendly environment with the boarders doing lots of interesting activities and going on trips.

Benenden School

Cranbrook Road, Benenden, Cranbrook, Kent TN17 4AA

Ages 11–18 **Pupils** 555 **Sixth form** 190 **Boarders** All full **C of E**

Fees: Boarding £37,950 pa

01580 240592
www.benenden.kent.sch.uk

Headmistress: Since 2014, Samantha Price, 40s. Attended Malvern Girls' College (now Malvern St James), so knows about life at a girls' boarding school from both sides. Read history of art at Edinburgh University and began her career in the Tate Britain marketing department, but soon felt office-bound and switched to teaching. Worked at Reading Blue Coat School, King's Canterbury and Hereford Cathedral School before taking up her first headship at Godolphin School in Salisbury, from whence she was headhunted for her present post. Leaving was a very difficult decision, she says, but she has no regrets: 'Benenden is my dream school, and full boarding is in my DNA.' Married to Iori, an army chaplain, with a young daughter and son.

A passionate devotee of girls' education, and a powerhouse of ideas and energy underneath a warm and civilised exterior. 'I'm very proud of this school. It's a wonderful place to be.'

Academic matters: In 2018, 81 per cent A*-A/9-7 at GCSE and 63 per cent A*/A at A level (A*-B 86 per cent). Pretty much always in the top 50 independent schools nationally. Everything you'd expect on offer, with breadth prized as much as depth: girls study a good range of languages, both modern and classical, and DT, art, music and drama are compulsory throughout the lower school. Science very popular, and is taught in truly amazing science block, all glass and blond wood: a floor per science, and at least three laboratories per floor, plus designated experiment rooms just for sixth formers, and a 150-seater lecture theatre which hosts a rolling programme of visiting speakers. 'My daughter's teachers have inspired her to be really passionate about science,' wrote one happy father, 'and she has really enjoyed science club.' Classrooms are large, modern and well-equipped, and superb library offers space and quiet.

No plans to introduce the IB: A levels are taught as part of a refreshingly commonsense yet innovative approach which makes any such change unnecessary. Girls can almost always study the combination of subjects they want, and the EPQ is offered to provide additional academic challenge. Lots of skills and vocational courses on offer which sound genuinely appealing rather than drearily functional. For instance, 'I don't think we'll do a food technology A level,' says head, 'but we might run Cordon Bleu courses, and I'd like to run the Leiths Diploma. Being realistic and practical will be increasingly what gets you ahead.' No danger of gender bias in this forward-looking school, however: DT is one of the most popular options, taught in an excellently-resourced technology block which even sports its own ICT suite. The school has introduced a Professional Skills Programme for the sixth form, which enables girls to work alongside professionals in a variety of fields and develop real-life experience of eg reading balance sheets, developing ideas into business proposals. Year 10s can take a course in finance and for younger pupils there's the Benenden Diploma (years 7 and 8) and real life problem solving linked to different aspects of service for year 9s.

The tutor system allows for a lot of contact time, and parents and students alike praise the caring and friendly approach. SEN department supports those girls diagnosed with dyslexia and dyspraxia, and students can have weekly individual lessons if needed (as with most independent schools, these are chargeable). That said, the school acknowledges that this probably isn't the school for those with more than mild difficulties. Extension programme for gifted and talented throughout the school.

Wherever we looked we saw girls relishing the curricular opportunities on offer. As one put it, 'At a school like this, you get to try everything!' A parent added, 'Academically, my daughter has come on amazingly since she joined the school.'

Games, options, the arts: 'You've got to involve yourself,' observed our tour guide, and there's so much to do here that it really would be crazy not to. Loads of traditional girls' sports, with lacrosse, netball and tennis topping the list; but more niche activities such as scuba diving and pool also popular. Dance is big here: there's a lovely dance studio where girls can learn tap, ballet and contemporary dance, plus a rather ace fitness suite for those wishing to acquire the body beautiful (or just keep fit), and dance GCSE is a new addition. Newish all-weather sports pitch and pavilion.

Fabulous theatre was opened by Helena Bonham Carter, staffed by two full-time technicians from whom the girls can learn lighting, sound and set construction. Professionals would kill to have facilities this good. Drama is concomitantly lively with at least two major productions a year and lots of student-led performances. LAMDA also flourishing. Music block was built in the 1960s and in another school would be something to boast about, but here looks down-at-heel and indeed an ambitious rebuild starts in 2019. Masses of music going on notwithstanding – instrumental lessons, ensembles, orchestra, choir, the works. Art and design is particularly impressive, with wonderful work on display: etching, lino printing and some whacky sculpture rubbed shoulders with really beautiful embroidery. How refreshing to find a school where girls can still learn such things if they wish to.

Lots of trips both home and abroad. Good range of weekend activities appreciated by students and parents alike. 'My daughter has thoroughly enjoyed the weekend programme,' said one grateful mother.

Boarding: All students here are full boarders. School is relaxed about letting girls go home at weekends. Boarding rooms are colourful, light and homely – perhaps a little crowded for some tastes, with up to five girls in a room for the lower school, but all the girls we spoke to insisted they liked it that way. Older girls can choose to have smaller rooms and fewer room-mates, and all sixth formers have their own room in a deluxe modern block built especially for them, designed to be a halfway house between school and university. Fully equipped and spotlessly clean, we couldn't help thinking that most university accommodation would be a bit of a come-down afterwards.

Background and atmosphere: Started in 1923 by Miss Sheldon, Miss Hindle and Miss Bird, three teachers from Wycombe Abbey, the school moved to its present site in 1924 and has flourished ever since. Held in immensely high esteem by its alumna, many of whom had gathered to pay it affectionate respect when we happened to visit. Many girls here whose mothers – even grandmothers – attended the school.

The original house, Hemsted, still serves as the school's main building, and must be everyone's idea of what an English boarding school looks like. The magnificent wood-panelled entrance hall and staircase are hung with portraits of the Earl of Cranbrook's family, and coats of arms are etched upon the stained glass. It was actually built in the 19th century, but was designed to look much older, and the effect is frankly gorgeous. We found ourselves thinking of Daisy Pulls It Off, and apparently most newcomers cry 'Hogwarts!' as soon as they get through the front door. It's still possible to board in Hemsted, and the girls that do told us they absolutely love it.

However, a massive programme of refurbishment over the past 20 years has ensured that Benenden can more than hold its own in the 21st century. All the facilities here are stunningly good, and the whole is set in 240 acres of exquisitely landscaped grounds: beyond the playing fields, where we saw girls desporting themselves at lacrosse, are lawns, roses, woods, water features, flower beds, a walled garden, lime tree avenue, all overlooking miles of hills and greenery beyond. 'I love it!' confirmed a cheerful sixth former, adding in proper Benenden patois, 'and you can walk into vill whenever you like.'

Excellent school shop, where students can buy everything needful from shampoo to study aids, and an air of unfussy practicality throughout. Food universally praised (we can confirm the chocolate brownies are to die for), and girls say that their suggestions for the menu are listened to. Impressive building programme has added eight new staff houses to overcome issue of local property prices deterring many good teachers from applying. Construction about to start on new school hall and music school. This is a school that takes people's everyday comfort seriously, and puts its money where its mouth is.

Pastoral care, well-being and discipline: No real behaviour issues – this is a happy ship, and the care and support given to the girls were praised everywhere. 'It was a big move to the UK for my daughter,' wrote an overseas mother, 'and the house staff looked after her as if she were their own, giving cuddles and love whenever she needed it. They still do so now.' And everyone we contacted said something similar. In addition to her tutor and housemistress, each girl is allocated an older girl or 'big sister' to look after her, and girls spoke to us with fondness about the friends they'd made across the different year groups.

Rules are enforced with a light touch. One mother commented, 'I like the fact that they teach the girls the right thing to do rather than impose really strict rules, eg they don't ban access to the internet – even for the younger girls; they spend time teaching them about internet safety instead.' Girls said again and again that they felt able to be themselves, and mothers frequently commented that their daughters hadn't felt pressured into growing up too quickly.

Considerable privileges and latitude given to sixth formers, who really value the increased independence and are consequently less likely to switch to co-ed at this stage. The school has opened a new café bar where sixth formers can buy a glass of wine on a Saturday night (with parental permission). All the girls wear uniform, even the sixth, but it's an unfussy uniform and the girls honestly didn't seem to mind – it's a community that fosters a sensible and pragmatic attitude to life's challenges. As one parent enthused, 'Everything at Benenden is done so smoothly and efficiently. Our daughter loves it and so do we. We are struggling to find a school as good as this for our son!' Another wrote, 'My daughter speaks of being school-sick during the holidays, the opposite of homesick, because she loves everything about the school so much – she is very, very happy at Benenden.'

Pupils and parents: Fees are high, and Princess Anne may be Benenden's most famous alumna, but this is not a school for snobs. About 12 per cent from abroad, many of them expats. Otherwise, families are solid professional London and home counties people who want the best for their children and 'work their socks off to send their girls here,' according to head. Bursary assistance ensures at least some social diversity: one girl on a 110 per cent bursary spoke movingly to us about her own experience: 'The school has helped in every possible way. I've never felt out of place, and I owe them so much.'

Entrance: Forty girls join at 11 and 50 girls at 13. Both intakes oversubscribed, but not dauntingly so. Plan ahead, though: the lists can close a year or more in advance. Early offers programme means 13+ entrants can be offered a firm place in year 7. Girls have to achieve at least 55 per cent at common entrance, but in practice many applicants will, so the school also uses pre-tests and interviews and works closely with local prep schools to be sure they're getting it right. 'We're looking for sound academic competence and potential. We're a broad church.' Occasional places for other years – the school operates a waiting list. Entry to sixth form dependent on exam, interview and current head's report, but fantastic sixth form opportunities mean that very few existing students leave, so not many additional places available.

Exit: At 16, hardly anyone leaves: occasionally girls may opt for a co-ed experience at schools such as Charterhouse. At 18, eight to Oxbridge in 2018, the rest mostly to Russell group universities (half places are in UK top 10) to read a broad range of subjects – seven medics in 2018, engineering and physics currently enjoying a surge in numbers. London, Edinburgh, Durham, Bristol and Exeter all popular destinations; four off to the States to study liberal arts in 2018.

Money matters: Scholarships of up to 10 per cent for academics, music, art, DT, sports and drama. Those who've been awarded a scholarship can apply to the generous bursary fund: a number of girls here benefit from means-tested assistance of up to 80 per cent. The Benenden School Trust also offers up to three 110 per cent bursaries each year to girls coming from local state schools.

Remarks: Traditional girls' boarding brought radiantly up to date, jettisoning what was bad, retaining everything good and adding a huge amount more. An exciting and appealing place: if we were young again, we'd be clamouring to go there.

Bentley Church of England Primary School

School Lane, Bentley, Farnham, Surrey GU10 5JP

Ages 4–11 **Pupils** 211 **C of E**

01420 525010
www.bentleyschool.co.uk

Headmistress: Since 2012, Katy Pinchess (40s). Began her career as a children's book buyer at Waterstones before settling on teaching (it's in the blood, her mother was a head). Experience includes setting up CET Primary School Westminster, a free school in central London. Back to Hampshire, joining Bentley C of E after a stint as head of Bordon Infants. Keen to build on 20-year legacy of previous head Phil Callaway, who transformed Bentley from two-room village school into highly sought after primary through personal dedication and judicious financial management. Parents seem confident that she has stepped into his rather large shoes and say, 'Everyone's really pleased, she's a lovely person.' Energetic and hands on, she is married with two young children.

Entrance: Sought after primary school and always oversubscribed. At the time of our visit almost all places were taken by children from the catchment area of Bentley and Froyle. Any remaining out of catchment places usually go to siblings of a child already in the school. Routinely has a waiting list for reception and years 1 and 2.

Exit: As in previous years, about three-quarters plump for Eggars School in Alton (local state secondary). Others choose independent education; local private schools include Alton Convent, Churchers, Salesian College, RGS Guildford, Guildford High and Lord Wandsworth College.

Remarks: Founded in 1842, on land given by the Bishop of Winchester, Bentley C of E has been modernised and expanded several times since the turn of last century including a new reception classroom. Still sits in a pretty, bucolic location next to a winding country lane surrounded by cottages, fields and hedgerows. It's very easy to imagine how this typical village school might have looked in Victorian times. Charming it may be but any similarity to old fashioned education stops as soon as one crosses the threshold. Bentley is a vibrant, modern little primary school which punches well above its weight.

Eleven-year-olds regularly achieve outstanding results (well above the national average) in year 6 Sats tests. Some 97 per cent of students score level 4 or above in reading, writing, maths and science; the one or two that score below this almost always have statements. Two or three manage a stratospheric level 6; 100 per cent get level 4+ in maths and English. With a full-time staff-to-pupil ratio of 1:20 and average class sizes of 30 children, we conclude that Bentley is fortunate to have some excellent teachers, ably supported by learning support assistants in each year group. 'Teachers are so enthusiastic and their energy reflects on the children.'

Unusually in a state school, everyone learns French. Rest of curriculum as expected; topic work links the disciplines, especially literacy, science, geography, ICT and history. Although classroom atmosphere is relaxed and very friendly, children appear busy, engaged and enthusiastic. ICT provision is good; school has largely moved away from fixed terminals to laptops and tablets; contributions from very active Parent, Teacher and Friend Association (PTFA) keep these up-to-date. Wireless network throughout and interactive whiteboards are in every classroom (unusual in village schools).

Reporting system is fairly informal, via regular parents' evenings and written reports at year end. Head says, 'Meet and chat sessions for parents happen several times a year'. Parents add, 'There is very much an open-door policy'. School looks after the gifted and talented as well as those with special needs. Deputy head works with the most able in small groups in years 5 and 6; special needs assistant in every class works with children requiring extra help (almost always classroom-based).

Naturally, Bentley isn't blessed with acres of playing fields like many of its independent cousins. Reception and years 1 and 2 have their own playground and equipment, fenced off from the 'big children'; years 3 up use a separate courtyard playground at the front of the school. The 'back playground', a grass pitch at one side of the school, is marked out for games, eg football, cricket, tag rugby, athletics and rounders; sadly main focus is on boys' sport. School also enjoys the use of much larger, council-owned recreation ground for running and sports matches. The children showing us round said wistfully that they wished they had more access. Sighed the head, 'Health and safety doesn't allow us'. Swimming (at nearby Treloar School's pool) once a week for year 3; year 1s get a taste of tennis. Bentley has nonetheless notched up a respectable sporting record. Recent successes include: national six-a-side football championship runners-up, under-11 county football champions, Isle of Wight rugby champions, under-10 and under-11 country cricket champions; girls were Kwik cricket county champions and area winners of national dance and basketball finals. Those with a talent for sport get extra coaching sessions from specialists on Friday afternoons. Clubs include netball, fencing and gym.

Music has a higher profile here than at most state primaries with a dedicated, if cosy, music room. A big draw has to be the piano teacher, who plays in a rock band and seriously looks the part. No surprise, then, that at least 50 children play the piano plus a good handful learning violin, clarinet, guitar and various brass instruments. Small school orchestra and choir perform from time to time (lots of keyboards and instruments stashed in a cupboard next to the dining hall). A local secondary offers extra coaching sessions to musicians with potential. Two Christmas plays, plus a fully-fledged drama production in year 6 (Bugsy Malone recently) make full use of school hall. No dedicated art room but plenty of evidence of creativity on display, we saw Giacometti-inspired figures fashioned from coat hangers made by year 6. School puts on as many educational visits as possible and firmly believes in residential trips for juniors from year 3 up. 'They do a lot of off-site stuff and pull in experts regularly, such as sports coaches and authors,' said a parent.

Aims to promote a kind environment; regular anti-bullying days are reinforced by discussions in classroom circle time. School's close 'family' feel means that 'new children are treated like celebrities'. The vicar of Bentley (also a school governor) leads assembly once a week. Teachers take the lead in pointing out unacceptable behaviour (we observed a reception teacher doing just that) but no child is ever made to feel the black sheep. Staff will always listen to parental concerns. Classroom assistants are usually parents themselves and are quick to pick up on any problems. 'There's always someone there to look out [for the children] on a motherly level.' Older children are encouraged to take responsibility for younger pupils, eg year 6 students read stories to reception.

Good array of clubs on offer after school, from the musical (orchestra, choir, guitar, recorders) through sporting (judo, fencing, netball, gym, tennis, football, basketball) to ceramics and science. Keen swimmers in upper years can go to Treloar pool before school to train. School canteen provides hot meals to around three-quarters of children (food is fresh, varied and inexpensive). Wrap-around child care from 7.45am-6pm. PTFA raises money for the school (typically £15,000 per annum) which helps to fund new building projects, purchase new books and technology, part-fund the very popular bonfire night and run one of the school's two minibuses. 'This means we can take an entire class out for a day trip.' Two class reps in each year group organise regular social events.

Located in rural Hampshire, the majority of families are inevitably white middle class, although we did spot the odd ethnic minority face here and there. Parents are very involved in the life of the school, helping out in the classroom, library, after school, on trips and during sporting events. 'A lot of people are prepared to give up time and money to make sure we continue to do what we do.' They stress, however, that Bentley isn't overflowing with pushy types. 'The children all see the school as an extension of their family ... it's more than just a school.' Anyone with young children living within the catchment area and willing to get stuck in to school life will be fortunate if they gain a place.

Berkhamsted Pre-Prep and Prep School

Linked with Berkhamsted School

Doctors Commons Road, Berkhamsted, Hertfordshire HP4 3DW

Ages 3-11 **Pupils** 533

Fees: £10,365 – £14,970 pa

01442 358201
www.berkhamstedschool.org.uk

Headmaster: Since 2013, Jamie Hornshaw BEd MEd NPQH FInstLM (40s). Educated at Plymouth University, where he took his primary teaching degree; recently completed at MEd in education leadership at Buckingham. Intent that Berkhamsted prep no longer seen as an easy shoo-in to the increasingly competitive senior school, entry to which he wants to be 'seen as a bonus.' Investing heavily in freshening up both the site and the staff room – 'lots of rolling up sleeves and getting back to basics.'

Formerly head of the British School of Paris Junior School. Cut teeth as year 3 teacher at St Peter's Prep in Devon, followed by Hazelwood School in Surrey, teaching years 3 and 4 as well as running sports teams and directing plays. Joined Grove Place Prep in Hampshire as deputy head and head of English and drama before moving to Brentwood Prep as deputy head. Attracted to Berkhamsted by 'family and community ethos,' inheriting it after a shaky period following merger with Haresfoot Prep. Now in the process of 'taking school by the scruff of its neck and moving it up a division' – as stated in his recent prize-giving speech: 'Status Quo's a great name for a band but not an ethos for a running a school.' Parents in favour of improvements made so far. 'He has a great communication style,' said one, referring to head's introduction of weekly update to share successes, and his Twitter feed, which regularly reminds parents about calendar events and results. Lives on site with wife and two daughters, both Berkhamsted pupils.

Head of pre-prep since 2015 is Karen O'Connor BA, PGCE, NPQH, formerly acting head of The Rosary Roman Catholic School in Camden.

Entrance: Non-selective entry into pre-prep at 3+ and 4+ currently oversubscribed. Fifty-four places in nursery class and reception, with around half moving up from the on-site Berkhamsted Day Nursery. Six additional places in year 2 and a further 15 in year 3.

Entry into prep more selective, particularly as senior school places are becoming harder fought for. Standardised testing in English and maths for applicants from year 3 and up. Fifty children recently tested for year 5 with just 15 places offered – 'we don't want to be seen as a soft option any more,' says head. Most make successful transition from pre-prep to prep, with a tiny minority who it is felt won't be able to keep up supported in finding more suitable schools.

Exit: Almost exclusively to Berkhamsted senior school at 11+. A handful each year head off to state grammar schools and one or two to schools traditionally seen as more academic, eg St Albans.

Remarks: School split between pre-prep, for children from nursery to year 2, and prep, across two different sites, about a five minute drive apart and with totally different vibes. Visitors to the pre-prep, housed on the former Haresfoot site, can't fail to be charmed – if not stunned – by the picturesque setting and seemingly endless acres of land. Superb facilities and spacious classrooms sit amongst walled gardens tipping off into woodlands, home to the adventure playground and high wires course. And what could make spelling tests any sweeter than taking them in a 20 acre meadow? Huge sports hall dwarfed the tiny tots we saw rehearsing their show and a new reception classroom block (2015) is the cherry on top of this idyllic setting.

The prep has a business-like atmosphere and instantly gives the impression of a very large school – when pupils arrive here in year 3 they leave behind a dreamy country prep environment for one which feels so urban it could almost be in London. A recent facelift, however, has left buildings very smart with few tatty corners, and pupils continue to enjoy excellent facilities – as well as occasionally those shared with the Berkhamsted senior school, including theatre, pool, playing fields and new food tech room. Slight wistfulness about lack of prep fields to run on at playtimes.

Majority of pupils from two to three mile radius, with many moving to the area for the 3-18 education found here. Very little ethnic mix but demographically diverse – plenty of first-time buyers with a bit of old money thrown in for good measure. Lots of dual income commuting families keen to benefit from outstanding wrap-around care and new, modern approach to communication: 'Things like the introduction of electronic booking for parents' evenings make life so much easier,' said one.

Pre-prep offers a gentle and nurturing start to school life. 'We don't support cursive writing being taught from 5,' says head. 'The only benefit is marketing to parents.' Homework – or 'home learning' as it's known here – is optional and the focus is on 'being mindful of every stage of development,' and allowing children to grow at their own pace. Things step up in the prep school with a well-structured timetable and parents praising the fact that 'it suits all academic abilities – those who aren't super bright don't get lost,' and reporting that children are generally pushed to reach their potential and are 'well prepared' for examinations, especially those for entry to senior school. Head concurs: 'In a mixed ability cohort we provide for the strongest and the weakest.'

Traditional, formal curriculum with French from reception and twice a week from year 3, science 'going great guns,' according to head and history top choice with the children due to 'inspirational' departmental head, whose room is 'like a museum'. DT specialist taught from year 3 in well-equipped lab, complete with dye sublimation machine to provide greater links with the art department. Drama on curriculum from year 3. Tasters of Mandarin and Latin in year 6 give pupils an idea of what's on offer at the senior school. Children mainly class taught to year 3 with lessons almost exclusively specialist taught by year 5 in a format 'closely modelled on what they'll experience when they move up to senior school.' Subtle streaming for reading from year 1 and maths from year 2. Maths groups split into sets from year 3 with movement on a half termly basis so 'it's never a white rabbit moment to parents,' says head.

Team of five SEN experts – all dyslexia specialists – work across all Berkhamsted schools, with about 10 per cent of the cohort on their register. Although they are qualified to work across all levels, there is an acknowledgement that 'the pace is fast' once pupils hit the upper prep years and 'they have to be able to cope – it wouldn't be the right school for children with greater needs.' Able to deal with mild to moderate dyslexia, dyspraxia and children on the autistic spectrum. All children screened in year 3 with a mixed programme of in-class and one-to-one help, and those with the greatest needs removed from French.

Parents uniformly comment on 'huge range of opportunities on offer' and this is highly evident in music and drama. All children play a stringed instrument in year 2 with peripatetic lessons available from year 1. There are choirs, bands and ensembles aplenty from year 2 upwards and LAMDA on curriculum to year 6. Huge number of productions and recitals on the calendar, with every year producing its own show annually – recent successes: The Lion King, Little Mermaid & Return to the Forbidden Planet.

Alongside drama, pupils name sport as top dog – and honours boards around the school demonstrate commitment and excellence, not just in the usual suspects but also minor sports like tennis and swimming, although with two games sessions and one PE lesson a week there's not as much coaching as at some preps. It's football, rugby and cricket for boys and lacrosse, netball and cricket for the girls as major sports. Focus on making sport accessible for more children, with initiatives like 'sports pupil of the term' – a prize for endeavour, not necessarily achievement – introduced. Competitive successes are 'on the up', according to head, with teams reaching national finals in swimming relay, national champions Eton fives and county tennis players and cricketers amongst the cohort. Fixtures up 25 per cent in the past five years and external coaches brought in to re-energise teams. New Eton fives courts getting good use. Compulsory Saturday sport axed in favour of optional house sports festivals, 'where even a D team player can get a gold medal.'

'Fantastic' extracurricular programme, say parents, with clubs on offer three nights a week in the pre-prep (cookery, judo, nature) – mostly included in fees – and clubs from Eton fives to Spanish in the prep. Lots of trips, with pupils going further afield as they move up the school, culminating in a year 6 outdoor pursuits trip to Skern Lodge. Wrap-around care a major selling point for the hard working middle class parent cohort. Pupils can be looked after from 7.30am to 6.30pm up to 50 weeks a year, including the provision of breakfast and tea – a facility used by around 30 per cent of families who are, apparently, 'moving from north London in droves.'

Things are looking up for Berkhamsted Prep now that the head has his feet firmly under the table, major changes have settled and improvements to the sites are completed. A solid choice for parents looking for an all-through, thoroughly rounded education – not to mention immunity to the local 11+ frenzy – in a leafy suburban setting. Without the universal favourite topic of 'next schools' on the dinner party agenda, we wonder what on earth Berkhamsted parents talk about...

Berkhamsted School

Linked with Berkhamsted Pre-Prep and Prep School

Overton House, 131 High Street, Berkhamsted, Hertfordshire HP4 2DJ

Ages 11–18 **Pupils** 1,247 **Sixth form** 395 **Boarders** 48 full (from 16), 10 weekly (from 13), 39 flexi (from 11)

Fees: Day: £17,265 – £20,640; Boarding £27,635 – £32,880 pa

01442 358001
www.berkhamstedschool.org

Principal: Since January 2016, Richard Backhouse, educated at Cheam and Marlborough followed by Selwyn College Cambridge, where he read economics. From there, took a gap year teaching sailing in Dorset and skiing in the Alps, and was promptly bitten by the teaching bug: 'I was fizzing after my first morning with the feeling you get when you take a child from "I can't" to "I just did".' Decided at that point to teach 'just for a year or two', which led to six years at Oundle teaching economics and ultimately becoming head of year 9, followed by a stint at Bradfield as head of economics and politics, director of pastoral and extracurricular and head of a 'difficult' boarding house which, under his watch, became oversubscribed. From there he moved as principal to Monkton Combe School in Bath where he spent 10 years before joining Berkhamsted.

As principal overseeing both the boys' and girls' schools, is ably supported in day to day running by Liz Richardson, head of the girls' school (years 7-11), Richard Thompson, head of the boys' school (also years 7-11) and Martin Walker, head of the mixed sixth form. So more chief executive than managing director, days are less 'punctuated by parents' and more focused on 'getting on with strategy and innovation'. Despite the 'ivory tower' nature of his role, is frequently pitch side on match days, at concerts and other school events ('charming,' according to parents) and keeps finger on pulse of school life with celebratory soirées for winning sports teams and production casts at his house.

A holistic educator at heart, believes strongly in 'educating the non-cognitive areas of the brain as well as the cognitive' and wholeheartedly supports school's reasonably mixed ability cohort remaining just that: 'we want to deliver higher grades by improving teaching and learning, not by selecting brighter pupils.' Believes that 'a great school gives you the skills not just to get your first job, but to win that first promotion.' Inherited school with 'plenty of innovation and an energetic and interesting staff', but with his predecessor having acquired Heatherton House School, integrated a nearby competing prep, brought the whole lot together under a (somewhat corporate) umbrella brand, and reached a stage of considerable oversubscription at all entry levels, what comes next? 'Change

B

for the sake of it is pointless', he says but aspires to 'continue reading the future clearly enough so that other schools continue to emulate us.'

Lives on Castle Campus with wife Debbie and has two adult children. Loves skiing, sailing, gadgets and Southampton FC.

Academic matters: You won't find Berko showboating at the top of league tables but head and parents alike are totally fine with that, all focused on broader offering. With around 70 per cent of senior cohort joining from the prep – many having been there since nursery – and a host of hungry grammar schools in surrounding area snapping up many of the most academic 11 year olds, value added is king. Succeeds in delivering excellent results for pupils across the academic spectrum with parents saying it looks after both brainboxes and less stellar siblings equally well. In 2018, 68 per cent of all GCSEs graded A*-A/9-7. At A level, 42 per cent were graded A*/A, with 76 per cent at A*/B – that's grammar school results with a mixed ability intake; impressive. With 27 subjects to choose from at A level (all the usuals, plus sociology, media studies and photography), plus the option of either EPQ or school's own mini MBA, designed in conjunction with Ashridge Business School, it's clear to see that school is really walking the walk when it comes to providing the breadth expected by its parent cohort. The mini MBA covers not just business performance, marketing and strategy, but also places a focus on personal impact and presence, 'recognising a demand for business related education,' according to head.

Consistently good results from all departments, despite a few grumbles from parents about 'patchy' teaching in one or two. IGCSEs in English, maths, sciences and RS (compulsory) ensure pupils are challenged. Setting in maths from year 7, languages from year 8 and science and English from year 9 – parents say pupils are 'assessed correctly' and moved up and down as necessary. It's a traditional offering of French, Spanish or Latin in the languages department, plus Mandarin, with pupils advised – although not compelled – to take at least one modern language to GCSE. Those joining in year 9 may not take up a new language. Aside from trad academic subjects, food technology popular at GCSE, thanks to outstanding facilities on both campuses, and we were thrilled on our visit not only to find eight boys diligently preparing a caramelised goats cheese and red onion tart as part of their GCSE coursework but also a male teacher in the food tech lab.

Pupils effusive about support given during university application process and familiarisation trips to universities available to some from as early as year 10. Weekly careers lunches for year 12 pupils with visiting speakers from all walks of professional life, many of them old Berkhamstedians.

School clear that SEN pupils must be sufficiently able to access curriculum but good proactive learning support department assists pupils with additional needs (mainly dyslexia or slow processing) with years 7 to 9 withdrawn from a language class to attend targeted sessions with the SENCo if required and one-to-one specialist sessions from year 10. Wheelchair access 'not an issue' with majority of campus accessible and timetables tweaked to ensure inclusivity if necessary.

Games, options, the arts: Sport for all, and we're not just talking rugby, netball and lacrosse (although they play all of these – and jolly well too). Over and above the all-round excellent offering for sporty types, there exists (uniquely in the area as far as we know) a dedicated, three strong outdoor education department poised to scoop up not only the gung ho pupils who want to have a go at everything, but also those who, on arrival, purportedly 'hate' sport – and thrust them into the great outdoors. From high ropes to Nordic walking ('will they still be playing rugby when they're 50?' asks the head of outdoor ed. 'Unlikely, but they may well still be doing this') via kayaking and bushcraft, it's all here, with a genuine focus on getting absolutely everyone to find something they enjoy. Parents report 'outstanding' coaching for the traditional sports, although a few grumble about early morning training sessions for squads – and trophy cabinets groan with silverware. Pupils earnestly assured us that 'if you want to get into a team, you will,' with commitment reportedly as important as talent when it comes to making it onto the team sheet.

Flexibility offered to outstanding (county, club and national) sportsmen and women who may need time out from timetable to pursue their training – with some allowed to take fewer GCSEs. And school isn't above poaching talented girls to supplement the boys' teams where necessary. A recent former female pupil played A team and first XI cricket with the boys for the duration of her time at school. From year 10 pupils can choose from activities such as zumba or pilates to keep in shape if competition isn't their thing. Super facilities abound – a vast sports complex houses huge multi-purpose sports hall, well equipped gym and pool – sports fields, including Astro, that are slightly out of the way the only downside.

Strong music and drama with as many as half the cohort taking peripatetic music lessons and bands, choirs and orchestras galore (we love the idea of a barbershop choir for boys), and drama a popular GCSE option. Highlight of the performing arts year is talent show where all comers can sing, dance or play their way to school superstardom all in the name of charity. Senior productions are 'amazing' and for those who prefer to stay backstage, opportunities abound in set design and backstage technology.

Endless extracurricular opportunities, with CCF and DofE, both run in house, at heart of school and strong uptake of both. D of E happily non-selective, with a 99 per cent take up for the bronze award in year 9 and one of the UK's highest number of gold awards achieved year after year. Compulsory lunch time clubs in years 7 and 8 ensure newcomers are making the most of opportunities and last period on Monday is dedicated 'clubs and societies' time. Multitudinous trips, both curriculum and enrichment based, punctuate pupils' time at school. 'Just great,' say parents.

Boarding: Less a boarding school and more a school with boarding. Two large, comfortable boarding houses, indistinguishable from residential properties, are situated a stone's throw from either campus. Houses boast large and beautifully furnished common rooms, mainly single rooms (lots of ensuite bathrooms in girls' house) and a well-equipped games room for the boys, plus kitchens where boarders can prepare meals at weekends. Occupied almost exclusively by international boarders (Chinese or Nigerian) who tend to join in year 12 for A levels (though can now join in year 10), often to prepare for British university. Best suited to older, independent pupils – and a good steppingstone to university life – as there is no separate schedule of activities, and organised weekend outings are sporadic, although sixth formers are allowed to venture as far afield as London on Saturdays.

Pupils can flexi or occasionally board from year 7 – the latter sometimes used by pupils staying late for an activity or rehearsal and applauded by parents for being 'flexible in the truest sense of the word – you don't even need to give 24 hours' notice'. Weekly boarding from year 9 and full time from year 12 (year 10 for international students), but at the time of our visit houses were occupied exclusively by sixth formers.

Background and atmosphere: Very much integral to the smart commuter town of Berkhamsted, the two campuses sit astride the pretty high street and the boarding houses and principal's office are dotted around town, yet in its entirety, school has a totally cohesive, integrated feel. The Castle Campus, which houses the boys and the sixth form, dates back to 1541 and has all the hallmarks – in scaled down version – of a traditional public school. The main school building is built around a grassy quad with cloisters at the side leading to house rooms where pupils from years 7 to 11 congregate for a spot of table tennis, pool or just to chat at break times. A tour of this part of the school will also take in the beautiful, two floor vaulted library and possibly the archive room where the historic green baize door referred to by Graham Greene in his writing (Greene was a pupil and his father a former head) leads you into an archive space dedicated to all things Berkhamstedian, from old uniforms and sports kit to books. The Kings Campus, a brisk 10-minute walk from Castle and base camp for girls from years 7 to 11, is a far more modern affair, boasting a fabulous modern double height dining room (we can vouch for the fish and chips) and sports centre. Both campuses have all-singing all-dancing classrooms and super art rooms – although it's a pity none of it is displayed on the rather sterile walls at Kings.

School follows a 'diamond' structure with a fully co-educational preparatory section, boys and girls taught separately from years 7 to 11 (although trips, productions and performances are mainly joint) and then together again in sixth form. Male and female sixth formers move freely between the two campuses and can choose to use either library (books can be withdrawn in one and returned to the other) and eat in either dining room. Coffee and tea is served at break times in a stylish and comfy sixth form common room on Castle campus with rooms for quiet study above. The very embodiment of leafy suburbia, school has a safe, sociable and happy feel – pupils are chatty, smiley and conventional and its diversity lies far more in the breadth of its academic and co-curricular offering than in the ethnicity of its pupils.

Pastoral care, well-being and discipline: Diamond structure appears to be a winning formula as boys and girls are free to concentrate on their educations 'without distractions' (their words) until sixth form and yet have sufficient exposure to the opposite sex to forge good social skills via extracurricular activities, trips, etc. Parents and pupils applaud vertical house system which brings all year groups together on a regular basis, with parents of girls in particular reporting older pupils 'scooping up' their younger peers when the going gets tough and boys saying they see the older boys in their houses as 'role models'. Pupils clear on protocol to follow should a problem arise – 'there are people on so many levels to help you' – starting with selected year 10 peer mentors wearing smiley badges, there to support younger pupils through the highs and lows of settling in, whether it's friendship issues or not being selected for a sports team that's troubling them.

Expectations regarding behaviour are 'black and white' according to head, but 'we like to encourage a culture of acknowledging that mistakes will be made and we just have to learn from them.' Despite generally conservative feel of school – our search for hard edges was fruitless – head adamant that 'we want pupils to feel they can be who they want to be' and parents concur that quirkiness is definitely embraced and, in the main, differences in terms of sexuality, race or religion accepted as par for the course. 'There is definitely no complacency around such issues,' says head.

Pupils and parents: Pupils arrive on a fleet of coaches coming from areas mainly within a 40-minute radius of school. Healthy mix of first time buyers alongside more comfortably affluent – but has a grounded feel and is definitely in the 'private' rather than 'public' school bracket. With such a huge cohort moving up from the prep, are there cliques to worry about? Apparently not – 'even the most institutionalised mix well,' according to one happy parent.

Thriving OB association with regular sporting fixtures against the school, meetings with fellow professionals, reunion dinners and charitable events, and busy Friends' association, that organises well attended balls, quiz nights and Christmas bazaars.

Entrance: No longer a safe bet for those who didn't quite make the grammar school grade at 11+, school oversubscribed at both major entry points (11+ and 13+) and places sought after by bright and talented pupils from far and wide, looking for more breadth than the local grammars can offer, without the hothouse feel of some schools closer to London. Places even fewer and further between now there is an official year 5 intake (a whole extra class and well worth a look if you don't fancy taking your chances at 11+), with around 80 moving up from prep each year.

There are around 25 to 30 places for boys and about 40 for girls up for grabs in year 7 with a further 45 to 50 into year 9 for boys and 'just a handful' for girls. Hopefuls take the school's own exam (English, maths and VR plus an interview at 11+; the same plus NVR and a language at 13+). Around 30 per cent of applicants for year 7 places are from state primaries. Siblings largely accommodated provided they reach minimum academic standard. Around 45 new students admitted into sixth form.

Exit: A handful leaves after GCSE. Entry requirement for sixth form is 43 points and despite local coffee shop chatter, school assures us that anyone not expected to reach these grades is advised to seek alternative options 'well in advance – it should never come as a shock.' Majority leave after year 13 to higher education. A solid clutch of Oxbridge places in recent years – five in 2018, plus one medic – with Nottingham, Nottingham Trent, Birmingham, Bristol, Reading, Leeds and Oxford Brookes currently popular.

Money matters: Cost of extras considered reasonable – particularly outdoor pursuits, expeditions and D of E which are startlingly good value as run in-house. Academic, drama, art, music and sports scholarships available at 11+ and 13+, usually representing a 10 per cent reduction in fees, although means-tested bursaries also available.

Remarks: In the words of one parent: 'without a doubt, 100 per cent solid and safe.' Parents send their children here hoping that not only will they thoroughly enjoy their educational journey but that the final destination will justify the fees. And in the majority of cases, that's exactly what they get.

Bethany School

Curtisden Green, Goudhurst, Cranbrook, Kent TN17 1LB

Ages 11–18 **Pupils** 320; 212 boys, 108 girls **Sixth form** 87
Boarders 73 full, 31 weekly

Fees: Day £16,725 – £18,465; Boarding £25,950 – £31,500 pa

01580 211273
www.bethanyschool.org.uk

Head: Since 2010, Francie Healy. A graduate of Trinity College, Dublin, he began his teaching career at an inner city school in Dublin, before taking up a post as maths teacher at Bethany in 1989. He's never wanted to leave the place, and grew his role to head up the IT department, then through director of studies, academic deputy and deputy headship. He doesn't, however, plan to stay quite as permanently as two previous heads, who are buried in the grounds.

'Genuinely held in high regard by the students. He is also very funny,' commented one parent. A charity raffle resulted in him changing places with a pupil for the day. He rang the school's uniform supplier to ensure he could be properly kitted out for the day, and queued up with his tuck money at break.

Known for his friendliness to both parents and pupils, it's hard to imagine any stern reprimands delivered in his County Clare burr. As we wandered through the sixth form common room and the boarding houses where pupils were converging at lunchtime, we noticed how relaxed the children remained in the head's presence – there was no straightening up or jumping to attention.

Academic matters: Bethany is a mainstream school with a specialist learning support department; around one-third of pupils receive support for specific learning difficulties, and 45 foreign nationals have English language support. Its day intake is also skewed by the density of grammar schools in the region, which tend to cream off the top achieving pupils at 11. Given its broad ability range, it produced a decent 20 per cent A*/A grades (50 per cent A*-B) at A level and 26 per cent A*-A/9-7 at GCSE in 2018.

As a small secondary it also appeals to those not suited to the rough and tumble of bigger schools. 'The small class sizes and, therefore, closer relationships with the staff have really helped her find her feet,' commented one parent. One boy who moved here from another secondary told us, 'The difference here is the teachers spend more time with you'.

The broad ability range is catered for through setting and an individualised approach. 'Get to know and understand the child, then you appreciate how that child learns and thinks. Then you set targets, and as soon as those are reached, raise them,' is Healy's approach.

Those on full learning support are not expected to study a language. Others who don't have an aptitude for languages are free to choose an alternative subject for GCSE (dance recently introduced). Only those in the top two sets study English literature in addition to English language. 'Bethany treats its pupils as individuals and is really flexible, it will change the timetable to suit the pupils, not the other way round like most schools,' said a parent.

Setting begins in English, maths and science from year 7. We saw this at work in English classes, where one group was tasked with finding unfamiliar words in the dictionary, and composing a sentence with them. All were working on laptops. Another group were looking at how sound and visual effects were conveyed in a piece of writing. The EAL group meanwhile was working separately on language skills.

Strong scientists can do all three sciences, and those who are less keen opt for one or two subjects. There are two well-equipped labs each for biology, physics and chemistry. Pupils were working on decomposition – looking at bread under what they told us were the optimum 'wet and warm' lab conditions, as well as at a dead bird they had handily found outside.

Mandarin is introduced from year 7, and the school has an exchange programme with Taiwan. This, says the head, is because 28 per cent of the world's economy will be Chinese by 2050.

Food tech is compulsory for years 7 to 9 (split for half of the year with design technology), and in the sixth form, where they do a 'university gourmet for life course' to prepare them for living away from home. DT has a good following to A level, and the workshops are well equipped with all the kit to cut, stick and mould. A level students were hard at work on their final exam pieces, the range clearly indicating their own interests – a golf cart, electric guitar, go-kart, a desk with a built in fish tank, and a dog house.

The work on display in the art rooms is a joy to behold – some catwalk-worthy costumes on mannequins produced by the A level textile students, and tremendous portraits by the art students. Others working on installation pieces were allowed to take over whole areas of the art room – one based on the birth of a lamb, complete with sound effects, straw bales strewn with lambswool, and film footage.

There is no requirement at sixth form to stick to the traditional/academic subjects. Those wishing to take three creative subjects are free to do so, and the school also offers two BTecs, in sport and business. 'They truly do find what you are good at and therefore make the things you aren't so good at much less important,' said a parent.

Learning support is given either as full support (10 per cent of timetable) or part-time support (three per cent). This is all timetabled with no sessions outside of school hours; as Healy says, 'pupils with learning support work harder in lessons, therefore they are the last pupils who should be getting extra lessons'. So the support is given instead of French in years 7 to 9, and in place of one GCSE in years 10 and 11.

Support for external exams is reportedly excellent, and we saw a small group in the learning support room being coached in revision techniques. In year 9, the learning support team sifts through the whole year group to establish who should apply for exam concessions, and who might need to get an educational psychologist's report. All of the pupils have a laptop or iPad, so use of these in lessons is no big deal, and the school uses Dragon speech recognition and Read & Write Gold dyslexia software.

All children receiving support will have an IEP (individual education plan) which identifies strengths, weaknesses, strategies, and targets. Subject teachers can look up the strategies for that individual child – which might be asking short questions; looking at the resources they are giving out and ensuring key words are highlighted; using coloured overlays; using cards so the child doesn't blurt out the answer; and advising where they should sit in the classroom.

The school's specialism is dyslexia, so this is the area of need where you will find the best support, but parents suggest it is not as focused and effective for other areas of special need.

Parents commented on the stability of the teaching staff. 'On the very odd occasion that teachers have not been up to scratch, issues have either been dealt with, or the teacher has been replaced,' said one parent.

Games, options, the arts: There are compulsory activities four afternoons per week. Teaching finishes at 3.40pm, and after a 20 minute break, children go to activities which finish at 5pm. The wide range of options includes the likes of chef's school, bushcraft, horse riding, sailing, model making, symphony orchestra, lifesaving and pilates.

Those who like to tread the boards are well catered for. Ex-pupils include the Brit award winning music producer Charlie Andrew, who pops back to cheer on the pupils. Music productions are reportedly terrific – one father's voice was breaking with emotion as he recalled a performance from the previous evening.

Alongside the traditional team sports there's options to suit all including clay pigeon shooting, tennis, basketball, badminton and table tennis. It's an inclusive affair, with fixtures matched to schools of similar standard – one or two parental grumbles that standards in sport are not demanding enough. But Bethany also caters for hotshots, with current pupils including a boy ranked third on the European golf circuit, and a pupil placed 16th in the world for sailing. Arrangements are made for the sporting stars to catch up if they need time out of school to attend key competitions. As they were for a boy who had acting commitments, and was allowed to take his A levels over three years.

Sixth formers have a Young Enterprise Company – they sell shares in it, with the aim to give a dividend back. They choose a different product to sell each year, and outside advisers come in to give timetabled sessions on business strategy. Pupils learned an important lesson when they tried to sell scented candles at a Christmas ice rink at the wrong price point.

Boarding: Around one-third of the pupils board, and around 40 per cent of the boarders are international students. One weekend in each half term is designated as a 'home' weekend, but full boarders and overseas students can remain in school for these weekends.

Most weekends will find about 80 students in residence. There's no Saturday school, but Saturday activities – trips to Brighton, London, Thorpe Park, shopping trips, sporting activities – are compulsory. Sunday activities are optional.

Three boys' boarding houses, one for girls, and a co-ed one for the sixth form. In the sixth form block all rooms are singles with ensuite bathrooms, modern, and a reasonable size. Some sixth formers stay in the houses for younger pupils if they want a leadership role. Younger pupils' dorms vary from twin to five bed rooms.

The last ISI inspection report relayed pupils' complaints about the food – this has been addressed by a supper boarding committee, and greater sensitivity to the preferences of international students.

Background and atmosphere: None of the usual eau de cabbage, trainers and pencil shavings smells greet you here – instead you catch wafts of strategically placed aromatherapy diffusers.

The school is a mixture of the glitzy and homely. Classroom blocks are utilitarian – you could be inside a comprehensive school. 'We don't do posh,' says the head. You might beg to differ when it comes to the facilities – a swanky £1.7m swimming pool; a fitness room groaning with running machines ('five grand each'), rowing machines, weights and exercise bikes; the cricket pitch and pavilion, tennis and squash courts. A digital performing arts centre with a performance space, practice space, concert space, and the digital equipment to film, edit and make music is in planning.

The school has a strong Christian ethos, and chapel twice a week is compulsory. But head says the sermons have a moral rather than religious bent.

Pastoral care, well-being and discipline: 'Seem to have them on a long flexi-lead which they will let out quite far, but they know when to pull it in,' said a parent. There's no pussy-footing around on the serious issues, though – boarders are checked for drug-taking by random mouth swabs and the occasional appearance of sniffer dogs.

Pupils are made aware of their relative privilege, and duty to those less fortunate. The head reeled off a series of recent charitable events, including a tour to South Africa where pupils helped to build a school in a township.

'Bethany has the knack of bringing out the best in each and every child, not only academically, but by drawing out hidden talents, and recognising the gifts and abilities children have that are not measured by grades or traditional accolades,' summed up one parent.

Parents are given email addresses for all staff, including the head, and there's a policy to respond within 24 hours. Healy's first step as head was to make all his correspondences on first name terms. Parents agree this helps to build relationships, and that any issues are dealt with quickly.

Pupils and parents: The school is set in the middle of nowhere but a fleet of buses brings the day pupils in routes from Tunbridge Wells, Sevenoaks, Tenterden, Kings Hill and Frant.

About 15 per cent of pupils are international students. The biggest group – around one-third of the total – comes from Hong Kong and China, but the school keeps numbers in any particular year group small to encourage them to converse in English.

Its dyslexia provision is a lure, but its small and nurturing ethos also attracts those pupils who would find the hurly-burly of a large comprehensive too much to cope with, and the parents who want something more holistic, and to avoid the treadmill of the highly competitive schools. The head's own three children have been through the school. His daughter got 10 A*/As at GCSE, proof indeed that they cater for the high flyers.

There's a preponderance of boys, owing perhaps to its one-time legacy as a boys' school, or the fact that boys tend to be diagnosed with dyslexia more readily than girls. 'I would tell prospective parents of girls to check that there are enough girls in the year group, as some year groups have just a handful of girls which would have made our experience of the school very different,' advised one parent.

However we also heard repeatedly of the friendships that form between different year groups, perhaps making the girl issue less of a thing than it might be in schools where friendships stick rigidly within year groups.

The parent community is also warm and supportive, we were told – to the extent that 'a number of parents choose to remain involved with Bethany once their children have left'.

Entrance: Pupils wishing to join in years 7 to 9 take the school's own entrance assessments. Sixth form applicants need to be predicted at least four grades 4-5 at GCSE, although for some subjects a grade 6 is preferable. Overseas students can take assessments at their current school, and have an interview via Skype.

Where a student has additional learning needs, the staff will, if necessary, go and see them in their current school, consider school and educational psychologist reports, and sometimes suggest that the prospective pupil spends some time at Bethany. They will usually be looking for standardised scores no lower than 90 (where 100 is average), but this can be flexible where a child has a particular ability in some areas. Autistic students are considered if high functioning, and if they can manage appropriately in the school environment.

Exit: About 60 per cent of pupils stay on into sixth form, and at this point leaver numbers are matched with new entrants. Those leaving at the end of year 11 are usually those not best suited to an A level curriculum, and they go into higher level apprenticeships or further education courses. Joiners come from overseas, or for the curriculum choice, such as when their own school won't let them do three art A levels.

At the end of sixth form more than 90 per cent go to university with business amongst the most popular courses, and the school's creative bent also sees high numbers achieving places at the top art and design colleges – one recently grabbing one of only 30 places in the country on an automotive design course. A range of universities with Oxford Brookes currently the most popular; others to eg Bath Spa, De Montfort, UCL, Portsmouth.

Money matters: Scholarships (10 to 20 per cent of the fees) for entry into year 7, year 9 and the sixth form in art, dance, drama, music, technology and sport. Academic scholarships to a maximum value of 40 per cent of fees. Two special scholarships called Christopher Jackson Scholarships can pay up to 100 per cent of fees, and bursarial awards are available covering 30-50 per cent.

Remarks: We loved the sense of letting children be free to be who they want to be. There's no shoehorning into option blocks, or diktats about studying certain loathed subjects. If they want to do three art A levels, fine, if that's what they're good at. Dyslexic? Then no need to do a language. The result: happy children, free to do what interests them, and all the more successful for it.

B

If you have a creative, goes against the mould child; or the deep thinker who can't bear the hustle and hassle of a huge school; or a bright dyslexic; or you just can't stand the competitive treadmill of some schools – then you have found your place.

Bishop Luffa School

Westgate, Chichester, West Sussex PO19 3HP

Ages 11–19 **Pupils** 1,465 **Sixth form** 272 **C of E**

01243 787741
www.bishopluffa.org.uk

Headteacher: Since September 2018, Austen Hindman, previously head of Peacehaven Community School. Degree in English and philosophy from Keele; deputy head at Hove Park before joining Peacehaven.

Academic matters: 'Judgement on grades alone is unhelpful,' says the school. But the grades are excellent for a state comprehensive all the same: in 2018, GCSE: 85 per cent of pupils got 9-4 in both English and maths, 36 per cent of grades were 9-7; A level: 60 per cent of grades were A*-B, 29 per cent A*/A. Pupils say there is pressure to do well, but this is from themselves, not the school. 'At the start of the course they do say the grades people got at GCSE last time and you think you'd really like to do that too. I want to get a 7 to show my parents and teachers that I can do it.' The school says it's important to find the right pressure: these are important times, don't waste them. But it is not an exam factory.

Class sizes 25-30, and remain on the large size in the sixth form. A tribute, then, to the teaching staff that the pupils feel there is so much individual focus on their learning; and that the results are good. 'Inspirational teachers,' say parents. Pupils say teachers are friendly and approachable, and there are only two scary teachers (out of 95). Lessons are lively: there was a buzz of energetic industry, occasionally bordering on boisterous, in classrooms; attentive silence from sixth formers where the teacher was in full flow. The aim is to get pupils to think for themselves: critical thinking starts in year 7 with Edward de Bono thinking hats and is carried through to sixth form with critical thinking in the AQA Bacc. Lateral thinking plays a big part in end of term exploration days: year 7 designed an airline, working in textiles to design a uniform, in food preparation to make light food etc; sixth formers had a 'day of evil', exploring evil as a philosophical concept.

Curriculum not just aimed at those who are academic. Key stage 3 students cycle through all varieties of DT: graphics, product design, textiles, resistant materials and food technology. There are two food preparation rooms; in one, purring pupils constructed trifles from their hand drawn designs – some spoon it up on the way home. These rooms are clearly used to the full: cake making even plays a part in further maths, with a chocolate cake holding the current record for tallest further maths cake of the year. At key stage 4, those who want to pursue a different vocational path take day release to Chichester College.

The geography teacher is very popular and successfully converts non-believers – 'my son didn't like geography until he was taught by [the teacher]' – 'he's the reason my son's doing a geography degree.' Budding mathematicians – and those bored by the subject – will be happy with the innovative teaching of mathematics: results are outstanding and there is a high uptake of maths in the sixth form.

The learning support department supports not only children with statements, but any pupils with particular needs, including gifted and talented. The four dedicated teachers and nine LSAs provide individual support, group sessions and in-class support.

Librarians work hard to enthuse pupils and staff with e-research and internet safety lessons, as well as an imaginative programme of challenge and award schemes; some way to go yet: just 36 pupils and staff competed in a recent 12/12 Challenge (to read 12 books or write 12 stories). Professional writers present the awards: Andy Briggs and Vanessa Curtis recently.

Games, options, the arts: Two large playing fields, in constant efficient use. MUGA (multi-use games area), climbing wall, and newish gym. 'They really take sports seriously, I thought they wouldn't. It's as good as an independent school,' commented a parent. Year 10 pupils can get a Junior Sports Leader qualification by learning to teach sport to primary school children. Extracurricular activities open to all pupils irrespective of ability: despite high achievement on sports field (pupils compete and win at a national level, and the school has the Silver School Games Kitemark Award for PE) it's an inclusive club at Luffa. Several parents commented with appreciation that their children had been encouraged to participate: 'My son's rubbish at sports, but has become enthusiastic about them, because the sports coach is so encouraging.'

Plenty of non-sporty options: chess club three lunchtimes a week – 'I thought it would be – you know, lame, but it was quite fun' – two film-making clubs, economics society with regular outside speakers, small but lively debating society, and IMPACT-the Christian Union, led by sixth formers, meets weekly to discuss ideas about Christianity and God. Plenty of opportunities for those interested in music: individual tuition, choirs, an orchestra and bands, with concerts and recitals throughout the year.

Keen uptake of DofE, currently 10 gold, and 20-30 silver and bronze; demand exceeds places. Lots of trips, including French and German exchanges, ski trips, and field trips. Further afield for the sixth formers: Tanzania, Washington and Pompeii.

Arts thrive at Bishop Luffa (it has the Artsmark), and it's not just for those with a natural inclination: drama, for instance, is taught to all pupils across key stage 3 'to nurture confidence and sensitivity.' The new creative arts centre houses music rooms, recording studio, drama and dance studios, and hosts the Bishop Luffa Summer Exhibition: Fruition.

Background and atmosphere: Built in the early 60s with some modern additions since, uninspiring buildings disguise the excellent school within. Cramped conditions – in some corridors you can touch both walls – and it felt a bit dark in places. However, £2.5m programme of improvements underway. One parent commented that it is hard to find your way around: year 7s are allowed to be late to class for the first week while they get their bearings. There is a quiet area away from the whirl – 'a good place to go to sort out an argument with friend.' The sixth form area is scuffed and packed; a peaceful interior hub houses a small library with 40 computers (you can bring your laptop and plug it in to the network).

Fun displays of art and textiles: clothes made from anything and everything, a fabric chocolate cake and a pink ring doughnut sitting temptingly at the top of a staircase, while a swan made of white plastic bags flies overhead. As you walk down a corridor a florescent green 3D box appears to float in front of you, the word 'think' written next to it – think outside the box. A grubby green wall looks as though it's waiting for a display: actually it's a wall you can lean on to make shapes – a fidget mechanism for restless adolescents.

Recent work to bring the decoration of classrooms up to scratch – 'a few classrooms are still scruffy,' say the kids. The school is tremendously clean, which is much appreciated by children. Year 7 pupils are particularly impressed by cleanliness after recent exposure to evidently unclean primaries – 'there's no half-eaten pizza lying around here.' 'Lit pick' keeps the school tidy – a detention, but also something done during wet break times – 'it's quite fun really'; the head, too, ducks and dives when he spots a piece of litter on the floor.

No religious brainwashing here: the church background shows in the supportive atmosphere. Everyone is important, which is why the two youngest pupils raised the jubilee flag (50 glorious years of Bishop Luffa). The key element is respect, between staff and pupils and in pupil relationships. If you come to Bishop Luffa, you must respect religion, but it's not their brand of Christianity or damnation: the school does have Muslims and Hindus (they can opt out of communion, but must attend the daily act of worship). However, 'not for you if you are anti-religion,' said one parent thoughtfully.

Food is very healthy; too much so for some: 'it would be nice to have unhealthy stuff sometimes,' said one pupil wistfully; outraged, others responded: 'we do have chips on Fridays' – pupils are fiercely loyal to their school. 'The pasta is overcooked,' said a long suffering ex-resident of Italy. But this is lost on most of the kids: Pasta King is so popular it has its own queue. One pupil said, 'sometimes you can be hungry' – apparently what's left by the time the end of the queue is served is not so desirable. Year 7s have their own food queue away from the rough and tumble of the rest. No eating in the wrong place – you get a red slip – but dedicated place for packed lunchers inside, and nice new area outside.

Pupils make their own way to school, on foot, bicycle, or train – 'if I drop him off, it has to be around the corner,' said one parent in lowered voice. Pupils are clearly happy to be there; even if most of them would prefer to be there a bit later in the day. All the pupils we spoke to would like to change the early start time (school day: 8am – 2.30pm). 'It's very hard for teenagers to get up at 6,' said one boy in injured tones.

Pastoral care, well-being and discipline: House system provides a sense of belonging and helps children feel secure: support and congratulation at a low key level suitable to the self-conscious age. Pupils assigned to a tutor group in year 7, and stay in the same group until year 13. The day starts with tutorial time and includes a thought for the day. One pupil, who felt his head of house hadn't really appreciated his efforts to change his behaviour, said, 'but I can talk to my tutor. There is always someone to go to.'

Pastoral care is underpinned with imagination: time out of school to visit Dad who works in Gibraltar not seen as a holiday, but essential family time. One parent said, 'They are very sensitive to teenagers. At an options meeting, the talk was not just about options, but also about the fact that kids are growing up and need to have a social life and interests outside school lessons. They really are interested in the whole child.' New year 7s are paired with sixth formers for individual mentoring, and will be greeted by their sixth former outside school on their first morning, so no one goes in alone. One parent commented on her worry when her quiet son started at Bishop Luffa, but how, after a teary first few days, he is flourishing and gaining confidence in its supportive atmosphere. His tutor was in attentive email contact, she added.

Bullying is dealt with quickly, said a parent whose son was a victim, though the head is quick to point out that sometimes it's not so much bullying as thoughtless words. They have a toothpaste assembly to sort this out: it's quick to squeeze out, much harder to put back in again: it's easy to say words...

Disciplinary system: warnings, red slips, then detentions – 'you can get a room 10 for being late' – it's not quite a room 101: no rats or anything scary used to check behaviour at Bishop Luffa. Indeed, this school champions a restorative approach to wrongdoing (all staff have been trained), which works well – 'I used to bunk off last year, but I've really tried to turn it around this year.' There are the problems you get with any bunch of teenagers: occasional smoking in the quiet area, the nicking of valuables (one pupil told us your phone or wallet can get nicked during PE if you don't put them in the valuables locker), and some pressure to have the right gear. You can get a red slip for a uniform problem, such as hitching up skirts or under-age make up (light make up allowed from year 11). A Juliano approach to law enforcement – 'some of my friends have just stopped wearing make-up,' said one pupil rather wearily. A parent said, 'Not for you if you don't like your child to be pulled up on behaviour – children have to step up and behave.'

Exclusion for swearing at staff, persistent disobedience, smoking or drinking. Drugs at school would result in permanent exclusion – 'because it is important that all the children can feel safe at school.' Eight pupils have been excluded over the last year, with five permanent exclusions in the last 13 years (three of these for drugs).

Pupils and parents: A true comprehensive, it takes all types. Pupils come from the deaneries of Chichester, Arundel and Bognor, and Westbourne. Many middle class, but not exclusively so.

Past pupils include: journalists Jonathan Thompson, Amanda Ursell, Rupert Winfield-Hayes and Charlotte Hawkins (Sky News presenter); theatre director Paul Millar; actors Linus Roach, Rupert Holliday-Evans, Cara Horgan and Nimi March; footballer Joel Ward; investment manager and founder of the Thirty Per Cent Club Helen Morrissey; explorer Catherine Hartley; musicians Jonathan Ansell (of G4) and Zoe Rahman; Rob Shaw, co-founder of Jack Wills Clothing Co; and poet and novelist Sam Meekings.

Entrance: From West Sussex primaries, at 11, 220 places a year, oversubscribed. The vast majority (165) CofE: prospective parents and offspring need to be regular churchgoers for two continuous years – 'go from year 3 to be sure of it,' suggested one parent. Thirty places to churches of other denominations, 20 local community places (no church required) and five special places offered to those in particular emotional need.

Academic sixth form: pupils need to get at least 6s to enter. Around 140 from Bishop Luffa go on to the sixth form, 20 places for outsiders.

Exit: Careers sessions fortnightly from year 7; it's low key and kids can tune it out, say parents, but when you need it, it's there. Around half leave after GCSEs. Nearly all sixth form leavers to university to university; four to Oxbridge in 2018; seven medics; some take a gap year; others to St George's, London, Liverpool, Cardiff, Bath, Bristol, Imperial College, London, Exeter, Sussex, York, Durham.

Money matters: PFA (Parents and Friends Association) help the less well off pay for school trips.

Remarks: A church school, but not a God club. Principles no one would disagree with: respect for others and helping each person to shine. Excellent results for a non-selective school, but no feeling of being a hothouse. Pupils are friendly and polite. Only downside – the cramped school buildings. One parent said, 'I really feel grateful that my son can go to a school like it. More schools like Luffa are needed! They have a balance between pastoral care and learning, and that is fantastic.'

B

Bishop's Stortford College

Linked with Bishop's Stortford College Prep School

10 Maze Green Road, Bishop's Stortford, Hertfordshire CM23 2PJ

Ages 13–18 **Pupils** 587 **Sixth form** 241 **Boarders** 72 full, 8 weekly, 76 flexi

Fees: Day £19,839; Boarding £30,411- £31,923 pa

01279 838575
www.bishopsstortfordcollege.org

Headmaster: Since 2011, Jeremy Gladwin BSc MEd. Educated at The King's School, Worcester (chorister) and Whitgift School in south Croydon. Graduated from Durham in geography, taught at Shrewsbury School for 15 years, rising to become head of geography and housemaster, then deputy headmaster at the Royal Hospital School, and headmaster of St Edmund's, Canterbury. Decided to apply for second headship as 'the opportunity to lead Bishop's Stortford College was too good to miss'. Recently took a masters in education at Cambridge, focusing on 'educational leadership and school improvement', the completion of which has prompted his appointment to HMC committee for professional development. 'Heads are lonely,' he says; 'they need more support. That way we might be able to tackle the current high rate of attrition.' Also an inspector for both ISI and Ofsted (boarding). Married with grown-up son and daughter. A keen walker, enjoys watching rugby and plays tennis at club level. Loves music, especially sacred choral (weekly attendance at evensong at St John's College, Cambridge is his de-stresser) and classical. A fine pianist. Mild-mannered, considered, down-to-earth type. 'Runs a tight ship; proactive and forward-thinking,' say parents.

Academic matters: Academic results have soared in recent years – unrecognisable in comparison to the college of 10 to 15 years ago. Head attributes this to the arrival of girls when the college went fully co-ed in 1995 – not only did they bring self-motivation but they raised the academic bar. A concerted effort to improve results through academic rigour, targeting and 'working smarter' has paid off – now among top 20 UK co-ed independent schools. In 2018, 52 per cent A*/A (82 per cent A*-B) at A level. Maths, history, English literature, psychology and physics are most popular subjects, with strongest showing in theatre studies, art, and geography. Out of the running for GCSE league tables due to IGCSEs, which parents gladly accept, but a commendable 65 per cent A*-A/9-7 in 2018. Prestigious '10 club' – tie for at least 10 9-7 grades at GCSE. Language provision has broadened – on joining senior school, pupils choose two modern foreign languages (most having been introduced to French, German and Spanish in the prep, not to mention Latin, which will return as an A level subject in 2019). Pre-empts the changes to GCSEs which head fears will discourage language take-up.

Streams and sets for most subjects meet needs of all, including the gifted. A dedicated learning support team of three sensitively supports 30 students with specific learning needs (charged as an extra), including dyslexia and Asperger's. All international students are offered one or two EAL lessons a week and reach IGCSE level (required for university admission). However, this is not solely an academic day school – head recoils at the suggestion of a hothouse. 'We won't sacrifice the breadth that comes with a boarding school curriculum – we just want to do everything well and keep some balance.' Broad-based academic intake – 'results are due to the quality of teaching and learning,' emphasises head.

Games, options, the arts: Successful sports: unbeaten seasons in rugby and hockey now the norm – several ex-international players offer top level coaching and inspiring role models. County hockey and district netball and swimming champions – swimming a major sport in fabulous pool; tennis and water-polo also popular.

Music important – around 10 per cent of pupils perform to grade 8 or beyond. Pianos in most boarding houses, plenty of airy practice rooms. Much-appreciated resident college musician supports in readiness for exams and accompanies. Orchestra and all manner of ensembles large and small. Twenty concerts a year, including choral work for pupils, parents and staff, plus a couple of ventures into the world of opera. Well-equipped theatre provides venue for some stunning musical and dramatic performances (set for recent production of Cabaret still in evidence when we visited, though slowly transforming into Scottish heathland for next epic – Macbeth). New art centre with stunningly mature GCSE and A level work on display in spacious ateliers.

Trips and tours across the globe including India, New York, Malawi, South Africa, Barbados, and a fair few closer to home too. Wide choice of extracurricular activities including DofE (the college is the leading school in east Hertfordshire) debating (standing room only for some hot topics) and community work.

Boarding: Full, weekly and flexi boarding, the latter most popular. All boarding houses new or refurbished, all en suite. Saturday lessons and sport mean everyone is at school till Saturday afternoon. Most go home on Saturday nights, but eg paintballing and visits to theme parks organised for those still in school. Own comfortable boarding house for prep pupils. Few full boarders but 50+ stay a minimum of two nights a week – most popular Wednesdays (sport after school) and Friday (Saturday morning lie-in for mum and dad).

Background and atmosphere: Founded in 1868 as a non-conformist boarding school, with aspirations of securing an effective and Christian education on terms that should not be beyond the reach of the middle class generally, originally sited on the outskirts of Bishop's Stortford. Once boys only, now 45 per cent girls. Full-on Saturday school for all from 8.20am until 3.40pm has its detractors, but most accept it's necessary if children are to make the most of all that's on offer.

Despite recent new developments and proximity to town, the 130 acre campus still has a rural feel. Governors canny through the economic downturn and fees have remained relatively low. Indeed, the ambitious programming of upgrading all the boarding houses will culminate in the original 19th century school building providing new classrooms and admin space.

Despite these physical changes, 'We are a large school, but we retain the small-school feel,' says head, and unabashedly goes on to describe Bishop's Stortford College as 'cuddly'. 'A really positive environment,' suggested a parent. Certainly the all-pervading ethos is one of kindness, caring and humanity – a quality the head has discovered is neatly defined by the Zulu word 'ubuntu' (which we went home and looked up – perfect). 'Pupils here are mutually supportive,' says head. 'They work hard. When asked why, they simply reply "why not?"' Head is keen to resist the spoon-feeding culture in favour of promoting independent learning in preparation for life. EPQ is popular in the sixth form as is the college's own research project programme – no UCAS points but an academic challenge and something to talk about at university interviews and mention on personal statement.

Superb library with two-storey bow windows, well stocked with books, DVDs (multi-lingual) and CDs. Ferguson Lecture Theatre is a cosy additional space, where assemblies can be relayed from Mem(orial) Hall, the original, atmospheric school hall. Sixth form Stars in their Eyes a sell-out. Sports hall with fitness suite in the gallery. Five all weather netball/tennis courts. Two floodlit Astro pitches.

Dining hall large and functional; food plentiful and tasty, on a three-week menu rotation (our sixth form guides tell us the pupils' request for 'chicken zinger' through the school council was provided by the catering manager and it was very tasty).

Pastoral care, well-being and discipline: Few discipline problems – head likes 'to give pupils a chance to get it right'. Strong house system offers support. 'The school expects a lot from the children and as a parent that is exactly what I want,' said one parent.

Pupils and parents: 'There really is not a type of child or parent,' said a parent. 'Plenty of commuters as London is so close, but there are farmers and scientists and just about all professions going.'

Pupils 'normal, not arrogant,' says head. 'I'm not keen on elitism.' Most from within daily travelling distance; about 65 per cent of boarders from overseas, including Europe and the Far East. Parents described by one of their number as 'friendly, sociable, aspirational, encouraging of their children'. Appreciate weekly contact by e-newsletter and the twice yearly news magazine.

Long list of distinguished former pupils includes presenter Andy Peebles, rugby player Ben Clarke, writer Dick Clement and educationalist Professor John Ferguson. The world of espionage features prominently via former heads of MI5, Sir Stephen Lander and Sir Dick White, and Peter Wright, author of Spycatcher.

Entrance: Via interviews, entrance tests and school references; takes a range of abilities, not just academic high-fliers. At 13 majority come from the prep school but also takes some 12-15 external entrants annually; small number join at 14, in time for GCSEs. Some 30-40 join in the sixth form – entrance is by interview and written tests; need at least five grade 6s at GCSE with 6+ in A level subject choices.

Exit: A handful – some 15 per cent – leaves after GCSEs to study A levels elsewhere. Nearly all sixth formers head to university. Five to Oxbridge in 2018, plus two medics. Bristol, Durham, York, Edinburgh, Loughborough, Bath, Manchester, UCL, Exeter, Warwick and Imperial College currently popular.

Money matters: Assistance for those in financial need. Academic, music, art and sport scholarships offered. 'A considerable proportion of our income goes on bursaries and scholarships,' says the head. 'If a child is talented but his or her parents can't afford us, we will do what we can to help.'

Remarks: Without five centuries of history to draw on, Bishop's Stortford College isn't widely known, but is among the generation of schools founded in the Victorian era that are quietly succeeding. Local word-of-mouth is enough to keep it oversubscribed – without needing to worry about recruiting for tomorrow, the head and governors can look further into securing the college's position well into the future.

Bishop's Stortford College Prep School

Linked with Bishop's Stortford College

Maze Green Road, Bishop's Stortford, Hertfordshire CM23 2PH

Ages 4–13 **Pupils** 585 **Boarders** 14 full, 2 weekly, 44 flexi (from 9 years)

Fees: Day £9,090 – £15,729; Boarding £21,102 – £24,102 pa

01279 838607
www.bishopsstortfordcollege.org

Headmaster: Since 2013, Bill Toleman BA MSc FRGS (40s), previously head of Yarm Prep School. Before that, deputy head at King's Worcester. Read geography at Nottingham University and has since added an MSc in educational management and leadership and fellowship of the Royal Geographical Society. Affable and so unassuming that when we ask him to describe his leadership style he calls in his PA, settles her in an armchair and closes the door on his way out. 'Approachable and informal,' she smiles, as soon as the latch clicks; adjectives bandied about by parents include 'child-centred', 'fair' and 'proactive'. Certainly in his tenure to date he has systematically swept away all signs of stuffiness – entrance exams are now sat in a multiplicity of cosy classrooms rather than in serried rows in one huge daunting sports hall, for example, and parents and pupils alike pop in at all hours, keen for a chat. 'If people want to come and see me I'm very happy to see them,' he says, although when the queue becomes too long or other matters are too pressing his PA honours visitors with an appointment in the head's diary. 'The children love that,' she laughs. To his regret, no longer has time to teach his beloved geography, although helps out with fieldwork (recently accompanying lower third to Walton-on-the-Naze). Enjoys surfing in north Devon and still plays occasional cricket and Sunday rugby. Married, with three grown-up sons.

Entrance: Entrance to the pre-prep is by an informal group assessment session and there is a long lead-in for tinies registered to start reception ('messy play' session in progress when we visited). External candidates for the additional 20 places made available at 7+ must sit the entrance exam to the prep school (English, maths and reading), spend a morning in school and are encouraged to meet the head with parents; no assessment required of existing pupils. A further 20 places offered at 10+ and 20 more at 11+ (academic and music scholarships available) to give a total of 100 pupils per year group by lower third (year 7). No sibling discount or preference given.

Exit: Some 95 per cent plus straight to senior school. Remaining handful to other, further-flung boarding schools (in recent years Harrow, Stowe, Millfield, Uppingham, Shrewsbury, Benenden) and a few to state at 11+. As Bishop's Stortford College is selective, prep parents are given plenty of advance warning if their child's ability to keep up after transfer is in question. Other suitable schools, recommended. Fairly rare occurrence as school prefers to tackle underachievement to keep pupils under its wing.

B

Remarks: Stunning green and leafy setting right on the edge of town extending in all to 130 acres of rolling Hertfordshire. Accessed via a lane of warm, red-brick Victorian houses and school buildings, some sensitively modernised, others waiting. Nearly all with privet hedges and ancient roses. Prep and senior pupils co-exist harmoniously on the site. Main prep building now all sparkling glass and purple carpet, thanks to £3m extension and refurb. Super reception area, hall with stage and roomy classrooms. Art rooms, including kiln, plus science labs across the attractive brick courtyard (complete with happy preppies chatting on steps, idyllically). Wonderful new library with floor-to-ceiling vistas. Shares with seniors music facilities, super 50-metre indoor pool in own timber-clad edifice, sports hall and hard courts, plus pitches as far as the eye can see. No wonder prep children look relaxed, contented – and well-exercised.

'This is a purposeful, happy place to come to school – it has to be,' says head, 'because we're here for a long time.' Pre-prep for age 4 to 7, prep for 7 to 13s. While pre-prep makes use of national curriculum year group terminology, traditional names still charmingly in use in the prep – so lower and upper shell are followed by forms 1 and 2, then lower and upper third (continuing into the senior). Although less than 20 per cent of prep pupils board, school operates a boarding school week for its pupils aged over 7, with long weekdays until 5pm for the eldest and Saturday morning school for all, afternoons for form 1 and above.

'Children work hard here because they want to, not because we make them,' says head; said a parent, 'My son has been coaxed, encouraged and inspired to push himself and achieve the best he could.' Academic streaming begins in year 4, plus setting for maths. Classical civ for years 5 and 6, Latin to add to Spanish, German and French for years 7 and 8. DT and drama on the curriculum from year 3 up. Lots of visits and trips, as well as speakers in – curricular activities included in fees. Bring Your Own Device recently introduced for top two years – prep pupils say they use iPads and equivalent in 80 per cent of lessons and that they really help with self-organisation.

Sport serious here and all involved. National finalists in pretty much everything – rugby, hockey, cricket, netball, even football, although only an after-school club. Standout individuals too, notably swimming and tennis. Lots of music – choirs, groups and tours.

'Have-a-go' culture is alive and well. One afternoon each week devoted to a 'wheel' of activities which changes with the term (street dance and yoga to survival skills). All pupils allocated to a house (either at random or according to family connection) – fierce competition through all manner of contests and quizzes. Highest achieving house wins supper with the headmaster. Fundraising through teddy bears' picnics, film nights, doughnut sales and auctions in aid of the annual chosen charity – £10,000 plus donated every year. Head meets prefects for 'biscuits and a chat' half-termly, and drops into lessons and activities unannounced.

Strong pastoral care network begins with form tutor as first port of call for parents, then heads of year. Pyramid above of senior teacher (pastoral), director of studies, operations, then deputy head and head. 'Compassionate' teaching and learning support for those with mild SEN much praised by parents of children who have benefited – IEPS, one-to-ones, additional time in exams.

Own comfortable boarding house for prep pupils. Few full boarders but 40+ stay a minimum of two nights a week – most popular Wednesdays (sport after school) and Friday (Saturday morning lie-in for mum and dad). Vast majority of pupils throughout school very local and only half a dozen international students in the prep – EAL support offered.

Parents in the main professionals or city, some farmers – same as in senior as pupils grow up through the school with few additions. 'There really is not a type of child or parent,' said a parent. 'Plenty of commuters as London is so close, but there are farmers and scientists and just about all professions going.'

Prep head's relationship with college head 'mutually supportive' and clearly on the same page.

The Bishop's Stortford High School

London Road, Bishop's Stortford, Hertfordshire CM23 3LU

Ages 11–18 **Pupils** 1264 **Sixth form** 370 (114 girls)

01279 868686
www.tbshs.org

Headmaster: Since 2014, Dale Reeve, previously deputy head of Leventhorpe School, and a maths specialist. He attended a state comprehensive in Harlow, after which he did a maths degree at Essex University and a PGCE at Leicester University. This is the sixth school he's worked at.

Lives locally with his wife and two young children and comes across as an affable and traditional family man, who is firm but fair. Certainly never one to keep students at arm's length, often getting stuck right in with their activities. 'It's brilliant that he coaches. My son is a very shy boy and he connected with him straight away,' said one parent. Other remarks from parents include, 'He has a great manner with the boys and parents' and 'Everyone likes and respects him.'

He takes an 'If it aint broke, don't fix it' attitude to leadership. Word on the street (well, at the school gates, anyway) is that he watches quietly, including sitting in on classes, rather than bringing in changes for the sake of it. 'One shift I am making is on discipline, though,' he says. 'Discipline is good here, but it could be even better. So we are focusing on things like low level distraction.'

Academic matters: There have been peaks and troughs over time' when it comes to GCSE results, says the head, but on the whole it's positive. In 2018, 35 per cent 9-7 at GCSE. At A level 25 per cent A*/A grades and 55 per cent A*-B. Chemistry, English language, theatre studies, PE and history are particularly strong.

Class sizes hover just under 30 in the early years, falling to 13-22 for A level. Expect fast-tracking of able students from year 7 in maths. ICT is a cornerstone of the school, with lots of great facilities across all subjects, and maths is the clear stand-out subject when it comes to success, with around eight Maths Challenge gold winners annually.

The school is heavily research-based, with one member of staff dedicated entirely to encouraging teachers in the area of research and development, with the ultimate aim of innovating their teaching. One pupil said, 'We are encouraged to be creative and challenge, which makes for lively classes,' whilst another reported, 'There's no spoon-feeding here.'

There are 97 students with SEN and they tend to do well, as do the less academic, despite the school's above-average ability intake. Parents and pupils are particularly keen on the so-called clinics at break and lunch times, aimed at pupils who struggle in specific subjects. 'These have saved my child,' said one parent. 'It's great that the children get a chance to speak to the teacher about what they're not grasping, with the aim that the teacher can hone in on that area in the next class,' said another. A third said, 'Certainly no need for tutoring, even if your child isn't as clever as others.'

'Enabling the less able is an area we have really focused on improving,' explains the head. But don't bother applying for sixth form unless academic – anyone seeking below level 3 should look elsewhere. Usual subjects offered at this level, plus philosophy, film and Latin. Speakers who have come to the school include Lord Rowan Williams, Alistair Campbell and Boris Johnson.

Games, options, the arts: It's hard to think of an extracurricular activity that isn't offered here, with everything from the normal (and highly successful) rugby, football and cricket fixtures (pupils regularly play against top private schools) through to go-carting, student-led charity groups and even a pupil-led class in IT skills for senior citizens. In fact, it's not uncommon to see large numbers of students still at school at 6pm, with many also coming into school early in the mornings. 'If there's a club that isn't offered that a few of us want, we pretty much know it will be brought in,' explained one pupil. Expect weekends to be taken up too. Saturday morning rugby training is 'expected but not compulsory' for year 7s, for example, with parents watching from the sidelines.

Music and performing arts are both strong, with imaginative and inspiring staff. Facilities, including recording studio and impressive music technology, enable the school to double up as a Saturday morning venue for budding musicians, whilst the orchestra pit allows for live productions and the impressive-looking drama hall encourages professionalism. Concerts and festivals happen all year round, not just at Christmas, and art is also taken seriously, with pupils regularly encouraged to apply for national competitions. School trips are often cited as the best parents have ever heard of, with recent examples including a rugby tour to Australia and a geography trip to Iceland. 'They're not cheap and that can be hard,' said one parent. 'But they're worth it.'

Background and atmosphere: There are some sports facilities, including a large sports hall that's thronging with basketball players at lunchtimes, but it's the extensive playing fields and an excellent sports ground (35 acres) some three miles away that students and parents rave about. Main school was built in the 1950s for a lot fewer students and although there have been many add-ons since, the school is bursting the seams in places, especially in sixth form centre. 'In the winter, the boiler can be weak and children have been known to have to stay at home if it's been on the blink, but that is rare,' said one parent. Some areas lack displays and need a paint job, but others are spot on and all have a strong welcoming vibe. The school claims to have a strong Christian ethos, with Jerusalem as the school hymn and close links with nearby St Michael's Church, but the emphasis is by no means in-your-face, with plenty of room for other religions and non-believers.

Pastoral care, well-being and discipline: 'There's no room for silly haircuts, trainers or shirts hanging out here,' summed up one parent. She's not wrong – these boys look super-smart all the time, thanks to the high standards of dress, including compulsory blazers, which are expected from the pupils. 'So embedded is the level of formality around dress that my son even keeps his blazer on until after he's done his homework!' laughed one parent.

There's a similar attitude towards behaviour, which the head sees as closely related: 'If we let these small things slip, then everything slides,' he explains. Should any boys fall foul of the clearly set-out disciplinary procedures, they find themselves in a small isolation room with plenty of posters of the school rules to remind them while they're there. But few spend more than a day or so in isolation and critically, the school's excellent counsellor (also available for staff) is based just outside the room and is well-known for supporting any boys who find it hard to conform.

Indeed, this is by no means a school ruled by fear, with boys seeming as positive as they are polite. Tellingly, they look adults in the eye when speaking and seem to be as at much ease chatting to the teachers as amongst themselves. Parents and pupils alike put it down to a structured pastoral set-up, mutual respect between staff and pupils and a bottom-up approach that enables pupils' suggestions to be listened to and acted upon – mainly through the school council. 'A while back, they put in a bully box and it just made the bullies tease you even more if you were seen putting a note in there,' said one pupil. 'But as soon as we explained that, alternatives were looked into.'

Year 7s may struggle, due to the culture shock. 'They really crack down on them straight away, with an instant no-nonsense and zero tolerance attitude,' said one parent. 'It can be quite hard on some of the children at that age, particularly the sensitive ones.' Pupils of this age say some teachers can get a bit too caught up in the discipline side of things and fail to praise enough. But again, it's generally agreed that this is balanced by an open-door attitude among staff. 'One of my friends had a son who loathed a particular subject and had nightmares about it. He went to see the head of year and he was completely understanding, and they came to an agreement about a solution. Ultimately, you feel they want the kids to be happy.'

Pupils and parents: This school is in an affluent part of town and the parental mix echoes this. Parents see this as a cheap alternative to independent education and by and large remain satisfied throughout. 'If you say your children go to this school, the normal reaction is, "Oh aren't you lucky?" and that's pretty much how we feel,' said one parent. Sociable parents are kept happy – there's a PSA (Parent Sports Association) and PTFA (Parent, Teacher and Friends Association), both of which plan regular events including bingo nights, candle-lit suppers etc and raise serious funds. Even outspoken parents are generally content. 'There's a minority who are not afraid to speak up, but we don't shy away from them,' explains the head. 'We're all for parental involvement.' Former pupils include Ben Skirving (rugby) and Greg James (Radio1 DJ). The 120 or so girls in the 350-strong sixth form bring balance and breath, as well as maturity.

Entrance: This is the kind of school that people move to the area for and even then, many boys don't get in. Places are awarded firstly on the basis of compelling medical reasons, secondly by sibling link. Ten per cent of places are also allocated 'to pupils with a proven aptitude in music or sport,' although with 170 boys recently applying for eight places on the back of their sport and 135 for seven places on the back of their music, there's stiff competition to prove yourself. The rest of the places are based on where pupils live (there's a traditional catchment area, defined by postcodes) and primary school attended.

The co-ed sixth form has 100 places open to pupils who have not attended the lower school – good results with minimum grade 6 in subjects chosen for A level essential.

Exit: Around a third leave after GCSEs for local colleges or to pursue vocational courses; a minority go directly into employment. Nearly all sixth formers move on to university, around a third to Russell Group institutions. Three to Oxbridge and five medics in 2018. Some students gain apprenticeship contracts.

Remarks: There are five secondary schools in the town, all rated by Ofsted as good or outstanding. Parents who opt for this school tend to do so because of the emphasis on respect and working hard, as well as the plethora of extracurricular activities. And despite the reputation that it has for serving the more naturally academic, we found the less able are also encouraged to shine, thanks to the drive to maintain standards and provide outstanding support for all.

Bloxham School

Banbury Road, Bloxham, Near Banbury, Oxfordshire OX15 4PE

Ages 11–18 **Pupils** 441 **Sixth form** 138 **Boarders** 154 full, 9 weekly and 254 flexi

Fees: Day £17,985 – £25,785; Boarding £25,785 – £33,675 pa

01295 724301
www.bloxhamschool.com

Headmaster: Since 2013, Paul Sanderson (40s), previously a deputy head and director of curriculum at Gordonstoun. Originally from Northern Ireland, he was educated at Banbridge Academy before studying evolutionary biology and genetics at St Andrews University. Postgrad qualifications from Oxford (PGCE) and Cambridge (MPhil). Taught at Lancaster Royal Grammar, Oundle and Carr Hill High before joining Gordonstoun as housemaster.

Drawn to the school's modest size, where children are 'less likely to disappear', he has made great strides in raising the academic profile of the school. Ambitious and determined, with a refreshing heart-on-his-sleeve honesty (a few watery-eyed moments when recounting the achievements of his pupils), Mr Sanderson's mission is to redefine what makes a Bloxham education.

A rugby enthusiast, with a passion for ice climbing and skiing. Runs a climbing wall class and recently took a group of students alpine climbing. Married with three young children.

Academic matters: In 2018, around 90 per cent of grades at A level C or better; small numbers taking most subjects but business studies and maths top the popularity polls. Teaches BTecs in sport and hospitality and a CTec in business. IGCSEs currently offered in English, geography and sciences; food tech and computing also available; won't publicise results.

Management restructure has introduced new deputy and five new heads of department and there's a definite sense that the bar has been raised when it comes to teaching standards. Staff:pupil ratio average is 8:1 and progress is measured across the year through a challenge grade system. Length of lessons has recently been increased from 35 minutes to an hour and music and drama have been shifted to the afternoon in response to latest research that children become more creative as the day goes on.

While Bloxham is quick to point out that it is not a special needs school, it does have a good reputation for nurturing able pupils with mild to moderate dyslexia who have become demoralised in more competitive arenas. A specialist dyslexia course is offered for up to six pupils a year in the third, fourth and fifth forms, focused on improving their reading speed and accuracy, spelling and study skills.

The Eunoia Society (ancient Greek for 'beautiful learning') provides an intellectual 'stretching' beyond the academic curriculum. As well as offering prep for Oxbridge entrance, it boasts an impressive programme of events, with trips to exhibitions, opera and ballet, and recent visiting speakers have included an art historian, a US diplomat, a professor of biophysics and a senior civil servant.

Games, options, the arts: While there's been some rebalancing of a historic bias towards sport, the school still takes great pride in its achievements. Rugby and hockey are particular strengths (girls reigning county hockey champions at time of visit). Regular rivals include Stowe, Warwick, Marlborough and Wellington and competition is taken seriously. Coaches use iPads to record games for post-match analysis.

Facilities are excellent. In addition to two all-weather pitches, the school boasts extensive playing fields, two squash courts, two fives courts, six outdoor netball courts (doubling up as tennis courts during the summer) and a 23m indoor swimming pool. The Dewey Sports Hall has a well-equipped fitness suite with yoga and an assortment of classes also on offer. Sailing takes place on a nearby reservoir. Recent national successes in both clay pigeon shooting and equestrian competitions (twice national schools eventing champions). No stabling at school but pupils may arrange to bring their own mounts for twice-weekly tuition. Those who don't own their own horses can arrange to hire from local stables.

Bloxham is fast gaining a reputation for its drama programme. Since his appointment in 2013, the director of drama has increased the number of productions from one to eight a year and all pupils are expected to take part, either front of stage or behind the scenes. The school recently staged its first original production (about Bloxham boys who fought and perished in the Great War), selling out all four performances to rave reviews: 'as good as the West End', commented one enthusiastic parent. The Great Hall stages the major productions, with the rest at the Wesley Theatre (a former Wesleyan Chapel).

The music department is housed in the Sam Kahn Music School and there's a new orchestra – quite an achievement given the size of the school's population. Fifty per cent split across music and music tech subjects. We dropped in on a lesson about film scores and learned of an impending visit from an old boy who now works as a film composer in Hollywood – such 'value-added' is much in evidence. Lots of rehearsal rooms support a busy performance schedule and there's the added bonus of a school radio station, run by pupils. Art provision is equally impressive. Sixth form students benefit from dedicated personal workspaces in a charming room that resembles an artists' garret, complete with sloping eaves.

'We want kids who are hungry and ambitious inside and outside the classroom', says Mr Sanderson and Bloxham's enrichment programme is extensive. As well as the Eunoia Soc (see above), pupils can choose from clubs ranging from astronomy to knitting as well as a wine society for sixth formers. Animal club is offered once a week for pupils keen to help look after the school's resident lizards, snakes, hermit crabs and beetles.

'We have students competing at international level for rugby and kayaking, a world champion shooter, a national champion clay pigeon shooter, a Formula Ginetta driver, diploma musicians, eight students in National Youth Theatre and 164 DofE participants,' says school.

Boarding: First and foremost a boarding school; day pupils (known as day boarders) make up half the population and can stay until 10pm, and the school opened a new day house in 2017. There's also the option of flexi-boarding (pay per night). One local parent said her son doesn't want to come home for fear of 'missing out on the fun'. This flexibility was a big draw for a number of the parents to whom we spoke.

Seven boarding houses are clean and bright with large communal areas – a bit dated in places but a rolling programme of refurbishment is under way. Weekly and flexi boarding in years 7 and 8, with own lower school boarding house. Full boarding from year 9. Thirteen per cent of boarders from overseas. Maximum of three beds to a room, full boarders have their own room from year 10.

Background and atmosphere: With its picture-book cluster of buildings in honey-coloured Horton stone, manicured lawns and homely atmosphere the school blends harmoniously with beautiful Bloxham village. The lower school (Exham House) is actually situated in the former village pub.

Originally known as All Saints School, Bloxham was founded in 1860 by The Reverend Philip Reginald Egerton who wanted to establish a school that embodied the high church values of the Oxford Movement. In 1897 it joined the Woodard Foundation, the group of schools founded by Canon Woodard to promote education in an actively Christian environment.

Food excellent (we took full advantage of visiting on Curry Thursday). Great choice and emphasis on healthy eating. Sociable lunchtimes with teachers sitting happily alongside pupils.

Pastoral care, well-being and discipline: Self-proclaimed 'gold standard' of pastoral care is justified. Multiple systems in place to ensure children's emotional welfare, including a team of 'peer listeners' – sixth form student volunteers with formal counselling training. Small size of school promotes healthy mixing and solid friendships between girls/boys and different year groups. Head meets daily with head boy and girl, helping to keep abreast of any grumbles or issues. School refreshingly honest about (infrequent) incidents of bullying; intervention swift and effective, according to parents. Keen sensitivity about emotional needs of pupils: 'let's face it, the teenage years are difficult', says head.

Holy communion for all once a week. School doesn't shy away from talking about the importance of spiritual development in education but head recognises need for religion to 'translate into the 21st century'. It's less about doctrine and more about getting children to think about their place in the world, 'To be a giver, rather than a taker'.

This ethos is reflected in service initiatives such as Reading Club, where older pupils help children from local primary schools with reading difficulties. According to head this has inspired at least one student to go on and train as a primary teacher.

Pupils and parents: Bloxham has long been a popular local option and is now increasingly so for London refugees looking for a smaller, more 'gentle' boarding school. Recent push to improve parent-school communications has been warmly welcomed. Very informative parents' handbook published annually; newly established parents' association. Saturday matches are well attended and there are plenty of opportunities for parents to get involved if desired. Former pupils include impressive numbers of high ranks from all three forces plus novelist Tom Sharpe and journalist John Sergeant.

Entrance: Candidates for lower school (age 11) via school's own exam (maths, English and verbal reasoning) and interview; CE for 13+ entry. Sixth form requires minimum six GCSEs at grades 9-5, with at least a 6 in chosen A level subjects (7 grade required for maths and physics). Lower school intake is from state primaries or independents such as Carrdus; at 13+ pupils from preps including Ashfold School, Beachborough, Bilton Grange, Swanbourne House and Winchester House.

Exit: Small leakage (around 10 per cent) after GCSEs. Post-A level, varied subjects and destinations; Bristol, Nottingham and Loughborough currently popular. Law, veterinary science and politics all 2018 choices.

Money matters: Parents say flexi-boarding option and late stay for day pupils represent value for money. Scholarships (20 per cent fee reduction) for academics, sport, DT music and drama. Means-tested bursaries can be combined with scholarships; limited number of full-fee bursaries.

Remarks: Successfully combines academic challenge with plenty of sport, service and practical life skills. A perfect environment for happy all-rounders.

Bohunt School

Longmoor Road, Liphook, Hampshire GU30 7NY

Ages 11–18 **Pupils** 1855 **Sixth form** 116

01428 724324
www.bohunt.hants.sch.uk

Headteacher: Since 2009, Neil Strowger BA (Keele, European Studies), MA (Sussex) PGCE (Oxon). Born in Norfolk, educated in the sort of comprehensive where bright kids played it safe and kept it low. The memory burns, fuelling his determination to make Bohunt a 'nurturing place' where students can work hard for the sheer love of it and grow their other talents. Began teaching in 1997, appointed to the headship of Bohunt in his early 30s in 2009. He's also the CEO of the Bohunt Academy Trust. Married, three young children. A self-confessed and bashful workaholic, he relaxes by visiting nice places of a Sunday and, when he can, skiing.

Bohunt back in 2009 was an unassuming, underachieving comprehensive with the second lowest funding in Hants. Mr Strowger has piloted it into the stratosphere. Now it's an academy enjoying a high profile nationally and internationally. It sent a delegation of students to No 10 to coach David Cameron in Mandarin ahead of a visit to China. It has been TES School of the Year.

So, you may think, Mr Strowger is one of these mythical superheads we've read about: supercharged ego, command and control, school uniform overlord, relentless disciplinarian, radiates a force field of charisma and menace, a tiger teacher. And there you'd be plumb wrong. Just as, if you judged his school from what you saw on the telly in that 'Are Our Kids Tough Enough? Chinese School' documentary (2015), you'd also be plumb wrong. Far from being terribly pleased with himself, Mr Strowger gave us every impression of never surrendering to satisfaction. No, he's a man whose best is never good enough and who speaks of 'the constant need for improvement'. Softly spoken, a thoughtful and open-minded listener. Not into status statements – inhabits an office conspicuous by its ordinariness. Not the sort to play hey-look-at-us games with eye-catching press releases and suchlike PR cock-a-hoopery. His leadership credentials are borne out by the school's achievements but, because his exclusive focus is improving the school experience of young people (rather than bigging up his profile), he is secure enough in himself to appoint and develop extremely able senior managers and work with them in partnership towards wherever their common vision takes them. As big a believer in developing his staff as in developing his students; they're all on the same learning journey and Mr Strowger expects this to nurture mutual respect. He hit a low point after that TV documentary (our view: a stitch-up) when some of his students were being beasted on social media. He seriously thought about stepping down. It was the advice of one of those students that he took, advice he had previously given her: learn from your mistakes and bounce back.

Parents we spoke to hold him in high regard and speak of his 'passion'. We are aware of dissenting voices – there are always some – who regard his management style as overly controlling, centred on making the school look good. For any head there will always be a tension between reputation management and standing by wayward students. We reckon his heart is in the right place.

He's out of school a lot on Trust business and clearly feels torn by that. He's reluctant to relinquish the headship because (nodding at students through the window) 'they're what I came into teaching for'. Among parents there remains a strong sense of 'l'ecole, c'est Mr Strowger'. One said trustingly, 'He'll get it right'. His deputy, Neil Pittaway, steps up as required. We like Mr Pittaway a lot: a warm, upbeat man who connects with the students.

Academic matters: Exam results feature front and centre of Bohunt's crowded shop window where you'd expect, placing it in the top 20 per cent of non-selective schools nationally. Progress (value added) scores above the national average and for disadvantaged students some way above, testament to the school's values of which these results are a happy byproduct. In 2018, 80 per cent of students got 4-9 in both English and maths at GCSE, with 29 per cent A*-A/9-7 grades overall.

The question uppermost in your mind is quite rightly: yes, but how did they come by these results? Silent classes? Teaching to the test? Rote learning? No on all counts. Again, it's all about values: 'serving the best interests of the students', getting them ready for the world as it will be, certain, as one parent put it, that 'You can only learn if you enjoy going to school'. This is a school that wants to enable its students to become 'game-changers, innovators and leaders'. So collaborative creativity trumps obedient conformity. And as with so much else here, there's no playing safe. We toured classrooms and remarked on the bubbly interactivity within. A student exclaimed, 'Yes, that's Bohunt'. The focus is preparing students for jobs that may not yet exist – the sorts of jobs that can't be done by gifted and talented computers – ie, jobs calling for soft skills: problem-solving, lateral thinking, teamworking. Challenge-based learning, they call it: the route you choose to get to an answer is as important as getting it right. A parent told us, 'They're on the ball about how kids learn, there's lots of encouragement'. Another praised the way the school 'relates education to real life', underscored by partnerships with local industries including Surrey Satellites and Siemens. The school is also an Apple regional training centre. Big emphasis, therefore, on STEM (science, technology, engineering & maths) and within that an agenda for empowering girls. Annual STEM festival attracts 3,000+ and more than 60 exhibitors. Students are regular national finalists of the BP Ultimate STEM Challenge.

It's in its language teaching that the school is at its most innovative – stunningly so. Again, the emphasis is real-world. Everyone studies a foreign language from the word go and almost everyone sits one at GCSE. Choice of French, Spanish, Mandarin, German. At year 7 tasters in two or three. One class per year takes the immersion route, studying a third of their subjects in one of three target languages for five years, knocking off the GCSE en route at year 9 and then a higher qualification in year 11. We watched an immersion class in Mandarin. Blew our socks off. There's a happy spinoff: students taught bilingually do better in all subjects.

One thing that pleased us: the spectacle of a boy outside a classroom receiving a meticulous and unyielding critique of his behaviour. There's rigour here. Parents we spoke to say yes, 'the children know the boundaries' and the reason they listen to their teachers is because 'teachers here like kids, they talk to them, they're on the ball about how kids learn and encourage them'. There's a general understanding that 'you get out what you put in' together with a widely expressed view that the school 'is definitely not just all about exam results'. Rewards for exceptional effort irrespective of ability named after the school's motto, 'enjoy, respect, achieve': ERAs.

One parent said of the teachers, 'they're just so committed.' We sign up to that in spades; the dedication and professionalism we saw are on a par with the best schools we've ever visited. All parents have their child's teacher's email address and get a rapid response to concerns – even, to one parent's embarrassment, on a Sunday. Another parent told of her daughter arriving home on the last day of term 'in tears because there would be no school in the morning'.

Special educational needs are addressed in conventional ways and of course 'within the constraints of finite resources'. SENCo liaises with feeder primaries before entry to ensure smooth transition. All students tested in year 7. Intervention weighted according to need ranging from from class teacher aware, to withdrawal from a foreign language GCSE, to small group work in the special needs department. The parent of a boy who just doesn't get on with school and may be borderline ADHD told us, 'They try really hard to find him things to do that he will like and where he can enjoy some success'.

Bohunt sixth form opened in September 2017. No A level results yet but EPQ successful.

Games, options, the arts: Art, music and drama are bundled under the title 'expressive arts'. Plenty going on in all areas inside and outside the timetable. Music especially strong; 20 per cent learn an instrument, free for pupil premium students. The Bohunt spirit of innovation is pervasive, of course, and in this area of ops begat the iPad band, which other schools are now going crazy for. It enables musical duffers to play along with accomplished instrumentalists and singers to create great sounds. We heard them. Blinking brilliant. There's ambition. Guys and Dolls, for example, is no pushover. And there's variety – breadth. Ensembles play lunchtime concerts weekly, everything from posh to pop: brass and string ensembles, choir, year 9 ska band, singer songwriters, full orchestra, dance and annual art exhibition. Arty types of all persuasions are well served by the exceptionally rich – 'amazing,' said one parent – co-curricular activities programme.

Sport is strong and getting stronger. Boys' basketball and girls' netball especially vibrant just now. Good range of team sports on offer supported by the co-curricular programme including before-school coaching. Inter-school fixtures. Well resourced, artificial pitches and a sports centre that is also open to the public. Outdoor ed includes thriving DofE up to gold. Plans afoot to develop the experience by bringing in scuba diving, sailing and expeditions to remote places.

Astonishing range of trips to more or less everywhere all the time. Most ambitious are expeditions to places like Greenland to do work on radiation levels for CERN/Cern or Kyrgyzstan to teach nomadic herders English. Pupils get two years to raise the £3K+ it costs using their own initiative.

Background and atmosphere: From Bohunt Liphook grew the Bohunt (multi-academy) Education Trust, which now comprises five schools in total: Liphook, Petersfield, Southsea, Worthing and Wokingham; and a franchise in China, Bohunt Wenzhou, a private boarding school opened in 2018. The latter is the first-ever branch established by a state school and takes its place alongside branches of top independent schools including Harrow and Wellington College. Profits will be repatriated to support the Trust's UK schools. It's all happened fast, this expansion, so it's bound to make some people a bit anxious. We were seriously impressed by the quality of all the teachers and senior leaders we met. They are clearly values-led and feel empowered; all are committed to collaborative leadership and shared endeavour. They swap good ideas (share best practice) and spark off each other. An English teacher told us, 'We are free to be creative'. Another: 'The culture of innovation here means that no one ever says "That's the way we do things here".'

The campus feels modern and comprises many single-storey buildings, so the scale is unintimidating. Functional mostly, not prestige but handsome enough. Doesn't feel like a school of 1,800+. Flows well, very little jostling. Inspirational quotes on the outside walls which students assure us they like. It was a wet day when we visited and – note to architects – muddy puddles had formed on the walkways compelling everyone to play Bohunt hopscotch.

Much excitement about the new sixth form in its separate building on the main campus. It offers a 'higher level of support and nurturing' from 'staff who know you best' than local sixth form colleges, we were told. The quality of applicants for teachers' jobs has risen in response to the inclusion of sixth form teaching.

Pastoral care, well-being and discipline: House system breaks the school down into manageable social groups. Students guided by tutors and achievement coordinators. Week-long induction including get-to-know-you summer camp. Welfare officer highly spoken of. Our favourite: the head of discipline, a man of arcane detective powers spoken of with hush and awe – 'I definitely wouldn't want to cross him', our guide told us. He's quick to nab anyone seen with a mobile phone in school time unless you need it for a lesson. Third strike and your parent or carer has to come and collect it. Well-being promoted by sessions in exam stress and strategies, plus mindfulness and learning from failure. One parent we spoke to said, 'They responded very fast when I raised concerns about teasing, and it worked'.

As visitors we were pretty much on a par with newbie 11-year olds and felt entirely safe and comfortable – no knots and clusters of cool kids lording it or being conspicuously different. We asked about that and students told us that yes, you get groups of friends of course, but no, now that we mention it, not cliques. Individuality is accommodated – one student told us: 'You have freedom to find your own way'. Our prevailing impression was one of really nice, happy kids. Emblematic of this: no swirling eddies of sweet wrappers at the school's entrance. Students are encouraged to speak out. There's a thriving StudentVoice which feeds back to senior management on policy issues and stages events. Students are involved in interviewing new staff and elect the head boy and head girl.

Pupils and parents: Ethnically not especially diverse, reflecting the demographic. For the same reason, lower than national average number of students on pupil premium. With just one London train an hour Liphook lacks the commuter magnetism of, say, Haslemere. Not a tile-hung English idyll sort of a place, more a big sprawly village with a lot of through traffic which often grinds to a halt at the start and finish of the school day. Estate agents locally report growing demand for houses driven by buyers wanting to live safe inside the school's catchment area.

Some parents told us that communications from the school can be somewhat last-minute. By the same token, at the time of our visit the school's website had a number of pages which launched moths. These are symptoms either of a school at full stretch or one that's gone off the boil. We reckon the former and judge that the school will not see this as an excuse.

Entrance: Bohunt draws students from as far afield as Surrey and Sussex. For every good reason we can think of it's massively oversubscribed. Priority to looked after children, siblings, those living in the catchment area then by distance. For sixth form entry, grade 5s in Eng and maths plus three other 6s. Come for a taster day if you want. Transition from linked primaries carefully managed.

Exit: So far around 50-60 of the 300+ year 11s have stayed on for the new sixth form, with most others to the outstanding sixth form colleges in Alton and Godalming and FE at South Downs. The first sixth form leavers will be off to university in 2019.

Remarks: A quarter of parents hereabouts go private, something that really gets Mr Strowger's goat. He reckons his school offers an independent-level education for free and he'd like to make a big dent in that percentage. Given that a state school gets to spend less than third of what an independent school spends per student, that's got to be a tall order. Or is it? Money on its own can't buy you Bohunt's wholehearted, highly professional teachers; they're easily as good as the best you'll find in the most successful fee-paying schools. Money can't buy you Bohunt's spirit of innovation and creativity, its kids-first ethos, its culture of 'we're all in this together'. And money can't buy you Bohunt's bottom line: independent-minded students who get great results.

Box Hill School

Mickleham, Dorking, Surrey RH5 6EA

Ages 11–19 **Pupils** 420 (298 boys, 118 girls) **Sixth form** 108 **Boarders** 124 full, 21 weekly

Fees: Day £17,850 – £19,710; Boarding £27,510 – £39,930 pa

01372 373382
www.boxhillschool.com

Headmaster: Since 2014, Corydon Lowde BSc MEd NPQH (40s), previously school's deputy head who took over following sudden departure of predecessor. Before that, nearly three years' handy overseas experience in similar role at British International School of Boston, preceded by seven-year stint at Hampshire Collegiate School, starting career at large state comprehensive.

'Has a vision he wants to share' and 'never tires of talking about what we're doing.' Hours he's putting in (lots of them) paying off, thought insider. 'School is going up.' Was 'gutted' that had to speak on the phone (in hospital having wonky knee put right on day of visit) as meeting best way of 'understanding where all that energy is coming from and where the school is going.'

Felt to be doing as good a job as anyone could manage in difficult circumstances, style reserved but friendly, reviews cautious but generally positive. 'It's new thing but I feel that Cory is on the right track,' thought one parent, speaking for pretty much everyone. Overwhelming desire is that he keeps school atmosphere just the way it is. Nobody is hungry for change.

A teacher from the off (management, part of his degree, was the career that got away), he comes across as quiet, mild-mannered and slightly quirky with self-deprecating Brit humour (honed, no doubt, during own schooldays at Dragon and Frensham Heights) that must make international parents want to take him home gift-wrapped in a Burberry bag. (Should really be Duchamp, says Mr Lowde, a loyal fan of their ties, socks and, indeed, 'pochettes'.)

Goal is school that reflects the world when it comes to nationalities (they have around 30 but no monocultures) and ability range. Would like more Brits – 'who wouldn't?' he says – and is hoping rising tide of Londoners is high enough to lap against admissions desk.

B

When not headmastering, follows sport. Was British Karate Champion in the 1990s (not an Olympic sport – down to international wrangling). Karate, he says firmly, is all about 'turning search for perfection into your own personal journey – not about aggressive confrontation' – a nothing-to-prove message that's not million miles away from how would like school to see itself.

Academic matters: That increasingly rare sighting in them thar Surrey hills – senior school that has continued to welcome the all and sundries who, these hard-nosed, results-driven days, wouldn't necessarily gain a place elsewhere. In circumstances, 40 per cent A*-B at A level in 2018; average 30 points for IB; and 27 per cent A*-A/9-7 at GCSE a tribute to quality of teaching.

While near neighbours have sought solid A grade glory, here they've carried on with broader ability range (many are around the national average). But school's frequent self-referencing as 'non-selective' needs grain of salt. Minimally selective, yes, but everyone accepted as 'greenies' (blazer colour worn to year 11) needs to be capable of passing eight or nine GCSEs.

Able pupils who do deliver top grades (parents pinching themselves at children's better than predicted results aren't hard to come by) won't, however, be held up as only aspirational model worth pursuing. 'Am great believer that competition crushes one's self-esteem,' says head (though not when it comes to sport, where all-out drive to win is 'about character'...).

Academically, it's about 'my growth, learning and success [being] made greater by your learning,' sentiments that do him credit, as does desire for kind, empathetic colleagues. They're well up to the job, say pupils, and palpably keen to get everyone involved. Maths department gets X Factor squared award for pupil recruitment, department head 'a genius.' Similar stories elsewhere. Even visitors may find themselves dredging up rusty French and Spanish greetings, courtesy of bustling, friendly language teachers who won't take non for an answer, while we assume whiteboard spelling of 'clergimen' [sic] in otherwise pacey English lesson was designed to test pupils' eye for detail.

Ethos derives in part from membership of Round Square group of schools, linked to ideals of eccentric but hugely influential educationalist Kurt Hahn, who stressed compassion coupled with 'just do it' mentality. (We quizzed tour guides who, impressively, were able to cite every one of key principles – and swore they hadn't mugged up in advance...).

Extreme cleverness catered for but also support 150 pupils with SEN, from mild dyslexia to school refusers – 'though we're not special school,' says head and pupils must be able to access curriculum. Helped by lowish pupil to teacher ratio (nine to one) and small class sizes (average 15 to 18 up to year 11, as few as two pupils in EAL and ISC lessons). Support includes one-to-one specialist help (normal maximum of an hour a week, mostly maths or literacy focused) and multi-sensory teaching. Will also try to help those (often with high functioning Asperger's) struggling with social communication.

About 70 of 110 EAL pupils follow mainstream syllabus, 50 in sixth form, English studied at range of levels, from IB diploma level to IGCSE, ESOL and IELTS. Others are found among 40 plus pupils at International Study Centre who can chose from four courses aimed at 14-16ish age range, most popular the one-year intensive GCSE programme (also marketed as pre-IB).

Some ISC pupils start a year or so behind peers, about half eventually joining 'mainstream' pupils (school's words, not ours). All 'fully integrated into school life...' says glossy literature (repeated several times for added emphasis) though some national groups stick together and school pupils can feel onus is on them to make first contact and bridge the cultural gap.

School's best recent curriculum decision has been reintroduction of A levels, reducing at a stroke post-16 departures of the IB-averse who 'want to stay but don't want to take six subjects,' says head, though they're encouraged to opt for extras such as IB theory of knowledge, extra maths and creativity, action and service – and some do (one keen A level student was even doing IB Spanish module out of love for the subject, though skipping the exam). Staff, insouciant about extra workload involved, see dual system as best way of boosting numbers studying top subjects at top unis, particularly maths and straight sciences.

Games, options, the arts: With practice rooms open all hours (7 in the morning till 9 at night) and free instrumental taster lessons, no shortage of opportunities for 100 or so budding musicians who hone skills, some to diploma level – one so impressive that visiting top musician offered tuition on the spot.

Other hands-on subjects housed in range of (mainly original) buildings including small, cobble-paved stables minimally converted to create atmospheric and fitting home for DT, every tool's home marked by pencilled outline on wall behind – very Patrick Caulfield. Visual arts headed by practising artist, who, paintbrush in hand, was adding final touches to own masterpiece as pupils worked around him, inspiring similarly accomplished work (our favourite among many featuring off-duty angels enjoying an off-duty cig).

Sport key to 'holistic' approach, though girls enjoy pinker-shaded version – holassism, perhaps? – and do netball and rounders (rugby and cricket for boys) with hockey and football in common, though pupils confident that if school would happily accommodate changes if demand was there. Frank acknowledgement that team sports 'not for all'; room to improve, thought parent, as not viewed as top priority, perceptions rubbing off on potential staff recruits (lure not yet sufficiently great to attract top talent). Results, which tend to align with levels of each intake's innate talent, can fluctuate fairly widely from year to year. That said, manifest advantages for the keen who, with minimal numbers of school teams, can get their fill of matches, though accepted that anyone requiring high quality sporting fix and nothing but will probably end up elsewhere. However, swish new sports hall with courts and fitness areas, plus MUGA and Astro outside.

Sensible decision to offer individual fitness from year 10 when 'almost anything is possible,' says school, the more so as sport happens twice a week, Tuesdays and Thursdays being reserved for school activities including magic club, sign language and – a rare treat – corsetry and dressmaking class which teaches traditional panelling and boning skills and is run by passionate devotee, enthusiasm largely responsible, as with fashion and textiles GCSE, for bringing in impressive numbers of boys.

Boarding: With large numbers of full boarders (around two-thirds boys), spending priority is six boarding houses, four in the grounds, two across the (quiet) village road. House names, though full of meaning to school, have certain random quality for outsiders, Constantine named after eponymous Greek king – school patron; Ralph apparently commemorating past VIP (though sounds like rakish English take on IKEA furniture policy).

Plenty to help boarders take mind off décor difficulties. After prep on Saturdays, seniors can travel into London. Must be back by '2230' [sic] (time rather than century, we assume), shopping trumping culture every time. Excellent range of trips including 'experiences' (Jamie Oliver and Harry Potter). One houseparent (male) runs regular pizza-making sessions ('leave dough to rise during the day, cook in the evening.') 'Never a dull moment,' insists school, firmly. Boarders agree. 'Can be almost too much going on,' said one.

Background and atmosphere: Word du jour, judged to pack a punch in terms of punter appeal, is 'inspiring', writ large throughout new school video, overlaying jolly images of suitably fired up pupils fencing on the school lawn (a summer term reality, not just camera-friendly set up) or putting up tents at summit of Box Hill, buffeted by gale force winds.

There's also much talk of holistic approach, though 'mindfulness', other all-purpose buzz word of choice, appears to be the meme that got away – so far. 'Not sure why aren't using it,' says member of staff.

'Stunning' is other obvious candidate, given village setting in Mickleham, between Dorking and Leatherhead and about 20 miles from London. As pretty as they come, main building once private gothic revival Victorian house with aspirations to grandeur, full of delightful stained glass biblical scenes and window seat epidemic (even modern boarding houses are rotten with them). Newer wings tacked on at the back sufficiently sympathetic to keep the charm intact though some more elderly stand-alones have their work cut out. 'Has the smell of an experienced building,' says one of tour guides of modern languages block.

Original grandeur belies school's relative youth, founded only in 1959 by Gordonstoun housemaster on principles inspired by inspirational educationalist Kurt Hahn, with much emphasis on whole pupil development (and plenty of non-Hahn inspired beatings for those failing to progress along right lines, according to one rueful 1970s-vintage OB). Now, pupils 'will all excel at something,' reckons school, while extending talent range to include high profile qualities such as friendship and general good egg-dom, which are 'acknowledged though not in OTT way,' says member of staff.

In any case, it's Hahn-lite (don't set them loose in all weathers on high seas: land-locked setting on Surrey Downs is against them) but ticks off must-dos: democracy, environment, adventure, leadership and service – with whole school activity week in September with camping, canoeing and rock climbing for all in Wales or New Forest. DofE – closely linked in ethos – from year 9 and just about everyone takes bronze. 'No reason not to,' says school, though silver and gold recruited on opt-in basis. Star attraction is trip to Philippolis, South Africa, where pupils have helped add new buildings including crèche and classrooms. 'Proof of faith in school,' said mother, whose son, just turned 13, had spent a month there.

Luxury goods on offer to counteract struggle with elements – 90 inch TV in new sixth form common room used for films and for pupils to 'enjoy live streams from the Royal Shakespeare Company,' trumpets prospectus. We're sure they do little else (sotto voce giggling when we asked undoubtedly down to recollection of Bard's many bon mots...). And when Titus Andronicus palls, there's always fun of watching vast tame rodents (gerbils not rats, despite unnerving tails) rolling around in exercise balls.

Overall impression is of well-tended school with little evidence of slight messiness reported by a couple of visiting parents – nothing to do, we're sure, with sign reading 'GSG visit [today]. Rooms have to be very tidy...' And so what if it's not immaculate? 'Don't send son to school for the décor,' commented mother.

Grounds undiluted gorgeousness (impressive mown stripes of grass that continued either side of small pond on back lawn giving unnerving impression that Jerry – the groundsman, and noted duck whisperer; pupils say he's followed by family of mallards each year – can walk, or at least ride, on water).

Golden glow set to spread as governor-sanctioned spending spree continues, aided by canny bursar who 'always has six months of staff salaries in the bank,' and is clearly a dab hand at curbing any headmasterly dash over cash tendencies. 'We're strong and robust – though hate that word, makes me sound like politician,' says head.

Now well on the way to transforming slightly dismal befores to far nicer afters. Rooms where clutter of tables and beds currently fight yellowing paint for supremacy slowly but surely transformed by attractive furniture, much of it custom created 'by our own maintenance team' and essential as most non-standard alcoves aren't compatible with off the peg designs.

'Work in progress,' says head. New sports hall will be followed by more space for creative arts ('absolutely not forgotten,' says head). Some Portakabins – some exteriors slightly shabby, interiors as well as can be expected and could be far worse – will remain.

Pastoral care, well-being and discipline: 'Willing to cherish the children for what they are – don't treat them as a commodity,' thought feeder school registrar. 'Very open and honest, don't sweep things under the carpet,' agreed parent. Example is alcohol policy. If over 18, boarders can purchase but 'carefully monitored' – to ensure any headaches are admin, not consumption, related.

Quality of communications only widespread complaint, described with single-word pithiness by several parents fed up with night-before notifications of matches and recent music event. (Though full marks to music staff for re-running one child's performance so late arriving mother didn't miss out.)

Other parents, however, reckoned that greater attention to termly calendars and school website would iron out most of the difficulties. Fortnightly newsletter from head also generally going down well, while more text alerts and email updates should take uncertainty out of nitty gritty-ness of who is doing what and when.

Nurturing element otherwise practically perfect, attended to with care and sensitivity. One pupil, bullied elsewhere and finding settling in hard, was cajoled out of foyer into class by head of year, now thriving. 'Helped him become accustomed to school until he was able to let go of that helping hand for a day or two.' Unpleasantness does happen but quickly and effectively dealt with, think parents whose children have been on receiving end. School's 'expose and eradicate,' approach includes ambassadors – 'our eyes and ears,' says head – who report any hint of transgression, backed up by anonymous online whistleblowing.

Boarders send two reps from each of the six houses to discuss issues – often food related – with school headed by 13-strong syndicate who supervise breaks, administer tellings off for minor uniform infringements and are led by head boy and girl, known as Guardians, superhero connotations a highly successful recruitment tool. Handover speech to successors an annual tear-jerker, with one post-holder 'talking to her parents through the speech and saying how grateful she was,' said mother, welling up all over again at the memory.

Unlike other top dogs we've encountered, not shy about using superpowers and will impose detentions, though not often and mainly for repeated rudeness. 'Know when someone's just being cheeky.' Given incumbents' nicknames (President Nice and Madame Fuhrer), we thought they showed commendable forbearance, though all pupil behaviour witnessed, in and out of lessons, was universally immaculate.

Pupils and parents: Parents range from diverse international community to ecstatic locals, often first time buyers, thrilled about what school has done for their children. All aware that school still seen as second choice. 'Wrong postcode for some Reigate mums,' said one. General sense that won't last, though nobody's in a hurry to add more competitive feel to a place felt to run on happiness. Boy numbers (outnumber girls two to one) and international element (around 84 per cent of boarders) also put others off, though seeing real life consequences of world events played out – one parent cited falling out of former best friends from different war zones – provides 'amazing' insights.

B

Monthly Friday teas for parents when school provides the cakes but 'doesn't overpower with teachers,' said mum. Later life reunions all over the place – Hong Kong the latest when checked bustling Facebook page (as well-tended as the grounds), though plenty of alumni stay don't move far away, careers covering eclectic range from surveyors to musicians and authors.

Entrance: Officially take into years 7 (40 places), 9 (20 places) and 12 (variable) but if there's space, will take at other times.

Majority of pupils from 10-mile radius though extending, Kingston and Horsham (as well as thriving metropolis of Nork) all now within reach thanks to extensive bus network (6.45am start for furthest flung locations). Micklefield, Downsend, Reigate St Mary's, Chinthurst, Aberdour, Priory Prep and Kingswood House among preps sending pupils, though no official feeders. Local primaries also well represented.

Exit: Many schools have much-trumpeted cohort who leave post-16, recognise error of ways and stage tearful prodigal son (and daughter) return, accepted with nary a 'we told you so'. Here, parent confirms it's the real McCoy with mother phoning Mr Lowde to ask if could have place back. 'Missed it so much.' Other post-16 losses, often to local sixth form colleges, partially staunched but trickle will continue, think parents, as pupils cast off 360 degree care for grittier experiences elsewhere. 'Not a criticism of the school but tribute to confidence-building,' pointed out mother.

Of the 40 or so per cent who stay on, university entrance for most, over 80 per cent to first choice, no Oxbridge currently but aiming for one or two a year – no special department as 'we're small enough to personalise timetable where needed.' 2018 students off to eg Exeter (film studies), Warwick (psychology), Nottingham (politics and economics), Southampton (physics and astronomy), Loughborough (graphic design), Surrey (accounting and finance) and Central St Martins (fine art), plus Madrid, Moscow, St Petersburg and Munich.

Money matters: Generous support for deserving families whose income range isn't cosily clustered at top end of £ dial. Warmth of welcome and matter-of-fact help with bursary application process felt to speak volumes about school's ethos.

Remarks: Warm-hearted, encouraging school that's easily overlooked in favour of guarantees of undiluted top grades elsewhere. 'Not right for families who want everything in neat and tidy boxes,' thought mother. 'It's not draconian here. You're doing it because it's what you need to succeed.'

Bradfield College

Bradfield, Berkshire RG7 6AU

Ages 13–18 **Pupils** 778 **Sixth form** 316 **Boarders** 710 full **C of E**

Fees: Day £29,925; Boarding £37,404 pa

01189 644516
www.bradfieldcollege.org.uk

Headmaster: Since 2015, Dr Chris Stevens MA DPhil (early 50s). Previously second master at Marlborough College (from 2011), he started his career in prep schools as a (very) young man. Brambletye, briefly as a gap student, and then Ashdown House as a young master where he split the year in half, six months at Ashdown (where a lot of the time was spent establishing the Ashdown château in France) and half the year studying for his doctorate. He finally firmly established himself in the boarding senior school world in 1997 when he started at Uppingham, where he was master-in-charge of cricket and housemaster for nine years. Educated in an all boys' environment at Tonbridge School, Dr Stevens read modern and medieval languages at Caius College, Cambridge and researched Italian literature for a DPhil at Oxford. This is where he met Helen, now associate professor of English at Corpus Christi, Oxford. They have school age daughters.

A highly intelligent man; sometimes you have to run to keep up with Dr Stevens in conversation. He thinks fast and talks fast, everything spoken in a mellifluous voice, however, and everything considered and thoughtful. He made the decision to work in schools rather than devote himself to academia largely because, despite his intellect, he loves the rough and tumble of life in a boarding school. Thoroughly unpretentious, he scoffs at the hierarchies that can divide the prep and senior school worlds and values the time he spent with much younger children and the very different challenges that are found in prep schools. Both he and his wife missed the boarding house atmosphere while they were at Marlborough and both are relishing being back in the fray and at the heart of things. They are still in the process of getting to know all the pupils, which he is determined to do. Sixth formers are regularly invited to dinner at their house, and a privileged few in lower years are also invited to dine with him and his wife. Otherwise it's at breakfast in the dining hall that he seizes the opportunity to eat with the more junior pupils and get to know their views on life at Bradfield and beyond. 'Best insight into who are the best teachers are too', he confides.

The 'beyond' is something that he holds very important. An outward looking man, he celebrates the influence of families from different cultural backgrounds – often each parent from a different country, and shudders at what the landscape may hold post-Brexit. An international outlook and mindset he considers to be essential, particularly in the face of how easy it could be to reflect a pocket of little England, given the picturesque, chocolate boxy location of the school.

An inclusive man, he has changed the staff photo so that it genuinely incorporates the whole staff, not just the teaching staff. Everyone is invited for hog roast and ice cream in his garden. He is passionate about avoiding pretension and a sense of entitlement. While keen to maintain the sense that Bradfield is a warm, relaxed and caring environment, he is concerned that this should not be mistaken for a lack of ambition. Students here are to be challenged without becoming stressed. Stretched in order to be stimulated, alive and curious. Parents approve, while noticing a shift towards heightening the academic standards. 'Fabulous,' said one; ' very sensible,' another.

Academic matters: A school that is, without question, on the up. A real contender now, academically, and firmly on the radar of aspirational parents as well as those who have always wanted a rounded and broad education for their children. A levels back on track after a disappointing 2017, with 76 per cent A*/B grades and 41 per cent A*/A grades in 2018. IB cohort got an average of 35 points (out of a maximum of 45). Pupils normally take 10 GCSEs; In 2018, 61 per cent A*-A/7-9 grades. Economics continues in popularity; business studies, film studies, textiles and photography all offered alongside the traditional subjects. One took Latin A level in 2017, none Greek (though a small number take the Latin certificate at GCSE, and an even smaller number do Greek) but five took Russian A levels. Large take up for EPQ; wide range of projects from 'Aid or trade in Africa, which is better for development?'; to 'To what extent is diversification the main reason for Apple's success?'; and 'Was the Lance Armstrong scandal beneficial for the sport of cycling?'

The Blackburn science centre is a hugely impressive. As well as being eco-friendly and thoroughly up to speed with technology, it is beautiful to look at and ergonomic. Ten classrooms and laboratories, spaciously spread out on each of the two floors. What goes on inside is also impressive. Parents regard it as one of the stronger subjects. 'Fantastic,' they said. The library, on the other hand, is reassuringly old school. Constructed of the local flint and brick with diamond paned windows, it is properly stocked with books as well as decorated with looming portraits of former heads and wardens. Not a high tech environment, but a refreshingly studious atmosphere prevails, young men and women working and collaborating in here. Comfortable areas filled with smiley faced emojis to escape to with a good book.

Large study skills and support department (SSSD – SEN to you and me). About 150 receive support; caters for everyone from those who require minimal support to those who need a reasonable level, but no specialist unit to cater for extreme needs. Would not automatically turn away someone with specific difficulties but will always ask the question, 'will they be happy here?' says head. Vast majority who use the SSSD have had a history of provision in their previous schools, but teachers can refer individuals, initially to houseparent.

Help given across the board at key pressure points. 'Extra lessons to help with GCSEs have been phenomenal,' said a seasoned parent with children at other schools. However if a child is not responding to being pushed, then the pressure drops. 'You have to want to do well, and what is brilliant is that it's cool to work hard and to get good results,' confirmed another parent. Grades given each side of half term. Reassuring to parents who like to feel on top of how hard their child is working.

Games, options, the arts: Bradfield is a football school, no rugby here at all. They are good – and known to be good. A recent captain of the first XI played for England in an international match against Scotland, we were told by our proud sixth form guide (who was a water polo aficionado himself). 'If you're good,' he said, 'opportunities open up for you at international level, but if you just love to play you can play at any standard that suits.' A wide range of teams means everyone can take part but a competitive edge survives. Boys' major summer sport is cricket; for girls it's lacrosse (there is also mixed lacrosse, and girls can play in boys' teams) and netball in the winter, tennis in the summer. Hockey and swimming are also major sports for both boys and girls. 'There is a team for everyone who wants to play and the B and C teams will get the same rewards as the A team. No elitism,' said a parent. Lush facilities from acres of green sports fields as far as the eye can see, to splendid indoor tennis courts, as well as outdoor courts, dotted around the grounds. Lots of sports tours to as far afield as Sri Lanka (cricket) and Singapore and Malaysia (hockey).

One of the most enticing range of minor sports we've seen. The school website reads like a highly exclusive action-packed adventure camp. From clay pigeon and rifle shooting (school has its own ranges for both) to zumba and yoga, with fives, real tennis, dodgeball, sailing, canoeing and polo as well as water polo and golf. A nine hole golf course is nestled towards the end of the games pitches. Water polo takes place in the glistening 25 metre pool that forms part of the swanky sports complex. CCF compulsory for year 10; Duke of Edinburgh also has a high uptake – our guide had just achieved gold. Standards are high here – both in the quality of provision, the teaching as well as facilities, and in the quality of commitment and enthusiasm from the pupils.

A Bradfield flagship is its Greek theatre, Greeker, as it's known. Recent performances include Antigone (in the ancient Greek). Theatre has been carefully restored and is sheltered in a shady bower. It is well used, whether it be for Shakespeare (Midsummer Night's Dream), a rock concert, or the whole school prize giving, which involves the famous handshaking ceremony ('a chance to test my knowledge of each child,' winks the head).

Music thriving, as is the art. Music is housed in a spacious building with two large classrooms, a concert hall and plenty of practice rooms. 'I'm enjoying coming here to play and practice,' enthused one sixth former; 'everyone is so friendly here.' A plethora of groups and choirs, jazz and classical, some pupil led, some staff led. We watched year 9s having rowdy noisy fun with steel drums, shakers and tambourines. The art rooms are tucked away on the other side of a brook in a delightfully separate, rustic cottage-like building. Everything is tidy and organised here but without losing a sense of spontaneous creativity. Well-thumbed art books are scattered amongst the workstations. A welcome relief to see them here rather than neatly stacked and barely touched in the library. Art is popular; students like the teachers as well as the subject. We saw monochrome butterflies on wire in the textiles department and an oil painted elephant on newspaper. Photography, sculpture and screen painting all in interconnecting rooms. One particular talented student had their work exhibited at the Tate Modern.

A plethora of societies from the religious (Swinbank) to philosphy, debating, drama and feminist (Neska).

With so much available you would have thought some students might become overwhelmed and not do anything at all. Not possible here. The Bradfield Diploma, a qualification pursued in years 10 and 11, involves pupils being assessed according to their co-curricular pursuits, and quite apart from that, affirmed one student, 'the Bradfield ethos is about getting involved; it is a family community and you get out what you put in.'

Boarding: Let there be no mistake, Bradfield is a boarding school. There are only 70 day pupils. However, with most families living within a 50 mile radius, only about 150 out of 750 pupils will be in on a Saturday night. 'We only have them home from Saturday tea time until Sunday evening, but it's a much needed chance to recover,' said one mother (although they are now able to return on Monday morning); 'it's so full on during the week.' Pupils will make the effort to stay in for a particular event, like the famous Michaelmas Goose weekend – a weekend packed with an interhouse riot of a competition which includes 'total wipeout' style water and inflatables obstacle course as well as dodgeball, debating, dancing and singing ('very raucous, and loud,' warned a student). The summer term sees more people opting to stay, and the further up the school they are the more they choose to enjoy the freedom to finish work and socialise with friends. Year group dinners are organised for Saturday nights and the unschooly feel to the place helps attract pupils into staying. Blundells Bar plays a large part in this, open in the evenings for sixth formers on Saturday nights (as well as two weekday evenings), this is the real deal with comfortable leather armchairs and pool table, doubling as a café in the day time for all year groups with proper coffee machines and muffins. With its decked terrace overlooking the cricket pitch, it's perfect for long summer evenings.

Faulkners – the mixed house for the whole of year 9 – is a Bradfield triumph. Not many schools do this, but the idea is to weld the year group together so that as they branch off to their different (single sex) houses in year 10 (all of which have been selected before they even arrive at the school), everyone will know each other and there will be less scope for cliquishness. There is the added advantage, suggested the super impressive and engaging housemaster and housemistress of Falkners, that

B

the young 13-14 year olds don't have to navigate what can be an intimidating hierarchy of older boys and girls. Most parents remarked on how much their children's confidence grew throughout the year, although inevitably we heard the odd case of difficult relationships, particularly among the girls. The building itself is modern, functional but attractive. Neat little drawers with names attached for mobile phones to go to bed in at the end of the day, very comfortable and tasteful common rooms on each boys' and girls' side, and a place in the centre where they can all gather to play games and hang out.

First class boarding accommodation – some of the most comfortable we've seen. Many of the study bedrooms have ensuite bathrooms, two or three to a room, there is a kitchen on every floor, and the comfortable common rooms are not the tatty stinky ones of olden days. Well upholstered sofas, pool tables and table football in good condition with all the pieces still intact, and best of all, when we visited at least, a lovely fresh smell of clean laundry.

Attempts are made to avoid houses becoming stereotyped – 'the sporty one', 'the nerdy one', although those trends can creep in without some social engineering.

Background and atmosphere: Founded in the 1850s by Thomas Stevens, lord of the manor and local rector, as a choir school for his church, Bradfield may not have a long sweeping drive, a grand central building, miles away in the middle of nowhere, but it is nonetheless a rural school. A picturesque one to boot, with its flint and brick buildings and sloping roofs. The village and the school are one and the same. There is no bank, post office or pub, but a fabulous arts and crafts manor house with stunning quadrangle and beautiful gardens, complete with astronomy hut for stargazing as well as the school chapel at the heart of the site. Here children have a chance to be children for longer, and there is not much to distract them from all that is available to do at school. Lots of walking to and from lessons, and that enticing sixth form bar is quite a hike. Faulkners eat in their house with some senior pupils. Others eat in the main dining room.

Plenty of quirky old fashioned public school traditions, including the many nicknames for things (glossaries are distributed on arrival arrive at Faulkners). Kitchens are Brewers, prefects, Beaks, Rux is the outdoor space near your house where you can kick a football around. The headmaster is the headman.

Day pupils fully integrated – sometimes leaving as late as 10 in the evening. They can leave after lessons but are encouraged to do their prep at school. In the sixth form they can get permission to drive themselves to school. All day pupils have a desk in a dormitory. Flexi-boarding arrangement is available, but not encouraged and not many take it up.

One housemaster (and ex-BBC sports commentator) observed that the fact that Bradfield is a football school, rather than a rugby school, allows it to lend itself more readily to a healthy, collaborative co-education environment. He may have a point. Relationships between the genders here certainly seem to be positive. Neither wary nor subservient but natural and enjoyable.

A strong community spirit, manifest in its educational partnership with Theale Green Academy, a local school which has gone from being in special measures to 'improving' and, 'we hope, to good,' says head. Pupils from Theale Green can come and learn science in the splendid labs here, but largely it's about sharing knowledge and expertise and providing support for their teachers. Continues to nurture the more than 100 year old relationship with Bradfield Club, a youth club in Peckham.

Pastoral care, well-being and discipline: Dr Stevens has a broadminded and sensitive approach to punishment. Highly experienced (chief disciplinarian was one of his major roles as second master at Marlborough), he recognises the difference between 'naughtiness' and 'nastiness'. As much of a concern as drugs now, in all schools, is the abuse of social media. While you need clear boundaries on the former, 'if you had zero tolerance with regard to social media you could empty a school,' he observes. One bad post may amount to stupidity, however three may well amount to bullying. Dr Stevens encourages an approach that helps pupils learn from their mistakes.

Faulkners students hand in their phones at night (quite apart from the threat to well-being caused by social media, the use of phones affects sleep, which is an even greater threat, he points out). Policies on phones and screens vary from house to house for year 10 upwards, but a heightened awareness of the effect – positive and negative – of screens is universal. 'The only criticism I have of the school is that they don't remove the phones of all pupils at the end of the day,' remarked one parent. Clear lines are drawn on intimate sexual relations as well as on using drugs in school – it's automatic expulsion. 'We don't have open season'.

Effective mentoring and support system between the sixth formers and newbies. Sixth formers eat lunch with year 9 in Faulkners and monitor their homework time. Complicated system of appointing head girl and boy, prefects, heads of house. Not all parents and pupils are fans, not least as some teachers can be indiscreet and partisan. It involves applications with references, an interview process, with some selection by the head boy and girl and some by the teachers. Within each house pupils are appointed to particular roles – head of academic, head of media for example, not difficult for the odd person to slip through the net and find themselves without a role.

Well-being is part of the curriculum for years 9 -11. This takes place in the Well-being Centre, a comfortable place among the roof beams where pupils can sit on beanbags, in chairs around a circle or at a large table to talk about difficult issues. A recent discussion was 'what does cancer mean to you?' They also do yoga, mindfulness and relaxation. The cynic may detect the influence of their grander neighbour up the road, but well-being is – or should be – firmly on the map in all good schools and this is just another indicator that Bradfield is keeping up with the times.

Tutors (all teachers also act as a tutor), attached to the houses, are assigned eight students. They will mentor, support and keep an eye on their progress – including their study skills and prep. Keen to strengthen and capitalise on this personal, focused support, Dr Stevens has freed up more time for tutors to meet their tutees so that as well as keeping a watching brief, they can take a more active, inspirational role. Some parents observed that their child had had four tutors since they started. Delicate balance struck between sticking with a tutor to form a solid relationship and moving on when the dynamic is not working.

We heard some reports that a high turnover of staff, particularly housemistresses and masters in the past, meant that not all holes were plugged soon enough when they appeared; however, it would seem that things are settling down now, and the atmosphere we experienced was purposeful, collaborative and stimulating.

On the whole a tolerant, unpressurised environment. 'You're always busy at Bradfield,' said a sixth former. 'If you're not doing something then something's wrong.'

Pupils and parents: Large London and local – Reading-Windsor-Ascot – contingent. About 10 per cent international families, based overseas. 'We keep an eye on numbers of particular nationalities, just to avoid cliques,' says head, but there is no quota at all, no missions to the East (or anywhere else) to recruit. Some Europeans – Spanish, Danish etc – but a more English flavour to it than many boarding schools. Certainly not flashy nor grand. Families here are pretty comfortable in their skin and with their lot. 'Impossible to pigeonhole,' commented one parent. 'There are foreign royalty, the odd celebrity, some very ordinary English folk and a few on full bursaries, a well-rounded community.' Boys still outnumber girls, about 60 per cent boys, but number of girls continues to grow.

Within those parameters, the pupils too are diverse. This is not a sausage factory. Dr Stevens values what he describes as 'the integrity of difference – one of the great strengths of a boarding education.' Pupils come from 60 different prep schools. No one school ever sends as many as 20. Among the prep schools that send numbers in double figures are Cheam, St Andrews, Lambrook, Northcote Lodge and Broomwood. Siblings are welcomed and their assessment looked at favourably: 'it would be wrong to turn them away on the basis that they scored a few percent less than they should have,' says head. Bradfield remains a broad church and under the current leadership will continue to do so.

Former pupils include politicians, Lord David Owen and Sir John Nott, authors Louis de Bernieres and Richard Adams, cricketer and broadcaster Mark Nicholas, actor Claudia Harrison and astronomer Sir Martin Ryle.

Entrance: Main entrance point is into year 9. Selection criteria are 'attitude, character and potential for happiness,' says head. School increasingly selective as demand for places has shot up in recent years. CE pass mark is 55 per cent (no slippage). Introduction of a pre-test in year 7. School considers prep school heads' reports and on the basis of that invites pupils for assessment in years 6 and 7. All candidates interviewed and tested. School works closely with prep school head with borderline candidates especially. The main aim is to find candidates who will be 'net givers' to the school.

First step is to see the school. Tours every Saturday morning and head makes himself available for personal meetings at other times. Occasional places do arise in year 10 and between 50 and 60 places in the sixth form. English and maths tests plus two interviews in November before year of entry into year 12. Minimum of six B/6 grades with at least Cs/4-5s in English and maths GCSEs.

Exit: Very few leave after GCSE. Practically all sixth formers go on to university. Current popular ones include Exeter, Edinburgh and Oxford Brookes. One medic in 2018; usually one or two to top arts or music colleges. Increasing numbers head for US universities and European ones, with 2018 leavers off to Indianapolis, Redlands and st Bonaventure, Moscow and Amsterdam. Three to Oxford in 2018. A very few (though school feels this is likely to increase) go straight into employment or on apprenticeship schemes.

Money matters: Although lots of scholarships awarded – including academic, sport and music – a fee reduction is only available with means-testing. The school is a charitable trust and provides bursary support, from anything from 100 per cent of fees to one per cent.

Remarks: Thoroughly unpretentious yet with lots to boast about, Bradfield is a heavenly place to learn and to grow. Very difficult to imagine who would not thrive here. There's something for everyone and lots for all.

Brambletye School

B

Lewes Road, East Grinstead, West Sussex RH19 3PD

Ages 2.5 -13 **Pupils** 300 **Boarders** 65 full, 41 flexi (from 7 years) C of E

Fees: Day £9,615 – £20,730; Boarding: £24,705 – £25,275 pa

01342 321004
www.brambletye.co.uk

Headmaster: Since 2015, Will Brooks BA (Durham), in tweed and pink (Brambletye's colour). Started by teaching maths and English at Bruern Abbey, where he was promoted to deputy head, followed by two more deputy posts at Sunningdale and Port Regis; glad now to be in a cosy family school and determined to keep it that way: knows all the names, addresses groups with 'Hello rascals', and wants to extend childhood for as long as possible; encourages children to build dens in the woods, and when a child knocked on his door to say 'come and see our den, we've just finished the second floor...' did so with alacrity... ('children need make mistakes...but we're not reckless...').

Parents gush about Will and his wife Amelia: 'great having a younger team with loads of energy and ideas'; '[they've brought] new vitality to school...[they] really encourage the children'.

Pupils approve too: 'nice and fun'; 'easy to talk to' and 'always involving us in his problems', said one to general hilarity of the rest, clarified to 'he wants our opinions about things' (and indeed has changed homework in response to criticism from pupils).

Entrance: Light touch assessment and interview.

Exit: Children depart for a wide range of destinations, with King's Canterbury, Benenden, Chrltenham College and Cheltenham Ladies all featuring (13 scholarships in 2018). Head emphasises the importance of children flying into the right senior school in the middle or top of the cohort.

Remarks: An old country retreat in the Sussex countryside with views over Ashdown Forest that stretch out into forever. Described by one parent who chose it over a place at a desirable London prep as a 'school in the woods' – 'how could any child not love it...[there are] trees to play in...' Inside, panelled walls, wood fires, a strolling sausage dog (Hercules) and comfy sofas. A stately home with pupils lounging happily by the fire, as if they were at home; which, of course, they are, pupils telling us it feels like a 'big family'.

Academically 'a real mix of kids,' said a parent at the this lightly selective school. 'High expectations', said the head, 'but plenty of support if necessary'.

A pupil told us, 'it's different to other schools because the teachers help you so much', another saying, 'you can give your opinion... a different opinion is not wrong'. Special praise for the maths teacher who 'makes it really clear', and for IT, a parent commenting, 'it could be desperate, but it's fun and creative...' The Latin teacher rewards full marks with a turn on the zipwire – an effective incentive for most.

'No one slacks in year 8', said a pupil, 'you're too scared', but the head makes no assumptions; he has introduced 'how to revise' for pupils to engage with what they know, don't know, and how to learn most effectively: 'they won't all be up all night before their finals when they're 21', says the head ruefully.

Smart new labs following a recent refurbishment, with the academic space to one side, practical to the other. The new library, art and debating chamber space is due to be completed in 2019.

Communication is 'excellent', say parents, with a new website, parent zone, and effort and attainment grades fortnightly. 'If a child gets a C3, a member of staff will call to discuss'.

A flexible approach to those with different needs – 'excellent to all its students', said a parent, describing how her fidgety son in pre-prep was allowed sit under his desk provided he would listen. 'Beautifully managed, no-one bats an eyelid'. A pupil of high ability with poor writing skills and a need to move around sits on a movement cushion (as do several others), has pencil toppers and wrist things on which to chew, is being taught touch typing, has a scribe in the meantime and is, said his mum, treated as an individual. Bored with history, he has been given a special project on WW1 propaganda and time to discuss it with the head of history. '[They] accept pupils as they are...'.

Around 20 per cent of pupils have extra learning needs, and most learning support is free of charge, provided in small groups or in class support. Where one-to-one support is necessary, this is charged as an extra.

It's a long day here, with day pupils being dropped off at 8am, and picked up at 6pm, or 7.10pm if they have activities, but all work is completed at school (very popular with parents). Saturday school on alternate weekends, lessons in the morning, matches in the afternoon – 'allows it to be a proper boarding school...keeps it alive at weekends...', said a parent.

'Strong, nurturing care – confidence building', said a parent, describing how her nervous son has gained a natural sense of confidence through drama, music and giving presentations; another told us her children's senior schools have said children from Brambletye are 'not daunted'.

Changes to pastoral care under the current head. The traffic light system moves pupils with pastoral needs to an amber light, which kickstarts a process with their tutor, and gets parents involved. Tutors are 'very, very vigilant and know of children's niggles,' said a parent, but children can also speak to a school listener, or a counsellor.

Generally 'children respect each other and are kind', said a parent, fresh from helping with school trip to Lords, but when there are problems between children ('not really bullying, but unkindness', said a pupil), parents say they are dealt with quickly and throughly, one telling us her daughter's problems were dealt with 'sensitively and discreetly'. The school's approach, said a parent earnestly, is that the bully needs as much attention as the victim – they address the problem, rather than handing out punishments. 'You're always given a second chance', said a pupil.

Amelia is always standing outside to greet the children in the morning, notepad and pen in hand to jot down any concerns. 'I feel I can really trust the school – and thank God we're not in this alone as parents'.

Pupils take real pride in the house system with discipline minuses and credit pluses contributing to the inter-house contest – 'it really works, they take responsibility', said a parent. Pupils get to know everyone in their house – 'younger pupils do talk to us about upsets...or just anything,' said a year 8.

Children are not allowed phones, and are not bothered – 'we manage time better without them', said a pupil, but older children would like more daytime access to computers and email (windows and iPads are lesson specific). The head works hard to help pupils understand their digital footprint, recommending that if they wouldn't be happy to show their grandparents, they shouldn't post it.

A domestic and international boarding community includes pupils from Russia, France and Thailand. Flexi-boarding is available from year 3, and is used by many local parents, who like to be able to just pop in to school. Years 7 and 8 have to choose between weekly boarding (opting in or out of weekends as they wish) or day; most board, with just three of year 8 remaining day pupils.

Dormitories for up to nine with bunk beds, old and quirky rooms for boys, a modern wing for girls, but all recently refurbished to a high standard. The most extraordinary views to wake up to. All dorms named after flowers and trees, and thank goodness for a school that doesn't think it detracts from boys' masculinity to sleep in Tulip.

Between 50-90 pupils stay at weekends, and enjoy trips out, such as go-karting or trampolining, or mucking around at school – a slope outside turns into a water slide in summer and snow slide on rugby tackle pads in winter.

No one goes hungry here – fruit is always available in the dining room, and 'grub' is available every evening until 8.30pm: toast, cereal, fruit, sandwiches. A parent told us how hard the school worked to help her fussy child to eat normally, emailing the parent every day with progress.

'Music and drama are exceptional', said a parent, describing the musicals in the school theatre as 'like West End productions' and an 'enormous pleasure'; another saying her child who didn't want to do a play was 'nearly jumping off the stage with enthusiasm'.

The standard of art here is exceptionally high for a prep school – 'amazing', said a parent, and they've had 180 art scholarships to senior schools in the last 20 years. 'Second to none, the teacher cares so much', said a parent whose unartistic son is slowly developing confidence and enjoyment.

Sport every day for an hour, and activities on top of this, although an extremely musical child who wanted more practice time for a music scholarship was allowed time off games – no rules for rules sake at this flexible school.

'Not so many to pick from [for teams] but we punch above our weight', said a pupil, another adding, 'If you're good at sport it earns you enormous respect'.

Girls have been in both cricket and football teams, and the first girl on the rugby team has apparently 'played a blinder' – but there's 'not been a boy in the rounders team', said a parent thoughtfully (although all pupils play in interhouse rounders). Hockey is now included on the curriculum for boys, who will soon play their first fixtures.

Pre-prep is described by a parent as 'so nurturing...a really safe space to hold the children as they grow'. Pupils have a great affection for their exceptional head – 'Mrs Atkinson, I love you a lot...' said a child, arms flung around her knees, and it's the first head we've seen invited on a sleepover.

Golden leaves for kindness fill a tree in the entrance hall and jewels are handed out for good work. Lots of time outside, pupils wearing their all weather muddy puddles. Growing boxes for each year (for outdoor maths), plants in wellies, two enormous rabbits (Moonbeam and Paddington) and a proper hobbit hole. A jolly nursery filled with happy busy tinies – 'George cries on the day he doesn't go to nursery', sighed a parent.

The head says Brambletye wouldn't suit a child with a flat learning curve, or one who never gives anything back – they need to engage with what's on offer. Parents thought reserved children might struggle, but pupils said that shy children will develop confidence, one year 8 telling us she was 'quite timid' in year 4, but 'it's small, everyone is welcoming and you get used to school quickly'.

Brentwood School

Middleton Hall Lane, Brentwood, Essex CM15 8EE

Ages 3–18 **Pupils** 1,600 **Sixth form** 313 **Boarders** 69

Fees: Day £7,236 – £18,945; Boarding £37,128 pa

01277 243243
www.brentwoodschool.co.uk

Headmaster: Since 2004, Ian Davies PGCE MA (50s), theology degrees from Oxford and Cambridge. Previously head of St Dunstan's College. Taught religious studies at Sackville School and became head of year and head of RE at The Latymer, Edmonton. He sees the school as 'educationally... more sophisticated than most' thanks to its diamond structure, educating boys and girls in separate gender classes from age 11 to 16, but together at other ages. So the school employs all 'the benefits of single sex education' while enabling pupils to 'also get the social benefits of choir, orchestra, combined cadets.. as part of a co-educational environment'. He adds, 'Nothing pleases me more than having a girl who is great at maths and physics go off to university to do engineering.'

Retiring in July 2019. His successor will be Michael Bond, currently vice principal education of Berkhamsted Schools Group, a family of six schools in Hertfordshire and Buckinghamshire. History degree from Liverpool and PGCE from Newcastle. Has taught at RGS Newcastle, Merchant Taylors' School (head of sixth form) and Christ College Brecon (head of history and housemaster). A keen sportsman with an interest in football (he says he is a long-suffering supporter of Newcastle United), skiing and fitness. Married to Suzanne; they have two sons.

Preparatory school head: Since 2011, Jason Whiskerd BA PGCE. Previously head of Aldenham Preparatory School in Elstree, Hertfordshire and deputy head of the King's School (junior) in Chester. Read history and politics at Trinity College, Carmarthen (University of Wales) and serves as an ISI inspector of other preparatory schools. A keen sportsman, having played cricket and rugby at regional level and, as testament to his Welsh roots (he attended Llandovery College as a boy), Welsh rugby and Swansea City are his passion. He is married to a junior school teacher and has three daughters attending the prep and senior school. A friendly man: extended a hearty welcome and warm handshake when we visited.

Academic matters: They start learning oral French from year 1. Verbal reasoning is taught from year 4 and Latin from year 6. There is emphasis on 'learning habits for life' so lots of push to get children to think for themselves, ask questions and 'look at things in detail'. From year 3 they are introduced to a house system so they can build relationships with older pupils. By the time they get to year 6 pupils take on roles as prefects, house captains, council representatives and more. Plenty of preparation for the move to senior school including a Q&A session with year 7s. Able children also well catered for with plenty of challenging extension opportunities. A couple of parents described how their children labelled as 'slow' and 'easily distracted' at previous schools, only discover that the real problem was that they had been bored, understimulated and capable of more.

I/GCSE results in 2018 were 60 per cent per cent graded A*-A/9-7. Alongside critical and creative thinking and the core subjects, they study French and Latin in year 7, and choose from German, ancient Greek or Spanish in year 8.

At A level in 2018, 44 per cent A*/A grades and 78 per cent A*-B. School offers 26 curriculum subjects, plus other activities such as law, cooking at university, Italian, peer mentoring training and sports leadership. IB scores averaged 36 points in 2018.

School encourages creative and critical thinking across all subjects, whether improving goal-scoring in sport, performing West Side Story in German, or applying maths in the composition of music. The syllabus is 'flexibly adapted to suit all pupils' needs' and 'able pupils do not get bored here', says the school. Parents agree with this, saying that although children are set early in year 7 in French and maths, these groups are not set in concrete and support is available if needed. 'I think it really is important that the children are not stuck with a label of being really clever or really daft,' said a parent. 'That doesn't happen at all. It is very, very flexible.'

EAL support provided to some 35 pupils, largely through teachers that have lived and worked abroad. The learning and development team also provides support to around 50 students with special educational needs. This includes an Individual Education Plan, one-to-one tuition, subject support and lunchtime drop in sessions. The department is very successful – some who receive additional support make such 'good and exceptional progress' that they 'sometimes outperform their peers', noted the ISI.

Games, options, the arts: This was one of three independent schools selected as an official 2012 Olympic training venue and it made world headlines when it opened up its doors to rescue an African Paralympic team left stranded at the airport with neither host nor facilities after a funding promise failed to materialise.

Coaches often successful sportspeople. Pupils have played at national and international level in fencing, water polo, cricket, football, squash, tennis and netball; fencing and athletics teams very successful. Alongside sports hall, pool, gym and dance studio, there are glass-backed squash courts, fitness suite and a fencing salle, plus extensive playing fields and a full-size running track.

Many pupils' works are exhibited at the annual art exhibition and school also tries to instil appreciation for art whether pupils 'consider themselves to be "arty" or not'. Various competitions include the popular water colour competition and the head's sculpting competition. DT and ICT are taught with art and food tech in the Hardy Amies Design Centre, equipped with its own library and computers. Recently a group of students scooped the top prize in an international design award with their life-saving 'glow' glove. 'We thought about different things and narrowed it down to safety as during the dark people don't see cyclists very well.' Their winning design went on display at the Design Museum in London.

Music and drama building equipped with rehearsal studios and practice rooms. Many students get involved in the school symphony orchestra, big band (which creates its own CDs), choir or choral society, and the regular musicals and house music concerts. A number of ex-pupils are exhibitioners at London music colleges or hold organ scholarships at university; there's an organ in the music hall and another in the chapel. Prep school has two orchestras and a junior choir that rehearses weekly. On the day of our visit many of the prep school classrooms were empty – our guide seemed baffled by this and was somewhat relieved when we happened upon a very noisy music lesson where children were exploring how to synchronise sound for a silent film. They were clearly having fun with flute, cymbals, drums, voice and more, but we got the feeling that the cover teacher may have pulled the short straw.

Similar story with drama: three major annual productions covering every genre from musicals to comedy to classics. Macbeth featuring video clips showing the war in the Middle East; Antigone performed with modern ballet choreographed by a student; a third year production of Arabian Nights; and West Side Story in German, all performed in the school's 400-seat auditorium. Mainly girls, but a few boys too, take part in dance showcases including tap, jazz and street.

Too many extracurricular activities to name: Trivial Pursuits, cross-country, table tennis, chess, D of E, Cine & Literatura, a Spanish film club, public speaking. 'You have to choose at least three; it's compulsory now,' we heard a year 7 pupil tell a sixth former. The Sir Antony Browne Society invites guest speakers on a wide range of current political, financial and medical topics. One of the most popular activities at the school is the 152-year-old CCF, which really creates a buzz in the atmosphere on Fridays when its 500-odd members come to school dressed in combat gear, ready for the afternoon and weekend activities, from hill walking to skydiving. Other pupils join the community service unit and help raise thousands for charities in the local area and abroad.

Boarding: The two boarding houses are a 'home from home' for the small boarding community, 60 per cent of whom are from overseas. Both are situated off campus, 'so you don't feel that you're there all day'. They are run like a 'well-oiled machine,' say the husband and wife houseparents, with regular routines (for homework, bedtimes and activities) and good links between houseparents, teachers and parents. As well as email, the 'children are Skyping every single night and we are Skyping with parents almost on a daily basis. I go into the rooms and they say, "Say hello to my mum".'

Background and atmosphere: During the English reformation a 19-year-old Protestant was burnt on order of Sir Antony Browne, then acting as a magistrate on behalf of Queen Mary. He purchased Weald Hall and land for the school in 1557 as an act of penance. The school received its motto in 1622 from the pen of John Donne, dean of St Paul's. Was a boys' grammar school, principally boarding, for many years. Admitted girls into the sixth form in the mid 1970s and into the main school in 1988.

The prep school was established in 1892 and moved to its present site at Middleton Hall in 1949; became co-educational in 1999. Pre-prep (ages 3 to 7) opened in 1995 and has its own grounds and buildings. In 2013, the pre-prep and the prep were amalgamated under the one headship of Mr Whiskerd, providing a seamless progression from 3 to 11, and are currently undergoing a multi-million development. There is a strong sense of the traditional alongside the modern – bright and lively classrooms, decorated with pupil's work, are housed in both 19th and 16th century buildings. In the gorgeous chapel (1868), pupils listen to biblical stories with a modern twist, for example, an account from one of the gospels about the danger of judging others, delivered alongside a screening of the Susan Boyle audition on Britain's Got Talent. Art and science is taught in an old stable block and Middleton Hall itself features stained glass windows and stucco ceilings. On the wall in the reception area is a large, colourful picture illustrating what it means to live by the Brentwood School motto of Virtue, Learning and Manners: 'We teach our children that the opportunities we create are best enjoyed when others benefit from them too'.

Set in the heart of the Essex town of Brentwood, across the road from the cathedral, the school stands on a 72-acre site. Not much is left of the Weald Hall save a few ruins. The Old Big School, built in 1568, still has the original front door and is used for lectures, meetings and discussions, and there's a beautiful Victorian chapel.

Pastoral care, well-being and discipline: Parents say 'pastoral care here is excellent' and that 'the older pupils help the younger pupils'. They value the peer mentoring room where sixth formers make hot chocolate for younger pupils, who can sit and talk if they have a problem. Year 6 pupils are trained in peer mediation and this helps 'pupils to resolve their own problems in the playground'. Bullying is rare, and the few 'misunderstandings' that do arise are 'nipped in the bud by the school very quickly,' say parents. One, whose daughter had been home educated and found the first few weeks a little daunting, commented on how well she had been helped to settle in.

Pupils have good relationships with their form tutors and teachers – 'everyone is helpful here', said a year 7 pupil. 'The teachers do tend to treat the children as adults,' said a parent. 'They communicate openly with them, so the children are not frightened to say, "I want to speak to you about something".'

Pupils and parents: Parents are mostly professional, with the majority being white English. 'Although we are a Christian school we welcome pupils of all faiths,' says the school. Many pupils move from the prep to the senior, others come from local independent and state schools. The school also has a number of international students (about 60 per cent of boarders, plus a few day pupils) from the Ukraine, Russia and other Eastern European countries, Central Europe and the Far East including China.

A number of notable former pupils including Douglas Adams, author of the Hitchhiker's Guide to the Galaxy, Sir Hardy Amies, couturier and dressmaker (he designed the school uniform), Lord Black of Brentwood, executive director of The Telegraph, Frank Lampard, footballer, Jack Straw, former lord chancellor and secretary of state for justice.

Entrance: Pupils assessed on language and dexterity skills for entry into the early years (about 40 places). Twenty places are available for external year 3 entry (age 7); entrance test in English and maths.

Year 7 entry by maths, English and verbal reasoning exams examination and interview. Sixth form entrance by interview and successful GCSE results (generally at least six grade 6s).

Exit: Over three-quarters of prep school pupils go on to senior school. They sit the same 11+ exam as external applicants and are prepared well (parents are warned a year or so in advance if the school perceives any problems). Candidates are interviewed for a potential academic scholarship or if they have struggled on the day. A few go on to local grammar schools.

Most – about 80 per cent – of senior school pupils stay on to sixth form. In 2018, eight to Oxbridge and three medics/vets. Four off across the Pond, including one to the Parsons School of Design on a scholarship and another to the American Academy of Dramatic Arts.

Money matters: A good variety of academic, art, drama, music, choral and sports scholarships, plus means-tested bursaries and six form scholarships offered via a two-hour critical thinking paper.

Remarks: Strong on values and has all the facilities and opportunities needed to provide a child with a rounded education. Very impressive.

B

Brighton and Hove Prep

Linked with Brighton and Hove High School

Radinden Manor Road, Hove, East Sussex BN3 6NH

Ages 3–11 **Pupils** 175

Fees: £7,191 – £12,261 pa

01273 280200
www.bhhs.gdst.net

Head of prep school: Since 2011, the sparky yet realistic Mrs Sian Cattaneo BA (Sussex) Cert Ed (50s). Came from over nine years as head of St Ives School, Haslemere, before that 16 years in Nairobi at the Banda School. Her son and daughter are now in their 20s. She was attracted to the Girls' Day School Trust by the attitude and dynamism of Dame Helen Fraser (the former chief executive of the GDST) and now 'I'll never go and work in a mixed school again!'

Parents say she 'has a heart of gold and cares deeply about every child' and that she works very closely with her deputy, creating 'a family atmosphere with kindness and grace'. She sees herself as a 'green hat' thinker (Edward de Bono's Six Thinking Hats) while her team puts her creativity into practice. Her office is set up with space for parents and children to come in and talk – she's gathered opinions on what is felt is important about the school and worked hard to reinforce and build on them.

Entrance: By tests and observation. Eighty per cent are referred by current and former parents.

Exit: By entrance exam to the senior school (around sixty-five per cent move there); or to other independents such as Roedean, Hurst or Brighton College (where parents say academic teeth are bared).

Remarks: Staff seen as the lifeblood of the school – and their friendliness and understanding of the need for flexibility given parental challenges is really appreciated by the parents. All teachers have email addresses for parent contact, there's a weekly newsletter, virtual learning platform for curriculum enrichment and source of information for parents and the nursery and reception have interactive learning diaries that can be added to by parents online.

Two classes per year all the way up the school. Reception has free flow to extensive outside space with an outdoor classroom. From year 3, the girls are taught by specialist teachers in specialist rooms – accustoms them to independence. We saw Victorian washing strung across the classroom, butterflies in remembrance of the suffragettes, all these part of the creative curriculum. Head is keen to ensure pupils are not too cosy; instead they are put in situations where they have to make their own decisions.

Year 5 and 6 use individual iPads for each pupil – staff are hot on training to ensure pupils use them to create presentations, share ideas and carry out research rather than just delight in the flick of the technology.

SENCo's 'learning differences' focus is about supporting girls with an empathetic approach and regular training for staff. There's a full time learning support assistant and she is used for individual and small group support.

The pupils are bright, interested and kind to each other – they reckon they all know everyone's name. Any 'friendship mishaps', as the children call it, are dealt with quickly. By year 6, they enjoy pouring milk for the nursery at break time and putting all the equipment away in the shed at the sound of the bell – as well. Others love to be in charge of logging books in and out of the friendly library; school council also very active.

Some great art on the walls and in process – ranging from Mexican Day of the Dead inspired foil skulls to precise drawings of the back view of the hairstyle of a friend in your class. Also examples of business enterprise eg creating the marketing, organisation and fundraising for Children in Need. As in other GDST schools, great outreach to local charities through visits to community, Guild Collections and music performances. Currently one of only two independent schools in Sussex that have the green flag of an eco-school, takes energy saving, Fairtrade, bio-diversity (raised beds in garden and allotment off site) and bikeability very seriously. Food is locally sourced and now cooked in house, salad option and no packed lunches. The staff supervise (and eat with the girls).

Attitude to games more focused now with new head of sport (previously taught PE by class teacher) and 60-80 external fixtures a term; netball, athletics, hockey, running, swimming, gym. PE hall (also assembly), new Astroturf, netball and tennis courts. Head of dance comes in to teach from senior school – this is very popular – while music is fabulously taught with three school choirs, a ukulele group, orchestra and 70 per cent of years 1 to 6 learning at least one instrument. Performances of all kinds in assembly, old people's homes and whole school shows and strong emphasis on music technology.

Brighton and Hove High School

Linked with Brighton and Hove Prep

Montpelier Road, Brighton, East Sussex BN1 3AT

Ages 11–18 **Pupils** 360 **Sixth form** 54

Fees: £14,007 – £14,421 pa

01273 280280
www.bhhs.gdst.net

Head: Since 2012, Jennifer Smith MA MEd (50s), in post for the long haul after a series of two-to-three year predecessors. An engaging and sensible Glaswegian, she spent the previous 10 years rising to deputy head at Wilson's, a state funded selective all boys school in Sutton. She still commutes south from there, her husband goes north to his headship in London. Attracted to her first headship by GDST values. 'It's about building resilience in girls' learning and confidence, while also very important to give value for money. My main aim is for each girl to know that we care for her and about her progress.'

Earlier challenges include five years as a head of English at an all boys grammar in her late 20s (and the first years of GCSEs) and a vital role in the turnaround of the ranking of Wilson's results. She uses her daily train journey to Brighton to blog for the school website – part of the 'technical explosion' she spearheaded in her first year, with a new online portal and online reporting. She doesn't teach the timetable at present, but does cover lessons, watches teaching and does duty in the canteen, using that time to hear suggestions from the students – and act on them eg new transparency in the behaviour system and a consistent 'tariff of discipline'.

Academic matters: Academic results strong with 76 per cent A*-B grades at A level, 49 per cent A*/A, and 60 per cent A*-A/9-7 grades at GCSE in 2018; dedicated staff passionate about their subjects. Bright, stimulating, independently minded, confident girls – a description approved by parents, staff and the local general public. Pupils are very conscientious and pile the pressure on themselves, but are encouraged to progress as individuals. Parents wonder at the results without overt peer rivalry – they feel it is extremely supportive, all of BHHS want everyone to succeed.

Touchscreens or interactive whiteboards in practically every classroom, both of which enable and encourage pupils to share centre stage with teachers. Pupils say the use of these and the online portal with past papers and learning tools really simplify catching up on classes and revision. Assessments for dyslexia and dyscalculia provided by the school and support for moderate cases via the SENCo team. Online reporting should now ensure that a diagnosis of dyslexia is attached to pupils through all subjects; in the past communication about the need for extra support has broken down.

Science is very popular, young and dynamic rather than geeky – the worktops in the revamped labs wouldn't look out of place in a kitchen showroom in Hove. Each sixth former has her own tray of instruments and test-tubes, encouraging responsibility and continuity. Latin is taught all the way through, along with a choice of French or Spanish, while maths and English are also strong with great use of external resources, whether it is a Cipher Challenge, guest author or theatre visit. The combined alumni of the GDST help to encourage aspirational and concrete links with world outside lessons, the pupils are busy and keen on learning, aware that their choice of single-sex education may already have given them a leg up.

Careers programme impressive with close links with the local careers service and employers, free psychometric testing in year 11 and the school organises work experience at the end of that year too. There are enterprise activities in all years, the Temple Project Qualification (the school's version of an Extended Project Qualification) and an intensive programme of visiting speakers, all of which apparently makes writing your personal statement for university application easy, although it may take you until then to realise that all these experiences are rounding out your character...

Sixth form has the biggest space in the whole school – although the numbers are small at present. This means very focused teaching and a real family atmosphere for those that stay, with plenty of experience coaching and mentoring the younger girls. Traditionally over half leave, many to the range of great (free) six form colleges around Brighton where there are more A level choices on offer externally eg media studies and vocational ones. Many BHHS girls have been there since the age of 3 or 4, so are keen to spread their social wings and learn with boys, although some regret leaving when their A level results are not so impressive as those who remain. Ex-students, with their male friends, can pop (and sign) in to visit the sixth form centre from the nearest college, BHASVIC.

Games, options, the arts: Great modern sports hall with disabled access and the normal rainbow of court lines, layered nets and trampolines, also two outdoor netball courts and Astroturf at the junior school. Netball and athletics are the most successful teams, but the track record is spread like the matches between independent and state sector opponents. Sport is good but it wouldn't be the reason to come to this school. The pleasant walk to the courts in St Ann's Well Garden is enjoyed by tennis players, girls are minibussed to Brighton Swimming Centre to swim, and the fitness studio is hugely popular – especially with the sixth form. However, the dance studio next to it appeals across all years, with one mirrored and one glass wall and all dancers with their eyes on the highlight of the year, a performance in a central Brighton venue. Drama also well taught in dedicated studio with professional lights and mixing desk, which doubles as make up and dressing room in the whole school productions.

Art department is beloved and productive – a microcosm of the ideal atmosphere of the school where teachers listen to individuals and then encourage each one to stretch themselves beyond their own expectations. 'It doesn't feel like a lesson, the teachers let you decide.' Officially it occupies two floors in a separate building with a darkroom and a Mac for photography (at A level) but the students' work is placed all over the school, is changed regularly and entices visitors to follow it to the source. Design technology also impressive with great use of acrylics and projects that range from concept to marketing. Likewise, home economics projects are all-encompassing eg tasty biscuits in enticing packaging and a level 2 food hygiene award – very useful for a summer job in a café.

The music house has been revamped. Full range of peripatetics, three choirs, two orchestras and a jazz band – as well as a biennial school musical – and packed performances. Also hosts Springboard, the Brighton and Hove Performing Arts festival. Performances of all kinds in assembly, old people's homes and whole school shows and strong emphasis on music technology.

Background and atmosphere: The original building (the Temple) became part of the GDST schools in 1880 – still central to the site, with pillars said to represent inverted cannons. Cluster of contemporary extensions spread out from this, wonderful height and light in the science block, other subjects spread between new and old buildings. Year 9 has a separate block near the netball courts and the sixth form centre and canteen are over a (narrow) public road from the main house. Main hall, used for two assemblies each week and performances, has retractable seating – when we visited, a vicar had just given a thoughtful address; apparently she has to be good since there are a fair few sceptics in the student body.

Main library is peaceful, with high ceilings – sixth formers can work there or in their own centre, computer access to the online portal as well as shelves of books. Sixth formers are allowed phones but the younger ones are not allowed to use theirs during the day – it is a busy site, so there wouldn't be much chance in the five minutes when the girls flood the corridors and stairs between lessons, racing back to the basement locker room to get more books or their sports kit. Uniform for the younger years, with small earrings and no bracelets – sixth formers can wear what they like.

A strong ethos of charitable giving with a Guild collection every Wednesday, where pennies are collected by reps in each form room. This all adds up and is given to two chosen charities per year. The charities are pitched by the girls at an assembly, so almost always have a personal motivation behind them, and the students use all their initiative to raise funds through other events eg a fashion show.

School council is also influential, with suggestions and complaints fed up through reps in each form. The same system operates in the GDST as a whole, so a case for change in BHHS would be pitched by a student rep to the GDST governors. Food is locally sourced and now cooked in house, salad option and no packed lunches.

Pastoral care, well-being and discipline: Strong pastoral support system with form teachers and sixth form tutors and year heads – set up for easy communication and accessibility. A mentoring service for younger girls – BLOBs – is an old acronym for Best Listeners of Brighton Schools. This really works, and is made easy by the amount of inter-year, inter-house contact through drama, sport competitions and end-of-year entertainment. Imaginative PSHE – we have encountered this in other GDST schools: the special events and whole days given over to topical issues all help to raise awareness and assist pupils with self-expression on current affairs.

School nurse on site, at the heart of the school near the basement locker room – parents and girls really value that common sense support; it eliminates the drama from long-term health conditions. Families really appreciate the frequent personal letters home from the head celebrating individual achievements. At the other end of the spectrum, some parents talk of bullying not dealt with swiftly enough in the past; however, the head appears to have it under control.

Students see themselves as a recognisable type, 'a BHHS girl through and through' – plenty of room for spirited girls but everyone is aware of the opportunities that the school gives them, so they are ambitious, organised and self-motivated. The head girl team is an example of the way cooperation and communication is fostered within the school – and links to organisations outside it.

Pupils and parents: From Hove, Brighton, Pulborough, Eastbourne, Worthing, etc. Buses from Saltdean, Worthing and Lewes. A real social and ethnic mix – artists, creative industries, investment bankers, teachers – and, due to competitive fees, a good economic mix. Busy parents, both normally working to afford the fees, or taking some help from grandparents.

OGs Karen Pickering MBE, Olympic swimming gold medallist, Claire Hicks MBE, director of Impact Foundation, businesswoman Heidi Cooper, several recent University Challenge competitors.

Entrance: At 11+ from a wide range of local maintained and independent schools and also the junior school. A recent rise in the intake at year 7 is hoped to swell the sixth form numbers. GDST entrance assessment for the main school – selective, but not super selective. Entry at sixth form requires five GCSEs at 5 grade or above, with 9-6 in subjects to be taken at A level; girls come from The Towers, Warden Park, Shoreham College.

Exit: Some 70+ per cent leaves post-GCSE, often for the sixth form college (less than half a mile away) BHASVIC – the very wide of subjects and boys in the classes are enticing and often it is a financial decision for the families. Recent university destinations include UEA, Oxbridge (two in 2018, plus three medics), Royal Holloway, Bristol, Brunel, Dundee, Imperial College and Belfast.

Money matters: Means-tested bursaries at year 7 normally awarded in rank order of performance in the entrance exam (50-100 per cent of fees); academic and music scholarships (10 per cent of fees) also available, plus Temple scholarships for all-round performance. More bursaries at year 12 and also another eight scholarships (10 to 30 per cent discount).

Remarks: Parents say it produces empowered, confident, clever girls – but not cocky ones – 'education rather than status'. Has suffered in the past through comparison to its noisy neighbour, Brighton College, both by staff and onlookers – now hopefully in an era where it is certain of its own value and ethos, with individual encouragement producing fantastic results and grounded girls.

Brighton College

Linked with Brighton College Prep and Pre-Prep School, Handcross Park School

B

Eastern Rd, Brighton, East Sussex BN2 0AL

Ages 11–18 **Pupils** 1,095 **Sixth form** 214 **Boarders** 142 full, 253 weekly
C of E

Fees: Day: £23,160; Boarding: £33,390 – £37,470 pa

01273 704200
www.brightoncollege.org.uk

Head master: Since 2006, Mr Richard Cairns MA (Oxon) (40s) His path to Brighton was via a law firm in Australia, a Palestinian refugee camp, Stewart's Melville in Edinburgh, The Oratory in Reading and the deputy headship of Magdalen College School, Oxford. Staggering list of achievements/accolades includes the opening of Brighton College, Abu Dhabi; a rise from 147th to top 20 in the UK academic rankings; doubling boarding numbers; trebling applications; a huge new building programme; the acquisition of Roedean Junior and Handcross Park Prep Schools; ISI inspection report with outstanding in every category; The Sunday Times Independent School of the Year.

Keen not to take sole credit for this, he has built a teaching and management structure to ensure that ideas and initiatives can be sparked and grown – inside and outside the student body. This attitude is magnetic – for pupils, parents and staff. He sees himself and the college as a mix of tradition and modern. 'I want every pupil to be who they want to be – as I say to them in assembly [pupils agree he does, and they remember it ...] "If I try to be him, who will be me?".'

Plenty of other schools try to tempt him away – the governors recently agreed a 10 week international trip, he says, 'to give me thinking time for the next seven years'. It was a global reconnaissance mission, visiting universities in the US and Canada as well as potential twin schools in Finland, Sweden, Singapore, Ontario and Hungary. Such symbiotic connections are characteristic of this head – and they appear to stem from a dedication to improving education wherever he can use his influence or initiative. He kicked off his tenure with compulsory Mandarin lessons but also connected with Kingsford, an East London school that was doing the same. Out of this link grew the London Academy of Excellence (LAE) in Stratford, East London, the first new sixth form free school academy in the country, helping children from disadvantaged backgrounds to get into university by making sure they pass the right A levels.

Has high expectations for his pupils, wanting them to be excited in the classroom. Teaches history to the fourth form. They report creative punishments from him for inattention eg writing a whole story about a turtle, or a poem about the girl the note was being passed to. Less formally, he has breakfast with the prefects and invites sixth formers to dinner. The pupils love getting to know the head in this way (one of seven children, he certainly knows how to cope with a large dinner table) and they discuss everything from divorce to cricket. He's not shy of involving the pupils in practicalities – from how much the new boarding developments cost to how much he would need to be sponsored to run the Big Balls relay for charity.

Academic matters: Shining results: in 2018, 90 per cent A*-A/9-7 at GCSE, 99 per cent A*-B and 83 per cent A*/A at A level; this is up with the best in London too. One of top value-added schools. Twenty-six subjects offered at A level. Biology, chemistry, economics and maths are particularly popular (the latter taken by about two-thirds of the pupils). About a quarter take four A levels. Outside speakers (John Major, Boris Johnson, Viv Richards, David Dimbleby, David Starkey, Jeremy Paxman, Michael Gove, Matt Prior..) visit in a Wednesday afternoon slot. Each department runs both a course-specific and a general Oxbridge activity, which obviously pays off, with a record number of pupils heading up to Oxford or Cambridge.

Staff are sparky and motivated – attracted by the charms of 'London by the sea' and being part of a school that's going up and up. An appraisal system of teachers by pupils is at the heart of the classroom. Pupils evidently respect quirky and effective teaching – whether it is their Mandarin teacher throat singing on YouTube or a video of a worked through past paper for maths A level revision. The Story of Our Land course combines history, geography, philosophy and religion for the third form (year 7s), who study the geography of the cliff an invasion force climbed or debate the merits of the Muslim or Christian standpoint while looking at the Crusades.

Languages popular, not just through the Mandarin innovation – compulsory in the pre-prep since 2007 and now a GCSE option (mostly A* grades so far), with graduate students from Chinese universities to assist – but also Latin, French, Spanish, Russian, Italian, German and Greek. The burgeoning Mandarin option is a USP, with the school being awarded Confucius Institute status by the Chinese government as a centre of excellence for the teaching of the language – the first such honour for a UK school.

All new pupils attend a literacy class and the dyslexia centre is nationally famous, specifically helping around five per cent of pupils. Some have English lessons here in small groups instead of a second modern language, individual help available in sixth form. School actively seeks out and welcomes bright children with dyslexia, dyspraxia or dyscalculia. Entry based on recent education plan report, CE assessment morning (observed in groups) and interviews by head and excellent head of centre. Approximately 50 taught in centre, which also supports the prep school students.

The bright library has a mezzanine level used for quiet working space for the sixth formers. Dedicated sixth form centre also has computers but is generally more social. Saturday morning revision classes on offer in the holidays, mostly to boost confidence before exams. Class sizes average 18 up to GCSE; after GCSE, the average is eight.

Games, options, the arts: Everyone has to do dance, PE and drama. House drama, house song and up to 15 different productions a year (including visiting companies, A level and GCSE performances and Commedia dell'Arte). Dance achieves nearly 100 per cent A*/A at A level and at GCSE happens in performing arts studio (outside classes offered to the community). Six-strong faculty teaches over 70 dance classes a week. Examinations in ballet, modern, tap and jazz, and the school boasts boys' street dance, modern and tap groups from junior to senior level.

New music school. Half of the pupils have individual music lessons, from more than 40 visiting music teachers; 22 music groups: choirs, orchestra, rock groups, concert band and various chamber groups, with participation in the National Chamber Music Competition as well as tours to Prague and Moscow. Ex-parents miss going to the performances.

Two hugely popular and innovative sixth form house competitions stem from the entrepreneurship programme and Strictly Come Dancing. The former gets academics and creatives developing a business plan together, each team competing to win £3,000 to commercialise their idea – previous winners have been a parking app and a device to stop babies knocking hot tea over. Strictly ensures boys are valued for more than just sport – the biggest applause in Monday morning assemblies goes to most unconventional achievements.

Purpose-built spaces for art, photography and DT make for beautiful art and design – there are still some lessons when the pupils watch a video for low maintenance inspiration but the proof of the art is hanging on walls around the campus.

Sport is enormously important here, all pupils taking part in games twice a week – rounders, netball, tennis, cricket, swimming and rugby possible on campus, otherwise it's a minibus to the college's Jubilee Ground, with six rugby pitches or two cricket grounds, further floodlit netball courts, a pavilion and three hockey Astroturfs nearby. Withdean's athletics stadium also hosts fixtures; each weekend sees some 300-400 children involved in competitive matches. National trophies in rugby (1st XV has particularly strong record of victories in Sussex) and netball (Sussex champions and national finalists), and leads the county in athletics. Cricket for both sexes a great strength – three former pupils have gone on to play for England women's team.

Community service a vital part of school life: pupils visit elderly people and help disabled children or teach pensioners how to use a computer; Make a Difference Day (MADD) sees every member of the college serving the community in more than 100 different activities, from cleaning beaches and clearing scrub to sorting clothes for charity. School raises money for local charities (including Whitehawk Inn, Rockinghorse, Chestnut Tree House) and those further afield (Romania, Kenya, Sri Lanka, India).

Boarding: Weekly boarding extremely popular – no Saturday school; many go straight home after Saturday morning matches. Full-time boarders can avoid the school curfew at the weekend if they stay with local families who take responsibility. Pupils can return from home by 9.30pm on a Sunday night or on a Monday morning – buses from outlying towns.

Five boarding houses for years 9-13 – two for girls and three for boys – plus a junior boarding house for 11-13 year olds at Handcross Prep and a new co-ed sixth form boarding house. Plenty of inter-house competitions, plus lectures, debates, music evenings, quizzes etc, and the after-school use of all facilities eg swimming pool and art department.

Background and atmosphere: Compact campus in Kemp Town, just four blocks from the sea front. Imposing 1840s buildings by Gilbert Scott (designer of St Pancras Station and the Albert Memorial). Award-winning buildings include School of Design and Technology and the Smith Café, where boarders can meet in the evening. The most popular part of this are the places where the boys and girls get to hang out casually together instead of signing in and out of each other's boarding houses.

Sited to the east of the landmark pier and pavilion, the school succeeds in being fashionable, practical and innovative – no Saturday morning school means that everyone has a full weekend and the chance to be part of the town instead of just being educated within it. This could put some parents off, since Brighton and Hove, like many seaside cities, has its fair share of addicts, drunks and loons. However, we've heard no disturbing reports and most sensible local parents realise that their children are going to come to Brighton at the weekend anyway and it is far better that they feel comfortable in their favourite cafés, bars and shops rather than loitering round Churchill Square.. Officially, there is a square patch of Kemp Town streets where pupils can stroll for 20 minutes of an afternoon, in a group, as long as they sign out. However, some definitely sneak a walk to the beach – they feel it's their right considering the prospectus proudly features pupils enjoying this out of bounds place.

Pupils are thoughtful and articulate – we visited on the day of Margaret Thatcher's funeral and got into a discussion with a group of 13 year olds about whether people would dislike her so much if she had been a man who had implemented the same policies. The head picks an individual each Monday to share a random act of kindness in assembly – this type of awareness is at root of the school's ethos which goes a fair way to balancing the social mix here. As in all schools, cliques could be found if you looked for them but the most popular are not necessarily the richest or prettiest; difference is respected and often admired. The pupils are aware that they are privileged. Has now scrapped its uniform code for 11-16 year olds in favour of a 'skirt uniform' and 'trouser uniform', with either sex able to wear either. The sixth form wear smart business-like clothes with some restrictions that are flouted when girls fancy tottering on high heels. They can drive themselves into school but must use street parking – high council charges are unpopular, with parents driving to attend chapel as well.

School benefits from a sense of the outside world, whether through exchanges with schools in Russia, Africa, America and Australia, the perspective offered by pupils from an inner-city school or the opportunity to twist their tongues round a year's worth of Mandarin Chinese. Link with Kingsford Community School in Newham, East London, beginning with heads' shared desire to make Mandarin mandatory, has grown into an HSBC sponsorship of three Newham pupils' education in Brighton for a year. Sixth formers buddy up with pupils at the London Academy of Excellence and share study tips via Facebook (boarders allowed 10 minute slots) and email.

The chapel, just big enough for the whole school, used three or four times a week for secular and multi-faith assemblies as well as Christian ones. Tradition still holds firm here (the oldest public school in Sussex), yet the chaplain is entertaining and eccentric – a new hymnal was an opportunity to get each house to prepare a song and belt it out in competition.

Pastoral care, well-being and discipline: As the head comments, this is 'a town school that is part of the real world, not apart from it'. At the beginning of every term he reiterates the ground rules on theft, bullying and beyond: expulsion and no second chances is the line on drugs and the security at the school gates is tight, yet cheery.

Report emailed home every three weeks and there are parent meetings – although some parents report not much time for parent feedback. Those needing the most help definitely get it – those who are motivated enough to dance between options will attract it too.

Head of lower school and the headmaster meet every registered pupil in their own school before they enter Brighton College. This reduces the fear of attending a new school and gives the pastoral staff a heads-up on what house and friendship group might suit a newbie. The little ones arrive three days before the rest of school and go on a treasure hunt to help them get their bearings. The transition to the upper school is another focus point for the empathetic head of lower school – moving from being one of 40 to one of 150 under the shared care of tutors and houseparents.

One lower school house and 13 others when the post-common entrance cohort enter, 325 boarding and 650 day – about 70 children in each so a good chance to develop cross year relationships. All of the youngest year in each senior school house share a tutor – as pupils grow they are matched with another for GCSEs and then A levels. Majority of housemasters and housemistresses are married and parents report incredible empathy for the fallout from tricky family and financial situations. Pupils learn how to iron a shirt, sew on a button and hold their own at a dinner party through house activities – really useful preparation for university admission and beyond.

Any bullying is dealt with speedily and with emotional intelligence – no homophobia or racism, some teasing but real respect for individuality. Two options at meals and dishes containing wheat are labelled, the school is nut free. Food is also available in the Smith Café and Café de Paris below the dance studio – and the houses all have kitchens for an emergency stack of toast for a starving teenage boy.

B

Pupils and parents: A great social mix from the children of butchers to highbrow TV presenters, successful entrepreneurs and a smattering of Conservative MPs; 33 per cent boarding, most weekly but seven per cent overseas (five per cent Asian). Lower school just under 50 per cent from Brighton state schools, also many from London schools that stop at 11. Head ensures that useful parent contacts are wound into life of school in way that benefits both – from Leon providing soup recipes for sidelines at matches to a stylist helping with a fashion show. School buses from towns ranging from Crowborough to Eastbourne with express services for weekly boarders Friday evening and Monday morning from Tunbridge Wells and Chichester. Pupils are cheerful, enthusiastic, friendly and polite and have an easy, relaxed relationship with teachers – at the top end of the school they feel part of a wider community; again, good preparation for life outside.

Entrance: Eleven plus entry via maths, English and verbal reasoning tests. Dynamic head of lower school has worked hard to build brilliant enrichment days for Gifted and Talented at local primaries – practical lessons in science labs, language work and unique experience of a senior school. All of this very attractive alternative to Brighton state school ballots.

Pre-test assessment for 13+ entry; CE pass mark now 60 per cent – whether from coming from prep school or externally – with a minimum of 55 per cent in English and maths. Emotional intelligence used in assessment of intake for prep so a maximum of five out of 60 each year do not go through to the college – they must be the bright side of average or they will not be happy here – and those who disrupt the learning of others won't fit in either. Around 45 from the prep join 40 already in the lower school. Seventy more from 54 other preps including St Christopher's, Hove and Handcross (now run by Brighton College).

Around 70 new pupils at sixth form (at least grade 6s at GCSE are essential), mostly from Burgess Hill, Brighton and Hove High School, Eastbourne, Hurst and Lancing.

Exit: A handful after GCSEs to local sixth form colleges, almost always for financial reasons. All A level leavers to university. Twenty-nine to Oxbridge in 2018, and 18 medics/dentists/vets; UCL, KCL, Bristol, Imperial, Durham, Manchester, Exeter and Leeds all popular. Three off to the US in 2017, five to Hong Kong (engineering, business, medicine and dentistry) and one to Dublin (medicine). Famous Old Brightonians, including Peter Mayle (writer), Lord Alexander of Weedon (lawyer and banker), Lord Skidelsky (historian and politician), Laurie Penny (writer), David Nash (sculptor), Matt Prior and Holly Colvin (cricketers), Sir John Chilcot (chairman of the Iraq Inquiry), Sir Michael Hordern (actor) and Jonathan Palmer (racing driver), testify to range of successful careers which may ensue.

Money matters: At a recent open morning, parents were wondering about what extras Brighton College might offer to justify its fees being higher than rival local schools' despite its limited campus space – half an hour later they were totally sold, having been treated to a Commedia dell'Arte take on the drama, a taste of Strictly Come Dancing by sixth formers and the heads of schools speaking about the high quality lessons. Bursaries and up to 20 academic awards (5-50 per cent off basic fees), five music scholarships (up to 30 per cent off), art, drama,

B

dance, sport, chess and all-rounder awards (up to 25 per cent off) and a DT scholarship (up to 15 per cent off) are available.

Registration fee and hefty deposits for accepting an offered place, into five figures for overseas boarders. Only refundable if pupils don't pass the entrance exam. Deposits retained to cover extras charged in arrears, balance refunded on exit from the school.

Extras include dyslexia support and EAL tuition.

Remarks: Happy, broad-minded town school for children and families who are keen on learning – producing fantastic results and sparkling individual success stories. Pupils are encouraged to achieve as much as they can, so you'd never be bored, but you could end up with too much on. Bold ideas fostered in student, staff and parent body, all the while anchoring the opportunities enabled by the fees in real world experience. Detractors of the school (often parents of ex-pupils at the prep or pre-prep) see it as too results focused, with some families turning to outside tutoring to enable their children to get into the college. Raising of CE pass mark to 60 per cent fuel for the fire of those who judge the school to be top-slicing to climb the results ladder, explained transparently by the school as a tool to manage the high volume of applications.

Brighton College Prep and Pre-Prep School

Linked with Brighton College, Handcross Park School

Walpole Lodge, Walpole Road, Brighton, East Sussex BN2 0EU

Ages 3–13 **Pupils** 516

Fees: £10,050 – £19,350 pa

01273 704343
www.brightoncollege.net

Headmaster: Since October 2017, John Weeks, previously head of the London Academy of Excellence, and deputy head of Brighton College. Read economics at Durham then qualified as a maths teacher at Sheffield. He arrived at Brighton College soon afterwards, where he has been maths teacher, housemaster, head of year and head of maths before becoming deputy head.

Entrance: Main entries at 3+ and 6+ with assessment in maths, English and verbal reasoning plus observation. Special arrangements for dyslexic pupils, with recent educational ed psych report. Travel via the same buses that serve the college– a third of the children live in town, a third from Hove and the rest come from Lewes, Worthing, Shoreham, Hassocks etc.

Exit: Over 90 per cent to Brighton College, having taken CE on a par with outsiders. The rest to eg Bede's and Battle Abbey. About four children a year leave early, 50 per cent financial reasons, 50 per cent deciding to settle into a school that is not so academically ambitious, with advice from the school. We have reports of the school assessments assuming increasing importance, with some pupils having a tutor – many of whom chose the school because of its excellent learning support.

Remarks: Compact, busy campus near the college; the two are very closely linked – the little ones walk across in reflective silence for lunch, chapel and games. The children are focused and engaged, polite and sparky – the eldest ones very aware of regular exams and what hangs on them. 'Why are we doing this when it has nothing to do with CE?' asked one, when being taught some tools for writing an essay. The school uses a metaphor for twice yearly exams as series of little hurdles rather than the Grand National. The achievement grades have been rejigged recently, aiming to make them more easily comparable with CE percentages; it may feel a bit bumpy initially for the kids who are struggling to hit the marks necessary for entry to the college.

They have an enormous amount of fun too; the teaching is inspiring and embellished with plenty of non-curriculum activities – from sleeping overnight on the Golden Hinde II in London to dancing with Kenyan Maasai. Three forms per year from year 2, each with 20-22 pupils. Latin for top set in years 7 and 8. A buddy system makes for good cross-year peer support; prefect and pre-prep reading groups cover wet break in classrooms. Normally they are outside on the playgrounds, kicking balls and shrieking about – although lunches are also used to squeeze in a mime class (60 per cent of the school do LAMDA), or to catch up on some work in the ICT room.

Four houses compete in sport, drama, debating etc. Pastoral care is well organised, with spreadsheets covering achievements, pastoral concerns and public recognition, ensuring that every child gets an acknowledgement – whether it is the Pelican Feather for kindness for the little ones or a Headmaster's Show up in the weekly newsletter. Some parents feel the flip side of this effective documentation is a tendency to pigeonhole or label kids, whether as dyslexic, dyspraxic, having a processing problem or as a scholar. All of these are well catered for here – there is a small dyslexia centre and two full time SENCos as well as strong connections to the main centre in the college. A maximum of nine pulled out third set English or French lessons for each SEN group, with 12 or so students left, so both clusters benefit from more focused attention.

The children begin their days with assembly in the main hall four mornings a week. It is also used for rehearsals, art displays and, when we visited, storing the Christmas shoeboxes for communities in Eastern Europe as well as local hospices. Music is marvellous here – from the accomplished chamber choir rehearsal we heard in the main hall to the junior wind group squeaking their way through Jingle Bells. Recent choir trips were to Disneyland and Barcelona.

The nursery and pre-prep has its own building (ex-St Mary's Hall, ex-Roedean Junior). Gorgeous light classrooms, well-stocked library and IT room, a big playing field as well as a playground out the back, and all look jolly in sweatshirts for nursery, smart uniforms for reception and upwards. Specialist teaching includes music, PE, art, Mandarin and French. Weekly swimming from year 1 up, competitive matches for year 3 and a huge variety of clubs run by outside coaches and teachers. Among the school council's achievements has been the idea for three new after-school clubs (Horrible History, singing, and calligraphy) and adding chicken curry and treacle pudding to the lunch menu.

The little ones in year 4 do projects every three weeks, getting passionate about making a video on volcanos erupting or designing a tooth hygiene poster. The library is a converted chapel, bright and well used as an alternative ICT room and for English lessons, children reading on the beanbags in the corner (as long as you write a book report...) One of the two science labs has a veritable menagerie of pets – from snakes to rabbits. Pet club members love to take some home at the weekend. There's a wonderful home economics room, with tasty ingredients laid out and recipes published in the weekly newsletter– as ever, the most popular is pizza.

The art and DT departments are also impressive, with projects including a clock for the playground and a sign for the revamped Brighton train station (the children wrote a letter and got shown around). The work looks fabulous and the kids seem to love it – they are aware they may get an art or DT scholarship if they put together a portfolio.

Sport is spread all over the town but minibuses nip back and forth and there is a huge range of team abilities – one main sport for boys and girls each term but always clubs on offer, with boys and girls recently playing hockey on the Astroturf. New climbing wall. The director of sport organises several football tournaments and athletics matches each year for boys and girls from local primary schools. You couldn't possibly try everything that is available, since the buses leave at 4.45pm each day. Homework is restricted to two subjects for 30 minutes each for years 7 and 8 (less for the other year groups), with one additional Latin prep at the weekend. A prep diary ensures that this is documented for parents and teachers – it also helps the children learn self-organisation.

Brighton Hove and Sussex Sixth Form College

205 Dyke Road, Hove, East Sussex BN3 6EG

Ages 16–18 **Pupils** 2,900

01273 552 200
www.bhasvic.ac.uk

Principal: Since 2016, William Baldwin – late 30s but could be mistaken for one of his students. Took his A levels at Strode College, Somerset and read psychology at Goldsmiths – 'an exciting place to be during the Britpop era of the mid-1990s.' Worked for The Children's Society and Childline for a year and planned to be an educational psychologist, which required a PGCE and two years' teaching experience. Part of his training at the Institute of Education was a work placement at the edgy and urban Barnet GfE college and this inspired him to go into teaching. Says this was challenging, but a good place to cut his teeth, and students taught him a lot. Moved to Godalming Sixth Form College in 2002 as a psychology teacher and was promoted to assistant principal (curriculum and quality) via middle management roles.

Also managed to fit in voluntary work as vice chair of the Independent Monitoring Board at Feltham Young Offenders' Institute and taught post-PGCE teachers at the Institute of Education – says it was a great opportunity to tap into the best talent for Godalming College (the IOE, not Feltham). Had no plans to leave but saw an ad and got offered the job here.

He is hip and cool – on the day we visited he was wearing purple trousers and a tweed jacket. He is a visible presence around the college and is a good speaker; 'he is approachable and motivating and a delight,' said a parent. Charming and open, he is an accomplished multi-tasker – he gets to work very early so he can leave on time to have tea with his young children: says it is good for his yin and yang of the day. He loves Arthouse movies and good food as well as cooking for showpiece events.

Never one to sit still, he has rebranded the college in his vision of a 'contemporary, creative learning environment' and redesigned the website – one of the best we have seen. Says the environment must be visually relevant to attract students, and the reception area and front corridors are now bright and light. He wants the college to be known for its creative approach to teaching and learning and says he was 'blown away' by the dedication and commitment of teachers – his life has been made easy by the high calibre of staff. Wants students to have a 'first class educational experience where they can feel safe to take risks' and 'where innovation meets excellence.'

Academic matters: Courses carefully considered at interview and enrolment and most students take three A levels or the equivalent – not encouraged to do a fourth unless it's further maths. Offers 31 subjects at A level and nine BTecs, and students can do a combination of both – over 20,000 subject combinations, apparently. A levels include psychology, PE, textile design, environmental science and business studies. Good take up of French and Spanish, and about 30 students a year take German. Particularly strong on maths and science with consistent praise for inspirational chemistry teaching. Gender champion project running through STEM provision. Maths and sciences popular with the girls and there is a healthy gender balance in the creative arts and drama. Subject extension sessions offered and teachers go beyond the curriculum to make sure students really understand their subject – biologists take part in a photography competition and physicists get involved with a green car project. Range of portfolio courses offered in second year, some for fun and interest and some for a qualification, and include the Extended Project Qualification (EPQ), Young Enterprise, creative writing, financial education and journalism, to name a few.

BTecs include health and social care, creative media production, performing arts and sport. In 2018, 40 per cent A*/A (70 per A*-B) at A level and 79 per cent of BTecs awarded distinction. Students can also resit English and maths GCSE if necessary.

BHASVIC has an aspirational culture and is a place where it is cool to work hard and do well, and high expectations are set from the start. Students given support in managing their time and working independently and safety nets in place to monitor progress with follow-up grades, tests and homework, 'which make it difficult to fall through the cracks,' thought a parent. Students can keep track of their own progress through their personalised online account.

Huge range of trips including visual arts to Barcelona, film and media to Budapest, geography to Croatia and New York, psychology and sociology to Berlin and scientists to Stemfest.

High calibre of teachers encouraged to look at different ways of doing things and are given a fairly free rein. 'Teachers do best when they don't feel constrained,' says the head, 'but college deals with underperformance.' Maximum class size is 22 with an average of 18. Tutors act as guides and mentors with one-to-one discussions and weekly group tutorials. Offer extensive help with UCAS forms, study skills, and even how to budget your student loan and deal with landlords as well as citizenship and personal well-being. Two careers advisors help with everything from form filling and interview techniques to job vacancies, gap years and work experience.

Space is at a premium and there is a shortage of places to study – students are seen working in every available corner. A seat in the silent study area is the 'hottest ticket in BHASVIC,' said one student.' Some go to the library in Brighton to work. A new £8.5 million building is due to open in spring 2020 to help address this.

Additional Learning Support (ALS) consists of a SENCo and eight staff, and can offer support to those with a high level of need and EHCPs, including a personal teaching assistant in class and assistive technology. 'My son is a wheelchair user,' said a father; 'he knows someone is looking out for him and feels supported throughout.' ALS can include help with essay writing, note taking and organisational skills.

Games, options, the arts: Offers an 'indulgent breadth' of extracurricular activities and 'there is something for everyone,' said a parent.

Good facilities on site include sports hall (also used for exams), dance studio and fitness centre and adjoining field shared with another local school. No one has to do sport but healthy lifestyles encouraged and many play sport for fun and exercise. Range of team sports including basketball, football, rugby and netball. Many successes in the sporting arena: the women's football team reached the National Cup final in 2017 and 2018, BHASVIC produced the English junior national squash champion, the rugby team are Sussex league winners and the men's basketball team is in the elite national league. Coaching qualifications offered in several sports on top of academic courses. For those less team minded a different exercise activity like yoga and dance is offered every lunchtime.

'Creative arts are part of the heartbeat of the college and creativity encourages learning,' says the head and creative arts types are in plentiful supply in Brighton. Impressive annual arts festival 'celebrates creativity in all its forms': music, dance, art, photography, media, film and drama.

Music offered at A level and BTec with many opportunities to sing in the choir or join a song-writing workshop as well as play in ensembles, the session band and the chamber orchestra. Several talented musicians involved with Brighton Youth Orchestra. The Christmas concert and annual musicals are open to all including staff. Multimedia and web design offered as a qualification and college has a media editing suite, two large photographic studios and its own dark room.

Dance popular and the studio works with dance companies in London – one male student recently taken on by Ballet Rambert. Duke of Edinburgh gold award offered to those who have already completed bronze or silver at previous schools. All are encouraged to join societies and get involved with charity and outreach in the community and many help with reading at local primary schools. Students here are politically aware – the feminist society is popular with both sexes and there is an active LGBTU.

Background and atmosphere: The college was founded in 1859 as the Brighton Proprietary Grammar and Commercial School and became Brighton, Hove and Sussex Grammar School. It moved to its current site in 1913 but the buildings were requisitioned as a military hospital during WW1 and the beautiful painted central hall was turned into a ward – now used as a social and working space and for exams. It became a sixth form college in 1975 when the education systems in East Sussex were reorganised. A lot fits into a constrained site and the college is a mixture of architectural styles. The main building is Edwardian red brick and the newest block, the copper building opened in 2014, is all plate glass and steel.

Relaxed and informal atmosphere with students huddled in groups and sitting on the floor outside lessons. Students are on first name terms with their teachers and are allowed to wear what they like as long as it is not offensive, and excessive tattoos and piercings not allowed. Most wear jeans and hoodies and individuality is expressed through vibrant hair colours. 'It is a very cool college in a very cool city,' said a parent, and 'is seen as the place to go in Brighton.' 'It is very Brighton,' said another, 'pushy, academic and buzzy, but it is also inclusive and diversity is celebrated.' College is a trailblazer on tolerance and transgender issues – you can be who you want to be here. It has been judged grade 1 outstanding by Ofsted in all four inspection areas.

Pastoral care, well-being and discipline: Although the head is trying to dispel the myth of a 'ruthless exam factory', this is a fast-paced environment and students are expected to work hard and take charge of their education. This is made clear at induction and interview so there are no surprises. There are plenty of safety nets and people to talk to and 'kids know who to turn to if there are problems', said a parent. No-one is left to flounder and students are taught skills 'to learn to know what to do when they don't know what to do.' Parents get a text if their child misses a lesson but the first point of contact is always the student. Personalised approach to education means the college is able to accommodate the super brainy and those with learning difficulties. Most of the college is wheelchair accessible. The parent of a wheelchair user commented that 'the college has gone out of its way to make sure he is included – he has been treated with care and sensitivity and the college has given him back his pride.'

Zero tolerance of drugs and alcohol on site – expulsion for anyone found in possession within the college. Tutorial programme encourages students to make educated decisions and be aware of the risks. 'Cyberbullying is rarely an issue,' says the head. Students are free to come and go into Brighton when not in lessons.

Good hierarchy of pastoral support from form tutor upwards, including a team of counsellors and guidance managers. 'The fantastic referral system to outside agencies is breaking the stigma of mental health,' said a parent. Student services team can offer advice about anything from anxiety and stress to substance and alcohol misuse, sexual health and relationships, and refer on as necessary. They also offer group work around self-esteem and how to cope with stress.

Active student union with 16 elected students including a welfare and charity officer. They organise social events including freshers' week and the Christmas talent show and charity fundraising events. Also have representatives on committees to ensure student voices are heard.

Pupils and parents: Produces 'confident, hardworking, colourful, independent thinkers,' and most parents are motivated and aspirational. About 60 per cent come from Brighton and Hove and the rest from East and West Sussex.

Most parents say that feedback is good and 'tutors are easy to contact, supportive and approachable'. They can track their child's progress online and through termly subject reviews. Two parents' evenings in the first year offer parents the chance to meet their child's personal tutor and course teachers.

Former students follow a range of careers and alumni include television presenter and actor, Jamie Theakston; Conservative MP, Michael Fabricant; film critic for Radio 1, Rhiannon Dillon; and comedian, Tony Hawks.

Former students of the Grammar School keep in touch via the Past and Present Association and ex-students of the college can keep in touch via the alumni network linked from the website.

Entrance: Entry via a guidance interview and is essentially non-selective and open to all who can cope and benefit from a course. Specific GCSE grades needed for certain courses – to study three A levels a student will need six GCSEs – five at 4 or above and one at least a 6, and must include a 4 in English and maths and at least a 4 in the subjects to be studied. Always oversubscribed but can usually offer to all who apply in time – if not will apply catchment area.

About half come from schools in Brighton and Hove and 10-15 per cent from independent schools like Hurst, Roedean and Brighton College. Independent school pupils come with a good work ethic and love the independence but often need some adjustment to working on their own.

Exit: Some 75 per cent of second year students apply to university with about 85 per cent of applicants securing places – 57 to Oxbridge in 2018 and 30 to vet and med school. About 20 per cent take a gap year. Huge support for students applying to Oxbridge and vet and med schools, with specialist tutor groups and help with applications and interview practice. Support for those wanting to study abroad with good links with top universities in the Netherlands and USA and information evenings for parents and students. The college is a SAT centre for entrance to American universities. Specialist programme for those wanting to go to art college – help with interviews and portfolio preparation. Equally supportive of those who want to go straight into apprenticeships and the workplace with strong links with local providers – the college works with local employers and helps with job applications and interview practice. Good record of degree achievement and completion (87 per cent get a first or 2:1 compared with 80 per cent from the independent sector).

Remarks: A busy and buzzing sixth form college with high expectations and a strong work ethic where students are expected to be self-starters and independent learners, but with excellent pastoral care and support at all levels. It probably would not suit those who need a lot of structure and guidance, but for the right student it offers wonderful opportunities both inside and outside the classroom.

Brockwood Park School

Linked with Inwoods Small School

49

Brockwood Park, Bramdean, Hampshire SO24 0LQ

Ages 14 –19 **Pupils** 74 **Sixth form** 60 **Boarders** 74 full

Fees: Boarding £21,900 pa

01962 771744
www.brockwood.org.uk

Principal: Since 2015, Antonio Autor. Principal by name only: there is no hierarchy here; everyone has a voice and is heard, and everyone has the same salary, from cleaner to principal.

Antonio has the still presence of a mountain or deep water. Here is someone who seems remarkably free of ego or any sort of push; and yet, astonishingly, he had a previous life as a professional footballer. He has a BA in business and has studied English at Cardiff, Brighton and London. He joined Brockwood Park in 1987, and his jobs have ranged from gardener to teacher.

Students: 'love' him; 'above everything, you can go to [him] if out of control'; '[I'm] really comfortable talking to him – normal conversation without having to fake adult and know everything.'

Dr Gopal Krishnamurthy, previously co-principal, stepped down in July 2018.

Academic matters: 'A way of education which is rare and original', said a parent, and completely different to traditional education, dismissed as 'academic memorising'; or as Krishnamurti (founder) put it: '...education [is]...not merely transferring what is printed on a page to your brain. Education may mean opening the doors of perception on to the vast movement of life.'

No small task and certainly not an easy option for student or teacher. Students are encouraged not just to accept what they read or are told, but to inquire into it themselves: we saw a group of students on the lawn, attempting to get a solar panel working again so they could charge their mobile phones on a camping trip; we have never seen a teacher so alertly attentive, but silent, as students worked it out. 'Right education is a mutual task demanding patience, consideration and affection', said Krishnamurti, and this is evidently so at Brockwood Park.

The only common courses here are inquiry time and human ecology. At inquiry time, the school meets to discuss the way we live our lives – '[my son] seems to find it valuable for sorting issues out'. Students said they felt listened to: 'space to speak,' said one. Human ecology is the study of our home in its broadest sense, recognising that we all share the responsibility to care for the planet. Students might work in the kitchen garden, eco building or observation: giving full attention to the world outside and, during inquiry time, to the world within.

There is a large element of personal decision-making in the curriculum, greatly appreciated by students: 'I learn something I want to learn; do what I want to do'; and to some degree by parents: '...students invest in what they are doing with choice', but 'I would like them to insist a bit more in academic matters'. Another said: 'I'm not sure [my son] is applying himself properly...I think he is challenged, but only if he is interested'.

At Brockwood Park they have their own way of getting people interested in things. Nothing is forced, but a pupil who doesn't like maths can expect to spend a lots of time exploring why. As a parent put it: 'If a student doesn't want to study, they discuss and discuss and discuss...'

Those under 16 take three core courses: science and mathematics, humanities, and arts and crafts. The focus, in each, is on learning through firsthand experience. Described by the principal as being 'the roots of literacy...getting them to think for themselves...[where] not knowing is a vital point of departure'.

Topic courses are also available, which enable students to explore issues in much greater depth: the teacher introduces a topic, such as 'movement of humans', and after a few weeks, students determine their own specific area of exploration.

Languages are taught organically, depending on the skills of the staff at the time. There's always a lot of support for them in this international school: Italian, French, German and Spanish are being taught at the moment. English as an additional language (EAL) is highly successful: a French speaker told us he was confident in English after only three months at Brockwood Park. 'Learning English is easy here. Even if I make a mistake, I don't mind. If you say something stupid it doesn't matter'.

Lessons are usually with six or seven students, 10 at the most, with teacher and teacher apprentice present, which allows students to 'work more deeply in the subject', said a dad who felt that a big class would have no time to divert from the programme. There are no year groups: 'even young ones help older ones sometimes', said a parent.

Students can develop their own projects if their proposal is approved by the teachers' group, which will choose an academic adviser to support the project for the year. It's a bigger, tougher version of the EPQ with 'a sense of excellence for its own sake'.

Those coming here from traditional environments can have some 'unlearning to do', often lacking original thought or vitality. We were given the example of a student who arrived with a long list of A*s at IGCSE: 'It took a lot to get her to ask questions or disagree with me – but now she says "I don't want you to help me".'

They're not against traditional achievement here, but it's a byproduct. '[We] do think exams are important, but not as a reflection of worth or learning. They are what you've done, in a particular direction, according to certain criteria. Academic success should not be confused with excellence'.

Some students take A levels and the mock exams are often the first exams students at this school have ever sat; they also have a pre-exam intensive study week with the aim of building

B

a sense of confidence in their own work: 'It's a game – we want them to play it well'.

Students can take IGCSEs if they want to; although it was clear that the principal couldn't really see why anyone would want to: 'an easy option'.

There are students here with dyslexia, dyspraxia and ADHD, but they do not like labelling students SEN: each student has their own programme, and the whole curriculum supports the special needs of each student. No extra charge for one-to-one unless help from outside is necessary.

Games, options, the arts: Exercise is important here, and students spend two afternoons a week playing games, but not games as you know it. Games are played for the pleasure of the movement, for the beauty of the shot, with 'heart [and] everything in the game', but not for the winning.

A couple of students who had tasted the joys of competitive sport missed the adrenalin, although they do play friendly football with local schools and the farmers. Netball, basketball, yoga (naturally) and hockey are also available. There are plenty of opportunities for long walks and orienteering: 'the need to finish together and take care of the team is a substitute for the team spirit of games', said a parent.

The art barn with its curved windows contains a pottery studio, darkroom and Mac suite. Textiles are popular – students used a Japanese manual dying technique on old sheets, before making them into clothes.

'Words have limitations', said Krishnamurti, so music, with the harmony it brings to body and mind, is very important at Brockwood, where regular informal concerts take place.

Boarding: This small school is a boarding community, roughly a third British, the rest international.

'[It is] intense to live with people, but beautiful to share all your day. Your whole life in this amount shared with all these people', said a parent. Another said it is an 'intense social life. [My son] is thrilled at this'.

Girls board in the main house, with single rooms for older girls, and large rooms for two or three younger ones. Students arrange furniture how they like it, some making their views clear from their door decoration: next to a picture of a cow: 'Not your mum, not your milk'. Bathrooms are elderly but clean.

Boys are in the cloisters, a 70s add on around a square of grass and trees with teachers living on the corners; this accommodation was described by one parent as 'adequate': his son will opt for the pavilion next year. The pavilions are very grand indeed: oak framed with underfloor heating and glass topped roofs, fragrant herb gardens outside; a wing each for girls and boys.

Students have to be in their rooms by 9:30pm and are now allowed smartphones, but only in their rooms. TV is not much of an event here; students generally spend more time in the sitting room: a grand old room in the main house, with sofas, grand piano and wood burner in the old fireplace, for staff and students alike.

Students may catch the bus into Winchester at weekends, and go away for the weekend if they seek permission first ('they're on top of their game for safeguarding', said a parent).

Wifi is in a particular corner of the school, and otherwise not easy to locate; apparently there's one spot up a particular tree, but use of devices is not encouraged...'beneficial to be starved of it for some time', said a parent hardily.

Background and atmosphere: '[It's an] interesting way of living – fantastically beautiful', said a parent, who was enchanted by his first visit to Brockwood Park – ' [We] discovered the ambience and the liberty of the students'. The school is run on the basis of collaboration, not competition: an atmosphere in which all sorts of students thrive: '[They] don't judge you here... [I] feel more open. Better for you: to love yourself and feel more confidence', said a student.

This school is about learning to live, and understanding yourself as something worthy of inquiry: '[It is] very challenging for the student; not an easy way', said a parent. Students have to learn about responsibility; or, as one parent put it: 'the capability of everyone to be response-able in a situation...what [they can] do to contribute to the world'. It starts in small ways here: a student described how she has come to realise that washing up is part of life: at home, it just happens; at her old school, there were cleaners. Here, everyone has to pitch in, or it doesn't get done.

'[It's] very challenging for parents to have children at this school. Questions raised with the students touch the parents: about the future, human beings and existence...I am educated by my kids by their education at Brockwood Park...for some, it is difficult to accept this', said a parent.

The strength of community here is something students were keen to talk about: 'everyone is open to know you'; 'after only four months, I have found a way I like of having relationships – I enjoy them; even if I don't like the person'. A wide sociality is encouraged, both in terms of the Brockwood community (exclusive relationships are frowned upon), and in terms of being part of a worldwide community: time is devoted to exploring social and political crisis.

Different faiths are tolerated, but if you follow a particular religion, others need to be free to ask questions of it and you. 'If there is a God, find him for yourself', said Antonio.

Many of the buildings are beautiful: the elegant main house; the assembly room with its beautiful wooden roof and a grand piano; and the study with cream carpet and wood panelling: morning meetings take place there every day – 10 mins of quiet time to start the day. As you walk around, you can feel how much this school is cared for: it is not, here, just a collection of buildings which serve as a shell to house those within.

The school sits in 40 acres, including the original kitchen garden, where students have human ecology lessons, and the head gardener works with the head chef to grow seasonal produce for the kitchen. All food at Brockwood Park is vegetarian; on the day of our visit a delicious lentil bake, a fresh salad from the garden with flowers, and fruit, students spilling out of the dining hall to eat lunch on the lawn.

Pastoral care, well-being and discipline: Understanding discipline at Brockwood Park is best done by considering the words of Krishnamurti: 'After all, discipline means resistance... Do you think resistance will bring about understanding, thought, affection?... Discipline is always exclusive, whereas understanding is inclusive. Understanding comes when you investigate, when you enquire, when you search out, which requires care, consideration, thought, affection'.

There is, however, no absence of rules or agreements as to how to behave; students sign a contract on entering the school, committing to the curriculum and caring for each other, and agreeing not to smoke, drink alcohol or eat meat (no sneaky bacon butties in Winchester at the weekend, either). Parents are convinced by the school's approach: 'Brockwood Park is the safest school to grow up a teenager that we know'.

Dealing with each breach of rules will be different, emphasises Antonio, but there will be a process, which will involve talking with teacher, student, tutor, and pastoral coordinator. It's an 'opportunity for learning', he says, and much depends on how the student responds to the process. An action plan for drinking alcohol might be for the student to investigate how alcohol attacks the body and mind, and share it with the school. 'Troubles with kids doing forbidden things [are] dealt with in a peaceful way; [they] awaken responsibility in kids', said a parent.

The gentleness of this school does not mean that there are no consequences for actions. Students will be suspended if a habit needs to be broken. Expulsion can happen, and has, for drug and smoking offences. 'I understand that a firm message has to pass on to the children, and it is slowly dawning on [my son] that he cannot act in any way he pleases'.

Another parent told us that his son had admitted to having an unsmoked joint in his room. The consequences were daily discussions with Antonio for 15 minutes every morning – for months. The parent had the impression both quite enjoy the chats now...

Agreements are settled between students and teachers about lesser matters, such as hairstyles and tummy rings; although a determined Mohican lasted out his time without changing his hair: agreements are not rules, but students wishing to flout them should expect a lot of discussion.

Students, asked to describe the best thing about the school, described their relationships with teachers: 'teachers look at you like a person'; 'chat any time'; 'someone, always, has an ear for you. Always.'

Bullying is not a problem here, say students and parents. Students agreed that some people are popular; 'but not better, or of more consequence,' pointed out another.

Pupils and parents: Many students are ex-Waldorf, said a parent; have already opted for this sort of education, and are 'mostly thrilled at what's offered [here]'.

Parents receive two detailed observational reports a year. Communication varies, with dates for events sometimes communicated rather late in the day, but pastoral communications are good. Parents can come and stay in the area for the weekend, and meet their child's academic adviser and tutors.

Entrance: Students attend a prospective week before they sign up to the school, so they know what to expect. Non-selective.

Inwoods Small School, a 10 minute walk away, is a junior school run by the same Krishnamurti Foundation, but few children come from there.

Exit: 'You will leave education here with a set of questions – with uncertainty', said the principal. More reassuring is the fact that most students leave to continue their education somewhere in the world, previous destinations including Bennington and Vasser in the US, Quest College in Canada, Lancaster and Sheffield Universities and the Guildhall School of Music and Drama in the UK. Entrance is secured on a mixture of exam results, interviews and coursework/portfolios. Others depart for gap years or jobs: one student went on to train as a chef and works in one of the only vegetarian restaurants in Italy – she is 'well balanced; well in her basket', said her father.

Money matters: Bursaries are available from seven to (exceptionally) 100 per cent of the fees. Around 15 per cent of the fee income is available for bursaries.

Remarks: Parents think it wouldn't suit a very competitive child, or one who comes from a rigid background – 'where are the instructions?' 'Great for creative types, artists and musicians'; 'A child needs to be independent in character – you need to "be an actor in your learning".'

This extraordinary school is not for those who want to purchase an off-the-shelf education with the assurance of a clutch of academic certificates to match, but for families who are willing to risk exchanging the bland safety of traditional education for something more real and exciting.

Burford School

B

Cheltenham Road, Burford, Oxfordshire OX18 4PL

Ages 11–18 **Pupils** 1,384 **Sixth form** 217 **Boarders** 98 full, 2 weekly, 1 flexi

Fees: No day fees; Boarding £9,900 pa

01993 823303
www.burford.oxon.sch.uk

Headteacher: Since 2008, Kathy Haig BA MEd (40s). Educated at Burford School herself, followed by Leeds University (food science and nutrition). Taught at schools in Hull, Keighley and Preston before moving to Ellesmere Port Catholic High School in Cheshire. Spent 12 years there, rising to be deputy head. Made a point of focusing on teaching and learning from the minute she arrived at Burford. When it comes to making decisions she always asks 'does it improve the teaching and learning?' If not, the school doesn't do it. Her approach has paid dividends. GCSE and A level results have risen year on year over the last seven years and the school was congratulated by the schools minister for making the top 90 secondary schools – for sustained improvement – in England.

Outgoing, full of ideas and a good listener, she says that 'the culture of inclusivity and mutual respect' is key. Parents told us that she is 'very down-to-earth,' 'easy to approach' and knows every pupil by name (no mean feat in a school this size) and if her door is open pupils can stop by and chat. When a group of boys mentioned they'd like to play chess at lunchtimes, it happened instantly. Now there's a chess league four times a week and they compete against other schools. She still teaches five hours a fortnight (child development GCSE to year 11 pupils). 'I love teaching and I think that it does the staff good to see that the head still has to do reports.' Married to a management consultant and has two teenage children, both at the school.

Academic matters: A large, rural comprehensive that takes boarders (one of only 30 state boarding schools in the country). Offers wide range of subjects to wide ability intake but expects everyone to work hard and fulfil their potential – in line with head's belief that if you have high expectations then 'children will live up to what you expect of them'. Curriculum is mainly academic plus a small number of vocational qualifications. Most pupils take nine or 10 GCSEs and homework plays an integral part, with parents asked to sign children's student record books once a week.

Exam results are very good – in 2018, at GCSE 25 per cent at A*-A/9-7 and 80 per cent 9-4 in both English and maths. At A level, 29 per cent at A*/A and 51 per cent A*-B. Thirty A level and BTec subjects on offer – all the usual, plus economics, psychology, media studies and photography. EPQ and AS critical thinking also available. Lessons are largely taught in form groups, apart from maths and French, which are set according to ability. Class sizes of 26 up to GCSE (20 for practical subjects) and average of 12 to 14 in the sixth form. Languages compulsory at key stage 3. All students do French in years 7 to 9 and can add a second language in years 8 and 9.

Learning support is housed in own block – The Learning Zone – and deals with a wide range of needs, from dyslexia through to the autistic spectrum and including social, emotional and mental health needs. Help given to children who arrive with lower than average literacy and numeracy and those with EAL requirements as well as the gifted and talented. There's also an inclusion room called The Bridge for students who temporarily need to study away from the main classroom. A mother whose daughter had to undergo spinal surgery was full of praise. 'Lessons were brought to her there,' she said. 'Potentially she could have had four months being home-schooled but thanks to The Bridge she only missed two or three weeks of school.'

In keeping with its rural setting, there is an outdoor classroom called The Acre. As well as being a base for a GCSE course in environmental land based studies it has chickens, ducks, rabbits, two miniature donkeys and a veg patch.

Games, options, the arts: Acres of green space encourage the pupils to be very sporty. PE and games are compulsory – sports offered include hockey, football, rugby, netball, tennis, athletics, keep fit and dance. As well as games fields (including a cricket square and pavilion), there's a gym/sports hall and netball and tennis courts. Loads of matches with local state, independent and international schools: Argentina and Australia send rugby, hockey, netball and cricket teams each year. School has its own equestrian team and runs an inter-house riding competition in the grounds every summer. If there's a sport pupils want to do, 'we will try and put in on,' says the deputy head, citing girls' cricket and volleyball as recent examples.

Music is fantastic. Around 300 pupils have instrumental lessons – 'you name it, we play it,' said one of our sixth form guides. Wide range of orchestras, string ensemble, wind band, jazz band and rock school plus a residential, summer music scheme for 100 pupils in North Wales. School hopes to build its own concert hall and recently became music hub for the area, offering workshops by visiting specialists, the chance to play in professional concerts and master classes at St Anne's College, Oxford. They rotate a musical with a drama production every year. 'We try and involve everyone.'

Well-equipped art block, with different areas for art, design, photography and textiles plus tech stuff that professional studios would give their eye-teeth for. Loads of voluntary extracurricular activities – during lunch breaks and after school (late buses put on so everyone can attend). DofE and Young Enterprise and lots of trips to foreign climes. The school is rightfully proud of its 20-year tie with a school in Uganda and there's an annual exchange. Burford pupils visit partner students in Uganda one year, then host them in Burford the next. Along the way they raise money for everything from a library and computer room to two cows.

Boarding: The head says she could fill boarding places twice over and we're not in the least surprised. Parents pay for children's accommodation but their education is free. 'State boarding schools show that you can have it all but at a fraction of the price of independent schools,' the mother of a sixth form boarder told us. 'We loved the feel of the place from the start. There's no keeping up with the Joneses. It's very diverse and there are people from all walks of life.'

The 90 boarders (half boys/ half girls) live in Lenthall House, a listed building down the hill in Burford itself and a 10-minute walk from the main school. As we said last time, it's a bit of a Tardis – a maze of interconnecting buildings with bright, newly refurbished rooms and excellent facilities. The school has created a flat within the boarding house for five sixth form girls – to help them prepare for university. Boarders come from all over, down the road in Oxfordshire to Hong Kong and China. Most are full boarders (a couple of weekly boarders when we visited) and staff put on loads of evening and weekend activities. Everything from go karting and ice skating to theatre trips and craft sessions. Supervised prep every night and in-house structured revision during GCSE and A level study leave.

Pupils eat breakfast (full English on Saturdays and croissants on Sundays) and tea at the boarding house but lunch at the main school. Boarders can invite day pupils to tea and there's a formal dinner at Christmas plus monthly lunches for local OAPs. Six live-in staff, including head of boarding and his wife. Boarding head moved to Burford from the independent sector and says: 'There is more drive and purpose among the boarders here. They are keener to do well and to take advantage of all the opportunities we offer.'

Application form on school website for boarding places. School asks for reference from children's current school and prospective pupils are invited to attend a taster day during term time. Students from overseas (30 per cent of boarders) welcome as long as they have a relative or host family living in the UK.

Background and atmosphere: Founded as a grammar school for boys by charter in 1571 and still celebrates Charter Day in October each year. Main school is situated on the busy A40 on the edge of the beautiful Cotswold town (an hour from London, traffic permitting). Moved to its present 36 acre site in 1960. School still maintains many old grammar school traditions, including house system, prefects and smart uniform (blazer and house tie) for all but the sixth form (who wear their own clothes but are expected to dress appropriately – no ripped jeans or Ugg boots). This year's first XV rugby team have opted to wear smart suits when they travel to matches – a custom they reckon will continue.

Sixth formers have their own block, with common room, study area and more freedom. Year 13s are allowed off-site at lunchtime and if they don't have lessons. Some drive to school. 'We get treated like grown-ups,' an appreciative youngster told us. The only grumble was not enough parking places. Students keen to be head girl or head boy write their own manifestos, take part in hustings and are voted for by staff and fellow sixth formers. Like the pupils themselves, the atmosphere here is busy and purposeful. Ofsted's 2014 report judged students' behaviour to be outstanding and when we visited we were impressed by their politeness, charm and enthusiasm for the school.

Pastoral care, well-being and discipline: Well-defined rules set out in excellent student record book – smart hardback given to each pupil at the start of the year, with ruler and whiteboard they can hold up for plenary sessions in class. Contains everything from equipment needed for school to spelling lists and what to do if the school bus is late. School's core tenet is that 'everyone will act with care and consideration to others at all times,' and it clearly works. School governor told us that Burford is 'very caring' and 'takes great pride in how we look after our youngsters'. There's a strong Team Burford ethos, with students keeping in touch for years after they leave.

Excellent induction programme for new pupils. Year 7s are mentored by trained year 13s and also get a three-day residential trip early in their first term to help them settle in. Year groups are divided into seven or eight forms, each with own tutor, who's also responsible for registration and PHSE. All pupils belong to one of four houses named after school founders and benefactors – Falkland, Heylin, Warwick and Wysdom. House competitions, from rugby and netball to art and even forensics, are fiercely contested. School council with four reps from each year group. Pupils have assembly twice a week – once for the whole school and once for their year group. Pupils say the food has improved a lot and offers a daily choice of hot meals, pasta, salad bar, vegetarian option and baguettes. Cashless canteen – biometric system reads students' thumbprints.

Pupils and parents: A real mix. Pupils come from a wide variety of backgrounds, ranging from disadvantaged to quite posh. Some have lived in the area for years, others have parents who commute to Oxford or London every day. Steep house prices mean few come from Burford as properties tend to be owned by older residents and second-homers. School gives financial support 'very discreetly' to pupils whose families can't afford to pay for school trips. Old pupils include Gilbert Jessop (cricketer), Simon West (film director) and Alice Freeman (rower).

Entrance: Children living in the catchment area and attending one of Burford's nine partner schools are virtually guaranteed a place. Thirty-five to 40 per cent of pupils come from outside the catchment area, from as far afield as Hook Norton, Faringdon and Bourton-on-the-Water, with priority given to those with siblings already at the school. Additional pupils arrive in year 9, including up to 30 a year from local private schools. 'We've had to put in an extra year 9 form,' says the head. Up to 20 new pupils a year join the 220-strong sixth form (minimum of two B/6s and four C/5s at GCSE required by all, plus some subject-specific requirements).

Exit: Around 40 to 50 per cent leave after GCSE – for vocational courses at local FE colleges (including Cirencester, Abingdon, Witney and City of Oxford) or apprenticeships/employment. Three-quarters head to university after A levels – to study everything from biomedical science to fine art. One to Oxbridge and one medic in 2018; others to eg Bristol, Loughborough, Royal Holloway, Plymouth, Sheffield, Warwick. School has a full-time careers adviser – professionally qualified and very experienced – who organises higher education and apprenticeships evenings, mock interviews, a careers convention and work experience (for year 10s and year 12s) and sees students one-to-one. School is also creating strong links with local businesses.

Remarks: A happy and successful comprehensive school with an impressive 'can-do' attitude. Pupils are keen to succeed and rise to the challenge admirably.

Burgess Hill Girls

Linked with Burgess Hill Girls Junior School

Keymer Road, Burgess Hill, West Sussex RH15 0EG

Ages 11–18 **Pupils** 470 **Sixth form** 66 **Boarders** 45 full, 2 flexi

Fees: Day £14,550 – £19,200; Boarding £28,050 – £34,200 pa

01444 241050
www.burgesshillgirls.com

Head: Since 2017, Liz Laybourn (BEd in PE and maths, Dartford College). She is devoted to Burgess Hill school; joined as a newly qualified teacher in 1986 and never left, becoming deputy head in 2006 and interim head after the retirement of the previous head due to ill health.

Liz is combining her headship with a master's degree in educational leadership, and is a vigorous champion of outdoor life and healthy living – she says she would have been a farmer in another life.

Academic matters: Generally excellent results; 55 per cent A*/A at A level in 2018. Parents are very satisfied with their children's progress. Consistent achievement at GCSE, with 75 per cent A*-A/9-7 in 2018.

GCSE maths and IGCSE science are high performers, alongside success in English, humanities and the arts. A good variety of mostly traditional subjects, with plenty of languages, both ancient and modern. Lovely language suite, with laptops which rise from the desk lid when required.

Small class sizes in sixth form (3-12) mean the girls have plenty of attention in class. Around 40 per cent of entries at A level are in science, maths and technology, and girls achieve excellent results in these subjects, with plenty of experience in using them: 'engineering experience day made me realise that engineering is not just about fixing things but about being creative and making a difference'. There's also an engineering education scheme, in which lower sixth pupils have a seven month project working alongside a company.

A parent commented that the range of subjects on offer at A level is not extensive, but she was satisfied that the it was best for her daughter to concentrate on 'bread and butter' subjects now: she could always specialise at university. 'Traditional values and methods here,' she added, but this school comes across as modern and engaged. Value added is carefully monitored using CEM, which shows that GCSE performance is on average one grade higher than of children of a similar ability: girls certainly thrive academically here.

There's a good mix of male and female staff, and the dedication of these teachers is, parents say, extraordinary. Extra clinics and one-on-one support means no one falls behind – pupils say it's easy to ask for help.

There's a new focus on SEND, until recently ad hoc in different rooms, but now in a dedicated room. Parents say help is very good, and are pleased that the support in small group sessions (in English, maths and science) is free of charge. (One-one is charged as an extra, as it uses outside support.)

A beguilingly named head of futures advises on A levels, university and careers, and will go over personal statements umpteen times until just right. There's lots of careers advice, and parents are encouraged to participate in 'take your daughter to work day' – all part of the head's drive to get the girls out there.

Decent size library, open 8.30am-6.05pm. Super computers sunk into the desks, screens visible through transparent desk top, key boards pulled out for use as required.

Games, options, the arts: Teams here do very well, girls saying being a small school means that they get more time from coaches. The girls excel at netball, hockey, athletics, rounders and horse riding. Facilities are not quite as extensive as parents might like – a field, five floodlit hard netball courts, also used for tennis, and floodlit Astroturf – but size of school site limits expansion. Pupils are bused to Ardingly reservoir for water sports, and use excellent local facilities for swimming and hockey.

Girls enthuse about extracurricular sports for all ethos at lunchtime, with clubs in badminton, ultimate frisbee, and fitness and dance. If there's demand for an activity, the school will do its best to provide: polo club started recently.

Creative arts events for all to enjoy – 'they don't chose the in-your-face confident girls to do everything here', said a parent approvingly. Busy drama and music departments, with regular productions ranging from Euripedes to Playhouse Creatures (a play about the struggles of actresses in a men's world). A big musical every year, last year The Shot Heard Round the World – written, composed and directed by three girls in upper sixth (one of the girls is now at Berkeley USA studying music and song writing). Croft II Drama is a circular soundproof room with good acoustics which serves as a drama studio, recital room and place for parents to mingle during the interval of events held in the hall.

Art is housed in a prefab block with a flat roof (bane of the bursar's life), surprisingly light around the edges, with a dedicated room for sixth formers, who can leave work undisturbed.

Textiles are taken seriously here, and it's a very successful department. Material here is used for anything and everything, from the practical making of device cases for laptops, to a handbag styled like a pocket watch, with an opening clock face (the maker winning national handbag designer of the year aged just 15).

Plenty of extracurricular, from law society and public speaking to DofE and Young Enterprise. But, the girls say, if don't want to be busy, that's fine. OMG here (not the expletive – Only Motivated Girls), but 'in our own particular little ways'.

Boarding: Boarders live in one of the two elegant Edwardian boarding houses, which house girls of mixed ages. Alongside full and weekly boarding, there are two flexi boarding spaces. Boarding available from year 7 upwards, occasionally year 6 depending on the maturity of the child.

Most boarders are from overseas (Hong Kong and China), with around eight nationalities in total (no wish to increase overseas numbers, says the school). One parent told us he would prefer boarding to be less of an overseas service; but it has meant his daughter has a best friend from Madrid and a desire to learn Mandarin.

Describes as a day school with boarding, and this felt like the case. The boarding house we visited felt quiet: the girls don't return to houses during the day, so there's not the busy to and through evident in many big boarding schools. But boarders are very happy here, and call the houses home. One parent told us, 'The care and attention from the staff is exemplary. I feel my daughter is extremely well looked after'; another, that 'boarding has had a huge and positive effect'.

Inviting trellis covers the entrance to a boarding house; inside, a comfortable common room with TV, table football, books and games; kitchen with fruit and cereal always available. Games room, with a church pew to perch on – makes lingering games seem unlikely – and large screen in front, also used for dancing with the Wii. One of the messiest bedrooms we have ever seen, but we are told this is unusual, and a reward scheme is in place to encourage tidiness. Fresh decoration, with bathrooms recently redecorated and deep cleaned.

If parents are late picking up day girls, they simply go over to the boarding house. Burgess Hill Girls is well situated in town, so if boarders haven't got a club, they may go into town in small groups after school. Supervised prep, then down time in the boarding house until bedtime, with years 7-9 handing in electronic devices before lights out at 10pm. Wifi is turned off at midnight and comes back on at 6am. Boarders contact home via Skype or internet phone, with the office phone or computer available as back up.

Activities organised for each weekend, both trips out and on site. Pupil feedback is important: there is a suggestion box, and a weekly discussion between pupils and catering; and although parents told us the quality of evening meals is not the same as lunches, the school says suggestions for changes to food are acted on immediately.

Background and atmosphere: Set back from the road in a leafy suburb of large houses and big old trees; we had to peer up driveway to be sure it was the right place – planning permission is being sought for an 'illuminated totem' (a bright sign you can see from the road) and new entrance railing. Buildings are a mixture of old Victorian villas and modern, with a slightly colonial feel; beautifully kept grounds, encircled by trees gives an immediate sense of safety and seclusion. But the girls here are not cosseted; school feels the most important thing is to 'get the girls out there' – and they are out there a lot.

Entry through glass doors, a large navy sign fronted with gold chairs, and a vertical radiator. Everything about the entrance says up to date. Parents describe the buildings as 'clean, crisp and fresh.' Decor inside varies from swish purpose built to elderly, with traditional moments: portraits of heads decorate an old staircase, much like 10 Downing St.

The food is tasty, agree the girls, and the chef takes on board suggestions from the box in the dining hall. There are old fashioned school desks filled with fruit (described in several languages), a spoon and fork clock, and a good selection of food, to which soup is added midway through the autumn term. In the annual poverty lunch, pupils lunch on soup, with one piece of bread and a piece of fruit: a reminder of how fortunate they are.

Most of the parents we spoke to were not specifically looking for a single sex school, but chose Burgess Hill Girls because it was school they liked most –'it felt the most authentic', said one; 'plain speaking', said another. The school believes being away from boys allows girls room to develop, to be themselves – and the necessary strength, resilience and broad shoulders to cope and be the best in a male dominated world. The girls we spoke to agreed; one girl who came from a mixed sex school said she was not afraid to shine here – 'boys interrupt,' she added. One parent admitted her daughter did find life at university a bit of a shock, but added that the sixth formers are well prepared, and have workshops on everything...including boys.

Girls here are encouraged to step out of their comfort zones: on Roche days, twice a year, pupils spend a day pushing their boundaries – we saw a group learning to plaster, patiently working their way up four columns planted in the lawn (no chance of contamination, with hooded plastic space suits and plastic goggles). Roche day ends listening to motivational businesswomen, encouraging the girls to take risks to succeed.

Kilt and pinstripe uniform, with sixth formers in suits.

'I am, I can, I ought, I will' are the words of the school motto, and they pop up all over the place. There is a strong moral tone about this non-denominational school, with a focused time to reflect on moral messages during a period of silence on arrival and departure from assembly, and healthy links with the local community. This is one of the few schools we have visited which views community service as an essential part of life balance, alongside academic work and play, rather than an optional extra, and it appears in many areas of life at Burgess Hill: from raising money for local charities, to holding an annual pamper day for local carers, and helping children with their reading at a local primary school. The whole school takes part in the Sports Relief Mile, and on an international level, the school supports Plan – a charity to raise the profile of girls across the world who do not have access to education.

Pastoral care, well-being and discipline: Parents say the staff work 24/7 for the girls 'above and beyond the call of duty'. 'If you send an email saying you're worried about something, you'll be at school at 8am the next morning chatting about it'. The school is excellent at keeping in touch, and parents emphasis the all round care – one described how she was chatting to a teacher about her worries about her daughter's anxiety, and the next day received a handwritten card through the post suggesting websites that might help. Girls agreed that they all knew who they would go to with a problem, from the head to favourite teachers, or the nurse (much loved by all). Sixth form mentors help younger girls, and all girls meet their teacher mentor every fortnight, to discuss work and anything else.

Bullying is dealt with straight on, and rapidly, said a parent. Both parties received counselling, and, most importantly to the parent, her daughter was taught strategies for dealing with bullies.

The honesty of this school is much appreciated by parents, who feel that problems here are dealt with head on: they are very engaged with the problems that can assail girls, and often make their appearance in years 9 and 10 – for example, obsession with image and being skinny, and rare instances of self harm. 'They are right on it', said a parent. A comprehensive drugs policy, within which each case will be carefully and individually assessed.

This feels like a place where a high standard of behaviour is expected, and by and large adhered to by the girls. Parents felt that poor conduct is very unlikely and would be much more of an issue here than poor performance.

A lively house system; though a little strange, you might think, for a modern girls' school to name its houses after dead male poets. A little bit of left over tradition, says the head. Lots of inter-house competition throughout the year, from public speaking, chess and sports, to performing arts day.

Pupils and parents: Parents are a mix of wealthy and not: city professionals, businesspeople, and working several jobs to keep their girls at Burgess Hill. Some are competitive – 'keen to ensure their daughters are achieving and being seen to achieve'.

Parents receive a grade sheet for attainment and attitude to learning every half term. Year 10s upwards receive working at and working towards grades. Two parents' evenings and one full report per year.

The school bus service is popular – a year 6 girl described her bus driver as one of the nicest things about school. It covers eight routes around Sussex every morning, children coming from as far afield as Horsham, Crawley and Uckfield. School is three minutes walk from Burgess Hill station, and just 45 minutes by train from London.

Communication with parents is excellent, and there's no prolonged email back and forth with parents: the school encourages teachers to invite parents with a concern or issue to come in, or pick up the phone.

Entrance: Most senior school entrants (80 per cent last year) come from the junior school, though this is not automatic. A good number also from local state primaries and preps in the south east and London. Skype interviews for overseas students.

Exit: Nearly half leave after GCSEs. Two to Oxbridge in 2018, plus two medics and a dentist. Other popular destinations Edinburgh, UCL, Reading, Sheffield, Exeter, Bristol, LSE, Durham, Liverpool, with one off to read English in Australia.

Money matters: No charge for pre and after-school care, from 8am-6pm, including breakfast. Academic, music, art, sport and drama scholarships, up to 40 per cent of fees, awarded at 11+,13+ and 16+. A number of significant bursaries (which do not take account of academic standard). Great value for money, say parents. 'The John Lewis of education,' says the school.

Remarks: This nurturing school puts time and thought into finding the best in each girl. Its excellent academic standards do not make it intellectually exclusive – parents felt it would suit all sorts, one saying that it suited both her very academic daughter, and the one whose talents were more middle of the road.

Burgess Hill Girls Junior School

Linked with Burgess Hill Girls

Keymer Road, Burgess Hill, West Sussex RH15 0EG

Ages 2.5–11 **Pupils** 185

Fees: £7,800 – £14,250 pa

01444 233167
www./burgesshillgirls.com

Headmistress of the junior school: Since 2011, Heather Cavanagh, previously head teacher of Dover College Junior School. Popular with pupils – 'nice and really kind', 'always listens to you'. Good relationship with parents, who says she's approachable, and always with the children. She's now also deputy head of the whole school, and heads year 7 and 8.

A hanging on Mrs Cavanagh's wall says THINK. She clearly does, a great deal. The head encourages her staff to always deal with pupils and parents with thoughtfulness and compassion, explaining that if you build trust and faith in parents, this works better if the road gets bumpy; and parents really appreciate being sent handwritten notes capturing moments of significance to children.

Background and atmosphere: Very new nursery and infant building providing excellent facilities for the students at the lower end of the school.

Entrance: Non-selective entry for nursery. Reception to year 2 assessed informally by spending part of the day at school. For year 3 upwards girls sit written papers and the school likes to see any current school reports, but looks beyond just academic ability. A few scholarships for academic and musical ability. They will admit mid-year if there are places available.

Exit: Almost all (over 90 per cent) go on to the senior school; automatic entry unless headmistress feels any girl may not cope with the workload.

Remarks: Burgess Hill is a school with academic focus, so it is no surprise that most girls move seamlessly from the junior school to the rigours of senior school. But this is not what parents appreciate most about the junior school: 'They support confidence and emotional well-being first, before moving on to the complexities of work', said a parent; and this certainly seemed true. The girls were happy and relaxed – 'I love being with my friends', 'everyone is so kind', 'people always help you'. Parents emphasised the thoughtful and detailed approach to care of their children, one describing how the school worked with her daughter, who had a stammer, for 10 months for free before she even started at the school; and how once she was there, she received extra care and work, with a daily update to the parent.

Another described her daughter's anxiety at going on a school trip away in year 4. The teacher chatted with child before the trip, and worked out a bedtime strategy: if the girl became anxious she would move her soft toy to certain position on the bed so teacher would know she was worried without her having to say anything.

Parents feel very involved with school life, and are invited to Friday assembly every week. All superstars go up and describe their piece of work – excellent for building confidence, say parents.

So these happy girls take academic work very much in their stride. Mostly single classes of around 13; years 3, 4 and 6 are currently double classes. The head says, 'If they don't get it [academically], that is our responsibility, not theirs. Girls should not feel it is their fault that they don't understand'. And they don't. One pupil told us 'I'm not good at spelling – they help me, and not in a mean way'. The school takes a wholehearted responsibility for pupils' academic development – a parent told us about her concern that her daughter just wasn't engaged with school work, particularly maths; and her relief at their response – don't worry, we will deal with it. They managed to engage the girl with maths – took her into the garden to count seeds, mum said vaguely – and it worked.

Outside activities are taken into account by school: three tasks to be completed over the course of each week, so prep can fit in with a child's out of school activities. Optional prep club available every day – teachers always help if you need it, and then you get tea and toast. 'My mum really likes it...'

Great focus on SEND, spotted both though baseline assessment and other data, but also through constant discussion between staff. In-class support, and dyslexia and dyspraxic specialists. One-to-one charged as extra. Also booster groups for things any student might be struggling with, such as cursive writing. They're aware that the most able sometimes need help – 'if they feel they need to succeed all the time, girls can avoid doing things differently, or taking risks' – so aim to build resilience in all their girls.

Pupils felt confident about who they would go to for help: form teacher, TA in the playground, a sixth former – 'if there's no-one else around'. Girls choose a member of staff to be their mentor, with meetings weekly, but daily if needed.

The approach to bullying is to always first listen to kids and parents until they have talked themselves out. Most incidents turn out to be friendship issues, rather than systematic and sustained behaviour, says the head, and we need to ask why a child is lashing out.

School minibuses take pupils to Ardingly reservoir for water sports, and to the Triangle for swimming: the juniors had just returned on the day of our visit, and hair dryers buzzed from each classroom – 'so they're not actually dripping down the chairs'. Girls play tag rugby and football, alongside all the usual sports. Extracurricular is led by girls' interests – scrabble and dance are popular, as are sports clubs, orchestra, and quilting bee. Seniors run drama club and textiles club for juniors, which are enjoyed by both age groups.

'Food is amazing', say pupils: macaroni cheese and Wednesday roast are favourites. Pupils told us they had felt concerned when it turned out that an apparently plain cookie had coconut in it; but their complaints were listened to, and now everything is properly labelled with ingredients.

This is school with strong moral direction. There is no particular faith affiliation, but there are moments of spiritual reflection in assembly, where girls think about what have done well this week, about being kind and saying thank you. All sorts of different religions send representatives in to talk to the girls. The children are well aware of life beyond school, sending two pupils to the town's youth council (the only non state school to do so), and fundraising for local charities, with a popular delicious dress up day for a children's charity.

Caldicott

53

Crown Lane, Farnham Royal, Slough SL2 3SL

Ages 7–13 **Pupils** 245 **Boarders** 111 weekly

Fees: Day £16,833 – £18,780; Boarding £24,918 – £27,687 pa

01753 649300
www.caldicott.com

Headmaster: Since April 2018, Jeremy Banks, previously headmaster of Beachborough School. His own mother was a headteacher, and having realised relatively young that he too had a way with children, he subsequently did a degree in education studies and geography at Warwick University and a masters in educational leadership (distinction) at Buckingham. Spent his first 10 years as a teacher at Dulwich Prep London, where he was director of studies and housemaster as well as teaching geography, maths and games. Joined Beachborough as deputy head in 2006 and became head in 2013. Now gently guiding Caldicott, this most traditional of preps, towards the 21st Century (school's first ever head with an active Twitter account). One of his first wins has been to review and overhaul the way boys are prepared for pre-test and secondary school interviews (cue rounds of applause from parents). We don't doubt that many more positive changes are afoot – watch this space.

When time allows, can be seen running through Burnham Beeches in an effort to get his 5k time below 19 mins. Married to Sophie, also a Warwick graduate (education studies and music) and also a prep school head. They have three daughters.

Entrance: One form entry in year 3 becomes two in year 4 (legacy of Bucks middle school system) and year groups usually grow to three forms thereafter. There is a short formal academic assessment plus an opportunity to meet other pupils and teachers and there is an open day in June. Though still a far cry from the London 7+, boys do get turned away for not being sufficiently academic, although the cohort is comparatively mixed ability.

Exit: Nearly all at 13, mainly to trad boys' boarding. Harrow and Eton get the most (12 and 11 respectively in 2018), then it's Wellington, Radley, Charterhouse, St Edward's, Winchester, Bradfield and Stowe. Ones and twos to eg Marlborough, Uppingham and Tonbridge, plus occasionally to day schools like Merchant Taylors' or HABS. Record scholarships in 2018 (16) plus school's best ever CE results, including three starred passes to Eton – the fruits of the appointment in 2015 of an excellent deputy head, academic, coming to bear. Definitely not a school for those with eyes on the Bucks grammars (or any other school with 11+ intake for that matter) at 11.

Remarks: Caldicott sits on top of a wooded escarpment with views down to Windsor; 40 acres of prime Bucks real estate adjoining beautiful Burnham Beeches. The school was founded in 1904 by Heald Jenkins who named it after his new bride, a Miss Theodora Caldicott Ingram. The school and its wonderful Harrison Harrison organ (recently restored and residing in the chapel) moved from Hitchin to Farnham Royal in 1938.

Perfect pitches extend as far as the eye can see, busy with grounds staff rolling and mowing grass that already looks like a billiard table. We defer to one of our guides who observed, 'I can't think of a prep school with better pitches.' Cricket and rugby are a big deal here with up to eight teams (is there really an 'H' team?) ready to take on all comers at all levels. Oxford's Dragon School, as its name suggests, is their fiercest opponent. And what about that H team? Do its duckers and triers really get the same standard of coaching as the Olympians in the As? Certainly, says school. 'We want everybody to take part; the coaches aren't baby-minding. The challenge can be finding other schools ready to field as many opposing teams.' When it comes to sport for all, noble aims such as these are often at odds with the grass roots actualities. Not so at Caldicott. Parents of unsporty boys do not find them swinging round the corner posts while the A team triumphs on a distant pitch. 'If the A team is playing then so are the Bs, Cs and Ds.' And it's the same with other things, drama for instance, lots of groups (teams) at all levels to 'keep everyone improving'.

Music (once the school's weak spot) and the other performing arts are gradually becoming more valued and significant parts of life at Caldicott. Boys benefit from an experienced and dedicated teaching team of peripatetic teachers and the music department delivers over 200 instrumental and singing lessons a week. All boys receive a class music lesson every week up until their final term. Although still very much second fiddle to sporting endeavours, there are low key choirs and instrumental ensembles which provide a variety of opportunities for collaborative music making, along with a range of performing opportunities throughout the year from informal, small-scale beginner platforms to whole school occasions such as carol services, charity concerts, and instrumental recitals. The musical and educational experiences of the whole community are enhanced by regular visiting performers, collaborative projects and outings to public venues. Boys have recently gained music awards to Eton College and Uppingham. Drama greatly improved with recent productions ('superb' say parents) including Beowolf, Guys and Dolls (dolls played by the rugby team's front row), The Gentlemen of Verona (musical version) and a play penned by the head of drama on the life of Roald Dahl.

Half the pupils are local, the other half come in from the capital on the 7.30am Caldicott express. School claims to have 'invented' busing in from west London – we hope the other busing Bucks preps pay a copyright fee. 'The service is incredibly efficient, the buses run like clockwork, they're travelling against the traffic,' we were told. Youngest go home at 4.30pm but rest stay until 6pm up to three afternoons a week – it's a long, active day, but at least there's no homework 'apart from a few spellings or a bit of reading' until the last two years (and the boys are all boarding then). Saturday school is 'proper' with lessons until 12.30pm for all and matches in the afternoon for the older boys. London parents just as visible on sidelines as locals. Is there a divide between the local and London boys, we asked? 'Not at all, the boys don't even notice,' said one mother, although she conceded that the London chaps seemed 'a bit more polished and prepared' when they joined.

All boys in years 7 and 8 board Monday to Saturday, no exceptions, and school has now introduced optional boarding (still weekly, no flexi) from year 4. It's an integral part of their preparation for senior schools such as Harrow, Eton and Radley. Dorms are upstairs in the main school building – clean, bright with home duvets, photos and posters. Evenings and weekends are busy with dedicated clubs including fly tying and model making, and competitions and activities such as fondue nights (boys have to go and buy the cheese as well as cook it) and a Caldicott Bake-off. New boarders are given an 'uncle', an experienced boarder in the same dorm who will help him settle in. Senior houseparents live on site with their family and all full-time staff do boarding duty. Our sixth form (year 8) guides, almost ready to leave for senior school, were waxing nostalgic: 'There's so many people around, it's a community,' said one. What would they remember, we asked? 'Summer evening cross-country runs through Burnham Beeches; after-school swims in the outdoor pool; the boarders' Christmas party with carol singing around the huge tree.' Sigh.

Teachers are called 'sir' and 'ma'am' and year round uniform of shorts (with boat shoes in summer) is de rigeur but that apart, education is firmly in the 21st century with bright classrooms, smartboards, well-equipped labs and lots of techy stuff. We loved the screens outside the DT studio flashing up individual photos of every boy proudly holding his finished work.

One way in which Caldicott is untraditional is its neatness – it's the tidiest prep we've ever visited. In fact it was a relief to see some naughty geranium cuttings sprawled muddily beneath a windowsill in the biology lab. Even the art room, usually reliable as a haven of creative chaos, was ship-shape. Parents describe the school as 'incredibly well organised' and it really does seem that no corner of the place is overlooked. Very reassuring.

Boys are set in maths from the start and in other subjects later on. Apparently there's 'much less setting than of yore', but several parents commented that the system wasn't clear and didn't seem that flexible. Average class size is 16, there's a good mix of staff – old and new – and about a third of teachers are women. The lessons we peeped into were lively and interactive, boys bursting with ideas and eager to contribute. Some grumbles in the recent past that school was slow to pick up SEN but this no longer seems to be the case; several new parents said teachers had been very quick to act on potential problems.

Monitoring is generally regarded as good and communication as excellent; 'Teachers are all contactable by email and usually reply within a couple of hours.' Pastoral care and school counsellor came in for high praise; wobbly new boarders are ably helped through those tricky first few weeks. Several parents remarked how thoughtfully boys in different year groups (so often tribal) related to each other.

Boys say food is 'so much better'. Chicken Kiev is top choice, closely followed by the Thursday roast and cooked breakfast. We were, however, told to 'avoid Saturday lunch at all costs.' We couldn't find out exactly why, but you have been warned. On the wall of the school dining room we were shown the honours boards and there he was, Nicholas Clegg, the only head boy in the school's history to hold the post jointly. The Caldicott coalition – you couldn't make it up.

The word we keep reaching for is 'traditional', but in its best, unstuffy, sense. Parents who choose Caldicott told us they do so because it has secure values: courtesy, fair play, loyalty, regard for others. 'When the boys leave they are young gentlemen,' one said. All in all, this is a cracking prep that will play more than fair by any boy lucky enough to get a place.

Carrdus School

Overthorpe Hall, Blacklocks Hill, Banbury, Oxfordshire OX17 2BS

Ages Girls 3–11, boys 3–8 **Pupils** 111 (15 boys)

Fees: £10,800 – £11,625 pa

01295 263733
www.carrdusschool.co.uk

Headmaster: Since 2012, Edward Way BSc (40s). Educated at Radley College and King's College, where he read geology. After a stint in the film business, he decided in his late 20s to follow in the footsteps of his teacher wife, Georgina (now SENCo at the school). PGCE at University of Bath, followed by posts at Cothill, Chandlings, Cheam School and Lambrook School, then 10 years as head at Great Tew Primary School, 12 miles away.

A self-proclaimed 'hardcore educationalist' ('I had to be to turn around a struggling state school'), one gets the impression that he spends a lot of time shaking off the 'muddy boots at the expense of proper learning' (as one parent put it) reputation Carrdus used to have. So far so good, with parents – who mostly describe him simply as Ed – loving the fact that he's upped the focus on academics 'while still keeping the unique ethos of Carrdus,' as one said.

His lack of airs and graces extends to pupils too. 'It's not like at other schools, where you're scared of your headmaster – ours is really happy and friendly,' one girl told us. As head of science who teaches regularly and does his fair share of break and lunch duty, he's certainly not one to shy away from front-of-house duties and his rapport with pupils balances informality and respect in a way many heads would envy. Shame, though, that some pupils told us that popping into his office without invitation 'would feel a step too far' (given that it's right next to classrooms).

Lives near Chipping Norton; he and his wife have three children. Loves gardening ('I'm almost an obsessive about it'), dinghy sailing and surfing.

Entrance: Junior school is currently full to bursting – tribute, says school, to the amazing staff. No entrance test – 'It's first come, first served'. Very broad intake. Majority of pupils come from Banbury and surrounding villages, with parents registering children up to three years in advance. Most common entry points are nursery, reception and year 3 (state school girls at this age – 'the state till 8' phenomenon, says head), but it's worth trying in between too. No scholarships offered but means-tested bursaries sometimes available.

Exit: About a third of girls to 'big sister' Tudor Hall. Rest to a wide range including King's High Warwick, Rugby, Oundle, St Mary's Ascot, Bloxham, Headington and Oxford High. Boys head at 7 or 8 to preps eg Cothill, Warwick Junior, The Dragon and Winchester House.

Remarks: School started in 1952 and moved to its present site in 1970 when founder Kathleen Carrdus bought Overthorpe Hall for the princely sum of £22,500. Has always had strong links with Tudor Hall, which bought school in 2011. Union seems to have worked well and Carrdus staff say they consider Tudor Hall their 'big sister'.

Main building a rambling 1880 hunting lodge, set in 11 acres of exquisite grounds – not in the fancy sense, but just dreamsville for little people, with magnificent, mature low-hanging trees practically screaming out to be climbed on (and which they are, joy of joys, allowed to do) and all the hidden spaces you could want for outdoor classrooms, bush craft, den-building etc. The hum of the A422 dual carriageway – and the rule that you can't play in the woods every break time (not enough staff to supervise all areas) – are about all that stop it being utopia for outdoorsy kids. Even the heated outdoor pool (always set to an agreeable 30 degrees) is in a charming walled garden, bursting with peonies, vines and fig trees when we visited on a glorious summer's day.

Lots of fresh air, smiley faces, slightly grazed knees and heaps of praise are order of the day at this unpretentious school that is anything but precious. Teachers are friendly, children are happy and secure and the atmosphere is casual yet stimulating. School's academic record is impressive, even more so in recent years, with hugely experienced staff – many brought in by current head. One class per year group, with a maximum of 20 per class. No setting, but the most able get the chance to move faster, while those who struggle get extra support as required. French from reception and Latin for last two terms of year 6. No scholarship stream – school prides itself on giving everyone the chance to shine. Homework for all – reception children take reading books home while year 6 pupils get 30 minutes' homework a night. Thousands of books, all colour-coded for different reading abilities – 'we're big on reading here,' says head. 'I'm always nagging the parents – read, read, read. If you can read and write, you can inherit the earth.'

Around 10 per cent of pupils with mild dyslexia, developmental coordination disorder (dyspraxia) and/or learning difficulties. One-to-one help available from led by headteacher's wife (15 years' teaching experience and AMBDA) or in small groups, often at start or end of school day. 'The support for my daughter has been fantastic – she's been nurtured and given all the practical support we need in a very gentle way,' one parent told us.

Musically strong, with around 75 per cent of pupils learning an instrument with a periplectic teacher, including piano, violin, guitar, saxophone, flute, cello or drums. Junior and senior choirs, orchestra, band and ensembles galore. Grand displays of arts and crafts taking up practically every bit of wall space throughout the school ('We used to have brightly coloured walls, but then we went neutral so we get the colour from the kids' work,' says head), with every class getting a whole day of DT taught by a Tudor Hall teacher twice a term – we saw year 5s creating delightful Victorian-style toys. Drama a firm favourite among pupils, with a specialist drama teacher on staff. Annual winter performance from lower school; a spring one from middle years; and year 5s and 6s do a summer one. Older girls we met on our our visit were buzzing about their forthcoming Robin and the Sherwood Hoodies play.

Hockey, netball, athletics, tennis, gymnastics, dance, cycling proficiency and swimming are taken by all and enjoyed by most. Cross-country a particular strength; one girl, in her break time, even insisted on showing us just how fast she could run, to the cheers of her peers. Justifiably proud of their wins (they'd just beaten the much bigger, Oxford-based Headington in hockey when we visited), but never smug. All sports take place onsite, with the exception of hockey, which involves girls travelling by minibus (the school has two) to Tudor Hall, 10 minutes away.

At least two trips a term per year group – to places like Stratford-upon-Avon, Oxford's Ashmolean Museum, Warwick Castle and the Roald Dahl Museum.

Registration is at 8.45am and there's a staggered finish of either 3.30 or 3.40pm, but to help working parents children can arrive from 8am and stay on any time up until 6pm (costs extra). In addition, there are before- and after-school clubs a plenty – arts and crafts, karate, roller skating, gardening, IT, messy science and sports, to name a few (also for an additional fee). Nutritious, wholesome lunches cooked on-site and served by friendly dinner ladies who know all the children's names. Extensive salad bar, while at break time youngsters help themselves to cheese, crispbread, raw vegetables and fruit (they can bring in their own snacks on Fridays – no chocolate, though) before racing off to play outside in all weathers.

No school uniform, apart from games kit. Dress code is 'not smart, not scruffy', with parents advised to send children to school in comfy, machine-washable clothes. No jeans, bare midriffs, nail varnish, mobile phones or chewing gum and jewellery only in year 6. Children are encouraged to be children, not mini-adults. Delightful (and short) list of school rules advises pupils: 'No sticks, no stones', 'Only climb as high as your friend's head' and 'It's only fun if everybody is enjoying it'. Pupils are well-behaved and discipline is not an issue because, say pupils, 'we understand the point of the rules.' Buddy system works well, according to pupils, and so-called 'Carrdus pathway' means confidence, imagination, aspiration, residence, independence and empathy underpins everything they do – from the rewarding of house points to going on a school trip.

Roomy and homely classrooms, mainly in the main lodge, boast high ceilings, blue carpets, grand views, fireplaces and the occasional 'secret doorway,' as one pupil excitedly told us. One recently turned into modern science lab. Smallish welcoming library, dining hall, large separate sports/assembly/drama hall (soon to be refurbished with new curtains and lighting, thanks to the PTA), separate DT building and inside/outside classrooms for nursery and reception provide all the learning space these 125 children need.

Parents – a broad mix of the extremely wealthy to those working all hours to pay the school fees – rave about the school. 'Sending our kids here is the best thing we've ever done.' 'The kids are so happy that sometimes they don't even want to come home.' 'Half the time, the kids don't even realise they're learning.' 'Carrdus picks out children's assets and builds on them and if they're lacking in confidence in any way, they subtly find ways of boosting them.' Active PTA, with activities ranging from new parents' breakfasts to annual bonfire party, Christmas fair and spring sale. Instead of standing in the car park, parents arriving to collect their children gather in the large entrance hall, complete with huge, welcoming sofas and, from November to March, a roaring log fire. If they'd change anything, say the parents we spoke to, it would be making it co-ed all the way through – but, says head, that ain't going to happen anytime soon.

Children have a lot of fun here, while achieving good results along the way. Pupils – boys as well as girls – keep in touch for years after they leave; we met one ex-pupil who left the corporate rat race of London to retrain as a teacher at her childhood school. A characterful, relaxed and genuinely child-centred school where what you see is what you get – happy-go-lucky kids both working and playing hard and getting outdoors a lot. You'll find no shouty teachers lurking round corners here; instead, say kids, it's like one big family.

Caterham Preparatory School

Linked with Caterham School

Harestone Valley Road, Caterham, Surrey CR3 6YB

Ages 3–11 **Pupils** 288

Fees: £9,210 – £15,060 pa

01883 342097
www.caterhamprepschool.co.uk

Headmaster: Since April 2019, Ben Purkiss, previously deputy head at Bede's Prep. After an injury ended his dream of being a professional rugby player, he did a degree in ocean science and geophysics, then returned to his old school as a science teacher and housemaster. He and his wife-to-be moved to London and he dabbled in the City, but working with younger children as a supply teacher made him realise where his real talents lay. They have since worked in prep schools including Cottesmore, King's Hall and the New Beacon, joining Bede's in 2015. They have two young sons.

Entrance: Oversubscribed at main entry points by at least 3 to 1; register early if you can. Twenty places in the nursery for children aged 3 rising 4. Then another 20 places in reception. Informal assessment only at this stage, intended to flag up any children with conspicuous learning or behavioural difficulties that the school can't help. No additional intake at year 3. The odd place higher up the school – always worth asking. At this stage applicants are assessed during a full day spent as part of a class at the school.

Exit: At least 80 per cent to the senior school. 'There's no weeding out. We do advise parents in the very rare event we think a child won't flourish – but it's advice only.' Small numbers opt for the local single sex alternatives eg Trinity, Whitgift, Woldingham, or for state schools.

Remarks: Absolutely glorious setting. Originally a boarding house, the pre-prep (nursery to year 2) nestles at the far end of the campus, approached by what is to all intents a country lane: it passes between privately-owned fields, home to a couple of quietly grazing cobs, an old bath, and a broken truck marked Horses. Apparently, it's been like this since the 1930s. No traffic, and all so peaceful. Have no fear that the school has been similarly stuck in the past, however: it absolutely hasn't. Lots of investment evident: super wet-play area in front of the school building, and lovely classrooms within – large, light, cheerful, well-equipped. Restful but busy, the nursery struck the Caterham note from the off: one 3 year old slept peacefully on the gaily-coloured carpet while others worked purposefully and quietly at painting – achievement without undue pressure. Sensible approach to uniform: the little ones wear PE kit until year 1, when they adopt smart maroon uniform. Impressive IT suite, with benches built 8 inches lower than usual so that the infants can sit at them in comfort. 'It cost more to get the benches in than the computers.'

Retrace your steps to reach the prep (years 3-6), located in a pleasant and welcoming red-brick building next to the senior school. For years 3 and 4 teaching is classroom based, then subject taught once the children reach year 5, so that they're confident with moving around for lessons by the time they're at the senior school. The prep has its own science, art and DT rooms, plus an excellent purpose-built drama studio and access to senior school facilities such as the recently-opened teaching kitchen. Work on display is of a high standard, and we were moved by some really excellent poems by the year 5s, evidence of the high quality of teaching that goes on here – the ISI described it as 'excellent… thoughtful, interesting and challenging.' We missed a proper library, however, and thought it a shame that there were only what the school calls 'small sub-libraries' dotted about the place. Full time SENCo supports the 20 or so children with mild SEN – dyslexia, mild autism, etc. Not the place for anyone with more than minor issues.

Regular drama productions, and the children often score successes at the Shakespeare Schools Festival. As you'd expect, terrific sports provision, with a great range on offer and everyone encouraged to join in. Lots of time spent outdoors, and everyone gets match practice. Music here is taken seriously and done very well indeed. The whole of the top floor is given over to it – we passed a splendid rack of double basses, and heard some ace flute playing drifting out from a practice room. In addition to two music classes per week, year 3 pupils spend the autumn term trying out stringed, woodwind and brass instruments free of charge, guided by the school's team of visiting music teachers. The children finish the term by giving a concert, and the parents are told how their offspring reacted to the different instruments. In this way, everyone make an informed choice about what they want to learn, which we thought admirable. In year 4, everyone learns guitar and in year 5, percussion. In year 6 it's music tech. Piano is also taught – in fact, the children can

C

learn pretty much anything (eg there are harps up at the senior school, and prep pupils can learn on them if they wish). The result is a really buzzing music community with lots going on: orchestra, ensembles, and at least two choirs, one of which had just got back from a trip to Prague.

As in the senior school, parents value the friendly and informative communication from staff, and appreciate the many opportunities to get involved as well as the after-school care available up to 6pm – 'A godsend!' cried one grateful mother. Caterham Prep children are friendly, sparky and good fun – as well they might be, given the range of what's on offer here and the kind, encouraging ethos. A happy and successful school.

Caterham School

Linked with Caterham Preparatory School

56

Harestone Valley Road, Caterham, Surrey CR3 6YA

Ages 11–18 **Pupils** 950 **Sixth form** 308 **Boarders** 141 full, 19 weekly (from year 9)

Fees: Day £18,045 – £18,900; Boarding £30,936 – £36,570 pa

01883 343028
www.caterhamschool.co.uk

Headmaster: Since 2015, Ceri Jones (40s). Attended Nab Wood Grammar (now the Samuel Lister Academy) in Bradford, which had already turned comprehensive by the time he started, then read history at Fitzwilliam College Cambridge. Went into teaching straightaway because he loved his subject. Began his career at Godolpin & Latymer, then Bancroft's, then joined Caterham as head of history. Left to take up post as housemaster at Tonbridge, where he stayed for 11 years. During that time he rose to become deputy head, and was seconded to run the Marsh Academy in the Romney Marshes. Returned to Caterham because he liked the quiet confidence of the students – 'they were all very different, very assured, but not arrogant.' Married to Kay Moxon, head of politics at Tonbridge, and they have two daughters.

Unlike many heads we meet with similarly glittering credentials (he has a masters in educational leadership), Mr Jones impresses as a very human headteacher with his feet firmly on the ground. With his kindly energy and soft-spoken manner, he is clearly popular with parents. 'An excellent head, and a very clear and intelligent thinker,' said one; 'he is definitely a doer, and we can all see positive changes and improvements.' 'We really appreciate that he's passionate about education being holistic, and not all about academic achievement,' said another. Manages to fit in some football in his spare time (he played for Cambridge), still teaches A level history. Runs the Accelerate and Access Foundation, a charity which helps bright children from disadvantaged backgrounds in the south east.

Has no wish to change the ethos and values of the school, but is a skilled moderniser – he introduced the policy of issuing all Caterham students with iPads.

Academic matters: Impressive. In 2018 83 per cent A*-A/9-7 at GCSE, and at A level 85 per cent A*/B and 60 per cent A*/A, putting it comfortably in the top 100 independent schools in the country.

Class sizes in first three years around 20-24, dropping to 15-20 for GCSE teaching and usually 8-12 for sixth form. Broad curriculum, with core subjects supplemented by Latin, philosophy & theology, computer science, 3D design, all the usual creative arts, and a good modern languages offering: French, German, Spanish, and, from year 9, Italian.

We particularly liked the Davey Building, home to the science departments, which had a real buzz about it. A biology teacher clad in brilliant pink lab coat and blue trainers saluted us with great good cheer, thoughtfully cradling the departmental mascot, Buffy the bearded dragon, as jazz drifted out overhead. The skeletons in the labs wore Jack Sparrow headscarves, and it really did seem refreshingly unstuffy.

Lessons universally praised as lively and interactive. 'My daughter has been inspired by the teachers' love of their subjects,' wrote a mother. 'The teaching standard is of the highest quality at Caterham,' wrote another; 'our son has blossomed in all subjects, making his choices for GCSEs even harder.'

The key note here seems to be approachability. One sixth former thought the best thing about Caterham was 'the relationship between staff and students – I've never seen anything like it. They're incredibly supportive and happy to give up their free time.' School introduced iPads for all its students in 2015, and is formally accredited as an Apple Distinguished School. Parents approve. 'The iPad use for school communication for the children is excellent, both for homework and for keeping in touch with what is going on in school,' observed one parent. 'I was sceptical at first, but have been proven wrong,' a father was happy to admit. 'I've seen how it allows the students to embrace technology as a great medium for learning.'

Full-time SENCo (here called the assistant director of learning and teaching), aided by two teaching assistants, offers support to the 15 per cent or so of pupils who need it – dyslexia, processing difficulties, the occasional high-functioning autistic student – mostly in a classroom setting. 'There is one-to-one support, but it's not the bulk of what we do. Otherwise I'd become a crutch, and we want them to be independent,' commented the SENCo, whose office was decorated with reassuring posters of celebrities with SEN – Daniel Radcliffe, David Beckham and the like. This is an academically selective school, however, and they were keen to stress that it's unlikely to be suitable for pupils with more than mild difficulties.

Games, options, the arts: Strong on all fronts, and superbly well-resourced: almost the first thing visitors see as they approach the school is what impresses as a Wembley-sized brand new Astroturf. Dual approach to sport: elite athletes go onto the Caterham Programme, where top-class coaching pushes them to their limits. But everyone is encouraged to have a go, and the school works to ensure that no one is left out. Rugby, hockey and cricket are the main sports for the boys, lacrosse, netball and tennis for the girls, and school has invested heavily in the coaching and facilities for these. It struck us as a rather traditional delineation, but the girls we spoke to liked it, praising the 'community feel' of lacrosse – something we couldn't remember about the game, frankly, so it's good that times change. There's also sixth form girls' rugby, synchronised swimming in the school's own magnificent pool, and a myriad of other exciting things to try, from horse-riding (the school has its own equestrian team) to judo, archery, golf, fencing – etc. Splendid sports hall the size of an aircraft hanger is open to the public, and the English hockey regional training team uses the facilities here. The Wildcats Adventure area, a woodland paradise of treehouses, ropes and zipwires, looked like every child's dream.

Performing arts has its own thriving centre. Drama has upped its game, with the opening of a new dedicated studio theatre in 2016 supported by full-time theatre technician – who also runs the Humphries Theatre, the large multi-purpose space across the foyer – with a strong team of tech enthusiasts drawn from the students. Annual shows for both senior and lower school pupils – 'I don't think I can count the number of things I've done in the drama department!' beamed a stage-struck sixth former. Recent productions include Grease, Les Misérables and Our Day Out. Lots of other things going on, including a trip to Edinburgh in summer 2017. Fabulous new air-conditioned dance studio – 'Dance is big here,' confirmed a male student, who praised the way the school encouraged both boys and girls to get involved. Annual MADLive dance performance showcases the students' achievements. Music department is lively and busy: orchestras, ensembles, concerts, choirs, and lessons on almost any instrument you can think of.

As you'd expect, visual arts are well-resourced, and we liked the textiles area – a pleasure to see sewing machines in a school in this day and age. However, the work on display, whilst stylish, didn't strike us as particularly inspired or visionary – perhaps there just isn't much creative angst at this down-to-earth, affluent school – and it's probably no coincidence that the only negative feedback we received concerned this part of the school's provision: 'I would pick out art as an area of weakness,' wrote one parent, bluntly.

D of E and CCF are flourishing, and there are dozens of extracurricular societies catering for every taste. Of particular note is the Innovations Centre, where pupils can play and experiment with all things digital and robotic, and home also to the film club, where pupils have access to their own Green Screen room and Mac editing suite for creating special effects.

Boarding: We thought the boarding pretty special. Houses are comfortable, spotlessly clean, light, modern in feel and attractive. In addition to everything you'd expect, girls' boarding house boasts a beautiful dining room with oak panelling and a rather lovely Positive Message Tree in the corner, which could have been tacky but simply wasn't. The boys are housed in equal comfort, and are about to get their own kitchen. Bedrooms are for four or two students in the lower years, then single rooms for lower sixth formers and single with ensuite for those in their final years. Good number of live-in staff, and a team of matrons are on site from 7.30am until 10pm.

Nearly 90 per cent are full boarders, mostly international students who do the IELTS (English language learning) programme on Saturdays. Weekly boarding introduced in 2016, and is attracting UK families – numbers small at present, but school hopes to grow them. However, now offers boarding from year 9 only (previously from year 7). Lots of trips and things to do – and a nice leisurely 10am breakfast on Sundays. The boarders we met struck us as a thoroughly happy and well-adjusted lot, and, as a student confirmed, 'the boarder and day pupil relationship is really good.'

Background and atmosphere: Founded in 1811 to provide a boarding education for the sons of Congregational ministers – William Wilberforce was one of the school's first governors. Moved to its present lovely site in the wooded Surrey North Downs in 1884. Even then the school was a forward-looking place. The main building, a beautiful late Victorian red-brick and terracotta affair, was the height of modernity for its time, with the heating being provided by circulating warm air through the Hare Stone Tower, now long gone. The school maintains its links with the United Reform Church – bursaries are available for children of URC clergy – but now describes itself as 'multi-faith' and welcomes children of all faiths and of none.

Lots of new buildings, all of them practical and most of them tasteful, and astonishingly well-equipped and extensive outdoor areas – playing fields, woods, bridle path, you name it. With 200 acres to play with, space is not an issue, and the students move about with an air of confident purpose, smartly dressed in their businesslike uniform. Co-ed really works here. The boys aren't loutish, and the girls aren't cliquey. More than anything, they're just themselves. 'For me, it's the most natural environment,' observes the head, and everyone we spoke to agreed. Students work hard, but are encouraged to play hard too and take advantage of the many opportunities on offer. 'Both my children find the school environment positive,' wrote a mother, 'and it's been a place where we've seen them develop. We cannot ask more from a school as we watch our children grow into young adults.'

Pastoral care, well-being and discipline: Universally praised for being a caring place that nurtures the whole child, and this is shown in lots of small ways rather than anything obvious. One such that impressed us was that boarding house prefects are there simply to support the younger students, not to discipline them – the house staff do the latter, so relationships between older and younger pupils remain friendly. Students appear confident without being arrogant, ready to have a go at anything, and really did come across as keen to serve the wider community. Behaviour throughout is lively but courteous.

Across the school, the words that kept coming up were 'approachable' and 'welcoming'. 'An unstuffy, happy school where the children do really well without being highly pressurised,' was one parent's verdict. Another wrote, 'There have been a couple of occasions when our circumstances have meant that the children needed some extra care and I found the school and staff incredibly helpful, and very swift and ready to offer and provide sensitive and genuine care for them.'

Form the top down, the school seems to have got the work-life balance right, and the result is a sane and kindly place where people have room to look about them. 'The school leadership at all levels seems genuinely to be on the watch for pupils in need of support and then deliver this in a sympathetic manner,' wrote a parent. A member of staff commented, 'People are nice to each other, because we're given the time to be nice to each other. We're valued by both leadership and parents. It's busy here, but we're not pushed to the limit.'

Pupils and parents: Parents are a grounded lot, mostly dual income and working hard to give their children a Caterham education. Supportive of the school, and very much involved, turning out in great numbers for sporting fixtures and other school events. School works hard to include them, running a lively programme of talks – Revise Like A Champion was aimed at parents wanting to help their children – and putting at their disposal an amazing hospitality suite complete with terrace overlooking the playing fields. Pupils are level-headed, proud of their school, very happy to be here.

Entrance: Around 90 places at year 7, a third of which go to children coming up from the junior school. Others come from a range of local schools, both state and independent: The Hawthorns, Hazelwood, Oakhyrst Grange, St Mary's C of E Junior School, Sevenoaks Prep, New Beacon School, Copthorne School, etc. Fifty additional places in year 9 to pupils coming from preps, either via year 6 deferred entry or standard year 8 route. Some additional places available in the sixth form, but almost everyone stays on, and, very commendably, the school doesn't weed out: the threshold of six B/6s at GCSE is 'a discussion point, not an ultimatum'.

Exit: A very small number after GCSEs, mostly for financial reasons. After A levels, the overwhelming majority to university; 12 to Oxbridge in 2018, plus four medics. Popular destinations include UCL, Exeter, Bath, Leeds, Birmingham and Manchester. A Study Abroad evening was recently offered for students looking to go overseas (including the USA). Vocational courses also becoming increasingly popular, and the head is currently in discussion with at least one high-profile financial company about apprenticeships (three on KPMG and Deloitte apprenticeship degrees).

C

Money matters: About a third of pupils on some form of financial assistance. Bursaries of up to 100 per cent available for pupils from low income families. Academic scholarships at 11+, 13+ and 16+ can be worth up to 50 per cent of fees. Broad range of 25 per cent scholarships offered in specific areas: sport, music, drama, science, art and design, all rounder and boarding.

Remarks: A traditional yet innovative school offering all that's best in modern independent education, both day and boarding, without putting its students through the mill. 'Caterham's one of the best schools in the country already,' the head told us proudly at our meeting. We're inclined to agree.

Chandlings Prep School

Linked with Cothill House

Bagley Wood, Nr Boars Hill, Oxford, Oxfordshire OX1 5ND

Ages 2–11 **Pupils** 345

Fees: £12,300 – £15,870 pa

01865 730771
www.chandlings.org.uk

Head: Since January 2018, Christine Cook, previously head of Cokethorpe Junior School for 11 years. Educated Westminster College, Oxford. Formerly director of studies at Chandlings, teaching houseparent at The Dragon School, head of year at The Oxford Academy (formerly Peers School) taught at Guildford Grammar School, Western Australia.

Entrance: Main entry points are nursery and reception, but children are accepted into all year groups if space allows. Chandlings takes a broad range of abilities; candidates are assessed to see where they lie within their cohort and places are offered 'provided the school can accommodate their needs.'

Exit: Chandlings goes up to 11 so the majority of leavers are destined for Oxford and Abingdon day schools: Abingdon School, Magdalen College School, The Oratory School (boys); St Helen and St Katharine, Headington, Oxford High, Wychwood (girls). Co-ed destinations include Bloxham, Cokethorpe, d'Overbroecks, Pangbourne College. Some girls head for boarding schools: Cheltenham Ladies' College, St Mary's Ascot, St Mary's Calne, Tudor Hall and Wycombe Abbey. One or two boys may join boarding preps such as Cothill for years 7 and 8. Very impressive record of prizes and scholarships – 24 in 2018, including eight to Abingdon and three to Magdalen College School.

Remarks: Our visit started with a tour of some mini museums. Children from year 3 had set up exhibits in the sports hall and were giving presentations on subjects as diverse as the Beano, crystals, kittens, Star Wars, African animals, riding, Chelsea FC and sloths. Many were dressed to represent their interests and all had written speeches. 'Have you ever wondered what happens to astronaut poo in space?' was a particularly well-received rhetorical question. Next on the itinerary was year 1 French: all were enjoying a game of passez le chien (soft toy) and learning numbers at the same time. Pre-prep get a French lesson once a week and from year 3 pupils get one lesson each of French and Spanish a week. Latin and Mandarin are offered as clubs. Twice weekly science lessons from year 3 onwards in properly equipped labs.

Parents we spoke to were all extremely happy with the 'fantastic' teaching – from nursery right through to year 6. 'The children are happy, they enjoy learning. Yes, they're pushed, but never too much – the balance is just right.' We dropped in on lots of lessons during our tour, enjoyed the delicious aromas in the cookery room and admired creative endeavours in art and DT. In a year 6 English class we were treated to pupils performing the war-time songs they'd written – and they'd composed the music, too. Places (let alone scholarships) at schools such as Magdalen College, Abingdon and St Helen and St Katharine are not easily won, but there's no sense whatsoever of Chandlings being an exam factory.

Extra help in class for any pupils with mild SEN, those needing more support have up to three one-to-one sessions a week plus in-class help as necessary. Parents were pretty positive about school's SEN provision but one observed that it probably wasn't the place for a child with significant problems. EAL teaching well established and lessons (individual or very small group) timetabled. In class support also available in, eg, English or science lessons, if necessary. Link with nearby BMW plant in Cowley brings a number of German pupils to the school; they join in with lessons but also have a specialist teacher so that they can keep up with the German curriculum.

Sport described by one parent as 'genuinely meritocratic' – that's not something we hear very often. Others agreed that the teams were flexible and players were moved around based on performance. 'They all get to play whenever possible.' Another said, 'the children's expectations are managed very well; they talk to them about how to improve.' Great emphasis on sportsmanship, behaviour at away matches, supporting fellow players etc. Chandlings has recently started playing in IAPS (Independent Association of Prep Schools) tournaments with strong debut performances in boys' U11 hockey and cross-country and girls' U11 netball and hockey. Boys' rugby and football teams also fare well in inter-school fixtures. In addition to netball girls play football and tag rugby plus rounders and cricket in the summer term. Riding lessons have are on the list of extracurricular options and all pupils have a weekly swimming lesson in the lovely warm indoor pool.

Parents and pupils told us how the profile of music and drama has been raised. LAMDA preparation and a public speaking club have been introduced, as have more opportunities for even the youngest to stand up and speak in front of their peers – the mini museums we saw were part of this initiative. Year 3 put together a 'play in a day'; year 4 pupils put on a musical – we could have spent the whole afternoon enjoying rehearsals for Joseph and the Amazing Technicolour Dreamcoat. Year 5s do a workshop production and year 6 'unite' after exams in an ambitious play, recently Emil and the Detectives. Well-equipped music rooms, weekly class music lessons, peripatetic teachers give around 170 instrumental lessons a week. Christmas carols held at nearby Dorchester Abbey, concerts and plays are performed in the sports hall – one pupil said he thought the school could do with a 'proper chapel' and also a theatre.

Chandlings opened in 1994 with just nine 'tinies'. The Cothill Trust had long thought there was a gap in the market for a co-ed prep and when the previous owner of Chandlings Manor was obliged to leave in a hurry, the trust stepped in. Chandlings Manor. The name conjours up ancient stones, mullioned windows, the faded grandeur of an ancient aristocratic line. The reality is more of a 62 acre Southfork Ranch/nouveau Cotswold mash-up with added fountains. Rumours about the former occupant abound. Whether he was in oil or arms dealing, one can only imagine the parties this house witnessed when it had 25 bathrooms, silk canopied ceilings, crystal chandeliers, a 30-seat cinema, small bore shooting range and, best of all, a casino. Parents be reassured, these well-appointed low-rise buildings do, in fact, lend themselves very well to a school. The fact that it was originally a house, albeit on a lavish scale, means there's still a comfortable, domestic atmosphere. Several parents commented on how they liked the fact that the school didn't feel (or smell) 'institutional.' Splendid grounds provide many opportunities for outdoor learning – there's a pontoon for lake dipping, bird-watching hide, wildlife night camera, not to mention mindfulness and listening walks and den building in the bluebell woods at break.

Chandlings is one of eight schools in the Cothill Educational Trust. The trust started in 1870 with nearby Cothill School, one of the few remaining boys' boarding preps, and in addition to Cothill and Chandlings owns four other prep schools plus The Old Malthouse, an outdoor education centre on Dorset's Jurassic Coast and Chateau de Sauveterre in SW France. Pupils from Chandlings and the other preps attend courses at The Old Malthouse and can spend a term at Sauveterre for total immersion in French language and culture.

The Bagley Wood address may sound like something out of Tolkein, but while there is a secluded air about Chandlings' bosky corner of south Oxfordshire, remote it isn't. School's location is incredibly convenient for Oxford, Abingdon and villages between. Demographic is quite an interesting one, noticeably more international than nearby preps. Several parents said they'd liked Chandlings because, 'it's less narrow' and 'not burdened by history'. Another told us, 'I like the fact that my children are making friends from all over the world.' The popularity of 'International days' is testament to this. Pupils are issued with 'passports' and families introduce travellers to the culture, traditions – and food – of their country.

Four classes of 14 -16 per year group, year groups kept together in same part of the building; classrooms are mostly light and airy and there seemed to be no shortage of space. A few years ago there was a five class year group and general consensus from parents was that this was 'too much'. No plans to significantly increase pupil numbers in the future, but we did hear parental concerns that staffing has not kept pace with current growth in pupil numbers. School is boy-heavy in some years – quite noticeably so in one or two of the classes we observed – but overall the split is around 60:40.

Long-standing tradition of Chandlings providing bed and breakfast for year 8 Cothill boys. Most parents seemed unconcerned about this, several of the boarders have siblings at Chandlings so it's quite nice for them to catch up briefly in the morning before minibus takes them back to Cothill.

Parents really like the different ways in which Chandlings works with pupils to prioritise values such as kindness and empathy. They were confident about the school's pastoral care systems and those who had experienced problems said that they had been dealt with sensitively and extremely swiftly. Teaching staff were described as 'amazing', 'they work so hard' and 'they respond to emails or calls so quickly.' School cook also singled out for praise by parents and children, apparently in addition to delicious lunches she also 'makes fantastic cakes'.

We'll leave the last word to the parents: 'It's so friendly – there's no particular type of person here', said one. Another added, 'It's full of happy children, enjoying themselves and learning, we're thrilled to have found it.'

Charterhouse

C

Admissions Office, Godalming, Surrey GU7 2DX

Ages 13–18 **Pupils** 810 **Sixth form** 431 (142 girls) **Boarders** 787

Fees: Day £32,364; Boarding £39,165 pa

01483 291501
www.charterhouse.org.uk

Headmaster: Since January 2018, Dr Alex Peterken BA MA DEd (30s), previously head of Cheltenham College and returning to his roots. Before joining Cheltenham in 2008 as deputy head he spent 12 years at Charterhouse, as head of higher education and careers and latterly housemaster of Saunderites. Educated at The Prebendal School, Chichester where he was head boy and head chorister, thence to Eton College as a music exhibitioner. BA in theology from Durham, MA in educational management from London and a doctorate in education from Surrey. Married to Henny and has six children; he enjoys choral singing (bass) and walking.

Academic matters: Most take either the Cambridge Pre-U or the IB diploma. A levels survive in four subjects, the most popular of which is government & politics. The Pre-U still seen as controversial among parents, who worry unnecessarily that universities are bemused by it. IGCSEs taken in preference to GCSEs in most subjects.

The mix of curricula here make judgements about exceptional performance in specific subjects difficult. Maths, history and economics are the stand-outs in terms of sixth form popularity. Art does well and many minority subjects shine. IGCSEs sparkle and demonstrate the value added by good teaching and individual attention. 2018 results saw 75 per cent of IGCSEs A*/A; 92 per cent of Pre-U/A level exams achieved distinction or merit (or A*-C) in 2018 and 56 per cent distinction (or A*/A). Average IB point score 35. This has to be impressive for a school which requires only 60 per cent at CE.

'Not frighteningly academic if you've come from a pushy London day school,' we were told by one parent, while another said, 'It's far more academically rigorous than we'd expected.' A third felt that, 'A lot of the seriously bright chaps are the international students.' However, 'There's a culture of trying hard and achieving,' another observed. We deeply approve of the first year's geography and history syllabus being largely focused on the rich history of the school. Not here do you meet pupils with no idea of the key figures and moments in the story of their alma mater. Careers provision and university preparation, having been described as 'needing a kick' by several parents, now rapidly improving, and school is building on Old Carthusian networks and willingness to support current leavers.

System of 'Calling Over' – boys get praised for effort or pulled up for lack of it publicly in class four times a term – is controversial. 'It's brutal,' complained one parent while acknowledging that 'it does mean they are doing something if a boy isn't pulling his weight.'

Very few with recognised or serious SEN of any kind. No withdrawal from classes for individual support. 'We subscribe to the idea enshrined in current legislation that all teachers must be teachers of special educational needs. The best person to support a pupil's needs is his or her subject teacher. All teachers receive regular training in supporting pupils' individual needs. We individualise learning as much as we can.'

Works with local Broadwater School to share staff development, learning opportunities and best practice.

Games, options, the arts: Everything done with vigour, dedication and enthusiasm. Ben Travers Theatre – opened by the great farceur himself in 1980 (at 93) – now looking a little tired, but still an excellent performing space with a cosy foyer. Lots of productions. Surprisingly small proportion learn an instrument but the standard of those who do, and the intensity of participation in multiple performance opportunities of all kinds, is exemplary. Very lively and creative art and DT ('someone made a motorbike') – each sixth form artist has their own space and we admired the flair and scope of work. Super ceramics, collage and painting, especially. Two new 3D printers.

Enormous sports complex with everything you'd expect and used, out of lesson time, by the general public. All-weather pitches, courts, fields and tracks in all directions plus a nine hole golf course. A famous football school – Spurs 'Legend' directs the game – with seven teams in each year and masses of matches for all. Sporting opportunities and achievements here of all kinds and hard to better. 'And if there's something you want to do which they don't offer they will try and set it up for you,' we were told. Also a famous CCF and formidable pioneering expeditions to all kinds of high up and far away places.

Boarding: Some 80 per cent board, and everyone is a member of one of the 12 houses, though girls sleep in their own 'hostels'. The new houses – 'architecturally weird and further away from everything' – are preferred by some as more functional, better resourced and nearer to sports facilities. Eating in the new houses is communal, so 'You can't go down in your pyjamas – such a shame,' thought one parent. Four girls' 'hostels' but they study in the boys' houses until 10pm when they trot demurely home. Boys not allowed anywhere near girls' hostels – ever. Girls' hostels felt to be better – all rooms have en-suite bathrooms, are very cosy and their rooms are only for sleeping. In the older houses en suites are scarce, some rooms are tiny, though no more than two share.

Most weekends, pupils may go home after sports fixtures on Saturday afternoons and return for chapel on Sunday evening. For those pupils who remain in school overnight on Saturday (around 20 per cent), there's now a full programme of weekend activities. 'There used to be absolutely nothing to do at weekends,' a sixth former told us. 'Now there's loads.' Most staff live on site – many in a strange tower, nine floors of a highly eccentric 1970s folly – and all live within a mile of school.

Background and atmosphere: Thomas Sutton (1532–1611) made his fortune from coal mining, endowed a hospital on the site of the London Charterhouse and left a legacy to maintain a chapel, almshouse and school. A foundation was set up to run a home for 80 pensioners (gentlemen by descent and in poverty, soldiers that have borne arms by sea or land, merchants decayed by piracy or shipwreck, or servants in household to the King or Queens Majesty), and to educate 40 boys.

The school moved to its present home in stockbroker-Surrey in 1872. The main school building, a substantial gothic statement of purpose, cannot fail to awe. Its post-WW1 chapel is vast, stark and sombre; no mistaking the genuine horror and grief at the nearly 700 lost Carthusians which inspired it. Many more buildings – some of less obvious architectural merit – have since accrued. Super library – subdued lighting, comfortable sofas, tables with laptop points and exemplary stock; a library that has been nurtured and loved. The site has grown to 250 acres with fields and pitches stretching away into the landscape. Trees, little gardens and courtyards humanise it and pathways meander about to give the impression of a sizeable and complex school 'village'.

The advent of sixth form girls into what many still feel is a very male establishment is a source of joy for most. 'The boys love it when the girls arrive,' one seasoned father of boys told us. 'It gives them the best of both worlds.' Some stress 'it takes a certain type of girl – they have to be confident and not stand any nonsense.' Sporty girls go down particularly well, it seems. And, inevitably, 'They do rank us on prettiness so you have to be robust'.

An overtly Christian school – for all its inclusiveness. Parents comment on that old-fashioned thing, the school 'spirit'. 'There's a strong sense of loyalty. They engender it very quickly. Loyalty to both house and school.' A seriousness about the place reflected in its publications, its sending of expert teachers to support the teaching of individual subjects in local state schools and in the appointment of a likeable 'director of social responsibility'. We like this.

Going fully co-ed and will take first girls into year 9 in 2021, with school roll gradually increasing to 1,000 to accommodate them and new girls' houses planned.

Pastoral care, well-being and discipline: Vertical tutor system described as 'brilliant!' – one tutor for two boys from each year, meeting at least weekly. Parents feel 'My son's tutor is on his side – we can't fault the system'. Very much a school for joiners-in. 'They do their best to make them try out everything. So even lazy boys get really pushed to try things.' Pupils are polite and charming and discipline is good, though parents tell us of the odd drink smuggling escapade. 'It's really not a problem here' though, affirm sixth formers. Junior boys wear tweedy jackets, older boys wear blue blazers and girls seem uniformly to have long hair and short black skirts. No pushing at boundaries to be seen anywhere.

Most housemasters accorded warm praise, though one or two houses described by parents as 'out of control'. School assures us this is being tackled – and we gather there have been several recent changes in the pastoral team. Boarders are 'very well supervised,' in their leisure time and 'the school is very sensible about absences and so on,' assert parents. Matron is especially highly praised. Most teachers described as 'incredibly kind' and as being a good mix of 'nice young ones – sharp-witted and impressive – and safer, older pairs of hands'. 'Kindness' was a word we heard a lot from parents. School seen by almost all as collaborative and encouraging mutual respect between staff and pupils.

Pupils and parents: About 80 per cent from London or the home counties. Twenty per cent made up of around 37 nationalities – a few have some EAL support but this is not the norm. Presence of overseas pupils is not new: Charterhouse has a relationship with Hong Kong going back 200 years and has long valued its international reach and reputation. Some sense that being sporty is valued more highly than being arty, and some creative but left-footed types take a while to feel at home.

Immense list of notable Old Carthusians includes poets Richards Crashaw and Lovelace, writers Joseph Addison, Richard Steele, WM Thackeray, Max Beerbohm, Ben Travers, Robert Graves, Simon Raven, Frederick Raphael, publisher John Murray, classicist Henry Liddell, actor-manager Johnston Forbes-Robertson, founder of the scouts, Robert Baden-Powell, cartoonist and wit Osbert Lancaster, composer Ralph Vaughan-Williams, historian Hugh Trevor-Roper, sculptor Anthony Caro, politicos and journalists James Prior, William Rees-Mogg, Dick Taverne, the Dimblebys, Jeremy Hunt, Duncan Carswell, philosopher Don Cupitt, pop impresario Jonathan King, the rock group Genesis, composer Rachel Portman and innumerable venerable ecclesiasts (among them, John Wesley) and redoubtable military men of high renown.

Entrance: About 125 places in year 9. Houses matter here. Parents and boys visit two or three, meet housemaster and staff and boys and have a good poke about. All are interviewed in the first house they visit – a record is kept for other housemasters to see if necessary. Parents then choose their preferred house – but they don't always get it.

Candidates now sit the ISEB common pre-test in the autumn of year 6 at their current school. Boys (and, in future, girls) invited for interview and activity afternoon in spring term and close contact maintained with prep schools. A few places not dependent on pre-testing remain for late applicants and exceptional cases. In the autumn of year 8, preps send updated reports – this can result in some boys being asked to withdraw. CE pass mark of 60 per cent expected. They don't over-offer, which is refreshing.

At sixth form, 75 girls and 30 boys come, most as boarders and a few as day pupils. Admission by competitive examination, school reports and interview. Offers of places are unconditional but high proportion of GCSE 9-7s are expected. Little choice of houses.

A few places reserved in years 9 and 12 for overseas candidates. Quite diverse admissions systems, depending on where you are from. 'It doesn't suffer from being too fashionable,' one wise parent ventured. 'It is good at choosing the boys who will suit it.' And from, 2021, year 9 girls.

Exit: Seven to Oxbridge in 2018, plus five medics; large numbers to Bristol, Durham, Exeter, UCL and, increasingly, to prestigious colleges in the US/Canada – 18 in 2018, including NYU and Berkeley, plus others to Italy, Spain and Hong Kong. No narrow range of subjects studied but a bent towards economics, politics and business management perhaps. No silly subjects pursued by anyone.

Money matters: Not a rich school. Most fee assistance now in the form of bursarial help rather than scholarships. Scholarships and exhibitions – academic, art and music whether at 13+ or 16+ – more for glory than dosh. However, can be topped up by mean-tested bursaries up to the value of full fees.

Remarks: An all-round impressive school – confident of what it does and doing it well. Pupils genuinely value what they are given here. As one, thoughtfully, expressed it, 'You feel you're part of something that should continue'.

Charters School

Charters Road, Sunningdale, Ascot, Berkshire SL5 9QY

Ages 11–18 **Pupils** 1,659 **Sixth form** 373

01344 624826
www.chartersschool.org.uk

Head: Since 2009, Richard Pilgrim (50s). Until 2018 he was co-head with Martyn Parker, who has now retired. Degree in physics with music from University College Cardiff (he also teaches physics here), PGCE from Leeds. He has been at Charters since 1984, previously as co-deputy head, and proudly declares, 'I can honestly say the school has never been as good as it is now.' Married with three teenage children, likes reading and the outdoors and describes himself as 'a lapsed French horn player'. ('He's very talented!' puts in a colleague.)

Academic matters: Extremely good, and getting better all the time. GCSE and A level results consistently put it in the top 20 per cent of state schools nationally, and that includes the grammars. In 2018, 63 per cent of A level grades were A*/B and 33 per cent A*/A; 83 per cent of pupils got 4-9 in both English and maths at GCSE and 40 per cent of GCSE grades were A*-A/9-7. All the more creditable, given the non-selective intake: children with a reading age of 6 rub shoulders with potential Oxbridge candidates, but, says head, 'it's really important for us that we cater for all abilities; the school is comprehensive and will remain so.' Curriculum is therefore very broad. Traditional GCSEs and A levels still very popular, but are offered alongside BTecs and NVQs, with the less academic KS4 pupils able to study off-site subjects such as motor vehicle technology and construction. French and Spanish are both taught to years 7-9, and we liked the way that all signage in the school was trilingual. Latin offered to G&T students.

Facilities in all teaching spaces are up to date, with both Macs and PCs available for students to use. New STEM building with maths teaching rooms and science labs. Really excellent library and sixth form study area, accessible to students from 8am to 6pm, and guarded by the thoroughly lovely Miss MacDonnell, who, our guides assured us, was the reason that 'it's always this quiet.' Everyone we spoke to lauded the staff as enthusiastic and knowledgeable, with one boy falling over himself to give praise: 'The teachers here are really up for giving everyone and everything a go.' He went on to describe how one of the English teachers, who happened to be a law graduate, was teaching him and his friend GCSE law as an extracurricular, simply because they'd asked if they could do it. Parents confirmed that 'studious children are accepted and congratulated by other children.' A sixth former commented, 'The school doesn't put you in a bubble; they emphasise independent learning here.'

Games, options, the arts: Charters became a sports college in 2002 as part of the specialist schools programme, which entitled it to receive extra funding for sports-specific teaching and facilities, provided this was used to drive the whole school forward. The programme was axed in 2010, but sport remains central to Charters' success and the facilities are excellent: seven tennis courts, full-sized hockey pitch, two Astroturf pitches, and two sports halls including basketball court and weight-training facilities. Every year group has 10 hours of sport per fortnight, and out of 70+ extracurricular activities offered each week, 40+ are sports and dance related. As well as the more traditional football, netball etc, sports such as golf, trampolining and skiiing are all available to do off-site. Although the school scores some impressive successes on track and field, much of what's on offer is intended to be fun rather than competitive, so that all pupils are catered for. It clearly works. As one satisfied parent observed, 'My daughter loves the sports. She's never home from school!' Head is very positive about the value of sport to education as a whole, adding, 'We don't have an obesity problem here!' And we could see, as we walked about, that they really didn't.

Annual drama productions in purpose-built drama studio are popular, and music is strong too, with choirs, orchestras and a broad range of instrumental lessons. Extremely varied programme of trips, both day and residential: the school jointly owns Tirabad Outdoor Educational Centre in rural Wales, and sends parties there throughout the school year. All the pupils waxed lyrical about the good times they'd had at Tirabad, with several calling it the best thing they'd done at Charters. Other destinations have included Spain, the USA, Sri Lanka, Beijing, Rome and Paris. Strong DofE programme, and lots of clubs – science, creative writing, debating, chess, etc.

Background and atmosphere: Established in 1958 as a secondary modern with 400 children, Charters became comprehensive in the 1960s to cope with increased demand and remains committed to comprehensive ideals. Became an academy in 2012, says head, 'because of the benefits of self-determination. We're less subject to the whims of education.' Since its beginning, the school has occupied the same site in an affluent, leafy suburb of Ascot. The uniform is sensible and unfussy, the modern(ish) buildings clean and businesslike, and there are a number of very pleasant green spaces in which pupils can sit and chat. Highly regarded by locals throughout its history, the school exudes purpose, cordiality and calm. All the students we spoke to said that they'd made plenty of friends here and that it was a very welcoming place. 'The people are open and friendly here'; 'The teachers help you get to know people'; 'My son has had a good time at Charters'; 'My children love all their teachers and find them very approachable,' were typical comments.

Pastoral care, well-being and discipline: Outstanding on many levels. The Maine Centre offers on-site support for any child with medical, social, bereavement or emotional issues and is fully staffed throughout the school week. Any pupil can drop in there with or without an appointment; students praised it as 'fantastic'. The school has also been a centre for physically handicapped pupils since 1981, and is fully equipped with ramps, lifts, etc. It works closely with a nearby autistic school, and provision for its high number of statemented children is excellent. Horizontal tutoring system, with tutors remaining with their charges from year 7 through to year 11 wherever possible. School has been nationally recognised for the leadership opportunities it provides for its students. Incidents of bullying are 'quite rare', according to the pupils, who also said that such occurrences were dealt with 'very well, very quickly and with an iron fist'. 'I've never, ever felt unsafe at this school,' added a year 9 girl. Year 11 prefects are all encouraged to take pastoral responsibility and, say parents, develop into mature and thoughtful young adults. A concern about discipline in their child's tutor group was raised in one quarter, but this appears to be exceptional: sixth formers we spoke to emphatically denied that there had ever been such issues during their time at the school and seemed genuinely shocked to hear otherwise.

Pupils and parents: Very much a product of the locality, with about 87 per cent of students from white British families, but high employment in the area has meant that families from all ethnic backgrounds are moving here in increasing numbers. Very broad social diversity, with deprived Bracknell pupils being bussed in alongside those from advantaged Ascot. Very strong parent support for the school.

Entrance: With some 500 applicants for 270 places, the school is heavily oversubscribed. As an academy, Charters is now its own admissions authority, but it buys in admissions admin procedure from local authority and the usual criteria apply: statemented children, proximity, siblings, etc.

Exit: After year 11, up to 40 per cent per cent to local colleges or to employment. The rest continue into the Charters sixth form, where 90-95 per cent go on to a wide range of universities, including Russell Group ones. Several Oxbridge successes each year – five in 2018, plus two medics. Popular destinations include Bristol, UWE, Exeter, Portsmouth, Southampton, Nottingham and Bournemouth.

Money matters: Government bursaries available to disadvantaged post-16 students who would otherwise be unable to continue their education.

Remarks: An admirable and humane school, with some of the sparkiest, brightest, most articulate and most delightful students it's been our pleasure to meet. Successfully holds its own against its glossy independent neighbours, and is preferred to same by many parents. If we hadn't lived in Crystal Palace, we would have sent our own children here.

Cheam School

Headley, Newbury, Berkshire RG19 8LD

Ages 3–13 **Pupils** 391 **Boarders** 50 weekly, 150 flexi **C of E**

Fees: Day £11,940 – £21,285; Boarding £23,520 – £27,630 pa

01635 268242
www.cheamschool.com

Head: Since 2016, Martin Harris BSc (50s). Previously head of Sandroyd for 13 years. After missing out on the RAF (too tall) started in the City only to realise that catching the same train every morning for 40 years wasn't for him. Coached children at holiday camp, loved it, gained PGCE and hasn't looked back. Had two spells at Ashdown House, first as a teacher (1991-1996), returning as deputy, then acting head (1998-2003), with a stint as deputy head at King's Rochester in between.

Two children with wife Catherine, who traded physiotherapy career for role here as an informal conduit for staff, parent and pupil concerns. Family completed by obligatory dog – a terrier rather than standard issue labrador.

With little time off (Sundays often filled with paperwork and marking – Mr Harris teaches history to top two years) school can be 'all consuming' – in a good way. Describes it in newsletter as 'exciting', staff 'passionate,' and pupils 'ebullient'. Even school's location and buildings are 'a great metaphor for prep school life,' though fortunately thoroughly tangible for review purposes.

He's felt to be fair and approachable. 'Spends time with the children, not in his office and I feel closer to him,' said pupil. He's relaxed into the role, say parents – not easy given of massive popularity of predecessor.

Few drastic changes. 'One of the great schools in the country,' says Mr Harris. 'Like a jumper, you don't want to start unpicking a few areas and find that everything unravels.' So far, IT has been upgraded, reasoning added to the curriculum, the uniform tweaked, and coaches more evenly distributed so Cs and Ds don't always get the gap students.

He's liberating staff to teach more creatively. 'Not [...] trendy or different but to open children's eyes so they're not just sponges regurgitating facts.'

Food is the most commented on development where Mrs H is introducing healthier options. Parents were pleased with sensible balance – an avocado on toast short of the full Naturally Ella, but a definite step up from previous stodge-heavy diet. (Decline of God's great chip not as popular with pupils.)

Also repainting some walls white (keeping enough Cheam dull red to please the traditionalists) and stepping up displays (miniature dressing gowns, giant toothbrushes for boarding) though school museum, complete with unsettling mannequin in vintage uniform, is staying.

'People are pleased,' we were told. 'Together, Mr and Mrs Harris are a considerable force for good. Very important for the pastoral side that you see the head and the head's wife together.'

Entrance: Popular with waiting lists in every year group. Broadly selective – must be able to access curriculum but few turned away. Entry by date of registration. Attend familiarisation day – reading, reasoning and maths with time in class – before place is confirmed. Main entry points at reception, year 3 (15 added each time), plus another 10 in year 4. A few places in year 7, rare in years 5, 6 or 8. No feeders – mix of state primaries, London preps and former locals, now returning home). Most live within 20 mile radius. Currently no EAL or overseas pupils.

Exit: One size fits most. 'At Cheam we are preparing your child for their future senior school which will probably be full boarding,' says the school. Every top name, every year, with Bradfield most popular recently, followed by Marlborough, Radley and Eton. Harrow also popular for the boys; girls to St Swithun's, St Mary's Calne, Downe House, Sherborne Girls. Wellington and St Edward's Oxford among other co-ed choices.

Nice mix of awards (19 in 2018) spread evenly through the range, couple each for academics, music and art – though stand out success recently is DT.

Remarks: Easy to pre-judge clientele by tweet congratulating 'former Cheam parents HM The Queen and Prince Philip on the birth of their Great Granddaughter.' That, and winning entry in sandcastle competition – a 'multi-storey mansion' – plus prevalence of cast iron titles among the old boys. Viscounts, barons, HRHs (UK and overseas), politicians. (Also John Michell, 'writer and esotericist': ask for details).

Boasts (in poshly understated way) gold-plated 17th century provenance, founded in (then) quaint Olde World village of Cheam in 1645.Moved to current 100-acre site in 1934, just in time to set up local Home Guard platoon and host 21st Tank Regiment in 1941 (tank rides offered as an after-class treat).

Added girls and day places in the 1990s to overcome, as in 18th and 19th centuries, significant money troubles (one financial crisis per century isn't bad).

But despite all this (and the names of pupils, rich on Florences, Allegras, Orlandos and Fredericks), school community stresses social mix. While not exactly drilling down into the deprived underbelly of the nation, rather more diverse – and infinitely more welcoming – than appearances might suggest. 'We came from state school – everyone is down to earth,' said parent.

Lots of earth, too, courtesy of splendiferous site with lakes, formal gardens and fountains, 'an awesome sight,' said parent. Traffic noise well damped down, replaced by gentle smack of tennis of balls on the all-weather surface (pupils' complaints of running track deformed by slope, tree roots and 'little frogs' not substantiated by school...).

Little of the original main house remains (two mega rebuilds in 19th and 20th centuries) and modern extras include the Duke of Edinburgh building (powered by geothermal energy), home to pre-prep, art and DT and a new kitchen area.

Space well used. 'Something for everyone' boasts the website of the extracurricular activities (most free) – including Greek and German as well as extra enrichment for scholars.

Gender stereotypes are being put to one side. Despite online images of ballet club, all pink tutu-wearing girls, biggest success is former (boy) pupil, a rising classical dance star. Membership of sewing, Sylvanians, Jedi and Lego is (often) similarly mixed.

Former sports inequality has also been addressed. Boys and girls play football and cricket, for example. Plenty of co-ed sports including cross-country (masses of prizes), athletics, shooting, fives and swimming (outdoor but no indoor pool – on the wish list).

Performing arts similarly varied, though limited purpose built spaces, including fab productions (regulars at Edinburgh Festival) and wonderful selective choirs. Two music lessons a week for all pre-prep pupils with tasters in recorder, strings and brass in year 2 (individual lessons from year 3). Well over half the pupils learn some of 17 instruments on offer, with lessons and (for boarders) practice sessions timetabled – impressive string quartet whizzing, unsupervised, through repertoire (snazzy Pink Panther theme). Drama, isn't taught in years 7 or 8, (some parents and pupils would like as an extra) though school points to showcases including soirées and full-blown shows.

Impressive emphasis on pastoral care – parents felt recently improved, especially for youngest; bullying minimal. Staff are all being trained in mental health first aid. Also staff mentors – pupils can request any teacher – prominent displays and emotional tracking (asking same, simple questions twice a year can help predict child's resilience level). One pupil we talked to was movingly open about how school had supported him through family crisis.

Boarders, from year 4, are up at 7am, lights out at 8.15pm for juniors, an hour later for the oldest. ('Sweet dreams' says the timetable). No mobiles – payphone and email only. Weekly, flexi but no full boarding, so everyone goes home on Saturday afternoons. Fluctuating numbers means, said some pupils, that could be on their own. Mr Harris qualifies this as 'not with their friends...they would never be on their own in a dorm.'

Parents couldn't fault the boarding organisation or the 'super energetic' staff who make it 'so much fun that everyone wants to board,' though our girl guides (who hadn't seen boys' quarters before) lambasted perceived inequalities, refrain of 'We don't have that!' prompted by everything from bigger hanging spaces for clothes to bed frames (some metal in girls' dorms, 'which rattle'). Even the disinfectant-filled jar for boys' combs got an envious look...

But it's the academic fare that really appeals. 'All learning should be fun,' says the school. Confirmed by parents who praised 'magical' teachers – recruitment boosted by staff housing in 'Cheamville'. New recruits with ultra-serious outlook (several 'worryingly young' – though average age is 37) are encouraged to lighten up. 'All seem to get the same principle which is that...if you can't have a laugh in prep school years, good luck to rest of your life,' said mother.

Pre-prep head, Mrs Marriott, praised for warmth, ability (and dressing up costumes – 'have seen her in more than any teacher should have to wear,' said mother). She presides over bright classrooms with fabulously inventive displays – teachers clearly arrive with A* skills in transformatory foil wrapping. Admirable fusion of fun and learning – on day of visit, reception pupils were busily chalking planets on courtyard paving stones.

Homework isn't daunting, with light reading, emphasis on key words and writing practice in pre-prep. Twice-yearly reports, plenty of informal contact encouraged while colourful, detailed newsletters (pre-prep has its own) fill in any gaps.

After gentle step up from year 2 to 3, pace increases from year 4, non-stop from 8.15am assembly to end of prep (attended by all) at 6pm – later for top years – and a no-concessions full day of Saturday school.

Well staffed (teacher to pupil ratio of one to six in prep and one to four in pre-prep) and smallish classes – 18 official max, smaller for French and maths, and setting generally left to year 5.

Plenty of interesting things to do, from hatching butterflies to investigating the contents of owl pellets (rather them than us). Numerous subject-related trips (history, geog, French) plus culture (theatre, ballet, museums) sweeten the pill.

Main focus, though, firmly on CE preparation in key subjects (English, maths, science, French, Latin, history, geography and RS). Less academic are, say parents, never made to feel like lesser mortals and subject popularity spans the ability range. Favourites include science – pluses the breeding colony of stick insects, minuses the paucity of labs (on the wish list) – plus DT and history. 'I love the Black Death,' said cheery pupil.

'Behind the scenes they are pushing as much as they can but aren't making them feel that academics is the be all and end all,' reckoned parent. 'People say it's so competitive but I haven't found that in any way shape or form.' Pupils agreed. 'So supportive about everything, in and out of lessons – may as well be my family,' said one.

C

If teaching is good – inevitable tutoring, with or without school's blessing, does go on – learning support is 'brilliant,' says parent. Issues quickly identified, up to two sessions charged for but anything extra normally isn't. Academic support also there if needed. Currently some 54 pupils receive some form of learning support in prep school, with one-to-one, group lessons and in-class support. 'Really good at helping the ones who struggle as well as the ones at the top end,' said parent. 'Half of these have a diagnosed condition (dyslexia etc) while the others need a little help with spelling, writing and maths,' says the school.

While growth in the 1990s was helped by mergers with two other less successful establishments, school's continued success is down not to establishment credentials: plenty, including David Cameron's old prep, have failed to survive. Instead, it's about ensuring that excellent results aren't achieved at the expense of fun. 'A little piece of heaven,' said one parent. But definitely not a metaphor.

Chelmsford County High School for Girls

Broomfield Road, Chelmsford, Essex CM1 1RW

Ages 11–18 **Pupils** 967 **Sixth form** 242

01245 352592
www.cchs.co.uk

Headteacher: Since 2007, Nicole Chapman (50s). Brought up in Burgundy, France, but says she feels 'like a local girl', having relocated to Essex soon after gaining her licence ès lettres (BA honours equivalent) in English with Spanish and French at university in Tours. Further qualifications gained since her time the UK include PGCE, NPQH and MBA (Leicester). She has a son and two stepchildren and joined CCHS after six years as head of a girls' grammar school in Gravesend, Kent – prior to which, she worked at a mixture of challenging and high-achieving grant maintained and foundation schools – both mixed and girls'.

Perspicacious, dedicated and single-minded, she is certainly a safe pair of hands for Chelmsford's stellar girls' grammar and is revered for her tough stance on standards ('Girls here are delightful, but they will take advantage if you let them'), inspiring them to greatness ('Being the leaders of tomorrow is something of a mantra here.') She tirelessly scours the state's coffers to make sure that her super-bright girls have access to the best possible facilities and resources, and has a long wish list for what she wants next (a new sports hall is at the top). Doesn't teach – 'I did do it one year, but my job is so big and I only have a small senior leadership team,' she explains. 'Plus it's not fair on the girls to teach without being entirely committed to all that goes with a teaching role.' But girls say she is a visible presence – taking assemblies, observing lessons and inviting selected girls to join her for drinks and biscuits to congratulate them on hard work. Parents describe her as '101 per cent committed,' 'exacting' and 'driven,' although some feel she could relax slightly with the girls over more pedantic matters, such as make-up. That said, she has been praised for bringing in a more relaxed uniform in suffragette colours.

Keeps fit through tennis, and loves reading and theatre, along with holidaying in France, where she has a house. Lives in Brentwood.

Retiring in July 2019.

Academic matters: A real star of the league tables, twinkling brightly among the UK's top 10 state girls' schools – and outshining all but the most hefty-fee-ed of the public schools. 'We benchmark our practice with the 19 girls' grammars around the country with similar intake to ours – and this year we came fifth,' says the head. Indeed, the academic achievement is famously sky high, with 11 A*/9-8s at GCSE common and regular achievers of four As at A level. In 2018, 87 per cent A*/A grades at GCSE. At A level, 75 per cent of grades were A*/B and 49 per cent A*/A. Results strong across the board, with no one subject area standing out.

Students praise the high quality teaching – all of which is done by subject specialists, who are passionate about their subject, as well as being acutely aware of how girls learn. 'There is no didactic approach to teaching here – it's a real mixture of styles including interactive, more formal presentations and encouraging independent learning,' says the head, who herself recruited the vast majority of teaching staff. 'It's very much my school, in that way,' she says. Teachers are as accessible outside lessons as in them, say students, offering workshops for those who run into difficulties, as well as 'access lessons' for sixth formers who struggle in any one area of a subject. Targets for girls are minutely detailed, so there's no slipping through nets, and girls also cite the single-sex environment as a factor in their willingness to throw themselves into the more traditionally male technological pursuits, without fear of opprobrium. 'The only thing I'd say is that there's too much homework,' one student told us, while another said 'I do feel the tests are too close together.'

No setting – 'there's no point with a range of ability so narrow,' says the head. Languages are taken seriously, with a fabulous new foreign languages block, complete with cutting-edge language lab, a great source of pride for the girls. 'It's pretty incredible, isn't it?' smiled one. French and German compulsory from years 7 to 9, with girls then picking up Latin from years 8-9. Spanish is an option from year 10 – and Mandarin is offered as an after-school option from year 9. Italian and Russian available in sixth-form. All girls have to take at least one language for GCSE, plus English, Maths, three sciences, a humanity and a creative 'to give their academic studies balance,' says the head. No longer offers technology.

Very small number of SEN – only eight when we visited, all of whom are supported in the classroom for their mild to moderate needs. 'Staff are aware of their needs and use specific strategies,' says head. 'The public profile of the school is quite scary, so we weren't sure it would be right for our daughter – but actually they've been amazing, with every teacher in completely in tune with her needs and the smallness of the school meaning that she never feels lost,' said one parent of a child with SEN. Wheelchair access throughout, although no students with mobility issues when we visited.

Twenty-three A levels on offer – mainly traditional, but with a few more unusual ones, including philosophy and classical civilisation. IB phased out but it's changed the way CCHS teaches, claims the head, with sixth formers now increasingly challenged to question what they're learning, with no danger of any girl being spoon-fed.

Games, options, the arts: Despite the academically-biased two-week timetable, less bookish pursuits are also encouraged at CCHS, with a cross-curricular enrichment day every half term seeing students off timetable, working on an extended project or activity, often off site. Examples include year 7s teambuilding at Mersea Island; year 8s being shown how an enigma machine works at Bletchley Park (an old girl worked there during WW2); a Holocaust survivor giving a talk to year 11s; and year 10s visiting Cambridge.

The list of lunchtime and after-school clubs is long and well taken-up – every department makes a contribution. French film club, football, netball, musical theatre, hockey, cross-country, netball, junior choir, history society, henna club and debating (particularly big here) are just a fraction. Student-led societies for future doctors, lawyers and the like are also evident. Lunchtime is nearly an hour so plenty of time for a 30-40 minute activity and then food, though girls often combine to save time.

PE is compulsory all the way to the top – years 7-11s have two one-hour lessons a week and sixth formers do sports for one afternoon a fortnight, either in or outside the school grounds. At least one sporty club every lunchtime and every day after school including gymnastics, fencing, table tennis and trampolining, alongside the team games. Tennis, netball, hockey and athletics are particular strengths – collects trophies from national and district competitions, and many do less traditionally girly options including tag rugby, cricket and football. 'We get a lot of individual successes too – one girl recently reached international level in taekwondo, and another in pentathlon,' says head. All-weather hockey pitch and playing fields, plus refurbished swimming pool, although everyone agrees there's a desperate need for a sports hall. 'The gym was built for a school of 450 girls and we now have twice as many,' says the head.

A quarter of the school learns a musical instrument – the orchestras, choirs and ensembles are of a frighteningly high standard, with girls regularly reaching finals of competitions such as Music for Youth. A welcoming music block – packed with instruments galore (from drums to glockenspiel) – is home to two large classrooms, practice rooms and recording studio. 'At Christmas, all the year 8s recorded a version of Do They Know it's Christmas?' our guides told us, with great excitement. The performing arts block is a real asset with a large drama space – we saw girls doing mesmerising solo performances to their peers in here. Annual whole school performances alternate between more serious literary productions and fun musicals, such as Jesus Christ Superstar. 'You audition for the main parts, but anyone can be in the chorus,' a student explained. Art is also pursued with enthusiasm and amazing talent, with some gifted paintings on show throughout the school – although the two art rooms don't provide the space the girls really need.

CCF is available – run by King Edward VI Grammar School down the road, although we were surprised the two schools don't team up over more school activities (there is a disco, but apparently the girls tend to dance, while boys stand on the other side sipping coke). Long and commendable tradition of community service, with almost all sixth formers involved and girls forming strong bonds with local special schools and retirement homes, often giving up their free time to continue beyond the prescribed sessions. Links with a school in Uganda, which a group of sixth formers visits every two years to do building work and teach classes. Other regular trips and visits include Latin students to Bath, geography students to Wales, plus French, German and Italian exchanges, just to name a few.

Background and atmosphere: A traditional red-brick Edwardian grammar school on one of the main roads into the county town of Essex, which will bring back memories for any grammar school girl of the last century. Opened in 1907, it has remained largely unchanged since, save for some tacked-on additions and the impressive music centre, languages centre and performing arts block. Sixth formers have their own house – including a very pink common room downstairs, and quiet study area upstairs. A café has been set up to encourage girls to eat food cooked on site, and the school serves decent enough food – we enjoyed a lovely roast – although students told us 'the eating area is too small and can get a bit squashed.'

The atmosphere is, as you might expect, ordered, focused and disciplined, but it's also lively, uplifting and supportive – lots of smiles and laughter in lessons and at lunchtime when we visited, there was a great raucous in the main hall as the girls performed dances for the annual house karaoke competitions. 'We make sure girls get lots of opportunities to let their hair down,' explains the head.

Not a school for girls who can't keep up with a fast pace of learning – although students insist all personalities fit in, including the very shy. 'I remember one particular girl who wouldn't say boo to a goose when she started here – she went onto be a medic at Cambridge and is a great public speaker now. And that's the thing here – it doesn't matter if you arrive without confidence because that's the bit we will transform,' says head. Debating clubs, Model UN and an internal programme called 'Find Your Voice' all help.

Pastoral care, well-being and discipline: In a close-knit community of fewer than 900 girls – who feel grateful to be here – discipline is hardly an issue, 'although I'm tough when I need to be,' says the head. Girls showed us the green cards they have to carry about – with black marks given for infringements such as chewing gum or wearing too much make up. Three infringements equals an after-school detention, but not many get them. 'They're held once a week, and the maximum we get is half a dozen,' says the head.

Stress, however, is an issue for some. 'It's not necessarily the school. Many of the parents have very high expectations, as do the girls themselves – and there will be times when they find it all too much,' says the head. No wonder the pastoral programme has been heavily invested in during the last decade, with the girls we spoke to knowing what teachers they can turn to for support, and there's a visiting counsellor and nurse too. Peer mentoring has been trialled, but isn't really taken up. Head also points to their growing emphasis on close monitoring, confidence-building and occasionally making adjustments to individual curricula. 'We have to make sure that the girls enjoy being here and do well. They need to cope with being among very bright girls, so we sometimes have to work hard to build self-esteem,' says the head.

Unusually, both the head and the girls are adamant that bullying is not an issue. 'Of course some girls are nicer than others, but we watch them carefully and intervene where necessary,' says the head.

Pupils and parents: Hard working and very able girls come from supportive homes – although 'supportive' is perhaps too soft a word for some of the most demanding parents. 'Let them have some downtime!' the school has been known to bark at some who request ever more homework. Around half the girls are white British; there's also a high Indian contingent. The school is crystal clear on the characteristics the girls should leave the school with – articulate, principled, knowledgeable, enquiring, resilient, reflective and creative – and girls are encouraged to look for opportunities in areas where they are weaker. All pretty fitting descriptions for the girls we met.

Old girls worthy of particular note include the United Nations' first woman under-secretary general, the late Dame Margaret Anstee, Dragons' Den dragon Rachel Elnaugh, sculptor Catharni Stern, Bletchley Park's Mary Kenyon and BBC correspondent Emma-Jane Kirby.

Entrance: Admission is no longer by the CSSE 11+ exam, but instead by tests 'designed to measure comprehension, vocabulary, verbal reasoning, non-verbal reasoning and

C

numerical reasoning skills', prepared by Durham University's Centre for Evaluation and Monitoring, and intended to be tutor-proof ('I adamantly disagree with tutoring,' says head). Tests held in September, with initial results in October. Places are offered through the local authority on national offer day in March to the 150 girls who have performed best in the selection tests and not been offered a place at a higher preference school. A waiting list stays open all year. Occasional vacancies further up the school are filled by inviting all girls on the waiting list to sit a test ('to see where they are in their foundation subjects,' says the head). The result? More girls coming from the state sector (there are now less than a quarter from preps – much lower than previously), as well as from more deprived areas of Essex – and the ability range has also gone up. 'All this is as it should be – grammar schools exist to provide an education for the very brightest, whatever their background,' says the head.

Another new admission rule is that 80 per cent of the year 7 intake must now live within 12.5 miles of the school (which takes you up to the M11 and down to the M25). 'We were finding that some girls were travelling up to three hours a day,' says head.

Vacancies in the sixth form – of which there are always 30, plus extra to replace any girls that leave after their GCSEs – are readily filled. These girls need an average score of 6.4 in their best eight GCSEs (see school website for details on how to work this out), and at least an A in the subjects they want to study at A level (except in humanities, where you can get away with a B).

Exit: Generally, around a quarter are tempted away after GCSEs by mixed sixth forms. Vast majority who stay go on to higher education. In 2018, 10 to Oxbridge, plus 16 medics. Nottingham, Southampton, Durham, Exeter, Bristol, Warwick and London unis also popular. A wide range of subjects are studied, with popular ones including languages, sciences, engineering, economics and business.

Remarks: An intellectually stimulating environment that gives a flying start to the brightest of girls. There's room to let your hair down, which seems to lead to few instances of teenage rebellion – certainly within the school gates – but there can be pressure, meaning it's not for the faint-hearted.

The Cherwell School

Marston Ferry Road, Oxford, Oxfordshire OX2 7EE

Ages 11–18 **Pupils** 1,983 **Sixth form** 625

01865 558719
www.cherwell.oxon.sch.uk

Head: Since 2016, Chris Price BA PGCE (40s). A local boy, grew up and was schooled in Oxford then read politics and international relations at Warwick before heading to the Manchester Institute of Education for his PGCE. A rare example of a head who has progressed from within, he was appointed at Cherwell as an NQT in 1992 teaching history, and over the course of over 25 years has progressed through the ranks of school teacher to headmaster.

Moderately spoken with no sign of ego and no snappy soundbites or corporate patter up his sleeve. A quiet, effective operator who, in his own words, 'embodies the school', commanding huge respect from his (excellent and dynamic) senior leadership team as well as pupils and parents, who describe him as 'warm, present and encouraging' and 'very focused on the children – a teacher at heart'.

So, with 25 years under his belt, doesn't he feel a bit complacent? No chance, he assures us. The leadership team uniformly models the 'vibrant and exciting' environment that's 'constantly changing' and he describes himself as 'outward looking,' constantly visiting and learning from other schools.

A family man and former captain of Oxford Harlequins Rugby Club – alas, plays no more but now lives his sporting ambitions vicariously through his three children, all of whom attend local state schools.

Academic matters: Holding its position as one of the best state maintained secondaries in Oxfordshire, and state school of choice to the great and good of Oxford's academic and medical set, Cherwell's results belie its entirely mixed ability cohort. Although its size looks a little overwhelming on paper (year 7 comprises anything from 270 to 285 pupils), parents uniformly report that school 'does the primary to secondary transition really well', spending most of year 7 developing pupils' social skills and resilience. It's this sheer scale, too, that enables school to offer a broad ranging, albeit mainly traditional, curriculum, with pupils taking up to 12 GCSEs and able to choose almost any combination they like (no compulsory languages, humanities or sciences) when it comes to GCSE options, and even successfully lobby for courses to be run for small numbers, as one pupil we interviewed did with dance.

Citizenship GCSE taken by all in year 10 and study skills on offer as a non-exam subject to those in need of more support. 'Success for all' is school motto and key driver and this is delivered – for most if not absolutely all – in spades. 2018's GCSE results look more like those expected from at the very least a semi-selective cohort with 44 per cent graded A*-A/7-9 and 84 per cent of cohort achieving grades 9-4 in both English and maths. There's still a strength in science left as a legacy of school's former official specialism, and head says modern foreign languages are also notably successful (pupils take either German or Spanish in year 7 – school chooses which – and can add French in year 8). Pupils we interviewed chorused 'history' when we asked them which department stood out for them, with a smattering of 'English' thrown in for good measure. All subjects taught as mixed ability in KS3 other than maths, which is initially set from pupils' KS2 Sats scores in year 7.

Around 70 per cent stay on to sixth form to pursue purely academic courses, school having now phased out practical BTecs and NVQs. Those that head off at 16 generally choose the 'really excellent' City of Oxford College, 'which can do vocational courses far better than we ever could,' says head. With over 250 pupils each in years 12 and 13, attracted by the diversity of A level subjects, the sixth form is almost like a separate entity, but with the pastoral care offered by a school: 'they feel cared for because they are,' says head. Results are solid with 32 per cent of A levels in 2018 graded A*/A and 59 per cent A*-B, with outstanding results reported by maths, art, DT, English and history departments. All year 12s take the EPQ now – 'it's a great vehicle for academic development.'

'Clarity' is buzzword used by staff at all levels. School vocal on its major focus on pupil premium and SEND students and takes a proudly 'simple' (but, we are assured, not basic) approach in the classroom, with strictly 'no gimmicks'. 'We believe in doing less and doing it well,' a senior staff member told us and this pared back, 'knowledge first' approach clearly pays dividends with pupils at both ends of the academic spectrum, as demonstrated by well above average Progress 8 scores. Parents we spoke to concur that this approach is effective and didn't have any concerns about their 'average' child getting lost in the middle of the very gifted and the strugglers. Teachers aim to give students a 'rich academic vocabulary', for example not just teaching the set texts in English, but giving them colour by teaching about the historical period and political/ social landscape. Austerity measures in place when it comes to use of technology in the classroom. Not a flashy piece of kit in sight and it's good old-fashioned handwriting all the way when it comes to homework. 'We occasionally use iPads for an art project,' one staff member told us, 'but we know what works and there's no need to fix something that isn't broken'.

Large and busy learning support department known as The Base looks after the 13 per cent of student cohort on the SEND register. Two specialist resource bases, for hearing impairment and communication and interaction (autism), run within – and as an integral part of – the school and are filled by referrals from across the county. Pupils from both bases can attend mainstream classes with additional support as required and are supported right from the moment they begin to transition from primary. With a specialist in charge of inclusion, the bases 'contribute to the diverse culture,' according to head. Parents say school is 'very patient' with the behaviour of the most challenging pupils, with those who need them being allowed to use 'time out' cards when classes become overwhelming or use the Base as a 'safe place'. Parents say that on the occasions they have not been happy with provision, SENCo 'always listens'. The Base also operates as a go to centre for other pupils feeling generally overwhelmed or concerned and is lauded by their parents as a safe haven during the transition period. Good EAL for eg the children of overseas Oxford academics and, although previous reviews questioned the effectiveness of dyslexia support, the ingredients, including discrete groups taught by literacy specialists and the 'reading recovery' system – an intensive provision if pupils' reading ages are low – are all there.

Games, options, the arts: 'We're a very sporty school,' our pupil guides told us and the plethora of team photos adorning the walls in the South Site sports hall concur. There are fixtures for A to C teams and the spectrum covers all major sports including rugby and football for girls and boys, basketball, badminton and cheerleading, with training for all taking place after school. Not a finely tuned machine of a department – sometimes it's the pupils that pull together teams for matches and parents say pupils can be notified of a fixture last minute – but it all seems to work fine and is a clear defining element of the school. Facilities are multitudinous but very basic and mainly in dire need of some TLC: three gyms, hard tennis/ basketball courts, generous fields for such an urban school and, most surprisingly, smart games kit for all, which seems at odds in a school so resolutely uniform free. Also access to the nearby Ferry Leisure Centre, just a short walk away – although sadly not its pool.

Art, music and drama on curriculum for all year 7s although the latter two not especially popular with those we spoke to and reasonably low take up at GCSE. Extracurricular music, however, thrives and there is a multitude of choirs, bands and orchestras in which to participate and perform at local venues or the Christmas concert. Major biennial whole school production is usually a musical – recently Guys and Dolls – with everything from scenery and costumes to orchestra led by pupils. From year 8, pupils participate in a carousel of DT options including food technology, textiles, woodwork and graphic design, although not all available at GCSE. Extracurricular is mainly sport focused, with a few artsy options, drama and debating.

Background and atmosphere: Despite its attractive leafy environs, Cherwell's never going to win any beauty contests – especially given the local competition. A mainly low-rise collection of very tired buildings date back as far as 1963 when the school was founded. The head says 'space and infrastructure' are his greatest challenges and a multi-purpose area is top of his wish list, but whole school is in desperate need of a serious facelift. Parents, however, are relaxed: 'Yes, we could complain about the fabric of the school, but it's not the most important thing,' said one. Split over two sites on opposite sides of a main road; the South Site houses years 7 to 9 and has the homely feel of a large primary school. Through a frescoed underpass is the North Site for years 10 to 13: rambling, bustling with groups socialising in every available corner at break times. Pupils of both age groups appreciate this segregation: 'it's like the school grows up with you,' said one. Two aesthetic anomalies are the new (2017) garden on the South Site, a lovely, ergonomically designed space with an artificial lawn, colourful planting in raised beds and timber seating areas, and the smart sixth form block with its café, common room and quiet work spaces.

School has been non-uniform wearing for some 30 years, but ironically pupils seem less fashion conscious than most schools with strict dress codes – no need to rebel with skinny ties or too short skirts: it's an androgynous dress code of hoodies and jeans for all. Despite the casual clobber and scruffy buildings, the school has a purposeful feel and in addition is a leading light in the Oxfordshire Partnerships drive with active programmes to share expertise with other local schools and raise standards in primaries. It's also a leader in the Oxfordshire Teaching Schools Alliance, with the majority of trainees keen to be kept on permanently at the end of their training contract (although one parent described it as 'a really demanding place to teach'.)

It's all about wheels when it comes to keeping on the move, with vast majority of pupils travelling to and from school by bike and secure sheds bursting at the seams in the corner of every playground.

Pastoral care, well-being and discipline: Culture of school is 'palpably strong', according to head, in relation to staff:student relationships, which makes for a happy ship. Such is the extent of this that sixth formers reported 'missing school' in the holidays. There's a clear 'behaviour for learning' policy in place, comprising a simple consequences and rewards system, the latter resulting in Amazon vouchers which 'judging by our bill at the end of the academic year, really works,' says head. Consequences result in sliding scale of punishments from detentions to a day-long isolation. Pupils admit an element of disruption in classes 'depending on the teacher – some are better at crowd control than others', although this is reportedly constantly improving. Parents say that when they raise concerns about such issues, school is grateful for insight and 'deals with it within a matter of hours'. Annual parent forums are well attended and school is 'really open to taking questions', according to parents.

Students in real need of assistance when it comes to focus invited to join the Night Club where they can crack on with their studies outside of school hours under the watchful eye of a teacher plying them with pizza. Fab. Pupils totally clear on procedure in the event of bullying or unhappiness and although there's no house system, the pastoral hierarchy is well understood and includes trained student counsellors. Points of difference in relation to race, religion and sexuality very well tolerated – 'the lack of uniform probably helps', pupils thought. Sexuality and gender issues openly discussed (school has Stonewall status) and pupils are well educated about using 'kind language'. Pupils known to move to Cherwell from other schools for its culture of inclusivity, and hard as we looked there was no sign of the racial cliques so often found in multicultural schools – a glance around the dining hall saw pupils of all races and genders merrily chatting over their canteen fare: 'everyone finds their group', pupils told us. No smartphones allowed to be used in school for KS3 pupils. Gadget lovers needn't fear, though – there's a 'nerd corner' (their words, not ours) for keen gamers who can bring their DS into school and compete against each other thanks to the magic of Bluetooth. Old fashioned tactics working well, eg recent focus on readiness to learn, with pupils made to enter classrooms calmly and silently in single file and being reminded of the importance of eye contact and attention to detail in routines.

Pupils and parents: Diversity in evidence at every turn as students buzz around school, and although the cohort is largely (65 to 70 per cent) middle class, with parents working at the university, hospitals, NGOs and the professions, school also serves some of Oxford's most vulnerable families and it's all in a day's work to integrate pupils arriving from overseas. Parents report 'a significant number of issues caused by colourful characters,' but in the main see this as a positive learning experience: 'my daughter is receiving as much of an education in keeping good relationships across the full social and academic spectrum as she is in the academic subjects,' said one. And the 'remarkable thing' is that friendships seem to cross all these boundaries too.

Well known old Cherwellians include model Yasmin le Bon, professional footballers Canice Carroll and Miles Welch-Hayes (both formerly Oxford United) and novelists Rachel Seiffert and Will Wiles.

Entrance: Non-selective. Oversubsubscribed from within catchment and around a dozen local feeder primaries, apart from the two resource bases which take students with EHC plans or by referral. Sixth form attracts students from local state and, surprisingly, independent schools looking for a step closer to uni (up to 30 some years migrate from schools including Abingdon, Headington Girls, Oxford High and Magdalen College). Four 6s and four 4s minimum entry requirement to enter sixth form.

Exit: About 65 per cent stay on to the sixth form. Around half of those to Russell Group, with 14 to Oxbridge in 2018. Smaller numbers to employment, apprenticeships and art college.

Remarks: 'Truly comprehensive and proudly so,' says head – and to us this sums up Cherwell. Yes, the academics are good but crucially, in the words of one parent, 'Cherwell students really get an education in what society is actually like.' Coupled with a dynamic academic faculty, more sporting and extracurricular opportunities than they have time for, and an open minded and supportive student cohort, it's definitely one for the list.

Chesham Grammar School

63

White Hill, Chesham, Buckinghamshire HP5 1BA

Ages 11–18 **Pupils** 1,277 **Sixth form** 371

01494 782854
www.cheshamgrammar.org

Head: Since 2015, Annmarie McNaney BA PGCE (50s). Educated in Coventry and Bristol (theology and sociology). Having sworn never to follow her mother's footsteps into teaching, she nonetheless stayed in Bristol to do a PGCE 'just to fall back on.' Bitten hard by the bug the first time she stepped into a classroom and turned down graduate traineeships with the NHS and M&S to take up first teaching post at Backwell School – 'a fantastic place to cut my teeth' – where she was promoted to assistant head of sixth form.

Joined CGS 20 years ago to the day we visited, as head of sixth form – a job she planned to do 'for five years'. Promotion to assistant head and then deputy head followed. Part of team that moved the school from a satisfactory Ofsted rating in 2005, via good in 2009 to outstanding in 2014. 'Expectations weren't high enough – but we could all see the potential'.

What next? 'Outstanding doesn't mean perfect,' she says. 'Now we need to move the school from outstanding to exceptional – it's not just about ticking Ofsted boxes.' Down to earth and popular with pupils and parents (her window ledge is stacked with thank you cards from departing year 13s – one of whom writes she hopes to send her children to CGS), still teaches critical thinking to year 7 and A level sociology – says 'I'll always be a teacher first'.

Lives in Berkhamsted with husband and two sons, one at CGS ('I'm constantly asking myself how I perceive things as a parent, not just as head,' she says) and the other at a local prep. Loves France and watching her boys play sport.

Academic matters: Competition's stiff on the academic front in grammar school country and with its tech college past, school has had to work hard to shake off its 'also ran' status. What's crystal clear, though, is that complacency is not a word in Chesham's vocabulary and it's steadily inching up the academic league tables, sitting comfortably now within the top 100 state schools. 'Once upon a time the school was happy with 44 per cent of GCSEs at A or A*,' says head, 'but now we want the main point of difference between us and our competitors to be whether parents want single sex or co-ed'.

And, thanks to a shift in focus 'from teaching to learning', things are moving forward apace, with an impressive 80 per cent of GCSEs graded A*-A/9-7 in 2018. History, geography, English and maths top performers with social sciences doing 'fantastically well' at A level. Similarly solid 2018 A level results: 42 per cent A*/A, 74 per cent A*-B. Ten GCSEs the norm, with majority taking three A levels, plus around 30 taking the EPQ.

Broad curriculum with focus on a mix of traditional subjects (hoorah for the recent reintroduction of Latin) plus others including photography, politics, sociology and psychology at A level plus, unusually, economics at GCSE as well as at A level. All take French and Latin in year 7 plus either German or Spanish in year 8. Setting in year 8 for maths only. Triple science for all but a few at GCSE. The onerously named 'more able and talented programme', which uses pupil data and teacher recommendation to identify potential superstars, aims to provide activities to benefit not just the top few but the whole cohort. Initiatives run across all year groups, from aspiration days – where former pupils share careers advice with year 7s – to Elevate sessions – six hours of training on exam preparation and technique by external speakers during years 12 and 13.

Superb SENCo supports pupils needing additional help – several with EHC plans and approximately 100 on SEN register, mainly due to dyslexia or processing issues. Also equipped to work with children with ASD and because of the broadly flat site, school's a feasible option for pupils with physical disabilities. Aim is to keep pupils in the classroom, but one-to-one and small group work provided when necessary.

Games, options, the arts: It's rugby, football and cricket for boys and girls luck out with the same three on their sporting curriculum, plus rounders and netball, with games compulsory to year 12. There are also options for basketball, athletics, lacrosse and tennis plus zumba, which takes place at the community leisure centre that conveniently opens onto school grounds, providing school with its gym and sports hall facility. Sport for all ethos seems genuine – our guide assured us that sports staff were 'very inclusive' and that trials for teams took place each term – no shoo-ins. Limited fixtures, although school puts out A and B teams for most matches and a C team wherever possible: 'you're more likely to get a match if you turn up to training religiously than if you're talented but not committed', pupils told us. Parents too seemed satisfied that their keen but average sportsmen and women were getting a fair bite of the cherry.

Sports staff highly focused on excellence and there's plenty of silverware in the school trophy cabinet to prove it, despite the fact that there are relatively few pupils to make up teams due to co-ed factor. Recently year 9 were district basketball winners; year 10 smashed the County Cup basketball finals to a degree where they stopped keeping score; the U13 girls' footie team won the county championships and school has held the Chiltern District Athletics Championships title since 2012.

Music reported by parents to be 'amazing' with performances aplenty (major productions Easter and Christmas), plus chances for everyone to get involved with a general choir and 'men's choir' (we assume for tenors), orchestra and house performing arts, encompassing drama, choir, solo performances and musical theatre. Perhaps not the broad spread of groups and ensembles found in some schools but we are told that the standard is 'exceptional'. Stand-alone music block should be finished in 2019. Sixth form produces an all-school annual play, recently The Tempest, run with parallel casts to increase the options for participation. Drama taught in a superb and very well-equipped studio space.

Fabulous art department run by 'inspirational' departmental head according to our guide. We were blown away by the standard of A level work on show in the art mezzanine – and, although there's plenty of IT in evidence around the school, the good old DT labs still survive in their original form: saws and lathes aplenty and subjects include food technology, engineering, textiles, electronics, product design and systems control.

Loads of extracurricular for keen participants in every mainstream sport from badminton to riding (school owns five ponies) – and academic help sessions, societies and catch-ups for just about every subject going. Other options are limited (although mindfulness about to be introduced) and occasional grumbles from parents that clubs are cancelled 'a bit too often'. Plenty of trips and tours, both curriculum linked and for enrichment. World Challenge has taken students to Madagascar, Cambodia and Czech Republic in recent years. Also link schools in Ghana and China, exchanges to Italy, France and Germany, not forgetting departmental trips to eg USA (politics), Vietnam (history) Iceland (geography) and Netherlands (art).

Background and atmosphere: What's in a name? Rather a lot, apparently. Founded in 1947 as the all boys' Chesham Technical School, later becoming Chesham Technical High School, then Chesham High School when it went co-ed in the 1970s. Finally cemented place as a credible player in the south Bucks grammar school scene with yet another – its final – change of name in 2010. Buildings wouldn't win any architectural awards – and decorators clearly had a job lot of drab, grey paint to use up – but the collection of low rise, red-brick buildings hang together as a functional whole, there's building work going on to extend the maths block, and school doesn't have the overpopulated, cramped feel of many local grammars. The jewel in the crown is the wonderfully bright and modern sixth form centre with its floor to ceiling architectural glazing and fair trade coffee shop and snack bar. Canteen also gets the thumbs up: an appealing area, designed by students as another modern, social space offering hot food and healthy salads as well as all the usual pizzas and sandwiches.

Pastoral care, well-being and discipline: Head describes school's pastoral ethos as 'unique' and parents generally concur. Bullying – even 'friendship issues' – almost unheard of, as are exclusions, and heavy handed discipline rarely required. Vertical tutor groups enable pupils to build relationships with others from all year groups, meeting daily for 20 minutes to catch up on timetable changes and forthcoming exams, share revision tips and achievements, as well as home-made cakes and Haribos. Everyone from year 7 upwards gets a voice and the youngest tutees speak confidently in front of the most senior. Pupils uniformly clear that they can 'be who they want to be' and head reports that tolerance of all differences and preferences is extremely high, with 'nothing considered a big deal by the end of year 7'. Plenty of leadership opportunities falling out of strong house system – heads of house, senior prefects, learning leaders, and head boy and girl elected by peers and teachers.

Pupils and parents: Around 15-20 per cent from local independents, mainly Chesham Prep, The Beacon, Berkhamsted Prep and Heatherton House, with the majority from a host of state primaries. Increasingly popular for its nurturing, less pressurised vibe than the Challoner's schools. Ethnic mix reflects local community with around 15 per cent mainly of second or third generation Indian origin. Pupils we met were perfect ambassadors for school – quietly confident, understatedly charming and not remotely precocious. One mother we spoke to had recently hosted a party for 80 CGS sixth formers and couldn't express strongly enough how well behaved and at ease they were with one another.

Entrance: Buckinghamshire Transfer Test in early September of year 6 (register during May/June of year 5). CGS doesn't fill from catchment most years so hopefuls from across the Bucks/Herts borders usually find themselves in luck on allocation day, travelling on a fleet of coaches from Berkhamsted, Hemel Hempstead, Tring and Bovingdon plus the Chalfonts and Gerrards Cross. Ones and twos from as far afield as Harrow via the Metropolitan line.

Around fifty additional places in year 12 makes for a buzzing sixth form of around 400 pupils. Some 100 applicants for these, from a variety of state schools and small – mainly single sex – independents (regular applicants from Thorpe House, Claire's Court, Piper's Corner). An average of eight grade 6s required at GCSE.

Exit: Around 85 per cent stay on for sixth form. Vast majority to higher education, around two-thirds to Russell Group (Birmingham, Bristol and Nottingham all popular). 'Several' to study medicine and veterinary science and five to Oxbridge in 2018. Applications supported by a dedicated team, praised by pupils and parents. Small handful to degree apprenticeship programmes with eg PwC, Deloitte, Dyson, again well supported with their applications by school.

Remarks: In the south Bucks microcosm of pushy parents, competitive children and a focus on academic excellence at any cost, here you will also find an overwhelmingly kind, nurturing and in many ways relaxed school, coupled with a clear focus on excellence and getting pupils to achieve their very best. Steadily climbing the local academic ladder without having to jeopardise its pupils' happiness – in the words of one parent: 'I decided I wanted my daughter to come out of school with her mental health intact. That's why we chose Chesham.'

C

Chigwell Junior School

Linked with Chigwell School

64

High Road, Chigwell, Essex IG7 6QF

Ages 4–13 **Pupils** 389 C of E

Fees: £13,485 – £17,985 pa

020 8501 5721
www.chigwell-school.org

Head: Since 2016, Andrew Stubbs BA PGCE, previously deputy head of junior school, who joined the school in 2005. History degree from Sheffield.

Head of pre-prep is Evelyn Gibbs PA, PARICS, PGCE. Previously acting head in St Mary's Catholic Primary School, Chingford. Did her degree in history, then became a chartered surveyor, retraining as a teacher, after which she worked in the state sector, teaching year 6s and under, before moving into educational leadership. A friendly and softly-spoken woman, she doesn't have an obvious air of leadership, but make no mistake – she is largely responsible for the pre-prep having hit the ground running and staff, pupils and parents praise her for achieving the 'perfect balance of making the children feel nurtured, whilst also getting them academically ready for the junior school.' Lives locally with her husband, and has two grown-up children.

Entrance: Competition is fierce. For entry into the pre-prep at 4, around 140 applicants for the 40 places, with young candidates evaluated via an assessment based on the EYFS curriculum and is primarily play based. 'They come from around 26 nurseries,' says Mrs Gibbs. Meanwhile, external entry for 7-year-olds to the junior school sees eight times as many applicants as places, with all applicants going through an assessment, interview, classroom experience and report from their previous school. By 11 years old, there are nearly 10 times as many applicants for the 40 new places in year 7, weeded out by an exam and interviews. About 10 academic and music scholarships offered and a growing number of means-tested bursaries also available.

Exit: Most parents send their children here hoping they won't leave until after sixth form, and indeed only a handful choose to send their child to another junior or secondary school, though all are now reassessed at 11.

Remarks: Less than a stone's throw from the senior school, and set on the main school site, the junior school is integral to the Chigwell community and adds to the all-pervading family feel. Its educational philosophy, academic and pastoral structures are the same as those in the senior school, supporting the school's aim to 'provide a consistent approach to education throughout the child's school career'. Plenty of joint activities bring juniors and seniors together, easing the passage through the school, and some teaching staff and major facilities are shared, including the dining hall and vast sports facilities, plus the impressive art, music and drama departments. That's not to say the junior school doesn't have good facilities of its own, however, including a dedicated playground, plenty of airy and modern classrooms, ICT lab and a spacious library.

'Despite pre-prep being separate, Mrs Gibbs works very hard to make sure it is part of the bigger school, bringing juniors over to read to the children, organising joint assemblies and events and running a buddy-system, just to name a few initiatives,' added one parent. This pre-prep, which takes 4 to 7-year-olds, is set in a stunning, state-of-the-art, purpose built building a few minutes' walk from the junior school – more of which later.

Back in the junior school, expect academic rigour at the core, so that children leave well-equipped at 13 to go into the senior school, but with an emphasis on fun in learning, with interactive, interesting lessons by well-qualified teachers that the pupils describe as 'firm but fair'. Enrichment includes the likes of day trips, visitors running workshops, presentations and taking part in regional and national competitions, whilst clubs range from animation and astronomy to debating, gardening clubs and BBC School reporting – plus all the usual academic and sporting clubs you'd expect. Plenty of opportunities to take part in activities in partnership with the seniors, and there are visiting speakers for year 6s and over. 'We want children to seize opportunities and really find and develop their interests.' This means that whilst the school day starts at 8.20am, with a staggered finish time from 3.05 to 4pm, many end up staying on – and there's also after-school care until 6pm for an extra cost (and a breakfast facility from 8am). 'Literally, whatever you're interested in, there's a club,' said one pupil, although one parent pointed out the clubs can be a victim of their own success, with disappointment felt due to many of them inevitably clashing. Plenty of school trips, mainly day trips into London, but some residentials further up the school.

Follows national curriculum. Languages strong, with French from pre-prep right through, and Latin from year 7; pupils are offered a choice of either German or Spanish from year 7. Mandarin offered as extracurricular. Setting in maths from year 5 and French from year 7. Pupils taught mainly by their form teachers in year 3, but they have a growing amount of specialist teaching as they move up the juniors, and all lessons are with subject specialist teachers from year 7. 'If you need an extra session with the teacher, that's always fine,' said one pupil. Homework only given 'if it has a clear purpose and links with learning,' with a maximum of one hour a night.

Sport is strong, with pupils fortunate to share the 100 acres of playing fields of the senior school, including Astroturf, well kept courts with all-weather nets, outdoor swimming pool, as well as rather less fancy indoor facilities, which are steadily being improved. Boys mainly play football, hockey and cricket, whilst girls play netball, hockey and rounders, along with some cricket and football in the summer. Other sports on offer include swimming, futsal and tennis. School does well in competitions, with the U11 football team reaching national finals for independent schools, and regular appearances from teams across all sports at regional finals.

Weekly music lessons for all up to year 8 and every other pupil learns an instrument, making for an impressive sounding 40-strong junior school orchestra, which regularly performs concerts. Year group concerts for everyone else. The Primary School Music Festival is a big event here, in which over 100 pupils learn three pieces to participate.

Drama facilities are outstanding, with the state-of-the art drama centre boasting a foyer big enough for pre-theatre drinks receptions; 170-seat theatre designed for use by the whole school community; green room; rehearsal and teaching spaces; and dressing rooms. All pupils have weekly drama lessons up to year 8, with a biannual play performed to parents, with cast of over 100. Drama club particularly popular and around 100 pupils take LAMDA, with 100 per cent pass rate, and plenty of distinctions.

Art and DT are of a high standard, with both visiting artists and creative teaching staff helping pupils develop their skills and individual flair, with some extremely skilful work displayed around the school.

Pastoral care is taken seriously here, with each form tutor knowing their pupils well. School counsellor also available, and there's lots of regular contact with parents, who know they can email any time. The junior school has its own house system, with house points and competitions, while opportunities for leadership include heads of house, prefects, librarians and catering committee. House points aside, pupils' stand-out behaviour and work is also rewarded via Chigwellian of the Year award and a golden time system. Meanwhile, bad behaviour (mostly forgotten homework and escalating misbehaviour) results in lunchtime detentions. 'We like discipline, but it's more a case of high expectations than lots of rules.' Temporary exclusions have happened (for example, for misuse of social media), but no permanent exclusions recently. A culture of kindness – plus a behaviour log which tracks any emerging patterns – helps prevent bullying. School council meets fortnightly.

Over in the pre-prep, which is located behind a coded gate, life is rather more lively, as you might imagine. But the extremely well-thought-of head keeps the 40 pupils in each of the three years (two forms in each) in check in a manner that the rest of the teaching staff mirror – that is, never shouting and with a nurturing and soothing manner, but with clear boundaries and expectations. 'I love coming to school. It's nearly as good as being at home,' one pupil said. The building itself is spectacular, both inside and out, with a large welcoming foyer. Even the toilets are beautifully decorated, with a sense of fun at the core. Some use of the main school, including the chapel and swimming pool. The pre-prep curriculum is creative, including forest school type events, and highly practical. French from reception, an emphasis on art and drama and two hours of sport every week, including by specialist coaches. Seventeen extracurricular clubs ranging from computers to ballet, with 80 per cent of pupils staying on after school every week. Enrichment includes workshops and visits, ranging from animal workshops to Indian dance sessions, and lots of trips to the likes of Bethnal Green Museum of Childhood and the National Maritime Museum.

SEN provision across both pre-prep and junior schools involves one full-time SENCo on hand to help children cope with the academic pace here. Dyslexia is screened for on entry, and any necessary mechanisms in place for this and any other issues, such as ADHD, autism or dyspraxia (although none with an EHC plan when we visited). TAs help too, with most help classroom based. Plenty of provision for gifted and talented, both in the classroom, and via (for juniors) literary or science workshops, links with the senior school and trips open to the Scholars' Group to places like the Royal Courts of Justice and Royal Observatory. For pre-preps, extra provision is regularly provided for any speech issues.

Pupils mostly wealthy and generally hail from a five mile radius, with a few starting to come in from east London, and many are the offspring of Old Chigwellians. 'The reason most of us want a slice of the Chigwellian cake isn't just it's the academic excellence, but the outstanding personal development,' said one parent.

Feeling cheerful and nurtured really matters here and the creative displays and smiling faces prove it. Once you get through to juniors, though, it's not for the fainthearted, but there's plenty of monitoring and help to make sure nobody gets left behind – there are even lessons on how to think constructively. This is a school where minds can and do grow in the widest sense possible and it all happens in a warm atmosphere where a happy mix of ages and cultures work together harmoniously and develop a genuine love of learning.

Chigwell School

Linked with Chigwell Junior School

High Road, Chigwell, Essex IG7 6QF

Ages 13–18 **Pupils** 440 **Sixth form** 178 **Boarders** 21 full C of E

Fees: Day £17,985; Boarding £30,885 pa

020 8501 5700
www.chigwell-school.org

Headmaster: Since 2007, Mr Michael Punt MA MSc PGCE (40s), a physicist who lives on site with his wife Gill and their three sons, all of whom attend the school – a fact that many parents say 'keeps him in tune with pupils' and parents' experiences of Chigwell.' His calm and positive influence is palpable throughout the school, with parents describing him as 'approachable,' 'well-liked' and 'respected.' In fact, many were swayed against the local competition purely on the basis of meeting him. 'He doesn't just talk at you in some grand hall – he chats with you in a relaxed way and seems to know exactly what you want to know,' said one.

Pupils also speak enthusiastically about him. 'He knows every one of us, as well as taking an interest in us,' one pupil told us. Not for him a chief executive type headship, but rather a personal touch that's helped by the size of the school and the fact that he and colleagues interview every child that comes here. Mainly, though, it seems to be down to his hands-on approach – he teaches pupils, does a lot of mock interviews and is often seen around the school. The week before our visit, he'd had all the prefects round for a meal and he eats regularly with the boarders.

Having grown up in nearby Brentwood, he did his degree at Oxford and his masters at Imperial, then worked at St Dunstan's College as a physics teacher, working his way up to head of year and head of physics, after which he did a stint at The Perse School, Cambridge, as deputy head (academic) where he continued to climb the ranks until moving to Chigwell.

Academic matters: Excellent results, which have risen steadily – 73 per cent of GCSE grades were A*-A/9-7 in 2018. Head puts this down to pupils' positive and conscientious attitude to learning and an excellent relationship with teachers, both points which the latest ISI inspection praised. ' 'I was amazed when my son emailed teachers about his essay during half term and got detailed feedback the same day, but that's how it is here,' said a parent. The tone of the communication seems to be spot on, too. 'In many schools, it's either too matey or terribly stand-offish, but they seem to have got the balance just right here,' said one parent. Lessons interactive and busy, with plenty of IT embedded across all subjects – and a pilot of tablet-embedded learning going on in years 9 and 12 when we visited. 'We'll see how it goes and may well expand it in future,' says head.

Low turnover of teaching staff, who must be willing to teach beyond their subject and get involved in extracurricular activity. 'It's not unusual to see maths staff getting stuck into games or English teachers helping to run chess clubs here,' says the head. 'It's the Chigwell way, this family-type approach.' Head regularly observes all teaching staff and has implemented a rigorous structure that ensures constant reflection and sharing of good practice.

On entry, four classes of 22 maximum, although class sizes drop considerably at GCSE level and to around a dozen at A level. Latin and French taught to all year 7s, and all try German and Spanish in year 8. In year 9, all pupils continue French and select one or more of the other three languages, with all pupils doing at least one modern language for GCSE. Mandarin also taught as extracurricular from junior school upwards. Setting in French and maths from year 7 and some in German from year 9. English and sciences set from year 10. Regular testing means there can be movement between sets to start with, although this is uncommon later on. Homework taken seriously, although it's never set for the following day.

At GCSE, all students take one modern language and the vast majority do the three sciences. Other popular options include geography, history, RE, with a strong interest also seen in other languages, drama, DT and music. 'We don't have option blocks – we make the timetable work around the pupils' choices,' says head, who adds that there are no early GCSEs taken here, although the top maths set in year 11 takes additional maths.

Wide choice of subjects at A levels. Economics, maths, sciences, geography and English are strong, but psychology, drama and DT are on the rise too, enforcing Chigwell's reputation as a place for the all-rounder. In 2018, 81 per cent A*-B and 49 per cent A*/A at A level.

Plenty of extension opportunities, including EPQ and HPQ (latter at GCSE level), essay competitions and Olympiads. Enrichment programme impressive and includes subject-specific groups, such as law groups, medics' groups, social sciences groups etc. University preparation stunningly good, with guidance for UCAS applications starting in the February of the lower sixth, with plenty of targeted guidance and support, and mock interviews aplenty.

Junior school pupils screened on entry for SEN, with further testing in the senior school. Learning support provided throughout the school as necessary either inside or outside the classroom. Not a school for severe learning disabilities, however, with only one statemented when we visited.

Games, options, the arts: Mass participation in sport does what it says on the tin here, with the possible exception of football, which one parent told us is all about the A team. Core boys' sports include football (first term), hockey (second term) and cricket and athletics (third term). For girls, it's hockey (first term), netball (send term) and rounders and athletics (third term), along with some football and cricket also in the summer term. Other sports include golf (played at nearby club), swimming, basketball and badminton. School punches above its weight in competitions, regularly getting through to regional finals, along with national finals for football and hockey.

Outdoor facilities are vast, with 100 acres of playing fields, including Astroturf, surrounding this small school, and indoor facilities are being steadily improved through an ambitious development plan. Pupils particularly keen to have an indoor pool, rather than just the small outdoor pool they currently have, and many want to see the unfancy sports centre updated – both projects under consideration.

The drama centre is an eye-catching red-brick building with professional facilities, including a foyer big enough for pre-theatre drinks receptions. All children use it for weekly drama up until the end of year 9 and it's also a popular GSCE option, with around a dozen taking drama at A level with great success. Related subject areas, such as theatre make-up and costume design, also taken seriously here, and the centre is used for public speaking, debating and LAMDA. Numerous productions. 'It would be rare to find a child who isn't somehow involved in drama,' says the head.

Music very inclusive, with every other pupil learning an instrument (over 300 lessons per week from 23 visiting music teachers), some of whom play to incredibly high standards (usually one a year to Oxbridge as a choral music scholar). Plenty of opportunities to perform in ensembles, with a wide range of musical tastes catered from swing bands to string bands, as well as rock and pop. The chapel choir, an elite choir for 40 odd students, performs regularly in the likes of Westminster Abbey, Canterbury Cathedral and Yorkminster, and there are plenty of other choirs too. 'Every aspect of music is amazing here, from the singing right through to every instrument you can think of, along with many you didn't even know existed,' said one parent.

Art and DT work closely together in the spacious and hi-tech facilities, with graphics offered as a GCSE option and many pupils going onto study architecture and fine art when they leave. Phenomenally good artwork displayed throughout the school, much of it in 3D.

Huge choice of extracurricular activities, from D of E and scouts to art exhibitions and the inspiring and thought-provoking talks on everything from evolution to restorative justice for schools. 'I haven't had a free afternoon in the last three years – but in a good way,' laughed one student. A seemingly infinite amount of trips, including French and Spanish homestays, hockey tour to South Africa, scout trip to Switzerland, annual ski trip to France, along with smaller scale trips including activity weekends in the likes of Wales and the Lake District. 'We are conscious that there is a broad mix of wealth and make sure we do not offer all five star trips,' says head.

Boarding: Sixth-form only boarders, of whom there are 30 living across four equal-sized boarding houses, either on the school site or just across the road. Hailing from around 16 countries – mostly central and Eastern Europe and China – the boarders are almost all international, and no two boarders who share a language share a room. 'The boarders help give the school a homely feel,' reported one student.

Boarding houses are more inviting than institutional. Rooms mostly twin, although the odd one has three beds, and boarders told us 'there's a good balance between houseparents letting you get on with it, and providing clear boundaries.' 'In our house, the parents have children aged 4 and 6 and we always love hanging out with them,' said one student. Curfews are 10.30pm on weekdays; 11.30pm at weekends. Daily study time between 7-9pm during weekdays – 'Even if you don't have work to do, you have to respect that others have and be quiet,' one boarder told us.

No shortage of events – the week we visited, they'd just had Divali weekend celebrations and a film night – which day pupils also join in, but boarders welcome the opportunity to be allowed to be self-reliant too. Boarders told us they'd formed close friendships with both other boarders and day pupils and already felt sad about the prospect of leaving the school.

Background and atmosphere: Founded in 1629 by the Reverend Samuel Harsnett, the local vicar, who became Archbishop of York and Chancellor of Cambridge University. Today the original red-brick schoolhouse, which is located on the approach road to the historic high street, forms the centrepiece to this pretty village of neat buildings, punctuated by gardens, blooms and trees. The surrounding playing fields stretch towards Epping Forest and give a rural aspect to the school and some lovely views from the windows of the attractive, low-rise teaching blocks. Buildings all kept up to date, with sixth form centre, dining hall extension, new sports hall and indoor swimming pool next on the agenda.

Of particular note is the 1920s chapel, which was built in tribute to fallen alumni and is a mainstay of life here. Pupils usually attend at least once a week for a service (and another weekly service at the local church).

All have lunch in the Harry Potter-esque dining hall (where teachers eat on the stage) and students can have tea at 4pm for no extra cost, as well as breakfast, for which they can bring parents and siblings. 'Every Thursday, our whole family has breakfast here – we love it,' said one parent. Food is plentiful and very good (we tried it). The uniform is smart and sober – kilts or plain trousers with a navy blazer, though the sixth formers wear office attire.

No need for intrusive bells here to mark the change of lessons, with pupils making their way around the school in an ordered fashion, and newbies of any age wear a plain tie so they can be spotted and helped when in need. 'This is a harmonious school, with really lovely young people who, in the majority of cases, you'd be proud to have as your own children,' says the head. Indeed, 'happy' was a word used a lot by the pupils we talked to, with several referring to it as one big family. No wonder old Chigwellians feel such a sense of loyalty, with growing numbers willing to come into do talks, mock interviews and offer work experience.

School council meets regularly, but achieves little more than the usual increase in number of water fountains. There's a strong charitable culture.

Pastoral care, well-being and discipline: The transition from junior to senior school is gentle, with parents praising the 'seamless process.' A strong four-house system, and staff who 'really know their pupils', according to the head, mean students are comfortable in the knowledge that they are being 'looked out for'. 'There are lots of personalities among the teachers here, but we all have someone we know we could speak to – a teacher that really stands out for us,' said one pupil, with many of the younger pupils talking about how friendly the older ones are. A school counsellor is employed for two days a week.

Discipline system highly structured, with detentions the most common sanctions, typically for late homework, missing chapel and being late. 'They're not given out willy nilly, so you take it seriously when you get one,' said one pupil. 'The pupils aren't saintly, and they've got a twinkle in their eye, but they're also hard working and really nice. We don't have many behavioural problems,' says the head. Current head has only made one permanent exclusion, although occasionally there are temporary ones, for instances such as smoking and repeated misbehaviour. Bullying rare, with pupils pointing out the 'confide' button on every school computer, where you can report issues anonymously at any time, or talk to a staff member confidentially.

Pupils and parents: This leafy suburb is spoilt for choice education-wise, with several good fee-paying schools on the doorstep and some of the best grammars in the country a short hop on the train away. Even Old Chigwellians admit to investigating the competition before signing up their offspring, but the school still wins people over with its ability to develop not just academic success, but confident, well-rounded people. 'One of the things that swung it for me was the way pupils talk to adults in a sophisticated way, but not without respect,' said one.

The parents – around two-thirds of whom are middle-class white British, with the remaining third mostly British Asian – praise the sense of community. 'My children have always said they felt they belong to something here – so much so that my daughter felt a real sense of loss when she left, and the same can be said for many parents,' said one. Most live within a five mile radius, although there's a growth in the number coming in from East London. Mainly affluent, although not exclusively rich kids and Landrover-driving parents. Lots of socialising – breakfast get-togethers and afternoon teas etc, as well as the programme of social events put on by the Friends of Chigwell PA.

Girls and boys attend in equal numbers. We found them relaxed, confident, articulate and witty. Five school minibuses available for pupils, with others using public transport, notably the tube or bus, whilst many get dropped off by car.

The list of distinguished alumni includes William Penn, Sir Arthur Grimble, Sir Austin Bradford Hill, Sir Richard Dales, Col Bob Stewart and Sir Bernard Williams.

Entrance: Most junior school pupils move up to the senior school, forming about half of the year 7 entry, with the other half from a wide variety of local prep and primaries. 'It's very welcoming, so my children took to it like a duck to water, despite not coming from the junior school,' said one parent. Around 300 apply for these 40-odd places; assessment by interview (separate ones for pupils and parents), and English, maths and verbal reasoning papers. Small number of vacancies at 13 (English, maths and a modern foreign language exam). At 16, those moving up within the school are joined by around 10 local entrants as well as around 14 overseas boarders. Entrants to the sixth form are expected to have achieved at least four A/7s and two B/6s in six GCSE subjects and A*-A/9-7 in their A level choices.

Exit: Hardly any post-16 leavers (usually around 10 per cent) and 95 per cent of those who leave after sixth form move on to a degree course at university, or music and other specialist colleges. In 2018, four to study medicine, four to Oxbridge and one to Harvard; some 70 per cent to Russell Group universities, notably Exeter, Nottingham, Bristol, Leeds and LSE. Popular degree subjects include economics, English and humanities.

Money matters: Academic scholarships available at 11 and 13 years; scholarships for art, drama and music offered at 16. Increasing number of means-tested bursaries available. 'I visit every family we are considering for bursaries,' says the head.

Remarks: A happy, nurturing and busy school with a genuinely family feel and an emphasis on creating caring all-rounders. Academically, pupils are put through their paces, but it all seems to be done in such a civilised and pleasant manner that you're far more likely to hear pupils talk about opportunities and prospects than pressure and stress. 'Anyone that wants to do well will do well here,' said one student, 'and I can't think of a nicer place to succeed.'

Christ Church Cathedral School

3 Brewer Street, Oxford, Oxfordshire OX1 1QW

Ages 3–13 **Pupils** 150 **Boarders** 20 cathedral choristers (from year 4)
C of E

Fees: Day £7,689 – £16,569; Boarding choristers £10,458 – £11,559 pa

01865 242561
www.cccs.org.uk

Headmaster: Since 2014, Richard Murray BA MA PGCE. Educated at Bradfield College – a 'profoundly inspiring' experience which sparked his realisation that teaching was 'one of the most important things a person could do' – and Durham (English, history and philosophy). PGCE from Magdalene College Cambridge. Arrived at Christ Church after a 14-year stint at Teddies (10 as housemaster) to find a school with a 'lovely, warm atmosphere' – a palpable feeling that he has grasped and built upon. Staff and parents agree that 'kindness has come to the fore and filtered down the school' under his leadership. Has raised school's profile, as well as the aspirations of the senior pupils, and built academic focus and rigour to create 'a serious prep school'. Describes himself as a 'choral music junkie', just one of his cultural addictions; the other is reading (a passion evidently shared by the whole school).

Married with three sons; one at Magdalen College School, one off to Harrow where Mr Murray's wife teaches classics, and another at Orley Farm School.

Entrance: Majority of day boys fairly local and enter from nursery or reception in a steady stream until year 3. A handful of girls in nursery. Assessment by participation in class for younger boys and academic tests for the older years. Cathedral choristers often (although not always) come from further afield and generally join in year 4, frequently having participated in one of school's 'chorister for a day' events and been bitten by the bug. From there they are required to pass a voice trial and academic assessment. One parent made the point that even with the necessary skill set in hand, it is imperative for cathedral choristers to be 'kind, generous, easy going and from a stable family background' due to the pressures of being part of such a small, hard-working boarding community ('it can have a negative tidal wave effect if not'). Full boarding for 'made up' cathedral choristers compulsory from year 5. Cathedral covers generous portion (sometimes 100 per cent) of choristers' fees as well as associated international tours. Cardinal's Scholarship for up to three year 3s who are expected to achieve well academically.

Exit: A handful of leavers most years at the end of pre-prep to local day schools – Magdalen, Abingdon et al. At 13 boys to a range of day and boarding schools including MCS, Abingdon, Cokethorpe and Teddies as well as Eton, Harrow, Radley, Shrewsbury and Haileybury on the boarding front. Cathedral choristers almost always win music scholarships or exhibitions, many with generous bursaries to boot. Non-music scholarships on the up – school now has a dedicated master in charge – although some parents commented that, when it comes to sports awards, success is driven by them.

Remarks: Tucked away in a historic corner of Oxford, linked to the college itself by a small courtyard garden and under the imposing gaze of Christ Church Cathedral just over the road. Born from Henry VIII's charter of 1546 which established the education of eight boy choristers and a master for the cathedral. Very much an urban school – and a totally different proposition to its local competitors with their magnitudinous acreage, muddy knee ethos and 'something for everyone' approach. Every available nook and cranny used and most drenched in history; buildings include the original Tudor residence of Cardinal Wolsey. Newer additions include a bright new classroom block and drama studio named for old boy (composer) William Walton. The net result is a cosy warren of surprisingly spacious and unsurprisingly characterful classrooms, labs and play areas.

Recent renovation programme has given school a bright, cheerful feel and there's not a tatty corner, chipped skirting board or malodorous dorm in sight. Formerly down-at-heel boarding accommodation now sparkles with pristine paintwork, funky lighting and squidgy sofas and a delightful common room, packed with musical instruments, has a stunning dual aspect of Christ Church College. Pool table hosts 'hotly contested' tournament. Pianos litter the school – an antique Steinway positioned unceremoniously at the top of a back stairwell just par for the course. Food has reportedly 'improved a lot' too and boarders look forward to the weekend chef who whips up 'beautifully presented' fare. Outside space would be top of boys' wish lists if they could wave a magic wand, but although playing fields are not on site, they're just a short walk away and – overlooked by the dreaming spires of Magdalen and Christ Church – are more than worth the journey. Dilapidated pavilion, but watch this space for news of an upgrade. Adventure play equipment recently added to the school's courtyards for use at break time, but there's no chance of muddy knees outside of games periods.

School's raison d'etre is to supply the cathedral with its choristers and although this absolutely pervades the school we didn't get the feeling that it defines it; one parent commented that it runs almost like 'two parallel schools'. Pupils fall into one of three camps: cathedral choristers, a minority group of up to 20 boys in years 4 to 8; Worcester choristers: day boys selected to be part of the Worcester College choir (approximately another 20, viewed by many to have 'the best of both worlds'), and the remaining cohort of around 110 boys who have varying degrees of musical interest or, occasionally, none at all (although in the main 'music is just what you do', says head, adding that there are 'more peripatetic music lessons per week than there are pupils'). All benefit from the school's bijoux size and its 'tailored education – our size is the clue to everything'.

Cathedral choristers start their commitment aged 8, when they join school as weekly boarding 'probationers'. From year 5 they operate as professionals, singing in up to four services almost every weekend, including religious holidays such as remembrance, Easter and Christmas when they stay in school until they have sung both at matins and the eucharist services (games socks hung up on Christmas Eve and filled by matrons a lovely touch and 'loads of fun and games' in the lead up). Demanding rehearsal (up to three hours a day) and performance schedule means no exeats but there are 'out' weekends where they can go home from Friday afternoon until Saturday afternoon. We arrived for our visit wondering if it was a somewhat niche existence for boys of such a tender age, and left at the end of the day convinced that the discipline, patience and concentration instilled in them during the course of their time of a chorister ('so often lacking these days', pointed out head) would set the right kind of boy up for life. With all musical commitments taking place outside of curriculum time, though, it's a rarefied existence and not for the faint of heart. With a requirement to study two further instruments (compulsory piano and one orchestral) on top of choir commitments, academic studies, sport and other selected activities (one chorister parent told us his son had a total of just 60 minutes unscheduled time a week), boys' hearts need to be absolutely entrenched in their music and the journey needs to be driven by them alone in order to be a happy and successful one. International tours during school holidays are part and parcel (recently China and USA) and boys are constantly photographed by tourists as they process to the cathedral in their Tudor style caps and gowns. Too much pressure and responsibility? For an average boy, undoubtedly. But the choristers we met were extraordinarily mature and self-assured for their years ('10 going on 19,' said one parent – our thoughts exactly), although still with broad smiles, tousled hair, wonky ties and the occasional untied shoelace. Their outstanding achievements infuse the entire school: 'all our pupils aspire to that excellence in whatever they do', says head, and school aims to relieve pressure when the heat is on at the cathedral.

Seamless transition into reception for littlies from the idyllic nursery setting, with parents praising the teaching that 'borders on individual tuition' in tiny classes (seven in reception when we visited). Trad curriculum, with French and Latin in the languages department, plus now Spanish and Greek as clubs. And what better way to incorporate all the languages spoken at the school by learning carols in as many as possible – even Korean? 'We like to celebrate diversity,' says school. Teachers are 'most brilliant' and 'fantastic', say parents – particularly head's newer appointments. Regular off timetable themed days, recently focusing on WWI with an animals at war workshop, trench digging and an insight into the German side of the conflict. Proximity to Oxford's wealth of offerings maximised with trips and outings, and visits from fascinating academics are the norm. Programming recently introduced to curriculum and IT, French, art, DT and games all specialist taught from reception. Reasoning on curriculum in year 5 to ensure boys' readiness for ISEB pre-test. With 10 per class, 'they have to knuckle down and can't get lost', say parents – some of whom (delightedly) report dramatic turnarounds in academic achievement having moved their son from larger preps or state primaries: 'Christ Church picks up their potential'. Head says success is due to the 'family atmosphere – we really know the boys.' Those at top of academic heap are sometimes working up to two years ahead of their age. School experienced in managing mild SpLD and makes good provision for a variety of SEN children, with a full time SENCo plus three TAs who are assigned where needed.

Atmosphere 'not testosterone fuelled' – boys participate in two games afternoons a week. Cricket and football fight for top popularity ranking depending on who you speak to (cricket: the head; football: everyone else) and boys also play rugby. The beauty of school's size is that everyone who wants to can play on a team and often it's whole year groups rather than just an elite group that get on the school minibus hoping for glory at inter-school tournaments. Although some parents feel that their boys are often outclassed on the sports field by larger schools, results are respectable considering the limited number of boys from which to choose; the CCCS A team will sometimes play others' B or C team to ensure a fair match. One dedicated full-time games coach, now supported by a part-time colleague (a professional football coach) and some 'very solid' members of the academic faculty, but families with the mindset that boys, like puppies, need to be rigorously exercised daily, should probably look outside of school for their sporting fix. Clubs take place as part of the school day. Real tennis hugely popular, as is chess which is played 'seriously' and to a very high standard. The 'herd energy' of the choristers also drives excellence in musical performances by orchestras, bands, choirs and groups for every instrument going. An art room festooned with props and canvases and DT lab homed in a charming former stable block testify that the creative child is well catered for and although there's no drama on curriculum, thespians are kept busy with bespoke plays often written by head of drama with particular pupils in mind for key roles.

Renewed focus on pastoral care recently: 'it's much better organised now', says head. Three resident dogs including one trained in literacy support and one in pastoral. 'Well used' counsellor visits one day a week and staff are all made aware of children on the red or amber lists that may need extra pastoral support or just a close eye. Boys understand the disciplinary code and in the main commit only minor transgressions, with the result being conduct cards to be carried for a week. Bullying a rarity but relationships between boarders can occasionally become 'explosive' due to the intensity of their living and working relationships. Older boys noticeably nurture and mentor the younger. Houses named after dignitaries associated with the school: Carroll, Wolsey and Sayers. Fiercely fought house competitions include enterprise day, music, sports, merits and prizes and, as culmination, the Dean's Cup. Parent association reportedly 'a lovely group and very organised'.

With boys from all backgrounds, many from hard working, dual income families, plus a range of cultural origins (more than half are fluent in another language), Christ Church offers what the head calls a 'unique educative experience' that sets it apart from the other local options. One parent described it as 'really normal and grounded with just the right set of values' – we agree. For an affable chap who would benefit from life in a tight knit community with intensely focused academics, provided he can either fulfil his sporting ambitions outside of school or has a limited need for such rambunctious frolics, then Christ Church might just fit the bill.

Christ's Hospital

Horsham, West Sussex RH13 0LJ

Ages 11–18 **Pupils** 907 **Sixth form** 281 **Boarders** 815 full **C of E**

Fees: Day £17,790 – £22,422; Boarding £34,440 pa

01403 211293
www.christs-hospital.org.uk

Headmaster: Since September 2017, Simon Reid BA (50s), previously principal of Gordonstoun and housemaster here for six years earlier in his career. A South African who read English at the University of Witwatersrand. Came to Britain in 1985 because he 'wanted to teach English literature in the country where it was written'. Has also been deputy head of Worksop College, having started his UK teaching career at Brentwood School, thence Stowe. His wife, Michele, is French, the family bilingual. Two grown up young.

Academic matters: Junior class sizes up to 25, 20 in core subjects at GCSE and fewer in option groups, 10 or 11 for A level or IB. Latin compulsory for first two years, second foreign language for one. Pupils say staff try exceptionally hard to incorporate exams in unusual first languages. IB becoming established. Take up was slow initially (28 in first year but now rising) – partly concern over importance of the decision (no future financial buffer if not right choice). In 2018, 67 per cent A*-A/9-7 grades at GCSE, 53 per cent A*/A at A level; IB average 34 points.

Campus arranged by subject blocks, all with high ceilings and plenty of space and equipment, including science and language labs. The ugly sister IT department (formerly known as Grange Hill by the students), replaced with a new classroom block, library and resource centre. A new sixth form and careers centre with a focus on careers and vocations – the thinking is that Old Blues can provide enough mentoring and connections for some pupils to enter a profession in the City without going to university. Art and humanities have their own specialised libraries (open for evening work, as are all academic departments, providing support).

The SEN unit has one part-time and two full-time SENCos – support ranges from mild to a tailored IEP if SEN is profound. Everyone with SEND gets a laptop. The whole campus has Wifi and all the IB pupils and upper sixth are offered a laptop too – these can be taken home. Parents appreciate 'equality of provision and equality of access to provision'.

Weekly chapel and tutorial periods; upper sixth get weekly lectures on topics ranging from photo-journalism, through medicine, dentistry and accountancy to Tom Avery's experience as a polar explorer. There is a huge amount on offer here and as pupils grow older they tend towards the management of their own studies, as they would at university, an enormously important piece of preparation for life after CH. Houseparents and staff who supervise prep periods play a great role in advising children on study choices as well as pastoral issues.

Games, options, the arts: Main sports are hockey, netball, football, rugby, cricket and tennis, with a decent fixture list against local co-ed schools, winning about 60 per cent. Blue Coats sports centre – 25m pool, double-sized sports hall, six squash courts, spin bikes, split-level fitness suite, vending machines and a café – is used by the public 60 per cent of the time, although the school has its own changing rooms. More

C

esoteric sports such as fives also on offer. DofE and CCF very popular.

Scout hut now converted to a multifunction theatre seating 200. A 500-seat theatre, modelled on Shakespeare's Globe, with padded red benches instead of the standing yard, is used by travelling drama companies too (contemporary dance as well as curriculum-relevant plays). Open access to these performances endears the school still more to Horsham residents. The debating society and the Model United Nations give student speakers more confidence in competitions inside and outside school.

The music department is a popular target for donations such as harps, bassoons and French horns. Listen to, play or sing in any one of the 43 ensembles and the joyful noise is gorgeous. There are chapel and symphony choirs (both restricted to a maximum of 150), a gospel choir, a junior choir and the Big (jazz) Band. Most pupils love to sing and the cathartic feeling of their voices joined together, soaring past the frescoes in the chapel, is one of the moments they squirrel away in their hearts – the BBC was hugely impressed that it could record them in just one take. Lots of Macs enable bedroom producers to hone their skills with music technology at A level.

Energetic art department – successful and focused on working on pupils' own ideas – produces an enormous range of work. Three floors of bright and naturally-lit space, an artist in residence, art historian, two full-time staff, sewing room, computer suite (although the primary source of each project is drawing, digital images are always involved) and a library full of glossy books – all open from 7.15am to 10pm. DT department occupies another large space and is equally well-equipped with computers, AutoCAD, laser cutter, graphics area etc and admirable focus on SMART objectives for each project. One pupil won the sculpture category of the new HMC schools' art competition with his remarkable recreation of a Brazilian favela as well as gaining the top Pre-U art mark.

Boarding: Sixteen single sex boarding houses along The Avenue and two newish upper sixth co-eds. Nearly all are looked after by a married couple (most of the 110 staff live on site, often with their own families), so every child gets a taste of parental and sibling relationships that may well be lacking in their own home. A recent revamp has left these boarding facilities sparkling – maximum three to a room, big common rooms with ping-pong and snooker, bright kitchens, a phone room (for the first two years no mobiles until 2pm). Every new arrival gets a nursemaid in the year above – they write letters to the new students the summer before they arrive; this relationship produces a family tree stretching across year groups. Ingenious support where need arises – matrons giving hugs, cleaning staff joshing the dedicated student and the head of learning support teaching a tai chi course.

In the two senior, Grecian (the name a hangover from compulsory classics) houses, rooms would be the envy of any university student. A double-height communal area, bowls of fruit, kitchens shared between eight, a BBQ on the deck, a little library area with a piano and students' art displayed. A quarter of the Grecians might be in long-term (more than a year) relationships with each other but no peer pressure to do this. The proximity of co-ed living space means that sex could be a problem, but the co-ed nature of the full school normalises boy/girl relationships. Lovely story of a Valentine's Day charity fundraiser, pay a penny for a snuggle – really inclusive. Matches on Saturday afternoons while Saturday evenings feel good with discos, theme nights or just a fun time in each house – watching football, a film or playing a game devised by the seniors with a slapstick pie in the face for those who mess up.

CH runs in three-week blocks before a leave weekend – some children don't want to or can't go home; they can stay in or get matched with a friend and spend the weekend with their family. 'There's no one way to be a CH pupil,' we were told. This diversity is the school's strength – whatever obstacles or advantages your home life might present, everyone is equal as soon as they tie on the bands of their uniform. The new 'deps' (deputy Grecians, lower sixth) probably find the acclimatisation most difficult. Pupils learn within the first year to live with a huge range of personalities, which stands them in good stead in later life.

Background and atmosphere: School was given its Royal Charter by Edward VI in 1553 to help orphan children of London. In 1902 the boys moved to the current purpose-built campus in Horsham (designed by Sir Aston Webb, architect of the façade of Buckingham Palace and King's College, Cambridge). The girls rejoined in 1985 to make it co-ed once again. Nowadays the demographic is much more mixed, but the uniform is still resolutely Tudor – mustard coloured socks and long blue coats. The pupils love the warm 'Houseys' and although the younger ones choose their 'civvies' carefully after lessons are over, the older ones default to school tracksuits. A refreshing lack of emphasis on trainers as a signifier of social tribe.

Progress supports the heritage showcased by the plaque-studded cloisters – from the plasma screen with BBC news and current school photos in the reception to the skylight-lit food hall. Six days a week, barring rain, the entire school marches to lunch from the quadrangle, house by house, to the accompaniment of the parade band. Parents and pupils say 'butterflies in the tummy' are caused by this sharing of 'music, ambience, exhilaration, aesthetic, ceremony, tradition and spirit' on a daily basis. Mingling tradition and technology is characteristic of the school. It may appear incongruous yet, in truth, it is inspirational. The food (delicious and varied), is eaten under the longest oil on canvas in Christendom. One of the best bits of the school is reported to be the spread at breakfast. They need that as fuel to get them around the huge campus – by the upper sixth you earn the privilege of a bike.

The pupils are proud of their uniform, don't mind being taunted as Harry Potter lookalikes on trains (they prefer references to The Matrix), are delighted to be recognised by Old Blues on the tube and smile wryly when confessing to smelling like wet dogs after marching in a rainy Lord Mayor's Show. They pour through the cloisters between their lessons, some holding the lead of a master's dog for a treat. The whole school meets in the chapel on Sunday morning. Stained glass windows (some Victorian and a couple of 14th century Flemish) came from the earlier campuses, but the Sir Frank Brangwyn frescos were commissioned for the Horsham site. Whole school assembly is conducted every week by the head in Big School, under the largest unsupported wooden ceiling in the country.

Pastoral care, well-being and discipline: All the pupils gather for chapel on Tuesdays and Sundays. The school was founded partly in response to a sermon preached by the Bishop of London and sermons are still powerful today. Lots of children here whose parents or carers are ill or struggling, so faith can be a real touchstone. School council is very thoughtful, student-run although spearheaded by an English teacher. Recent topics include racism – considering the effect close groups of international students (Hong Kong Chinese) can have in a community. Empathetic research came up with how tiring it was to speak in your second language all day long, therefore what a retreat your own culture could be.

Minor misdemeanours mean getting up for 7.15am and a dress parade. Mini-detentions on Sunday am, the big one is on Saturday night, and a card system which restricts free time by having to sign in (for smoking, bullying, drinking alcohol.) Internet access fairly unrestricted (you often can't get onto useful sites with blanket bans) but it is monitored – a 14-year-old looking at porn will lose his/her laptop and school email account. 'Swearing at the staff is unacceptable' (suspension) and continued difficulties will result in a behaviour contract between the pupil, parents and school – a line drawn in the sand. Drugs – class A or supplying – mean police involvement and immediate expulsion; for cannabis there will be one chance, after which the ongoing drug testing policy is implemented. Family circumstances are always taken into account. Parents really appreciate consistent and accessible staff.

Pupils and parents: The pupils know they're lucky to be here – four or five turned down for each given a place. Although accepting pupils from all over the UK, in reality about 30 per cent from London (Hackney, Tower Hamlets, Islington, Acton), 30 per cent from Sussex, 30 per cent south west and home counties, rest from Scotland, Wales, north of England (mainly sixth form entry and only if they have some extended family in the south east). Historical links with Richmond, Newbury, Reading and Twickenham – the towns on the route of John and Francis West (17th-century scriveners) to Christ's Hospital.

Eleven per cent international pupils – mostly Europe or the Far East. Lots of second and third generation Nigerians and Gambians, Hong Kong Chinese (attracted by CH's status as The Royal Mathematical School) and German anglophiles who love the school's excellence and tradition while valuing the fact that it is not an enclave of privilege. Since 2011, five per cent each from the UK, Europe and the rest of the world pay full fees, having made a conscious choice to pay for an egalitarian ethos. It has not been easy to change the pupil profile and great care was taken over admitting a small number of international pupils. Now students appreciate the still wider diversity; it's easier to chat in German with a friend who is a native speaker or swipe some Asian cooking tips in the house kitchen.

Lots of aspiring middle class and freelancers. Only about 40 per cent of pupils have both parents resident at home so houseparents try to help by encouraging communication between parents and new pupils. Pupils are drawn from all walks of life and the majority enjoy some form of means-tested bursary. If CH does its job, then former pupils will be ineligible to send their children to their alma mater, unless they pay the full fees.

Notable Old Blues (the dead ones have boarding houses named after them) include Coleridge, Middleton, Peele, Barnes Wallis, the cricketer John Snow, comedians Mark Thomas and Holly Walsh, the academic Alan Ryan, conductor Sir Colin Davis, Martin Linton MP, England Rugby Union second row Joe Launchbury, Baroness Ruth Deech, Lord Simon, former Chairman of BP, and General Sir Garry Johnson MC, strategic adviser to the MOD.

Entrance: Most at 11+, 25 to 30 at 13+ and 45 to 50 after GCSE. No feeder schools, but a very good relationship with south of England primaries and preps. Fifty heads came to a recent open day so they can see what type of child will thrive at CH. Not on the public school radar, so not much cachet on the dinner party circuit. The initial application form elicits lots of information about family circumstances and finances – from previous school, local church, social services. The staff in the admissions office are at the end of the phone to answer questions and baffled or swamped parents really value this.

Exit: Some 10-15 per cent leaves after GCSE for vocational courses. More than 90 per cent of sixth formers to university – the Upper Grecian houses are a real stepping-stone to life there. In 2018, eight to Oxbridge and three medics. Exeter, Durham, KCL, Bristol and Warwick popular; others to Germany, Italy and British Columbia. Engineering, archaeology, classics, law, music, maths degrees. Artists seem to take it in turns to go in a posse to Camberwell, Falmouth and Central St Martins.

Money matters: Currently 14 per cent pay nothing, 34 per cent pay less than 10 per cent of full fees, 72 per cent per cent receive some level of bursary support and 19 per cent pay the full boarding fee. Of the £301 million allocated to means-tested bursaries by ISC schools last year, £15.5 million of that was at Christ's Hospital alone.

Parental contributions are assessed on the total family income of the home in which the child resides, interest and dividend payments plus a percentage of any financial and other assets above £25,000. Most DSS benefits are included, but not housing benefit, disability allowance and carer's allowance. Reviewed each year. Discounts for siblings within school. Tudor-style uniform is free. Extras include £20 pocket money per term, music contributions (means-tested again), a dictionary and a bible. CH has a big endowment but, like every other school, lives beyond its means.

Curriculum-based trips are partially funded by the foundation (means-testing applies). Old Blues provide travel grants for gap years etc.

Remarks: Well-adjusted, confident and accepting children who look forward to coming to school. This is the only independent school that escapes the state school prejudice when attracting principled teachers. The Old Blues are incredibly loyal and you can see why – with 75 per cent of them in the top quartile of income in their later life, CH turns many lives around in an unpretentious and joyful manner. Admirable work.

Churcher's College

Ramshill, Petersfield, Hampshire GU31 4AS

Ages 3–18 **Pupils** 1,090 (225 junior, 865 senior) **Sixth form** 246

Fees: £9,915 – £15,420 pa

01730 263033
www.churcherscollege.com

Headmaster: Since 2004, Simon Williams BSc (biology, Durham), married to Alison, with three children. Started teaching career at King's College Wimbledon, where he taught biology and rugby, progressing to head of science at Newcastle under Lyme school, then deputy head at Warwick school.

Parents say he's 'lovely; very approachable'; 'great at listening'; 'children wouldn't want to go and see him about a disciplinary matter – they're slightly in awe of him, but he's approachable too'.

Lives on site – almost lives the school: he has black tie dinner parties every Friday for sixth formers to practice making small talk, and is there at every match and event. Described by pupils as 'very fair; very motivating; very involved in school life'; 'knows all the names...' ; 'takes a great deal of pride in the school'.

Head of junior school: Since 2016, Ffion Robinson BA (Cardiff) MA (Kings College, London), previously head of the junior branch of Lady Eleanor Holles, Twickenham, and deputy head of King's House, Richmond.

Popular with pupils: 'takes our ideas forward'; 'can bring anything up'; 'feel she cares about you'. A parent told us 'less is more' with this quiet head, who is warm, caring and 'brings a progressive air to the school'. Parents feel she listens to them, and are delighted with breakfast club, and the up coming tea club which takes the school day to 5.30pm.

Academic matters: 'Fairly academic, very supportive', said a parent, 'not a hothouse. They want to get the best out of everybody.' Results are impressive: in 2018, 55 per cent A*/A at A level, 87 per cent A*-B; 66 per cent A*-A/9-7 at GCSE.

Not hugely selective: ability ranges between 100-140, with most pupils being in the 105-110 range. 'If you're not A* you don't feel like a poor student', said a parent, whose son is in a bottom set but 'doesn't feel rubbish about it'.

Value added is impressive: one whole grade at A level higher than ALIS value added expectation. Taken as a group, pupils here want to succeed, says the head, so, much like those walking down Oxford Street, joiners go with the flow.

'A good environment', said a pupil, who likes the fact that it is selective and competitive. 'Teachers will push you towards your potential', said another; 'no cruising, he added feelingly, or as another put it: '[they] facilitate those who are less competitive' and make sure you reach your potential. Report card system if grades drop: teacher and parents sign off work; not so much punishment as tool to address the problem, say pupils, adding that parents here 'care a lot about grades'.

'Teachers are lovely – amazing', said a parent, and 'very efficient if you have an issue', recounting a well thought out, same day response to an email sent on a Friday evening. Pupils say 'staff are very supportive. If you have a problem with a topic, they always make sure you understand by the end of a session'. Those higher up in the school describe a more interactive relationship with teachers; pupils attend parents' evening from year 4; a year 3 told us he felt they too should be allowed to go.

There are plenty of extra sessions at lunchtime for those who don't understand something, from catching the A train – for sixth formers who are less applied than they should be, or hard workers who are not making headway – to the springboard club: strong encouragement for those lacking academic confidence.

Pupils can struggle to fit in all the homework if they have activities after school, and then a commute home, but 'bright sparks do some homework at lunchtime', said a parent. 'It's all about learning time management skills'. Pupils say 'if you can't fit it in because of commitments, you can send an email, and they will accommodate you'.

Science and maths popular high performers, with history and geography also coming in for much praise. Subjects mainly traditional fare.

A parent whose mildly dyslexic daughter had a meltdown during mocks reported sensitive and efficient handling by the school: they tested the pupil again, diagnosed processing issues, and ensured she had extra time put in place during exams. Churcher's supports mild conditions in one-to-one sessions, charged as extra. No classroom assistants in the senior school. Dyslexics have the same level of attainment as mainstream.

SEN unit also offers spelling and handwriting clubs during lunchtimes, and workshops to help with exam anxiety, with a Firefly online version for those too shy to attend (80 workshop attendees; 320 Firefly listeners).

A few head off after GCSEs to sixth form college, for financial or freedom reasons, but those who stay are glad they did, enjoying the delights of Ramshill, the sixth form centre, the toast (20 loaves a week), and the opportunity for more self direction; although one told us that she gets more supervision than her friends who have gone to college, and will get better grades by staying at school: 'it's easier to fall under the radar at college'. A life skills course for those heading to university concentrates on practicalities such as financial management and encouraging your child to do the weekly shop (perhaps stock up on loo roll before this experiment). The head takes every opportunity to find sixth formers roles of responsibility and leadership with younger pupils, including being a science aunt or uncle to a first former.

The junior school is a 'pacy environment', says Mrs Robinson, and pupils give generally positive accounts of their lessons, in particular maths, with a teacher who makes everything 'fun and interesting'; pupils were delighted with an Easter egg hunt where the colour of the egg you found dictated how many minutes you had to answer questions.

For those at the gifted end of the spectrum, there are extension tasks in each lesson, but no labels within the class: 'divisive for parents and kids', says the head. Mild special needs are catered for with one-to-one support, learning support to be rebranded as 'learning enrichment'. Dyslexics will be encouraged to learn to touch type, and Chromebooks and iPads are available to support lessons – 'given the skills to be successful'.

Head has removed annual exams for all but year 6, to the great delight of pupils and parents (parents said it was the best email they had ever received), and the amount of homework (30-60 mins a night depending on the year group) is under consideration: 'downtime is important; they need to refocus on enjoying life'.

The school nursery opened at the beginning of 2017 and currently has 20 pupils (owls or pussycats, depending in age). The nursery is a beautifully converted bungalow, complete with handcrafted nursery furniture and a low bench in the kitchen for cookery lessons. Plenty of outside space with thriving courgettes and sunflowers, grown from seed; a bandstand and mud pie station.

Games, options, the arts: Pupils say this is a school for children who are 'open to trying new things and excited about doing things', and the vast array of extracurricular attracted many of the pupils we spoke to. There's no compulsion to join in, but everyone does something, and virtually everyone does a lot; over 700 pupils do D of E, and virtually all the year 2 pupils are involved in OSCA (an in-house version of D of E for younger pupils).' We encourage children to have fingers in lots of pies', says the head, '[and] keep breadth for as long as possible – children tend to perform best across the piste'.

Music and art were described by a parent as 'phenomenal'; art is particularly fabulous, and displayed all around the school, even outside; one student used her experiences windsurfing to capture beautifully the vitality of wind and wave in her GCSE artwork on extreme weather; another was shortlisted for the 2017 Saatchi gallery international art prize. Art is increasingly popular at A level, with over half of entrants achieving A*/A. Many pupils are involved in drama, GCSE, A level and LAMDA, and the annual musical is very popular.

There's lots of focus on art in the junior school too: piles of snozcumbers were lying around for an evening with Roald Dhal; hand-printed T shirts were hanging to dry; clocks designed on Dell laptops on the laser cutter; and Segal inspired butterflies and flowers decorated a window. Each class in the junior school produces a play, and around two-thirds learn instruments – there are so many pianists they have a piano gala.

Competitive, said a parent, particularly at sports, but 'you don't need to be competitive to be happy here'; another parent explained that Churcher's gets the best out of individuals, who then go on to do well, rather than it being a school which aims to win everything.

There's a diplomatic flavour to sports provision here: rugby can be full contact form or tag (no compulsory violence here); and no purchasing cricket whites unless your child is in a team. How practical. All first years play in matches, and all those who want to represent the school have the chance to do so, even if in the C and D teams: 'the development leagues'. Girls can play cricket, football and rugby at junior and senior schools.

Background and atmosphere: 'Weren't intending to go private, but really liked it', said a parent, who wanted a balanced school which would suit her very academic and less so offspring, and was attracted too by the pupils: 'the children are polite, courteous, confident...nice human beings...'. Another said there's all the 'academic stuff', but what really attracted her was the 'thirst for grabbing life and enjoying it'.

Pupils describe the atmosphere as 'encouraging'; in this friendly school 'everyone seems to get along', said another. 'I love the way they applaud each other', said the head, recounting how the maths challenge winner gets as warm applause as rugby team; when we met pupils we noted how respectfully they let each other speak and listened to each other. In this environment it is no surprise that the house system is for fun, and friendly competition on sports day.

It has a different profile to other private schools – 'not a public school feel', said a parent, who liked the mix of parents, with lots of dual income professionals; some posh, some not.

The core building is 19th century, supplemented by a wide array of lovely new ones. The library isn't a hushed space – it's alive and noisy at break times on the basis that it's better well used than a place of holy quiet.

'Size right; not enormous', said parent. 'Don't want to be bigger', says the head. Not a drop off school, says the head – you need to be involved.

Many of the junior school buildings are new, with large purpose built classrooms, one of them even en suite with large doors onto the playground, flung wide on the sunny day of our visit. All of the classrooms had space for sitting on the floor; years 4 and 5 graduate to proper desks you can put things in. At break time they have a great big field to run around on, an adventure course (if in trainers with teacher present) and sensory garden for those seeking for a calmer environment, with lavender, a music area, and a large egg to crawl into.

Pastoral care, well-being and discipline: This school is 'discrete and private' in the way they deal with pastoral matters, agreed pupils, who said they would tell their form tutor about any problems in the first instance, and 'if teachers think there's something going on, they chase it down'. Pupils can also speak to their personal tutor, counsellor or the school nurse : she's 'so lovely', said a parent, 'never turns them away', describing her son sitting in tears in the car on one of his early days at the school; the remedy: hot chocolate with the school nurse, followed by delivery to a favourite lesson.

Parents describe a school which deals efficiently and thoroughly with pastoral issues: a parent whose child was bullied on Facebook said it was dealt with 'immediately and well'. Pupils were confident that persistent bullies would be excluded. Naive behaviour will be addressed with education; malicious behaviour with sanctions, says the head. The biggest problem is finding out, but pupils will often blow the whistle. At the junior school, pupils said 'tell the teacher and they deal with it instantly', and that they would go to their class teacher or the head with any problem.

'Quite strict', said a parent, 'a tuck your shirt in' sort of school (although another bewailed girls rolling up their skirts). Good behaviour is important, and pupils are expected to be polite and respectful to support staff and teachers, say parents.

As for drinking and drugs, pupils understand that these grave offences could result in exclusion, but are confident that the school will investigate the why of misbehaviour. No evidence of a drug problem in school, but things happen outside school; a parent said Churcher's actually 'courts' information from parents about what's going on beyond the schools gates, takes what parents say very seriously and 'does what it can'.

No recent exclusions, but a few 'managed moves', where a cumulation of misdemeanours meant children would do better starting elsewhere with a clean slate.

Pupils and parents: Some families are 'loaded; others scraping to get the kids through'. The PA is very active, with lots of social events – the parents' ball is sold out within two days.

Communication from school, via app, website, email and occasional hard copy letter is good.

Entrance: No formal assessment for pupils joining nursery and reception; tests in English, maths, spelling and reading for entrance to other years, and also writing from year 3 upwards.

At 11+, exams in maths, English and verbal reasoning, and the head interviews every child, seeking both the loud and the quiet, the academic, musical, artistic and/or sporting: the better the mix, the better the dynamic works. What pupils must have is a passion for something.

Ninety-five per cent of junior school pupils progress to the college, and they make up 30 per cent of the year, the rest coming from 140 other different feeder schools, both independent and state.

Exit: Around a quarter leaves after GCSEs. Most to Russell Group (Exeter, Bristol, Cardiff, Bath and Nottingham currently popular) or specialist art or music colleges, such as the Central School of Art and design. Three medics and a vet in 2018. Generally a few a year to Oxbridge.

Money matters: '...really good value for money', said a parent, '[and] this is one reason it is so popular'. Sibling discount and scholarships available.

Remarks: This school achieves balance very well, so a parent of four very different children told us that she didn't think there is a child Churcher's wouldn't suit: 'so broad, easy to fit in'. 'It's a boisterous, active kind of school', said another parent, and those happy keeping busy in a lively environment will enjoy life here.

City of London Freemen's Junior School

Linked with City of London Freemen's School

Ashtead Park, Ashtead, Surrey KT21 1ET

Ages 7–13 **Pupils** 398

Fees: £13,398 – £14,742 pa

01372 277933
www.freemens.org

Headmaster of the junior school: Since 2014, Matthew Robinson (40s), previously deputy head. BA from Plymouth, MA from Surrey, QTS from Institute of Education, MEd from Buckingham. Has also taught (English, Latin and humanities) at Cranleigh Prep, King's College Wimbledon and, mostly recently, at Junior King's School Canterbury. Amiable and approachable, but not a man to let grass grow under his feet: has been boarding tutor and coached football, rugby, hockey, cricket and golf as well as directing various school plays and editing school magazines. Married to Victoria, also a teacher; they have four children while also finding time to go to the theatre, walk, play golf and squash and listen to music. Highly rated by parents, who called him 'an excellent leader, very open to feedback and discussion but making his own views clear.'

C

Entrance: Sixty places available at 7+, and a further 20 at 11+, making up a school of 400 pupils. Places occasionally available in other years if families have to relocate – always worth checking. Maximum class size of 20, and gender balance is even across the school.

Selective and competitive at all stages. Children sit tests in maths, English and non-verbal reasoning. Results are considered together with feeder school report, and all applicants are interviewed regardless of how they scored. Always oversubscribed, particularly at 11+ when at least six pupils apply for every place. However, parents confirm that whilst their children work hard to win their way in, once they're there the atmosphere is unpressured.

No pre-prep and no plans for one. The school is proud of its all-through route for academically able pupils, and has no wish to jeopardise this by taking younger children who are necessarily more of an unknown quantity.

Exit: Virtually everyone to senior school. No entrance tests are required of the junior pupils, and the transition is seamless and well-managed. 'Once you're in, you're in,' confirmed the head. 'The children arrive at 7 and our expectation is that 10 years later they'll still be here.' The same is equally true for children who joined the junior school at a later date.

Remarks: The all-through route right up to year 13 takes the heat off the juniors once they arrive and ensures a calm, unpressurised atmosphere throughout. (We were touched to see a photo display of the children's recent holiday homework: to climb a tree!) Lessons are sound and solid, and children are motivated and engaged. 'The junior school is very welcoming and the emphasis is on trying hard, enjoying learning and experiencing new things,' wrote a mother. 'The school has a talent for making potentially challenging things seem very normal.' Another observed, 'Freemen's primary school children can enjoy life like real children. I think it is a very healthy environment.' 'The academic standards are high, yet there is a lot less stress and pressure compared to what I hear of other prep schools,' was another comment. Just occasionally, the atmosphere struck us as a little too comfortable, and it may be no coincidence that one member of staff observed to us in passing, 'The pupils are so bright and motivated that the academics almost look after themselves.'

A smattering of students with mild SEN are supported by a team of four SEN teachers across the junior and senior school. Support is 'done quite subtly' – at breakfast and lunchtime clubs, for instance – and students with dyslexia will do one foreign language rather than two. However, this isn't the place for more than a low level of need, and parents should check that the school is able to support their child.

Housed in the purpose-built Kemp House, the junior classrooms look out onto the foyer space, attractively furnished with armchairs and scatter cushions. Very inviting library at the heart of the school, well-resourced and colourful – we liked the Shakespeare display in particular. Excellent IT room, cool and spacious – again, lots of good work on the walls. Junior school boasts its own science lab, art room, music practice rooms and assembly hall, and also has access to some of the senior school's teaching facilities and fabulous outdoor spaces – rolling greenery as far as the eye can see. Additionally, there is a lovely adventure playground exclusively for the juniors. As the head remarked, 'We have the strength of a junior school and the resources of a senior school.' All the parents who contacted us praised the activities on offer, calling them 'fantastic', 'outstanding' and 'superb'. Sport is taken very seriously, but the emphasis is on participation and enjoyment. 'Probably not as competitive as some schools, but my children get to do more sport as a result,' thought the mother of two not-very-sporty children, although another parent felt that there was too much emphasis on participation at the expense of results. Boys do football, rugby and cricket, the girls do hockey, netball and rounders (a very traditional offering), and everyone does swimming – new six-lane pool. Other sports on offer include fencing, athletics, running and tennis. Boys get more squad time and matches, we are told.

Drama is seen by many as one of the highlights of the school – Romeo and Juliet was a year 8 production – and the school enjoys regular success at the Shakespeare Schools Festival, with everyone encouraged to get involved. Music is also popular, with a variety of orchestras, bands, ensembles and choirs (plenty of boys in the latter, always a healthy sign), and regular concert opportunities, but again the emphasis is on inclusion. 'If children are complete beginners, the staff will write the music part for the notes they know so that they immediately enjoy playing in a group,' wrote one mother.

Broad enrichment programme gives children the chance to try all sorts of things they might not normally sample eg mountain biking, Bollywood dancing, martial arts, photography. Younger children recently spent a term learning sign language, rounded off by using their skills to converse with a hearing-impaired visitor to the school.

Rules are clear, children know what's expected of them, and the absence of undue academic pressure seems to result in a happy and relaxed school community. Most parents say that staff are open to discussion if they have concerns or questions, and that any incidents are handled with discretion, sensitivity and kindness. However, we have also had a worrying report of bullying incidents badly handled, leading to a parent removing their child from the school. There is a strong and unapologetic emphasis on independent study and organisational skills, with all pupils expected to think for themselves. If your child requires a high level of nurture and shepherding, therefore, this school may not be the best fit. The parents we spoke to, however, were well satisfied with the confident and capable individuals their children were learning to be. As one parent put it, 'The school trains children to study on their own gradually. By the time my daughter was in Y7, she was very organised and now does what she needs to do independently.'

This is classic commuter country, and Freemen's families are mostly professional, but from a range of backgrounds nonetheless; some affluent, some making large sacrifices to pay the fees. Parents' Association is proactive and supportive of the school. Pupils predominantly from surrounding Surrey towns of Ashtead, Epsom, Banstead, Leatherhead, Esher and Cobham, and school offers a return coach service to these areas and more. Shuttle bus to and from Ashtead station also a great help, particularly to those travelling from further afield. The junior students we met were able, cheerful, polite and grounded. Very little ethnic diversity, reflecting the area's demographic, but all the children we saw were mixing happily together regardless of difference.

'We are delighted with the school and both our children actively look forward to going back after the holidays,' was a very typical parental comment. For those seeking a solid, reliable all-through educational route for their academically able sons and daughters, this is an excellent choice.

City of London Freemen's School

Linked with City of London Freemen's Junior School

Ashtead Park, Ashtead, Surrey KT21 1ET

Ages 13–18 **Pupils** 526 **Sixth form** 229 **Boarders** 57

Fees: Day £18,243 – £18,279 pa; Boarding £27,906 – £30,816 pa

01372 277933
www.freemens.org

Headmaster: Since 2015, Roland Martin (40s), cheerful, communicative, intellectual, and thoroughly likeable. Grew up in a council house and won a Foundation scholarship to Rendcomb College in Gloucestershire, where he was a boarder, got involved with everything and had a wonderful time. Read English at York and was about to embark on a PGCE when he was offered a job at Newcastle-under-Lyme School and decided to learn on the job instead. Six years there were followed by 13 years at Eton, where he taught English and drama, and was also head of year 11 and a housemaster. Returned to his alma mater Rendcomb in 2011 as headmaster, so well versed in the demands of the role before moving to Freemen's four years later. Married to Kerri, who works at the school as outreach officer, with two children.

Thinks that if he hadn't become a teacher he might have chosen to be ordained as a minister ('And I still might be!' he adds), and certainly feels that teaching is a vocation. Delighted to be at Freemen's – 'This school gets under your skin really, really quickly.' A theatre lover and true scholar, whose passion for all things 18th century was so infectious that we wanted to join his sixth form classes on tomb sculpture ourselves. Popular with students, who describe him as 'humble', 'down-to-earth' and 'involved'. Parents concur, grateful for improved communication and commenting that he is 'quietly confident and very approachable, with a clear vision of where he wants to take the school,' and 'incredibly kind'.

Academic matters: Extremely good results year on year at both GCSE and A level – in 2018, 83 per cent A*-A/9-7 for the former, with 66 per cent A*/A and 88 per cent A*/B for the latter.

Viewed by parents as pretty much the best in the locality, and students say that the school 'feels very academic'. No feel of being a pressure-cooker, however, and parents and pupils alike praised the way that academic performance was achieved without undue stress. 'You don't feel that you're lacking if you're not in the top set. The teachers always encourage you to do well.' Independent study skills a priority: 'They give you the tools you need to work with, but they don't spoon-feed you,' was a typical comment. 'My history teacher is so interested in everything about history, and is always up for a chat – it led to my choosing history,' enthused one sixth former. 'The opportunities for my son to challenge himself academically both in school hours and in terms of extracurricular provision are excellent,' wrote a mother, 'for example maths challenges, literary society, science and technology seminars. The small classes and tutorial group system work well and the children are all very motivated.'

Curriculum is traditional but broad, with all the usual subjects taught and enjoyed. School offers French, Spanish, German and Latin, and is looking at introducing Mandarin ('We're behind the curve on that one,' admitted head). The lessons we attended were sound and solid, with all students keen to participate. Head not especially a fan of giving out iPads, but felt that the school was behind the times on the ICT front when he arrived and has worked to modernise the provision.

At sixth form the school offers A levels, plus the Free Minds programme, a kind of internal baccalaureate introduced by the head and aimed at helping students to go off-piste intellectually. 'It has helped my children to broaden their interests and thinking,' wrote one mother. Unless they're taking double maths, all sixth formers have to do the EPQ.

A smattering of students with mild SEN are supported by a team of three SEN teachers across the junior and senior school. Support is 'done quite subtly' – at breakfast and lunchtime clubs, for instance – and students with dyslexia may do one foreign language rather than two. However, this isn't the place for more than a minor level of need.

Games, options, the arts: Sport is very strong here and the facilities are stunning – huge hockey Astro is very impressive – but the emphasis is on inclusion, with a number of grateful parents praising the participation and enjoyment fostered by the school's culture. 'My son chose to play down a team in rugby because he was frightened of tackling and the school was happy to accommodate this, as the focus is on building the boys' confidence and enjoyment of the game,' wrote one mother. Boys do rugby, football and cricket, girls do hockey, netball, tennis and rounders. A very traditional divide, and one mother, who was effusive in her praise of the school, did comment, 'My only gripe is that the boys have no choice in the lower school other than to do football, then rugby, then cricket and don't have the opportunity to experience tennis or hockey – which would suit some of them far better.' Varied programme of extracurricular sports eg fencing, squash, pilates, kickboxing, archery, and coaching for these described by parents as 'outstanding'. Ski trips highly rated by students. Cracking gym and fitness suite, where perspiring young men were pumping iron under the guidance of a trainer when we passed by.

Music taught in excellent purpose-built block, complete with recording studio, Live Room for pupils' own band practices, Mac suite and all the practice rooms you could desire. Orchestras, choirs, ensembles – always plenty going on, including collaborations with the other City of London schools and the chance to play at venues such as Milton Court and St John's Smith Square. 'The music at Freemen's is excellent, with very high standards of concerts and individual music teachers,' wrote one parent, adding, 'It is a shame they don't offer a music tour abroad as other schools do.'

Drama is accommodated in the Ferndale Theatre, which is an odd shape but very well-equipped and staffed. Lots of scope for getting involved. School plays are 'amazing!' according to pupils – previous productions have included Phantom of the Opera, Evita, Romeo & Juliet and Laura Wade's Alice set in a prop cupboard. School has recently appointed a dramatist-in-residence to help extend the clubs and activities on offer. School scores regular successes in the Shakespeare Schools Festival.

Art is flourishing, although the work we saw struck us as enjoyable rather than particularly inventive. CCF and DofE offered from year 9. Generally, both parents and students were full of praise for the enrichment here, although a couple hinted that some of the opportunities on offer looked better on paper than in actuality.

Boarding: New and spruce boarding house can accommodate up to 30 boys and 30 girls in years 9 to 13. Attractive floor-to-ceiling etched glass entrance doors give immediately onto a big open plan common room, light and airy, although not, one imagines, particularly private. Students share two to a room until the sixth form, when they can have a room to themselves.

Two kitchens for boarders' use, plus very nice laundry facilities. Full, weekly and flexi-boarding are all offered.

The school was founded to care for orphans, so boarding is part of the original statute and must be provided. However, it's fair to say that the current residents are rather different to those in 1854. Almost all today's boarders are paying full fees and hail from overseas eg China, Hong Kong, Malaysia, Kazakhstan. They have to have good English to start with, and a specialist EAL teacher visits three times a week, ensuring they make rapid progress. A very small number of weekly boarders, and these are usually from the UK.

Only two live-in staff, supported by a day matron and other assistants. This is a small community, and reading between the lines, a quiet one. We didn't get to meet or talk to any boarders, and couldn't detect the kind of buzz so palpable in other boarding houses we've visited.

Background and atmosphere: The second of the three City of London schools to be created, Freemen's opened its doors in 1854 with a remit to educate 'orphans of the Freemen of the City of London'. Housed originally in Brixton, it could accommodate up to 65 boys and 35 girls – applicants had to be aged between 7 and 10 and could stay until they were 15. So whereas many schools have added on boarders, girls and junior-aged children in order to survive economically, Freemen's took them all from the off. In 1924, the school relocated to the 57-acre Ashtead Park estate in Surrey; fee-paying boys were now also admitted, with fee-paying girls joining them in 1933.

Oddly higgledy-piggledy entrance gives little indication of the beauty and space that awaits just around the corner. The main house, built in the 17th century and given the Bonomi treatment in the 18th, is flanked by Palladian balustrade, topiary, manicured lawns and is simply gorgeous. 'It's a very nice place to be,' agreed our tour guide, as we paused to admire the wonderful wood-panelled entrance hall. Despite this, the campus has a modern feel to it: lots of new buildings – the Haywood Centre is the hub of the school and bang up to date. Even more is planned: a huge overhaul of facilities is set to take place over the next 8-10 years. No danger of anyone feeling cramped, though: there are space and green fields in abundance, stretching far away into the distance. We walked about at lunchtime and saw both girls and boys charging hither and yon in what seemed like a civilised pastoral idyll, laughing, shouting, playing, generally being active, healthy and noisy.

House system helps to build positive relationships across the school. A pupil told us, 'I absolutely love it here. It's really friendly and welcoming,' and another added, 'Everyone's really open-minded. It's a happy school.' A parent wrote, 'There is none of the razzamatazz and sales manner of some other schools.' We agree – if anything, the school was a little too unconcerned about showing us its best side, with the result that it came across as successful and contented, rather than dynamic and self-searching.

Pastoral care, well-being and discipline: Universally praised as a kind, non-judgmental place where children can flourish. 'I am a single mother and the school has been nothing other than supportive to myself and my sons, who have had a massive adjustment period over the last year,' was a particularly heartfelt testament we received. This is all the more praiseworthy given that it runs alongside the school's longstanding emphasis – commented upon by many – on students thinking for themselves. 'Freemen's children are expected to be independent from arrival in year 3 onwards and as a result in the main the school produces very confident, organised individuals and we feel that our children have benefitted from this,' wrote a parent, adding, 'There is little hand holding though, and the onus is on the child to seek out help.' Students agreed: 'There's a lot of support in place if you ask for it.'

Behaviour is like the uniform: sensible and smart. Tutor system ensures that everyone is known and supported, rules are clear, and children say they know what's expected of them. Pupils can bring their own lunch, but most choose the school meals, which are very good ('much better than they used to be,' confided a sixth former), and served in the main house dining room under the beneficent painted gaze of former school dignitaries.

Head has open door on two mornings a week for staff and two mornings a week for pupils. A delegation of girls came to talk about their concerns for PSHE – they'd felt the school was stuffy on topics such as sex and sexuality. Head listened and acted – 'We've worked a lot on pupil voice.' No issues with transition from junior to senior – Freemen's operates as one all-through school, and the younger children are familiar and comfortable with the site and senior staff well before they move up at 13.

Students say: 'The balance is good here. It's academic, but they let you get on with it. The homework load is manageable. Most people do stuff outside school and the teachers are aware of this.' 'My children have thrived since joining the school and are very happy there,' was a typical parent comment.

Pupils and parents: This is classic commuter country, and Freemen's families are mostly professional but from a range of backgrounds nonetheless; some affluent, some making large sacrifices to pay the fees. Parents Association is proactive and supportive of the school. Pupils (apart from boarders) predominantly from surrounding Surrey towns of Ashtead, Epsom, Banstead, Leatherhead, Esher and Cobham, and school offers a return coach service to these areas and more. Shuttle bus to and from Ashtead station also a great help, particularly to those travelling from further afield.

Freemen's students are able, cheerful, polite and grounded. Very little ethnic diversity, reflecting the area's demographic, but all the children we saw were mixing happily together regardless of difference.

Entrance: At 13+, the overwhelming majority come up from the junior school. There is absolutely no academic barrier between junior and senior school, something which is a huge draw for parents: entry from year 8 to year 9 really is automatic. 'Once you're in, you're in,' confirmed the head. 'The children arrive at age 7, and our expectation is that they'll still be here 10 years later.' An additional 20 places for outsiders, all keenly competed for – applicants mostly come from local preps eg Downsend, Danes Hill, Cranmore and Lanesborough. At sixth form around another 20 join, including overseas boarders. Sixth form places for UK students are offered on current academic performance (applicants must be sitting at least eight GCSEs), school report and interview, although offers are conditional upon GCSE grades achieved. International students sit papers in January in English, maths, non-verbal reasoning and the A level subjects they wish to study.

Exit: A small number at 16+, either for financial reasons or because they fancy a change. At 18+ the majority to Russell Group unis. In 2018 the most popular destinations included Birmingham, Exeter, Newcastle, Loughborough and LSE. Ten to Oxbridge, nine medics, and one each to Hong Kong and California.

Money matters: Fees are competitive alongside other comparable schools in the area. Academic and music awards at 13+ and sixth form available to current pupils and incomers. Means-tested bursary awards, sponsored by the City Livery Companies and often tied to certain professions. A very small number of children of Freemen who have lost one 'family breadwinner' parent attend completely free as Foundationers, whether they are day pupils or boarders.

Remarks: A school that produces confident, motivated, happy young achievers. A blessing to parents looking for a high-quality stress-free educational route that will take their academically able sons and daughters from age 7 right through to 18. Almost unique in this neck of the woods.

Cobham Hall

71

Cobham, Brewers Road, Gravesend, Kent DA12 3BL

Ages 11–18 **Pupils** 180 **Sixth form** 43 **Boarders** 65 full, 14 flexi

Fees: Day £18,231 – £22,203; Boarding £27,546 – £34,551 pa

01474 823371
www.cobhamhall.com

Headmistress: Since September 2018, Maggie Roberts BA. Degree from Birmingham; she has taught English and history to sixth form level in the UK – at Wellington College and Queen Anne's School Caversham – and Germany, at Schule Schloss Salem, one of the Round Square founding schools. She has run two Round Square International Conferences and has led Round Square International Service Projects in South Africa and Thailand. She has also been a boarding housemistress.

She enjoys quilting and cross-stitch, reading and walking. A member of a walking club, her greatest challenge to date was to complete a Moonwalk in aid of Cancer Research, and is proud to have completed a walking marathon. She has two grown up daughters and two dogs, and can often be found wandering around dog shows and other similar events.

Academic matters: The IB was introduced in 2009 and A levels phased out at the same time: however, this has now reversed, and the current year 13s (2018-19) will be the last to take the IB. The results reflect the wide range of abilities within the school, with the 2018 penultimate IB average point score of 30; 33 per cent A*-A/9-7 grades at GCSE. All girls take at least eight GCSEs and most do 10. Girls setted in maths, English and science from year 7 and sometimes in other subjects depending on the size of the year group. 'Girls generally do better than expected,' says the school. Class sizes up to 20 in the lower years with an average of 12 and no more than 12 per class (and some much smaller) in sixth form. One parent said that she was concerned about the small classes before her daughter started but added: 'the brightest girls are stretched and encouraged'. The teachers are a 'good combination of the homely and the vibrant and dynamic' – about half are male.

French, Spanish, German and Latin offered at GCSE and A level. Science is popular and most take three separate sciences at GCSE although dual award is available – 'girls are braver about sciences in a single sex school.' Computer science, film studies, drama and PE are all A level options. The small size of the school means that they can be 'reactive to demand and flexible with the timetable'.

Cobham offers a pre-A level course and girls joining this for the year have the option of sitting up to five GCSEs. Many join for only one or two terms to brush up their English or as preparation for the sixth form at Cobham. They are taught separately in most subjects but may join the school's GCSE students for sport. They live in Main Hall with the other GCSE students.

About 60 girls need help with English and the EFL programme is tailored for each girl. Girls joining in years 10 and 12 need good English and will generally study the English B qualification (English for non-native speakers). The school is a registered centre for ESOL exams but not IELTS.

The school is CReSTeD registered – about 20 need some sort of learning support. Much emphasis on inclusivity; girls offered one-to-one support to develop strategies and there is good support for teachers in the classroom to enable them to get the best out of students. Occasionally have to turn a girl away if the school feels they cannot meet her needs.

Girls offered careers advice from early on: via PSHE in the lower years and are then help with interview technique before work experience in year 10. They take part in the Big Business Pitch, a two day event where girls learn about starting and marketing their own business. Year 12s attend a higher education fair and an Oxbridge conference. Plenty of help with personal statement and university choices. The school also belongs to the ISCO which, for a fee, offers girls individual interviews and career profiling until the age of 23 – most sign up to this.

Games, options, the arts: Sport has come on by leaps and bounds in recent years; 'it was at the egg and spoon race stage when I arrived,' said the previous head. 'Now we have girls trialling for the England U18 hockey team, the Kent County Schools show jumping champion, a girl in the South of England eventing team, finalists in the National Biathlon Championships and an Elder (old girl) headed for Rio with the modern pentathlon team.' Good links with local hockey club – some county hockey and netball players and a girl training with the girls' U16 West Ham football team. All girls up until year 11 have to take part in team sports two or three times a week and sixth form have to take some exercise – zumba and yoga are popular. Indoor heated swimming pool with swimming coaching twice a week. Duke of Edinburgh compulsory in year 9 – most do bronze and a good number do silver, some start gold at school but complete it at university.

Impressive artwork displayed around the school reflects the internationalism of the pupils. Photography popular and school has its own darkroom as well as a suite of Apple Macs for digital work. One photography student invited to exhibit at the Royal Academy. Ceramics and sculpture particularly dynamic under the tutelage of the 'legendary clay man'.

The school has a fully-equipped drama studio, but the magnificent Gilt Hall is often used for productions and everyone has to take part in the inter-house drama competitions. One whole school play a year and girls do well in LAMDA exams.

The school fosters a spirit of adventure and leadership – girls encouraged to take assemblies and stand up in public, and about 20-30 attend the Model United Nations each year. Trips and expeditions all over the world as part of the Round Square – conferences and exchanges, usually for three to four weeks but sometimes for a whole term, and involvement in international projects working with students from other Round Square schools.

Ambitious head of music who previously worked in Barbados 'pushes the boundaries and has got the choirs going'. The school has links with Rochester Choral Society and the chamber choir has recently returned from a trip to Poland. About half the school takes individual music lessons in the music wing with nine practice rooms, a recording studio and digital music suite. 'It's a small, lively department – not that many do music, but those who do are very good and into it,' according to one girl.

Boarding: About 50 per cent board, mostly full with a few weekly and flexi-boarders – school is very accommodating

C

but likes 24 hours' notice unless there is an emergency, and charges accordingly. The younger girls sleep in Main Hall in bright light dorms of two to five. Two sixth form houses – Bligh and Brooke – with single and double rooms, many ensuite. All boarding houses have kitchens and common rooms with large televisions.

Sixth form boarders can eat breakfast and cook supper in their houses – they have a weekly visit to supermarket and are taught about food hygiene. 'We have a lot of fun in the boarding houses and boarding makes you learn how to rub along with people,' said one girl. Girls have genuine friends in different year groups and it really does seem to be a 'home from home'.

No Saturday school, but day girls have to come in on some Saturdays for activities, project work, and some school trips. 'My daughter sometimes asks to stay in for the weekend as the boarders have such fun, especially if there is a tip to Bluewater shopping centre,' said a mother. Cookery club runs on Saturdays: girls cook a meal and eat together in the evening

Background and atmosphere: The school is housed in a grade 1 listed Tudor mansion complete with turrets and chimneys and set in 150 acres of parkland between Gravesend and Rochester, about 30 miles from London and 10 minutes from Ebbsfleet station, with Eurostar connections to mainland Europe. Built for the 10th Baron Cobham in the 16th century and sold to the earls of Darnley in the 18th, it remained their family home until 1957. Often used as a film set, including for the Hetty Feather BBC series by Jacqueline Wilson and feature film Tulip Fever, as well as weddings and conferences. The school was opened in 1962 by Mrs Bee Mansell as an international boarding school for girls where they could enjoy the same education as boys. Cobham joined the Round Square in the early 1970s and was the first girls' school to do so. The name comes from the Round Square building at Gordonstoun, one of the original member schools where the first RS conference took place in 1967. Everyone given a map on arrival but girls quickly get used to their stunning surroundings – the ornate fireplaces and plasterwork ceilings and the glorious Gilt Hall complete with an 18th century organ soon get taken for granted.

Pastoral care, well-being and discipline: The Round Square philosophy 'there is more to you than you think' and 'education through experience' underpins everything the school does. 'It is only when girls step out of their comfort zone that they truly discover themselves.' Girls given a lot of autonomy and encouraged to use opportunities and 'they seem genuinely to care about the Round Square programme,' said one mother. 'Girls want to do well and we put so much pressure on ourselves – it is important to make time for yourself,' said our guide. Girls are trained and expected to take part in the running of the school and all staff and girls vote for the Guardian (head girl).

Older girls very supportive of younger ones and everyone is given a 'big sister' when they arrive; the mixed aged tutor groups in each house means there is good mixing between year groups. 'Everyone is very kind and my daughter and I both felt part of the Cobham family from the start,' said a mother. Years 7-11 have their own common rooms with kitchens, which encourages mixing between day girls and boarders. Weekly 'family lunch' when girls sit in tutor groups and practise their conversation skills. Bullying rare but nipped in the bud and restorative justice applied. Automatic suspension for drugs or alcohol – not that it is an issue here – and repeat offenders would be asked to leave.

Community service involves anything from visiting old people's homes and collecting food for food banks to helping out in local primary schools and youth clubs. There is a Christian Union group within the school and those of other faiths are encouraged to worship locally – there is a Sikh temple, mosque and synagogue nearby. Good communication between staff means any problems are picked up quickly

Pupils and parents: About 40 per cent of pupils are foreign nationals, rising to about 60 per cent in the sixth form, with increasing numbers of Europeans. No one nationality dominates; 'girls really do mix' and integration taken seriously – no two girls of the same nationality are allowed to share a bedroom and there are 'small sanctions, like kitchen duty, if you are caught speaking your native language during the day,' said our guide. Day girls come from as far afield as south east London. The school turns out girls who are 'confident and worldly-wise, who are keen to get involved and tend to be quite adventurous. The girls don't grow up too quickly and there is no need to yank up your skirt or slap on the make up as no one is going to see..They are more likely to be seen chatting in Lady Darnley's garden or swinging on "the branch".' 'Turns out confident and beautifully eloquent girls,' said one mother. The girls all see themselves as global citizens and have no fear of travel – 'the Round Square network means they have friends all over the world,' said a parent.

Elders, as the old girls are known at Cobham, are hugely loyal to the school and include Mishal Husain, news presenter, Olivia Graham, archdeacon of Berkshire, journalist Alex Crawford, Francesca Amfitiahtrof, creative director at Tiffany's, Princess Antonia, Duchess of Wellington and Kate French, who was part of the modern pentathlon team at Rio.

Entrance: Entry into years 7, 8, 9, 10 and sixth form via tests in English and maths and an interview with the headteacher in the autumn before entry. International students can either take the school's own tests or apply via UKiset. A taster afternoon and sleepover can be arranged at any time and parents are also given the opportunity to get to know each other. Main feeder schools are Steephill and St Joseph's at Gravesend, Pointers in Blackheath and south east London preps and local state primaries – the school runs a minibus service as far as Sevenoaks.

Some 10-20 join from abroad for the increasingly popular one year pre-A level course.

Exit: Around a third to half leave after GCSEs, mainly to larger co-ed schools, local grammars and sixth form colleges. For those who stay on for the sixth form, great trouble is taken to choose a course and university that is right for each girl. Around a fifth to Russell Group universities; art foundation and business courses popular as are eg criminology and biomedical sciences. Growing expertise in helping girls with the process of applying to foreign universities including Australia and the US – the school is able to help with SATs – and one off to Switzerland, another to Canada in 2018.

Money matters: Art, drama, music, sport and Round Square scholarships by application, and general (academic) scholarship by invitation only – identified through the entrance assessments. Means-tested bursaries are available for up to 100 per cent of fees.

Remarks: A small, truly international school which turns out compassionate and adventurous global citizens.

Cokethorpe School

Witney, Oxfordshire OX29 7PU

Ages 4–18 **Pupils** 666 **Sixth form** 151

Fees: £12,600 – £19,200 pa

01993 703921
www.cokethorpe.org.uk

Headmaster: Since 2002, Damian Ettinger BA MA PGCE (50s). Educated at St Joseph's College in London and the universities of Manchester and Surrey (theology and philosophy). Former head of theology and housemaster at Downside and before that at Prior Park College, Bath. Enthusiasm apparently unwaning after so many years in the job; the evolution of Cokethorpe continues with seemingly boundless momentum on his watch. So – he's not resting on his laurels then? 'What next is a constant concern', he assures. 'There's still a job to be done here, and I'm excited by it...although I don't want to be compared with Arsene Wenger'. Confident that Cokethorpe now 'cemented in the market as a credible alternative' to the great and the good of the Oxford school scene: 'we're not a highly academically selective school – but we are an academic school.'

Parents say he's 'quite a character' and 'a bit off the wall'. Says he 'likes people complaining,' and, five years since our last visit, is still waiting for pupils to launch an underground newspaper. Looking at the squeaky clean faces moving around the leafy campus, we doubt they ever will, but we respect Mr E just a little bit more for his subversive optimism. 'Knows all the children,' say parents, who like the fact that he's there to see them off on trips whatever time of day or night their departure. Keeps his hand in in the classroom by teaching civics programme and will quite happily step into handle a maternity cover if required. Married with five children – one still at Cokethorpe; jazz buff and classic car enthusiast.

Head of junior school: Since September 2018 is Nicola Black, formerly head of Dulwich College Kindergarten and Infants' School and before that director of studies at Hornsby House School in London. Recently appointed to the IAPS pre-prep advisory group.

Academic matters: National curriculum with extras followed in the junior school. Specialist teaching from reception for music, art, drama, languages and sport. Pupils rave about class teachers' creative approaches to teaching. We loved the Jurassic Park year 6 maths topic which covered the all too often punitive topics of area, perimeter, circumference, pi and money all in the guise of a clever, pupil-centric business game. French from reception, with tasters in Italian, German and Spanish in years 4 to 6. Latin in years 5 and 6, now continued to A level. Mixed ability classes of up to 20, with setting for maths and spelling from year 3. Accelerated reading programme throughout junior school and into years 7 and 8 with special prizes for word 'millionaires' and treats for those achieving full marks in the post-read quizzes. Newly introduced Cokethorpe Diploma ties together different aspects of the curriculum and enables progress to be tracked and rewarded, from reading to IT skills, academic engagement to academic outcome. Parents delighted with junior school from start to finish: 'wonderful', they say, 'can't fault it'.

Public examination results respectable, inching up year on year at GCSE and moving up in leaps and bounds at A level. Most take ten GCSEs. In 2018, 57 per cent A*-A/9-7 at GCSE; 44 per cent A*/A and 70 per cent A*-B at A level. Local state secondaries are good so parents want to know what they're paying for – but Cokethorpe is now delivering results that are comfortably ahead of these and most other local co-ed independents, although the single sex Oxford schools aren't yet quaking in their boots. Pre-U studied for history with good results. Despite upward trend, head isn't complacent. There's now a target of getting Oxbridge success to 10 per cent (six or seven per year) of cohort and 75 per cent to Russell Group, although 'there's no fixed mindset,' he assures; 'we're just as happy for our pupils to go to Harper Adams if that's right for them.'

There's a way to go but watch this space – greater numbers of pupils choosing traditional academic A levels (maths, physics and economics all currently top choices) should help pay dividends in this regard. BTec in business (four days in school and one day on work placement) now available to a maximum of nine pupils for whom A levels are not the right path. 'Many schools wouldn't have the confidence to offer it,' says head, 'but we see BTec as a great opportunity to offer an alternative route. It gets you places.' Participating pupils agree: 'phenomenal' and 'amazing' they say. Their A level counterparts give the history and drama departments top marks as departments with best teachers. Parents 'can't say that absolutely all the teachers are fantastic' ('mediocre' was a word we heard from several): 'they're not uniformly up there with teachers at the top Oxford schools,' although a few departments received praise as having 'pockets of excellence' amongst teaching staff. Physics, English and maths top performers at A level. Sociology and psychology both available at A level. Value added in top eight per cent nationally.

SEN department now shifting away from calling themselves 'learning support' to becoming 'learning development': 'the point of the department is to develop the skills necessary to successfully access the curriculum'. Around eight per cent of cohort on register – and although one-to-one tuition does take place, integration is always the objective. Can support pupils with mild to moderate SpLD and 'mainstream' ASD. Progress of all pupils carefully tracked and when things go wrong school says first conversation is with the pastoral team, then action plans with objectives and timeframes are put in place: 'we put the responsibility for learning on the pupils.'

Games, options, the arts: The fabulous grounds are put to great use for all major sports – rugby, football and cricket (plus some hockey in recent years) for boys, and hockey (year 8 were 2018 county champions), netball and either tennis (national finalists in 2018) or cricket for girls ('huge'). All that's missing is a swimming pool – but nobody seems to mind and lessons take place at Brize Norton. Director of sport ensures four hours of physical activity per week for every pupil. School has own boathouse for kayaking (but alas no rowing) and there's a new nine-hole par 3 golf course. We could only see fixture sheets for A and B teams in junior school, but senior pupils were keen to assure us that 'if you commit to a sport, you'll be in a team', plus there are tons of inter-house competitions to ensure everyone gets stuck in. Strong record of national competition successes in clay pigeon shooting and kayaking. A few grumbles from parents that sporting standards have slipped in recent years – although coaching standards are 'very high', they say, school struggles to attract sufficiently talented pupils. Disappointingly 2018 didn't see the 1st XV win a single match, although pupils assure us that 'rugby's a really big thing'. For the elite, tours such as rugby to Biarritz are the cherry on top.

Director of co-curricular position created in recent years to preside over the 180 activities (or AOBs as they are known) available per week in the senior school (some pupils manage up to six per week), all taking place during the school day. A long lunch break of 95 minutes and buses that leave the grounds at 5pm facilitate participation and pupils in years 7 and 8 are expected to do a minimum of two per week. Higher up the school, one compulsory academic clinic is added to the schedule. Annual curriculum enrichment week sees pupils head off to anywhere from Thorpe Park for a business course to Auschwitz for history.

'Very active' drama department, with termly whole school productions (recently Oliver Twist, Grease and Lord of the Flies), with extra parts written in for keen participants if necessary, taking place in the performing arts space in former lawnmower shed. School boasts own wardrobe mistress and pupils can manage lighting and sound. Formerly weak music department now 'absolutely thriving' under entirely new staff. Profile of singing raised throughout whole school – all choirs open to everyone with no audition – and with tours to destinations such as, recently, Cologne, we're not surprised by their popularity; bands galore, including award-winning jazz band, and 350 peripatetic lessons every week. Music for all to a very high standard – we liked the way it is unavoidable even for those who do not play or sing: pupils give lunchtime music recitals, madrigals on May Day (happily we were there to witness these), a singing category for all in the inter-house competition, and the choir sings grace from the gallery to dining pupils below every Wednesday. DT and art benefit from spacious well-appointed workshops. Art, photography and textiles offered at GCSE and A level.

Background and atmosphere: It's not often that a seasoned Good Schools Guide writer pauses to gasp upon entering a school estate, but by golly when we drove into Cokethorpe, we did stop and draw breath. Granted, the weather gods had smiled upon the school on the day of our tour, but we cannot recall visiting a more picturesque or well-groomed school setting on our Thames Valley travels and parents describe it as 'an amazing learning environment'. The Cotswold stone Queen Anne building housing the junior school and offices presides serenely over vast striped lawns, littered with ancient trees, meandering pathways and eclectic sculptures (the giant peacock in pride of place on the front lawn was crafted from trees ripped from the ground by a tornado in recent years). Upon entering the Vanbrugh-style mansion, where the first Viscount Harcourt entertained literary fellows Swift, Dryden and Pope, you could almost forget you were entering a school (save the chattering throng of year 5s excitedly bustling past on their way off to PGL). Not a tatty noticeboard or dusty trophy cabinet in sight.

Reception to year 6 are taught in an array of spacious and characterful classrooms arranged over three floors (we loved the cosy attic feel of the year 6 rooms) and benefit from sharing the grounds, dining hall, sporting and academic facilities (science labs and IT suites) with their senior school comrades. Beyond the main building lies an array of equally enchanting features: a round a cobbled mews is the main academic quad, one-to-one learning support rooms in converted stables, a roundhouse and clocktower. The red telephone box book exchange (suspiciously tidy) is just one of head's quirky brainchildren; 'if one day he put a plane in the middle of the quad and said it was the new history classroom, I wouldn't be surprised,' quipped our (staff) guide. Sixth formers have The Grove, their own coffee shop, serving free drinks and snacks, also used as an alternative to the staff room by teachers: 'great for modelling adult behaviour and keeping channels of communication open,' we were told; 'our students are people people – it's perfectly normal to them to chat casually with teachers.' Sixth form centre, atop the trendy glass and metal library, designed to merge seamlessly against the trad buildings, a jewel in the crown for older pupils, although some parents felt that sixth formers are not given the freedom they deserved to study wherever they please. Further riches outside: on top of the fabulous pitches, Astroturf and forest school, there's a new clay pigeon range, air pistol range and climbing tower.

Pastoral care, well-being and discipline: School is joint Roman Catholic and C of E foundation and pastoral care has long been viewed as a pillar of the school, although parents we spoke to had polarised opinions, with some having total confidence in the school's ability to guide their child through the teenage years and others left feeling disappointed that their child had not received the support they needed through tricky times. We heard of a few nasty examples of bullying at the top of the school – again with mixed views on how they were dealt with. Possibly not the obvious choice for children that are quirky or have an obviously unusual character. The sample of pupils we met seemed happy, however: 'there are loads of siblings here so everyone knows everyone else – there's a real family feel.' Despite improving academics, head keen to continue taking less academically able younger siblings: 'other schools could learn from our good practice'. Pupils well informed about safeguarding and there's a new peer mentor system with selected pupils trained by school counsellor. PSHCE provides pupils with a well-being and integrity toolkit that 'creates constructive dialogue and educates pupils about their choices'.

Pupils and parents: 'Not a pretentious school,' the head told us. And not a diverse one either. Parents looking for a slice of real life grit for their offspring, move along please. Steadfastly Caucasian and middle class, pupils delivered daily into the 'Cokethorpe bubble' (in the words of one student) on a fleet of coaches covering over 20 routes encompassing Swindon, Oxford, Brize Norton and Didcot. Parents the usual mix of professionals, academics, medics and city workers, and pupils a conservative bunch.

Entrance: Deliberately tiny reception class – just 10 pupils at the time of our visit – with a maximum of 12. Pupils arrive in increasing numbers throughout the junior school, with two forms of 16 by the time they reach year 6. Assessments in maths and English for places in reception to year 2, plus an assessment day and report from previous school in years 3 to 6. Up to 72 places available in year 7. Half of these taken by pupils moving up from junior school, with the remaining places going to applicants from over 20 prep and state primary schools. Preps sending pupils in numbers include Chandlings, St Hugh's, The Manor and New College. Competitive entry (maths, English, interview and observed activities) for external candidates with about four applicants for every place. Sibling rule applies as long as they are suited to the school and although pupils passing through the junior school are not guaranteed a place, it's rare for school not to move them up. Candidates at 13+ offered provisional places on basis of pre-test, subject to performance at CE. Sixth form entry (about a dozen places available most years) requires 9-4 in maths, English and science plus decent grades in subjects to be studied at A level.

Exit: Almost none leave after year 6, although parents given heads up in year 5 if child not thought to be suited to senior school environment. Between 10 and 15 per cent leave after GCSE, mainly for local colleges. At 18 to a broad range of universities reflecting the broad academic intake and range of academic ability. Durham, York, Exeter, Warwick, Edinburgh and Nottingham are popular university destinations, also agricultural college and a few gap years. One to Oxford in 2018 and one medic. One or two most years to drama or art college – including two in recent years to RADA. Refreshingly, school HE fair now includes not just universities and colleges but also degree apprenticeships ('quite embryonic, but we want to make sure that everyone's aware of all their options'). We approve. Careers talks for sixth form every Friday, covering everything from student finance or UCAS application to career insights from old pupils or parents.

Money matters: Fees around the same level as nearby independents. Plenty of means-tested scholarships and bursaries for all manner of talents: academic, art, music, sport, drama, classics, modern languages and all-rounder. Points mean prizes with the introduction of new (and we think unique) 'academic and leadership grants'. Pupils earn points for pre-assigned achievements from year 7 onwards: think major contributions to sport (at national, regional or county level; high involvement inside school); academic excellence (calculated by average grades at GCSE), awards in high grade music or LAMDA exams) or participation in eg D of E or World Challenge. These are totted up and converted into discounted fees for sixth formers of up to 20 per cent. We're not sure that we like such a blatantly transactional incentive – good old-fashioned school spirit is the best driver of excellence in our book, but school says the scheme aims to 'celebrate successes' of pupils across the ability range, not just the most able.

Remarks: A spectacular learning environment that can cater for children of all abilities if they fit the Cokethorpe mould. Not the obvious choice for families made up entirely of brainboxes, and worth keeping an eye on academic trends and an ear to the ground regarding pastoral care, but one for the list if the single sex Oxford powerhouses are not your cup of tea or if your offspring span the academic range.

Colchester County High School for Girls

73

Norman Way, Colchester, Essex CO3 3US

Ages 11–18 **Pupils** 971 **Sixth form** 220

01206 576973
www.cchsg.com

Executive principal and CEO: Since 2010, Gillian Marshall MSc BSc (biochemistry) PGCE NPQH. Previously deputy head at the mixed comprehensive Notley High School, Braintree, for 11 years. Prior to that teaching posts at Bishop's Stortford High School for Boys, Townley Girls' Grammar School in Bexleyheath and Davenant Foundation Christian Ecumenical School in Loughton. A biology and chemistry specialist, she says she has 'always loved teaching and never considered doing anything else'. Keen on all sport, particularly running. Mrs Marshall has three children.

She and her SLT are on a mission to take the school 'beyond outstanding', by 're-evaluating its vision' and making sure that its precious cargo of some of the country's brightest students are instilled with a 'world-class education', and the self-belief and resilience to use it to make a real difference.

Academic matters: A regular feature in the UK's top 10 high-achievers for both attainment and value added, CCHSG attracts the cream of the crop with ease. These bright students have fought their way through the rigorous consortium of selective schools in Essex 11+ exam and are veritable sponges for the stimulating, thought-provoking, multi-faceted education that awaits them. French and German are begun in year 7 and Latin kicks in in year 8. Students must take at least one of French or German to GCSE. Sciences are taught separately from year 7 and are popular A level options. Technology lessons for years 7, 8 and 9 are run in conjunction with Essex University where the students learn a variety of skills in state-of-the-art facilities.

School achieved its 'best results ever' in 2018: 90 per cent A*-A/9-7 at GCSE and 62 per cent A*/A and 88 per cent A*/B at A level. Maths regularly delivers at least an A/7 grade for 90 per cent of those taking it. Sixth formers mentor the younger ones. Everyone studies creative and critical thinking from year 7.

Such stellar achievement in all areas may cause a few anxieties, but parents applaud the school's ability 'to achieve excellent exam results without the students being stressed' and the 'serene atmosphere'. The quiet expectation is that students will be independent, organised and, adds a parent, 'achieve high grades from year 7 onwards'. Indeed the most recent Ofsted report was tantamount to flawless. 'Students here enjoy being successful and achieving,' explains the headteacher. Lessons encourage the deeper exploration of knowledge through lively debate, challenge and innovation. Ever-present is the necessity for all learning to have a real-world application.

The school has a small number of students on the SEND register and the SENCo ensures that appropriate support is offered both on an individual basis and via in-class assistance where necessary. Staff themselves are constantly updated on individual students' needs, and the school works closely with students, parents, and external agencies.

Games, options, the arts: The headteacher's drive for 'excellence in everything' really does extend to everything. Numerous musical groups, ensembles and choirs, many instigated by the students themselves, are all of exceptional quality. Drama is traditionally strong, with two major whole school productions each year and year 7 students also taking part in annually in performances of Shakespeare and Dickens. Art shows great depth of sensitivity, maturity and complexity for students of such relative youth and – typical of the CCHSG approach – projects are seen as an opportunity for general education as well as refinement of artistic technique. Works are displayed in galleries and exhibitions across the region and in London, on a regular basis. 'Creativity should be in every lesson,' says head. The school has the Artsmark award.

CCHSG students have dominated Colchester Blackwater School Sports Partnerships competitions of all kinds – netball, hockey, basketball, athletics in particular – for the past 25 years. Gym and dance are on the PE curriculum for all year groups. Elite athletes are picked and trained in squads, but those with more enthusiasm than talent have many active clubs to choose from every lunchtime, including very popular before, during and after-school swimming in the school pool. An impressive range of subject based and other extracurricular clubs run throughout the week, some of which are run by senior pupils; staff are generous with their time and encouragement. D of E is thriving with over 100 students participating each year. The school has accreditation to run bronze, silver and gold awards in-house. Sixth form students are involved in the European Youth Parliament and in developing their entrepreneurial skills through the Young Enterprise Scheme. Inspirational speakers (eg first British woman to reach the top of Everest, Rebecca Stephens, and Paralympian Steve Brown) emphasise the 'I can do anything' ethos that pervades all aspects of the school.

Background and atmosphere: Founded at the turn of the century but relocated to its current site, a campus setting on a quiet road a mile from the centre of Colchester, in 1957. Aims to be the 'new generation of grammar school' – free of the shackles of traditional Victorian architecture and atmosphere that

C

pervades some of our longest established state selective schools. The building has been much upgraded with the replacement of all the once rattly metal framed windows with fresh energy efficient panes and painted panels. Brings the campus into the 21st century. More than a million pounds have been spent on upgrading the facilities here (including new and refurbed science labs) to ensure they do justice to the quality of teaching and learning at one of the UK's very highest achieving schools. The Big Build project has provided an extension to the sixth form facilities and a new classroom block to replace the tired portacabins; a new multi-functional sports hall is currently being constructed.

Extensive playing fields on site, and green spaces between the teaching blocks have been much improved with fencing and picnic benches for students to gather on at breaks.

Students rave about the food – a dedicated catering manager buys fresh ingredients every day and with his team of staff even tries out recipes suggested by the students. Bright dining space – recently expanded – serves hot and cold food, and students who have lunchtime clubs can request food to be speedily collected and eaten wherever is most convenient. Payment is via a biometric system (fingerprint recognition). Breakfast club operates from 8.00am, which is particularly helpful for the many students who travel a considerable distance to school.

Pastoral care, well-being and discipline: With so much talent in a relatively small space, CCHSG could be something of a pressure cooker environment; however, the strategy is to use PE and PSHE lessons to teach coping skills, approaches to revision and even breathing exercises at crucial times. Students themselves say they feel well supported by form tutors, who move up through the years with their charges as far as year 11. Very many opportunities for students to act as role models – year 10 Literacy Leaders run sessions on eg the proper use of the apostrophe and give literacy lessons to local primary pupils, Junior Sports Leaders and Youth Health Champions offer lifestyle workshops. Charity work is intrinsic – students choose good causes to support through cake sales, non-uniform days etc and raise around a whopping £10,000 a year. Students appear to get along happily together and self-discipline is exemplary – detention rarely resorted to. Students recently prompted an overhaul of the rewards system – merits in years 7 and 8 and now 'R awards' in year 9, with the names of those receiving them entered into a raffle for a tasty prize (recently an iPad), plus pens, pencils and Amazon or book vouchers along the way. Years 10 and 11 receive commendations. Every half term each member of staff recognises a pupil for achievement and another for endeavour with a congratulatory letter home – seniority of staff member signing denotes the magnitude. Also rewards for attendance, community service and many Jack Petchey. Grade for 'attitude to learning' now replaces 'effort' in reports.

Pupils and parents: 'Self-awareness, self-esteem and self-discipline' are key attributes here, and students grow up in a supportive environment that nurtures confidence, maturity and the belief in oneself necessary to achieve any chosen goal. Joining CCHSG from around 65 different primary schools across central and north Essex and south Suffolk, students are from varying home backgrounds, a handful with English as a second language (although their fluency has enabled them to get through the entrance exam).

Lots of leadership roles: as well as head girls and deputies, there are form prefects, literacy and sports leaders. Student Voice members meet weekly with a vice principal to discuss student matters and well-being and work on projects eg improving facilities, healthy canteen food, school reward policies and nominating candidates for the Jack Petchey Awards.

Keeping in touch with parents is not easy, given the geography, but there's a half termly e-newsletter celebrating the many achievements and a weekly information bulletin to parents and students (also published on website); parents also increasingly engage with the school's lively Facebook page and Twitter account. Parents are largely supportive of school events and the PTFA has grown in recent years, running a series of successful fundraising and social events across the year. A welcome guide for new year 7s is prepared by older students who identified a need.

Old students include plantswoman, garden designer and author Beth Chatto OBE, Olympic gold medal-winning sailor Saskia Clark and MP Stella Creasy.

Entrance: One of the top-performing schools in the UK, it's no surprise that places are highly sought-after. Entrance is granted to those 160 students who perform best in the consortium of selective schools in Essex 11+ exam – maths and English. For all students joining the sixth form, minimum entry requirement is four 7s and two 6s, including English language and mathematics and 9-7 in the subjects to be taken at A level. Many travel from far and wide, some lodging in Colchester for convenience.

Exit: Around 20 per cent leave post-GCSEs – mostly to co-ed sixth forms or Colchester Sixth Form College. Nearly all year 13 leavers to university, generally several to Oxbridge, with a few to art college, music conservatoire or higher level apprenticeships. York, UAE, UCL, Sheffield and Bath recent popular choices. Law, medicine and academia established career paths.

Remarks: A place of education that is not just a beacon nationally, but also internationally, delivering a world-class education to students equipped with the drive, intelligence and integrity to take the lead in any chosen field and to make a rich contribution in life.

Colchester Royal Grammar School

6 Lexden Road, Colchester, Essex CO3 3ND

Ages 11–18 **Pupils** 957 **Sixth form** 381 (112 girls) **Boarders** 30 full (sixth form, currently boys only)

Fees: Boarding £13,200 pa; Day: free

01206 509100
www.crgs.co.uk

Headmaster: Since 2015, John Russell BSc MA ARCS, previously deputy head of Cranbrook School. Physics degree from Imperial College; first job in a Loughton comprehensive school before becoming head of physics at Ilford County High.

Gracious, unintimidating and refreshingly honest and transparent, he is a hands-on head, who teaches physics to at least one year group every year, and has plans to do more. Students regularly pop into his office unannounced, usually to tell of their successes. 'If I grant them a leave of absence – which I sometimes do for competitions as far away as Poland – the criteria is that they have to tell me how it went afterwards.' We noticed he pays the same level of respect to students as they give to him in conversations – it's all very mutual, with no draconian rules around standing up when he walks into a classroom etc. 'He's not like a headmaster – he's one of the team and the students love him for it,' a parent told us. He has a weekly drop-in session for parents and staff say he is highly supportive and consultative.

He lives five minutes' walk away with his wife, Michelle, a chemistry teacher, and their three children, two of whom are at the school. Describes himself as an enthusiastic sportsman if not a very accomplished one, with a particular enjoyment of football and racket sports. Also has a passion for music.

Academic matters: Extremely high academic standards, with the school's A level results nearly 72 per cent A*/A and 93 per cent A*-B in 2018 – having made them number one in the government league tables for most of the last 10 years. 'One student recently got nine A*s and 2 As, and that was at A level,' says the head. At GCSE, 80 per cent A*-A/9-7 grades.

No setting in years 7 or 8, French and maths setted from year 9 – 'but this is only a question of pace,' says school. 'Set 4 pupils will still be expected to achieve 9-8 at GCSE.' French and Latin in year 7, plus additional choice of German or Greek in year 8. One of the very few state schools to offer Greek to A level – for a state school, an above average number go on to study classics at university. No areas of weakness to speak of at either GCSE or A level, with particularly outstanding results in humanities, maths, sciences, DT and economics. 'We have lots of further maths students,' says head. If the school doesn't teach a subject that a student desperately wants to do, they'll try to provide one lecture a week if the student agrees to self-teach the rest. 'We've done this with government and politics, Mandarin and a number of other subjects in the past,' says head.

So what's the secret of their success? One word – teaching. Students rave about the teachers here, notably their commitment to keeping every single pupil intellectually stretched and on track to meet their targets, providing extra support and revision clubs as necessary, and being available out-of-hours via email. 'There's lots of talk about where you should be at and how to achieve it.' Then there's the sheer quality of teaching. 'They keep it imaginative, fresh and innovative at all times.' 'They're not afraid to throw the textbooks aside.' 'You are never bored in a lesson.' 'Their enthusiasm is contagious.' Etc. Not a single inattentive expression spotted during our visit – these youngsters are hungry to learn and the teaching is a feast, in every sense. 'It's made very clear that it's ok to fail – that's how you learn – and my son has thrived because of it,' said one parent. 'It's not just intellectually rigorous and stimulating, it's relevant too – showing boys how what they're learning fits into today's world,' said another. 'It's more than about getting these youngsters to pass exams – it's about where this learning is going to take them in life.' Homework levels are, according to students, 'reasonable – and if you haven't been able to do it, there's a culture of support, rather than an immediate sanction.' Maximum of 30 in a class lower down; 25 at GCSE; and 20 in sixth form.

Some SEND pupils with physical disabilities, including visual impairments, and a fair number of Asperger's, plus a few dyslexic. Support is mainly classroom-based, and parents could not praise it more highly. 'With our son, they have taken a difficult autistic boy and grown him into a wonderful young man – coping with his complexities and outbursts in their stride, and celebrating every minor success. The staff should be getting an OBE, in my opinion,' one parent told us. Any EAL pupil will have had a high enough standard of English to pass the selection tests.

Games, options, the arts: Cricket and rugby strong. Regular fixtures against state and independent schools, with some representation at national level. Increasing strength in athletics. Netball, and now rugby, for sixth form girls. 'That's the one thing I'd change – I really think there could be more on offer for girls,' one told us. Other sports available as extracurricular activities, including sailing and weight-training. 'Sport here is inclusive – it's not all about the top players,' parents assured us. Extensive playing fields five minutes' walk away – 'less than ideal, but that's the way it is,' says head. Within the school, there's tarmacked playground, which is regularly used for sport, plus a heated outdoor pool.

Exciting music department, which takes up a whole (on site) three-storey house, with loads of opportunities for any pupil with any musical ambitions. 'Our son is musical, but I didn't know what to expect with this school because it's better known for the academia, but the opportunities for learning and performing have massively impressed us,' said one parent. No shortage of instruments (many donated by old boys) and break-out rooms. Live music in every assembly; choirs and school orchestra; ensembles and bands, many student led; and 200 learn an instrument with a peripatetic teacher.

Drama only offered as extracurricular, but popular, with a much-talked-about annual performance, with examples including Fame and West Side Story. Rehearsals for a French play when we visited, as part of French lessons, highlighting their commitment to cross-curricular teaching. Spacious and light art block where – joy of joys – average work sits side-by-side the obvious greats. 'If I'm honest, art is not my son's strongest subject, but he still wanted to do it for GCSE and he's been encouraged at every turn – the school understands that the benefits of art aren't just for those who are brilliant at it,' said one parent. Around 12 do art GCSE art, and similar figures for A level. DT rooms also spacious, and clearly well-used and loved.

Lots of sport and music themes among the clubs, plus the likes of BBC Young Reporters' Club, right through to more obscure ones such as Rubik's cube club, Swedish club and even a colouring club. Many are student led. Very strong public speaking society, which regularly competes. 'You should see them – watching one of the boys talk is like watching Tony Blair,' says the head. Students enter so many competitions that even the head loses track, although he's now got himself a 'little black book' to record them in. Day trips to London for cultural days out and year 7s were at Colchester Zoo the day we visited. Plus residentials eg classics trip to Italy; languages trips to Germany; sports tours to Italy. 'We do bonding trips too, including taking all year 7s to the cinema at the end of the first term, and we recently took year 12s on a bowling night,' says the head. Plenty of charity work, including an award-winning mental health charity, Time to Talk, which was set up by students themselves.

Boarding: Two boarding houses for sixth form boys (school is currently developing girls' boarding provision), both with a mixture of single and double bedrooms (generally, you share in year 12 and get your own room in year 13). There are cooking facilities and a communal area in each house, and four resident staff members for the 30 boarders. Boarders mainly those who would have too far to travel to school each day and pupils from abroad; particularly popular in Hong Kong, where a member of staff visits each year to interview potential sixth formers, with these students now making up around half of all boarders.

After school finishes at 3.40pm, there's free time, followed by dinner at 6pm and study time from 7-9pm. Lights out at 10.30pm on weekdays and 11pm on weekends. Plenty of freedom to go into town, albeit with a strict signing in and out system. 'Some go into London too, as well as to stay with local friends, although we need permission from their parents for that,' the housemaster told us. Organised trips out include cycling and visiting Cambridge. But, for the most part, they seem content to hang around school, where they are permitted to use school sports and music facilities during evenings and weekends. The gym – which had unfortunately flooded when we visited – is also popular. 'Staying here also gives us a chance for a weekend lie-in,' one boarder smiled.

Some of the rooms could do with a bit of TLC, but then again this is state boarding. And with bedrooms not quite as tidy as in many schools we visit, we weren't surprised when we were told by the housemaster that 'we do guidelines, rather than rules.' 'These are young men, and we treat them as such – but with the pastoral structure very firmly in the background,' he explains. Lots of transition work, especially for the Hong Kong contingent, where boys get to meet each other before they arrive and are given plenty of information to help them prepare.

Background and atmosphere: Directly descended from a Colchester town school that existed in 1206 and was granted royal charters by Henry VIII in 1539 and Elizabeth I in 1584. Set in an affluent residential area of Colchester, the main buildings date back to the late 19th century. These are home to some classic grammar school classrooms, with big windows overlooking the shiny floored corridors, plus a very traditional, well-stocked library, complete with oil paintings of old headmasters on the wall, and additional silent room at the side. Newer additions – which include blocks for science and engineering, computing and art and renovated music and drama facilities – fit well with the attractive old school buildings. Wonderful to see sixth form engineering students hard at work on imaginative projects (top secret, we were warned when we busily scribbled down the details – but all proper real world stuff that could potentially change lives). The sixth form centre is home to a lively common room, with a large, all-school, cashless refectory to the side. Lovely, well-tended gardens of a standard unusual in a state school, featuring quiet and private sitting areas for students – in full use when we visited. Head admits he'd like 'more room for sixth form private study, but I think we're lucky with everything else.'

Despite the emphasis on academic brilliance, the atmosphere here is supportive, caring and – according to some students – 'almost family-like.' 'Everyone assumes it's a hothouse, but it's really not. And we have such a diverse range of people – some are natural brainboxes; others have to work really hard to get on.' The common denominator, they say, is that everyone is a self-starter and highly motivated. We encountered lots of laughter and fun banter, including with teachers. 'There's something very special about the ethos here that quite a few of us parents get quite emotional about,' one parent said.

Everyone welcomes the addition of girls at sixth form. 'They settle in very quickly and tend to be very sociable, bringing the boys out of their shell,' explains the head. Uniform includes a vivid purple blazer, and for sixth formers, it's smart dress. Loud, old-fashioned bell system that's a bit of a bone-shaker until you get used to it, but it certainly gets kids moving swiftly.

Pastoral care, well-being and discipline: Excellent standard of conduct and not many discipline problems, yet nobody describes this as a 'strict' school. 'There's nothing onerous about the discipline here. In fact, there's plenty of space to make mistakes and learn from them,' said one parent. 'They have this gentle, reward-based, quite soft culture that brings out the best in everyone,' said another. Punishments, when they do happen, include loss of privileges and lunchtime and after-school detentions. No permanent expulsions in the head's time at the school, although around three temporary ones. Zero tolerance of drugs – possession leads to expulsion – with no cases in recent years.

Lots of staff leadership roles, which helps create a strong pastoral system. Beneath the deputy head is the head of lower school, head of sixth form and heads of year. Big focus on promoting mental health and healthy lifestyles. Buddy schemes; part-time school counsellor; plenty of emphasis on transition to make sure year 7s and new year 12s settle in well. Minimal bullying. A fair amount of stress, particularly around exam time support, but there is support. 'My son had a wobble due to the pressures of work and the school dealt with it very compassionately, gathering together the relevant teachers to support him and keep us informed.'

Pupils and parents: Years 7-11 mainly from Colchester and surrounding area, but students travel up to an hour each way each day, including from Ipswich and even east London. Students come from a complete mix of families, both ethnically (including international, especially in the sixth form boarders contingent) and in terms of wealth and class. All feel extremely grateful – rarely have we come across such an appreciative bunch. Very active parents' association (called CRGSA).

Old boys include Telegraph columnist Giles Smith, economics commentator Tim Congdon, costume designer and double Oscar winner Jim Acheson, founder of Freeserve, John Pluthero and former BBC education correspondent Mike Baker. 'Our alumni are very supportive,' says the head. 'If we have a big project on the go, they always try to help and they are very keen to support anyone who is in a financially vulnerable position – those who would otherwise miss out on an opportunity. They are also supportive when it comes to careers, helping sixth formers move on, offering internships, interview advice and networking.'

Entrance: Highly competitive September 11+ exam, made up of English (including verbal reasoning) and maths papers. Places are awarded in rank order to the top 120 boys who have named Colchester Royal Grammar School as a preference (the school is expanding, so while there used to be 850 students, they're increasing that figure to 1,000). Candidates do not have to live in Essex. Around 450 apply. Head discourages tutoring your way in, although isn't blind to the fact that it happens anyway – is trying to offer more support to able local primary school students who can't afford it. No preference for those on pupil premium.

Minimum of four grade 7s and two 6s at GCSE for entry into sixth form for internal and external candidates. 'But because places are awarded in rank order, in reality they'll need a lot of 9-8s,' says the head. Around 450 external entrants apply for the 100 or so places (half of them girls), who also require a school report and must satisfy the school's academic requirements. Candidates for sixth form boarding places must meet the academic requirements first. Overseas boarders must be British or EU passport holders.

Exit: Some 90 per cent stay onto sixth form – 'the five or so boys who leave usually do so because we aren't offering the courses they want,' says head. Sixth formers virtually all to university, mostly to Russell Group including Imperial, LSE, Durham, Bath, Bristol and increasingly, St Andrews. Also MIT and Hong Kong. Popular courses include sciences, economics, history, English and languages. In 2018, 29 to Oxbridge, 21 medics/vets.

Remarks: 'This is the best education that money can't buy,' was a favourite expression of the head's predecessor – and we think that's still the case. One of the country's top selective boys' state schools, which rivals many independents, but without the hard edges that schools of this calibre can have. 'It's exceeded our expectations,' was the most common phrase we heard from parents. Any academically able and hard-working boy (and sixth form girl) should thrive here.

Cothill House

Linked with Chandlings Prep School

75

Cothill, Abingdon, Oxfordshire OX13 6JL

Ages 8–13 **Pupils** 204 **Boarders** All full **C of E**

Fees: £27,660 pa

01865 390800
www.cothill.net

Headmaster: Since 2011, Mr Duncan Bailey (30s). Educated at Cothill and Eton then Manchester University (French) and Vienna University (German). Bitten by teaching bug during year abroad but harboured ambitions to nurture passion for sport, particularly tennis, and moved into sports management. 'Fell into teaching' after being asked to stand in for head of modern languages at Eton, where he spent two years. Prior to taking headship at Cothill, ran Sauveterre, the Cothill Trust's French outpost, for eight years.

Married to Maria (his 'secret weapon' according to parents), lives at heart of school with two daughters. A hands-on couple, the Baileys are in true loco parentis – head says he is 'a parent above all things' – taking full responsibility for the four year groups housed in the main school building. Maria 'does everything,' from rolling up her sleeves to help with cooking, cleaning, teaching and running the school if required, right down to marching boys back to the salad bar if they don't have enough veggies on their plates.

Relaxed and approachable, with the chameleonic ability to switch between the persona of favourite uncle and respected leader, and not averse to taking pupils on at table tennis or joining in with an after-hours skateboarding session, head says he 'likes boys to be happy, expects them to be busy and insists they are polite.' Parents consider him 'very dynamic, involved and committed to the school' and the few that were 'worried he might be a bit green' when appointed have climbed firmly back into their boxes.

Entrance: Recruits about 20 boys with a 'fairly broad brush' into year 4, with intakes in both September and April, numbers swelling to between 25 and 30 by end of year. Parents and boys interviewed together ('we choose the whole family') to establish fit rather academic ability. Boys assessed rather than tested, in English and maths. Majority at this point from London preps with just a few local boys in the mix. Good number of Forces' children and between 10 and 15 per cent international (Spanish, Russian, Chinese and Thai) although head insists on fluent English as no EAL on offer ('they have to be able to survive in the boarding environment').

Oversubscribed from year 5, with head looking for 'boys who are prepared to roll up their sleeves and get stuck in' above all else. Drop-out rate of less than one a year. A number join in summer term of year 5 to settle in before real focus on destination schools starts in year 6.

Exit: About 20 to 25 per cent each to Eton, Radley and Harrow. Smaller numbers to Winchester, Marlborough and Wellington, plus Sherborne, Stowe, St Edward's and Malvern. No fall-out to day schools. Huge focus on 'negotiating' places with destination schools with evidence of heart and soul going into making sure boys land in the best places. 'A good handful' of scholarships most years, most notably in art and music.

Remarks: Steadfastly traditional and so discreet you could miss it altogether in its picturesque village setting. No grand buildings or flashy reception. Visitors arrive directly into the heart of the school (the dining room) – giving the first clue to school's substance over style ethos. Main building is a large country house with later additions nestled in 26 acres of grounds, playing fields and woodland. Sports and leisure facilities include a 15 metre indoor pool, six all-weather tennis courts, a nine-hole golf course, a somewhat shabby, albeit well used squash court cum table tennis room and a fleet of shiny BMXs for tearing around the woods. Equally appreciated by pupils is the wealth of retreats where they can spend as much free time as they like indulging creative passions such as woodwork (a real favourite with boys, guided by former police officer known as 'PC'), pottery and art. There's also a large, modern library and gleaming ICT suite for, amongst other things, Skyping home, although a handwritten letter once a week is compulsory.

No common, bar a pool room, and no significant evidence of televisions (junior movie nights and major sporting events only are hosted in head's sitting room) or other passive distractions. Parents report boys roaring around on scooters in their pyjamas before bedtime rather than gluing themselves to screens. And therein lies the magic of the place. Macs and iPads do have a home here but what Cothill really offers is a Swallows and Amazons style education. It's a school where boys can 'have a childhood,' say parents. They can build dens or bird boxes, go pond dipping or interpret Notre Dame Cathedral in clay to their hearts' content. Parents and boys also firmly supportive of full boarding ethos (two exeats per term), which makes for fun-filled weekends jam packed with activities for all, not just those who live too far away to make a weekly journey home. Broad geographical spread, from Scottish Highlands to Norfolk as well as overseas, makes for a collegiate bunch.

Majority of parents from upper echelons, most of whom have gone 'through the system', with titles aplenty. Car park generally occupied by ancient mud splattered 4x4s rather than gleaming Maseratis on match days and supporters, who are encouraged and welcomed to visit twice a week, tend to be of the green welly variety, with the odd royal godparent thrown in for good measure. In the words of one mother, 'definitely not the facelift and white Range Rover crowd.' That said, head reports increasing numbers of professional, middle class London parents, keen to escape the hothouse London day school scene and allow their boys the space and roundedness offered by a country prep. One such parent reported that without exception the children are just from 'incredibly nice families who want the very best education.' Boys confident, smiley and polite and, with shirts untucked and ties askew, the slightest hint of Just William.

Strong artsy feel around the place with examples of boys' work festooning every spare wall and surface. Music, art and DT highly praised and head's bet with us that 'about 70 per cent' of boys would say their favourite subject was history appeared to be bang on the money. A visit to the history room demonstrated what teaching at Cothill is all about – getting boys out of their seats and experiencing things firsthand. A mini Battle of Trafalgar was laid out across pushed together tables, complete with tablecloth sea and stacks of wide, slim drawers opened to reveal other famous (mostly French) battlefields to enable boys to visualise and act out events. Another recent highlight for history department was the re-enactment of the Dambusters raid on the school field. No wonder it's top dog, although this kind of thing is apparently all in a day's work for most departments here, with teachers described as 'inspiring' and often 'quirky – in a good way.'

The star draw though, has to be Sauveterre, Cothill's unique French chateau outpost near Toulouse where all year 7 boys spend a whole term immersing themselves in French language, culture, food and sunshine. Parents evangelise about the benefits of this, not only where tipping the balance at CE is concerned but in terms of an unforgettable life experience.

Boys 'loosely set' from the outset for all subjects with maths more tightly so, but flexible according to exam results. Class sizes between 10 and 15 at the bottom of the school, gradually shrinking to seven or eight from year 7 onwards, consistent with head's belief that 'success at common entrance comes from small classes at the top of the school.' Each subject teacher reports to head on every boy on a weekly basis, resulting in a score out of 10 read out in Friday's assembly. High running totals at the end of term lead to treats and trips. Although school not equipped to deal with serious SEN, superb support in place for those who need a bit of extra help with a highly experienced, passionate SENCo who spends time with every boy before they join the school.

'Spectacular' drama, with frequent plays and shows, including original works written by Cothill teachers. And yes, boys do take on the female roles ('mainly with enthusiasm,' they told us). Around 80 per cent of cohort plays a musical instrument and there are bands and choirs galore for them to showcase their talents. Sport every day, with a focus on health, fitness and everyone getting a go at representing the school. Lower teams celebrated as vigorously as superstars – a recent fixture saw the bottom football team allowed to wear the first team strip as a reward for thrashing the opposition in their previous match.

Parents moving 'overeducated' children out of London preps shouldn't be surprised if boys cruise a bit academically initially. Year 4 is all about getting to grips with boarding to set the foundations for future success and happiness. Tidy, basic dorms for about eight boys, adorned with all the usual football paraphanalia, house years 4, 6 and 7 in the main school and year 5s are split between here and 'the bungalow' – a cosy outpost across the games field where, according to parents, boys feel 'terribly grown up.' Action-packed weekends mean boys become wistful when they are at home, missing the mix of organised activities – an optional trip out every week and free time on their rollerblades, ripsticks or exploring the woods.

All year 8s minibussed out after supper each evening to sleep at nearby Chandlings School, which looks disastrous on paper but in reality 'works brilliantly' and gives boys 'the space to be pre-teenagers.' Weekends also spent there, in the care of an 'extraordinary' house couple, with boys given their own activities and free run of Chandlings' facilities. Formerly sceptical parents now evangelise and are insistent that this part of Cothill life should 'never change.'

Unsurprisingly top notch pastoral care with parents reporting that school 'celebrates high spirits' and 'really understands each boy's potential and how to get him to reach it,' with more than one parent telling us their son had been 'turned around.' Very impressive, albeit informal, daily staff meeting where issues or concerns are raised (from which boys need to be reminded to wear their spectacles to who is struggling with the pressure of scholarship exams) leads to holistic care for every pupil. Boys know they can confide in whomever they wish, whether it's their tutor or junior matrons (usually gap year girls). Parents report boys returning to school 'without a backward glance' – and our guides themselves encapsulated the spirit of the school by telling us that the only kind of boy they could imagine not liking Cothill would be 'an iPad lover.'

Cottesmore School

Buchan Hill, Pease Pottage, West Sussex RH11 9AU

Ages 4–13 **Pupils** 175 **Boarders** 120 (from 8 years) **C of E**

Fees: Day: £9,597 – £17,973 Boarding £27,285 pa

01293 520648
www.cottesmoreschool.com

Headmaster: Since 2008, Tom Rogerson, married to Lottie, with two small sons, Wilf and Bear. Cottesmore runs in the family (grandad and dad were heads before him) – 'I've been quietly planning to take over since I was 17', said the head. Routed via other schools (Ludgrove, Eaton House and Broomwood); his dad wouldn't let him take the headship too early. Quite right, dad.

Articulate and thoughtful, focuses on each pupil and knows them all – they chatter away happily with him. A strong team with Lottie, who provides ballast for the head's lively energy.

Parents like him – 'He's a warm guy, easy to talk to, and always there when I pick up and drop off from exeats'. Another: 'A school derives its culture from the head – and I like its culture. It places emphasis on traditional Christian values: kindness, courtesy, honour and fair play.'

Entrance: Pre-prep: taster day, during which prospective pupils will do a piece of work assessing English and maths. Prep: English and maths tests, interview (children need to be 'interested and interesting') and head's report from previous school. UKiset test for non-English speakers.

Exit: To many of the more magnificent public schools: Eton, Charterhouse, Benenden, St Edwards and Marlborough popular.

Remarks: Approach the school past towering rhododendrons, lawns mowed to velvety smoothness, golf flags, the fragrance of flowers and hedges. Cottesmore is a stately Victorian pile – enter through the heavy wooden door carved with mischievous sprites. Wood panelled walls, stately hall with minstrels' gallery; fishing rods leaning casually against the wall in a corridor. Things here are orderly, but it's not an institutional tidiness: there's a feeling of a home, where places for things arise organically and become established through habit.

Grounds which beg to be played in: climbable trees everywhere, from 'the monkeys' – a cave of under rhododendron/tree branches – to the hollow oak: climb its ancient trunk in a circular direction (teacher present, and only up to a certain height). Bamboo for forts and den making – so popular here that it occasionally has official activity status. A parent said to his wife of their son, who had fallen out of a tree and was limping towards them on the last exeat – 'he's having a childhood and that's wonderful.'

Children here are bubbling, confident and eager, so keen to tell us about their school that we hardly needed to ask questions. They happily fill their own skin: we've rarely met a group of children so content to be themselves. Some bounced up to say hello and give their views; easily said, in front of their head, what they didn't like about school (the chairs are too low and they want new showers).

We met too, quieter introverts, busy with the library and their model railway in the basement. They've started their own after-supper library lecture series ('tea' was exceedingly popular). Not so likely to bubble eagerly about the things they love; but no hesitation in expressing their views, and total confidence in their value. Geekiness is certainly not frowned upon – 'they're lauded for loving the library', said Lottie.

The head said, 'we're a family school', then chuckled; whether this is a good thing clearly depends on how dysfunctional the family. Certainly the warmth and care seen here must exceed what many families experience at Christmas. ('Beautifully small', said a mum).

Broad church here – which means chapel isn't optional. Cultural Christianity, whose values informally underpin the community, but 'we go about it quietly'.

An academically rigorous school – 'rigour balanced with fun', said the head. A flamboyant fashion designer to be is celebrated; but 'he has to be good at maths by the time he leaves'. Lack of endeavour here would be a problem – 'that's not an option'.

'Not a pressure cooker', said a parent who has experienced the hothouse of London preps, '[and] notches up in balanced and useful lives'.

Small classes, no bigger than 14. Single form entry until year 4, then double form entry, finally splitting in three in the final year. Pupils are streamed (but not labelled) and set within those streams. This school does extremely well at enthusing its pupils: they showed a keen interest in Latin, eagerly pointing out Latin in the roots of words, and telling us their favourite myths.

Maths lessons have been transformed by new IT (iPads, Chromebooks and a Raspberry Pis). Pupils were whizzing through tables on iPads – less time marking means more time teaching; or 'connecting', as the head likes to say. Excelling at maths is something this school particularly prides itself on: the head has increased the number of maths teachers and seen CE scores soar.

A geography teacher was enthusiastically making geography pertinent to the real world: 'What are the pros and cons of building a Tesco in the Cottesmore grounds?' (The head's smile became a little fixed at this point...)

Learning support helps students who have mild dyslexia, dyspraxia and dyscalculia, also those with speech and language difficulties. Ten to 20 per cent of pupils receive one-to-one help, and in-class assistance (charged as an extra). The fact a child has SEN doesn't make any difference to attainment here, says the head.

Behind a glass panelled door is pre-prep, the colour and liveliness evident through the glass panels. Coloured cellophane hung from the ceiling in strips – 'we're doing under the sea at the moment'. Single form entry, around 10 per class, children seated at round tables, doors in each class opening onto the lawn: a much more relaxed, crazy colour atmosphere than on the other side of the door, but a similarly high standard evident from the written work in displays. A parent told us that Cottesmore was the only school they visited which was more interested in the child than the parents: Lottie got right down to her daughter's level – 'so, do you like spiders?' And off they went to find one.

A large array of sports on offer: 33, including all the usual major sports, as well as the less usual: archery, shooting and billiards. Pupils of all abilities play in matches, and even the C and D teams play a good number of fixtures. They win plenty of matches and get plenty of support – Danish housekeeping team take great joy in waving their pompoms in support of the third X1.'It is competitive – they care a lot for sport, but they know they have all types, and encourage and get the best out of everyone.'

Houses here are called sets, and there's plenty of friendly inter-set competition. A parent, commenting on the set dash, said 'The whole school cheer each other, particularly the useless ones...To be very kind is to be very Cottesmore', he added.

Plenty of clubs, from real tennis to fishing for carp in the pond – 'the film club is just the best', said one girl. Chess compulsory for two years – it's taken very seriously here (under 11 girls champs).

Music is strong, with 80-90 per cent learning instruments; there are three choirs, including the chapel choir, which often tours abroad. The head of music is also head of drama, so every play tends to be a musical, said a parent: Oliver! was described by another parent as 'excellent – my quite shy son volunteered for it...'

Everyone in the prep has a bed and boards to some extent: around 80 per cent full time, everyone else up to four nights a week (must stick to chosen nights). In this small school, there are no separate boarding houses: everyone just troops upstairs to bed, the matron's flat situated between the boys' and girls' dorms.

Large dormitories for 8, three per room for older pupils, the usual is six. Pupils wake to music – the latest charts.

'Palatial since my day', said a parent; but actually they're mid renovation – decoration of some rooms is a bit tired.'It's all going', said the head briskly; although the parents we spoke to were happy with it as it is.

Year groups take it in turn to occupy the drawing room in evenings (music, piano, chess, Wii dance), other year groups spilling out into hall, library and ICT room, playing ping pong or snooker. Children here flow everywhere – no feeling of being penned into a particular area.

Lots of activities at the weekends: Saturday morning school, then matches; trips on Sundays – children talked with great joy of a trip to Brighton Pier, when older pupils were allowed to go off in groups of four, and told us how much they love the independence – 'at my last school they never stopped watching us', said one, impatiently. 'Here, they trust us'.

Each class sends a rep to the school council and food committee – a food committee board in a class room simply stated 'BETTER BURGER'; but they don't have much to complain about: they've won awards for their food, which a parent described as 'brilliant'.

The children's happiness is testament to how well they are cared for – and indeed the school Happiness Charter is on the wall of every room. A parent described the school as 'gentle'; they chose Cottesmore for its rounded, happy pupils, and nurturing environment. Easy for pupils to speak to staff here – they're all out in the hall at break time, accompanied by their coffee trolley.

Certainly the best mannered children we've met at a prep, leaping to their feet if we so much as glanced over, opening doors, shaking hands. Watching the children, it seemed evident that the respectful environment influences how they treat each other.

Time out area on a wooden chest in front of the study – pupils who've been a bit rowdy perch there until they've calmed down. A clear bullying policy: the one incident a parent described to us was 'clamped down on quickly'.

Pupils from London, home counties, and abroad, including expats and diplomats (about a third of boarders from overseas). A parent from London told us he looked at 20 prep schools, and Cottesmore had the best combination of options one could get: 'A* in all the things that really matter in life'.

C

Coworth Flexlands School

Chertsey Road, Valley End, Chobham, Surrey GU24 8TE

Ages Girls 3–11, boys 3–7 **Pupils** 121

Fees: £8,730 – £13,710 pa

01276 855707
www.coworthflexlands.co.uk

Head: Since September 2018, Nicola Cowell, previously deputy head of teaching and learning at Surbiton High Girls' Prep. Degree from Oxford Brookes University; BA in primary education. Started teaching in the state sector in Oxford before moving to St George's School, Cologne, Oakfield Prep in Dulwich and then to Surbiton High.

Entrance: Into the Skylark nursery at 3, first come, first served, with more joining further up the school, mainly in reception and year 3. Completely non-selective, although a very disruptive child with severe behavioural problems might stretch such a small school too far. Definitely a local school, 'almost all parents come from within 10 miles', some only recently decamped from west London. In the past they kept very quiet as word of mouth – together with a large proportion of siblings, including boys up to the age of 7 – easily filled the places. Now, due mainly to parents being under greater financial pressure and opting for the state system, they are being forced to advertise the hidden secret of their existence.

Exit: To an extraordinarily wide range of senior schools: recently the girls have had offers ranging from the airy academic heights of Wycombe Abbey and Cheltenham Ladies' College through Downe House, Godolphin, St George's Ascot and St Mary's Ascot to the less hothouse local alternatives. The boys tend to move on to Papplewick at 6+ or Sunningdale or Woodcote House at 7+.

Remarks: The slightly cumbersome name, more aircraft industry than education, came about from the amalgamation of two tiny local schools needing the economies of scale, and this is still a minnow in prep school terms.

The motorway madness of the nearby M3 and M25 is swiftly left behind on arriving at this commutable oasis, think silver birches and bracken not palm trees and sand. Turning off the busy road, we passed the forest school, an unsurprisingly woody corner, extremely popular with pupils, both in term time and during the summer holiday camps. Soon faced by unpretentious brick buildings, decorated with jolly mosaic murals, we drew up to the shrieks of girls on break floating from behind a high brick wall, making our first thought 'this is definitely not a repressive regime'. Once inside, the interior is cosy and practical, more Famous Five than Hogwarts, house shields on the stairs and a well-stocked library full of beanbags for relaxed reading.

The Skylark nursery occupies two cheerful rooms with doors opening out onto a separate playground with small people streaming happily in and out, clad in a delicious mix of apparel from full-on princess mode, complete with muddy hem, to Oshkosh dungarees. You could be forgiven for thinking this was just a glorified play school, but there is a subtle but certain focus on future essentials, such as motor skills and manners, from the infinitely patient teachers and assistants. Relaxed they may appear to be, but the basics of music, writing, maths and computing are slotted into the daily schedule so that the first building blocks needed for 'big school' are all in place.

Once in reception, the dressing up is over and uniform is donned, but the atmosphere remains the same, with the trust between teachers and children obvious as soon as you enter the classroom. Classes are small, eight to 10 for core subjects, and groups are taught simultaneously. One form was taking a test but instead of being stressed, they looked up happily from their individual encampments constructed from educational books. As you move up the school, the air of concentration increases but an element of fun still appears to remain on the agenda. Happily, a science class in year 5 were allowed to let out their stick insects, which they had hatched from eggs, showing that they were sophisticates at handling them compared to us, although the enjoyment quotient was probably similar.

If you wanted to judge the school purely on academic success you would be lavish in your praise, as they have achieved 12 scholarships in the last two years from a mini cohort of less than 20 girls each year. One parent told us that the teachers are a comfortable mix of about 25 per cent who have been here for a long time and relative newcomers chosen because they are 'best for the job' and 'do everything right'. We felt that this was fair comment and, when we had talked to them, came away pretty certain that they also felt this was an extremely good billet. However, this is not a school that only concentrates on success at exams. Their ability to gently tease the best out of each child and prepare them for senior school at social as well as academic level is a quality that several parents remarked on.

Pupils talk of loving 'the space', all 13 acres of it, with raised beds for veggies tucked in a corner and a new outdoor classroom. This is embellished by a rustic bench donated by last year's leavers and endearingly engraved with their names. The games fields, slightly more St Trinian's than All England in feel, now include popular football pitches. The U10s even managed to win a cup, fairly remarkable considering the numbers the coach had to draw from. Netball and athletics also have fans and the school is bringing in more coaches from outside to stem any parental fears that latent talent on the sports field is lying undetected. Apparently last year's leavers were a sporty lot with one girl winning a sports scholarship but this, whilst not as rare as hens' teeth, is probably not going to be a regular occurrence.

The children's art is on full view, from a pinboard on a staircase covered with drawings of skeletal trees to an eye-catching portrait in the head's study: 'that's my next art scholar'. Artistic themes crop up all over the school, from seasonal autumn leaves being carefully studied for a lesson in shading, to paintbrushes being used as measuring sticks in a maths class.

Music is everywhere, from a small girl having an individual singing lesson to year 2s practising their version of Que Sera Sera for their class assembly, slightly struggling to fit in their own lyrics and sway together at the same time. The school choir takes part in the Chobham Festival of Music and to great excitement (parents as well as children), all went to Wembley earlier this year to sing on stage (one of only four schools nationwide to be chosen) for Voice in a Million.

Ignoring the size of the talent pool, drama is enthusiastically taught by an actress when she is not playing the principal girl in Christmas panto and the performances were judged 'surprisingly professional' by one parent and 'a real highlight' by another, with all the girls having a significant part in a school production every year. Almost 80 per cent of LAMDA pupils gained distinction last year, so their teacher's time away from the green room was certainly well spent. One ex-pupil won both a drama and a performing arts scholarship and her parents said that the teachers were 'incredibly supportive over the application process'.

After-school clubs go down well, particularly amongst those who are kept at work beyond pick-up time. One mother was particularly impressed that they taught a very popular robotics club in her daughter's rather than her son's school. There have been slight mutterings from parents in the past about the standards of some of the clubs, but school is encouraging new external talent to help make the options more attractive. It must be working, because a current pupil agreed with the general consensus that things are looking up, saying that they were 'great, particularly the one run by the Surrey Academy of Musical Theatre'. Homework can be done at school and they are very flexible about early drop-offs, another boon for modern hard-pressed families.

Even under pressure, the nearest we could get anyone to tell us of how they might deal with any negative attitude from pupils was the admittance that they could issue a pink slip for non-completion of homework. This is probably not the ultimate deterrent, but it is obviously the maximum needed in a school where they appear to have eliminated unkind or thoughtless behaviour.

To encourage responsibility, every girl in year 6 is given a bespoke leadership role that suits her talents and she can slot into easily. This initiative does make staff remark that coming up with suitable roles and job descriptions can take imagination when there are more than 20 girls in year 6. One of the current favourites is eco captain, who has set up an environmental science project with Royal Holloway.

The green theme is a mission: they are aiming for an Eco School Green Flag (you actually get one to fly) and the forest school plays a major role. Tinies go there for the modern equivalent of nature studies whilst older girls do more in-depth scientific projects. 'It's not just a frolic in the woods; we want them to consider this area as a serious study option later on.' The outdoors is not the only game in town as they also run a Food Waste Week, a house competition organised by the eco captains to encourage the least amount chucked out at lunch, which judging by the yummy food on our plates can't ever be very much.

Perhaps fortunately, they have abandoned the old motto of 'love conquers all' with its definitely dated 60s feel, but this is still the ethos of this charming place, albeit with a 21st century gloss on it. Once allowed through the front door, the temptation to curl up in a corner and stay for life is hard to resist as Coworth Flexlands is, in every aspect of its set-up and approach, the scholarly equivalent of a much-loved and needed comfort blanket. We wondered if this might just be us on a mushy day, but the evidence that staff and pupils feel the same is omnipresent.

Cranbrook School

Waterloo Road, Cranbrook, Kent TN17 3JD

Ages 11–18 **Pupils** 839 **Sixth form** 285 **Boarders** 250

Fees: Boarding £13,362 – £16,032 pa

01580 711804
www.cranbrookschool.co.uk

Headmaster: Since 2012, Dr John Weeds MA MPhil EdD (50s). Read classics at Pembroke College, Cambridge and his academic studies have long been part of his life. He jokes that he didn't want to be outdone by his talented micro-biologist wife, but the letters after his name attest to a driven and committed educationalist.

His most recent thesis was on the subject of the gifted and talented, which will come in useful here. But having consciously chosen to work in the state sector, he is very concerned with equality of opportunity too. He has an eye on rebalancing Cranbrook's increasingly independent school intake; he has ensured there are some less financially demanding school trips and wants to see the girls at Cranbrook given more of a voice too.

He found the school somewhat laid back, and hasn't been afraid to grapple with it – 'some traditions I'm prepared to take on,' he told us. One of the contentious changes was suits for sixth formers five days a week. 'It's created a different feel – more businesslike and focused,' he says. Understanding that parents 'really do want best grades,' he aims to deliver consistency of performance and to retain the focus on the academic. 'I don't want to lose sight of the diverse extracurricular offer, but we need more balance,' he says.

The parents we spoke to are right behind him. One told us: 'He is not a slick performer but the benefit is that I believe he listens and engages with both students and parents.' Another said: 'I feel his quest to raise results is to be praised and supported.'

He has three adult sons.

Academic matters: A level results 61 per cent A*-B, 33 per cent A*/A grades in 2018. There have been tweaks all round, including a new approach to mock exams. Pupils know what is expected of them and are fired up to achieve it.

Some subjects notably outperform others by a mile, namely the large cohort of talented mathematicians. The school was a specialist science school for years and has a new observatory equipped with telescopes. A third of pupils take science A levels, with chemistry particularly popular with the girls, and almost all taking single sciences at GCSE. Strong humanities, but English seems to be a weak spot. Head says the new assessment framework is challenging. Numbers taking languages fall off at A level, to only 10 per cent. Most seem pretty focused on traditional curriculum subjects but a sixth form enrichment programme offers additional choices such as astronomy, sports leadership and psychology.

At GCSE in 2018, 53 per cent A*-A/9-7 grades. Pupils study 11 or more (mainly academic) subjects at GCSE, excelling at maths, physics, Latin, IT, French and art. Maths and RE are out of the way a year early. A third of maths whizzes currently take home an IGCSE too, with year 9 and 10 students winning a clutch of gold medals in national maths challenges. Languages on offer are French and Spanish, with Chinese for native speakers.

More than a third of teachers have been at the school for longer than 10 years. The head assured us that only two staff left last year but parents are less concerned about turnover. They approve of the new focus on performance and are keen on removing the few 'dead wood.' One told us: 'There are a handful of teachers who struggle to control the class and some who could explain their teaching and homework better.' Other teachers singled out as inspirational. The pupils we spoke to said teachers will stay behind to explain things if they don't understand something, while RS and physics teachers were praised for their revision guides and pre-university preparation. The brilliance of the maths results is due quite simply, says the head, to 'the best maths teacher in Kent.'

Parents seem split between those who think the amount of homework is about right and those who think there should be more, particularly in the holidays. A pupil said: 'Teachers will always give you more if you ask for it' – clearly a loophole for the less inclined, but there don't seem to be many of those here. The online parent portal keeps parents up-to-date with progress and there are half-termly assessment records for effort and attainment.

Two full-time student support assistants offer additional support for specific difficulties (outside the classroom). SENCo is a dyslexia specialist and admin assistant is also listed as having mentoring skills. Between 10 or 20 pupils each year with special educational needs (whether or not recorded by the local authority as such).

Head told us with feeling: 'We're very committed to supporting those with particular needs. We will do just about everything we can.' If pupils need a laptop they don't necessarily need to bring one – the school will find one. Pupils won't slip under the radar here, he said, and added: 'We will pick up those who can become hard on themselves and down, and won't forget other children who can achieve great things.' A handful with EAL needs – EAL tuition is offered free of charge for anyone who needs it.

Games, options, the arts: School has a strong sports tradition. Fifty acres of sports fields and everyone participates. High-calibre cricket and rugby teams, with a growing fixtures list. One pupil told us he'd left a prestigious local grammar specifically to join the Cranbrook rugby first XV (he'd played against the team and admired it). Hockey and netball strong too. Some pretty glamorous sporting tours – South Africa for cricket, Fiji and New Zealand for rugby. A team of U15 girls recently became British fencing champions. Facilities include an outdoor heated pool, squash courts, Astroturf, plus sports hall with dance studio (currently offering Bollywood classes), climbing wall and gym (popular in the evenings with sporty boys).

Not much consensus about music here. Head claims it's the 'story of the year' but some parents not so ecstatic. One told us: 'One concern is that the extracurricular music programme is not as strong as it could be. There are great facilities and talent but this is not always harnessed effectively.' It's certainly a well-resourced and vibrant part of school life, with several choirs, an orchestra, jazz and rock bands, folk, string, sax and brass groups, charity concerts and community carol services. Total of some 150 students take individual instrument lessons, with many learning more than one and working on higher grades. Lots of pupils trying an instrument for the first time. Live music at every assembly and whilst pupils still seemed a little wrapped up in their early morning fugs we saw teachers toe-tapping along to a jazz band which could easily take a turn at Ronnie Scott's. However, no longer offers music GCSE or A level due to funding cuts.

The more artistic may be in the minority – only a handful taking art A level. Having tackled exam performance as her first priority, art teacher is encouraging boys into the classroom (now one third of pupils). Art room is open all hours and cool graffiti art pop-ups grab the attention of everyone as they move around the school. Large, well-used facilities for DT and food technology.

The Queen's Hall is the home of the drama department and is a fully equipped and recently refurbished theatre – largely run by the pupils, but also used by outside touring companies. Annual house plays as well as junior, senior and whole school productions.

What Cranbrook does well is encourage pupils to be self-reliant and take responsibility, whether that is through CCF or DofE, fundraising for the charities they care passionately about – no standard Sports Relief here – or being given the freedom to set up any clubs they're interested in (40 at the last count, including curling club which promptly won a county-wide competition).

Annual trip to Tanzania to work on health and education projects is a stand-out opportunity. Pupils compete for a place and work hard to raise the money themselves. 'It was the best thing I have done in my life,' said the head girl. There's also an exchange partnership with a school in Kerala for two weeks at the end of the autumn term. All richly eye-opening, and no doubt contributed to the school's International Schools Award from the British Council.

Enrichment programme for years 9 and 10 means pupils go off timetable for two weeks. 'We take them out of their comfort zone,' said the head. 'They have to research and do presentations on what they've learned. This year they met everyone from a policeman to a prisoner. It gets youngsters who are bright to think.'

Boarding: Boarding houses are a bit of a lottery architecturally – some old, some modern. The year 10 dorms we visited in one house were more like tiny ships' cabins, with multi-tasking bunk-beds/desks, but as pupils get older they often get more space. There's a rolling programme of new carpets, curtains and bathrooms and we were impressed by the accommodation – squishy sofas, polished wood, no institutional paint colours (tasteful greys). Washing gets turned around in 24 hours – setting the bar quite high for when pupils return home – and there wasn't the slightest whiff of a less than fresh sock. Boarding pupils can invite day pupils over after school and it's easy to see how self-sufficient youngsters can be here, without the need of the rural parental taxi service.

Background and atmosphere: Founded in 1518 and given a Royal Charter by Elizabeth I in 1574. School's buildings straddle the main road into the pretty Kent town of Cranbrook and are a jumble of every architectural style, from 1970s accommodation blocks to a fine Georgian mansion. Local church of St Dunstan's is in the middle of the campus – very much part of the community.

The fact that Cranbrook is a selective state school with a large boarding contingent gives the place a unique feel. The alumni society is awash with hugging groups from reunited houses. Total of 12 houses – seven for boys and five for girls. Day pupils are grouped geographically to start with to help out of school socialising.

A parent told us that the school offers 'a balance of high academic achievement and extracurricular activities that is the equal to many public schools.' Another described Cranbrook as 'a very intriguing mix of competitive and laid-back.' They added that 'it places responsibility on the students rather than spoon-feeding them, which means that students need to step up.' Pupils want to go places here – it's not uncool to be clever.

Pastoral care, well-being and discipline: Pastoral care is highly praised. On arrival each child is allocated a tutor who will monitor their academic and activities programme, social progress and work with their head of house. As one parent pointed out, the houses and tutor groups are something of a haven. Pupils return to their houses regularly throughout the day – which helps to prevent the build-up of any bullying.

Mentoring is a word that crops up a lot (peer to peer, sixth form to younger pupils, staff to pupils). There is a smart new medical centre (like a mini hospital, with beds for sick boarding pupils), and counsellors offer appointments four times a week. Head has tightened up on discipline and believes the behaviour of pupils is now excellent (a view backed up by parents). Good liaison with parents, plus contracts for good behaviour.

Pupils and parents: Head says that youngsters who are 'particularly interested in learning' and have 'a real spirit of enterprise and adventure' will thrive here. Parents reckon school is ideal for self-motivated, well-rounded pupils who have capabilities beyond the academic, and are organised, not overly sensitive or under confident – or 'the engaged, interested and aspirational'. The place 'may not be suited to students expecting to be hand held,' although quieter children have found their niche too. Independence is held in exceptionally high esteem.

Parents tend to be less the super-rich and more middle class professionals with increasingly high expectations. Definitely a varied bunch, suggesting there's a good chance of finding like minds. Some parents are reputedly stirred up and vocal about the recent changes, whilst every other parent we spoke to was quick to say they liked to be 'hands off.' Head cites strong relationships with parents and a tradition for supportive involvement, particularly with careers teaching.

Notable alumni include Es Devlin, superstar stage and costume designer of the 2012 Olympic closing ceremony, Tim Smit, founder of the Eden Project, astronaut Dr Piers Sellers, comedian Harry Hill, designer Ptolemy Mann, journalist Sir Charles Wheeler and sports commentators Peter West, Brian Moore and Barry Davis, plus many high up in the Forces.

Entrance: Selective, catering for the top 20-25 per cent of the academic ability range. Has historically started at 13, but had first 11+ intake, of 30 day pupils only, in 2017. This will gradually increase to 90 places from 2021 (all day pupils), whilst the 13+ places decrease (from 162 to 72, including 52 boarders).

There is an 8.5 km preferred catchment, pushing up house prices even further nearby (inaccurate addresses taken very seriously). Applicants previously often came from the Cranbrook state secondary, The High Weald Academy. Now the competition has shifted up a gear – a strong intake from prep schools such as Marlborough House, Dulwich Prep and St Ronan's. Boarders mostly come from just outside the catchment area – most within 40 miles, including London and the home counties. About one third are based overseas – they must hold an UK or EU passport.

The 11+ admissions are via the Kent test – multiple choice English, maths and reasoning papers, plus a writing exercise, held in September of year 6 with the results given before the local authority application deadline. Sign up in June of year 5. The 13+ entrance exam (day pupils in January, boarders in November) is a three-hour, multiple-choice verbal reasoning test, plus the school's own papers in maths and English. As for some other Kent selectives, now a more rigorous English entrance exam, including 20 minutes of free writing, looking for flair beyond the basics. The maths test is based on the national curriculum, but designed to root out those performing at the higher and lower ends.

Only room for a few new entrants into the sixth form – 16 or so day students and a few new boarders. They require 11 points at GCSE (or equivalent) with A*=4, A=3 and B=1 point, but given lack of spaces, likely to be far more demanding in reality. Anyone who does not achieve the 11 points at GCSE is asked to leave.

Exit: Under 10 per cent leave post-GCSE. Parents and pupils feel the school prepares well for university, and helps with gap years too. Around 95 per cent of sixth formers head to university. Three to Oxbridge in 2018, plus three medics/vets. Large contingent to Russell Group, popular destinations include Bristol, Nottingham, Leeds, UCL, Warwick, Exeter and Birmingham. Many traditionally academic subjects, but also Asian studies, criminology, anthropology, product design and psychology.

Money matters: New academic scholarships for year 9 entry – 'identifying those who are not just just strong at their subject, but passionate as well'. Small financial reward but inclusion in high achievers' scheme.

Remarks: Recent changes have definitely left everyone a little shaken and stirred, but if the school's recent results are anything to go by Cranbrook is raising its game nicely. As an alternative to the high pressure Kent grammars, with the facilities and atmosphere of many private schools and the fun of boarding too, it's an excitingly different proposition for the adventurous young teen.

Cranleigh Preparatory School

Linked with Cranleigh School

Horseshoe Lane, Cranleigh GU6 8QH

Ages 7–13 **Pupils** 347 **Boarders** 50 weekly/flexi

Fees: Day £15,480 – £20,085 ; Boarding: £24,255 pa

01483 542058
www.cranprep.org

Headmaster: Since September 2018, Neil Brooks BA QTS (late 40s), previously principal of Fulham Prep Schools and before that interim CEO of the Cothill Educational Trust. Read geography and PE at Warwick University; spent his 20s as a 'soldier', as he puts it, a British army officer serving in an airborne unit in Northern Ireland and Bosnia.

After a 'disastrous' year in industry, he was told by a friend that he 'needed to get back into an institution, preferably without the need to wear a straitjacket'. After writing over 100 letters he came to teaching by chance (it was much more difficult to change course and get a late foothold in the profession then, he avers) and started his career at Cothill, where he stayed for many years before becoming head for eight years from 2003. He then embarked on a project with his wife to set up the The Old Malthouse in Dorset, affiliated with the Natural History Museum and Pimlico Academy in London (his two sons were at school at Canford at the time). However, after five years he 'hungered for a more traditional teaching environment', and his appointment at Fulham was aided by a long friendship with Jane Emmett (the former head and owner of Fulham Prep).

Thoroughly direct and down to earth, with an engaging, self deprecating sense of humour.

Entrance: The main entry point is at 7+, with another chunk of pupils wanting to join at 11+, enough to add one or two more classes. During the assessment day for entry at 7, children complete comprehension, maths, spelling and reasoning on computer, plus a handwritten piece of creative writing; they also take part in art and PE sessions. Quite a day for a 6-year-old, although the school does 'try to make it as relaxed as possible'. For entry at 11 children come to an 'activity morning' for an interview plus art, sports, problem solving and team building sessions. They then return a few months later for computer based maths, reasoning, spelling and reading plus handwritten comprehension and creative writing. At this stage children are being assessed on whether or not they would thrive academically and socially at the Cranleigh School across the road. However, this is not a pre-test for the senior school; pupils still need to take common entrance and go through the formal admissions process at Cranleigh School.

Exit: Around 85 per cent move 'across the road' (an oft used phrase here) to Cranleigh School. The links between prep and senior schools are increasingly strong and up to a third win Cranleigh scholarships. However, it is quite accepted that others will want to move elsewhere and they are given equal support and advice. Those who do move go on to a wide range of public schools including Wellington College, Charterhouse, Millfield, St Catherine's Bramley, Prior's Field.

C

Remarks: A traditional prep school with an outdoorsy, sporty feel. Whilst it's co-ed, the boyish culture seems to dominate somewhat. Parents describe it as 'busy, robust and challenging' and those children who enjoy life here are energetic, sporty and have a sense of humour about 'banter' from other pupils and younger staff. Families are generally well-heeled, some extremely so, mostly from the surrounding countryside and villages. They pitch up to school events and matches, often more dads making an appearance than at other schools, and describe themselves as a pretty vocal and often demanding lot.

Academically inclusive with the range of abilities catered for by extensive setting within classes and, in the top two years, streaming into one scholarship and three or four common entrance forms depending on numbers. 'Academics have been upped, which is no bad thing,' reported a parent of long standing; another told us her scholarship form daughter gains confidence from being at the top here academically. Learning support is 'at the centre rather than a satellite' with dyscalculia, dyspraxia and dyslexia all catered for and just under a fifth of pupils receiving some level of support. Needs are spotted early on and thoroughly addressed with classroom assistants and interventions in small groups or one-to-one. All pupils' progress is closely monitored via a thorough record system with inputs from all staff.

Art is of an amazingly high standard. The head of art is confident and enthusiastic about children's abilities and she seems to get fantastic work out of everyone. The art room is stuffed full of current projects by pupils of all ages, including some really unusual ceramics, textiles and sculptures alongside more expected drawing and painting. Talented artists could find the perfect niche here.

Drama and music are also well covered; both are part of the curriculum for all ages with numerous performances each year. Individual instrumental or singing lessons are held in the music school, recently enlarged with the addition of a practice room for ensembles and choirs. Talented musicians benefit from a programme called Cranleigh Music 7-18 in which music teachers work at both Cranleigh Prep and Cranleigh School and the most able musicians play in ensembles across the age range.

Sport is a major focus of school life, whether you ask pupils, parents or staff; it's timetabled every day with matches mid-week and on alternate Saturdays. Rugby and hockey are big, but there are less usual options including riding over at the senior school's on-site stables. The Cranleigh Sport 7-18 programme brings sports staff over from the senior school to spot talent and coach at all levels. Parents expect their children to be able to represent the school in matches and teams are fielded from A to D to give everyone a good chance. Of course pupils know who will be in the As but they say, 'it's possible to get places in other teams'. Non-sporty or quiet bookish children may well find this whole active vibe just too much; as one parent says, 'it's horses for courses'.

Pastoral care is the remit of the deputy head; she has been at Cranleigh Prep for over 20 years and is familiar with the ups and downs of life here. Incidents are tracked and dealt with pragmatically, parents are phoned, high jinks are recognised, punishments are taken and pupils move on. An annual anti-bullying questionnaire identifies any new issues – such as social media, which has been addressed using a visiting outside agency to talk to children and parents. A few parents have told us about persistent unkindness from other children which has left their own feeling upset and unsupported; the deputy head responds that bullying and unkindness are taken seriously, efforts are focused on changing unsociable behaviour and pupils have been suspended in the past. She points out that she recently asked staff to send her any notes from parents praising their children's care and her file of these is much thicker than her file of dissatisfied and problematic correspondence.

The great outdoors is what defines Cranleigh: acres of grassy pitches, an Astro pitch, tennis courts and netball courts. The senior school across the road dominates the views, keeping that future option ever in mind. The buildings are a mix of Edwardian and a hotch-potch of newer, including a recent one providing three more classrooms and a common room. Some are a bit disappointing inside, a few rather poky classrooms and a sports and performance hall which felt like a cavernous shed; others are good, eg the well-stocked library, a couple of IT suites with new desks and integral computers and the welcoming, very comfortable reception area.

Boarding houses are traditional, or somewhat old-fashioned depending on your view. The girls' boarding house we visited (some two-thirds of boarders are boys) had dorms for four or six, high windows, firm mattresses and lots of Justin Bieber and 1-Direction posters. Two matrons are always on hand to keep an eye on things for boarders and day pupils; they offer TLC in their cosy room or the next door sick bay or in the brightly furnished sitting room cheerfully labelled the Ikea Room. Boarding is weekly or flexi with a minimum of two nights a week; there are no weekend boarders. Although day pupils hugely outnumber boarders, the daily routine of late finishing, prep at school and Saturday school on alternate weeks feels rather more like a boarding school.

A few scholarship awards are given to exceptional candidates at 11, nothing earlier. Sibling discounts are available for third and subsequent siblings.

In short, a sporty co-ed school run on traditional lines in a glorious rural setting with strong links to its senior school. A good choice for a broad education, less academically pressured than many others and with plenty of learning support for those who need it. Robust and energetic pupils preferred.

Cranleigh School

Linked with Cranleigh Preparatory School

Horseshoe Lane, Cranleigh, Surrey GU6 8QQ

Ages 13–18 **Pupils** 654 **Sixth form** 240 **Boarders** 467 full **C of E**

Fees: Day £31,170; Boarding- £37,705pa

01483 273666
www.cranleigh.org

Headmaster: Since 2014, Mr Martin Reader (40s). Brought up in Orpington and attended St Olave's Grammar School, which he describes as 'an academic school that also offered breadth of sport, art and music.' Thence to University College, Oxford where he read English, played lots of rugby and stayed on for an MPhil (his dissertation was on an 'anonymous early Scottish poem'). Also has an MBA in school leadership. Harboured early ambition to be a television presenter and has the look – think twinkly but unimpeachable silver fox.

First teaching post and first experience of a boarding school was at St Edward's Oxford, from there he went to Oundle and then to Reigate Grammar where he was senior deputy head before taking up headship of Wellington School in Somerset, where he spent eight years. Loves the boarding ethos, 'Boarding gives us time to develop deeper trust and partnership. Nothing is more rewarding than having time to talk to children.'

He describes his headship as 'coming home' and says he has found Cranleigh parents to be 'very grounded.' They in turn describe Mr Reader as 'a very good fit', 'approachable', 'diplomatic' and 'visionary'. Changes he's made have been generally well received: lessons are now 50 minutes instead of 35 ('gives pupils more time to think and encourages problem solving', he says) and there's a drive to get pupils going with independent learning skills from the prep school up. His mission to 'ensure we are current' has lead to the appointment of a head of contemporary music to support 'non-traditional' musicians. Art provision has had a makeover and the new head of DT is a robotics specialist. What makes Mr R's heart sink is 'constant measuring'. He fears 'the enriching cultural experience' that lies at the heart of a good education is in danger of being sacrificed on the academic altar. 'It is possible to do both and be successful,' he says.

Head feels school needs to 'burst the Surrey bubble' and to that end has encouraged the Beyond Cranleigh programme. Pupils help the local community, litter picking, working in local schools and staging joint concerts. He is developing an exchange with a Chinese school and building on longstanding links with a community primary school in Zambia. His wife, Amanda, who is head of careers, is also very involved with this project. The Readers have a son at the prep and a daughter in the senior school.

Outside school Mr Reader enjoys cooking and he also preaches in the local church. He's a trustee of the Hawk and Owl Trust and hopes to encourage barn owls to nest on campus (maybe he should offer a barn owl bursary...). Favourite book? 'Crime and Punishment. It's got everything – violence, love, tragedy, morality.' No owls, though. When asked to sum up the Cranleigh ethos he says, 'It's a competitive school. We love to compete but we play for the shirt, not individual glory.'

Academic matters: One competition school doesn't enter is the race for exam league table glory – the Cranleigh way is educational breadth rather than narrow academic focus. Nevertheless, the healthy spread of exam grades from A* to Cs and Ds, not to mention a good handful of Oxbridge places every year, confirms that teaching covers the spectrum of ability. In 2018, very creditable 68 per cent A*-A/9-7 at GCSE; at A level it was 42 per cent A*/A (79 per cent A*-B). General feeling is that Mr Reader will tighten academics where necessary. The newly-appointed director of teaching, learning and innovation (who also teaches physics) told us about plans to build up the EPQ and a school-wide drive to embed independent learning and thinking skills.

We sat in on a fourth year art lesson where not everybody was as engaged as they might have been, but it was just before lunch. Fair to say this is not a school where you will find silent concentration behind every classroom door – we got the feeling that while most eyes were on the board, more hearts were outside on the pitch. A level options pretty standard but also include geology and Greek (as two-year AS courses) and, unsurprisingly, PE. English, history and economics are the most popular subjects at A level, followed by maths and sciences. Very small numbers for music and languages – as elsewhere. Pre-U so far only for maths and further maths. Cranleigh also runs its own specially designed EPQ courses with everyone taking perspectives on science or culture and humanity course.

Around 100 pupils with SEN, mostly mild dyslexia etc. Some receive one-to-one tuition (extra cost) but most are supported in class. Parents were keen to tell us how well their very different children have done, 'Pupils are treated as individuals academically,' and 'There are lots of subject clinics and if a child needs some hand-holding they'll get it.' One mother said that the teaching at Cranleigh had 'absolutely been the making' of her daughter. Longer lesson times took a while to bed in, 'My children complained at first but they appreciate them now.'

Games, options, the arts: Cranleigh has 31 sports pitches and appears to be outstanding on all of them. This success is all the more impressive considering that the school is half the size of its closest rivals; 'We have to play big schools to get all our teams matches,' the deputy head told us. He added, 'Sport here is about participation, not just about the elite. Everyone is expected to be involved, staff as well as pupils.' Recent silverware includes National Rugby 7s schoolboy champions, Finegold Cup (riding), U16 girls' indoor and outdoor hockey champions and Devizes to Westminster (international kayaking challenge) title holders. There will undoubtedly have been more wins since so best see school website for latest. Average of 29 teams playing on match Saturdays which doesn't leave many to cheer from the sidelines. More than 20 sports are on offer, there's a nine hole golf course – golf mainly played for relaxation pupils told us, but that doesn't stop the golf team winning inter-school tournaments – several Astros and a conditioning room. Two physios, a sports doctor and strength and conditioning coaches on hand to tailor individual fitness and nutrition programmes. Equestrian centre has two all-weather arenas and 60 acres of grazing and riding land. Pupils may bring their own ponies; those without learn on the school ponies.

Music and drama are tackled with typical gusto. According to the school's handy infographic, Cranleigh in Numbers, there are nine plays and 70 concerts (home-grown and visiting talent) a year. The arts certainly aren't a competition-free zone with keenly fought contests for house dance, singing and drama. Strings and woodwind also compete (separately), as do poets and creative writers. Speech Hall is the largest performance venue, seating up to 500, and there are two smaller studio theatres. When we visited one of these was being very creatively fitted out for a junior production of Treasure Island. The Merriman Music School (named after first headmaster) has a 100 seat auditorium and 14 practice rooms. School bands can practice in the fully soundproofed 'rock room'. New head of contemporary music adds another, possibly louder, string to school's bow. 'Spine-tingling' congregational singing is more than fully supported by splendid three manual-pipe Mander organ in chapel. Organist in residence gives lunchtime recitals and organ lessons are available. Much participation at all levels, but as elsewhere, small uptake for music and drama A levels.

Plenty of extracurricular options, including visiting speakers and lecture programme for A level students. Timetabling genius ensures CCF and DofE don't clash. There's so much going on it's hard to see how pupils fit everything in; little wonder day pupils stay until 9pm several nights a week. Might it all be too much for some, we asked one mother. She thought not: 'Yes, it's full-on but the children are so happy and if they're happy, they perform better.'

To conclude, Cranleigh is a very sporty school but, as parents and staff were at pains to tell us, it's not just a sporty school. Message received. Even so, perhaps not the confirmed ball dodger's first choice.

Boarding: Four boys' and three girls' houses (forth due to open in September 2019). No flexi boarding, day pupils are fully part of boarding houses and have a cabin desk in boarders' rooms – it's their 'centre of gravity' within the school where they do prep, get changed for sport, make toast and drinks and take part in house activities. Day pupils can sleep over occasionally if activities such as school plays or trips finish very late and 'we will always scoop up in an emergency.' All do prep in their rooms 'with doors open and prefects in corridors.' 'We expect proper, disciplined work,' said housemaster. Tutors are on hand to inspect and any slackers can expect a short sharp spell at one of the 'naughty boy desks'.

Boys' houses are, inevitably, older and, though clean and bright, looked pretty worn out. Grubby polystyrene ceiling tiles rarely enhance a room and walls looked as though they'd been crashed into by generations of schoolboys – probably because they have. Common areas very lived in; walls decorated with team photos and vintage style black and white shots of heroes: Mohammed Ali, Steve McQueen, James Dean. Dorms of up to four for first years, single study bedrooms for sixth formers. Very few personal touches (artistic arrangements of massive shoes don't count), but that's boys' boarding for you. Sixth formers' single study bedrooms looked better – more in the way of photos and posters. Matron's room is the focal point on the ground floor from where she keeps an eye on comings and goings. Nice big garden for kickabouts and barbecues. All upper sixth formers are prefects – 'they're positive role models' – and year groups are mixed (not segregated by corridor). The housemaster stressed how 'integrated' the year groups were and how seriously his sixth form prefects took their house responsibilities. 'We have a beer and a chat with the prefects, they're quick to notice if things are getting a bit scratchy.'

All in all one feels that the concept of gender fluidity has yet to find a foothold in Surrey. Girls' houses are modern, done out in pinks and purples and considerably better provided for on the soft furnishing front. Perhaps they could loan a few beanbags or pom-poms to the boys? Matron ('She knows everything,' our guides said) resides in a room just like a family kitchen, with sofas, throws and lots of photos. Girls can make drinks and snacks and talk over the day's events in comfort. Study bedrooms (most are doubles, some ensuite) are tidy and colourful, bedecked with bunting and fairy lights. Girls are 'affiliated' to boys' houses – 'it fosters co-ed spirit', we were told – and join them for activities such as plays, music and themed socials (wine and cheese, jazz).

Staff reassured us that houses are competitive 'but not tribal' and that the school works very hard to mix pupils up, especially important when so many come from the prep across the road.

Background and atmosphere: Founded in 1865 by George Cubitt, MP for West Surrey, and Rev John Sapte, who decided that what Victorian Surrey needed was 'a public school for the education of the middle classes.' The school was to 'provide a sound and plain education ... for the sons of farmers and others engaged in commercial pursuits.' The Surrey County School, funded by public appeals, was built on eight acres at the top of a hill just outside the village of Cranleigh. As the school grew to its present 280 acres, neighbouring farms were gradually acquired, remembered only in names such as The Butts (a sixth form café). If the original red-brick buildings embody the school's founding ideals, 'sound and plain', their elevated position at the top of a short avenue lends a certain aspirational grandeur. Most recent addition, the Emms Centre, houses modern foreign languages, science labs and IT, its double height atrium, flooded with natural light, was being well used by pupils revising for exams when we visited. The new humanities teaching block with dedicated business and careers centre is definitely not last in line.

Transition to co-ed, which started in the 1970s, was finally realised in 1999, but numerical equality of boys and girls is not on the cards. A ratio of 60:40 in favour of the chaps is the desired aim and the fourth girls' boarding house should help achieve it. No plans for significant increase in pupil numbers and parents certainly think school is 'just the right size'.

Parents told us they felt Cranleigh's reputation as a school that was just good for sport was always unfair and has, finally, been laid to rest. 'The school itself hasn't changed but the mindset of some people has', one told us. In our last review we noted that Cranleigh had become 'fashionable'. The school is undoubtedly still fashionable but its enduring popularity owes more to highly satisfied pupils and parents than any transient modishness. A 'sister' school, Cranleigh Abu Dhabi, was opened in 2014.

Pastoral care, well-being and discipline: 'Houses are everything' at Cranleigh, both academically and pastorally. 'Returning to your house should be like coming through a family door,' we were told. Each is almost like a mini-school but they 'aren't empires' and are run on consistent lines. Houseparents have a detailed overview of every aspect of a pupil's school career and tutors, teachers and prefects form 'layers' to catch problems. The parents we spoke to were very positive about all aspects of pastoral care, several commented on how well the school had dealt with 'difficult' teenage moments. 'They're so supportive, whatever the problem,' said one parent. Another told us, 'they expect the pupils to be independent but they know exactly when to step in.' Tutors are very quick to pick up on and let parents know about missed homework deadlines – whether the child is a boarder or day pupil, 'they want to work with parents'.

Pupils told us that their opinions were listened to although the democratic triumphs we heard about were small and mainly food based: Weetabix is now served every morning, spaghetti hoops are on the Wednesday menu and pepper is back on the tables (we couldn't find out why it disappeared). More significantly, after some wrangling, a termly teaching feedback survey will be implemented. 'It will improve communication', our guides said. Teachers weren't available for comment.

We heard several observations to the effect that expectations were higher for girls and that it was possibly bit easier being a boy at Cranleigh. These weren't criticisms, consensus is that school is right to make allowances for chaps' 'rough and tumble', although the interior décor of their boarding houses might disagree. Relationships between pupils are 'few' but 'managed extremely well'; the rules are crystal clear and it's not the Cranleigh way to break them – apparently 'you just wouldn't do that.'

Pupils and parents: Very much a local (home counties and London) boarding school – nearly all parents live within a two hour drive and matches, plays and concerts are very well supported as a consequence. 'I love the fact that my children get a great education and also have local friends', a mother told us. While school didn't seem to us as high end as its popular reputation suggests, a quick count of the Range Rovers doing Sunday night drop off will give you the superficial demographic. That 'Surrey bubble' may be in Mr Reader's sights but perhaps he's going to need a bigger pin.

Pupils are relaxed, confident and friendly, 'not overly sophisticated', said one mother, approvingly. There appears to be some leeway when it comes to hair and uniform (especially skirts below the knee rule) and many of the boys looked like they'd be much more comfortable in sports gear than suits. Very small number of international students, mainly from Russia and Poland. Former pupils include numbers of successful sportspeople, fair few military types plus Patrick Marber (actor, director, screenwriter); actors Julia Ormond, Laurence Naismith and Michael Cochrane; historian Andrew Roberts and former editor of the Guardian, Alan Rusbridger.

Entrance: About half come at 13+ from Cranleigh prep. Also Feltonfleet, Aldro, Danes Hill, Godstowe, Amesbury and Windlesham House. Majority of outside 13+ places offered in year 7: applicants are invited for an assessment day with a short test in English and maths and an interview to make 'an informal assessment of their interests and abilities.' Conditional offers made on the basis of this and reference from current school. Offer dependent on performance in CE or other assessments. School says it is looking for children who will thrive academically but also those who will make the most of the many opportunities on offer. All schools say this but oversubscribed Cranleigh means it and can afford to be choosy.

A few places are available at 16+ but competition is strong. Candidates should be predicted 9-7 grades at I/GCSE and must sit verbal and non-verbal reasoning papers and submit an essay. Interview and reference also required.

Exit: A few leave post-GCSE, mostly to pursue courses not offered at school. University destinations and courses of those who stay on are as diverse as one might imagine. Lots to Bath, Birmingham, Bristol, Exeter, Durham, Newcastle and York. Handful to Europe and North America. Six to Oxbridge in 2018.

Money matters: Fees broadly in line with similar schools. Day fees towards the upper end of the scale but you are paying for six long days a week. Variety of scholarships on offer (music, sports, all-rounder) and these can be supplemented by means-tested bursaries.

Remarks: Cranleigh's motto, 'Ex cultu robur' (From culture comes strength), is a potent and timely reminder that education is about so much more than just exam results. This is a school where the team is defined as much by its fellowship as its success, although it helps that team Cranleigh does win quite a lot of the time. Mr Reader has distilled the famous Cranleigh ethos into five words: wholeness, time, family, love and hope. We think he's got it about right.

Cranmore School

Epsom Road, West Horsley, Surrey KT24 6AT

Ages Boys 2-13, girls 2-9, becoming fully co-ed **Pupils** 430 **RC**

Fees: £12,000 – £15,000 pa

01483 280340
www.cranmoreprep.co.uk

Headmaster: Since 2006, Michael Connolly BSc BA MA MEd (50s). Scottish, quietly confident, straight bat, no nonsense. Years of experience as teacher, housemaster and head in a number of HMC senior and prep schools. He keeps active with squash, tennis and dog walking; reads something philosophical or theological most days (his arts subjects) and enjoys a broad musical taste. Mrs Connolly is a qualified teacher who also works in the school in the marketing department and shows prospective parents around. They have three sons, all in their 20s.

Thoughtful and considered, he tackles difficult topics up front and head on. Parents describe him as 'reliable', 'straight talking', 'unassuming' and 'trustworthy'. Under his leadership, Cranmore is widely inclusive while maintaining high academic and social standards, with many opportunities for individual success.

He has limited contact with junior pupils (this is left to Fiona Nicholson, the very experienced head of the junior department), increasing as children progress through the school. In their final two years he teaches weekly lessons and gets to know them really well.

Entrance: Not-selective and proud to be so. Prospective pupils spend a session in class and are assessed to ensure they would be happy and successful. Assessment definitely not competitive; head reassures that 'the average child will be fine', so long as they are prepared to 'get stuck in and have a go'.

Co-ed nursery, reception and years 1-4. The school will gradually become totally co-ed. Academic, music and sports scholarships awarded for entry at 7+. Means-tested financial assistance potentially provides, at most, a free place.

Exit: Pupils move on to a wide variety of senior schools, reflecting the non-selective intake: eg Brighton College, Charterhouse, City of London Freemen's, Cranleigh, Epsom, King's College Wimbledon, Lancing, Millfield, Reigate Grammar, Royal Grammar School Guildford, Reeds, Sherborne, St George's, St John's, Tonbridge, Wellington, Winchester, Worth.

Around third to half leave at 11, mainly to avoid pre-testing and/or common entrance. Of those who leave at 13 around a quarter win scholarships, awards or exhibitions (24 in 2018).

Remarks: A genuinely all round school. Parents feel 'it's very balanced between academics, sport and music' and 'ticks boxes in lots of different areas'.

Located deep in Surrey's green commuter belt, on a large site with spacious, well-equipped playgrounds and a forest school. Nursery in the original Victorian building tucked away around the back; the rest of the buildings are modern, spacious and purpose built, with impressive teaching facilities, particularly for science and IT. Nursery, junior and senior share all facilities but at different times, so it is not overwhelming for the youngest.

High expectations, and for the most part the children 'surprise themselves' with their achievements. Mr Connolly aims to limit the inevitable academic pressure; he is 'not a big fan of homework' and believes 'if pupils come to school fresh and get engaged while at school that should be enough to realise their abilities'. A long-standing Cranmore mum explained, 'He tries to educate the Surrey parent not to get too worked up about academic success'.

Parents tell us Cranmore 'turns out pupils who want to learn', and that their children have been 'well challenged and tutored' by 'talented teachers' who 'know what buttons to push'. They feel 'the school sticks by all the pupils throughout and has great belief in the mix of abilities', and their children are 'monitored and assessed so there are no surprises'. Mr Connolly meets every parent during year 5 to discuss aspirations and manage expectations for suitable senior schools.

Broad range of subjects taught, although recently Latin has been dropped from the CE syllabus, with Mr Connolly reassuring that it is not compulsory for most senior schools. He teaches senior pupils on a carousel of (non-examined) Latin, Greek and philosophy, two terms of each over the final two years. Pupils are set in English and maths from year 4; years 7-8 each have one scholarship and two CE classes.

Post-CE programme is 'fantastic, every day is jam packed,' say parents, who are pleased their children stayed on to enjoy final two prep years with smaller teaching groups, prefect responsibility, exclusive blazers and a common room with play station, pool table, air hockey and table football.

Sport is the 'wow' factor which attracts lively, active types. The facilities are 'amazing' and coaching is 'totally professional' with a 'squeaky clean sporting ethos'. By the time pupils leave they will have had the opportunity to try over 20 sports, including climbing, rowing and skiing (with ski club lessons at Sandown Park for pupils and families). There are plenty of clean, flat pitches, including all-weather pitches, sports hall with squash courts and fitness room, gym with climbing walls (laid out for lunchtime judo club when we visited), a 25 metre indoor swimming pool. There's enough indoor sporting space to accommodate all, so rain never stops play. Huge number of teams are fielded; however the less sportingly inclined may not feel entirely comfortable in this super-active environment.

Music has 'incredible facilities' coupled with an 'exceptionally good head of music'. It forms part of every day in assemblies, performances and curriculum, and there are over 250 individual instrumental or singing lessons each week.

Catholic ethos runs through the school; head explains: 'It's a Catholic community and everyone does everything, it's fundamental to the school. If you want to come to Cranmore you accept this'. Having said that, the majority of families are not Catholic, and feel perfectly comfortable with daily prayer, half-termly mass and Catholic RE syllabus. Pupils are 'not indoctrinated' and parents recognise solid, Christian values that 'do pupils quite a bit of good'. They feel school focus is on 'confident, well-rounded children, who care about each other and are allowed to be individuals'.

On the whole, pupils work calmly within clear, tight boundaries and are well motivated to please, earning merit points for their house. Much parental praise for the deputy head, who deals with occasional episodes of bullying. Pupils are helped with coping strategies and parents are involved. Discipline is about learning and moving on with 'no labels for bad children'; the aim is to educate children to make the right choices via drip feed over a long period. Mr Connolly is onto the dangers of cyber-bullying: his approach is zero tolerance to any cyber-messaging he deems inappropriate, and he has suspended pupils.

Cranmore families are hard working, busy, 'definitely Surrey people'. Most can comfortably afford fees, a few making financial sacrifices. Plenty of stay-at-home mums picking up or watching matches in muddy Hunter wellies. Active parents' association provides friendly socials and fundraising. Pupils' classes are changed around each year so children, and parents, get to know all in their year group.

An all-round school maintaining high standards and impressive results from a non-selective intake, gradually becoming co-ed, with so much on offer that every child can find something in which to succeed.

Cumnor House Sussex

82

Danehill, Haywards Heath, West Sussex RH17 7HT

Ages 2-13 **Pupils** 380 **Boarders** 16 full, 17 weekly, 36 flexi (from 7 years) **C of E**

Fees: Day £8,985 – £19,530; Boarding £22,635 – £23,250 pa

01825 790347
www.cumnor.co.uk

Headmaster: Since 2001, Christian Heinrich BA PGCE (40s). Degrees from Kent and Oxford. Previously housemaster, then deputy head, at Summer Fields. ISI Inspector, IAPS appraiser of fellow heads, and chairman of the Boarding Schools Association in 2013, so plenty of insight into schools at all levels. Confident, and very sure of his approach to childhood and education: 'If a child is happy, education takes care of itself.' Described by pupils as fair, fun and someone who 'doesn't get unreasonably cross.'

Parents are very enthusiastic about him: 'Incredibly kind and supportive of kids – particularly those who struggle'; 'Easy to see when you want to'. 'Radical and brave...in that he works for the kids and not the parents,' added one parent thoughtfully. Parents might find it difficult to accept the extraordinary level of pressure to succeed that can be absorbed by children – but the head and pupils here are fully cognisant, and the head does what he can to relieve the pressure.

Married to Belinda, who teaches French in the pre-prep; they have four children.

Entrance: Non-selective in early years; thereafter selection of those most likely to be fully involved in school life. Taster day for all, and interview for years 6 and above. Two full means-tested bursaries for talented (academic and/or sport and creative arts) pupils joining year 4, covering 100 per cent of fees up to 18 at one of the partner schools (these are Ardingly, Benenden, Eastbourne College, Hurstpierpoint College, King's Canterbury, Lancing College, Mayfield, Radley, Roedean, St Mary's Ascot, Sevenoaks, Tonbridge and Worth) – apply by April to join in September.

Exit: To a large variety of senior schools (30+), with Hurstpierpoint most popular recently, then Cranleigh and Brighton College, Ardingly and Charterhouse. In directing children towards schools, considers not just whether they can meet the academic requirements, but also whether they're sufficiently emotionally robust to cope with life at the school in question.

Remarks: Beautiful setting in the Sussex countryside overlooking the downs. Buildings range from the charming to the unremarkable, in a village-like cluster. Lush green grounds, and large pond to row over in the Cumnor boat, or swing over on a rope (it's drained and cleaned and carefully tested for any virulent bacteria first, assured the head's wife).

Main entrance has been recently modernised and leads into the slightly scuffed country house hotel-type interior – parquet floor and log fire, and a few Famous Five books on a window sill by a sofa. Lego table and 70s sweets jigsaw on the go. 'Another genius from Cumnor' cushions – to reassure existing parents, or perhaps tempt prospective ones?

Common room with a log fire, couple of pool tables and newspapers (including Times and Independent). Award-winning art work on the walls, and a long piece of paper where pupils had drawn self-portraits in the style of Quentin Blake to celebrate World Book Day.

Pre-prep is a cosy separate entity that particularly attracted one mum, who remembers fondly the special mothers' day celebration in reception, children presenting mums with handpicked flowers wrapped in foil, then escorting them into school for special cakes and poems – 'very simple and lovely.'

Nursery open 7am-7pm 50 weeks a year, available to the whole community. Pyjama-clad children can be delivered in time to have breakfast alongside the older boarders and then picked up ready for bed at night.

'Academic, but not pushy academic,' says the head. Certainly a school which achieves a goodly number of scholarships, but not, in atmosphere or method, like a prep with an eye on the prize for the duration. Many parents fresh from pressurised London preps may struggle initially with the comparatively relaxed Cumnor environment – 'you don't know at what level everyone else's child is reading,' said one startled mum. No constant testing. I have to tell them to trust us, says the head – 'children are meant to be enjoying themselves and having fun.'

Careful consideration of the timetable, which is broken up so kids are not using their brains in the same way for long periods of time – pre-prep dance outside before each maths lesson. No one model fits all – so if there is good reason for the usual school curriculum not to apply to a child, then an exception will be made.

Not much prep until year 7 (when pupils start preparing for scholarships and CE): just vocab and spelling, which could be learnt in the bath or around the dinner table, and reading, occasionally left undone – 'I don't read on Friday nights as mummy and daddy have gin and tonic,' said a child in year 1.

Year 7 and 8s all have iPads for use during lessons, purchased by parents in an optional scheme ('you didn't have to sign up, but if everyone else was going to have one...'). No social media or unsuitable apps.

Learning support is excellent, and not only provides support to (around 30) pupils with special needs, but also to those who just need a bit of extra help now and then. There's an educational psychologist on the staff, who observes classes, and deals with any emotional problems suffered by pupils which may be exacerbated by school, from separation anxiety to bereavement. No extra charge for counselling or one-to-one learning support. Additional charges for extras such as speech therapy.

Saturday school on alternate weekends, which children seem happy with (though some parents would prefer a lie in, and more family time).

School motto – 'aim high, be kind and dare to be different' – permeates everything, said one parent: apparently the head girl's and boy's job is to make sure everyone is happy at break time, and no one is being left out; so it comes as no surprise that the pastoral care is very thorough: regular full staff pastoral care meetings where every child's name is read out, and their welfare considered, and a new well-being curriculum programme. Form teachers are the first port of call for difficulties until year 5, after which each child has a tutor whom they meet twice once a week to talk about everything and anything. School policy on bullying is to make sure children understand what bullying behaviour is, and ask them to blow the whistle: senior children attend the ABC committee (Anti-Bullying Committee) every week to report on anyone they are worried about. One parent whose child experienced bullying behaviour said it was dealt with quickly and efficiently, and also praised the presence of 'gappers' (gap year students), who she said could pick up on things teachers might not get to hear.

CofE, but not evangelically so. Exposure to the most valuable tenets of faith with a bohemian touch: daily prayers described by head as also a school silence – a time for a loud school to be silent and consider things.

The school shares facilities in the local community, and links with a local primary each year. The head is setting up the Cumnor certificate (own brand DofE), which will involve years 7 and 8 working in the local community, and being part of drama workshops with younger pupils from local primaries.

Food is 'amazing,' say kids – apparently there are no adjectives which can do justice to the wraps. In-house custard creams and jammy dodgers bulge with cream and jam and were startlingly yummy to those of us used to the pedestrian version (they've got an award winning pastry chef).

Occupations, as clubs are called at Cumnor, range from boules to calligraphy, and vary each term. Cinematography described in detail by enthusiastic kids – 'it makes you look at films in a completely different way.' There's a waiting list for cooking, but everyone gets a turn eventually. Year 8 learn to cook a three course meal as a post-exam treat.

The 'co-curriculum' (sports and arts) is given equal rather than ornamental value here ('they find out what every child has going for them,' said a parent).

Sport is for awareness, commitment and health – and everyone: a poor, enthusiastic player will be in teams all the way through, playing matches most weeks. 'It's nice to win,' said a pupil; but it's not the only or main purpose of sport here. No A, B or C teams until year 7: teams change from week to week, and the make-up of teams depends on whom they are playing.

Art is 'exceptional,' said one parent. Housed in a barn-like room with high beams, glass doors and space to hang strange colourful objects. All learn a musical instrument – it can be dropped in year 7 to make way for the demands of common entrance and scholarships, though many continue.

Each year from year 3 upwards does an annual production, Shakespeare being the year 8 remit to be performed in the mossy green outdoor theatre.

The uniform and sports kit is good quality but expensive – one parent complained indignantly at the cost of school sweatshirts; but there's some second hand provision in the uniform shop. Sports kit is laundered by the school, much to the joy of parents.

Boarding is possible from year 7: full timers, who all go home every other weekend, weekly and flexi-boarders, who spend a few nights every week at school. 'They are completely flexible,' said one grateful parent. Tremendously popular with pupils, several of whom commented on their difficulty persuading their mums they were old enough – 'but it's so fun.' Lots of activities: preparations for Dragons' Den were under way, not to mention Marlborough Murders, Friday night is magic night and day trips at the weekends.

Rooms are for five, and cosy: four beds at ground level, and one bunk. Bathrooms are clean and up to date. Parents like the proximity of houseparents (described by parents as 'warm and welcoming' and 'extremely efficient'), and the easy access pupils have to gappers, who have rooms on each corridor, and are the first point of call in the night.

Fruit is always available, and there's a pantry where boarders can make tea, toast and hot drinks (with gappers' help). Obligatory weekly letter writing, and phones available for making calls in the evening or at break time – parents and pupils were happy this was sufficient. No Skype, iPads or mobiles allowed ('they get technology soon enough,' said one parent). Currently no overseas boarders.

Parents around 30 per cent London, the rest local, mostly professionals or city types. Not cliquey, said one parent, outgoing and sociable, inclusive of newcomers, with a buddy system to match new parents with old.

Dame Alice Owen's School

Dugdale Hill Lane, Potters Bar, Hertfordshire EN6 2DU

Ages 11–18 **Pupils** 1,451 **Sixth form** 424

01707 643441
www.damealiceowens.herts.sch.uk

Headteacher: Since 2016, Hannah Nemko (early 40s). MA (Nottingham) MeLtrs (Stasbourg) PGCE. Married to a teacher, with two young children, Ms Nemko was promoted to the top job from her role as senior deputy here. She joined the school in 2015 from Yavneh College, where she was deputy head and helped set up the college. Prior to that she taught for two years at the Royal Grammar School in High Wycombe and at Immanuel College for five years before that. Born and brought up in Essex, Ms Nemko was, by her own admission, dedicated to her studies and a model schoolgirl. Head girl of her High School (Beal High School), she confides that she loved playing schools as a child and was the first in her family to go to university. She recalls her father telling her that her primary headteacher said she would never amount to anything as she couldn't master fractions, and quietly smiles at the thought that she is now a headmistress ('with A level maths!' she adds).

Tall and svelte, with soft brown eyes and stylishly short dark hair, Ms Nemko looks more like an A list celebrity than a headmistress. As we wander through the school, nothing escapes her notice. Some boys jostle with each other over their packed lunch, she firmly takes control. An apple core obstructs the path, she swiftly scoops it up; a boy sits looking glumly in the distance, she stops to enquire and give comfort. Warm, unaffected and natural, Ms Nemko is also disarmingly self-deprecating.

She regards her pupils with sharper clarity, however. 'A typical Owenian', she says, 'is someone who has a natural interest in the world around them and wants to explore all avenues. Students here are intellectually curious and this becomes self-perpetuating.'

Ms Nemko is hugely popular with the students; the senior boy who showed us round seemed positively envious that we were about to spend two hours in her company. Not, by any stretch, a backroom head, she is very present and particularly enjoys teaching maths to those who struggle with it most at GCSE level (she baulks at talking in terms of sets); 'being taught by the head can give students – who can feel frustrated at not being able to achieve as quickly as their peers – a lift, and it sends a message that the school will invest in them as much as anyone to help them achieve.' 'Maths was not a subject that ever came easily to me.. but I worked hard at it and succeeded well at A level, so I know how to communicate with others who find it a struggle.'

Always busy doing things that matter, Ms Nemko also oversees all the appeals and admissions and prioritises anything that affects the students. Staffing is also a priority: 'I spend a lot of time with the head of pastoral...it's very difficult to get good staff' – a cry from the top that is becoming increasingly, and disturbingly, familiar to us. 'I work hard to look after my staff as much as my students, and try to do all I can to ensure that their working life is balanced, and employ as much of a "yes" policy as I possibly can.'

An unusual appointment in the eyes of some. Her youth and lack of experience as a head ruffled a few feathers. However, Ms Nemko's extensive experience of both pastoral and teaching and learning furnishes her with the tools she needs for any fine tuning that is required here. She inherited a well-oiled machine from her highly esteemed predecessor – also her mentor – and, say parents, there should be no need for dramatic change. The mantra that she recites to her students – 'Be the best you can be. both socially and academically' – she clearly applies to herself too.

Academic matters: A partially selective intake (about 40 per cent) raises expectations and standards across the board. Parents choose the school for its academic aspirations and excellent teaching, and those that have got in through other channels – musical talent, postcode, sibling and a large dose of luck – largely share the same ethos. Results are impressive by any standards. In 2018, 60 per cent A*/A grades at A level and 69 per cent 9-7 grades at GCSE.

A specialist language and science school, students can choose between French, Spanish and German (two of these languages are taught from year 7 and many do two at GCSE); in addition Italian, Russian, Japanese, Mandarin and Latin can often be arranged as an extracurricular pursuit. Fourteen science labs spread across two floors in the impressive science block opened by Lord Winston in 2014. Judging from the rapt faces of the year 7 pupils we observed, science is popular and well taught.

Laptop stations throughout the school for students to borrow with simple finger identification. No one is allowed to feel at a disadvantage. Lots of overseas trips – staying with host families in year 9 and study trips abroad in year 12.

More boys than girls do maths at A level, especially further maths. Setting for maths and languages from year 8, but Ms Nemko is determined to keep setting to a minimum and works hard to get rid of any stigma of being in the 'bottom set'. Computer sciences now offered at A level. History department particularly strong; history is the most popular subject at GCSE and, together with maths, at A level. Unusually, economics and business both offered at GCSE as well as A level. Some do the EPQ.

Focus is not only on the pure academic subjects (phew): DT textiles, graphic products, resistant materials and food technology offered at GCSE, with textiles and product design at A level. Subjects we see diminishing at an alarming rate in the maintained sector and a luxurious by-product of not having to rely solely on government funding. No BTecs.

Not the school to choose if your child needs a lot of extra support, although they do have a few on EHCPs and they do the best they can for each one. The SEN department is small and not especially well resourced – 'we don't need a lot from it,' says head. A number of pupils here have high functioning autism – they 'will do fine. we don't think it's fair to take on pupil unless we can fully support them ...the strength of the school lies in the quality of teaching in the traditional academic subjects,' says Ms Nemko. 'Teachers will refer pupils with specific learning profiles to the SENCo and look at strategies to support those children but EHCP parents need to understand who we are and the limits of what we can offer.'

Maximum class size in years 7 to 11 is 32, with seven or eight groups per year. In the sixth form they range from between 12 and 20. Culture of support throughout the school includes sixth formers giving support in the class room to pupils further down the school. High praise for teachers from parents and pupils, as well as Ofsted. Very committed and hardworking. Our sixth form guide commented on the amount of support and help he received with his UCAS application and with his Oxford entrance exam.

Games, options, the arts: We were impressed by the art. Four studios with an array of work on display. Fifty-seven pupils took art GCSE in 2017, over half got A* grades and no one got below a B. Some A level art students go on to do foundation courses at, eg, Central St Martins and the Royal Drawing schools and others to fashion design courses or to eg read architecture at Cambridge.

Sport is plentiful and your sporty child will thrive here. Excellent sporting facilities including acres of pitches (the site occupies 35 acres of grounds), a large sports hall and floodlit Astroturf. They play a lot and there are regular fixtures every Saturday. More football than rugby. The 1st XI won the Herts County Cup recently. Both boys and girls play football and hockey, girls also play rounders and netball. There are also badminton, cricket, basketball, athletics and tennis. Good-sized gym stuffed with equipment – mats, trampolines etc – and the school frequently produces impressive cross-country runners. Many succeed at national and county level in a number of sports.

Music is 'phenomenal', the adjective used by nearly all parents we spoke to – and music is a passion of Ms Nemko's. Historically, too, it has always been a strength of the school. School celebrated its 400th anniversary in 2013 by hosting a sell-out concert at the Royal Albert Hall. A plethora of orchestras (a total of five, including full symphony orchestra), ensembles, choirs and bands, all of high standard and everyone, not just the super talented, gets the chance to perform. Enthusiastic and supportive music teachers create an environment where students want to take part rather than feel forced to do so. Exceptionally well resourced with a concert hall (outstanding acoustics), three specialist classrooms (one with networked Sibelius 7 and LogicPro X software), and a fully-equipped modern recording studio, rehearsal and recital studio. Tickets to the Soul Band are always a sell out.

Drama takes place in the sparkling new Sir Alan Parker building. There are three productions a year including separate upper school and lower school plays. Recent performances include Grease and Alice in Wonderland. All pupils do drama in years 7 and 8, and it's available at GCSE and A level. Drama teachers praised for their enthusiasm and energy and lots of pupils choose it as an extracurricular option.

An abundance of trips – including a recent football tour to South America, historians visited the Somme and every two years there is an offer of a trip in the summer holiday to 'somewhere wonderful' to open the windows onto the wider world. Not part of any curriculum, but pupils and staff value it enormously. Recently those lucky enough to get on the trip went to Namibia. There are also regular language exchanges with partner schools in France, Spain and Germany. D of E (22 achieved their gold award in 2016-17), as well as over 140 extracurricular activities to choose from.

Background and atmosphere: Originally founded in Islington in 1613 by Dame Alice Owen, the school was entrusted with its leadership to the Worshipful Company of Brewers and they continue to be trustees of the school today. Born Alice Wilkes, she narrowly missed being struck by a wayward arrow when she was young and vowed that as soon as she was rich enough she would do something for posterity as a mark of gratitude. Fifty years on and thrice widowed, she used her wealth to establish a school for 30 boy scholars from Islington.

A girls' school was added in 1886, and in the late 60s a search was made for a new location. The school moved to its present site on the edge of Potters Bar in 1973. To this day Dame Alice Owen's takes immense pride in its history. All pupils receive 'a crown for annual beer money' at a ceremony at the Brewers Hall in the City of London. Year 7s receive a £5 commemorative coin, years 8s receive £1, rising to £6 for year 13. Dame Alice originally instructed the governors to visit the school annually to inspect the pupils' progress and this still forms part of the annual open day and prize-giving. In the early days the scholars collected flowers to make buttonholes; today pupils in years 7 to 11 wear white carnations while sixth formers sport red carnations.

When we visited we were struck by the stillness of the place. Nestled amongst acres of green fields and trees, it is peaceful despite the M25 thundering around its edges. There is a calm sense of purpose. Images of Dame Alice are dotted about the school, a stained glass window in reception, a portrait complete with ruff in the hall, a statue in the canteen.

A mix of modern buildings from the 70s low rise to more recent blocks. Maths, science, drama and technology all now housed in their own ultra-modern blocks and there is another exciting project in the pipeline. The central focus of these hotch-potch buildings is the Brewer's Garden – a jungle of large grassy mounds, circled by winding paths. Our guide thought that they were deliberately designed to stop football being played at break in that central space, and remarked on how 'chilled' the area is. Vast outside space beyond – Astroturf, tarmac, fields and woods, as well as the lake, concealed by bamboo and reeds, situated at the top of a hill overlooking Brewer's Garden. Close to the pond is the moving WW1 memorial, and each year on Remembrance Day a number of people stand around on the top of this hill and remember those who died. At other times of year a football is kicked about during break and lunchtimes. There is plenty of opportunity to let off steam, and shrug off the academic concentration that takes place most of the day.

A corridor in the main building holds all the honours boards – complete with gold leaf on wood – dating back several decades. As well as football and netball captains it also lists those who achieved first class honours degrees at their various universities. However the school has moved with the times, a sixth form boy assured us; it is not just sitting on the laurels of the past.

While years 7 to 11 eat in the main hall behind the reception building (a space that has a number of uses including exams), the sixth form have their own swanky dining room, which is open all day and where many of them choose to work as well as eat. No more lunch money and all the problems that can be associated with it – payment is made by fingerprints and parents are able to see what their children are eating when they receive their statement.

A distinct atmosphere pervades the school, partly on account of the unusual admissions criteria. There is a healthy mix here of the very able and a broad range of ability. Students are aware of this and say they like it. A 'partially selective system raises the ethos of the whole school,' says Ms Nemko.

Pastoral care, well-being and discipline: Behaviour is excellent on the whole. ' You need to come here with a good attitude,' said one boy, earnestly. ' People feel pleased to be here and want to do well, as you are admired for doing well.'

Pastoral care is very much a priority of the current head and under her leadership the students get a voice. Effective school council run by a team of 10 senior boys and girls, including the head boy and the head girl, is concerned with student well-being (as well as other things). They meet Ms Nemko once a week to discuss concerns and school improvement. Students want to be on the school council and feel proud of their position.

An unusual feature of the pastoral care here is that the form prefects – selected from year 13 – and form tutors work together to educate younger students about issues ranging from sex to social media. This happens in a designated form period once a week.

Strong culture of helping others less able than yourself. Sixth formers go into lower year lessons to help with maths, for example, and the same expectation extends to helping peers in your own lessons. A lot work very hard to get here, which creates a self- perpetuating sense of intellectual curiosity and endeavour, as well as high expectation.

'The one thing all pupils are encouraged not to talk about is how they got into the school – it all works its way through. It doesn't matter how you got here: the only important thing is that you are here. We are all Owenians striving to do our best,' says Ms Nemko.

Pupils and parents: A more prosperous school than most of its kind, Ofsted remarks (the most recent inspection was in 2009) that the number of pupils on free school meals is 'very low'. Practically all pupils are fluent in English and the numbers with special educational needs is also low.

Pupils travel from far and wide – a good number commute on the train from Islington, large numbers from Potters Bar, Enfield, Barnet, Hatfield and South Mimms.

Plenty of distinguished former pupils, including Gary Kemp (and three other members of Spandau Ballet), Madness guitarist Chris Foreman, Sir Alan Parker, Dame Beryl Grey and Joss Ackland. A framed letter from Gary Kemp on the wall in reception declares he's 'proud to be an Old Owenian.' Spandau Ballet gave its first performance in the school hall and a commemorative plaque is planned.

Parents are an eclectic mix – from media types and factory workers to company directors and teachers. They are hugely supportive (hosting fundraising events, quiz nights and a summer ball) and all keen on the idea of an academic, non-exclusive school.

Entrance: Two hundred places in year 7 are competed for by over 1,300 applicants each year. The admissions process is complicated in that it is semi-selective. Home address must be within one of the listed areas at date of registration. Sixty-five places by academic selection, with tests in maths, English and verbal reasoning – currently a student needs to score over 115 to be in for a chance of a place. Ten places reserved for applicants with musical aptitude. The school serves 15 parishes within Hertfordshire, nine postcodes in boroughs of Brent and Enfield. Twenty places a year are reserved for pupils educated or with a permanent address in Islington. Priority given to looked after children and to those with special needs, then 22 who live closest to the school and siblings of pupils already at Dame Alice Owen's. Children taking the entrance exam and music tests must live in one of the school's designated priority areas.

Around 500 apply for 30 places in the sixth form. Applicants come from local state and independent schools and the same entrance criteria applies to externals as to those who wish to stay. Minimum of five grade B/6s at GCSE and grade 5 in English and maths if they are not included in the five. Priority given to existing pupils. Slightly more girls than boys in the sixth form.

Exit: Around 15 to 20 per cent leave after GCSEs. School requires minimum same GCSE grades as for external candidates to enter the sixth form. After A levels virtually all go on to higher education with 80 per cent to Russell Group universities – lots to UCL, and other London colleges, including LSE, King's and Imperial. High numbers to Bristol, Durham, Nottingham and Warwick. They read all manner of subjects from aeronautics and astronautics at Southampton to criminology and sociology at Liverpool and fashion and textile design at Portsmouth. More traditional courses include medicine and engineering (nearly half go on to study science), economics, politics and history. 'Our students are eclectic in their interests.' In 2018, 29 to Oxbridge, 12 medics and one to USA (Stamford).

Money matters: Funded by government as an academy but also gets money from the Dame Alice Owen Foundation (The Worshipful Company of Brewers is the trustee), fundraising events and donations.

Remarks: A purposeful school that manages to combine excellence across the board – particularly academic and music. Parents, staff and pupils here are all rowing, and rowing hard, in the same direction. If you have managed to get a place, congratulations, you have won the lottery.

Dame Bradbury's School

Linked with Stephen Perse 6th Form College, Stephen Perse Senior School, Stephen Perse Pre-Prep (City), Stephen Perse Junior School, Stephen Perse Pre-Prep (Madingley)

Ashdon Road, Saffron Walden, Essex CB10 2AL

Ages 3–11 **Pupils** 269

Fees: £11,175 – £13,800 pa

01799 522348
www.damebradburys.com

Head: Since 2015, Tracy Handford, previously head of St Hilda's Prep in Bushey. Educated at Lancaster Girls' Grammar School and the University of Leeds, where she read applied biology. Followed this with an MA in curriculum studies from the Institute of Education, University of London. Began career as a boarding tutor at Taverham Hall School, Norwich, then Holmwood House, Colchester. Moved to become head of year and head of science at Bishop's Stortford College Junior School before becoming director of studies at St Faith's School, Cambridge. Status as ISI inspector should mean she has her eye on the competitive ball and her experience means she is au fait with the Cambridge school scene. Likeable, down to earth, 'professional and knowledgeable,' say parents. Committed to providing her pupils with 'more than a set of qualifications'. Lives in rural Cambridgeshire with her husband and daughter.

Entrance: Waiting list with sibling preference. For the kindergarten and reception, informal visit with head of early years. Later entrants, depending on age: chat/observation in the classroom/tests in age appropriate core skills of maths and English. School purports to be non-selective, but says children are accepted on the basis that they can access the learning – gives school some wiggle room.

Exit: School starts talking to parents about next school when their children are in year 4. Over 90 per cent get their first choice. Stephen Perse Foundation senior school a favourite – helped by tempting early offer process which removes the need for entrance testing and SPF having gone co-ed in September 2017. By no means the only option, though, with large numbers boarding the so-called Hogwarts Express daily from Saffron Walden to schools in Cambridge (Perse Upper, The Leys, St Mary's Cambridge, as well as SPF) and others to board further afield (Cheltenham, Oakham, King's Ely, Oundle, Cheltenham Ladies). Academic, music, art and sport scholarships frequently awarded. A handful to Saffron Walden and Linton state schools.

Remarks: Dame Johane Bradbury is named after its founder – the sister of an early 16th century rector of Saffron Walden. Today the school is situated in a quiet suburban street not far from the town centre. Slightly dour late Victorian edifice belies the modernity inside – all white walls and funky accent colours since becoming part of the Stephen Perse Foundation in 2013 and the arrival of Mrs Handford. Parents have appreciated the step change and note improvements to the facilities, administration and academic rigour. 'Being part of a bigger foundation results in a scrutiny that previously did not exist apart from ISI inspections, and I feel much more comfortable knowing that the future of the school is secure as part of Stephen Perse,' commented one. Foundation offers CPD opportunities for staff and central administration, giving more time for teachers to teach and to develop curriculum approaches.

Mrs Handford is credited with 'taking the school forward', boosting academic standards through specialist teaching, IT and creativity across the board. Commitment to instilling values, developing integrity and personal qualities continues with added oomph. 'Children are encouraged to make good choices in their learning and behaviour,' says head and this is quite strategic, with classroom displays focusing as much on 'learning habits' and 'what makes a good monitor' as examples of (extremely) good work. Useful, according to our guide, when you're struggling in a maths test and catch sight of the word 'determination' writ large on the wall behind your teacher's head. Every pupil holds a position of responsibility at some point and super 'YAK' accreditation for those identified as 'being yourself, aiming high and being kind' – school's key aims in a nutshell – while the house system 'gives a real sense of pride,' exclaims our guide.

'Hard to find children sitting down at a desk – they're outside dragging a branch or using technology,' says head, and indeed a sparky and innovative approach to learning when we visited with pupils actively engaged in purposeful activities – from 'office' role play in kindergarten, to learning Spanish while studying Miro, to a soundtrack of the Gypsy Kings in year 4. Says head, 'investigation is integral' to the curriculum, which is devised by SPF and reviewed regularly. Thematic learning is the key with a four year theme cycle in pre-prep and two years in the juniors to keep things fresh. 'We're moving away from the curriculum being driven by content and instead taking a skills based approach,' head explains. Much use of digital technologies with Macs and iPads all around – ideal for in-class support as well as extension. Google classroom for years 5 and

6. Homework only in English, maths and science – parents encouraged to take their children out instead, 'to satisfy intellectual curiosity'.

Collaboration across the foundation gives scope for enrichment activities (recently pre-prep multicultural day in Cambridge on understanding diversity, World War Two workshop for upper juniors). Specialist teaching for music, science and languages – French and Spanish for all, and Latin from year 5. Learning support has made great strides – the focus is on inclusion, ensuring pupils are supported within the classroom. Room and capacity for increased roll but 'space is a benefit,' says head. Two form entry with pre-prep classes of up to 16 and the rest to 20. Kindergarten for around 22 rising 3 to 4s, awash with wellies and sharing 'big gym and little gym' outdoor play and learning area with the two reception classes and all of the school's facilities. Large kindergarten classrooms have plenty of corners for creative play – on the list for refurbishment. Parents invited in to watch lessons including music, languages and weekly forest school. Year 6s help as buddies.

Fab new brightly coloured art room is an inspiring work space. Innovative library with lit, carpeted shelves, dominated by central 'reading tree' with nooks and crannies filled with books and places to sit. Graphs of most popular reading and pupils' own reviews. Very tempting. Rainey Hall opened in 2013 by Earl of Wessex, indoor sports facility presided over by no fewer than eight PE trained members of staff (a record for this size of school?) offering rugby and netball, athletics and cricket (two girls' teams wiping the floor in local fixtures). Outside 184m track and Astro as well as playing fields. Also a teaching garden complete with pond for dipping.

School's own theatre is the venue for assemblies – raked seating for privileged year 6 – and annual productions for every year group from kindergarten and reception nativity to year 5 shortened Shakespeare and year 6 musical. Also houses lively music department where year 2 up learn the recorder and year 5 the ukulele. Thriving orchestra open to all when ready.

'The provision of extracurricular activities is second to none,' asserts a parent, and certainly the wide choice of clubs runs the gamut from STEAM (STEM plus arts), to iPad photography and ceilidh band. Sports clubs change every term (all welcome unless squad training). Residential trips much anticipated, building from four days in York for year 4 to five day trips in year 5 (Cornwall) and year 6 (Snowdonia). Different years take on different projects – last year's Snowdon visitors produced an iBook.

Fresh fruit and a carbohydrate are the usual breaktime snacks supplied by the kitchens and there's a choice at lunch of the cooked meal, vegetarian option or salad, followed by a hot pudding or yogurt plus fruit. Breakfast club is popular for the hot chocolate. Dining hall doubles as an arena for critical thinking – enormous green board invites mind maps and the articulation of thoughts and ideas.

Any type of child is suited here, says head. All we met presented as enthusiastic learners with a solid work ethic and an appreciation of worthwhile personal qualities and values. Refreshing. 'You can be a great learner but you need to know how to use what you've learnt to get the most out of life,' says head. Pupils are assessed on their engagement with learning and all make good progress, she adds.

Parent profile has changed somewhat in recent years due to the establishment of local science parks and greater commuting to London or Cambridge. Invited in to school often, including to help with clubs. Working parents booked in in advance. Parental trust in the school runs high.

An exciting and enormously positive prep school which inspires children to learn independently and enthusiastically and to develop the skills and qualities to apply their learning in life. Quite likely the shape of prep education to come.

Dane Court Grammar School

Broadstairs Road, Broadstairs, Kent CT10 2RT

Ages 11–18 **Pupils** 1,256 **Sixth form** 368

01843 864941
www.danecourt.kent.sch.uk

D

Executive Headteacher: Since September 2018, Kate Greig, previously headteacher of King Ethelbert. She has several leadership roles in Kent education and is also an education advisor for the Royal Shakespeare Company.

Ms Greig is executive headteacher of King Ethelbert as well as Dane Court Grammar School: these have been federated schools for 10 years. Dane Court is a member of the Coastal Academies Trust, a small group of local primary and secondary schools working together to improve the educational chances of all children in Thanet.

Academic matters: The school converted entirely to the IB in 2012, 'because A levels have proved not fit for purpose, and IB students are more likely to gain a place at the best universities'. Students can choose between the more academically focused diploma or the careers certificate, which is a vocational version and offers courses such as applied business, sports science, and health and social care, alongside the core subjects.

It's an intense programme but school says: 'Busier students get better grades. They will only have two to three free study periods per week, but once they get into the rhythm of working at that pace they really enjoy it.'

Not all parents were happy about this change. One commented: 'It feels as though the sixth form has suddenly gone comprehensive, offering vocational courses as well and I feel our children are ill prepared for the IB through our style of education which is not European style. They have been narrowing their studies and heading towards specialisation since year 9.'

English, science and maths departments are strong, and sixth formers rate the history and politics departments. Parents say languages are an area of concern, and school agrees, calling that a 'fledgling' department. A recently appointed languages head and staff are charged with turning the department around. French, German, Spanish, Italian and Japanese are on offer. For years 7-11, there's a new skills and character-based curriculum, called ICE (Independent Cultural Enrichment).

Results 'reflect the community'. In the Thanet area, there are around 40 more grammar places than children reaching the required standard each year. Some pupils have not in fact passed the Kent test.

Given that context, the school delivers well – 2018 results show 41 per cent of GCSEs at A*-A/9-7. Sixth formers take their studies seriously – 'You're expected to work hard here', they say – and a couple make it to Oxbridge most years. In 2018, average IB point score of 34.

Games, options, the arts: Arts are a real strength, reflecting a community where many musicians and artists make their home. There is exceptional art on display, and photographs outside the theatre show professionally costumed and staged productions of Grease, Annie and Midsummer Night's Dream.

Broadstairs has a big reputation for folk music, hosting an annual festival and performances in its pubs every night. Lots of musicians among the parent body and lessons on a wide range of instruments available.

Overseas tours include a 10 day sixth form trip to teach in Namibia, a pastoral trip to Bonn for year 8s, skiing, and departmental trips to Valencia, Iceland, Ypres, Paris, and New York.

Sporting teams do the school proud – both girls' and boys' football teams regularly reach the Kent Cup final, girls are successful at rugby and the school table tennis team are national champions. Those who aren't selected to play for the school have an opportunity to compete in house sporting events and there are extracurricular sports such as rowing, rock climbing, orienteering and mountain biking.

D

Background and atmosphere: A £20 million rebuild and refurbishment completed has created a spacious and natural light-filled campus, which appears at once industrious and serene. The aim was to create inspirational buildings to make pupils feel valued and worthwhile – and in this case it works. The central atrium looks more like the offices of a prosperous technology company, and it's not hard to see how this motivates children more than the grimly oppressive Victorian architecture of many schools.

At break time we saw students milling around the big central space or queuing at the coffee bar, sitting in comfortable chairs chatting in groups, looking over their notes prior to exams. There's no regimentation, and they look more like university students.

There are six open plazas, each hosting a house base and a curriculum area base, with labs or classrooms leading off from a large central study space. The plazas are open at break for their house to eat lunch in, play games, or do homework.

The sixth form has a distinct area in each house plaza and in the central atrium, but there's been a deliberate decision to integrate them more with the rest of the school, and now they help with supervision. 'Everyone mingles more now,' agree the students.

Pastoral care, well-being and discipline: There's no uniform for the sixth form – depending on the day, a mixture of 'smart business wear', jeans and shorts can be in evidence. Younger pupils are in uniform, with a simple 'black, white and gold' theme: white shirts (sometimes hanging out) for all, tartan skirt (sometimes hitched up) for girls and black trousers for boys. Black and gold ties are optional for girls, and black blazers with a gold badge are worn by all. 'Our students are not always the neatest, but they're happier for it.'

Recently established house system is used to entrench a sense of community, and the first thing pupils see as they walk through the front doors is a screen displaying live house point totals. A house cup and book tokens are awarded to top performers.

Students who cross the line are dealt with by a restorative justice system. 'It's not a punitive approach, we urge people to do the right thing. We talk to them, and we listen to them'. Lots of the students have had training in peer mentoring. One student who transferred from another school found the atmosphere very different. 'Everyone here is a lot nicer, and there's a lot more respect,' she said.

Pastoral care is delivered through a mentoring system that is popular with both students and parents. 'I really like mentoring, it allows us to have time with our form tutor and if you have a problem you can go to them about it,' said one girl. A parent with two children at the school concurred. 'The pastoral care is excellent, they are supported really well,' she said. Another parent wished more detail was conveyed home, saying: 'I don't feel we get enough information. There were plans for a computer system, where parents would be able to see for example if their child had been late for a lesson, or got a house point, which looked like it was going to be good but it never got off the ground.' School says this system will be introduced. But one mother had found staff 'very accommodating' when she had needed to discuss anything.

Pupils and parents: The deprivation in the area and scarcity of jobs – 3,500 applied for 180 jobs at Primark – means that students see no future for themselves, and 'we have to do a lot of work on confidence building'. These social problems are compounded by London boroughs buying up cheap housing in the area for their overflow social housing tenants, and clusters of Eastern European immigrants settling in the area 'which causes some tension and resentment. We have to do a lot of work with students on equality and understanding'.

Mixed parent body, with some finding themselves in challenging circumstances, the vast majority supportive. A parent commented: 'I work in a junior school and I always recommend it to parents there'. Pupils agree that it's a pleasant environment. 'It's a nice community, everyone is happy and friendly,' said one.

Entrance: There are two grammars in Thanet – this is considered the better one and is oversubscribed. Students come from more than 30 feeder primaries.

School is currently over planned admission numbers in every year group, so joining mid-way depends on a place coming up. Pupils can join in the sixth form, and need six 6s and two 4s at GCSE to do the IB diploma, and three 6s and two 4s to do the IB Careers Certificate.

Exit: Around 25-45 per cent leave after GCSEs. Three-quarters of sixth form students go on to university – was 80 to 90 per cent but numbers have dropped since the increase in fees. In 2018, three to Cambridge, and others off to Madrid (dentistry), Bulgaria (medicine) and Utrecht. Some to Russell Group universities, over half to top 25, lots staying in Kent; courses range from sports psychology at Bournemouth to integrated engineering at Cardiff to international development at UEA. 'There's a lot of support to help them make university choices,' said a parent.

Remarks: This would be a great fit for the child who doesn't respond well to authoritarian, old school regimes. Everything about the school speaks of treating the pupils respectfully, on the assumption that they will behave maturely.

Children are not publicly bawled out for misdemeanours, instead they talk through their actions with their peers. Expensive equipment isn't locked away – why should it be, there's no assumption that the kids will damage it. And the physical space looks more like a university, which in turn creates the expectation that this is a place for serious learning.

Danes Hill School

Leatherhead Road, Oxshott, Surrey KT22 0JG

Ages 3–13 Pupils 860

Fees: £6,615 – £19,281 pa

01372 842509
www.daneshillschool.co.uk

Head: Since 2007, Willie Murdock (50s), BA PGCE from Queen's University, Belfast where studied Latin. Previously deputy head who stepped into the breach following sudden death of charismatic predecessor. CV short to extinction. Arrived at school as Latin teacher after qualifying in 1980s, loved it and simply never left. Though not one for introspection, career choice just might, he thinks, be down to desire to rework deficiencies in own education in N Ireland state system – rigour first class, teacher empathy rather less so.

Wife teaches here (one of several married couples at the school) and all three of offspring went through, again common practice. Would send out worrisome message about the school if shunned by own staff, he says. Decent discounts help, as does staff-only early morning crèche down at the pre-prep, a 10 minute drive away, but universal staff enthusiasm for school (and regret from teachers whose older children missed the boat) would disarm all but most hard-bitten of cynics. Though a stayer himself, supportive of wanderlust in others. Funds training and, if can't provide appropriate hike in responsibilities (though often can), gives blessing to search for more senior roles elsewhere, five or so deputy heads and heads amongst them.

Size may make this an empire worth having, but job is no sinecure. 'Think of him as being administrator rather than educator,' reckoned one parent. Something he's definitely good at and given school this size, way with spreadsheets an essential core competency. Ditto ability to engage talented staff – interviews will seek to weed out any 'two-dimensional characters' and will always ask how they fill leisure hours (he admits to love for shooting and fishing, assisted by German shepherd 'who thinks she's a labrador').

Though has a lighter side, takes some digging to uncover. While won't ever make heads' year book as most likely to 'roll his sleeves up and josh with the kids,' reckons one parent, he is 'jovial and approachable' – as well as running very popular camp for year 8 leavers in his own garden. Those who ski will see a fair amount of him. Also teaches Latin and 'definitely knows us,' reckoned older pupils, though they felt that form tutors would be place to go for problems (head of pastoral care runs regular surgeries for those with less run of the mill issues).

Relaxed about partial knowledge of parents. 'May not know every name but know a teacher who does,' he says. Deals effectively with battalions of challenging mums, described by one local as 'the Marbella mob' and by a current parent as 'the black Range Rover brigade' (certainly well represented in car park). Perhaps, theorised one mother, has made sensible decision to resist demands to set up PTA, so can 'bat parents away one at a time', rather than cope with a whole classroom of opinionated and occasionally disgruntled customers. No, he says firmly. 'PTAs can create conflicts of interest' – so trustees say 'no', though Friends of Danes Hill 'organise social and charitable events,' stresses school.

Unlikely to make drastic changes. With excellence the order of the day, results excellent and pupil numbers at capacity, why rock the boat?

Entrance: Highly popular; particularly oversubscribed in year 2. Anyone joining in nursery or reception will go straight through, year 1 and 2 hopefuls observed, taster sessions with literacy and numeracy tests for year 3 and above, though stressed that 'we are looking at the whole child.'

Billed as virtually non-selective and inclusivity is the name of the game, range of mild to moderate needs catered for in and out of class courtesy of well-staffed SEN team. A busy bunch with 90 children alone who have SpLD. School takes it seriously with SENCo part of senior leadership team, plenty of training to ensure good, school-wide understanding of SEN – a real strength. No-go area, predictably, behaviour so challenging that would disrupt learning of others.

Increasing numbers now coming through pre-prep (Bevendean). Has recently added new mornings-only class for children turning 3 in academic year but too young for kindergarten (follows pleading from parents keen to avoid multiple morning nursery drop offs) and ends at year 1, numerous visits to main school minimising worries about move to year 2.

Priority in all year groups given to returning families (fair few start, are posted abroad, and then move back again) and siblings. Feeders range from local primaries and preps to city centre establishments. No waiting list – easier to give straight yes or no decision, says registrar, who is now so attuned to London school stress that can identify family location by tones of desperation alone. Inroads into SW London reflected in extensive bus route services (everywhere from Leatherhead to Wimbledon, Weybridge and Richmond).

Trad families remain but now equalled by influx of new blood, much from City, plus other assorted sources of wealth (several well-known footballers are current parents, though 'don't big themselves up, you don't know they're there,' said relieved parent) while growing international component felt to add welcome richness and variety to school community.

Exit: You name it, they send someone there. Guildford High, Sevenoaks, RGS all feature together with local faves (Epsom College, St John's Leatherhead, St Teresa's). Plenty of scholarships to the latter two and one to Eton, part of 57 total in 2018 (results in glut of honours boards overflowing into dining hall, another couple in hall foyer, would make for entertaining I Spy game). Good on school, too, for praising hard work of scholarship candidates 'who did their best and came so close' (which would also include the children diplomatically referred to in prospectus as 'yet to find their talents...')

Once rather reluctant to prepare pupils for year 6 exams – inevitable given siren call of 11 plus – school now phlegmatic about manning up to slight loss. Stresses (quite hard) that 'we do not have a big drop-off' with around 90 out of the possible 100 year 8 seats filled and that runs 'established programme that produces a great success rate [in year 6]'.

Remarks: Not a school that hides its light under a bushel. 'Practically perfect in every way' screams banner outside (well, almost – we paraphrase), greeting motorists on the main Oxshott to Leatherhead drag. Given the early morning queues caused, according to one local, entirely by fleets of parents blocking the only through road, they'll certainly have time to digest every syllable.

What school is trumpeting (could do so literally, what with 300 plus pupils learning instruments and the 13 ensembles available for them to showcase talents, from chunky orchestra to assorted string, wind and brass groups) is recent all-outstanding inspection. Given just how much of the school there is, pride understandable.

While site, at 55 acres, may not be the biggest in the area (though lavish by London escapee standards), it's pupil numbers – larger for a fair few than the senior schools many will eventually go on that cause jaw to drop. 'Dread it when it's first question parents ask,' says registrar.

Even inspection team was giant-sized – needed to be, what with viewing 100 lessons in two days. Biggest prep in the country, thinks school. Would have been bigger still had previous head realised dream of ramping up to 1,000 pupils and extending leaving age to 16. No longer. School size just right, thanks, says head, ditto leaving age – school not temperamentally equipped to handle fallout from any heavy duty teenage angst. Why so big? Undoubtedly makes good financial sense – economies of scale are 'awesome' but main benefit is creation of 'a senior school for little people,' says senior teacher.

Some may balk at notion of teenies mustered into maturity beyond their years but, with exception of very early GCSEs taken by year 8 scholars for fun – not our idea of jollity but takes all sorts – it's not about hothousing but giving primary

D

aged children access to range of opportunities and subjects that come with giant-sized staff roster. Means more esoteric languages can be taught, vast range of school trips organised, recently including visits to Liverpool to watch tide washing over Gormley figures, all courtesy of staff pool, deep and talented enough to resource the lot.

Pupil largesse does come with inevitable logistical problems. 'You'll ask one child if he knows another and because he's in a different class, he'll never have heard of them,' says local. 'Can be hard to find your friends at break,' agreed pupil. And while we loved the school mag (who wouldn't, given lookie-likey resemblance to iPad, all gloss and cleverness?), with under a handful of entries from each year group (three for year 4, for example – four if you count pictures as well) we couldn't help wondering if there were times when opting for quantity over quality would improve otherwise microscopic chances of being one of the favoured few to be featured.

Newer parents are more accepting of the scale. Some, with several children and longer term experiences that span rise and rise of pupil numbers, are less sure. 'They can feel it's not the school they signed up to,' said one. Biggest question mark was how well school managed the invisible middles. 'Can go unnoticed,' thought parents. Difficult for any school, accepts Mr Murdock, well behaved average pupils with talent for inconspicuous survival all too easily camouflaged when flanked to one side by the troublesome, to the other by the super able.

But however thick the bushel and deeply buried the light, school adamant that will be discovered, even if it takes years. There's even special group, Big Foot Club, that acts like living pending file, where simmering potential gets extra encouragement to come to the boil – one pupil went from hating sport to captain of rowing.

Other secret weapons include delightful librarian. 'Knew she was right for the job as soon as walked into the room,' says head. No wonder. 'Job means I have fun all day,' she says and clearly means it, running parent and child reading-and-hot-chocolate sessions (sports-mad dads and sons make up sizeable chunk of regulars) relegating useful reference books to lower shelves and making fiction the star of the show, array of colourful spines as appetising as they come.

Very littlest also well catered for in pre-prep, popularity enhanced by jolly staff, imaginative outdoor learning with wonderful dipping pond (part of main school grounds) and thoughtfully expanded site featuring swimming pool, jigsaw-shaped mural, seasonal chickens (one recently – and usefully – completing circle of life by going from egg to extinction) and cheerful long, low building, each window adorned with different coloured shutters.

For the keen, able or talented anywhere in school, finding niche unlikely to be a problem. 'If you have a child who is very good at something, they will fly,' said mother. For one, joining from tiny school, 'It was like he'd always been there,' agreed another. Cracking organisation is glue that holds the fabric together, courtesy of terrific, friendly backroom team, say parents, with admin staff who 'do a fabulous job,' said one. 'Because it's so well managed, you just don't feel it is such an enormous school,' felt another.

Effective split into lower, middle and upper schools, who eat, play and leave together, means that though it is huge, 'they manage the size extremely well,' said mother. So small are many of the classes, the result of setting (starts year 2 with English and maths, more subjects added each year) or splitting (half will take DT, half drama, for example) that it's a rare class with more than 10 or so pupils (official class averages are between 16 and 20, maximum 22, with overall teacher to pupil ratio of one to eight). Teaching praised for overall quality across the board, small amount of slightly dull lessons compensated for by the many that aren't.

Level of light-touch but effective behind the scenes management reinforced by relaxed-looking pupils with impressive manners and well-controlled volume (enjoyable impromptu version of 'Let it go' from Frozen in the distance was as loud as it got).

Site structure also helps, varying gradients working in school's favour as without resorting to aerial view, it's just about impossible to see the entire place in one go. Only time you get sense of scale is at lunchtime, as one third of pupils, swapping places with the next, tumble out of dining hall to enjoy masses of well-supervised activities outside, from zip wire and small climbing frame, rota ensuring fair use by all, to ball games and den building in woodland or, in case of two small girls, madly rushing round in circles on the path.

Strong house system (points accrued for academic and sporting success, flag of current leader displayed in school hall) and masses of loyalty-building competitions also do wonders for sense of togetherness, enhanced by involvement through school council which petitions for changes. Some, such as marine biology club and more water fountains by sports pitches 'where we really get thirsty,' points out year 8 pupil, successful. Others, notably own common room for year 8 pupils, mentioned by at least 10 of the children (appeal of own area in the woodlands understandably sags in winter months) are pending, though Mr Murdock seemed to be giving off buying signals.

In general, however, facilities are so good that parents touring future senior schools prone to regular 'is that all there is' moments. Upgrading required here and there, notably sports hall (adequate but lacking in appropriate bells and whistles) and indoor swimming pool (current version achieves all-weather status by virtue of marquee topping during winter months. 'So English,' says member of staff.)

School stresses opportunities – no mountain too high, no valley too deep, expanding exponentially in line with numbers. Thus curriculum can be broader, specialist staff more numerous, speech, music, art and drama more ambitious in scope. Summer concert is 'highlight of the year,' reckoned mum, with 'energy rolling off the children as they perform,' while even the kinetically challenged have gentler option of tea time concerts, beginner performers welcomed with enthusiasm.

No doubt that list of can-dos is impressive, sport taken very seriously with pitches to make spectators pinch themselves – 'feeling of space when you're watching a match is unbelievable' – nearing 20 different sports, games grouped by ability A-F squads from year 2 (those losing their places in teams 'will have reasons explained to them,' says literature) parents similarly invited to keep comments about the ref to themselves – children ditto, and should be thanked after the match, urges literature. Extra tuition on offer for the keen, while, from year 6, pupils can ditch ball games altogether for something completely different, such as rowing.

Staff roster even runs to full time head of swimming. Individual sporting successes impressive. Same names tend to crop up across the sporting range 'to the point where it's tedious,' thought one parent – three of four names cited for tennis brilliance all belonged to the same boy, for example. 'Maybe games staff are under the cosh for timing but sometimes would be good if looked beyond the obvious,' thought parent.

Large (predictably) amounts of team triumph (boys score with county football, girls currently ahead on national honours in IAPS hockey, netball and skiing, both sharing honours for indoor rowing).

All adds up to pupils who, says school, 'often lead the way'. Less charitable might think that on probability alone, given numbers, so you'd hope. Children themselves, however, many who had ended up here following bad experiences at smaller but palpably less nurturing schools, were clearly having a whale of a time. 'You don't need to be any sort of character to succeed here,' said one year 8 pupil. 'They'll help you find your strengths. You can just be yourself.'

You might not have to top the ebullience charts to be happy here, but an excess of confidence certainly isn't going to hold you back. Inspectors noted school's aim of turning out 'well-rounded and self-assured individuals who enjoy succeeding.' Locals can be a bit (but not much) blunter. 'Occasional whiff of arrogance,' reckoned one.

Those braving it are buying into largesse of opportunity doled out to bouillabaisse-like mix of abilities. Few subjects come without some added buzz, from geography department's new weather station to DT's 'outdoor kitchen' – in everyday parlance, a garden – where grow things and then cook them.

You go in expecting to be confronted by pupil-rearing on an industrial scale and leave with senses nicely stimulated rather than overwhelmed. Though a big, bouncy, confident school that won't appeal to everyone, worth leaving preconceptions at the gate (along with the traffic jam). Despite yourself, you're likely to end up being charmed.

Dolphin School

Waltham Road, Hurst, Reading, Berkshire RG10 0FR

Ages 3–13 **Pupils** 209

Fees: £10,170 – £14,070 pa

01189 341277
www.dolphinschool.com

Head: Since September 2018, Adam Hurst, previously housemaster and English teacher at Dauntsey's. BA from Reading; married to Jo, head of English.

Entrance: The vision of the founder, who started this alternative (then Montessori) school in 1970 from the gardener's shed in the grounds of her house (which remains adjacent to the school and where she still lives), was for Dolphin to cater for the more academically able. And while the school is still well suited to brighter children (and the Montessori approach still shapes nursery and reception learning), the pupil demographic has changed, with Dolphin now welcoming a wider mix of ability. Non-selective for entry into nursery and reception; pupils entering from age 5 upwards are assessed during a day of tests, including maths and English. Traditionally, parents have been largely academics, visiting Europeans and artists who are attracted to the school's free-thinking ethos, but equally expect their children to gain places, if not awards, at top independent and grammar schools. Today, though, they're just as likely to work for IT companies in the Thames corridor.

Exit: Roughly a quarter of pupils leave at 11 for local state and independent schools, the rest stay on until 13 for common entrance. The vast majority, according to the school, gain places at their first choice schools, which include Abingdon, Queen Anne's, Wellington College, Reading Grammar, The Abbey, Gillotts, Leighton Park, Sir William Borlase, Reading Blue Coat, Pangbourne College, Headington, Holyport, Luckley House, Shiplake College, Rugby and The Piggott Academy. 'There's no snobbery here about secondary school choices,' reported one parent, who was opting for one of the many good local state schools. 'Our options have been treated with the same respect and dignity as any fancier private school.'

Remarks: You don't have to spend more than about 10 minutes in this school to realise it's unique, yet defining exactly what its magic ingredient is remains a challenge even the head teacher can't rise to.

The first thing you'll notice is the lack of uniform, with staff also casually dressed and most addressed by their first names – both approaches that provide a taster into the broad-mindedness and rejection of rigid educational ideology that mark this school out. 'We take the view that at the centre of our job is providing an environment that feels comfortable because if children are comfortable, they're much more likely to be engaged and confident.'

And engaged and confident these youngsters certainly are – no doubt helped by the fact that throughout the school is a total immersion approach to learning, the polar opposite of spoon-feeding pre-chewed lumps of facts that can characterise the national curriculum at its worst. In every lesson (all taught by subject specialists in dedicated classrooms from year 3), pupils are encouraged to take the scenic route down their own 'avenues of thought', with learning regularly going well beyond the usual boundaries. It's the children who take the lead here, asking questions and discussing their ideas in a forum that gives them space to really be themselves.

Besides the usual range of subjects, there's French from nursery and classics from year 3, which becomes Latin from year 4. Spanish and Greek are available from year 7, with other extra subjects including architecture, astronomy and – most recently – earth studies.

Although this is not a hugely techy school (staff are more interested in getting children outside in muddy fields than getting them to tap away on iPads in classrooms), there's a good IT suite and – joy of joys – touch-typing is taught from year 3. Maths is a stand-out subject and juniors and seniors regularly arrive home counting awards won in the UK Maths Challenge. Reading is another big focus, with 15-25 minutes a day dedicated to heads in books for children and staff alike. Homework is set weekly, with pupils expected to do four to six hours of homework per week by year 8. Exams are held off until the end of year 5.

Drama is big, with pupils often gaining drama scholarships to their senior schools. Almost every year group is involved in some kind of annual performance, and there's great excitement among pupils about the annual production put on by years 7 and 8 at the Edinburgh Fringe Festival. Many of the plays are written by the drama teacher and they're often thought-provoking, with one recent example being These Fragments, a poignant production about refugees. Around 10 peripatetic staff teach the usual range of musical instruments and there's a school choir, ukulele band and various ensembles, with children regularly performing during assemblies, house music competitions and a concert in summer.

Then there's the school trips, of which there are at least three a term from nursery upwards. Forming the very cornerstone to the school's unwavering approach to experiential learning, the pinnacle is the year 8 Alps trip – an eight-day hike, which involves pupils warming up several years beforehand. Field trips are also common – building up from a three-day trip to Sussex in year 3 to a nine-day trip to Italy in year 8. All trips except foreign ones (where parents pay about half) are included in the fees, with the occasional contribution to food requested on top.

In terms of SEN, the school is relatively inclusive, taking on the usual range of dys spectrums, plus mild ADD, ADHD and ASD, although it's honest about what it can't cope with and does turn children away if it feels they won't keep up. Pupils and parents praise the diagnostic abilities of the SENCo, as well as the one-to-one support provided in break-out classrooms, which is used to supplement what goes on in the classroom.

Sport is more about cooperation than competition. That said – and despite Dolphin's numbers – it competes successfully against some much larger schools, and some children achieve regional and national representation. Boys mainly play football, rugby and cricket, whilst girls focus on netball, hockey and rounders, using the two on-site tennis courts and three grass pitches, as well as the school hall and Hurst Cricket Ground, a two-minute mini-bus ride away. Tennis is a strength too. Twenty after-school clubs supplement the timetabled sport along with the gentler exertions of yoga, ballet and dance.

Don't expect wonders when it comes to facilities, which – with the exception of a shiny new science lab – are pretty average, with some on the shabby side. Parents are also unflashy, with only a sprinkling of the big black 4x4s that you get at many local preps – many work their socks off to get their children an education here. For those who want to be involved with school life, there's no shortage of opportunity to volunteer on the school trips, even driving the minibus, as well as getting stuck into fundraising via events such as curry nights and the annual summer fair.

Pastoral care is highly praised by pupils and parents alike, with the school appearing to achieve that tricky balance of being nurturing, yet also encouraging maturity and independence. In addition to the form teacher, who is seen as the primary conduit for pastoral care, pupils in year 6 upwards have a mentor – someone who, ideally, isn't their form teacher and who doesn't teach them at all, whom they meet every other week informally over lunch. It also helps that the school is small – with two classes per year, with an average of 12 children in each (although one class had 19 when we visited). This, together with a buddy system, leads to cross-year friendships, as well as helping to prevent bullying. There are clear warning systems for poor behaviour – of which the worst tends to be around missing homework, being rude or unkind and not putting in enough work – which culminate in breaktime detentions.

No wonder the pupils we talked to – all of whom were eloquent, chatty, sharp and witty – were familiar both with the word 'kinaesthetic' and its meaning. Also no wonder that so many parents are evangelical about this school, with many moving to the area solely to get the kids in.

All schools say that they treat every child as an individual but this school actually does it, producing cheerful, humane, confident, mature and thoughtful children with a life-long love of learning ahead of them. As one parent put it, 'They bring education alive.' 'If schools got stars for children's engagement and happiness,' said another, 'they'd be off the scale.'

Dorset House School

88

The Manor, Bury, Pulborough, West Sussex RH20 1PB

Ages 4–13 **Pupils** 144 **Boarders** 49 weekly/flexi (from 9 years)

Fees: Day £8,982– £17,850 pa; Boarding £105 per week (4 nights)

01798 831456
www.dorsethouseschool.com

Headmaster: Since 2017, Matt Thomas, formerly deputy head of Moulsford, and previously taught in two challenging comprehensives 'where you need a huge box of skills'. Degree in PE, geography and education studies from St Luke's Exeter. Married to Julie, with two children. The head was attracted to the school by the mud – 'it's outdoorsy – how schools should be'.

The head's most important quality for pupils to gain at DH is confidence. He's by the gate every morning to greet the children – just as important is for them to return his greeting, and make eye contact; pupils are expected to shake hands firmly each Friday before they receive their tuck voucher. The emphasis on manners and respect is matched by a warm friendliness between pupils and head, pupils saying: 'the head will sit next to you and ask what you're doing'; 'gets involved in everything we do...' ; 'he always helps'. The head teaches RS to years 7 and 8, which he loves – 'the highlight of my day'.

This open-door policy also applies to and pleases parents, who describe him as 'warm and friendly'; 'in the fabric of the place'.

Entrance: Non-selective, entrance on the basis of a taster day and school reports. In-house nursery is not part of the school but supplies around half of reception entrants.

Exit: Sends pupils to a wide range of senior schools, in particular Brighton College, Hurst, Lancing, Ardingly, Seaford and Marlborough.

For 2018, Hurst most popular, then Brighton and Wellington; six scholarships taken up.

Remarks: Dorset House seduces at first sight. Set on the banks of the Arun with views over the Downs, its ancient buildings (a 12th century manor house at its core) are surrounded by lawns, walled garden, woods and an amphitheatre. A parent said, 'You walk through the grounds and feel that idyllic childhood memories could be created. It took my breath away a bit...'

Beyond the stunning grounds, what immediately strikes a visitor is children having fun – when we arrived a group of girls were giggling, elbows digging into a tub of fruit – 'trying to get their snack without their hands', explained the head. It's a school where you hear laughter and see children playing as well as learning – as a parent said, the attraction is in the 'joy that the school creates'.

In this small family school, there's lots of mixing across year groups – it's not unusual to see a year 8 holding hands with a 6-year-old. One parent said her son loves its size because he's a worrier- '[he] feels safe and contained'.

Many are attracted to the sense of children having a traditional upbringing – 'they're allowed to be children for a lot longer', said a parent, another saying, '[my son] has rosy red cheeks and muddy kit every day...nonstop chatter and always saying how good lunch was...so bubbly and enthusiastic...'

This school listens and cares, but the head is keen to equip pupils to cope rather than resolve all their difficulties for them; one parent described how her daughter was given 'coping strategies' to help with a problem with peers, and how much this helped – 'she understood what was going on and how to deal with it'.

Pupils said they would talk to a teacher or gap students if they had a problem, and pupils can request a session with the independent listener, described by a pupil as 'a comfortable and supportive experience'.

Punishments here are proportionate and rare. You get the feeling that they're not often necessary. When Ds (detentions) happen, they generally doing something useful – cleaning up a classroom or picking up litter. Or so pupils have heard.

It's small, relative to some of the preps in the area – 'not for those for whom huge grounds and the best facilities are essential', said a parent, but the head is keen to make both pupils and school the best they can be. A 'boutique class act', said a parent firmly. It really is.

Sports lessons follow the usual gender divide, but girls have played on the cricket team – 'it's a very flexible school, no hard and fast rules', said a parent.

A small school means fewer teams, and one parent suggested it wasn't the school for someone who 'wants to be always on the winning team'. But, parents and pupils insist, there is an upside to being small: everyone has to take part so everyone has a chance; a mixed ability team brings out the best qualities in all players; and those who excel can be a big fish in a small pond – or play for the team in the year above for more of a challenge.

A parent who described his daughter as a 'lazy socialiser' said this has gradually changed in the world of Dorset House. She did one-night boarding, and is now asking to do more, and wouldn't say this unless she was really happy – 'she loves to sleep'.

Praise for boarding was common to all the parents we spoke to, in particular, the warmth and care of the houseparents. Boarding is available Monday to Thursday, and there is competition for places, which are allocated in as fair a way as possible. Large dormitories (six to eight) nestled under the eaves, each bed with a reading lamp. 'Buns' before bed (not actual buns anymore, but toast, fruit and cereal). An attractive common room with packed bookshelves, a pool table overlooking the Downs, and a piano and squashy sofas, with a pile of soft blankets to snuggle under to watch a film. '[They] love being with friends...never in a hurry to come home', said a parent.

Homework is contained at Dorset House: half an hour to an hour, completed at school. Only in year 8 does it overflow the school slot, with French and Latin vocab to be learnt at home, and essays to write over the weekend. Some of the usual worry about CE, but pupils are well supported by teachers and the independent listener – 'not a hothouse', says the head firmly.

Science and English were repeatedly mentioned by parents and pupils as exceptionally well taught, the science teacher described by one as 'barmy – in brilliant exciting way', and indeed we have seldom met a more enthusiastic teacher, describing humans as 'scientists from the moment we're born...', and keen to describe the delights of blowing up jelly babies in the fume cupboard (to show how cells use energy).

There's a large selection of books in the English classroom and the boarders' common room, but no library as such; neither pupils or parents feel this is of concern; 'the kids read relentlessly', said a parent.

Class sizes have increased a bit, now up to 22 in the upper part of the school, but this has meant TA support has increased, so the child-teacher ratio has improved.

Learning development (LD) in the pre-prep involves lots of movement – a pupil was happily engaged on a wobble board during our visit. The LD teacher brings her old camper van to school in the summer, and pupils love popping to the van for lessons. A more formal approach in prep, but a gentle switch when pupils are ready during years 4 or 5.

Pupils can have up to two sessions of support outside class, and support in class too. Assistance is flexible, pupils can have just half a term of support if that's all that's needed. In-class support is included in the fees, one-to-one is charged as an extra. Parents say the support is good, and like the fact sessions are integrated into what's going on in class and the curriculum – 'a very holistic approach'.

The head gives year 6 and 7s test interviews for senior school, each pupil having to make their appointment to see him – 'it's all about soft skills and taking responsibility', says the head. One parent said her son was set up well for his large senior school – 'learnt great values, how to speak to people and be confident, to look out for others – it's been a smooth transition'.

Music is a particular strength, described by a parent as 'amazing'. The music director follows the Kodaly approach from Hungary, and enthuses about children's inherent musical ability 'which they all have in their DNA'. Drama has less focus, felt one parent, but there is LAMDA, drama clubs and various school productions.

The most recent ISI Report awarded the school an 'excellent' for the quality of pupils' academic and other achievements and `excellent' for the quality of pupils' personal development.

The pre-prep building is separate but proximate to the prep, and filled with light, colour and joy. The head (Sarah Hobrow) is a dab hand at making up songs for learning, the hokey-cokey now the maths doubling song, pupils in both schools often eager to set her another challenge.

During our visit, half of reception were squeaky clean and making buns, the other half were outside, happily filthy, in head to toe wet weather gear, making a dinosaur family comfortable in sand and mud. It is difficult to imagine happier 4-year olds.

Children learn through topics, the year 3 classroom transformed into a chocolate factory, huge sweets hanging from the ceiling, children relishing learning about chocolate with Willy Wonka, the Aztecs, and chocolate fudge, then running a chocolate museum to teach their parents all about it.

D

Dover College

Effingham Crescent, Dover, Kent CT17 9RH

Ages 3–18 **Pupils** 302 **Sixth form** 71 **Boarders** 99 full, 4 weekly, some flexi (from 11 years) **C of E**

Fees: Day £7,725 – £16,050; Boarding £21,000 – £31,500 pa

01304 205969
www.dovercollege.org.uk

Headmaster: Since 2015, Gareth Doodes MA. Educated at Eastbourne College, where he boarded in sixth form, then St Andrew's (history) and Cambridge (PGCE). Taught history at Taunton School, followed by a stint as housemaster at Oakham. Joined Milton Abbey School as deputy head, but after six months (and aged only 32) was offered the top job, a role he filled for five years. Then briefly principal at George Heriot's School in Edinburgh, but realised he preferred to be back in Blighty and accepted the headship at Dover College, whose governors fell on his neck with cries of joy after what had been a challenging few years. Married to Jess, who works in the school's marketing department. They have a young son and daughter, both at the school.

First job was to move head's study from its former remote location at the top of a boarding house to a lovely light ground floor room at the heart of the school where he is much more visible and in touch. 'Whenever you walk past his office he waves!' say students affectionately. A fabulously energetic man, however, who is just as likely to be out and about teaching the year 6s, taking A level history ('it's so important to get into the classrooms'), leading assembly and fully involving himself in school life. 'Constructive and friendly' was an opinion echoed by everyone we spoke to, and parents enthusiastically praised his vision for the school and the staff appointments made to date.

A former choral scholar and still a keen musician, playing organ, piano and violin. Other interests include cycling and running and is a self-confessed 'current affairs and politics junkie'.

D

Academic matters: That most refreshing of things in this county, a non-selective school and pleased to be so. The school slogan is 'think differently', and from juniors up to GCSEs, teaching is delivered via themes eg 'coffee, tea and chocolate'; 'war and peace' or 'two thousand years ago'. What children learn across the subjects is therefore inter-connected, and they're encouraged to debate and discuss. It's an approach similar to the IB, and it's no surprise to learn that the school will introduce an IB-inspired curriculum across the school in September 2019. To be clear, the IB itself won't be offered: the school doesn't want to stop teaching A levels and its small size puts offering both beyond its reach. Instead, sixth form students will choose an academic or a vocational pathway alongside a 'thinking differently' course, a 'leadership and skills' course and the EPQ. 'We liked the IB, and wanted to take the best parts of it whilst not disenfranchising the UK market,' says head, 'We feel our bespoke curriculum gives the best of all worlds.'

School insists that they have the full ability spread, including the very able, although their exam results reflect the diverse intake: 38 per cent A*/B and 24 per cent A*/A grades at A level; 22 per cent A*-A/9-7 at GCSE in 2018. High praise everywhere for the value-added: students who came to Dover College because they'd failed the Kent Test often leave with better A level grades than their friends who passed it. We spoke to one such sixth former in receipt of offers from two excellent universities, who confirmed, 'the academic support I've had from all the staff here has been absolutely fantastic.' Extra lessons routinely offered in the evenings, at weekends and even in the holidays for students who need them.

One small class per year in the junior school, rising to two per year in the senior school – usually between 10 and 15 students per class. Setting from year 9 in science, maths and English. Languages taught are French, Spanish, Mandarin – a slightly narrow provision in a school that's so proud of its international connections, particularly the number of German students who come here. Latin was recently introduced for pupils in years 7 and 8. Very good range of subjects on offer at both GCSE and sixth form, commendable in such a small school.

The lessons we saw in both junior and senior schools were lively, enjoyable and expertly taught. The head of science shares her teaching space with fish and guinea pigs – 'I like to have live animals in a lab, it reminds us of what we're here for' – presided over by a cheerful, white-coated skeleton sporting goggles. We liked the French class where the teacher had put photos of her own family up on the board and invited students to identify 'ma soeur' 'mon pere' etc – so eager were the children to put their hand on the correct photos that they kept knocking them off the board. Being able to see France from the classroom windows is especially motivating, perhaps? Junior school history class was immaculately behaved but full of vim and vigour, a pleasure to watch. At the time of our visit, not the most glittering dynamic intellectually – triple science GCSE was only introduced comparatively recently, suggesting that the school's expectations of its students may once have been too low – but the staff are now working tirelessly to raise the game in this area and the pupils everywhere struck us as confident and keen to participate. Pleasant learning resources area, but the library was disappointing – small, not many chairs (suggesting few linger here), rather bare and drab; lacking a dedicated librarian, and we thought it showed.

Parents raved about the learning support, which here is called individual needs. 'Sending our children here was the best thing we ever did,' 'The help we get for our son and his dyslexia has just been above and beyond.' School keen to stress, however, that it isn't geared up for more than a mild level of need. Study skills – organisation, prioritising tasks, time management – are taught to all students as part of the curriculum.

Games, options, the arts: Drama facilities currently rather moth-eaten, but the school's 150th aniversary is approaching and celebrations include an entirely revamped creative arts centre, to be run by the school's director of performing arts, a recent appointment intended to expand the provision in that area. 'The key thing in a school is creativity,' says head, himself a devotee of all things artistic, 'and I want to re-establish creativity at the heart of the curriculum.' Regular productions – we looked in on an animated rehearsal of Scrooge, where the children were clearly having a whale of a time – and school is happy to send students interested in lighting and sound on technical enrichment programmes at eg the Gulkenkian Theatre in Canterbury. The Minerva Club offers an excellent programme of theatre trips; around eight per year.

The chapel is at the heart of the school's music-making, and choir is especially strong – we thought the standard of part-singing really fine. Other events include concerts, recitals and competitions. Art is lively and popular, and the art block is a hub of focused creative calm, with photography, fine art and textiles all offered at A level. 'My son has really been brought out of himself by the art and the music here,' commented a mother.

Very strong emphasis on charity and community work, with all students taking this very seriously – recent appeal for shoeboxes filled with presents was so successful that when the Christmas Child charity reps turned up to collect same they couldn't get them all in the van. DofE has had variable take-up in the past, but is now reinvigorated and growing in popularity. School is also in the process of joining Round Square, a network of schools worldwide that all sign up to founder Kurt Hahn's six ideals: internationalism, democracy, environment, adventure, leadership and service. For the pupils, this will bring increased opportunities for overseas exchange and community projects.

Under new leadership, sport here is impressively varied and the approach is entirely inclusive: recently every single pupil in years 7 and 8 played in at least eight fixtures for the school, making this an excellent place for children who want to get involved. 'We're fostering that participation culture,' said the sports director with relish, a man who leads the 6am sessions in the fitness suite, 'We celebrate excellence and we've got some great individuals who are exceptional, but the guy who plays for the U13B team is equally important to me.' Rugby, cricket, athletics, cross-country, hockey, netball, tennis, basketball and rounders are all on offer, plus swimming, squash, sailing and horse-riding. Football is flourishing: the boys recently did a football tour to Germany, and the girls countered with one to Holland. The school's Eton fives courts have been refurbished and put to work, and the Astroturf laid across the Priory's old burial site is in constant use. The monks slumbering below would surely approve – laborare est orare and why shouldn't the same be true of playing soccer?

Boarding: Available from year 7 upwards. Around a third of the students here board, and about two-thirds of the boarding community are from overseas and board full-time (the UK boarders tend to go home at weekends). The school works to keep a good balance of nationalities – it's popular with European students because of its location – but doesn't have quotas. The price of flexi-boarding has been slashed, and the result is a much higher take-up: recently, for instance, a number of day pupils opted to stay over at the school after returning late from an evening theatre trip to London. How sensible is that?

Boarding houses are, according to the students, 'really family orientated'. Students share in threes until they reach year 11 when it drops to two, and only upper sixth formers are guaranteed a room to themselves. Accommodation is homely, bordering on shabby – utilitarian furniture and a washbasin is the norm here rather than fitted wardrobes and ensuites – but is warm and comfortable and characterful: lots of light, views of Dover Castle, potted geraniums at the entrances, cheerful common rooms equipped with games and coffee machines, and clothes lines strung across the laundry room ceilings in the basement – 'Every single child here gets their shirts ironed!' beamed the matron. It struck us as more genuinely cosy and welcoming than some schools we've visited, whose boarding houses may have been smart but had all the ambience of a motel. The boys have an excellent kitchen for their own use, and the girls are getting something as good very soon. Prefects get first pick of bedrooms in exchange for responsibilities: organising rotas, tidying the common room, supervising the younger ones, etc.

Unusually, no official exeats, although students can go home if they wish. Every weekend here is staffed, and, according to students, choc-a-bloc with things to do. Saturday programme of trips – cultural, sporting, shopping – plus fun activities such as Quasar. Older students can opt instead to do supervised study. Sundays are relaxed and the emphasis is on winding down. Staff universally praised for their kindness and hard work – 'they're always there for you,' said a year 8 boy.

Background and atmosphere: Built on the site of the 12th century Benedictine St Martin's Priory, Dover College was founded in 1871 by a group of local businessmen who wanted the town to have its own public school. In 1958 the then-headmaster Alec Peterson opened an international faculty in the sixth form before going on to help create the IB. The school has maintained proud and strong international links ever since. Originally for boys, it became fully co-educational in 1974, opened the junior department in 2001 and its own nursery in 2009.

Many buildings have been patched on down the years, but there's still a wonderful sense of history everywhere. We passed the remains of the original priory on our way to the junior school – two Victorian houses knocked together – and were given coffee in the barrel-ceilinged dining hall, which happens to be the oldest working school refectory in the UK. At the heart of the school is the chapel, which is simply lovely, with white crumbly walls that put us in mind of Caerphilly cheese, and timbered beams – a kindly, mellow, peaceful place. 'We're proudly Christian. It's our absolute moral compass here in the college,' affirmed the head, and who wouldn't feel the same in such a place? The school welcomes children of all faiths and of none, but everyone must attend chapel twice a week. For the seniors, this is formal worship, but for juniors, it's more like an assembly – we watched certificates and house stars being given out for reading, progress, courage, enthusiasm, etc, to children who were chatty, articulate and beautifully well-mannered. Evensong is held every Friday – parents are welcome to attend, and can also come along to assemblies: we spotted several rows of them at the back of the chapel smiling proudly at their offspring, before they headed off to the refectory to chat over tea and buns laid on by the school.

There are currently around 300 students on the roll for the entire school ie from reception to year 13. The aim is to increase this to 350 by 2020, but the school is keen to keep the sense of personalised education that is its USP, and class sizes will stay at a maximum of 15. Lots of integration between juniors and seniors – it really is one school. At mealtimes children sit in houses rather than year groups, to encourage a family atmosphere. A member of staff eats with them at the head of each table, and judges competitions such as 'who can eat the most vegetables'. It seemed a very happy ship to us. All the staff we spoke to expressed great satisfaction at working here, and a number also opt to send their children here. Great sense of loyalty to the school amongst Old Dovorians, many of whom play an active role in fundraising and development. 'We love the family feeling here,' said one mother. 'It's like a prep school that goes all the way up to 18.'

Pastoral care, well-being and discipline: In many ways, the teacher we spoke to summed up the appeal of this likeable school as we strolled across the beautiful old college green, dotted with junior pupils having a kickabout: 'In three years, I've never had to raise my voice. The children are fantastic, and there are are no discipline issues, so you can get on and teach. It's a wonderful place to work.' Parents agree. 'There's a very high standard of nurturing and care'; 'It's a real family atmosphere'; 'The communications are excellent'; 'Since coming here, the improvement in my children's confidence has been amazing'.

House staff are proactive in mending any broken friendships, and well-being is taken seriously. PSHE is taught throughout the school and carries a high profile. 'It doesn't have a chance to fall out of favour here,' according to deputy head. Pupils feel happy, safe and free to thrive. 'I haven't experienced any bullying here – the culture is not fostering of it,' asserted a sixth former. 'Compared to my old school, the bullying is none, non-existent,' said a younger student firmly.

The food used to be a source of unhappiness, but school has listened, created a student food council and appointed new chefs. Results are now 'massively improved' according to students, and we thought it excellent, one of the best school lunches we've had. Arriving on a Friday, we were offered a choice of four hot main courses: traditional fish and chips that wouldn't have disgraced an East End chippy, some thoroughly appetising smoked haddock and potatoes, rather excellent local sausages, and an inviting chicken curry. Unusually on a school visit, we really were hard-pressed to decide what to have. A visiting speaker who came to give a talk on the tea business liked the school so much that he offered to mix a blend especially for them, taking into account the particular chalkiness of the area's water. We can report that Dover College tea makes a most refreshing cuppa, inducing a mood of tranquillity and reflection.

Clear rewards and sanctions policy, but amongst both children and staff the overall feel here is a peaceable one. 'Every pupil here will have an opportunity to lead because of the school's size, but they also need to learn how to follow,' was a remark of the head's that impressed us. Students here combine both roles with warmth and composure.

Pupils and parents: Day pupils drawn mostly from a 20 mile radius – Canterbury, Ashford, etc, ferried hither and yon by network of school minibuses. Predominantly Caucasian demographic of these reflects the area, but strong international intake ensures diversity and balance.

Many parents here are first-time buyers of private education, and show enormous support for and commitment to the school, actively involved in fundraising and helping out. 'We're just lucky to have our daughter here, and we'll help with whatever we can,' was a typical comment.

Entrance: Non-selective academically, and with every intention of remaining so – 'It's one of our great strengths.' Instead, the school looks for potential, and a willingness to fit into the school environment and contribute to its ethos: 'Pray together, stay together, eat together.' In the older children skills and aptitudes are always of interest – arts, sports, etc.

Happy to admit into most year groups and at any point in the academic year. Largest intake is into year 12, when a lot of international boarders join them, plus a 'surprising' number of local day pupils, often those whose grammar schools have rejected them for sixth form. Very small numbers in the infant year groups, but increasing thereafter as parents get stressed about the upcoming Kent Tests.

Exit: A few head off to grammar school after year 6 having passed the 11+, and a similar exodus after year 11. 'Our parents are not rich,' reflected the head. At 18, recent destinations include Reading, Dundee and Royal Holloway to do courses both academic and vocational. International students often return to their own countries for university. Art foundation courses also a popular choice.

Money matters: Fees are extremely reasonable: weekly boarding here will set you back less than a day place at one of our leading London schools. A range of scholarships available at 11+, 13+ and 16+: academic, art and DT, drama, music, sport and all rounder. Means-tested bursaries available for those who need them.

Remarks: Excellent value for money, something we don't often say in our line of work; sending your child here will genuinely set them up. But also a place that is human in its outlook: healthy, kind, and vigorous in its quest for excellence. As one student put it, 'I love it at this school, and I feel privileged to be here.'

Downe House School

Cold Ash, Thatcham, Berkshire RG18 9JJ

Ages 11–18 **Pupils** 590 **Sixth form** 169 **Boarders** 570 full

Fees: Day £27,495; Boarding £37,530 pa

01635 200286
www.downehouse.net

Headmistress: Since 1997, Emma McKendrick BA PGCE FRSA (40s). Educated at Bedford High and at the universities of Liverpool and Birmingham (German and Dutch). Previously at The Royal School, Bath, where she had been i/c careers and sixth form, a housemistress and deputy head before becoming head in 1994. Remarkably young when appointed to her first headship – that this was so is to the credit of the school's governors. She is soft-spoken, stylish, somehow very grown up, calm and relaxed. Her office and the room in which she receives visitors is a joy – windows on three sides so she can 'see everything', bright, light and tasteful. Parents – who tend to be deeply passionate about the school and many of whom are old girls – sigh with pleasure: 'She is excellent, on top of everything'; 'She is miraculous – I can say nothing against her. She is so professional, warm, and has a sense of humour. One cannot but be in awe of her, but you love her too'.

Academic matters: Had opted for Pre-U in preference to A levels in all but a few arts subjects – 'It really has made a difference to my upper sixth,' said the head. 'They are forced to be more independent. They are far better served by the Pre-U in terms of coping with what they will get at university.' However, with demise of AS, now returning to A levels for most subjects.

In 2018, at A level and Pre-U, 60 per cent A*-A, D1-D2 and 89 per cent A*/B. Maths very popular, with biology and English close behind. Good numbers for Latin and the odd taker for Greek. Politics, photography and economics offered along with history of art, plus all the trad subjects. Wide range of languages including support for home ones. Eighty-four per cent A*-A/9-7 at GCSE in 2018. Blissfully small classes – this is nurturing indeed.

Most teachers highly praised, many seen as 'inspiring'. Learning skills support given to those with mild dys-strata plus those who need extra help with organising themselves or time management. Also stretching help for the most able. Hopeless site for anyone in a wheelchair – the buildings are too scattered and the site is too up and down for this to be possible. EAL support given where needed – 35 in receipt of individual help when we visited.

Games, options, the arts: That the extracurricular life of the school is run from its own sizeable woodland cabin in the heart of the site with designated staff tells you everything. Every kind of opportunity is offered here – from trips to The Royal Opera House to playing lacrosse for Berkshire, to preparing soup for hungry people in South Africa from sackfuls of bones fresh from a slaughterhouse during a trip to a link school there. Lots of visits from outside speakers, who clearly inspire and motivate. Much lively and imaginative charitable activity – often with the boys from Radley. Excellent drama – again, often with Radley – generously supported by old girl Geraldine James, who opened the performing arts centre and has been known to take aspiring actresses under her wing. Two recent successful auditions for the National Youth Theatre. Successful and popular debating.

Sports are many and varied and include, for older girls, pilates, fencing and golf. Several girls are England lacrosse players – lax taken more seriously here than other sports. Internal competition between houses seemingly counting more than fixtures against other schools. Art is lively, though housed in the least attractive building on site – great range of activities: we loved the individuality of work in textiles, ceramics and woodwork, along with truly impressive painting. Ballet, modern dance, tap and hip hop on offer and around half the girls take speech and drama. Practically all of them learn at least one instrument. 'They all do so much extra,' a parent told us, half-admiring, half-concerned. 'They do whack on the pressure – the girls themselves, that is.'

Houses clearly of immense importance here – friendly but significant rivalry in all areas of school life. Lots of trips at home and abroad – all with sound educational or charitable purposes. Most exciting, memorable and generally aaaahed over is the term spent during year 8 at the school's own converted farm in the heart of Perigord. Those who join the school in year 9 seem to spend the next five years biting their lip at having missed an unforgettable experience. A seasoned sixth former told us – as if it were obvious – 'Oh, we never stop talking about it.' It's about French and French life, cuisine, charity work, community and living ensemble. On top of that, the expanded Global Schools Exchange Programme means girls now have the opportunity to take part in exchanges with fifteen partner schools across five continents – combined with international sports and curriculum-related tours and links with international charities.

Boarding: All but a handful of local day girls are full boarders. One boarding school veteran told us that the boarding staff were much the best she'd ever come across. The boarding houses themselves are much loved. We relished the dressing up boxes in the junior houses.

New lower school house for all year 7 and 8 girls, providing a sheltered introduction to boarding life. Older girls are in mixed age houses – dorms are mostly spacious; singles and doubles for the older girls are homely and attractive. Everywhere is properly carpeted and curtained. Fresh flowers abound – no sense here that 'nice' areas are just for show – this is home and it feels like it. All houses either wireless or with network points.

Sixth form houses are exceptionally well designed and furnished. Pigeonholes for girls' post and newspapers; sofas, careers areas, meeting rooms, kitchens. Girls can be independent here, if they wish – no wonder so few leave after

GCSEs. All have a personal safe in their rooms. Further extension to and enhancement of the boarding facilities planned.

Lessons until 12pm on Saturdays are followed by sports, so everyone signs up to the full boarding life. Saturday evenings are spent in rehearsal, at concerts, trips to theatres, cinemas etc. Sundays include trips, D of E activities and chillin'.

Background and atmosphere: Founded in 1907 by Olive Willis, its first headmistress, as an all-girls' boarding school. Its first home was Down House in the village of Downe, Kent – formerly the home of Charles Darwin. The school outgrew the house so Miss Willis bought The Cloisters in Berkshire – its present home – on a high ridge which provides occasional views over distant downs. The Cloisters – still at the heart of the school – comes as a surprise. Built by Maclaren Ross for an order of Spanish nuns, who named it The School of Silence, it has an arched walkway linking most of the classrooms which – with its white walls, arches and terracotta pantiles – is incongruously Moorish in the heart of Berkshire.

However, the school has grown many newer buildings – boarding houses, specialist blocks etc – around the main building and the site is now extensive – many buildings nestling amongst trees, woody areas and neatly planted beds. Most recently, the Murray Centre – a wonderful new building which sits in the heart of the campus and serves the whole community. The space combines a new library and collaborative learning areas and seminar room, as well as a highly flexible performance space, gallery area and coffee shop. All maintained by 'little green men' who hover around the site on electric car-lets. No architectural gems here – nor any monsters – though a few blocks lack charm. The whole has a sense of modest purposefulness – described by one mother as 'almost spiritual'.

The uniform is standard school green skirt, shirt and jumper, though the sixth form still cling to their floor length black skirts – 'They wear them so they can keep their pyjamas on underneath,' one mum told us.

Pastoral care, well-being and discipline: 'Completely faultless,' a mother said of the pastoral care. 'The house staff are very responsive and email you back at once.' 'When people complain, things do get done,' another vouchsafed. 'We've been bowled over by the pastoral care,' said yet another. 'The attention to detail is extraordinary – almost obsessive. Nothing is too much trouble.'

The loveliest school dining room we have seen in over 100 schools – proper tablecloths on round tables seating six to encourage time over meals. Food – 'We make all our own bread and sausages and buy in the absolute minimum' – which occasions rhapsodies in the girls.

Some sense that the sixth form centre separates older from younger girls and work still to be done on integrating those who arrive after the first year, but this is tricky in girls' schools everywhere. Very few discipline problems – smoking sighed over as 'an occasional safe rebellion which one wishes they wouldn't do', and illicit drinking looked upon as a threat to a girl's personal safety – 'You need to be safe, to look after yourself and to preserve your dignity,' the head reminds them. No drugs incidents within memory and the very rare girl who 'cannot stop being unkind has to go'.

Pupils and parents: Girls from all over the UK and beyond; increasing numbers of daughters of alumnae. Seven per cent from overseas – mostly from the Far East but also the US, Nigeria, Kazakhstan. Parents solid middle class, usually with boarding backgrounds.

Exceptionally impressive list of notable alumnae includes: chemist and educator Rosemary Murray, Geraldine James, Clare Balding, Mary Midgley, Elizabeth Bowen, Priscilla Napier, Anne Ridler, Audrey Richards, Sophie Conran, Lulu Guinness, Fru Hazlitt, wildly different comics Miranda Hart and Laura Solon, Hannah Wright – pioneering barrister, Jenifer Hart – pioneering civil servant and Oxford don and Aileen Fox – pioneering archaeologist. Oh – and Kate Middleton. A rare degree of loyalty amongst alumnae – few schools excite more affection, it seems, and many keep in touch. Mrs McKendrick fosters this in imaginative ways, enlisting old girls to support newbies in their professions, eg an established barrister mentoring a recent alumna in her pupillage. A considerable attraction to potential parents.

D

Entrance: Lists close at 110 applicants and head interviews all those over four days, during which all are tested in maths, English and reasoning. They also participate in drama and sports activities et al to see whether they're happy and likely to fit in with boarding life. Eighty then invited to sit CE for the 60 available places. At 13, around 65 are assessed similarly for the 35-odd places. Girls from 180+ preps/primaries have joined Downe in recent years – from all over the UK. From 2018 girls can apply for a place up to three years in advance for entry at 13+. Extra-early assessment in year 6 and early assessment in year 7 for these places.

At 16, it depends on how many are leaving but usually around 8-10 places for the 'huge' number who apply. Applicants sit the school's own papers and the strongest are then interviewed, the best offered conditional places. Seven I/GCSEs at 6 or above expected including 7+s in sixth form subject choices.

Exit: Good post GCSE retention – around 10 per cent leave after GCSEs, often for co-ed sixth forms. Most to top UK universities, eg Bristol, London, Warwick, Exeter, Leeds, Edinburgh, with six to Oxbridge in 2018; some overseas (seven in 2018 to the US, Canada, Switzerland, Netherlands). Almost 20 per cent pursue STEM subjects at university, with other popular choices including psychology, history of art, MFL, economics, politics, RS, business related degrees plus music and creative arts.

Money matters: Scholarships for sports, arts and academics more of an honour than a significant contribution to fees. Bursaries up to 100 per cent of fees plus additional help available for the right applicant.

Remarks: Archetypal traditional girls' full boarding school turning out delightful, principled, courteous and able girls who go on to make a significant contribution to the world. As one parent said, 'We couldn't be more thrilled.'

Downsend School

1 Leatherhead Road, Leatherhead, Surrey KT22 8TJ

Ages 2–13 **Pupils** 419

Fees: £11,535 – £15,435 pa

01372 372197
www.downsend.co.uk

Headmaster: Since 2013, Ian Thorpe BA MA (40s). Previously four years as headmaster at Chinthurst School and before that head of junior school at City of London Freemen's, preceded by stints all over the place, from Caterham Prep, where he was deputy head, to Witham Hall (deputy head and housemaster).

Married to 'very patient' wife, a teacher at Caterham, attended by two sons. A former grammar school boy, he's bright, jovial and energetic (looks exactly like sportsman he is, PE his main degree subject at Exeter). Refreshingly candid about strengths. He's a 'good all-rounder,' he says, with knack of getting what he wants – likely to come in handy for persuading 'supportive' bosses at Cognita, school's owner, to declare corporate wallet open.

Trilingual in French and Dutch (expat upbringing in Belgium) – results in excellent conversion rates for overseas families delighted to find head able to talk the talk in own language. Works wonders with Brits who have only to hear strains of unknown tongue (all but their own, generally) to assume 'you're really clever.'

Parental niggles leave him unfazed – most logged and being sorted, including pressing need to visit senior schools further afield to plug the knowledge gaps. 'Want more than helicopter perspective,' said a father. Just as well he's dynamic and good at disseminating the corporate message, think parents. While some 'see his style as slightly in your face,' supporters praise energy levels and hours worked. 'He's always there,' said one.

And while not necessarily quite such a details man as his predecessor (reckoned he knows about two-thirds of pupils' names though had 100 per cent strike rate during our visit) his verve and vision felt by others to be just the ticket. 'Has shaken things up (in a good way),' reckoned a mother. Easily bored, and enjoys a challenge. Just as well, what with numbers declining slightly in recent years following big rise about five years ago which saw school creaking at the seams, leading to some parents who bemoaned lack of intimacy voting with their feet.

Now St John's Leatherhead and Epsom College offer 11+ as well as 13+ entry, he has a fight on his hands to hold on to pupils in top two years. Currently loses a third after year 6 and, if parents desert wholesale, thinks Mr Thorpe, area as a whole could be the poorer, smaller preps taking only to year 6, only a few larger schools, this one included, able to finance the CE years; school has announced it will expand to senior level, taking its first year 9s in 2020.

Officially, it's stiff upper lips as usual, helped by increased pupil numbers and a big drive to proselytise benefits of the traditional prep school model, though behind the scenes furrowing of brows likely to be the in look for foreseeable future. Efforts to increase year 7 recruitment and build better links with traditional public schools (Wellington is starting to appear on parents' wish lists) continue apace.

Thus far, head has tended to stay four years in each post before moving on. His clear relish for fight to demonstrate, in the face of substantial reasons not to, why it's worth staying for the whole prep school experience, means that he's unlikely to be getting itchy feet for some time to come.

Entrance: Mixed ability and proud of it, declining to offer places only if child's behaviour or learning difficulty outside school's ability to cope. Otherwise, possession of place in nursery or reception usually leads to automatic passage through the school. Informal assessment for entry in year 2, tests in English and maths in year 3, ditto for other occasional places, may also be interview with the head. Pill can be considerably sweetened by interspersing exams with a spot of art or sport. Scholarships on offer in year 3, sibling discounts up to 15 per cent.

Prep packs them in from assorted points close to school locations, many local. Recent decision to provide return buses as well as inward bound ones a boon to growing numbers of working and longer distance families. Many originally from London, dual-income professionals increasingly the norm, making school's early morning, after school and holiday care between 8.00am and 5.30pm (and even later during term time) even more a boon. 'We really only close over Christmas,' says staff member.

Exit: Very rare that pupils don't make it from pre-prep into year 2 though occasionally happens if felt that won't manage the pace. Some parents take it badly, others are more pragmatic. Better the conversation now and support to find another school than 'drifting through, hitting year 6 and not have a place,' thought one mother.

Big senior school menu features occasional guest appearances by Hampton, Harrow and Guildford High but most senior schools – like many of delicious school lunch ingredients – are locally sourced, St John's heading destinations, Epsom College entrants dipping slightly, Reigate Grammar increasingly popular. Scholarships – around a quarter academic – steadily increasing. From 2020, pupils will be able to stay on for GCSEs.

Remarks: Founded in 1891 and fully co-ed since 2001. Snapped up by Cognita in early noughties and one of the largest schools in the group.

A mini-brand all on its own, extending tentacles (albeit embracing ones) into other regions of Surrey, courtesy of three additional pre-prep outposts, nearest just a few doors down from the prep. Were called lodges, name ditched after school sensibly worked out that associations with retirement homes, hunting and freemasonry rather than exuberant education of the very young were very possibly unhelpful. Though size and layout varies (Leatherhead, most generously endowed with space, has delightful tree and topiary-edged field off to side, so able to host own sports day rather than holding it at prep). Each offers small-scale cosiness, Ashtead notable for tiny reception classes of no more than 10, lunch fresh-cooked each day on all three sites, regular visits by minibus to prep for concerts, swimming and sport (including matches between the three), ensuring fear-free transition in year 2.

Parents tend to choose pre-prep that's an easy buggy stroll away, confident that curriculum and ethos will be pretty much identical in each. Some variation in specialist teachers and ways of doing things, though parents feel convergence of management styles is on the way in.

Pre-prep heads also bring stamp of individuality while sharing honours when it comes to warmth – we liked Ashtead's entrance featuring a beribboned tree next to weeny placards, each announcing birth of a new baby.

Pre-prep numbers on way up, Ashtead full, Leatherhead close. Epsom, the outlier (it's about five miles from mother ship) and located at end of private road close to well regarded state primary, currently siphoning off a fair few pupils in reception, has more work to do. With new wildlife and woodwork-mad head, bursting with ideas, from bringing chick from home on first day of autumn term to transforming part of playground into woodland paradise, we suspect they'll be hanging on to many more.

As for the prep, it's seen as the well-balanced option for those searching for something in between colossus and boutique establishment – neither over wood-panelled nor fetishistically au courant.

In an area bristling with good schools this one stands out as happy medium in terms of ethos, achievements and family background. 'More balanced than other schools – some parents aren't short of a penny, others are scraping the kitty to pay the fees,' thought one father. Balance applies equally to look and feel of the place.

School has willingness to accommodate those whose interests don't follow those of the common herd. You don't have to love rugby, for example – table tennis or badminton enthusiasts are catered for with equal dedication, while one upper school basketball fanatic dreamed of dedicated hoops that 'didn't wobble.'

Hard to argue with sporting success that regularly makes local headlines – it's a rare year when school doesn't secure national title somewhere along the line, swimming the biggest strength. 'Can't remember the last time they lost a match,' says father. Girls' sport as strong as boys – revved up following slightly lukewarm comments in last inspection.

Generally good, too, with SEN pupils – over 150 receiving some form of support in slightly bleak room slightly apart from main drag, though help is limited to mild difficulties only. Parents praise openness to new ideas such as allowing laptops for those with SpLD, though one mother felt had needed to push to ensure that SEN awareness and approaches make it into collective staff consciousness. Head, who agrees, is bumping up admin team so SENCo can spend more time working with class teachers.

The school isn't right for everyone. 'A bit of a hothouse,' thought local senior school insider, though tutors hired to plug specific gaps rather than as a permanent accessory, as elsewhere. Parents a motivated bunch and it's a rare child who isn't read to at night, thinks mother. Teachers impressive, too – though these days unlikely to hang around for long if they're not, think parents. Though the head couldn't possibly comment, he has made expectations clear. 'I've used the words "uncompromising standards..."'

Well-structured curriculum, where academic focus, though sharp, isn't allowed to blot out cookery and sewing, both on offer all the way to year 8. Enjoyable lessons include junior pupils writing letters to favourite authors in English and upper school science lesson practical comparing exhaust fumes of (teacher's) Jaguar (good) with school minibus emissions (sootier). Lots of praise from pupils, all mentioning 'happy' teachers who 'have lots of friends' (always nice to hear). They tell terrible jokes too, to relieve entrance exam pressure – 'so bad that they're funny,' say pupils.

Teaching staff donate minimum of an hour a week to run lunchtime or after-school club (includes green-fingered nurse and science technician who recruit helpers to tend idyllic garden haven). Fab range of activities, now free of charge.

'Hats off to school for exam preparation,' said mother, child in proud possession of several excellent offers. Results aren't trumpeted perhaps as much as they might be elsewhere, despite goodly number of scholarships, though new, modernistic honours boards may help.

As with youngest pupils, attention to detail is good, from homework – 'just enough to stretch you,' said year 7 pupil – to carrot-focused discipline, detentions possible but rarely necessary, credits and house points the norm (with highly desirable trip to Guildford Spectrum for the winners).

Successful occupation of middle ground makes for very happy pupils, think parents. Possibly too much so, reckons head, who has found school's oft-published desire to produce 'children who enjoy life' a bit much to bear, especially when proffered as excuse for iffy behaviour and appearance, something he's cracking down on (two message-bearing boys, both barefoot after PE, were swiftly returned to sender). 'It's like saying we're a school for children who breathe air,' he says. While head may want to tweak the recipe, no doubting parents' happiness with the basic ingredients. 'It's about having fun,' said mother. 'Sounds a bit twee but that's the core of what they do.'

Dr Challoner's Grammar School

Chesham Road, Amersham, Buckinghamshire HP6 5HA

Ages 11–18 **Pupils** 1,356 **Sixth form** 427 (73 girls)

01494 787500
www.challoners.com

D

Headmaster: Since 2016, David Atkinson (40s), previously deputy head. Geography degree from Oxford; joined Challoner's in 1996, becoming head of geography and director of sixth form on his way up. A chartered geographer, appointed to the Royal Geographical Society in recognition of his work in geographical education, including texts on geomorphology. Has worked to promote wider access to higher education, especially in STEM subjects; leads the Astra Learning Alliance, which provides training and development for teachers in Bucks and Herts.

Reserved, unassuming and thoroughly likable, he keeps a hand in teaching – 'Contact with grass roots is essential and teaching is what the school's all about.' Has enhanced the staff well-being and mental health offering so much that they've won an award from MIND (one of only two schools to do so) – 'Happy, healthy staff provide a better service,' he says. Continues to develop the pedagogy. 'He's a lot less formidable than the last one,' said one parent. 'He's was one of the reasons we moved our daughter here in the sixth form; he knows the school inside out and is really approachable,' commented another. Pupils say they see him regularly during the school day and feel his dedication to mutual respect 'very much sets the tone of the school.'

Lives locally; enjoys cricket and music.

Academic matters: Remains Bucks' top performing boys' grammar school, regularly appearing in the top 20 state schools nationally; no wonder the Challoner's brand is synonymous far and wide with academic excellence. In 2018, 74 per cent of GCSE grades were A*-A/9-7; with 56 per cent of A levels graded A*/A, 80 per cent A*-B. Don't believe the hype about it being overly pressurised, insist pupils, although they quickly add, 'some of us do put a lot pressure on ourselves' and admit that 'a B can be disappointing.' Others say they find themselves 'comparing our results to others – which can be a good or bad thing, I suppose,' while parents told us, 'It is results-driven, so while not the hothouse it's often made out to be, it isn't for slackers.'

Majority take 10 GCSEs. Maths and science shining particularly bright; no obvious weak areas. Around two-thirds do four A levels; remainder does three, plus EPQ, which gets some terrific results across a wide range of topics, including our favourite, Royal Spouses in Tudor Times (must have been a juicy one to study). Traditional-ish curriculum focuses on the solid, academic subjects required by top universities with no media studies and not an 'ology' in sight. But they have added computer science at GCSE and, unusually, the school offers electronics at both levels too. Success attributed to school's emphasis on learning habits and skills as well as the hard academics, plus engaging, lively and interactive classes and an extremely strong team of staff, with a good number of young innovators in the staff mix. Testament to their calibre of staff here is the fact that so many move into senior leadership roles at other schools – 'I'm one of three heads locally that all worked here at the same time,' says head. 'In most schools, you get a few bad teachers – we've found none here,' a parent told us.

Setting from year 9 in maths, year 10 in science and at GCSE in English, with the top and bottom sets kept small – sometimes 12 to a class. French plus either German and Spanish from year 7, at least one of which is taken at GCSE – and the language exchange programme gets rave reviews. Perhaps surprisingly, no Latin, except as a club. Homework not for the fainthearted – around an hour of 'really focused work' for year 7s, up to 1.5 hours by GCSE, and yet more for A levels.

Lots of praise for the SENCo and specialist SEN teacher (who takes a national lead around improving exam arrangements), with help both in and outside the classroom available for mild end SEN – 'learning support spot on,' said one parent. Quite a few pupils with ASD ('particularly those that fit the Asperger's profile,' says head) are also served well here.

Wifi favoured over fixed IT equipment; classrooms and study areas awash with students using laptops and iPads to aid their learning (year 12 politics students were googling federalism and Obama's influence in politics when we visited). All pupils from year 8 have iPads, brought from home. And if parents don't have one? 'By hook or by crook, the boys get one,' says head, but year 7s have to sit tight for a year – 'they have enough to cope with academically and socially; throwing a device into the mix isn't helpful,' believes head.

Games, options, the arts: This school is proof that an elitist approach to sport can be turned around into an offering so inclusive that pupils don't remember it any other way, even just a few years later. Thanks to a strong partnership between the school and a group of passionate parents, everyone now gets a chance to represent the school as long as they 'show commitment to training.' 'You still get the really good people winning us loads of trophies, but there are A to D teams in most sports and if you're not in them, you get to do games outside Challoner's,' a pupil said. A recent highlight was the U15s rugby team making the national Vase competition at Twickenham – the whole school, in 27 coaches, went to watch. Rugby, football and hockey are the three main winter sports; cricket and tennis in the summer term. For sixth form girls, there's competitive netball. There's also fencing, mountain biking, golf, sailing and fitness; badminton increasingly popular. Although lacking the sprawling grounds of its privately funded rivals, school makes effective use of the fields it does have and boasts a climbing wall, spacious sports hall, two new championship tennis courts and a multi-use Astroturf which pupils told us 'is in full use practically every lunchtime and after school' as the sporty squads train and take full use of the clubs.

Other popular clubs include debating, Model UN, journalism club and drama. Most do at least one club, although head admits 'you do sometimes get a drop off in the middle years; for example, the keen 11-year-olds doing Lego club come back to robotics club when they're teenagers and keen on programming.' School enters a lot of competitions, with particularly success in Apps for Good, whereby students think of an app, then code, market and advertise it. DofE gold recently launched.

Music and drama flourish; often involves teaming up with sister school Challoner's High. Orchestras, choirs and ensembles aplenty performing to exceptionally high standards. Lunchtime concerts at the local church and music tours from juniors upwards give pupils regular opportunities to perform. Around 10 peripatetic teachers come in to teach instruments to hundreds of pupils. Impressive productions, most recently Dirty Rotten Scoundrels (which Robert Lindsey, who was in the last West End version, came to watch). Lots of discos, balls and other social events provide further opportunities to socialise with the girls.

Perhaps not the first choice school for DT fanatics or really arty types, with the well-equipped graphic design suite having superseded DT – some seriously outstanding work leads many to head down this avenue at university. 'Not a big hitter in terms of GCSE take-up, but certainly stable,' says head. Recently refurbished art block is airy and light, but traditional rows of desks and copying from the whiteboard when we visited meant it lacked the more laid-back, bohemian vibe that art departments so often have. It would also have been nice to see more art work exhibited around the school. Cookery on curriculum in years 8 and 10 as part of PSHCE, taking place in a gleaming kitchen space, complete with flat screen televisions to walk boys through recipes.

Trips and tours for both academic and enrichment purposes, including a popular ski trip, Iceland (geographers), Washington DC (historians), Namibia (biologists), as well as the golden ticket – the biannual cricket tour, recently to Sri Lanka. 'I do worry if everyone can afford them, though,' says one parent.

Background and atmosphere: Founded 1624 under the will of Dr Robert Chaloner (sic), former rector of Amersham and Canon of Windsor. Moved to present site on the edge of Amersham High Street in 1905, when it became co-ed. Due to expanding numbers, girls got their own premises a few miles away in Little Chalfont in 1962. The original fascia lends the school a reasonably attractive frontage – particularly in comparison with the majority of grammars thrown up in the decades that taste forgot – and the campus, although now a smorgasbord of architectural styles spanning the decades, feels spacious, well-organised, accessible and remarkably pristine. The jewel in the crown is the spectacular newish sixth form centre which includes buzzy lounging area and Café Africa run by a local not-for-profit organisation on the ground floor, a group study area on the first level and the cherry on top: an airy library with small break-out study areas. Pre-sixth form, boys lunch in a modern dining hall with good food and plenty of wholesome, healthy options.

Purposeful is a word you'll often read in our school reviews, but it's as if the word was made for Challoner's – every classroom and learning space seems to be packed with utterly absorbed, attentive and driven learners, some (quite a lot, actually) in silence; others (usually the older ones) engrossed in intellectual debate.

Uniform of blazer and tie is worn with pride (woe betide any boy that doesn't have his shirt tucked in) until sixth form when boys can wear their own suit and tie; girls similarly smartly attired. At this point, students given considerable responsibility and freedom. Morning attendance is compulsory then free to go if no timetabled lessons. The addition of girls in the sixth form – now accounting for around a fifth of the cohort – has created a different ambience, with sixth form boys telling us 'it's made the boys work even harder because the girls are so clever.' 'But you have to be the kind of girl that can just get stuck in,' one told us.

Pastoral care, well-being and discipline: Mental heath and well-being are buzzwords here, with a student development team providing counselling and support on tap. 'I don't think there's a single issue I couldn't talk to one member of staff about on that very day,' said one pupil, while a female sixth former with experience in several previous schools told us, 'I've never seen a school where the staff get so involved in the extracurricular, which I think really helps them to get to know you outside the classroom.' Parents agree that pastorally, the school stands out, many seriously impressed that the senior leadership team knows so many of the boys so well.

It all kicks off with a very well-liked head of year 7 visiting each and every one at their primary school, while a well-attended summer sports camp before they join gives those joining in ones and twos from village schools a chance to make friends before term starts. Huge number of official roles higher up the school with up to 80 elected prefects, house captains and senior prefects give older students a sense of responsibility. The girls are well represented in these leadership roles. Six houses drive the school's competitive spirit, fighting it out throughout the year at 'virtually anything you can name.' Plenty of friendly interaction between year groups: sixth formers apply to be mentors to year 7s, visiting their classrooms with fun activities up their sleeves or just to chat and listen. Year 10s pulled in to advise year 9 pupils on their GCSE choices and pupils drew up the anti-bullying charter, displayed in every classroom ('You're not seen as a snitch if you report bullying here,' said a pupil). Resilience classes for younger ages – 'I believe in equipping pupils with the capacity to cope with the ups and downs they will inevitably face,' says head. Tons of fun student-initiated fundraisers – both for charities and school – range from 'peg the teacher' to teacher/student penalty shoot-outs or designing and selling Challoner's beany hats.

Boys generally well-behaved, with minor transgressions punishable by a tiered system of detentions (lunch time, after school or head's). Lots of rules; 'You do wonder if some of them a bit petty – more than once, I've thought, "Really?" when my son had a sanction for a very minor issue,' said one parent, but others approve: 'The rules are consistent and the boundaries clear,' commented another parent. One permanent exclusion in the last few years – drugs related; 'Any head that says drugs is a non-issue isn't telling the truth, but we won't tolerate it,' says head. Plus a few temporary exclusions most years, usually for 'minor scuffles that get too physical' or 'general teenage defiance.'

Pupils and parents: Most parents are affluent middle class, many of whom, were it not for the god of catchment areas smiling on them on school allocation day, could ably pay for their sons' schooling. Around 20 per cent from ethnic groups, predominantly Asian, with a tiny number on free school meals. Coaches from all directions.

Boys and girls here have a natural confidence and erudite chatter; sit them in a room of public school pupils and we defy you to tell the difference. Where other grammars have whole programmes dedicated to convincing boys that they are good enough to try for Oxbridge, Challoner's students feel (and some grumble) that's just what's expected of them – nice problem to have. Alumni include Roger Moore (actor), Matt Watson (cricketer), David Wands (academic and educator), Justin Robertson (DJ), John Shepherd (scientist), Dominic Raab MP, Rick Warden (actor) and John Mousinho (footballer).

Entrance: Challoner's widely considered the hot ticket and, as such, massively oversubscribed. Applicants kick off with the Buckinghamshire Transfer Test – usually at their primary school – in early September of year 6. Those who pass (usually around 30 per cent) are entitled to a grammar school place. Selection then comes strictly down to distance from candidate's home to front door of school. And don't be fooled into thinking that living in catchment (which stretches as far as eight miles in one direction) will entitle you to a place. Offers can extend to about six miles from school, but this varies from year to year. And no more can savvy north London parents sneakily rent a flat in Amersham with the aim of popping their little darling on the Metropolitan Line each day – you need to have lived at your home address for 18 months before applying to the school. And yes, they do check...

Around 42 feeder schools in total; a third join from local preps (mainly The Beacon and Chesham Prep), but these are indistinguishable from their peers who join from state primaries in leafy commuter villages.

Occasional places crop up further up school, and at this stage, catchment goes out the window and the place goes to the child with the highest score in the entrance exam. Around 25 new places open up in year 12 and are offered to the candidates with the best GCSE results, mainly from local state schools, occasionally defectors from the private sector. Sixth form co-ed.

Exit: A handful leaves after GCSE. After sixth form, most to Russell Group universities, notably Nottingham, Durham, Exeter and Bristol. In 2018, 21 to Oxbridge. Increasingly to high-profile overseas universities, such as Stanford. Wider range of courses than you might expect eg computer games design, paramedic science – 'We hunt out the little nuggets right for each person,' says head. Sixth formers concur that support around university applications is 'very strong, regardless of what course or where you want to go.'

D

Money matters: Like other grammars in this part of the world, it is neglected by state funds in favour of schools in run down areas, so generosity of parents is leaned upon, albeit with no pushiness. The active friends' association raises over £30K a year via various fundraisers. Regular parental contributions are 'solidly reliable,' raising around £125K each year.

Remarks: Many Challoner's parents may argue that they are essentially paying for their offspring's education with their house price premiums, but staff describe the school as 'the best education money can't buy' and it is certainly as good as it gets for able and driven boys (and girls in sixth form). Think ahead, buy near the school and get that 11+ super tutor booked.

Dr Challoner's High School

Cokes Lane, Little Chalfont, Buckinghamshire HP7 9QB

Ages 11–18 **Pupils** 1,223 **Sixth form** 339

01494 763296
www.challonershigh.com

Head: Since 2015, Alan Roe, previously a member of the senior team at Chesham Grammar School, which he helped towards its outstanding Ofsted rating in 2014. A geographer, he initially taught at the Downs School in west Berkshire, and became head of humanities at Dr Challoner's Grammar School, where he worked for nine years before joining Chesham Grammar in 2011. Teaches geography to year 11s and mainly sees students by appointment and for informal chats around the school – as well as offering birthday teas to year 10 girls in his office (in small groups).

Fairly reserved and not a man to waste words, he is nonetheless engaging and utterly passionate about the school, particularly its mission going forward. In fact, he kicked off his tenure by working with some parents (management consultants, working with the likes of Costa and BA) for six months to create a one-page vision – no mean feat for a school that 'was traditionally unable to describe itself very well. Now, it can.' Parents describe him as a 'strong and visible leader,' 'a man with real presence' and 'someone with huge emotional intelligence.' 'He recognises and respects in a very public way the contribution of all stakeholders to the school,' adds another parent. Students applaud how he celebrates individual successes and say he is 'clear on expectations' and 'very approachable.'

Lives near Aylesbury with his wife and two daughters, both of whom are primary school age.

Academic matters: Regularly hovers around the top of regional and national state school league tables. In 2018, 76 per cent A*-A/9-7 at GCSE; at A level, 49 per cent A*/A and 77 per cent A*-B. Six classes of 30 in each year group, with setting from year 9 in maths – although it's purely about pace, as one student explained: 'I was in the bottom set for maths GCSE, but still got a 7. Most of us did.' Indeed, maths is one of the greatest academic strengths of the school at all levels, with over 100 mathematicians in year 13 testament to this. 'This department is a machine – maths is easily our most popular A level,' says the head – although one parent said he'd like to see girls competing in more inter-school competitions.

Also super-strong in languages. Unusually, pupils take three in year 7 – French, German and Spanish – and not just as taster courses, with 1.5 hours per week dedicated to each language. From year 8, they pick two of them, as well as taking up Latin. Parents say it 'takes away the difficult decision about which two to go for when girls join the school.'

Good breadth of subjects available at GSCE, with most popular non-core subjects including RE, geography and history. An impressive 25 subjects are taught at A level, with the most popular including biology, chemistry, English literature, geography and history – plus, of course, maths and languages. Less traditional offerings at A level include Latin, classics, psychology and graphics. No gender stereotypes – with around 30+ typically doing GCSE computing and 20-30 doing physics A level. 'It's part of the joy of being an all-girls school. They just find their passion and get on with it,' says the head.

Recruiting and retaining good, experienced teachers is prioritised within the school's budget, leading to an 'expensive, but stable and outstanding 70-strong team', according to the head – with a healthy staff turnover of seven or eight leaving per year, while others stay as long as 30 years. 'Our philosophy is that the best schools have the best teachers.' Parents praise the 'extremely supportive' relationship between teachers and pupils, which 'involves lots of mentoring and coaching.' Students describe teaching as 'collaborative' and 'inspirational.'

The school is widely praised for its depth of learning – girls here don't just learn about the subject itself – they drill down deeper, making links with other subjects and doing their own investigations. Target setting is high on the agenda, with formal monitoring every term. 'These teachers know your precise strengths and weaknesses and how to overcome the latter – it's astonishing,' one pupil told us. There are a few bad apples, say parents – 'my daughter is damning of a few of her teachers, but you get that anywhere.' Homework typical for a Bucks grammar – an hour a night in year 7, reaching up to two or three hours a night by year 13.

Dedicated SEN team, this team supports pupils with a wide range of needs ('not just mild and moderate,' says head – although only two with EHC plans when we visited), both in and outside the classroom. No wheelchair access, however.

Head keen to point out that despite the school's strong academic reputation, 'this is an A*-C school. So while the majority of our grades are A* and A, our staff battle hard for the girls in their best, worst and middling subjects. In fact, their eyes often gleam the brightest for those hard-sought Cs.'

DCHS regularly hovers around the top of regional and national state school league tables. In 2017, 74 per cent A*-A/9-7 at GCSE; at A level, 47 per cent A*/A and 73 per cent A*-B. Six classes of 30 in each year group (phasing out the old intake of five classes), with setting from year 9 in maths – although it's purely about pace, as one student explained: 'I was in the bottom set for maths GCSE, but still got an A. Most of us did.' Indeed, maths is one of the greatest academic strengths of the school at all levels, with the number of year 12s choosing to take further maths testament to this. 'This department is a machine – maths is easily our most popular A level,' says the head – although one parent said he'd like to see girls competing in more inter-school competitions.

DCHS is also super-strong in languages. Unusually, pupils take three in year 7 – French, German and Spanish – and not just as taster courses, with 1.5 hours per week dedicated to each language. From year 8, they pick two of them, as well as taking up Latin. Parents say it 'takes away the difficult decision about which two to go for when girls join the school.'

Good breadth of subjects available at GSCE, with most popular non-core subjects including RE, geography and history. An impressive 25 subjects are taught at A level, with the most popular including biology, chemistry, English literature, geography and history – plus, of course, maths and languages. Less traditional offerings at A level include Latin, classics, psychology, graphics and textiles. No gender stereotypes – with around 30+ typically doing GCSE computing and 20-30 doing physics A level. 'It's part of the joy of being an all-girls school. They just find their passion and get on with it,' says the head.

Recruiting and retaining good, experienced teachers is prioritised within the school's budget, leading to an 'expensive, but stable and outstanding 70-strong team', according to the head – with a healthy staff turnover of five or six leaving per year, while others stay as long as 30 years. 'Our philosophy is that the best schools have the best teachers.' Parents praise the 'extremely supportive' relationship between teachers and pupils, which 'involves lots of mentoring and coaching.' Students describe teaching as 'collaborative' and 'inspirational.' The school is widely praised for its depth of learning – girls here don't just learn about the subject itself – they drill down deeper, making links with other subjects and doing their own investigations. Target setting is high on the agenda, with formal monitoring every term. 'These teachers know your precise strengths and weaknesses and how to overcome the latter – it's astonishing,' one pupil told us. There are a few bad apples, say parents – 'my daughter is damning of a few of her teachers, but you get that anywhere.' Homework typical for a Bucks grammar – an hour a night in year 7, reaching up to two or three hours a night by year 13.

Dedicated SEN team includes an experienced SENCo, who (significantly) is the deputy head. This team supports pupils with a wide range of needs ('not just mild and moderate,' says head – although only two statemented when we visited), both in and outside the classroom. No wheelchair access, however.

Head keen to point out that despite the school's strong academic reputation, 'this is an A*-C school. So while the majority of our grades are A* and A, our staff battle hard for the girls in their best, worst and middling subjects. In fact, their eyes often gleam the brightest for those hard-sought Cs.'

Games, options, the arts: PE mandatory from years 7-11, with 20 sports taught to a high standard by enthusiastic staff – netball, hockey, athletics and cross-country at the core. Sport popular off curriculum too, with a sports leadership programme in place for those competing at country, national or international level – which involves DCHS girls having worked with over 2,000 primary school children. DCHS successfully competes at a high level across the board, including more marginal activities like fencing, basketball and rowing in its armoury. Cricket is on the up, and there are non-competitive exercise options including pilates, yoga and boot camp. Majority of sports clubs are free, with just a handful (such as rowing and fencing) charged as an extra. 'While there's lots in place to ensure the elite thrive here, sports at DCHS is also about participation, with a staggering 110 year 7 girls doing after-school netball this year,' one parent told us – although another pointed out, 'There's no full-size hockey field – you can't deny that's a weakness.'

Huge range of music, drama and art-based extracurricular activities on offer (again, mostly free), with 370 girls involved with one of the many ensembles, orchestras and choirs when we visited. Choirs alone range from the all-school, 60-strong junior and senior choirs through to the elite 12-strong Con Brio choir. A favourite is the swing band, which tours with the boys' school biennially – just one of many opportunities for musically-able girls to perform publically. Some 500 girls learn an instrument with a peripatetic teacher – a huge number for a school of this size. And music lessons are also built into the curriculum up to year 9, after which it is optional. Decent numbers take it as GCSE.

Budding actors are also in for a treat here, with two main school productions performed joint with the boys' school every year – one senior production; the other open to all. 'Normally, one of these is student led,' says the head. 'Last year, year 10 wrote Lady of the Flies, which was phenomenally good.' In addition, girls can apply to be in the boys' school performances. Opportunities for girls to learn technical sound, lighting and set building. Strong arts and technology faculty, with quality work festooning the immediately surrounding area, although it's a pity this doesn't make its way further into the school. Other extracurricular options of note (most of which take place at lunchtimes or after school) include Mandarin from year 12; DofE; the fiercely contested debating, with regular trips to the Oxford Union; and the economics society, which attracts external lecturers from the worlds of business and government. Many of the clubs and societies are student led – and some are run joint with the boys' school, including the English society and the award-winning Young Enterprise. In short, something for everyone, although some parents told us they'd like to see the girls pushed to do more. 'That's improving, but not fast enough,' said a parent.

Unbelievably long list of school trips for all year groups, from curriculum based and language exchanges to an activities break for year 7 and a visit to Tanzania for year 12 (with girls expected to raise funds to travel and work for charity). There's a year 9 residential enrichment week, with a choice of 5+ options including to Iceland and Germany, and plenty of one-off trips, such as music and sports tours. Start saving your pennies, though – these trips 'cost anything from £200 to over £1,000,' says the head.

Background and atmosphere: Founded in 1624 by Dr Robert Chaloner (sic), becoming co-ed in 1906. Girls hived off to Little Chalfont in 1962 (the boys' school, Dr Challoner's Grammar School, is a few miles away in Amersham). Tucked away amongst prime South Bucks real estate, visitors may feel transported back to the 1960s as they drive in, although the mix of tired-looking, no-frills buildings from this era includes some smarter additions from the 1990s. Plus points include the feeling of spaciousness – although not by any means a vast campus, the school is surrounded by mature woodland. We also like the outdoor amphitheatre, used for summer term performances, and new courtyard café, where students can socialise and study. There's an impressive number of multi-purpose spaces including a large, modern sports hall, assembly hall, gymnasium and sound-proofed drama studio, all excellent for the school's large and active performing arts community.

And while the fabric of DCHS lacks many of the gleaming facilities one might expect in a leading school, it's worth noting that the school is in the midst of a five-year premises plan, which includes a new sixth form common room and study rooms and two cutting-edge science labs (already complete) and general improvements throughout the school. Food is good, say students, albeit served in a rather overcrowded dining room.

Despite fierce competition for places at this hard-working school, there is an informal vibe, although the consensus is that unmotivated souls might struggle. 'If you are not a self-starter or naturally curious, I think you could feel uncomfortable here,' one parent told us. Pupils say they are given 'a lot of freedom' and there is a feeling of trust and ownership around the school, with girls given free rein of the buildings – including the computer labs – at break times.

Pastoral care, well-being and discipline: The school day – which runs from 8.40am-3.35pm to fit in five one-hour lessons – includes tutor time both at the start and end of the morning. 'We wanted to make sure there are two key points of contact for the girls every day – important from a pastoral perspective,' says the head. Other key features of the excellent pastoral system here include the strong relationships between the teachers and girls; the fact that girls generally have the same academic tutor from year 7-11 at the school; the non-teacher student support officer, who is available at all times for both academic and emotional support; the two part-time school counsellors; and full-time matron. There are also befriending schemes between year groups and a 'big sister, little sister' initiative, with older girls able to mentor junior sports squads or tutor younger ones if they are struggling academically. 'My daughter had some anxiety problems, which became quite serious, and they were brilliant at dealing with it quickly and well.'

Hugely successful house system encourages mixing and co-operation between year groups. A head girl team is elected each year, with one head girl and 11 deputies, each looking after a specific aspect of the school ranging from innovation and student voice to press and PR. Very professional glossy school magazine, put together by pupils, showcases girls' talent in writing features, poetry and short stories as well as photography and artwork. Popular termly discos with the boys' school enable them to let their hair down in a safe environment.

Bullying 'practically non-existent,' according to the girls. 'It's not like my last school – it's so friendly,' is a phrase you'll hear over and over again. Poor behaviour also 'very rare', says head – with girls getting the odd detention, but generally no more than one or two during their entire school careers. 'I've never seen anything like it – the behaviour is ridiculously good,' says the head. 'The girls police themselves – there isn't a need to be heavy handed,' said one parent. No permanent exclusions in living memory and no temporary exclusions during the current head's time.

Teacher/parent communication has 'greatly improved', with parents now able to email individual teachers via the school office. Parents also praise the weekly newsletter.

Pupils and parents: Families mostly middle-class, with around a quarter of girls joining from local prep schools and a negligible number eligible for free school meals. Most live within six miles; the furthest currently come from 10.5 miles away. Excellent bus service, but parents need to be on hand to collect after later activities. 'Increasingly, girls use the Met line, with Little Chalfont tube station only a seven or eight minute walk away,' adds the head. 'It's particularly popular with our sixth formers.' Good ethnic mix for the area – typically 67 per cent white British, with a wide variety of ethnicities represented among the remaining girls.

We found the girls polite, well-turned out (the school cuts no slack around the uniform looking smart) and confident. 'When you meet girls at the open day, you can't help but think, "I want one of those!"' said one parent.

Parents are a sociable bunch, compared to many state schools, and parental expertise highly welcomed. 'We currently have two architects helping us, as well as financial and legal support, just to name a few – we're very lucky,' says the head.

Alumni include Amal Alamuddin, international human rights barrister (married to George Clooney); Olympian Clare Cunningham; television presenter Fern Britton; actress Carey Mulligan; editor Lisa Markwell; and Lucy Winkett, canon at St Paul's Cathedral (first female).

Entrance: Highly selective, with entry dependent on success at 11 plus, administered by a conglomeration of the county's grammar schools following collective achievement of academy status. As you might expect, there's no shortage of tutoring (often for years in advance) by hopeful year 6 parents for those 180 coveted places. The two largest feeder schools are Little Chalfont Primary School and Maltman's Green School in Gerrards Cross, after which there's around 50 different feeders, with many girls joining in ones or twos from their junior schools, forcing them to integrate and make new friends quickly. Even the largest feeders only send between 10 and 15. After looked after girls, preference to those living in the catchment area, then those on free school meals, then siblings, then medical or social need.

D

The vast majority stay on to the sixth form ('the ones who leave either want to study different courses or the tight-knit community isn't for them,' sixth formers told us), with around 40 additional places open up in year 12, attracting girls to apply direct from other grammars, independents and the brightest from the upper schools. This is oversubscribed and girls are selected on GCSE results (minimum of two 7s and four 6s required, with 7s or 6s in chosen A level subjects).

Exit: Ninety-six per cent on to higher education – around three-quarters of them to Russell Group universities; 14 to Oxbridge in 2018. No one course is particularly popular, and only six or seven go to any one university. 'Our girls head off in every single direction under the sun – and we are very proud of that,' says the head.

Money matters: State maintained. Parents invited to make a voluntary contribution per year to the Challoner's Girls' Foundation to enable the school to fund a variety of initiatives such as pupil laptops.

Remarks: Full of bright-eyed go-getters who give their private school peers a real run for their parents' money. The Challoner's brand continues to live up to expectations for parents lucky enough to have both 11 plus results and the moveable feast of distance in their favour, although those who have been pushed through the 11 plus may face a tough challenge. An outward-looking school that supports and inspires, stretches and challenges, and frees up bright minds.

Dragon School

Bardwell Road, Oxford, Oxfordshire OX2 6SS

Ages 4–13 **Pupils** 825 **Boarders** 229 (from 8 years)

Fees: Day £11,988 – £21,135; Boarding £30,615 pa

01865 315405
www.dragonschool.org

Head: Since September 2017, Dr Crispin Hyde-Dunn MA (Oxon) PGCE MA (Ed) NPQH, PhD (40s). Read history at Oxford. Previously head of Abingdon Prep. Before that was deputy head of King's College School, Cambridge and earlier still was head of history at New College School in Oxford. Wife, Lucy, is a medical research fellow at Oxford.

Entrance: Register early – as early as you like post-conception. The school is full and there are waiting lists at all stages. However, spaces can be available at any time as pupils move away to another area or country. Potentially easier to get in as a boarder but this depends on the year group. Non-selective entry although the school assesses maths and English to check that a child will be able to cope. Up to 100 per cent means-tested bursaries are available from year 4 for the full five years. Not based on academic merit: the school states that they 'start with need' but have to be sure the family is able and willing to commit to the Dragon way of life – Saturday morning school, extracurricular commitments etc.

Exit: Frequent destinations include Abingdon School, Cheltenham Ladies' College, Eton College, Harrow School, Magdalen College School, Marlborough College, Radley College, Rugby School, Stowe School, St Edward's School, Wellington College, Winchester College and Wycombe Abbey. No favourite school, but 'we have a strong working relationship with St Edward's', as the two schools have a similar ethos and are co-ed day and boarding. Pupils are supported but not intensely prepped for pre-test at 11 or entrance exams at 11 – would not want a child to get into a school on the basis of excessive prepping. Senior schools take note of the Dragon's reports and trust their judgement but this isn't a school whose priority is to get children into the most academic local seniors. Bucket-loads of scholarships won – 40 to 50 per year. Famous Old Dragons include Sir John Betjeman, Leonard Cheshire VC, John Mortimer, Antonia Fraser, Alain de Botton, Rageh Omaar, Hugh Laurie, Tim Henman, Tom Hiddleston and Emma Watson to name but a few.

Remarks: The Dragon, so named after an early school football team called Dragons, is as sought-after as ever. Originally founded as the Oxford Preparatory School by a group of dons who wanted a progressive, liberal school for their sons where learning would be fun. Once avant-garde, education and society have caught up with these principles so that today the Dragon can only aspire to unconventionality. It has resisted formality and retains the ethos of ordered disorderliness – a charmingly unpretentious, relaxed atmosphere. The school confesses they are relaxed about petty issues – untucked shirts, scruffy uniform and clutter – while concentrating on the things that matter, such as learning. Like an upturned swan – feet paddling busily on the surface whilst the underlying systems are serene and quiet. Unconventionality, or 'colouring outside the lines', has always been and still is encouraged, although school admits it is 'a balancing act' between risk-taking in schoolwork, striving for imagination and curiosity on one side, and discipline and toeing the line on the other. The Dragon aims for and encourages both.

Broad curriculum with a huge extracurricular programme including languages such as Mandarin, Japanese, Arabic and French as well as 'toast and translation' (a Latin club), music and drama etc. Most subjects are setted with scholarship classes at the top of the ability range. Learning support needs are screened in year 2 or on intake and help is available at extra cost. Dedicated learning support unit with five full- and three part-time members of staff who advise and update colleagues and draw up individual education plans. Additional groups provided at no extra cost for handwriting, reading comprehension and social skills.

Breadth is key at the Dragon with excellence across the board – outstanding sport with fantastic facilities and accolades too numerous to mention. Non-sporty children can find refuge in music – equally successful and receiving high praise from parents. Over two-thirds of pupils take individual music lessons. Fantastic art work in light airy art rooms and space in the Forum for the annual art exhibition – check out the school magazine – worthy of any secondary school. Facilities in general match those at many senior schools with science labs, impressive library (look out for dragons etched on the glass fronted mezzanine), 25m swimming pool and playing fields stretching down to the river and boat house. A mini-campus with happy free-range children roaming around, unrestricted by petty rules and health and safety, having a jolly time; play by the river still possible as long as a child can swim two lengths of the pool fully clothed. Traditions such as this survive along with others – female teachers are called Ma, bun break at mid-morning and tea in the afternoon. The blue cords of yesteryear have stood the test of time – for boys, shorts in summer, longs in winter plus polo shirt and jumper; for girls, a kilt and bright yellow shirt, summer plaid dresses.

The Dragon is large (800+ including pre-prep, a mile or so up the road). Boys outnumber girls still. Some grumbles about middle of the road children lost in the masses and unable to find a niche if not sporty or musical. School says that the children are separated into smaller units so that they operate within age-related spheres at any one time without being overwhelmed. Good pastoral care – children are discussed weekly and communication is paramount. The school takes its privileges with responsibility and is committed to raising money for charity through entrepreneurship which starts with the concept of the 'little society' and the teaching of philanthropy to children, and extends to ventures such as the locally renowned Dragon sale which raises tens of thousands of pounds. School is lead sponsor of a new multi-academy trust which includes three Blackbird Leys' primary schools. The primaries can use the school's science, art, music and sporting facilities, while Dragon teaching staff are developing initiatives within the new academies. The Café Dragón brand of ethically-sourced coffee is sold at school events.

Boarding houses, separated by sex and age, run by married couples with a homely atmosphere and individuality. Bun breaks and tea in the houses with supper in the dining hall. Children can pop in and out of their house during the day. Day pupils often invited back. Full boarding means that the boarders are 'the heartbeat of the school'. Weekends are packed with activities and many day pupils opt to board – one boarder walked from his boarding house past his family home every day. Day pupils easily fielded until 6pm, playing with boarders or participating in the huge number of extracurricular activities.

It was once established for dons, but they have largely been priced out of the market (in line with many independent schools). Lots of London money and business parents buying up north Oxford but professions also in evidence – many medics, lawyers, as well as a few academics (wealthy ones or few children). Lots of Old Dragon children. The Dragon remains the choice for the social elite of Oxford – if you want to be invited to the smartest dinner parties, this is your school. School says there is still plenty of mix and parents agree that everyone can find their level and this is not necessarily a school full of nannies in the playground. Boarders local and international, with no particular country in predominance. Around 30 pupils have EAL lessons.

The Dragon is still the prep school in Oxford, in sound heart as ever, chosen by parents for breadth of education, good old-fashioned freedom and encouraging a 'can do' attitude. Lifelong friends and contacts start here.

Dulwich Prep Cranbrook

Coursehorn, Cranbrook, Kent TN17 3NP

Ages 3–13 **Pupils** 510 **Boarders** 100 flexi (from 9 years)

Fees: Day £5,970 – £18,390 pa; Boarding £28 – £42 per night

01580 712179
www.dulwichprepcranbrook.org

Headmaster: Since 2010, Paul David (50s) with a BEd in maths and PE from St Luke's, University of Exeter (he grew up in Cornwall). He taught at the City of London Freemen's School in Surrey, where he was housemaster, prior to becoming deputy head of St Paul's Juniors. He also taught maths at St Paul's. He was appointed headmaster of Eaton Square School in 2002. We meet in his comfortable panelled office in The Manor and find him to be very well turned out and easy to talk to but are most impressed with his ease with the younger children.

He is a keen sportsman, and whilst his rugby playing days are behind him, he's now a keen skier and tennis player. He is married to Nicky, a prep school teacher, and they have two children. Parents describe him as an excellent leader, appreciating his dedication: 'he's very visible – gets involved with school life – playing in charity hockey matches, school panto, coffee mornings, and I think I've even seen him playing the trumpet...' Yes indeed, Mr David is a trumpet player.

Perhaps his biggest challenge is the changing nature of exits with pre-testing and more 11+ leavers (especially to the now 11+ Cranbrook School). Mr David sees this as an opportunity and is already planning to introduce the Dulwich Diploma to augment common entrance and scholarship preparation. The school's shape may change ultimately so that it will have a 'slimmer top and fatter middle'.

Entrance: Unconditional offers for children joining nursery to year 2. Main entry points 4+ and 7+. Not oversubscribed. In years 3 to 8, children sit an assessment and spend a day at school. Most live within 15 miles but families come from all over the Weald of Kent and as far away as Maidstone and Ashford.

Exit: Around a quarter of pupils exit at 11+, but this will inevitably rise now that local state grammar Cranbrook School has a year 7, and 11+ entrance is on the rise everywhere. A couple to Sevenoaks most years, a handful to Sutton Valence and Tonbridge and others to a wide spread across Kent and Sussex: Benenden, Bethany, King's Canterbury, Eastbourne College, Roedean and others of the Kent grammars. A high number of scholarships usually, often with top academic scholarships to Tonbridge and Benenden.

Remarks: Nash House is for 3 to 5 year olds, Little Stream for those aged 5 to 9 years and the Upper School for pupils in their final years of the school.

The only aspect of the school which did not garner 'excellent' from the latest ISI report was the teaching, graded as 'good', much to Mr David's disappointment, but he has wasted no time making the minor adjustments needed to the staff room and points to the scholarships indicating that 'it's clear there is differentiation and stretching going on'. One father felt: 'Maths has a reputation amongst some parents for being less strong, particularly at the lower end.' Otherwise, we hear nothing but praise. One long-standing parent told us: 'The quality of teaching has been excellent across the curriculum and in many areas exceptional.' Recent migrators say: 'outstanding' and 'the standard is high'.

Nineteen teachers have been at the school for longer than 10 years. Standard curriculum. Latin commences in year 6 and is led by a passionate recent recruit. French is taught from Little Stream with Spanish added in years 7 and 8. Late joiners may play catch up with languages not encountered before. Personal tutors monitor progress of children in years 7 and 8 as well as acting as mentors.

IT is well integrated within the school. Each pupil in years 7 and 8 has personal ownership of an iPad which has just become part of their pencil case – the head describes a textiles project in which students used their iPads to record from start to finish with time-lapse photography. The library is large with a full-time librarian and boasts some 7,000 titles.

Plenty of dressing up days in Little Stream and Nash House: on Egyptian day they mummified a member of staff. As well as form teachers, subject specialists for maths and science. Very ordered, bright and inviting classrooms with tortoises in the science room. Children seem smiley and chatty and teachers are thrilled with the building they had input into designing. Plenty of individual attention. A mother having observed her children learning through play in the initial years: 'It is obvious great care has been given by the teaching staff to establish a curriculum which suits the children both academically and emotionally.'

This is a school which places an emphasis on 'oracy' – standing up and speaking well is all part of the school's effort in developing socially confident individuals. Several parents credit their children's flourishing independence to the school. Some testing lower down the school, then more of an emphasis on twice yearly exams from year 5 – the children we met about to sit them said they were used to testing and it was no big deal.

'The kids at Dulwich are so fit,' enthused a parent and the first thing one notices about the school are the extensive, manicured acres. Every child plays sport and everyone in year 3 and above plays in a match against other schools. From year 4 children must be available to play in Saturday matches. A mother whose daughter is a talented sportswoman said: 'the opportunity given to her to excel at any of the sports really is hugely impressive.' There are also Tribe (house) fixtures for each age group. Girls play netball, hockey, lacrosse, rounders and tennis, also taking part in cross-country, track and field events, triathlon and swimming. Boys take part in these too and play football, rugby, hockey and cricket. The pool is outdoor and the children tell us it's warm, but we witnessed boys clutching towels and shivering. There are additional options such as badminton and orienteering for the non-rugby devotees.

A parent said, 'Sports coaching, particularly for those not in the first team, needs to be improved', but Mr David seems particularly hot on inclusivity and says that every child in years 5, 6, 7 and 8 plays a match, they do 'bottom up' house sports tournaments and the specialist coaches and gap students are shared around teams of all abilities. As if anticipating our question, the school plans to start a girls' cricket tournament and aims to find more matches across the board. The school has hosted IAPS and national cross-country competitions, the under-13 lacrosse team were the only one from a prep school to reach the last 16 of the national championships and the schools boasts handy table tennis players too.

Sixty per cent take instrumental lessons.Taster music lessons are available to children in year 3 on a wide range of instruments from the kinderhorn to the ukulele. Some attend the Junior Royal College of Music on Saturdays. Children play at regional festivals such as the Hastings Music Festival and musical ensembles have toured Prague and Italy. The Tribe music competition, performed in front of the whole school is a highlight: last year pupils chose to perform One Direction songs. There is a string orchestra in Little Stream and a senior orchestra, percussion groups, woodwind ensemble, Stringcredibles, jazz band and choirs.

Drama is timetabled. Each year group performs annually, whether straight plays or musicals such as Grease or The Sound of Music. Performances, musical and dramatic, are spectacular according to parents who if they appear windswept it's because they all report being so frequently 'blown away'.

We're pretty sure that every school we now visit will have its art compared to the benchmark of Dulwich Prep Cranbrook: truly stunning from the earliest beginnings in Little Stream to the beautiful scholarship work that to our eyes easily compared to GCSE projects elsewhere. Leavers were working on a sculpture project making a flock of porcelain Matisse inspired doves (there are two kilns) holding bundles. The head of art conceives of new projects every year, so year 4 does not always do X and year 5 Y but says much is child-led.

There are trips relating to every subject, ranging from visiting Lullingstone Roman villa, to trips to the West End for drama and a residential geography trip to Felixstowe. In Nash House all classrooms have an outdoor learning area (under a retractable roof) leading onto the playground. Little Stream enjoy forest school activities and from year 5 start there camping in the grounds progressing to a full week in Snowdonia by year 8. Teachers with a passion run clubs, most included in the fees. New this year is on-trend coding and Mandarin. Clubs that caught our eye: rock club, mah-jong club, water polo and DT jewellery.

An hour from London by train, rather more by car, the school resides in 50 beautiful acres of Kent countryside. The school has a charming history – Dulwich Prep London (DPL) evacuated its 300 boys by train to Cranbrook at the start of World War II, setting up in huts in the headmaster's orchard, and after the war remained as a separate school. The two schools are still linked and are run by The Dulwich Preparatory Schools Trust. It became fully co-educational in 1975.

The school buildings are so nondescript we barely noticed them. However, the pre-prep resides in a stylish new-build, with the same architect as DPL – a wooden exterior, fabulous in and out spaces and a large soft surface playground. Classrooms are vast by metropolitan standards and every inch looks fun. Little Stream also has use of a heated swimming pool.

Parents praised the pastoral care as 'excellent', 'impressive' and 'thoughtful' and there has been a move towards developing the softer, pastoral side. The head places an emphasis on nurturing self–confidence but says 'you don't need to be "robust" to do well here'. All new children have buddies. The Head attends all of the pastoral meetings and says he's never before worked with 'staff who are so attuned to children'. Everyone is delighted with the recent partnership with Place2Be for one-to-one counselling and group sessions.

In addition, the school provides learning support for approximately 170 pupils. As well as dyslexia and dyspraxia a wide range of other needs such as maths, sensory processing, or speech and language difficulties; hearing or visual impairment and complex medical conditions are also catered for. SEN provision in small groups and occasionally one-to-one. Some withdrawal, some in class. All learning support is included, not always the case elsewhere.

New extended day care options – a choice of breakfast and after-school clubs. Day boarding is available until 8.00 pm for year 5 and above and year 4 siblings: includes tea, supervised prep and an activity. Then there is flexi-boarding from one night to full weekly boarding. The girls' boarding house is The Manor with beams aplenty, fresh new carpet in the common room, flags and fairy lights in the lovely high-ceilinged bedrooms and standard issue pine bunk beds. Everything very ship shape. The boys' boarding is housed at Lodge, a modern building set in the grounds. Recently refurbished with a red, white and blue theme. Dorms of six sleep in year groups and all bring their teddies. Lobby full of tennis racquets and cricket bats, overflowing bike shed, boarders' fire pit.

British, no overseas pupils. No EAL. One mother: 'It is a real mix from the creative industries, doctors, finance, and farming.' 'Not all bankers, lots of business owners,' said another. Lots of events, a real community, friendly to newcomers. 'There's a real sense of goodwill and warmth,' said a new mother. One parent concluded: 'it definitely feels like great value for money'.

Eagle House School

Linked with Wellington College

Sandhurst, Berkshire GU47 8PH

Ages 3–13 **Pupils** 388 **Boarders** 10 full, 40 weekly, 50 flexi (from year 3) **C of E**

Fees: Day £11,580 – £18,105; Boarding £24,330 pa

01344 772134
www.eaglehouseschool.com

Headmaster: Since 2006, Andrew Barnard BA (50s). Educated at Christ's Hospital and Sheffield University (archaeology). Joined Eagle House to teach English and history, becoming head of history before moving to Heath Mount School as housemaster and head of English, followed by deputy headship at Winchester House, then back to Eagle House as head. Ably assisted by wife Sarah who fulfils hands on role as trad headmaster's spouse as well as teaching French and EAL. Their three adult children are all Old Wellingtonians and two have followed their parents into the teaching profession.

Relaxed, warm and highly personable; on the door every morning and visibly thrives on the hustle and bustle of a busy prep. Throws himself into the daily fray whether teaching history or playing an ugly sister in the annual staff panto. Has collected strength and depth around him during the course of his tenure with an outstanding staff that parents describe as 'seasoned, but not too seasoned'. Keen to keep school's independent identity and protect position as feeder to many schools, whilst acknowledging the obvious benefits of close relationship with Wellington College. Leads a 'welcoming community' where 'those who opt in, thrive'. School holidays see him heading to his home in France: 'we've been doing it up for twenty years – it's the most therapeutic thing'.

Entrance: Pre-prep: trial day and usually automatic progression to prep. Prep: trial day, copies of reports and a reference from current head. Prep relatively non-selective but pupils 'expected to be able to cope with the school's academic course'. New class added in year 5. Year 7 entrants are tested in English, maths and reasoning.

Exit: Average of nearly 60 per cent to Wellington College over recent years, making it the top feeder by some way. Head assures us that entry requirements are the same as for other preps but 'good discussions' take place when considering applicants and assessment day 'feels like a home match'. Solid numbers (some 10 per cent) to Bradfield College, around six per cent to Lord Wandsworth College (a handful each year at 11+), plus ones and twos to Canford, Charterhouse, Marlborough, Eton, Radley, RGS Guildford, Sherborne, St Edward's Oxford, Luckley House, Downe House, St Mary's Ascot and St George's Ascot.

Remarks: Nestled in woodland between Crowthorne and Sandhurst, school was founded in Hammersmith in 1820 and has been on current site since 1886. Owned by neighbouring Wellington College yet manages to avoid a corporate feel and – for now at least – successfully hangs onto its own identity. Around the main mock-Tudor school house, with its panelled entrance hall (complete with roaring fire on the day of our wintry visit, and setting for school's 'legendary' match teas), sit a number of additions. These vary in architectural style from ultra-modern (the Golden Eagle Centre, housing the drama studio and enviable sports hall, and the design lab with its robots, laser cutters and 3D printers) to tired portakabins (music centre and pool) – although head assures us that the end of these is in sight with plans afoot for a new music centre. Stunning modern library. We loved the maths classroom with writeable-on walls and swanky new science labs with their space age work stations. A stroll past the pretty memorial garden leading to the quaint chapel with its stained-glass windows (see if you can guess which one was designed by a pupil) reminded us that despite all these whistles and bells we were still at a traditional prep school – albeit one that is not just moving with the times but ahead of them.

E

Delightful pre-prep department with outdoor spaces mirroring the classrooms within. Child led teaching in the early years (recent question 'how do you ride a unicorn?' answered beautifully with the help of hobby horses): 'it's not the same old ideas coming out of the cupboard every year,' smiled one staff member, 'it keeps us fresh'. Amen to that. From nursery, children take turns to prepare snacks for the rest of the class and join school lunch in the (recently refurbished) main dining room. Pencil skills taught one-to-one and phonics and maths in small groups from reception – and what 5 year old wouldn't want to start penning their first novel in the enchanting indoor 'writing den', draped in toile and festooned with fairy lights? Years 1 to 4 mainly class taught (class size max 20) and follow International Primary Curriculum, which 'finds common ground between rigour and enjoyment' and means subjects, other than English and maths, are taught thematically around topics such as chocolate or fashion ('brilliant,' say parents). Each topic has a 'wow' entry point (think chocolate workshop) and 'knowledge harvest' at the start to engage pupils and set the direction of learning. The 'exit point' often sees pupils' work showcased to parents.

Pupils follow traditional academic model from year 5, with reasoning for the ISEB pre-test covered in English and maths, and all lessons an hour long (although 'it can be a bit hard to concentrate that long', admitted pupils). First school we've ever visited where pupils decreed Latin their 'most fun' subject; 'science experiments in the dark' a close second. School stopped following CE curriculum for humanities in 2017, enabling it to deliver greater breadth. Momentum in these subjects kept right up to the end of the summer term in year 8 with pupil-led cross curricular projects covering subjects from Nelson Mandela to Mexico. From 2020 school will no longer follow CE curriculum at all and its year 8 pupils will not have to take the examinations regardless of which senior school they are moving to. 'Data tracking and monitoring is so much more helpful than CE exams', says head. Where they lead, others will (we hope) follow.

Inviting 'extra learning' classroom is the hub for two full-time SEN staff who work with pupils with mild to moderate SpLD, in a combination of one-to-one and group work. Six hours a week spent in pre-prep supporting eg development of fine motor and social skills. One full time EAL teacher.

Compulsory Saturday school now on alternate weeks, comprising two academic lessons followed by Golden Eagle activities which focus on either service in the community or teamwork and leadership; head 'very proud' of service ethos – an excellent example of school's 'joined up thinking with Wellington'. We asked pupils of which of the holy prep school trinity – drama, music and sport – they were most proud. Drama was the hands down winner: 'amazing' they chorused; 'it's the really cool thing to do here'. Inspirational head of drama 'really pushes us,' they told us. Parents say he doesn't mince his words and 'gives them a really hard time' when drawing the very best performance out of his cast members (the maestro himself told us 'we're not really trying to do a school show – it's got to be better than that – it's more about youth theatre'). Such pursuit of excellence draws auditionees in droves, with 150 pupils across the school signing up to audition for a recent production of Joseph – 55 of them gunning for main parts. Up to three productions in rehearsal at any one time, plus an annual trip to perform at the Edinburgh Fringe. LAMDA taught by Wellington's drama coach. Music also shines and is on curriculum to year 8. Ninety pupils are part of senior choir, and with a thrilling repertoire including rock, pop, gospel and world music – as well as international tours, most recently to Holland – we're not surprised. Some 85 per cent of cohort take peripatetic music lessons and showcase their talents at local care homes as part of the Golden Eagle programme as well as informal lunch time concerts and larger termly performances.

Sport every day. Boys play half a term each of football and rugby (some said they would prefer a greater focus on one or the other), followed by hockey after Christmas and cricket in the summer term. For girls it's netball, hockey and now cricket rather than rounders as main summer sport (cue delighted cheers). School all for mixed gender teams and predicts there will be female players in the first cricket team within two years. Watch this space. Some matches played on Wellington's pitches and everyone participates. Is it important to win? we asked. Surprisingly, the reply was 'not really – we just like to enjoy it'. Some parents grumbled that the sporting ethos could be more competitive but school takes pride in its inclusive ethos and concurs that enjoyment is the number one factor. Despite this, trophy cabinets are far from empty and 'school hits nationals most years in one sport or another'. Specialist sports teaching from reception and timetable has now been rejigged to ensure that top coaches, including a pro London Irish rugby coach, train all pupils, not just the elite. Biennial sports tours – netball and cricket to Antigua, hockey to Holland and football in the UK. Thirty sports on co-curricular list, from fencing or karate to laser clay pigeon shooting and roller skating. Huge extracurricular programme takes place at lunch times and after school with around 60 activities on offer every week and pupils in year 6 and below expected to participate in one a day. If it all gets a bit much, those seeking quiet time can retreat to the library for 'colour, chat and chill' time during the lunch break. Pupils love the activities fair that takes place at the beginning of every term.

Flexible boarding model can accommodate up to 70 pupils from year 3 from two to five nights a week in lovely spacious dorms. Girls' dorms, of course, are adorned with personal effects and boys' rather bare; gender stereotypes are hard at work with pink and blue everything respectively. Gorgeous newly renovated common room with cushy sofas makes a cosy hub for evening down time and boarding parents are 'brilliant', say parents who love the weekly boarding newsletters that keep them informed of their children's activities.

Learning for Life programme (PSHE) covers all matters pastoral, including SRE, well-being, mindfulness, feelings and emotions. 'We make it relevant the whole time', says head, 'pupils know that people here have their backs'. Pupils who had experienced significant family events told us openly and with staggering maturity how supportive school had been in supporting them through difficulties. Many schools say they're like a family but Eagle House palpably feels like one; a recent year 7 joiner told us 'he'd never felt more welcome anywhere'. Whether your sights are set on increasing the odds of a place at Wellington several years hence or you're keeping your options wide open your child can't fail to enjoy his or her journey through this progressive, kind and buzzy school, described by one parent as 'a beating heart that just doesn't stop'. Sounds like win win to us.

Eastbourne College

Old Wish Road, Eastbourne, East Sussex BN21 4JX

Ages 13–18 **Pupils** 630 **Sixth form** 280 **Boarders** 287 full **C of E**

Fees: Day £23,130 – £23,505; Boarding £35,250 – £35,655 pa

01323 452323
www.eastbourne-college.co.uk

Head: Since 2016, Tom Lawson (PPE Oxford), married to Jessica with two children and adored Boxer dog Roy. Previously deputy head at Christ's Hospital, and a 16 year stint at Winchester.

At Eastbourne College (EC), the head has found his fit. He looks back wistfully to a time when public school was about becoming a balanced human being, not hitting the top of the league tables; his primary aim for pupils: to be good people other people want to be with – 'they come out really nice'...

Loved by pupils, who smile when they think of their head: 'great guy – decent sense of humour'; 'modern – bringing EC into the 21st century'; 'really nice...witty...makes an effort to know us all'. Tells great stories in assembly, which always start, 'So there I was...'

Parents like him too: 'really approachable... very jolly'; 'highly intelligent...great business acumen...'; 'will look at each child...understand that kids can have a bad day'.

Academic matters: Pupils head down in quiet concentration. Is it always like this? In maths, mostly, but not when it doesn't need to be. Not in English, said our guide, people talk non stop in English. And in economics – which the head teaches.

A largely traditional subject offering, including classical civilisation, Greek and Latin, but politics have made it onto the curriculum and the school is open to offering other subjects where there's demand. Desire to study non-curricular languages is accommodated wherever possible.

EPQ or the Gold Arts Award available to supplement A levels. The head is also introducing an online passport, to ensure pupils are on track for life, to include skills from cooking, driving and finance to team work, charity and resilience. By the time they come to fill out UCAS, these pupils will be ready, as will macaroni cheese and a balanced bank account.

An excellent level of high end results at this lightly selective school: A level 38 per cent A*/A in 2018; at GCSE, 69 per cent A*-A/9-7; science and maths are particular strengths. The head is keen to increase academic results, but says he will do this with better teaching and learning, not by becoming more selective. '[They] work twice as hard because it's not selective', said a parent, who added that this comment could apply equally to teachers and pupils.

One parent said her above average son thrives at the EC 'because of the nurturing approach, and their kind, gentle way of getting results'. Another described the teaching as 'on the whole good', others commenting on the 'spectacular teachers', in particular in science and music. There is the odd bit of home tutoring here and there, but extra sessions are also provided at school.

Two reports a term, achievement and effort grades; tutors go through reports with pupils, who add their comments and targets, before the report is posted online for parents. Feedback in report cards is very helpful, said a parent; '[they're] on top of it all the way'.

Saturday morning school, lessons from 8.40-12, is seen as part of the boarding ethos by pupils and parents (one commented that otherwise their children would have to 'fill in time'), although those with sporting commitments like it less.

Learning support help with a broad range of conditions, but not at the severe end of the spectrum. Out of class, one-to-one assistance, charged as extra. Parents are very happy with support, one saying the head of learning support is 'approachable, helpful and great at communication'; another that her dyslexic son has had 'phenomenal results'. All year groups scanned.

A head of futures has just started, and sixth formers are delighted: one told us careers advice used to be 'nothing much', but now they have someone to help with university, careers, and skills; 'very good news', said a parent. There's no point going to an event if you can't go up to someone, shake hands and introduce yourself, says the head of futures, fresh from a lesson on communication skills and year 9 pain at having to stand before their classmates and say their name and what they love doing.

Games, options, the arts: There's space every afternoon for co-curricular activities (although we have never seen detention listed as such before): games, service or creatives.

'It's a very sporty school', said a parent, and they play everything, the girls excelling in tennis and hockey, the boys at rugby, which is the major boys' sport here (football is classed as one of the many 'other options'). 'Hockey is excellent', said a parent, whose son plays for England, and says the school is very flexible about time away training, and helping him catch up with work afterwards. A girls' cricket team is just starting up, and the school will accommodate any girls who want to play football. The school is very proud that 93 per cent of pupils represented the school in teams last year, believing that team play is one of the best things about sport. The aquathalon (swimming in the sea, then running along the prom) was only cancelled because of stormy seas...but the whole school was steeplechasing across the downs....

The school has just completed £33m worth of works – Project 150 (that's how many years they've been here); they have 'enhanced how [my daughters] feel about [school]', said a parent. It's top class stuff – not just a big swimming pool, but one with Olympic training pads at the end of each lane; the ballet studio even has a raised roof for those high leaps across the centre. Dry changing rooms and wet; everything a sporty person could desire. DofE too, with the highest rate of gold awards in Sussex.

Service starts in year 10 with CCF for all; not all are keen, but school is enthusiastic about the opportunities for challenge and teamwork. Some continue with CCF, while other year 11s learn the skills to go out into the community. By year 12 and 13, pupils are volunteering in charity shops, schools and old people's homes.

The creatives option ranges includes all things musical and artistic, from the Gold Arts Award (an arts alternative to the EPQ) to singing with the Decibelles or Testostertones.

Parents comment on the 'amazing art and music depts', with a 'standard of professionalism [that is] wonderful'. Art exam work is displayed in the Birley Centre and is of a very high standard – pupils regularly obtain top grades here. The art department is rich with works of the imagination, and lively with challenge, a teacher describing with enthusiasm the reward of life drawing without looking at the paper.

We loved the innovative work in textiles, projects showing the meticulous care taken by pupils, one considering a 'communion of threads'; we particularly liked the map dress, cut to a figure and a landscape.

A parent described the musical talent at EC as 'unbelievable'. There aren't any foreign music tours (unlike sports and arts), but plenty of domestic performances, and 'standards are incredible...' at school open concerts, say parents. There's a lively drama department, with productions ranging from Peter Pan to Chorus Line, and a small group performing at the Edinburgh fringe.

Boarding: Around 45 per cent of pupils here board, with three boys' and two girls' boarding houses. They cross the age range and pupils form small families who look out for each other; it works really well. International boarders come from a range of countries, and make up 15-20 per cent of the boarding community.

Parents describe strong teams in the houses, from matrons, who 'really look after them', to 'the housemistress [who] couldn't have done more to help my daughter settle', said a parent, admitting it was hard, but saying they give plenty of individual attention, and the housemistress was 'amazing – dealt with issues before they became issues'. Another described her son's housemaster as 'absolutely brilliant...slightly disorganised...it's quite endearing... he needs a nap now and then'. Her weekly boarding son has learnt to be very organised, but there are prompts – 'they don't expect complete self sufficiency', said the parent.

Spacious, colourful common rooms, with a constant supply of fruit, and kitchen for toast and drinks. Own ensuite room from year 11, spacious shared study bedrooms in year 9 and 10; no choice over room mates – pupils don't seem to mind. 'If girls don't get on, they will be thrown in together; they will press on through difficulties by getting to know each other', said a parent. 'They don't shy away from problems'.

'Flexibility makes it what it is', said one parent. Boarding can be full or weekly and there's odd nights in for day pupils in Arnold Lodge; they really cater for all, with some obligatory community weekends in ('a good thing' said a parent).

Matches on Saturday afternoons, and trips on Sunday – Thorpe Park, Harry Potter World and the like.

Saturday nights on the town for upper sixth until 10.30pm. A two drink limit, supposedly, but sensibly enforced – 'providing you're not wobbling or vomiting, no one's going to breathalyse you', said a sixth former; they appreciate being treated as responsible human beings, and behave accordingly.

Background and atmosphere: The thing about Eastbourne, said a parent, is that it's actually 'not that far'. It feels like a peaceful backwater, but is only an hour and half away from London, a seaside town with its broad streets and bracing air. EC was described by a parent as having 'a public school, traditional feeling'; there are old flint buildings that fit this description nicely, but it is an indisputably modern school, with new classrooms and sports facilities to prove it.

One parent chose EC because of its intimate size; 'it feels like a close family. Everyone knows each other'. The head describes a 'confident, calm community' where there is space for fun, and this seemed almost exactly right. There's chatter, but no rowdiness (though year 10 can be a bit wild, say sixth formers...'that was a good year', said a year 11 nostalgically). There is a feeling of competence and organisation; pupils who know where they're going and what they're doing. 'Both girls feel quite special being there...If it wasn't warm, relaxed and efficient, they wouldn't cope with the long days...' said a parent.

The pupils we met were friendly and unassuming; not much arrogance here, and it's difficult to imagine these modest pupils bragging about their achievements (might need to practise a bit of this before those university interviews...)

The school is part of the Eastbourne Schools Partnership, which involves local schools getting together to benefit all, activities ranging from digital workshops to community orchestras, and Roy's homework club, where EC sixth formers – and the head's dog – tutor struggling GCSE pupils from partner schools, with both tutor and tutee benefiting hugely.

House feeling is strong; houses are homes in a school with a boarding atmosphere, even for day pupils, and pupils go back to their houses during break times or free lessons. We saw a fantastic boys' day house, with table football, pool, and ping pong, and thought the girls might like some of this in their houses too...the boys even had an Astro with floodlighting in the back garden for football. Apparently the girls do come over sometimes, and use it for hockey...

An active school council make members' voices heard: complaints about too long lunch queues have lead to staggered intake, and girls requested and voted for trousers, now part of the uniform.

'What's your favourite colour?' asked the head, and the ceiling of the smart new dining hall glowed red in response. The food consumed in it has 'massively improved', said a parent, and we hear fine things of breakfast – 'best meal of the day'. There's a cafe, which can be used by sixth formers during free lessons, bringing something of a university feel for the upper years.

Pastoral care, well-being and discipline: 'Brilliant pastoral care', said parent, 'tutors will call just to say how things are going', another parent telling us the school identified and told her about a problem with her daughter before she knew anything was wrong; this seems typical of this vigilant and proactive school.

Care begins in the houses, and parents report close relationships with house mistresses/masters, one describing a housemistress as 'very caring, very prompt in all queries, seeks opinion if unsettled. Really on top of things. Keeps things in proportion'. House structure can vary a bit, said one parent, whose son's current head of house is '... caring, but doesn't command respect'.

The non-hierarchical house structure promotes friends through the year groups, and this helps prevent bullying, say parents. 'Really like a family – what you want when you hand children over to an institution – [that they] have child's interests at heart'. One described a bullying incident – 'ragging'- dealt with thoroughly through the house system, and says small issues are efficiently dealt with this way.

Certainly a school for second chances, agree head and pupils, a parent commenting that, 'the school really makes the effort...' to involve them in education about mental health for teens, and is 'very open about drink and drugs': drug users will have to submit to a testing regime, sellers will be out. 'It's more what goes on at home that is the problem', says the head, who tells parents they have to develop a 'digital spine'. What happens out of school certainly counts, whether in uniform or not.

Pupils and parents: Mostly local middle class professionals and quite a few old boys; 'down to earth parents', said one. 'Everyone welcome', said another, describing a parent community which is – 'as strong as you want it to be'. An ex-state school parent said he 'sometimes feels like the hick cousin', but that his children have not felt this at all and settled easily.

Parents and pupils agree that it would suit a wide variety of children, and, said a parent, 'would sort out disruptive kids'. Lots of siblings at this family school. One parent chose because she wanted mixed sex, mixed ability for her non-alpha oldest son, but has also found it right for her highly self sufficient second son too.

Very efficient school buses, 'so many routes...bend over backwards to help.'

Entrance: Lightly selective. Pupils from the allied St Andrew's Prep, with whom EC is working on a bridging curriculum for years 7-9, and other prep and state schools. EC now accepts pupils on the basis of school report, CAT scores and reference in year 6, the head seeing no point in the CE, or putting year 6 pupils through the stress of a test.

Exit: Around 20 per cent leave after GCSE. At 18, most go to Russell Group universities, Exeter and Bristol particularly popular. Four to Oxbridge in 2018 and one medic.

Money matters: Scholarships from 5-20 per cent of fees. Means-tested bursaries of up to 60 per cent.

Remarks: This is a friendly, down to earth school which, as a parent said, 'thinks...about the whole person...the roundedness of the individual...' Hard workers will thrive here, and relish the great opportunities available.

Edgbarrow School

Grant Road, Crowthorne, Berkshire RG45 7HZ

Ages 11–18 **Pupils** 1,414 **Sixth form** 332

01344 772658
www.edgbarrowschool.co.uk

Headteacher: Since September 2018, Stuart Matthews, who joined the school in 2012 as deputy head. He has also been assistant head at St Crispin's School, where he spent 12 years. Studied international economics at Loughborough and has a PGCE in economics and business from Warwick. Still passionate about teaching and takes two year 13 economics groups. Big sports, and particular Spurs, fan, mostly from the armchair.

Academic matters: Plenty of top teachers (staff to pupil ratio is around one to 16, average class size of 21) to ensure that those capable of it get the grades. Impressive A level results with 37 per cent of grades at A*-A and 58 per cent A*-B in 2018. GCSEs also very respectable with 31 per cent of all grades at 9-7, and impressive 83 per cent of pupils achieving 9-4 in both English and maths.

Pupils put in an intensive day to get there, with four one-hour lessons every morning – worth it for easier afternoons, reckoned pupils, just one lesson taking place after late lunch that starts at 1.30pm. 'Friends ask if we get hungry, but you get used to it,' said year 8 tour guide, who praised well-ordered lessons, manageable homework and sensible deadlines.

No subject laggards, with languages, geography and history all extolled, while maths, biggest subject at A level, is 'pushed', thought one parent – though in good way. 'Gave my child some extra lessons to bring her up (before GCSEs) and is now storming on.' RE, however, gets the most praise, with colourful lessons (discussion about avatars well under way on day of visit), enticing display cabinet stuffed with crucifixes and figures of Buddha and Durga and provocative quotes on walls '...of all the things which have been permitted, divorce is the most hated by Allah...'

Setting starts early, three weeks into year 7 for science, maths, English and languages ('lets you get to know your form first,' said year 8 pupil) but will take individual aspirations into account – optional Latin taught by Wellington College staff member (several send own children here) and we heard of one budding scientist with borderline grades given lots of support so could take triple rather than dual science at GCSE.

Much praise for attention to detail – pace noticeably quicker in top groups but, said one pupil, 'priority is to make sure we understand.' Out of lesson meetings encouraged if pupil needs help, rapid response to parent queries. 'Sometimes disagree with comments on homework reports. Teacher will email straight back to arrange meeting,' said father.

One parent wondered if chilled-out coasters sometimes get away with it, citing bright child guaranteed Cs and not particularly inclined to push for greater grade glory. School points (literally) to pinboards lining wall-and-a-bit in office, filled with postcard-sized pictures and predicted grades of all year 11 pupils, who also get a copy. Goal is to move as many could-do-betters as possible along wall till hit five 9-4s with English and maths or better section. Not all will manage it, but won't be for want of trying.

For the 80 plus SEN pupils (100 have EAL) there's progress department which caters for moderate learning needs including SpLD, BESD and language and communications difficulties. May be withdrawn from languages (bottom sets in any case will often take one rather than two), instead receiving literacy, numeracy or social support. School praised for speed in picking up undiagnosed needs and fighting for support, thought parent, even to extent of matching child and key SEN staff member. 'If don't feel the connection, will find you someone else.'

Games, options, the arts: Talented well catered for (several subject teachers are qualified coaches/referees), kind but determined staff also determined to ensure that those whose natural roosting spot is spectator side of the touchline don't miss out either. 'Daughter doesn't like games but is never left alone or pushed aside,' thought one mother. Masses to do after school, too, from trampolining to badminton.

Parents aware of living in shadow of Wellington College where 'if you're good, get into England and under 18s squads,' said one; staff welcome collaboration – both schools are part of local trust which funds deserving students – but clear that 'we're not in competition.' Mild – very mild – grumbles aside (one over academic support being timetabled during PE – now changed; other relating to difficulties for working parents with 4.00pm match timing), contentment is again the norm.

Similarly the case with music. Helps if brass is your thing, with touring swing band a star attraction, though numbers are currently down and cooler guitars attract more interest. 'Would be nice if had own group,' thought parent. Once approved by teacher, enthusiasts have open access to practice rooms. 'Incredible and brilliant – if are going to turn into good adults, need to be trusted,' said mother.

Bustling activity programme includes DofE – no limit on numbers (around 55 do bronze, 10 sixth formers working on gold) – language trips to Germany, France and Spain, though proposed US skiing trip for year 8 children cancelled – without fuss – when families told school that was a continent and financial commitment too far.

Background and atmosphere: Huge friendliness of the place is a hallmark. This is a school tangibly operated by real people for the benefit of real students – to extent of putting end-of-term lost property on hangers for easier identification and retrieval (worlds better than slightly sordid looking – and smelling – lucky dip boxes elsewhere). 'Even if reception is busy, they'll welcome you with a smile,' said mother.

Setting, just outside small village of Crowthorne, more unobtrusive than pupil numbers might suggest, many buildings – mostly low rise in compact group – as well as can be expected, all immaculately tidy (staff pick up stray bits of litter, forms take turns to carry out more extensive sweep).

Grounds extend to new, lovingly tended Astroturf (funding provided on condition that, like sports centre, is open to public out of school hours), two large fields – shortly to be drained and relevelled – bordered by woodland. Dog walkers are most frequently spotted wildlife, though deer and red kites have occasional walk/fly on roles (assertive seagulls, automatically reset to British Summer Time, form orderly rooftop queue at lunchtime). Low-key security balances protection and sense of independence. 'School doesn't want us to feel trapped,' said pupil.

Wonders done with limited resources: long, potentially dingy corridor transformed with artwork (picture of girl meditatively demolishing gingerbread man one of many attention grabbers), lines of lockers sprouting clutch of fanciful ceramics.

School's wish list inevitably huge. Attractive sixth form centre with vast atrium area shows what can be done – member of staff there 'conscious of how lucky I am compared with colleagues.' Focus for much study and limited loafing – 'if we see someone who's been sitting around doing nothing for ages, will remind them to get out books.' (They do, too – and it works).

Other top areas singled out by parents include canteen (meals served in hall used also for drama, assembly and exams) where, boon to working parents, can pre-order family evening meal for four (giant pizza a bargain £8), all boxed up ready to come home with child. Few complaints about menu offerings. One parent thought could ease up on the carbs but tour guides quick to explain that even the Slushies (bright blue) 'now made with much healthier ingredients...'

Pastoral care, well-being and discipline: Traditional-sounding sixth form organisation, with head boy and girls, five deputies and six captains for customary sport and performing arts to fundraising and debating. Also a tuck shop manager and two freshers reps. Total of 30 posts – with more to come as create subject ambassadors.

Bullying, virtual and otherwise, not felt to be huge issue – many parents unaware of any problems, those who were praised school's efforts to reduce incidence: running pupil talks, sending regular updates on new, potentially worrying apps. 'I probably get three emails a week,' said father. Families realistic about technology-related difficulties. 'Peer pressure very different from when we were at school – cyber-bullying did spoil child's enjoyment of school,' felt parent. Student support, well known as place to go for the sad or troubled, offers counselling, mentoring and, in one instance, special notebook for 'timid' pupil to record concerns.

Numerous chances to shine, not just academically but through SPEAK awards, which recognise sterling all-round qualities – the A stands for 'Above and beyond'. Correspondingly brisk sanctions policy, with failure to get homework diary signed or being late for lessons (there's latitude for new year 7s) resulting in warnings and detentions, Friday break the one to avoid, said one pupil, as 'teachers have cake and you have to watch them eating it.'

School's excellent online behaviour policy uses pictures and simple language to spell out exactly what each rule means in practice and they're felt to be fair, nothing heavy handed or draconian about application – pupils even respond with occasional touch of humour. 'Get to know your teachers and find out how lenient they are,' features on display of pupils' year 9 survival tips. Eases off in sixth form (no uniform as would require policing and 'they've had bellyful in lower school,' said sympathetic member of staff).

Care over smallest things felt to be exceptionally good. After child had nasty but accidental spill on stairs, family received several calls (unprompted) outlining efforts to check cause. Girls' friendship issues imaginatively tackled – school encouraging self-help, one child ostracised by reigning queen bee enfolded by willing alternative group.

Ethos helps even the shy to flourish – no mean feat for the many swapping from minute primary schools for seven form entry. Some use as opportunity to reinvent themselves. One child, formerly known as 'the shy one', has become dynamic form rep – revelling in chance to ditch preconceptions, courtesy of encouraging tutor. 'Got behind her and really brought her on,' said approving parent.

Pupils and parents: Catchment area that spans mansions to mid-terraces, ladies who lunch to 9 to 5ers, results in varied social mix, seen mostly as desirable melting pot – 'kids count the person more than the money,' thought one mother – though one father reckoned could lead to occasional awkwardness. 'One of child's friends asked me, "Do you always drive old cars?"'

E

Entrance: Via LA (Bracknell); is its most oversubscribed secondary – around 600 apply for 210 year 7 places. Priority for looked after children and those with medical or social needs followed by those in catchment area, siblings and linked primary school. Distances 'calculated using Pythagoras' Theorem,' says LA website, with 'measurement in metres is then multiplied by 0.000621317 to convert this measurement to miles.' Impressive stuff. We're sure parents would settle for nothing less.

Exit: Around a third leave after GCSEs. More careers guidance would be appreciated – though felt to be good support for helping sixth formers prepare for world of work. Two to Cambridge in 2018, plus three medics and a vet; Russell Group is well represented. Southampton, Cardiff, Edinburgh and Surrey popular destinations. Sciences dominate with sprinkling of arts and humanities (history, English) though also plenty of excellent artists coming up through school, many aiming for foundation courses at nearby highly rated Farnborough.

Money matters: Help for those in difficulty felt to be well handed, with all school trip notification letters urging parents to come forward if will struggle with finance. For 16-19s, bursary scheme offers maximum of £1,200 pa. Shame similar option not open to school itself, which has (reluctantly) asked families for optional financial payment of five pounds a month to keep things ticking over. Some parental unhappiness, directed not at school but at government decision to solve sixth form colleges' financial woes by cutting schools' budgets to match, leading to permanent million pound hangover. 'You've got Wellington costing £9,000+ a term yet we've got to pay money to our school just to help it out,' says father.

Remarks: Big school, individual approach, stemming from can do everything, open all hours headship style. 'Your school is successful because it is very well led,' says succinct Ofsted report.

Edge Grove Preparatory School

99

Edge Grove, Aldenham Village, Hertfordshire WD25 8NL

Ages 3–13 **Pupils** 502 **Boarders** 40 flexi and weekly (from 7 years)

Fees: Day £12,660 – £16,935; Boarding +£1,545 – £6,215 pa

01923 855724
www.edgegrove.com

Headmaster: Since 2012, Ben Evans (40s). A Devon lad (mother still breeds Dartmoor ponies there) with a love of all things country. Head boy at Bramdean School before heading to Exeter University to read history and archaeology. Returned, armed with his degree and PGCE, to Bramdean where he 'learned to teach,' before taking up the post of head of history at Brighton College, later returning as deputy head to his alma mater.

Had a 'now or never' moment before hot footing it to Sri Lanka to teach at the junior school of the British School in Colombo, Sri Lanka, where he served a total of six years, the final four as head. Returned to the UK following the birth of his first child and found love at first sight with Edge Grove – 'exactly what I wanted.' Lives in the main house (his living room doubles up as a meet-and-greet office for visitors like us and parents) with wife Alex – 'an absolute gem,' according to parents – and their two young sons, both at the school. A dynamic, likeable and plainspoken couple, they run the school very much as a partnership, albeit with clearly defined roles – his realm being all things educational; hers being the person to say, 'And why exactly are you doing that?' (along with helping the admin team, co-ordinating the uniform shop and PA and organising events eg a recent science conference for year 8s). All this, and she also completed a PhD while in post.

He has made dramatic changes, including scrapping Saturday school, 'upping the ante' on the academic front and growing the school both physically (acquiring an extra 20 acres, adding to their existing 28 acres) and in numbers (from 320 pupils in 2012 to current 500 – 'it stops there,' says head). 'You can see he has everyone pulling in the direction he wants the school to go in – from the top to the bottom of the school, there is a solid consistent message about doing your best, being a risk taker and having fun,' one parent told us. Just what Edge Grove needed after an unsettled patch with a revolving door of head teachers.

When not immersed in running the school and family life, the great outdoors beckons. 'I try to run marathons,' he says; 'and I try to stop him,' laughs Alex.

Entrance: More selective than it was, 'if only because we have more interest in the school and fewer places,' says head. But assessments and parental interview still relatively relaxed by north London standards. School says it would rather take someone with lower IQ who plays an instrument and has parental buy-in than someone very bright with no passion for the school's ethos. Little ones at 3+ and 4+ come for a short session where staff engage them in an activity and observe their skills in, for example, sharing and socialising. Currently oversubscribed for nursery and reception. Occasional entry at 7+ and more at 11+ – an assessment day and verbal/non-verbal reasoning tests before spending a day in class to see how they fit in.

No bursaries in the lower part of the school apart from those offered to military families. Scholarships for existing pupils in years 7 and 8 to 'acknowledge their contribution to the school.'

Exit: Majority of girls leave at 11; others and most boys leave at 13 – although it's a movable feast, depending on the year. Girls to St Albans High School for Girls, Haberdashers' Aske's School for Girls, Abbot's Hill and Downe House, with St Albans Boys, Merchant Taylors' School and Harrow popular for boys; plus both to a range of co-ed schools including Rugby, Haileybury, Uppingham, Berkhamsted and Aldenham. A good handful of scholarships achieved annually, ranging from academic to sport, art and music. Conversations about next schools start with parents in years 5 and 6.

Remarks: When you arrive at this idyllic country prep, it's hard to believe that it's just a stone's throw from north London and less than five minutes from the M25. Set in grassy parkland (even more of it since the school acquired extra land) with the requisite cows grazing next to the drive, Edge Grove – formerly the home of JP Morgan – is a world apart from many of its concrete-clad urban rivals.

Smiling boys and girls (school is now firmly co-ed, though older pupils told us you still get the odd class with less than a handful of girls) in bright red uniforms give an impression of a happy, down to earth and confident cohort. And, really, who wouldn't be smiling with these big skies, beautiful views, open spaces and walled gardens ('we get plenty of freedom to use it all,' say pupils) to greet you every morning? Not to mention the beautifully maintained outdoor swimming pool (lessons are weekly, weather permitting) and well-used forest school, plus separate facilities for science, home economics, art and creative arts for older ones. When head gets his long-awaited small rare breeds farm (they already have chickens), it really will be seventh heaven for outdoorsy types.

Families are a real mix – the predictable 4x4s, some discreet old money and plenty of dual income families who work hard to pay the fees. The latter are particularly grateful for the wrap-around care (breakfast club from 7.45am and activities from 4.30-5.30pm daily, with children also able to stay for prep and supper – 'if you get stuck on the train, it's no problem,' said one). About 20 per cent London based with the rest from around Radlett, St Albans, Elstree, Stanmore, Edgeware and Borehamwood. Ethnically diverse, far more so than the competition: 'wonderful,' say parents. Four minibus services ferry years 3 to 8 to school if they choose.

Head 'aiming for excellence in all subjects,' with parents praising the 'academic rigour while keeping learning interactive and fun.' 'Sometimes, you don't even realise you're learning, especially with forest school,' said one child, incredulous that education 'can be so entertaining.' Plenty of kinaesthetic learning in evidence – not a whiff of chalk and talk when we visited. School day structured with English and maths in the mornings, when the children are most receptive, followed by a superb lunch (literally no complaints – almost unheard of), although dining room's proximity to (stunning) library made for loud background noise for readers when we visited.

French from pre-school and classics from year 5 with setting starting in year 3 for English and maths, then for French and science from year 5. Years 7 and 8 see pupils split into three classes – a scholarship set (scholarship or CE); CE only set; and everyone else. So streaming, then? 'I like to think of it as tailoring,' retorts head, who sees no point in children doing CE for the sake of it. Edge Grove Baccalaureate completed by all year 7s and 8s as part of the school enrichment programme – taught by head. Mandarin, Spanish and Italian offered as after-school clubs for budding linguists. Massive push on digital technology. SEN provision for the milder end and no plans to increase provision. 'I'm dyslexic and get all the help I need, mainly in the classroom,' one girl assured us, while a parent said, 'They put a lot of things in place to help my son, including some extra lessons – they were really good.'

Outstanding art taught in inspirational atelier style space with first class work in genres ranging from ceramics (every pupil was creating a ceramic poppy for remembrance Sunday when we visited) to textiles, on display. Lots of cross-curricular. Home economics also on the curriculum. Classrooms alive with sound of music (we saw year 3s do an enchanting stone age song and dance) and wonderfully decorated practice rooms (over 180 peripatetic lessons each week) with posters on the doors, exclaiming things like 'Rubbish! Sorry! Terrible! Are all words banned in here.' A lucky few get to try their hand in the school rock band or the award-winning junior jazz band. 'And there are three choirs, plus orchestra and ensembles!' one of our guides added, excitedly. Plenty for budding thespians too – every child gets a chance to perform in the modern, airy theatre.

Sport taken seriously, with around 800 fixtures a year and specialist teaching from reception, and coaches with top-notch credentials on board. 'They're getting better at integrating the genders,' said one parent, although one girl told us, 'they still don't do football for girls, which is a shame.' Core sports are hockey, rugby, football and netball – and cricket, swimming, tennis and athletics are also played to high levels, with squads who reach regionals if not nationals. Cross-country, table tennis and archery added to the mix to enable children who don't take to team sports to find their sporting prowess. Basketball increasingly popular. Inter-house matches and tournaments (especially swimming) are considered highlights of the year among pupils and ensure everyone gets a go. 'Shame there's no full-size Astro pitch, but you can't have it all,' said one parent. Clubs galore – many of which are included in fees – from gardening and chess to taekwondo.

Around 40 flexi boarders. On the downside, very little wardrobe space (one wardrobe for seven girls) and no lockers (leads to lots of lost socks), but it's worth it, say pupils and parents, for the nurturing, cheerful environment and brightly decorated dorms which sleep up to 14 pupils, with seniors (years 7 and 8) having their lounging and TV area incorporated into the dorm. There's also a games room in an annexe with snooker, table tennis and table football. Head, determined to avoid 'sleepover culture,' insists that boarders stay for a minimum of three nights a week from year 5, although they can stay for one in years 3 and 4. 'We only live round the corner, so never even thought of boarding, but our child insisted and loves it,' said a parent, echoing others.

Pastorally strong across the board, with head of well-being (qualified life coach) and non-teaching head of pastoral care on staff. Parent workshops on offer, and children have an emotional barometer in their planner. Minimal misbehaviour and bullying because 'we're big on respect,' says head; pupils concur. No school rules for the same reason – 'if you respect the school and others, you shouldn't need rules, although we do have golden moments which are read out in assembly,' he says.

This is a delightful prep with an ethos of discovery and learning through doing – no drilling facts and boring worksheets for these lucky things. Both aspirational and fun, it's a school that enables children to go onto a wide range of first choice schools, without the pressure that's so prevalent in this north London bubble. And the children seem to genuinely appreciate the big skies, lush grounds and round-the-clock activities.

E

Elstree School

Woolhampton, Reading, Berkshire RG7 5TD

Ages Boys 3-13, girls 3-7 **Pupils** 240 **Boarders** 15 full, 95 weekly/flexi C of E

Fees: Day £11,550 – £21,000; Boarding + £1,620 – £6,300 pa

01189 713302
www.elstreeschool.org.uk

Headmaster: Since 2013, Sid Inglis BA (40s), previously headmaster at Ludgrove. Uncertain as to career until taught English in Chile (where met wife Olivia) and realised that as professions go 'there is no finer job.' Appointed at exciting if nerve-wracking time following wobbles in leadership, parent confidence and pupil numbers. It's now all go again, with school at capacity, no need even to contemplate going fully co-ed (girls leave at 7), scholarships back to full honours-board levels – and all right in world.

Mr Inglis's first name is unusual and, even more unusually, shared with last head but two. Would be karma except that real name is Andrew. All the other more predictable essentials are also in place: labrador ('though had her before we arrived,' says equally charming Mrs Inglis), three cherubic offspring (two still at the school) and website must-have – photograph capturing whole shebang smilingly disporting themselves on well-positioned, sunlight-drenched bench if human (and beside it if not).

Would take a mean-spirited reviewer to deny that Mr Inglis exudes winning headmasterly qualities of authority and personability. Out and about like nobody's business. 'Very much a figurehead,' said parent. 'I don't know how he can be in so many different places all the time. He and his wife go around like a pair and are very supportive of one another.'

E

Even slots in weekly story-reading session to different pre-prep class each week (we encountered him en route with book, wondering if would require 'funny voices'). While parent approval can reach adoration levels, pupils' response more down to earth. 'Lets us get on with life as long as we're sensible,' said one. 'Doesn't feel special – acts just like a normal teacher.'

Relaxed, too – when this reviewer turned up at the very last minute for an open day visit, he (and all colleagues) were genuinely welcoming (if there were any less positive feelings, were fathoms deep).

He thinks it's part and parcel of the ethos that made this a dream job. Does a spot of teaching (RS, his degree subject, has yielded to classics here) and loves it. Aim, as laid out in prospectus, is to discover 'how a child is intelligent rather than how intelligent a child is' – while still preparing them for range of senior schools.

Translated, means that 'don't want academic success at the expense of muddy knees,' he says. 'If a child is confident and happy in their own little shell, academics will follow.' School, he says, isn't for chest-beating alpha males, jostling for position (or females, either). Will have a few who struggle academically but exude sense of purpose elsewhere, shining on sports field or stage. Combination of variety, straight-talking pupils and enjoyable challenge of (successfully) giving school boost it needed makes this a role he relishes. 'Love being busy.'

He is passionate about sport, particularly rugby and cricket, and enjoys playing golf and fishing. He took over after the school spent a year under an acting head, after the abrupt and unexplained resignation of the previous head, and brought with him parental hopes for stability after troubled times.

Head of Home Farm School (the pre-prep), Kay Markides, arrived 2009. Graduated in science, married with a family (including a son who attended Elstree) before deciding to train for teaching young ones. Taught for a while at another school nearby. Thrilled to be involved with Elstree, and it shows. Warm and at ease with the children ('I love them') she is clearly not only very competent but also exudes calm dependability. Presides over a talented young staff who clearly relish the company of their young charges, patiently explaining things and then rushing around with them in the grounds of the prep school.

Entrance: Non-selective into Home Farm, the pre-prep (nursery to year 2), whose 60 pupils are accommodated in next door farmhouse and converted outbuildings, with own separate entrance and playgrounds but overlapping grounds. Co-ed but boy-dominated as 'people are signing up for the whole school'. Taster day plus informal assessments for entry into year 3 upwards. Growth of waiting lists (in almost every year group) means that while ability range is wide, 'we have become gently selective,' says Mr Inglis.

Exit: Good links with Bradfield (former head, now at Eton, sent all his brood here), most of first rank southern staples represented. Eton and Radley also top choices, then Winchester, Stowe, Pangbourne, Marlborough and Wellington. Seven scholarships in 2018.

Year 3 girls to St Andrew's Pangbourne, Cheam, St Gabriel's, Marlston House and the Manor, Abingdon.

Remarks: School that likes life in duplicate. Pre-prep's 60 pupils have large magical woodland area (annexed from prep), paths canopied with intertwined branches or bordered with wild grasses (there's even a troll bridge) – and a second mini wilderness for everyday, star attraction a palatial roofed sandpit big enough for whole class to enjoy. Even Mrs Markides shares year 2 teaching duties with colleague (though second best rule undoubtedly doesn't apply).

Appearance, in pairs or otherwise, is winningly green and traditional. School's 150 acres include two lakes, one used for Elstree Award activities (like DofE but bespoke), croquet lawn with wire sculpture of (Lewis Carroll inspired?) flamingo, courts and pitches (including full-sized Astro), dog-walking parents and staff adding homely touch.

Though vibe is venerable (pre-prep uniform list specifies named napkin ring), mood is progressive. 'Lots of tradition and trust, but we're well aware it's a modern world,' says Mrs Inglis. Mr I stresses importance of charitable activities that open pupils' eyes 'to the wide world away from idyllic leafy confines.'

'Pushes children hard but pleasantly so,' thought prospective parent. 'It's not "you will learn 10 verses by Tuesday".' By way of proof, there's combined staff and pupil YouTube version of Happy to mark departure of recent batch of girl leavers, treat for dad dancing (or teacher equivalent) connoisseurs and anyone needing lesson in chutzpah.

Full boarding the only traditional element that isn't faring so well, hanging on but only just. Now a minority occupation for 15 out of the 100 or so boarders, mainly overseas (Russians, sprinkling of Spanish) plus odd Londoner, though most stay for at least three nights a week. They 'get used to it,' thought pupil. Not most ringing of endorsements, even backed by run of grounds at weekend.

However when it comes to flexi or weekly stays, 'boys are clamouring to board,' the head told us firmly, reeling off vast list of evening activities on offer when they do – from bridge to fantasy football, debating and improvisation. School now so 'full to bursting' from Monday to Friday that it's a case of joining the queue with waiting list in operation. No quibbles with boarding logistics, which work a treat, year 4 to 6 dorms to the side – we liked their emergency cuddly toy cubby hole to keep homesickness at bay – while years 7 and year 8 have separate quarters in main building.

Dorms on large side – eight to 10 not uncommon – but with spacious, pleasant rooms and friendly, uncrowded feel. Décor variable, one room a shrine to Shoot! magazine, plastered floor to ceiling with pictures of footballers, another, the former ballroom, featuring stucco storks looking down from ceiling in gentle amazement at year 8 pupils' beds in formation on parquet floor. Possible setting for new reality TV show, 'Come boarding,' perhaps?

If full boarding continues to decline and parent vibe suggests it will – 'strong majority who like the day aspect,' thought one – Big Weekends could be the future, with 40 or so other pupils piling in for fun and games including Laser Tag and exciting Indoor Lions, inside version of Stuck in the Mud played in the dark for added thrills. Extremely popular (currently free of charge, so no wonder) and means 'full boarders have more company,' says school. Also an organisational cinch as Saturday school – a full day with lessons and afternoon games – is in full force from year 4. And without Saturday school, 'weekends are too long,' thought pupil.

Best teaching (and there's lots of it) combines humour and memorability. One English teacher (a school favourite) known for quick draw funny pictures – enthusiastic year 7 boys (like all other pupils smilingly standing up for adults) praising memorable stick person imagery that instantly conjured up poetic protagonist 'swimming against tide with heart sinking...'.

Open to learning needs including ADHD. Key is ability to keep up academically and impress with right attitude: prospectus stresses that 'effort is king'. While teachers sometimes sorely tried, rare that won't make a go of it, helped by much-praised learning needs department. Will, though, review progress in years 4 and 6 when long-term compatibility of child and school will be weighed up, says headmaster. Thus far, nobody has been asked to leave.

Impressively inclusive, say parents, with children's confidence boosted by lessons cannily pitched at challenging rather than daunting. 'My son thinks he's brilliant because they've given him the work that's appropriate,' said mother. Even less inspirational teachers – maths felt to be slightly variable – usually get the results in the end. 'If you get something right, you get a point. Didn't like it but it does work,' thought one pupil.

Pre-prep pupils similarly keen on lessons and given undiluted praise from parents – staff 'can't do enough, there morning, noon and night, so happy and 100 per cent involved with the children' – no wonder. One small maths fan was full of praise for 'hard sums', another extolled virtues of recent pirate topic because 'they kill people' – before being gently shepherded into more wholesome approach by teacher. 'Our pirates wouldn't do things like that.' (He didn't look totally convinced).

Music 'absolutely thriving,' says head, with 200 individual lessons timetabled each week, top performers reaching grade 8, two recent scholarships (Radley and Charterhouse) and department 'always full of boys.' Prep choir (one of three) is 30-deep, recent delights including choral evensong at Bath Abbey. Music school now includes a rehearsal studio and music technology room.

Drama similarly successful with boys happy to take female roles and lack of self-consciousness that comes with single-sex environment. Parents thrilled with gentle encouragement that sees the formerly un-keen blossoming into performers. Talent search starts early with violin (free lessons for all in year 1) and recorder (year 2) – parents apparently thrilled with results, performers shining in end of year concert.

Sport equally strong and inclusive (goes down to E teams and 6th XIs). Fine summer evenings an enthusiast's delight, with croquet on front lawn. Lots more – from swimming to shooting, golf and judo, as well as school staples – athletics, football, rugby, hockey, cricket (coach, current Berkshire captain, also teaches pre-prep pupils, one mightily impressed to find his teacher known to Lord's).

Plenty of informal activities, too; one tree full of roosting boys, like giant navy blue rooks. Though staff presence seemed to us to be relatively hands-off, some parents and pupils feel free time can be over-supervised. 'Always a teacher walking round.' Reasons for adult presence well understood – 'it's so someone doesn't get hurt,' and by year 8, said pupil, things improve. 'They accept you need some time alone.' Greta Garbo tendencies no doubt forgotten in excitement of table football matches and hotly contested corridor cricket. Boys very keen, though one thought teachers possibly less so when caught in path of oncoming cricket ball during evening rounds.

Gentle pace gets up speed through the school, senior school entrance exam pressure an inevitable fact of life for year 8 pupils, though teachers do best to defuse the tension, felt boys. Weekly form time used to air difficulties; friendly gap students a more informal source of support, comfort food – evening bowls of cereal – provided for boarders.

Pastoral care generally felt to be good, from daily staff briefings to half hour catch up sessions at lunchtime. Pupils urged to use common sense if someone is feeling left out of activities – 'they expect us to find something that fits,' said pupil. Bullying clearly well managed. 'Issues dealt with very quickly with children pulled in. If you overstep the mark there's a punishment and everyone knows that,' said parent. Pre-prep opts for circle time and golden rules. Staff had slight struggle to remember them but do appear to work, parents full of praise at absence of problems in any age group.

Highly organised parents notable for efficiency and ability sweep up newcomers – 'integration' events include lunches for the mums and curry nights for dads (or vice versa one progressive day?). Praise, bar mutterings about over influential queen bees from former parent, was universal, school community the icing on the cake. Attracts London exiles as well as locals, drawn by welcoming culture and lots to keep sporty and arty happy.

'Son has been pushed where would like to be pushed and pushed along where needed to be. An amazingly efficient school that continues to surprise me,' said mother.

Epsom College

College Road, Epsom, Surrey KT17 4JQ

Ages 11–18 **Pupils** 897 **Sixth form** 328 **Boarders** 145 full, 187 weekly **C of E**

Fees: Day £18,765 – £25,266; Boarding £33,849 – £37,263 pa

01372 821234
www.epsomcollege.org.uk

Headmaster: Since 2012, Jay Piggot BA MA PGCE (50s). Previously headmaster at alma mater Campbell College, Belfast between 2006 and 2012, and, before that, put in 17 years at Eton (clearly a hard place to leave) starting as assistant master in 1989 and becoming housemaster 10 years later. Not bad going given that it was only his second teaching job: his first, immediately after completing his MA in English Renaissance literature at Liverpool, was at Millfield, where he taught A level/Oxbridge English.

Career success undoubtedly assisted by personality and appearance – quietly dashing, though doesn't overdo the leading man business. Gimlet vision, too – noticed and swiftly dealt with errant piece of rubbish, a very small plastic wrapper, only one in otherwise immaculate grounds.

Lordy, lordy, what a popular man he is. Pupils – 'a joy,' he says – say he makes an effort to know names, comes to matches and makes with the social chit chat. Biggest vote winner, however, are the birthday cards – otherwise sophisticated international pupil clearly thrilled with his, particularly handwritten signature – cynic had checked authenticity with damp finger just to be sure. Parents also like what they see. Innovations all welcomed. 'Very proactive behind the scenes and has pushed through some sensible changes,' said one. Definitely a step up from predecessor. 'School ran well but didn't have the personality.'

College was already known to him before the headhunters came a-callling, and found vision, ethos and commitment very much to his taste. Younger son, a keen golfer, moved with him (older brother is going great guns at Eton).

'Would love' to teach again and might when has got through current to-do list, which is lengthy. Getting shorter by the minute, though. Popular changes include axing of seasonal timetables, originally to make most of winter light, but cause of mega all-round confusion to all.

High profile reintroduction of matrons into the houses was an Eton-inspired development that's brought a caring, maternal touch (thus far, all women) to details such as tracking down missing shirts and sewing as well as control of rowdy element. Of even greater significance has been academic shake up, still ongoing, starting with observation of every member of staff since he arrived, followed with ISI-style feedback. 'A privilege,' he says. (We're sure they feel the same). Many stay for years. No wonder, with perks headed (for many, though not all) by housing either on-site or within a few minutes' walk. 'My wife told me we're not going to move,' said one. Given Epsom property prices, you can't blame her.

E

In addition to the introduction of heads of year, designed to add missing link identified in recent inspection, he's also not going to stand in path of old-timers who could be moving on to greater things elsewhere, while rejigging weak spots including A level languages and biology and GCSE English literature. Dynamic incomers, including former Uppingham head of modern foreign languages – similar developments in science – are being brought in together with fledgling new generation of bright young things adding oomph to lessons (occasional dullness one of few inferred criticisms in last inspection report).

Still more shaking up to come, however, essential given school's previous sleepiness and 'red-hot' competition – Wellington, Cranleigh and Charterhouse as well as St John's Leatherhead and Reed's School. Bumping up interior life of school is part of the process, with Eton's dawn to dusk (and beyond) intellect-boosting programme the inspiration for mind-expanding programme – expect more pupil-organised drama, musical and debating activities (medical, history and politics societies are already on the go) sparking impassioned discussions that ramp up the intellectual temperature from tepid to mercury-busting.

Mark of success? Would like popularity of places to increase to the point where competition for boarding places as strong as for day hopefuls.

Academic matters: One of formerly mid-ranking schools to have substantially upped game in recent years. Fun lessons got pupils on the go, literally so, with movement minus the music, A level students standing up for miracles (theology) and marginal cost (economics) – everything, in fact, but their rights.

Parents, while agreeing with head that some teachers are 'past their best', think generally offset by vast majority who are 'engaging, personable and, most importantly, able to motivate. They appear to love their subjects and to enjoy teaching and the company of the children – none of these are a given, in my experience.' Megawatt enthusiasm often a game-changer, especially at sixth form level. Sciences score particularly high conversion rates. 'Was my dream to be a translator – now it's chemistry,' said pupil.

Ability to devote time to all (an impressive 55 hours contact time a week) means that 'there are no lost causes,' says head. Plentiful tracking and feedback means pupils know where they are and how they can improve, feedback seamlessly integrated in lessons. 'We put down our comments when we've had a test and it gives teachers a good idea of where we are,' said sixth former.

Though class sizes aren't teeny tiny – average 20 for GCSE (maximum 23) and between 10 and 12 at A level (15 max), with pupil to full time teacher ratio of 8:4 – school is consistently good when it comes to added value, setting in maths, banding in languages and sciences (where small group of less able students might do GCSE dual sciences rather than IGCSE triple). No-one takes 'silly' numbers of GCSEs, says senior teacher – aim is to ensure good grades in manageable quantities.

Currently, results generally very good given relatively mixed intake, with 77 per cent A*-A/9-7 grades at GCSE; 87 per cent of A level entries graded A*/B and 57 per cent A*/A in 2018.

Good, largely traditional subject range, almost ology-free – 'nothing against psychology but it just isn't us,' says teacher – though language options now include GCSE Mandarin, originally for overseas students but now open to all. However, MFLs not the strongest suit, with few takers at A level – maths and economics much the most popular.

Hugely dynamic head of DT is also bumping up recruitment, particularly amongst girls, by ensuring that environment, full of technological marvels – though it's pupils' superb mortice and tenon joints and chamfering skills that help pull in the A* grades – is also tidy ('was grubby and fragmented') with plenty of wood-turning (apparently the secret of cross-gender appeal).

Big feature is EPQ, a mini-dissertation that, at best, combines originality and staying power (recent topics include carcinogens in food and madness in Henry VIII's court – separately). Worth the effort. One pupil, down an A level grade and out of university course, called department head and used hers to talk her way back in again. No doubt that attracts the very able – one pupil, exile from leading girls' school, delighted to be somewhere that praised good work rather than training spotlight on pupils only when failed to deliver top grades – though one parent queried its suitability for the truly brilliant. 'Might be a bit too comfortable,' she thought. 'It's a broad church and some kids are too bright [and] shouldn't be there.'

Extra scaffolding where needed, with clinics all the way through the school in all key subjects and teachers not just present (many live in) but in many cases 'always available.' That said, school isn't geared up to cope with anyone with more than mild learning difficulties. Of the 100 or so pupils with SEN, none currently has EHCP, SpLD the overwhelmingly dominant need, though have coped with (mild) ADHD as well.

Plenty of emails home and 'progress reports every three weeks,' ensure that everyone knows what's going on, while lengthy school day (finishing 6.00pm) incorporates sufficient free periods for the organised to sock it to the homework.

And though initially gentle pace startling to alumni of non-stop pushy preps, school gets praise for stress-appropriate levels of pushing tailored to each child. 'They know which way to push,' said mum of recent leaver. 'The teacher told my child that she "might get an 7 in biology GCSE, but I don't think so".' Nettled, daughter was spurred on to do just that.

Games, options, the arts: Sport success plentiful – boys' and girls' rugby VIIs regular regional winners, lots of post-school success, too (five OEs play for Harlequins), ditto hockey (mixed seniors won Surrey U18 competition), as do minors with recent captain of golf driving his way to Stanford golf scholarship (first European for over 10 years, says school) and shooting. Facilities generous – including swimming pool – and, in case of one of two sports halls, close to giant-size (even better with new sports pavilion up and running), two cracking sports halls, one giant sized, six squash courts, a swimming pool and a fencing salle. No partridge in pear tree (but would undoubtedly be doing a few press ups if there were).

Outside, timetable pushes variety – first years have both outdoor and inside sports in an afternoon and, further up the school, non-standard sports can be done off site – riding, for example and climbing, though school now has its own climbing wall. Range ensures that 'you're not penalised if you're not sporty,' thought a mother, with matches for all. 'Sport is very important, whether you're A team or D/E/F team material,' agreed another parent. Sports captains, rated by the rank and file – 'positions are well earned,' thought one – have a real say in team structure. 'You can discuss team composition with the coach and that's good,' thought pupils. Termly activity sheet encourages pupils to experiences shock of the new. One boy, initially dreading jive dance, discovered instead that he was 'that sort of person' – and loved it.

Plenty head for DofE, room for all (can add more staff if demand is high). CCF feather in school cap – one of oldest and biggest in country, teeming with facilities, (we liked esteem-heavy 'confidence' rather than assault course). Wears success lightly – numerous impressive sports cups casually behind bars with the guns).

Arts also attacked with relish. Music felt to be 'on the ascendant,' thought teacher, with lots of instrumental lessons – drums, singing, electric guitar and piano the biggest sellers, some reaching diploma level; challenging, performance opportunities ranging from low stress impromptu recitals to high quality productions including The Cunning Little Vixen and excellent chapel choir, masses lining up to audition – a macho-free area, reckoned year 9 and 10 pupils. Those not making the grade can 'let voices develop' in non-selective Glee Club instead.

Visual arts, recently upgraded, feature confident, instantly recognisable year 9 pictures of Kew Gardens – one of many trips. Everybody gets out a lot, DT excursions to real factories (Brompton bikes to Henry vacuum cleaners) so popular that school staff sign their Sundays away, too, school chef enjoying outing to Cadbury's as much as pupils.

Boarding: Similar numbers for full boarding and weekly. Boarding houses, dotted round the site, now all done up to the nines – matching up to head's aspirations to equal best in Britain – with decking and glass snazzy-ness. Sensible trouble-preventing measures include half-termly dorm swaps and plenty of weekend activities for full boarders, from trips to Thorpe Park to house evenings and bowling. 'Never lonely because lots going on,' said sixth former.

Buddy system helps combat homesickness (most reckoned that worst was over within first week), one house even creating own surrogate family, one year group per generation and organising popular old fashioned sports day as an ice-breaker. Here, too, matrons, add much appreciated extra tea and sympathy layer (housemistresses – always academic staff – can 'sometimes be more of figure of authority,' thought sixth formers).

Background and atmosphere: Altogether a civilised place to be, starting with laid-back parking regime, permitted along one side of the one way road that winds round the lush green campus (new upper sixth drivers are vetted by the head), imposing chapel at its heart. Though patron is HM the Queen, not a high-society institution. Started life as the Royal Medical Benevolent College, a charitable Good Thing, helping the relics of deceased impoverished medics. Strongly Victorian in spirit and execution – most buildings completed between 1850s and 1920s. School wasn't welcomed by all, overt charitable status 'distasteful' to recipients, reckoned contemporary letter to Lancet.

Took only boys for the first 120 years or so (sisters presumably expected to marry their way to economic success); girls added 1996 largely as emergency recession-busting tactic (local area had suffered heavily and pupil numbers had plummeted). Now, of course, school wouldn't be without them and they're on almost equal terms in the sixth form, though minority partners in other years. Desired ratio is 60:40 is, thinks head, about right, ensuring girls have the same options as boys, particularly when it comes to games. 'All get the chance to contribute,' he adds, firmly. No complaints from girls themselves, or parents, so seems to be working. Added a lower school – years 7 and 8 – in 2016.

Though it's all 19th and early 20th century authenticity from the front with 'real wow factor,' thought parent, sold on first visit, tasteful modern extensions stretch back a considerable distance to the rear (current bursar, a woman, was a former architect, and it shows). Behind public face is 'pupil world', the second sweep of buildings where most of the teaching takes place. Modern additions – humanities building particularly palatable – don't jar (though some areas, like maths and theology blocks, could be nicer, and almost certainly will be when funds permit).

When it comes to décor, different departments exhibit endearing idiosyncrasies – from pot plants in chemistry lab (and sign announcing 'nudisme interdite au delà de cette limite') to blue-painted English rooms (also notable for friendly clutter of framed posters and attractive display boards already filling up nicely in second week of term) while modern languages is all-purple (even down to lampshades). Black wall in one of physics labs, however, is for sensitive experiments and 'not because we're pandering to goths,' explains larger than life department head.

Technology warmly embraced with Wifi throughout (and 'extreme' internet safety settings triggered by word Middlesex) and the Hub, new high tech room where lessons can be recorded for posterity. Tradition equally enjoyed but not pointlessly so – most of original medical artefacts and stuffed animals that once dominated science rooms have gone. 'Antiques dealer took the rest,' says teacher, cheerfully.

Big plans include new careers centre, lecture rooms, art gallery/café and social areas for sixth formers.

Pastoral care, well-being and discipline: Seniors a strong force (and will be even more so once head succeeds in replacing current sixth form block with something altogether spiffier). Take turns to lead assemblies that are so far removed from commonplace fare that we had to double check that searingly articulate reflections on 9/11 were being delivered by sixth form girls. It appears effortless. No wonder – it's been in rehearsal since June, points out the friendly chaplain. Older pupils keen to stress that 'hierarchical system associated with traditional English boarding school, pitting year group against year group' is 'a terrible idea' and will pitch in to take sides if older boys show signs of picking on younger ones. 'It's part of our role and it works.'

Little in the way of serious misbehaviour, however, with just two pupils 'withdrawn by parents' (expulsion by face-saving euphemism) in senior teacher's 15 years. Drugs issues in both cases, though it's very rarely the end, behind the scenes second chances often possible. Day to day, class silliness and late homework the main issues, reckoned pupils, with escalating sanctions – lines, notification of tutors, warnings, departmental then school detentions – rattled off by all.

Lots of rewards, too – from pizza or chocolate for work-related merits and distinctions to privileges of seniority – sixth form day girls cited joy of leaving sports kit on shelves in study rooms instead of trekking, when younger, to go to separate storage area.

And though house system (separate for day and boarding pupils) engenders ferocious sense of competition (choir contest in particular), it isn't carried over into lessons, 'which stops it becoming tribal,' reckoned parent.

Pupils and parents: Predominantly local intake with vast majority of pupils, including 95 per cent of UK boarders, living within 10 to 15 miles. School keen to expand the range but, meantimes, results in happy fusion of streetwise Londoner with leafy Surrey-ite, reckoned teacher – cool without the ennui.

Many staff have own children here (has peaked at 40 or so). One parent we spoke to who'd opted for local alternative thought numbers were excessive – though appeared to be a lone voice. Working mums – far more these days – were something of a feature to the point where socialising tends to feature nights out to ensure 'you don't feel out of the loop,' thought career-driven mother.

Cosmopolitan feel added by international component (largeish at 20 per cent) drawn from Hong Kong, Malaysia, Russia and Korea, though many more from western Europe. For the 10 per cent who are non-native English speakers there is a structured EAL programme in place, but they're fully integrated into the curriculum says the school, 'right from day one'.

Malaysian numbers probably not affected by opening of sister school in Kuala Lumpur in 2014 – first foray into pastures new, as 'there will always be pupils who want a UK education,' reckons school.

Entrance: School is after all-rounders with several strings to their bow and 'fair share of the bright pupils'. Once a second choice regular, increasingly a bill-topper, recruiting from over 40 preps and state schools, likely to increase as it extends reach (Danes Hill and Downsend, Shrewsbury House, Aberdour and Feltonfleet feature prominently though no official feeders). Full-on charm offensive attracting south west London schools.

New 11+ intake via maths, English and VR tests plus interview in January of year 6. Second intake into year 9, with January pre-test in year 6 (VR – scores of around 118-120 the norm – NVR, English and numerical skill plus interview), same again (minus NVR) for non-prep candidates in January of year 8. Once 'day pupils were brighter and more studious' than boarding pupils, thought one insider. No longer the case.

If no joy at 13+, small number of places at 14+ (three to five only, English, maths and NVR tests). Second biggest influx is post-GCSE with 45 to 50 joining the sixth form, following VR, NVR and numerical skills tests plus interview. Push to up state school numbers (currently around 20 per cent of the total) as a way of 'supplementing the ratios'. Some haggling after year 12 for a handful of pupils whose progress gives cause for concern. Repeating year not an option, dropping a subject can be the solution.

Exit: No shortage of ambition, most achieving first choice unis; Exeter, Nottingham, Durham, UCL, Oxford Brookes, Edinburgh and Manchester in top 10 destinations; four to Oxbridge in 2018 and eight medics. Economics and finance followed by business, geography and sociology popular.

Money matters: Annual bursary spend close to £750,000 on up to 100 per cent of fees. Possible additional financial support for families with medical connections through the Royal Medical Foundation, based at the school, though since 2000 a separate legal entity. Lots of scholarships on offer, academic and headmaster's (for 'a wide range of disciplines' from drama to chess) at 11+ and 13+, sports and music at 16+ too.

Remarks: With demographics and parent power going his way, head's boarding aspirations could well be realised. 'A brilliant school for my son,' said mother. Another commented that school had got 'everything there was to get' out of her child. 'You really can't ask much more than that'.

Eton College

Eton, Windsor, Berkshire SL4 6DW

Ages 13–18 **Pupils** 1,320 **Sixth form** 537 **Boarders** All full **C of E**

Fees: Boarding £40,668 pa

01753 370611
www.etoncollege.com

Head master: Since 2015, Simon Henderson MA PGCE (30s), previously head of Bradfield College. Educated at Winchester College, followed by Brasenose College, Oxford, where he read history. Teaching career started at Windsor Boys' School, thence to Eton in 2001, where he was a deputy housemaster and head of history, and on to Sherborne School in 2009 as deputy head (academic). Married to Ali with four young children.

Mr Henderson has the impeccable manners, inscrutability and cerebral acuity generally alleged to distinguish the man who's been to Winchester, but in our experience also common to many heads of senior schools. But he has, too, the aura of serene composure and mastery of self that Betjeman mocks, gently, in his poem, The Wykehamist: 'It's something too to know your wants/And go full pelt for Norman fonts.' We strongly suspect that Mr Henderson's equivalent of Norman fonts is schools and teaching. Of his own education he says, 'I loved school – it was dynamic, exciting and vibrant.' His first experience of teaching was in South Africa on his gap year; 'I absolutely loved it.' His vocation was confirmed by a spell doing corporate internships in the City ('awful').

Does being head master of Eton leave any time for teaching? 'The unpredictability means I can't commit to any formal teaching, but I make guest appearances.' He says he has 'plans to get back into the classroom,' but in the meantime is making a 'conscious decision to be here as much as possible.' That must be hard when his presence is expected at so many events – 'I go to lots of dinners,' he says somewhat ruefully. 'Schools are big communities of people, it's so important to make personal connections.'

In any large boarding school it will be housemaster, rather than headmaster, who is pupils' day-to-day influence and whom pupils and parents know best, so it was perhaps unsurprising to find that almost all of the many parents we spoke to had had no contact with Mr Henderson. 'He holds lunches after games on Saturdays but we haven't been to one yet.' 'My son says he sends cards to all the boys on their birthdays and they sometimes meet him if they've won a prize.' And what do the boys think of their 'head man'? 'He's nice, but he seems quite strict.'

When we met Mr Henderson, his mind was on the role of technology in the classroom. Eton's Tony Little Centre for Innovation and Research in Learning is at the forefront of developments in this field, working in partnership with education technology firms and also pursuing its own ventures. The centre's aims are to take this expertise beyond the school gates and make it available to its state school partnerships, local education authorities and the wider world. Interestingly, Mr Henderson sees this as Eton's virtual version of other schools' overseas franchises. Eton itself, he believes, cannot be replicated, but the school's approach to education can.

Does he foresee a time when Eton's beaks (teachers) can stand down? 'Technology is changing what happens. For example, if there are 20 pupils of broadly the same ability in a maths set, computer programmes can be used to detect areas of weakness and generate questions that consolidate or extend learning, but they will never be a substitute for human interaction.' He believes that this kind of personalised learning will free teachers to concentrate on higher order work – spending more time with individuals rather than generating questions. 'Technology will enable teaching in schools to become similar to that in universities – with a mixture of small classes, online courses, set-piece lectures, time spent on individual study and more fluidity between year groups.'

Every Eton head appointed in recent years must surely have pondered at the start of his tenure whether or not he had the stomach to go down in history as the barbarian who consigned the school's world-famous uniform to the archives. Mr Henderson was touted as a moderniser, just the sort of chap who might actually do this deed. Not that he's ever said as much, naturally. In an early press interview his answer to this predictable question was, 'Well, I'm not getting rid of the uniform this week', accompanied by a photograph of him sporting chinos, a linen jacket and a slightly casual shirt (with tie, of course). Several years on, and despite moving headmaster HQ from traditional study to a studiedly modern office, in sartorial matters at least he appears to have gone native. No doubt the tailors at Eton town's four (yes, four) gentlemen's outfitters have decided it's safe to go ahead and splash out on new tape measures.

Mr Henderson is one of the school's youngest ever heads, so perhaps donning the armour of the uniform each day makes it easier to inhabit such a huge role. Not that he seems to need any help, as anyone who heard him being questioned by MPs from the Education Select Committee inquiry into 'exam integrity' will know. Completely unruffled, his answers were eloquent and precise and there was no doubting his resolve that such a thing (boys seeing material that later appeared in exam papers) would never happen again.

So where, beyond his new office, is the evidence of Mr Henderson's promised 'modernisation'? After all, he taught here for eight years so must presumably have identified things that could be improved. He has made half term holidays longer to bring them into line with other independent schools and banned mobile phones for boys in F block (year 9). He told us that he wants to continue the school's work to broaden opportunities and access – long term commitments include sponsoring nearby Holyport College (a state boarding school) and the London Academy of Excellence, a state sixth form college in East London. Eton's famous Universities Summer School has been running since 1981 and provides expert subject tuition to pupils from state schools who are applying to top universities. Mr Henderson says that he shares his predecessor's ambition for access to Eton to become 'needs blind'. 'We spend around £7m on means-tested bursaries and most of that money has been given by former pupils for this purpose.'

Access to Eton may one day become needs blind, but it's unlikely to become gender blind on Mr Henderson's watch. He told us, with just a hint of impatience, 'There's too much focus on whether a school is single sex or co-ed; what matters most is whether a school is good or not.' Adding, 'Young people feel under more pressure to conform to gender stereotypes at co-ed schools.' Women teachers are still in the minority at Eton, but the appointment of the first female lower master (the senior deputy head) is a good sign.

We were interested to get the head's take on the public perception of Eton and the way the school is portrayed in the press. 'We must not be defensive, we need to engage with our critics. Pupils who have been educated here should never feel guilty, but they must be aware of their good fortune and responsibilities.'

We doubt Mr Henderson has much in the way of spare time, but what he has is reserved for his family (he has four young children) and golf. And supporting QPR. Favourite writer? Thomas Hardy. Regrets? Giving up on the piano and clarinet.

Rather than headline-grabbing attempts on the superficial, one gets the impression that Mr Henderson has addressed himself to Eton's internal workings, adjusting the calibration of its doubtless Byzantine ancient mechanisms. 'I think he's probably making subtle changes,' one father told us. 'Subtle changes' can be hard to spot, even for a Good Schools Guide writer, so thank you Eton parents for your help and all those insightful, robust and sometimes contradictory opinions.

Academic matters: Parents think teaching staff (known as 'beaks') are 'exceptional', but not without exception, and those we met lived up to such billing – deeply knowledgeable about their school and delighted to tell visitors about its past and present. Eton must be a great gig – not just for the kudos of working in the world's most famous school and the resources and opportunities it offers, but also the intellectual challenge of teaching a carefully hand-picked selection of the (mostly western) world's sparkiest young men.

The deputy head (academic)'s introduction for new parents sets a certain tone, 'When all is said and done, a boy is not coming to Eton simply to earn a set of qualifications.' But exams are exams and even Etonians must jump these trifling hurdles. They do so hardly putting a foot wrong. IGCSEs for most of the core subjects; nine languages on offer in addition to French and Spanish including Mandarin, Russian, Arabic, Italian and Japanese. Considerably more opt for classical Greek and Latin than for drama, DT and music. Most boys take 11 subjects and gain top marks in all – 96 per cent A*-A/9-7 grades at I/GCSE in 2018.

Though still impressive, A level results spread a little beyond the first letters of the alphabet (or their Pre-U equivalents) – in 2018, 77 per cent A*/A at A level and 50 per cent D1/2 at Pre-U but there are also on occasion Cs, Ds, Es – even, gasp, a couple of Us. Most popular subject by a considerable margin is maths, followed by economics, history (both of these offered as Pre-U), religious studies, physics, further maths and chemistry. Further maths garners the highest percentage of A*s along with fine art. Only a handful of takers for drama and DT, much better news for the oft-beleaguered modern foreign languages – particularly Spanish – but more opt for Latin than French.

Small classes and setting for all in most subjects ensure teaching is precisely targeted and boys' progress is extremely closely monitored – any falling off is brought to the attention of tutors and housemasters. Several parents thought it is the combination of great teaching and competition between the boys themselves that keeps academic standards flying, 'they learn so much from their peers.' Clearly understood and immediate sanctions for work submitted late or sub-par. Parents marvel at the beautifully written and minutely detailed termly reports – each arrives accompanied by a two- or three-page letter from the boy's housemaster and tutor.

Full boarding means a different shape to the school day, with lessons (known as 'schools') following afternoon sports activities at least three times a week. We sat in on several late afternoon sessions: computing, Spanish and F block (year 9) divinity. As they mustered and spread themselves out, waistcoats and hair somewhat dishevelled, the older boys could have passed for weary ushers at the end of a particularly gruelling society wedding. And notwithstanding all the high-powered goings on in the Tony Little Centre for Innovation and Research in Learning, the lessons we observed would have made perfect sense to any shades of beaks long dead – books, pens, questions, answers, discussion, testing, checking and a bit of good-humoured banter (though we're not sure what they'd make of laptops, Google and interactive whiteboards).

Well-resourced and highly professional SEN provision and staff. Around 50 to 60 boys receive regular learning support for mild to moderate dyslexia, dyspraxia, dysgraphia – either one-to-one or in small groups (charged as an extra). All boys assessed during their first term and any whose results give cause for concern get extra help, either from their tutor or the SEN unit.

In 2017 Pre-U candidates in economics and art history had their marks disallowed by the examination board after evidence of questions being leaked in advance came to light. In the case of art history there was no evidence of Eton pupils or staff having done anything wrong, but this was not so for economics, where the revelations lead to the departure of the head of economics, who was also deputy head (academic) elect. The school dealt with these matters swiftly and openly, but it makes one wonder under how much pressure teachers feel to produce top results in their subjects.

Games, options, the arts: How long have you got? It is surely impossible for any boy to have a go at all the opportunities Eton offers in a five-year school career, but the message from pupils and parents is that the school does its utmost to foster and support boys' interests and ambitions. 'Whatever the talent or interest, school will do all it can to enable boys to make it their thing.' 'Eton encouraged me' was a phrase we heard several times, not necessarily in relation to extraordinary achievements but, for instance, performance opportunities for keen but far from concert level musicians. Co-curricular programme includes CCF – Eton's was founded in 1860 when the country was threatened by Napoleon – community service, and over 50 'societies', nearly all established and run by boys, including debating, comedy, Orwell (described as 'left wing'), cheese and wine (these last two are not held together). Meetings, many with visiting speakers, take place in the evenings.

E

School playing fields, with evocative names such as Agar's Plough and Mesopotamia, used for football and rugby matches in the Michaelmas half (term), rugby and hockey in the Lent half and cricket and athletics in the summer. With up to 16 teams fielded for a particular sport at any one time, a parent told us that sometimes two opposing schools are invited so that everybody gets a game. On match days there can be up to 40 teams competing. Even the least sporty boys will play in house and inter-house competitions. A parent told us, 'Sport is important, but it doesn't dominate school life; it's just one aspect of the boys' development – like music and drama.' Another observed, 'Even if your son was in all the A teams at prep school, he probably won't be when he gets to Eton – it can come as a bit of a shock when they find out how many boys are better than them!'

Eton also has its own unique version of football, 'the field game', but since no-one else plays it these matches are entirely home affairs. Another unique sporting tradition is the 'Eton wall game', a version of rugby played between Collegers (scholars) and Oppidans (rest of the school) on a narrow strip of ground adjacent to a brick wall. Nearly all matches, entirely organised by the boys, appear to result in goalless draws, but the rules and vocabulary are so esoteric and confusing we can't comment further. Suffice it to say that Boris Johnson was a keen player. Rowing takes place at Dorney, with superb facilities developed for the rowing and canoeing events of the 2012 Olympics. One or two parents (presumably not parents of rowers) thought that investment in Dorney had been at the expense of other sports. Huge range of minor sports including rackets, fives, golf, shooting and sailing. While lack of stabling means you can't bring your horse to Eton, school has thriving polo and eventing teams.

Over 1,000 individual music lessons a week, splendid facilities for teaching and concerts, eight (yes, eight) organs, and a hierarchy of orchestras: symphony orchestra for the best, chamber orchestra for string players from the symphony orchestra, concert band for wind and brass players plus junior versions of all these. Smaller groups such as piano trios, quartets, jazz and rock bands get the chance to perform at events organised by the school, houses or boys themselves. Audition-only College Chapel Choir sings three times a week at services, tours abroad and has produced nine CDs, but there are also plenty of opportunities for keen but less exquisitely musical voices to be heard.

Of all Eton's many strengths, it was drama that parents singled out for particular praise: 'stupendous', 'phenomenal', 'as good as West End productions.' The Farrer theatre has 400 seats and there are two smaller venues. 'It's not exclusive, there are so many opportunities to get involved – not just acting but on the technical side'. What with whole school plays, house plays, and productions written, produced and directed by boys themselves, it's perhaps understandable that relatively few boys feel the need to choose GCSE and A level drama.

The large numbers of art GCSE and A level A*s are nurtured in the light-filled Drawing Schools, home to teaching expertise and superb facilities for painting, drawing printmaking, photography, computer graphics, sculpture and ceramics. Each year a different artist in residence is invited to set up an open studio, produce and exhibit their work.

Boarding: Eton has 25 boarding houses, mostly located in historic buildings throughout the town. Each is home to 50 boys (exception is the scholars' house, College, which has 70). Every boy has a single study bedroom – no dorms or sharing. Rooms we saw were pretty standard issue boys' boarding school – relatively unadorned apart from large shoes. Several parents mentioned that the quality of the mattresses left a lot to be desired.

Around half the houses have their own chefs and dining rooms; boys from houses with no catering have their meals at Bekynton, the college dining complex, eating in house groups together with their housemaster and other house staff. According to boys, the main pro of a catered house is 'not having to dash down the street for breakfast on a cold, rainy morning.' One parent suggested that because Bekynton offered a wider choice of food, a non-catered house could suit a boy who is a 'picky eater.' We enjoyed a delicious lunch in Bekynton's staff dining area where the food was, we were reassured, exactly the same as the boys were getting (but with added napery).

Meal times seem to be more formal affairs than at other boarding schools. A member of staff told us, 'Eating in house groups is important for strengthening the relationship between staff and boys.' In addition to three main meals, all boys are provided with morning and afternoon drinks and snacks in their houses (breaks known respectively as 'chambers' and 'messing'). And if they're still hungry they can forage at the school shop or those in the town.

When it comes to choosing a boarding house the unanimous advice from school and parents is to keep on open mind, 'Don't get fixated.' Do your homework, visit at least three, rank them in order of preference and the 'vast majority' will get a place in one of their choice. Everything will depend on parents' (and boys') rapport with the housemaster and also the dame (responsible for domestic arrangements, health issues etc). One mother advised, 'Trust your instincts; if you really don't think a housemaster is going to get the best out of your son then it's better to go back into the pool.'

Housemasters are in post for 13 years and in addition to the housemaster and his family, there will be a deputy housemaster and two assistants, the dame and her assistant, plus domestic staff. Boys also have responsibilities – every house has a house captain and a captain of games. Eton provides all teaching staff with accommodation, so boys' tutors will live only a short distance away.

While boys arriving from prep schools may at least be accustomed to boarding, message from parents is that the very long, full days are quite a 'gear change' for new boys – more so for those coming from state schools. Some housemasters hold events such as barbeques or football games over the summer for those joining in September. New boy integration is, apparently, 'very good' – housemasters are 'incredibly observant and always contactable.' In addition to standard holidays, boys can go home after commitments on Saturday until Sunday evening.

It's perhaps inevitable that over 13 years a housemaster will shape the 'character' of his house and as a consequence houses may 'collect boys in the same mould.' Accordingly, some houses will become known as, for example, 'sporty' or 'musical'. Several parents thought there were ongoing 'power struggles' between senior management and housemasters (such tensions are not uncommon in boarding schools). While everyone was overwhelmingly supportive of the 'federal' status quo and utterly loyal to their own sons' housemasters (all 'fantastic', 'indefatigable' and 'inspirational' to a man), one or two conceded that 'a degree of uniformity' might keep accusations of fiefdoms at bay.

Background and atmosphere: Eton is a small and charming Thameside town, not unadjacent to Slough and a bridge away from Windsor. It also just happens to have the world's most famous school attached. This makes it somewhat atypical, with its three art galleries, gunsmith, four gentlemen's outfitters and any number of restaurants and cafés. At least some of the latter should be applauded for having resisted the temptation to mine the rich and apparently inexhaustible seam of school related names. No-one but tourists and the occasional nervous prep school boy visiting with his parents looks twice at the tail-coated pupils and teachers as they stride up and down the high street between boarding houses and main school.

On arrival we were made very welcome in the porters' lodge, wood panelling decorated with framed personal photos of the royal family (princes William and Harry were pupils here – it is their local school, after all). Royalty or not, Eton's front of house staff are charming and friendly to deal with – in person or over the phone; quite an accolade when you consider just how busy the world's interest in its most famous school must keep them.

The school was founded by in 1440 by King Henry V1 to provide free education for 70 poor boys, but his ambitious building work stopped (the chapel, though fine and large, is considerably smaller than planned) and the school lost many of its original endowments when Henry was deposed by Edward 1V in 1461. Records from the 16th century show pupils had a pretty tough day – lessons finished at 8pm and there was only an hour of 'play'. The school's history lives on in its language – terms are 'halves' because there used to be only two three week holidays a year; 'oppidans', from the Latin for word for town, refers to pupils (originally from the nearby town) who, unlike the scholars, did not live at the school. Now it means all pupils who are not scholars.

Eton has two superb libraries, a huge collection of fine and decorative art including works by Sir Joshua Reynolds and JMW Turner, and no fewer than three museums. The Natural History Museum contains material from botanist and Old Etonian, Sir Joseph Banks, who sailed with Captain Cook; the Museum of Antiquities has a particularly fine collection of ancient Egyptian artefacts and there's also a Museum of Eton Life. All three are open to the public on Sunday afternoons.

Until the late 19th century boys at Eton could wear pretty much what they liked, although the upper-class monoculture at that time probably ensured they all looked fairly similar. When uniform was introduced it appears to have taken its first breath and dived into a vat of aspic. Top hats and cropped jackets may have been shed along the way, but what message do tail coats and white collars have for the 21st century? Pride in tradition and the confidence to follow one's own path, or outdated fancy dress, preserved because it distinguishes the members of a privileged club? The answer will be down to the politics of the observer.

Ironically, egalitarianism Eton style means boys and (male) teaching staff wear pretty much the same costume, with subtle distinctions of hierarchy such as patterned waistcoats and silver buttons for exalted members of Pop (sixth form prefects). Such uniformity may be why the issue of uniform is less pressing than one might imagine. Despite it being an outfit that flatters just about anyone who wears it, boys shed their uniform double quick once the school day is done.

Pastoral care, well-being and discipline: By all accounts the house and tutor system works powerfully well to ensure that despite the size of the school, no one is overlooked – 50 boys in each house means only 10 of each year group. Boys are encouraged to discuss social and health issues; the house dame deals with minor medical problems and school has three doctors, a psychiatrist, two psychologists and a counsellor. Honourable mention goes to the multi-denominational chaplaincy team in this context too. We heard mixed reports of peer support – some say that there's a strictly observed hierarchy of age, but we also heard that members of B block (sixth form) are assigned to look after younger boys. Like so many things at Eton, this seems to vary between individual houses.

Eton is a demanding school, 'very much into the pursuit of excellence in every field', but it is also very good at choosing boys who will thrive in such an atmosphere – robust self-starters who want to take every opportunity offered: 'It puts a lot of trust in boys and treats them as adults from the word go.' Parents describe it as 'surprisingly meritocratic' and 'very comfortable with difference.'

While appearances would suggest that the school doesn't sweat the small stuff (things like hair etc), one parent sounded a word of caution. 'They have their own way of doing things which is fine when all is going well, but if you come up against the system it can be pretty inflexible.'

Pupils and parents: Cast your preconceptions aside: families from all walks of life can, and do, send their sons here. Name down at birth has long gone and now around 60 per cent of Etonians do not have any family connection with the school. We heard from lots of parents who had plenty to say about the school they had chosen for their sons; they were as interesting, non-standard and off-message as we could wish, but all were convinced that though demanding, an Eton education was the very best choice they could have made.

As for Etonians themselves, many are super talented, most are charming, but once you become 'uniform blind' (and because nearly everyone is wearing it this doesn't take very long), they're reassuringly just schoolboys of the scruffy hair, doodles on hands and scuffed shoes variety.

The term 'old Etonian' has of late become something of a knee-jerk pejorative shorthand for posh, wealthy and privileged, indiscriminately applied to the relatively small number of alumni prominent in public life – from David Cameron, number 19 in the list of British prime ministers educated at Eton, to actors such as Eddie Redmayne, Damian Lewis, Hugh Laurie and Tom Hiddleston. The reality is that you're more likely to have encountered Etonians unknowingly as they quietly get on with doing their professional thing in journalism, medicine, education, law and the arts. Before them came centuries of soldiers, including 37 holders of the Victoria Cross, explorers, novelists, sportsmen, poets, politicians, academics, philanthropists and the odd ne'er-do-well (ancient and modern). Fictional OEs include James Bond (expelled), Bertie Wooster, Lord Peter Wimsey, Mark Darcy and that old crocodile-phobe, Captain Hook.

Entrance: You might think that all Eton has to do is to sit back and wait for the world to beat a path to its door, so when we met the director and deputy director of admissions we were surprised, and delighted, to find two scholarly Indiana Joneses. As they spoke we had a vision of them in pith helmets, enthusiastically navigating roads less taken to discover new talent for their school. With around five applicants for each of 250 places, you don't need us to tell you that getting a place at Eton is tough, but it's reassuring to know that the admissions department is equally rigorous in seeking out the 'right' candidates.

This is an academically demanding school, but a place depends on much more than getting all the right answers in tests. Eton looks for that extra je ne sais quoi – a quality that is more about character and personality than bolt-on achievements. Parents who believe they can play the system by forcing their son to memorise War and Peace, making him practise the harpsichord until his fingers bleed and drilling him to say that his favourite leisure pursuit is calculus, do not generally prevail. Of course, if your son willingly does this kind of thing he's probably in with a chance.

All applicants are assessed in year 6 – verbal reasoning, numeracy, perceptual potential, interview and school report. School recognises that pre-testing may penalise late developers, so stays in touch with school heads and gets feedback on near-miss candidates. Just think for a minute of the amount of work that assessing and interviewing 1,200 10-year-old boys involves – a five-strong committee spends two days considering the candidates, and places offered are conditional on passing CE or, for boys at state schools, Eton's own exam in year 8. A further 80 names go on the waiting list.

And what about the prep school baccalaureate? We asked knowing that a kind word from Eton would cheer its champions in prep schools up and down the land. The Indiana Joneses morphed back into tail coated Etonians: 'We still like CE; CE is the right foundation, it covers all the core areas of the year 8 curriculum.'

Scholarship boys include 14 King's Scholars (decided on academic merit alone), plus New Foundation scholars (boys joining Eton from state schools) and many more.

Minimum of six grade 7s at GCSE needed for entry to sixth form, not much of a hurdle at a school where the majority get 10 or 11 GCSE 8-9s. Twelve sixth form scholarships a year for boys from state sector or independent schools lacking sixth form provision.

Exit: One or two may depart for co-ed or day schools post-GCSE, but after A levels almost every boy will be headed for university. Eton has in the past been inexplicably coy about its leavers' destinations, keeping information on their website that is several years out of date. But no more! Perhaps they have listened to prospective and current parents' views. Maybe, ahem, they took heed of our comments about how unhelpful this was. Whatever the reason, we welcome the new spirit of openness. No more 'ball park' figures for us: in 2018, 60 Oxbridge places (38 Oxford, 22 Cambridge); three to UK medical schools. Rest to the likes of Durham, Edinburgh, Exeter, UCL and Bristol.

Really impressive numbers to Ivy League and other prestigious colleges in the US (40+). School says: 'There continues to be strong interest in applying to the US with a high percentage of those applicants ultimately choosing to attend US universities. The vast majority of boys apply in their final year, with only a few opting for the US route in A Block after leaving Eton.'

Money matters: Indeed it does, and school remains determined as ever that lack of it should not be a barrier to any boy who is offered a scholarship. Currently around quarter of boys receive some form of financial support – still a way to go before Eton reaches its stated goal of being 'needs blind'.

Remarks: As George Orwell definitely didn't write about his alma mater, some schools are more equal than others. Eton is an extraordinary place, like many of England's institutions it's a misunderstood mass of contradictions – ancient and modern; exclusive and accessible; liberal and exacting; loved and hated; formal and eccentric; hierarchical and meritocratic. And though it sounds counter-intuitive, somehow these traditions, formalities, rules and hierarchies harmonise, allowing 1,300 tail-coated flowers to bloom.

Farleigh School

Red Rice, Andover, Hampshire SP11 7PW

Ages 3–13 **Pupils** 450 **Boarders** 100 full/weekly, 40 flexi (from year 3) RC

Fees: Day £10,770 – £19,590; Boarding £21,990 – £25,485 pa

01264 710766
www.farleighschool.com

Headmaster: Since 2004, Father Simon Everson BA cert theology (50s). Educated at Caterham School and then spent a year working as an auxiliary nurse. 'It was the most formative year,' he says. His parents weren't churchgoers but he studied theology at Leeds Collegiate, followed by a three-year certificate in theology awarded by the University of Oxford. He spent 13 years as an Anglican curate and vicar in south London, first in Rotherhithe and then in Kennington. 'I couldn't have enjoyed it more,' he says. 'The people were so warm and welcoming.' He took a keen interest in local schools (he was chaplain and governor of Archbishop Michael Ramsey Technology College in Camberwell) and when the opportunity to become senior chaplain at Hurstpierpoint College came up he jumped at it. Following his conversion to Catholicism he was asked to apply for the role of chaplain at Farleigh and he became head five years later.

Thoughtful, enthusiastic and engaging, he's determined that children should enjoy their time at Farleigh – and they clearly do. He recently gave an assembly about the 10 things he hoped an ex-Farleigh child would say about the school. They included the following: 'Here people believed in me. Here I was listened to. Here I was understood. Here I was given the best possible start in life.' He attributes the school's success to three things – having a clear vision, recruiting the best possible staff and having 'utterly supportive families'.

He enjoys teaching this age group because of the children's openness and lack of cynicism. 'I feel completely energised by them,' he says. He's adamant that the school should be inclusive and ensures that every pupil represents the school in sport every season. Parents say he is an outstanding head. One told us: 'He is an amazing and very unique man. He is very approachable and understands how parents think. The children highly respect him.' Another explained that the ethos of the school 'comes primarily from the headmaster, who is the most remarkable exemplar of a decent man. He is an inspirational headmaster who imbues the school with his values.'

He is certainly busy. As well as his headship role, he's the school chaplain and teaches RS to years 7 and 8 and PHSE to years 6, 7 and 8. He also celebrates Sunday mass, baptisms, weddings and funerals in the school chapel. He tells the children they can ask him anything they like and is constantly surprised by their insightfulness. Nevertheless, he was taken aback when a child asked him if his dog collar was 'bolted on'. He ensures that pupils are grounded and aware of what is going on in the wider world, from Syria and Iraq to the local community. 'We are always trying to look away from ourselves,' he says. Pupils visit homes for the elderly in Andover and he was delighted when a 100-year-old woman imparted her tip for a happy life to them. 'Don't bear grudges against anybody,' she said. The school also has a long-standing relationship with a local special needs school.

Head's wife Gail is immersed in school life – one parent described her as 'an unsung heroine, always smiling and very caring'. A qualified nurse, she is part of the learning support team. They live in a house on-site and have two daughters, one at college and one at university. Asked about his hobbies, the head answers with one word: 'Italy'. Passionate about music (Wagner in particular), he used to play (and teach) the cello and hopes to take it up again when he has time.

Entrance: Non-selective. No formal assessment for entry into kindergarten and the pre-prep but pre-prep joiners are invited to spend a taster morning with their peers. 'We don't really turn children away,' says the pre-prep head, 'as long as we feel this is the right place for them.' Virtually all pre-prep children transfer to the prep.

Informal assessment for prep school places. Priority to practising Catholics (40 per cent of pupils are Catholic), boarders, siblings and children of former pupils. The school offers a 15 per cent discount to full or weekly boarding children of Forces families. Bursaries are available on a means-tested basis. The school has partnered with the Royal National Children's Springboard Foundation, the boarding school bursary charity, to offer means-tested, 100 per cent bursaries to two children from disadvantaged backgrounds. It recently launched its own bursaries programme – The St Theresa Fund – for year 7 and 8 boarders.

Exit: Most prep pupils stay till 13, although a few leave at 11. When we visited, Westminster, St Paul's and Wellington College had recently announced plans to drop CE from 2021 and rely solely on pre-tests. 'I can see the advantage of it because the children can then enjoy the rest of years 6, 7 and 8,' the head told us, at the same time expressing concern about those who don't get through the pre-test and have to do CE as well. An impressive number of children gain scholarships – 19 in 2018.

Year 8 leavers go to a host of schools – 21 different destinations in 2018. Popular choices include Marlborough (eight out of 53 in 2018), Sherborne, Sherborne Girls, Radley, Godolphin, St Mary's Ascot, St Mary's Calne, Ampleforth and Downside. Some boys to Eton, Harrow or Winchester most years. The school makes a huge effort to stay in touch with former pupils, with a thriving Farleigh Society and regular reunions.

Remarks: Founded as a school for Catholic boys at Farleigh Wallop near Basingstoke, it moved to its current location in 1982 and became co-ed. The heart is a magnificent Georgian house set in 70 acres of sweeping Hampshire parkland with a landscaped arboretum. On the day we visited the head pointed out a glorious red maple tree, its leaves glowing in the autumn sunlight. Despite its rural setting, the school is only five minutes' drive from the A303 (very handy for London parents). It has grown over the past years but the head doesn't want it to get any bigger than it is now. Average class sizes of 14 in the prep and rarely more than 18.

The house has been sympathetically adapted to school life, while retaining much of its original charm. The elegant drawing room is used as a common room and the ballroom is now the chapel, recently extended so it easily seats the whole school. 'You can come into the chapel and have a quiet moment any time,' our young tour guides told us. A variety of new buildings, including a modern science and food tech department and a swish music block, complete with a stunning recital room, 12 practice rooms, recording studio and rock room.

Subject specialists from year 5 (French and PE from reception and Latin from year 6). There's an annual week-long French trip for year 6s. Pupils are set for maths from year 3, English from year 4 and science from year 6. Science is taught in three ultra-modern labs, with circular fixed benches with gas taps, electric points and circuit points. Everyone does ICT – an hour a week in years 1 to 7 and 30 minutes in year 8. Teachers can book iPads for younger children but year 7 and 8 pupils are provided with their own by the school. Everyone learns to type and the children learn coding from scratch. 'Someone left with a typing speed of 82 wpm last year,' said our awestruck guides. Year 5 pupils and up create their own e-portfolios – a record of their work and a useful revision tool. Four classes per year group in the prep (around 60 children in each year). Saturday school for years 3 to 8. Learning support is free, provided one-to-one or in small groups and very well integrated into the fabric of the school. Well-stocked library – all pupils have a library lesson and a reading lesson each week. School has also introduced a 20-minute 'drop everything and read' session every day. Assembly is held every day, either in the chapel or the theatre.

The music is 'extraordinary'. Three-quarters of the pupils play an instrument and there are plenty of opportunities to join orchestras, bands, groups, specialist ensembles and choirs. Several rock bands and three jazz ensembles, including the Thundering Herd Big Band, Five Foot Six traditional jazz band and Green Shoots. Piano is popular and every pianist gets the chance to play in public at the annual piano festival. Programme of 50 to 60 musical performances each year, plus regular informal concerts. New head of drama is continuing the focus on public speaking, regarded as an invaluable skill for the future. The school excels at debating, regularly winning the prep schools' debating competition at Marlborough and elsewhere. Myriad opportunities to act in plays and musicals, all performed in the well-equipped theatre. Annual dance show and school recently introduced an arts festival, with a street piano, concerts, outdoor science laboratory and a Bake Off competition.

Art and DT departments pride themselves on discovering pupils' talent – often when the children themselves had no idea. 'It's the sheer, raw pleasure of a child finding that they could do something that was completely unknown to them before,' says the head. The head of DT (wearing an apron emblazoned with the words 'epic DT teacher', which he hastened to explain was given by a parent) says he is constantly surprised by the children's inventiveness, whether they are making 'wiggly wooden snakes' or building bridges – yes, literally.

Sport is important. Games on four afternoons a week, with matches on Wednesday and Saturday afternoons. Vast expanse of playing fields, plus a 22m indoor pool, sports hall and an all-weather pitch. PE curriculum includes dance, gymnastics, life-saving, fitness and leadership/team-building. Boys do football, rugby, cross-country, cricket, athletics and tennis and girls do hockey, netball, cross-country, cricket, rounders, athletics and tennis. Notable successes include the U12 netball team winning the IAPS national finals in 2018 and recent U13 rugby team unbeaten in five years and 55 matches at Farleigh. Tennis is popular – two-thirds of pupils have lessons.

The school offers flexi-boarding up to the summer term of year 7, when children either revert to day or convert to weekly or full boarding. The boarders include a cohort of four or five children from Madrid, who spend three terms at the school. Boarding is well organised, with junior (years 3 to 6) and senior (years 7 and 8) boarding houses. Larger and very wholesome dorms for youngest while older pupils are housed in twos and fours. Children are encouraged to bring photographs and posters from home, all adding to the cheery atmosphere. The school has its own 24/7 surgery, complete with a brightly coloured model skeleton to explain the parts of the body ('we call him Nelson,' the senior nurse told us with a smile). GPs from nearby Andover Health Centre visit twice a week. Children eat all their meals in a light, airy dining room. At lunch there's lots of choice, including a vegetarian option, plus salads. Boarders have high praise for the breakfasts – they can have a cooked breakfast every day if they choose. Plenty of opportunities for pupils to air their views – a pupil from every class represents their peers on the school council.

The Catholic faith is at the school's core and Sunday mass is open to all. The head aims to keep faith enjoyable and contemporary and members of other churches say they never feel left out. At mass children of other faiths 'come up and receive a blessing'. Parents praise the school's pastoral care – 'it's why we chose the school,' said one mother. We were impressed by the buddy system, whereby younger children team up with older buddies. We spotted pairs of intertwined butterflies woven into the hedge – depicting each pair of buddies.

Most live within 15 miles of the school, including villages around Andover, Basingstoke, Romsey, Stockbridge, Salisbury and Winchester, while some come from near Alresford, Devizes, Marlborough and Newbury. The school runs minibuses on three routes. Parents are a mix of locals, Londoners and Forces families – all hugely supportive of the school. 'Farleigh creates very unique children,' said one. 'The kids are really grounded and unspoilt. They are taught that the most important thing is to be kind.' Another parent concurred. 'In this day and age Farleigh does something remarkable,' he said. 'The children it spits out at the other end are by the standards of their peers remarkably well-adjusted and thoroughly decent and kind.'

The pre-prep is based in its own spacious building on the school site, with two classes per year group. We arrived at 4pm, with excited children pouring into after-school activities like yoga and sewing. Pre-prep opens its doors for breakfast club at 7.30am and an after-school club runs till 5.45pm.

Farleigh is an outstanding school and we aren't in the least surprised that parents go into raptures about the place. 'Ah, lovely Farleigh,' mused one father. Children, teachers and parents extol its virtues, its academic success, its beautiful grounds and its prowess at everything from music to sport. But above all, it's a happy school, led by an exceptional head who's determined that every pupil should be listened to and understood. He wants children to be given the best possible start in life – and they really are.

F

Felsted Preparatory School

Linked with Felsted School

Braintree Road, Felsted, Essex CM6 3JL

Ages 4–13 **Pupils** 515 **Boarders** 10 full, 36 weekly/flexi (from 9 years)

Fees: Day £9,285 – £17,820; Boarding £23,250- £24,465 pa

01371 822610
www.felsted.org

Head: Since September 2016, Simon James BA PGCE (40s), whose degree is in history. He moved from Chigwell Junior School, where he was also head, before which he was head of Rossall School, Lancashire. Prior to that, he was director of studies at Kings School, Chester, a post he took up following various teaching posts at key stage 2.

He's relaxed, easy going and chatty – definitely more of a carrot than a stick man, and with an open door policy for children, parents and staff alike. But don't be fooled – despite his warm and cuddly exterior, this is a head that kids don't want to disappoint and who is not afraid of being proactive when it comes to improving school processes and strategies. 'He's out and about every morning at the school gates, which is a really nice touch,' one parent told us, and he teaches games and history 'to keep in touch with pupils.'

He lives a 10 minute drive away with his wife, Jill – who joined Felsted as a teacher four years prior to him – and their two daughters, who joined the school when their mum did. 'It made this a very easy move for me,' he smiles. A keen cricketer and ex-rugby player, he enjoys cooking and travelling with his family during school holidays.

Entrance: Various entry points including 4+ and 7+, with big intake at 11+ when prospective pupils submit a confidential report from their previous school and undergo interview and assessments in English, maths, non-verbal and verbal reasoning. 'Entrance isn't overly selective, but it is rigorous when it comes to the process involved,' one parent sums up. Entry lower down is less stringent, although interview and taster day still a must (and a school report, if they're moving from another school). Academic scholarships are available, covering up to 20 per cent of fees. There's also the Mary Skills award (a convenient surname, if ever we heard one) for talent in subjects including music, sport, art, design, technology and engineering, which covers up to £2,000 of fees. Some open bursaries are also on offer. Unlike many other preps, classes continue up to the end of year 8.

Exit: More than 94 per cent proceed to the senior school, often to join older siblings. 'Caters for all types, so why look elsewhere?' The remainder head to other boarding schools, overseas or move for financial reasons (to state schools).

Remarks: The prep school is made up of a hodge-podge of buildings (some beautiful; some less so) directly across the road from its big sister, the senior school. With a few exceptions, these buildings are divided into four separate areas – each home to the school's four 'phases,' which move the pupils on towards greater self-reliance, focus and specialisation. Each phase has its own head, who – together with the director of learning and deputy head – make up the senior leadership team. Stewart House – home to reception, year 1 and 2 – is a contemporary, purpose built two storey building with lots of sunlight and stunning views, not to mention a huge, cuddly 'FelsTed' in the reception area. The classrooms are spacious and colourful, with plenty of imaginative artwork adorning the walls, and there's a library, multi-purpose hall and wide, bright play spaces instead of corridors. Years 3 and 4 are based in Frome Court – a series of prefab buildings, where pupils can use the dedicated contained playground or venture out into the bigger green space, shared with the older children. At this age, children start to be mainly taught by subject specialist teachers. Years 5 and 6 move up to Cloisters – based in (you guessed it) the old cloistered part of the school, and finally, there's Courtauld House for years 7 and 8, which includes a sociable common room. All share the new and shiny science labs, spacious ICT suite, Ross Hall (for assemblies, performances and some games) and art block as part of their impressive facilities.

As with the senior school, parents here recoil at the thought of huge pressure. Every pupil and parent we spoke to believes the balance is just right and we were impressed with the school's commitment to that overused term, 'holistic education.' Indeed, Felsted claims one of the biggest co-curricular programmes in the country, with LAMDA, golf, riding, cooking, gardening, Mandarin and judo just a few of the wealth of opportunities on offer for these lucky young things. There are also lots of trips – the head was about to introduce a bushcraft trip for year 6 when we visited.

The three classes per year group are kept to a maximum of 18 students up to year 3, which then rises to 20, and there's setting in languages, English, maths and science – usually with five tutor groups per year, with some exceptions (eg there are four groups for maths in years 6 and 7). There is plenty of personalised learning on offer for SEN, usually outside the classroom and for half hour lessons – as many as necessary per week. 'Welcome to my box,' laughed the head of SEN when we met her. But although her office is indeed compact, there are two other dedicated learning support rooms upstairs and children seem to like the environment – no stigma attached. Extension lessons for the very able. 'I've got a very intelligent child, who is also very strong-minded, and they've dealt with him brilliantly,' one parent told us.

Languages are strong, with all pupils learning Spanish, to which they add either French or German from year 6. The brightest kids also take Latin from year 7. Homework is given twice a week from year 5 and three times a week from year 7 and woe betide anyone who hands it in late. 'They cut you no slack,' one student told us, despite the long school day. Indeed, while year 2s and under finish at 3.30pm, year 3s start to be introduced to lengthier days that, by year 8, last from 8.20am-5.55pm – that's longer than a lot of adults spend at work in a full-time job. And there's Saturday school – optional for years 5 and 6 and compulsory for years 7 and 8 – although most youngsters love it. 'You get to do activities like forest school and golf,' one student explained.

Drama is taught weekly, with good take up at extracurricular level too and a much talked-about school performance every year. Ditto with music – as in all students do it, and many do extra, including belonging to the orchestra, chapel choir or one of the many bands and ensembles ranging from the jazz band to steel drum group. Plus, around 60 per cent learn an instrument via peripatetic lessons. We love the two art rooms – an Aladdin's cave of opportunity for budding young artists, who can try their hand at everything from textiles to pottery – 'and even making props for the school plays,' the art teacher told us, pointing to the huge elephant's head from the Lion King performance.

Sport – of which the core for boys are rugby and hockey, while for girls, it's netball and hockey (and cricket for both in the summer) – seems to strike the right balance between healthy competition and inclusiveness, with regular fixtures for A-G teams in many sports. And with players reaching county level in cricket and rugby – plus national finalists for hockey, netball and horse riding – there's plenty of silverware to keep the school cabinets glistening.

Boarding is a major part of school life here, with Felsted Prep boasting its own – very uninstitutional – boarding house, which has a capacity for 64 students: one floor for boys, the other for girls. In reality, some 10 use it full time, while there are some 36 weekly or part time boarders, where parents commit to three specific days a week. Bedrooms have between two and eight beds, with children encouraged to personalise their space, and each floor has its own common room. The boarding day begins at 7.45am for breakfast, while evenings include homework time, activities ranging from ICT to football (with different choices each night), and weekends include trips out ranging from cinema to the beach. Even the so called 'domestic fairies' get stuck into the community feel, with lots of friendly notes from students to them, and vice versa, left on doors. Communication with parents is encouraged, with animated videos regularly sent home and unlimited phone calls allowed during sociable hours.

Pastoral care is a key strength back in the daytime part of school too, with each head of phase tasked with ensuring the children are happy, while a tutor system for the older children means those in years 6, 7 and 8 have their own personal tutor for three years. 'These tutors know us well and make sure we feel comfortable talking to them,' one student told us. There's a matron available too, as well as mindfulness classes.

While rewards are seen as being more effective than punishments to keep kids on the straight and narrow, misdemeanours are certainly not overlooked. Indeed, each child carries round two cards in their pocket, reminiscent of an old train ticket from the 1960s – green for good deeds and cream for bad ones. Teachers sign them when either happens (holding doors open might be a good one, while running in a corridor a bad one) and three signatures equals a house point or, conversely, a detention, either on a weekday – or for serious transgressions, a Saturday one with the headteacher.

This is a school with an outdoorsy focus, complete with outdoor pizza oven, outdoor classrooms and mini Duke of Edinburgh style award activities outdoors one afternoon a week. Links with senior school are on the up, including joint academic ventures, such as years 7 and 8 working with seniors on science projects and use of sports facilities. Food is good – we tasted it – although the dining space options aren't great for the younger ones.

Despite the school being located in rural Essex, it feels part of a much bigger world rather than existing as a primary school bubble – no doubt helped by things like their 'global centre,' complete with a skype wall, which enables pupils to communicate with a school they support in India. Families – who are a mixture of traditional farming families, the super wealthy, entrepreneurs, middle class professionals and no shortage of dual income families – can't get enough of it. 'Felsted is more of a way of life than a school,' one parent told us. 'And it's one the children know they are very lucky to have.'

Many schools claim to be child centred, focusing on each individual across a wide ability range, but not all achieve it. Felsted does, providing a busy, bustling and largely fun environment, where the ethos is all about doing the very best you can and finding your key strengths.

F

Felsted School

Linked with Felsted Preparatory School

Felsted, Great Dunmow, Essex CM6 3LL

Ages 13–18 **Pupils** 564 **Sixth form** 244 **Boarders** 121 full, 105 weekly, 189 flexi **C of E**

Fees: Day £23,550; Boarding £29,010 – £35,985 pa

01371 822605
www.felsted.org

Headmaster: Since 2015, Chris Townsend BA PGCE (40s), previously deputy head. Classics degree from Oxford, where he was an exhibitioner and won three cricket blues. First teaching post at alma mater Dean Close, then housemaster and head of boarding at Stowe, then to Felsted in 2010 as deputy head.

Students and parents alike revel in recounting the story of the moment his appointment as head was announced. 'The whole school – including staff and pupils – erupted into applause, which lasted for about 10 minutes!' we were told, with all parents, staff and pupils we spoke to enthusing about how 'excellent,' 'inspirational' and 'nurturing' he is. Teaches when he can (Greek and Latin), plays piano at school concerts, referees some of the rugby, as well as doing the corridor rounds and attending some school trips, including one to Uganda and

Malawi in the summer holidays. But despite his larger-than-life reputation, he is not extrovert, loud, opinionated or loquacious; instead, he is mild-mannered, quiet and unassuming – just the kind of chap you'd feel safe leaving shy, petrified little Johnny with on first day of boarding school. Not that he's afraid to discipline, as any student will confirm.

He couldn't live closer if he tried, with a door behind his office desk leading straight to home, where he resides with his wife Melanie (assistant head at another local school), their two children (both at Felsted) and a red setter.

Academic matters: Not overly selective, but each year a solid cohort achieves top grades across the board in both GCSEs and A levels: 48 per cent A*-A/9-7 at GCSE and 65 per cent A*-B and 27 per cent A*/A at A level in 2018. The broad ability range is big pull to many parents, including one who told us, 'My son got into a top grammar school, but I didn't want him in a highly pressurised, "work-work-work" environment – Felsted still gets good results, but it's more fun, offers a more holistic education and has a mix of people that better reflects real life.'

At GCSE, the strongest subjects are maths, English, sciences, RE and languages, with other popular options including geography and history. There's also a good creative uptake, with decent numbers of students and grades in DT, music and drama. At A level, students do particularly well in psychology, geography, RE and history – and, increasingly, maths and science. Other popular options include business studies and economics. 'This part of the world is known for its entrepreneurial buzz,' points out the head. More generally, the school has a reputation of bringing out the best in all and IB is taking off even among quite conservative local families – currently about a third of the sixth form opts for it: 35 average point score in 2018.

Year 9s all learn Spanish (the core language here), plus French, German or Latin, then in year 10 they can take up to three languages, with other options including Italian. Other languages also on offer as part of the IB, where they can be self-taught, with past students having done just that with Japanese, Russian and Mandarin. Parents praise the 'native speaking language teachers and high number of classroom assistants to make sure everyone stays on track.'

Setting (up to six sets per year) in maths, English, sciences and languages and class sizes are kept small, between 15-20 up to GCSE, and often considerably smaller in sixth form. Staff development encouraged, with both peers and pupils invited to provide feedback on selected lessons and suggest what constitutes good or outstanding teaching – all part of the collaborative ethos of the school. Projects with other schools also exist, with a view to sharing best practice. Teachers – all of whom are involved in pastoral care and who really get to know the children – are known for being a thoroughly committed bunch, with a positive and engaged staff common room.

Homework isn't for the faint-hearted, although for the younger ones, homework sessions are built into the school day – a welcome relief, say parents, given that the school day lasts from 8.15am to 6pm and there's also Saturday school. IT is embedded into learning, with pupils encouraged to use Chromebooks, Google Classroom and even smartphones in some lessons (more of which, later).

SEN pupils, of whom there are many (albeit at the mild to moderate end – mainly dyslexia, dyspraxia, ADHD and autistic spectrum), have personalised support from the learning department, which has no stigma attached, not least because it's open to everyone, offering everything from intensive one-to-one tuition to drop-in sessions to help with prep. 'Why wouldn't you want extra support to help you do your best?' one student asked, rhetorically. 'My son has dyslexia and he wound up with As and A*s, thanks to the personalised support he got behind the scenes,' said one parent. EAL teachers also on hand, also in a specialist department.

Games, options, the arts: Traditionally sporty, with the school producing some outstanding cricketers and Olympic athletes, and there were three boys signed to professional rugby teams when we visited. In fact, hockey, rugby, netball and cricket (including for girls, now that it's replaced rounders) are all strong, with regular success at regional and national championships. Partnerships with professional clubs such as Saracens Rugby, Essex Cricket and Blue Hornets Hockey. But fear not if your child doesn't make the teams as the emphasis is very much on participation. Lots of other alternatives to keep you fit and occupied, including swimming, badminton, squash, show jumping, water polo and tennis, to name a few. Games fields and facilities stretch as far as the eye can see across the school's 80 acres and include 12 pitches, nine cricket squares, two floodlit AstroTurf fields, 10 hard courts, squash courts, gym, weight training – and the rather less impressive and tired-looking sports hall and indoor swimming pool, the latter of which was mentioned by almost every parent we spoke to as the 'main downside of the school.'

Pupils are all expected to have a crack at music, in one form or another – and few complain, with lots of pride around the many choirs (including the elite chapel choir that sings at main services) and orchestras. The House Shout singing competition is a favourite event, and all students sing in chapel. Quite a few learn an instrument via a peripatetic teacher and there's an emphasis on percussion, including marimba players (a marimba was donated to the school by Dame Evelyn Glennie, who performed here). Regular opportunities for overseas tours – the choir was going to Italy at Easter during the academic year we visited.

Everyone does drama in year 9, then it's an option – but a popular one, with a few students going onto study it at university. Easily the best school play posters we've ever seen displayed on the walls – including Jesus Christ Superstar (which around 120 pupils took part in) and Joseph. Parents rave about the quality. Every two years, the school takes a production to America, including a past performance in a maximum security women's prison.

The art school, which is based in the old school laundry, is fabulously quirky and practical, with plenty of great facilities (although no dark room, we noticed) and an authentic feel. Extracurricular possibilities are plentiful, including weekly life drawing sessions. Evidence of some serious talent.

Foreign exchanges to a wealth of countries and residentials to practically everywhere you can think of. Biologists and geographers go to Bali; tennis players to Portugal; business studies students to New York; other sports tours to Australia etc etc. Back in the UK, geography field trip to rather less glamorous Swanage and plenty of cultural trips to the likes of Cambridge and London. Charity volunteers to Uganda, their partner school in Ethiopia and a former pupil's Magic Bus, which supports children in the slums of Mumbai – and there are links with Royal Docks Community School in the East End, which pupils regularly visit.

You won't find many schools with a longer list of extracurricular options – we felt exhausted just looking at the 50+ options including academic society, charity projects, amateur radio club, astronomy club, beekeeping, bridge, Greek club, life skills, Model United Nations, science film club. Huge take up of D of E – at the last count no fewer than 12 gold awards in the upper sixth – and 237 enrolled in CCF. Very much accords with Round Square school promoting IDEALS – internationalism, democracy, care for the environment, adventurous pursuits, leadership and service. Felsted has been a global member since 2010.

Boarding: Some 80 per cent board – full-time (mostly international and expat families, with a sprinkling in the UK), weekly (usually, when both parents work) or three-nights-a-week (mainly local families). 'We live in the village, but I asked my mum and dad if I could board as you get the best of both worlds,' one student told us. 'There's always a waiting list – the boarders are really happy,' said a parent.

Two day and eight boarding houses, five for boys and five for girls – plus co-ed boarding in the prep school from 9 years upwards. Separate upper sixth form boarding houses. Here, students get their own room and more freedoms – seen as good preparation for university. Each house has its own unique feel and ranges from being in the main building of the old school (traditional rooms – almost an Oxbridge feel) to the brand new, open-plan girls' boarding house. Ongoing investment means that a seven-figure sum was also about to be spent on upgrading one of the boys' houses when we visited. Dorms range from singles up to eight beds. 'They're pretty strict on tidiness, but it's more a case of matron having a quiet word, rather than draconian room inspections,' a student told us.

While the boarding timetable is highly structured (in evenings, it's supper in main school, back to your house for prep, then quiet time, while weekends have a full activity programme, with chapel on Sundays), there's also 'lots of chances to catch your breath,' as the head puts it. Boarders particularly like the independence – for example, being able to walk to the local shop or getting a Chinese take-away from the village – which is well balanced by the feeling that this is a really supportive environment, with many of the houseparents having young families. There are no restrictions on parental visits and robust measures in place to help new and international students settle in.

Background and atmosphere: Traditional, yet progressive, it feeds off its history but is not hidebound by it. Founded in 1564 by Richard, Lord Riche, Lord Chancellor of England, the school's original Guild Hall is still in use with other, later, attractive grade I and II listed buildings scattered throughout the village, interspersed with well-tended lawns and sports fields and cut through by the quiet Dunmow to Braintree road. Most recent additions include the music school, the Bathurst gardens for socialising and outdoor performances and the sixth form centre – a great space to hang out, play pool or enjoy regular social events where the odd glass of wine is permitted. Pupils particularly like the coffee shop – open to all in recreational times, although only sixth formers are allowed to work in there.

Some areas could do with an upgrade, notably the swimming pool and sports hall – and we'd hoped for more of a wow factor in the library. 'My husband went to Felsted and much of it doesn't feel look like it's changed from 30 years ago – but then again, it's not the facilities that make a great school,' said one parent. Food is good, with unlimited helpings. As a C of E school, the chapel is at its heart and Felsted is one of only two remaining independent schools to have its own mission church in the East End of London, with links to the church and the young people in the surrounding area.

Overall impression of being a happy, happening place with parents content to be swept along for the ride. 'I'd be amazed if you found a Felstedian who wakes up and thinks, "I don't want to go to school today",' said one student.

Pastoral care, well-being and discipline: This is a school with big expectations around behaviour and uniform, which seem to be unanimously welcomed by parents and local businesses – and even the children agree it's 'all pretty fair.' 'You're as likely to get rewarded for good behaviour as you are punished for misdemeanours,' one told us, explaining the school's card system, which involves each pupil carrying two small cards in their pocket – one for good deeds to be instantly recorded by teachers ('If we carry books for a teacher, for example') and one for transgressions ('If our uniform is really scruffy or we talk in class, for instance'). A full 'good' card gets you housepoints, while a full 'bad' one lands you in detention. Around a dozen temporary exclusions in the year we visited, mainly for serious bad language, bullying and alcohol abuse.

Lenient with mobiles phones. 'They are part of modern living. So there seems nothing to be gained by denying their existence, and much more to be gained by embracing them and it's for this reason that we sometimes ask students who have one to produce them during a lesson and use them to assist with learning,' one teacher told us.

Pastoral care highly praised and attributed to a range of factors, including an atmosphere of openness and purpose; the house system that 'means everyone is close – and not just with people in their year,' said a student; peer counselling; and prefects being trained in child protection. Bullying minimal, doubtless for all the same reasons – and when it happens, it's dealt with swiftly on both sides. A life coach and a counsellor are on hand, and there's a new well-being centre 'at the heart of the school'.

Pupils and parents: Felsted produces self-starting, entrepreneurial and independent spirits – characteristics that are immediately evident among the ambitious, self-motivated and self-aware pupils, who have some of the healthiest can-do attitudes we've seen. The mix of students – who range from the highly-driven and academically-oriented to the more fun-loving and easy-going – is a breath of fresh air. And they are all pretty down to earth. Ditto for the parents, who are expected to get stuck into school life. 'We're only into the second week of term and already we've had harvest festival and a charity event – and that's not including Saturdays spent watching sport,' laughed one parent, but with no irritation. 'I love it – we all do.'

While most families live within a couple of hours of the school, it is increasingly attracting London-based families. Taking advantage of its proximity to Stansted Airport, international students make up some 18 per cent of pupils. Long list of notable OFs includes English test cricketer John Stephenson and General Sir Richard Dannatt, until recently chief of the general staff.

Entrance: A hundred pupils – split across three classes – come in at year 9: around 70 come up from the prep (having passed a transfer exam), with the remaining 30 from feeder schools including Holmwood House, Heathmount, Orwell Park and Edge Grove. Those taking CE are required to obtain 50 per cent in each paper. Others take a verbal reasoning test, interview and submit a confidential report from their current school. They may also take tests in maths, French and English for setting purposes. The same is true at 14+ entry. At 16+ (when the year group increases from 100 to 125), there is a similar entry procedure and pupils are required to obtain five GCSEs at grade B/6 or better including B grades in the subjects being pursued. Pupils who do not have English as their first language will be assessed by the head of EAL.

Exit: Around 80-90 per cent stay on to the sixth form. After A level, most to good universities such as Exeter, Durham, Nottingham, Cardiff, Liverpool and King's London. Three to Oxbridge and one medic in 2018, plus one off to ESCP Europe Business School to study management. Business-related subjects, humanities, law and the sciences popular.

Money matters: Academic, music, sport, art, design and technology or drama and all-rounder scholarships offering up to 20 per cent off the fees are available at 13+ and 16+. There are some assisted places up to 100 per cent on a means-tested basis or via open bursaries.

Remarks: At one time, the focus on catering for a wide ability range meant this school's reputation in the academic stakes wasn't as high as it could have been. Not so now, with a renewed focus on academic performance striking just the right balance with valuing individualism and quirkiness. No wonder there's such a sense of excitement as this school becomes increasingly recognised as a leading independent boarding and day school.

Feltonfleet School

106

Byfleet Road, Cobham, Surrey KT11 1DR

Ages 3–13 **Pupils** 398 **Boarders** 10 weekly, 50 flexi (from 7 years)
C of E

Fees: Day £11,799 – £17,325; Weekly boarding £21,051 pa

01932 862264
www.feltonfleet.co.uk

Headmistress: Since January 2018, Shelley Lance, previously deputy head. Theology degree from King's College London; began her teaching career at Alleyn's, then taught at Whitgift, where she was head of lower school and responsible for the school's pastoral care provision. She joined Feltonfleet in 2010.

A self-confessed 'reluctant head' – 'I love the frontline coalface interaction, which can very easily be squeezed out when you're leading a school,' she explains. So she teaches RS and mindfulness, as well as sitting in on other classes, including in pre-prep, and doing gate duty every morning. 'It can mean long days and be exhausting, but it pays dividends because I know all the teachers, children and parents, which facilitates easy communications and means I sense frustrations and know when changes are needed'. Charismatic, grounded, gutsy and highly articulate, she has certainly not shied away from making changes, including a major rebrand, replacing compartmentalised learning with a more thematic approach and moving away from common entrance towards 'the equally rigorous model' of the Prep School Baccalaureate. Plus – and this is the real biggie – a major expansion of pre-prep. Parents call her a 'natural leader', 'responsive', 'phenomenal' and 'everything you could want in a head', while pupils say she's 'fun' and 'very involved'.

Married to Ed, head of lower school at Epsom College, they have a young son, Henry. Enjoys family time, the great outdoors, skiing and reading.

Entrance: Largely non-selective, the pre-prep works on a first-come-first-served entry basis which means, says the school, that 'broad range of ability inevitably comes through.' A phased pre-prep expansion from 86 to 160 places will make competition less of an extreme sport than it was, although parents are well advised to bag one of places by registering at birth. Further external places available for year 3 entry, when you can expect border controls in form of maths and English assessment plus interview 'to search out character and enthusiasm for learning'. (Own year 2 children aren't tested.) Occasional places also crop up, including in year 7 following a few post 11+ departures at end of year 6.

Exit: Epsom currently most popular followed by St John's and Wellington. Other destinations include Eton, Harrow, Brighton, Charterhouse, King's College, Hampton, Cranleigh and Reed's. Good guidance on future schools, and school has right connections, reckon parents; scholarships across the board for art, drama, DT, music, sport and academic usually in the early 20s.

Remarks: The swish, modern and airy reception area makes for a grand entrance. We could almost have imagined ourselves in an upmarket corporate establishment until we spotted a pile of pencil cases on the floor and a procession of boys and girls in their smart blue blazers. On the left is a stunning performing arts centre and dance studio (a joy to see the little ones tap dancing); on the right, the vast glass walls frame a striking view of the main prep building (mid-19th century gothic), which you loop round the corridor to get to. Here you are met with yet more stunning interiors, this time more traditional, including the head's designer office – think interior magazine-worthy grey armchairs, orchids, scented candles, beautiful art (one by an upper school pupil, the rest by the school's art teacher) and – reflecting her approachability and transparency – a new glass-fronted door. From this sun-drenched room (even on the January day we visited), you get a panoramic view of the sweep of green stretching away down a gentle slope towards the grass pitch, idyllically bounded by woods and dipping pond much used by all year groups, plus the very popular treehouse now complete with slide ('the children begged for one for three whole years!' says head).

On both sides are the learning blocks for year 3s upwards – soon to be joined by new labs, teacher rooms and a whole new teaching block, which have now passed planning stage. Plenty of idiosyncratic charm throughout, from revamped lower school block classrooms with winning cosiness, colour and light to seniors' French classroom with miniature shop and restaurant, much used for role play. Calvi, the separate pre-prep building across the road, is also winningly equipped, from own hall to shaded play areas (trees a feature everywhere) with big sandpit and marked out scooter track. Plentiful wildlife, too, some guinea pigs, available for cuddles, and tadpoles, who aren't.

At one time, the school was known locally as one of the less academic; no longer, with a strong and dedicated staff cohort and ever-enhanced strategies to ensure the curriculum and its delivery are top notch. Parents generally delighted with academic running – 'there were some weaker teachers, but they've been weeded out – I'd say they are all good to very good now,' said one. Maximum class sizes of 20 (occasionally 22), optimum size for lively classroom atmosphere, reckons school. We saw pupils crawling around a lab in the dark with torches (studying how shadows work), younger ones gleefully playing in a recorder group and the DT lab ready for pupils to make the likes of mood lights and rulers; this is a bustling, engaging environment. Specialist teaching for French, PE, swimming and music from year 1, when they get shot at DT and digital learning too. Options grow with age and by year 5, all subjects are taught by specialists. Setting from English and maths from year 3 and in science and French from year 7. SEN and gifted and talented provision overseen by the four-strong learning enrichment department who use an integration model as much as possible; one parent told us, 'It's fine and certainly better than it was.'

Strong range of sport on offer (netball, hockey and cricket basic range for girls, football, rugby, hockey and cricket for boys, swimming, cross-country and athletics for both). Fab facilities too in the 25-acre estate, including indoor swimming pool, Astroturf, yodelling-quality sports hall, hard surface tennis courts and two rifle ranges (air and.22) on top of scenic sports fields. Strategy is to seek out challenge, everyone representing the school regardless of talent, although some parents feel 'girls' sport isn't taken quite as seriously' – a view not lost on the head, whose prep school district meetings often involve fighting for sporting equality via a more varied fixtures model. 'Bottom line is we're on it and we've added two more sports coaches to add to our own depth of expertise.' Plenty of tolerance for the rugby-averse – not the case elsewhere. Mega results in shooting – teams beat everyone everywhere, including older siblings in senior schools (Wellington and Epsom College). Coach, who travels here from Wales 'because he likes us', secret weapon.

Drama popular – it would be hard not to be enthusiastic about performing in the swanky theatre. Parents describe the performances as 'outstanding' and impressively, drama is also used for raising serious issues such as bullying and gender wars. Good collaboration with music department, the head of whom has an exceptional reputation – 84 per cent of pupils learn an instrument here and well over half are in one of the five school choirs (junior and senior), with the 15 single-instrument ensembles also popular. Year 2s went off to sing in an old folks' home when we visited. A welcoming and well-equipped art room is a haven for the creative, with iPads used to photograph all work – 'it gives me an opportunity to give feedback actually on their work,' explained teacher.

Weekly and flexi plus day boarding options from year 3 – latter can include a full boarding day without the sleepover. In reality, it's only a handful that weekly board; much more popular are the one, two or three times a week flexi options which parents use for helping prepare their offspring for senior school, encouraging greater independence or simply because their children 'want nothing more than to stay over at school with their friends, despite us living 10 minutes away,' as one parent put it. Homely dorms (though pink for girls' dorms and blue for boys' seems outdated) with 46 beds in total. 'Trial nights' are popular, say pupils – themed nights encouraging pupils who haven't stayed overnight before to have a go. A good programme of activities, the opportunity to mix with pupils across the years and a much-loved matron are all part of the pull. 'I wondered how much homework my son would actually get done, but it's tightly monitored, followed by the fun stuff in the sports hall,' one parent said. Here, as elsewhere, essential to shut ears to competing clamour of A3 that borders one side of site, though pupils oblivious.

Rigorous pastoral system subject to routine interrogation, with frequent dedicated meetings and an emphasis on staff accountability. Pupils told us, 'We all have a favourite teacher so that's the first port of call for most of us'. Impressive focus on mental health, including from outside speakers. 'Every child knows every child, so the younger ones grow up knowing it will be their job to take care of the newer ones later on,' said one parent. 'They take their leadership responsibilities, like being prefect, very seriously,' said another. Unusually, pupils told us there's 'no bullying'; head wise not to make such bold claims, but all can list a whole bunch of prevention policies that, as one pupil put it, 'stops friendship fallouts turning into anything worse'.

Behaviour good, with pupils reporting that strictness increases as you get older – 'it's always fair and good preparation for your next school,' said one. Pupils we met (there's a pretty equal gender split) were lively, happy and comfortable in their own skin. And although we arrived at drop-off time to a sea black Range Rovers, school says (and parents agree) that families range from the very wealthy to those who 'really work hard to get their children here.' Most hail from Weybridge, Cobham and Esher, although there are some groans about growing numbers from London – 'I think the school should set their cap as to whether they're a local school or not. The big increase has changed the dynamic for the school, especially for playdates,' said one. Food good – that hasn't always been the case, say parents. Ditto with affordability of uniform – this was a major gripe in the past.

From an already strong base, this is a school that feels on the up and for a prep, it takes an impressively long-term look, preparing children not just for their next school but for life. All this in a happy, positive – not to mention immaculate – environment.

The Folkestone School for Girls

Coolinge Lane, Folkestone, Kent CT20 3RB

Ages 11–18 **Pupils** 1,160 **Sixth form** 237

01303 251125
www.folkestonegirls.kent.sch.uk

F

Principal: Since September 2018, Mark Lester, previously assistant head and vice principal.

Academic matters: Just over half of GCSE grades A*-A/9-7 in 2018. 'Each year we have a group of at least five girls who in other schools would not get their GCSEs. We make sure they do.'

School is passionate about creating equal opportunities for children from less advantaged backgrounds – from using its own entry test alongside the Kent test in an attempt to weed out raw talent rather than coached performance through to providing this group with extra resources. It is troubling that the value added score is lower for pupils in receipt of free school meals. Again, this is far higher than national averages but they think it isn't acceptable. 'We have to do the best we can for all kids. We have identified a small gap in progress between those receiving free school meals and other students. We have paid for individual tuition in English, maths and science for every underachieving free school meals child and we pay for revision guides. We try to do the bits a middle class parent does – that is, buy books for their children, pay for tuition if they are behind, take them out to places.'

The other reason behind the great progress is a determination to ensure that all teaching is excellent. Teachers carry a lanyard around their neck with the school's four tenets for outstanding lessons: engagement, challenge, independent learning, and feedback. 'We have training sessions around those four things.' A teacher who fails in any of these areas gets six weeks of coaching and if they are not at the right standard after that 'we would start to move them out of school.'

The result is 'the best education in the area,' parents told us, with some 'charismatic and inspirational' teaching. In 2018, a third A*/As at A level and over half A*-Bs. Most popular subjects at English, maths and psychology.

Maths is the strongest department. Children are set from year 7 (seven sets). 'It's a mistake to mix ability. You need to teach at pace and you can't do that if half the kids haven't got it.' Girls do maths GCSE a year early, then do further maths or statistics in year 11. Science and English set from year 9.

All have to do the EBacc (taking science, maths, English, a language, plus history or geography to GCSE). Students pick two languages from French, German and Spanish in year 7, then can keep both going in year 8 or drop one. Languages identified as a failing department and the results are changing now. We witnessed one French lesson where the energy almost visibly burst through the door. Girls were singing a French song using karaoke equipment – lots of hilarity, but the notes on the board showed that they were learning to conjugate verbs. A parent told us this was a regular event, with verb tables on one occasion set to a One Direction song.

In other classrooms the atmosphere was quiet and studious, with desks in rows. The students say that 80 to 90 per cent of the teaching is good – they were able to reel off the names of teachers whose lessons they enjoyed, including a history teacher who often performs in costume from his dressing up box and is, one said, 'the most passionate teacher I've ever come across.'

Games, options, the arts: We didn't get a sense of this being a very sporty school. Vast playing fields, but indoor facilities are meagre and the gyms look untouched in 30 years, save the addition of a lonely exercise bike. Girls are often bussed up to the sports centre in town for better facilities. 'Sport hasn't particularly impressed me,' said a parent. 'A lot of parents don't see it as a priority and often clubs don't run because no-one turns up.' However, the tennis courts are now a multi use games area, and there's new fitness suite packed with everything from treadmills to cross trainers plus kettlebells, medicine balls, dumbells and stability balls.

Staff confirm that the first priority is academic but say other schools in the area put up little sporting competition, with Folkestone girls winning all their matches. One parent wished the school would raise its sights and play more competitive teams in Canterbury and Ashford. Sports day is apparently a highlight, though – a relaxed event with the head of history providing hilarious commentary.

Music is 'a great department', according to one pupil – regular concerts and musical productions and girls can qualify for a BTec by managing their own production (from fundraising to selling tickets and overseeing lighting and sound). Art department has a darkroom and green room and studio with sea views and quite a few go on to art college.

Overseas trips include a biennial four-week expedition for years 11 to 13 to eg Borneo or Ecuador with a focus on volunteering and environmental studies. Girls may build bridges or converting buildings into a nursery or village hall, alongside activities like scuba diving. During year 11 girls do internships, where they spend one day a week throughout the year in an industry related to their career aspirations.

Background and atmosphere: School feels like a happy ship; staff passing in the corridors greet each other by first names – no stiff hierarchy here. 'The leadership team is confident,' a parent told us. 'They are in a comfortable place because they have done well, so they are not trying to put in knee-jerk policies or react to inspections. They can take a considered approach.'

Girls seem very relaxed – they turn out the results but don't have that glassy eyed look of industry we've seen in some schools. None of the parents we spoke to thought it was an overly pressured or competitive environment. Social skills are good, too – girls gave us a confident account of what they were doing, and why.

The school is on a leafy road in the posh part of Folkestone, a stone's throw from the sea. Sixth form has its own cliffside terrace off the common room, with views to France on a clear day. It's considered the best school in the area, although it faces competition from Canterbury grammars. Unjustly so, said one parent. 'At our village school the playground talk was that Canterbury was the place to go, but those of us whose children went to Folkestone are all delighted with it.'

Current campus was created when the Victorian girls' grammar merged with the next door technical school, so there are now double-sized areas of playing fields and two school halls. The Victorian part has had recent facelift and benefits from wood panelling and curved staircases, giving it a hint of grandeur. The modern half has the dated and knocked about décor sported by most of the county's grammars.

Pastoral care, well-being and discipline: No behaviour problems according to the girls – 'no one would dare,' said one. Staff disagree, saying the school encounters the usual range of rebellion and personal problems, all dealt with through support and sanctions. Each of the school's four houses is headed by a student development leader who has no teaching commitments and whose role is to oversee well-being and academic progress (and is also the first point of contact for parents with any concerns).

There are quite a few luscious lashes and blushed cheeks in evidence – staff say they take a pragmatic approach to this. 'They are not supposed to have a lot of make-up, but we're moderately relaxed about it. What's going on in lessons is much more important.' Sixth form dress is liberal – jeans and trainers allowed, but a bare midriff might result in being sent home to change.

Pupils and parents: Broad mix of backgrounds, with 20 per cent of pupils receiving free school meals. Number of pupils from non-British backgrounds, including several Nepalese girls whose parents are stationed at the nearby Gurkha regiment barracks. Around half of parents have been in higher education. The school desperately wants to change perceptions among some local parents who don't have this background. 'Parents think it's snooty and not for them. They put limits on their children and lots who don't do the Kent test are capable of passing.' Even with newspaper headlines proclaiming that the school was first in the county for GCSE results recently, there were still empty places at first round offers in March.

Entrance: You get two shots at it, via the Kent 11+ test or through success in the school's own exam. The latter comprises verbal and non-verbal reasoning, English and maths. It's not uncommon for girls to pass one and fail the other. It's a lot easier to get in here than in other parts of the county – only 15 per cent of the local children will pass the Kent test, compared to 38 per cent in the pushy parent enclaves in the west of the county. Entry at sixth form requires six GCSEs at 9-4, with at least four 6s.

Exit: Most girls stay on for the sixth form, with about 10 each year moving on to vocational courses. After A levels more than 90 per cent progress to higher education (usually one or two to Oxbridge, and around 25 per cent to Russell Group). The school regularly invites back old girls in professions like law, medicine and banking to develop pupils' ambitions.

Remarks: You can't argue with the results – or with the school's zeal to ensure that every girl gets the results she is capable of. What's particularly good is that they seem to achieve this without the girls feeling under great pressure. Yes, they know they have to work hard, but not to the extent that parents worry about them overdoing it. It's 'quite rounded and balanced,' one mother told us. We like the school's determination to weed out poor teaching too – it's something a lot of schools would be all the better for.

Forres Sandle Manor School

Sandle Manor, Fordingbridge, Hampshire SP6 1NS

Ages 3–13 **Pupils** 203 **Boarders** 75 full, 25 weekly (from 7 years) C of E

Fees: Day £8,400 – £16,905; Boarding £18,940 – £23,550 pa

01425 653181
www.fsmschool.com

Acting head: Jody Wells, deputy head, is holding the fort.

Entrance: Most at age 3 or 8, boarders from 7. Non-selective but works from premise of 'Will a child be happy here?' Stomping grounds include New Forest, Avon Valley and environs of Cranborne. Predominantly white British with a handful of short-stay pupils from Norway and Spain. Boarders a 50-50 mix of expats, mostly Forces, and locals. Around half are first time buyers. Start when you like, if room (pressure on boarding places – must pay for full even if weekly board). Means-tested bursaries and discount for Forces.

Exit: Over 25 different schools in the last four years, including Canford, Bryanston, Sherborne, Sherborne Girls, Clayesmore and Dauntseys. Eminent old boys: Michael Foot (Forres), Alec Guinness (Sandle Manor).

Remarks: Set in child-friendly grounds, centred around an elegant Jacobean manor, a stone's throw from the New Forest. It's hard to imagine a more captivating environment for the tweenager. Delightful pre-prep with inspirational head who ensures learning is child-led, fun but pacey. Super pirate ship playground and forest school ensure year round fresh air and plenty of boisterous play.

All 6 year olds screened for reading delay – those found in need are given booster sessions till back on track. 'We never guarantee a child will improve but are yet to have one that doesn't.' Fans of Ruth Miskin's Read Write Inc, which promises every child a reader by age 6. Imaginative teaching and learning captivates the spellbound youngsters. We especially liked the 'naughty bus' that hides on a daily basis and had been found encased in ice on our visit. Even an errant bus can't compete with the excitement of making stinky, brown poo – a simulated investigation which begins with crushing of digestive biscuits (to mirror crunching of teeth), mixed with water (replacing saliva), washing up liquid and vinegar added (enzyme and stomach acid), then squeezed through grandma's stocking, simulating the intestine and final movement: learning at its gory, imaginative, and experiential best.

Fairly relaxed approach to learning in the prep school – not a soft option, but perhaps uniquely, youngsters say they'd like more prep sooner, 'The year 8 workload is a shock and we could be better prepared for it'. Gifted children pepped up via PACE activities; some, such as Green Giant, an eco project examining biodiversity and recycling with hands-on fun – chopping bamboo, mixing smoothies and making wool – open to all.

Learning support encompasses wide range of cognitive ability. 'We have children who cannot read/decode but are L4 and L5 national curriculum in some subjects, so we have to help and support'. Parents enthuse, 'My child struggled at his previous school, but since he came to FSM and got the support he needed, he has never stopped smiling.' Another added, 'It's a long day yet my child is never tired. Somehow they work it just right.'

Most teachers deliver multi-sensory lessons geared to active learning. English, drama and science top the popularity polls; 'Our science teacher respects us – he's not patronising, we do lots of experiments, it's fun and there is practically no writing,' cooed one boy. History, geography and RE depart from confines of CE, a conscious decision to develop skills of enquiry and investigation. Testing topics include Smuggling in Fordingbridge. Senior schools approve and see some seriously good work – not that fun doesn't come into it: we spotted a wall of history jokes, our favourite, 'Who built the Ark? I have Noah idea!' Post CE youngsters hone their practical and problem-solving skills – changing a tyre, wiring a plug, ironing shirts or finding the scariest ride at Thorpe Park.

Most lessons take place in The Barn with scattering of specialist buildings for art (we loved the bronze Olympian action sculpture), DT and music. Sports hall and climbing wall on wish list, but grounds contain heated outdoor swimming pool, courts for netball and tennis plus myriad of pitches. Ennui not an option – daily sport and afternoon activities as diverse as scuba diving, golf (even for the tinies) and banana boating, alongside annual trips and tours to everywhere from Iceland to Africa. Project week and cub-camp, with Boy's Own firelighting, knife-skills, cooking and camp craft, perennially popular. All lower school do ballet (a good way to spot potential dancers and dyspraxics) – optional classes for seniors. We listened to the fledgling Exterminators jamming and spotted imaginatively named groups, eg Flute Pastilles, and fabulous fiddlers. School has a competitive edge: thrice finalists in the Junior Memory Championships and recent debut as finalists in Kids' Lit quiz.

Seemingly parents equally competitive when it comes to teams, with boarder parents saying, 'Local parents seem to have everything sewn up – it can be difficult for the boarding fraternity to get a look in, especially for parent fixtures,' adding, 'Communication could be better – they're great at reporting on the kids but not on activities: we need time to schedule and plan'. Parents kept busy with quiz nights, football, hockey, plus 'maths for mums and dads', courtesy of Friends of FSM – hardly surprising they jest that an in-school Costa Coffee concession is on their wish list.

Meals are table served in one of two dining rooms, the mantra to always try a little, including experimental offerings such as beetroot brownies and soup concoctions dreamed up by the youngsters. Sports teas are legendary and, as we flicked the last melt-in-the-mouth crumbs from our lips, could only nod in heartfelt agreement as our trusty guide declared them 'outstanding!'

A boarding school that welcomes day children – 'It's a family-friendly community, flexible when we need it'. Fairly healthy weekend boarding numbers though parents of full boarders say to check the age and gender of those who stay, if this is important to you. Cheery boarding accommodation with ongoing renovations – though we were a tad overwhelmed by the swathes of bubble-gum pink adorning the girls' dorms. We loved the 'getting better bay' with healthy doses of TLC for the homesick and panaceas for the poorly. Seemingly all want to try boarding, so expect up to 11 per dorm and the odd grumble that it can be difficult to escape, 'Sometimes you need time or space but they can be hard to find'. Nothing too heavy-handed on discipline front: naughty boarders are red-carded and miss the coveted Wednesday special boarding night or put on dreaded laundry duty, sorting socks, folding shirts. Matrons praised, 'You can tell them things because they have seen it all before and know what to do', ground-staff lauded as cheery and fun, 'They have a nickname for everyone'.

Focuses on developing happy, confident children. Takes a broad range, delivers the goods, 'One minute you are watching a really talented child, the next someone who is just keen to join in'. Children are respected and 'feel part of the gang,' say parents. Children candid, 'It can be a bit difficult for those who are naturally loners or need quiet space.' Not posh or pushy. A happy, homely school with a sunny disposition, going from strength to strength. Turns out friendly, confident, quietly ambitious youngsters.

Frensham Heights

Linked with Frensham Heights Junior School

Rowledge, Farnham, Surrey GU10 4EA

Ages 11–18 **Pupils** 391 **Sixth form** 75 **Boarders** 37 full, 52 weekly

Fees: Day £18,330 – £20,430; Boarding £26,370 – £30,810 pa

F

01252 792561
www.frensham.org/

Headmaster: Since January 2019, Rick Clarke, previously deputy head at Warminster School. Born and raised in South Africa (his father was a teacher and his mother an ed psych), he has a degree in English and psychology from the University of Natal and a PGCE. Has taught English in South Africa and the UK; posts include head of English at St John's College in Johannesburg and at Brighton College and housemaster at Wellington College. A keen runner, he is training for his first half marathon. His wife, Natalie, is an artist and art teacher and they have two children who have joined the school.

Academic matters: Not 'selective' as normally understood – this school is more concerned that you join them for the right reasons than because you will help them soar to league-table-topping prominence. A smallish school, so not the hugest range of subject options at GCSE or A level. Very high pupil:teacher ratio makes for lots of small group and one-one support. Impressive results in Eng lit; the three sciences, when taken separately, also impress though most take IGCSE double award. Blissfully small classes for eg RE, ICT (computing GCSE, computer science A level). No Latin, no Greek. Photography taken – spectacularly – as an extracurricular GCSE with huge numbers and great success – see below. All A level subjects taught in small groups – much appreciated by students. English, maths, geography, history, art most popular. Only a few take langs, including some native speakers. Sixth form seen by some as being less rigorous academically than it might but the newish head of sixth is 'driving up standards,' we were assured. And 'we are upping our game in stretching the gifted and talented'. Parents concur. 'Not hothousing doesn't mean they can't achieve highly,' affirmed one. In 2018, 30 per cent A*-A/9-7 at GCSE and 33 per cent A*/A grades at A level (64 per cent A*-B). Disappointing library which doubles as café and place to sprawl in breaks with little evidence of its books being used. Recent expansion of science block to create six separate labs.

Loads of support – eg maths clinic each lunchtime. Not great for wheelchair users as the site is huge, bumpy and has steps. Main House not wheelchair-friendly at all. But school will try to take anyone they feel will benefit – mild SEN are catered for with enthusiasm and dedication and some families shared between Frensham and nearby More House for those with greater needs. 'My daughter had one-to-one for her reading and her reading age jumped two years in a term.'

Games, options, the arts: Think, Create, Explore is inscribed around the school and the vast menu of extracurricular options should tempt the most sluggish teenager to do just that. Bike maintenance, American football, boules, tap dancing, barbershop and various dance forms – before, during and after school and at weekends. Excellent new music block; around half learns at least one musical instrument in school – 'Frensham bends over backwards to find teachers if you want to learn some different instrument,' a budding soloist enthused. Masses of bands, orchestras, ensembles, choirs and performance courses through the veins of the school. Dance much praised and popular. Drama is well-provided for and central to the school. The theatre is a wonderful asset – it has everything and does everything – and is well used, as are the two drama studios and the little wooden outdoor theatre on the front lawn. Performance values are high with a healthy, pervasive culture of it being OK to perform. Creative drama team under innovative long-serving head of dept.

Outstanding photography under even longer-serving, inspirational leadership and now with unique facilities for techniques old and new. Brilliant, diverse and poly-faceted artwork – we were truly struck by the rigour and values underpinning the skills and the freedom pupils were given to develop as they needed. Witty ceramics, clever textiles, wood and resistant materials productions with mind-opening themes explored with structure and solidity. Arguably, the most impressively led art dept in the country.

Sports are enthusiastic, various and 'improving', according to parents, though some feel they could and should be better. School points out that they are now competing against much bigger schools and taking part in various national cup competitions. 'Outdoor education' is important – there is forest school, the outdoor Terrace Theatre, the swimming pool in the walled garden and loads of activities to develop outdoor skills – DofE gold award taken here and the whole school breathes in its own glorious 'outdoors'. Facilities – indoor and out – are certainly conducive to performance but one senses that real energies go into creativity rather than goal-scoring.

Boarding: Hamilton House accommodates the 11-13 year-old boarders – boys and girls housed on different floors. They share a breakfast room/kitchen and a large garden. Main House houses the older boarders – girls and boys in opposite wings and with entry codes. Roberts House, the sixth form centre, is everyone's base all day: day pupils share studies and workspace. We knocked at a random door and found two lads in hoodies actually working and blinking at the disturbance. Whole school on fibre-optic broadband and Facebook etc blocked till tea-time. Boarding is good – decent sized rooms in the main though some singles are tightish; nice, bright shower rooms and good kitchens. Exceptionally welcoming sitting rooms – especially The Sit, which looks like home. Food – very good, we tried it – served in big dining room with tables and banquettes and everyone eats ensemble. Around a third stay in at weekend and are busy – see note about extracurricular above. Powerful cleaning fluid smells almost knocked us over in several buildings.

Background and atmosphere: Charles Charrington, the brewer, acquired Fir Grove House on the edge of Rowledge village, overlooking a panorama of Surrey woods and hills and transformed it into Frensham Heights – an imposing gothic red-brick residence with turrets, leaded lights and stained glass, splendid Georgian-style interiors, cornices, architraves, fireplaces – the lot – in 1902, as a would-be ancestral pile. Alas, the First World War intervened and the house became a military hospital and, as the old order changed, was reinvented as a school by three redoubtable women – Edith Douglas-Hamilton and joint headmistresses, Beatrice Ensor and Isabel King. Ensor, an early proponent of Montessori education, was a theosophist, a vegetarian and an anti-vivisectionist. But the school's progressive credentials, being coeducational and liberal, were integral to its ethos from the first. Strangely, every head since its pioneers has been male.

Set in extensive woodlands and the older children trail 10 minutes through the woods to the village with its supermarket and sweetshop. Immense and meticulously kept grounds – school pays tribute to the excellence of the financial management and, indeed, it is admirable that the place is so well maintained with so small a population of fee-payers. Newer buildings nestle in trees and witty sculptures sprawl on the lawns and in foyers – we loved the slumbrous wire rabbit ('the little kids curl up in its ears') and the jokey wax mushrooms, as well as the huge black panther.

No uniform – so everyone bar a few in uniform of hoody, leggings/jeans, sweatshirts, boots/trainers. It looks relaxed and sane – enhanced by the amount of linked arms and hugging we saw – more like a bunch of French children, we thought. Central to the ethos is personal maturity: 'They are given real responsibility,' one parent told us, 'and can take the initiative – the school's approach to that is excellent.' This extends to falling in and out of love, which, of course, they do, but we were impressed by the compassion and mutual respect with which this is handled. 'It does happen but anything more than a hug or kiss in public is frowned on and people are respectful of what others want to see.. if people break up, we look after each other,' a wise mid-teen averred. 'It's not for everyone,' said another. 'If you need real structure and routine it's not for you.' 'Conventional parents need to look beyond the informality and recognise that the pupils respect the teachers because of the way they treat them rather than because of the rules,' a less conventional parent asserted.

Pastoral care, well-being and discipline: Everyone agrees about the staff: 'It's almost personal tutoring – they know how I learn so they explain it to me how they know I can understand,' a bright sixth former told us. 'They encourage pupils to excel in music, art, sport – whatever they're good at,' said a parent. Also a sense of a recent tightening of discipline – especially on illicit fags and booze. 'Some people were getting cocky – they've cracked down on it now,' we were advised. But pastoral care universally praised: 'They're not heavy-handed over minor transgressions – they see them in a learning context but if you cross a line you'll be suspended.' And another parent: 'If you've got that much freedom you need the support to go with it.' A strong sense that mutual respect and mutual support is central to the ethos of the place.

Pupils and parents: Around 75 per cent day pupils who come from a radius of about 40 miles – Petersfield, Goldalming, Farnham. Boarders are weekly eg from London or from overseas and school has wise policy of not taking more than four pupils who speak any one language into any senior year. So penny nos from eg Russia, Germany, Croatia, Spain. Intensive EAL available though needed by very few. Notable Old Frenshamians include performers Bill and Jon Pertwee, Jamie Glover, David Berglas, Rufus Hound, Hattie Morahan; also Sir Claus Moser, Noah Bulkin (Merrill Lynch, Lazard, now entrepreneur) and uber-fraudster, Edward Davenport.

Entrance: All candidates for years 7-9 are interviewed. Exams a week or so later – 11+ tests in reading, writing, spelling, maths and non-verbal reasoning. Same plus a science test for 13+ candidates, though pre-testing in year 6 for boarding year 9 places available on request. 'We are not only interested in academics. Our selection process is also based on performance in a group interview.' Sixth form places require six GCSEs at 4+, ideally with 6s in A level subjects, 'but we're flexible,' says Andrew. School also sets its own papers for sixth form entry. Oversubscribed by 4:1 at this stage.

Exit: Around 50 per cent leaves at 16 – mostly to the several large state (free) sixth form colleges round about, some few for the IB or for subjects not on offer here. Nearly all who stay get to their first choice university which suggests good guidance and realistic applications. To one of the widest range of tertiary education establishments we have seen. Many to creative courses – arts, design, music – but also the odd Oxbridge entrant (one to Cambridge – architecture – in 2018, plus one off to study graphic arts in New York) and others to study everything from architecture at Nottingham to geography at King's, London. Different, diverse, distinctive.

Money matters: Sibling discounts for third and subsequent children of 10 per cent. Scholarships and exhibitions in academics, performing arts, creative arts and sport up to £750 pa – so glory rather than gold. Means-tested bursaries in case of need but school has no endowments so not plentiful.

Remarks: A place to grow up in. Every kind of opportunity to become the person you are meant to be and to learn about others while you're at it. Civilised, liberal values with wraparound care and support. We loved it.

Frensham Heights Junior School

Linked with Frensham Heights

Rowledge, Farnham, Surrey GU10 4EA

Ages 3–11 **Pupils** 129

Fees: Day £6,900 – £12,765 pa

01252 792561
www.frensham.org/

Headmaster: Since 2005, Nic Hoskins BA (40s), who also acts as assistant boys' housemaster in the senior boarding house. Previously deputy head at Willington Prep, Wimbledon. Cheery, energetic Cockney, Nic's degree was in primary music, art and drama and he has 'a passion for the arts'. His weekly newsletter to parents is, as you'd expect, reflective, creative and very much in keeping with the 'thinking' ethos of the school. He clearly loves his job and seems as thrilled now to have it as when he first arrived. Nic teaches music to children from nursery through to year 3 and IT from years 3-6. 'How can you mould children if you don't know them?' Quite!

Entrance: Entry to nursery in the term of 3rd birthday (16 places) or the following year to reception – assessment done by informal observation during a visit. Years 1-6 take one or two more – roughly two apply for each place. Candidates spend a day with peer group and are assessed in reading, spelling, maths – while having a fun day.

Exit: Vast majority to senior school and why on earth wouldn't you?

Remarks: Junior school in two buildings: nursery to year 3 in sunken single storey, red-roofed accommodation with attractive, good-sized classrooms full of attentive, relaxed looking tots and really interesting activities going on. Light, airy rooms and space to explore and breathe. 'Flottage' (apparently a contraction of 'The Flat Over the Cottage' – but irrelevant now) houses the upper years and sees that time as very much preparatory for the senior school. One form in each year. Rooms arranged very intimately – though teachers have free rein over this – but we liked the shell-like arrangement with little tables in a curl around the teacher's desk in one year 4 room. School has its own SENCo who gives small group support where needed (known, appealingly, as 'clubs') and one-to-one (charged extra) if necessary. 'We could take anyone whose presence wouldn't be detrimental to the rest of the class,' says Nic.

Good junior playground with lots of different surfaces, play equipment and a glorious redwood at its heart. We enjoyed boys and girls playing football together and harmoniously – not a common sight. Much shared with senior school including sports facilities and staff and the dining room: 'It's a beautiful thing to see 3-year-olds and 18-year-olds eating together,' enthuses Nic. Senior pupils love coming back on visits and have fond memories of what they learned where and with whom. 'It was magic.'

Gayhurst School

Bull Lane, Gerrards Cross, Buckinghamshire SL9 8RJ

Ages 3–11 **Pupils** 320 **C of E**

Fees: £12,159 – £15,438 pa

01753 882690
www.gayhurstschool.co.uk

Headmaster: Since 2016, Gareth Davies BA PGCE MEd (40s). Previously head of Alleyn Court for eight years, before that deputy head at Rose Hill, Alderley, prior to which he taught in various preps (mostly maths). Originating from the Swansea Valley, he studied HR management at the University of Glamorgan, but a free Friday spent in his aunt's primary school during the last year of his degree lured him into teaching and he's 'never looked back.' PGCE at University of Wales, Aberystwyth. Since then, MEd in educational leadership and school improvement at Cambridge.

Gets brownie points from all parents for meeting and greeting at the gate every morning and running regular parental forums. But has something of a Marmite effect overall, with some lapping up his 'clear commitment to mental health and well-being and his strategic plans for the school,' while others grumble that 'he isn't very inspirational or dynamic' or disagree with the changes he's made (more of which later). Pupils say he's 'nice' and 'friendly,' but some (particularly lower down the school) say, 'we don't see him much.' Higher up the school, this is not an issue – he teaches three or four lessons a week to year 5s.

Married to Lisa, a nursery nurse, with whom he has three daughters (two at the school; third, no doubt, to follow). Commutes from Haslemere, where they live with their sproodle, Humphrey. A season ticket holder for Swansea City and an ardent follower of the Ospreys and Welsh rugby, he also enjoys playing golf and cricket when time allows – 'not as often as I'd like, believe me,' he laughs.

Entrance: Non-selective up until year 2, after which there are tests for reading and maths and a 'gentle' interview 'to check social fit.' Nursery can take maximum of 25 pupils; after that, it's three-form entry from reception with scope for four-form entry from years 3 to 6, dependent on numbers, with class sizes peaking at 16 (occasionally 18). Originally a boys' school, it became co-ed in 2008 – welcomed by most, although some say 'there's an overemphasis on the girls and the attention and awards they get, relative to their overall numbers,' which currently sit at around 28 per cent. While there used to be waiting lists in younger years, that is no longer the case; and with 20 per cent movement in the local area (mainly due to job relocation), spaces often appear higher up the school. There's a means-tested 100 per cent bursary for one child in each of years 3 to 6.

Exit: Majority to local grammar schools, including Dr Challoner's Grammar, Dr Challoner's High, John Hampden, RGS High Wycombe, Beaconsfield High, plus independents, notably Berkhamsted, Royal Masonic, Wycombe Abbey, Haileybury, Pipers Corner, LVS Ascoy, Merchant Taylors', Claires Court and Shiplake. Note: school has phased out years 7 and 8. So if there's any chance at all that you might want a 13+ common entrance public boarding school straight from here, this isn't the school for you. Worth noting the mass exodus of around 16 boys to The Beacon around about the time the current head joined, and a few still move there, though most agree this is related to the 'axing of year 7 and 8' and/or the fact that 'some parents just don't like change' (last head was there 23 years). Five scholarships in 2018.

Remarks: Nestled between houses on a residential lane, this is not a school that wows you with a grand manor house, pristine front lawns and elegant hall. Yes, there is the original Georgian-style house (since extended), but there's a car park in front and the low-key side entrance leads you into a reception area that's more functional than frills. But inside the five-acre site, which the school relocated to in 1930, the large well-kept field provides an impressive centrepiece for the whole school. In front lies the all-weather Astroturf, while at the back there's a pretty woodland (also home to an adventure playground) and three large rugby fields. Nursery has its own building with inside/outside space on the left, with a cluster of junior buildings on the right, while all senior classrooms are in the main building, including dedicated IT, art, science and music facilities. There's also a traditional-style wooden pavilion (also used for LAMDA) and sports hall (by the head's admission, 'an area of weakness for the school'). The uninspiring junior library seems to have fewer books than most households, while the senior library becomes a noisy thoroughfare between lessons, but overall there is a feeling of space, airiness and ample amenities – and some classrooms are truly loved ('our labs are great, especially in year 4 as you get to use the Bunsen burners,' said one pupil).

This is a school on a journey, say parents, with the head having made some big changes, including an extension to the school day to fit in more lessons (well received), three periods of form time ('a bit overkill,' believe some) and a staggered finish to accommodate the 'horrendous traffic and parking situation,' as one parent put it. To cries of delight and horror (in equal measure, from what we can gather) from parents, homework was ditched – or at least, is now done in the form time ('which, let's face it, makes it not homework at all'). School insists feedback has been 'almost entirely positive,' but particularly tetchy parents from year 6, anxious about the shock of homework in year 7, are relieved there's now up to an hour's homework a night. Some rules were relaxed under the new head too – 'children used to be asked not to play outside the head's office, for example,' he says – again, mixed reactions to this more relaxed attitude.

But the school's academic robustness without the pressure-cooker ethos is still its big pull. Most get into their chosen school and around five a year win scholarships, both academically and in the arts and sport. National curriculum is followed, with extras such as dedicated weeks to science and arts, and the children are taught by subject specialists in all but maths and English from year 4, then everything from year 5 (with the moving around to different classrooms 'great preparation for year 7,' say parents). Spanish from year 1; French from year 3. Setting from year 4 for maths and streaming in years 5 and 6 for English and maths – not popular with all, though, with one parent saying, 'If your child is great at English, but not at maths, it just doesn't make sense.' (School insists, 'Two specialist teachers for both maths and English teaching across the year group have the expertise to support all the children regardless of their ability').

Some say teaching is 'less rigorous than it was' and believe 'it's time some teachers to move on,' but others disagree and pupils we met were quick to tell us what they loved about teachers ('maths is so fun here'; 'all the teachers dress up on World Book Day' etc), though a few were frowned upon, 'especially the ones that shout.'

Strong on SEN – plenty of early assessments and intervention, along with close working relationships between SENCo and SEN specialist (both full-time) and teachers and TAs. Small group work or even one-to-ones where necessary, at no extra cost. No statements when we visited.

Sport gets the thumbs up from children – 'I don't even like sports and I love PE here,' said one. Rugby, football, cricket, athletics, cross-country, hockey, netball and rounders all on offer, with matches spread across weekday afternoons. But children would like the trophies they win 'to be more visible – most are tucked away in corners of the school we're not allowed in,' and some parents would like to see more trophies generally – 'there's a wonderful range of sports, but no proper focus on producing a winning team,' said one. Swimming lessons at Chalfont Leisure Centre for reception to year 2s and extracurricular clubs makes for an impressively long list – everything from chess to knitting, plus all the usual sporty ones.

A real strength of the school is the inclusive approach to music and performance. 'If someone wants to get up at a concert and sing a solo or play their instrument, they're allowed to, however terrible they are – which makes for some really charming little concerts,' said one parent. Nearly half learn a musical instrument and there are junior, senior and chamber choirs, plus music ensembles, with music theory a popular extracurricular club. There's a big passion for art too – everything from textiles to intricate paintings were displayed when we visited. School trips often combine both and include such far-flung places as Rome, Florence and Vienna. Other trips include skiing (with parents and teachers so that all years can go) and adventure camps.

Pastoral care has always been the cornerstone of the school – children feel able to approach form teachers and the 'share' box (where children can post worries and acts of kindness) is well-used 'and acted on,' according to one pupil. Unusually (uniquely, perhaps), the head told us, 'we don't have any bullying'; but one child told how he was persistently picked on by another boy, although 'the school did deal with it well.' Parents had similar tales – 'I think it's more accurate to say they nip things in the bud,' said one parent. 'Ethos more supportive than strict' and 'no formal sanctions,' according to head; pupils' version is that 'some teachers are extremely strict' and described how they sometimes have to 'stay behind at the end of a lesson, are kept in at break or have a note sent home to be signed by your mum.' No packed lunches allowed; school food popular among some pupils, while for others the mere mention of it led to a grimace (top tips from pupils: 'never choose the quiche').

Families span from the very well-heeled to first-time buyers, with a significant growth in dual income and less wealthy families. Mainly white British, followed by British Asian; rest a melting pot from Nigeria, China, America, Russia and more – 'a cosmopolitan mix that well reflects the area,' claims school. Mainly local families, but some travel 10 or so miles from places including Amersham, Uxbridge, Penn and Stoke Poges.

Pupils are bubbly, articulate, polite and refreshingly at ease among adults. There is an overall sense of fun without raucousness and a purposeful buzz. Plenty of leadership opportunities, with some rotated on a termly basis to give more children a go. Parents are a sociable bunch, with an active PA. General communications can be 'atrocious' and day-to-day interaction with teachers 'isn't there unless you request it,' say some.

This is a school that's been on a bumpy ride, but still excels at finding children's strengths and building on them, as well as enabling children to enjoy things they may not excel in. 'So if, like me, you have one who's academic and one who's not, they both shine,' said one parent. A mixed ability but aspirational school with a strong sense of community and where children are happy and relaxed – though perhaps a little too much so for more traditional parents' liking.

G

George Abbot School

Woodruff Avenue, Guildford, Surrey GU1 1XX

Ages 11–19 **Pupils** 1,992 **Sixth form** 495

01483 888000
www.georgeabbot.surrey.sch.uk

Headteacher: Since 2016, Kate Carriett BMus MA NPQH, previously principal of Kings College Guildford, which is part of the same multi-academy trust, GEP Academies. Studied music at Royal Holloway and Bedford New College and trained as a secondary music and English teacher at Birmingham. Was head of music in Warwickshire and Staffordshire before moving south to become head of year in Surrey. Her first headship was at Kings College.

'Education is the most important leveller in society,' she declared in response to our question about what drew her into education – and true to her principles, she's only ever worked in the state school system. Warm but no-nonsense, parents call her 'impressive' and 'refreshingly objective,' with one 'half expecting a defensive reaction when I went in to complain to her about a teacher, but what she actually said was, "Children are generally right about these things – we will of course follow it up." I was impressed.' 'She's proud of the school's academic record but makes it very clear that's not the be-all-and-end-all, with resilience and happiness also high on her agenda,' said another pleased parent.

Currently doesn't teach (although will in future), but pupils say she's regularly seen around school (we spotted her in a corridor telling a group of pupils off for not queuing in single file). For the most part, say pupils, she's 'friendly' and 'approachable.'

Lives with her husband and two sons; pursues her love of music and literature in her spare time.

Academic matters: GCSE results are tremendous for a comprehensive – in 2018, 83 per cent of pupils got 9-4 in both English and maths, and 39 per cent of grades were A*-A/9-7. Setting for maths from year 7, science and languages from year 8, and English from year 9 ('lots of movement based on regular test results,' say pupils) – everything else is mixed ability. Year

7s choose one modern language from French, German and Spanish, with top linguists (around 100 out of the 300 cohort) picking up a second from year 8. GCSE options selected at the end of year 8, 'but we only guide students to do the government-promoted Ebacc if it feels right for the individual.'

Each year around 38 A level courses are offered, as well as five BTecs/diplomas in sport, science, business studies, child development and performing arts. In 2018, 62 per cent of A level entries received A*-B grades and 34 per cent A*/A. The most popular A levels are maths and sciences, with almost half of the sixth form choosing maths, and options in this subject include further maths and STEP (which uses questions similar to undergraduate level maths, and is used by Cambridge for conditional offers). Other popular subjects include economics, photography and psychology. Students who take four A levels have the option to drop to three at the end of lower sixth.

G

The rigorous attention to the quality of teaching is the USP here, with a thorough and ongoing 'reflection and review programme' which includes every teacher being observed at least once a term. Where a performance issue with a teacher is picked up, they quickly improve or leave, although in reality that's rare – the school's reputation means they attract the best teachers and hang onto them with their hot CPD offering. 'Obviously, you get a few bad teachers along the way, but it doesn't amount to many,' one pupil told us. 'Bottom line is nobody slips through the net,' they added, reeling off a list of approaches used by those falling behind including emailing teachers, subject clinics, revision sessions etc. Interactive, practical-based teaching helps raise standards too, say pupils – 'science is full of really fun practicals, which don't even feel like lessons, and you leave some maths lessons feeling like you've played games whereas actually you now know a whole new theory,' one pupil told us. 'My son never reads – he's more a maths person – but they've taught him English in such a way that he's sailing through the exams,' said one parent.

New 'show my homework' hub praised by the head – 'it's a huge step forward, whereby pupils can see on their phone or computer exactly what they have to do by when, with things like pop-up reminders for tests.' Pupils we met were less enthusiastic, reporting 'a recent spike in homework levels that sometimes feels unmanageable' – 'I think all teachers feel they have to be seen to be setting it now,' said one.

The school excels at special needs, with its own unit for 12 visually impaired pupils, including some braillists. 'The portacabin could do with a lick of paint, but what goes on inside is excellent, with an ambitious, knowledgeable support team and a joined-up approach with the rest of the school and pastoral system to match,' said one parent whose daughter is completely blind. 'And it's not just hand-holding – they push the children forward to constantly challenge themselves academically as well as physically and emotionally.' Children with learning difficulties also well catered for, according to parents – we heard rave reviews and tales of extraordinary achievement from parents with children with the likes of dyslexia. There are also dedicated members of staff overseeing gifted and talented pupils, who get masterclasses in subjects such as forensics, hieroglyphics and tessellations, and are encouraged to enter national competitions.

A dedicated careers advice team helps with UCAS applications and we were pleased to hear pupils talk ardently about apprenticeships too – we see too many schools undervaluing these. Also great to see year 10s immersed in the annual 'interview day,' with a hall packed full of local businesspeople through to parents from the business world doing mock interviews and CV checks with pupils, then giving detailed feedback – 'you learn so much,' one awestruck pupil told us.

Games, options, the arts: Dynamic head of PE supports a large team including top-notch sports coaches, renowned for pushing even pupils at the top of their sporting game – 'We have quite a few children here representing Surrey and indeed their country in everything from athletics to running, and more.' Does well in matches against other schools, particularly in football and rugby – 'and that includes the private schools; we played netball against Wellington last week,' says head. Some niggles from parents that there aren't enough teams – 'My son loves football, but they only have an A team in his year, which is really disappointing,' one told us.

Facilities include Astroturf pitch, sports hall with two full-sized basketball pitches and performing arts centre with mirrored walls for dance teaching; larger pitches in nearby New Inn Lane also used regularly, including for some fixtures. For the non-sporty (of which there are many, judging from the parents we spoke to), there's everything from table tennis to mountaineering – and, according to one pupil, 'we even play quidditch.' 'For me, breadth is important, and that goes for all extracurricular activities so if, say, a pupil is appearing in a West End show, which does happen quite a bit, I'm more than happy to support that,' says head.

With that kind of talent, it's no wonder school drama productions are considered of such high quality – 'You'd think you were in the West End with some of them,' said a parent. Visual arts also strong, with some stunning A level textile works on display, with intricate embroidery. Fabulous dark room area for photography and clearly committed art teachers. 'The exhibitions are amazing,' one parent told us, while another said, 'My daughter isn't actually that arty, but they've supported her in choosing it as a GCSE subject and I couldn't fault their methodical training.'

Music boasts some great software, according to our guides, and there's a long list of orchestras, bands, choirs (including all male sixth form choir) and ensembles. Plenty of opportunity to perform publicly, with the chamber choir and rock choir frequently on tour. But peripatetic teaching only takes place after school hours.

Excellent clubs, extracurricular activities and trips. 'The opportunities are phenomenal, and my daughter is signing up to things I'd never dream she would,' said one parent, although pupils and parents warn, 'it's not handed on a plate – you have to be the kind of child that will put yourself forward for things.'

The school has a partnership with various overseas schools in China, Canada, Tanzania, South Africa and India, and reciprocal visits are arranged.

Background and atmosphere: The school was built in 1976, and looks like a typical 1970s comp. Nothing to write home about then, and the most appealing part is the sixth form common room, which has a café area designed in the same way as a high street brand, with lots of space for lounging. Facilities are not lacking, though, with plenty of study space and multiple libraries, science labs etc. But there's no denying some are in need of sprucing up, with the school about to embark on a campaign to rejuvenate the entire arts area when we visited – 'we're aiming for a new-build to house arts, graphics, photography and exhibition space,' says head, who also has a new gym, another Astroturf and bigger dining facilities on her wish list (parents we spoke to were desperate for a better canteen – 'both my kids have actually given up on the long queues now and ask for daily packed lunches, even when I can't find anything interesting in the fridge,' said one).

The school is huge, with 10 forms to a year, but still manages to tend to the individual, according to parents, with 'a strong culture of respect.' Regular surveys undertaken by the school to investigate areas of concern for students, parents and staff and pupils we spoke to said 'we definitely feel listened to here.'

It is in partnership with Fullbrook, Guildford Grove, Losely Fields, Kings College Guildford, Boxgrove Primary and Sandfield Junior, the seven now known as the Guildford Education Partnership.

Pastoral care, well-being and discipline: Those trembling at the idea of letting loose their sweet 11-year-old into a community of 2,000 will be especially cheered by year 7 arrangements. They are cocooned in their own block, with their own toilets, they have their own sculptured playground (designed by students) and eat lunch separately. Two heads of year (academic and pastoral) are dedicated to year 7. 'I couldn't believe how, on the very first term's parents evening, teachers were saying "hi" to my son and using his name as we walked by – he's a shy boy and it's a huge school; there's no chance of children feeling like a cog in the wheel here,' said one parent. After this they are passed on to another pair of heads of year who stay with them through years 8 to 11. 'They get to know their students very well,' said one parent. Much is made of leadership opportunities and ensuring these aren't restricted to the sixth form, with student leaders and well-being ambassadors appointed (and given training) from year 7.

It's a disciplined environment, though pupils we met couldn't quite decide whether to go as far as calling it 'strict' – 'they are exacting on things like uniform and homework, and lots of detentions are handed out, but the teachers aren't patronising and controlling,' explained one of our guides. Year 12s have to 'earn the right' to go off site during the school day between lessons. Strong agenda for mental health and well-being – a good thing too, with pupils we met telling us they knew of those with 'anxiety issues,' as well as pupils who have self-harmed or suffered with eating disorders. 'I guess it happens everywhere and the good thing about this school is that they don't shove these issues under a rug and there is a counsellor if we need one,' said one pupil.

'We had one bullying incident that turned into a big drama, but the school tackled it well,' one parent told us, although three pupils told us the anonymous reporting system can be treated as 'a bit of a joke' – 'you get people threatening, "I'll just put you on bully alert," or putting false accusations in the box.' One pupil said, 'I even had someone report me as bullying a teacher I'd never even met, as a joke – it was horrible.' School, however, says, bullying is rare and 'the email bullying alert system is one of a number of ways that students can communicate concerns – the system is used appropriately in 99 per cent of cases and is an important "instant" way for students to access support should they need it.' Drugs, alcohol and smoking 'not an issue in school,' according to the head. No permanent exclusions in the last few years and school unwilling to provide the number of temporary exclusions, but says it's 'below average' and 'firm action is taken to support the respect agenda.'

Some parents criticised reports as 'unsatisfactory – no comments, just tick boxes' – but the school does better than the average secondary school parent evening experience of five minutes per year, they added.

Pupils and parents: 'Skewed towards the able and motivated,' says school. 'It's not overly competitive, but there's a good attitude to study – kids are not embarrassed to be keen to achieve,' said a parent. It's a predominantly wealthy area and many parents choose to send children here who could afford independent education. But with 10 per cent on pupil premium, it feels genuinely comprehensive. 'This is the school everyone wants to get into and we are proud to be here,' one pupil told us. Parents equally appreciative – 'What more could you ask for out of the education system than this school?' said one particularly happy customer. The PTA is strong and the parent community friendly.

Entrance: Nearly 1,000 applicants for 300 places. Places are allocated first to looked after children, to those with exceptional need, and to siblings, and then on proximity, which for a first round offer means you are likely to need to live within two miles of the school. No priority for those at one of the GEP Academies primary schools. An average year sees around 10 appeals lodged, of which one-third likely to be successful.

Students wanting to stay on or join the sixth form should check the differing criteria for each subject, but school says 'you need a grade 6 or above' in many subjects. A maximum of 50 sixth form places are available for external candidates each year, and a significant number of these new joiners come from the independent sector, often attracted by the wide range of courses on offer. Requirements are lower for BTec courses.

Exit: Around 60-70 per cent stays on into the sixth form; those who leave usually do so to go in search of more vocational study. Around half of sixth formers go on to Russell Group universities. Three to Oxbridge in 2018, plus six medics/vets (one in Poland). STEM subjects and economics/business most popular choices; among the current university favourites are Birmingham, Royal Holloway, Portsmouth, Bournemouth, Bath, Exeter and Durham; Surrey increasingly popular too – 'probably to do with cost of accommodation,' said head. Others off to the Netherlands and Japan.

Remarks: Utopia made flesh – the kind of school successive education ministers and parents have dreamed of, but which rarely comes to fruition. A school that gets its fair share of Oxbridge offers in any one year, but also offers a fantastic package of education for students with special needs. Staff, pupils and parents are a thoroughly likable and grounded bunch, as well as being aspirational and genuinely excited about meeting full potential. Perhaps most impressive were the number of parents we spoke to with tales of the school having teased out interests they never knew their children had – then supporting them to excel. The downside – trying to find a house within its two mile bull's eye.

Godstowe Preparatory School

Shrubbery Road, High Wycombe, Buckinghamshire HP13 6PR

Ages Girls 3–13, boys 3–7 **Pupils** 435 **Boarders** 70 full, 5 weekly, 23 flexi (from 7 years)

Fees: Day £10,800 – £16,620; Boarding + £8,025 pa

01494 529273
www.godstowe.org

Headmistress: Since September 2017, Sophie Green (40s). Warm, serene and so glamorous that we wondered if she was off to the opera after our visit. Previously head of Herries School in Cookham. She has also been director of studies at St George's Windsor Castle, where she prepared pupils for scholarships and was involved in the demanding boarding life of the choristers. She is an ISI inspector.

Ask anyone, pupil or parent, to describe her and we'd put money on them using the word 'calm.' 'I like the fact that she was in no rush to make a big show of making a difference when she joined – she just calmly gets on with doing a great job,' one parent told us. 'She's quietly spoken but make no mistake

G

– everything she says is calmly and carefully considered and usually spot on,' said another. Admired for being a good role model to the girls, regularly using examples of strong females from history in her (very well received) speeches. 'And she's a real listener,' one parent enthused, telling how some families grumbled about parking – 'so she spent two mornings from 7.30am in the car park and then made the necessary changes.' Pupils like her 'emphasis on wellbeing' and that 'she's always reasonable and never raises her voice.' But, most of all, they love her black lab, 'Meg the celeb', as she is affectionately known, who – when not being walked by pupils – lies peacefully in the head's elegant study.

Lives onsite with her two teenage sons. Enjoys dog walking, reading, meeting friends and travelling.

Entrance: Despite Godstowe's popularity, school is adamant that it will remain 'first come first served', non-selective. Entry to pre-prep The Lodge (boys and girls) at 3+; most girls move up to the prep (100 per cent the year we visited), with a third class opened up for newcomers in year 3. Other main entry points are years 5 and 7 but girls join all the way through from a variety of local prep and state schools (space permitting) and boarders (who can join from year 3 onwards) from further afield. Boarding can be full time or flexible with many day girls choosing to try it in years 7 and 8 as a taster for senior school.

Exit: Not a specific feeder, with girls heading off to a range of senior schools notably Wycombe Abbey, Cheltenham Ladies', Queen Anne's and Downe House; others to eg St George's Ascot, Rugby, Wellington, Stowe, Haileybury, Tudor Hall, Oundle, Uppingham, Pipers Corner, St Edward's, Bradfield, Millfield, Headington, Heathfield and Marlborough. A handful leave for local grammars at 11.

Remarks: England's first girls' boarding prep school and Enid Blyton's inspiration (though not the only contender) for Malory Towers, purpose built in 1900. The grounds make excellent use of a hilly, if a little blustery, site overlooking High Wycombe, with the original pretty Virginia creeper-clad buildings now housing years 3 to 8, plus The Lodge and nursery buildings. The few boys in pre-prep, mostly siblings, move on at the age of 7.

The airy atrium style reception building (buzzing at pick-up and drop-off times – 'we want parents to really feel at home here') is a more modern addition to the more rustic Victorian buildings and has a gallery-like atmosphere, setting the tone for the rather artsy feel of the whole school. It also gives a flavour of the wholesomeness that abounds, from the display cabinet of ceramic teapots (year 6) to the fresh-faced girls beaming from the 'Godstowe in Iceland' photobooks on the large oak coffee table. As if on cue when we arrived, a teacher practically skipped through reception humming a song from Beauty and the Beast; another walked through with a box of pompoms; and the girls actually curtsied when introduced to us.

We found Godstowe to be jolly hockey sticks without the plums in mouths. That's not to say all the girls are from well-heeled backgrounds, but that they have the boisterous enthusiasm and excitement with very traditional (some might say old-fashioned) manners while remaining thoroughly grounded. Definitely not a school placing importance on hushed tones, girls dash about chatting noisily (we even heard screams of exhilaration in the nursery playground) and when you ask them what a Godstowe girl is, they practically sing in unison, 'well-mannered, happy and successful.' Not that girls here are taught to follow the crowd – far from it, they're encouraged to value their uniqueness and to find the thing(s) they're good at.

Non-selective it may be, but success is in the air here. Minority (about 15 per cent) peel off at 11 to local schools (parents have to 'opt in' to 11+), but unlike many prep schools in the area which hothouse pupils for the sought-after Bucks grammars, this is a true 3-13 establishment, feeding its post-CE alumni into a heady mix of top day and boarding indies, many with scholarships. Which are pretty abundant, by the way, with the current record for one year standing at 54, to 20 different schools. School puts this down to 'commitment and dedication of staff, who provide quality teaching and know the girls really well' and is proud not to share the pushy reputation of some of its competition.

French is taught from reception, Latin from year 6 (plus Latin and Spanish as options from year 7) in creatively themed classrooms. Classes in pre-prep school 'subtly' streamed, with a maximum class size of 18. Formal setting in maths from year 3 and in all academic subjects from year 6. Girls stay in form rooms for lessons in years 3 and 4, after which they start to move around the school for individual subjects. We saw as many girls learning on their feet and interactively as we did staring at talking teachers. Science particularly exciting, say girls – 'especially when you get your Bunsen burner licence in year 5.'

General acceptance that everyone learns differently and SEN is all in a day's work rather than marginalised. Two dedicated SEN staff in place and an excellent EAL programme that we saw in action – mostly for those boarders from the Far East and Spain, with girls' needs assessed upon entry to the school and timetabled to meet their specific requirements. 'My daughter has dyslexia and it's been a complete non-issue getting her the support she needs,' one parent told us.

Creative pursuits are well catered for, with a dedicated sewing room in DT where girls knock up skirts and dresses for the year 7 and 8 fashion show ('the highlight of the year,' said one pupil). Large, bright and airy art room a joy to visit – we saw girls getting messy and smiling from ear to ear as they worked, with every nook and cranny (along with much of the rest of the school) displaying arts and crafts in just about every form you can think of, from glazed sweet packets and shoes to life-size papier-mâché humans that wouldn't look out of place in a GCSE exhibition. Head of art considered something of a legend and her specialisation of 3D work is welcomed. Food technology centre opened in 2017 by Mary Berry.

Some 300 girls learn musical instruments and practise daily in bright, well-equipped studios.

Parents say the standard is 'incredible.' 'It is not unusual for me to give out certificates for grade 8 with distinction in assemblies and we have two pupils currently working towards a diploma too,' says head. All pupils are encouraged to participate from the age of 3 in regular recitals and choir is compulsory in years 3 to 6. JK Theatre is used for music concerts, as well as plentiful drama productions.

Sports – for which there's plenty of outside space, plus £2m sports hall – includes the usual suspects (netball and lacrosse) taking centre pitch, all to a high competitive standard. Athletics and rounders are also on offer, as are ballet, gymnastics and dance, and new pool will doubtless put swimming back high on the agenda. 'It's a bit gendered,' criticised one parent, although cricket and indoor football are available as school after school clubs. Some parents feel the A and B teams are a bit exclusive.

Parents say boarding is 'exemplary.' 'It's an extremely caring, nurturing and organised environment – you know they'll get all their prep and music practice done and you also know they'll have fun,' said one parent, while another told us, 'They make me feel very much part of the school even though I'm hardly there.' Boarding facilities homely, albeit in need of a lick of paint in places, with dorms (sleeping between four and eight), cosy common rooms and homely kitchens. All have their own large gardens with plenty of outdoor equipment. Newly appointed head of boarding and housemistresses are non-teaching staff, leaving them free to focus on girls' pastoral care. Good mix of full, weekly and flexi-boarders, with strong international mix – some 40 per cent from overseas. Weekend activities keep boarders busy, many of which take place off site (bowling, skating, theatre, cinema etc). 'I found it hard when I arrived as I missed home, but everyone was so lovely that it was soon ok,' one pupil told us.

The mobile phone arms race was stopped by the clever acquisition of 100 bog standard phones (yes, these do still exist) into which girls can insert their own SIM cards to call home. Thursdays are 'no go gadget' evenings in the boarding houses to further encourage those old-fashioned skills, reading, conversation and game playing. Girls say the best thing about Godstowe is 'everyone is happy all the time' – future careers in PR await. Food considered 'great' but uniforms (well, the cloaks anyway) are a sticking point for some parents as 'it's so impractical in the winter' (head says it's on her list).

For day girls, early drop-off plus breakfast (7.30am) and late pick-up plus supper (7pm) is available for day girls at low cost and the 'enrichment curriculum' (that's after school clubs in old money) offers up to 50 options. These range from the traditional sports, LAMDA and wind band to Mandarin, politics and yoga, with up to 100 girls staying for these. Post CE, year 8s are given a lifestyle crash course to prepare them for a less cosseted existence. Includes classes in self-defence, internet safety and relationships, charitable works, trips out and visiting lecturers. Overall behaviour very good, with LOFT (loss of free time – again, in old money that's detentions) for misdemeanours – 'very rare,' say girls.

Families hail from a 20-mile radius for day girls, with minibuses servicing three routes. Friends of Godstowe (FoG) organises the usual fairs, cake sales and coffee mornings etc, though one parent felt 'there's less of a community than I've experienced at other preps'.

This is a school with energy, where girls are lively to the point of effervescent and focused but not pressured. A passion for creativity is also bred into the core of this traditional school and latent talent is drawn out of those who didn't even know they had it.

Gordon's School

114

West End, Woking, Surrey GU24 9PT

Ages 11–18 **Pupils** 839 **Sixth form** 241 **Boarders** 187 full, 51 weekly

Fees: Day £5,790 – £7,614; Boarding £16,134 – £17,235 pa

01276 858084
www.gordons.school

Head teacher: Since 2010, Andrew Moss BA MEd NPQH (50s). Started teaching in 1992 and has worked in a variety of boarding and day schools, including most recently a headship in a Cognita independent school. Before that he was a deputy head in Hampshire, and deputy director of studies and housemaster at Wymondham College (also a state boarding school).

He's 'businesslike' and 'no-nonsense', say parents. While insisting he is 'approachable' and 'responsive', one summed up, 'I wouldn't want to mess with him' while another voiced, 'He's straight talking and demands a high level of commitment from both the students and families – that is not for everyone so don't even think about coming here unless you're prepared to go all in.' One recalled an information evening aboutthe sixth form, in which his message was, 'If you don't want to work, don't come here – it's that simple'. Students say he's 'interested', 'visible' and 'knows us by name'. Known for his signature stern, tough chapel talks; one student said, 'He is assertive and authoritative, but he's also friendly.' We found him old-school when it comes to manners and rules, but modern in his outlook for the school – pretty much the perfect combo for this military influenced school.

Despite his strong ideas, he is big on using staff and parents as a sounding board ('you can't build capacity all by yourself') and takes feedback seriously, with one student telling how they recently 'blocked a change that the school wanted to make around the structure of prep time – it did not suit us and he heard us.' Regularly meets with parents at everything from tea and cake afternoons (before exeats) to information evenings. Keeps a finger on the pulse by standing in for teachers when he can.

Has two children of his own (both attended the school) and is a keen skier in his spare time.

Academic matters: Among the very best state offerings in the country, with an academically rigorous curriculum. It is an all-ability school, for which students are not selected via entrance exams, yet its results are top notch. In 2018, 94 per cent of pupils got 9-4 in both English and maths, with 40 per cent 9-7 grades. At A level in 2018, 47 per cent A*/A and 76 per cent A*-B grades. Value added is also a stand-out point, with the school in the top one per cent for progress from GCSE to A levels.

Head believes in putting progress under the spotlight. 'Attainment will take care of itself if progress is prioritised, so tracking is our number one thing.' Nobody slips through the net here, say students. 'If someone isn't keeping up, there are lots of interventions to help get them up to scratch,' said one. While the school has always had a real push on effort and working hard, they are now even more forensic about ensuring everyone is reaching their potential and the students (who even get ranked in their year on effort) literally refer to their efforts in decimal points. Students also get target and working grades, and every half term they receive significant feedback on what they need to do next. 'You can't be brilliant at everything but the beauty about effort is that you can control it,' says head. Message is clearly getting through, with one student telling us, 'It's not all about As and A*s here; it's about doing your very best, whatever grade that might mean.'

Teachers 'really care', say students. We were told a story of one 'who'd been a bit of rogue' walking into his maths exam: 'He said to his maths teacher, "I'm going to get a B for you" The teacher told him to get the B for himself, but the student was insistent. "No, miss, this will be for you." That pretty much sums this school up.' Parents praise the 'strong and disciplined' teaching team and their 'high expectations for students'. Lessons are fairly formal – nearly all desks were facing forwards in the classrooms we visited and behaviour was impeccable in all but one classroom where a boy threw his pen at a classmate then looked very sheepish when he spotted us.

Everyone is set for English, maths and science (six sets per year group) and also for languages in years 7 and 8 – a language is compulsory at GCSE; either German, French or Spanish. Lowish requirements for additional support; some seven per cent have one-to-one EAL help and four per cent have EHC plans, led by full-time SENCo and delivered in small groups and individually. 'We don't have a big learning support department,' admits head and parents told us they 'haven't been great around SEN in the past' but insist that is no longer the case. 'They've helped my son through his problems with English because they know his success in that subject will impact on all his subjects,' said one.

They plough through the work here, books filled at a pace, and there are plenty of practice papers and timed tests to make sure everyone is well prepared for GCSE. 'It can be daunting at the time, but when it comes to the exams, you're so well prepared,' said one student. 'The new linear exams suit us,' says head. Homework diaries are an important part of keeping on top of everything, really well used, signed every week by parents and school. The diaries are used for merits too, as well as warnings.

Sixth formers take mainly traditional A levels ('those with gravitas, the ones that open doors') although there are now three BTechs available in sport, ICT and business. Parents like it that sixth formers are not allowed off-site during teaching hours (although they are able to go home early if they don't have a last lesson), so are more likely to work during their 'study periods' (they are not called free periods here). Around 10 per cent do EPQ.

Although two-thirds of its pupils live at home, the school is structured as a boarding school, with these 'day boarders' (as they are known) organised the same way as the wholly residential boarders in an extended school day. So everyone is in a house, with houseparents, and following the same programme, including after-school clubs, supper and supervised homework, until 7.30pm (or 6.45pm for some of the younger ones), and everyone attends Saturday morning school. These are covered by the 'day boarding' fee of £7,000+ a year.

Games, options, the arts: Everyone here burns the candles both ends and that's just how they like it – 'we all know busy people achieve more,' explains head. After what would be the end of the school day at most state schools, the compulsory extended day here begins with 'period 7' – anything from sport to cooking, bagpipe lessons, golf, equestrian team training or ICT coding. After that, it's tea and then prep.

Masses of sport on offer, with good facilities on site – more than 40 acres of playing fields, and all the usual football, rugby and hockey pitches, to the less usual (for a state school) shooting range, Astroturf, BMX track, rowing centre and indoor heated swimming pool. Gordon's teams are happy to take on the toughest opponents and often play independent schools. The first football team had reached the semi-finals of the English Schools FA Cup when we visited. But it's not just about the elite, with all students encouraged to participate and there's an impressive engagement rate for older girls (who often drop out of sports at other schools). A much awaited new sports hall will be ready in 2020. Over 100 students do DofE every year, including a striking number of golds. And all three Forces are represented in Gordon's combined cadet force – quite a feat to manage a naval unit in landlocked Surrey.

Great tradition of hard-fought inter-house competition gets everyone involved, regardless of ability (boys' rugby is a highlight of the year), not just in sport but also in art, music and drama, with specialist facilities for all. Music very big here, with a junior boys' choir the newest kid on the block, joining the orchestra, choirs (including male teachers' choir) and concert band, as well as the pipe and drum band which, together with marching practice, is a major focus on the school. LAMDA has grown in recent years and there are junior and senior productions every year too, plus drama ambassadors who direct, stage and light their own smaller productions. In fact, student led initiatives more generally are on the up, with a growing number of societies such as eco society and global social leader programme, as well as the Sudan Society (Gordon's is the only European school ever to have gone to Khartoum). Runs a Model United Nations programme and is the only state school to host its own MUN conference. There are two annual art exhibitions, with improving take-up for art at both GCSE and A level, following a dip in numbers.

Boarding: There are six day houses and four residential houses – all well used by both day and full boarders, who mix well. From 2019, there will also be a new co-educational house for year 7s. Boys and girls are allowed freely in each other's houses, but no boy is allowed upstairs in the girls' boarding houses and vice versa. Common rooms are spacious yet cosy – like genuinely lived-in homes – and are kitted out with the likes of pool and table tennis tables. All sixth formers have study rooms, even in the day houses – around two to four desks in each room, with some particularly swanky new ones. All understandably more relaxed than other parts of the school, there is nothing sterile or pristine about these boarding houses. Ofsted's inspection of boarding facilities pronounced them 'outstanding' in every respect. Boarders say 'it's home from home'.

Background and atmosphere: Ceremony and discipline are in the DNA of Gordon's, which was founded in 1885, at the behest of Queen Victoria, as a national memorial to General Gordon who was killed at Khartoum. The reigning monarch has been the school's patron ever since and every teaching block is named after a country he visited.

Every student learns to march and takes part in every one of the eight parades and chapel services held each year, accompanied by the pipes and drums marching band. There is marching practice every Friday, and once a year students go to London and literally stop the traffic when they march down Whitehall past the Cenotaph, ending up at the bronze statue of General Gordon on the Embankment. Although right up the street of the keen musicians in the band, it can be rather a chore for some of the others. 'It's not exactly my favourite thing, but it's just part of school life so you get on with it and actually you become more fond of it as you get older,' said one student. 'Well, it's no bad thing for students to do things well that they don't necessarily want to do – it's a good lesson for life,' retorts the head, adding that it gives 'a great edge' and 'story for interview' when applying to uni. Definitely part and parcel of what makes this school different, it is also seen to encourage camaraderie and is part of the discipline that feeds into the classrooms.

Day to day things are rather less regimented, but all very orderly – head describes atmosphere as 'purposeful calm'. The school is built around a large quadrangle, where the students hang out during break and lunch if they are not in their houses. Alongside the original Victorian buildings are some less pretty 1960s additions, and (much better) 21st century facilities, including the new music and drama centre, science block, sixth form centre and (most recently) maths centre. Classrooms are large, light and spacious, in both the older and newer buildings, and well resourced. Stunning chapel, built in 1894, which houses numerous school treasures, including a book which lists the names of all the Gordon's boys killed in the two world wars. Pupils are never for a moment in any doubt about their school's heritage.

Pastoral care, well-being and discipline: Houses form the backbone of this school and the fact that they are physical houses helps create a genuine village culture. Very close companionship among students, including across year groups – 'houses are like a brotherhood,' one student told us. Every residential boarding house has two houseparents, a day matron, two residential tutors and a graduate assistant tutor 'so we are spoilt for choice about having someone to talk to as you'll always get on really well with at least one of them, probably more,' said one student. Plenty of peer mentoring. Counsellor available, to which students can and do self-refer. Full mental health agenda, including guest speakers and mental health ambassadors, and the school is about to start benchmarking for happiness and wellbeing.

There's not much allowance for anyone stepping out of line at this highly disciplined school, but for those obedient souls happy to stay within the set boundaries there are plenty of rewards and responsibilities on offer. Pupils quickly pick up on what's expected of them and are generally hardworking and appreciative of what's on offer. Simple good manners are prioritised and it shows. Similarly picky about uniform. If a girl's skirt is deemed too short (and we didn't see any) she will be given a week's grace to get a new one. Sex, drugs and rock and roll? 'It's a residential school, so I can't say it doesn't happen but instances are very, very low,' says head.

School admits they 'are not without bullying incidents, but what we don't have are repeat incidents', which he puts down to the (you guessed it) house system, plus anti-bullying ambassadors. Very clear sanctions system with the first offence a verbal warning, followed by a bad comment in the diary – usually that's enough, but if not, it's a detention which is seen as a very big deal here. Around seven or eight temporary exclusions a year – 'it would be lower if we did not choose to have such a high bar'; permanent exclusions very rare.

Pupils and parents: Although it's a state school, most parents have money, certainly parents of boarders who have to cover the boarding fees. Parents of day boarders must be able to afford the £7000+ day boarding fees and will be in a certain socio-economic demographic to live in the catchment; of necessity they must live practically next door and some move house to get this education for their children. Aside from these locals, parents are a huge mix of professional, diplomatic and Forces. Weekly boarders typically live within an hour's drive, full boarders come from all over the UK, with about 15 per cent from overseas (expats).

We found students friendly, polite, happy and very proud of their school; all regular young people, not quiet and cowed by the rules and regulations, but confident and ambitious types who seem to thrive in the order of everything.

Entrance: Tough. There are typically 400 applications for the 116 year 7 places on offer (of whom around 32 board) and around half of these are generally swallowed up by siblings. Non-selective, so no entrance exams. Full or weekly boarder places prioritised by 'need to board'. This usually means children from Forces families from the UK and overseas.

For admission as a 'day boarder' think purely of location. Catchment varies but typically you'll need to live no further than 1km from the school. Needless to say, school is popular among local estate agents. A small number of places allocated each year to children with statements of special educational needs.

Between 30-40 additional places available for the sixth form, where the entry requirement for both existing and new pupils is five GCSEs at 9-4 (including English and maths) with 6s or 7s (depending on subjects) for chosen A levels.

Exit: Around 40 per cent leave after GCSEs, most wanting a wider breadth of courses. Most sixth formers on to university; around half to Russell Group. Two Oxbridge places in 2018; three medics. Universities in the west country currently popular (Exeter, Bath, Bristol etc) and just about every course you can think of, with STEM on the up.

Money matters: The education is free, but parents pay for the boarding and parents of day students must pay for the after-school activities, house staff, Saturday school and meals. Around 10 per cent of places funded by means-tested bursaries and there are 12 sixth form scholarships in sports and creative arts.

Remarks: A very different state offering – more like a private school without the price tag and elitism. Committed to traditional values, high standards, good discipline – doesn't share its 'semper fidelis' motto with the US marine corps for nothing. Those happy with the 'heads down and work' ethos are rewarded with an all-round, top notch education, pastoral care par excellence and enviable opportunities for sport. Suits focused, self-directed types and is definitely not a soft option.

Great Ballard School

Eartham, Chichester, West Sussex PO18 0LR

Ages 2.5–13 **Pupils** 124 **Boarders** 1 full, 30 flexi (from 7 years)

Fees: Day £8,580 – £15,310 pa; Weekly boarding (4 nights) £17,010

01243 814236
www.greatballard.co.uk

Headmaster: Since 2015, Richard Evans BEd MEd (management) (50s). He was educated at a grammar school in Wales and did his teacher training at St Paul's and St Mary's in Cheltenham (where he met his wife Carol) and spent five years at a state secondary school before joining Eagle House prep school. He then held several prep school posts before spending five years as head of St Andrew's in Surrey, a further four as head of Bromsgrove Prep and three as head of Craigclowan, Perth before moving south to Great Ballard.

He took over after a period of uncertainty when the school had two headmasters in three years and has now set it on an even keel. 'There has been a great change since Mr Evans took over,' said a parent. 'The school used to be a well-kept secret, but he is brilliant at marketing and raised its profile in the local area and on social media.' There is a brand new star-studded website (the school is in an International Dark Sky Reserve) and the school 'feels a much more self-confident place,' said a parent.

He loves all things sporting and used to be a keen cricket and rugby player – he played rugby for Saracens for four years. He also loves golf, has recently taken up fly fishing and is outdoors whenever possible, walking or cycling on the downs – and having owned a few himself, he enjoys sports cars. He is also an ISI school and boarding inspector.

A visible presence around the school – he is always out on the steps in the morning and his door is genuinely open for parents to call in. 'He seems to care about the children on all levels and gets to know the whole family,' said a parent, and 'we love the fact that he knows everyone and what's going on in your life,' said a pupil. His year group annual dinners for parents and teachers are extremely popular, as are the special lunches he lays on for the children in his drawing room. He is a stickler for tidiness and good manners and anyone with muddy shoes is sent to polish them.

He and his wife Carol are very much a team – she is in charge of pastoral care and boarding and teaches geography and maths. They have two sons in their 20s.

Entrance: Almost non-selective – all have a taster day with informal assessments when teachers look at behaviour, confidence and integration. Entry from year 3 is via spelling, reading and non-verbal reasoning tests and references from the child's current school. If the child has learning difficulties the school will ask for a more formal assessment with the head of learning support. Most join in nursery or reception, with other entry points in year 3 and year 7, when children often come from local primary schools, but entry possible at any time, even mid-term, if there are spaces. All new children are paired up with a buddy to help them settle in.

Exit: The school takes great trouble making sure that children move on to a secondary school which is right for them, works closely with senior schools and recently hosted a senior schools

G

fair. Seaford College the most popular (five scholarships, one of them academic, in 2018) with others off to Priorsfield, Lancing, St John's Southsea and Midhurst Rother College in 2018. Very few children leave at 11+.

Remarks: The school was founded in 1924 in New Milton in Hampshire and – following moves to Stowell Park in Gloucestershire during the war and 12 years in Camberley – it moved to its current location at Eartham House in 1961. Built in 1743 as a summer retirement house, the main building was remodelled by Edwin Lutyens in 1905 and is set in 30 acres within the South Downs national park – you couldn't really imagine a more wonderful place to grow up. It still has the atmosphere of a family country house, complete with a large teddy bear in the hall and a cannon in the garden. The headmaster's study is an elegant drawing room and only the prefects are allowed to walk down the sweeping staircase.

G

Most of the classrooms are in purpose built cabins in the garden and are all light and airy. The gym is used for assemblies, concerts and school plays and can just accommodate the whole school. The headmaster would dearly love to build a sports hall but the strict planning laws within the national park won't allow this; parents who send their children here value the ethos and atmosphere far more than swanky facilities.

The school is owned by Sue Jay whose father, John Chedzoy, rescued it from almost certain closure in 1990, when it was the only school in the area that would accept her child, who had a disability. Her husband and son are both on the board of directors and Sue is involved with the day to day life of the school.

Single form year groups throughout the school with a wide range of abilities in each class and an emphasis on personalised learning and care for all, with effort is valued equally with achievement. 'Expectations are high both in and out of the classroom, but in a nurturing and encouraging way,' said a parent.

Average class size is 12-13 with a maximum of 19, often with setting for maths and English in the larger classes. Children gradually introduced to testing – exams at the end of every term from year 6 means they are well prepared for scholarship and common entrance exams in year 8. The more able children are stretched and those aiming for academic scholarships take extra science and maths as an activity. Children are encouraged to discuss current affairs and to take an interest in the world beyond the school. Cooking is part of the curriculum – 'we love it when we can eat our own prep,' say the children.

Average age of staff dropping due to natural fallout and is now late 30s. Several new heads of department have reinvigorated the school and nearly half the prep school teachers are men. All staff get involved in boarding duties and activities.

Ongoing standard assessments for dyslexia, and any learning difficulties picked up early and support put in place. Full time SENCo and part time assistant as well as a teacher who is trained in SEN, and school can cope with a broad spectrum of difficulties. Many taken out of class for one-to-one tuition, some in class help and one child with an EHC plan has a teaching assistant.

Well-established forest school for all year groups where children can build dens, make mud sculptures, learn crafts and toast marshmallows over a campfire as well as learn about the natural world. Children put on their boiler suits at break time and head into the woods to play, and can climb trees to the height of the tallest teacher. Who needs a climbing frame when a fallen tree is much more fun? An outdoorsy school where children can go mountain biking on the downs and sail and kayak nearby, and there's a whole school camping adventure in the grounds every summer. 'Children can be children for longer here without the outside pressures', said a parent.

Pre-prep and nursery have their own buildings with an enclosed play area in the old kitchen garden, but are very much part of the school and use the grounds, forest school, swimming pool, cookery room and other facilities. The pre-prep is headed by a man who provides a good role model for boys to look up to. Specialist prep school staff teach music, sport and dance and pre-prep children can take part in after-school clubs. It is a happy and cosy environment, and often children come for the nursery with plans to move on to primary school and then end up staying until they are 13. 'My son would not settle at any nursery until we discovered Great Ballard – he loves the outside space', said one happy parent.

Indoor heated swimming pool, an Astro and tennis courts with playing fields at the top of the hill with views to the coast. Boys can do winter cricket net practice at Arundel. Everyone needed for matches and the less sporty have to take part. This gives all children a chance to shine – 'my daughter was never really interested in sport but has had to take part and now she really enjoys it – that would never have happened in a larger school.'

Music increasingly important, especially singing, and all have to sing in one of the three choirs until year 5 – director of music is a semi-professional singer. 'We love singing,' said a pupil, 'and hymn practice is such fun.' Children take part in the Young Voices school choir concert at the O2 and in the Chichester Festival and sing at the Christmas carol concert as well as lots of informal concerts and performances in assemblies. Growing numbers learning an instrument and there are now two percussion ensembles and other instrumental groups, and children can compose their own music on a suite of computers.

Dance including ballet, tap and zumba popular, and school has its own dance and drama studio in the main house. Weekly drama lessons from year 3, annual prep school musical and the pre-prep has its nativity play and termly concerts. Many take LAMDA exams and all are confident to stand up in public by the time they leave.

Busy art department with its own kiln – it was van Gogh term when we visited so there were sunflowers everywhere and year 8 had made some fine sculptures of their heads. Artists who show potential are singled out for extra lessons in the evenings and usually stay the night afterwards – the school gets at least one art scholarship each year.

Good range of clubs after school and on Saturday mornings – gym, dance and sport are the most popular. Much interaction and collaboration between year groups through sport and activities, reinforced by the keen competition between the three houses – Romans, Spartans and Trojans.

Year 7 trip to France and the year 8 outdoor pursuits to Dorset after common entrance. Children also get involved with fundraising in the local community and support charities including St Wilfred's Hospice, Chestnut House and the Stone Pillow a charity for local homeless people.

'The great strength of the school is the tight knit community and the strong pastoral care,' said a parent. 'Everyone knows each other and the older children naturally look out for the younger ones.' There are clear rules and boundaries and an emphasis on respect, good manners and consideration for others means bullying is rare, and when it happens it is dealt with immediately. Cyber issues carefully monitored; years 5 and 6 take part in an e-safety workshop with a follow up session offered to parents. There is always someone to talk to, staff, peers or an external 'listening ear'. Emphasis on well-being and mindfulness for senior pupils. Staff know whole families well and 'support and nurture them in everything they do,' said a parent. 'My daughter settled in immediately and has never been happier – I wish we had found the school earlier', said a mother.

Elegant dining room lined with honours boards and shields and children's artwork. Cafeteria system with lots of choice –

staff eat with children to supervise table manners, the chefs know every child and everyone we spoke to praised the home cooked food. 'It's the only school where my child hasn't complained about the food,' said a parent.

Seven dorms, all with fab views, and children often see deer on the lawn in the early mornings. Girls' rooms decorated with posters and fairy lights and the boys' with the usual sports posters. Nearly all boarders are flexi except for a group of children, mainly from France, Italy and Spain, who join the school for half a term in the summer. They have intensive English teaching in the mornings and then take part in the full range of activities in the afternoons. Boarders have their own social area with a pool table, ping pong tables and a television and can take part in activities and outings like bowling and indoor rock climbing.

Parents mainly local professionals from a 20 mile radius. Active parents' group organises events like the Christmas fair, summer fete and Valentine's day disco as well as street dance classes. 'Parents have lots of opportunities to be involved but there needs to be a balance,' says the headmaster. The school runs a minibus service and is very accommodating of working parents with breakfast club, after-school clubs and supper for non-boarders, and can usually fit in an extra boarder if there is an emergency. After-school care till 5.30pm; the nursery is open all year and older children can join activity camps here during the holidays.

Alumni include: actress Honeysuckle Weeks of Foyle's War fame; naval officer Captain Nick Cooke-Priest OBE; professional cricket coach Julien Fountain; former British defence attaché, Patrick Tootal. Michael Morpurgo taught here in the 1960s.

A charming small school in an idyllic location where children have the freedom and space to grow up slowly. The only complaint we could elicit from any parents was that children cannot stay there until they are 16.

Guildford High School

Linked with Guildford High School Junior School

London Road, Guildford, Surrey GU1 1SJ

Ages 11–18 **Pupils** 726 **Sixth form** 188 **C of E**

Fees: £17,214 pa

01483 561440
www.guildfordhigh.co.uk

Headmistress: Since 2002, Fiona Boulton BSc PGCE MA NPQH (early 50s). Read biology at Cardiff University, followed by a PGCE at Oxford. First teaching post was at Stowe, where she taught biology and chemistry and became housemistress of a sixth form girls' boarding house. Spent five years at Marlborough, where she was a teacher and housemistress. She then moved to Surrey, teaching part-time at Guildford High while studying for her MA. Appointed as deputy head in 1996 and became head six years later. She is also a National Leader of Education, a role that involves helping other schools to raise standards and develop a self-improving and sustainable school system.

Guildford High is oversubscribed (three applicants for every year 7 place) so while she is in no way complacent about pupil numbers she has been able to concentrate on 'the teaching and learning, the extracurricular and everything else' – the areas she considers most important in a school. 'By doing that I can make sure we are excellent at what we do,' she says. She still teaches five lessons a week, including year 9 biology and year 7 current affairs. 'I enjoy teaching and I'm good at it,' she says. 'It means you've got your finger on the pulse. I'm currently teaching 90 pupils so I'm writing reports and meeting parents too. It means that as you walk round you know your school. I try and know every pupil.' She invites every pupil to a form leaders' lunch (every girl gets the chance to be a form leader between year 7 and year 9). She meets every year 9 one-to-one to discuss their GCSE choices and sees every sixth former individually when they're writing their UCAS personal statements.

She insists there isn't a typical Guildford High pupil. 'They're an eclectic mix of personalities,' she says. 'They're all bright and busy in different ways. It's the culture of the school.' Parents are very impressed by her approach. 'She is fantastic, very involved in everything,' one told us. Of all the school's myriad achievements the head is most proud of the school's pastoral care. A parent said that when problems arise the school is outstanding in its support. We visited during the annual Well-being Week, which featured yoga sessions, mindfulness, dancing, a magician's show and a juggling display. The head was totally unfazed at the sight of 'a guy juggling on a unicycle outside my office' as she arrived for work.

Interestingly, she doesn't believe that girls learn best in single sex schools – or vice versa. Interviewed by the Daily Telegraph in 2014, she said: 'I think if you create a really great environment then pupils do well. I don't sell a school on it being single-sex. I sell it on the fact that we set out to be excellent in all that we do and that's why you should choose us – not because it is an all-girls school.' Her views haven't changed in the intervening years. 'I think we are a really good school because we set out to be outstanding in everything we do,' she says.

Married to a QC, with three children (the youngest is a pupil at Guildford High). In her spare time she enjoys reading, playing the piano and walking in the Lake District.

Academic matters: Academically outstanding. In 2018 83 per cent A*/A grades at A level and 97 per cent A*-A/9-7 at GCSE. In years 7 to 9, pupils study two languages from a choice of French, German and Spanish, plus Latin. Separate sciences from the start, taught in 12 labs, one of them painted a dazzling purple. Lots of STEM trips to inspiring places like NASA and CERN. Girls also take DT (resistant materials, textiles and food and nutrition). Philosophy, psychology and digital arts are covered on a carousel basis and girls have weekly current affairs lessons, where they are encouraged 'to think on their feet and voice their opinions'. As the school says: 'From the outset, girls are taught to think for themselves, to analyse and question and we instil a genuine love for learning.' Parents bear this out. One mother told us: 'I'll never forget my 15-year-old daughter coming home and saying "I've had the most amazing chemistry lesson". She was literally on fire with enthusiasm.'

Parents like the fact that no homework is set in the holidays, allowing everyone a complete break from school. The mother of a year 7 said: 'I'm blown away by the school. I was slightly nervous that it would be all about the academic side but my daughter skips into school each day and skips home. It has been the making of her.' Another told us: 'The teaching is outstanding, stimulating and the girls don't feel pressurised. I don't know how they do it. You don't have to be a superstar to fit in. Everyone finds their niche.' The pupils reiterated this view. 'People say it must be pressurised here because the school gets really good results but it really isn't,' said one.

Eighty per cent of pupils take 10 GCSEs, 10 per cent take 11 subjects and 10 per cent take nine. All the usual subjects on offer at A level, plus economics, PE and psychology. Relatively small number of pupils with SEN needs. Girls are rarely taken out of lessons for learning support; teachers support them in class instead. Girls are enthusiastic in their praise for teachers. 'We can email them and they are very willing to help if you have any questions,' a sixth former told us. She particularly appreciated teachers' lunchtime lectures – on everything from Victorian graveyards to Einstein.

Games, options, the arts: Sport is truly exceptional. At the time of our visit 27 girls were representing the country. The school's executive director of sport was recently awarded the MBE for services to education and former pupil Emily Appleton, who left in 2017, is now a professional tennis player, Sky Sports Scholar and rising star. Unwavering in its support for her, the school even allowed her to take one of her A levels in Paris, where she was competing in the French Open. 'Everything is bespoke,' says the head. 'We like to do everything we can to support our pupils. I say "yes" to everything. When you have opportunities like this you have to grasp them.' In the same vein, a year 7 girl is currently appearing in School of Rock in London's West End and a girl in the junior school is about to appear in Roald Dahl's Matilda the Musical.

G

Sports facilities are fantastic. Newish sports centre houses a 25m swimming pool with touch-pad timing, sports hall, fitness suite and vast social area for match teas, lessons and meetings. It overlooks five netball courts, a lacrosse pitch and neighbouring Stoke Park, which the school uses for cross-country. Youngest girls do curriculum sport – main sports are lacrosse, netball, gym and swimming – but year 9s and above can choose from a vast list, including rowing, volleyball, badminton, synchronised swimming, zumba and yoga. Sixth formers have options like ice skating, squash and golf too. The go-ahead director of sport (who played lacrosse for England herself) is keen for girls to 'have a sport for life'. As she says: 'If the girls want to do something, we'll put it on. The key thing is not to restrict them. It's for them to choose what they want to do.' Some girls arrive at 7.15am for first team lacrosse practice, then have breakfast before lessons start. More games practices at lunchtime and after school.

Eighty per cent of girls in the senior and junior schools have individual music lessons. Music is a big part of school life, with opportunities to join choirs (there's even a parents' choir), orchestras, ensembles and bands. Joint chamber choir with boys from the Royal Grammar School has sung evensong at St Paul's Cathedral, Westminster Abbey, Chichester Cathedral and St Mark's Basilica in Venice. New recital hall can seat 200 people and there's also a recording studio and teaching studios. Up to 25 girls a year take GCSE music and up to eight do A level. Art is stunning, showcased in sleek display cabinets (the head of art spotted them at the V&A and ordered some for the school). When we visited, an A level student was busy photographing the head of politics – clad in a jacket painted with famous logos to illustrate the theme of 'limitations and freedom'. Drama is huge. Every year lower sixth form girls write and produce a panto for year 7 girls to perform and there's a plethora of other performances, including a Shakespeare Festival for years 8 and 9 and drama productions and musicals for all.

As the head says, this is a busy school, with a vast range of activities from dawn to dusk (including European Youth Parliament, Young Enterprise, DofE, inter-house cupcake baking, Monopoly and football). Close proximity to London means that it attracts the most inspiring speakers around. On the day of our visit girls were looking forward to hearing a lecture by historian Suzannah Lipscomb. Girls are encouraged to take part in extracurricular pursuits. They fill in feedback forms at the end of each half term about what they're involved in, how happy they feel and how lessons are going.

Background and atmosphere: Guildford High School is the jewel in the crown of United Learning, which owns 13 independent schools and more than 30 academies across the country. The school is run by the head and her team, but with the advantage of a wide group of other United Learning heads to consult over best practice as well as a central budget to draw from for major projects.

The school opened at Haydon Place in the centre of Guildford in 1887 and moved to its current site in 1893. By the mid 1920s there were around 200 pupils and expansion was rapid after the Second World War. The school is located on the north-east side of Guildford, where the town centre meets leafy Victorian suburbia. Buildings are a mix of old and new – all very wholesome and well maintained. Sixth formers have their own sixth form centre in the heart of the school. Sixth form class sizes are smaller, teaching is more informal and they are allowed to walk into the high street during their free time. There are plenty of opportunities for pupils of all ages to air their views, including a school council. Head girl and prefect candidates write a letter of application and those who are shortlisted give a three-minute presentation in front of the head and teaching staff. Girls belong to one of six houses, Amethyst, Emerald, Opal, Ruby, Sapphire and Topaz – the names were chosen by the girls and are 'very bling', jokes the head.

Plenty of opportunities to mix with boys from the Royal Grammar School. Many travel in by train together and there are joint music and drama activities. The two schools also share general studies lessons and mock Oxbridge interviews in the sixth form.

Pastoral care, well-being and discipline: Pastoral care is second to none. Girls' first port of call for help and advice is their form tutor, then their head of year and then the dynamic deputy head pastoral ('the most vibrant person you'll ever meet,' says the head), who has introduced a host of innovative, original and creative ideas to highlight pastoral care at the school. The deputy head pastoral and her team drove round the Surrey countryside making a James Corden-style Carpool Karaoke film to introduce themselves and then played it at assembly. She even organised a live nativity scene at Christmas, complete with real donkeys. Parents approve wholeheartedly, one describing her as 'cheerful, positive and kind'. A trained nurse is always on site and the school doctor and school counsellor are available every week.

Year 7 to 11 girls wear smart navy uniform (striped shirts and no ties, which they approve of) while sixth formers can wear their own clothes, plus a jacket. Rules are clearly laid out but girls say they don't think anyone breaks them. If pupils have a problem with organisation they are assigned a teacher mentor to help them.

Pupils and parents: Around 80 per cent of senior school pupils get the train to school, from places like Weybridge, Woking, Farnham and Wimbledon. London Road station is a handy 40 metres from the school – 'if I could hug the head who had the foresight to move the school here in 1893 I would,' smiles the present head. New year 7 pupils are allocated to the same forms as girls from the same area so they all travel in together.

Notable old girls include playwrights Ella Hickson and Lucy Prebble, actresses Celia Imrie and Julia Ormond and Mumsnet founder and chief executive Justine Roberts.

Entrance: Girls from the junior school take up 40 per cent of senior school places at 11 (they don't sit an entrance exam for the senior school). The others (from around 90 different feeder preps and state primaries) sit written papers in English and maths. They also have a one-to-one interview – the head describes it as 'a friendly chat about yourself'. The process is transparent, aiming to create a level playing field for applicants of all backgrounds. Parents we spoke to said their daughters had been daunted at the thought of it but the school quickly put them at their ease.

Up to 10 new girls join the school in the lower sixth. Candidates sit three papers in subjects of their choice, plus a general paper and an interview. Entrants are expected to have a minimum of six A*/A or 7 to 9 grades at GCSE, passes in English language and maths and A*/A or 7 to 9 grades in their chosen A level subjects.

Exit: A handful of girls leave after GCSEs. At 18 virtually all go to top universities (one or two do art foundation courses and the aforementioned Emily Appleton became a professional tennis player). In 2018, 14 girls headed to Oxbridge, with others going to the likes of Durham, Bristol, Birmingham and Exeter, plus one off to Vermont. A considerable number study medicine (eight in 2018) but there's a 50:50 split between the arts and sciences. Lots of support when it comes to UCAS forms and the careers room is always open. Alumnae who return to speak to pupils comment on how well the school prepared them for university.

Money matters: Academic and music scholarships are available at 11+ and 16+ and can be up to a third of the fees. Assisted places are available at 11+ and assessed on financial need, as well as bursaries for daughters of the clergy. Sibling discounts of five per cent for second daughters from the same family and 10 per cent for third and subsequent daughters.

Remarks: An outstanding and nurturing school that provides a superb education across the board – academically, on the sports field and in the performing arts. This is a place where bright, hard-working girls develop a positive and enquiring approach to life and learning and set off for university full of confidence and enthusiasm.

Guildford High School Junior School

Linked with Guildford High School

117

London Road, Guildford, Surrey GU1 1SJ

Ages 4–11 **Pupils** 274

Fees: £10,584 – £13,743

01483 562475
www.guildfordhigh.co.uk

Head of junior school: Since 2016, Mike Gibb BA PGCE NPQH (40s). Educated at Taunton School, followed by Royal Holloway, University of London, where he read economics. After graduating he went to Sandhurst and spent seven years in the army before deciding to retrain as a teacher. Did his PGCE at Canterbury Christ Church University, then taught geography, RE and maths at Westbourne House School, becoming head of boarding and a member of the senior leadership team. Was deputy head here for five years before being appointed as head.

He describes the school as 'really vibrant and exciting, with a lot of laughter and fun', adding that 'it isn't a desks in line sort of place'. He still teaches 'a little bit' – mainly computer science and humanities.

His wife is head of a Dorking comprehensive and they have two grown-up children. In his spare time he enjoys singing in his church choir, golf and walking.

Entrance: Selective entry by assessment and interview. For entry at 4+ girls visit the school twice. During their first visit their language, number and general cognitive skills are assessed. On their second visit teachers look at their social skills in a group environment. 'We try and make it as gentle a process as it can be,' says the head. 'They are not expected to read and write. We are looking for children who are ready to learn.' The entry process for 7+ places is more formal. Girls take written papers in English and maths, have lunch with their peers, tour the school and take part in fun activities. Competition for places is undoubtedly stiff. Around 60 to 70 girls compete for 32 to 36 places in reception every year.

Exit: Ninety-five per cent of juniors progress to the senior school. There is no entrance assessment at that point – once girls join the junior school the expectation is that they will go right through. Of the very few who leave after year 6 some choose boarding and one recently went to ballet school. If there is an academic issue the school flags it up as early as possible, certainly by year 5.

Remarks: The junior school is housed in a separate building on the senior school site. Junior girls frequently visit the senior department (they have lunch there every day) and the two buildings are so close that as they come down the stairs they can spot senior girls working in the science labs. Every corner is well used – the art room recently expanded into the eaves – and the science lab is spacious.

The school prides itself on being 'a lively, vibrant place where girls blossom personally, intellectually and socially'. When we visited the place was a hive of activity. Girls were busy rehearsing for their inter-house music competition and everywhere we looked small groups were enthusiastically practising their song and dance routines. The school walls are full of artwork and motivational posters – we spotted one declaring that 'mistakes are proof that you are trying'.

Teaching at this high-achieving school is a combination of traditional and innovative, offering academic rigour, practical work and a lot of fun. The Sunday Times placed it top of the prep school league tables recently although the head stresses that these aren't the be-all and end-all. 'Yes, league tables are great,' he says, 'but it's not why we come to school every day. We are far more interested in the development of the girls and the characters they are turning into.'

Girls study 14 subjects, with Mandarin taught in key stage 1, Spanish introduced in year 1 and French from year 3 (languages are all taught by specialist teachers). 'The girls are very enthusiastic,' says the head. 'They think it's cool to learn and they want to learn new things.' The girls work hard in school and with that in mind the junior school has endeavoured to reduce pupils' homework. 'They take their reading books, spellings and tables home but when they get home they need to be going to Brownies or ice skating – things like that,' says the head. Strong emphasis on reading. All pupils have a reading journal and the school is keen on encouraging girls to read the classics. The current year 6 cohort have discovered a penchant for Agatha Christie, says the head. We particularly liked the mural running the length of the main staircase, spiralling through centuries of monarchs, wars and historical events. A few girls have learning difficulties or special educational needs – such as dyslexia and dyspraxia – but 'not a huge number,' says the head, 'because the pace is so fast here.'

Everyone is involved in drama productions and most girls play at least one musical instrument, many of them performing in a group or orchestra. Years 5 and 6 recently sang Berlioz's Te

Deum at the Royal Albert Hall, while the Festival Choir sang Wassail in Southwark Cathedral. Sport is a key part of the school right from the start. The youngest girls do gymnastics, dance, games, athletics, mini tennis and rounders. Swimming is introduced from year 2 (using the school's 25m indoor swimming pool) and from year 3 girls have five PE lessons a week, including swimming all year round, netball, cricket, tag rugby, football, athletics, rounders and tennis. Netball, gymnastics, athletics and swimming are particular strengths of the school, with girls regularly winning national and county championships. There's a raft of extracurricular activities, with more than 80 clubs (everything from chess to yoga to IT) each week. In year 2 girls go on their first residential visit while year 6 girls get a trip to France at the end of their time at the junior school.

All the girls belong to one of four houses. As they progress through the school they get the chance to sit on the school council and year 6 girls take roles as prefects and house captains. As in the senior school, pastoral care is the number one priority. A peer mediation scheme encourages pupils to use listening and negotiating skills to resolve 'any small difficulties' and teams of peer mediators take responsibility in ensuring that playtimes are happy and disagreements are defused before they can escalate. Girls wear a smart but practical uniform of tartan pinafores (skirts for year 5 and 6), pale blue shirts and navy blazers.

Pupils come from Guildford itself, as well as towns like Woking and Esher – mostly places within a 20-minute drive. A few travel in by train with older siblings but the majority are brought in by parents.

A top-notch, happy and caring school. Bright girls who are keen to learn and want to get involved in everything from the performing arts to sport will thrive here and go right through the senior school to boot.

Haberdashers' Aske's Prep and Pre-Prep

Linked with The Haberdashers' Aske's Boys' School

Butterfly Lane, Elstree, Hertfordshire WD6 3AF

Ages 5–11 **Pupils** 270 **C of E**

Fees: £15,339 – £20,346 pa

020 8266 1700
www.habsboys.org.uk

Executive Head: Since September 2018, Matteo Rossetti, an Oxford classics graduate and formerly head of prep at The Harrodian. Most recently, he has lived in Morocco with his wife, who was deputy ambassador there, and their two young children.

Entrance: Selective entry at 5+ and 7+. Pre-prep: first round of assessments in age bands; tasks aim to 'identify potential'. Those called back for second round have individual 45-minute assessments. Parents interviewed by head, though that's by no means a decision maker. Thirty-six places in total, with five or six chasing every place.

Prep: around 120 take reading, writing, maths and verbal reasoning tests, competing for 18 7+ places; some 48 invited back for further assessments and interview. No sibling policy as such but having a sibling in the boys' or girls' school, or being the son of an Old Haberdasher, may help in a tie break.

Exit: Automatic entry from pre-prep to prep. The majority of prep school students continue on to the main school – no need to take the 11+ any more. 'You could practically hear the collective sigh across north London when we announced it We wanted to make a commitment to children from 5-years-old to 18.'

Remarks: Entering the school through the elaborate gates off Butterfly Lane in leafy Hertfordshire and up the winding drive, you feel as if you're going on an exclusive spa break than arriving at a school campus.

The prep and senior school share 100 acres of parkland with the adjoining girls' school, separated by a fence lovingly nicknamed 'the passion gate,' although there are few links between the boys' and girls' schools. In the heart of the grounds (once the rival of Kew Gardens) stands Aldenham House, a grade 2 listed building dating from the 17th century and home to the senior school. But before all this, on your right, is the prep school. Originally a bland, purpose-built 1980s block, it has undergone a massive refurbishment so that all learning areas are bright, airy and well-equipped – classrooms adapted for advanced IT systems, CO2 detection, ventilation, state-of-the-art desks from Germany, plenty of natural light etc. The ceiling lights even have acoustics built into them 'so teachers don't have to bellow.' A dusty old prep school, this is not.

There are 12 classrooms with around 18 pupils in each class and three classes per year group. There is a specialist science lab, an art and design room, impressive new library and a large multi-functional hall. Expect pristine, shiny floors, immaculately presented pupils' work adorning the walls, displays of historical facts, stunning art work and stories written in handwriting of which a secondary school pupil would be proud.

Academia is by far the biggest priority at this school, with Sats results consistently outstanding. Slackers need not apply. Twice winner of the Sunday Times' Independent Preparatory School of the Year, and the only boys' school to have won at all. But parents reject the 'hothouse' reputation: 'Other schools let it be known that average will suffice and the children consequently plateau, which doesn't help anyone – just because Habs pushes them harder doesn't mean they don't have fun too,' said one parent. Specialist teachers for languages, music, art, science, drama and PE – for everything else, boys are taught by their class teachers until year 5, when all teaching is by subject specialists.

The boys are encouraged to think creatively. Stimulating lessons can involve making motorised cars in design technology, and flying hand-made helicopters from the hall balcony when learning about weight and force; younger boys design and produce their own version of Mr Men books with their own characters. Outside learning on the up. Homework levels are high.

Accommodates children with mild learning difficulties eg dyslexia or dyspraxia, and will give some one-to-one specialist help if necessary at no extra cost. 'We must assume that we're all on the SEN spectrum, so we focus on the individual more than the label' – although greater difficulties may entail a move elsewhere and there seems to be some stigma attached to SEN, with one boy visibly upset that his peers had discovered he was receiving learning support.

First rate art, with teaching combining strong basic skills with experimentation, breadth and understanding – all of which involves boys working with a vast range of materials, with some stunning results and much of it cross-curricular. For example, they'd just done a big project on India, which included making a huge tapestry. No getting away with sticking pasta on paper at this school. Music also a crowning glory of the school – everyone tries out an instrument in year 5, 'even if it's trumpet lessons that only last three weeks.' Seventy-five boys are taught by peripatetic teachers. Three orchestras and a chamber choir. Drama popular, with boys using the senior school's theatre – two big annual productions, plus smaller ones by individual year groups.

The prep shares an all-weather pitch, athletics track, extensive playing fields, new sports hall with covered swimming pool and tennis courts with the senior school, with rugby, football, athletics and cross-country the main sports for prep boys. Emphasis on sport for all – 'It's more about teaching sportsmanlike behaviour and letting the boys let off steam than we're in it to win,' insists school, although they don't do badly at fixtures, with a couple of strong years in rugby and athletics behind them when we visited, as well as a respectable cricket scores. But, said one year 6 boy, 'When oh when will we get our football goals in the playground? We've been asking for years.'

Clubs aplenty, with staff expected to run at least two each and all boys encouraged to attend at least two. Ranging from Japanese to scuba diving and badminton to mime, boys raved about the opportunities. 'When they put details of the mime club up, it was full within 20 seconds,' one said. Chess taken very seriously, with a specialist coach provided from pre-prep. The school has won the English primary schools chess title several times, and many boys have been selected for the England squad.

School not exactly known for encouraging individuality or anything remotely left of centre so we half expected a bunch of sullen-looking military-types (bearing in mind the school crest and motto 'serve and obey'), but we met spirited boys, all seemingly relaxed and happy and chattering away, although one pupil did mention that he would 'like less homework.' To call the boys competitive feels like an understatement – 'I'm the most competitive in the class,' one boy told us; 'No, I am,' insisted another, oblivious to the irony.

Pastoral care is the untold story here, claims school, and parents concur, describing the school as 'caring' and 'nurturing.' House system at the centre – each boy's house leader stays with them through the entire prep school. But it's strict too – 'the shame of having your name in the report book is usually enough to keep the boys in check' (there's also an excellence book).

Families come from a wide radius, reaching as far as Berkhamstead, St John's Wood, Welwyn Garden City and Enfield. The almost legendary coach system (mentioned in former pupil William Sutcliffe's book New Boy) will transport any child from the age of 7 from these far flung towns and is shared by both the boys' and girls' schools. The school has a large cultural mix, with some 20-30 per cent each of Jewish and Asian families, and students are actively encouraged to learn about other faiths.

'The distance to the pre-prep is not ideal, but we've come to see virtue in it,' said the school before we embarked on the six mile journey from the main Haberdashers' campus. 'It's a safe enclave and the boys feel special having their own patch.' The school, situated at the bottom of a residential street (a nightmare to find), looks like a scout hut from the outside, albeit made more upscale by the gravel driveway. However, we were immediately drawn to the large playground, with an adventure climbing area surrounded by beautiful woodland, as well as the colourful and bright classrooms within the prefab. There's also a multi-purpose hall and kitchen (boys get a daily hot meal).

The boys play weekly games at the prep school, and have sports events and cross-country there at least once a term. They also use the prep school hall for concerts and productions. The idea, explained one teacher, is to integrate the pre-prep students slowly into the prep. We found the pre-prep boys attentive, bright and hungry to learn, lapping up the kinaesthetic teaching style. As for the families, 'There are lots of 4x4s, but not a lot of Bentleys,' as one teacher put it. 'The pre-prep is lovely – they really are like a little family,' one mother said.

The Haberdashers' Aske's Boys' School

Linked with Haberdashers' Aske's Prep and Pre-Prep

119

Butterfly Lane, Elstree, Hertfordshire WD6 3AF

Ages 11–18 **Pupils** 1,144 **Sixth form** 310

Fees: £20,346 pa

020 8266 1700
www.habsboys.org.uk

Headmaster: Since September 2018, Gus Lock MA Oxon (late 30s), previously head of Warwick School. Educated here at Habs', he read ancient and modern history at Oxford. First teaching post was at The Manchester Grammar School, thence to Merchant Taylors' School in Northwood, where he became head of middle school and met and married Alison (a French and Italian teacher). Mr Lock then moved to Warwick School, where he served as deputy head before taking on the headship. Gus and Alison have three young children.

Academic matters: 'Exams aren't the most important part of education,' said no Habs boy, or parent of a Habs boy, ever. 'Exams are the number one priority for parents – they know that top grades will open more doors to their sons,' says the school, unapologetically. And there are certainly few that aren't flung wide on the basis of this top-of-the-league school's consistently high results – in 2018, 81 per cent of A levels A*/A, 96 per cent A*/B. GCSEs are seen merely as 'a hurdle to get over' (boys soar over the bar, with 93 per cent of GCSEs A*-A/9-7 in 2018). Quality not quantity, however, is the guiding principle – exam numbers are kept to a manageable nine or 10 at GCSE, three at A level. ('Unless you're taking further maths, they discourage you from doing four,' said one sixth former.)

The school is also traditional as far as the curriculum is concerned, undistracted by the IB, the Pre-U or the EPQ: 'We don't muck around. A levels serve boys very well.' That said, all boys do an independent study project in both year 9, then have the option to do another in year 12 ('We like our own versions because they are a free choice and less guided'). All subjects do well at GCSE, with maths exceptionally strong; geography, history and sciences also stand out. At A level (of which there are 25 subjects on offer), maths, economics, English and languages (against the national trend) are the top performers and most popular subjects.

Four languages offered from year 7 (Latin, German, Spanish and French). Italian, Russian and Arabic are added for GCSE, with Japanese and Mandarin available as tasters in the sixth form. Setting in maths and languages from year 9 and in a wider range of subjects in year 10 – a good thing, say parents: 'There are boys here who are just light years ahead.' Boys say there's no stigma about being in 'the bottom set' etc – 'this is the bottom set at Haberdashers', after all,' said one.

Year 7 can be tricky for those not already in training for the school's intensive regime and those from homework-free primary schools can sometimes feel daunted. They soon learn, however, to take it in their stride. And if they don't, there's help on offer from the learning support team to academic clinics. 'Nobody here could get away with saying, "I didn't do as well as I could because I couldn't get the help I needed,"' said one boy. SEN firmly at the mild end, also helped by the learning support team, while the gifted get extra work as and when they require it. One parent, with a child who had more than one need, said, 'The support in all areas could not have been better.'

Teachers described as 'exceptional' and 'inspiring.' 'Some are more old school than others, but they're all good,' said one boy. 'Teaching here is not about lecturing boys, who take notes – it's about going on a journey of exploration with them to tease out their academic excellence in whatever way it takes. It takes a special kind of teacher to let them go and see what wild and wacky ideas they come back with,' says school, although they have few problems recruiting. 'Whatever we advertise, we find.' Armoury of teaching weaponry includes all the latest technology, some traditional methods, but mostly debate and increasingly outdoor learning. Boys told us you can go at your own pace in lessons – 'but you must work to the best of your ability.' A level class sizes can be as few as three or four students – 'we are very lucky,' said one sixth former. No weaker departments, agreed all the boys we spoke to, 'and history and politics is among the best in the country, taught by some of the best minds around that could easily be at a top university but have chosen to stay here.'

Games, options, the arts: Extracurricular taken seriously, with a strong work-hard, play-hard ethos. 'The word on the street is that it's nose-to-the-grindstone as soon as boys get through the gates, but that couldn't be further from the truth,' says school. 'We are encouraged to do three lunchtime and two after-school clubs,' one boy told us – with no shortage of brain-stretching opportunities ranging from Sudoku to robotics. Plenty of chess champions and debating cup winners. 'Our boys can talk for England,' says school; we concur. Many of the clubs are student led. Community service is given a strong emphasis – 'We try to make them realise that being gifted brings the responsibility to put something back into society.' Good take-up for CCF.

Sport is played enthusiastically and competitively – excels at cricket, athletics and water polo (national champions). In winter, all boys play rugby and soccer; in spring, hockey and soccer; in summer, cricket and athletics. Individualists can enjoy orienteering, badminton, climbing, shooting and golf. New sports centre used by whole school.

And if you're absolutely not into any sport, which many boys aren't, then you can just opt for fitness for exercise and focus your efforts on music, drama or art instead. Over 600 learn a musical instrument, with four orchestras, three wind bands, three big bands and jazz ensembles, choral society, chamber choir and largest school guitar ensemble in the UK – and many boys play and learn outside school too. 'Music is absolutely my favourite department,' said one boy, with his sights firmly set on becoming a doctor. Art and DT are thriving departments – both busy and popular, 'a sanctuary for many people' – there's huge crossover between maths, physics and DT for those who want to become architects etc. Some adventurous art work, too, with a series of individually painted cow sculptures (each following a particular artist's style) dotted round the site.

Drama enjoyed both academically and as an extracurricular subject, with some impressive whole school, house and form performances (think Brecht, Arthur Miller and Shakespeare, rather than High School Musical). Excellent facilities include one of the country's few operational fly towers and a well-used drama studio. The school has a notable history of creative talent – recent alumnae include Matt Lucas, Sacha Baron Cohen, David Baddiel and Booker nominee, A D Miller.

Around 300 trips and tours a year ranging from cricket in Sri Lanka to model UN in Paris and from history of art in New York to geography in Iceland. Plus a popular annual ski trip.

Background and atmosphere: School's namesake, Robert Aske, was a wealthy merchant haberdasher who opened the school in 1690 for the benefit of less fortunate members of his profession. Founded in Hoxton, it moved to Hampstead in the early 20th century and then, in 1961, to its current spacious 100-acre site in the grounds of Aldenham House in Hertfordshire. The attractive 17th-century red-brick mansion, once the residence of banker and influential botanist Vicary Gibbs, remains the focal point of the school. As well as the undoubted delights of its rolling rural expanses (the house and grounds served as the backdrop for '60s television series, The Avengers), it is notably well-equipped, with a medley of well-planned and well-laid out buildings. But boys agree there are departments that still need renovating, notably English, 'where the rooms can get really stuffy.'

The newly-extended library is spacious, attractive and bright, with enthusiastic and knowledgeable staff, while the swish new sports centre would give a David Lloyd fitness club a run for its money. Complete with indoor swimming pool, squash courts, climbing wall and gymnasium, it's also got Joe's café which does a great toastie (outside sports facilities are impressive too – all the pitches, Astroturf and courts you could want for). School's secluded location gives the luxury feel of a country boarding school. It also keeps distractions at bay: with the exception of a few sixth form drivers, most boys arrive in the morning and stay firmly put until ferried home by parents or coaches at 4 or 5pm. Forest school facilities, including a woodland nature trail with 18 stations, where boys learn to gut fish, light camp fires, mountain biking etc. 'A lot of kids live an urban London life – it's the first time they have climbed a tree.'

Very strong house system, particularly in the lower school, where boys are taught by house. Diversity strong – the entire spectrum of belief is celebrated weekly with 12 individual assemblies covering everything from Hindu, Buddhist and Jain, to Jewish, CofE and secular. Most are led by the boys themselves and all pupils, whatever their persuasion, are welcome to attend whichever they choose. 'The school is very good on being multicultural, with strong friendships across the board and no ethnicity or religion based cliques,' one parent told us. Food ranging from formal sit-down to grab-and-go is available from a number of outlets – but while it caters for all tastes and religions, some boys said the veggie options can be dull ('You wind up having pasta every day').

Atmosphere purposeful and stimulating, with boys so absorbed in their lessons that many didn't notice us come into the classrooms – but they can let off steam too, with a reassuring amount of hullabaloo at break times. And while boys are supportive of one another, they're fiercely competitive too. 'Everything at Habs is a competition,' one parent said. 'For some boys, this is exactly what they want and they thrive on it. For others, it can seem overwhelming at times.' Boys and parents told us they'd like to see more collaboration with the girls' school – at the moment, it's mainly for music, drama and the coach to and from home.

Pastoral care, well-being and discipline: A ferocious work ethic is essential to survive happily at this school and the push from parents, particularly of the tiger variety, tends to be as strong as that from teachers – 'We have no arguments about homework here'. Boys don't generally wilt under the pressure, but for those who do struggle, pastoral care kicks in at an early stage from house tutors and form tutors – and there are also counsellors and a chaplain. 'We only lose one or two every other year and that's after a lot of intervention.' PSHE and assemblies cover mental health issues such as self-harm and eating disorders. However, one parent felt there 'is a disconnect between the extraordinary level of care and attention that comes from the leadership team and the individual members of staff, who you feel are judged on their own results and take no notice whatsoever if a 13-year-old is completely overwhelmed.' Another said, 'If you have a child who lacks confidence and is prone to worrying that everyone else is better than them, for God's sake send them somewhere else.'

These are bright, well-behaved, motivated boys – 'mucking around just isn't part of the culture.' Discipline is firm, however, with detention for minor misdemeanours like forgetting your swimming costume and homework not done to a satisfactory standard. 'Boys like to have boundaries.' London's usual temptations tend to remain safely outside the gates – 'If they're brought in, there's zero tolerance. The boys know what's expected'. No permanent exclusions for several years, with less than a handful of temporary one for things like insolence, cyberbullying and fisticuffs. 'Better that they make mistakes here than working for Lloyds bank, though.' Big on anti-bullying strategies – 'they talk about it on day one in year 7, then every term after that,' one boy told us.

Pupils and parents: Most families are from the aspiring professional classes, many of them dual-income, reflective of the north London/Hertfordshire borders in which the school sits. (An extensive network of coaches with 110 stops imports boys from a 30 mile radius, from St John's Wood to Luton, Harpenden to Ruislip.) The school has traditionally had a significant Jewish core, who still represent about 30 per cent – now Asian families make up a similar proportion of the intake. Whatever their ethnic origins, these are families where the mantra 'education, education, education' is not simply spin. Boys are positive and polite, self-assured without being self-regarding. The long list of illustrious old boys includes Simon Schama, Sir Nicholas Serota, Sir Martin Sorrell, Damon Hill and Brian Sewell. Strong alumni network good for work placements and careers advice for current boys and lifelong friendships for ex-Habs' boys. 'It's unusual for those from a boys' day school to remain so closely in touch – it's not as if they shared dorms.' Communications with school better than they used to be, say parents, with a regularly updated online newsletter having had 200,000 hits since it was launched three years ago.

Entrance: Main intake is at 11 from a wide range of prep and state schools. School sets its own exams in English, maths and reasoning. About 600 apply for 100 places (in addition to those coming up from the prep school); 300 recalled for interview, which takes place in groups and individually. 'We don't mind crooked profiles. If someone is outstanding at maths, we can cope with the fact that they're less good at English.' That said, it's a school where a high percentage of successful candidates will already be at, or near, the top of their class. At 13 plus, 70-80 apply for 20 further places, with exams in English, maths, science, French, humanities and an optional Latin paper. At 16 maybe a handful of places to cover gaps left by leavers, but the school does not actively seek newcomers into the sixth form. Entry by interview, a general essay and – for those wishing to study maths – a maths paper; minimum of six 7s or above required at GCSE.

Exit: A handful leaves at year 11. After sixth form, all to university – 28 to Oxbridge in 2018; Bristol the most popular destination then LSE and Imperial. Increasing numbers to Ivy League universities – 'still less than a handful a year, but growing'. Large numbers into the professions – medics, lawyers, vets and dentists. 'Parents want practical careers for their boys,' said one father.

Money matters: Fees not outrageous, but extras are added regularly to the bill. Some 200 boys are on scholarships of between 10-30 per cent of fees. Bursary help also available, ranging from five to 100 per cent. 'We are not the last bastion of the mega-rich by any means, but I'm also aware you have to be pretty affluent to live in north London.'

Remarks: A school that identifies talent and builds on it, Habs is a passport into a prosperous career, provided your son likes swimming in this type of pond – that is, big, busy and with a relentless pace. Indeed, we lost count of the number of parents who, when asked what they loved about the school, began with the phrase, 'For the right child...' by which it transpired they mean a bright-eyed boy who thrives on filling his time, toeing the line, being inquisitive and constantly pushing himself. For these boys, Habs is an outstanding offering.

Haberdashers' Aske's Junior School for Girls

H

Linked with Haberdashers' Aske's School for Girls

Aldenham Road, Elstree, Hertfordshire WD6 3BT

Ages 4–11 Pupils 319

Fees: £16,104 – £16,980 pa

020 8266 2400
www.habsgirls.org.uk

Executive head of junior school: Since 2015, Robert James-Robbins, who is also senior deputy head of the whole school. He was previously interim head of the junior school for 18 months, and has also worked at JAGS, as English teacher and senior teacher. He has an English degree from King's College London and a PGCE from the Institute of Education.

Entrance: Two reception classes. Selection is a careful process and girls have to demonstrate their 'Habs-ability' to win one of the most coveted school places in the area, if not the country. Girls are observed and chatted to within small groups with similar birth dates. Of some 250 who apply for around 40 places, the parents of about 80 will be invited to meet senior staff to talk about their daughters and why they might suit the school.

School is looking primarily for 'personality, teachability and sociability,' as well as 'some evidence that the girl is more advanced than usual' and 'chatting to parents is useful.' To weed out the pushy, we wonder? No comment.

All 7+ applicants come to a group activity session in December, with a select number invited back to sit the entrance assessment in January (around 100 girls compete for up to 10 places, taking papers in maths and English) and their current schools asked for references. Some return, with their parents, for a meeting with the executive head and deputy head of the junior school.

Exit: Vast majority of pupils go to the senior school with just a handful each year moving to pastures new, mainly for financial reasons (local grammars beckoning) or to boarding school, with girls very occasionally advised in year 5 that they may not flourish in the fast-paced environment that is the senior school. Year 6 girls are no longer asked to sit the 11+ senior school entrance exam.

Remarks: A wonderfully modern, spacious building attached by a corridor to its equally stunning big sister school. No sense of it being a waiting room for the real thing – this school is special in its own right. Easily navigable even for its youngest pupils, with large classrooms displaying uniformly excellent work. Super art room displaying some outstanding work, plus own gym, music room, a cheerful library which can be used by girls at break from year 3 up and state of the art ICT suite. Fabulous adventure playground, used by year groups on rotation.

Readers sceptical that such an academically successful school can also be fun should think again. Habs girls are down to earth, noisy and animated and clearly love every minute of the school day. Although many parents naturally reassess whether to move on to the senior school at 11+ or look elsewhere, they uniformly give a clear message that their daughters would never speak to them again if they were moved. Rather than pushing girls, school aims to 'nurture a love of learning' and focuses on 'resilience, self-esteem and risk-taking' as keys to success, noting that 'very able children put enough pressure on themselves.' Girls say school is 'five out of 10 for strictness'. At 25, classes are quite large compared to other preps but parents say it's not a problem as school attracts girls who want to learn. Girls add: 'We know that if we're sensible, everyone has a nice time.' Enough said.

Families generally from surrounding area as there's no school transport until year 3, with the odd girl travelling from as far afield as St Albans. Demographic reflects diverse local area with large Jewish and Asian contingents, although 'cliques don't divide on cultural grounds,' according to the head. Plenty of wealth, but also a strong contingent of parents making sacrifices to offer their girls this top opportunity, and parents say school is sensitive to families' differing situations.

French and Spanish are introduced in years 1 and 2, French and German taught formally from year 3. Specialist music and PE teachers from reception and for science from year 3, when girls start to move around the school for different subjects. Setting in maths from year 4. Individual music lessons on offer from year 3 with around 40 per cent taking up an instrument. School 'wants music and sport to be for everybody,' and girls agree that they are. A and B teams compete in all the main sports (including football) against other schools, but less starry enthusiasts can follow their sporting passions at a recreational level if they don't make the team.

Part time SENCo works with girls needing extra help due to mild dyslexia or dyscalculia. There is routine screening for this.

Good pastoral approach, with school 'keen to hear children's voices' – one girl per class elected by classmates as representative on student forum. Bullying has to be dealt with on 'a very occasional basis,' and school places a particular emphasis on educating girls in how to avoid cyber issues. All year 6 girls are prefects, with two elected captains for each of four teams (houses) which compete – although not fiercely, according to parents – throughout the year for team points, with the prize of a mufti day in the summer term.

Overall, a best in class girls' prep and first step on the ladder to reaping all that the Habs' brand has to offer. With this start, these girls are undoubtedly on course to be the movers and shakers of tomorrow.

Haberdashers' Aske's School for Girls

Linked with Haberdashers' Aske's Junior School for Girls

Aldenham Road, Elstree, Hertfordshire WD6 3BT

Ages 11–18 **Pupils** 859 **Sixth form** 222

Fees: £18,393 pa

020 8266 2300
www.habsgirls.org.uk

Headmistress: Since 2011, Biddie O'Connor MA (50s). Educated at St Helena School, Chesterfield followed by St Hugh's College, Oxford (classics) and Sidney Sussex Cambridge (PGCE). A doyenne of girls' education, she cut her teeth teaching classics at Francis Holland. Joined Haberdashers' Aske's (Girls) as head of classics and sixth form before becoming deputy head, then head at Loughborough High School, where she spent nine years before, as one parent put it, 'coming home'.

Inheriting a flourishing, massively oversubscribed school when she joined Habs' as head, she was 'able to take time to assess the changes needed,' before putting in place a 15 to 20 year plan to improve the site. She recognises that these days her main competitors are the state grammars and is focused on outperforming them not just in the classroom but by 'building resilience,' and turning out 'happy, adaptable girls,' ready to take their careers and lives 'global'. Parents describe her as 'thoroughly sensible,' saying she 'works hard to tone down the panic' that can arise (mainly amongst parents) in highly academic environments.

Retiring in July 2019. Her successor will be Rose Hardy, currently head of St Margaret's Bushey. Read history at Oxford, then studied for a PGCE at London University and more recently completed an MEd in educational leadership. Spent 10 years at St Albans School, latterly as second master (sic).

Academic matters: School continuously shows its gleaming metal, flying amongst the top schools in the UK in all league tables with year after year of outstanding results. In 2018, 94 per cent of A levels were graded A*-B with 71 per cent A*/A. GCSEs equally impressive with 94 per cent A*-A/9-7. Five forms of 25 girls per year group with class sizes shrinking to 15 for GCSE and sometimes just five or six for A level. Ten GCSEs taken as standard with four full A levels commonplace.

Balanced curriculum with no particular bias – in popularity or results – although strong take-up of sciences at A level as well as English, history, maths and economics. Girls report 'quite a bit' of homework, with about an hour and a half a night by year 10, but say the deadlines are long and some subjects are heavier than others. They claim that school discourages homework on weekends and is lenient if pupils are feeling the pressure. School keen to maintain balance between strong academics and nurturing a love of learning and doesn't constantly test girls.

Recent appointment of new ICT co-ordinator aims to push school towards the 'progressive' bracket by moving towards technology becoming part of day-to-day lessons rather than a specialised subject.

All girls assessed for SEN on entry to senior school, with mild dyslexia the most common issue but school also experienced in dealing with profound visual and hearing problems. Two SENCos cater for individuals' specific needs with customised learning plans, and 'lost sheep,' albeit a rarity here, are dealt with empathetically. Exceptionally gifted girls are nurtured in a 'very low key' manner, according to head, monitored 'by sleight of hand' through cosy chats with heads of department, and scholars are, in the main, anonymous. Roundedness is the name of the game with school ensuring that even top brainboxes participate in a broad spectrum of extracurricular activities.

Games, options, the arts: High octane sports programme 'to cater for all tastes and abilities' according to girls and parents, with five star facilities across the board. Seven new tennis courts and one of the best swimming pools; train as a lifeguard or join the synchronised swimming squad. Super fitness suite, great sports hall and separate gym but no dance studio. Sporting prowess in abundance – lacrosse is the main winter sport, accompanied by all the usual suspects – but it's not the school's sole raison d'être and girls preferring more artsy or academic pastimes are equally well catered for: 'we want sport to be for everybody, not just the elite,' says head.

'Outstanding' music, perceived across the board to be 'just as cool as sport' with the vast majority of girls learning at least one instrument, and reaching grade 8 is a normal event. Choirs, elite as well as non-selective, cater for all abilities and there are opportunities aplenty to perform in bands, ensembles and orchestras covering all tastes and abilities. The 50-strong symphony orchestra is the cherry on top, with 'phenomenal' performances not just at school but on international tours and at prestigious venues such as the Barbican, often in conjunction with the next door boys' school.

Art, led by a 'charming' departmental head, according to parents, is equally impressive, with the whole school festooned with work of an exceptionally high standard and some outstanding three dimensional projects displayed in a wonderful atrium. Although eyes are firmly on the academic prize, a good number take art at both GCSE and A level. DT also alive and kicking and a surprisingly popular exam choice, even amongst the most academic girls. A full programme of drama completes the set with a major play each term (sometimes with the boys' school) and opportunities for everyone to get involved, whether on stage or behind the scenes. Proof in the pudding that roundedness is a genuine ethos at Habs'.

Background and atmosphere: Established following the bequest of £20,000 in 1698 by Robert Aske, Master of the Worshipful Company of Haberdashers, to found a school and almshouses in east London. Moved to its current site in the early 70s to join the boys who had taken over Lord Aldenham's – rather grander – estate a few years earlier. The happy co-existence of two single sex (each with their particular needs) schools provides the best of both worlds for many, although parents uniformly agree that the cultures of the two schools are totally different. Pupils love the fact that they can collaborate and socialise together (including informally at lunchtimes) but learn totally separately.

Set amongst vast grounds just minutes from the roar of the M1, the Habs' campuses offer the unique balance of a leafy country feel for the London set and something a bit edgier for those hailing from the comfy home counties. A reasonably uninspiring exterior compared to the grandeur of the neighbouring boys' school, but functionality is top notch and the interior of the school feels light, clean and wonderfully spacious.

The atmosphere is nicely cool for such an academic powerhouse. Girls move cheerfully and noisily from class to class with not a bluestocking among them. In many ways the feel of the school – first class facilities aside – is that of a top notch grammar rather than an elitist girls' school, testament to the down to earth approach of the head and her staff. Year 13 girls said that with all the new developments planned for the coming years, they wished they could have their time all over again.

Pastoral care, well-being and discipline: Staff and parents agree that school is 'happy and supportive' and girls concur, describing the cohort as 'really friendly' and appreciating the fact that they 'can always talk to girls in other years'. Girls in year 8 are 'amigas' to year 7 newbies; relationship starts with a personal letter offering helpful tips on settling in. Girls claim that 'the whole atmosphere is relaxed' and staff say they aim to 'inspire not push'.

Rare incidents of bullying taken seriously with form prefects the first port of call in helping to deal with friendship issues, but teachers fast to mediate ('always with a box of tissues,' said one) should the need arise. Older girls help educate their younger peers on bullying, with a recent year 9 drama production focusing on the issue. Parents happy with pastoral care, which includes a counsellor available on appointment, with girls saying 'there's always someone for you to talk to'. Lots of pupil-led charity initiatives with girls showing their wit and putting their creativity to the test to put on shows for the school and, recently, tongue in cheek 'Made in Elstree' T shirts for sale.

Pupils and parents: The vast coach network ferrying girls in from far and wide makes for a truly diverse and varied cohort with pupils travelling to school from across north/north-west London and Hertfordshire. School caters for the spiritual needs of all religions with weekly Jewish, Hindu/Jain/Sikh, Muslim, Humanist and Christian assemblies; girls allowed to choose which to attend regardless of their own faith. No place for the cocksure or work-shy – parents say they are 'paying for the peer group' – it's cool to study and hit top grades and the girls drive each other on to achieve great things. Girls need to be 'energetic not timorous,' according to head, to cope with the long school day followed by 'loads of activities'. Old girls include BBC's Charlotte Green, Vanessa Feltz and fashion designer L K Bennett.

Entrance: Ferociously competitive – over 600 hopefuls. Fifty move up from junior school; applications for the remaining year 7 places from approximately 50 per cent state primaries and 50 per cent prep schools, with feeders including Manor Lodge, Radlett Prep, Orley Farm and Beechwood Park. A new format sees girls tested in English (including reading for understanding), maths and verbal reasoning. Applicants spend a whole day in school and are looked after by older pupils.

They are looking for about 80 girls who can 'think on their feet'. All prospective parents meet the head and although the school 'likes' to take siblings, they 'won't break the rules' if they think a girl won't fit. Girls coming in ones from state primaries benefit from an extra induction day where they can get to know others in the same boat.

Between 10 and 20 join in year 12 from a range of state and independent schools, largely to benefit from the support around higher education applications. School equally scrupulous in selection at this stage: 'girls are jumping on board a moving bus,' says head. About three applicants for each sixth form place; head says there's no quota but that school is 'looking for a good social fit'.

Exit: Very few leavers after GCSEs (some 10-15 per cent) – Habs' girls know when they are onto a good thing. Dedicated head of careers and higher education oversees every university application, with the department also boasting an Oxbridge tutor, interview tuition ('although we don't want universities to criticise us for over-preparing candidates') and guidance in international applications. The process starts in year 11 when girls are exposed to the choices on offer to them with a programme of organised careers events (some organised by old girls) and university visits. School supports and encourages 'meaningful gap years' and offers hands-on guidance with girls' UCAS applications when they return.

About a quarter to Oxbridge (12 in 2018) with the remainder mostly to top universities. Bristol, LSE, Birmingham, Warwick, Nottingham, Edinburgh and Edinburgh popular destinations. Medicine currently most popular subject (18 medics/dentists/vets in 2018) followed by economics, history and English. One off to Dartmouth in 2018. Usually one or two to drama or art colleges.

Money matters: Up to £6,000 a year means-tested financial assistance for a limited number of pupils, including full bursaries. Academic and music scholarships for up to half fees.

Remarks: Undoubtedly best in class girls' education. Turning out super accomplished, confident and thoroughly likeable young women with their feet on the ground and their eyes on the prize; the brand continues to go from strength to strength. School recognises that its charges' careers and lives are going to be global, and directs them accordingly towards excellence across the board – not just in academia. Parents concur that 'what makes Habs' is the range of opportunities on offer'.

H

Haileybury

Hertford, Hertfordshire SG13 7NU

Ages 11–18 **Pupils** 833 **Sixth form** 317 **Boarders** 540 full (from year 9) C of E

Fees: Day £17,031 – £25,620; Boarding £21,837 – £34,422 pa

01992 706353
www.haileybury.com

Master: Since September 2017, Martin Collier MA, previously head of St John's School Leatherhead. He read modern history at St John's College Oxford, followed by PGCE from London University. His first 10 years of teaching were in the maintained sector, at the 'fantastic' Thomas Tallis in south London and the 'tough' Weavers School in Wellingborough. He then moved into the independent sector and Oundle School, where he worked through roles of head of history, director of studies and second master. He also has many years' experience as an examiner with different boards, has been involved with the Qualifications and Curriculum Development Agency and has appeared as an examinations expert before the House of Commons select committee on education. He is also chair of the Headmasters' and Headmistresses' Conference (HMC) academic policy group.

No extrovert, but quietly impressive and we loved his sing-song intonation and commanding hand gestures that have an almost sermon like effect. Not the warm and cuddly type, but genial and passionate about getting the best for every pupil. Big on vision (in his wider roles, discussions stretch as far as 'curriculum planning for 2035') but also detail ('schools are all about detail,' he says). 'Some say he's scary, but he's not once you get to know him,' insist pupils, who say they see him regularly around school (no wonder, when he spends three days a week showing prospective parents round) and value 'the way he asks for feedback and acts on it.' Has made 'plentiful changes' including around timetabling, recruitment of new staff, tightening up lesson planning and use of reflection within lessons; parents see it as 'upping the ante academically' and it's gone down a treat. 'I think he will do tremendous things,' mused one; clearly the general consensus.

Married with three older children, he lives (as all masters have since time immemorial) onsite but is the first not to use its tucked-away sitting room as his main office, which has now been moved centre stage to the picturesque quadrangle where 'I see everything, and where pupils can see me.' It is, he says, the 'best view in the school.' We agree.

Academic matters: A famous name in public school education, Haileybury has become equally renowned for its enthusiastic participation in the IB, which was launched in 1998 'to provide a broader curriculum' and continues to flourish here despite floundering elsewhere. About 110 sixth formers (over a third) follow the diploma programme, with about 40 arriving each year specifically to do it. 'The IB is engrained into our culture and we embrace it philosophically, including the individual thinking, lateral thinking and pupil driven learning,' says head. A levels, however, are still very much on offer and the school does very well in both sets of exams, with 36 average IB points and 36 per cent A*/A in 2018. English, history and drama notably strong; ditto for maths ('if you can do maths, everything else follows,' believes head). Highly-qualified staff (including a hefty sprinkling of doctorates) generally teach across both systems. 'The teachers are amazing – they go above and beyond,' said one pupil.

Lower down, IGCSEs in just about everything, with 68 per cent A*-A/9-7s in 2018. Here, all do a compulsory core of maths, English language and science. From year 7, pupils pick two languages from German, French and Spanish and one from Latin or classical Greek – compulsory until the end of year 8, when pupils are 'strongly encouraged' to continue at least one. German and Italian also taught to the native speakers taking the IB. Setting in maths and languages from year 7, science and English from year 9.

All pupils are screened on entry 'to understand how they are as a learner' and as such, learning support is not an add-on but an integral part of education, although typically around 50-80 have a diagnosed SEN (mild to moderate) and get more help than others; a small number, too, have extra help with English as a second language. School has one of the most sophisticated tracking systems we've seen – 'we get to know the pupil first, then the data helps us understand how to tailor their learning.'

Overall high expectations, with sane expectations. 'It's not uncool to be clever or try your best but it's very unpressurised,' said a parent. 'My son got amazing GCSE results, much better than we expected, but without any stress and hassle,' said another. Parents appreciate the teaching recruits – 'the majority were good before, but certain departments were stronger than others, whereas now it's good across the board,' said one.

Games, options, the arts: Co-curricular activities are very much part of Haileybury's raison d'etre and for many families it's why they choose the school. 'Both my children have learned to become their true selves and that's a direct result of the school stretching them in all directions. This, for me, is the biggest stand out point,' one parent told us. School says it helps that 95 per cent of staff live on site – 'they're committed and involved at every level.'

The school has an outstanding reputation for sport, which is compulsory for all throughout, with games afternoons twice a week and matches on Saturday. Plenty of teams too, often from A-D, so everyone gets a chance to show their mettle. And those who aren't fans of the playing field can do 'something less taxing,' with options including aerobics, badminton, trampolining, rowing, rackets, golf and sailing, among others – although pupils told us these never get taken 'anywhere near as seriously as the core sports.' Though boys triumph in hockey and football (where the school plays in the Boodles Cup) and girls in tennis, hockey, netball and lacrosse (competing at county and national level), rugby and cricket remain the 'communal sports' and it's not unusual for the whole school to turn out to cheer on matches played on the front field. Some niggles from parents about girls' sports playing second fiddle, but pupils we spoke to were having none of it ('lacrosse is massive,' laughed one). Facilities out of this world, with a bright, modern pool, two Astroturf pitches and a professionally operated tennis club in the grounds (but another parent niggle here – 'lower school aren't allowed to use it, which is a bugbear,' said one). The rackets court is also considered one of the finest in the world and plays host to the world rackets championship. High Performance Programme (including training and lectures) aims to help talented sportspeople raise their game. Proper physio support and hi-tech fitness monitoring equipment is business as usual here.

Music out-of-this-world. The school has a 30-year tradition of exceptional choral singing and won the BBC Songs of Praise School Choir of the Year some years back (it has reached the semifinal twice since then too). Practically every parent we spoke to mentioned the head of music by name, describing him as 'charismatic' and 'phenomenal.' 'He's so inclusive too, it's not just about favouring the best,' said one. Chamber choir of about 30, plus larger chapel choir of about 90. Wide range of other musical opportunities, from jazz bands to concerts and musical theatre. Twenty peripatetic music staff, with pupils studying everything from harp to bassoon and from organ to jazz piano.

As with music, art has its own purpose-built, spacious and light-filled building – open seven days a week and in the evenings, regardless of whether you're doing a GCSE or A level. Offers 2D and 3D, print, ceramics, photography and textiles, with exams tailored to individual interests. Stunning works on display. Drama renowned for bringing in a whole host of pupils out of their shell who may never have acted before. It's not the same children on the stage every year, confirm parents, and again it's not just about those doing a GCSE or A level (although both are available). Some pupils said they'd like 'a bigger and better theatre.' Dance lessons on offer for about 100 keen participants in jazz, ballet, street and tap, plus an annual dance show. Trips galore, as you'd expect, as well as more modest outings to battlefields and cultural events.

Community service is huge – everything from digging gardens for the elderly to helping in local primary schools. School is particularly proud of being the single sponsor of a local academy which, says head, 'is improving significantly as a result – it's one of the most important things we do.' Wednesday afternoons devoted to D of E, CCF and adventure training for years 9 to 11, broadening out in the sixth form to take in activities like photography and web design. 'I'm not convinced it's the best thing in sixth form, though – we barely have enough time to study as it is,' one pupil told us; some pupils down the school also mentioned the need for 'more free time' with one girl looking completely dazed when listing her activities.

Boarding: From year 9, about 70 per cent of pupils board, with a sizeable chunk of weekly boarders who leave late on Saturday and return on Sunday evening or Monday morning (except for five or six weekends annually, when all remain). Opportunities too for flexi boarding in years 7 and 8 and taster boarding (three days a week) in year 9. Unusually, a boarding ethos for all, with an opportunity for day pupils to stay until 9.30pm (though most leave at 6.30pm) and some have their own beds; fewer, though, with the recent spike in boarders – 50 more in the year we visited, bucking the national trend. School attributes it to their location and modern family friendly approach and the boarders lap it up – 'we're like brothers and sisters.'

Seven boys' houses, five girls'. Four more recently built, with light, bright rooms, the rest older but updated. 'The house personality literally becomes the housemaster or mistress's personality and I love that,' said one parent. A couple of eight to 10 bed dorms in younger years; for the rest (and all from year 11), single or shared rooms – some with military-precision neatness, others in the kind of disarray you'd see in normal homes. Active inter-house social life and plenty of weekend activities for full-time boarders, with Saturday film nights and Sunday trips. Plus 'a lot of people have flats in London' or visit local pupils (with beneficent parents).

Background and atmosphere: The school was designed in 1806 for the East India Company by William Wilkins (also responsible for the National Gallery and Downing College, Cambridge) as a training college for civil servants bound for India. In 1862, after the closure of the college, it was taken over by Haileybury, to be transformed into a public school for families in the professions and services, amalgamating, in 1942, with the Imperial Service College. The first girls were admitted in 1973. Today the school continues to occupy an impressive slice (550 acres) of rural Hertfordshire, complete with magnificent neo-classical buildings constructed round a traditional quadrangle. Later additions include modern, purpose-built buildings which sit surprisingly well amongst the more established architecture, with favourites including the DT centre (easily the best we've seen) and regularly revamped science block (with wildlife documentary showing in lobby). Interestingly it was the domed chapel (more like a full-on church) that came out as the best-loved space in a recent pupil survey. All must attend services there four times a week. Beautiful, well-stocked library. 'If they don't have a book, they will order it for you.'

Not a grand school in atmosphere. Manners are formal (new pupils jump to attention, teachers are addressed as Sir) but not stiff. And despite the pupils' full timetables it's surprisingly calm, not a bit frenetic. 'You see these happy, helpful children wandering around and you realise what good individuals they're producing – what more can you want for your kids?' said one parent. International vibe is celebrated, with around 20 per cent from abroad.

Food comes highly commended; three compulsory self-service meals a day in the mammoth oak-panelled dining room, though parents and pupils say the favourites can run out fast.

Long tradition of charity work. The Haileybury Youth Trust, first set up in the East End in 1890 by old boy Clement Attlee, has been working with impoverished Ugandans since 2006. It receives grants from both UN and EU and has even patented a brick now used for building schools, kitchens and water towers.

Two further Haileybury branches operate in Kazakhstan, the first British public schools to be opened in Central Asia, with plans for more international schools. These help underwrite bursaries for UK-based students.

Pastoral care, well-being and discipline: The pastoral ethos is central to everything – 96 per cent of pupils said they have an adult to talk to at school in a recent survey. The chaplain (known as 'the reverend') is seen as a particularly key pastoral figure – 'everyone trusts him,' said one pupil. Lines of communication with parents praised, as is the school's frequent tweeting – 'it means I can always see what my son is up to pretty much all the time,' said one.

Parents have mixed views on the transition from lower to upper school – everything from 'my children were the only ones from the country we came from and they felt so included so quickly, there seem to be no cliques at all' to 'my son had a tough time at first and didn't easily settle but they didn't get to know how to handle it. The housemaster seemed out of his depth.' Parents say the school essentially operates as two schools, a more-or-less self-contained lower school, running as a day prep from 11 to 13; and an upper school, from 13 to 18, which is very much a boarding school, with a full day of lessons and sport on Saturday; older pupils also told us they have 'very little to do with the lower school.' But school insists there's more integration these days, drawing the lower school into the upper 'as we didn't want the lower school to be a holding pen.'

Discipline standards are tighter under current head, whom parents describe as 'no nonsense' but 'not draconian'. Sanctions run the usual gamut from detention to permanent exclusion, of which there have been a handful in recent years, plus around 10 temporary exclusions ('typically a day or two to make a point,' says head). Zero tolerance to drugs, but not enough of a problem (pupils concur) to do random testing (although they reserve the right). Bullying policy clear and pupils adamant strong community spirit prevents it. Strong prefect system.

Pupils and parents: Mainly from the nearest home counties – Hertfordshire, Essex, Buckinghamshire, Cambridgeshire – and it's easily commutable from London too. In general parents are 'City folk, business people, successful professionals' and as most live reasonably nearby, more involved than usual at boarding schools. Large numbers from Europe for the sixth form, particularly Germans and Italians. Pupils seem happy, confident, friendly and balanced.

Entrance: More academically able applicants than in the past, though school won't be pinned down to saying it's more academically selective. Cohort of 65 in year 7, a further 70 in year 9. Unusually, also a healthy intake (20) in year 10. Typically, 70 new pupils enter the sixth form, including about 40 from overseas. At this juncture the school is heavily oversubscribed, with about three applicants for every place. Entrance tests at all levels in maths, English, verbal and non-verbal reasoning. Year 9 entry pre-tested by negotiation with the prep school 12 or 24 months in advance and entrance exam used for setting. 'We are looking for somebody who wants to do their best, is B+ to A* academically and will throw themselves into the co-curricular.' Wide range of feeders including Heath Mount, Duncombe, Lochinver House, Beechwood Park, Davenies, St Josephs in the Park, St Hildas & St Faiths.

Exit: About 15-20 leave after GCSEs, often for local day schools. Post A levels and IB, it's mainly to Russell Group universities (most popular choices include UCL, Warwick, Durham, Nottingham, Leeds, Bristol and King's College London). Five to Oxbridge in 2018 and three medics. Wide range of subjects, the sciences and maths being most popular. Good specialist advisers, but some parents would like more support for North American and European universities, which pupils are increasing choosing ('everything is geared to Oxbridge applications and medics,' said one); head says he's addressing this. Three or four to art college.

Money matters: Academic, music, sport, art, and all-rounder scholarships form a complicated system, in addition to a range of (generous) means-tested bursaries.

Remarks: A vibrant and busy school set in exquisite surroundings, with a long established, successful IB diploma programme and an exceptional co-curricular offering. Great fun for those who want to be involved in everything it has to offer, although you might want to look elsewhere if you have a child who burns out easily.

Hall Grove School

London Road, Bagshot, Surrey GU19 5HZ

Ages 3–13 **Pupils** 442 **Boarders** 2 flexi (from year 7)

Fees: £10,800 – £14,700 pa; Boarding + £3,975 pa

01276 473059
www./hallgrove.co.uk/

Headmaster: Since 1981, Alastair Graham (early 60s), son of the founder, who took over soon after his father died. He started his own education with the shortest of school runs (just down the stairs), continuing at Bradfield (the Greek theatre there may explain his enthusiasm for drama and for the classics) and then to Reading University. After obtaining a degree in estate management he set off for the great outdoors, an experience that has clearly influenced his approach to developing the Hall Grove ethos.

More country squire with Tattersall shirt and cords than gowned academic, pastoral care was always top of his agenda and he worked as a shepherd in both Scotland and New Zealand before exchanging his flock of sheep for a classroom of children. The external difference is that he swapped collies for labradors, the internal one that he sees himself more pater familias than farmer.

He says that he felt like a 'prodigal son' returning from the other side of the world to take over the school after his father's unexpected death, but now feels 'blessed that he was given such an opportunity' to develop Hall Grove, overseeing on his watch a fairly stratospheric rise in pupils from 130 to nearly 450. Although this number would have astonished his parents facing their original class of six, they would surely have felt that his decision to move out of the fields and into the schoolroom was a sound one. Whilst keen to say that he is 'not a one man band', he tries not to have too many administrative staff: 'we are not a bureaucracy'. With no governors, the school is still very much his baby and he sees it as an extended family for which he is responsible, although one parent said he was finding this more difficult now that the school has expanded.

Passionately keen on 'taking learning outdoors,' he hosts a conference on bolstering happiness and academic learning with a greater knowledge of the natural world. This concept is explored in theory and practice throughout the school and enforces his individual approach to the prep school experience. His love of the wild has even led him to become a Conservative candidate in the Highlands, where Tory voters tend to be badly outnumbered by sheep. Married to Catriona with four children.

Entrance: The Barn (early years), offers places after seeing parents and discussing the child's current development. There is a main intake at 3+, although this is a non-selective school at this stage and also embraces a sibling policy. The children from pre-school get first crack and now make up over 50 per cent of the reception class, which, according to Catriona, leads to the newbies settling down very quickly. In year 3, the expansion to three forms allows room for an additional 20 children, who take tests in maths and English at the school. At the beginning of year 7 the upper school replaces any leavers (mainly girls going to a school where the intake is at 11+). At this stage, potential pupils spend a day at the school and are assessed to help confirm that they will fit in with their peer group.

Exit: Girls tend to leave mainly at 11 and boys mainly at 13, though some girls do stay on, usually heading to co-ed senior schools. Wellington and Hampton appear the first choice for more academic pupils, probably partly on proximity grounds, but children also go to a wide range of both private and state schools, often fairly local.

In terms of destinations, then, Wellington and Bradfield are tops, St George's Weybridge, Charterhouse and Hampton close behind.

The head or the head of the upper school starts a dialogue with parents about senior schools in year 5 or 6, but encourages parents not to close doors by making a final decision too early. They have an excellent record of matching children to schools and can only remember 'one or two in the last 13 years' who failed to get into their first choice. The children in year 8 were confident that they had been prepared properly and spoke highly of the support given.

Remarks: Despite London being just down the road, this is more Wind in the Willows than Wandsworth. Forget the tarmac drive, cause of a twice daily logjam, 'complete mayhem and madness': this is in every sense a country school, complete with cheerful rosy-cheeked children.

Bought by the head's parents in the 1950s, Hall Grove, once a small estate set in Surrey countryside, has grown somewhat organically from an unpretentious Georgian house into an educational hub, and although the ice house is fenced off (not a health and safety winner), the gardens, grounds and stables (moved but fully inhabited) are still there. Forty acres of land, still displaying a hint of an agricultural past, now includes the old walled garden recently restored to its former glory. The wish to stock it with pigs as ambulatory waste disposers may not go down too well with modern regulations, but if porkers don't make it there are plenty of plump ponies, serenading cockerels and labrador puppies to ensure that the atmosphere belies its slightly suburban situation.

The original house, home to both the Graham family and the flexi-boarders, has a hall dominated by a fine 'school of Thomas Lawrence' painting, portraying a Byronic figure staring into the distance, presumably not sure what to make of the current inhabitants. The four boarders' rooms (mainly used on a one night basis but available for longer stays if necessary) are bright and cheerful, with a funky communal space under the roof and smart new showers; but, inevitably, the traffic of so many feet leads to more well-worn carpet than shiny new floors – no sign of a trendy decorator's hand here. The academic side of life is scattered in rather random fashion through converted outbuildings and log cabins, disparaged by a few parents but clearly enjoyed by the children. All the classrooms have fresh displays of work in progress, there is a huge adaptable space for IT (two new IT rooms recently added in fact), separate rooms for art, pottery and DT and generous space for the thriving music department. It may not be the tidiest of lay-outs but the various components all appear loved and well cared for, in particular the new(ish), imaginative building for the early years.

Two classes at reception increase to three from year 3 to year 7; in the final year there are two sets plus a scholarship stream. The last is not universally popular with parents, who say that it can lead to divisions in the year group, but the head of the upper school points out that the scholarship exam requires a different syllabus. All children fill in a daily diary charting progress, open to staff and parents and monitored in the beginning by the form teacher and after year 5 by the child's study tutor, basically a liaison officer. There has been a report of holes in this system, in particular with children in the middle school who might need additional help, but the head says that further training is being given to teachers and there is evidence of one-on-one tutorials to tackle the problem. The school has a SENCo, is open to children who have mild educational problems and tries hard to help them. However, it does not appear to have the back-up to manage any child who has serious problems in keeping up, and one parent was not entirely happy with the support given. Although 'not an academic sweatshop', the upper school succeeds in hitting a high mark on a regular annual basis.

Sport is taken seriously: 'mens sana in corpore sano' definitely features amongst the head's axioms along with 'the busier they are, the better they do'. This can result in sending them out to run through the snow if the games pitches are unplayable, a practice one parent thoroughly approved of. 'Sport for all' is not just a slogan and the less talented receive equal encouragement from young enthusiastic staff and gappers, often past pupils. Lots of trophies line the sideboard and both sexes punch above their weight in several conventional sports, such as rugby, hockey and tennis, as well as the more unlikely golf and judo. On an ambitious note they are aiming high and have built up relationships with Chelsea Football Club and Harlequins to help spot and nurture future stars.

An annual art exhibition proves that attention is not only focused on the games field and the children's artwork, including desirable pottery, is visible all over the school. Drama and dance fill the seats regularly and the smiley faces of the casts speak for themselves. The head believes that 'music helps brain development' and music scholarships to senior schools are won almost every year. Over 200 individual lessons each week, leading to both classical success outside the school and the formation of a popular jazz band. Singing, a highly praised choir and composing, using music technology, also rate positive feedback from pupils. After-school clubs satisfy most interests, ranging from Lego (for littlies) to Lab Rats (for the scientifically mad) via Pony Grove (for the horse mad).

The majority of parents have a business background, so aware of the fairly common need for two salaries, maybe partly to pay the school fees, Hall Grove tries to help by offering not only a bed for the night but also early breakfast and late tea: 'can be a godsend,' said one over-stretched mother. Finally, the star turn for the children, even above the highly competitive Masterchef competition, is the annual outing by year 4 upwards to the school house and farm on the Devon coast. It's universally loved by pupils, who describe it as 'the best thing'; teachers also rate it highly, saying that it can help flag up hidden talents which might slip under the radar in the classroom, but often show up in the lambing shed or when paddling a canoe.

H

Halliford School

Russell Road, Shepperton TW17 9HX

Ages 11–18 **Pupils** 402 **Sixth form** 67 (4 girls)

Fees: £ 15,960 pa

01932 223593
www.hallifordschool.co.uk

Headmaster: Since September 2017, James Davies BMus LGSM FASC ACertCM PGCE. Degree in music from Sheffield and a postgrad from Manchester; first post was assistant director of music at Ashville College, becoming a day housemaster. Director of music, boarding housemaster and later deputy head at Scarborough College, then deputy head at The King's School, Tynemouth, where he found himself in his second term running the school with his fellow deputy head during an interregnum. Then to St Bees in Cumbria, which despite his best efforts closed in 2015. He worked as a consultant and inspector before joining Halliford. Until recently a serving RNLI lifeboat crew member; his father and sisters were Olympians but injury prevented him from following in their footsteps.

Academic matters: May not be super-selective, but is a school where achievement matters. 'Had perception of the school as non academic but that was completely wrong,' said parent. As long as pupils demonstrate that drive to succeed is there, teachers work with what they've got and often do very well. In 2018, 46 per cent of GCSE grades were A*-A/9-7; at A level 59 per cent A*-B and 31 per cent A*/A. Because of inclusive sixth form admissions, admits some onto A level sciences and maths without the A* or A grades at GCSE that are a non-negotiable elsewhere. 'We won't turn them away,' agreed teacher. It's harder all round – but worth the effort.

They know how boys tick. Science, like maths, mega at A level (have had 20 plus in lower sixth taking physics). Big on physical activity – younger pupils, for example, exploring senses by buttering slices of bread blindfold. Ditto French, where prepositions were memorably demonstrated by photos of pupils enjoying a bit of licensed mucking about – 'Ethan est dans le pull de Joshua' – though we never got to grips about just how they make language exchange trips so amazing that several parents (and pupils) told us that they didn't want to come home...

Pupils were universally positive about teachers. 'We've recently had our best GCSE results ever and I knew that mine were the best I could have done – it's a very fair reflection on the teachers.' Ideal, says school, for 'sort of pupil who wants to be in a smaller environment and do their best.'

Parents generally satisfied, particularly those with able sons, though one felt that tricky middle achievers could do with an occasional prod. School agrees that 'people at the top will always shine, people at the bottom will always make themselves known and it's the people in the middle you've just got to continue to care about.' Staff encouraged to see 'if they can do one thing better in their everyday life' – so motivating the mid-rankers might just feature.

Growing emphasis on tracking progress should also help, with pupils assessed in year 9 and 12, though not year 7. 'Don't believe in testing them to death,' says school. There are formal staff meetings to discuss progress and informal note swapping, venue the pleasant teachers' room river views as eye-catching as attempt at casual seating – eight identical, upright teacher-ly armchairs in a circle round a very small table.

Similarly, parents felt they were kept in the picture, with updates provided at least every eight weeks. 'Slippages would be known to us quickly,' said mother. Extra sessions can often make the difference, and not just at A level. 'It's all tailored,' agreed sixth former. 'Teachers are prepared to help you do well – everyone has a personal connection.' Even our earnest year 8 tour guide regularly took himself off to optional French clinic '...if I feel I haven't performed as well as I should.' Sensibly issues what amounts to check-list for parents in year 10, so are aware of what needs to be done for controlled assessments. (Sixth formers are 'deemed capable of doing their own organisation,' – and don't get one.)

You'd expect them to be good with SEN, as indeed they are, recently recruiting first full time learning support coordinator and supporting around 80 pupils who don't have formal identification of SEN. A further 26 have small group teaching and three get one-to-one support – nothing offered in class. Some have high functioning autism, other needs include ADHD. Approach praised by parents. 'Son was struggling with literacy and they've picked up on that, though doesn't have a diagnosis – have him on their radar,' said one.

Male staff in the majority (just over 60 per cent) and a mix of long stayers, relative newcomers (several with dashing facial hair) and a (young) old boy now returned to run the library. 'Quite a few of my old teachers still here.'

Games, options, the arts: It's all about participation. School may never run to an orchestra or lay on 25 plays a year, but everyone who wants to can be involved – far better than numerous plays restricted to a select few, says the school.

Take sport (all the mains), coached mainly by subject teachers and running to D or even E teams so everyone has a chance, though fixtures can be on the sparse side (one D team had just two in a term, both cancelled). It's a bit different for sixth form girls. A budding showjumper has permission to train off site and pilates is also an option – but inevitably not much in the way of team sports.

Parents, though hankering (mildly) for spot of rowing (shame to waste Thames on the doorstep) and a 4G pitch, are realistic about what's achievable in a small school. Otherwise, praise encouragement, range and facilities, which include decent sports hall (large but modestly positioned so doesn't dominate) and pitches: fore (behind the school) and aft, closer to the river, very occasionally flooded, though Weybridge Vandals and London Irish will loan theirs.

What they have, in any case, translates to impressive success, up and coming rugby star James Gulliver among former pupils whose framed shirts are on display by way of inspiration.

And in any case, while sport, for some, matters more than anything else – 'my favourite thing in life,' said (boy) sixth former – those who aren't as keen don't feel penalised. Parents are particularly thrilled at school's ability to fire up love of the arts and plenty of pupils have a foot in each camp (world champion go-karter took us through his GCSE art sketchbook). Annual year 8 Shakespeare Schools Festival is particular highlight. 'Amazing,' said mother, whose non-thespian son had taken to the boards (in female role) with panache.

Music may be something of a minority activity, with around 15 per cent of pupils learning instruments, but still plenty to do for those who are so inclined. Stand up and swing event in nearby restaurant, with 20-strong band, was a two-night sell out, while the Christmas choir rehearsal we witnessed was impressively well attended, with solid tenor and bass sections. 'No audition – emphasis is on participation,' says school.

But it's in visual arts where school at least matches sporting achievements (and school inspectors lavish praise). Quality and range hits the visitor like a wave, from colourful, forest-like fronds that run length of the corridor ceiling to large slab of shattered concrete (either work in progress or an accident) that oozes slowly down the wall. (Works well as either...).

Teen artworks are unusually low on introspection that runs like an existential thread in many other schools. It's angst-lite – minimally tortured self-portraits, masses of wonderful ceramics (department is regularly written up for quality and rarity), plus gorgeous painted boxes by the front door and – the highlight – a rainbow coloured frou-frou of paper and plastic that explodes in a rainbow froth down a lightwell. 'Because we're small, they're not pigeonholed,' says school.

'Perhaps it's being close to the river,' mused the head of art, as we admired one of a number of highly competent pastoral scenes that evoke unalloyed feelings of general contentment (the trained eye could discern a bit of a dark cloud in the middle distance but it could as easily have been going as coming). And did he mind the fact that many of most talented pupils headed off to do other things – one recently study architecture at Cambridge? Why, no, he was just happy to have facilitated their passage along the way.

Care for others also reflected in extensive community involvement. Year 9 pupils help in local park while sixth formers work at special school. For proof of commitment, trophy cabinet, packed with all the glittery stuff you'd expect, also features an oddity – a wooden castle made by pupils at school in Ethopia and presented to the sixth formers who'd worked there.

Other interests well catered for with extensive range of clubs, from debating to chess, music tech, a reading circle and – our favourite – model engineering, offering the irresistible chance to build own tiny steam engine. Everyone is encouraged to join at least one and most do, reckoned pupils. For extra yomping, there's always DofE (bronze and silver managed by school, some pupils go on to gold under own steam).

Background and atmosphere: Pretty original house was home of Lady Hamilton of Lord Nelson fame (though with very considerable alterations since).

School exudes financial probity today, but it's been a close call over the years. Only emergency measures by the first chair of governors, Mr Greville-Giddings, stopped it from going under in the 1950s. One of the houses now bears his name, though they've changed so often – from water themed (Dolphin, Heron and School) to trees (Ash, Elm, Oak and Yew) to royalty (Sandringham, Balmoral, Buckingham and Windsor) to the current batch (Desborough, Greville, Russell and Wadham) that it's anyone's guess as to how permanent a tribute it's likely to be.

Main buildings are arranged in a rough square – just about qualifies for name of 'quad'. There are the inevitable alterations and additions – old stables have gone, for example – though newer buildings are perfectly serviceable and could be even more so with makeover for the occasional blank-ish wall, one bare except for two pictures huddled together for company above turn on the stairs.

Departments are laid out with the odd quirk – science (old wooden lab benches in most labs relentlessly traditional) paired with Latin. Architectural star undoubtedly the sixth form centre with own bright café area (though, despite rumours, serves same food as rest of school – much of it sourced from local suppliers, including Shepperton's high street butcher), also home to art and music departments. Overall feel, from library (runs pick-a-book sessions for boys, many readers, others 'who would prefer to be doing sport') to roofed semi-cloisters – ideal for bag storage (odd drop and bolt manifestation elsewhere) is pleasant throughout, without – unusually – single Portakabin of shame.

Pupils, gently chivvied outside by staff at lunchtimes – some prefer conviviality of art and music rooms – were busy playing tag in paved courtyard area on day of visit. 'We encourage traditional games,' says school.

Bar absence of cap-doffing (not worn here) and winter warms all round, you could have slipped back in time, particularly when it comes to manners – impeccable, agree parents. 'It's quite staggering how polite all the boys are,' said one. 'You don't expect that in teenage boys.' 'Gentlemanly,' was verdict of sixth form girl (a word we'd not come across for a long time). Several teachers are even waging against 'like' as a filler word, though may be a losing battle. 'Everyone who used it five times had to leave the class – and soon there was nobody left,' said pupil.

Pastoral care, well-being and discipline: In plenty of schools, happiness is on the elusive side. Here, it's taken for granted. Boys, even some natural slug-a-beds, spring out of bed at relatively early times of day (an essential, given the slow to sluggish stopping train service), packed and ready to go. 'Alarm goes off, he's up and in his uniform, bish bash bosh,' said one parent.

At its heart is a highly effective tutor and house system, together with top-rated matrons who dispense kindness along with the band-aids for the inevitable sports injuries. All were praised by parents (senior leadership team, in contrast, was so low profile that one mother had to ask son for names).

Head is on hand for less tractable problems and school's clear cut sanctions process is there on the website for all to read. Pupils are very occasionally asked to leave, but it's a rare event (recent placard-wielding father's demo after son's withdrawal even rarer – and not supported by parents we talked to). For top three years, obvious carrots (and sticks) are dispensed with. Instead, they're assumed to know how to behave.

Generally, school's emphasis on mutual respect works. Older boys mentor younger ones and school urges parents with problems to get in touch, sensibly pointing out that 'if the school is not aware of a concern it cannot deal with it...'

Year 7s get transition tutor, a kindly teething problems expert, followed by same tutor for years 8 to 11. Expect emails to be answered within 24 hours (and often almost instantaneously) and problems, including low level unkindness, usually resolved quickly. 'Jumped on it as soon as they knew and were very supportive,' said parent.

Pupils and parents: New parents get a 43 page alphabetic guide (ends on U for uniforms). Most pupils are pretty local, either arriving by train from Hampton, Teddington and Twickenham way or from Staines and Ashford, or by school bus (currently four routes – Kew, Walton, Woking and Staines). Majority white – ditto the area (keen to encourage more diversity). No EAL pupils currently.

Families will generally have had a nose round some of the better known alternatives including Hampton (independent) and state sector, which is brilliant for Catholics (St Paul's, Sunbury) and girls (Waldegrave), less so for agnostic families with boys.

Our tour guides – unusual but sweet combination of tall lower sixth boy and quite diminutive year 8 – were polite, nice and chatty. Had chosen school because 'seemed normal,' said one. 'Down to hearth, friendly, community feel.' Goodness was just the normal side of eerie – 'no restrictions on lunchtime conversation but are remarkable quiet,' says school (and, by Timothy, they are – one even picking up a sweet wrapper en route and then apologising for brief departure to deposit in a litter bin).

We were curious as to why girls would sign up for sixth form when there are so few of them – none at all in some years and never more than 20 per cent: ideal percentage, thinks school. First wave arrived as refugees when local girls' school closed – arrived 'out of expediency and has continued.' May sound several pantones short of a red carpet welcome but don't be put off. Girl we spoke to was having a ball. Friendly atmosphere and gentle boys (once have nerved themselves to make conversation – takes about a week) both attractions, though abundance of loos also a big selling point. 'Really clean and you tend to get them to yourself.'

Entrance: 'Comfortably full' in most years with more interest in year 9 entry 'probably due to going round prep schools and reminding people we're here.'

Selective (probably in top 50 per cent of population) but not massively so. Average score 115, realistically unlikely to be offered place if less than average (100). Offers 60 places to year 7 and around 12 in year 9 (English, maths and reasoning) – when adds extra class (from three to four) and reduces numbers (drops from 20 to 18). All about fit, though, so previous reports matter and family commitment is essential (all candidates get interview, with parents, before they sit the exam). Won't take anyone who, regardless of home support, is unlikely to make it through GCSEs and into the sixth form, (minimum five at 9-5, including English and maths required).

Exit: No post-GCSE cull though substantial numbers (around 50 per cent) head off to some of popular local sixth form colleges post-16. Sport and art doesn't currently translate directly into courses, though design emphasis undoubtedly supports engineering applications and STEM subjects generally rule OK. One to Cambridge in 2018; Birmingham, Oxford Brookes, Coventry and Portsmouth currently popular.

Money matters: Scholarships (academic, sport, music, art and drama) worth up to 10 per cent of the fees, reviewed annually, though also encourages bright but financially challenged families to apply, occasionally offering 100 per cent bursaries. Would like to do more but as has to come out of income, inevitably limited.

Remarks: A friendly place where everyone is known. Bar child in search of the comforting anonymity of a bigger school, or girls not keen on the full Zuleika Dobson experience, few it won't suit. 'There's room for everyone,' said parents. 'We've never had any doubts at all.'

Halstead Preparatory School

Woodham Rise, Woking, Surrey GU21 4EE

Ages 3–11 Pupils 216

Fees: £7,500 – £14,400 pa

01483 772682
www.halstead-school.org.uk

Headmistress: Since 2013, Mrs Penny Austin BA. Age not disclosed so we'll hazard 40s. Previously head of Walthamstow Hall Junior School, which she joined in January 2004 after working for 10 years at Ardingly College Prep School, starting off as class teacher and promoted to deputy headship in 2002, when she also became an independent schools inspector. Musical training – was a professional singer – took her into schools where she was willingly subsumed into world of education. Led inexorably to a PGCE followed by two years as class teacher in state primaries in Brighton and East Sussex before move to independent sector.

Whether in academic dress for special occasion assemblies or – admirably – working as a teaching assistant with all year groups (ensures she knows pupils and staff inside out), style is 'me being me,' she says. These days leaves the school music to others, though still runs a chamber choir with husband close to their Sussex home. Certainly works for parents, who rate her as approachable and aeons away from previous twinset and pearls approach to leadership (though we can testify that she's peerlessly smart). 'She's brought a warmth to the school,' said a mother.

Bar a few instant, unilateral changes when she first arrived, like ditching the compulsory school napkins ('didn't get washed very often'), her approach is consensus-based. Involve everyone and listen to ideas, she says, and changes will be faster and happier. With new uniform, building, lunch menu and timetable all under her belt in the first two years, clearly she knows what she's about.

Girls think she's 'amazing'. Older pupils may come to her office for help with reading, tinies can confide problems to the big, friendly teddy there. Either way, 'You don't ever feel uncomfortable,' said year 6 pupil. Firmly committed to single sex education for girls, she is working hard to ensure that niminy piminy aspects kept under control – she's aware of the dangers of the school being seen as pocket of beribboned niceness.

Sweet it may be, but it's the sort on the golden syrup tins, deriving from strength rather than sickliness. Thus the new mission statement namechecks self belief and love of learning and reins back the references to homely, caring feel. Football and judo enjoyed as much as origami and cake decorating, she says – important that everyone realises it.

Entrance: Most families within 10 mile radius of Woking, just under three-quarters white British, around 10 per cent Asian. A small number (currently seven) have EAL requirements, just over 30 multilingual.

Pupils largely come as they are to nursery (from age 2). Later, they need to attend a taster day and from year 2 upwards, pupils are asked to do maths and English assessments to gauge strengths and weaknesses.

Unusually, offer academic and music scholarships, sat by all current year 2 pupils as well as by external candidates and worth around 10 per cent of the fees. No public announcement of winners and successful families 'asked to be discreet,' says head, keen to mute the competitive parent rumour mill. (Most are.) Sound financial management and some tough decisions (no sibling discount, for example, though do have priority in the applications process if oversubscribed) also enables schools to offer means-tested bursaries (up to 100 per cent) for new and existing families. Real hardship has to be demonstrated, stresses literature. Frequent or expensive holidays and luxury cars and a second home are among lifestyle choices unlikely to give you a head start in the applications process (criteria still come as an occasional surprise to some, says head).

Caters for 15 pupils with SEN, three with statement or EHC plan, one receiving intensive one-to-one support and LEA funded, some with more than one disability. Can manage specific learning difficulties to processing and speech and language, ADD/ADHD (as long as no severe behavioural difficulties) and other conditions including epilepsy and physical difficulties.

Exit: Most nursery joiners stay all the way to year 6, when leavers almost exclusively head for single sex senior schools. Good years (and most are) see significant (high single numbers at least) to Guildford High School and St Catherine's, Bramley as well as Sir William Perkins' School. Tormead, Prior's Field plus a selection of Catholic schools (St Teresa's, Farnborough Hill, Notre Dame) also feature. There were 18 scholarships in 2018.

But don't get the impression that fuss is reserved for high flyers. All abilities enjoy same levels of care. 'Staff told me that they'd get her into the right school for her – and they did. I trusted them and was right to,' said mother.

Currently no word on future career success ('none known' says school) though it's busy attempting to fill in the gaps.

Remarks: Founded as boarding school in Kent in 1927, evacuated to Wiltshire in World War II before popping up in 1947 on current site as a day school. Became a charitable trust in 1970s with what's described as 'Christian, non denom ethos...' (sensibly hedging bets, perhaps) for next phase in almost 90 year history.

Site, in quiet residential road a mile from Woking, is the perfect size – Goldilocks would have a ball. With just under 220 pupils (numbers impressively constant, even during worst of recession), it's small enough to 'know where everyone is,' says head but big enough for pitches, lots of greenery, delightful enclosed nursery and reception playgrounds packed with fun and educational goodies (they can't get enough of junk music kit, sounds of rhythmic bashing carrying beautifully all the way up the road).

Has even managed to buy extra land from neighbours to create a secret garden, one half green and tranquil, the other featuring blinding white gravel and diamond, L-shaped and triangular wooden planters at different angles, less Frances Hodgson Burnett than a non-verbal reasoning problem reimagined by Alan Titchmarsh. 'Maths teacher did have an input,' says head.

Older part of school, the original Edwardian house, is home to well-stocked library on top floor, cosy SEN room – 'wanted it in centre of school,' says head – and older pupils, top years somewhat compressed, though clearly very happily so, into compact classrooms.

Easy on the eye recent wood-clad building, nicely slotted in without jarring, is spacious in looks and feel – showpiece vast first floor picture window, adjoining and apparently inaccessible windowsill that runs above steep staircase used as display area and crammed with delightful ceramic pots with paper flowers. 'Teacher pushes them along with extra long ruler,' explains pupil.

Small size really matters to pupils and parents. 'Came from school with 30 in the class,' said pupil. 'Nothing was a challenge – now everything is.' There are just 33 in the biggest year group and 21 in the smallest (tinier still for chicks and ducks, the two nursery classes). Means lots of delightful family touches that include stirring of school Christmas pud by every child in the school in assembly.

Clearly good at ingredients in general, given end result – girls who are a credit to their parents and teachers – even more so following Mrs Austin's directive that all shall stand up for visitors (a few parents were initially unsure but now won round, and we admired year 5 group placidly carrying on with needlework while waiting to be told to sit down again).

But though they show up at senior schools as 'nice, polite, well-behaved little girls,' says one registrar, don't get the impression that only the instantly compliant are welcome, stresses Mrs Austin. 'Strong characters learn that there's a time and place for everybody.'

They're smart, too, even more so following a uniform redesign, feisty triumphing over fusty, drab brown blazers and skirts consigned to the great secondhand uniform shop in the sky and replaced by smart toning blues (tartan even features on cushions in reception, no doubt an effective aide-memoire). It's an example of Mrs Austin's ability to steer a canny line between the new and outré. There may be a new games skirt (great favourite with pupils) but there are still three Alice bands on the uniform list and compulsory panama hats continue to line the cloakroom shelves, brim up (and huge on 'aaah' factor when worn by nursery children on visit to local farm).

Similar balance struck elsewhere. Handbell rung by senior pupils (a favourite duty) marks the end of lessons that may feature iPads, used tactically, never slavishly, or handwritten work (pen licences are much coveted). Even the parents' association has changed name from 'Ways and Means' (suggests stay at home sewing circles) to the altogether more businesslike Halstead Preparatory School PTA. It's far more in keeping with growing numbers of dual income parents – and school looks after them with excellent value out of hours care (7.30-8.00am, including breakfast, for under a fiver) and reassurance. 'If someone's stuck on a train and can't collect on time, we will always manage,' they say.

It's all achieved, say parents, by team of happy, well led teachers with enough time for every pupil. No compromise on recruitment, says Mrs Austin, who'll advertise as often as it takes to get top quality candidates through the doors. While academic ability is generally above average on arrival, school boosts pupils' appetite for learning – inspectors highlight progress made by both SEN and G&T pupils is impressive.

Class size maximum of 16 to year 2 and 18 for other years. Staff ratios are generous (one for each 10 pupils) without being lavish, overwhelmingly female. Cosy, long term team – average age mid 40s, nine staff who've been here for over 10 years.

Plenty of specialist staff (PE, drama, dance and music from nursery with art, DT and food tech, ICT and French added from reception and year 1). Maths and English specialists introduced in year 5 when both subjects are set. Academic support either in class or one-to-one provided as needed.

There's no shallow end stuff here – topics are in depth, with cross curricular weeks for years 1 and 2 (The Circus, Under the Sea), recent food-themed special offering chance to make own vegetable character (politicians presumably off limits).

Results, given range of ability, extremely impressive, from year 6 pupil-designed science experiments – one feeding snails different diets and mapping preferences, another swabbing different areas of the school for bacteria – to group recital of poetry, diction, sound effects and sophisticated choreography all created without any input from teachers.

Throughout, fear-free originality is a real feature – easy to understand why recent latest inspectors went positively gaga about educational wonders that had come their way. 'Genuinely inclusive,' felt a parent. 'Celebrate success without quietly stressing the girls out.'

Hallmark was enthusiasm for all pupils for maths – including those happy to admit they struggled. Voted a top favourite courtesy of buzzy teachers who stop at nothing to help, from motivating 3D stickers and Percy Pigs – 'We go mad for them...' – to personalised revision material. One keen young cook even had a term's worth of problems recast as numbers to be fed and cost of ingredients. 'Was so touched,' said mother. 'Made her realise why she needed to do maths and it changed her.'

Numerous – and largely voluntary – opportunities to shine range from Owl Awards against the clock times table competitions (three minutes, perfect answers or no award), to celebration assemblies where good work means house points, as do out of school triumphs – even budding dog trainer had moment of glory. And once given, points are for keeps, say pupils. 'Nothing can be taken away because you've [already] earned it.'

Encouragement to try new things extends to delicious food (chef busily but largely unsuccessfully encouraging pupils to essay an asparagus spear on day of visit) and residential trips – not just for leavers, who head for France, but for years 4 and 5 who enjoy UK-based residential stays. There's an equal sense of adventure closer to home. Over half the girls learning an instrument, some to grade 4, encouraged by timetabled taster sessions on different instruments – no faffing about with recorders, either, with girls lugging trombone cases round the place (tips on knee-bashing avoidance covered in first lesson, says teacher). Enthusiasts, some beginners, others 'incredible,' said mother, can perform at tea time concerts – and then graduate to orchestra, run as a club, as are the four choirs.

For the sporty, plenty on offer, from athletics and rounders to football, matches achieving variable success, upside the number of ABC teams and guarantee that 'your daughter does get to play in matches no matter how appalling she is,' said parent.

While pupils pride themselves on good sporting manners – 'We're not sore losers,' said one. 'We just say 'OK, we tried our hardest' – one parent reckoned an occasional prompt from the school was needed when it was clear they were 'not very pleased the other team have won.' Particularly true on sports day, when house rivalries reach fever pitch. If they cheer when other houses have lost, 'the teacher will say "that's not very Halstead, is it?"' said mother. 'They're encouraged to support everyone, and I like that.'

For a very few parents and pupils in need of a broader canvas, it can feel slightly too compact. For most, a combination of imaginative teaching across the ability range and confidence-building delivered in an atmosphere that's cosy rather than cloying is hard to beat.

Mrs Austin stresses that this isn't a school full of 'frightened little rabbits – we don't want to be the sweet little girls' school but the excellent girls' school where they grow up into confident young ladies ready for the next step.' Year 5 pupil, diligently putting final touches to delightful Father's Day specs case, very definitely no Cottontail. 'I'll expect something in return,' she said. 'This has taken all year.'

Handcross Park School

Linked with Brighton College, Brighton College Prep and Pre-Prep School

126

H

Handcross, Haywards Heath, West Sussex RH17 6HF

Ages 2–13 **Pupils** 382 **Boarders** 55 (from 7 years) **C of E**

Fees: Day £9,690 – £19,080; Boarding £16,110 – £38,010 pa

01444 400526
www.handcrossparkschool.co.uk

Headmaster: Since 2016, Richard Brown MA, who lives on site with his sons. Previously head of Dorset House School, with a stint before that as housemaster at Pangbourne College. Five years in the army are not immediately apparent in this head, who likes best to spend his free time writing or walking. Was a 'tennis parent' and understands parents getting a bit twitchy about teams. His most important qualities to inspire in pupils: love of learning and kindness.

'Bent over backwards to help us', said parent seeking urgent places for her four children mid year, '...transition was incredibly easy'; another said, 'one step ahead and always thinking about what needs to be done' (passing places appeared on the drive as if by magic...). A bit more traditional than his predecessor, thought another, explaining that he has introduced grace before meals, and increased the emphasis on manners. Parents appreciate the well attended surgeries the head has introduced for the parents of each year group, and say he is at his best one-to-one.

Following an adored predecessor has its challenges, but most appreciate his ideas: 'The...leadership programme is brilliant,' say pupils, and his busy programme upgrading facilities is very popular. He's good at focusing on children's abilities, said a parent – '[he] makes a point of telling a child if they're doing well'.

'I like his different approach – more focused on academics', said a year 8 pupil thoughtfully. A boarder told us, 'he's really friendly; comes and chats at lunchtime and visits boarding houses....helps with maths'.

Entrance: By one or two-day taster experience including English, maths and reasoning assessments and interview, plus reports and references from previous school. Remote assessments and Skype interviews possible for overseas applicants. Pupils come from local nurseries and preps, but with expansion of boarding the catchment area is widening to Brighton, Crawley, Haywards Heath and London. Boarders mainly from London, Forces families, a few from Europe.

Exit: About a third to Brighton College, another 20 per cent to Hurstpierpoint, rest scattered between eg Wellington, Marlborough, Winchester, Oundle, Dulwich, Epsom, Charterhouse. Twenty-one scholarships in 2018.

Remarks: A parent told us 'the culture [of this school] is to do with the magic of childhood'; or perhaps the magic of how we think childhood should be, with acres of green on which to run around, ancient trees to climb, and teachers who say, how about doing this lesson outside in the sun? Children seem young here compared to city schools, and the head aims to extend childhood for as long as possible (whilst of course preparing pupils for senior schools). It's impossible to resist the happiness of this place, and this reviewer received more random smiles in corridors from children here than at any other school; a tribute not just to their politeness, but to the genuine warmth and friendliness which seems to fill this school.

It's not selective, but parents say it's an academically challenging school: 'we joined the school for more academic stretch', said one; 'the bright are well challenged', said another. Parents say teachers are as the best thing about Handcross, and feel that its small size means they know teaching staff well: 'The teachers are very inspiring – particularly...in English and science', said a parent, relaying her surprise when her son, enthused by science for the first time, and talked about time and black holes the whole way home.

'Teachers are kind', agree pupils, one commenting that English has become less scary because the teacher uses her own stories and experience; a year 3 pupil said of the history teacher, 'he tells wonderful stories...and they're all true!'

Handcross is a Google reference school, and a lot of academic learning here is through this medium. Pupils start using Chromebooks in pre-prep, and have their own from year 5 of prep school (although not to the exclusion of using a pen). Parents and pupils are enthusiastic: revision notes and homework are all detailed there and pupils can email the teacher if they're not sure about a topic. In Spanish, Chromebooks mean that each table can be doing something different; in the class we saw one group answered questions on a video, others were translating, others practised conversation.

'[Google Chrome] works across so many different things', say pupils, who particularly love the multiple choice Caboodle. Google expeditions mean pupils can travel the world in geography and history – 'so amazing', said a pupil, enthusiastically recalling a virtual trip to the theatre to see Lincoln die. GoGuardian means teachers can see whatever pupils are doing on screens – 'so they know if you sometimes look at the football scores...', said a pupil feelingly.

Learning support has been transformed here in the last year, with parents and pupils bubbling over with enthusiasm for the wonderful staff in the 'dairy'; '[My son's] self confidence has soared...', said a parent. Innovative thinking in this unit: there are no desks, but beanbags, a ball to lounge over and wobble boards; a teacher may well say, 'let's do our half an hour of English walking among the trees': they understand here that dyslexic children need to move while they learn. Dyslexic pupils were using tweezers to move dinosaurs from bowl to bowl to increase their dexterity – a fun way to improve handwriting; a pupil struggling with maths was using a toy horse rider and jumps to learn his four times table (four faults every time you knock down a fence).

Around 20 pupils receive regular support (one-to-one charged as an extra), but this is a department with school wide relevancy, a parent telling us that any pupil who feels 'flaky' about exams can do them in the dairy instead of the school hall, and in this friendly environment feel more confident and do better.

Handcross is part of the Brighton College family, but is no back entrance to the college; pupils must hit same standards as other applicants. The link provides a quality standard, and staff throughout the family share best practice.

Pastoral care is a particular strength. The head is keenly aware of the mental health issues which can assail young children, and is keen to increase pupils' resilience to life's knocks. If pupils have a problem they will talk to their tutor or the deputy head (pastoral), loved by pupils and parents alike, and pupils can also talk to an independent listener. Random acts of kindness are rewarded with kindness bands, on the day of our visit for handing in money, helping a younger pupil find their parents and for lending someone shin pads.

Parents say that complaints of unkindness or bullying are dealt with quickly – '...same day, took seriously, dealt with it discreetly. School investigates misdeeds, doesn't jump to conclusions'. This school is upfront when things go wrong: an incident was dealt with 'head on...in a mature manner...and avoided the school gate gossip', said a parent; 'they allowed children to make a mistake and be helped rather than punished. Their way of dealing with the situation made me feel we're at the right school'.

The usual sports, and gorgeous grounds to play them in, with an indoor pool too. Chances for all in A-E matches every week, and a celebration of the less able in the 'Be Trewe festival' where the D and E teams play other schools. Girls and boys play football, cricket and rounders (which gives every player a chance to play – unlike cricket, which favours the strong few).

Most pupils here learn instruments, and music lessons are an energetic business: shoes were in a scruffy pile at the entrance, pupils were sitting on the floor, drums and other instruments between legs, singing and playing with gusto. It's a traditional set up musically, which one parent thought could benefit from some street dance and hip hop. More than 70 pupils do LAMDA exams, with drama lessons and annual productions for all year groups.

The swish new art and design centre houses art of all sorts, including pottery, textiles and photography. Music played as pupils practised watercolour techniques; next door in woodwork, pupils were turning recycled wood into flags and making plastic coffee containers into Christmas bells.

The lavish range of clubs includes pig care; despite calling them Thing One and Thing Two, the field to plate scheme didn't work out, and the pigs look set for a long and happy life at Handcross.

Around a quarter of years 5-8 do some sort of boarding, with full, weekly and flexi available. An international presence, with boarders from Spain, China, India and more. The varied activity schedule at the weekend always includes a trip; Thorpe park, laser quest and the shopping centre are all popular. Day pupils can join boarders for breakfast at 7.15am for small extra fee, and can stay for supper until 6.30pm. 'Takes the pressure off if you're both working', said a parent (pre-prep also provides wrap around care for 50 weeks of the year).

Boarding facilities are of a very high standard, and 'sensible bedtimes,' said a parent approvingly. Food is equally good, and pupils enjoy food from around the world on Tuesdays – a taste from home for overseas boarders.

The best things about boarding is the freedom they get compared to home, pupils agree. Phones were banned a few years ago, and for a few days, boarders didn't know what to do with themselves. Now they're up and out, involved in sport or drama or watching a movie. 'We can interact with friends more'.

Pre-prep is headed by Mr Gayler – 'a big kid at heart; throws himself into everything', said a parent. It's set in what would once have been the walled vegetable garden, now a magical place of willow arches, cherry trees and every sort of adventure equipment. The children make full use of the surrounding woods in their forest school lessons, and on the day of our visit, reception, all in pjs, were about to take a magic trip on a bed to a jungle.

Communication is good ('to the point of saturation', said a parent), by email and text; not just if matches are cancelled, but even if a road is closed that might be a problem on the school run. Parents are confident of quick response when they contact the school.

One means-tested bursary, virtually 100 per cent, and one free place in nursery.

No average family, say parents, but it wouldn't suit 'someone overly aggressive or full of their own importance and abilities', said a parent crisply.

'Believe the advertising,' said one parent earnestly. 'Its very welcoming, very kind'. 'Scatter kindness' is a sign which appears all over the place at Handcross, and it seems that everyone here has taken this to heart.

Headington Preparatory School

Linked with Headington School

26 London Road, Oxford, Oxfordshire OX3 7PB

Ages 3–11 **Pupils** 250 C of E

Fees: £9,315 – £14,082 pa

01865 759400
www.headington.org/prep/head-s-welcome

Head: Since 2014, Jane Crouch BA, MA (40s). Studied French and geography at Keele. Her masters, in educational management and administration, is from the University of London. Was previously head of Dame Bradbury's School, Saffron Walden and before that head of Ashford School, Kent and deputy head of Great Walstead, West Sussex. Mrs Crouch had the confidence of parents we spoke to and her easy, friendly relationship with the girls seems well established. Tempting though the calm of her study must be, she told us that she 'loves getting into the classroom' and was 'determined to fit some teaching in'.

All possible building work having been done, we wondered whether Mrs Crouch wanted to redevelop any other aspect of the school. While not hatching plans for revolution, she told us that she hopes to extend the range of after-school activities and has her sights set on the prep becoming an 'eco' school. She's also keen to up the involvement of sixth formers from the senior school, 'helping with assemblies and other activities'.

Mrs Crouch and her husband are keen coastal walkers but, since coastline is in short supply in Oxfordshire, they are enjoying new vistas in the Chilterns. As if running a school wasn't enough she enjoys zumba, spin and step classes and visiting art galleries. On her Kindle you'll find Swedish crime fiction.

Entrance: From age 3. Early years foundation stage is formed of two year groups, nursery and pre-kindergarten. Early application recommended, in any case at least one year in advance of entry. Offers are strictly in date of registration order with priority given to applicants with sister(s) already in the prep or senior school. Occasional places for older children; those aged 7+ attend assessment day and are tested in mathematics, creative writing, reading comprehension and spelling.

Exit: Around 90 per cent to senior school. Parents are given plenty of warning if a girl looks unlikely to pass the entrance exam. Senior school looks at applicants in the round so a talent in music, sport or drama may boost chances.

Remarks: Headington Prep is based just over the road from the main school in a large Edwardian house (once upon a time it was boarding accommodation) with generous gardens. Stunning curved glass atrium is the impressive culmination of several years' refurbishment work to build what is, in effect, 'a new school inside an old building.' On a large board just inside the entrance, photos of girls were displayed alongside their 'hopes and dreams'. If all goes to plan these mini Headingtonians in their smart blue pinafores will become the film directors, nurses, actors, civil engineers and prime ministers of years to come. Nor do we need to worry about a shortage of ice cream shop owners or cup cake bakers.

It must have tested the architects' ingenuity to fit everything in but these lucky girls now have a dining room, the floor of which depicts a river and meadows (could this be a ploy to get them thinking about rowing?). Apparently the food has improved along with the accommodation. There's also a gym, dance studio, music rooms and, drum roll, a proper theatre with retractable seating. So, no need for girls to go over to the senior school for PE, drama or music but they do head that way for swimming once a week. Musicianship starts young – reception and year 1 learn how to read music and play the keyboard. Singing and orchestral days are a great way for older players to workshop and develop ensemble skills. The library has been extended and is a bright and cheerful place to curl up on a beanbag and read.

H

So pristine was the remodelled school that we were beginning to wonder whether the girls felt able to let rip, but an art room full of plaster and paint be-smattered girls enthusiastically constructing props for a forthcoming play dispelled our concerns. Small classes (average 16) allow pupils to develop at their own pace, as do 'flexible' maths groups in the older years. Years 4, 5 and 6 get two hours of science a week in a proper lab; 'We do as much hands on stuff as we can.' In the grounds there's a greenhouse, pond and plots for growing plants and vegetables. Girls also enjoy visits to the Oxford University farm at Wytham where they learn about agriculture on a larger scale.

School says it will make 'reasonable adjustments' for pupils with mild SEN. Dedicated 'learning enrichment' department supports girls who need a little extra help as well as stretching the most able.

We've seen some forest schools in our time and it has to be said that this is one where the word 'forest' is stretched rather thinly. Headington Prep is officially so designated (to be fair they also have the run of senior school's ample grounds). Buses are certainly commoner than beech trees on Oxford's busy London Road but we're sure that girls enjoy their outdoor learning. Mrs Crouch is a fan: 'It increases independence and helps develop a genuine interest in nature.' She wants her pupils to 'have time to play, make mud kitchens, just to be in the woodland.'

Sport came in for particular praise (prep has a Sport England Activemark gold award), all girls get the chance to represent their school in team games and extracurricular activities include cricket, dance, fencing, trampolining and cross-country. Older girls use the senior school's all weather pitches for netball and hockey. Parents help out at after-school clubs and other events.

Lessons end at 3.30pm then it's clubs until 4.30 or 5.00pm, there's also after-school care until 6.00pm – children are given tea and can play or take part in extracurricular activities. Given the school's location, we wondered how parents managed to drop off and pick up their daughters safely. Mrs Crouch revealed all, 'We have an arrangement with the pub across the road and parents can use the car park.'

This friendly and extremely well resourced prep would be a fine place for any girl to begin her educational journey – and for most, the next stage is only a short walk away.

Headington School

Linked with Headington Preparatory School

Headington Road, Oxford, Oxfordshire OX3 7TD

Ages 11–18 **Pupils** 800 **Sixth form** 246 **Boarders** 166 full, 29 weekly, 12 half-weekly **C of E**

Fees: Day £17,652 – £19,251; Boarding £24,015 – £38,286 pa

01865 759113
www.headington.org

Head: Since 2011, Mrs Caroline Jordan (50s). A local girl, she was educated at St Helen and St Katharine in Abingdon, read geology at Oxford and did her PGCE (science) at Manchester. Previously head of St George's Ascot and before that spent 10 years at Wycombe Abbey where she was head of sixth form and deputy senior housemistress. Lives on site; married to Richard, a company director, one adult son, two border collies. Currently president of the Girls' Schools Association.

Before going into teaching Mrs Jordan ran her own business. She says that heads 'need those skills'; they do, and indeed we could imagine her as one of the dragons on Dragons' Den – not that she's scary, but she is direct and, well, businesslike. As one parent said, 'definitely not fluffy'. She's forward thinking and ambitious, hyper alert to social and educational change and ready for whatever the future holds in these areas. Parents describe her as 'really on the ball' and 'ahead of the game' and are mostly in favour of the changes she's making. 'She's mad about rowing,' we were told; 'you should hear her shouting from the riverbank when her crew are racing!' Another was impressed by Mrs J's energetic networking when she accompanied crews to a competition in the US. 'She took the girls round as many universities as she could, making contacts.' We anticipate US college scholarship offers rolling in for Headington rowers.

Parts of the school are being seriously revamped – not just bricks and mortar but also Headington's Achilles' heel (rowing excepted): sport. Mrs Jordan is frank about this; historically lack of opportunities and support meant that girls had to join outside clubs to progress in team games such as hockey. A complete overhaul of facilities and teaching will see the 'inspirational' head of rowing become director of sport, no doubt expected to do his magic in other departments.

Favourite childhood reads were Dorothy Dunnett's Scottish historical novels but these days Mrs J enjoys quick crime thrillers on her Kindle. Down time is spent 'mixing concrete' – she and her husband are restoring a 500-year-old house in France.

Head of junior school since 2014, Mrs Jane Crouch BA MA (40s). Studied French and geography at Keele. Her masters, in educational management and administration, is from the University of London. Was previously head of Dame Bradbury's School, Saffron Walden and before that head of Ashford School, Kent and deputy head of Great Walstead, West Sussex. It was early days when we visited but Mrs Crouch had the confidence of parents we spoke to and her easy, friendly relationship with the girls already seemed well established. Tempting though the calm of her study must be, she told us that she 'loves getting into the classroom' and was 'determined to fit some teaching in'.

All possible building work having been done, we wondered whether Mrs Crouch wanted to redevelop any other aspect of the school. While not hatching plans for revolution, she told us that she hopes to set up a breakfast club, extend the range of after school activities and has her sights set on the prep becoming an 'eco' school. She's also keen to up the involvement of sixth formers from the senior school, 'helping with assemblies and other activities'.

Mrs Crouch and her husband are keen coastal walkers but, since coastline is in short supply in Oxfordshire, they are enjoying new vistas in the Chilterns. As if running a school wasn't enough she enjoys zumba, spin and step classes and visiting art galleries. On her Kindle you'll find Swedish crime fiction.

Academic matters: In 2018, 84 per cent A*-A/9-7 at GCSE. At A level, 54 per cent A*/A (78 per cent A*-B). Maths, economics, sciences, fine art and English literature notably successful. Languages don't seem to attract many (as is so often the case).

More than respectable IB average of 38.5 in 2018. Take-up for IB roughly 20 per cent and growing – Mrs J certainly thinks it is a more secure option at a time when 'A levels are up in the air.' She's particularly keen on the IB theory of knowledge course and this is now being offered lower down the school. We're sure the girls benefit but it's also a canny and not so subliminal bit of IB marketing.

Gone are the days when girls ploughed through up to 13 GCSEs; it's 10 now with increasing number of IGCSEs. Choice of one language from French, Spanish and German; surprisingly there's no Mandarin GCSE although it's offered as an after-school club, as is ancient Greek. All do Latin in first two years.

Twenty-nine subjects to chose from at A level including fine art, photography, computing, law, psychology and government and politics. EPQ encouraged but there's 'not much time' in term and research and writing during the summer holidays post year 12 can be a big ask. Oxbridge, medicine and veterinary hopefuls get application support and so do girls applying for architecture. The latter receive specialist lectures and help with portfolio preparation – must account for the unusually high number of Headington girls accepted to study this oversubscribed subject.

Special mention here for ICT – girls learn to code in Python and apply this and other skills to robotics. Not content with winning 'best rookies' and 'first moves' prizes at recent Student Robotics Competition, the Headington team (one of just two all girl teams) designed, built and programmed an autonomous robot from scratch to become champions. 'It sent a real buzz through the whole school,' the head girl told us proudly.

School says it makes 'reasonable adjustments' for girls with mild SEN including one-to-one weekly support for girls in the lower school and drop-in sessions for the middle school and sixth form. EAL tuition also provided.

Games, options, the arts: The 'inspirational' leadership of Headington's South African head of rowing has brought the school national and international success on the water (most recently the J8 crew won the Henley women's regatta). Girls start training in the summer term of year 7 and some parents think this is too young (boys generally don't begin until age 13); school says the programme is run in conjunction with Oxford Brookes and everything is very carefully monitored. Compared to the riverside facilities enjoyed by other notable Oxfordshire rowing schools such as Abingdon, Headington has it tough – they row out of a couple of portakabins shared with St Edward's School. 'Our success is all down to inspiration,' says Mrs Jordan.

School boasts over 30 different sporting activities (many are lunchtime or after-school clubs) including fencing, synchronised swimming, dance and cheerleading. It's also pretty horsey, despite the urban setting. 'It's a side branch of the Pony Club,' we were told. What if you don't have a horse? We asked. 'Oh, someone will lend you one,' came the airy reply. Girls compete in blue Headington silks and bring back plenty of rosettes.

Mrs J acknowledges that there's still work to do when it comes to 'sport for all'. 'Every girl should have her own regime to stay fit and healthy, whether or not that includes competitive sport. We should expect these things from a school.' She wants team sport to be 'for everybody', not just the chosen few. With this determination and the new facilities taking shape in the grounds, Mrs Jordan's ideal of 'scholar athletes' may soon be realised.

Singing and orchestral days are a great way for older players to workshop and develop ensemble skills. Budding artists, actors and musicians are spoilt for choice – facilities include a 240 seat theatre complete with box office and professional backstage team. The seriously well-equipped music school, opened by Brian Eno, a former parent, provides ample teaching, practice and recording space. Girls must participate in some musical activity during their first two senior school years – the emphasis is on taking part and most choirs, orchestras and ensembles are audition free. Music for all is the message with break and lunchtime concerts and, recently, a Garsington opera workshop.

Pupils' paintings of a very high standard are proudly displayed all over the school, including the head's office. A level results for fine art should also be put in a frame – almost every candidate is awarded A*. As we marvelled at the work in the splendid double height art building our guide confessed that it was 'a bit overwhelming for those who can't draw.'

CCF (from year 10 upwards) is 'huge' and girls love the camps – whether in Dartmoor, Scotland or the school grounds. D of E attracts good numbers too. Tempting range of trips from geography in the Alps and diving in the Red Sea to expeditions and charity work in Ethiopia, Kenya and Zanzibar.

Boarding: About a third of pupils board, either full time or weekly. Head is not a fan of flexi boarding (describes it as 'bed blocking') but school may accommodate pupils for one offs (plays, trips) or family emergencies. Year group boarding houses are cheerful with plenty of home comforts. Most have double study bedrooms with good storage and room mates are swapped around each term (sixth form can choose). For those who don't go home on Fridays there seems to be plenty on offer – we saw sign up sheets for strawberry picking, a day trip to Brighton and a make up workshop. Sixth form boarders have kitchens and may cook for themselves as long as they ask in advance – enables house parents to be sure girls aren't missing meals. They can also go to parties and stay over with school friends – parents are emailed for permission.

Background and atmosphere: Founded in 1915 by a group of evangelical Christians to provide a 'sound education for girls to fit them for the demands and opportunities likely to arise after the war.' Occupied various houses in the area, trading up as it grew from 18 to today's 1,000 (including 280 in prep school). Present main school was built in the 1930s in a sharp-edged, no frills style described (rather kindly) as neo-Georgian. Set in 23 acres just off Oxford's busy London Road, it's right next to the hospitals and ambulance sirens lend it an extra urban edge. Despite its town site there's a sense of space, and plenty of greenery remains undeveloped. Newer buildings are very well appointed, especially the Diamond Jubilee Building – home to large, modern teaching rooms, ICT and that award-winning robot.

Lessons we observed were challenging but not intimidating, girls were contributing enthusiastically and seemed keen to have a go and share opinions. In an A level English 'taster' class we were impressed by how quickly students got to grips with new ideas. A brief introduction to the principles of critical theory and they were off, producing Marxist and feminist readings of Where the Wild Things Are. The library is all you could ask for and dedicated librarians also provide a cuttings service – filing cabinets hold the latest journal or newspaper material for over 250 subjects. This resource, hand in hand with Google, introduces girls – particularly sixth formers tackling the EPQ – to university style research techniques. 'They know everything here', said our guides.

Pastoral care, well-being and discipline: Parents and girls we spoke to were generally very positive about pastoral care, but the school is large and busy and we did wonder how quickly a quiet or unhappy child would be noticed. This is where the sixth form prefects come in. Each class of around 20 is allocated two prefects, whose job is not only to be a friendly non-teacher face, but also to get to know the girls and alert staff if they suspect a girl is struggling socially or in any other way. There is also a drop-in counsellor. Prefects are elected by peers and candidates for head girl and deputies have to make speeches at hustings before those on the chosen short list go before senior staff for final interviews. Win or lose, it's all very good experience. Sixth form common room was looking rather forlorn when we visited, but it's since had a make over and is now, apparently, much more inviting.

Some concerns expressed about the lunch arrangements – feeding 800 girls in an hour and a half must be quite a challenge. Sittings are by year group, but with only five minutes in between, one pupil acknowledged that lunch break was 'a bit of a mosh.' Staff 'bouncers' are positioned outside for crowd control and 'when it's raining you push.' All good fun when you're used to it but 'quite intimidating' for newbies. Once you're in, though, food is seriously good, varied and plentiful. We enjoyed a delicious meal in the large, modern dining hall decorated with huge canvases of old school photos – all the food is serve yourself and girls help themselves to as much as they like of everything.

Pupils and parents: 'Not too posh' – nice, swishy-haired girls who don't seem to kick too hard against uniform, skirt length and make up regulations. Most families from Oxford's private and public sector employers – medics, lawyers, academics, IT professionals. Head says, 'girls understand that parents are making an investment'. Growing cohort of weekly boarders commute from London on the Oxford tube (stops outside). International students from 47 countries – IB and rowing reputation are attracting more Europeans. Zealous overseas recruitment in the past led to large groups of one nationality (evident when we visited the sixth form Costa café). Parents say that this has been 'a big issue' and they would like to see better integration. Head acknowledges these concerns and says things are now being managed. OGs include Baroness Young, Julia Somerville, Lady Longford, Christina Onassis, Emma Watson and Lily van den Broecke

Entrance: Several applicants for every place (but bear in mind that girls will be sitting for other schools too). For entry at 11+ girls sit papers in English, maths and non-verbal reasoning and have an interview. Prep school candidates (13+ entry) come for an interview and taster day after the pre-test. Sixth form entrants sit exams at Headington in the November before their proposed entry.

Exit: Inevitably some girls depart post-GCSE (31 per cent in 2018), lured to local co-ed sixth forms, although we hear that it's not uncommon for there to be a return to the fold after a few weeks. Nearly all sixth form leavers go on to university, including usually several to Oxbridge – six in 2018, plus 21 medics, dentists and vets; LSE, UCL, Durham, Bristol, Bath, Birmingham trending currently, with six per cent off to study abroad in 2018: Europe, USA, Hong Kong, Japan.

Money matters: Academic, music, art, drama and sports scholarships (£300 per year). Means-tested bursaries of up to 100 per cent of fees plus help for Forces and clergy. Of course there are extras but parents told us that these weren't unreasonable; they also said that they approved of the sensible and inexpensive uniform.

Remarks: This dynamic school is going from strength to strength. True to its founders' aims, nearly a century on it is still sending out girls ready and able to tackle whatever the future has to hold.

Heathfield School

London Road, Ascot, Berkshire SL5 8BQ

Ages 11–18 **Pupils** 181 **Sixth form** 56 **Boarders** 150 full **C of E**

Fees: Day: £22,185 – £22,800; Boarding: £35,760 – £36,630 pa

01344 898343
www.heathfieldschool.net

Headmistress: Since 2016, Marina Gardiner Legge, previously director of studies. MA in English literature from Oxford and PGCE from the University of Hong Kong, where she started her teaching career relatively late, having previously worked in business marketing, the charitable sector and teaching horse riding to disabled children. Head of year and assistant head at Rutlish School, a boys' comprehensive in south London, before joining Heathfield in 2013.

Go-getting, no-nonsense, earnest, engaging and frank, she is on a clear mission to change the school's reputation (parents told us that girls are known as 'clotted cream' among some local schools – as in, thick and rich). 'I'm sick and tired of hearing people say this school isn't for clever girls,' she says. 'We are easily comparable to Downe House, yet often seen as its poorer cousin.' With dwindling numbers in some year groups presumably reflecting her fears, it's no wonder her first job in post has been heading a mammoth marketing campaign, albeit with some hiccups as the school's introduction of a weekly boarding option caused such uproar among traditionalist parents that it was promptly reverted.

Girls claim she's a visible presence (often out and about; teaches English once a week) and that she 'commands respect while being incredibly supportive.' Parents seem keen too. 'She's picked the school up and is running with it – great to see.'

Lives on site (having previously commuted from Fulham). Has three grown-up daughters and hobbies include writing poetry and running. 'I ran a marathon, having never been a runner until after I got over two bouts of cancer 10 years ago. I'm all about perseverance and resilience.'

Academic matters: Aims high across the subject range, with parents certainly getting their money's worth when it comes to added value (Durham University research puts school in top 12 per cent schools nationally and in the top 17 per cent of independent schools nationally for pupil progress) and generous staffing levels (one to every four pupils), which result in small class sizes with average of 15 and maximum of 19, often single figures for sixth form.

Top line results mostly good overall. In 2018, 32 per cent A*/A grades at A level. Spikier profile for individual subjects – strong in art and design, photography, psychology, biology, English literature and RS, but sprinkling of D grades in some facilitating subjects. Total of 24 subjects on offer, mostly traditional, with economics and film studies recently added. Slightly mixed results at GCSE, too (41 per cent A*-A/9-7). Strongest GCSE subjects include RS, English literature, geography and history, with most popular subjects include history and geography. Photography a new addition.

Setting? 'Absolutely!' exclaims head, although it starts from form 3 (year 9) upwards in English, maths and science. Languages kick off with Spanish and French from form 1 (year 7), Latin from year 9. Current push on sciences, off to high profile start with Lord Winston opening new STEM building, boosted by lively lessons, although it's proving a slow burner, with A level take up improved but still some way to go.

Girls asked to set their own targets (under supervision), which are reviewed every half term. 'Teachers know you well, so they know what makes you learn best,' one girl told us. 'And there are subject clinics if you feel you are falling behind.' It's no exam factory, though – 'it gets great academic results without being a pressure cooker,' summed up one parent.

SEN (15 per cent when we visited) well-resourced though Spectrum centre (an unfortunate name if ever there was one, although the name is intended to evoke rainbow shades of pupil diversity rather than autism) is widely used as drop-in service for walking worried, as well as those with identified need (headed by dyslexia). 'There's no stigma,' a pupil assured us. But SEN pupils must be able to follow the curriculum and cope socially and nobody misses lessons, with some in-class support from higher level teaching assistant as well as group or one-to-one sessions, some after school.

Games, options, the arts: Strong on sports, with an emphasis on team sports, matches often twice a week. Regularly attended by parents and staff, including head ('I go to as many off-site matches as possible'), with some of sportiest playing across several year groups – only drawback the minnow vs shark issue if facing opponents from far larger schools. As for those who aren't sporty, 'they're expected to get stuck in anyway, and it's a jolly good thing too,' one parent told us.

Lacrosse popular, no doubt helped by decent tours – USA, Canada among them – and pupil success (regular selection for county and regional squads and one girl picked for great glory with England's development squad). Netball, rounders, tennis and swimming do well and prominence also given to fitness, with one housemistress being trained up in zumba when we visited. Strong equestrian resources coordinated by dedicated staff member, adept at finding good livery stables and organising dashing events (like military riding with swords) – and the school has its own polo league too. Don't expect ponies on the front lawn, though – all off site. Everything else – including courts, indoor swimming pool, sports hall, fitness suite and playing fields – on site.

Outstanding art department, with some spectacular work dotting the walls (although the three most notable canvases 'have been there for years,' say pupils) plus impressive textiles adorning mannequins, including a ballgown made from intricate layers of denim, with red sequin Nike logo on the bodice. In fact, one of the things the school is best known for is nurturing BRIT style talent in the arts, bolstered by close ties with London College of Fashion, which provides proactive course and careers advice to interested sixth formers. We were particularly blown away by an impressive rail of avant garde garments ready for the school's annual fashion show (the hottest date on the school calendar, say pupils) which teams up with music and drama department (think actors juggling and live music). Very well-resourced photography department (with two staff and a dark room).

Drama department thriving, with whole-school Christmas performance (the likes of Lady Windermere's Fan) and LAMDA is strong here too. Good at knowing who'd rather take a back seat, though nobody escapes altogether, with termly chapel reading for all, even the shyest accepting it as the norm. Plenty of opportunities for the musical too, from audition entry chapel choir to choice of bands including orchestra and flute ensemble for instrumentalists. Sixty-four girls currently taking peripatetic instrument lessons.

No shortage of clubs – mainly sports, but academic and arts based also popular, plus debating. Head also keen on girls suggesting and running their own – recent examples include gardening club and new online newspaper called the Heathfield Hub. Plentiful day trips ('Tomorrow we're off to a climate conference,' one sixth former told us) plus some residentials, including the form 3 'rite of passage' trip to Barcelona, part of a geography and classics syllabus.

Boarding: No boarding houses as such. Instead, the upstairs of the main building is dedicated to bedrooms – shared (up to eight girls) for younger years, then own rooms from form 3 upwards (en suite for head girl). The ones we saw were roomy, light, homely and tidy, but with reassuring pockets of clutter and little touches like teddy bears and blankets turning beds into dens – no military style scrutiny here. A gizmo a year policy means you get toaster and kettle from year 10, dishwasher and sandwich maker a year later etc – causes great excitement for the girls. But despite close proximity of bedrooms, girls encouraged not to use them during the day. 'We want them to feel they're going home after school.'

Levels of off-duty shrieking suggested that good times were demonstrably had by all, though 'not definitely not like a sleepover,' we were told by a pupil. (As one dorm is directly above head's study, probably just as well...)

Super-efficient and kindly housemistress manages it all, helped by team with background in childminding, nannying or youth work rather than academic background. 'You can talk to them about anything and they're so helpful,' a pupil told us. 'One girl in my daughter's room couldn't sleep and they got her a sleep therapist and yoga – nothing is too much trouble,' said a parent.

Two closed weekends a term, otherwise first two years who want to can go home after Saturday sport, returning Sunday evening – similar freedom of choice for sixth formers. No weekly boarding – parent power soon stopped that, even though the school had printed it on their school sign (some felt it took away from the traditional boarding school image; others worried it was a sign that the school was facing financial difficulties – hotly denied). Many suspect weekly boarding will eventually be phased in discreetly.

Weekend activities mainly include sports (swimming pool, tennis courts and the sports hall 'in constant use,' says school literature) and there's also dance and music, craft, cookery and discos, bands, quizzes and competitions in the evenings. 'The themed dinners are good too – everything from Alice in Wonderland to Harry Potter,' one girl told us. Outings as well – cinema, museums etc. Older ones do less, with licensed lazing about, along with some socials with local boys' schools.

Background and atmosphere: Heathfield is just one of a number of tiny, charming girls' schools in the area that, to the untrained eye, can seem pretty much indistinguishable. But

H

what sets this one apart is a particularly happy and homelike feel with a dash of top school trimmings. (That and the penny-sized home-made biscuits and meringues served with tea to all visitors.) It's as if someone has carefully curated a best of boarding school experience, from the tiny, bow-fronted Harry Potter-esque tuck shop (where, said sixth former, 'hordes of first formers run to get strawbs and ice cream and eat them in little groups on the pitches') to the occasional water fight and spontaneous dancing, both popular exam pressure relievers. In short, it's a bubble – so much so that you might wonder how it's managed to survive in today's fast-living society. And there – explain parents – lies its appeal. 'I'm not saying it's cut off from the real world – it genuinely isn't – but these aren't streetwise girls and they stay children for longer, while getting an excellent academic grounding and holistic education. If you like the sound of that, this is the school for you.'

There's not a hair out of place (and if there were, it would be cashmere) on the 36-acre site; pupils wear their uniforms with pride; and we're met with a look of horror when we asked if there are assemblies on issues such as self-harm or anorexia ('We're all about prevention here – so we'd make sure they ate healthily in the first place').

H

Originally founded in London by Victorian educational bigwig Eleanor Beatrice Wyatt for the disadvantaged of South Ken (doubtless a more substantial group in 1882 than today), school moved to current site in 1899 when she decided to concentrate on training future educators in greener surroundings. In 2006, gained pupils and financial boost after merger with St Mary's Wantage, commemorated in attractive performing arts centre, old honours boards displayed in foyer. Wyatt would have no problem recognising the school today, down to high church accoutrements that include a termly candlelit mass once a term (white dresses on the uniform list) in tiny chapel, pews bearing engraved names of all leavers and heads. But that's not to say facilities are lagging behind – those of note including the dazzling shaker/Laura Ashley style fifth and sixth form common rooms leading off old assembly hall, plus well-stocked pristine white-shelved library, uber-modern science labs and playing field where groups of friends congregate in summer.

Pastoral care, well-being and discipline: Strong nurturing culture. 'But without the cotton wool,' adds the head firmly. When asked who the girls talk to if they're unhappy, the consensus was there was nobody they couldn't talk to. 'You could even go to the head if you wanted,' said one, with more common sounding boards including the housemistress, teachers, counsellor (two days a week), 'independent listener' ('hardly used, but important they are there,' says head) and the girls themselves (with an unfortunately named 'crush' system, whereby a sixth former becomes a younger one's crush to help look out for them). Small size means school tends to function as a family ('including inevitable sibling rows'). Alpha personalities probably better suited to larger school.

Traditionally, more carrot than stick when it comes to behavioural policies, although everyone agrees the current head has stepped up on strictness – with detentions now set for poorly worn uniform, lack of punctuality, misbehaviour in class etc. Parents clearly pleased that girls who see it as 'cool to continually misbehave' get their just deserts (22 temporary exclusions in just over two years). A number of girls have also been expelled or given the option of going quietly during the last few years, say parents, although school insists it's actually just one girl. Smoking in school grounds historically an issue – and some parents stay it still is, although school reports that current head 'has clamped down hard on it.'

Pupils and parents: Almost one in 10 mums are old girls, which adds to the already strong likelihood of being invited to socials (mass pub lunches before exeats), as well as to the fiercely strong school loyalty. Indeed, plenty of old money keeps on rolling down the generations as satisfied customers send on their daughters and granddaughters, although head insists it's a more mixed bag than in the past.

Balance is firmly in favour of 'British girls' (just under 80 per cent of total, a fifth from expat families, international pupils largely from Europe, Russia and Far East). Old girls include designer Nina Campbell, actor Sienna Miller, polar explorer Rosie Stancer and the late Isabella Blow. In fact, so many famous names that aren't so much dropped as infused into school literature. When you've so many celebs that Mrs Le Bon judging the school fashion show merits only a (large) postage stamp-sized picture in the school mag, you've got nothing to prove about your connections.

Current pupils feature Emilies, Kathies, Charlottes, Daisies and Roses in abundance – a roll call of reassurance. These are the kind of girls who look you in the eye, who are confident, chatty and generally likeable.

Entrance: Offers (mainly in form 1 but quite a few in form 3) are conditional on passing school's own entrance papers (English, maths and non-verbal reasoning), taken in November with places offered in December. Places also available in the sixth form – interview plus minimum five grade 4+ GCSEs with 6s in A level subjects. School is looking for girls who are ambitious, good communicators, team workers and have creative potential.

Majority of pupils within 50-mile radius, mostly from country preps ('we are seen as a nice continuation – now that I've got my fire working, I just need the black lab,' laughs the head), although some from west London, with Hyde Park School, Knightsbridge Prep, Finton House, Fulham Prep, Eaton Square, Pembridge Hall, Garden House, Broomwood Hall and the Thomas's trio – Clapham, Fulham, Battersea – the biggest feeders. Others from Surrey, Sussex and nearer bits of Hampshire (Ashdowne House, Cottesmore, Daneshill, Farleigh, Godstowe, Wellesley House). A few from East Anglia, Yorkshire, Scotland. Bright locals interested in day places also encouraged to get in touch as this offering is proving more and more popular.

Exit: Some – perhaps 10 per cent – leave post-GCSE. 'Co-ed is a big call,' says head. Of those who stay on, vast majority go to university or college, with one or two off abroad in 2018 (St Petersburg and the American Academy of Dramatic Arts) and the rest to a range including Exeter, Bristol, Durham and Edinburgh, plus art at Bournemouth, Camberwell and Leeds and textile design at Falmouth. One medic (Plymouth) and one vet (Surrey) in 2018.

Money matters: Discounts of 10 per cent for children from diplomatic, 20 per cent for Forces families (five children max in each case) down to five per cent for siblings (flat rate).

Music, drama art and sport scholarships offered at 11+, 13+ and in sixth form. Also academic, by invitation – top 40 per cent of entrants sit extra tests. Confer lots of glory but, at £750 a year, little in the way of spondoolies. Also means-tested bursaries covering all fees ('The bastion of privilege is changing,' insists head). Helping hand extended to existing pupils if family finances hit a crisis.

Remarks: Enchanting and quintessentially British boarding experience with chocolate box-esque quality, though works hard to ensure that it never tips into cutesie. And while this small school produces rounded, ambitious and highly capable girls thanks to its good academic grounding and outstanding opportunities in the arts, one can't help but wonder about its long-term future unless the die-hard traditionalist parents are dragged kicking and screaming into the 21st century.

Heathside School (Weybridge)

Brooklands Lane, Weybridge, Surrey KT13 8UZ

Ages 11–18 **Pupils** 1,260 **Sixth form** 202

01932 846162
www.heathside.surrey.sch.uk

Head of school: Since 2018, Tracy Dohel BSc (maths with economics), MA (maths education), NPQH. Started her working life in the City – 'I wanted to use my maths degree in a way that wasn't number crunching, but with a sister already in teaching there was no way I was going to do that,' she laughs. Soon realised her passion for imparting knowledge and inspiring people, however, so teaching it was. Taught across schools in various London boroughs, most recently Pimlico Academy and City of London Academy, Islington, as vice principal. Prior to coming to Heathside, she was principal at Ark Helenswood Academy in East Sussex, where she got the school from 'requires improvement' to 'good' within two years – 'mainly using a coaching model for staff that I am now introducing here.'

Calm, easy going and razor sharp, she has a rapport with students, six or so of whom she invites for weekly breakfasts with croissants and fruit (seen as a huge treat – they earn merits for the privilege). Had brief jaw dropping moment when we asked her if she teaches – 'Of course!' came the reply. In fact, she particularly relishes the challenge of '14 or so year-olds who don't like maths', getting a real kick out of bringing them back on board. As with most secondary schools of this size, many parents have not had personal dealings with her, but those that have speak highly – 'I had absolutely no problem getting in touch with her, she's very quick to respond and positive too,' one told us. Lives locally with her husband, with interests including fearless pursuits such as open water swimming and motorcycling holidays.

Previous principal, Anne Cullum, is now executive principal of both this school and (when it opens in 2020) Heathside Walton on Thames, which will have 900 students aged 11-16, with 'the same principles but its own identity'. Less soft-around-the-edges, but still very well thought of by parents, she will retain financial control of the school while Ms Dohel will cover the day-to-day running – although during our meeting, she appeared to retain a more governing role than we had anticipated (that said, it was Ms Dohel's first term in post).

Academic matters: Gets very good academic results which put it up with top-performing schools nationally, and it's in the top 10 per cent for value added too. From a non-selective intake, 89 per cent got 4-9 in both maths and English GCSE in 2018, 38 per cent of grades A*-A/9-7. At A level, 68 per cent of the grades were A*-B and 40 per cent A*/A.

Students put it down to 'amazing teaching staff,' who they say 'go above and beyond at every given opportunity.' 'I've never been able to fault them; they have so much time and energy and are so inspiring – and that goes for whether you're a straight A student or you struggle academically,' said one. Another student told us, 'A few times, I've had a good half-hour chat with the teacher after the lesson finishes. It's never a case of, "Lesson done, that's it".' Lots of specialist teachers, even in physics where there's a national shortage, although parents and pupils say business studies is currently suffering due to two staff having been on long term sick leave. Staff are skilled up, valued and consulted – with a particularly impressive menu of CPD offerings, including intensive coaching – with the result that they generally only leave to take up promotion or if moving aboard. Parents pleased that teaching is consistently good, homework always marked, and describe staff as 'enthusiastic' and 'great'. School was praised by Ofsted for its 'meticulous systems to assess and track pupils' progress regularly,' something we saw in action and which stops anyone falling behind.

French and Spanish from year 7; students continue at least one of these languages from year 8, with some setting at GCSE level. Setting also in maths from year 7, while English is taught in mixed ability until year 10. Huge emphasis on English and maths, which are seen as absolutely core; anyone who joins sixth form without maths or English GCSE will have to add it to their timetable – 'they do it until they pass it,' is school's attitude. Good take up of solid traditional subjects like history, geography and single sciences at GCSE, of which most students take nine in total. 'We encourage them to choose subjects that have credibility,' says school.

Sixth form is up against strong local competition but has a reputation for high-quality teaching. Great take up of science and maths at A level, as well as politics; only English lit, no English language. Pupils in search of vocational courses head next door to Brooklands College and other local colleges – the sixth form offers 'academic' A levels only, of which most students do three and some (around 30 the year we visited) do the recently introduced EPQ. Dedicated sixth form block, newer than the main building, ground floor shared with main school.

H

The SEN team helps students with additional needs in a multitude of ways, including screening on entry and support both in and outside the classroom. Clinics offered to sort out subject-based learning needs and dedicated tutors in English and maths are on hand to help any student. One parent told us how this included her daughter, who is in the top set of maths. 'Sometimes, children at the top get forgotten because they'll get through no matter what, but not at this school – they make sure everyone reaches their full potential.' Another parent reported, 'The SENCo is amazing. My son was on her radar straight away and she put so many things in place, including avoiding crowded corridors which can be a trigger for anxiety, and making a reward chart themed on one of his key interests.' That said, one parent told us how 'some older members of staff aren't so open to children with additional needs – one made us feel like we weren't parenting well and had a naughty child and that hasn't been easy at times.' Can cater for most needs, including visual and hearing impairment – some classrooms equipped with induction loops. Access for the physically disabled, including a shower and treatment room, dedicated loos and lift, ramps everywhere – aiming to make whole school accessible, although there were no physically disabled students when we visited.

Games, options, the arts: All valued and well executed. Sport locally renowned, with the school doing well in rugby, football, cricket and netball regionally and occasionally nationally. Also on offer is everything from yoga to cheerleading and table tennis to volleyball. Canoeing on the up. PTA has recently funded the return of sporting colours and the school supports students who play, for example, in football academies. One student was recently named the most up and coming sports personality of the year in London; another plays for Brighton and Hove Albion; while another is a Team GB member for ice hockey.

Drama available at GCSE, but school no longer gets the numbers to justify running it at A level. A play or musical is performed annually (alternating each year), most recently Grease and A Christmas Carol, with students raving about the behind-the-scenes (eg hair and make-up or stage design) opportunities for those not wanting to be in the spotlight. Music very good – hundreds of students get involved, everything from individual lessons to Young Musician of the Year to school orchestras and choirs and after-school clubs. DofE very strong and completion rate good. Fantastic trips including annual ski trip, sports tours in Europe and lots of theatre visits, and the gifted and talented are regularly off to special events. Always loads going on and students encouraged to give it all a go, with financial help available for those on pupil premium (about 10 per cent). Everyone does some community work, eg in a retirement home, other school, or hospice. Art is popular at both GCSE and A level – one student showed us an intriguing portfolio based on the theme of self-injury – 'this student has been predicted a B but this is A standard work – she's come on a treat,' said the teacher.

Strong links with industry and business. For example Glaxo Smith Kline helps with science and local businesses and parents support a work experience day, conducting mock interviews with students, mentoring and giving help with CVs etc. Lots of (Ofsted highly praised) governors drawn from local businesses. Geographically fortunate, also has links with local businesses like Mercedes, Honda, McLaren.

Background and atmosphere: The school is located down a quiet lane, opposite a cemetery and playing fields, surrounded by trees. No access down the lane for drivers at school start and finish times – parents are asked to drop at the top. Fifteen minutes from station, lots walk – the lane is awash with a sea of students in their cobalt blue blazers at the start and finish of the day.

Most of the buildings date from 1966, when the school was built for just 500 students. This is the main beef for most parents ('it's so outdated', 'many of the facilities could do with updating, some are very old' etc) but a new year 8 classroom block and relatively recently refurbished sixth form centre provide more fresh-looking buildings and there have been other more minor refurbs, for example downstairs in the main school. But the students seem to barely notice (except for the graffiti in the toilets, although there is less than there was, they told us) and even those that do aren't fussed – 'facilities don't affect the teaching, so it really doesn't matter to us,' shrugged one. A few had niggles about the music facilities, but there's a new building project in the pipeline. We loved the buzz of the food tech rooms – year 8s making delicious-smelling pizzas – and the welcoming vibe of the sixth form common room with café, with quiet study room with computers for those who want to knuckle down. The library is pretty average and we'd like to have seen more science practicals in action, although we were assured there are many.

This is a happy and caring school where staff are committed and students generally enthusiastic, all packaged in a wonderfully calm atmosphere. And despite large numbers, it's not a scary place for year 7s, with a two-day induction for all newbies and a series of visits throughout the summer for the more vulnerable ones to get used to their new learning environment. There's a good feeling of community around the place – echoes of a primary school atmosphere where key staff know the students and really engage with them. 'We tell them they can achieve whatever they want.'

Pastoral care, well-being and discipline: Plenty of non-teaching pastoral staff on hand, and reassuringly the students seem to know who to go to in times of need. 'Teachers regularly check in with you, asking you how you are and making sure you're not stressed or worried about anything,' one student added. Instead of a counsellor, there's a well-being lead who takes a more holistic approach and works with both students and staff, doing questionnaires, giving assemblies on mental health issues and was in the midst of a community-wide pilot project on mindfulness when we visited. Parents who have needed to call on the school pastorally say it is 'exceptional in its support – they go over and beyond what they need to do.'

Strict? You bet, but students take it in their stride, all agreeing the rules are fair and sanctions (mostly detentions) explicit. Most parents are in favour too – 'you do get some that don't like it, but for me it works, especially with teenagers who need clear boundaries,' said one. Only one full-time exclusion in the last year and none in the two years prior to that, although there are around five temporary exclusions per term – 'generally of students who don't do what's asked of them.' But whereas students in isolation were previously based in a room on a main corridor, attracting too much attention, they've now been moved right out of the way and have no chance to revel in their notoriety. The school's code of conduct, 'Give respect/gain respect', is well known to all. The eight-strong senior leadership team is seen around the place. Plenty of praise, with the merit system rewarding students with things like jumping the lunch queue. Mobiles allowed in some lessons, but otherwise must be hidden at all times. Bullying not seen as much of an issue and dealt with promptly when it does rear its ugly head.

Generally pupils' behaviour and attitude to learning are good – it's OK, even cool, to be clever here. School repays that with ethos of 'listening to the student voice', with a lively student impact team. Head girl and boy, prefects, librarians and house system all in full swing. Successful mentoring programme. Pupils fairly smart – less so in sixth form, where jeans, t-shirts and hoodies become a uniform all of their own.

Pupils and parents: Middle class, reflecting local area. Lots could afford to send their children privately but choose Heathside instead – whole families go through. Engagement from parents is outstanding, with 100 per cent attendance at last parents' evening. Friends of Heathside, the PTA, raises between £30-40k a year for the school, plus all the usual mix of quiz nights, parties, murder mystery events and so on. Students we met were polite, mature, friendly and motivated to achieve – the kind any parent would be proud of.

Entrance: A real scrum to get in here from Weybridge, Walton and Hersham area. Parents prepared to go down the private route will try their luck here before shelling out fees. School is also the state school of choice for families coming from abroad. Average of 700 plus applications for 210 places – 'my parents were very, very happy when they heard I got in,' said one student. At 11+ students join from up to 20 primaries, but predominantly from Ashley CofE (Aided), Cleves School, St James CofE. Strong links with its primary feeders – employs staff to go into them on a weekly basis. Otherwise usual sibling and distance criteria in operation. No longer selects a percentage by aptitude.

To join the sixth form (and this goes for existing students, as well as new ones – around 10 a year join from outside), students need five subjects at grades 9-5 including English and maths plus special entry requirements for individual subjects eg 7 for maths.

Exit: Surprisingly (although perhaps less so when you look at smaller numbers in sixth form compared to lower down) up to half leave after GCSEs – to study either for more vocational qualifications or at the lower colleges. Sixth form leavers to a range of universities. In 2018, four to Oxbridge and two medics; others to eg Exeter, Durham, Warwick, Southampton, Birmingham, Nottingham, Leeds, Bristol, Cardiff, Sheffield, Edinburgh, where they study everything from engineering to the arts and lots more besides. Parents told us careers advice is excellent in sixth form, but one or two felt it could be stronger lower down the school.

Remarks: An unpretentious, welcoming school with high standards and high expectations, offering its students a good all-round experience. Winning combination of committed staff and eager students – state education as it should be.

The Hertfordshire & Essex High School and Science College

Warwick Road, Bishop's Stortford, Hertfordshire CM23 5NJ

Ages 11–18 **Pupils** 1,295 **Sixth form** 404 (98 boys)

01279 654127
www.hertsandessex.herts.sch.uk

Executive Headteacher: Since 2009, Cathy Tooze MEd (Cantab), previously head of Hadleigh High School in Suffolk. Positive and authoritative, her manner is relaxed, though you feel she can be firm when the situation demands. Instantly likable, and both interesting and interested, pupils wax lyrical about her approachability, fairness and commitment to not letting a single student slip through the net. 'She'll always give you a smile, and if she's strict about something, you know there's a good reason for it,' said one student. A National Leader of Education and Ofsted inspector, she is often away from the school, but has created a strong leadership team to ensure she's not indispensable. 'I'm not a massively hands-on type of head anyway,' she says, pointing out that she doesn't teach much (an hour a week of maths to years 8 and 9 when we visited) and she doesn't pretend to know all the students by name. That said, she eats with students in the dining hall daily, as well as taking assemblies and regularly visiting classrooms. 'Students often pop into my office unannounced,' she adds, 'asking anything from "Can we do a cake sale for charity?" to "Can we tell you about something we did today?"' Parents describe her as ambitious, aspirational and sincere. 'She's a really good role model for the girls because she's so driven, but also such a nice person, and she absolutely practises what she preaches,' said one.

Co-headteachers since September 2018 are Emma Kirkham and Richard Vaughan.

Academic matters: A very successful school, a particular feat given the fact that it is totally non-selective. In 2018, 92 per cent got 9-4 in both English and maths; 41 per cent A*/A grades. Executive head (EH) puts it down to 'exceptional standards of teaching and learning' and the very positive work ethic, along with ensuring the school is not a mere exam factory. 'We realise that the greatest gift we can give our students is a fantastic CV, but you can't do that if they're not happy and enriched,' she says.

Certainly no glazed eyes or yawning in classes when we visited. Chalk and talk is out; hands-on, interactive teaching is in. The curriculum itself is traditional, with modern aspects, including technology, with one computer to every three students, although iPads only regularly used in sixth form.

First two weeks in year 7 are spent rigorously but pleasantly assessing students, then setting them individual and detailed targets, with progress tracked three times a year thereafter. Targets regularly notched up to help raise expectations, although they never come down, with students provided with peer mentor and/or one-to-one catch-up teaching to get them back on course if they stray. 'I've had three daughters at the school and they're all quite different academically, but have all thrived,' said one parent.

Generously staffed (80 teaching staff when we visited) and good admin support allows teachers to spend more time in the classroom and less on pen-pushing. All teach their degree subject, which, the EH says, means they are focused, committed and keen to broaden the students' experiences through a huge variety of trips and extracurricular activities. Regular out-of-hours email communication between staff and students and relatively little staff turnover. 'All the teachers are involved in research into pedagogy,' adds EH. School has a partnership with Cambridge University for the Initial Teacher Training Programme, and is an experienced provider of placements for trainees. Also works with other local secondary schools (Leventhorpe, The Bishop's Stortford High School, and Presdales) to deliver its professional studies programme, which develops trainees' understanding of research and pedagogy.

As a science specialist college, it's no surprise that many students take triple science, which stands them in good stead for A levels. School has been chosen as one of 34 Maths Hubs across England and leads a number of work groups across Essex and Herts to develop outstanding practice in maths teaching, making this another strong subject. Languages growing in popularity. French and Spanish compulsory until year 9, and Mandarin and German have recently been introduced. For many, the technologies are a good contrast to the more academic classes, and there are some unexpected GSCE subjects including astronomy. Setting for languages, maths and English from year 7, although 'the setting is not particularly tight, with lots of moving around.' Top sets can number as many as 28, but the lower classes are often much smaller.

Very wide choice of subjects at A level – all the traditional academic options, plus more unusual ones including Latin, photography and government and politics. Also offers further maths. In 2018, 70 per cent A*-B and 36 per cent A*/A grades. Sixth formers have a half-day of enrichment on Wednesday, which includes DofE, extra languages and sport, and also listen to struggling readers in year 7. Cambridge Pre-U global perspectives and research course gets intellectually bright students studying hard and thinking outside the box, and stands them in particularly good stead if applying for Oxbridge.

Able, gifted and talented students are identified early on, in addition to those who will benefit from individual learning plans, including SEN (66 when we visited). With students arriving from around 40 primary schools, the number of students requiring such help is often quite large, especially at the beginning. Among these are the average of five students in every year 7 who require some catch-up time with the school's visiting primary school teacher on areas like phonics. The cognitive ability tests in year 7 can also highlight issues like dyslexia that may not have previously been identified. Other students have particular needs such as visual impairment and cerebral palsy, which can require learning materials being adapted accordingly and staff training put in place so that they can continue to ensure these students fully access the curriculum. The base for all this is The Lodge, an on-site converted house with living rooms and bedrooms that have been transformed into welcoming looking breakout rooms, although help is classroom based where possible. Impressive number of staff, including five teaching assistants timetabled to offer both in-class support and some small group literacy sessions, SEN learning manager, two learning coaches and one counsellor. Ground floor access is good throughout the site. Where some of the school buildings are inaccessible to wheelchairs above ground level, rooming considerations are taken into account when timetabling.

Games, options, the arts: Netball and cricket are the strongest sports, with the school boasting county champions in both. Tag rugby, basketball, volleyball, trampolining, water polo, futsal and judo are also popular, with plenty of gold, silver and bronze medals from the Herts County School Games, and indoor rowing is an unusual forte. Facilities good, although tired in places, including hard courts for tennis, netball and basketball, four rounders pitches plus a football pitch on site, as well as a 25m indoor pool and dance studio. Has its own large playing fields with hockey pitches and a grass running track five minutes' walk away plus a brand new sports hall complex complete with floodlit Astro and six netball/tennis courts. Plenty of extracurricular sporting opportunities, with sixth formers continuing an interest in sports, at which point the boys compete well on the football and rugby fields. Links with the Jacqui Ison School of Dance, Bishop's Stortford Volleyball Club and Hertfordshire Cricket to bring coaches into school and develop school-club links. 'It doesn't matter if you're not sporty, though, as they're inclusive, but not pushy,' said one student.

Art and DT taken seriously, with students inspired to produce work that is original, skilful and personal. Facilities excellent and welcoming, including industrial lasercutter and 3D printer. Makes use of the Rhodes Centre in the town for exhibitions, raising the school's local profile. Exceptional work displayed in public places throughout the school too.

The music block across the road is a hive of activity, with the two big teaching rooms and several break-out rooms all in full use when we visited (one small group performed a Coldplay song for us, having only practised for about half-an-hour). One of four local schools to give entry to eight pupils who show exceptional musical aptitude at age 11 – 'It's about an innate aptitude for music, not experience'. Plenty of other students with musical ability entering through usual channels, though – 10 per cent learn an instrument. Concerts described as 'breathtaking.' Several choirs, an orchestra (for students with grade 5 minimum and includes a harpist) and ensembles for regular playing practice, including junior strings, jazz band among others. Combines with drama for whole school performances, with recent examples including Hairspray; new drama studio plus film and media suite.

School has the British Council International Schools Award and, as such, has a genuine focus on global citizenship. Close links with Eden High School in Uganda for over a decade (teacher exchanges and an annual trip for year 12s and 13s, where they build a house, work in a nursery and teach English) and a science exchange programme with a school in Germany. Other trips include Cambodia and the school had just established a partnership with a school in China when we visited. Interact Club for young Rotarians run in sixth form, which had raised £13,500 for charity the year we visited (overall, the school had raised £17,000).

Background and atmosphere: The original buildings, which date back to 1909, have the look and feel of a grammar school in a leafy and private residential road a mile or so from the town centre (it's a dead end so hardly any traffic). In fact, The Bishop's Stortford Secondary School for Girls was initially founded to prepare girls for a career in teaching for a fee of £3 a term. In 1944 fees were waived and the school was granted self-governing status by King George V, who presented a portrait of himself that still hangs in the impressively panelled school hall.

New teaching blocks have been added in the intervening years, all of which have generously sized classrooms and other teaching spaces (no bursting at the seams here) and a house over the road was acquired to make an impressive music school. Decent sized science labs and a well-used library, open from 8am-5pm, with a 40-strong book club and 26 active student librarians. 'It's not a geeky library, but a really lively hub,' said one student. Whizzy new sixth form centre with café, IT centre and library.

Plenty of clubs, including astronomy club, media club and jazz, so although the school day is officially 8.40am-3.40pm, many students arrive earlier and leave later (although generally not beyond 5pm). Sixth formers can leave the school for one hour at lunchtimes, with many driving into town or having a driving lesson. 'But as the food is so good, many stay,' said one.

A student reception, run by years 7 and 8, gives students a chance to learn valuable skills, whilst visitors get greeted by the girls themselves. Atmosphere around the school is laid back, yet purposeful. Strong links with local primary schools.

Pastoral care, well-being and discipline: Coaching and mentoring are big here, with trained coaches offering one-to-one coaching sessions and sixth formers trained as peer mentors who support pupils lower down the school by acting as 'buddies'. Leadership also strong, with a head boy and girl as well as a swathe of prefects and a school council, who have achieved such things as improved student toilets and better cooking facilities in the sixth form common room.

Form teachers send postcards home to parents if students do particularly good work, go out of their way to help another student etc, with five postcards resulting in a letter home. No real discipline problems, with less than a handful of students, if that, attending Friday afternoon detentions, mostly for uniform infringements (four of these gets you a detention), chewing gum or forgetting homework three times in a row. An immediate one-day exclusion rule for use of bad language, and EH says she would exclude for bullying, but in reality everyone is so disapproving of it (students looked aghast when we asked if there was any) that any problems are nipped in the bud. School awarded a Stonewall School Champions Bronze Award – given to those with good policies to tackle homophobic and transphobic bullying.

A form per year for each of the five houses, with half-termly competitions in sport, music and others such as best hamper for Harvest Festival. 'The house points system creates healthy competition.'

Pastoral care second-to-none, according to the parents we spoke to, one of whom has a daughter who's suffered extreme mental health problems, including the need for an ambulance at school. 'They could not have been more amazing with her, with staff putting in a lot of time and effort to help and providing a complete open-door policy, as well as special measures and contacts where necessary.'

Pupils and parents: A half-an-hour's drive is the maximum distance that students tend to travel, with the majority much closer. On paper, local competition is hot, with parents spoilt for choice amidst excellent state secondaries in Bishop's Stortford, but the traditional approach to education and single-sex environment makes this school particularly popular for parents of girls (and boys at sixth form). Indeed, it is often picked ahead of the local fee-paying institutions. 'This means we are very fortunate in having many families that have the same vision of education as us, which makes for an easy partnership,' says EH.

Students here are keen to learn; they are determined, sensible and savvy learners. Boys enter at sixth form; 'It was so easy to fit in,' one boy told us.

Active PTA, a proactive governing body and a parental forum. Parents are kept in touch with weekly news updates and newsletters roughly once every half term; requests to see the head are usually granted for the next day.

Entrance: Non-selective, except for five per cent of places reserved for students with an aptitude for music, and another five per cent for sports. Amounting to eight students in each discipline, these places are highly sought-after, with around 200 students applying. Regularly three times as many applicants as year 7 places, with children in the looked after system/SEN prioritised, followed by siblings and staff children, then it comes down to where you live. All students are visited in their primary school prior to joining the school.

Around 450 applications for 190 sixth form places; about a third currently boys. Five 6s or over, with a minimum of 4 in English and maths, to succeed – plus 6 or 7 in selected A level subjects. Existing students who meet this criteria are prioritised. Each year, around 70 students who have achieved seven 9-7s at GCSE are supported towards an Oxbridge or Russell Group destination, with courses including the Cambridge Pre-U global perspectives and research course.

Exit: Around 40 per cent leave after GCSE, primarily to do a BTec, performing arts qualification or vocational qualification. Of those who stay on, 85 per cent go on to university, the rest to prestigious apprenticeships or performing arts courses. Two to Oxbridge in 2018, plus three medics. Many to other Russell Group universities; East Anglia, Kent, Nottingham and Reading the most popular destinations recently; several off to study psychology, with others doing eg physics with theoretical astrophysics, ancient history, midwifery and automotive engineering.

Remarks: This school manages a clever combination of being laid-back and fun, whilst at the same time focused and resolute in striving for the best. Coupled with the school's astonishing attention to detail in the assessing, motivating and monitoring of each and every student, it's no wonder that there really isn't a type of character or learner that won't fit in here – and more than that, has every possible chance of flourishing, with the school regularly appearing in the top three of the comprehensive school league tables. An exceptionally well-oiled machine, this school embraces new attitudes towards education whilst holding onto strong traditional values and, in doing so, provides a dazzling learning environment for hard-working pupils.

Highfield and Brookham Schools

Highfield Lane, Liphook, Hampshire GU30 7LQ

Ages 3–13 **Pupils** 465 **Boarders** 130 full, 7 weekly (from 7 years)
C of E

Fees: Day £11,100- £21,525; Boarding £23,850 – £26,250 pa

01428 728000
www.highfieldandbrookham.co.uk

Head of Highfield: Since 1999, Phillip Evitt, MA (Cambridge) and previously head of history at Dulwich College (50s). Brainy, articulate and a dead ringer for Tony Blair in his glory days, reckon a fair few parents (particularly the mums), some staff and probably pupils too, if able to connect with dim and distant political past.

Personable (head, that is – we can't comment on T Blair) with smile, voice, animation and epic hand gestures to the fore, but very much his own man. Attractively self-deprecating – 'It's very sweet of you,' he says when complimented. Emphatically not a spin doctor, he's 'totally genuine' thought a parent (coal-effect gas fire in his study was only non-authentic accessory).

He's good with the 'pushy, intelligent, successful parents,' said a dad and even better at cultivating highly effective relationships with senior school heads, securing places through 'amazing contacts to enable you to get what you want. If school's operating well, that's really what you need at the end.'

Leads a happy band of teachers who have 'a strong sense of unity – they're all good mates,' thought one, though it's taking a few turns of the wheel to secure uniform quality across the subject range. Maths and sciences 'excellent' but 'weaker in languages,' reckoned one parent, though 'not borne out in the sets the children are placed in at senior school,' says school.

Lyrical about post, for which he was head(master)hunted despite having no plans to go to the country and prepare for government. 'I never aspired to headship.' Drove down 'on a profoundly unpromising late April day' battling new baby sleeplessness (last of four children, all – impressively – home births, now aged from teens to their 20s, who came through the school), and was instantly captivated by pupil élan as future charges played in the rain with evident enjoyment. 'I thought "how intriguing." These were children who felt comfortable being children, they didn't have that world weariness of the south London streetwise 13 or 14 year old.'

Modestly assumed he wouldn't suit. Of course he did, and still does. Now well into his second decade, he's sixth head since school's foundation in Southampton in 1892, though far from being its longest serving (number two, member of family that still owns the school and responsible for move to purpose-built accommodation in 1907, clocked up a staggering 49 years).

Not much given to imposing his own world view, he lets school success (and its originators) speak for itself (we particularly liked school's weekly parish-style newsletters, featuring ads from local business amidst the reports of sporting and musical successes).

Relishes all that school has to offer in the way of tradition but is careful to keep the pace of innovation ticking over. Year 7 and 8 pupils have iPads which talk to school whiteboards and can store and file homework. May sound fancy but well in keeping with school's reputation for doing things earlier than most (it's been co-ed, and taken day pupils, since the 1970s).

He's taken difficult decisions from the off, starting by axing the 'madness' of compulsory boarding which was putting off many a parent who loved everything else about the school. To traditionalists, 'I was the hunter who'd shot Bambi's mother.' Many others approved and ultimately it proved a vote-winner. Now it's boarding because you want to, not because you have to – and, combined with sterling exam success, school is packing in the numbers, helped by increasingly popular pre-prep incubating the next generation.

Feels it's vital to listen to parents. Schools were 'conceited and arrogant' for too long, the experts in education who kept their customers at arms' length. These days, with successful, highly educated parents, 'you ignore what people have to say at your peril'. Suiting action to the word may make him 'possibly too accessible,' thought a parent. 'Does well to keep himself slightly aloof because otherwise, he'd end up having to get involved in every single micro issue that every parent had.'

Radiates clearly heartfelt belief in role of schools in providing not just rigour but also 'joy and wonder, enchantment, delight, challenge, excitement, fun.' Collect the set and learning becomes 'something you get out of bed to do, like turning a page in a book and wanting to move on to the next page.'

Despite rumours that he was considering his options as he approached his 10th anniversary, we weren't picking up any sense that he was off to scribe his memoirs (or indeed, set up a Peace Foundation). Just as well, then, that there's no Gordon Brown figure lurking on the premises.

Best bit about the top slot? 'Genuinely, I want to make things better.' We feel a song coming on. Could it be D:Ream circa 1997? We think it could.

Head of Brookham pre-prep: since 2015, Sophie Baber BA PGCE postgraduate diploma in psychology, who previously taught at Marlborough College Malaysia.

H

Entrance: First come, first served until year 2 when school is 'sightly more cautious, as we need to ensure we can support pupils.' That said, there's not much that can't be handled in the way of learning needs, including one pupil with an EHC plan and fully LA funded – very much not the norm; school's deep regret that school is a postcode's throw from special needs switched on Hampshire.

Access all pupils largely down to owner says yes approach. Grandson of the founder, he has children at the school and what appears to be fairly substantial behind the scenes presence. 'When I first arrived, I asked, "Do you want me to be very tough in who we take on?" He said, "I want you to take them on and make a difference",' said previous head.

Most proceed from pre-prep to prep, though parents think number told they may not make the cut is rising (there's also no automatic rite of passage for siblings.) 'Definitely raising the standards,' reckoned one parent. 'When we first started, you had to have a severe problem not to get in.'

Most families within a 25 minute drive, Haslemere, Liphook, Liss and Petersfield the norm, Midhurst and Farnham at a stretch, augmented with influx of well-heeled Londoners, offspring increasingly the products of Thomas's and similar ultra-smart establishments.

Atmosphere is changing too. Once 'a bit chaotic and very friendly', it's now 'much slicker' – bemoaned by some though 'not necessarily a bad thing,' thought one mother. Though on the rise, the pushy, assertive contingent ('mums who wear hats at matches,' according to a local – we're keeping a watching brief on this one) is small enough 'to be squashed' by fellow parents. Tutoring, so far at least, remains a minority out of hours occupation 'and only if your child is really struggling.'

Exit: Move to prep is viewed as an exciting prospect by year 3s. 'It feels you can be free, because you get to walk around by yourself without a teacher following and there's much more playing area,' said one.

Prep school has opted for laissez-faire approach to departure age, loosening the ties by offering preparation for 11+ (and even 12+) as well as common entrance. It's proved a smart move, parental freedom of choice coming down strongly in favour of staying the course, with what head describes as 'a small attrition rate' – as few as four leaving at end of year 6 and senior boarding for most. Widespread destinations, with Marlborough currently the most popular then Cranleigh, Canford, Churcher's College, Bryanston, Eton, Prior's Field, Sherborne and Wellington College. Scholarships, being pushed hard, thought parents, are going great guns (11 in 2018).

Other local schools, wrestling the will they, won't they stay on beyond year 6 conundrum, must envy top years stability here. Though a few do leave early (some, reluctantly, because of financial pressures) seniors-only delights lure vast majority, headed by wonderful trips – voluntary year 7 trip to remote Scottish island to build own camp (look, no adults) one of the most memorable.

Parents feel breadth of talent and characters in top years something to celebrate. 'You've got people who are going to Eton, people who are struggling ...but who might be the best at sport or the best at music, and they can accommodate that,' said parent.

Remarks: Approached through prosperous Liphook, school looks a treat on a sunny spring day. Picturesque brickwork casts early morning shadows on a sea of green, pitches everywhere, side order of bluebell-carpeted woodland (provides fuel for new biomass boiler as well as home for achingly on-trend forest classroom), all 175 acres well-used by mothers who 'turn up in their lycra and go running with their labradors,' said former parent who also bemoaned the fact that 'it's easy to start feeling a bit smug.'

Top-up scenery fix every Wednesday when there's post-match 'car park time', families enjoying picnics together (courtesy of Messrs J Sainsbury – branch a short 4x4 schlep away), invitations to international boarders from local families ensuring nobody is left out.

Interiors are corridor heavy, twists and turns best tackled with an expert guide – star turns include attractive, solemn (but not sombre) chapel (nearby plaque commemorating school's founder must be touched if passed – brings luck, say older girls), nice, bright main music room (with a second for composition); excellent library, walls stuffed with reading lists, each personalised with jacket illustrations as effective aide-memoires – a time-consuming but worthwhile labour of love that ensures everyone broadens literacy horizons, say staff – and one of the small details that shows just why, academically, the school shines.

Layout on Venn diagram lines, pre-prep largely self-sufficient but overlapping with prep when it comes to music, art and some sport, especially for older children. Cosily named nursery classes, Little Bears and Big Bears, lead a more self-contained existence, with attractive classrooms and separate, secluded and well-equipped play area. Integration starts early through treehouse families, small groups that span the age range and meet to share worries or good news, enjoyable sessions in forest school for all, and mealtimes, with older bruins having lunch in Highfield dining hall (Little Bears bring packed lunches instead), fajitas much enjoyed, 'salty' ham one of few dishes that wasn't.

Reception pupils start off in similar seclusion, though by the end of their first year, they're enjoying substantial tumbling about green space featuring gorgeous (though rather ignored) outdoor xylophone, as well as more conventional but attractive equipment, mad galloping in tentative sunshine seemingly the main amusement, though with behind the scenes staff presence to suggest games. Space gorgeous, only drawback ease of mislaying possessions: 'That sports jumper was there yesterday,' said pupil, with interest.

Inside, every inch of relatively compact and modern building is used to maximum effect. New and grandly named research area (library with computers – touch typing is taught in reception) was recently added, entrance area come assembly hall occupied by high flying and wonderful woven willow dragon spouting red velvet fire. Onesie design, though highly efficient, means some areas, such as nursery/reception music, are also through routes to somewhere else. Not a problem as remains '...a nice quiet place though sometimes people go through it,' said pupil.

Everywhere is extremely neat with not an inch wasted and loads to see and do, including rocket in reception class, less final frontier than cosy den, though strange lifeforms, courtesy of tank o'tadpoles, had already been discovered. Classrooms for older children, all interesting spaces and angles, were big on colourful, extensive and up to the minute displays (including some gorgeous monster poems).

Parents rate academics. 'We want our kids to have been pushed to the level where they can achieve either common entrance or scholarship to one of the major public schools,' said one. Achieved with no setting to speak of until year 3, maths the sole exception. 'If we have a big enough spread, might do it in year 2.' Anything but laissez faire, however, with lots of monitoring and no automatic move up between years, those who would benefit from 'spending extra time at a stage' as it's diplomatically phrased, doing just that. School also has a fair few of the extravagantly bright, who get fair share of extra support and encouragement – including peer socialisation (occasionally tricky for those punching above their weight conversationally).

Big thing is the creative curriculum, introduced several years ago as a way of avoiding national curriculum ennui by adding all round oomph. Takes a theme such as 'Day at the sea', 'Knight in the castle' (pun intended), launches it with wow factor event (Sir Teach-a-lot knocking thunderously on pre-prep door to invite pupils to visit castle for a spot of princess rescuing) and ends similarly, with parents invited to share the fun by coming to medieval banquet or turning school into Brookham-sur-Mer, complete with donkeys and sand.

Subjects are knitted in en route, some national curriculum must-dos covered off-piste. While not everything can be shoehorned in (many science discoveries, for example, having inconveniently post-dated Round Table days) it's amazing how many dots can be joined. Would an exciting display of ultra-tactile rocks in year 3 classroom be followed by a snazzy volcanic eruption? Of course it would.

Huge staff enthusiasm provides a welcome outlet for pent-up creativity and they are encouraged to give full rein to creative instincts. Children are pretty sold on the idea (even if you did get the impression that overlaying a narrative element was even more popular with staff than their pupils) with activities, many hands on, doing wonders for confidence, one dyslexic child 'growing about three feet' after trebuchet improvement tip dramatically improved its destructive powers during siege weapon-making session.

With or without fun element, lessons are generally enjoyed, science for strong practical dimension, art at least in part because of resident dog, asleep in corner, music for charismatic teacher, whole-school favourite. Spanish, taught from year 3, seemed to be the only laggard – 'I just don't get it,' said pupil.

'What we do – I'm sure all schools say this – is absolutely aim to add value,' says prep head, disarmingly. Boasts 'unbroken record in getting everyone to first choice senior school'. Trickier these days because of the rise of pre-assessments, think parents, which has pushed up academic standards, and a tribute to what one described as 'fantastic' teaching across the ability range. So far, no sense of pressures feeding through to pupils, let alone creating the 'pale, wan' types that one parent reported seeing at other, more academically-focused hothouses closer to the capital. Indeed, this bunch were notable for good cheer (and delightful manners, too) though some parents felt that a few families have increasingly to be restrained from ramping up the anxiety levels at home.

Pupils, though reassuringly relaxed, have no doubts as to expectations, though lead-in is gentle, usually (though not invariably) mixed ability teaching for everything in year 4, maths set in year 5, when there's across the board specialist teaching, academics ramped up several notches in year 6 with three sets for everything, strengths in English, maths and science determining who you're with for everything else, including music and sport. Fourth set is added in year 7, and scholars identified. 'They try to give them other names,' say pupils, 'but we know exactly which group we're in.' (School, which sticks to 'obvious' one to four numbering, was slightly baffled by this.)

Staff, reckons one of their number, are 'lifers, not bolters' who '...all like children, and that's not always the case with some teachers,' says head (laughing, but we don't think he's joking). This lot include many clearly in love with their subject – head of maths was happy to deliver short tutorial on iPad geometry apps, their habits and haunts to this reviewer (only flaw the occasional unintentional transmission of scrawled notes to mothership whiteboard in classroom, visible to all).

Year 8 pupils, with impressive maturity, were quick to acknowledge that though some teachers were clearly more down with the kids than others (sports teachers and witty head of music particular favourites) even those with a less obviously child-pleasing style 'could turn a good pupil into an excellent one,' said one – and had the scholarship to prove it.

Most commonly school can cope with mild to moderate dyslexia, dyspraxia and dyscalculia, speech and language, auditory and sensory processing difficulties, fine and gross motor skills, Asperger's and mild ASD. Support one full time plus assorted specialists – ranges from study skills to specific help with literacy and maths. Seen as part and parcel of daily life by pupils – 'helps you write and read if you are having a problem,' reckoned one – support is regularly reviewed and, in the case of one rapidly progressing pupil with ADD, withdrawn altogether.

Though parent felt that SEN support could be even better, it's generally still felt, however, that full time SENCo, five other therapists and positive attitude from owner, a brilliant and dyslexic businessman (sister was a highly-rated teacher here until recently), creates haven for those with mainly mild learning needs. Children are 'never made to feel persecuted' and '...one of the great glories of the place in that we are a very broad church,' says head. Especially good with late developers, giving them the confidence to bloom in senior school – and many do.

With increasing numbers testimony to school's appeal there's the inevitable fraying at the edges. It's all change, however, with new sports hall planned, together with major surgery to senior teaching block including two additional science labs. Parents, while praising efforts, keen to see replacement of 'old fashioned' kitchens which, though good for terrific range of break time snacks and 'lovely' lunchtime fajitas as well as recently introduced salad bar, can be slightly over-reliant on stodge for afters.

Boarding has also had a fairly substantial shake up following period when lack of feedback made parents feel uncertain about pastoral care. New houseparents have 'definitely breathed new life and energy into our boarding.' Parents agree. Now 'hand on heart I'd say boarding is excellent whereas before I wouldn't have been able to recommend it,' thinks one.

Stalwart adult presence reassures – you're never more than two dorms away from a houseparent – as does good communication including separate boarding email updates and mobiles 'strapped to us,' says houseparent, whose cosy office becomes an informal meeting place for 'tea and gossip' and who has custody of special huggable piggy which 'slots round stomach' and is loaned out to ward off homesickness blues. Approachable matron, meanwhile, full-on mending session under way when we visited, is 'always here at breaktime for chats and spare clothes.'

There's considerable smartening up (showers in reds and pinks, girls' dorms very fetching – Tom Daley pin ups adding final touch) with more to come. Loss of linen room, imminent, will be mourned by the heat-starved Spanish boarders who 'go in to soak up the warmth,' says houseparent. Biggest casualty, though, will be boys' shower golf, fondly imagined to be a secret from staff, ball propelled round vast, old-fashioned, Carry on Camping style washroom course, bonus points awarded for sinking hole in one into tooth mug.

Has all made boarding wildly popular. Pupils plead to start – 'mine were supposed to be day,' said one mother, resignedly – and is almost universal in top years. Who can blame them when evening cricket calls (there's always a summer term surge in numbers) and lures include guinea pigs and climbing frame in juniors' cosy cottage garden, as well as dress down Sunday morning breakfasts and highly rated cook your own supper sessions for years 7 and 8, run by Mrs Evitt who, though a vegetarian, gamely tackles hard core red meat dishes including 'delicious' burgers stuffed with mozzarella.

Day pupils, however, get fair share of the action, staff interests swiftly channelled by head into delightful range of clubs. School boasts of 'enough to experience something different every day of the week' – probably an understatement, given range extending from recently introduced Hyperdrive after school talks (history of flight the ambitious inaugural topic) to the remote control club which races model boats across smart swimming pool, as well as bushcraft group (one for the Bear Grylls wannabees, if ways with newly defunct wild rabbits anything to judge by).

Bonds are further strengthened by compulsory Saturday school in prep, well tolerated by all (marginally later starting time sweetens the pill – just – for sleep-starved parents), as allows five clear afternoons of sport a week, Thursdays reserved for Highfield Keys – school's own DofE equivalent with 'spectrum' of activities ranging from 'charity outreach to outdoor pursuits.'

Big programme of optional Saturday sports undoubtedly helps, as do popular after-school clubs (majority sign up for at least one), judo, gymnastics and orienteering amongst the options, street dance, pottery and chess ringing the changes and 60 per cent of pupils also learning an instrument. Animated children also encouraged to look outside immediate surroundings, worthy swapsies with London multi-cultural Catholic school – a valuable eye-opener for all. 'I suddenly realised that there's all these other people like me,' said one of few non-white pupils.

House on house whomping is a big thing (not for nothing do their names commemorate famous English victories). Ranges from the big set piece pomp and ceremony of sports day, where knights set forth from separate marquees to do battle, to Bonfire Night guy contest, Lady Gaga a recent winner (Bradley Wiggins would have been a strong contender but 'his head fell off' – rarely a recommended tactic). If there's no house to duff up, 'we can turn anything into a competition,' said year 8 pupil, citing tidiest dorm, cleanest teeth and best veg plot by way of proof.

Officially, 'we aim to teach pupils that it's all about taking part.' However, 'Life is competitive.' And while prospectus may highlight 'development of fine and gross motor skills', pupils, organised on mainly traditional lines (cricket, football and rugby for boys, rounders and hockey for girls, swimming for all in decent pool) are in no doubt that purpose is to form ace teams and slaughter the opposition. 'We've only lost one match this year,' say 7 and 8 year-old football and rugby stars. Matches are, naturally, played to win with staff who are proud that their own teams regularly trounce those of other schools setting high class example. School says that it's emphatically not out 'to win at all costs' and stresses that all pupils shall have team games and represent the school in matches, whether endowed with athletic superpowers or not. Good sportsmanship comes with the territory and 'full respect is given to other teams in defeat and in victory. It's not personal.'

Parents agree that victory never comes shorn of good manners, which are emphasised throughout the school, year 8 monitors supervising younger pupils at break and lunchtime.

School, as a result, is a breeding ground for 'amiable killers,' says one parent, with netball stars known for pausing as they streak to victory to voice tender concern for opponents after collision. 'My daughter stops to say, "are you OK?" if she treads on someone's feet,' said mother. Boys' sport is 'excellent – I would say they win three-quarters of their matches,' reckoned dad. One parent felt girls' sport was a bit undernourished compared with boys'. Absolutely not so, says school, which puts it down to perceptions that girls currently 'don't win as many of their hockey matches because they are less experienced on Astroturf than other schools' teams,' though will all change when they get their own.

All in all, a super school that radiates enthusiasm and good cheer. Head says it's the happiest place he's ever worked in, felt previous GSG description 'tradition with a twist' summed it up to a tee. Aim is for greater cultural variety in the future, particularly in the top years, 'because it's good and healthy for the children.' Track record of all round success makes it a safe bet that it will add extra flavour to the mix.

Hillview School for Girls

Brionne Gardens, Tonbridge, Kent TN9 2HE

Ages 11–18 **Pupils** 1,200 **Sixth form** 298 (63 boys)

01732 352793
www.hillview.kent.sch.uk

Headteacher: Since 2016, Hilary Burkett. Came from Rainham School for Girls in Medway, where she arrived as a newly qualified teacher and spent 16 years working her way up to head of school. It had an overall executive head, and she thought the time had come to run her own ship.

Listen hard and you'll hear the trace of an accent from her upbringing in a small town in the Pennines. Certain teachers there 'who inspired every step of the way' were what attracted her to teaching, but she says they probably wouldn't have predicted her reaching the top of her profession. She was a shy child, who had to be encouraged to put herself forward. Took her degree in 3D design, and was an art teacher in earlier days. Still teaches graphics, and time away from school finds her camera in hand, searching out angles in urban landscapes, or shopping for more photography equipment.

'Clearly passionate about the school and its achievements and seems highly motivated to improve every aspect of the school, particularly the academic side,' said one parent.

Burkett says her early focus has been on improving standards within lessons, both in behaviour, and allowing staff to attempt more creative pedagogy. Staff well-being is another point of focus. 'I want to be a school where people enjoy coming to work, feel supported, and enjoy teaching students.' This policy encompasses everything from giving them cake on the first of the month, to allowing them time out of school to take part in the Erasmus programme.

'I love it that the head still teaches so she knows what it is like to teach the new curriculum – that must support and inspire her staff,' one parent said.

Academic matters: Turns in a decent set of results for a non-selective school. In 2018, 64 per cent of pupils achieved 9-4 at GCSE in both English and maths, and 21 per cent of grades were A*-A/9-7, while A levels saw an impressive 57 per cent of entries receive an A*-B and 38 per cent A*/A. Excellent Progress 8 of +0.44.

There's no house style to the teaching, Burkett says, but it's not formal. 'We've been looking at creative approaches where the student is active in learning, and we've been doing a three year project into how students learn, with the aim of empowering them rather than them being reliant on staff.' Lots of group work and peer assessment.

In maths and science, much work goes into developing confidence. We see this in action in a maths class studying interest and depreciation. A girl asks how to go about the equation, and rather than telling her, the teacher suggests she tries to work it out. 'It's teaching them to take a leap of faith because they lack confidence to try,' Burkett explains. The theory is it gives them the confidence to attempt tricky questions in an exam. In another class, the pupils have completed some exercises and the teacher reassures them, 'It's better than yesterday, and it will gradually get better throughout this week.'

Burkett is refreshingly honest about the problems in science and maths teaching, which is an endemic feature of state schools but not always acknowledged. 'If any school says maths is fine they are in denial,' she says, 'given the combined problems of recruiting maths teachers, and the increase in difficulty in the new curriculum, which shakes pupils' confidence.' Her answer is to over-staff in maths and give extra responsibility to the subject team to support improvements and try new things. They run skills sessions where they break maths groups up to focus on particular areas of difficulty.

In science she says part of the problem is how difficult the subject is; students lack confidence in it and often don't want to take it, it's hard to teach, and most parents say they found science difficult. Again, developing confidence is the holy grail. We watch a class which produces shrieks of amazement when colourless liquids change colour as the bottles are shaken. There follows a call and response of 'What do we call that energy?' 'Kinetic.' 'What are the particles doing?' 'Colliding.' 'What do we need for successful collision?' 'Activation energy.'

Most students take the dual award, but a few do three separate sciences. Higher up the school we watch a year 12 biology class on formation of tissue fluid with some really engaged questioning from pupils. The science labs in a swanky new block rival those at independent schools – bought at a bargain price in return for allowing the installers to show other potential buyers around. It's a growing department, with 60 applications to take biology A level this year.

Other subjects are kept up to scratch with three formal observations per year and casual drop ins where staff can critique each other's work and learn from others. Parents we spoke to named one or two staff who their girls groaned about, but felt that the teaching was largely good. Art and PE departments have particularly inspiring staff, one said.

History is a popular subject, and unusually for a comprehensive, offers both modern and ancient curricula (one teacher is an ancient history specialist). Alongside the EBacc subjects, other GCSE options include dance, drama and graphic communications, and there are also BTecs in business studies, travel and tourism, and health and social care, and vocational qualifications in child development and music technology. One parent said a real strength of the school is that it allows pupils to change subjects without hassle.

At sixth form there are three pathways – three A level courses for more academic students; combined programmes taking in a mix of A levels, applied general courses, and enrichment qualifications; and a 16+ programme which combines applied general qualifications, work experience, and English and maths resits if necessary. Students usually need a minimum of five GCSEs at grade 4 or above to stay on.

There's no requirement to take a tranche of academic qualifications. Students set on performing careers can take A levels in dance, drama and music, and a BTec in musical theatre.

The learning support department has a SENCo supported by two higher level TAs and five TAs, with the Lilac Room providing a retreat for a child who needs some time out. Learning support is well managed and effective, according to one parent. 'At the first parents' evening I was so impressed by how all the teachers knew about her learning needs, and they all informed me about how it was handled specifically for her in each lesson. She needs to repeat an instruction back in order to understand it. The teachers have been great about this, not making her feel stupid or disruptive when she does this. They also encourage her to use her phone to photograph written instructions, so that she doesn't have to try to copy it down and make sense of it in the rushed environment of the classroom.' But another wondered if her daughter's difficulties passed them by, saying: 'Although we'd been offered an assessment and support for dyslexia, in years 7 and 13, this was never followed through.'

Autistic students need to be able to manage in the main body of the school, 'but we know their comfort zones'. Students with higher levels of needs are accommodated in the Sapphire Group – which can be just one person in a year group. 'It's not something we officially offer, but when we have students with low cognitive abilities and high level needs we provide a curriculum dealing with core life skills – how to cook, look after their health, manage money. We put them in for a different qualification in maths so they can feel they've been successful.'

Games, options, the arts: Has a box office on its website, and West End-worthy show pictures in the corridors – for a recent production of Cats, a professional make up artist taught the girls how to do their feline faces, which peer out from a smoke-swirled stage in the production shots. They are all ambitious productions – recently Sister Act, which had 100 performers. Anyone who wants to be part of a show can be.

It's a performing arts specialist, and wandering the corridors after hours is like stepping into an episode of Fame. Lots of ballet buns and girls working out their moves in rehearsal rooms. The facilities are tremendous – there are dance studios with sprung floors, a recording studio where they produce CDs for remastering in London, and a studio theatre equipped with an arts technician, who teaches pupils to weld and construct their own sets and run the lighting and sound gallery. They use a selection of local theatres for the big performances.

Twenty year 7 places are given each year to girls with aptitude in dance, drama or music. They get additional support and dancers become part of the dance company – year 13s use year 7s in their exam pieces, and they put on cross-age performances. Great for the talented, but it can make others feel distinctly B list. One mother said her daughter felt overlooked, convinced the teacher thinks she has no talent as she is not in the top dance ability.

These scholarships aren't a straitjacket – one parent said that although her daughter joined on a dance scholarship, she decided not to take this for GCSE and this wasn't a problem. Students are allowed to take time off to do auditions and be in shows – several have parts in pantos, a couple are in the English National Ballet. Others have modelled for French Connection, Gucci and Prada.

The biggest extracurricular club is cheerleading, and the team of 160 students are national champions at every category for schools, head says breezily. Their coach used to be a national cheerleader – she trains sixth formers in coaching qualifications.

Over in the textiles room, we're shown the work of a pupil who has just won young fashion designer of the year for the southern region – 'we win most years,' the teacher said. Preparations are under way for a combined fashion show and art exhibition. We see some mature work, and hear of more stars in the making – one student's painting is on show at the Turner Contemporary in Margate.

Biggest sports are handball, athletics and netball, and the showbiz razzamatazz even comes to sport with the school's own Sports Personality of the Year event. 'Really good fun. Everyone gets dressed up and it is done in a very Oscars way,' said a parent.

There are also Stars in their Eyes singing events, dance platforms, concerts, and the school's own Hillfest showcase festival. A girl who loves putting on the greasepaint will be in her element. 'She is involved in many clubs at school – netball, trampolining, athletics, dance, choir, art and cheerleading and has so much fun,' one parent said.

Background and atmosphere: The school's history dates back to 1854, but it has been on the current site since 1936. The original building saw further additions in 2004 and 2010. The new buildings have wide corridors and high ceilings, while the schools sits on a hill with fantastic views across the county – there's a great feeling of calm and space.

It's in much better nick, and better equipped, than neighbouring state schools. It's a single academy trust, and the school employs its own canteen and cleaning staff, and the caretakers do a lot of the maintenance work.

'There are always new things going on which make it feel fresh and innovative. I don't feel it is stuck in its ways like many other schools,' said a parent.

In this fiercely grammar county it has suffered from some snobbery, but those who've tried it have no doubts. One mother said: 'My older girls were able to work at a fast pace in the grammar schools, and my youngest daughter can work at her own pace here at Hillview and still feel that she is bright, and is inspired to believe she can achieve anything she sets her mind to. Great, great school. I would recommend to anyone.'

Another said: 'Most girls do not follow the performing arts at the school, so it is a conventional secondary school in all other aspects.'

There's a gloriously guff-free website: clear, easily navigable, and all the facts you need are there. Shouldn't be such a rare beast among schools, but it is.

Pastoral care, well-being and discipline: 'Strict about correct uniform and no makeup,' said a parent. Head describes short skirts as the bane of her life; her latest measure is a compulsory kilt-style skirt, which is harder to hoik up.

Missing a single piece of homework will result in a detention – 'this ensures they just do it,' head says. There's a maximum of an hour a night, but usually a week in which to hand it in.

There's a strict discipline policy, which escalates for misdemeanours through warnings, breaktime detentions, after-school detentions on a Friday, being put on report, and finally to internal exclusions, where they are sent to another school for a day.

The school is little troubled by pupil pregnancies – none in the last eight years – and head says there are no drug issues. The school supports a few pupils with gender identity issues. Where possible they draw in older girls to help younger pupils through emotional or mental health difficulties.

Rather than houses, there are three 'communities' – Austen, Hepburn and Westwood. Children meet in their communities every morning. 'A very good idea,' said one parent. 'My daughter meets every morning with others from her community from years 7, 8 and 9 and this is not only an opportunity to form friendships with other years but also adds to the community feeling of belonging.'

Parents say a student support system means they always know who to contact if there is a problem. They receive three reports per year which detail their child's strengths and two ways of improving in each subject.

Pupils and parents: The intake is skewed by the locality. There are two girls' grammars within a stone's throw, sucking up higher achievers, while the wealthy area also supports a number of private schools. The mainstay of the school is middle to lower ability, but there are a clutch of academically able girls, some drawn by the performing arts offer, some who may have narrowly missed an 11+ pass.

The school opens to boys in the sixth form, and male numbers have steadily increased. Some come specifically for the performing arts, others often have a sister here and the family like the school.

Gripes from parents include the school canteen, 'never enough food to go round', requiring the bane of packing lunches, and some think communication could be improved.

Entrance: The catchment area varies according to the number of applications each year. On average, those within eight miles will get in, though put your bags down no more than six miles away if you want to be sure of a place in the first round. Later allocations have taken the distance up to 14 miles in leaner years – the school encourages parents to appeal and says that most who want to get in will, and they are occasionally able to add an extra form to cope with demand. Recently the intake has been affected by the birth dip (now receding), and by the expansion of nearby Weald girls' grammar.

There are usually around 50 applicants for the 20 performing arts scholarships, and siblings take priority.

This year 40 external students (boys and girls) joined the sixth form, but that is likely to double in the next round. Some come for the performing arts, others taking refuge from local IB schools. Otherwise the big attraction is the widest range of choices. 'Other schools have been cutting courses, we've tried not to because we believe students should be able to specialise in whatever they want,' Burkett says.

Exit: About 50 per cent stay on into the school's sixth form. Around 30 pupils per year move on to specialist performing arts schools, and some into performance careers – former students are in the national tours of Shrek and Cats. Some 50 per cent of sixth formers to universities ranging from Oxford Brookes to King's College London to University of the Arts; others to FE colleges, gap years or apprenticeships.

Remarks: Go and have a look, because otherwise you may be missing a neat trick. In this fevered patch of west Kent there's an attitude that if your child doesn't make the grammars, then you must go private. But you'll find here facilities from science to music and dance which match many an independent school, as do the rolling grounds; and a nice bunch of disciplined kids, seemingly undisturbed by social ills. A girl who yearns to tread the boards will be in seventh heaven, and parents saving on fees will find plenty to make a song and dance about.

Hockerill Anglo-European College

Dunmow Road, Bishop's Stortford, Hertfordshire CM23 5HX

Ages 11–19 **Pupils** 839 **Sixth form** 250 **Boarders** 174 full, 121 weekly, 80 flexi

Fees: Day: free; Boarding £7,210 – £16,752 pa

01279 658451
www.hockerill.com

Principal: Since 2013, Richard Markham MA. An Oxford historian and former international hockey player who represented Wales, he began his teaching career at Marlborough College in 1994, where a variety of roles (including teacher of history and history of art, deputy housemaster, master in charge of hockey and IB coordinator) culminated in director of studies for his last four years. Insists the differences between Marlborough and Hockerill are 'not as pronounced as most people think', with key similarities including boarding and academic rigour. Whilst he inherited a school that was by no means complacent about its continued success, staff and students agree that he has pushed for a rounder education than his predecessor, believing that 'exam results are important, but a good education is about so much more.'

Relaxed but self-assured, he manages that winning headteacher combo of putting people immediately at ease, whilst still retaining a clear air of leadership. Staff clearly feel valued, able to explore innovative teaching techniques, and are never micro-managed, but woe betide any who go to him with a problem rather than a solution. Regularly dines with groups of students to seek their feedback, pointing out that with 92 per cent of day students eating lunch on site, the refectory is 'a good place to keep your finger on the pulse.' Meanwhile, year 12 students in his history class are taught at the conference table in his magnificent, spacious office.

Married with two children, he lives on site; interests include reading history, as well as playing and watching most sports, notably cycling, golf and hockey, the latter of which he coaches at Hockerill. Favours the term principal over head.

Academic matters: One of the most successful comprehensives in the country. In 2018, 51 per cent A*/A grades at GCSE. Also one of the top non-selective state school post-16, with an average IB point core of 35 in 2018 – excellent by any standards.

Part of the DNA of the school is to bookend GCSEs with the IB, with an IB middle years programme that means all pupils continue with a language, arts and technology. Class sizes average around 24, dropping to 18 at sixth form. Setting in English and maths from year 7 and science from year 9. Students expect to (and largely do) work hard and study hard, with Saturday morning school compulsory and plenty of prep (two hours a night by year 10). But this isn't just a school for the academically gifted; it has a wide mix of ability. 'You're not pressurised to get good grades, but you are expected to do your best,' said one student. Another, who has now left to study A levels at an independent school, said, 'Unlike my current school, which is all about teaching you how to get top marks, learning exam techniques, and basically being an alpha student, Hockerill's ethos is that education should be much broader, and I love that I left with so much more than a bunch of qualifications.'

Head claims the biggest change for him was 'coming to a school with a curriculum model I had not seen anywhere else.' Indeed, even in the gilded private sector, you'll be hard pushed to find a school where years 8, 9 and 10 are taught geography and history in either French or German – a programme with 80 per cent participation and which really sets the pace for this truly international school, where languages are genuinely embedded in the curriculum. Seven languages as separate subjects also currently on offer, including Japanese and Mandarin, with less than a handful of students doing fewer than two languages.

Truth be told, nothing here is taught in siloes, with students expected to link humanities with languages, languages with art etc. Teachers are particularly praised for making subjects exciting and offering careers support in their topic area. 'There's a real passion among teachers about preparing us for both university and life beyond university,' said one student.

The college had 15 children with a statement of SEN when we visited, including one wheelchair user, extreme dyslexia and Asperger's, all of whom are dealt with by the SEN co-ordinator, both in and outside the classroom. 'The transition in year 7 was faultless, with the school knowing all about our daughter and her needs before she'd even started,' said one parent, who added, 'The reviews are excellent, the head of SEN is accessible and there's a great emphasis on any extra help being made to be enjoyable.' Meanwhile, the EAL co-ordinator helps the international students who need assistance with language and settling into a different way of teaching. 'We keep abreast of teaching styles in the countries these students come from,' explains head.

Games, options, the arts: The IB requires a mood of involvement and pupils here lap this up, with over 70 popular clubs, including fencing, public speaking, knitting and dance. 'Younger students really get stuck in, trying new things out before they find where their interests lie,' said one student. Sport is strong, with girls playing mainly hockey, netball, rounders and athletics, whilst boys are largely drawn to rugby, cricket and football. Fixtures against both state and private schools, and there's some exceptional individual talent too, with national champions in golf and karate, among others. New sports hall will soon supplement the pitches and courts.

Music, drama and art part of the curriculum until year 10, with plenty of individual musical instrument lessons, including the organ (the director of music is an organ scholar). Regular performances from the popular orchestras and choirs, with a good balance of classical and modern, of which one parent said: 'You always go away with goosebumps because they're just so good.' There's a rotating pattern for drama performances – one year, there's a whole school production; the next, there's a dance show; and the next there's an art-based competition. Art and DT boast good facilities and interlinked rooms.

Given the global theme of the school, it will come as no surprise that there are some impressive international trips, including to India and Uganda, as well as language exchanges in years 8, 9, 10 and 12, whilst in school pastimes include Amnesty International and Model United Nations.

Boarding: Alongside full and weekly boarding, there's a flexi boarding option from 7.15am till post-prep 9pm with a requirement to stay 7-10 nights per year. 'You do everything the boarders do, except actually sleep here,' explained one student.

Six single sex boarding houses for different age groups, where teachers also have flats, all bright, well-maintained and welcoming, with all pupils having a study bedroom, sharing until year 12, then winning their own private space in their final year. Downstairs reception rooms in Thames boast polished floors, leather Chesterfields, beautiful fireplaces and large windows, whilst the other more modern boarding houses include comfortable and homely reception rooms.

All boarders are cared for in relaxed manner by houseparents, some with own family. Supervised prep sessions for all boarders, as well as plenty of opportunities for clubs and organised activities, events and trips. In fact, boarders enjoy the vibrant lifestyle so much that many choose to hang around even on exeat weekends. School prides itself on constantly evolving its boarding offering according to student feedback, and there are several forums (eg entertainment committee and food committee). Pastoral care praised. 'My eldest was horrendously homesick for a very long time, and the school was brilliant,' said one parent. 'They make sure there's a real sense of community among the boarders,' said another.

Background and atmosphere: Compact and leafy site close to Bishop's Stortford town centre with an attractive mix of arts and crafts, 1930s and contemporary buildings, and new science labs in the offing. The school's calendar is similar to a conventional independent boarding school, with longer holidays to allow boarders to return home for two weeks at October half term, three weeks at Christmas and nine weeks in the summer. Pupils make good use of the extra time – 'It allowed me to go to China,' said one. Classrooms are quiet, teachers politely addressed. Very strong community feel, with everyone getting involved. 'Not just a place to be – a place where you grow up,' said one remarkably mature young man. Strong sense of mutual respect between teachers and pupils: 'Teachers give a lot. We want the knowledge and the teachers help us to learn'.

Pastoral care, well-being and discipline: A traditional but non-denominational school, where teachers are called Sir or Ma'am and everyone has sensible haircuts and wears uniform (blue in the lower school, black and white in the sixth form). Not excessive on school rules, though, with more of an emphasis on expectations of politeness, kindness and punctuality. 'If you set the right tone, you avoid major issues,' says the head, with low level prep-related detentions about as harsh as it has to get on the discipline front. Attendance problems and defiance non-existent, which students attribute to being well aware there are 10 applications for every place. 'There's an ethos that we are fortunate, and with that comes responsibility,' explained one. Incidents of bullying extremely rare, with incidents of unkindness dealt with quickly. Pastoral care is praised.

Pupils and parents: Some 40 per cent of boarders (who are required to hold an EU passport) come from overseas, with significant numbers from eg Spain, Germany, Italy and France. Twenty-four nationalities altogether. Weekly boarders generally from 1.5 hours travelling radius. Pupils are articulate, mature, friendly and confident, appearing genuinely to enjoy interaction with adults. 'I walk into school knowing I'll be stopped and asked how I am and that they really mean it,' says head. Hockerill Parents and Friends Association, which includes both current and former parents, is an active fundraising and social community responsible for changes such as refurbishment of the library and chapel, and which runs staff bids in the summer term which have resulted in eg 3D printers and a camera for sixth form.

Entrance: Eight hundred plus applications from over 60 primary schools for 120 places in year 7. Hertfordshire residents are allowed four choices at year 7, and you can use two of these to apply for both a day and boarding place. Places are allocated on the basis of siblings, language and music aptitude tests, children of staff and distance. For boarders, priority is given to Forces and diplomatic personnel plus boarding need. Those looking to board are interviewed – away from their parents – to assess how well they would adapt to life away from home. Boarders pay for board and lodgings but not tuition. About half of the 130 places in year 12 are reserved for boarders.

Exit: Around 40 per cent leave post-GCSE, some because they prefer A levels, some because they don't meet the entrance criteria and some because they fancy moving to a sixth form college or other local school. Post IB, over 90 per cent get first choice of university, with around three-quarters to Russell Group universities including three to Oxbridge in 2018 plus one medic. Quite a few to a range of overseas universities, mostly in Europe, but also one to Tokyo in 2018. 'We get lots of help to apply for universities, both here and overseas,' said one student.

Money matters: Boarding fees far cheaper than a conventional independent boarding school, starting with a flexi boarding option at £7,000+.

Remarks: 'There is no such thing as a typical Hockerill student,' the head girl wrote in a speech she was about to deliver when we visited, and you really do feel variety is the spice of life at this extremely well-run school, where students are encouraged to gain a genuinely holistic education, but with enough opportunity to follow real passions. For students who are willing to knuckle down (and this doesn't necessarily mean they have to be highly academic), this is an exciting and dynamic place to learn and grow up, knocking the socks off many fee-paying sc hools.

Holmewood House School

Barrow Lane, Langton Green, Tunbridge Wells, Kent TN3 0EB

Ages 3–13 **Pupils** 450 **Boarders** 34 weekly/flexi (from year 3)

Fees: Day £8,520 – £18,885; Boarding £21,870 – £23,850 pa

01892 860006
www.holmewoodhouse.co.uk

Headmaster: Since September 2017, Scott Carnochan, previously head of Sedbergh Prep in Cumbria. Degree from Heriot-Watt University and postgrad from Nottingham. Has taught at Hillcrest Prep in Nairobi, been housemaster at St John's College School, Cambridge and head of boarding at Repton Prep. He played 1st XI cricket at school, was captain of rugby at school and county level and played international rugby, representing Scotland at U18 and student level.

He and his wife Kate have two young children. Kate is also the new head of marketing for the school.

Entrance: For nursery and reception it's first come first served, and entry into the pre-prep is non-selective, although informal assessments will ensure the child can keep up. Around 15 children join at year 3, and for this stage onwards prospective pupils take tests in maths, reading and spelling, plus there's an interview, and reports from the previous school are considered. Academic scholarships, which can be topped up with bursaries, are available from year 3.

Exit: Has previously had a reputation for not supporting children aiming to take the 11+ and for frowning on departures before 13. (A thorny issue indeed in the grammar school hotbed of Tunbridge Wells, and that policy has now changed.) School now says it welcomes children intending to leave at 11, and although it does not provide bespoke 11+ tuition, the preparation all children receive for secondary school entrance and common entrance pre-tests will be relevant. It's likely to take a while for this change of heart to filter through both in local reputation, and through a cohort which entered before this policy was in place. Not that it was ever impossible to move to a grammar – parents have previously organised their own tuition, and the last few years have seen many pupils move on to grammars.

At 13+ the school has a reputation for harvesting a good crop of scholarships. The range of schools children go on to has broadened – majority to Tonbridge, with Sevenoaks and Eastbourne also popular, then a scatter to Eton, Benenden, King's Canterbury, Charterhouse, Ardingly etc. Music, sport and drama scholarships.

A roadshow with 20 senior schools is held every two years to help families decide schools.

Remarks: No doubt about it, the facilities are fantastic with £4.5 million building project adding among other goodies new classrooms, science labs, learning hub, digital library, enrichment centre as well as a modern cloister.

It's one of very few prep schools with its own 20 metre rifle range – and the pupils are champion shooters among English schools. There's also a 25m indoor pool, squash courts, a climbing wall, and a snazzy sports hall. Lots of sporting success at county and national level. But we like the fact that the non-sporty don't get it rammed down their throats as much as in some other prep schools – there are two afternoons of compulsory team games, but on the other three they can choose drama, music or craft activities, or individual sports instead.

There's a 350 seat theatre and lots of big productions – and treading these boards launched the careers of old boys actors Dan Stevens of Downton Abbey and Tristan Gemmell (Casualty and Coronation Street). More remarkably, perhaps, Shane McGowan of The Pogues was also here.

All this, alongside what the school claims is a high staff to pupil ratio (1:9), and the number of specialist teachers, comes at a cost. You know what you're in for when one of the FAQs on the website is 'Why are your fees relatively high?' School has deliberately narrowed the fee gap with neighbouring preps, but it's still about £1,000 a term higher than others in the locality. We heard talk of school gate grumbles about fees funding large numbers of bursaries; whether you applaud that or not will be a matter of personal conviction.

They do a great deal to ease the way for working parents. There are minibuses at 4.30pm and 6pm to accommodate different finishing times through the school, and children can be looked after until 7pm. There is also a health centre staffed by nurses between 8am and 7pm every day. It means they can manage complicated medical regimes, but also look after a child who just needs to rest for half an hour before bouncing back, rather than having to call parents to collect them. Saturday morning school has been abolished.

Full-on timetable with the aim to be the top academic prep school, and to ensure that children in common entrance forms (year 6 to 8 have two of these and one scholarship form) are well prepared enough to get into their chosen school without any doubt. 'The last thing we want is them sitting the common entrance exam with everything crossed.'

Has put back creating the scholarship class to the start of year 6, believing they can better identify the children suited to this class after they have had a year working with subject specialist teachers, which begins in year 5. 'It's not a designer accessory. It's hard work and the last thing we want is a child in there who is struggling. Parents perceived that they got the best teachers, but we have deconstructed the idea that you get a better deal in the scholarship class. Now we get children or parents who turn it down because they don't want to be put under increased pressure, and scholarships are not worth much financially these days.'

From year 5 there are two periods a week of Latin, and scholars can also do ancient Greek. There's also Mandarin philosophy in year 8, a Spanish option from year 6, and French from nursery.

The seniors get Christmas and summer term exams in every subject, although for year 5 this has now been cut down to just English, maths and science exams in the Christmas term. Teaching is generally very good; the children learn a lot and are pushed quite hard, parents told us.

There are two full-time specialists and three part-time learning support assistants, and parents reported being very impressed with this input. It was highly visible on our visit, when a number of children were receiving individual or small group tuition.

In the junior school, years 3 and 4 are classroom-based with a form teacher, although they go to music, art, DT and science in dedicated classrooms. There are three proper science labs, complete with a skeleton, and the art department has specialist equipment for etching and a kiln for pottery work. Interesting work on display included flint knapping and cave art.

The pre-prep curriculum includes timetabled IT, and everyone starts an instrument in year 1. This, along with a specialist music teacher just for the pre-prep, enables them amazingly to have a pre-prep orchestra. Reception, year 1 and year 2 have a separate block with their own dining room. Posters around the building ask: 'Do you have good manners?' They're big here, even illness isn't an excuse, as another poster in the health centre asks children whether they have said please and thank you.

Boarding is available to children from year 3. Currently majority of boarders are flexi, but school aims to bring the weekly ratio up to half; some 50 per cent of boarders are from overseas. Boarding accommodation underwent a recent refurbishment, and there is scope to increase the places to 50. Dorms are six-bedded and there's a combined games room. It's loved by the children – the two houseparents are 'really kind', they say, and they enjoy activities such as playing It, having a pizza party, or playing outside on skateboards.

There's a new energy about the place as reforms are working their way through. 'We have deconstructed the atmosphere of elitism generated by a very competitive scholarship stream and attitude to sport; it is wholly inclusive and there is no-one outside looking in.' Whether your child is a scholar or needs extra support, a sporting whizz or an arty type, they'll find their place here.

Holmwood House School

H

Chitts Hill, Lexden, Colchester, Essex CO3 9ST

Ages 3–13 **Pupils** 250 **Boarders** Up to 60 weekly/flexi (from year 4)

Fees: Day £10,140 – £17,895 pa; Boarding £35 per night

01206 574305
www.holmwood.essex.sch.uk

Headmaster: Since 2009, Alexander Mitchell, 50s. Originally from Perthshire, though he worries the burr is fading, having spent more of his life down south than north of the border (not to Essex ears, it isn't). Educated at Napier in Edinburgh, with a degree in music from Colchester and PGCE from Reading. Has taught in the state and public, single-sex and co-ed, day and boarding sectors, most recently for three years as head of the music school at Loughborough Endowed Schools and 10 years as director of music at Haberdashers' Aske's School for Girls. ISI inspector for 10 years. He's only the fifth Holmwood head in its 90-year history and the first ever not to have any past association with the school. 'Underneath his friendly, easy-going exterior there is a respected, efficient, deep-thinking workaholic,' notes a perceptive parent. Lives on-site ('handy for fire drills,' approved a pupil) with his wife Helen – head of PSHCE and registrar – and their two children, all in the school and ranging from year 4 to year 6. Conducting was his love, but he says he doesn't miss the music – 'I have plenty to be getting on with here as headmaster and our head of music and drama is outstanding; I'm very lucky to be doing what I feel I was meant to be doing, it's the best job in the world.' Still finds time to play bass guitar in the school's jazz band. 'Happiness is the key to progress,' he says. 'I can't promise a perfect school but I can promise a happy one.' Chimes with Holmwood's Latin motto, which translates as 'I was glad'.

Entrance: A third from the school's own nursery, which takes 53 children from 6 months and is set in an attractive rural building a few miles from the main school. The rest go off to good local primaries. Usual entry point to the main school is at age 4, straight into the dedicated reception, which takes two classes of 18 in each year. A handful more pupils arrive at throughout each year. Boys in the majority.

Exit: Year 8 children largely depart for Felsted, Framlingham, Ipswich or Oundle. One or two to Uppingham and Rugby and a similar number to Royal Hospital School, Culford, New Hall and Greshams. School proud of range of scholarships won (23 in 2018). Occasional places at eg Eton, Harrow, King's Canterbury, Benenden, Ampleforth, Brighton College, Millfield, Stowe.

Remarks: The principles of the school have remained the same since it was founded on this very site, two miles from Colchester, in 1922 by a Mr and Mrs Duggan, whose aim was 'to develop the individuality and abilities of each child, to make him self-reliant and adaptable and to help him face reality.' A collection of semi-rural buildings punctuated by courtyards and outside spaces that cleverly maximise the opportunities for outdoor education (we've never seen so many woodland classrooms, play areas and nature trails in one prep school). Garden Block arranged around a tranquil garden in memory of a former pupil and treated by all with respect.

H

The Holmwood day is divided into lessons until tea at 4pm and then prep and activities until supper for boarders and more activities until lights-out. Flexi-boarding – minimum one night – is popular and most take advantage by year 8 ('I tell parents their children will let them know when they want to board,' says head). Houses are named after the elements and there are competitions and challenges all year round. Intriguing range of reward systems – golden leaves, superstars, as well as 'showups' and 'showdowns' for older pupils with the requisite number of showdowns leading to a detention ('I had one once,' confessed our guide. 'I'm not getting another one'). There's 'a week for everything' – English, Maths, Mental Health and Well-being, and when we visited a celebrated scientist was setting up ready to give a demonstration as part of Science Week.

Reception children have their own little world, across a path from the main school. Cavernous for the two classes of 18 in the early years department – with airy classrooms and intriguing corners tailored to computer play and dress-up – it also has a lovely outside play area with a patch of age-appropriate, safe woodland to explore. The main pre-prep department houses years 1, 2 and 3 in spacious, modern, purpose-built accommodation. Moving into the prep, pupils are arranged by ability in English, maths, French and science and in years 7 and 8 into a scholarship and three further sets. A few new arrivals, but the head points out 'as the year group gets larger, the sets get smaller'. The scholarship set is made up not just of the brightest but those who have the 'emotional maturity to cope with the stretch and challenge'. Pupils from year 4 begin to move to specialist classrooms – 'you're exhausted for the first few days but you soon get used to it,' reassured our guides. Year 6s learn Latin. French in reception then a carousel of French, Spanish and Mandarin. A few drift off into the strong local state selective system at 11+ but the vast majority press on to 13.

Music and drama is 'about to explode' under the direction of the new head of department, predicts Mr Mitchell. Matilda being rehearsed with years 6 and 7 throughout our visit and, recently Pirates of the Curry Bean. Art room described (accurately) as 'humongous' by our guide, and full of unusual projects including animation installations by year 8s, who all received a still turned into a souvenir picture. DT is offered as an activity in a fully-equipped studio. Sport every day for those who want it. Rugby, hockey and cricket are major for boys, while girls play netball, hockey and rounders. Some 20 acres of the 34 are given over to sport, plus a vast newish sports hall and indoor swimming pool. On-site Lexden Rackets Club – financed by compulsory purchase of school land for the A12 decades ago – is heaving with fit young retirees on a dreary Wednesday morning, but also a superb resource for the school at other times. School has its own tennis and squash coaches.

Library with 12,000 books and an intriguing colour-coded filing system, presided over by the school librarian. Red sofas for the exclusive use of year 8 are as close as they come to a common room. Science labs in converted stables. Jubilee Hall with tiered seating for nearly 200, backed by professional-looking exhibition space – self-portraits when we visited. Dyslexia unit recently renamed learning support (although the sign-maker hasn't yet caught up). Excellent provision for SEN. 'We make progress here,' says the head. 'That might be a scholarship for one child, or an improvement in reading for another. We nurture strengths and support weaknesses and develop young people who are confident, and above all comfortable with whom they are.'

Boarding house open from Monday evenings to Saturday mornings – no full boarding. As well as using school sports, art, music and cooking facilities, boarders have a games room with pool, table football, table tennis etc in the main building cellar for evening recreation. Has abolished Saturday school.

Courtesy and respect are still ingrained at an early age and children here are at ease with anyone (the head swears by the 'train to Norwich test' – in a parallel universe as the proprietor of his own company, he would be sufficiently confident to put any Holmwood pupil on a two-hour train journey with his best client). 'Every child is well mannered and friendly,' agrees a parent. 'Even on the sporting field – win or lose, the children are always gracious.'

Surrounded by its own playing fields, Holmwood has the feel of a much larger school, but at its heart it's a small community of some 300 pupils which extends to embrace their families too. Holmwood is now part of the Bellevue Education Group.

Holyport College

Ascot Road, Holyport, Berkshire SL6 3LE

Ages 11–19 **Pupils** 540 **Sixth form** 188 **Boarders** 224 full

Fees: Day free; Boarding £13,100

01628 640150
www.holyportcollege.org.uk

Head: Since the school's foundation in 2014, Walter Boyle MEd NPQH, previously deputy principal at Wymondham College, England's largest state boarding school. Raised in Belfast, Mr Boyle initially failed the 11+ but was later admitted to Grosvenor Grammar School in Belfast thanks to the intervention of a sharp-eyed teacher. Read French at the University of Strathclyde in Glasgow then, after teacher training at Queen's Belfast, taught for 11 years in Northern Ireland including at Strangford College, a school set up to educate Protestant and RC youth together. Assistant head of Prince Rupert School for Forces families in Germany before heading to Wymondham.

Laser focused on exam results, and unapologetic about his goal of 'getting as many Holyport children as possible into the best universities'. And beyond uni, a career: 'I've got that always at the back of my mind. Straight As are not enough – interests and co-curricular are important, and our longer day here helps.'

Academic matters: Purposeful. Prefers to offer a traditional, fairly narrow, Ebacc-centred, academic curriculum rather than to faff about on frippery. No IB, Pre-Us, IGCSEs or BTecs. Offers Latin, but no DT. Single sciences, but no business studies. Second set of GCSEs were taken in 2018 with superb results, especially in sciences, Latin and – surprisingly – art. Seventy-seven per cent got 9-4 in both English and maths (57 per cent got 9-5). A third of all results were at A*-A/9-7. First A levels will be taken in June 2019. STEM subjects are big here: 50 per cent of sixth form uptake is for maths or sciences subjects. Also offers economics, government & politics and sports science.

Carefully chosen staff, many from independent schools or state boarding. 'They listen to, act on and are very open with parents,' said a mum whose child joined the school upon its opening in 2014. 'It was a leap in the dark deciding to send our child as first cohort into a new school,' she recalled. 'I cannot express enough how impressed I am by them'.

Afternoon prep sessions supervised by sixth formers. Pupils we spoke to praised the SEN provision. Art therapist and a counsellor visit the school each week.

Games, options, the arts: The extended day – 8.30am-5.30pm for all pupils, boarding and day – is the school's secret sauce. The long afternoon allows time for a phenomenal co-curricular programme with offerings ranging from Mindful Colouring to Real Tennis, Young Enterprise and ballet. 'And it's a bonus for working parents too', a mum reminded us.

Games and sport rule, and no excuses. Games and PE three or four times a week in the younger years (less after year 9). Main sports for girls netball, hockey, tennis and athletics. For boys football, rugby, cricket and athletics. Loads of lesser sports; can't be many other schools – state or private – where every child learns to play Eton fives and does a PE module of rowing. 'When we first set up the school, Eton didn't push anything....' recalls the head, 'But they did ask if the children might perhaps learn to play Eton fives'. Regular team games also flourish (LVS and Marist College are arch-rivals). Saturday morning matches against independent schools (day pupils come in for these), some held at Eton; Wednesday matches against state schools. All that said, it's perfectly possible to be a non-sporty soul and thrive here.

Some 40 per cent learn a musical instrument. Three choirs; one gets the opportunity to sing at Windsor Castle and at Holyport's Christmas carol concert held at Eton. Art popular ('It's costing me a fortune,' sighs the head). Annual college musical is performed in Maidenhead Town Hall. D of E thrives and awards are presented at Eton. Older pupils may take part in some Eton societies. Boys can now take part in CCF with Eton (and girls from Sept 2018)

Boarding: Almost equal numbers of boy and girl boarders are housed directly above the classrooms in a school version of 'living over the shop'. Certainly unique: day pupils walk through the boarders' common rooms to reach their study area on the floor above. The biggest dormitories house five; sixth formers room in pairs. Fourteen staff, plus their families, live on campus. Post-university 'gap students' assist. No mistresses here: female heads of houses are referred to as 'housemasters'. Boarders can arrange to spend a school night at home each week eg to attend to take part in a local activity or sports team. Also allowed to go home on Saturdays after their sports obligations (if any). About 60 per cent stay in school all weekend

Background and atmosphere: The 'first boarding free school' opened in September 2014, with much ado and a visit from the Queen, Prince Phillip and Theresa May (the school's in her constituency). Set snugly on Ascot Road in affluent rural Berkshire ('If you want a mix, it's easier to get less-advantaged families to come to a school in an affluent area than to get well-off children to attend school in a poor area', explains the head).

A compact school – it began with 68 day pupils and 55 boarders in years 7-10, and enrolled its first lower sixth year group in 2017. Its smallish numbers make many things possible (discipline, personal touch, small class sizes) but create some limitations (range of sixth form subjects). Also small physically, with minor irritations (parking, shortage of music practice rooms) already seeping in. In the running for our coveted 'most hidden school office' award – reception is tucked behind the main school (took us nine minutes to find, had to employ satnav, step-counter, and phone-a-friend). This beating heart of the school, 'the SNW', is named for Sir Nicholas Winton who rescued 699 children, most of them Jewish, from Czechoslovakia on the eve of WW2. Sir Nicholas attended the school's opening (at the age of 105) and pupils strive to carry on his altruistic example through community service and links with a school in Gambia. New-build school quad is functional but dreary. We were there on a stuffy winter day: a bit of ventilation in some of the classrooms would work wonders.

May not look like a private school, but it many ways it runs like one: scholars programme with talks and events to stretch the clever clogs. Lord Adonis handed out prizes at prize-giving. Some pupils had recently attended a lecture at Eton by former US Secretary of State and presidential candidate John Kerry when we visited. The pupils are proud of the schools' relationship with Eton and there's no chip on shoulder weirdness about it. Indeed the relationship seems to work both ways, with Eton and Holyport now learning from each other.

H

Pastoral care, well-being and discipline: Drugs and alcohol haven't been major problems – yet. But staff are rewriting school policies in anticipation of the school's first 18 year olds attending from Sept 2018. Pupils can used mobiles between lessons but if used in class 'they're gone'. All pupils are assigned to a house (girl day pupils join a boys's boarding house; boy day pupils join boarding girls). Most recent Ofsted report is so gushing it makes one blush: 'The exceptionally skilful headmaster...', 'Pupils' conduct throughout the school is excellent and their behaviour is impeccable', 'The school is a harmonious community'..

Pupils and parents: Feel lucky to be here. The requirement to be at school until 5.30 of an evening filters out most slackers and compulsory sports scares off the rest. Aspires to being a carefully orchestrated melting pot of abilities, ethnicities and social backgrounds, and comes darn close. The school has the highest percentage of looked after and adopted children in Windsor and Maidenhead LA and over 12 per cent of pupils are on free school meals (roughly the national average). That said, more children come from Privet Lane than Benefits Street. Children's behaviour that we witnessed was impressive. 'It's an academic school,' a parent told us, 'but what I like most is that they're expected to say please and thank you, to tuck in their shirt, to clean their shoes, to show respect.'

Entrance: Horrifically, shockingly oversubscribed: received 376 applications for 26 year 7 day places in 2017. A meagre 26 day places and 18 boarding places available in year 7 and the same again in year 9. One family we spoke to had moved from London for no reason other than to be near enough to qualify for Holyport.

Day places are literally gold dust: academically non-selective but 'priority is given to so many children that there's barely any space left for locals,' grumbled a parent. The parade of priorities includes the usuals – looked after or adopted children, those with a special medical need, siblings – but also children of the school's founders (!), children receiving pupil premium (up to 20 per cent of intake), children of staff and, for year 9 entry, children moving up from Windsor middle schools. Only then does proximity come into play.

Boarding places require an interview to establish 'suitability to board'. Then priority is given to boarding 'need', with Forces families at the top of the pack.

A few sixth form places for external candidates. Minimum requirement (for internal and external candidates): seven A*-C/9-4

GCSEs, including English and maths, of which five must be B/6s. GCSE A/7 grades are required in subjects to be studied at A level.

Exit: Too soon to say. In 2018, 50 per cent of 16 year olds stayed on to join the school's new sixth form. Some did not make the cut, others chose to move elsewhere to pursue less traditionally academic subjects or vocational courses. Pupils can attend careers talks at Eton.

Remarks: A school with the modest aim of transforming lives. Much has been invested in this school – not just money but reputations. So far, so excellent, especially STEM.

Horris Hill School

H

Newtown, Newbury, Berkshire RG20 9DJ

Ages 7–13 **Pupils** 120 **Boarders** 90 **C of E**

Fees: Day £16,800 – £20,400; Boarding £23,850 – £27,450 pa

01635 40594
www.horrishill.com

Headmaster: Since 2011, Giles Tollit BA (40s). Tall and lean, reminded us a little of Bryan Ferry in his salad days. Seems reserved at first but soon unbends and shows a nice, dry sense of humour. Initially destined for a career in the military, he studied classics at Bristol on an army bursary. Took gap year job at a prep where he was expecting to teach Latin in a fairly junior capacity, but before term started found himself head of classics. Such a fiery baptism would have been enough to turn a lesser chap off teaching, but it had the opposite effect on Mr Tollit, and Sandhurst's loss turned out to be preps' gain. Ten years at Caldicott and thence to Bilton Grange as deputy head. He's 'delighted to be back in an all boys boarding school' (he loved his own time at prep) and certain about the positive benefits of a sector he believes suffers from outdated stereotypes. Not that he has to sell boarding to the parents he meets; they've all done it themselves. Describes school, memorably, as being 'not dissimilar to a cruise ship; doors close at the start of each term and off we go.'

Mr Tollit teaches Latin and Greek and helps the scholars polish their skills in debating, logic and philosophy, he 'mucks in' as necessary and takes year 8 camping at his house in north Wales after exams. Describes HH as a 'seven day a week' school and is unconvinced by flexi-boarding, which he feels is sometimes the worst of both worlds. A former UK shot, he has introduced clay pigeon shooting and a rifle range is planned. He's also a keen photographer and, because 26 miles just isn't enough of a challenge, an ultramarathon runner.

Married to Molly, also a classicist, whom he met at university. It seems that three young sons aren't enough for Molly, who has turned her energies to transforming part of a field in the school grounds into a thriving kitchen garden. Establishing one at their former school, Bilton Grange, taught her 'what works and what doesn't' and HH is reaping the rewards.

Parents think the Tollits have brought energy to the school and like the fact they have their own family. They have total faith in Mr Tollit, think he knows their boys incredibly well and praise his (and rest of staff's) swift response to calls and emails. Boys think head needs to be 'a bit more relaxed' but like the fact he's introduced clay pigeon shooting.

Entrance: From age 7. No exam 'as such'. Head meets all prospective parents. Boys have informal interview with the head, simple maths and English assessment and spend a day, a year before entry for those pre-registered. Mr Tollit says he's 'not looking for superstars'; boys are observed to see how they interact and whether they are comfortable being 'in the academic spotlight' of such small classes. Years 3-6 can be day or boarding; years 7-8 boarding only (does not take new entrants to year 8).

Exit: Nearly all to senior boarding schools. Recently: Winchester, Radley, Eton, Harrow, Sherborne, Marlborough.

Remarks: Founded in 1888 to prepare boys for entry to Winchester, Horris Hill is set in 80 acres of wooded heathland on the borders of Berkshire and Hampshire. You'll need your satnav first time round so as not to miss the quaint wooden signpost directing you down an unpromisingly narrow lane; it's almost as though only those who need to will find their way here.

One of Horris Hill's idiosyncrasies is that it doesn't do year groups, it does 'termly remove'. Boys are placed in small classes (average 12) according to the progress they are making and remain there until they have mastered all their subjects to the requisite level. It might sound like a nightmare to organise but head says the maximum discrepancy between similar age boys is 'a couple of terms either way'. A boy's performance is reviewed via 'form order' (mark, position and effort grade) every three weeks, and at the end of term he stays or moves up accordingly. It's an unusual (possibly unique) system and only feasible in a school of this size (max 130) and age group. Besides accommodating summer birthdays, advantages are no B stream, no individual subject setting and ongoing challenges for both brightest and less able. According to Mr Tollit, it's as close as you can get to an education that is customised to each boy's needs. Arrangement is only for academic work; boys are grouped by age for sport, dorms etc. Parents all in favour, say it's great both for confidence and humility as boys are usually towards the lower end during first term and nearer the top in the second. The consensus is that the system works, even if one or two parents admitted they didn't entirely understand it.

Lessons we observed were fun, inclusive and challenging – a hard trio to achieve but less so with a class of 10, perhaps. Subject classrooms are named after senior schools: Winchester, Harrow, Eton, Radley etc. It took a bit of getting used to seeing such an age range, but the boys' enthusiasm and rapport with teachers was inspiring. In geography, impressive answers to quick fire questions were rewarded with chocolate; in the next classroom we thought we'd come across boys being punished but discovered that immersion in French pop music is a great way to practise listening and vocab. In the DT workshop, small boys in enormous aprons were busy sanding and drilling – some with more finesse than others. Was there anything, we asked, that they would like to change at their school? Extra free time was one suggestion, as was getting rid of second prep (senior boys do this after supper). Most popular idea was being able to bring small pets to school, something we mentioned to Mr Tollit, who promised to consider the proposal. Few boys with SEN – dyslexia, dyspraxia – receive support but this isn't the place for those with more than mild problems.

The no mobiles, laptops, iPads (basically, no screens) rule is, as far as we could tell, no big deal and so much easier than trying to control limited access. Boys write weekly letters and may email/Skype from the house computer. As a teacher observed, if the no screens policy were to change, 'it would mean more rules.' Boys accept the policy and parents love it. They're not quite so keen when, for instance, CE results come out and they can't talk to their sons because the boarding house telephone is engaged – surely room for a little more 21st century communication technology here? This is a school where 'live' notice boards mean that someone changes the pictures and display on the wall in the dining hall corridor several times a day. There aren't smartboards in every classroom, although those we saw were being creatively employed; boys treasure the one or two teachers who spurn their use. Science labs, art and DT rooms have all the necessaries in a charmingly scruffy, no frills style. By contrast, a high tech rooftop weather station relays the prevailing conditions to a screen outside the geography room.

Sensible uniform features navy blue cords – either trousers or shorts, boys can decide. Apparently 'some boys wear shorts even when it snows.' Sartorial democracy extends to choice of tie as well. Long morning and lunch breaks allow plenty of time to work in the kitchen garden, ride bikes (boys can bring own), play outside in the meadows, make dens and have adventures in their own bosky dominion (known as Spain because it's roughly the same shape). Nowhere is out of bounds but pupils mustn't go off alone. Camping out and cooking in the woods is one of the ultimate post-CE treats. Juniors have their own wood, 'too tame for us,' said our super confident year 8 guides. One of the characteristics of HH is the amount of personal freedom pupils enjoy, finely balanced by the equivalent expectation of personal responsibility. Boys organise their own activities (or sign up), recording where they are on a notice board so that everybody knows.

Youngest boarders (age 7-9) have lovely rooms in the 'private side' above the head's family quarters, with teddies on beds and lots of posters. Evening activities include silent reading, film nights with popcorn, board games and even shoe polishing (try suggesting that at home...). Numbers are small so things are flexible; if it's hot they can have a swim, if everyone's exhausted they go to bed early. Gappies 'bridge the gap' between boys and staff and are, as always, very popular. What about the homesick, we ask? Of course it happens, but staff are vigilant and boys support each other, telling tutors if they're worried about someone. 'You feel awkward at first,' our guides said, 'but it only lasts a week.'

Lots of younger teachers with families live on site, married couples head up the boarding houses, but after the junior forms most of the teaching staff are men. This notwithstanding, the traditional boys' own atmosphere prevails and is what many, especially army families, treasure. There are a few local day boys who are 'building up to boarding', rest may go home after matches on Saturday until Sunday evening (except first and last weekend of term) but most stay, 'or you miss too much fun.' That fun includes cross-country cycling, tree running, kite flying and ghost stories round the campfire. A parent praised the 'pater' system that pairs new boys with older boys and said that these cross age friendships are kept up throughout school. Older boys move on to one of two Edwardian houses a short walk across the playing fields. Four bed rooms are very comfortably furnished with home duvets, posters, beanbags and lovely soft carpet. Fruit bowl and toaster fill the gaps between meals, all of which are eaten in school dining room. Everyone, staff and pupils, sits down together at large tables, boys serve the food. Head v keen on benefits of 'interaction across a table'.

Spacious and well designed music school can accommodate all for studio theatre or concert performances. Twenty-six practice rooms means there's no excuse for not getting down to scales and arpeggios after breakfast. Parts for all in 'fantastic' music and plays. Main venue for drama, assemblies etc is rather tired windowless sports hall, not enhanced by pervasive whiffy trainer smell, but never fear, Mr Tollit is on the case and this part of the school is undergoing complete refurbishment. As he says, 'HH is not a flash school', but a shooting range, climbing wall and upgraded squash courts are on the way. Interestingly, it seemed to us that there was less of an obsession with organised sport and winning here than at other similar schools. Plenty of options: usuals plus hockey, squash, tennis, sailing, golf, fencing. Boys think cricket and football are what they're best at and all get to represent school in something. Parents come and watch matches, although it's a long round trip if you live in London. Swimming pool is outdoors (very) with wooden changing huts – all a bit basic but doubtless character building. One of the school's 'quite old fashioned secret things' is the modelling and train room, a glue and paint besmattered garret where Warhammer enthusiasts create their miniature worlds and model railway buffs of all ages can operate trains and signals.

With a maximum of 130 pupils, quite a few who are siblings, the parent body is small, self selecting and fiercely supportive. Although it's in a wealthy part of the country, HH is definitely not (outwardly at least), a smart school. Parents are welcomed to plays, concerts, matches and Sunday evening chapel and there are social events such as fathers' and sons' cricket matches and mothers' and sons' tennis, but there's no PTA, sports day or speech day. One father, who had considered London day schools for his sons, spoke of the way in which HH 'preserves innocence' – not just by absence of personal technology but also because full boarding means boys develop a camaraderie that is not influenced by each others' possessions or houses. On a more practical level, parents love the fact that all sports kit is provided, washed and maintained by the school.

Horris Hill is such a distinctive school it's unlikely you could choose it by mistake; proud to be different, it epitomises the very best prep school traditions without being pompous or rigid. HH boys are confident but not precocious; they think for themselves but aren't arrogant. There's room for big characters but a shy child won't be trampled underfoot; academic success is important but not to the exclusion of other talents. As another happy parent told us, 'it's a hidden gem.'

H

Howard of Effingham School

Lower Road, Effingham, Leatherhead, Surrey KT24 5JR

Ages 11–18 **Pupils** 1,580 **Sixth form** 354

01372 453694
www.thehoward.org

Headteacher: Since 2012, Helen Pennington BSc NPQH, previously deputy head. A hands-on and a long-serving teacher with more than a decade's experience at the school; a year-long absence in 2009 to 2010 on secondment to Ofsted, followed by troubleshooting support at assorted struggling schools has given her a breadth of experience. We found her chirpy, down-to-earth and no-nonsense, while parents who know her (not all parents that we spoke to did) describe her as 'a positive force', 'a good listener' and 'easy to talk to.' While she doesn't teach (except on an ad hoc basis when necessary), students told us she's a visible presence in the school.

Since 1999, the school has been overseen by Rhona Barnfield MA BSc CBE (for services to education). She is CEO of the Howard Partnership Trust – a not-for-profit, multi-academy trust made up of nine local primary and secondary schools, including Thomas Knyvett College in Ashford and Oxted School. She chairs assorted education-related committees in Surrey, and is a member of the Regional Headteacher Board, a group elected by professionals who support the regional schools commissioner in his work in overseeing the performance of academies in south London and south east England. She is 'more of a figurehead than anything else now,' as one mother put it, rarely even attending events at the school.

Academic matters: Long-held reputation for excellence, managing consistently good results against stiffish local competition, including from independents. In 2018, 83 per cent of pupils got 9-4 in both English and maths GCSE, with 26 per cent A*-A/9-7 grades. At A level, 55 per cent of grades were A*/B and 27 per cent A*/A.

School takes considerable pains to choose high quality teaching staff who are passionate advocates for their specialist subjects. 'They make sure every child reaches their full potential, no matter what it takes,' one parent told us. We wondered if the first class we passed – in which excitable, but immaculately behaved students were thoroughly engaged in a fun subject quiz – would be a one-off; but it wasn't, with every teacher we saw using imaginative techniques. 'You'll rarely see a science lab without a practical going on,' one student told us, while another added, 'The teachers are so supportive – you never feel you're getting in the way if you knock on their office door and they'll think nothing of spending an extra half hour with you if it's needed.' Strong academic results also helped by 'the fact that we've worked so hard on behaviour and attitudes,' believes the head. 'It means teaching can be a real joy here, with extremely positive relationships with students.'

There's constant feedback, with students kept informed about where they stand and what they should be capable of, while parents get three reports a year. If any student's work slips, they're given a mentor and strategies are put in place – whether that's a revision course or one-to-one support. Teacher training is superb, with inset days maximised – for example via a 'best practice festival,' in which teachers showcase examples in under two, four or six minutes. 'We create a video and blog so teachers can go back to it. It's inspirational seeing the techniques,' says the head, who adds that there's also a lot of sharing of best practice with other schools in the Howard Partnership Trust.

Academically strong across all GCSEs, with stand-out results in English, maths, science, history, technology and drama (which are also the popular options, with the addition of PE). Practical GCSE options include food preparation and nutrition, and there's also a good range of vocational qualifications offered by the school as GCSE alternatives/additions, including BTecs in business, sport and a technical award in textiles. Everyone takes at least one modern foreign language GCSE – with language teaching beginning in year 7, when almost all students take two languages out of French, Spanish and German. 'In year 9, the ones who appear to have the least aptitude for languages drop one,' says the head, who adds that they also offer 'express languages' to students who show the most aptitude. Latin available as an enrichment option for the most academically able from year 9. With early setting (for maths and languages in year 7 first term and English and science added in year 8) the aim is for each to receive according to need.

An impressive 37 A levels available, with maths, sciences, social sciences and humanities attracting the highest numbers of students – while the strongest results are in maths, sciences, psychology, media studies, history, geography, geology, product design and graphics. Languages have a relatively low take-up, but they do run here. School listens and will add new subjects if demand and resources are there.

Not a high proportion of SEN, but there's the full range of mild, moderate and severe – who are helped both inside and outside the classroom with tailored help. 'The SENCo is extraordinary – she and her very caring team work really hard with the children,' said one parent. 'I was advised that my son should go to a specialist school because of his needs, but he wanted to come here because all his friends were – and it was absolutely the right decision. He's loved it and passed all his GCSES, which I would never in a million years have thought possible,' said another. 'You wouldn't know the difference between students with and without SEN in this school – and that's the way we like it,' says the head.

Games, options, the arts: Two hours a week devoted to PE. In winter, the core sports are netball, hockey, rugby and football, while in summer, it's tennis, athletics, cricket and rounders – but there's plenty more variety besides, including gymnastics, badminton, trampolining and dance. Extracurricular sport is high on the agenda, and there are regular tours, for instance for rugby and football – plus, the school supports individuals whose talents lie in more unusual sports, such as ice skating, rowing, sailing etc. Lots to brag about when it comes to sporting successes, both from individual students and school teams – and indeed the school does just that every week on the PE faculty's twitter feed. 'To my great delight, we hold up well against our fee paying neighbours,' smiles the head.

Students reassured us that sport isn't just for the elite; parents not so sure, with one saying, 'Some of the PE teachers do seem to have their favourites, who get picked for everything.' Another believed the issue is more the lack of PE staff, 'which means they can only run an A team and sometimes a B team.' Facilities include a big sports hall (which doubles as a dance studio), plus a gym. Outside, there are hard courts and a field, but as it's not the best quality, the school also rents the King George V Playing Fields in the summer, just a minute's walk away. For home rugby fixtures the school uses Cobham RFC, which parents and players love.

Slick annual productions from the drama department, some with huge casts. 'The last production, Evita, was amazing – they put so much work into it,' a parent told us. Drama is increasingly popular as a sixth form option (boys as well as girls).

Richness of offerings inside art and DT departments reflect willingness to invest in pupil creativity. Students can choose from GCSE options of art and design, fine art, textiles, product design, graphics and food preparation and nutrition – while at A level, there's art, textiles, fine art and photography in the art department and graphics and product design in DT. Some stunning work is displayed throughout the school, as well as some more average work – always a good sign that art is recognised as beneficial to all, not just the extremely talented.

Music is a major part of school life, with a whole school orchestra, chamber orchestra, jazz bands and various choirs including a pop choir. Some of the performances (eg rock and pop concerts) are co-managed by the students – while other regulars include summer and winter concerts, an annual music festival with a local primary school and students going out to sing in local old folks' homes at Christmas. Peripatetic teachers come in to teach over 100 children everything from drums to trumpet.

Masses of trips. Natural History Museum, Kew Gardens and Barton-on-Sea are just a few of the day trips on offer. Language exchanges, including to Switzerland (which covers French and German). Sports tours to various countries. Even Disneyland Paris is a potential destination for students here, while sixth formers studying science are invited to expeditions to the likes of Honduras or Mexico, where they do real research work. There is also a trip to Cern.

Background and atmosphere: Set in the east of the village of Effingham, the school first opened in 1940, when it was built for 240 pupils. It's a good job facilities have since expanded (including a sports centre, purpose-built sixth form block, new senior canteen and some specialist science facilities) as the school now has in excess of 1,500 students. 'You do feel the squeeze in some departments, such as drama, and in some corridors,' one student told us – although sixth formers say there's no lack of private study areas, which is the most common complaint around physical limitations in secondary schools. Nor is there any shortage of outside green space, certainly at the front (lots of grass and a playing field) – although tarmac prevails round the back, including a bleak-looking netball court, albeit with a fair few mature trees dotted around.

There's no frills when it comes to facilities – and many look tired and run-down. We spotted two half-eaten apples on the floor of one corridor, despite the bin being just a few metres away. What's more, our guides didn't pick them up as they passed. That said, it is, by-and-large, kept tidy and this school is proof that outer appearances do not have to be a guide to inner beauty, with students clearly bursting with pride about their school, which seems to strike just the right balance between a pervading sense of order and a feeling of overall cheeriness. In all classrooms we visited, engaged students looked absorbed in their study. And it's not as if the students are particularly interested in having shiny, new state-of-the-art buildings. 'More than once, I've said to my children, "Surely you'd like newer buildings and more space?" but they defend it to the hilt,' one parent told us. The library is lovely – a large, open-plan space that includes a library garden, while the computer suites are plentiful and well-stocked. Art – including DT – also spacious and well-equipped. Two separate canteens serve different age groups, with students reporting positively on the standard of the food.

Pastoral care, well-being and discipline: Highly rated by parents. 'My child had the same form tutor from year 7 right up to her GCSEs, and she was wonderful,' said one parent. Year 7s are eased in very gently, with support from trained-up year 9 mentors, their own area at break time and earlier lunchtime to give them a few minutes' head start on the mêlée. Refreshingly, there's also lots of work on resilience in these earlier years – the theory being that students may encounter fewer problems if they are more resilient. At the other end of the age range, sixth formers start by having to be in at the same time as younger pupils, though later on, after demonstration of requisite commitment, they may enjoy a lie-in if they don't have early lessons. They wear own clothes and can melt away into own common room for R and R, bizarrely furnished with railway platform style slatted metal benches on one side, soft seating on the other.

Strong pastoral structure means there are 'lots of different channels you can go down,' say parents. 'The first point of call would be the form teacher, then you've got head of year, head of subject, deputy head and then the head.' Pupils, too, praised staff accessibility – felt to be good throughout the school and exceptional in the sixth form. 'You can go to anyone,' said one. 'They're very sympathetic.' Flexible, too. And there are part-time counsellors.

Parents say it's a kindly place, with plenty of rewards for effort – including house points, postcards home, green cards, headteacher's commendations and achievement assemblies. But the school is no pushover, with high expectations, particularly around good manners, uniform and deadlines. 'The big step change with good behaviour was us deciding that if we modelled it – treating the students in exactly the same way we would want to be treated – then it might be copied, and it has been,' says the head. 'Behaviour here has improved dramatically,' agree parents.

Students are crystal clear on the rewards and sanctions ladder system – which include B1-3 cards (1 for low-level behaviour like talking in class, while 3 is for serious stuff like bad language). 'Students tend to get the most detentions in the earlier years,' students told us – and even these are tiered, with the two-hour Friday headteacher' s detention the most shameful. Fixed-term exclusions have declined dramatically within the last five years, although unusually the school refused to provide any figures. No permanent exclusions at all – although very occasionally (again, they won't provide figures), students are referred to off-site provision (mainly for physical violence, although it would be unfair to suggest this is a problem here. Nor is drugs – there have been no issues at all in recent years).

Not bullying free, but trained student anti-bullying ambassadors and the promise of prompt response to any issues all help. 'My daughter was on the receiving end of some nasty behaviour and it was stopped immediately,' said one parent. Another told us, 'I've had a couple of issues, but I emailed teachers on a Sunday night and got a phone call back on the Sunday night. They are keen to nip things in the bud.'

Student voice reasonably strong, while the head boy and girl also chair a primary school confederation council made up of representatives from the main feeder schools.

Pupils and parents: Lots of affluence (local property prices have gone up, largely thanks to this school), with some having used the independent sector for the primary years, but this is by no means the case for all. 'In fact, one of the reasons I love this school is because it's socially varied and not all one type,' one parent told us. The furthest come from 10 miles away, with most pupils getting one of the seven contract coaches, while others get public buses, cycle or walk. Families are 90 per cent white British – a reflection of the area. Great sense of community for such a large school.

Notable alumni include Tom Felton (played Draco Malfoy), Tom Shanklin (rugby union), Emelia Gorecka (athlete) and Dan Gallagher (footballer).

Entrance: Predictably oversubscribed for 240-place year 7 entry, with over three applicants for every one place. The seven-tiered local authority entry criteria is pretty standard and basically means that anyone living in Horsley (East and West) is in; ditto Howard-facing Fetcham inhabitants. Those with siblings at the school are in with a stronger chance, though priority status is given to those living within catchment area. Combination of proximity and attendance at feeder primaries (Oakfield, Eastwick, St Lawrence, The Raleigh, The Dawnay and The Royal Kent, among others) is the next best bet.

For sixth form – which sees between 20-30 students joining from other schools – net is cast a bit wider. School welcomes applicants from a range of private and state sector – and gets them. 'Normally, we expect the equivalent of five 4s at GCSE and at least a 6 in the chosen subjects,' says the head.

Exit: Around 25-30 per cent leave at 16, many for sixth form colleges – although interestingly, a number of these students (some years, as many as 10) return to the school during the academic year. Of those who leave after sixth form, over 95 per cent stay in education. Assortment of subjects studied, including STEM, psychology, geography, business and economics. Destinations also varied, with current popular ones including Nottingham, Southampton, Leeds, Bristol and Exeter. In 2018, three to Oxbridge and three medics.

Remarks: High-quality education from a serious-minded and effective school. Minute attention to detail and inspired teaching ensures that, for a large school, nobody slips through the net, with strong results in both absolute and value-added terms. A well-oiled machine that students are rightfully very proud of.

Hurstpierpoint College

140

College Lane, Hurstpierpoint, West Sussex BN6 9JS

Ages 4–18 **Pupils** 826 **Sixth form** 319 **Boarders** 404 weekly & flexi (from 13 years) **C of E**

Fees: Day: £9,060 – £23,850; Boarding: £27,825 – £29,955 pa

01273 833636
www.hppc.co.uk

H

Headmaster: Since 2005, Tim Manly (Oxford, LSE and Cambridge), married to Henny with four children. Abandoned a career in commerce to teach, first at Sevenoaks, then as deputy head at Oakham School before joining Hurst. The only head we've come across where pupils gave an audible 'aaaah...' when asked for their views: 'the best head'; 'respectful of us as pupils....makes the effort and knows all names'; 'not scary...you can have a conversation with him'. The head likes to keep teenagers busy and expectations of pupils are high, said another, who described the head as 'a man of boundless energy; always there, always visible... who is very engaging as an individual. [He] takes every opportunity to include parents in what the school is thinking and intending'.

Head of prep and pre-prep: Since 2013, Ian Pattison (chemistry, Southampton), married to Janina with one son at the prep. Joined Hurst as a chemistry teacher in 1997, and became a housemaster in 2006. This warm, enthusiastic head loves hockey and cycling up mountains; no surprise, then, that he wants his pupils to be ready to take on the world. 'Not a place for children who just want to turn up to do lessons and go home'. A head pupils can go and talk to about anything.

Academic matters: 'Pupils are well taught and achieve their academic potential', said a parent. '[It] does its core purpose brilliantly'. In 2018, 54 per cent A*/A at A level, 84 per cent A*/B. At GCSE, 67 per cent A*-A/9-7. Sciences and maths are popular high performers.

No IB takers in the current cohort, but the door isn't closed to those keen to take the IB in future years. A good range of subjects available, including BTec in business and sport, though pupils felt media studies was a noticeable omission from the list. The head initiated dropping from four A levels to three, with all pupils doing the EPQ.

Results have gone up in the last four years: parents speculate that this is partly due to a more selective intake, partly due to a change of staff – 'it's a very quality staffroom now', say staff. Parents told us there has been a tightening up of academic standards: 'If pupils don't engage academically, there will be more and more supervision to ensure they do engage and get the grades they are capable of getting', said parent. Some 'disquiet at new rules', with a few parents expressing concern that Hurst might be edging into the territory of the local high flying competitor, but things have settled down, and parents are delighted by the new regime for Oxbridge (five places in 2018).

Hurst has a challenge grade system, which means that each child's performance is assessed according to the challenge set for them: tick is on target, +1 exceeding target, -1 falling short. There are no comparisons between pupils, and a parent commented that she likes the fact that a very academic child can get minus marks because they're not achieving their potential. There are frequent reviews under the challenge grade system, and teacher comments are 'thoughtful, personal and helpful' said a parent. It certainly works for pupils, with Hurst in the top 10 per cent nationally for value added. 'Academic performance is not the be all and end all', said a parent, but her child 'achieved more than she thought she would achieve'.

One hour lessons and a longer school day means there is a steady pace, said a parent, but expectations are in accordance with your abilities: 'you are recognised and supported as a person'. Parents describe great support from staff – 'happy and willing to work incredibly long hours', said one appreciatively; 'they make it easy to catch up if you fall behind,' said a pupil.

iPhones are allowed in the senior school: the school is strict about usage, and pupils generally keep them switched off when they're meant to be. Pupils in years 9-11 have MacBooks, and iPads are frequently used in the prep, which one parent said has made a 'huge difference [to her son's] learning and confidence'.

Hurst is described by the head of prep as 'a genuine through school', and it works hard to ensure continuity between prep and senior school: a single deputy head academic covers both schools, and any change to the college curriculum will result in changes all the way down; for example, the introduction of Spanish GCSE means that this is now taught in years 7 and 8 of prep.

Year 8s take exams before leaving prep; it's not the CE, but there is a ritualistic formality about them, and all the frisson of results in envelopes. Pupils want to do well, though not through fear of failure: all progress to the college (the few whom it is felt would not thrive there are told in good time). The absence of CE frees up the curriculum – year 8s spend time doing a presentation and essay on a topic of their choice.

The learning support department provides mostly one-to-one support for pupils with mild learning difficulties. A parent described how their unconfident dyspraxic son turned into a different child at Hurst – 'he didn't feel a misfit anymore'. He was assessed straightaway, and the parent was asked how her child learned and what worked for him; her advice was forwarded to all her son's teachers and has been every year since.

Games, options, the arts: One parent said what she liked best about Hurst was 'the sheer level of opportunity and encouragement. Everyone has a go and gives everything they've got. Whether you're good at something or not doesn't matter – everyone will support you. That's what you're paying for...'

The wide range of co-curricular activities here includes dissection, mechanics, environmental conservation, CCF and DofE (silver for all). 'They encourage anything which enthuses the kids', said a mum, describing how her chamber music loving daughter was encouraged to create a group.

Music is a popular pastime, though numbers taking A level are few, and every taste is catered for; there's a huge non-audition choir of 160, and a selective one too. A lively outreach programme sees Hurst musicians entertaining the local community: the Big Band playing for village pensioners at Cake at the College, and the brass group playing festive music for the WI in the village.

There are a great number of dramatic performances every term, from Cabaret to Titus Andronicus and Lord of the Flies (by the prep), now in the new theatre. 'It's better to do lots, than one Barbican level performance a year', says the head, and this means that performers include both the experienced and novice at this school which champions 'give it a go', regardless of ability.

A rugby school in the main, with just a couple of teams giving a nod to football. Netball is strong for girls, and both girls and boys play hockey and cricket. '...[there are] isolated moments when rugby comes first, netball second...but girls' sport has come on tremendously and does extremely well', said a parent. A school with an inclusive sports ethic: a parent said her son is in a D team, but still enjoys matches every other weekend. 'You can't tell which team they're in on the basis of enthusiasm', says the head of prep.

A flexible approach to sixth form games – you can do what you want three times a week, and games haters can do yoga instead. Even lower down in the school, there is a humane quality to games here – a parent told us how her son, rugby hater, joined Hurst prep, and was immediately allowed to do kayaking, rock climbing and orienteering instead.

Art is displayed throughout the school, in beautifully mounted neat and tidy style. Standards are high, and facilities have recently expanded to include a printing press and textiles room, in which pupils used wax and sewing to produce a mixed media hanging exploring man's impact on the environment. Only a handful take A level, but GCSE is more popular, with most pupils achieving high grades.

Boarding: A strong house system here with separate houses for day pupils and boarders. A parent described their child's house as 'a refuge, not just a place to leave books': there are homely common rooms, cosy bedrooms with bunkbeds or studies for day pupils, and kitchens ('for cookie baking', said a parent).

'Care is extremely good', said a parent, who added that on the odd occasion her daughters had had problems with girls they roomed with, the housemistress had listened, and switched the girls' rooms.

Pupils are together with 10 or so others in their year group, and form a really strong bond: their 'own clan', said a parent. 'It's the main way you make friends', said a pupil, and they evidently enjoy much lively inter-house competition, including house water polo.

St John's is the sixth form boarding house, and popular with parents and pupils alike. 'St John's is brilliant', said a parent, 'a good step up towards university...but still well monitored and controlled'. Individual rooms at St John's mean pupils can sleep during the day if they want to; the head is evidently not speaking lightly when he says 'it's a busy place, pacy – pupils need some stamina'. School no longer offers full boarding in the sixth.

Currently no prep school boarding, but plans to introduce this soon for years 7 and 8.

Background and atmosphere: Parents choose Hurst because they feel it provides something more than an academic education: 'We want [them] to do well academically but not as an expression of everything else... we want them to be brought on as people...'; 'we wanted the children to be themselves'. Seen, then, as a holistic educational experience by parents, it is no surprise to hear the head say, 'I don't want to win everything, it's not healthy...'. Learning here comes from many different angles, and the school is loyal to its pupils – 'Anyone who is in the school can stay. We will back them. We always take siblings if we can...'

School buildings of grand old Sussex flint walls, draughty cloisters surround a courtyard, and Grimm's fairytale windows. Gorgeous grounds – 140 acres of them, but they are not the main pull for pupils. 'I fell in love with Hurst', said a pupil. 'It was the atmosphere, everyone was involved'. Pupils have friends across the year groups, a sixth former proudly telling us 'younger pupils are often disregarded in other schools, but not here; younger pupils can have leading parts in plays'.

Prep buildings sit alongside the college, surrounded by play areas, including a wooden adventure climbing course, and woodland school for outdoor education.

Chapel – 'the still place' – was named as a favourite place of many (dining hall, with its delicious food, and the rugby pitch also figuring). 'Chapel', said a pupil, 'is where we consolidate the week. The whole schools gathers'. The head gives a thought for the week, pupils are recollected – there is no feeling of piety at this school, but weekly chapel evidently plays its part in drawing the community together.

Uniform: smart navy for boys, and a lovely tartan skirt for girls (though ending at a troubling mid-calf length). Once pupils reach year 7, they get college blazers – quite a milestone. Sixth form must wear suits, can choose the colour and must look smart – 'to match the work ethic', said a pupil gravely.

Pastoral care, well-being and discipline: The head is well aware of the whitewater nature of adolescence – 'it's all about the speed of turnaround after a dip', and whilst this school works hard to try and keep children from vulnerable situations, there are good support networks in place to support pupils: houseparents, tutors, staff and school counsellors. 'It really is a fantastic community', said a parent. '[A] strong culture, and out of this, children support each other. Problems are addressed and dealt with swiftly'.

A parent described the effective support given to her child, whose friend suffered serious trauma: counsellors provided 'what she needed'. They are very aware that some pupils might suffer from anxiety, said another, and are 'right on' in their support of pupils. Counsellors give advice and talks to pupils on mental health issues, and although one parent felt that there is not enough work done with pupils about knotty life issues such as consent, others felt this was dealt with adequately.

Tutors are the first ports of call for pupils with difficulties in prep, but they are happy to extend support to whatever is necessary, including family therapy or a life coach.

House guardians (pupils) regularly meet to discuss anyone who might be in distress, at both the prep and senior school. Bullying is discussed a lot – 'the school have a firm grip on it...and my son is ripe for it...' said a parent. Pupils were very clear that incidences of bullying could result in suspension or expulsion: not harming others or self is evidently a mantra they have absorbed.

There's careful education about what constitutes bullying and how to form positive relationships with each other (boys, in particular, sometimes don't even realise they've upset someone, says the head) and creating an environment where children feel they can talk about problems. The head has, and will, suspend or expel pupils for being unpleasant to others.

The head, said a parent, is 'almost Victorian' in his laying down of the rules: the Big 12. Parents say everyone knows what they are, and the disciplinary consequences of breaching them. 'It's strict', said a parent, 'which is a good thing...'

Rowdy pupils will have a bumpy ride here. 'Not a school for second chances', said another, 'though punishment is about trying to educate and improve'.'What you do at the weekend does matter', say pupils. 'Particularly if there might be photographic evidence', one added feelingly.

Pupils and parents: Hurst feels like a local school in its intake, said a parent who likes this, and the typical Hurst family consists of the upper middle class white professionals who live in the area. School buses serve the local area, Chichester and London.

A parent told us this is not a school for those who want to fly under the radar and just get to the end of their school days: 'the thing you do at this school is engage – it can be anything, there are endless opportunities'.

Day-to-day communication is good, confirm parents, and the views of parents on teaching and pastoral care are sought regularly.

It's a long school day with a 6 o'clock finish, which can be tricky for parents collecting day pupils – 'we moved to be close to the school', said one. Prep school day finishes at 4.20pm, but with after-school care (included in fees), can run until 6.00pm to match the college day.

Entrance: Not aggressively selective, but recruits better than average. Those joining from outside take ISEB pre-test in year 6 for year 9 entry and need to get over 55 per cent in maths, science and English, 50 per cent in other subjects at CE. Hurst prep year 8s make up less than half of year 9: there is a big intake from outside at this stage which 'avoids stagnation', says the head of prep.

At prep, most pupils join in reception, year 3 and year 7 (which, like year 9, is oversubscribed).

Exit: Most depart to Russell Group universities; Edinburgh, Bristol, Loughborough and Exeter are popular choices. Five to Oxbridge in 2018, and two medics.

A handful leaves the prep school for other local senior schools.

Money matters: Academic bursaries from 11+.

Remarks: Parents are clear why they chose Hurst: '[It has the] right balance... the right direction, the right balance of pastoral and academic. Our four very different children have thrived there. [There's] lots going on and it's very inclusive'. 'It's a good time to have kids here', said another. 'It's hitting a high – and Tim Manly is inspiring for kids'.

Hurtwood House School

Holmbury St Mary, Dorking, Surrey RH5 6NU

Ages 15–18 Pupils 340 Boarders 300

Fees: Day £28,950; Boarding £43,428 pa

01483 279000
www.hurtwoodhouse.com

Joint headmasters: Richard Jackson MA (70s), originally an English teacher, is the founding head. Richard's (we are all on first name terms here) soft-spoken and understated manner belies the weighty and imposing presence of a man who has lived and is still living a remarkable dream, a dream he and his team bring about daily for their privileged students.

Mr Cosmo Jackson BEd (40s) and son of Richard was appointed 2004 to do the main day-to-day running of the school. An alumnus of Charterhouse, Cosmo spent two years at Bristol University not enjoying economics and thence to the University of the West of England to do his – perhaps inevitable – BEd. He was, in all senses, to the manor born, as were the majority of his siblings, their spouses and, quite possibly, ultimately, their offspring as Hurtwood is, triumphantly, a family concern and four other Jacksons are on the staff. Parents seem a little bemused. 'He's very charming but the students don't see much of him once they're in. He doesn't teach anyone.' A pity as he is easy to talk to, smilingly enthusiastic and loves his job.

Academic matters: Contrary to popular opinion, this is not just a school for arty/media types. Sciences are strong and the results across the whole range of subjects are uniformly starry. A levels offered include all three sciences, economics and sociology. Some students yearn for more eg philosophy. Most popular are, unsurprisingly, drama, media, English, maths and psychology. Fine art and textiles an astonishing stand-out success.

Average class size is between eight and 12, often smaller. Teaching is, according to parents, 'pretty excellent' and the students we spoke to were extravagant in their praise, admiration and, in some cases, hero-worship of teachers. The Jackson philosophy is all about bringing in the best and assiduously monitoring both staff and students to ensure that no slacking, laurel-resting or coasting occur. Parents know what they are paying for: 'They're spoon-fed to a terrible degree,' said one, 'but that's why the fees are so enormous.'

According to the Jacksons, success depends on kindness and monitoring. 'Socially and pastorally we are the friendliest school in the world but we're strict when it comes to work.' Cosmo says, 'We have the cosy feel and intimacy of a prep with the academic rigour and maturity of a university.' Weekly staff meetings to check on anyone whose performance causes concern. Everyone graded A1-U5 and staff swift to pick up on anyone not meeting expectations. In 2018, 85 per cent A*-B and 58 per cent A*/A at A level.

No SEN dept – Richard talks of 'enthusiastic amateur support' and acknowledges that among such creative people, the 'dyses' are bound to be common. But, he feels, 'they should, by now, have learned the strategies and techniques to manage their difficulties'.

Games, options, the arts: The glory of Hurtwood and at the heart of its ethos. Arts and media all to professional standards – largely because the teachers are West End/media pros absolutely on top of their game and all the latest in production. And this is the great attraction. We spoke to numerous academically-minded students who had come to Hurtwood because their previous schools offered the chance of one or two productions each year in which they might, or might not, get a part. Here, productions, films, videos of all kinds and sizes roll off the blocks constantly and, if you are of a mind to, you can be constantly engaged in them. Acting 'company', a film 'academy' and a dance 'company' are elite groups restricted to a dozen or so devotees.

No glitzy performing arts centre such as are now routinely found in 'top' schools. The theatre is good, of professional quality and seats 180 though with little backstage or flyroom/ wing space. The students learn the design and building of sets not by doing, but by seeing it done by the pros, very expensively, brought in. This a positive policy decision of the Jacksons. They do learn lighting though, again, lighting pros brought in to do the actual biz in the 'jaw-droppingly good' concerts and shows, as parents concur. 'They walk out of here and could manage a BBC studio,' one thought, 'and those who go on to media courses find they know pretty much everything they do in the first year, at least.' New TV studio complex and edit suite the envy of many strapped production companies.

Around a quarter learn an instrument. A further quarter take singing lessons and a sixth take dance. Music tech is, inevitably, a big deal here with two tech rooms plus recording studio. Art is rich and varied – impressive and imaginative portfolios emerge from the small studio down the track through the woods. Costume design makes practical use of textiles skills and the results are stunning. Monthly newsletter produced in-house and largely by students is a slick, cool number.

Games an also-ran. It's just not why you come. 'If you want to do a sport, you're pretty much in the team,' we were told by an enthusiast who gave up his place in his elite's school's elite first XI to come here. There's a football pitch, all weather-hockey/ basketball pitches, two tennis courts, a new sports pavilion, so it's there if you want it. Pool and table tennis around the place as well.

Boarding: Around 50 boarders live in the upper floors of the main building. Not over-roomy or over-appointed but perfectly adequate and with inspiring views. The rest in houses within a short bus ride – school keeps a fleet of buses which shuttle to and fro. All boarding houses are attractive and interesting architecturally though the loveliness of the interiors varies according, as much as anything, to taste. But most parents agree, 'it doesn't worry the pupils,' and 'the house staff are lovely.' Assuredly, here are not the dinky study bedrooms with en suites and all mod cons found elsewhere. As one parent opined, 'They haven't chucked money at the accommodation, but I'd rather have good teaching than smart bedrooms.'

Background and atmosphere: Richard Jackson conceived his school way back in the late 1960s and it bears the stamp of those idealistic, anything-is-possible, heady and experimental days. Hurtwood's first incarnation was in a building rented from the National Trust and he looked for three years until he lighted on this lovely house in its perfect spot. It was always to be a 16-19 school, GCSEs being, for Richard, 'the absolute natural breaking point.' And so it has proved.

Set in 25 acres of stunning Surrey rural idyll, the house is a 1900s late arts and crafts, genteel mock Tudor fantasy, beautifully sited on the hills overlooking the North Downs. Getting here is a challenge as the road darkens and narrows, winding though and over the wooded hillsides – reminding one just how rural Surrey can still be, though each bend has a gated entrance with entryphone – this ain't your hill-farming sticks. The place is beautifully kept and the car park must have one of the most privileged views in the country. Downstairs is lovely – a huge and inviting drawing room with coffered ceiling, grand fireplace, sink-into sofas and lots of warm limed oak. Similarly, the library has a wondrous ceiling and, when you look down, a jolly good stock of books, periodicals etc. Dead posh loos too. Less artistically pleasing outbuildings house various subjects and classes, common rooms etc.

Food is 'out of this world'. One parent marvelled at 'the amount they must invest in the kitchen. It's all cooked there – nothing is brought in.' Another enthused, 'I turned up one day out of the blue and there was a dressed salmon!' Breakfasts apparently so good, superlatives fail. Much-loved ice cream machine and barbeque bar.

Pastoral care, well-being and discipline: Pupils and staff on first name terms – works fine although those who come from stiff public schools never quite get used to not saying 'Sir'. Parents praise the 'very secure environment'. Residential 24/7 but students are free to go home at the weekends with permission and around 75 per cent do. No rich programme of activities over the weekends as elsewhere because those who do remain – or come in especially – have rehearsals, projects etc they just can't put down. Occasional weekend activities include hiking, camping in Snowdonia, paragliding, powerboating, high ropes courses and paintballing. School runs buses into Guildford and Cranleigh for shopping etc.

Very strict regs on smoking, drink and drugs. On our trail down to the arts block we met the 'smoking teacher' ready to ambush those having a sneaky drag but, although some parents sighed over these perennial problems, most felt it happened at weekends out of school and school is absolutely resolute against all such folly. Lots of counselling given when needed; random testing for drugs. Mixed boarding houses though sexes on separate floors or wings and 'very-strict no-go areas'. Girls wear black leggings, ankle boots and hoodies and boys wear skinny jeans, trainers and hoodies. Very little self-expression via 'see-me' garb. Sensible attitudes seemed pervasive. If there are any worried parents, we did not find them.

Pupils and parents: Approximately two-thirds are British, mostly from London and the home counties. Rest from, well, everywhere – nationals from 33 countries at the time of our visit. Sixty with EAL needs supported by specialist department. We did hear knots of students talking Chinese but mixing is better than at many schools – largely because productions bring people together. No distinction made or felt between day and boarding students, those who drip wealth and those on scholarships. 'There is,' a clear-eyed student told us, 'an ever-present sense of being part of an elite, but most people are very grounded and it's only with some of those from overseas where you really sense loadsamoney.' Everyone says how well everyone mixes.

Parents also a good mix – many in the arts. School/home links not touchy-feely. One parent said, 'They don't do parents' evenings – such a relief as we're not hands-on parents.' On the other hand, another said that they'd like the teachers to be around when they pick up on Friday evenings and a third echoed the feeling that she didn't get a chance to know her son's teachers.

Notable former pupils include Nikki Amuka-Bird, Emily Beecham, Phoebe Boswell, Emily Blunt, Amelia Brightman, Ben Chaplin, Amelia Curtis, William El-Gardi, Edward Fox, Aidan Gillen, Sam Harrison, Jack Huston, Tom Mison, Leah Wood, Hans Zimmer, Hannah Herzsprung.

H

Entrance: There are 150-170 vacancies each year (55 per cent girls and 45 per cent boys). No open days, it's much more personal here. School says, 'We are looking for students who are going to make a positive contribution to our community. Character, personality, willingness, cheerfulness, liveliness, helpfulness, maturity, a sense of responsibility and a strong sense of purpose are all qualities that we are looking for.' Admissions criteria like these – in all their triumphantly civilised vagueness – are not found everywhere.

Parents and prospective pupil are seen by the head and the interview usually lasts over an hour. Then, if you are still keen, you register and apply. What matters is whether you will fit in and make the most of the opportunities on offer. Some turned down at that point, a few, obviously outstanding, applicants are offered an immediate place, subject to reference, at that stage; the rest are put in a 'pool' for selection later in the year. Oversubscribed and currently a waiting list of around 50-60, entirely acceptable, hopeful would-bes. Places not dependent on GCSE results (except for eg the sciences and maths).

Exit: To a surprisingly mixed bunch of courses at a very wide range of unis from Oxbridge (four in 2018) to eg Bristol, Nottingham, Bath, UCL, with several off to the US, one to Hong Kong and one study hospitality in Switzerland. Music, art, drama and film courses, as you'd expect, but maybe fewer than you'd expect. Quite a few engineering and business management degrees and one medic (Malaysia) in 2018. School runs its own agency, now headed by Emily Blunt.

Money matters: Famously and unashamedly expensive. Until you get here and sense the quality it's hard to gauge quite why. Two performing arts scholarships on offer annually worth 50 per cent of fees; two more at 25 per cent. Jacksons use their discretion to support those who deserve it and need it. Definitely worth trying, especially if you are local and utterly determined to succeed.

Remarks: Unique and impossible to label or compare. If you're talented, hard-working, collaborative, appreciative of opportunities and in love with performance and production, you'll have a stunning time.

Immanuel College

Elstree Road, Bushey Heath, Bushey, Hertfordshire WD23 4EB

Ages 4–18 **Pupils** 681 **Sixth form** 101 **Jewish**

Fees: £9,990 – £17,670 pa

020 8950 0604
www.immanuelcollege.co.uk

Head master: Since September 2017 Gary Griffin, who previously worked as an educational consultant for various schools, including Immanuel. Degree from Exeter in economic and social history and politics, PGCE from the Institute of Education. He spent nearly 30 years at City of London School, joining as a history and politics teacher, rising to become second master (deputy head) and acting headmaster in 2014.

Although he is not Jewish, he is a former governor and chair of the education committee of a Jewish school, Naima JPS.

Prep school head: since 2012, Alexis Gaffin BEd (Cantab). Educated at Haberdashers' Aske's School for Girls, South Hampstead High School and Homerton College, Cambridge, where she read education and religious studies. Worked in state primaries in Manchester, before spending three years in Israel. Took some time out when her four children (now aged 14 to 21) were young, before returning to Noam Primary in Wembley, where she went from 'very part-time' to 'very full-time' as deputy head. An Ashdown Fellowship raised her sights to 'team leadership', and a subsequent visit to Immanuel changed her life: 'I said I've found my job...Thankfully they found me, too.' An early years specialist, she continues to take all children for PSHE: 'I may not know everyone's reading level, but I know their personality, know who needs support.' Judaism is fundamental to her educational world view. 'I am as Jewish doing maths as when saying my prayers.' Competent, clear-sighted, caring and efficient, she believes the school is very much an extension of the family: 'A postage stamp of my philosophy: build whole, happy people'. Parents praise her highly: 'She cares passionately and gets things done.' Married to a teacher at Hasmonean, in her (limited) free time, she loves to read, cook and bake and 'spend time with my family'.

Academic matters: Prep school teaching largely follows the national curriculum. 'You don't have to reinvent the wheel,' says the head, 'but you shouldn't see it as straitjacket either.' The academic emphasis is on 'structured learning', with a mixture of 'teacher-led' and 'self-initiated' activity. During our visit, activity of the self-initiated sort seemed purposeful and enthusiastic, with two keen 5 year olds rushing to play 'spot the matching words', while, over in the 'vet's corner' a busy crowd was tending its stuffed animals. A further pair tested the sands of time with the help of the head. 'Shake the glass harder. Is the sand going faster?'

The school provides a 'modern Jewish orthodox' education and, as well as a class teacher and teaching assistant, each year group has a designated rabbi to help develop understanding of Jewish customs and practice, as well as an appreciation of biblical and rabbinical texts and love of Israel. Daily morning prayers, plus weekly Sabbath assembly. Specialist teaching, too, in modern Hebrew from year 1, expanding to three full periods of modern foreign languages (two of French, one of Hebrew) in year 3. The head is also contemplating an after-school club in Mandarin (learning herself in order to test-drive the experience).

A part-time SENCo helps provide 'structured intervention' where necessary: 'If we can, we support pupils and provide for their needs,' says the head. More complex matters are addressed by external specialists (at an additional cost).

At senior level, 'We specialise in those pupils who don't believe in themselves as robustly as other children. Anyone can take in A* kids and get A* kids at the end. We spend a significant amount of time in the value added band.' And yet despite this, and the school's historical reputation as being for the wealthy but less able, several years of good, solid results mean that Immanuel can sit proudly alongside its competitors. In 2018, 62 per cent A*-A/9-7 grades at GCSE and 51 per cent A*/A at A level. Though it is selective at 11, the academic range is reasonably broad, albeit skewed to the more able. Small class sizes, sometimes as few as 10 in a class, depending on set, means the teachers really have the chance to get to know pupils as individuals. School probably works best for the child who needs close care and attention, rather than the one who needs academic extension. That said, one parent told us: 'One of my children is very academic, the other has mild dyspraxia. The school caters amazingly well for both.' Another parent said: 'What is so nice about the school is that pupils can naturally achieve their potential. There is no sense from the school that you are a failure.'

An independent learning project in year 8 develops research and study skills. Years 10 and 11 setted and top two sets (of four) take IGCSE in English, maths, history, music, and triple science.

Jewish studies forms a fundamental part of the curriculum. Modern Hebrew is taught in years 7, 8 and 9 and students have the option to study biblical Hebrew as well as textual Jewish learning. There are three religious options for sixth formers: A level RE with Judaism and ethics; preparation for Jewish life and an intensive textual course (some pupils go on to study at Yeshiva and seminary); or a course about Jewish wisdom for life called Chochma. Secular A level options include sociology, theatre studies, PE, maths and psychology. A kosher bar/bat mitzvah is a condition of college membership.

'Relationships between staff and pupils are excellent' (ISI), and teaching has been much praised by parents as being very nurturing, caring and aiding in emotional development: 'I've had follow-up calls from teachers to my home', one parent told us. Once appointed, teachers (half of whom are not Jewish) tend to stay. Good and caring special needs provisions for both physical and learning difficulties are another reason why parents choose this school. Despite the upstairs-downstairs site, a specially adapted lift makes all things possible. Outstanding and specialised support and individual learning plans are used as necessary.

Games, options, the arts: Art is a biggie here and for many the reason they chose this school above others – good numbers of sixth form pupils awarded places at Central St Martins, or other high profile art institutions. The art we saw was imaginative and innovative, with students enthusiastically explaining to us the thought process behind their work. A few art scholarships for 11+ entry.

A vibrant drama department produces two productions a year, and students excel in their musical theatre examinations. The chief examiner of the London College of Music was 'blown away' by the talent and application of the entire cohort, we are told. Music is part of the core curriculum, but only a handful take it at GCSE. There are three concerts a year.

'We're not hugely well known for our contact sports..but that might be because our children like to keep their teeth!' This is not a school where parents prioritise sport, and high level competition is certainly not part of the creed, although in the last five years 'increasing success has been earned by a dedicated and skilled PE department'. Older pupils have access to a small but well-equipped gym, and football, basketball, tennis and netball are played with enthusiasm and success. Immanuel Sports Award evening sees district trophies were awarded for all the fore-mentioned sports. Football, basketball, tennis, athletics, cricket, badminton and trampolining all available, plus netball and dance (very strong) for girls. One mother told us: 'Because of the class sizes, my daughter gets exposure to all sports which perhaps she might not get in a larger school where she wouldn't necessarily make the team.' The college has adequate rather than inspiring facilities; prettily positioned running track, well used tennis courts.

There is a strong and enthusiastic following for debating, and indeed when we visited, the debating society were about to discuss the motion 'why homework should be scrapped.' (Sadly, we couldn't hang around to see the outcome). There is full participation in awards schemes such as Young Enterprise and Duke of Edinburgh awards, and the students are exceptionally ambitious and entrepreneurial: three recent ex-pupils have appeared successfully Dragons' Den, and another is currently working with a winner of The Apprentice. 'We have a phrase here called Tottenham Chutzpah, and it means that an Immanuel pupil really punches above their weight.'

Plenty on offer at the prep beyond the school day, with clubs in arts and crafts, chess, choir, football, board games, gardening and drama. Individual music lessons, too, in guitar, violin and piano from year 1, and LAMDA qualifications from year 3. Whole school 'musical extravaganza' held annually, and school play now in the pipeline.

School trips are definitely a strength – the whole of year 9 to Israel for four weeks, the entire year 12 to Poland. One student wrote of his experience to Auschwitz: 'It was a truly powerful moment and helped us to begin to comprehend the scale of our people's tragedy.' Suffice to say, these trips are life-long bonding experiences between the pupils.

Background and atmosphere: Founded in 1991 by the then chief rabbi, Immanuel Jacobovits, who wanted to establish a religious school to rival some of north London's most famous academic names. The core of the building is a magnificent, turreted Victorian pile (formerly a convent school) described by Pevsner as sitting atop its 11 acres of Hertfordshire green belt like a Harrogate Hotel. Plenty of later additions, including the recently opened Bet Knesset (synagogue), funded by one of the parents, which means pupils now have a place to worship on site as well as facilitating those who are shortly about to undertake their bar or bat mitzvah. When we visited the school, the new science block was due to be unveiled in the next couple of weeks – a large, sparse space with functional classrooms (not yet decorated with pupils' work). 'Apologies for the industrial look of the new block. This is what comes with having to be bomb-proof, bullet-proof, earthquake-proof..everything proof.'

Sadly, these added security measures were perhaps never more pertinent then during our visit, which followed a spate of antisemitic attacks in France and the threat of more local ones. We noticed a heavy security presence patrolling the entrance of the school, where parents are no longer allowed to park their cars or loiter. We were told that a new, heavy duty gate was in the process of being built. One parent told us: 'You do worry that sending your child to a Jewish school can potentially put them in a dangerous situation. But the school is doing everything they can to make it as safe as possible like doing regular drills, and parents are kept well informed.'

Once you get past security and enter the school, you are confronted with a bit of a mish-mash – rather like a comfortably shambolic family house. This is definitely no pristine show home like some of its private school contemporaries, and whilst this arguably lends itself to the homely vibe, we couldn't help but feel that a fresh lick of paint, or a few more displays of students' work (particularly the wonderful art), would work wonders to brighten up the place. Clearly, it is not the school's priority, but we wondered if parents were concerned about this at all. After all, this school is still as costly as many of its private contemporaries. One parent told us: 'The building is a bit tatty, but it was the grounds I was impressed with.' Another said: 'It's not something that really bothers me or my daughter at all. It's the privilege of having very small classes with individual attention that we're paying for.'

The students we spoke to seemed to agree. One told us: 'I got offered a place at Haberdashers' and City of London, but chose this school because class sizes were so small and it felt very welcoming.' Another said: 'This school really seems to have the ability to get the best out of us and it caters for everyone.' The pupils we met were a very astute, friendly and well-mannered bunch. 'Happy' was the word banded around from head, to parents, to pupils themselves. 'Because of the size, it has a real family feel,' said one parent.

The prep school shares the senior school's leafy, well-equipped and well-protected campus, but has its own light and spacious new building with a separate playground. Generously-scaled classrooms provide ample accommodation for 20-22 (max) in each year group. Founded in 2011, it is increasing classes yearly. The gaps are filled in as younger ones progress upwards.

Unlike some of its orthodox state school competitors, Immanuel has a relatively modern approach to the faith: 'This school, after all, was founded on the belief that girls should have the same chance as boys.' The school aims to turn out young people who are 'kind and confident, know themselves and help others. They understand where they are going, have a loyalty to being Jewish and a relationship with their faith that is going to continue.' Food is kosher, healthy and appetising (schnitzels on the day we visited). Staff share pupils' dining rooms which, from what we witnessed, are places of eager conversation and thoughtful dialogue.

School does a very good job of involving parents. Every couple of years a trip solely for parents is organised to Auschwitz, which, as one parent told us 'bonds us completely.' Regular coffee mornings and quizzes also organised. Programme of social action in Jewish and wider community a high priority, and a long list of funded charities.

Pastoral care, well-being and discipline: Second to none at this school, and the reason most parents we spoke to chose it above others. One parent told us: 'My son was quite badly bullied in his former school, so we removed him and chose Immanuel because we had heard it was a very nurturing school. He's a completely different boy now and is very happy.' Others said that Immanuel has a reputation of being a 'safe haven', with children joining at random times if they don't get on at their current school.

Two co-heads of year plus four tutors in year 7; designated pastoral leaders in years 8 and 9. Deputy heads constantly available to pupils and parents. Prefects are self-elected – those who are keen to take on the responsibility apply for the post and are interviewed. Once appointed, they play a large part in the life of the school, helping younger people to read Hebrew, organising social events and charity fairs. Jewish identity and prayer is very much part of the ethos. Boys are expected to wear a kippah (head covering) at all times, and years 7-11 have compulsory prayers before class. For sixth formers, prayer is primarily voluntary, but compulsory before the major festivals. It's not a problem for the pupils, we were told; 'This is a school where it is cool to be observant, but by the same token, nobody makes anyone else feel embarrassed if they are less observant.'

Discipline not particularly high on the agenda, although uniform rules becoming stricter, primarily for religious reasons; 'If a female pupil has her skirt rolled up, she is told to roll it down straight away', one parent told us. However, another parent bemoaned the lack of discipline in other areas, particularly the fact that her daughter seems to be allowed to chew gum in class, or certainly during school hours, 'which amazes me, and I'm not sure why.' No serious concerns about drugs: 'this is an amazingly innocent place, and although we are not blind to it, we have never had to worry about drugs being an issue. Pupils who have a bit more money would prefer to spend it on FIFA World Cup tickets.' Exclusions are virtually non-existent; only three pupils have been suspended in three years, and those were due to 'technology related issues.'

Pupils and parents: Applicants must complete the standard certificate of religious practice form designed by the office of the chief rabbi, but after that the school takes in the full spectrum, from the seriously observant to those who don't attend synagogue, but have an attachment to the Jewish way of life. Immanuel is particularly popular with Sephardic Jews. Pupils tend to be 'very friendly, welcoming, and self assured.' (ISI). While there are many affluent, professional parents from a broad sweep of north London and Hertfordshire, there are also a large number of families assisted by scholarships and bursaries, and modesty, respect and consideration of others are the watchwords. One parented commented that 'you really don't get the feeling here that these kids have it all.' A coach service available, which brings pupils from as far as St John's Wood.

The school prides itself on its family atmosphere and communication with parents is excellent. 'We always feel we know exactly what's going on,' said one. A weekly newsletter keeps them posted on what's happened in class and regular invites are sent out to celebrate religious festivals. Working parents, too, can avail themselves of the before- and after-school clubs.

Entrance: From small beginnings, Immanuel Prep has quickly become oversubscribed and selective. 'We've grown from a few little people and some adults to a highly sought-after school,' says the head. She is, however, still very much looking for a mixed-ability intake. Most new entrants arrive from nursery school, an increasing numbers of siblings among them. The admissions procedure aims to establish 'school readiness': 'We want to see how sociable they are, whether they can listen to instructions.' Not every small child, of course, can, and the head is happy to be flexible. 'They may just be nervous. I'm willing to visit them in their own setting.' Children transferring into existing classes have formal interviews and tests in maths and English. Year 6 applicants are jointly assessed by staff of the senior school. Siblings are given priority throughout, though not guaranteed entry. 'We're not doing a favour to the family if we don't have the facilities to help the child reach their potential.' Some scholarship and bursary funding available.

Selective entry to the senior school, but not overly so – prospective pupils have to sit the college's own 11+ exam, with scholarship papers available in Jewish studies and science, and the school is looking for pupils who can pass GCSE at grade C/4 or above. However: 'We don't always take students who score highly in exams. We take on board other factors, and in that respect we're no different from Eton.' Willing to consider pupils for admission at any point. There is small external intake into the sixth form by interview, GCSE results and suitability for A level courses.

Exit: The vast majority of parents her are looking for a reception-to-sixth-form education and most pupils will proceed seamlessly to the senior school, but not without first demonstrating their capacity to 'access the curriculum'. The head is firm that preparation for senior schools elsewhere is not on offer. 'I'd like everyone to go all through.' That said, each child is given a firm grounding. 'Are we facilitating the child to fulfil their potential? Yes. Are we giving them practice papers? No.'

Around a third leave post GCSE. Good preparation for university – series of seminars, plus tailored individual advice. 'No stone is left unturned. We find courses that suit pupils' strengths'. Also prepares students for any additional tests required for medicine or law. Birmingham tends to be much the most popular university followed by Nottingham; others to a range from Imperial to Reading, with about 60 per cent to Russell Group. Occasional Oxbridge place (two in 2018, four to the USA and one medic). Many do a gap year in Israel.

Money matters: Not a rich or well endowed school, largely because any extra money raised or donated contributes towards scholarships and the four week trip to Israel, which some pupils can't afford: 'We currently offer nearly 25 per cent of students scholarships in some form or other, either in full or part payment, but we are constantly striving to offer more,' the school told us. Immanuel Jakobovits academic, Jewish studies and science scholarships at 11+; exhibitions worth £2,000 in art and music; means-tested bursaries.

Remarks: Produces confident and well-qualified young people with a deep understanding of their faith.

ISL Surrey Primary School

Old Woking Road, Woking, Surrey GU22 8HY

Ages 2–11 **Pupils** 90

Fees: £10,450 – £15,500 pa

01483 750409
www.islsurrey.org

Principal: Since 2015, Richard Parker (50s); started work in a law firm in the City, which may have been the inevitable job choice for a Cambridge graduate in history, but trained as a secondary school teacher at the Institute of Education and taught in London before he and his wife worked in international schools in Spain, Argentina, Hong Kong, Portugal and Brunei. He knows what it is to be an expat and this experience of different cultures brings a wealth of understanding to the development of International School of London in the Surrey countryside. Two children (one of whom attended the school); he lives locally and is committed to making the school a friendly place for families coming in as well as innovative and open. He gives the school a 'sense of community' with Buddy Parents (who help settle new parents in), a transition programme (allowing for easy entrance and exit for pupils) and values other cultures with every child given language lessons in their mother tongue. Weekends are spent in galleries as a restorative relaxation. Also in charge of the International School of London in west London.

School leader is Sarah Partridge, who joined the school in 2011 and was most recently early years leader and head of marketing. She started her career in a London primary school over 20 years ago, and has taught at primary level in international schools in Lesotho, Peru, Argentina and Italy.

Entrance: Admissions officer looks at previous school reports, interviews prospective pupils and their parents and tries to match the needs of the child with the school's resources. Tours of the school throughout the year and entrance and exit is flexible, with places coming up mid year sometimes. Expect to meet the head, who likes to know all pupils and is active in admissions.

Parents believe that the inclusive nature of the school enhances the children's education and adds to 'the soft stuff that you can't put your finger on like the warm atmosphere'. Children with learning differences are accepted wherever the school can meet needs – experience of cerebral palsy, speech and communication difficulties, dyspraxia and dyslexia. Fees are all inclusive – no extra charges for the mother tongue language lessons, learning support, day outings, most clubs – and have been reduced to be more affordable for locals.

Exit: The life of a Third Culture Kid almost inevitably involves moving school frequently, though many stay right through to 11 unless the family is relocated. Leavers off to eg ACS Cobham and Egham, Box Hill, LVS Ascot, Frensham Heights, including some scholarships.

Remarks: Modern low level buildings set in wooded area of suburban Woking. Large playing fields and woods around the school with new building projects all round – new theatre, community café for parents, specialist dance studio and music room. Airy and modern inside, with practical spaces – almost all wheelchair accessible. Informal and open, no uniform and everyone on first name terms. The relaxed approach can unnerve some parents who have tight schedules and expect super efficiency, but was seen by one parent as a school that tests and improves systems and they liked the idea that 'it is a growing school and our kids are growing with it'.

Privately owned by the Lebanese family who started the International School of London, bought the Surrey school and also run an international school in Doha, Qatar. The Makarem family members are on the board, have weekly updates and visit regularly.

Early years department set up originally for siblings, but growing as a viable alternative to local nurseries thanks perhaps to its extensive outdoor play area. In the garden space for early years they have exchanged all their plastic equipment for more sustainable materials – we loved the play kitchen with copper, steel and wooden utensils and pots. The first indoor sandpit we have ever seen – very well used, not just for decoration.

Primary classes round an airy atrium with access for each class to an outside play/study area. Small classes with teachers and assistants as well as specialist teachers coming in for music, PE, performance, language acquisition and mother tongue language learning. A bank of iPads per class that was used in several of the classes as children typed out work they had previously written and edited. English of varying levels depending on child's level of fluency on arrival with the emphasis on language development and vocabulary followed by more phonic-based work. Maths at a good level and other subjects taught using primary years programme – topic-based work covering history, geography, technology, science and art and as many other subjects as can be included. Rainforest corners in several classrooms when we visited, with children preparing a jungle performance, learning songs from the Jungle Book, and fabulous 3D constructions of four levels of the jungle ecosystem. Education through as many styles and strategies as possible – outdoor work, experimentation, technology, performance, debate. This multi-sensory enquiry based learning learning ideal for a school where children join from so many different countries. Parents spoke of having chosen this school for its ethos of embedding learning 'in a real world context' and 'the creative approach to teaching and the flexible curriculum'.'Kids feel they are developing not being pushed,' according to one parent. 'They are academically stretched but in a nurturing way'.

Pupils say that the school is teaching them to be individuals and preparing them to be able to study independently. The fact that each child will bring their own language and culture is acknowledged in a basic tenet of 'individualised learning' whereby each has their own starting point and goals. Eventually the aim is for each – not only special needs pupils – to have their own learning profile, as each pupil has their own learning aims. There are individualised learning coordinators who support children with needs in individual lessons but mostly by giving in-class support plus giving teachers strategies for differentiated teaching.

Exciting artwork considering it is a small school, developed by teachers who are clearly motivated and passionate. Emphasis on ideas and self-initiated work in all the arts and options.

Sports with specialist PE teachers in the large areas outside the school. Swimming weekly at local baths. Netball, football, basketball and dance offered, while a partnership with a specialist, local acrobatics club – Prime Acrobatics – means lessons from the more traditional gymnastics through to circus skills. This is an inclusive school, where all children have the opportunity to represent the school, regardless of ability, with matches and tournaments with local schools, though parents have suggested more inter-school sporting events should be the goal of the PE department. The attitude here is to 'have a go' and sports events range from fencing and archery, to tag rugby, to tennis and cricket as well as alternative sports such as a Tri Golf Tournament and Frisbee Festival. There are generous amounts of outside learning – weekly timetabled forest school sessions and there's a new permaculture garden area.

Music teacher with passion and commitment bringing more music into the school in a large new music room – school choir and a band play in assembly as well as during shows and performances that are whole school affairs of some importance. Timetabled twice weekly class music lessons. Individual instrument lessons possible.

Pupils we spoke to said that there were not as many extracurricular options as in a larger school but that 'you were involved' and that 'the school has a family feeling'. There is an award-winning 'transitional programme' which helps support on entrance and exit. Value placed on moral education and wider learning seen with awards being given for, amongst others, adaptability, resilience, co-operation, morality and thoughtfulness.

Student voice heard loud and clear through student government with reps from all classes and several subcommittees for culture, sport, events etc. Much debating in student government, then voted on in school assembly, then taken to senior management who say their job is to make these decisions reality.

Pupils said the school was 'nice and caring' and the family atmosphere they spoke of was apparent in the way mixed ages were seen outside playing together and looking out for each other. Pupils appreciated that 'you learned in lots of different ways – not just writing' and that what you learned was related and 'everything fits together'. Confident and socially aware pupils spoke of the school helping them understand 'what I am good at'. Pupils said there was no bullying or unkindness, but the school has an anti-bullying policy so they are not oblivious to the possibility. A full-time school counsellor with an open door available for pupils, parents and teachers.

Very international school but with a growing number of local students who come for the small classes, language learning and innovative style of learning. Largest proportion of students are from the Netherlands (partly because it used to be a Dutch school for children of Shell employees). But wide number of other countries represented – Arabic speakers, Russian, Spanish, German. Parents very involved in the school and use it as a start to their integration in the UK and a social hub. Regular talks on bilingualism and TCK (Third

Culture Kids). Parents appreciate the relaxed approach and the emphasis on education in its broadest sense, and rather than being pressurised with teaching to exams had chosen the school because it made their children 'enquirers' and gave them 'skills of how to learn'.

Invicta Grammar School

   144

Huntsman Lane, Maidstone, Kent ME14 5DR

Ages 11–18 **Pupils** 1,481 **Sixth form** 314 (27 boys)

01622 755856
www.invicta.kent.sch.uk

Headteacher: Since 2009, Julie Derrick (50s). Not a hair out of place in an immaculate bob, not a chip in her nail polish, well-cut clothes on a tiny frame. Very few papers on her desk, and these are all neatly squared to their neighbour. According to her deputy, she's a stickler for attention to detail. Ask her any fact about the school, and a spreadsheet or printout is there in a flash. But she's no ice queen – she's warm, chatty, curious. And under the serious side there's a lover of musicals and Bridget Jones novels.

Parents say she's highly visible and involved in everything at school, and girls say she's 'really nice' – they respect her, but aren't scared of her, they say.

She joined the school as head of business and enterprise, being promoted to deputy en route to the headship, and is now also joint CEO of the Valley Invicta Academies Trust. She began her career in management consultancy, working for Holiday Inns, before training as a teacher in her late 20s. Early postings took her through a series of comprehensives in deprived areas of London, including Sir John Cass and Catford Girls' School, 'a tough introduction to what education and social mobility is all about'; and Aylesford Sports College in Kent.

There's shop talk at home, as her husband is vice principal at a high school, and the elder of her two daughters is in teacher training – the younger is at university, and was formerly a pupil here. And Derrick herself is an ex-pupil of the school.

Academic matters: Recent results put the school as the best in Maidstone, with 74 per cent A*/B and 40 per cent A*/A grades at A level and 65 per cent A*-A/9-7 grades at GCSE in 2018. 'We're giving as good an education as the super-selectives, but the delivery is far more creative; it has to be as we have a broader ability range, so our curriculum offer is far more exciting,' says Derrick.

We were impressed with the rigorous attention to quality of teaching. Staff have regular inspections to ensure they are up to scratch, with the deputy head observing the 'pace, variety and challenge' of lessons, and grading them as outstanding, good or requiring improvement. It's all part of an accountability they call Metal (monitoring and evaluation of teaching and learning) – which also includes student interviews, parental surveys, and interviewing other staff. The result – parents say the girls never complain they've had a boring day. 'There's lots of hat wearing and role playing, for example they did Lenin's funeral in history and they all had to wear something black. And my daughter loved it when they put a mobile phone in a microwave to see the waves in science. Every lesson has a creative and a serious element,' said one mother.

Derrick makes no apologies for doing her best to ape the independents. 'If we can give as near to a private education as possible without the parents paying for it then I'll be very happy,' says Derrick. As indeed will the parents, we suspect.

The majority of sixth formers take the AQA Baccalaureate (which comprises three A levels, an Extended Project Qualification, work experience and community service). Maths, biology, politics, and history are popular choices. The sixth form here is no place for slackers; those lacking in work ethic, or top grades ability, advised to move elsewhere. The requirement of minimum C in every subject in year 12 to progress into year 13 is rigorously applied, and can result in relatively high levels of departure at the end of year 12. 'Superb for coasters who need spurring on, and at getting pupils to perform to the best of their ability, but you have to be able to run with the pack,' said one parent.

It's rare for a pupil to become disaffected or disengaged with the curriculum, says Derrick, but in the odd case where this has happened the school has devised a package for that pupil where they do fewer GCSEs, put in place work experience, and develop their leadership skills to prepare them for employment.

The classrooms are informally arranged, and most are buzzing with chatter. There's lots of discussion, and you're allowed to help each other, the girls say. Sets are based on learning style. 'They never have a feeling that they are not good at something, because the school does psychometric testing and divides them into learning styles, so they might say you are a visual learner, and we'll put you in a set with similar learner types,' said a parent.

All of the pupils study Thinking Skills and Habits for Success – 16 characteristics shared by successful people, such as persistence, thinking flexibly, communicating clearly and taking responsible risks. Business and enterprise is timetabled from year 7. 'I felt strongly that we should be giving this to everybody: no matter what you do you will be in the world of business,' says Derrick. There's also an hour per fortnight on 'academic discipline', which includes some literacy, Latin, topical issues, and memory techniques.

In languages, year 7s are allowed to make their own choice from French, German and Spanish, with a second choice introduced in year 8.

Homework is given in three categories: must, should, and could. Most want to do all three, we're told, but it means they can choose how to spend their time, and if they attend a club one evening they won't be punished for dropping the optional homework.

Games, options, the arts: There's a big choice of interesting clubs and societies – beekeeping, equine, debating, astronomy, boxing, pre-med, and Moda fashion magazine are just a flavour. Music is growing: 'They got rid of the whole music department and brought in a new one about two years, ago; since then the choir has really taken off,' said a parent. There's a big school production every year and the school says that everyone who auditions gets a part. Those not in the production get involved through enrichment days, designing costumes or making goodies to sell in food tech.

Art is well resourced, with a huge, light filled studio and a broad range of options including art and design, photography, fine art, graphics, and textiles, which has enabled students to gain places at art colleges without the need for a foundation year.

It's not a sporty school. 'I don't get the impression there is very much focus on sport; it doesn't seem to feature,' said a mother. Derrick says it is under development: 'Sport is not as high profile as in other grammars, but we recruited a new head of PE last year to improve competitive sports. For the first time this year 40 students went on a sports tour of Spain.' Indeed, there is a brand new all-weather pitch, plus eight tennis/

netball courts and cricket facilities, and a sport hall is under construction.

Background and atmosphere: There's some clever use of budgets going on here. It looks very swish indeed compared with the majority of old-fashioned and crumbling grammars in the region. In what could reflect Derrick's early years in hotel industry, reception wouldn't be out of place in a mid-range hotel chain, and there's more idea about branding than we usually see in schools. The girls' maroon blazers are reflected in a lighter shade in the carpet, while a deeper shade on the walls sets off huge oil canvases highlighted with pinpoint lighting.

The artwork looks professional, but has all been produced by the pupils. There's a strong creative bent here – the walls also showcase impressive textiles work the girls have produced for school fashion shows. There are well-used noticeboards everywhere, with all the posters neatly aligned and current. Everywhere is very clean. 'Even at 3.30pm the toilets are immaculate,' said a mother. You almost expect to see a housekeeping trolley down the corridor, and it's all deliberate. 'The learning environment is key – we keep it as fresh and modern as we can within the confines of a school budget,' says Derrick.

The school converted to an academy in 2011, and picked up an Outstanding from Ofsted in 2012. It previously had a pressurecooker reputation, which Derrick is keen to dispel, and we're convinced this is more than just lip service. 'When I took over we had an accelerated curriculum, and they took all their GCSEs at the end of year 10, it was a one size fits all, and could be criticised as very much an exam factory. Now they are on individual programmes, and they will all take GCSEs at the end of year 11 with some acceleration where it is right for them,' she says.

'The head's changes have made a difference, the atmosphere has changed,' said one parent. But another is sending her second daughter elsewhere. 'It's a very good school for the academic child. It's very efficient. My elder daughter has been happy, it has served her well and she is staying on at A level. My younger daughter is more middling, and I don't have that warm, fuzzy feeling about it for her, although if I had another like my elder daughter I would send her to Invicta,' she said.

Another mother judged the balance is right. 'They are quite pushy, they want to get results, but there's extra support for the girls where they need it. It's not over the top,' she said.

One parent particularly liked the fact that when her daughter was struggling with maths, part of the package of support included a mentor from the year above who helped her twice a week.

Pupils say they are encouraged to do lots of clubs and develop a broad range of interests. And pushing an all-round education extends out of hours. 'One thing I really like, they do expanding horizons trips – to the theatre, ballet, art exhibitions – which are open to whole family. They hire a bus and you have an opportunity to go to the West End at reasonable prices,' said a parent.

There are regular Women in Profile days, attended by businesswomen in everything from finance to personal bodyguarding, who hold workshops and encourage girls to realise they can do these jobs. 'Invicta is great for the businesswomen of tomorrow. I expect a few power brokers will come out of it,' said a mother.

Pastoral care, well-being and discipline: This school has the best approach to transition we've come across, which puts to shame the half-day in July preparation for the big bad world of secondary school more commonly offered. It begins in year 5, when prospective pupils are invited in for maths and English workshops, and subject-based days such as performing arts, business studies, geography or team building. Girls who have a confirmed place take part in a series of events over the next six months, including a languages day when they will choose their first to study, and receptions where they can get to know each other. 'It means they start in September knowing where the toilet and the medical room is, how the dining hall works, and they hit the ground running,' says Derrick.

'Transition was amazing,' confirms one year 7 parent. 'My daughter went to so many workshops, meetings, and events, from the start of the summer holidays she was an Invicta girl, and she settled in incredibly well.'

Early into year 7 they have a one-to-one meeting for staff to find out about them, their hobbies, whether anything is worrying them. 'They get to know your child phenomenally well. There is a huge amount of tailoring to your child,' one parent commented.

Parents say that Mrs Derrick knows every child personally, and one parent whose children have also been in the independent sector says: 'My children have been at four different schools and I would say on pastoral care, this school is in a league of its own.' Derrick was at pains to tell us that she places an equal amount of importance on the care as the academic results the school delivers. 'I look for a certain type of staff; their care has got to be as good as their qualifications,' she says.

Parents reeled off examples of the school responding quickly to parental wishes and concerns. 'We weren't happy with the long bus journey to school,' said one. 'So Mrs Derrick called in the bus company. We managed to reroute the bus, so the journey time has now been reduced from 80 to 40 minutes.'

Another added, 'They had a medical club for year 10 onwards. We asked why there wasn't one for younger pupils, and within three weeks they had set one up for the lower school.'

Girls say there isn't much in the way of discipline because they don't get a lot of bad behaviour; teachers are strictest about uniform, they say, with the usual groans about restrictions on earrings and make up. There are lots of reward trips to Thorpe Park, Disneyland, the cinema, they report.

Pupils and parents: The pupil body is predominantly white middle class, but there are 126 pupils whose first language isn't English, including Nepalese pupils whose parents are stationed with the Gurkha regiment at Maidstone's barracks. Girls come from a wide catchment extending to Hawkhurst, Ashford, Sevenoaks and Tunbridge Wells, and from around 70 feeder primaries.

Entrance: Girls must pass the Kent 11+ in order to apply. In case of oversubscription, priority goes to those with siblings in the school and then those living nearest, not to those scoring highest in the exam. For entry at sixth form, pupils must have six GCSEs at A*-C/9-5. Around 40-50 students, including some boys, join the sixth form each year.

Exit: Around 10-20 per cent leave after GCSEs. On average, 90 per cent go on to university, and half to top 25 universities (a quarter to Russell Group). Three to Oxbridge in 2018 and six medics. The University of Kent, Canterbury Christ Church and the London universities are all popular destinations, as they enable students to economise by living at home. But some are going much further – the school has developed links with Harvard and Yale, which deliver presentations to pupils each year, and an increasing number of the school's pupils are applying to them.

Remarks: Strikes us as a place for the more serious-minded and less worldly-wise girl – as one mother put it: 'If you've got a girl who is into boys, ahead of her years, gobby, with a rolled up skirt, she'll go to one of the other schools.' And we'd pinpoint it for the creative rather than the sporty – the work on show points to some seriously good art and textiles teaching. Its importance in the life of the school is clear, from the hardback books of pupils' work available to browse in reception to the properly lit and displayed work throughout the school. Head is on the ball, so we'd say it's a safe bet as long as she's there.

Inwoods Small School

Linked with Brockwood Park School

Brockwood Park, Bramdean, Hampshire SO24 0LQ

Ages 5–11 **Pupils** 47

Fees: £6,200 pa

01962 771 065
www./inwoods.org.uk/

I

Head: Since 2005, Mary-Ann Ridgway, known as Mary-Ann (Montessori diploma in eduction, and diploma in higher education, Chichester), whose partner Loic is also involved at Inwoods. Mary Ann has been at Inwoods since its inception in 1998, and worked before that at the Montessori school in Grenoble, France.

Mary Ann is uncomfortable with the title head: the team run the school, design the curriculum, and make decisions together. Warm, gentle, and sure of what Inwoods is trying to do for its pupils: find the right attitude to living and learning, with respect and love, for self and others.

Entrance: Non selective. Taster days, as many as needed.

Exit: To mainstream or independent schools. In 2018 to Dunhurst, Ditcham, Perins and The Petersfield School. Sometimes Bedales. A few return, age 14, to Krishnamurti education at Brockwood Park.

Remarks: The sounds of children – chatter, squeals and laughter – drift through the woods before you see the school, and these are the sounds of the school at work. Inwoods sits in woodland, sung around with birds rather than traffic. There's a miscellany of buildings: two converted barns, and a straw bale house built five years ago, with its truth window allowing a glimpse of the straw walls within. There is simplicity to these structures; like the teachers here, they do not present themselves with status or intimidation. Interiors are calm: this is not a school where the value of work is illustrated by packing walls with its colourful products. Inwoods shares the process of learning rather than giving emphasis to an end product. At one end of a barn is a kitchen area for preparation of the vegetarian lunch, and fruit and oatcakes for snacks: preparing a meal becomes part of life, not something for someone else behind a closed door.

Outside, the ruins of an oak tree have been left for children to scramble over. There's some adventure playground equipment – the children recently had great fun laying the woodchip beneath it. Rain water is collecting in the well, and will soon flush the toilets. There's a pond, where children learn quickly how to take great care with small creatures: 'questions come alive at the pond'. A large wooden nest made of sticks, whole school size, is under steady construction, vegetables grow in boxes, and there's a small field/football pitch – whichever is called for. Children can climb trees up to the ribbon wrapped around its branches: safe loving limits, says the school, while allowing for a healthy amount of risk taking which develops wisdom of the body and the ability to safely control physical motion within their surroundings.

Time for quiet is important at Inwoods. Every morning, the children walk over from Brockwood Park, and when they are close to Inwoods, a teacher will raise their arm: a signal that the rest of the walk will be in silence, everyone sitting in a quiet circle on arrival. Occasionally a grown up will be lightly directive – 'feel the sun on your face'; 'notice the snowdrops...' – attempting to bring the children into their senses. '[It is a] pause for watching and observing rather than reacting', says Mary-Ann.

Education here is discovery of this extraordinarily world; at Inwoods, subjects become investigations, pupils adventurers. During our visit small children were grouped around a tree trunk with an adult, magnifying glasses in hand, discovering. A child broke off to run, then returned to the group; no problem, no yelling, no telling off.

This school is not about coercion or control, and it is only on visiting this sort of environment that it strikes you how much traditional education relies upon hierarchy and domination. A child here can say, 'no' without punishment. Some newcomers enjoy this assertion of self so much they say no an awful lot at first, and are occasionally told kindly but firmly, 'sometimes there is no choice'. With patience and time cooperation naturally comes about. Directive and non-directive teaching happen here: there is a feeling of freedom, but actually tremendous care and thought goes into preparing areas and activities: 'Engagement from children also comes from offering something interesting and inviting', says Mary-Ann.

Children are divided by age: the little ones are oaks, middle years are apple or cherry blossom, and the eldest redwoods. In these groups, the children engage in morning activities, from maths to craft, with the aim of making learning as meaningful and hands on as possible. For instance, in maths the emphasis is on conceptual understanding, first achieved through concrete materials (clay, origami, body movements, Montessori materials...), then pictorial representation and finally abstraction. 'His teacher finds maths everywhere she looks and [my son] is fascinated to discuss this with her, even ideas that are way beyond his current level – he is not afraid or worried by not understanding'. A child has mastered a concept if they are able to teach it to another, and this is much encouraged. One redwood might be teaching another to make a kite, another how to multiply using the chequerboard.

No IT classes here; but, as Mary-Ann pointed out, they get plenty of that at home. A few laptops are available for the older children to use for project work, and there is limited internet access.

Afternoons are free choice: when pupils choose an activity and choose to learn, they engage in a different way. Choices include painting, using the Arno Stern method. No comments on paintings are allowed, so children paint with uninhibited freedom, exactly how and what they want.

Education is learning of all sorts: every Tuesday the whole school has a nature morning, which involves gardening and looking after the grounds; exploring pond life and insects; and bushcraft and woodcraft – blossoms and redwoods recently whittled wooden butter knives, and one boy made a bee house.

This environment, which allows pupils to pace themselves and values them for being where they are, lends itself naturally to those with special learning needs. In a creative approach to learning, pupils who struggle with spelling learn a word using clay, modelling each letter and its meaning: 'because' was illustrated by one child as two people, a piece of wood on the ground, and one tripping over it. These processes produce a deep understanding of a word which is mastered rather than memorised.

School trips are often walks – 'Children naturally enjoy being out of doors, but if we don't continue to nurture [this] then they lose that connection'. There is a rare commitment to establishing intimacy with nature: on a recent walk, each child was blindfolded and led to a tree to get to know it through touch. They were then returned to their starting place, blindfolds removed, and challenged to find the tree that they had touched.

In this unhurried way of education, there is little regard to national targets. Education here is not about fitting a particular mould, but about finding out, having an easiness with mistakes and seeing how this helps one learn. A parent told us her son had started to compare himself to his peers at his previous primary school; said, 'I can't read' and disengaged from the process. With gentle encouragement and hands on methods at Inwoods it all clicked – 'with no anxiety, no fear'.

Leavers will have gaps in national curriculum knowledge because they have engaged in so many other areas of learning, but they will have a sustained interest in learning, and a strong sense of what they feel good at and enjoy doing. Teachers will prepare pupils for entrance exams for another school if the pupil is clear that this is what they want. Children become self-directed and confident in engaging with adults, says Mary Ann, which are good tools for entering mainstream.

There is a sports day, including a treasure hunt, and egg and spoon races, but no first or last – it's just for fun. At Inwoods they are uneasy about ambition: often success comes at the expense of others, and if you always need to achieve, you will also often fail. But if you do something you love doing, this produces its own species of ambition: to get better at it because you love it doesn't depend on rewards or praise, nor is it at the expense of others, or dependent on another's performance. There's plenty of outside exercise here; pupils go up to Brockwood Park to use the tennis courts and enjoy playing football, though this can dissolve into competition. Adults try to promote a gentler approach, and those with sporting passions are encouraged to pursue them outside school.

There are rules: not to hurt, damage, destroy or disturb others; and agreements: decisions reached by adults and children together – for instance, when it is ok to go barefoot, when tidying up will be done....

Great care is taken to encourage consideration for others: children think about how to explore something or someone new with sensitivity and care, considering questions such as 'how do we know what's fragile inside someone or something new?'

When the children are in conflict, the emphasis is on talking, listening to both sides, and then trying to understand each other's feelings. If there's a real problem, children will be lightly shadowed. Great care is taken not to label a child 'bully'. A child has been excluded for bullying, but this is rare. Discipline here is largely about understanding the consequences of your actions: for instance, if you break an agreement and throw sand at another, you will not be allowed in the sandpit for a period of time.

It is an individual approach to education, yet there is an emphasis on community, with work parties and responsibilities: pupils will be made aware that sometimes individual needs must make way for those of the community. Parents, too, must volunteer (for community reasons and to keep down fees), and help out for 35 hours a year: kitchen, weeding or maintenance.

Every week the entire teaching team meets with one set of parents to share their observations of their child, and listen to what's going on at home. There are regular exchanges during pick up, and parents and teachers meet as a group twice a term.

Inwoods is a local school, unlike its big brother Brockwood Park, but it attracts pupils of all nationalities, some of whom even move country or county to attend: current pupils are from India, Spain, Greece, Italy, Portugal and Canada as well as the UK. Of the 36 children, 28 are full time and eight come for just one day a week (because they are being home schooled for the rest of the time, or are reluctant school goers starting gently). No problem taking a holiday in term time here: this school values learning beyond school walls.

Not many attend both Inwoods and Brockwood, partly because of the gap between 11-14, where there is no Krishnamurti education available; partly because the fees at Brockwood are much higher.

John Hampden Grammar School

Marlow Hill, High Wycombe, Buckinghamshire HP11 1SZ

Ages 11–18 **Pupils** 1,076 **Sixth form** 317

01494 529589
www.jhgs.bucks.sch.uk/

J

Head: Since 2016, Tracey Hartley, previously deputy and interim head of Nonsuch High, where she worked for 10 years. The first ever female head at the all-boys grammar in High Wycombe, she has also been head of history and head of sixth form in various co-ed schools. Originally from Canada, she started out at Mr Kipling delivering cakes around the country, with her first job being in south Bucks, before turning to history teaching.

Not as front-of-house as some heads, we gather ('I haven't had anything to do with her,' was a common phrase from parents we spoke to; some students felt similarly, although others told us she does do the rounds of the school reasonably regularly and 'we see her at assembly.') And her speech at the open evening we attended suggested that she is not a natural orator, but seems warm and friendly. Students told us she's 'nice, but stricter than the last head' and 'gets involved when she can, but she's got a really busy job.'

Sport and the arts fill her spare time: having lived in Scotland and Manchester, she has spent Saturdays at Murrayfield and Old Trafford.

Academic matters: Don't be fooled by hard data which doesn't place JHGS at top of local league tables – this can be skewed partly by those of mixed sex cohorts, boosted by girls' results, and partly by more affluent catchments. School is now competing ably against its closest rivals and stands out when it comes to value-added, with the measure for this at A level the highest of Bucks grammars and among the highest nationally.

Solid and constantly improving academics should help doubters sit up and take notice, with 52 per cent of all GCSEs taken in 2018 achieving A*-A/9-7. Boys take between nine and 11 GCSEs; the majority take 10. A level results also consistently robust in recent years – now just about neck and neck with the nearby rival RGS, with 64 per cent at A*/B in 2018, 38 per cent A*/A.

'But it's not an exam factory,' insists head, 'and it's not a pressurised environment.' Parents agree – 'You get a virtual hand round your back, as opposed to the Challoner's push,' says one. Lots of young, male teachers are 'great role models for boys,' say parents, and 'lessons are interactive and really well planned,' report boys. 'You get the odd teacher that the kids say are rubbish – I remember one young form teacher in particular, who was a bit insipid, but most are great.' Lots of debating in the classroom, which goes well beyond the confines of the national curriculum, and school 'constantly tries to recognise achievement,' with honours for everything from academic or sport achievement to community work.

Pre academy status, school held specialisms in design technology and science, sport and art and modern languages, with these still strong suits. Boys choose two out of French, German and Spanish in year 7 and all take at least one for GCSE (around 10 per cent do two). Plenty of language trips – we saw lovely displays of students visiting German markets. Science 'packed with practicals,' one student told us; we got a demo in one of the swanky new refurbished labs of an acid/alkaline test. Form sizes between around 30 with most GCSE classes capped at 24. Boys set from year 7 for maths and year 8 for English. Setting for languages if the need arises. EPQ classes offered all through lower school to develop the necessary skills for later success.

Expected grades set at the beginning of each year and monitored digitally to make sure boys stay on track. Parents appreciate the half termly reports on pupils' achievements and attitudes to learning – 'they are brilliant because you can always see where your child should be with their work.' School steps in quickly if performance or motivation starts to slip, with catch-up classes in all subjects at lunch times and after school keep standards high. 'My son is academic, but not uber bright, and they put on lots of extra tutoring and help in class for him,' one parent told us. Less enthusiasm for parents' evening – one parent said she turned up and one or two of the teachers didn't even know who her child was.

'Gifted and talented' outlawed as label, with school preferring 'high achievers,' to place a higher emphasis on hard work. Learning support department has specialised staff on hand to help those who need it with personalised learning plans.

School is currently re-evaluating use of iPads. Back in 2013, iPads were standard issue for all boys from year 7 to use in class and at home (parents can buy or lease from school at preferential rate). But teachers and students alike are now questioning whether it really brings anything to the table (check out the brilliant news report done by students on the issue, available on the school website). 'It's great for video projects – but it can be really distracting for homework,' said one boy.

Games, options, the arts: Lots of sport played at competitive level but it's not just for the elite, with nearly half of all year 7 students having represented the school in fixtures against other schools. Regular wins at regional level for football, athletics, swimming, squash and table tennis; and at county level for rugby, hockey, handball and cricket. Recent national success includes squash national finals (second and third place in U13 and U15) and current students represent the country in swimming, hockey, table tennis, rowing and GB SkiX. One former student competed in the Rio Olympics. 'But we're not obsessive about winning,' insists the sports teacher we spoke to. 'The main thing is to introduce a lifelong love of sport.' There are some impressive CVs in the department, including an ex-professional football coach, premier league hockey player, national title winning table tennis coach and level 3 squash coach. Great sports hall – in which we saw badminton and table tennis in full swing – plus an older hall with climbing wall. Immense newish Astroturf – a shared project with the neighbouring community sports centre – bound to be the envy of the competition.

Plenty to choose from on and off the sports pitches on the extracurricular schedule too, with over 100 clubs and activities on offer – and there's good take-up, with 73 per cent of all year 7s taking part in at least one after-school club. 'Huge' emphasis on leadership, with plenty of opportunities for boys to participate in weekends away and international expeditions from year 9. 'My son went on a leadership course at Wycombe Abbey – he absolutely loved it.' Debating and public speaking thriving, with regular wins at national level. Usual array of trips; one year 13 boy said he'd been to seven countries during his time at JHGS – 'it's fun, but more importantly, it gets you out of your comfort zone,' he said. And a year 7 boy raved about his camping trip in his second term – 'it rained the whole time, but we still loved it.'

Both music and music technology on offer at A level. Professional standard recording studio where boys can cut their own tracks. Oodles of bands – wind, jazz etc – plus choirs, orchestra and ensembles going on every lunchtime. Musical production staged annually, most recently Little Shop of Horrors, following in the footsteps of Miss Saigon. Uniquely, school allows only pupils to play instruments in productions – professionals, parents and staff strictly banned – and performance and backstage roles are open to the whole school. Top musicians are recognised each year at an awards ceremony with prizes for both excellence and improvement and boys perform nationally – one had been picked to feature in the BBC proms season at the Royal Albert Hall when we visited. We heard a year 9 saxophonist play so beautifully it stopped us in our tracks.

High performing art department. Not the most inspirational atelier we've seen, but outstanding work on display including pop art, street art, some experimenting with spray paint and plenty of fine art. Good take-up at both GCSE and A level and school boasts several former pupils who have moved on to study art at top establishments including Central St Martins. DT extremely popular, with roomy, well-equipped workshops and a recent partnership with Furniture Makers Livery Company, which the school hopes will lead to 'innovative projects'. 'So far, I've made a stylish fish model, a bottle opener and a model of a Shanghai building,' one year 7 boy said. The gleaming food technology lab hosts cookery lessons for years 7 and 8 that are extremely popular with boys ('making pizza is the just the best,' said one boy) – we even got to taste some of their Italian food creations, along with tasty mini-ice pops. Delish.

Background and atmosphere: Founded in the early 1890s as an art and technical school to support children of High Wycombe's traditional craftsmen and known as High Wycombe Technical High School, before achieving grammar status in 1984. Boasts an eclectic list of alumni ranging from chef Heston Blumenthal to author Terry Pratchett, as well as a number of sportsmen including mountaineer Kenton Cool and swimmer Simon Burnett.

Fabric of school has little of the polish of its nearby competitors, with buildings in the main pretty scruffy and some areas crying out for licks of paint. The dining room, stunning black and white library, a few of the science labs and 'not sexy but important' sixth form centre are the exceptions.

Vibe is surprisingly calm and relaxed for an all-male, high-performing grammar and there's a strong sense of community. 'We work together by supporting each other,' says head. Boys talk about school's 'friendly atmosphere' and 'mutual respect between staff and boys.' Few complaints about the food – 'the chicken tikka curry and bacon and cheese bagels are amazing,' one boy said. The new 'no bag' rule (bags go straight into lockers at the start of the day) helps with congestion, say boys.

Pastoral care, well-being and discipline: With a welfare officer, two counsellors, a school nurse, form tutors and heads of year on hand – plus sixth form mentoring available to younger boys – students here get a tip-top pastoral package and they're not afraid to use it. Bullying 'very rare,' boys told us, and parents concur that any incidents are dealt with proactively and quickly. Zero tolerance of drugs and alcohol even if it's outside school; ditto with cyber issues – rarely issues in reality. House system brought in surprisingly recently and there are 'achievement points' to motivate individuals and 'behaviour points' to keep them on the straight and narrow. Detentions rare, especially higher up the school ('I haven't had one since year 7,' one sixth former said) but 'the school takes no nonsense,' say boys. Just check out their pdf on school rules (available on the school website) to see the exacting standards on issues like haircuts. 'You don't really get very naughty kids here – just a few on the cheeky side, but they don't get away with much,' one boy told us.

Pupils and parents: Although 95 per cent from a 10-mile radius, students come from some 40 feeder schools (majority from state primaries; under 10 per cent from preps) across the county spanning High Wycombe, Marlow, Bourne End and as far afield as Denham and Farnham Common. Buses run from Maidenhead, Gerrard's Cross, Stoke Poges and Denham, says school, but we spoke to some parents who were so fed up with the length of the journey – 'it stops everywhere' – that they got together to organise their own private minibus at a cost of £6 a day.

Broad range of socio-demographics and in the main more grounded than neighbouring grammars, with families hailing from urban High Wycombe as well as leafy south Bucks villages, and around 22 per cent of the cohort from ethnic groups (mainly Pakistani). Tiny minority eligible for free school meals, but we were impressed with the head's emphasis at open evening on ensuring less well-off parents were not put off applying – 'we have funds to ensure you can get everything you need for your son to flourish,' she said, pointing to factors like uniforms and trips. Parents praise the 'vastly improved communications from the school.' Boys come across as serious and focused, down to earth, respectful and well-mannered, although some were less comfortable with looking us in the eye than others.

Entrance: Selective, but school is expanding from 150 to 180 for year 7 entry in 2019 and is considered by parents as easier to get into than other Bucks grammars. 'I put JHGS down over Challoner's because my son was borderline 11+ pass,' is a common comment. Applicants must have passed the Buckinghamshire 11+, taken in the September of year 6. 'You should not tutor your boys,' said head at latest open evening, 'but you probably didn't hear that so I'll leave it up to you.' This is despite the new 11+ format, introduced in 2013, apparently aiming to identify potential and weed out heavily tutored candidates. Later, she explained to us, 'Parents might not listen to me because they are more influenced by their friendship circles and social media chatter.' School not filled within catchment so definitely worth an application if your heart's set on a grammar and you're outside the stipulated area.

Exit: Vast majority (some 80 per cent) enter sixth form, the rest mostly to vocational courses. Most sixth formers go onto university with around 50 per cent to Russell Group universities. School proud of the vast array of – not always obvious – courses chosen, with recent examples including cellular and molecular medicine, marine technology, offshore engineering and security. Others (increasingly) into higher level apprenticeships. In 2018, two to Oxbridge – medicine and dentistry. Boys speak highly of careers advice on offer and help with UCAS and enjoy frequent visits from professions.

Money matters: Ongoing fundraising via PTA events – some better attended than others.

Remarks: A purposeful school where pupils can be themselves and achieve personal bests in a focused but supportive and friendly environment. Much more on the radar for middle-class parents than it used to be – and preferred by some for its relatively relaxed environment – it's not overly macho, celebrates pupils for everything from sport to debating and beats the other grammars hands down on value-added.

The Judd School

Brook Street, Tonbridge, Kent TN9 2PN

Ages 11–18 **Pupils** 1,150 **Sixth form** 249 (87 girls)

01732 770880
www.judd.online/

Headteacher: Since September 2017, Jon Wood, who moved up after four years as deputy head. His watch has brought a modernising scythe – the website and newsletters for example looking distinctly fresher, alongside developments in the intake – but much of this was planned in conjunction with the outgoing head, rather than leapt upon as he took the reins.

He's a career teacher; during his own schooldays at a Norwich independent he imagined going into the City or becoming an actuary in order to earn a lot. Post-maths degree, though, he decided to do teacher training, and within a week decided it was for him. 'I like young people, academia, the buzz of someone getting something.' He doesn't regret eschewing the big bucks, appreciating the time with his family he gets in return.

J

Prior to joining Judd, he was deputy head at Wirral Grammar School for Girls. Likes to keep a hand in now by teaching year 7. 'Means I get to meet everyone. They get to know me and that I'm not a scary headteacher.' He teaches them 'learning development' – an introduction to the school's 'student vision' – of which more later.

If grammar schools are a hot potato, tutoring for the 11+ test is even more of a prickly subject, but Wood openly and unashamedly says he is coaching his own primary aged children. He believes candidates are at a great disadvantage if they come across the papers for the first time when sitting the 11+, and that this tutoring divide is one of the biggest barriers to entry to grammars for children from lower income backgrounds.

Keen on sport but claims to be hopeless at it. He coaches football and has seen it recently introduced at what was previously a fiercely rugby school.

Academic matters: No place for also-rans. In 2018, more than a quarter A* grades at A level (85 per cent at A*-B), and at GCSE, 73 per cent of entries were graded 9-7.

Wood says he is keen to make it even more of a scholarly environment. 'I want to be surrounded by interested and interesting students, talking in the playground about something they've seen on the news,' he says. Central to this is the school's Student Vision. This has been created by examining the qualities seen in the most successful year 13s; distilling this into six core learning skills; and working out how best to teach to enable students to develop these skills. The key characteristics sought are reasoning, reflection, inquisitiveness, courageousness, collaboration and empathy.

'It's easy in a high ability school for children to concentrate on doing well in exams – absorb lesson content passively, and reproduce what has been shown in lessons in exams,' Wood says. 'The students who do very well at GCSE and fall short at A level are the ones who never had to do much to pass exams. The ones who do better at A level have a genuine interest in subjects, and we are trying to foster those traits. It means making sure assessments don't reward skills which we are not seeking such as factual recall which they can do easily.'

Parents who want to do a compare and contrast will have to back off, though. Reports to parents will tell you only how your son is doing against expected performance. 'If students are below our average when they are working at their best, it's not relevant to know they're below average – if their commitment to learning is high, then parents should accept their grades. If they want to know their position in class, go to another school.'

A parent reported to us how Wood stood up for boys against overbearing parents. 'At the GCSE options evening he told the parents in no uncertain terms that the choices should be those of the boys – as they were going to be the ones studying them – and that the options were not about an outmoded view of what are worthwhile subjects.'

The only setting that goes on is for maths from year 8; and in the GCSE years, languages are split into two streams. Food tech isn't offered after year 8, but DT is popular, with around half the year group taking DT at GCSE, and around 15 candidates through to A level. Wood bemoans the narrowing of the national curriculum, which has come about as a result of a focus on Ebacc and Progress 8. To counter this, younger students will in future sit 11 GCSEs rather than 10, and they will be required to choose something from a pool of art, music, DT, PE and computing, to provide some breadth. It will be achieved by a cracking pace of delivery – for example pupils here are typically timetabled for six 50 minute lessons in maths, where a lot of schools would provide eight.

At A level, we're pleased to see a state school still expecting everyone to begin with four (where others have reduced this to three as a cost-cutting measure). There are a couple of exceptions for elite sportsmen and those with medical issues. Maths A level courses are heaving – out of a year group of 180, usually 160 will continue with maths, and 60 will take further maths. This, Wood believes, is because the 11+ tends to self-select pupils with these leanings as it is highly based on maths and reasoning. Other big departments at A level are physics, chemistry, biology, economics and history. A few all-rounders leave to take the IB at Tonbridge Girls' Grammar, while girls wanting to specialise move over to Judd (and most often for the sciences).

School faces the ever-present difficulty in recruiting science and maths teachers – and for an additional reason. 'Some are scared to apply because the children may be better mathematicians than them. These kids will eat you alive if you are not able to take them up to Oxbridge levels. A handful could do without us, and in those cases we are guiding them to go beyond us, and trying to help them mature as young people.' But we had good reports overall on the teaching, with parents able to rattle off several whom they felt were inspirational and creative teachers.

A learning support team of five supports around 30 pupils, some with visual or hearing impairment or physical disability, but of which two-thirds have needs associated with autism. The school is going a step further in supporting highly academic students with autism, and plans to open in 2019 a Specialist Resource Provision (SRP) in association with the local authority, which will provide places for 20 students who have an EHC plan for autistic spectrum disorder.

Games, options, the arts: Shock horror, they have introduced football for the first time in 80 years. 'But I don't want it to detract from rugby,' head says hastily – the neighbouring grammars, with whom there is a bitter contest for rugby supremacy, will be hoping it will.

Elite athletes among the pupils – some chosen to represent England in cross-country and athletics, one boy getting a wild card entry to Wimbledon, a team reaching the national U18s quarter final in rugby, and a swag bag of 22 medals at Kent Schools' Athletics. There are cricket tours to Barbados, rugby tours to South Africa – parents expected to cough up for these.

Usual music offer but drama is rather lacking – none on the curriculum, no performing arts space, and one annual production – extra productions only put on when there's a keen group of sixth formers organising it. School keenly participates in linguistic, chemistry and physics Olympiads.

Background and atmosphere: Something of a centaur about the building, with both swanky science facilities in a new building and 1950s style labs in the wood panelled original school building – authentic enough to give you a shudder if they weren't the scenes of your finest endeavours at school. 'We're a traditional school with a modern twist. Things like this remind us that the school is 130 years old,' Wood says.

A surprise touch for a venerable old grammar school is the rainbow horse which greets you in reception. It signifies a commitment to support LGBT people in the school community. Staff had training, which included 'reflecting on our attitudes to difference,' Wood says.

It's a rare beast among state schools with 26 acres of playing fields and seven rugby pitches (and has recently been able to buy more land where other schools have seen theirs sold off). It benefits from a wealthy parent body – their donations contribute about a quarter of funds for new buildings – and the school is much better resourced than other state schools as a result. Some parents grumble about quite how often the collection tin is rattled, and the hefty price tags for overseas trips.

Like many other state schools, Judd has had to expand as a means of counteracting squeezed budgets, and several parents reported consternation at this. 'It does feel at times as though the place is full to bursting in terms of shared resources, and some of the teachers are not quiet about their workload and feeling put upon,' one said.

There's also parental disquiet about the 10.10am start every Monday. This was introduced to give staff time for meetings and lesson planning, and to counter financial pressures, but it's a headache for parents whose own working day means they have to leave before their child, or for those in the villages who have no public transport at that time. 'To teach a generation of students that the working week begins mid-morning on a Monday is short sighted and goes against those traditions that seems so valued and worthwhile in other elements of the school,' said one parent.

Pastoral care, well-being and discipline: Along with many other secondary heads, Wood finds mental health their biggest pastoral issue. Support for struggling pupils comes through tutor groups, and through a team of trained student listeners and mentors. Prefects and heads of houses wear 'listener' badges and staff a room where pupils can go during lunch to play board games or to discuss problems, while a professional counsellor comes into school every week to offer sessions by appointment.

Boys need to be fairly robust to withstand the transplant shock which comes from cruising at the top of their form in primary school, but finding themselves distinctly average or trailing others in a school of this nature, which can knock confidence.

Minor infringements such as on uniform tend to be dealt with by a stint clearing lunchtime tables; for drugs – where there have been a few incidents recently – parents will be involved, and the ultimate sanction is exclusion. Wood had to deal with some dinosaur attitudes among the pupils, which made sixth form an uncomfortable place for some girls, with the result that word got around and girl numbers temporarily dropped off. 'We have challenged poor attitudes and behaviours, and put at the centre of our culture a sense of mutual respect and understanding, and making people more ready to stand up for differences.'

The autism unit set to open in 2019 will aim to bring its pupils fully into the main body of the school over time, but will enable new joiners to have anything from none to half of their timetable in mainstream lessons, and the rest of their lessons in student support. There will be pre-emptive care, so that if staff know that any lessons that day will be taken by a cover teacher, they will have a plan for that. They will have key workers to help them plan their day to minimise anxieties.

Pupils and parents: A well-heeled bunch. Changes to entry criteria in the last couple of years, with more pupils drawn from the local area, has reduced the ex-private school quota to around one-quarter (from one-third). But the five places offered to pupils in receipt of free school meals have not been fully taken up – head blames the local authority's refusal to allow any preparation for the Kent Test in its primary schools for the slow steps towards greater social diversity.

Entrance: Bulge year 7s in 2017 and 2018 entries have resulted in a permanent move to six forms of entry (180 pupils) from the 2019 intake. Now you need to concentrate hard. The school has two catchment areas, an inner and an outer. The inner area is a jagged flower shape, which extends further to the north and west of Tonbridge than it does to the south and east – check it out before talking to estate agents. For 2018 allocations the inner area provided 157 places, including five for those on free school meals, while a further 23 places were offered to 'outer' area candidates. In both divisions places are offered in rank order according to 11+ scores. Cut-off scores vary from year to year, but are around 364 for the inner area and 395-400 for the outer area. However pupils joining under the free school meals criteria, and those who will join the autism provision, need only score a pass (320 marks).

About 70-80 external candidates join at sixth form, around three-quarters of whom are girls. Current students must have achieved a minimum average grade of 6.5 in their best 10 GCSEs, including a 5+ in maths and English language. But 2019 will see the introduction of a new method, where students will apply and register their interest; on results day the school will rank all applicants, and make offers down to the 75th person. It will be nerve-wracking since 250 apply every year; Wood's argument is that GCSE predictions are too arbitrary a basis on which to select pupils – being right only about 60 per cent of the time. Counting 10 subjects instead of looking for six good results stops boys writing off certain subjects, he adds.

Exit: Post-GCSEs around 10 boys choose to leave for new pastures, including the IB, a similar number miss the grades and go elsewhere. At 18, virtually all onwards to university – 75 per cent to Russell Group, 21 to Oxbridge in 2018, and around a dozen to medical school each year.

Remarks: Top option for a studious boy – a school where it's fine to be a geek and growing brains will be well fertilised. Its prestige means it's top of many a parent's wish list, but you should think hard before pushing a borderline student through selection tests with high levels of tutoring – will they keep up once in?

Doing well at spinning plates in a cold financial climate with the result that boys enjoy superior facilities and options to those in most state schools. Many parents pinching themselves at getting this on a free – but donations invited – basis.

The Junior King's School

Linked with The King's School Canterbury

Milner Court, Sturry, Canterbury, Kent CT2 0AY

Ages 3–13 **Pupils** 349 **Boarders** 64 full (mainly years 6–8) **C of E**

Fees: Day £11,145 – £18,735; Boarding £25,710 pa

01227 714000
www.junior-kings.co.uk

Head: Since September 2017, Emma Károlyi, previously deputy head and director of studies at Loretto. She has a degree in classical studies and ancient history from St Andrews, is married to Julian, also a teacher, and they have two children. A keen viola player, she hopes to get involved in music and orchestras in Canterbury.

Entrance: Most join in nursery and reception but major intakes into year 5 and year 7 when extra classes are added and occasionally into year 8 for CE if trying for King's. Younger children have a taster day and informal assessments; from year 5 children tested in English, maths and non-verbal reasoning.

Means-tested bursaries available from year 7 for up to 100 per cent of the boarding fee. Academic scholarships offered at 11+ for new joiners and children already in the school – worth a max of five per cent of fees. Additional bursary support available.

Exit: About 85 per cent go on to King's Canterbury. Others to eg Benenden, Eastbourne College and St Edmunds. A few leave for the grammar schools at 11+ – some after-school coaching provided but parents usually get their own as well. Scholarships to King's Canterbury every year. Those considered borderline for King's required to sit a pre-test and parents are given plenty of advice if it is thought a child might not pass common entrance to their chosen school.

Remarks: Founded in 1879 as the prep school for The King's School, Canterbury and spent its first 50 years in the precincts of the cathedral. Boys were known as 'parrots' because of the noise they made and houses are still named after parrots. Moved to current site in 1929 when Lady Milner gave Sturry Court, an Elizabethan manor house, together with the Tithe Barn, in memory of her husband. It was opened by their friend Rudyard Kipling. Two miles from the centre of Canterbury, it is set in 80 acres of grounds and playing fields with the River Stour running through the middle.

Has a reputation for being quite competitive and according to the prospectus 'endeavour and success are held in the highest regard'; however, the number one golden rule is 'Do be kind, gentle, helpful, respectful and polite' and there is great emphasis on good manners, tolerance and friendliness. Parents full of praise for the school: 'My children are all very different and have all been happy – you don't have to be very sporty to have fun here'. 'The competitive environment has brought my daughter out of herself and given her confidence.' All agree that this school is 'best for children who are good at something' and that 'there is a very nice balance between academia and other things so children can build confidence in different areas'.

J

Strong Christian tradition with weekday and Sunday services at the village church and confirmation and carol services in the cathedral but all faiths made to feel welcome. Full-time and weekly boarders (mainly from year 6+) cared for in two immaculate houses: Kipling (boys) and Juckes (girls). Local children often ask to board for the last year and one mother commented slightly wistfully, 'my daughter wants to be at school more than she wants to be at home'. Lots of evening and weekend activities plus Saturday school with lessons in the morning and sport in the afternoon means there is no time to get bored or homesick.

Relationships with staff relaxed but respectful and there is always someone to talk to – year 5 upwards have two class teachers, one male, one female. 'The teachers seem interested in developing my child as a human being not just on an academic level,' said one happy parent. Bullying rare and dealt with swiftly via detailed anti-bullying policy.

School supports a variety of charitable causes and all children expected to be involved at some stage during the year – sponsored walks, donations to Salvation Army, the school fête, visiting old peoples' homes etc. They share their sports facilities and theatre with local groups; school is keen be part of the local community. Junior King's provides funds for a school in Malawi and children are encouraged to take an interest.

Average class size 15-16, max 18. Three parallel forms with setting in maths from year 5, English and languages from year 6 and science in year 8. Separate year 8 scholarship class. French from reception, Spanish and Latin from year 5. Greek offered to scholars. Special provision for French, Spanish and Chinese bilingual children. Separate sciences taught in specialist laboratories from year 7. Children learn IT programming skills eg making computer games as well as spread sheets, presentations and website design. 'Everyone is expected to participate in class and it is a fast-paced academic school which does not suit everyone'. Very occasionally, it is suggested tactfully that a child might do better elsewhere.

Bright, sunny library central to main school with 14,000 books and run by a part-time librarian – the most widely-read children are appointed to The Most Honourable Order of the Book. Experienced staff of 'inspiring and dedicated teachers' as well as talented young graduate assistants who come to work for a year before going to train as teachers. Much more attention given to SEN in recent years, about 10 per cent with some sort of learning support, either withdrawal or in-class help – system of monitoring and referrals means problems picked up early. Two dyslexia teachers, one full-time, one part-time plus a graphologist. EAL support if required.

Sport taken seriously and the school likes to win. Superb facilities, here and at King's. Rowing an option from year 7 plus a cricket pro and winter coaching and squash offered at King's. Floodlit Astro (funded by a parent) means hockey now a major sport for boys and girls. Girls have been IAPS champions three times in recent years. Huge galleried sports hall and 14 tennis courts. LTA tennis coach recently appointed and school usually sends a team to the national IAPS tournament at Queenswood. Heated outdoor pool for fun but serious swimming taught at the King's recreation centre. Fencing particularly strong and a number of international fencers started at Junior King's. Inter-house competitions give everyone a chance to take part and new talents often emerge at the summer sports day when a huge variety of sports are contested.

Performing arts take place in the Tithe Barn. Music is central; over 60 per cent learn at least one instrument and the choir is a special part of school life. Range of bands, choirs and ensembles cater for every age and ability and with at least one big concert each term, 'music is never far from your ears.' Advent carol service and sung evensong at the end of the summer term are held in the cathedral and there are music scholarships to King's senior most years. Drama part of the curriculum from year 3 and just about everyone has a chance to get up on stage at least once a year.

Busy art department – photography, film making, art history, graphic design, pottery, textiles – the sort of opportunities you would expect to find at a senior school and children can use the facilities at King's as well. DT from year 3 includes racing car design when children build and race a car in the Kent championships, jewellery making and T shirt design and a Dragons' Den type competition when children form teams to solve problems.

Annual Spanish exchange, skiing, weekend in Normandy, post-scholarship trip to Greece, the much looked forward to post-CE jaunt to Cornwall, rugby to Paris, hockey to Holland, cricket and choir tours to Brussels – European destinations which do not put too much strain on parental pockets.

Activities most afternoons and evenings, dozens to choose from (some charged for), everything from animation, circus skills and bushcraft to debating, gardening, jazz dance, riding and photography (digital and dark room).

Pre-prep housed in the Oast House with own hall and library. Seven classrooms with up-to-date ICT provide a colourful and stimulating environment. Children learn PE, French, dance and music from reception onwards and use the prep school facilities – sports hall, Tithe Barn, sports fields and dining hall. Accredited forest school in the grounds where children were making nettle pancakes over a camp fire on the day we visited. Nursery now housed in newly built Swiss-style chalet known as Little Barn with all the mod cons and under floor heating – a busy, happy place with guinea pigs and fish tanks.

Day children from up to 40 minutes away via minibus service or accompanied train from Ashford. Most from professional families – doctors, medics, lawyers and City and creative types. About 45 per cent of boarders are foreign nationals from a variety of countries; strong links with Brussels and the Foreign Office – many parents choose the school for its global outlook. Active Friends' Association has weekly breakfasts and organises social events such as hog roast and Christmas bazaar to raise money eg funded the new adventure playground.

Alumni include: former Olympics minister Hugh Robertson, actor Orlando Bloom, Commonwealth Games president Tunku Imran Ja'affar, ceramicist Edmund de Waal and cricketer Freddie Kemp.

Kendrick School

London Road, Reading, Berkshire RG1 5BN

Ages 11–18 **Pupils** 740 **Sixth form** 160

0118 901 5859
www.kendrick.reading.sch.uk

Head: Since 2012, Christine Kattirtz BA PGCE NPQH. Having studied history and politics at Salford and doing her PGCE at Bath, she started her teaching career in 1981 in Leicester at Sir Jonathon North Community College. Joined Kendrick as a history teacher in 1985, working her way up the ranks to deputy head in 2001, then associate head in 2007. 'I feel that the school is the way it is largely because of the things I've done over the years,' she says, promptly revealing a gushing letter from a former student.

As well as extremely self-confident, we found her commanding, astute and formidable – a woman with serious presence, although girls told us 'she can be lovely' and 'softer around the edges than you might think.' And it's worth noting that before she became head of department, she was head of pastoral – 'which was my natural inclination. I would always want to be seen as kind and understanding.'

'An inspiration' is the most widely used description among parents and students alike and there's no doubting her and her senior team's abilities. Staff, meanwhile, say she is fair, transparent and open – putting the girls at the heart of everything. Teaches A level history and regularly sees girls at break times, as well as popping in and out of lessons.

Academic matters: Outstanding results across the board, with the school consistently among the top performing selective schools in the country. In 2018, 86 per cent A*-A/9-7 at GCSE – and school also shines when it comes to value added, featuring in the top five per cent of schools in the country in terms of progress of students between key stages 2 and 4.

School attributes its dazzling results to girls being 'bright, enthusiastic and curious, with a love of learning,' coupled with 'teachers' unwavering commitment and lack of complacency when it comes to new ideas in teaching.' Teachers, say students, are available 'as much as you need them,' including drop-in clinics, one-to-ones and email communication, while also delivering 'very interactive lessons.' Noticeable mutual respect between teaching staff (where we saw a good gender split and mix of ages) and girls, with a few exceptions ('A few teachers could be nicer,' one girl told us). 'They're very able students who enjoy the challenge – they're a joy to teach,' one teacher told us.

Despite the (perhaps inevitable) hothouse reputation, girls and parents insist it's unfounded. 'They actually build you up quite gently from year 7,' said one girl, 'although expect a lot of tests and homework and you do notice the acceleration in learning in year 9.' Girls split into three sets in maths from February of year 7, which divides into four sets in year 8 (top two with around 30 pupils each; bottom two with around 18 each). Tracking of students achieved with military precision.

German or French from year 7, with the other one added in year 8, along with Latin – and all girls take at least one modern foreign language at GCSE, with around 20-25 girls also choosing Latin. Among the 11 GCSEs that all girls must take are at least one humanity (history, geography or RS) and all three sciences, where girls praise the 'high level of practical lab work.' Certainly no shortage of Bunsen burners fired up when we visited. SEN policy all pretty standard (23 students on the SEND register when we visited – mostly dyslexic; one statemented), with most help within the classroom setting itself.

In sixth form, all girls take three A levels (out of 18 on offer) and most take four – in 2018, 68 per cent A*/A (88 per cent A*-B). Historically, class sizes haven't tipped much above 20, 'although numbers are creeping up in some subjects due to budgetary constraints,' one teacher admitted. 'But once numbers tip over 30, we'd usually have a discussion about the possibility of splitting a class up.'

An enrichment programme ensures sixth form students develop further skills, with volunteering highly encouraged and a focused PSHCE programme supported by a range of external speakers. One period a fortnight is also dedicated to joint activities (such as team building, mentoring and current affairs debates) between years 12 and 13, designed to get the two year groups to bond in a non-academic setting.

Games, options, the arts: Wide range of sports on offer, including swimming, netball, badminton, dance, gymnastics, fitness, tennis, hockey, rounders and athletics, with keener girls participating in fixtures, with – as a PE teacher told us – 'reasonable results.' Sport mostly takes place on site, thanks to facilities including a vast sports hall (one of the newer additions to the school), plus modern dance and fitness studio, indoor pool, tennis courts, gym and front lawn 'which is just about big enough for rounders and basic athletics,' as one girl put it. For more serious athletics, girls use Palmer Park and Reading University sites.

Music strong, with peripatetic teaching on offer in practically every instrument you can think of – a harpist was practising when we visited. Chamber, vox, junior and senior choirs, plus the usual range of school orchestras and ensembles for wind, chamber and ukulele, among others. Regular performances include junior and senior music concerts, spring music concert and house music competition – plus an annual air ambulance concert, joint with Reading School (boys), following a student (whose life was saved by one) making the initial request.

Drama practice takes place in two main drama rooms with occasional whole-school performances (Guys and Dolls and Oliver! are recent examples), house drama competitions (a firm favourite among students) and Shakespeare Schools Festival all significant annual events in the drama department calendar (some overlap with music and drama for bigger performances). Around 9-11 girls do drama GCSE and although the school is open to offering drama A level, there hasn't been enough take-up for several years.

Art and design thriving, with particularly impressive textiles displays, plus canvases and paintings on display throughout the school.

An eclectic mix of clubs (many student-led) come and go, depending on demand, and currently include gardening, chess & Scrabble, European film club, LGBT, chicken club (girls were enthusiastically handling chickens when we visited), robot club, space society, UN, first aid, book club, among others – plus all the usual sports and subject led ones. Geography club set up by year 12 girls the week we visited. Politics high on the agenda, with mock elections to coincide with real-world ones and high-level political debates encouraged from the off. 'This is an outward looking school, which I think is reflected by their relationships with local schools right through to them constantly reminding the girls of the context of the wider world,' said one parent.

Frequent charitable events (raised £8k the year we visited) – also largely student-led. 'A couple of students approached me recently, concerned about the homelessness issue in Reading, so we put them in touch with the local charity Launchpad,' says head, adding that the sixth form raise in the region of £3,000 for Comic Relief. Young Enterprise Company scheme provides sixth formers with the opportunity to run a fully-functioning trading company to help develop business potential.

Regular residential trips include Isle of Wight (year 7), PGL to North Devon (year 9), Germany and France (modern languages trips for years 10 and also years 12-13), Malaysia (or elsewhere such as Nepal or Cambodia, year 11 – for 3-4 weeks), skiing (year 9-13) and German Christmas market trip (years 11-13). 'My trip to Cambodia was one of the most rewarding experiences I've ever had,' one girl told us.

Background and atmosphere: The school's namesake is John Kendrick, a Reading cloth merchant who died in 1624 – and whose oil painting still hangs in the school hall. He left a substantial bequest to provide local employment and education for the poor, and the money was initially used to set up a workhouse (called The Oracle – the name now given to the shopping mall that's been built on the original site), hence the inscription on the painting which reads 'John Kendrick, founder of this workhouse.' Then, in later years (after an unfortunate blip in which Kendrick funds were mismanaged), the remaining bequest was used to found both Kendrick Girls' and Boys' Schools (the latter of which later merged with Reading School). In its current form, the school was founded in 1877 in Watlington Street, where it remained for 50 years – moving in 1927 to its current site on the corner of Sidmouth Street and

London Road (a one way street near the town centre which, as locals will tell you, is generally bumper-to-bumper traffic).

Main building is grade II listed, with extensions from seemingly every era added on since, some more attractive than others. Latest additions include the sports hall/canteen in 2005 (former huge; latter tiny beyond belief – 'many of us eat lunch in our classrooms,' explained a student) and the library and sixth form block in 2009, both located by the school's side entrance. Meanwhile, recent renovations include some of the science facilities. Although the site is small, every inch is optimised, with everything from tennis courts squeezed between buildings to allotments and chicken coop (former used for gardening club; latter for chicken club). In the main, corridors and classrooms have a 'no frills' feel, but are enhanced by the outstanding noticeboards celebrating students' work. No shortage of IT, with 40 interactive whiteboards throughout the school, plus 300 computers, iPads, Chromebooks and more.

The Kendrick 'pledge' of friendship, kindness and respect are taken seriously here and you'll be hard pushed to find a girl who doesn't reel them off at some point in her sales pitch of the school. Girls belong to one of three houses, competing not just in sport events, but drama and music – and even Scrabble and University Challenge. Housepoint system also in place (head can give a five housepoints in one – a very big deal if you get one), with house captains in year 12 and vice captains in year 10. The school's birthday is celebrated every year – 'I wanted there to be a day every year in which former students could come to the school if they want to,' says head.

K

Pastoral care, well-being and discipline: From the finely tuned transition process to the key role of the tutor (also accessible for parents) throughout each girl's school career, the pastoral infrastructure is a well-oiled machine. 'There's a close-knit and caring relationship between girls and their tutors,' parents told us, while the school points to the regular tutor meetings, documentation of all information, formal and informal discussions, regular one-to-one student profiling, reports and tutor involvement in their form's PSHCE programme. Mental health and well-being are words that pop up reassuringly frequently among both staff and students and there is a student-led mental health week. Head clearly open to new ideas regarding pastoral care too – 'One parent suggested a whole day every year in which year 7 students and their parent have a 15-minute interview with me, my deputy or a head of year to talk about any concerns, and we're about to start that.' Likewise, she has made adjustments to the curriculum by reducing homework in the lower years and minimising work during school holidays to help prevent mental health issues arising.

High expectations (to work hard, behave impeccably, have a positive attitude to learning, be polite, turn up on time etc) keep the sanction of detentions from rarely having to be implemented. 'Barely anyone gets one,' say girls. Bullying also infrequent, thanks to the emphasis on supporting your peers and mutual respect. 'Friends will always have your back here and stick to you like an octopus right the way through Kendrick,' said one girl.

'Girls can be themselves in this school. They don't have to hide their intelligence. It's cool to be clever,' says head – and students concur. Cross-year friendships common, thanks to house and mentoring system. Busy student council, with recent triumphs including the installation of the new food technology lab and the upgraded Faraday science laboratories. 'The student voice is at the heart of everything we do,' insists head.

Pupils and parents: Multi-ethnic population (with Indian the most dominant group after white British) a great source of pride for the school, which celebrates this rich diversity in everything from assemblies to individual projects. We found students self-assured and articulate, with a thirst for knowledge and an impressive depth of thinking – and although not the smiliest we've seen, they certainly don't lack optimism. Ditto for parents, although some of them remind you why the pastoral system needs to be so strong ('My daughter is going to be a doctor' is not an unusual comment, even among some parents of year 7s, although it is firmly discouraged by the head – 'Let them be children, I say'). The KPS (Kendick Parents Association) provides a strong social and fundraising network. Most girls travel in on foot or by bus or train – very few by car (and who can blame them, with that crawling traffic?).

Former pupils include Beryl Cook (artist), Chi-chi Nwanoku (musician), Janet Reger (lingerie designer), Yasmina Siadatan (winner of The Apprentice, 2009), Jessica Swale (theatre director and playwright) and Claire Taylor (England cricketer).

Entrance: Brace yourself – this school is heavily oversubscribed, with 1,000 girls applying for 96 year 7 places (three form entry). Entry by 11+, using a common admissions test that girls take in September to apply for schools including Kendrick, Reading (boys) and others in Slough and beyond. Those who get in come from within a 15-mile radius and once in, they don't leave. An additional 40-50 girls join at A level, mainly from local schools including Reading Girls' School – for which girls need eight GCSEs grade 5+s, including English and maths (and 6 or above in subjects studied); also expected to attend an interview and written test.

Exit: Rare for more than 10 girls to leave at GSCE ('Why would you? This is Kendrick!' says a parent), with those that do mainly heading off to local co-ed or independent schools. 'Sometimes, they want to do a course like psychology that we don't offer; sometimes they just want a change,' says head. Post A levels, girls go almost exclusively to Russell Group universities, with current favourites including King's, UCL, Warwick, Bristol, Nottingham, Birmingham, Edinburgh and Exeter – plus, of course, Oxford and Cambridge (12 to Oxbridge in 2018; 15 medics). Top subjects include engineering, medicine, finance and law. 'And with the surge in interest in business and economics here, we've also noticed more girls incorporating these subjects into their degree,' says school, which adds that they are 'not opposed to girls doing apprenticeships and integrated courses at non-Russell Group universities.' Students point to 'excellent careers advice,' plus 'brilliant mentoring through the UCAS process, including by the head.'

Remarks: With a reputation as one of the finest schools in the country, entrance into Kendrick is your daughter's ticket to a flying career, with the proviso that she's prepared to work extremely hard both academically and in extracurricular activities. A school where passions are encouraged and nurtured, we found girls are free to be who they really are and are well supported by peers and staff alike. A go-getting and inspiring education for very bright girls.

Kent College

Linked with Kent College Preparatory School

150

Old Church Road, Pembury, Tunbridge Wells, Kent TN2 4AX

Ages 11–18 **Pupils** 529 **Sixth form** 110 **Boarders** 51 full, 13 weekly, 20 flexi

Fees: Day £20,571; Boarding £25,710 – £32,778 pa

01892 822006
www.kent-college.co.uk

Headmistress: Since 2016 Julie Lodrick BA (music, Chichester), MA (educational leadership, OU). Previously principal of the The Mount, the Quaker school in York, deputy head at Farlington school, house mistress at Queenswood school, and director of music at St Margaret's in West Sussex. Abandoned a career as a singer to teach – 'there was always something missing'. Loves being head of Kent College (KC) – 'I don't feel like I've got a job... it's a fantastic way of being'. Married to Andrew with two grown up stepchildren.

Believes that appearances matter, as well as substance: parents think the head wants to 'produce nice young ladies who can present themselves to the world', not a million miles from the 19th century KC aim: to educate girls 'having regard to the cultivation of a Christian and ladylike deportment...'.Tips from Debrett's appear at assembly, and startled pupils are learning the importance of good posture, etiquette, and looking your best – and when to use a mobile phone on a train (don't, in case you were wondering); though the head points out that this is all about being dressed and behaving appropriately for the environment you are in. The parents we spoke to, impressed by the head, were quite enthusiastic – 'great to prepare the girls for the outside world'; not all the girls were so keen – 'it doesn't matter how you look', said one indignant child to mother.

On a practical level, parents say that when you ask for things to be done, the head listens, responds quickly and sorts the problem out. Less popular is the perception that she is trying to make the academic profile 'sharper', though we were assured that she has no intention of creating a hothouse, believing it is far more important to focus on the good mental health of pupils, and the potential each child has to develop their abilities.

Academic matters: 'Not a hothouse', said a parent, 'but they will make the most of your child's talents, and get the best out of them academically'. Results are consistently creditable: in 2018, 62 per cent A*/B grades, 33 per cent A*/A grades at A level; GCSEs: 57 per cent A*-A/9-7 grades. English is popular, with most pupils receiving top grades (it makes a difference having published authors on the staff, says the deputy head), and geography, with its 'fantastic teachers' is one of the most popular GCSEs. RS is compulsory at GCSE; parents could opt their kids out, but none do.

Plenty of traditional subjects here (options include classical civilisation, Latin, ancient Greek and history of art), but psychology, the new kid on the block, is very popular with pupils, and heeding pupil suggestions, sociology is now available. This school prides itself on making any combination of subjects work – the deputy head here is a timetable mastermind.

Teaching is good, say parents and 'what a nice bunch of teachers...it's not so long since they were young'; ' [They're] in touch with kids' lives, very committed, hard working...know my child... I'm very pleased'.

Maths is the one area of concern, parents worrying about staff turnover and inflexible teaching styles of new teachers, high levels of tutoring, and the best teachers teaching the top sets – 'they should be good all through', said one indignantly. KC points out that pupils achieve good results in maths, and a new head of maths will be starting soon.

This school emphasises that ability is not fixed, and all have the potential to grow, which is evident in their superb value added: MidYIS data shows that KC adds at least a whole grade per GCSE; and, more remarkably, a further grade at A level: BBB to ABB can often make the difference between Russell group and non-Russell group, points out the deputy head. KC achieves this by placing girls in small classes with focused teaching, and constructing classes around individuals: this is not a school which unquestionably follows the same pattern year after year.

ICT is under review, and developing: the VLE now live, and there's Wifi throughout site. There are six dedicated computer rooms, and laptop suites.

The SEN unit supports mild difficulties, in one-to-one and group sessions (extra charge for one-to-one). One parent described excellent support from the unit for her daughter's problems with processing, and the 'amazing change in [her] grades'. The unit will support any pupils who need extra help, from those with gaps in knowledge to those struggling to engage with lessons.

Parents describe a school which is very attentive to learning styles: one said her daughter was upset because she seemed to make no progress; the school suggested a mentor: 'Now she has a learning support journal; can see the progress she is making, and is learning to organise herself'.

Sixth form can feel like relentless pressure, and parents feel KC is a listening school on this: one who emailed the school to report a daughter in meltdown over the amount of homework said it all eased up the following week. Pupils say the deputy head has an open door so you can 'just go and vent' when it gets too much.

There's lots of support with UCAS, although a parent suggested there could be more interview practice for university and jobs. The head's push on developing a global mindset means more visits from inspirational speakers, talks ranging from apprenticeships to Cambridge.

Games, options, the arts: Games at KC was what drew one parent to the school: she described visiting as the parent of a child on an opposing team and noticing the rapport of the girls with their sports teacher; a pupil challenging the teacher to a race, and 'the joy they both experienced'. The humane quality which runs through KC penetrates even sports, pupils commenting that the head of sport is 'so endearing, completely understands that some [pupils] hate it, but her enthusiastic approach makes even haters optimistic...'

The sports department has grown in the last four years: there are more teams, more matches and more specialist coaching. KC runs specialist academies in gymnastics and swimming, and gymnastics is a particular strength here, with national and individual team successes.

Everyone who turns up to training gets included in matches, and pupils told us the school doesn't get miffed if you want to play out of school – '[they're] really flexible with everything'.

KC excels at drama: they have a 300 seat theatre in which they run a theatre academy, and drama is often one of the most popular options, with pupils achieving top grades. Parents told us of the magic effect drama has had on their shy offspring – 'she's always laughing and confident now' – one pupil telling us that she had been painfully shy when she arrived at the school, and probably still would be but for the enthusiastic support of the drama teacher: one word well uttered felt like an achievement.

Music is housed in a purpose built centre, complete with drum studio and Apple Mac suite. Musicians play a crucial role in the success of the school annual productions, and recently performed the Marriage of Figaro, complete with guest professionals.

Activities are compulsory until year 11, and the girls have a fine array to choose from, including beekeeping and fencing. A popular option in lower sixth is the Leiths course: 'you get a knife set and a chef's uniform', said a pupil with enthusiasm, 'and two times a week you can forget all about work'. It's also rather nice having children who can come home and cook a good supper...

Textiles is big here: KC hosts and often wins prizes in the Young Fashion Designer of the year. Photography now a full A level, and is now more popular than fine art.

Boarding: 'It's very important for the girls to feel cherished', said the head of boarding, '[the boarding] house needs to feel like home'. A parent told us: 'My girls loved boarding; they made it fun for them. [The girls were] very much at home [and staff were] very attentive to their needs'.

There are some 85 boarders, including flexi boarders – on regular nights, just during exams or when parents have a last minute work crisis: popular with parents and pupils alike. Around a quarter from overseas (China, Hong Kong, Europe, Africa). No real divide between day pupils and boarders, say the girls, though the Chinese/HK pupils do form strong friendships within their community. UK boarders tend to go home at weekends, but there's a full programme of activity for stay behinds.

Around 35 of the boarders are juniors (years 4-9), mostly weekly; but Saturday activities are so popular that some parents take home their child on Friday and drop them back on Saturday morning so they can join in (trips to trampoline parks or castles) and stay Saturday night.

Juniors are in rooms of around six (which change each term); no bunkbeds, and facilities are clean and well kept. There's a comfortable common room and kitchen where they can make toast or help themselves to fruit.

Seniors are in double rooms, with single study bedrooms for upper sixth. Rather more substantial kitchens than in the junior house, and grown up feeling common areas. More freedom for seniors, who can take the 15 minute walk to the farm shop on the other side of reservoir, but no wandering around in the woods on their own. Buses into Tunbridge Wells are organised for girls in year 10-13, and weekend trips to theatres and shops might go to Bath or London.

Lots of special boarding community events, such as the boarders' international evening to celebrate every boarder's culture with food and performances, and the leavers' BBQ – 'we hire inflatable things', said head of house – an assault course last year. The leavers' bag includes university essentials: an adult colouring book, fairy lights, a mug and a rose.

Background and atmosphere: Pupils describe a school of strong family feeling – '[we're] like a bunch of sisters'. Biscuits are put out for the girls at the end of the day: 'all the girls in happy chatter', said a parent. Not cliquey, say pupils, who told us they could happily sit down to lunch with over half the year. Although one parent commented it would be nice to see someone at the front of the school to say hello in the morning, pupils here have strong relationships with teachers, one telling us it is the best thing about KC – 'I can go to [to them] with any problems or personal issues. A friend in grammar school has one teacher she can go to with problems – here, there are many'.

A girls only environment is a grade enabler, says the school; a STEM subject enabler too, and no worries about fitting the box and behaving a certain way. 'They can roll over and over down [a slope in] the grass', said a teacher, 'which wouldn't be cool with boys [present]: they can be children for longer'. One pupil told us the best thing about the school was 'how comfy I feel... but not babied or hand held'.

A Methodist school, but welcomes all faiths or none; though the John Wesley prayer about doing all the good you can is part of daily conversation here. The chaplin is always available for a chat, and leaves chocolate outside his door.

The main building is a Victorian manor house set in beautiful Kent woodland, surrounded by a miscellany of other buildings and styles: the new Walker building 'is amazing' say pupils: arts and textiles have their own space, and the new library is great (though we never quite got the bottom of the body outlined on the floor in tape...). Pupils would like more infrastructure improvements, and work is on the cards, but even the older buildings here were well cared for.

There is a house system (Celts, Danes and Saxons), with all the usual inter-house sport, drama and quizzes, but the girls weren't very engaged with it: 'it could be improved', said pupils.

The uniform is basically blue, and has been through a few changes: the plain version made the girls look like cadets at Hendon police college, said one parent, and others say the current blouse reminds them of toothpaste: we rather liked it. Sixth formers wear a suit (skirt or trousers), and are pleased to be relieved of the need to choose what to wear.

Pastoral care, well-being and discipline: One parent described KC as an 'extremely caring small community' where 'teachers genuinely care a lot what happens to girls'; it was chosen by another because she felt her daughter would get a good education in a small class environment, but be more nurtured than at a grammar school, where 'middle of the road can get a bit lost': 'Both girls came out really believing they can achieve – and having achieved academically'.

The school takes a pastoral approach to disenchanted pupils, which, the head says, is usually due to lack of confidence: 'We need to unpick the reasons why a pupil cannot engage'. They will talk to the pupil and parents and provide a huge amount of extra support to help resolve problems.

KC has a good eye for pastoral care: a parent told us about the lovely change in her daughter, who found it difficult to make friends at her old school: chocolate club, run by the learning support team, gives pupils who struggle socially practical help, for instance suggesting ways to open a conversation; other support includes the buddy system, ensuring that nervous girls have someone to walk with to the bus stop, and to sit with at lunch time, until they are confident they can manage on their own.

Bullying is dealt with effectively, though the head is quick to point out that long, targeted bullying campaigns are very rare; problems are more likely to be the small tiffs typical to childhood, which are quickly resolved by talking; and in fact a parent whose daughter received unpleasant texts from other pupils said it was dealt with within half an hour of her phone call, and there have been no further problems. The school counsellor will help both pupils and families if necessary, a service described by a parent as 'very, very subtle'.

A parent described a school that is 'good at spotting what happens', and communication is good – 'brilliant at responding to telephone/email queries'; 'oh yes, grades all the time'.

Pupils and parents: Parents range from extremely wealthy to those making sacrifices for fees. Parents agree that this is not a school for very pushy parents or children who are only interested in work (go to a grammar). Eleven different bus routes around local villages and beyond; most pupils from East Sussex or Kent.

Entrance: One hundred or above on standardised scores, leeway for those from state primaries. Feeder preps: Sevenoaks, Derwent Lodge, Dulwich, Wallyhall junior. Fifty per cent of intake from own prep.

Exit: Around half to Russell group, with Birmingham and Nottingham popular destinations, but a range from architecture at Edinburgh to events management at London Met. Two medics in 2018, St George's and the other at Rijeka Medical School, Croatia. One off to the Glion Hotel School, Switzerland.

Money matters: Means-tested bursaries, and scholarships of up to 10 per cent of fees.

Remarks: The word parents use most to describe KC is 'happy'; next up is 'all rounder'. 'They will make the most of what your child is good at, whatever it is', said a parent.

Kent College Preparatory School

Linked with Kent College

151

Aultmore House, Old Church Road, Tunbridge Wells, Kent TN2 4AX

Ages 3-11 **Pupils** 210

Fees: Day £9,990 – £16,011; Boarding £25,236 pa

01892 820204
www.kent-college.co.uk

Head: Since 2016, Nicholas Pears (music degree, Cambridge), married to Emma, with two children. Previously head of music, then head of junior school at Sevenoaks Prep, with a few years off in the music industry in between roles. It is rare we meet a head who has so quickly inspired love in his pupils – 'The girls absolutely adore him', confirmed a mother, and eager smiling faces greeted him in every classroom.

'Mr Pears has presence', fanfared one parent, who was also pleased that the new head is present – living on site, there in the mornings to greet children, and around in corridors, happy to be accosted for a quick chat.

The head believes single sex education enables girls to say ' I can', and this is his aim for pupils; though 'not yet' is fine too.

Entrance: From the age of 3. If spaces, girls may join at any time and are encouraged to come for a taster day beforehand. Entrance tests in English and maths taken from year 3.

Exit: The majority of pupils make the transition to the senior school at 11+, with the rest going on to the grammars. The school has a good track record in the Kent Test and also prepares girls for the entrance exams to other independent schools.

Remarks: On a parent's first visit to the school, they reached the door at the same time as a couple of year 3 girls. The girls said hello, made eye contact, and held open the door – 'they had a real confidence...a lovely confidence and were totally comfortable in their surroundings...'. The two year 6 girls who then showed the parents around gave a real sense of how much they loved their school; happy and confident children, an intoxicating blend for parents.

The proof of the pudding has been evident in a shy daughter who is now 'head up and brilliant with adults', the parent pointing to lots of gentle exposure in assemblies and tea time music concerts, along with a safe school environment and kind relationships between girls.

Wellbeing is the first concern at this school, and is evident in the mechanisms put in place to support children, such as the buddy system which connects an older girl with younger one, or in the school e-safety ambassadors – pupils trained by Kent police in keeping safe online. It's also clear from the relaxed and happy children; parents comment on the 'exceptional care' at this school, from the head, the teaching staff and from the 'gang of ladies' who care for children before and after school (wraparound care from 7.30am-7.30pm includes breakfast club, after-school club – including activities – and supper club) – 'if we're stuck, or running late...if anything happens, we know the girls will be fine...' Pupils can board from year 4, but in practice prep school boarders are flexi-boarders from years 5 and 6.

The support from teachers and SEN staff is supplemented by the school counsellor, who is on hand to help girls with any problems, ranging from marriage breakup to death, Olive the dog helping girls who find it difficult to open up. 'School becomes family', said the head earnestly, and this was evidently so in some cases, a tiny tot in reception who regularly stays to supper club and eats with the head and his family greeting him with beaming affection on our tour.

This small school with its small classes gives teachers the time and space to unpick problems, so disruptive or disinterested behaviour will be addressed by asking why, looking for the story behind the difficulties and ways to address it.

The prep school feels quite separate to its senior counterpart, although the aim is to make the schools feel increasingly one, with pupils going through from 2-18. To this end, prep pupils use the college pool, gym and theatre, and increasingly share specialist staff; early years performed their nativity at the college, and 6 years olds were excited to see sixth formers coming to assembly and performing arias from the Marriage of Figaro. It hasn't quite seeped through to parents yet, one describing the prep school, approvingly, as 'a bubble' (with all the safety and security that this suggests), but who added that she would be looking for different things in a senior school – 'there are a variety of great schools in the area'; this includes, of course, grammar schools, which syphon off some of year 6. Parents who take this route tend to tutor their children and the mental health of his pupils is clearly something that concerns the head: tutoring children unlikely to make it through the 11+ places them under undue pressure: 'worlds can fall apart at 10'.

Pupils no longer take an exam to progress to the college, though some will take the entrance exam to the senior school for the chance of a scholarship (10 per cent of fees). For the few for whom the college is not right, the head will talk to parents in year 5.

The ability range for the school is wide, with most pupils in the above average range; but those of less than average ability who can cope with the curriculum with additional help are welcome. Small classes (of no more than 18), so it's easy for teachers to differentiate between ability in a mixed class, though maths is set from year 4.

Parents describe a school which is very attentive to pupils and the way they learn, one telling us that the school noticed her child worked a lot on her own, and referred her to SEN to check all was well: that it was a learning style, rather than a learning problem. The SEN unit may support any child with a particular problem at any time, and help children with mild learning difficulties in one-to-one and small group sessions.

The modern light school buildings are filled with colour, in displays on walls, sometimes ceilings, and, on the occasion of our visit, in year 1 – who were preparing their assembly on the eclectic mix of Christopher Columbus and Neil Armstrong in a wonderful and bewildering combination of outfits. All the usual sports here, with dance as part of the curriculum rather than just an add on. Gymnastics and netball are particularly strong (gymnasts are national champions and the netball team were in the IAPS finals).

A good all round school which suits all comers, with a mix of parents: 'Appeals to all sorts'; 'The girls are happy at the end of the day; so are we'.

King Edward VI Grammar School, Chelmsford

Broomfield Road, Chelmsford, Essex CM1 3SX

Ages 11–18 **Pupils** 1,102 **Sixth form** 382 (121 girls)

01245 353510
www.kegs.org.uk

K

Headteacher: Since 2014, Thomas Carter MA PGCE NPQH (40s), previously deputy head and associate head. He read maths at Clare College, Cambridge and worked in management consultancy and strategic development before changing to a career in teaching. He also has an MBA from Warwick and a PGCE from the Institute of Education and holds a diploma in French language and literature. Before coming to KEGS in 2001, he spent five years at Westcliff High School for Boys.

Affable and frank, he is also ultra-efficient. Says his three key principles are excellence, equality and compassion – and students agree: 'He achieves very high standards within a culture where everyone is treated with dignity and respect.' He's big on leading by leading by example too. 'He speaks to us in the same way he expects us to speak to him and he is as quick to pick up a litter as we are.'

Teaches far more than most heads – around an hour a day of maths to the upper school. 'It's partly to connect with students – I don't want to be too remote. And I think teaching is important if I'm to have credibility among the staff.' Impressively, he tries (and succeeds, according to the students we spoke to) to get individual time with all 150 year 7s, if only for a few minutes. 'He's very fair – he'll always stand back and listen to your side of the story,' we were also told. Parents describe him as 'approachable,' 'enthusiastic' and 'quietly authoritative.' 'He's just perfect for the school.'

He is married with two sons, both of whom are at KEGS. His wife has two careers – a professional singer and a garden designer. He has a serious interest in music (violin, piano, singing) and enjoys learning languages and skiing.

Academic matters: In terms of academic achievement, one of the top 10 state grammars. In 2018, 90 per cent A*-A/9-7 grades at GCSE and 63 per cent A*/A at A level (not including general studies, which is taken by the majority of students). Outstanding commitment from staff who, according to a parent, 'go a thousand miles beyond the call of duty and don't just stick to the curriculum. They give a proper education.' 'Teaching isn't obsessively focused towards exams,' and a love of learning is engendered right from the word go. 'I just spent an hour with one of my teachers, who is known for giving up pretty much every lunch hour to help students – and that's not unusual among staff here,' one student told us. Younger boys enjoy creative lessons – Blackadder used to illustrate a point and volcanoes made from bicarb of soda – and all are stretched and challenged, with target setting and monitoring all busily happening behind the scenes. 'There's almost a university ethos in terms of levels of enquiry and intellectual curiosity – but with a safety net if any boy struggles,' said one parent. Lots of CPD for staff, with younger ones supported to do extra qualifications. 'There's a lot of research on how people learn best – and just as doctors are expected to be up-to-date with medical advances, we ensure our teachers are kept up-to-date with these,' says the head.

Known for sciences, although GCSE results are also particularly strong in maths, Latin, geography and history. Languages popular. At A level, art, chemistry, English, geography and geology do particularly well, while maths is also popular (many do further maths). History and English at Pre U, with very successful results for English. Some sixth form classes feel a bit too big, say students – 'hovering at around 20' – and some would like a wider A level curriculum, perhaps with less traditional subjects such as psychology and business studies. 'But the teaching at this level is phenomenon.'

Setting from maths in year 8, 'but it's fairly fluid and boys are never far from the top set,' says head. Year 7s all take French or German, which they learn at a fast pace – then they take their GCSE in that subject in year 9. In year 8, all boys also take up Latin, which they can continue for GCSE if they choose, and they pick up a second modern foreign language in year 9 too – either the one they didn't do in year 7, or Russian or Mandarin. 'All language teachers only speak in that language, which is daunting at first, but a great way to learn,' say students. Head explains, 'Learning a language isn't just about passing the exam here – we want students to leave knowing how to converse in a second language because that should be a normal thing to do.'

IT embedded in all subject areas. Awards for those who tot up the most effort marks. Homework starts at around 1.5 hours a night in year 7, then builds up slowly, peaking in middle school at around two hours a night. 'It is intense and if you don't like homework, this is not the school for you,' says the head. 'We hope by the sixth form that students have learned to plan and manage their own time.'

A few have special educational needs – a SENCo oversees these students, who generally have visual impairment, dyslexia, dyspraxia or Asperger's syndrome. 'Understanding, inclusive approach,' according to parents, whilst students told us the pupil support unit is 'discreet.' 'There's not a stigma, but you don't shout about going there,' one said. That said, there's great support for those at the more severe end of SEN, 'with real cheers in assemblies when they are singled out for achievements.' 'This department worked with our son's care team – they really did everything they could to make sure he could reach his full potential. I can't praise them enough.'

Games, options, the arts: Not known for its sporting prowess, 'but it should be,' believe many parents. Rugby fares well and full range of fixtures in all major sports. Students also win competitions in basketball, badminton, table tennis and tennis. Sport is compulsory up to end of year 12, and optional in year 13. Sixth formers get the chance to play squash or swim at the local sports centre. Lots of house competitions – particularly popular among those who aren't so good at sport. 'It's fine if you're not that great as you play other people who aren't that great,' said one student. 'There's definitely a have-a-go culture, rather than just focusing on the elite.' Most sports take place at Bedford Fields, an impressive 30-acre site four miles down the road, although the main school site does have some tennis courts, a playing field – albeit a bit tired – and a new sports hall.

Welcoming, modern art department is veritable Aladdin's cave (albeit with a lot of natural light) rammed with lively work, especially by the younger ones. Music block is also new and there's plenty to write home about from this department, not least the commitment for 30 year 7s to learn an instrument free of charge in lessons of three. 'It's partly to build our orchestras of the future, but also because learning an instrument isn't always affordable,' says the head. Ten peripatetic teachers on hand to teach instruments to other students, for a fee. Three orchestras, wind band, jazz band and various choirs, with concerts every term and lots of participation (40 for the wind band alone when we visited). Plenty of music tours. 'My goodness, the music opportunities are fantastic – there is literally something for everyone,' one parent gushed.

The students also take great pride in their drama department, with one big production taking place every year – usually a musical one year, then a straight play the next. 'The standard is breathtaking,' one parent told us. 'I was one of the 150 students involved in Les Mis and it really helped me build friendships, as well as allowing me to experience a high quality production,' one student said. Smaller scale productions – with some of the plays written by students – run throughout the year.

D of E, CCF and good selection of clubs enrich beyond the curriculum – including sport, music, drama, chess, maths clubs, three debating clubs, computing clubs, young engineers, school newspaper, just to name a few. Many win national competitions and most are student-led – the newspaper, for example, has no input from staff whatsoever. Most take place at lunchtimes – some boys fit two in their lunch-hour, although a few told us it can be a squeeze to fit one in, 'especially if it involves changing clothes.' Medical society particularly popular – 83-strong when we visited. Charity work managed by the student-led charities committee (again, student-led). 'Extracurricular life here is so diverse – you can be anything from a young engineer to a keen actor to a maths mentor – or, more likely, all three. The added extras beyond the academics is a huge pull of the school.' 'A lot of these very bright boys could easily be one-dimensional, but the school ensures that never happens. I don't know anyone who doesn't do anything extra.'

Trips to just about everywhere you can think of – Alsace, Boulogne, Iceland, New York, China, Rome, Paris, Barcelona and Kenya are all visited most years, with KEGS Foundation and school funds available to help those who can't afford it.

Background and atmosphere: Founded in 1551, nearly 350 years before it settled on the present site close to the town centre. Last 100 years have seen numbers increase eight-fold and buildings, permanent and 'temporary,' added behind the original low-key red-brick frontage. Absolutely no frills and some students said they can 'feel a bit cramped indoors,' but there are impressive features, including the grand, stain-glass-windowed and well-stocked library, housed in the school's first hall; and the Darwin Centre – sixth form centre – which is a three storey state-of-the-art building containing a spacious study area oozing natural light, a classroom and colourful and roomy sixth form social area on the top floor. The fabulous new art centre is 'a joy to work in,' according to students, and we also like the Oxbridge-esque feel of the outside cloistered quad areas that sit within the figure-of-eight shaped original buildings. Science labs could do with a face-lift, but surprisingly this doesn't seem to bother students one iota – 'It doesn't impact on our learning,' they told us, and the results speak for themselves.

Despite the ferocious competition for places and intensive pace of study, students are clearly happy. Parents agree: 'this is no exam factory', 'with a real emphasis on creating a positive environment,' although everyone we spoke to said boys who are over-tutored to pass their 11+ can struggle once they get in. 'It seems a shame as you can tell another learning environment might be better for them.' Strong sense of community where the acquisition and sharing of knowledge exude from every pore, and where the atmosphere is generally calm and concentrated.

Uniform is standard white shirts, ties and black blazers, customised with a bright red stripe round collar – and it's an instant detention for any top button undone. Plain blazers for boys and girls in the sixth with a free choice of shirt colours.

Pastoral care, well-being and discipline: Counsellor on hand if help is needed, although some students we spoke to had no idea about this, and the ones who did weren't aware of where you'd find her. 'But the fact that we haven't needed to see her could be seen as telling in itself,' pointed out one student, with all parents agreeing that the school is generally nurturing and that teaching staff are on hand to help iron out any problems. 'Any difficulties are identified early on and strategies are given to help,' say parents. 'This is a school that really listens and they act quickly.' The pastoral structure is certainly strong, starting with form tutor and rising up five levels to the head, although many students told us that in reality, 'you just find the staff member that you've most bonded with if you need someone to talk to.' 'The fact that many of the older children mentor the younger ones is also relevant, say students – 'you can confide in them if you've got any worries you don't want to talk to staff about.'

Slightest sniff of bullying is instantly investigated – but it's rare. 'It's ok to be quirky or different here – I don't know anyone who feels they can't be themselves,' said one student. Strict on mobile phones (where and when you can have them – they're not actually banned) and uniform, but it's not a school brimming with rules and an active school council encourages a high level of civilized co-existence. A new-ish strike system means that if you get four strikes in less than five weeks in any one of the three areas of equipment, homework and behaviour, and you get a detention. 'It's not unusual to get a detention at some point in your school career, but lots of boys get no more than that,' says the head. High expectations of conduct in the classroom – full engagement and no chit-chat at all in the ones we saw. No permanent exclusions in the current head's time – although he has 'helped move one student to another school, following an incident' – and there are a handful of temporary exclusions each year, usually as a result of physical violence.

Pupils and parents: Pupils from as far afield as some London boroughs, but most much closer – with students mainly travelling in by train, bus or on foot, a few cycling or dropped off in the car. Diverse parent body – range of occupations and backgrounds. Good ethnic mix – around half white British, while the rest include Asian, black, Eastern European and more – 'a glorious mix,' says the head. Old boys include Lord Fowler, Simon Heffer, Grayson Perry and Alex Dowsett. A lively PA and parents tell us there's good communication from the school.

Entrance: Hugely competitive. In recent years, over 1,000 of the brightest examined for the 150 places. Lots of tutoring goes on to help smooth the process, although the school has got rid of verbal reasoning in the 11+ in an attempt to create a fairer playing field – and it's true that there are small, but growing, numbers on pupil premium: four per cent of years 7 and 8 when we visited. Wide catchment area with over 60 feeder schools – prep and primary – but 80 per cent of places are reserved for those living within 12.5 miles.

Almost all stay onto sixth form. Minimum of five A/7s and three B/6s to do so, with at least an A/7 in the subjects to be studied. 'In reality, lots have seven or eight A*s or more,' says the head. External applicants (who include girls – increasing numbers of them) come from a mix of other grammars (including the girls' grammar across the road), private and comps.

Exit: Virtually all to university – 24 to Oxbridge in 2018 plus one to Harvard. Around three-quarters of the remainder to Russell Group universities, with a sprinkling doing gap years or apprenticeships. Good spread of locations and courses, with Warwick, Exeter, Bath, UCL, Kings and Imperial among the favourites. Lots of medics – 23 in 2018.

Remarks: Inspired approach towards teaching and while it's clearly an intensive environment in which to learn, the pastoral care is outstanding and students are generally a very happy bunch. Staff are passionate about their subjects and students thrive in an atmosphere where it's cool to study. Beware of over-tutoring to get your child in, however – they could struggle to keep up.

King Edward VI School (Southampton)

Wilton Road, Southampton SO15 5UQ

Ages 11–18 Pupils 953 Sixth form 227

Fees: £16,050 pa

023 8070 4561
www.kes.hants.sch.uk

K

Head: Since 2002, Julian Thould MA – Pembroke College, Oxford (50s). Surprisingly, for this overtly scientific school, his subject is history with a passion for medieval castles, evidenced by some detailed scale models in his office, including an intricate one in chocolate, that he was judging for a year 7 competition. Worked in industry before a teaching career in some top schools, Westminster, Cranleigh and King's Worcester, until appointed to his first headship at King Edward VI. Impressively well organised but definitely approachable, he believes children do best when they are happily occupied. Hence the exciting co-curricular programme, which not only attracts some to the school but also encourages enthusiasm, enjoyment and ambition that spills over into academic work.

Retiring in July 2019. His successor will be Neal Parker, currently vice principal and head of the senior school at The Grammar School at Leeds. Educated at the British School in the Netherlands and The Purcell School of Music, he read music at Oxford, and has a masters in educational leadership from Newcastle University. Started his career at King's College Wimbledon; has also been director of music and head of performing arts at Newcastle Royal Grammar School. Married to Sarah, a deputy head at Harrogate Ladies' College, and they have one son, Joe. As well as his passion for music in all its many forms, Neal is an avid sports fan and lover of the outdoors, particularly hiking in the Lake District.

Academic matters: 'All our pupils are bright enough to do three sciences and a language,' says the head, and certainly exam results speak for themselves. The swathes of top marks at GCSE are in maths and the sciences (73 per cent A*-A/9-7 grades overall in 2018), with maths also multi-starred at A level, but there is a fair sprinkling at all levels in every subject in the wide and demanding curriculum (A levels 85 per cent A*/B grades and 54 per cent A*/A in 2018). In the lower school everyone has a go at two mod langs and Latin and carries on with one modern plus at least one other (either modern, Latin or Greek) until the end of third year. At GCSE everyone takes RS early (a bit reluctantly at present, though with tip top results – this is due for a change). All do three sciences and a language with the option of three further subjects, adding up together with maths and English subjects to a total of 10.

There are routes to either three or four A levels in sixth form with everyone doing 'foundation studies' as well. Pupils can do subjects not taken at GCSE, except of course in maths, science and languages, where knowledge is cumulative. Despite the excellence of the arts and humanities, most choose maths and science. In one group of 10 pupils, all but one claimed maths a favourite subject and, incidentally, RS as the least. 'You can get maths done and either you understand it or you don't.' Work ethic is strong with pupils saying, 'it's great if you do well but no one is afraid to ask if they're struggling with something'. Possibly science and maths are so popular because there are so many medical/scientific families, and it's what the school is known for. But the head says, 'Look at the results. There's a better success ratio.'

Sixth formers clearly have high expectations and are appreciative of the support the school gives them. The classes we saw had a quiet buzz of interested discussion and pupils talked about their work with serious enthusiasm.

Games, options, the arts: Art is exciting with masses of multi-media, sculpture, abstract, photography flourishing and expanding with the advent of a head of art with an impressive photographic career. Some really good art going on; also some frustration within the department that comparatively few take it beyond GCSE.

Music certainly lively and enthusiastic. A very impressive a capella choir organised by the sixth formers was rehearsing during our visit as well as the strings boning up on Prokofiev for an orchestral concert. Lots of pop and light music as well, and students doing music technology on equipment resembling aircraft consoles. A few get to National Youth Orchestra standard and there are lots of tours, concerts, festival triumphs, high-powered workshops and masterclasses etc. Drama also popular with several performances annually, musical and other. Some are in the lofty great hall with its airy but formal atmosphere and acres of honours boards and some, such as a recent History Boys, in an intimate theatre in the round, professionally lit and equipped and due for expansion soon.

The importance of sport is emphasised by the school being fronted by sports fields, both grassy and green Astroturfed. The cavernous sports hall is flanked by a dance studio much used by the girls, though even the boys do a dance module in the third year. Fantastic record in netball (girls), hockey (both girls and boys) and cricket at county and regional level. Rugby is less strong, 'but a keen coach'. Masses of individuals achieve in fencing, sailing, rowing, swimming etc and there's strong support for athletes of all varieties. Double Olympic sailing gold medallist Iain Percy was here, also Keith Wiseman (past chairman of the Football Association), John and Simon Francis (county cricketers), Dudley Kemp (England rugby cap and past president of the RFU) and Rob Moore (hockey Olympian). Parents like the Saturday fixtures – they keep 'em out of town.

Fifty-plus clubs, many as intellectual as the most academic parent might hope, but some with a distinctive King Edward's twist to them: the Byron Society, the German Magazine Club, the Scamp Club (concerned it seems with codes and code-breaking). The Green Team is busy planting veg and its work has now been crowned by the award of a Green Eco Flag. The appointment of an assistant head of co-curricular to coordinate it all demonstrates both how important this aspect is to the school and how incredibly well organised – essential if pupils are to fit it all in.

Real training for social awareness too, with masses raised for charities by the 'charity commission' – £25,000 plus per annum in a huge variety of enjoyable ways – and pupils enjoy the contact they have through educational programmes with local primary schools: 'It's a real pleasure to be able to help someone with reading or science'. Lots of DofE – gold awards – and a plethora of trips enthusiastically promoted by staff. 'Good staff – good at their job,' a parent commented.

Background and atmosphere: A historic foundation funded by William Capon for the poor scholars of Southampton, under royal charter from the boy king, it opened a year after his death in 1554. The present buildings date from its return from evacuation in Poole during WW2. From the outside it still looks like a post-war grammar school, despite acres of grass and smart blue railings all round – a recent really efficient security and check-in system is in place. Inside, it feels distinctly sophisticated and academic, with the acres of polished lino and slightly institutional coat of arms set into the front hall floor. Everything is geared to a comfortable, work-friendly environment. The atmosphere in the attractive sixth form centre, with its elegant metal arches, break-time snack bar and constantly manned careers offices, positively invites hard work. 'You can get more done here in an hour than in a whole evening at home,' an upper sixth boy commented.

Lots of recent refurbishment in the science zone part funded by the Abraham Trust. No shortage of money, so a new all singing and dancing technology centre and of course appropriate IT everywhere – iPads just coming in for the art department.

Recently acquired the Stroud School in Romsey, one of its main feeders, now known as Stroud, the King Edward VI Preparatory School.

Pastoral care, well-being and discipline: Terrific rapport between pupils and staff, especially amongst sixth formers. Prefects, known as Prepositors, and heads of houses patently feel part of the team running the school, and the head boy talks as eloquently as the head in the video clips on the website. Collaboration is key, with school council having a say in major decisions and undertaking research into pupils' needs. They take credit for the streamlined but inviting dining arrangements. Good healthy fare with svelte sixth formers tucking into old-fashioned nursery puddings – too busily occupied to put on weight. Rules on uniform etc are strictly observed, keeping the confrontation points at a superficial level. It must work since they look pretty smart, including the non-uniformed, 'dress for work' sixth form. Pastoral care run through tutor groups drawn from one or two years depending on age and stage. PHSE stresses intelligent responsibility. Lots of drugs education. Head more concerned about 'legal highs' – alcohol etc – and pupils' awareness of what they are doing to themselves. Sanctions range from detention for minor infringements of rules to expulsion, short suspension and investigation, testing for drugs. All staff get pretty extensive pastoral training and meeting times to coordinate concerns. The school assumes an intelligent attitude from pupils, and all rules and policies are clearly laid out with relevant explanation in the student diaries.

Pupils and parents: It's efficient and serves the large proportion of local medical and academic families, with very small ethnic minority proportion. The huge catchment area is right up to Andover and Winchester to the north and edging Portsmouth and Bournemouth east and west. Seventeen bus routes, all energy-savingly full, with major routes doing a second evening run for after-school activities. Locals, including the head, use bikes. Lots of community-minded parents run a PTA (the KESSoc) with second hand shop, social stuff etc. Most can't find anything but good to say of it.

Recent old Old Edwardians range from Hugh Whitemore (playwright and dramatist) and Michel Vickers (pop group Manfred Mann) to Michael Langrish (Bishop of Exeter), Ian Bruce (ex-president of the RNIB) and Sir Edward Abraham FRS (Oxford academic – ground-breaking work on penicillin and synthetic antibiotics). Also His Honour Judge David McCarraher, Sir Michael Bichard and Her Majesty's Ambassador Richard Kinchen MVO.

Entrance: Known to be hard enough to put off unrealistic would-bes but still about two try for every place. Exams in maths, English and reasoning plus interview and report from previous school. Half from state primaries, and around 25 local independents. Sixth form entry asks for six GCSEs at grade 6 including English and maths but possibly getting a bit more competitive after a bumper crop of super bright applicants. Pupils from the recently acquired Stroud prep school compete on equal terms with the other entrants – no special preference.

Exit: About 70 per cent go through to sixth form. Almost all of these to Russell Group universities – the cream. Nine to Oxbridge in 2018 and 11 medics.

Money matters: Bursaries, means-tested, 100 per cent remission for the most deserving. Scholarships, academic (up to 10 per cent of fee), creative arts (up to five per cent of fee) and sports. Entry at 11, 13 and sixth form. A tight budgeting school with a policy of never borrowing to build. Always has enough cash in hand to cope with any eventuality

Remarks: At first sight a juggernaut of a school, but definitely more upmarket than its grammar schoolish image. Everything done thoroughly and well, as its confident, lively and hard-working pupils attest. Certainly worth the commute from Andover.

Kingham Hill School

Kingham, Chipping Norton, Oxfordshire OX7 6TH

Ages 11–18 **Pupils** 339 **Sixth form** 108 **Boarders** 144 full, 54 weekly

Fees: Day £17,220 – £19,620; Boarding £24,390 – £33,045 pa

01608 658999
www.kinghamhill.org.uk/

Headmaster: Since 2008, Nick Seward MA BEng (40s). After a fairly international childhood, he boarded at Millfield School and went on to do aerospace engineering at Imperial College. His interest in the dispossessed and the homeless in particular, however, led him to work with homeless people in Blackburn and London; after a year travelling he went to Durham to study theology including a masters with a thesis on CS Lewis. He worked as a curate for four years but eventually moved to teaching at Magdalen College School (it was that CS Lewis connection that attracted him – Christianity with literature and deep intellectual curiosity). He was mentored and inspired by the head who 'celebrated eccentricity' and he saw that 'hard work, rigour and routine delivered challenges and results for the bright boys'. It must have been a transformative teaching experience, where he saw how school could encourage and channel individual interests.

He has brought the same ethos to Kingham Hill, which he joined because he was drawn to its 'Christian ethos, strong heart and the non-selective admissions policy', and he believed it was a school where he could make a difference. And it would appear he has. The parents, teachers and pupils are 'impressed' and 'adore' him for his commitment, his humanity and humility. Interests include go karting, sea fishing, camping holidays with his family and running the local football club. And this on top of teaching (economics) up to a quarter of a full teaching timetable and preaching or taking services in the local church.

He brought in big plans ('Realising our Vision') and has delivered well before schedule – increasing pupil numbers, improving exam results, raising funds to build fabulous new facilities (library, maths and science block), and all these improvements whilst sticking faithfully to an inclusive admission policy. He would like to increase bursaries and maintain the founder's intention to provide 'education for the poor'.

Married to 'the lovely Hannah – the clever part of the marriage'. She was previously a director of music (explained one child who is a chorister). She helps out as informal school matron and joins on the joint annual skiing trip with Magdalen College School. They have one daughter and three sons.

Academic matters: Small classes, traditional teaching, an emphasis on handwriting and ethical behaviour over technology, and a very individualised level of input gives pupils clear boundaries. It means that lessons are calm and directed. Some limited setting in classes; pupils learn tolerance and teachers manage to differentiate. Science and maths results lifting: wonderful light and airy new building specifically for these subjects. Fantastic science labs – a science trip to CERN was a highlight for one student doing physics. Languages and humanities in the old school, wood panelled classrooms where history lessons referred to pupils from the First World War era who had sat in the same rooms and belonged to the same school houses.

K

The size of the school and close teamwork of teachers (several live on site) allows for some cross-curricular work – French/history trips, biology/sports, English/music. Evidence of interactive whiteboards but education here is more about discussion and explanation than technology. French or Spanish compulsory initially, but currently not a very high take up at GCSE or A level (nearly all A level linguists take Chinese or Russian). Good GCSE results – especially for a non-selective school. Forty-seven per cent A*-A/9-7 grades at GCSE in 2018. Popular subjects are maths, sciences and history. And very good and improving A level results – 46 per cent A*/A grades, with mathematics, government and politics, economics and business studies very popular and maths particularly successful. Now offers an animal management BTec, with practical learning on the school farm. Students spoke of 'wide opportunities' and having 'more ways to choose' because of the breadth of opportunity.

The brightest children from each year are invited to join the Octagon society, where they can discuss philosophical and ethical questions. Students felt that it 'allows us to really push our thinking' and teachers enjoyed the chance to 'motivate' and 'enrich outside the usual school curriculum'. Several pupils we spoke to felt very proud and privileged to be part of the Octagon society, which 'pushes me'.

The school has a successful learning support department with students given both individual and group support (sometimes instead of taking a foreign language), and some choosing to go along for extra homework help, study skills, revision help and advice about technological support for learning. In-house assessments possible and extra time for exams and laptop use for those with dyslexia where needed.

This has the 'vibe of an international school but is still very British,' explained one student. It is accredited by New England Association of Schools and Colleges and is recognised by the US Department of Education. This means that US pupils can gain American school credits alongside the British curriculum and, if they stay to the end, can graduate with a US high school diploma. Also provides SAT preparation classes. Perfect for students moving to and from the States.

Games, options, the arts: Acres of space for exercise – we were pleased to hear from the girls that their sports are taken just as seriously as the boys'. Fencing, hockey, basketball, watersports, climbing, mountain biking (all those wonderful rolling hills and forests). Rugby very popular with boys we spoke to. Girls in the football teams. Lots of matches against local school teams, but room for those who want to pursue individual sports – swimming, gym, long distance running. The warmest school swimming pool we have come across with pupils also gaining certificates in lifeguarding and being able to earn money and experience doing this at weekends. The pool is open to pupils' families – parents reported using it regularly in the morning after dropping children off at school, and at the weekends.

Years 7 and 8 have the opportunity to learn a new musical instrument with free music lessons, and then often join the school orchestra or one of the ensembles. Singing is part of chapel service every morning ('it sets the tone for the day') led by school choir and backed by an organ scholar from Oxford. A 'taste of the Anglican choral tradition,' according to the head, as well as four different choirs including gospel.

Art is in an older workshop – creative chaos with many media including the rare treat of a pottery studio with kilns. DT (resistant materials) led by very long-standing teacher who clearly loves the fact that students explore and lead the learning. His own background in aeronautical engineering is evident from the many large model planes made by students as well as metalwork, 3D digital printing, woodwork. We saw garden benches that transformed into tables, book cases and finely jointed boxes. Hugely practical and creative.

Performing arts in a good drama hall – musicals, speech and drama, straight acting – any chance to perform welcomed and is the highlight of the school according to one pupil we spoke to. Drama scholarship pupil has 'new confidence since joining the school', and drama awards announced in assembly alongside sporting achievements.

The school farm, run by the chaplain's wife, is a real asset – 'my son's favourite day is when he has farm club after school'. We saw a child leading a pony round the school, we met Casserole the rabbit, saw the new lambs being fed by bottle, and were introduced to the one-eyed horse. And this is a real little farm, not a petting zoo – pupils are taken to the abattoir when the time comes and learn about real agricultural practices, not just pet keeping. A touch of sanity and a chance to keep pupils' feet firmly on the ground and in the mud.

Boarding: Some 60 per cent of students board (almost entirely termly boarders, though a smattering of weekly boarders too) in a range of small houses. A maximum of 33 pupils to a boarding house with resident houseparents. These houses are their home, with clean, bright bedrooms and sitting room areas. A house for day pupils too, so they have a space to gather together each morning, leave their bags and get changed for sports. Boarding houses used in the morning for house meetings (aka checking diaries, reminding about music lessons and special notices), at lunchtime to collect themselves and their books, and after school for homework and recreation. Slightly more boys than girls board, but this is slowly equalising, especially with creation of the Lodge for more independent living for sixth form girls, which is a highly prized destination – day students stay occasionally too if they have evening practices or activities. Students in the Lodge do their own laundry and have more freedom than those in other boarding houses. Both parents and pupils reported that there was no division between day pupils and boarders. Local parents regularly welcomed boarders from further away for long weekends or exeats.

Background and atmosphere: Purpose built in 1886 by a philanthropist who wanted to educate the poor from the East End of London and get them out into the country, the wooden beamed chapel and mixed outbuildings still feel more like a country manor than a school. Well kept grounds and buildings, but not precious. It is set high in the Cotswolds with views all round of rolling hills and distant villages mid way between Stratford upon Avon, Cheltenham and Oxford. A hundred acres of grounds allows for wonderful playing fields and space to breathe. Chapel central to the school with daily services and the chaplain a big presence in the school. 'Atheists a minority at Kingham,' according to one parent, but pupils were encouraged to explain and discuss their points of view; 'free thinking encouraged' and 'no indoctrination'. Pupils expected to 'back up their ideas' rather than repeat dogma. Christian values 'core to the school' with prayer central too.

Pastoral care, well-being and discipline: Pupils call the close-knit community that exists at the school the 'Kingham bubble', and we can see why – set in some isolation in the countryside, with older and younger pupils mixing unselfconsciously and both adults and pupils 'treated with respect as individuals whose opinions are valued'. No teachers on first name terms, but no pupils called by their surnames either. Pupils 'on a par with teachers' who 'chat to them', and pupils say they 'feel listened to'. This school is 'more about the whole child' and is 'not pressurised'. The teachers 'find out about the kids' and 'interact with the children'. There is 'an ease between teachers and pupils, it is respectful but jovial at the same time'. Parents like the fact that the school is 'warm' and 'happier' than most and reckon that teachers must be better because the school is not selective but get such 'good added value in terms of academic achievement'. Parents spoke of pupils not being pushed but of being 'given opportunities and encouraged' and of choosing the school precisely for that reason.

Pupils and parents: Famous old boys include Andrew Adonis, Pink Floyd's Guy Pratt and even an air-vice marshal. This range of interests and careers sums up the school – space for pupils to be individuals. Approximately 15 per cent of students from families in the Forces or Foreign Office, with 10 per cent American students (state department or embassy families), some 70 per cent of students British and 20 per cent overall international. School works hard to ensure no large groups of international students so a medley of some 20 nationalities (we met a German student, a boy from Uzbekistan and a Chinese girl just for starters). British students primarily fairly local. There is no pressure to be a 'cool kid' at this school, which 'doesn't attract the more pushy parents'. Parents spoke of the joy at finding an alternative to the very academic and driven schools that abound in the area, where pupils have time and are encouraged to have extracurricular interests rather than focussing entirely on academic studies.

Entrance: No academic selection and the school will take children needing learning support but 'rarely' those with ADHD, autism or behavioural difficulties. Head meets all families when they visit and/or apply and then there is an assessment in English, maths and reasoning, as well as sight of previous school reports. Assessment by agents if pupils from abroad. Taster days possible for prospective pupils – so reassuring for parents and pupils to know the school before committing.

Exit: Around 20 per cent leave after GCSEs and around 15 per cent after year 12. Serious effort goes into career guidance, with presentations and careers evenings – attendance, needless to say, by MOD and agricultural colleges, but also a wide range of other careers talks. Americans tend to go back home for university, though none in 2018, with the only international destination Paris (biochemistry). Others to eg Exeter, Bath, Birmingham, Oxford Brookes, York. The school is very proud of several past students who came from backgrounds in care to go on to Oxbridge.

Money matters: Fifteen per cent of revenue from the school is spent on concessions and school bursaries (means-tested bursaries of up to 50 per cent are available and a generous 100 per cent of school fees for able sixth form pupils). Scholarships of up to 25 per cent of fees for academic, art, performing arts and sport and at sixth form, one 50 per cent organ scholarship and three 75 per cent academic scholarships. The school has a proper set of 12 governors – rare and reassuring in a private school, as well as trustees who oversee Kingham Hill Trust. At present, building projects are funded from revenue, which appears solid.

Remarks: The overriding approach is 'what can the school do for the pupil rather than what will the child bring to the school'. The Kingham bubble is a supportive community of pupils and teachers treating each other with respect and kindness in this area of outstanding natural beauty. A traditional English boarding school with Christian values and prayer at its core, giving a solid education in its widest sense to both English and International pupils.

King's Rochester

Linked with King's Rochester Prep and Pre-Prep

Satis House, Boley Hill, Rochester, Kent ME1 1TE

Ages 13–18 **Pupils** 256 **Sixth form** 92 **Boarders** 50 full, 1 weekly, 1 flexi **C of E**

Fees: Day £19,320; Boarding £31,590 pa

01634 888590
www.kings-rochester.co.uk

Principal of King's Rochester and head of the senior school: Since April 2019, Ben Charles, previously second master (senior deputy head) at Portsmouth Grammar. Music degree from Exeter and PGCE in music from Durham. He has been director of music at Chigwell and Millfield, and joined Portsmouth as deputy head in 2009. His wife Helen is also a teacher and they have four young children. Ben is an experienced choral conductor and singer, and also a huge sports fan, particularly offering support to teams from his native city of Leicester.

Academic matters: Caters for a wide range of academic ability from 'Oxbridge to average'. In 2018, 26 per cent A*-A/9-7 at GCSE and 25 per cent A*/A at A level (50 per cent A*-B). All do RS and ICT at GCSE. PE, music, classical Greek, Russian and German are among other subjects offered. Business studies, government and politics and history of art amongst 24 A level offerings. Will run an A level class for as few as three pupils and 'will go to great lengths to tailor the timetable to suit the children'. EPQ also offered alongside A levels – another feather in your cap for university entrance.

An extraordinarily dedicated team of teachers – a good combination of some who have been in the school for many years and bright, young, newly qualified staff. 'The levels of devotion are extraordinary – they even ran revision classes on Easter Monday,' said one parent. 'The teachers really seem to care how we do,' said a pupil. Dedicated careers department – 'school has beefed up advice for university and beyond,' said a parent. An old boy has set up Jobs Network to provide advice and work experience to current and former pupils and help with interview practice and technique. Current and former parents encouraged to offer help with work experience or as a mentor. All upper sixth have mock job interviews with feedback and lower sixth have cv writing clinics.

Team of qualified SEN teachers – mainly for mild dyslexia, although school happily accommodates those with greater needs where possible. Pupils assisted in class, through withdrawals and with IEPs.

Games, options, the arts: Sport on the up helped by the introduction of sports scholarships and the new facilities. School took over the Stirling Sports Centre and adjoining Holcombe Hockey Club from Medway Council, now refurbished and renamed the King's Rochester Sports Centre, a 10 minute walk or short minibus ride from the school. Olympic standard Astroturfs and new outdoor tennis and netball courts plus indoor hockey, badminton and cricket nets and a fitness suite. Free membership for King's parents and open to the general public too. Some team sports still played on the pitches within the school grounds. On-site netball means the girls now get match teas – has made the 'netball mums' very happy. Rowing from the school's own boathouse on the Medway near Maidstone – 18 rowing boats and five large canoes. School very supportive of outside achievements eg national level pentathlon plus sailing and skating, and several pupils play cricket, rugby or hockey at county level. Strong tradition of fencing – fencing master was involved with organising Olympic competition. DofE popular and 10-15 do gold each year. CCF offered in all three services – compulsory for the first two years and many keep going. Our guide had learnt how to fly a plane with the RAF division.

Impressive music – the prep is a cathedral school so the choristers (boys only 8-13) are part of the school and the chapel is Rochester Cathedral. Choir trips all over the place and they make recordings for Radio 3. Several choirs, orchestras and ensembles, a wind and jazz group and inspirational and 'brilliant' director of music. About 50 per cent learn at least one instrument with several reaching grade 8 each year, and a number go on to study music, often with organ or choral scholarships; pupils recently won scholarships to the Royal College and Royal Academy of Music. On a lighter note, the annual house music competition and popular termly Open Mic night give pupils an opportunity to perform in public.

Busy art department with photography, sculpture and fine art offered – product design particularly popular and pupils often go on to art college. Three major drama productions a year, numerous theatre and opera trips to London, and visiting theatre groups organise drama workshop within the school.

Numerous after-school clubs and societies with 'something for everyone' including bell ringing, debating, ICT and chess. Ballet popular throughout the school: some up to grade 8, and a handful keep going into sixth form. Lots of trips and outings – choir to Vatican and China, Physics to CERN, maths to NASA and World Challenge to northern India.

Boarding: About half of the boarders from overseas – some 14 different nationalities and school works hard on integration. Boys' boarding house (recently refurbished) for 43 and girls' for 25. Start off in small dorms, and sixth form and most of fifth form have their own room with ensuite bathroom. School sports facilities available in the evenings. Always something organised at weekends eg shopping and cinema trips and children are expected to take part.

Background and atmosphere: Part of the Foundation of Rochester Cathedral, the school was founded in 606 AD at the same time as the cathedral and re-founded under Henry VIII in 1541 when the monastery at Rochester was dissolved. Prefects wear a gown and carry a cane but the school is certainly not old fashioned and inward-looking. A great sense of history here with the buildings clustered round the cathedral and next to the Norman castle; Charles II spent his first night in England at Restoration House on his return in 1660 and Queen Elizabeth I is rumoured to have stayed at Satis House (now the school administration building). A range of buildings from the medieval cathedral to Georgian, Victorian and 21st century, with Watling Street running down the high street. An unexpected and peaceful oasis in the middle of the bustling Medway towns. One of the few co-ed independent schools in Kent which offers a seamless education from 3-18 years.

Pastoral care, well-being and discipline: Strong Christian ethos; the cathedral is the centre of school life and the service held four mornings a week is a period of quiet reflection before the day begins. All faiths and backgrounds welcomed. All are expected to come to the services in the cathedral but do not have to participate. A tangible sense of community where everyone knows each other well and it is 'a very family oriented school where there are genuine friendships across year groups and kids look after each other,' said one happy mother. 'It is a close knit community that produces confident, self-reliant children who are not cocky,' said another, and 'It really does try to cater for all, and they are very personal in the way they deal with the kids'. 'My son has at last found a school where he is happy – it offers the best pastoral care I have come across. Most schools say they treat every child as an individual but King's Rochester really does,' said a father. School takes a firm line on drugs and runs a programme of drug awareness through PHSE but has not had any issues.

Pupils and parents: Big range from traditional to first time buyers and some who make genuine sacrifices to send their children here. Some come from the Medway towns and villages, some from 25 miles away and some come down on the train from SE London, Bromley and Blackheath. Extensive minibus service from as far away as Tonbridge and Sevenoaks. Children generally 'down to earth and engaging – they exude confidence and are compassionate, sociable and great fun to be with'.

Former pupils known as Old Roffensians and are hugely supportive with a great sense of loyalty to the school. They go on to follow a variety of careers and include surgeons, musicians, authors, artists and poets. Alumni include Prof Sir Derek Barton, who won the Nobel Prize for Chemistry, John Gummer, former Conservative cabinet minister, Pete Tong, Radio 1 DJ and Matthew Walker, professional cricketer.

Good communication with parents who say they feel involved. Moodle, a virtual learning environment where children can access classwork, homework and notes is proving popular with parents, who can keep an eye on what is going on.

Entrance: Broad ability intake but children are expected to be able to take 9/10 GCSEs and 3/4 A levels. Summer exams for those coming up from junior school are used for setting purposes and very few fail; and school will give plenty of warning if this is likely to happen. Entry from other schools at 13+ via common entrance or school's own tests. Occasionally spaces in year 10. Very few leave after GCSEs. Another 20 per cent join in sixth form and are expected to get at least five GCSEs at grade 5 or above and 6+ in subjects to be studied at A level.

Exit: Small fall-out after GCSEs. One to Cambridge in 2018, and one vet. Bournemouth, Brighton, Hull, Portsmouth, Reading, Southampton and St Mary's Twickenham currently popular.

Money matters: Offers sports, academic and music (including organ) scholarships worth up to 30 per cent of fees which can be topped up with means-tested bursaries up to 75 per cent of fees. Discounts for clergy, Forces families and siblings.

Remarks: A warm and caring family school with some of the best pastoral care around where children can grow up in the shadow of the cathedral. A wide ability range but all made to feel valued and the brightest get into the best universities. Going from strength to strength under the dynamic head.

King's Rochester Prep and Pre-Prep

Linked with King's Rochester

St Nicholas House, King Edward Road, Rochester, Kent ME1 1UB

Ages 3–13 **Pupils** 375 **Boarders** 3 in top prep years

Fees: Day £7,125 – £14,955; Boarding £21,960 pa

01634 888590
www.kings-rochester.co.uk

Headmaster of Preparatory School: Since September 2018, Tom Morgan, previously deputy head of the Prebendal School in Chichester. A cathedral chorister, he is a graduate of the Royal College of Music where he met his wife, Camilla, and together they have four children. He has also worked at Swanbourne House, Ashdown House and Chafyn Grove.

Headmistress of pre-prep and nursery: Since 2009 Sarah Skillern MA BA NPQH (late 30s).

Entrance: Most join in the nursery at age 3+ and move on to the pre-prep the following year. Places allocated on a first come first served basis. Entry into the prep is via an interview with both parents and the child and a report from the child's current school – most join at 8+ and 11+ but will take children at any time if there are spaces. Large intake at 11+, particularly from primary schools and independent schools which finish at this age – testing in English, maths and non-verbal reasoning; this also guarantees them a place in the senior school. Will only not offer a place if a child needs more help than the school can offer – mild to moderate dyslexia no problem. Choristers (boys only) admitted via a series of musical and academic tests and join in year 4, and are offered music scholarships worth 30 per cent of fees which can be topped up with a bursary if necessary and 30 per cent off (compulsory) music lessons.

Exit: Almost everyone (currently 95 per cent plus) moves on to the senior school. About six a year to local grammar schools. Support and help with maths and non-verbal reasoning but do not coach for the Kent Test. Entrance to the senior school is just about automatic but all have to take a set of exams in the summer – mainly for setting purposes.

Remarks: Prep and pre-prep very much part of the whole King's School. They are all part of the strong Christian community with the cathedral at its centre, but all faiths made to feel welcome. Prep and pre-prep are both self-contained but use the senior school facilities including the swimming pool, art and DT room, games pitches and sports centre. Purpose built pre-prep has bright and colourful classrooms and its own play area. Prep school is a cluster of modern buildings surrounding the paddock (used for rugby and cricket) and shares a large hall with the pre-prep. Light and airy with photographs all over the place.

Children streamed from year 6 and setted in some subjects. French introduced in year 5, PSHE taught from year 6 and Latin and DT from year 7. All three sciences taught separately in year 8, and can use the senior school labs. 'Kids gradually prepared for senior school and are encouraged to take responsibility for themselves'. About a quarter of lessons taught by senior school teachers in the last year, some in the senior school, and top two years can play in the senior school symphony orchestra. German introduced in the nursery via fun-based activities with songs and puppets, and continues into the senior school – taught by a native speaker. Years 7 and 8 do an exchange with a school in Munich every other year. Head of IT 'very forward thinking' and IT is integrated into all lessons and taught as a subject throughout the prep school. The library is the centre of the school and younger children are taught how to use it – a bright light space.

Good learning support – one full time and three part time SEN teachers. Offers mostly in-class support, mainly for mild to moderate dyslexia and mild behavioural issues, and has a 'joined up approach'. Staff often go into English lessons to look for issues. The school no longer has CReSTeD status. Light touch EAL when required.

Boys play rugby, hockey and cricket and some football, girls play netball, hockey and rounders as their main sports, and everyone swims all year round in the school's own pool. Fields up to four teams per year group so everyone has a chance to play in a match. Strong musical tradition as you would expect with a cathedral school and about 40 per cent learn an instrument – taken out of lessons on a rota basis and most practice done at home. All do class music and singing as well as some theory and composing. Good range of bands and orchestras including wind band, string orchestra and quartet and fiddle groups, with termly concerts in the school hall and a celebration of the performing arts in the summer term. All children in the pre-prep have the chance to perform in a concert. One lavish theatre production each year and plenty of opportunities to perform in public; poetry festival, LAMDA exams and informal concerts as well as visiting theatre groups and drama workshops. Choir trips all over the place and they make recordings for Radio 3. Recent netball and cricket tour to Barbados. Good range of after-school clubs including ballet, Irish dancing and trampolining. Children made aware of the environment and their impact upon it and there is a master in charge of the school's carbon footprint.

Pupils come from a 25 mile radius from as far away as Sevenoaks, Tonbridge and Bromley and increasingly from south London. Good network of school buses. A very inclusive school where parents are encouraged to get involved, they 'feel part of the school and integral' to their child's education, they 'come from all walks of life and everyone is made to feel they fit in'. All new children have a buddy who contacts them in the holidays and looks after them when they arrive. The school 'has a very good pastoral feel and you feel you are really listened to as a parent – I only moved my children recently and wish I had done so earlier,' said a delighted mother. Before and after-school care very helpful for working parents, and anyone who arrives before 8.15am is offered breakfast.

Kings' School (Winchester)

Romsey Road, Winchester, Hampshire SO22 5PN

Ages 11–16 **Pupils** 1,692

01962 861161
www.kings-winchester.hants.sch.uk

Headteacher: Since 2013, Matthew Leeming. Educated at Westminster School and St John's College, Durham. He taught geography at schools in Liverpool, Lincolnshire and Peterborough before moving to Hampshire. After spending six years as deputy headteacher at Brookfield Community School, he was appointed headteacher of Crofton School in Stubbington. Married, with two children, Mr Leeming lives in Chichester, which has a similar school system and his family experience confirms his view that secondary 11-16 school followed by sixth form college is a very beneficial arrangement for pupils. Friendly, unpretentious and easy to talk to, he evidently loves Kings'. Describing himself as 'the cat that got the cream,' he believes it is an exceptional school and seeks to maintain its outstanding academic standards and well-ordered discipline, perhaps 'softening it a little to make it a more nurturing atmosphere for 11 year olds'. He exudes pride in the school, and this attitude is shared by many of the staff (there are an exceptionally high number of staff children in school), and this clearly rubs off on the confidence and motivation of his pupils. Under his guidance Kings' has become the lead school in the Winchester Teaching School Alliance, which includes all the Winchester schools and the university. It has resisted academy status, regarding Hampshire as a very education friendly local authority.

Academic matters: Results rival those of grammar schools, which is impressive for a school with a totally comprehensive admission, and one which accepts a high number of disabled and special needs pupils. In 2018, 82 per cent of pupils got grades 9-4 at GCSE in both maths and English and 36 per cent of grades were A*-A/9-7, an achievement which would be considered gratifying for upper streams elsewhere. Business studies, which moved to a new business suite in late 2016, is key to the curriculum (but is no longer compulsory). GCSE core subjects are maths, English and science (plus PE and PHSEE) for all. Since all the staffing concentrates on only five year groups with 336 in each, Kings' is able to offer and a bigger and more flexible group of options than most. Pupils are divided into bands for two groups of subjects – maths/science and English/humanities. Other subjects are taught in mixed-ability groups. This gives a combination of setting and streaming which allows all pupils to be in appropriate groups even if they happen to be brilliant at one subject but struggle with others.

All but one humanities group are encouraged to take at least one modern foreign language and some encouraged to take two, so the languages are better served than in many schools, with French, German, Spanish and Italian on offer from first year. Pupils who request a particular language normally get it, and can add a second language from the second year. Native speakers of other languages are given help to tackle GCSE in their own language and get consistently high results. No Greek at present but Mr Leeming wonders if they are missing a trick there, as Latin is popular – so watch this space. Science can be taken as a double GCSE or three separate subjects depending on the pupil's band and science, English and maths are sometimes taught in single sex groups depending on the needs of each group.

Results for the separate sciences demonstrate quite how well Kings' does for able students: 9-7 grades are achieved consistently by about 60 per cent of biology and chemistry students, and over 70 per cent in physics, with a regular 100 per cent 9-4 in all three. More than 40 option choices including child development, photography and a BTec in PE among the less common.

Since the school is a centre for access for physically disabled pupils there is a huge allocation of 30 or more staff, who provide extra help in class for a variety of needs. SEN pupils can have up to three hours individual support teaching or get support in lessons, and every assistance is given so that only in exceptional cases are pupils excluded from a subject of particular difficulty. Both the SENCo and pupil support teachers ensure that all aspects of pupils' needs are met including sport for physically disabled pupils.

Some parents worry that Kings' may not develop academic strugglers as well as high flyers, but as one parent pointed out, 'outcomes for lower streams are exceptional' – and the figures certainly confirm this view.

Games, options, the arts: Art, music and drama all do respectably as exam subjects with good sized groups. Music is immensely well served as an activity with choirs, orchestra and groups for classical and popular music, and there are annual drama productions and performance nights – The Crucible was in rehearsal at the time of our visit. Kings' now incorporates the Tower Arts Centre with theatre and dance space so has use of some professional facilities.

Sport is definitely a key feature with lots of post-school and lunchtime extra sport – cricket nets, tennis etc and boys' and girls' teams for major sports. Stopping at 16 means they don't get the national accolade that some all-through schools manage, but the girls proudly announced that they had been second nationally in U16 girls' football recently 'and it was all decided in a penalty shoot-out at the end. Half the school went up to Manchester to watch'. One sporting publication judged them as best comprehensive school for sport. Teams do pretty well locally with a star player nominated by the school after each match, and there are regular tours abroad for netball and football. The impressive sports hall and pool are a shared with the local community and there is generous provision of Astroturf and other playing facilities.

Though there is not the huge diverse range of activities that some independent schools offer there is definitely something for most interests, with maths, science and other subjects running teams in national challenges. (Maths does particularly well.) Activities are mainly in the lunch hour and before 4.30pm with a second fleet of buses provided for those who stay on. Homework club offers a chance to get it done before going home with a bit on help on hand, and there is a catch-up homework session in the lunch hour. Theatre visits bound plus exchanges to Spain, Germany, France and Italy, and subject related-trips to Iceland, Germany and even New York.

Background and atmosphere: The spacious green site originally harboured a girls' school and a boys' school – both rather rocky. Their visionary amalgamation into an 11-16 mixed school over 25 years ago created an exceptionally well-organised and thus academically fruitful academic atmosphere. The buildings are harmoniously set round courtyard spaces amid green pitches and park-like grounds. It feels like an independent school, except that Hampshire manages to maintain the grounds as fit for purpose but not to manicured garden standard.

Wheelchairs and walking frames cause no comment and there is a special wheelchair-friendly space in the dining room. On our visit the dining room was functioning as the floor of the stock exchange in a noisy and extremely enthusiastic business studies day, but was miraculously restored to function in time for lunch. Pupils say food is OK and appreciate the summer ice cream and winter hot drinks stalls run as business enterprises by senior pupils. Work experience is compulsory for everyone in year 10, while younger pupils have activities week.

Pastoral care, well-being and discipline: Uniform is pretty smart on the whole with very few ties at half mast. A parent commented that this is a place where it is definitely OK to do well. Pupils say there are few rebels and hard working responsible behaviour is so much the norm that it is definitely 'uncool' to flout the rules. This was very evident on our visit when an unscheduled fire alarm had 1,700 pupils standing in perfect silence for 10 minutes while well-oiled procedures checked the buildings. Everyone was accounted for within eight minutes – quite a feat in the middle of lunch break in so large school with so many wheelchairs in evidence and some groups miles away on the games field. The support team was noticeably watchful for anyone who might have problems standing long in the sun and everyone had an extra bit of time off to make up for missed lunch break.

Pastoral care is mainly through tutor groups of about 30. Discipline is traditional and strict, though Mr Leeming is very aware that children also need kindness and a bit of freedom, so there is a distinct and possibly necessary softening of atmosphere in favour of really good pastoral care. Pupils said there was little or no bullying and Mr Leeming said that the inevitable few issues were quickly pinched in the bud.

There is strong leadership from the year 11s, who considered they had a good social life and were looking forward to their leavers' prom. They told us that they enjoy the disciplined atmosphere and consider the rules sensible, saying that very few pupils don't really buy in to the Kings' mindset.

Pupils and parents: Catchment includes some outlying villages but mainly local housing which has quite a wide social mix; some quite downmarket as well as the academic shady suburbs. Pupils are friendly and articulate. The prefect layer gains from responsibility earlier than in an 11-18 school, so that they are confident and definitely proud of their school.

Until recently there was a small boarding house mostly for pupils from abroad. There are still a few pupils who lodge in the town to attend Kings' but the emphasis is now on children from the locality.

Alumni include comedian Jack Dee, actor Colin Firth and footballer Wayne Bridge, though the first two date from before the current amalgamation.

Entrance: After looked after children and those with medical needs, priority to siblings, those in the catchment area (mostly south and west of the school), those from linked primary schools, children of staff.

Exit: The vast majority (about 70 per cent) go to Peter Symonds, with the others spread between Barton Peveril, Sparsholt and Eastleigh Colleges for sixth form. A few go to vocational courses.

Remarks: An exceptional school. One parent told us that she and her children were proud and privileged to belong to such a great school – and all for free. Definitely Kings' has all the characteristics of a good school, whether maintained or independent: academic excellence, strong leadership, sound and enlightened discipline and wonderful facilities. No wonder some parents are prepared to pay by accepting Winchester house prices.

The King's School Canterbury

Linked with The Junior King's School

25 The Precincts, Canterbury, Kent CT1 2ES

Ages 13–18 **Pupils** 853 **Sixth form** 373 **Boarders** 681 full

Fees: Day £27,495; Boarding £37,455 pa

01227 595579
www.kings-school.co.uk

Headmaster: Since 2011, Peter Roberts MA PGCE (50s), previously head of Bradfield College for eight years. First in history from Oxford followed by a PGCE at London Institute of Education. Started teaching career at Winchester as head of history, then also as master in college. Always immaculately dressed – 'sometimes a vision in tweed and sometimes besuited'. He is super brainy and regarded as 'quirky and eccentric but with a good sense of humour and perfect for the job – we would not want anyone who was run of the mill,' said a happy parent. A thoughtful academic 'who works unbelievably hard and is always out and about with his dog.' He attends every play, recital and concert and even the matrons' meeting, describing his job as 'vastly enjoyable.' Teaches the Shells (year 9) 'when he can'.

Describes the ethos of the school as 'interactive osmosis'. 'It is the richness, the diversity and range of our lives here that makes it distinct and special.' He feels the school 'gives a strong sense of belonging, a realisation that King's helped to make them (the pupils) what they are' and 'this creates the wish to give something back in return' and sees the atmosphere of the school as 'like a massive confidence-building machine'. Expects very high standards from the children at every level. Each week the Robertses invite 15 different pupils, one from each house, to lunch in their private dining room. Much expected, too, from staff and light being shed on the few pockets of less than good teaching.

Married to Marie, an elegant and accomplished Frenchwoman who was head of department at two large state schools and, in addition to playing an active part in school life, is also a harpist. They have three daughters. They enjoy spending time in France where he sails, and they both practise calligraphy and paint watercolours – helping to uphold the renaissance ideals of what is technically the oldest school in the country.

Academic matters: The pursuit of academic excellence is at the heart of everything the school does but co-curricular activities given equal weight and pupils have a 'rich' day. The brightest take some GCSEs early, allowing a head start on A level subjects; the less academic may drop a subject at GCSE. Pupils encouraged to take a creative subject like art, drama IT or music alongside academic subjects. In 2018, 57 per cent A*/A at A level, 73 per cent A*-A/9-7 at GCSE (IGCSEs for most subjects). Strong across the board and languages particularly good – mainly taught by native speakers and housed in the Old Palace. Most subject combinations can be accommodated even if some have to be taught outside the timetable. School always looking at ways to stretch the most able and curriculum constantly adapted. Currently 27 subjects to chose from at A level (including geology), including seven at Pre-U, and advanced extension awards in most. Astronomy offered as a

GCSE along with Italian, Russian and Mandarin GCSE ab initio in sixth form. Strong work ethic and 'Children do not seem to realise how much they cram into the day, it is just normal for them,' said one mother.

Pupils encouraged to think about their broader academic profile and alongside A levels there are enrichment subjects such as critical thinking, perspectives on aesthetics, globalisation and science and the extended project. Careers advice starts in the first year on a drop-in basis and fifth form have timetabled careers periods to help with A level choices and beyond.

Stunning William Butterfield designed library (1848) is centre of academic life with a hushed and studious atmosphere and combining the best of the old and new with 30,000 books and a range of periodicals and European newspapers as well as DVDs and online reference sources. It is a great source of pride and always staffed and open every day until 10pm and at weekends. Somerset Maugham and Sir Hugh Walpole both left their personal libraries to King's.

About six per cent need extra help, mainly for mild dyslexia, and any pupil can ask for help with study skills. Probably would not suit anyone with bigger difficulties and some parental concerns that children do not get as much support as they need. EAL for a handful of pupils but all must be fluent on arrival.

Games, options, the arts: Acres of playing fields about 15 minutes' walk away as well as a modern sports centre incorporating pool, indoor courts, climbing wall, café and gym – more akin to the smartest private leisure centre than the school sports department. Huge choice of sports – girls' hockey thriving with 15 girls in the English hockey training system. Cricket and rugby going from strength to strength and several boys have been selected to play for Kent U18s; school has also produced several international fencers. Rowing on the up for boys and girls after a period in the doldrums and old boy Tom Ransley won gold at Rio 2016. Sports coaches include an England cricketer and an Olympic hockey player. Not everyone represents the school in matches but still play sport for 'fitness, health and fun' and most people find something they enjoy. Everyone is expected to get involved and participation is everything – 'you don't have to be brilliant but just give it a go and have fun.' Sporting trips all over the world – rugby in Argentina, cricket in Grenada and netball in South Africa.

Long tradition of excellent drama and music and anyone involved is definitely awarded 'cool status.' Fab new junior music school opened early 2016 and new performing arts centre in former Victorian malthouse due 2019. Symphony orchestra plus numerous bands and ensembles; the pupil-run jazz club is particularly popular. Plenty of choral groups, from the Crypt Choir which tours annually, most recently to China, to the choral society which is open to anyone who enjoys singing, including parents and staff. 'Wherever you go around the school there is always music coming from somewhere'. Masses of drama both on and off the curriculum – house plays, GCSE and A level productions, drama competitions, fashion shows, full school plays – 'Wherever there is a quiet corner, you will find a rehearsal going on,' as well as regular theatre trips to London. Busy art department housed in 12th-century priory has a different artist in residence each year. Photographic studio and pottery centre opened by old boy Edmund de Waal.

Huge range of activities continues into sixth form – anything from academic societies with visiting speakers to mountain biking, cryptic crosswords, debating and the Model United Nations. CCF once again a popular option. Community work and volunteering are central to school life, often part of DofE, and include teaching science in local primary schools, riding for the disabled and help with swimming for handicapped children.

The famous King's week at the end of the summer term is the highlight of the year for pupils and parents alike and is a festival of music, drama and dance with events being staged in all corners of the school every day for a week – parents and friends come bearing picnics and it is a major social event culminating in Commem Day and the leavers' ball. 'The quality and variety are phenomenal' and there is everything from Shakespeare, classical concerts and jazz as well as a lighter touch provided by the house harmonies. Those not involved do not feel excluded and have as much fun as those taking part.

Boarding: Six boys' and five girls' senior boarding houses (latest, Kingsdown House, for girls, opened in 2015). Half the houses clustered round the cathedral and the other half across the road on the St Augustine site where they have their own dining hall. Pupils equally happy to be in houses in either location, most popular houses booked up years in advance. Boarding houses friendly and welcoming with areas where pupils can make their own snacks and relax. Small dormitories for younger children and individual study bedrooms for sixth form. Large and popular social centre open for the whole school during the day and for sixth formers in the evening.

Background and atmosphere: Set in the shadow of Canterbury Cathedral and part of a World Heritage Site, this has to be one of the most inspiring settings for a school. Founded in 597 when St Augustine arrived in Canterbury and then re-founded as The King's School during the reign of Henry VIII after the dissolution of the monasteries – not many schools can produce a list of headmasters going back to 1259. Beautiful ancient buildings and cloisters and immaculate gardens with the busy city life going on just beyond the gates. Pupils enjoy the contrast and the fact that the city with its shops and cafés is on the doorstep and say, 'it makes us feel part of the real world'. The headmaster says the combination of the cathedral and a vibrant student city 'grounds the children in a wider reality'. The school sponsors the Folkestone Academy and lends its facilities to the wider community.

Took girls into sixth form in 1970s and went fully co-ed in 1990. Boarding houses plus day houses and a smaller sixth form girls' house in a variety of architectural styles from the 13th century Meister Omers to 21st century Grange. A close knit community, 'it's got everything, the spiritual dimension from the cathedral and a sense of beauty and history'. Former pupil Michael Morpurgo said, 'King's is like a university designed for younger people.'

Pastoral care, well-being and discipline: Smart uniform worn throughout the school, pinstripes, wing collars and a jacket – and a brooch for the girls. All look very professional and businesslike; monitors wear purple gowns and are, unsurprisingly, known as Purples. Astonishingly busy day – one of the first lessons the children learn is how to plan their time – but there is still room for lots of fun. Strict rules and punishments regarding drugs, alcohol and parties and children know where they stand. Strong Christian tradition and moral values. The main school services held in the cathedral but different religious and cultural backgrounds recognised and valued.

Children have a healthy respect for each other and are generally self-regulating regarding bullying and other misdemeanours, and honesty and integrity are highly valued. Pastoral care comes in for particular praise from the inspectors. Big effort to address everyone's happiness with several staff/pupil committees to ensure all have their say.

Regular communication with parents especially through housemasters and house mistresses. Good interaction between year groups facilitated by mixed age tutor groups and mentoring from older pupils. New Shells have a top year mentor. Day children and boarders mix well and 'you can't tell the difference,' according to one pupil.

Pupils and parents: A good mix socially and culturally with a wide catchment area – popular with locals, London and county sets and Foreign Office families and increasing numbers from abroad. About 20 per cent foreign nationals. Doesn't really produce a type but pupils are articulate, well rounded and very supportive of each other, appearing genuinely to celebrate each other's achievements. 'The finished product is amazing,' according to one mother. 'The boys and girls are charming, personable, not shy or arrogant and have a great sense of fun but are still ambitious'.

The recently formed King's Society, a cultural, social and educational society for parents and friends, now comprises over 300 families. Members organise lectures, music recitals, tours of the cathedral with the dean and social events. Old boys and girls include potter and writer Edmund de Waal, astronaut Michael Foale, Patrick Leigh-Fermor, Christopher Marlowe and William Somerset Maugham, supermodel Jacquetta Wheeler, Olympic silver medallist and world champion rower Frances Houghton and Anthony Worrall-Thompson.

Entrance: At 13+ by common entrance. School's own exam and an interview for those who have not been prepared for CE. Occasionally spaces in year 10. About a third come from Junior King's but they still have to take the same exams as everyone else; rest from a range of Kent and Sussex prep schools and London day schools. Pass mark has recently been raised to 60 per cent but school likes to keep families together and takes an enlightened view if someone is borderline. It is also possible for pupils to take an entrance exam to Junior King's at 11+ which would guarantee entry to the senior school – they would still have to take CE for setting purposes. About 30 join in the sixth form with entrance by competitive exam and interview in Nov before entry with minimum of seven 6s at GCSE – also required of current pupils.

Exit: Those who leave after GCSEs (very few), usually go to local schools or London day schools. Vast majority of sixth formers depart to top universities – 19 to Oxbridge in 2018, with UCL, Exeter, Edinburgh and LSE all popular. Increasing numbers to American universities (two to UCLA and two to NYU in 2018). Languages, sciences and economics/business management most popular degree subjects recently.

Money matters: Up to 20 King's Scholarships and exhibitions as well as music and sports and art scholarships, all with a rigorous selection process and worth up to 10 per cent of fees. Three or four sixth form scholarships awarded for outstanding performance in the sixth form entrance exam. Greater emphasis on bursaries – the King's foundation has been set up to fund both scholarships and bursaries and allocated over £1 million a year. Parents means-tested annually and can receive up to 100 per cent of full boarding fee.

Remarks: Thriving academic school with highly motivated pupils. 'The children never stop – I do not know they fit everything into their day and still have time for a busy social life,' said one parent. Not a heavily religious school but the Benedictine tradition of care for body, mind and spirit is very much in evidence.

Lambrook School

Winkfield Row, Nr Ascot, Berkshire RG42 6LU

Ages 3–13 **Pupils** 549 **Boarders** 10 weekly, 30–40 flexi boarders
C of E

Fees: Day £12,312 – £19,737; Boarding £22,098 – £23,664 pa

01344 882717
www.lambrookschool.co.uk

Headmaster: Since 2010, Jonathan Perry, previously head of Kingsmead School in Hoylake, and before that senior housemaster at Monkton Combe, Bath. Degree in religious studies and history from Gloucestershire; PGCE from Cambridge. With a family made up largely of teachers and clergy (father was a bishop), public service is clearly in the blood.

Personable, chatty and very much a double act with wife Jenny, a gentle and hospitable woman who works one day a week as a clinical pharmacist at a nearby hospital; their own children attended the school and have since progressed to Wellington and Downe House. 'I only got the job because of Jenny,' he jests. 'But a headmaster's wife's husband, he is not,' points out Jenny; indeed, her role is limited to meeting prospective parents with him (most mornings), helping pastorally with the school nurses, overseeing the school's second-hand shop, match teas and liaising with the PTA.

Doesn't do timetabled teaching ('I'd constantly have to find cover'), but does current affairs sessions for older pupils when he can. Says his door is always open, although pupils told us they 'wouldn't dream of going over to that side of the school unless invited'; they did add, however, that he's 'approachable,' 'fun' and 'often out and about' and they are clearly at ease in his company.

Described by parents as 'the perfect fit' and 'always willing to go the extra mile – the type of head who gets into costume on Greek day and who is the first to start clearing up after a social event.' And it is testament to his modesty that it took parents to tell us how he greets them every morning, is present at most matches and, as one put it, 'finds exactly the right school for your child to move on to.' Mixed feelings about his decision to increase pupil numbers, but he promises 'no more.'

A keen sportsman, he enjoys golf, tennis and cricket, 'but more often these days from the sidelines.' Cornwall is where the family go to get away from it all – sea being practically the only thing lacking in Winkfield Row.

Entrance: Mostly at 3, 4 and 7 years. School meets all prospective pre-prep families and there's a formal assessment day for entrance to the prep, up to a year before prospective entry. Assessment criteria include academic ability, wider interests, character and behaviour. With around four to five applications per place in some years and growing waiting lists, parents are advised to clock an interest a good few years in advance.

Increasingly favoured by west London parents (for which school runs three minibuses, but is capping it there); while home counties parents hail from Ascot, Windsor, Eton and Henley, as well as villages right across Berkshire, Buckinghamshire and Surrey.

Exit: All to first choice senior schools including Wellington, Bradfield, Eton, St George's Ascot, Downe House, Harrow, Marlborough, Charterhouse, Radley and Stowe.

L

Remarks: If you're lucky enough to visit this magnificent white Berkshire mansion on a sunny day, it is a glorious site. And if you pick a day to see the school's 52 acres of lush prime estate at their peak of green and pleasantness, expect to see children playing under trees, with the cricket pitch and nine-hole golf course (yes, really) looking like velvet and birdsong coming from every direction.

The front door of the original house leads to a grand hall and staircase, with stylish reception area and headmaster's study; pupils and parents enter through a modern foyer which bridges the old and new builds. The library is gem, with gothic wood panels and shelves, plus comfy seating for children to use anytime (which they do). Double glass doors lead from here into the spacious, conference style Churcher Room, where we saw pupils working away on iPads. The dining room, although large, is homely and unintimidating. Here, as elsewhere, historic photographs of the estate's history and past pupils – teams, plays etc – form part of the fabric rather than a separate archive. Founded in 1860, Lambrook is alma mater of, among others, Lord Alfred Douglas (Oscar Wilde's downfall), Queen Victoria's grandsons Prince Christian Victor and Prince Albert, W C Sellar and R J Yeatman, authors of 1066 and all that. More recent alumni include actor Alex Petyffer and rugby internationals Max and Thom Evans.

The fine chapel with its gleaming brass and polished pews can no longer accommodate everyone, so whole school assemblies and inter-house competitions (singing etc) take place in the performing arts auditorium (a 2013 building that is also home to swish music facilities), while other newer buildings of note include the sports hall and spectacular indoor swimming pool (2015).

The boy:girl ratio here is 60:40, but the feel is thoroughly co-ed. And despite the step up in academic rigour in recent years (including more testing), Lambrook lessons genuinely seem fun, with relaxed but respectful relations between pupils and staff, many of whom live on site. 'I can't think of a single teacher that has been substandard,' one parent told us; and teachers (a good mix of male, female, old and young) praise the CPD they're offered. Many pupils (and some parents) would gladly give their right arm to give up Saturday school (compulsory for years 5 and above), although will have to grin and bear it as head says, 'I'm proudly holding onto it – it's what most will be doing in senior school so it prepares them well.'

Four form entry from year 3, with maximum of 18 to a class. Setting from year 3 in maths and English (five sets); from year 5 in French, Latin and science (four sets). Lots of fluidity, agree all, and there's some informal banding for humanities too. French taught from nursery; Spanish from year 7 (Saturday school); German for scholars; Latin from year 5; Greek for the most able year 7s. Mandarin as extracurricular. Homework on the heavy side – 40 minutes a night from year 3, moving incrementally up to an-hour-and-a-half by year 8, but with compulsory daily prep sessions that finish at 5/5.30pm, pupils don't usually have to take any home – 'such a boon,' said one parent.

Milder cases of SEN well catered for, with support in the classroom where possible. No stigma, with pupils chatting away about their various needs, while parents rave about open minded approach: 'The school is very mindful that dyslexia is not one thing and are happy to try one thing and move onto another if it doesn't work, as well trying out approaches I've read about,' said one.

Music is flourishing; 85 per cent of children learn at least one instrument up to and including grade 8 (420 performing arts lessons each week) and there's a wealth of school bands and ensembles, as well as a full symphony orchestra. We were privy to choir practice in the chapel at lunchtime – a sonic sensation; no wonder they are regularly invited to sing at Eton College and St George's Chapel, Windsor and have also performed at Notre Dame Cathedral. 'It's not just the acting we get involved in, but the backstage tech stuff too,' pupils told us excitedly. Art also flying, with the school currently building a bigger department for art, design and technology.

Grounds and facilities are a sports person's paradise and while it must be tough to do them justice (and, apparently, the match teas), the boys' and girls' teams regularly bring home gold and silverware – school currently county champions at hockey and first 11 football team has been unbeaten for three years straight. Main sports (played four afternoons a week) are football, rugby, hockey, tennis, cricket (boys) and hockey netball, lacrosse, tennis, rounders (girls). 'But we don't just play to win,' say pupils, with A-E teams ensuring everyone gets to represent the school. Don't like sport? 'You still play!' pupils told us, but breadth of activities thankfully mean most are lured by something – trampolining, skiing, basketball, fencing, diving, sailing, polo (well, this is Ascot). Impressive choice of clubs include creative writing, beekeeping, debating, astronomy etc, with school often busy until 8pm. Equally exciting range of expeditions, with highlights including canoeing in Sweden and bi-annual cricket tour to South Africa, all with a strong sense of public service included.

Proactive pastoral care, with form tutors and heads of year meeting with pastoral head every week to identify children in need of support – 'anything from a friendship group regularly falling out to someone whose father has just died.' Matron, counsellor (visits every Thursday) and Mrs Perry also involved. 'It's a busy, pressured environment and we have to back that up with support,' she says, with staff themselves attending mental well-being courses. 'There's no teacher I don't feel I could talk to,' one pupil told us. High expectations (rather than lots of rules) set the tone for the good behaviour and most pupils go through school without a detention. 'There's room to slip up, with most teachers giving multiple warnings before you get a punishment,' one pupil told us. Two temporary exclusions in the last few years. 'Bullying doesn't exist,' pupils told us; head knew better than to make such assertions, 'but we're on the front foot, identifying and keeping a close eye on children with sharper elbows.' No-phone policy.

We visited the nursery, separate from but close to the main school, just before lunch (meals on wheels from main school kitchen). Tinies sitting on the floor were engrossed in a singing session. All downstairs classrooms boast fenced in outdoor areas to encourage freeflow, while outdoor classroom with tepees and a sensory walk is also used regularly. Pre-prep has its own hall, used for before (from 8.15am) and after (until 6pm) school care – a bonus for parents, especially if they have older children at the main school.

Boys' dorms (two to 10 beds per dorm) are located at the top of nursery, all with homely touches and contemporary colours, plus a common room packed with table football and other active indoor games. Girls' dorms (two to eight beds per dorm) are back in the main house, with similar set-up but far more pink and a common room more focused on seating ('We chat and watch telly more,' explained one girl). Boarders' kitchens are large, sunny and refreshingly un-institutional. Boarding (available from year 3 upwards) is either weekly or flexi; the latter is particularly popular at the end of the week – parents certainly appreciate it – with 220 different children having boarded during the last year. 'It's really good fun – you get a great mix of scheduled activities and free time with your friends,' one pupil told us.

Lambrook is a happy, dynamic and unstuffy prep school in an idyllic pastoral setting where children are educated to the best of their potential. Providing a fabulous range of opportunities to broaden horizons and instil new interests, it's best suited to the academically able and (ideally, but not exclusively) sporty boys and girls.

L

Lancing College

Linked with Lancing Prep Hove, Lancing Prep Worthing

Lancing, West Sussex BN15 0RW

Ages 13–18 **Pupils** 591 **Sixth form** 257 **Boarders** 351 full **C of E**

Fees: Day £24,570; Boarding £35,985 pa

01273 452213
www.lancingcollege.co.uk

Head master: Since 2014, Dominic Oliver MPhil (40s). A grammar school boy who read English at Sheffield before spending a decade forging a sterling academic career at Oxford (specialising in Shakespeare). Edited the Longman School Shakespeare edition of Richard III, which garnered very favourable reviews. Eventually, wanting a less narrow life ('the bit that really excited me was teaching students'), took a post at the Royal Grammar School in Worcester. Three years as head of English at Malvern College followed, then a four years as managing head of Bedales School, before he settled into the top job at Lancing. Married to Lydia, a psychoanalyst, with two sons, both of them pupils in the Lancing family of schools.

'Approachable and visible,' was the verdict of parents. Head and school seem to be a particularly good fit; he brings insight and genuine scholarly radiance to the relationship, Lancing provides history and warm-hearted Woodard-style Christian ethics, and both exude silver-haired distinction. A real marriage of true minds.

Academic matters: Lancing is less punishingly selective than (at least one of) its nearby competitors, and this is reflected in its results, which are nonetheless very creditable. In 2018, 53 per cent 9-7 grades at GCSE; 55 per cent A*/A, 76 per cent A*-B at A level.

Make no mistake, however, there is some real scholarship going on here. In 2017 the school set up The Heresy Project to celebrate the anniversary of Martin Luther nailing his articles to Wittenberg church door and to encourage Lancing lower sixth formers to challenge orthodoxy. They did, and we thought the resulting essays were impressive examples of coherent and independent thinking. How does the school achieve this in its students? According to the deputy head academic, by placing a high value on intellectual joy and curiosity. Year 9 students, for instance, come off timetable for a week each year to write a dissertation on something that interests them; half a term prior to this is spent learning how to amass and assess information. The head himself teaches the skills of parliamentary debating and integrating quotation into argument. Lucky students, we thought, who seemed to take all this for granted, praising the lessons simply as 'really enjoyable'. The classes (average size 18, smaller in the sixth form) we saw were teacher-led and traditional, but friendly and relaxed with good student input. 'Exceptional and dedicated teachers' according to one parent.

Languages offered include French, Spanish, German and Mandarin. One parent lamented that compulsory Latin had been phased out for the year 9s. Excellent science facilities, although the physics class we saw were gleefully piling outdoors to launch water rockets. Learning everywhere is purposeful, calm and undertaken with satisfaction. Superb library is open seven days a week – strict silence rules, but there is also a seminar room for collaborative work and plenty of computer workstations.

Two full-time and one part-time SEN teachers support the small number of students with mild dyslexia, dyspraxia, slow processing, etc. 'The school was able to accommodate my son's additional needs beautifully, enabling him to shine in the areas he loved, and he is now at a top university,' wrote a grateful parent. International students must already have excellent English and are screened for this on application, but once here, they receive regular EAL support.

Games, options, the arts: One of the best programmes of extracurricular activities we've come across anywhere with facilities and staffing to match. The one-word question 'Sports?' to a group of students received an universal exhalation of satisfaction. 'What's great about Lancing sport is that it really is for everyone, and you can find your level.'..'The range of sports here is just ridiculous!'. Main ones are football, hockey, netball, tennis (on both hard and grass courts) and cricket. One student we spoke to relished his place in the 6th football team, playing twice a week for enjoyment; his friend in the 1st team practised four times a week and received regular professional coaching. Even this unathletic reviewer thought the football pitches were amazing – 'As school pitches go, this has to be one of the best in the country'. Cricket is also strong – Mason Sidney Crane was an OL. Excellent swimming pool, used by locals as well as school community. Endless list of more niche sports includes sailing, squash, basketball, riding (brand new equestrian centre), Eton fives, golf, fencing, badminton, water polo and aerobics. CCF also popular, we witnessed a boy being awarded an enormous trophy for success in target rifle shooting.

Lancing's farm provides a refreshing alternative for those who want to get their fresh air and exercise off the sports field. Run by the estates manager with two part-timers and an abundance of student help, there are lots of ways to get involved. Would-be vets learn to give injections to animals, and anyone who wants to gets to bottle-feed the lambs – or even to get up in the night to help deliver them.

Music here is 'unrivalled' and we thought that outside of a specialist music school, you'd be hard-pressed to do better. Wealth of opportunities includes orchestras, choirs, a cappella club, Big Band, rock music workshops, conducting classes, improvisation workshops, composition lessons and a full programme of chamber music coaching. Between 30 and 40 concerts each year ensure that everyone gets plenty of chances to perform. Instrumental lessons offered on practically anything, 'including Chinese flute'. Masterclasses and professional recitals are common, as are visits to concerts and opera. The chapel is home to no fewer than three organs, and the chapel choir and choral scholars sing evensong at major cathedrals across the country.

Drama is popular and well-resourced – 'outstanding,' wrote one parent – with around 10 events a year including productions. There's even an open air theatre, opened by Agatha Christie in 1960, where the Founder's Day play is performed every summer term. Dance is also offered – ballet, contemporary, street jazz. Art is very big here, and we thought the work on display was superb. 'The art department is wonderful and full of happy, enthusiastic teachers,' wrote a parent. Now offers photography GCSE as well as Pre-U. Busy calendar of community service includes DofE and the outreach programme for sixth formers. Lots of school trips – recent destinations have included Malawi, Germany and Iceland. 'It's been brilliant,' said an upper sixth former; 'I've got involved in so many different things and I've loved them all!'

Boarding: Some 60 per cent of the students board and boarding is very much the school's ethos. Seven of the nine houses are for boarders: four for boys and three for girls, reflecting the slightly boy-heavy intake (which school is working to address); new co-ed day house. Full, weekly and flexi options and free boarding for day pupils if an activity goes on past 9pm. Of the day pupils, half stay over regularly and it's not uncommon for there to be 280 pupils in school over a weekend.

All houses are for the full age range of students from years 9 to 13. No separate sixth form accommodation, but they have their own corridor and common room and the students said they preferred the resulting age diversity. On entry, pupils generally share in pairs, threes or fours, but two to a room is standard in year 10 and single rooms by year 11. The rooms we saw were spacious and neat, although the lad who declared that 'coming down here is a breath of fresh air' might well have been referring to the wintry interior temperatures. All houses have a matron and, say students, 'they're all welcoming!' 'Our second mum!' Some 70 per cent of teachers live on site and involve themselves in the school, meaning that there are lots of activities and socialising in the beautifully furnished and well-equipped communal areas – 'There is SO MUCH to do!' was a comment echoed by many.

Everyone we spoke to agreed that boarding, even if it was part-time, enabled them to get the most out of being here. 'You're more involved,' 'It's easier to work.' As the head put it, 'For me, it's the logical extension of educating the whole person. Who wouldn't want to live here? I wake up every morning and feel that. And that's the experience of the vast majority of people at Lancing.'

Background and atmosphere: Traces its origins back to 1848, but on the present site since 1857. There can scarcely be a lovelier school approach anywhere. Emerging from woodland, the road opens out onto the astonishing prospect of the school chapel: 90 feet of soaring Victorian gothic in Sussex sandstone, crowning the rolling grassland that slopes gently down towards the coast. Nathaniel Woodard, the founder, built some cracking schools, but knew he was on to something special with Lancing chapel, insisting that it was built to its full height at one end first, so that if he died before completion the proportions couldn't be cut down to save money. So from the outset, perhaps, the Lancing principle was to put beauty before profit, and it doesn't seem fanciful to say that the benign effects of this are perceptible throughout the school.

Consider the light and airy art department (with sea view), bursting with imaginative work, the wonderfully high-ceilinged library or the working farm with its programme dedicated to the reintroduction of the grey partridge. Lancing impresses as a place where creative thinking is encouraged – or rather, where creativity grows and thrives by itself, because the soil in which it's planted is so good. 'Lancing allows for the eccentric,' as one pupil put it. 'It's about giving them the time to stand and stare,' affirmed the deputy head. 'Relaxed, friendly, a happy school,' said a parent, more prosaically.

Lancing welcomes those of all faiths and of none, but Christian values underpin the school and are made flesh by the chapel. Long, thin, vaulted – and chilly – it's the only space large enough to house the whole school community. Everyone has to attend college eucharist on Wednesday morning, as well as on one or two Sundays each term, but the approach is inclusive. All the students we spoke to loved it and insisted it was part of what made their time at Lancing unique. 'The chapel remains to our whole family as a very special and emotional place,' wrote a mother.

'It's an honour to be at a school this pretty,' and 'I've loved the look of Lancing since I was little,' were comments echoed everywhere. But this is also a busy, bustling community that buzzes with purpose and activity, and perhaps the real beauty of the place lies in the equilibrium and sense of sanity that the school manages to achieve. 'The school is really excellent at putting eggs in different baskets,' thought a younger pupil. 'The first time I came here I knew this was the school for me – it was the balance,' said another. 'It's such a family feel,' said our tour guide, as we passed a tabby cat washing itself contentedly outside the piggeries.

Pastoral care, well-being and discipline: Housemasters and mistresses are the first point of call for parents. 'I cannot praise my son's housemaster enough for the support he offers to both the young men under his care and their parents!' wrote one mother, and all the parents we contacted concurred. 'Housemistress is extremely kind with a lovely family'; 'Always approachable'.

Long-established peer support scheme is also highly valued, with over 50 students applying each year for the 18 or so places. Those selected spend over 16 hours being trained by the school counsellor in skills such as listening, confidentiality and dealing with homesickness. No restrictions on phoning home, we were relieved to hear.

Surprisingly, a couple of parents whose opinion of the school was very positive nonetheless murmured that they weren't entirely satisfied with how the school had dealt with issues around bullying: 'We've found that the school policy on this doesn't match up with our children's experiences'. The pupils we spoke to, however, insisted that bullying was rare and that instances were dealt with swiftly. Certainly behaviour around school appeared excellent and parents report that the discipline is 'firm but fair'. The attractive dark blue uniform is smartly worn and gives way in the sixth form to equally smart business attire.

Catering has changed recently and there is now much praise for the food, served up in a magnificent dining hall reminiscent of an Oxford college. 'Healthier,' 'Nicer,' 'Plenty to eat,' say students. We ourselves were served a delicious lunch so can only agree.

School operates a six-day week with Saturdays being given over to a mixture of lessons and extracurricular activities. Day pupils have to be in school by 8.15am and must stay until 6pm so it's not the place for those with a busy life outside school. A few complaints persist from parents of day pupils that they're not always kept fully in the loop regarding events and fixtures. Inevitable, perhaps, in a school as energetic and bustling as this where the mindset is primarily boarding.

Pupils and parents: Accepting of difference and encouraging of resourcefulness, the school suits all sorts but is very much for those who like to keep busy. Around 25 per cent of boarders from overseas. Parents are hard-working, professional, aspirational, successful. Bus service covers a wide area and there's a shuttle between Lancing College and the preps. New London bus serves those needing to get back from the capital on a Sunday evening. Alumni include Evelyn Waugh, Sir David Hare, Peter Pears, Tim Rice, Christopher Hampton, Jan Morris, Tom Sharpe, Jamie Theakston and Sir Roy Calne, pioneer of liver transplantation.

Entrance: Selective. At 13+, about 100 places on offer, with around 20 to 25 per cent of these usually going to pupils from the school's own preps at Hove and Worthing. A few places also available at 14+. At 16+ an additional 40 or so places. School looks for 'academic crunching power', but also for a wide-ranging and diverse school community – 'a willingness to give, and a wish to participate in a broader kind of life.'

Exit: Small number (some 10 per cent) leaves after GCSEs, but school insists it doesn't cull. 'We have an academic bar, but it's administered humanely. If you take someone at 13, you have a duty to look after them.' At 18, mostly to Russell Group universities; London universities, Newcastle, Cardiff, Bath, Leeds and Nottingham currently popular, with others off to the US and France; three medics in 2018. Art, design and architecture are all popular choices – a love of beauty, perhaps, being a happy side effect of living on this ravishing campus.

Money matters: Scholarships available in all the usual fields – sports, drama music, academic, all-rounder – plus, more unusually, an organ scholarship for Y12s and the Peter Robinson Cricketing award, which in 2017 was won for the first time by a girl. 'Owzat'!

Scholarships are worth between five and 10 per cent of the fees, and students who achieve one can then apply to the bursary fund for further assistance. Commendably, school is currently fundraising to create 25 'Foundationer' places by 2022, enabling students from poorer backgrounds to access full-fees assistance. 'It's important that we have a mix of students, not just the very wealthy, and it's making everybody here think about what education is for.'

Remarks: A truly beautiful school where the upward spaces encourage students to reach for the skies whilst keeping their feet on the ground. As one parent put it, 'Lancing is wonderful, and has given my children such a positive start to their lives.'

Lancing Prep Hove

Linked with Lancing College, Lancing Prep Worthing

The Droveway, Hove, East Sussex BN3 6LU

Ages 3–13 Pupils 245 C of E

Fees: £9,060 – £15,975 pa

01273 503452
www.lancingcollege.co.uk

Head Mistress: Since 2016, Kirsty Keep BEd. Educated at Bournemouth School for Girls and Homerton College, Cambridge where she gained her BEd. She started her career teaching English at Edge Grove and was promoted to senior mistress with a remit to integrate the newly arrived girls into what had been a boys' school. She then spent 11 years as head of the lower school at Downsend Prep in Surrey before moving to Lancing Prep at Hove. She and her husband Ed grew up together in Bournemouth and both taught at Downsend; he now teaches maths here and they have a daughter in the pre-prep, so a real family affair.

She is the first female head in the history of the school, and says she has the best of both worlds as she has the autonomy to run her own school but with the support of the wider Lancing family. 'Kirsty took on a good school and is improving it – it feels like a school in the ascendant,' said a parent. She has embarked on a major refurbishment programme but the aims and ethos of the school remain the same. 'Family values are at the heart of everything we do and all are nurtured through their childhood so they are ready for the adolescent years. We want every child to find something at which they excel.' All are encouraged to be brave and independent and to focus on being the four Rs – Resourceful, Resilient, Reflective and Relating – and are rewarded for demonstrating these qualities.

She describes the school as free thinking and free flowing and has a genuine open door policy, so parents and children can walk in for a chat without an appointment. 'You can talk to her mother to mother and she is always happy to have a chat and a bit of a laugh.' 'She always makes time and is never in a rush,' and 'does her homework before a meeting and has the data to hand.' She teaches critical thinking to years 3, 5 and 7 and one of her great pleasures is listening to the Archers on the way home from work – 'It is the secret to finding a balance in life,' she says. When she is not working, she loves skiing, reading, swimming and the theatre.

Entrance: Non-selective on academic grounds but it is sometimes suggested a child might look elsewhere if it is thought they would not thrive. All have a taster day and for those not joining in nursery or reception, the school asks for a reference from the child's previous school. The main entry points are nursery, reception and year 7 (often from state primary schools) but can join at any time, even mid-year, if there is a space.

Exit: Over 75 per cent of year 8s to Lancing College (often with awards) but only after discussion with parents – entry via 11+ testing followed by CE at 13+ mainly for setting purposes. The others to a variety of schools, the most popular two being Hurstpierpoint and Bede's. A small number leave at 11+.

Remarks: A modern, forward looking school with a delightful old fashioned feel where children can grow up slowly. Formerly known as Mowden, the school was founded in 1896 for boys only at Mowden Hall, Essex by the Snell family who ran it for three generations until 2002. It moved to Hove in 1901 and to its current purpose built site in 1913. The pre-prep opened in 1997 and the last boarders left in 1999. On the retirement of the Snells in 2002 it was bought by Lancing College, became Lancing College Prep and started taking girls. The school is aiming for a ratio of 60:40 and although some years are still a bit boy heavy, it no longer feels like a boys' school with girls but a proper co-ed school. It became Lancing Prep Hove when the college bought what is now Lancing Prep Worthing. Major recent refurbishments included a large multi-purpose hall which doubles up as a dining room and assembly, performance and sports hall, and the ultra-modern Snell library – all plate glass and blue furniture.

The school is set in seven acres of grounds in a prosperous area of Hove, eight miles from Lancing College. It is part of the Woodard group of schools with strong Christian roots and welcomes all faiths, and none, and aims to instil in children the importance of contributing to the community inside and outside the school.

Several of the classrooms are in cosy pre-fab buildings outside the main house and much outdoor learning takes place in the grounds. Classes average of 14, and are mixed ability until year 7 when a class is created for potential scholars. 'I get so much more attention than at my last school', said a newly arrived boy. French taught from year 1 with Spanish and Mandarin offered as clubs. Latin added in year 6, German and Spanish in year 7, alongside optional Mandarin.

One full time SENCo and an assistant – children either taken out of lessons or given in class support, whichever works best. Can accommodate mild learning difficulties – mainly dyspraxia and dyslexia; no blanket testing for dyslexia but the small class sizes mean everyone can be closely monitored. Not an ideal building for wheelchair users 'but would always work with prospective parents of a disabled child to explore how we could meet their needs'.

The school is not an exam factory and wants children to be creative, curious and independent, to enjoy learning for its own sake and not be funnelled through the syllabus. 'It is a kind, gentle school, which has a certain magic that raises the children's game and gives them the confidence to aim high,' said a parent. 'Male teachers can be difficult to recruit,' says the headmistress, but the deputy head and several teachers and games coaches are men, so there is a significant male presence to provide role models.

Offers all the usual sports and the school fields enough teams for everyone who wants to play in a match. Girls' cricket recently introduced and increasingly popular. Also offers tennis, basketball and athletics; swimming lessons for everyone at Lancing College, with golf and squash available there too.

Music taught from nursery upwards and is 'huge', said our guide, and about 75 per cent learn at least one instrument. The music department is housed in a warren of rooms on the top floor. Most start with the piano or guitar and every child is offered the chance to play the violin or cello in year 3. Children can take part in a variety of ensembles and play in school concerts and in the local community. The choir sings regularly in the local church and the parent-teacher choir takes part in school events.

Residential trips from year 5: year 7 to France, year 6 to PGL and year 5 to the New Forest, plus a year 7 geography trip to Dorset and year 8 outdoor adventure trip to Wales after CE. Most children have the chance to be in a play or musical every year as well as take part in poetry readings and drama awards, and the weekly drama club is open to all.

Dance popular with both boys and girls with three dance clubs a week which include contemporary, tap, ballet and street. An annual highlight is the Strictly Dancing at Lancing competition and children also take part in an annual dance show at the college.

Busy art and DT department housed in the old squash courts – 'there is lots of freedom to do your own thing and add your own touch,' said a pupil. The school takes part in the annual children's parade in Brighton and a huge spider was being made for this when we visited. Year 7s make and race rocket cars and can sometimes use the DT rooms at Lancing College.

'They offer loads of activities and there is something for everyone,' said a parent, including ninjutsu, climbing and even a Lego STEM after-school club. Debating and chess are popular and debaters visit the House of Commons to see how it is done for real.

Each child has a cultural passport with a list of goals to tick off. It might be baking a cake or recommending a book to a friend, taking up a hobby or making a difference to someone less advantaged. Older children get involved in the Christmas shoebox collection for the local homeless in Brighton and Hove – pupils learn to appreciate and not to take for granted how fortunate they are by talking to homeless young people only a few years older than themselves.

'The school nurtures every child but does not wrap them in cotton wool', says the head mistress and there is a strong system of pastoral support. The form teacher is the first point of contact and the matron is ELSA (Emotional Literacy Support Assistant) trained and looks after the physical and emotional health of the children. 'She is easy to talk to and there are lots of people to make sure you are ok,' said a pupil. A school counsellor from Lancing College comes over as needed and can offer counselling to year 6 and above on referral. PSHE is incorporated into the academic curriculum and children are taught how to stay safe and behave appropriately online and how to spot fake news. The school works closely with parents on e-safety and offers parents PSHE so they can help their children with issues such as study skills, self-harm and relationship problems.

Buddy system for all new children and 'you often forget someone is new after a couple of weeks,' said a pupil. Lunch is served in the new multi-purpose hall – the menu has been overhauled and children are encouraged to try new things. Teachers eat with the children to keep an eye on table manners and add to the family atmosphere. There is a whole prep school assembly four mornings a week.

The pre-prep is very much part of the school with classrooms in the main house. Lots of outdoor learning for the younger children such as drawing on the garden paths and outdoor phonics lessons. The nursery is housed in a bungalow next door, bought in 2013 and entered through a gate made of giant coloured pencils. The emphasis is on fun and story-telling and they have a mud kitchen. They go for nature walks and visit the Lancing College farm. PE and music from nursery upwards. 'It is like a home from home,' said a mother, 'my daughter cried when she was ill and couldn't go to school.'

Most families live in the Brighton and Hove area and many walk to school, but there is a school minibus, which also calls at Lancing College, and a subsidised taxi service for those who live further afield. It is an arty, creative area and not many parents go to work in a suit. Some children are bi- or even trilingual but none need extra help with English. Wraparound care from 8am-5.30pm and children can do supervised prep at school – useful for working parents.

Parents regularly updated with photos and emails of what their children are up to. Active PTA runs events including a quiz night and comedy night, and helps with the fête and the shoebox appeal, and the dads have a golf group known as the lapdogs – history doesn't relate how they got this name. The school's best known old boy is England cricketer Mason Crane.

Lancing Prep Worthing

Linked with Lancing College, Lancing Prep Hove

Broadwater Road, Worthing, West Sussex BN14 8HU

Ages 2–13 **Pupils** 176

01903 201123

Head: Since 2014, Heather Beeby MA PGCE. She was educated in the state system and did her PGCE at Roehampton and her masters at the Institute of Education (science education). She started her career with ILEA (the then Innter London Education Authority) and then spent nine years at Thomas's in Battersea, finishing as senior mistress. This was followed by four and a half years as deputy head of Brighton College Prep and then head of St Christopher's Hove, another Brighton College school, and seven years as head of Hurstpierpoint Prep. After a stint as director of communications at Hurst she joined the prep at Worthing soon after Lancing College took it over (it was previously called Broadwater Manor School).

She loves the humanity and integrity of the Lancing family of schools. It is not an exam factory and although the school has grown by 50 per cent since she took over, it is still small enough for her to get to know all the children and their families, 'and even the names of their dogs.' She loves a new challenge and says that as the children are expected to learn new things, so should the staff. She has recently taken up playing the trumpet and plays in the school band, and her handmade pheasants won the staff art competition. She also teaches some French and directs the annual musical.

She says she always acts with the ethos of the college in mind but has the freedom to make her own mark on the school and has the mutual support of Kirsty Keep, the headmistress of Lancing Prep at Hove. She says she is in a position to make an impact on the children and their lives – teaching them to love learning and to be kind, and helping them to believe that they can make a difference by encouraging them to go out into the world and do good.

She is always looking at ways to bring about positive change; she wants the children to be excited about coming to school and looks for innovative teachers with interesting ideas. 'The school came alive when she joined,' said a parent, 'and the staff have been given a shot of energy and enthusiasm.'

On the rare occasions when she is not working she loves to walk on the South Downs and to spend time at the family house in France. Married to Nick, who is director of drama and dance at Lancing College; they have two adult daughters.

Entrance: Non-selective as long as the school can cope with a child's needs. Cognitive ability tests (CAT) for entry into year 7 used to indicate the progression required for a pupil to join Lancing College in year 9. The main entry points are nursery, reception, year 3 and year 7, but will take children into any year where there are spaces.

Exit: Some 75 per cent to Lancing College and the rest to local independent schools such as Christ's Hospital and Brighton College, and local state schools including Steyning Grammar, at 13+. Very few leave at 11+. Many get scholarships to the college and there's one recent all-rounder scholarship to Brighton College.

Remarks: Formerly known as Broadwater Manor, the school was founded in 1930 with five boys. It grew steadily and in 1968 opened the pre-prep and started admitting girls. The nursery was opened in 1981. It joined the Lancing family of schools in 2014 and became known as Lancing College Prep at Worthing, and is now very much a first choice school for parents.

It is set in a wisteria-clad Georgian manor house in two acres of grounds in the Broadwater area of Worthing. The school has managed to cram a lot into a small space and it has its own sports field, cricket nets and recently resurfaced netball courts, as well as a small sports hall. 'Lancing College has spent a fortune since they bought the school – it has been rewired and generally spruced up,' said a parent.

The multi-purpose hall is used for assemblies, concerts and art exhibitions and doubles up as the dining room. The Foundation Library opened in 2017 is a bright, welcoming space with green furniture, beanbags and masses of books. All children encouraged to read through the Drop Everything and Read scheme (DEAR).

The pre-prep is very much part of the school with bright airy classrooms. The nursery is more self-contained and most but not all the children move on to the pre-prep. They have their own nursery garden fenced with giant pencils but have lunch in the main hall.

The head describes the school as a 'happy thriving community of learning – an academic school where children want to do well.' 'Teachers really care and go the extra mile,' said a parent. Average class size is 14 and while not quite there yet, the school is aiming for two classes of 16 per year – big enough to challenge in class but small enough to give everyone enough time. Foreign languages a particular strength and reception and year 1 offered tasters in French, Spanish and German; they start French in year 2. Latin from year 4 and in year 7 children can choose to study either French, German or Spanish. Older children now take part in the modern foreign language programme at Lancing College reintroducing Spanish and German alongside French. Science is taught in old-fashioned labs in the former cricket pavilion – soon due for refurbishment. All are set in core subjects from year 6 and in all subjects in years 7 and 8. Potential scholars taught separately in year 8. 'The school is brilliant at bringing out hidden talents and will stretch or support as necessary', said a parent.

Everyone screened for dyslexia and bright dyslexics do well here but must have the desire to achieve, says the head. One full-time SENCo and a teaching assistant who helps with in class support. About 10 children have one-to-one help in a range of subjects. 'Any learning difficulties are picked up quickly and dealt with,' said a parent. Not much call for EAL help but school can provide it if required.

'The school punches above its weight in sport,' says the head. Senior children play most of their games and matches at the college. Boys play football, hockey and cricket but not contact rugby. The girls play hockey, netball and rounders and sometimes mixed football and hockey. Swimming from nursery upwards at the college and tennis played at a local club. Inclusive approach to matches and everyone has the chance to play in a team if they want. Football particularly strong and players have been signed for Brighton and Portsmouth.

Music is important to the head and 'the school buzzes with music and children are excited by the opportunities.' Music taught from nursery upwards and the new director of music is a classical clarinettist who makes music fun; she has increased the range of lessons in woodwind, brass and guitar and has introduced voice and percussion. There are many musical opportunities including junior and senior choir, and most children have the opportunity to perform either in the annual musical, in termly soirées or in the pre-prep summer concert.

A new and shiny drama studio in the grounds was given to the school by a generous benefactor. The annual musical is open to all abilities and is a great confidence builder – 'my son was too scared to say a word in public and now has a major speaking part in the school play,' said a mother. Masterclasses are held at the college and a visiting drama teacher prepares children for LAMDA exams, and almost all get distinctions. Numerous opportunities to stand up in public: children can read at the big services at the college and at the weekly eucharist service, they can lead assemblies and can take part in poetry reading competitions and in the Worthing Festival as well as the Strictly Come Historical Dancing competition.

Vibrant art department – children were making shoes out of clay when we visited and many get art scholarships to the senior school.

Pastoral care has always been strong. 'An ethos of kindness pervades the school,' said a mother. There is a palpable family feel, staff know the children well and any problems are sorted out quickly. There is also a sense of fun: 'we laugh a lot here and children and staff laugh together,' says the head. There is always someone to talk to – the first port of call is the form tutor and the senior master has overall responsibility for pastoral care. Good manners are important; children stand up when an adult comes into the room and staff and pupils eat together at lunchtime. Lancing is part of the Woodard Foundation which educates children in a broadly Christian community with a strong moral framework and a sense of service to others. Each house comes up with innovative ways of raising money for their chosen charity which include Open Arms, Malawi, The British Red Cross, The Snowdrop Trust and Great Ormond Street Hospital.

Children are taught about food and nutrition in PSHE and can learn to cook as part of culinary activities. Popular food and nutrition activity for year 8s culminates in a formal dinner for parents cooked by their children.

All children have a cultural passport where they set out their goals and ambitions – maybe speaking in assembly, reading a particular book or helping someone less fortunate than themselves.

Supportive group of parents – mostly hard working professionals who want to be part of their children's lives. They have chosen the school for its small size where their children can be happy as well as academically challenged. 'It is a major part of our lives and home and school have morphed into one', said a parent. Active parents' group the LPW Association runs the Christmas and summer fairs and raises money for extras like the third generation day – an annual event designed to give the children such happy memories that they will pass them on to their grandchildren; recent third generation days include an outing to Kidzania in London, a code-breaking day designed to rescue the bursar who had been 'kidnapped' and a Harry Potter day when the college allowed owls in the dining room and Quidditch in the lower quad.

Very supportive of working parents with wraparound care from 8am to 6pm and holiday clubs and a minibus service which also stops at Lancing College.

Lanesborough School

Linked with Royal Grammar School (Guildford)

Maori Road, Guildford, Surrey GU1 2EL

Ages 3–13 (3–11 from 2019) **Pupils** 359 **C of E**

Fees: £10,890 – £15,270 pa

01483 880650
www.lanesborough.surrey.sch.uk

L

Head: Since 2007, Clare Turnbull, previously deputy head for three years, but after a decade here she has no itchy feet, she assures us. 'I have no desire to move on to another headship. Here I can still teach, and that matters, and every year I have done new things,' she says. It was always her ambition to work in a cathedral choir school, following a childhood in which she was immersed in Canterbury Cathedral, where her father is a retired honorary canon. Mrs Turnbull is herself a lay canon at Guildford Cathedral. Previous posts include director of studies and head of French at Maidwell Hall School in Northamptonshire.

Outside the school gates most evenings, having informal chats with parents and boys, we're told. Plain speaking, and wants to know about it if parents have an issue. 'If they've got an anxiety, let's talk it through, or it will bubble through to the boy,' she says. Not that an issue is likely to pass her by, according to parents. 'We find it incredible that she knows in such depth what our sons are doing well at or are struggling with – her attention to detail is astonishing,' said one.

'Very enthusiastic and clearly born to teach. She communicates well, is highly visible around the school, and accessible,' is another parent's verdict.

Entrance: Focus on the key entry points (nursery, reception and year 3) to give yourself the best chance of a place. The school is currently full with a waiting list, so otherwise you are relying on someone leaving. However, increasing from three to four forms in year 3 from 2019 alongside becoming a 3-11 school.

Mrs Turnbull describes the school as 'unashamedly selective' – and more than half of the boys each year go on to the Royal Grammar School (RGS) Guildford, which is one of the top performing boys' schools in the country. So you'll want to be sure your boy can keep up. 'Is your boy going to love it academically, and thrive?' Mrs Turnbull asks.

For nursery and Shell (the school's name for reception), selection involves a boy coming in for an hour as part of a little group. The school will look at how he responds to a set of tasks, and his social skills. For entry into year 3 boys will first come for a familiarisation afternoon of sport, music, team building and social activities. Academic tests will follow. 'We are looking for a boy who loves learning, who asks questions: why, how is that happening?' says Mrs Turnbull. 'It's not necessarily about levels. You might get a wonderfully quirky boy who may not get level 4 writing but will get level 6 maths, but one would think carefully, are his issues in English going to stop him loving the whole curriculum?'

Exit: Strap in for the long haul financially. It's rare for a boy to go on to a state school (one every few years). Around 55 per cent go on to the RGS, where they form up to one fifth of the pupil cohort. Recently, others to St John's Leatherhead, City of London Freemen's, Reigate Grammar and Reed's. Of those going on to RGS, typically about one-third went at 11, the rest at 13, but that will change when years 7 and 8 close in 2019.

Remarks: A common thread in parents' comments is that the school really 'gets' boys, and structures its approach accordingly, in aspects such as boredom thresholds and length of breaks.

Parents say it's first and foremost an academic school, and one best suited to boys who are willing to knuckle down. 'There is fierce competition among able students,' one parent told us. 'Boys are definitely stretched academically, and I am pleased that there is often extension work particularly in maths and English,' said another.

Nevertheless, parents say it is a nurturing environment. 'It is competitive, and the work load is pretty high, but allowance and time is made for those who find it more of a challenge; they will be split into a smaller group and helped,' one told us. Another insider said: 'I know several parents of boys who are not academic and who would still be very positive about the academic training that the school has provided, so I think it is fair to say that it caters for boys of all abilities.'

There is setting for maths from year 4, and other subjects in years 7 and 8, but there is no scholarship stream bagging every place in the top set, allowing boys to be placed according to strengths in individual subjects.

The style is fairly traditional – most of the classrooms are organised with desks in rows, although the atmosphere is lively within. We saw year 8s enjoying a debate on whether RE should be taught in schools; the fact that the 'yes' camp won may be testament to the school's RE teaching. Science teacher sometimes brings in her snake and duck, the latter waddling happily around the lab. Boys are taught from the age of 8 in a proper science lab. 'The boys often come home full of chatter about a lesson or activity during their day,' a parent said.

Children study three languages from year 5 – French, Spanish and Latin – although occasionally boys with dyslexia, or who are struggling, drop Latin. Pupils with dyslexia or other difficulties can have one lesson per week with a specialist at no extra charge.

From year 5 all teaching is by subject specialists, and exams are introduced. 'We spend a lot of time teaching them how to learn, and getting them ready for the mental and emotional side of life and exams,' Mrs Turnbull says. Parents praise the preparation for senior school entrance exams.

The school is easily accessed from the A3 with no winding country lanes to negotiate – the corollary to this is that it doesn't have the easy parking and rolling fields of the preps deeper in the country. Hence the two parent gripes (pretty much the only ones we heard) are over the lack of sports facilities and the nightmare parking. With two other independent schools in close proximity it's havoc at drop off and pick up times. The school does its best to ease this with a one hour window for morning drop off between 7.30 and 8.30am, a breakfast club for early arrivals, and children of all ages able to stay until 6.30pm.

The pre-prep department is based in another Edwardian house in a parallel road. It has attractive play areas, including an outdoor classroom called Boyzone. This has its own bird hide, wooden staged seating for drama, and playground toys. The main playground has wooden trains and boats to play in, a covered cave area, and a planting area for the popular gardening club. The pre-prep has its own dining room, and everyone from reception up is expected to scrape their own plates.

Lessons showed high levels of engagement on our visit. In a year 1 maths class a boy told us solemnly, 'We are learning to use a ruler, follow instructions, and make predictions'. Another group was studying Scott of the Antarctic. 'Conditions were very bad, and they ran out of food,' one boy told us.

The pre-prep curriculum includes French from reception, and swimming from year 1. The school provides the choristers for Guildford Cathedral (boys are invited to join at age 7 in year 3, and receive a bursary which reduces their fees). Hence the sub-organist from the cathedral works with and talent spots from the year 2 chamber choir. The 18 choristers aside, it's a musical school. There are 100 boys in the school choir, 60 in the chamber choir, and more than 70 per cent learn an instrument. All boys in year 4 play a violin or cello provided by the school.

Bursaries are available up to 100 per cent from 7+. The head is assiduous about keeping these confidential. Nobody besides herself and the financial director know who is on a bursary. And she is acutely aware that some parents will be stretching themselves to pay the fees, so she gives you the reassurance that there will be no slips in the book bag asking you for more money. 'We promise there will be nothing over the compulsory extras; everything is very transparent,' she says. Costs for summer term residentials and extras are split across the year to help parents budget.

In sports 'we win more than we lose,' says Mrs Turnbull, but it's not elitist: 'Having a go is avidly encouraged, and B/C/D teams get plenty of matches,' parents told us. There is some feeling that sports staff are overstretched as a result of this and the amount of options on offer.

There are around 50 extracurricular clubs. Favourites among the big boys include an astronomy club, which even enables them to take a GCSE in the subject after one year; baseball club; and senior classics, based around a computer programme designed by a member of staff, in which they take control of a Roman state and lead armies. Airfix club is a top pick among younger boys.

There is lots of promotion of responsibility. Year 2 boys each have a buddy in Shell, and they take them out at playtime and keep an eye on them, and read to them. Year 8 boys are assigned a younger form, and they take morning registration once a week, and help with that form. There's lots of interaction between different ages in the school – we saw year 5s working on their own version of an Aesop fable which they were later going to read to the year 1 and 2 children. 'What I particularly like is that the senior boys go into pre-prep and read to the younger ones, making a great connection between the two ends of the school,' said one mother. This rids any sense of scary big boys – as we toured the school the younger boys called out delightedly to our year 8 guides.

And the parent body is friendly too, we're told. There's a good number who have moved out from London, and one parent told us: 'Having arrived in Guildford knowing no one, we found the parents very friendly and welcoming, helping us all to settle in to our new town.'

Langley Grammar School

Reddington Drive, Langley, Slough, Berkshire SL3 7QS

Ages 11–18 **Pupils** 1,141 **Sixth form** 320

01753 598300
www.lgs.slough.sch.uk

Head: Since 2010, John Constable BSc (50s), an affable man who has lived and breathed the grammar school system for most of his life. Having attended one himself as a boy in Suffolk, he then had physics teaching posts at Aylesbury, Watford and Sir William Borlase (Marlow), before becoming deputy head of Wycombe High School. This wasn't Plan A, he admits, which was to work as an engineer for a decade after graduating from his degree in engineering science and management in Durham. 'But I didn't enjoy it and probably wasn't very good at it, so I moved the teaching plan forward and did my PGCE after two years,' he says. Was told that choosing the grammar system would mean he 'wouldn't get very far', but he happily proved them wrong.

Not the kind of man to beat around the bush, he says it how it is, but does so with both warmth and charm. Known for being a consultative leader, although directive when required, with the main changes under his reign including a greater focus on the well-being and mental health of pupils; more systematic monitoring and tracking of students' individual progress; and ensuring students are better supported to achieve the grades they are capable of ('before, they were rather left to get on with it in many subject areas,' he says). Pupils say he's 'often seen in corridors' and is 'very approachable'. 'Children respect him, but are not intimidated by him,' said one parent. Seen as a perfectionist who strives for the best in everything, pupils overwhelmingly agree that the ethos of the school comes directly from him.

Lives in nearby Herts, with his wife and their teenage son and daughter. Sails, and is a qualified dinghy instructor, as well as enjoying hill walking and photography.

Academic matters: Among the top state grammars in the country and a beacon of pride locally, this is a school where expectations are high and students are serious about their studies (we saw heads down or hands up in every classroom we visited, bar none). Sixty-eight per cent A*-A/9-7 grades at GCSE in 2018 and 37 per cent A*/A at A level.

A former specialist maths and computing school, there remains an emphasis in the curriculum on acceleration in ICT/computing and enrichment with additional year 11 qualifications in maths. Science also strong, with students expected to take three separate sciences at GCSE. In recent years, English has also come into its own, thanks to a fresh, more dynamic approach. 'Parents nearly always value maths and sciences, but arguably not always English to the same extent, so this has been a challenge,' admits head. French and German taught from year 7 (one of which all students take at GSCE), along with basic Latin, and classical civilisation is an option for GCSE and A level. All the usual suspects when it comes to A level choices, with popular options including maths, sciences, geography, psychology, economics, history and English, with uptake of languages at A level small, reflecting national trends. Sixth form boasts a broad enrichment programme, including a LAMDA public speaking qualification taught by the head and head of drama. Independent learning encouraged, particularly

L

in sixth form. 'Even in the first two weeks of term, they treat the year 11s differently, which is great,' said one parent.

Class sizes are 30-31 (dropping to mid 20s for GCSE subjects), although these large numbers seem to pose no challenge to learning. Setting from year 9 in maths and year 10 for English, maths and science. Mutually respectful relationships between staff and students, particularly noticeable in sixth form, although a few pupils told us they feel the custom of standing up when a teacher walks into the classroom is 'outdated and disruptive.' Oodles of admiration for teachers' willingness to go beyond the call of duty. 'Nothing is ever too much trouble in helping you reach your potential and that includes giving up lunchtimes to help you get the grades you want,' said one pupil. Parents agree. 'Students have access to teachers by email and they often answer late into the evening or during the holidays,' said one.

Frequent linking of lessons to the world of work, whilst students also praise the cross-curricular links. 'If you go from an English lesson into a history one, there's an expectation you'll link the two and build on what you just learned,' explained one. 'We had one science class in which we studied butterflies, then an art class where we turned them into detailed posters,' said another.

Huge success in the use of iPad technology in lessons – with year 8s the latest to join the school's rolling programme, which already involves years 9, 10 and 11 regularly making use of them in school. 'We disagree with the government that mobile technologies are disruptive,' says head, and pupils concur that it encourages innovative ways to enhance learning. 'We're not exactly pioneers because we learn from others, but we are considered a leader in the field,' says head.

Small number (22 when we visited) on the SEN register, mainly due to dyslexia, learning impairment and Asperger's. Support is provided by an individual needs co-ordinator (SENCo qualification, as well as being a psychology teacher), who also helps with wider issues like disorganisation and lack of social skills, mainly outside the classroom (working in conjunction with the school's learning mentor and the school counsellor). Parents largely impressed with the 'proactive approach'. 'The school has made lots of suggestions and facilitated everything my son has needed. We haven't had to push for anything,' said one. 'Our son has been well supported all the way through,' said another. On entry to the school, around 50 per cent of students speak English as a second language, although intervention work in English (especially in essay writing skills) goes a long way to addressing this.

Plenty of school trips, including short residential trips for year 7s upwards. Pupils speak particularly highly of the language trips to France and Germany, whilst geography field trips have included visits to Slapton, Northern Ireland, Sicily and Iceland, and classic civilisation students visited Pompeii. Older pupils can also get involved in expeditions to the likes of Morocco, Jordon, Ghana and Zambia.

Games, options, the arts: Despite the school's hard-working ethos, there's no shortage of encouragement for pupils to take up less academic subjects. Good sports facilities, notably a main four-court sports hall that can accommodate the whole school (and which the community also uses), several outdoor courts and a floodlit, all-weather pitch. There's access to the park next door, too, and there's also an old gym to complement the new sports hall. The sheer variety of sport rules it out of being known as 'a rugby school,' 'a hockey school' etc, but this is considered a positive. 'There's something for everyone,' explained one pupil. Two hours of timetabled sport a week is strengthened by plenty of lunchtime and after-school activities and matches, with particular successes against private and other state schools in cricket and basketball (including girls' basketball). Retaining interest in sport higher up the school can be a challenge, however.

Music a growth area, with over 250 individual music lessons taking place each week, plus weekly lessons for years 7, 8 and 9. All the usual orchestras and choirs, plus some student-led groups, which include a lot of girls with guitars. Plenty of opportunity to showcase talent in assemblies, concerts and productions, with recent examples including Beauty and the Beast (juniors) and Blood Brothers (seniors). Drama (for which there's a spacious purpose-built studio) part of the curriculum up to year 10 and a popular GCSE choice, although interest fluctuates year-on-year as an A level option. Art is encouraged, sometimes even pushed, and includes plenty of visits to galleries. Some impressive artwork adorns the corridors and head's office (interestingly, we noticed no work from other subjects prominently displayed around the school, with the exception of canvas photography prints showcasing pupils doing different activities across subject areas).

Background and atmosphere: Nestled among quiet residential streets of red-brick semis, this isn't an aesthetically pleasing school from the outside, with the core block a giant box-like construction, typical of 1950s Brutalist architecture. That said, it has softened with age and paint and it is surrounded by plenty of green space and more attractive modern buildings (some of which were financed by selling off a 'redundant' strip at the edge of the site about 10 years ago). Moreover, it's kept scrupulously clean and well-maintained, both outside and in, with areas of note in the old block including the colourful and welcoming dining hall and the well-stocked and spacious library. In fact, given that this main block has suffered some serious structural problems (which has meant erecting some unsightly pillars throughout the interior), the school has done very well to keep it looking as neat, tidy and welcoming as it does. Only the science labs stand out as being particularly tired, and the pupils certainly have no beef with their facilities.

Alas, structural issues continue. 'As far back as 1966, the HM Inspectorate acknowledged that whilst the school was built to an experimental design, it had not been entirely successful,' points out the head, with a raised eyebrow. The second reason is that Slough Borough Council wants to support the expansion of the intake by an extra 30 pupils in response to pupil numbers rising in Slough. The main part of the school will be rebuilt during 2019/21 to include new science, tech, art and computing areas, then hall, library etc.

The purpose-built sixth form building, on the other hand, is light, spacious and welcoming, with facilities including a well-used 220-seat lecture theatre and several airy sixth form classrooms and common room. Built in 2007 to have a university feel, it has stood the test of time. Meanwhile, the not-very-imaginatively named '1996 building' has decent sized, airy classrooms and is home to music, drama, English, history and maths. Other separate blocks include the sports hall and single story building for food tech and textiles.

If there's one overriding atmosphere in the school, it is one of calm. There are no bells, no boisterousness (even at break times) and between lessons, students walk purposefully and quickly to their next lesson, chatting in groups. Green blazers with the school insignia for boys, green jackets for girls, traditional enamel badges for positions of responsibility worn proudly.

Pastoral care, well-being and discipline: Exceptional transition programme for year 7s, largely because pupils enter from over 80 primary schools across a wide geographical area and across varied cultural backgrounds. 'Around half of the students come here knowing nobody,' explains head. 'Not that this is a disadvantage as we find it means they make a real effort to make friends and build relationships.' Pupils agree, with older students fondly remembering the efforts the school made to settle them in. When we visited, one corridor displayed post-it notes that new year 7s had posed anonymous questions on, ranging from 'What if you're late?' to 'How do you know where you have to be?' which teachers had answered in pen underneath.

Pastoral care offered mainly from form teachers, phase leaders and school counsellor. Religion(s) a key part of school life, with lots of visiting speakers and everyone taking RE at GSCE (typically 65 per cent or more get top marks, which head sees as proof that students enjoy it and take it seriously).

Anti-bullying initiatives considered successful, including a telling atmosphere, trained anti-bullying mentors, restorative justice, a school counsellor and a clear no-tolerance policy. Pupils say diversity also helps. 'I think it's because we're all so different that we learn to respect differences early on,' explained one. Lots of cross year friendships, helped by the wide range of after-school clubs.

Traditional house system, which provides the framework for all manner of competitions, ranging from music to sport, with the annual sports day held at Thames Valley Athletics Stadium, an event that causes great excitement.

A clear set of expectations, rather than school rules, with the usual range of sanctions for those who break them. The head rarely has to implement them, though, and even mobile phones are allowed to be used in school, provided they're not used in lessons or with headphones.

Pupils and parents: Pupils enter from as far as west London boroughs (although entrance criteria now focuses on being more local) and typically from over 80 primary schools. Students (of whom 94 per cent are minority ethnic and two-thirds are from Asian/British-Indian backgrounds) are articulate, respectful and polite, although some are quite passive, with staff having to work hard to encourage more lively participation. Currently no PA and parents rarely get together, except at school events, although attendance for these is high. No school bus, with pupils arriving by train into Langley, by public bus, car share scheme, cycling or walking.

Entrance: Slough is not a fully selective authority, so parents must opt in for their children to take the test (CEM – Centre for Evaluation & Monitoring – 11+) set by the four Slough grammars acting as a consortium. This test is taken in September. Places have historically been allocated according to rank order of performance. But now all places go to pupils in the three Langley Priority Admission postcode areas who achieve 111 or above, with priority to those in area 1, then to those in area 2 on pupil premium, then children of staff, then those in area 2 by ranking order. Intake increased to 180 over six classes. Head is under no illusion about the prevalence of tutoring, but does point out that CEM was selected over the previous GL Assessment on the basis that they are more guarded about the information in the public domain and won't release practice papers. Minimum of 20, and maximum of 45, sixth form places for external candidates, with admission on the basis of general standard of GCSE grades and some specific criteria for A level subjects selected.

Exit: Around 20 per cent leaves after GCSEs. Russell Group universities, particularly the London colleges, are favoured (45 per cent), with four Oxbridge in 2018, six medics and four dentists. Popular subjects include maths, science, engineering, medicine, law and business, accounting and finance – nothing remotely fluffy. Support for pupils continues after they leave, especially if they delay university entrance, although gap years aren't common.

Remarks: This is a school that takes the top 30 per cent of ability range, so rather than being super selective, it's built on the noble ideal of the Bucks/Kent grammar school model (it was a Bucks grammar school until the 1970s when the local authority boundaries changed). And perhaps because of its location, it manages to avoid sharp-elbowed parents after a private education on the state. But make no mistake, this is a serious-minded school, where students are hungry to learn and highly focused. 'You never go home at the end of the day without feeling you've learned a lot,' said one student. 'Nothing is ever stagnant and no one is ever lazy,' agreed another. But whilst you feel some of the students could do with giving themselves a bit more downtime, this school could never be accused of being an education hothouse, with staff doing all they can to encourage a holistic education and produce rounded individuals.

Leighton Park School

Shinfield Road, Reading RG2 7EE

Ages 11–18 **Pupils** 462 (300 boys, 162 girls) **Sixth form** 118
Boarders 92 full, 41 weekly, 3 flexi

Fees: Day £17,618 – £21,978; Boarding £24,364 – £35,746 pa

01189 879600
www.leightonpark.com

Head: Since September 2018, Matthew Judd, previously second master at Haberdashers' Aske's boys and executive head of its prep. Degree in geography from University of Wales and teaching qualification from Cambridge. Started his career at Habs in 1993, becoming head of department and housemaster; moved in 2005 to be principal at MPW college in London before rejoining Habs five years later as second master and then later head of the prep and pre-prep. Also an ISI inspector and was motivated to apply for the job after inspecting the school. Grew up in Crawley and was the first person in his family to go to university, having attended the local comp in the shadow of Gatwick airport – 'if you were a boy, you went into baggage handling; if you were a girl, you went into duty free.' Lives on site with his partner Ian; a keen musician, and enjoys travel and fitness.

Academic matters: Academic work is taken seriously and pupils strive for success – as they should – although not, thankfully, a results-driven school. In 2018, 51 per cent A*-A/9-7 at GCSE. New GCSE offerings include dance, engineering and food tech. A level and IB offered though IB numbers not yet on a par with A level takers. In 2018, 33 per cent of A levels gained A*/A. Overall IB average 30. Very strong added-value – top school in Berkshire. IB retained partly because 'its values are so much those of the school'. Useful cross-fertilisation – IB and A level languages often taught together in year 12 and all take an EPQ for its educational value. Good languages. BTec in creative digital media available in years 10/11. Very good teacher:pupil ratio at 7.5 pupils to one full-time teacher and some sixth form classes with only one or two students. Small but well-stocked library and much praise for the range of visiting outside speakers. Interesting displays of work – we were moved by the WW1 montage of Old LPs fallen in battle which made it all pathetically real.

Parents, for the most part, praise the teaching – 'My son is enthused by everything – especially the Mandarin' – while there is some sense that a little more rigour, vigour and initiative might not come amiss here and there. School counters that its added value shows great rigour. Very much a school for joiners-in and those with breadth and brain.

EAL classes for small number of students who need them and school prepares them for FCE and IELTS exams. They don't take an additional language and use one of the class English lessons to boost their language skills. Some 15 per cent on the SEND register – surprisingly few for a school with such a good reputation for supporting those with an educational special need. Individual learning centre and all staff involved in support. No in-class assistants unless provided by the pupil's LA. Helpful and flexible approach, as parents attest, and 'they are quite relaxed about Ritalin, they take it in their stride'. A sense that the large and highly-regarded SEN team are there to make themselves less and less needed.

Games, options, the arts: Large and beautiful site, with fields, pitches, courts and tracks which positively set your muscles aquiver. 'My son is not sporty but they have really got him to love it,' a mother marvelled. Music is big here and no other house activity compares with the annual House Music, which is taken very seriously – 'almost too seriously,' we were told, 'as everyone gets really into it and the noise is louder than at a football match'. Good number learn an instrument in school and remarkable cohort of fine musicians – ie beyond grade 8 – practise here. Art exceptionally varied and imaginative. We loved the year 10 work on 'Surfaces, facades and veneers' and the sixth form studio was full of mind-stretching, clever creativity, alongside examples of the crucial skills of drawing and painting. Pottery, photography, textiles and DT work provide evidence of novel, individual ideas being fostered. DT provision newly enhanced by laser cutter, CNC router and 3D printer. Drama also lively – big productions, mostly musicals, in attractive, flexible theatre, its regular seating arranged, interestingly, in the guise of a Meeting. Also small drama studio in stand-alone brick building, formerly a squash court.

L

Lots to do. And lots of encouragement to try things out. Huge range of clubs and activities and masses of space for them all. Young Enterprise, DofE, trips of all kinds but no CCF, of course.

Boarding: School would not claim that boarding accommodation is up-to-the minute. Rooms are spacious enough. Most younger years share in 3s and 4s. Sixth formers in singles but not an en-suite or even a bedroom with basin anywhere on site – yet. All houses well-provided with table games, TVs and sofas – they feel like home only with more fun. Many day pupils stay until 7.00pm or even 9.00pm, thus getting the best of two worlds.

Many staff live on site and have boarding duties. Head's modest house, also on site, all adds to the sense of community and pupils love that 'our tutors are in the boarding houses after school and we can just chat to them'.

Background and atmosphere: Situated in the centre of 'the park' – an apt name for this spacious, meadowed site with hundreds of mature trees, garden areas, large reedy pond, generous planting and low-rise blocks – is the main building, an elegant 1850s white house. It was bought by an earlier incarnation of the school in the 1880s and more land was donated by the Reckitt family – the aim being to educate Quaker children for Oxbridge. It remains a Quaker-run school as the majority of governors are Quakers and, although no member of the Friends remains on the staff and only penny numbers of pupils are Quakers, the school lives by and exudes those gentle, civilised and socially responsible values. Few who leave here take nothing of those with them, and many see them as a guide for a healthy life. A palpable sense of calm pervades the place – you feel it as you drive in and your shoulders drop as you step out of your car and breathe out.

This is not just another school and it is best not to approach it as such. Nor is it 'alternative', though the pupils and teachers being on first name terms can deceive you into thinking so. The Quaker philosophy is central and, although it is never pushed at you, its calm wisdom steals gently into one's consciousness. 'When you're in year 9, you don't really get the meaning of it,' one soon-to-be-leaver told us, 'but, by the end, especially when life is hectic, you really appreciate it. It helps you find quiet time to clear your thoughts.' Weekly Meeting for Worship and monthly Meeting are the overt Quaker practices but, in the diverse mix of today's population, no particular faith dominates and everyone brings to the sessions what they wish. In practice, this approach changes relationships. 'Calling teachers by their first names makes you treat them as people – you don't have to be on your best behaviour and it makes you more inclined to learn,' we were advised. And, of pupil:pupil dynamics: 'If we fall out we tend just to fix it and hug it out.' The Peace Pole – an extraordinary carved wooden column visible from most parts of the school – enshrines these principles, as do the many examples of pupil creativity – benches, tables etc carved from fallen trees on the site – around the place.

Lots of buildings of all eras, little of startling architectural merit though the Oakview restaurant is cleverly designed and a popular addition. We were very impressed by the food – its freshness and variety – and deeply regretted not being able to stay to sample it. 'Theatre Special is when they cook it in front of you – like a performance; pork baguette is a thing of beauty,' apparently.

Some splendid individual rooms, especially in the main building. New all-singing-all-dancing music and media centre with rehearsal and performance rooms plus a fully-equipped media suite. We were repeatedly struck by the good order of the site – not an instance of peeling paint, a shabby carpet or a stained wall met our eye and, over an extensive tour, we saw not a shred of litter. Signing is useful and not municipal in style.

Houses, named after notable Quakers, matter but not too much – except at House Music. But the traditions and values of the place inspire spontaneous, unaffected loyalty.

Pastoral care, well-being and discipline: Discipline maintained with a light touch and some incomers given refuge after mishaps elsewhere become model citizens here. Historically great place for deserving second-chancers – 'The only people to get kicked out are complete idiots as they'll have had several warnings'. However, is now taking a firmer line under new leadership, we are told. A parent told us that 'they encourage them to become self-reliant and independent' and 'unlike at other schools, they can pick up their own clothes and make their own supper'. 'They are good at integrating kids who've been fish-out-of-water at their previous schools.' More rules than you might expect – no eating while walking around, no use of mobiles during the school day – but all designed to consider others and to maintain the peace. And school is subtly stiffening the teacher-pupil dynamic to remind all that, in the classroom, work is what matters and discipline is there to protect that principle.

Pupils and parents: Day pupils outnumber boarders 3:1. Full boarders outnumber weekly/flexis by 4:1. And boys outnumber girls – as in most co-ed schools – by 2:1. Some 72 per cent are UK nationals, the rest from everywhere – 29 nationalities at time of our visit, so no cliques and enclaves. Vast majority of UK students are local or local-ish. Healthy 75 per cent of boarders in school at weekends. Old Leightonians: Sir David Lean, Sir Richard Rodney Bennett, Jim Broadbent, Laura Marling, Eliza Bennett, Michael Foot, Lord Caradon, Lord Frederick Seebohm and a fair clutch of MPs plus Rowntrees, Cadburys, Clarks, Reckitts, Morlands and Frys.

Entrance: Online entrance tests in English comprehension and maths, plus creative writing exercise and short interview in the January preceding entry for years 7-10. Entry to sixth form conditional on GCSE or equivalent results, plus interview. At 11+, 95 apply for 40 places; at 13+, 35 apply for 15-20 places. At year 10, 20 apply for 10-15 places. Year 11 is a 'pre-sixth' year for overseas students. There are six applicants for each of the 20-30 places in the sixth form. Second language speakers sit an EAL test.

Exit: Some 40 per cent leaves after GCSEs. Roughly similar percentage of sixth form leavers to Russell Group universities, a third off to do creative degrees. One to Oxford in 2018, one to the US and three to European universities. One parent enthused, 'we liked the fact that alongside the leavers who read medicine at Oxford they celebrate those who go and learn circus skills'.

Money matters: Not an immensely rich school but a decent amount of money available for bursaries. Emphasis on enabling those whose financial situation would not allow them to attend, to do so, so most recipients on awards of 50 per cent or more. Robust mean-testing and assessment of income/commitments/assets etc. Six on 100 per cent bursaries at time of our visit. Scholarships mostly worth 10 per cent.

Remarks: A school in which to grow. Not for hustlers, bustlers and takers but great for thinkers, makers, givers, be-ers.

Leventhorpe School

Cambridge Road, Sawbridgeworth, Hertfordshire CM21 9BY

Ages 11–19 **Pupils** 1,200 **Sixth form** 290

01279 836633
www.leventhorpe.net

Head: Since September 2018, Malcolm White, previously deputy head. A Leventhorpe teacher for over 18 years by the time of his appointment, he led the business studies department and then the social sciences faculty for more than seven years before being appointed assistant and then deputy head.

Academic matters: Traditional timetable caters for mixed ability cohort, who join as six form entry in year 7 and are set for maths from their Sats results. Setting flexible and parents 'really impressed with levels of communication' when pupils moved up or down. Results respectable, with 83 per cent getting 9-4 in both English and maths at GCSE in 2018. At A level, 48 per cent of grades were A*/B. School reports star subjects to be English and social sciences, plus 'spectacular' results at both GCSE and A level for technology (students also uniformly declare this department 'inspirational') and maths, where parents report 'variable quality of teaching', reportedly 'on its way up'. Science has been 'a weakness to date' but a new departmental head is on track to boost results – so watch this space. It's French and Spanish for all in years 7 and 8, and compulsory to continue with one (or both) in year 9. Parents praise teaching of languages, which incorporates creative methods such as film and music rather than just text books. 'Student choice comes first,' so no compulsory language at GCSE: 'If a student is able to choose subjects they like as their options, they are more likely to do well in these, hence their confidence and self-esteem will benefit and they'll do better all round.' Financial literacy qualification offered as enrichment subject alongside GCSE and A levels is popular with brightest pupils.

Majority of pupils take 10 GCSEs, with brightest adding one more if they take triple science. Less traditional routes on offer for those of a non-academic disposition, with students able to choose fewer than four GCSE options to lighten the load and – where appropriate – day release to attend vocational college courses. Recent increase in SEN provision – now a full time SENCo, one higher level TA and eight TAs to offer support to those on the register. Focus on early intervention for students falling behind in literacy and numeracy in years 7 to 11, with withdrawal from other subjects for special booster sessions run with the aim of getting them back on track and able to keep up with the cohort. No fixed approach to nurturing pupils at the top of the academic spectrum – 'we teach a growth mindset. Anyone can achieve if they work hard – that's the philosophy of the school.' This reflected in the replacement of an elitist speech day with 'achievement awards' – 25 per year group up for grabs at the end of each year to celebrate endeavour as much as – if not more than – results.

Games, options, the arts: Compulsory sport to year 12, with four periods per fortnight. Unsurprisingly, school is 'more rugby than football' and is 'coming on' in competitive fixtures with year 7 finalists and year 8 recently winning the district plate. Keen competitors are selected for an A or B team, and school says that 'everyone who turns up regularly to training will get a match,' even relative beginners if they are keen, according to parents. Football popular with both sexes too, although with more talent to choose from it tends to be harder for hopefuls to make the squad. Strong cricket, thanks to an arrangement with Sawbridgeworth Cricket Club, and netball and hockey for girls. A and B teams for girls' rugby, football and cricket on top of trad sports, with increasing competitive success at district level.

Sports tours moving up the agenda, with a rugby tour to New York and girls' sports tour to Cyprus timetabled for 2019. Plenty of other trips tick the academic and enrichment boxes: skiing in Switzerland, language trips to France and Spain, battlefields trip to Belgium and business studies to Disneyland Paris, to name a few.

Drama, newly on curriculum for years 7 to 9, and run by a former head girl, thrives with strong results at GCSE and productions aplenty for budding thespians of all ages. Shows tend to be more Oliver! than Othello and in recent years have included The Wizard of Oz, Grease and West Side Story. Parents report ethos to be 'very inclusive' and quality to be high – and our musical tour guides said that playing in the orchestra pit would be their overriding best memory of their Leventhorpe years. Lack of swanky music centre more than compensated for by wildly enthusiastic and talented teaching staff ('fantastic' say parents). Grant funded free instrumental lessons for all year 7 and 8 pupils requesting them – with funding continuing to year 13 if pupils choose music as GCSE or A level option. Lower and upper choirs, orchestra, folk band and even an accordion ensemble (the only one we know of in the area) all strut their stuff at termly concerts, with beginners and improvers given the opportunity to show what they have learned at termly chamber concerts. A music tour to Germany is a highlight of this active department.

Background and atmosphere: Although your heart may sink when you pull up outside the drab low level 1960s blocks that front the main road through Sawbridgeworth, the moment you step into the recently refurbed reception area, all high ceilings, glass and colourful displays of artwork and textiles, you get an inkling that there's something special beyond. And although the majority of classrooms tick the 'tatty' box, in the main they are large and light – and we've never seen so many computers. The wow factor really hits you when you step into the learning resource centre and library (2013) – an airy, double height space, flooded with light and punctuated by bright colours, beanbags,

L

plus a beautiful mezzanine study area for exclusive use by years 12 and 13 (complete with yet more IT). By the time you walk across the piazza to the fabulous, architecturally stunning leisure centre (2012), you'll have forgotten that the 1960s ever happened. Equipped with everything from trampolines to cricket nets and a state of the art dance studio and gym that's open to pupils before and after school, plus an outside viewing balcony overlooking a vast Astroturf, playing fields and beyond as far as the eye can see across farmland. All that's missing is a swimming pool. But that's just next door.

The artsy side's well catered for too, with a superb drama studio and buzzy art rooms displaying huge canvases and pottery designs. Super food technology facility, with equally appealing textiles room showcasing high quality creations from fleece hats, shorts and dresses. And with pupils telling us 'there are just so many' clubs and societies to choose from, we're not surprised school is becoming so popular.

Pastoral care, well-being and discipline: School says 'mutual respect' is the driving force behind a culture of good behaviour in school, with little need for heavy handed discipline beyond 20 minute lunch time detentions and a weekly after-school detention which rarely sees more than 15 pupils in attendance. Recognises that 'mental health is a growing concern' amongst young people and is making it a key priority for next three years, with a 'mental health first aid' programme aimed at educating pupils and parents of warning signs. Differences of race or sexual orientation are reportedly well tolerated. 'Students feel safe here to be who they are. It's genuinely not an issue. We like to give pupils the chance to let us know about bullying if it occurs.' Trained 'active listeners' in years 10 and 11 are on hand to address concerns raised by their younger peers and school works closely with parents on current issues, eg cyber bullying, with 'eye opening' seminars and briefings. Pupils describe school as 'really friendly – we all really look out for each other' and parents say bullying is 'taken very seriously' and 'jumped on quickly' when it occurs.

L

House system pervades all and is manifested through house ties for boys and coloured blazer badges. Pastoral care channelled through heads of house, with year group heads now taking responsibility for academic progress and parents have an email address for every teacher – and, importantly, report receiving fast replies – making communication simple. Inter-house competitions for absolutely everything, plus house points as rewards for endeavour and achievement in the classroom.

Pupils and parents: School's geographical location – wedged between middle class Bishop's Stortford and less affluent Harlow – makes for a totally mixed parent demographic, from city workers to manual labourers. An aspirational choice for Harlow parents, and an increasing favourite with the Bishop's Stortford crowd if they're looking for co-ed. The melting pot seems to work – school has a friendly, stress free vibe and pupils we met were a delightful combination of articulate, inquisitive and quietly confident. Because of musical aptitude entrance criteria, there's a fair bit of talent knocking about too (anyone who has attempted to learn piano will understand our awe at our tour guide modestly saying he was 'struggling' with grade 4 having been learning for just a year. That on top of grade 8 violin) which adds to the generally diverse and convivial feel to the school.

Entrance: Priority given to pupils attending one of eight feeder schools in surrounding villages and their siblings. School has filled from these in recent years. Eighteen places held back in each year group for applicants not at these feeders showing exceptional musical aptitude, with test taken in consortium with two other local secondaries.

Exit: Around 70 per cent stay on after year 12. Thereafter 'the landscape is changing', with increasing numbers of pupils – around a third – choosing straightforward or degree apprenticeships or management training schemes with companies ranging from M&S to HSBC, Deloitte and PwC, rather than the traditional university path. Of those heading to university, popular destinations are London colleges and Nottingham with large numbers also stay closer to home, heading to Anglia Ruskin University – up to 20 in some years. Two or three to Oxbridge most years, notably Robinson College Cambridge.

Remarks: In a survey carried out recently by school, over 95 per cent of parents said that they would recommend Leventhorpe, with its super facilities, community spirit and strong discipline all top reasons. With a young, purposeful head who parents say 'never lets things stand still' as its driving force we predict it will go from strength to strength, giving pupils of all abilities abundant all round opportunity and positive attitude towards learning. In the words of one parent: 'They celebrate success, whether it's 10 top grades at GCSE or a pupil who has simply exceeded their expectations; it's just what they do.'

Lochinver House School

Heath Road, Little Heath, Potters Bar, Hertfordshire EN6 1LW

Ages 3–13 **Pupils** 340

Fees: £11,175 – £14,685 pa

01707 653064
www.lochinverhouse.com

Headmaster: Since 2011, Ben Walker BA PGCE CELTA. Educated at Lochinver House (head boy in 1977 – tie, badges a photo 'of when I had more hair,' proudly displayed in his office), St Albans School and Reading University where he read English. Joined retail group C&A as a management trainee after university. Realised after a year that the commercial world was 'not really for me' and took a PGCE at the Institute of Education. Spent 13 years in inner city state secondary schools, rising through the ranks, before he and his wife sold up and moved the family to Kenya in 2002, where they spent three years starting a school, coordinating health care projects and working as Church Mission Society partners. Towards the end, took a post at St Andrews, Turi, a prep school for expats and wealthy nationals, which led him, on his return to the UK in 2005, to the role of deputy head at Swanbourne House in Buckinghamshire. Came full circle and joined Lochinver House as head six years later.

Imagine the kind of person you'd want around in a crisis and chances are this is it – naturally serene, unflustered, friendly, frank, jovial, a natural communicator and, perhaps most importantly, knows how to get things done. 'He's amazing,' enthuse parents – 'a perfect mix of all the qualities you want in a headteacher.' 'He knows exactly what he's doing so even if you don't agree with him, you just trust him.' Pupils call him 'kind,' 'wise,' 'enthusiastic,' 'fair' and 'not strict..well, maybe sometimes when he needs to be.' If an invitation to his 'headmaster's hot chocolate' (a Friday event for those with the most house credits that week) is considered a golden ticket, then his termly 'head's pub lunch' (a treat for boys who get a 'thumbs up' award – given to those 'who are golden in the less predictable ways') is platinum. We hope the head's PA gets to go along sometimes too – she got a special mention from practically every parent we spoke to – 'she's the school's secret weapon,' summed up one.

Married to Jill, head of St Nicholas Prep, Kensington, with whom he has three grown-up children. Cycles to work every day ('2,000 miles a year'), swims a mile on Saturday ('with my wife') and plays badminton every Tuesday ('events permitting').

Entrance: Currently oversubscribed and 'gently' selective. Candidates at 3 and 4 assessed informally in small groups ('a fun day,' say parents) to check suitability and potential. Boys entering higher up the school, some from state primaries and some new to area, spend a day at the school with a 'buddy' and are tested in numeracy and literacy, with competition often stiff for these occasional places. School retains two form entry format (maximum class sizes 21) to the end of year 6, with years 7 and 8 splitting into three smaller classes of 12, including an accelerated group.

Exit: Around 80 per cent stay to year 8, with the usually less academic remainder taking different 11+ paths to avoid the common entrance hurdle ('we are happy to prepare for 11+ and don't get uptight about it,' says head) or leaving for financial reasons. A few to selective state schools. Others join in year 7 ('the transition for my son couldn't have been smoother – they really take these boys under their wing,' said one such parent). Leavers go on to a variety of independent schools, including Haberdashers' Aske's Boys' School, St Albans School, Merchant Taylors, City of London, UCS, Haileybury, Aldenham, St Christopher, St Columba's, Mill Hill, Oundle, Stonyhurst, Charterhouse. 'Historically, guidance around senior school choice hasn't been great, but it's vastly improved,' one parent told us.

Remarks: 'I didn't realise it was quite so big,' says practically every prospective parent. Located in an eight-and-a-half acre site tucked away in residential suburbia, Lochinver House won't seduce you with its good looks, but in true ugly duckling style it could well win you over with its hidden beauty which manifests itself in a warren of practical facilities and decent outdoor space, all aimed at squeezing excellence out of its young charges.

Pre-prep block unlikely to win any beauty contests but has its own small library and the walls are cheered with art and written work, as well as a 'giving tree', which gives a clue to the supportive nature of the school, with kind deeds posted as leaves on a daily basis. Also has its own garden – a haven in the north London urban jungle – where the youngest pupils grow vegetables, build, dig and have story time when weather permits. Playtimes are spent in the enclosed adventure playground (made less alluring by proximity to car park) or, for older boys, it's a choice between tarmacked area in the middle of the school (complete with basketball nets, skipping ropes and other good old-fashioned toys 'for the boys who don't like football,' whispers the head) or the huge Astroturf, which doubles up as sports field and cricket pitch (although not for A and B teams for fear of nearby windows). Sports fields are split between the main site and additional space across the road, offering plenty of options for matches and games practice. And for older boys, there's a lovely eco garden, complete with bug hotel and swamp-like pond.

Other stand out facilities include a theatre (we saw a delightful rehearsal of a harvest festival assembly from year 4s), light and bright dining room (with superb artwork on the walls), even lighter and brighter art studio (plus DT lab upstairs), modern well-equipped science labs (where boys were acting out the relationship between the voltage, current, and resistance in one lab and pouring and examining liquids in another – 'there's loads of practicals,' say boys) and sports hall. Mundane-looking library surely misses a trick, but recent cash injection has boosted and expanded main classroom block and there's a new reception and admin building ('a good welcome is so important,' says head). Coach house recently remodelled for provision of extra support.

'Maths is amazing, science is out of this world and while English used to be the weakness, that's shining bright now too,' one parent told us, echoing others. Languages department another star player, with French from year 3, Latin from year 5 and two year courses in Spanish and Russian from year 5. 'My son joined in year 7, with no French, and was in top set soon afterwards,' said one parent. St Albans school reportedly considers Lochinver boys amongst its best linguists. Setting from year 3 for maths, year 5 for French and from year 7 for sciences. IT, music and games taught by specialists from reception up and drama from year 1. Majority of classes held in form rooms until year 3, when boys graduate towards moving around school for specialist teaching in all subjects – great preparation for next school. Verbal and non verbal reasoning embedded in the senior curriculum – 'preparation for tests is a key focus.' Good scholarship output with around a dozen most years to a variety of next schools (25 the year we visited). IT embedded into lessons, with all boys getting own iPads with 'army-grade cover' from year 6. Excellent CPD for teachers, who we saw engaging pupils in a multitude of ways. Notable lack of pupils being tutored outside school, compared to other local preps, say parents – 'hurrah for that!' says head.

No statemented children but a number with learning difficulties and these, along with gifted children, are supported in various ways, with a combination of booster sessions, guidance for families and involvement of external agencies where necessary. 'My son was completely left behind at his state school, but within four weeks of being here, they identified his exact strengths and weaknesses and developed a support programme – he's since had the right diagnosis and is starting to fly,' said one parent.

Musical pursuits so absorbing that your son will probably leave with more strings to his bow than you'd thought possible. Two-thirds learn an instrument and half of those learn two. Bassoon, oboe, harp – you name it, there's probably a peripatetic teacher for it. Compulsory recorder in year 3 and between six and eight musical recitals every year. All the usual choirs, orchestra, ensembles ('and rock band,' added one pupil, excitedly) you could shake a stick at, but it's the musical composition that really sets this school apart, with the musical score for one recent school play written and performed by boys (another time, a professional quartet came in to perform boys' compositions). Opportunities for the thespian community to shine too, with performances for all, with almost everyone getting involved either on stage or behind the scenes. Art projects so enticing, it was all we could do from sitting down and getting stuck in too.

Core sports are rugby, football and cricket. First ever prep school finalists at U13s ISFA cup, with repeated success at U11. Biannual football tour to Portugal and rugby tour to South Africa. Basketball on the up – 'we beat Milfield last year – a real David and Goliath job,' says head. Less competitive boys able to sample the likes of sailing, golf and taekwondo. A-C teams in all sports and A-F in football, but, said one parent, 'More credit for lower teams, though, please – even if an E team wins 12-nil, it doesn't get celebrated.' Shame there's no swimming pool, say others, but school utilises nearby pool for lessons.

Clubs aplenty from year 1, including chess, Lego, animation, Roman mythology and creative arts. Plus wrap-around care (costs extra) from 7.45am to 6pm (including tea for those that want it) and homework club for older boys. School minibuses ferry children from Finchley, Southgate, Totteridge, Hadley Wood and Barnet directions for a small daily charge, mornings only. All valued by 'very grounded' families – majority professional, many dual income. Large catchment area, some as far as Crouch End and Welwyn. Intake reflects the north London multi-cultural mix.

Relaxed, happy vibe. Lots of vertical relationships, largely thanks to houses, buddy schemes and pupil-run ABC (Anti-Bullying Council) and school council with reps from reception up. Immense leadership opportunities on offer and impressive charitable works. New 'been there, done it' project – a kind of mini DofE. One permanent exclusion in living memory; most years, no temporary ones. Fees considered excellent value – low for the area and includes almost all trips and excursions, moderate learning support requirements and many clubs. Very active PTA. Food excellent; 'cook's biscuits are to die for,' said one parent – we can vouch for that.

This is a friendly prep that really 'gets' boys. They get them moving around in lessons, give them bursts of fresh air between lessons, as well as lots of wellie time. And while it's no picnic academically, it's no pressure cooker either – 'boys get a long way without realising it,' as head puts it, with challenging open-ended tasks given from the off 'so they become critical thinkers'.

Lockers Park School

L

Lockers Park Lane, Hemel Hempstead, Hertfordshire HP1 1TL

Ages Boys 4–13, girls 4–7 **Pupils** 175 **Boarders** 14 full, 29 weekly/flexi (from 7 years) C of E

Fees: Day £10,950 – £17,385; Boarding £25,050 pa

01442 251712
www.lockerspark.herts.sch.uk

Headmaster: Since 2013, Chris Wilson BSc PGCE Cantab (30s). Read rural economics at Newcastle before moving to Cambridge to take a conversion course to enable him to teach maths to A level, followed by his PGCE at Homerton College.

Returned to alma mater Winchester House for first teaching role, where he spent 11 years teaching maths and running first XI cricket and colts rugby, heading the boarding house for 10 of them. Moved to Lockers in 2012 as deputy head, drawn by its rigorous sporting culture, boarding heritage ('boarding is infused through the school,' he says) and pastoral approach, as well as its superb musical offering (although he cheerfully describes himself as 'woefully inadequate' in this respect). Headship came after a period which was, according to parents 'turbulent', with three heads of school in six years. He has reportedly 'steadied the ship brilliantly' and restored confidence to staff, with parents describing the change in mood after his appointment as 'palpable'.

Still teaches years 7 and 8 maths and revels in being able to 'physically see the path of the boys' development' in a prep school and having 'involvement in all spheres' of their lives. Parents describe him as a 'fantastic communicator' and say that he has returned a focus on academic achievement which had formerly been 'slightly lost'. A cricket fanatic, he likens the patience and thoughtfulness required for the game to his role as head. Intent that his charges will remember the fun side of school, believes in 'freedom within boundaries' and aims to 'fly in the face' of pushy parents to 'ensure Lockers boys have a childhood'.

Engaging and likeable with a relaxed persona, and ably supported by wife, Hayley, who fulfils a traditional head's spouse role as well as caring for their two young daughters.

Entrance: Pre-prep welcomes girls as well as boys – most go to local girls' school Abbot's Hill at 7.

Not currently oversubscribed, although at highest ever numbers. Main intake into year 3 with a 'low key' assessment day including tests in verbal reasoning and maths. Scholarship day in February with applicants also observed in music, sport and a fun activity such as a treasure hunt. Head says they are 'not only looking for academic strength' but for children who can bring 'that certain something' to the school.

Pupils join mainly from state primaries, occasionally other preps (a large influx recently from Berkhamsted Prep), within a 20 to 30 minute radius of the school. Approximately half the cohort are day boys, with the rest doing 'some form' of boarding (two nights minimum). About 50 per cent of full time boarders are overseas pupils (typically Russian or Chinese) and some Forces.

Exit: In ones and twos to a broad variety of schools. Most recently to Aldenham, Harrow, Rugby, Eton, Bedford, St Albans and Winchester; in other years Berkhamsted, Stowe, Shiplake, Haileybury, Bradfield, Radley and Shrewsbury also popular destinations. The occasional one to state grammar at 11+, although this is 'definitely not encouraged,' says head.

Remarks: Adamantly traditional in its fabric but with a subtly modern feel (thanks to a rolling programme of improvements), Lockers was purpose-built in 1874 and sits atop 25 glorious acres of woodland – a boys' own oasis in a drab Hemel suburb. The heart of the school is undoubtedly the stunning, light-flooded panelled dining hall, which typifies Lockers' success in juxtaposing the modern with the school's rich history, the names of alumni etched on its walls. Everything is focused on bringing out the best in boys – from the 40 minute morning break where they can tear around fields and woodlands with just enough time for a bit of den-building, to the pristine well-structured classrooms (if there was a GSG award for the cleanest prep, Lockers would be in with a good chance) and predominantly male staff. Staff know all the boys and are '100 per cent accessible,' say parents – 'clearly visible and just a phone call or an email away.'

The spacious, well-stocked library has a cosy feel, with armchairs and banks of computers, and the chapel can house the whole school at a squeeze. Art room large and airy with its own kiln, although feels suspiciously tidy – and whole school could benefit from more artwork on display, especially as standards are high enough to win a senior school art scholarship most years. DT recently rehomed into a modern block with two super rooms – one for design and one for work. A comfortable boarders' common room is supplemented by the 'boys' hall' and the old gym, home to table tennis and pool tables. Engine enthusiasts will adore the 'train room' – a dedicated space for a huge model railway. Pianists practise on a baby grand situated in a very public space rather than tucked away in a practice room – 'great for getting them used to performing,' says head.

Tousled boys bomb happily around between classes with plenty of cheery greetings for staff and visitors. The uniform – or lack thereof – comprising a check shirt of the boys' choice and a pair of navy cords, sums up the collegiate learning environment where the endgame is reached via a path punctuated with a lot of good, wholesome fun as well as academic rigour. 'Best' is when the jackets and ties come out – again the boys' own choice of jacket – reserved for school outings, concerts and away matches. School committed to small class sizes with between 10 and 15 in most forms – parents feel that school's bijoux size is its 'true strength'.

Long days – sometimes up to 11 hours for older boys – with all allowed to arrive at school from 7am and stay for breakfast and supper at no extra charge and with no prior arrangement, all of which helps to cement the seamless boarding vibe – parents say it's like 'one big family.' Boarding house is part of main school, with boys split over two floors according to age and presided over by a housemaster who is supported by a team of live-in matrons.

Bright, functional dorms housing four to six boarders slightly lack the personal touch, although boys can bring their own duvet covers. Exeats every third weekend, unusually from Friday lunch time until Monday evening, with Saturday morning school still going strong on non-exeat weekends, optional for pre-prep.

Setting from year 7 in preparation for CE with specialist teaching across all subjects from year 5. Modern languages exceptionally strong, with head describing French as school's 'stand out' subject and parents adding history and geography to the list. A brief audience with the head of modern languages certainly confirmed his passion for language and inspirational teaching techniques. Latin and ancient Greek also on the menu, although not considered by parents to be school's strongest suit. Maths and English 'on the up,' says head, due to recent staff changes.

Music 'firing on all cylinders', according to head, led by the 'most dynamic, committed' head of music who secures a music scholarship for at least one boy each year. Violin for all from year 3 and at least 96 per cent of boys continue with an instrument, some playing two or three. Choirs, ensembles and bands galore with an invitation to join the 'intensely serious' main choir considered a real accolade (dare we say cool?). Drama on curriculum from years 3 to 5 (replaced by Latin in year 6), with opportunities galore for budding thespians to perform in plays, poetry competitions, debating etc.

Sport not the school's raison d'être but a good ethos in place – head laments the demise at some fixtures of the traditional post-match tea in other schools ('a bag of crisps and box of juice – just not the same') – and places huge emphasis on fair play and sportsmanship, fielding A-E teams whenever possible so everyone gets a trip on the bus whatever their ability. Sports department is making the most of its not inconsiderable facilities, including cricket nets, a renovated outdoor pool, tennis courts, and putting green. Sport every afternoon for all boys, with the timetable adjusted seasonally to allow for more light for outdoor fun. Occasional parental grumbles that less sporty boys are 'labelled' in the early years and don't get the same coaching opportunities as their more able peers. Tons of extracurricular from chess club to year-round skiing at the nearby snow dome. Lockers' own cub and scout packs thrive, and boys who take part generally stay the night afterwards.

Chapel every morning takes a 'general studies' approach and acts as a 'reflective, calming exercise' to start the day. Boarders' fun nights well attended by day boys and the anti-health and safety Dark Tower night, an unlit night time treasure hunt around the school, hugely popular. In summer, day boys stay over after evening barbecues and are 'swept along' with boarding activities throughout the year, some parents saying their boys never want to come home. Action-packed weekends for full-timers with activities split three ways between the cultural, educational and purely fun. All prep done in school – a popular move with boys and parents. Parents report that any incidents of bullying or upset are dealt with effectively in a 'supportive and understanding' way.

In all, a small but perfectly formed school which gives boys all the tools they need to continue on to top public schools. Lockers offers the best of both worlds – boarding for those who want it, with all the benefits plus their own beds at home for those who don't. In the words of one happy parent who moved two boys from another prep: 'boys are known and valued at Lockers, rather than unknown and undervalued'.

Long Crendon School

Chilton Road, Long Crendon, Aylesbury, Buckinghamshire HP18 9BZ

Ages 4–11 **Pupils** 212

01844 208225
www.longcrendon.bucks.sch.uk

Headteacher: Since 2010, Sue Stamp BA (60s). After completing her degree in English Lit at Westfield College, London, she gained her teaching qualifications from the now defunct Philippa Fawcett Teacher Training College. Was then offered a place on the Selfridges training programme, 'where I stayed until I had my first child in the late 70s,' she says. When she did finally take the plunge, jobs included working in international schools in Africa for 10 years, where she climbed the ranks to middle management. Began teaching in Bucks in 2003 (also becoming SENCo) and from there, became assistant head into Bearbrook School, Aylesbury, then deputy head at Waddesdon School, before moving here.

Any staff member who's been at this school longer than Mrs Stamp will tell you that it has been on 'quite a journey' since her arrival – priorities are clearer, staff work more collaboratively and outdoor learning (more of which later) is integral to the curriculum. Doesn't teach regularly, but gets 'stuck in if required,' and she has a clear open door policy ('actually a closed door doesn't stop the pupils here!' she laughs), with children popping in to tell her anything from a new idea for an after-school club to concerns around friendship issues. We found her dedicated, no-nonsense and perceptive. 'She's not touchy-feeling, although she is approachable,' said one parent. 'She is not a big, gregarious character that you rally behind, but I think it's great we have someone who is more interested in pushing children forward, than herself.' Others describe her as 'no pushover,' 'disciplined but fair' and 'unbelievably supportive, when you need her behind you.' Pupils say she is 'strict, but nice at the same time.'

Lives locally, and hobbies include reading, walking and making the most of her National Trust membership.

Entrance: Admission by means of the local authority criteria – which means that, in order of priority, it's looked after children, SEND, living as in catchment and siblings of children already at the school. In practice, that means the vast majority of families live in the village, no more than half-a-mile away and many year groups (of which there is single entry in each one) are oversubscribed. 'If you're on the outskirts of the village, there's a chance you won't get in,' admits the head.

Exit: Grammar schools in Bucks are popular – notably Aylesbury High, Aylesbury Grammar and Sir Henry Floyd – and many parents tutor their offspring in preparation of the 11+. Lord Williams's School, Thame, is the nearest comprehensive – 'it's a great school and many of our children go there,' says the head. Occasionally, children move into the private sector, usually in the Oxford area.

Remarks: Staggering commitment to outdoor learning, which has had a direct impact on academic results. It all started when foundation teacher Simon Poote, who won the 2015 award for Best LOtC (learning outside the classroom) Innovator, worked with the children to create a special outside space from a neglected area of the school site. The children helped him to build hills and landscapes, sow wild flowers, build a veg plot, add ropes, pulleys and water channels, create a fire pit, bird hide, camp out tent and even a mud kitchen. There's a wooden outdoor learning lodge, plus wet weather gear for the whole school, and the school has also formed a strong link with a neighbouring teaching farm, where the children spend time looking after animals, collecting produce and cooking the food they harvest. 'Writing results from the foundation stage children dramatically improved as the children are desperate to write about what they are experiencing,' reports the head, who adds that children are also 'much less likely to give up and more likely to undertake challenges across the curriculum as they have experienced what hard work can achieve.' 'You're always out and about here,' one child told us, with others pitching in with example upon example – 'We get to make jam!' 'The bug hunting is awesome.' 'We did apple pressing!'

The school – which was originally built as a secondary school in the 1960s – certainly has no shortage of outside space, including a huge sports field, tarmacked playground, plus the outdoor learning spaces. Inside, there are big, light and airy classrooms galore – with one class getting two classrooms all to themselves – a sliding door between them. There's a spacious art room, sadly devoid of artwork on the walls, perhaps simply because it's already been pinned to every other school wall. Indeed, rarely have we seen such imaginative, colourful and spectacular wall displays – a real showcase for the school's creative side. Sports/assembly hall is huge, with a lovely big stage; music room is also large – and jam packed with instruments; and we also like the conservatory for one-to-one work and small groups. Facilities could do with an upgrade in places, but what they lose in aesthetical décor, they gain in sheer space. Indeed, there's still room left for the school to rent out space out to a private onsite nursery and charity pre-school.

L

Teaching staff are praised for being 'fun' and 'engaging' and are given freedom to try out new and innovative methods – although some parents would like to see more male staff. We heard from one child about how they recreated the Great Fire of London, taking their miniature replica houses outside to burn. 'Every bit of learning seems to be brought to life,' said one parent.

French from year 3 and Spanish for year 5 only. No setting – 'A rising tide raises all ships,' says the head, who is also big on the growth mindset. 'The children are really encouraged to have a go at things – they're never afraid of failure,' said a parent. School strong on CPD for teachers, helped by the fact that they're part of a federation of schools (local comp, plus eight primaries), who share best practice, training days etc and have strong networking links.

The school has a history of turning out children who excel in reading, grammar and punctuation – head puts it down to a combination of children regularly visiting the school and local libraries; guided reading all the way up the school; plus plenty of stories read by teachers. Homework kept to a minimum.

No statemented children when we visited, but around 10 per cent have more mild to moderate SEN at any one time – dyslexia, dyspraxia, ADHD and autistic spectrum, in the main. All get class-room based help, while some get extra help in small groups in the conservatory.

Sport has become more competitive under the current head's leadership ('Parents told me this was top of their wishlist when I joined,' she says), with Friday afternoons now dedicated to house sports, overseen by the specialist sports teacher. Football, rugby, netball, cricket, hockey and basketball are all played with gusto – and the school does well competing against other schools. There's plenty of sports-based extracurricular clubs and no shortage of facilities including three football pitches and an outdoor swimming pool that's used from May to the end of September. 'All classes swim twice a week – we don't have any children leaving this school unable to swim,' says the head.

Music also has a specialist teacher, with singing and instruments a big part of life for everyone here – with a school band (The Brass Snakes), which plays at events. Seven peripatetic teachers also come in. Drama – taught in the main hall – is a favourite among pupils, with plenty of productions.

Art seeps into practically every subject. Pupils regularly exhibit at the Roald Dahl Festival in Aylesbury, making puppets and suchlike. Extracurricular clubs include all these areas, plus the likes of dance, comic club (requested by pupils) and science club. Outings galore and residentials for year 4 upwards.

Parents say this is a nurturing and friendly school, where teachers really get to know the children and one of the teaching assistants is a trained counsellor. One child had struggled with going to school for over a year, and it was this school that turned him around – 'they could not have been more supportive,' said the parent. Pupils feel comfortable approaching the head and there are robust rewards systems – dominated by house points system and the much-loved Smartie Awards, in which pupils or staff can nominate a child for effort in anything at all. Selected pupils are trained as play leaders and foundation children are buddied up with a year 6 student. This is a school that lives and breathes its values, keeping them fresh by changing them every half-term – when we visited, they were resilience and determination. Bullying rare. 'We get the parents in straight away,' says the head. Student council is a big deal.

Parents mainly middle class – many dual income (grateful for the optional before and after-school care). Strong PTA keeps things sociable. Reflecting the local village's ethnicity, the vast majority are white British.

This a true village school with a friendly, values-driven community that families move to the area for – and they're not disappointed. The dedicated teaching staff are focused on the whole child, rather than ticking boxes, and there seems to be no end to the lengths they'll go to in order to bring teaching alive. 'My children skip to school – who could ask for more?' summed up one parent.

Lord Wandsworth College

Long Sutton, Hook, Hampshire RG29 1TB

Ages 11–18 **Pupils** 614 **Sixth form** 149 **Boarders** 78 full, 66 weekly, 185 flexi

Fees: Day £20,430 – £23,460; Boarding £24,780 – £33,900 pa

01256 862201
www.lordwandsworth.org

Headmaster: Since 2015, Adam Williams (40s). Born Down Under, he went to Bradfield then Durham University. Previous job was deputy head of Glasgow Academy; has also been head of geography at Bradfield and Oakham. A neat man with an open face and the hint of a twinkle, he honed impressive cricketing and golfing skills, making it into national teams at schoolboy and university level. Out of school he still keeps his skills up to scratch, preferably on some windswept Scottish course more easily reached from his last job. His Australian start may have led to his love of travel and he rather endearingly admits to having used his geography classes as an excuse to bring out the holiday snaps.

Feeling that his first task on taking over was to thoroughly understand the school staff from groundsmen to departmental heads, he shed the suit and successfully donned the overalls. He was also pretty sharp over his pupil homework: one recent leaver was 'bowled over that he knew my name the first time he met me'. Described as an 'absolute legend' (a term more usually handed to brilliant steeplechasers), he plans to set this down-to-earth, country school firmly in the educational firmament, an approach that is steadily gaining appeal with local parents and is endorsed by his regular, witty, self-deprecating letters about life as a headmaster.

Married to Karen, a busy medic who tries hard to be on tap as much as possible; three children.

Academic matters: They work hard at the three Rs and it clearly pays off with GCSE results 42 per cent A*-A/9-7 in 2018. The results at A level also solid but not stellar, 41 per cent A*-A and 68 per cent A*-B. However, bright children feel sufficiently stretched: for some Oxbridge is a definite possibility not a dream and the remainder speak confidently about reaching the next step, whatever it may be.

The 60:40 boy:girl split may partly account for maths and science having tended to be the school's forte, and the new building for the former backs up the quality of the teaching. One sixth former said he was so well taught that he'd moved from a doubtful pass at GCSE to a predicted A* at A level. A concerted move to change this bias is in progress and parents report that arts-orientated children are flourishing.

All pupils take one or two languages at GCSE and a new outing to France takes place 'pour encourager les autres'. Latin is compulsory for the first two years and either this or classical civilisation is taken by 35 per cent at GCSE. Language numbers at A level are quite small (19 last year) but in a French oral class a valiant attempt to explain why the French are so French was being combined with politics in the shape of Marine Le Pen. BTec sport is a new option.

Screening for dyslexia takes place in the first and third years and again in the lower sixth. All teachers are aware if there is a problem and the nine per cent who need it have weekly one-to-one sessions. Strong encouragement to hand in original work and not to succumb to the temptation of Wikipaedia is given to pupils and parents. There is also a popular tutorial system ('they become friends when you're in the sixth form and even stay friends after you've left').

Across the board the staff training budget has been doubled and the slight tendency to have brilliant sportsmen/women who can teach a bit is being reversed by sourcing teachers who are also sporty.

Games, options, the arts: Famously strong at rugby, they don't just pay lip service to a wide range of other sports but are winning prizes, particularly at girls' hockey and cricket. As well as providing several club and county level players on the turf, they have even managed to switch surfaces and pull an international ice hockey player out of the bag. There are plenty of teams across the sporting spectrum for the less starry, who can also choose anything from yoga to rock-climbing or riding. The system works well, parents happily reporting that they 'run them ragged on the sports field'.

There are chances to give almost anything a go at the beginning: 'All schools say that they try and bring out your strengths, but here they really do it'. Saturday morning clubs, including options for the arty, sporty and those keen to fill academic gaps, are so popular – particularly the destruction and reconstruction of electronic or electrical objects – that parents are prepared to make sure day children don't miss out. 'He might even be able to mend the Hoover at the end of it so it's well worth the drive.'

Lots of takers for DofE, and the possibility of taking to the sky in a glider is a strong card for the CCF, with the added draw of yomping in the wilderness far from tidy, cultivated Hampshire.

Art is important, both visibly around the school ('he tends to claim any empty space,' said a teacher wryly) and because it is a favoured subject for exams as well as a good fun co-curricular activity.

The new teaching centre topped by a mirrored dance studio for zumba fans and Strictly wannabes is run by a head full of energy and ideas, attracting an increasing number of students from senior scholars to shy first termers. Choirs cater for all abilities, 'even the tone deaf are encouraged to give it a go', an admirable if slightly worrying thought. The practice rooms are full all week and the department head 'beams with pride', not only at the mastering of Scriabin but also at the squeaky rendering of an Abba tune.

The drama department is flat out all year round, tackling everything from Sheridan to Lloyd Webber, plus clubs, technical workshops and sorties into the outside world. The only negative is the lack of a dedicated auditorium, richly deserved, according to parents.

Boarding: Enormous flexibility is the key, a policy very popular with hard-working parents whose life is made easier by the ability of the school to scoop up their children when necessary, rescue only an email away. The eight boarding houses, one co-ed for the first two years, three for girls and four for boys, are run by multi-tasking houseparents. A rigorously enforced tracking system prevents chaos and assures parents that their offspring's whereabouts are known at all times.

Background and atmosphere: The century-long transformation from farming orphanage to present day public school began in 1912 with the bequest of Sydney Stern (the one and only Lord Wandsworth), a wealthy playboy turned Liberal politician. For the son of a Victorian banker buried in the Balls Pond Road it was rather an odd choice as a memorial, but due to the financial ability of the foundation trustees it turns out to have been a wise one. The school motto, 'perseverantia vincit', was taken most literally by the redoubtable Scot Sandy Henderson, headmaster from 1943-1968 (25 years of perseverance), who inspired the metamorphosis from agriculture to academics.

Still surrounded by the original farm, the school may have a rustic setting, but once through a surprisingly pompous, arched entrance there is a view of neat brick buildings and a shiny tarmac drive bordered by expectant playing fields. This is not a school with architectural pretensions, and one of the boarding houses was described as a 1960s disaster. However, a flight of fancy that one might have stumbled onto a low budget film set is swiftly squashed at the sight of lively teenagers purposefully swopping classrooms. No slacking here, as one day pupil put it; in fact the only negative point she could raise was how tired they were at the end of a packed day.

There is now a firm, securely financed, 10 year plan for change in place, including the completion of all brand new classrooms over the next five years as part of a concerted effort to modernise the school. Part of the regeneration, the new maths block – kitted out with wickedly clever whiteboards – and an assembly hall are finished, and the creaking science block is next on the agenda. The junior boarding house has girly curtains and rows of cuddly toys in the dormitories, and although the senior houses seem a little bland, long on new bath and shower rooms but low on cosy clutter and smelly socks, reliable information reveals that they can also look as if 'regularly burgled'. Maybe it's all squashed into the huge cupboards when the GSG comes round?

The head is determined to stop it being pigeonholed as a rugby crèche (all the fault of poor Jonny Wilkinson, who heads a list of high flying alumni so long that it seems as if LWC rugby has seen more dramatic conversions than the road to Damascus).

Pastoral care, well-being and discipline: One parent described the pastoral care as 'second to none', a claim backed up by ubiquitous signs in a boarding house reading 'I am available 24 hours a day, in or out of term'.

Hot on bullying in every form with notices everywhere, and all pupils have to carry a laminated card with examples on one side and how to get help on the reverse. Practical emails about cyber-bullying and internet dangers are sent to parents, giving detailed instructions that even confirmed Luddites can follow.

The rules don't come to parents as a surprise but are applied on a fair, case-by-case basis and not necessarily sticking entirely to the book. No outward evidence of teenage rebellion – these are not students likely to sport green hair or facial piercings. Some parents have a minor niggle that the younger ones can look pretty scruffy, particularly in comparison to the exceptionally tidy sixth formers.

A strong impression is created that most (not too wacky) ideas from the pupils will be seriously listened to, and that the head's statement 'their ideas and views are at the heart of the school development and planning' is no vain promise.

Pupils and parents: The distinction between day and boarding students is blurry as they seem to morph from one to the other pretty seamlessly, and lots of supposedly day pupils stay on to work or play long after the academic stuff is finished. Up to five per cent international students and the head plans to recruit more into the senior school. The Sternians' Association, with its deliberately rustic (covered in tractors) website, encourages parents to muck in and even make fools of themselves at the Santa Dash, a charity run started by the head.

Entrance: Almost all from prep schools including Yateley Manor, Eagle House, St Neot's and Hall Grove, with a few from local primaries. Selection at 11 through school's own tests in English, maths and reasoning, aiming to identify a bit above average pupils who will fit into this tight community. Thirteen plus candidates need 50 per cent at CE; mid-range GCSEs, a school report and an interview to join the sixth form. 'All along we are looking for pupils who will get stuck in and put their hand up.'

Exit: Some 30-40 per cent leave after GCSE to go to one of several excellent state sixth form colleges in Hampshire, usually for budget reasons. One medic in 2018; destinations included destinations include Exeter, Edinburgh, Bristol, Bath, Manchester and Leeds. Good next step communication with students, who say that the well-informed careers adviser 'will always find out if she doesn't know the answer'.

Money matters: Eight per cent of pupils are supported by The Foundation; means-tested awards restricted to British children who have lost the support of one or both parents through death, divorce or separation, and whose surviving parent (if there is one) has not formed a new relationship. The order of priority is: 'children who have an identifiable boarding need, the need for pastoral care and support, the need for stability and security in a structured environment, the candidate's home and family situation, the ability to cope academically, integrate socially and contribute to the college community, the family's financial circumstances'.

Remarks: Until recently a bit under the radar but worth watching this spot. An impressive head, smarter buildings, improving results and a firm set of values should encourage more potential parents to key this postcode into their sat navs.

L

Lord Williams's School

Oxford Road, Thame, Oxfordshire OX9 2AQ

Ages 11–18 **Pupils** 2,134 **Sixth form** 508

01844 210510
www.lordwilliams.oxon.sch.uk

Headteacher: Since 2005, David Wybron MA (50s). Read history followed by PGCE at Swansea University then taught in Cambridgeshire and Great Missenden, Bucks before joining LWS as head of humanities. Formerly deputy head of lower school then deputy head of school. A firm believer in mixed ability state education (regarding his own children's grammar school education: 'it wasn't for want of trying to get them in here – we were out of catchment') who sees his biggest challenge currently as navigating pupils successfully through the 'mess' the government has made of GCSEs. Is 'energised by the funding battle' and passionate about primary school links – chairs the Thame partnership with local primary schools and instigates partnership events such as science festivals with a focus on space. Still turns hand to teaching history GCSE and is heavily involved in DofE. 'There at the right times,' say parents; he's a 'clear leader' and 'seems in control'. Plays golf ('badly') and squeezes in the occasional half marathon when time allows. Serious, business-like demeanour. Lives in nearby Haddenham and is married with two adult children.

Retiring in July 2019.

Academic matters: Strong academics given head's assessment that school is 'a proper comprehensive'. Most take eight GCSEs – results in 2018 saw 76 per cent of students getting 9-4 in both maths and English, with 19 per cent of grades A*-A/9-7. At A level, 55 per cent were graded A*-B and 40 per cent A*/A. Wide range of subjects at both levels, plus options such as ASDAN to offer practical skills-based courses from year 9 to students not taking languages. Alternative packages also available at KS4 for those not choosing the academic route, eg TRAX, a motor mechanic qualification. Particular strengths in history and government and politics at both GCSE and A level. All take either French (the class we saw was being taught by a native – nous approuvons) or German in year 7 and can add another (usually Spanish) in year 9. No Latin. Setting in maths from year 7 as well as in languages from October half term. Sciences and English set from year 10 and, unusually, pupils also set for PE. Between 60 and 70 per cent of pupils stay on for sixth form, which is the largest in Oxfordshire, and are joined by students from other schools who are attracted by the size of the school and range of courses, which includes health and social care, psychology, sociology and media studies as well as all the usuals.

Strong faculty culture among staff, with a positive buzz around the staff room from teachers who seem genuinely happy to be there (and we are delighted to report that those we met had far better general knowledge than us, as demonstrated by their casual lunch time quiz). Many longstanding members of staff (we met one who had done a decade yet described himself as a 'newcomer'), peppered with some younger blood. 'There's a great sense of commitment to the school from staff', said one. 'Things just work here, because we expect them to'. Parents broadly happy with teaching with just a few grumbles about miscommunication of A level syllabuses and slightly 'non-adaptive' teaching styles for the eldest pupils in some departments. Pupils report that most teachers are happy to provide extra help and support outside of lessons and parents of pupils of all abilities – yes, even those who could have gone to grammar school – say that school 'exceeds expectations' on the academic front.

Weighty SEN department, with over 400 students on the register and 30 specialist teaching assistants. Two inviting classrooms, well equipped with computers and comfy areas (as well as Charlie, the therapy dog, whom we were thrilled to meet on our visit) serve as the learning support base. School 'proud' of its transition arrangements for pupils joining from year 6 – parents concur these are 'brilliant'. The 'pioneers programme' works with year 6 primary teachers to ensure pupils in need of extra support receive all the help they need when they arrive. This is augmented by a summer school, run by a mixture of school staff and sixth formers, to help newbies settle in. School has experience dealing with moderate dyslexia, dyspraxia and dyscalculia as well as partially sighted pupils, cerebral palsy, hearing impairment and pupils in wheelchairs (site is fairly flat and largely accessible). Pupils on the register have their own 'pupil passport', provided to every teacher so they are aware of their educational needs. Parents report communication to be frequent (face to face updates with pupil present every term) and regular updates home as and when appropriate. There's an onsite communication and interaction (autism) base with its own admissions process from where ASD pupils can access the main school timetable as appropriate for their individual needs. Crucially, there's also a 'more able' programme for high achievers with two dedicated co-ordinators who engineer masterclasses, special projects and attendance at special events outside of the curriculum, recently a STEM trip for year 9 girls.

Games, options, the arts: Formerly a sports academy and pupils say sporting offer remains 'great'. There's hockey, football (both sexes), rugby (tag for girls), cricket (school still the only state school to play an annual match with the MCC, to head's delight) and rounders, plus commitment to supporting minority sports such as swimming or riding. Two sessions of curriculum PE per week plus training at after-school clubs. Does everyone get a chance to play in a match? 'Definitely', we were assured by pupils, with staff adding, 'there's a lot of rotation', with inclusivity sometimes at the expense of competitive success. Not always the case with football, apparently, where school likes to play to win, say some parents. Strong fixtures list including matches with local independents although all are painfully aware of the clear difference in training when they come up against private schools. Happily, they still emerge victorious much of the time, however. Enviable space for sporting endeavours – acres of fields, plus three Astroturf pitches, an athletics track, rugby pitch and spin studio. Thame Leisure Centre adjoins the upper school site so pupils can also pop in there in their lunch hour and for year 7 swimming lessons.

Performing arts also popular and school holds Artsmark awards for these. There's a smart performance studio for concerts and plays. Dance praised by parents as 'really inclusive': clubs for all levels in every year group and a dance company by audition for those with more experience. It was great to see some older students (boys as well as girls) really enjoying a dance class in the studio when we visited. Major biennial whole school productions, recently Oliver!, see students both performing and stage managing the production. The GCSE artwork was on display at the time of our visit and we were impressed by the individuality of what we saw. Peripatetic music lessons are on a rotation scheme, but although the music facility was spacious and inviting, we didn't see much evidence of take-up – just a short list of classes on a fairly tatty notice board. Singer of the Year is an annual highlight, as is Gambia Night – LWS's take on Britain's Got Talent in aid of a sponsored school in Gambia. There's an orchestra and a few musical ensembles for older students, and we loved the sound of the non-selective choir which sings mainly popular songs from the likes of Ed Sheeran or Abba.

Mixed reviews of clubs depending on age groups. Younger pupils we met looked blank when we asked them what was on offer at lunchtimes. Homework club, anyone? After school, it's mainly sports training. Older students agreed that you had to 'sniff out' clubs in the lower school but that once you moved up to the upper school there were 'rich opportunities' to occupy their time. DofE 'a real strength,' says head, with 300 students participating at the time of our visit, 35 of whom were working towards their gold award. Head rolls up his sleeves and accompanies the troops on expeditions (which, on occasion, have been known to include students in wheelchairs), along with between 70 and 80 'really impressive' parent helpers. 'The school gives literally thousands of hours in voluntary service each year through DofE', says head. World Challenge displays school's breadth of vision, offering the chance for the older students to experience a trip to overseas destinations including India, Africa and Far East, to the envy of the parents. Special outdoor pursuits trips for vulnerable learners help build rapport with parents and increase attendance figures.

Background and atmosphere: Established in 1559 by Lord Williams of Thame, school still has connections with New College, Oxford. Portraits of former heads still gaze out from the walls of the older, upper school building and antique scholars' boards add a sense of heritage. History kept alive by an active alumnae association, The Old Tamensians, who meet annually on the founder's day weekend. School split over two sites, a couple of miles and approximately seven minutes by car apart – inconvenience or advantage? The jury's out: 'It's not such a shock when you move up from primary school,' say pupils, and parents we spoke to broadly see it as an advantage: with 300 pupils in a year group it makes sure nobody gets lost and also enables school to acknowledge the seniority of year 9s with prefectships in their last year at the lower site. Equally, the academic rigour really starts to build once pupils move up to the senior site, again seen as a positive 'new phase'. It is, however, a factor that very much dictates the school's daily running. Lessons are 65 minutes long each, with a 20 minute break between them to allow teachers to commute between sites. It's no issue for most families, many of whom cycle to school on the Phoenix Trail. School ends half an hour later twice a week to allow an extra lesson to be squeezed in after all those long breaks.

The two sites have entirely different vibes. The lower school is a typical 1960s low rise affair with a variety of add-ons from across the decades. No gleaming new showcase architecture; it's functionality all the way, albeit there's no lack of space and the wide, bright corridors are adorned with pupils' artwork, which gives it a lift. The upper site is set around a stately old schoolhouse surrounded by newer buildings, a bit like a university campus, and is lifted by a very swanky new science block – The Clark Building. We loved the sixth form library which, with its honours boards, was like a step back in time and reminder of school's long heritage. Smart new uniform introduced recently after student feedback via the school council that they 'wanted to look proper, like the grammar school'. So now blazers and ties have replaced the ubiquitous sweatshirts of yesteryear – and jolly smart they look too (although girls still able to choose own skirt within the 'pleated' category which is causing consternation amongst parents).

Pastoral care, well-being and discipline: Head describes pastoral aspect of school as 'a real strength' and parents and pupils we spoke to unanimously agreed. From day one there's an emphasis on a smooth transition from primary school for 'wobbly' joiners and throughout the school the Learning for Life programme covers aspects including cyberbullying and self harm as well as broadening horizons with talks about the Middle East or university applications. There's a weekly 'fast forward' meeting for staff from every year group with the head of year, senior teachers, SENCo and school counsellor in attendance, to pick up any new or ongoing issues and action them as fast as possible. Pupils say 'there are so many people to talk to' if problems arise and they're 'fantastic' – the pastoral support office has an open door policy during school hours and pupils said that when bullying occurs, school is 'very good' at dealing with it, parents adding that pupils aren't afraid to speak out. Supportive culture is driven by tutor groups; students are in the same tutor group for years 7 to 9 and possibly for the rest of their time at the school, depending on tutor's location. 'We all grow up together', said one happy pupil.

Parents and pupils both love school sending home postcards congratulating them for outstanding work – one parent told us that the deputy head had emailed when her daughter had done especially well in exams. Staff seemed to genuinely care for pupil body; we visited during the GCSE period and witnessed a teacher deal with an anxious pupil in a highly empathetic and gentle manner that we wouldn't have expected in a school with over 2,000 students. 'Behaviour is strong', according to head. There's a good warning system and few exclusions – 'although we will exclude if it's merited,' says head – he has recently had to exercise this for minor drugs offences. Pupils report that disruption in class, although occasionally 'massive' is dealt with well in the main, and 'that's real life', say parents. Poor behaviour, after a series of warnings and detentions, could incur a day in the 'isolation unit'. A group for young carers provides support for around 30 students, taking them on special trips eg Chessington in the summer and a panto at Christmas: 'you always have friends here,' one member told us: 'if you need support, you'll get it'. Diversity embraced: 'if two girls are walking around holding hands, nobody bats an eyelid,' said head. With less than five per cent of cohort non-British Caucasian, we were impressed to see special arrangements being made for a student to have access to a room for prayer during Ramadan.

Pupils and parents: Reflective of the local community in that social backgrounds are varied: some middle class, some from estates. Statistically lower than average numbers on pupil premium. Students we met were extremely likeable, articulate and bright. Many parents are former pupils. Head says that some parents who could have chosen a grammar school for their child still choose LWS; 'it really narks when they say they'll send them here if they fail the 11+', he says. The Resource Base means that there are higher than usual numbers of pupils on the SEN register. New parents encouraged to join the Lord Williams's Association and to get to know one another and senior staff at the meetings.

Entrance: Non-selective. Oversubscribed from local primary schools within Thame and Chinnor, as well as applicants from Buckinghamshire over the county border. The Resource Base is filled by students with statements and by referral. New sixth form entrants (still non-selective) arrive from a range of state and independent schools.

Exit: Between 60 and 70 per cent stay on to sixth form each year. Others leave for FE college or apprenticeships. Around two-thirds of sixth form leavers go into higher education, about a quarter of these to Russell Group. One to Oxford in 2018 – 'we're working on making it less of a lottery,' says head – plus one medic and two vets.

Good careers provision starts in year 10 with work placements for all students, co-ordinated by dedicated careers advisor, and there's Future Fest, where a variety of regional companies and organisations come to school. The relationship with New College, Oxford is put to good use with career-focused visits and workshops.

Money matters: School 'very honest', say parents, about the shortfall in funding and has a donation scheme to encourage families that can afford it to give what they can on a monthly basis.

Remarks: Considering its financial boundaries, Lord Bill's does 'a magnificent job' with pupils from all backgrounds and of all abilities, with parents uniformly telling us it 'brings out the best' in their children. Yes, the pupil body is enormous, but in the words of one happy parent: 'in a school of that size, you can always find a friend who's just like you, no matter what you're like'. Silver linings.

Ludgrove

Wokingham, Berkshire RG40 3AB

Ages 8–13 **Pupils** 185 **Boarders** All full

Fees: £27,450 pa

01189 789881
www.ludgrove.net

Headmaster: Since 2008, Simon Barber BA (40s) following six years as a teacher here and, before that, at Ashdown House. Mr Barber, who grew up here (and has fond memories of watching cows being milked in what is now the art and carpentry block), completed teacher training at robust state school Cranford Community College with aplomb, tweed jacket and Eton education no barrier to pupil acceptance – when asked where he was at school 'I said, "down the road, just south of Slough".' Spell teaching geography at LVS Ascot was followed by short digression 'as junior squit' in corporate finance – quickly realised not for him.

Headship shared until 2013 when joint incumbent moved on to school of his own. After initial parental nerviness, Barbers now universally reckoned to be bit of all right, having grown into role. Mr Barber teaches Latin, PSHE and Greek myths – 'so important, you can see their little minds buzz.' He's nice but strict if necessary, thought pupil – 'if people are talking after lights out.'

Mrs Barber ('Sophie' to all) sorts domestics – 'kitchens, matrons, nurse, cleaners' – as well as being first point of contact 'for mothers' worries' and prepping boys for first phone calls home. '[Mr Barber] likes children, enjoys their company and knows how to make them feel good about themselves,' said one parent. 'As a team, they are superb,' agreed another.

Barbers' immersion in school life is almost total (though Mrs Barber does get short daily break to collect youngest child – they have two daughters and a son – from local school). Instead of separate house have own (though separate) quarters in the main building, but appear miraculously claustrophobia-free. Mr Barber, in particular, can go for days without leaving the building. 'I love walking round the school and thinking about creating an environment that is fun, safe and full of opportunities,' he says.

Entrance: Takes 30 in year 4 when it's completely non-selective – unless you count speed of registration as competitive sport.

L

'Don't believe in testing boys at 8,' says school. After initial enquiry (at birth) parents receive letter from head (handwritten) with registration form (printed). Two years before joining, there's a fun day for boys with confirmed places, followed by final make-your-mind-up time.

For occasional places (around eight in year 5, four in year 6 and even a couple in year 7 – generous bursary scheme helps bright boys fill gap between state primary and common entrance), hopefuls sit English and maths tests 'to be sure they can slot in easily.' Duvet changing and tie-knotting practice before start of first term also urged.

No official feeders, but road here well trodden by families moulded in traditional cast (plenty of second generation pupils or better). Around 40 per cent from well-connected pre-preps (Finton House, Thomas's Fulham, Eaton House, Knightsbridge and Broomwood Hall in London, Pinewood and Farleigh outside), many escaping competitive inferno of London school entrance.

Around half of places to country dwellers, most within two-hour commute (Wiltshire, Hampshire, Berkshire, Northants). A few from further away (East Anglia, Scotland). Remaining 10 per cent overseas, split about equally between expats (FO, MOD) and international pupils from all over – India, Thailand, Ukraine, Russia, Spain, China, Nigeria, Korea. A few arrive for year's immersion in penultimate year then head for home. DBS-cleared drivers (ideally same one both ways) on tap to do the airport run.

Exit: Given diverse input, rightly proud of output – reckon to get around three-quarters, sometimes more, into Eton, Harrow and Radley. Mr Barber's expert knowledge of all four won't mean special treatment at CE, though word dropped in admission tutor's shell-like can't go amiss if results an unexpected disaster. Others to eg Winchester, Marlborough, Tonbridge, Charterhouse, Wellington and Sherborne. Six scholarships in 2018, including one each to Eton and Radley and two art scholarships to Marlborough.

Best-known OBs are Prince William, Prince Harry and Bear Grylls (who recently waxed lyrical about his experiences in print). Very occasionally head may suggest specialist school. One dyslexic pupil has recently gone to Bruern Abbey, though 'welcome back at any time,' says Mr Barber.

Remarks: Mood is determinedly upbeat...'a belief that one should always look on the bright side of life,' says prospectus and reflection of Mr Barber's philosophy. May not sing the Monty Python song but lives it. 'The eternal optimist,' says Mrs Barber.

So at their best, teams 'are a match for anyone.' School trips – a range, from Devon (leavers and geographers) to Sauze D'Oulx (skiers) – return having learned that 'a sense of humour can see you through most tricky situations'. Torrential rain makes sports day 'a memorable occasion.' Breakages in Roman-themed pottery session 'added to the authenticity.' Boys ward off looming homesickness by 'thinking of funny things and looking forward to the next lunch,' said one.

Upbeat approach translates into academics. Teachers are 'amazing,' say parents, talking round subjects and knowing their pupils. 'They work you hard but within your ability,' thought pupil. 'I wasn't clever when I arrived – now I am.' 'Never gave up on my son...and he flew,' said parent.

Small classes (average 12, maximum 15, minimum eight) undoubtedly help. So does overall staff to pupil ratio of just under one to seven (and that's not including the nurse and six matrons; all live-in). Streaming in English and maths from the beginning, lessons lively – new boys attacking Venn diagram in geography with enthusiasm; ditto 11 year olds discussing perils of 16th century religious affiliation. (Can read on in cheerful, traditional library, popular titles enticingly face up in long rows, pupils trained in old-fashioned referencing using real encyclopaedias.)

Boys go through order papers with division master (form tutor) so clear on how to improve. Ups and downs caused by small class sizes and narrow range of marks (can shoot from second to eighth place) can cause occasional jitters among success-focused parents who need lots of reassurance. 'Boys pick up on their hopes and fears,' says Mr Barber. While coming top is well and good, the message that endeavour counts is received loud and clear. 'Trying hard is better,' said top year boy firmly. Workload in and out of lessons bearable, adjusted if necessary. No shame in saying you're struggling – teachers will set less and help with catch up, thought boys.

Individual excellence (good work) commended by head and rewarded with sweets. Plus marks also awarded, best performing house rewarded with special (and, needless to say, 'delicious') tea. The naughty get minus marks – occasional detentions. Boarding runs its own rewards system, giving angels, however dirty their downstairs wings, a second chance at redemption

Parents get emails summarising life in and out of the classroom and can phone child's class during a 40 minute slot at lunchtime to speak to son. Resulting free-for-all generally works (a bit of muttering about parents who go beyond allotted five minutes) though substantial redialling sometimes required. Alternative – giving boys mobile phones – felt by all to be far worse. Some – 'particularly sweet boys who want to make sure their parents are all right,' said mother – also send emails.

Daily staff meetings, attended by boarding nurse, ensure whole-school awareness of any issues. Wobbles impressively dealt with. 'Support without throttling,' said parent. 'Nurtured from the start but guided towards independence as they get older.'

Solid assistance for pupils with learning needs – around 30 or so in the school – includes academic support (booster groups for spelling, maths, reading) as well as help with handwriting, one-to-one EAL lessons and esteem and confidence-building sessions – we liked King of the Shelves award for better organisation skills. Four specialist teachers develop programmes for pupils with more complex needs – speech and language or specific learning difficulties – and ensure that subject teachers know how to implement it. 'Have been called a rottweiler,' says jolly but firm head of learning support. Younger pupils have support sessions during art, drama and music while older pupils can opt to miss occasional rest period or break so don't lose out on favourite subject.

Merely mastering school's year group numbering system must be considerable source of pride. 'Sixes are year 4; fours year 5, threes year 6, twos year 7 and top year is year 8,' says school handbook. And those missing fives? 'Not a year group but a game with a small ball and leather gloves,' it adds, helpfully.

Uniform options similarly quirky. In addition to giddy whirl of jacket choices (a tweed spotter's dream), school jumpers offered not just in navy, but rather more exotic pink and green, adding welcome flash of colour to massed gatherings.

Great outdoors spread over 130 acres includes usual playing fields as well as nine-hole golf course and plenty of space for building camps. Every parent commented approvingly on boys being out in all weathers. 'All is underlined and bold and caps,' said one. Sports rampant and not just for current pupils, either. Most recent alumni calendar featured five matches and just one drinks party.

However, quantity doled out can be varied to taste. Everyone, talented or otherwise, gets shot at glory of minibus trip and match tea. How much glory is a tad confusing to decipher, what with online match reports dating back to 2013 with tendency to linger on the glories of game well played rather than the score.

Deadline for posting team lists is 7.00pm the night before, seemed a bit tight in giving parents sufficient time to change all arrangements and rush up to watch their son score the winning try/goal/run – but felt largely to work as most teams, once settled, there for the duration. Parents in broad agreement, biggest issue we encountered relating to yawning gap between the keen and talented – who get lion's share of training and interest – and keen but less so, who don't and can be completely overlooked. More matches on the cards for every shade of ability, says school, while swimming notable for squad training that's open to all.

The less athletic joyfully opt for extra art, pottery or, top favourite, carpentry/DT, where Portuguese fishing dinghy, owl nesting box as well as enough chairs and tables to equip several classrooms are among impressive projects to have helped school to several DT scholarships in recent years.

Music busy, with choirs, open access music block, numerous ensembles and vast majority (85 per cent) playing at least one instrument (bagpipes, tuba and bassoon adding interesting new timbre to conventional choices). Not as busy as drama, however, now in impressive new theatre (none of that 'performing arts centre' nonsense here...) where according to prospectus, boys 'have been on stage non-stop...' Crumbs. Our visit clearly took place during one of brief periods of non-occupancy. (Drama teacher was having lunch at the time, explained school later, keen to ensure nobody got the wrong end of the stick, and theatre 'has had a tremendous impact on provision of music and drama'.) No wonder exeats billed as a time to relax. Happen every fortnight, so not too punishing for the youngest recruits.

Attractive 19th century building was purpose-built as school and it shows. Dorms, all south-facing with attractive big windows and same gorgeous view over greenery as from head's study but a floor up, hold four to 10 pupils from single year group, some in bunk beds, each with top year monitor, honoured with different coloured laundry basket (vibrant pink in one case). Every pillow adorned with loved, often dilapidated soft toy, resident seamstress ('crucially important,' says Mrs Barber) on hand to work miracles when teddies' arms come adrift or eyes go missing – 'upsetting but it's the smell they like...' Matrons much praised. 'Never shout if you do something wrong,' said pupil. 'Say it doesn't matter, don't worry.' Occasional accidents sensitively sorted – boys squeeze matron's arm when woken up, signal for sheets to be unobtrusively washed and replaced.

Dedicated maintenance posse roams school, killing at least 99.9 per cent of all known germs dead and rounding up errant possessions. Basins, loos, baths in communal washroom all radiant; boys' clothes and towels a tribute to precision folding, cloakroom a thing of wonder, coats and shoes lined up as if on parade – a daily, 90 minute task undertaken with pride.

Not a job for the boys, though perhaps it should be, joining list of well-organised activities carefully balanced to ensure that everyone is just busy enough and thus avoiding too much time for introspection, particularly for newbies (who have dedicated matron and allocated 'shadow' to help them settle in), but ensuring 'can flop if they want to,' says school.

Saturday is the faster-paced weekend day, with lessons till lunch, matches afterwards followed by free time, film screenings and a spot of X-Factor if in season. Sunday has fixed slots: chapel and assembly to announce the day's happenings. Otherwise less structure, with activity staples (swimming, art, films) and specials (visiting climbing wall, circus workshop and – occasionally – ice cream van) but also potential for spontaneity – boys will organise own games of cricket, five-a-side football or make camps. Less official dorm raids and stair run (down one, up the other at night without being caught) also happen but 'I know nothing about it...' says Mr Barber.

For youngest, there's comfort zone story time with Mrs Barber, 'special half hour when they're piled like puppies on the sofas and all over the floor.' Tuck, in the form of sweets, isn't allowed. Instead, school suggests packing 'useful and fun' – but inedible – items such as bluetac, string, stickers and playing cards.

School-supplied treats appeared attractive replacements for missing goodies, particularly birthday ice cream cake with choice of five flavours, multi-coloured remnants being solemnly enjoyed by small break time group on day of visit. Similarly colourful foodfests celebrate pupil nationalities (Ireland with mandarin, whipped cream and lime jelly...). Match teas a more restrained mix of sandwiches and cakes (parents) with doughnuts, crisps and juice for boys. Pupil committee gets unpopular dishes pulled and replaced (fish pie with scampi).

Other trad preps can feel as if saturated in own past. Here, though pride in history is evident, it's not overwhelming, with few pictures of ancient OBs. Instead, names of new boys are added to the honours board within a few weeks of start of first term – simple but effective way of generating pride and self-confidence and looking ahead.

'You've got to look at what you're doing – and how to do it better,' says Mr Barber. 'It's amazing,' said one parent. 'The camaraderie amongst the boys is one of the key things and they leave with lifelong friends. I couldn't fault it at all.'

LVS Ascot (Licensed Victuallers' School)

London Road, Ascot, Berkshire SL5 8DR

Ages 4–18 **Pupils** 822 **Sixth form** 169 **Boarders** 190 (from 7 years)

Fees: Day £9,990 – £17,907 pa; Boarding £25,566 – £31,464 pa

01344 882770
www.lvs.ascot.sch.uk

Headmistress: Since 2010, Christine Cunniffe BA MMus MBA. After university, had close brush with the law (professionally speaking, that is), securing postgraduate traineeship with Slough-based legal practice only to succumb to alternative role as pianist to fashionistas and London high society (think white baby grands and late nights in plush hotels). Four years later, she put aside renewed yearnings for law when husband-to-be pointed out years of study ahead and tried her hand at teaching instead. Loved it from the off, going straight in as head of music, first at a Stevenage school, then St Bernard's, a selective co-ed grammar school in Slough. Joined LVS Ascot as ambitious director of music in 2003 (school, which had no choir when she arrived, was performing Vivaldi's Gloria at Eton College Chapel just two terms later).

Personable, laid-back and quietly assured, she has an unusual (if not unprecedented) openness for a head, which she feels sends useful message to pupils. 'If I have self-doubt, I admit it – children are going to face problems in life, so why pretend it doesn't happen?' Lives on site with her husband and youngest child, who attends the school (the two older ones have now left for uni) – all three regularly feature in conversations. 'I am very honest about my experiences of parenting; I want parents to know I understand I know what they're going through.'

She's clearly nailed it, with parents describing her as 'empathetic' and 'understanding.' All parents are given her email address and she doesn't shy away from criticism. Runs the parent staff choir, 'which is tremendously good fun and a good way to encourage bonding.' 'There's no superiority about her – she doesn't swoop in with the, "I'm the principal" look,' one parent told us, while others point to her strategic prowess:

L

'She knows her stuff and is very strong on where she wants the school to go.' Pupils keen – juniors practically hugged her when they saw her – but some seniors told us they rarely see her except at assemblies. Doesn't have time to teach, she says, but steps in when needed. Is something of a TV celeb in the headteacher world, regularly appearing on programmes such as ITV's This Morning to debate topics ranging from back to school stress to whether there should be homework in the holidays ('yes, definitely – a little each day is no bad thing').

Academic matters: Non-selective, but no easy ride – 'we think like a grammar school and that means knowing when to put the pressure on and turn it off to get the best results.' Expect multiple retakes, for example, if your child gets lower than their predicted grades in their mocks. But it's no hothouse, say parents – 'children generally reach their potential happily and the school seems to know the best way to respond to each child.'

Mission in junior school is to ensure that no child is left to languish in educational no man's land; regular meetings picking out those 'falling below or zooming ahead'. Favourite subjects among pupils include literacy (popular library-based reading scheme, which carries on into main school, tests comprehension rather than merely rewarding headlong dash for the last page) and science in year 6 – where, joy of joys, 'you get to light the Bunsen burner'.

There's a pick and mix approach to national curriculum – used or modified where it works, ditched if it doesn't – and everything is seasoned with welcome dash of carpe diem flexibility so teachers can go off piste if it's deemed appropriate. Subject specialist teachers in most subjects from year 5. Setting in maths and English from year 3 and science from year 7. Class sizes average at 13-15, with a maximum of 20.

Children's progress is well ahead of national averages and exam results are good for a non-selective school, let alone for one so large. In 2018, 24 per cent A*-A/9-7 at GCSE. Nine or 10 the norm, selected from around 20 subjects – no Latin or classics, but there is law, psychology, PE and media/business studies – and RS recently changed to philosophy. Wide range of BTechs are popular. Everyone has to take at least two sciences, but languages (students choose two from French, Spanish and German from year 7) are not.

Around 65 per cent stay on to sixth form – more than in the past, no doubt partly due to jazzy new sixth-form block with swish study areas that top businesses would be proud of and 30 wide-ranging courses, including law and psychology. In 2018, 39 per cent A*-B and 13 per cent A*/A grades.

Scholars programme run by vice principal for the gifted and talented. Those with SEN on the rise – 'as long as they only need a maximum of one hour of additional help each week in addition to in-classroom support, that's fine; any more than that and they'd struggle to keep up with the curriculum,' says head. 'The school doesn't pretend they have all the answers, but they're willing to try new things and are incredibly open,' said one parent with a child with more complex problems.

Games, options, the arts: School's sports philosophy is that there's something for everyone – 'we are not all about boys' rugby and girls' netball; in fact a popular sport at the moment is boys' hockey, great for boys who are less keen on contact sports,' says head. Team sports are favoured, though, and compulsory for all, including sixth formers – 'what we want is for them to leave here with a love of sport for life, not give up on those who aren't the very best.' Inevitably, there are moans and groans – 'you do see kids who stand on the side with their arms crossed, but most are keen,' one parent told us.

Cracking facilities including two games halls, the larger with climbing wall and cricket nets, the smaller with cushioned floor for happier landings in judo and high impact sports. Enticing heated pool is well used, offering all-ability training at 6.30am three times a week, while thumping pop music makes well-equipped fitness suite even more inviting for youngsters. Elite golf academy for sixth formers, which combines coaching at a nearby club with a BTec in sports science. Plenty of wins against other schools in rugby, football, netball and hockey; school also competes in athletics and swimming.

Drama a joy, with every parent we spoke to praising the slick performances – 'it's lovely to see the ones who get stuck into lighting or directing praised just as much as the performers,' said one. Plenty of signs of artistic talent and spacious studios to work in. Music (as you might expect, given the head's background), is strong, with three choirs, numerous ensembles including rock school and jazz band, and around a third of pupils learning instruments, some to diploma standard. Whizzy music tech studio adored by students, a couple of whom were enjoying a working lunch in the recording studio when we visited.

Boarding: Boarding houses are homely, yet practical, with plenty of leather seating and welcoming photos in the spacious communal areas, while the comfy carpeted dorms sleep between one and five. 'I came to England two years ago and settled so much quicker than I thought – they make it so easy,' one student told us. Experienced boarding house staff are experts at sidestepping homesickness and are enthusiastic, friendly and forward-looking (one recently introduced the digital Reach system that means staff and parents can keep tabs on students at all times).

Keeping idle hands (and brains) busy is the priority, with a steady but not relentless stream of activities. After school, it's free time from 4pm-5.50pm (usually a club or, for year 9s up, going into Ascot), then dinner, prep and finally an hour more free time before winding down for bed at 9.30pm. Weekend minibuses, booked by the hour, swap returning sports teams for boarders off on assorted excursions (shopping, cinema, bowling, walking in Windsor Great Park, go karting and paintballing all popular, with some trips further afield to eg Portsmouth) with departures and arrivals as precisely coordinated as flight control at Heathrow. Laminated sheets stating 'This dorm is too untidy to be cleaned,' spotted in pile on the side, are mercifully rarely needed, say staff.

Polite reminders in the common rooms for international students to speak in English – a world map on the wall reveals the vast breadth of countries they all come from. In fact, the large international contingent helps explain why most boarders are full time, but increasingly flexible options are available – and day pupils can also cross to other side by signing up for occasional one-off boarding sessions. 'Out of the nearly 200 boarders, around 120 are here any one weekend,' one housemaster told us.

'If you want the manor house boarding experience, this isn't for you, but people need to see past the buildings to see the phenomenal time they have here,' one parent told us. 'In my son's boarding house, they have such a great mix of international students, kids from brewery trade, from the military and families who are just minted – and in true LVS style, they keep them all completely equal.'

Background and atmosphere: Site was formerly home to Heatherdown, an ultra-traditional prep school for chaps and David Cameron's pre-Eton alma mater, with own miniature steam railway. It was demolished in 1982 after Licensed Trade Charity (LTC) – which was founded 200 years ago to support drinks trade employees and now runs school – made such an advantageous sale of previous premises in Slough to well-known supermarket chain that could fund construction of what prospectus claims is the 'most modern boarding school in the UK'.

And although the thoughtful layout of 80s red-brick buildings may no longer be the cutting edge of school design, it still manages to look surprisingly contemporary and the fundamentals still apply, noticeably the way space-intensive subjects like performing arts get the room they need in central location rather than being consigned to outer reaches of site, while related subjects are housed together making navigation a breeze. The whole place has a small university campus feel, with a rolling refurb programme ensuring facilities stay up-to-the-minute. Massive recent investment in new dining room to provide restaurant standard space, complete with booth seating and natural lighting, where everyone eats together. Sports department has also had a complete face lift. Outside, there's 25 acres of grounds with oodles of sports grounds and rustic bridge spanning small but perfectly formed lake.

Junior school is vibrant and colourful, with good-sized infants' play area with buddy bench (hardly used, though, say pupils, because nobody gets lonely) and lots of sturdy wooden equipment to climb and balance on. Year 3s and up enjoy scaled up versions in adjoining area, separated by unmarked but universally recognised boundary line. Reception also has smart outdoor classroom and cheerful playhouse, starting point for innumerable let's pretend games.

Atmosphere throughout is surprisingly laid-back, despite the hard work – no mean feat. Youngsters are encouraged to ask questions and thought processes, and lesson bell abolished after it broke five years ago, ending mid-sentence rush for the door and making teachers so happy that was never reintroduced.

School houses, originally named after major drinks brands such as Guinness and Carlsberg, were in process of changing when we visited – 'It was a nice link to LTC, but would you call houses after cigarettes? Anyway, some of the breweries don't exist anymore anyway,' explains head.

L

Added flexibility with extended day, including meal and the run of learning resource centre, popular with working parents.

Pastoral care, well-being and discipline: Highly regarded pastoral focus is a tutor group system, with same teacher responsible for child's well-being throughout school career. 'I've been blown away by the quality of individual care,' said one parent, while another points to the way 'they hand out so many awards in assemblies – and it's not just the predictably clever ones.' Students say reformed Horrid Henrys stand as much chance as card-carrying Perfect Peters of getting their day in the sun.

Head's own experiences make her sympathetic to late developers. 'I experienced problems at about 13 and it's made me passionate about not giving up on a child until we have exhausted all areas.' She believes some children 'need to test boundaries, but they also know the security of knowing those boundaries don't shift.' Usual hierarchy of detentions, Saturday morning ones being the worst – and if that doesn't do the trick, the student is sent home and brought back in only on contract. 'I don't think twice about asking students to leave for anything such as misuse of social media or bringing alcohol on site, where a second chance is not warranted, although I've only ever had to do it three or four times,' says head.

School brings dogs in two or three times a year for random drugs checks, but nothing has ever been found – 'the kids actually love it when they see the dogs,' laughs head. Zero tolerance to bullying – 'I was bullied as a child and take a very firm line. Thankfully, the students are real heroes when it comes to reporting any unkindness.' Asked if they knew of anyone with eating disorders or who had self-harmed or been bullied, one student said, 'I personally don't know of anyone, but I'm not stupid enough to think that means it doesn't happen because it can happen anywhere' – suggests it's not just the staff that lack complacency. Students said they'd like to see more consistency among teachers, with regards to sanctions – 'you do get much stricter teachers than others,' said one.

Pupils and parents: A friendly, un-showy and straightforward bunch, pupils are thoughtful rather than introspective, articulate but not glib, and fond of school without the kind of gushing that makes us suspicious. Start of term, said one, 'feels like you're going home rather than just going back.' Families have historically covered socially and economically broad spectrum from royalty to socially deprived, although there's been a noticeable shift towards more 4x4s lately, suggesting greater affluence.

Catchment area extends 15-20 mile radius or so to Reading in west and Maidenhead up north, compass points ably covered by seven school bus routes (some oversubscribed, so worth checking). That said, families from London fringes and deepest Berks and Bucks are on the rise. These 'locals' form large proportion of the clientele and, while job mobility means some degree of coming and going each year, there's not as much as you might suppose. Some expat families, mainly in Forces, and there's a fast-growing international component. Alumni include Holly Tucker, co-founder of Not on the High Street, Simon Cowell and Tracey Ullman.

Entrance: Most children arrive at junior school in reception (single form to year 2) or year 3 (two forms to year 5). At 11+ majority from school's own junior department with assorted state and private schools supplying the rest. Around 35 places become available at sixth-form; students will need GCSE grade 6 or better in chosen subjects though vocational courses such as ICT and sport also available for those of a more practical mindset.

Exit: Up to half leave after GCSEs. Nearly 90 per cent of sixth formers to university, with courses ranging from the solidly academic – philosophy, business and maths currently popular – to the more vocational, including sports studies, film production and nursing. Remainder enter a variety of apprenticeship schemes and jobs. Massive breadth of 33 universities, roughly 20 per cent Russell Group, with largest numbers currently to London, Surrey and Winchester.

Money matters: Ten per cent discount for siblings (only third child onwards, but discount applies even if first or second subsequently leave), 15 per cent off for MOD and diplomatic service employees, including five per cent early payment discount and a 20 per cent reduction for anyone who has worked in the licensed drinks trade for five years or more.

Scholarships – academic, music, art, drama and sport – all worth up to 50 per cent off fees. School tries to keep budgeting simple with many senior school clubs and activities included in the fees – rowing, riding, sailing and ballet plus individual instrumental lessons and one-to-one language or learning support are the main extras. Means headline fees are just that, with minimum of extras, although brace yourself for the big school trips to the likes of South Africa and Brazil – but again head tries to keep these to a minimum and plans them at least a year ahead so you can dust off your piggy bank.

Read terms and conditions carefully: has unusual policy of retaining acceptance deposits, plus payment for bus transport for the next term, if pupils decide to leave the school, even when a term's notice is given. Only exceptions are if the child leaves at end of year 6, year 11 or year 13.

Remarks: Families are attracted to the all-through co-education in this well-equipped, welcoming and unpretentious school. We particularly like the university campus style, modern layout and the fact that non-selectivity is seen as the starting point for success rather than a justification for its absence. The strong results prove it works.

Magdalen College School

174

Cowley Place, Oxford, Oxfordshire OX4 1DZ

Ages 7–18 **Pupils** 904 **Sixth form** 309 (96 girls) **C of E**

Fees: £17,130 – £17,784 pa

01865 242191
www.mcsoxford.org

Master: Since 2016, Helen Pike MA (40s). Previously head of South Hampstead High. Born in Preston, state educated and was first in her family to go to university. After studying modern history at Christ Church, Oxford she looked set for an academic career, but teaching claimed her for its own while she was on a masters scholarship at Ann Arbor, University of Michigan. After a short stint lecturing at the University of Warwick she went first to Westminster School where she taught history, thence to City of London Boys (dep head of sixth form), St Paul's where she was head of politics, and RGS Guildford (deputy head). That's a high-octane progression through some of the country's most academically demanding schools.

Credits 'inspirational' history and English A level teachers at her sixth form college and says she was torn between these subjects when deciding what to study at university. History won, but she also took a masters (yes, this master has three masters degrees) in creative writing at Birkbeck and in 2011 published a novel, The Harlot's Press, about a female printer in early 19th century London. Says her creative energies are currently deployed in speech writing but could well return to fiction when time allows.

Some may have been concerned that the appointment of a woman as master would change the character of the school or spell the end for one or two of its benign and much-loved eccentricities (and eccentrics). They needn't have worried. Staff traditionally put on a mini Christmas panto at the end of term and several pupils mentioned how brilliant it was when the master unexpectedly burst into song. Parents seem pretty positive, 'approachable' seemed to be their adjective of choice, 'I feel I could go in and speak to her if necessary'.

Razor sharp, opinionated (we love heads who tell it like it is), with a keen sense of humour and of the absurd. Not an iconoclast – she is a historian after all – she describes the school as 'conservative with a small c', adding, 'we have a very settled culture of expectation and we know what we're doing.' Her modus operandi is to 'analyse carefully and be bold' and now that the latest building project is finished she is gearing up for a huge drive for bursaries. When she describes herself as 'messianic about the transformative power of education', you know she really means it.

Almost uniquely among the senior school heads we've met, most of whom say regretfully that they simply don't have time to do any formal teaching, she has timetabled lessons with A level historians, introducing lower sixth pupils to political thinkers from Hobbes to Marx. She keeps an open-door policy for all pupils and meets regularly with prefects and sixth form girls (one of whom described her as 'a blast'). Her partner is Professor George Garnett, the sometime senior proctor at Oxford, and she has three stepchildren, two of whom studied at MCS. She's a keen runner and recently completed the Oxford half marathon. Favourite book when growing up was Jane Eyre: 'all of Charlotte Bronte's novels are about education in some form or another.'

We found the master delightful company, wearing a historic role respectfully, but with a colourful flash of her own stylish insouciance. It's hard to imagine her being fazed by anyone or anything, but she says she is 'in awe' of the multiple talents of her staff, describing the MCS common room as 'the best.' It seems to us that she has found her people.

Head of junior school: since 2012, Tim Skipwith, previously head of the middle school (years 9-11), a biology teacher who has been at the school for over a decade. He is 'a wonderful guide for parents on the 11+ process' and reputedly very hot on pastoral issues.

Academic matters: Not much scope for subject by subject analysis when it comes to exam results. Even for such an academically selective school they're seriously impressive: 96 per cent A*-A/9-7 at I/GCSE in 2018 and 84 per cent A*/A at A level. The boys who join at 11 are by definition able but according to the master, 'we make them cleverer' (a claim backed up by 'statistically significant value-added data').

The challenge at I/GCSE is to 'keep the boys' interest' and make the curriculum 'less sloggy'. All do 10 subjects including three separate sciences and a modern foreign language (French, Spanish or German). Greek, Latin and computing are also options, as are art and music (no drama or DT). Twenty A level subjects offered in the sixth form, that's only four more than at I/GCSE, the newbies being politics, philosophy, economics and further maths. Pre-U for English, history, French, German and Spanish. School very much not at home to 'ologies', as the rather crisp comment on the website makes clear: 'Subjects which might count against an applicant to top universities are generally avoided.' Parents tell us that pupils are advised to 'choose A level subjects they really enjoy' rather than the ones that fit a particular mould, but then again, they can't go far wrong with what's on offer. Maths and further maths are overwhelmingly the most popular choices, followed by sciences, economics, English and history.

M

All study at least four A level subjects in the lower sixth and around half continue with four (or more) throughout. In addition, all lower sixth pupils undertake a personal research project known as Waynflete Studies – a bit like the EPQ but with extra added Oxford. Pupils choose a topic in consultation with teachers and attend lectures and seminars; they are then matched with an academic from the university for paired or individual tutorials. The programme culminates in the Waynflete Studies evening at which pupils present their research to fellow students, staff and parents. Projects are marked internally and then go before an external panel who choose the winners for each subject category. This is an invaluable, not to say unique opportunity for pupils to enhance their subject knowledge and fantastic preparation for university interviews – it must surely have a bearing on MCS's consistently impressive Oxbridge success rate.

We sat in on lessons: first was sixth form politics where different voting systems were being investigated. Two pupils presented their research to the rest of the class, answering questions and explaining complex details – all very serious. Then, by way of contrast, it was second year (year 8) Latin where a large class, most dressed in hockey kit, rattled off nominative, accusative and gerunds with enthusiasm. No call here for the gentle narratives of the Cambridge Latin Course: this was old school, verb learning, Kennedy's Latin Primer territory – and the boys were loving it. Pretty impressive, especially since many of them only started to learn Latin when they arrived at MCS.

Yes, the pace is fast and expectations are high, but academic success is not at the cost of fun and interesting digressions. Very little setting, just 'loosely' for French and maths from year 8. Lots of young teachers as well as what were described to us as 'legendary dinosaurs', and all seem to have more than several strings to their bows ('polymath' may as well be on the job description). Parents marvelled at how well their children were known as individuals and how alert staff were to even subtle changes in mood or performance – 'they pick things up so quickly'. Subject clinics are readily available and there's no stigma attached to those who need help of any kind. Junior school boys are screened for SEN in year 5 and there is one-to-one and specialist support available for senior school pupils. 'You don't have to be the brightest', said one mother (hmmm, it's all relative), 'they just want pupils to do the best they can – not for the reputation of the school, but for themselves.'

Girls who join the sixth form, mainly from nearby single-sex schools (much to the latter's great regret), notice a culture change as well as an increase in pressure. 'The philosophy seems to be to keep us as busy as possible; there aren't nearly as many private study periods as you get at my old school.'

Games, options, the arts: We lost count of the number of times pupils, parents and staff told us, 'actually MCS is a really sporty school' or words to that effect. Do we think they protest too much? They're certainly fielding strong opposition to those who still believe you can't be clever and sporty. Tennis (current year 11-13 students national champions), cricket, hockey, football and rugby have all 'really come up'. City centre site lacks the acres of pitches enjoyed by rivals, but then how many schools have their games fields and pavilion on an island? Magdalen's School Field sits in the middle of the Cherwell, connected by photogenic 'willow pattern' style bridges which feature heavily in marketing material. Good use is made of adjacent university facilities including swimming pool and the track where Roger Bannister broke the four-minute mile. While having a river running through your grounds appears not to guarantee rowing success, sailing is a real strength and MCS has won the National Schools Team Racing Championships for six out of the last nine years. Master told us that over 80 per cent of pupils get to represent the school in one sport or another: 'we're in to win' and the Saturday match programme is 'huge'. Everyone agrees that sport is now taken much more seriously, but as one parent put it, 'sport has its place, but it doesn't rule.' Unique to the school is the game of Kingball: it's derived from fives but the rules are highly complex, changing with each new influx of boys.

M

The school was founded in part to educate the choristers of Magdalen College Chapel, and 16 boys from the school sing at daily services in a tradition unbroken since 1480, crossing under Magdalen Bridge via a special tunnel to bypass the traffic. They also sing from the tower in the city's famous May Day celebrations, tour the world and make recordings, including the soundtrack to the BBC's Blue Planet series. The choral foundation keeps music at the heart of MCS and there over 60 concerts a year featuring choirs (including a parents' choir), small and large instrumental ensembles, three orchestras, two jazz bands and a samba group. Ambitious whole school productions such as Orff's Carmina Burana are staged at the Sheldonian Theatre.

Drama may not be on the curriculum but that doesn't stop it from being enthusiastically pursued in after-school clubs, whole school productions and house plays – as well as an annual jaunt to the Edinburgh Fringe. Dramatic highlights include open air Shakespeare on the school's island (villains may end up in the water) and performing at the Pegasus Theatre and Oxford Playhouse, with whom the school shares a resident director and producer.

Tremendous selection of lunch time and after-school clubs runs from anime to Warhammer by way of bridge, DT, coding, comic book illustration, Lego and debating. The aim is for pupils to have fun and enjoy school life, though one parent thought younger boys in particular sometimes struggled to fit eating into these busy lunchtimes and felt school could be more vigilant about this. It's one reason that lunch is served from 11am.

'Huge' programme of outreach, coordinated by deputy head of educational development – a post created by the master shortly after she arrived. Includes helping local sixth formers with university admission (especially medical school) and homework clubs for secondary schools. All lower sixth formers do an afternoon of community service every week and some opt for extra on Saturdays. Oxford Festival of the Arts was founded by MCS in 2008 and is a highlight of the year. Local schools, the university and community groups collaborate with arts professionals in a programme of music, theatre, literature and film events. More than 100 performances, lectures and workshops attract over 23,000 visitors to venues all over the city.

Background and atmosphere: Established in 1480 as part of Magdalen College by William Waynflete, bishop of Winchester, Lord Chancellor of England and also school master – he was the second headmaster of Winchester College and possibly also the first head of Eton. Waynflete came from relatively humble origins and entered the University of Oxford from one of the town's grammar schools. He founded his school to offer similar opportunities not only for the boy choristers who sang in the college chapel, but also for able boys from the town.

The school occupied various parts of the college, finally moving over Magdalen Bridge to its present site on the Plain in the late 19th century. No grand entrance; an awkward turn off a busy roundabout at the bottom of the Iffley Road takes one to a familiar mix of school architecture from the last 100 years – some parts wearing better than others. The rather charming 1920s bungalow classrooms along Cowley Place which used to be the sixth form common room are now rehearsal rooms named after one of the school's former pupils, Ivor Novello; junior school is across in School House (1893). New Building (2008) still looks very smart but no longer lives up to its name since the recent arrival of the Richard Record Sixth Form Centre (named after a former pupil) with 'quiet' and 'silent' study rooms, a café and lots of social space. The master's offices are also here, on the top floor with a tremendous view out over School Field to spires beyond. Tremendous, yes, but temporary – St Hilda's College, the junior school's immediate neighbour, has demolished one of its buildings but construction is underway. As the master pointed out, with rather pleasing symmetry the new principal of this former women's college is, for the first time in its history, a chap. He is erecting a tower.

Pastoral care, well-being and discipline: School very proud of its pastoral care and rightly so, according to parents: 'they know the pupils so well – not only how they perform academically but also what makes them tick, what their interests are.' It can be an intense atmosphere, especially for the younger boys, and parents say staff are watchful in case things get too much. There's a social club 'with very good cake' at lunchtime to which new boys who 'aren't quite ready to brave the playground' are gently directed. Sometimes all that's necessary is a few quiet moments stroking the master's rescue dog, a beautiful golden retriever cross who tones perfectly with the pale wooden surfaces of her office and, rather spookily, arrived with the name of Lily (MCS motto is 'Sicut Lilium'). Three full-time matrons care for pupils, including triage from a mental health lead practitioner who liaises with two counsellors.

Interestingly, pupils are allocated to one of six houses according to where they live. Some travel in by train or bus from quite far so this is a great way of making friends who share the same journey. New boys are paired with buddies from the year above, and sixth form mentors are on hand. A mother told us, 'my son and his buddy were chalk and cheese, but they got on brilliantly. There are lots of characters in this school, no one type, that makes it very tolerant of difference.' Other parents said much the same, 'there's no dominant, cool set – it's fine to be small and weedy.' The 90-100 or so girls who join the sixth form seem to do so with few problems – we imagine school is as careful at picking the 'right' candidates for this end of the school as it is with the younger boys. Sixth form described to us as 'very sociable – they like to have fun.'

Detentions tend to be for 'cheek or talking too much' and 'leaving bags around'. In the case of the latter crime this doesn't seem to be a successful deterrent: there were bags everywhere – decorating the base of columns outside in a way we're sure the architect did not intend, and strewn about hallways. Teachers conscientiously move them to one side as they walk past, muttering about the bag problem. There are plenty of lockers – we could just about make them out through the abandoned bags.

Food is 'amazing' according to one of our sixth form guides. She thought it was better than what she'd had to eat at the Cambridge college which had just offered her a place. It was only 11am when we passed the dining room but it was full of boys (sixth formers have their own café) tucking in to fish and chips. 'Some of them get to school pretty early' we were told. There's also a tuck shop that was just about managing to keep a ravenous crowd supplied with toasted sandwiches.

Pupils and parents: There is undoubtedly a certain cachet attached to one's son or daughter getting a place at MCS, but it's intellectual, rather than social. One mother nailed the demographic thus: it's not the 'kind of school where people dress up for parents' evenings'. Another said, 'it's not snooty, people from all backgrounds fit in.' Such is the pull of an MCS education that pupils travel in from as far as Newbury and even Northamptonshire and some families will move house if their son or daughter gets a place. Fairly typical Oxford mix of lawyers and medics, usually with both parents working; not as many dons as before – fees are out of the reach of many academics these days. It was suggested to us that there is a larger than average proportion of only children at MCS – interesting if true. Former pupils, known as Old Waynfletes (OWs), include St Thomas More, William Tyndale, John Foxe (as in Foxe's Martyrs), Ivor Novello, the Oscar-winning director Sam Mendes, Misha Glenny, Ben Goldacre, Nobel Laureate Tim Hunt and Noel Chavasse VC & Bar, the most highly decorated soldier in British history.

Entrance: Two-class entry to junior school from year 3 upwards. At 7+ entrance is by maths and English papers plus a half day of group activities. 'Attention is paid to each child's co-operation, enthusiasm, self-discipline and ability to concentrate.' At 8+ and 9+ by maths, English and verbal reasoning papers plus interview. Auditions for choristers in October and January. Also run pre-assessments giving feedback on suitability. Junior school pupils all take the same 11+ exam as outside applicants to the senior school (almost all pass). Parents assured us that tutoring isn't necessary for boys applying from state primary schools. Around 50-60 places each year for girls in the sixth form, minimum of six 8-9s at GCSE required although reality is that nearly all candidates will far exceed this.

Exit: A few (perhaps 3-5 per cent) leave after GCSEs, mostly 'for financial reasons' or to study A levels not offered by the school. Persistent rumours that pupils who underperform at GCSE are kicked out were firmly quashed by the master: 'We absolutely do not cull.' Forty-four to Oxford and Cambridge in 2018, plus 27 medics. Nearly all to top universities, including Bristol, Exeter, UCL, Durham, Edinburgh. Others off to Harvard, Berkley and ESCP Europe business school in 2018. Sciences marginally more popular than humanities, anything from aeronautical engineering to cognitive neuroscience. We were told that school does not 'push' Oxbridge and counsels pupils to choose universities based on the type of course they want to study.

Money matters: Despite its ancient foundation and top-notch connections, this is not a rich school. Modest scholarships and exhibitions for academic and extracurricular can be topped up by means-tested bursaries – master is on a mission to boost funds for these. Will generally try to help families who fall on hard times.

Remarks: We're tempted to say that an MCS education has nothing to do with exam results, but that would be misleading. Nevertheless, for most pupils a clutch of A*s will prove to be but one among the many lifelong benefits of learning here. A powerful place in which intellectual curiosity, creativity and individuality all flourish in the pursuit of excellence.

Maidstone Grammar School

Barton Road, Maidstone, Kent ME15 7BT

Ages 11–18 **Pupils** 1,305 **Sixth form** 327 (78 girls)

01622 752 101
www.mgs.kent.sch.uk

Head: Since 2012, Mark Tomkins BSc NPQH PGCE (40s). Grew up in Cheltenham, where he was educated at Arle Comprehensive and Pate's Grammar. Read maths at Birmingham University and went home to Cheltenham to do his PGCE. Has spent almost all his working life in Kent boys' grammar schools, the first nine years at Dartford Grammar and latterly six years as deputy head at The Judd, Tonbridge. Says he knew MGS well before he applied for the job and felt part of the school within a couple of weeks. Tall and enthusiastic, he feels that the headship is the 'best job in teaching – it is such an honour and a privilege to be able make a difference in a big way'.

Highly regarded by everyone we spoke to, he is 'friendly, welcoming and approachable and will stop and have a chat,' said one pupil, but 'he has an air of authority when he walks into a room'. 'He talks to the kids as young adults and asks what people think and listens to their views – an absolute inspiration, who has re-energised the school,' said one mother. He says it is 'not just about raising expectations but also giving children the knowledge and skills to succeed', and he wants pupils 'to be interesting and interested, self-assured and with a strong work ethic'. He is also an inspiring maths teacher.

He took up rowing about 10 years ago and it has become his passion. He has twice competed at Henley Regatta and is a member of Maidstone Invicta Rowing Club, where the school keeps seven boats. He coaches when he can and rows with the boys, and has recently rowed the length of the Thames. He loves travel, especially if it is rowing related.

Academic matters: In 2018, a disappointing 30 per cent A*/A at A level and 38 per cent A*-A/9-7 at GCSE. All take 10 GCSEs – top two sets take maths a year early and then take further maths GCSE the following year. All study at least one modern foreign language and can choose from French, German, Mandarin and Spanish, taught in well-equipped language labs. Latin also offered. Media studies available at GCSE and A level and all have to do courses in religious studies, personal development, careers and citizenship. The school offered IB for a while; no plans to reintroduce it, but does offer enrichment sessions similar to CAS element of IB. Group work and individual research encouraged in homework. Years 7 and 8 take part in applied learning days

M

where they learn teamwork and project management skills. Well-used library with 15,000 books, 10 networked computers, newspapers, magazines and journals as well as the careers library.

Careers guidance praised in recent parental survey – careers education in tutor periods and pupils encouraged to listen to guest speakers and informal lunchtime talks; all have a careers interview and are supported in their subject choices at GCSE and A level. Everyone is expected to find work experience at the end of year 12 – school will help with contacts if someone is struggling. Old Maidstonians offer mentoring scheme for sixth formers and guidance on job opportunities and university selection as well as help with contacts for specific careers. School keen to promote Oxbridge. 'I thought it was only for private school kids,' said one boy, 'but the school took us to the open days and gave us lots of support and encouragement and six of us got offers at Cambridge.'

A good balance of age and experience amongst teachers, but most in their 40s. 'Teachers are approachable and genuinely seem to care,' said one girl, who had recently arrived in the sixth form from another school and was pleasantly surprised by the good rapport with teachers.

Some 45 students have some SEN, mainly mild dyslexia. All staff dyslexia trained and track children and a team of teaching assistants available to give in class help – no withdrawal from lessons. No official Gifted and Talented programme; Ofsted, which recently downgraded it to Good, recommended that teachers 'challenge all pupils, particularly the most able pupils, to think deeply and explain what they have learned precisely'.

Games, options, the arts: Sport taken seriously, especially rugby; the school has won the Kent Cup two years running and when we visited the rugby team had recently returned from a training trip to Portugal. Cupboards of silverware proudly displayed around the school. Girls' rugby team also popular and successful. Sport compulsory in lower years – year 7 fields C and D teams, although further up the school there are the usual grumblings that it is always the same boys who are picked. Extensive extracurricular programme for sport with inter-house, club and team practices at lunchtime and after school six days a week. Good facilities with refurbished sports hall, gym and weight training room and indoor and outdoor cricket nets, tennis courts and sports pavilion. Pupils also use Maidstone Leisure Centre and Cobdown sports centre. Some sports fields on site but no floodlights (neighbours) so rugby and hockey teams train off-site in the winter. Rowing also popular on the Medway at Invicta rowing club.

M

CCF a big part of the school culture – about 250 take part in army, navy and air force, learn about 'camaraderie, service and leadership' and are given the chance to do adventurous things like abseiling, climbing and sailing. The RAF section offers flying scholarships and the opportunity to train for a private pilot's licence. Most of year 10 takes bronze DofE but popularity of CCF does not leave much time to take it further.

'The music scene is buzzing,' said our guide, and there is a wide repertoire. Instruments and ensembles for beginners to advanced: full orchestra, symphonic wind band, teachers' bands and students' bands which play alongside each other, four-part choir and pupils encouraged to form their own ensembles and pop groups. All have the chance to perform in concerts locally and further afield, including regular lunchtime concerts and at least one major concert each term to which parents are invited.

The school play has been relaunched under the direction of an inspirational English teacher and the school has recently staged Oh What a Lovely War! and Oliver! – large cast plays which draw from all year groups. Pupils can get involved with stage management, sound and lighting as well as acting. Shakespeare Day and workshops for year 8s to encourage younger boys into acting, and regular theatre trips to London, especially the Globe Theatre.

Impressive array of artwork in a range of media, techniques and styles and annual art exhibition coincides with summer concert, a 'cultural extravaganza' when parents can come and picnic.

Extended Learning Week takes place in the summer term for years 7-10, when children can follow their own interests for a week – anything from foreign residential trips and educational visits to putting on a pantomime for local primary school children. The aim is to extend cultural and social experiences through teamwork and interaction between year groups. Very popular and particularly praised by parents. The school recently sent a group of pupils to take part in the Model United Nations in New York and Harvard.

Background and atmosphere: The school was granted its first charter in 1549 and has had an unbroken existence since, apart from a temporary closure in 1554-8 due to Maidstone's connection with Sir Thomas Wyatt's Rebellion against Queen Mary. A second charter was granted under Queen Elizabeth in 1559. It was founded to teach the boys of Maidstone and in 1818 had 10 day boys and 15 boarders; by 1914 there were 139 boys, and now there are 1,300+ pupils. It moved to its current, purpose built site off a quiet street on the edge of Maidstone in 1930. Eclectic mix of architectural styles from mock-Tudor quad – used for concerts and speech days, cloisters and assembly hall; and imposing gatehouse – 'the most iconic part of the school,' said our guide – to some less beautiful 1960s structure. These are gradually being replaced by well-designed 21st century buildings including the applied learning centre (2010), the sixth form and food technology centre (2011) and the science and computing building (2018). Sixth form block a social space with computers where students can work, make snacks or just chill – has good views of the playing fields so a popular place for watching matches. (Some sixth formers complain that they do not have anywhere quiet for private study.)

Strong sense of history and tradition here and the school motto can be translated as 'One day it will be a joy to look back and remember'. All former pupils become Old Maidstonians (OMs) when they leave and 'the allegiance is incredible, the strongest I have ever seen in a school,' says the headmaster. OMs hold open evenings for year 7s and sixth formers to talk about the motto and being a Maidstonian. Pupils value the traditions and woe betide anyone who tries to stop them: there was outrage when a previous headmaster stopped ringing the big bell for assemblies – it was immediately reinstated. The school song, written in 1908, is still sung in Latin on speech days and the beginning and end of term. When the headmaster arrived he asked the pupils and teachers to help design a 'word cloud' depicting the core values of the school, like enthusiasm, achievement, integrity, community, but at the centre of the poster in the largest letters is 'tradition'. This has been turned into a poster and displayed around the school, lest anyone forget.

Pastoral care, well-being and discipline: 'Pastoral care the best I have seen,' says the head, and the school is a 'community within a community'. Full-time student services department, described as 'fabulous' by one parent, where students can go for advice and guidance, but all teachers have pastoral responsibility. Pupils have the same form tutor for the first five years, which gives consistency of care in a big bustling school. Parents encouraged to contact school as soon as there is a problem. Bullying issues taken seriously and punishments are severe, but school want bullies to learn from mistakes. They are made to write a letter of apology and to try to understand what effect their behaviour has had. 'Parents want a firm line on discipline,' says the head, and he will excluded pupils permanently if necessary. 'I do not apologise for this – boys know there is a line they cannot cross'. Having said this, exclusions have gone down year on year since his arrival.

House system reintroduced in 2007 with pupils choosing the names of the six houses, which include Hurricane, Endeavour and Invincible, all suitably galvanising, each with its own identity and all arranged vertically to enable pupils to get to know different year groups.

Younger boys wear black trousers and jacket with the school badge and white shirt with the house tie. Sixth formers are expected to dress in a businesslike way and to set high standards, with a jacket and collared shirt for both boys and girls, and a beady eye is kept on skirt length – not that many seem to want to push the boundaries. Everyone expected to show respect for all members of the school and wider community, and sense of pride pervades. Over 20 senior prefects and a captain and vice-captain help run the school, and all wear their badges with pride. All have to apply for positions of responsibility and are interviewed by current prefects and the senior teachers.

Good food served in the new refectory run by an independent catering company, but still about half bring in packed lunches.

Pupils and parents: All sorts, but mainly white middle class, with majority from professions. School founded to teach the 'boys of Maidstone' and doesn't want to move far from this ideal. Most from local primaries and small handful from prep schools. Some from Maidstone housing estates, others from prosperous surrounding villages. All seem to have a strong allegiance to the school and are incredibly proud to be there, and are generally a well behaved and polite bunch. Does not produce a type – stress on boys being comfortable in their own skins and not having to fit into a mould. Only a small proportion receive the pupil premium and a handful need EAL help.

Parents generally very supportive and are made to feel welcome from the start: head has reintroduced well-organised parents' evenings and open mornings – previously many parents never met their child's teachers. Parents kept informed via the parent portal where they can check subject and tutor reports, attendance record and the timetable. They receive a full school report once a year and two academic progress summaries. All parents automatically made members of the parents' association and are asked to contribute £30 per pupil per year into the amenities fund to raise money for activities. They also raise money via social events for school improvement projects.

About 40 girls join the sixth form each year, often for the wider choice of subjects, and settle in quickly. 'My daughter was pleasantly surprised how easily she settled in and felt part of the school from the start – the best decision she ever made. The more laid back approach and increased freedom encourages the kids to work hard'. 'It felt quite daunting, but also exciting. The boys involved us from the start, but you do need to be the sort of girl who puts herself forward; it would not suit someone who was very shy'. Plenty of opportunities for girls to take on positions of responsibility, and one was recently appointed vice captain of the school.

Entrance: Via the Kent Test in September of year 6. Not super-selective, but a complicated oversubscription arrangement for boys living in named parishes as school wants to be able to continue to draw from the villages it served originally. Oversubscribed, and very few appeals successful, but they do run a siblings policy.

To enter or join sixth form pupils must gain at least 45 GCSE points including at least a 4 in English and maths. About 40 girls and 10 boys join in sixth form, mainly from Invicta Grammar, Maidstone Girls' Grammar and a handful from the high schools.

Exit: Up to a third left after GCSEs in 2018 – some to move to local girls' grammars which take boys in sixth form, others to colleges or work. A small number fails to get the required grades to stay on. To a wide range of universities – a lot of trouble is taken to get the course and the university right. About a third to Russell Group universities (one to Oxbridge in 2018, plus two medics), the rest all over the place including occasional one or two to the US and Europe. History, engineering, economics and maths always popular, but some study more vocational courses like property development or event management.

Remarks: School now back on track and is again healthily oversubscribed under the inspirational headmaster. Strong sense of tradition, and extraordinary allegiance and loyalty among its pupils and alumni, make this a very special school.

Maidstone Grammar School for Girls

Buckland Road, Maidstone, Kent ME16 0SF

Ages 11–18 **Pupils** 1,211 **Sixth form** 313 (45 boys)

01622 752103
www.mggs.org

Head: Since 2015, Deborah Stanley BSc ARCS, educated at Highworth Grammar School in Ashford, as was her mother before her. She made up her mind to become a teacher aged 6 when she realised that she would be much better at getting the children to sing in assembly than the grown up in charge. Her ambition had always been to teach in the Kent grammar schools so, following a maths degree at Imperial College and a PGCE at Christchurch Canterbury, she did her teaching placement at The Norton Knatchbull boys' grammar in Ashford and ended up spending eight years there. She then spent five years as head of maths at Simon Langton Girls' Grammar before moving to Rainham Mark Grammar as assistant head. Joined MGGS as deputy head in 2007.

She is well liked and respected, very cool, calm and caring and dedicated to the school, but also 'full of creative ideas', as well as approachable – her door is always open to staff and pupils. She is 'quiet but does not miss a thing and is also financially astute and on top of the budget'. Very involved with her local church – particularly with young people, where there is frequent banter about her being a head teacher. She loves gardening and walking holidays along the south coast – especially walks involving tea shops. Has taught maths to boys and girls and says maths and science need to be taught differently for each: 'girls need to be taught to believe they can do it. We have high expectations and set high standards, and work hard to build self-confidence and leadership skills'.

She still teaches and is highly regarded by the pupils. She has restructured the leadership team since her appointment and takes huge trouble over recruitment – she would prefer to manage without than take someone whom she did not consider up to scratch. Does not shy away from discipline but is very perceptive and aware of children's backgrounds, and adapts pastoral care accordingly.

Academic matters: Thirty subjects offered at A level, the most popular being psychology, biology and mathematics. Computing, PE, drama and health and social care also on offer. 'Economics A level popular with the boys and encourages them

M

to come,' said one of the girls. In 2018, 29 per cent A*/A and 58 per cent A*-B at A level.

Girls are not afraid of science nor mathematics and school takes these subjects seriously. Girls are streamed in maths and most take three separate sciences at GCSE. 'There are often more girls doing physics than at local boys' schools,' said a parent, but school offers a broad curriculum including food technology, business studies, drama, music and PE. All study two foreign languages from year 7 and French, German and Spanish offered at GCSE – French taught by a native speaker. A French exchange with families in Perpignan has been started. In 2018, 53 per cent A*-A/9-7 grades overall at GCSE.

Annual STEM week dedicated to science, technology, engineering and maths – anything from a visit to Kew Gardens and science careers guidance to the Big Reptile show which generates enthusiasm in the lower years. Annual inter-house maths and science competitions, mathematics days and science themed assemblies. 'We are committed to nurturing the scientists of the future,' says the school. 'We do masses of practical work which helps you remember the theory,' said one girl and 'we get lots of extra support with maths,' said another.

Plenty to stretch the gifted and talented who have their own co-ordinator. Increasing numbers take the Extended Project Qualification (EPQ) 'which challenges the girls to make sure they know what they are talking about', says the headteacher. Debating competitions with other schools are popular and the most able work independently with a mentor on Oxford University degree modules. The school has its own observatory and about 20 of the brightest girls study for an astronomy GCSE – completed in one year with lessons outside the timetable.

One of the school's stated aims is to develop a lifelong love of learning and there is an emphasis on fun eg games for literacy and numeracy: WOW (word of the week) and POW (puzzle of the week). 'English teaching is outstanding,' said our guide. 'The teachers recommend lots of books and it is important we enjoy literature'. 'All the teachers are incredibly supportive and we can email them at any time'. 'The sixth form office is always open and you can talk to anyone – we get lots of support from subject teachers but we are not spoon fed. You are on your own at uni and the sixth form is a bridge.'

M

Enrichment courses in sixth form include personal finance and spoken English. Community sports leadership course popular with those wishing to develop leadership skills and is especially useful for potential teachers.

MGGS is an accredited Advanced Thinking School and pupils are taught to ask perceptive questions and think laterally. Full time careers and higher education co-ordinator and a well-used careers library. Pupils have careers interviews in years 9, 11 and 12 as well as talks by outside speakers, including local engineering firm BAe Systems and a recent visit to King Digital Entertainment (of Candy Crush fame) to find out about jobs in creative digital industries and computer science. Interview prior to sixth form application to make sure subjects match career plans and great trouble taken with timetable to try and enable pupils to take the combination they want. All year 11s are expected to do work experience after GCSEs, with help from an outside agency if necessary, and workplace shadowing offered in year 12.

A small number needs EAL assistance but usually for technical language. Some 60-70 need some additional support, mainly for mild dyslexia and dyspraxia, and one-to-one support given outside lessons. Good mix of teachers, some of whom have been at the school over 30 years, but also take on three or four NQTs per year – one boy who joined for sixth form returned as a teacher after reading history at university

Games, options, the arts: 'The holistic approach to educations helps pupils see the bigger picture and there is a focus on fun', said a parent. Fab new sports hall opened in 2016 and named after Molly Tipples, chairman of the governors, who had been instrumental in the fundraising; used for volleyball, badminton, indoor football, etc. Netball the most popular sport – the school has five courts (also used for tennis), girls play at district and county level and school is currently U19 Kent champion. Indoor rowing in the gym – they take part in national rowing championships and can also row on the Medway at Maidstone rowing club. Boys play full-side football outside and 5-a-side football indoors and also get involved in tennis and rounders clubs.

All year 9 expected to take part in bronze Duke of Edinburgh Award with an 'if not why not' approach. About 20 achieve gold each year. Vibrant music department and MGGS has set up Kent initiative to get pupils started with small group music lessons to share the cost, and has instruments available to borrow. Two music studios with editing suites and individual practice rooms. Lots of music clubs including year 7 band, wind band, samba band, brass band and clarinet choir as well as numerous other choirs – pupils and staff sing together in the chamber choir. Pupils perform at assemblies, at lunchtime charity concerts and other concerts throughout the year – the carol service being the highlight. Not forgetting the year 9 concert which raises money for charity.

Dance particularly popular and school has on site dance and drama studios but no theatre. The main hall, equipped with a new lighting system, is used for the annual dance show and whole school production – recent plays have included Oliver! and Grimm's Tales.

The house arts day in the autumn term has been going since at least the 1930s – totally student organised on a three year rotation between music, drama and art – 'phenonemal,' said a parent; 'I was wowed'. 'I love the school get togethers like house arts and assemblies – it gives you such a sense of belonging,' said a year 9 pupil.

Artwork all over the school rotated fortnightly with a wonderful display in the reception area. Textiles particularly impressive – when we visited the theme was Titania, using recycled fabric. 'Sewing is a skill for life,' said our guide, 'and I now make a lot of my own clothes' Fine art and graphic design offered at A level, but ceramics and photography not an option, which is a disappointment to some. Regular subject-based trips including geography trip to Iceland and psychology trip to Auschwitz.

Background and atmosphere: Founded in 1887 with funds from the Wardens of Rochester Bridge, the school opened in 1888 in Albion Place with 18 pupils and moved to its present site in Great Buckland in 1938. It is up on the hill above Maidstone set in 16 acres and surrounded by woodland and grassland, but within walking distance of the town centre and two mainline train stations. Eclectic mix of buildings: Buckland House houses the main teaching block and sixth form centre and has wide, bright corridors and a hushed and studious atmosphere with a self-contained area for the sixth form with a café and private study area. Then there is the T (for temporary) building which is the science block, put up in the 1950s and still standing – although the actual labs have been refurbished in the meantime. 'No frills – you get what you see – but it is still a school that shines,' said a parent. Two lovely courtyards filled with roses, refurbished with money raised by the parents' association and with much input from the students, great places to sit and revise. It is still possible to visit the tunnels where the girls sheltered and had their lessons during air raids in World War 2.

Brown uniform not the most flattering, but has been the same for 100 years and girls like the continuity: 'At least it's not going to affect your adult wardrobe,' said one girl. School is 'hot on uniform transgressions'. Sixth formers allowed to wear own clothes but are expected to dress decently – may wear jeans but no bare shoulders, sandals or crop tops and girls respect this:

'It's more like uni – we can express our personalities; the school trusts us and it works well'. School keeps a stash of suitably modest tops in case a girl arrives at school indecently clad.

Charity fundraising embedded in the culture; each year group holds one event a year and can choose the charity – can be anything from dressing up to cake stalls to 'crazy sporting events'. Last year the school raised £19,000. Close links with two schools in Nepal, sends old computers to them and pupils keep in touch via Skype. Longstanding tradition of Rag Week held just before Christmas, which raises at least £4,000 per year for charity. Entirely organised by the four head students, it includes lunchtime performances, fancy dress day and a rag ball. 'It is very hard work but lots of fun', said one senior girl. Strong links with local primary schools, with pupils coming in for masterclasses in maths, English and PE, and senior girls helping with French and reading.

The house system, with six houses and including all staff, is about community values – strong house loyalty, and old girls always remember which house they were in. Girls encouraged to develop leadership skills – each house has three house leaders and pupils have to put themselves forward and make a case for election and are then given a mentor if they need one – 'this creates and brings leaders to the fore', says the head.

Pastoral care, well-being and discipline: High levels of discipline 'but not in a shouty way' – eg mobile phones confiscated for a day if pupils caught using them without permission. Girls stand up when a teacher comes into the room and are taught self-discipline and respect. The senior leadership team is highly visible – all teach and there is always someone at the school gate at going home time. Teachers are good role models and have high standards and expectations of pupils. It is a school which is proud of itself. Pupils mostly well behaved – transgressions generally dealt with by 'direct and redirect', but depends on the scale – occasionally have to be sent home for the day but exclusions are rare.

The school motto is 'non sibi sed omnibus' (not for oneself but for all) and pupils encouraged to be aware of others – kindness awards are announced at speech day. Strong pastoral system – form tutors the key source of support from year 7 upwards, student leadership team is responsible for each year group and sixth form management team offers academic and pastoral support.

'My daughter knows she can go to anyone for help if she needs it and feels someone always has tabs on her, teachers are honest with her and only give praise where it is due but she always feels she matters'. 'There is a limit on the amount of homework set in the lower years and exam pressures are well managed; my daughter has never felt overwhelmed'. Parents given information and advice about how to support their children. 'As a parent I have always felt included – before my daughter went into sixth form we were invited to hear about the syllabus and I always felt part of the learner's journey'.

Pupils and parents: Parents are from a wide range of backgrounds, with many in professional jobs either locally or in London – the high speed train has changed the area. Generally loyal and supportive, and active fundraisers through the parents' association. About seven per cent are on pupil premium, and although pupils are still mostly white British, the increasing ethnic mix reflects the Maidstone area and the school has strong links with the local Gurkha community. Girls are 'hard working and want to do well and are concerned for their friends and peers', says the head, and they go on to a huge range of careers. Old girls are very loyal to the school and many come back for speech day. They include: Lizzie Yarnold, winter Olympic gold medallist; Josh Zare, X Factor contestant; Carol Goble, professor of computer science at the University of Manchester; Dame Karen Dunnell, national statistician and registrar general at the Office for National Statistics; Mia McKenna-Bruce, actress (Penny Branning in EastEnders).

New pupils who join for sixth form made to feel welcome, and one became head student. ' Everybody has been so lovely and welcoming and I have had no problems settling in', said one. 'Moving into the sixth form is such a change and the boys diffuse the girls,' said another. Boys usually come from other selective schools, either because they want a change of scene or because of the subjects offered. 'The boys integrate well and the girls love having them around', said a parent, and they are in great demand for plays and drama groups.

'The bit I valued most about MGGS', said one old girl, 'was the strong sense of community: it's like one massive family and you really get to know other years – all normal, lovely, funny people.' Strong sense of tradition amongst the pupils and the leavers' celebration is always a children's party with pass the parcel and ice cream – and also a prom at Leeds Castle.

Entrance: Year 7 entrance via the Kent Test taken in the September before entry, which involves tests in English, maths, verbal and non-verbal reasoning. Almost all come from primary schools with only about five a year from prep schools – partly because there are very few prep schools in the immediate area. Tight catchment area and those in villages outside Maidstone vulnerable to boundary changes. Occasional places in years 8 and 9 – tests for these year groups taken at the school.

Some 50-60 join the sixth form, mainly from other grammars and high schools, and include about 45 boys. New applicants and current students have to fill in online application forms and places are awarded purely on academic merit. Internal and external entrance criteria exactly the same – six GCSEs at 5 or above including English and maths and at a least a 6 in subjects to be studied at A level.

Exit: Over 80 per cent of students go onto university, an increasing number taking up degree apprenticeships. About 25 per cent to Russell Group universities. Keen to promote Oxbridge – about 10 per cent apply and about one or two per year usually go (two in 2018, plus two medics).

Money matters: Government funded bursary fund is available for sixth formers in the greatest need. Old Girls' Society gives annual £50 prize to the pupil the school considers has contributed the most to school life and also makes donations to the cost of various activities.

Remarks: A compassionate and caring school with a strong community feel and good academic results.

M

Maltman's Green School

Maltmans Lane, Gerrards Cross, Buckinghamshire SL9 8RR

Ages 2–11 **Pupils** 400

Fees: £11,160 – £15,270 pa

01753 883022
www.maltmansgreen.com

Headmistress: Since 2005, Joanna Pardon MA BSc PGCE (50s). Educated mainly in France, with A levels at Folkestone Grammar School, followed by London University, then a masters in environmental studies (still her passion – Maltman's is a leading eco school) at Wye College. Has had a varied career teaching in schools including Riddlesworth Hall, Norfolk (history, technology and director of studies), Ashford School, Kent and, prior to landing at Maltman's, Gateways Prep in Leeds, where she held her first headship. If there's such a thing as a headmistress aura, Mrs Pardon has it in spades, oozing something of the 'old school' surrounded by a halo of calm, coupled with healthy dollops of common sense and a purposefulness only found in truly vocational teachers.

Understands her audience to a tee and refuses to be drawn into conversations about pushy local parents. 'The flip side of an ambitious parent is that they are totally supportive of the school,' she quips. And in this most aspirational of suburbs she is, in the main, keeping parents very happy by 'producing girls that senior schools want.' Revered by the majority, who describe her as 'very approachable, if not overly hands on', with just occasional mutterings from some that too much air time is given to the most demanding parent voices. Head says she is more than happy to stand her ground – and frequently has to. Even those who vent frustrations with the school (mostly in relation to relentlessly driven helicopter parents dominating the scene) concur that Maltman's has been the making of their daughter.

Strongly rebuts local rumblings of staff jumping ship, saying although a number of senior staff have left of late, these were almost exclusively retirements. A number of recent staff appointments include a new deputy head, head of junior school and head of professional development – 'crucial', she says.

Presides over her domain from a splendid drawing room, littered with personal effects giving clues to her role as doting aunt and keen fell walker, and dominated by Malty, an enormous old English sheepdog rug sprawled in front of the fireplace. From here she tutors hopeful scholars, holds lunches for year 6 girls and heads off on her various duties around the school, stepping in for absent staff members whenever necessary. Lives on site with husband and spends school holidays walking in Devon, where she also has a home.

Entrance: Non-selective and generally not oversubscribed for entry into day care, nursery or reception. Occasional places higher up the school dependent upon year group – definitely worth a call if you're moving into the area.

Exit: Careful placement at senior school a huge strength, with conversations starting with parents in year 4. About a third to local grammars, mainly Dr Challoner's High or Beaconsfield High, depending on the current catchment lottery.

On the independent front, feeds a large number of girls to The Royal Masonic School, Piper's Corner and Berkhamsted, with several to Wycombe Abbey and others off in twos and threes to eg Queen Anne's Caversham and St Mary's Gerrards Cross. In 2018, 19 scholarships.

Remarks: Situated in the leafy super-affluent enclave of Gerrards Cross, somewhat unexpectedly down a residential lane lined with prime South Bucks real estate. The original house dates back some 300 years and is now a very attractive combination of arts and crafts and art nouveau with modern additions. From the moment you set foot on the highly polished tiles in the entrance hall, dazzled by the silverware displayed in the entrance's trophy cabinet, you know that what will follow can't fail to impress. A private house until 1918, the school was founded for young ladies from Yorkshire and had boarders until the mid-1990s. Nowadays it's attended by immaculately turned out stockbroker belt girls – noticeable by their purple wool coats, impressive array of hats for all occasions and unwavering eye contact.

Super facilities abound from the charming and spacious nursery, housed in a former stable block, upwards. Large, brightly decorated classrooms proudly display girls' work with barely a centimetre of bare wall on show – a theme continued throughout the school, which is festooned from top to bottom with high quality artistic endeavours from screen prints and puppets to hand made pop-up books. Two inviting, well stocked libraries, gleaming new labs, a pottery room and kiln, lovely art room and DT lab, used by the whole school. The jewel in the crown is currently the stunning indoor swimming pool complex (the grapevine tells us the water's a bit chilly but our guides, ever on-message, disputed this), plus the multi-purpose gym and performance space. Not the most spacious prep school campus we've seen, but grounds well utilised with separate, well-equipped playgrounds for junior and senior girls, a discovery garden (part of head's eco push) and decent playing fields.

Given the non-academically selective nature of Maltman's, its results speak volumes about a school rich in educational and extracurricular opportunities ('our outcomes are those of a selective school', says head). Feeding an array of senior schools across the academic spectrum from the lofty heights of Wycombe Abbey down, girls are taught by specialists for all subjects from year 4 and parents praise the quality of teaching at all levels, as well as an extracurricular programme that spans the usual sporty and artsy suspects as well as opportunities such as RSPB Club (run by head) and woodland detectives. School's reputation for pushiness precedes it but parents aren't complaining – 'my daughter has loved every minute,' said one – particularly when the secondary school offer letters drop on the mat en masse.

Roundedness may be the official Maltman's mantra, but parents and girls say sport is still top dog, with Maltman's girls – or those of them that make the rather exclusive A or B teams anyway – regularly trouncing the competition in everything from netball to gymnastics. A coveted place in the gym squad is akin to membership to an exclusive club. Taking on all-comers in national competitions, the Maltman's Army, as it's known by parents, only slightly tongue in cheek, is drilled and rehearsed to within an inch of its life – an ethos which pervades the school. Parental ambition appears to be a major contributor to this excellence, and although parents say the girls are 'driven to win', it can be an exhausting regime for those who are putting in up to nine hours training a week outside of school to keep their place in the squad, although school says they do not encourage this. Head says she is tirelessly focused on 'balancing excellence with participation', although it seems that the former still often trumps the latter. That said, sports day is reportedly only 'quite' competitive, according to girls, with everyone able to take part and some fun races as well for those not in the elite athlete bracket.

Girls' voices heard loud and clear, evidenced in the wonderful Malty's News newsletter, brainchild of a year 3 pupil and written exclusively by pupils for pupils. Another suggested an 'act of kindness week' which was duly implemented. Girl power at its best. Pupils also elected to sit on the school council and the eco-council.

Music another strong suit with around 50 per cent of girls playing a musical instrument and choirs, bands and ensembles galore. Parents with boys at many a nearby school sigh that their sons just can't compete with their sisters' school performances. Drama on curriculum and, in true Maltman's style, productions are exceptional – a recent rendition of Bugsy Malone was close to professional standard. In addition to this, there are four nativities for staff to put on at Christmas, plus carol service, lots of LAMDA and numerous other opportunities for budding thespians to strut their stuff. Lapraik Hall now boasts latest lighting and sound equipment plus retractable seats. Notably, at prize giving, six girls are selected to speak, with head saying she makes an effort to choose those who don't always get the opportunity to shine.

Quality rather than quantity in the languages department, with French from year 1 but no Latin on curriculum. Mandarin, Spanish and German on offer as clubs or for private tuition and girls say top subjects are science and maths. Three classes of up to 18 stay together from reception to year 2, at which point there's a reshuffle into four classes of max 16 with occasional movement thereafter if the need arises. Setting for maths and English (two sets, politically correctly coined 'regular' and 'upper') in year 5. Eagle eyes are peeled for SEN and a robust approach is taken to providing appropriate help with one-to-one support taking place in an inspiring dedicated room. Head of learning support is qualified educational psychologist and is supported by a specialist literacy teacher and team of support staff who tackle girls' needs at no extra charge.

Very few discipline problems and head empathises that when things go awry it's often because 'something else has gone wrong,' hence a light touch employed in most cases ('I'm not into retribution,' she says). Despite the competitive ethos fostered less in school than in some of the families, the atmosphere is purposeful and friendly. A few question marks over how effectively 'friendship issues' are dealt with, particularly in the lower part of the school where parents feel the school could do more to foster kindness in the playground.

Good work and high achievement praised at all levels. Exceptional work rewarded with a Malty's Favourite certificate, prized by girls of all ages, and headmistress commendations given out for 'really special work'. As well as external awards for regional and national excellence in all things, the trophy cabinet shows how school values and rewards girls for everything from academic progress (not just achievement – we approve) to consideration, enthusiasm and love of learning.

Head says, 'we will do our girls proud' and of this there is no doubt. Shrinking violets should proceed with caution – and some do head off for gentler pastures along the way – but send your daughter to Maltman's and watch her sing, dance and cartwheel her way towards secondary school success...and quite possibly, with her eyes fixed determinedly on the prize, world domination.

Manor House School, Bookham

Manor House Lane, Bookham, Surrey KT23 4EN

Ages 2–16 **Pupils** 300

Fees: £9,255 – £17,403 pa

01372 457077
www.manorhouseschool.org

Headteacher: Since 2016, Tracey Fantham BA MA NPQH, previously headteacher of Blenheim High School in Epsom, one of Surrey's leading state schools. Prior to that, at The Howard of Effingham, another of Surrey's best state offerings (which happens to back onto Manor House), where she joined as head of PE then moved up to assistant head. Childhood dream was to be a PE teacher ('My dad was a professional sportsman and I was inspired by my own PE teachers'); did BA in PE at Carnegie Sports College (as was then) and PGCE at Loughborough.

Progressive, serene and glamorous, parents are suitably wowed. 'She's amazing – I don't think we knew what we were missing out on until she arrived.' 'She's superwoman – I doubt you'll find anyone who isn't delighted with her' (we didn't). You wouldn't know it from the photo on the headteacher's welcome section of the website (where the girl sitting next to her looks terrified), but pupils are impressed too – 'She's modernised everything from a new uniform to more iPads into lessons,' said one. Widespread praise for her decision to raise the bar academically ('They were letting anyone in before,' bemoaned one parent) and that she's brought enrichment and (you guessed it) sport to the fore. When she's not in her plush office with open fire, sink-into white sofas and vast bay window overlooking an impossibly green lawn (girls are only allowed on it in the snow), she teaches GSCE PE – and, say girls, 'does the rounds, often popping her head in classes.'

Lives in Guildford; sport and walking the dogs on the beach both feature prominently in her spare time.

Academic matters: Pitches itself as a school for those with average or above average intelligence (which wasn't always the case), looking to progress without the stresses of a pressured environment. GCSE results do well against local competition – 64 per cent A*-A/9-7 grades in 2018. Around half of pupils take nine GCSEs; the other half (who take triple science) take 10. Breadth of subject areas encouraged, with most popular GCSEs including art, Spanish, French and geography. Plenty of vocational GCSE options too – food and nutrition, child care, music, PE and drama.

'The teaching style is the stand-out point here – they really engage the children by bringing the subjects alive,' said one parent. 'Last year, my daughter studied the Tudors and when I picked her up from school, she would talk about it non-stop for about an hour.' Many give thumbs up for 'the small classes' (maximum number is 20), along with 'the very open lines of communication with the school' and the fact that 'they extend classroom work for the brightest girls.' Being clever is not geeky here, pupils told us – 'and everyone loves the way they make lessons as interactive as possible.' We saw iPads being used in several classes – in maths, year 7s were making short tutorial videos explaining the theory they'd just learned, while a drama class involved small groups of juniors running around the grounds filming each other. Teachers are bright-eyed and cheerful – 'Because we know each girl well, we can work to their unique set of strengths and weaknesses accordingly; as a teacher, that's extremely satisfying,' one told us, while another gave us a long spiel about teaching highlights almost without taking a breath, finishing off by simply saying, 'I love my job.'

Thematic, cross-curricular teaching is common in the prep (the Tudors project, for example, spanned art, geography, history and English). Subject specialist teachers from year 5 in around half of subjects, building up to all by year 7. Setting from year 4 in maths and English, plus science from year 7. School was trialling setting in PE from year 7 when we visited, which school says has been successful as 'those with less confidence are now excelling.' French from nursery, Spanish from year 5, taster sessions in German in year 6, with year 7s choosing two out of the three languages, which can be then dropped after year 9 – 'I don't believe in forcing children to take a language at GCSE if that's not where their strengths lie,' says head. Latin and classical civilisation from year 5, with pupils choosing one or the other from year 7. Increasing focus on STEM subjects and themed weeks with names like Girl Power all part of a wider effort to show they are no longer a school catering for 'girly girls.'

No SEN assessment on entry, however all families are asked to detail any learning support being received, and all year 7s are screened for dyslexia as a matter of course. Any pupils requiring more than a couple of learning support sessions (13 per cent of girls when we visited) are charged extra. 'We're mainly talking about the mild end of dyslexia here,' says head – very few EHC plans. One parent whose daughter does have one was full of praise, though – 'the school has been brilliant, helping us every step of the way and it's now looking as though she will exceed expectations.'

Games, options, the arts: A school on a journey when it comes to sports, with specialist coaching increasingly invested in and games teaching praised, but some parents feeling they 'haven't quite got where they need to be.' Girls compete in hockey, netball, tennis (particularly strong tennis academy), athletics, gymnastics and swimming; also hosts triathlons. Matches most afternoons for A through to C teams whenever possible, so most gain match experience, much appreciated by parents and girls. Additional opportunities in lacrosse, golf, soccer and taekwondo (GB coach gives taster sessions during day, with chance to take it up after school). We also saw girls whooshing past the large bay window in the head's office – 'part of our run-a-marathon scheme in which girls get the chance to run a mile each day for 26 days,' explained head. 'Sporting excellence is important and we enjoy competing, but equally important, in my view, is creating a wide range of sporting activities for girls to take forward in life,' she says; parents think the balance is spot on. On-site outdoor facilities (including outside pool, which head plans to replace with indoor one as her next big project) and sports hall good; changing rooms for each year dotted around school.

Drama popular, including at GCSE, although drama studio disappointingly small, so girls usually use hall (except for LAMDA and small group practice). Every girl gets the opportunity to get involved in prep and senior productions respectively, including sound and lighting. Seniors were rehearsing for My Fair Lady when we visited, but performances are not always so traditional, with We Will Rock You and Billy Elliot past examples. 'The girls take on boys' roles with grit and determination,' says head; parents say the resulting productions are of 'stunning quality.'

M

Busy, inspirational and buzzy art room, where year 8 girls told us with great excitement about their annual fashion show, in which they make clothing creations from old rubbish and exhibit them on a catwalk. Classrooms double up as hubs of artwork too, particularly in the prep – we saw year 4s drawing with perspective and skill well beyond what you'd normally expect for that age. 'They really encourage you to express yourself in your art,' say parents, and it certainly made a refreshing change to see displays filled with a rich diversity of work rather than almost-identical pieces of art. Not unusual for girls to gain art scholarships into sixth forms at other schools.

Music also part of the have-a-go ethos here, with violin for all in reception (free paracetamol available for that teacher, we hope) and individual music lessons taught by a variety of peripatetic teachers throughout the year groups. With junior and senior choirs (plus parent and staff choirs) and orchestras, there's lots of opportunity to perform. One year 11 girl – 'a female Ed Sheeran' – recently raised £1,000 for the homeless through selling her CDs in the school.

Extracurricular activities keep most girls busy at least one lunchtime or after school a week – all the usuals (sports and arts), plus a few more innovative examples, especially in the prep: bridge, photography and young engineers among them. None are student-led, though – a missed opportunity, perhaps? Trips a plenty – every year group from year 3 goes on a residential, building up from one night away. Aim is mainly to enhance learning, plus a few sports trips including a new ski trip, a trip to Iceland and the odd biggie such as a one-off year 11s trip to Peru.

Background and atmosphere: Housed in a classically beautiful Queen Anne house set in formal gardens and parkland, tucked away in a surprisingly quiet and leafy Surrey lane close to the busy A3 and M25. The house can be (and regularly is) hired as a wedding venue. The picturesque walled gardens, sweeping lawns and the 'safe' location are much loved by parents and many of the girls. Inside, the house feels like a rather grand home, with large, welcoming hall enjoyed by the girls as much as visitors (so nice to see one girl warming her hands on the open fire without being shooed away in favour of visitors), while the central staircase leads up to cosy, carpeted upper prep classrooms (with flamboyant floor-to-ceiling displays of pupil's work) on the upper floors. Behind the main house is a number of newer blocks housing the art room, school hall (doubling as a theatre and gym), three science labs, music room, home economics block and classrooms for the oldest girls. Purpose-built nursery facilities sit alongside the prep classrooms, both with extensive outdoor play areas. The whole place has a quiet, country feel and exudes positive vibes (even in the loo there was a reminder displayed in pretty pastel colours on the door that 'positive thoughts generate positive feelings').

Truly a through school – little, if any, separation between early years, prep and seniors: it is one community, a major USP the school uses to differentiate itself from the competition. Although the prep and senior girls do have some separate playing areas, they are involved in each other's school lives on a daily basis (including whole school assembly twice a week), with most of the senior girls having a role – prep and subject prefects, house and sports captains – with responsibilities across the whole school. 'The leadership roles are like what you get in the sixth-form in other schools – we're really lucky,' one girl said, the lapel of her blazer dazzling with badges. 'You know every girl here, even those in the nursery,' we were told more than once.

Pastoral care, well-being and discipline: The word 'nurturing' cropped up in almost every conversation with parents. 'An individual approach to academic success' is the school motto and with teachers knowing the girl inside out, not much gets past them. Parents are divided on whether the school is cosseting – 'There's definitely a Manor House bubble, but I love it – the girls have plenty of time to venture further afield when they're 16,' one parent said, while another said, 'I'm not so sure that's accurate – it's an outward looking school, always focusing on where the girls are going next.' Many speak of it being the right place for 'quiet' girls, with the school excelling at building up confidence. 'Our girl was never the one to put her hand up in class, yet now she's form captain,' said one. Not for the wild child, the rebel or rule breaker: she would stick out like a sore thumb. And perhaps not even the gutsy and spirited, judging from this parent's comment, which suggests this isn't a natural fit for those who want their daughters to strike out independently and make their mark: 'We get the odd few feisty girls coming in from other schools, but they soon conform because the majority of girls aren't like that – they're just nice and caring.'

Strict on uniform (new, more modern blue one to replace the 40-year-old green one) and no make-up or mobile phones. Those who do transgress get detentions, 'but most go through school without one,' girls told us. 'Behaviour is exceptionally good,' confirms head, saying their secret is to work 'with clear policies and consistent boundaries' and discuss bad behaviour and its effect. Bullying? 'Touch wood, I haven't had to deal with anything at all,' says head – and pupils are equally dismissive of it; are they in denial or is this really the first ever school to never encounter pupils mistreating others?

A counsellor visits for one day each week, providing confidential advice and support for both girls and staff. Issues of potential teen angst – alcohol, drugs, eating disorders, cyber-bullying, self-esteem – are covered in class.

Pupils and parents: Parents choose it to avoid the academic pressure and competition of the 'Surrey schools mafia' and many make their decision the moment they step into the school: 'The welcoming feel is like no other school we visited,' said one. A sociable bunch that go out of their way to welcome newbie parents, conversations with them are heavily peppered with use of words like 'delightful,' 'sweet' and 'charming' and they feel Manor House suits families who are 'not too pushy' and like the 'innocence, warmth and friendliness.'

Pupils come from around a 15-mile radius from Epsom to Guildford to Wimbledon. School minibuses run in the mornings and afternoons with a minibus running to Effingham Station before and after school. The girls we met were charming, polite and confident without a hint of precociousness. They looked fresh-faced and tidy, with swinging pony-tails and sensible skirt lengths and always looked us in the eye when talking.

Entrance: Baby and toddler group once a week helps ease children (boys and girls) into Manor House before they can remember anything else. Nursery, also co-ed, starts from age 2. School proper, with uniforms and for girls only, at age 4 in the lower prep, moving through into the upper prep at age 7. Entry assessment for juniors – English, maths and interview with a teacher – plus school report and reference.

Almost every girl moves seamlessly through from the junior to senior school here; the largest external intake is at reception, years 3 and 7, with pupils coming from a scattering of local state and independent schools. An entry testing day is held in January prior to entry in September for 11+ – SPaG, English, maths and science and an informal interview with head/deputy head. This is a growing school, although head is keen to cap it around 320.

Local reputation of catering to a wide range of academic abilities is lagging behind reality, says head. 'We now want girls who are meeting expected levels of progress or above.'

Exit: All girls leave after GCSE, mostly to study for A levels, at eg Reed's School, Hurtwood House, King's College Wimbledon, Epsom College, Esher College, Godalming College, Howard of Effingham, Prior's Field, St John's and Tormead. Very small numbers jump ship along the way – 'but for some, the small size or all-girls environment just doesn't suit them,' one pupil said.

Money matters: Four academic scholarships (two 50 per cent, two 40 per cent) open to internal and external applicants. Other scholarships in sports and the creative and expressive arts are available on a case-by-case basis (around 10 some years), at 10-30 per cent of fees. Annual means-tested bursaries, in line with the school's charitable status, for new and existing pupils, theoretically covering up to 100 per cent of fees, though the school is keen to manage expectations. Applications for bursaries need to be made by November for the following September.

Remarks: Wholesome, unpretentious girls embrace learning in this homely environment within stunning surroundings. Unpressurised (for the most part) and friendly, but this is no soft option – the school is increasingly selective and academic and the girls both work hard and play hard, with results to match. Absolutely no fear of girls leading each other astray and they form friendships for life. A school which though forward-thinking in so many ways, also hints back to a bygone era.

Manor Lodge School

Rectory Lane, Ridge Hill, Shenley, Hertfordshire WD7 9BG

Ages 4–11 **Pupils** 439

Fees: £10,320 – £12,300 pa

01707 642424
www.manorlodgeschool.com

Head: Since 2018, Mrs Alyson Lobo, previously deputy head and at the school since 2005. Prior to that she taught and was deputy head at a local infant school.

Entrance: Selective 'to a certain extent' at 4, with more than three applicants for every place. Assessment takes about an hour, and is equal in importance to interview with candidate and parents: 'We're looking for children with character and parents who recognise the importance of partnership with school for 11+ success,' the previous head told us. Automatic entry for siblings, with around 25 per cent from the sibling-only nursery on site. Waiting lists for every year group, with those entering post-reception, mainly from state sector or due to relocations, invited to spend a morning in school and tested in maths and English.

Exit: Strong record of feeding to the south Herts/north London plethora of academic powerhouses including St Albans Boys and Girls, Habs Boys and Girls and Merchant Taylors. Those not reaching such dizzy academic heights well catered for too, with movement to St Columba's, Aldenham, Haileybury, Queenswood and St Margaret's. Hardly any to boarding and an average of five per cent to state schools, including Dame Alice Owen's. Outstanding scholarship record: 48 in 2018.

Remarks: Nestled at the end of a country lane in a rural setting of fields housing the local pony population, the only clue to the urban environs of Manor Lodge is the M25 sign just visible on the horizon. Excellent use has been made of the grounds surrounding the 300 year old former country house, which has a colourful history as health spa, film set (notably A Clockwork Orange) and the private home of double agent Eddie Chapman. Wonderful grassy outdoor spaces include two adventure playgrounds, one of these exclusively for reception children, two sports fields and a large wildlife garden ('a great privilege to visit,' say children), often used for science lessons and complete with well-populated swamp and observation hut. Outdoor learning also takes places in the newly created forest and woodland gardens, and the more exotic Japanese garden: quite the place for horticulturally inclined, as well as the young.

The main building provides an impressive façade for the school but the classrooms, which include a dedicated dojo for martial arts, don't quite live up to the grandeur of the exterior, although there is a quaint charm to the winding staircases and narrow panelled corridors. Thankfully the 'new block' (2003) with its brightly painted corridors bedecked with fruits of the children's labours and large airy form rooms, delivers light, bright classrooms with a more modern feel. The Grand Designs style dining room added in 2008 plays a starring architectural role and multi-tasks as dance and gymnastics studio. Newish sports hall/theatre (2015) with rooms for music and drama, plus all-weather multi use games area.

Former head constantly referred to Manor Lodge as a 'family school' and it benefits in atmosphere from its co-ed pupil body which gives off a friendly, relaxed vibe. Boys and girls mix freely and provide 'healthy competition' for one another in the classroom, according to parents, and pupils say that although the school has high standards, it is 'not super strict.' School community, from the north London/south Herts environs, is 'very demanding' in its expectations according to previous head, although children come over as earnest and serious, many articulate beyond their years but not precocious. Very few super-affluent families, with the majority hard working middle class and many first time buyers. Diverse ethnic and religious mix representative of the local area.

Quality rather than quantity in the language department, with French from reception and Spanish from year 5. No Latin or classics but specialist teaching for music, art, CDT, IT, PE, drama and languages from the word go. Around 25 per cent of teachers are male (including one in infant department) lending a healthy dose of testosterone to the mix. Pupils continuously assessed using PIPS scheme. At the top of the school, children benefit from a tutorial system 'almost like university,' where they are given instant feedback on all work, with 'some responses from teachers almost as long as the child's essay,' according to previous head. All year 5 and 6 pupils receive a mini report every four weeks to track progress and constantly reassess targets. 'Thorough preparation' for 11+ is the name of the Manor Lodge game, with all year 6 pupils receiving interview technique coaching from a former top senior school admissions tutor.

Pupils mixed mainly according to geographical location in reception and classes are shuffled in year 3. Setting in maths from year 2 and English from year 5, when children start to move around the school for individual subjects. Previous Head cautiously picked out English as the school's 'greatest strength' but quickly added that most scholarships achieved are all-rounders. Parents say that children 'hardly know they're learning' lower down the school and that pressure 'steps up just a little bit each year.' More than lip service paid to focus on independent thinking, with all pupils working towards completion of their 'thinking skills passports,' focusing on creativity, independence, collaboration and persistence. Extremely close bonds in evidence between staff and children, with teachers referring to the 'sheer joy in learning' they hope to give their young charges and even reception staff showing clear affection for pupils.

M

Not much in the way of heavy duty SEN, but that said, there is very little call for it – just a handful of pupils per year group receive extra help from the part-time SENCo to iron out minor issues. Maths and English specialists join classrooms to provide support to those who need it, and those with specific talents, either academically or in music or art, receive accelerated tuition outside classroom time.

Art room on the basic side but one of the most orderly we've seen – 'you can't create in chaos,' according to the art teacher – and pupils enthuse about the teaching in this area, with evidence of their work displayed around the school. DT also a firm favourite with both sexes, with pupils describing their teacher as 'passionate,' although facilities in this area are not the star attraction. Music lessons take place in a room with spectacular views across the countryside and are very popular, with 50 per cent of junior pupils taking peripatetic lessons and a host of bands and choirs on offer for budding performers to display their wares. Previous head reckoned 'nobody leaves Manor Lodge without being a performer,' with frequent recitals on all scales, ranging from class assemblies, which 'quietly teach confidence,' according to parents, to musical productions, most recently Charlie and the Chocolate Factory. Year 6s bow out of the school each year with a major production at the Radlett Centre.

The trophy cabinet in reception tells visitors all they need to know about the sporting culture of the school which has, according to parents, 'hugely improved,' in recent years. Two dedicated sports staff (one male, one female) run the show and have helped school inch its way up league tables and earn its place in a competitive local fixtures list. A-D teams are put out wherever possible with cricket and netball being standout sports – teams in both finished the season unbeaten recently. Girls' football on the up and cricket also popular with the female cohort, although no fixtures – yet. Trophies and accolades also up for grabs for less sporty ones, with annual awards for everything from maths and handwriting to reading – and even one for 'good egg.'

Hugely popular (and competitive) house system and pupil body vociferous in school matters with the school council. Two councillors elected from every year in the school attend monthly meetings to put forward ideas and suggestions for improvements. School introduced badges for those on school teams, choir or bands and holding responsibilities such as librarian as a result of council discussions –many pupils now proudly weighed down with these. School presidents from each gender are elected by the pupil body ('they always get it right,' says head) and lead council meetings. Pupils proud of school's Green Flag status and boasts an eco team, recycling club and bird watching amongst its enrichment programme. No specific anti-bullying measures in place but head says that 'children know they can talk to any adult,' adding that incidents of unpleasant behaviour are 'pretty rare.'

The Manor Preparatory School

Faringdon Road, Shippon, Abingdon, Oxfordshire OX13 6LN

Ages Girls 2-11, boys 2-8 (becoming co-ed throughout) **Pupils** 355 (281 girls, 74 boys) **C of E**

Fees: £12,780 – £15,570 pa

01235 858458
www.manorprep.org

Head: Since January 2018, Alastair Thomas, previously head of The Elms School near Malvern. A degree in French from King's College, London was followed by a brief stint at John Lewis before he joined Kingshott Prep School, where he became head of French. Moved to The Downs School nearby as head of French and Latin before becoming deputy head at Lambrook in Ascot. A very social animal, approachable and full of energy, very keen on sports and music. Married to Hannah; they have two daughters and a labrador collie cross, Barney.

Entrance: 'Virtually non-selective'. Informal visit with parents for youngest, trial day for pupils entering years 1 to 6.

Exit: No formal links to any senior schools but pretty seamless progression of girls trailing scholarships and awards – majority (around 40 per cent) to St Helen and St Katharine; Headington and Rye St Antony also popular, some also to Oxford High.

Boys have left at 7, most to Abingdon Prep where they have a 'reserved' but definitely not 'guaranteed' place, also The Dragon and Magdalen College. Becoming co-ed throughout gradually, starting with year 3.

Remarks: Approach via the educational super-highway that is the Faringdon Road in Abingdon and just when you think there can't be another school, take a sharp turn into The Manor. We arrived at drop off time and bravely nosed the modest GSG-mobile between the juggernauts of the Oxfordshire school run. One of the sensible benefits of the Abingdon4Education partnership (or 'soft federation', as the school calls it) is a joint bus service that ferries children in from all points of the compass (Henley the latest to be added) and serves Abingdon, St Helen and St Katharine, The Manor and thence (by minibus) Abingdon Prep. Apparently, even The Manor's tiniest will soon have their own dedicated bus with age-appropriate booster seats and school staff to accompany them on their travels – this should ease car park congestion.

Our visit began with assembly and a rousing blast of Land of Hope and Glory from the small but perfectly pitched orchestra, segueing into Dancing Queen – a fine start to anyone's day. An inspiring talk on heroic failure was illustrated not only with famous examples (Eddie the Eagle) but also anecdotes from staff and pupils. The most frequently cited experiences were riding and skiing challenges – doubtless a reflection of the school's demographic, but one brave soul claimed to have 'weeded the garden in the rain'.

The friendly, relaxed but orderly atmosphere of assembly set the tone for the work and play we observed. Manor Cottage is the first stop on the 'chronological horseshoe' plan of The Manor estate, the charming home of the pre-nursery Manorites, brightened outside with little pots and wellington boots full of pansies. Up to 16 boys and girls come here for anything between one morning and five full days from the age of 2. Play, gardening, stories, cookery – children make their own snacks once a week – this is very much a home from home.

The nursery block has an enclosed garden with space to ride bikes; 'we do as much learning outside as we can'. Eager beavers in smart bottle green sweatshirts were having break when we visited, excited about making jam tarts after break – part of the term's jubilee theme. For nursery children who do a full day a mezzanine area allows a soft space, if not for sleep, then quiet rest according to parents' requirements. We thoroughly approved of the 'Ask me about...' whiteboard at the entrance to the building – staff write up some of the day's key events so that parents can ask their forgetful darlings leading questions and maybe even receive answers.

More formal teaching begins in reception and, as in other schools, hard stuff goes on in the morning. In every classroom we visited busy hands were doing: in one class pupils were sitting on the floor with little whiteboards practising writing numbers; in another fractions were being explored by folding sheets of paper. Lessons start with a mental maths warm up, move on to practical work and finish with 'recording'. In each room thinking skills boards pose problem-solving challenges. 'What we don't do is spoon feed.' Indeed, independent learning and 'risk taking' are built into the teaching programme right from the start. Pupils are set from year 2 in maths; an extra set means that each gets exactly the support or extension work they need. All the requisite technology is in place and IT lessons are once a week; screens are mostly in dedicated areas, actively used for research but not dominating classrooms. The hands-on approach to learning persists in the science lab: we saw enthusiastic year 6 girls pile in from the grounds brandishing newly captured mini beasts in magnifying jars, ready to be drawn, described and then released... until next time. The library has had a recent refurb with some wonderful hidey holes created in which to curl up and read.

The learning support department is at the centre of things, in the manor house from which the school gets its name. 'We can cope with anything, from a pupil needing a bit of extra help with maths and reading, to severe dyslexia.' Parents we spoke to endorse this, describing the learning support team as 'fantastic', 'working wonders.' Three dedicated teachers assess all children and offer support individually, in small groups or in class; this is free up to the end of year 1. According to one parent whose child needed significant support, 'costs can escalate but the school advised us what to expect so at least we didn't get any nasty surprises.' A private speech therapist is also available and the school has accommodated children with hearing and sight problems. Support is tailored to the individual: 'we are flexible according to need'. EAL also on offer and pupils often go from speaking no English to fluency in an astonishingly short time. Impressive gifted and talented programme also in place.

And now to sport. Lucky Manor sports staff (all specialists) are based in a splendid stone barn. There's plenty of green space for running around; additional specialist netball and tennis take place at the nearby White Horse Leisure Centre and swimmers get to use the splendid pool at Abingdon School. When asked about Manor sport, there was a temporary modesty lapse, 'We win everything!' Can this be true? We checked: from cross-country to equestrian, tennis to biathlon, Manor girls leave others standing and compete at county and national levels. Part of the secret of the school's success could be the fact that one member of staff is employed solely to coordinate matches and ensure that all clubs, sporting or otherwise, run and run smoothly. If The Manor says it offers a club, it really does; 'we're not half-hearted' (as if).

Mainstream offerings are free, specialist options such as Spanish or Mandarin are charged and pupils can pursue interests from golf to face painting, chess and touch-typing. Instrumental lessons (including harp) are supported by before and after-school music clubs including guitar, chamber group, singing and wind band. The dreaded music practice is encouraged by an awards scheme; teachers set weekly goals and give practice tips. Our charming guides were looking forward to the year 6 Stratford visit (a post-entrance exam treat) which includes a trip on the river, a play and the chance to romp through the Bard's home town in Elizabethan costume and duelling scars (courtesy of a former head of wigs and make-up at the theatre). Other excursions include camping on the Ridgeway, outdoor pursuit adventures on the Isle of Wight and a week in Normandy.

Some of the parents to whom we spoke described how The Manor had 'rescued' their children from unhappy schooling elsewhere and 'returned the smiles to their faces.' Others praised home/school communication, saying that queries were always answered promptly and parents felt that dialogue with teaching staff was genuinely encouraged. A few had concerns about how the pace accelerates in year 5 in advance of entrance exams but said that their daughters, having been 'thoroughly manored', took this in their stride.

So, what manner of magic goes on here? Does the studious atmosphere of those high-octane senior schools waft along the road? Perhaps, but that doesn't quite account for the enviable results achieved by this happy, unpressurised, non-selective school. The head defines it thus, 'We want to cultivate bright-eyed enthusiasm, to say "let's go for it and play with heart"; learning should be linked to the fun of life.'

M

Marlborough House School

Hawkhurst, Cranbrook, Kent TN18 4PY

Ages 3–13 **Pupils** 335 **Boarders** 25 flexi (from year 4) **C of E**

Fees: Day £8,730 – £18,060; Boarding £39 per night

01580 753555
www.marlboroughhouseschool.co.uk

Headmaster: Since 2013, Martyn Ward, married with two girls at Marlborough House School (MHS). Went to Westminster College

Oxford, then taught at The Hall and Cothill House, before becoming deputy, then acting head of Eastbourne College Prep.

Warm and personable, much liked by pupils – 'he's fun, and interested in us' – and parents – 'he's a breath of fresh air'; 'always around when you want to speak to him'; 'knows the children and is genuinely interested in them' (he sends birthday cards to all the children, which is much appreciated).

Entrance: 'No type it wouldn't suit', says the head. Broadly first come, first served, with taster days and soft touch testing so they know where pupils are and can monitor development. A parent thought that it wouldn't suit children who don't recognise discipline – pupils here need to be respectful of all ages.

'Took a long time to get in', said a parent who waited two years to get a place for her daughter, but it's evidently worth the wait. 'Our experience is overwhelmingly good at many different levels...'.

Exit: Large number to Cranbrook (which started 11+ entry in 2017); Eastbourne College, King's Canterbury, Bedes, Sutton Valence and Tonbridge are also popular. A few to Eton, Harrow, Winchester et al. In 2018, a big wadge of scholarships taken up, a mix of academic, sport and drama.

Remarks: Some children really do skip between lessons here; it's a very buoyant place. Elegant buildings, beautifully kept. Gravel crunches under foot. Mature trees (no climbing); but under the rhododendrons at break time, flashes of uniform and scrambling limbs. A plastic cow peers around the edge of the bushes, a school jumper draped around its head.

'When education looks [this] good and learning is [this] inspiring, how can you not choose it for your children?' said a parent. When the head arrived, he replaced some of the old guard with a young, lively staff which transformed the school academically – 'fun and active lessons'; 'inspiring', say the children (yes, the children). 'The staff the head brought in are utterly amazing', said a parent, 'and anything you might wince at occasionally is overwhelmed by their reinvention of lessons'. One teacher blows a bugle of brilliance if he reads something fabulous in class; another gives top gun award for great work: aviator shades and a moustache for the day. 'They enthral the children', said another parent, in awe. Dull or mediocre will not be tolerated from teaching staff here; an assistant head's role is continuous assessment and improvement of all teaching staff (360 appraisal is coming, and these articulate pupils will welcome the opportunity to make their views known).

The curriculum in year 5 starts to prepare pupils for both CE and 11+, the focus being on maths and literacy – 'this is what gets pupils into senior schools', says an assistant head. Commenting on the atmosphere, a parent said ' it's not wholly laid back; but [doing] the best you can do is perfect'. Both the very able and those towards the middle of the pack thrive here, bright pupils being stretched with extension work.

The SEN unit is open door to anyone, including those who just want a chat and some reassurance. They help those with a variety of needs, including severe dyslexia. Most support is offered in groups of up to six (the dynamic is better in small groups, they say, and it's more fun for pupils). One-to-one help is also available, and is charged as an extra.

The school is divided into nursery, pre-prep, middle and upper school, with separate buildings for pre-prep and nursery. A jolly nursery, with children learning to care for rabbits, guinea pigs and giant snails. A quiet area behind ribbons, for snuggling down for a nap or quiet time.

MHS is often chosen by parents and children for the happy comfortable atmosphere that pervades the school, one parent adding that it is 'neither as clinical or feral as other independent options in the area'. Another was attracted by the respectful interaction between staff and children, and described the role modelling by staff as 'exceptional'. 'It does feel like a special greenhouse environment', said one parent who worries a bit that her children won't be able to cope in the real gritty world, and would like more integration into the local community – 'but they learn great values [and] they have found [my son's] areas of potential and fanned them'.

MHS promotes British values, says the ISI (tolerance and respect, in case you were wondering). Officially non-denominational with a Christian ethos; it actually feels distinctly Christian, with a sung grace (lovely chime-like responses), and chapel twice a week. One parent said, 'I like the fact that it's not afraid to have a Christian ethos: in word and genuinely in spirit it is a kind school'.

The uniform is moving from navy to grey tweed, 'curiously old fashioned', said a parent: the school listened to pupils and parents about the faults of the current uniform (itchy jumpers and tricky tracksuit bottom linings), but parents don't feel they were sufficiently consulted over the new design. Pupils do feed back their views on school through the class rep to the pupil forum twice a term, but these very vocal pupils were clear that they would like a greater voice, particularly to make suggestions about food: puddings are excellent, first courses variable, and some outrage that only year 8 get to visit the salad bar. More outrage that burgers and doughnuts have disappeared (quiet hurrahs from the parents), and disgust at the courgette buns and beetroot brownies which have appeared in their place. Thank goodness for much loved fishy Fridays.

Sport every afternoon from year 6 upwards, with lots of pupils saying that sport is their favourite thing about MHS. They excel in many areas, often achieving national level: quite something for a small sized prep. But there is a pleasing emphasis on sport for all, with an approach that highlights enjoyment, inclusion and effort: coaches focus on the bottom teams, with most parents and pupils saying that everyone gets a regular chance to represent the school in matches.

There is the traditional sports gender divide along cricket and rounders lines, which causes a little parent discord – 'as a progressive prep, they should have girls' football'. The school is not averse to girls playing boys' sports, but it can be hard to find other preps for them to play against.

Forest school for pupils up to middle school, and it's very popular – 'you can see the kids' shoulders going down', said a teacher.

Music is really lovely – pupils benefit from a comprehensive programme, which evidently fosters a real love for music: an ad hoc group was singing a pop song at break, accompanied by the year 5 music scholar on the piano (blimey), while pupils passing the room in the corridor outside joined in with the odd phrase as they went past. Various instrument and vocal coaches from illustrious stables such as the ENO and the Globe.

Pupils here love drama, and would just like to do more of it (a play a term in pre-prep, but only in year 6 and sometimes year 8 in the rest of the school, say parents; school insists that there are annual plays for all middle school children and more informal plays and recitations higher up).

A wealth of clubs, including philosophy in the forest and theatre make up. Must be one of the only schools with a permanent indoor maypole, children learning that the important thing is to keep smiling merrily, even if the ribbons are getting in a frightful tangle.

'Good manners cost nothing but mean a lot', says a notice on a door. 'Are you looking as smart as you could be?' says another. Respecting self and others is the theme which runs through this school from nursery to year 8, with much of the system of rewards and sanctions being tied into this ethos. Bad marks may well land you in the reflection room to consider the impact of your behaviour and what you might do differently in the future.

Most pupils said that they would go to their form tutor if they had a problem, one shyer pupil saying he would rather use an independent listener box so he wouldn't have to talk in front of others. 'It's a very caring school', confirmed a parent whose daughter needed a lot of support after her father died: the school made sure there was a safe person to go to if she was upset, and weekly meetings at SEN to talk about her dad. A parent whose son experienced bullying at his previous school said he was 'brought back to life' by MHS. There have been one or two incidents at MHS which caused concern, but the school sat the boys down together and talked things through – 'it was dealt with thoroughly and communicated well', said the parent.

'The best club is boarding', said one boy, who has finally persuaded his mother that he should have one night a week at school. Twenty-five boarders over the course of a week. Last minute requests for boarding will be accommodated if there's a space. Pupils can board from year 4, but most are older.

Comfortable common room with sofas, TV and table football. Evening activities are popular – laser guns and throwing marshmallows into a bucket are recent hits, and pupils enjoy roaming the grounds. A nice supper for boarders – 'pitta bread things, and hot chocolate or milkshakes', said one boy with enthusiasm (no kitchen for snacks at present).

Rooms with bunk beds, mostly for six; cosy, but not cramped. Ample bathroom facilities in good condition. Blue sheets for boys, pink for girls; but white provided to older girls who asked. Boys' dorms named for sport, mostly skiing, with the black run stairs (roped for safety) down from their top floor dorms; girls' dorms named after flowers and bubbles (pupils chose dormitory names a few years back).

Parents are diverse: city, professionals and business, old money, and 'just working hard to get them through school'. A very parent-friendly school and the friendly parent group quickly scoop up newcomers.

Mayfield School

182

The Old Palace, High Street, Mayfield, East Sussex TN20 6PH

Ages 11–18 **Pupils** 398 **Sixth form** 184 **Boarders** 164 full, 20 flexi **RC**

Fees: Day £21,000; Boarding £32,925 pa

01435 874600
www.mayfieldgirls.org

Headmistress: Since 2008, Antonia Beary, previously deputy head here, and before that at New Hall, Ampleforth and The Leys. Read English at Cambridge. Devoted to the school and its pupils, and determined to inspire her girls to do anything: 'they don't have to be something safe or obvious [in their careers]'. Hear hear.

In assembly, challenges Britain's Got Talent as lamentably failing to model good behaviour or taste; in fact, encourages the girls to challenge lots of things on a regular basis. Parents are confident that she handles the school well, and impressed at her knowledge of every child. 'Delightful head...very professional', said one; 'slightly eccentric...has helped us so much', said another. 'Girls like her, but have a healthy respect for her', said a dad, adding that his daughter is happy to write or speak to the head if things go wrong.

Academic matters: 'Some absolutely amazing teachers', said a parent, who told us about staff who have 'engaged and enthused' her daughter in subjects she didn't like. 'I feel that teachers really know my children', added another. A good number of top end results at this gently selective school – nearly 60 per cent A*/A at A level, 71 per cent A*-A/9-7 at GCSE in 2018. The school is in the top 20 per cent of value added schools, adding at least one grade onto pupils' expected scores.

Maths, chemistry and biology are very popular here, determinedly bucking the trend for girls to choose more humanities. The head says it is important to create an environment where girls can make mistakes, and the approach to learning maths at Mayfield is based on this: 'Maths is brilliant', confirmed a parent. Geography is also a favourite – 'we're evangelical about geography...' RS is 'very lively', say the girls, and a parent who described herself as a committed atheist said how much her children enjoy this subject: plenty of challenge and discussion.

Lessons of quiet, determined concentration; though an excited physics teacher showed us a burst of air pinging out of a bucket, to the slight embarrassment of our guides.

Most pupils take 11 GCSEs, which must include a language. Class numbers in lower school are up to 15, with up to 12 in A level classes.

Pupils here happily mix subjects, splitting their time between sciences and arts, for instance, and the school prides itself on not labelling pupils and persuading them to choose options accordingly. One parent felt that that girls should be guided towards studying their strengths, but other parents like the open choice at A level – 'I knew the girls would struggle to choose, but it was important it was their choice'. We love the idea of the subject fair, with teachers pitching their subjects to girls. A wonderful way of keeping teachers on their toes. (As is their habit of getting girls to help interview new staff.)

One parent said she was 'worried they wouldn't push kids enough', but they have been 'brilliant at handling different levels of maths, and pushing them where necessary'. Subject clinics are open door and well attended, and pupils describe teachers willing to put in extra time. New sixth form enrichment programme with options ranging from global perspectives to farming and land management to diploma in culinary skills and the art of effective communication, plus an Erasmus research project.

Small library lower school library, much liked by the younger girls, who felt that the upheaval of changing schools was helped by having their own safe area away from the rest of the school, and a well-stocked main library for years 9 upwards (New Scientist, Psychology Review, Pharmaceutical Tech and The Tablet).

Swish new sixth form centre, complete with kitchen and 'friends' common room'. Lovely views over the countryside, study rooms with designated desks, and intimate classrooms. Own clothes for sixth formers, but no jeans or leggings. A small room overlooking the chapel with beanbags and candles for quiet moments of reflection.

Around 40 pupils receive SEN help, which in this school can be anything from assistance with a particular problem, to help for dyslexic pupils or extra work for gifted and talented. 'No extra time in the real world', says the head, and the unit aims to give pupils strategies to deal with and make the most of their talents. A parent whose friend's daughter attended the unit raved about it: 'They have a very practical way of helping with difficulties'.

'No negativity smudge', said a parent; 'so many use [the unit] one way or another'. Help is usually on a one-to-one basis out of class. Charged as an extra. Dyslexic pupils achieve at the same rate as other pupils.

Games, options, the arts: Sports are extremely popular, and there's everything imaginable here, though some, such as football, are extracurricular options. The usual compulsory sports in years 7- 9, with free choice after that (pilates, fitness room and zumba become options at this stage). Girls decided they wanted to learn kickboxing, and a couple of months later it was up and running – 'an incredibly responsive school', said a parent. Cricket now an option with coaching by a former England player. Riding is immensely popular: pupils can bring their own horse to school, or take part in a horse share. Fabulous equestrian facilities on campus – pupils ride at national level. All have a chance to represent the school in matches if want they to, and netball is popular even with the girls who find it difficult. One parent described how her daughter was awarded a muffin when she scored in netball – 'her ball skills were so abysmal', she cheerfully explained, 'they didn't think it would happen again'.

Plenty of trips, including one to Cambodia to teach children English – 'an extraordinary initiative', said a parent, with teachers managing to fit teaching TEFL to pupils into the school day. 'I was gobsmacked', said a parent, who said the trip has led on to so many things, such as designing a t-shirt, and a video workshop so that pupils could compile video libraries while away.

Two-thirds of pupils here learn an instrument, and many play them in the orchestra. Several choirs, the more selective ones singing at illustrious venues, such as Westminster Abbey. Regular school productions, and both LAMDA and GCSE drama are popular, though there are fewer takers at A level.

A vast range of options available, with activity sessions built into each school day – compulsory down time. There's even a farm club with livestock – though the last residents have just been eaten.

Food and nutrition is 'quite splendid,' said a parent, and compulsory in years 7-9, on the basis that however brilliant your mind, you can't function in life without a healthy body. There's a session every Saturday morning for boarders, and how to eat well on a budget it is part of the life skills course for sixth formers (roux sauce and making bread – no white slice at uni for Mayfield girls).

M

Exceptionally beautiful artwork on display around the school, with some lovely ceramics: a pot modelled on church architecture captures the feeling of a soaring church roof, and butterflies fly from the edges of a ceramic gold fish bowl. A dress inspired by WW1 is made of teabags and luggage labels; a half decomposed shirt shows the stress and texture of the material.

Boarding: Around 50 per cent of pupils are boarders, divided into four houses by age. 'The school is ultra flexible about adding extra nights', said an appreciative parent. Junior houses have comfortably sized rooms for two, three and four, with beds for anyone who boards more than two nights a week, bunkbeds for the odd night flexi boarder. All rooms have basins. Common room of colourful squashy sofas, Wii and TV; lovely to see a dressing up box.

Plenty going on: a crammed notice board includes details of a trip to the Harry Potter studios and an animal rescue centre, and Pride and Prejudice catch up night; two-thirds of boarders are around at weekends to enjoy activities. Fruit, toast and cereal are always available in the kitchen, where a map of the world – 'where do you come from?' – shows a wide spread of flags.

'Rooms are quite nice,' said a parent, 'but it's the personalities that make [the boarding experience]', describing his daughter's slightly eccentric housemistress who enjoys extreme sport – 'a great role model', he said with enthusiasm. 'They love and respect her in equal measure'.

Sixth form boarding, in St Dunstan's, is spread across the top floor of the old school in four areas, with around 20 pupils in each. Over 60 sixth form boarders, of whom 50 or so are full time. (Anything over three nights is full time, because this encourages pupils to stay for the weekend, which makes a better atmosphere.) Good-sized individual study bedrooms. Considerable freedom and responsibility for sixth formers, who are allowed up to London at weekends, and into Tunbridge Wells by bus.

No work on Friday night – movies, popcorn and mocktails... 'food is important to these girls', said the housemistress. Brunch in house on Sundays: pupils turn up in their pyjamas for waffles and eggs of all sorts.

Laundry is done for younger ones, with pupils gradually assuming more responsibility, until they are doing their own in sixth form.

An overseas parent was full of praise for the care her homesick daughter received from the housemistress: she was confident that the school would email her straight away with any problems, and they respond immediately to any emails from her. Her daughter keeps in touch by telephone and Skype (mobile signal comes and goes). Transport home is arranged well.

Background and atmosphere: One parent said that the moment her girls walked into the site they loved it: 'They saw the school in action and were enchanted by it'. It offered something to both her girls, the more academic and the less so. Another said that the surroundings and small size of the school attracted them – 'everyone knows each other'.

The religious backbone of this Catholic school underpins the supportive, caring atmosphere. Pupils are of any or no faith, but they do have to attend liturgy (some think it's boring; some like the space to be quiet and think), and boarders must go to mass on Sundays. But the Catholic ethos is applied gently, and often with cake – the history teacher described attending mass at a church in France on a school trip, and the delight of going to the patisserie next door for cream cakes afterwards.

Community service, in the Actions not Words programme, is 'a fundamental part of who we are', says the head. This sees girls working at a local primary school or an old people's home, or helping with riding for the disabled. 'I think they benefit more from doing it than the people they help', said a member of staff thoughtfully, explaining how important it is for girls to look beyond themselves.

Most parents are happy with the single sex environment, one saying that she felt girls don't want to appear cleverer than boys – 'I don't want them to have to bother to look after male egos...' The head says the girls value the space to be themselves, and they also have social and academic engagement with nearby boys' schools. But it's not exclusively female here: there are male teachers in nearly every department.

Plenty of smiles and good manners from pupils. 'They develop the whole person', said a parent, who felt that girls from other schools are not as well rounded or comfortable with themselves and adults. They are good academically, but there is not too much pressure', said another. Girls here are competitive, and there is certainly vigorous competition between the houses, but 'resilient, not bloodthirsty', said a member of staff.

Food is good: since the new chef arrived 'they come home raving about it'. Changes are made in response to suggestions in the food comment books: the request for savoury snacks at break time resulted in the delights of cheese scones and sausage rolls.

Beautiful buildings and grounds, once a palace for an archbishop, discovered by the school's founder when she took her girls on a picnic from the school, then situated in St Leonards. The chapel is ancient and movingly plain. At Christmas, the village cluster in for the live crib – baby, donkey and all, the angel Gabriel singing from a balcony. The Hub (café) is the centre of the school, and many pupils' favourite place (for good reason: deluxe hot chocolate, doughnuts, and blue raspberry slush, with healthy snacks besides).

The school puts itself out for parents – one parent said that when they were unable to make the last parents' day, the school gathered all the teachers for a tailor-made alternative meeting. Another confirmed that 'if we're unhappy about anything, an email or phone call gets an immediate response'.

Pastoral care, well-being and discipline: Pastoral care is the particular responsibility of the deputy head, who is quick to point out that actually it is a responsibility of each teacher here. This works, emails shooting around between teachers, boarding mistresses and parents so that any problems are quickly picked up. There are plenty of people for pupils to talk to: tutors, the head of pastoral care, the school counsellor, the chaplain – and two members of staff additionally trained in counselling, one in CBT, the other a humanist. 'Care of pupils here gives stability. I feel teachers will listen to any problems they have', said a parent.

Tutor groups in the middle school stay the same for three years, which means the eight girls get to know each other really well. Girls are good at looking out for each other, one teacher telling us that some girls came to see her, anxious that one of their friends was skipping meals. This school is extremely aware of the various conditions which can affect teenage girls, and staff are ever vigilant.

The head is keen to teach girls coping skills – 'in the real world they are going to meet difficult and dominating people... if they're wrapped in cotton wool, they won't be able to cope'. True to this, a parent said bullying behaviour is often 'cut off at source by the girls'. But systems are also in place to capture anything untoward, from general unhappiness onwards – 'they're very vigilant', said a parent, who described a conflict between girls, efficiently sorted out by the housemistress.

Disciplinary measures are rarely needed here, though accumulated bad marks would result in detention, where you sit in silence and consider the implications of your crime. No one has been excluded in the past year, though persistent disruptive behaviour could lead to a mutual conclusion that a girl would be better placed elsewhere. Selling drugs would result in immediate exclusion; a contrite drug user would probably be given a second chance. Behaviour out of school must be as responsible as in, and things that happen out of school will have implications inside.

Pupils and parents: 'You won't find old girls on the cover of Hello', said the head. 'They will be influential, but this is not the cult of the celebrity'. The large variety of families at this school is reflected in the mixed entry, with 50 per cent from state primaries and the rest from local preps, with a small number from overseas.

Entrance: At 11+, 13+ and 16+. Gently selective, but largely on the basis of fit: pupils attend a two day assessment, which includes papers in English, maths and verbal reasoning, and fun activities. Less good performance in one area can be compensated for by excelling in others.

For sixth form entry, pupils take exams in two of the subjects they wish to study at A level, and a general paper. Pupils must get at least six GCSEs at 6+, with 6+ in the subjects they wish to study at A level.

Exit: About 15-20 per cent leave after GCSEs. In 2018, three to Oxbridge, including one off to study linguistics at Cambridge on a choral scholarship, medics to Bristol, Shanghai and Hong Kong and a Polish student heading for NYU Abu Dhabi on a full scholarship to study engineering. Plus one going to the Scandinavian Academy of International Fashion and Design in Copenhagen.

Money matters: Seven full bursaries, one in each year group, and scholarships worth 10-20 per cent of fees.

Remarks: A great all-round school with high academic standards, extensive extracurricular and the outward-looking expectation that its pupils will enrich the lives of others, both at school and beyond. A parent said: 'They get so much right. Would recommend to anyone. Sheer awe...'

Mayville High School

35-37 St Simon's Road, Southsea, Hampshire PO5 2PE

Ages 2-16 Pupils 500 C of E

Fees: £7,635 – £11,235 pa

023 9273 4847
www.mayvillehighschool.com

Headteacher: Since 2014, Rebecca Parkyn (40s) MA French and German (Oxon) MA PGCE MCIL. Mrs Parkyn was a past pupil at Mayville and is now both the head and a parent of a child at the school. She originally left Portsmouth for Oxford University where she studied at St Hilda's and then went to University College London to do an MA in philosophy. She gained a PGCE at the Institute of Education, London and her first teaching post was at St Benedict's, where she taught languages up to A level. She became head of German and head of philosophy at Bedales, which must have suited her well because she stayed for eight years before moving to become head of the languages faculty at King Edward VI in Southampton.

Her first few years at Mayville have been marked by building a senior block, developing the curriculum (ICT, food technology, sports), modernising systems (especially monitoring progress), and employing a nurse – not only for first aid but also for counselling and addressing emotional and mental health needs. Neither she nor governors appear to have any desire to change what they see as a successful school, but there is potential to take on more pupils now the premises have been extended and perhaps eventually develop a sixth form.

She lives in Portsmouth with her three children and maintains her interest in philosophy.

Academic matters: Early years have their own block, with a small playground for outside learning as well as use of the large junior playground for trikes when the juniors are having lunch. There are rooms for more formal learning as well as rooms for crafts and messier activities – and evidence abounds of creative learning with the nursery following the early years foundation stage curriculum. Very open access for parents, who appreciate the good communication with well-qualified teachers and assistants. French starts in nursery and goes all the way up to senior school, with Spanish, Latin and Philosophy for Children now taught in the junior school too.

Two form entry from reception creates a system of 'co-education separately' with boys and girls learning core subjects in different classrooms, joining for break times and some specialised subjects. The idea is that they have different learning styles but that they get the benefit of shared common time and space. Classes of no more than 12 mean that pupils get lots of attention, everyone feels that they can succeed and 'teachers know us well'. Weekly library lessons encourage reading and used for research. No KS2 exams and laptops used where needed.

The single sex classes continue in the senior school, with small classes – getting even smaller as children choose GCSE options. If necessary, individual lessons (especially for unusual languages). Parents felt that teamwork is encouraged: 'If my child is struggling, seems like the others step up, and she can support others in her areas of strength'. Limited subjects, according to pupils, but 'the teachers know what they are talking about' and the results speak for themselves, especially when you look at the range of IQ and the value added scores, which are impressive for some pupils. Some take triple science, almost all take French, religious education popular with good results, the odd few take sociology, functional skills, Spanish, drama or dance. More taking graphics or design technology than art recently.

The mixed non-selective intake and numbers with dyslexia reflect on the GCSE results with some pupils achieving nine GCSEs with grade 7s, while others are very happy with their five 9-4s. Latest results in 2018 show 24 per cent A*-A/9-7 grades. One parent explained that her son had been dropping behind severely at school and losing confidence, but on moving, 'Mayville worked with him and within two years he was back on track with his peers, ultimately achieving grade 6s in both Englishes at GCSE. I know that if I had left him in his previous school this would be a different story.' Some bright pupils also, who flourish in the quiet, small classes and get excellent results. Suits families who want a school that can cater for their children's range of abilities.

All children assessed both in junior and senior school both for dyslexia and gifted and talented. Two full-time staff work in the dyslexia unit, as well as four part-time staff. Specialises in dyslexia, but with resources and staff who can also work on dyscalculia and dyspraxia. The role of the dyslexia unit is not only to take children out for individual or group lessons, but also to assess and to disseminate summaries of the needs of all the children with SEN, encouraging the use of laptops and multi-sensory learning, and thus supporting classroom teachers. Speech and language therapists taken on when needed but 'we prefer to employ therapists and have them in house'. Plenty of differentiation in class (no one-to-one support). Able, gifted and talented programme (often resulting from the school assessments) ensures challenges, leadership roles, an enrichment programme.

Games, options, the arts: The 20 acres of fields 10 minutes' bus ride away provide space for team sports (hockey, netball, rugby, football, volleyball according to season). Separate boys' and girls' teams, with fixtures against other local independent and state schools. 'Rugby teacher really nice,' according to one pupil, but 'shame we don't have a girls' football team'. Sports increasing in popularity and importance, with pride in pupils who got to ISI finals, though perhaps still not a school for those wanting endless competitions and team sports. Swimming at local pool is compulsory up to year 7.

Performing arts a very big attraction of the school – drama, dance, singing all expected from pupils who sometimes choose the school specifically for this strength, and who not infrequently go on to perform in the West End. Pupils have joined the English dance squad, performed in Billy Elliott and gone on to study drama. Well-equipped music department where we saw pupils composing using Sibelius software and enthusiastic music teacher working with choir in preparation for Mayville's 120 year celebrations.

Specialist art teachers ensure serious artwork, and the good grades at GCSE reflect this. We loved pottery jars made as part of Egyptian studies in year 4, and the generous number of computers in the art room for research and for their photography. Pupils said they had never been able to express their creativity before coming to Mayville but now they can. They said, 'Everyone knows your talents here and you get invited to perform in assembly.' Rock Challenge seen by some pupils as a highlight – an inter-school performing arts competition (dance, music, choreography, drama). New Charlotte West Centre for music and art.

Food technology a busy centre where 'we make loads of things like cakes, sauces, pastries', and clearly inspiring because an enormous Bake Off competition provides cakes for end of term celebration.

Good selection and spread of clubs across the year groups – sports, music, science, crafts, eco car (competition in Goodwood in the summer term) etc but, particular to the school is the St John Ambulance clubs that include first aid training from year 1 upwards; older pupils find the skills useful when applying for summer jobs. Schools trips start with junior outings to local museums and adventure centres, going further afield and for longer as they get older (eg skiing, Barcelona, language trips, Hay Festival).

Background and atmosphere: School's spread over five blocks up and down the street makes timetabling complicated, but allows each house to feel like a small school in its own right. The senior blocks are much like a sixth form college with small outdoor space and kitchenette, the nursery is in a separate house with its own playground, but all join for assemblies and the canteen cooks and serves all the pupils. Mayville works hard to juggle and combine the best of all worlds – small spaces, but shared facilities, separate boys' and girls' teaching but shared activities. Classrooms are small, but then class sizes are small too. Traditional feel, smart uniform strictly maintained (too strict, according to boys who 'wish we could wear shorts', and 'we are always told off for having shirts hanging out'). But despite the traditional feel of the school, pupils described it as 'unique, unorthodox, and not solely focussed on academics'. House system for galas and matches. A school council – though pupils unsure when this met or how they could get ideas put forward.

Practical support for parents in terms of before and after-school care with tea provided, and extensive holiday camp provision (the school is only closed for two weeks a year at Christmas) allows for working parents and helps with commuting, and this flexibility is appreciated by parents, many of whom both work.

Links with St Simon's Church – they attend termly services there and use the hall for dance. There is a Christian Union which the youth pastor from the church supports and the vicar comes to assemblies occasionally.

Pastoral care, well-being and discipline: Despite small class sizes, there is some formality and clear rules and regulations. 'We can't cross the road between houses to go to lessons without a teacher, and sometimes this makes us all late for lessons.' Pupils said bullying was dealt with well (what honesty when a school recognises it and deals with it rather than pretending it doesn't happen) and most spoke of the great relief of moving to Mayville where people are 'welcoming and friendly and we all know each other', and 'teachers give more help'. They told us that the school 'embraces your strength'. Both parents and pupils commented on strength of pastoral care, maintained by meeting in tutorial groups at the beginning and end of the day to check on homework, well-being, issues of the day – and communication 'almost instant' between parents and school. Parents said, 'My children are happy, and once they are happy, everything else follows'.

Pupils and parents: Children often arrive somewhat bruised from larger schools and find the small class sizes a welcome relief. 'One pupil comes from Winchester, over an hour's journey each way,' we were told by one pupil, 'though I live two minutes away'. Very wide catchment area served. Minibuses pick up pupils from the Isle of Wight ferry and other transport hubs round Portsmouth. They come from both independent and state schools where they struggled and told us they get 'more help here' and that they like the 'quiet classes'.

Some Navy families or sailing families, some from IBM and local firms, with less than 10 per cent EAL (Danish, French). Parents we spoke to had moved one child to Mayville High because they were not getting support for their dyslexia and ended up sending non-dyslexic siblings because the children wanted to feel unpressured.

Entrance: Very open to visits by prospective families – some arriving mid year if they are relocating. School reports looked at, children attend a taster day and are tested for reading, spelling, maths and comprehension. School is selective but mostly wants a 'real world and inclusive' mix in each class and to ensure that they can meet the needs of the child. Waiting list for boys usually. No child on an EHC plan and whilst they clearly have excellent support for dyslexia, they only take mild to moderate cases. There are induction loops in new classrooms for hearing impaired children and disabled access in some buildings.

Exit: About 85 per cent go to state sixth forms – eg Chichester College, Havant and Portsmouth FE colleges; a few move to Portsmouth Grammar School or other independent schools for sixth form.

Money matters: Big capital projects often supported by trustees, who have libraries and buildings named after them so clearly involved in more than just termly meetings. Fees reasonable but extras include learning support lessons, lunches, trips, music lessons, before and after-school care and tea. Sibling reduction goes up to 50 per cent for third and subsequent children.

Remarks: An interesting mix of traditional values and standards alongside plenty of support for the individual pupil in both academic and creative endeavours. Very small class sizes with the opportunities of larger school facilities and specialist teachers seem to 'give pupils confidence and allow them to be successful and happy,' say parents. Good incorporation of specialist dyslexia unit within the school for individual and group lessons. Impressively reasonable fees whilst class sizes remain a maximum of 12 pupils.

Michael Hall School

184

Kidbrooke Park, Forest Row, East Sussex RH18 5JA

Ages 0–19 **Pupils** 463 **Sixth form** 43 (11 boys, 32 girls) **Boarders** 7 full with host families (from 14 years)

Fees: Day £4,875 – £12,670; Boarding + £7,000 – £8,065 pa

01342 822275
www.michaelhall.co.uk

Director of Operations: Davina Skinner. No head, instead a education management team currently consisting of nine, including the director of operations: joint college chairs, the upper school faculty chair, the lower school faculty chair, the early years faculty chair, the bursar, the compliance officer and the SENCo. UK Steiner Waldorf schools are strengthening (or implementing) their management structure partly in response to government-led policies. Some parents would like to go the whole hog and have a head teacher, one that was freed from the teaching load to manage and concentrate on staff development and appraisal – and to deal with tricky parents. Someone who was totally supportive of the school but would take ultimate responsibility for issues that arose and ensure they were dealt with quickly.

Growing percentage of the staff come from mainstream private or state schools and say the varied educational changes that are going on externally give the Steiner faculties more confidence in their own stable approach. Weekly faculty class teachers meetings to look afresh at the curriculum, gain advice from peers and share research. School reception well-ordered and professional with a cupboard marked PE kit for sale.

A charity, with its only trustee a company called Michael Hall School Ltd; the trustees and directors (council of management) are split between parents, teachers and independents – all elected by members of The Michael Hall Association. Independents contribute a range of perspectives from Forest Row, mainstream schools and retired Steiner teachers. As the oldest (90th birthday in 2015) and largest Steiner school in the UK, best practice and more mundane admin are shared with the rest of the Steiner Waldorf school fellowship, while city Steiner school kids in particular are welcomed to share the fantastic grounds.

Academic matters: Kindergarten feels like a farmhouse kitchen, homey and calm. Earthy rather than bright colours are used in the decoration, pictures are taken home rather than being put up on the walls – children are encouraged to find their own level of creative play and imitate the adults with plenty of repetition and ritual. Each of the six classes (age range 3 to 6.5) has access to its own garden (and a bread oven, built by the older students), where apples are peeled, crushed and juiced in the autumn – a strong seasonal rhythm. Books on the window sill; children can take one down if they are interested but stories are told and not read, pictures are used to feed imaginations. Same principle applies to toys – all unformed with no detail. Early years provision rated outstanding in most recent inspection, with other features judged to be 'good'.

Ideally the same class teacher from 3 to 7 and then 7 until 14. In reality, staff's modern personal lives mean that this post held by one teacher 50 per cent of the time; recent council consideration to reduce the length of these sole class teacher years but current consensus against. Range of ability is huge – one parent complained that are all taught at the pace of the slowest pupil, resulting in bored bright ones, while another delighted that her bilingual children get to expand their language skills creatively while less fluent children are coached. This variety of experience must stem from the skill of the teacher, which used to be a bit of a lottery, less so nowadays with tighter appraisals and continuous training; new teachers also have mentors.

By age 13 some specialist teachers for maths, English and languages (French and German from 7, Spanish from 12). Parents have reservations about size of teaching body, sometimes only enabling one specialist teacher per subject. Class size about 18 with a traditional layout, a rolling blackboard, games and music used in lessons. Children taught to write before they read (7 or 8 – usual in mainland Europe, startling in the UK); they learn manually and are encouraged to do before they understand. Never just sitting at a desk, instead alternating with the left and the right side of the brain, encouraging both intellect (singing times tables) and body (crochet and knitting) nimbleness. Parents take great joy in the students' 'whole body grace'.

Not suitable for a child with serious learning challenges for whom a group learning experience would be difficult. Staff say it is tricky for a child to get an EHC plan here since it is privately funded and council prefers to provide support in a mainstream school where staff skill set can be shared with a group of SEN pupils. However, three SENCos teach in small groups or one-to-one with word processors, a reader and scribes available for exams. Square pegs thrive within a huge range of different language and abilities – kids who would have been eggheads elsewhere are running, skipping and hopping and grounded within their bodies. Overtly intellectual kids will not be pushed to excel in one area, aiming to round out the individual rather than just concentrate on documented strengths.

Mnemonic power of free-ranging discussions and holistic links cannot be underestimated – walking from Forest Row to the seaside during geography main lesson, through landscape showing signs of smelting, charcoal burning and shipbuilding; chemistry experiment allowing a child to explore tens of different types of mould on own initiative. However, when the children get to GCSEs (first external targets or tests), they are doing the work for these exams in 50 per cent of the time that their mainstream peers get. Extra main lessons on practical numeracy and literacy. Whether a child stays for A levels or not depends mostly on their strengths and the family's finances – one parent says no dilemma for creative child, but another that is interested in all things mechanical may need more technical resources to explore her passion eg at present lasercutting done out of school through teacher's contacts.

Such organic schooling relies on a three-way partnership between the child, the teacher and the parent – communication between these is vital for success. End of year reports are ramped up to come out twice a year in the upper school. Some parents have been frustrated during parents' meetings (once a term) by the lack of focus on individual children – now scheduled time for each child common in upper school parent evenings, spreading to lower school as well. Lower school teachers frequently do home visits to enable a good dialogue to take place between parents and teacher about the child. Staff see themselves as meeting their children's developmental needs as opposed to mainstream schools which they see as swimming apart from them eg post-GCSE work experience at Plaw Hatch Farm, midsummer play and talks about e-safety and drugs awareness to balance teens' tendency to look inwards.

M

Upper school (14-19) now in the main mansion (feels more like a traditional sixth form transition); maths is streamed while A level choices mean more select groups, even though the main lessons can be in a community of around 30. These operate concurrently with A level choices – each one lasts a shorter time than they did in the lower school, but the curriculum still covers a huge range of topics (eg ecology, meteorology, economics, gym, drama). Subject cross-pollination is ubiquitous. Product design is fabulous – mat that responds to heat of food, nautilus shell light – coming out of well-led department with 10 PCs with AutoCad and Google sketch up, technology here is a mere facilitator and not ubiquitous. The purpose-built library (non-computer catalogue) is well stocked with old Steiner favourites and eight computers available for project work during the middle and upper school, the ICT department has 24, the art and photography department have four. Wifi in two rooms in the mansion, phones and Macbooks can be used, five school laptops in a cupboard, five desktops and a printer. Students say lack of computers is due to school finance rather than Steiner restrictions.

The breadth of education is really appreciated by the upper school – they feel it is one of Michael Hall's USPs. They also comment one of the few areas kept unexplored is the Steiner Waldorf philosophy itself – upper school wait until the year 12 conference for the big reveal of the education theory – some feel they could cope with that knowledge earlier. One suggested filming a nature documentary on the relationship between staff and pupils but at present no video cameras available for that. A relatively traditional range of A level choices on offer, no media, film, technology or textiles – 'quality rather than quantity,' say teachers. Exams certainly not the be-all-and-end-all but in 2018 85 per cent of GCSE grades were 9-4, whilst at A level, 36 per cent A*/A, 57 per cent A*-B grades.

Games, options, the arts: Balance between practical and academic disciplines is the aim, constantly linked into physical changes of a growing child: each class of 12-14 year olds has a chance to cultivate a bed in the two and a half acre walled biodynamic garden, literally grounding an emotional wobble with earth. Seasons run through the timetable too: whole school assemblies mark natural festivals as well as the end of term – Michaelmas, Advent. Initially, class teacher on stage with little ones, snapping fingers, clasping legs, stamping feet and singing rounds, soon poems are learned by rote and recited, costumes, lighting and sets designed for productions in the theatre. Pupils don't choose drama over sport or art or vice versa, everything is a whole class activity which bonds them socially. Midsummer play is a great example of this, post-GCSE kids put together costumes, dialogue, music and staging for a performance in a just one week – The Tempest, the Conference of the Birds.

No competitive games until middle school and then only ones that use the hands – three outside tennis/netball/basketball courts and a multi-purpose gym with lots of imaginary narratives to link different disciplines together – balancing, climbing, skipping, trampolining, trapezing, rock climbing, athletics, gymnastics, archery. Swimming only for the upper school during a three week rotation at a local sports centre, also squash. External matches in basketball, netball and volleyball with both private and state schools; 'we win more than we lose'. No football since the Waldorf Steiner development philosophy encourages upright throwing of a ball rather than kicking and heading – but one talented boy who played for Brighton got day release to train there.

At age 11 (apparently the peak of athletic fitness before puberty and lumbering teenage years), everyone takes part in the Olympic Games (this coincides with the study of ancient civilisations in the curriculum). Steiner schools from all over the UK and Europe come and camp and compete – but with enough categories to ensure everyone receives a medal. The GCSE years are bookended by an earth stewardship apprenticeship camp (bushcraft, tracking, a woodland sauna) at the beginning and, after the exams, external work experience work projects that benefit the school (bread ovens, boat climbing frame, environmental classroom).

Everyone learns woodwork and bookbinding as well as to knit and sew, moving from a gym bag to their own shirt. Impressive pottery, drawing is integrated into all topics – eg, while studying the Renaissance, everyone will draw a room with perspective. Initially art has a uniform 'Steiner look' – this stems from wet on wet painting and colour being the essence of the work until the age of 15, when a period when only black and white is used – to link in with the 'I love this, I hate this' period of development. However, individual styles, talents and mediums are breathtaking by GCSE and the older ones return to help the younger pupils post-exams before a trip to Italy where they sing in churches and look at art. Photography one of the most popular and much the most successful A level.

Finally eurythmy – described by Rudolf Steiner as 'visible speech and music'. At first glance it looks like a bunch of kids clanking metal pipes to the accompaniment of a piano, kept in check by a softly spoken lady. However, no denying that it aids the development of rhythm, teamwork and coordination – and it's fun. Nowadays there are two terms of ballroom dancing (more circle dances than cha-cha-cha) which probably coincides with when the children get fed up with it, but by the upper school they appreciate the measured left brain exercise during peaky adolescence – and the cheeky ability to spell out insults in dance to non-Steiners.

Background and atmosphere: In 1919 the Austrian philosopher and scientist, Rudolf Steiner, began a school in Stuttgart for children of the workers at the Waldorf-Astoria cigarette factory, using a curriculum based on nurturing emotional and cognitive intelligence. Today 1,000 schools and 2,000 early years centres in over 60 countries now use this holistic approach, making it the fastest growing independent education system in the world. Their curriculum is unique and, in the lower school, all teaching is done 'through the teacher and not via text books'. Michael Hall, founded in 1925, is the longest established of the 35 UK Steiner schools to offer national curriculum exams. NB do bone up on Steiner philosophy of Anthroposophy before signing up.

Many families move to Forest Row so their children can attend, as local estate agents well know. This makes for a community feel with school buses to Tunbridge Wells, Lewes, and Brighton and East Grinstead train stations, allowing children to come from far and wide – you can walk down the hill (the estate consists of 60 acres of parkland) from the A22, along the Cow Path, to the main building (Georgian listed). An ongoing plan for site development, many of the buildings are modern and distinctive, eg the kindergarten (Hobbitshire-like – the Waldorf Steiner font on all signage begs more Elvish references), the gym, the theatre. Pupils build climbing frames, edge a path and help to maintain the garden – this produces food for the kitchens (hearty and healthy), sells to the community and feeds a compost dragon each year.

The site and school do feel magical and slightly removed from reality – gloriously green – classroom blocks with art on walls and stained glass (created by a former parent) lit stairs encircle natural play areas. Some families see it as a refuge from mainstream education where children are 'criticised and their self-esteem damaged', 'like workers in an intellectual factory'. A few Forest Row residents call it 'Sandal City' (a lot of the villagers own a pair of Birkenstocks too), full of 'Michael Hooligans', although the monthly mansion market, school performances and Christmas fair go some way to demystifying the school community with outreach. The small number of detractors 'feel sorry' for the children who, if their parents cannot afford the fees any more, end up at the local state school 'unable to read or write' and see the children as unruly and hippy rather than confident and open. Upper school might kick off their shoes in summer (not policy) but they also hold open doors and give polite directions and make sure they don't call the play ship a 'pirate ship' in the little ones' hearing, keeping it open for their imaginations. Pupils say that outside reactions include 'oh, the special needs school' and 'you don't do any work' – they do think they can spot other Steiner pupils at 50 paces though, 'a bit rainbow hippy, a bit knitted'.

Pastoral care, well-being and discipline: Class teacher is first point of contact in the concerns procedure, followed by the chair of faculty. Each upper school child also has a class guardian and a tutor – he or she can request a particular teacher for this latter role, choosing one to suit a particular subject choice or emotional support. Ideally the one class teacher for eight years in the lower school should be a constant, could well see you through your parents' divorce, puberty, your gran's death. Obviously character clashes – children go through love and hatred of parents and class teachers – and this system teaches you to confront the things you don't like, instead of turning away from them. If open and honest conversation fails, the child may move into the parallel class (in the lower school) or leave. Peers also learn to provide support: when a best friend going abroad left one child lonely, the other class mates took turns to play with her, since she found it hard within a large group; when a stammerer was teased by a parallel class, his classmates fetched the teacher to help sort it out.

Three parent evenings a year and a year end report written by the class teacher; no ranking within the class, instead a good understanding of how they thrive. Education is matched to the development stages of the children to avoid unnecessary friction. A pastoral care team helps with techniques, even the capacity for an extra teacher for a limited period to support the social aspect of the class – less experienced class teachers have permanent mentors, which reassures parents. An Anthroposophical doctor sees the children for pedagogical related issues but a qualified nurse manages day-to-day medicines and conditions.

Kindergarten parents are impressed by the self-possession and responsibility of upper school kids; they look out for the little ones both in and out of organised school. Any smoking is done outside the grounds, there isn't really any underage drinking and the norm is to be single although there are some couples. No phones for youngest children, progressing up the school to having them switched off in a bag, then not being used in spaces were the little ones can see. Pedagogical stories are used a lot in the younger years – remarkably effective (obviously this does not work so well in mid-teens). A system in upper school for behavioural, alcohol or drug incidents – resulting in anything from detention through a behavioural contract and finally to exclusion.

Pupils and parents: Practically all local families – some as far as Brighton, Tunbridge Wells, Nutley and London. Twenty-five per cent non-UK born, around five with EAL and a few boarding with local families (Ofsted outstanding). Can be roughly divided into three groups – the New Age-ers (instinctively want their children to have as much of a childhood as possible before being forced into tests and bombarded by materialism), the Anthropops (done a lot of reading on the Waldorf Steiner philosophy) and the cosmopolitans (moved from a country where their children attended a Steiner school or kindergarten). Lots of Steiner pupils send their children to a Steiner school and many return to teach or volunteer, to help 'create innovators'.

M

Lots of small to medium sized business owners, educated parents making an educated choice – natural risk-takers, musicians, feng shui consultants, architects, lawyers, teachers, equity analysts, bankers. Self-selecting one income families since the slow build up to a full school day means one parent must be around for pick ups and drop offs for years – school is well aware that this restricts part-time working and now starting three long days by age 9. Expensive holidays are often sacrificed for this Steiner education, in practically all families a measured and happy decision; parents thrill in children's ability to entertain themselves with their imagination, pen and paper, no recourse to an iPad.

Those parents who are frustrated with the unconventional way the school is run are those who are least involved. Parents organise advent fair, mansion markets, donate their expertise – 'most of us parents have the equivalent of a masters in event management by the upper school' – craft mornings, gardening and building a new bread oven. The community surrounding this school looks after its own – but the outside world can be a bit of a shock for some pupils. By upper school many non-Steiner friends have fallen away. A girl who left to go to Lewes Sixth Form College wanted to return after three weeks – no exercise, she missed mixing with a wide peer age-group and she didn't like the regimented way subjects were taught.

Past pupils: Oliver Tobias, Sean Yates (international cyclist), Bella Freud, Esther Freud, Marty Boysens (mountaineer), Prof John Pearce (author and professor of child psychiatry at Nottingham University), Stuart Korth (Osteopathic Centre for Children), Frank Dillane (actor), Oliver Chris (actor), Rowan Harrington (DJ and producer).

Entrance: At no specific age – 'the younger the better'; natural breaks in the Steiner curriculum occur at 6 and 14 years old. Non-selective in academic sense, although much effort to ensure class communities mesh. Mild dyslexia and dyspraxia fine (often diagnosed and always supported by learning support department) – more severe conditions sometimes OK as long as children are in system from kindergarten and their needs do not detract from quality of whole class education. Class teacher will interview potential parents/pupils – previous experience of French or German and music an advantage. Brighton Steiner and Waldorf School of south West London are main feeders at age 14. Sixth form entry by interview.

Exit: Up to 15 per cent leave at 12/13 to enter mainstream schools. Some 30-50 per cent after GCSE for sixth form college in order to take more vocational A levels. Most upper schoolers go on to degree courses: two to Oxford in 2018; others to study eg illustration at the University for Creative Arts, Edinburgh, law at Nottingham, outdoor adventure and environment at Cumbria, physics at Durham. Many European universities take Steiner pupils without external qualification. Subjects include music, architecture, history, psychology, drama and art foundation. Some take gap years to improve language skills and cultural appreciation.

Money matters: School runs a bursary scheme through which families on lower incomes are able to pay lower tuition charges. To qualify, a detailed statement of income has to be provided to the school. Discounts on fees for siblings. Extras: organic two-course hot lunch, charged for each day of the week it is eaten, individual music lesson and instrument hire.

Remarks: A gentle school which aims to keep children from rushing into adulthood before they're ready and parents value for 'creating innovators'. This education will not work for every child, nor every parent – both would need to be tremendously involved in the educative process. Very difficult to explain a Steiner school without direct experience or attending an open morning – hippy stereotypes abound and you might find a compost bucket resting on a photocopier – yet this school is a beacon of professionalism among UK Steiner schools and the children who emerge are confident, articulate, international, open-minded and grounded. Lucky them.

M

Milbourne Lodge School

Arbrook Lane, Esher, Surrey KT10 9EG

Ages 4–13 **Pupils** 280 (238 boys, 42 girls) **C of E**

Fees: £12,240 – £15,390 pa

01372 462737
www.milbournelodge.co.uk

Head: Since January 2016, Judy Waite BA, previously deputy head. Educated at The Tiffin Girls' School in Kingston upon Thames, then read modern history, economics and politics at London University, followed by a PGCE at the Institute of Education. She started her teaching career in secondary schools, teaching history and politics at Croydon High School GDST, then at a variety of comprehensives. Her twin sons (a lawyer and a banker) attended Milbourne Lodge and she liked the school's ethos of 'work hard, play hard' so much that when a job came up she made the switch from secondary to prep school education. She started as an English and history teacher in 2010, was deputy for three years and then became head. 'It's great to lead a school whose values I absolutely believe in,' she says.

She loves teaching and still teaches English to year 5 pupils and history in the upper school. 'I can't imagine doing anything else,' she says. 'I want to give the children a thirst for knowledge.' She believes that teaching enables her to see the curriculum from the inside and to know all the children well, which helps when it comes to advising parents on future schools. Excellent connections with schools like Westminster and St Paul's (she predicted both of these would abandon common entrance before the official announcement). She's also a firm believer in children having 'a balance of studying and physical activity every day' and all the Milbourne children get this. 'If it rains we just carry on,' says the head. Often playful and fun when she leads assemblies, she's a stickler for hard work and excellent behaviour in the classroom. 'If they cross the line I'm terrifying,' she jokes.

Warm, dynamic and fizzing with ideas, she's very visible around the school. Parents say she is 'a good leader' and 'very much embodies the Milbourne spirit'. One told us: 'She's a great ambassador for the school and she really embraces and supports the school's idiosyncrasies and quirkiness.' Another remarked on her approachability – 'she's very often on the gate in the morning.' In her spare time she enjoys studying historical battles and archaeology and goes boogie boarding in Cornwall. Her husband Rob is a retired engineer and often helps out around the school, taking on everything from odd jobs to coaching rugby. He also referees rugby at St Paul's School.

Entrance: Entry to the school is selective. Children registered for reception entry are invited to an informal activity session 18 months before they join the school. Around ten to 12 new entrants start in year 3 (the whole year group is about 40), following a November assessment in maths and English and an informal discussion with a senior member of staff, plus a games session with sports staff.

Exit: The majority of pre-prep children move to the prep (they don't have far to go – everything is on the same site). Most prep pupils stay till 13, although girls opting for all-girls' schools tend to leave at 11. The wooden boards in the entrance hall bear testimony to an impressive array of leavers' destinations, with scholars' names engraved in gold lettering. Popular destinations for boys include St Paul's, Eton, Westminster, Tonbridge and King's College School, Wimbledon while girls often head to schools like Downe House, Wycombe Abbey and Lady Eleanor Holles. Those who want co-ed choose schools like Epsom College, St John's School, Leatherhead and Charterhouse (which will admit girls from year 9 from 2021).

Remarks: Founded in 1912 by Harvey Wyatt, Milbourne Lodge built up a formidable academic reputation under the classicist Norman Hale, who was owner and head from 1948 to 1998. In 2007, the school became part of the Cognita Group, which owns and manages 70 schools in Europe, Latin America and Asia. The School Inspection Service judged it to be 'outstanding in all areas' in 2017.

The school has remained on its original site, set back from a quiet, leafy lane in Esher. The main building is a converted Victorian mansion – very charming and busy, with every inch of space used to maximum effect. Recent additions include a stylish new building complex, named after Norman Hale and comprising six new classrooms and a swish science lab equipped with Bunsen burners and microscopes. There's a new music block and a resources centre, which the pre-prep uses for assemblies. Four classrooms are housed in a large wooden hut in the garden – they look fairly basic but the children love them. Extensive playing fields are a short walk away but still on the same site. The heated outdoor swimming pool is used from just after Easter to the October half-term. There's also an award-winning garden, where the children grow their own produce.

Milbourne Lodge offers a traditional, very personalised education for energetic, bright pupils in pursuit of excellence. The school motto says it all really – 'ad optima petenda', in other words, 'strive for excellence'. English and maths are set from year 4 but it's 'very flexible' and children frequently move sets. French from year 2 and Latin from year 4, plus Greek for scholars and separate sciences from year 5. Parents says the school's size means that the education is 'tailor-made' for every child. A mother told us: 'Every child is known – and their strengths and weaknesses are known.' Everyone is encouraged to read widely. The school shadows the annual Carnegie award and the staff talk about their own favourite books in assembly (the children have assembly four times a week). They were gripped when the head of sport recalled excitedly queueing up at midnight as each new Harry Potter book was published. 'They found it really funny that you had to wait,' smiles the head. Each year has two forms, with a maximum of 40 in each year group in the prep.

Art and IT are exceptional. In 2018 the school was one of 15 finalists in the David Shepherd Wildlife Foundation's Global Canvas children's art competition – chosen from 4,500 worldwide entries – and was invited to exhibit at the Natural History Museum. The art and IT departments, located at the top of the school, work closely together, sparking off ideas and capturing the children's imaginations. They take on a different theme each year and when we visited pupils had just started a project entitled Money Can't Buy. Their first task was to think of 'something that makes them incredibly happy and doesn't cost anything'. They wrote these on Post-it notes – everything from hugs to friendship – and created a vast poster. We were struck by the children's creativity and ingenuity, particularly a leavers' book with self-portraits in the style of Julian Opie and QR codes linked to videos of the year 8 children talking about their time at the school.

Pupils do sport every day and the school fields loads of fixtures. Despite its size there have been notable successes in rugby, football, cricket and netball. 'Gosh, we are feisty,' says the head. Boys do football, rugby, cricket, swimming and athletics and girls do netball, hockey, rounders, swimming and athletics. A mother whose sporty daughter stayed on till year 8 said she'd had fewer competitive matches in her last two years but she'd also played football with the boys and done lacrosse out of school. She promptly sailed into the hockey A team at her next school. Plenty of opportunities for music and drama, including the Dickensian Evening, where a play is performed in the school's Centenary Garden in December (yes, December), with fairy lights woven through the trees, mulled wine for parents, hot chocolate for the children and a recitation of Benjamin Zephaniah's Talking Turkeys. At the time of our visit the child chosen to read the poem was excitedly planning to wear an inflatable turkey suit for the occasion.

Girls are greatly in the minority. We wondered whether they need to be robust here but a year 8 girl told us that Milbourne suits all types. A parent with three daughters told us: 'It cuts out the princessiness that you get in some all-girls' schools. We absolutely love it.' Pupils say the school is friendly and that they all know everyone. An engaging year 8 boy had made it his mission to know every year 3 child by name by the end of the autumn term. Most pupils come from within a 35-minute drive (the A3 and M25 are within easy reach). Some are very local and walk to school, others are driven in by their parents (no cars allowed on the school site) or get the bus from places like Guildford, Oxshott, Horsley and Cobham. The school runs a return minibus from Wimbledon and Putney.

The school is 'digital-free', which the head says gives the children an extra couple of years of childhood. Some pupils who travel to school by themselves have mobile phones but they hand them in when they arrive. The school day is a long one, from 8.15am to 4pm or 5.05pm for the upper school, but the children said they loved being busy. 'You get tired, but in a good way,' one boy told us. 'And we get lots of breaks.' The school runs a breakfast club from 7.45am and there's a sibling club for children waiting for older siblings to finish lessons.

Milbourne is big on traditions, including games like Ambush, Puttocks and the Mornington Mile. 'I couldn't tell you what the rules are,' laughed one mother. 'None of the parents understand it but the children know exactly what to do.' Strong emphasis on PHSEE, with outside speakers invited in to talk to children and parents. Tutors are children's first port of call and there's also the Bob Box, where pupils can post a letter if they are feeling worried about something. Every child belongs to one of four houses and there are house competitions galore as they compete for points for the highly prized house cup, presented in the summer.

Attractive nine-acre grounds, with gardens, woods, sports pitches and an eight-lane athletics track. Older pupils do cross-country runs. Younger ones play Ambush in the Woods (unique to the school and invented 40 years ago by a teacher). 'The children are out in all weathers,' a mother told us approvingly. The food is managed by Cognita's supplier and everything is cooked on-site. The menu always includes a main course, a meat-free option and a snack bar – the children told us they like the curries and the gammon best. Pupils wear dashing magenta blazers, piped in white braiding, and the older children's lapels are laden with badges for sporting and leadership achievements.

The pre-prep opened in 2009 and is housed in the former headmaster's house, stylishly brought up to date with bright, airy classrooms opening on to the pre-prep garden. Prep teachers teach subjects like French and RS in the pre-prep – which all adds to the school's family atmosphere.

Last time round we described Milbourne as a boys' school with girls – but things have definitely moved on. Girls are still greatly in the minority but this feels like a co-ed school, with opportunities for everyone to thrive. Best of all, the children are industrious and engaged, with a sense of purpose and clearly having the time of their lives. As one parent put it: 'They are comfortable in their own skin.'

Moulsford Preparatory School

Moulsford, Wallingford, Oxfordshire OX10 9HR

Ages 4–13 **Pupils** 367 **Boarders** 39 flexi/weekly (from 10 years)

Fees: Day £11,415 – £17,055; Boarding £21,360 pa

01491 651438
www.moulsford.com

Headmaster: Since 2014, Ben Beardmore-Gray (40s). Educated at Ludgrove (where his father taught) and Ampleforth. After history degree at Newcastle he trained as a lawyer and worked in the City, but the lure of the family business was too much for him and he succumbed to teaching. Back he went to Ludgrove where he gained his QTS, thence to Farleigh Prep as deputy head followed by seven years as head of Mowden Hall School in Northumberland.

Mr B-G is a huge fan of boarding. He and his wife, Sarah, have done a stint as houseparents and he also ran boarding at Farleigh. While the majority of pupils at Moulsford may be day boys, the small Monday to Friday boarding community is 'key to the school's ethos,' he says. He sees weekly boarding as 'dynamic' and 'forward thinking' and believes it could well be the future for schools like his.

Boarding also 'draws staff' who are enabled, courtesy of the school's staff flats and houses, to live in what could otherwise be a prohibitively expensive part of the country.

By all accounts Mr B-G had a job of work to do in his first headship at Mowden Hall, so he must have been glad to find his next school in such rude health. He pays tribute to his predecessor (who retired after 20 years) and says, with some relief, that he inherited a 'cracking school' that was 'running very nicely' and 'fantastic' staff. He also seems to have been bowled over by the support and dynamism of the parent community.

Having 'spent his first year observing' and consulting parents, Mr B-G has exciting plans for Moulsford's future. The school already has a deservedly strong reputation for sport; Mr B-G wants to raise its profile in other areas, particularly the performing arts. Hence forthcoming redevelopment of the theatre and music school – cue more plays, ensembles and concerts. He wants Moulsford boys to enjoy breadth of opportunity in as many different areas as possible. All this, we were assured, will not come at the expense of sporting excellence. Some parents we spoke to hoped that leadership change would also herald ethos change in this area. While no one wanted the school to be less successful on the sports field, quite a few wanted more opportunities for chaps who are never going to make the A teams.

Mr and Mrs Beardmore-Gray, who met at university, both hail from this part of the world. The couple have three children plus the standard issue black lab. Down time is for cricket, golf, tennis and cycling.

M

Entrance: Main entry points are reception (for pre-prep) and year 3 (for prep). One pre-prep class; expands to three in year 3 when boys join from schools such as Rupert House (Henley), Cranford House (just across the road), The Manor (Abingdon) and Harriet House (Frilsham), which all kick boys out after year 2.

Entry to reception is first come, first served. Assessment day in October for following September's year 3 applicants. School says it's not 'overtly academically selective' but paucity of boys' prep options in Henley area means a scramble for places.

Exit: Abingdon takes the lion's share of day boys followed by Readley, Pangbourne, Bradfield, Shiplake, Marlborough, The Oratory and Magdalen College School. Boarders to Radley, St Edward's Oxford, Marlborough, Wellington, Stowe, Harrow and Eton.

Remarks: Moulsford and its eponymous village sit on the banks of the Thames just outside Wallingford in south Oxfordshire. Fast rail links to the capital make this picturesque area attractive to London escapees with young families (and deep pockets). The school has always been popular with locals; its distinctive red blazers and caps give chaps a retro Just William charm and make for great free PR in Waitrose. The strange dearth of boys' preps in and around Henley is Moulsford's gain – about a third of the school's pupils come in from there by coach (about half an hour each way).

Before Moulsford took up residence in 1961 the Victorian red-brick building at its centre was a private house and subsequently the boarding accommodation for Cranford, the girls' school across the road. It sits, high and dry, on top of a steep bank overlooking the Thames. Lush water meadows at the foot of the bank do their job if the river floods and the rest of the time accommodate a fire-pit, camps and the school's fleet of river craft.

Head's study and front of house admin are downstairs and boarding accommodation is upstairs. The library occupies what must have been a delightful drawing room with bay windows overlooking the river. Room and contents have been completely refurbished and there's a new librarian to go with the new reading material.

No Saturday lessons but extensive programme of matches demands attendance. Boarding starts at age 10 and is Monday to Friday only. Flexi boarding parents must commit termly in advance to minimum of two nights a week. 'Day boarders' can stay until 8pm. Dorms sleep up to 13 and were, at the time of our visit, looking rather down at heel. We're pleased to report that these have now been refurbished from top to toe, including new mattresses (the latter were previously source of some parental grumbles). As we looked through the dorm windows we wondered if the occupants were inured by familiarity to the priceless view of river and water meadows so charmingly framed by Virginia creeper. We hope these lucky boys remain blithely ignorant for as long as possible of the hours they would have to slave in order to open the curtains onto such a vista as adults.

About 35 boys board at any one time and those we met were keen to tell us how much they enjoyed the experience. 'There's so much freedom. After prep and supper you can kayak or go in the pool and in winter there's movies'. Food – especially fish and chips – got the thumbs up apart from 'something like couscous'. We certainly enjoyed sharing the boys' riverside barbecue lunch.

General consensus from parents is that teaching is 'brilliant'. Just recently, there has also been a major overhaul of the curriculum with a move away from the traditional common entrance exam.

First on our tour was an inter-house maths challenge in the multipurpose hall with stage, retractable seating and very impressive lighting gantry. Small groups of boys, the 'top two or three from each house', were tackling maths problems in a relay. Later on the whole school (including staff) gets involved. Apparently it's very entertaining although we remain to be convinced by the dramatic potential of equations.

Next stop was a year 6 class in the rather swish ICT suite. Boys were learning how to select and export images for use in the picture books they were designing for young children. By way of contrast we also saw little year 2s who were learning to tell the time in a reassuringly hands on and low tech style.

Top set French was a hoot. An inspiring teacher, a bag of props and imaginative use of the interactive whiteboard kept everyone on their toes. No 12-year-old boy should be without the ability to say 'There is a stain on the pillow' or 'The mini bar is empty' and these chaps (according to our notes they were all called Henry or Monty) could bandy such useful phrases with Gallic gusto.

Science labs and art rooms are in good shape and we loved the new stand-alone classroom, all cedar and glass, topped by a living roof – it's been commandeered by geography, which considering the riparian views, seems fair enough. Music and drama are tackled with typical enthusiasm. There are currently two choirs and an orchestra; parents said that music had improved 'hugely' in recent years and all supported head's plans to raise the status of the performing arts.

After-school clubs used to be limited, something parents felt needed addressing. A new 'head of activities' was therefore appointed and lo and behold, a new extracurricular programme of activities has now been rolled out.

We mostly heard praise for Moulsford's approach to SEN though there were one or two grumbles about cost and how out of class support timings didn't always fit in sensibly with lessons. 'Little and often' is the mantra and whether it's help with motor skills, speech and language or handwriting the school will provide support from in-house or external experts. 'Come and talk to us' if you're worried, the head of SEN tells parents.

And so to sport – acknowledged by everyone to be Moulsford's forté. Cricket, rugby, football, hockey, tennis – courts and pitches are tip-top. 'Rugby is our best sport,' boys told us, but added that the school isn't 'just about rugby'. School says all teams get expert coaching and plenty of matches against rivals such as the Oratory Prep, The Dragon and Caldicott. Some parents say this isn't the case for the boys in teams C-F and felt boys who weren't natural athletes not encouraged enough to try different sports such as hockey or tennis. Moulsford is also a top judo school (came joint first in recent IAPS championships) and offers trampolining, fencing, gymnastics, a climbing wall and 'wonderful match teas'.

Canoes, kayaks and dinghies are launched from the school's own creek for expeditions upriver to Goose Poo Island. Forest school, camping in the tepee, bows and arrows, fire building and whittling – plenty of opportunities to make the most of school's dampest asset. Not quite Swallows and Amazons though – participation is limited by the number of craft so not everyone gets a go. Nevertheless, by the time they leave boys should be pretty handy around boats of all kinds – great for those heading to rowing schools such as Abingdon, Eton or Harrow.

The legendary post-CE tradition of throwing each other in the river, beloved by former pupils (known as Old Moles), was retired with the last head. Now boys can enjoy multiple goes at hurling themselves down a huge water slide while parents drink champagne and try not to watch. We imagine most are secretly relieved that their sons are in no danger of a ritual ducking in the Thames

What did they think of the head, we asked a group of boys enjoying their riverside barbecue? 'He's lively,' we were told. And what should he do for the school? 'Make it more famous, not enough people have heard of it.' Other boys were keen to add to Mr B-G's to-do list with requests for a retractable roof for the outdoor pool (parents echo this one) and loos on the far pitches. The cricket nets are, apparently, fine for fast bowlers but too low for spinners. Several boys were very keen to see fishing reintroduced as a hobby. Greatest consensus was over the inverse relation between the expense and quality of the special school socks. 'Six pounds a pair and look!' (They fall down.)

With a loyal crew and new captain at the helm the good ship Moulsford is steaming ahead. Yes, things will change but from what we heard the head's plans are in harmony with parental consensus. Mr B-G told us his favourite book is The Great Gatsby but parents can be confident that under his leadership Moulsford will most definitely not be 'borne back ceaselessly into the past.'

The New Beacon School

Brittains Lane, Sevenoaks, Kent TN13 2PB

Ages 4–13 **Pupils** 400 **Boarders** 16 flexi (from year 5)

Fees: £11,100 – £15,885 pa

01732 452131
www.newbeacon.org.uk

Headteacher: Since 2008, Mike Piercy BA (40s). Read English at Leicester; two headships prior to this one – Moor Park Prep in Ludlow and Dunhurst, Bedales Prep, where he loved the liberal ethos. Previously deputy head at Forres Sandle Manor. He teaches English to all year 5s and runs a weekly drama activity group; 'a natural teacher,' said one parent. 'He's relaxed and well in control, popular, fair and a good speaker,' said another. Skilled at managing parental expectations. 'Very approachable and personable,' said one parent, 'but he is tough when he needs to be and knows what he wants.' Another added that he is 'adept at managing high achieving parents with opinions and quietly sticks to his guns on a non-confrontational way.'

Wife, Lucy, teaches senior music; they have four children between them and live in a house in the grounds.

Entrance: Most join in reception where entrance is non-selective and on a first come first served basis; tends to be oversubscribed so worth registering boys as soon as possible – occasionally a third reception class can be added if there is space. About 60 per cent of boys do the full 9 years. Selective entry from year 3 with testing in reading, reasoning and maths. Those entering in year 5 are expected to commit to stay until 13+. Opening co-ed nursery in September 2019; the main school will remain boys only.

Exit: Send to a wider range of schools than in the past, but Tonbridge then Sevenoaks are still the most popular, with increasing numbers to Caterham and a few each year to King's Canterbury, Sutton Valence and Eastbourne. About 20 per cent leave at 11+, mainly to the grammars and a few to Sevenoaks. 'The teachers are very good at talking to parents and choosing schools and take great trouble to get the school right,' said one parent. Impressive list of scholarships including academic, sport and music scholarships to Tonbridge for the last couple of years – all displayed on the boards in the dining room.

Remarks: Founded in 1863 at St John's Road, Sevenoaks and moved in January 1900 to its present purpose built site in 21 acres on the outskirts of Sevenoaks. It stayed put during the war and even admitted girls for a while. The school was ahead of its time in many ways and introduced a pre-prep department and science, languages and maths laboratories as well as a parent-teacher association long before other schools in the area.

Everywhere well maintained with a rolling programme of refurbishment. The school makes good use of its relatively small site and the latest addition is a swanky new sports, arts and media centre for sports with auditorium, gallery, activity studio and technology zone. The chapel, built in 1912, only holds 100 boys; Friday evening service is compulsory for years 7 and 8 and includes a talk from a visiting speaker, often a from a senior school.

The school is proud of its academic tradition and has high standards and expectations. 'We ask boys to strive for personal excellence,' says the headmaster, but the school 'caters for all and boys are taught at the level they need,' said a parent. Boys don't feel 'over-pushed,' said another. 'They get used to working hard and playing hard but they never feel under pressure; the school is very good at tailoring to an individual boy's needs'. Parents say it is 'very annoying' that the school has a reputation in the area for being a 'bit of a hothouse' as it is 'simply not true and there is a very good level of emotional and academic support'. The school works hard to develop confidence and self-belief and is good at spotting potential – 'my son would not get on the stage when he joined but now has the main part in the school play', said a mother.

Pre-prep and reception housed in bright, airy purpose-built block with their own Astroturf playground. Some 14-16 per class and two members of staff – around half of all teachers are male. Specialist teachers in music, ICT, swimming and games. High expectations and firm boundaries and boys taught to respect each other's opinions from an early age. Taught health and hygiene and given a sticker for eating their veg. Good communications with staff mean parents feel they know how their children are progressing. Early years highly praised by the inspectors, who say all teachers have a good understanding of how young children learn.

The prep school is divided into three distinct sections: the junior school for years 3 and 4 with its own building, the middle school for years 5 and 6 and the senior school for the top two years. Usually about 45 boys per year group with an average class size of 15, but sometimes up to 20. Streaming from year 5, but flexible approach and movement between streams if required. A scholarship class is added in year 8 and the high achieving common entrance boys are streamed, with the other two classes being mixed ability. Boys have specialist teachers from year 4 and are given increased independence from year 5, when they start moving classrooms for lessons. ICT ties in with all subjects and 'it's fun,' said a boy. French introduced in year 5 and the brightest start Latin in year 6. Classical Greek offered as an after-school club from year 6. Although some of the language teaching further down the school can be 'a bit hit and miss', according to one parent, most do very well at common entrance, with over 90 per cent getting an A. Sciences taught separately in well-equipped labs from year 5. The headmaster appointed three new heads of department soon after he arrived, and a female deputy head, and the staff are a good mix of age and experience. The teachers know the boys well, said a parent, and the reports are very 'insightful'. 'The teachers are very open', said a boy. 'We can ask questions and they don't bite your head off if you get it wrong'. 'I like the fact there are no girls around – it is more relaxing and it means the teachers focus on you'.

Well-used and well-stocked library in what was a 23 bed dormitory, headed by a librarian and assisted by a team of pupil librarians. Boys are encouraged to do their prep at school. Wide range of outings, including history trip to the National Portrait Gallery and Canterbury Cathedral, geography trips for all year groups and the year 8 trip to France includes visits to Agincourt, Crécy and the Somme battlefields.

N

One full-time SEN teacher and two part-timers a well as EAL and maths specialists, and others brought in as required. About 60 boys need some sort of help, and emphasis is on identification and support in the lower years – all are tested for dyslexia in year 2. A handful has one-to-one support in year 5 and above.

Sport taken seriously with the usual rugby, football and cricket and the recent introduction of hockey on the new floodlit Astroturf (also used by the local community). Inevitably more focus on team than individual sports, although school trying to address this with some recent additions to the fixtures including inter-school swimming. Specialist teachers brought in for minor sports like judo and fencing, and sailing offered at a local reservoir. School works hard to find fixtures for the lower teams so everyone has the opportunity to play in a match. Loyal and enthusiastic bunch of parent and staff supporters. Sporting etiquette taken seriously and woe betide any boy who argues with the referee. 'The facilities are not the best in the area due to the limited space', said a father, 'but the boys still win most of their matches', as is demonstrated by the abundance of silverware on display in the entrance hall.

Mike Piercy's particular interests are music and drama and these have come on in leaps and bounds, but not at the expense of sport. The school aims to develop a love of music in the boys, most learn an instrument and all sing – 'it is part of the culture; there is always something musical going on,' said a parent. Two lessons a week starting with the recorder in year 3 and the ukulele in year 6, and boys can learn to compose their own music from year 5. Purpose-built music and arts centre with space for whole class teaching and smaller rooms for individual lessons and rehearsals. Wide range of ensembles including woodwind quintets, percussion groups and string quartets as well as the big band – boys get the chance to perform in all three parts of the school, with informal concerts most weeks and three big ones a year. Two choirs in the middle school, one inclusive and one selective, and year 6 and above can audition for the chapel choir. Choir trip every other year – boys have sung in St Mark's Venice and at St Peter's, Rome. Each part of the school puts on a production once a year with everyone involved. Lots of opportunities for standing up in public, including poetry recitations and debates, and the senior boys hold a Question Time.

Busy art department with its own kiln and opportunities for litho and screen printing. Artwork displayed around the school includes some impressive Dale Chihuly-esque installations in the dining room, made from recycled plastic bottles and painted in the house colours. The art room is well used and always open at lunchtimes. Well-equipped DT room including a laser cutter.

Varied extracurricular activities include chess taught by a grand master, model making, photography, shooting and athletics. 'It is not all about sport,' said a parent, and 'helps boys appreciate and respect different talents'. Strong sense of community and boys appear to genuinely celebrate each others' gifts. Bullying is rare and is dealt with quickly and effectively and boys know who to turn to if they need support.

Boarding offered from Monday to Thursday with space for 18 boarders – just a handful stay the full four nights. 'It's so civilised,' said a boy. 'It's just like home'. The boarding master runs a tight ship and boys do prep and music practice and take part in a well-structured evening activity programme. 'My son gets much more done than he does at home', said one mother.

Many parents 'high achieving, aspirational professionals who drive large 4x4s'. They choose New Beacon because it is clear about its mission of high expectations and academic tradition – there are very few unhappy parents here. About 30-40 foreign national children, mostly of City workers who have been posted to the UK. About 50 speak English as a second language and a handful need EAL assistance.

Early morning club from 8am to help working parents and after-school club until 5.25pm.

Active parents' association puts on two or three events a year, including a summer ball, which give parents the opportunity to get to know each other. Old boys include high court judge Sir Guy Newey, ambassador Sir Sherard Cowper-Coles, England cricketer Sam Billings, Siegfried Sassoon and Vice Admiral Sir Tim Laurence.

New College School

Savile Road, off Mansfield Road, Oxford, Oxfordshire OX1 3UA

Ages 4–13 **Pupils** 161 **C of E**

Fees: £9,870 – £15,951; Choristers £5,763 pa

01865 285560
www.newcollegeschool.org

Headmaster: Since 2008, Robert Gullifer MA Cantab FRSA (50s). Educated at Bristol Grammar School, choral scholarship to St Catharine's College, Cambridge, where he studied English. Somewhat unusual in that his teaching career has encompassed both senior and prep schools. Previously head of English and under master at KCS Wimbledon, deputy head at the Dragon and deputy head at his alma mater, Bristol Grammar School.

He shares his comfortable study with a baby grand, many books and a beautiful double bass on which he's recently passed his grade 3 (with distinction). He sings, plays the piano and the organ ('a bit'), has a fondness for Chaucer and 18th century literature and loves the poetry of Carol Ann Duffy and UA Fanthorpe. So far, so donnish, and he's unlikely to be asked for his passport in this particular corner of Oxford, but Mr G wears his considerable learning lightly and cuts a sprightly dash in a sharpish suit. Parents sing his praises in unison and described him as: 'so kind', 'very understanding', 'lovely', 'understated', 'gentle but firm' – a raised eyebrow maybe; never a raised voice.

He's been at the helm for nearly 10 years but his enthusiasm is undiminished – several parents described him as 'very forward thinking.' The glint in his eye as he explained why NCS has recently abandoned common entrance in favour of the Prep School Baccalaureate (PSB) was that of an unlikely rebel, albeit with a cause: 'CE is narrow, old fashioned, it's losing currency.' He was won over by the breadth of the PSB and the way in which it values all aspects of a pupil's school career: 'It's a flexible, intelligent response to education.' He says his staff are 'delighted' at the change and parents are enthusiastic too – quite a vote of confidence; Oxford mummies and daddies are no pushovers when it comes to the important matter of exams.

As a former boy chorister (local church choir) and undergraduate choral scholar, Mr Gullifer understands the hard work and sacrifices that lie behind the sublime music and more glamorous aspects of the chorister's life, such as making records and tours abroad. He has done all he can to ensure that singers miss as little 'normal' school as possible. Sitting in on a lunchtime practice was a great privilege: the absolute intensity of the boys' concentration belied the seemingly effortless perfection of the sound they made.

Mr Gullifer has two adult daughters and is married to an Oxford law don. One might imagine that they spend their leisure time enjoying the cultural and social opportunities that college life affords – and undoubtedly they do – but only when not undertaking intrepid expeditions, most recently staying with nomads and riding wild horses in Mongolia.

Leaving in July 2019. His successor will be Dr Matthew Jenkinson, currently deputy head academic, head of history and senior English here. He's also one of the chorister tutors. Has a DPhil from Oxford, having won the Thompson Prize at the University of Durham. He also holds masters degrees in historical research and educational leadership and is a fellow of the Royal Historical Society. The author of several books and hundreds of articles on a range of historical and literary topics, his outside interests are – as one might surmise – mainly cultural, though he has a weakness for Italian crime drama and most things Italian.

Entrance: This is a small school with only one class only per year group, so if your heart's set on it for your son it's best to get his name down as early as possible – and yes, we do mean birth. Entry to pre-prep (age 4) is essentially first come, first served and assessment is described as 'gentle and informal.' Entry to prep (age 7) is more competitive and candidates take part in an assessment day, overseen by head and/or deputy head, with tests in maths, reading, reasoning and creative writing. Priority given to siblings at both entry points. Candidates for choristerships (fee reduction of up to two-thirds) are heard at the age of 6 or 7 by the organist of New College. No special preparation necessary; the organist can 'tell straight away if they have what it takes.'

Exit: Majority go as day pupils to Magdalen College School, Abingdon School or D'Overbroeck's. Regular handful to boarding schools such as Eton or Radley (currently less frequently Winchester, despite ancient links). Around 70 per cent awarded scholarships or exhibitions.

Remarks: New College School was founded in 1379 along with New College itself, by William of Wykeham, Bishop of Winchester. According to New College statutes the school was to provide 16 'poor and needy boys less than twelve years of age, of good standing and honest conversation...to assist with serving, reading and singing...in the Chapel'. Wykeham's motto, Manners Mayketh Man, is in English, rather than the customary French or Latin, reflecting the founder's relatively humble origins. We're sure he'd be delighted to see that it now adorns not only school and college crests but also the smart navy blue jumper of the NCS teddy bear. Unlike New College chapel, which is built into Oxford's ancient walls, the school has had several addresses in this corner of the city over the centuries, finally coming to rest at its present site in 1903.

The school's history may be imposing but its public face is anything but daunting. Tucked in securely at the end of a quiet cul-de-sac, the scale is domestic and unpretentious with not an inch of space wasted. Ditto the front of house car park – a challenge to even the most skilled tessellator of vehicles. All drivers hand their keys over on arrival so that reception staff can reconfigure cars at a moment's notice. Parents who bring their sons in by car told us that drop-off by 8am (school day starts at 8.15) 'just' beats the traffic. School bus service extends to Banbury, Chipping Norton, Stanford in the Vale and Henley. The city's park and ride scheme is also recommended by parents of older boys: 'It's brilliant, we drop them off and they get the bus in – they enjoy the independence.'

Cheerful, busy boys in grey and red rush about between lessons and let off steam in the playground or adjacent garden. Pre-preppers have a separate recreation area with well-designed wooden climbing structures. Not a huge amount of space for running around but enough if you factor in the extensive New College playing fields a short distance away (school has its own pavilion). Actual running is done around the nearby University Parks; 'You have no idea just how big they are,' we were told. No wonder NCS runners do well at county and national level. Big emphasis on fitness as well as competition. Plenty of rugby, football, cricket and hockey going on (the latter with notable recent success), all get a chance to play in a team and those teams hold their own against much larger schools, but one feels that ball sports don't dominate here as they can do in other boys' preps. Several current and former parents mentioned that this was a deciding factor for them. Our delightful guide confessed he was 'perplexed' by the lack of swimming. 'We could at least have a club,' he said. Astroturfing the playground is, apparently, also high on boys' wish list.

Head maintains that his is a 'relatively unselective' school, but this is Oxford so the parent demographic probably ensures a ready supply of curious minds and high expectations. The Pitt Rivers Museum, Sheldonian and Bodleian are among three of the city's world famous institutions that are minutes away – there can't be many schools that run a Friday after-school museum tour club. New College chapel is used for weekly services, the pupils are regular visitors to the college and attend special events there. Nevertheless, despite being surrounded by the sublime in all its cultural and intellectual manifestations, 160 boys in a fairly small space ensure that the prevailing atmosphere at NCS is robustly (and delightfully) 'skool'.

One class (max size 20) per year group means inclusive teaching is a must and parents were unanimous in their praise for how the staff manage both to stretch the most able and help those who need it. Children with mild to moderate SEN (dyslexia, dyspraxia, Asperger's) receive 'fantastic' specialist support, custom-built around individual needs. 'Mr Gullifer is so helpful,' we were told, and 'teachers understand – nothing is too much trouble.' However, while the school goes out of its way to be flexible, the pace is fast and boys with SEN need to be able to keep up with their classmates.

Modern science lab, different science taught each term with practicals 'most weeks'. School generally well supplied with technology including not one but two 3D printers, used to produce board games, cups and even a VR headset out of biodegradable material. Latin taught from year 3, so too is coding; ancient Greek offered as extracurricular option. We put our head round the door of the DT room, full of boys enthusiastically sanding and hammering some interesting, if not immediately identifiable, creations. Pupils' written work, art and pottery nicely displayed around the building and corridors feature well maintained boards dedicated to subjects, current affairs and trips. We loved the photos on the noticeboard in the English classroom: boys had been asked to take snaps of their parents reading for pleasure (not on screens and not for work). 'Parents are important reading role models,' we were told.

Internet safety club members, known as 'e-cadets', make presentations to other classes on topics such as fake news. Very entrepreneurial eco committee runs weekly shop selling environmentally friendly pencils, rubbers, folders and biodegradable rulers, plus the 'famous' NCS water bottles, made from recycled plastic. Lots of other lunchtime and after-school clubs include LAMDA award preparation and twice-weekly cookery.

It's certainly a busy life for the 24 choristers but their routine is less demanding than that of other cathedrals (hence no boarding). Boys are not required to sing at Christmas, Easter or Sunday morning services, but they sing the daily services during university terms and also have a full programme of recordings and concert tours – at home and abroad. Being a chorister is a big commitment, but the rewards of such an intense and professional musical training are lifelong. 'It's a privilege to be a chorister parent,' we were told. The training 'enhances' every aspect of school, 'boys recognise the rewards of consistent hard work.' One or two find missing lunchtime clubs 'hard at first' but soon adjust.

N

While boys don't need to be musical to join NCS, the professionalism of the choristers and calibre of music teaching mean that it's highly likely they will be by the time they leave. From year 5 upwards Saturday morning is dedicated to music; the extra time enables the school to have a large orchestra as well as individual instrumental ensembles. Plenty of opportunities for all boys to sing, both at hymn practice and in junior choir, chamber choir or the choral society, all of which can be heard at school concerts and venues around Oxford.

Even the tiny pre-preppers have two music lessons a week (one singing, one 'formal') and perform in their own nativity play and annual 'showcase', so naturally by year 3 they're ready for Gilbert and Sullivan. The G&S tradition had been sacrosanct for years but, shock, horror, comic opera has lost out to splurge guns and parents can look forward to seeing their 7- and 8-year-olds giving it the full gangster in Bugsy Malone. Our guide had fond memories of performing in The Mikado but added thoughtfully, 'I don't think we'll do that one again.' Could Nanki-Poo, Yum-Yum and friends have been silenced by sensitivities around cultural appropriation? The drama continues in years 5 and 6 with a French play, and it's Shakespeare (school's own adaptations) for years 7 and 8. Theatre may not be West End standard but the beautifully designed posters for school productions which line the walls nearby certainly are.

Parents summed up NCS as 'inclusive', 'immensely kind' and a 'close-knit, family school'. They described the atmosphere as 'supportive, not competitive' and 'hugely encouraging'. Staff are 'very quick' to respond to queries and problems are 'solved very fast and at the right level'. Pastoral care is 'excellent', extending at times to parents as well as their children. The only tiny grumble we could elicit was about the food – not quality, but portion size. Fear not, it's hardly Oliver Twist, but several felt the older boys could do with a third sausage.

The motto, Manners Mayketh Man, might sound rather starchy and at odds with such a friendly, inclusive, school – but Mr Gullifer interprets it thus: 'How you behave makes you who you are as a person.' He wants 'every boy to leave here thinking all doors are open', an aim that sums up the essence of a well-rounded education and one which parents, boys and this reviewer agree that NCS achieves.

New Hall School

Linked with New Hall School Preparatory School

The Avenue, Boreham, Chelmsford, Essex CM3 3HS

Ages 11–18 **Pupils** 1,209 **Sixth form** 202 **Boarders** 242 full, weekly and flexi **RC**

Fees: Day £18,546 – £19,878 pa; Boarding £24,579 – £30,681 pa

01245 467 588
www.newhallschool.co.uk

Principal: Since 2001, Katherine Jeffrey MA PGCE MA (EdMg) NPQH. Previously an RE teacher at St Mary's School, Shaftesbury, head of RE at Woldingham School, deputy head at The Marist School, Ascot before coming to New Hall as its first ever lay principal and teacher of theology. Awarded the Institute of Directors' East of England Businesswoman of the Year Award, followed by a national Independent Schools Award for Outstanding Strategic Initiative. Since 2010 she has been a committee member of the Catholic Independent Schools' Conference. Mrs Jeffrey is married with four daughters – all educated at New Hall School.

Making the change from dyed-in-the-wool Catholic convent girls' boarding school of variable academic results to one of the UK's foremost successful pioneers of the 'diamond model' (co-educational prep school, single-sex teaching for ages 11 to 16, returning to co-education for the sixth form) took Mrs Jeffrey a speedy five years. Presumably also nerves of steel, which we don't doubt pulse beneath her polished exterior. 'She oozes confidence and enthusiasm,' swooned one impressed parent, and many laud her 'efficiency'. Indeed, the school comfortably met all the targets it had set itself when adopting the 'diamond model', notably a student body of exactly half girls and half boys. When we visited, New Hall had recently trounced Harrow at rugby and Eton at tennis – to the transparent delight of Mrs Jeffrey. However, amid all this blatant success, at its heart – and its principal's – New Hall remains a Catholic foundation Christian community with core moral values to impart. 'My aim is to shape the adults of the future, form their characters as people of integrity and kindness,' says Mrs Jeffrey. 'We are a community – no-one is here in isolation.'

Academic matters: In 2018, 37 per cent of A level grades were A*/A and 72 per cent A*-B. Similarly impressive results at GCSE – 55 per cent A*-A/9-7. Interestingly, the genders at New Hall are on a par results-wise at GCSE, bucking the national trend for boys to fall behind by 10 per cent. More grist to the mill of the 'diamond model', allowing the teaching between 11 and 16 to be tailored to gender-specific learning styles, with co-ed lessons in the prep and sixth form.

French and Spanish are taught from year 7. Theology is compulsory up to year 11. Computer science for all in years 7 and 8. In year 9, classics, Latin and critical thinking are introduced. GCSE students have timetabled religious studies, English, maths, science and a choice of modern language with Greek a new option. Head of science has the final say in who takes separate sciences and head of languages gives the 'oui or non' or 'si or no', to students opting for two languages. Most students take 10 or 11 subjects, a few more or a few less according to ability. Each student in years 10 and 11 follows a tutorial programme including 'life skills' and careers education. HPQ and EPQ available. Staff reputedly bend over backwards to make sure students shoehorn in their favourite subjects – one parent reported the head of PE giving up his lunch for individual lessons with her son whose GCSE timetable was already full to bursting.

Gifted and talented is taken seriously with accelerated and differentiated learning in lessons and encouragement to take part in enrichment opportunities. The DELTA club promotes scholarly habits (including 'challenge', 'persistence and big picture thinking', 'intellectual courage' and 'metathinking'), and the OMEGA club is for the several each year with sights set on Oxbridge.

Games, options, the arts: 'Our co-curricular programme is not an add-on,' emphasises principal. Sport in particular is taken very seriously. Income has been ploughed into facilities – sleek, purpose-built gymnasium block stuffed with cardio machines and weights overlooks a sweep of sports pitches, 10 courts for netball or tennis (full-time tennis pro nurtures future stars), 400-metre cinder running track and chlorine-free pool in its own block with changing room facilities (also used by the Essex swim squad). A former equestrian arena is now an indoor sports hall with state-of-the-art flooring, while the many horse-related activities take place off-site. County and national athletes in many disciplines, including UK independent school golf and equestrian champions, not to mention star swimmers, cricketers, tennis, hockey and rugby players. A New Hallian athlete competed in the latest Commonwealth Games.

The first time we've come across a choir that's compulsory – year 7 boys and girls enjoy or endure a year before being given the option to remain. 'We have discovered some great voices that way – people who wouldn't have put themselves forward,' says head of music. Choice of choirs for those inclined, including Voces for the broken-voiced, plus instrumental ensembles of all kinds and the occasional rock and pop band. Organ lessons on the restored Norman & Beard organ in the school chapel. Many informal as well as the formal performances. Despite a good take-up at GCSE, a small handful study A level music and the odd one or two each year progress to conservatoires.

There are regular – and by all accounts, spectacular – drama productions all year round and involving all ages, and the Walkfares Centre is the venue for all performing arts. Annual dance show is a highlight and dance A level popular. Own dance company takes students from year 10 upwards and crosses over with the local community. ESB and LAMDA thrive. Around 30 a year take art A level – working away in a warren of atelier-style studios – and about a third continue beyond, though architecture tends to win out over fine art.

In keeping with the school's focus on community and charity, all pupils are heavily involved with the New Hall Voluntary Service, which for many becomes a way of life. One pupil recently received the Princess Diana award – for swimming the Channel to benefit Great Ormond Street Hospital – but all make a contribution of some kind.

Eight houses – unrelated to the boarding houses – contest in competitions of all hues.

Boarding: Cream sofas? Cushions? Can this be a boys' boarding house? For 7-13 year olds? Indeed it is at New Hall. Quite apart from Earle House's jaw-droppingly ornate cornicing and mouldings worthy of a royal palace, the place is spotless in the face of a most unforgiving neutrally toned décor – not a muddy rugby sock nor a mouldering trainer to be seen. Either the staff deserve a medal or this is a new breed of boy. The usual entertainment – large-screen TV, Xbox etc – but arranged in such civilised, convivial surroundings that one could happily invite one's grandmother for a spot of GTA. The dorms too are a revelation – again tidy beyond belief with all belongings stowed neatly into storage compartments hiding behind the ladder treads of ingenious high-sleeper beds, designed by the former New Hallian director of boarding and incorporating a study space underneath. Magdalen House, for girls in years 3-8, is more the usual fayre – though rooms for ones and twos rather than the multiples for boys (full boarders usually roomed with the flexi-boarders) – and a comfortable lived-in look with cheery décor chosen by the girls themselves. Four other houses – two for boys and two for girls as they progress through the year groups – accommodating the 33 per cent who board on a flexi, weekly or full-time basis. Up to 16 reserved places for junior (full and weekly) boarders from year 3 onwards.

Background and atmosphere: The original Palace of Beaulieu, ancestral home of the Boleyn family and thought to represent much of the attraction to King Henry VIII of his second wife (beheaded), perhaps with good reason. Henry expanded the existing building to create a most imposing and gargantuan edifice, with eight courtyards behind a 550-foot wide red-brick frontage and two enormous gatehouse towers. Channel 4's Time Team dug up evidence of the foundations of what appears to have been a nursery for Henry's first-born, Princess Mary. Having passed through a few hands (including those of Oliver Cromwell) after Henry's demise, in 1799 the palace became occupied by the Canonesses of the Holy Sepulchre, one of the most ancient orders in the Catholic church, established in Europe long before the English Religious Community was founded in 1642. Forced out of their home in the Low Countries by the French Revolutionary Wars, the Canonesses brought their school to the Palace of Beaulieu with the intention of offering a Catholic education to girls denied this in England in the Post-Reformation period. Thus, New Hall is the oldest Catholic girls' school in England.

Today's New Hall is (in terms of footprint at least) but a fraction of Henry's pile, but breathtaking nonetheless and approached via a mile-long avenue at the end of which one fully expects a National Trust ticket booth to appear. Perhaps one of the most impressive interiors is the chapel, with its original solid wood door and Henry VIII's coat of arms over the main entrance.

Behind the long façade of the main building, which houses an impressive entrance hall with waiting room, the chapel, classrooms and a boarding house, there is a dedicated arts block incorporating two large studio spaces (which host the school's popular Saturday dance and drama schools as well as lessons throughout the week). The Eaton Theatre seats 210 and is used for productions as well as lectures and year meetings. Large library with study area for all-comers and hanging with Apple Macs. Eight science labs. Spacious refectory reminiscent of the restaurant in an upmarket London department store with a choice of three hot options (the traditional fish and chips on the Friday we visited), plus a salad bar and other cold choices.

Sixth form is a tight-knit community of 200, presided over by staff other than those that continuing pupils will have met in their junior years. Sixth formers have their own wing of the arts block, with study space and chill-out zone including snack kitchen.

New Hall hit the education sector headlines when it became the first independent school in the country to enter a partnership with a struggling state primary school. The school now lends its expertise and guidance to Messing Primary School, 15 miles away – management input, plus New Hall pupil-run events, such as an international day and community carol service.

The new science centre on Mrs Jeffrey's wishlist starts construction in 2019.

Pastoral care, well-being and discipline: 'Parents remark on the smiles here – on the faces of pupils and staff alike,' says Mrs Jeffrey and this does appear to be a rather serene community. Personal qualities, kindness in particular, are recognised and drawn out, and pupils we met were certainly happy in their own skin. This is a Catholic school and although those of all faiths and none are welcome, Christian values are at its core. Support and care for others, both in school and outside it, are fundamental to life here for even the smallest New Hall pupils. New Good Hope café donates proceeds to For Jimmy charity.

Parents too are comfortable in the fold. 'The school has always encouraged parents to give feedback and support the development of the site, by running parent forums and questionnaires,' said one satisfied parent.

Pupils and parents: One clearly in touch with her target market, Mrs Jeffrey appreciates the fact that her school is surrounded by a changing profile of local parents – from the traditional farmers and professionals to city commuters and the grammar school educated. 'Some have attended the historic Catholic schools such as Stonyhurst and Worth themselves and are now looking to us for their children,' she says. Being Catholic is not a prerequisite, but engagement with the religious life of the school very much is. 'If you come here you sign up to the whole package,' says Mrs Jeffrey. 'I would hope that our pupils would leave here well-informed on matters of faith, and that they would have absorbed our core moral and spiritual values.'

Buses zero in on the school from a myriad directions daily and boarders come from all over the south east, many from London thanks to the fast and frequent commuter train service – 35 minutes from Liverpool Street to Chelmsford, four miles away. The rumour is of a proposed new mainline station right at the end of the New Hall drive (no prizes for guessing Mrs Jeffrey's preferred name for it). Long a favourite with overseas pupils, about 45 per cent of boarders, who represent more than 30 countries.

Entrance: Year 7 has 120 places – usually three times oversubscribed. Around 40 pupils come up from New Hall's own year 6, although they too must go through the same entry procedure as external applicants – papers in English, maths and verbal reasoning plus a three-minute presentation to members of the senior school SLT. Lengthy admissions preamble – families have usually visited for at least one open day as well as a group tour including the opportunity to ask questions of the senior leadership team before beginning the formal application. Lower sixth has 150 places, with new entrants needing two 7s and four 6s at GCSE to be in with a whiff. 'Our A level classes are very fast-paced,' says principal, 'with pupils aiming for A* to B grades.'

Exit: Some 30-40 per cent leave after GCSEs. Three to Oxbridge in 2018, plus one off to the Royal Veterinary College. Sixty per cent to Russell Group unis.

Former pupils are automatic members of the Old Fishes' Association (being rebranded as New Hallians) and this association numbers many notables, including international fashion designer Anya Hindmarch, CNN international correspondent Christiane Amanpour, artist and novelist Leonora Carrington, opera singer Stefanie Kemball-Read and Horrid Henry actor Theo Stevenson.

Money matters: Scholarships for Catholics, academic, music, all rounder, sport (general) and tennis, plus means-tested bursaries.

Remarks: There is the feeling that New Hall is much more than the sum of its parts, with personal qualities and integrity as central to the ethos as an application to study and success.

New Hall School Preparatory School

Linked with New Hall School

The Avenue, Boreham, Chelmsford, Essex CM3 3HS

Ages 3–11 **Pupils** 345 **Boarders** 6 full, 10 weekly, 8 flexi (from year 3) RC

Fees: Day £9,801 – £14,478; Boarding £19,761 – £21,531 pa

01245 467 588
www.newhallschool.co.uk

Principal: Katherine Jeffrey MA PGCE MA (EdMg) NPQH. Previously an RE teacher at St Mary's School, Shaftesbury, head of RE at Woldingham School, deputy head at the Marist School, Ascot before coming to New Hall as its first ever principal and teacher of theology. She has overall responsibility for New Hall School, both preparatory and senior. (The prep school is split into two divisions: pre-prep is headed up by Robin Field, while the preparatory division is run by the head of years 3-6, Alastair Moulton. Both of whom were teachers at New Hall prep before taking on more senior roles).

Katherine Jeffrey was awarded the Institute of Directors' East of England Businesswoman of the Year Award, followed by a national Independent Schools Award for Outstanding Strategic Initiative. Since 2010 she has been a committee member of the Catholic Independent Schools' Conference. Mrs Jeffrey is married with four daughters – all educated at New Hall School.

Making the change from dyed-in-the wool Catholic covent girls' boarding school of variable academic results to one of the UK's foremost successful pioneers of the 'diamond model' (co-educational prep school, single-sex teaching ages 11-16, returning to co-education for the sixth form) took Mrs Jeffrey a speedy five years. Presumably also nerves of steel, which we don't doubt pulse beneath her polished exterior. 'She oozes confidence and enthusiasm' swooned one impressed parent, and many laud her efficiency. Indeed the school comfortably met all the targets it set itself when adopting the 'diamond model', notably a student body of exactly half girls and half boys. When we visited, New Hall had recently trounced Harrow at rugby and Eton at tennis – to the transparent delight of Mrs Jeffrey. However, amid all this blatant success, at its heart – and its principal's – New Hall remains a Catholic foundation Christian community with core moral values to impart. 'My aim is to shape the adults of the future, form their characters as people of integrity and kindness,' says Mrs Jeffrey. 'We are a community – no one is here in isolation'.

Entrance: Earliest joining point is at 3+ into the pre-reception class. Assessment is by nursery reports, parent interviews and trial sessions, but the school also carries out home visits and nursery visits, 'so that we can build strong relationships with our families and ensure that a child's start at New Hall is as smooth as possible'.

Exit: Some 70 per cent move up from New Hall's year 6 to the senior school; the rest waylaid by the chart-topping state selective schools in Chelmsford and Colchester, one or two to other independents, and a very few to other state secondaries. Even New Hall prep children must take the year 7 entry exam in English, maths and verbal reasoning and give a three-minute presentation to members of the senior school senior leadership team to secure their transfer.

Remarks: Shares the sweeping mile-long avenue approach to the main school, with a quick swerve to the left to reveal the self-contained wing that is the preparatory school. A more functional building than its palatial neighbour, the prep school is an elongated brick-built edifice with a central corridor on both floors, with spacious classrooms leading off either side, all with large windows drinking in the surrounding acreage.

Although this may appear to be a bricks-and-mortar learning environment for boys and girls aged 3 to 11, it is in actuality a vertex of the much-vaunted New Hall diamond model – pupils are taught co-ed for the preparatory years, split for single-sex lessons from 11 to 16 and brought back together again for the mixed sixth form. New Hall has been a well-publicised pioneer in this arrangement and recent academic results are certainly testament to its success.

Indeed, no sooner had we stepped across the threshold of the prep school than a display case fairly brimming with gleaming cups drew our eye, and our young guides were more than happy to rattle off the most recent accomplishments – many county and national – of young New Hall academics and athletes. A member of the school council was in our midst and, on passing a board featuring his own beaming face and those of fellow councillors, he explained that the school is on the face of it run by the head and the teaching staff but that the school council also in fact has quite a say in what goes on around there. He did, however, lament the veto of a recent request to reinstate crisps as a breaktime snack. 'Worth a try,' he shrugged, philosophically. Yet more cups proved the point that the house system (houses Matthew, Mark, Luke and John) provides scope for countless annual competitions and opportunities to rack up hotly contested house points, including house singing, book week (poetry recitals etc), swimming galas, general knowledge quizzes and sports days. Every Friday, the week's house points are awarded to the house captains during the whole prep school assembly. Annual house cup presented at prize giving. Serious stuff.

A large assembly-cum-sports hall is central to the school. New St Francis Chapel in the grounds, in its own garden with rabbits and chickens. This is a Catholic school and although those of all faiths and none are welcome, Christian values are at its core. Support and care for others, both in school and outside it, are fundamental to life here for even the smallest New Hall pupils. New Good Hope café donates proceeds to For Jimmy charity.

Pre-reception, reception and infant classes – two-form intake all through the school – line the ground floor corridor, all spacious rooms with their own outdoor fenced play and learning space. Usual maximum class size from reception to year 2 is 20. In years 3 to 6, classes can increase to 21 or 22 pupils, primarily to allow for reserved places for 7+ boarders – up to 16 reserved places for junior (full and weekly) boarders from year 3 onwards in two recently refurbished junior boarding houses. Popular with London families. 20 per cent overseas boarders.

All aspects of the curriculum start in pre-reception – science, maths, English, music, PE, performing arts, ICT etc. All learn French from a specialist. At KS2 English and maths are divided into ability sets of around 13 pupils to allow the delivery of a more detailed and bespoke curriculum. Latin once a week in year 6; Latin club open to all in years 3 to 6. Educational visits, workshops, residential trip for year 6, bring classroom learning to life. 'Consistent high quality teaching with a vibrant, engaging, relevant curriculum ensures that our children exceed all expectations, develop a wide range of knowledge, skills and understanding and build a firm foundation for future success.'

A well-stocked and meticulously organised library is arranged with corners for each age group – colourful stools for little ones to perch on while reading – and a suggestion book for titles the librarian said she would be happy to 'investigate' before stocking. No plans to move to e-readers as yet – 'you can't beat the feel of a book,' says librarian, who has a band of year 6 volunteers to help scan in and out. Art rooms are cavernous and newly renovated and there is space for music practice – more than half of pupils learn an instrument and there's a 35-strong, full prep school orchestra. Top musicians get to grade 5 with distinction by end of year 6. Lots of performance opportunities (recently at the O2 and the Royal Albert Hall) and three choirs – infant, junior and chamber (chamber choir has won the Stratford and East London Music Festival for nine years running; junior choir recently won its category too). Impressive.

Prep has its own games teachers but these are bolstered on games' afternoons by specialists from the senior school who coach pupils in specific sports, with great success in local derbies.

'At the preparatory school, we aim to prepare our pupils for the future world; to be independent learners, able to adapt to different situations and of course literate in ICT in order to prepare them for the technological age in which they live.'

Indeed, a thorough, academically focused preparatory school education, enhanced in depth and integrity by the Catholic ethos.

Northbourne Park School

191

Betteshanger, Deal, Kent CT14 0NW

Ages 3–13 **Pupils** 177 **Boarders** 48 full, 5 weekly, 5 flexi (from 7 years)
C of E

Fees: Day £7,632 – £16,755; Boarding £20,985 – £24,300 pa

01304 611215
www.northbournepark.com

Headmaster: Since 2015, Sebastian Rees (40s), a prep school man through and through. Attended Cumnor House and Cranleigh, and describes his time there as 'the best school years you could have.' Read languages at UCL, did his PGCE in primary education, lived in Spain for three years as an English teacher, then returned to England for a spell as assistant head at neighbouring Northbourne Primary before joining Junior King's School, Canterbury as director of studies. After six years he took up the post of head of prep at Seaford College, before the headship at Northbourne beckoned. No plans to move on – this is 'the dream job'. Married to Gillian, the head of the pre-prep here, with four grown-up children scattered hither and yon.

His mother is German, and his interests have always included languages, 'the value of which', he says, 'is immeasurable'. Also likes making things eg furniture, and even a swimming pool, and renovating anything broken. May well have spent hours as a child tinkering with his father's radio set. Thoroughly engaging, he comes across as both thoughtful and down-to-earth, completely on the wavelength of his young charges and in his element at this rural but outward-looking school. Parents report themselves very happy, reassured that the school has lost none of its essence under his leadership and that numbers are increasing. 'A fantastic man for the job,' was a typical view.

Entrance: Twenty-four into the nursery at 3+, of whom between 50-75 per cent usually move up to reception (some leave for the state sector at this point). School is one-form entry with a maximum class size of 20, so not too many places available at 4+. Occasional places in other year groups – always worth checking.

The head likes to meet all applicants initially – happy to Skype those from overseas if this is a problem. Specifically looking for two things: can the school meet the needs if a child requires learning support? And behaviour – 'We're a happy ship, and one child can make a big impact. Above all, we're looking for children who want to be here.'

Children are then invited to a taster day during which 'low level' assessments will be made of their academic ability – ethos is non-selective, but school points out that as a prep school their focus is on preparing pupils for the Kent Test and common entrance, so children need to be able to cope. School also looks for how they fit in with their peers and engage in class.

At year 7, healthy numbers of overseas children apply to join the French programme, replacing the gaps left by those who jump ship for grammar schools at this point. International applicants have their level of English assessed and sit papers in English and maths.

Means tested-bursaries available from reception upwards, usually up to a maximum of 50 per cent. Scholarships available for sport, creativity (art and drama), music and academic excellence. Sibling discount of 10 per cent.

Exit: A number pass the Kent Test and leave at 11 for the local grammar schools. ('I'd like to lose none of them,' comments head, ruefully.) The majority, however, stay on to sit common entrance at 13+. Destinations are diverse, reflecting the intake, and include St Edmund's Canterbury, The King's School Canterbury, Kent College, Benenden, St Lawrence College, Worth, Tonbridge and Dover College. One King's scholarship to Eton, plus a drama scholarship to King's Canterbury in 2018. Most of the overseas pupils go back to their original lycée, but a few stay on in England.

Remarks: Set in 100 acres of beautiful landscaped grounds and approached via a quiet wooded lane, Northbourne is pretty magical, especially on a blustery autumn day with leaves swirling about. The large, grey and honey coloured house, finished in 1845 and looking all chimneys and inglenooks, became a school in 1936 and the current Lord Northbourne was one of the first pupils. He still takes a keen interest in the school, and has been known to take year 8 pupils to tea in the House of Lords.

Dotted around the estate are the Old Rectory, now home to the pre-prep and nursery, and the Church of St Mary the Virgin, aka the school chapel. The Christian ethos is integral to the school and service is held every other Sunday. Attendance is not obligatory, however, and a current Muslim pupil does supervised Koran studies during chapel time. The head and his wife live in the old head gardener's house, complete with walled garden – 'The dog thinks he's in heaven.' Children can go sledging when it snows, and even in September a big pile of wood was in preparation for the traditional Guy Fawkes bonfire.

With some 175 children on the roll and no plans to increase to two-form entry, this is a small school with a family feel. What lifts it above similar schools is its remarkable languages programme. For over 20 years Northbourne has offered a unique provision: at age 11, French and French-speaking Spanish children can join the school's Section Française Bilingue and continue on the French curriculum for years 7 and 8 (Sixième and Cinquième in the French system). Taught separately by French staff, they follow the French national curriculum in history, French and maths – the exams are ratified by the Lycée in London and monitored by the CNED in France, so that pupils can slip seamlessly back into French education when they leave at 13. However, they're taught science, music, art and geography in English, and come together with all the other Northbourne students for sports, art, music, socialising, etc. Meanwhile their English counterparts have been learning French from the nursery and Spanish from year 5 – 'it's very hands-on and completely immersive,' said a parent proudly.

The result is something rather wonderful: an international, open-minded, happy, diverse community, where everyone really does speak each other's language. It's not uncommon for children to leave here trilingual, effortlessly switching between French, Spanish and English. 'The languages are taught brilliantly,' affirmed one English mother. 'Most children who've been through Northbourne will do French and Spanish GCSE early, and many of them will do A level as well.' 'It's been so much easier for my children to pick up French and Spanish because they hear these languages spoken all the time, it's not a big deal here,' said another. 'There were many opportunities for my children to travel abroad. It gave them huge confidence and a massive head start when they moved on to senior school,' was a further comment.

In addition to the languages, there's a broad curriculum for both English and international pupils, covering all the usual subjects. Most classes are taught in beautiful old Northbourne House, skilfully put to use as a school. We liked the science lab in particular. 'We try and keep things as hands on as we can,' beamed the teacher. 'We're currently growing rocket plants from seeds that Tim Peake took into space,' although it seems that micro-gravity took its toll on these – 'They flopped over!'

School operates a two-week timetable with Saturday school on the middle weekend. The lessons we saw were purposeful and focused, but also lively, bubbly and highly enjoyable. 'I still find maths really, really, really, really fun,' said one young year 5 pupil who seemed to speak for many, and the history teacher was dressed up in a crown and sword when we met her, to the children's evident delight. Pupils with additional needs supported by full-time SENCo and team of teaching assistants. School approach is to give support in the classroom wherever possible, rather than taking children out of lessons.

Loads to do here. ('In England you do so many more games!' enthused our Spanish tour guide.) Sports are high quality but inclusive – 'Excellent,' according to a mother; 'the sports teachers have totally inspired our children.' Football, rugby, cricket, hockey, netball, rounders, athletics all on offer, plus swimming, volleyball and cross-country. Outdoor education is also a big part of the school's provision, with opportunities to build shelters in the grounds, spend the night therein and cook breakfast on open fires in the morning. There's a policy of encouraging tree-climbing, although children must stick to trees that are no more than twice their height. 'I love the Broken Bone Tree!' one little girl told us cheerfully – no broken bones in evidence at our visit, however. We loved the notice in the main entrance, 'You may go into the woods today – take care!' Next on the head's wish list is an on-site organic farm and a chicken coop.

Music is 'absolutely exceptional,' 'off the scale,' say parents, 'and other prep schools are in awe of how good it is here'. (Old boys include the composer Sir Richard Rodney Bennett and the concert pianist Freddie Kempf.) Some 70 per cent of pupils can take singing and a wide range of instrumental lessons, and take part in an excellent array of orchestras, choirs and ensembles. At least two annual productions, a senior and a junior one, performed in the sports hall. LAMDA exams also popular. 'The music and drama here changed me! There's so much to do,' said a French student.

As many as 18 clubs on offer at any one time, among them Lego, junior chess and fencing, needlework, yoga, music enrichment and French Ciné. Plenty of residential trips eg kayaking in the Ardêche. Well-used table football in corridor.

The boarding community is mostly international and full-time, although there are a few London children who go home at the weekends and flexi-boarding is popular amongst the day pupils. Girls live in a modern building in the grounds, the boys are housed in the old school where the rooms open onto a corridor replete with stained glass skylights. Facilities in each are comfortable and well-equipped, with dedicated lounges and kitchens for the children and ensuite bathrooms in many of the rooms. Beautiful views from the windows abound. Unusually, there are no official exeat weekends, but the school organises Eurostar trips every few weeks. Parents are allowed to call every day on the boarding house phone (not on the pupils' own mobiles) and time is rationed to 20 minutes each. Boarders are 'thoroughly happy,' according to parents. 'I'm never homesick!' said a French year 7 boy, 'and I love the countryside here.'

The pupils are put into one of four houses, Nelson, Drake, Wellington and Marlborough – all famed, ironically, for licking the French. Any disputes these days are dealt with kindly and swiftly, however, and the head personally makes sure that every incident is resolved satisfactorily. No issues with social media, and access to mobiles and iPads strictly limited, both for day pupils and boarders. Smart grey and navy uniform is worn proudly, and behaviour is excellent. 'The children are all brought up to be incredibly polite – they open doors, stand aside in the corridors, and are so courteous!' confirmed a parent.

The head has shortened the school day – 'Some children were finishing at 6pm when I joined. I felt it was too late for children this age' – but working parents can use the breakfast and after-school clubs, and a shuttle bus means that they can drop off to either the pre-prep or the prep – a godsend for families with a child in both. Indeed, kindness and common sense are the keynotes here. Birthdays are celebrated at lunchtime when the whole school sings Happy Birthday! and Mr Rees personally delivers birthday cards. 'It's wonderful here, the teachers are so kind!' was a typical pupil comment, and a French lad added, 'For me this is a beautiful school and I love the teachers here.' All the children struck us as self-possessed, healthy, confident and chatty. A mother wrote, 'Northbourne has been a total antidote to the whole selective school treadmill. They help children hold on to their childhood and look after their emotional well-being.' Vigorous and articulate, the children had no difficulty criticising the food, however, and as a veteran of school lunches we confess we didn't think it up to standard for a boarding school. School dismayed to hear this, and contends: 'Since your visit we have spoken to many of the children at mealtimes and monitored what they eat and leave behind and it does appear that overwhelmingly they enjoy the food.'

Many parents here are buying into the independent school system for the first time and working hard to put their children through. Others, particularly those from international families, are from quite privileged backgrounds. The children, happily scrambling into their boiler suits and rubber boots (on the uniform list) to go outdoors, seem genuinely and blissfully unaware of any difference. Who wouldn't like it here, we asked them. 'Someone who didn't like to be outdoors,' was the unanimous opinion.

For children lucky enough to come here, this is the most lovely school. 'It's been brilliant for my children, a really special place, completely magical,' was one mother's verdict, and everyone we spoke to agreed. A happy and well-adjusted child told us, 'Wherever you go, Northbourne is your home. I sometimes talk about going home and I mean Northbourne.'

Notre Dame School

Burwood House, Convent Lane, Cobham, Surrey KT11 1HA

Ages Girls 2-18, boys 2-7 **Pupils** 600 **Sixth form** 70 **RC**

Fees: £10,710 – £16,770 pa

01932 869990
www.notredame.co.uk

Headteacher: Since 2013, Anna King MEd MA PGCE FRGS, previously deputy head of the senior school and before that, a teacher in middle management at St George's, Ascot. A Cambridge geography graduate and Fellow of the Royal Geographical Society, she has 20 years' experience of secondary education. She has also written for Oxford University Press secondary geography publications department. Teaches some geography and history to year 7s 'as it's a good way to get to know the girls' and pupils clearly relish the fact that she knows most of them by name, although girls further up the school told us they 'don't see her that much except for assemblies and sometimes in the corridor.' Noticeably youthful and fresh in her attitude, she has brought about significant change to the school and is much liked by parents and pupils alike. 'It's a different place – much more focused and academic, with a far bigger sixth form, and facilities have dramatically improved too,' summed up one pupil. Lives in west London with her husband and two teenage daughters.

Head of prep: Since January 2019 is Amelie Morgan, previously assistant head at St George's College Junior School in Weybridge. History of art degree from Newcastle and PGCE from Brunel; she also has a masters in educational leadership.

Academic matters: Lessons are pacey but not pushy, and that goes for the prep too, where class sizes are usually 15-20, but occasionally peak at 23. The prep humanities curriculum has been overhauled to fit the so-called TASK model (Thinking and discerning; Active participation; Skills for learning; and Knowledge with understanding). 'We have high expectations of the quality of work here,' says school – these girls really won't get away with simply printing out internet 'research' they have not really read or understood. Teachers are careful to ensure no girl leaves a class without having grasped the topic, say pupils. 'There's lot of holding up of hands in lessons,' one explained. Prep pupils have specialist teachers in Spanish, IT, sport, music, drama, Latin and food, and there is a challenge coordinator for the prep. IT embedded throughout. Hefty amounts of homework – praised by parents, although some pupils feel 'there's just too much of it.' Pupils love the cross-curricular approach – 'For example we're learning about World War 2 in history and just did World War 2 landscapes in art.'

Spanish from nursery. 'Not only is it an easier language than many, but we have a number of Spanish schools in our federation, so pupils Skype and make penpals with some – there's a genuinely international focus from early on,' says school. Latin from year 6, French and German from year 7. Plus some extracurricular language options at various points, including ancient and modern Greek and Italian.

Around 50 of the prep school children speak a second language, with some trilingual – school sees this as an asset. Two staff (one for prep, one for senior) lead SEN, with a team of specialist tutors, providing one-to-one extra lessons if required (nothing extra in class). But while the school was once seen a top choice for struggling children, numbers of SEN have gone down and mild dyslexia and dyspraxia is about as severe as it gets now. 'We need the girls to be able to cope with the curriculum,' says school. School is wheelchair friendly in all but a fraction of the facilities, but this was not being taken up by anyone when we visited.

In year 7 the girls are taught in three groups (class sizes around 20-22), apart from maths where they are set in four groups, and English, languages, art and humanities where they are in four mixed ability groups. Then from year 8 they are set in maths, science, English and languages. They can take up to 11 GCSEs; most take 10. At GCSE 52 per cent A*-A/9-7 grades in 2018. Theology is compulsory and most pass with A*-A grades. Other strong subjects include art, maths, English lit, geography (for which the department has won awards) and history. Drama is increasingly popular and Latin is an option but only a handful takes it. At A level, 52 per cent A*/A grades and 78 per cent A*/B in 2018. Of the 26 subjects on offer (for which girls can choose any combination), most are traditional, with some less common offerings including history of art, Latin and classical civilisation. Maths, psychology, English, biology, geography and history among the most popular and successful.

Games, options, the arts: Lucky prep and senior pupils get full use of school sports facilities, which include a new floodlit all-weather hockey pitch and four netball courts; 25m indoor heated pool; full-size sports hall; and 25 acres of grounds (they recently acquired 7.5 acres over the lane). All the usual contenders, including hockey, netball, rounders, swimming (compulsory up until year 9) and cross-country, with girls often competing both internally (house competitions) and at country and regional level. Plenty of teams (A, B, C, D and E for netball and hockey) and indeed of silverware to prove their prowess. School ski trip is hugely oversubscribed. Football, gymnastics, badminton are among other sports on offer.

Drama facilities have a wow-factor, notably the 370 seat Elizabethan-style theatre, which is nonagon shaped (best for acoustics so picks up even the tiniest voice from a nervous performer). Parents have come to expect polished productions (of which there are many – recent examples including Daisy Pulls It Off and Oklahoma) from Notre Dame and over a third of girls take external LAMDA exams. Music also big here – 80 per cent do extracurricular lessons in the prep school, and over 30 per cent in seniors. In prep, there are two choirs, fledglings strings, flying strings, concert band and music maestros (for gifted musicians). At senior level, there are another two choirs, chamber orchestra, string ensemble, concert band and a new rock band. Merits and distinctions abound.

Standout GCSE results in art and design, with all students generally gaining top grades. Their work, which is displayed around the school, includes mosaics, sculpture and paintings – all of a spectacular level.

Clubs aplenty – over 50 a week in the prep alone and many more in seniors. Ukulele, sprinting and chatterbooks (junior book club) popular in prep, and there's even a scissors club for little ones. At senior level, coding and creative writing get big numbers, plus all the music, drama and sports clubs. Lots of 'oohs' and 'ahhs' among pupils and parents when you mention the trips, of which there is a long list including day visits to all the usual suspects, plus camping on the field for year 4s, PGL week for year 5s upwards, and language exchanges, history and art trips to various countries.

N

Background and atmosphere: Opened on its current 25 acre site just outside Cobham in 1937, where it is set in attractive parkland on the banks of the River Mole, with the hum (and view) of the motorway in the distance. School buildings comprise the magnificent Georgian Burwood House, with a maze of modern buildings running off it. All is tidy, well-maintained and resourced with plenty of space. An air of calm pervades.

School is part of the Company of Mary our Lady, a worldwide educational foundation and the oldest recognised order for teaching girls in the world. It was founded in Bordeaux in 1607 and current pupils, staff and governors still pilgrimage there today. The vision of the order's founder, Saint Jeanne de Lestonnac, is embodied in the school's mission statement, and the school has lots of 'special places' including the chapel, which can take the whole prep or senior school, and the La Mothe prayer garden – you will be in no doubt that your daughter is at a Catholic school. The prep motto is 'love, learn, flourish' and the girls are involved in pastoral projects which encourage their personal development.

All starts with 80 children, including boys, in the nursery, which has been cleverly refurbished to be bright, colourful and welcoming. Parents particularly like the wrap-around care on offer – Early Birds and Owls breakfast and tea clubs can provide care from 8.15am to 5.30pm. Like the whole school – the rest of which, after year 2, is girls only – it has dazzling facilities (including colourful and spacious library, music room, science lab and ballet hall, while classrooms are all nice and light) and the children look busy and content. Outside the prep, there are planters for young gardening enthusiasts, adventure playground and treehouse, where lessons are sometimes taught as part of the emphasis on outdoor learning. In seniors, it's the learning resources and sixth form study centre (complete with sixth form parking out the front) that stand out – a shame that more students don't stay on to take advantage of it. 'I think the sixth form is amazing – they get so many opportunities and the careers advice is second-to-none,' one parent told us. School says average size of sixth form fluctuates, but is expected to be around 70 across both years.

While the dining room used to be seen as separating the prep from the senior school, much effort has gone into making it feel as if the two schools are joined by the dining room. Prep girls we spoke to certainly feel part of the big picture here, drawing on all the school's facilities and enjoying interaction with older girls, making the transition at 11 relatively stress-free. The whole school – in its slightly out-of-the-way location – feels safe, away from it all. And even though a significant percentage of families are not actually Catholic, they sign up for the school as if they were – accepting that the belief system is very much part of the set-up here. Girls told us they join in with the morning and evening prayer and grace before meals, attend masses four times a year, study theology and undertake days of reflection. 'Pupils and staff come back to work with a fresh mind. Young people don't generally have enough proper quiet time.'

We can vouch for the fact that food is good. Good job really as it's obligatory to have it until year 9. 'It's all part of our focus on building a sense of community among the girls,' says the head.

Pastoral care, well-being and discipline: Pastoral care definitely not an add-on here. 'I've lost count of the number of parents who say, "My child has never had an unhappy day here",' one parent told us, and every parent we spoke to, bar none, used the word 'nurturing' when describing the school. Gospel values are at its core – 'respect, honesty, forgiveness, kindness, patience,' says school. Lots of peer mentoring and 'big sister' schemes, while praise and reminders about 'desirable behaviour' are drip fed by staff. 'No child is invisible here,' one parent told us. No school counsellor, but there is a school nurse and chaplain. Parents and pupils told us girls are supportive of each other ('lots of high fives and wows when friends do well in something,' said one) and it's not a big or intense place. 'I think it's probably a combination of all this that means bullying never seems to be an issue,' said one parent, although sensibly, the heads won't go as far as saying it doesn't exist.

Discipline is not a word you're likely to hear. 'We are less about punishment and more about expectations,' explains head. 'Girls are keen and want to do well and if they make a mistake, we take the time to work out what went wrong – sometimes that might mean talking it through, sometimes it might mean a warning and sometimes it might mean a detention.' Girls concur that reward schemes are more of a priority than sanctions, except when it comes to uniform. 'And we do have a warning system for things like talking in class and forgetting homework – if you get five, it's a detention, which is seen as pretty shameful.' Meanwhile, in the prep, 'the worst you'll get is a hard stare'. Drugs, alcohol, smoking? 'Oh gosh, no.'

Tradition of pupils helping with a pilgrimage for sick people to Lourdes and sixth formers working in a local home for the elderly and contributing to a project for disadvantaged students in Albania or Spain.

Pupils and parents: A supportive bunch of largely local professional and business families, including a scattering of celebrities among the parents and actress Ruth Wilson and hairdresser Sacha Mascolo-Tarbuck among the old girls. Parents' association, Friends of Notre Dame, is busy and well supported, organising plenty of events – all the usual from quiz nights to golf days.

Neat and tidy uniform is adorned by polite pupils (business wear for sixth formers) who take manners very seriously, holding doors open for each other, no pushing or charging about. But they're reassuringly vocal, with no shortage of chit-chat, although one parent told us alpha females might struggle here.

As the school is tucked away at the end of a long narrow lane, access is by car or school coach only. Rapped knuckles for parents attempting to drop their daughters off to take a walk or cycle up to school – deemed unsafe. Last coach now leaves at 6:10pm to cater for those attending after-school clubs.

Entrance: Juniors from 2+ (early years) 4+ (reception) and 7+ (prep). Occasional places at other times – worth asking. The children attend an observation/assessment day at the school before offers are made – 'We look for a competent grasp of basic skills at a level appropriate to their age,' says school. 'Not ruthless, but working with parents to help them make the right choice.'

At 11, entrance assessment in English, maths and non-verbal reasoning. School says it is looking for talents that already exist that they can foster. Fifty per cent of places go to girls moving up from the prep school. The rest from all over, including St Paul's, Thames Ditton; Holy Cross, Kingston; Ursuline Prep, Wimbledon; and The Study, Wimbledon. A handful of girls join at sixth form, where there are approximately 70 girls in total across the two years – criteria for them (and for existing pupils) is at least a B/6 in any subject they want to study at A level (and an A in some subjects, including maths). Dedicated to Catholic faith, but welcomes those from other faiths or none provided they are 'sympathetic' to the school's ethos.

Exit: Boys leave at 7. The majority of prep school girls (80 to 85 per cent) stay for the seamless transition to the senior school – far more than there used to be. But it's not automatic – girls retain their place through assessment of their progress during years 4 and 5. Those wishing to apply for an academic scholarship are still required to sit the entrance exam. Around half stay on to sixth form, with the other half leaving to do vocational courses or academic subjects the school doesn't run, board or (most popular) attend a co-ed school. High flyers off to read eg business at Surrey, maths at Warwick and psychology at Durham in 2018. School says university admission tutors report back that the quality of the students' personal and school statements is frequently the deciding factor for choosing a Notre Dame student.

Money matters: Bursaries throughout and scholarships for year 7, year 9 and the sixth form. Remember to include extras when budgeting – trips and coaches, in particular, said one parent.

Remarks: We'd be surprised if many girls didn't reach their full academic potential here – and many come away with a love and decent skill set in at least one of the arts too. It's a school that feels small and this, together with the strong Catholic influence, gives a sense of being quite protected from the outside world – a pull to some parents, but may put off others. Girls are busy, focused and happy.

Oratory Preparatory School

Linked with The Oratory School

Goring Heath, Reading, Oxfordshire RG8 7SF

Ages 2–13 **Pupils** 442 **Boarders** 21 full, 4 weekly, 20 flexi (from year 3) RC

Fees: Day £10,266 – £16,443; Boarding; £21,153 – £24,522 pa

01189 844511
www.oratoryprep.co.uk

Headmaster: Since 2017, Robert Stewart (40s) BA PGCE. Educated at Dragon School and St Edwards, Oxford then theology degree from Durham followed by PGCE at Queens', Cambridge. First post at Ampleforth before moving to Eton in 2001. During his tenure of some 16 years he coached rugby and cricket, was head of divinity and ultimately a housemaster and master in charge of Roman Catholics. Open and businesslike, still with shades of public school formality but on his way to getting to grips with the cosy charisma required of a seasoned prep school stalwart. 'Sincere, highly visible and approachable', say parents.

Was 'immediately impressed' by staff upon arrival, so was it a case of a new broom doing the proverbial at this well established local favourite? Reportedly more of a gentle (but thorough) spring clean. The big – and surprisingly controversial – news was the scrapping of compulsory Saturday school in favour of a voluntary programme of enrichment activities, with pupils from years 6 to 8 able to join for some or all parts, or not at all. Following the initial parental protests from a significant, vocal minority though, it's actually gone down rather well – try as we might we couldn't find a pupil who missed it and even some of the most vehement protestors have performed a volte face after trying the new arrangement.

Introduction of hot snacks – sausage and bacon sandwiches – at morning break also a hit, 'a bit like scoring a hat trick', and report cards are just twice termly now – a popular move with staff. High on mid-term agenda is retaining more girls in years 7 and 8, a strategy kicked off with a brand new Astro in 2017, lending itself beautifully to netball and hockey, and an 'absolutely superb' new head of girls' games, 'crucial in creating a sense of being genuinely co-ed.'

Head still teaches RE to years 4 and 6 and English to year 7. Lives on site with wife, Sam, a GP, and their three children – two daughters and a son – all now installed at OPS. Full time dad in holidays, oft found at the family home in Somerset, either cheering on Chelsea FC or dreaming of finding the time to train for his fifth marathon.

Entrance: Non-selective, although tinies now moving up to reception in numbers from on-site nursery, Little Oaks, established 2014, makes it worth getting names down early as most year groups oversubscribed. Assessment morning and report from current school for entry to pre-prep and prep.

Exit: Conversations start as early as year 4, particularly for girls planning to leave at 11. Parents say school 'does not encourage' departure at the end of year 6 so don't expect tons of coaching for 11+ entrance exams. A small handful of boys leave at 11+ bound for local day schools, with now about a third of girls choosing to stay put and numbers rising. Despite boarding angle, parents mostly want co-ed day schools next. Between a quarter and a third of boys move seamlessly up to the Big O, with Abingdon and Radley popular alternative single sex options, St Helen and St Katharine or Queen Anne's for girls and Pangbourne, Wellington and Bradfield on the co-ed front. Broad range of awards: all-rounder, drama, art and multiple sports.

Remarks: Approached down a seemingly endless drive that winds through some 65 acres of grounds, before opening out to reveal the lovely arts and crafts main school building, with its wealth of original features including oak staircase and panelled, Hogwarts-esque, dining hall. Modern additions from assorted decades, the most recent a beautifully designed wood clad nursery for pupils from 2+ set in the heart of the woodland. Pre-prep housed in former stables with top notch outdoor facilities and jolly classrooms adorned with examples of pupils' written and artwork. Outdoor learning, including forest school, strongly in evidence with an enviable abundance of fields, ponds and woodland lending itself beautifully to the cause.

With just 35 per cent of the cohort RC, it's catholicism with a small c: 'parents buy into our strong pastoral ethos and we're keen to make the school as accessible as possible to all religions and cultures', says head. Daily prayers, hymns in assembly and the charming Father Ken – also chaplain at the senior school – are the only obvious indications of school's religious foundation, although all pupils attend mass once a week in delightfully compact school chapel (termly for pre-prep). Parents praise the overwhelmingly 'kind and thoughtful' culture of the school, streaming down from a number of 'genuinely spiritual' senior staff members modelling Christian values. Any pastoral issues reportedly ironed swiftly out with parents 'impressed' by the way things are dealt with.

Surprisingly, boys outnumber girls two to one; school has genuine co-ed vibe, and the girls certainly make their presence felt. This helped by uplift in those continuing into year 7 (over 30 girls in combined years 7 and 8 at the time of our visit), who operate as single entity for sports and social events and 'really have each others' backs'. 'Not a glitzy school,' according to head, with large number of first time buyers and a down to earth feel, pupils coming from a radius of up to 30 minutes. Little racial diversity (less than 10 per cent non-Caucasian) and head says there are 'occasional issues' amongst pupils reacting to difference, but all faiths are represented in (sometimes very) small numbers.

Solid academics in classes averaging 16. Pupils couldn't choose a particular favourite department, just that 'whatever your favourite subjects are, you can be sure they're covered well'. In the languages department it's French from reception, with two native speakers on staff, Spanish in years 3 and 4 and Latin from year 6. Mandarin on offer as a club. Setting for maths from year 3 with 'plenty of movement', and thereafter in year 7 when a small scholarship set is formed. Parents report 'incredibly high' workloads for the most able pupils – 'a great deal is expected of them' – with a far more nurturing approach to those less academically inclined. Technology used lightly where appropriate – pupils love the 'pebble pads' voting tool in history as well as mathspace on the school iPads. The upside of a very long school day (8.15 am to 5.00 pm including a compulsory hour of prep, followed by optional activities until 6.00 pm) is that very little work goes home – a great relief for parents.

Two dedicated learning support teachers in prep school and one in pre-prep offer extra one-to-one lessons up to twice weekly for pupils needing SEN support, charged as extra. Parents describe department as 'a supportive constant in the background – always there to help'. School can support mild to moderate dyslexia, dyscalculia or dyspraxia and mild ASD. Excellent EAL provision offers eight hours of specialist integrated teaching per week for international (mainly Spanish) boarders who typically join for year 8. Performance 'a big thing'. 'Almost everyone' sings in the non-selective senior choir, although choristers, of course, audition and 'are quite another thing altogether'. We loved the fact that music department (described by head as 'very inclusive' and parents as 'incredible') embraces imperfection with its 'beginners concert' for new instrumentalists, and experienced musicians are inundated with opportunities to perform. Orchestras and bands abound; there are numerous music practice rooms and many pupils achieve at least grade 5 in an instrument by the time they leave. Drama 'really fabulous', according to parents. Senior pupils take a play annually to the Shakespeare Schools Festival and there are combined plays for years 3 and 4, and 5 and 6.

As at the Big O, it's mostly about rugby for boys, although footie results are not too shabby and cricket's also big. Definitely one to beat on the fixture list. Director of sport told us it's 'sport for all', sometimes with two fixtures a week and as many as six teams fielded in years 7 and 8. Parents less convinced that quality coaching is 'for all', though, with grumbles that C and D teams tend not to benefit from the outstanding instruction on offer to the more able players and are often lumped with an inexperienced gappie: 'not a very encouraging message'. Football and cricket also for girls alongside netball, hockey and rounders, now with fixtures and, on occasion, girls playing on boys' teams. Additional options including tennis, athletics, triathlon, darts (darts!) and recently a mini mudder mean that even the most comfortable of couch potatoes should find something to float their boat. According to pupils, though, it's the co-curricular opportunities that are the real cherry on top of the OPS pie. Unashamedly 'outdoorsy', according to head (thank goodness for the sensible winter uniform of roll neck jumper atop shorts and kilts rather than shirt and tie), a plethora of activities awaits pupils at the end of their school day and if that's still not enough older years can choose to take part in the optional Saturday morning enrichment programme that offers everything from talks on philosophy and climate change to visits from senior school heads to three or four weekly modules run by teaching staff on eg cookery or upcycling.

Boarding totally flexible, with all boarders having their own bed, regardless of how many nights they choose to stay and the majority, living locally, doing it 'just for fun'. Boarding houses in main school building, with boys on one side of the staircase and girls on the other. Lovely quirky dorms with up to 10 beds get top marks from us for decoration – unusually, even on the boys' side. Cosy common rooms offer both mixed and single sex socialising areas and are kitted out with table football tables, air hockey, board games and TVs. Quite the most inviting san we've ever seen – and house staff of matrons, nurse and gappies give the place a happy family feel. There's 'loads to do' for the international full timers who get trips to local attractions at weekends.

Prefectships galore for top two years – compulsory duties assigned to pupils according to their interests: art, music, class, ICT, library. Minibus routes morning and afternoon from Reading, Shiplake and Henley. Active parents' association (FOPS) organises coffee mornings, fundraisers and class reps. In the words of one parent: 'OPS is a school for all sorts of children'. A place with a palpable buzz and vibrancy that gets the balance between giving children the freedom to be themselves, whilst maintaining a focus on traditional values, excellent manners and respect, absolutely spot on. No longer a 'boys' school with girls' but a truly co-ed option, one for the list for parents of boys and girls who want their children to reap all the opportunities that a genuine 13+ prep can offer.

The Oratory School

Linked with Oratory Preparatory School

194

Woodcote, Nr Reading, South Oxfordshire RG8 oPJ

Ages 11–18 **Pupils** 250 **Sixth form** 83 **Boarders** 131 full, 14 weekly, 6 flexi **RC**

Fees: Day: £16,917 – £24,966; Boarding: £22,695 – £34,299 pa

01491 683500
www.oratory.co.uk

Head Master: Since 2016, Joe Smith BA PGCE MEd (40s), formerly head of Oratory Prep since 2010. Educated Liverpool University where he got a first in English, PGCE at Brunel, followed by his first teaching post at Colfe's School then 12 years at Monkton Combe, Bath where he became head of English and housemaster.

Sees his role as 'a huge honour and privilege' and, armed with intimate knowledge of the perception of the so called Big O (thanks to candid parents at the prep), has pruned dead wood ('who you put in front of boys in the classroom is crucial') and formed a (mainly) young and dynamic senior leadership team – some existing staff, some newly appointed – with a strong focus on the senior part of the school, particularly the sixth form. Next on the list is the introduction of girls to the school from 2020, with the aim of a 60:40 ratio in years 7 to 9 by 2025.

Youthful, extremely personable and popular with parents and boys, who parents say 'hugely respect' him. Apologised when we arrived for the smell of bacon in his office – he'd just finished breakfast with a group of pupils, a weekly event ('getting to know them is incredibly rewarding'). Always 'out talking to everyone', say parents – and even occasionally serves coffee at school events. Lives on site with wife Debbie, his three children, two boys at the school (one at the OS; one at OPS) and a girl at nearby St Helen and St Katharine, and two dogs.

Devoted foodie, wannabe chef and has recently and reluctantly retired from village cricket.

Academic matters: Unashamedly gentle on the grey matter and results are a bit of a mixed bag – not surprising given the mixed ability intake. Head acknowledges middle ground school status ('we know our niche') but keen to up the academic ante and has appointed new academic deputy to make it happen, and some new young staff who, according to parents are 'spicing things up'. He remains insistent, however, that he won't alienate the less academic all-rounder and will continue to accept some boys achieving 40 per cent at CE (50 is the usual requirement) provided they have 'something else to offer.' Pupils now sit the more challenging IGCSE in English language and lit, French, Spanish and sciences. Most take 10 GCSES, and although in 2018, 46 per cent of these were graded A*-A/9-7, this stat is heavily skewed by stellar performance in art department, with 6 the most prominent grade across the board of subjects and a fair number of 3s and 4s in the mix – particularly, and somewhat bizarrely, in RS.

Parents, however, praise teaching staff – in some cases for helping their son pull a grade 4 in maths out of the bag when they never thought he would – and, uniquely for this most academic of geographical enclaves, are fully accepting of the mixed bag of innate ability. The bright and focused, however, are not an endangered species and we spotted one or two boys who had achieved seven or more 9-8s (identified by their special striped blazers, known as 'deckchairs') during our tour. Head explains ethos thus: 'Boys in our top leagues would be average elsewhere – but we believe that to be a big fish in a small pond can be incredibly beneficial for many children's confidence.' Also: 'We do really well with boys who need a bit more time to mature'.

Trad curriculum with French, Spanish and Italian in the languages department, plus ancient Greek and philosophy to A level. Computer science GCSE now on offer to lower sixth formers. RS (Catholic syllabus) compulsory at GCSE and into sixth form, when boys do not have to work towards an A level but have 'a carefully designed scheme of work on theology taught by Fr David and other members of staff'. A level results, as with GCSE, are representative of the mixed ability cohort: 40 per cent were graded A*/A in 2018 and 62 per cent at A*/B. No significant change to trends in results over the years – we'll watch with interest to see how, as head 'raises expectations of staff and boys', things ramp up. Just one or two take the EPQ each year.

No makeshift former broom cupboard for the learning support department here – it actually is, well, a department. And one that means business too – with 29 per cent of boys on the SEN register it needs to be. A full time SENCo, supported by eight subject-specific part timers, who use a combination of in-class and one-to-one support strategies – and where appropriate a reduced timetable – to bring boys with mild to moderate learning difficulties, dyslexia or ASD up to speed. Super EAL teaching for international pupils – we met several (one who had just achieved an 8 in his English GCSE having arrived from Germany with 'school English' in year 9) who could pass as natives.

Games, options, the arts: Historically synonymous with rugby of the 'guts and glory' variety (is there any other kind?), but look a little closer and you'll find that there are plenty of alternatives for boys less inclined to 'drive for the line' (their words not ours). Nestled amongst pitches and fields galore that fall away into glorious woodland, plus 90 minutes of sport at the end of the day four days a week (the fifth day is CCF – compulsory to year 10), any boy would find it hard not to throw himself into the plenitude of games on offer. There's everything you would expect (rugby, football and cricket are major sports) plus seriously competitive shooting, rowing, badminton and tennis, plus activities including basketball (coached by head), swimming (in super modern indoor pool complex) and golf (school has its own 9-hole course, natch). A separate mention for real tennis: Oratory has one of only five courts in UK schools and has hosted the national championships – get any member of staff talking on the subject and take your seat for a comprehensive education, all the way back to Henry VIII. All abilities represent school in fixtures: 'We're great for the keen but average as well as the superstars', says head; 'our size means we need everyone to play to make up team numbers.' There's that big fish/small pond advantage again. Head says that past marketing focusing heavily on sport 'is a problem' and assures us that school has 'loads of gentle, arty types' but it seems to us that even those boys tend to enjoy casting the paint brush aside and getting stuck into something physical – and if they really don't then this probably isn't the school for them. A full programme of sports will be in place for girls by 2020; hockey, netball, tennis and rowing will be major sports (years 7 and 8 will train and compete with girls at the prep school) but football, touch rugby and a host of minor sports will also be offered. Dance will be added to the curriculum and homed in a new fitness centre and dance studio.

Back on the subject of paint brushes, we were welcomed to the creative oasis (the words 'art department' simply don't do justice) by the positively effusive head of art with the words: 'Why give a boy a paintbrush when you could give him a powertool...or a mop?' And why indeed, when with such tools and alternative techniques such as collage, printing presses, 3D photography, ceramics and modelling can deliver such masterpieces as those by the swathes of boys who choose to take art GCSE, A level and Pre-U? 'We take students much wider than mere draughtsmanship – if they can't handle representation, we get them into abstraction and really engaging with the materials – it's very much a boys' course'. And not a still life in sight. With this ethos in place, results unsurprisingly outstanding. Around half the sixth form cohort take the Cambridge Pre-U rather than A level, with the vast majority achieving D3 or A*/A. Several each year to art college or degree courses – most skipping the foundation stage having surpassed the standard in school. DT adjoins art and is similarly impressive both in terms of facilities and teaching – 'another of our crown jewels' according to our pupil guide. Using industry standard software and equipment, boys are encouraged not to merely design products but to make and, crucially, sell them too, with entrepreneurship encouraged to the extent that more than one boy has a business running on the side outside of school. As with art, exam results are superb and the half dozen or so who choose to pursue the subject after school are typically given very low offers from colleges and universities keen to snap them up.

Dramatic productions performed in very smart recently renovated studio, complete with soundproofed prop room and swish sound and lighting suite. Lots of music too: the inclusive Schola Cantorum sings at masses, vespers and school functions (plus international tours) and all the usual bands, orchestras and ensembles are present and correct. Plus one for bagpipes. Nothing out of the ordinary on the extracurricular activities list – although we love the sound of the very popular ballroom dancing class for sixth formers in conjunction with Queen Anne's which culminates in a ball.

Boarding: Junior boys (years 7 and 8) housed in St Philip House which has its own recreation, social and teaching areas. Boys join one of four senior boarding houses in year 9: Faber in the main building is 'more like a family' with its smaller numbers, according to our guide; Norris, FitzAlan and St John are purpose built, the former two modern, well kitted out (table football, table tennis and darts) and spacious (if a little soulless) with younger boys four to a room, doubles for GCSE students and singles for the sixth form. Housemasters deliberately mix nationalities, and boys' rooms are moved every term. Boys in senior boarding houses expected to manage their own laundry – even the ironing (taken particularly seriously before a social, apparently). Quality and quantity of food a common grumble by parents and pupils and the pizza delivery scooter is not an uncommon sight – tuck box required. Girls joining in 2020 will be able to board from year 9 in a new boarding house – Wootton – named after school's first 'dame'.

Full schedule of evening activities on week nights: sports, public speaking, debating or academic societies; day boys welcome. Wednesday is house night with trips out to cinema, go-karting or trampolining. Weekend activity schedules for the hundred or so who stay are kept deliberately light, although some parents would like to see more on offer. As all boys finish their week after Saturday fixtures, on Sundays there's compulsory mass followed by brunch and then they are free to do their own thing – either relaxing in school or taking a bus into Reading.

Boarding is full or weekly, no flexi, although school has recently introduced occasional boarding – a maximum of 10 nights per half term.

Background and atmosphere: Founded 1859 by Cardinal John Henry Newman, Christian thinker and educational pioneer (beatified in 2010) to create a Catholic boarding school along the lines of the major English public schools ('Eton minus its wickedness') to serve the Catholic community. He provided the school with its motto: 'cor ad cor loquitur' (heart speaking to heart). School remains proudly Catholic ('Catholicism is central and fundamental to our identity – it affects our pastoral and moral side', says head) although there are none of the ostentatious shrines or symbolism so often found in Catholic schools on show, pupils from all faiths and none are equally welcomed. Head too refutes any trace of a formerly austere reputation and institutionalisation: 'I want school to be joyful – formality's really not my style.'

Twenty minutes from Reading and situated just off a main road, and yet the setting is the quintessential best of Britain: rolling hills, woodland and playing fields tipping off into farmland. The 400 acres of grounds are spectacularly well maintained and atop it all is the Queen Anne style manor house which has homed the school since 1942. Beyond the rather severe marble foyer and 'black room' used for concerts and teas, corridors and classrooms rather wash over you – remarkable only in their ordinariness – and for a school so prolific in producing outstanding art work, the main buildings are somewhat bereft of displays of creativity ('the art department probably wants to keep it all', said one of our guides). Safe as houses for any parent concerned about errant sons tripping off to the local – there's not so much as a shop for miles around and school and overall feel is of a slightly other-worldly, idyllic and wholesome bubble – we wonder whether this is at the expense of preparation for real life, though.

Turning co-ed from 2020.

Pastoral care, well-being and discipline: School 'really excels' in pastoral care according to parents, to the point of staff supporting not only the child but the parents and visiting family homes in extreme cases. The four senior houses engender 'incredibly strong house affiliation', says head, to the point that sixth formers recently rejected the idea of their own separate house, although a sixth form centre is in the planning. The Rose Bowl competition – the annual house competition comprising everything from drama and music to sport and debating – is

0

fiercely fought and the most common reason for day boys to take up the occasional boarding beds. Relationships between pupils and staff 'really strong,' say parents – we lunched with a number of senior staff members and can concur we would be happy to entrust our male offspring to their care on the grounds of inspiration, enthusiasm and humour. The resident priests are praised as approachable sounding boards for both parents and boys in need of a chat.

Daily masses and other services in St Joseph's Chapel. Daily prayers in houses, Sunday masses with RC and non-RC boys welcome to serve at the altar.

Few sanctions required, according to head, and traditional methods when they are: head's detention on a Saturday night pretty much as bad as it gets, and there's 'not a huge amount of drinking or smoking' but occasional suspensions for eg violence or repeated defiance. All sixth formers given the honour of prefecture 'unless they have seriously blotted their copybook'. Very little in the way of bullying: 'we are such a small community, the bully themselves would be ostracised', one pupil assured us and boys said that diversity in terms of race or sexuality was well tolerated, although head admitted to school being 'a bit behind the times' when it came to supporting any LGBT pupils.

New appointment of girls' school co-ordinator aims to build strong and meaningful links with the likes of Downe House, Queen Anne's and Rye St Antony. Events include language dinners, guest speakers and rowing competitions (oars not arguments) as well as 'good old socials', where the boys get to showcase those ballroom dancing skills.

Pupils and parents: Traditional with the proverbial capital T with not a shaggy head, thin tie or pointy shoe in sight. If you like boys clean cut and preppy then look no further. We are told that quirky boys do exist here but failed to spot any. Established, professional parents in the main with fewer first time buyers than many other schools. Twenty-five per cent of boarding cohort is international, with boys from European Catholic countries, Russia, Nigeria and Asia. Locals come from around Reading and south Oxfordshire villages – a radius of up to one hour.

Entrance: Entry not very academically selective. Around 15 to 20 places at 11+ with boys tested in English, maths and VR/NVR plus informal interview. Applicants largely from state maintained sector at this point, plus 11+ preps like St Piran's, Chandlings and St Edward's in Reading. ISEB pre-test introduced for entry in 2018 and beyond with around 50 per cent CE pass required at 13+ plus prep head's report and interview. Around 25 out of 35 boys move up from the Oratory Prep school each year, accounting for about one third of year 9 cohort (head aiming to up the numbers to half). Other feeders are Moulsford, Woodcote House, St Andrew's Pangbourne, St John's Beaumont and Papplewick. Scholarships at 11+ and 13+ for academic, music, sport, art and all-rounder.

Will turn co-ed from 2020, with girls' entry at 11+, 13+ and 16+, or other years if space available.

Exit: Between six and 10 leave after GCSE, mainly in search of a co-educational existence, with nearby Henley College a big draw: 'They are attracted by the lack of uniform and co-ed culture, but it's a battle we'll win,' says head, and parents in the know say the boys in question often miss the 'roundedness' of The Oratory.

Not vast numbers to Russell Group universities (around 25 per cent) and only the occasional one to Oxbridge; one to medical school in 2018. Popular destinations over past few years include Bath, Exeter, Oxford Brookes, Royal Holloway, Swansea and West of England. All manner of subjects with a strong bias towards vocational over academic.

Money matters: Full boarding fees in line with top public schools, now topping £30K. Generous scholarships and exhibitions up to half fees, plus means-tested bursaries.

Remarks: Now's the time to look again. Still not the obvious destination for a single-minded scholar, but for the arty, sporty, late developers and just those who prefer a lower temperature environment, definitely one for the list.

Our Lady's Abingdon

Linked with Our Lady's Junior School Abingdon

Radley Road, Abingdon, Oxfordshire OX14 3PS

Ages 11–18 **Pupils** 310 **Sixth form** 79 **RC**

Fees: £16,050 pa

01235 524658
www.olab.org.uk

Principal: Since 2012, Stephen Oliver BA MLitt PGCE (50s), previously deputy head of St Benedict's, Ealing. Educated at the universities of Birmingham (Latin with Greek), Cambridge (PGCE) and St Andrews (ancient history) and has taught at Stonyhurst, the Royal Grammar School, Guildford, Uppingham and Haberdashers' Aske's School.

Was a novice monk at Downside Abbey for a year and a half in his 30s in between teaching posts. Enjoys cricket, jazz and writing – has published Smoke in the Sanctuary, a comic novel set in a Catholic parish in the west of England, and is currently writing his second novel. Frequent, erudite blogs on the school website clearly demonstrate his literary leanings.

O

This is his first headship, and he says that he was drawn to OLA's 'calm atmosphere' and 'nurturing quality'. He enjoys the variety of the job, keeps his hand in teaching Latin and is 'never bored for a second.' Although business-smart with impeccable dress-sense and manners, he fervently denounces the 'creeping corporate culture' increasingly apparent in many of today's independent schools. Married to Caroline; three young children, all at the junior school.

Academic matters: The school motto is 'Age quod agis' (Whatever you do, do well) and while grades are strong, emphasis is on cultivating confident, well-balanced members of society rather than Nobel Prizewinners.

Students take an average of 10 GCSEs, with 50 per cent of grades A*-A/9-7 in 2018. The school follows the AQA syllabus for science and additional science with further enrichment and practical assessments helping ensure that over half the students take one or more science subjects at A level – with solid results.

At A level, 21 per cent A*/A grades in 2018 and 49 per cent A*-B. As more boys filter through to sixth form (the school turned co-ed in 2009), the range of subjects on offer is evolving to reflect this demographic shift. For instance, product design has just been added at A level to run alongside food and textiles design and technology subjects. Now offers EPQ. As you might expect at a Catholic school, religious studies is a core subject and all pupils take it at GCSE – they've got a new suite of classrooms together with the PE department, as well as a new science lab.

Touring the classrooms, we saw obvious efforts made to inject imagination and fun into learning. One year 8 Latin class in the middle of learning about Pompeii had just scattered outside to start building volcanoes. As one student remarked, 'The teachers work hard to make sure lessons aren't boring'.

Games, options, the arts: School has a long-held reputation for the quality of its art, design and technology, and as you enter through its light and lofty Mall, walls are adorned with quite breathtaking artwork. There is good take-up of art and DT at GCSE and A level.

OLA has its own drama studio, equipped with Wifi, audio-visual equipment and professional video cameras. Regular drama performances take place in the school auditorium, which has a seating capacity of 400. On the day we visited, pupils were rehearsing in glorious sunshine for an upcoming outdoor production of Wind in the Willows. Music provision is also strong, with five rehearsal rooms and an ICT suite equipped with the latest music-writing software. The whole school takes part in the annual house singing competition, and carol services often take place at Dorchester Abbey.

The roomy and well-stocked Ratcliffe Library also incorporates a sixth form study centre. Recently renamed to commemorate former pupil, first world war veteran and military cross recipient, Bertram Ratcliffe, the library is also at the heart of the school's very successful annual Festival of Reading.

The school has an impressive 25m pool located between the junior and senior schools. Tennis and netball courts are on the main school site, while playing fields and athletics facilities are just down the road at Barton Field. Hockey is played at nearby Tilsley Park, recently taken over by Abingdon School. However, as parent of a year 9 boy pointed out, the school is perhaps best suited to 'boys who have other interests than playing rugby every five minutes'.

The extracurricular offering is impressive. Students are expected to get involved in at least three lunchtime and after-school clubs every term, with choices ranging from chess to judo to Young Enterprise and justice and peace group. Duke of Edinburgh is particularly strong. Trips outside school are an important part of the educational experience and expeditions have included climbing Mount Kenya and working in an orphanage in Patagonia. The sixth form was in the middle of its annual enrichment week, and we witnessed clouds of icing sugar in the auditorium during some enthusiastic cake decorating, while other students were preparing to embark on a treasure hunt to Oxford.

Background and atmosphere: The school was founded in 1860 by Sister Clare Moore, a nun from the order of the Sisters of Mercy who worked closely with Florence Nightingale in the Crimean War. The Sisters are still represented on the board of governors and visit on various occasions during the school year.

The school went co-ed in 2009, largely due to demand from parents at the co-ed junior school who wanted their sons to stay on past year 6. To reflect its evolving character, the school has recently undergone a brand makeover. A new logo with a greater emphasis on the acronym 'OLA' and an altogether fresher, more contemporary feel, reveals the school's desire to move away from a convent girl image while still celebrating its Catholic heritage.

A centrepiece of the school is the 1907 chapel, where solemn carvings and sacred adornments co-exist with brightly-coloured prayer cards and hand-made paper flowers that dangle in strings from the balcony. It's an image that sums up the essence of this school – a happy and nurturing place built upon strong historic and moral foundations.

Pastoral care, well-being and discipline: Around a third of the intake is from Catholic junior schools, and the school welcomes children from all or no faiths. Senior school masses are held at regular points during the year and on particular feast days – 'We want the link to the Catholic school tradition to be explicit but in an inclusive way,' explains the principal. 'For most people, the Catholic ethos is an attractive feature of the school.' This was generally echoed by the parents The Guide spoke to, who were impressed by the school's emphasis on moral education.

The head of year 7 doubles up as the induction tutor, making sure that all new students settle in well, and small class sizes help to cultivate a distinctive family feel. Bullying is 'minor and infrequent'; 'we nip things in the bud'. Pupils we spoke to agreed, saying any bullying is stamped out pretty quickly. The school has been 'building up' its special needs provision and a designated head of learning support leads a team of five. One parent of a dyslexic son described the learning support as 'absolutely fantastic'.

Pupils and parents: Not an ethnically diverse mix, but reflective of the area's wider community. Gradually increasing proportion of boys. During a sunny lunch break, this reviewer observed a fevered game of footie in the playground, with a solitary girl in goal, while an impromptu game of basketball saw a mixed gathering of girls and boys from different age groups.

A recent survey conducted by the school showed that parents felt communication could be improved, an observation repeated to us. One parent felt that children were entrusted with too much information to relay home, while another commented that 'there isn't a great deal of social interaction between the school and parents.' But overall, parents were full of praise for the school, approving of its small size and a 'family' atmosphere between staff and pupils.

Entrance: Roughly 25-30 per cent of senior school entrants from local Catholic schools (eg St Edmund's and St Amand's), some from as far away as Newbury and Swindon. Around 80 per cent of the OLA junior school leavers move up to the senior school. Main intake at age 11, following exam and interview and at sixth form minimum of five GCSEs at B/6 or above. One parent of an existing OLA pupil who failed to make the grades for sixth form felt the admission policy was 'confused', with the school initially refusing entry but then changing their minds and offering a place.

Exit: Around three quarters stayed on post-GCSE in 2018. The size of the school means that A level students benefit from very small classes with plenty of individual attention and advice. Leavers to a range of universities, popular destinations include Newcastle, Bristol, Nottingham, Royal Holloway, Swansea, Birmingham.Usually several to art foundation courses. None to Oxbridge in 2018.

Money matters: Fees are on a par with the other local independents. Lunches are extra. Academic scholarships and bursaries are available for entry to years 7, 9 and 12, providing up to a 60 per cent reduction in school fees. Special consideration for bursary funding is given to children whose parents are practising Catholics and who attended Catholic primary schools.

Exhibitions are also awarded in art, drama, music and sport, providing some financial assistance with purchasing relevant kit, equipment and materials.

Remarks: This is a school that treats education as an exciting journey, not just a means to an end. Parents of academic high-flyers or sporting champs will probably look elsewhere, but worth serious consideration if you want your child to experience a well-rounded education and the freedom and encouragement to develop their strengths, whatever they might be. Its Catholic ethos has helped create a happy, nurturing school where pupils' spiritual and emotional needs are valued as much as their academic ones.

Our Lady's Junior School Abingdon

Linked with Our Lady's Abingdon

196

St John's Road, Abingdon, Oxfordshire OX14 2HB

Ages 3–11 **Pupils** 75 **RC**

Fees: £9,474 – £13,149 pa

01235 523147
www.olab.org.uk

Headteacher: Since September 2016 Ms Erika Kirwan, previously a member of the senior leadership team at St Mary's Catholic Primary School in Hornchurch, Essex. Before this she was acting deputy head of New Hall Preparatory School in Chelmsford. She has also taught in other countries including Egypt, Poland and Portugal. Classics degree from Cambridge, PGCE in primary education and masters from the Institute of Education.

Entrance: Children are accepted into the school's nursery class at any point after the beginning of the term in which the children reach their third birthday. Flexible about entry at other stages. From years 4 and above children are given short written assessments to determine their academic ability.

Currently 50 per cent local (Abingdon), 30 per cent slightly further (Didcot, Wantage) and remainder up to 20-30 miles away.

Exit: Usually 80-90 per cent of year 6 goes on to OLA's senior school. The two head teachers meet every week and there are shared facilities with senior school for science and DT and shared staff for PE. But an element of distance between the two schools is encouraged to create 'a nice balance between familiarity and mystery' for children moving up. One parent of a pupil with learning difficulties spoke with high praise of the 'smooth transition' from junior to senior school, with the senior school learning support team receiving a 'thorough briefing' about her daughter's needs. Pupils also head off in ones and twos to eg Abingdon Boys', St Helen and St Katharine, Faringdon Community College, Kingham School and Wymondham College.

Remarks: A happy, lively place to learn. The school incorporates the original convent buildings and the charming nursery is housed in the nuns' old laundry room. Red brick, leaded windows and giant arch doorways lend an atmosphere of quaint gothic.

Teaching loosely follows the national curriculum: 'we adapt it to our needs'. In the classes we visited, we didn't see a single teacher behind a desk but instead often huddled down at eye level with the children, friendly enthusiasm combined with focused attention. Older children were quietly sitting down, hands up and no nonsense.

Sees itself as an 'all-round' school, although perhaps not for the super sporty. 'We don't shine at sports', especially when pitted against the many local preps. 'We often come away bruised but happy'.

Not so with the arts. Colourful artwork adorns the corridors and walls and we eavesdropped on a delightful class guided reading of Ted Hughes' The Iron Man. We had a fright upon discovering a full size coffin laid out in one room, only for the drama teacher to pop up and explain its presence as a prop for the summer performance of Oliver! 'One of the dads is an undertaker – very handy!' she exclaimed with glee. The lovely library is run by the aptly-named Mrs Storey and a well-equipped computer suite is available to children from reception age.

Parent-teacher communication is excellent. 'The teachers are kind, responsive and open at all times', said one parent. Every class teacher writes to parents at the beginning of each term, and in the morning the school operates an 'open door policy', where children can be dropped from 8am and parents chat with teachers. As a result, parents are very engaged, the PA is thriving and a number of parents run after school clubs.

There's a big emphasis on extracurricular activity with after school clubs every day until 4:00pm (and the option to pay for after school care until 5:30pm). Forest school is a big hit, and recent school trips included Marwell Zoo and Sulgrave Manor. At the time of our visit, year 2 children had just spent the night in the school gym to prepare them for their first residential.

A focus on pastoral care is obvious throughout, underpinned by the school's Catholic ethos. Pupils spoke enthusiastically about the annual 'animal blessing', where children bring their pets in to be blessed. 'We had horses in the gym!' shrieked one.

A centrepiece of the school is the 1907 chapel, where solemn carvings and sacred adornments co-exist with brightly coloured prayer cards and hand made paper flowers that dangle in strings from the balcony. It's an image that sums up the essence of this school – a happy and nurturing place built upon strong historic and moral foundations.

d'Overbroeck's

333 Banbury Road, Oxford, Oxfordshire OX2 7PL

Ages 11–18 **Pupils** 600 (inc. 67 in International School) **Sixth form** 343 **Boarders** 225 (in sixth form)

Fees: Day £17,730 – £23,850; Boarding + £9,000 – £14,850 pa

01865 688600
www.doverbroecks.com

Acting principal: We heard as we went to press that Jonathan Cuff is holding the fort after the departure of Emma-Jane Henry. English literature and African & Caribbean studies at Kent after a gap year teaching in Jamaica, which inspired her to do a PGCE at the Institute of Education after a year in IT recruitment. She has taught in state and private schools, including Surbiton High and St Christopher, where she was deputy head. She read.

Academic matters: Sixth form offers 35 subjects at A level (all the usual, plus others like film studies, history of art, philosophy, sociology and photography). Unlike some schools (and thanks to nifty timetabling) students can choose virtually any mix of A levels. 'The key to students' success is getting the subjects right,' says the school, which encourages students to choose the subjects they'll enjoy and do well at. 'There is no subject combination that we rule out,' says the head of sixth form. Alongside their A levels some sixth formers do an Extended

Project Qualification (EPQ). In 2018, 78 per cent A*-B and 54 per cent A*/A grades at A level.

The principal says the school appoints teachers 'who know their subjects inside out,' are enthusiastic and care deeply about teaching. Lessons are relatively informal, while being highly engaging and interactive, with teachers constantly checking that everyone has 'got it' before moving on. The students we met were unanimous in singing their teachers' praises. 'You won't find better teaching anywhere,' one girl told us appreciatively. 'I switched to economics quite late and my teacher stayed behind for an hour every week to help me catch up, from the day I started till the week my exams began. I've never found teachers who care this much.' Another said: 'The teachers want the best for you and it makes you want the best for yourself.'

GCSE results are good too. In 2018, 58 per cent A*-A/9-7 grades. Successes in biology, chemistry, physics, maths, English and art are particularly notable. Most students take 10 GCSEs, including three separate sciences and at least one language. French, Spanish, Latin and classical civilisation are on offer but school can organise German, Italian, Japanese, Mandarin and Russian if required (the benefits of having the dreaming spires of Oxford close by).

Academic ethos is the same in both sections of the school. 'We are an academic school,' Mark Olejnik, the genial head of years 7-11, told us, 'but we want children to enjoy their learning. Happiness is the very essence of what we do here.' Learning support offered for mild dyslexia and dyspraxia at no additional charge. Sixth form teachers have been known to spot issues that have been missed by previous schools and target appropriate help for students. Class sizes are small – no more than 15 up to GCSE and up to 10 at A level. There's an emphasis on discussion and confidence-building throughout, with pupils encouraged to offer their views.

Games, options, the arts: The school has worked hard to offer a broad range of sports and activities. Sport isn't compulsory for sixth formers but students are expected to do at least one extracurricular activity in the lower sixth – everything from hockey, rugby and netball to film club, yoga and first aid, plus Young Enterprise and D of E. Lower sixth students also have a compulsory enrichment programme – a variety of outside speakers, from university professors and admissions tutors to writers, scientists and entrepreneurs.

d'Overbroeck's doesn't have its own playing fields but makes the most of the extensive facilities across Oxford. This seems to work well, with students being ferried by minibus to a number of excellent sporting venues including Oxford Brookes (which has an Astroturf, fully equipped sports hall, fitness gym, squash, badminton and basketball courts, climbing wall and more). Year 7 and 8 pupils get three hours of games a week while those in years 9, 10 and 11 have two hours and 20 minutes of timetabled sport.

Drama is a delight, with younger pupils teaming up with sixth formers to stage major productions like Les Misérables and Peter Pan. In years 7, 8 and 9 pupils have a double lesson of art and a double lesson of music each week. When we visited, a group of year 8s were studying 'impossible architecture,' designing fantastical creations that would give our most eminent architects a run for their money. Many go on to study art in the sixth form and one parent told us: 'I am an artist myself and can say that my daughter has been brilliantly taught.' Eighty students take individual music lessons – all levels (beginners to grade 8) and everything from the violin to electric guitar. Recitals by pupils are often held at the Jacqueline du Pré auditorium at St Hilda's College, as well as regular concerts for students of all ages in the school hall. Music and music tech are popular at A level too.

Debating and public speaking are hugely popular. A couple of years ago, a team of year 9 pupils reached the national final of the Youth Speaks public speaking event. 'Opportunities are thrust on you here,' one of the team told us. 'It really makes you want to participate.' Loads of school trips, including recent summer expeditions to Namibia, Iceland and China for year 10 to 13s, annual ski trips and visits to theatre productions in London and Stratford-upon-Avon, science visits to the Rutherford Appleton Laboratory, one of the UK's national scientific research centres, and much else besides.

Boarding: Most lower sixth boarders – full and weekly – live in one of two co-ed boarding houses close by (60 places at new Islip House, opposite the new sixth form building, and 18 places at Hayfield House). Double rooms with en-suite bathrooms at Islip, singles with shared bathrooms at Hayfield. Girls and boys live in separate 'zones', but meet up in communal areas for meals and socialising. Houseparents cook supper, lend a friendly ear to boarders, oversee the 7pm to 9pm study periods and make sure everyone is in by the 10.30pm curfew (11.30pm on Fridays and Saturdays). There's also a small girls' boarding house – Benson's.

Most upper sixth boarders live with host families, all carefully vetted and regularly inspected, though they may live in a boarding house if space allows.

Background and atmosphere: d'Overbroeck's is 'a mushroom-shaped school' – the place gets bigger as it progresses up the age range. It started out as a sixth form college, founded in 1977 by French and Spanish teacher Malcolm van Biervliet, who was head of languages till he retired in 2007. Invited to speak about the school's ethos he said: 'Friendship is a cornerstone in the d'Overbroeck's structure, contributing to the happiness of staff and students alike, and thus making the process of teaching and learning a more enjoyable and symbiotic experience.' Staff and students agree that his vision still holds true today. Was purchased in 2014 by the Oxford International Education Group.

Brand new sixth form centre on Banbury Road brings all facilities onto one site including science labs, a 180 seater auditorium, performing arts suites, library and common rooms.

There's a real buzz everywhere you turn – lots of lively chatter, teachers and pupils on first name terms and an informal and energetic atmosphere throughout. New caterers based in the sixth form centre provide meals for students throughout the school, including dinners for boarders. Some students stroll up to M&S or Taylors in Summertown to buy lunch – they're spoiled for choice. 'This is a relatively informal environment. We don't stand on ceremony but there are clear boundaries and we have high expectations of the students.' Youngsters heartily approve. 'It's not stuffy here at all,' a girl told us.

d'Overbroeck's opened its lower school in 2005, snapping up a Victorian building in nearby Leckford Road previously occupied by Phil and Jim's, a local state primary. A 10-minute walk from the sixth form, the years 7-11 site is compact but makes the most of every inch of space. The lower school now boasts an ingeniously designed main building, with a galleried library resembling the upper deck of a ship, light and airy classrooms and a social area with a vivid pink wall, café tables and glossy blue lockers. The original school hall next door is used for lunch, assemblies and theatrical productions. Numbers in years 7-11 are now pretty much on capacity at around 175, with two forms in years 7 and 8 and three from year 9.

No uniform for sixth form but year 7 to 11 pupils wear smart navy polo shirt or jumper with school logo. 'Apart from that they can wear their own clothes,' says the head of years 7-11. 'As long as they are reasonable. No purple hair, hoodies, hats or nose piercings.' He admits that being called by his first name took a bit of getting used to though the school and students reckon it enables everyone to be themselves.

Pastoral care, well-being and discipline: Pastoral care is widely praised. Sixth form students are assigned their own director of studies (universally known as a DoS) – usually one of their subject teachers. Youngsters talk to them about academic and pastoral matters, with academic progress, attendance, punctuality, work rate and general well-being closely monitored. 'I see my DoS every day,' one boy told us. Parents get a progress report by email every six weeks. Pupils can also talk to a trained school counsellor if they prefer and many turn to the school's dynamic young social organiser – a huge asset to the school, who organises everything from film nights to barbecues. 'We are strict about the things that we need to be strict on,' says the school, and students and parents agree.

Firm rules on alcohol, drugs and smoking. No drugs tolerated – offenders asked to leave immediately. Students say bullying 'just doesn't happen here' and that unlike many other schools 'there is no sense of being considered cool or not cool.' 'Everyone is included,' a sixth former told us. 'It's a really friendly place.'

Sixth formers say that d'Overbroeck's has got its priorities right and appreciate the fact that it doesn't impose pointless rules and regulations. 'If you want a school that makes you go to chapel and has an army of prefects this probably isn't the right school for you,' one boy remarked. The school is firm about pupils being prompt for lessons and handing work in on time. Students who are 10 minutes late aren't allowed into the class at all and an email is immediately sent to their parents. The only gripe we heard from sixth formers was the lack of lockers – a perennial whinge.

Form teachers are the first port of call in years 7-11, with tutor groups meeting every day and staff holding a meeting every week to discuss pastoral issues. The head of years 7-11 stands at the school gate every morning to greet pupils – 'even in the pouring rain,' said one girl. 'It makes you feel really welcome.' Younger pupils we spoke to praised everything about the school, from the small class sizes, 'fair' rules and chocolate cake ('it's not overcooked') to being able to email teachers for help and getting answers back in double-quick time. 'You rarely have anyone in a bad mood here,' said another pupil. 'And I'm not just saying that.' The school has its own car-themed house system – Cooper, Morris and Austin – but unlike more traditional establishments, these focus on environmental matters and fundraising for charity as well as competitions and sport.

Pupils and parents: Pupils are an eclectic mix of high achievers and grafters. Year 7 pupils generally arrive from local primary schools while year 9 entrants tend to come from Oxford preps like Christ Church, the Dragon and New College. No boarding at 11-16 – most live in Oxford and surrounding villages, but some travel from as far afield as Wantage, Faringdon, Swindon and even Warwick. More boys than girls in lower years, but a few more girls than boys in the sixth form. Post-16, equal numbers of day pupils and boarders. UK students come from a vast range of schools (both state and independent) while international students fly in from more than 30 different countries, including Italy, Spain, Russia and China. A handful of very clever Thai government scholars every year too.

The school makes a big effort to keep parents in the loop. Parents we spoke to appreciated its 'modern, unstuffy approach,' 'family atmosphere' and 'emphasis on the important things.' 'My son never enjoyed school until he came to d'Overbroeck's,' one mother told us. 'But he has thrived and been happy here right from the start. He'll be very sad to leave.'

Entrance: The school is selective but emphasises that pupils should have 'a reasonably wide range of abilities.' Alongside the academic requirements staff are looking for students 'who will enjoy the environment and make the most of it.'

Main entry points are year 7, year 9 and sixth form. At 11 and 13 applicants take internal assessment tests in English, maths and non-verbal reasoning, plus a short interview and reference from current school. 'We are looking for potential,' says the head.

At 16 prospective students have an informal interview (they can also sit in on a few lessons if they wish) and need eight 9-4 grades at GCSE, including maths and English. The school also stipulates that pupils need at least a 6 in subjects being taken at A level while those doing maths need at least an 7 at GCSE (further maths needs an 8/9). International students sit written English language test (and maths test, where appropriate) and their level of English must be strong enough for the courses they want to do.

Exit: At 16, around two-thirds of year 11 pupils progress through to the sixth form (a few head to local state schools like Cherwell and Cheney and in recent years a few girls have moved to Magdalen College School's co-ed sixth form). At 18, virtually all go to university – five to Oxbridge in 2018; other top destinations include UCL, Exeter, Bath, Leeds, City University, Bristol, Imperial, King's College London and LSE.

Money matters: A range of academic, art and performing arts scholarships for pupils entering years 7 and 9 (up to 20 per cent of tuition fees). Academic, art and performing arts scholarships available at sixth form level (up to 40 per cent of fees).

Remarks: d'Overbroeck's has made its mark in Oxford as an exciting and forward-thinking place to be, with a lively, happy environment that fizzes with energy and ideas. Along with top-notch teaching and rigorous academic standards the school helps students to achieve impressive results and make lifelong friends along the way.

Oxford High Preparatory School

Linked with Oxford High School

1 Bardwell Road, Oxford, Oxfordshire OX2 6SU

Ages 4–11 **Pupils** 300

Fees: £9,000 – £11,667 pa

01865 515647
www.oxfordhigh.gdst.net

Head of junior school: Since January 2019, Jessica Williams, previously deputy head and head of girls at Ashfold Prep. Born in Wales, educated in Northern Ireland, Cyprus, Hong Kong and England, she has a first class degree in physiology and psychology from Southampton and a PGCE in secondary science and biology from Homerton College, Cambridge. She began her career at Aylesbury Grammar (biology teacher and then head of year 7); has also been head of boarding at Lucton School and a science teacher at Llandovery College. She describes herself as a keen runner and occasional tennis player. She enjoys walking with her husband, also a teacher, and the family Jack Russell, Pippa; they have three teenage daughters.

Entrance: First come first served into reception, then selective; year 3 other main entry point. For entry to years 1-6 girls spend an observed assessment day with tests in maths, English, reading and spelling. School says it tries to give positive individual feedback to parents of girls whose applications are unsuccessful.

Exit: Vast majority (currently over 95 per cent) go on to senior school (same exam as external candidates, but this is not the sole deciding factor). Will advise parents in good time if senior school not appropriate and help find alternatives eg Wychwood, Rye St Antony, Tudor Hall.

Remarks: School believes that girls benefit from being taught in a single sex environment because they are usually ready to engage with academic study more quickly than boys. Not, thank goodness, that we saw tinies doing anything too academic in their characterful Victorian house on the busy Woodstock Road (which even boasts a parent café). Jolly outside space with canopied play area and 'nomow' turf. Youngest start on ground floor and ascend as they grow. Infants now get a hot lunch; other parents must provide packed lunches. Rather neglected feeling library and music room on top floor plus multi-purpose space – one of the benefits that came from the school's decision to close small nursery dept. Another is that reception children now have improved ground floor facilities with more access to the outdoors.

Early years and national curriculum followed but with plenty more added in. Specialist teachers for science, art, music, PE, ICT and foreign languages (Mandarin now taught reception to year 6). School hopes to supplement the ICT provision with iPads – much more mobile and versatile than desktop terminals. Parents we spoke to were all pretty happy with facilities, even more so the teaching and staff. There was a lovely display of photos showing mums and dads sitting at tiny tables trying out some of the activities their children got up to in a normal day. SEN identified early and teaching then 'goes at the pace of the child.' Peripatetic SEN specialists provide one-to-one support as necessary but fewer than 20 at any one time receive extra help. School can (and does) accommodate bright girls with eg Asperger's, but 'parents send their girls with a view to them entering the senior school so they must be able to cope.'

O

We were shown around the Bardwell Road site (years 2-6) by two very self-assured year 6 girls in smart kilts. Lower years wear pleasingly timeless navy blue tunics. Everywhere we looked girls were busy, busy, busy: happily creating delicious-looking Plasticine cupcakes in the big messy art room; doing cartwheels in the gym (it's a red letter day when the wall bars are pulled out apparently, but 'it only happens once or twice a term'), learning about mad Tudor instruments in music; doing 'lots' of experiments in the science labs. System of different staircases operates to avoid rush hour chaos at lesson change-over. General air of make do and mend; nothing at all wrong with that although the library (doubles as venue for music lessons), seems to be in a corridor, with a few uninvitingly deflated beanbags for seating. Hardly the place for those OHJS voracious readers to curl up in bookish quiet. School says that big plans are afoot, 'parents, girls and governors have been consulted about how to make best use of the sites and develop them for 21st century learning.' Our unfailingly diplomatic guides said the food was 'sometimes nice, sometimes nasty', but appreciated the option to have a jacket potato on the nasty days (who doesn't?).

School very proud of the new 'nomow' (do they get commission?) grass quiet area outside a year 6 classroom with its coloured benches and tables – guess this is where girls go to read in peace. Playground is larger than expected, plenty of space to run around and let off steam; includes a netball/tennis court, raised beds, a pond and fountain. Juniors also use sports facilities (swimming pool etc) at the nearby senior school – now have own head of sport. All the usual after-school stuff (art, chess etc) plus the delightfully unusual and popular Morris dancing club. Girls from the senior school come over to help with reading and run activities. Our guides said that they thought their school was 'more intellectual' than others and that there was 'a lot of homework' in year 6 but that it was 'manageable'. Parents (usual Oxford mix of professionals, academics, medics) we spoke to were a pretty satisfied bunch. Lots of praise for the excellent teaching and support and, perhaps, a sense of relief that all being well their daughters were launched on their way to the senior school, the universe, and beyond.

Oxford High School

Linked with Oxford High Preparatory School

Belbroughton Road, Oxford, Oxfordshire OX2 6XA

Ages 11–18 **Pupils** 600 **Sixth form** 123

Fees: £15,546 pa

01865 559888
www.oxfordhigh.gdst.net

Headmaster: Since September 2017, Dr Philip Hills, previously deputy head at Hampton School. First in classics from Cambridge, where he also directed plays and played football (he still coaches sports teams) before going on to write a PhD on Horace. Stayed on at Cambridge as a lecturer and research fellow, then began his teaching career at Eton, moving on to head the classics departments at Bristol Grammar and then St Paul's. He introduced mindfulness to the Hampton curriculum and set up a Latin outreach programme with local state schools. Married to Professor Alison Hills, an Oxford tutorial fellow; they have three children.

Academic matters: Girls study for 10 GCSEs (none taken early) and in 2018 an impressive 90 per cent of grades were A*/A/9-7. Triple award science and iGCSEs. Eight language options including Mandarin and Russian. Responsive and flexible when it comes to A level choices; girls choose from 26 subjects and staff timetable around them. In 2018, 63 per cent of grades at A level were A*/A. Very strong science, plenty go on to study medicine and up to 30 per cent in any year head for Oxbridge.

Teaching is taken 'beyond the curriculum' and staff enjoy the opportunity to lead (or possibly follow) girls off piste academically. The 360 Programme encourages a broader outlook with leadership opportunities, lectures and elective courses. OHS is the first school in the UK to partner with FutureLearn on an online course and runs scholarship programmes with some of its London sister schools including Wimbledon High.

Lessons we saw were a teacher's dream – bright, curious girls excited by their subjects and full of questions and ideas. And what of the perennial problem, girls' reluctance to take risks and get things wrong; how does the school encourage courage? School is on the case. 'We want to help girls develop a core, an inner strength, a sense of self.' There's a drive to foster bravery, of setting the bar higher and higher, either literally in PE, or metaphorically. 'We get girls to talk about the fear, to confront the worst that could happen.'

Games, options, the arts: Inspiringly messy art rooms with very high quality work on display, likewise textile creations of an impressive standard – OHS girls have gone on to the Ruskin and the Royal Academy.

Masses of musicians, as one might expect, with choirs, orchestras, ensembles and bands for all levels of ability. Girls benefit from Oxford's cultural venues and OHS performs in the Sheldonian and various college chapels. Music and drama enthusiastically and successfully pursued as extracurricular subjects but penny numbers taking them at GCSE and A level – not quite academic enough, perhaps.

Clubs are, with exceptions such as bridge, CCF and knitting, subject or sport based. Thus: engineering club, dissection club(!), biomedical club – all serving to extend studies beyond the syllabus. But lest you think OHS girls are living up to the school's bluestocking reputation by being worthy but dull, take a look at the school magazine: it's one of the most witty, affectionate yet wickedly irreverent we've read (and we've read a few...). The rules from 'Top 10 secret tips for writing articles about school trips' should be carved into the desks of all school magazine editors: 'Thou shalt not murder... us with boredom' being the first.

We have heard mixed reports about sport, some feeling that it doesn't quite match up to the standard of academics (rather a tall order) but girls have represented their county and country in a range of events, notably hockey – U16 and U18 county champions – swimming and cross-country. Indeed, swimmers from OHS were selected for British Olympic and Paralympic trials. Girls pursing individual sports at national and international level are fully supported eg exam timetables adjusted to avoid clashes. Sixth formers may take a sports leadership course. Super swimming pool, standard issue sports hall, but on a 10 acre town site space is pretty limited. Fortunately OHS has an arrangement with the nearby Dragon School for use of its playing fields. Partnership with Oxford Hawks hockey club means girls get specialist coaching and use of their pitches. Fair to say, we think, that sport gets A-, rather than an A*. School adds that it now has established partnerships with Oxford United Women's Football Club and the Oxfordshire Cricket Board which have resulted in 'huge number of girls participating and winning tournaments.'

Background and atmosphere: Tucked away unexpectedly behind dons' grand Victorian villas (school is somewhat at odds with local vernacular), the site is currently undergoing a multi-million renovation programme to provide new sixth form facilities and an arts centre (due to open 2020). Bold metal sunflower centrepiece outside reception is an effective focal point and is illuminated at night, thus delivering school's motto 'Ad lucem' (To the light) at all times. Founded in 1895 with just 29 pupils, the school has moved between various North Oxford venues and settled in Betjeman's 'bonny Belbroughton Road' in 1957. It was a direct grant school and head is committed to continuing the meritocratic tradition by beefing up bursary coffers.

The dining hall is a bright and welcoming space with glass walls overlooking outdoor space for al fresco lunch, but with its determinedly jolly coloured plastic chairs looks as though it was designed by adults to be 'down with the kids'. Ditto the reception area in grey and lime green: it's smart but we hope it will stand the test of time. Sixth form cyber café with laptops open all day. Girls say that the food has improved and all usual options – baked potatoes, pasta, salad bar, etc – served up. We were surprised to see beanbags lining the walls of the corridor outside the dining room. 'What are these for?' we asked, imagining perhaps wearyingly long queues for baked potatoes. They are, apparently, a relaxation area for sixth formers, rather popular and thus much hijacked by other years.

Inevitably, given its central Oxford location, OHS has a reputation for being the bluestocking school. And what's wrong with that? It's hardly an insult to be linked to a movement that championed women's education and no one could accuse OHS girls of being dull or frumpy. The uniform is comfortable and low key with sunflower logos on navy blue sweatshirts. Sixth formers wear their own clothes and do not, thank goodness, have to adhere to the style black hole that is 'business dress.'

Pastoral care, well-being and discipline: There doesn't seem to be an OHS 'type'; several parents told us they were surprised to find 'a real mixed bunch.' School says that it is important for OHS not to have a 'house style'; they want all pupils to find someone to whom they can relate and we can report that the phrase most often used to describe the girls is 'really friendly'.

Parents praise the way in which staff treat pupils as individuals, giving positive encouragement to the less confident and helping to bring out the best in every girl. Particularly important at a school where there is bound to be a vocal 'hands up' team in every class. Discipline low key, bullying or other friendship group problems headed off at pass or dealt with promptly. Usual range of sanctions for smoking, alcohol (short-term exclusion), drugs (exclusion).

Pupils and parents: Broad international mix of cultures, especially for a day school; some families are connected to Oxford University or the nearby hospitals. Not snobby; school is keenly aware that parents make significant sacrifices to send their daughters here. They've probably seen the list of former pupils. Deep breath: Dame Maggie Smith (actress); Sian Edwards (conductor); Elizabeth Jennings (poet); Emma Bridgewater (potter); Ursula Buchan (journalist); Sophie Grigson (cookery TV/writer); Louise Williams (violinist); Dame Josephine Barnes (first woman president BMA); Miriam Margolyes (actress); Dame Rose Macaulay (novelist); Anne Pasternak-Slater (academic); Julia Hollander (director); Harriet Hunt (international chess grand master); Joanne van Heningen (architect); Cressida Dick (first female commissioner of the Metropolitan Police); Martha Lane Fox (lastminute.com); Gemma Mortensen (co-founder, More in Common), Sarah-Jayne Blakemore (Royal Society University research fellow and professor in cognitive neuroscience at University College London). OHS girls are most definitely not highly-strung thoroughbreds – these tend to be stabled elsewhere.

Entrance: Main senior school entry at 11, 13 and 16. Year 7: own assessments in maths, English, reasoning and interview. Parents say that the entrance test is a good filter and doesn't disadvantage bright girls from state primaries, but don't imagine that these children aren't given a little coaching. Year 9: assessments in English, maths and a language during year 7. For sixth form entry, admissions interviews and at least grade 7 in most GCSEs, and certainly for chosen subjects. Academic potential and ability looked for.

Exit: A small percentage decamp elsewhere (local co-eds, boarding, state) post-GCSE. Some 14 to Oxbridge in 2018; others to eg Exeter, UCL and York.

Money matters: As other GDST schools, regarded as good value for money. Fees include day trips and ISCO test in year 10 (many other schools charge this as an extra). Variable number of scholarships awarded at 11 and 13 (academic, music and head's scholarship). Scholarships also awarded at 16 (academic, head's, art, sport, music and drama). Bursaries, up to 100 per cent of fees (based on financial need), available at age 11, 13 and 16.

Remarks: Oxford High manages the seemingly impossible task of turning out confident girls with exemplary academic results without turning up the pressure. Serious matters are certainly taken seriously but there's also plenty of fun. 'When the time comes we want them to be ready to burst out of the doors, but we want them to look back with a tear in their eye.'

Pangbourne College

Pangbourne, Reading, Berkshire RG8 8LA

Ages 11–19 **Pupils** 432 **Sixth form** 132 **Boarders** 85 full, 12 weekly, 143 part

Fees: Day £17,655 – £24,885; Boarding £22,170 – £35,190 pa

01189 842101
www.pangbourne.com

Headmaster: Since 2005, Thomas Garnier BSc PGCE (50s). Educated at Sandroyd and Radley, read physics at Bristol and was a seaman officer in the Royal Navy for seven years. He left the navy 'for love' after meeting his wife Alexandra (who's also very involved in school life, including running events such as an annual piano festival) and trained as a teacher. Did PGCE at Oxford, followed by first teaching job at King Alfred's, high performing state school in Wantage, Oxfordshire. Spent 10 years at Abingdon School, where he progressed to housemaster and then head of boarding.

We found him – sporting traditional attire with socks that Jon Snow would be proud of – animated, affable and reassuringly enthusiastic about students having their say (which made it all the more surprising that the ones we met seemed cautious of telling us anything they thought could be deemed as even vaguely critical of the school). We were also struck by how willing he is to adapt, constantly reconsidering the school's policies – he recently, for example, decided to trial a partial mobile phone ban 'in light of what is emerging about their effect on young people's mental health'. Students describe him as 'tall' (he really is), 'well-respected' and say 'he knows all our names – amazing, really'. But although he occasionally manages to fit in some physics teaching, rowing coaching and is involved in the naval section of Pangbourne's CCF, they said 'you don't see him much'. Parents agree: 'You don't have much contact with him, but you can always get a meeting if you need one'. 'I think he's just the right balance of intimidating, which a head should be, and approachable,' said one parent, while a student told us, 'He's friendly, but you wouldn't make too silly a joke around him.'

Has two sons, both educated at Pangbourne (one still there). A firm believer in 'lifelong learning,' he took up the flute again after a 25-year gap, passed his grade 8 with ease and has since done the same with piano.

Academic matters: School welcomes a wide range of ability, although says it has 'become more discerning about only taking students we feel we can genuinely support without it having too much of an impact on others' (the idea being that everyone gets a slice of the pastoral cake, not just a needy few). Head agrees that Pangbourne is sometimes perceived as being 'for the less able' (particularly in the context of the surrounding selective schools) but is vexed, claiming they do a very good job for academic children (there's a gifted and talented programme for the most able) and parents agree: 'We've got one child who is really bright and another who is a bit slow with processing, but they've supported both brilliantly,' said one (and most families we spoke to said they send all their children here because of this).

Setting in maths, science and French from year 7 and English from year 10. Students get a taste of French, Spanish and German in year 7, then most pick one for GCSE (although it's not compulsory). Eight or nine GCSEs is the norm here, including IGCSE English language, English literature and maths.

Students choose between combined science and two or three separate sciences. Latin is offered as an additional extra, despite small numbers. In 2018, 41 per cent A*/A/7-9 grades at GCSE, with strongest results in English and maths.

Around 25 A levels offered (popular ones include maths, English, geography, economics and business studies), plus BTecs in sport, music tech and DT – 'great for the less academically focused students or those who find exams stressful'. In 2018, 54 per cent of A level grades were A*/B and 21 per cent A*/A. School says some of the most heartening performances are found among those who worked tremendously hard to secure Bs and Cs – 'We take real pride in these.'

Tracking data used extensively by teachers; students get 'heatmaps' to highlight their strengths and weaknesses. 'There's been a big push on helping student take greater ownership over their learning and students talk about their work in a much more reflective, positive way now,' says school. Students say teaching staff (two-thirds male and a third female, half of whom live on site) keep most lessons lively, 'but even when the lesson is boring, you do learn,' said one. Good mix of experienced and newly qualified teachers (school has links with teacher training departments at universities of Buckingham, Reading and Oxford Brookes). One parent told us, 'The teaching level has fluctuated a bit and there have been complaints, but latterly they've really upped their game and got some really good new ones in.' Staff hold regular academic clinics and students can also email their teachers.

Learning support available for students with minor learning difficulties – individual lessons offered at extra cost, 'although for most, it's a case of making sure their teachers know how to go the extra mile for them.' School works hard to identify those whose SEN hasn't yet been picked up.

From September 2019, no more academic lessons in Saturday school (there will still be sports and activities) – one parent wondered if the cheers could be heard the other side of Berkshire. No loss of teaching time, though, as lessons will be moved into the week.

Games, options, the arts: A very sporty school, with at least an hour a day spent exercising, with plenty of wins against other schools especially in hockey and rugby; the school's size means virtually all get the chance to represent it. Pangbourne boathouse is a mile from the school, on the scenic banks of the Thames, and school has won the Princess Elizabeth Challenge Cup at Henley four times. Unlike some schools where pupils drop sport in the sixth form, everyone keeps it up here: 'I'm a firm believer that you learn so much on the sports field or hall or in a boat,' says head. Main boys' sports are rugby, hockey, rowing and cricket while girls do netball, hockey, rugby, rowing and tennis. Lots of equestrian enthusiasts – riding popular. One parent told us, 'Initially, it was hard for my son to settle because he wasn't that sporty – thank goodness for the hockey, which he did like – but he's at the top of the school now so that may have changed.' School insists it has and students agree: 'It's really ok not to like rugby – I don't,' said one, while another said, 'The increase in breadth of sports means there's pretty much something for everyone'. Decent facilities, including newly refurbished open-air pool, but students said the Astroturf and hockey pitches need updating.

Terrific music school houses recital hall, recording suite and 10 practice and teaching rooms, as well as four prized Steinway grand pianos – 'I practically live in here,' beamed one student.

Around a third of pupils take individual music lessons, with brass, drums, guitar and singing leading the pack. Loads of musical groups to join, including orchestra, jazz band, choirs and a marching band. Performing arts are on the up with a variety of college productions, theatre trips and drama workshops. Three drama studios and pupils encouraged to take Trinity exams. Everyone does CCF for at least a year and DofE is compulsory in year 9, with three-quarters of students doing silver and a third doing gold. Spectacular art and DT spaces, with healthy numbers taking subjects at GCSE and A level and some mind-blowing work displayed throughout – some of the most imaginative we've seen, including large 3D installations.

Relatively few clubs and societies – school feels that after DofE, music, drama, sport etc, 'the week is already well filled'. All the usual day and residential trips, including to far-flung places such as New York (academic) and South Africa (joint rugby and hockey).

Boarding: Four boys' houses and two for girls (with another one in the pipeline for around 2024), integrating both day and boarding students ('the day boys and girls are very much included as part of the boarding ethos', said one parent). Just over half of students board – around a third of these are full boarders while the rest are either part boarders (Monday, Tuesday, Thursday and Friday) or weekly boarders (introduced in 2017 as a third option). The latter two options grow in popularity as the students move up the school – by sixth form around 70 per cent board. 'We don't actively push boarding,' says head. 'It's a natural phenomenon.' No flexi-boarding, although school offers parents chance to buy 15 extra boarding nights a year per student. Houses are functional, with some homely touches and dorms ranging from single bedrooms to those housing four. Pupils eat breakfast, lunch and supper in the central mess hall. Boarding staff praised by parents for being 'very nurturing' and 'genuinely caring'.

The youngest pupils (years 7 and 8) are housed in Dunbar, a detached red-brick house with its own garden (loads of space to play football, jump about on the trampoline and catch up with friends). Lower school lessons take place in the main school, but the rest of the time students make their way back to these cosy environs. Students told us how students are divided into four 'watches,' (Port, Starboard, Forward and Aft), each with their own 'watch captain'. Capacity for 22 in Dunbar, with around 16 beds taken up when we visited – generally larger dorms than for senior boys.

New life has been injected into the boarding programme in the last couple of years, say students, who cite comedy evenings, magic evenings, Come Dine With Me house competitions ('the food was good – surprisingly good,' says head), among others. 'It's more exciting than it used to be.'

Background and atmosphere: School is set in 230 acres ('half an acre per student isn't bad,' laughs head), in an area of outstanding natural beauty. Founded in 1917, Pangbourne's aim was to prepare boys for service in the Merchant Navy and Royal Navy. In 1969, however, the school was established as a charity, with a similar curriculum to other schools, and these days only two or three leavers a year join the Forces. Even so, Pangbourne prides itself on maintaining many of its original traditions and is the only school in the UK where students wear Royal Navy officer cadet uniform every day.

Students parade in their number one (ceremonial) uniforms eight times a year, with practice every Friday morning. Uniforms have to be immaculate and shoes polished. A guest of honour inspects the whole school on the vast parade ground and takes the salute as pupils march past. Head says Pangbourne's parades are an integral part of school life and help to develop self-discipline (pupils have to stand still for 15 to 20 minutes, often with a biting wind whistling across the parade ground), confidence, teamwork, leadership – 'and above all, a community spirit.' 'It's not always massively popular with the younger ones, but the older ones start to realise what an amazing thing it is and the pride really kicks in,' a parent told us.

Pangbourne has its own distinctive vocabulary, much of it nautical. Study bedrooms are cabins, house common rooms are gun rooms, the dining hall is the mess hall and casual clothes are always referred to as scruff. Current head introduced 'flag values' – kindness, integrity, industry, moral courage, selflessness, resilience and initiative – and students are urged to display them throughout their time here. Chapel is a key part of Pangbourne life, including 'congers' (Saturday morning congregational practice), reflecting the school's firm Christian ethos with a 'forthright and challenging' chaplain (although students tell us 'it's fine to be atheist'). Many services are held in the Falkland Islands Memorial Chapel, opened by the Queen (who has visited the school five times). The rest of the extensive campus is a mixture of buildings, some in need of updating (eg labs) but most on a rolling programme and everything is fit for purpose. Food good – we enjoyed a hearty roast on a frosty day.

School has been fully co-ed since 1996 (it's now approaching 4:3 girls). Lots of student committees, including boarders, food and general student councils. Very inclusive Team Pangbourne feel to the place and pupils are fiercely loyal to their school. All students expected to greet everyone they walk past – 'it can get tiring, but I can see why they insist on it,' said one. Sixth formers can apply to train as peer mentors. Raft of prefects – called cadet captains – chosen by head and senior staff. Lower sixth pupils take leadership course in readiness for their responsibilities in the upper sixth.

Pastoral care, well-being and discipline: 'Happiness' is a word you hear a lot here, the ethos being that if youngsters are happy then their self-worth and academics will follow. The main vehicle for the pastoral care is the house system, with weekly meetings among staff using a traffic light system for all students. School counsellor is well-used – students self-refer. Growing emphasis on mental health, including outside speakers. Sixth formers have their own bar (Medway), which is open for soft drinks on Thursday evenings and pizzas and beer/lager (strictly limited) on Saturday nights.

There's a feeling you can make mistakes here – 'everyone makes mistakes', points out head. But there are 'crystal clear' policies on everything from boy-girl relationships (PDAs banned) to bullying and drugs, alcohol and cigarettes. All have caused issues at one time or another, admits school, with one or two permanent exclusions a year, most recently for substance abuse or 'inability to reform bullying behaviour'. Around 10 suspensions a year, 'usually for inappropriate, offensive or unpleasant behaviour'. Less serious sanctions include the 'sin bin' – a kind of mini-detention for failing to produce prep or applying yourself in class – while Saturday detentions are for repeat offences or more grave misdemeanours. An equal emphasis on praise means positive input is also rewarded.

Strict uniform policy. Students must need hefty trunks to pack all their kit, though – list includes number one uniform (jacket, trousers/shirt and cap with badge for Sundays and ceremonies), number two uniform for every day (trousers/skirt, navy jersey, epaulettes, beret and Dr Martens shoes), and recreational rig (known as 'rec rig') for social occasions and away matches (sixth formers may now wear suits instead). And that's before they even think of throwing in games kit and weekend clothes. Trousers only to be offered as an alternative to skirts from September 2019 – surprising to us that it took so long, though seemingly not to students who are also fine with the strict 'not too long, not too short' haircut rule (questioning societal 'norms' doesn't seem to feature highly among students here).

Students say it's 'a caring, friendly school' and that it's easy to settle in.

Pupils and parents: Fleet of minibuses brings day pupils in from as far afield as Basingstoke, Newbury and Highclere, with bus routes also now offered from Henley-On-Thames, Wargrave and Twyford. Majority of boarders live within an hour's drive. Around 11 per cent from overseas (including the Far East and Germany). Despite school's naval associations, only around 20 youngsters from Forces families. Families mainly hard-working – 'you get the odd child picked up in a Lamborghini but plenty of VWs like ours too,' one student said. Former pupils include the late film director Ken Russell, Olympic gold and silver medallist sailor Andrew (Bart) Simpson (a sailing foundation was set up in his name after he drowned whilst training for the America's Cup), motorcycle racer Mike Hailwood, hedge fund founder David Harding, former Second Sea Lord Admiral Sir Michael Layard and Dazed & Confused founder and journalist Jefferson Hack.

Entrance: Students come from a host of state and prep schools, including Brockhurst, Moulsford, Thorngrove, St Andrew's, Pangbourne and many more. Main entry points are at 11, 13 and 16. At 11 and 13, admission is by school's own entrance exam or CE (interview and head's report taken into account too). Pupils joining sixth form (up to 20 a year) must have at least five good GCSE passes, including English and maths.

Exit: Some leave after GCSEs (usually around 15 out of 80), mainly to do subjects not offered here or 'just for a change'. Around 90 per cent go on to university – around 40 per cent per cent of those to Russell Group, the rest to so-called 'selective' universities or the newer ex-polys. Cardiff, Exeter, Leeds and Bristol are recent big hitters; Birmingham, Oxford Brookes, University of the West of England and Nottingham Trent also popular. In 2018, one to Oxbridge, on an organ scholarship. Subjects are wide ranging, including more vocational ones like agriculture, accounting and sports science. Apprenticeships growing in popularity and a handful go into the Forces.

Money matters: Not a rich school, but a significant number receive some help with fees. Means-tested bursaries are available from 10 per cent upwards, with around 10 to 12 students receiving 100 per cent. Scholarships include academic, music and sport at each entry point – not very significant in value so means-tested for those who need help.

P

Remarks: A small, distinctive, grounded and family-oriented school that puts huge emphasis on self-discipline, teamwork and leadership. Caring and supportive, Pangbourne buzzes with activity and encourages every pupil to have a go.

Papplewick School

Windsor Road, Ascot, Berkshire SL5 7LH

Ages 6–13 **Pupils** 215 **Boarders** 128 (from 9 years) **C of E**

Fees: Day £16,455 – £22,845; Boarding £29,745 pa

01344 621488
www.papplewick.org.uk

Headmaster: Since 2004 Tom Bunbury BA PGCE (50s). Educated at Woodcote House Prep and Millfield before heading to read law at Durham and ultimately returning to Woodcote to try his hand at teaching. Landed at Papplewick in 1993 after completing PGCE at Homerton College Cambridge, and has remained ever since. Route to headship included spells as head of maths, housemaster and deputy head.

Quite the most genuinely charming head teacher we have ever met. Jolly (we were reliably informed by a pupil that 'head's detentions are actually fun') yet utterly sincere; a wry smile never far from his face. At heart an educator in the most holistic sense: he speaks of the 'luxury of inculcating the values required to be a really good human being' upon his young proteges and turning them into 'leaders...but compassionate ones'. 'Kindness' is also a buzz word around here. We don't doubt that under his influence they emerge with such attributes in spades. Firm believer that 'prep school should be fun – but with some really high standards.' Parents say that he 'knows every boy' and is 'headmaster first, businessman second'. During his tenure has made enormous investment in the staff team (evidenced by eyewatering fees) – says 'there's genuinely not a weak link'.

Entrance: School 'passionately non-selective – but character counts', says head, as do reports from former schools, and no offer will be forthcoming 'if there are any worries on a behavioural front'. School structure is an 'inverse pyramid'. Up to 16 boys join year 2 from a mixture of local pre-preps (Upton House, Coworth, Lambrook) and state primaries. Class splits into two smaller forms in year 3 when more come from the surrounding areas and there's another significant intake into year 4 when the London boys start to appear, transported by the Papplewick Express that whisks them away from the academic pressure-cookers of west London (stops are in Brook Green and Chiswick) in a mere 40 minutes. A good handful join in years 7 and 8 and 'integrate seamlessly,' according to parents.

Exit: Feeds all the biggies – Eton takes the largest number then Harrow, Charterhouse, Winchester and Wellington as well as all the other great and good in smaller numbers. Between 10 and 15 scholarships most years (10 in 2018), across the board from academic to sport and art, with a King's Scholarship to Eton not considered an anomaly (there were two, in fact, in 2017 and another in 2018).

Remarks: We're trying not to think of Papplewick as the Prince Harry of the school world but if it were human you'd definitely be attracted to its quirkiness, sense of humour, wit and kindness (may we add slightly dishevelled appearance?) rather than any trace of flawless beauty. A surprisingly urban campus directly opposite Ascot racecourse, with 'the square' – a concrete playground littered with lethal looking ripsticks and scooters (anyone for 'ripstick wars' at break?) at its heart, surrounded by a jumble of buildings of various architectural styles. None of the superficial beauty boasted by some of the local competition, but things are getting smarter with the addition of a new, purpose built year 8 boarding house atop two year 5 classrooms and the airy newish entrance hall: part entertainment space, part art gallery to showcase boys' masterpieces. And anyway, Papplewick parents say they value 'culture and staff above new facilities'.

Despite the rather ramshackle – and in some parts shabby – school fabric, all mod cons are incongruously present and correct. But it's the innately confident buzz at Papplewick that blows any comparison with more pristine schools out of the water. Boys whizzing past on scooters? Check. Teachers strolling around in fancy dress for a themed language day (the first time we've ever been introduced to a teacher as 'the school dragon')? Yup. Seven year-olds casually sporting living, breathing royal pythons around their necks? Well, yes – and more of that later. 'Infused with kindness and understanding,' said one happy parent. Another: 'Teaching is just a small part of what Papplewick is all about'.

Plenty of first time buyers take away any sense of old school stuffiness, with a healthy mix of entrepreneurs, professionals and dual income families thrown in with the more trad boarding prep sort. Boys unassumingly charming and totally down to earth. It's been a while since we've been asked over lunch whether we have any brothers and sisters or pets, but ask they did with a disarming innocence and then told us all about theirs. No script or message, just good old fashioned small talk, and parents love the way their children's eccentricities and individual character traits are embraced.

'We genuinely don't want to be known for anything in particular', says head. Papplewick has the nonchalant air of an all-rounder about it ('we are absolutely a boys' school to our core – but not macho,' says head). 'Deliberately' trad curriculum ('it's evolution not revolution here') including French (taught by a native speaker), Latin plus Greek for scholarship candidates. It's a six day a week timetable with Saturday school, followed by assembly, chapel and sports fixtures. Never fear that you'll barely see your boy at weekends, though – parents, siblings and even grandmas and grandads are invited to join for proceedings from chapel onwards, including lunch which 'makes for a big family feel,' says head.

With such an elite list of destination schools, surely there must be some sneaky outside tutoring afoot? Not much, apparently, and it's 'actively discouraged', according to school. Parents say 'they just don't feel that pressure'. Preparation for the pre-test is covered in English and maths and 'thinking skills', including verbal and non-verbal reasoning, is on curriculum in year 5. 'What we do in school is sufficient,' says head. 'There are many layers of preparation for common entrance and above all you need to be interesting to get into Eton or Winchester. You can't tutor that.' Well said. Parents concur that 'there's real intellectual rigour' in the upper years.

Not an obvious choice of school for a child with anything above mild to very moderate SEN. All pupils screened for dyslexia with a small number benefiting from two additional support lessons per week (charged as extra). 'We don't write anyone off', director of studies told us – 'there's no sense of not being able to do it and our potential scholars pull up the 50 per cent CE candidates'.

Boarding compulsory – absolutely no exceptions – from the summer term of year 6, with a few full, part-time or occasional boarders beforehand in years 5 and 6. Official visiting is Wednesday afternoon but it's a 'modern, family friendly model of boarding' these days according to head and 'parents can drop in whenever – we make sure they know they're not being a pain'. A compulsory, non-stop merry-go-round of activities in the first two weeks of boarding life wards off homesickness and boarding parents report that thereafter, although allowed mobile phones in the evenings, their offspring are 'too busy to call home'. There are 'lots of fun and games' right up until bedtime, when tutors scoop up their charges for hot chocolate and a chat about the day. On top of that, 'babies and puppies help,' says head, and with two-thirds of staff living on site, there are plenty of each. Photos of matches and other activities emailed to parents unable to make it in person. Colourful, cheery dorms, walls adorned with murals of snowboarders and surfers, are reached via a narrow staircase in the main school building. Unusually for boys, it seems to be cool here to have plenty of personal effects around your bed, although that might just be because storage is minimal – just a few hooks behind the bed, with 'home clothes' kept in a separate location and handed out by matron as needed. Importantly, boys know exactly who to call if they need an 'outside listener' – posters are prominently positioned in each dorm. Full boarders are treated to outings on Sundays, or are just able to 'chill out'.

'Very good' drama, according to pupils and parents, with recent productions including A Christmas Carol and Macbeth and all parts covered by boys. Director of music (Classic FM's 2017 Music Teacher of the Year, no less) is breathing new life into the department. All year 4s now learn whole class recorder and year 5s a brass instrument. African drumming is another new addition to the music curriculum, inspired by music director's recent past teaching in an inner London school. Music technology on curriculum for all in years 7 and 8. On top of all the funky stuff that's going on there are three choirs – non-selective for the younger pupils, and the first of which sings in chapel every morning. Wind and brass bands plus a string ensemble give the 70 per cent of pupils taking peripatetic music lessons the chance to brush up their performance skills.

Over 600 fixtures a year on the sporting calendar with 'opportunities for all' and A to D or sometimes E teams fielded most weeks. 'Being in the A team is really played down', said one parent, 'to encourage kindness'. A legacy of a former ex-pro director of sport, it's football rather than rugby in the long Michaelmas term ('it plays to our international strengths', says director of sport – 'our Spanish boys, for example, have never picked up a cricket bat before they come here') followed by rugby then cricket, but there's also croquet (including fixtures), golf and basketball. Boys say 'it's quite important for us to win', but school feels that its 60 per cent win/draw hit rate is just the ticket to teach boys how to lose with humility too.

And so to extracurricular. In true Papplewick style this is stuff boys' dreams are made on. There are, of course, other schools that can match the karate, fencing, chess, Airfix and Lego activities on offer here. Perhaps a few can also offer shooting and polo (played off site). But we are yet to find another that can boast herpetology – known to Papplewickians as 'snake club.' Less of a club and more of a school obsession, herpetology takes place in a science lab with wall-to-wall cages homing reptiles of all shapes and sizes, plus the crickets and new born chicks needed to feed them. When we visited, the club was in the ongoing process of breeding 'the most orange' snakes (and bearded dragons, of which they hatch around 40 per year) possible. Breaks and lunch times see boys in their droves head off to handle and care for their reptiles – 'these are the eco warriors of the future,' we were told. True enthusiasts are presented with the covetable 'herpetology colours' – a tie featuring a serpent coiling one of its stripes. Well if that doesn't make a boy interesting enough to nail the Eton interview, we're not sure what will.

Parkside School

The Manor, Stoke D'Abernon, Cobham, Surrey KT11 3PX

Ages 2–13 **Pupils** 274 (16 girls in co-ed nursery)

Fees: £12,165 – £16,692 pa

01932 862749
www.parkside-school.co.uk

Head: Since December 2018, Nicole Janssen, previously director of training and development here, and the school's first female head. Music degree and PGCE from Kingston; leading maths teacher for Newham, deputy head at a London primary school, head of upper school then deputy head at Longacre School in Surrey. Joined Parkside in 2016 as a specialist teacher.

Entrance: Boys in the co-ed nursery can move seamlessly to the pre-prep and prep. External entrance to pre-prep and 7+

dependent on an assessment day held in November, which includes tests in English and maths. Any SEN issues will be taken up then too. Perhaps less choosy than some of its rivals, but if boys are rude and disrespectful on assessment day – 'some are,' admits the school – then they will be turned away.

Boys join from a wide local radius including Wimbledon, Kinsgston, Esher, Claygate, Weybridge, Oxshott, Byfleet, Cobham, Stoke d'Abernon, Fetcham and Leatherhead. Mainly English, some Korean, Russian, American, South African and Australian. Most year groups full, but occasional gaps appear – always worth a phone call – and if there is a place, it is dependent on maths and English tests, plus spending time with the head to check 'fitablity'. Limited number of means-tested bursaries available, covering up to 80 per cent of fees.

Exit: From nursery, 70 per cent of boys move on to pre-prep – others to the state system (Royal Kent, St Matthews) or co-ed preps such as Danes Hill and Feltonfleet. School not geared towards pupils leaving at 11 and very few do. At 13+ boys depart to an increasingly wide range of senior schools including Reeds, St John's Leatherhead, Millfield, Sherborne, Stowe, Charterhouse, Epsom College and Lancing. Occasionally to Eton or Harrow. School well practised at matching each boy to the right school – it's all handled gently and kindly and the school works hard to provide firm links with schools across the south east and south west, as well as providing an annual senior school exhibition, boarding school evening etc.

Remarks: This is a happy school, set in stunning grounds, which is strong academically, but without the pressure-cooker ethos of some other schools in this moneyed area of Surrey. 'There's no doubt my sons are challenged in the classroom and reach their full potential, but it's no hothouse,' one parent told us.

Teaching staff (a good proportion male) are a healthy mix of NQTs ('they bring fantastic ideas straight from college'); those with two or three years teaching experience ('they bring new ideas, plus a bit of experience); those from industry ('they bring great experience'); and longstanding staff ('they bring continuity'). There's clear target setting for each boy and, according to pupils, 'Teachers always offer extra support if you don't understand something – nothing is ever too much trouble.' A few parents feel the school may not be right for the super-bright, 'but that's not to say the boys don't do really well,' said one. School keen to point out that the top sets (of which there are three from age 9 in maths and English) are now exclusively for scholarship applicants from year 7; other sets reasonably fluid. French from nursery and Latin from year 5. Two classes of 20 per year, but with the setted subjects, the average teaching group is nearer 12.

Boys have a lot to fit in their day, with a pacey 10 35-minute lessons a day timetable. It's not quite as frenetic as it sounds, though, with some double periods (and even triple for art and sports). Homework kept to one or two 35-minute assignments a week (term time only) and there's no Saturday school. General subject teachers in pre-prep, then subject specialists in French and music from year 3, after which they pick up more and more so that by the time they're in year 5, they are taught entirely by subject specialists. IT embedded into learning – coding, programming, touch-typing all part of everyday life here.

Good provision from quite a large SEN department – 19 per cent of boys SEN when we visited, albeit at the mild to moderate end. These boys receive varying levels of support, including up to two one-to-one support lessons a week if they need it, plus extra support from a classroom assistant – and any necessary classroom adaptations eg wobble seats for pupils with dyspraxia. Learning support centre accessible to other pupils too eg to improve handwriting or deal with anxiety issues.

Music strong, with weekly classes described by boys as 'really exciting,' and plenty of extracurricular on offer, including choir, big band, rock group and ensembles. A third of pupils learn an instrument with a peripatetic teacher. Current push on strings to be taken up by more boys. Pupils regularly perform at music festivals.

Art and DT are outstanding – studios are jam packed with talented paintings, textiles, pottery etc and boys were busy making scaled-down bedrooms, complete with furniture, when we visited – enchanting. Historically, drama has not been a strong point. Not so now, with a new teacher – 'she used to be an actress,' we were told in awe by one boy – brought in to shake things up. Lots of clubs and activities on offer (eg fencing, cooking, chess, golf, skiing and supervised prep) with everything finished by 5pm.

Famously sporty and well used to picking up county and national trophies in U11 and U13 competitions. Core sports are football, cricket and hockey, the latter being extremely popular and successful. Rugby an option in years 7 and 8, with other key sports on offer including athletics and swimming. Super sports facilities set in school's 45 acres of parkland include a 20m swimming pool, a splendid cricket academy, tennis courts and even a river (the Mole runs through school grounds) used for kayaking. 'There are some really good coaches,' pupils told us. More than one parent we spoke to felt sport here could be more inclusive, but school insistent that 'one of the things we have put a lot of effort into in the past two years is to achieve a fair chance for all levels.'

At the centre of the striking grounds is the historic manor house, with decorative ceilings, pillars and panelling, which houses the head, staff rooms, boys' dining room and a magnificent salon, complete with Rococo fireplace, used for school assemblies and functions. The classroom block is a newish, well-designed and airy space. A 100 seat performing arts hall, lecture room and art block have been added since, plus a superb library for the prep school (pre-prep and nursery have their own libraries). This has become rather the hub of the school, hosting talks by visiting authors and there are fun competitions held here too, including the 'Who can read the most words in a term?' The current winner managed a whopping two million. Separate languages block. The nursery building, a converted barn, is appealing, colourful and brimming with activity – all safely cordoned off from the bigger boys. Parents appreciate the after-school care available at the nursery and pre-prep. Picturesque church (and hall) on site, which the boys attend for a service every half term.

As you would hope in a smallish operation like this, pastoral care is first class. Staff are approachable and boys in the top year wear white shirts so that the younger boys (in grey) know who to ask for help and advice. Plus, there's a worry box. 'My son has had a few rocky terms on and off and when he's struggled, they've noticed and really supported him,' one parent told us. Boys seem proud of their school and loyal and kind to each other and there's lots of cross-year friendships. If a bullying occurs, they tackle it quickly and firmly – there was one temporary exclusion for it the year we visited. Strong student council. There's a well understood framework of discipline, but not masses of rules and no naming and shaming. When asked what they would change if they were headteacher for the day, we got the best answer ever – 'We do get to be headteacher for the day!' 'Everyone loves it,' say boys.

En route to the school, we passed flash cars galore, yummy mummies and houses belonging to Chelsea footballers (the school backs on to the club's training grounds). But Parkside aims to play down this aspect of the area and some families choose the school precisely for this reason. 'People are surprised by the range of backgrounds, with lawyers and bankers, electricians and plumbers,' said one. Parents a sociable bunch, with thriving PA.

A good traditional prep school, described by parents as 'friendly' and 'warm,' where boys enjoy an all-round education and are friendly, polite and confident.

Parmiter's School

High Elms Lane, Garston, Watford, Hertfordshire WD25 0UU

Ages 11–18 **Pupils** 1,455 **Sixth form** 412

01923 671424
www.parmiters.herts.sch.uk

Head: Since April 2018, Michael Jones, previously head for nine years of Holmer Green School in Bucks. Previous roles include head of drama at Francis Combe.

Academic matters: Heady mix of the extremely able (our guide, Cambridge offer under belt, proudly introduced himself as 'self-proclaimed nerd'), 25 per cent of whom were selected on academic ability (albeit reportedly vast majority heavily tutored), the musical (10 per cent of cohort get in on musical aptitude) and after that a mixed bag. As you would expect, exam results are solid: in 2018, 92 per cent achieved 9-4 in both English and maths and 53 per cent of grades were 9-7. At A level, 79 per cent A*-B and 52 per cent A*/A. Value added scores are high – one parent we spoke to said their child, now Oxbridge bound, merely 'scraped in' on academic aptitude but was 'brilliantly supported' through any crises of confidence and 'encouraged rather than pushed' to reach his goals. Two or three subjects a night as homework seems heavy but parents say teachers are sympathetic if parents send a 'ran out of steam' note. For lovers of league tables, school hovers around the top 100 state schools in the country.

Seven form entry makes for a large cohort, with numbers increasing further in sixth form. All classes mixed ability in year 7, with setting ('fluid and reviewed frequently,' according to school) introduced for maths, languages and science in year 8. No early GCSE entries – 'we prefer to keep breadth for longer', although A level mathematicians can take the A level in one year and follow it with further maths in year 13 if deemed sufficiently able. It's nine GCSEs for most, plus a short course in RS and one extra if sciences being studied separately. School has specialisms in music and languages – French from year 7 with either Spanish or German added in year 8 and one language compulsory at GCSE, although academically weaker pupils may be allowed special dispensation in this regard if struggling with literacy. Latin, Mandarin and Japanese on offer as extracurricular. Sciences, maths and English are most popular at A level. But it's not all about exams. The popular (compulsory) liberal studies course for sixth formers brings in outside speakers on a weekly basis to cover practical topics such as tenancy agreements, bank accounts and UCAS applications. There are also visits from prison inmates, holocaust survivors and a Red Arrows pilot.

Over 100 pupils (around seven per cent of cohort) on SEN register at any one time, with provision praised by staff and parents alike. Full time SENCo, supported by team of TAs, can accommodate a range of needs from dyslexia, dyscalculia and ASD to physical or severe visual impairments through a mix of withdrawal and specialist intervention in class.

Games, options, the arts: The students raved not just about one thing that made the school tick but a range – sport, drama, music and art all got a mention, and the word most frequently used? Opportunity. With 60 acres of grounds more akin to a private school, pupils are spoilt by a full-sized Astro and seven (no, that's not a typo) football pitches, floodlit tennis and netball courts and a sports hall equipped with gym and dance studio, the tone is set for a culture of participation and not inconsiderable success. Despite the measly standard two periods a week of PE on curriculum (compulsory to year 11), pupils can take advantage of sports clubs every lunchtime and after school, with options including girls' cricket, rugby and football. Fixtures aplenty but these are mainly for elite players and there's rarely anything below a B team. Perception of sport variable among parent cohort depending on ability of child. Those with elite performers clearly delighted but gripes from others with less talented (although equally enthusiastic) offspring who felt that team selection ('ruthless,' according to one) was not always handled fairly, with commitment and determination not receiving just recognition. Plenty of accolades trip off the tongues of enthusiastic pupils when we ask how successful their teams are – some seemed almost embarrassed: U12s were recently second in district hockey, U13s won the district basketball league and came second in district rugby league and the trophy cabinets in reception are groaning with silverware awarded at other events.

Music also high on extracurricular agenda with all manner of ensembles, orchestras and choirs to cater for different instruments and ability levels. Lavish annual productions will appeal to budding thespians, with recent shows including Les Misérables and Little Shop of Horrors and a recent Fringe Festival inspired by a sixth form drama trip to Edinburgh receiving top reviews from our pupil interviewees. The annual gym and dance show has gained such popularity that it now takes place at the Watford Palace. On top of that, pupils can choose from cerebral pursuits such as femsoc, chess, engineering and coding to name a few. D of E open to all with strong take-up – around 120 currently working towards Bronze Award as, true to Thomas Parmiter's will, 'service is a big feature of school life'. Short answer is they're spoilt for choice.

Background and atmosphere: Founded 1681 in Bethnal Green with funds left by wealthy East London silk merchant Thomas Parmiter in his will, which is now framed in all its glory on the wall of the head's office, along with a couple of charming pictures of the original all-male cohort, numbering about 10. Became a boys' grammar but turned comprehensive and co-ed when it moved to Hertfordshire in 1977.

Fabric of school now is typical 1970s comprehensive with few aesthetically redeeming features but retains reminders of its history, with features such as the stained glass remembrance window, and tradition with its wooden honours boards and portraits of former head teachers. Very little to write home about in terms of gleaming facilities – a complete overhaul of the science labs is top of current wishlist and some rooms are multi-purpose, eg textiles classes in home economics room – but for a school that has been forced to grow in pupil numbers there's a great feeling of space and somehow it all just works. Two well-stocked libraries, one for years 7 to 11 and one for sixth form, boast smart fleets of desktops and areas for quiet working. Plenty of space for sixth formers to hang out and socialise or work, with the cherry on top being their own super café run by a former member of the main catering team that offers freshly made cakes, lunches (taco chilli and Penang curry on the blackboard on the day of our visit) and snacks in a buzzy, basement style area.

The queues for the main canteen – even at break time – indicate that the pupils appreciate the quality of the catering (all scratch cooked on site) and although it was full of hungry students chatting, the atmosphere was extremely civilised and calm. In fact, the word most pupils used to describe the feel of the school was 'friendly and social' – apparently even the teachers are 'nice, approachable people.'

Pastoral care, well-being and discipline: Staff talk about school in terms of the 'Parmiter's family' and describe pupils as 'the most motivated group of young people we have worked with,' so there's reportedly little in the way of major transgressions – mainly just the usual friendship issues and not handing in homework, although there are up to a dozen fixed-term exclusions each year, usually for 'continued defiance'. Pupils give discipline a rating of four out of five: 'strong but fair'. Uniform policy is strict even in sixth form where boys are expected to wear suits and girls to 'dress appropriately', although there's a current pupil-led uprising against girls not being allowed to wear trousers with an active campaign in place – watch this space.

Pastoral care receives high praise from pupils who are clear on who to speak to when things do go wrong and say things are dealt with 'sensitively'. They describe school as 'extremely inclusive' in all matters relating to race, religion and sexuality, including current transgender issues. Parents agree that there's 'no labelling' and rave about their children's 'fantastic, multicultural set of friends.' One also commented on children dealing with bereavement receiving excellent care using 'tried and tested' methods. A whole double notice board in a main corridor is dedicated to diversity, including a calendar covering festivals of all religions and artwork on gay role models, and head describes mental health as 'very high on the agenda.' School is 'adaptable' regarding moving pupils' forms if there are clashes and there's a peer mentoring system in place. Mutual respect between staff and pupils is a recurring theme: 'They always take our feelings into account,' said one happy pupil; 'they try to solve problems at the beginning and always think like humans.' House system isn't pastoral but is competitive with competitions from sports day to house bake-off and pupils 'at their most animated' when positions are read out at the end of term.

Pupils and parents: 'Pretty mixed socially and culturally,' says school and with a fleet of 11 buses transporting pupils from the likes of urban Harrow and Stanmore to Hemel Hempstead and leafy St Albans, that's not surprising. Small Caucasian majority with healthy mix of all other races in evidence and around nine per cent EAL. Pupils feel that it's this diverse cohort that makes it tick along so happily. Former pupils include Roger Tilling (the voice of University Challenge), England cricketer Steven Finn, Swansea footballer Tom Carroll and rogue trader Liam Neeson.

P

Entrance: There's a long list of criteria: looked after children are first priority with around a dozen in school at time of writing. The next 10 per cent of places go to those living in closest proximity; then it's siblings; compelling medical reasons; 25 per cent academic selection (VR and maths); 10 per cent musical aptitude (test and audition); then children of staff who have served at least two years; and finally remaining places by proximity. Currently heavily oversubscribed with around 1,400 applicants for 208 year 7 places. Around 400 applicants for approximately 50 year 12 places each year, with offers made to about half.

Exit: Roughly a quarter leave after GCSEs, mainly to employment or vocational college courses. Around 90 per cent of sixth form leavers go into higher education to a huge range of new, redbrick and Russell Group universities. Twelve to Oxbridge in 2018 plus seven medics. There's a full time careers co-ordinator and a database of former pupils able to offer internships: 'helping our students with networking is crucial'. School keen to promote alternatives to university: 'encouraging increasing numbers into apprenticeships, particularly in fields such as engineering, is a no brainer'.

Money matters: School not a great subscriber to controversial compulsory parental donations and 'there's certainly no hard sell' in this regard, although a letter is sent to new parents at the beginning of year 7. Happily, the parents' association is very active on the fundraising front and school also gets funds for capital works from the Parmiter's Foundation Charity.

Remarks: Purposeful, friendly and inclusive semi-selective state school with a truly inclusive feel and a sense of both history and progressiveness. In the words of one happy parent: 'Parmiter's makes absolutely sure everyone gets on the education bus. Nobody is left behind'.

Peter Symonds College

Owens Road, Winchester, Hampshire SO22 6RX

Ages 16–18 **Pupils** 3,975 **Boarders** 74 full

Fees: Day free; Boarding £14,490 – £15,600 pa

01962 857500
www.psc.ac.uk

Principal: Since September 2018, Sarah Russell BA (history, Reading), previously deputy principal and then principal of Alton College. Lengthy experience in sixth form education and sits on several policy groups.

Academic matters: Often chosen for academic prowess, results here are excellent: in 2018, 62 per cent A*-B, 34 per cent A*-A; 'head and shoulders' above other options, said a student. This largely non-selective college achieves impressive value added: up one grade across three A levels. 'Education is most important here', said a student, describing, wearily, how in some schools everything is important; 'here: education', she said simply.

Students said they would like more information on non-secondary school subjects and methods of teaching before they start – 'can go in and love or hate'; but they do have a taster day, when they try each of their subjects and get a course overview; they can also take four subjects with the flexibility of dropping one after the first year.

A good variety of A levels on offer, including the less usual environmental science and commercial art. A few BTecs available. Only maths and science are selective (7+ at GCSE), with students in maths and biology consistently achieving top grades. Students report some subject gender divide, more girls taking sociology, English, classics and law; more boys taking economics and computer science; but sciences and maths are well balanced. The EPQ is available...'ah, love it', said the group of students we spoke to, 'if you have a burning passion...'. Nice to escape the 'write this argument' restrictions of A level, said one student; '[I got a] reduced offer from university because of it...'.

Classes are mixed ability, with 16-20 students. An experiment putting maths strugglers into small sets with the best teachers showed they did no better; the conclusion: that working with peers who are motivated and succeeding does more for struggling students. Additionally there are three sorts of workshops in every course: support workshops, for the struggling (attendance might be obligatory); extension workshops, to push the able; and structured workshops for exam revision.

There's not the coercion you get at school, say students, who like this: 'Because you choose the subject, failing is only your own fault. So pull yourself up – and people do'. It's a different vibe to school, one explained: 'it's cool to do well'. In this supportive student body 'uppers help lowers,' said a student, or teachers will help out. Study support is very good, said a parent: 'Grand at helping you study independently...if you seek it out'. It's not a place for those who need hand holding, parents agree.

The SEN unit supports 900 students with mild-severe physical or sensory impairments, or mental health needs. 'This college places great value on SEN and the tools we need to do the job', said head of SEN gratefully. '[We are] very, very supported by senior management'. Range of support includes one-to-one sessions, in class support and other assistance: the physio room with plinth means that students in wheelchairs can come and take a rest; a frame allows another student to work in a standing position. 'We work hard to find creative way to meet student needs...'.

The unit will help any students who want to develop independent study skills – 'not just a special place for special people', said head of SEN earnestly, but the onus is on the student to seek help. One parent told us her mildly dyslexic son gets extra time in exams, but that's it. The help is there if he asks for it, thinks the parent, but her son is 'slightly embarrassed and lazy...'.

Careful preparation for competitive university entrance, with interview practice for anyone who needs it, and a dedicated Oxbridge tutor. The independence and responsibility of college prepares pupils well for university, and parents report a smooth transition between the two.

Students can make an appointment to explore their career options, but a certain amount is laid on for those who aren't likely to do this, such as careers week and the careers fair.

Games, options, the arts: Students must take part in one activity, and there are plenty to choose from, including rock challenge, national dance competition, colouring club and young Liberals. The college supports many activities which are set up by students: Symonds Speaks, the debating club, recently beat Winchester College, which the head understandably finds pleasing.

A number of students do community service as part of the DofE, but the head would like there to be more of it; a programme to encourage volunteering will be launched soon.

Peter Symonds is home to Hampshire Specialist Music Course. Just 12 places on this highly selective course, but it is the cream of music provision: students get one and half hours of individual tuition a week, as well as opportunities to form chamber groups and orchestras.

Peter Symonds is the national leading sixth form for games, and if you excel at sport, the chances are you will quickly be in a team, but just the one team: keen sportspeople must choose their favourite sport. It can be a shock for those who were a big shot on the school rugby team to arrive at Peter Symonds, compete against 500 others, and not make even the fourth team. One parent told us her kids opted to take up lacrosse: a new sport to most, so an assurance of a place on the team.

Sun pours through the slanting glass roof of the art block, which has doors that open out onto grass; a nice space to work in, though no designated spaces for individual students, so work can't be left out.

Boarding: '[It's a] boarding facility, not a boarding school', said head of boarding firmly. 'Not like the packed schedule for boarders at Winchester College, and students should not have these expectations', said a parent, although boarders are taken out for a team building day at the beginning of the year, and have various themed dinners. They can use the gym and sports hall three times a week after school hours.

Students here are treated as young adults; time is not structured, although they are expected to study during quiet time from 6.30-8.30pm. Safeguarding is taken seriously: students are always monitored in house, and day parents get students up – or attempt to – if they've got an 8.30am lesson. Each boarder has a care plan, which records everything that happens to them. But you 'don't have to go out; don't have to go to dinner', said a student who'd experienced independent school boarding, with evident relief. Students don't have to sign out to leave the campus, and just need to be back by the generous curfew times: 10.20pm during the week, 11.00pm on Friday and Saturday for lowers, 11.30pm for uppers. ('Many of the students have part time jobs', explained the head of boarding.)

Peter Symonds is the sixth form for the Falklands Islands, although they account only for a small number of the 75 or so boarders, who come from the Forces, and across the country.

'[There are] close communities in both boarding houses, particularly the smaller house', said a student, and they try and match students up to their preference after visiting. School House is smaller and older; Falkland Lodge distinguished by its ensuite twin rooms and a feeling of Premier Inn. Each house has its own study room, common room and kitchen, where students help themselves to breakfast. There are rotas for kitchen duty (only the odd prompt necessary, say houseparents), and students do their own laundry.

Background and atmosphere: The college sits in an expanse of daisied green, a mixture of the old grammar buildings and modern additions, the swish and the less so. One pupil compared its vastness with the size of a small town, but said that the numbers mean that you can act as an individual: you don't have to fit; 'cat girl', mentioned a student; 'oh, cat girl,' chorused the others: ears, eyeliner, tail 'n'll; but there are communities of people within the vastness, which come down to subject passions: '[with] such diversity of subjects... you can find someone whose views and interests are like yours. No one goes through without making a friend'.

The atmosphere here is relaxed, though purposeful and confident. '[It's a] stepping stone from school to university, freer and more open than school', says college. One parent told us her daughter opted to leave private education for Peter Symonds; her daughter likes the informality, and 'being in control of her own destiny'.

As at university, there's a student union, which 'is prominent and has a strong voice', said the elected members, who meet with SMT – and would like to more frequently.

The college is packed with technology, with no suggestion of any shortages: 'austerity is not an issue here,' said a student: there are 211 PCs and 170 laptops in the library alone, and a huge range of magazines, journals and newspapers. They will get hold of any book a student needs, either buying it in, or by inter-library loan.

The biggest problem here has been finding space to study. The library fills quickly and early, particularly in the exam season. There are lists of free classrooms and the new Hopkins Study Centre should alleviate matters.

The food is good: chicken and chips are popular, as are the cookies. It's rather pricey: around £5 for a good lunch, and lots nip to Tesco for a £3 meal deal.

Pastoral care, well-being and discipline: 'The support service is belittled, but actually it's fantastic,' said a student who told us that if you have a problem, you can drop into the Hub (a centre developed for the 'worried well,' says the head), talk to your tutor, or any teacher. 'If you need help, look for it. You're treated like an adult – peerless, fantastic advice'.

The Hub was a response to the tsunami of low level mental health problems, such as anxiety and low mood; its aim is to increase student resilience; 'a lifesaver for my daughter', said a parent; 'cool about everything', said a student. About seven pupils drop into the Hub every day, which is staffed by one full-time mental health specialist and a team of five counsellors. They also provide classes on mindfulness and well-being, and have introduced a therapy dog: Haatchi has just three legs, looks large and vicious, and is a real poppet.

There's a nurse and sexual health clinic – 'very discreet', say students. Free condoms (six a week) and chlamydia tests available from student services, and the college can send students to a pharmacy for free emergency contraception: students here don't feel the need to titter embarrassedly about sexual health.

At this huge college, you wonder how shy introverts might fare, but they do well, insist both head and students: you quickly form bonds in your small subgroups of subject or activity. Bullying not a problem, say students; 'rare', agrees college: 'something students have left at school'.

Parents are largely not involved, but would be contacted early with any concerns, whether pastoral or academic.

Behaviour outside of college is only a matter of college discipline if it brings the college into disrepute; 'we're acting on bluff really', with few sanctions available in this quasi grown up environment; suspension is the best they can do, pupils knowing that it will be on their record and references. 'But there is little call for sanctions.'

The college works hard at drugs education, and second chances are possible here; but students will be asked to leave if not attending, not doing work, or behaviour is distracting others from learning (just a couple in the last few years).

Pupils and parents: Parents and students here generally reflect the white, middle class make of up the Winchester area.

Communication home is mostly through students, so is reliable as your child, but the parent portal shows details of homework, progress, effort and attendance.

Progress reviews show grades and effort, one parent commenting that it would be helpful to have more feedback if your child is less able. Parents are only invited to parents' evening if there's a problem, and none of those we spoke to felt this was ideal '...would like more parents' evenings, or a detailed report'; 'can go through the whole thing with seeing anyone...'.

P

Students say many are late to lessons because of poor public transport; the popularity of the college is such that students come from near and far, one travelling one and half hours in from the New Forest. For those driving in, parking is tricky.

Entrance: No defined catchment area, but priority goes to those closest; offers will continue to be made in an ever increasing circle around the college until they run out of places. One hundred and fifty feeder schools, a small number from independent schools.

Base entry is five 4s at GCSE, but most have considerably more than this. Students at the lower end of entry will be advised to take a combination of A levels and BTecs. Students can restart and do something different if subject choices really aren't working out.

Exit: Ninety per cent of pupils go to university, 53 to Oxbridge in 2018 (in the top five Oxbridge feeder schools, in the illustrious company of Eton, Westminster and Hills Road Sixth Form College in Cambridge) and 52 medics. Around a quarter to Russell Group. One to Harvard. As with other sixth form colleges, students here are more likely to get first class and upper second degrees.

Around 100 drop out each year, often going to other sixth form colleges, agricultural college or vocational college.

Remarks: This college is a wonderful opportunity for those ready for independence: 'always a step forward; always working towards where you want to be'.

It's quite academic, said a parent, and those who are have no notion of independence, aspiration or good work habits will struggle here. But even these students can come through at Peter Symonds: 'They enter a class [here] and see what it looks like to work hard and succeed'.

The Pilgrims' School

3 The Close, Winchester, Hampshire SO23 9LT

Ages 4–13 **Pupils** 270 **Boarders** 90 full/weekly (from year 4) **C of E**

Fees: Day £11,055 – £19,245; Boarding £24,330; Choral scholar £14,598 pa

01962 854189
www.thepilgrims-school.co.uk

Head: Since 2015, Tom Burden (40s), previously head of Hereward House in London. Originating from the Isle of Wight, he won a scholarship to Oxford to study theology. Teaching after graduating while considering careers, he realised that education was for him and so stayed for five years at Alleyn Court in Southend. He followed this with five years at Lockers Park boarding prep in Hertfordshire, as head of English, in charge of scholarships and doing lots of sports coaching. He 'loved every minute', realising 'that boys should be boys, enjoy their precious childhood and grow through being trusted with responsibilities'. A sportsman and fanatic about Southampton FC, fascinated by ecclesiastical gothic architecture, his passion is nonetheless for education. He believes that Pilgrims' is first and foremost an all round academic prep school with strong sport, music and other activities, which happens to have two professional choirs. There is no hierarchy in the school even though the choristers – who sing in Winchester Cathedral – and quiristers – who sing in Winchester College Chapel – rank among the best in the country. He is adamant that these years, which will give boys the memories and foundations for their whole lives, should be inspiring and enjoyable as well as industrious for every boy in the school.

Entrance: Boys are assessed in individual taster days, designed as much to gauge whether the boy will take to Pilgrims' life as to establish educational ability. Pilgrims' is selective but interested in boys who will do well there rather than just academia alone. Entry to the pre-prep is by fun activity mornings, and there are 10 or so places available at 7+and 8+, and a few at 11+ for preparation for senior school entry at 13+. Boarding is from 8 and boys can come in for trial stays.

Applicants for the choral scholarships are auditioned in November and voice trials include a prepared piece, aural tests designed for those who may not have musical experience and academic assessment. Most choristers and quiristers join in years 4 and 5. Boys come from far and wide, including abroad, as well as from local nurseries, primaries and independent schools.

Exit: Pilgrims is not the prep school for Winchester but enough families see it as a route for there to be a separate form in year 8. Winchester exams are earlier and different from common entrance, which accounts for another form, as well a third group for scholarship candidates. Prepares scholarship boys very specifically and successfully for the academic requirements of other major schools. Unsurprisingly, music awards and exhibitions are also plentiful.

Those going to Winchester College and Eton account for about 50 per cent each year. Remainder range from co-ed (like Canford or Marlborough) to single sex (like Radley or Sherborne); both full boarding (Charterhouse, Harrow) and day (King Edward's Southampton and Portsmouth Grammar School).

Remarks: Strong academically with Latin as well as French, which is started from reception and later benefits from trips to France. Science in impressive labs, with some serious scholars on our visit assiduously absorbed writing down observations on an experiment. Teaching looked to be fun and boys clearly enjoyed an English lesson while a maths group we saw was involved in establishing the purpose behind algebraic calculations and definitely getting the point. The head says he has struck lucky in having remarkable teachers. Art, including some pottery, computing and CDT all well equipped too. Parents report pupils work conscientiously and one commented that the school is right for all of her boys although they are widely different in abilities and inclinations. SEN stepped up recently with screening from the beginning with plenty of expert support on hand, with the occasional pupil needing one-to-one but more benefiting from in class support. Plenty of prep but boys taught not to exceed allotted time for it, one parent gratefully explained. The pre-prep has its own new purpose built centre tucked lovingly in between the school and the deanery garden, which is generously open to them as a forest school, clearly much enjoyed by the muddy group we saw. Though pre-prep is a separate unit, it feels cosily within the main school and its staff value sharing the common room above it, which definitely facilitates coordination of curriculum and info.

Music is central to the curriculum with pretty distinguished senior and junior choirs and chamber choir, as well as the two professional choirs. A huge orchestra was successfully tackling Beethoven 'on sight' in the medieval Pilgrims' Hall (also used for assemblies) when we visited, while the Big Band was swinging away in the music department. Nearly everyone learns an instrument and the boys said that both music and games are 'cool' here. Lots of opportunities for small groups and supervised practice for boarders. Music school in the converted stables bulging with pianos (even one tucked into a practice cupboard under the stairs), rehearsal space and equipment apart from designated chorister rehearsal room. The high musical standard enhances productions such as the Mikado. Drama is on the curriculum, but there are masses of events like the Christmas cabaret as well. Other activities range from Latin and Greek speaking workshops and trips abroad to wetter pursuits such as wakeboarding and angling.

For a smallish school Pilgrims' fields an astonishing number of teams. Sport is cleverly timetabled so that choristers do not miss main sports for rehearsal, though sometimes musical team players have to bow out for a professional engagement. Football boasts 20 and rugby 18 teams for the various different age groups while cricket has nine, though not all play very frequently. Lots of sporting activities, sailing, hockey, water polo, though as yet listed building planning has prevented cover for the outdoor pool. Boys also get plenty of supervised kick about time on games pitches where, one pointed out, Henry VIII might have watched events from Wolvesey Castle, which forms a stunning backdrop.

Being in the middle of the close in largely medieval buildings, Pilgrims' has managed to expand into three attractive courtyards, one grassed with a pretty little pepper pot venue for small performances, one Astroturfed for play with a climbing wall, and one tarmac, where parents collect day boys and mingle with boarders up to all sorts of intriguing after-school pastimes. Lovely light and spacious purpose built classrooms and library cleverly harmonise on the outside with the medieval and Georgian close.

Pastoral care is mainly through form teachers until the last three years, when boys are in tutor groups of up to nine. Fortnightly progress bulletins to parents now 'thankfully online', said one parent, no longer drowning in paper. Very prompt action on behavioural and other issues with parents kept in the loop.

Boarding, 90 strong but expanding by parental demand, is available from year 4. The two houses originate from the choristers' and quiristers' needs, which form the core of boarding life. The increased number of main school boarders means that activities, which can sometimes be a little denuded by choral demands in the lower years, will become more viable. Dormitories must be the nicest anywhere. Six or eight on bunk beds with cunningly themed rooms amazingly decorated – the Beano room even has comic strips revealed when the blinds go down. Pristine decoration, though the head feels they should not be too unnaturally tidy. Teaching houseparents, with their own boys in school, make it seem like a family, and three professional nurses are all approachable, parents say, and happy to keep in touch over the smallest thing. Particular concern given to supporting troubled or anxious pupils to the extent of appointing a new director of well being, available to all. Parents can visit whenever and apart from the demands of the choirs and overseas boarders it is all pretty flexible. Wrap-round care from breakfast with boarders and supervised prep until 8pm for families that need it for a 'small fee'. Choristers who have to stay on over Christmas and Easter for choir weeks get a pretty good time as well as working hard and one mother told me her son couldn't wait for his first Christmas.

Uniform is informal and comfortable with jerseys, red for choristers and blue for quiristers, while year 8s wear hairy tweed jackets. Food ok with formal dining and grace before meals as well as a much loved new tuck shop. Parents from all walks though still pretty well to do, with a good sprinkling of musical families. Boarders from abroad (10 per cent), Hong Kong etc plus some expats. Past pupils include Patrick Gale, Jack Dee, Jon Snow and four BBC choirboys of the year since 2000, with at least one finalist almost every year.

Choral scholars get 40 per cent off fees and free tuition on one instrument. Bursaries and music awards means-tested up to 100 per cent, with first school uniform free to holders.

Altogether a stunning and distinctive school, gracefully combining an up-to-date outlook with ancient traditions, now becoming more cohesive and adventurous under Mr Burden's guidance. There's something special here for almost every boy.

The Portsmouth Grammar Junior School

Linked with The Portsmouth Grammar School

206

High Street, Portsmouth PO1 2LN

Ages 2.5–11 **Pupils** 355

Fees: £10,233 – £11,352 pa

023 9236 4219
www.pgs.org.uk

Head: Since 2010, Peter Hopkinson, married to Michaela, a TA here, with two children. Read communication studies at Sheffield, and was previously head of the junior department at Abbey Gate College, Chester, and Arnold Junior School, Blackpool (now AKS Lytham).

Parents say he's very visible, and they wouldn't hesitate to go to him with a problem: 'Very approachable and friendly'; 'an able leader'. He does circle time with all the children over the year – 'a really good way to get to know all the kids,' he says, discussing themes such as awareness of world with the little ones (a teddy also attends), and developing philosophical thinking skills with older pupils.

Entrance: Most join the nursery, others in reception, year 3 and increasingly year 5. Entry to nursery through observed play; to reception by informal assessment; to year 1 upwards by tests in maths, English, non-verbal reasoning, and spending time with peer group to observe sociability.

Exit: No 11+ to progress to senior school for pupils already in-house. Very few in each year don't make it on to the senior school, usually those with severe SEN.

P

Remarks: 'I don't believe in private school', said one devoted PGS parent, who feels that the advantages of PGS weigh decidedly in its favour against even outstanding state primary schools in the area, commenting on the combination of welcome, friendliness, mixed demographic and outstanding resources which make PGS unique: 'I stopped looking for houses back home up north...' Summed up succinctly by another: 'What you get for your dollar is incredible...'

Community is strongly encouraged here, both at school and outside the school gates. 'What we picked up on when we visited was its feeling of happiness, [a] feeling of cohesion and working together...', said a parent. Democracy gets things done here, pupil council members seeking suggestions to write in their special notebooks: successes include a new junior school playground (including a hobbit house); refurbishment of the boys' and girls' loos; and packed lunchers shedding their isolation and being able to sit with those having school dinners. Outside school there's a termly beach clean, and the brass band and strings orchestra perform frequently. 'Not for someone not keen to be involved', said a parent.

Parents too, have their say: the parent forum deals with whole school issues – 'parents really feel like stakeholders', said one, describing how they were instrumental in changing the layout of canteen for juniors, so they have to queue past little pots of crudités and fruit. The kids like their smallness; take and eat: parents are happier.

Small classes (from 12 in reception, triple entry, to 15-20 from year 2 onwards). 'You don't need to be academically gifted, but average plus, and need to work hard, or you'll struggle with the pace', though the deputy head was quick to point out that those who can't cope with this can get help from learning support.

Nursery to year 4 are situated on the main school site. Years 5 and 6 are housed over the road in the original Victorian school, where classrooms conditions are a bit tighter, but pupils benefit from their own set of specialist classrooms, including DT, drama studios and cookery. The walls are full of neat displays of work, and photos of school trips: happy memories described in some affectionate detail by our guides. School trips range from year 3's recent trip to Ufton Court to experience life as Anglo Saxons, complete with Saxon banquet and stories from Beowulf, to the ski trip – fabulous skiing, bumboarding in the evening and 'a hotel with a bar and everything,' said a year 6 guide enthusiastically, to the nervous laughter of a teacher – 'they had great hot chocolate,' he added, slightly bewildered. Residential school trips get going in year 2, and a worried parent told us how much she appreciated the teachers tweeting photos – 'I couldn't speak to [my daughter], but I could see she was happy!'

There was a lively buzz in most lessons we saw, hands springing up to answer questions – 'What's the opposite of a synonym?' 'A cinnamon bun?' suggested one bright spark, to the chuckles of her classmates.

Education is based on the PGS Connected Curriculum, the head's brainchild: a model of thematic topic-based learning, which interconnects disciplines to encourage transferable and flexible skills. It's similar to Primary Years IB, but 'avoids its wooliness', said the head: not every subject fits every topic, but connections will be made where they are relevant, and enhance learning. Year 4's current connected curriculum topic is Mighty Mountains, launched with learning survival skills in the wooded area behind the playing fields.

Pupils are set for maths from year 4, but are otherwise in mixed ability groups. iPads are in frequent use for all years, and regular lessons in the computer room, with its coloured keyboards, ensure everyone can type by the time they get to year 6.

Pupils are continually appraised, and may have an SEN assessment if necessary. Around 34 of the junior school receive learning support, mostly in small groups out of class, but also through in class support by TAs.

The creative curriculum covers food tech, DT, drama, music and textiles, the textiles room piled high with coloured cloths and wool, one of our guides pointing out the beauty of the colours in the sunlight pouring in from the window. This room is the base for the sewing machine club, which makes clothes to send to PGS's connected school in Uganda.

Music is important here, and most pupils learn an instrument, with a flying start from the school: in year 3, each pupil gets a term's free tuition on a string instrument, then on a brass instrument. Junior school music week saw the school alive with the beat of Indian dancing and drumming workshops. PGS is the cathedral choir school, and pupils can audition for the boys' or girls' choirs: boys from year 3, girls from year 5. Drama is popular too, with LAMDA available from year 1, and an annual production each year from year 2. The year 6 production is a lavish affair, costumes and backdrops designed and made by teachers, the score composed in-house for the instruments played by year 6.

A big nursery, in spacious purpose built classrooms, with between 40-60 children and lots of staff: 15 working at a time means they are always well staffed. Trips to the beach (PGS has beach school status), yoga and dance, and a role play room which transforms into pet shop, café or realm of snow and ice, depending on the theme. A darkened room with a tower of glowing lights for sleeping or calming down. Joint ventures with reception make the transition to school easy. It has an excellent reputation locally, and is oversubscribed, one parent putting her son down for a place when he was 6 weeks old.

The sporting year starts with a talk by head of sport about the school's philosophy of sport: inclusivity, and being happy putting your trainers on. Ask if they enjoyed the match, not who won, exhorts the school (the newsletter no longer includes results). 'One or two of the parents are...enthusiastic...' on the touchlines, said a parent – teachers will have a quiet word.

'It's really splendid,' said parent, 'because everyone is in teams from the beginning, everyone is good enough to play, no one inadequate'. In this school, membership of teams depends on sportsmanship, not just performance on the pitch. The usual gender divide in sports: rugby and football for boys, netball for girls, but girls here also play football and cricket. The PGJS cheerleading squad is southern champion.

One parent commented on the great use of twitter by PGS – if a match is cancelled at the last minute, the school will tweet. 'Communication is excellent, sometimes too much!'

A thorough pastoral system, with each child's well-being regularly assessed by teachers. The pastoral team includes two counsellors, who also do circle time with all the children at some point, and run special groups. All counselling services are included in the fees.

'Great pastoral care', said a parent, extolling the care given to pupils following a parent death, adding that teachers always email back quickly to queries, and it's easy to have quiet word at end of the day. One parent described how carefully the school look out for one of her children who is 'painfully shy', and was very upset by a mild telling off from a teacher which resulted in panic attacks. The school took this very seriously, and has now included dealing with anxiety as part of PSHE.

Pupils are encouraged to look out for each other, and to spot and report bullying behaviour. Playground pals (special friends in lower years), mean that those who have no-one to play with can go to the friendship bus stop, where special friends will scoop them up. Bullying is dealt with 'very carefully', said a parent, whose daughter was on the receiving end of some of the subtler forms of emotional bullying often particular to girls. The teacher started with general conversations with the whole form about friendship and kindness, moving on to specific conversations with the girls concerned, which resolved matters. '[My daughter] wasn't belittled or made to feel it wasn't important. She really trusts her teachers'.

The Portsmouth Grammar School

Linked with The Portsmouth Grammar Junior School

High Street, Portsmouth PO1 2LN

Ages 11–18 **Pupils** 1,070 **Sixth form** 355

Fees: £15,951 pa

023 9236 0036
www.pgs.org.uk

Head: Since September 2018, Dr Anne Cotton, PGS's first ever female head. Studied classics at Christ Church, Oxford, where she was awarded a double first and later completed her DPhil. Was head of classics at The Henry Box School in Witney before joining Magdalen College School in 2009, where she was head of lower school, head of upper school and assistant head. She became director of Oxford Festival of Arts in 2013, forging partnerships with creative partners and businesses, as well as launching an extensive programme of outreach with Oxfordshire schools.

Married to John, who is assistant director of music at Abingdon School, with two young children. Her interests include voluntary work, swimming, and walking, and she continues to enjoy research: wrote Platonic Dialogue and the Education of the Reader.

Academic matters: Most parents are attracted first by PGS's stellar academic reputation, and results are consistently excellent: in 2018, 52 per cent A*/A at A level, and an average of 38 points at IB. At GCSE, 67 per cent A*-A/9-7. Maths and sciences are particularly high performers, but excellence across the board here. The line locally is that it is terribly selective; but one parent said, 'not as much as all that', and the parents we spoke to agreed that average or better would thrive here. Pupils describe a strict working environment, where you are encouraged to work hard. 'That's how we want it to be', one added seriously.

Pupils and parents appreciate the availability of both IB and A level, although A levels are a great deal more popular: around 50 do IB, 250 A levels. The IB is seen as more challenging and rigorous ('definitely harder', said a parent), and A levels as a safer option. But those who take IB are glad they did: 'a global and outward looking course,' said a parent, while a pupil described how easy it had been to move to the IB from the US system. Another described the IB as 'pressured, but valuable', adding that her 'daughter got a tremendous amount out of it'.

PGS Extend takes place over the summer break between lower and upper sixth, similar to the EPQ, but this in-house version allowing greater flexibility of approach – recent entrants included a presentation on the Tanzanian health care system, a composition based on musical styles from around the world, and the creation of an animatronic hand.

The school produces a rough guide to sensible subject combinations to help pupils take the right subjects for particular career paths, keen to help pupils consider not just which university to attend, but where they will be at 25.

Both pupils and parents commented on the calibre of teaching and commitment of staff: 'I've experienced no better', said one pupil who had arrived for sixth form; 'It's incredible how hard the teachers work', said a parent; 'the quality of teaching is amazing'. This is a school which invests in its staff, and has developed a bespoke leadership course with the university.

A wide range of subjects from ancient to modern: 'we are committed to providing minority subjects', and those who take Greek do extremely well; though there is appetite for even more, one pupil suggesting that the curriculum could benefit from the inclusion of Mandarin. RS here comes with a P – philosophy: 'It really encourages kids to consider ethical conundrums of modern life', said a parent. Maths and sciences are very popular, pupils relishing the smart new science labs. Pupils from year 9 upwards use mobile devices, which are particularly useful for collaborative work in lessons, and homework is often set in google classroom. Every break time there are clinics for the struggling, and pupils are comfortable emailing teachers if they need extra help.

Lessons have recently got longer, and the six 50 minute lessons have apparently lead to a calmer pace of day, much praised by a sixth former – 'It allows you time to get into a subject'.

Once a year the timetable is suspended for enrichment week, this year's curriculum enhancing activities including a mini Apprentice style competition to market a new drink for year 9 money management pupils, and a year 8 trip to a theme park to design and programme a new ride, combining business, ICT and physics.

Years 7 and 8 have much less to worry about than their peers at prep school, who are busy preparing for the CE. The focus in middle school here is on learning how to be independent: working out strategies for learning, and taking responsibility for themselves, and a reasonable amount of communication home to parents. One parent commented that her year 7 son initially struggled to fit in rugby matches, rugby training and all his homework, but as year went on, he worked out better how to organise himself.

The SEN unit assists pupils with mild to moderate dyslexia, although it is possible they could meet the needs of a pupil with severe dyslexia. No extra charge for SEN help, including one-to-one. There has been a lot of work done to ensure access arrangements for exams meet individual requirements.

Games, options, the arts: Pupils are bused to the Hilsea playing fields for most of their outdoor sport, around four miles from school. 'Bit of a trek', said a parent, 'but it's an inner city school'. The legendary Hilsea match teas take the edge of the drive ('I don't have lunch on match tea days', confided a parent). One pupil wistfully told us how much he would love a pool on site (the school uses the local Navy pool); but it is likely that the school will benefit from any new university facilities in the vicinity.

Not a football school: there are a couple of club options, but serious football players play outside school. Boys at this school play rounders as well as cricket – a rare thing. For those less keen on teams, beach running is available.

'Grades open doors', says school, 'but often pupils are more inspired by their co-curricular activities'. Pupils are encouraged to join at least two clubs in middle school, and keep up their extracurricular until they leave. Options range from the stock market club to Pride, with over 50 activities to chose from.

Music is a focus at this school, with an array of ensembles and orchestras. 'Children are taken very seriously as musicians', said a parent; 'the first violin is always introduced at concerts'. They will find a teacher for whatever instrument your child wants to learn, and the music school has ample practice rooms and a beautiful wooden ceiling rotunda. PGS forms partnerships with other musicians, composer Alexander Campkin challenging the choir with high notes and close intervals in his new work World of Merriment, while the London Mozart players do masterclasses for pupils. PGS is the choir school for St Thomas's cathedral.

Annual drama productions are immensely popular with pupils. Performances often take place in Portsmouth theatres, giving productions a professional edge, a parent commenting how much her daughter relished being part of the tech crew in productions.

A sculpted plaster head with a lollypop in its mouth stands near the door door of the art studios. Art is not splashed all over at this school, but there's an impressive array in the art department. We watched year 10s drawing dead things, Death in Venice playing in the background to get them in the mood. Art GCSE is heavily dominated by girls – 'boys don't quite get its purpose,' said art teacher; although the A level class is more balanced. Teachers are introducing more graphic design at GCSE, which they say boys relate to better.

Background and atmosphere: The energy and friendliness of PGS are what strike you first: 'It's a buzzy, vibrant place', said parent, another adding that 'it's a big school, but doesn't feel like it, with small tutor groups helping pupils feel secure, and always plenty of people around that you know'. The strong feeling of community was mentioned by several parents, and indeed it was one of the few schools we have visited where one of our guides intervened with some younger pupils' misbehaviour. There is nothing lax about this school.

Pupils dress in different combinations of the school colours of black and red, depending on their house and seniority, the blazers black with red piping (somehow avoiding the feeling of public school precious that often accompanies piping). Even sixth formers wear some uniform here, the girls apparently loving the sixth form tie (which they can pair with any smart jacket). In a piece of open discrimination, sixth form boys have to wear a blazer.

The house system is very lively here, the 'healthy rivalry' reaching its peak in the house croquet tournament, with other competitions throughout the year, and each house having its own base within the school.

'C of E, but not pushily so', said a parent. There are services at the cathedral a couple of times a term, but 'it's more about decency, and a moral framework', nowhere more evident than in the enormously popular club PGS Pride, busy changing minds in the three years since its inception: now 69 per cent of pupils think it would be easy for a pupil to come out (just 47 per cent in 2013). Pride has hosted speakers on living with HIV; being Muslim, gay and a drag queen; and being gay, a priest and a dad. 'It's had a tangible impact on self worth', say staff, embraced school wide, the canteen even producing rainbow cup cakes. Diversity is accepted here, a parent happily describing her three very different children who were, or are, all very happy at PGS.

Food is excellent – not a single criticism to be found. Pupils can pay by card or thumbprint, which impresses everyone, the system also recording what kids choose to eat for the benefit of parents. Breakfast is available from 7.45 every morning.

Splendid old buildings mingle with the modern (though the one time barracks are a little foreboding from the street). The new sixth form centre is the glassy jewel in the crown, with sixth formers enjoying their own café, library and a glass bridge which connects to the rest of school, so the sixth can keep their gadgets dry while the rest of the school scurry across the playground in the rain. There are plenty of places to work, from the project room designed for collaborative work, its walls lined with research books, to the senior library, and strictly no talking Memorial library, pin drop silent, sixth form and teachers only – or with special permission. Well cared for interiors, everything spic and span. PGS is home to the first twinned toilet we have ever visited, its sibling a remote latrine in Uganda.

PGS plays an active role in the Portsmouth community: it runs the Portsmouth arts festival with a range of local partners; organises a community beach clean every term; its ensembles play out and about; and it connects with local state schools – a number of sixth form pupils join PGS on bursaries every year, and they exchange staff to develop experience and expertise. The PGS gap year programme attracts applicants from across the country, gappers combining teaching with singing daily services at the cathedral.

Pastoral care, well-being and discipline: 'It's known as an academic school', said a parent, 'but it's the pastoral care and extracurricular which make [it]'; 'it doesn't sacrifice children's well-being for the need to do well academically', said another. Parents are pleased at the new emphasis on PHSE as a specialist lesson, not just a chunk of tutor time (whose quality depended on the skills of your tutor).

Tutors have big role in pastoral care, and are likely to be the starting point for a child with a problem: 'I feel they really "got" my kids', said a parent. 'There's always someone looking out for them, usually their tutor', said another, commenting how the school made sure things ran smoothly for her children when she was unwell.

Pupils can also talk to a peer listener (selected and trained sixth formers, who attach to tutor groups between years 7-9), or a counsellor. Children can be referred, or refer themselves by email or telephone. Counsellors can meet with families if this would be helpful and will deal with any issue which effects a child: we heard how helpful they had been to a pupil coping with bereavement, and a sixth former struggling with anxiety.

Pupils said they would go to their tutor with any concerns about bullying behaviour, and parents feel that any problems are dealt with promptly. Incidences of bullying, both homophobic and other, have fallen since PGS Pride came into being: it has helped foster an atmosphere of tolerance and equality – for instance, pupils are clear that saying 'don't be such a girl' is not acceptable.

Drug related problems are rare. They will test if necessary, but haven't had to for a few years. If perpetrators show remorse, respond and learn from their mistakes, they will probably be given a second chance. Parents think that bad behaviour and don't give a damn will be asked to leave, and indeed the only recent (temporary) exclusions have been for antisocial behaviour.

Pupils and parents: Traditional types, said one parent, with lots of hardworking professionals.

Stations are 15 minutes walk from school, and pupils travel in from all over the south coast, from Petersfield, Haselmere, Guildford, the Isle of Wight and Chichester. A private coach service brings pupils to the door.

Communication from school is good, say parents, and although information coming via children has a less reliable arrival rate, but there's always plenty of warning by direct methods about trips and concerts.

Entrance: Most pupils at the junior school progress to the senior school, without exams, and make up around 50 per cent of year 7. The rest come from state primaries and local independent schools.

For external candidates, at 11+, assessments in English, maths, comprehension and non verbal reasoning and interview. At 13+, as above, with additional assessment in a modern foreign language.

For entrance to sixth form, at least six GCSEs at grades 9-6, to include 9-7 in the subjects to be studied at A level or IB higher level, and at least grade 6s in subjects to be studied at IB standard level. External candidates also sit papers in non-verbal reasoning and comprehension.

Exit: A handful leave in year 11, mostly to sixth form colleges. In 2018, 70 per cent of year 13 leavers to top universities, with four to Oxbridge and 14 medics (including one to Universidad de Navarra, Spain). One off to South California University to read economics.

Money matters: Means-tested bursaries may be awarded to those with outstanding academic potential, and may be up to 100 per cent of fees. Scholarships are typically 3-6 per cent of fees, but more significant awards are made on a discretionary basis. depending in the level of achievement.

A parent told us, 'You can really see where your money is going – on things which directly benefit the children, like quality teaching and food'.

Remarks: 'Come here for the variety', said a pupil, and those who like to be involved would certainly thrive at this busy school, which succeeds across the board, excelling academically, and in sports, music and drama. But more than this: PGS is a school where diversity and tolerance are part of its lifeblood, not just a tag line. As one parent said, 'The school makes its claims, as they all do, but here they are all true'.

Portsmouth High Prep School

Linked with Portsmouth High School

36 Kent Road, Southsea, Hampshire PO5 3ES

Ages 2–11 **Pupils** 120

Fees: £7,500 – £9,888 pa

023 9282 4916
www.portsmouthhigh.co.uk

Head: Since 2014, Paul Marshallsay; studied physical education at Exeter University. Joined the school as deputy head in 2011 and became acting head in 2013. He started his teaching career at Victoria College in Jersey before becoming head of department at Burgoyne Middle School in Bedfordshire, followed by deputy head at Yorston Lodge School in Cheshire. Has taught all age groups from reception to sixth form, specialising in a variety of subjects including physical education, mathematics, geography and computing. He is married with one daughter.

Entrance: Prospective pupils are informally assessed in maths, literacy, English and non-verbal reasoning. There's also an informal interview with the head.

Exit: Ninety-nine per cent to senior school (automatic entry, but may sit entrance tests if they want to try for scholarship/prizes).

Remarks: Junior school is located in elegant house, five minutes' walk from senior school. Slight feeling of other worldliness, perhaps engendered in part by being a single sex school, with an emphasis on old-fashioned good manners, perhaps because the entrance is so non-institutional – a high ceilinged white entrance hall, full of light, with white frescos dancing around the top of the walls. Brightly coloured seating and papier mâché hens, along with a suggestions box.

One parent told us that she walked through the door and knew it was the right school for her daughter. Girls are articulate and charming, and a real tribute to their school. The school's focus on speech and drama purports to develop confidence, and certainly the girls we met, from reception upwards, were keen to share their thoughts about their school. They like an awful lot of things, from fraction Fridays (a chocolate or fruit cake is divided into fractions before consumption) to their favourite teachers. Most of the girls' criticisms concerned lack of space and décor. 'The paintwork in the hall is wearing away', said one. 'It gives it an old sort of feel'.

School buildings are a combination of styles, including the lovely main building, a purpose-built pre-prep and what was a rather down-at-heel, converted Victorian house with squashed classrooms for years 3 to 6. Girls, parents and school alike keen to gut and redo this building. 'It's a bit crowded and it's difficult to focus when the window rattles sometimes', said one girl. Although the walls were painted in bright colours, displays were rather limited in this part of the school. School has now invested in a new building with three classrooms and PE changing room.

Lovely outside space with an outdoor classroom and Astro, also mini gardens, beast areas and a chick house with a webcam so pupils can see the eggs hatch. Also an area known as the dell (looks like a miniature assault course – it's not all so ladylike).

Girls are encouraged to take care of each other's feelings, and older children are very solicitous of younger pupils. A newcomer told us: 'I don't know why, but I don't fall out so much with my friends (here)'. Everyone we spoke to was happy to be at an all-girls school. Why? Because 'boys are annoying, loud and noisy'.

Girls are very well behaved. Extraordinarily quiet line of nursery pupils were waiting for instruction in their ballet lesson – girls have clearly absorbed the adage that manners maketh (wo)man, and apply it fully. Meanwhile year 6 pupils applied lively energy to their science lesson, responding to the question about 'upthrust' by saying in a delighted chorus – 'that means you can pick up Daddy in a swimming pool'.

An enquiry-led curriculum, including beach and forest school outside and all sorts of things inside – year 2 children returned to school at start of term to find 'an alien called Zapper' had arrived on the classroom ceiling, complete with a letter of introduction saying that the creature only appeared at night. They were encouraged to ask questions – so they wrote to the head of ICT to request a camera to record Zapper's night-time activities. No flies on year 2. In a maths in motion project girls run a virtual Formula 1 car, measuring the angles and length of the track and checking tyre pressure and gradients.

Music is strong, with 90 per cent learning an instrument. Art room packed with papier mâché heads, gauzy fish and skydiving figures. Lots of clubs – 'always something going on,' say parents.

School council sessions are chaired by the head girl, with the head as minute taker. Meetings discuss things pupils want to improve, though it seems unlikely they will be getting that zip wire any time soon.

Communication with parents, by email, is prompt and efficient. Parents very involved in school and are welcome to attend a celebration assembly every Friday. Girls take turns to perform, which gives parents a snapshot of what they are doing in class.

The senior and junior schools are increasingly close. Parents told us that the junior school is more under the senior umbrella since the arrival of current senior head.

Pupils come from the surrounding area, the Isle of Wight, and from as far afield as Chichester and Petersfield.

P

Portsmouth High School

Linked with Portsmouth High Prep School

25 Kent Road, Southsea, Hampshire PO5 3EQ

Ages 11–18 Pupils 350 Sixth form 80

Fees: £7,500 – £13,986 pa

023 9282 6714
www.portsmouthhigh.co.uk

Headmistress: Since 2011, Jane Prescott BSc PGCE NPQH. Was deputy head of Leicester High School, then deputy head of Loughborough High School, with a background in the army. Energetic and engaging, she is liked and admired by parents and pupils alike. Feels that the girls' well-being is the most accurate indicator of the school's success.

She is 'very hands on', one parent told us, and has open door to pupils, staff and parents (apparently fully used). 'She is very approachable and comes to everything,' said one pupil approvingly.

A devoted advocate for single sex education: 'Boys shuffle for the top of the pack while girls tend to take a back seat', she told us. 'Girls feel the benefit here – there is no subject stereotyping'.

Academic matters: Results are good, though not as good as they have been at A level: 30 per cent A*/A grades in 2018 (62 per cent A*/B). GCSE results remain steady at an excellent 65 per cent A*-A/9-7 grades. This head believes in the prime importance of pastoral care for wellbeing and achievement. Invigorated staff and pupils aim for outstanding, but pupils report a surprising lack of pressure to get those A*s. 'It's very caring', said one girl. 'I got a D in my mocks, and they said, "let's work out what went wrong". I got an A in the actual exam – but there wasn't pressure to get an A'.

Parents talk of nurture and 'support without pressure'. One said that a D grade would be celebrated as much as an A grade if that was the best a girl could achieve. 'The competition is for the girl, not the school'. Parents say the school is less fiercely competitive than the nearby grammar and that there's no pressure here to retake disappointing grades to tweak those league tables. 'Move on', says the head firmly. 'All things are explainable'. (Even if the explanation might be laziness and recent reformation of character.)

A smaller selection of subjects on offer than at larger schools, but staff will do their best to accommodate a girl's urge to learn something in particular. Most girls take a language up to GCSE, but a few struggling with the basics can drop their language to focus on maths instead. Over half of pupils take maths at A level. Pupils who arrive with little English are supported to learn the language.

Spacious labs, which after the £1.2 million refurbishment (amongst other things) allow pupils to use the data feed from solar panels on roof. When we visited, upper sixth pupils were just off to hear Lord Winston speak. 'We try to give the girls all the opportunities we can – as much extracurricular as possible to make science relevant to the rest of life', says the school.

RS is popular – we observed a lively GCSE class doing some bartering (a slight relief to hear the noise after the sheer concentrated effort of most classes observed). The topic was economic trading with ethical dimensions. 'They are trying to solve world poverty', explained the teacher. 'They haven't done it yet,' she added dryly.

Constant data collection on performance, so those falling behind are quickly spotted. Immediate redress, starting with a chat to pupil and parents. Annual parents' evening, half-termly report cards and one full report a year.

All pupils are screened for SEN, but just a handful with special needs. SENCo for the whole school and special individual and group sessions where necessary. One pupil has been given an iPad of her own to assist her learning.

Games, options, the arts: Sport taken seriously and despite small urban site, the school will soon have a multi surface Astro and offers almost everything, including football and tag rugby. If there is a criticism from the girls, it is that they don't get enough games lessons (although most years have five sessions a week).

Wide enrichment programme includes sailing, Amnesty and ever popular DofE.

Strong music department, and plenty of public performance, including overseas tours and the Royal Festival Hall. Drama studio, plus larger stage in the hall next door. Girls have performed at the Edinburgh Festival.

Lovely art space – central atrium flooded with light from glass ceiling. Art courses cover ceramics, textiles, photography and fine art, with girls dictating the content as they get older. DT room packed with exciting equipment and a Tiggerish devotee of DT for a teacher. Rows of tiny models lined the shelves when we visited – a mini-me project for year 7s.

Background and atmosphere: Buildings are a hodge-podge of styles. Old buildings are lovely, particularly the sixth form house, though some of the new buildings look a bit like Tesco. Interior is mostly well cared for. New catering manager has improved food dramatically. Eating in the dining room compulsory for year 7 (tables laid and waiting), but optional from year 8 onwards, so many opt for the school café. Parents astonished that their daughters choose to sit next to a teacher and chat at lunch time.

'You are known for who you are here', said one girl, adding that she felt 'anonymous' at the local grammar. Class sizes of around 20 for years 7 and 8, 15 to 20 at GCSE. A level classes vary in size. Parents feel that school's small size is its strength – girls can't get lost, literally or otherwise. Numbers on school roll are down – head reckons this reflects economic climate but bewildered parents suggest more marketing might work. School wouldn't want to be larger than 500 though, says the head. Small numbers mean staff and girls know each other well, and the curriculum can be tailored to individuals.

School is calm – difficult to imagine extremes of behaviour here. One parent told us that girls have 'confidence without cockiness', while another commented that her shy daughter was transformed after a couple of years here.

'It's nicer without boys – boys are disruptive', said a year 8 girl firmly. This seemed to be the prevailing view of pupils, and the school attracts a few disillusioned escapees from the local grammar. One parent who worried about single-sex education before she sent her daughter here said: 'I thought they would be, you know, bitchy, but they are almost too nice to each other. They are very caring.' With two boys' schools nearby, girls have plenty of opportunity to socialise on the way to and from school and during activities like the cathedral choir. Sixth formers share a few lessons with boys from St John's, too.

The sixth form centre is part of the school, but sixth form girls get far more independence. Head girl and senior prefects (elected by peers) have lots of responsibility. School has tried to create a college atmosphere for the sixth form, and succeeded. Sixth formers attend house meetings and assemblies first thing, then come and go as they please. If they abuse the system, they have to stay in school, but this is very rare. No uniform, but smart dress with the silver Portsmouth High badge – no jeans. They are self assured, polite and friendly. The sixth form house has a white seating area, very tidy kitchen (with its own dishwasher) peaceful study rooms, small library, computer room and conservatory. 'When things are stressful at home, I just want to get to school and be in the sixth form centre', a sixth former said.

Officially it's a non-denominational school but in practice it's mildly Christian. Morality is a general approach, not religion-led. Lots of community activities too. Girls contribute to local charities, volunteer at the local food bank and at beach clean ups and are part of the British Council's Connecting Classrooms project.

Pastoral care, well-being and discipline: An emphasis on pastoral care under current head. Girls feel that they can talk to the head, that they will be listened to and that their efforts are appreciated. 'You get a handwritten card the day after you are in something – a proper one, not just one of those ink print things'. If something is wrong, the girls had no doubt to whom they would turn – 'the deputy head ... she's like a mother hen'. School also has a welfare officer.

Bullying very rare. Girls supported through any friendship problems by deputy head. Pupils can become peer supporters in year 9 and receive training in confidentiality. 'You have to fill out a proper application, like a job', a pupil gravely assured us. Great care taken in smoothing the transition from junior to senior school for year 7s. Girls appear to have good relations with teachers – 'not invasive, but caring', said a sixth former. Another girl told us: 'If you are struggling (with work), it's caring... how can we work together, how can we sort this out?' This is certainly not a rap over the knuckles, must do better, sort of place.

Pupils and parents: Pupils travel in by school minibus, public transport, hovercraft from the Isle of Wight, by bike and on foot. Parents are a broad church. 'I thought it would be all Boden mums, but it really isn't', one mother told us. Parents say it's for those who value education and are prepared to invest. 'We don't go on holiday much,' said another.

Famous old girls include Dame Mary Donaldson, the first woman Lord Mayor of London, Dr Jane Collins, chief executive of Marie Curie Cancer Care, author and broadcaster Jane Hill, MP Meg Hillier, TV presenter Charlotte Jackson, Dr Katharine Vincent, an expert on sustainability and climate change, Dr Frances Saunders, president of the Institute of Physics and actress Denise Black.

Entrance: Most girls start senior school in year 7, but pupils can join in any year. Standard entrance exam in English and maths. Seven or eight pupils join at sixth form level.

Exit: Roughly 10 per cent leave after GCSEs, mostly to sixth form colleges. None to Oxbridge in 2018. Destinations included Bath, Birmingham, Bristol, Edinburgh, Cardiff, Durham, East Anglia, Exeter, King's College London, Loughborough, Manchester, Newcastle, The Royal Agricultural University, Royal Holloway, Sheffield, Warwick and York.

Money matters: Much cheaper than most schools of its ilk – great value for money. A number of small scholarships and bursaries (a couple of which pay the fees in full).

Remarks: A super no-frills choice. School is big enough to appeal to almost any girl, but not at the expense of the personal touch. Pupils and parents agree that all girls would thrive here and that it's a place where timid souls will flourish. Prestigious local reputation and a member of the GDST sisterhood.

P

The Prebendal School

52–55 West Street, Chichester, West Sussex PO19 1RP

Ages 3–13 **Pupils** 160 **Boarders** 16 full, 2 weekly (from 7 years) **C of E**

Fees: Day £8,160 – £15,495; Boarding £18,975 – £22,290; Choristers £11,145 pa

01243 772220
www.prebendalschool.org.uk

Head: Since 2017, Louise Salmond Smith BA (East Anglia), MMus (Hull), PGCE (Gloucestershire), Keele (MBA). Previously head of junior school at Tormead School in Guildford and the school's first female head. Plain talking, feisty and a virtuoso on the recorder. Has introduced hot chocolate at Bill's as the termly treat for pupils with the most pluses, this replacing a book token; her parish is wholly convinced by the wisdom of this move, and all aspire to join her.

Pupils say she's 'really nice' and that they see a lot more of her (than the last head): 'she's a lot friendlier'. The children seem to appreciate that they don't have to leap to attention when they see her around the place; a small child, post music lesson, saw the head with relief and gave up her private battles with the timetable to ask for help.

Stands up for children, and refused to remove from the classroom a child with SEN who was, a parent complained, disturbing her child's learning. The complainant and her children departed, the other parents appreciating that lessons of the classroom are not just those found in books.

Parents are very enthusiastic: 'brilliant...knows every child's name...speaks in a way they can understand'; 'a doer...not full of bluster. Has great ideas and is interested in the children themselves'.

Entrance: Non-selective. Testing for bench marking and setting purposes. Taster day for prospective pupils. Auditions for choristers, boys only.

Exit: Mainly feeds Lancing, PGS and Seaford, with the odd pupil to Eton and Harrow; the head is keen for parents to expand their horizons.

A small number leaves after year 6 for state schools.

Remarks: This is a school of sounds. Children move through corridors at their own pace, making their own noises, from chatter, to sung snatches of anthems, to an odd experimental mixture of the two: children finding and expressing themselves by voice. Music is a way of life at this school; virtually all the children learn one instrument and many learn more, and each year there are a clutch of music scholarships to senior schools.

School buildings range from ancient to modern, but it's the old ones that arrest you: the curved classroom doors off a spiral staircase; the jail from the old magistrates' court (now storage behind bars); the cavernous old kitchen in the Bishop's Palace, used for band practice and drama. The Prebendal is as old as the cathedral (1100s), and was founded as its song school, with its first head listed simply as John. To be in these buildings is to feel centuries peeling back around you; teachers say to children: 'this room was here when...' Pupils are sitting in time, and this is something they are very aware of – 'I can feel it in English when the windows rattle as a bus goes past', said one pupil: history shaking down through the centuries.

P

Pre-prep is the modern part, full of light and colour; but from its playground the cathedral arches up, ancient behind modern. The school treats the cathedral as its chapel – 'but we let them use it for other services', said the head kindly. Pupils say it's a religious school, with lots of prayers and services (they quite like the ritual of it), and parents like that the children get used to talking in cathedral assemblies; 'not arrogance, just what they do...'

The divine sound of the choristers comes at a cost: 23 hours of practice and services a week; like having a part time job on top of the full time job of school and being a kid. Asked if he would recommend it, a chorister said, 'only if you like life very hectic'. But if you love singing, this is a chance to be part of a professional choir, with the cathedral paying 50 per cent of fees, and there's topping up if needed. It's boys only, and there's no prospect of a Prebendal girls' choir in the near future; funds only run to one professional choir, and a girls' choir instead of the boys' one would be a radical step too far.

A mix of abilities at this non-selective school, the very academically able and those that just 'muddle through', said parents. 'No divide or distance between them', said another, they all mix, and pupils from the state sector comment with pleasure on teachers who focus on all, not just those at the lower end.

Teachers know the children well, one parent describing how her son's teacher approached her at the end of his first week at Prebendal – 'this is how I am thinking about teaching [your son]....'

Prebendal follows the CE syllabus, but also the pre-senior baccalaureate, which focuses on skills rather than spoon feeding. It's a great idea, and parents feel it will set pupils apart, but it hasn't really kicked in yet, and pupils would like more time to talk in lessons; a teacher pointed out that both pupils and teachers have to get used to a different way of being. But we saw some lively lessons, a year 8 pupil standing on a chair to work out an equation in blue marker on the window to the encouragement of her peers; scribbling on windows during lessons is encouraged here.

Most people are attracted to Prebendal by its small size and family feel, and describe the school as gentle and nurturing – 'they won't shut your kids down, judge them for being dyslexic, or anything else...' Learning support staff are 'on it', said a parent, describing how they read with her dyslexic son daily, and provide extra in class support free of charge (one-to-one sessions are charged as extra).

Beach school fortnightly for the little ones, the head saying she would rather they are learning their letters outside, with a stick in the sand, than a pencil on paper inside. On the day of our visit, year 2s were finding things, man made or natural, then building them into castles (this term's project). It is difficult to imagine a happier place for children to learn.

The boarding here is mostly weekly or flexi; only the 11 choristers and a couple of international pupils are around at weekends, when it is very quiet, said a chorister, although there is a family feel to Sundays, when the families of choristers join the school for Sunday lunch.

A dormitory (of 14) with old wood panelling has ancient graffiti, carved into it by pupils long gone; pupils of the present day are allowed their own graffiti, by pen not penknife, on the wall of a tight spiral staircase. Dormitory numbers shrink as pupils get older, to three for year 8s. Bathrooms are clean, sometimes elderly (when did you last see a wall mounted cistern and chain?)

Pupils describe the school as 'strict but friendly'. Bullying is 'taken quite seriously' said a pupil, and the head says they encourage snitches. Pupils say they talk to both sides, but there are not always evident consequences for the person doing the bullying, and things can recur. System of pluses for all things good, comments for the bad, with three comments getting you a detention – this might be copying out a portion of an encyclopaedia, or some Mandarin. Parents report prompt dealing with pastoral concerns; the form teacher or school chaplain are usually first port of call, 'but anyone passing would help...'

A playground big enough for break time football, tennis and hen coop; the rescued factory hens have nearly all their feathers now, and Vera, the bravest, enjoys cuddles at break time (two pupils at a time in the hen coop only), and has braved the hen swing (who knew).

There's a new outdoor classroom with wood chips underfoot (year 8 patiently pick up the ones that get away), and a more informal area called the amphitheatre: a circle of wooden benches with a fire pit at the centre (a wise head prioritises toasting marshmallows).

They have their own entrance to the Bishop's Gardens from their playground, where they can climb trees – to a certain point. At night, after the gardens are closed to the public, boarders use the garden for manhunt in the dark.

For a small school, there is a vigorous programme of sports, and parents think this is probably the only element of the school that feels really competitive; but they read both losses and wins out in the cathedral, and no-one holds it against those who haven't achieved on the sports field, added a parent earnestly.

One pupil told us how wonderful it feels to play cricket on their pitch next to the cathedral – it is the backdrop to their lives here, and gives great pleasure. Girls are pleased they now have opportunities to play cricket, and football too, but want to keep playing all their traditional sports as well. In some years there are cool kids and it's the sporty ones who get the kudos (not any nastiness, we gather, more 'idols...'); a bemused shake of the head from a chorister at the thought that his status might command any admiration from his peers.

Parents like the long school days, and the flexibility, geared for working parents – 'they will keep children if you're late to pick up...I've picked up at 9pm...' It's a friendly, busy parent group, with nearly all parents working (lots of professionals); 'no one has time for bitchiness...'.

Pupils agree that the food is OK, though not up to home cooking: 'main courses packed with mushrooms, puddings packed with raisins', said a pupil resignedly, but compared to his old school, it's really good.

A girl who likes her skirt gravely told us that she still thinks there should be the choice to wear trousers, and the boys were very clear that they would like to wear shorts in summer. A sympathetic shudder from all at the requirement for pre-prep boys to wear shorts all year round. Some pupil uncertainty as to whether using Pupil Voice (their council), makes a difference, but the head is keen to change this; she has refurbished the girls' changing rooms, and the pupil who suggested a zip wire over to school from the cathedral wasn't all that surprised it was turned down.

Parents say Prebendal would suit all, from the really sporty to the meek and mild. 'It looks very traditional, but the thinking is new', said a parent. 'Not that it's Bedales', she added.

Prior's Field

Priorsfield Road, Godalming, Surrey GU7 2RH

Ages 11–18 **Pupils** 445 **Sixth form** 81 **Boarders** 51 full, 14 weekly, 26 flexi

Fees: Day £17,700; Boarding £27,900– £29,925 pa

01483 810551
www./priorsfieldschool.com

Head: Since 2015, Tracy Kirnig, 50s. Born and brought up in London, she ventured to university in Aberystwyth, reading RE and philosophy. Ms Kirnig was never in doubt about a teaching career and returned nearer to her roots to take a masters in education at King's London and then a PGCE at Lancaster before working in both the state and private sector. Her interests in music and travel are re-enforced by the scaling of Mount Kilimanjaro last year, particularly impressive as she admits to being a late-comer to the joys of climbing. Moving here from her last job as deputy head of co-ed Caterham school, she is noticeably happy in her own skin with a firm belief in the worth of her school and in particular of the girls in her care. Married to a geo-technological engineer with a side-line in potting.

Academic matters: An academically selective school, although not generally in the high-flying category; in 2018 grades at GCSE were 57 per cent A*-A/9-7, with record-breaking 50 per cent A*/A and 76 per cent A*-B at A level. There has been a noticeable, recent, attempt to redress the balance away from the arts, with around half the year taking one or more maths and science subjects at A level. Languages are not an obviously strong point, but they make a great effort to find outside teachers if pupils voice sufficient interest in a language outside the fairly narrow choice on the core curriculum of French, Spanish and Latin at GCSE. Everyone takes one or two of these at this stage and recently up to 20 per cent have taken at least one language at A level.

The average class size in the early years is 18, reducing to 15 as they move up the school and six in the sixth form. Setting takes place on arrival at both 11+ and 13+ for English and maths and later in the first term for science, MFL and sport. The girls speak of flexibility and are confident that they will be moved up or down rapidly if it appears necessary.

The staff, with a ratio of one teacher to eight girls, have a relatively high average age but, as the head says, 'this brings a wealth of experience,' 22 of them having been at the school for more than 10 years. Despite this statistic, she feels that there are plenty of younger members and promotes them on the basis that 'they are old enough if they are good enough'. Certainly, on our visit, the enthusiasm and interaction with the pupils was noticeable with plenty of young faces and absolutely no stuffed shirts in evidence. It may be a smallish school but the determination to help each girl reach her academic potential is clearly evident.

The staff and pupils are confident about the SEND provision; it appears to be handled efficiently and sensitively, although they admit that they might dissuade a parent from sending a child with problems that would prevent her from coping fairly easily with the school's academic expectations. However, one parent told us that they were 'great about accepting my very dyslexic daughter' and that the SENCo was 'fantastic'. One-on-one help is available, if necessary, at an hourly rate.

Games, options, the arts: A surprisingly sporty school despite its size. Netball, hockey and athletics tick the most boxes and teams compete locally and nationally. Tennis is huge; they even run to a tennis academy (complete with a permanent coach), which paid off recently in the Surrey U15 championship and with their first tennis scholar having her pick of American universities. At a more achievable, if slightly wacky, level the inter-house cross-country competition last year had an underwater theme, with the girls sporting mermaid tails; it may not have increased their speed but it was good for a laugh.

Clubs and activities are a big deal, meriting their own brochure, and are often free, although if you're into creating Funky Food, not surprisingly, you have to pay for the ingredients as well as persuading your parents to eat the results. Rugby and cricket now available, the latter becoming popular after the successes of the England women's team. In a nod to the country, you can go riding after school, or if you're a home bod, you can get into knitting and crochet, of which we saw an imaginative, if eccentric, example in the making.

Completely unsurprisingly given the school's arts and crafts heritage, there is a major emphasis on art, music and drama. The art rooms are designed for people taking it seriously, with sixth formers each having their own space that fills up with imaginative work during the year. The result is that several girls go on to art college and a high proportion of alumnae make it a career. They mean what they say about encouraging talent, as one girl with a natural bent for photography persuaded them to add the course to the GCSE curriculum. New music rooms encourage even the less musical to give an instrument a go, whilst the more gifted are nurtured carefully. Drama is definitely front stage with brave large cast musical productions, entry in the Shakespeare Schools Festival and popular LAMDA and RADA classes.

Boarding: About a quarter of the girls board but increasingly this is on a weekly or flexible basis rather than full time. At weekends the school can seem a little empty lower down as only around seven to eight board full time in the first two years, but further up the school the percentage increases to 50 per cent in the fifth year and up to 60 per cent in the sixth form. One parent was a bit unhappy and thought that her daughter lacked supervision, but this was contradicted by several of the present cohort.

The younger girls are up in the attics in cosy if slightly cramped quarters of up to four in a room, but it feels cheerful and there was no griping when asked if they had enough space. You wouldn't want to be a budding fashionista with a lot of frocks as the hanging space is strictly limited, but there are lots of drawers for 'stuff' and you are encouraged to make it as personal as possible. The bathrooms looked newish and were pretty spotless, a nice cleaning lady telling us they had a 'really good go twice a week'. The sixth formers all have larger rooms with good work space, the upper sixth even having their own bathrooms – a much appreciated luxury. The general consensus was that there was plenty to do out of school hours and some of the day girls would love their parents to come up with the cash so that they could board.

Background and atmosphere: Prior's Field nestles in a hidden corner of leafy Surrey, just out of sight of the London hubbub. A rather surprising unicorn- themed advertisement for the school is squished on a small roundabout off the A3, but the tree-lined road leading off it soon reveals a pebble-dashed, beetle-browed arts and crafts set of buildings. The original 1900 house, designed by CFA Voysey, has grown since through the addition of convincing fakes and the whole ensemble fits happily into its surrounding acres.

The founder, Julia Huxley, was related by blood, marriage and proximity to the intellectual and educationally passionate giants of the Edwardian age. You could not dream up someone more suitable to start a school than the granddaughter of Dr Thomas Arnold (the Rugby legend), niece of Matthew Arnold (the poet), wife of Leonard Huxley (a Charterhouse schoolmaster himself before becoming an important literary figure) and friend of Conan Doyle. Her children, Julian, a scientist and director of UNESCO, and Aldous, author of Brave New World, provide further evidence of why she was the perfect person to run a school based on moral philosophy and forward thinking. There is a brilliant photograph of her in the hall, hand on chin, glasses slightly skew whiff, with her ample successor, Ethel Burton-Brown, sitting at her feet, made more touching by the fact that she died a year later aged only 46. Conan Doyle sent his daughter here and the germ of the idea for a short story entitled The Adventure of Priory School must surely have come from his knowledge of Prior's Field, although the plot is not exactly an advertisement for pupil care.

The slightly labyrinthine layout of a turn-of-the-century house is not ideal for a modern school, but a newbie told us that despite getting lost frequently for the first two weeks she had quickly learnt the necessary shortcuts to make it everywhere on time. Again surprisingly, the interior, whilst a tad scruffy, is not as dark as you would expect and is greatly improved by art on every available wall as well as impressive displays of textile work for which the school is justifiably famous. Amongst the newer buildings, they are proudest of their pristine science, technology and music centre, which manages to be light and attractive inside despite its folksy exterior. The area at the front of the school is cramped, but the back opens up to a wide green space, a new all-purpose Astroturf pitch, several tennis courts and woodland beyond.

P

Pastoral care, well-being and discipline: This side of the school was high on the head's agenda when she took over and she has changed the structure so that now there is one person responsible for the emotional development of each individual, separate from the person in charge of checking whether they've got the right tights on. PSHE is not just an acronym here but built into the whole workings of the school, and the result hits you straight on, all the girls we talked to genuinely appearing to put helping each other above being competitive. The school has definitely got across their belief in moral welfare but it is not heavy handed; common sense rather than a set of rules is the order of the day. With her philosophical background, the head also wants to broaden awareness and a series of talks on mindfulness are scheduled, the first one being given by a Buddhist nun. Zero evidence of wrongdoing: the head girl sounded puzzled when we asked her if she had to discipline the younger ones.

The beautifully presented food (think huge Moroccan bowls of salad and a bread offering that would challenge a trendy London bakery) is seriously yummy, one girl giggling that it was much better than her mum's. Being allergic or just fussy is not a problem, a non-gluten pupil telling us that there was masses of choice and they were 'really helpful about it', and teachers seem very aware of any potential problems.

Not the smartest of schools in terms of uniform, but this is being remedied with major input from the pupils who, slightly to our surprise, actually want to wear blazers with badges to show off where they come from.

Pupils and parents: Majority of day girls bussed in from all points of the compass, increasingly from nearer London as parents turn away from the capital's pressure-cookers and look for an academically competent school with an individual flavour. Some 10 per cent from a wide range of foreign countries; these, when asked, said that they had settled in straight away, and certainly all had smiley faces. Parents' backgrounds are as diverse as the children's ambitions but they say that they feel fully involved with the school via personal contact and email communication as well as the PSA.

Entrance: An open morning or a pre-arranged 'Meet the head' coffee morning plus school tour are followed by a taster day in November and an exam in January. The school is oversubscribed at 11 and 13 but they don't just go on exam results. Rather, they try to find girls who are 'sparky, curious about life and learning and want to get involved with everything on offer'. A genuine effort is made to determine whether this is the right place for each individual and they're pretty good at it, judging by the great attitude of the present lot.

Exit: In this tough financial climate and due to the school's location, it is hardly surprising that a large number (upt o half) leave after GCSEs, a percentage of which are replaced from outside. We suspect that affordability is the major reason, but the assumption that life is more 'real' in a co-ed still attracts a proportion to either private school sixth forms or state colleges with good A level results. No Oxbridge entrants recently but Nottingham Trent, Cardiff, Bath, Lancaster, Leeds and Nottingham popular; several off to study sciences alongside those starting art or graphic design courses – plus the first tennis academy graduate on a full scholarship to Iowa. Grandparents will be thrilled that Enid Bagnold (National Velvet) was an old girl, watchers of Netflix will know of Victoria Hamilton (the queen mother in The Crown), and others will be encouraged that Baroness Mary Warnock was at the school.

Money matters: Plenty of scholarships and bursaries; academic, sporting, musical, artistic and dramatic abilities are recognised by an award which equates to between £250 and £1,000 per term. One or two exceptional tennis players are awarded a place in the tennis academy, with coaching costs fully funded by the school. A handful of foundation awards (100 per cent bursaries funded by parents, alumnae and friends of the school) are awarded each year and a 20 per cent discount on the fees is given to the daughters of parents in the Forces.

Remarks: A century may have passed but the aim to turn out resilient young women, capable of achieving the maximum possible in the outside world, remains the same. It is still a school where 'it is cool to try out new things', and the head is confident that the well-equipped young adults that leave are recognisable as the children that arrived five or seven years earlier. The school is also long on charm and good at detail, winning us over immediately by giving us a car parking space with our name on it.

The Purcell School

Aldenham Road, Bushey, Hertfordshire WD23 2TS

Ages 8–18 **Pupils** 180 **Sixth form** 84 **Boarders** 138 full

Fees: Day £25,968; Boarding £33,156 pa

01923 331100
www.purcell-school.org

Head: Since September 2018, Paul Bambrough, previously vice principal at the Birmingham Royal Conservatoire, where he also, inter alia, taught in the vocal and operatic studies department and contributed to the orchestra conducting course. Whilst director of music at the Sixth Form College Farnborough, he created the largest A level music department in the country of 500+ students. He has sung at most of the UK's foremost concert halls and cathedrals, is a harpsichordist, organist and pianist and has worked as a repetiteur with some of the world's finest singers. Away from music he enjoys the countryside, architecture and maintains a (largely) enthusiastic fitness routine.

Academic matters: Not an obvious place for the academic scholar who also happens to be a musical prodigy, but then again this is not a place pretending to be a one stop shop all for the all-rounder: far from it. 'Music colleges don't require academic excellence ... but we do want parents to trust that the academic side can be delivered.' Public examination results variable from year to year: 51 per cent of A level results graded A*/A in 2018 and 71 per cent A*/B. Subject range limited, and unsurprisingly by far the greatest number of takers are in the artier subjects (English literature, art and music tech consistently most popular), although the diminutive number opting for sciences tend to do quite well. School encourages pupils to take three A levels 'unless performance requirements get in the way'. Cambridge pre-U qualification in music now offered in place of A level music.

GCSEs respectable, with 56 per cent graded A*-A/9-7 in 2018, consistent with previous years. Pupils generally take no more than seven or eight subjects (compulsory music, maths, English language and science) – 'our pupils undertake a huge amount of practice; there simply isn't time'. There are so few pupils in years 5 and 6 that they are taught as a single group, and classes throughout are comparatively very small, but increase gradually towards the upper end of the school. Teaching staff vibrant and engaging in the main (occasional parental rumblings that some have been there too long) – with some new appointments really upping the ante. 'The academic side isn't stellar,' say parents (and it's true to say that it doesn't come close to measuring up to other nearby independents in that regard, either in terms of facilities or teaching), 'but it's getting better all the time'.

But ultimately it's all about the music. Pupils' days begin bright and early with pre-breakfast practice, and continue with instrumental tuition and rehearsals interspersed throughout the day, with supervised practice for the younger pupils. Blessed with music rooms containing two grand pianos apiece and genuinely inspirational music teachers, most of whom also have professorships or senior teaching posts at top music academies and colleges. Having observed one such maestro in action, we are hard pushed to think of a single more dynamic teacher of any subject we have seen (and the pupil was nothing short of breathtaking). Pupils have up to two hours of academic music lessons a day, around two hours weekly of individual instrumental tuition plus between three and (in the final years) up to five hours of timetabled practice per day. Theory not taught as a matter of course beyond grade 6 – a cause of consternation for some parents. School adamant, though, that it is on offer 'on demand' up to grade 8 for those who wish to continue (with exceptionally high results for those who do), and the recent accolade of the Incorporated Society of Musicians' Gold Award for the highest achievement at GCSE music (taken a year early at The Purcell) should give comfort that school has the academic side of music covered.

With one-to-one relationships so fundamental to teaching music, what happens if a pupil and teacher just don't click? 'School is amenable to change,' the parent of one such child told us, 'but parents need to be prepared to intervene.' Abundant performance opportunities from lunchtime recitals under the discerning eyes of peers and teachers to the full symphony orchestra at Cadogan Hall, and chamber ensembles series at London recital venues (Wigmore Hall, St Martin-in-the-fields).

Dedicated SENCo works with the 50+ pupils on the register, the majority requiring help with some degree of dyslexia, dyspraxia or dyscalculia but also some ASD (two statemented at time of writing) and ADHD. Assistance also provided to pupils with general organisational and planning skills, particularly around exam time. One-to-one support provided in lessons when required.

Games, options, the arts: Never have we been so reassured by the sight of a boot rack laden with well-worn football boots. Despite the all-pervading musical focus hanging in the air, and only one timetabled PE lesson per week, pupils still enjoy a range of sports including badminton, volleyball and football, mainly of the rather jolly, participative, uncompetitive sort, with the exception of one annual fixture against the Yehudi Menuhin School (the Purcell usually wins). Recent appointment of an enthusiastic young sports teacher has been met with rapturous appreciation. 'He asks the pupils what they want to do, then organises it for them'. Perfect. Sports facilities rather sparse – we were not voluntarily shown the ancient, draughty sports hall (cobwebs present), but see it we did and frankly it does the job, as does the very generous field at the school's rear. Yoga a regular and organised activity to benefit the young musicians' core strength and posture and help avoid injury, and those who wish to are able to use the gym and pool at nearby Bushey Leisure Centre.

Other options vary wildly as there's such a constant intake of new pupils with differing interests, but those with a specific passion are encouraged to start their own club, be it debating, chess or ping-pong. Choir is compulsory, art pursued to a high standard in the delightful stable block atelier adorned with cellos and bicycles hanging from the ceiling and some inspirational two and three-dimensional work – much of it music themed – on display. A dedicated art technician supports the teaching staff and keen photographers and potters can use the dark room and kiln. Drama 'very good' (and now on curriculum) according to parents, with pupils entering into the spirit with great enthusiasm and delivering some 'highly entertaining' performances.

Boarding: Majority of pupils involved in boarding life to some degree and they enjoy all the creature comforts of smart, cosy boarding houses. Littlies in years 6 to 8 are in homely co-ed Avison House, just a hop, skip and jump from the main school building. Run with a true family atmosphere, with its own garden, well kitted out common room (anyone for table tennis?) and spacious twin bedrooms ('we do have one single, but nobody ever wants it,' the housemistress told us). Accommodation has been designed to be totally flexible, thanks to a clever system of locking doors on the bedroom corridors to allow for fluctuations in the male:female ratio. Full programme of activities runs for these youngsters, including team building at the start of each year.

Sunley House, upstairs in the main school building, is where you'll find some of the girls from years 9 to13 (as well as Rupert, the house labrador), and offers modern rooms, lovely views – and pianos in the bedrooms of sixth form pianists. Peachy. The large, well-equipped common room doubles as venue for film nights, food nights and craft activities (dreamcatchers and crochet recent hits). Gardner & Graham offer the same high quality accommodation for years 9-13, arranged in single sex corridors. Parents praise house staff as 'wonderfully supportive' and 'so kind', with the only real grumbles relating to the food which, we must agree, was not up to scratch for a boarding school. Tuck box definitely required.

Weekly boarders head home Friday afternoon and the programme for those staying for the weekend is a mix of performance classes, practice and rehearsals with homely activities (baking, takeaways) in the house when time allows. So integral is boarding culture to the school that parents tell us their day pupils can 'feel a little bit out of it' at times.

Background and atmosphere: Not as old as one might expect, despite being the UK's first and oldest specialist music school. Founded in 1962 by Rosemary Rapaport and Irene Forster as The Central Tutorial School for Young Musicians and residing first at concert venue Conway Hall then Morley College in London before relocating to Hampstead. Renamed in 1973 and relocated to its current site – formerly the Royal Caledonian School – in 1998. The drab environs of Bushey and austere Edwardian façade of the school do no justice to the lightness (actual and metaphorical) and vibrancy that lie within. The pristine main school corridors are bathed in natural light and schools with three times the number of pupils would envy the space. First stop on our tour – via a welcoming modern reception area showcasing some 3D artwork – was the coffee shop, frequented by both staff and pupils, and decked out with brightly coloured sofas, tables and chairs. Spacious classrooms, kitted out with all the latest IT equipment, look out over a vast field that could almost fool you it was countryside. The icing on the cake, however, is the fabulous modern music centre at the school's rear with its multitudinous practice rooms, teaching spaces, studio theatre and concert hall. Even for a music school, though, we found the library somewhat lacking in...well, books. Pupils can take out any music score you could think of, but those looking for the latest David Walliams will need to consult Amazon.

So why choose a school like this over a mainstream school with a cracking music department? It's simple, according to the pupils, who are not just mainstream kids with a cracking aptitude for music: 'everyone here is like us.' And if ever a real life school could mirror the Hogwarts wizards versus muggles effect, The Purcell is it. Pupils have often felt 'different' in their former schools and joining The Purcell has enabled them to live, breathe (and probably dream) music in a school where everyone's agenda is the same. Even their senses of humour have a musical slant. Unexpectedly for a hotbed of such great talent, the temperature is pretty low and overall vibe laid back and friendly – pupils told us: 'everyone in the school is a friend...even the teachers'. Lack of uniform underscores relaxed, creative vibe and parents say 'it feels more like a college than a school.' Performance is all part of a day's work – our tour included a lunch time recital by a trio of year 13s, and nothing could quite have prepared us for the standard of music – we were buzzing for hours afterwards.

Pastoral care, well-being and discipline: Crucially, staff:pupil ratio is such that in the event of an issue they have ample time to spend resolving it. Pupils say that bullying is out of the question: 'Everyone respects each other and we're such a small community that a bully would be socially ostracised'. Homesickness in the boarding houses is dealt with 'with incredible patience and kindness', say parents. Despite vast talent pool, school assures us that 'pupils are no more neurotic than other kids', but that the necessary systems are firmly in place to support the pressures, which are different to those experienced by most young people: 'We ask them to work at adult level and need to be aware of the demands that are placed on them'. Pupils say school is very helpful with time management challenges and that they have 'lots of free time' to unwind from performance pressures. School 'extremely firm' around transgressions, according to parents, and alcohol or drug use results in expulsion.

Pupils and parents: Families from all walks of life and social backgrounds, some from the music world, many (around 40 per cent) from other creative industries and occasional bewildered parents who have no idea where their prodigy's talent came from. Tiger parents not an endangered species. A little less than 20 per cent of boarders come from overseas, with largest numbers from Korea and Singapore. Pupils bright and breezy, funny and articulate – totally at ease in this environment with their talent, commitment and work ethic. Former pupils include Oliver Knussen (composer and conductor), Nicholas Daniel (oboist and first winner of the BBC Young Musician competition), Catrin Finch (former harpist to the Prince of Wales), Lara Melda (winner of 2010 BBC Young Musician), Janice Graham (leader, ENO Orchestra), and Yiruma (Korean pianist and composer).

Entrance: Audition season runs weekly between September and March. Prospective pupils come for a preliminary, one-to-one audition and are invited back for a thorough going over by a panel if they are taken to the next stage. Key criteria is not what grade candidate has achieved but how committed they are to a career in music. About half those who audition are offered a place – staff talk about the 'wild glint in the eyes' of the selection panel when they see an outstanding talent. No academic threshold but school 'must be able to cater for them' and numbers for entry into any year group are a constantly moveable feast. The tiny numbers at the lower end of the school (10 pupils in year 6 at time of writing) quadruple by year 12, and there's a large intake post-GCSE.

Exit: Almost all to the great and good of music colleges, top universities to read music, and conservatoires. Strongest numbers to Royal Academy of Music, Royal College of Music and Guildhall School of Music and Drama; several to study abroad (Europe and USA). King's College and Royal Holloway

College, London frequent choices; usually one or two Oxbridge: two in 2018 and one to Harvard. The occasional pupil goes completely off piste and chooses to read anything from history to aeronautical engineering – no trends here, but we're talking one or two per year. Occasional premature departures back to mainstream education – often because families with more academic children struggle with the balance being so enormously in favour of music.

Money matters: With boarding fees now comfortably topping £30K it's up there with the top public schools, but very few pay full fees. The majority of places (currently over 140) are funded by the brilliant government music and dance assisted places scheme, school bursary or scholarship.

Remarks: In the words of one parent: 'proof that specialist music schools can work'. Not to be entered into lightly – particularly at the younger end of the age range – but here is a greenhouse of a school, providing exactly the right environment for its brilliant young students to flourish amongst like-minded individuals.

Queen Anne's School

6 Henley Road, Caversham, Reading, Berkshire RG4 6DX

Ages 11–18 **Pupils** 460 **Sixth form** 137 **Boarders** 136 full, 34 weekly, 32 flexi **C of E**

Fees: Day £24,135; Boarding £32,070 – £35,580 pa

01189 187300
www.qas.org.uk

Headmistress: Since 2006, Julia Harrington BA NPQH (50s). Educated at grammar school in Lydney and Exeter University (history and politics). From a family of teachers, decided to break the mould and work in the media before accepting her vocation and training as a teacher and psychodynamic counsellor. Having seen the array of dazzling facilities at QAS, we wonder whether she's actually a wannabe architect. 'No – but I am passionate about creating the right learning environment'. Clear that exam results are not enough to get girls where they want to be as adults: 'they need creativity and resilience too – and their inner compass needs to be set firmly'. Parents say she's absolutely 'pro empowering women'; she's a born marketeer (but don't let that put you off) and, with her game face on in full sales pitch, she'd get our vote if she went into politics. There's a psychologist fighting to get out too; conversation is littered with references to school's proprietary neuroscientific study with the University of Reading into how people learn – BrainCanDo. Says she's 'very aspirational for the girls', and for the school too, in our opinion, and clear that she 'recognises the importance of self-esteem'. Charismatic, energetic and extremely likeable – parents say she 'really listens'. So, some years into the job, what's next on her undoubtedly forward-looking wish list? Making the most of school's geographical location by building strong links with local tech giants, and a multi-use sports pitch. We have no doubt that with Mrs H and her 'can do' approach at the helm these won't remain on the list for long.

Academic matters: Solid results, especially given mixed ability intake. In 2018, 69 per cent A*-A/9-7 at GCSE with excellent outcomes in sciences, languages and the humanities. At A level, a respectable 40 per cent A*/A and 70 per cent A*-B. Biology, maths, chemistry, psychology and economics most popular choices in recent years; just tiny numbers choosing languages. Strong added value, with pupils adding between one and three grades to results. Smallish take-up of EPQ with around 18 per cent completion in 2018.

Head says academics are 'critically important, but we'll make sure we get there holistically'. On the subject of exam results, what's her take on the mixed bag of academic ability amongst the pupil cohort? 'We've got the medics and the lawyers and vets and the straight stars,' she says – 'but that's not for everyone'. In truth, those 'straight stars' are in the minority. But the beauty of QAS is that it takes girls of all academic abilities and works hard to get the best out of them and, head says, is 'quietly measuring and assessing all the time'. School has been working for some years alongside Reading and Goldsmiths Universities to develop research into what makes the brain tick with its BrainCanDo project to enable staff and girls to understand the science of learning. Such initiatives notwithstanding, the teaching we observed was basically what we see in good schools everywhere: small classes, engaged pupils and plenty of audience participation. Crucially, 'girls are able to access real learning strategies', according to head. Students say their teachers are 'passionate' and parents, with only a few exceptions, agree. The A level economics class we sat in on was buzzy and interactive with state of the art classroom technology being used to full effect.

Girls set for core subjects in year 7 and progress is 'carefully tracked from the moment they arrive', says head. E-learning is a major focus, sending message to students that 'tech is cool'. Collaborative working facilitated with access to OneNote and areas of the school (notably the 'study pods' in the sixth form centre) have their own mini Wifi zones to enable students to share ideas and projects. Touch typing taught as 'a tool for life'. We approve. Visits from eg leading artificial intelligence companies and programming masterclasses reinforce the message and participation in fun Bebras computational thinking competitions ensures that technology 'is not seen as too geeky'.

SEND support provided in class wherever possible with individual sessions (additional charge) available if required taking place during the (extra long) lunch break to avoid 'counter-productive' withdrawal from classes. Around 15 per cent of cohort on SEND register, with about nine per cent receiving support at any one time. Subject clinics praised by students. School has experience working with mild dyslexia, dyspraxia, ADD and hearing impairments. Much of site, especially the newer parts, wheelchair accessible. 'There's absolutely no stigma to SEN', school assured us, 'but girls have to be able to pass the entrance exam'. EAL taught in place of MFL or Latin.

Games, options, the arts: And so to where the school truly shines – and where to begin? Super sports facilities, including 25m pool, fitness suite, sprung floor dance studio, climbing wall, squash courts plus loads of tennis and netball courts means there's something for everyone. Even girls who hated sport before they arrived at QAS 'love it here' and there's a 'culture of being active', says school, whether it's a sponsored charity walk to Botswana (the distance, not the actual route), yoga, meditation and pilates or fiercely competitive games. Known for outstanding lacrosse (despite the sloping pitch – soon to be levelled, much to the delight of all – school has five girls who play for England and ranks in national top eight), and netball also strong. Fixtures for everyone in years 7 and 8 with A-E teams and from year 9 there are still C team matches most weeks, with 'incredible' sideline support from the parent body, and girls giving the thumbs up for fair team selection.

Dance is 'huge', with three-quarters of students taking dance classes and in 2018 150 ISTD dance exams taking place in school. Stunning annual dance show (we were blown away by video clips pinged to us by glowing parents) to an almost professional standard, often fully choreographed by the girls themselves. Rowing ('very strong') is coached by a former Olympian. Plenty of fun as well as serious sport – sports day is 'for everyone', with highlights including a flag relay race (flags designed by pupils) and a capture the flag competition organised by sixth form. Ballroom dancing lessons for sixth formers with boys from The Oratory – with whom they also play mixed tennis and go on a ski trip – culminates in a summer ball, eagerly attended by almost everyone ('it's a rite of passage', says school).

Clubs galore at lunch times and after school, and double period lunch break enables girls to take part in activities as well as eat. Fabulous art department – 'creativity happens here' announces a trompe d'oeil splashed across floor and entrance. One of the most imaginative arrays of A level art we've seen, from intricate hanging installations to the imaginary office of Kim Jong Un's head of propaganda. DT absorbed into art ('we don't do technology, but we have technology,'), with super equipment including 3D printers and a laser cutter enabling the focus to be 'career focused, not airy fairy' according to staff. Ceramics teacher recently appointed. With such riches in terms of facilities and an inspirational departmental head, no wonder so many girls choose art as GCSE and A level options (25 at A level in 2018) and many head off to study product design or architecture at university.

Drama, too is 'a big subject' according to school. How do they choose what productions to stage? 'We look at what the girls will be good at'. So sometimes it's Shakespeare, sometimes a musical. Music taught in the gleaming new music centre (2018) which, from a grand piano to a fleet of state of the art iMacs, has whistles and bells and then some. On curriculum from year 7, pupils work on projects such as writing advertising jingles to creating soundtracks to short movies. Beats scales and arpeggios any day of the week. Over 300 peripatetic lessons take place each week and year 7s all sing 'whether they like it or not', although with whole choir trips to destinations including Washington, New York or Rome, we suspect that 'like it' they mainly do. Chamber choir is unauditioned (there is a consort choir for elite songstresses) and with bands aplenty from jazzabelles to saxaholics there are informal performances every week.

Boarding: If it's possible in the boarding world to be all things to all girls, QAS has it sewn up. Day girls, full boarders and everything in between all rub along easily together. Flexi is just that. One night a week? No problem. Full boarders are treated to a range of weekend activities and if the plan sounds like fun, day girls are welcome too. Four smart boarding houses are mainly purpose built, well kitted out and beautifully decorated with squidgy sofas and stylish fabrics in communal areas. No poky kitchenettes – the hubs of the houses are spacious home-style kitchens, complete with farmhouse table and chairs as centrepiece for girls to gather round in the evenings. The houseparents we met were just the ticket – friendly and approachable but no nonsense – and many houses have a four-legged resident. Upper sixth girls are based in Michell, slightly separate from the main cluster of buildings to give them peace and a degree of independence. Day girls have (slightly scruffy, very untidy) rooms with desks and lockers.

Background and atmosphere: Set amongst 34 acres of prime Caversham real estate. The handsome ivy-clad Victorian brick pile belies what lies beyond: not the usual melange of low rise horrors from the decades that architecture forgot, but an aesthete's dream collection of facilities (fit for a capital F if only our editors would allow it) to rival any we've seen. The Space, home of the brand new sixth form centre plus dining hall, is a triumph of glass and stainless steel, complete with Café 6, the bright, stylish in-house eatery serving hot snacks and proper coffee to sixth formers, who relax in leather upholstered booths or outside in their own charming courtyard area. Atop this are flexible classroom spaces (we loved the writable-on walls) and themed breakout rooms decorated in the style of eg Central Park (Astroturf carpet, skyscraper mural and park benches), Big Ben or theatre. The female chaplain performs services in the galleried chapel for lower and upper school several times each week. Food gets the thumbs up; breakfasts are 'amazing' and good old fish and chips on Friday is top lunch. Queen Anne's is part of the Westminster Greycoat Foundation and was established on its current site in 1894. Historic links with Westminster and the Abbey remain. Between head and her marketing department there's plenty of buzz around school with initiatives (mostly linked to BrainCanDo) such as the recent week-long experiment allowing sixth formers to sleep until 10am before starting their school day. We wonder whether parents buy into such non-curriculum focused initiatives. The jury's out amongst those we spoke to, but our advice is not to not get distracted by all the spin and fluff – everything you expect to get from a school with boarding fees well north of 10 grand a term is here, and more besides.

Pastoral care, well-being and discipline: Long days (8.00am to 6.15pm) but prep is completed under supervision at school and tea is provided, so quality time at home is, in theory, just that. School transport includes coaches with flexible routes, taxis and minibuses to ship girls from up to an hour away to school each day. Pastoral care praised from the rooftops by parents and pupils and there are not many schools we have visited that have such a relaxed atmosphere and 'hardly any peer pressure,' according to pupils. Problems can be taken to housemistresses ('really approachable', say girls), tutors, independent listeners or fellow pupils from year 10 upwards, trained as part of the peer mentor team. 'Families' are akin to vertical tutor groups; newbies are given a 'sister' in the year above when they join, and girls clearly appreciate the strong inter-year group relations.

Uniform rules 'have got really strict recently', say girls (shorter skirts and more more earrings high on their wish lists). Sixth formers allowed the dreaded 'smart business' mufti (it didn't look all that smart to us, but to be fair it was exam season). The distinctive red hooded cloaks are no longer compulsory uniform but are still worn at formal events, eg carol services and the biennial service of thanksgiving at Westminster Abbey. Not an obviously diverse community but school does run an annual LGBT week with special assemblies and talks and there's a diversity noticeboard highlighting different sexualities. Misuse of social media results in immediate suspension (enforced a few times in recent years), but the usual drinking, drugs and smoking transgressions are few and far between. Low incidence of serious mental health problems rife in some girls' schools – 'we're very hot on intervention', says head, and houseparents eat all meals with girls to keep an eye on healthy dietary habits. Well-being programme has replaced PSHCE recently and is now delivered by a dedicated team to tutor groups in years 7-10, covering issues such as relationships, friendship and social media. Pupil well-being ambassadors 'make such a difference,' says school.

Pupils and parents: Girls we met were down to earth, articulate and chatty. Majority are reasonably local, with boarders and day girls living up to an hour away. Sixteen per cent overseas (including students from over 15 countries, Forces and expats) with the remainder mainly a mix of entrepreneurs and City workers. Increasing numbers from London who see it as an alternative to the ferocious London school scene and, after all, Paddington is only a 25 minute train ride away.

Entrance: Girls join at 11 from a large number of prep schools and state primaries. Tests in maths, English, verbal and non-verbal reasoning and a group interview. Recommendations of help required for girls with SEND made in offer letter. For entry into year 12, there's an entrance exam and requirement of minimum six GCSEs at grade 4 or above (including English and maths and 6 in subjects to be studied at A level.

Exit: Around a fifth head off after GCSEs in search of co-ed sixth forms or to local colleges. Those who stay move on to a range of universities: Bristol, Cardiff, Edinburgh, Leeds and Newcastle all popular destinations in recent years, as well as a number of new universities and in ones and twos to degree apprenticeships. Degree choices range from the traditional academic to fashion marketing or mechatronic robotics. One or two to Oxbridge most years (one in 2018).

Money matters: Boarding fees as expected and in line with local competitors. Day fees not too painful considering extended school day and access to boarding perks. Scholarships for art, music, drama, sports and all-rounder at 11+ and 13+. Foundation generous in the case of hardship or support needed by less wealthy families.

Remarks: Cut through the marketing blurb and you'll find a school where you can be a star without being an academic whizz. 'There's something magical about the place', said one parent; 'it's as much about life preparation as academics'. And with such an array of first class facilities, tip top pastoral care, plus a culture of female empowerment, we think it's definitely one for the list of any parent for whom happiness and roundedness are top priorities.

Queenswood

214

Shepherd's Way, Brookman's Park, Hatfield, Hertfordshire AL9 6NS

Ages 11–18 **Pupils** 434 **Sixth form** 107 **Boarders** 119 full, 35 weekly, 75 flexi

Fees: Day £20,925 – £24,825; Boarding £21,525 – £33,750 pa

01707 602500
www.queenswood.org

Principal: Since 2016, Joanna Cameron BSc PGCE (40s). Educated at St Stephen's College, Broadstairs where she was a boarder from age 7 (pony in tow) followed by A levels at Moira House School, Eastbourne. Degree in environmental science from St Mary's College, University of Surrey, where she stayed to complete PGCE with specialism in biology. Considered a career in either the RAF or police force, but was 'inspired by my own love of school' to eschew a life in uniform and pursue the path of teaching, firm in the belief that 'every girl should have great opportunities'. First teaching post was at St Mary's, Wantage, where she became head of science, followed by a stint at St Gabriel's, Newbury, before becoming deputy head at Ipswich High School in 2013. Headship of an all girls' boarding school seemed a natural next step: 'I'm so at home in this environment'.

Was impressed by 'phenomenal' pastoral care and has now improved it further by cementing the structure rather than relying on individuals. Says school is 'passionate about every girl exceeding her expectations, not only celebrating success at the highest level' and keen to communicate that, despite continued uplift in registrations, Queenswood 'will never be an academic hothouse – we get results without tears'. Parents concur that their daughters are 'part of a community that's not just about exams' (perhaps that's why the jungle drums tell us that Q scoops up a fair number of refugees from nearby girls' schools that are found to be either too academically pushy or unfriendly). Exudes a sensible and purposeful aura; parents say she's 'full of determination' and has focused on 'evolution not revolution' since her arrival. All this, wrapped up in a friendly and down to earth demeanour. Says Q has 'such warmth' and seems to embody this herself.

Lives on site with husband, David, a software engineer, and two sons currently schooled at Lochinver House and St Columba's. Entire family visible around campus, often all going to school supper and performances together. 'I want to show our girls that women today really can have it all', she says. Keen sportswoman – runs, plays hockey and still competes with her horse.

Academic matters: Strong results, especially given broad intake. In 2018, 65 per cent of A level/Pre-U grades were A*-B, and 40 per cent A*/A. Although these don't place school at top of local league tables (the competition is, to be fair, on the stellar side), few can touch it when it comes to value added. Parents pleased to see the academic ante being upped – science and French reportedly showing marked improvement. Strong modern languages department, with French, Spanish, Italian and Japanese all available up to A level (Japanese increasingly popular partly thanks to a cultural visit to Japan) and Latin from year 7. Chinese GCSE and A level for native speakers if requested. Nine or 10 GCSEs taken by the majority, but the most able can take up to 12, plus the optional HPQ (Higher Project Qualification) which counts as a half. In 2018, 58 per cent of GCSEs were graded A*-A/9-7. Outstanding GCSE results in maths and science – maths also very popular and reports top results at A level. Psychology A level now available – a bid to stop girls looking elsewhere.

'Gentle setting' in year 7 for maths and English, then science from year 10. Teaching 'aims to be bespoke and individualised' says head, 'all teachers aim to inspire one or two girls every single day' – and with the luxury of a staff/student ratio of 5.5:1 and class sizes never higher than 24 (often smaller), the formula to achieve this is spot on. 'Our USP is that we have time for every girl,' says head. Relationships palpably strong between students and staff and an 'open door' culture pervades: 'my teachers work around me', one sixth former told us. Trad teaching, although technology well used – all girls have a laptop and google classroom is being 'gently' introduced.

Newly launched personalised learning hub (2018) has replaced the traditional SEN department and brings girls with IEP reports, academic scholars and Oxbridge candidates together under one roof 'to get rid of any stigma and ensure all needs are met', says head. 'It sits nicely with who we are'. Around 10 per cent of cohort are on learning support register at any given time – and are kept on it even after 'graduating' to ensure no slippage. School now aiming to avoid withdrawal altogether and keep support for those with mild to moderate SpLDs as much in the classroom as possible.

Games, options, the arts: 'Queenswood's good at everything,' one proud pupil told us. And who are we to disagree? Sport tops the list and it's a battle between hockey and tennis for starring role, parents marvelling at how decidedly unsporty prep schoolers have become passionate sportswomen during their time at Q; 'it's the give it a go attitude that we love,' said one. On the tennis front, school is national LTA clay court centre, hosts the annual national schools' championships, is recommended by the LTA as a destination for wannabe tennis pros and offers tennis-specific sports scholarships. It boasts no less than 25 courts – 12 clay and 13 all-weather. New sports hall has replaced antiquated indoor tennis centre. Hockey played competitively for two terms on the impressive Astroturf; tip-top coaching sees many girls reach county and some national level and trophies and cups abound. Students can also choose options including athletics, gymnastics, fencing, swimming in modern indoor pool, sailing, badminton and tag rugby. Football less popular but sometimes played if demand is there, school is a UK hub for girls' cricket – a recent masterclass with former England captain has left girls 'absolutely inspired,' say parents – and the recent introduction of a dance scholarship has put that firmly on the school map too.

Elite athletes across all disciplines are carefully mentored; fitness coaches devise bespoke programmes, advise on diet etc and school accommodates external training and fixtures for these high flyers (a GB skier, a GB sailor and a GB tumbler currently in their number). Parents of less elite players report delightedly on emphasis is on health, nutrition and fitness too. Tons of sports tours, recently tennis to Catalunya and Rome, years 7 to 9 hockey to Barcelona and biennial senior hockey to eg South Africa and Sri Lanka. Well-being introduced in year 11, with options including yoga, couch to 5K, boxercise, riding, golf and basketball. Up to six sporting activities on offer every lunch time: 'it's the rich non-academic life that makes all that maths and physics worthwhile', quipped one parent.

'Amazing' music department, according to girls, more than half of whom learn at least one instrument, some more. Inspirational departmental head says, 'if they have a talent, I'll try to find it', and 'anything goes in terms of style – as long as it's good'. Q songwriters are frequently highly ranked in the Amnesty International Protest Song competition – with one recent overall winner. Bands, orchestras and ensembles for every instrument and genre, from percussion band to flute choir. The school CD with performances recorded at Angel Studios we were given to take home made the journey fly by. Plenty of opportunities for international showcasing here too – orchestra and choir tours to destinations including Venice and Florence allow students to perform in world class settings – next up is Hong Kong in 2020. Drama equally strong, making excellent use of super facilities that include a studio theatre with a full time dedicated two-man stage crew. Lower and upper school plays are open to all, with girls forming strong friendship bonds across year groups. Recent hits have been Les Mis and A Christmas Carol Gone Wrong (the latter a comedy penned by school staff). Large LAMDA take-up with excellent results.

Buzzy art department with artist in residence on hand. We loved the way that art scholars of all ages are brought together to create paintings and installations for display around the school – when we visited they were working on a collection for the new library. Decent take up of art A level, with a few girls each year heading off to art school. Super textiles too, starting simple with jazzy pencil cases for younger pupils, building up to wedding and evening dresses by senior girls. Leiths cookery course run in preference to food tech (sounds like a good trade to us), taught as a timetabled lesson to years 7 and 8 and as a club thereafter. An abundance of clubs at lunch times and after school – girls encouraged to do at least three per week – and even sixth formers pack their schedules with pursuits including Model United Nations and debating on top of their academic and sporting commitments.

Boarding: At its very core a boarding school, although day pupils well integrated ('they are good at discouraging a boarder/day girl split', one parent assured us) and all manner of flexible options, from one to four nights, now in place as well as full boarding (mainly international students, who account for about a quarter of the school population) and occasional boarding too. Majority of accommodation over two floors in main school building. More functional than inviting with very little personal decoration in place and no sign of a tidy dorm policy – perhaps Queenswood girls are so busy they don't have time to hang around and enjoy their dorms, although when we popped in at break time, rooms were awash with girls hungrily getting their morning social media fix. Decorative improvements are afoot, however, so watch this space. Sixth form accommodation is better, with bright and cosy common rooms, views across the rolling hills and playing fields and a full kitchen for students preferring to prepare their own meals. Two staff members live in each house. Very small boarding numbers in years 7, although recent dramatic reduction in boarding fees for these years (now cheaper to weekly board than travel on some bus routes) hopes to see this change. Almost half board in some capacity in year 8. Lively programme of activities for full boarders, with cooking, crafts and trips – often making the most of proximity to London – and sixth formers are allowed into London in pairs, although older girls in particular appreciate 'lots of free time'. Day girls can stay for any meal with no charge.

Background and atmosphere: Founded in Clapham Park in 1894 before moving to current location – a purpose built neo-Tudor building, set amongst 120 acres of sports fields, woodland and immaculately clipped gardens – in 1925. Rarefied in the extreme. Just two miles from the M25 but still somehow in the middle of nowhere. Passing through the monogrammed, wrought iron gates the real world is left behind and immersion into a pristine, wholesome universe feels absolute. Rolling programme of improvements keeps things fresh – there's no particular jewel in the Queenswood crown but perhaps more a tiara of equally shining attributes. Sixth formers now have their own centre with smart studies shared between three or four students, social area and well stocked kitchens. Super theatre with all mod cons and stunning new library – an airy, vaulted art deco affair housed in the Old Pool Hall.

Girls, smart in grey and purple, are friendly and down to earth. There's an air of innocence about them – not a spiky edge in sight. All appreciate the 'immense trust' that pervades school: 'we can leave our stuff around and know that it will be safe,' one told us.

Pastoral care, well-being and discipline: Pastoral care uniformly 'phenomenal', according to parents. In a competitive landscape of academic hothouses and sharp elbows, Queenswood seems elevated to a higher stratosphere permeated by kindness and support. Sure, there are 'friendship issues' like everywhere else, but students told us that anything over and above day to day spats 'gets shut down really quickly'. Head describes communication between staff as 'phenomenal' and mental health issues amongst the students such as anxiety or eating disorders are 'few and far between'. Parents rave about 'proactive approach to teenage mental health'. 'We have so many pairs of eyes on them,' says head, 'and the staff operate as one large team.' Girls say they 'go above and beyond' to help one another – demonstrated by excellent mentoring programme with A level students supporting GCSE strugglers where needed. Sixth form students are able to choose their personal tutor and meet with them weekly to discuss progress or concerns.

Almost every dietary requirement imaginable catered for by an outstanding canteen staff, delivering top notch cuisine morning, noon and night. Although a reasonably conservative environment, head says 'we don't shy away' from issues with eg sexuality: 'differences are totally accepted and the vast majority are really accepting of one another'. But is all this kindness and such a heavily rarefied environment really preparing students for the big bad world out there? Head believes so: 'we actively encourage risk taking and failure, to develop resilience,' she says. Transgressions? 'Very few. I'm lucky', says head. No drugs enforcements on recent record and just one alcohol related misdemeanour, resulting in exclusion. Mixed views on socials with boys' schools. Some girls we spoke to wanted more, some none at all. Lochinver's on the dance card for the younger girls, with Bedford and Radley for the older ones. Thankfully, some bright spark did away with the year 7 disco recently and replaced it with a mini Olympics style team building event: 'much more fun,' said one attendee.

Pupils and parents: Around half of all pupils board, with a quarter of these from overseas, largely Hong Kong and mainland China, and all continents represented. Increasing numbers of first time buyers plus north London families looking to escape the hothouses by taking advantage of Q's bespoke transport service. Active parents' association organises plenty of social activities throughout the year and helps with fundraising efforts. All sixth formers awarded a silver Q brooch – presumably to help them identify one another in the 'real' world. The Old Queenswoodians' Association is some 4,000 members strong and branches across the globe in readiness to support and advance its members whatever their location or chosen field. Speech days are attended not just by current pupils and their families, but also a handful of old girls – some in their 80s – who come to socialise and share in the successes of current pupils. Carol Thatcher's an old girl, as are tennis ace Naomi Cavaday, actress Helen McCrory and TV presenter Lady Georgie Ainslie.

Entrance: Increasing competition for between 50 and 60 places at 11+. Candidates take school's own exam; all applicants are interviewed and seen by head. 'References and spark as important – if not more so – as academics,' we are assured, although school expects successful applicants to be 'at least average or above'. Top feeders are Stormont, Duncombe, Devonshire House, Edge Grove, Heathmount and Manor Lodge. Strong sixth form intake. Candidates must have six GCSEs at 6 or above and 7s in their chosen A level subjects.

Exit: Up to a quarter leave after GCSEs, mainly lured by co-ed or to experience life outside of the ivory tower. 'Retention into sixth form is tough,' admits head who is upping the ante to try to hang on to older students – not just with the new sixth form centre on the edge of the site to give it a slightly separate feel, but also with focused events such as talks from eg Tom Kerridge and Clare Balding. Careers department, however, thought to be 'really good' and mirrors school's open door policy for meetings or CV checking as well as organising careers and networking evenings with OQs and current parents. Majority at 18 to wide range of solid universities – over a quarter to London colleges, a couple each year to American universities (often with sports scholarships in hand). Pleasingly broad range of subject choices – no trends. One to Oxbridge in 2018.

Money matters: Day fees on the high side compared to local competition – and that's without the pricey, albeit bespoke, door to door transport service. Occasional means-tested bursaries and discount for Forces families. Majority of scholarships are honorary, offering additional support or training rather than monetary value.

Remarks: Pushy parents move along – this is not the place for you. But if you want your daughter to experience all the sport, arts and extracurricular that Queenswood has to offer, whilst securing some pretty decent grades (and staying sane in the process), we strongly advise a visit.

Radley College

Radley, Abingdon, Oxfordshire OX14 2HR

Ages 13–18 **Pupils** 696 **Sixth form** 282 **Boarders** 696 full **C of E**

Fees: £38,325 pa

01235 543000
www.radley.org.uk

Warden: Since 2014, John Moule MA (40s), previously head of Bedford School. Educated at a Telford comprehensive and sixth form college, he won a history scholarship to Lady Margaret Hall, Oxford and left with a first. Refreshingly atypical background for a post like this. Taught history and politics at Dean Close, Cheltenham, moved to Stowe as head of history and became housemaster, then senior housemaster. Perhaps it's Radley's proximity to Oxford but we thought Mr Moule had a little of Laurence Fox's (aka Sgt Hathaway in Lewis) lean, pale intensity. This impression only somewhat dampened when we learnt that pallor was a result of his 'feeling under the weather'.

He seems to have made a very favourable impression and was described to us as a 'brilliant' speaker, able to hold an audience of parents and boys simultaneously. 'He's very visible and really involved' one mother told us, 'He drops into Socials (Radley-speak for boarding house) and plays chess with the boys.'

Married with three children, his eldest daughter is a veterinary student, his son is finishing A levels at Bedford School and the youngest is at a girls' day school nearby. Having worked in medical research his wife completed a second degree in maths and now divides her time between the many and varied duties of a head's spouse and teaching at a school in Oxford.

Like so many heads Mr Moule claims to have 'fallen' into teaching. (Watch out, there must be a huge and cunningly disguised hole somewhere designed for just this purpose.) It goes like this. He was all set to study for a PhD in 16th century English theological history but the grant-awarding bodies had other plans and chose this moment to withdraw the financial support that had hitherto been awarded to arts students with first class degrees, 'You could say that I was saved by lack of funds'. At a loose end in Oxford, someone inevitably suggested he try teaching. 'I'd never set foot in an independent school but after two weeks I knew it was right.'

Of course Mr Moule is convinced of the benefits of a full boarding school. 'It fosters strength of character and independence'. He goes on, 'The 24 hour culture is hugely creative, it allows teachers to develop boys' genuine interests beyond the classroom.' He describes the 'powerful' triangle formed by the school, the parents and the boy, 'all have to buy into it', he says. For fee paying parents that is both metaphorically and literally the case.

Since becoming warden Mr Moule has done a great deal of observing. Not only has he dropped unannounced into lessons and watched every don (Radley-speak) teach, he also shadowed pupils throughout their day (including late afternoon and evening) to learn more about their experience as well as the school's 'flow'. And what were his conclusions? He was seriously impressed by the variety he found but felt some lessons were rather too teacher led. We imagine it can be hard to avoid in a school full of bright boys who for the most part will arrive having had eight or more years' listening and learning in prep school. We saw some young hopefuls during our visit, serious little chaps wearing polished brogues and tweed jackets – just like the fathers accompanying them.

He wants to do more to raise boys' awareness of the world beyond Radley's 800 prime Oxfordshire acres and has also told parents, and boys, that he intends to 'wage war on teenage apathy'. While acknowledging that every day should still contain a little time for creative boredom, he says boys have a tendency to do 'just enough' and feels this should be challenged. When he's sorted that one out perhaps he could let us know.

His plans for the school itself are well underway. The website has already been improved beyond recognition – it's now (fanfare) welcoming and informative – and the college's famously esoteric ('mystical' was how the warden described it) entry procedure has been revised. It used to be the case that if you had to ask Radley how to apply then you were probably too late. The process is now more open, in line with other, similar schools, though the 'List' remains and is an advantage for those who want to sign up early. Increased bursarial support is another target, as is 'careful' recruitment of applicants from beyond (even far beyond) the home counties.

Mr Moule's strong Christian faith means Radley's timeless tradition of whole school chapel four times a week is in safe hands. Boys 'love' chapel he told us, 'especially as they get older', and indeed this was borne out by those we spoke to. Of course it's important to the 'sincerely spiritual' but it's also valued by chaps who just want a bit of peace and quiet, or 'separated space' as the warden puts it. It may not be as fashionable, but perhaps this is mindfulness, Radley style.

When not wardening Mr Moule says he is an 'avid' armchair sportsman and enjoys a spot of golf or real tennis. Reading is, naturally, another recreation and favourite books include Wilkie Collins' The Woman in White and P G Wodehouse's classic, The Mating Season. Box sets are also high up on this warden's list, especially The West Wing and the US version of The Office. And if he hadn't so carelessly 'fallen' into teaching? Journalism, the law and the church are all the poorer for his stumble.

Academic matters: Even with the recent changes to its entrance procedure Radley is not a school that selects solely on academic ability; excellent GCSE and A level results stem from fine teaching and staff who don't think their job is done when the lesson finishes. Recent reintroduction of the linear, two year A level has proved that Radley wasn't so maverick after all when it held out against AS levels being taken at the end of the first year sixth. We did detect a certain quiet satisfaction that the rest of the country has finally come into line. Sixth formers sit three or four A levels, a fourth subject is generally one that contrasts with the other three. All will also do an extended project.

R

In 2018, 78 per cent A*-A/9-7 at IGCSE/GCSE; particularly strong results in, well everything, but also some C-D/5-3s, even an E. At A level 65 per cent A*/A, most popular subjects history, maths and English literature followed by sciences. Notable proportion of A* in art and English lit. Nice to see decent numbers taking classics, languages and geology too. While maths and further maths are very popular, Radley has always stood apart from the overwhelming science/maths dominance so commonly found in boys' schools and we're glad to see this remains the case.

Teaching in the lessons we observed was of the tried and tested sort – a fast pace and lots of quick fire questions kept everyone on their toes. Very clearly exam focused. However, despite adding a distinctly scholarly air, gowns didn't seem to make Radleians any more elevated or less prone to muttering at the back than their non-gowned counterparts at other schools.

Latest ISI report called learning support 'exceptional' and parents are in agreement. All boys have to meet the entrance criteria to get into the school but once there SEN support is extensive and lacks stigma. Individual and small group sessions are arranged according to need. Some take place during what is known as 'central hour' (1.30-2.30 daily), time set aside for relaxing, working, music lessons, extracurricular activities etc.

We met some really amusing and inspiring dons who just seemed to love their jobs (less jobs, more way of life, we thought) and the very stones of the place. Good mix of ages and lots of women among teaching staff. Dogs seemed to be part of the package too – that explained the water bowls we'd wondered about in some of the classrooms. All dons and their families live on site.

Much talk of efforts to 'learn from other schools and widen diversity'. Strong links with local primaries and a Maidenhead secondary school; some exchange of teaching staff but latter a little too far away for frequent activities. Closer to home the warden hopes to further develop joint academic extension activities for A level subjects such as music, English and geography with Headington School. There are links for the scholars with St Helen and St Katharine's and plans for 'ambitious extension days' with Oxford High School. Lest we get too carried away by all this talk of diversity, at Radley take your dog to work day is unlikely to be joined by enrol your daughter day any time soon.

Games, options, the arts: All rather civilised. Manages to maintain a creditable sporting reputation without the ruthlessly competitive atmosphere than can prevail at boys' schools. We got the impression that the disinclined to run are not regarded as also rans. Rugby is main game of Michaelmas term – around 20 separate teams do battle every Saturday.

When it warms up the 'wet bobs' row; 'dry bobs' play hockey, fives, cricket or tennis in the summer term. Boat house on the Thames is 10 minutes away and those wet bobs are usually up there with near neighbours Abingdon and rivals Eton and St Edward's during the Henley Regatta and head of the river competitions.

Twice weekly so-called 'minor sports' include swimming, golf (there's a course on site), fives, squash, real tennis, cross-country, rackets, tennis, badminton. Those who wish to can do a spot of beagling. Alternative sports programme (ASP), is a circus of different sports for boys (remove upwards) who don't take to rugby. Sixth formers can choose which sport they want to play.

Art school, complete with rather cool gallery space, is in Clocktower Court. Pupils' work, paintings, ceramics and photography, not confined to here, it's all over the school – eerily lifelike papier mâché boys peer down from beams in the library. Ambitious projects undertaken in DT include surfboards and a rather spectacular trebuchet. Once again, facilities lack for nothing and are open late into the evening and at weekends. Nine or 10 boys take art or DT at A2 with creditable results.

Large chapel choir with trebles from local primary schools and preps sings at services and evensong in chapel and elsewhere, including Oxford colleges. Weekly concerts in the school coffee shop, house and college concerts give boys as many solo and ensemble performing opportunities as possible. The music school is open until 10.15pm and boys are expected to organise their own practice although a member of staff is on hand to help. Just one or two doing music at A level despite high profile of music in the school – theatre studies more popular option.

Inter-house competitions and endowed prizes are great motivators and boys take to the stage for such keenly fought contests as the part song competition, debating, declaiming, battle of the bands, piano and percussion trophies. The legendary Piano Extravaganza featured, most recently, 91 players from age 6 upwards (under 13s are dons' children) playing on eight pianos. The Silk Hall is school's premier music venue and next door is the theatre where college and year group plays are performed as well as A2 drama devised pieces. Parents rave about the drama at Radley; even shy boys take to the stage. No reluctance from boys to take on female roles but every so often school puts a 'Girls wanted' advert in the local paper if the production requires the genuine article. Warden told us he directed several plays at his former school and might be tempted again.

CCF compulsory for removes, fifth form do community service and sixth formers can choose enrichment activities such as opera, film or cooking. Couple of parents thought a few more 'life skills' wouldn't go amiss at this stage. Seriously impressive calendar of visiting speakers including WW2 RAF hero, Auschwitz survivor, scientists, authors, journalists, MPs and members of the clergy. Vast array of trips – theatre in London, art in Florence and music tours (singers and instrumentalists) to America. Energetic fundraising for variety of good causes including partner school in Tanzania and Christian Aid.

Boarding: Boarding houses at Radley are known as 'Socials' and Socials are distinguished by letters of the alphabet (A Social, B Social and so on). First years ('shell') have curtained 'cubs' or cubicles with a sink and cabin bed. Apparently Radley was the instigator of this arrangement that affords pupils some degree of privacy within a dormitory. It caught on and can still be seen in many prep and senior boarding schools. From removes (second year) on it's single study bedrooms. In typical boarding boy fashion these were all rather tidy, noticeboards generally unadorned by photos, posters and the like. Our guides told us they liked the busy, structured days at school and appreciated the relative freedom of home life all the more for it. 'We probably take Radley for granted,' one added.

Boys may buy uniform, stationery, tuck etc in school's shop (known, wait for it, as 'Shop'). Card system for purchases in Shop or coffee shop; 'jam account' (upper limit of £60 per term) for tuck. One parent thought it was a shame there was no opportunity to buy secondhand uniform, sports kit etc.

'Oxford leave' allows boys (mostly sixth formers) to travel into Oxford (by bus or taxi). Upper sixth chaps may spend Saturday evenings there as long as they're back in Social by 10.30pm. Quite a restricted regime for boys of this age, although exeats and privis allow a few slightly longer Saturday nights out elsewhere.

Background and atmosphere: In the quartet of boys' full boarding schools (first violin Eton, second violin Winchester, cello Harrow), Radley would be the viola – less frequently played ('mystical' entrance requirements), smallish solo repertoire (690 boys), confident, necessary, but unflashy (low profile) and so on. It's also the newcomer, having been founded by Oxford movement devotees, The Revs Sewell and Singleton, in 1847 to 'provide a public school education on the principles of the Church of England.'

The founding Revs organised their school along the lines of colleges at the University of Oxford, hence some of the nomenclature: warden, dons etc. Indeed, Radley still has that slightly separate feel of an Oxford college, enhanced by the sight of boys rushing to and fro, gowns billowing behind. Last vote saw proposal to do away with gowns defeated by 95 per cent. Daily choral services were, and remain, a key aspect of the school.

It was believed boys' minds and souls would be improved by learning in a beautiful rural setting and well-designed environment. Shades of William Morris perhaps. School motto is the succinct, Sicut Serpentes, Sicut Columbae ('Be ye wise as serpents, and harmless as doves'), and these creatures appear on the coat of arms – with the cross keys of St Peter, to whom the college is dedicated, safely between them.

Radley College is neither overwhelmingly grand nor intimidating. Reception is small and unpretentious, seating would indicate that they do not expect more than three people to arrive at any one time. Reception staff friendly, but appeared to be fighting a losing battle to stop the office becoming overwhelmed by online delivery packages. 'Radley boys keep Amazon in business,' said a long-suffering voice from behind a pile of boxes.

School originally occupied the Mansion, an 18th century house that belonged to the Stonehouse, then Bowyer families. This rather elegant building with grand panelled reception rooms is now home to admin and the warden's offices. Other parts are usual mix of charming and slightly less charming additions. Wide vistas, generous lawns and paths are another great advantage of a large, rural site. The grounds were by laid out by Capability Brown and some features of his design remain visible. Many trees, looking especially lovely on the golden autumn day of our visit. Immaculate pitches (delightful cricket pavilion) stretch into the distance.

Queen's Court (aka the Doughnut), opened by Her Majesty in 1997, may dominate aerial views of the college but we were rather taken with the inside, which seems to have stood the test of time. It's home to maths, economics, biology, geography and geology and the communal space outside the classrooms is full of fascinating natural history specimens and large tanks containing turtles, scorpions and cockroaches. Members of the animal society come here to get up close with reptiles and snakes, if not doves.

Pastoral care, well-being and discipline: The tutor (housemaster) is the key figure in a boy's life at Radley. He oversees the boys in his Social along with sub-tutors and pastoral housemistresses (PHMs) – the latter come in for particular praise from mothers of younger boys. Form masters monitor academic progress. Boys in the first two years also have a lower sixth mentor. Cocoa at 9pm every night is a chance for all the boys in a Social to meet up and chat about the day; this and other activities help blur year group hierarchies. Boys are expected to help with the running of their Social: shell do chores such as collecting post; sixth form house prefects supervise prep and bedtimes. Parents all praise dedication of Social staff and say that any enquiries are dealt with 'by return', they also like the regular progress reports.

Two exeat weekends per term and boys earn 'privis' or privilege weekends for good behaviour, work etc. On 'Sunday outs' boys can go out with parents or a friend after chapel for the day. One mother lamented, 'My son doesn't take his privis, there's too much going on at school to miss.' Rather sweet little handbook sent to boys before they join includes useful advice such as, 'Bring more tuck. Most don't bring enough,' and, 'If you are lost, confused or unhappy don't be afraid to ask for help.' Information about who to ask (both in and outside college) and how to do this is also included.

School places great emphasis on tolerance, kindness and manners. Biggest crime, according to new boys' handbook is, 'to be rude to a cleaner, a member of catering staff, the ladies who help you in Shop or any other member of the College staff.' This is not intended in a de haut en bas way – as the Warden says, 'we discourage any sense of entitlement or arrogance.'

School is keen to enhance the quality of social activities with girls' schools. Shell still get the chance to disco with the likes of Wycombe Abbey, but older boys now join girls from St Mary's Calne, Tudor Hall, Headington and St Helen and Katharine for dinner and discussion or joint theatre trips.

Pupils and parents: The warden describes a Radleian as 'civilised, friendly and engaging, in short, good company' and all the boys we met lived up to his definition. He also debunks a commonly held myth (that may stem from former entrance procedure) that most boys are sons of former pupils. 'It's 15 per cent', he told us. Seems that the lower sixth drama group we had spoken to where all but a couple were second or third generation Radleians was just a blip. 'Most people find out about us through word of mouth,' continued the warden. 'They've met and liked a Radleian at work or university and think of us as a possible school for their own son.'

Even so the hour has arrived to tweak what school describes carefully as its 'cultural variety'. Don't expect a revolution, or a rainbow nation – it'll be a while before the grain of truth packs its bags and departs from school's nickname, 'Ra Ra' Radley. Change will happen, carefully, in Radley's own time, and it will most certainly be for the (even) better.

Former pupils (ORs) include Andrew Motion, poet; Sir Clive Stafford Smith, human rights lawyer; Lord Wilson of Dinton, former cabinet secretary; Peter Cook, comedian; Sandy Nairne, former director of the National Portrait Gallery; Christopher Hibbert, Historian; Ted Dexter, Andrew Strauss and Jamie Dalrymple, England cricketers; Sir Charlie Mayfield, chairman of John Lewis; Lord Wolfson, CEO of Next. And many other actors, writers, lawyers, engineers, sportsmen, clergymen and public servants of all kinds.

Entrance: Still the forward planner's choice. Radley remains loyal to those who register early and 'conditional' offers are made three years in advance to boys on 'Provisional' and waiting lists. Subject to interview and ISEB common pre-test results, they will get firm offers on 1 March of year 6. No open days, individually arranged visits all through the year. Friendly and approachable admissions staff will explain system.

Admissions procedure is changing but up until 2018 boys not already registered may apply for one of around 40 'Warden's List' places. Radley puts 'much emphasis' on candidate's performance at interview and head's report when assessing applicants for these. From 2019 onwards, after offers are made to boys on the 'Provisional' list, there is an open entry system whereby all interested candidates are first asked to sit the ISEB common pre-test in year 6 and send a school report; interviews will be offered to shortlisted candidates and offers made in June of year 6.

Few (around eight) places at 16 + but on the whole this is a settled community and there's not much movement.

Exit: Bristol, Durham, Edinburgh, Exeter, Leeds, Manchester, Newcastle and UCL hoover up most of Radley's leavers. Regular 15–20 boys to Oxbridge every year – mock interview exchange scheme with nearby Abingdon School seems to benefit both sides. School's university entrance team recently expanded to integrate expertise in applying to universities in North America, Europe and beyond.

Money matters: Cheapest of the quartet (no viola jokes please) but there's barely a gnat's crotchet between them. Uniform requirements less painful on the purse – parents told us that suits, shirts etc can be bought from high street. Gowns aren't expensive and, look on the bright side, might save on jacket dry cleaning bills (and they cover books if it's raining, boys told us). Sports kit will cost you, but then it does everywhere. Lack of coffee shops (or indeed any shops) in immediate vicinity looks promising but remember the Amazon overwhelmed reception desk ...

Scholarships of up to 10 per cent off fees awarded annually at 13+ and can be topped up to 100 per cent with means-tested bursaries. Foundation awards enable boys from state system to attend a prep school for two years before admission. Armed Forces Fund provides assistance to boys from Forces families. All very clearly explained on school website.

Remarks: In our last review we said that Radley was the connoisseurs' choice; this remains the case. Yes, it's traditional, but it's utterly unstuffy. Like the serpent and the dove in the coat of arms, respect for tradition lives harmoniously with tolerance, intellectual curiosity, humour and humanity. Radley provides boys with an immersive education of the highest quality and a strong moral and spiritual core.

R

Reading Blue Coat School

Holme Park, Sonning Lane, Reading, Berkshire RG4 6SU

Ages 11–18 **Pupils** 761 **Sixth form** 253 (88 girls) **C of E**

Fees: £16,695 pa

01189 441005
www.rbcs.org.uk

Headmaster: Since 2016, Jesse Elzinga, previously director of studies at Harrow. BA in comparative religion from Harvard and MSt (as a Rotary Ambassadorial Scholar) from Oxford. The only student ever to go from his Detroit state school to Harvard, he captained varsity lightweight rowing there, twice winning the national championship in the eight. His first job was teaching theology and philosophy at Whitgift, later becoming assistant head of sixth form, before moving to St Edward's Oxford as head of RS, later becoming director of studies.

Suave, erudite and philanthropic (see Money matters); staff say he is also consultative and efficient. 'Listening is imperative, but I don't like to waste time so once I've got the picture, I say, "Ok, I understand, let's do this",' he told us. Parents like his 'inclusive approach' and 'focus on marginal gains.' Students like his sportiness ('It means he gets really involved in our sports,' said one) and say he 'often pops into lessons.' But although he told us the door to his vast study is always open, students told us they wouldn't dream of going in. Teaches when he can (A level politics).

Lives on site in the headmaster's house with his wife Elaina and their two young daughters. 'I'm so lucky – I have a key to the gate to the tow path, which makes for wonderful walks, and occasionally I can pop back and give my daughters a kiss and pop them down for their nap at lunchtimes.'

Academic matters: Academic, for sure, but not overly pressurised. 'The school takes education to a whole new level in terms of engaging the children in learning,' said one parent. 'You get a lot of PowerPoint presentations and very well-designed projects,' agree students, who also approve of the boy-friendly 35-minute lessons. In 2018, 69 per cent A*-A/9-7 grades at I/GCSE (currently IGCSEs in maths, English, geography, science, history, modern languages and ICT) and 75 per cent A*/B and 44 per cent A*/A grades at A level. Maths, English and sciences do particularly well at GCSE, with no real areas of weakness, while for A level (of which 23 are on offer), sciences, maths and economics are the shining stars, with takers of English, art and languages also successful, though fewer in number. Less usual A level choices include classical civilisation, DT, government and politics, drama and theatre, physical education and psychology.

Setting in maths and languages from year 7 ('but only part-way through the year as we do our own testing rather than going on previous attainment levels,' says school) and in sciences for the GCSE years. For languages, boys choose two from Spanish, French and German in year 7 – and Latin is optional from the start of year 8. All take RS GCSE in year 10. Enrichment opportunities in the sixth form include visiting speakers and the school's own PLUS course, which covers giving a presentation, writing an extended essay and effective note-taking as well as careers, personal statements, finance etc. Half of year 12s do an EPQ – high by national standards.

The world of geology has much to thank Reading Blue Coat for – the serendipitous result of a former teacher's passion for rocks is a dedicated lab full of fascinating specimens in the geology and psychology centre (a sympathetic but modern refurb of a 18th century building). Boys take a taster course in year 9 and many go on to study geology (via a Welsh exam board) for GCSE and beyond.

Support is very much tailored towards the individual here, say parents. 'I have three boys of completely different abilities and each of them have had the support they've needed to reach their full potential.' School rebuffs target setting. 'You can get complacent if you're already an A student and you're given a target grade of A; and it can cut aspirations to tell a student their target grade is B just because they usually get C. We aim to get everyone up to A and A*s – it's just a case of finding the best way to suit that child.'

Teachers mainly friendly and unpretentious. 'They really get to know us,' report students, although some said they'd like to see greater consistency. 'Some are quite old-fashioned and have very different standards than others.'

All are screened at 11 and 16 and the learning support department (a team of three based in the converted stables) provides assistance for those with mild SEN (dyslexia mainly) and students who require it are given extra time in the entrance exam. 'I have three sons, two of whom have SEN, and every single member of staff has been informed about their specific needs and they've had all the support they've needed and more,' said one parent.

Games, options, the arts: Given its Thames-side location and fine boathouse, the school's rowing glory will come as no surprise, with the head reeling off details of every recent local, regional and national win. One boy represented Great Britain in rowing the summer we visited. They're no Abingdon and Eton, mind. But, as head points out, 'That's an unfair comparison – Eton has an Olympic rowing lake on the school site!' Main three sports are rugby, football and cricket, all of which have a number of boys playing at county and national level – and the school does well in fixtures, holding its own against some of the big schools, with crowds of parents (and often the head) attending matches. Head says his proudest sporting moment was delivering 33 match reports in football in one week in a Monday assembly. 'Thirty-three!' he repeats, incredulous. Sixth-form girls happy with the sports on offer to them, notably hockey and netball. Some stand-out elites, including one boy who plays badminton for England and a girl who does figure skating at national level – school willing to be flexible with timetable. But the less sporty aren't ostracised – 'My son will never be a natural athlete, but he's always been encouraged to stay involved.' That said, some parents say it's a shame the department 'has its clear favourites and makes that very obvious.'

Shooting, bushcraft, archery, politics, Young Enterprise, DofE, scuba diving, creative writing, journalism and technology are on offer alongside drama productions and sports activities. Sixth formers help in local primary schools and with sports coaching as part of the Sports Leadership Award. CCF is very strong and popular with both boys and girls and cadets have represented the whole movement at national remembrance events. Impressive public speaking record – junior and senior teams have orated their way to become local, national and world champions in recent years. Charitable works encouraged. 'I like our students to do more meaningful things in the community – working in a Sue Ryder home, for example, not just bake sales,' says head. Residential trips galore – recent examples include Ghana, Uzbekistan, Pompeii, Milan, Barcelona, Pembrokeshire. 'You go away at least once a year with the school,' one student told us.

Music is at the heart of the school – all boys are auditioned for the choir and learn a musical instrument for the first two years, and there's a strong orchestra and all the usual ensembles. But it's jazz and contemporary music that really shine, with band practice for the popular Swing into Summertime – in which parents picnic on the lawns and listen to the latest talent – going on when we visited. 'I've never come across a school where music is so cool,' says the head. 'When I hear bands blasting out music at 5pm on Fridays, I refuse to kick them out because they're having so much fun.'

Drama also strong, with separate performances from lower, middle and upper school – including a much talked about recent performance of Grease – and a well-liked head of department.

Art (also popular) is, says head, 'the one area I wouldn't touch when I came to the school.' GCSE and A level exhibitions on when we visited, revealing some talented work, especially on canvases, with a long-standing art teacher himself a working artist who was commissioned to present Theresa May with a painting for her 60th birthday.

Background and atmosphere: Located in the chocolate box village of Sonning-on-Thames, home to Theresa May and George Clooney and full of ancient bridges, half-timbered and thatched houses, tea shops and, at certain times of the day, gridlock in its narrow roads. Founded in 1646 by local merchant Richard Aldworth to offer education for the poor children of Reading, the school moved to its current site 300 years later. 'It's one of the best things the school ever did,' says head. Indeed, unlike many of Reading's best schools stuck on small town-centre sites, this one boasts 50 acres of playing fields (on which nine football matches can be played at once) and wooded grounds which roll down to the Thames and boathouse. 'We're also next to Reading rugby and hockey clubs, so we get to use all their top-notch facilities as spill-over and Astroturf pitches,' adds head.

The classical proportions of the Regency mansion that once stood here fell victim to a serious case of Victorian mock gothicism and sprouted towers and mullions. Not at all sinister on a bright summer's day, but could be rather a brooding presence on a winter's afternoon. Nevertheless a striking building with brick and flint exterior, which is now home to head's office, some teaching areas, IT suite and library (historically not enticing 'due to demands for silence,' say boys, but open door policy and new young librarian means that's set to change). We were delighted to open a door off the library and find a several boys relaxed on beanbags reading. Once a week for the first two years all boys read books of their choice in these peaceful surroundings.

The rest of the site is a mix of newer buildings and facilities including sixth form centre, science centre, sports hall/gym (which hosts two assemblies a week), Richard Aldworth Building (main teaching block with middle school common room), canteen ('where the food could be better,' more than one student told us) and, most recently, the new DT block and a multi-use games area. 'My first son started here in 2003 and the school site is literally unrecognisable from when he started,' one parent told us. Everything is extremely clearly signed ('We have a joke that if you stand still long enough, the bursar will put a blue sign on you') and the interiors of blue carpets, coupled with light oak and glass, gives a fresh, modern feel, although we would like to have seen more examples of students' work through the corridors. The only remaining eyesore is the drama centre ('It's a real shame my boys haven't had access to a proper theatre,' one parent said), but planning permission is in place for a new performing arts centre.

The traditional uniform of long blue coat (hence the school's name), breeches, yellow stockings and buckled shoes is now only worn on high days by prefects – girls and boys. The rest of the time, it's a more typical grey/navy combo and for sixth formers, smart business wear. Some parents are irritated by growing number of days being shaved off the summer term.

Pastoral care, well-being and discipline: The school has active and well thought through policies to foster vertical as well as horizontal bonding. Students see their tutors twice a day and if there's a problem that needs input, it goes to head of year or even head of section, all of whom are trained in child protection. 'So it rarely gets to the deputy head, let alone me,' says head. Two chaplains and a part-time counsellor also available. 'It's a big school, but it's caring,' more than one parent told us. 'We chose the school because we'd heard the boys are happy and that has held true for ours,' said another. Parents describe the school as 'strict' – 'sometimes I've questioned whether it's overly so,' one told us, but most happy with the regimented approach that 'keeps otherwise easily distracted boys in tow.' 'Probably not the best school for a child who likes freedom to do their own thing, but for those who thrive on clear structures and guidance, coupled with a culture that allows for creativity, it's wonderful.' Detentions rare; a handful of temporary exclusions most years; no permanent exclusions in the last three years. Bullying rare. 'If they get a sniff of it, they're in there like a shot,' one parent said. Four houses, named after the school's founders and benefactors, are the focus for competitive sport, music – house singing – and charity fundraising. Girls coming into the sixth form have at least three taster days and get to meet their subject teachers and fellow pupils.

Pupils and parents: 'In a civilised area like this, we are very lucky with the nice middle-class families whose children are polite and very well-behaved,' reports head. From roughly a 25 mile radius, taking in Reading, Maidenhead, Wokingham, Camberley, Wallingford, Fleet, Twyford and villages between. Around half come from state primaries; the rest from local preps including their main feeders of Crosfields and St Piran's, along with St Edwards, Holme Grange and Lambrook among others. Girls come from schools with no sixth form such as Cranford or for a change from single sex education, a number from The Abbey and Queen Anne's. Fees roughly a couple of thousand per annum lower than local competition, but this is regarded as a nice bonus rather than a deciding factor for most parents.

School buses available from Reading, Wokingham, Henley, Maidenhead, Marlow and Windsor. Former pupils (Old Blues) include television presenters Jeremy Kyle ('not an alumnus we are particularly proud of,' admits school) and Matt Allwright (Rogue Traders), Reading West MP Alok Sharma, round-the-world yachtsman Mike Golding OBE and the actress Natalie Dormer (Casanova, The Tudors).

Entrance: Just under three applicants for every place at 11 and just over three at 16. Interview (for both students and parents) with headmaster or senior colleague, entrance examination in January comprising English, maths and verbal reasoning plus reference from current school. A further competitive intake at 16+: around 40 girls and 10 boys enter the lower sixth each year. Entry at this age requires verbal and non-verbal reasoning tests plus a minimum of seven GCSEs grade C and above, with at least As (or numerical equivalents) in most subjects to be studied at A level. From 2018, students will take online assessments and written English tests.

R

Exit: About 85 per cent go through to sixth form. Nearly all to first choice university – Exeter, Leeds, Cardiff, Birmingham, Southampton and UWE currently popular. Most, but not all, to study heavy duty subjects such as aeronautical engineering, dentistry, maths, modern langs and physics. Sports science and, not surprisingly, geology also popular. In 2018, one to Cambridge and three medics.

Money matters: Cheap-ish, as Basil Fawlty would say – fees lower than at a few prep schools in the area and head keen to keep it that way. 'The value for money is notable,' one parent told us. Scholarships for art, music, academics and sport – up to five per cent of fees (used to be 25 per cent 'but it struck me as wrong to give discount to millionaire families, rather than those who couldn't otherwise afford to come here,' says head). Two foundation scholarships awarded annually on merit and means-tested (100 per cent of fees). In addition the school awards roughly half a dozen bursaries per year group ranging from 25 per cent to 100 per cent. Watch this space for more bursaries becoming available in the next few years – it's one of the head's main focuses, which he spoke passionately about at length to us.

Remarks: No shortage of other good day schools to choose from in this area, state and independent, but academically this hovers at the top and it also stands out for the vibrant, friendly, family-oriented feel and extracurricular offering. 'It's not just a school, but a way of life for the young people. It's a whole community,' summed up one parent. A school that remains true to its founding principles, continuing to put all its efforts into providing a first class all-round education for the boys and girls fortunate enough to go there – and one which is increasingly keen to be financially accessible.

Reading School

Erleigh Road, Reading, Berkshire RG1 5LW

Ages 11–18 **Pupils** 1,032 **Sixth form** 334 **Boarders** 76 weekly

Fees: Day free; Boarding £11,248 pa

0118 901 5600
www.reading-school.co.uk

Head: Since 2012, Mr Ashley Robson BA NPQH MBA, previously deputy head since 2005. History degree from Newcastle-upon-Tyne; first jobs at Princes Risborough School and Royal Grammar School, High Wycombe before becoming head of history, head of house and assistant headteacher at Aylesbury Grammar School.

With the demeanour of a jovial uncle, he's a big hit with the pupils, who describe him as 'really friendly and funny' and 'the ideal headmaster because you know he really cares about us.' He teaches most of them history at one stage or another and often pops in and out of other lessons, as well as supporting sports fixtures where he can. A humble man who is big on praising staff ('This teacher is amazing,' he says, introducing us to one of them. 'How would we manage without you?' to another), he's also popular with parents – no mean feat given some of their sky-high expectations. 'He is an exceptional man, who is not interested in standing still, but only moving the school ahead.' 'He holds himself to very high standards and expects his staff to reflect those in everything they do. But he is also a human being and understands that boys make mistakes.'

Lives an hour's drive away in Bucks with his wife, with whom he has three children – Dominic, who works at NHS England, Joseph, who's at Oxford University, and Harriett, who is studying for her A levels. Enjoys sport, particularly football, and travel.

Academic matters: For intellectually inquisitive, naturally bright and highly motivated boys, this school is likely to feel a very natural fit. And thanks to a combination of academic rigour and inspirational staff (whose sharpness, energy and wisdom almost make you want to sit down and get stuck into the lesson yourself), there are no real areas of weakness, with stand-out results across the board – including in value-added. At GCSE, 87 per cent A*-A/9-7 grades in 2018.

Setting in maths from year 8, with class sizes for top sets capped at 32, while bottom set numbers tend to hover between 10-12. No stigma 'as everyone gets A* anyway,' say pupils. New language strategy not for the fainthearted, with German, French, Spanish and Latin all studied in year 7; then Latin and two of the others in year 8; and at least one language to be taken at GCSE (Latin and German most popular). Teachers all subject specialists. 'You can't pass on what you haven't got – but even that's not good enough on its own. Teachers also need passion and the ability to inspire,' insists head, and pupils say they do this with bells on. 'Every teacher here goes the extra mile, not just in the classroom, but in terms of extra help including subject drop-in clinics and one-to-ones if you need them,' said one. Rapport between teachers and boys notably good-humoured and mutually respectful. 'I can't think of one teacher that doesn't allow you to have a joke in the class – they like making learning fun,' said one boy.

In sixth form, boys choose four A levels from a largely traditional mix, including (unusually) Latin and ancient Greek if numbers permit. In 2018, 92 per cent A*-B and 75 per cent A*/A grades. Most popular subjects are maths, chemistry and economics. Boys also expected to enrich their sixth form timetable with one of these three options: first, student charity committee, which raises around £10k for charity (past examples include Syrian refugees and partner school in Kenya); second, the Future Stories Programme, which aims to increase social mobility by boys teaching and mentoring disadvantaged children in local primary school; third, the student-led Dementia Champions programme, whereby boys become 'dementia friends' and roll out what they've learned across the school. 'Boarders visit local care homes as part of this programme – it's great for intergenerational bonds,' one boy told us. Formal extended project qualification (EPQ) also available.

Less than 1.5 per cent with SEN (one statemented when we visited) – most on the autistic spectrum or dyslexic, whose additional help is mainly provided outside the classroom by the SENCo (who only works one day a week – she teaches the rest of the time), supported by part-time (2.5 days a week) learning support adviser and SEND governor. 'The SENCo is not backward in coming forward and really champions the boys, recognising that some staff get their needs and some don't,' one parent of a child with told us, adding, 'She is very collaborative with parents too, even letting me run a session with staff to explain what my son's condition is like to live with.' One parent with a child with dyslexia, however, told us, 'I notice it gets forgotten sometimes, for example when he needs extra time in exams.'

Games, options, the arts: For parents that treat this school as an alternative to a high performing independent school (many do), sports will be your wake-up call. With no acres of rolling green fields, rows of pristine tennis courts or swimming pool, it is fair to say that nobody is blown away by the sports facilities – or indeed successes – here. But the boys don't half do badly when they put their minds to it, holding the titles of U18 county rugby champions and KS3 and KS4 national badminton champions when we visited. As for local fixtures, there's no school they like thrashing more than Blue Coat ('They're our local rival,' say boys). Core sports are rugby (autumn), football (spring) and cricket (summer), with lacrosse and badminton also growing in popularity. Amenities include sports field (picture perfect when we visited, with clear blue skies and boys playing in their cricket whites), refurbished gym and three pitches 400 metres away on the other side of the Royal Berkshire Hospital. There are plans to build a sports hall and multi-use games area – though nobody dares guestimate a completion date.

Music a real strength and considered a good alternative for the non-sporty in terms of encouraging teamwork. Orchestras, ensembles and choirs galore, with the house music competition the highlight of the musical calendar. 'Even if you're not mega into music, like me, it's a great night – we all love it,' said one boy. 'Close your eyes and you could be listening to professionals,' gushed a parent.

Drama facilities nothing to write home about, but that doesn't stop it being a popular at GCSE and there were just enough boys to do A level the year we visited. Practice for a student-led extravaganza (the first in years) in full swing when we visited – We Will Rock You. 'I don't know anyone who doesn't like drama here – it's not even like a lesson, but a way to express yourself and let off steam,' said one boy.

Art offered at GCSE and A level, though numbers not high and DT facilities recently scrapped to make way for a computer science block. 'Let's face it, the arts are not a big selling point – people don't come here for that. But at the same time, the school doesn't completely ignore them,' said one parent.

Copious amount of clubs and societies, many student-led. Chess (considered a sport here, albeit tongue-in-cheek) does particularly well – national schools senior chess champions when we visited. Ditto with public speaking. 'I was sent out to Hong Kong to represent the school in a public speaking competition and felt physically sick when it came to the actual moment of speaking, but I wound up reaching the finals,' one boy told us, understandably proud. Trips aplenty, with recent examples including football tour to California, cricket tour to St Lucia, language exchanges to Germany and France. Boys on pupil premium (around 1.5 per cent when we visited) financially supported so nobody misses out.

Boarding: Boys wear their boarding identity as a kind of badge of honour. But, points out one, 'It couldn't be further from the traditional public school boarding experience, what with the family feel and older boys taking the younger boys under their wing. My son wasn't great at maths and an older boy took such delight in helping him,' said a parent.

Two boarding houses (some friendly rivalry between them) accommodate a maximum of six boys each per year group. Most boys' families live within the M4 corridor and because only weekly boarding is on offer here, the majority go home after school on Friday, returning Sunday night or Monday morning ('although a few stay on Friday night if they've got a fixture the next day').

Décor no-frills but comfortable, with boys touchingly proud of the space spread among the eight common rooms (complete with pool tables, table football and TVs – 'particularly great fun when we all get together to watch a game'), as well as kitchens, music practice rooms and study spaces. Singles up to three bed dorms – space and privacy increase as boys get older. All impressively tidy (rooms are scored for tidiness daily and the weekly winner gets an extra £5 on their refectory card) – and although boys admitted 'the shared areas can quickly turn into a tip, we do tidy them up regularly.'

Boarding staff are second-to-none in terms of their 'commitment, enthusiasm, motivation, morale and belief in the boarders,' according to Ofsted – we agree. And because both housemasters have young families, there are often young children about too. 'My first sight when I open my eyes in the morning is usually of the housemaster's 1-year-old daughter waving at me,' laughed one boy. After-school life is tightly timetabled – clubs from 4pm (at least three on offer per evening) then dinner at 5.30pm and finally shared study time from 6.30-8pm. Much anticipated bi-annual boarding trips in summer and winter include the likes of theme park and West End theatre.

Background and atmosphere: Founded as part of Reading Abbey in 1125, the school is estimated to be the 10th oldest school in England (though some argue there may have been a school running in Reading prior to this) and the 20th oldest in the world. Moved to current site in 1870, where it now consists of an attractive red-brick grade 2 listed building with two wings, in

R

front of which sits the beautifully manicured field. Expect all the usual grammar school features – parquet flooring, green tiles on the corridor walls, windows into the classrooms etc. Other notable additions to the campus include a snazzy new science block (a joy to watch boys excitedly making benzoic acid), Page building (art, computer science, maths and IT), John Kendrick building (library plus more classrooms), the music school (far end of the field) and South House (one of the boarding houses – the other, East Wing, is attached to the main block). Newly refurbished refectory (where they do darn good quirky cakes – beetroot and chilli among them – students say the rest of the food is good too). Also recently refurbished are four of the computer science labs (replacing the old 1950s DT room) and lecture theatre. Although some areas look more pristine than others, 'there's nothing we want for when it comes facilities,' say boys.

School values of excellence, integrity and leadership are brought to life not by predictable assembly orations, but by real-life responsibilities (one boy carried out a remarkably professional student survey, as just one example). And it is this, together with the scholarly yet relaxed vibe – and the leafy green campus – that gives an almost university-type feel to the place. 'Atmosphere can get a bit competitive between the boys, though,' said one boy. 'I sometimes wish there was a bit more "we're-all-in-this-together",' agreed another, though another disagreed. Strong partnership with Kendrick School (local girls' grammar), with joint concerts, annual prom and some societies such as the economics discussion group.

Pastoral care, well-being and discipline: Definitely more carrot than stick, with the tiered detention system rarely used. 'When boys mess up here, it's usually just a silly mistake – and the school wants us to learn from it, rather than warn us that severe punishments are waiting around every corner, which would just make us disenfranchised with school life,' one boy said. Seemingly endless (as you've probably gleaned) examples of student-led activities and policies – school believes that giving students responsibility over their own school is a better way to get them to respect it than strict rules.

Anxiety can be an issue, especially at exam time – and that's just the parents. When boys get worried, their first port of call tends to be head of house (five houses in total), or – in year 12/13 – their head of year. There's also a counsellor who visits one day a week ('he's busy – and I see that as a good thing,' says head), plus there's a day matron, two boarding matrons and a new medical centre. PSHE classes, described by boys as 'insightful,' also help raise awareness of mental health issues – and there's a (student-led again) mental health action plan committee. Once-weekly visits to chapel help pupils explore moral dilemmas (as a non-denominational school, this is with a secular emphasis).

R

Bullying rare, although a couple of parents told us about 'a cyber-bulling incident, which the school dealt with brilliantly – getting the boys to do a presentation to parents on the dangers of social media.' No permanent exclusions since 2013 and less than a handful of temporary ones each academic year. Everyone agrees the school is fair and 'works on logical argument and persuasion, which the boys are perfectly adept at using themselves to probe the senior leadership team if they don't agree with their punishment!'

Pupils and parents: Catchment area for day pupils roughly equates to a 15 mile circumference, with the majority of day boys coming from Reading and Wokingham; furthest points reaching as far as Maidenhead, parts of Slough and Newbury. 'Most boys travel in by bus or train and the journey is under an hour,' says head. Boarders' families tend to live in the M4 corridor, within a couple of hours' drive.

Parents a pretty vocal lot. 'Some have very, very high expectations of their sons and we have to help them manage that with the reality of the situation,' says head. Active PA.

Rich ethnic mix, with white British and Indian backgrounds dominating, but plenty of others besides. Old boys include Christopher Renshaw (theatre director), Damian Green (Secretary of State for Work and Pensions), Ross Brawn (Formula 1), William Laud (Archbishop) and Joe Eyre (actor, writer and theatre director).

Entrance: Highly competitive 11+ exam, comprising of two separate multiple choice papers, each lasting around 50 minutes. Provided by the Centre for Evaluation and Monitoring (CEM) at the University of Durham, each test assesses verbal, non-verbal and numerical ability. No practice papers available (an attempt to stop over-tutoring, although you won't stop local parents giving it a go), although there is a familiarisation sheet on the school website and on the school website. Over 800 sit the entrance test for the 138 year 7 day boy places and a similar ratio for the 12 boarding spaces – you can only apply for one or the other. Having a sibling here already is no advantage and rarely do more than a handful of boys come from a single primary school (and even that's considered a lot). Registration window opens in May with a closing date around mid-June.

To stay on into sixth- form (or join as a newcomer) boys need the equivalent of at least 54 points across eight GCSEs, and at least a B/6 in the subjects chosen. Around 150 apply for the 70 or so additional places.

Exit: Nearly all stay on for sixth form – 'The boys who leave after GCSE tend to go to a sixth form college nearer where they live in, say, Basingstoke or Henley, or they don't make the grades,' says head. Sixth formers almost all to university, 70 per cent to Russell Group, with Bristol, Warwick, Durham and Imperial currently featuring highly. In 2018, 29 to Oxbridge, 26 to medical school. Very strong numbers to read economics-based subjects, with second most popular course engineering, followed by medicine in third place. Also prevalent, but in smaller numbers, are history, English, classics and maths.

Remarks: Although it's been a while since the school was given the prestigious State School of the Year 2010 award by the Sunday Times, it is still recognised as one of the leading state schools in the country due to its exceptionally high academic standards and strong emphasis on personal development. What we love is that it achieves this with a good dose of merriment and 'own-your-own-learning' treatment – a testament to the teachers and leadership team who do not seem to apply undue pressure or strictness and who hand out student-led projects like Smarties. For erudite boys who want to be given wings to fly, your future starts here.

Reeds School

Sandy Lane, Cobham, Surrey KT11 2ES

Ages 11–18 **Pupils** 721 **Sixth form** 266 (80 girls) **Boarders** 72 full **C of E**

Fees: Day £19,740– £24,675; Boarding £26,310 – £31,800 pa

01932 869001
www.reeds.surrey.sch.uk

Head: Since 2014, Mark Hoskins BA MA MSc (50s). Previously second master (senior deputy head in modern currency) at RGS Guildford between 2005-2014. Before that, spent eight years at

Whitgift, starting as head of economics and business studies in 1997 and then becoming head of middle school. First posts were in highly regarded maintained schools – two years apiece at Rosebery (comp, girls) and Wilson's (selective grammar, boys). Mixed sixth form here first foray so far into co-education.

Praise from parents comes thick and fast. 'Impressive'; 'A lovely guy'; 'Has accelerated the academic side without losing the breadth.' Ditto for wife Sharon, whose diligent attendance at events has been approvingly clocked. Has two children, son (at the school) and daughter (distinctly miffed she isn't as too young).

Though an able sportsman (coached soccer in US during gap years), Mr Hoskins talks down his successes – becoming modesty a given, he says, when working in schools with world-class pros on the staff. Nobody, though, likely to call him out on academic qualifications, what with two masters, a second in economics from the University of London, accomplished post-marriage with small children and combined with full-time teaching. 'When you're teaching bright pupils, they push you and so you want to push yourself.' Still fits in some teaching currently economics to upper sixth, switching effortlessly between different roles – father to head – without breaking step, with son's friends at ease within minutes.

Parents who already know (or have heard tell) of previous achievements at RGS are quickly converting others. He's taking the school by stealth (as well as charm) and doing the evolution not revolution thing. Latest inspection praises democratic, light touch management style, with teachers regularly observed but encouraged rather than censured while management structure is being reworked to give more opportunities to the talented.

He's forceful where necessary. 'Don't ever want to be on his bad side,' says pupil. Not out of fear but because 'wouldn't want him to lose his respect for you.' Not a hacker and slasher, think parents, whose perception is of new talent being grafted on to the staff team (average age early 40s) and tired areas jazzed up with a bit of extra colour – chaplain impressively also a maths teacher and rugby coach, a case in point. School was 'ripe for a shake up,' said one mother. Mr Hoskins seen as the person to administer it.

State educated himself and with a strong moral purpose, he'd like to up numbers of foundation places for disadvantaged pupils.

Academic matters: Edging ever closer to nearby powerhouses like Hampton and RGS as locals wake up to educational excellence on their doorstep and, in small but growing numbers, start to make this their first choice. Elsewhere, pupils' brilliance polished till it shines but personalities remain unchanged. Here, parents feel pupils' characters have room to grow, too.

Pupils, particularly those living some distance away and involved in matches, clubs and events will, however, need to arrive with a few ready-to-wear sterling qualities, headed by keenness and motivation. Disorganised types can end up trailing home to face sizeable quantities of homework ('they do get quite a lot,' said mother) and a few, say parents, may not last the course. School disagrees. 'No-one has left due to being disorganised,' says Mr Hoskins.

Won't be for want of numerous helping hands from the school, reflection of high staff to pupil ratios – just over one to eight – and reasonable class sizes (17 up to year 11, 10 in sixth form). Following substantial makeover, there's more setting, regular testing and additional feedback on academic attainment with boys awarded bronze, silver and gold grades for effort as well as achievement. 'Have no worries about where son is going academically – am more than comfortable,' said parent.

School is notable for quality of support – currently offered to around 80 pupils, vast majority with assorted dys difficulties, and very small numbers with ADD, ADHD, ASD, visual or speech and language issues. Just under 20 with EAL are supported individually or in small groups.

Regardless of need, pupils must be able to thrive in relatively (but not ridiculously) fast-paced environment. 'If they need so much support that it would be difficult to access, this wouldn't be the right place because your confidence takes an absolute hammering,' says Mr Hoskins. If make the grade, progress is often exceptional, helped by well thought out support including ADR (assess, do and review) programme.

While overall pass rates remain pretty consistent (at A level, A*/A grades 41 per cent, 78 per cent A*/B in 2018, with 71 per cent A*-A/9-7 at GCSE) subject popularity ebbs and flows. A few more girls taking A level physics would be good (numbers are very small) though those we spoke to felt were well supported whatever their interests.

Subject choices are fairly standard up to GCSE (electronics is about as outré as it gets), though there's a research project for year 9s. Post-16, there's an impressive 27 A level options include graphics, taken by around 10 each year. Will also keep subjects going for very tiny numbers (one or two year each year taking computing, for example, slightly more taking art). Most now take three A levels, plus additional courses from a range that includes music technology, general studies and further maths.

It's reinforced by boundless staff enthusiasm. Every subject gets own write up – 'It's been another bumper year in the world of physics,' burbles school mag – as well as appetite-whetting extras such as recently-formed medical society where would-be doctors justify career choice to peers. Most mentioned by parents, however, is fabulous Futuretech programme – DT reimagined to give free rein to 'what if' projects linking STEM subjects. DIY model wind turbines created by second years and visit from TESLA among the many highlights.

Games, options, the arts: Old Reedonians' website may convey message that life without sport is one wasted ('injury, marriage or the arrival of children...' quoted as distinct inconveniences) but school these days is natural home for those eager to improve pen or bow hold as well as racket grip. Head, with consummate diplomacy, felt by parents to avoid any suggestion of sports vs the rest, drama and music sharing equal place on the rostrum. Agreed, says teacher. 'You just don't win world titles for them.' (Just as well given that sports trophies take up almost enough space to host own open day.)

Ham-fisted, two-left feet or otherwise, everyone will have talent, however limited, coaxed out of them. Parents and pupils stress effectiveness of school's approach – a fine balance between compulsion and encouragement. 'Do something whether you like it or not – and you mostly do,' said sixth former. Activities – 75 plus, ranging from archery to golf and judo to silk painting – cater for dabblers as well as enthusiasts. Sixth form boys – who have fourth X1 fixtures – organise 'not very good' gentleman's hockey team just for the fun of it. 'We just want to play,' said one.

There's also popular DofE (with strong philanthropic dimension) and CCF. Don't neglect social skills either, with everything from debating club (so can participate in discussion) to Toastmasters for older pupils (where discover how to lead it). Many new sixth formers, compelled to try previously hated activities (two a week in years 11, 12 and 13; three to year 10) converted into fans. Brilliant for bonding even if not, thought pupil.

Strength of arts, performing and visual, particularly impressive, from scale of ambition to levels of investment and numbers involved (over 200 individual music lessons each week and a fifth of all pupils taking part in recent concert). Sixth form technicians, recently rewarded with two RADA technical course places, work into small hours to put final touches to lighting for major productions (created a big top – inside – from scratch for The Impresario), while music scholar who complained about piano quality wasn't just listened to but flown to Germany to help choose brand new Steinway.

Whatever your specialist interest, facilities excellent, packed in on relatively compact site. Trees know their place – confined largely to the perimeter so space can be given over to cricket, rugby (big and little pitches), two Astros and tennis courts. Whole shebang has accolade of being accredited by Tim Henman Foundation as model primary school outreach programme for others to follow.

Inevitably, sport remains biggest selling point for some families. 'Why we chose the school,' said mother. Biggest lure for the ultra-talented are three academies (golf, tennis and skiing) offering elite coaching (every major sport comes with own professional), flexible timetable and extra training (before or after school and – in case of skiiers – sent off to the snow), plus osteo clinic and sports injury rehabilitation. Youngest sports scholars enjoy substantial perk of all day trackies to avoid frequent changes of clothes, school adamant that no wizard/muggle divisions exist. No swollen heads either – 'they've lovely boys,' said parent. Individual successes at national and county level are copious across range of age groups and sports (including 26 for hockey). Ditto stonking team triumphs (tennis – three consecutive wins in World Schools' Championship; golf – regular national finalists). New indoor cricket centre, available to outsiders as well as pupils, includes system that 'combines motion tracking and video analysis'.

System relies on, and gets, happy cooperation between academic and sports staff, particularly in sixth form with pupils allowed to devote some private study time to sport ('a privilege and must be able to invest time to catch up on work,' stresses school). Significant weapon is sizeable number of teachers so blessed with charm that can even make punishments a laugh a minute. 'If we forget our kit, coach makes us run and touch all the lines on the pitch – there are about 500,' said junior pupil, chortling at the very memory. 'Makes it so funny.' You probably had to be there.

Smaller numbers mean fewer limits, thought one mother. 'At other schools you have to make choices early on, here they can do anything.' One originally sports-centric boy was also singing and acting at every opportunity – slightly to his own surprise, as well as that of parents. 'Confidence has gone through the roof.'

Boarding: Though only 15 per cent board, juniors in The Close, seniors in School House, sixth formers upstairs in own courtyard block (currently under refurbishment to provide glassed-over study area and café) complete with lecture theatre, they're a happy clan, with a strong and oft-(very oft) mentioned sense of community. Sixth form girl boarders, a particularly minuscule group (under a handful in upper sixth), flock together and take pleasure in niche status, downstairs common room a homely oasis of papers and possessions. Offers full, weekly or occasional B&B – a boon to any child with a late finishing match or parents with work commitments. Despite low numbers, school rarely feels empty, say pupils.

Accommodation is spick and span, white and magnolia the prevailing signature décor, eye-catching touches headed by world's reddest kitchen in School House, neon signs and slinky bar-style seating for its 36 year 9-11 boarders. Elsewhere, communal areas are businesslike rather than breathtaking, though as long as there's space enough to pack in the crowds for must-watch TV (usually matches, we'd assume), pupils clearly don't mind.

Tempo of life is exceedingly brisk and a marvel of logistics, junior boarders showered and powered into breakfast in just 30 minutes – even faster when bacon's on the menu (food – bar some evening meals – generally excellent) – while all-action weekends for everyone are filled with (more) sport, mixed age cinema trips, shopping (in groups of three, one phone compulsory) and doughnutting (descending Sandown Park's dry ski slope in rubber ring).

Pace accounts for absence of personal touches. Some pinboards stay empty because there's just no time to unpack. 'Too much to do,' said pupil, who'd had initial reservations about absence of down time. No longer. 'Now realise that being busy is perfect.'

Cheerful matrons keep everything ticking over, washing machines permanently on spin cycle (18 loads of laundry in one day a personal best), aided and abetted by thoughtful, compassionate houseparents proffering small hours hot chocolate and DVDs when homesickness strikes and with welcome ability to tread the fine line between firmness and latitude. 'With boarding you try to make it like a family,' says one. 'When someone's done something wrong you try to think if they'd be in trouble for something similar at home and separate something that's annoying – like being too loud or watching TV too late – from something that merits a detention.'

Background and atmosphere: Founded in 1813 by Andrew Reed, social reformer, minister and serial setter upper of charitable institutions (and upsetter of fellow trustees), but the only school to survive intact, discounting change of name (originally the London Orphan Asylum), location (arrived here via Clapton, Watford and – briefly during WW2 evacuation – Totnes), and financing (fee-paying pupils first admitted 1950s, though charitable focus on foundationers has never changed).

Handy for M25 and with Gatwick and Heathrow just a 30-minute drive away, it's a cinch to get to, as long as you avoid rush hour and don't take address too literally (says Cobham but actually in Oxshott – it's a postal area thing).

Heart of the school is restored arts and crafts building, home – among other areas – to attractive chapel and library, surrounded by separate music school, labs, classrooms and airy sixth form block with lecture theatre which doubles as venue for film screenings. Packs a lot on to 40-acre site – including mysterious amounts of lost property, despite school's comprehensive naming service. 'Usually get it back but can take a very long time,' said mother. 'In my experience, much better than other schools on this,' says Mr Hoskins.

Overcoming pupil/space dilemma by corralling outside areas and roofing them over – small courtyard is now a conservatory-style dining hall extension while The Close boasts an impressive stretch reception, 100 or so tennis balls trapped on the roof a happy reminder of previous incarnation as impromptu sports pitch.

With master plan now agreed, there's plenty of development happening. Likely to be equally imaginative and ambitious, says Mr Hoskins, though won't put up buildings all over the place and ramp up pupil numbers as 'would ruin what we have.'

Pastoral care, well-being and discipline: Cordial relations between staff and pupils ensure that lines are clearly drawn, usually toed and rarely crossed, mild eccentricities tolerated while not actively encouraged. Year 11 boy, dealing with exam tension in his own way by sporting a rolled up trouser leg, was clocked by adult tour guide – 'High spirits' – then left to own (if rather more self-conscious) devices. Headmaster has flexed disciplinary muscles for serious breaches (as with other schools, drink and drugs the main culprits) – offenders likely to be asked to leave.

Everyone very much at home here, much emphasis on age-appropriate three-day induction programme. For year 7s includes on-site camping and games of chubby bunnies ('See how many marshmallows you can get in your mouth and still say "chubby bunnies",' said pupil – well, of course). Activities for new sixth form girls include rather more sophisticated (and confectionary-free) meal out in Kingston.

For first two years, The Close, a separate building, is a world in miniature. 'Opportunity to settle very well without being overwhelmed – a home away from home,' said parent. Have own houses, games, activities and responsibilities, plus quality pastoral back up from sixth form mentors, a high profile and popular presence, who dispense quiz questions and chocolate brownies, organise house drama and deal with acts of minor unkindness.

System works exceptionally well, houseparents keeping a close eye on charges, say parents, but not exclusively so. 'Everyone needs to have an idea of collective responsibilities,' said pupil. 'If they're not willing to put in the effort, they wouldn't be suitable.' For the majority who are, individual record books – an initiative from the chaplain (he's buzzing with them) – will be a chance to list golden deeds of compassion and virtue as well as mere academic success.

Pupils and parents: With just a handful of expats and around 12-15 international students, 80 per cent from Hong Kong, most families are UK-based Brits living maximum of an hour's travel time away, network of school bus routes reading like estate agent's bumper book of desirable destinations (Putney, Richmond, Wimbledon and Guildford).

Foundationers, some with traumatising early life experiences, are painlessly absorbed. 'Ensures other children don't live in a bubble,' says school. Parents agree, though one warned against excessive hikes in school fees. 'Run the risk that end up with two categories, those who can afford it and foundationers, with a gap in the middle.' Mr Hoskins points out that 'in the last two years, fee increases were less than many of our competitors.'

End product includes plenty of high-grade sportspeople (Tim Henman most glorious example), though crop of musicians, actors and entertainers is almost as substantial. One 1980s batch (they organise alumni by decade here) yielded two opera singers, an art dealer and a Jordanian prince. Plenty of somethings in the City as well.

Sports, arts or royalty, Old Reedonians stay in touch. 'Keep caring and giving to family long after graduation,' said one. 'Once a Reedonian, always a Reedonian.' Partners, we were told, like to swap notes, finding ORs nicer and gentler than the common herd.

Judging by today's happy mixed age lunchtime throng, pupils impressively (and unusually) relaxed about talking about their feelings, oldest pupils encouraging the youngest to speak, everyone giving strong impression of liking everyone else, nothing much has changed.

Entrance: At 11+ English and maths tests plus VR, all (normally) taken at school in January for entry in September. For 13+, register a good three years in advance, pre-test in year 6, CE in June if at prep school. Other candidates sit English, maths, science, modern language and VR papers. Sixth form hopefuls have observed lesson to judge teamwork and two subject-based exams – superior ability mentioned by inspectors.

Foundation pupils – some referred by own school or children's charity – have range of difficulties, from financial hardship to loss of a parent or seriously ill sibling. Need to sit entrance exams and will also have home visit.

While greater competition inevitably means more able applicants achieving well beyond pass mark, head doesn't go by grades alone. Good relationships with prep heads essential for CE so can consult 'if they bomb because of real pastoral issues,' and may still take, with academic support to fill in gaps.

Children of former pupils urged to identify themselves at registration. Won't give you edge over competition, says Mr Hoskins – but bad news is more likely to be accompanied by a phone call.

Exit: About 11 per cent exit post-16 – fewer each year – freedom offered by local sixth form colleges ('longer hair and earrings,' says Mr Hoskins) the main lure. If shy of required GCSE grades (around eight grade 6s) school will help if possible, though substitute subjects may be imposed (DT rather than physics, say). Also possible to repeat years.

Translates into gamut of places: Bristol, Exeter, Leeds, Loughborough, Newcastle, Oxford Brookes, Southampton feature most years. Courses ditto – modelmaking to nutrition, speech and language to quantity surveying and design in every permutation. One medic and one vet in 2018; others off to California, Colorado and Eindhoven.

Money matters: Bursaries for foundationers up to 110 per cent of fees. Also range of scholarships – DT and drama at 13+ and in the sixth form – also open to existing pupils, plus headmaster's award for able but not quite scholarship level candidates at 11+ and CE; additional scholarships awarded to existing pupils during school career if merited. Fees steep but include majority of extras – meals to choir tours so 'looks more expensive than it is,' said mother.

Remarks: One parent equated school to post-privatisation Jaguar – took a while for shift in quality to be recognised. 'Took years for prices to catch up, but they did.' With Mr Hoskins in the driving seat, this revamped model is definitely proving an all terrain winner.

Reigate Grammar School

Linked with Reigate St Mary's School

Reigate Road, Reigate, Surrey RH2 0QS

Ages 11–18 **Pupils** 1,018 **Sixth form** 263

Fees: £18,600 – £18,720 pa

01737 222231
www.reigategrammar.org

Headmaster: Since 2012, Mr Shaun Fenton MA PGCE Med NPQH (50s). Formerly head of Pate's and founded and chaired National Grammar Schools Association. Educated at Haberdashers' Aske's, then PPE at Oxford. Started and ditched City career for education, first in west London comprehensive until drawn by challenge of The Ridings School in Halifax, labelled worst in Britain in TV documentary. Exhilarated by challenge of working with one of the first superheads, who achieved rags to riches magic, forged in hotbed of innovation. 'If something worked here, would work anywhere.'

Much in demand to repeat the process, quickly promoted to first deputy headship in Hertfordshire, followed by spell as troubleshooter injecting aspiration into other troubled schools that had shed senior management following inspection failures. Tough, energetic, enthusiastic and 'comes up with about 1,000 ideas a week,' said member of staff. 'A very nice young chap,' reckoned a paternalistic local.

His arrival has had a mixed reaction from parents, who seem to be holding back while they gauge the measure of the man. They love his God particle-like ability to be in several places at once (one had recently come across him at a hockey umpiring class – his latest qualification) and the way he's handed out his email address and positively implored parents to get in touch – no issue too small. 'I love to hear from them,' he says (he also likes to use them to gauge temperature of public feeling – the words 'focus group' crop up, in other contexts, more than once).

Particularly good at unpicking existing school practices and refashioning with more stuffing. Sixth form mentors don't just talk to pupils but are also charged with speaking to their families. Scholars are challenged from day one, with a programme designed to shape talents into Oxbridge-friendly material if academic and all-weather leadership fabric (sport) with captaincy a managed exercise in building relationships, helping develop struggling teams and nurturing individuals. 'No point just getting them to play matches – it's about the psychology.' Lots of praise, too, for innovations to date, notably reintroduction of house system.

Parents worry that new system of offers to some prep pupils as early as year 5 could reduce numbers making it through to senior school. But though one parent felt it had 'put the cat among the pigeons', head was clear that 'it means offers for the vast majority of Reigate St Mary students and not just the high performers'. Overall, 'admission at age 11 is approximately half from excellent local state primary schools and half from prep schools.'

Conundrum for some might be why, with solid A* career, he has opted for first time move into independent sector instead of carrying on down the path to government darling roles as a superhead's superhead, advising the great, good and better on how to do it. But it's simple. As at Pate's, he can educate society's leaders himself and cut out the middleman. As to why here – it 'was the only school that stood out for its ambition to make a real difference.'

Nervous to start with (he says), he certainly isn't now. Has been charged by the governors with providing education 'the way it should be, with no short cuts.' Slow cook approach lets top grades rise from teaching that lets pupils live their subjects – converting hall into mini Parliament to explore legislative process, for example. 'This could not be further away from a hothouse approach but can deliver stunning, authentic learning,' says head.

Wants to make school one 'you drive past others to come to'. And, yes, he does want to get results up, though refused to be drawn on any specific targets, or schools he'd measure himself against (Caterham is the long term rival at the moment). He also wants staff asking 'what excellence looks like... what are the best teachers and schools in the world and doing? What does it mean to us?' Too many schools coast, he thinks, relying on showy but shallow academic gimmicks, where pupils, drilled to the test, fetch up as 'charlatans, not historians.' As to 'outstanding' inspection ratings, pretty much waved aside as something that for any really good school is the starting point.

Will know he is hitting the sweet spot when shared language of excellence permeates the building and crosses the departments. No wonder 'some staff feel they have been hit by a tsunami – need to hold on tight,' thought insider.

Pupils, meanwhile, see a lot of him as he beams out from airy office overlooking playground. He somehow manages to pack in a bit of teaching, too. An RE teacher originally, he takes 1675 (school's foundation date) as starting point for philosophical debate about pupils' place in the world. Lively charm makes him a winner. Jolly, determined and, through previous posts, has seen it, done it and got the results to prove it, leaving no doubt that this head will make his mark on every area of the school without, despite recent appearance in full Darth Vader regalia, necessitating a walk on the dark side.

Married – wife Anna works part-time at the school – with two sons at linked prep.

Academic matters: 'Not a hothouse, but academic,' is the view of one prospective parent who, like others, reckons head has been charged with ramping up results. Sciences and maths top the popularity chart, history close runners up, geography, government and politics and RS leading second wave, while marginals include music and Latin (13 taking music A level a couple of years ago was 'exceptional', says department director, who is happy with small exam numbers and big involvement).

Much that's good, little bad and nothing ugly, with GCSE and A level grades both onwards and upwards. In 2018, 81 per cent of GCSEs A*-A/9-7 and 70 per cent of A levels A*/A grades. Expect best feet to be put forward and pips squeaked, all, however, without imposing undue stress. Direction of travel is gladdening head's heart. Ten subjects taken by most, with IGCSEs for sciences, Eng lang and maths, where very able whizz through a year early. Maths is only formally set subject apart from languages, grouped to allow later starters (often from state primaries) to catch up with early adopters.

Has introduced High Performance Learning: 'an innovative, world-class education profile that helps students become enterprising learners, advanced performers and global citizens'. Teaching we saw of a fairly formal nature (and some classrooms plain rather than purl when it came to display) but judging by interest levels – front-facing, engaged pupils clearly absorbed in subjects – it's quality stuff. 'Not every single teacher is brilliant,' felt parent, though praised the many who were. 'There's lots of laughter and interaction.' And while teenagers 'might moan, they do get on with lessons.' Plenty of oohs and ahs in year 8 chemistry class, as teacher created solid. 'I love chemistry – teaching is brilliant,' said Oxbridge hopeful. Computing another winner – first year pupils animatedly creating crests and GCSE candidates' amazing robotic creations proudly on show (top grades the norm).

Relaxed pupils clearly weren't feeling the strain. Big benefit – plenty of time for non-examined goodies on offer during the normally exam-dominated GCSE years of fourth and fifth form as electives ensure there's no lull in the pace of learning. Result is sense of open house, with teachers welcoming followers in and out of lesson time, subject loyalties very keenly felt and endearingly expressed. 'It's my third home,' said year 9 enthusiast of computing. 'Music's my second.'

Games, options, the arts: Something for everyone, even down to flourishing forensic club (DNA testing one of covetable skills covered) with music, drama and sport taking joint curtain call in neatly blended annual summer festival featuring show-stopping goodies like fashion catwalk, school v MCC match and assorted productions and concerts.

Extracurricular, indeed, is 'the heartbeat of the school,' says head (who should know, what with taking games lessons on a Wednesday afternoon and being brains of the enterprise). DofE, CCF and many, many trips – 'more than we need,' thought one parent (but in a good way). Clubs and activities get a brochure of their own.

Sport big but not bloated (offers 'the opportunity to play both winter sports simultaneously' – now that's what we call co-ordination), and gets unusually modest showing in school literature. Success, though substantial (fourth form rugby team stuffed with county players) isn't a front, back and middle pages splash.

The talented are well catered for, now girls too (their sixth form rugby team 'popular,' reckon pupils), as well as enthusiastic triers. 'My son had a fixture practically every Saturday, daughter hardly at all,' said parent – now approaching equality for both. Particularly strong in athletics (dogged too – one national biathlon finalist swam and ran in below zero temperatures) as well as cricket (impressive wins against strong schools).

On site facilities stretch not just to sports hall but very snazzy swimming pool (open to parents every Sunday). Focus for games is 32-acre site (stonking but chilly, 'about four degrees colder than everywhere else,' thought staff member'), just 'five to 10' minutes away (15 in rush hour – we tried it) and worth a Saturday visit for the bacon butties alone.

Arts, performing and visual, cast equally long shadow. Supercharged head of drama reaches across age and interest range. Pulsating productions including puppet play, Animal Farm and A Winter's Tale complete with revolving clock – 'bonkers but really good,' thought pupil. Breathtaking in both scope and ambition, with talented individuals scoring places in national youth ensembles of every type, including largely undergraduate-level festival.

With strong singing (many prep choristers move up to senior school), you'd expect super music and you get it. 'Jaw-dropping,' said parent. Around 50 per cent have individual music lessons, some reaching diploma standard. Once a year giant orchestra (participants numerous rather than Goliath-proportioned) scoops up local junior school performers. Normal sized version for daily use plus concert band, intermediate versions too, for those en route to grade greatness but not there yet. Add free theory/aural classes, five choirs, most audition-free, one open to staff and parents, new house music competition and evening soirées in head's garden, and it's a wonder the director of music isn't fraying at the edges. 'Music is so relaxing,' he says, however, smilingly picking way round percussion break-out sessions in attractive (and tactically soundproofed) building.

Background and atmosphere: Despite 17th century foundations, it's the 19th century that dominates, with up to the minute additions nicely accommodated (delivered via smart new Ballance building with change in floor covering only hint to seamless welding to existing block). New £8m learning and resource centre provides (inter alia) a library and sixth form centre surrounded by landscaped gardens.

Close to centre of Reigate, market town made good thanks to commuter-friendly train connections (and very slow level crossing). Canny land acquisition almost allows stroll into town to be accomplished entirely on school land. School has personable, unintimidating, family-centric feel. Its two sites are mere yards apart.

Atmosphere nicely inclusive, and not just for pupils – support and academic teachers, who share common room, all muck in, clearly feeling both wanted and involved. They include head of IT, former City type, running lunchtime talk on morality of banking, and head of catering heavily involved in ICT. Until recently, 'was nice but a bit sleepy,' thought school insider. 'Not any more – there's something new happening every week.'

Has announced it will open five co-ed, all through boarding schools in China for Chinese children, in conjunction with the Kaiyuan Education Fund. The aim is to promote character development as well as academic success and to use part of the income to fund bursaries in the UK.

Pastoral care, well-being and discipline: Pupil happiness and pastoral care is the priority and carries all before it, says head. Get it right and you 'can light the touch paper of success in all other areas of their life.' Parents confirm school's fleet-footedness in troubleshooting and what mother described as 'open door feeling' to problems. One girl's friendship issues reported to teacher who 'sorted it' effectively. 'Unique' staff lend an ear with problems, with form tutors (who move up with pupils) as well as sixth form mentors and listening service run by chaplaincy.

Poor behaviour a minority interest, serious problems almost unknown, reckoned pupils we talked to. Detentions 'for cheekiness' and late work, rewards via on-line credit system.

Pupils and parents: Mixes 'indigenous Surrey with incomers,' said local. Lots from south west London. Some grew up here, went off to work and then came back, said local estate agent. 'I know lots of families.' As to children? 'A credit to the town,' he reckoned. Most famous old boy is David Walliams, who was recently doing a spot of filming at the school. Other alumni include Trevor Kavanagh, Keir Starmer, Susan Gritton and Ray Mears.

Entrance: For the right candidate, computer doesn't invariably say no, even out of season. 'Come and talk to me,' says head. Entrance isn't 'just about testing and measuring,' he adds. Teacher feedback and reports count too. He's after children 'who will make the world a better place,'. Choristers, though welcome, subject to same criteria as the rest. Now pre-tests for 13+ entry in year 6 (maths, English and reasoning).

For sixth form, grade 7s at GCSE in subjects to be studied at A level and an overall tally of at least four 7s, four 6s and no grade lower than a 5. Some parents worried that entry requirements were being toughened up but school again works on case-by-case basis resulting in 'a number without the full requirement coming back,' says head. 'I see any individual leaving because they are without the grades or even grades close enough as really sad' – and where possible, 'will waive the requirements'. If it isn't possible, 'they are a very, very small minority.'

Also notably brilliant at resolving year 12 nightmares. Head 'hugely supportive' when things go wrong, agreed parents and pupils, moving mountains to keep pupils at the school, sometimes repeating year or dropping a subject.

Exit: Some 80 per cent stay on to the sixth form. Eleven to Oxbridge in 2018 plus seven medics. Highly rated for quality of HE destinations by Sutton Trust which placed school in top two per cent of all UK co-eds – Durham, Bath, Loughborough, Exeter, Nottingham and Edinburgh most popular destinations currently, with one off to the US in 2018. Saturday morning help sessions for leavers needing help with deferred entry post A level a real boon.

Money matters: A scholarship programme (about 150 awards across the school), with awards of 30 per cent, potentially 'significantly more' at head's discretion. Also head's scholarship – for children bringing a je ne sais quoi activity or interest which offers 'value to the school community – scholars are expected to give back.' And, a nice touch, all those with straight A*/9-8s at GCSE automatically get £1,000 off the sixth form fees (parent to child bribe chats, you'd imagine, are rife as a result).

Remarks: Hothouse ethos not on the agenda but, given the head's success at Pate's, where similar approach had transformational approach on results, we'd predict similar marvels here. Definitely one to watch.

Reigate St Mary's School

Linked with Reigate Grammar School

Chart Lane, Reigate, Surrey RH2 7RN

Ages 3–11 **Pupils** 344

Fees: £12,000 – £14,850 pa

01737 244880
www.reigatestmarys.org

Head: Since 2005, Marcus Culverwell (40s). Previously deputy head (joined school in 2003). Before that, head of science, then director of studies, then deputy head at Lancing College Junior. A local boy, he was educated first at Caterham, then Archbishop Tenison's sixth form after squeeze on family finances. Sporty, science-y and spiritual. 'Very Christian,' says a parent.

Teenage years dominated by dreams of joining Aviation Mission Fellowship – dashed when failed final stage of commercial pilot training. Studied aeronautical engineering at Hertford followed by MA at Brunel. With dearth of jobs in industry, teaching was originally intended as stopgap career but rapidly became something far more. He realised that he wanted to work with younger children when, while combining teacher training with spell on staff at Cardiff FE college, he was unable to comfort weeping student encountered in corridor.

Personable, child-friendly (has three of his own, two at the senior school, one here) and pupils rush to talk to him, clearly confident of sympathetic hearing. No wonder, given approach to playground duties (takes guitar and sings – though 'not a musician') as well as breaking out into the occasional assembly rap. Keeps staff on their toes and though 'we never sit still', potentially exhausting pace is tempered with generous dollops of non-teaching time to regroup for the next big think. It's a work in progress that started with Mr Culverwell's first inspection, five weeks into the job, when he produced rationale of planned curriculum development, now on overhaul number three, each marked by progressively closer ties to senior school.

Desire to make a difference is manifest – has recently completed book on educating children for social responsibility. A committed eco school with Green Flag status. The school embraces a growth mind-set ethos which promotes resilience amongst the children and a desire to seek new challenges in an atmosphere where hard work and determination to succeed are rewarded. The aim is that the children develop 'can do' attitudes and the ability to bounce back from failure enabling them to reach ever-higher levels of achievement. Parents acknowledge value of approach but aren't always receptive to newsletter homilies exhorting them to 'down tools and cuddle the children – hard when you're trying to pay the school fees,' said one.

Academic robe on one side of study, Captain Considerate outfit (worn by pupils to deliver hi-tech homilies on behaviour) on the other sums up approach – relaxed gravitas. Ultimately perception is that it's Mr Fenton down at the big school who rules the roost and makes the big decisions. Thumbs up, however, for being well intentioned – and, overall, 'a nice man.'

Entrance: Non-selective at 3 – first come first served and increasingly over-booked, almost reaching London frenzy levels (including occasional pre-pregnant enquiries). Sympathetic attitude to SEN, permeating from knowledgeable head and increasing resources – SENCo, until recently an add-on responsibility for class teacher, now a separate post. Covers the works, including EBSD, ASD, ADHD, severe dyslexia and those with physical disabilities – rated 'brilliant' by senior school specialist on recent visit.

Gets our vote for recently revised curriculum and brilliantly humane transitions between stages. 'Our ethos is that happy children learn,' says nursery manager. One and 2-year-olds have regular playdates with parents, getting to know big, bright nursery up to two years before they start.

Atmosphere 'moves from buzzing to calm classroom by end of reception so ready for change in pace in year 1,' says staff member. Class sizes rise from maximum 15 in reception and below to maximum 22 in years 1-6.

Choristers (now girls and boys), original reason for school's foundation, have voice trials at 6 or 7 and, if successful, become probationers.

Exit: Vast majority – some 80 per cent – to senior school (11 with scholarships in 2018). Other destinations include Dunottar, Ardingly and Worth. Parental anxiety following decision to offer firm places to many in year 5 considerable but misplaced, thinks school, as around three-quarters will end up going on to the senior school while those without guarantee can still sit the exam in year 6 and take chances with other outsiders. Much better this way as avoids previous misery of sitting and failing entrance exam, says school, when children can be guided to a better place instead. Some playground gossip means pupils aren't as blissfully unaware as parents would want and 'if you're just one of a handful not to go through to the senior school it can be hard on the individual,' thought one.

Remarks: Originally founded as choir school by Godfrey Searle, canny chartered stockbroker and musician who calculated (accurately) that selling off small area to council for municipal bowls green would avert desire to run bypass through grounds.

Unusually, a cathedral choir without portfolio, though makes up for it with regular appearances at Chichester and occasional visits to St Paul's, tradition starting in the Second World War when regular choir was evacuated. Commercially in demand, too, for Disney amongst others. Choristers' robes line corridor, atmospheric practice room, low-tech shelves bursting with music-stuffed folders, fruit and biscuits laid out for after-school rehearsal – a bit like a time capsule (laptop apologetically to one side the only modern note).

Acquisition by senior school in 2005 was a relative no-brainer, once established that decline in pupil numbers was reversible. Now healthy enough to justify recent £4.5 million investment on impressive glass and brick main teaching block for years 1 to 3, which rears up behind original building, partially concealed on far side by man-made hill, demanded by planners to avoid upsetting locals' sensibilities and incorporating splendiferous downstairs sports hall. Years 4 to 6 are quartered in less plush but perfectly acceptable older-style block. Bright kindergarten (corridor a cheerful clutter of wellies) taking up the ground floor.

Hard-surfaced games area close to school. Attractive, undulating grounds beyond, partially wooded (lots of den building in warmer months) and with beautifully planted memorial garden where head boy and girl lay wreaths in front of school. Assorted pitches (four football, two multi-surface) plus athletics track and cricket pavilion are attractively set in the greenery, all well used and supplemented with additional sessions at senior school and trips to playing fields a short coach ride away.

Though there's some parental moaning if children don't make top teams, school makes efforts to secure fixtures for Bs and Cs as well 'so there are games for all.' Sport broadly split along trad gender lines, but it's permeable – current year 5 rugby and football star player is a girl (while zumba and gymnastics clubs also attract small numbers of boys).

Staff work hard, lessons supported by what head describes as 'phenomenal' planning. All expected to run a popular club two terms in three (free unless run by outside experts). Start in modest way from year 1 (reception parents clamour for share but 'they've had a busy day and need to go home,' thinks head). Really gets going in year 3 with waiting lists 'for everything' and impressively wide ranging, from a thriving Lego League team who compete at national level, to a popular Outside Club making good use of the school grounds. Good range of popular trips, too, from bushcraft – a current fave rave – to even more rugged Snowdonia and Mont Blanc.

Ever closer links with senior school sees growing number of specialist teachers (maths the most recent addition, as well as music, games, art, IT) making short walk over. Curriculum consistency between two schools means not just singing from same song sheet but with barber shop harmonies, too.

Academic focus on continuous assessment is seen as quite intense by parents – though doesn't necessarily permeate through to children – with charismatic staff implementing sensible rewards system (golden time is king) that helps to produce confident, courteous children. 'I hope you have a lovely afternoon,' was heard from one 6-year-old. Smart too – dress code is nostalgic (caps and trad hats for younger pupils, grime-management grey shirts for boys).

Innovative language teaching keeps French as the big one with Spanish and German each taught for a term in year 6. Though maths only subject with formal sets, year 1 has informal streaming, while differentiation is 'part and parcel of lessons' aided by excellent staffing ratios – younger children have full time TA as well as teacher. Classes notably calm though not at expense of fun, reception children listening, rapt, to end of day story, year 1 pupils falling over themselves to show delights of science lessons – leaves 'that were crispy and brown if didn't have enough water,' flowers with ink-dyed petals. Favourite subject? 'It is now,' said one.

Big on purposeful technology – Wifi up and running, iPads for all children in years 4 to 6, 'a tool we use everywhere,' says head; deliberate mix of Macs and PCs 'so children bilingual' and Kodu so widely used that 'should be official foreign language.'

Now offers wrap-round care from 7.30am-6pm.

Lots of pride in past and at least one eye on the future. Parents of the vast majority of RSM pupils (not just the dead certs) will find passage to senior school eased. For a small number aim is managed and failure-free exit elsewhere. Being a pupil here 'makes it much easier to get to the grammar school, not for the few but, in the future, for almost every St Mary's child,' says school. Means you know what you're buying into. 'You have to live with it or move on,' says parent.

The Rochester Grammar School

Maidstone Road, Rochester, Kent ME1 3BY

Ages 11–18 **Pupils** 1,213 **Sixth form** 333 (30 or so boys)

01634 843049
www.rochestergrammar.org.uk/

Head of school: Since June 2017, Clare Brinklow, previously assistant principal here. History degree and masters in professional practice from Kent; after a year teaching history at Bordon Grammar School Trust she joined Rochester Grammar in 2009 to teach history, sociology and politics, rising to assistant director of sixth form and then assistant principal.

Executive principal is Mr G Bassan BA NPQH. CEO is Mr S Gardener.

Academic matters: In 2018, a quarter of GCSEs were A*/9-8. At A level, nearly three-quarters of grades were A* to B, and IB students averaged 37 points. The school has specialist status for maths, ICT and music; history, English and science are all strong departments. Modern foreign languages haven't matched up so new language teaching methods introduced. Students in years 7 and 8 learn languages through drama workshops and role play with no written work, with the aim to build their vocabulary and confidence before moving to the next level. 'The brain is wired to learn languages orally first. The worst that will happen is that students will get Bs, but they will be able to order sandwiches confidently and catch a train using that language. Language teaching hasn't worked for so long. We have watched children dumbstruck in France and Germany, asking "do you speak English?" in English. If we see a problem we get to the bottom of it and we're prepared to take a bold step to make a difference.' The school also offers Latin, which unusually is oversubscribed. One parent explained why her daughter loves it: 'They also cover the civilisation, history and literature. It's a good option if you're not a good linguist'.

As we walk the corridors there's a hubbub coming from all the classrooms. Pupils are animated, some half on their feet. Tables aren't arranged in serried ranks, but in blocks or U-shapes and there's much collaborative work and discussion going on. 'There's lots of guided discovery. We are told a limited amount, and we are supposed to find out the rest, we're not spoon-fed', say the girls. Thinking and memory skills are big buzzwords in the school, or, as the students explained to us, 'We focus on how to learn, not just what to learn'. They all know what type of learner they are, and how they work best. 'I'm a logical thinker', said one. 'I can't understand diagrams', said another, 'so the teacher gives me an explanation in words'.

Sixth formers speak of an individuality in teaching styles that makes lessons lively and interesting. 'History and politics are fantastic, the grades are consistently amazing and the teacher has such a passion for the subject he turns bright red when we're having a debate', said one. Another, who transferred from a different school, said the gap in expectations between the two is huge. 'It's very demanding; the school expects you to be on top of your game'.

No teaching slackness tolerated. 'If a member of staff, after appropriate support, is unable to demonstrate an ability to improve, they move on. It's the same with supply teachers covering sickness absence: we might have two or three supply teachers in quick succession which concerns parents, but it's important to get the right one.' You can't argue with the success of this strategy.

One parent called the school 'a jewel in Rochester'. But the other side of the coin is that the pace is fast and your daughter will have to be prepared to work hard. The school follows a two year compressed KS3 to enable some accelerated students to sit English, maths and science GCSEs in year 10. One parent related that when her child took three GCSEs in year 9, 'She got three As which she wasn't happy with, so she retook them to get A*s'. The pace and quantity of work can impact on family life too, as one parent explained: 'Some parents find it quite hard to accept the amount of work their child has got to do'. Her daughter worked a couple of hours a night in year 7/8, and all evening in year 9, but willingly, she said. The school expects around 14 hours of homework per week to be completed in the sixth form, but many students go beyond this of their own volition. Parents report one or two girls who have left because this environment didn't suit them. But they stress that children are not left to flounder. 'There are lots of support clubs, they don't just write them off,' said one.

Speaking to sixth formers, it's apparent that the vast majority develop a self-belief that they are capable of anything, rather than being flattened by the expectations. 'It does get to the stage that you think a B is not good enough. But that's how life is', one told us. 'When I got a B in a mock I was distraught, I didn't deserve a B. Then I think, if they're getting A, why can't I? If she can do it, I can, and I ask other students how they are doing it.' Another girl told us, 'I don't want to go to Cambridge, but I know that if I did, the school would enable me to get there.'

Games, options, the arts: Lack of green fields equals lack of serious sporting provision. Football and athletics are the school's main areas of competitive success. An old girl made the GB synchronised swimming squad, another's an international skier.

The school has the largest girls' DofE centre in the country and opportunities include a three week trek in China. Takes part in the Comenius project, promoting European culture. Individual trips encouraged to develop the girls' personal interests and career intentions. One girl is going to the student UN in Geneva, with the school matching her fundraising, another has been to CERN for an extended project.

'Join the choir, see the world', they say – anyone can be in the choir, which has taken them to the Vatican City and the USA. Music concerts on a termly basis, international musicians brought in to perform in the school's Thorndike Arts Centre. Two governors' places for musicians – students get bursaries to spend on music lessons, in return they give back to the whole school by running extracurricular activities – one girl runs two choirs, another a quartet.

Language exchanges to France, Germany, and Spain. 'We believe in exchanges and immersion, spending a week with a host family, we do not believe in day trips.'

Background and atmosphere: No dreaming spires, it's a functional building, but it's modern and in a good state of repair by the standards of state grammars. 'A bit soulless,' said a parent.

The school moved to this new building in 1990, having opened in 1888 with a then progressive aim to educate young ladies. Became an 'academy of excellence' in 2011. The school is a combined mathematics/ICT and music specialist school, a Thinking Foundation school, and the first 'Memory' school accredited by Exeter University – teaching students how to learn and memorise is a priority.

It's a powerhouse for women. Houses are named after an eclectic group of women such as Jane Tomlinson, Eva Cassidy, Ella Fitzgerald and Hildegard (of Bingen). Corridors are lined with posters detailing the most powerful women in the UK today, as well as the illustrations of ex-pupil Evelyn Dunbar, held up as a beacon for forging her way into the entirely male dominated theatre of war when she became the only female commissioned war artist during World War II.

Work is under way on developing an old girls' network. 'In public schools the former students associations can be very powerful; we want to give our students that same advantage. There are still some industries where it matters who you know, and we would like our young ladies to look after each other.' Its young alumni group, now 100 strong and growing, brings back former pupils to help current students see themselves five years down the line, and to give them contacts to go to for advice.

Everything reinforces a message to be the best, which concerned one parent, who said: 'One thing I didn't like when we looked around, there were so many lovely displays and all the work was excellent; other schools had things up which weren't quite as good, but where people had done their best. I wondered, if you weren't quite up there, how would you feel?'

R

Pastoral care, well-being and discipline: Discipline? There's quite a pause before the sixth formers respond, 'People don't really go out of line here'. It usually only comes into play for uniform infringements, for which the girls have to do community service, helping out the teachers.

Pastoral care thrives on teachers knowing their pupils very well indeed. Girls have the same head of house and the same form tutor for six years, which means problems are spotted and interventions organised early. There are vertical form groups, with years 7 to 12 mixed together, and family groups of five or six within each form. Younger girls like this because they can ask senior students for help with their homework, or advice on which options to choose, and it means they don't find the big girls so intimidating. All new girls are mentored by a girl a year older. For year 13 they are put in subject specialism forms – those headed for medicine in one, musicians in another, for example.

Parents speak highly of the school's rapid identification of and solutions for any learning difficulties. One recalled: 'Soon after she started the school, her CAT tests showed a big discrepancy. The school arranged further testing and we found she was dyslexic with processing difficulties. I was astonished because this had never been suspected before. They've given her a range of strategies to help her cope, and it's not holding her back in any way.' School is 'very proud of the special educational needs provision at this school; we find a lot of students have SEN which wasn't identified before'.

To deal with the pressures they are under, the school has introduced a Sumo initiative, to develop 'bounce-back ability'. 'It's about developing their resilience to take the knocks when they occur'. It takes students through a series of responses, such as: How can I change this situation? What can I learn from it? Is there anything positive about it? Am I responding appropriately? and how important will this be in six months' time?

Pupils and parents: No question about the added value here. From a school community where just 25 per cent of parents are graduates, it delivers one in three pupils to a top 10 university.

The pupil body is a true social mix. Some parents are not working and are in difficult circumstances, some are doctors and lawyers. Some children live in public housing, around 10 per cent were privately educated at primary school. One in 10 pupils are from non-white backgrounds. What they have in common, say pupils, is that, 'everyone really wants to do well'.

The pupils feel it's an extremely supportive community. 'There isn't a person who won't help you', said one. Another said she has experienced 'overwhelming kindness' from fellow students. A third needed to raise funds for a work experience placement at the United Nations and was humbled that with fellow pupils' help, she managed this in one week.

Entrance: There's no catchment – entry is entirely based on scores in the local 11+, the Medway test. The pass mark for this fluctuates around 509 and last year students needed 514 or higher for a place at Rochester Grammar. There are two music scholarships and five places are held for appeals. 'Some of our greatest successes didn't pass the test.'

Around 30-40 places become available in the sixth form, when entry also opens up to boys. Some 12-18 boys join the sixth form each year as the school achieves better results than any other in the area. Minimum entry requirements are 5+ 9-4 grades at GCSE, with grade 6s in all courses to be studied at A level or IB except maths and the sciences, which require a grade 7.

Exit: Around 80 to 90 per cent stay on into the sixth form when they can opt to take either A levels or the IB. There's a tailored programme for students wishing to apply for Oxbridge or medical school. Two to Oxbridge in 2018 and five medics/dentists. All are expected to go on to university and the school does a great deal of work on guiding pupils' choices; many of them will be the first in their family to take a degree. A virtual university week is held in year 12, when pupils are taught in university format and given advice on UCAS applications and accessing bursaries.

Pupils looking at wackier courses are likely to be discouraged. 'We engage in a lot of research with the students, looking at where that course is likely to take them, and the value of investing in their education. A student might say "I want to do X course at Y university, I like the tutor, and the facilities are really nice." We unpick that. Where do people from that course go to post-university? What percentage gets full-time employment at a certain level of money? We make them understand, it's not just the next three years, make the wrong choice now and you play catch up for the rest of your life.'

The result is that nearly one-third of pupils go to a top 10 university, one-half to a top 20, and 80 per cent to a top 40.

Remarks: The poise, focus and articulacy of sixth formers here is incredible – it's like talking to young graduate professionals rather than a bunch of schoolgirls. So is their work ethic. 'I want to stay in and study on Friday nights, I'm not forced to,' said one, as the others nodded in agreement. The school is determined that the girls will make the best use of their intelligence and take their rightful place at the high table of professional life. You'll be hard pressed to find a school more likely to steer your daughter on to great things. But you need to be sure she'll cope with the pressure.

Rochester Independent College

Star Hill, Rochester, Kent ME1 1XF

Ages 11–19 **Pupils** 308 **Sixth form** 215 **Boarders** 80 full, 10 weekly (from 16 years)

Fees: Day £12,600 – £18,900; Boarding + £12,000 – £13,500 pa; International Non EEA Boarding £33,000 – £37,800 pa

01634 828115
www.rochester-college.org

Principal: Alistair Brownlow MA (St Andrews) MPhil (Glasgow) in English, joined as a new graduate in 1997. He's a great communicator, bouncing with enthusiasm like Tigger, and expressing the school's beliefs and methods with an articulacy which backs up his reputation as an ace English teacher.

Academic matters: There's no uniform or dress code, and the teachers are just as likely as pupils to be wearing a hoody. Everyone goes by their first name. So far so hippy – until you walk around the building during lessons. Hush has descended, and opening a classroom door reveals silent pupils, and desks in rows. Alistair says: 'People try to place us in the progressive/alternative mould, but we're not. It's common sense; small classes, good teaching, and an informal but ordered and respectful atmosphere.'

The next surprise comes in the teaching methods. 'We teach-test-teach-test,' says Alistair. The idea that testing thwarts children gets short shrift here. 'A lot of schools don't do enough regular testing. At A level we do a test every week in each subject. If we're going to put something right we need a rigorous diagnosis of what is wrong,' Alistair says. There's no objection to this degree of testing from pupils – in fact the students seem to welcome it. 'Testing means you can't get delusions, you really know where you are at any point,' said one. Another, who was told by her grammar school that she needed to 'lower her sights', said: 'The teaching style is completely different, we are tested all the time and my grades have gone up consistently.'

There is a firm concentration on exam technique, but still the school isn't seen as an exam factory. One sixth form pupil said: 'The focus is on exams, but it is still enriching. We get a two hour lesson for everything which means the teachers can drift off topic which helps a lot with general knowledge and essay subjects.' Teachers are 'very passionate about their subjects,' say parents, and another pupil, comparing the teaching to that at his former grammar school, said: 'The teaching is of a better quality and the teachers know their subject to a greater depth.' And a pupil at the lower end of the school said: 'You don't get to the end of one lesson without doing something fun.'

Many students transfer here after poor progress elsewhere and the effect can be dramatic. One said, 'In my first two weeks here I learned more than I had in the whole previous year.'

There are three pathways through the sixth form, mainly set in different teaching groups. There are those doing a two year A level course through the school; students who have transferred here for year 13 after a disappointing year 12; and those who have done two years elsewhere and are doing retakes. The A level programme is flexible with no option blocks, and students can do speed courses in a new subject to complement retakes. Results for 2018 A levels show 29 per cent of entries achieving A*/A and 63 per cent A*-B. Maths is the biggest A level subject. English literature and film studies are also strong departments, both having received Good Schools Guide awards in recent years.

At GCSE, biology, chemistry and physics are taught at IGCSE level for those aiming to study sciences at A level, and students also take the IGCSE in English and English literature. Languages on offer include German, French and Spanish, but it is not compulsory to take a language. Pupils can also take subjects such as astronomy, film studies and photography at GCSE. In 2018, 19 per cent of GCSEs were A*-A/9-7 and 38 per cent were A*-B/9-6.

Parents especially appreciate the efforts made to ensure each pupil gains the best possible grade. One said: 'There are a lot of extra lessons before exams, in the holidays and so on. They will do as much as they can if they think you can improve your grade.'

Another praised the fact that they don't charge for extra tuition in the evenings and holidays, adding: 'I was concerned about my son's maths and suggested getting him some tuition. They said it was their responsibility, and I should not be looking for tutors. They did some extra work with him and he got an A, so I was ecstatic.'

Now offers an apprenticeship course in boatbuilding, enabling students to gain City and Guilds qualifications up to NVQ level 3.

Games, options, the arts: Sport is growing, but the school doesn't have the infrastructure to provide serious provision. There's a newly created rugby team for year 11 to 13s, which uses the facilities of a local rugby club and is coached by a player from England's women's team. It also supports those playing at higher levels – one sixth former trained with a London football club, and the school enabled him to fit lessons around his sporting commitments. Another sixth former hoped to compete as a sprinter in the next Paralympics. But as one student points out, it is not the type of school which tends to attract the sporty, and so PE provision tends to be more activity based, like ice skating, sailing, self-defence and climbing.

Lower down the school the students play in mixed teams, so boys say games have to be less rough.

It would be hard to find better provision for an artist. GCSEs are offered in six disciplines – fine art, graphics, photography, textiles, ceramics and 3D. Some students take three of these to A level, which enables them to bypass a foundation year. There is terrific work on display. Two students have won places on the prestigious fine art degree course at UCL's The Slade School. Dominik Klimowski, former BBC online picture editor, teaches photography, and local artist Billy Childish is a visiting lecturer.

There's a rich cultural programme – a drama theatre hosts visiting theatre companies and art shows, and the school's on-site cinema regularly hosts the National Schools' Film week.

Boarding: Boarding is only available to students of 16+. Virtually all students have single rooms. Some have a very small 'pod' ensuite, otherwise it's shared bathrooms. Furnishings are basic but the Georgian high ceilings and big windows add light and space, and all rooms have a phone and internet point. There's a big common room with a pool table and comfy chairs, and a study for quiet work.

Currently some 40 per cent of boarders are from the UK, 11 per cent from Europe, and the remainder from countries including Canada, USA, Thailand, China, Russia, Nigeria and South Africa.

Background and atmosphere: It started as an A level college in 1984, and extended to take pupils from year 7 in 2007. Bought by Dukes Education in 2016.

The campus is as unique as the school. It started as one terraced house, but as the school expanded, it gradually bought up 13 properties in adjoining roads, including a Georgian terrace which houses the boarding accommodation. What would once have been the back gardens to these houses now form the grounds with ancient apple trees and wild garden areas, paths to secret nooks and crannies, a viewing platform to climb – and an oversized garden shed where founder Brian (Pain) likes to hold his maths classes. Students work on garden projects such as the allotment as part of their DofE award, and the gardens have won a Kent Wildlife Trust Gold Award.

Mid-career, Brian took time out of teaching to become an architect, and the campus reflects this interest. The theatre in the grounds is known as the Womble building – the theatre space is underground, whilst over the top there's an outdoor seating area which can be used as an open-air auditorium.

An igloo-like structure in the garden is used as an outdoor classroom, shelter, and quiet space. Intended to inspire and motivate, it has a central roof opening for cloud watching.

When we visited the school was awaiting delivery of some steel sculptural musical gates – an art installation created by Henry Dagg, who plays with Icelandic pop star Bjork, and has transformed his garden fence into a glockenspiel. You will be able to play three octaves on these gates, sufficient to pass your music A level, according to Brian. Reflecting on the £100,000 price tag of these gates, Brian says, 'I'm committed to culture'.

Pastoral care, well-being and discipline: A level students have one-to-one meetings with a personal tutor every couple of weeks, more frequently if they wish, and pupils lower down the school have individual meetings every half term.

Parents receive formal reports once a month, which are 'meaningful, not full of euphemisms, and not from a software package'. Younger pupils have a parents' evening, but in the sixth form tutors deal directly with the students as young adults, and reports only go home once students have seen them first. 'We promise there will be no surprises through that feedback,' says Alistair.

R

A number of the pupils have been labelled as bad apples or having limited prospects in previous settings, but have quickly turned things around at the college, where they are free from discipline based on minutiae. One such pupil, previously at a girls' independent, said: 'I was constantly getting picked on by teachers and getting detentions for stupid things, like going to the toilet'.

They are strict about homework and behaviour, but removing petty rules means the rapport between pupils and teachers is much better. Or, as one pupil put it, 'The only thing to rebel against here is education itself'.

Other pupils have come from grammars where they felt under too much pressure, or from large schools where they felt overwhelmed, and all say they are learning better and enjoying school more here. 'I worried a lot at my old school, here it's a better environment,' said one. 'At my old school if you improved, they didn't notice,' said another.

Parents all speak highly of the pastoral care, and the growth in confidence they have witnessed in their children. One has three children at the school and she said: 'They are all very different but they are spot on about all of their weaknesses and strengths.'

Pupils and parents: Local pupils form 70 per cent of the cohort and come from a wide catchment – there are minibuses from towns including Tonbridge, Tunbridge Wells, Maidstone, Ashford and Sevenoaks, and the train station opposite brings pupils from Bromley and London. A further 15 per cent come from elsewhere in the UK, and 15 per cent from overseas, including Thai government scholars (who tend to be very high performers, often ending up at Oxbridge).

Numbers lower down the school are small. It starts with around 10 pupils in year 7, who have deliberately opted for a small and different type of school. These are added to over the years, generally by pupils who have been disaffected or haven't thrived in other schools, to numbers in the mid-20s for GCSE years. By sixth form it grows to 50 in year 12, and 130 in year 13/14. This is something to consider in the younger year groups, especially as currently two girls are each the only girl in their years. The flipside is it makes for more natural relationships between the boys and girls and less of the gender division that you see in big schools – they are clearly relaxed in each other's company. None of the pupils or parents we spoke to saw the small year groups as a problem – there's much more mixing between years, and pupils keep up with other friends in their neighbourhood – and many see this as a plus.

The students are a strikingly nice bunch. It's a place for individuals, and there's a lovely air of tolerance and warmth between the pupils – many of whom seem relieved to have found a home among other square pegs. 'They look after each other, and if someone does well they are pleased about this,' said a parent. Those whose strengths lie outside the traditionally alpha areas of academic or sporting have their own kudos. 'There is a lot more respect for art and creativity,' said one pupil.

Students say it is not competitive, and that there's a huge range in academic ability and ambition. 'If you work your hardest and get an E that's fine,' said one. 'Stronger people help the weaker people; no-one's struggling because everyone helps each other,' said another.

Parents love the lack of school gate competitiveness: 'That playground talk, everyone wanting their child to be in the top set, you don't have that here,' said one relieved mother.

About 50 per cent of pupils have been previously in the independent sector, but a lot of pupils come from families with no tradition of private education.

Entrance: It's non-selective in that there's no entrance exam for children joining at 11 or 13, and there's no minimum GCSE grade requirements for sixth form entry. But every prospective student is interviewed, and the principals say they do turn some away.

Direct entry into any year group at any point in the academic year is possible, and places can be secured in the short gap between exam results and the start of a new term. Around 60 students join each year, either to retake their A levels having completed two years of A levels elsewhere, or directly into year 13 after disappointing results in year 12 elsewhere.

Exit: Around half leave after GCSEs, and many join the sixth form. The courses students go on to reflect the broad range of abilities and interests catered for: some go on to read law, maths, medicine or classics; others have taken up courses in animal behaviour, film studies, marketing, photography or midwifery. One to Cambridge and two medics in 2018; Exeter, Cardiff, Sussex, Newcastle and Essex popular destinations.

Money matters: Around £100,000 per year goes into means-tested bursaries, which are awarded not on academic ability, but 'if we think they'll make a good contribution'. Scholarships include the Ralph Steadman Art Scholarship, which offers a two year full scholarship for A levels.

The school has a policy to keep extras to the minimum – music lessons, buses and exam fees are extra, but extracurricular trips are kept deliberately modest. 'We don't take for granted that parents have bottomless pits of money,' says Alistair.

Remarks: This won't be one that sits on your shortlist and you can't make up your mind about. You'll either love or hate this place. Your money won't buy the trappings of a public school – no mahogany-rich headmaster's study, certainly no suave head in a handmade suit. No pupils with collars and lips firmly buttoned. No PTA committees or fundraising balls. For some that will be a blessed relief.

You'll get that warm buzz in your heart when you recognise your kid in the personalities here – or not. That might be one of several types we saw – the quirky one, condemned to be picked on in an average school; the fiercely intelligent, who has rubbed teachers up the wrong way by being too smart for his own good in other settings; the kid whose education got derailed by too much focus on petty rules and discipline.

It won't suit sporting jocks – facilities are meagre, and there are rarely enough pupils of the right age and inclination to make a team.

But it's a great option for the cash-strapped; many parents with only enough gold in the pot to fund a couple of years in the independent sector buy in for the last year of GCSEs, for the A level course, or for retakes. And it's a sound investment – most improve considerably on expectations at their previous school.

Roedean Moira House

    223

Upper Carlisle Road, Eastbourne, East Sussex BN20 7TE

Ages 1–18 **Pupils** 227 **Sixth form** 34 **Boarders** 58 full, 1 weekly (from year 5)

Fees: Day £9,345 – £18060; Boarding £21,915 – £33,420 pa

01323 644144
www.moirahouse.co.uk

Principal: Since July 2018, Andrew Wood (BA, biology, Durham). Formerly deputy head at Newington college prep in Sydney, director of studies at Bede's prep and faculty lead of science at Roedean. A resident of Eastbourne, Mr Wood previously cycled every day to Brighton; girls are fascinated that he's super fit, said a parent, who described him as 'engaging, willing to listen and takes points on board'.

When Moira House joined the Roedean Group of schools in September 2017, Elodie Vallantine – previously acting principal – took up the position of head of school. Oliver Blond is executive head of the Roedean Group, and parents say he has dealt with the changes well, and given them a lot of confidence.

Academic matters: This school pays scrupulous attention to every pupil: 'they know each girl's capabilities', said a parent, another saying that 'you feel it's only your daughter in the class when you speak to staff'. Class sizes are small (around 10-12); the intention is that the school will grow a little, but there will not be more than 18 in a class.

Solid results for a non-selective school: in 2018, 32 per cent A*/A, 46 per cent A*/B at A level, 52 per cent A*-A/9-7 at GCSE. No pressure for everyone to achieve top grades, a parent saying, 'girls are well supported to do as well as they can do'; a pupil that 'people get the grades they deserve'. Some results were a little erratic prior to Roedean's arrival; there was a period of rapid staff turnover, including the previous principal, but Roedean are confident that results and consistency will improve with their input.

The atmosphere in class is animated in the junior school; a bit more low-key in the senior school, but this seems likely to change, with Roedean inputting both staff and vitality. Indeed transformation is underway: teachers from Roedean are popping over for revision sessions; nine new teachers have been appointed; and the two nearly antique science labs replaced. The principal is keen to have flexible furniture, so rooms can be arranged to encourage collaborative working. Parents are pleased at the prospect of the school raising their game academically, and innovation increasing under new management.

The most popular academic subjects are psychology, philosophy and photography, subjects which also tend to command the best results. Performance in maths is consistently good at both GCSE and A level. A good range of subjects at GCSE, with plenty of languages available: French, Spanish, German, Latin and Mandarin. A smaller range of A levels, but the bonus of very small class sizes: providing there is staff capacity, A level courses will be run with a minimum of two pupils.

Roedean Moira House will also house Roedean International, a one year gateway programme specifically designed for East Asian students to gain the necessary level of fluency in English to access the British curriculum.

Fitting in with their ethos of holistic education, all pupils will be required to complete the Roedean Moira House diploma, with the aim of helping pupils develop a wide portfolio of skills. All the academic elements, including an independent project, are compulsory, and pupils are required to complete at least one element in the other sections, which include community service and life skills.

Pupils are taught in mixed ability classes with differentiated teaching, and are involved from a young age in the junior school in selecting the level of task that will challenge them most, and moving between tasks if they have picked the wrong level. Children with extra needs will usually be assisted in class with extra help from teaching assistants. Those who need more help – generally for dyslexia, dyscalculia or ADHD – can have small group or one-to-one sessions with the SENCo, at no extra charge.

A well stocked library with the sort of atmosphere that makes you want to sit down and read, no doubt largely fostered by the wonderful librarian: 'It brings joy to my heart when I come in the morning, and it's messy! It means it's used'.

Games, options, the arts: An extremely sporty school: there's sport every day, including cricket, football and swimming in the indoor swimming pool, used by all, from nursery upwards. Tennis is a serious undertaking here, and there are not only hard courts, but grass courts too, used by the professionals for practice during the pre-Wimbledon international tournament in Eastbourne; a significant number of senior pupils serve as ballgirls during the tournament, a high point of the year for many.

Performing arts have become a strength in the last few years, and it is extraordinary to watch a child perform a vigorous tap dance, pause to sing (with no apparent shortage of breath), then keep dancing. Pupils from pre-grade 1 through to grade 8 receive

R

excellent results in their Trinity theatre exams, and there's an additional course available in musical theatre. This year's big production is a Midsummer Night's Dream, complete with rock n' roll band and glee club, and there's the less highbrow and decidedly intriguing 'We are going to get a little bit naughty with Matilda'. Choirs range from the a cappella vocal group to all comers cantabile, and there's a proper recording studio, open not just to the elite vocalists but also those who want to record their latest ukulele composition.

Photography is one of the most popular subjects here; pupils learn to communicate ideas and feelings though the lens while learning key skills, and produce some innovative work.

Inspirational teaching of textiles, which lets girls proceed in whatever way their imagination proposes: we saw everything weird and wonderful, from a skirt of balloons, to an embroidered jean jacket to wear with wings of coloured silks, and a strange insect in black tie from a girl who hates things pink and girly.

Every day there are activities scheduled, which include fencing, archery, singing, horse riding and DofE, and there's a new adventure playground.

Boarding: Full, weekly and flexi boarding available, and odd nights possible if there's space. In the midst of a boarding refurbishment when we visited – 'smell the carpets', said our guide ecstatically. It's all new and very swish, and the girls are pleased that it is no longer just clinical white – there's a splash of colour in each room, whether it be a red chair, or green wall. Rooms are generally for two or three students, some of them with gorgeous views out over the sea – and grass courts – both pupils and staff appreciated a good view of Djokovic from the boarding house last summer. There's a kitchen for snacks, toast, fruit and biscuits, and a common room – boarders tend to be older pupils, so this pleases all.

Plenty of trips at weekends, from the usual museums and shopping, to watersports on the Cuckmere. Boarders enjoy weekday evening jollies such as hot chocolate Wednesday and Friday film club.

Background and atmosphere: Parents are attracted to this school for its strong community – 'it's very family orientated, very personal'. One said all her daughters have flourished there, 'it's like joining a doctors' surgery...a joined up feeling'. The community is underpinned by the pyramid house structure, and pupils have an intense allegiance to their house: Merlin, Excalibur, Pegasus and Vulcan. The head girls are known, gallantly, as knights, and it does seem that there is something both of old England and dedication about this school.

For an independent school, it is remarkably free of the anxiety and stress of achievement and constant measure that plague many. A parent described it as a happy relaxed school, where 'if your daughter has something, they will find and nurture it'.

Girls who have been at a co-ed school appreciate the single sex environment – 'boys seem to triumph more', said one; 'I'm more confident here,' said another. Sixth formers assured us that they do mix with boys outside of school, and are not worried about entering a co-ed environment at university.

From the tiny 4 year old girl bubbling over about her day to the unassuming sixth formers, the girls we met here seemed very natural, and answered questions with frank spontaneity. They seem comfortable in their own skins, and without city gloss. Indeed, this was a school with an old fashioned feel, although there are plenty of modern elements, and no attachment to traditions empty of meaning: trousers now an option.

Parents and girls appreciate the advantages of joining the Roedean family, and the head of the Roedean Group is keen to reassure them that they will keep all that is best about Moira House – 'we will not change the nature of the school or its legacy'. Its ethos of promoting strong women ('be what you want to be...be an astronaut,' said one parent) fits well with Roedean. There were a few tears from girls when the Moira House signs came down, but the process has been done well, with both parents and pupils reporting a lot of listening before changes are made.

Pastoral care, well-being and discipline: 'Nothing short of a miracle', said one parent, describing the transformation of his shy daughter to 'outgoing'; she even 'performs on stage'. There's plenty of opportunity to perform, whether it be in a play, or doing a presentation in assembly which, parents feel, 'helps you to believe in yourself'.

Form tutors are on hand to sort out difficulties, a parent confirming, 'if there's a problem, they will do their utmost to sort out as quickly as possible' and, 'there's nothing raised that hasn't been dealt with'. The school nurse doubles as counsellor for more serious problems.

Girls are encouraged to blow the whistle on bullying, and reeled off a list of consequences: isolation, detention, exclusion...'generally it gets sorted', said one; 'friendship issues dealt with so well', said a parent.

Discipline is light touch here – it doesn't seem to need to be more. Pupils generally behave well, and are clear that behaviour out of school as well as in matters, whether you're in uniform or not. If it hurts someone or you, then the actions matter, say pupils.

Pupils are encouraged to care and look out for each other; older pupils have angels and cherubs training, angels being trained to look out for their cherubs, with practice sessions on knotty problems such as self-harm and eating disorders. Younger pupils in the junior school are encouraged to be cool cats, and use their whiskers to sense if something is not right with their peers.

Parents talk a lot about the 'caring, nurturing family' at this school; it is one whose members receive careful individual attention and care. A pupil who wasn't wearing her glasses and was getting headaches was reminded to wear them in every lesson after her mum mentioned the problem to her tutor; a child in the junior school who struggles to concentrate is helped by wearing headphones to block out noise when she is doing a task; a girl who lost a close relative was given a time out card, so if she felt wound up and stressed during a lesson, she could use the card to leave and calm down: they have 'a great deal of emotional understanding', said a parent.

Pupils and parents: Plenty of local families, including those who had no plans for independent schooling, and those who weren't looking for single sex education, all of whom loved Roedean Moira House when they saw it. People stay here for the long term; whole dedicated families pass through, loving it.

Entrance: Much more exciting than the usual taster day: prospective pupils attend rockpools day on Eastbourne beach with a focus on marine life conservation, followed by a discovery day at school a few months later.

Entrance exams, but not for purposes of selection (unlike Roedean). Pupils join from many local state schools, also St Andrew's prep, Bede's, Eastbourne College and Lewes Old Grammar.

Exit: Around three-quarters leave after GCSEs and around 15 per cent after year 12. Career talks beyond the usual – not many schools tell pupils about opportunities for women in construction, and this blue sky thinking is reflected in destinations and subjects. One medic in 2018, destinations included Bournemouth, Canterbury Christ Church, East Anglia, Manchester, Oxford Brookes, Portsmouth, Reading,

Southampton, St Andrews, St Georges, Surrey, University of the Arts, London; one off to Harvard and one to Paris.

Money matters: Fees are dropping under Roedean's management, and are impressively low for the south east; 'making independent school affordable', says the head of the Roedean group.

Roedean has founded the Eastbourne Scholarship, which can give a substantial fee reduction, for academically able girls from state schools.

Remarks: A small, nurturing school known for its meticulous care for its pupils, now underpinned with academic rigour by Roedean. A place of great opportunity for girls, particularly in sport and performing arts.

Roedean School

Roedean Way, Brighton, East Sussex BN2 5RQ

Ages 11–18 **Pupils** 602 **Sixth form** 169 **Boarders** 257 full, 51 weekly, 10 flexi **C of E**

Fees: Day £16,440 – £21,495; Boarding £23,640 – £38,565 pa

01273 667500
www.roedean.co.uk

Headmaster: Since 2013, Oliver Blond (40s). Previously head at Henrietta Barnett School, one of top selective state girls' schools in the UK, for seven year stint – perfect for seeing through a generation of pupils without starting to repeat himself, he says. Before that, deputy head, North London Collegiate, so something of an expert in all-girls education. Not certain post here was natural fit until visited, when was instantly won over by school's charisma. So far, the feeling seems to be mutual. 'Aspirational, sweet and delightful,' said old girl.

Busy, busy, busy – as well as teaching (English, drama, philosophy) also academic director of the Princes' Teaching Institute charity, as well as raising two young children with wife Helen, teacher turned successful children's author. Highly articulate (goes with the headship territory), he's also soft-voiced and a great listener (both rarer commodities). Forthright mothers, old girls and especially pupils who 'know everything that I took six months to learn': he listens to the lot.

Formerly forbidding mood amongst tight-knit school community, including a few who were a tad suspicious to find bloke in charge, now one of almost palpable relief, with rave reviews for speed with which Mr Blond tackled perma-complacency that dominated teaching and attitudes. School is going back to roots – academic, all-round school for British girls with a smaller percentage of international students, though with many more day students and total numbers increasing to more than 500, building on an already healthy surplus.

While working on amplifying siren call to Londoners, even contemplating lowering weekly boarding prices so a closer match for day school fees in the capital, he's also ensuring locals start to see school not as impenetrable posh fortress but accessible Sussex place offering warm welcome on the cliff tops. They're coming round, brand starting to feature on trendy Brighton ravers' educational wish lists, with admissions team fielding 300 per cent increase in enquiries from locals and over 170 families attending recent open day (one of three).

Integration by stealth should help. Girls and boys from local schools now involved in co-ed go-karting to hip-hop curriculum enrichment, while sixth form Wednesday afternoon community service includes sessions in local primaries. School is also pushing bursaries for local state school pupils. And, yes, though previous attempts have been made to bring in bright but financially challenged, with slightly sporadic results, we'd back Mr Blond to make it happen.

Longer term, would like a third of places offered to UK pupils on needs-blind basis (school already offers some support to similar proportion of existing pupils). Will only work, though, if pupils and families, with or without scholarships, have evidence of change. 'A school that's waiting to be different just isn't enough,' he says. 'That's why we've gone at it really quite quickly.'

Presciently, Mr Blond's first choice career was, apparently, Spiderman. Scaling the heights and accomplishing the impossible? No wonder he's proving so successful.

Academic matters: Formidable competition from other local independents including Brighton College and Lancing, and any number of London options, has made school necessarily self-critical about results. Things now very definitely on the up, with 72 per cent of GCSE grades coming in at A*-A/9-7 in 2018. At A level, English, humanities (with exception of history) and languages currently minority interests, and of the star subjects, maths is outstanding year in, year out. Further maths also highly successful. Almost the cue for spot of subtle back-patting, A*/A grade percentage at A level at 54 per cent in 2018, 77 per cent A*-B. New one year GCSE course to encourage very bright European girls to stay for a year or longer.

Parents are hugely relieved that school's previous shortcomings have been addressed. The fear had been that essence and iconic status as landmark British girls' boarding school were in danger of ebbing away, with rise in international pupils and non-negotiable format – full boarding or nothing – putting off many potential customers. And while nothing wrong with cultural diversity – 'you get a huge level of tolerance for other people and ideas,' thought insider – proportion of international pupils had caused sense of alienation, numbers of OGs sending own children dropping like a stone.

Focus has been to seek out 'dynamic, inspirational and energetic staff with new ideas and teaching methods,' head says. The ones we saw in action certainly lived up to their star billing, with head of drama scoring bonus marks from pupils for wearing 'Vans with a suit' (must play well in Brighton). Parents approve of youth and energy. Girls agree. 'They make you feel you can do anything,' said one.

School is also recruiting master teachers, heroic role and a half involving mentoring, studying for extra qualifications and doing a spot of original research on top of normal teaching duties. Rethink of mixed ability teaching under way following parental concerns about sluggish pace in English lessons. Those needing additional English help in sixth form able to take pre-A level course to bring them up to scratch, parallel streams operating in earlier years.

School also offers strong support for pupils with learning difficulties, staffing recently bumped up with appointment of new head of English with extensive experience of dyslexia. 'They push the message that dyslexic children are taken on the same basis as everybody else,' said parent. Engagement in lessons the only line that must be toed, says Mr Blond. Otherwise, school will do best to help, working with parents to put extra support – as needed – in place.

Million dollar question is how much can be achieved without recruiting more able pupils. Parents like current mix. 'Varied – not just full of professionals' kids who all want to go to Oxbridge,' said one. Mr Blond adamant that most important point is that 'girls at all levels will thrive here, though standard of entry is rising already with increased interest in the school.' Aspirational, yes, but 'won't become some hothouse and wasn't the case in last school.' Get encouragement and self-confidence right, with school 'a platform for women to go out and feel that anything is possible,' and good exam results will be the by-product with no need to go out and trawl for straight A grade students.

Key to success, he believes, is ensuring that pupils are listened to – he's very hot on fatalistic tendency of girls to see low grade as final judgment. Wants teachers to say less, listen more and help pupils articulate sometimes hidden ambitions so can be helped to achieve them.

Creation of more shared meeting areas – teachers' own dining hall has been sacrificed to the cause; common room with outstanding sea views is on its way out – will mean better communication. School, though, already good at 'finding people's strengths and helping them patch the weaknesses,' reckoned insider. 'Their drive is to make bring out the best in everybody, no matter what it is.' Girls all – unconsciously – smile when asked about life at school. Endorsement doesn't come much more authentic.

Games, options, the arts: A place that allows unforced blossoming amongst kindred spirits. 'Whether you're a singer, guitar player or sports player, it's very good to have social identity around the stuff you're interested in,' said mother.

No them and us divisions between sport and arts, and 'not too binary,' reckoned parent. Pupils full of praise for school's desire to cater for budding polymaths, from rescheduling some after-school events to offering subsidised or free overnight stays to ensure music or sports enthusiasts have the after-school opportunities they need, to new co-curricular programme for pupils in years 7 to 9, which offers two afternoons a week physical and intellectual stretch (car mechanics to Russian literature). Can result in unexpected blooming – only girls' team to reach national finals of programming competition, for example. Head's push for more community involvement is also building Brighton connection. 'The girls want to pitch in and go and visit old ladies in the sixth form, so there's very much a sense of community,' said OG.

Sports increasingly busy and competitive – 'come back in three years and we'll be winning everything,' reckoned girls, grounds at the front pitch-perfect with all the trimmings and added sea views; new floodlit all-weather pitch; fixtures lists, previously on the empty side, busily being filled (and such a priority that features in new sports teacher's title), teams running to D in some sports. As elsewhere, nothing appears too much trouble for highly motivated staff, from developing tempting options for the less enthusiastic (zumba, synchronized swimming) to encouraging links with outside clubs, planning training programmes with external coaches for some of the sports scholars, even finding assessor for pupil working towards umpiring qualification.

Creativity, arts and music consistently good, even through leaner academic times. Art winds way into much of life there, with works on display as beautiful as design of original art room, partially glassed roof letting in northern light – 'the best,' says teacher – tiles with scenes of 1930s school life and, our favourite, a stove featuring heaven (gates and kettle stand), purgatory (oven) and hell (fiery flames), which broke in 1960s and hasn't (sadly) been used since.

Performing arts a particular strength, vibrant new drama team shaking things up, replacing previous worthy performance choices, all bang on syllabus but distinctly lacking in clap-along appeal, with a few more popular options. 'Was Chekhov before,' thought distinctly envious sixth form tour guides, watching infectiously toe-tapping rehearsal for open day, featuring selection from Hairspray.

Encouragement a feature of the process, with talented instrumentalists working with others who can't read music, for example. 'The degree to which they are supportive of one another is very striking. Has nice moral effect,' thought parent. Latent talent encouraged by trumpet, clarinet or violin lessons for all in first two years and around half the pupils have individual music lessons in school.

School trips extensive, masses abroad.

Boarding: Boarding – four houses each named for a colour and decorated to match – is wonderfully homely, rooms prettily proportioned and furnished, teapot lights hanging cosily down over breakfast bar to add domesticity to giant-height ceilings.

Boarders enjoy busy weekend activities such as visits to Buckingham Palace and local animal sanctuary, which day pupils can also sign up for. That said, with tunnel down to the sea (much enjoyed) and stile onto the South Downs (blank looks when mentioned to pupils, despite mention in school literature), staying put isn't half an attractive option.

Background and atmosphere: Founded by pioneering Lawrence sisters in 1885, heavy financial lifting courtesy of bunch of Midlands industrialists and friends, brilliant connections including artist Sir George Watts. Apart from brief reincarnation as HMS Vernon during the war, when was filled with Royal Navy electrical specialists while school was evacuated to Keswick, has been making stand for girls' education here for well over 100 years.

Like Eton, name has entered national consciousness as shorthand for certain type of education (school is commonly – though not uniquely – thought to be inspiration for Enid Blyton's Malory Towers series). Reality is 'consistent' finished product, thought parent: 'Articulate people who think for themselves and are conscious of the community.'

School now reacquiring spring in step, as increasing numbers of parents discount siren call of nearby co-eds whose idea of success is founded on 'noisy alpha male overachiever,' said parent. Like others, finds this a less stressful enclave for her 'un-pushy' child. 'My daughter's not one who'll walk in and want to take over socially, but she's managed to have very strong identity here.'

Ditto school itself. 'Looking outward, aiming high,' says sixth form prospectus, with literal accuracy, dainty Oxbridge-style mini cloisters conveying – perhaps – subtle message about founders' higher education aspirations for pupils. Cosy-looking it ain't, at least from the front, with cliff top, slab-like buildings (think turreted Kendal mint cake) menacing coast road to Brighton, 45-acre site on permanent collision course with the elements, salt spray countered by special rations for plants, bracing winds the stuff of nostalgia for past pupils.

Odd Portakabin aside, much to enjoy, including cheery dining halls (youngest two years have small scale version of their own, formerly staff area, table cloths in cupcake pinks and reds) while Horizons café, small box of lettuce aside, concentrates on essential sugar-rich snacks. Now developing a school farm (16 sheep and lambs arrived recently).

Inside, makeovers are transforming the place. Pupils have also been refurbished, with eccentric uniform policy (comfy in the week, smart only on Sundays) now reversed. Most now reconciled to house tie (initially a sticking point for a few) but all like smart, tailored blazers, badges crammed onto lapels recording sunny hours of school lives.

Pastoral care, well-being and discipline: You want it, they've got it, from excellent health centre taking range of difficulties such as diabetes in its stride, hot chocolate and chats available for as long as needed to help boarders settle in.

School listens and responds to problems. 'Has been really easy to get help,' said parent. Bullying isn't tolerated – will expel – while effective peer listening programme, backed with proper training so sixth formers know when adult assistance should be sought, stops anyone suffering in silence. 'If someone is sitting alone in the dining hall, you'll tell them "you're going to sit with me – you're not going to be on your own",' said sixth former.

Big feature of success is open door policy that sees day girls on the premises, with school's blessing, well past advertised hours every evening and welcomed back at weekends.

'They are very clear that you are part of the school whether a day girl or boarder,' said mother. Integration is something school has always done well. 'In my day, we were from very different backgrounds and just mulched along together and I'd be very surprised if there was a huge amount of perceived difference between day and boarding pupils now,' agreed OG.

Pupils and parents: 'Sweet, polite girls,' was one comment, though OG pointed out that niceness often comes with 'let's have a pop at it' attitude. 'Makes you more robust so perhaps you do a few more things you wouldn't have done.' Certainly borne out by career choice dilemmas faced by pupils, one agonising over whether to opt for being a barrister or singer, a second torn between primatology and acting...

Pupils feel liberated by school's approach. 'When I came here I was quite a pessimistic, glass half empty person. Here, you feel you've got another chance to get things right if they go wrong, without feeling judged,' thought one.

Once part of the place, it doesn't let go easily, old girls busily spreading the word, enthusiasts one and all – and 'a mighty source of strength,' according to school literature. Old Roedeanians see school days as 'catalyst' for happiness and success in later life and very special part of lives. 'Felt I should be at the back giggling with my mates,' said one OG, who'd been back for recent visit.

Currently some 70 per cent of boarders are international. While 'it's always been quite an international school,' points out one (ample proof in OGs' website, with thriving communities all over the place), increasing recruitment of London and local families is creating a balance everyone is happy with. Mix and match in every sense 'and I like that.'

Entrance: Numbers rising, with year 7 intake now likely to be around 60. Majority from local schools, state and independent. Further 20 to 25 pupils join year 9, up to 60 admitted in sixth form.

Exit: Around half leaves after GCSEs. Two to Oxbridge in 2018 and one medic; others off to the US (three) and Australia, with UCL, Birmingham, Bristol, Edinburgh, Imperial, Loughborough, LSE and Royal Holloway popular British destinations. Turns out girls with 'a bit of purpose in life,' thought OG. 'We're very good at being able to slightly reinvent ourselves and get on with just about anybody.'

Money matters: With £10 million foundation endowment, able to offer considerable help and scholarships worth up to 40 per cent of the fees, bright locals, in particular, should be making a beeline for the place. Brighthelm awards at 11+ and sixth form of up to 100 per cent for extremely bright girls from local state schools, who must be nominated by their current head.

Remarks: No danger of sun setting gently on past glories. This is a school that's going places. Sixth formers leaving as the tide turns would gladly do it all over again. 'Wish my daughter was starting there now,' says mother. 'It's a fabulous place.'

Rowan Preparatory School

6 Fitzalan Road, Claygate, Surrey KT10 0LX

Ages 2–11 **Pupils** 335

Fees: £11,190 – £14,850 pa

01372 462627
www.rowanprepschool.co.uk

Headmistress: Since 2014, Susan Clarke BEd, NPQH University of Southern Queensland (primary and psychology) (late 30s); appointed deputy head in 2012 following West Acton primary school headship. 'I wanted a solid grounding in an independent school,' she explains. After previous head's early retirement, she became acting head then head in April 2014. Mrs Clarke believes her independent girls' boarding school education helped prepare her for her present role whilst gaining 'valuable operational experience' in a state school which was part of the community, a feature of the Rowan with its close village and church links. 'I have thoroughly enjoyed leading the school, seeing the prep develop from two to three form entry.' Living in Claygate, with a supportive husband who works in the City, she shows no sign of moving on; her own daughter attends the school and son is nearby. Her Australian accent is barely discernible, nonetheless she shared with us her love of sunny days and BBQs. To relax, she cycles, walks and enjoys cooking family meals.

No longer teaching, Mrs Clarke ensures plenty of pupil contact by leading assemblies, sharing Friday scones with girls and manning the school gate whenever possible. Parents describe her as 'progressive and forward-looking', confident she will ensure their daughters are equipped for life. No stranger to working parents' demands, she has ensured supervised prep sessions are available as well as increasing holiday provision. Aware of ambitious parents' expectations, she is on hand to advise parents about senior school choices as well as listen to any girl who might have a concern. 'I want all the girls at Rowan to love learning whilst enjoying their childhood.' Parents admire how the head and her team provide cohesive leadership and respect 'a head who does what she says she is going to do'.

Entrance: Non-selective throughout, offering girls taster days to ensure they can access the education on offer. The nursery accommodates 18 girls from age 2 with priority for joining kindergarten with 10 additional pupils. Kindergarten splits into two reception classes equally dividing joiners with those who remain until year 3 with its three classes. Many join from local nurseries or pre-preps such as Shrewsbury House, Glenesk, Jack and Jill, The Rowans plus state schools including Thames Ditton Infants, Long Ditton Infants, St Matthew's Downside, The Orchard and St Paul's Esher. Entry at 7+ involves an activity day with year 2 girls, all completing maths, reading and writing tasks plus craft with year 3 teacher. Parents have a range of business and professional backgrounds. The means-tested Pell Assisted Place Award benefits prospective year 3 pupils with other bursaries available for unexpected emergencies.

Exit: Most popular destinations in 2018 were Guildford High, Surbiton High, (fellow United Learning schools), St John's School, Leatherhead, St Teresa's School, Effingham and Tormead School. 30 scholarships offered in total. Rowan has an enviable reputation for securing places at diverse schools, the majority independent girls' day schools and these sparkling results are one reason parents choose the school. Other regulars are Notre Dame, St Catherine's, Bramley, Lady Eleanor Holles and Wimbledon High with a sprinkling to board, usually Benenden or Wycombe Abbey and a few to state grammar Tiffin Girls' in Kingston. Parents state there is 'plenty of hand holding by the head and her team, providing bespoke expertise to ensure the appropriate destination for individuals'.

Remarks: In 1936 at Rowan Brae, in leafy Claygate village, 16 miles from central London, founder Katherine Millar admitted her first young pupils. The motto Hic Feliciter Laboramus (Here We Work Happily) encapsulates the school's ethos. Rowan Hill, the preparatory department, followed and the school became a charitable trust in 1961. Now a member of United Learning, Rowan shares its objective of encouraging 'the best in everyone' and benefits from ongoing investment, the use of sports facilities and staff training. Parents comment, 'The school has a grasp on reality, so important as we are incredibly lucky to live in Surrey. Home and school life are balanced with the emphasis on the children, not on the business.'

Rowan Brae houses nursery to year 2, overseen by one of two deputy heads, who when we visited was moving to her own headship in Oxfordshire after 11 years. Parents feel confident the many long serving staff will provide continuity, and that the school will employ an excellent successor; a true sign of trust in the leadership. Just as there has been investment in the Hill, so there will be refurbishments to Rowan Brae, providing a welcoming front entrance with ground floor medical room, as well as hall, music and technology rooms, making best use of the space available. Classrooms lead out into the playground and the light, spacious rooms are filled with imaginative, artistic displays, including a wonder wall showing impressive handwriting progress over time. Jam-packed with equipment including computers and banks of iPads, the Brae has its own kitchen with food prepared on the premises, so there's no to-ing and fro-ing to the prep site. Outside is an eco garden room with natural wood and greenery 'to get away from the plastic and bright colours'. Cleverly refurbished classrooms have displays and sinks at child level with plans to extend the colour scheme and ideas elsewhere.

We saw inventive topic lessons, girls preparing for sports day in the playground, and others enthusiastically discussing their jungle animal parts in a forthcoming production. Year 2 pupils were happy, engaging, confident, describing trips and activities they enjoyed and excitedly anticipating their first sleepover at school. They proudly explained how good behaviour is rewarded with the presentation of the class bear to go home overnight and displayed Rosie Rowan (an 80 year-old school doll), who presents weekly pre-prep awards and celebrates her birthday with a party every May. There is a sense of purposeful activity and girls collaborating, supporting one another, so it is perhaps no surprise the recent ISI inspection found the school to be outstanding.

Nursery hosts a Friday toddler group. Brae parents describe it as 'nurturing as well as structured'. Comparing it with their sons' schools, they find Rowan more formal in approach, especially for younger pupils who start their day in the playground, taken up to their classrooms by teachers. Parents can view each girl's 'learning journey' folder at any time, attend parents' evenings, concerts and assemblies; additional meetings are by appointment. All value the role play approach to teaching involving song and dance, and the extracurricular activities in reception. Versatile hall is used for gym with dedicated spaces for music and technology in the pre-prep. A little reading each night and a page of tricky words based on sounds is given for homework. Several parents applauded how teachers encourage the girls to use their imagination. Year 2s are carefully prepared for a smooth transition to the prep, with anxious ones invited for lunch and to use iPads to photograph their new building to lessen anxiety. Several teachers work in both buildings so girls see familiar faces and go to the Hill for lessons, such as art and computing. The head of inclusion learns all she can about the girls moving up and works across both sites.

Parents applaud the motto 'I can, I can, I know I can' taught to the girls to help them cope with challenges and become resilient, both inside and outside school. The school is a close community, collaborating to bring out the best in everyone. The balanced curriculum was judged 'outstanding' by inspectors. We saw Mrs Clarke lead assembly awarding certificates, praising not only academic, music and sporting prowess, but the 10 star qualities which include kindness, cooperation, courage, perseverance and resilience. The prep pastoral deputy head has counselling skills and teaches every class social and emotional well-being, and parents praise the 'well rounded education' their daughters receive and consider 'all teachers are approachable and all girls are cared for'. Communication systems work well, with weekly Friday Notes from the head, email contacts with prompt responses, as well as prep book notes. There are no serious discipline problems and friendship issues are quickly resolved with honesty and empathy.

Specialist teachers in pre-prep for music, art, computing, French, ballet, PE, games and swimming extends to all specialists at the prep. Latin from year 5 with Spanish and German available as additional language clubs. Philosophy and mindfulness for all, with engineering and technology in recently opened rooms including 3D printers. Year 6 study life skills and learn about careers, businesses, even undertaking risk assessments.

Learning outcomes are excellent for all and effective assessments and monitoring ensure everyone is supported. Currently three girls receive English as their additional language support, primarily in class but also with one-to-one help where appropriate in partnership with parents. The experienced head of inclusion works closely with her team, utilising in-class strategies with intervention groups for those in need.

Year 1 girls receive a free cello or violin lesson, sponsored by the parenting body. Some 80 per cent of girls in years 2 to 5 take instrumental and/or singing lessons with regular senior school music scholarships awarded. Choir and ensemble instrumental groups are timetabled before school and during lunch breaks. A dedicated arts festival, throughout spring and summer terms, celebrates creative and performing arts.

Year 6 girls chatted confidently over French Friday croissants and lunch. They feel safe, part of 'a family where everyone knows one another' and wish their teachers could stay for ever and drama lessons were longer. They enjoy playing in the woodland spinney, although, some parents commented sadly, 'not in the wet'. Their gazebo and outside musical instruments at pre-prep and prep were funded by the Friends of Rowan, parenting body, which provides social events and raises finances for eg retractable seating plus adventure play trail.

Sports include netball, hockey, lacrosse, cricket, gymnastics, dance, swimming, athletics, tennis, cross-country and biathlon, with judo, badminton, football, Sh'Bam and tag rugby clubs, plenty of fixtures and facilities closeby. Girls excel at gymnastics, hockey, athletics and swimming. Grumbles are very few but some parents would prefer the girls to play sport daily and wish there could be more space, suggesting this is not the best choice for a very sporty child. Sports clubs before school using a fleet of minibuses ease early drop offs in a residential side road.

A school with a forward-looking but traditional head, where polite, biddable girls look impeccably neat and tidy in their smart red and green uniform. 'I would never question choosing the Rowan where I have three really happy girls, one dyslexic, one bright and one in every team, as there is something for everyone.' A vibrant, high-achieving school, Rowan manages to be fun-loving and unpressured, ideal for determined triers, keen to do their best.

Royal Grammar School (Guildford)

Linked with Lanesborough School

High Street, Guildford, Surrey GU1 3BB

Ages 11–18 **Pupils** 948 **Sixth form** 272

Fees: £18,285 pa

01483 880600
www.rgs-guildford.co.uk

Headmaster: Since 2007, Dr Jon Cox BSc PhD (40s). Educated at St Mary's College, Southampton, then studied physiology and biochemistry at Southampton University. Postgrad course at Royal College of Music (French horn is his instrument) and toyed with becoming a professional musician before deciding on a career in teaching. Joined Whitgift School in Croydon as a biology teacher in 1992 and stayed for 14 years, rising through the ranks to become deputy head before his appointment to the RGS in 2005 as headmaster in waiting.

Hasn't frightened the horses with wholesale changes to what was already a very successful operation, but neither has he rested on the school's considerable laurels. He began with a long 'to-do' list, which he still runs today. 'Every time I cross off a job done, I add something new to the bottom. It's just like a house, something always needs doing,' he says, brandishing another long list of 40+ points he's jotted down to mention during our interview. It covers all sorts – everything from academic innovations, creation of new staff roles, building programmes, community links; the list literally goes on – he's a man on a mission.

Affable, down to earth, buzzing, you sense his delight at having what he calls 'the best job in the country – fantastic boys, inspirational staff, parents on side and appreciative'.

RGS is very much his show and he's great at managing parents – they don't run this school. 'He's very much in control and you don't get the impression he would welcome a waste of his time,' said one mother. 'But equally he's approachable and I wouldn't hesitate to speak to him if necessary'. 'He's very at ease in his role and really cares about the school,' said another. 'A fabulous figurehead for RGS,' agreed a third. 'I've heard him talk to prospective and current parents many times and he's a good speaker, witty and easy to listen to, he handles all that side of things very well'.

Pupils like and respect him – 'he's a nice guy' and 'smart' they say – and seems to know what they are about; writes a comment on every boy's report. 'He never talks down to them,' said one parent.

While absolutely mindful of his school's many strengths, not least its academic prowess, Dr Cox says he takes most pride in the fact that RGS is 'a wonderful community. Mostly you'll ask your son if he has had a good day, not for details about his maths test,' he says. 'There's a great, supportive atmosphere here that really enriches the boys in all aspects of their lives'.

With his own son having recently joined the school, he understands the anxiety parents feel around the admissions process. 'I was out of school when my son did his test and interview, but it was agony nevertheless, so I do empathise with parents.'

He's working hard to overcome the school's elitist tag and dispel two main myths about RGS – that it's a hothouse and not for the sporty; 'Neither are remotely true,' he says. 'I want people to recognise that we are a school for bright children, irrespective of their backgrounds'. To this end the school entertains children from local primary schools every Monday to do Tudor project work (buildings reflect school's Tudor origins and Dr Cox's office includes a Chained Library) and runs Saturday masterclasses and a summer school. Service to the local community is a big theme at RGS.

He is married with three children, still plays the French horn and is a keen amateur magician. Also a governor of a school in Watford.

Academic matters: Outstanding in all respects and very much the academic school for boys in the area. RGS features in top 10 or 20 of league tables of all variety. Pupils are selected from the top ability band, working far above the national average. Maths and science very popular and two-thirds take maths a year early. Maths is also the most popular option at A level, followed by physics, economics and chemistry. Pre-U offered in chemistry and the school has great success with this subject – at recent Chemistry Olympiad RGS achieved five gold, 10 silver and seven bronze awards. English and humanities give equally good accounts of themselves; philosophy and theology a new Pre-U offering. Modern languages (French or Spanish from 11+ or German at 13+) compulsory to GCSE. Arabic, Chinese, Russian and Japanese also available. Latin a popular option and Greek also on offer. PE a new GCSE option. Positively dizzying success in exams overall – in 2018, 89 per cent of grades at GCSE were A*-A/9-7 while at A level 81 per cent of grades were A*/A (95 per cent A*-B).

Head has conducted an enormous push on teaching and learning, including lowering the pupil/staff ratio. We've heard nothing but huge parental praise for 'exceptionally good' teaching staff. 'Teaching is inspirational – absolutely no dead wood,' they say. The boys are encouraged to be self-motivated, independent learners, and the lessons are intensive and conducted at a brisk pace. It's cool to be bright at the RGS and the boys set themselves high standards as they jostle for position. 'My son was surprised to find himself towards the bottom of the class having been top dog at his old school,' said one parent. 'I really wouldn't coach a boy to come here as it would be no fun if you were struggling', said another, more seasoned parent. 'These boys are a competitive bunch and frankly anything less than an A* is a disaster for them. But that's really not because it's a hothouse – it isn't – it's simply that they do so well on their own abilities'.

It's a can-do culture – the school talks of 'strengths' and 'development areas' rather than 'weaknesses'. Extra work on offer to help anyone falling behind. 'I know they keep a watch on grades and are absolutely on top of everything,' said one mother whose son had slipped a little. 'He got all the help he needed to get back on track'.

On average two to three homework assignments an evening of around 30 minutes each – 'nothing too onerous,' parents feel. Support available for the handful of boys with a learning difficulty or disability.

Games, options, the arts: A broad and balanced offering. DT a popular subject choice (a pupil proudly showed us a 3D laser cutter, and the new John Brown building – linked to the main school by a stunning, architecturally distinctive glass bridge – provides inter alia a purpose-built DT centre). No drama taken at GCSE (though Dr Cox is now promoting drama lower down the school). Not huge numbers doing art either, but what there is is remarkably good.

Most sport is off site at Bradstone Brook, the school's 20-acre playing field and pavilion a few miles away. School rails against its reputation for being less sporty than some of its heavyweight public school neighbours in the area and can in fact hold its own. Rugby, hockey and cricket on offer, but football is lacking. 'Such a shame good footballers cannot represent the school,' moaned one miffed mother. But lots do play at break on the Astroturf and Dr Cox points out that 'We do run football very successfully in the sixth form with A to D teams'. Shooting range is popular. Facilities not whizzy – no swimming pool for example, so boys troop down to the local Spectrum swimming pool (a bit downmarket for some) and to Guildford Lido for the annual gala. 'Actually the boys love getting off site for this,' said a mother. 'It's only 10 minutes away and the walk warms them up – plus they get to run past Guildford High (School for Girls)!'

Music now has the space it deserves –a fab new music centre, including a recording studio and rehearsal space.

There's an extensive timetabled programme of extracurricular activities, known as Period 8, which includes all sorts of clubs and societies, house competitions in an array of sports, plays and musical performances, CCF, D of E and even a scout group. It's a school where things happen, lots going on, often until about 7pm.

Background and atmosphere: Historically a grammar school and still a grammar school at heart. The school was founded in 1509 under the will of Robert Beckingham, and became 'Royal' in 1552 by charter of King Edward VI. Was run as a state school for 30 years after the war, but returned to the independent sector in 1977 rather than become non-selective. Charming tall, white 450 year old building on one side of Guildford High Street (includes Chained Library and various public rooms) while on the other side of the street the school buildings date mostly from the 20th century, although pleasing facades mean there's no horrid 60s look to them. The site is a little cramped, but fortunately RGS boys have manners and respect, otherwise it could be mayhem. Pupils are respectful of staff, hold doors open for each other and parents say they relish knowing where the boundaries are and settle into what is expected of them. 'The school understands them, how they learn and gets through to them in a way that switches them on and makes them responsible for their own studies,' said one parent. 'They really play to their strengths.'

Pastoral care, well-being and discipline: Although a non-denominational school, its ethos is firmly based on sound Christian principles. Parents describe the school as very supportive. Senior staff operate a pastoral data base and a 'care list' of boys to keep a special eye on. Parents feel their sons form good relationships with each other and across the year groups. 'They bond really well', one parent told us. 'And it's a joy to see'.

R

Dr Cox claims to have improved the behaviour of many a 'scallywag' – 'I'll give them some responsibility, that generally turns them around'. In the grand scheme of things any bad behaviour is of the mild variety. These are regular boys, school appears very on top of things and is quick to clamp down on anything untoward with the occasional incident of the argy bargy variety firmly and quickly stamped on. Nothing serious enough to warrant exclusion in the last few years. A benevolent atmosphere, with no hint of a heavy hand. 'I think we do a good job of selecting them in first place and sussing out their attitude to work', says Dr Cox, who for all his bonhomie, is no soft touch – 'They really don't want to come to me for a telling off,' he acknowledges. 'But I think they know I am basically on their side. These are impressionable young men, finding their feet in the world. I see our job as being to correct their behaviour. I'd rather they made their mistakes here, before going off into the world'.

Pupils and parents: School's town centre, close-to-station location means it attracts families from some distance away, involving a few quite complicated train journeys. Some parents are really discerning (there are plenty of good independent schools in the area, although no other single sex boys' day schools). For others RGS is their only independent option and if their sons don't pass the exam, they will stay in the state system.

Latest parental survey attests to parents being happy with their choice. 'There's a pretty good mix of boys here, with the extremes probably drawn to the centre by the camaraderie and sense of "we are grammar school boys with a shared identity",' said a long-standing parent. 'No outlandish types among boys or parents' – although some quite quirky, dare we say eccentric, boys find a happy home at RGS. Generally a nice broad spectrum of society, all bright, but a mix quite reflective of life generally. 'The longer he's there the more I am happy,' a parent told us. 'The school seems to have had a very insidious effect that has turned him into a lovely young man. They're not swotty and snobby, but a down-to-earth, nice group of lads'. Boys we came across were very courteous, not super smart, just regular teenage types, but seemed friendly and happy as they milled around.

Parents pleased that they don't have to crack the whip at home; it seems that the school sorts their sons out to be completely self-sufficient. 'These boys are the real thing from an academic point of view – they are not arrogant and don't grow up believing the world owes them a living,' says Dr Cox.

Entrance: Tough – has one of the highest academic hurdles in Surrey. On average there are 350-400 applications from boys from almost 100 local schools for 140 places. All sit exams in English, maths and verbal reasoning plus an interview: 'We're looking for potential,' school says. Advice from everyone we spoke to is 'don't coach, other than a little exam practice'. 'You'd be miserable here if you'd just scraped in,' summed up one parent, speaking for many. 'Even a bright boy who was absolutely top dog at his old school might well find himself 25th in the class here'.

By and large the school is happy that they get admissions 'spot on'. Dr Cox can only recall one or two boys who subsequently couldn't cope with the academic rigour of the place. At age 11 the majority come from the state sector, reflecting the relationships built up with local schools. Then at 13+ another 45/50 boys join from prep schools, with Lanesborough the major feeder school, sending around 30 boys a year.

Don't expect red carpet treatment when you visit. 'Everyone is very nice and it's well-organised, but they don't have to try very hard', one mother said. 'We visited other schools where we got more special treatment because they really need to fight to get families to choose them – RGS is in a strong position because it doesn't have local competition.' Dr Cox sees all prospective parents himself – can be 20 or so a week – and unsurprisingly he has a great conversion rate. NB After an interregnum of a couple of years when no sports scholarships were awarded, RGS reintroduced scholarships for sport and 13+ places offered from September 2020 will be unconditional.

Exit: Almost all to their first choice of university. Twenty-seven Oxbridge places in 2018, and six medics. Many to Imperial and Durham (which can be harder, Dr Cox points out) and the rest as you would expect to other Russell Group heavyweights including notably Bath, Birmingham and Exeter. Three overseas in 2018 – to Yale, Harvard and Sciences Po (Paris).

Money matters: Lower than average fees, with the school working to keep them low. Appeals to parents who don't have the funds for more expensive schools. 'Proper' bursaries include money for uniform, sports kit and books; 'There's no point otherwise,' says Dr Cox. A few years ago RGS could not give bursary money away, but now there's a good take up following the establishment of better links with other schools.

Remarks: One of Surrey's most highly regarded and sought after schools. Cutting edge and working hard to keep its top spot as the best school for boys in the area. It's an environment where boys spark off each other and learn at a fast pace, so it's not for a worrier or a 'scraper-in'. A school for bright boys, who don't have to have been overly prepped or privately educated at primary level.

The Royal Grammar School, High Wycombe

227

Amersham Road, High Wycombe, Buckinghamshire HP13 6QT

Ages 11–18 **Pupils** 1365 **Sixth form** 369 **Boarders** 14 full; 54 weekly

Fees: Day free; Boarding £13,020 – £14,673 pa

01494 524955
www.rgshw.com

Headmaster: Since 2015, Philip Wayne, previously head of Chesham Grammar. He studied at Manchester University and the Royal Northern College of Music. Following a number of years as a freelance organist, pianist, conductor and lecturer, he qualified as a teacher and held several leadership posts in the Midlands. He moved to Buckinghamshire in 2004 as deputy head of John Hampden Grammar and became head of Chesham Grammar School in 2007.

Pragmatic and plain-spoken, he's widely considered to be exactly the breath of fresh air the school needed. 'He had his work cut out as the school had been resting on its laurels, but he's risen to the challenge, bringing renewed energy and direction,' said a parent, while others report that 'he's very much in touch with the pupils' and 'has his finger firmly on the pulse.' Pupils describe him as 'approachable' and 'inspirational' and like that he turns up to so many events and sports fixtures; he also runs student conferences and sees every boy on his 12th birthday. Has humility (quicker to praise the boys and staff than himself) and while all heads speak about their school with pride, his loyalty seems particularly heartfelt: 'I didn't enjoy my own secondary schooling,' he admits. 'In fact it was only when I got to university, I realised what a phenomenal education everyone else had had. But if I'd come to a secondary school like this, with its academic and sporting focus, I'd have absolutely loved it.' Big on the independent school mindset, but devoted to the state sector.

Lives in a nearby Buckinghamshire village with his wife and teenage twins (son at the school). Passionate musician and loves watching sport, family life and cooking.

Academic matters: Consistently delivers a good showing in national league tables for academics and although hasn't quite caught up with the area's top performing grammar for GCSE results (72 per cent of GCSEs graded A*-A/9-7 in 2018), they are only a whisker behind at A level (74 per cent of A levels at grades A*-B and 48 per cent A*/A in 2018). Value added on the up. Currently phasing out IGCSEs, 'which have not been compatible with league tables.'

Majority take 10 GCSEs, with modern languages, history and geography among the most popular and top performing subjects. Wide-ranging but traditional curriculum, including computing (stunning results), classical civilisation and Latin, with school making no apology for not offering the likes of economics and business studies. 'We offer a good solid curriculum that doesn't close doors unwittingly to the best universities,' says head. A language (French, German or Spanish) is compulsory and there is large take up of all three at both GCSE and A level, with Mandarin, Italian and Japanese available 'on tap.' Music thriving, with a one-year course for those that don't want it to take up an option space.

All boys expected to start with four A levels – 'partly for breadth, partly to minimise impact of unwise choices,' but school is open to boys dropping one if it all gets too much. Sciences (physics Pre-U and A level), maths, further maths and economics all popular and do very well. Classics, Latin and modern languages also strong. Good take up of EPQ.

Six classes of 32 in each year group, with setting in maths, English and languages from year 9, when boys are taught in groups of around 25 for most subjects. In years 7-9, boys are offered a carousel of music, art, drama, cookery (not food tech – boys made pizzas rather than design them), DT, computing in smaller groups. School 'goes in heavy with homework from the word go', according to parents, with at least three 30-minute pieces per night (all set online), but boys seem to take this in their stride – as they do the rigorous tests they take in every topic. 'School is excellent at monitoring progressing and acting on it,' said one parent. No coasting here. Boys use a range of technologies including iPads and the VLE is well-used.

Teachers' passion for their subjects is evident as you walk round the school; noticeable lack of bellowing, with positive staff/pupil relationships – 'you really feel they want the best for you,' said one boy. Some pupils would like email contact, 'but most teachers make themselves available at lunchtimes – they definitely go the extra mile,' said one. That said, a few boys with heavy extracurricular programmes (eg rugby takes up three lunchtimes a week) said they find it harder to track down extra teacher support. Some parents alluded to a few substandard teachers 'and you do wonder why they are still there, but on the whole, the teaching is phenomenal.' Some parents told us they tutor their boys outside school, but school insists this isn't necessary. Lots of practicals in science – 'I haven't had a chemistry lesson without a practical this term,' one year 9 boy told us. Good staff retention; CDP exceptional; and most teachers visit other schools 'to get new ideas'; and in keeping with the independent school ethos, they are encouraged to get involved in sport and/or school trips.

SEN at the milder end, with strong learning support department, which helps boys in and outside the classroom. 'It's all very discreet,' says the head – 'No waving inclusion banners here – we just get on with offering what help is needed.' School is also adapted for wheelchair use – 'also handy for the grandmas who want to come to the concerts,' says school.

Games, options, the arts: Rugby, rugby and more rugby, with over 400 boys regularly involved and playing top independent schools, as well as local fixtures. 'It's important to have a USP,' believes head. But this is by no means a rugger-bugger school, with 14 other competitive sports, and many more non-competitive ones, on offer. Hockey has taken off considerably since the installation of a new floodlit, all-weather pitch; cricket involves regular fixtures, with boys playing in prestigious festivals; rowing (they use facilities in Marlow) is popular, with around 50 boys performing well in regattas; plus Eton fives, squash, tennis (burgeoning), table tennis, karate all offered. Some pupils and parents grumble other sports don't get the same quality fixtures or kudos as the rugby teams, and boys in these other sports should certainly not expect the same hero-worship in the playground. That said, there are sighs of relief from some non-rugby parents as it's a 'major commitment' with training five times a week and fixtures most weekends in season. 'Still no football and that won't change,' says head (to the inevitable disappointment of some boys). And if you're not sporty? 'That's ok-ish,' was the response from parents and pupils.

Indeed, Thursday afternoon activities (TAA) allow boys to choose from a vast array of sporting or academic enrichment activities ranging from Japanese or Mandarin to social services. This is in addition to after-school activities and indulges boys' passions for more marginal activities like climbing (the school boasts an impressive 40ft climbing wall in main sports hall) and astronomy or endeavours like the Caterham Project which sees year 13s building a car from scratch. D of E and CCF also extremely popular from year 10, with 200 boys taking part in the latter. Boys enthuse about extracurricular at every given opportunity, listing everything from Model UN and debating to Dr Who club and RGS Has Talent. 'Not expected, but encouraged – and, really, you'd be mad not to,' said one pupil.

Music 'really, really strong', according to parents, with the charismatic director of music running a large number of ensembles including symphony orchestra, massed choir, wind, string and jazz bands, close harmony group. Biannual shows such as Les Mis and My Fair Lady (which has got two million hits on YouTube), both in conjunction with local girls' school. Most orchestral instrument lessons on offer (around a quarter of boys learn one or more instrument), plus singing, guitar, piano and organ, with top professionals including BBC big band leader and West End singer forming part of the peripatetic team. Plenty of opportunities to get involved for non-performers too, with the school's stage lighting and sound team proving hugely popular.

Art improving, thanks to new leadership, with students creating everything from fine art to 3D work and decent take-up at GCSE, plus collaboration with Wycombe Museum.

Trips, tours and exchanges galore. World Challenge scheme starts in year 7 then branches out globally higher up the school, with destinations in recent years including China, Vietnam and Belize.

Boarding: Boarding offers great value for money, with full boarding costing less than most day school fees. Some 70 boarders (full boarding only from year 10, with the odd exception in year 9 – weekly up until then) reside in the bright, modern boarding house (1999), located in the heart of the school campus. Boarders say 'it's very relaxed and homely' and the boarding house has an upbeat vibe, partly dictated by the energetic and approachable head of boarding. 'If you miss home, they are onto it immediately,' one boy told us. Each academic subject has a pupil champion that younger boys can approach if they need guidance with any part of their studies and the pupil food and boarding council electorate voices collective opinions about how the boarding house is run.

Younger boys are housed in spacious four-man dorms, decorated with personal effects to varying degrees. Years 12 and 13 are in cabin-like single rooms with en-suite shower rooms and the communal areas are peppered with boy toys like pool tables, table tennis and air hockey tables and flat screen TVs. No wonder most years are oversubscribed.

Boys return to the boarding house after school to get the blood sugar levels back up with a snack then participate in organised group activities on two or three afternoons a week. All meals are taken in the boarders' own canteen ('better food than in the main school', agree pupils) and prep takes place after supper from 7.30 to 9pm ('either doing supervised prep in the computer room, great for keeping on track, or doing prep in our room'), while the sixth-formers can manage their own study time.

The majority goes home at weekends, with around 20 – mainly international pupils – staying. The schedule at the weekend is 'pretty relaxed' and boys are allowed into town in groups of two or three. Half-termly big trips – paintballing, go-carting and Thorpe Park are annual highlights. Note you can't convert a boarding place to a day place until the end of year 11; and you must have a valid British or EU passport to be eligible for a boarding place.

Background and atmosphere: Founded in the 12th century and given a royal charter in 1562. Centred around an attractive red-brick Queen Anne style building, although someone in the 1960s thought it was a good idea (it wasn't) to obscure this from view with a new block that, as one pupil puts it, 'is unfortunate to look at, especially from the street, but with good practical space inside.' An interesting mix of ancient (the oldest classrooms recently had their 100th birthdays) and modern, including a bright, modern canteen, cookery suite and fitness suite with panoramic views of the beautifully kept sports fields. Outside, there's plenty of pitches and the fives courts have been refurbished; there's a new all-weather pitch; and the sports hall has a swimming pool with retractable roof which, despite its 40-year vintage, still knocks spots off many we've seen. Large airy library with plenty of space for quiet study and there are plans to build a new sixth form centre. Size of the vast music block gives away the school's collective passion for music, which includes a music technology centre. 'Not exactly your most up-to-date, modern school in terms of facilities – and some of it looks really tired,' said one parent (and boys say 'some of the toilets are disgusting'), but there is a rolling programme of refurbishment.

Overall vibe of the school is traditional, with a modern twist and 'the roundedness of public school,' as one parent puts it. The majority join from state primaries, however. A true camaraderie between year groups is immediately visible in the playground and boarding house and we found boys polite, fun and confident. 'Perhaps not as embracing of issues like gender fluidity and being gay as other schools, though,' said one parent; and one pupil told us, 'The fact that so many pupils excel here can feel like a double-edged sword – it can mean it's hard to get recognition when you do really well as something.'

Pastoral care, well-being and discipline: A positive culture of praise and heads of year meet weekly to make sure no pupil is missed if they're wilting under the pressure. Boys we spoke to were aware of mental health risk areas from self-harm to eating disorders, with mindfulness classes available (also to staff), plus chaplain and three part-time counsellors. Good induction routines for year 7s, followed by mentoring systems. Surprisingly new house system. Full care for boarders from matron, housemasters and tutors.

Generally a well-behaved bunch – largely complying with the zero-tolerance policy on drugs, drinking and smoking; those that don't are hauled before the head and face exclusion, as they are for insolence, fisticuffs and bullying (around 20 temporary exclusions in the last two years; less than a handful of permanent). New sanctions system, which includes a detailed list of unacceptable behaviours and their consequences, was surprisingly well received by pupils. 'It's now completely consistent whereas before some teachers were much stricter than others,' one explained. Parents informed even when pupils get a first warning, three of which mean a detention. Strict on uniform. 'Some older boys throw their weight around a bit, but the school does clamp down on bullying,' one pupil told us.

Pupils and parents: Boys come from leafy south Bucks villages and a range of suburbia on the way to High Wycombe. Fewer come from the town itself, but school has outreach programmes to address this. Ethnic mix changing rapidly and school is now about 30 per cent non-Caucasian (higher in lower years), reflecting the local community. Parents of boarders lean towards the middle classes, often professional dual income families, and internationals. About half a dozen girls join for specific lessons (Greek, classics) in year 13. Parents report excellent communications with school, but one unimpressed that 'you have to choose six teachers to see on parents' evening – at other schools, you get to see every teacher.'

A plethora of high profile alumni from the sporting, political and showbiz worlds England rugby players Matt Dawson, Nick Beal and Tom Rees; GB hockey captain and Olympian Jonathan Wyatt; professional golfer Luke Donald and, representing the artsy crowd, pop stars Howard Jones and the late Ian Dury and comedian Jimmy Carr. Many are very supportive of the school and visit

Entrance: Places highly sought after, with selection subject to success at the (new, more rigorous) 11+ exam and Buckinghamshire criteria, including the ever-moveable feast of catchment. School has its own testing process after 11+, with a waiting list of around 80. Little movement out of the school these days, but they do expand in years 8, 10 and for the sixth form. Around 40 places for the latter, about 10 in the boarding house, with around 60 applications – you need eight Bs or above (Or numerical equivalent) and As in certain subjects to be studied at A level.

Worth considering boarding at 11 if a day place looks unlikely and candidate has a high 11+ score. Forces families and boys in care are prioritised and these are mixed with some overseas pupils (although they must have a British/EU passport) and locals keen for the boarding experience.

Think twice if you have to tutor your son to death to get him in. 'It's not a school for scraping by,' say pupils.

Exit: Over 90 per cent stay on to sixth form. Majority straight into top universities – Durham, Exeter, Birmingham, Leeds are popular, as are music colleges. Between 15 and 20 into Oxbridge most years – 14 in 2018. Good university advisory provision in place, with specialist support for those hoping for entry to international universities. 'I've got three tutors helping me with my Cambridge application and I can't believe how much time they're giving up,' one pupil told us.

Money matters: Proactive approach to state grants through the Condition Improvement Fund have enabled capital projects to take place. PA active and successful in fundraising. Parents are generous in their support of the 'annual fund' and the various 'friends of' groups (rugby, hockey, rowing, cricket and music). Old boys also generous donors.

Remarks: Don't believe the hype pitching The Royal Grammar School as a hotbed of rugger boys. Yes, they play rugby to an exceptionally high level, but there are 14 other competitive sports, as well as outstanding music, drama and academics all wrapped up in a supportive, friendly package. Parents at other local grammars might consider it 'a bit God and country,' but the traditional values that have the school competing ably with its independent and state maintained neighbours – and thrashing many top public schools on the sports field – mean boys (and their parents) benefit from a private school ethos without the hefty price tag.

Royal Masonic School Cadogan House

Linked with Royal Masonic School for Girls

Rickmansworth Park, Rickmansworth, Hertfordshire WD3 4HF

Ages 4–11 **Pupils** 240 **Boarders** 8 full, 8 weekly/flexi (from year 3)

Fees: Day £11,475 – £13,290; Boarding £20,115 – £21,225 pa

01923 773168
www.royalmasonic.herts.sch.uk

Head: Since 2014, Ian Connors BA PGCE TEFL MBA (in education management) NPQH (40s), previously head of primary at Harrow International School, Bangkok. Degree in English and American history and literature. Has also been director of studies at King Edward's School, Bath and head of a Cambridgeshire primary school.

Informal, warm and unguarded, this is a truly hands-on headmaster. As often as he's in his surprisingly modest office, he's actually teaching ('I can't create a happy, successful school if I don't even know what it's like at the coalface'), as we saw for himself when we observed his lively ICT class, where he won instant brownie points among the girls for teaching the educational version of Minecraft. 'He's all about getting the children to engage,' say parents – so while more old-school parents admit they'd like to see a bit more traditional discipline ('I preferred it when there was more focus on being strict about uniform, for example,' said one), others gush that 'It's the fizz and excitement of learning that he wants to impart – wonderful!' Praise across the board for the fact that he's 'completely transparent about challenges and never afraid to accept criticism' and his 'excellent strategic plan going forward.' Girls call him 'friendly' and 'really funny.'

Keen sportsman – Arsenal supporter – and loves walking, cycling and travelling abroad with his family. Married to Ingrid, a teacher who runs her own phonics company; they have three daughters at the Royal Masonic School.

Entrance: Two-form entry at 4. Academic ability is 'just a part' of the selection criteria, with the way candidates approach tasks and interact with other girls during the gentle half day assessment held in equal regard. Abound half come from the on-site pre-prep, Ruspini House, though places not guaranteed. Around half a dozen join year 3. Entry from year 1 upwards involves a full day assessment including English, maths and reasoning tests.

Exit: Girls are guaranteed a place at the Royal Masonic School and about 85 per cent take it. 'It's an utter joy not to worry about entrance exams, especially when I see the stress that puts other families under,' said one parent. Those that do move go mostly to local grammars for the obvious financial reasons. Hardly any to other independents.

Remarks: The creative displays of artistic endeavours and handwritten work, along with educational themes that are imaginatively brought to life in every inch, are like nothing else we've seen. We walked through World War I trenches in one corridor, only to find a classroom-come-rainforest. We saw the cosiest, most welcoming book-corners known to mankind and ancient Egyptian art practically jumping off the noticeboards. Everything is in 3D and bursting with colour and textures, while other senses were awakened, for example via soft classical music playing in a whole-class reading session. 'It was a real selling point for me,' one staff member admitted. Outside is an enticing adventure playground, large grassy play area, wild flower garden and beyond that an outside learning facility, part of the forest school initiative, 'great for bringing children out of their shells.'

Located on the same campus as the Royal Masonic School, Cadogan House opened in 2011 as the gleaming, newly refurbished home for its pre-prep and prep. Enviably spacious facility, in its own lush grounds, it mirrors the grandeur of its big sister but maintains a safe and nurturing vibe. It benefits from a few shared facilities (dining hall, swimming pool and breathtaking sports hall), as well as some staff, which gives girls a seamless and comfortable transition into year 7. Own art and DT rooms, ICT suite, a well-stocked library, hall and soon-to-be science lab (although shame it will have to double up as a regular form room).

Girls, with their boaters and tidy plaits, are polished, polite and confident but very down-to-earth – and super keen, barely drawing breath as they wax lyrical about this field trip or that teacher, though the school has a surprisingly tranquil and studious (albeit relaxed) air compared to the chaotic clatter of many prep schools. Not too many raised voices here, with an innate respect embedded – 'sometimes a challenge with new girls until they get used to it.'

Academically robust across the board, with phonics going from strength to strength, leading to standards of reading and writing well above the average, though some parents would like to see more emphasis on maths ('next on the agenda,' insists school). Strong languages – Spanish from reception and French from year 3, with extracurricular clubs in both also on offer. Classes are mixed up at the end of years 2 and 4 and girls get a taste of senior school life by starting to move around the school for some lessons in year 5 and 6, including cookery, textiles and DT. Setting in maths from year 4. Homework given out every Monday, with a full week to complete – 'a godsend for busy families and there's a sensible amount too,' said one parent. Teachers comprise a good mix of age and experience, though not gender (as ever at primary level, it's mainly women).

EHC plan children a rarity here, but full-time SEN co-ordinator plus three part-time assistants on hand to assist those with mild to moderate needs with a creative, friendly approach. There are options for paid-for one-to-one sessions if required, and parents praise how 'the SEN team and class teachers work very closely.'

R

Artistic skills are taught to a high level, with art scholarships offered most years and a blended curriculum where relevant (pottery Tudor miniatures, for example). 'Very strong' performing arts, say parents, with girls clamouring for parts in the annual (usually musical) production – it was all go with Aladdin practice when we visited. Musically, there's been a big jump forward with high take-up of instruments and the ukulele played by all in year 3, plus a thriving prep orchestra (with wind and string sections) and two choirs – one chamber (by audition) and pre-prep and prep choir (open to all).

Competitive sport from year 4 (with a few events for year 3) and a host of extracurricular clubs and activities to choose from, including skipping, kickboxing, maypole dancing and fencing. Plenty for less sporty types too ranging from yoga to drawing to film making. Annual residential trips from year 3 onwards allow pupils to spread their wings outside the campus bubble, while day trips include the likes of Windsor Castle, Harry Potter Studios and Stonehenge.

This is a nurturing school, where teachers get know the children well, consolidated by presence of peer mentors in year 6 to act as 'big sisters' to the younger ones. Trained by the school counsellor, they are on hand to support and guide through any minor personal or friendship issues. Girls' concerns can also be anonymously posted into a 'worry box' ('mostly about friendship concerns') and are then addressed by the relevant form teacher. Bullying largely avoided by identifying 'mean behaviour' early on and having a clear process to deal with it – parents say it 'works a treat.' PSHE extends to parents, who are brought in for seminars on subjects ranging from internet safety (all girls are given a school email address from reception) to coping with bereavement or avoiding 'helicopter' parenting.

The number of full-time boarders is dwindling – down to about eight among the over 200 children – but weekly and flexi or ad-hoc boarders are on a steady incline (around six to eight each so far). About a third of full-timers are international (from Asia and Russia) with a few of Forces families in the mix. Junior boarding house, a wing of one of the three senior boarding houses, is available from year 3 and has good facilities and plenty of space, although parents are hoping for a refurb soon. All meals (apart from weekend breakfast, when girls can pad downstairs in their pyjamas) are taken in the senior school. Food is reportedly 'outstanding'. Boarders take advantage of the full array of after-school activities, plus games, in-house events and an extensive DVD collection. Weekends see them participate in creative activities and on outings such as local bowling, shows and rollerblading or further afield to the seaside. From year 3, day girls can stay until 5.15pm for supervised prep and can also stay for supper (until 6.15pm).

Though not lacking in the yummy mummy stakes, families are from a surprisingly wide range of social backgrounds – many local, with some from further afield (Gerrards Cross, St Albans) taking advantage of the excellent coach services, available from year 3 up, that run from the Chilterns, Hertfordshire and north London areas. Girls travelling from London hop on the shuttle bus that runs from the nearby station. Parents invited to get involved – reading to children, assist on trips etc – but no guilt necessary if you're working too hard to pay the school fees.

A tip-top girls' school for those that favour the less pressurised, warmer and more friendly feel over a relentless pursuit of all things academic – but which still manages to get good results and, perhaps best of all, a free pass into RMS senior school.

Royal Masonic School for Girls

Linked with Royal Masonic School Cadogan House

Rickmansworth Park, Chorleywood Road, Rickmansworth, Hertfordshire WD3 4HF

Ages 11–19 **Pupils** 676 **Sixth form** 159 **Boarders** 68 full, 19 weekly, 6 flexi

Fees: Day £17,475; Boarding £27,495 – £29,835 pa

01923 773168
www.royalmasonic.herts.sch.uk

Head: Since January 2017, Kevin Carson BA MPhil PGCE (40s), previously co-interim head at The Grammar School at Leeds. Has headed up the English and drama departments at Cheltenham College and subsequently Abingdon School, also taking on the role of resident tutor in boarding houses in both schools. He particularly championed equal opportunities for his female tutees within Cheltenham's co-educational environment.

Original plan was to go into academia, but after spending 'more time in the library than with people' while doing his postgrad, he 'realised a more sociable career might suit me better.' Became so passionate about teaching as soon as he'd tried it that 'friends said I talked about nothing else – not even small talk,' he laughs. Still teaches year 7s and 8s and sixth formers. 'It's absolutely the best way to get to know the students,' he says.

With his broad (by southern standards) Scouse accent and laid-back demeanour, he's certainly not your stereotypical headteacher of a home counties private girls' school, but parents and pupils are thrilled with him. 'Make no mistake, he had big boots to fill,' says one parent, 'but I think everyone would agree he is absolutely dedicated to the children and it shows.' Girls say he is 'around a lot, whether teaching, doing lunch duty or assemblies and sometimes he just pops into lessons – we really feel we know him.'

Married to Sarah, with two daughters, both in the junior school. Outside of school, the family pursues a wide range of sporting and cultural interests.

Academic matters: The school does academically better than it's sometimes perceived to. In fact, it's turning formerly dismissive heads and winning more and more parental votes with persistently improving results. In 2018, 49 per cent A*/A grades at A level and 60 per cent A*-A/9-7 at GCSE. Small class sizes (maximum 20) across the board and teachers who 'go the extra mile', with lots of clinics, email correspondence and one-to-ones during lunchtimes where necessary. 'They really get to know us individually and what makes us tick– nobody slips through the net here,' said one pupil. Setting from year 7 in maths and French, with fewer than 10 in some lower sets. More setting (English, science) from year 9 but these are very flexible and it's not unheard of for girls to move from the bottom to top of six sets in the space of a year. Everyone does one modern language from year 7 (out of French, Spanish and German), then in year 8 they pick an additional one (Mandarin and Italian also on offer by this stage). Latin for all from year 7.

Parents say it's a 'good all-round school' where their children get to 'have a go at everything.' 'They are spectacular at finding each child's strengths across the board and then relentlessly nurturing them,' was a typical parent comment. Girls told us they don't feel under pressure, even though homework levels 'can feel very heavy in the upper years.' History by far the strongest department, say pupils ('they just make learning so fun and have so many great staff'), with sciences and maths coming to the fore at A level.

At A level, everyone starts off taking four out of 30 options (all the traditional, plus the likes of psychology, sociology, photography and creative arts). But those taking two A levels in photography or art are treated with as much support as mathematicians and scientists taking four and in any case, three-quarters of pupils drop an A level and pick up an EPQ, whose results are impressive. Handful of BTecs also available, for example in food and nutrition and performing arts. Plus a plethora of non-examined courses in subjects ranging from history of feminism to the more practical cooking at university. Good parent networks mean plenty of top business leaders come in to do one-off talks.

Excellent on SEN, according to parents, with individual lessons on offer (at extra cost) to girls needing support – around 60 in total when we visited, though none with EHCPs. All pupils screened on entry. Specialist EAL teaching for overseas pupils (again, charged as extra). 'It helps that the school is so transparent and accessible,' said one parent, who claimed her daughter had 'become a different child – so happy and well supported.' School claims to cater for the gifted and talented, although a parent said, 'if I had an academically brilliant child – I mean, really at the top end – I have no doubt a more selective school would be better.' Reporting system could be improved, say some parents – 'they give them such good grades that you sometimes are led to believe they're doing better than they are, so it throws you when the exam results come through.'

Games, options, the arts: Gymnastics, trampolining, dance, squash et al take place in a jawdropping double sports hall. Acres of playing fields, great for cross-country and adventure training, and all-weather pitch, with football, cricket and rugby most recently on the up. Trophies galore for the competitive, especially in hockey, netball (internationally), gymnastics and swimming (nationally). Big push on inclusivity to give the less naturally sporty a love of physical activity (including PE lessons for all including sixth formers and alternative options such as zumba, pilates and yoga on offer).

School has strong artsy feel, with some beautiful pieces peppered throughout the pristine corridors. There's a well-used photography studio and dark room, drama studio and plenty of musical and theatrical productions throughout the year, many performed at the Watersmeet theatre in Rickmansworth. Great excitement about new performing arts faculty opening in 2019 with dance studio, drama studio, music areas and all-new recording studio. Musical opportunities abound, with 300 girls learning an instrument and concert orchestra, various ensembles and choirs, along with an emphasis on jazz groups.

Trips and tours of all sorts and vast array of extracurricular activities, including very popular DofE and cadets, means the school continues to buzz after lessons are over. Girls enthuse over chess and Chinese clubs as much as astronomy (in school's own planetarium – there's an astronomy GCSE on offer too) and taekwondo. Plenty of charitable works, with prefects nominating a charity for the school to support each year.

Boarding: Three boarding houses with most boarders in years 10 to 12. Around 40 per cent of boarders from overseas – Europe, the Far East, Russia and further afield. Also popular with Forces families.

Boarders are treated to an outing every Saturday (bowling, cinema, horse riding, theatre, London attractions etc), with occasional trips further afield, with recent examples including Brighton and to Harry Potter studios. Older girls allowed to London in groups for shopping and lunch and in years 12 and 13 to the cinema in the evenings. 'It's incredibly warm and welcoming, and they get the balance just right about how much independence you get,' one girl told us.

We visited the most newly refurbished house which, like the rest of the school, was spacious, clean and well-equipped, as well as being cosy and homely with all the mod cons. Dorms with up to four girls per room in younger years; and up to two for sixth formers. Tidiness clearly not a priority for some, suggesting more lenience on that front than at some schools we visit. Light, bright and modern dining room, where boarders and day girls take all their meals, feels like a hub of chatter at lunch time, with girls seated at sociably round tables, enjoying freshly cooked meals which are, according to all, 'outstanding'.

Background and atmosphere: Founded in 1788 to educate the children of masons who had fallen on hard times, the current 150 acre site, built in the 1930s, is the school's fourth home. A vast campus, more akin to a redbrick university than a suburban girls' school, with smart, identikit buildings surrounding two quadrangles ('teeming with girls chatting in the summer term,' said one), and the longest teaching corridor in Britain. Became an independent school, open to all, in 1978.

Great sixth form centre – comfortable common room, complete with black and pink sink-into sofas, and café area. Girls describe guidance at this stage of their education as 'excellent', with teachers giving up free time to help with UCAS applications, although some parents said they would like to see 'more emphasis on Oxbridge applications.' Spectacular rotunda library, one of the nicest we've seen, with plenty of space for quiet study. Atmosphere is serene (so much so that you sometimes wonder where all the girls are) and purposeful, but with a good dose of fun thrown in the mix, although girls told us there could be 'more integration between the year groups.'

This is a forward-looking school, but with a strong sense of tradition – RMS is the only school in the country still to do 'drill': a spectacle of pinafored girls with pinned back hair performing something akin to synchronised swimming but without the water (they recently appeared on The One Show). Places in the squad are highly sought after, with dozens volunteering even for the reserves.

Pastoral care, well-being and discipline: Often chosen by parents precisely for its pastoral focus, the school is regularly invited to talk about their tactics at national conferences. So what's their secret? 'Time,' says the head – every teacher has enough time to support the individual girls, as well as to bring up issues, no matter how small, during weekly staff meetings. 'She's loving science but is worried about her French vocab test' and 'She's had a fall-out with her friends but worked it all out now' etc. Sixth formers are trained as peer mentors by the school counsellors, with year 9 girls taking on 'big sister' roles to new year 7s. School acutely aware that friendship groups formed in year 7 sometimes breaking up in year 8 or 9 and on the ball in how to deal with it, with specific friendship mediator on hand. 'It means it rarely turns to bullying,' girls told us.

Behaviour is excellent – girls put it down to mutual respect with staff. Parents add that school has never been afraid to 'take a hard line' when necessary and has even been known to call in police to educate girls on the outcomes of certain scenarios if they rear their ugly heads. School claims alcohol, drugs etc are 'not an issue'; girls concur. On a more micro-level, girls say the school 'isn't strict, but there are a lot of rules, especially around things like uniform.' Detentions aren't as readily handed out as at some schools, though, with a whopping five black marks before one is handed out.

Pupils and parents: For over 200 years, this was a school for families facing hardship and although it's now fee-paying, the culture seems to have stuck, with girls well-grounded and grateful to be there. Seemingly younger and fresher than their more streetwise grammar peers, RMS girls are nonetheless confident and articulate too. Ethnically reflective of the local area – mainly white, with a large British Indian contingent and sprinklings of other backgrounds.

Parents – an exceptionally sociable bunch – from all walks of life from the well-heeled to hard working, dual income, first time buyers. 'But as a working mum, I'm still a minority,' said one. Some expats and international parents, largely of overseas boarders. Many from across the Chilterns and Hertfordshire, with an increasing north London crowd. The school provides an excellent coach service from all these areas, with the London brigade able to take advantage of the shuttle bus from the tube station. Parents of girls at smaller prep schools reported a bit of a culture shock when their daughters joined this vast establishment, but added that they felt totally at home 'after just a few weeks'.

Entrance: Increasingly selective (but nowhere near as much as some local schools), RMS is seen by more and more parents as a desirable option. Majority join at 11+ but some places are also available up to 14+. Online test in maths, English and reasoning. There's also a creative writing exercise, group activity and group interview. School looks closely at report from current school as well as test results. Candidates for entry in later years sit tests in English, maths and non-verbal reasoning.

Around 170 girls compete for approximately 60 places. About a third come from state primaries; a further third from local preps (Maltman's Green, Charlotte House and Orley Farm are main three feeders); and the final third from school's own prep Cadogan House (guaranteed entry, making for a mixed bag academically). Good sibling policy – a relief if younger ones aren't as starry as big sister. Around 25 new places are available in year 12, with girls being selected on GCSE results and extracurricular achievements.

In line with its charitable ethos, school offers a limited number of assisted boarding places to disadvantaged children from London boroughs of Hillingdon and Tower Hamlets and (surprisingly) Norfolk. Head says that integration of these girls, and that of the mainly international boarders, is 'fantastic'.

Exit: A small exodus – around 15-20 per cent – at 16, to local grammars, state schools and college. Majority of those who stay the course go on to university, with around 40 per cent to Russell Group; Leeds, Exeter, Nottingham Trent, Royal Holloway, Bristol, Birmingham and Nottingham all popular. One to Cambridge, one to Melbourne, plus two vets and a dentist in 2018. Huge breadth of subjects studied – 'and you get no less attention if you choose to study marine biology than law,' said one pupil.

Money matters: Capital expenditure is underpinned by an endowment set up by the Masons and the school is a tenant of the site. Multitude of scholarships and exhibitions available at 11+ (academic, all-rounder, art, music and sport) and sixth form (performance arts added) typically offering 25 per cent discount on fees. Five per cent discount for siblings and 10 per cent for Forces families. Means-tested bursaries available.

Remarks: Academically on the up, RMS is now a serious contender in the competitive local market, with top notch facilities also a pull for many families. Teachers adept at drawing the best out of everyone, whatever their abilities, and the emphasis on the arts and extracurricular means girls leave well-rounded and confident. Nurturing, but not to the point of being a bubble, this is a school that walks the walk when it comes to focusing on the individual. 'I can tell you about my experience here, but it won't be the same as anyone else's and that's the great thing about this school,' was the kind of comment we heard time and time again from girls, although pushier parents might still prefer some of the more selective local schools.

Rupert House School

90 Bell Street, Henley-on-Thames, Oxfordshire RG9 2BN

Ages 3–11 **Pupils** 153 (131 girls, 22 boys)

Fees: £11,469 – £14,130 pa

01491 574263

Head: Since 2013, Clare Lynas MA PGCE NPQH (50s). Previously deputy head at Thorngrove, Newbury. Before that, taught at assorted independent preps across London, Berkshire and Hampshire. Studied English at St Andrews, then did primary level PGCE at Edinburgh, initially with the aim of becoming an educational psychologist, 'but I fell in love with the teaching,' which – true to her word – she says she still does. 'It's essential

R

to teach because part of caring for children is knowing and understanding them.' Later did a masters in child development and a secondary level PGCE.

No-nonsense, candid and big-hearted, she strives for a non-hierarchical atmosphere – 'We're a small school so all staff get stuck into duties that need doing, including wiping tables, and I'd like to think I'm part of that,' she says; staff concur. Pupils say she's 'strict' ('You always behave when she's around') but 'fair,' 'welcoming' and 'great at telling stories.' Parents call her 'aspirational,' and 'straight-talking' with particular praise for her transformation of sports (although some parents would still 'like it to be more competitive').

Lives with her husband and three boys in Newbury, but stays in Henley during the week – 'It's important to be part of the community.' Enjoys long walks, birds and wildlife.

Entrance: Now co-ed to 11, entry points are mainly in nursery (called Rupert Bears, age 3+), reception (age 4+) and year 3 (age 7+), although pupils do join at other times 'if there are spaces' (there usually are). For the lower school, expect a trial day and informal assessment by class teacher; for the upper school, children do written assessments in English and maths. But it's non-selective throughout, 'so we're looking for socially cohesive children first and foremost,' says head. 'With English and maths, we're looking for potential to ensure they'll be able to keep up, rather than existing achievements.'

Exit: St Helen & St Katharine (Abingdon) and Queen Anne's (Caversham) take the lion's share of girls, closely followed by The Abbey (Reading) and Headington (Oxford). A few to boarding schools and less than a handful to state sector, mainly Sir William Borlase's (Marlow) and Gillotts (Henley). Scholarships on the up, including academics, all-rounders and in the arts. Some leave earlier, mainly due to relocation. Watch this space for boys' destinations as they move through the newly co-ed school.

Remarks: Blink and you miss it. Seriously, if you don't drive straight past it on your first visit, even with good directions, you're doing well. Founded in 1924 for just 10 pupils (three of whom were the founders' sons), the school moved to its current location in 1942 – a site comprising two red-brick town houses in an impossibly quaint part of Henley. The move led to a change of name too – from St Joan's to Rupert House, its newer namesake being one-time neighbour Rupert, leader of the king's cavalry. It can only be due to the mercifully large gardens that they've managed to stay put, with the original outdoor space now home to two additional buildings – one for the lower school (with fenced in early years playground plus adventure playground for all) and another for art, science and SEND department; they've even managed to squeeze in a greenhouse, gardening club and mud kitchen area. In short, the school is something of a Tardis, albeit with some inevitably elbow brushing and a need for backs to the wall when a whole class piles past.

Don't assume sports are a write-off as a result, though, as it's only a short walk (almost all off-road) to two courts, grass football pitch/running track, pavilion and parking area, all owned by the school. Behind this is a fabulous forest school area, and there's a licence for outdoor education in the woods beyond. Pupils also get use of a hockey pitch and the rugby club next door, while swimming is provided in local pools, using minibuses. 'Sport wasn't prioritised in the past, but it's great now – the children get loads of outdoor time,' one parent told us. Core sports are netball, hockey, rounders and athletics, all of which pupils compete in, as well as getting involved in one-off events such as aquathons.

Back at base camp, we found pupils engaged in a wide range of learning styles – everything from lively discussions about wind pollination (with pictures they'd taken of wind pollinated flowers on iPads) to older girls giving eloquent speeches in preparation for the compulsory English Speaking Board exams (which all pupils do). When quizzed by us on their favourite aspects of each topic, we wondered if they might actually jump out of their seats, such was their enthusiasm to reel off example upon example – no more so than in science, with answers including making parachutes ('which we used to transport our teacher's egg for her lunch'), insulators ('we got to store chocolate in it and eat it afterwards'), boats ('to do a race – that was when we learned about streamlining') and even 'elephant foam that hit the ceiling.' Woe betide any child that isn't able to instantly assess how their current learning fits into the Prep School Baccalaureate (a programme of study for children that aims to develop and track knowledge, skills and attitudes), though 'The PSB is important to us because if you get two great people being interviewed for, say, Cambridge, this could be the deciding factor,' believes school.

In lower school, pressure is minimal, with barely any homework ('mostly spellings,' say parents) and all learning, with the exception of English and maths, focused around a topic – round the world, animals, space, ocean and seas, water, to name a few. Lots of parent involvement, class assemblies (reception were practising for a delightfully musical around-the-world one when we visited) and practical learning, including horticulture, DT and cooking. But it's all change in upper school, say parents, when girls are expected to hit the ground running. Setting in phonics in lower school; maths from year 4 or 5 (changes each year according to pupils); English and science from year 5. Two languages taught – French from reception; Mandarin in year 4 and 5. Class sizes are a maximum of 20 in lower school and 16 (after boys leave) for upper school, although some are much smaller – one class had just eight when we visited. Subject specialist teachers in PE and music from nursery; French and games from reception; art, science, DT, food technology, horticulture from year 3; Mandarin from year 4. Outdoor learning embedded, with year 3s just about to head off into the woods to find woodlice when we visited.

SEN not historically a strong point, say parents. But learning support team now offers in-class support from nursery upwards (mainly literacy, some numeracy), plus one-to-one if you're prepared to pay for it. Around 16 per cent of pupils have SEN, mainly at the milder end (with many more using learning support).

Teachers are 'in the main, nurturing' and 'go above and beyond,' say parents. 'They are really helpful and even when they get cross, they're never shouty,' say children. Staff turnover? 'There isn't any,' one teacher told us – 'honestly, teachers who come here, stay.' Those that do leave tend to be the younger ones ready for a new challenge. As with many preps, noticeable lack of male teachers, but disappointing complacency about it during our visit (although school later told us they would 'love to have more male applicants').

Musically strong, with junior and upper school choirs (open to all), chamber choir (by audition only), orchestra, string group, vocal group, plus groups for saxophone, guitar and drumming, harp ensemble, musical theatre group and music theory club. Drama so popular that it gets even the very quiet ones performing with confidence – 'everyone gets a go on stage,' say parents. Vibrant art studio – what it loses in natural daylight, it makes up for in cheerful colours and art displays, with some exceptionally impressive year 6 art scholarship work exhibited. Nearly 50 extracurricular clubs – all the usual suspects, along with everything from film animation to 'think tank' (strategic board games – 'very good for children's logic,' says head). 'Boyish experiences also catered for, including martial arts some terms,' says head, 'as we don't want them feeling like passengers in a girls' school.' The growing number of dual income families are grateful for the wrap-around care available, with school open from 7.30am until 5.50pm daily for those willing to pay.

Only a light touch is needed with regards to discipline – 'even I was surprised – they really don't like getting in trouble,' says head. No kidding – a 'debit' is given out to those who fail to adhere to a warning, with three debits leading to 'reflection' time, but rare is the child who even gets past one debit, pupils told us, wide-eyed with horror at the mere thought. Manners are big here – pupils stand up when teachers walk in and you can expect doors to be held open well before you're anywhere near passing point. Compliant these pupils are not, however – we found them confident and chatty, with individual personalities shining through. And – almost unheard of – every pupil looked us in the eye when talking.

Pastorally, it's all hands on deck, with form teachers the first port of call for children. An 'independent listener' (think shoulder to cry on more than trained counsellor) comes in once a week, while a robust anti-bullying policy helps keep unpleasantness at bay, although parents and pupils say school isn't immune to big friendship fall-outs. 'You have to be very forgiving here,' one girl pointed out, astutely. Small class sizes deemed too small by some for this very reason – 'There might be some children who need a bigger base from which to form friendships or elsewhere to turn if friendships go wrong,' said one, although another pointed out that 'it makes for more cross-year friendships.' Parents pleased that boys no longer have to leave at the end of year 2: 'it gives a lovely family atmosphere when they join lower school.'

Families span an eight-mile radius, but at least two-thirds are from the town centre – a good job, given the lack of parking (although you can drop-and-go in the mornings). Ethnically, it's nearly all white (this is Henley, after all) and while there's a more of a mix in term of wealth than you might expect, there's still plenty of the yummy mummies and green welly brigade (again, this is Henley).

This small but ambitious prep is nurturing to the point of feeling 'like an extension of home,' as one parent put it. Not for parents who hanker after a flashy country house and grounds, and the smaller classes won't suit everyone. But for those who want a friendly community school, which prepares pupils well for secondary school without undue pressure, this is a jewel.

Ryde Junior School

Linked with Ryde School with Upper Chine

Queen's Road, Ryde, Isle of Wight PO33 3BE

Ages 3–11 **Pupils** 242 C of E

Fees: £7,635 – £12,795pa

01983 612901
www.rydeschool.org.uk

Head of junior school: Since 2015, Linda Dennis, previously deputy head at St Faith's School, Cambridge, where she held many roles over 25 years, including curriculum co-ordinator, deputy head (pastoral), head of drama and head of languages. She is an ISI inspector.

Winchester born, Mrs Dennis grew up on her parents' dairy farm, near Andover, before attending La Retraite School, in Salisbury, and graduating with a BEd from Southampton University. She began her teaching career in Dorset before moving to Cambridge in 1990. Her husband, Philip, is a history teacher and she has two sons, one of them also a teacher.

Entrance: Non-selective. Tested in English, maths and non-verbal reasoning higher up for placing purposes. IQ test for those for whom English is not first language. The closure of state middle schools on the island has resulted in a steady stream of pupils into years 3, 4, 5, and 6, although there has not been a marked increase in overall numbers. Academic scholarships available for entry into year 5.

Exit: Typically 95 per cent goes through to the senior school with rest going to island state schools or occasionally an independent school on the mainland.

Remarks: The junior school is on the main school campus, a cluster of unremarkable buildings to one side. Nicely kept, and feels safe and secure – definitely separate from the senior part of things.

Two or three classes a year, size 14-18. Set for maths and English from year 4. There's the usual love/hate split for maths, but even the haters say the teachers are really nice and helpful if you don't get it. And for those who love it – 'we have maths challenges as well as sports fixtures', said one boy proudly.

There was a huge basin of conkers in the science lab: year 3s were finding out whether size and shape have an impact on strength in a very joyful conkers experiment. New focus on languages, with Spanish becoming the second language, and Mandarin or Latin being taught from year 6. A nice emphasis on creativity – not always the case in through schools with an eye on the end results: year 4 write a story or poem every week, and after their trip to the Amazon World, wrote stories about the Amazon in geography. Plenty of monitoring and the school will do everything and anything to help children falling behind.

Reasonable size library, where pupils can do prep after school. Not loads of room to run around at break time (year 6s look forward to using senior school playing fields), and the children would like a bit more interest in their playground, although the climbing frame is a fairly recent addition. Break times could be longer, say pupils – 'we spend a lot of time in the classrooms. I think we need longer to refresh our brains.' (Currently 15 minutes twice a day, plus an hour for lunch.) However, now more outdoor learning with forest school and beach school teachers.

Ethos of hard work, and rewarding positive behaviour. Children behave to meet expectations, says the school, and it largely works: about five detentions in the last 16 years. Not the right school for those intent on disruption; but they do an excellent job with those who were disaffected in their previous schools. Bullying happens – as it does everywhere – but is dealt with efficiently.

Lively children who express a bubbling enthusiasm for their school, which they clearly love. After meeting a group of juniors, we were met by beaming smiles and hellos when bumping into them later, a step beyond the usual compulsory politeness. School says it is the norm for pupils to behave quietly and well, and the pupils we met were certainly polite; although this is not a leap to your feet school.

As you would expect in a school this nurturing, parents are encouraged to come up to classrooms – 'it's important to know if the hamster has died'. Community and family are important words here. Constantly in contact with parents by text and email, and there is very little that they rely on children to tell parents; although parents who are used to the gold standard communication at Fiveways infants section sometimes find the move to a bit less information challenging – apparently a Facebook group has been set up, and parents remind each other of things they need to remember for school trips.

Smart uniform – a fair amount of the usual grey. The girls dislike the stripy summer dresses, although actually they look quite nice: but the full skirts can blow up the waist in a fresh breeze. Girls would be happy to design a new dress, and actually they'd like a pinafore: an aqua pinafore. Great kit-bags on wheels – no back problems developing here.

Pupils eulogise about the food, in particular Thursday roasts (which came into being after feedback from the class food reps – food feedback is paid proper respect here). There's a good range on offer daily, including two puddings; although one boy, when asked what he would like to change about his school, said in a pained voice: 'It would be good to have seconds. At the moment we have to fill up on bread and butter.'

The three houses compete vigorously, not just on the sports field, but also in the sailing challenge and the inter-house sandcastle challenge – you would expect no less from an island school. The usual range of clubs, plus ASC (Adventure Service Challenge) which is like a mini DofE for years 5 and 6. A very few boarders at the top end of the school share the Bembridge boarding house with senior school pupils.

Children from nursery to year 2 are at Fiveways, a separate campus across the road. Mixed ability classes, although teachers will hand out work of differing levels within classes. Children work in quiet deep concentration, slightly startling in children so young. Classes of 14-16. Pupils read with a teacher or teaching assistant every day. For all that, a surprisingly small library. Mandarin and Spanish from age 4, two lessons in each language every week.

Playground with new climbing equipment, noisy plants which come to life when the wind blows through them, and a fragrant herb bed (the herbs are used in school kitchen). Not huge, but classes take break in turns, so there's plenty of room to run around.

Parents couldn't say enough about how great this part of the school is; one just wistfully commented that it would be nice if they had a few more male teachers. Although there didn't in general appear to be a distinction drawn between girls' and boys' activities, the club set up has some divisions: Rainbows is a Brownie group for the girls (arts and crafts, cooking etc), Only Boys Allowed for boys – where they do things like make codes, modelling and camping, and sign in with a thumb print: sounds super, and possibly quite a few girls might think so too? Though questionable whether many boys would fancy joining Rainbows...

This is a CofE school, with a 'pervasive' religious approach. Attendance at church services is not compulsory, but actually all elect to attend. When the children reach year 2, they are encouraged to take assemblies themselves, as solo or collective attempts: assemblies this term have included a visiting hamster and dog. Pupils can also bring in a parent to give an expert talk: last term the children learnt about Scotland and developed a clan Fiveways tartan – scarves all round.

Parents praise the detailed and thorough communication from Fiveways: the Fiveways' flyer comes out every Friday; parents receive emails and texts, and the flipchart in the foyer makes sure that parents are kept informed about everything including the menu for the day. If they know their child is going to loathe everything, they can sign up their child for a sandwich or a bowl of plain pasta.

The most notable thing about this part of the school is the detailed thought and attention given to the pastoral care of each child. Fiveways understands all the nuances of bullying; how it differs between the sexes; and how, for little girls, this could amount to a look passed during a lesson (the seat plan would be varied accordingly). A similar level of detailed consideration would be given to get to the root of bad behaviour, in order to resolve the problem – 'we will do whatever is necessary, even if it means involving an educational psychologist'. One parent commented on how well her child's learning difficulty was spotted and dealt with. SEN provision is excellent. No stigma here – everyone is happy to visit the SEN teacher.

Ryde School with Upper Chine

Linked with Ryde Junior School

Queen's Road, Ryde, Isle of Wight PO33 3BE

Ages 11–18 **Pupils** 523 **Sixth form** 141 **Boarders** 49 full, 11 weekly, 6 flexi **C of E**

Fees: Day £13,230; Boarding £26,010 – £29,160 pa

01983 562229
www.rydeschool.org.uk

Headmaster: Since 2013, Mark Waldron. Previously head of the English College in Prague, deputy head of Sherborne, and taught at The Leys School and Radley College. Mr Waldron is keen to prepare pupils to compete internationally, and has shaken up language provision to support this. Parents find the head approachable, are impressed by his priorities.

The head encourages his teachers to think about the potential for creative and independent thought when planning their lessons: could the lesson take place without the pupils? Mr Waldron teaches maths – always the bottom set, so he knows the lowest common denominator. Regularly turns cakes into fractions; and what are the chances of getting that elusive blue in a tube of Smarties?

He is learning to sail, and currently classes himself as incompetent crew; is a politics junkie and devotee of the races. Likes pub quizzes. You can see how he might.

Academic matters: Good solid academic results for a non-selective school. In 2018, 34 per cent A*/A at A level. At GCSE, 41 per cent A*/A /7-9. IGCSE also available, and the head has introduced the vocational IB (IBCP) alongside the IB. In 2018, average 32 IB points. Ryde is chosen by some parents for its consistently good results, which give a 'degree of assurance': it is in the privileged position of being virtually the only independent mainstream school on the Island (the other is very small), and Island state secondary schools do not rank highly in the league tables. One parent said that he feels his children 'have the chance to excel and achieve their full potential'.

Class sizes at A level 8-14, a maximum of 22 at GCSE. There is a strong work ethic at Ryde – the classes we saw were almost universally heads down, working hard, the concentrated effort almost palpable – 'It's not something that you get teased for: it's actually cool to be clever', said a pupil.

Maths and science are popular – due in part, says the head, to the large number of doctor parents; and illustrated by year 10 turning the whole periodic table into cupcakes in the school bake off. The head has come from a school where students were studying in their third or fourth language, and firmly subscribes to the saying 'if you only speak one language then you can only live one life'. Spanish is the new second language at Ryde, and Mandarin and Latin are also finding a place in the curriculum. Alongside GCSEs pupils study one of global perspectives, arts award, science CREST award or informatics.

With Mr Waldron has come a new emphasis on the sixth form: there's a new sixth form block on the main campus, and a new emphasis on career planning and lifelong learning. It's about destinations, says Mr Waldron: pupils needs to understand where they want to go, and how to get there. IB students know what they are doing and why; not always the case for those studying A levels. So at Ryde even A level pupils will do the theory of knowledge core of the IB, so they 'get an idea of what it means to think.'

The sixth formers we met were polite and articulate, although they didn't quite have the spit and polish you might encounter in some mainland independent schools: perhaps this is because the Island and school constitute a secure and more laid back environment. Mr Waldron is well aware that his domestic pupils might lack some of the edge which is evident in his international students, particularly those from the eastern block.

Parents receive mini monthly report cards detailing effort and progress, until GCSE, when this turns into attainment, and predicted and target grades – to flag up any problems with work. Focus on praising effort: merit badges worn on blazers, like awards for courage under fire, are awarded entirely for effort. When the school as a whole has achieved 2,000 efforts there's a mufti day.

Strong SEN provision: around 15 per cent of pupils here have special needs, and the school makes provision for up to moderate dyslexia. Aim for SEN pupils: to make all capable of independent learning.

Games, options, the arts: Music is super here – our tour guides, neither of whom were taking music A level, said their happiest hours at school were spent in the music block. The teaching inspires a real love of music, and pupils relish the joys of the annual Global Rock – an international dance competition. Students put together routines and costumes themselves: parents describe the results as 'incredible'.

Not a school, says the head, for a top sportsman or woman: two pupils left at 16 to attend schools with more focus on hockey and rugby (although sailing is thriving). The sports provision is decent, but it's difficult to get good mainland schools to come and play on the Island, and as a small school, there's a limited choice of pupils for teams. But if you're good at sport you get to be a big fish in a small pond and have opportunities you might not enjoy at a larger school.

Grand DT room in the predominantly glass block. 'If I get them in year 7, they stay,' said the DT teacher with a smile; and indeed both our guides expressed huge enthusiasm for the subject, and remembered with affection their first task of designing an insect in year 7. Roof terrace with lovely view out over the sea – it's made full use of for parties – and a few beds of weeds which apparently have an eco purpose. The art rooms have the hushed atmosphere of a cathedral: any talking is done is whispers, pupils concentrate hard.

Both CCF and DofE are popular here; a parent commented that it is the good provision for music, arts and extracurricular that give children here such a good level of confidence.

R

Boarding: The main boarding campus is some 10 miles from the school, but there's a daily bus service and the school pass can also be used to obtain free travel on public transport on the Island. The boarding house is beautiful arts and crafts buildings, sensitively restored and converted. Admiring the lower gallery, a long elegant sitting room with squashy sofas, packed bookshelves and piano, you might think you are being shown around a rather lovely National Trust property. Then you would spot the drum kit and TV and know you're not. The upper gallery above has been turned into double bedrooms surrounding a living area for year 10 girls – an idyllic set up, flooded with light from the long windows. Sixth formers get single rooms, unless they request to share. There's also a sixth form boarding house in Ryde within walking distance of the school for those who want to live more independently.

Ryde chosen by one parent for the strong sense of family in the boarding houses, compared to other schools where boarding provision seemed like 'housing for battery chickens.' His children are happy; any minor issues arising have been dealt with successfully, and he has 'absolute confidence in the boarding set up'.

The large site is shared with an activity centre, so there are plenty of outdoor facilities for boarders to enjoy – anyone for after-school caving? Indoors there's a room with pool, table tennis and table football. Pupils say the boarding experience is sold on the basis of lots of activities, but really some of them rarely happen: quad biking, for instance, only happens during the first week of term. (There is, perhaps, a particular push on special activities at the beginning of terms to help new kids to bond.)

Boarders can roam the 100 acre grounds more or less as they please, providing they sign out first. Must keep in sight of the drive on dark winter days, and need to seek permission to go the beach, which is off campus. The youngest boarder is currently year 6 – there isn't an age restriction, but the head of boarding likes there to be boarders of a similar age to keep each other company.

Pupils comment that the food in the boarding house is 'awful' (in comparison, food at the school is 'gourmet'). School is well aware of the problem, which is tricky to rectify since the catering facilities at the boarding house are shared with the activity centre. But there is a gorgeous mural in the dining room of animals waiting to board Noah's ark, a pair of black cats, tails held jauntily high, leading the way. The mural remains unfinished: the painter pupil didn't return from the First World War to finish it off; but it must be lovely to look at while wading through the substandard grub.

Boarders set up their own clubs – cheesy Tuesdays (the cheese on toast club) and the Coco Pops club – foodie clubs popular for obvious reasons. They make good use of the kitchen facilities, and can cook as they please – there's plenty of fruit and cereal available at all times, and a Tesco run every Friday night (no Red Bull allowed).

Background and atmosphere: A school surrounded by stunning scenery – how lovely to sit in the library and stare out at the picture postcard view over the sea. Venerable main building with nondescript (but well cared for) adjuncts, plus renovated science labs.

The advantages of attending school on the Island are clear: it is safe, secure and beautiful. The counter to this is perhaps an element of complacency born of isolation: the head is keen for pupils to look beyond the Solent – pupils must not be limited by the stretch of water: they will need to be able to compete nationally and internationally. Mr Waldron intends to ensure they can.

Pupils are friendly and polite (although this is not a leap to your feet place) and clearly enjoy being at school – one who transferred to Ryde from a local school commented how good it is to be at a school where he actually wants to stay and do activities, just because it's nice to be there. One parent said the best thing about Ryde are its pupils: 'grounded, mature; and nice kids to be around.'

A traditional environment – although surprisingly pupils are allowed to use mobile phones in class for task-related research: one parent commented that he is not happy with a rule so open to abuse. CofE but with a light touch – prayers at the end of assembly, because that's just what happens; much like a full stop at the end of a sentence. But Mr Waldron is keen for religion to play a larger part, and has introduced compulsory church as a fortnightly event. Sixth formers are unimpressed: they've been told that this is reflection time, but don't quite see why it should have to take place in church.

Parents are happy with communication levels, and reaction to complaints (which are rare): when one did have a problem and raised the issue with the head, it was dealt with swiftly and well.

School council of pupil representatives who have been feeling a bit disenchanted with the slow reaction to their views and requests: for instance, the school council requested a shelter outside the canteen, so that pupils waiting in the lunch queue on rainy days didn't get wet. A sensible request – but it took a couple of years to happen. The head says this has been addressed: democracy has come to Ryde, and the school council is operating under a new pupil-run system.

End of year trip to somewhere theme parkish has been replaced by an activity week focusing on life skills. This has not been uniformly welcomed by pupils, the majority lingering on the side of 'not fair.' Lower sixth, in particular, felt they might have had more fun on a roller coaster than learning to tidy and clean – although there must have been a number of grateful parents, and those changing a tyre skills may well come in handy.

Uniform is the usual fare, but some parents, apparently, are obsessed with wanting a 'trendy exclusive uniform' – think black blazers with yellow trim; although one parent we spoke to observed dryly that 'Ryde kids don't actually want to stand out on the bus.' Quite.

Pastoral care, well-being and discipline: Parents view the pastoral care at Ryde as exceptional – 'they do a terrific job' – and describe the advantages of a small school where staff know all the pupils and their families. Parents like the strong community atmosphere at school, and comment on the extraordinary level of support and counselling from the school following the tragic death of a pupil, both to the immediate family, and to other pupils.

The head is keen for his pupils to achieve a balance in life, and there is new emphasis on life skills and mindfulness to emphasis the importance of enjoying and experiencing the present (involves controlled breathing – even those who were sceptical beforehand were happy to admit that this was super – one admitted to taking relaxation as far as sleep). Indeed, there is a new health and well-being centre. This does not feel like the sort of school where grades will be achieved at the expense of well-being; indeed the head muses on whether the Norland nanny in last year's batch of sixth formers, who worked hard to achieve her two A levels, will be happier than the Cambridge mathematician.

Pupils confident that there would be a teacher or form tutor they could talk to if they had a problem. There is a move to involve sixth formers more with younger years, and prefects now wear listener badges, so kids have an obvious person to go to if they want to talk to someone other than a teacher. Any bullying occurs is dealt with properly – 'sensitively and appropriately' said a parent.

Pupils and parents: Large number of parents scrimp and save to get their kids to Ryde. Around 80 per cent of boarders are international; also pupils from all over the Island, DFLs, and those from Portsmouth who commute over on the ferry. More pupils arriving across years 9/10/11 since Island middle school closure. Parents range from fish and chip shop owners to medics.

Entrance: Interview with head for all prospective pupils. Most pupils stay through to the sixth form.

Exit: The majority of sixth formers to a range of universities, particularly King's College London, Southampton and Loughborough. One to Oxbridge in 2018 and two medics; others to Canada, Madrid, Vienna and Hong Kong.

Money matters: Wants to keep fees affordable for Islanders. Scholarships open up means- tested bursaries. Academic scholarships are available for entry into years 5, 7, 9 and the sixth form with sailing, music and sports scholarships also available for entry into years 7, 9 and the sixth form. McIsaac scholarships also available and some HMC scholars are placed at Ryde.

Remarks: A school distinguished by its strong community, set in beautiful surroundings with solid academic provision. Not somewhere you are likely to encounter unscheduled exuberance, but vitality is likely to increase with Mr Waldron at the helm. Clearly the best option for many Islanders.

Rye St Antony School

Pullen's Lane, Oxford OX3 0BY

Ages Girls 3-19, boys 3-11 **Pupils** 322 (39 boys) **Sixth form** 39 **Boarders** 29 full, 8 weekly, 6 flexi (girls from year 5) **RC**

Fees: Day £9,870 – £15,330; Boarding £21,000 – £25,935 pa

01865 762802
www.ryestantony.co.uk

Headmistress: Since September 2018, Sarah Ryan, previously deputy head of Mayfield School in Sussex, and only the fifth head in the school's history. English degree from Oxford and MA from Goldsmiths. Began teaching at King's School Bruton, became head of department, then moved to The Oratory. Returned after a career break to the post of director of boarding at Leweston. She is married to Paul, also a teacher, and they have a daughter.

Head of the pre-prep and prep departments: Emma Coode, who joined the school in 2012. The inclusive philosophy of Rye starts from the get-go: 'everyone here is valued for who they are', she says.

Academic matters: You won't see Rye hovering around the top of the league tables alongside the academic superpowers that populate the local school scene – but that's just fine with them. And with their pupils' families, for that matter. 'We value the mix of ability', said one earnest sixth former; 'it's not judgmental and we all help each other'. 'Very nurturing', say parents. 'What you see is what you get and it's all about what's good for the pupils not about what they can do for the school.' School allowed to steer its own course – 'we are unique in a different way'. As focused on instilling 'a sense of duty and community' in its pupils as sending them off in the right direction when it comes to higher education – which incidentally covers anything from Oxbridge to secretarial college in any given year group. 'Parents want a school that can look after all their girls, whatever their academic aptitude'. To this end, school is constantly seeking ways to enhance and expand opportunities with options such as a BTec in business option for sixth formers or the Leiths Food and Wine course, on curriculum for years 12 and 13. Parents of the brightest girls 'choose Rye with every confidence it can deliver on the academic front' but are also attracted by the unique quality of 'valuing the idea that happy people are the most successful.'

Public examination results bear out the soundness of this approach with usually solid outcomes. In 2018, 19 per cent of A levels were graded A*/A with 53 per cent grade A*/B. At GCSE in 2018, 28 per cent were graded A*-A/9-7. Fairly respectable given the thoroughly broad church intake. Breadth of subjects on offer impressive given school's size, with maths and history top A level choices. All the usual suspects on offer at GCSE, plus food and nutrition, drama and Latin. At A level, girls can include Chinese, classical civilisation or government and politics in their choices should they be so inclined. Timetable almost entirely – and uniquely – flexible, again a benefit of school's size, with girls able to combine any mix of subjects without the restrictions of fixed 'blocks'. A level classes tend to be tiny – just four girls were studying French and two religious studies when we visited – and it's no sweat if just one wants to take any given subject at A level: 'we just make it work'.

Class sizes in the senior school up to GCSE average 16 and with a pupil to teacher ratio of 1:5 there's little chance of any strugglers slipping through the net. When it comes to SEN, 'we have catered for the needs of the extreme and the mainstream'. Those needing the most support are given the flexibility to complete their schooling in the most appropriate way and emerge with a skill set that equips them for life. Learning support (charged as extra) is available to any pupil who needs it but outside of formal intervention little touches such as the fact that there are four maths sets help iron out any minor issues without a fuss. Strong links with several European countries means that specialist teachers support a significant number of pupils with EAL, with outstanding results: 'sometimes after a couple of terms you can't tell they're not English', enthused one pupil of her international peers.

Games, options, the arts: 'When it comes to games, we're never going to win all the trophies, but we're enthusiastic and inclusive and that's what counts'. It's a traditional roster of netball, hockey and athletics at Rye plus a super range of clubs. An outdoor heated pool provides a popular summer term lunch time club for pupils from year 3 up. Some success in fixtures – occasionally against much larger schools – but winning at any cost is not Rye's raison d'etre, which is better described by one pupil as 'competitive and fun'. Parents say girls are always a bit surprised when they win a fixture. School has grounds rather than acres of playing fields, but as with everything here, it does the trick and there are ample facilities for pupils to get sporty. School boasts 'serious' rowers and horsewomen amongst its cohort and celebrates victories won outside of school in assemblies. In fact, parents say school 'celebrates everything'.

Punches way above its weight when it comes to extracurricular activities with a good array on offer for all ages. Books feature widely, with A Book A Month and Carnegie Medal Shadowing Club building on the fantastic foundations laid in the junior school by Rye's devoted librarian (when we visited she was outside with some of the youngest children drinking pumpkin soup and reading Halloween stories). For prep pupils there's forest school, indoor climbing, small animal care and even a festive decorations club (Christmas is huge at Rye, but more of that later). Seniors throw themselves into everything from dissection, mindfulness and Minecraft to psychology, DofE and Young Enterprise. There are choirs aplenty (happily, almost all non-selective) as well as an orchestra and chamber music group. Additional optional activities for boarders cover baking, power walking and climbing and there are further opportunities to join external clubs such as the Oxford Fencing Club and Oxford Isis Korfball Club. No wonder school feels the need to produce such a beautiful booklet to showcase its plethora of activities.

R

Arts taken seriously and 'very strong'. Drama on curriculum from reception, LAMDA and ABRSM results alike are very good and there's no shortage of opportunities for pupils to flex their performing muscles. From termly teatime concerts for novices to drama festivals the halls of Rye are certainly alive with the sound of music. And it's not just local performances on the agenda – notice boards in the smart music block advertise past and future musical tours to far flung regions including Paris and Venice.

Lovely drama studio gives girls all the space they need for performances with the light and bright art studio, festooned with high quality paintings, 3D work and textiles, the cherry on top of the arts offering.

Boarding: Boarding officially available for girls from year 5, although when we visited the youngest were in year 7. The idyllic Croft, boarding house for girls up to year 10, is straight out of Enid Blyton with its parquet floors, sweeping staircase and spacious dorms. Communal areas are vast and beautifully furnished, years 7 to 9 are in mixed age dorms and the eldest girls aspire to quirky attic rooms, up endless flights of stairs, sleeping just two or three and with panoramic views of the grounds. Years 11 and up are housed in The Cottage – also home to the sixth form centre – in single study bedrooms with a halls of residence feel, perfect preparation for uni. Maximum 65 boarders at any one time and there's full, flexi or weekly boarding on offer – even occasional nights if beds are available. Good chunk (70 per cent) of boarders are from overseas – lots of South East Asian names on study doors, particularly in the upper year groups, but also a few Europeans (mainly Spanish) – three or four per year. Girls really value the opportunity to build international relationships: 'it makes for the best friendships', they told us. Breakfast and lunch taken in houses, with dinner for all boarders in the main school dining hall. On top of special boarders' after-school clubs, good provision over weekends with school making the most of proximity to London and Oxford, plus sports, art and drama, film or cinema nights. Each year kicks off with a team-building weekend away and girls can venture into Oxford in groups from year 10 upwards.

Background and atmosphere: One parent told us 'there's a little bit of magic at Rye', and we definitely sensed a special and unique 'girls own' atmosphere – an inexplicable feeling of sisterhood that can clearly be traced back to the founder and very first headmistress, Elizabeth Rendall, of whom a wonderfully atmospheric photographic portrait (complete with packet of cigarettes in foreground) presides over the entrance hall. She and Ivy King started the school in a house on the Woodstock Road in 1930. Many saw out the war here, growing fruit and veg in the gardens and taking fire warden duties at night. Girls learned to scull on the Cherwell and swimming was taught at Dame's Delight (ladies' counterpart to Parson's Pleasure). Miss King took over the helm on Miss Rendall's retirement, succeeded by Miss Sumpter, from whom Miss Jones took the reins in 1990 and Ms Ryan in 2018. It is from these formidable females that the school still takes its lead and the bravery and progressiveness of the founders – who were as competent in site maintenance as teaching Latin, all whilst persuading parents to allow their daughters to go to university – lives on. It's no wonder that Old Ryes are so dedicated to their alma mater to the point that there were, at time of writing, five on staff.

Oft described as a 'hidden gem' and very different to the first impressions made by the heavy hitting schools in the area, but this is where books by covers should never be judged, as past the little car park lies a charming, leafy – albeit bijoux – campus. The main school building is a fine example of late Victorian splendour with immaculate modern additions nestled amongst beautifully tended gardens and ancient trees. Signs of investment and updates abound. A lovely new reception area provides a warm welcome to the main school building with its tall ceilings and wide, light corridors, bedecked with works of art and colourful notices. The modern library, among the most inviting we've seen, is well stocked and furnished with a mix of cosy beanbags and more formal tables and, presided over by a dedicated (and dare we say dynamic) librarian, is hub to the many literary activities (author visits, creative writing workshops, book clubs, trips to Oxfordshire Author Awards) on offer. Plus the views across the lawns are to die for. Other new additions have been skilfully integrated, delivering the necessary facilities without ruining the quaint original architecture. Hopefully next up for some attention are the rather basic science labs.

School has a genuine 'all-through' feel, with juniors and seniors taught in a collection of charming buildings separated by just a winding path. The nursery is housed in King House, in quirky, rambling classrooms up in the eaves that can't help but inspire young imaginations. Nursery open from 7.30am to 6.30pm – useful for the working parents that largely make up the Rye cohort. Juniors housed in Langley Lodge, part of the original collection of school buildings that retains its Victorian charm with winding staircases (complete with colourful giant papier mâché giraffe at the bottom), giant sash windows, fireplaces and high ceilings, yet with all the requisite classroom technology present and correct.

Pastoral care, well-being and discipline: School has a lay Catholic ethos, meaning that while Catholicism is integral, it is outward looking and inclusive of all religions (or none) and cultures, and focused on spirituality rather than doctrine. Indeed, staff reported one Muslim girl 'gaining the confidence to wear the full hijab' in sixth form, thanks to her supportive experience at Rye. In this vein, pupils are expected to understand and observe certain principles of tolerance and consideration to prepare them for adult life. There are no frocked clergy or nuns on the teaching staff and the lovely little chapel is an understated stand-alone building open throughout the week and used in particular for the weekly Sunday mass.

A more contented cohort you couldn't hope to find. Absent are signs of pressure, stress and ferocious competition, and instead smiles abound. There's a genuine feeling of girls looking after each other, but the support infrastructure is built upon a friendly and down to earth (largely, from what we saw young-ish) staff room: 'the support we get from teachers is amazing', said one pupil. Patricians (senior prefects) are trained in basic child protection and advise staff and governors as well as organising a mentoring system for all new pupils which involves each girl being allocated a 'housemother' – an older pupil – to help her to adapt to school life and answer any questions or concerns. And for when things do go wrong, there's an 'independent listener' – a retired teacher at the end of the phone – to help put things in perspective.

Girls say they know every other pupil at least by sight, if not name, and talk about the school's 'family atmosphere'. 'We love it when the whole school comes together', they say. Which, as promised, brings us on to Christmas. As with any family, it's the unrivalled highlight of the calendar, and even on a dull day in early November, enthusiasm effuses from staff and pupils at the mere mention. Girls say they're 'hoarse by the end of term' with all the singing that goes on, from the staff panto (male teachers in drag an apparent highlight), the Christmas lunch, classroom décor competition, traditional 'tangerine party' and carol service. Much enthusiasm too for the house system ('house points really matter,' according to one earnest year 7) with its many year-round competitions from charities day to sports day with the top house winning a house barbecue.

Discipline takes a magnanimous approach with head often consulting with offenders' peers to 'get an insight into family matters' and 'steadily unpick the issues to find the reason'. Open discussions are key and resolution rarely involves suspension or harsh sanctions. Even detentions are unheard of.

Pupils and parents: 'Representative of local fluid population.' Happy mix of locals and overseas pupils with many parents working at nearby BMW, the university or John Radcliffe Hospital. Largely down to earth, dual income – plenty of first time buyers mixed in with old farming money and the children of old girls. Strong links with European countries (Italy, Spain, France and Germany), with pupils visiting from these countries for part of the summer term most years.

Entrance: For entry into all year groups, parents and prospective pupils are interviewed together. It would be 'hypocritical and silly' not to admit all girls from the prep school. So parents can happily buy into Rye safe in the knowledge that it is a genuine all-through offering. About two-thirds of girls of the 30 or so moving into year 7 join from a mix of local state and independent schools – no particular feeder.

Exit: Boys peel off at 11 to a variety of local preps and secondary schools with almost all junior girls moving seamlessly up to the senior school. Up to half leave post-GCSE and, due to the broadest church of intakes, impossible to identify trends when it comes to higher education, with girls off to study eg evolutionary biology (St Andrews), sports management (Cardiff Met), fashion photography (Southampton Solent) and art and design (Istituto Europeo di Design, Rome) in 2018.

Money matters: Fees comparative with nearby 'league table' girls' schools with all their gleaming facilities might raise eyebrows from some. Scholarships and some means-tested bursaries available at 11+, 13+ and 16+. Pupils can apply for a King Award for up to £300 to enable them to further an interest or learn a new skill.

Remarks: Above all, a most civilised and humane school which achieves good individual outcomes for its girls wherever they sit on the academic spectrum. Although not an obvious choice if your girls are all high academic flyers, parents select Rye for all the girls in their family, safe in the knowledge that their daughters will have their individual potential developed whatever their ability. In the words of one happy sixth former: 'Rye accommodates everybody. We all have a chance to shine.'

Saffron Walden County High School

Audley End Road, Saffron Walden, Essex CB11 4UH

Ages 11–18 **Pupils** 2,114 **Sixth form** 653

01799 513030
www.swchs.net

Headteacher: Since 2016, Caroline Derbyshire MA (in English Lit from Cambridge). Previously executive principal of the Chilford Hundred Education Trust for 10 years, and before that deputy head at Saffron Walden for six years. Although she is executive head of the Saffron Academy Trust, which includes three other local schools, students very much see her as 'their' headteacher and this is where she spends most of her time. Known for being both strategically astute and working closely with students and staff, she feels strongly that 'I don't want to be a faceless or nameless figure' – and students concur that she's not one to hide away in her office. 'As a headteacher, I believe you have a significant influence as a role model and in the tone you set and optimism that emanates from you,' she told us. We certainly found her cheeriness infectious, and she's fantastically easy to get on with too – down-to-earth, warm and amiable. 'What's not to like?' said one student, while others describe her as 'bouncy,' 'inspirational' and 'very visible.' Parents say she's 'friendly' and 'never makes you feel like it's a them-and-us experience. It's more like talking to a friend.' Make no mistake – she runs a tight ship, but she achieves it with more carrot than stick.

Lives locally with her husband and two teenage children, and interests include reading, theatre, musical concerts and playing tennis.

Academic matters: Rigorous setting across all core subjects, with 10 sets per year group. Pupils set for maths and English from year 7, for languages (all study French and German from year 7; Spanish from year 9) from year 8 and for sciences from year 9. Tracking is as thorough as it gets, with one parent reporting, 'The best thing about this process is how much they engage the students, with the result that they own their own targets, as opposed to having them imposed on them. It makes such a difference in them being determined to meet them.' A graders felt to be A* students get just as much attention as D students who are believed to be capable of Bs and every department is kept on its toes. 'It's pretty forensic,' says the head – and nobody slips through the net here, agree students.

GCSE results good. In 2018, 38 per cent of grades were A*-A/7-9. Students choose their options (usually eight or nine subjects) in year 8 and then start their courses in year 9, rather than the usual year 10. Everyone takes English and English literature, and a very high proportion chooses triple science, while other popular subjects include history and geography. Results strong across all subjects, with particularly outstanding results in humanities, DT, classics, languages (especially German), drama, PE and computer science. Unusually for a state school, County High (as everyone calls it) offers Latin to more able linguists at GCSE as well as A level. A few take BTecs in vocational subjects, such as hospitality and health and social care – but, says school, 'as part of a balanced academic curriculum.'

Sixth formers follow one of three routes – one for the most academically able and requiring at least five GCSEs at 6+ (including maths and English) and at least 6s in chosen A level subjects, another for those with five GCSEs at 4+ and a third for those with five GCSEs at 3 or above. Students choose from a vast array of subjects – all the usuals, while classical civilisation, media studies, philosophy, PE, psychology, criminology, film studies, music technology, government and politics and sociology among the less obvious. 'There's plenty of guidance about which ones to choose,' one student told us. A level results impressive, with 40 per cent A*/A grades and 67 per cent A*/B grades in 2018 – and the sixth form is in the top one per cent in the country for A level value-added performance (ie progress made from GCSE to A level).

Dedicated teaching staff of 140, with good mix of ages. Strong links with Cambridge University's education faculty, and every subject department has at least one trainee teacher. There is a culture of professional development and staff are keen to enhance their skills, with many taking education masters degrees in their spare time. School leads a teaching group alliance too, which involves providing support for teaching across other schools, among other things. 'Bottom line is staff here are incredibly focused on reflecting on their own practice,' head told us. 'Teachers are always trying out innovative new techniques, and their passion for their subject really shines through,' one student told us, while others gave examples about how staff go 'above and beyond to make sure we keep up – whether that's in lunchtime, after school or even in holidays.' Communication with both students and parents is excellent – via email, student planners, yearly reports and parent evenings. 'It's not just seen as acceptable to contact teachers directly – it's encouraged,' one parent said. In fact, the only thing students could criticise about lessons here is the lack of use of phones – 'I know other schools incorporate them and I do think there's a place for it in today's teaching,' said one.

SEN team of 22 offers one-to-one support and in groups to pupils needing extra help. Additional challenges provided for gifted and talented. 'Our daughter, who has special needs, has gone from a quiet, shy girl to someone who puts her hand up in class and feels confident. I can't speak highly enough of the learning support team,' one parent told us, clearly delighted.

Games, options, the arts: The music department is the beating heart of this school, boasting two orchestras, a concert band, jazz band and a myriad of choirs and ensembles – all performing to an exceptionally high standard, with around six sell-out concerts a year. 'Students perform at various levels, but the result is astonishingly good – honestly, it's amazing to hear,' one parent told us. More than 400 pupils have individual music lessons in school and the multi-million pound Saffron Hall concert hall has become an acclaimed international venue with artists specialising in everything from classical music to jazz regularly visiting to play alongside the students, as well as providing music masterclasses. 'This term, the National Youth Jazz Orchestra played alongside our jazz band, with our students performing solos in their concerts – you can imagine how much our students learned,' the head enthused. The school has also launched a post-16 music academy, 'which attracts talented young musicians from the local area'.

Art is also strong, evidenced by the sheer volume of students' artwork displayed throughout the corridors – including everything from giant 3D creations to finely detailed textiles. Literally every art room was a hive of excited activity when we visited – from students getting messy with clay to youngsters experimenting with pastels for fine art. A large proportion of the students who take A level art (there are three to pick from) gain A*s.

Drama was also in full swing on our visit, with all three drama practising areas (the two school halls and blackened 'Pit') revealing some clear talent and a great deal of fun. Popular at both GCSE and A level. Film studies also an A level option, and the school runs the Gordos, an annual short film competition for budding Steven Spielbergs. School productions taken seriously (Twelfth Night and Goodnight Mr Tom were performed the year we visited – plus a bespoke opera written for the school entitled The Glass Knight, based on local legend). 'The productions here are very slick, both thanks to the hard work the students and staff put in and the professional-quality production facilities,' one parent told us.

Lots of clubs at lunchtime and after school – debating, sport, chess, film club, LGBT group etc – and trips galore, ranging from cultural visits to China and Africa to exchanges to France, Spain, Germany and Chicago. Strong emphasis on green issues and charity work, with sixth formers running an annual charities week every December, raising money for global, national and local causes chosen by them.

The array of silverware on display in the hi-tech sports centre is testament to the sporting prowess of this school, whose Saturday morning fixtures include frequent wins (to the head's delight) against independent schools. All students play sport up to 16 – mainly the usual suspects of rugby, hockey, netball, cricket, tennis and athletics. Outdoor facilities include huge fields, grass cricket square, pavilion, tennis courts and Astroturf – impressive for a secondary state school.

Background and atmosphere: Located on the edge of the pretty market town of Saffron Walden, in north east Essex. Extensive grounds, including own farm with cattle and sheep (and a highly successful farm club), and plenty of trees. In springtime pupils can see lambs gambolling in the paddock from the rugby and hockey pitches. Main building dates back to the 1950s with plenty of modern add-ons since – all kept in pristine condition. Classrooms mainly bright and airy, with lovely wide corridors, and stand-out facilities include Saffron Hall, a truly world-class venue, and the Hartley Learning Centre, an uber-modern library of the likes we've never seen. Pupils fiercely (and understandably) proud of the school, with the students we spoke to unable to think of a single facility they are left wanting.

Extremely strict on uniform ('I don't think there's any point in having one unless it's going to be worn properly,' says head) – blazers, black trousers and ties for boys and blazers and tartan kilts for girls, up to the age of 16. Sixth formers can wear what they like, within reason, and get their own block, with study centre (silence during lessons) and common room (the only disappointing room we came across – roomy, yes, but homely, no). Over half the students have school dinners in the cashless cafeteria or on the hoof from the other café – while the rest bring in packed lunches.

Pastoral care, well-being and discipline: 'One of the things that has astonished us about this school is the quality of the pastoral provision,' was reflective of several parent comments we heard. 'You're never short of someone to talk to if you have a problem here, either academically or around well-being – and no matter how small it is,' a student concurred. Each year group divided into 10 tutor groups and children stay with the same tutor up to GCSEs. And as well as their tutors and heads of year ('both of whom really get to know you,' say students), youngsters can talk to one of the school's full-time counsellors, who are trained in areas including cognitive behaviour therapy. Students say it's easy to settle in too – thanks to a special induction programme for newbies, maps and mentoring from older students. Bullying rare and quickly nipped in the bud, with preventive work including a recent focus on celebrating student 'acts of kindness.' 'We wanted more emphasis on the positive, less on the negative,' explains the head – there's that carrot again.

Instead of having a head boy and head girl, there's a team of 10 head students – each one tasked with an area such as fundraising or student council. Year 11s are appointed prefects and encouraged to mentor year 7s and 8s. School also keen on 'student voice,' which is split into three areas (green voice team, well-being team and teaching and learning team). Recent successes include a campaign for a better outdoor eating area and improving the way electricity is used in the school.

Not the kind of school with traditional rules, not least because the head dislikes both words. 'I prefer "code of conduct" because I think it encourages self-discipline, and I don't think a lot of people know what "traditional" really means in this context. So I'd say instead that we have high expectations around good manners, as well as about being positive and community minded,' she says. It clearly works because run amuck these students do not, with exemplary behaviour throughout. Many students go through the entire school without a detention, and there tend to be less than handful of fixed term exclusions each year, with no permanent exclusions at all under current headship. Drugs, smoking or alcohol are all met with zero tolerance (and no excuses), but again there have been no problems for years. 'We recently delved deep into year 10s' behaviour in class and given that age 14 can be the most colourful of the teenage years and that some of our students have complex needs, we were delighted to find that not one student was off-task in any lesson,' says head.

Pupils and parents: Pupils come from a mix of rural and urban backgrounds, with more than ever from Saffron Walden itself since the town's expansion, including extensive new housing. Many walk or bike in, while others travel by bus from surrounding villages. Ethnicity reflective of the area, with a whopping 88 per cent of families white British – and the majority are middle-class, with only a small proportion from disadvantaged families. Parents and pupils feel a lucky lot. 'Whenever I meet a parent, the first thing they say is how delighted they are to have a child at the school – in fact, even when they are objecting to something, that's their opening gambit,' says the head. Students, meanwhile, are engaged, motivated learners – and we were struck by their high aspirations and articulate and engaging conversation. 'They're a joy to teach,' smiles the head. Ex-pupil Ben Maher was part of the gold medal winning GB show jumping team in the 2012 Olympics and also rode at Rio 2016.

Entrance: Heavily oversubscribed, with over 600 fighting for 290 year 7 places. Siblings get priority, followed by residents of 12 listed parishes. Further three criteria, but the vast majority of places are offered on the first two, so if you don't live in catchment, forget it. No feeder primary schools as such – that's not how Essex entry criteria works. More than three-quarters stay on for sixth form, when they are joined by 100 newcomers a year, making for a mammoth 630-strong sixth form, which many locals see as a kind of sixth form college in its own right – and a popular one at that, with many more applications than places. 'We get a lot of children who don't get a year 7 place going off to other local state schools and independent schools, then coming back to reapply to do their A levels here,' says head.

Exit: About a quarter leave after GCSEs, mainly to do vocational courses or apprenticeships at local colleges including Hills Road Sixth Form College and Harlow College. 'We don't lose many who want to study academically,' says the head. Around 85 per cent of sixth formers go on to higher education; the rest are 'supported by the school with their progression into employment or other educational opportunities'. Four to Oxbridge in 2018, with around half to Russell Group; Durham particularly popular. Students get loads of one-to-one help to guide them through the complex UCAS maze and parents and pupils alike rave about the Oxbridge preparation course. 'You hear reports that state schools don't prepare kids for Oxbridge – well, this one does. They do everything imaginable to help them,' one parent told us. Popular courses include sciences, classics, history, English, law, psychology and medicine (two medics in 2018).

Remarks: A vibrant, fast-moving local school of outstanding quality, with innovation in teaching and great facilities. It buzzes with activity from dawn till dusk – ideal for children who want to work hard and play hard. Even though it's a big place (with all the advantages of the breadth of opportunity that brings), students say it feels small, thanks to every child being treated as an individual. If anywhere will make a high achiever of your child without undue pressure, this is it.

St Albans Girls' School

Sandridgebury Lane, St Albans, Hertfordshire AL3 6DB

Ages 11–18 **Pupils** 1,215 **Sixth form** 250 (7 boys)

01727 853134
www.stags.herts.sch.uk

Headteacher: Since 2010, Margaret Chapman BSc NPQH (40s). Educated at the University of Wales, Aberystwyth before teaching geography, geology and ICT and ultimately becoming deputy head at Mill Hill County High School. Moved as deputy head to The Priory School, Hitchin.

Indefatigable on the subject of STAGS, brimming with opinions on all things educational. Sets high standards of

S

behaviour and work for staff and students alike. Believes in teaching staff taking ownership of student pastoral care rather than just academic success and has aimed to empower all members of the school community – including support staff – to create a dynamic, democratic environment. Focused on turning out 'articulate and confident women who are ready for society and the world of work.'

Definitely not the soft and cuddly type ('Believe me, the children know who Mrs Chapman is,' says deputy head), but most certainly a contender for hardest working head award, should one exist, as she can often be tracked down to her office at 9pm. Parents like her – 'I've never met someone more efficient'; 'She runs a tight ship and is very much in control, but she's approachable too'; 'She's one of the reasons we came to the school, having heard her inspiring talk at the open day' etc. Students in the younger years told us they'd barely seen her, even at assemblies ('She's mostly in her office and only seems to come out for prestigious events and fire drills,' one told us) whereas older ones report more frequent contact ('She helps us with GCSE choices and starts off exams,' said one student). She's 'strict, but in a good way' and 'firm but fair,' they told us. One thought she'd 'get suspended for being caught mucking about. But I just wound up getting a telling off and I think that sums her up – you think she's scarier than she really is.'

Lives locally with husband and grown-up children. A geologist at heart, is the proud owner of a large rock collection and loves the outdoors, particularly the sea.

Academic matters: Robust results, particularly given school's non-selective intake and broad range of abilities. In 2018, 89 per cent got 9-4 in both maths and English in 2018, 38 per cent of grades A*-A/9-7. At A level, 68 per cent of the grades were A*-B and 40 per cent A*/A. Smallish take-up of EPQ but good results.

There's a mandate for success here, regardless of ability, with tailor made learning programmes for students rather than a one-size-fits-all approach. In practice, this means huge flexibility around GCSE options, with students taking between eight and 11 depending on ability, along with seemingly no end to the support laid on by teachers, whether that's during the class or by email or in one-to-ones or small groups afterwards. 'Sometimes my daughter hasn't understood something and the teachers are amazing about ensuring she gets it,' said one parent. For those who struggle with the challenges of academia, the school also offers specialised programmes to help with life skills and build self-esteem and confidence. Consortium and partnership arrangements with other local schools and colleges enable students to take vocational courses from year 10 during school hours, although in reality there's very little take-up (the more likely scenario is students from these other institutions taking advantage of what STAGs has to offer). Students and parents alike rave about the teachers' 'enthusiasm' ('although you do get some that just write on the board and get you to copy it – that's quite boring,' said one student), with school offering impressive CPD and a 'well-being week' for staff where they get offers to have their car washed, nails done, massages and even a round of golf.

S

Tight setting in maths and broader setting in modern languages (French and Spanish on offer) from year 7. Some banding within form groups for English and science from year 8 and tighter setting in those subjects for GCSEs. Languages, history and geography popular at GCSE with dance, media studies, food technology and textiles available for those looking for diversity in their choices. Results particularly strong in English, science and Spanish. At A level, there is plenty of breadth when it comes to pathways, with most popular options including Spanish, sociology, economics, English, history, geography and psychology. Some 60 per cent of students take STEM subjects (with data showing that nearly half of them go on to study STEM subjects at university). In terms of results, shining stars include the 'ologies', business, economics, maths and English. There's a 'little and often' approach to homework – 'we do not want them to drown'.

SEN all in a day's work for the 12 per cent of school requiring additional help, with policy of 'inclusion' into classrooms. Five full-time SENCo teaching assistants cover one-to-one classroom support. 'We get to know them and their parents and then come up with a personal programme that every class teacher is made aware of – that's how we break down the barriers.' Strong gifted and talented programme touches 15 per cent of pupils, with enhanced activities such as science workshops to stretch analytical skills and get them thinking outside the box. 'Very early on, we introduce high aspirations, such as Oxbridge,' says head. Some 20 per cent of EAL students, although school says the figure can appear misleading as most are fluent in English.

Games, options, the arts: School is well equipped for sporting excellence, with nine tennis courts, three hockey pitches, a cricket square, athletics track, heated outdoor pool and purpose built sports hall complete with multi-gym for staff and pupil use. STAGS families can buy summer membership to use pool in evenings and weekends for the princely sum of £55 and many do.

List as long as your arm of available sports – all the usuals, plus skiing, equestrian, judo and chess, among others. Teams successful at district, county and national level (packed trophy cabinets adorn the school entrance), with students saying 'if we want to play, they make it happen'. Particular strengths in swimming, athletics, football, rugby and netball. Girls' accolades out of school also celebrated – current champions in chess, judo and swimming. Dance and gymnastics extremely popular, with a very well used dance studio.

School is 'a hotbed of creativity,' according to staff, with drama and music both 'excellent' and around 16 per cent of girls taking individual music lessons in school, using the new private practice rooms (although students told us 'you used to be able to get in one for practice time but we never seem to be able to now'). 'You name it, they play it,' says school, with students telling us about the plentiful opportunities to perform publicly, including in the abbey. Two well-used drama studios, with girls constantly preparing for performances, including an annual musical (High School Musical when we visited, while smaller performances tend to be more highbrow). Large, inspiring art department with an impressive and diverse array of work on show, to a notably high standard, throughout the school. DT going from strength to strength. We saw year 7s busy at work in the food tech rooms – on the tatty side, but students told us that's next on the PTA funding list.

Good range of extracurricular from year 7 up, ranging from the intriguingly named Spitfire and Battle of Britain club to more predictable drama, textiles and sports activities. There are also clubs for film, philosophy, debate and Jewish club, Pride and more – 'there really is something for everyone,' a student told us. Girls rewarded for regular attendance and parents happy that they are 'actively encouraged to do two from year 7.' DofE taken very seriously – over two-thirds of year 10s do the bronze award. Trips and tours galore, with favourites including the annual ski trip, year 9 Belgium trip, year 10 Spanish trip and geography trip to Naples. Charity work is 'an enormous focus' for the girls, says the school; 'they really get their teeth into it,' raising tens of thousands every year for their selected chosen charities.

Background and atmosphere: Founded in 1920 as a girls' grammar, STAGS shrugged off its selective mantle some time ago in favour of status as a business and enterprise college. Located in the north of the city, it appears – from the front – to occupy a ubiquitous low level 1960s warren of buildings, but a multimillion pound project means that behind the uninspiring front there are now multiple building works going on, with latest additions including sixth form centre (with bright common room and two large study rooms – one with chatting allowed and one for silent study), three new Mac suites and purpose-built music and drama department, while a two-storey, eight-classroom block is currently being built, and the dance studio relocated and refurbished. All is a buzzing hub of enthusiastic, independent learners turning out commendable results. The well-stocked, spacious library provides more space for quiet study and handy types should be impressed by the superbly equipped DT lab.

Staff are militant about tidiness and order, so there's not a spot of litter, and there are thoughtful touches such as covered picnic areas and plenty of outdoor seating, to ensure the girls have somewhere to loll during break times. Dining room (sorry, 'restaurant', as students have to call it now) spotless and ruthlessly efficient, and a 'snack shack' for those preferring to grab something on the hoof – we did not, however, spot a healthy item among the supersize cookies, chicken nuggets, pizzas and wedges (although, to be fair, the catering staff hadn't finished putting the food out). Woe betide anyone who fails to wear their uniform correctly – 'we don't do short skirts,' says head; sixth formers can, however, wear smart businesswear.

Pastoral care, well-being and discipline: Directors of learning for each year group ensure that girls are kept on track academically, socially and emotionally. Lots of emphasis on teaching resilience. The student welfare office is a welcoming space which students can pop into anytime, and there's a full-time school counsellor, as well as peer mentoring in place. Hugely successful house system, with eight houses named after influential women. Good work and behaviour rewarded with house points, with girls working hard to keep 'consequences' (minus marks that can lead to detentions) to a minimum for the greater good of their housemates – which ultimately leads to the winning house getting a much sought-after pool party and BBQ. 'It's not always easy, though, as there's a lot of inconsistency in how easily the teachers give out consequences – some give one for forgetting a book and other teachers don't mind at all, for instance,' one student told us. Heaps of house events, from competitions, plays and challenges to a plethora of fundraising efforts, with each house choosing its own charity – lots of cake sales attack the staff's waistlines with ruthless efficiency.

Parents told us 'the pastoral care is excellent,' with lots of examples to back it up. One told of how all her daughter's classes were moved downstairs 'because she'd had an injury – she'd have hated a whole half term without interaction with her student friends and they made that happen.' Another told us, 'The school had more understanding of my daughter after one meeting than her primary school had over her whole time there. They talked me through what they could do and what they couldn't – it's been life changing.' Leadership is a 'big deal' here, says head, with girls offered opportunities to show their metal at all stages; there are two heads of house per year group from year 7, captains of everything, from games to charities.

'There's a great sense of community here and I haven't dealt with bullying for a long time,' says head. Students we met agreed about the sense of community but disagreed about the bullying – 'bullying happens in the shadows, you just don't report it because you know the people in charge of pastoral care will say it's not bullying,' said one. Further up the school, students told us bullying was less likely, but said they'd still like a bigger push on preventing and dealing with it. Another told us that she'd like to see 'more linking up of the different year groups, which I think would help'.

'Strict' is a word you hear a lot here. 'The girls know what's expected of them and I think it makes them feel safe,' said one parent. Alcohol, drugs and smoking are 'not an issue', with staff describing the girls' behaviour as generally very good. No permanent exclusions in living memory; usually one or two a year temporary ones 'for a whole host of different reasons.' Staff ensure an 'on the table' conversation before offenders return, offering them holistic support and guidance to make sure they feel part of the school community again.

Pupils and parents: Fresh faced, immaculately turned out students move excitably around the corridors but it's heads down for lessons, where you've never seen such concentration. A few boys filter into year 12, looking for 'an enhanced educational offering', and integrate well with the girls, according to staff. We found students articulate, polite, respectful and forthright – surely set to be the movers and shakers of the future.

Majority from St Albans and surrounding towns, although a few from as far afield as Borehamwood and Hitchin. Broad socio-demographic, ranging from affluent families choosing STAGS over fee-paying alternatives to less well-off but aspirational families, seeking a traditional yet forward thinking education for their girls. Head says she is happy – and has been known – to knock on doors to engage the few parents who are 'scared to aspire.' For the most part, it's not an issue, however, as there's good parental engagement, with Show My Homework and talks on everything from safety to understanding teenagers helping to keep families closely involved in school life. About 11 per cent qualify for free school meals but staff say they are 'hard to spot' even in this middle-class setting. About 27 per cent from ethnic minorities. Regular PTA meetings with the school's senior team ensure parental voices are heard and that, in line with the ethos of the school, things keep moving forward. Some complaints from parents about transport from areas such as Harpenden – 'three or four busses pass and claim they are too full to allow the girls on,' said one.

Entrance: Parents move heaven and earth (not to mention house) to get into STAGS, with over 1,000 applications for 240 places. 'We get a lot of upset parents calling in on 1 March,' admits school. Majority enter at age 11, coming from around 60 feeder primary schools. It remains non-selective, with admissions still administered by the local authority despite academy status, and there are no plans to change this, although it is reviewed by the governors every year. Waiting lists in ever year group. Around 50 extra places available in year 12, with applicants required to achieve a minimum of five 4+s at GCSE and grade 6 or higher in their chosen A level subjects.

Exit: Around a quarter leave at 16 as mixed gender environments or vocational courses beckon, with the odd one seeking out subjects not on offer at STAGS. 'Some just want a change,' a sixth former added. Vast majority who leave at the end of year 13 go straight on to higher education. Two to Oxford and four medics in 2018. Others to universities including Warwick, Leeds, Nottingham and the London universities. Huge variety of courses including geography, media, psychology, history and, increasingly, sciences.

Masses of careers advice which trickles down as far as year 7. 'Right from the off, the world of work is exposed as the goal and the curriculum exists to support that,' says head. One parent told us, 'My daughter wants to be a vet and right from year 7, she was talked to about what she'd need, as well as other potential jobs. No girl does a subject for a subject's sake here.'

Money matters: PTA is 'very involved – and then some', says head, raising over £40,000 a year for the school with various events. Around 10 per cent of parents make a voluntary contribution to bolster coffers towards rolling improvement programme.

Remarks: This is a school where everyone seems to get swept along with the culture of learning – 'it's not just about the high achievers here, it's about making sure everyone flourishes,' said one parent. Strict, but fair, safe and positively bubbling with opportunities, this is a school where everyone can shine.

St Albans High School for Girls

Townsend Avenue, St Albans, Hertfordshire AL1 3SJ

Ages 4–18 **Pupils** 1,065 **Sixth form** 179 C of E

Fees: £14,970 – £18,795 pa

01727 853800
www.stahs.org.uk

Headmistress: Since 2014, Jenny Brown (40s). Educated at North London Collegiate before reading English at Oxford. With both parents English teachers 'it was the very last thing I wanted to do,' she says, instead taking a job at Robert Maxwell's publishing house (thankfully too young to invest in pensions) – 'the last word in really dull jobs'. Escaped to teach English at Cranleigh ('like coming home'), followed by Highgate School, South Hampstead High, Channing and St Paul's Girls where she was director of senior school. Still adores the 'sheer joy' of teaching and takes a 'gluttonous' approach to indulging this passion, teaching year 7 creative writing ('she makes girls really think', say parents), and parts of the A level syllabus to sixth form: 'incredibly useful to keep in touch with what's going on around school...and for my sanity'.

Fell in love at first sight with the 'extraordinary combination of high achievement and civilisation' she found on arrival at STAHS, notably the distinct lack of 'neurotic' girls. Feels that school's geographic location plays large role in comparatively pervading grounded atmosphere: 'It beats with the same energy and ambition as a London school, but being that little bit further out lowers the temperature a bit'.

Statuesque, stylish (a coincidence that her outfit was colour coordinated to her office accessories?) and, according to parents 'ferociously intellectual', looks for girls 'with headlights on' to join school. With this as benchmark, she is on full beam. Prolific member of the twitterati and frequent commentator on all things feminist, oft quoted in national newspapers on subjects such as sexism in the workplace. One half of the Good Schools Guide's first set of identical twin head teachers – her sister, Jane, is head at Wimbledon High ('it's lovely to be able to share ideas'). Lives in Highgate with playwright husband, Ben, and enjoys theatre, literature (muses 'who would I head towards first in Heaven – Shakespeare or Donne?') and a weekly swim in Hampstead Ponds. Writes poetry 'when creative space allows'. Two children, one in sixth form, one at university.

Leaving in July 2019 to head City of London School for Girls.

Head of prep: Since September 2015, Mrs Judy Rowe (40s). Educated at North London Collegiate School and Durham University. Formerly head of lower school at Belmont, Mill Hill Prep. Businesslike, chatty and in the running for sportiest prep head of the year – running, canoeing and cycling are just a few of her weekend pursuits. Parents say she has opened formerly firmly closed doors to them ('we are actually invited into the classroom now – before, there was a line in the playground that we weren't allowed to cross') and changed prep beyond recognition –all for the better.

Academic matters: With girls selected from 4+ and places fiercely fought over at 7+ and 11+, school is firing on all academic cylinders from the get-go and is certainly not for the faint of heart. Even the youngest pupils buzz with intellectual curiosity and are stretched accordingly. And STAHS girls don't all wait until they get into the senior school to start notching up achievements: 2016 saw them win the Creativity in Science prize at the eastern region Big Bang Science Fair; in recent years school has been placed second and third out of 600 entries in the GSK Science Competition and every girl for the past three years has successfully gained the Bronze Crest Award from the British Science Association, generally for students in years 7 to 9. All that and they still manage to squeeze in an impressive number of music and LAMDA exams.

French from reception and Mandarin on curriculum from year 4. Specialist teaching for science, ICT, languages, music and PE from the start sees girls moving independently around the junior school from a young age. Parents, 'blown away' by science teaching, say staff can get even the most reluctant scientist 'totally absorbed'. Class sizes slowly expand from a maximum of 20 in reception to 24 in years 3 to 6. Unsurprisingly 'very low' numbers on the SEN register but school able to support mild dyslexia, dyspraxia or dyscalculia through mix of one-to-one and class based work. 'ACE' (additional curricular education) groups not only support girls in need of extra help but also push the top half dozen or so girls in each year group with a focus on additional problem solving and advanced reading. All girls also screened upon entry to year 7, with general approach to SEN mirrored in senior school.

Sensible approach to homework in junior school, with between 20 and 40 minutes of 'research based' homework most evenings. Head takes dim view of tutoring and holiday hothousing, instead encouraging parents to lighten up by providing list of suggested activities – making scrambled egg or writing a thank you letter as arduous as it gets. Senior girls report homework to be 'reasonable', as are staff when it comes to endorsing the occasional extension.

Scholarship is the first of school's three key values and can be found in spades in senior school. Despite (or perhaps due to) head's determination for girls to 'keep it real' and focus on things other than just academic studies (as if to prove this point one of our guides had just got her busking licence, with plans afoot to hit the lucrative South Bank on weekends), results are stellar. Twenty subjects on offer at A level. In 2018, 70 per cent of all A levels were graded A*/A and 92 per cent A*-B. History, RS and maths most popular subjects; surprisingly small language take-up. GCSEs no less impressive, with nearly 85 per cent graded A*/A or 7-9 in 2018. IGCSEs in all core subjects, plus history and modern languages. Mandarin available as twilight option with GCSE taken in year 9. At least one language compulsory at GCSE and most also choose a creative option. Most take nine or 10 GCSEs with average class sizes at this stage between 15 and 18, becoming much smaller at A level.

Newly appointed director of higher education and careers ensures girls are pushed 'out of their comfort zone', with all departments teaching 'university stretch' at A level and 'second to none' Oxbridge preparation according to head. Girls declare support during the university application process 'amazing', with each being allocated to a specialist in their chosen subject for bespoke guidance throughout: 'invaluable', said one grateful sixth former. Next step is 'to invest in tapping into our alumni to boost careers offering,' says head.

Games, options, the arts: Where does school's heartbeat lie, we asked, sport, drama, music or academia? None of the above, according to girls – but all are drawn together by a common thread of enthusiasm and a 'can-do' attitude. Sport high on the agenda right from early prep days with 'very broad' offering not just of netball, lacrosse, athletics, dance and gym, but also karate, fencing and ballet, giving girls a competitive edge when they move through to the senior school. Despite the fact that games pitches are a 10-minute walk from senior school, girls manage to participate in every sport imaginable, with the focus 'heavily competitive' when it comes to lacrosse and netball.

Unusually, compulsory games all the way through to sixth form. Whilst not nestled amongst vast playing fields, impressive facilities for an urban school include new sports pavilion, dance studio, fitness suite, large, traditionally equipped sports hall, netball courts, lacrosse pitches and 25m swimming pool, also used by prep pupils. Prep has own cross country course – with pre-lesson runs three mornings a week (run on Tuesdays if you want to try to beat head). Competitive fixtures for all produce all manner of silverware year on year.

Drama also extremely popular at all levels. Major school productions – which tend to err on the side of mainstream – draw girls to participate with great gusto in all elements, from costume, make-up and tech to performing in the orchestra pit ('always amazing'). Annual house drama competition follows a theme, recently children's literature, and is scripted by year 12s, with all year 7 girls in the cast. Senior performances take place in Jubilee Hall which can seat up to 350, with prep pupils strutting their stuff in the beautifully adapted Lodge building developed from a former caretaker's house, now home to many junior concerts and year group plays where, we are assured, 'everyone gets a good innings – nobody's stuck in the chorus'. At time of writing, school boasted two members of National Youth Theatre. Super serious music in very smart senior music block, with girls streamed according to musical aptitude from year 7 and top set taking early GCSE in year 10. Over 500 senior girls take peripatetic instrumental lessons each week, with plethora of choirs (chamber, gospel and everything in between), bands and orchestras in which to showcase their talents.

Superb art displayed in bright, inspiring studios – with A level artists benefiting from their own serene space, akin to a London art college. Is art allowed as a third A level? We are assured this is not frowned upon: 'that's something I feel strongly about,' says head, 'it's a discipline.' Similarly high standard on display in prep school, where every spare inch of space is adorned with a delightful junior masterpiece. Outside of the classroom, co-curricular programme doesn't disappoint, with girls able to spread their creative, sporting and intellectual wings to their hearts' content plus CV boosters like D of E, Model United Nations and EPQ. Prep boasts impressive range of options, with outstanding forest school provision (on and off curriculum) the jewel in its crown, thanks to its stunning wooded grounds and dedicated outdoorsy staff.

Background and atmosphere: Founded in 1889, school moved to current site in the centre of this popular commuter town in 1908. Close links maintained with both the diocese and St Albans School (boys). Quirky mish-mash of buildings from trad Victorian to uber modern, plus one or two less appealing 1970s additions, straddles a quiet residential road, with girls moving seamlessly and sensibly between the various sites. A tour of the school takes in an impressive mix of facilities from the separate sports complex to stunning rotunda building – all floor to ceiling glass – where pupils can work, socialise and treat themselves to something from the on-site Starbucks or sandwich bar. Super library for years 7 to 11 has studious feel and is extremely well resourced. Sixth formers have own kitchen and common room, plus library offering selection of newspapers, magazines plus copies of all A level texts. Smart, navy uniform worn by girls up to sixth form, when pupils are allowed to dress 'appropriately' down.

Head hits nail on head, describing atmosphere as 'relaxed formality'. Less rarefied than expected given lofty league table position – possibly because of urban location: head says girls 'live with in-built risk all the time'. In fact, were it not for the glittering facilities one could almost mistake it for a top state grammar and indeed head encourages collaborations with local high achieving state schools such as STAGS, QE Boys and Loretto College: 'we are perceived in community as a pillar', she says.

Prep occupies spectacular rural site in village of Wheathampstead, a four mile drive down country lanes from its big sister. Stunning country house setting nestled amongst 18 acres of lawns, woodlands, adventure playgrounds and a meadow. The only school we have visited where head keeps spare pair of (spotty) wellies for visitors.

Pastoral care, well-being and discipline: Much focus placed on ensuring mental well-being and happiness and girls show strong understanding of the balance between 'competitive edge' and being more relaxed. Head highlights relationships between pupils and staff as 'exemplary' and a key factor in school's positive atmosphere. House system integral to pastoral structure – starting in the prep and travelling all the way up – with housemistresses key points of contact on all matters pastoral. Pupils assure us that they are in no respect of the 'cookie cutter' variety, in fact that they are 'positively encouraged to be quirky' and that 'school accepts differences both inside and out of the classroom'. 'Supportive' used time and time again to describe overall ethos of school with all differences of race, religion (assemblies are multi-faith) and sexuality (LGBT Society present and correct) seemingly taken in its stride. In addition to staff, there are external counsellors two days a week and pupil mentors aplenty from the raft of school and house officers, plus head girl and three deputies, voted by a combination of pupils and staff to trained and signposted youth health champions.

Likewise in prep, environment strikes balance between high achieving and nurturing, with buddy systems and buddy families, a playground squad to ensure everyone's joining in and a school committee which meets fortnightly. And better food than the senior school (apparently).

Pupils and parents: Majority of pupils from hard working, often dual income families from across the demographic range (lots of professions and City) but, quips head, 'certainly not oligarchs.' With disproportionate number of only children amongst the cohort, prep parents can be somewhat 'tigerish' according to one parent – and as for the prolific class Whatsapp group? You have been warned. Localish contingent still in majority but around one third of applications now from families living in London boroughs eg Finchley and Totteridge plus as far afield as Luton, Hitchin and Potters Bar. These pupils arrive on one of a fleet of 10 buses. Those we met showed a delightful mix of intellect, empathy and groundedness – and not a jolly hockey stick amongst them.

Entrance: Oversubscribed (applications on the increase and a very high acceptance rate) and highly academically selective with main entry points 4+, 7+ and 11+. For entry into reception, girls assessed in an informal multi-task session. Head adamant that they are 'not looking for girls who are pushed, prepped or tutored'. Additional class added at 7+, with online assessments in maths, English and reasoning and school looking for 'girls who will do well at 16 and 18'. Thirty-five per cent of joiners at 11+ come in ones and twos from state primaries and independent feeders include Beechwood Park, Manor Lodge, Radlett Prep, Holland House and Palmer's Green to name a few.

Senior school unashamedly a place for 'very able girls who can engage intellectually'. There are 120 year 7 places up for grabs with about 40 moving up from prep and around three applicants for each remaining place. Prep pupils sit the same exam as external applicants for the purposes of scholarship selection. Came out of North London Consortium in 2015 ('we have to make very fine judgements and the papers were not interesting or lively enough to discriminate', says head). Candidates sit English and maths papers, with the former including 'a task that absolutely cannot be prepared for' and around two-thirds are interviewed before final offers made. Around 15 places up for grabs in sixth form, with minimum of

A grades at GCSE in chosen subjects required and A* for those taking maths A level.

Exit: Almost all from prep to secondary, with just a small handful each year to boarding or state. Early heads up if staff feel pupil unlikely to thrive in fast paced senior school (usually a good handful are advised to look for pastures new – but parents say it's rarely a surprise). Around a fifth leave after GCSEs, heading for co-ed, boarding or just a change of scene. At 18 all progress to higher education, with nine to Oxbridge in 2018 plus three medics. Other popular destinations are Leeds, Bristol, Durham, Exeter and Nottingham.

Money matters: Means-tested bursaries up to 100 per cent available. Scholarships for academia and music from year 7 and academia art/DT, games and drama in sixth form. Prep parents delighted that majority of after-school clubs now free of charge and speak highly of good value before and after-school care offering (7am to 6pm). Many grumbles though about high pricing of school coaches and recent hefty annual fee increases (particularly painful for those with multiple daughters), and although senior school fees now in line with other comparable schools, prep fees comparatively on the high side – perhaps the price of (hopefully) avoiding the 11+ mayhem.

Remarks: Under the driven eye of Jenny Brown, STAHS has become a genuine competitor in the London day school scene with results and Oxbridge success on the up. Send your daughter here and watch her soar, but keep fingers firmly crossed that school's new highly competitive agenda doesn't override the 'nurture factor' that makes it currently stand apart from the hothousing rest.

St Albans School

Abbey Gateway, St Albans, Hertfordshire AL3 4HB

Ages 11–19 Pupils 863 Sixth form 310 (80 girls)

Fees: £18,600 pa

01727 855521
www.st-albans.herts.sch.uk

Headteacher: Since 2014, Jonathan Gillespie, previously head of Lancing College for eight years. Read modern and medieval languages and did a PGCE at Cambridge; taught at Highgate School and Fettes College before joining Lancing.

Doesn't teach pupils on timetabled basis ('the demands of a head mean I couldn't give it my all'), but gets stuck into Oxbridge trial interviews, assemblies, giving out weekly commendations etc. A more consultative leader than his predecessor (brought in the first parental questionnaire the school has ever seen), but believes in 'evolution not revolution' in terms of making changes. Pupils describe him as 'approachable' and not somebody they want 'to let down.'

We found him amiable, chatty and excitable, but also traditional and authoritative. Keen sports coach, especially hockey (he umpires at national level), and has been involved in CCF. Other interests include hill walking and golf, and he celebrates family's Scottish roots by playing the highland bagpipes. Married to Caroline, former civil servant, with whom they have two sons, one at university and one in school.

Academic matters: In 2018, 82 per cent of GCSE grades A*-A/7-9, placing the school in upper echelons of league tables with no weaknesses at either GCSE or A level. Home grown sixth formers average points score equivalent to 10 A grades or nine A*s at GCSE. Top performing subjects are English, maths, history, music, design technology, sciences and classics. IGCSEs in maths, sciences, languages, history, music and English. In 2018, 66 per cent of A levels were graded A*/A. Maths popular and successful, with strong showings in sciences, art, classics, geography, drama, economics, DT, RS, history, ancient history and English. Languages less popular but interest increasing. French, German and Latin are on an equal footing in year 7; top sets take French in year 10 and international O level in year 11. Setting from second term in the first year in maths and from the start of year 9 in other core subjects. 'A bottom set here is still well above average,' says head. Many take an extended project qualification (EPQ) in the lower sixth. Typical titles include 'Is the creation of Chimeras ethical?' and 'Was Cicero as influential an orator as he thought?'

Traditional, didactic lessons, although plenty of room for interaction and work in small groups, as well as creative ways of learning, with evidence adorning many of the school corridors (one exceptionally well presented science display was complete with flashing lights). 'My son comes home itching to research more about the subjects he's taught,' said one parent. Drop-in subject clinics at GCSE and A level for most subjects at least once a week. Teaching staff highly praised, with the latest inspection report noting that they are an 'inspirational force in and beyond the classroom.' 'You can email them at any time and they get back to you promptly,' said one parent. Homework taken seriously, with at least one hour a night in first form, moving up to two hours a day in sixth form. No room for complacency or coasting. 'There's a strong expectation that you do your best and nothing less,' one pupil told us.

Not the best place for heavyweight SEN, but the learning support unit (which is located centre school) employs good, competent staff who cheerfully and successfully handle bright pupils with processing or other difficulties. 'Our admissions process is good at finding those who will thrive here, so it's generally a smooth process getting them the help they need once they join,' says the head. Parents concur. 'We knew our son was dyslexic, and whilst it was not really recognised by his primary school, this school picked it up in a single test at the application stage and has been fantastic in ensuring he gets all the support he needs now he's a pupil, including special lessons in the school day.' Mostly dyslexia, dyspraxia and Asperger's. School speaks of the 'gift of dyslexia' and how it enables the world to be accessed in a different way. Learning support also organises mentoring for those struggling to maximise their potential, as well as help around resilience, relieving stress, facilitating study skills etc.

Careers guidance from the fourth year; detailed help with university applications, including Oxbridge. 'This starts early and is incredibly detailed and individual,' said one parent.

Games, options, the arts: Sport has a strong reputation here, but non-sporty types need not fear, say parents. 'Everyone has to take part in sport because it keeps you fit and healthy, but there's no ethos of "You will enjoy sport, no matter what!"' Excels in rugby (D teams in most year groups), hockey, cricket and cross-country for boys and netball, lacrosse and tennis for girls. International reputation in cross-country. Other major games also on offer, along with sailing, squash, badminton, aerobics, golf, athletics, climbing and table tennis. School owns a 400 acre farm – Woollams – about a 10 minute drive away, with 75 acres dedicated to world-class, jaw-droppingly impressive pitches (including Astroturf) and courts, plus a spacious and modern pavilion, where pupils who do commit to sport are expected to spend most Saturdays. These dazzling

S

outdoor facilities are complemented by a state-of-the-art sports centre on site, which includes stand-out climbing wall and swimming pool (where sixth-formers can train to be lifeguards and then get a job at the pool in the summer) and even an endless pool with motion-capture technology to analyse style, strength, conditioning etc (the sports hall also has cameras throughout for analysis of sports play).

Outstanding coaching, and national and international sporting honours, plus numerous school representatives in county teams, across many sports. In the English Schools AA national cross-country championships, half the county senior team come from St Albans and the intermediate team are current national champions. School are 10 times winners of the King Henry VIII relays and recently notched up fourth place in the world cross-country championships. But whilst the school enjoys its winning, head insists this is not at all costs and fixture list constructed to ensure a balance of easier and more challenging matches.

Music on the up, with 185 lessons taught by peripatetic teachers every week and many pupils play to a very high standard. Now a Steinway school, it's no wonder that piano is increasingly popular. Inclusive school choir (which includes some teachers) performs at the abbey twice a week, and there are plenty of bands, ranging from jazz to rock. Drama collaborates with music department for some impressive whole school performances, whilst the drama department (located opposite the school) puts on regular smaller plays. Art and DT boast some real talent, with excellent facilities to fuel passions, although some pupils express disappointment that there is no food technology. Outdoor team-work fostered through robust and popular CCF and D of E. Army and air options available, though parents say RAF wing plays second fiddle to Coldstream Guards – despite the former offering opportunities to take off and fly.

Extracurricular clubs mean the school day is regularly stretched beyond the official 8.35am-4pm. 'There are so many clubs and everyone feels really encouraged to try them out,' said a pupil. 'Special transport is provided, so nobody misses out and they often lay on food for them,' added a parent. Trips could hardly be more diverse, including to Pen Arthur, a rugged farmhouse in rural Wales, which is owned by the school and used for various activities and field work. Triennial charity visits to an orphanage in Tanzania (one of many charitable ventures), while sporting trips to the likes of Sri Lanka (cricket) and southern hemisphere (rugby). 'You name somewhere, we'll go,' says a smiling head, although he quickly adds he's aware of potentially mounting costs for parents and so they're always optional and there are plenty within the UK.

Background and atmosphere: There's a real buzz here, with a purposeful, dynamic and friendly vibe, where students are hungry to learn but don't take themselves too seriously. Originally founded in 948, this is one of the oldest extant schools in the country (so ancient that the first pupils did not speak English) and this sense of history is a great source of pride to pupils. Adjacent to the abbey, the school has some extraordinary rooms and nooks with gothic windows and yard-thick walls. One such is home to the school's small museum. In contrast, there's the light, contemporary Aquis Court building (former home to KPMG), which the school has acquired and uses for art, with five studios including ceramics and kiln, sixth form centre with private study area and classrooms, with other buildings nestling among well-maintained gardens. Facilities are all outstanding, with some particularly well-equipped science labs and a spacious junior and senior libraries.

From fifth year, pupils can go into town for lunch (although the privilege is quickly removed if they're not impeccably behaved), keeping the school from feeling remote and elite. That said, the on site cashless refectory serves an excellent array of food (some of the best we've seen) keeping younger ones happy. Breaktimes usually spent in class common room and outside in the abbey orchard (with teachers on duty) at lunchtimes.

Boarding went in the 1950s, direct grant in the 1970s – girls arrived (mainly from local independents and states) in the sixth in 1991. 'It's a wonderful co-ed school for girls to enter from a single-sex school because all the girls are new together,' said one parent. 'I don't know any of the girls who don't love it here,' said one female pupil, although it's generally agreed that girly-girls may struggle amid the testosterone. Boys say the presence of girls 'makes us more mature.'

Lots of outreach work (school motto is translated from Latin as 'Born not for ourselves'), involving pupils going into care homes, working with children with learning disabilities etc. Children from local state schools enjoy some of the facilities, including pool and science labs. In fact, exceptionally strong links exist with local state schools, with sixth formers mentoring primary school children and together with staff providing masterclasses in maths, sciences and drama. Student voice traditionally weak, but improving, with recently formed student council having brought about more water fountains and refurbished toilets. 'I think they're really working on this area, but there's still some way to go to ensure pupils are instrumental to what goes on in the school,' said one parent. Despite the obvious links with the abbey, pupils say religion is low-key.

Pastoral care, well-being and discipline: Horizontal tutorial system, plus prefects, full-time school nurses, school counsellor, chaplain, two heads of sixth-form and lots of senior staff with pastoral roles reflect the emphasis on pupil support. 'My son says you can ask the prefects anything and that you never feel silly,' said one parent. 'Initially when my son started, he was a little bit quiet but his confidence has really grown, all thanks to the pastoral care,' said another. Traditional when it comes to discipline, boundaries and order, although there's room for boys to learn from their mistakes and we witnessed usual boisterousness at break. Entrance into sixth form earns a whole new level of respect and grown-up facilities, including an on-site Starbucks (not surprisingly, also used by staff).

Bullying? 'Yes,' says head, 'because every school does. But if you're asking me if it's persistent, then no.' This, he puts down to both strong sanctions and encouraging pupils and parents to report any unpleasantness early on. 'I always think youngsters are like pebbles on a beach – when the tide comes in, they inevitably bump and give each other a polish. But we have to make sure that's all it is.' Legal highs had just been added to the list of drugs for which pupils are expelled, when we visited.

Pupils and parents: Over 70 per cent of pupils from local Herts area and about half of those from St Albans itself. The rest, including quite a few Jewish pupils, from north London, mostly from Enfield. Smaller number from other ethnic minorities or families where the first language is not English. Boys come into the first year bright-eyed, bushy-tailed and in the main, grow into interested, sharp, articulate young people who are, on the whole, grounded, not pompous. School works hard to integrate girls but it remains steadfastly a male environment, attracting resilient and robust girls into the sixth form. Eight school bus routes bring the majority of children to school, whilst others walk or get the train.

Parents are ambitious – mostly professional, many first-time buyers, plus a handful whose children would otherwise qualify for free school meals. Good sense of community among parents, if that's what you want, but easy enough to opt out of the events and parent get-togethers if you don't. Some parents say the school could be better at communication with them, particularly electronically. 'As it is, I have to get my son to take a picture with his phone of the fixtures information,' said one parent. Very strong Old Albanians, many of whom send their sons here and, later, their daughters. Only 13 schools have produced more Fellows of the British Academy and Royal Society. Notable former pupils go back to the year dot but recent ones include Sir Tim Rice, archaeologist Lord Renfrew, film producer Mike Newell, General Sir Richard Lawson and Prof Stephen Hawking.

Entrance: 'Unashamedly a selective school, but not ultra-selective,' insists head, although it is seriously over-subscribed, with more than three applicants per place. IQ of 125+ at 11+ and 127+ at 13+ (say discrepancy is due to tutoring, not innate ability). At 11, tests in English, maths and VR and interviews, all on the same day. At 13, apply early, conditional offers made following assessments in Y7; late-comers compete for the few remaining places. Tests as at 11+: three interviews and entry dependent on CE results. Around 100 applicants for 40+ places at 16 – with minimum grade 7 required in A level subjects and a grade average of 6.6 or over at GCSE for both external applicants and those moving through from GCSEs.

Exit: A laudable 78 per cent go on to Russell Group universities, notably Birmingham, Bristol, Durham, Exeter, Nottingham and Warwick, with popular subjects including economics, engineering, history, law, maths and the sciences. Regular success with medicine and veterinary science applications (11 in 2018) and six to Oxbridge.

Money matters: Academic scholarships, for absolute excellence, worth five per cent of fees awarded on the basis of performance in the entrance tests at 11 and by separate exam at 13 and 16. Choral scholarships by audition at 11+. Art, music and sport scholarships at 13+. Currently 42 bursaries, 20 full-fees remission. Bursary funds equivalent to five full fees pa allocated by combination of need and merit so if top three pupils require 100 per cent bursary there will be little left for anyone else, but school usually manages to offer something to almost all who need it.

Remarks: Hovering towards the top of the league tables, this is a friendly, outward-looking county school where academia comes first, and sport a close second. Fear not if your son (or sixth form daughter) isn't sporty, however, as the 'work hard, play hard' ethos of the school can (and frequently does) mean pupils are drawn more towards drama, art or music than sports, in addition to their more intellectual studies. Traditional, disciplined and highly structured, this school demands high standards from all, but its emphasis on a rounded education means it is not the academic pressure-cooker that so many London schools are.

St Andrew's School

Buckhold, Pangbourne, Reading, Berkshire RG8 8QA

Ages 3–13 **Pupils** 285 **Boarders** up to 30 flexi

Fees: Day £10,860 – £18,150 pa; Flexi boarding + £3,360 pa

0118 974 4276
www.standrewspangbourne.co.uk

Headmaster: Since 2015, Jonathan Bartlett (40s), previously head of Moor Park School in Shropshire for seven years. Read PE and history at Brunel University. The youngest of seven children, he grew up on a pig farm but also 'loved' his time at a boys' boarding school in Wiltshire, so much so that his first job after university was at Papplewick, one of the boysiest of boys' boarding preps. Took off on a round the world trip which included setting up an online education company in America, where he also met his wife. All very entrepreneurial and exciting but he still missed Papplewick, eventually returning there and becoming deputy head.

When we met he was beaming with pride at pupils' CE results ('I can take very little credit for these'). Given school's size and non-selective admissions policy, the scholarship haul was certainly worth smiling about. Says he was drawn to St Andrew's because of its 'country prep values' and 'relaxed, informal feel'. He has plans, of course, but there's no revolution on the cards (and none necessary). Somewhat overdue improvements to sport and drama facilities are underway and longer term he's keen to 'build boarding'. On the academic front he has appointed a head of learning and reintroduced Latin (year 6 upwards).

Mr Bartlett, who says he 'hates being behind a desk,' takes year 8 scholars for problem solving and reasoning. His wife, a linguist with a masters in health education, also teaches. Favourite books? Animal Farm (unsurprisingly) and A Prayer for Owen Meany.

He describes the school's demographic as 'quite diverse' (emphasis on 'quite', we think) and definitely 'not stuffy'. And what do parents think about the Bartletts? 'It's so exciting, they're absolutely fantastic for the school,' said one. 'Mrs Bartlett is really involved and easy to talk to,' said another, who thought Mrs B's being American was a 'breath of fresh air'. Several others commented that they felt the head was genuinely listening to parents' ideas and had a clear vision of what needs to be done. Children were won over almost at once by the zip wire and climbing frame that were installed at the same time as their new head.

The Bartletts live on site and have three children (one at Moor Park, one at Malvern and one at St Andrew's) plus two of the obligatory prep school head labradors – 'heads have them because they're bombproof,' countered Mr B. Down time is for sport (cricket and golf) and family bolthole in Pembrokeshire.

Entrance: Mainly from local nurseries and primary schools or families relocating from London. Admissions ethos couldn't be simpler: St Andrew's is 'a family school which offers places to children who will be happy and thrive academically'. That all sounds lovely but remember, it's also a popular school that receives many more applications than it has places. Main points of entry are at ages 3, 4 and 7 although places may become available in other years. Younger children invited to spend a day or half day in the school; older children sit 'short' tests and year 7 candidates are assessed formally. Priority given to siblings and children of former pupils.

Exit: Mainly all over (the home counties). Co-eds Bradfield College and Pangbourne scoop up the majority; one or two each year to Wellington and Marlborough. Fair few boys head to Abingdon, Magdalen College School and Radley; girls to Downe House, Tudor Hall and Queen Anne's Caversham. Head says they lose 'a few' girls to day schools at age 11 but can sometimes arrange 'deferred places.' Good spread of academic, sport and music scholarships – an impressive 11 in 2018.

Remarks: St Andrew's motto is Altiora Petimus ('we seek higher things') and this is certainly the case as one ascends the steep hills of the Thames valley in search of the small village of Buckhold. School occupies a rather delicious gothic revival pile designed for Herbert Watney (of the brewing family) by Alfred Waterhouse, better known as architect of the National History Museum. Not all parts of the school building are by him – no prizes for guessing those in which he didn't have a hand. Lawns roll down to meadows and woodland, in total 54 acres of greenest Berkshire, where Buckhold birds do their best to drown out the persistent hum of the M4 – a reminder that less pastoral regions (Reading and Newbury) are close by.

Not a school with ancient lineage, it opened in 1934 under joint heads. Two heads may be better than one but this was somewhat over specified considering the inaugural page of the register runs to eight boys. First girls were admitted in 1971. At just over 290 pupils it's comfortably full and while head acknowledges it 'could expand', he says there are no plans to stretch numbers beyond 300. Parents will be relieved; several told us that they chose the school for its size. 'We looked at bigger preps but felt that our child might get lost.'

Our visit started with a walk through the dining room, worth a visit if Royal Doulton tiled panels are your thing (they are ours). Then it was out and over to the cluster of modern buildings housing nursery and pre-prep. Up to year 2 children are taught by stage, not age, we were told as we tiptoed past a group working hard on their phonics. Adaptable multi-purpose conservatory with small cookery area was lovely and bright (though we wondered if it didn't get a little warm in summer). Specialist teachers for French, music, PE and swimming. Parents told us that pre-prep was 'on top' of the basics such as reading, spelling and times tables and aimed to get these 'out of the way' before move to prep.

Some parts of the pre-prep looked in need of a revamp – outside areas in particular were a bit scruffy and didn't appear to make best use of extensive space available. Staff acknowledged things could do with 'sprucing up' and told us that future plans include opening up the reception class and extending the indoor/outdoor space with a canopy.

Some of the forest schools we've seen are a challenge to the conventional meaning of the word 'forest', but with 50 bosky acres St Andrew's isn't one of them and outdoor activities, rain or shine, have always been a big part of the school day – whether it's collecting bundles of 10 sticks for maths or going on a 'shape hunt'. Each child plants a tree on arrival and sees it grow as they move through the school. All-in-one waterproofs and wellies hang in the cloakroom and get a lot of use. 'We love the fact that children can play and explore in the grounds. They're encouraged to be bold and enjoy the freedom.'

Independence is the aim and even the youngest are expected to dress themselves, use knives and forks and pour their own milk or juice at break; some parents take a little convincing, especially if they have to wash the aftermath. We loved the noticeboard in the nursery cloakroom which had a filthy shirt pinned to it with labels pointing to each stain reading, 'I'm sorry that my uniform got dirty today but this shows that I have been learning x.'

After-school provision has been beefed up for all age groups. Equestrian skills are honed at the next door stables. The summer bike ride club has been a huge success: 'We weren't sure if parents would want to bring their children's bikes into school, but they love it.' (Preponderance of 4x4s may be a factor.) Pupils learn cycling safety via the 'bikeability' scheme and the course culminates in an Enid Blyton style group ride and picnic.

We came across a group of pupils (according to our notes they were all called Daisy, Harriet or Freddie, but surely that can't be right) enjoying their morning break 'squash and bs (biscuits)' outside and conducted a quick vox pop. What did they like about their school? 'We have two breaks every day and you can climb trees, it's just amazing.' 'Everyone can be in a team; no one is left out. And everybody cheers.' And what about their new head? 'He's SO nice and really friendly. He chats to us about football during supper.' 'He's strict, but not mean strict. He's only strict to keep us in order.' 'We've got more freedom to climb trees, as long as you do it in threes so that if someone hurts themselves there's one person to tell the teacher and one person to calm them down if they're upset.' So, all good – especially on the tree climbing front.

Next stop was year 5 history and pupils arrived, sorted out their seats and were ready to work in double quick time. It was an enjoyable, pacey lesson based around interpreting portraits and every pupil got to contribute their ideas. Teaching style seems to be fun – hands on with lots of activities and trips – but also rigorous. None of the parents we spoke to thought it was an academically pushy school, instead they used words like 'intense' and 'thorough.' Science labs are pretty trad, with specimens in glass cases and stuffed alligators; pupils told us that they really enjoyed all the practical work.

Learning skills (no longer known as learning support, 'everybody decided on the name change') steps in quickly if necessary, whether for short-term confidence building or extended help for pupils with mild SEN such as dyslexia. Focus is on individual, rather than group, work and the approach is holistic – children are taught relaxation techniques and staff are vigilant for signs of stress. Parents say homework 'not excessive, just a bit of reading or spelling until year 6, unless there's a test coming up'.

'We're quite sporty,' a pupil told us, modestly. In fact St Andrew's, though small, is a big player. Hockey was described to us by one parent as 'phenomenal' – recent achievements include girls' team getting to the national finals and boys' team winning the county championships. School orienteering team are also national champions. Swimming, tennis, lacrosse and equestrian also enthusiastically and successfully pursued. One of our guides was glad she could now play cricket instead of rounders but thought that girls should also get a chance to play rugby (not yet on the cards). Fantastic new sports centre with swimming pool and climbing wall.

Drama lessons take place in the rather small studio – lots of lighting equipment but no actual stage. After-school drama club is popular and there are regular productions (performed in sports hall) but head and parents acknowledge that the subject has been something of a Cinderella. New specialist teaching has already improved matters and plans for a proper stage and better facilities are afoot. Pupils may work towards the LAMDA grades and several have won drama scholarships to senior school.

While drama may be playing catch up, music at St Andrews is in a class (in fact a music block) of its own. Head told us he was 'blown away' by the high standard. A quick look at the noticeboards revealed three recent grade 8s and even a diploma, not to mention a range of individual instrumental lessons that started with bagpipes and, for all we know, ends with xylophone. Three choirs (plus one in pre-prep), a full orchestra, a string orchestra, big band, jazz band and concert band and any number of ensembles. Parents of musical children are delighted with the provision but we did hear one or two mutterings about (almost inevitable) music/sport timetable clashes. The sporty and musical child might be stretched rather thin here, given the predominance of both.

Boarding (Mondays to Thursdays) increasingly popular. Accommodation is up in the eaves of the main house (boys at one end, girls at the other and a sensor alarm between) and preponderance of beams and wood give the space rather an alpine feel. Small numbers make for comfortable and homely arrangements, dorms spotless but not at all institutional. Boarders love the experience – hot chocolate and toast in the common room, summer evenings playing tennis, swimming or 'just lying on the grass talking'.

No house system; school has 'sections' distinguished by colour (red, blue, green etc). 'It's a bit boring but that's the way it's been since the beginning', we were told. Parents confident that pastoral care system would pick up any problems early on and also praised home-school communication, 'Teachers respond very quickly'. Chapel (can just about seat whole school) three times a week; 'it's a buzz when everyone is singing,' said our guide; Christmas carol service is held at Bradfield College. When asked about food the pupils were very keen to share: curry Mondays and chicken in barbecue sauce are firm favourites; rocky road and chocolate brownies are top puddings. Opinion sharply divided as to whether macaroni cheese was best or worst.

Families live within 45 minutes' drive and are mostly long-term local or London escapees. Parents, many both working, appreciate the improved after-school care. Very active parents' association, FOSA (Friends of St Andrew's) arranges social events such as pub nights and charity fundraisers. 'It's not a cliquey school,' we were told, 'there's a really good mix'. While this is undoubtedly true, it's worth bearing in mind that the 'mix' doesn't have that many different ingredients ... Former pupils include author David Cornwell (aka John le Carré); broadcaster Adam Hart Davis; artist Sir Howard Hodgkin; actress Emily Bevan and, wait for it, James and Pippa Middleton and their sister, Catherine, Duchess of Cambridge. Apparently it was at a hockey match on the fields of St Andrew's that Prince William, then a pupil at Ludgrove, first saw his future wife. All credit to the school for not overplaying this particular connection.

Many of the parents we spoke to had looked at larger or better-known schools before choosing St Andrew's. 'It's a little gem,' was a phrase we kept on hearing. The fact that it has been below the radar appeals to some, rather like that favourite, 'unspoilt' holiday destination. One mother said, 'I don't really want to tell my friends [about St Andrew's]; it won't be so unique and special.' Er, sorry about that. School's relative youth means that some founding old boys from the 1930s are still on the mailing list. The registrar told us of one chap who, at nearly 90, loves to come back and visit. And his verdict? 'Yes, it's changed, but the magic is still here'.

St Catherine's Preparatory School

Linked with St Catherine's School

Station Road, Bramley, Guildford, Surrey GU5 0DF

Ages 4–11 **Pupils** 255 **C of E**

Fees: £8,985 – £15,180 pa

01483 899665
www.stcatherines.info

Headmistress: Since 2012, Naomi Bartholomew MA BEd Cantab (40s) who was educated at Portsmouth High School and went on to read English and education at Homerton College, Cambridge. She spent two years in south west China with the VSO, then taught in state and independent primary schools. Five years as head of English at Yateley Manor was followed by the deputy headship at St Catherine's in 2009. We previously called her 'calm, clever and warm'. Think Miss Honey, if Miss Honey were the extremely effective head of top girls' prep. Smiles start here, with the head, and radiate down through the charming head of the pre-prep to the teachers to the girls. Or maybe it's the other way round. Either way, what a lot of smiles!

Entrance: Roughly 50 applicants for 32 places at 4+. A few more join in years 1 and 2, but entry is most competitive at 7+ when the school has only four official new places. A few certified brainboxes join in year 5, often from local state schools. Apply by October of the year before you'd like your daughter to start.

Exit: Roughly three-quarters (some years more) will proceed to the senior school after sitting the 11+ (maths, English and, somewhat unusually, science) alongside all other applicants. Others aim for local schools like Prior's Field, Cranleigh and Tormead, or to board further afield. The head meets all year 5 parents to discuss future schools. 'There's no weirdness about it – it was really useful,' said a mum.

Remarks: The fun starts in the bright and welcoming pre-prep with two small classes of 16 and specialist teachers for music, games, ballet and computing. Learning taken seriously, but never dreary. Weekly pre-prep assembly bestows Kindness Awards. Class sizes expand slowly as the girls move through the school.

Academic focus gradually ratchets up as girls approach 11. iPads compulsory in years 5 and 6, with parents voicing the usual pros (they've gained so many skills!) and cons (they're addicted!). SEN department, known as Academic Mentoring, serves around 20 girls with mainly low level problems, from organisational challenges to mild dyslexia.

The school's neat as a pin outside appearance belies a labyrinthine interior, with the feel of a medieval town of courtyards, gardens, walkways and overlapping buildings. The senior school across the road serves as a steam valve with prep girls shepherded back and forth for swimming, dance, chapel, lunch and some games. Some snazzy spaces, like the stylish purple and green IT room and the new science lab opened in 2018 by (local) educator and broadcaster Maggie Aderin-Pocock.

Dance is fabulous and the teaching inspirational. Reception and year 1 have ballet timetabled. Thereafter, the ambitiously named St Catherine's School of Dance offers a wide range of lessons and coaching. 'It's my belief that dance, like French and music, contributes to their education,' says the head. 'We're not necessarily about creating ballerinas.'

Music is for both the expert and the merely eager. Everyone tries a string instrument for a term in year 2, then recorders in year 3 (plus a go at some brass). The result is that well over half the girls play an instrument and there are loads of informal concerts spread through the year. NB The school hall now possesses a glorious pipe organ donated by a local music-lover.

More drama offered than when we last visited. It's taught weekly to years 3-6. Big 'play with music' ('not a musical!' the girls insisted) is a very large deal for year 6 in their final term when entrance exams have faded into the mists of time. Girls (and parents) think there's still room for more.

Games are a big part of life for many of these competitive girls, and standards are high. Lacrosse is introduced in year 6. Swimming is a major sport, and the girls use the senior school pool once a week from year 1. Efforts have been made to include one and all, but match selection remains selective, according to parents of less gifted sportswomen.

Immense range of clubs from construction to knitting to music tech helps augment the shortish school day. 'Girls need to stay for after school activities if they want the full education the school offers,' a mum told us. And most do. Nice to see chess taken seriously. The resident international chess master holds a weekly session and the school hosts a national girls' chess competition which recently saw the largest number of girls on record in the UK gathering to play the game of kings.

Parents are universally grateful their girls are here. The school is popular with families fleeing London who may prefer St Catherine's to the more citified Guildford options: 'If you're moving out of London, you're really not looking for an urban school,' one parent explained. 'You join a nice, welcoming community,' said another. Coaches bring girls from Farnham, Haslemere, Woking, East/West Horsley and Clandon. School opens at 8am but parents can drop off at the senior school from 7.50am. Boarding showing green shoots, with a few occasional year 6 boarders and increasing numbers of parents asking about it.

S

St Catherine's School

Linked with St Catherine's Preparatory School

Station Road, Bramley, Guildford, Surrey GU5 0DF

Ages 11–18 **Pupils** 653 **Sixth form** 170 **Boarders** 79 full, 39 weekly
C of E

Fees: Day £18,375; Boarding £30,285 pa

01483 899609
www.stcatherines.info

Headmistress: Since 2000, Alice Phillips MA Cantab (50s). Educated at Kendal High School, then read English at Cambridge. First teaching post was at the Royal Masonic School, Rickmansworth, where she rose to be head of English. Thence to deputy headship at Tormead in 1993. Understands young people. As a boarding school brat – Mrs Phillips' father was a housemaster at Sedbergh – she 'grew up with 68 surrogate brothers and four natural ones'.

Mrs Phillips impresses at once as being full of brisk common sense, good humour and get-up-and-go. But she is also super-bright, super-articulate and super-focused on the highest of standards for her staff, her charges and herself. 'She is utterly determined for her girls,' one mother told us. And this blazes forth in her dedication to the job of equipping them for the future – 'girls need to be in an environment which demonstrates that there's nothing you can't do'.

Back in the saddle after a few years of cross pollination as President of the Girls' Schools' Association (GSA) in 2014, which took her out of school three days a week, and then vice chair of the Independent Schools' Council 2015-17. Now busy directing the school's next phase of physical development – rebuilding part of the sixth form boarding house ('we're not going for luxury en suite' but comfortable, practical and home from home) and replacing a time-worn teaching block with a whizz bang new one dedicated to science, technology, maths, digital learning and independent research.

No plans to go anywhere for now, but if retirement should beckon, feels the school is firmly on its rails come what may – 'If I went under a bus the rest of the management staff would keep the ethos going without a hiccup'.

Academic matters: A level results excellent across the board – no weak areas. Over 90 per cent of subjects taken at A level in 2018 were graded A*-B, 66 per cent A*/A. Maths the most popular A level, by far: 60 per cent of girls do it in sixth form. No other subject has even half as many takers. Greek and German surviving alongside shiny sixth form ab initio subjects like business, economics, history of art, psychology and photography. Sixth form enrichment programme includes advice on higher ed and interviews, healthcare and citizenship issues. No plans to bring in the IB diploma: 'By the time they're in sixth form they're ready to specialise,' says the head. All girls start sixth form with four A levels and around half drop a subject after the first year. Some sixth formers may do another GCSE, add a language or work on an EPQ.

IGCSEs in most core subjects, with GCSEs for the arts (art, DT, drama music, textiles) and fringes (Greek, Latin, PE). At I/GCSE in 2018, over 83 per cent A*-A/9-7 grades. All girls do an IGCSE in French, German or Spanish. Italian an option in sixth form. Food and nutrition available as a GCSE (some girls' schools have dropped this) and all girls participate in cookery lessons in the first two years, rotating with art, drama, DT, textiles and music. Most girls sit one GCSE, plus an RS short course, one year early.

SCAGS – tracking tests for every subject every term – keep the flames licking at the girls' heels in the years leading up to GCSEs. 'They let you see where you are within your year,' a girl told us earnestly. Academic extension programme for years 11-13. Lots of options, lots of opportunities – real education takes place here. Sensible system of sixth form subject mentors.

Embraces technology, but not naive. Parents are required to supply iPads for their daughters from year 5 up – yippee, if that's your thing. Google classroom used for notes/prep. At the same time, the school advises parents to purchase phone contracts with minimum data, and the library remains well-stocked. 'We have literally every book,' our guide gushed.

Parents unlikely to zero in on this school for its SEN provision. Girls with only mild dyses likely to be able to stand the heat. 'We pride ourselves on our tracking system,' says head, 'and on spotting any late-emerging problems'.

Games, options, the arts: A 'busy' school. Music, dance and performing arts particularly shine. A ton of music on tap and standards are high – over 600 individual lessons are taught every week through the senior and prep schools, and Mrs Phillips has been a governor of the Yehudi Menuhin School since 2009. The list of ballet/dance lessons available at school is as long as your arm. LAMDA too. Lively art in many media. Lots of clubs, and girls can start their own, eg this year's Medical Reading Club(!)

Games important – a bit jolly lacrosse sticks – and more inclusive than in the past. Lots of opportunities for those less than Olympian in prowess – 'I'm on the fourth lacrosse team!' a girl told us brightly (there are five). Guildford High are the arch rivals (Benenden for lacrosse). Meanwhile, sports hotshots fulfil their destinies – county and national finals places in several sports and stellar showings in swimming, tennis and – especially – lacrosse. Usual range of sports on offer, and excellent facilities, plus equestrian team, and lots of individual success in non-mainstream sports eg ice skating. DofE thrives and produces a surprising number of golds. Excellent outside speaker programme, sixth form lectures, and lots of stimulating trips.

Boarding: Boarder numbers start slowly in the younger years but work up to over a third of the sixth form – around 125 boarders all told. Around half of boarders are full, half weekly – the boarding fee is the same either way. Occasional boarding also an option. Half of boarders are from international families (either expat or foreign). Big concerts, productions and lectures are streamed online so that overseas families can tap in. No Saturday school, but plenty of activities offered, plus sports matches. And, in case you're wondering, the admissions requirements are exactly the same for boarders and for day pupils.

Bedrooms and dorms are spacious enough, welcoming and homely. Most in two-bedders, often with a third bed for occasional boarders. Even sixth formers mostly share. Boarders encouraged to invite a day girl friend to board on a Friday night once a term, and are invited out at weekends in return. NB The school can accommodate a few boarders from the prep school across the street – hugely handy for a few parents.

Background and atmosphere: Established in 1885, this is a school with a proud tradition (only seven heads in its 130+ year history) which, unusually, has grown and developed all on the one site. Set in a leafy village 10 minutes south of Guildford and smack in the centre of a private school nirvana, with girls' schools Guildford High, Tormead and Prior's Field, co-eds

Cranleigh and Charterhouse, and boys-only Royal Grammar School all within five miles.

Snug and compact, the school makes a tidy footprint surrounded by playing fields. At the centre is a humongous £15 million complex – the 125th Anniversary Halls with a dazzling auditorium (seats 300 and has 'better acoustics than the Barbican') plus music practice rooms, a recording studio and other spaces, which segue into the sports hall, gyms, changing rooms, dance studios and a single squash court. All fits ingeniously under one roof ('it's great, we can avoid the rain'). Indoor swimming pool. Science labs a mix of old and new. 'University style' sixth form study centre, designed with input from the girls.

Strong house system – girls are allotted to houses aiming for a mix of abilities and interests in each. Strong ethical dimension to energetic charity work – includes toilet twinning with a loo in Africa. Food has improved – salads particularly praised – though it has not reached the Michelin star quality of a few girls' schools we have visited.

The school's web site is succinct rather than ostentatious – an apt reflection of the school.

Pastoral care, well-being and discipline: 'Lovely dedicated staff,' universally praised. A sense that all girls can fit in and do well here – whatever their aptitudes, enthusiasms, personality – something to which all parents we spoke to attested. 'It can be a bit full-on for some of them,' one parent admitted – and others agreed: 'the girls themselves push themselves to the limit – the atmosphere makes them want to be the best of the best.' 'They do the best they can,' another said, 'but they do it while looking after each other.' All that said, this is not the Kew Gardens Palm House, and a few girls have decamped here from the most sizzling of hothouses (Wycombe Abbey, North London Collegiate?) and thrived in the slightly lower temperature.

Worship once a week for each year group in the gothic style chapel – splendid Kempe stained glass windows celebrating notable female saints, fabulous rose window and Willis organ. Uniform dropped starting in the spring term of the upper fifth on through the sixth form.

Pupils and parents: Attracts bright berries from Guildford and surrounds plus south London, and overseas boarders. Locals come from everywhere but mostly the school's own prep and from Haslemere, Midhurst, Farnham, Guildford, Godalming, Cranleigh, Woking, Esher, Oxshott, SW London. Overseas pupils predominantly English with some EU nationals. Full boarders from, eg, China, Taiwan, Nigeria, Hong Kong, Russia, Malta, Korea, Ireland, Latvia, Estonia, Moldova – aiming for a wide blend. Lots of old girls' daughters. Middle class and comfortable backgrounds, in the main.

Notable old girls include Francine Stock, Juliet Stevenson, Elizabeth Beresford, Zena Skinner, Davina McCall, UA Fanthorpe, Dorothy Tutin, Elinor Goodman, Isabel Hardman, Abi Dowling, Lily Travers, two ambassadors and legions of academics and other high flyers.

Entrance: Entry by academic selection, using St Catherine's own assessment. Eleven plus candidates take papers in English, maths, science and verbal reasoning. A few places at 12+ and 13+ – papers in English, maths and reasoning. Reports from existing schools. Sixth form general paper, tests in A level choices, verbal reasoning and predicted GCSE grades – 7s expected in A level subjects. Interview for potential sixth formers (in person or via Skype). Roughly 1.5 applicants for each 11+ place – about 90-100 enter at this age and 6-9 more boarders at 13+. Around 70 apply for the 10 or so annual places in the sixth – they can afford to be very choosy. School flexible and helpful – happy to interview via Skype if you're abroad.Not a school for anyone with less than fluent English. The few internationals who need help are offered it long-distance in the summer before they join the school.

Exit: Some 10-15 girls leave after GCSEs – mostly to co-eds or to state sixth forms. Sixth form leavers to top unis – three to Oxbridge in 2018 and three medics, with five off overseas.

Money matters: Four scholarships available at 11+ cover 10-20 per cent of fees. More of the same ilk at sixth form. Music awards include the esteemed Jennifer Bate Organ Scholarship, offered in conjunction with Guildford Cathedral. A few bursaries covering up to 100 per cent of fees for the bright broke at 11+ and sixth.

Remarks: If you want convincing that girls only education is the right and modern way for your bright and motivated daughter, go and look. This is as good as it gets.

St Christopher School

Barrington Road, Letchworth Garden City, Hertfordshire SG6 3JZ

Ages 3–18 **Pupils** 552 **Sixth form** 92 (61 boys, 31 girls) **Boarders** 16 full, 29 weekly, 10–15 flexi (from 11 years)

Fees: Day £10,890 – £18,075; Boarding £19,950 – £31,650 pa

01462 650850
www.stchris.co.uk

Head: Since 2007, Richard Palmer (50s), who first went to St Christopher as a gap student and then went on to get a first in education at Nottingham. He taught science, drama and design technology at several schools, eventually becoming head of DT and housemaster at St John's College School, Cambridge before finding his way back to St Christopher. He became head of the junior school in 2004 and has been head of the whole school since 2007.

Previously chair, now on the committee of the Society of Heads, he is also a school inspector with the Independent Schools Inspectorate, giving him an opportunity to see other schools in action. His office is full of mechanical toys and old cameras – a man who loves design and technology still managing to teach it to all in year 7.

Described by parents as well respected, level headed, genuine and a little shy. He does not overwhelm with charisma or charm but is clearly confident in his decision making and that clear decisiveness feeds down to the school. He allows for things to be liberal without being in the least slack. He wants the school to 'remain distinctive' with a breadth of education and for 'pupils to be able to work and live with difference'. He has some freedom to do this since pupils do not do Sats and they follow the national curriculum only loosely. He wants to create more dynamic middle school years and allow topic work and individual work to continue in those years before exams set in. He is keen to find ways to bring drama and philosophy earlier on in the school. So far from a complacent head, but one with vision and goals.

Academic matters: Not narrowly academically selective, yet clearly a school with an expectation that each child is hungry to learn and participate. Independent learning is encouraged

S

throughout the school by teachers who are enthusiastic, energetic and creative.

Nursery has more space than usual with plenty of outside play areas – grassed, soft surfaced and a covered 'outside classroom' with lots of equipment clearly being well used for learning. Historically Montessori, so lots of practical learning, playing and making but now following the EYFS curriculum with clear evidence of more formal phonic learning and number work. Children seen in wellingtons in the garden as well as in wonderful fairy dressing up clothes. Reception children well prepared for reading and writing when they are ready and lots of trips to the junior school in preparation for year 1 transfer.

In the junior school, topic based learning and much creative planning seems to allow students to develop and research ideas, which allows for more independent learning than usually seen in a junior school. Topic learning across all subjects very much in evidence – stretching the topic to music and maths not just in humanities. Small classes – 20 is the average – with a teacher and teaching assistant in each airy classroom. Desks grouped – a sign of collaborative learning with lots of space for carpets, beanbags, making and creating. Early introduction to democracy with class rules and ethos very much child instigated. The junior library is extremely well and widely resourced – a joy in this technology based era – with pupils and parents encouraged to take books out at any time even if the enthusiastic dedicated junior school librarian not available. Interesting to see extension maths in this non-selective school, allowing for more challenging work. Learning support staff (two) in the junior school take pupils out of class but pupils also given in class support.

Five one hour lessons each day in the senior school so no rushing between lessons with bags full of books, and as a result much less tension all round. Extra impressive therefore that they manage to give such a breadth of subjects (though no Latin or RS). Spanish and French expected for all students, where appropriate. Language exchange trips considered a rite of passage and something to look forward to in year 10. Geography trips also popular as is the history war graves trip to Northern France. The trips get more exotic as the students move up the school – Rajasthan one of the most original we have seen. Creative English learning involving role play, drama, filming, and journalism work. Setting in maths from year 7 then more subject setting in year 9. Separate sciences from year 9.

Sciences and maths get particularly good GCSE results as do English, arts and crafts and DT. Parents and students appreciate being able to choose whatever combination of 18 GCSE subjects they want with no timetable limitations or restrictions. Subjects include film studies, additional science, PE and Spanish. At A level there are even more subjects to choose from with the arts and sciences getting particularly impressive results. Career evenings and seminars to help students from year 11 onwards with choices for further education. Extension classes for Oxbridge candidates and extended project qualification for those with particular interests. In 2018, 30 per cent A*-A/9-7 grades at GCSE and 31 per cent A*/A at A level, with 45 per cent A*-B grades.

Dedicated learning support staff in both junior and senior parts of the school take students out of classes for extra (paid for) lessons as well as supporting in class. Touch typing taught before school if desirable from year 5 onwards and we saw several students with laptops as well as having amanuensis (teaching assistant writing for them – particularly useful in exams). The school takes some 25 per cent pupils with special needs, though these places fill early with cognitively bright dyslexic pupils and a few with autism spectrum disorders or ADD. Pre-screening for children with special needs, so apply by November in order to make sure the school has enough provision in place for individual needs.

Games, options, the arts: St Chris is often chosen is for its wider curriculum offerings. Art, music and drama not considered soft options but very valued subjects. A very lively music department with practice rooms for individual instrument learning as well as much music creation in music technology suite. Bands and groups abound – some students we spoke to were delighted to go to a gig in a north London pub and see one of their school bands on stage. Plenty of opportunities to perform at weekly Morning Talks. More jazz and rock and small ensembles than classic orchestras, although these too exist. Junior school choir and some singing.

A large theatre building ideal for drama classes and huge annual musical productions. All the school involved in these extravaganzas, and if you don't like to be in the limelight, lots of opportunities backstage, in production and stage management.

This school is well known for its visual art department which is marvellously well resourced – sewing machines, pottery studio, printing room, woodwork, metalwork, fine art in very mixed media. A whole room dedicated to displays of their work – and one rather wonderfully designed piece of woodwork even ended up in a shop window to display shoes.

The forest school site is generous and gloriously muddy and wooded and well used.

Despite the non-competitive ethos, successful sports teams despite that definitely punch above their weight for such a small school. Everyone is involved and the theory is that this brings up the weaker sportspeople – evidently it works. Matches against local teams and county games. Netball, rugby, football, tennis, volleyball etc. Swimming pool used from early years up – for swimming lessons and fun swim club as well as squad training. It is also an opportunity for older students to obtain a lifeguard certificate so they can work at school or outside in the holidays. Heaven to find a pool with a very civilised and warm temperature of 28 degrees. More sports in lunchtime clubs and after school – rambling, cross-country, cycling, jogging, dance, canoeing, trampolining, athletics and fitness training. Their spacious green fields much in use when we visited for an inter-school football competition with five games going on at a time.

An impressive climbing wall up the whole of one side of a classroom block. But there are also trees in the grounds that are specifically 'climbing trees' – any child welcome to climb in break time if they think they can get up and down. Such a joy to see kids climbing trees in these health and safety conscious days. Plenty of fruit trees and others growing in the extensive grounds. The apple trees are picked and juiced in October by the students who get a bottle to take home. Other growing areas including a wormery from which compost is made and sold locally or used here. Nothing wasted from vegetarian school lunches. A garden shed designed and built by students made from recycled plastic bottles and bamboo sticks provides a good greenhouse for seeds and plants before planting out. And the role of food is not only evident in the growing and composting, but of course in the cookery suite. The Vege Centre is a serious part of the school curriculum where students are taught to make meals not just bake scones. The enthusiasm for all these extracurricular activities was brought home, according to one mother whose son came home eager to show off his cooking skills one day and another time wanting to make a board game.

Once a week there is an enrichment programme allowing students to choose an activity to explore – film making, jewellery, yoga, tai chi, philosophy, dependent on the interests and skills of current staff, supplemented where necessary by external tutors. These are across the age groups so give an opportunity for different years to get to know each other and perhaps explains the familial atmosphere.

Boarding: Extremely flexible boarding available from year 7 upwards. Where there is space and availability, pupils can choose between 'day boarding' between 7.30am-7.30pm which includes breakfast, supper and supervised homework, flexi boarding just for the odd night, weekly boarding from Sunday evening to Friday afternoon or full boarding. Inevitably more full boarders as the students move up the school, especially international students. Three boarding areas according to the age of the student, with some 20 year 13 pupils in a separate house on the school grounds, year 11 and 12 students in a very modern and light extension, and younger years in cosy traditional rooms in the heart of the school. Many of the rooms are single ones – privacy being part of the respectful ethos of the school.

Kind houseparents and gap students involved in weekend activities, and each teacher also responsible for one Saturday activity a year. Weekly evening activities available include movie night, cookery, games nights. Weekend activities almost always involve a trip away from school. Cooking facilities for snacks available to students, though older students have a good kitchen and cook for a weekly supper club. Meat meals are available for boarders after the vegetarian only daytime school canteen. Despite separate boarding areas, it felt very family-like, with older students and younger all hanging out together. We liked the rule that phones were taken away and charged overnight and only returned in the morning once beds were made (something to start in all homes, perhaps?).

Background and atmosphere: Founded during the First World War, this school aims to treat children as individuals, to be non-judgemental and to encourage independence. The Quaker origins of one of the first heads are reflected in Morning Talk three times a week that always involves a period of silence. This opportunity for silence was also seen when we visited: in the middle of a lively lunch, one student rang a bell, the hall fell silent for a moment, and the pupil thanked the hall and the day continued. The right to ring the bell is clearly a privilege allowing for a moment of calm.

Large grounds and airy classrooms with plenty of space also add to the atmosphere of calm. Set in a quiet road in Letchworth, and based around an arts and crafts building with wood panelled rooms, several newer buildings and extensions: a slightly ramshackle group of buildings, with plenty of opportunity to walk outside between classes. Immaculate grounds and planting and freshly painted and very clean rooms despite the fact that many of the buildings are old. The school exudes clean orderliness, which is surprising in view of the reputation it has for being liberal. Students wear their own clothes, call teachers by their first names, are all doing projects and exploring ideas, and there are no bells between lessons, little noise and a great sense of purpose. Teachers appear passionate and engaged, as do pupils. The friendly and efficient catering staff, ground staff and administrators all spoke of loving their jobs. One doesn't sense hierarchy here at any level. Parents said that they appreciate that the school concentrates on things other than uniform and it was one less thing to pay for and worry about. A parent said the school 'has fantastic facilities, is not selective and is all inclusive. What's not to like?'

Pastoral care, well-being and discipline: You wouldn't choose this school if you wanted a safe route or wanted to impose on your child, said one parent, but it really works if you trust your child to make their own choices and the school to nurture and empower them. Parents described it as 'non-pushy and non-selective but allows the child to pursue what they most want to do'. The pupils do choose – their subjects, the direction they want to take and how they work best. Classrooms were busy with students carrying out their own projects and working at their own pace. This is possible because the teachers work hard and there is so much mutual respect. First name terms with teachers – we saw pupils open doors for teachers and teachers waiting for pupils in the lunch queue. No pushing and shoving. Older pupils making allowances for younger pupils and sitting together at lunch. More like a family rather than exclusive year groups.

Dedicated head of pastoral care who liaises with heads of year, who in turn meet with advisors or tutors. The fact that students meet their advisors every day means that issues are fed back quickly up the school, and students and parents feel that they always have someone to speak to. Parents we talked to all knew exactly who they could speak to or email with questions or complaints or concerns.

Self-government (a way of introducing democracy and ensuring students are totally engaged in the school) is an important feature of St Chris according to students we met. Anyone can attend the school council, at which student representatives can vote. Any proposals that get passed by the school council go up to a meeting of the entire senior school where each student can vote. Resolutions passed by the school are enacted unless vetoed by the head (which almost never happens). Pupils we met loved the fact that even the youngest child in the senior school could make large things happen – like the building of the cookery Vege Centre.

Pupils and parents: Quite a large proportion commute from north London thanks to trains from Finsbury Park and school buses. Also some from Cambridge, and more who are either local or move to be near the school. A growing number of international students, especially higher up the school, who tend to be boarders. This is not a narrowly academically selective school and students and parents really reflect this – some making sacrifices to have their children at St Chris, some second generation St Chris families, some bursary students, some with quite significant special needs, some with multiple strengths and huge academic ability. Ideal for a family with several children of mixed interests and abilities – how rare to find a school to suit both the artistic child and the mathematician, the reader and the doer, and to value them all equally. Parents said they are 'encouraged to be involved' and 'can pop in at any time to ask questions'.

Entrance: The school has wonderfully popular open days (the head thinks the free lunch helps keep everyone cheerful for the day) and many parents visit several times to get a feel of the school. Applications are followed up with an interview – both of parents and, separately, the child – to make sure that expectations match. All applicants over year 4 are given cognitive ability assessment which is age related. They aim to accept 25 per cent with special needs if the school can match child's needs to school resources. Since all applicants are interviewed, the school looks for a match of school's ability to match the child's needs. Mild dyslexia well supported with extra individual lessons, high functioning verbal pupils with autism spectrum disorder seem to do well, and especially good for anxious children. The head says that 'some children need to be here', and they may well be given a place even if they don't meet the requirement that 'all prospective students need to show cognitive ability of at least 100 standardised score'. Oversubscribed senior school, and years 5 and 6 generally full too. Children with individual needs must apply by early November for the following year.

Exit: All early years move onto junior school, and almost all move from junior to senior school. Quite a bit of movement at 16 (50 per cent in 2018) as London students get weary of the commute and move to sixth form colleges in the big smoke, and some are just ready for a change or move to technical colleges.

As for higher education, interesting split between the large number who go on to do art (around a quarter) and those who do engineering, science and maths. The art teacher was very proud to show that every single child who applied to art college was offered a place (including Parsons in New York, Bournemouth College, London University of the Arts). Some applying for foundation art courses were offered the degree course directly since they were so well prepared by St Chris. A good range of universities – including Russell Group. A special extension group prepares sixth formers for entry into the most demanding courses.

Money matters: This school is built on solid foundations with good transparent governance provisions in place. Financially stable and well supported. The facilities show recent and regular investment and maintenance. Despite having to pay for extras like music lessons and individual learning support lessons, parents say that the school does its level best to keep costs to parents down as much as possible. There are some 100 per cent bursaries and small allowances (10 per cent fee remission) for art and academic scholarships for pupils at years 7, 9 and 12.

Remarks: Calm and orderly, busy without feeling hectic. Palpable sense of mutual respect between pupils and teachers, between pupils and other pupils and a sense of confident self-respect in the pupils themselves. Passionate, quietly self-confident and articulate students suggested that this was because everyone felt empowered thanks to their role in the school council and self governance. The ethos of respect included the school buildings – extremely well cared for with interesting wall displays, spotless toilets and no sign of writing on desks or chewing gum under desks. The pupils are given a voice at this school so there is no need for graffiti.

St Clare's, Oxford

139 Banbury Road, Oxford, Oxfordshire OX2 7AL

Ages 15–19 **Pupils** 270 **Boarders** 240 full

Fees: Day £19,878; Boarding £41,375 pa

01865 552031
www.stclares.ac.uk

Principal: Since 2017, Andrew Rattue MA PGCE (50s). Formerly head of King's College, the British School of Madrid, and prior to that head of RGS Worcester. Read English at Brasenose, Oxford and later Victorian studies at Birkbeck before nailing the hat-trick with a PGCE from King's College, London. Says teaching was 'the last thing I wanted to do,' but following a postgraduate stint working in a school in Thailand, and there discovering that he possessed that rare and fearless quality of enjoying the company of teenagers, his destiny was sealed and his career has seen him teach English at Mill Hill and Haberdashers' Aske's (including a sojourn as a Fulbright exchange teacher in Dallas, Texas), become head of English at Highgate and second master at RGS Guildford. Joined St Clare's 'at an important time', he says: 'we represent the polar opposite of the Brexit mentality'. Parents say he has brought 'a different presence' to the school and is 'very involved' with the progress of every student.

Married to Jacky, currently training to be a careers advisor, with three grown up sons and a daughter, all accomplished linguists. Self-confessed 'frustrated thesp' (career highlights include directing Matt Lucas as Mr Hardcastle in She Stoops to Conquer during his Habs days); lover of theatre, cinema, walking and travelling. Governor at nearby Rye St Antony School and the Oxfordshire Hospital School, and trustee of the Alliance Française in Oxford.

Academic matters: St Clare's is all about the IB and students come from the world over (48 different nationalities at the time of our visit) to study here for the two-year IB diploma. The first school to offer the IB in England and over 40 years' experience, plus consistently high results, means that St Clare's is more than able to compete with the many top public schools now offering the IB. 2018 saw an average score of 36 points and 20 per cent of students passing their diploma with 40 points or more (one with 45 points). Impressive given the non-academically selective intake and rigorous demands of the diploma: three subjects at standard level, three at higher, including mother tongue and English, a humanities subject, science and maths. Not forgetting the compulsory theory of knowledge course, extended essay and community, activity and service (CAS) programme. Makes A levels look like a walk in the park – one of the reasons St Clare's claims it has the edge over schools that offer both routes: 'when pupils realise the continuous academic rigour required to do well in the IB, there can be a disastrous temptation to quit and jump across to A levels for the wrong reasons,' said one senior staff member.

Students report high standards of teaching and praise school's internationality as a major benefit: 'we're very open minded and willing to share different views which means a broader range of conversations.' Parents say that excellent teaching is a given but also that 'nowhere else can you learn such tolerance by living with such a diverse group of people.' Relaxed approach to numbers needed to run a course: if one pupil wants to study eg Mandarin, then study it they shall (and most likely be roomed with a native speaker to help with tricky homework to boot).

Those too young to commence the IB course (UK year 11) or who need to brush up their English language skills can spend a year in the school before the IB course proper starts, studying the pre-IB. This is flexible in length, up to one year, and can be joined at any time to bring students up to speed before starting the core subjects at diploma level. Despite the fabulously international teaching staff (literature must be taught and studied in mother tongue, so individual tutors are recruited from all manner of local and worldwide institutions), all tuition (collaborative and informal; no chalk and talk in evidence) is in English and class sizes average 10 to 12, sometimes fewer. Languages – unsurprisingly – are the star turn, with maths and science departments also 'outstanding', according to head. Economics and business strong, and psychology 'charismatically taught'. History and global politics 'well taught and popular'. No dedicated SEN department but mild to moderate learning difficulties catered for by an LDD coordinator, and school has experience with students with ADHD, ASD and hearing impairment.

Games, options, the arts: Sport at St Clare's is a totally different proposition from the usual independent school formula, with no PE on curriculum but sport falling under the 'activity' banner of the mandatory CAS module of the IB. No playing fields – all students have membership to the swish Nuffield sports centre and pool in nearby Summertown, and other facilities are a short minibus ride away at other local schools or Oxford Brookes University. Boys' and girls' football teams use the Astroturf pitches at Oxford City FC grounds, and rugby teams use nearby Oxford Harlequins ground. The walls of the 'covered way' showcases the multitude of sporting activities on offer – from badminton to meditation. There are so many activity options that one pupil even saw it as a negative: 'team sports suffer'. Football (both sexes) popular.

The creative part of the programme offers up music, drama, dance, writing, debating and Model United Nations (prizes for anyone who can find a school better qualified to excel in the latter). Pupils describe director of music as 'incredible' and head delights in the eclectic range of musical instruments that arrive amidst luggage from far flung corners of the globe: 'our concerts are remarkable: epiphanies of international culture that nowhere else in the UK could deliver'. Not a huge uptake in peripatetic lessons – flute, piano and violin dominate – but school will arrange tuition in instruments of pupils' choice and many musical pupils use the practice rooms in their free time. Drama smaller scale to what's on offer in many other independent schools, but performances do take place on high days and holidays and there's an annual musical production. The CAS programme also involves community service, which takes the form of charity work in local shops, visiting the elderly, wildlife conservation projects or helping at local schools. A personal tutor is on hand every week to monitor progress and offer advice.

Pupils report 'loads of freedom' to explore the city and its rich cultural offerings: free lectures at the university as well as the local shops and cafes of Summertown which is just a five-minute walk away ('The Italians like to go there to smoke,' the head told us. 'That, and apparently the pasta is cooked more to their liking than ours'). The exception to the freedom rule (curfew at 11pm on weekdays and midnight at weekends) is for the pre-IB students who have compulsory weekend excursions on Saturdays. Grumbles from those concerned, who said they would like weekends to be more relaxed, although we think if they were dropped into a trad public school they'd have more gripes on that front. Fewer major international trips than some other schools (eg no rugby tour or ski trip).

Boarding: Almost all students board full time. Fifteen boarding houses – all single sex – within a short stroll of one another and teaching facilities. All pre-IBs and younger IB1s (year 12s) housed in the stunning '121' – an architect designed, oak-clad collection of modern cubes sensitively adjoining a Victorian frontage, each housing two students, with picture windows onto the grass quad and art studio. Others dotted amongst the Victorian villas – all rooms we saw were extremely spacious and well furnished, many full of Victorian character, some with own showers and all with safe and Wifi. All IB1 students doubled up with another nationality and disagreements are, apparently, very rare. IB2s (year 13s) can choose to share with a friend or take a single room. All houses have residential warden in charge of general well-being of students, who must text their warden at 7pm each evening to let them know where they plan to be that evening – 'wardens run the houses with a light touch,' parents report. Curfews are generous (11pm week nights and midnight at weekends) but rigorously enforced. Those over 18 are allowed to drink 'but with care,' those ever-sensible students told us. Party animals 'so rare they go down in history', said one parent. Day students allocated a house and able to stay one night a week with no additional charge and can also take all meals in school, seven days a week.

S

Background and atmosphere: In head's words: 'There's only one St Clare's.' It would be wide of the mark to agree that other independents are 'samey' in comparison but his observation that there are 'several genuine USPs here' rings true – and it would certainly stand out amongst local IB sixth forms to those on a tour of UK education options. An 'extremely' international cohort is just the start of it – some nationalities with numbers in 20s or 40s, many with under five and several with just one: 'Nobody stands out', one (Swedish) pupil told us: 'we all do.' No uniform and first name terms between teachers and students. Parents say school doesn't have a brand, rather a culture. Prefects? No. Many pupils are offspring of former St Clare's students who met at the school and what the head calls the 'small, human scale touch' is in plain sight. Founded after World War II by visionary educationalist Anne Dreydel (portrait looms over reception area) with the motto 'to advance international education and understanding', St Clare's was a pioneer in establishing exchange opportunities for German students. Recognised with an OBE and the German equivalent, her cultural olive branch towards international peace has evolved – via a stint in the 1960s at a 'posh girls' finishing school' ('Old Etonians in their 50s still blush at the mention,' chuckled head) – into a thriving sixth form for around 265 students. There's 'still a sniff of the slightly alternative atmosphere,' says head, but there's certainly no whiff of eau de party school in the air – the vibe is studious, and students are mature and sincere. 'There's a lot of focus on studying,' our guides assured us.

Fabric of school lends itself well to collegiate feel, with a collection of 27 Victorian villas set amongst prime north Oxford real estate, providing boarding accommodation and classrooms: 'we get to live in this amazing city, not just our school,' one student raved. Buildings are Tardis-esque, with spacious gardens to the rear and quirky touches such as red telephone boxes dotted about. Three meals a day taken in the canteen (standard quality school fare with an international twist) or school coffee shop (the delightfully un-PC named Sugar House), which serves up coffees, teas, paninis and cakes all day (although not at the end of the day when it's most needed, some students complained). Pamela Morris building (2015) is home to several laboratories and maths rooms, as well as being base camp to the 'pets and plants' club (that's rats and snakes to you and me). Breathtaking purpose designed art studio with bi-folding doors onto a grassy quad and optimum north facing light, plus dark room for budding photographers, and one of the loveliest libraries we've seen (and certainly the most diversely stocked).

Pastoral care, well-being and discipline: With 270 15 to 18-year olds thrown together so far from home, what could possibly go wrong? Well, not a great deal, says head. School apparently 'reads the riot act' when pupils arrive and thereafter works on the basis that open channels of communication and lashings of trust go a long way to keeping teenagers on the straight and narrow – and when trouble does rear its head, clear consequences are set in motion. 'There are very few rules, but they are strongly enforced,' say parents. Pupils respond well to this: 'it feels like home. There's very little we can't do – it allows us to be independent and find our way in life'. Lateness or poor behaviour results in loss of free time, confinement to the library or house. Those who fall off the study wagon made to attend compulsory supervised study. Zero tolerance of drug use, transgression resulting in immediate suspension and expulsion for a second offence– school maintains right to drug test students at random. Sex possibly a bigger (although not major) issue: 'we have strict rules and education in place but can't stop the students having relationships,' sighed one senior staff member. Liberal environment makes for high tolerance of any differences relating to sexuality: 'there are possible issues with acceptance amongst some nationalities,' says head, 'but it's seldom discussed; just not an issue.'

Parents love the fact that 'everybody is new – so there are no cliques'. School admits it has its 'fair share' of mental health issues to deal with, particularly anxiety, perfectionism and eating disorders, and has 'beefed up' pastoral support system with the appointment of a counsellor on staff to support the house wardens and trained peer mentors who 'actively seek out' homesickness. Families praise the 'incredibly serious' approach to supporting affected pupils. The new weekend activities programme also attempts to keep possibly homesick younger students busy with trips to football matches, theatre trips and shopping outings to eg Bicester Village. Students meet with their personal tutor on a weekly basis to cover pastoral and academic issues. Open channels of communication between parents and staff – parents invited to email their child's tutor or teachers at any time. Reports and test results viewed electronically via the parent portal.

Pupils and parents: Not the usual international boarding crowd. St Clare's is less of a global brand than many public schools scooping up the progeny of the global elite, so appeals to a different market. Head describes the typical St Clare's parent as 'discerning, intelligent and ambitious', drawn to the school not only by the rich opportunities but also by the fact that it's 'part of the real world'. Italians are the largest group, followed by Germans, Russians ('we are still very much open for business to Russia,' says head) and British (who although significant in number make up just eight per cent of the school community). Parents see the total lack of their own group presence around school as the only downside: 'a bit strange'. Brits – as with other nationalities – often join from international schools overseas ('an easy transition,' say pupils), but some simply have an interest in the IB. Around 10 per cent are day students with parents working locally at the university, hospitals, BMW or similar businesses. In a round table scenario, they are disarmingly mature, serious and erudite. Around 18 scholars each year, some on full bursaries, 'set the tone of the school,' according to head. A 60/40 girl/boy split.

Entrance: Semi but not overly selective. Word of mouth is St Clare's secret weapon and most students have links through friends or family. Conversion once families have visited is 80 per cent. Majority join in UK year 12 (just 45 pupils in the pre-IB year when we visited). Placement tests in English and maths marked whilst the potential student is still in the building and if they pass muster at interview stage – enthusiasm for the IB being number one criteria – offers made on the spot. A four-day induction programme for newcomers is supported by senior students. Fluent English a necessity.

Exit: Majority straight to higher education – about half to UK universities. Popular choices include London colleges (LSE, UCL, Imperial) as well as many Russell Group and new universities. Others to Europe, the US and elsewhere.

We've seen a few careers departments and, with its in-depth knowledge of destinations and courses that other schools are unlikely to have even heard of, plus online tracking system covering everything from research and applications to offers from institutions in multiple countries, we've yet to see one better. 'They guide you every step of the way,' glowed one student. Recent alumni have headed to diverse destinations such as Harvard (one on a 'full ride' scholarship), Bocconi and the elite World Bachelor in Business course at the University of Southern California. St Clare's Connect (like a private version of LinkedIn) ensures St Clare's alumni continue to benefit from global networking opportunities even after they leave the school.

Money matters: Generous means-tested bursary scheme for around 30 promising students. Day fees reasonable especially considering their inclusive nature.

Remarks: A perfect stepping stone (for suitably mature and motivated students committed to the IB) between school and university. A real sense of turning out not St Clarians but global citizens – with these girls and boys as our future world leaders, there is hope after all.

St Clement Danes School

Chenies Road, Chorleywood, Rickmansworth, Hertfordshire WD3 6EW

Ages 11–18 **Pupils** 1,463 **Sixth form** 336

01923 284169
www.stclementdanes.org.uk

Head: Since January 2018, Toby Sutherland, previously deputy head. Formerly at Queen's School, first as a business and economics teacher, later becoming assistant and then deputy head. Responsible for day to day leadership of the school; previous head Josephine Valentine is now executive head of both St Clement Danes and Croxley Danes.

Academic matters: Consistently impressive results at all levels and Ofsted outstanding. In 2018, 91 per cent achieved 9-4 in both English and maths at GCSE; 44 per cent A*-A/9-7 grades. At A level, 38 per cent A*/A and 69 per cent A*-B, which the school is quick to point out are similar grades to the famously good nearby Bucks grammar schools. Rigorous attention to detail in the tracking of all students means personalisation at student level is strong. This kicks off in year 7 with cognitive ability tests, among others, which give the school a flavour of the type of learner each pupil is – 'essential as we're an all-ability school'. 'The targets are just right- stretching but not stressful,' said one parent. Good results also attributed to the purposeful, 'can do' culture. Indeed, we found classrooms full of happy, attentive learners and dynamic teachers, although a few parents told us they feel middle-of-the-road pupils can fall off the radar a bit. 'You'll breeze through if you're bright and quick, but it can be more tricky if you're average, below average or lazy,' said one, although others disagree. 'I'd never have thought my daughter would go onto A levels and university, but she excelled in her GCSEs and A levels and is now at a great university.'

High calibre teachers and good staff retention, both helped by the fact that this is a National Support School, which leads the Herts & Bucks Teaching School Alliance – a group of over 20 schools, universities and local authority learning trusts who collaborate to promote exceptional standards of education. 'The alliance has a massive role in helping us to keep our talent, because staff get training opportunities well beyond the school itself'; it also enables the school to remain at the forefront of research and development. In the English department, when we visited, there were three ex-heads of English teaching, two of whom are specialist leaders in education. 'You come away from parents' evening buzzing from how passionate the teachers are about what they do,' said one parent. 'I think the kids feel that too and it inspires them to go above and beyond.' School also known for strong cross-fertilisation of teaching.

No specialist subjects at this school. 'We aim for excellence across all subjects.' French from year 7 and German or Spanish from year 8. Italian had just been dropped when we visited, to the disappointment of some pupils. 'I wish they'd add in another language in its place,' said one. Most popular GCSEs tend to be the humanities. Setting for languages, maths, English and science from year 7, although there's plenty of movement. Subject clinics across all subjects, as well as study sessions during the Easter holidays for pupils with upcoming exams. Technology embedded into lessons, although school insists on there being good reasons for it, rather than 'for the sake of it.' Pilot scheme of iPads being used in year 7 when we visited.

Majority of pupils stay on in sixth form, choosing from 26 A levels, the most popular of which are science, maths, English, economics and business studies. Plenty of help in transitioning from GCSE, as well as lots of monitoring and assessment to keep students on track throughout the two years. Comprehensive guidance for university applications including Oxbridge, as well as job applications, and an impressive programme of external speakers. 'This year, these have included people from Warner Brothers, RAF and people talking about how to set up your own business or go into football management,' said one pupil. Extended Project Qualification increasingly popular, with 50-60 pupils doing it per year on average.

Students who are identified as gifted and talented go on the Exceptional Performance programme for the duration of their time at the school, which involves being given a mentor (staff member) to champion their needs. Meanwhile, SEN (seven statemented when we visited) mainly includes dyslexia, autism and ADHD, all of whom receive mostly classroom based help. 'We look at every child on a case-by-case basis and are very honest about how we can help and where we'd struggle'; although they've never turned anyone away, some parents do decide to go elsewhere – for example, although the school has accommodated three wheelchair users in the past, they might struggle with some of the narrow corridors in a school which was originally built for 821 students and now serves 1,400.

Games, options, the arts: Rugby, football, tennis and athletics are the strongest sports, with teams regularly competing at a high level, including against independent schools and Bucks grammar schools. District and county champions in athletics, with particularly talented students getting their picture framed on the school's honours wall (seen as a majorly big deal among pupils). Facilities include an all-weather flood-lit pitch, hard courts, gym and sports hall – all more than adequate. The annual gym and dance display is a highlight of the year. Hockey is weak, according to some parents, and there's no swimming, although the school supports the swim teams that practise outside school. In fact, they had just made the national finals when we visited.

Swish new art facilities. Evidence of some strong artistic talent – mainly fine-arts based, with photography also becoming increasingly popular. DT and food tech facilities impressive. Two areas for drama practice, with whole school performances and junior school productions put on alternative years. Examples include Macbeth, Les Misérables and Joseph.

Music flourishes here, with well-equipped facilities and no shortage of enthusiasm among both students and staff. Ensembles include two orchestras (around 70 in the main one and 60 in the junior one), two choirs and a jazz band, which provide opportunities for beginners through to National Orchestra members. Regular concerts, including the prestigious annual Commemoration Service in St Clement Danes Church in London, are described by parents as 'stirring stuff.' Student-led music groups regularly set up, including flute, folk, guitar and brass groups. 'I'm in the gospel choir, chamber choir and first orchestra and I love them all,' one pupil told us.

S

Extracurricular clubs plentiful and although some parents say they're mainly sports based, the school is clearly open to new ideas, including student-led clubs. 'A mother wrote in asking if we did a pony club – we didn't, so we set one up.' Sixth formers expected to get involved in community service – anything from working in a local charity shop to running a brownie pack.

Over 70 national and international trips per year, including London museums and galleries; annual activities week to Bude for year 7s; music tours to Paris and Barcelona; annual athletics training camp in Lanzarote; football tours to USA; language exchanges to Lyon, Bilbao and Potsdam; art trips to New York and Venice; and World Challenge expeditions to Cambodia, Vietnam, South America and Africa. Because the school receives the support and financial backing of the St Clement Danes Holborn Estate Charity (established in 1552 to support the education of the children of the parish of St Clement Danes Church in England), pupils rarely miss out on relevant activities, even if affordability is an issue.

Background and atmosphere: Founded in 1862 as a boys' grammar school in Houghton Street, London. Relocated to Hammersmith in 1928, before transferring again in 1975 to its present location in Chorleywood, where it became an all-ability, co-educational school. Its reputation has since gone from strength to strength and it's largely responsible for soaring house prices in the area. Became part of an academy trust in 2011.

All the original 1970s buildings remain, mostly in surprisingly good nick, with other buildings – including the maths and languages blocks, Barbirolli Hall and Carey Sixth Form Centre – added more recently. Barbirolli Hall (named after Sir John Barbirolli, an Old Dane who went on to conduct the Halle Orchestra in Manchester for over three decades) given a facelift in recent years, with £20,000 of the funds raised by the pupils themselves. 'They were each given £10 and told to invest it in fundraising,' explains the head. Meanwhile, the Carey Sixth Form Centre has been extended. With the feel of a halfway house between school and university, it has well-equipped classrooms and three types of self-study areas – café; quiet study area; and silent area. A £7m grant, to provide space for the extra 30 pupils it is admitting to year 7 between 2016 and 2020, has also enabled the school to rebuild maths and art areas (including a gallery area for permanent art displays), remodel the original centre of the school (previously cramped) and increase the number of study areas and sports facilities. Recently opened is a new science lab plus a suite of rooms for food technology, a new technology computer suite and a large open space to help pupil movement through the school. 'There's always plans for the future, although beyond the hall is an area of natural outstanding beauty, which can limit our building aspirations.' Next on the list is a brand new learning resources centre.

Each block has shared study areas in addition to the classrooms, with the English block boasting a central, roomy IT room. Some classrooms and walkways could be bigger, but clever timetabling and classroom allocating, along with a strictly enforced one-way walking system, helps prevent any overcrowding. Library disappointingly tired, but pupils assured us it's a lively and popular hub. Some parents feel the food could be more nutritious, and many take in packed lunches. Not a single piece of litter in sight during our visit, with everywhere spotless. 'You have to love your learning environment,' says the head. We found the atmosphere calm and structured, with a reassuring amount of liveliness at break times. Pupils articulate, confident, curious and happy.

Leadership opportunities include a prefect system, peer mentoring, Franklin Scholars and a strong student council, with five subgroups ranging from fundraising to student welfare. 'Sixth formers help the younger years a lot – there's no feeling of them being cut off in any way,' one pupil told us. Eight houses, with plenty of inter-house events throughout the year, culminating in Sports Day.

Celebrating success is literally centre-stage at this school – with prize-giving ceremonies, a sea of silver trophies adorning the long cabinets outside the head's office, along with the honours wall. Also a house point system and plenty of daily praising of students in various forms.

Pastoral care, well-being and discipline: Pastoral care has always been notable here, even in the 1970s, with every student supported by form tutors, pastoral leaders and the senior management team, in addition to a full-time matron who doubles up as a school counsellor and part-time welfare worker who goes out to families when necessary. School also leads pastoral care for the South West Herts group of schools to share good practice. Particularly big on transition, with every pupil visited in their primary school and a huge focus on settling new pupils in.

On the strict side, with clear expectations around behaviour and detentions for things like regularly disrupting class or persistently failing to hand in homework for no good reason. That said, school insists they allow for grey areas. 'Take bad language, for example. A pupil using it when they're not expecting a teacher to hear is very different from someone swearing at a teacher, for instance – although both would be punished.' There has to be room to make mistakes. 'If you can't learn from your mistakes as a teenager, when can you?' No mobile phone policy, except in sixth form.

'Oh yes,' was the answer when we asked if there was bullying. 'Every school has it', but a restorative justice programme called Learning Together, which is led by the deputy head, and clear anti-bullying policies and e-safety evenings for parents, all help prevent it. Most parents we spoke to hadn't encountered any bullying, although one parent we spoke to felt that in her case, it wasn't taken seriously enough.

Suspension rate generally low, with some peaks and troughs. Very low exclusion rate, with school preferring to work with other schools to provide a student with 'a fresh start' if needs be – with no more than one case per year on average. 'We also take in children from other schools on this basis from time to time'.

Pupils and parents: Most families from within a five-mile radius – mainly Chorleywood and Rickmansworth. Most pupils walk, many across Chorleywood common or through residential areas, whilst those from further afield generally get the bus. Some sixth formers drive, but few parents drop their children off, not least because parking can be a nightmare.

'People see this is a very middle-class school, but in fact there's a big range,' says school. When we visited, 24 pupils were on free school meals. Seventy-eight per cent white British students, the rest a wide range of other nationalities and ethnic backgrounds.

Parents talk of feeling 'privileged' their children got into the school and many are very involved in their children's education, with 100 per cent attendance at parents' evening. Active PTA, with a small band of very dedicated parents (mostly mums) fundraising and organising social events, such as comedy evenings and wine and nibbles evenings.

Entrance: Heavily oversubscribed, with nearly 1,000 applicants for 240 places. Non-selective, except for 20 per cent of places, which are reserved for students with an aptitude for music (10 per cent) and academic ability (10 per cent). The furthest these students tend to come from is Watford or Pinner, although the places are highly sought-after. For the remaining 80 per cent of places, children in the looked after system/those with an EHC plan which names the school are prioritised (following the admissions code), followed by siblings (usually amounting to half the cohort every year) and children of staff (around 2-3 pupils every year), then it's down to distance, with priority given to a WD3 postcode.

Not many pupils leave, so very few spots open up in other year groups. Around 80-85 per cent of pupils stay on for sixth form, although they need to get 6 or above in the GSCE subjects they choose at A level, which some parents complain is too strict and excludes pupils who'd really like to stay on. An additional 35 places are opened up for external applicants, usually attracting around 160 applicants who are assessed on their GCSE average points score.

Exit: Around a third leave after GCSE, most for BTech courses, performing arts or vocational qualifications. Of those who stay for the sixth form nearly all go on to university with popular recent choices including Nottingham, Exeter, Southampton and a good number of other Russell Group universities (usually about 30 per cent). Four to Oxbridge in 2018 (one offered a place chose a US university). Popular subjects include English, history, maths, physics and psychology. Around 10 per cent go into high level apprenticeships or directly into employment.

Remarks: This is a school that aims to be good at everything, refusing to pigeonhole itself into excelling in certain areas over others, making it a great place to study for pupils, no matter where their strengths lie. Embracing new innovations in teaching, it is also a school that feels progressive, whilst still retaining traditional values. Above all, it stands out for being a place where most children are happy and, in the main, reach their full potential. No wonder it's a school that parents move to the area for.

St Edmund's College

Old Hall Green, Ware, Hertfordshire SG11 1DS

Ages 3–19 **Pupils** 838 **Sixth form** 146 **Boarders** 89 full, 16 weekly, 17 flexi (from 11 years) **RC**

Fees: Day £11,025 – £17,805; Boarding £23,460 – £30,915 pa

01920 824247
www.stedmundscollege.org

Headmaster: Since 2012, Paulo Durán BA MA (London). Educated at the London Oratory, King's College London and Heythrop College. Married to Alice, a teacher, with one daughter at St Edmund's. After spells at South Hampstead and Alleyn's, he took up a post as head of modern languages at Mill Hill School where he stayed for six years, before moving to St Edmund's as deputy head in 2009. After three years he was offered the headship, and, he says, would like to stop here. Parents hope so too. 'A very warm, very charismatic man and a very strong leader,' said one mother. 'Please don't leave!' But he is leaving, in July 2019.

Prep school head: Since 2013, Mr Steven Cartwright BSc. Joined the school in 2009 as deputy head and became acting head before taking up the post of headmaster. Married with two daughters, one at St Edmund's. Interests include squash, climbing, running, 'my family, my school!' Popular with parents, who describe him as 'lovely'. 'He's such a nice man, very approachable,' said one. 'He's really good with the children,' said another. An enthusiast who wants the best for his students. 'I am passionate about this school. I do sincerely believe that we strive for the best, and we've got a very nice community.'

Academic matters: Broad curriculum in the prep, including French, with a learning support manager to provide help for those who need it; we liked the learning support room, which was welcoming and cheerful. At the other end of the scale, a child who was particularly gifted in French attended lessons over in the senior college, and all the children go there for science. 'The teachers always encourage the children not just to learn, but to understand and ask questions,' said one satisfied parent.

Generally a sound performance with top grades consistently accounting for around a third of results. In 2018, 46 per cent A*-A/9-7 at I/GCSE and 41 per cent A*-A at A level. 'Results are very good, and I want them to improve,' says head, but aims to achieve same 'without changing the children or the school. It's about moving up those league tables the hard way.'

Broad curriculum comprises all the usual arts, humanities and sciences, with maths being a particular favourite. 'I like maths, purely for the fact that the teachers are so willing to help you,' said one boy, and his friends agreed. French, Spanish, German, Latin and Italian are on offer. All students learn French in year 7 and study an additional language throughout year 8 and 9. As you'd expect in a school of this ethos, religious education has a high profile, and RE is compulsory up to and including GCSE. The pupils aren't bothered by this, because 'the RE teachers are really good!' Bang-up-to-date ICT suites, and well-resourced classrooms and science labs. Food tech a popular option, and the children were proud of their achievements in the school bake-off. Lots of good quality work on the wall displays, and we were pleased with the standard of writing and spelling. The handsome library is surprisingly small for a school this size, but was lively and welcoming and regularly hosts visits from the likes of Kevin Crossley-Holland and Dave Cousins.

Our young tour guides were upbeat about lessons and about the amount of individual attention they got from teachers; the average class size is 21 (14 in sixth form). Parents described the teaching staff as 'really fantastic' and 'always there for the pupils', and praised the unwearying help given, in any subject, to students who needed it. 'If you're in the top set, you're pushed just as hard as you would be in a top academic school,' commented one sixth former. But a broad range of abilities is catered for here. Pupils with SEN requirements are well-supported, both in class and at homework club, which happens four afternoons a week. EAL available and IGCSE second language English is offered to overseas students where appropriate.

The intake is only gently selective, which may account for the odd unexpected hiccup in student knowledge here and there. Talking to us about the school's history, a year 9 pupil told me, 'France wasn't Catholic back then, which is why the school moved here.' But the school's history is quite long and involved, and we were impressed by the pride with which the children talked about it. Everyone was adamant that the school fostered a strong work ethic and helped all students to achieve their best.

Games, options, the arts: One happy parent, a musician herself, described the music as 'fantastic', and we certainly liked what we heard. Schola Cantorum regularly gigs at the likes of Canterbury and Westminster Cathedrals; chapel choir sings on Sundays during term time, and the chamber choir is much in demand for more secular school functions, such as weddings and dances. New music recording studio and vocal booth. Lots of ensembles including an orchestra and jazz band, ably supported by a 21-strong team of peripatetic music teachers. School is particularly keen to build on choral scholarships 'and to see where that takes us.' There's a musical production every year; Our House by Madness is a recent example, and Half A Sixpence at the nearby Broxbourne Civic Hall. 'They're a lot of work and a big commitment but they're absolutely wonderful!' enthused one student. Drama is also popular, with lots taking LAMDA exams, and student-directed productions such as – amazingly – One Man, Two Guvnors.

Last period of every school day is given over to extracurricular activities, so all pupils participate in something. An extremely wide range of arts, crafts and other interests are offered, including CCF, D of E and Model United Nations. There are also some pretty special opportunities for travel. 'The trip to Thailand was one of the most amazing things I've ever done,' said one girl, and other pupils were starry-eyed about their experiences in India, America and Barcelona.

Wonderfully spacious campus means lots of playing fields plus tennis courts and Astro. Girls' sport is strong and includes hockey, netball and football. The boys' provision for traditional team games appears to be something of an issue. 'I'd like to see more organised compulsory training for the top teams,' said one boy, diplomatically. Parents (eager in their praise of all other areas of the school) were more forthright, criticising what they claimed was a 'lazy' lack of coaching for school teams who then had to 'go out and get slaughtered every week against better-trained sides.' Students confirmed that rugby/football practices were sometimes scheduled after the school buses had left, so that pupils, who travel in from an unusually wide geographical area, had no choice but to miss the sessions if they wanted to get home. The school counters by saying that the after-school clubs, targeted at mass participation, were scheduled at the request of parents, who had seemed happy to collect their children themselves. A sports academy focuses on the development of elite players in years 7 and 8. The less traditional sports – table tennis, golf, badminton, aerobics – are all flourishing, and there can't be many schools which can offer their students fishing (in the school pond) as an option.

Plenty of extracurricular activities at the prep too, with music and drama flourishing, and lots of sports (football is particularly successful). 'This is a very sporty school!' said one little boy, enthusiastically. Children can use the senior school's sports facilities.

Boarding: Boarders (full, weekly and flexi) are very well looked-after, with lots of staff living on site, and the school counsellor is always on hand. 'Bullying here is mercifully rare, and we set the bar low,' said head, firmly. One boys' and one girls' boarding house (twin or single rooms), with a communal common room where they can socialise together after prep. The usual weekend theatre, cinema and shopping trips for boarders, who include pupils from 20 different countries; activities include themed cultural evenings.

Background and atmosphere: Founded in France in 1568 as a seminary for English Catholics when the Reformation's prohibition of Catholic education forced Cardinal William Allen to decamp to Douai in Flanders. A couple of hundred years later in 1793, the French Revolution had professors and scholars packing their bags once again and moving to the village of Old Hall Green just north of Ware, where a small (and very secret) Catholic school had formerly acted as a 'feeder' for the Douai seminary. On 16 November 1793 – the feast of St Edmund – the school was created. It weathered various changes of fortune during the 19th century, but celebrated its quarter centenary in 1968, admitted girls to the sixth form in 1974 and has been fully co-educational since 1986. The school lists 20 canonised saints and 133 martyrs amongst its alumni, and is proud of its history, which it commemorates throughout the building in drawings, paintings and artefacts. Now occupying the whole of the village of Old Hall Green, the site is spacious (440 acres), wooded, and stunningly beautiful.

If Catholic iconography makes you uneasy, this ain't the place for you. Pictures of popes, archbishops, cardinals and saints are everywhere, along with statues, shrines, relics, holy paintings, and even a graveyard, containing, said an earnest pupil, 'people who died for the school'. It was something to see students lining up, in their own free time at their own volition, to use the Scofield Chantry for a few moments of candle-lit private prayer. The prevailing mood throughout the school, even at its liveliest times, was one of calm benevolence and order. 'We pride ourselves on the way we talk to our students and the way they talk to each other,' said the head, and all the young people we spoke to were in agreement. 'Everybody is nice, everybody respects each other,' 'I love it here, all my friends are nice,' 'The atmosphere is lovely,' were typical comments. Prayers are said before every lesson, 'And some of the prayers are really nice!' cried a pupil, who then recited one for me with great affection, adding 'You don't have to join in, but everyone respects it.' The school's Pugin chapel is lofty and awe-inspiring, and is used for weddings, funerals and baptisms as well as for school services. It's flanked by the smaller shrine chapel, built to hold St Edmund's left fibula that was presented by Cardinal Wiseman in 1863.

The college is overseen not by a specific order but by the Archdiocese of Westminster, and the Roman Catholic ethos is completely central to the life of the school. Even the year groups are named after Catholic principles: Elements, Rudiments, Grammar, Syntax, Poetry, Rhetoric I and Rhetoric II. 'We're proudly and unashamedly Catholic,' as the head put it, but added, 'We're also proud of being inclusive.'

Located on the same beautiful campus as its big brother, the junior school benefits from an enviable degree of space and wooded tranquility. Whereas the main senior school building is grand and imposing, the prep is a smaller, cosier affair, housed in a former family home designed by Pugin and containing many of his hallmark features. The prep children have their own very appealing little chapel, which is in daily use, plus an outdoor amphitheatre.

Pastoral care, well-being and discipline: Everyone we spoke to was especially warm in their praise of this aspect of the school. 'The school is very nurturing,' 'A very, very welcoming place, my child settled in straight away,' were some of the comments, and the last ISI inspection report praised the pupils' spiritual and personal development as outstanding. The house system is the main source of pastoral care with each pupil having a tutor and head of house.

The prep school children we met were relaxed, happy, well-mannered and fond of their school. 'They're really kind here, and I've made a lot of friends,' 'I prefer this school to my old one, there's so much to do,' were typical comments. As one parent added, 'There's a very nice atmosphere within the school. We're really pleased, no complaints at all.'

A number of pupils and parents commented on the lunch queues, which, they alleged, were not always well-managed. Some children spoke of having to miss lunch if they needed to attend clubs, or even if the queue just was too long. 'She loves the meals, but doesn't always get to eat them!' said one mother, 'I can't understand why they haven't nailed that problem.' School admits that the situation needs addressing, and says it is working on ways to improve things. On the plus side, boarding means that all pupils can stay for supper at the school when they need to – when there are concerts or parents' evenings, for instance. Spacious, well-kept environment seems to create a relaxed and happy community of individuals, quirky and otherwise, with a refreshing range of aspirations: one student hopes to set up a museum dedicated to vacuum cleaner parts.

Pupils and parents: Day pupils make up the majority of students, and are bused in from all over Hertfordshire and beyond via a network of 17 different routes. Excellent scholarships and bursaries ensure wide social diversity. Significant community of international students – many from eastern Europe, Africa and Asia. About 40 per cent of pupils are from Catholic families. The rest are from other Christian denominations, and from 'all other faiths and from none'. Notable alumni include William Scholl the sandal designer, perfumiers James and Robert Floris, and Ralph Richardson.

Entrance: Entrance to nursery from the term following children's third birthday. Further admissions at 4 and at 7 by interview ('crucial,' says head) and informal assessment. Around a third of the children are from Catholic families, the rest from all faiths and from none. The school's popularity is rising, and they recently went to two form entry from year 3 in response to demand.

About 20 a year of the senior school entry come from the prep, for whom entry is automatic, provided they joined in year 4 or below. External candidates sit entrance exams in maths, English and non-verbal reasoning. However, the report from the child's previous school is just as important, along with the St Edmund's interview. 'We interview everyone for at least 30 minutes, and for as long as it takes, really,' says head. The school's popularity continues to rise and they are now oversubscribed, with around 220 applicants for the 80 available places. Small additional intake at 13+. Some join the school at 16+, for which they need five A*-B/9-6 grades at GCSE with at least B/6 in their chosen A level subjects.

Exit: Nearly all prep school pupils move up to the senior school. At 16+, around 40 per cent to state sixth form colleges, or, very occasionally, to other independents. The rest stay on for sixth form here. At 18+ mostly to university: Manchester current front runner, with Hertfordshire Uni another favourite, alongside several London universities. Two to Oxbridge and one medic in 2018.

Money matters: Academic scholarships at 11+ and 13+, awarded on performance in the entrance exam. Music, art, sport and all-rounder scholarships also available, often in combination with academic awards. Total awards can be extremely generous – we heard from one parent whose child's scholarship was worth 90 per cent of the annual fees. A few sixth form scholarships. Limited number of means-tested bursaries, covering up to full fees.

Remarks: A successful, flourishing, dependable school with real spiritual heart. Well worth considering.

St Edmund's School

St Thomas Hill, Canterbury, Kent CT2 8HU

Ages 3–18 **Pupils** 576 **Sixth form** 126 **Boarders** 140 (including 24 choristers, from 8 years) **C of E**

Fees: Day £7,647 – £20,466; Boarding £24,267 – £34,968; Choristers £23,427 pa

01227 475601
www.stedmunds.org.uk

Head of school: Since September 2018, Ed O'Connor, who has been deputy head here since 2013. He has a degree in history and an MEd from Cambridge and a MPhil in international relations from Oxford. He started off working in the City before joining St Albans School as head of history and politics, thence to Sutton Valence (director of sixth form and head of history) and then head of sixth form and politics and history teacher at The Perse School.

Academic matters: The strong Perse connection is bound to have an impact, and the school makes no bones about increased expectations. 'Perse is in the top 10 academically, St Edmund's will never be that, but we are looking to raise the bar so that people feel tested.' Rebranding means the school is no longer marketing itself as a music and drama school, and no longer describing itself as non-selective.

S

But while all the families we spoke to were aware of the change, none felt that a more academic bent was at the expense of less able pupils, or non-academic activities. 'I think this is an additional benefit to the school. The music and drama department is just as excellent as it was,' said one parent. 'It's a great turn around, without losing the school's comprehensive ethos,' said another. 'There is no feeling that you can settle for what you get – if you are predicted a C you have to try to get a B or higher.' Sixth formers told us that they would be heartily congratulated for a C grade if that was the best of their ability. 'Everyone has their own target grade which they are pushed to exceed,' said one.

We heard particularly strong praise from parents of dyslexic children. 'They are very good at identifying but not labelling,' said one. Another described a child who was struggling with the GCSE curriculum, but through what was described as 'learning tailor-made to him' went on to win a place at Cambridge. School expects higher academic standards to result in more pupils with special needs, as it will encompass more students with Asperger's, many of whom are in the highest academic band nationally.

Should your child fall behind, it won't be seen as your problem. In this instance, school says they find out what is behind it and put in a lot of pastoral and academic support. 'We don't say to parents you are going to have to supervise this, we make it our business to turn things around.'

When some pupils were struggling in French, the response was 'Let's throw Arabic at it'. These pupils took a Cambridge Certificate in Arabic and Middle East studies instead. 'Four kids got distinctions. It's a Perse way to take something which looks higher end and give it to kids who are struggling, it builds confidence.'

As well as Arabic other new subjects introduced are economics, politics and Greek. At A level there are 26 subjects to choose from, the EPQ and an option to do the AQA Baccalaureate. The most popular A levels are biology, history and photography. Maths and theatre studies are also strong departments. In 2018, 22 per cent of A level entries achieved A*/A grades, 44 per cent A*-B; at GCSE, 44 per cent of entries were A*-A/9-7.

There's no hiding place for teachers. Teachers are left to their own styles, as long as it works. Music teaching is said to be 'inspirational' and the head of junior school music was running a lively class investigating scores from Bond films when we visited. A sixth form economics class was studying the cement market, and the teacher was relaxed about some having earphones plugged in as they worked, as he said they were all turning in A*/B grade work.

'There are some fabulous teachers, and there have been some teachers whose tenure has been short because they just weren't up to the job. That's what we call progress. They use different techniques for different children – above all it's not a one size fits all school,' said a parent.

S

The junior school has its own bright and cosy classrooms, and the curriculum includes swimming, music, dance and French from the earliest years. In years 3 to 5 subjects are extended to include geography, history, IT and Latin. There is some streaming – we saw year 5 maths groups tackling number problems on paper in one set, while another was learning weights and ratios through making biscuits. The artwork on display in a variety of media is notably good.

In the upper half of the junior school – years 6, 7 and 8 – lessons are taught in a separate block in the upper school, where they can use the senior's science, art and design technology rooms, and all lessons are taught by subject specialists.

Games, options, the arts: Go in with your eyes open. It's a small school so you can't expect to have top flight teams. Some parents mourn the lack of rugby – the school plays football and hockey instead, which works better in a mixed year group of just 65. 'There's lots of sport there if you want to do it, but you have to be realistic, they are not going to beat the massive teams,' said one parent. For the top level players it can be frustrating, but a parent of one of these is pragmatic about it, saying, 'Even in big schools they are only going to get one or two county level players. And they are doing a lot to improve, such as getting in professional coaches.'

Music is strong, as you might expect in the school which educates the choristers of Canterbury Cathedral. There's a purpose-built music school with a recording studio. It's big on theatre too, with theatre studies well subscribed, and a full size, refurbished theatre with five wings and a green room to perform in.

Some parents would like to see more trips, though one reeled off an impressive list her children had taken part in – skiing in Italy, drama trip to New York, music/language trip and watersports to Spain, Rua Fiola survival adventure, Christmas trip to Lille, language trip to Switzerland, and history trips to Portsmouth.

Saturday morning school is now optional. It's not charged for, pupils don't have to wear uniform, and the activities are the likes of international cuisine, technology, art, film making, sport, and music. One-third of day pupils come in for it.

Boarding: Over half of the boarders are from overseas. There are flexi, weekly, and full boarding options. Junior boarders (11-14) live in School House, a newly refurbished wing of the main school building. Senior boarders live in the main school building or in the nearby Clare, Sunfield and Gorsefield Houses. Boys' dormitories have views over the fields to the cathedral, through arched mullioned windows. Girls overlook the changing rooms. Boys have ensuites, girls don't. The boarding rooms are fairly cramped, but there's a big common room/kitchen and sixth formers have separate studies shared between three or four people. After optional morning school on a Saturday, afternoons are free, and Sundays see outings to London museums, Bluewater, ice skating and so on. The 23 choristers (boys only, from 8 years) live separately in Choir House within the cathedral precincts, with a timetable which includes 20 hours singing, attending evensong six days a week, and recordings.

Background and atmosphere: The school is centred around a High Victorian building with its own chapel. The exterior is grand, and there are commanding views across the fields to Canterbury Cathedral. But the senior school interior has stained carpets, holes gouged out of plaster, some cramped classrooms shoved into unlikely parts of the old building, and is frankly scruffy. If you're doing the circuit its shabbiness will be evident among the more glitzy schools; but current parents don't notice it and see it as all part of the warm, family atmosphere. Staffing and small class sizes a recent priority, school says increased pupil numbers in the last few years are funding fund refurbishment, including a new academic hub building and overhauled library.

It's a school with a smile on its face, a great sense of ease and happiness pervades. 'It's as friendly and warm as a prep school. Every single teacher knows me and you just feel welcome,' said one parent.

Will you fit in? One parent described it thus: 'It's not a competitive school. If you want to be told that your child is number one at everything, don't come here. If you get your kicks from being told you're better than everyone else, it's not for you. If you are a show off, don't come here. There's no pride in being better than someone else here – it's about being better than your own expectations and about being part of the school.'

Pastoral care, well-being and discipline: Praise for the pastoral care from parents was overwhelming. One child missed several months of school owing to health problems in his GCSE year, and he was given one-to-one teaching on his return to enable him to catch up. We also heard about a teenager who had derailed; the response, as the parent described, 'Spending days after talking, planning, resetting goals and wiping the slate clean for a new start. At all times protecting his dignity and his self-esteem. Within days all teaching staff adopted a completely different set of rules for him, and never mentioned earlier failings.'

Another family had to deal with bereavement, and the parent said: 'I can categorically say that had it not been for the pastoral care and time and attention the head and his housemaster provided to him, and what he gets out of the school community, his world would be a far worse place than it is today. I am eternally indebted to St Edmund's School.'

Pupils and parents: People tend to stick with the school. At transition recently, 52 out of 54 came up from the junior to senior school, and around 10 new pupils join at this point.

International students represent 28 nationalities – there are larger groups from China and Germany, but kept no bigger than 15 students, and also students from Thailand, The Congo, Kazakhstan, Russia, Nigeria, Poland, Belgium and France.

It's not a school where you need designer clobber for the school run. One parent described the parent body as 'trying to do the best for their children. Very mixed finances, not all necessarily finding the school fees that easy, and not doing it for the social cachet of being an old boy. Very few pushy parents, certainly not seeking advance for their own child at the expense of another.'

Another described the school gate as 'friendly, warm, no parents whinging in your ear "my child wasn't the shining star ..."'

Entrance: Usual entry points (3+, 7+, 11+, 13+ and 16+) plus choristers at 8+ via voice trials, and other year groups when places available. Junior school entry is based on assessments on a taster day to gauge academic levels; nearly all juniors move up to the senior school with no entrance test. At 11+ entry for outsiders (a few join at this stage) there are formal entrance tests (verbal and non-verbal reasoning) and consideration is given to Kent Test results. Year 9 entry involves tests in maths and English, and a guideline requirement would be common entrance marks of around 60 per cent or above (although you don't have to pass common entrance). Sixth formers need 9-6 at GCSE in the subjects they wish to study.

Exit: Nearly all juniors join the senior school. All sixth formers go to higher education including conservatoires and drama schools, and popular university destinations are Manchester, Reading, Exeter, UEA, Sussex, Durham, Bristol and Canterbury. One medic and one vet in 2018.

Money matters: Scholarships of varying value for both day and boarding pupils are awarded in academic, music, sport, art and drama categories. These can be topped up by means-tested bursaries for those currently at the school. Discounts offered to children of clergy, members of the armed forces, and third and subsequent children, and choristers.

Remarks: Which of the effusive quotes to use? We've seldom seen such overwhelming praise for a school, and for pastoral care, from parents. Nor such a sense of a cohesive parent body without factions. Not for you if you want a school high on social cachet and entry to society by school tie, or smart teas after thrilling wins against top flight teams. But if you want a school which is going to take great care of your child, and get the best out of him/her, whether s/he's a Cambridge or C grade student, definitely one for the shortlist.

St Edward's Oxford

Woodstock Road, Oxford, Oxfordshire OX2 7NN

Ages 13–18 **Pupils** 692 **Sixth form** 277 **Boarders** 578 **C of E**

Fees: Day £30,285; Boarding £37,845 pa

01865 319200
www.stedwardsoxford.org

Warden: Since 2011, Stephen Jones MSc MLitt (50s), previously head of Dover College. Educated at both Hurstpierpoint and Lord Wandsworth Colleges. Erudite, a man of many degrees, went to Durham to read maths and physics but graduated with a rare first in philosophy, then read maths before embarking on research in philosophy of maths. Was an assistant housemaster at Cheltenham College, head of maths at Berkhamsted School and a social tutor at Radley before his appointment at Dover. Married to the delightful Katie, who has her own successful career in the church – no mean feat alongside being a headmaster's wife. They have three children, two of whom have flown the nest.

We're told he is a good sportsman, keen on staying in shape, enjoys fives and sailing and has a keen sense of humour; 'His student house was dubbed Front, so he could talk about going back to Front'. An accomplished mathematician, he loves poring over the figures and has a brain that specialises in pure logic, in whatever discipline. Parents say, 'Youngsters respect him, he is easy to talk to.' When we meet he is chatty, relaxed, enthusiastic – 'I don't have all the answers, what head does?' – but stresses that 'I want to engender a culture of academic excitement, sharpen things, raise expectations tempered with understanding of what the world is really like'. He is realistic, too, and under no illusion that keeping St Edward's on top of its game and rubbing shoulders with competitors will demand toughness and vision.

Academic matters: Most take nine or 10 subjects at IGCSE/GCSE, all the usual plus Latin or classical civilisation and Greek alongside PE, DT and drama. In 2018, 58 per cent of GCSEs were graded A*-A/7-9, a touch down on last year. Philosophy/ethics/political literacy courses for lower school pupils and all sixth formers study for an EPQ or equivalent: 'Great preparation for independent study at university and beyond,' says warden. In 2018, 76 per cent of A level grades were A*/B (40 per cent A*/A) and the IB average was a creditable 34. Scholars' societies – OX2 for lower school and The Woodstock Group for seniors – stretch the able. Parents say science teaching is variable: 'Joint offering of IB and A level has resulted in good teachers being stretched too thinly' – school says IB/A level combination 'is now a fundamental part of school life and timetabling, and has impressed the IB Schools and Colleges Association. I don't think parents would see it this way now.' At A level, biology and art & design popular and successful.

Good for self-esteem: 'Those who can, will, those who can't will be encouraged to be independent, guarding against learned helplessness. We are an inclusive school so classroom teaching is at the forefront of supporting all pupils. All pupils have learning challenges at some point; learning development staff can monitor, assess and advise on the best way forward.'

Has a reputation for being gentler on the old grey matter – both entry and exit – than many of its near competitors yet, in these league table propelled days, parents may seek a school that is 'forgiving' on entry but don't want an apology on exit – nor do they get one. Teddies (as it is affectionately known) has been shimmying up the league tables: not via hot-housing – 'There are enough schools in the locality doing that,' says school – nor by upping the entry ante (though scholarships have been expanded and a new girls' house, Jubilee, helpfully nudges boy-girl ratio close to 3-2); rather the main thrust has been to eke more out of everyone, think good breezy airing, rather than squeezed through the wringer. Pupils write A* and keep in their pockets; IGCSEs introduced; IB now taken by around half the sixth form. A levels remain, though no Pre-U, the tougher alternative to A levels; 'Not really the thing for our cohort', said warden.

However the biggest buzz (and buzz-word) is meta cognition ('know about knowing,' said our young informant). Warden wanted children to develop intellect, to reason, question and enquire. 'Some children arrive browbeaten through CE; we have to rebuild their confidence, inspire and invigorate them'. Working on the youngsters meant developing staff. 'I appointed a new academic director who encourages staff to share good practice, go off-piste, explore and enjoy their subject,' says warden. A move that appears to be working: 'Teachers love the curve ball question but some had lost their nerve, teaching only to pass an exam rather than exploring their subject,' says academic director. 'That is changing'. Dead Poets Society this isn't, there is still a generous nod to the syllabus and ticking boxes – plenty of routine revision, past papers, chalk and talk during our spring visit, but our guides said they're treated to discussion-based, interactive, active lessons. Parents approve: 'It's a happy, friendly common room with a great vibe that rubs off on kids'. Academic push still a work in progress but generally all things learned are looking up and bucking up.

Games, options, the arts: Fabulous facilities – 100 acres of prime north Oxford; outdoor courts, cricket pitches, a new cricket pavilion (Hampshire County Cricket Club runs a satellite academy at the school for pupils and local juniors), a nine hole golf course, boathouse. Indoors there is a superbly equipped, sparkly leisure centre – the hub of middle class Oxford mummies working off their lunches – shared with, and leased from, the school, providing a fantastic gym, indoor and outdoor pools, indoor tennis courts and fitness and dance studios. Pupils win accolades – cricket team undefeated, have their fastest first eight ever, runners up at National Schools' and Henley; several GB junior oarsmen and county cricketers; girls' hockey teams particularly successful. Rugby less robust: 'We take a few hits,' confess boys, though tide is turning. First ever female director of sport is working hard to tempt talent of tomorrow to Teddies – with an array of special events. Not that those who wince at the thought of catching a ball should worry: 'They will find a sport you can not only do but do so proficiently; it's all about building confidence. Staff get involved too – it's lovely to see their commitment – it rubs off on the youngsters.' Only moan is expense of sports kit: 'Always something else on the bill; they must be in-league with the supplier,' joked one parent.

S

Art good with results to match, especially at A level with facilities for jewellery making, ceramics, sculpture and large fine art displays. The North Wall Arts Centre (enjoyed by the local community – hosts visiting artists and theatre groups) boasts exhibition galleries, drama studios and a cosy 250 seat theatre. Parents say dance has come on in 'leaps and bounds' and music is on the up (new music school features, inter alia, recital and rock rooms plus a recording studio), with something for everyone regardless of where you sit in the talent pool. 'Kids try hard, there's a huge number of bands, plus excellent choirs including one for parents and the community.' Excellent extracurricular provision including ever popular Duke of Edinburgh and CCF.

Boarding: Boarding houses have own identity – quad or field side: choose quad for a disorganised child, field for those who relish open space. New girls' house, Jubilee, is, according to warden, 'more like an upmarket hotel than a traditional school house'. For most of the rest, including odd Cinderella house ('about to improve,' say school) it is standard, homely rooms – shared save for the older years, with an assortment of communal facilities. A further boys' boarding house planned with co-ed sixth form.

Cohesive boarding houses provide welcome support and foster inter-year friendships. Good food, all dine centrally, pupils say it's fun to mix with friends from other houses, parents rue table manners: 'They're noticeably very much "bolt-food" variety.' Safari suppers, ice-skating and discos are a sample of the many weekend jollies.

Boarders may go home on Saturday evenings after sport or other commitments, or stay for Saturday night activities and to explore the local attractions. 'Lots of boarders go home on Sunday after chapel, leaving school feeling somewhat empty and unloved for those forced to stay in,' said one parent, but another added, 'I like that they can come home on Sundays; we relish the family time.'

Background and atmosphere: Situated in leafy north Oxford, the setting is privileged indeed. Much akin to an Oxford college, the main buildings surround a lawned quad. Recent additions include an eco-inspired life sciences building – solar powered with 'more technology than you could wish for'. School isn't the grandest we've seen: it may lack the edge of some of its established upper-crusty rivals, but while we might think it has enough of everything, work has started on a major development to include a new library and 1000 seat assembly hall. Simple peaceful chapel, compulsory on Sundays for boarders, C of E but all faiths welcome. Day pupils may go home at 6.30pm, but the majority stay until 9pm to do prep and extracurricular activities with their friends; all can have a bed in the boarding houses and sleep over if they're too spent to go home.

Pastoral care, well-being and discipline: Parents say pastoral care is excellent, only caveat, 'We'd love our child to have the same tutor throughout, someone who can help and support when pressure builds or child overloaded, overwhelmed or overwrought'; school counters, 'structured tutor system for continuity of tutoring in lower school and in sixth form is ideal for a boarding school'. Still has its fair share of rich kids, some with arguably too much pocket money at their disposal.

Tough on drugs; warden says, 'If we suspect, we test; if positive, save the most exceptional circumstances and I can't think of any of those, they're out.' Punishments for smoking, parents say booze handled brilliantly for the child. 'Quite a number drink and smoke in younger years (same everywhere?), they push boundaries but school pushes back.' Local pubs policed, those aged 18 get a pub pass but other savvy sixth formers sneak off to Summertown for their Saturday night tipple. 'If they get caught they get bust but it doesn't stop them,' said our mole, adding, 'You must be able to say a lucid goodnight to your HM, otherwise it's a night in the san and the ignominy of being woken every 30 minutes.' School adds, 'All have cheese and biscuits and spend an hour with HM when they return; it's great fun for HM and means we get to keep a friendly eye.' Despite tolerance, some parents feel school needs to be more trusting, offer more privileges to older ones, with a long rein tugged hard for those who rail against.

Pupils and parents: Parents a mix of academics, professionals and business. Fifteen per cent of boarders from overseas, from a huge variety of countries. Most of rest from Oxford, home counties or greater London. Has a local reputation of privilege and at times pushing the boundaries – Teddies' girls in particular – yet the pupils we met were grounded, down to earth and friendly, a view shared by others we spoke to. 'They're clubbable, they've had to live with people in close confinement, they learn how to get the most out of others,' says warden, with a student adding, 'My parents gave me The Good Schools Guide and I chose Teddies; it has lived up to all in the review but especially on the friendship and friendliness front.' Notable former pupils include Kenneth Grahame, Laurence Olivier, Douglas Bader, Guy Gibson, Jon Snow, Emilia Clarke and Sam Waley-Cohen.

Entrance: From a range of prep schools, majority of day from Dragon. Skype interviews possible for those based overseas. Gently academic 55 per cent at CE, non CE candidates take the school's own exam. A handful sit an exam at 11+ to guarantee a place. Runs an academic challenge day for local year 6 pupils, with diet of philosophy, Arabic, economics, architecture and politics, to spot scholarship potential and encourage applications.

Exit: Handful (some 10 per cent) leave post-16 to pursue courses not offered here or to save on fees. Three to Oxbridge in 2018, rest to eg London, Exeter, Bristol, Leeds and Edinburgh. Six to the US and 2 to European universities. Two medics in 2018; other popular subjects include geography, biomedical sciences, engineering, maths, modern languages and history. Inspiringly, St Edward's doesn't view the path to university as job well done: 'We look to the bigger picture, the young employable 25-year-old making strides in business, commerce, enterprise and academia. Understanding the cut and thrust of the world beyond university is paramount.'

Money matters: New scholarships introduced – academic, music, sport and all-rounder can be means-tested to a maximum of 100 per cent. From 2019, a STEM scholarship for girls at 13+. Sizeable number on bursaries: 'Often the most able,' says warden. 'Attracting bright pupils is good for the school, good for the teachers and good for results.' All are considered annually for an honorary scholarship. Minor scholarships available for drama, art and dance.

Remarks: For those uncomfortable with ultra prestige, the trappings of the old and bold, or the sheen of highly-polished academia, St Edward's offers an established, acceptable, dependable alternative. Those who seek out Teddies will either be judging it against day school rivals or other co-ed boarding schools; it doesn't sit at the top of either pile but it holds its own, taps on elbows and keeps them on their toes. All-round broad education with plenty of nurturing, perceptibly raising expectations and results while maintaining its discernible cheer and friendliness. A busy school with a rosy outlook, ideal for a broad range of academic abilities, the late bloomer, the all-rounder and the high-flyer who doesn't wish to be a mere pebble, fighting for survival, in the tidal wave of Oxford's academic powerhouses.

St George's College, Weybridge

Linked with St George's Junior School

Weybridge Road, Addlestone, Surrey KT15 2QS

Ages 11–18 **Pupils** 920 **Sixth form** 250 **RC**

Fees: £16,845 – £19,185 pa

01932 839300
www.stgeorgesweybridge.com

Head: Since 2016, Rachel Owens MA PGCE NPQH (40s), previously headmistress of St George's School Ascot. Has also been vice principal at New Hall School and, before that, head of history at Prior Park College, Bath, following spell in career-nourishing environment of North London Collegiate School. First female head of St George's.

State educated (former grammar turned comp), Oxford history graduate who started reading for the bar, realised wasn't for her and instantly got teaching job near home town of Bolton, in part to alleviate guilt towards perennially-supportive parents. Has not looked back since. Poised, super bright, smiley, energetic and highly pragmatic, she radiates quintessential head qualities. Trustee of an HMC scheme that brings talented Eastern European sixth formers to British schools.

'I inherited a very traditional school,' she says ('more like stale,' said one parent), but has worked hard on modernising it and has swung her door wide open to parents, which has gone down a treat – and her chocolate sessions with a handful of youngsters at a time means 'I eat my way through students,' she laughs. Also coaches netball. 'Oh my god, she's been such a breath of fresh air,' was a typical parent comment, while students describe her as 'driven,' 'grounded' and 'open to suggestions, no matter how minor.'

Lives onsite with husband Tom, who teaches at RGS, and their two children, who both attend St George's.

Academic matters: Good results – 75 per cent A*-A/9-7 grades at GCSE in 2018 (their best yet). Similar story for A levels with 53 per cent graded A*-A in 2018, something that puts them among area's stronger performers (and local competition, state and private, is fierce).

So how's it done? Selective entry aside, there's a noticeably enthusiastic and dedicated team of teaching staff – we saw one in action making the marking of countries on a map appear electrifying. Much hand-clapping for head's decision to recruit 10 more of them ('they were too highly geared when I arrived – they needed more time to plan lessons, mark and talk to the children'), as well as her decision to, as one parent puts it, 'get rid of the deadwood.' 'There is still something of a lottery when it comes to really excellent teaching, but there's no doubt the head is on top of it,' agree parents.

Head also attributes the Josephite ethos, 'which staff buy into, Catholic or not, about always going above and beyond and enabling children to be supported.' Overall, there's sense of constant nudging to bring everything on that bit quicker and better, although it's 'definitely not hothouse,' insist parents.

Emphasis on scholars is palpable – they cropped up in almost every conversation we had with students and parents. Fear not if your little cherub didn't make the cut on entry, though – head's new policy enables current students to apply at 13+. But, says school, it's not just the gifted and talented cohort that get their turn at the more imaginative and challenging projects – 'the best geographer in the year might not be a scholar and that is recognised here.' Students concur.

Setting from year 7 in maths and modern languages (students choose from French, German and Spanish from year 7, then add a second in year 9). Latin for all from year 7. English language IGCSE taken a year early by everyone, sensible as capitalises on two years of timetabled library sessions where 'we can direct pupils' reading'. Strongest performing I/GCSEs include maths, English, languages and RS (latter both compulsory), with the most popular subjects including history and geography. At A level, maths, history, business and economics get the most uptake, with maths and languages the show-stoppers in terms of results. While in the past the 'ologies' haven't got a look-in with the ultra-traditional curriculum, that looks set to change, with psychology recently introduced to the 22-strong A level options, of which all students take three (four for the super-bright) plus an EPQ. 'I know of young people who left the school because there were no modern A levels, so I hope this continues to change,' said one parent. Here as elsewhere, language take up falls off sharply post-GCSE, something school is keen to reverse.

Policy is emphatically not to throw weakest to the wolves but catch problems early; students agree that when things go wrong, school acts quickly. First port of call is often the academic support department which also helps those with specific learning difficulties (dyslexia, affecting 50 or so pupils, by far the most common, handful of pupils have ADHD, ADD and ASD, only two EHC plans). 'My son is dyslexic and completely disorganised and they've turned him around with their support,' one parent told us. Weekly 'surgeries' available in every subject. 'I'm struggling with maths and don't mind holding my hands up to admit it – and the surgeries and teachers' extra time with me have both really helped,' said one sixth former. Some criticism for current (lack of) careers advice, but two part-time (between them, available full time) specialist careers advisers had just been appointed when we visited.

Games, options, the arts: Would be criminal if sporting results didn't live up to glorious facilities (so many pitches, courts and nets that you could play somewhere different just about every week of the academic year). Fortunately they do, with whacking great double-fronted trophy cabinet stuffed with silverware – a challenge to even a posse of cat burglars – as proof. Hockey does particularly well, closely followed by rugby and netball – and the school is one of the top co-ed rowing schools in the country

It's all set in 100 acres, vast for home counties, let alone within M25 – property developers must salivate every time they drive past – and comes with a delightful 19th century cricket pavilion, a boathouse on the Thames and even a brace of rivers running through the grounds (why stop at one?).

Triple-colour awards are a regular phenomenon, as are small but steady numbers of rowers, cricketers and netball players cherry-picked for regional and national squads. But enthusiasm as well as talent is rewarded – 'every child gets the chance to represent the school,' says head. 'Obviously, the A teams get the most coaching and attention, but I'd say they're pretty well committed to all teams here,' one parent said. New 'activity centre,' of which we saw gleaming new plans, is carefully named so as not to alienate those more interested in gymnastics, yoga and pilates and live up to school's dedication to be 'all things to all people.'

With school offering 100 activities every week, most included in fees, no shortage of opportunities to find your inner sporting hero – or indeed cook, artist or musician. And for the less conventionally-minded, there's the likes of Land Rover 4x4 programming, French cookery and Greek clubs. Volunteering ethos very strong and often with religious dimension. Highlight for many is oversubscribed week in Lourdes where lower sixth volunteers become full-time carers for disabled children – 'life-changing,' say many. Every year 9 student spends a week in summer volunteering in local community. Standard fare of DofE and slightly more glamorous World Challenge also on offer. Predictably long list of trips, including overseas, range from subject based to annual ski jolly; 'you could go away every year if you could afford it.'

Musically robust (school won prestigious BBC Songs of Praise Senior School Choir of the Year the first time it entered), balancing highly selective with audition-free; even the whole school choir, open to all comers, tackles demanding choral works with panache (although some would like to see more modern singing opportunities too – 'it's all very choral and traditional'). Refreshingly, school is unfussed by smallish numbers taking GCSE or A level music, even in an age when there's increasing sense that if you can't measure it in exam results it's scarcely worth doing. Staff get stuck in too – 'we had staff singing practice on our last inset day,' says head.

We don't use the world 'phenomenal' lightly when it comes to art in schools, but some (not all) breathtaking pieces (all fastidiously framed in white and silver frames) adorn the corridors and offices, while the art rooms exhibit everything from huge traditional oil canvases through to the more avant-garde (including an intriguing rack of butcher-themed sculptures of hanging raw meat). Decent numbers for GCSE and A level, with one A level student telling us, 'This department is my sanctuary.'

Performing arts good – there's even a wardrobe mistress, with facilities including a large drama studio and theatre, but some parents think they're 'missing a trick with potential in this department. They could be doing so much more.'

Background and atmosphere: You'll hear a good deal of the phrase 'politesse and douceur'. Hard to pin down but think Arthurian knightly values (the good ones) given a 21st century co-educational makeover and you're probably not far off. And despite sounding highfalutin, it clearly goes in – pupils behave exceptionally well, with doors routinely held open a good 40 feet in advance in longest of corridors.

Ethos stems from Josephites, a small Belgian educational Catholic order dating from early 19th century, which founded school in 1869. Though declining in Europe, order is vibrant in the Congo and blessedly scandal-free everywhere (only hint of controversy is at US school run by similarly named though unrelated order which is fighting, with strong parental backing, to retain corporal punishment – 'nothing at all to do with us,' points out St George's). Don't expect an old-school Catholic culture, though; only a third of families are even Catholic and several students told us they were agnostic or atheist and that it wasn't 'remotely frowned upon.' 'The Josephites don't impose their religion and they're modern and un-shockable – I think that shines through here,' says head.

As the UK mother house, the school is home to elderly priests who, like everyone else, must relish the space at their disposal. For vista-starved visitors from London it's a breath of fresh air (quite literally), with many pretty traditional buildings, some Victorian, others a slight mish-mash of periods, and the widespread use of gorgeous, unifying and beautifully tended greenery to bind everything together. There's a green and pleasant quad for the youngest pupils and, amongst many other areas, a sixth form garden – though if the school put its mind to it, pupils could all have their own plot and you'd scarcely notice. Many of the classrooms are refurbished (shame, though, that the doors were all firmly closed), with overall effect smart and welcoming – lots of shiny oak wood and toning shades of school burgundy.

Newest building is the 2010 Henderson Centre which geography and history departments share with sixth formers, who have their own study rooms, café-style common room complete with balcony and mood lighting. Also home to sixth form only subjects like economics.

Not pressurised, exactly, but slackers need not apply and there's some antagonism among some parents about what they see as an 'over-emphasis' on Oxbridge. 'I've sat in meetings thinking, "I really don't want to hear about Oxbridge yet again".'

Pastoral care, well-being and discipline: Six-house system, and the 'families' within it (grandma/pa in sixth form, followed by mum/dad/children/grandchildren in younger years) form the anchor of the caring culture of the school, as well as being the focus for inter-school competitions. Heads of year may have a 'light touch,' but are also' highly supportive and nurturing,' say students, who particularly praise their 'effective approach to bullying.' 'They've really cracked down on it and one of the first links you come to on the school website now provides an opportunity to report any unkindness, anonymously if you prefer,' a student told us (head confirms it's well used – and, impressively, often about unkindness to others not themselves). Counsellor and chaplains available on tap and parents we spoke to with children with specific issues (one with a mental health issue; another with a medical condition) can't praise the school enough. 'Our daughter's sense of belonging to the school – which is largely thanks to the understanding, compassion and dedication of the teachers – has enabled her to keep up educationally and she is so much happier.' 'Our daughter says the teachers in the school are her greatest support system' etc.

More carrot than stick when it comes to tackling behavioural issues, of which the head says there are mercifully few; 'the worst I tend to see is laziness.' Plenty of warnings for minor misdemeanours, say students, rather than instant punishments, with parents called in for meetings where themes emerge to try and 'nip things in the bud.' Next come lunchtime detentions followed by after-school ones, and finally suspensions for repeated offences (less than a handful a year). Strict on uniform. Zero tolerance for drink, drugs and smoking.

Pupils and parents: This is deepest Surrey, so don't expect much of an ethnic mix (fewer than 20 pupils non-white) and only very slightly more diversity when it comes to English as a second language. Families cover more of a social mix than the area might suggest, though, with a predictable number of marble hall dwellers, but plenty who don't need to plug in sat nav to borrow cup of sugar from neighbours. Lots of social events to help them mix. Students we met were serious and sensible, with impeccable manners, but we also noticed a reassuring hullabaloo and chirpiness in the corridors between lessons.

Entrance: Junior and senior school combined dominate independent education locally, with 90 per cent coming from within 10 mile radius, subsidised coach services doubling the distance for remainder (school open to suggestions for new routes if there's sufficient demand) and convenient rail links making commuting a doddle.

Large numbers of places – 110 on offer at 11+ – sounds good on paper but half (and rising) are collared by own junior school pupils, and three times as many children sit exams as get places. Additional 44 places at 13+ are in equally hot demand. In total, there are around 30 or so feeder preps, Bishopsgate, Cranmore, Feltonfleet, Hall Grove and Hoebridge among them, others as far away as Kingston/Twickenham and southern side of Guildford. 'We are looking for a bright all-rounder – energic, resilient kids, not overly tutored ones,' says head, although more than one parent told us there's a feeling that as the school becomes increasingly academic, they weren't even sure their child would get in now given their time again.

Around 15 join at sixth form, for which a total of 9-10 GCSEs are required, including 7s in chosen subjects. Maturity and commitment also considered. Further down the school exam success is just one of the factors too. Siblings accommodated wherever possible.

Exit: Around 10 per cent leave post-GCSE and for post-A level students, university places are the norm. Steady numbers to Oxbridge (four to Cambridge in 2018 – sprinkling of choral scholarships too, often, and lots of support – and one off to study neurobiology at Harvard) and around three-quarters secure Russell Group places, with Birmingham, Nottingham and the London universities currently in vogue. Geography and history well represented as are business and management, but almost everything from law and medicine to architecture featuring somewhere. Careers followed later are just as diverse – including respectable numbers of first grade sports stars amongst the old boys and girls, including Anthony Watson.

Money matters: Scholarships capped at 10 per cent of the fees. A separate means-tested programme provides full funding for over 40 local children (some of whom are scholars), while hardship bursaries help struggling families in 'torrid times'.

Remarks: A school with vigour and ambition that does a grand job on bright, motivated pupils with its nurturing atmosphere and wraparound pastoral care. Parent after parent told us of their diverse mix of offspring all having their very different needs met so that they were able to grow into 'the very best version of themselves.' Especially suited to gung-ho multi-taskers – those who can handle 10+ GCSEs, but also love to embrace extracurricular to a high level and who will step out of their comfort zone with glee. Clearly a hard place to leave – 'I know I'm going to go through a bereavement this summer,' was one quote, and that was just from the parent.

St George's Junior School

Linked with St George's College, Weybridge

Thames Street, Weybridge, Surrey KT13 8NL

Ages 3–11 **Pupils** 619 **RC**

Fees: £10,170 – £13,965 pa

01932 839400
www.stgeorgesweybridge.com

S

Headmaster: Since 2003, Antony Hudson MA PGCE NPQH (50s). Previously deputy head at Prior's Field. Before that, worked at assorted independents, all secondary and in Surrey or close, bar a three-year stint as housemaster and sixth form head in deepest Derbyshire to get taste for rural lifestyle out of system.

The first layman in the post, he nevertheless has an air of a man of the cloth and mentions of God are scattered into most conversations. In fact, he told us, a couple of years into teaching career he was within a whisker of following in footsteps of an older brother (he has four) and entering the priesthood, when doubts set in. Instead of taking his vows, he opted for marriage and a family. Very much to the community's benefit as he and his wife Helen (a teacher at Ryde's Hill in Guildford) play a huge part in church life. Their two sons, now grown-up, were both at St George's College.

Mild-mannered, kind, sincere and open-minded, it's hard not to warm to him and parents and pupils simply adore him. 'We are left in no doubt that he genuinely cares about each child,' one parent told us. But doesn't dissemble – you'll get the truth from him, even if it hurts, say parents, and, fittingly, his office alone would win awards for transparency, with doors or windows on three sides. One of them, nearly always open, is on route for pupils visiting the library – handy for making himself a visible presence.

Prides himself on knowing every pupil by name which he achieves by teaching RE, as well as coaching football; known for being an extrovert type who's always happy to dress up in the line of duty or get his guitar out for a sing-song.

Entrance: Other school bursars must look at the rising numbers and weep. 'At 650, I'd say we've reached our optimum, although not our maximum of 688, which I just feel would not be good news for our clubs or the lunch hall,' says head.

Entrance is selective all the way through, with behaviour and social skills assessed for nursery places ('Get in there at least 18 months ahead if you can', advised one parent) and academic tests added at appropriate levels from reception onwards. No scholarships but assisted places (usually two per year) are available from year 3, potentially covering 100 per cent of the school fees.

While it's not essential to be a Catholic, sympathy with the belief system undoubtedly helps, as does realisation that while the Josephites who founded the school have a child-centred and kind approach to education (rare in 19th century circles), it doesn't preclude weeding out children who struggle academically.

In the past, the academically able could get unconditional offers of senior school places as early as year 2, but the 7+ assessment has now been ditched. Instead, all pupils take the 11+; invariably, over 95 per cent pass ('There's a lot, and I mean a lot, of preparation for it,' one pupil bemoaned).

Exit: Plenty in (usually some every term) and plenty out, too, with a whopping 40 per cent change from year 2 to 6. 'It's the Weybridge phenomenon – lots of relocation,' says head, who adds that finances (or lack of them) and falling behind academically in spite of support are further causes. For those who stay the course, three-quarters transfer to the senior school. Of the remainder, most head off to other independents – Hampton, SWPS, RGS and Reeds among them.

Remarks: The new fancypants Ark building for the lower years has transformed this large school site, taking it from old-school shabby to 21st century chic. Cosy classrooms (which peak at 20 pupils) boast more glass than wall space, with daylight flooding in, and there are vast balconies with enviable views. The word 'corridors' doesn't even feel right here – the inviting spaces between classrooms are bright, colourful and airy and double up as cheery break-out areas, with one spacious enough to hold whole-year assemblies. Here, as with all upper years, all pupils get their own locker. Nursery, meanwhile, is located in an attractive side-wing complete with indoor/outdoor learning space and years 3 to 6 are housed in the main four-storey building. While nowhere near as plush, it's appealingly traditional in places, with a notable 18,000-volume library with animated librarian, who even organised their own literature festival (other local state primary schools also invited). Everyone, from tinies upwards, has minimum of one library session a week. Large, light lunch hall also a boon.

The third of the three main buildings, the performing arts centre, includes bog-standard main hall (showing four annual plays – every child goes on stage at least once a year) and impressive music centre (where every child in year 3 or 4 gets a go at learning an instrument either individually or in pairs). 'Music is a wonderful department – I asked if my child could learn the French horn and just 10 days later the lessons were happening,' one parent told us. Whole school orchestra and senior, junior and chamber choirs all popular. Spacious arts studios (there's even a kiln) housed in portakabins. Next on the building wish list is a sports hall.

If the site was big before, it's now huge, having recently grown to an attractively laid out, mainly grassed 50-acre area. There's an eco-garden in memory of a pupil who tragically died in 2014, two forest school areas (outside learning is on the up here, as in so many schools) and seemingly endless play areas with enticing-looking apparatus.

Not the school to choose for educational fads and fancies. Focus is always on keeping in step with the senior school (staff and pupils visit regularly) and parents are never in any doubt, for good or ill, about how pupils are doing. French taught from year 1. Setting in English and maths from year 5, with specialist teaching for small groups in years 3 and 4. Subject specialist teaching in all subjects by year 5. Plenty of homework from the off, capped at an hour a night by year 6, although Wednesday is no homework night. Is it pressured? 'Nos' and 'Yeses' were called out simultaneously by the pupils we met.

Learning support team offers group support from nursery upwards (mainly literacy, some numeracy), then there's a programme for shared support from year 3. Around 12 per cent of pupils have SEN, mainly at the milder end, with four per cent receiving one-to-one support. 'You get very good and imaginative support,' according to one parent with a child with dyspraxia.

Teachers, who span the experience/age spectrum (but are mainly female until you get to, you guessed it, management level – 'it's the nature of the beast,' says head), win pupil approval and come across as completely devoted. 'You do get some shouty ones, though,' one pupil told us. In classroom-based subjects, lots of traditional teaching from the front though plenty of hands-on involvement elsewhere. Science and art rooms are open at break-time.

School's sense of tradition is inescapable but not over-weighty and inextricably bound up with religious dimension, centred on imposing chapel with a weekly mass. In a nod to the sensibilities of the softer 21st century child, though, there's an element of sugar coating, with some crucifixes round the school depicting cheerful Holy Family rather than the agony of Christ. And children told us 'it's fine if you don't believe – nobody minds, as long as you show tolerance to all religions.'

Sport department has improved, say parents – everyone in junior school plays in at least one proper match regardless of ability, and while there continues to be an inclusive touch throughout, there's also plenty of fodder for the more competitive, with U11s girls' hockey current national champions ('We almost have to scour the land to find a team to match us,' says head). Similar picture for rugby and cricket has come on big time, including for girls, while swimming and gymnastics are represented in both local and national competitions (leotards encrypted with school badge reassure parents gymnastics is no bolt-on here). 'Whether you're middle of the road or have a real passion for a particular activity or sport, they'll cater for you here,' said parent. Excellent facilities include heated outdoor swimming pool, courts, pitches, all-weather surfaces for hockey and tennis and – with opening aimed for September 2019 – activity centre with climbing wall, dance studio and LED flooring with can apparently transform from netball to hockey at the flick of a switch.

Every pupil is expected to do at least one club from year 1 (and every teacher expected to run at least one) and with French, cake decorating, book club, Mandarin and chess on the menu, it's no wonder some kids fill up their whole week. But woe betide the parent who tries to use clubs as 'free' childcare – 'that's absolutely not what the clubs are for,' warns head (although some parents remained flummoxed as to why the school doesn't offer wraparound childcare options for the growing number of dual-income families – 'we'd gladly pay for it,' said one).

The robust pastoral system is a well-oiled machine, the upshot of which is that there's a strong emphasis on belonging here; wearing the school badge 'means something'. That said, yellow and red caution slips are regularly used for those who step out of line ('the likes of overt unkindness or deliberate lying are not tolerated,' says head). We found pupils delightful and polite, but not stifled by manners – there was plenty of chit-chat and talking over each other in their eagerness to tell us about school life.

Rare is the school that doesn't claim to tease out every child's strengths and weaknesses, but this one seems to genuinely excel at it, with no child finishing their primary education 'without knowing they shine at something, probably many things,' say parents. 'I want to hear every child's voice by the time they're in year 6 – I mean, really hear them and who they are,' says head, with real emotion in his voice.

St George's School (Ascot)

249

Wells Lane, Ascot, Berkshire SL5 7DZ

Ages 11–18 **Pupils** 261 **Sixth form** 75 **Boarders** 92 **C of E**

Fees: Day £22,800; Boarding £33,570 – £35,460 pa

01344 629920
www.stgeorges-ascot.org.uk

Headmistress: Since 2016, Liz Hewer (only just 40s), two children, one dog. Destined for pointer and whiteboard from the cradle; her mother taught special needs. A brief flirtation with the financial world before and during her Cambridge career but back there for her PGCE. Relaxed, friendly, very sporty, captained the women's hockey team at Cambridge and won two half-blues for cricket. She comes here from literally just down the road as she did seven years as deputy head at St Mary's Ascot, but plenty of other top schools on her CV, including Marlborough.

Supporters are vocal and enthusiastic; she has taken time to understand the workings of the school ('she turns up for everything' and 'meets questions head on') before she makes too many changes. There's obviously much more going on inside both her head and the school, but the hot topic now is the introduction of traffic lights on the way to the car park, not ground-breaking but a jolly sensible step. She lives happily on site, finding 'going home to be mum helps me switch off'.

Academic matters: LH is confident that the balance of teachers – average age early 40s – is correct, and there was no mass exodus at the end of her first year in office. Our impression was plenty of younger faces amongst the staff, and the girls said they liked the variety of teaching styles. A new academic deputy head has been brought in to ensure that all levels of ability are catered for, as there had been some intimation from parents that the most able were not being stretched enough. Small classes in the first years, a maximum of 20, but more usually 15 or 16 are reduced to 10 for GCSE courses and often single figures at A level.

Setting starts from day one in maths, followed by Latin, French, science and Spanish in the third year and English at GCSE. Monitored twice a term, pupils say they are happy with the flexibility, confident that the staff are on it. One pupil told us that she had moved from the bottom to the top set at exactly the right speed.

You have to get your beauty sleep here because there is a deliberately long day; starting at 8.15am, it's pretty full on until the end of prep, which varies from 6.15pm for the younger ones to 6.45pm for the sixth form. If they add in other activities or clubs it can often be a 12 hour stretch before the day girls get home. Despite the long hours, the format appeals to both boarders and day girls because it means that they can chill when the school day ends with homework out of the way.

At present, but undergoing review, the lessons are only 35 minutes, which elicits the odd grumble but means they fit in nine lessons and slot in one more for A level students. The average number of entries for each girl at GCSE is nine or 10 with the occasional super-bright spark taking 11. The majority of students in the sixth form take three A levels plus an EPQ in the lower sixth. Some of this year's entry were not entirely convinced that they had sufficient time to do the extra work needed for an EPQ, although LH contends that it is becoming a valuable source of content for UCAS personal statements and interviews.

The 10 per cent or so of the school who have special educational needs, mainly dyslexia, speak highly of the SEND provision. One pupil told us that her problems had been so well dealt with that they no longer existed, and another that her only gripe was that she was limited to 25 per cent extra time in exams. Equally, a mother said that they had 'bent over backwards' to make her dyslexic daughter's life as easy as possible. Any girls who want or need that little bit extra can attend clinics, often with one-to-one teaching at no extra charge, which were described as 'brilliant' by one parent. After consultations with parents they also have the option of calling in the nearby Helen Arkell Institute, one of the UK's leading dyslexia centres.

We left feeling that there was a high level of satisfaction with the teaching although there does not appear to be one particularly outstanding academic area. A more accurate evaluation might be the across-the-board added value (GCSEs average a grade higher than expected at entry level). The impression is that they are trying hard to raise the academic bar and their results are very consistent. In 2018, 61 per cent A*-A/9-7 at GCSE, with a dip to 35 per cent A*/A, 58 per cent A*-B at A level.

Games, options, the arts: The head certainly has all the right sporty qualifications and seldom misses turning out to cheer them on.

In the summer the outside lacrosse pitches turn into tracks for athletics and the six netball courts magically grow into eight tennis courts. You can play everything from badminton to squash in the sports centre, which incorporates a viewing balcony for fans. Lower down everyone gets a chance to be in a team, but further up participation becomes more focussed and the teams more competitive, with one parent commenting that 'the coaching was second to none'. One of the results of all the hard training has seen them crowned Small Schools Lacrosse Champions two years in a row, but they don't just cater for sporting heroines. On top of the daily offerings they can provide private coaching for everybody from wannabe ballerinas to polo players.

There is a mass of popular options when it comes to out-of-school activities, including a surprisingly oversubscribed ukulele club. The older girls are fully involved and often run clubs for the younger lot. The only negative was a mention from a boarding parent that there was 'too much knitting club'.

The arts are another example of how this school refuses to be limited by the small number of pupils. There may have only been two sixth formers in the art room but their work was colourful and accomplished. An indication of how seriously they treat the subject was the presence of the artist-in-residence as well as a new young art teacher who has taken over from a Georgian legend.

The music department is headed up by a long-term, much praised contributor who twinkles at the new enthusiasm for the flute amongst the possibly less talented pupils but also helps the very able to move on to specialist establishments, such as the Royal Northern College of Music. The choir is 'so good', according to parents, that they regularly sing in public, including in the Albert Hall and with the BBC Symphony Orchestra.

Drama and music for all is the guiding principle and serious time and effort goes into carrying this out through inter-house drama and music competitions, LAMDA exams, the opportunity to take drama at GCSE and A level and even a theatre director in residence. They recently staged a production of Cats involving over 80 girls.

Boarding: The balance tips more towards boarding as they move up the school with only 20 per cent full-time boarders in the first two years but increasing to nearly 50 per cent in the sixth form.

The formal stairs out of the main hall lead up to cheerfully decorated, cosy dormitories for the first two years, 'deceptively spacious' in estate agent speak; we liked the look of them and believed the assurance that they were 'always that tidy' was down to a daily vetting. Sensibly, they mix up the first and second years so that there is an experienced old hand around if it all seems daunting to begin with. The number sharing diminishes as you go up the school with the upper sixth having their own room in a separate house. This is a bit dingy at the moment with strange 80s wallpaper in the passage and rather depressing ex-bedrooms used as studies by day girls. Staggered improvement here is next on the list and due to start soon.

One parent felt that full boarders were quite often left to their own devices and that it was more a school for free spirits than girls who needed a lot of TLC; having said which there was strong confidence in the house system and that the older girls looked out for the new intakes. Parents speak highly of the flexibility on offer: 'if she wants to stay for dinner, she can stay for dinner'.

The food is win, win all round, being both gastronomic and healthy; one parent said it was so good that she was moved to write a thank you letter. The only eating problem might be avoiding the temptation to want seconds of everything. Day and boarding pupils all muck in together, which is another way that the school avoids barriers springing up.

Background and atmosphere: Originally a boys' prep, until it went bust in 1904 despite having Winston Churchill as a pupil. After a sex-change into a girls only establishment it continued on surprisingly strongly through two world wars, thanks to an air raid shelter enterprisingly built at the start of the second.

This tiny kingdom lies down a lane only a short canter from the finishing post at Royal Ascot. The main circle of buildings crowns the top of a steep hill, guarding the green lawns and well-tended playing fields below from the encroaching hordes of modern houses. The original Victorian house grew over the years with the most obvious additions of more classrooms, a chapel, labs, music rooms and a sixth form house, all built in the 1980s. Later buildings include a technology block, a sports complex, a performing arts centre (no prizes for guessing that it was opened by the Duke of York) and, most recently, an imaginative, light new library complete with a feisty librarian: 'she was part of the package'. Next on the list is to be a swanky new swimming pool tucked under the hill, opening in September 2019.

Once past the intercom and the keypad, the modern sentries of scholastic establishments, you find yourself in a large entrance hall, bedecked with trophies, cups and futuristic fashion. The centrepiece is a splendid flower arrangement distracting your attention from the friendly ladies on reception (not there at weekends) sitting beneath a board listing the names of the school's head girls, past and present. As in almost all buildings that have evolved over time, the rest of the layout is slightly confusing to the outsider but poses no problems to its inhabitants who all talk of its 'homely atmosphere'.

Pastoral care, well-being and discipline: LH's ease with social media means lots of communication with parents, which goes down well. She is quick to tweet praise and encouragement and parents feel they are kept in touch with their children's progress on all fronts. The school has a pastoral deputy who deals with petty disciplinary problems quickly and efficiently and there is no evidence of serious issues. This is a school that takes modern dangers seriously, and he also oversees the successful blocking of social and streaming media for older girls during lessons; younger girls have zero access.

The pupils now have a clear structure of authority, with the head girl supported by a team including a group of peer mentors; girls in the lower sixth who choose to undergo formal training with the school counsellor so that they can offer a friendly shoulder to lean on or even cry on if necessary. This format works really well, according to parents, with the inevitable odd grouse being sorted out so discreetly that the original sufferer is only aware that the problem is no longer there. Members from all years are elected to take part in a school council where they can air their ideas or their moans, and the sixth form has its own separate version.

Pupils and parents: As with so many similar schools, the evolution from the days of old school parents (who dropped their children off at the beginning of term and picked them up at the end) to present day parents (who prefer them to sleep in their own beds) is almost complete. High earning, mainly very local parents of both sexes drop their children off before they go to work for the rest of the day, thankful that they can arrange for sleepovers if they are still chained to their desks or stuck on an aeroplane.

A large number of pupils lives locally but some are bussed in from as far away as Chalfont St Giles and a smaller number come from west London, often on a school bus that operates at weekends. Some 10 per cent come from international families spanning the globe from Mexico to China with the occasional Russian or European.

Entrance: Described by one parent as 'pretty much non-selective', intakes are at 11+, 13+ and into the sixth form. At 11+ admission is by exam, interview and report from current school. Pre-assessment operates for 13+ entry with exams in maths, English and verbal reasoning plus an interview. Access to the sixth form requires a minimum of six 9-5 grades at GCSE and at least a 6 in any subject to be taken at A level. There is a wide variety of feeder schools including local preps such as Lambrook, Upton House, Godstowe and Coworth Flexlands and local primaries. Some also come from west London schools including Thomas' schools, Knightsbridge, Broomwood Hall and Garden House.

Exit: Around 15 per cent leave after GCSEs, girls tempted by the lure of co-ed and parents by the savings made if the move is to a sixth form college. Leavers after A level in 2018 went on to a variety of destinations: one medic (UCL), another off to study musical theatre (Guildford School of Acting), and another business with marketing (Edinburgh).

Money matters: Academic, music, art, sports, performing arts and all-rounder scholarships available at 11+, 13+ and 16+, all offering up to 10 per cent off the fees. In addition they offer a limited number of means-tested bursaries.

Remarks: As with their equine counterparts on the racecourse across the road, careful attention is paid to each well-bred individual, persuading them to give of their best. However, it is done in a spirit of camaraderie and they are actively discouraged from being academic know-alls, bullies on the games pitch or divas on the boards. Old-school tradition meets 21st century sensibilities to turn out intelligent, civilised, young women proving that the Georgian formula continues to work.

St George's School (Harpenden)

Sun Lane, Harpenden, Hertfordshire AL5 4EY

Ages 11–18 **Pupils** 1,375 **Sixth form** 403 **Boarders** 118 full

Fees: Day free; Boarding £12,210 pa

01582 765477
www.stgeorges.herts.sch.uk

Head: Since September 2017, Helen Barton, previously deputy head and geography teacher here. She trained as an accountant before seeing the light, taking a PGCE and teaching at state and independent schools in Herts and Beds, joining St George's as assistant head in 2005. She studied for a masters in education and became deputy head in 2008.

Academic matters: As a totally non-selective school regularly delivering high results, parents can bank on St George's knocking it out of the park when it comes to value-added, with 57 per cent of GCSE grades 9-7 in 2018 and 93 per cent of pupils achieving 9-4 in both maths and English. School is clear to point out, however, that this is not just in the realm of academia, but also in 'confidence, values and esprit de corps' that the students outperform expectations, acclaiming staff's 'ability to instil a sense of can-do' in its charges. Top A level grades are similarly commonplace. In 2018, 73 per cent A*-B, 43 per cent A*/A at A level.

Ten to 11 GCSEs are the norm, with compulsory RE amongst them, leading, unusually, to a full class at A level. Parents appreciate flexible approach to timetabling at GCSE. Maths, 'without reservation', is the jewel in St George's crown and the most popular A level choice by both sexes – 'it's phenomenal to see how much they enjoy it.' Art also outstanding with school boasting the highest percentage of top grades in county at both art GCSE and A level. Setting in maths and science from end of year 7, with English set for GCSE.

French from year 7, German and Spanish from year 8 and all on offer at GCSE but, disappointingly, only French at A level. Mandarin available to all, although not examined, and school is one of just 45 Confucius Classrooms across the UK, meaning that it has Chinese firmly embedded in its own curriculum and strong links with China, including a popular exchange programme. Also has International School status.

SEN all in a day's work for the full time SENCo and seven teaching assistants on staff. Plenty of experience dealing with statemented children, and learning support ranges from helping with a few extra spellings to an individually planned timetable. Large percentage of cohort identified as gifted and talented, with extension work provided accordingly both on and off curriculum with Science Olympiads and Maths Challenges.

Games, options, the arts: Sport taken seriously but 'not elitist', according to school, with all abilities trained together. Rugby and cricket are main boys' sports, with A-C teams playing competitive fixtures most weeks in all year groups. It's lacrosse for the girls – St George's is the only state maintained school in the south of England to play, so all fixtures are against independents, hence often at weekends. Other popular options are netball, rounders, basketball, tennis, athletics and, to a limited extent, dance. Compulsory participation to year 13, with more casual mixed classes in sixth form that encompass table tennis, badminton and trampolining. Indoor games take place in the impressive newish sports centre, also home to an attractive and well-equipped gym and weights room.

Possibly the best art department of any school for miles around – 'the pride of the school,' say pupils. Every inch of the art corridor walls and ceilings festooned with breathtakingly creative and technically exemplary work also spilling over to cover most walls throughout school. Huge (four foot) three dimensional papier mâché masks welcome visitors into this showcase area, and from that point on it's hard to know where to look, as outstanding paintings, drawings, sculptures and installations – no two the same – assault the senses. Creative facilities also superb, with three huge DT labs – again with some wonderfully turned work on display – and two huge art rooms provide yet more exhibition space for pupils' superb creative endeavours. Textiles, photography, sculpture and graphic design all on offer.

Music provides St George's heartbeat. Choirs, orchestras and bands galore and so much talent to display that annual house music competition now takes place in Watford Colosseum. One major annual drama production – Scrooge, Fame and Hairspray in recent years – in which all year groups can participate as well as smaller shows throughout the year.

Plenty of extracurricular activities from sewing and gardening to chess or curriculum based classes take place before and after school – excellent for boarders and day pupils alike. Well-attended ATC as well as World Challenge expeditions to far flung destinations from Argentina to Mongolia. School's connection with Gansu Province, China, has yielded exchange trips and a small team led by head to lecture at University of Beijing. Other trips include educational expeditions to Washington (politics), Space Camp (maths) and a popular biennial ski trip.

Boarding: Despite the small number of boarders (maximum capacity 135, with anything between five and 15 each of boys and girls in any given year group), they are very well integrated into the school. Friendships between day and boarding pupils flourish and visits to day pupils' homes encouraged. Far from feeling like a minority group, boarders take pride in their status to the point of having requested their own, slightly different, tie. Relationships between year groups are forged through fun activities such as 'speed dating' – an in house way of getting to know newcomers.

Boarding houses have friendly family feel, thanks in no small part to the young (40s), bubbly director of boarding who lives on campus and oversees the pastoral welfare of her charges full time. 'She really understands what makes teenagers tick,' said one happy parent. Girls from years 7 to 12 are housed in the old school building – safely tucked away up what seems like 15 flights of stairs – in dorms which sleep anything from two to six: 'we tailor it according to intake from year to year and girls' individual needs,' says director of boarding. Year 13 girls have the run of a swish new house with single rooms and en suite bathrooms. Boys are in a stand-alone block with a less cosy, more practical feel – though we are assured that the sparse decorations in dorms and common room are purely by choice ('it's not cool to have posters up,' said one of our guides). Both houses have tons of communal space – massive common rooms furnished with plenty of squashy sofas and other nooks and crannies around the house with beanbags, armchairs and computers for boys and girls to congregate outside of school hours. Both houses have well-equipped kitchen areas for boarders to make themselves snacks – and there are baskets of goodies out to keep them going after school.

Boys and girls are allowed to visit each other but only in common rooms – although apparently romantic liaisons are incredibly rare: 'There is a strong sibling-like feel amongst the boarders,' say pupils. The terms 'flexi' and 'weekly' are not used and, although some boarders go home more frequently than others, all pay the same fees (less by some stretch than most private day schools) and have the same status. Around half stay for weekends (more boys than girls), with all meals apart from weekend breakfasts taken in the main school dining room. Pupils from year 9 allowed into Harpenden with permission in twos and many attend classes such as yoga or dance in the village. Pupils grumble that school is too strict about them leaving the premises – parents breathe secret sighs of relief.

Channels of communication to home left wide open with boarders allowed phones, handed in at bedtime, although they are trusted to keep iPads and laptops 'to keep it as much like home life as possible.' Weekends bring Friday night football club, competitive matches for many on Saturdays, cinema trips and one big trip each term (paintballing, Thorpe Park, Brighton have featured recently). Boarders also have their own formal dinner or ball each term, organised by senior pupils. Younger pupils have a fixed programme of after-school activities including boarding skills – learning how cook, do their laundry, make jam etc.

Background and atmosphere: Feels more like a private school than some private schools we know – and certainly wins the prize for smartest comprehensive school uniform with its green Harris tweed blazers for the boys and pleated kilts for the girls. Situated a stone's throw from Harpenden High Street, school was founded in 1907 by the Rev Cecil Grant as a non-denominational Christian foundation with its own Anglican chaplain and weekly Sunday chapel service, which occasionally hosts up to 400 members of the school community and their families. One of the longest established fully co-educational boarding schools in England, the school retains many of its historic traditions, with pupils taking great pride in their house competitions, formality of chapel, speech days and all the different ties awarded.

S

The original Victorian gothic-style building still provides the heart of the school – and girls' boarding house – with various additions and extensions which run the full gauntlet from occasionally gleaming (sports hall, language block) to downright shabby (most of the rest). Despite its somewhat down at heel sum of the parts, however, the whole hangs together with a feel of purposefulness and functionality and is actually part of the school's overall charm. Sixth form common room and study areas in dire need of a refurb, but nobody seems to mind – the overall feel of the school is welcoming and contented – 'children can grow up at their own pace,' say parents. A new link with nearby Batchwood Tennis Academy hopes to attract talented players from all over the country to boarding houses.

Pastoral care, well-being and discipline: Very little need for strong discipline – hard to believe that 'chewing gum' is the worst that happens but that was all our guides would confess to. Occasionally pupils 'don't work out' on the boarding side but in the main 'they feel very lucky to be here – there's no sense of entitlement,' says director of boarding. 'Traditional values and caring ethos,' makes school tick, according to head with strong support from parents. Pupils rewarded for demonstrating school's core values of courtesy, integrity, manners and discipline. Houses presided over by a head of house, assistant and team of tutors. The arrangement of tutor groups gives pupils very little room for manoeuvre when it comes to bad behaviour. An 'excellent' student services department supports children with welfare or emotional needs with its qualified counsellor, to whom pupils can self-refer, and a pastoral support worker.

Pupils and parents: Affluent Harpenden and its surrounding villages provide the vast majority of day pupils with boarders coming mainly from further afield, and around 55 per cent of these from overseas. Cohort is hence naturally inclined towards hard work and success upon which school can build. A highly involved and vocal parent body turns out in droves for matches, concerts and shows and the Sunday service in chapel is very well attended. Alumni include philosopher and political theorist Michael Oakeshott, classicist and writer Rex Warner, actress Laura Haddock and rugby player Owen Farrell.

Entrance: The most oversubscribed of Harpenden's three secondary schools, with a complex admissions process run by school. No academic selection but a series of priorities including catchment (currently extending to around 800 metres from school), regular church attendance for at least two years (minister's letter required), and siblings receiving priority. Genuine devoutness not put to the test – local parents can cynically choose to pray rather than pay as long as they think ahead and accept that their child will have to attend chapel at school on at least three Sundays a term. A handful each year from local prep schools.

Boarders must be EU resident or hold British passport and are interviewed by head and director of boarding to assess suitability, as well as provide a good reference from their previous school. 'Need' also comes into play – for example children with both parents working or in the Forces, with occasional children switching from day to boarding places to save time on the daily commute. Applications should be in a year in advance, although boarding places not currently oversubscribed. Very occasional charitable places but no bursaries offered.

Exit: Around three-quarters stay on into sixth form after GCSEs – leavers generally move to other schools and colleges. More than two-thirds to Russell Group/other top universities, with 14 Oxbridge places in 2018 and five medics. Occasional students to US universities.

Money matters: As a voluntary aided school, St George's buildings are owned by the school's Foundation, which has to find 10 per cent of the cost of all capital projects and on-going building maintenance from very limited funds. 'There is a lot of do-it-yourself work here'; school enlists the assistance of its active parents' association for fundraising support throughout the year.

Remarks: A real gem of a local secondary school with plenty to offer pupils whether they want to paint, study or play their way to success. Riding high as one of the top non-selective state schools in the country, St George's can boast a secure, Christian community as well as top notch results.

St Helen and St Katharine

Faringdon Road, Abingdon, Oxfordshire OX14 1BE

Ages 9–18 **Pupils** 734 **Sixth form** 192

Fees: £16,470 pa

01235 520173
www.shsk.org.uk

Head: Since 2015, Rebecca Dougall BA MA (40s), previously head of the Royal High School, Bath. Has also taught at Wycombe Abbey and Oxford High, where she was deputy head. An English literature specialist, she is chic, youthful and dynamic, as well as being passionate about single sex schools, having attended one herself.

Doesn't teach, but not a CEO type head and is known among pupils for being personable and approachable, regularly popping into lessons and having an open-door policy. 'She doesn't just know our names – she knows what our interests are, often stopping us to ask us about them,' said one pupil, with another adding that she gives 'great thought-provoking assemblies that we genuinely look forward to'. Parents also impressed. 'She has her finger on the pulse and you absolutely feel you can trust your daughter to do her very best in her care,' said one. Impassioned about the school without being dewy-eyed, she is as focused on the girls' achievements and aspirations as the practical steps and vision needed to make these possible.

Lives locally with her husband, who teaches history. Extracurricular interests include medieval literature, design, property, travel and absorbing other cultures – in style.

Academic matters: Unapologetically selective and academic. In 2018, 87 per cent A*-A/9-7 grades at I/GCSE, and while the girls would probably be too modest to say out loud that 'St Helen's girls don't get Bs [or 6s]', this perfectly respectable grade doesn't seem to see much light of day here. Head puts this down to the traditional recipe of good teaching, hard work and high expectations. There's a fizz and energy about learning, along with a refreshing lack of cynicism, which was palpable in every classroom we visited and among every conversation we had with pupils. 'It's cool to learn here and that comes across very quickly,' said one parent. Teachers, too, have a fire in their eye, with pupils referring to 'their first rate subject knowledge' and dedication, which often involves them putting in a lot of extra hours.

Most girls do 10 subjects and choices include DT, drama, Latin, Greek and computer science. Spanish is the lead language from year 7; then in year 8, pupils add a second language of French, German or Mandarin. Additional language options at GCSE include Mandarin and there's an Arabic course for sixth formers. Take up for separate and dual award sciences roughly equal. A level results also fairly lofty (75 per cent A*/A grades in 2018) with sciences, maths and English the most popular choices closely followed by geography, history, art, and religious studies. Some subjects (government & politics and theatre studies) are taught jointly with Abingdon boys. Small junior department (years 5 and 6), which is by no means a 'light' version of the senior school, but rather its own operation with dedicated teachers, but which accesses many of the senior school facilities.

School wants girls to develop as 'active, independent learners, able to think for themselves and prepared to take risks' and to take a 'broad and balanced approach' to their education, says the head. 'We're not grade hunters,' she insists, although there are lots of tests and exams. Lessons we observed were indeed stimulating and interactive, with plenty of questions and debate – no sign of young brains being crammed with facts. 'Flipped classroom learning – currently all the rage – is what we've been doing here for years,' explains the head. Indeed, pre-reading and extra resources being provided to students to study at home before the class session, which then is devoted to exercises, projects and discussions, appears to be business as usual here. Sixth form teaching, in particular, goes above and beyond the syllabus requirements, providing a depth of learning that gives girls a real edge. EPQ a significant feature of sixth form life; coding recently introduced; scientists take an ethics course; practical art, craft and design workshops.

The learning support co-ordinator is praised by parents for excellence in diagnostic testing and support for the few girls with mild dyslexia/dyspraxia or who are on the autistic spectrum, with the head ensuring that every staff member is on board when it comes to any special needs, along with extra pastoral care, which she firmly believes should be at the heart of any SEN provision. 'What's particularly impressed me is the effort that all staff have gone to, whilst keeping it all very low-key so as to prevent my daughter feeling fussed over or stigmatised,' said one parent.

Games, options, the arts: Art and DT facilities are bright, spacious and well-equipped – the former comprising of sky-lit, atelier-like studios in the old building, the latter housed in the new 3D design centre. Innovative results are to be seen throughout the school, with a particularly striking ceramics display when we visited, although one parent with experience of other local schools told us, 'I don't think there's as much opportunity for keen artists here as there is at Headington and Oxford High.'

Plenty of ambitious music and drama productions including Anything Goes (senior school), Alice in Wonderland (middle school) and The Lion King (lower school), often in conjunction with Abingdon School. Performance spaces are the intimate, round studio theatre, a larger stage in YPH and Abingdon School's Amey Theatre. The annual playwriting competition creates quite a buzz, with the winner directing her own piece.

Practice rooms in the music department are in constant use for singing and instrumental lessons (450 per week) and, unsurprisingly, school musicians do well in local and national competitions. Four orchestras, eight choirs, two wind bands, a big band and more than 20 smaller ensembles. 'My daughter didn't go down the exam route, but has been given a love of music that I think will last her for life,' enthused one parent. Large and successful uptake for DofE and Young Enterprise,

Sport facilities never stand still here. That was literally the case when six outside courts were moved from one side of the playing fields to the other so that they could be floodlit (houses overlooking the old spot weren't keen). There's an extra 12 acres of playing fields just across the road and the new sports centre includes a large hall (able to host international competitions), improved gym, indoor rowing facilities and dance studio. For swimming, climbing wall and more courts, girls use Abingdon School.

Although we saw for ourselves fixture lists with A, B and C teams – and the head vouches for the fact that she's stood and watched C teams competing – a recurring grumble is that less attention is paid to the B and C teams. Girls who start school keen to have a go at, say, lacrosse (the only school in Oxfordshire to offer this sport) or play in netball matches can feel sidelined if they don't make the As, according to some parents.

Regional, national and even international representation across several sports, particularly equestrian and great excitement about the netball team having reached national level for the first time when we visited. Additional opportunities for football, rugby, trampolining, cheerleading, Frisbee, sailing and golf, plus gym and dance.

Extracurricular ranges from knit chic to Christian club, and every department runs subject-based clubs, some of which are student-led. School trips aplenty, including an annual ski trip for lower and middle school and residential team-building trip to Somerset for year 7s, plus foreign exchanges to France and Germany. Also, geographers to Iceland, historians to Berlin, artists to Cornwall and (every three years) lacrosse players to the USA.

Background and atmosphere: The distinctive main red-brick building is original to the school's 1903 foundation by nuns of the Community of St Mary the Virgin, who wished to provide a 'liberal and advanced' education to the young ladies of Abingdon. Behind reception, the central atrium, once the dining room, is now used for little more than lunchtime cake sales and provides the walkway through the junior department to the shiny new palace of science – a striking facility with 12 spacious, colour-co-ordinated science labs (where we saw girls enthusiastically dissecting pigs' hearts in biology), a hall/theatre complete with stylish break-out areas, as well as contemporary kitchen and dining facilities.

Thanks to a very generous private donor, study facilities are superb throughout, notably the stunning library in the Jean Duffield building, with curved bookcases arranged spaciously in circular sections, comfortable seating, Farrow & Ball tones and glass walls and doors leading to silent study areas. 'I love studying here – even more so than at home because the dedication to study is infectious,' one pupil told us. Natural light is amplified by a central well and a winding staircase leads to a ground-floor fiction section, a university-style 120-seated lecture theatre and café with opening hours to cater for early birds or girls staying on for the numerous clubs and after-school activities. Other facilities of note include the large, well-equipped IT suites, modern (and reassuringly chaotic) sixth form common room, and delightful chapel.

There's a core spirit of endeavour and enthusiasm and, as you might expect, tradition is big. Plenty of rituals, such as 'the bonkers school hymn' (head's words) and the 2p race on St Kate's Day, whereby girls, in their year groups, compete to line up 2p coins on the tennis courts for a chosen charity.

The school day begins at 8.30am, with eight lessons kicking off at 9.10am, including a decent stretch for lunch and finishing at 4.15pm – unless girls stay on for clubs. A joint bus service with various local schools delivers from as far as Reading, Oxford, Thame and Faringdon in the morning. Separate ride home at the end of the day, including for those staying on at 5.20pm. Food is great – 'the best ever,' exclaimed one girl.

Pastoral care, well-being and discipline: 'We talk a lot here – pupils and teachers, teachers and the rest of the staff, staff and parents, all of us really,' reports the head (and pupils agree), claiming that this – above all else – means problems are generally prevented or nipped in the bud. 'But no head should think they've cracked pastoral care. It should always be developing.'

At the centre of the current pastoral care system are the form tutors and heads of section, and there's also a full-time chaplain, health centre staff and part-time counsellor (employing a second was under consideration at time of our visit). Friendship fall-outs are tackled quickly, thereby helping to prevent bullying, with the other main issues they face including problems at home and balancing aspirations of parents with those of the children. Then there's the academic pressure. While girls are trained to handle it well, there are inevitably moments when it all gets on top of them, and molehills can become mountains, particularly around exam time. Parents say support for this (offered to whole family, not just the pupil) is 'phenomenal' and communication more generally is excellent too.

All the usual responsibilities for students, including prefects (who proudly don boaters and blazers for big occasions), house captains (there was a new house system when we visited as the previous one wasn't encouraging enough cross-year bonding), school council and mentors – along with plenty more besides. In lower sixth, every single girl has a role of responsibility, such as charity or sports rep.

Discipline requires a light touch. The expression of disappointment by a highly regarded teacher goes a long way here, along with a firm set of rules that mean everyone knows what's expected of them in the first place. 'I'm not saying I haven't had girls here on a Saturday morning, for instance for misuse of mobile phones, but discipline really is a nominal part of my job,' says head.

All girls attend chapel once a week, although school life itself is becoming increasingly secular. Girls are enthusiastic and aware charity fundraisers, busy with lunchtime cake sales and other enterprises; many serve in the school chapel as sacristans, readers or choristers.

Pupils and parents: Bright, ambitious girls. Ditto parents. About half come from local primaries and the rest from feeder preps – around 25 in total. 'There's a sweetness about the girls here,' adds the head, while parents are, she says, 'level-headed and interested'. There's a lively PA, which does fundraising for charity and the school, as well as fostering friendships among parents. Almost all white British, reflecting this part of Oxfordshire, although there is a sprinkling of African-Caribbean, Indian, Sri Lankan, Turkish, Chinese and Japanese, among others. Former pupils include Samantha Cameron and her sister, deputy editor of Vogue, Emily Sheffield (both decamped to sixth form boarding at Marlborough), Alice Thomson (leader writer the Times), Belinda Bucknall QC, Lindsey Russell (Blue Peter presenter) and Becky Wait (author).

Entrance: Entry at 9, 10, 11, 13 and 16, though the majority come in at 11. Maths and English tests and informal interviews for 9+ and 10+ candidates, who get automatic admission to senior school, though they take a transfer test for the school's records and possible scholarships. Exam at 11 (maths and English) plus observed 'taster days' and informal interview with head; roughly three candidates for every place. 'We take a long time over admissions,' reports the head, who says she's looking for potential, not overly coached children, as well as a 'confidence hook.' 'If they're passionate and brilliant a particular subject, or they love singing in the choir, for example, we know that can boost their confidence at times when it may fall in other areas.' Girls who get a place go into one of four classes per year, each with 22 or 23 places (maximum 24).

Existing pupils gain entry to sixth form even if they have wobbled at GCSE – there's no weeding out to 'bump up' A level results (not that this seems necessary). Candidates from other schools – of which there are usually anywhere between 15 and 20 each year, and who come from both the state and independent sector – chosen via pastoral and academic interviews and verbal reasoning test. They will need good I/GCSEs (at least five A*-A/9-7 grades, including in subjects to be studied) and a positive reference.

Exit: Around 10-20 per cent leave post-GCSE, and roughly the same number join, but most stay on – no uniform and shared teaching with Abingdon boys does no harm to retention figures. Eleven to Oxbridge in 2018, the rest mainly to first choice Russell group institutions, Bristol, Exeter and Cardiff being favourites, plus two off to the US. No significant subject bias, though 12 medics/vets in 2018; we can look forward to Helkat doctors, lawyers, engineers, vets, musicians and psychologists in years to come.

Money matters: Fees relatively low, with the school featuring in the Telegraph's top 10 schools offering value for money, but extras (including lunch) can soon mount up. Small number of scholarships: academic scholarships awarded according to performance in entrance exam and, at 13+ interview; music scholarships (free tuition on one or two instruments) on basis of audition. Approximately 10 per cent of students currently in receipt of financial support. Hardship fund available to support families whose financial circumstances change suddenly mid-year.

Remarks: A school with outstanding teaching, a go-getting culture and breathtaking facilities and opportunities. Produces confident, spirited girls with fine minds, but who aren't afraid to roll up their sleeves and get things done. The pacy environment – school really does move at a brisk speed – isn't for everyone, but fastidious admissions procedures and ongoing support and encouragement enable girls (aka 'Helkats') to fly high, with few, if any, wilting. If your daughter is bright, energetic and curious, then a St Helen and St Katharine education could be the golden ticket to Oxbridge and beyond.

St Hilary's School

Holloway Hill, Godalming, Surrey GU7 1RZ

Ages Girls 2-11, boys 2-7 (becoming co-ed throughout)
Pupils 198: 153 girls, 45 boys

Fees: £10,092 – £14,850 pa

01483 416551
www.sthilarysschool.com

Headmistress: Since 2012, Jane Whittingham (50s), previously deputy at nearby Rowan Prep in Esher, with particular interest and qualification in dyslexia. Came somewhat late to her first headship due to time spent with her own family; her four children are now grown-up.

She is positively glowing with kindness, but not afraid to speak her mind even when it goes against the grain. 'She's not one of those heads that's constantly schmoozing parents – in fact it's the children she talks to when she's on the gate every day and every decision she makes is in their interests, no matter what,' said one parent. 'She knows every single child and their character,' said another.

Which probably explains why her open-door policy is just that. Nearly all heads, especially at primary level, claim to have one, but in our experience pupils often don't even know where the head's office is. Here, children regularly follow the famous 'big red staircase' to her exceptionally child-friendly study (complete with play corner) to show her their latest great piece of handwriting (one did just that when we were there) or just for TLC and encouragement dressed up in fun sessions such as reading with Bella, a teacher's black lab (standing in for the head's dog, who is now in 'semi-retirement'), Ludo and lemonade, dodgers (jammie) and dominoes. Groups of year 6 girls are regularly invited to lunch here with wine glasses (of juice) and 'posh cutlery'.

Doesn't teach but does regular reading and assemblies, which cover meaty topics ranging from dementia (they're a dementia-friendly school) to same sex relationships. 'She attends absolutely everything – even the dads' camping, where she rings the bell and tells all these hedge fund managers and suchlike to go to bed,' said one parent.

Not one to rest on her laurels, she continues to move the school forward: 'I have one idea a day while driving up and down the A3.' Most recently, she launched STEAM (STEM plus the arts) across the school.

Entrance: Entry to nursery at age 2 now allows unfettered progression throughout school for boys and girls, as it is gradually becoming co-ed – boys can stay for (or join) year 3 in 2019 and move up from there with the girls. 'There's been a bit of controversy around it, especially among parents who chose the school because it was single sex, but nobody's pulling out and most are thrilled,' one parent told us. 'Parents used to say to us, "You say you're family-oriented but then you split us up" – now we don't need to do that,' says head.

Other entry points at reception and at 7+, when quite a few join from local state infants' schools. No academic selection, prospective pupils and their parents meet the head and the child spends a morning in school so staff can benchmark their current attainment and give them a taste of life at St Hilary's.

Handful of scholarships up to 30 per cent. Means-tested bursaries available, mostly 10 to 50 per cent, including very occasional full bursary. Scholarships at year 3 entry, in-house scholarship tests for those already at St Hilary's; 'they write a story and do a maths paper during a lesson and don't really realise so there's no pressure'. Current pupils can apply for academic, art, sports, dance, swimming, music or drama scholarships, although they only get them 'if there's real potential and talent', says head, with successful pupils often going onto get scholarships into senior schools in the same subjects – 'and, because we track, we know they often wind up studying them at A level too', says head.

The whole entry and scholarship process is, say parents, 'very low key.'

Exit: Boys have previously left aged 7, two-thirds to nearby Aldro, a couple each to Lanesborough, Pennthorpe and Cranleigh Prep. The vast majority of girls leave at 11. Prior's Field, Guildford High, Tormead and St Catherine's most popular recently. Also occasional one or two to Churcher's College, King Edward's, Amesbury, Frensham Heights, Farnborough Hill, St Edmund's, St Teresa's and Wycombe Abbey.

Head meets with all parents to help parents find the right senior school, who appreciate her honesty about choices. They note how work ramps up at the start of year 6 with a focus on English, maths and science, plus verbal and non-verbal reasoning. Children are, they report, 'very well prepared for their next step'.

Remarks: Founded in 1927, St Hilary's is perched on a hill accessed via a steep country lane on the outskirts of Godalming. The original main Victorian house looked an absolute picture with its traditional Christmas decorations when we visited, despite it being the worst of British weather, while inside the mix of 19th and more 20th century additions are surprisingly seamless, albeit a bit warren-like in places. The overall feel is so welcoming and homely that the lack of anything stupendously modern doesn't feel remotely detrimental, and in any case it's all thoroughly fit for purpose. Classrooms, science lab, music, art rooms – and even the ICT suite – are interesting and colourful, interlinked with lots of open doors in the younger age groups. The nursery section, taking boys and girls from age 2, is bright, fun, well organised and with fabulous outdoor area. Older pupils can come here for half an hour before school and have breakfast (as an extra, from 7.45am – it used to be 8am but the train timetable changed; they can also do clubs or after-school care until 6pm). The library is among the most inviting we've seen, with animal-themed cushions dotted around the genuinely relaxed seating areas. Stunning wall displays throughout the school.

The ethos of St Hilary's sets it apart from some of the other prep schools, offering encouraging but unpressured prep school education. Parents feel the school is 'happy' and we found smiling, carefree pupils learning and playing in a buzzy atmosphere – 'the teachers like us to be buzzy bees,' one girl said, as if reading our minds.

The lack of pressure doesn't mean lack of academic success. Despite the non-selective entry and mixed-ability teaching (although there is setting for maths from year 3 – and even year 2 if it works for that cohort – and in comprehension from year 5), parents told us the children 'reach their full potential' and that it 'has become steadily more academic under the current headship'. 'One of my children is incredibly academic and the other isn't and the school is ideal for both – and that's the great thing about it as it pushes everyone to achieve their best. If anything, they get more excited for my younger one doing well because he makes bigger jumps,' said one. Indeed, value added takes centre stage here – the child who can't put a toe in the big water who goes onto compete in a swimming gala etc. French taught from reception (and Spanish, as an extracurricular club for years 1 and 2, and from year 3 as part of enrichment), philosophy from year 1 and everyone has 'HOT' (higher order thinking) – 20 minutes a week to focus on problem-solving skills. Forest school also part of the curriculum.

Specialist teachers in French and music from kindergarten and sport from reception, then in everything from year 3. 'Some primary heads are averse to employing senior school trained staff, but we're not – they bring a whole new breadth and dimension, and it's not as if the curriculum stops at 11,' says head.

Around 40 children with SEN, 'although a lot of these needs wouldn't feature as such in a state school – they may be under the radar there,' says head. Clearly no stigma, with pupils proudly showing us the learning support unit and talking at length about 'how much it helps'. 'My daughter was in the state sector and seen as a naughty child, but within a week of moving her here I had a phone call saying they'd noticed some issues with her learning and they called in the ed psych to do a report and sure enough she got a diagnosis. They've now put in everything and more that she needs and she's completely taken off – she's a different child,' said one parent.

Kindness is a recurring theme: children are aware of each other and the need to be good citizens. Pupils told us, 'If you have friendship fallouts, you'd never know a few days later – it's a very friendly place.' Pupils celebrate friends' achievements via a kindness bucket outside the head's office and there's a much-coveted True Friend wrist band awarded to pupils who have been particularly kind and helpful to others. Lots of integration between older and younger pupils, with paired reading, a buddy scheme and 'helping hands' which involves year 6s accompanying the same child to each assembly.

These children are not the sort to be bothered by fashions and fads; there's a charming innocence about them; the school feels something of a sanctuary in our fast paced world. 'We want the children to feel comfortable in their own skin,' says head, though there's the usual emphasis on polish that preps are renowned for – shaking hands, eye contact and using cutlery properly, for example. Behaviour good – if a child runs in the corridor, you only have to look at them and they melt – 'the most we need to sort anything is a chat,' says head.

Music and drama form a core part of daily life, with 'wonderful musicals', according to parents – Sister Act a recent triumph. Every child is in a major production every year – usually two year groups per play, plus a whole school carol service. Lots of instruments learned as part of the curriculum (violin in year 3, clarinet in year 4, African drumming in year 5 and 'we write our own song for the carol service in year 6,' said a pupil), plus a variety of musical clubs, groups and orchestra. The art room, in the converted barn, is a treasure chest of textiles, ceramics, oils and watercolours, with some fabulous results adorning the walls. 'You're allowed here in lunchtimes and lots do,' a pupil told us.

Sport involves mainly cricket, netball, hockey and football (for girls and boys), as well as swimming at the local pool. Recent increase in squads, with everyone who wants to getting a chance of playing matches in a team. School does well in competitions, sometimes reaching national level.

Families tend to be classic middle-class professionals and although they've historically been more laid back and less demanding than the Surrey stereotype, one parent told us, 'There is a new breed of parents who are a bit more pushy.' Lots of stay-at-home yummy mummies, but most years have their fair share of dual income families. Most pretty local, with furthest coming from around 12 miles away. Three bus routes (with option to do drop-offs and pick-ups for siblings at other local schools en route) mean parents don't have to drive. PTA is active with lots of social events, all the usuals.

Overall, happy, charming and a little bit old fashioned; academically successful and, above all, unpressurised.

St Hilda's Preparatory School for Girls

High Street, Bushey, Watford, Hertfordshire WD23 3DA

Ages 2–11 **Pupils** 185

Fees: £12,012 – £12,843 pa

020 8950 1751
www.sthildasbushey.com/

Headmistress: Since 2015, Sarah Jane Styles, previously head of Francis Holland (Sloane Square) Junior School. BA, QTS in theology and MA in philosophy of education. Has also been director of studies at Wheathampstead House (now St Albans High School Prep).

Seen by pupils as 'fun,' 'creative' and 'excitable,' she certainly has vivacity and sparkle. 'She has a very clear vision of the direction she wants the school to go in,' add parents, who describe her as 'focused,' 'dynamic' and 'straight talking.' 'She's not your cuddly, nurturing head who all the kids go running up to hug, but nor is she at the other end of the scale of being all businesslike and authoratitive – I'd say she's somewhere in between,' said one. Does guided reading with younger pupils and teaches mindfulness and English to older ones. 'It's important to keep your hand in,' she says. Has plans to introduce philosophy lessons, having done so successfully in her last two schools.

Lives in St Albans and enjoys cycling and walking. Was a member of the royal navy and now a member of the royal naval reserve at weekends and in school holidays.

Entrance: Up to half of the 20 reception places are filled from the school's co-ed Bluebird nursery. But there's no automatic entry, with both Bluebird pupils and potential newcomers all assessed to ensure good fit (sociable, keen to learn etc). Occasional places further up the school, with girls joining from a mix of local state and private schools as parents are increasingly drawn to the academic outcomes of St Hilda's, along with the small, nurturing, family feel.

Exit: Despite its membership of the Aldenham Foundation, this school is completely independent and does not act as a feeder to any particular school, with girls leaving at 11 to an enviable range of top-notch local independent and selective maintained schools including North London Collegiate, St Albans High, Haberdashers', St Margaret's, St Helen's and Royal Masonic. Multiple offers and several scholarships across the arts and academically are the norm most years. Boys leave the Bluebird at 4 for nearby schools including Northwood Prep and St John's.

Remarks: Founded in 1918, moved a few years later to current location in Bushey High Street in an unassuming Victorian house (originally the home of artist Hubert von Herkomer), which has since had a number of more modern add-ons crammed into the site. The result is a compact, urban feel, more akin to a London school than a leafy suburban prep. But boy, does it use every inch of its grounds, with pupils in waterproof onesies climbing trees and scanning the woodland for acorns, pinecones and suchlike in the 'outdoor classroom' when we visited, while den building areas for older girls are in full use most break times. Other outdoor highlights include hard and grass play areas, adventure playground paid for by the PTA coffers, and willow den 'where younger ones can go at playtime if they're feeling overwhelmed or shy' – also used for guided reading in the summer.

The whole scene is testament to the essence of the school – a stimulating, energised place with a real family feel (helped by maximum class sizes of 20 and one form entry). Girls are studious and mature – not a hint of precociousness – but they also have a glint in their eye, are hardy and have plenty to say for themselves. 'You see every girl's individual character flourish here rather than them turning into some homogenised prep school mould,' one parent told us. 'You'll be hard pushed to find a girl that doesn't run in happily through the gates in the morning,' said another.

As for the buildings, don't be fooled by the view from the street. Although nobody could argue the school is large, it is something of a Tardis, with a labyrinth of well-equipped classrooms. The hard-working hall doubles up as a dining room (head chef knows all the girls by name, plus their dietary requirements, and delivers crowd-pleasing lunches every day) and there's also Whitby Hall, an 80s construction which houses a well-equipped gymnasium. More surprises lie behind the façade of the swimming pool building – recently refurbished – which somehow hides a good sized, indoor heated pool and spacious and pristine changing areas. The library and science room (you can't really call it a lab – not a Bunsen burner, microscope or test tube in sight) and music rooms are spacious enough, if not a little bland (but next on the list for refurb), and the classrooms have small windows, many of which look straight out onto hedges, but they are cheery and inspiring, full of examples of girls' work. There's also an art room and IT suite.

St Hilda's punches well above its weight when it comes to academics, ably competing with its neighbouring hothouses. 'The girls have such fun that they don't even know they are learning half the time,' said one parent. Certainly not a yawn or glazed look in sight when we visited, although inevitably the 11+ preparation class wasn't quite as animated as others. Girls encouraged to learn how to fail 'because out of failure you learn,' says head, one of whose (many) favoured acronyms is GRIT (Get Really Into Trying); girls were certainly unfazed in giving us examples of work they'd done that hadn't worked out as planned. Light homework is set from nursery; 10-15 minutes a night from year 3, rising to an hour in year 6. The after-school homework club, supervised by teaching staff, can help ease the pressure at home. School doesn't believe in setting pupils, believing it's important to allow for a child's different capabilities within a subject (although some differentiation for some maths projects for older years).

Specialist teachers for Spanish, French, swimming, forest school, PE and music from nursery; science from reception; and English, maths and humanities from year 4. All teachers know the girls 'inside out' say parents. 'This was the thing that really won us over when looking at local schools – the pastoral care that stems from this,' said one parent. Others point to the teachers' 'approachability' and 'open door policy for parents,' while girls also have access to a part-time chaplain (from Aldenham School) and their housemistress, plus younger ones get a buddy from an older year.

The school's size also means that SEN (head prefers 'ACE' – accelerated education – 'because we focus on stretching, challenging and supporting those at the top end as much as those with extra challenges') usually mainstreamed into the classroom. Plus a range of friendly-sounding 'clubs' for areas such as spelling and language enrichment allow pupils who need it to receive extra help without feeling marginalised. Recent scholarships (from all-rounder and academic to sport, music and art) are the proof in the pudding that good things can come in small packages.

This is the kind of school where, on snow days, children pile outside rather than kowtowing to health and safety, which parents feel is an accurate reflection of the school's home-like culture. In its quest to produce all-rounders, girls are encouraged to do at least one extracurricular club (most do more), with quirkier examples including water polo, pilates, debating, food club and yoga.

Sport is wide-ranging – netball and athletics (girls represent the borough, and sometimes nationally, in the latter) are flagship sports, with supporting roles from rounders, lacrosse, tennis, hockey, gymnastics, ballet and dance, and year-round weekly swimming for all from nursery up. Facilities include two hard courts and, of course, the pool, with sports fixtures requiring more space now taking place at Aldenham School, 10 minutes away. These boast a 400m running track, sports hall and long-jump pit. More competitive fixtures than previously and the provision of Aldenham's minibuses has made this previously prohibitively expensive exercise feasible, resulting in a more sporty outlook.

Art produces some wonderful results, on display throughout the school. Music goes from strength to strength, with all year 3s learning violin (let's hope the teacher has a good supply of paracetamol) and 60 per cent of the upper school learn an individual instrument across the range of strings, wind and piano. Orchestra, choir, string groups and ensembles. No whole school production, but plenty of nativity productions, music recitals and plays, with year 5/6 performances taking place at Aldenham, with recent examples including Daisy Pulls It Off and Joseph. English Speaking Board available for years 3-5. Bin Bag Assembly an annual highlight for year 6s, who each design an outfit out of rubbish bags then turn the lot into a fashion show. Day trips in abundance – year 6s were off to Houses of Parliament just after our visit – and residentials include bushcraft camping trip, Swanage, Cornwall and France.

Not a strict school – think values, not rules; 'We do it like this' posters, not 'Do not do this' ones; but high expectations around uniform, manners, not distracting others in class etc. Some friendship issues – several girls told us about experiences of 'feeling left out' or someone 'being mean to me' and tried to go into great depth about the detail – but head says they work hard to unpick the triggers 'as no child is naturally mean' and they work with families where necessary.

Most parents are from the hard-working middle class, many stretching themselves for their daughters' education. Lots of first time buyers and a variety of ethnicities, reflecting the local area, although some come from further afield – stretching as far as Kenton, Wembley, St Albans and Chorleywood.

Busy families benefit from the Bluebird nursery which offers wrap-around care 50 weeks a year. Parents of nursery age children can select term time, state school or St Hilda's school terms to fit in with their situations and deliver flexible childcare. This ethos also spreads up the school with breakfast club (from 7.30am), free early drop off (from 8am) and late pick-up, including tea (up to 6.30pm).

Not a school for parents seeking to be wowed by state-of-the-art facilities and the acres of fields that many preps boast, but expect to be seriously impressed if you're looking for a small, caring, family-like atmosphere where girls' strengths are played to and the girls' capabilities – academic and otherwise – can and do shine. As one parent puts it, 'The school is small, agile and focused on outcomes which they achieve by fitting the school around the individual girls, not the other way round.'

St Hugh's School, Oxfordshire

Carswell Manor, Faringdon, Oxfordshire SN7 8PT

Ages 3–13 Pupils 350 Boarders 15 weekly, 105 flexi (from 7 years)
C of E

Fees: Day £11,655– £20,085; Weekly boarding + £3,930 pa

01367 870700
www.st-hughs.co.uk

Headmaster: Since 2006, Andrew Nott BA (early 50s). Son of a bishop, educated at The Beacon Prep and King's, Taunton. Studied history at the University of Wales, PGCE Westminster College, Oxford. Worked for the Church Commissioners where he met his wife, Sarah. First teaching post at St Andrew's School, Eastbourne, rose to deputy head. Thence to Davenies for his first headship prior to St Hugh's. Parents describe him as 'amazing' (adjective also frequently applied to Sarah) on a personal level; one or two said they found him a little shy on more public occasions.

Mr Nott is proud of his scholars' achievements but he is also a true champion of the strugglers and late bloomers who are inevitably part of the cohort of a non-selective school. He told us that he had thoroughly enjoyed his time at prep and it is this 'carefree' existence that he wants children at St Hugh's to experience. He loves sport, especially cricket (he is a member of MCC and had a bookcase dedicated to copies of Wisden) and is determined that all the children at St Hugh's get a match, including the E and F teams. He vividly remembers 'the boys who weren't in the A team picking daisies on the boundary' during his prep school cricket matches, and though St Hugh's may be a traditional school in many ways, this is one bit of history Mr Nott does not want to repeat. His mantra is 'excellence and inclusion' and he's also a big champion of kindness, a 'hugely important virtue' that he believes is undervalued these days.

School has acquired five acres of adjoining land for additional games fields, but although the roll is full there are no plans to increase numbers of pupils significantly. Mr Nott says, 'We could be a lot bigger but I want to keep the character of the school, to know every child.' Sounds pretty definite to us but a few parents expressed worries about the school getting bigger. Development on this beautiful rural site is no doubt a planning nightmare, but the newish Cannon Building – named like other parts of the school after a former head – is a superb facility housing science, art and DT, and there's the new Dovecot library. The heads of these departments worked with architects to design their ideal rooms and are still purring contentedly.

Mr Nott and his wife Sarah have five children; four attended St Hugh's and the youngest is still there. Sarah is responsible, among many other things, for the tastefully low key marketing and excellent newsletter. The Notts live just over the lane from school; it's not much of a boundary but just far enough to allow time to switch off and enable the head to enjoy planning the family's next trip abroad and practising creative cookery. Though usually pretty competent, he admits to a recent disaster courtesy of Heston Blumenthal (who doesn't?). He's also fascinated by the academic side of leadership. Favourite childhood reads? Tintin and the Willard Price series of adventure stories.

Retiring in July 2019. His successor will be James Thompson BA QTS, currently head of Royal Russell Junior School. Previously at Ardingly College Prep School and before that at Kingswood Prep in Bath. Dream was to be a professional sportsman, but opted for teacher training (with PE specialisation) after coaching at own prep in Kent and loving it. If he needs a second opinion, family is riddled with teachers, while Viv, his wife, is head of a Notting Hill nursery school. Two daughters no doubt also provide feedback as required.

Mr Thompson remains big on sport (cricket, hockey, golf, skiing), even writing anon column on umpiring for The Telegraph (if you need an insider's slant on the shoulder height rule in lacrosse, he's your man). He's 'very kind, prefers being in PE kit, hates suits and wears pink trousers and odd socks,' say current pupils.

Entrance: Non-selective, non-competitive, it's first come, first served. Mr Nott likes to meet parents as well as children. Prospective pupils spend a day; those entering year 3 or above have assessments in English and maths. Main entry is into reception (up to 26 places), year 3 (up to six places), year 5 (up to eight places). Nursery takes up to 25 a year.

Exit: To schools all over home counties; most popular destinations: Abingdon, Headington, St Helen's & St Katharine's, Cheltenham College, Marlborough, St Edward's Oxford.

Over 95 per cent of girls stay on until age 13; apparently this is very popular with parents – perhaps because their girls stay children for that little bit longer.

Remarks: We arrived on a perfect English summer's day and Carswell Manor, which looks like a bijou country house hotel, seemed to glow with the golden warmth of Cotswold stone. On closer inspection much of façade is pebbledashed but somehow still pretty classy. The Manor was once home to the Niven family and it seems fitting that David Niven, the quintessential English gentleman, was born here – the old place even gets a mention in his autobiography. St Hugh's is without doubt the tidiest school we've ever visited and it's not just the buildings and grounds that are polished and groomed: the teachers too were quite remarkably elegant – not a baggy cardigan or tatty sandal in sight.

Founded 1906 in Chislehurst with three pupils and co-ed since 1977, St Hugh's is now very much a family school – nursery was established in response to parent demand and the minute it opened was 'immediately full with younger siblings.' Mothers walk their dogs in the grounds after morning drop off. Indeed dogs are a bit of a feature: they kept trotting by or popping out from under tables during our visit – all glossy coated and impeccably behaved, of course. Though we saw no ponies we hear that they also loom large here – jodhpurs (very much not pyjamas) are what the busy St Hugh's mother wears first thing in the morning.

Small classes (average 13), spacious modern facilities and glorious surroundings are enough to inspire any child to reach their full potential, and while not all will be scholars and high flyers, everyone is encouraged to find their talent. Much is expected of these children and sometimes Mr Nott's role is to manage expectations; by their second or third child old hands know they can relax and put their trust in the school. Parents we spoke to felt that Mr Nott's advice about senior schools was excellent and absolutely right for their child; the broad spectrum of schools St Hugh's sends to bears this out.

Maths and English set from year 3, French from year 6; rest of subjects taught in mixed ability groups but this can and does vary from year to year according to cohort. French and Latin for all, optional extracurricular Spanish and Mandarin. Greek for scholars. Middle school pupils (years 3 and 4) have their own teaching block and activities such as drama, choir, sports day etc – a nice way to let the youngest take centre stage. Low turnover of staff apart from gappies (usually old boys and girls) who stay for a year. In lessons we observed pupils were quiet, engaged, working hard individually and in pairs. Small class sizes mean teacher can tailor tasks according to ability; they also make it hard to mess around at the back (not that there seemed to be any such tendency). Parents describe SEN support as 'brilliant'; the head of the service told us that the aim is for it to be 'flexible and fluid', to give pupils a boost when needed and then 'launch them back, even if they need to be picked up again later.' Support is either individual or in booster groups and is not charged as an extra. Pastoral care also came in for high praise – merest whiff of bullying is dealt with at lightning speed.

A school tradition and one of the highlights of year 8 is a week's post-exam adventure trip to Wales, during which Mr Nott gives the children their CE results over fish and chips on the beach. Once back in Oxfordshire as part of an extensive leavers' programme, pupils are initiated into important life skills such as how to tie a bow tie, polish shoes and iron shirts; they also create and stage a fashion show for a local children's charity.

Excellent sporting facilities both inside and out (new swimming pool complex under construction) host sport for all, every day. All main ones plus squash, basketball, tennis and introduction to lacrosse. Head confirms that every child gets to represent the school in matches. Notable recent success in riding, tennis (and real tennis) and cross-country. Large number of sports scholarships awarded to St Hugh's pupils every year. Music and drama are also inclusive with enough plays, choirs, bands and ensembles to accommodate the full range of abilities and a new music block. Outdoor production of A Midsummer Night's Dream staged around atmospheric ivy clad 'temple' in the grounds. St Hugh's seems to produce thinkers and listeners (as opposed to shouters) and recognition for this comes in the form of a clutch of top awards for debating and public speaking. Art and DT thriving in their new building – art room boasts a large walk-in kiln, ready to receive the most ambitious ceramic creations and electric windows that can be controlled to provide optimum natural light conditions.

Pre-prep is housed in the old stable block with classrooms round a flexible central space that can be divided up and used for small group work. Rooms are carefully decorated with colourful posters and children's work and, as in the main school, the atmosphere seemed to be one of gently restrained exuberance. Or so we thought until we came across a monsieur from the big school delighting the pre-prep pupils with his all-singing and dancing weekly French lesson. Literacy taught via Read Write Inc phonics programme and for this children are grouped by their stage of development, not age. Official forest school: pupils from nursery to year 6 get to do lots of messy learning in the woods (last two years have bushcraft). As one member of staff remarked, 'Some children come to life outside.' Parents promised us that pupils really are allowed to get muddy.

Youngest (age 3 upwards) start in The Cottage nursery, a charming house that originally belonged to the groundsman (he is happily accommodated elsewhere). On our visit we saw determined excavation in the large sandpit that is, fortunately, six feet deep. Children sign in for their sessions on the interactive whiteboard and there is an ICT suite upstairs along with a rest room for pupils who still need a nap. Same phonics programme as pre-prep used to introduce letter sounds etc. Specialist teaching for music, dance, ICT. Introduction to French is via croissants and chocolat chaud.

Flexi and weekly boarding – parents pre-select boarding options at the start of term. Those wanting a full week get priority, those who want a couple of days are most likely to get them if they are consecutive. As a rule can't do sleepover style occasional boarding but will work something out in an emergency. Boarding is very often 'children driven', it's the parents who need persuading. Comfortable, characterful dorms up in the eaves (the boarding house has recently been refurbished), all very civilised – common room with original John Piper on wall (sigh). Matrons inspect every morning to ensure that boarders live up to the St Hugh's standard of tidiness. Day pupils can stay until 7.30pm for prep and supper (no extra charge) and about a third do. No Saturday school. Wednesday evenings are reserved for 'fun' things and there's no prep. Parents pre-select home time but emergencies and late changes accommodated. Sensible uniform and termly bill low on the dreaded 'extras'. Fees include all trips (including trips abroad) and SEN support. Means-tested bursaries of up to full fees available.

So, what's the demographic? Put on your deerstalker and consider these clues: nearly all the pupils are children of privately educated parents; a school bus scheme was discontinued after a couple of terms because no one used it (private lift sharing arrangements more popular); mussels are a favourite on the scrumptious lunch menu. So far, so county, but though the social profile be small, parents say it's neither snobbish nor exclusive and the children we met were down to earth, funny, normal kids.

St Hugh's is seemingly a school with nothing to prove. It doesn't advertise and prospective parents are not bombarded with glossy anythings. For a flavour of the place, ask to see a copy of the beautifully produced half-termly magazine, St Hugh's News. Such understatement, coupled with fees that are higher than local average (but are all-inclusive and considered 'good value' by the parents we spoke to), might seem counter intuitive in an area that is not under served with preps, but St Hugh's is always full, courtesy of the low tech marketing marvel money can't buy: word of mouth. Happy parents, happy children, happy dogs – what could be better?

St James Senior Boys' School

Linked with St James Senior Girls' School, St James Preparatory School

Church Road, Ashford, Surrey TW15 3DZ

Ages 11–18 **Pupils** 417 **Sixth form** 62

Fees: £18,930 pa

01784 266930
www.stjamesschools.co.uk/seniorboys

Headmaster: Since 2013, David Brazier BA MSc PGCE. Studied English and American literature at the University of Kent; MSc from Reading University. Previously head of Long Close School, Slough, where application numbers tripled during his six-year reign (and which some boys left to follow him to St James). Prior to this, he was head of English and drama at Crosfields School in Reading and assistant headmaster at Davenies in Beaconsfield, Bucks.

Chatty and amiable, he makes no secret of his clear intention to advance the school dramatically, particularly academically. 'The previous head was Margaret Thatcher's speechwriter, so he wasn't an educator, whereas my background is in school improvement,' he says. So far, so good – applications for year 7 doubled within his first three years and there is a waiting list for the first time in the school's history.

He is the first head with no connection with School of Economic Science (SES), the philosophy that the school was founded on – although he insists he is spiritual. What he's done, agree parents and staff, is take the founding principles and 'sharpen them up for the modern world.' 'His arrival felt a breath of fresh air,' said one parent. 'He's progressive and outward looking, but has kept everything that's important about the school.'

A hands-on head who knows every boy by name, he teaches philosophy to year 9s, including a course he has written on 'Love, relationships and sexuality,' and drama periodically across all year groups. 'You get the feeling he's a teacher at heart,' said a parent. Has an abiding love of the performing arts (especially Shakespeare) and he has written three plays that have been performed in schools. Having played for Berkshire Schools and Hurst in the Thames Valley League, he is also passionate about cricket and is a qualified coach, which the boys benefit from. Wife, Lizzie, is a leadership and management consultant; two grown-up children, one a maths teacher.

Academic matters: Despite the selective entrance criteria, academic promise has never been the be-all-and-end-all here, with the school valuing boy's strengths, wherever they may lie. All teaching is underpinned by a philosophical and spiritual ethos that means boys are encouraged to focus constantly on wholeness ('not being stressed and managing your energies well,' explains the head) and harmony ('ensuring you get on with others and are at one with your environment'). In practice, this involves a big push on mindfulness (which boys are taught from year 7), meditation and quiet time, which is a major feature at the start and end of every day.

In 2018, 36 per cent A*-A/9-7 grades at GCSE. At A level, 38 per cent A*/A grades (76 per cent A*-B). Traditional range of subjects on offer at both levels, with the addition of business studies BTec for sixth formers. Allows pupils to specialise early, following their individual bents. Spanish, German and French introduced from year 7 and everyone takes one of these modern languages for GCSE. Unusually (uniquely, believes the school), Sanskrit – the Indo-Germanic language pre-dating even Greek and Latin – is introduced to year 7s (those coming up from the junior school have already learned some) and continues for those who can manage it until year 9, becoming an option thereafter. 'Sanskrit used to be seen as the language to do if you wanted to be spiritually enlightened,' explains the head. 'But we've taken the mystical mumbo jumbo out of it, with a university-based teacher coming in to teach it.' Heartening to see Greek and Latin as relatively popular GCSE options, though few continue classical or any other language to A level. Year 7s are set in maths and Sanskrit; year 8s in maths, French, Latin and Sanskrit; and by year 9, boys can expect to be in one of four sets in these subjects, the weakest of which has around 10 pupils. Homework in abundance (one-and-a-half hours a night in year 7, up to four hours a night in sixth form) and if it's not up to scratch, boys can expect a detention.

No talking down to pupils whatsoever during our visit, although some parents told us that while there are plenty of stars among the staff, a handful are old-school 'and not so well-liked'. Help instantly and easily available, with the option to email teachers when on study leave, or come in for support. They respond readily to parental emails too. The school is aiming for teachers newly employed under current headship to have a masters or PhD, and all now use a rigorous monitoring system to ensure all boys are on track, as well as undergoing weekly teacher training themselves.

SEN (which includes the usual remit of dyslexia, ADHD, autistic spectrum etc) pupils have historically been so numerous and well-supported here that the school started to get a reputation as being a special needs school – something the head is keen to change. 'When I joined, we had a third SEN, now it's a quarter, with far fewer EHC plans,' he says. It's not that he's any less dedicated to the school's 'lovely bespoke SEN department, with the caring ladies that run it,' he says. 'But most of the extra assistance from the SEN department now happens in the classroom itself, embedded into the lessons. That makes us much more mainstream.' Parents say it works well.

All boys work towards a St James Baccalaureate, recognising the breadth of education as well as academic success.

Games, options, the arts: Hearing some of the younger boys sing in the chapel stopped us in our tracks. Singing is, in fact, so established here that when we asked some of the boys if they enjoyed it, they looked confused – as if we'd asked them if they enjoy getting dressed. In the old days, it was strictly classical, but nowadays boys are just as likely to sing gospel or pop – a welcome change, they say. There are the usual school choirs, orchestras, ensembles and bands and around a fifth of boys learn an instrument with a peripatetic teacher. Electric guitar and drums particularly popular, although head is pushing for less gender stereotyping (which basically means more strings). Opportunities to perform publicly, including the much talked about annual concert in Hammersmith Town Hall.

Drama mainly takes place in the studio called The Empty Space after Peter Brooke gave his support for it (a deliberately minimalistic rendering of 'creative space'), although we also saw boys performing Shakespeare (well) in the roomy school reception area on our arrival – a joy to watch. Performance is important, as is speech itself. 'If you have not mastered speech by the time you leave here, then those who have will master you,' is a maxim quoted at the boys. 'Makes them talk and engage in conversations,' say parents. Serious annual productions in collaboration with the girls' school in Olympia, with everyone making light of the considerable amount of inter-school ferrying this involves.

Art facilities decent enough, with two roomy, well-lit studios, although we'd like to have seen more examples of pupil work around the school. DT facilities impressive, shiny and well-equipped with new workshop and computer lab – an increasingly popular GSCE option and now also offered at A level.

Sport is pushed hard, with facilities including lake, tennis courts, rugby pitches, cricket squares, Astro and football pitches – practically all in full use on the sun-drenched day we visited. Kept beautifully (not a weed in sight), these form a striking backdrop to the main school building and can be seen from most classrooms. Inside sports facilities less notable though a sports hall is under development. Rugby, hockey, cricket and cross-country are the big sports here, with football on the up, although not quickly enough for some boys we spoke to. Plenty of minor sports and opportunities too – everything from martial arts to kayaking or open swimming in the school lake and climbing (particularly popular). Boys regularly go on to get sports scholarships. But some feel there's still too much emphasis on rugby; 'If you don't like rugby, where do you go?' said one, as if he hoped we might actually have an answer.

Wednesday afternoons are dedicated to clubs run by a mixture of staff and sixth formers – magic club, comic club and military history clubs among the less predictable. 'Boys suggest a club and we make it happen,' says the head; pupils concur. Then there's the before and after-school programme of activities – everything from sports clubs to philosophy club. Around a quarter takes up the cadet force; a popular DofE scheme attracts others. Around three-quarters of the school takes up one or other of these outdoor options. Some charitable and social activity, but less than we'd expected.

Plenty of leadership and team-building days. In year 8, they have a service day in which they assist the groundsmen with practical tasks like fence-building and gardening, while in year 9, a Stepping into Manhood formal dinner allows the boys and their fathers to experience formal dining with an inspirational after-dinner speaker. A trip to Lucca, Italy, presents a scenic opportunity to year 10s and there are lots of other school trips besides. 'My exchange programme in Montpellier was one of the best experiences of my life,' one boy told us. On offer to all boys are twice-yearly lectures at the RSA given by everyone from eminent physicians to ambassadors. The Ficino Society is a programme of academic talks designed to foster and care for potential Oxbridge candidates, which adds to the intellectual life of the school and thus meets its requirement to nurture the gifted and talented.

Background and atmosphere: The school was founded in the 1970s within the bosom of SES, which itself was founded in 1937 as a means of exploring through the study of the world's great religions and philosophies what it is to be fully human in a spiritual way and, in so doing, what goes to make a spiritually healthy and prosperous community. But whilst the SES flame burned high back then, it has attracted increasing controversy over the decades, with some even calling it a 'cult'. Particularly since the current head's appointment, the school has distanced itself from the movement, now describing itself as 'a philosophically inspired school whose roots are in the SES, but which has grown and evolved, with the philosophy and ethos made available to all.'

Originally based in Twickenham, the school moved west in 2010, now occupying a truly beautiful site in the West London Lake District, in stunning buildings erected by The Society of Ancient Britons in 1857 to house the Welsh Girls' School. They have been well renovated to make a spacious and light environment, although facilities are not quite as glossy as at some neighbouring schools.

Pastoral care, well-being and discipline: The boys' form tutors are at the heart of pastoral care. 'I've never experienced such understanding and support from a teacher,' said one parent, while a boy told us, 'I had some issues at home and my teacher really helped.' Buddying system between sixth formers and year 7s popular and a school counsellor was about to be employed on a part-time basis when we visited. 'It's ok to admit vulnerability here,' said one pupil.

Misbehaviour and anti-social behaviour not tolerated and a yellow and red card system culminating in after-school detentions, along with high presence of staff including head in corridors between lessons and in breaks, ensures it stays that way. Strict on uniform, with staff regularly uttering the words 'Shine your shoes' on the gate in the mornings, whereby boys are sent to the dedicated shoe-shining room (yes, really). Bullying a bit of a problem in the past, but current head claims to have cut it by half, having 'moved a few pupils on' early in his role and introduced new, stricter-than-ever policies around it. Drugs a non-issue to date.

Lots of leadership opportunities, thanks to the prefect system, class representation on the school council and the sixth-form run clubs, among others. 'Manhood', 'character' and 'character-building' are terms much in evidence here. 'Gets teenage boys, all noise and go and fast paced, to meditate in silence,' said one parent. School food is vegetarian (those SES foundations again) and we enjoyed a mean vegetable lasagne and salad. Some boys love it; others are less keen.

Pupils and parents: All but one pupil came west when the school moved, and the catchment area still stretches far to the east, with school run buses helping to keep it that way. The rest use public transport, with three-quarters arriving by train (the station is opposite the school) or public buses, which stop right outside. Hardly anyone dropped off by car. Ethnic and social mix is typical of the area – predominantly white, with some Asian, African-Caribbean and Chinese, among others. A mixture of different faiths, notably those (Hinduism, Buddhism) on which the SES drew heavily. SES a non-issue among parents these days, though, with only a couple of members left. Parents range from the super-rich to those working all hours in modest jobs to get their boys in. Lively and sociable PTA, including annual ball, quiz nights etc. 'They want the parents to be part of the school,' said a parent.

Boys are lively, confident and sparky, but well-mannered and disciplined when they need to be, with lots of heads down in the classes we observed. No talking over each other, with listening skills clearly deep-rooted. 'Boys here are kind, generous and determined – it's the reason I chose the school,' said one parent. 'My son has blossomed. No more hunched shoulders. He walks square,' said another. There is, say boys, 'a spirit of looking out for each other – it's very supportive, almost like a big family.' Not for the kind of child who thinks they can do it all on their own, this is a school for those who are willing to ask for help.

Entrance: Around 160 applicants for 70 places in year 7. Selection on the basis of entrance tests in English, maths and verbal reasoning plus interview with the head. In fact, the interview can outweigh the entrance test if it is felt the boy has 'character' or other gifts which the school feels would benefit from its distinctive educational approach. 'We're looking for a renaissance man vibe – boys who like singing, sport, leading, speaking confidently and valuing what others say too,' says the head. Thirteen plus entry by similar tests in year 7. Pre-tests available at both stages (in year 5 and year 7) for those prepared to commit to a place here.

Entry into the sixth form requires a minimum of grade 6s at GCSE plus interview with the head of sixth form and headmaster. This also applies to boys already in the school, and some are encouraged to look elsewhere or helped into more vocational areas if the school feels that A levels are not appropriate.

Exit: Between a third and a half leaves after GCSEs for a clutch of comfortable reasons – access to the IB, wanting more practical courses, or just having been there since age 4. Majority who leave go on to colleges or co-ed school sixth forms. Occasional sixth form Oxbridge or medical places; otherwise to a range of courses from acting to actuarial science.

Money matters: Not a rich school, with lower-than-average fees. But whilst the pot for scholarships and bursaries has historically been correspondingly small, it is growing, with five academic and sports scholarships in the year we visited. School aims to support with means-tested bursaries those who could otherwise not come or who have financial problems once accepted.

Remarks: Although not as distinctive and different as it was in the SES-focused days of old, this relatively small school is still set apart from the norm, with spiritual principles influencing every aspect of curricular and extracurricular life. That's not to say it isn't academic – the current head makes sure of it – but it's about helping boys grow into the best adult men they can be, both spiritually and intellectually. Two pieces of advice for parents – first, acquaint yourself thoroughly with the ethos and second, take note that the head, who has brought about sweeping changes, sees the school as being very much on a journey. 'Come back in a few years and I think you'll find something really magical,' he told us. We think he could be right.

St John's Beaumont School

Priest Hill, Old Windsor, Berkshire SL4 2JN

Ages 3–13 **Pupils** 290 **Boarders** 25 full, 25 weekly/flexi (from 7 years) RC

Fees: Day £7,353 – £18,733; Boarding + £3,893 – £9,995 pa

01784 432428
www.sjb.community

Headmaster: Since 2006, Mr Giles Delaney (40s). Educated at Hereford Cathedral School, studied music and psychology at Cardiff (instruments are the not-at-all-easy French horn and organ). PGCE at Cambridge and thence to St John's Beaumont. Became deputy head three years later before being catapulted at a very young age to headship on sudden death of his predecessor. He seems so at one with the school, staff and boys that we wonder if it was always his plan to stay at the old place for so long; his answer is a wry smile.

St John's Beaumont, like other RC schools, has a reputation for being pretty disciplined, although Mr Delaney is anything but a martinet. He sees no reason why boys can't be expected to give their very best in a caring and nurturing environment. He's extremely interested in research on how boys learn, especially the importance of pupils' relations with staff: 'boys don't learn subjects, they learn teachers.' In a boys' school 'everyone will have a go at orchestra, choir, dance. They will give everything a shot and smile if it doesn't work.' Certainly when it comes to the importance of context, relating academic subjects to the real world, it seems that Jesuit schools were there long before the educationalists.

Mr Delaney, who looks a bit like a young Colin Firth, is modest and charming. He told us that he had taught 'most stuff', still teaches year 5 ('getting them ready for pre-tests surreptitiously') and is looking forward to a new challenge: introducing the pre-prep boys to music. We weren't taken in by his self-deprecating answers. Boys and parents say his teaching is 'absolutely brilliant', 'fantastic', 'the best'. Loves preparing assemblies and shares a keen interest in medieval history with his wife, Katie, who teaches in a school in north London. He is currently studying for an MSc in education at Oxford. They have four daughters – must be something of an antidote to life at SJB. And if he hadn't gone into teaching? A conductor, he thinks, or a graphic designer, 'something not in an office.' Favourite book? Solzhenitsyn's One day in the life of Ivan Denisovich: 'It's about endurance, valuing the smallest things.'

Entrance: There's a waiting list so plan ahead. Most boys enter at age 4 after attending a taster session (no formal entry test) to assess suitability – looking for boys who will 'thrive' here and 'play an active and positive part' in school life. Parents and children interviewed by the head. Further small intake at year 3 (dependent on performance in school's own assessment and reference from current head). Priority given to practising Roman Catholic families, siblings and applicants with connections to St John's or a Jesuit education

Exit: To all the big beasts and all the more impressive given non-selective intake: Eton, Harrow, Tonbridge, Winchester, Wellington, Charterhouse, Ampleforth, Downside, Stonyhurst, Hampton. Notable record of academic, sport and all-rounder scholarships.

Remarks: St John's Beaumont sits in red-brick gothic grandeur on a hill overlooking Old Windsor, surrounded by 70 acres of grounds (which now contain an outdoor theatre in the wood) and playing fields next door to Windsor Great Park. Designed by John Francis Bentley (also responsible for Westminster Cathedral) and opened in 1888, it was the first purpose-built prep school in England. Tucked behind the Victorian edifice are recent additions: a fine sports centre with vertigo-inducing climbing wall, music, science and art departments, a theatre and the pre-prep block (complete with a new STEM room and the addition of very popular school guinea pigs), all on a rather more human scale. The huge reception hall, hung with portraits of old boys and next door neighbour Her Majesty the Queen, sets a rather formal tone. Classical music playing discreetly in the background only just takes the edge off what could be an intimidating first impression for some prospective parents and their boys.

Our visit started in one of the original high ceilinged classrooms with a year 8 maths lesson. Considering it was nearly the end of term and these boys had done CE (many had won scholarships), their quiet concentration was remarkable. Working in pairs, they applied themselves to bisecting a line so that they would 'impress maths teachers at their next schools'. In accordance with the principles of Jesuit education, they then discussed context, suggesting where this technique could be applied in real life. Maths is a particular strength of SJB and the best take part in national competitions and maths challenges, winning medals at all levels. Three finalists recently gained distinctions in Junior Maths Olympiad. Science very hands-on; boys told us that a highlight was 'setting custard powder on fire' and went on to explain the theory behind the conflagration. Latin from year 6, Greek for scholars.

Having learnt (and swiftly forgotten) how to bisect a line it was off to year 6 history in a slightly less lofty Portakabin. After the maturity of the mathematicians we were relieved to find a sparky class tackling the causes of the First World War. Their presentation skills may have been a work in progress but there was no doubting their enthusiasm and depth of knowledge. Here, context was relating 1914 alliances to the current situation in Afghanistan. Distracting them from the task in hand, we asked what one thing would improve their school. The answer was unanimous: girls! Apparently girls would 'make the place tidier' and 'help with questions'. Dream on, chaps.

Golf, cycling, climbing, sailing, skiing – SJB boys pursue and excel at all kinds of sport, but rugby rules. They regularly field 16 teams and successfully play David to some much bigger Goliaths. Most recently the 1st XV was undefeated in all but one match. Usual parental grumbles that it's not much fun in the lesser teams who don't get any of the specialist coaching. Football gets a proper look in, too. There's an impressive swimming pool (the older boys recently did a diving course) and a climbing wall in addition to all the usual facilities. Proximity to the Thames doesn't always guarantee a commitment to rowing but in this case it does and there are 50 boys in the squad netting a haul of medals in regional and national championships. For years 6, 7 and 8 it's sport every day plus matches on Saturday. It's a long day too: years 4 and 5 finish at 5pm, for older boys it's 6pm or later if they're doing extra activities (wraparound care available for younger boys). One of our guides said he thought parents should know that 'it's quite tiring'. Music, art and drama don't seem to be overshadowed by the sports behemoth; that long day means there's time for both.

Fifty or so boys board (one junior and one senior dorm). Full weekend programme of activities, many chosen by boys on the boarding committee, includes paintballing, tank driving and trips to Windsor Castle and the Science Museum. Weekly boarding also an option. Interesting animal themed house system engenders keen rivalry for 'TYE' points (Tiger, Yak and Emu). Junior uniform (navy blue Bermudas until year 6) looks smart but several parents still reeling from eye-watering cost of anything crested, including jumpers and shirts.

Approximately 60 per cent of boys come from RC families but don't imagine this leads to monoculture – a peek into any classroom will dispel doubts on that score. Parents unanimously praised the pastoral care and the way the school welcomed diversity. One who was not Catholic said that religion was 'not an issue' but described the RE curriculum as 'very truly Catholic, up to and including creationism', so SJB unlikely to be destination of choice for Dawkins minor. School's view is that they welcome boys of any faith or none but those who join, 'join a community', and must play their part, including attendance at mass. Admissions process wise to parents who are only interested in the school for its CE results. The scholarship boards provide a record of the school's evolution. Thirty years ago practically all went on to Catholic schools such as Stonyhurst, The Oratory, Ampleforth; today's scholars are just as likely to be bound for Eton, Winchester and Wellington.

Mr Bentley the architect obviously believed in giving boys lots of space and air, hence the wide corridors and high ceilinged classrooms, and the generosity of his design, while unmistakably Victorian, stands up pretty well to the demands of the 21st century. His intimate and beautifully decorated chapel, bearing the scars of wartime bombs, only seats 60, and at Christmas there are several services so that all parents can enjoy the special atmosphere and 'magical music'. Whole school events take place in the somewhat less atmospheric sports hall. Part of the Jesuit educational ethos is that a child should be 'well rounded and worldly wise' and to that end SJB boys go far and wide; not only history and sports trips to France and Italy but also swimming the Midmar Mile in South Africa to raise money for charity. They're also stretched by the school's impressive Magis programme; senior boys have weekly lectures from visiting speakers, parents and members of staff and are also encouraged to present talks themselves. Recent subjects include deafness and language acquisition, Battersea Dogs' Home and space exploration. Lots of fundraising to support a sister school, St Rupert's, in Zimbawe.

Day boys come in from a 10 mile radius (bus service operates from Chiswick and Maidenhead); about 40 per cent of boarders from overseas. Parents a mix of trad Windsor and glossy Middletonshire (or as someone put it, those who have Wentworth membership and those who don't). Their sons are commendably oblivious to such pigeonholing and there's a great sense of camaraderie; boys are proud of their school and its traditions. Mr Delaney describes St John's Beaumont as a community that asks its members, 'What can you give?' It expects the very best but also give boys the confidence to try new things and learn from mistakes. As a parent remarked, 'It can appear prescriptive but the boys don't see it like that, they thrive on structure and clear rules. My son loves going to school.'

St John's School (Leatherhead)

Epsom Road, Leatherhead, Surrey KT22 8SP

Ages 11–18 **Pupils** 803 **Sixth form** 262 **Boarders** 32 weekly, 135 flexi

Fees: Day £19,200 – £24,300; Boarding + £5,130 – £6,405 pa

01372 373000
www.stjohnsleatherhead.co.uk

Head: Since September 2017, Rowena Cole (40s) BSc PGCE MBA. Educated at Exeter University (biology). Drawn to teaching by her own experiences; 'it saved me – I loved all those little bits of school life like DofE and could never imagine myself sitting behind a desk'. Has taught in both the state and private sectors: Howard of Effingham and City of London Freemen's followed by a deputy headship at Guildford High School before taking the reins as head at Dunottar School in Reigate. Parents love the fact that she's a local – 'I really wanted to lead a school in the community I grew up in', she says. Relished the opportunity to take the helm as a female head of a traditional public school.

First job was to do away with the dusty tomes and leather wing back chairs in the head's study ('I didn't want to be that kind of head') and now presides from a serene minimalist oasis of calm in soft, monochrome grey where pupils can feel at ease and the Surrey mums can try to work out which shade of Farrow and Ball paint is on the walls. Parents say she has 'a big job' to do to really make the major changes made by her predecessor (introduction of girls and entry at 11+) work properly. Keen to continue sharpening the focus on academics, although adamant that it won't be at the expense of breadth; 'we want every child to achieve as much as they can but have no plans for the school to become more selective' (thank goodness: the area doesn't need another highly selective school) and says the plan is to continue 'placing equal value on everything and staying genuinely broad in outlook and interest'.

Married to Alistair with whom she has two young children and a menagerie of pets. Lives on school site during term time and enjoys adventure travel when time allows.

Academic matters: Not renowned locally as stiff competition for the top Guildford schools, although parents who may formerly not have bothered looking here for their bright child are starting to think again. Academics 'better than we thought', according to parents and results now coming to bear after a strong push on academics in recent years. League table watchers will still note that St John's sits way below the lofty likes of Guildford High and RGS, but considering its far gentler admissions policy, output is testament to (mostly) strong teaching and belief that academic success goes hand in hand with pastoral care. Is it cool here to work hard these days? 'We're well on the way – there's been a big shift, and it's definitely cool to be involved,' says head.

With a host of new academic societies and external scholarship pages on pupil intranet, the message is certainly out there. School notes that girls' academic work and success helps to pull the boys along, although by the sixth form they are equal. Looking around at A level classes, we wondered whether certain subjects were biased towards one gender; boys currently outnumber girls in A level subjects such as chemistry and DT, for example. School says rather that it reflects the imbalance of the sexes at the top end of the school than any latent gender stereotyping – and was fast to point out the large number of girls taking A level maths. Worth asking the question if gender neutrality is high on your wish list, however. Parents praise staff as top notch role models, not just taking pupils in hand when it comes to curriculum based learning but also in life skills, eg what colour socks or tie to wear with which shoes or suit.

Trad curriculum, with French, Spanish and German all on offer in the languages department, plus Latin and Classical Greek. At GCSE in 2018, 74 per cent graded A*-A/9-7, with top performers English, maths and humanities (particularly RS). Twenty-seven subjects available at A level; all the usual suspects plus classical civilisation, politics, psychology and business. Maths, psychology, economics and English are top choices, with solid results across the board: 47 per cent graded A*/A in 2018 and 84 per cent A*-B. Smatterings of C and D grades noticeable at both A level and GCSE, although not in any particular subject. EPQ taken by over one third of year 12 cohort, with solid results. All take three A levels, along with a core curriculum covering political thought, philosophy and finance ('extremely practical').

All pupils screened on entry to identify any additional needs. Four full time learning support staff work with the 10 per cent of pupils currently on the register who are also catered for by teaching staff (there are no TAs), small group sessions and one-to-one classes where necessary. 'Our job is to remove barriers', they say. The small number of pupils with EAL have flexible, small group provision alongside support from tutors.

Games, options, the arts: All additions to the academic curriculum taken very seriously and highly valued; school places equal value on sport, drama and music to academia. Sport 'riding high', says head (her following comment that they recently 'smashed' Blundell's at rugby confirmed how seriously competition is taken here). Facilities all present and correct, plus a 'very glamourous' new swimming pool set to open in 2019. There are A-D teams in most years so everyone gets a chance to represent the school and there's a high standard of coaching across the board, including ex-All Black rugby player who not only takes a broad range of rugby teams but also the U12 girls' netball team. Moreover, pupils uniformly felt that the standard of coaching was high regardless of the players' level. The usual suspects (rugby, football and cricket for boys and hockey, netball and rounders for girls) are on the roster for lower years and year 10 and up have a range of choices including tennis, athletics, cross country, yoga, pilates and baseball too. Trophies aplenty – in recent years St John's has won the Rosslyn Park National Schools Sevens for rugby and the National Independent Schools League for football as well as multitudinous accolades for county hockey and netball. School also features annually in The Cricketer magazine's list of top 100 cricketing schools.

If sport flies high, in our opinion music soars. We were fortunate enough to be treated to a lunchtime recital on our visit and would rank what we saw as some of the best school music around (a special bravo to the oboe teacher who is clearly outstanding, judging by his pupils' performances). Around one third of pupils learn a peripatetic instrument and several pupils play outside of school with national orchestras and ensembles as well as the many taking place in school. We loved the fact that games kit clad pupils turned up to watch their friends perform along with parents and teachers in exactly the same way they would go to cheer on a sports team. On the pop front, school supports pupils creating their own rock bands. Senior school musical – most recently Legally Blonde – is a highlight, but according to pupils nothing eclipses 'congers', the whole school hymn practice, which is apparently 'the most fun ever'. Drama also well represented with plenty of opportunities for the thespian community to throw themselves into a variety of school productions. More prizes won at the Leatherhead drama festival and several pupils belong to National Youth Theatre.

Good art and DT facilities are housed in a modern block with a reasonably high standard of work on display, although again art seemed to us to be a 'girl' subject (boys we spoke to felt the type of work was more focused on female aptitudes) and DT had a distinctly male flavour.

CCF compulsory (and 'massive' according to pupils) in year 10, and many continue beyond; 'significant' community service and DofE, involving challenging activities and trips. Evening activities, lectures, rehearsals and concerts can all be demanding on pupils' time, although their take on it is 'we're really well rounded'.

Boarding: If we had a pound for every parent who told us St John's offers 'the best of both worlds' we'd (almost) be able to afford the fees. Although not a viable option for those who need full boarding, flexi-boarding flourishes, with nights spent at school increasing as pupils reach GCSE and A level (about 40 weekly boarders at the time of our visit and 'loads' two to three nights a week). Lower school (years 7 and 8) can now board four nights a week and with such delightful accommodation on offer – spacious, colourful modern rooms with characterful period fireplaces, bunks and central sofas (far better than the bedrooms of any 11-year old we know), who wouldn't want to? One enthusiastic year 7 boarder described it as 'just the best'. Senior boarding accommodation has similar, albeit more traditional, appeal with tidy corridors and rooms for up to four in the younger years. Twin or single rooms with small ensuite loos and showers are the privilege of sixth formers and all boarders can grab fruit on the go from the generously laden bowls in the corridors and snacks from the small kitchens. Model is totally flexible and much loved by working parents: 'You can ring in the morning if you need last minute cover; it's great when you have breakfast or dinner meetings in London'.

Background and atmosphere: Imposing building on the outskirts of Leatherhead. Enter through the wrought iron gates (if you're very fortunate you might be directed by the utterly charming grounds staff) and watch the school open up Narnia-like as you walk into reception and gaze out through the floor to ceiling windows onto the main quad. The look of the school reflects its character. It comprises a splendid (immaculate – try as we might we couldn't find any shabby corners) Victorian building with cloisters running around the quad and an imposing panelled dining room used by everyone for all meals (and rumoured to have been a potential set for Hogwarts). Beyond are other newer buildings including the terrific classroom, art and DT block, a new science centre and a very attractive modern new boys' house plus a new boarding house for girls. Plus the stunning modern chapel – one of the loveliest we've seen. Pupils required to attend daily chapel as well as Sunday evening services with their house once every half term, at which parents are also welcome.

Very much a local school with the majority hailing from within a 15 mile radius. Trad environment (head only recently inadvertently overturned an archaic rule that only allowed prefects and staff to walk on the central path in the main quad), providing a safe and wholesome education that's 'genuinely broad in outlook and interest'. Initial impression is of a conservative (big and small c) and somewhat squeaky clean bubble; definitely not for those looking to give their offspring a healthy dose of gritty reality (this is deepest Surrey, after all). But despite this, there's a definite feeling of acceptance for anyone who might not quite fit the typical mould (we met one or two) and sixth formers assured us that they were well equipped to tackle the 'real world' (although we couldn't help but wonder what they'd make of the average digs in a northern university city). Girls now take up 50 per cent of places in year 7, so the culture shift from 'boys' school with girls' is as good as complete, although parents (and, we are told, some boys) said that some still see it as just that (glorification of the 1st XV named as a factor). Barely any trace of former die hards lamenting the loss of Saturday school or arrival in the 21st century, though; we heard nothing but positive remarks about school's metamorphosis and parents we spoke to were looking forward to embracing further developments when they arise; 'we haven't changed the value set,' says head. No changes in the house structure, around which pupils' lives revolve: the day start and ends there, their tutor is to be found there and studying and socialising takes place there.

Pastoral care, well-being and discipline: House system is key to school's pastoral success ('so strong' say parents), with almost every staff member a tutor to a small number of pupils. Loyalty to houses runs deep and pupils will support their house/matron/ prefects to the hilt to an extent not seen in siblings' schools. Now that girls are just part of the furniture, plans in pipeline to forge links between boys' and girls' houses to create brother/ sister relationships for sport and other competitions, which are numerous and include a house pancake race around the quad on Shrove Tuesday. Any bullying (rare) kept in check by house system ('sixth formers step in if we see anything going on,' one told us.) Older year groups mentor the younger, forming genuinely supportive relationships. Fairly strict mobile phone policy – years 7 to 11 have to hand them in at the start of the day. Year 7 and up bring their own laptop for use at school and we are informed that the Wifi is 'absolutely amazing'. Disciplinary issues are, unsurprisingly, 'very limited'. No LGBT+ society but there are openly gay staff members (both sexes) as well as a few pupils, and in the interests of 'walking the talk' a member of staff has been open in assembly with their own experience of depression to encourage pupils to seek help should they need it.

Pupils and parents: Boys still just about outnumber girls but the overall imbalance is not particularly noticeable. Pupils describe school as 'a real community' and note that the integration amongst members of the same houses forges strong ties between year groups. Families are typically well-heeled middle-class professionals ('we're definitely not glitzy or glamourous,' one mum told us) but hold a happy middle ground of being generally more down to earth than parents at many of Surrey's flashier boarding schools – and bit more relaxed than those at the day schools. St John's suits pupils who can cope with a fast paced and busy environment, Saturday sport and Sunday chapel included. Be ready to relinquish weekends away and lie-ins – or if your child has multiple commitments outside school they may not be prepared to sacrifice. Pupils we met were charming but not smooth, well-spoken but not posh. Notably (in the words of a particularly sparky year 7 boy), 'everyone is smiling'.

Entrance: One of the head's questions to self when we met her was 'how do we run admissions to make it a more emotionally intelligent process?' We'll watch with interest to see what changes in the coming years, but for now it's fairly standard. There are 80 places available at 11+, with applicants required to take maths, English, reasoning and an informal interview. No major feeders at this point and plenty from state primaries. At 13+ (year 9 entry), a further 45 places open up and offers are made on the basis of a report from head of current school plus a pre-assessment taken in January of year 6, after which unconditional offers are made, with CE no longer required. Feeder preps include Danes Hill and Felton Fleet.

Entry to sixth form is now selective, with about 30 places available. Applicants sit an assessment and interview in November of year 11, plus report from current school; places are confirmed by GCSE results. 'Co-curricular strengths are taken into account.' At 16, lots of girls come from nearby Manor House, and a few boys and girls wanting a change from local state schools or other independents.

Exit: Over 85 per cent to first choice of university in 2018, with a good handful taking gap years. Most popular recent destinations: Nottingham, Birmingham, Exeter, Durham and Bath. Two or three to art foundation courses. Three to Oxbridge in 2018 and five medics. Degree apprenticeships 'pushed quite hard' but few are attracted to them; parental aspiration is definitely for university. Parents report 'a pretty robust system' in place when it comes to university guidance – in fact sixth formers given so much help with university applications that parents told us they didn't even need to look at at the form. Tutors lead the process and there's a series of lectures plus trips to Reading, Surrey and Portsmouth universities.

Money matters: A little bit pricier than most local day schools. Scholarships available in music, drama, art, design and technology, sport, academic and all-rounder, at 11+, 13+ and sixth form entry, worth 5-10 per cent. Means-tested bursaries and grants available, including up to 100 per cent of fees for children of Anglican clergy, foundationers, reflecting the school's foundation.

Remarks: Safe as houses. A school that recognises the value of tradition (upper case t), family and good manners and genuinely values roundedness as much as academic success.

St Lawrence College

College Road, Ramsgate, Kent CT11 7AE

Ages 3–18 **Pupils** 653 (200 junior, 453 senior) **Sixth form** 131
Boarders 191 full (from 7 years)

Fees: Day £7,695 – £15,999; Boarding £29,985 – £35,835 pa

01843 572931
www.slcuk.com

Principal: Since 2013, Antony Spencer MA (Oxon) ACA (early 40s). Read PPE at Oxford. Previously spent five years as academic deputy head at Clifton College and before that director of studies at Denstone College in Staffordshire. Offered numerous jobs when he left Oxford, including a place on the police graduate scheme, a place at Sandhurst and the civil service fast

S

stream but chose to train as an accountant at Ernst and Young. The draw of teaching was always there, and after seven years in the City he answered an ad for a job at Eastbourne and has never looked back.

Enthusiastic, energetic and very chatty and easy to talk to, he 'lives and breathes the education system'. He has 'added a bit of contemporary oomph and is just what the school needed,' according to one parent, and is looking at new ways of doing things. He says he has arrived at an exciting time when the school is poised for growth, and it has grown by 10 per cent in his first year and is now nearing capacity. He is raising the profile of the school, has upped the marketing locally and internationally and redesigned the website. He feels the 'great strength of the school is its size – the optimum size for a close community', small enough to have strong links between year groups but large enough to be able to afford good facilities.

Well-liked by the children, who say 'he is friendly and makes us feel comfortable, and understands what we are talking about and listens to what we say'. They are particularly pleased that he has moved boarders' Sunday chapel to the evening, which means they can have brunch and a lie-in on Sunday mornings. Married to Suzanne, who he met at Oxford, they have four children at the school. She previously taught history but is now an EAL teacher. They live in a house in the grounds and spend much of the holidays at their house in France.

Head of junior school: Since 2016, Ellen Rowe BA PGCE, previously head of Haddon Dene Prep in Broadstairs. Geography degree from Sheffield; worked for her local authority then for Shelter before turning to teaching. Has taught at state secondary and independent prep schools, including as director of sport at Spring Grove Prep in Wye. Married to Adam; they have twins who are both at St Lawrence.

Academic matters: In 2018, 18 per cent A*/A and 40 per cent A*-B grades at A level. At GCSE 37 per cent A*-A/9-7 grades – not bad for a non-selective school with quite a few EAL pupils, and good value added. As well as the usual subjects, psychology, music and music technology, PE, ICT and theatre studies offered at A level – 24 subjects in all, plus sports BTec and EPQ. AS photography proving very popular. German A level available for native speakers. Pupils do particularly well in history, maths, economics and psychology. Science offered as dual or triple award at GCSE and taught by young and enthusiastic team in old-fashioned but redecorated science labs across the road, complete with small science lecture theatre. Popular science and engineering week and science lecture in conjunction with the Royal Society of Chemistry. Maths and science clinics for anyone who is struggling. Non-examined RS course for all. A number of foreign trips including geographers to Iceland and physicists to CERN.

S

About 10 per cent need some SEN help, one-to-one coaching as well as support alongside lessons and some small group teaching with focus on inclusion to make sure pupils do not feel pigeonholed. Head of department a mainstream teacher who has specialised in SEN plus two part-timers. School has CReSTeD status. About 60 pupils receive some EAL support with a determined focus upon integration; now offers intensive EAL course for lower sixth entry. Lots of support tailored to individual needs, most take English GCSE and a few do ESOL. IELTS offered for university entrance.

Careers centre open every afternoon; careers programmes for years 9 and 11 and sixth form – seminars, lectures and group sessions and one-to-one advice about higher education.

Saturday lessons and afternoon sport from year 9 upwards, with years 7 and 8 doing activities on Saturday mornings. Years 7 and 8 taught separately in Kirby House but by senior school teachers, and can use the other specialist facilities. One lesson a week of thinking and study skills and ICT incorporated into core lessons.

Games, options, the arts: Wide range of sports offered and both boys' and girls' hockey particularly strong. Cliftonville hockey club has its home at St Lawrence and a number of old Lawrentians are in the team. The principal is a keen player and trains with the local side when possible. School brings in additional outside coaches and runs a cricket and netball academy during the winter, and several pupils train with the Kent squad – 'sports coaching is exceptional,' said a parent. Growing sporting reputation is attracting more local families.

No-one made to take part in team sports, but everyone has to do some sort of exercise – the mirrored dance studio is popular with the less sportily inclined. Keen to encourage an ethos of sporting achievement and a healthy lifestyle beyond school. 'They like to keep you fit and active,' said one boy, and many day children stay on to exercise in the evenings. DofE popular and several gain gold each year. CCF compulsory in year 9 and many carry on. Juniors can use the sports centre and theatre, indoor heated pool, Astroturf and games pitches and have plenty of sport and fixtures against other local schools.

Music part of the curriculum for years 7 and 8 and also offered at GCSE and A level. A number of bands and ensembles including rock, jazz, samba and concert band as well as various sixth form bands outside school, and school has its own recording studio. Regular music trips at home and abroad and school has invested in instruments for children to borrow.

Has a 500 seat multi-purpose theatre with specialist lighting and sound equipment, with seats that can be covered so it doubles as the examination hall; everyone has a chance to take part in major productions, either on stage or behind the scenes. Drama part of curriculum until year 9 and also offered at GCSE and at A level. Enthusiastic head of drama gets everyone involved.

DT taught by inspired teacher and pupils undertake projects for real clients – we saw a fine chair which had been designed and made for the local council. A number go on to study product design at university. The school has recently bought a 3D printer.

Good range of activities including maths and science club, chess, musical theatre, various minor sports and debating society. Extended school day available for juniors, from 8am to 5pm, at extra charge. After-school activities for reception to year 2, whilst years 3-6 can take part in optional Saturday morning activities – these are popular with the children and can range from scuba diving to computing to play rehearsals.

Boarding: One girls' and two boys' boarding houses all with common room, kitchen and tuck shop. Girls' house newly refurbished, light and bright with comfy sitting area, galleried atrium and en-suite bathrooms. House kitchens closed at lunchtimes to make sure pupils eat a proper meal. Year 7 and 8 boarders and day children live and learn in Kirby House, a light, modernist building with a glass atrium and a library which is housed in what looks like a large blue pottery chimney – inspired. All junior school boarders sleep here too. Large bright common room area with sofas, table tennis, a piano and a large television and 10 five-bed dorms with en-suite bathrooms and two flats for resident staff. Pupils allowed into Ramsgate at the weekends and some activities organised.

Background and atmosphere: Founded in 1879 as a boys' boarding school with the purpose of combining 'careful religious training with a sound, liberal education'. The college was incorporated as a public school in 1892 and went fully co-ed in 1983. It is set in 45 acres of walled grounds in the middle of Ramsgate and within walking distance of the sea. The Virginia creeper clad main building, complete with towers and turrets, is a monument to muscular Christianity. Inside it is all panelled corridors and sweeping staircases. The chapel, with its beautiful stained glass windows and fine organ, was built to commemorate the lives of over 130 Old Lawrentians who died in the First World War. Impressive 19th century dining hall decorated with portraits, shields and silverware. Major investment in building projects in recent years including new science, art and design technology theatre.

Pastoral care, well-being and discipline: The strong Christian ethos of the school underpins its religious and spiritual life. Chapel services three or four times a week and on Sundays for boarders help maintain an ethos of consideration for others and moral values – one of the stated aims of the school is to encourage 'a sense of serving others as a source of personal satisfaction'. The popular chaplain, often with iPad in hand, 'makes the services interesting', according to the children. All major world faiths are represented within the school; Jewish pupils can attend the synagogue in Ramsgate and Muslims can observe Ramadan.

Strong house loyalty and plenty of friendly inter-house rivalry – plays, matches and singing competitions. All houses have live-in houseparents and a resident tutor. School takes firm line on bullying – principal believes in restorative justice and likes to get to the root of the problem. Instant expulsion for the supply of drugs – children know where they stand.

Good food with plenty of choice including a salad bar and can cater for special diets and allergies. Food committee made up of pupils and staff and meets regularly to make recommendations. Coffee shop open at break time, evenings and weekends – also popular with parents at drop-off time. Lots of interaction with the local community – children from nearby schools invited to watch plays and the Chemical Magic show and take part in the annual science and engineering challenge.

Pupils and parents: A big range: traditional families from local prep and primary schools, a number of first time buyers and first generation immigrants who are aspirational and ambitious for their children. Popular with the arty crowd moving down from London – high speed railway means it is just over an hour to St Pancras. School prides itself on its internationalism and 30 per cent of pupils are foreign nationals from 27 countries including a sizeable contingent of Nepalis from the Gurkha barracks in Folkestone. Strong Nigerian connection and particularly popular with the Germans in sixth form. Children generally integrate well, although some say there could be more interaction between boarders and day pupils.

'Relaxed yet respectful' relationships between pupils and teachers. 'I love the way the children are treated like young adults,' said one parent. 'Everyone is respectful of everyone else, it is a very caring and supportive school.' 'My son joined for the sixth form and felt welcome from the start – sending him there was the best thing we ever did'. A very loyal team of former pupils – successful businesspeople and entrepreneurs who help with work experience. Pupils are 'natural and friendly and unpretentious' and very supportive of each other. Lots of mixing between year groups, helped by the house system. Parents encouraged to get involved, and are pleased with principal's improvements in communication, particularly the parent portal where they can view their children's marks, teachers' notes and homework.

Entrance: Just about non-selective but needs to ascertain that a child would be able to cope with the curriculum, and international students tested in English and maths. Entry to junior school via meeting with head for parents and child plus taster day and report from child's current school, and sometimes an assessment if there is concern a child might not be able to cope. Very few take common entrance – usually just reports from a child's current school and an interview. Will take children at any stage including occasionally into year 11. About 50 per cent of senior school entrants come up from the junior school, others from a range of state and independent schools – they have a big primary school engagement programme. Some transfers from local grammars. Around 15-20 join in sixth form – assessed on GCSE performance (normally five passes) and must have adequate English.

Exit: Automatic transition from junior to senior school and some three-quarters stay on – the rest mainly to grammars and non-selective state schools. Preparation for the Kent Test is part of school life, but some parents still get outside coaching. Scholarship and a discount in fees for those who pass Kent Test but choose to stay on at St Lawrence. Around 40 per cent leaves after GCSEs, either for financial reasons or to take vocational courses. Most go on to university, with UCL, Bristol, Warwick, Durham, Queen Mary London, Leeds, UEA, Royal Holloway and SOAS currently popular. Others to a wide range of careers: one recently went on to train as a yachtmaster and another to join the band of the Royal Marines.

Money matters: All-rounder, academic, sporting and music scholarships offered at 11+ and 13+ – worth up to 50 per cent of fees. Sixth form scholarships for up to 50 per cent of fees for academic, arts, music and sport. Also means-tested bursaries, and special bursaries for Forces families who qualify for the Continuity of Education Allowance. Generous sibling discounts.

Remarks: A school on the up with a new energy and buzz since our last visit, all helped by the raising of standards in all areas, especially sport, and the influx of London commuters taking advantage of property bargains. 'The school has so much potential and is just beginning to realise this,' said one parent.

St Mary's School (Gerrards Cross)

Packhorse Road, Gerrards Cross, Buckinghamshire SL9 8JQ

Ages 4–18 **Pupils** 350 **Sixth form** 50

Fees: £8,085 – £16,980 pa

01753 883370
www.stmarysschool.co.uk

Head: Since September 2018, Patricia Adams MA, formerly academic deputy head at Blackheath High. Degree in modern languages from Oxford, masters in applied linguistics from Essex, and returned to Oxford for her PGCE. Has previously worked in senior leadership at Norwich High, been head of upper school and head of Spanish at Oxford High School, and head of modern languages at Headington School, Oxford.

S

Head of prep: Since 2013, Mairead Carney BA DipHE (late 40s). Educated at University College Galway where she read English and French, followed by a higher diploma in education. Afterwards worked with disadvantaged local children before moving to London to pursue a career in investment banking. Had calling to teach after 11 years in business, so volunteered at Manor House School in Ealing, where she spent six years as a year 2 teacher, followed by another six at St Helen's Hillingdon. Joined St Mary's (as did her daughter, now in the senior school) as a form teacher in 2009 before becoming head of prep department following her predecessor's retirement.

Academic matters: 'Good teaching across the board,' according to prep school parents. French from year 1 and Mandarin club on offer at lunchtimes for all year groups. Maths department 'vibrant' and 'becoming more challenging', with a weekly 'I can do maths' initiative in place which sees pupils split by ability rather than year group. No setting, but innovative approaches – such as stacking 'traffic light' cups on pupils' desks to let the teacher know how they are feeling about the work – means everyone can go at their own pace.

Results solid though disappointing dip recently. In 2018, 45 per cent A*-A/9-7 grades at GCSE. At A level, 55 per cent A*-B, 31 per cent A*/A. Unlike most other schools, St Mary's bijoux stature (30 to 40 girls per year group) enables it to cater for the broadest of academic spectrums, from Oxbridge types all the way down. Some take Bucks 11+, although even those who pass tend to stay put in the main.

All the usual subjects offered at A level, as well as theatre studies, PE, media studies, health and social care and most recently government and politics. French from year 7, with German or Spanish as options in year 8 and free choice of language at GCSE. Latin recently discontinued on curriculum (although available as a club) and replaced with thinking skills to help girls move away from rote and towards independent learning – study skills also offered in year 7. Setting in maths from mid year 7, for French from year 8 and science from year 9, when girls make an early start on their GCSE course. Science department 'amazing', according to head, with 'really exceptional' teaching. Girls report great teaching all round.

Excellent SEN, holistically incorporated into curriculum by head of learning support appointed. Girls speak openly about their (usually mild) dyslexia or dyscalculia, thanks to an overwhelmingly friendly and supportive school ethos – and possibly the clever 'cake club' where extra help is administered over home baked patisseries.

Games, options, the arts: Prep school seems more artsy than sporty in general with ballet on curriculum from nursery and LAMDA a popular option from year 1. Each key stage performs an annual drama production and there's a strong take-up of music, with around 50 per cent of the cohort taking advantage of peripatetic lessons. Art classes take place in a dedicated room and DT – covering everything from sewing to mechanics – follows the design process used in industry, according to a parent who designs aircraft. Wonderful works of girls' art festoon the corridors and shown in art exhibition.

'Amazing' head of senior creative arts faculty has 'transformed art department,' according to parents, getting to the nitty gritty of what kind of work inspires girls. Superb fashion drawings recently led to a show with girls modelling recycled or upcycled garments made with their own fair hands. Wonderful works of all genres are displayed on every spare inch of wall around the school, and the overall feeling is of a culture that truly values creativity and artistic endeavour. Music and drama 'needed a boost' and recent Christmas Extravaganza saw girls singing, acting and dancing their way through a packed programme. Other recent performances have included Mary Poppins and Romeo and Juliet, and 'legions' of peripatetic music lessons take place each week as well as 'good quality' efforts from the choir, chamber choir and orchestra.

Plenty of sport going on, although it's definitely not school's raison d'être. Occasional competitive fixtures come into play in years 5 and 6 with prep school turning out A and B teams for netball matches, but sometimes it's 'a bit of a challenge to get a team together as the school's so small,' according to parents. PE taught four times weekly, though, so girls are no couch potatoes, with swimming at the local sports centre for one term each year. Sport lovers craving more can sign up for dance, gymnastics or various sports clubs at lunchtimes or after school, many of which are covered by fees.

Senior school fixtures for netball, rounders and tennis, and school says 'every child competes if they want to,' although it's a struggle to get enough girls together for a hockey team. Numerous individual sports on offer from fencing to badminton, with dance a very popular option now, thanks to state of the art sports hall, leading to a biennial gym and dance show in which the whole school participates. Flexibility and support offered for those with talents which require time out of school.

Previous head launched 'mission to take girls out of themselves' on arrival, introducing the St Mary's Challenge, requiring compulsory participation in at least one extracurricular activity. School happily reports that formerly quiet girls have discovered debating, others football or rugby, and girls agree that the new approach is paying off as they enthusiastically reel off lists of clubs to which they now belong.

Background and atmosphere: Founded in Paddington in 1872 as a school for girls, run by Anglican nuns; moved to current premises in 1938. Senior school housed in an Elizabethan manor house, feels more like a cosy prep than a senior school – until you spot the purposeful teenagers moving between classes. Closure of nursery has given more space to reception and a new library; pre-prep now has its own centre, Paddington House. Small numbers of keen learners able to flourish in classes the girls uniformly describe as 'fun.' No whistles and bells when it comes to facilities, and the fabric of the school is all rather higgledy piggledy, but somehow it all just works and even little ones talk about the school community as being 'like a family.' Very much a school where staff and girls are known to each other (most know every other girl in school by name) and girls of all ages describe the cohort as 'like a family.' Newcomers say they are made to feel one of the gang within days and that there are absolutely 'no cliques.' School uniformly described by pupils as 'unique', and girls quick to dismiss questions from friends at other schools about how it feels to go to such a small school. Facilities nothing to write home about, but somehow it all pulls together nicely – sixth formers proud of their new centre complete with common room.

Pastoral care, well-being and discipline: Refreshingly un-pushy compared with many in the area. Nurturing not pressurised, focused on gentle encouragement towards the best outcomes for individuals rather than mass league table glory. That's not to say school doesn't give girls a bit of oomph when it's needed though, with ambitious targets set across the board for all. Very little goes unnoticed ('the joy of a small school,') and reputation for caring well-earned in the locality and responsible for luring many a parent through its doors. Worry box present but rarely used, and each class has a sixth form prefect, trained to advise in the event of minor difficulties. School council, made up of two girls per form and chaired by head girl, has drawn up charter against bullying.

Astoundingly happy prep pupils skip (literally) around the school, with some saying they never want to go home and many resisting parents' suggestions of taking the 11+ as they 'never want to leave St Mary's.' Size of prep school means that very little passes by unnoticed, and although there are initiatives such as buddy systems to help keep harmony in the playground, the compact critical mass makes being friendly easy, and girls say they know the name of every other pupil in the school. Bijoux size also enables sharing facilities (the science teacher cited the school skeleton as an example) with the senior school a straightforward process.

Praised by parents for zero tolerance approach to negative aspects of social media, with active monitoring of Facebook, Twitter et al and parents and girls educated to give it a wide berth for as long as possible. School's size makes it easy for such messages to hit home, and although electronic devices are sometimes allowed for correct usage, they're not compulsory – 'we're not ready to go there yet,' says school.

Strong 'mysteriously named' house system rewards girls for everything from academic excellence to kindness, ensuring all feel valued, and frequent competitions from the swimming gala to the house quiz, where the pupils 'raise the roof', offer an element of non-threatening competition.

Pupils and parents: A diverse social mix, given affluent environs, with most very local – often within walking distance – but a smattering from surrounding areas including Bourne End, Farnham Common and Denham. Ethnic mix reflective of local area with around 25 per cent non-Caucasion, mostly Indian. Parents want 'challenge but not pressure' for their daughters, says school. Many girls a bit unpolished in their appearance with lots of un-brushed heads of hair and the odd pair of ripped tights in evidence – very different to some of their pristine local competitors – but somehow this all adds to the unpretentious charm of the place. Very active parents' association welcomes all-comers and active social scene described as 'a real community.'

Entrance: Entry into reception at 4+ by visit to class to 'assess their suitability'. Class sizes remain very small in the lower years (some as low as nine), growing as girls move up, where by years 5 and 6 they generally reach – or are close to – capacity. Girls joining post reception, typically either new to the area or refugees from either the state system or other pushier preps, are gently assessed in English, maths and – from 7+ – non-verbal reasoning.

Senior school entry by assessment and interview. Vast majority join year 7 from prep department; the fact that there's 'no cut off point at the end of year 6' is key benefit to the school – girls sail seamlessly into senior school with no hiatus. New joiners at 11 are gently selected and come from a range of local state and independent schools into one of two classes of no more than 16. Form groups capped at 20 in sixth form, with maximum class sizes fixed at 12.

Exit: Around 75 per cent of prep pupils move up to the senior school, with a few off to local grammar schools. Around a fifth head to new pastures post-GCSE (mainly grammar or co-ed boarding schools) but most into year 12 to benefit from small class sizes and individual attention (some A level classes are as small as five or six). All to higher education to read a variety of subjects, around half to Russell Group universities and the occasional one to Oxbridge. Destinations in 2018 included one dentist off to Cardiff, others to eg York, Oxford Brookes, Exeter, Brighton, Loughborough, Birmingham, Liverpool, Queen Mary's London, Aston, Hull, Royal Holloway, Newcastle, Bournemouth, Royal Academy of Dance.

Money matters: No bursaries in prep department, though several all-rounder scholarships for year 3 entry. Not a rich school but academic scholarships available at 11 and 16 to existing and new pupils, plus a music scholarship at 11. Small number of means-tested bursaries available in senior school.

Remarks: A safe bet for parents who don't believe that bigger is necessarily better and are keen to avoid the trials and tribulations of the year 6 examination frenzy. Not the natural choice for alpha females or those who thrive on competitive sport, and doesn't offer the bewildering breadth of extracurricular or gleaming facilities of larger schools, but a happier school you couldn't hope to find, and academics are robust given the broad church intake.

St Mary's School Ascot

St Mary's Road, Ascot, Berkshire SL5 9JF

Ages 11–18 **Pupils** 386 **Sixth form** 118 **Boarders** 363 full **RC**

Fees: Day £27,603; Boarding £38,790 pa

01344 296600
www.st-marys-ascot.co.uk

Headmistress: Since 1999, Mary Breen BSc MSc (40s). Married, no children. Previously spent seven-year stint at Eton, where she ended up as head of physics. Before that, taught science at The Abbey School Reading.

Her career was kick-started by head at Wellington who, having appointed her husband to a teaching post, saw Mrs Breen's useful physics degree lying fallow and suggested putting it to practical use. 'A few months later, my first class was 22 Wellingtonians. I discovered I could do it and loved it,' she says. The rest, as they say, is history or, in her case, science.

The school's first lay head, she has commendably piloted St Mary's through the choppy waters of changing educational fashions without once changing course. The result is a school that has remained totally true to itself – and unapologetically so. 'We're not trying to be all things to all people', she says, 'but we've got a coherence that works'.

Smart, with a hint of va va voom (and no doubt requiring every ounce of it at times), she relishes the job and is reassuringly in control without anything of the martinet about her. Her genuine and purposeful charm is particularly effective when directed at parents. 'I say "we're Catholic. We're all girls. We're full boarding. We're a good medium size, with just under 400 and no plans to get any bigger or smaller. And we're very proud of our academic reputation. If that's a match for your daughters, let's take it further".' Most do.

Head is no slouch when it comes to heading off potential defection higher up the school. 'Having seen them grow up as teenagers, you want them as your gorgeous sixth form', she says. Plenty of official endorsement too. School recently breezed through visits from Ofsted and ISI (who decided to pop in at the same time) and scored glowing reviews from both.

Parents are universally full of praise, highlighting head's professionalism and nous. One father told us she should have a 'sainthood'. 'All you could ask for in a head', said another parent. 'She's the right person at the top to build the right team round her'. Admiration extends to 'excellent' communication following a one-off resignation of a member of staff found with inappropriate images on computer in an incident which was, the head is at pains to point out, 'unrelated to school'. Equal enthusiasm from pupils. 'She knows everyone's name and is personable, efficient and approachable', said one. Felt to be particularly good with family-related issues requiring delicate handling.

Wears regular questions about whether she's thinking of moving on with slight (and understandable) weariness. Her answer? Until she wakes up thinking she doesn't want to do this job, she has no intention of moving on, though she wouldn't be averse to a bit of industry-spokesperson duties on the side were the opportunities to come her way. Our advice to suitable bodies? Snap her up while stocks last. A natural in front of a crowd, she'd be jolly good at it too.

Retiring in July 2019. Her successor - and headmistress elect during 2018/19 – is Danuta Staunton BA MA PGCE. English degree and masters in Renaissance literature, both from York. Worked in publishing before joining St Mary's English department, and has been here ever since, as year coordinator, deputy head of house and then part of the senior management and education team.

Academic matters: All round excellence, helped by well-stocked staff room (overall pupil-teacher ratio of six to one). Class sizes average 16 up to year 9, 15 for GCSE years and seven at A level. Three in a class not uncommon for more rarefied subjects such as further maths.

At A level in 2018, 68 per cent A*/A grades and 93 per cent A*/B. I/GCSE results similarly classy – 98 per cent A*-A/9-7 grades. Head is keen to dispel the suggestion that results are easily come by or a foregone conclusion. While they may suggest highly academic intake at 11+, with the vast majority at the top end of spectrum, behind the scenes number crunching (school uses MIDYIS) tells a very different story. Pupils span just about everything from the mid-range and below to the giddy super-bright heights.

A well-managed process steers a careful line between encouragement and pressure. The universally cheerful and confident demeanour of sixth formers about to enter final preparation for final A level exams indicated that it was working. Pupils rated supportive ethos – 'It's cool to work', said one – and extensive out of hours access to staff. 'So many of the teachers stay late that it's easy to meet up with them', confirmed another. Well-structured lessons where peers, as well as staff, assist with problem areas are a boon, too, say pupils.

Transformation of geese to high-flying swans isn't lost on parents, who talk of being 'staggered' by strings of GCSE top grades achieved. It's something that the head, to her credit, doesn't care to over-stress, given that it's unlikely to do much in the way of improving pupil confidence.

Subject range, though not vast, is well chosen and augmented only after considerable deliberation. Religious studies a non-negotiable core subject at GCSE. Latin (taught like French from year 7) taken by around half the year group at GCSE, well ahead of Spanish, German, Italian (added year 8) and Greek (year 9).

Three cheers for science, a particular strength, with five well-equipped labs and surging physics numbers post-16 (head takes some classes) on a par with biology and chemistry. Around 20 per cent take science subject to A level.

Maths also has consistent numbers of fans, though broad sweep of subject popularity (English literature, politics and French all make an appearance in the top five most years) means most tastes are well catered for. 'There's no subject that's a no-go area. When people ask me, I'm really proud to say what I'm doing,' said a further maths and science star.

Games, options, the arts: 'We're academic but with lots of extracurricular activities', a pupil told us. 'The school encourages you to thrive'. And how. Being not just good but 'brilliant' at everything, including sport, drama and music, is the goal, though not easy in such a small school stresses the head. If anything holds them back, it won't be resources, with sports facilities positively glistening with new honed and toned additions. In addition to swimming pool, the Orchard Centre has a big sports hall, two squash courts and a dance studio. One of few girls' schools to have own 400-metre running track, green instead of customary red. Polo available, courtesy of local stables.

While there's a steady crop of outstanding individuals and teams at county level and above (tennis a particular strength), any lingering perception that the keen but hopeless are left to languish is out of date, says the head. All shall have matches (if not prizes). Team sport ceases to be compulsory post 16 but there's enough to inspire even the most sedentary-minded to stay happily active. Body conditioning, universally (though to official disapproval) known by girls as LBT (legs, bums and tums), particularly popular.

As with sport, the arts boast range of spaces that would be outstanding in a school with double the numbers. With its studio, full-size theatre, enormous green room (partitioned for girl/boy casts), bar and extensive costume room, the Rose Theatre is a budding thespian's dream. Many work towards LAMDA exams, gaining the full set by the time they leave. Productions every term, some girls-only, others involving other schools. Production of The History Boys featured an all-girl cast, apart from the French mistress, who was played by an Etonian. A sixth form group took its own play to Edinburgh Festival, gaining good reviews into the bargain.

Art, housed with textiles (DT, though not a GCSE option, is taught as a carousel subject in years 8 and 9) is terrific. In some schools, head of department's hand often all too visible in strikingly similar interpretations of GCSE/A level coursework theme: here, variety (including burqa-clad, slogan adorned figures in entrance) suggests pupils really do think for themselves. Quality is so impressive that you almost forget where you are and start peering for red spots. Portraiture wonderful – not surprising as school, in one of many go-ahead moments, offers life drawing. Here as elsewhere, school's decision to go its own way has left it ahead of the game. 'We stick to traditions worth sticking to', a senior teacher told us.

Music is a high-profile affair. Well-equipped recital room, numerous practice rooms (including one, doubly soundproofed, for drums), concerts also in the chapel to capitalise on 'wonderful' acoustics. Head of music who grows her own compositions is now inundated with requests for new works following première of spine-tingling Easter Story and also plans to up numbers taking subject at GCSE and A level (scant handful currently).

Activities provide outlet for girl power in every form. For younger pupils, few delights trump pet club housed in mish-mash of cages and runs. Hamsters and rabbits dominate, with talent shows featuring animals in natty little homemade outfits. Animal friendliness is a big thing generally and mercy dashes aren't unknown. 'Only this school would put a damaged pigeon in a taxi and send it to the only vet open on a Sunday,' said a member of staff.

Wide range of clubs and societies, from the mind-expanding (human rights, music appreciation, current affairs) to D of E, London theatre trips and upscale wine-tasting (upper sixth only). Born movers and shakers (and there are many) can hone their organising skills in assorted forums, from influential school council ('what we recommend gets done', say girls) to range of committees. Old girls regularly pop up to widen careers horizons as part of a programme that kicks in from year 9.

Boarding: Modernising elsewhere in the school has seen large-scale abolition of big dorms (mostly no more than five to a room). Top favourite, however, was blast from the past curtain-partitioned 'cubies' in year 8 dorm, voted the best fun, with last night of term midnight feasts.

Sixth form privileges include no uniform (pupils were delighted by this, some parents less so), permission to queue-barge at meal times and annual ball. Biggest perk is separate living quarters, away from main school hurly burly, circle of little homes corralled around own courtyard. Decent kitchens are well used (fruit and veg high on request list, adding to menu staples of toast, pasta – and chocolate crispie cakes). Entertaining is encouraged, with guests treated to more elaborate fare (visiting Etonians haven't thus far reciprocated in kind. 'They don't have the same facilities,' say the girls).

Multitude of house-organised weekend activities helps to dispel any boarding blues. Staples include mass pizza ordering as well as rare forays into deepest girly territory (nail decoration a favourite) and specials like St Patrick's Day marked with cookery (Irish potato scones) and crafts (shamrock felt jewellery).

Background and atmosphere: School was founded in 1885 by the Institute of the Blessed Virgin Mary (IBVM), a religious order begun by Mary Ward (1585-1645). Her dreams of founding a Jesuit-inspired apostolic women's order (she even crossed the Alps on foot to put her case to the Pope) came to nothing in her lifetime. Undaunted, followers continued to plead her cause, though it was 2009 before her 'heroic virtue' was recognised by Rome.

Catholicism defines the school, sweeping in the committed and the less so. Morning chapel compulsory for all while regular weekday masses are optional, attracting anything from a dozen to 60 just before exams. Houses take it in turns to organise mass and pick the hymns, the more rousing the better. The election of the current Pontiff greeted with huge excitement. 'Someone started screaming "white smoke!" – I had coursework to do but the Pope comes first', a sixth former told us.

School makes the most of its 55-acre site. Main buildings, some on gothic revival lines, go up rather than out, with long but not unfriendly corridors, helped by warm terracotta and mosaic tiles and a riot of gleaming staircases (some now adorned with essential if unattractive anti-slip edging).

We were the first outsiders to experience the gorgeousness of school's former concert hall, now transformed into a terrific new senior library (juniors separately and snazzily catered for). Nicer than many universities, say pupils. No wonder, with its curvy window seats, acres of bookcases and wonderful first floor curved ceiling. Café, complete with morning papers. No learning resource centre faffage here. Pupils can take in iPads and laptops but the printed word is definitely the star of the show. 'Books betoken silence', says head firmly.

Pastoral care, well-being and discipline: A little light rule-bending aside, few serious offences on this head's watch. Sanctions, when they do occur, are now consistent from house to house (just about the only minor imperfection found after recent inspections). Internet misuse would lead to merit-cancelling red ticket. Drink and smoking, almost unheard of, would result in suspension and 'you'd be out' for drugs.

Day to day, six heads of house have the biggest pastoral responsibility. They're considered mainly excellent. Praise too, for boarding. Inevitable beginner homesickness well handled with the help of older buddies and kindly boarding staff, vast majority of whom don't teach. 'They're lovely and very sympathetic if you say you have too much work,' said sixth former. Residential chaplain is mentioned by almost everyone as inspirational force for good and a multi-tasker to boot.

There's a fair bit of moving around which stems from a sensible desire to head off anything that could lead to cliques forming. Sleeping arrangements changed at least once a term and occasionally twice to mix and match the personalities. As a result, happiness tends to rule, and on the rare occasions it doesn't, there's a swift resolution of problems. Sixth form exceptionally strong, with friendships that often endure for life.

Pupils and parents: Around a third from London, a third within an hour's travel, a fifth from overseas (half non British) and the remainder from elsewhere in the UK.

Before head's arrival, vibe was a bit Frost in May, with slight sense that the very grandest of old Catholic families had a more exalted cachet than others. Now, though they're still represented, and anyone paying full fees needs to be 'mega rich' to afford them, there's a more egalitarian spirit abroad.

Increasing numbers are funded by bursaries, and though there's lots of emphasis on socialising with other top notch schools (Eton the top favourite) there's careful control of the trappings of excess. Nickames, amongst them Biggles, Squeaky and Booey, are plentiful and once bestowed are generally there for life.

Parents are a happy bunch. Not hard to see why, given the St Mary's effect, resulting in girls who emerge ready to subdue the world with charm, intelligence, confidence and poise. 'I think anyone in my year could stand up quite happily in front of 500 people and speak,' one former pupil told us.

Entrance: Selective but not awesomely so. Siblings, while favourably viewed, need good dose of what it takes to secure a place. School gives preference to girls who are Roman Catholic (nearly all pupils are). Many from bilingual backgrounds, though no formal support offered. Special educational needs geared towards those with 'generally mild' dyslexia, with learning support lessons and workshops.

Main entrance points are 11 (English, maths and general knowledge/intelligence tests) and 13 (English, maths, science, religious studies, history or geography, MFL, Latin). Feeder schools many and various (300 preps and maintained primaries); so oversubscribed that inevitably there will be some disappointments.

For the unsuccessful, there's another chance in the sixth form (test in proposed A level subjects plus general paper). Chances of success are diminutive though. The maximum new intake is just five, though in reality often fewer.

Exit: Virtually no fall-out after GCSEs. Nine to Oxbridge in 2018, plus 11 off to study abroad (US/Canada/Europe). Bristol, Edinburgh and Exeter also popular. Subjects range from sciences to languages, law to art. Numbers going into performing arts are increasing – one old girl is currently working with Steven Spielberg.

Money matters: Standard range of scholarships at 11, 13 and 16 on offer (five per cent reduction on the fees). Music scholarships include free tuition on up to two instruments.

Remarks: Catholic education at its best. So popular that when it comes to getting a place, faith may not be enough.

St Michael's Preparatory School

Otford Court, Row Dow, Sevenoaks, Kent TN14 5RY

Ages 2–13 **Pupils** 450

Fees: £11,850 – £14,400 pa

01959 522137
www.stmichaels.kent.sch.uk

Headteacher: Since 2013, Jill Aisher BA PGCE MCIL (50s). Read modern languages at Oxford. With 25 years of teaching experience, her career falls into two parts – working in a selective state grammar as a teacher of Latin, French, Spanish and English, followed by senior leadership in the independent sector. Deputy head at Newton Prep for six years, then three years as head at St Nicholas Prep, Hyde Park, prior to taking up a Kent headship (fulfilling a long-held plan to return to where her husband grew up and her children went to school).

Says she was drawn to the 'strong sense of emotional well-being' at St Michael's, as well as its stable population, where she

S

can prove herself. Pupils tend to stay from 2+ to year 8. Installed in her palatial office, with splendid views and a Hogwarts-type turret for her desk, she couldn't be more delighted.

Warm and friendly, a fast thinker and talker, highly articulate in her vision for the school. She is seeking to give it a more outward-looking view – both injecting a global perspective into the curriculum, often via ICT and connecting locally, and enabling children to master learning by understanding their own learning style and giving children more of a voice, as equals. Myriad ways for children to do just that from taking part in the newly energised school council to most radically, helping the head interview new staff.

Parents say that head is 'very efficient and pro-active.' 'My children say she is strict, but also sometimes very funny,' one told us.

Married for 30 plus years to Johnny, a senior employee of our nation's favourite department store, with three children. One son is studying for a second masters at the RCM, another a music producer and her youngest daughter is at King's Canterbury.

Entrance: The majority (intake of 40) enter the pre-prep at 2+, but there are additional entry points in reception, year 3 (and year 7). Prospective parents need to get on the waiting list as early as possible. Some sibling priority and an informal assessment day, but entry is not selective and places are offered to those heading the list in the June, 15 months prior to entry. The majority of pupils come from within a seven-mile radius.

Entry at 7+ is via a standard maths test, together with a school reading and English test. Entry into year 7 is via maths and English test and being observed participating in a normal school day. Bursaries from year 3 and scholarships and bursaries for year 7 entry.

Exit: Most popular destinations at 11+ : Radnor House, Sevenoaks, Weald of Kent Grammar, Walthamstow Hall and Trinity School. Most popular destinations at 13+: Caterham, Tonbridge School, Sevenoaks and Walthamstow Hall.

Head stresses that the school really prepares children for the 11+ or CE. Parents agree. 'I have total confidence in preparation for their next school,' one told us.

Of those who exit at 11+, almost all will be successful in achieving their first (guided) choice of school. 'We have all abilities,' says the head. 'We set out to prepare for a broad range of schools that will encourage and affirm. For some a slower pace is appropriate.' Between 40 and 60 per cent continue into years 7 and 8.

Remarks: St Michael's was founded in 1872 as a school and home for orphaned boys. In the 1980s the pre-prep was added and girls welcomed, and in the 1990s it became a day rather than boarding school. Prep is housed in a large red-brick Victorian gothic mansion, with an adjoining sports building. Inside, modern, bright spaces, smart purpose-built science labs and dining hall mix in a homely jumble with the chipped paint, Gothic panelling and stained glass of the old building.

This isn't the prettiest part of Kent, cheek by jowl with the M25, but the gain is swift commuting to central London. Less than four miles to Sevenoaks and once you have arrived at the school, the 90 acres of grounds, which swoop up and down before the main house are stunning. Wooded hills for bushcraft, camping and fitness runs, plus games fields and pitches.

The curriculum does not surprise, but ticks every box. The head singles out science and English, sport and art as particularly strong – and parents agree. In the modern science labs we watched white-coated children experiment with the boiling point of water and our enthusiastic guides ('science is really fun here') were keen to tell us all about explosions, trips and their participation in the national CREST competition (they designed a games console).

Despite the head's modern languages background, nothing too 'bold' on the horizon for languages. Focus is on consolidating current provision, with a Mandarin club set up in response to parental requests. A wonderful moment as the French teacher invited one of the boys to share his work with this editor – they were discussing which school subjects they preferred. 'Je déteste le Français,' he had written in immaculate French.

Nearly a third of staff have been at the school for more than 10 years. Parents say they are 'very caring and accommodating' and that there are 'some outstanding teachers,' though a couple would like more of an open door policy. Maximum class size is 20 in pre-prep and 18 in prep and setting is gradually introduced – for English, maths, science and French by year 7. One pupil we met told us the 'teachers are really supportive,' describing how they always have time to sit down with pupils if they don't understand something. Another parent said of her child: 'She's gone from feeling unnoticed and swimming in knowledge gaps from her last school experience to feeling totally included and valued in class.'

School says there are plenty of opportunities for gifted children to excel. Full-time SENCo, known as head of learning development here, who provides in-class and one-to-one support. Thirteen per cent with SEN and 13 pupils with EAL needs. Laptops can be used in classrooms. 'My son is still struggling with literacy, reading and spelling but he feels supported and not alone in his battles,' a parent told us.

Head is keen on the power of technology to 'transform and personalise learning,' so tablets and mobile devices are on their way. As always, the debate on homework rages but there is a feeling that it is quite intense in the upper years, with up to two hours a night by year 6. But a parent told us: 'When I feel that they are overloaded and not managing, the school immediately reviewed and reduced their homework.'

School has a strong reputation for its sporting talent and success. On the day we visited the school gates were being painted gold in honour of the school's golden girl, former head girl Lizzy Yarnold, team GB skeleton Olympic gold medalist. Swimmers compete in IAPS national finals, rugby teams punch above their weight against bigger preps, netball teams compete well and a year 8 pupil recently represented the UK at wakeboarding. Two games afternoons a week. One parent praised the excellent standard of coaching, another pointed out that if children are interested in something more unusual they will still need to find it elsewhere.

All pupils are given the opportunity to represent the school in major games every term. This seems transformative, at least to the children who had recently joined the school and described themselves as not particularly sporty. One said: 'I feel I can try my best, and I don't get shouted at.' Sports day is enjoyed as much for sitting around on blankets with friends between races as the competition itself.

Every pupil has a class music lesson every week. Around half receive individual instrument tuition, with pupils currently studying 11 different instruments. If a child has a musical whim ('anything other than the bagpipes') the school will strive to find a good teacher. Four choirs, two concerts per term, instrumental groups. Children also take part in the Sevenoaks and Royal Tunbridge Wells International Music Festival. Head of music continues to take things up another notch.

Much high quality art and design work on show – children had just completed their own take on Keith Haring canvases and were keen to show us their post-it note animation to rap music. Parents agree that drama is a relatively weak spot. No dedicated theatre, but the recent head of drama has big plans.

A wealth of arty, sporty, and musical pre- and post-school clubs including extreme collage, golf, Lego, dance and scratch programming. There is an after-school club to support working parents.

Pre-prep is housed in a spacious, light, purpose-built building, entered via a suspended walkway. Parents with a love of Grand Designs will adore it. Every class has outdoor access, wellies hang in little wooden houses ready for muddy play, Astroturf for wet weather and bulb-planting just getting under way. Maximum class size is 20, with two staff. Far higher ratios in the nursery and kindergarten years.

Whilst the children are meticulously prepared for every new experience, parents may need a little hand-holding in their transition to the (as yet) less swankily designed prep. As, one satisfied parent put it: 'The pre-prep is second to none.'

Parents speak very highly of pastoral care. Bullying not unheard of, but staff very quick to take action and empower children to handle it themselves. The children we met said they found the school 'cosy' and that they knew everyone because it wasn't too large. Many schools talk of 'the individual child' but St Michael's truly delivers on this. At every turn parents and pupils fell over themselves to paint a picture of inclusivity. One said: 'We've had four children at the school at various times over the past four years – all very different in abilities and personalities. The school has suited them all.' Parents said the school suits 'self-starters, those with special needs, the academic and less academic.' 'It is quite a big, bouncy school,' one added, 'but the staff take care of the less confident ones and help them come out of their shell.'

A huge mix of families. Parents with children higher up the school likely to be Kent families, but new families coming up the school comprise working parents, relocators (from London and internationally). Car of choice in the car park very definitely a shiny black Range Rover. Particularly glowing reviews from those arriving from or returning from abroad who remark on the warm welcome from other parents. Such are their numbers that they've recently set up their own international club (sounds a bit 'gin-slings and elephant polo' but is more about helping each other to settle into Kent life).

Saint Ronan's School

262

Water Lane, Hawkhurst, Kent TN18 5DJ

Ages 3–13 **Pupils** 437 **Boarders** 117 flexi (from year 4) **C of E**

Fees: Day £10,476 – £17,952; Boarding +£38 per night

01580 752271
www.saintronans.co.uk

Headmaster: Since 2003, William Trelawny-Vernon (early 50s). Very much a joint enterprise with wife Emma (she's the Trelawny, he's the Vernon) – who is both registrar and head of history. Known as Mr and Mrs TV to pupils and parents alike. The couple met at Exeter, where Mr TV read biology. Previously at Stowe School for 12 years, including posts as a biology teacher and seven years as housemaster of Chatham House. 'Universally loved', according to parents.

The business is in the blood – his father was head of Hordle House (now Walhampton) in Hampshire. Four children – the youngest at the prep, the other three have moved on to King's Canterbury. The family left the head's accommodation to move off site in 2005 and they eschew the parental dinner party circuit, believing it's important to maintain a distance. Parents think they get it right, as one commented: 'One of the areas in which the school excels is managing successfully the line between parental involvement and keeping parents distanced when necessary.'

Both grew up in a four-child family, and with their own gang of four have that deep respect for fairness and equality of treatment which comes from big families. 'Neither of us likes the concept of the alpha child,' says Mr TV.

School and family is everything to Mr TV – time off finds him socialising with the wider family, and stress relief comes by sitting on his tractor and mowing the grass, or researching the history of the two families. Both are content with home and hearth, or as Emma puts it, 'We're like labradors sitting in front of the fire'. Holidays take them to the West Country, home of Emma's ancestral seat (her brother John inherited the Salusbury-Trelawny baronetcy).

Entrance: All children attend a taster day, and children seeking places in year 3 and above are assessed by the class teacher and take verbal and non-verbal reasoning tests. Intake covers wide-ranging abilities, but all are expected to pass common entrance or the Cranbrook grammar tests, so 'There will be a couple of children where we will have an honest dialogue with the parents and tell them that their child's needs are not going to be met here,' says Mr TV.

Scholarships are available for academic, music, art and sporting talents, and there are means-tested bursaries. Minibuses bring children in from Staplehurst, High Halden, Burwash, Wittersham and the villages en route.

Exit: It's not the place to come if you have your sights on the grammars – despite these being within travelling distance, the school doesn't encourage exit at 11. Only one or two children per year sit the Kent 11+, so it'll be a lonely experience and you'll have to find a tutor.

The majority of parents are buying into private education for the duration, although a good proportion go on to Cranbrook grammar at 13. King's Canterbury, Eastbourne and Hurst are popular, and some go further afield. 'Since I've been head we have fed into 63 different schools,' says Mr TV. Parents say they are good at helping you choose the next school – the TVs visit a clutch of senior schools each term so they are well informed.

Generally a good number of scholarships (26 in 2018, around half for sport), and one or two parents admit to feeling some playground one-upmanship about places and scholarships secured. 'There is competition from some of the parents, which can make you feel uncomfortable if you let it, though not between the children,' said one.

Its quirkiness ensures there is no Saint Ronan's product – and the roll of past pupils is stuffed with the great and good. 'Just look at the alumni to see how successful it is in producing movers and shakers and Boy's Own heroes,' said one parent. Indeed the list reads like a fantasy dinner party guest list: BBC security correspondent Frank Gardner, spy Donald Maclean, MP Airey Neave, Olympic rower Matthew Parrish, and the late Mark Shand, travel writer (and brother of Camilla, Duchess of Cornwall).

Remarks: A what's-not-to-love campus. Gorgeous grounds with ancient, spreading trees, inspiring views, a fishing lake, and its own 100 acre wood. And there's even a farm with pigs, alpacas, and chickens – newborn piglets greeted our visit. The emphasis is on old-fashioned, wholesome fun, making every use of this natural playground. 'It's idyllic, they get to dam streams and play with pigs and chickens,' said one parent. Everything is named for Boy's Own adventures – there's the Gulch, an area around a stream ideal for making mud pies, the Saltmines, an overgrown area with secret pathways, and even the pitches have names, such as Timbuktoo (because it's a long journey to reach it). A classroom on the edge of the woods is the Hobbit House. As one parent put it, 'If Enid Blyton was still around, Saint Ronan's would be exactly the sort of school she would be writing about. We are buying a truly magical childhood experience, not just a superb all-round education.'

All this romping is made easier by probably the most relaxed and colourful uniform we've seen – corduroy trousers, skirts or pinafores, topped with school sweatshirts in a choice of colours – pink, green, red, purple, light blue and navy. There's a formal uniform which is worn on Fridays, key days and for trips out.

The pre-prep is in a separate bright and modern building (where a corridor poster advises on 20 things to do before leaving pre-prep, such as dam a stream, make a mud pie, and hold an animal). There's also a cosy kindergarten in the former headmaster's house.

Moving up to prep brings the grandeur of Tongswood House, a Victorian mansion built by an Oxo magnate, with original features including a sprung floor ballroom, where frescoes of semi-naked nymphs on the ceiling liven up assembly for the older boys.

There's wood panelling and grand staircases aplenty, and classrooms are eccentrically named, such as Old Bailey, 10 Downing Street, Lombard Street (because that's where the safe was), and Windsor Castle (once a lavatory). Children scrape to their feet as you enter – standing up for grown-ups is something the teachers are strictest about, say the pupils, along with manners, being kind, and being honest.

Kindness is the rule for staff too. 'If we heard a teacher shouting at a child, they would have to come into the office and explain why,' says Mrs TV. 'We like to treat them in the same way as our own children.' Prefects are elected by the children in a secret ballot 'which means they go for someone who is kind and gentle, not necessarily just one of the first XV,' says Mr TV.

In reception you're greeted by a wood fire burning in the hearth – where parents come to warm up for post-match teas – and a basket of free range eggs for sale. You can also pick up school produced pork and apple juice. The head's secretary is Mrs TV's sister, known as Aunty Amanda. Parents love the reportedly eccentric ways of school admin. They talk of things being done in a Saint Ronan's way, one of 'happy chaos', which 'wouldn't suit parents who want everything done in a completely perfect planned-out way'. It looks disorganised, but it works, they say. 'We do slightly chaotic and quirky with great aplomb,' said one mother proudly.

Prizes are given for contribution as well as achievement, and one parent said, 'although they are encouraged to achieve, this is not done in an over-competitive manner'. And pupils say that the teachers discourage any jostling for position. 'When we get exam results the teachers encourage us not to ask each other what we got, but if you get a bad mark people still always say you've done really well, or tell you what to do to improve. I once got 27 per cent but the others just said I was unlucky,' said one boy. Setting for subjects begins in year 4, with streaming in year 8. Latin is taught from year 6.

Parents praise the efforts made to find and develop talents, which may not be academic. There are 16 peripatetic music teachers, and a DT building which develops practical skills – it's equipped with laser cutters and scroll saws, and children take woodwork from year 3, making everything from working pens to cars for drag racing. 'We are so impressed that every child has something they will achieve in. It has been music for my daughter and sport for my boys,' said a mother.

There's a great range of sports on offer – an extras programme one afternoon per week offers archery, fencing, golf, sailing and lacrosse. The school's sailing team has been prep school champions, and one girl has made the GB U15 fencing team. There's other options on extras afternoon for the non-sporty, such as farming, funky dance, fishing, beekeeping and touch typing.

Much is made by the head and parents about keeping the pupils children as long as possible, and they are clearly successful at cocooning them. The year 8s seem younger than their peers we meet in secondary schools – no less articulate, but definitely less worldly. Parents report no divide between age groups, saying: 'You constantly see older children encouraging and playing with the younger ones, and children in year 3 aren't scared of the year 8s.'

Parents predominantly work in the City of London; others are doctors at the nearby hospital, or farmers. 'It is very inclusive and friendly with no social divides, and parents are always ready to help one another out,' said a mother. There are fitness groups for parents to join including zumba, Nordic walking and joggy-doggy.

The only gripe you'll hear from parents – and that's a mild one – is that they find it a long day for the prep school children (8.30am to 5.15pm, with prep afterwards at home or at school from year 5 until 6.30pm). A lot of children take up the flexible boarding option – 'really fun,' the pupils agree; around one-third of children stay for up to four nights per week. Rooms are up in the eaves, and again you wouldn't be surprised to find the Famous Five up there having lashings of hot chocolate. Boarders do supervised prep for one hour, then after supper, the options include swimming, singing, and playing outside. Matron Julie is reportedly 'nice to cuddle with'.

St Swithun's Prep School

Linked with St Swithun's School

Alresford Road, Winchester, Hampshire SO21 1HA

Ages 3–11 **Pupils** 189 **C of E**

Fees: £5,424 – £13,971 pa

01962 835750
www.stswithuns.com

Head: Since 2017, Rebecca Lyons-Smith (degree from University of Northumbria; PGCE, MBA from UCL). Previously, deputy head at Stroud, King Edward VI Preparatory School.

She sits on the governing body of a local state junior school and has recently become an inspector for the Independent Schools Inspectorate. Lives in the New Forest with her husband Trevor, a consultant gastroenterologist at Southampton General Hospital, and her two stepsons.

Entrance: Non-selective with two form entry. Girls with a co-ed nursery. When The Pilgrims' School (choir school of Winchester Cathedral) opened a pre-prep department in 2008 there was a natural single sex split between these two schools.

Exit: Usually more than half to St Swithun's senior school and a handful to Godolphin School. The rest in ones and twos to eg Alton Convent, King Edward VI School, Churchers College, Lord Wandsworth College. Wycombe Abbey, Sherborne Girls School, Downe House, Sir Henry Beaufort School, Eggar's School, King's School, Amery Hill.

Remarks: The ethos here is to have fun and make mistakes, no spoon feeding – it feels a very happy school, with the kids

S

joking and teasing confidently with the adults and each other without overstepping the mark. Form teachers are on top of the ins and outs of friendships; staff retention (female heavy) is excellent with lots of career development in house.

Daily assembly (separate for the nursery and the pre-prep), the nursery has outside free flow, the older ones help out at break. At lunch the littlest are served by the teachers and the older ones, while year 3 and above help themselves – cookery lessons and clubs enjoyed. New uniform takes its orange from the so successful senior school lacrosse team, shorts in the summer instead of dresses are great for climbing trees. Spanish and German for the youngest, a trip to a château in France on offer for older girls, skiing and sailing are off site sport options.

Four houses (named after birds) compete in swimming, rounders, netball and spelling – the head girl teams add up the house points and make a power point presentation for each Friday assembly. Head girl for one term (chosen by the teachers) and an apprentice for a year – the latter form the school council and are voted in by the children, they gather consensus among the kids and feed it back to the head and the deputy: names for school guinea pigs to an ambitious design for the new playground (they petitioned for a budget rise).

ICT goes from bugs for simple coding in nursery to podcasts for a humanities project on natural disasters. Topic-based curriculum feels exciting (war artists' sketches, air raid shelters in DT and war poetry in English) with off curriculum science days, one offering an insight into the trades of electrician, architect, project manager.

The school building is gorgeous, light and bright (huge argon-filled double glazing) with ethernet, Wifi, Chromebooks, underfloor heating, 21 square-metres of photovoltaics on the roof, a lift (school council requested music and a mirror!) and a separate external entrance for the nursery. It is all designed to reflect the school's teaching rather than the other way around, with the science room opening out into the shelter belt and nature trail, an open plan library at the entrance and all classrooms and staff training rooms with windows onto the internal corridors. Transparency for all.

Up to 16 per class in the pre-prep; 18 in the prep. Full time SENCo and team of classroom assistants for in-class support, outside agencies if required (experience in supporting Down's syndrome and cerebral palsy).

Shares a librarian, gym and pool with the senior school, as well as curriculum links and joint academic policy set by the governors. Enormously popular fame academy just for the junior school ends with a recording in a studio off site: the girls write a song together, perform it (eg dulcimer, drums, piano), entries whittled down by peer votes and creative teams grow as the field shrinks. Drama ranges from Shakespeare to the West Side Story with four performances a year, roles are auditioned for and Pilgrims' boys are asked in if needed.

Lots of medical professional families because Southampton hospital is so close, lawyers, accountants, HR, PR – down to earth rather than glitzy with the best marketing being word of mouth. One parent often commutes to work in London, sometimes a father in Russia or China with a mother setting up base in the UK with the kids.

St Swithun's School

Linked with St Swithun's Prep School

Alresford Road, Winchester, Hampshire SO21 1HA

Ages 11–18 **Pupils** 510 **Sixth form** 134 **Boarders** 110 full, 103 weekly
C of E

Fees: Day £20,565; Boarding £33,600 pa

01962 835700
www.stswithuns.com

Headmistress: Since 2010, the contained and cogent Jane Gandee MA (40s). Read French and Spanish at Girton College, Cambridge, then a local government accountant until she went into teaching (OU PGSE) at Lord Wandsworth College, Oakham, Queenswood and finally director of studies at City of London School for Girls. The stamina and thoughtful tactics that make her a successful athlete (represented Cambridge at athletics and cross-country, captained the women's football team) are combined with a rigorous passion in her stewardship of the girls here. She teaches Spanish in the lead up to GCSEs and speaks at two out of the five assemblies each week, finding raw material in books ranging from Freakanomics to Daphne du Maurier novels.

Proud of the expanded co-curricular and sport options ('she's got the place buzzing'), determined to open the pupils' eyes to a real range of issues via external speakers – John Humphries, Michael Portillo, Sir Ralph Fiennes, Laura Bates (Everyday Sexism) – so they can make their own decisions. Committed to developing girls' resilience and confidence – they once took the mickey out of her for her frequent championing of feminism, but now they join in.

Academic matters: Brilliant exam results, up in the dizzying thin air at the top of the league tables. How a relatively unselective school like this one manages it is mysterious and must drive the London hothouses – with their exacting entry testing of pupils from the age of 4 – around the bend. Parents say, 'They don't cream off the top of their applicants; they help girls reach their potential'. Famed for hotshot sciences (three floors of dedicated labs) and maths; English is just as impressive, even if pursued by fewer girls – pupils say teachers are great, 'no duffs'.

Psychology, politics and art history offered at A level (with art history lessons also on offer for parents). Compulsory GCSE subjects are English, maths, plus a foreign language and at least two sciences. Setting in maths and modern languages – with support (one full-time SENCo, part time assistants and outside support if necessary) an SEN child can still access the curriculum. French and German both studied to the end of year 8 when Spanish enters as an option. Most take (only) 10 GCSEs, and just French taken early – a strategy that produces few results below a 6. In 2018, 80 per cent A*-A/9-7 grades at GCSE. At A level, 66 per cent A*/A.

Parents report that teachers expect a lot and the girls push themselves, which means that confidence must be built elsewhere if not academically strong. The whole of the lower school enters the Maths Challenge, which encourages different ways of thinking. The Stretch programme helps put academia in perspective – a compulsory hour per week of a loosely cerebral activity for every pupil eg film clubs, music composition, chess, Amnesty international.

The timetable is in half hour units but most lessons are an hour; each A level choice has an hour of each subject per day for balance and to mitigate risk when missing a day. The light and warm library is used for study periods mostly by the sixth form, although whole classes can book out the IT area. In the upper sixth both day and boarding girls can return to their one dedicated house to study and hang out.

Careers fair annually in Harvey Hall with parents and old girls and speakers ranging from architects to philosophy teachers. Families report that careers advice strong on well-trodden paths such as medicine and Russell Group universities, yet quirky directions need more research initiative from home.

Games, options, the arts: Lacrosse is the strongest sport with a fixture every Saturday in both the two terms it is played, attendance at the nationals and amazing international tour a highlight. Conscious effort to broaden the range of sports – netball and tennis are on the up in terms of competition; also swimming, archery, golf, fencing, squash, scuba diving, badminton, cheerleading, football, polo, skiing, pilates. Some of these are only on offer as one of the 30 or so co-curricular choices, others have emerged into the fixture list. The pool is 25m with an Olympic standard diving board (Winchester residents use it too), stables are 10 minutes away and the sailing squad heads off most Sundays. Location in South Downs National Park means limited permanent floodlighting for sports pitches but play continues regardless through temporary arrangements. Early morning swimming popular until studying gets really serious in sixth form, and equipment has been recently updated so apparently girls watch The Big Bang Theory while running.

In the lower years there is an hour of art, drama and food tech each week. Very enthusiastic art team with a regular life model, Rosa Verloop inspired sculptures (stuffed tights), nominated desks and eventually cubby holes for A level students – DT floor just as sparky with electronics, laser cutter and Green Power car (has to be fast, green and involve good team) racing every year at Goodwood, but no A level take up at present. Amazing aromas sandwiched on the floor between the other choices, cooked up in the professional tech kitchen. Textiles popular too with A level newly on offer.

Performing arts centre provides a lively hub for music and drama in the school (and doubles as the venue for morning assembly). Drama studio backs on to the main stage and is used for lessons (no A level at present). Girls do plays on their own initiative too, inviting Winchester boys in for male parts (and vice versa) eg Alan Ayckbourn's Bedroom Farce. Recent joint performance of Oliver! with Winchester College, and more planned. Parents would like more academic links to Winchester College, but it plays quite hard to get; lots of local girls' schools would like to be partnered with it more closely.

Great range of orchestras, bands, ensembles and choirs – chamber, gospel and a capella – some open to all, others more selective. Music school houses practice rooms and an IT suite with Sibelius for composition, basic Cubase skills for recording performances. Around 75 per cent of pupils learn a musical instrument and some 215 candidates are entered for external music exams each year. Senior choir sings evensong each term in the cathedral and tours overseas every other year.

Boarding: Separate boarding and day houses until a single combined one for upper sixth; the latter are the only ones allowed to go back to their house to work during the day. The seniors do prep duty for the younger ones and there are clusters with a 'mother' in the sixth form and younger 'sisters' or 'cousins' in other years, a 'family' that looks out for each other. A race back to day houses for a hot chocolate made for the girls at break – and letter delivery for the boarding girls; day and boarding girls become less separate as they move up the school. Different nationalities are more likely to hang out with their own at the weekend – the balance is well set between cultural comfort and integration.

Initially Toblerone shaped dorms with equal sections under Velux windows, flexible boarding and school bed linen for the youngest, a single room for most from 12+ with a hand basin, useful essay quotes and posters on the wall. Each house has thoughtful inclusive touches that soften the necessary (safeguarding) communality – word of the week board for little ones, movie night, pool table, Wii, piano – as well as the vital drudge of learning to do laundry. Everyone sits around the breakfast bar at the weekend in their pyjamas and the houseparents make sure that full boarders keep busy with three activities during week nights and three at weekends eg a trip to the zoo, decorating your mobile phone cover, making gingerbread men, skating or music practice.

Background and atmosphere: Founded as Winchester High School in 1884 by Anna Bramston, daughter of the Dean of Winchester, who remained as school secretary for over 40 years – the dean, the headmaster of Winchester College and the mayor are still part of the governing body. Changed its name to St Swithun's in 1927 and moved to the present 45 acre site in 1931. Vast, intimidating, red-brick, Queen Anne style building with blonde parquet flooring, large windows and long corridors – girls learn to look up and smile as they pass each other rather than hold/avoid gaze as they approach from either end.

A tight community of supportive girls with a culture of 'go for it' rather than 'too cool' to join in eg minority of girls remain in normal clothes on dress up days. Flip side of this is the pressure for good results that they can exert on each other. Boarders and day pupils retreat to different houses for break but all eat together at lunch, and head girl team runs the school forum and instigates a school wide and term long game of tag. This has everyone searching for their targets, who in turn dye their hair, swap uniforms and even hide in cupboards – all for glory, chocolate and side effect of integration. Pupils give regular assemblies and topics range from Beyoncé to the Khmer Rouge, while the school forum has input to subjects as disparate as the air con in the gym and more tenor timbre in the hymns. Fundraising Friday is another equaliser, as money is raised for the voted annual charities, and some girls do EdClub, a worldwide initiative that uses Skype to encourage disadvantaged children (many in slums) to learn using broadband.

Winchester the town is important for the freedom it offers only 15 minutes' walk away – and usually a cab ride back up hill. Provides an opportunity to meet up with Winchester boys; the seniors can eat out or go to a play. The outgoing ones say it is very relaxed, no-one puts on make-up, they are all just a group of friends with about 20 per cent in relationships and many of the day girls knowing the boys from local life; the less confident ones mention a pressure to add the boys as friends on Facebook as soon as they return – yet all monitored (some girls reckon too closely) by the housemistresses and house assistants. Both have a reduced teaching timetable so that they can concentrate on the emotional temperature in each house – there is a health centre on site and a clinical psychologist offers discrete appointments in the old chapel; the whole school benefits from her years of experience of the lives and issues of teenage girls. The leavers' ball is usually just for the girls alone (their choice, no Winchester boys); that, and the singing of Jerusalem, is guaranteed to cause some tears to be shed.

Pastoral care, well-being and discipline: Houseparents are first point of contact for issues from homesickness through bullying to A level choices – although a form tutor is vital for the latter too. Parents feel everything is dealt with swiftly and sensibly; avoiding a before bed phone call can give both parent and child a less weepy night. Phones are used for email nowadays, particularly useful for older girls looking at timetables and emailing essays, restricted for the younger ones.

An art project of smiles photographed around the school has found a permanent home on the wall of the modern (2013) chapel – all full boarders and staff attend every Sunday, optional for the upper sixth. Over-indulging in alcohol the most common serious disciplinary issue – and that not very, if girls' shock at relaxed attitude observed in their visits to boys' or co-ed schools is anything to go by.

New Thrive programme for all years 'aims to inculcate the habits of good mental and physical health, and to prepare students for the world outside the school gates'. Lessons designed around 'real world' experiences have included year 7s trying out setting up a new community after a plane crash on a desert island, year 10s practising empathetic listening through role-play and year 13s taking part in a student survival programme including cooking and cycling.

Pupils and parents: Down to earth parents who value education; armed forces, businesspeople, diplomats, lawyers, doctors and parents of bright children working in less lucrative professions; four wheel drives rather than Bentleys. Over half are day pupils – school bus services are getting better after unflattering comparison with King Edward. Twenty (and rising) per cent of boarders from London, often with more local weekend houses – weekly boarders make up 20 per cent of the school. Heathrow is less than an hour away and Southampton airport only 20 minutes, so 16 per cent of boarders from overseas, range of 17 countries. Occasional international guest pupils come for a term from France, Germany, Spain, Czechoslovakia – must be fluent in English. Alumni range from actor Emma Chambers (Alice in the Vicar of Dibley) to journalist and radio presenter Fi Glover and Emma Walmsley, CEO of GlaxoSmith Kline.

Entrance: Main intake by pre-test, January 11+ and CE. Places offered on pre-test and reference from current head – no longer in order of registration. Everyone must pass CE, whether from state, private, or school's own junior school. The latter provides about a third of the intake, others from London day schools and local preps. About 20 more enter at age 13 with a pre-test 18 months before (can be taken overseas) and then a firm offer; if there is a crisis and they don't make the necessary 60 per cent at common entrance then there is leeway – occasional places further up the school. About 20 join the sixth form with own entry and test in November; a summer year 10 report is necessary before registration – very competitive.

Exit: Around 25 per cent leave after GCSEs, bound for the local sixth form college or for other co-ed sixth forms. Almost all the others go on to university, mostly the old-established ones, with Oxbridge (four in 2018), Exeter, Bristol, Imperial College London, Oxford Brookes, Edinburgh and Warwick being favourite destinations, sciences unsurprisingly popular (two medics in 2018). One off to ETH Zurich.

Money matters: One in six pupils has a means-tested bursary, an academic scholarship, sports scholarship or a music award (available at 11, 13 and 16). All scholarships are for up to 20 per cent of fees and based on the calibre of the applicant, rather than need. Bursaries are means-tested and available for 50 to 100 per cent of the fees. Music awards include free music lessons.

Remarks: Academic powerhouse with bluestocking reputation now widened into great co-curricular and sports options. Girls egg each other on to great results and fun too.

St Teresa's Effingham School

Effingham, Surrey RH5 6ST

Ages 2–18 **Pupils** 634 **Sixth form** 77 **Boarders** 57 full, 6 weekly, 11 flexi (from year 6) **RC**

Fees: Day £8,955 – £17,595; Boarding £24,300 – £29,955 pa

01372 452037
www.st-teresas.com

Headmaster: Since 2012, Mike Farmer (50s). First teaching job was as a sailing instructor, spending three years post-graduation in Greece and Turkey. He met his future wife Mary-Ann in Greece and looming marriage and family took him to a job in the real world at Godolphin School, Salisbury, where he taught economics, business and ICT. The head there, Hilary Fender, took him with her to be assistant head at Headington, Oxford in 1997. First headship was at Kilgraston in Perthshire (2003), where he achieved the gong of UK Independent School of the Year in 2011 and turned around a school that had been dubbed the Marie Celeste to achieve the highest growth rate in its sector.

He has a sound business head, the confidence of his governors and a clear sight of what he needs to do to ensure the school flourishes in a wealthy and highly competitive area for independent schools. Comes across as self-effacing and unassuming but what lies beneath is steel. Has taken bold risks to finance capital projects in order to boost the roll and scythed staff where necessary. Educated at a large comprehensive himself and not at all stuffy. 'He's a very humble man – he doesn't have that ego you see in some heads,' a parent told us.

Career paths of his children show that he pays more than lip service to developing individual talents – one is a theoretical physicist, one a theatrical agent.

Head of prep: Since 2015, Sarah Conrad, previously head of New Hall Prep School in Chelmsford. Having graduated with a BA in English, German and theology from the University of Durham and completed her PGCE, began her career in primary education teaching in a variety of schools including a four-year post in the renowned British International School, Tanglin Trust School, in Singapore. Returning to the UK, worked as director of music at top preparatory St Cedd's School in Chelmsford before moving to New Hall. Married with two daughters.

Academic matters: Prep school parents are impressed with the care and the quality of teaching. 'Our daughters bounce into school every day,' one told us. Another said: 'Our daughter had struggled at her last school. We felt she had slipped through the net and not progressed at all in years 4 and 5. We were concerned about how far behind she was when she entered in year 6. The prep school teachers were amazing. She caught up without feeling stressed or pushed at any point in the year.' Setting for English, maths and science. Pupils taught by specialists in some subjects from year 3. Science lab for the younger children within the prep and from year 5 pupils are timetabled to use the science labs in the senior school. Computer science including coding and robotics taught from year 1.

School is non-selective – head's aim is to boost its academic reputation, but not make it a hothouse. 'We have got to make sure we can stretch the top end,' he says. To this end, he has brought in an assistant head (academic) who runs the Oxbridge enrichment society and the gifted and talented programme. She is like a glamorous Miss Jean Brodie, brainy and geeky but with spiky heels and stylish clothes. Just the job to have teenage girls hanging on her every word and parents love her weekly 'All geek to me' emails, with their suggestions of enriching books, radio programmes, exhibitions etc. She also runs academic seminar evenings, where girls present findings in front of their peers, and brings in visiting speakers – recently a talk from the Nuffield Foundation on the ethics of treating dementia.

Most popular A level subjects are English, maths and science. Head has overseen the introduction of new A levels, including classics, classical civilisation, Latin, government and politics and music technology. In 2018, 64 per cent of entries achieved A*-B and 33 per cent A*/A at A level; at GCSE, 53 per cent A*-A/9-7.

Languages include French, German, Spanish and Latin, with Mandarin and Russian as after-school options. Double and triple award science on offer and there are visiting speakers of the calibre of Sir Robert Winston. The school is considered a specialist for art, especially in the overseas market, and each year pupils progress to fashion design and art foundation courses. We saw some fantastic textiles work and sixth formers deeply engrossed in their work in the art room.

Pupils talk of the individualism of teaching, so there is not one particular style. We saw a key stage 4 class dissecting a poem and noted the pupils' confidence in voicing their individual interpretation; nearly all had something to say and they were unabashed in front of a visitor. Loads of praise for the English department from parents – indeed, for most of the teaching – although one told us: 'There are still a couple of old retainers who some of us feel should be sent down the hill, but generally Mr Farmer has got a grip on what he expects from his staff.'

Games, options, the arts: Lots to appeal to tennis players or riders. Newly formed St Teresa's Tennis Academy is headed by former Wimbledon player Lee Childs. Four hard courts and nine artificial grass courts. Recently opened equestrian centre stables around a dozen horses and riding is offered as an after-school option. Head says it's an unashamed way to draw in new pupils and differentiate the school from the competition.

Sports hall has been redeveloped and a coach brought in to run a swimming academy. Is now the Surrey hub for Pentathlon GB, giving the school access to Olympic coaches. 'We will become a very sporty school,' says the head. A parent told us: 'Negative comments have been made about sport (or lack of it) by many parents but this has been addressed by Mr Farmer and a much more efficient PE timetable is now in place.'

Director of music effused enthusiasm as he showed us round the music department. A professional French horn player, he has performed with the most prestigious orchestras but is just as keen on bringing in local rock bands for the girls to produce in their own sound recording studio, or using digital technology. We saw one class composing on computers using serialism, a method often used to produce discordant film music. His contacts enable him to bring in professionals as peripatetic music teachers – cello teacher works at the Royal Opera House, flute teacher is in the BBC orchestra. Noticeboards are crammed with flyers for music events and pictures from overseas choir tours (girls have had the opportunity to perform in venues like Notre Dame Cathedral). School also hosts the Surrey Hills Music Festival, as well as numerous recitals.

Thesps can take LAMDA courses in public speaking, musical theatre and acting. Three achieved gold medals last year and some have gained up to 200 UCAS points from these qualifications. New arts centre on the way – old art rooms will be converted into an new sixth form study facility.

Week night activities for boarders range from pudding club to ice skating to picnics, with Saturday afternoon outings to theme parks, theatre, paintballing, bowling. On site activities include falconry and circus skills. Plus tennis, riding and other sports.

Boarding: Some 60 per cent of boarders are international students though school has set maximum of 10 per cent in school as a whole. Boarding accommodation recently refurbished, decorated in light neutral colours and homely touches. Rooms range from singles for the sixth form to dorms for three to six girls for the younger pupils.

Background and atmosphere: St Teresa's was founded in 1928 by the Religious Order of Christian Instruction, and the main house now forms the centre of the senior school. Other buildings have been tacked on over the years, and the former nuns' accommodation has been converted to classrooms. The prep school was newly built in 2009 (it moved here from another site). There's nothing to set an architecture fan's pulse racing, but the classrooms are bright and functional. The campus is a lovely 48-acre parkland with ancient trees, set in an area of outstanding natural beauty. Very secluded – it would be nigh on impossible for girls to sneak out for a night on the town.

When the head arrived he made wide-ranging changes straight away in order to turn around the school's fortunes. Rebranding meant changing the school's name, modernising the school's newsletter and bringing in a new uniform. It was out with the old and in with the new in key staff appointments – 'there was some staff movement,' he told us diplomatically. In one year he brought in a new head of prep, head of science, head of boarding and assistant head (academic).

It's been well received by parents. As one told us: 'I have yet to hear a negative comment about Mr Farmer. I think we are all astonished at how he has managed to turn the school around and increase the numbers in such a short time.' Another said: 'He has transformed it from a good to an amazing school. The children's view of the school and their pride in it has changed a lot.'

There's a buzz about the staff – they are clearly rejuvenated by the changes. And word is spreading. 'I was at a coffee morning for new parents and the vibe was amazing. People were saying it was their number one choice and were queuing up to get in – well, that's new,' said one mother. Year 7 intake doubled to four forms; plush sixth form centre can accommodate up to 120.

School's Catholicism comes in the gentlest form – as an ethos of kindness, supporting the weaker, and strong pastoral care. Around a quarter of the pupils are Catholic and there's no requirement for staff other than the head to be Catholic. Although certain feast days are celebrated, the school recently celebrated Diwali, led by an Indian member of staff. Mass on Sundays is compulsory for Catholics and all boarders attend twice a term. The chapel is modern, with some stained glass and soothing music throughout the day – a place to wander into for peaceful repose. The priest is reportedly young and trendy. There's nothing to frighten off those not of the faith, said one parent. 'The school isn't overly Catholic but it has a Christian way about it, which is a good thing. I know people are put off by it, which is a shame because it makes the school a more nurturing place to be.'

Pastoral care, well-being and discipline: In school, younger girls' well-being is monitored through a buddy system – sixth formers meet their charges once a week. Girls feel able to raise issues and know they will be listened to. "We can make suggestions and we will be heard and acknowledged,' said one girl. 'We weren't happy with the school food so we surveyed pupils and presented the findings and it has improved a lot since.' Head plans to introduce Big Brother style video diaries (which he previously ran at Kilgraston), where girls can raise any concerns.

Pupils and parents: Girls are wholesome looking – all pony-tails and make up-free faces. Wide range of nationalities – 15 per cent of students are international boarders from countries like China, Hong Kong, Mexico, Spain, Russia and Nigeria. Locals bus in from a radius extending to Guildford, Reigate and south London.

Most parents who choose the school haven't put academic reputation as their top priority. This means there's a blessed lack of competitive parent syndrome, we're told. Some very wealthy parents, but a mix of economic backgrounds. 'Those with limited funds will certainly not feel intimidated, although the arrival of the tennis academy and equestrian centre could change this,' said one mother. 'One prospective parent did ask me if a horse was going to be an option on the kit list.'

Entrance: Entry into the co-ed nursery is from the age of 2. Entry into the prep is by report and informal assessment during a welcome day, as well as references from previous school. The main criterion is whether the child is likely to cope in the senior school. In practice this only rules out those receiving high levels of learning support.

Senior school currently has a waiting list for the first time in many years. More top end girls have been applying, which means the academic standard for entry at 11 is now similar to an 11+ pass or level 5 in national curriculum tests. Canny parents who think their child may miss this mark are putting girls in the prep in year 5 or 6 as this gives automatic entry. However other talents can tip it. 'A girl may be very good at sport, art or music – we won't go just on the exam,' says the head. There's a big influx at senior entry – year 7 currently has 25 pupils from the prep and 35 newcomers. Virtually all year 6s progress to the senior school, many with scholarships.

When it comes to the sixth form, all current pupils are accepted 'as long as we can offer them a programme,' while incomers need six 6s and a 7 at GCSE.

Although the school is Catholic, there is no requirement to be Catholic. Children raised in the faith do not get priority, although it may be a deciding factor.

Exit: Vast majority of prep school girls move on to the senior school, with automatic entry, and usually several with scholarships. Recent higher education destinations include medicine at Leeds, human sciences at Oxford, accounting at Durham and Manchester, art foundation at Central St Martins and youth and community studies at Winchester. None to Oxbridge in 2018.

Money matters: Scholarships are awarded for academic excellence, art, drama, music and sport.

Remarks: Moves afoot to ramp up school's educational attainment by pushing the brightest, but not at the expense of the middling. We reckon that this is a school that truly can cater for wide ranging abilities. There's a lovely, gentle atmosphere – we saw no cliques of glossy haired alpha girls. A good fit for girls who want to take their time to grow up or those who need to know it's OK to be geeky.

The Schools at Somerhill

Somerhill, Tonbridge, Kent TN11 0NJ

Ages 3–13 **Pupils** Yardley Court 243, Derwent Lodge 139, Somerhill Pre-Prep 190

Fees: £10,050 – £15,465 pa

01732 352124
www.somerhill.org

Heads: Principal of The Schools at Somerhill and head of Yardley Court since September 2017, Duncan Sinclair MA HDE, previously head of Taunton Prep. Born in Zimbabwe, he moved to South Africa at the age of 7. Read English and environmental science at the University of Cape Town before completing a higher diploma in education. Began his teaching career in Cape Town, also coaching cricket, rugby and athletics. At the same time, he enjoyed a secondary career as a semi-professional rugby player representing Western Province as a second row forward. Moved to St Michael's Preparatory School, Kent, in 2002 where he was year 4 teacher, head of geography and PSHE and deputy head and completed his MA in educational leadership and management. In addition to taking part in competitive cricket and hockey, he plays the clarinet, trombone and tuba and is a keen chorister. Married to Georgina, a primary teacher with a PE specialisation; they have three young sons, who are all pupils at Somerhill Pre-Prep.

Headteacher of Derwent Lodge: Since 2016, Helen Hoffmann, BA MA Lit PGCE, previously director of studies at Vinehall. Helen has worked in independent education for over 15 years, holding both academic and pastoral head roles, exams officer, GCSE examiner and head of English and drama. A literacy specialist, she has taught eight different subjects at a senior level and has taught every year group from year 1 to 13. For Helen, the three 'R's of education are risk, resilience and reflection. Creative and dynamic, she has a passion for developing a growth mindset in those she teaches.

Head of Somerhill Pre-Prep: Since April 2019, Jacqui Marriott, previously head of pre-prep at Cheam School, having been head of early years at Dulwich Prep Cranbrook and Dragon School in Oxford.

Entrance: The schools describe themselves as mixed ability and the majority of children join Somerhill via the co-educational pre-prep (main entry points at pre-school and reception). Transfer to Yardley Court (boys) and Derwent Lodge (girls) is automatic at year 3. Those wishing to squeeze in at 7+ may sit a brief assessment. Prospective parents could get lucky with a place beyond year 3, but the numbers say if this is the school for you, you'd be wise to get in early. A few accepted in the final pre-exam years, space permitting. Discounts for siblings: five per cent for a second child, 10 per cent for three or more.

Exit: Girls are prepared to leave at 11+ for Tonbridge Grammar, Tunbridge Wells Girls' Grammar, Walthamstow Hall and Kent College. High number of boys, around 40 per cent, also exit at this stage for the Kent grammars, principally The Judd and Skinners. Principal is clear that Somerhill is 'not an 11+ factory', neatly illustrated by the pupil we met who was unfazed by having sat the exam the previous day. Nonetheless, results are strong with a 90 per cent success rate. Tutoring does go on – a sore point – but both heads see it as unnecessary and generally to be discouraged. Of the rest who stay on most go to Tonbridge, Sevenoaks or Eastbourne, many with scholarships and exhibitions.

Remarks: Traditional curriculum with plenty of active learning.

Plenty of long-serving staff with young male teachers significantly visible at Yardley Court. All expected to go the extra mile, such as those we saw on the day of our visit, cheerily preparing to take part in a school camp out. Parents describe the quality of teaching as excellent, with the inevitable few exceptions. Reports graded for effort as well as achievement, individual targets identified and timed so that parents have an opportunity to follow up quickly at consultations – not always a given.

Just over 10 per cent identified with special educational needs, mainly dyspraxia and dyslexia. Two full-time and three part-time staff across both preps, offering mostly in-class support. Dyslexic children using laptops during lessons were less visible on our visit than in some preps, but we were asssured that this is supported where beneficial.

Somerhill is a terrifically sporty school, with over 600 fixtures annually. It's not just about the A and B teams – boys and girls play in at least four inter-school matches a term, whatever their ability. The school is particularly strong in athletics, notably cross-country, with both boys and girls now national IAPS champions. They have a very strong swimming team, with Yardley Court placed 5th in the 2018 IAPS Swimming Nationals.

Inspirational sporting figures pop by – Bonita Norris, mountaineer and the youngest woman to reach the summit of Everest, recently talked to Derwent Lodge pupils. Paralympian swimmers Stephanie Millward and Claire Cashmore have visited, while Yardley Court pupils heard from Kenton Cool, who has scaled Everest 11 times, and old boy Ruaridh McConnochie, rugby 7s Olympic silver medallist in Rio.

In response to parental disquiet, homework – particularly holiday homework – has reduced significantly. Music teaching is singled out for praise, as inspirational, inclusive and fun (new music centre). The summer concert involves more than 300 pupils in both junior and senior choirs, as likely to include pop songs as the classics and recently featuring songs from Abba. Pupils can choose from more than 22 instruments for individual tuition and roughly two thirds do. In year 4 Yardley Court boys can take choral auditions for Tonbridge School's chapel choir.

The two preps share good size art facilities, high up in the attics, including two new pottery kilns. Art on display is of a very high standard. 'Some amazing work produced,' said one parent and we agree – we saw year 6 pupils animatedly discussing with their teacher how they were to build a life-size wire animal sculpture.

S

Clubs are squeezed into every moment. For the girls, active options include ballet, tennis, hockey and netball, or they might try knitting, ceramics, jazz and modern art, plus they can now join the boys in camp-building, LAMDA club, First Lego League, Young Engineers, Judo and more. Boys can start the day with a spot of Samba band, and end it with sport of every kind or, for the non-sporty, gardening or Cubs. Creative minds can try camera, animation or cookery clubs.

All three parts of the school are housed in a large Jacobean stone mansion, once a family home, set in 150 acres: part manicured lawns, part playing fields and extensive woodland. The school perches at the highest point, giving it great views over the Kent countryside. With the Derwent Lodge houses named after the Lake District, a dipping pond, den-building and sledging on snowy days and not one but two proper adventure playgrounds (which will sell the school in an instant to children), there is a definite whiff of Swallows and Amazons. Inside is a confusing maze of staircases and classrooms, some rather utilitarian, others all stained glass windows and polished wood. And, while there is a bit of chipped paint like any lived-in family home (the family feel is frequently mentioned by old boys and girls), the wood gleams and there's not a leaf out of place.

The preps seem right for parents and children wanting a single-sex environment – there are very different uniforms and separate play-times in addition to tailored teaching – but there is also a bit of mixing. Shared activities include taekwando and indoor athletics, choirs, cake sales, orchestras, theme days and trips such as ski-ing and sailing. Some parents would like the boys and girls to mix more; it's a balance the schools strive to get right. Parents agree they are hot on anti-bullying.

Somerhill seems particularly well-suited to the working parent. Not only does the single site mean a life-saving single drop off for most families, but the school day begins at 8am, and pupils can remain in school until 6pm. Breakfast club from 7.30am; after-school clubs run until 5.30pm (some additional fees) and then co-ordinate with tea if necessary and late supervision (small fee). Younger children can be supervised for free as they wait for their siblings.

Highly popular pre-prep: with three classes (20 max) in most of the years. It neatly slots into the former coach-houses, providing spacious classrooms with plenty of natural light. Younger children play in the soft-surface central courtyard, but also benefit from their own adventure playground and time in the grounds. The atmosphere is warm, calm and caring and there's a team of plentiful, long-serving staff. The twin focus on both academic achievement (SEN assistance where needed) and teaching of good behaviour was in evidence during our visit when children worked diligently in small groups, greeting us politely.

Pupils travel from Sevenoaks, Tunbridge Wells, Kings Hill and Tonbridge and surrounding villages, some by school bus. Mostly children with English as their first language, with no EAL requirements. Parents come here from all walks of life but are a well-heeled bunch in the main – plenty of takers for a £1,000 school trip to Bermuda in year 8, for instance. They describe their peers as friendly and supportive, 'very, very rare to hear any school gate carping'.

What kind of child would thrive at Somerhill? Apparently there is 'no set mould, you don't have to be a certain type, or to conform. A child who is happy in his or her own skin'. Parents say the school doesn't wrap children up in cotton wool, and while 'sporty kids would be in their element, it's also good for wallflowers ... the art room is open for all at break times as is the library'.

Seaford College

Lavington Park, Petworth, West Sussex GU28 0NB

Ages 13–18 **Pupils** 798 (524 boys, 274 girls) **Sixth form** 217
Boarders 25 full, 88 weekly, 75 flexi

Fees: Day £10,320 – £21,390; Boarding £21,510 – £33,090 pa

01798 867392
www.seaford.org

Headmaster: Since 2013, John Green. Background in professional rugby – he teaches the first team, donning wellies with suit. Taught previously at Barry Boys' School, Ardingly College and

Hurstpierpoint, before becoming deputy at Seaford. Married to Sîan with three children.

Tiggerish energy, staunch and unapologetic supporter of the underdog, with a clear vision of how he wants Seaford to be. Works hard to install a sense of value and self worth in all his pupils: A* pupils at Seaford now consider Oxford; BTec pupils are told 'you could be employing those A* pupils in a few years time'. Quality he most desires for his pupils: pride in self.

Academic matters: In 2018, good solid results: 33 per cent A*-A/9-7 at GCSE; 47 per cent A*-B, 32 per cent A*/A at A level. Judged on its place in a league table – unremarkable. But the remarkable exists within these figures at this non-selective school. The most able are achieving the high grades you would expect; but so are a good number of those of more average abilities: Seaford generally adding at least one grade to pupils' attainment.

New pupils at Seaford all have a data interview: a detailed meeting showing parents and the pupil their CAT scores and the national picture of attainment for someone of their abilities. 'Children in the middle can achieve highly and shouldn't put a ceiling on expectations'. Top grades can suddenly seem like something attainable: one parent told us about her son, told by his previous school that he was a no hoper. His confidence has soared at Seaford: he's predicted good grades at A level, and led Young Enterprise last year. When he went up on speech day for an academic prize, 'it was worth every penny'.

'Seaford was seen as a school for dunces,' said a parent who was initially dubious about the school, thinking it was a 'too relaxed environment.' On meeting the head, the parent quickly felt that things had changed. Rigour is now a word which could apply to Seaford. One parent described how her son did a mock paper which went wrong: 'they were all over it and him, in a supportive, but thorough way'.

There's a new focus on high flyers here: a head of enrichment now guides the Oxford application process, and an enrichment programme selects high performers in each subject and adds a layer on top of syllabus stuff – masterclasses in maths this term with lectures on chaos and infinity. Lecture doors are open to anyone truly interested (while trying to exclude crafty prep dodgers).

The head has made several staff changes, to the relief of parents: 'The dead wood's gone', said one briskly. There was a lot of praise for the effort put in by teachers: 'what makes this school special is its staff'; 'teachers go above and beyond to help failing pupils... three extra sessions a week to help my son get a pass'.

An extremely active tutor system, with a weekly meeting of an hour, and daily catch up of five to 10 minutes every morning. Pupils are also part of vertical tutor groups spanning year groups.

Homework is marked with comments, not grades – 'if pupils get a grade, they immediately want to know what their friend got'. Effort grades have been abandoned – only pupils can really know. Instead, effort and attainment have been absorbed into the Challenge Grade system: grades set are a indication of potential – what a pupil could achieve if they work hard. Different colours indicate how well they are progressing towards their challenge grades, from significantly underachieving red, through amber, green and gold to extremely high-achieving platinum. Challenge grades are set with tutors and can be upped by pupils if they feel the challenge is not sufficient (hollow laughs from students).

A good array of subjects on offer at both GCSE and A level, plus BTecs (most recent additions hospitality and countryside management) and EPQ. Most subjects have a spread of attainment in grade terms, with grades in English, history and maths clustering towards the top end.

Learning support here is done extremely well by a staff of nine specialist teachers, five full-time, four part-time. Nearly half the pupils at the school use the unit at some point, by teacher or self-referral. Seaford proudly locates learning support in the centre of the campus, 'not the usual broom cupboard under the stairs', said a parent wryly.

'I've been to a lot of schools who say they are good at SEN', said a weary mum, 'but here it isn't just a soundbite'. The unit describes an approach that involves nurturing and developing individual potential, working hard to increase confidence, by pointing out what's right, not wrong, and how to improve. High degree of joined-up thinking to enable dyslexics to access the curriculum, with the unit meeting with other teachers regularly.

And their approach yields results. A parent described how her severely dyslexic son 'changed overnight' here. He was told at his prep that he wouldn't be able to sit GCSEs, but is now at the school of architecture in Oxford, having left Seaford with three A levels and an EPQ. If things weren't working, Seaford always looked for alternatives which fitted him better, she explained.

Mild to moderate dyslexic pupils in general, though the door is not closed to those at the severe end of the spectrum if they have a high IQ or good underlying ability, but they need to be able to access the mainstream curriculum with the help available. The unit assists pupils with dyspraxia, speech and language problems, slow processing speeds and memory problems. Would consider mild Asperger's, but not the place for autism. Help also given for ADHD (experienced but not specialists in this).

There is one guaranteed one-to-one session a week (which is charged as an extra). Extra sessions are offered to pupils if they become available, on the basis of need. There is a little in-class support.

Seaford has had a number of high-achieving dyslexics, one achieving his eight As and one B at GCSE with the help of a scribe; another part of the current small group of high flyers trying for Oxford.

Games, options, the arts: A new focus on games with the rugby-playing head: hockey's always been strong here (county winners); now rugby's just as good. Girls were languishing behind the boys a year or so ago, but head has given girls' sport a new emphasis: hockey and netball are flourishing. Cricket and tennis for both girls and boys are taking off.

Teams for all, the best playing every week, less able around six times a term. Specialist coaching for all ability levels here; and it's not just the top performers who get the accolades: recent team of the term was the U14 hockey C team.

Music at Seaford is glorious.Singing is outstanding here – the head of voice is also head of voice at junior Royal Academy in London. The head soloist describes 'music coming up through my toes' – it's no surprise that she and the choir were selected to support Gary Barlow on the last night of his tour. The music block is all white paint and new wood – smooth, calm surroundings to complement the mellifluous sounds.

Not as great an emphasis on drama as music ('not enough,' said one parent bluntly), but drama is now part of the year 9 carousel, some pupils do LAMDA, and there are productions each year: Dr Faustus the last, a dyslexic pupil taking the lead part, learning his lines by drawing pictures.

Compulsory CCF in year 10: the parades are dull, say pupils, but CCF camp was a favourite memory. DofE also available.

Art here is superb, with a big range on offer, from fine art to creative media production. Exam work included dresses of balloons and feathers; curvy wooden speakers and fabric stags' heads (they look so much better in tartan). Ghoulish sci-fi heads in the animation area; a fabric prawn (Shaun), life-like and eerily huge, hung casually from the ceiling. Sixth form art students almost live in the block – there's even a kitchen so they can brew – 'we look after them', said the head of art, comfortably. Students depart for art colleges across the country.

Boarding: It's particularly nice here, and one of the nicest things is its lack of uniformity. The four boarding houses are all different, each with a strong sense of home. Most are weekly, full timers largely being international (10 per cent of boarders are from overseas). Flexi-boarding is also available, and it's usually possible to get a room at the last minute by emailing houseparents.

Boys (years 9-12) are in a crisp new building (which parents love), run by houseparents with fluent ease. Basket drawers for shoes as soon as boys come through the door – they generally remember: it's nice to walk around in socks with underfloor heating. If they don't – hoover duty that night. Rooms for two, with temperature gauges in each room and a sofa which can turn into another bed. New wood furniture, built in above bed lights. Rooms compact, but not tight. Worth getting the big jobs – head of house gets a comfy chair and ensuite, TV and fridge (wow).

Wifi throughout (indeed, throughout the campus), and a system so house parents can see if pupils are online when they shouldn't be (after 11.30pm); younger pupils hand in tech at bedtime. Comfortable common room, kitchen for snacks, fruit and toaster. Homework is supervised, houseparents pleased that their only niggle ('haven't got any homework sir') has been resolved by the internet site which makes it clear what everyone's got. A house mum bakes pancakes and fudge crumpets for movie night. Houseparent dogs bounce into the common room in the evening. The kids love it.

Girls in years 9-12 are housed in the Mansion: rooms of all shapes and sizes for one or two, some extremely spacious – elegant windows, dreamy views. Graceful spiral staircase up to the boarding floor. In various states of paint, just done and needs doing ('needs to be modern and fresher', said a parent). Good quality wood furniture, comfortable furniture, the usual kitchen provision.

Sixth form boys housed in what parent and pupils refer to as 'the youth hostel' (aka Hedon Hall); 'but the boys are all happy in there and love the housemaster'. The fabric is old, and inside it is painted lime green (gulp); but the furniture in bedrooms and common room is smart and new, bathrooms are clean, and the common room is decorated with sports paraphernalia, donated by past and present sixth formers. Residents have a fierce affection for the house and its head, who is a staunch supporter of them. He enforces an hour's leisure reading every afternoon in the winter term (proper books, not magazines), having found out that dyslexic commuters do better because they read on the train.

Sixth form girls live in a bungalow, well-mown lawn with gnomes out front, patio with BBQ around the back. Some feeling of arriving in antipodean suburbia. Scottish giant of a house dad, casually consuming his Magnum, showed us a bright pink sitting room with golden buddha in the fire place – teenage heaven. Kitchen and seated area – they can go to the dining hall for breakfast, but most prefer to eat 'healthy girly breakfasts' in house. Cosy rooms, with the usual high quality fittings. A warm friendly relationship between pupils and houseparents.

Plenty going on for boarders at weekends, with the Sainsbury's trip on Friday evening, sports and shopping trips on Saturday, and trips to places of interest on Sunday.

Background and atmosphere: A long driveway, past golf flags waving the in the breeze and ancient trees up to the mansion house: stately home turned school. Seaford College sits at the foot of the downs, wooded hills rising immediately behind it, mists caught in the trees on the drizzly day of our visit – brewers' dubbin, said the head of English dreamily. A beautiful flint chapel nestles in the grass behind the school. Compulsory weekly service, but all beliefs welcome.

Stately elegance mixes with old cottages and swish new build. A few tatty Portakabins, due to be ripped down soon. Most parents we spoke to would like things to be a bit smarter –'there shouldn't be peeling paintwork – it needs a bit more polish'; and the head is working hard to spruce up buildings as well as pupils. Manners are of the old-fashioned variety, and include standing up for visitors and handwritten letters of thanks.

There's an emphasis here on giving something back: community service activities every week, and community action day once a year, which includes activity programmes with local primary school children, or clearing beaches.

It would not suit a child who was full on academic with no other interests, said a parent. 'Very intelligent children will thrive there if they do other things...it could be a very lonely place for those just absorbed by maths and physics. Everyone's outside at the end of the day – you need to be able to mix and be a bit independent'.

Pastoral care, well-being and discipline: Pastoral care at Seaford is 'unbelievable,' said a parent, as she described the extraordinary level of kindness and understanding from the school when facing family tragedy. And they're very aware of the pressures of growing up. Staff in the Pink House provide a listening ear at any time – pupils can even ask to be excused in a lesson, and staff will email the Pink House to say a pupil is on the way. It's staffed by one full-time director of care and welfare, a part-time safeguarding officer, the rev, a counsellor and Poppy the dog (who is particularly busy in September helping homesick pupils). At least 10 pupils turn up at the Pink House every day, but problems can be also be picked up by phone, tutors or peer mentors. Any bullying is dealt with promptly, confirm parents. One described how her daughter would pop in to the Pink House to get some perspective on school squabbles – 'so and so's being a bit nasty, I'll go the Pink House and see what they think'.

In discipline terms, rules are firmly based on traditional good manners and strict enforcement of standards. No more easy-going Seaford: the head is ensuring the school is up to the mark, from looking smart to the top 10 rules: break them and you risk exclusion (interestingly, dishonesty is ranked outside the top 10 as a less serious offence, alongside chewing gum...). No second chances for sex or drugs (although first time joint users might get a managed reprieve, depending on the circumstances). And to make sure no one flouts the rules, sniffer dogs (a crazy spaniel and a labrador) check the lunch queue. They're much loved by kids – and have never actually found anything. Two exclusions in the last year: for persistent disruption, and bullying. No surprise, in this caring school, that those suspended or excluded can go the Pink House for a chat with support workers 'to feel the love.'

Delicious lunch served for us in the head's study – is it always this nice? 'It doesn't look quite like this', said the head boy carefully, regarding a swirl of purée, 'but it tastes good'.

Pupils and parents: Posh, and not, here – 'I know someone with a jet, and others working three jobs to get their kids through'. Lots of weekly boarders from London, and school buses serve the surrounding area.

Fewer girls than boys (around a third), but the head is keen to attract more, and ran an everywoman conference to provide aspirational role models for girls.

Parents are happy with a good level of communication, with frequent emails from school, and teachers letting parents know if there's a problem – 'in the past we'd have had to work this out for ourselves'.

Entrance: Fifty per cent of year 9 from Seaford Prep, the rest from a range of preps and local primaries. ISEB pre-test in year 6. Non-selective until GCSE; thereafter need 45 points to enter sixth form. Screening for SEN on entry.

Exit: Some 20 per cent to local sixth form colleges, usually for financial reasons. Around 20 per cent to Russell Group; Oxford Brookes most popular destination by far in 2018 with 13 students going there.

Money matters: Fees good value for money, said a parent; but she wouldn't want them to be any more. Means-tested bursaries; range of scholarships available at 13+ and 16+.

Remarks: A happy, exceptionally caring school, which strive to do well by all who cross the threshold, whatever their ability.

Sevenoaks Preparatory School

268

Godden Green, Sevenoaks, Kent TN15 0JU

Ages 2.5–13 **Pupils** 387

Fees: £10,350 – £14,295 pa

01732 762 336
www.theprep.org.uk

Headmaster: Since 2012 Mr Luke Harrison BA PGCE IAPS. Early 40s. An old boy of the school (along with three other members of staff), he was educated at Tonbridge and St Mary's College, Twickenham (University of Surrey) where he read English and drama. Did his PGCE at St Luke's, Exeter with his first job at the Weald of Kent Girls' Grammar, where he met his wife. He then taught English and theatre studies up to A level at Kingston Grammar. Joined Sevenoaks Prep in 2001, as he wanted the opportunity to get involved with all aspects of school life and had a brief to get drama back on track.

Married to Clare, a trained teacher who, among her many roles, is assistant head, in charge of admissions and teaches history to years 7 and 8 – 'they work well together and are a very effective team,' according to one mother. They have two daughters in the school. Considers the strong family and inclusive ethos a particular strength of the school and is always available to parents – prefers face to face meetings rather than emails – and will visit families at home if there are problems. High praise from parents, who say he 'is a good communicator who is highly visible and approachable, and seems to care and understands what parents are looking for, and is open to new ideas'. 'He knows the kids well and they respect him'. Parents also say he has a 'great approach' and they like his philosophy: 'If a child is happy, everything else follows' and 'Kids need resilience, and while success is always celebrated, they must take risks and learn to fail'. 'He has tightened things up and is on top of things,' said one mother, but he feels that any changes are 'evolution rather than revolution'.

Entrance: Non-selective means a diverse group. Nursery takes children from 2 years with intakes in Sept and Jan and build up sessions through kindergarten to be ready for full-time school in reception. Four children join in year 3 after a taster day and assessment in English and maths and an hour with the head of learning support. Another intake in year 7, mainly from local primary schools or those returning from overseas. Very rarely are there spaces at other times. Many children's names put down at birth and there are only places in reception if someone leaves. Most from nursery are guaranteed a place as long as the school feels they can cope with the curriculum. The emphasis is very much on ensuring that the school is the right setting for the child. No open days and parents always shown round by pupils 'so they can see school as it is'. School wants happy parents and families always encouraged to look at other schools in the area before making their decision.

Exit: In 2018, at both 11+ and 13+ stages, pupils went on to a rich array of schools, including Sevenoaks, Tonbridge, Caterham, Sutton Valence and Eastbourne College.

Up to half leave at 11+, mainly to the grammars and some to Sevenoaks. No specific tutoring for 11+ (Kent imposes strict rules against this) but, as well as ongoing maths and English lessons, there is a focus on reasoning skills in year 5. Many get outside tutoring as well.

All pupils are CAT tested and, as one parent commented, 'the head is very good at helping parents with the choice of senior schools – it is always about what is best for the child'. A good handful of academic and music scholarships each year, including to Tonbridge and Sevenoaks, as well as the occasional art and drama scholarship.

Remarks: Founded 1919 with six boys who were too young to attend Sevenoaks Grammar (now Sevenoaks School), the school moved to its present site in the 1960s and went co-ed in 1991. The original building is an old farmhouse just outside Sevenoaks, set in 20 acres of playing fields and backing on to the 1,000 acre Knole Park, which is used for nature walks and cross-country running. No grand central building but well-designed additions over the years including a large sports hall, also used for plays and assemblies, new classroom blocks and the architect-designed light and airy Oakery dining hall with drama and music upstairs.

Pre-prep school is a self-contained unit with a warm friendly atmosphere a few minutes' walk from the prep school and with its own hall, dining room and four new classrooms opened. All teachers and assistants are specialists in early years' education and work in partnership with parents. One particularly charming touch is the twilight nativity play with live animals.

Children move from the pre-prep into the prep school in year 3 and are taught in year group blocks with their own classrooms; years 3 and 4 have their own playground. Class teaching for core subjects and specialist teaching for drama, languages, music, PE, ICT and games. Specialist teachers for all subjects from year 6, when children start to move classrooms for lessons. French taught from nursery and Spanish from year 6. Normally 20 per class but smaller groups in top two years. Informal setting in class from year 3, setting in maths from year 4 and setting in all subjects from year 7. Potential scholars in years 7 and 8, and those who need stretching, offered special sessions before and after school. 'The school is very inclusive,' said one parent, 'and particularly supportive of high flyers and underachievers'.

Low staff turnover but enough to 'freshen things up' – good combination of consistency and new blood, most in their 30s and 40s; most who teach at the top end of the school are secondary-trained subject specialists. School has introduced Singapore Maths with an emphasis on mental arithmetic. 'It gives the children a deep understanding and is not just about learning by heart,' says the very enthusiastic maths teacher who gave us a demonstration. Maths Challenges popular and school does well in inter-school competitions. Geography quizzes each week and children are expected to keep up to date with news and know what is happening in the world. Recently refurbished science lab used by years 6-8 – masses of practical work, and we saw some fine models of energy-saving houses and watched some splendid erupting volcanoes. Emphasis on creativity and fun (but no games) in ICT lessons and children taught coding and programming.

One full-time and one part-time SEN teacher, mainly for mild dyslexia and dyspraxia; support in lessons or small groups and some one-to-one help, but 'don't want to make children feel different'. Teachers always on look-out for problems and children screened from reception upwards. EAL offered – children mainly taken out of class and are encouraged to celebrate their own culture and background.

Sport for all and puts out as many teams as possible – rotates players in Cs and Ds to make sure everyone can play in a match. The usual sports: football, rugby, cricket for boys and netball, hockey and rounders for the girls. Judo and fencing also popular and archery offered in years 7 and 8. Gymnastics club set up and lots of children are members of sports clubs outside school. 'It's not too competitive, kids want to do well and be part of a team but it's not all about the glory,' said one mother.

One hour a week of music for all and most try out an instrument, even if only the recorder or triangle. Vibrant music department with lots going on: rock band, orchestras, string quartet, brass groups and the 80 strong choir. Drama part of the curriculum, annual plays for each year group and all children encouraged to take part.

Good range of lunchtime and after-school clubs include judo, tennis, gymnastics, street dance, fencing and archery. Lots of outings and visits to help bring learning to life with an emphasis on learning through experience – some local and some further afield eg history trip to Bayeaux and the WW1 battlefields and a moving memorial service at Ypres.

Bushcraft course at beginning of year 8 when children spend several days camping in the woods. Staff on the look out for leadership qualities and heads of school and prefects are announced afterwards. Children taught that they are part of a wider community and pupils' charity committee an important part of school life – 'it's not just about raising money; kids spent some time at Age UK drop in centre'. Social entrepreneurship project after common entrance when children are given £10 by the Rotary Club to set up their own business and turn it into £100 or more. They have to design spreadsheets and a business plan.

Strong pastoral support aims to help parents and children alike and all treated with 'empathy and understanding,' said one mother. 'The school is very nurturing and really looks after the kids'. Good food with plenty of choice served in the Oakery dining hall, which was opened by Gary Rhodes and which our guide referred to as the 'restaurant'. Children sit in year groups with teachers and kitchen staff keeping an eye on healthy eating. Healthy lifestyles encouraged and discussed in lessons and reinforced by helpful messages on the dining room wall.

Top two years help run the school and have different uniforms with badges and ties for positions of responsibility. All year 8s become a prefect at some stage but have to earn their position. Coveted Oak Award given to those who play a particularly active role in the school community. Our guides felt that 'friendship issues were sorted out quickly' and they were 'given more freedom than at other schools and that 'personal responsibility makes people more organised'. School finishes at 4pm but many opt to stay till 6pm and do supervised prep (wraparound care now also available for nursery and kindergarten pupils till 6pm).

Most families live within about 15 minutes of the school and are mainly commuters, local professionals and medics – some very wealthy, others who require bursaries. Most are incredibly supportive of the school. Increasing number of double income families but also some stay at home dads. About eight per cent foreign nationals. Headmaster says he tries to 'get away from the elitist feel, and it is the broad spectrum which attracts parents'. 'A real mixed bag,' said one parent; 'all abilities, walks of life and family dynamics.'

Social events committee, with reps from each class, organise coffee mornings and nights out for parents as well as the Christmas bazaar, summer ball and family day – some purely for fun, some to raise money for charity. 'The school is very supportive of parents and it is a great way to make new friends – we are allowed to picnic in the grounds and use the tennis courts and treat the school as an extension of home.' Notable alumni include Ian Walker (yachtsman), Mike Conway (racing driver) and Daniel Collings (journalist).

Sevenoaks School

High Street, Sevenoaks, Kent TN13 1HU

Ages 11–18 **Pupils** 1,093 **Sixth form** 438 **Boarders** 347 full

Fees: Day £23,355 – £26,523 ; Boarding £37,296 – £40,464 pa

01732 455133
www.sevenoaksschool.org

Head: Since 2002, Dr Katy Ricks, 50s. Previously deputy head at Highgate School and before that posts at other top flight schools – St Edward's Oxford, where was head of English, Latymer Upper and King Edward's, Birmingham. Career choice clinched by first teaching role at St Paul's School for Girls where became clear that that 'talking to young people about literature' was going to give her more satisfaction than research.

Elegant with penchant for vivid colours, she lays claim to purple handbag, and pink and grey study described in previous review as 'minimalist' (no change there). Married to academic (at King's College London) and of course vastly intelligent (first from Balliol). Conversation is scattered with quotes – we were treated to Keats and Dr Johnson.

The first woman head in school's history has made this the place to be if you're after consistently top, top IB results (GCSEs are equally amazing). Fiercely proud of the school and bursting with ideas, she's engaging and charming – and disarmingly open about mugging up on previous Good Schools Guide's description of her 'infectious enthusiasm' and ensuring it came across just as strongly this time round. It did.

Headship is 'brilliant', biggest perk being in charge and 'making things happen,' she says. Point of education is about 'letting people feel free to be themselves in the best way that they can,' and giving them means of creating robust moral and intellectual framework for themselves – qualities enshrined in IB learner profile. Some parents see her as a CEO type rather than a hands on head but pigeonholes are unhelpful, she says. 'I'm simply myself.' They describe her as impressive, something she's aware of though feels 'completely un-terrifying'.

Pupils, particularly in senior years, say she's both inspiring and approachable. 'Barrier is still there but you feel comfortable to talk,' thought one. Another praised seamless transition from 'extremely personable' English teacher to school figurehead as required, though she's not heavy on the small talk – it's straight down to business.

Does she feel it's lonely at the top? Never. 'In fact,' she says, 'bring on the loneliness.' As to role models? 'I'm my role model.' The school feels smiley – and she is a very smiley head. Her pride and excitement in the school permeates the place. We felt it in everyone we met.

Returning to King Edward's School Birmingham as chief master in September 2019.

Academic matters: Not so much a case of getting down with these kids but scrabbling up to their level. Regardless of mother tongue, notable for gift of gab and desire to avoid muscular Christianity (or contortionist's pantheism) in favour of secular education that builds curiosity, creativity and critical thinking. They leave, says school with 'enlarged capacity for independent thought' – and without, as far as we could see, acquiring swollen heads on the way out. This despite evident brightness starting early, year 7 packed with top of their year types – no surprise given school's entry criteria: grammar school level or better (possibly a bit OTT, thinks Dr Ricks). 'Other girls took five lessons to learn something; I took one,' says typically bright 11 year old. Most pupils find flocking with similar high fliers an easy transition, though brilliance of plumage can be dazzling. 'It was hard at first,' said one recent leaver.

Being on the ball essential, what with just 45 minutes for breakfast and dinner (lunch is a more leisurely 90 minutes – though you'll be packing an activity in as well) and not a place for the vague, thought parents: something that this reviewer, who'd never been whistled round a school with such friendly but single-minded efficiency, or written notes faster, can confirm. Unquenchable sense of purpose the norm. 'A lot of people had very strong opinions about where they'd be in life in the next five or 10 years time,' said ex-pupil. (And you can probably assume they aren't thinking middle rank pootling with safe pension in Basildon.)

But while spreading a little zappiness throughout, school doesn't ramp it up to mind-blowing levels. Don't sit exams early – why spoil the pleasure of discovery? Staff lay on homework with a light touch rather than trowel – if not necessary, won't set. While around 10 per cent of pupils have some form of learning need, it's mild only for dyslexia, dyspraxia, dysgraphia, ADHD, Asperger's Syndrome and visual impairment. Only exception is hearing impairment.

Curriculum – naturally – is robust. Three sciences from the off, second language added in year 8. Most teaching is mixed ability – maths and languages the exceptions – sometimes adjusted instead for gender balance. For years 10 and 11, formulaic in the sense that these very bright children have only to be shown the way to strings of A*-A/9-7 grades at GCSE and it happens (92 per cent in 2018). Norm is 10, school teaching own English lit course to avoid dreary staples. ('Nobody wants to do Lord of the Flies,' said mother.) Ditto for art, music, drama, history of art and technology and critical perspectives course. New Middle School Diploma for years 9-11 records co-curricular and skills based learning. By sixth form, IB is natural extension of school's way of thinking, most pupils revelling in mind-stretching approach that's been their lot so far. It's about 'developing brain muscle so can frame an argument,' said upper sixth English teacher leading typically lively, interactive lesson. Intellectual weightlifting produced 39 point IB average in 2018. More than half of the cohort achieved 40 points or more.

Maximum class sizes sound large (24 to GCSE, 15 in the sixth form), but average is far lower (16 to age 16, and between eight and 10 in final years), with overall teacher to pupil ratio of one to nine.

Credit to Dr Ricks for staff team so strong that (unusually) parents and pupils couldn't name a single weak area (inspection accolades agree). 'Can go away and think about it,' offered recent leaver. Stable core of middle management reflected in average staff age of 41, with 55 notching up 10 years plus. Inevitable turnover of younger mob to more senior positions elsewhere (around 10 to headships in recent years). Not an issue, think parents, as quality replacements are lining up to take their places (final year Oxbridge undergrad sitting bolt upright in waiting room on day of visit).

Dr Ricks shortlists all staff applications herself, exercising football manager's eye for talent. Down to being 'a curious, observant person if you put it nicely or, if you put it nastily, a nosey parker.' Stand out staff quality she's after? Personable brilliance. 'If child was on a bus with this person for two hours, would they enjoy their company and be sparked by it?'

Games, options, the arts: Visitors might find numbers of events and activities almost overwhelming. Not so pupils, busily adding more, from coding to Middle Eastern Society, at a rate of knots. Others enter – and win – high profile competitions, one group snaffling £15,000 prize after developing app for autistic children. Overdoing things isn't an issue, they say. Can mean hard choices – some pupils (reluctantly) give up drama in the sixth form, and school keeps watchful eye on the ultra-active, though approach, ladling on the encouragement rather than activating the brakes, is distinctly hands off. 'If you feel you can cope, you probably will,' says pupil. Latest initiatives are three institutes – teaching and learning, service and entrepreneurship and higher education and professional insight.

Lavish facilities the norm. For sporty, substantial outside spaces supplemented by great indoors of Sennocke Centre – just lapping its three tennis courts, pool and giant sports hall probably enough to meet daily exercise requirements. With some international pupils completely new to team sports, hasn't been high profile area in the past, though recent successes – U14 hockey and U16 netball teams making national finals – could signal a change, achievements recognised by must-read authority, School Sport Magazine. Individual sports generally more popular – sailing especially so. However, numerous parents and pupils testified to star ratings for CCF, available from year 10, khaki-clad mob milling prior to drilling, rugged in tee shirts despite below zero temperatures on day of visit.

Performing arts impressively housed in The Space, with vast, acoustically advanced theatre that takes staging challenges in stride (pop up orchestra pit for Les Mis a doddle) and umpteen practice rooms for 750 weekly individual lessons. Very talented flourish (conductor Andrew Gourlay is a former pupil) with symphony orchestra, jazz band, gospel choir and song writing groups among many ensembles on offer, though 'have a go' spirit sees all abilities from virtuoso to enthusiast rapturously received when take to the stage.

Boarding: Until seventh and eighth boarding houses finished in 2019, sensible to book your place early – not easy to change to boarding later on and even sixth formers (house captains excepted) share rooms. Not that pupils mind, enjoying companionship and, according to one sixth former, preferring in any case to study in three-level, attractively nook-filled library, which like Sennocke Centre and practice rooms is open late. 'Less distraction as you don't have your stuff round you.'

Cleanliness comes as standard (a spot of stuffiness in one bedroom was nothing that open window or two wouldn't solve), ditto entertainment (TV/DVD, Sky, snooker or table tennis, Wifi) and bulk deliveries of bread, fruit and milk (sensible refrigerated dispensers).

Considerable variation otherwise. Sixth formers have International Centre (boys) and International House (girls). Then there's gorgeous Johnson's, one of six houses for year 9 to upper sixths, all early 20th century Agatha Christie-whodunnit-style fixtures and fittings. No longer offers boarding to years 7 and 8.

Some non-negotiables. No solo travel to more distant boarding houses regardless of age and, if late, with accompanying teacher. Youngest pupils have phones removed at night to begin with – and at any age if used after lights out (parents predictably thrilled that off this particular hook).

Otherwise, trust and flexibility dominate, from lockers (unlocked) to negotiated later bedtimes for older pupils if vital world events like US election intervene. 'About compromise,' says warm houseparent, who teaches ironing and cooking as university preparation, though washing happens, magically, off stage. House rivalry low key to point of invisibility – 'Children have to compete with the outside world, they don't need to compete with each other,' is parent's take on school's philosophy.

No them and us between day and boarder, local or international pupils – 'seamless,' said pupil of integration between the two (national groups split up, factions/combatants eg Russia/Ukraine brought together). House events include Valentine's meal (partners can be blind date, same sex, day or boarding pupils – one boy invited his best friend).

Around three-quarters of sixth form boarders stay on at weekends (it's half or so in other years). Home clothes allowed though if inappropriate will be 'sent home at the boarder's own expense...' (not a regular occurrence).

Sunday excursions enjoyable if not cutting edge (a liking for Lazer Quest definitely useful), but a welcome change from frantic pace of life in the week. School prefers parties for younger pupils when hosted out of school to be alcohol-free – and provides useful hints and tips including checking water bottles for vodka – though sensibly stops short of laying down law (impossible to enforce, we'd have thought).

Background and atmosphere: Given awe-inspiring prospectus – fabulously well written, slightly tongue in cheek self praise in vignette form – school could have work cut out just living up to it. For the most part, succeeds – triumphantly, even if tiny imperfections (like smeary bin in visitor's loo) are the more jarring by comparison. And though it comes with over 500 years of history – was one of the earliest secular school foundations in the country – and literary references in works by everyone from Daniel Defoe to Charlie Higson, isn't weighed down by it, with plenty of space, physical and philosophical, to let in plenty of fresh thinking and the odd bit of quirkiness.

'Wonderfully happy location,' thought pupil. Good for the area, too – Sevenoaks's biggest employer, owning substantial chunks of the high street (all pupils must use underpass – severe sanctions if they don't). Waitrose – appropriately – marks the boundary line. Most of 100-acre site, which backs on to Knole House, isn't visible from the road, though year 7s and 8s initially operate on a smaller scale for registration and break while are finding their way round the school's '...30 buildings, 107 classrooms, 14 sports pitches, 12 lawns, six ponds and thousands of trees.' Latest additions to bump up the numbers are science and technology and IB global study centres.

Each modern language merits own room off long corridor, the world in miniature, while English scores paved courtyard with baby olive trees and silver birch – a grove in the making – just needs own Muse. In the meantime, plenty of inspiration from works of art dotted around, many by teachers and former pupils. One orange sculpture is featured in nuts and bolts parent handbook, together with similarly toned handbag. Possible reimagining of lost property cupboard? 'Probably to give sense of scale,' thought sensible guide.

All well worth a look given that one talented sixth form artist (product of satisfyingly messy art room, complete with artist in residence and pile of larger than life-size clay busts) recently flogged one of own works for £1,000...

Pastoral care, well-being and discipline: Copers will thrive. 'You shape up pretty quickly,' said parent. Big on nurture in year 7 but given pace of life here, in other years best to get with the programme pronto. Plenty of help around. Daily meetings with tutors reckoned to be a good safety net, staff normally quick to respond to parent queries. Counsellor also well used – sometimes making appointments difficult but school is planning more.

Robust but not unkind sanctions for eg alcohol misuse. For drug use, possible that might be allowed back but would have to agree to random testing for remainder of school career.

Commonsense advice issued on everything from pocket money allowance (keep it sensibly low to avoid 'over-reliance on material goods' – nice thought, though we can't help wondering if that boat has already sailed – even recent lower school cake sales raised over £1,000) – to cases of bullying: rare, according to school surveys, but acknowledged to rear head now and again.

School sensibly quotes examples of nastiness: 'You've got no friends, you're fat/gay...' and urges telling at all times. One parent agreed that unkindness happens but room to escape the tormentors helps. 'You can breathe here,' thought pupil. Minor problems tend to work themselves out, school on the whole reserving its energies for coping with more serious problems – has fair share of mental illness including eating disorders and self-harm. 'Very on the ball,' thought mother.

Parents are also expected to behave. Don't expect leave to remove children in term time without a very good reason (weddings or funerals might just about hack it but little else). And as for taking unilateral decisions to run holiday of lifetime into first few days of term? No way. 'School holidays are fixed at the absolute maximum consistent with good learning,' says school. In contrast, an empty school is the goal at exeat weekends though pupils 'in real need' can stay.

One parent felt that a bit more approachability 'would make it a better place for parents and allow better communications.' Emails felt by several to be a bit too abundant (about 10 a week, more at start of term, thought parent) and hard to prioritise. Rethink is underway, says school.

Pupils and parents: Has always been cosmopolitan, first international pupil arriving in the 18th century. Currently international 175 pupils from Australia to Azerbaijan, Serbia to Singapore, Malaysia to Moldova – greater proportion further up the school, plus 70 expat families. Walls of vast dining hall serving quality food that even Italian tour guide, initially sceptical, was happy to endorse, decorated in a sea of flags representing every pupil nationality.

Sizeable numbers of local-ish families (Kent, Sussex and accessible bits of Surrey plus some Londoners). Can join popular parents' choir. Friends' organisation, recent innovation, going great guns with monthly drinks and cultural excursions.

Some parents reckon that small proportion of pupils – Londoners in particular – afflicted by sense of entitlement. Absolutely not, we were told, indignantly. 'We're grounded, also there's so much cultural diversity.' School's down-to-earth outreach programme (two pupils diligently sorting stock in local charity shop, medics putting in time at local school for the disabled) doubtless helps.

Entrance: At 11+, 80 places, same number again at 13+. For year 7 place, entrance tests in maths, English and VR, references, interviews and reports. Numerous local prep feeders. Rumour that state school entrants may be favoured if tie break for a place.

Applicants for 13+ entry take maths, English and VR tests in year 7, plus 40 minute group interview and reference. Unconditional offers made in June of year 7. Those at prep schools asked to aim for 70 per cent at common entrance (used for setting purposes). For sixth form entrance, when another 75-80 pupils taken in, tested in three proposed IB higher level subjects plus maths and English if not native language (high levels of fluency essential though can offer a session a week to 10 pupils needing short term boosters).

Exit: Vast majority (over 95 per cent) stay on into sixth form. Count down to UCAS form completion handled extremely well with teachers pitching their own degree subjects. Also 'how to' personal statement talks, coaching for US SAT tests and support if predicted grades don't work out quite as planned – school has talked near misses on to foundation places at desired uni.

Many offers from highly prestigious unis here, there and everywhere – many to US and Canada (19 in 2018), few to anything other than Russell Group or top international equivalents (10 to universities within Europe or Hong Kong in 2018). 'Work really hard to support them, in the end it's what you pay them for,' said parent. As a result, destination list tends to resemble a global best of higher education list, 37 Oxbridge places in 2018 plus Yale, Stanford, Berkeley, Brown, Duke and McGill. 24 medics and vets.

Money matters: At least five full bursaries at 11+ (may trickle up to year 9 if funds permit), some partial bursaries and offer of temporary support if difficult times strike existing pupils. Scholarships of up to 10 per cent.

Remarks: Exhilarating, immersive education that's ideal for intellectually voracious, organised, go-getting types. Less so for those in search of a more gentle voyage of self-discovery.

Shiplake College

Shiplake Court, Shiplake, Henley-on-Thames, Oxfordshire RG9 4BW

Ages 11–18 **Pupils** 478 **Sixth form** 200 (52 girls) **Boarders** 35 full, 96 weekly, 36 flexi (from 13 years) **C of E**

Fees: Day £17,700 – £22,230; Boarding £20,895 – £33,075 pa

01189 402455
www.shiplake.org.uk

Headmaster: Since 2004, Gregg Davies BSc Cert Mgmt (mid 50s). Married to Alison, who works in learning development here, and to whom he frequently refers in conversation. They have a daughter, who is an Old Viking (former deputy head of college), now at university. Mr Davies is, at once, intimidating and benign, humorous and serious, mischievous and earnest. His luxury is the speedboat he keeps moored just below the front lawn. He is direct, looks you straight in the eye, but has a light touch. Immediately likeable, he not only has a twinkle and warmth, but is the kind of man you would be pleased for your son (and daughter) to have as a role model.

Passionate about 'growth mindset' – 'I grew up dreaming of playing rugby for Wales or Scotland and at 36 I played for Scottish veterans – that's an example of growth mindset.' He coins words/phrases for the year. Last year it was 'yet', this term it's 'just try'. Mr Davies, with his two great bearded collies that share his office, is a man you could work with in a crisis. Parents describe him as 'very extrovert', 'going the extra mile', refer to his 'refreshing, individual approach' and a noticeably 'thoughtful, non-judgmental attitude but unafraid to say what he thinks.' He succeeds in treading the delicate line between being everyone's friend and confidante and that of esteemed and highly respected headmaster.

Retiring in July 2019. His successor will be Tyrone Howe, currently a housemaster at Uppingham. Went to school in Northern Ireland; studied German and international relations at St Andrews and has a masters in European literature from Oxford. He started his teaching career at Marlborough but left to play professional rugby for Ulster, going on to represent Ireland, the British and Irish Lions and the Barbarians. He then spent five years in industry before returning to education, coaching rugby at all levels at Uppingham as well as his teaching duties, and has been a regular Sky Sports rugby commentator.

He and his wife Alex, also a teacher, have young twins and two dogs.

Academic matters: Very small class sizes, maximum 16, allowing each child to get individual attention and creating strong value added scores. For science it's either double or triple award (even when small numbers choose the triple option, the school will support it); the modern language options are French and Spanish (but will facilitate the teaching of other languages such as Mandarin for an additional fee). No Latin or Greek. In 2018, 26 per cent A*-A/9-7 at GCSE and 42 per cent A*/A, 61 per cent A*-B at A level.

New sixth formers have a weekly lecture series and complete either an EPQ or a CoPE (Certificate of Personal Effectiveness). BTecs in business, travel/tourism, criminology, music and sports studies, the two latter available as A levels too. Proving to be popular as well as successful – particularly business. Computing, ICT, media studies, drama, philosophy, photography and psychology are also options. Results have improved enormously over the past few years; 52 per cent A*/A grades at A level in 2017, 72 per cent A*-B.

A school that celebrates its 'all ability' intake, Shiplake is creative and innovative in how it instils a healthy learning attitude in it pupils. The Shiplake Seven is a mantra engraved in the breast pocket of every maroon, black and gold striped blazer (curious, open-minded, motivated, reflective, determined, creative, independent). This is enforced and reinforced throughout the academic, as well as the co-curricula. In addition there is a highly developed programme of 'flipped learning'. Students are expected to have researched a topic before a lesson – frequently teachers will have created video presentations for the pupils to watch before the lesson begins – so that the lesson itself can be used for more in-depth exploration of the issues and themes.

The Thinking Space – what we would usually call the library – is modern and high-tech, but only two small neon shelves with books – this library is online. Brightly painted telephone boxes contain periodicals and store laptops. A canary yellow pod filled with cushions is where, one imagines, you might find a student or two curled up with a book (if there were many to choose from). Moving seamlessly through to The Quiet Space or Flow Room, a cool blue and white area, designed to represent the Henley regatta and the Thames. This is where students can tap away at their essays in silence and calm tranquillity.

Shiplake has long had a strong reputation for excellent provision for those with SEN and the support provided by the learning development department is exceptional. There is a definite drive, nonetheless, to diminish the understanding that this is Shiplake's strength. Any year 7 or 8 applicants who need this kind of support will be told that this is not the right school. From year 9 upwards, however, boys can receive up to four 50 minute lessons per week (at extra charge and always replacing a modern language lesson). Seven dedicated teachers as well as two support workers give a wide range of support from small seminar subject tutoring to one-to-one help as well as assisting with organisation and study skills. We witnessed years 12 and 13 benefiting from 'guided study', given help with structuring essays and proof reading. On average about 15 per cent of pupils have access to the LDD, with a range of conditions – most commonly dyslexia and dyspraxia but also a smattering of ADD as well as Asperger's and ASD.

Games, options, the arts: The focus on sport here is evident from the number of teachers who have some kind of physical education qualification and/or interest. Rowing is excellent.

The boathouse nestles below the main building and grassy slope right on the bank of a bend in the river Thames. The Lynch, the island beyond owned by the school, makes this area ideal for adventure, rafting and camping exercises. This isn't a large school, and yet the boys who row do very well, and it is a growing sport for girls. Three Vikings represented Great Britain in the European and World Championships recently, winning four gold medals. A lot of enthusiastic rugby, football, cricket, netball, hockey and tennis players too. Games sessions are timetabled and there is an emphasis on inclusivity. Plenty of pitches as well as an Astroturf, a well-equipped gym (especially for the rowers), with squash courts, charming outside pool and refreshed sports hall. Enthusiastic and popular DofE, community service and CCF.

Art housed in spacious beamed roof space in the eaves at the top of one of the modern buildings. Photography in the adjoining space. Lots on display around the school. Busy ceramics department; a stunning life-size ram made out of chicken wire and fur ushered us there. Large DT space, four rooms with capacious work stations. Large lecture theatre where the full orchestra practises and performs. Chamber choir and auditioned-for First VIII a capella group, as well as an HM choir for those who can't sing but want to, although it sounds pretty painful. One parent cringed at the idea of performing badly on stage – the headmaster's choir embraces it and works on the motto 'choice, risk, consequence' that permeates so much of life here. Plenty of jazz groups and string groups. Winter, spring and summer concerts give them a chance to perform. Music technology with all the gear – Macs and keyboards – takes place in the comfortable, new John Turner building. Lots of individual practice rooms and all overseen by an energetic and inspiring head of music. Atmospheric theatre in the Old Tithe Barn area, painted black, with black wooden floorboards and black stone walls, complete with old wood smell. We witnessed a red nosed group of year 8 boys bringing colour and humour to the place with their improvisations about the Olympics.

'One of the exceptional things about the school,' observed a parent, 'is the ability to find something in which a boy or girl can shine.' Singers emerge who never knew they could sing, and the same applies to drama, dance and all areas of school life. 'A lot of this is down to Mr Davies's influence,' commented a father. 'He knows the children so well and he learns what their needs are, how they can be motivated and inspired.'

Boarding: Five core houses from years 9-12, mixing day and boarders (though full boarders predominately live in Burr House). In addition there is a sixth form girls' house (Gilson), as well as a house dedicated to the year 13 boys (College House). Years 7 and 8 join Olympians or Titans, and attend the majority of their lessons in their house group. Some senior girls lucky enough to have ensuite bathrooms. Younger boys normally share their room with two or three others.

Boarding comes in all varieties here and is tailor made to meet the demands of the families. Far more weekly than full boarding pupils. 'We haven't done a full marketing push to attract overseas families,' says the school's communications director. The school feels relatively local. Flexi-boarding is popular and attractive to busy families where both parents work but can have quality time with their children at weekends.

Not a lot of pupils stay at school at the weekends, but a dedicated team of housemasters and teachers as well as matrons make sure that there is plenty to do for the few who are in. We were told of a particularly popular trip to Liquid Leisure in Slough, as well as enjoyable nights out at the local curry house. Each house is comfortably (and remarkably tastefully) equipped with sofas, kitchens and games rooms with, when we visited, a delicious smell of clean laundry, and the lubricated sense of being well run.

Background and atmosphere: Situated in the luxurious Oxfordshire countryside, on the banks of the Thames only a couple of miles from Henley, but far enough from the bustle of Reading to feel secluded and remote, Shiplake Court began its existence in 1895 as family home and farm. In 1959 it became a boarding school, and it has always been smaller and a more nurturing environment than many schools of similar ilk. The site has been very tastefully developed through the years, modern buildings and windows, blending with the old, and the red brick and flint atmosphere here is calm and well kempt. Church services are a short walk away in St Peter and St Paul. Daily services are short but an important part of the routine in keeping students focused, on message, and well clad – Mr Davies will pull anyone up for scruffy attire, let alone poorly polished shoes.

Mr Davies runs a tight ship. Staff are wholly committed and everyone rows together to achieve the best possible outcome for each student. He has recently bravely tackled the modern bane – mobile phones. Now every student has to hand their phone in at the beginning the day, to be returned in the evening. He was driven to do it after observing that young people 'rarely talk to each other any more'. The benefit has been palpable as chattering can be heard again over break and while walking down the numerous pathways.

Parents praise the communication. It's frequent, inclusive and inescapable, from everyone – the receptionist to the head – and covering everything from discipline to rewards and merits. Not a school for a fire-and-forget parent.

Sports fixtures happen on a Saturday morning – if Jack isn't in a team then he can find another programme to keep him busy (art club, LAMDA, for example). There are no Saturday lessons, allowing more family time at the weekend for day pupils and weekly boarders.

Pastoral care, well-being and discipline: Shiplake's reputation as having an exceptional standard of pastoral care is justified (we couldn't find anyone to disagree). This is founded on high teacher to pupil ratio (roughly 1:6), and a highly effective school chaplain, the Rev, who doesn't teach but is the pivot of the pastoral system. Even p go to him with their troubles ('He is your Rev too, I tell them,' says Davies). A strong system of tutors (primarily assigned to individual pupils for academic support and normally house-based, but sometimes work across houses for older students), as well as houseparent, matron and various support staff within the house. Parents warmly praise the extent to which the staff get to know their students and understand any difficulties. The school GP is excellent and is proactive about communicating with any external specialists. There is cross communication throughout the departments and houses and through to the head, and in turn excellent communication with parents. Pupils feel safe here. The structures are there to keep them so.

Quite apart from the structures, however, there is also a strong set of principles running from the top downwards. From growth mindset, the Shiplake Seven and the annual key words and phrases to mindfulness clubs and good old-fashioned exercise and fresh air, constant care and attention is given to the well-being of the students. The food is delicious – and there is plenty of it (one parent was delighted that her son eats six sausages for breakfast), with a wide choice in the wood panelled gothic great hall plus piles of toast back at the house. Mentoring – responsibility taken by the sixth formers for the new year 9s – is both popular with the students and an effective way to break down hierarchies. Bad behaviour not tolerated – from drugs to bullying – and the school will not accept children with behavioural difficulties. However, Mr Davies is remarkably open minded about young boys who come to him with a chequered past, always prepared to recognise potential and give people a second chance.

Pupils and parents: Set in the heart of shiny Range Rover well-heeled territory with sky high property prices, Shiplake has plenty of parents who live up to their environment. Most parents work, a lot are in business. Some are demanding and discerning, some completely hands off, and school prefers the former. Most parents share a balanced view about exam results, and while they want their children to flourish are not obsessively competitive about how they are performing academically. Not a smart or fashionable school ('no fancy airs and graces,' said one former pupil), parents here are grounded and practical, with sound middle class values and concerned more about the right fit for their children than brand. A few Forces children, but mostly local families (the majority live close enough to be day or flexi boarders). Only five per cent of families from overseas, school looking to increase that number. Most of the catchment is east of Reading (navigating Reading during rush hour puts a lot of people off).

Pupils here are allowed to be individuals. They are taught to be practical and hands on, encouraged to roll up their sleeves and get a Sunday job. Work experience ideally is in a builders' yard (no holding onto to mummy's and daddy's coat tails in a law firm here). The broadness of selection helps to contribute a colourful mix of ability and personality. They come in all shapes and sizes with a range of skills, from the uber rower, to a committed oboist, with no doubt some future actors, designers and entrepreneurs in between. We were pleased to meet Will Satch, Olympic gold and bronze medallist and old Viking, who was visiting his old school. Mr Davies, clearly proud of Will's rowing achievements, was equally full of praise for his communication skills (Will is regularly wheeled out to deal with the media). Other notable alumni include Nick Jones, Soho house proprietor, Alex Pettyfer, actor, Chris Standring, jazz musician and Jonty Hearnden, antiques expert.

Entrance: Assessment is thorough, takes a day and enables school to see 'the whole picture'. Numeracy and literacy is just one part of the jigsaw. Candidates participate in a group activity during the afternoon, they are interviewed by the houseparent and deputy and finish the day with a sports activity. The question staff ask themselves is would this child be happy here – the long days, the exercise (even for day pupils there is a strong boarding ethos) – and what will they contribute to school life? A mix of prep and state primary pupils enter at year 7; the main intake, however, is at year 9. The number of girls in the sixth form has doubled, now 50+. Incomers require 5+ GCSEs (with at least a 5 in English and maths) though they make exceptions for those they feel will fit in. 'We will let our own boys stay on if we can find something useful and enjoyable for them to do.' Will rescue those burnt out from (or shot out of) Thames valley swot-houses.

Exit: 'We get the pupils onto the right courses,' says head, 'played to their strengths.' A huge range of universities; Oxford Brookes, Bournemouth, Nottingham Trent, Newcastle and Exeter currently popular. Applications are starting to be made to US universities. Equally wide range of courses from law and mathematics to sports development, television production and maritime business and logistics. Around 25 per cent leave after GCSE but are replaced.

Money matters: Art, drama, music and sports scholarships awarded but more for prestige than pounds. Sixth form schols depend on general aptitude test, plus test results in two subjects to be studied at A level. Means-tested bursaries awarded at the school's discretion with small pot to assist existing pupils, should financial hiccups occur.

Remarks: Perhaps the only child Shiplake would not suit is the super clever nerd. Possibly the only parents not suited are those for whom brand comes before substance. It is highly unlikely that anyone will leave here with a feeling of having failed; some will shine more than others but no one will be made to feel less valued. The key to success, however, is a wholehearted commitment to contributing to the community – in whatever way suits.

Sibford School

Sibford Ferris, Banbury, Oxfordshire OX15 5QL

Ages 3–18 **Pupils** 399 **Sixth form** 62 **Boarders** 30 full, 10 weekly, variable flexi (from 11 years)

Fees: Day £9,180 – £14,739 pa; Boarding £26,154 – £28,644 pa

01295 781200
www.sibfordschool.co.uk

Head: Since 2016, Toby Spence. Joined from Greensteds, a British curriculum boarding school in Kenya. A Quaker by upbringing, his career has included a five year stint as head of history at another Quaker school, Bootham in York: 'I'm a late medievalist and it was a joy to see York Minster out of the window'. He also had the delicious experience of returning to his old school – King's School in Tynemouth – as deputy head, and as the boss of a teacher who had disliked him in his schooldays. 'We got on better as colleagues,' he says.

Toby is married to Jill and they have three young children, all providing proof of the pudding by being at Sibford School. They are a super sporty family, and Toby is something of an action man, with swashbuckling tales of paddling a sea-kayak with killer whales off Vancouver Island, making a number of first ascents of mountains in South America, and sailing Tall Ships around the coast of Australia. He has brought a fervour for triathlons to the school, with much excited chatter about one held earlier in the week when we visited.

A new emphasis on sport is at his instigation, as is a greater emphasis on the academics, although not to the detriment of those requiring learning support, he assured us robustly. His watch is bringing not quite a new broom – not the Quaker way – but rather a dustpan and brush to some dusty corners.

Parents told us he is 'inspiring to students and parents' and they felt confident Sibford was in good hands for the future. 'He's open to opinion and change,' said one. Others appreciated his deep involvement in helping sixth formers to secure university places.

Academic matters: Sibford has a long held reputation as the go-to school for the child who needs a little extra nurturing and support. Toby insists it will remain that way; but that he also wants to develop its academic offer. 'Sibford has an unfair reputation as warm and cosy, but not particularly strong academically. For me they are not mutually exclusive,' he says. Work is underway on what he terms 'rebalancing'. There's a director of learning and teaching, and a fresh tracking and monitoring system. There are working groups looking to build on good practice, and to deliver improved added value results. 'My expectation would be 0.5 on value added, so if you are predicted four Bs you would get two As and two Bs,' he says. In 2018, 52 per cent of A level grades were A*-B, a 30 per cent A*/A. At GCSE, 24 per cent of grades were A*-A/9-7.

The junior school is small – 90 pupils – with the majority joining the school at year 4 or above. Year 1 and 2 are in a joint class. Subjects are mainly class taught, with specialist subject teaching for music and PE. There is setting for English and maths. We looked in on a year 5 maths class, and received an unprompted chorus of 'We love maths' from the children. Learning is frequently taken outdoors – we saw a troop of little ones coming through the mist in their orange boiler suits, looking like a tiny chain gang. Reception parents spoke fondly of welly walks and forest school.

In the senior school there is setting for English, maths and science. Pupils can choose the dual award or separate sciences. The language choice is French or Spanish, with German as an extracurricular option. Numbers are higher in the senior school, with 46 in year 7, split into three teaching groups averaging 14 to 16 pupils.

There's a choice of 28 courses in the sixth form, ranging from traditional A levels to textiles or product design, as well as BTecs at levels 2 and 3 in subjects including business studies, sport, ICT and media. Courses will be laid on for small numbers, as one parent said: 'My daughter's French class has just two pupils. I had worried about whether this would work, but it does and the teachers respond well to any class size.' Sixth form is 'led by an outstanding head who knows all the pupils well. The sixth formers are encouraged to be young adults and provide leadership to younger pupils and amongst themselves,' according to a parent.

'We have lived in three different countries since my daughters began their education, and so far the teaching staff and experience at Sibford has been far superior to anywhere we've been before,' said a parent. 'My daughters have all had an excellent connection with their teachers, and I have felt that they quickly understand their learning styles, strengths and weaknesses, and work with them individually in the ways that motivate them best. The teachers at the junior school make it fun and engaging to learn, and they have been quick to see where they can stretch and encourage them to push themselves to work harder and excel.'

Around 20 per cent of pupils receive learning support for any combination of literacy, numeracy, fine motor, attention and focus, and speech and language needs. Children typically come out of language lessons for support, and in years 7-9 receive three hours per week. For years 10 and 11, it's two hours, and sixth formers have one-to-one for an hour or two. It's possible to have additional one-to-one on top. The learning support department is well regarded – one parent said it had given her child 'confidence and belief in her abilities'. And it is not restricted to those timetabled sessions out of class. 'My mantra is we are all in the support for learning department,' Toby says.

There's also extension work for more able children – one parent told us her child was in a small group having additional English to stretch them further.

Games, options, the arts: 'We tend to do better in the younger rugby teams,' said our honest guide, when asked about sporting wins. 'Sport is not all about winning, culturally we are more into full participation and giving our best,' is the head's take.

As a small school, and one with a contingent of children there for gentle nurturing, it wouldn't be the place if league-leading teams and dazzling matches are top of your requirements. But you can expect it to claw its way up the fixture lists under this sports-mad head – we did notice his eyes straying out of his office window to the rugby pitch conveniently in view when the 1st XI were playing.

And it can be a joy for pupils shunted to the sidelines at previous schools. 'I'm now in the 1st XI rugby team when I wasn't in a team at my other school,' one boy told us proudly. A parent concurred: 'At her previous school our daughter wasn't great at sport, didn't get into any of the school teams, and felt left out of sport generally. At Sibford the school finds sports that everyone can participate in, and everyone gets a chance to be on school teams. She has been much more sporty, doing swimming, hockey and netball, and representing the school in enthusiastic teams.'

From year 7 there is a sports carousel so if competitive sport is not your bag you can do other things. On our visit we watched a mixed sex group having a ballet masterclass with two male dancers. A new climbing wall adds to the options, and there's a recently formed equestrian team. Triathlon, swimming, hockey and cross country are the strongest sports.

Plenty of bands, orchestras and ensembles, and an egalitarian approach to performance opportunities. There's a dedicated drama studio, and the school gets a strong showing in LAMDA exams. The head of drama is RSC trained, and a number of sixth form leavers have gone on to production and acting careers.

Boarding: Around half of boarders from overseas (predominantly Asia, a few from Europe). There are three boarding houses – one each for 11-16-year-old boys and girls, plus a co-ed sixth form house – all with games rooms and quiet areas. Sixth formers have one or two to a room, in the younger houses it may be up to four to a room. Rooms are standard boarding fare.

There is plenty of flex – some pupils will board only one night a week, to tie in with after-school clubs or early morning swimming, or as a chance to sleep over with friends. 'There are always things to do,' one boarder said, and the sixth form girls assured us the presence of their friends meant that they often got more studying done than they might at home alone.

Boarding is for seniors only, but occasionally they will take a year 6 when an older sibling boards.

Background and atmosphere: It's a long wind through tractor muddied lanes to a bigger campus than you'd expect for the number of pupils. It sits in 50 acre grounds with an orchard, woodland and pond. The original manor was sold off, and the campus is now a hotchpotch of purpose-built blocks including the more recently added music and art blocks and a sixth form centre.

It was founded as a co-ed boarding school by the Quakers in 1842, with an ethos to find that of God in everyone. 'The way I interpret that today is finding the good in everyone,' Toby says. 'Our role is to find the talents and qualities in each individual and develop and celebrate it. At this school you don't have to be one type of person, or one particular fit. We talk about the three Rs but for us that means respect, resilience, and relationships.'

There are meetings for worship twice a week, where the community sit in silence, but anyone can speak or give a reading. Fewer than five per cent of families are Quakers, but the rest are drawn here for the values, and many more parents attend the meetings. 'No parent should be put off Sibford for a moment because it is a Quaker school – it is an entirely positive and largely benign influence,' one parent said. Our pupil guides told us that meetings were a nice time to reflect. 'Like walking into another world, it's beautiful,' said learning support head.

The use of Christian names for all children and adults, and the meetings, result in excellent relationships across the school, parents said. One commented that the sense of community means that teachers often stay for many years, giving tremendous continuity and commitment.

Pastoral care, well-being and discipline: 'Always believe you might be mistaken,' is Toby's starting point, meaning errant pupils always have an opportunity to speak in their defence. 'Let's hear, listen and understand. We look for the good in anyone; however bad has it been, we ask, where's the good in here?' Discipline mainly comes in the form of positive reinforcement and praise, but there are 'full sanctions if need be' which has included pupils being asked to leave.

This approach means they will consider pupils who may have gone off track in other schools. 'We are open to discussion, and we say if you want to come in these are our expectations. We have some real success stories.'

A parent commented: 'I have occasionally felt that sometimes staff, particularly in the junior school, are less strict with certain children who might require more discipline. They work very hard to support children through kindness and patience (living the Quaker values demonstrably). The senior school is firmer, which we recognise and appreciate.'

Two well-being counsellors are on site two days a week, and the school offers training for parents in identifying and supporting mental health problems. For children with autism or other needs who may need emotional support at any time, they will put together a timetable of key people who are free throughout the day. 'It needs as immediate a response as possible; after the event isn't good enough,' says the learning support head. Where children have social communication difficulties, learning support sessions may include coaching on strategies they can use in class.

A few pupils are transgender or gender questioning. 'Our senior leadership team is reviewing what we need to do to get it right. Our school community understands why this school is at the vanguard here – equality, tolerance, and liberal values are very important to us.'

'Peer relationships are very accepting,' parents said.

Pupils and parents: The school is set among the mellow Cotswold stone of the Cameron-Clarkson brigade, but pushy parents are a rare breed here, we're told. Those choosing it are like-minded, in putting equal store by the values a child will gain to the certificates they leave with. 'Not a yummy mummy brigade, you don't have to dress up for the school run,' said one mother.

Others love the mutual support, and lack of jostling over which set or which team your child is in. 'There's a big fan club if a match is on, and they'll be shouting for all the year groups, not just their own child's,' one parent said.

Another praised 'the inclusive manner of the school, where all ages mix frequently, and there are no groups of girls who exclude others from their circle. Everyone gets on very well, regardless of age, ability, background, etc.'

Entrance: Will Sibford's changing focus alter its intake? 'Early days,' says Toby. 'But the numbers coming to see us doubled last year.' There is now a formal assessment day in January for year 7 entry (before it was come when you like). However, he says, 'There is no bar to jump, no Sats, no 11+. Pupils take CATS tests, do some outdoor learning and ceramics. We are a non-selective mainstream school, so as long as the child can cope and thrive in this environment they will be offered a place. It might be more tricky where we feel we might not be able to meet needs.'

Progression from the junior to senior school is as good as automatic. For more academic sixth form courses they ask for five or six 6s at GCSE for externals taking up A level courses – for vocational courses that would be more flexible.

Exit: About 50-60 per cent of pupils stay on into the sixth form. Leavers include those who may move on to something more vocational; a few who want a more rigid academic focus; and a few who are seeking a bigger sporting offer.

The majority of sixth form leavers go on to university, and to a wide variety including King's College London, Warwick, Cardiff, Oxford Brookes, Royal Northern College of Music, Birmingham Conservatoire and Royal Agricultural University.

Money matters: There are academic, sports, music, drama and arts scholarships worth 5-10 per cent of fees, and means-tested bursaries covering up to 80 per cent of fees.

Remarks: One of the few schools which is genuinely all ability, in every meaning of the word. There's a place here for those who need learning support, and those who might apply to Oxbridge; for those who want to perform on stage, and for those who want to quietly contemplate; for those who've made teenage errors of judgement, and those who need cosseting. It's a great option if your brood all need different handling. You won't come here if a slick and shiny public school is what you are after; despite having an international contingent, the feel is more of a local school. However, if competitive parents and league table chasing turn your stomach, you will find your ilk here.

Sir Roger Manwood's School

Manwood Road, Sandwich, Kent CT13 9JX

Ages 11–18 **Pupils** 1,037 **Sixth form** 246 **Boarders** 55

Fees: Day free; Boarding £11,898 pa

01304 610200
www.manwoods.co.uk

Headteacher: Since 2013, Lee Hunter MA (Cantab) PGCE. Originally from the East End where his father was a docker, he was educated at Campion Grammar School, Hornchurch before it became a comprehensive and says it was this grammar school education which gave him the chance to go to Cambridge. Read natural sciences, turned down a research post and seriously considered making a career in youth work. He then took his PGCE at Durham and his first job was teaching chemistry at a truly comprehensive comprehensive where some pupils in his class were highly academic and others were illiterate; one of his rowing pupils became national champion. Three years at the small British School in Milan where he was promoted to head of chemistry, age 25; three at RGS High Wycombe as assistant head of science; 16 at Tiffin Girls', latterly as deputy head, before coming to Sir Roger Manwood's as head.

He has a keen eye for detail and, following some health issues earlier in his career, he says he has learned to appreciate every day as it comes. He likes to keep his hand in in the classroom and teaches science to year 9 and the EPQ to year 13 as well as games to year 7s. He knows most of the pupils by face if not all by name. His great love is travel and he has friends all over the world. He accompanies the pupils on as many school trips as he can and has been to Florence, Paris, India and China as well as on many DofE expeditions.

He is very supportive of the arts as part of his holistic approach to education and it is a great honour for pupils to have their artwork and textiles displayed in his study alongside the framed minutes from a governor's meeting in 1892.

Academic matters: In 2018 28 per cent of grades A*-A at A level (50 per cent A*-B) and 49 per cent A*-A/9-7 at GCSE. Offers German, French, Spanish and Mandarin at GCSE and many of those who get into Oxbridge are linguists; many of the language teachers are native speakers. A number of German and Spanish pupils come to board in year 12 and pair up with A level students to help with spoken language. Weekly taster lessons in Mandarin in year 7 and all study French plus either Spanish, German or Mandarin from year 8. Native speakers can take language GCSEs a year early.

GCSE options include computer science, music and drama. Science offered as three separate subjects and some years a few take the dual award. Technology taught as product design, and textiles offered through A level art.

Twenty subject options at A level including psychology, politics, business and film studies plus Spanish, German and French. The most popular subjects are maths, RS, biology, English and history closely followed by chemistry and physics. Students take only three A levels as the school feels that three good grades plus the EPQ are looked on more favourably by universities, and that students have more time for volunteering and other activities, tying in with the whole person ethos of the school. Sixth formers have their own study area with computers and Wifi. 'It is not an exam factory,' said a pupil, 'but it makes you driven to work.'

Class sizes range from 25-32 lower down the school with as few as five or six in some A level classes. Low staff turnover and the average age of teachers is 40s. 'All are well qualified', says the head, 'and most have a good 10 years' experience,' but there is also a handful of NQTs and four School Direct teachers who train at the school and bring fresh ideas. 'The teachers really care and want you to succeed,' say the pupils. 'It's not difficult to be passionate about this place,' says a teacher. 'It inspires confidence in the kids and they are not afraid to get things wrong'.

SENCo and four assistants cater for a range of needs from dyslexia and dyspraxia to ADHD and emotional difficulties – very few on the autistic spectrum. All year 7s screened for literacy and those with support needs have one fortnightly lesson and are tested again at the end of year 9. Older pupils act as maths buddies and reading buddies for years 7 and 8. 'It is satisfying for both and also helps to bond year groups,' says the head.

EAL offered on an individual basis, usually to international boarders – one TEFL trained teacher at the school. Gifted & talented identified early and challenged across the board, and offered extracurricular activities such as the science enrichment clubs and a visit to Cambridge in year 10.

Regular careers evenings and pupils encouraged to think about their future from an early age; careers boards are dotted about the school. Independent adviser comes into school one day a week and pupils can book appointments from year 9 onwards. Online Morrisby testing offered from year 9, year 10s spend a week doing business enterprise and year 11s do two weeks' work experience after GCSEs – school can help with contacts. Plenty of help with UCAS forms and interview practice and year 12s attend an annual university fair at Canterbury. 'The careers department is good at the bigger picture,' say the pupils. 'You are not pushed in certain directions or made to apply to university but the school works at the wider options and is very supportive of apprenticeships.'

Games, options, the arts: Sport mainly played in break time and lunch time clubs; most continue into sixth form. Many play for fitness and being part of a team; 'it is social and helps you make more friends,' said a pupil. The school has its own floodlit mini Astro plus cricket and hockey pitches on site, with rugby pitches a short walk away, but not enough capacity to host hockey matches, which are played at Canterbury hockey club. Huge sports hall used for indoor hockey and a range of minor sports as well as whole school assemblies. Swimming at Thanet swimming club in Margate. School's cricketers were recent Kent champions and pupils also play sport for outside clubs including elite Kent cricket teams. Girls' hockey very strong with two recent junior international players and one who represented GB in the Olympics.

Each year some 20-30 gain DofE gold and 60-80 are involved with the CCF and take part in adventure training weekends and the annual summer camp. The CCF band is in much demand at carnivals, parades and Remembrance Day services.

Only about 120 take music lessons, but music is the most popular club and it is offered at GCSE and A level. 'Musicians are a close knit group,' said a pupil. 'There is always something musical going on at the school,' said a parent. Something for all abilities, including the school orchestra, brass, jazz and rock bands and several choirs and ensembles. Concerts throughout the year; the orchestra has an annual trip to a European city.

Active drama department with a big production every year, either a musical or a Shakespeare play, as well as drama studio productions. Offered at GCSE but not A level.

Students' art displayed around the school and there are art and photography competitions throughout the year plus a competition to design a colouring book, and students exhibit at the Sandwich Art Society.

Trips abroad are referred to as Global Awareness and the ethos is 'let's go out and experience it'. Annual visits to twinned schools in China, the Gambia, Germany, India and Spain. Politics trip to New York and Washington, Geography trip to Isle of Arran, World Challenge expedition to Vietnam, the list goes on. Pupils have to self-fund the latter and can earn money through teaching English when they are there.

'We cram so much in and are encouraged to do as much as possible and try new things,' said a pupil, 'and there are prizes for everything.' Pupils take part in public speaking and debating competitions, produce an impressive school magazine and put together the sixth form fashion show; school recently won a grant to build a single pixel camera to investigate how insects see the world. Wide range of after-school clubs include particle physics society, fitness, gardening and DT.

Boarding: One of 35 state boarding schools in the UK; and eight of the 120 places in year 7 are reserved for boarders.

Two boarding houses in the grounds, one slightly bigger, so girls and boys swap round depending on numbers. Both houses are kept immaculately and run by dedicated houseparents, a matron and a tutor, who keep in close contact with parents. Both have a homely, family feel with a maximum of three to a room with some single rooms and year groups kept together.

Most are full boarders from abroad, but boarding increasingly popular with English families and majority are in school at weekends. Boarders and day pupils integrate well and boarders often stay with local friends at exeats. They leave their houses at 8.15am and only sixth formers are allowed back during the day.

Something is organised each weekend, maybe a trip to the cinema or the pantomime, and boarders can take taxis to sports clubs and the local swimming pool. Younger boarders have supervised prep. Both boarding houses run a spiritual, moral and cultural programme and are transgender accepting, and all cultures are celebrated through food and cooking. Birthdays are always celebrated with a cake.

The current boys' house has a panelled hall with a pool table and games room with a television and PlayStation. The girls have banished all institutional language from their house and so their common room has become the living room and the kitchen is the social centre of the house, with lots of baking and toast and pot noodles. The houseparents have a young son who is very much part of the house family. The two houses mix together at weekends for barbecues, activities and debating.

Background and atmosphere: The school was founded in 1563 by Sir Roger Manwood as a Free Grammar School to educate the townspeople of Sandwich; it moved to its present purpose built 30 acre site off a quiet residential street 1895. The main building is red-brick Victorian and has been added to in a variety of styles over the years. Busy, welcoming reception area decorated with silverware, sports photos and handbag art. 'The school is forward looking but has held on to its traditions,' said a parent. 'There is still a whole school remembrance service and two carol services that include everyone.'

Uniform worn until sixth form when students have to dress as if they were going to the office. 'The uniform code is quite strict and some try to push the boundaries,' said a parent.

Giving something back is part of the ethos of the school and the junior and senior charity committees raise about £20,000 per year. Sixth formers encouraged to take positions of responsibility as prefects and buddies to years 7 and 8; they host a lunch for 100 local pensioners, volunteer at local primary schools and run an annual maths competition and sports tournaments.

Pastoral care, well-being and discipline: Friendly community atmosphere 'with mutual trust between year groups,' said a pupil; 'you can leave your bag outside lessons, everyone looks out for each other and it is easy to make friends.'

Good support system with form tutors and year heads the first port of call. A counsellor comes in one day a week and all have access to a well-being coach who can help with anything from stress management to diet and exercise. Pupils generally well behaved; school works with transgressors and will apply sanctions and temporary exclusions if necessary. Outside agencies may become involved and there is an occasional managed move.

Food good, say the pupils, with cashless cafeteria system, and they can take food away and eat in the grounds or the courtyard. Sixth formers have their own quiet study area and café where they can buy hot snacks.

The culture is 'work hard, play hard' and pupils are encouraged to develop new interests and take responsibility, but the atmosphere is much more relaxed than in many of the local grammars. Strong house system with emphasis on community – 'it encourages you to get involved and have fun and is competitive in a nice way – inter-house sports are great for team building but are not taken too seriously,' said a pupil. 'You can do anything, get involved and get points for your house, including public speaking and the arts.'

Pupils and parents: Families represent the local population from middle class professionals to struggling single parents, with medics from the local hospital and creative types who have moved down from London. Many pupils become the first in their family to go to university. All parents automatically belong to Friends of Manwood and the PTA organises about four events a year. Old Manwoodians help with careers advice, interview practice and the CCF.

Former pupils include high court judges, bishops, senior military figures, international sportspeople. BBC's defence correspondent Jonathan Beale, Olympic hockey player Melanie Clewlow, England cricketer Tammy Beaumont, high court judge Sir Robin Knowles and child actor Jack Scanlon are all Old Manwoodians.

Entrance: Quite a broad intake for a grammar school: takes the top 38 per cent and pupils not under the same pressures as at the west Kent grammars. School still oversubscribed, but as long as a child passes the 11+ Kent Test, it is open to those who live closest and most come from within about eight miles. Preference to siblings. Most come from one of about 30 feeder primaries and local independent schools like Northbourne Park, Wellesley House and St Faith's.

Boarders and those joining in other years take the school's own tests in English and maths. Some 30-35 join the sixth form and require at least six GCSEs at 4 or above, with at least a 4 in English and maths and at least a 5 in most subjects to be studied at A level. International students need at least a 7 in the IELTs exam or IGCSE in English as a second language. Those not taking GCSEs sit school's own tests.

Exit: Some 25 per cent leaves after GCSEs – some don't get the grades to move into sixth form, others move elsewhere for vocational qualifications or because they can't study the subjects they want. Some go straight into apprenticeships with companies such as Network Rail or the Merchant Navy, others to a huge range of universities (about 50 per cent to Russell Group) to read anything from modern languages at Durham, English at Exeter, architecture at Edinburgh, journalism at Lincoln, sports therapy at Chichester to social work at Kingston. A handful to Oxbridge most years – three in 2018, plus three medics and a vet. Some have won scholarships to universities in USA; overseas boarders to universities all over the world.

Money matters: Government cuts have led to the school cutting out a lesson on Friday afternoon, sports provision has been reduced and parents have to pay for some after-school clubs. This has upset some families but allows school to offer wide range of extracurricular activities. The head says that this has enabled the school to offer more fixtures than ever before and more parents have got involved in coaching teams. Parents asked to pay £5 per month into the Manwood Trust to help fund projects like the library refurbishment and school minibuses. Sixth form bursary fund for students who would not be able to stay on without help with travel, books and equipment. Boarders pay a boarding fee but the education is free.

Remarks: A grammar school with an holistic approach to education where extracurricular activities are given almost equal weight with academic achievement. Pupils pride themselves on their individuality, are genuinely supportive of each other and there is a palpable sense of kindness and consideration for others around the school.

Sir William Borlase's Grammar School

West Street, Marlow, Buckinghamshire SL7 2BR

Ages 11–18 **Pupils** 1,070 **Sixth form** 409

01628 816500
www.swbgs.com

Headteacher: Since January 2018, Kay Mountfield, previously deputy head. Studied English and drama at Royal Holloway College and has been greatly involved in the work of the performing arts department, directing numerous school musicals. She founded and continues to produce and direct the Royal Borough Youth Opera at Eton College; many of its members and former members hail from Borlase.

Academic matters: Selective intake and consistent performance well above average across all subject areas, with the most dramatic hike seen in STEM subjects, where there is a big push to ensure girls are also on board. Although teachers can give plenty of examples of IT being embedded into core subjects, some pupils complain that computer technology as a subject in its own right is in danger of falling behind.

Historically, the school has been criticised as being an elitist, academic hothouse, but there is overwhelming agreement that is no longer true, with staff being pushy, but by not overly so. Less able students are well looked after, with parents of children of mixed abilities feeling satisfied. Less than a handful of SEN pupils, but significant resources and effort poured into ensuring they reach maximum potential.

Some mixed, but strong, views about homework, with a school survey showing that a third of parents think there's too much, a third think there's too little and a third think it's just right. 'Arguably, they are all right because each child's learning needs are different'; school feels its focus on personal learning programmes is critical.

References to some outstanding teaching and a robust learning mentor programme, in which staff and sixth formers ensure everyone is on track and sufficiently challenged. Big emphasis on student-led study, with the library dedicating significant space to entirely student-led societies in subjects such as medicine, English and physics. Great excitement from both students and staff about the evidenced impact on their learning and the fact that students from these societies have persuaded the likes of author Simon Singh and the chairman of the Institute of Physics to provide lectures. These societies also regularly persuade major companies to let them visit. Overseas trips are plentiful and open to all students, with recent examples including Uganda, Greenland and Iceland.

Independent learning is a major focus from an early age, which culminates in undergraduate level research carried out at sixth form, where dissertation titles include 'Is music therapy useful in the treatment of Alzheimer's?' And 'Do the laws of physics prevent the operation of time machines?' Meanwhile, events like Take A Risk Day, in which children do anything from cook something new to learn a new language, form part of the emphasis on encouraging students and teachers regularly move out of their comfort zone. 'One of the challenges of a grammar is that many children have never got stuck or failed and it's really important for all children – but especially these – to develop resilience,' explains school.

Most pupils take 10 GCSEs and in 2018, 67 per cent of grades were A*-A/9-7. At A level 77 per cent A*-B, 48 per cent A*/A.

Games, options, the arts: The school earned a specialist status in performing arts in 2005 and although the specialist school programme has since disappeared, the school's drive in this subject area hasn't, with very little resistance to it being compulsory from years 7 to 9. 'The reason we went for performing arts was to counter perceptions that we are purely academic and because we strongly believe that creativity helps students think laterally.' Big push for boys in drama and dance, which has been helped by a recent Strictly event and a popular all-boys dance club.

S

Impressive amenities, including a top-notch dance studio, theatre and cutting-edge recording studio, facilitate an innovative arts programme, where everything from Roctober to an annual Boscars (complete with red carpet and bronze statuettes) are the source of considerable excitement and pride. Regular productions of the likes of Kiss Me Kate, Forbidden Planet and Les Misérables involve pupils from all years, always with an eye to reinforcing different aspects of the curriculum and individual achievement. Students are particularly proud of a stirring play about World War I, which moved around the whole school and ended in a commemorative silence. Musical talent abounds and gets due recognition within the school and local press, with no less than 10 choirs, all conducted by students, not to mention the bands ranging from rock to jazz.

Strongest sporting activities by far are rowing and hockey, with two full international girl rowers and 40-50 county hockey players. But the school offers much more than that on the sporting front, with around 20 at any one time forming the Borlase Elite Sports Team (BEST). Extra clubs and competitions exist in pretty much every sport you can think of, including cheerleading, dance, table-tennis and girls' rugby. In fact, so popular are sports and performing arts that many students wind up overstretching themselves, with the school increasingly focusing on teaching time management. But there's no on-site swimming pool and students complain the gym is on the small side.

Background and atmosphere: The fact that the Hand and Flowers (the only UK pub to be awarded two stars in the Michelin guide) is right next door speaks volumes about the affluence and charm of the area, and the school's striking 17th century brick and flint buildings do not look out of place. Inside the school grounds, expect pretty cloisters, gardens and a feeling of space, with the more modern buildings towards the back of the school. A much-loved (but overstretched) café and outdoor areas are populated by relaxed and happy-looking pupils and the school is proud of the lack of corridors and the hustle and bustle that goes with them, instead providing lots of areas where pupils can be calm and quiet. It seems to pay off – even when the bell goes for lunchtime, students walk around relatively serenely.

On the downside, the school currently has capacity for 950, but actually contains over 1,000, which means there are buildings that bursting at the seams, notably sixth form facilities. That said, the school has plans to build a three-story development. Also disappointing is the lack of ethnic diversity, although that reflects the local area.

Pastoral care, well-being and discipline: Evidence of an ordered and respectful attitude when walking around, with rooms containing expensive equipment left open and low levels of bullying and other troubles. The school puts it down to a strong commitment to developing student voice, leadership and team skills, particularly among prefects, as well as a lot of both formal and informal mentoring. Vertical tutoring, a system of organising students into small pastoral tutor groups made up of pupils from different year groups, is highly praised by pupils and teachers alike. There are also regular surveys checking that students feel supported and have at least one main person within the school to confide in about any existing or potential difficulties.

Teachers on the strict side, particularly when it comes to uniform and homework deadlines, but with consistent and well-laid-out expectations, although low level disruption is an ongoing issue. There's a big drive on dealing with the behaviour not the child, with one sixth former reporting, 'One of the boys who was naughtiest in years 7 and 8 has just got an offer at Oxford, which I think says it all about the lack of labelling of students among both teachers and students.'

There's a sense that you can be who you really are at this school. 'There's room for every type of person,' confirmed one student. Parents agree. 'Whether you're in the nerdy academic bunch, the sporty lot or the performing arts bunch – or in no particular bunch at all – you are seen as equal,' said one.

Pupils and parents: Virtually non-existent parking ('I feel sorry for the Hand and Flowers pub!' said one parent) means parents don't feature at the school gates much, but many are very active when it comes to helping out with sport, music and drama. There's a good parent rep system that is particularly valued by parents in the first few weeks of joining, where quiz nights and other social events ensure those who want to socialise can do so, although there's no pressure. Communication between the school and parents can be hit and miss, according to some parents, but the new and improved website has helped. Pupils are respected in the community for being a well-behaved and polite bunch, and their aspirations tend to reflect their moneyed and ambitious parents.

Entrance: Catchment area shrank considerably in the late 90s and has remained relatively small, but the school is still heavily oversubscribed at 11+, with entrance by school exam. The admissions policy allows for 45 external sixth form spaces, but they normally accept 80, some from as far as Ealing. Selection on GCSE results and the school's assessment of commitment to their chosen subjects.

Exit: Some 10 per cent leave after GCSEs. Students are introduced to a wide range of professions and careers through presentations and workshops. Many go on to top level universities and colleges. Popular destinations include London, Durham, Warwick, Exeter and Bristol, across a wide range of subjects. In 2018, 11 to Oxbridge, plus five medics and a dentist. No shortage of support for students in everything from completing UCAS personal statements to ensuring leadership, presentation and interview skills. So much so that some students complain of preparation overkill.

Money matters: This is the third lowest funded of the 1,800 or so academies in the country when it comes to money per pupil. But because lack of funding not always immediately obvious, some parents complain of getting fed of being asked to do yet more fundraising. That said, 'Build a Better Borlase' has a strong history of mobilising financial and other support from current and past parents and pupils, resulting in great facilities.

Remarks: This is the kind of school that many of the parents wish they'd been to and that pupils are very proud of. Yes, there are niggles, but they are relatively minor and the focus on creating and celebrating confident and responsible, respectful individuals who do well in their subjects is abundantly clear throughout the school. Very much part of community life and yet it feels like something of a haven from many of the typical problems that beset teenagers.

Sir William Perkins's School

Guildford Road, Chertsey, Surrey KT16 9BN

Ages 11–18 **Pupils** 597 **Sixth form** 121

Fees: £15,915 pa

01932 574900
www.swps.org.uk

Head: Since 2014, Chris Muller BA (40s), promoted to the top slot five years after joining school as deputy head. Before that, at Kingston Grammar as head of classics for nine years, six as head of sixth form. Preceded by identical pairing one level down (classics teacher/deputy sixth form head) at RGS Guildford, with first teaching post at St Dunstan's.

Parents very happy with approach – forward thinking that stops short of the revolutionary, a moderate who'll keep the new buildings coming but the essential values the same and won't 'be too comfortable – or frightened of addressing challenges,' felt a mother. Packs a lot into his 11-hour day. Attends every event going ('girls like it that you're there'), teaches classics-related subjects to all year 7s, some year 9s and lower sixth and still manages the time for much appreciated corridor chats with pupils.

A bibliophile and burgeoning public speaker, managed to combine both interests in recorded online TEDx talk on the need to read, garnering 629 views (close to school numbers) but a solitary comment – 'Woo, go, Daddy' – (our punctuation) posted by a certain 'Got Mullered' (one of his two teenage children, who'll be 'thrilled' to be in print). Current affairs are another interest (he's a member of 1964 Club for Epsom and Ewell locals who 'share common values and objectives with the Conservative Party and wish to see them elected'). Currently a happy man, then. Dr Who is another interest (Jodie Whittaker for prime minister?), family skiing trips his escape.

Also, like other heads, writes blog which, again traditionally, is completely comment free ('Got Mullered' clearly needs to be pressed into action again) though one parent recently told him that 'it's the first thing I look at on Saturday.' (We're delighted for him).

Sees good pastoral care as the starting point for success. Have fun, enjoy your lessons and learning without tears will follow – and is at pains to point out to parents that perfection isn't all it's cracked up to be. 'Things go wrong and that's fine – it's working out what you've learned from that missed step, that's the important part of the experience.' Lives the message – won't ask anyone to leave post-GCSEs. 'If you come here, we're committed to you for life – not going to cull anyone at the end of year 11. The really bright pupils see that you're looking at girls as individuals with needs and realise that "that could be my daughter one day," and they're quite reassured by that.'

Academic matters: School's bloodless aims are to 'maintain high academic standards and encourage the enjoyment of learning and good habits of work'. But behind the primness beats a corporate warm heart. Yes, school pulls in the grades – 81 per cent A*-A/9-7 grades at GCSE in 2018 and 47 per cent of A levels A*/A (78 per cent A*/B). But achievements come without sense that they're the be all and end all of anyone's existence.

Parents are clear about who school is for – local bright, conscientious girls who'd wilt in heat radiating from area's famous all girls' academic sizzlers. 'Not about results to the exclusion of everything else,' said one. 'It's academics plus drama and dance.' One mother shook her head over friend busily cramming daughter for entrance exams elsewhere 'so could be stretched.' Challenge not lacking here but 'didn't want daughter to feel she had to run every day in class.' Another praised sensible approach to illness-related absence. 'Don't feel that world will come crashing down around their ears or that have to struggle in with a temperature.'

All about 'aiming for excellence, not perfection,' stresses Mr Muller in school magazine – worth restating in big letters over every classroom. 'We want them to like the challenge but not create such a pressurised environment that it almost paralyses them.' Lessons notable for easy rapport between staff and pupils, from year 10 girls enthusiastically leaping to their feet so could explain their approach to algebra problems, to biology teacher selecting 'victims' to label a heart. 'It's easy,' she enthuses. 'You say that...' replies pupil, grinning.

Encouraging feedback from parents on SEN support. Learning support coordinator (appointed to address shortcomings identified in last inspection) qualified to diagnose learning needs (mainly mild) and gently persistent in ensuring all staff see them as everyone's concern. 'Kills with kindness,' says school. Currently school supports 50 or so girls, two with mild physical difficulties. Ranges from withdrawal from lessons (usually a language), or extra help with organisation.

As with SEN, academic performance is a whole school issue, subject staff presented with results so can see struggles, strengths and anomalies – expect to add at least a grade at

GCSE over baseline assessments, traffic light system flagging up dips in performance – A grade students scoring B in a test will flash red. 'Might be issues, parental or personal, so don't use as be all and end all but it's a piece in the jigsaw,' says head. Leads to spot on grasp of strengths and weak points. 'Got the absolute maximum from my daughter,' said one. 'They've been right on the button with [exam] predictions.'

Won't shirk from hard-to-hear stuff – if predicted GCSE grades aren't good enough for A level sciences (7s needed to bridge difficulty gap), parents are told. A few don't like the plain speaking and move post-16 – with mixed success elsewhere. 'Changing your school to hear what you want isn't the answer,' said parent.

Bar occasional staff member who doesn't quite gell and moves on pronto, teaching gets good all round ratings. Class sizes hit 22, maximum 25 in years 7 to 9 then drop rapidly to maximum of 12 in years 10 and 11 and to as low as one for sixth form (maximum 14, depending on subject) with overall pupil to ratio of just under 10 to one.

Maths (like French, set from year 7 – though plenty of movement as natural ability becomes evident) a particular strength. Ditto science where heads of biology and psychology hold doctorates. 'Fantastic,' said parent. 'Good, solid and organised.' Borne out in results, bar recent A level physics blip, with two D grades out of just seven entries. A one-off that shouldn't be repeated, says head.

Post-GCSE, almost infinitely flexible course options in the sixth form. Most take three A levels plus life skills, leadership and PE/lectures in lower sixth plus options ranging from further maths to extended project or an additional AS or GCSE). More of the same in final year – six week student grub cookery course inevitably popular. If subject blend doesn't quite work for everyone first time round, school will keep on rejigging until it does.

For horizon widening, there's large, trad library. Oasis of calm (though 'don't want everyone sunk into stupor,' says librarian, who runs it on trust so no barriers come between girls and reading).

Little to complain of, bar one parent's sense that aspirations for top achievers could be ratcheted up a notch. 'Interesting,' said head, diplomatically, pointing to current results (eight per cent to Oxbridge) as proof that it's a far from neglected area. Academic pupils get 'stretch and challenge...to ensure fulfil undoubted potential.' Whole animal dissection is the big treat for budding medics. 'We've done a rat and a squid,' beams animated sixth former. Who could ask for more?

Games, options, the arts: Impressive numbers learning instruments (500 or so within school), with mega spring concert the annual powerhouse performance – though low profile among non-musical families.

Art harder to miss, vast, accomplished canvases everywhere. Pupils' depiction of withers-wringing emotions – stigmata-studded arms; a tear-stained child draped in Union Jack; supplicant girl, holding out cup and saucer at dining hall entrance – a tribute to catharsis, given cheery, turmoil-free public faces of their creators.

Sport dominated by rowing, involving 180 girls – the largest female programme in the country, says school. Win medals (national schools rowing championships) and have a new boat club on Laleham Reach. Other highlighted achievements all individual ones – badminton, sailing, ballet – which could also do with a tad more chronology, while netball and hockey are considered by pupils and parents to be the pick of the team sports.

Incentives include natty sportswear range (duvet coats for swaddling on match days) and stickers. Olden times silver and gold stars replaced by unicorn for creativity ('don't hand out many,' says games teacher, wistfully), pearl for grit and determination, dog (sociability), bee (organisation) and tree (reflection). Just needs addition of pulsating brain symbol for staff who memorise them all ...

Usual mutterings about time and effort lavished on top teams at expense of everyone else. 'If not in the A or B team, don't bother getting out of bed,' thought one disappointed mother. 'Turn up to practice and you're going to get a match,' insists Mr Muller, while acknowledging challenge of increasingly elite nature of sport as pupils progress up the school. 'Want them to enjoy camaraderie as well as enjoying sport, but finding fixtures for them is quite tough.'

We also heard reports of staff driving to local fitness centre and enjoying a coffee while senior pupils (who had walked there) were busy exercising – a 'do as I say, not as I do' approach that could benefit from a rethink, felt one parent. School points out that car needed in case of accidents to repatriate injured pupils.

Considerable energy, in contrast, expended in organising trips that include alternate years visit to Ghana – longstanding link with school there, themes woven into range of lessons (malaria nets in geography, for example) and generally impressive approach to the big issues. Problems faced by LBGT community addressed in recent newsletter – school also runs weekly 16+ Stonewall group.

Inspectors couldn't, meanwhile, get enough of DofE scheme, run largely by devoted parents, some now qualified trainers, who send decent cohort off to Buck House each year for gold medal presentations.

Background and atmosphere: Known informally by all parents we spoke to as Willie Perks (but, unendearingly, as SWPS to pupils), it's a jolly place that presents the journey to adulthood as something that, while challenging, holds the promise of being really rather fun.

Entrance exam experience is sweetened with chocolates dotted around. Sixth formers mastermind junior drama competition plays but also create eagerly awaited Christmas pantomime, lampooning the staff so effectively that several demanded meetings with (previous) head's doppelganger.

One parent wondered if school's defining Christian ethos was getting blurry round the edges and mourned passing of traditional hymn singing – 'good for the soul.' Mourn no longer. Never really went away and is undergoing a resurrection, says Mr Muller, who's also a fan.

Boys had first dibs on education when school was founded in the 18th century by successful merchant keen to give something back. Daringly co-ed from 1736 before move to present 12-acre site in 1819, becoming a girls' grammar from 1940s until the changing political climate led to independence in 1970s.

Completely rebuilt in 1914 and no problem getting to grips with school layout – just think of a figure of eight on its side. Got it? No, nor did we, but girls are quickly at home. Outside are two inviting little quads, one with a pond. Inside, subjects sensibly housed together (only anomalies are art next to science – airy windows the reason – and DT, which gets own little building, the former gym). Corridor displays bloom with beautiful handmade fabric books marking year 7 trip to Southall physics corridor and colourful paper flowers (biology project). Hearteningly, includes work that shows 'good practice' rather than highest marks.

Additional thoughtful details, from Muller TV (gives info on train times and events) to year 7 pupils' secure corridor (admin at one end, staff room at the other, for easy wobble containment) make this brilliant place to grow up – and grow out of, girls loving time there but raring to go by the end. Just what you'd want, it could be argued. 'I did enjoy SWPS, but equally I was quite happy to leave when I did,' said former pupil. 'It's a lovely school, but I found it got a bit small and familiar by the time I was in sixth form.'

New purpose built wing including spaces for drama workshops, music teaching, careers and sixth form centre with rooftop terrace should stop school bulging slightly at the seams – and may at least postpone ennui for future generations.

Pastoral care, well-being and discipline: School, like others, is picking up slack as government-funded services struggle. 'Difficult for teenage girl to walk into CAMHS and ask for help, so schools do need these services,' says Mr Muller. And it's not just girls who are helped. Parents are increasingly calling in for support, with school's blessing. 'We've realised that the more information we give them about the road bumps in the way of their daughter's journey at school, the more they realise it's not the end of the world.'

Former matron now relaunched as full-time counsellor, but known to all by previous title, though 'doesn't capture what she does,' says head. Doesn't sweat the small stuff (sore finger, said sixth former, greeted with a brisk 'what do you want me to do about it?') but brilliant with the big issues. Felt to be particularly good at developing rapport with vulnerable pupils, including those with eating disorders. 'Daughter will go to her if a bit wound up or needs some help,' said mother.

Teachers, particularly form tutors, also felt to do a pretty neat job in pastoral care. Pupils enthused about emailed reminders to take multivitamins, another teacher de-thorned roses at desk as a Valentine's Day treat. 'Just like a mum at school...'

Pupils also fully involved. Year 11s mentor year 7s and in turn have teacher to support them through horrors of GCSEs, while sixth formers take turns to run a listening room so younger girls can air problems. Seems to work, with bullying felt by pupils and parents to be a rare thing, friendship issues the normal bugbear. 'I feel they do have people they can talk to,' said parent.

While supportive of the needy, zero tolerance of the naughty, with detailed behaviour policy that would make any would-be transgressor think twice. Includes parents, who'll find their children excluded not just for drugs, violence and tampering with fire extinguishers (among other crimes) but also if fail to pay fees or are unreasonably snippy with staff. Sensible sanctions include carrying out 'useful tasks' for minor misdeeds (such as include eating food in classrooms or naughty use of make up, phones, cameras...).

Girls, in the meantime, able to be thoroughly themselves – one head girl praised for concentrated effort made in everything 'including wholeheartedly singing the wrong tune to a hymn in assembly'. Teachers, too, have a happy time here. One, formerly at tough-ish school, 'thrilled that can walk home thinking about physics equations rather than "why did the boy jump out of the window?"' enthuses head.

Pupils and parents: Other establishments notable for girls with glamorous hairdos 'sculptured into tousled creations,' thought mother. Here, you don't dress to impress. 'Not a lot of peer pressure on looks.'

Some parents sigh over lack of sixth form uniform and 'sloppier' appearance – less desirable role models for younger pupils. Head and pupils united in vociferous disagreement. 'Easier to learn in comfortable clothes – and it's good for us,' said sixth former. Girls look smart when need to, says head, but 'worrying about what's in their heads rather than how they look is really important – and I'm happy to argue with anyone who doesn't think so.'

Families geographically homogenous (most live within 15 miles of the school), culturally, too, affluent white Surrey dwellers and suburbanites the overwhelming majority.

Old girls in search of proper name – SWPSies? – meet up for annual catch-up and cream buns session and also help mentor current pupils. Careers impressively varied – one landing job at Network Rail following degree in ancient history (possibly researching origins of first BR sandwich...). Masses of science, too – again with welcome touch of levity – astrophysicist and BBC science broadcaster owning up in school magazine to intense boredom of PhD topic.

Active Friends of...hosts sell-out events and pulls in the donations – current target is £40,000. School also sends out leaflet with contact details for parent ambassadors, a great idea though not currently a well-used service. 'You're only call I've ever had,' said one.

Entrance: Main intake of up to 96 places in year 7, though offer some deferred entry 13+ places. Candidates (about two per place) sit English and maths exams. Have around 30 EAL pupils (rarely need extra support).

Sixth form places dependent on 9-7 GCSE grades in proposed A level subjects.

Exit: Around a third leaves after GCSEs. Big on science and maths subjects – three medics and a vet in 2018, with Essex, Birmingham, Nottingham and Edinburgh all popular. Some two-thirds to Russell Group; three Oxbridge in 2018.

Sports and arts scholars presumably account for the decent showing in related courses though music scholars seem to change course – few take on to uni. Many sixth formers were happily undecided about what to do and praised lack of pressure to make a decision – and unlimited support along the way. 'Wasn't a case of "don't be ridiculous" but "what can we do to help?"' said parent whose daughter went on to pilot school.

Money matters: Academic, music, drama and art scholarships offered in year 7 and sixth form (when sports is added), worth between five and 25 per cent of fees. Music specs come with warning to Mrs Worthingtons to 'consider girl's ability..to avoid unnecessary disappointment...'. Foundation bursaries cover up to 100 per cent of fees.

Remarks: Excellent results achieved with a big dollop of humour and humanity. 'If you don't excel at something, you're not going to feel that you can't achieve in other areas,' thought parent.

Would soon-to-qualify pilot daughter be tempted to complete victory roll over Chertsey on maiden flight out of nearby Heathrow out of sheer joie de vivre? 'Wouldn't put it past her,' said mother.

The Sixth Form College, Colchester

North Hill, Colchester, Essex CO1 1SN

Ages 16–19+ **Pupils** 2,930

01206 500700
www.colchsfc.ac.uk/

Principal: Since 1997, Ian MacNaughton BA (50s), read economics and social sciences at UEA. Previously taught at Brighton, Hove and Sussex Sixth Form College and Brockenhurst College. Also worked in a Hampshire County Council residential boarding house for 11-18 year-olds.

With his office based smack in the middle of the main college building, he is a visible presence around college, which is also helped by the fact that he usually teaches economics (although didn't the year we visited due to management and strategic demands). Students and parents describe him as 'approachable,' although inevitably in an educational institution of this size, many have no experience of dealing with him personally. Passionate about not just the college itself, but the wider FE sector – although we noticed he can be better at talking than listening when he gets going on a subject.

Interests include sports (tennis, football, cricket, running), current affairs and travel.

Academic matters: Achieves consistently strong academic results, especially given the context that Colchester has two super-selective 11-18 grammar schools that cream off the local top talent (that said, approximately 20 per cent of students from those two schools choose to transfer to the college for sixth form). In 2018, 50 per cent A*-B and 25 per cent A*/A grades at A level. But the real boon here is the value added – with the college having, for many years, achieved the best value-added scores for any sixth form in the country, with students' package of A level results regularly streets above their package of GCSEs achieved prior to entry.

A whopping 55 options on offer – English, psychology, maths and biology among the most popular. Sciences and humanities do particularly well in absolute terms, while subjects that shine from a value-added perspective include English and biology. Art related subjects are both popular and get great results. Four languages on offer – French, German, Spanish and Italian, along with introductory courses in Japanese, Mandarin, Greek and Latin. No subject combination is rejected – 'as long as you get the entry requirements, we find a way' – and if you do pick the wrong course, staff help you switch. 'Both my children made alterations to their courses and they felt senior tutors were both accessible and prompt in dealing with their concerns.' However, those choosing any numerate A levels but not maths or statistics 'are strongly encouraged to also choose maths studies'.

The extended project programme does well, as does IB – an average of 33 points in 2018. Students are also able to do a variety of courses leading to GCSE (usually retakes), including a one-year 'improvement' (Advanced Foundation) programme. Special programme available for those wishing to apply to Oxbridge, medical schools and other competitive career areas. 'My daughter wants to do medicine and the college could not have helped her more. She feels very prepared.'

Plenty of praise for the high quality and accessible teachers. 'If my daughter is worried about something over the weekend, she'll email her teacher and 99 per cent of the time, they'll email her back. Support seems to be around the clock.' 'They spend lots of extra time with students individually in college time to make sure they are on track.' Students told us, 'they don't force you to work like they do in schools – they gently motivate you through engaging teaching and high expectations.' Classes are lively and engaging – with students giving regular presentations in English lessons; lots of experiments in science; plays in history; debating in politics etc. 'You never get lessons where the teacher just talks from a textbook and you take notes.' Some students quibble that classes can feel a bit big at 20, but other classes have only a handful – with an average number per class of 17.5, according to the principal.

All students have access to one of 120 personal tutors, who are in turn supported by senior tutors, with other specialists on hand for individual counselling, careers and HE information. And all students get a regular (termly) review of their academic progress. There's also a student mentor programme, run in most departments. 'This is brilliant if you want someone to explain something to you in a different way to the teacher,' a student told us.

The learning support centre takes up a whole on-site house, where a team of 17 staff provide support for those with learning difficulties including dyslexia and dyspraxia, as well as physical disabilities or health (including mental health) needs. 'Some of our students have really quite high care needs,' says the head. Others use the centre for help with study skills, with regular workshops on issues ranging from coping with anxiety to creative writing. 'I came here to get help with handwriting – they were brilliant,' said one student. The buildings and outside areas are 99 per cent adapted for those with physical disabilities, and one student with complex medical needs told us, 'the college could not have been more accommodating with my regular hospital appointments and need to use the lift when in college.'

Games, options, the arts: Students are expected to embrace at least a few of the 100 extracurricular opportunities, which range from sign language to Shakespeare club. 'If you just want to study qualifications, this is not the college for you,' says the principal, although two parents we spoke to told us their children hadn't embraced this side of college life. For those do like the idea of a more rounded education, there's DofE, Amnesty International and plenty of outside speakers, in addition to the clubs. There's also a pre-teaching programme, which involves around 90 students going out for two-hour placements on a weekly basis. There's an active college council, with six main committees (social, arts, charities, sport, environment and international), and students can also apply to be student ambassadors and peer mentors.

No shortage of sports on offer both on and off the curriculum (with around 200 doing sport and PE at A and AS level), with facilities including an onsite sports hall and all-weather courts, in addition to which the students have access to a range of facilities around town – including Colchester Rugby Club, a local leisure centre pool and local squash, football and tennis clubs. Core sports are soccer and basketball, with a growth in volleyball, with the college regularly doing well all three at competition level – while the more unusual sports include boxing and tchoukball. 'We have a big push on getting girls more involved in sport, including in rugby, football, basketball, netball and hockey,' says the principal. Lots of sports programmes eg of team squads, community sports leaders awards etc.

Atmospheric art department, with a fabulous art school feel, including lots of natural light and impressive works on display. 'I just come in here to hang out sometimes – it's so relaxing and reminds you what else is going on around the college,' one science student told us. Courses include photography, art history, graphics, textiles and sculpture – all of which are also on offer off as extracurricular. Drama and art also popular, with courses including music, music tech, dance and performing arts – the latter of which is a popular option at university. 'I'd love to have a big auditorium for 1,000 people, but we have a very good drama studio for 300,' says the head. Students rave about the Shakespeare drama club, among others.

Long list of day trips and residentials, ranging from day trips to Stratford, Colchester Zoo and local nature reserves to history tours to Berlin, Holocaust memorial trips to Poland and a regular German exchange. There's also the opportunity to undertake voluntary work abroad, including to South India with the Russ Foundation to work with orphan children and blind women. The students raise funds to take over – often to the tune of £10,000, and even have a shop on site for this purpose.

Background and atmosphere: Located on a historic town centre site, right on top of Roman ruins – 'a boon for archaeology students.' A school occupied the site until 1987, using the original building which dates from 1912 – then the college took over, giving it a significant face-lift and large new extension, with a maze of newer buildings having been added onto the site in the years since. Now, the feeling is largely of a purpose-built college, with plenty of natural light and spacious classrooms and study areas – and generally well-equipped facilities. The most recent additions are the Pavilion facility, a uber-modern building dedicated to student study and social areas, and 58 North Hill – an house that was adjacent to the college, but which is now on site and has been converted into the learning support centre.

'There's a feeling that the facilities are really invested in, and that the site is constantly being updated, whether that's new desks or fans right through to whole new buildings,' said one student. Most departments have a glass-walled staff room by the entrance, so you can see who's in and who isn't and there's a noticeboard in each faculty, with named photos of all staff, 'which really helps when you're new.' The two refectories serve hot and cold food, although lots of students also head into town for lunch or to Starbucks, Costa etc when they have a free period. Well-stocked library, with an upstairs silent study area.

The atmosphere is relaxed and informal – with students wearing their own clothes and on first name terms with teachers. Corridors can get a bit congested with lively students, but inside classrooms, the atmosphere is calm and purposeful. 'It's not uncool to want to work and be involved,' one student told us, pointing out that they're expected to be in college five days a week.

Pastoral care, well-being and discipline: Not all 16-year-olds are self-motivated, natural self-starters – but if your child is, there is no reason they shouldn't thrive here, even if they have the odd wobble. 'If you have a problem, your personal tutor is always on hand and they sort things out quickly,' a student told us, adding that there is a very high level of individual guidance, 'which can help stop things escalating in the first place.' Also ensuring a strong pastoral system is a team of counsellors (some staff; some voluntary), a health worker, the study support centre and peer mentoring. And as staff only work with this limited age group, they come to know the kinds of issues they face, says the principal. 'We are very big on progression for students – and I think that helps too,' he adds. 'If students have a clear sense of where things are going for them over the next two to five years, it can help enormously with meeting short-term targets.' The main challenge pastorally is mental health, he says. 'It's a growing problem everywhere.'

Transition is well thought out, with new students eased into this more adult world with an induction day in the summer before they start. Meanwhile, the extracurricular focus helps them build friendships beyond their courses. 'Students tend to bring friendships from their previous school, but make many more during their time here,' says principal.

'They're strict on punctuality and deadlines, but that's about it,' said one student. 'Even then, they don't tell you off or chase you. They just make it clear that if you don't put the effort in, they can't help you and that, really, there's no point in you being there.' Principal claims to have 'virtually zero' discipline problems, with permanent exclusions non-existent and temporary exclusions very rare. 'When they do happen, it tends to be for not complying with work, rather than any behavioural issues,' he says. 'But generally, we tend to resolve those issues well before they reach the "You're not coming in, so what's the point of you being here?" point.' Good anti-bullying system in place.

Pupils and parents: 'There's a real mix of personalities and backgrounds here,' say students, and there's a higher ethnic intake than you might expect from the location, albeit still small – 12 per cent non-white compared to six per cent for the whole area. All come from with a 12 mile radius, mostly by bus or train if they live any distance. We found them a mature and dynamic bunch. 'They are keen to do well – they enjoy learning.' Past students include Dermot O'Leary (TV) and Joe Twyman (co-founder of YouGov). Parents feel involved via parents' evenings, reports, 'and we know we can call the teachers or principal too.'

Entrance: Students wishing to do A levels – who form the majority of the 3,000 students – generally need a minimum of two 6s and three 4-5s, 'but there's flexibility when it comes to individual courses,' says the principal. 'So you might have three 6s and not get on a course or one 6 and four 4s and get to do three A levels.' 'On paper, I needed a higher grade in art GCSE than I actually got because I missed my art exams, but they agreed to look at my portfolio and accepted me off the back of that,' said one student. For IB, students specifically need a minimum of three 6s from GCSEs in maths, English, a foreign language and a science. Vocational options vary but criteria is generally lower.

Applications available from the time of the open evening in October until the closing deadline in January. All candidates must be between 16 and 18 when starting at the college and all are interviewed face-to-face. College also requests previous school report. Fear not if you're worried about picking the wrong course – there's plenty of guidance and you can always change later if it really doesn't work out.

Around eight per cent from independent sector. Currently only fractionally oversubscribed, largely thanks to the college having expanded dramatically, although the principal expects this to change when the area comes out of its five-year demographic dip. 'Colchester is a popular growth town, with the biggest percentage rise in Britain,' he adds.

Exit: Over 80 per cent to university (some after a gap year or art foundation course), to a wide range of destinations. Essex, UEA, Leeds, Kent and Nottingham all popular. Eight to Oxbridge and 15 medics in 2018, plus about 20 off abroad.

Money matters: Parents are asked for £30 contribution for the two-year stint – towards facilities and insurance for school trips. A £20 refundable deposit also required for text books.

Remarks: An upbeat, hard-working, can-do culture exudes from every nook and cranny of this college. Not for students who expect to breeze through, but a fantastic option for motivated young people. We were left in no doubt about how well they respond to the high expectations of the college, which are well supported by a brilliant tutorial system and plenty of individual guidance and support. A highly recommended bridge between school and university.

The Skinners' School

St John's Road, Tunbridge Wells, Kent TN4 9PG

Ages 11–18 **Pupils** 1,060 **Sixth form** 300

01892 520732
www.skinners-school.co.uk

Head: Since 2013, Mr Edward Wesson MA (early 50s). Educated at Tonbridge, where he was head boy, and at Cambridge, where he read law. 'Dabbled in journalism' and worked on the Sevenoaks Chronicle before training as a teacher. 'I became a teacher because I knew it would be a lot of fun,' he was overheard telling a pupil. Taught at New Beacon, Sevenoaks and Wellington School, Somerset, followed by 12 years at Hampton, where he became head of sixth form and master in charge of cricket. Was deputy head of Reigate Grammar for four years and then head of King's Tynemouth for three years before moving into the state sector as headmaster of Skinners' – although he says Skinners' also has 'the DNA of an independent school'. He teaches history and politics and is married to Susie, also a teacher; they have two young daughters. He is a keen sportsman and still loves his cricket, and goes to the theatre whenever he can. Approachable and easy to talk to, although boys say he is 'quite low profile' and they don't really know him. 'He does not shirk discipline and is strict but fair,' said a parent. He presides over the weekly whole school assembly and attends matches and concerts, and 'he comes across well and makes a good speech and really cares about the school'. He attends the teenage forum (school council) and is heading a drive to limit the amount of time boys spend staring at screens. He is a governor at Skinners' Kent Academy which Skinners' sponsors and says both schools benefit from the cross pollination.

Academic matters: Specialist status in science and maths with best results in these subjects at GCSE, especially physics and maths, with maths, physics and geography being the most popular at A level, along with English and history. Sciences taken as three separate IGCSEs and some take maths early. In 2018, 68 per cent of GCSE grades were A*-A/9-7; at A level, 44 per cent A*/A and 77 per cent A*-B.

Works with a local school to increase the range of subjects, especially in sixth form. TWGGS (Tunbridge Wells Girls' Grammar) girls come over for German and PE and boys can go to TWGGS for Spanish and psychology. Dedicated languages building and all study French and German in Year 7; boys can do either or both for GCSE. French trips to the Loire, exchanges with schools in Vannes and Avignon, and a German exchange with a school in Bonn. Latin has been reintroduced at KS3.

RS GCSE for all with an emphasis on philosophy and ethics leads to some interesting discussions. Skinners' own tailor made course on thinking theories, techniques of problem-solving and evaluating ideas for all of years 7 and 8. Civics programme in sixth form involves critical thinking and gives space to discuss challenging ethical questions via lectures and visits from outside speakers; now offers EPQ. ICT and computing offered up to GCSE including website design and data handling, all in well-equipped IT suites, and there is a strong focus on internet safety in the lower years.

Well-resourced careers library with careers co-ordinator. Careers advice through PSHE in lower years and boys encouraged to find work experience after GCSEs. Sixth formers offered talks from visiting speakers and presentations on student finance, studying abroad and the UCAS form. Own biennial careers fair and all are offered a careers planning meeting with an external advisor.

Teachers hardly ever leave but attend regular courses to keep up to date; there has been a recent influx of new young teachers due to retirements and nearly half are now women – boys always address them as Sir or Miss.

Full time SENCo and a qualified assessor for dyslexia, dyspraxia and other difficulties– about 60 boys need some support; a few on autistic spectrum and currently two statemented children. Help tailored to individual needs with either one-to-one or small group work. A counsellor comes in weekly. Most able given extension work within the classroom and are stretched and challenged through a wide range of societies but otherwise no special treatment.

'Although the school is super selective, it is not a pressured environment, and individual targets are set for each child; boys never feel inadequate and streaming is very sensitively done,' said one parent. Another thought that 'the ethos of hard work and achievement can be quite daunting for some, and the emphasis on independent study can be difficult at the start', although 'we don't get tons of homework,' said our guide approvingly.

Games, options, the arts: Sports grounds at Southborough, 15 minutes' walk away with five rugby pitches and a football/cricket pitch and running track. Big emphasis on rugby, which is taken seriously, and good parental support at matches with teas provided by parent volunteers. Recent leaver playing for Harlequins and others go on to represent their county or region. Fierce rivalry with The Judd grammar school at Tonbridge. While some parents say that rugby is still a major focus of school life, another said, 'There is much more on offer now for non-rugby players' and there is a 'conscious effort to accommodate boys not into major sports', who are allowed to give it up after the first term. 'If a boy is not mega-sporty it is not an issue, as there are plenty like him,' said the mother of a boy who does not enjoy rugby. 'The school is putting more focus on the creative and sensitive aspects of being a boy and not just rugby'. All have to do a minimum of three hours of sport a week and there is something for everyone – the school is becoming increasingly good at badminton and basketball, in new sports hall with its own climbing wall and winter cricket nets. Good range of sports clubs, including tennis on own on-site courts, and shooting. Strong cross-country running – much of it done through local clubs. Football lower profile, and keen footballers tend to belong to local clubs. Hockey training at Tunbridge Wells Girls' Grammar and a local hockey club. Boys tend to be health and fitness conscious, said our guide, and the fitness suite is 'sixth form heaven' with weights and a cardiovascular section.

CCF, with its emphasis on self-reliance, teamwork and leadership skills, is popular and enables the school to offer outdoor adventures with the army's support. D of E recently established with huge take-up. Active music scene with about 60 per cent learning an instrument and a music room, bristling with computers, which is open all the time. 'Music is fantastic with a huge number of clubs,' said one parent. 'If a boy is musical he will be catered for'. Two orchestras, choirs, swing bands, big band, jazz band and chamber orchestra with regular concerts. Music offered at GCSE and A level and one boy doing grade 8 saxophone. Drama increasingly popular with three performances per year including a senior production in on-site multi-purpose theatre. They also team up with TWGGS for drama.

Art compulsory for the first three years and housed in a light, bright space with a wide range of media offered including installations, film, graphics, sculpture and photography. Parents' Association helped fit out the junior art room with digital cameras, a projector and a sewing machine. Art popular at GCSE with a high proportion getting A*s, and a handful take art A level – sixth formers have their own art room and recent trips have included visits to Berlin and Amsterdam. Impressive GCSE and A level art shows, art displayed around the school and art students also involved with stage painting.

Good range of lunchtime and after-school clubs including sports, music, debating and baking as well as academic societies, and year 7s are given tasters in their first term. Year 10 takes part in the BBC School Report at the Tunbridge Wells studio, and a sixth form group recently returned from a 10 day Model United Nations trip to Harvard and New York, and came within the top five internationally. Recent history trip to Krakow and Auschwitz. Others have included Morocco, Iceland, Madagascar and Ladakh.

Background and atmosphere: Founded in 1888 by the Worshipful Company of Skinners with 53 pupils. The burghers of Tonbridge were not happy that Tunbridge Wells had been chosen for the site of the new grammar school, and this led to the foundation of The Judd the following year; and so a fierce rivalry was born. The school still occupies its original site in Tunbridge Wells. Even in the 1930s space was at a premium, and there were plans to move to Southborough, but World War II got in the way and only some foundations were laid – still visible in the corner of the playing fields. Most of the architectural styles of the last 130 years are represented somewhere in the school. Main school is the original Victorian building, and there have been many additions over the years. The stark, concrete 1960s block still known as the New Wing houses refurbished science labs (new lab recently completed) and the dining hall, where whole school Monday morning assemblies take place. Then there is the 1980s Knox Wing classroom block and the 1990s Leopard Building, which houses maths and ICT. Byng Hall, an ex-Victorian church institute acquired in 2002, used for music and the performing arts, won an award for its sensitive conversion. The Cecil Beeby Building houses modern languages, and fine sports hall was opened in 2012. Planning permission has recently been granted to turn the little-used old gym into an art and literature building, new sixth form centre and library, but school is still hoping for funding, and it will be some years away.

Strong sense of purpose about the school; 'Boys are proud to be here and proud of what it stands for as part of the community,' says the headmaster. The school is proud of its green credentials and holds the eco-schools green flag for sustainability.

Pastoral care, well-being and discipline: Instant expulsion for transgressions beyond the pale eg supplying drugs. Our guide said he 'could not imagine anyone being caught with drugs'. Effective team of heads of year, tutor groups and teachers means that there are prompt interventions, and bullying dealt with quickly and effectively. Pastoral care consistently praised by parents: 'My son has thrived there and he has been really looked after,' said a mother. 'They focus on the child as a whole and embrace them for who they are. I always feel I can email or phone if I am worried and I feel I am listened to'. Others commented: 'The pastoral support is outstanding – if a boy needs help there is always someone to talk to'. 'It is a very inclusive school and the older boys look out for the younger ones'.

Sixth formers have a new common room with study area, and sixth form prefects act as mentors to years 7 and 8 and assist in the running of tutor groups. Senior boys have to apply for these positions and attend an interview and are then given support and training. They help year 7s settle in and explain to them what is on offer.

All look well turned out in smart uniform with blazers with the school emblem of the leopard and edged in the school colours, each slightly different to signify the house, school tie in house colours and dark trousers. Sixth formers wear a suit with collar and tie.

Four houses with strong house loyalty; inter-house competitions like sport and debating. The food is good with plenty of choice and a salad bar and there are often international themes. 'My kids love the school dinners and it's reasonably priced – very few bring in a packed lunch,' said a mother.

New boys are given plenty of support settling in – the head of year 7 visits as many boys as possible in their primary schools, induction afternoons and a parents' evening are held in the term before entry, and boys are likely to travel to school together are put in the same form. Year 7s start school a day early so they can learn how the school day works before everyone else returns.

Pupils and parents: Largely middle class parents with very few children eligible for free school meals – school is trying to redress this on entry. Parents generally very supportive as they are 'happy their kids are here and support the ethos'. 'Boys are spirited and happy in an unforced way, and loyal to the school and to each other,' says the headmaster. 'There are some real scholars but most enjoy school just as much for friends and the extracurricular activities as the academics.'

Famous old boys include Christopher Hogwood (classical musician), Nick Knowles (TV presenter), Bob Woolmer (England cricketer), Jamie Spence (golfer), Tony Eldridge (war hero – the 'human torpedo').

Entrance: Entry via the Kent Test, or more formally the Kent Assessment Procedure, in the September before entry – those with the highest scores offered places first and then those who live closest to the school. Ten pupils on free school meals admitted as priority if they have sufficient test scores. Oversubscribed many times over – four applicants per place. From September 2019, distance as well as a qualifying score will be incorporated into over-subscription criteria.

Some 85 per cent come from 75 different primary schools, with St John's being the biggest feeder, and the rest from local prep schools, especially Rosehill in Tunbridge Wells. The other 15 per cent come from up to 20 miles away. No siblings policy. 'The Kent test is now much more difficult to coach for but it doesn't stop people doing it,' says the headmaster. About 20 boys join the sixth form from other schools and need an average of 48 GCSE points (between A and B) from their best eight GCSEs. This also applies to those already in the school, and most progress to sixth form – priority is given to current pupils.

Exit: Hardly any leave after GCSEs (five per cent or so) or at the end of year 12. A handful go straight into work after A levels but most go on to university. Two to Oxbridge and three medics in 2018, rest to mainly Russell Group universities. Bristol, Leeds, Exeter and Nottingham very popular; biggest subjects, engineering, English and economics. Extra Oxbridge help and interview practice. One or two to art college most years. Most join the Old Skinners' Society when they leave and become 'Leopards'.

Remarks: A consistently high performing grammar school where boys are happy and well supported – they come out with good grades and go to good universities, from whence there is a well-trodden path into the professions and the City.

South Farnham School

Menin Way, Farnham, Surrey GU9 8DY

Ages 4–11 Pupils 817

01252 716155
www.south-farnham.surrey.sch.uk

Headteacher: Since September 2018, Claire Donnachie, who is also director of teaching school here. She has previously been director of school centred initial teacher training (SCITT) at George Abbot and director of teaching school at Esher High. South Farnham was one of the first Teaching Schools; she has several qualifications as a leader of education and has worked with Ofsted and the DfE on developing SCITT programmes and teaching standards.

Entrance: Non-selective, oversubscribed, sense of fabulous sweetshop surrounded by disappointed parents pressing noses to glass. Now 90 places at 4+, two more classes added at 7+, many from four feeder infant schools. After standard queue jump priorities – looked after children, siblings – success

S

hinges on home to school distance. Dozens of families, turned away outright, don't even get that far. No wonder local estate agent pays for website link.

Exit: Majority to highly thought of Weydon School; significant minority to leading independents including Salesian, Royal Grammar School Guildford.

Remarks: Currently one of the nation's top performing primary with 135 plus children – that's four classes' worth – regularly getting excellent Sats results. Puts boot in commonly held belief that with primaries, small equals beautiful, with consistent year in, year out demonstration that bigger substantially better. It's an elite national support/national teaching school, rated one of the best in the country for teacher training.

Detractors might point to affluent locale as significant unfair advantage – annual fundraising total of both parents' associations, separate for infants and juniors, now closing on £30,000, is a pointer. Surroundings undeniably attractive. Infants – sensitively modernised Victoriana – cheerful interiors, disabled lift. Tardis-like, appears tiny at front, opens up to reveal idyllic wooded valley setting and generous running around space, veg garden producing harvest soup for all, sensory garden and – a rarity – heated outdoor pool.

Juniors, spacious with enviable facilities '... better than some secondary schools, ' said parent. Architecture – best-quality 1930s municipal, topiary-fronted, much improved and deceptively square-shaped – 'It took me two terms to find my way round,' said year 6 guide. Grandfather clock and scholarship board residual reminders of pre-1970s incarnation as girls' grammar, Joanna Trollope rumoured former teacher.

Outside, seven acres of space with grass, Astroturf – school regularly does well in matches – dipping pond and attractive courtyard area complete with looming model heron. Inside, two floors of vibrant corridors with eye-catching displays – letters from linked Japanese school, all 42 Unicef Children's Articles, year 6s cover one a week – link classrooms, five libraries and six art rooms – some large, others bijou – well-equipped ICT suite that children – ultimate praise – vote better than home PCs. Jewel in the crown is the two dance/drama studios, gym, hall and practice rooms all much in use for large-scale, multi-cast Christmas/summer shows, plus spring concerts. New music block added in 2015.

But while it's lush, especially with surroundings, all pitch perfect winding lanes, detached homes (frequently bordered with vaguely intimidating noli me tangere high hedges) pupils come with normal range of needs – currently 147 with some form of learning difficulty, 87 with EAL needs. 'We take whatever the community gives us,' says head.

Educational community flocks to touch hems of these particular academic gowns, and no wonder, given way staff work with raw material, spinning it into results gold. Lesson quality outstanding but tip of the iceberg – it's the 90 per cent under the surface preparation that's magic weapon, achieved by talented, well-led staff, average late 20s, mostly women, cohesive, happy, talkative, incredibly hard-working – who are the true ingredient X. Inevitably many are high-flyers on way to greater things elsewhere – 'We've had people leaving here after three years to become deputy heads' – so high(ish) turnover. For occasional few the intensity, though undoubtedly rewarding, simply too much. No shortage of talented replacements, however, with first-class internal training programme helping many teaching assistants qualify as teachers.

Adds up to environment where no child in need of a helping hand allowed to slip through net. Junior class size of 35 headline figure but misleading. Emphasis is on differentiated learning, with 30 teaching assistants – all in training, many teachers in waiting – and seven personalised learning specialists making it happen and true child/adult ratio of 13:1. Is piloting super-size classes of 60, with experienced teacher backed up by two newly qualified teachers and two teaching assistants. Able pupils stretched – members of National Association for Able Children in Education – while from year 1, rigorous monitoring identifies any literacy/numeracy stragglers, 'Often the ones at back of class, not putting up their hands,' says teacher. They'll have separate sessions – up to five a day by year 6 in small focus groups, covering same work as higher ability group, nuanced to iron out any difficulties en route.

Forensic attention to detail sounds dry but translates into enthralling, nth-degree planned lessons. Even usually drab spelling notebooks burst with colourful doodles as children encouraged to create own aide-memoires for tricky words. Chalk and talk clearly discarded long ago in favour of lessons where individual work prefaced by engrossing group activity – 'soundscape' recreating Dickensian London for year 6 pupils, teacher stomping round room as plausibly crabby Scrooge – in costume, too, children in character as cringing street urchins – so riveted that, unusually, not a single head turns for visitors, though could have something to do with sheer volume of traffic as everyone from VIPs to visiting teachers beats path to this educational nirvana.

Other comprehensively scotched myth is that big means noisy. Lack of volume takes some getting used to – you almost welcome (rare) sight of child pushing ahead through doorway – though reassuringly less Midwich Cuckoo than well-tuned powerful car. Teachers uniformly soft-voiced, children ditto. Seeing them en masse, a blue-jumpered sea of tranquillity in assembly a revelation to anyone assuming that little eddies of fidgeting/chat, countered with mild adult irritation were an educational fact of life.

Inspirational teaching must help. Hand in hand with this is top-down faith in the children. Year 3s taste responsibility from word go as message bearers. 'We don't get that many notes home and it's left to the children to tell you,' said slightly shell-shocked mother.

There's unsupervised break time access to practice rooms – conflicting rhythms, keys and styles fight for supremacy in the corridors. Children get say in casting decisions for many large-scale, multi-cast plays that are highlight of school calendar. Also decide when to have lunch – delicious, freshly cooked, at least two mains and puddings, fresh bread on the side, unobtrusive wastage/veg consumption checks, standing invitation to parents to eat with child – late bell reminds latecomers to get a move on.

Instead of convoluted rewards vs sanctions system common elsewhere, trust is the big motivator. No house points, no 'honour of the school' sticks or carrots – indeed, children politely puzzled by notion. Result is children with quiet confidence of people who know what they're about, behave and do well because of 360 degree assumption that they'll want to. Tangible sense of purpose and pride in accomplishment. 'I don't know anybody in the school who isn't interested in something,' said year 6 boy.

So is this a one-off establishment or something others could replicate? 'Every school could be [as good]. There's many as good or better. When we work with other schools, the key element is the striving for success and the total belief that it can happen... You've got to have an ambition.'

This remains a jewel in educational crown, demonstrably good at what it does, fortunate in its focused, dedicated staff and making a virtue of its size, producing happy children whose quiet confidence and pride in their many achievements is a pleasure to witness.

Steyning Grammar School

Shooting Field, Steyning, West Sussex BN44 3RX

Ages 11–18 **Pupils** 2,237 **Sixth form** 427 **Boarders** 127 full **C of E**

Fees: Day free; Boarding £9,300 – £11,100 pa

01903 814555
www.sgs.uk.net/

Head: Since 2013, the energetic and insightful Nick Wergan (40s). He began his career in investment banking before retraining as an English teacher in 2004; then rose rapidly after being dubbed Outstanding New Teacher of the Year (2007) by the National Teaching Awards, through posts as head of English (Sackville School, East Grinstead) and deputy head (Blatchington Mill, Hove). He's resourceful and decisive, empowers his teaching team to lead and role model leadership for the pupils, and this delegation means he can also turn his powerful brain to looking at business partnerships to help with the funding crisis that dogs state schools.

He has a house on site in the Elizabethan part of the school, but also owns and lives on a vineyard nearby with his family – producing award-winning sparkling wine. This pragmatic mix of localism and global business is at the heart of his tenure. He looks to local secondaries (through Challenge Partners network) to keep Steyning Grammar striving to be its best, trumpets the school's 400 year tradition to make new legacy connections, has a conference phone on the table in one of his two offices to enable frequent management communication across two sites, and tweets and blogs avidly. He teaches English to year 7 once a week, and students say he pops in and out of classes, corridors and the canteen, working closely with the head boys and girls to take the temperature of the school too.

Academic matters: Reflections on learning are intrinsic to the school success – whether that is implicit in weekly year group assemblies (hall only holds 350); explicit in the title of the school's newsletter; or sustained through what has been created through the IB learner profile, even though the qualification is no longer on offer here. (Few state schools in the UK can afford it financially now after funding cuts.) The size of the school means that over 30 A levels and just as many GCSEs are on offer, class sizes normally 24 with 16 to 20 at A level. In 2018, 21 per cent A*-A/9-7 at GCSE and 65 per cent got 9-4 in both English and maths. At A level, 26 per cent A*/A and 52 per cent A*-B.

Years 7 and 8 are in the Church Street site, so their atmospheric classrooms have parquet floors and a maze of doorways leading to subject-based areas. Learning is far from low tech, though; there are banks of computers and we saw a fizzy drink can that had been rigged to record sound. At the other end of the tech spectrum, a class loved building the rock cycle using plasticine. The library was buzzy with authors visiting and pupil volunteers; an enterprise day involved a pitch to businessman Lord Sugar. However, by the time they have made their GCSE choices pupils are panting to get the open corridors and swell of new students in the Shooting Fields Site. The latter is dominated by the huge and successful A level specialist sixth form, which feels more like a college but with the pastoral support of a school – a real draw for the third of students who join in year 9.

Tutorials are one-to-one and a curriculum reform means pupils now do fewer topics but more richly. Project-based learning is electric here; the pupils love it and the opportunities it provides to anchor their academic subjects in the practical and take the experience back into the classroom: a trip to the European Organisation for Nuclear Research in Cern; Kimmeridge for biology and geology; the Globe Theatre; Oviedo for Spanish.

The learning resource centre is not just about books – a remote access system means students can log on at home and avoid emailing documents back and forth. The mezzanine level is the sixth form domain and students congregate here even in break time, a sure sign of their commitment to learning – they also gather in the canteen and a learning zone behind that.

A trial period of the 'show my homework' app pleases parents as well; they like to log in and see what needs to/has been done and by when. Kahoot gamifies learning in conjuction with an interactive whiteboard; apparently a warm up to a class can get pretty heated.

Engaging teachers make for the most popular A level subjects, maths, politics and chemistry at present – science labs have loads of space for practicals, which might have 16 in each class compared to 20 in extended subjects. The school is a member of 250 Challenge Partners, in a hub with three Brighton secondaries sharing constructive collaboration and challenge to improve practice and so the education of their children – the leadership team finds it a really valuable to have such critical friends. During the GCSE years the pupils become responsible for booking their parents' appointments and act as their guides on the parents' evening itself – family feedback is that this independence works well.

The Cuthman Centre is a separate building that acts as a haven for the more vulnerable students (category 3 SEN), eight at present with specific learning difficulties; they have roll-call or more casual tea and toast there when needed, and there are NHS nurses, a counselling programme funding by pupil premium and enabled by GP referrals. In-class SEN support with learning support mentors is targeted and the impact evaluated: it ranges from laptops in exams for those with illegible writing to an SEN passport created with parent and carers. The gifted and talented (now More Able) are supported outside lesson time with book clubs and an Oxbridge programme.

Games, options, the arts: Competitive sports are netball, rugby, football, rounders and cricket, with fixtures against both independent and state schools across the county – and the Marylebone Cricket Club. The site itself has two rugby and one football pitch; sixth formers have free access to the town leisure centre adjoining the school – they can use facilities such as the pool, squash courts and dance studio (external reputation for good boys' dance). They also love the chaos of the sixth form sports day with its wheelbarrow races and Fairy Liquid slide. The equestrian team (pupil-owned horses) trains at Hickstead. If PE is not a GCSE choice, then pupils have non-competitive sport a couple of times a week.

The music department is thriving with ticketed performances each season and some 20 A level students, but would love more space (who wouldn't). Logic is used for composition on Macs, there are opportunities for mixing with the use of the live room. Plenty of individual practitioners eg a boy playing the violin, guitar, piano; a ukulele and keyboard in a shared room in the boarding house.

Art and technology is exhibited throughout the halls of the school – and the drama hall is open to the public. The whole school competition is Steyning's Got Talent – some kids think it is profoundly uncool, others use it as a springboard to more public performances across the county. Full school performances such as The Wedding Singer might involve 300 people in the six-night production – set, backstage, make-up as well as performers.

The 50th school anniversary trip to the Norfolk Broads had just passed when we visited. Jailbreak is another riot of a challenge where the whole of year 13 is locked up and has to escape from the science department windows, source vehicles, collect permits and get to Horsham for their recapture. This, and other initiatives such as Macmillan coffee mornings, Pink Day, Comic and Sport Relief, all add up to raising around £15,000 each year for charity.

Wilton Park is nearby, the only branch of the Foreign Office outside London, and interns from there come to work with the More Able – this gives rise to a foreign affairs discussion group, tackling topics such as Syria and Ebola. For prospective medics and vets there are established links with Brighton University and timetabled prep. There are opportunities for students to become equalities, digital or eco-commissioners, do DofE and Young Enterprise, as well as lunchtime enrichment activities and independent learning working across year groups.

Boarding: On the State Boarding Schools Association committee and in the second tier of state boarding in terms of numbers. Judged outstanding by Ofsted. The boarders take enormous joy in their international mix, while grounding themselves by earning money on shifts in the canteen and volunteering.

Four boarding houses, two adapted and two purpose built, all with live-in houseparents. The pupils share rooms in the younger years, and are really joyful about the different cultural traditions that they get to experience, from jollof rice on Nigerian Independence Day to Chinese New Year; they promote their differences yet all order takeaways together. In the most modern house the year 13 pupils have a wet-room shower/ toilet ensuite; they prop their doors open to their shared corridors and apparently are very responsive when told to turn their music down – 10.30pm curfew in the week and 11pm at weekends. The (mostly) boys watch the Premier League on their laptops; they have an ironing board and a kettle in their shared kitchen; when fending for themselves they eat toasties and pizza since health and safety dictates there is no proper oven. The houseparents lend their kitchen when a bake-a-thon is organised for charity.

The girls have photos as well as their names up on their doors – the images are taken by a photography student, whose work also features on the achievement board; this is the most obvious sign of a real sense of supportive celebration of peers. One girls' common room is huge and more homely, with desks for quiet study places too, since this is a realistic experience away from home, with scheduled time for work, although laundry returned to your cubby within a day would be unusual at home...

Facebook photos posted (eg rocket club with powder paint ejected from a parachute) and well dones handed out by the houseparents for being tidy and general good, with prizes drawn at the end of term – once it was a helicopter ride! There is chance to pitch to a 'houseparents' dragon's den' for a new piece of equipment, whether a freezer or a pool table. As elsewhere, technology is used to facilitate rather than trumpeted for its own sake: Skype interviews for prospective boarders; applications scanned and emailed in; Wifi or ethernet with hotspots means that Skyping home via an iPad is easy; WhatsApp is used to tackle awkward time differences.

Background and atmosphere: Founded in 1614, turned co-ed in 1953 and now spread over two sites in the small Sussex town of Steyning with architectural styles ranging from chocolate box Elizabethan black and white, through classic 50s secondary modern school architecture, to the super functional and crisp boarding house, not yet a decade old. Character-based learning is at the centre of the curriculum – teaching, assessing and reporting home on learning characteristics like grit, growth mindset, curiosity and zest.

The 'Steyning family' is made up of children who are encouraged to take risks so that they are not afraid of failure, and staff who are set on preparing the next generation to take over – 'the sooner the better!' says the head. The ethos of the school is printed large on boards in both sites, and the children are resilient and well-supported through exam and everyday academic pressures. The infrastructure for boarding, with the 125 teaching staff and 150 support staff, helps to produce excellent outcomes for disadvantaged students in particular. The staff tenure is traditionally long (30 years is not that unusual), since it is a big school with plenty of space to develop and enough room for children to escape a parent/teacher's shadow.

Far from an inner city urban intake, but everyone is aware of where they stand in the wider society – boarders from the Caribbean come across occasional piercings and extensive LGBT support, the local village kids taste cultures from Barbados to Spain, and parents say, 'it opens up everyone's minds'.

Busy, big and teeming with children at break time – especially in wet weather, when they head to the gym, eat lunch in the classrooms or the school canteen. No hall large enough for a whole school gathering, but the split site means that the pupils have a real sense of progression and responsibility, from getting a key to their own locker in year 7 to wearing their own clothes in the sixth form, and using the canteen as a study space as well as one to eat in.

Independence is highly valued here, and pupils often ask teachers for help on what suits them best in terms of learning as an individual. The staff are committed and respond swiftly and with initiative; the 400 year heritage adds gravitas when looking for aspirational connections. Ofsted, the State Boarding School Association and CofE status are all three seen as important benchmarks, but by no means the most important measure of the school's success.

Pastoral care, well-being and discipline: Both school and year councils provide feedback on issues such as uniform, the colour of leavers' hoodies, the learning resource centre, internet access to YouTube research etc. Prospective head boys and girls write a letter of application, then the school participates in an online survey, meaning year 13s get some input even though they are leaving – then they must pitch with a speech to the whole of the boarding cohort.

Horizontal pastoral system through year head and form tutor; the tutors have 12 students each and the learning mentors 10. Their aim is to personalise the school – whether that is via checking in at the Cuthman Centre and munching a piece of toast or through Pizza and Paragraphs for English Support. Growing confidence is vital, and the classes of 24 are a practical maximum to enable that.

More casually, there is supported (by the heads of year) revision in the dual purpose school canteen – peer mentors enable paired reading and might meet for breakfast in Boltons (one of the boarding houses).

No truancy, no smoking on site and no drinking. If a kid impacts the learning in a classroom then they are removed from that classroom. The student could end up in the Cuthman Centre, then a follow up and reintegration. The range and policy of sanctions is reportedly reassuring for kids who have been beating at the boundaries at other schools; 'It's different here, you know what to expect'. The documentation and communication of the next steps is vital for everyone involved. Academic, social or emotional barriers are identified and everyone gets analysing, understanding and working together – parents and grandparents included – with reflection and using principles of restorative justice. Head says, 'we see the best of the students' behaviour at school...'

Pupils and parents: Local, rural and coastal catchment area encompasses a huge range of parental employment – multinational companies, small business owners, teachers; families will relocate and buy within the area to ensure they can get access to such a good state secondary education. A state boarding school can be a niche choice for many students – from Northern Ireland, Antigua, Denmark, to name just three.

Pupils arrange their own social lives, which is part of the independence that the school aims to build, and since so many walk, ride or bus into the school there is very little chance to of casual school gate friendships between parents.

Entrance: Strong relationships with local primary schools. Catchment is some 200 square kilometres encompassing Henfield to Rydon. The local authority handles the year 7 and year 9 intake. Only boarding is selective, and that is about balancing fit and gender in a year group, aiming for 50 per cent of each sex. The sixth form is amongst the largest in the south east of England. Admission is usually a grade 6 or above in the subjects of choice.

Exit: Up to half leave after GCSEs. After the year 13 leavers' celebration – they get into limos and head off to a club in Worthing, thrilled there is no room on site for something more low key – 70 per cent head off to higher education. Destinations and subjects range from Guildford School of Acting to history at Exeter; two to Cambridge in 2018 and two aspiring to be medics after a gap year.

Money matters: No fees for tuition, just for boarding; discounts available for up to three siblings.

Remarks: A grammar school by name only, non-selective with a huge sixth form and all the curriculum choices that size enables. Diversity of boarding provision enables the broadening of everyone's minds – from Sussex villagers to Caribbean islanders.

Stowe School

Stowe, Buckingham MK18 5EH

Ages 13–18 **Pupils** 800 **Sixth form** 340 **Boarders** 680 **C of E**

Fees: Day £26,355; Boarding £36,660 pa

01280 818205
www.stowe.co.uk

Headmaster: Since 2003, Dr Anthony Wallersteiner MA PhD (50s). Cambridge history scholar and art historian, married to Valerie, three children. Previously at the academic powerhouses of St Paul's and Tonbridge but in Stowe he has discovered his nirvana. He certainly seems a perfect fit for this unique school with his erudite and maverick charm and even his lack of a watertight educational track record. Indeed, his prep school report told of a time waster, a lazy boy who would never amount to anything, yet his final school report raved about a cerebral scholar off to Cambridge. 'Children need to find their passion and drive, to be inspired and to inspire, to appreciate the beauty of life, to be creative, to find their utopia. And that's what we do at Stowe, awakening pupils' enthusiasm and excitement and igniting the spark.'

A man with presence but also fun to be with. We found him irrepressibly talkative and have rarely come across such name-dropping (old Stoics and other famous visitors to the school; he even showed us a video on his phone of Supertramp's Roger Hodgson playing in their recording studio). Many parents enthuse that he has done wonders for the school, improving facilities through fundraising; some feel that he glorifies the benefactors at the expense of ordinary families 'who struggle to pay the extortionate fees.' Smiling staff bellow 'Ah, headmaster!' as he approaches while students are in awe of his knowledge of their lives.

Stowe was in the doldrums when he joined. It needed lifeblood and direction and he's made it his mission to return it to its glory days, but with a 21st century twist. 'We used to stand shoulder to shoulder with Eton, Rugby and Harrow and we were renowned for being idiosyncratic, for looking after the individual, allowing characters to emerge – Leonard Cheshire, David Niven – Stoics with an innate sense of confidence. Branson in the 60s probably typifies what it is to be a Stoic and that's what I wanted to inject into the place. Old Stoics have set the world alight; I want that to continue.'

Academic matters: Tasked with raising academic standards at both the point of entry and departure, Dr Wallersteiner has made the school more selective ('We lost the bottom 10 per cent') and moved academic rigour centre stage, with a particular emphasis on value added, with story after story of pupils who were predicted Cs or Ds, but wound up with As. 'At St Paul's and Tonbridge, pupils both come in and leave as thoroughbreds. But, sticking with the racing analogy, how much more interesting to come in as an outsider and win the race?'

A level results solid – 30 per cent A*/A in 2018; 41 per cent A*-A/9-7 at GCSE. Maths, sciences, languages and history strongest subjects at GCSE; Latin, Greek, English and chemistry at A level (unbroken 25 years of Stoics becoming Oxbridge chemistry graduates). Head insists once flakier departments have strengthened, but pupils told us maths, English and biology are still weaker than others and a couple of parents said year 9 teaching could be more rigorous overall ('they have a tendency to go over the same things the children learned in their previous school'). Teachers also a mixed bag, say pupils and parents, with excellent pockets of interactive, engaging teaching, 'but a few old-timers that seem to stamp out fresh ideas that the newer teacher come in with.' Subject clinics and extra tutorials for those who fall behind, plus a firm mantra that what goes on outside the classroom is just as important, hence encouragement to join and start up clubs, get outside speakers in, visit relevant museums and do a lot of work experience (with £100 prize for the sixth former who does the most work – we met the latest winner who did a whopping seven weeks across five different hospitals). 'It's one of the reasons our students do so well at interviews,' a teacher told us.

Sets (six) in most subjects, 'but with fluidity.' Spanish, French and German (plus Mandarin for those who want it) from year 9; one modern language compulsory at GCSE. Most take 10 GCSEs; 50 per cent take four A levels, while the other half do three and an EPQ.

Prominence is given to Carol Dweck's growth mindset theory, building confidence and marginal gains ('go to sleep 10 minutes earlier; do five minutes more exercise a day; spend 20 minutes less on social media a day' etc). SEN provision for mild to moderate cases thorough and 'second-to-none,' according to parents, with dyslexics enthusing about help not just from support staff but across the board. 'If anyone told me they have a child who is dyslexic but who is bright and determined, I'd recommend Stowe any time. They have been exceptional,' one parent told us.

Games, options, the arts: Whether running or reading, beagling or bugling, singing or shooting, there's something for everyone – and probably a lot you've never even considered. Sport up there with the best of them, with national representation in rowing, running, golf, cricket, rugby, fencing and equestrian events. Teams draped in accolades too – top of the national schools' league table for cricket and first division lacrosse champions, with similar levels of success for polo, hockey and rugby.

Facilities outstanding, including playing fields, assault course, a new golf course, sports hall, climbing wall, fencing salle, fives courts and pool. Latest offerings include a scrambling track (shiny motor bikes), athletics track (opened by Sebastian Coe – there's that name dropping again) and new equestrian centre with 20 stables. Bring your own horse or ride one of the rescue ones. Key winter sports of rugby, hockey and lacrosse cede to summer offerings of leather on willow, athletics and tennis, with polo, rowing, sailing, clay pigeon shooting and golf just some of the country club offerings. 'Gym is pretty poor, though,' say pupils.

Strong in art – several to art school. Some terrific work on display and in the making, in the now sun-drenched studios (mezzanine level removed to let in more light). Emphasis on cross-curricular, with examples of architectural drawings and geography-based paintings reminding pupils how art isn't an add-on. Art eclectic too – in a single lesson, you can go from post-conceptual abstract expressionism to figurative to neo-classicism.

Music popular, plentiful, oft polished with weekly summer al-fresco performances – the perfect backdrop for picnicking parents. New music school, with high quality performances coming from every nook and cranny – every year 9 pupil tries out a musical instrument. High number of music diploma students. Everything from bagpipes to violinists – 'The range is unbelievable,' said a student. Resident DJ nights in the weekend nightclub (kitted out from the remnants of Crazy Larry's in London).

Drama performances 'as good as the West End – just extraordinary,' say parents. Whole school production of 1984 in the making during our visit – 'but with a modern take to reflect the Trump era.' Annual arts festival encompasses science, sport, dance, music, art, drama.

All do CCF or DofE with push towards community work, plus endless charity involvement. It would be hard to find a corner of the globe Stowe pupils haven't had a chance to visit over the years on tours and trips. Some parents felt extracurricular provision could be more plentiful, 'particularly in the younger years'.

Boarding: Nearly 90 per cent board across 13 boarding houses, eight for boys and four for girls, including a sixth form girls' house, all comfortable with kitchens and communal rooms. Some boys envious of newer, purpose-built accommodation for the girls (one of them opened by the Queen, 'although I'm not sure she actually approved of the architecture,' says head), which boasts in-house gym, pool room etc, though a new boys' boarding house opened in 2018. 'The girls' accommodation is more like a hotel, whereas ours is really cosy,' one boy shrugged. Dorms of up to 10 for boys (although most much smaller) and up to four for girls; by sixth form, most in twos or singles. Colourful and comfortable common rooms and study areas throughout.

Care delivered in abundance with everyone from cleaners and caretakers, housemistresses and academic staff on hand to help, plus close liaison with parents, as befits a proper full boarding school. Buddy system ('which can feel forced') replaced by a new house family system, in which two pupils from each year group 'look after each other'. School strict on which weekends are for exeats; pupils would like more floater weekends. Also strict on routines – bedtime at 9.30pm for year 9s, moving up in 15 minute increments.

Each house has its own identity, say pupils – arty, sporty, academic, horsey etc. 'Although friendships are not confined to your house, there is a great loyalty towards it,' they told us. Day pupils (some 120, but rising) insist they aren't left out and are attached to a boarding house (including having their own desk); they are expected to stay for prep until around 6.30pm. Plans afoot to build two day houses.

Background and atmosphere: To say the physical environment is breath-taking feels like the understatement of the century. The 750 acres of parkland and sublime landscape gardens (owned by the National Trust since 1989) are widely regarded as the most significant in Europe and the embodiment of 18th century enlightenment. They include exquisite woods and waters, temples and gardens. Youngsters adore the place: 'Once you get here you never want to leave; when it snows, it looks more magical than Narnia.'

The school has occupied what was formerly the country seat of the Dukes of Buckingham and Chandos since it opened in 1923 with 99 boys. Girls were first admitted into year 9 in 2007 to expand numbers (previously it was only co-ed in sixth form), now up to 40 per cent and rising. The main building ('the mansion') is a splendid, neo-classical palace, largely modelled by Robert Adam in the mid-18th century and benefiting from the respective geniuses of Sir Johns Vanbrugh and Soane, William Kent and Capability Brown. The stone-flagged, below-stairs administrative centre includes the head's spectacular study – 'Sir John Soane in gothic fantasy mode' – a mini replica of Henry VII's chapel in Westminster Abbey with fabulous fan vaulting, lead canopies, brass screens and tracery.

Most recent renovations and additions include the theatre, music school, science block with sixth form study centre and new art school. 'I make no apology for inviting generous and friendly alumni to invest in our projects,' says head. He laughs that he'll probably be remembered as 'the king of stucco', such is his desire to ensure all buildings blend in architecturally – even the gardener's cottage now has columns.

Purposeful atmosphere with boredom-busting teaching injecting a good dose of fun. Practical teaching where possible – 'The upper sixth told me they were a bit rusty on a particular area, so I thought we'd do a quick demo to sort that out,' a chemistry teacher told us as we watched them create bubbling pink liquids. Pupils encouraged to be go-getting and they seem to think nothing of writing to the likes of Richard Branson and head of chemistry at Cambridge to help them with their EPQ – and they get answers (usually the ones they want) back. Nice to see a uniform that doesn't look scratchy. Nice too to spy unusual haircuts that suggest young people are able to express themselves. Self expression is one thing, but head is fanatical about length of girls' skirts: 'I've introduced a new one that goes to below-the-knee.' Pupils attend chapel twice a week (three times for boarders), but atheist views are accepted, say pupils.

Pastoral care, well-being and discipline: House parents and tutors, matron, counsellors and sixth formers who have been trained on the peer support group programme make up the strong pastoral team, which parents say is less strictly regimented than other schools ('no petty rules'). Head sees every child on their birthday 'to have a general chat and find out what's working and what isn't.' We quizzed the pupils on vices and sins: drink and drugs? 'Testing random and compulsory. Second chances may be possible but never a given'. Bar for sixth form but random breathalyser catches those who transgress. Eating disorders? 'PSHE lessons, external talkers and close monitoring is good at preventing this.' Cyber bullying? 'Zero tolerance, discussed openly and frankly in both assemblies.'

In the past, pupil transgressions at Stowe made regular headlines; less so these days. Fewer exclusions too, says head – five suspensions and two permanent exclusions in 12 months previous to our visit, mostly for sexual misconduct. For lesser offences, it's a sanction (early morning detention) or Saturday night grounding.

Pupils and parents: 'Accepting' and 'diverse,' according to pupils, although we saw little obvious evidence of that diversity. Around 10 per cent from outside the UK (below average for boarding schools). Attracts the solid and traditional types plus oddballs and those who might be overlooked elsewhere. Pupils, formal in approach, are charming, polite, grounded, confident and entertaining. Parents a mix of entrepreneurs, academics, old money (lots), new money (rising numbers), country and creative (plus a few celebrities). 'Stowe may look posh but most of us aren't,' say pupils; parents concur. Fascinating and diverse list of former pupils – aristos, artists, actors, academics, journalists, poets – the lot.

Entrance: More selective than in the past; no longer the 'back up plan' but a conscious first destination, particularly for girls. Pre-tests in year 6; looking for 55 per cent plus at CE. But, true to its founding principles, high grades aren't the be-all-and-end-all. 'They are welcome, but more important is a spark, something we can ignite – evidence of effort more than natural ability,' explains head.

Handful from state schools, rest from a range of preps, including Winchester House, The Dragon, Summer Fields, Ashdown House, Papplewick, Sunningdale and Windlesham. Around 50 additional pupils enter at sixth form (100-120 apply), for which entrance criteria (and this goes for existing pupils too) is minimum of six 6s, including 7s in subjects to be studied.

School caught up in a 'cash for places' scandal in 2016 when registrar told an undercover journalist that if there was a 'marginal decision' over whether to admit an overseas student, a six-figure donation from their family could help secure the place. Needless to say the registrar resigned, although head at pains to point out no money actually passed hands and was seemingly more incensed by the underhand journalist than the registrar 'whose career has now been unnecessarily ruined'.

Exit: Around 10 leave after GCSE, mostly to day schools, performing arts school or occasionally because they underperform academically. Of those who leave after sixth form, nearly all to university – three-quarters to Russell Group, especially Bristol, Edinburgh, Exeter, Newcastle, Warwick, Manchester, York, Kings and UCL. Usually a few to Oxbridge – two in 2018. Business-related courses popular. A considerable number to good art schools, with some going to highly-acclaimed music or drama schools.

Money matters: Eight per cent of income goes back into scholarships and bursaries – means-tested options for both, with a small number of fully-funded places for exceptional candidates with proven financial need. Additionally, Roxburgh 'schols' (named after Stowe's revered founding headmaster) awarded to outstanding all-rounders nominated by the heads of their previous schools. Stephan 'schols' available for bright day pupils from the state sector – worth up to 25 per cent of fees, with further support from means-tested bursaries as with other scholarships.

Remarks: What makes your child get out of bed in the mornings? What really interests them? What do they want to be good at? These are the questions Stowe gets to the heart of in its quest to nurture the individual. 'Stowe is the catalytic converter of education,' says head – and although it's a bold claim, it's not entirely unfair. Captivating, with something for everyone, this is a school that mixes the erudite with the sporty and studious, and in which the eccentric can shine. And it all takes place in stunning surroundings. A privileged education for those for whom more conventional schools might feel too much like a straitjacket. If your sights are firmly set on league tables and academic brags you may not have considered Stowe, but Stowe is most definitely ready for you.

Summer Fields

Mayfield Road, Oxford, Oxfordshire OX2 7EN

Ages 4–13 **Pupils** 250 **Boarders** 200 (from 8 years) **C of E**

Fees: Day £12,000 – £21,159; Boarding £30,360 pa

01865 454433
www.summerfields.com

Headmaster: Since 2010, David Faber MA Oxon (50s); came to Summer Fields as old boy; former parent and governor, as well as grandson of illustrious alumnus, Harold Macmillan PM. After Eton and Balliol, became a Conservative MP from 1992-2001, including Opposition spokesman foreign affairs (recently secured schools minister as a speaker for a meeting of prep and public school heads). A keen cricketer (sits on MCC committee) and has introduced new cricket nets to the fields; also referees boys' football matches.

Interesting appointment as not originally from a teaching background. Urbane and reserved in manner until on the subject of the boys' achievements – fond collector of past medals; 'sporting caps' and historical mementos of the school. Uses his experience as a historian and author (two books on modern history) in teaching history to the older years and lecturing on Appeasement and the Munich Crisis to public school history societies. Popular with parents ('dream headmaster'), who have seen him institute 'a lot of changes for the better, one thing at a time'. Makes himself available to the parents and appears to know the boys by name and character. Married to Sophie, not on school staff, with two school aged daughters and a son at Oxford University.

Head of the new pre-prep is Joanna Chapman, previously head of junior school and pastoral lead at Knightsbridge School, with degrees from Exeter and Winchester.

Entrance: Into the pre-prep by 'very relaxed and informal' assessment. Prep school 8+ entry assessment day includes written tasks (English, maths and non-verbal reasoning) and informal interview, along with an all-important report from current school. Early registration necessary, but occasional late entry places and mid-year starters also accepted. Special assessment day for the Maclaren Scholarship – up to 100 per cent bursary for a year 6/7 boarder given to a high-flyer, usually from a state primary. Academic and music scholarships at 8. Head refers to it as a 'national' prep school, with most coming from within an hour's drive of Oxford; some overseas and regular group of Old Summerfieldian sons. Previously thought of as upper crust, and hasn't entirely shaken off the image. Head disagrees, but one parent regretted the narrow social compass. No plans to take girls.

Exit: About 60 per cent to Eton, Harrow, Radley and Winchester. Lots of scholarships in recent years offered by Eton, Harrow,

Bedales, Wellington, Radley, Harrow and Oundle. They covered academic, art, sports and outstanding talent. Head maintains, 'Proof of the pudding is that the less academically able boys still get into public schools'. Parents like the fact that it doesn't feel like a 'feeder' but still gets great results.

Remarks: Set in over 70 acres of stunning grounds in the heart of North Oxford, the school is unremarkable from the front, but boasts a stately bow fronted building with fields, woods and river at the rear. Founded by Victorian educationalist husband and wife team, Maclarens, in 1864 and still conscious of its Christian traditions with Victorian chapel and oak paneled hall. However, there are more modern additions of several smaller houses along adjoining road; two pools (indoor and outdoor); a sports complex, Eton fives courts, a climbing wall, new all-weather tennis and Astroturf courts, as well as 9-hole golf course and cricket nets and relatively recent very large sports pavilion.

Very long day for both boarders and day boys, starts with whole school convening for chapel or assembly. Lessons in small classes (10-17) and early setting promote strong academic results at CE. Scholarship class in last two years given Greek, and Latin and French learnt by all. New DT and ICT suite and science labs, where boys encouraged to 'design your own experiments and make things pop', as well as large, busy library. Boys genuinely motivated by trips to Oxford museums and field trips, including to France. Teaching staff visible round school, as most live in, some of long standing (30+ years); 'most staff leave to become a headmaster somewhere else'. Academic success earns boys personal and house points which can be enjoyed by tangible rewards in the school shop (Buzzer) and a house feast. A staff of six for learning support, with some experience in EP support and statements. One parent felt that it was particularly good for boys who aren't particularly socially confident and so may experience difficulties elsewhere.

Lodges (boarding houses) for boys of same year group; run by husband and wife team and kept apart from the teaching rooms (no homework or dining in lodge). Remarkably neat dorms, sleep four to six boys, with effective in-house incentives for boys to change own sheets, polish shoes and tidy up. One parent commented, 'What I like is that Summer Fields doesn't smell like a school'. Weekend leave for boarders regularly throughout the year. Pastoral care is managed with a three tier 'belt and braces' approach. Lodge parent claims, 'Homesickness is more of a problem for the mums' than the boys, who are kept busy in the evenings with board games, computers and giant chess sets. Parent of a young boarder was hugely relieved how easily the youngest were settled in. Discipline maintained by healthy competition and withdrawing privileges rather than anything more gruelling. Boys appear to appreciate this.

S

Music is a strength, with a dedicated music block and theatre. Three choirs, one with adult voices, sing in Oxford colleges and on tour (Rome recently). Specialist music staff allow boys to take up to three instruments (we heard of a 10 year old playing four), ranging from conventional to electric guitar, even quirky. They recently hunted down a Marimba (eastern xylophone) teacher in Oxford for a lad from the Far East. Drama productions for different year groups from Twelve Angry Men to We Will Rock You, open to all those who risk taking time from their scholarship clubs. Sport is plentiful and all-inclusive; parents like the fact that all boys make the teams, which play twice a week. Football has recently had its best season since 1937; rugby and hockey also strong, with some players in county cricket and rugby teams. Prolific art and ceramics studio, obviously not PC – fantasy coats of arms and big game trophies made from papier mâché adorn the walls.

Boys emerge from lessons brightly but quietly. They are articulate and confident, although suspiciously neat and clean in brightly coloured shirts and sweaters. Parental niggle that boys were 'a bit too polished'. However, children appear kind and supportive – 'when you are in the third year you know everyone's names' – and a nice touch that both staff and children refer to the school as 'We...'. Boys don't seem fazed by formality or overt competition – academic progress bulletins are posted on the board every two weeks for all to read – but seem to enjoy it as 'healthy rivalry'. There is a wealth of extramural activities, spanning spiritual (Time for God group), sporting (fencing, shooting, polo) and more earthy interests (cookery and Adventure Quest – bushcraft-style camps – for handy skills in lighting the campfire and skinning a rabbit).

An appreciation of the school's history is encouraged with scholars' boards lining the walls of the hall; and a moving remembrance day service, when choral speakers read out names of the fallen alumnae. Boys follow this up with a trip to the Somme. Old Summerfieldians include generous helpings of baronets, colonial civil servants and military leaders as well as Dick Francis, who set one of his detective novels at the school. Active old boy links suggest happy memories.

New pre-prep in a converted boarding house in the grounds.

A small and cosy school, in a serene and beautiful setting, successfully eases a boy in to a boarding career. It provides a breathtaking array of sports and music facilities as well as being reliable in placing boys in top public schools. Sense that boys work hard/play hard and turn out to be happy, considerate and polite, if slightly formal. Not for Just Williams.

Sunningdale School

Dry Arch Road, Sunningdale, Ascot, Berkshire SL5 9PY

Ages 7–13 **Pupils** 110 **Boarders** 100

Fees: Day £18,180; Boarding £23,400 pa

01344 620159
www.sunningdaleschool.co.uk

Headmaster: Since 2005, Tom Dawson MA PGCE – and recent distinction in grade 1 piano (40s). Previously taught at Harrow before taking over the shop (school is fully owned by the Dawson family) inheriting headship 'because I'm the boy,' he jokes (slightly).

Family-run is understatement and a half. Wife Elisabeth, fellow modern languages graduate, is highly organised director of studies, garnering almost as much praise as husband. 'Lovely', 'kind' and their ilk crop up in conversation with parents with Swiss railway regularity.

Amy, a jolly Dawson sister, one of three (others educationally occupied elsewhere) runs high quality art department and masterminds school productions, more fulfilling than previous career as mural painter (only so many David Beckhams you can glorify on child's bedroom wall without spot of existentialist angst).

Also living and working on site are Mr Dawson's own parents and uncle, who acquired school as going concern in 1960s and are a genial background presence, mother putting final touch to colossal flower arrangements, father waving from ride-on roller. 'Keeps them going,' says their son.

We wondered about sotto voce presence of school parents, who don't, currently, have own association. 'Don't need one,' says Mr Dawson, who points to numerous 'meet the Dawsons' opportunities at well-attended matches, concerts and exhibitions. Parents, professing ardent faith in his leadership, fall over themselves to deliver several carillons' worth of ringing endorsement apiece. 'Exudes incredible values,' 'outstanding personality' two among many.

Mr Dawson, while amiable, is reckoned to miss nothing and parents felt that wouldn't shirk from tough decisions. 'If there's one super naughty boy in the school then I guess somebody has to be expelled, as in all schools,' thought one. Impressive networking skills don't go amiss either. 'I know a lot of people,' he says, and what a useful crowd they are. Barnaby Lenon, former Harrow head, extols virtues of pupils and school at length on school website. Mr D cultivates contacts through cricket – a predictable passion. Another – repairing pre-digital Roberts radios (impressive range neatly arranged in his study) – possibly less of an obvious social asset.

Entrance: Register at birth for one of 22 places, waiting list if full (as, increasingly, it is). Mr Dawson understandably hates putting up 'no vacancies' sign – 'don't want to be known for it,' – but is currently 'turning down a lot. It's a cosy, happy place and I don't want to get any bigger.'

While has plenty of high flyers, entrance requirements aren't stratospheric. School expects fluent reading and writing and grasp of basic arithmetic. May ask for report from current school and very occasional pupil is directed elsewhere.

Prospective pupils spend day at the school year before they join when sit short papers in maths, English and VR. Also attend music, art and sport workshops. Main purpose is to work out forms ('we don't really operate in year groups,' says school). Some scholarships available as well as means-tested bursaries. Weekly boarding available for the first three years. Also takes maximum of 10 day boys through the school, all locals, inherited by Mr Dawson who has 'just stuck with them.'

If you miss the boat, there's a diminutive chance of place or two in year 7 – 'incredibly rare for anyone to leave,' says Mr Dawson – offered after cognitive ability tests (though non-academic strengths also taken into account).

No linked feeders; elite London mob – Garden House, Thomas's, Eaton House – increasingly feature, as do old boys' offspring – at 10 per cent and rising, says school, which stresses that fees 'are kept as low as possible.' School buses to London at exeat weekends, long leaves and end of terms.

Gaps increasingly filled by international families – one boy we met saw family only three times a year – though school has recently started live feeds for concerts. Otherwise, pupils come from all over the country 'except Cornwall'. We were hoping for some ancient West Country vs home counties blood feud. Disappointingly, down merely to poor transport links.

Exit: Mr Dawson not a fan of serial entrance exams and suggests maximum of three senior schools, two aspirational, one 'a safer bet'. To most of major, trad names in south-east. Harrow often features prominently. Other usual (and desirable) suspects include Winchester, Eton, Harrow, Charterhouse, Uppingham, Oundle, Radley, Stowe, Tonbridge and Marlborough.

Remarks: Long the place where old money arrived as small change. Cricket commentator Henry Blofeld, Duke of Westminster, horse trainer Sir Henry Cecil – list of old boys says it all. All it takes is names of first two heads – Girdlestone and Crabtree – to know you're in the presence of Tradition, with capital (and gold-embossed, gothic-lettered) T. Would make a fine detective series title as well. Additional helpful pointers come by way of slightly fly-blown pictures of Victorian worthies in visitors' loos – OBs Duke of Marlborough 1893; Lieutenant the Honorable FHS Roberts VC, killed Colence SA 1899,

Scratch the surface and you'll find...more tradition, bookcase packed with Biggles, Worrals and even a Henty or two (remnants of old library) adorning the morning room – or, more prosaically to those of less gentle birth, the school office. Makes statement architecture of curved library – first building visitors see and the newest – the more startling by comparison. Accoutrements – refectory table and two sternly positioned sofas – are set off by glow-in-the-dark bright blue carpet (also a dormitory feature), bare walls crying out for some splendiferously mustachioed OBs, picture windows giving vistas not of bosky woods or slumbrous streams but cars approaching up the drive.

Shelves reassuringly weighted in favour of fiction, wooden blocks with school number marking borrowings, one per boy. And if you want to borrow two books? 'Two?' asked Mr Dawson, experiencing mild Beadle-like moment. 'Why would anyone want to read more than one at a time?' It's the hallmark of a school with a strong sense of its own place in the world, conventional yet not in thrall to crowd mentality. Summer half term, for example, happens a week later than normal. Trade off, with school taking strain of final revision for CE exams, worth hassle of arranging two sets of holiday activities for offspring elsewhere, reckoned parents.

Class structure, average size 12, also takes a bit of getting used to. Ability rather than age-based, so while nobody is ever moved down, brighter boys will go up a year, sometimes two, never more. In top years, carefully planned scholarship work ensures there's no 'here's one I made earlier' duplication.

From animated debate on how to stop extinction of coral reef in science – 'tries to make it as visual as possible,' said star pupil – to year 6 pupils reading (beautifully) extracts from end of year English exam, a 'do-able' past CE paper, impression was of willing learners enthusiastically taught. Bright, super-engaged staff, majority male and with average age of 39, includes several of distinctly young fogey-ish disposition and bouffant charm – Boris Johnston recast with auburn and brunette tresses.

Impressive commitment to pupils with SEN. One, with ASD, initially reluctant to attend lessons, supported with one-to-one help, funded by parents, 'fully integrated,' says Mr Dawson. More usual needs (mild dyslexia) respond – miraculously so, thought one parent – to small classes and skilled teaching without intervention. Head 'isn't a big believer in throwing tons of time and money at extra tuition,' said one parent. 'Because the classes are so small, and teaching so good, you don't really need it.'

Staff praised not just for ability to inspire love of learning – 'never did we expect such commitment,' said mother – but for reinforcing universally wonderful manners and behaviour. One parent thrilled when master told son to 'stand up and show the way for your mother.' Compliments, convertible to house points, awarded for the dutiful, complaints doled out for the untidy or overly chatty lead to writing out code of conduct.

Had been very slight relaxation in discipline, now checked, thought one pupil (like peers, a charming lunchtime host) and all to the corporate benefit. 'Wasn't working so well before – now good for the school but bad for the individual.'

Minor transgressors write out school code of conduct; serial offenders lose 'privs' for a week, part of plentiful school jargon that includes 'going across' (signals need for comfort break rather than deepening interest in spiritualism), 'grub' (sweets) and 'lemonade' (a generic term covering hot chocolate, juice and even cake).

Parents universally thrilled by restricted presence of i-anythings out of lessons, and tactical use within. Rather than mass breaktime retreat into solitary cyber universe, pupils here whizz energetically about in real time with friends. 'Really important because children become so addicted to these games that they don't interact with their peers,' said relieved mother.

Plenty for them to enjoy, from lovingly tended plots with courgette flowers and tomatoes to three Gloucester Old Spots, sensibly not named, bees ditto – though for logistical rather than emotional reasons. Other tucked away treats include shaded mini-adventure playground for first years and personable wood-panelled and colonial-style chapel, consecrated 1880 after arriving in kit form (so many identical labradors on site that you start to wonder if assembled in similar way).

While academic success is all well and good (and often very well and very good), school also does best to find ubiquitous spark. Music a strength, with 80 boys learning at least one instrument, variety of ensembles to play them. Many cheering examples of mild reprobates transformed by gift for singing (there's a queue to join the choir, say parents).

But whichever formerly dark area of the curriculum light of budding talent might illuminate, helps to have at least nascent interest in sport. Not for everyone, one OB recently describing it as 'an acquired taste', but for most, it's a way of inculcating right values, particularly as school size ensures participation by all. 'Perfect because even the boys who are mediocre at sports all get to make the teams – nobody gets left out,' said parent. Year to year results vary considerably – inevitable consequence of small size. One cricket and rugby team had been undefeated all season; others with less enthusiastic cohort won't do half as well.

In addition to big three (football, rugby, cricket), tennis, Eton fives (since 1892), golf and swimming are all provided on site. Five pitches (four multi-use) appear to stretch away into far distance, courtesy of clever landscaping that makes the most of stand out planting, including massed rhododendrons (Mr Dawson has sole pruning rights over favourite). Provides effective masking of more functional buildings including vast sports hall (for basketball, fencing, air rifle shooting and much more) and gives 25-acre grounds feel of something much bigger.

Sport, inevitably, dominates the summer term after school activities list, replaced in winter by idiosyncratic range that currently includes Warhammer and fly-tying (teachers, all required to take at least one sport or activity, encouraged to indulge own enthusiasms). All adds to the fun, as do the 'endless' activities (now that's what we call organisation). Being on the go essential (particularly for new boys) in helping to acclimatise to full boarding lifestyle – weekly an option in the first three years, though 'half full board from the word go,' says school.

In addition to two long weekends (Friday to Monday evening), a couple of bonus Sundays and half term, there's much anticipated treat of year group excursions to school/family-owned house in France. Icing on the cake (almost literally) is first class food prepared by Mrs Dawson Snr. One boy 'asked why I can't cook like that,' said mother.

School points out that boarding for all hurts parents far more than the boys – 'always rather sad for the mother,' agreed one, 'but we just knew they'd be so happy.' Also ensures a full house at weekends for Saturday film nights (no lonely minority waiting for life to start again on Sunday evenings) when all but first years, who have own small scale version, pile into theatre with pillows and duvets.

All happens within or next to main building, dorms six to eight-bedders, comfortable rather than haut couture ('they're nice, cute, small, humble,' said parent), possessions neatly arranged, pinboards sometimes rather sparsely filled. Bathrooms and loos clean, fragrant and hygienic – bar single cracked tile surround in need of repair. Most pupils in top two years enjoy additional privacy of individual cubicles (new arrivals will start off in dorm). Buddies take settling in duties seriously – 'boys were all waiting and had his bed made,' said parent, leaving son for taster weekend.

For the very youngest there are separate quarters with common room (reassuringly compact) and playroom (ditto – Hide and Seek games a non-starter) and own live-in matron, one of five, three full time, notable for reassuring names (Miss Turnball and Miss Foynes – yet another detective team, surely?) and a guaranteed presence on the touchline at matches.

Education here is all about bestowing resilience, self-awareness, realism and courage (fairy godmothers might blench). 'Finally and most importantly, pupils must learn to love life...' says website. If they don't while they're here, won't be for want of trying.

Parents are in no doubt they succeed. 'We put our trust in Mr Dawson,' says mother. 'We've been so incredibly impressed with the results.'

Sutton Valence Preparatory School

Linked with Sutton Valence School

Church Road, Chart Sutton, Maidstone, Kent ME17 3RF

Ages 3–11 **Pupils** 270 **C of E**

Fees: £9,420 – £13,830 pa

01622 842117
www.svs.org.uk

Head: Since January 2017 Claire Corkran BEd MEd (40s). Educated at Wycombe Abbey and Homerton College, Cambridge where she read theology and history and gained her degree in education. She also has a masters in educational leadership and management from the Open University. She started her career at St Aubyns prep school and then spent four years at James Allen's Girls Prep as head of history before moving to the British School in Houston as senior teacher and Common Entrance co-ordinator. She returned to the UK after another four years and joined Copthorne as Head of RS and PSHE where she started a thinking skills department. She joined Sutton Valence Prep in 2010 as deputy head and became head in January 2017. 'A complete natural,' says a mother. 'She is always good humoured and focused on the detail and you can ring her up and be put through immediately and everyone is as important as everyone else.'

Warm and chatty, she is an advocate of introducing children to philosophical thinking early on and aims 'to produce flexible thinkers who are self-reliant and strong.' She is introducing Curiosity Club – enrichment workshops to stretch the children beyond the usual curriculum. Has always taught English but sadly can't get to the classroom as often as she would like.

She lives in a flat in the school and her many godchildren think she is the coolest godmother as she has a playground and a sports hall in her garden. She says that the school is all-consuming and she only surfaces during the holidays when she can indulge her love of travel and the outdoors.

Entrance: Non selective until year 2 and then via tests in reading, spelling, maths and non-verbal reasoning and a taster day. Very inclusive with a good learning support team – it is rare for a child to be turned away. Children can join at any time – even year 6 if there is a space – but would still have to sit the entrance exam to the senior school. 'Children are very adept at scooping up new pupils and they settle in well,' says a parent.

Exit: Between 50 and 60 per cent to the senior school, a good number to the local grammars and a handful to local independent schools like Bethany and Benenden with a few to comprehensives. Families given a lot of support with their choice of secondary school – information evenings every term in year 5 to ensure parents are comfortable with their decision. Children supported through the Kent Test and 11+ common entrance and other entrance tests – a pupil recently won an academic and all-rounder scholarship to Brighton College.

Remarks: The school started life as Underhill Prep in 1958 and was amalgamated with Sutton Valence Senior School in 1994 when it became Sutton Valence Prep and Pre-prep. Hidden away off a small country lane, surrounded by orchards but only a mile or so from the senior school, it is part of the Sutton Valence family but also very much a school in its own right. The main building is a Victorian country house surrounded by modern additions with 12 acres of playing fields and an athletics track a short walk up the hill. The Bates Hall is used for sport, drama, concerts and assemblies while the pre-prep have their own hall and there is a soft playground and outdoor classrooms for the younger children.

Welcoming reception area with elegant sofas and chairs and a fine array of silverware. Large photos of the children in action displayed all around the school – not formal team photos but children having fun – and honours boards all the way up the stairs where they are fast running out of space. Everything immaculate wherever you go, beautifully expressed by one of the children who said 'the teachers put blood and sweat into making things look lovely.' Large, light dining room with good food and children sit with their teachers in house groups so can talk to different year groups and there is grace before lunch.

Strong sense of community. Children are accepting of each other and are taught that differences should be celebrated. Effective anti-bullying policies and children understand that it's not acceptable. School has a relaxed atmosphere but high expectations inside and outside the classroom, instilling traditional values and good manners, with the Christian foundation providing a moral framework. The message of making a positive difference in the world is constantly reinforced and children are encouraged to step out of their comfort zones and try new things, with a focus on leadership opportunities – a leadership week takes place at the end of the summer term. House cup awarded each week with points for all areas of school life including kindness, and achievements are celebrated in assembly. Year 6 start to talk about their online profile and behaviour and parents are included in discussions about online safety. All children moving up from the pre-prep are given a year 5 buddy to support them for the first year and one of our guides said that this was one of the best things about the school.

The elected school council helps decide which charities to support and a recent 24 hour sport relief basketball marathon raised £7,000.

Specialist teaching from nursery, increased as children enter the prep department in year 3 with all lessons taught by subject specialists by year 5. Children set in maths some time in year 3 when they are ready and for English in year 4 – all taught the same curriculum but at a different pace and ICT is used in lessons – even the children in nursery are taught on interactive whiteboards and iPads. The gifted and talented are stretched within the classroom. 'We don't raise the bar, we take it away,' says the head. Wide age range of teachers who have been with the school from between two and 25 years, as well as a couple of Australian gappies. No seriously old timers and lots have or have had children at the school. 'All bring something interesting and all are very passionate and creative about their subjects,' says the head.

Buzzing science department with a drawing of a heart on the floor so that children can follow the blood flow and 'walk our bodies' and some alarming pictures of the dangers of cigarettes and alcohol. And, most importantly, the ten school guinea pigs which are loved by everyone and are the responsibility of the science prefects and are the first port of call on any school tour.

Children who need extra help either taken out of lessons for small group or one-to-one sessions or are given in-class support and develop a learning style to suit them. All are screened for dyslexia on arrival and teachers are vigilant with a focus on early identification. The SENCo is very sensitive with parents especially if a special need is diagnosed or suspected. Reading for pleasure is taken seriously with designated reading time after lunch every day and children take part in the accelerated reader scheme with badges for the millionaire readers. Children taught how to use the library and school takes part in World Book Day and National Poetry Week. Our guides informed us that they are also learning 'tenacity'.

Individual targets set for each pupil and internal tests in English, maths and science at the end of each term. Grade cards sent home twice a year. By the end of year 5, exams are more formal to prepare children for entrance to senior schools. Homework starts with spelling, times tables and reading in year 3 and by year 6 pupils are expected to do up to an hour 4 nights a week.

Full range of sports offered – the prep has its own sports hall, pitches, Astro, netball courts and a small swimming pool as well as full access to the senior school facilities. Apart from the usual football, rugby, netball, cricket, hockey etc they also offer golf, judo, karate and street and tap dance through the activities programme. The aim is for everyone to have fun and to develop a lifelong love of sport and exercise. School fields as many teams as possible and all take part in keenly fought inter-house competitions.

Music on the curriculum with two half hour sessions a week which include composition, performance and listening with the emphasis on fun – children start by playing an ocarina and move on to a ukulele. Over 130 children take music lessons for at least one instrument. Three choirs open to all as well as the auditioned chamber choir and a range of musical groups including a full orchestra, string orchestra and brass and guitar group. Formal and informal shows and concerts throughout the year, some, including a rock concert, a joint effort with the senior school as is the large gala concert in the Summer term.

Busy art department with enthusiastic teacher – we admired some battery operated roundabouts and fish made from household objects when we visited. Children's work is displayed all over the school, which has its own kiln. 'We are very spoilt,' said our guides.

Children build confidence through public speaking and acting, with years 2-4 required to take the LAMDA exams and each form taking an assembly at the local church. Children can enter competitions and take part in the inter-school maths challenge held at the senior school. Drama part of curriculum and all of the prep school have the opportunity to be involved in a play once a year, either on stage or behind the scenes – the highlight being the leavers' play at the end of year 6. After school clubs every day include sports, gardening, cookery, art, music, singing and dance. Year 5 go on a three-day residential trip to Normandy and year 6 take part in a bushcraft trip to the Cotswolds.

A network of minibuses brings children from Kings Hill, Maidstone, Biddenden and Headcorn. Parents down to earth, hardworking, busy and very appreciative of the before and after school care (breakfast club at 7.30am, after school to 6pm). Parents Association is 'fantastic,' says head, organising social events, running fun activities for the children (like the Easter egg hunt) and donating funds both to the school and its selected charities.

Sutton Valence School

Linked with Sutton Valence Preparatory School

North Street, Sutton Valence, Kent ME17 3HL

Ages 11–18 **Pupils** 548 **Sixth form** 162 **Boarders** 41 full, 15 weekly, 57 flexi **C of E**

Fees: Day £16,395 – £21,405; Boarding + £5550 – £11,940 pa

01622 845200
www.svs.org.uk

Headmaster: Since 2009, Bruce Grindlay MA (Cantab) MusB FRCO (50ish). His family emigrated to Canada when he was 14 and he returned to England to take up an organ scholarship at Emmanuel College, Cambridge. He started his teaching career at Bedford School, where he was head of chapel music and housemaster, before taking up the post of director of music at Christ's Hospital in 2001. He is married to Elizabeth (Lilla), whom he met at Cambridge. She has a PhD in English from UCL, where she lectures, teaches some A level English and is in charge of the academic scholars. They have two children at the school, one of whom has been offered a place at Oxford.

They live in a house in the grounds, go to the theatre and opera whenever they can, and spend the holidays at their cottage on the north Norfolk coast or sailing in Cephalonia. Mr Grindlay is a keen cook and a Freeman of The Worshipful Company of Cooks (he doesn't like to do things by halves), and is never happier than when cooking a big dinner party. He also cooks the Christmas dinner for the 100 or so support staff at the school. Rumour has it that he is also rather good at golf. He is tall and immaculately dressed and is 'good looking and lovely,' say several mothers; 'he sets the bar high but he doesn't frighten you with his intelligence – if anyone comes to see him with a problem, he always looks into it.'

He describes the school as 'a community where individuality is cherished and where pupils have the opportunity to make better versions of themselves'. 'Education is about improving outcomes – all have different starting points but it is the length of the journey they travel that matters – the community is the most important thing and all bring something to the table'. 'A brilliant headmaster,' said a pupil. 'You see him every day and he always says hello and is easy to talk to.' He has tightened up all areas of the school and it has grown by 20 per cent since he arrived and now operates a waiting list.

Academic matters: Twenty-seven per cent A*/A, 56 per cent A*-B at A level in 2018, and 40 per cent of GCSEs A*-A/9-7. Some 25 subjects offered at A level with geography and business studies being the most popular. A wide range to suit different abilities including economics, psychology, media and film studies, sport and photography and can also offer Chinese and Russian. EPQ available. As well as the usual subjects, the school offers media studies, computing, photography, drama and sport at GCSE.

Impressive value added – something that the headmaster is particularly proud of. The improved results are partly due to pupils being made to realise they can do it and keeping them engaged. The top 30 per cent can be stretched and achieve A* and A grades, for others a C is a brilliant achievement – staff know the pupils well and so know what they should be aiming for; attainment and effort levels are reviewed half termly. Class sizes up to 18 in the junior years and as few as four in some A level classes.

The headmaster takes on one new young teacher each year for on the job training: they bring academic passion and energy and reinvigorate the staff room.

CV writing and interview skills part of the curriculum from age 11. Annual careers convention in lower years and all year 11s have individual interviews about their career aspirations – the head librarian has a masters in careers education. Plenty of help with UCAS forms – sixth formers attend a higher education convention at the University of Kent, lectures are offered on degree subject choices and extra support available for prospective vets and medics. The few not going to university are given help with job applications and interview technique.

Full time SENCo plus two full and two part-time teachers. Pupils either given in class support or withdrawn from lessons for small group or individual tuition and are helped to develop their own learning styles and coping strategies. About 190 on the register for concern but not many need extra help. All juniors take part in a study skills programme and all are offered help with stress, resilience and exam technique. About 40 need help with EAL and have 2-3 lessons a week instead of languages, unless close to native fluency, and can take an IGCSE in ESL and IELTS for entry to British universities.

Numerous opportunities for academic enrichment; the school has close links with the local section of the Royal Society of Chemistry. Debating and public speaking are particular strengths, pupils can take part in the Model UN, take courses in financial services and personal effectiveness and leadership, and join the philosophy club.

Games, options, the arts: Excellence, endeavour and discipline are the buzzwords of the Sutton Valence sports department and everyone expected to aim for their personal best. Some join the talented athletes' programme, others play for the fun and the exercise. Sport for all in major and minor sports and about two-thirds play in weekend matches. Higher up the school sport isn't compulsory but must take some form of exercise. Dance, aerobics and badminton popular among the less team minded. Pupils also encouraged to train as umpires and coaches. The school also has an equestrian team but you have to provide your own horse and transport.

All do bronze DofE in year 9 and about a quarter achieve gold before they leave. CCF is part of the curriculum in year 9 – all three services but army by far the most popular; can learn to fly in the RAF and take a BTec in leadership as part of the course, and the shooting team does well at Bisley. About 10 per year take part in the Young Enterprise scheme.

Not surprisingly, given the headmaster's musical talents, music has gone from strength to strength. About 200 learn an instrument and there are a number of formal and informal concerts. The chapel choir is a central part of the school community and has sung evensong at Canterbury, Cologne and Winchester cathedrals and performed at the Pantheon and St Peter's in Rome, and top singers can attend a masterclass at the Royal Academy of Music. Large variety of musical groups including the chamber orchestra and string ensembles and quartets, several pupil-run rock groups and there is a suite of computers for composition. The band has accompanied Jools Holland, toured Paris and Disneyland and played in concerts with the Gurkhas and several pupils are in the Kent county youth orchestra.

Drama at GCSE and theatre studies at A level, and several achieve gold in the LAMDA exams each year. A junior and a senior play each year – either a big musical or something more serious.

Art housed in a beautiful old church in the village. Everyone introduced to a range of different styles when they arrive and 'you are given the freedom to create what you want in DT,' say the pupils.

Numerous trips and visits throughout the year have included sports tours to South Africa and Canada, a camping and trekking expedition to Morocco, a ski trip to Italy and a visit to the Neeja Modi School in Jaipur, Rajasthan as well as CCF trips to Belize, Brunei and Malaysia and DofE expeditions.

Boarding: Boarding for three or four nights a week is popular and a godsend to working parents. 'You always have the same bed and can change nights,' said a pupil. Four boarding houses: junior boys and girls live in a large residential house a few minutes away and are housed in five small dorms, all with ensuite bathrooms, and there's a small five-a-side football pitch. 'It's like a large family,' said a pupil – 'we all eat supper together in the kitchen and then have to do supervised prep before free time'.

Two senior boys' boarding houses of about 55 each and a girls' house of 44. Younger pupils share, whilst upper sixth have their own study bedrooms and all can use the school's facilities at evenings and weekends. The girls' house is below the main teaching blocks and must have one of the best views in Kent.

Saturday morning lessons and afternoon sport for all, and movie nights, pizza evenings and kitchen cook ups are organised for the full boarders. All houses have a houseparent and a team of tutors and house prefects and new arrivals are teamed up with a buddy so there is always someone to talk to and 'matron is like a second mum,' said one girl.

Background and atmosphere: The school was founded by William Lambe, a London clothworker, in 1576 and the Worshipful Company of Clothworkers ran it until 1910, when it was transferred to the Westminster School Foundation (which also includes Queen Anne's Caversham, Grey Coats, Emmanuel and Westminster City School). Girls were admitted in 1983 and it is now fully co-ed. They have recently opened a prep school in China.

Built into the hill just above the village of Sutton Valence and with wonderful views over the Weald of Kent, the Virginia creeper clad main buildings, including a lead clock tower, dominate the skyline. Surrounded by immaculate lawns and flower beds and the acres of playing fields stretch out on top of the hill – it can be pretty windy watching winter matches. The Lambe's library, formerly the school dining hall, contains 11,000 books ranging from first editions to kindles and DVDs. Four day houses alongside the boarding houses, and the co-ed junior house for years 7 and 8 where children can find their feet before moving into the senior school at 13+.

House based charity work is overseen by the chaplain. The school has close links with Maidstone's Gurkha community and raised £60,000 to rebuild a school in Nepal flattened by an earthquake.

Strong sense of community with whole school chapel service every Monday and a weekly headmaster's assembly where sports results are read out and achievements celebrated. Leadership opportunities in all year groups and younger pupils take part in a leadership course and help out in prep school and in village community projects, whilst lower sixth take part in a community service programme. Positions of responsibility are keenly fought over and lower sixth have to write a letter of application for prefect positions and are interviewed by the headmaster. The prefects wear gowns and the Sutton Valence Blue – a dark blue gown – is awarded to those who make a major contribution to school life.

Pastoral care, well-being and discipline: The school is small enough for everyone to know everyone else and prides itself on picking up any problems quickly. Each house has a houseparent and house-based tutor groups which meet daily. These are arranged vertically so that year groups get to know each other and sixth formers can act as mentors and role models, and tutors are the first point of contact for parents. Needle sharp inter-house competitions, plays and quizzes, as well as celebrations, generate house loyalty.

Zero tolerance on drugs and pupils sometimes put on a contract (including random testing) if drug use suspected outside school. Vaping not allowed. School promotes the philosophy of growth mindset which encourages pupils to believe that they do not have a fixed ability and therefore create glass ceilings for themselves, but that with perseverance and encouragement they can improve. 'Once confidence comes, children achieve more than they ever thought they could,' says the headmaster.

School is very aware of mental health issues and pupils can talk to the two counsellors or the school chaplain, who is kind and down to earth, and school has set up a new mental health strategy 'can I have 10 (minutes)'. Pupils can choose a member of staff they feel comfortable with and talk to them at any time. The usual cyber problems – social media issues generally happen outside school but parents are given guidance on how to manage them.

Pupils and parents: A 60:40 boy girl ratio – would like to be 50:50 but lose a lot of girls to the single sex grammars. A stable nine per cent from abroad. Others from a 20 mile radius including a number of Gurkhas. A network of school buses brings children from Ashford, Hurst Green, Hawkhurst, Kings Hill, Sevenoaks, Tenterden and the edge of Tunbridge Wells.

Eclectic bunch of parents – lots of City workers and entrepreneurs, first time buyers and local farmers – generally down to earth, hard-working types. Some struggle to pay the fees and others are very rich – it is not unknown for a pupil to be given a sports car for their 18th birthday. The headmaster describes the pupils as 'charmingly confident but not arrogant, self-disciplined with a desire to please,' and his prefects as a 'ministry of talents'.

A very sociable school with an active PTA and 'there always seems to be something going on – which is great if you have just moved to the area', said a parent. Busy Old Suttonian Society with 4,500 members worldwide who hold regular reunions and an annual dinner, and offer advice and mentoring to current pupils. Well known Old Suttonians include: journalist Robert Fisk; GB hockey player and gold medal winner at Rio 2016 Susannah Townsend; BBC journalist Ben Brown; England cricketer Mark Benson; actor Peter Polycarpou; and painter Terence Cuneo.

Entrance: Main entry points are 11+, 13+ and sixth form but will take pupils into other years if there are spaces. For 11+ tests in English, maths, verbal and non-verbal reasoning. Children at prep schools are expected to take common entrance; others, including those from abroad, can take school's own tests. New sixth formers will need a minimum of five GCSEs at grade 6 plus an interview. Foreign students have to pass an English exam. The school is on the radar of heads of local preps eg Wellesley House, St Ronan's, Marlborough House, Dulwich Prep, St Michael's Otford, Sevenoaks Prep and the New Beacon

Exit: Most sixth formers go on to higher education to study a huge range of courses. Bournemouth, Bristol, Exeter, Liverpool, Newcastle, Oxford Brookes and UWE currently popular; others to Glion, Switzerland (hotel management), Bocconi University, Italy (economics) and University of Delft (aerospace engineering). About 20 per cent leaves after GCSEs either to go to state schools or because they are not A level types and want to take BTecs and NVQs elsewhere.

Money matters: Academic, music, drama, art, sport and DT scholarships – those who do well in the entrance tests are invited to sit the scholarship exams and prep schools can put pupils forward for 13+ scholarship. The Westminster Scholarship available for sixth form. Bursaries are at the discretion of the headmaster and can be applied for via the bursary committee.

Remarks: Now very much a first choice school which has grown in size and reputation under its inspirational headmaster. Can accommodate a wide range of abilities from the very bright to the less so and all are tolerant of each other's strengths and weaknesses. 'It embraces all types', said a mother, 'and you can try everything, don't have to be pigeonholed and the school is determined not to be a sausage factory.'

Tonbridge Grammar School

Deakin Leas, Tonbridge, Kent TN9 2JR

Ages 11–18 **Pupils** 1,182 **Sixth form** 287 (40 boys)

01732 365125
www.tgs.kent.sch.uk

Head teacher: Since 2005, Rosemary Joyce BA MA PGCE NPQH (40s). Read religious studies and history at Stirling, followed by a PGCE and MA at London. Previously deputy head of Nonsuch High School for Girls, Cheam; senior teacher at Clarendon School, Trowbridge; head of religious studies at Aylesbury High. A highly effective administrator who managed to get funding and organise the rebuilding of large parts of the school in record time. She is charming and businesslike and considers her role to be a privilege rather than a job, saying that 'education should be about transforming people's lives'. Teaches philosophy to the sixth form and takes assemblies, but some pupils and parents feel she cuts a slightly remote figure and they don't really know her. She has twin daughters in the school.

Academic matters: Has received the British Council's award for internationalism each year since the introduction of the IB in 2004 and has been top IB state school in the UK for several consecutive years. Ran IB and A levels side by side for a number of years and exclusively the IB from 2012 – caused a bit of a fuss as some families felt they had not been given any choice. However, this has settled down and school and teachers are fully committed to the IB; students who want to do A levels move elsewhere after GCSEs. In 2018, average IB points just under 37. Languages and sciences particularly strong with German, French, Italian and Spanish offered and regular foreign exchanges. Wide choice of subjects maintained under IB but sometimes a subject doesn't run if not enough takers. 'Natural sciences a more natural fit than than sports science' but film and theatre studies popular.

At GCSE, 82 per cent A*-A/9-7 in 2018. School works within the principles of the IB Middle Years Programme (MYP) but is not accredited and will continue with IGCSEs and GCSEs.

Co-ed sixth form since 2000 with about 20 boys in each year who appear to integrate well and 'add a new energy to the classroom'. Good support for Oxbridge and more pupils being encouraged to apply – help with choice of college and preparation for tests, Oxbridge tutors invited to talk to students. Reciprocal arrangements with local schools for interview practice. Medical and vet students come back to talk about the application process.

Good balance and age range of staff (respectable number of male teachers), from very experienced to newly qualified – extraordinarily dedicated team who give up their time to run clubs and sporting fixtures. Maths and chemistry teachers are old girls of the school. Class sizes no more than 30 or 25 for practical subjects with setting from year 8 for maths and French. Ofsted considers the teaching to be outstanding. Progress reports sent to parents and pupils are 'given the freedom to learn from their mistakes'. Form time every day and sixth form have daily contact with their learning mentor – three tutor reviews with learning mentor per year to review progress and set targets. House points awarded for good work.

Curriculum designed to stretch the gifted and talented – maths challenge in Holland and a national level language Olympiad held at school. Enrichment programmes include debating society and subject-led clinics at lunchtimes to stretch and support pupils. School sends a team to the Model UN; recent study trips to Iceland, Singapore and Swaziland. Good SEN support, mainly for mild dyslexia, either individually or small groups. Everyone, including sixth formers, screened on arrival; teachers alert for other difficulties. About one per cent need some sort of EAL help – families who speak another language at home or those who move into the area to join school for IB in sixth form. Increasing number from abroad who stay with local families.

Games, options, the arts: Music particularly strong and caters for all ages and levels of talent. About 300 pupils learn at least one musical instrument. Masses of group music and individuals can shine at house musical events. Three formal concerts a year, array of ensembles, swing bands and orchestras, often student run eg the ukelele orchestra. Three choirs, classical and contemporary – Motet choir won Barnardo's National Choir competition which led to an invitation to sing at the Royal Albert Hall, and were runners up in Songs of Praise Choir of the Year competition. Concerts at St John's Smith Square and at the Cadogan Hall with London Chamber Orchestra.

Active drama department. Whole school production every other year with annual smaller productions as well as some joint drama with Tonbridge School. Theatre studies is offered as part of the IB. New drama and dance studios. Vibrant art displayed around the school taught by 'enthusiastic and friendly teachers'. Art taken early with excellent results – textiles popular.

Team sport compulsory until sixth form and many continue as it forms part of the CAS element of the IB, but can be 'a bit patchy', according to the girls. 'There are not enough matches and sporty girls join outside clubs,' said one. Netball, tennis and hockey are the main sports; some hockey coaching on site and at Tonbridge School. Basketball popular with boys and girls in sixth form; boys have their own football team and many play for local clubs. School's own pool has seen better days and swimming now done elsewhere, but school says plans are afoot for 'an exciting new development project' on the site. Fab new sports hall and all-weather pitch. Action! on Wednesday afternoons for years 7 and 8 – anything from sports, first aid and glass painting to Indian head massage – but clubs 'peter out further up the school', according to some pupils. Some run by sixth form as part of the CAS element of the IB. Pupils also take part in the Young Enterprise scheme and run their own radio station, Radio TGS. They are involved in a community project in Africa – recently a group of about 20 raised money and built a library for a school in Swaziland – 'they lived in fairly basic conditions and it was a life changing experience for my daughter,' said one mother.

Background and atmosphere: Founded in 1905 on the top floor of Tonbridge Library with 19 girls and the motto 'Courage and Honour'. Moved in 1913 to current site,14 acres on a hill in south Tonbridge with great views in all directions. Recent redevelopments include new sixth form study and social centre, IBarn.

Strong sense of community with compulsory service activity once a week – younger children do something within the school, older pupils might help in a primary school or volunteer in an old people's home and sixth form do community service as part of the IB. 'We like to take pupils out of their comfort zone where they flourish and it helps them see themselves as part of a broader picture', says the head. In a recent project some senior pupils worked with children from a pupil referral unit using the photography and IT facilities at the school.

Pastoral care, well-being and discipline: Pastoral care seen as a whole school responsibility; 'we want to get the support right so pupils can be as successful as they can be,' says head. Programme of monitoring, tracking, support and interventions. Learning and peer mentors offer support to girls at form time, and 'there is always someone to talk to and the school wants us to be happy,' said one pupil. Dedicated student manager oversees the transition from primary school and provides a crucial link between home and school; children are put into forms with similar postcodes so they can make friends with girls who live near them. Years 7, 8 and 9 have registration together so they can get to know other year groups, and sixth form has mixed year tutor groups. Year 7s have a bushcraft camping week in nearby woods and new sixth formers invited for a bonding weekend at the University of East Anglia in the summer before they join.

Pupils and parents: A fairly middle class group whose parents take an interest in their education – fewer than 20 children on free school meals. Loyal alumni who come back and speak to pupils and often send their daughters here. 'Well-rounded, grounded children who are highly motivated with a good work ethic – we cannot believe our luck,' said one delighted mother. 'Our daughter is interested and happy and loving every minute'. 'The school has high expectations and the children have so many experiences and opportunities,' said another. The pupils have a 'privileged education but are not necessarily privileged; they push themselves in all areas and have a strong sense of being part of the wider community,' says the head.

Attractive uniform with blue jerseys and straight check skirts, and dress code for sixth form of dark matching suits with skirts as short as they can get away with. Alumni include Victoria Hislop (novelist and travel writer); Rebecca Stephens MBE (first British woman to climb Everest and the seven summits); Lynn Wallis (artistic director of the Royal Academy of Dance); Angie Sage (author of Septimus Heap series); Felicity Aston and Jo Vellino (polar explorers). Active and committed PTA involved with fundraising and social events.

Entrance: Entrance via the Kent Test at 11+ in verbal and non-verbal reasoning and maths, and places are hard fought. No allowance made for siblings. Area places (135) to those living within Tonbridge & Malling Borough, Tunbridge Wells Borough and Sevenoaks District; Governor places (35) to high performers living outside the area; 10 places to those on pupil premium living in one of the three local council areas, but whose scores weren't high enough for an automatic Area place.

Sixth form entry (including boys) based solely on academic results with a minimum of B/6 at GCSE or equivalent in English, maths, a science and a language (if studied) and guidance meetings offered at the school to discuss subject choices. Mainly from other grammars for the IB and East Sussex schools which finish at 16+. Occasionally spaces in other years – entry via school's own test.

Exit: Historically very few left after GCSEs but numbers have increased (now around 40 per cent) as those wishing to do A levels move elsewhere. Over 95 per cent to higher education and a huge range of universities, 80 per cent Russell Group. Durham, Exeter and Leeds current favourites. Eight to Oxbridge in 2018, plus two to the US/Canada and 13 medics/dentists/vets.

Money matters: Music bursaries available and awards in sixth form. Tradition of helping families where money is tight. Pitchford Fund set up by PTA in 1950s and enables those in immediate financial need to take part in activities.

Remarks: A remarkable school, and anyone who gets in here is very fortunate. Considered to be one of the most academic schools in the area, but pupils wear their learning lightly and have time for so much else. Everyone we met was self-confident and ambitious but down to earth and very much aware of the wider world beyond the school gates.

Tonbridge School

High Street, Tonbridge, Kent TN9 1JP

Ages 13–18 **Pupils** 788 **Sixth form** 332 **Boarders** 459 full

Fees: Day £30,342; Boarding £40,446 pa

01732 365555
www.tonbridge-school.co.uk

Headmaster: Since September 2018, James Priory, previously head of Portsmouth Grammar School (PGS). Read English at Oxford, before his first teaching post at Bradford Grammar School, moving on to PGS in 2000 as head of English. Remained loyal to PGS since, taking on posts as head of English, senior teacher, and assistant head of the sixth form before becoming head. Three children; loves the poetry of Edward Thomas, the downs and choral music.

Academic matters: Very impressive. In 2018, 69 per cent A*/A and 91 per cent A*/B at A level. Twenty-four subjects offered at A level and, apart from the usual, include Mandarin, PE, theatre studies, business studies and government and politics. Most popular are maths, economics and history, followed by physics and English – particularly good results in maths, English and economics. Boys still find time for further academic work – three presented their scientific research to an international conference in China and another has published a GCSE French text book.

Most take 10 GCSEs (mostly the more rigorous IGCSEs). In 2018, 92 per cent A*-A/7-9 – among the best results in the country. Science offered as dual award or individually – particularly good showing in individual sciences. All have to take a language at GCSE and a good range offered including French, Spanish, Chinese, Italian and German. Our guide singled out history and French for being especially well taught – 'the head of French is inspired'. Art GCSE offered as fine art or photography. All do non-examined course in divinity, which is largely discussion based and includes critical thinking. Everyone takes digital creativity (ICT) in three fab digital creativity labs. Voluntary Extended Project offered in upper sixth year.

Good liaison between teaching departments – very dedicated team of teachers 'who really seem to care and will go the extra mile for us,' say the boys. 'Bright young teachers [mostly male although there are now 15 female teachers] who are great role models for the boys.' Academic staff also involved with coaching sport and are 'passionate about opportunities available to the boys'.

Boys need to be organised and there is an emphasis on independence from the start, with all encouraged to find their own learning style. All boys screened for learning difficulties on arrival (mainly mild dyslexia and dyspraxia) and all are offered help with study and revision skills and note taking, essay writing, memory and organisational skills – boys often self-refer for drop in sessions or targeted help. Learning mentor training programme so boys can help each other. Novi (first year) dyslexic pupils trained as dyslexic specialist mentors and can help in partner primary schools. Two part-time EAL teachers mainly offer help with technical and scientific language.

Games, options, the arts: Huge range of opportunities help develop self-reliance and leadership skills. Long tradition of sporting excellence but ethos of participation by all, and everyone has the chance to play in a team. Truly superb sports facilities, and was a training venue for the London 2012 Olympics. A hundred acres of playing fields, all immaculately groomed, three Astroturfs, clay tennis courts and an all-weather athletics pitch. Sports centre with cricket nets, 25 metre swimming pool and climbing wall and a fitness suite to rival the swankiest of London health clubs. Membership open to general public. School has hockey, rugby and cricket academies, has produced county and international cricketers and has one of the best rugby sides in south east; recent leavers play for Harlequins and Saracens. Every imaginable sport including fives, ultimate frisbee, fencing and water polo and sailing – novi encouraged to try lots of sports so every boy should find something he enjoys. Weekly house leagues sports for those not in the top teams.

Increasing numbers involved in music, with about five boys taking music A level each year and over 50 per cent of all boys learning one of a huge range of instruments, including the Marcussen chapel organ, one of the best in the country. All Steinway status means top quality pianos in every practice room. Director of music a professional conductor. Wide range of orchestras, bands and ensemble groups for all musical styles including flourishing jazz and pop groups and thriving choral music. Numerous concerts and recitals, including the Octagon concerts, which feature a different instrument each week. Excellent facilities include two recital halls, a suite of teaching practice rooms, music library, soundproof room for jazz and percussion, and a state of the art recording studio. Often team up with musicians outside school eg a concert with Benenden at St Martin in the Fields and South Bank Sinfonia at the Royal Festival Hall; and choir has sung at St George's Chapel, Windsor and Chichester Cathedral, and deputised at St Paul's when the cathedral choir was away.

Drama also thriving, with about eight major productions a year in 400 seat EM Forster theatre (complete with orchestra pit and studio theatre), including three major school plays, with girls from local schools taking part in most productions. Boys get involved with all aspects of production including set design, stage management and lighting. Regular drama competitions and house plays, which are put together by the boys with drama staff acting as mentors, as well as other small scale productions and plays in Spanish, French and German.

Arts workshops by visiting professionals include street dance, masks, puppetry and film making and upper sixth boys invited to take a play to Edinburgh Fringe via the Hogshead Theatre Company. Boys also take part in the National Theatre's play writing competition. Varied programme of lectures by visiting speakers, and boys can choose from a huge range of societies: cultural, political, scientific and sporting, anything from bee-keeping, astronomy and wine appreciation to sub aqua and robotics.

Seminar programme in GCSE and lower sixth years encourages boys to question their assumptions and see things from a different perspective – eg sustainability in business or organ transplants. About 200 boys take part in CCF across all three services. Duke of Edinburgh Award also popular with about 20 achieving gold each year. Not forgetting numerous foreign visits and exchange trips during the holidays.

Boarding: There are seven boarding houses and younger boys start in small dorms of up to six. Older boys have their own rooms. Strong system of pastoral care. Housemasters seen as 'father figures' who get to know boys and their families very well. Aided by assistant housemaster and five tutors per house – boys have regular meetings with their tutors. During the week all boys eat in their houses but at weekends boarders eat together in the Orchard Centre. Most boys go home after games on Saturday, but have to be back in time for Sunday evening chapel. Although trips and outings are organised, it can be quite lonely for those who stay in.

Background and atmosphere: Founded by Sir Andrew Judde in 1553, the school still has close links with the Worshipful Company of Skinners, and Skinners' Day is celebrated each year at the end of the summer term. The school grew rapidly in the 19th century and has been rebuilt twice on the original site. Dominated by the fine rebuilt Edwardian chapel (it was gutted by fire in 1988), the school is set in 150 acres of immaculately kept grounds behind the not-so-glamorous Tonbridge High Street on the northern edge of the town, stretching down to the river and the railway line. The imposing Victorian buildings with tasteful, modern additions manage to combine a respect for tradition with the most up-to-date facilities. The Vere Lodge Centre for DT and art, with its spiral staircase and light-filled space for private views and exhibitions, is particularly impressive. Well-used library – built in 1962 and recently extended and refurbished – with 23,000 books, a number of which date from the 17th century, as well as the 1479 Jensen Bible – although boys seem to get most of their information online, and there's plenty of digital technology here too. Gleaming new science centre (2019) puts Tonbridge at cutting edge of school science; new classrooms and very latest technology juxtapose with original architectural features, aiming to modernise the way science is presented, learned and understood.

Pastoral care, well-being and discipline: Seven boarding and five day houses situated on the edge of the playing fields and along the high street (most recently refurbished), each with about 60 boys. Strong sense of belonging in houses helped by range of inter-house competitions in art, music, film, sport plus house plays and concerts, and close friendships are formed. School aims for as wide a mix as possible in each house and tries to split up boys from the same prep school to stop cliques forming. Good food – all eat in their houses, with grace before lunch.

Boys 'very driven – it's cool to work and there are not many problems on the behaviour front – the boys know they are there to work and are expected to work hard – the pace can be quite challenging for some,' said a parent. Mindfulness meditation is taught as part of PSHE to all boys in year 10 and is increasingly popular as an activity. Boys are taught to focus on the present and not worry about the past or the future – a skill for life which helps them cope with stress. There is an emotional literacy programme for senior boys and an on-site school counsellor.

All boys are expected to attend weekday chapel services four mornings a week, and other faiths encouraged to attend their own places of worship for special religious festivals. School is increasingly connected with the local community and there is a growing sense of social responsibility, with large numbers of boys involved with Tonbridge Community Action – boys help in local primary schools and hospitals and develop the skills and confidence to do things which make a difference. Local primary school children come to use the labs on Wednesday afternoons and hold inter-school sports days at Tonbridge. Recently, 150 boys spent the night under cardboard boxes and raised £5,000 for a homeless charity. Tonbridge has close links with The Marsh Academy at New Romney and is one of its sponsors – Tonbridge boys act as e-mentors and provide help and support to Marsh students, and Marsh students come to Tonbridge for practical science work in the labs. Gap year boys can also work at Marsh Academy for a term.

Pupils and parents: Most boys live within about an hour and a half of the school and it is becoming increasingly popular with London families. School describes the typical Tonbridge parent as 'understated and low-key' and the boys as having a quiet self-assurance – 'great team players who get on in all settings'. Alpha males thrive here and sport still dominant, but boys also admired for other things and music and culture increasingly important; it is 'a much more tolerant and a kinder place than it was some years ago'.

About 10 per cent foreign nationals from 33 countries, who are generally well integrated. Each house twinned with a house at Benenden for socials, restaurant outings and quizzes. Parents encouraged to get involved, and there is always strong support for Saturday matches. Most parents are members of the Parents' Arts Society, which organises cultural and social events each term, everything from private views at art galleries, theatre trips, wine tastings and lectures to weekend trips to Europe. 'It is such a fun way to get to know the other parents,' said one mother. There doesn't seem to be a typical Tonbridgian – some sporty, some less so, some musical, some not – but all seem to enjoy themselves, and the key seems to be to take part in everything. They have a keen sense of fun, demonstrated at the annual Pink Day when all boys dress up in pink in support of breast cancer charities with some very imaginative and outrageous outfits.

A long list of famous old boys includes EM Forster, Frederick Forsyth, all members of the band Keane, Vikram Seth, Patrick Mayhew, several generations of the Cowdrey cricketing dynasty, Dan Stevens of Downton Abbey fame, Tim Waterstone and Kit Hesketh-Harvey.

Entrance: Most join at 13+ from 50-60 prep schools. Computer based pre-assessment and interview in year 6 followed by common entrance (pass mark about 65 per cent) or the school's own exams in English and maths. School operates a reserve list and keeps in close contact with prep schools. A handful joins in year 10 and about 20 join in lower sixth. Sixth form entry via tests in subjects to be studied at A level.

Exit: In 2018, 25 to Oxbridge. Other popular destinations are the usual suspects: Durham, Bristol, Exeter, Bath, London unis and Nottingham, mostly to read hard academic subjects, but not all follow the herd – other destinations include film production at Bournemouth, golf management at Birmingham, land management at Cirencester and popular music performance at the Royal Northern College of Music. Full-time university and careers advisor widely praised, plus guidance and support from housemasters and other specialist staff. University and careers offices open all day – careers and higher education programme starts at end of first year. Good relationships with European and American universities and provide on-site training for SAT exams. Boys have recently gone to Harvard, Berkeley, New York, Queen's University Canada, Trinity College Dublin and Maastricht.

Money matters: A well-endowed school which offers numerous awards. Up to 45 scholarships offered at 13+ – academic, music, art, drama, technology and sport. Academic and music scholarships offered in sixth form. Top academic scholarship worth 50 per cent and all others 10 per cent, which can be topped up with a means-tested bursary. About 15 boys on full fee remission and a further 15 on 80 per cent fee remission. Means-tested foundation awards given to boys to help fund years 7 and 8 at prep school followed by a guaranteed place at Tonbridge.

Remarks: The prospectus says that 'Tonbridge seeks to excel in everything it does' and it certainly lives up to its aim. 'We have been delighted with the school and our boys have been happy and done well here, but you sometimes wonder if the next stage of their lives can live up to this amazing start', said one parent.

Tormead School

27 Cranley Road, Guildford, Surrey GU1 2JD

Ages 4–18 **Pupils** 730 **Sixth form** 84

Fees: £8,100 – £15,450 pa

01483 575101
www.tormeadschool.org.uk

Head: Since 2010, Christina Foord BA MPhil PGCE (40s), previously deputy head and head of boarding at St Catherine's, Bramley. Prior to this she taught English and history in a number of schools including The Queen's School, Chester. She takes a keen interest in music and sport of all sorts and is eager to provide her girls with opportunities to showcase their talents. Known throughout the school as being 'up for a challenge', she recently abseiled down the tower of Guildford Cathedral in aid of charity. Married, with two senior-school aged children and two dogs. Staff remark in admiration that she's ready to get 'stuck in' and when the new climbing wall was inaugurated, she was one of the first to scale it.

Academic matters: One of the high flyers in Surrey (and way beyond). Excellent academic results across a wide range of subjects – 2018 GCSE results were 79 per cent at A*-A/9-7; A level results 83 per cent A*-B and 58 per cent A*/A. 'Does really well even by less academic students,' said a parent. Plenty of scope for choice in languages at GCSE and A levels including Spanish, German and Greek.

Ten GCSEs is the norm. Refreshing to see that risk-talking is also encouraged – pupils who are keen to pursue a subject which may not be their academic forte are still encouraged to follow their dreams. No undue academic pressure ('not as pushy as other schools,' said a parent), and any worries about exams are sensitively handled by the school. Pupils are marked for effort as well as attainment, so the less academic still get plenty of credit for trying hard and 'you feel on top of how your daughter is really doing,' said a parent. Has 'embraced digital technology' with every teacher Apple qualified.

In the pre-prep, literacy and numeracy are taught in the mornings, when the little ones are fresh. Core English, maths, science and ICT, plus French from year 2 and Latin from year 5. Girls are gradually prepped for the entrance exam to the senior school, although everyone is keen to stress the lack of pressure – pupils included.

Much focus on thinking skills, learning attitudes, and encouraging the girls to take risks, both academically and physically, in the junior school. Ethos geared toward helping them to have confidence in their work and in their lives. Much effort to create a culture of thinking outside the box, exemplified in the Out of the Box Project in which pupils invent a 360 degree art project or answer questions such as 'what's inside Paddington bear's suitcase?' or 'what's Leonardo's next invention?

SEN provision recently upgraded from peripatetic support to a full-blown department, including a full-time member of staff in the junior school, offering not only dyslexia support but also study skills, maths clinics and acknowledgement of different learning styles. 'Brilliant,' say pupils, 'Extremely good at helping you out,' and no stigma here for anyone having extra help. Personal attention pays off. Pupils with dyslexia credit their teachers with helping them flourish – dyslexic pupils have achieved A*s and served as head girl.

Games, options, the arts: A school known for its gymnasts ('we're hot on gymnastics here,' said one pupil, proudly); specialist gymnasts' training hall with sprung floor. All sport is played keenly and to a high standard – including hockey, netball, rounders, swimming and tennis. New system of 'development squads' for the keen but less naturally able. Increased number of fixtures for the B and C teams after parental complaints that the A teams were stealing the show. From pre-prep upwards, games and gymnastics weekly with specialist teachers, with swimming added in year 3.

It's a small campus, but on-site facilities are supplemented by use of formidable local ones, such as the Surrey Sports Park at the University of Surrey – the school has an agreement that lets the hockey team use it as their home pitch, allowing the introduction of junior hockey; other sports include spinning, zumba, a climbing wall and squash. Tennis is on two on-site all-weather courts. Sporting success at county level and nationally, especially in swimming, gymnastics, biathlon and sports acrobatics.

Music mandatory until year 9, enthusiastic participation afterwards. Some 275 individual music lessons a week, plus two senior school orchestras, a jazz band (which tours Europe biennially), numerous ensembles and choirs. A programme of events throughout the year, including lunch time concerts and the inter-house music competition in which every girl takes part. The performing arts centre provides a modern and vibrant venue, with a proscenium stage and professional lighting and sound. LAMDA speech and drama awards are popular. Art is exceptionally strong here – wonderful examples are on display around the school and new art suite recently opened.

Much buzz around other extracurriculars, including additional sporting, language, film, art and craft activities, plus fencing, movie club, cake decorating, origami and debating (another school success story). Students regularly achieve recognition in DofE Award (multiple gold awards achieved each year), the Wings of Hope Achievement Awards, and others. School is one of only a handful nationally to have been awarded Star status by the British Schools Exploring Society. Past sixth form destinations have included Vietnam and Zambia, with plans for Ecuador and Galapagos and a partnership in Nepal.

Background and atmosphere: Founded in 1905, the school has made do in the past with a hodge-podge of classrooms and Hogwarts-style corridors tacked onto the original Victorian building ('Frankenstein's building,' quips Foord), but ambitious modernisation and expansion has seen, inter alia, numerous and well-equipped science labs (sciences very strong here), plus a dedicated sixth form physics room with a white board, computers, etc. An impressive art department and design and technology room. The library is new with sixth form area and resources accessible from home. Increasing uptake of the early morning breakfast club, which starts at 7:50am. IT provision good, with plenty of computers and internet connections.

The sixth formers have their own department (revered and envied by the younger girls), no uniform, and recently refurbished lair complete with kitchen facilities, groovy furniture and a clock designed by the DT teacher. Sixth form girls love their freedom and compliment the school on letting them organise charity events, discos, etc themselves. They are visibly proud of their achievements in maths and science and comment on how much extra time teachers spend to help students understand the material. Popular socials with local boys' schools – RGS, Lanesborough, Cranmore.

Nursery-aged girls have their own little domain, bursting with age-appropriate playthings and charming examples of artwork. They also have a dedicated playground apart from the hustle-bustle of the older children. Older pupils are encouraged to spend time with the younger ones, and they do, creating a nice atmosphere of community between the nursery and the rest of the school. Classrooms for the older junior pupils boast small library collections and projects cover the walls, into the stairwells and beyond. Art rooms and computer labs well kitted out and obviously well-used. Art lovingly displayed about the premises. Absolute discipline on the playground (the whistle blew and the children literally stopped in their tracks). World maps prominently displayed and highlighting a different country each week; geography a big part of the culture.

Pastoral care, well-being and discipline: Various problem-solving options start with the form tutor and a trained counsellor is on hand. System of 'aunts' whereby every new girl has another girl assigned to her to help through the first few weeks. Full-time staff member for university counselling and professional development, keen to refocus pupils not only on university entrance but also 'what they will be like when they're 35 and beyond.' 'Oxbridge teas' to link past and present pupils, higher education evening for lower sixth, even support for SAT tests for those pupils considering university in the US.

Pastoral care programme unanimously praised by parents as superb, for some the deciding factor in choosing the school. 'My daughter comes off the bus happy all the time. Nothing seems to overwhelm her,' said one parent. Another noted, 'Mine doesn't compare herself to others, but she used to in her old school. Academics used to be very hard, now she just takes it in her stride.' Less confident girls benefit from the caring and positive ethos; girls leave the school with self-confidence, good social skills and a dash of worldliness. 'Good at taking the timid and shy and making them blossom,' said a junior school parent. In addition to emphasising girls' independence and strengths, the junior school has a very proactive policy on creating a positive atmosphere and combating bullying in any form. It works this magic by focusing on the small things, whether it's a pencil case or an unkind comment, because for girls of this age, 'that's their reality'.

Parents 'have no hesitation' in getting in touch with the school. Any issues are dealt with promptly. PSHE lessons start in the junior school and extend, by the time they reach the sixth form, to discussions about substance abuse, personal safety, relationships and childcare. Assembly an important beginning to the school day, emphasis on care, respect and highlighting the six 'core values' of the school, which cover topics such as respect, academic excellence, a varied curriculum, and bringing out the best in the girls in preparation for life beyond school. Tough line on all transgressions – drugs possession a cause for instant expulsion, similar stance on persistent smoking or misbehaviour. Both pupils and parents say bullying is confronted openly and with great success.

Pupils and parents: Pupils are bubbly and enthusiastic, self-confident and friendly. They appreciate their all-girl campus ('You can come to school ugly!') and have a strong sense of their good fortune in being there. Neatly dressed in blue blazers, no ties but occasional personalised uniform in evidence. Happy chatter in the hallways between classes.

Parents' association has a co-chair for the junior school and the senior school. Parents mostly English or foreign nationals raised in the area, with a mixture of backgrounds – old girls, professionals, London-bound commuters, first-time buyers. Excellent bus service extends all the way to Esher and Haslemere (and beyond). Old girls include comedian Sandy Toksvig and Claudia Parsons, the first woman to circumnavigate the world by car.

Entrance: Junior school selective at 4 (by a 'party' where girls are observed by staff members) and at 7 by maths, English and reasoning tests.

Senior school entrance exam at 11, with pupils selected for academic potential (reasoning, maths and English), extracurricular interests and current school reference. No interview. Some 25 to 30 per cent from state schools. Sixth form entrance requirements include eight GCSEs, 9-5, with at least five at grade 7 or above.

Exit: The vast majority of the junior girls sit the entrance exam for the senior school and 85 per cent go on there, many with scholarships (including seven to the Elite Athletes programme in 2018). About sixty per cent stay on to sixth form. Three medics in 2018; Nottingham, Birmingham, Kings College London and Newcastle popular destinations.

Money matters: Parents remark on the 'good value' represented by the school. At 11+, academic, music, sport and art scholarships, worth 10 per cent of tuition fees. For sixth form, academic, music, and art scholarships, plus internal sport scholarships are available. Full bursaries available at 11+ and 16+ on a case-by-case basis.

Remarks: A nurturing, buzzy school with a tradition of high academic standards that is not content to rest on its laurels. New facilities bringing it in line with its aspirations. Opportunities for pupils to find their niche, whether in art, sport, drama or music, while still encouraging experimentation and maintaining an all-round approach.

Tring Park School for the Performing Arts

Tring Park, Tring, Hertfordshire HP23 5LX

Ages 8–19 (dancers can do 3rd sixth form year) **Pupils** 363 **Sixth form** 145 **Boarders** 210 full

Fees: Day £14,865 – £23,655; Boarding £25,275 – £35,760 pa

01442 824255
www.tringpark.com

Principal: Since 2002, Mr Stefan Anderson MA BMus ARCM ARCT. Fifties, single, no children. A highly personable man whose Boris Karloff-like photo on the school's website in no way reflects his immense charm and humour. A classically trained musician, he grew up in Canada and attended Carleton University, Ottawa; then moved to the UK and studied at the Royal College of Music and Emmanuel College, Cambridge, where he was an organ scholar. He spent 12 years at Wellington as assistant director of music, then seven years as director of music at King's Canterbury, before taking up the principal's post at Tring in 2002. Very much involved in education nationally: an executive director of the Boarding Schools Association, and a trustee of the National Schools Symphony Orchestra. Universally liked and admired by parents and pupils. 'I think he's wonderful. He's absolutely spot on with the kids,' said one mother. 'They all respect him, but they can have a laugh with him,' said another. 'Kind and courteous and very professional,' pronounced a third. 'Makes time for you, easy to deal with, very helpful and very fair,' added a fourth. 'He's brilliant, a character,' said a father, 'There's a great fun side to him.' The feeling is clearly mutual. 'I love it here!' Mr Anderson affirmed. 'The students can be high-maintenance, but it's never dull.'

Academic matters: Tring's results are proof that for the right children, the chance to do what they love actually enhances their academic performance. Only half the school day is given over to academic lessons, and the students here are selected solely on their performing abilities (if they pass the audition, applicants sit academic tests for diagnostic purposes), yet results just keep getting better. In 2018, 63 per cent of GCSE passes were A*-B/9-6. You could be forgiven for wondering if these results were made up of non-academic subjects such as drama and dance, but no: they cover the full spread including sciences and languages. In 2018, A level results were 25 per cent A*/A and nearly 53 per cent A*/B. BTec performing arts no longer offered. Solid spread of academic subjects offered includes English lit, French, German, RS, history, geography, IT, and all the sciences. 'We push the academic side hard,' confirmed the head, who was brought in to improve Tring's profile in that area. Active and successful learning support department caters for wide variety of SEN, and roughly a quarter of students have either one-to-one or small group support. Parents report themselves very happy with the provision. One mother whose child has dyscalculia reported, 'She really struggles with maths, but she's had excellent support.' A boy with dyslexia told us, 'I've never had so much help as I've had here.' 'The support for dyslexia is brilliant,' said a father.

Those of us who remember the days when stage school was more often than not a byword for poor education can only marvel. But then Tring isn't a stage school in the old-fashioned sense, as the pupils were eager to point out, but a heady mix of high-level vocational and academic education, where the two strands rub together to produce very bright sparks. The former head boy has gone off to Manchester to read medicine, and one Tring alumna, a physicist, has recently started her doctorate. As the director of studies, herself a Cantabrigian, put it: 'It's very exciting working with students who are engaged and passionate with their lives. There's a joie de vivre here that spills into academic lessons.' That said, it's important to remember that this is a vocational school, one of only eight such in the UK funded by the DfE as centres of excellence for exceptionally talented young dancers and musicians. Tring's remit is to produce highly-trained performers who've received a rounded education; not lawyers and doctors who like hoofing.

Games, options, the arts: Believe it or not, Tring had actually played a football fixture shortly before we visited. They lost 11-0. 'But,' assured the head, 'we played with great passion.' Students do get together for an informal kickabout, or walk down the High Street to the local swimming pool, but there are no organised games on Tring's timetable, because there isn't time for them. Instead, half of every weekday is given over to vocational training, and, say parents and students alike, it's amazing. 'Equal to the very best available in this country,' said one parent. 'Inspirational!' said another. 'Second to none, absolutely fabulous,' said a third. 'My son's physical fitness has improved dramatically,' said a fourth. And everyone else said something similar.

Children in the prep (years 4-6) receive training in acting, singing and dancing. Thereafter, students specialise in either dance or theatre arts. Dance training covers ballet, contemporary, tap and jazz; drama training does pretty much the same, but less intensively and also covers voice, improvisation, and other aspects of theatre technique. And of course there's musical theatre and singing too. Tring isn't a specialist music school – aspiring concert pianists would feel frustrated at having to break off and jeté every time they'd sat down to practice – but the music department is strong, with several excellent choirs and all students given the chance to learn instruments and play in ensembles.

Packed programme of shows, plays, musicals and other performances throughout the year, all of them done to an astonishingly high standard. Sometimes students have a chance to do external work – ballet dancers join English National Ballet for productions of The Nutcracker, for instance – but not that often. The school doesn't encourage students to be absent, and children wanting a school that will act as their agent and find them regular professional work should look elsewhere.

Boarding: With limited space and funds, the boarding provision was only rated 'satisfactory' by Ofsted in 2011, and we have to say we thought it pretty basic; we saw seven girls to a room, for instance. On the other hand, the 9-12 year old girls in question didn't seem bothered. 'It's fun! Like we're one big family! And if we're having a row, the houseparents sort it out and then we're all best friends again!' Pupils are encouraged to do what they think will make their quarters nice: thus the girls' accommodation was a profusion of heart-shaped pink fluffiness, whilst the boys' was as fresh and tidy as you'd expect rooms shared by multiple boys to be. New boarding house for 70 pupils opening in 2019. Feedback about the food was very mixed, with a number of parents expressing anxiety about how much and how healthily their children were eating, and several stories of boarders needing to pop into town to fortify themselves at McDonald's (a behaviour not confined to Tring students, of course). We ourselves were given a pleasant and nutritionally-balanced meal in the canteen, so it's impossible to comment on this further. Third year sixth formers (the sixth form dance course is a three year course) sort out their own accommodation.

Background and atmosphere: Today's Tring grew out of the Cone Ripman School, founded in 1939 and itself the result of a merger between two previous dance schools. Originally located in London, the outbreak of war forced a move to Tring where the school shared premises with the Rothschild Bank at Tring Park Mansion House (strange bedfellows they must have been). In 1941, the school was able to move back to London but kept its Tring premises as a second school where boarders could be accommodated, and in 1947 both places were renamed the Arts Educational School, to reflect Grace Cone's and Olive Ripman's commitment to a proper academic education for their stage-struck charges. Gradually the two schools diverged, with London becoming more focused on post-18 training, while Tring continued to develop as a vocational boarding school. Eventually they became completely independent and in 2009 the Tring school changed its name to Tring Park School for the Performing Arts, in order to avoid confusion with its former partner. Originally for girls only, one boy was admitted in 1993, 'and that opened the floodgates'.

Still housed in the gorgeously flamboyant mansion in which it took refuge over 70 years ago, Tring Park School literally sings with activity and joy. Half the stunning wood-panelled entrance hall is glazed off as a dance studio, and we arrived amidst cries of 'Five, six, seven, eight, and right! Two, three, four, and left!', while Guys and Dolls mingled jauntily with a more demure strain from the ballet class next door. Everywhere we looked, we saw children enjoying themselves and eager to tell us so. 'Life here is amazing!' 'You get here and everyone has something to give!' 'Everyone's really welcoming!' 'It's so creative!' 'It just makes you want to dance more, being here. You get to see everyone's talent!' 'You have more time here for what you love, you're more connected!' twittered a group of frankly adorable young things. Parents agree. 'If you have a non-academic child, as we have, the enthusiasm and the passion motivates them to do better at everything. Our son loves it, he absolutely thrives on it,' said one mother. Another commented, 'The children are lovely, all so dedicated, and it really is like a family,' adding, 'When my husband and I are walking round the school, we wish we were there!' 'Every child comes out with poise and confidence from that place, they all know how to present themselves.'

The mansion's grade II listed status has hampered some necessary modernisation – it took years to get planning permission for Wifi to be installed – but the school boasts an impressive array of newly-built dance studios. It has also received funding for an even bigger and better theatre to supplement the existing 176-seat Markova Theatre, while the new art centre will move from the site of Baron Rothschild's zebra cage to a new home next to the theatre. The surrounding tree-studded gardens provide a tranquil and soothing backdrop to all the artistic fervour.

Feathers do get ruffled occasionally. 'Inevitably at a school like this, there is competition, and I think there should be,' said one level-headed student. But everyone we spoke to insisted that the school also fostered care and affection amongst its students. 'We've always been taught not to compare ourselves to others, but to where we were last term,' said one sixth-former. 'If their best friend gets the part, the others still give her a hug,' said one mother. Another said, 'There is no real jealousy or one-upmanship over talent, and good performances are widely praised and discussed between pupils.'

Parents were less starry-eyed about school-parent communication, and everyone we spoke to agreed that it needed improving. 'Communications are not all they should be,' was a very typical criticism; 'they could be more regular and more informative.' Another said bluntly, 'We pay a hell of a lot of money for our child to go to Tring, and if I send an email I expect an answer.' The head acknowledged these criticisms with candour. 'I would absolutely agree. We need to upgrade our facilities so that we can have a parent portal. We email things weekly, but we don't have a newsletter as such. We have plans – our aim is to get a new iSAMs system (school information software). Staff are extremely busy here, but that doesn't excuse it, and I take it on board.' A new appointment, head of careers, was made recently to address concerns that families weren't getting enough information and help with students' UCAS applications.

We also heard disquiet from parents whose children hadn't been allowed to take the course of their choice at 14+ or 16+ after having already spent two or more years at the school. Specifics weren't forthcoming, but we gathered that this particularly applied to those with aspirations to a career in dance. 'This can be a more difficult adjustment than the school acknowledges, and it's you the parent who has to deal with your child's disappointment,' wrote one worried mother. But as other parents observed, a career in the performing arts is tough, and the head was adamant that the school always put the child's best interests first. 'I would dispute very strongly that we block anyone, but we try to get the child onto the course where we feel they'll succeed. If someone has unrealistic expectations, we speak to the child and to the parents. But 95 per cent of the time, parental, child and school expectations match up.' The great majority of parents we spoke to agreed. As one mother wrote, 'Tring provides a very supportive network for students who are struggling or who change their minds about whether vocational training is for them.' Another said simply, 'The support given by Tring's staff is exceptional. Our son is very happy there, and flourishing beyond our imagination.'

Pastoral care, well-being and discipline: Parents praised Tring's pastoral care, with the boarding staff particularly singled out. 'The housemother was wonderful, and my son settled in really quickly,' 'A houseparent in a million' 'The houseparents are so switched on,' ''The houseparents comfort you if you're homesick!' 'They're amazing! They do so much for us!' were typical comments. The medical unit was also very highly rated: 'Informs you immediately if there are any problems,' 'The medical staff were exceptional,' 'Both pastoral and medical care have always been exemplary.'

Behaviour at Tring is exuberant but respectful. There are the usual sanctions for infringements, but the students want to be here and are generally keen not to mess up. Many parents commented on the children's excellent work ethic, and one boy added, 'My time management has become fantastic since starting here. You really do become reliable, hard working, responsible. You have to work hard.'

Pupils and parents: From a very broad range of backgrounds, and from all over the UK. Some from overseas (around 10 per cent of boarders), and EAL help is there for those who need it. Many of them new to boarding, or to independent schools, or to the world of performing arts, but all of them united by a common ardour. Inevitably, there are more girls than boys, with the current ratio being more than 2:1. Do the boys mind? 'No, because I'm friends with all the boys in my year,' said one young lad, 'and my confidence with girls has increased!'

Entrance: Children can join the school from age 8 to 16, but the commonest entry points are at ages 11-13, 14 and 16. Applications are increasing, particularly at 16+, and overall the school receives seven applications for every place. One-day audition process at which children show what they can do in dance, drama and singing. They aren't expected to excel in all three of these – although many do – but the school is looking for great talent and potential in the candidate's chosen specialism, 'and they have to show a real desire to learn,' says head. If they're successful in gaining a place but need funding to take it up, they're called to a second audition. An online audition and screening application recently launched.

Exit: The majority of students continue on into the performing arts in one way or another. A few dance stars progress straight to major companies such as English National Ballet and Scottish Ballet; others might join the school's own dance company, Encore, for a rigorous third year of touring and performing, or take up places at dance schools such as The Place. Drama schools are also a popular destination: Laine Theatre Arts, Bristol Old Vic, etc. 'And we regularly turn out some good classical musicians,' adds head, although invariably these are singers – one recent alumna went on to train at The Royal Academy of Music and has already appeared with Garsington Opera and Opera North. Some go straight into professional work (Downton Abbey has mopped up several Tring alumni). And a number decide to go to university instead: Royal Holloway, Nottingham and Oxford Brookes in 2018, alongside eg New York University and the Juilliard performing arts school in New York some years.

Much praise from parents and pupils alike for the way Tring supports and guides students' career aspirations. 'I'd love to get a job in a ballet company,' said one young male dancer, 'but my body doesn't work that way, I'm not flat-turned-out. But the teachers work with you to find other ways you can do things, and they're brilliant.' A parent whose son was now at college told us, 'He knows he can still call on Tring for help and advice, a relationship he really values.'

Money matters: Stonkingly high fees, as you'd expect with all this specialist tuition, but around one third of students are on some kind of support. Dancers who join the school at age 11, 12 or 13 can apply for funding from the government's means-tested Music and Dance Scheme. Dance students joining at 16+ may be eligible for DaDA scholarships (Dance and Drama Awards, another source of government funding). And Tring has its own scholarship fund for musical theatre and drama pupils, to which families can apply. Many Tring students come from families on modest or low incomes. Up to 100 per cent assistance available for those who need it.

Remarks: An extremely impressive vocational school that gives its students an excellent and well-balanced education. Children for whom the performing arts are central to their existence will feel they've come home the moment they walk through the door. As one mother whose daughter had been there eight years said, 'We cannot fault it. She's had a wonderful time, and the training has been amazing. Her work ethic is fantastic, she's very well-prepared for auditions, she's made friends for life, and she's grown into a wonderful young lady.'

Tudor Hall School

Wykham Park, Banbury, Oxfordshire OX16 9UR

Ages 11–18 **Pupils** 328 **Sixth form** 98 **Boarders** 244 full

Fees: Day £22,095; Boarding £35,610 pa

01295 263434
www.tudorhallschool.com

Headmistress: Since 2004, Wendy Griffiths, BSc PGCE (50s). Educated at Queen Elizabeth Grammar School, Carmarthen, read zoology at University of Wales – still a trace of her Welsh accent. Previously head of sixth form at Tormead School, then director of studies at St Catherine's, Bramley. As a student she had plans to become a doctor, but while teaching in a Portsmouth comprehensive Miss Griffiths had an epiphany. After seeing how excited her class became during an 'ambitious' practical lesson she succumbed to pedagogy and has never looked back.

Before our meeting we'd already been entertained by the sight of Miss Griffiths dancing and lip synching to Chic's We are Family in a film made by the girls of Todd (year 7 house). There aren't many heads we can call to mind who would even consider doing this, let alone be able to pull it off with such groovy aplomb. The video was playing on a wall-mounted screen, somewhat at odds with the restrained décor of the entrance hall. It's also on the school website, along with others – they like making films at Tudor Hall.

With her sleek bob and leather skirt, Miss G is poised and highly professional (albeit with a twinkle). She was described to us as someone who 'never slows down', which may account for the fact that in addition to the responsibilities of headship she was also just coming to the end of a stint as chair of the Boarding Schools Association in its 50th anniversary year when we visited. What about boarding schools then, we asked, are they still necessary? 'Almost more than ever' was the not unexpected reply. A boarding school is able to inculcate so much more than narrow academics: 'Instead of sitting at home glued to social media, at boarding school children have to be be social, they learn how to get on with everyone'.

Miss Griffiths still interviews prospective pupils and teaches a GCSE biology class – that's four lessons a week, very unusual for a senior school head. She lives on site with her husband, who teaches history at Sibford School; they have one daughter. Spare time, should there be such a thing, is for dog walking – plenty of Cotswolds on the doorstep for that.

To conclude, here's a little list of the the words parents used to describe Miss Griffiths: 'Outstanding', 'astonishing', 'highly professional', 'diplomatic', 'inspiring' and (we heard this one repeatedly), 'a great role model'. 'She just gets it', said one.

Academic matters: Gradual upward trajectory of academic results is testament to small classes (average 15), plenty of individual attention and by all accounts, dedicated and inspirational teaching. In 2018, 64 per cent A*-A/9-7 at GCSE, and 74 per cent A*-B at A level (34 per cent A*/A). Top performers at A level are geography, economics and maths. That maths is one of the most popular A levels speaks volumes for the teaching – head told us with regret how girls continue to arrive from prep schools saying they 'can't do' it.

Innovative work to inspire girls to stay engaged not just with maths but also science subjects. Super new labs for exploding jelly babies as well as more serious experiments. We saw girls in smart red lab coats investigating their own cheek cells under the microscope. Lively programme of extracurricular science clubs, visits to science fairs and National Space Centre etc.

We shared a delicious lunch with girls who had very different and exciting plans for their future – lots of gap years followed by courses from criminology to drama. No sense that sixth formers are all expected to board the non-stop university express – one told us how much support she'd had for her decision to go straight into interior design rather than take a degree in the subject.

Visiting speakers widen horizons as does head's initiative, 'Tudor in three continents', which includes travel scholarships for girls to participate in projects in India, Cambodia and South Africa whilst at home the school has added a project that doesn't involve epic amounts of air travel: mentoring children at the Bolton Lads and Girls (sic) Club. Meeting less fortunate children in their own country, rather than thousands of miles away, has been a very profound experience.

Parents told us staff keep an eagle eye on each girl's progress and are quick to intervene if she appears to be lagging. 'Teachers work so hard to get the right results; if there's a problem they really drill down to find the root cause'. Girls love the fact that teachers are so accessible: 'there's always a subject teacher who can help if you're stuck on homework or revision'. What parents love is the individual attention given to their daughters' academic progress; all those we spoke to said they were confident no child would be allowed to struggle or fall behind.

SEN or EAL support provided individually or in classes but head says this is not the place for a girl with serious needs; 'we want all pupils to be able to participate fully in the curriculum'. Dynamic learning support team uses variety of approaches including latest educational technology such as iPad apps.

Games, options, the arts: School has put considerable efforts into improving sports provision and parents say that it's much better. Facilities are all present and correct including glass roofed outdoor swimming pool (not used in the winter) and plenty of pitches. Girls told us that a 'bigger gym' and a 'pavilion on the top pitch' would be great. Larger schools' A teams are likely to have the advantage so notable and sustained recent successes at county level in hockey and cross-country are all the more creditable. Individual talents in tennis (lovely courts in former walled garden), skiing and riding are well supported and a wider range of non-competitive options such as swim fit and zumba are offered in the sixth form. Girls also work with Carrdus School (Oxfordshire prep owned by Tudor Hall) and local primary schools to provide pupils with coaching and taster sessions in eg lacrosse.

Drama is offered at GCSE and A level but TH girls love to perform, whether or not they are pursing it as a subject option. Great results in LAMDA speech and drama exams too. Regular participation in Shakespeare Schools Festival, plenty of theatre trips and a choice of stages – newish studio theatre has eye-catching neon sign. Dance is accorded greater status here than at other schools and can be taken as a GCSE. Reaction, the audition-only school dance group, has been going for over 20 years; the house dance title is as keenly fought as house singing and drama competitions. Music, too, offers girls of all abilities the chance to perform – whether at school concerts, carol singing at care homes or carrying off trophies at Banbury Young Musician of the Year competitions.

The quality of the art, both in the studios and (perhaps a little infrequently) displayed throughout the school, fair took our breath away. Quite the best we can remember seeing anywhere. Likewise textiles and photography. Style and subject matter went from traditional to unexpectedly edgy and challenging. The textile and art rooms stay open into the evening and at weekends and girls love the freedom this gives them to work on their projects outside lessons. Textiles currently housed in Portakabin but purpose built studios are in the offing. Leavers regularly go on to art foundation and fashion design courses.

Extracurricular options encompass just about everything from Model United Nations to the very popular dissection club. It seems not only can a Tudor Hall girl address a crowd and whip up a soufflé (if she's done the Leiths course), she can also eviscerate a frog. Parents approve of the way girls are kept very busy lower down the school, gradually developing independent study skills as they approach the relative freedom of the sixth form.

Boarding: The full Monty – two exeats per term and no flexi or weekly. Saturday school with lessons until 1pm and games in the afternoon, trips, activities and down time thereafter. Boarding is arranged horizontally – ie by year group – meaning that everything (activities, bed times etc) can be tailored to the age group. Works especially well at exam times – much easier if everyone around you is revising.

Year 7 boarders and day girls are based in Todd (named after the school's founders), a charming house with a large peaceful garden on the edge of the school grounds. It's as uninstitutional as possible with a large family kitchen, colourful soft furnishings and lots of toys and games. And, when we visited, a body on the sitting room floor. 'Just step over it, we're doing first aid,' the housemistress told us. Todd girls love putting on plays and concerts for their captive audience, they also enjoy 'special breakfasts', baking and Sunday excursions (day girls can go too). Todd girls have lower sixth buddies, described to us as a 'big sister support system'.

Dorms vary from two to six cabin beds; bathrooms are clean but on the functional side. Apparently they're 'due for a refurb'. Personal technology at this end of the school limited to mobile phones for 10 minutes a day. Skype etc always available, 'we never stop a child speaking to their parents'. Glad to hear it.

T

Housemistress has set up a Facebook page for Todd parents who get daily photos and updates on their girls' activities.

Other houses (known as The 11s, The 111s and so on) are spacious and well equipped. Girls need no encouragement to personalise their space; walls were papered with photos, letters, bunting and many, many rosettes – plenty of keen horsewomen here.

Each boarding house has its own character and traditions so there's a real sense of progression through the school. Sixth form accommodation is designed as a halfway house to prepare girls for living independently. They can cook, are responsible for their own laundry and organise trips and activities. One such is the Christmas shopping trip to Paris (plus Disneyland Paris); no shortage of teachers signing up to chaperone that one, we imagine.

Background and atmosphere: One of the oldest girls' boarding schools in England, Tudor Hall was founded in 1850 by Rev T W Todd and his wife. In 1908 the school moved from London to rural Kent and on the outbreak of the Second World War it decamped to Burnt Norton, a small Cotswold manor house, to escape the air raids. Pupils, teachers and parents stayed here, even during the holidays, and old girls remember those times with great affection. It was a visit to the gardens at Burnt Norton that inspired T S Eliot to write his eponymous poem, a meditation on time, memory and original sin. Perhaps he would have penned something a little jollier than 'Garlic and sapphires in the mud clot the bedded axle-tree' if he'd visited a few years later when the Tudor Hall girls were in residence.

Surrounding area predominantly rural – grazing cows more common than passing traffic – but access to Oxford, London, Stratford and Bicester etc pretty easy. A great summer treat for the older girls is, we were told, to walk to the nearby farm shop, buy a picnic and eat it in a field. Wouldn't suit a committed urbanite, but that's not really the demographic which is, we suspect, one that is accustomed to town and country living and has the right shoes for both.

First time visitors may be surprised to find no busy reception desk; the entrance hall, with its bergere furniture, beautiful flowers and polished wood, is rather reminiscent of an exclusive hotel – but the welcome is warm and personal. Usual mix of buildings – not everywhere is country house gracious – but all well tended. School magazine and publicity material are similar – high production values but nothing boasty or brash. Come to think of it, that probably sums up the Tudor Hall pupil.

Pastoral care, well-being and discipline: Tudor Hall has long had a reputation for the highest standards of pastoral care, but don't confuse caring with soft. Yes, it's a nurturing environment, as all the best small schools are, but within that environment girls are encouraged and tested; challenged to overreach their own boundaries and try new things. All the parents we spoke to felt that their daughters were in the safest of hands and cited many examples of occasions when tutors or other members of staff had gone above and beyond to help or advise them. Day and boarding parents get a weekly update from tutors about what's been going on and home school communication in general receives nothing but praise.

A couple of people we spoke to thought the downside of year group boarding was that it contributed to a somewhat stratified hierarchical atmosphere, but we didn't feel this was the case. Vertical house system, not to mention the mix of different clubs and sporting activities, must go a long way to defuse this. Day girls are very well integrated and can join their boarding friends for trips and weekend activities, but it's a long day and, with Saturday school, a long week. Even year 7 day pupils don't finish until 6.45pm or later, although they will have had an hour or so's break, a snack and done their homework.

Regular socials with chaps from Radley, Eton and Harrow. The young gentlemen from Harrow are current favourites, but apparently this changes from year to year.

What do you gain from boarding, we asked a group of sixth formers? They all cited strong and lasting friendships; others valued the 'accessibility' of teaching staff and the fact that there's always someone around to help with academic work. 'It helps you become responsible and independent – and it stops you taking home for granted.' We like that last one but doubt it survives the summer holidays.

Pupils and parents: Most recent ISI report described Tudor Hall pupils as 'overwhelmingly positive in outlook', which sounds rather alarming – a posse of Pollyannas, perhaps. It would be so easy to fall back on the old stereotype of Tudor Hall girls as darling daughters of the home counties, what with Leiths, polo, doing the ski season, etc – but that wouldn't be fair or accurate.

The girls we met were friendly, thoughtful, comfortable in their own skins and definitely not the identikit result of an educational production line. There's no arrogance or sense of entitlement and definitely no hair flicking. Girls know they are fortunate and are very aware that the world beyond Banbury is considerably less shiny; it certainly won't be any the worse for having Tudor Hall alumnae in it.

Pride in one's school is not usually compatible with the teenage psyche, but Tudor Hall girls aren't too cool for that. Lots of daughters of old girls – always a good sign. Other old Tudorians include Katherine Hooker, tailor to Duchess of Cambridge; Cleo Barbour, shoe designer; Julia Peyton-Jones, director of Serpentine Gallery.

Entrance: Candidates for 11+ and 13+ invited for 'taster day' (or day and night for prospective 11+ boarders) and assessment days with tests in maths, English and verbal reasoning. The tests are to 'ensure girls are compatible with academic pace' of school. Girls applying for entry at 13+ offered conditional places dependent on outcome of CE. Sixth form entry by general and subject-specific papers. All candidates are interviewed by the head who told us she is looking for 'character.' She believes that girls who are 'sparky about something' succeed because the school can channel their enthusiasm into other areas.

Exit: Bristol, Birmingham, Edinburgh, Exeter, Leeds, Newcastle and Nottingham are current Russell Group favourites, with a couple to Oxford in 2018 as well as LSE and Sciences Po, France. Subjects studied are as diverse as the girls themselves: economics, biological sciences, law, architecture, languages, textile design, songwriting..

Money matters: Fees at the slightly less eye watering end of the boarding range; day fees look like good value considering time spent in school. Academic, music, art, drama and sport scholarships (up to £1,000 pa) available at 11+, 13+ and 16+. Also textiles and dance at 16+. Means-tested bursaries to support new and current parents in financial need.

Remarks: Leave your preconceptions at the door and prepare to be bowled over. Whether your daughter is headed for fashion design or Oxbridge, under Miss Griffiths' dynamic stewardship Tudor Hall deserves a place on everyone's shortlist.

Tunbridge Wells Girls' Grammar School

Southfield Road, Tunbridge Wells, Kent TN4 9UJ

Ages 11–18 **Pupils** 1,032 **Sixth form** 303

01892 520902
www.twggs.kent.sch.uk

Headteacher: Since 1999 Linda Wybar, 50s. Read English and took her PGCE at Hull. She also has an MA in education management from the OU, taken when her twin sons were toddlers. Linda's earliest ambition was to clean and tidy her parents' wool shop, but she soon decided she would prefer to be a headmistress and never looked back. She came south for her first teaching post and has taught in Kent schools ever since. Her first appointment, at a co-ed school, was a tough one where she 'learnt a lot about behaviour management and how to motivate young people'. Taught English for four years and then became head of department at Norton Knatchbull Boys' Grammar, where initially she was the only female member of staff, followed by deputy headship at Highsted Girls' Grammar, before moving to TWGGS as head teacher.

She still teaches English to a GCSE class. She says, 'The school prides itself on its blend of academic challenge and the wider life outside the classroom – expectations are consistently high but girls should still be able to pursue their passions where they can'. The school appears deceptively relaxed – 'there is lots of fun and laughter and we don't want girls to feel pressurised' – and she is proud of the exceptional pastoral care and guidance: 'a strong sense of community pervades the school; it is our greatest strength'. The girls say she is 'approachable and dynamic – she is very energetic and turns up to all the after-school stuff'. 'She is very passionate about the school and her assemblies are relevant, upbeat and encouraging, and she is in tune with the girls and well respected'. 'She is also quite strict and we can't get away with much', added a pupil. 'She is always available', said a parent, 'and you will always get an answer within 24 hours – you can feel the pride and pleasure she gets from the school'.

Married with two grown up sons, she has a cottage in Cornwall where she and her husband retreat whenever they can. She loves good wine and food and the theatre and is a regular visitor to Stratford.

Academic matters: An unashamedly aspirational school with the results to go with it; girls are not pushed but expectations are high. In 2018, 69 per cent A*-A/9-7 at GCSE; 51 per cent A*/A and 81 per cent A*-B at A level from a range including psychology, sociology, politics and economics, with biology, maths and psychology being the most popular. Younger girls are given a lot of help with time management skills. Setting in maths from year 8 and in science from year 10. Everyone learns French and German from year 7 and takes up Spanish in year 8, carrying on one or two languages to GCSE. RS compulsory – 'it makes the girls think – especially the philosophy and ethics element,' says the head.

Close co-operation with Skinners' boys' grammar across the road eg PE and computing A level is taken at Skinners' and Skinners' boys come to TWGGS for Spanish and psychology. Gifted and talented girls are differentiated in the classroom and some bilingual girls are allowed to take their own language GCSE early – but are not taught by the school.

Good age range of teachers, some of whom have been at the school over 25 years but also take on a few NQTs each year – most staff stay a reasonable length of time and are generally keen to embrace change. The small number of girls with dyslexia and dyspraxia are well supported in class; there are no special lessons or teachers. Support given to visually impaired and school can deal with mobility issues, but some of the older parts of the school can be quite difficult to navigate. A handful with EAL requirements.

Well-equipped careers department with an independent careers adviser and careers education integrated into PSHCE lessons. All expected to do two weeks' work experience after GCSE – most find it themselves but school has good contacts if needed. Well stocked and well used library overseen by a helpful and enthusiastic librarian, who also runs reading groups for all ages in partnership with other local schools.

Games, options, the arts: Sporty school with lunchtime and after-school clubs as well as timetabled PE lessons. Sixth form encouraged to do some form of exercise but have to organise themselves, although staff are involved with teams and competitions. Floodlit netball and tennis courts recently refurbished and school has its own Astroturf, which means most matches are held on site. Fine record of achievement in county and regional tournaments: recent U19 netball county and regional winners; U19 regional hockey finalists; regional finalists in gymnastics and cricket; and won gold in the U19 regional floor and vault competition. Supportive of girls who belong to sports clubs outside school and gives some leeway with homework if they are in after-school matches.

Drama a particular strength, and the school has its own performing arts centre with professional lighting and retractable seating, with numerous events throughout the year. Biennial whole school production and annual year 8 Shakespeare festival, year 9 drama festival and sixth form production. Drama and music departments work alongside each other on whole school productions. Girls also able to take part in workshops with professional actors and theatre companies and often team up with Skinners' for drama productions. Prefects run drama clubs for the younger girls. Drama also part of the curriculum in the lower years, albeit one lesson every other week. Girls can get involved in all aspects of production from costumes and lighting to script writing and scenery design. Drama offered at GCSE and A level.

The school's specialisms are English and music, and although it no longer gets extra funding, music is part of its DNA – 'there is music everywhere,' said our guide. About 400 girls have music lessons and take part in extracurricular musical events. Recently expanded music block with individual practice rooms and an ICT music room where pupils can compose their own music. Large array of orchestras, bands, choirs and ensembles and there are usually TWGGS girls in the National Youth Orchestra or Choir. The school gets involved with national music competitions, were recent national chamber music champions and take part in the National Festival of Music for Youth. Work hard on links with the community which enables girls to perform alongside other musicians like The Royal Opera House schools projects and orchestras in Tunbridge Wells. They also perform in local primary schools and in old people's homes. The staff choir sings regularly at school events. Usually a couple of girls a year go on to read music at university.

Good take up for art, although 'the equipment is not too elaborate,' say the girls; there are very few computers but they have their own kiln, and textiles particularly popular. All learn food technology for the first three years, along with graphics, textiles and resistant materials. Art displayed around the school and rotated regularly.

Huge range of clubs, many run by the girls, including the popular feminist society. Two of the most well-attended clubs are debating and CCF. Girls can join the debating society from year 7 and TWGGS is one of the strongest state schools on the debating circuit, taking part in many national competitions and often hosting the local rounds. TWGGS is the only girls' state school with its own CCF. 'My daughter loves the CCF and gets so much out of it in terms of leadership skills and working in a team', said a mother. 'It's another fun thing to do', said a pupil. 'You get to learn first aid and orienteering and it's a good way to get to know girls in other year groups'. A handful each year takes gold D of E and about 25 gain silver.

Masses of outings and trips – to museums and art galleries, history trips to Russia and Hampton Court, geography trips to Iceland and Devon and language trips to France, Germany and Spain. School runs an exchange programme with a school in India and has a regular expedition to Ghana – girls go to stay with a family in India for three weeks and Indian girls come back to stay with girls in UK and come to school. Places on the biennial trip to Ghana are keenly contested and girls have to take an assembly on their return. The school raises about £40,000-£50,000 per year for the Ghana Education Project and has built a girls' school there.

Background and atmosphere: The school was established in 1905 as an all-girls selective grammar. It is off a quiet residential street on the edge of Tunbridge Wells and backs onto open countryside. The original Edwardian buildings are solid and functional and visitors are greeted by cabinets full of silverware. Teaching blocks have been added over the years as well as a performing arts centre and music block and an attractive courtyard with flowering trees and benches where girls can socialise or revise. The school has its own Astroturf, tennis, netball courts and athletics field on site and a small gym and a large hall for assemblies – can't quite fit in the whole school. New sixth form block with a computer room and common room for each year group – sixth formers can also bring in their own laptops.

Strong links with the community and about half of the sixth form girls do some sort of voluntary community work: some teach a foreign language to primary children through music and others help with reading at local schools. Large numbers involved with fundraising for local, national and international causes – over £10,000 raised for charity each year; a different charity is chosen by the charity prefects each term. Younger girls wear tartan skirts and jumpers and there are strict rules about not rolling up their skirts, which staff enforce. Quite a relaxed approach to clothes for sixth form and they can wear whatever they like apart from crop tops, ripped jeans or sportswear.

Pastoral care, well-being and discipline: 'A highly successful and happy school,' say the inspectors, and the staff are proud of the high level of pastoral care. There is a robust anti-bullying policy with any problems being dealt with immediately; community and caring are regular features in assemblies and the school is 'big on respect'. No house system, but the strong pastoral care means no one gets left out – girls are encouraged to look after each other, with sixth formers offering help and support to younger girls and a prefect responsible for each form. Year 7s are each paired with a year 8 buddy, and take part in a bonding day at Carroty Wood activity centre soon after they start.

Close liaison between form teachers and tutors, who monitor academic progress and general well-being and who are able to offer support for friendship problems in the lower years. There is an external counsellor, in school pastoral support with a walk-in office, a school nurse, and mental health issues are discussed regularly. Good links with outside agencies if needed. Transgressions are few and 'a firm conversation usually does the trick'. The head has never had to exclude a girl permanently, but sometimes one might be sent home for a couple of days for a serious misdemeanour, 'often something daft and they usually turn out ok,' says the head. 'Discipline fundamentally self-imposed and based on consideration for others'.

About 70 per cent of girls eat in in light airy canteen – the food is good with plenty of choice. Sixth formers tend to bring in packed lunches and eat in their own kitchen, or use local facilities.

Pupils and parents: Families reflect the mixed social and economic background of the area within two or three miles of the school, but are mostly white middle class. 'Girls sparky but caring with a real ability to enjoy themselves inside and outside the classroom – they are determined and ready to work hard for their goals but also kind and supportive to each other and the staff'. 'There is no typical TWGGS girl', said a mother; 'the girls can become who they want to be and no-one is moulded'. There is a strong sense of community helped by the tight catchment area which means girls often know each other outside school. The head girl and her team of prefects play a significant part in running the school, including heading up some extracurricular activities as well as support for the younger pupils. Girls go on to a wide range of careers – a significant number into medicine, business and accounting but also design and the arts, plus some into teaching. Old girls include Jo Brand, weather presenter Nazaneen Ghaffar and tennis champion Virginia Wade.

All parents are automatically members of the PTA, which organises social and fundraising events like an annual quiz night, the biennial ball and a whole school sponsored walk, and also runs the second hand uniform shop. They contributed £50,000 towards the new performing arts centre. Good communications between school and parents and 'you feel you are with your daughter all the way through, and you can get as involved as you want'.

Entrance: Entry into year 7 is via the Kent PESE Test, which is sat in the September before entry with tests in English, maths and verbal and non-verbal reasoning. There are seldom spaces in other year groups; applications direct to the school. Over 80 per cent come from state primary schools and the rest from local independent prep schools like Rosehill, Derwent Lodge and The Mead in Tunbridge Wells. The catchment area is tight and is currently about a two to three mile radius, with preference given to those living in specific parishes, but this can change from year to year. There are also 14 governors' places for those in the wider catchment area who do very well in the 11+. Sixth form entrance depends on point score from the best six GCSE subjects (including a minimum 6 in English and maths) and a grade 7 in any A level subject. Twenty or so join the sixth form but it depends on spaces and courses; girls settle in quickly and are made to feel welcome.

Exit: Most go on to a wide range of universities to study a huge variety of subjects. Seven Oxbridge places in 2018 (three of these to study law, the others languages, land economy, geography and economics). Girls occasionally go to university in Europe but none have yet gone to the USA.

A small number leave after GCSEs, some to local FE colleges or vocational courses where they can work at a different pace and a few each year move to independent or other local schools for sixth form.

Money matters: Most parents contribute about £40 per year into the TWGGS Fund which is for extracurricular activities such as tournament fees and transport to matches as well as visiting group music teachers, score sheets for concerts and prizes for speech days. It also helps towards the cost of drama productions, pays for pupils to take part in debating competitions and pays into the Southfield Fund to help those who are struggling pay for school trips and other activities.

Remarks: A consistently high performing school with a tight catchment area which is always oversubscribed. It turns out confident, well rounded girls who are willing to take part and who have a strong sense of the wider community. 'All the promises have been fulfilled and my daughter is a different girl since she arrived at TWGGS – it has exceeded our expectations', said a mother.

Twyford School

High Street, Twyford, Winchester, Hampshire SO21 1NW

Ages 3–13 **Pupils** 395 **Boarders** 103 flexi (from year 4) **C of E**

Fees: Day £7,066 – £19,509; Weekly boarding £24,552 pa

01962 712269
www.twyfordschool.com

Headmaster: Since 2010, Dr Steve Bailey BEd PhD FRSA; educated at Kent College, Canterbury, Southampton University and St Paul's College of Education (50s). Born and raised bilingually in Hong Kong before teaching history (all levels) at Winchester College for 30 years; housemaster for the last 12. A Fellow of the Royal Society for the Arts, research fellow of the International Olympic Committee, author of six books and with an international reputation as a historian of sport and the Olympic Games.

Dr Bailey encourages teachers to deliver lessons beyond narrow CE requirements. Regularly observes teaching and makes no secret of his ambition for more creativity in the classroom; is keen to avoid 'death by worksheet.' Banished formal exams in the first two years of prep school and introduced extension lessons, known as Apprenticeships, in the timetable. 'Children are capable of far more than we sometimes offer.' Intellectual and erudite, is also a keen sportsman. Played hockey at county and regional levels and enjoys tennis, water polo and surfing. Wife Paula MSc (health psychology) has taught ICT as well as tutoring children with specific learning difficulties. They have three children, all in full-time education.

Entrance: Main entry points are nursery and year 3, although places are occasionally available in other years. Nursery places allocated according to date of registration; siblings have priority on waiting lists at other times. Short half-day assessment in November for those joining prep school the following academic year, which school says is 'not a rigorous hurdle.' Most pupils live within 30 mile radius, some weekly boarders further afield.

Exit: Many boys leave for Canford or Winchester College, a steady few with music and academic awards. Other boys and girls scatter far and wide, but most popular destinations are Bradfield, Godolphin, King Edward VI, Marlborough and St Swithun's. A clutch of academic, music and drama scholarships in 2018.

Remarks: Main school building, a beautiful Queen Anne house, is set in over six acres of playing fields and surrounded by the South Downs. Moved to its present location in 1809 from premises in nearby Twyford and can probably trace its origins back to the mid-17th century. (A Latin grammar book has turned up bearing the inscription 'Twyford School, 1775'.) Boarders still live in original house, which has a pretty Victorian chapel, oak-panelled library, atmospheric old school hall and large modernised refectory. Teaching takes place in a collection of modern buildings dotted around quadrangles.

Lots of hard work going on for CE when we visited; most pupils aim to sit level 3 in subjects across the board (some level 2 if appropriate). 'Dr Bailey has increased the aims and aspirations of the children.' All subjects are taught in forms until year 6, except for maths, which is set from year 4. From year 6, pupils are divided into three sets for all subjects; in year 8, they are divided into a scholarship and Winchester College entrance set, and two common entrance sets. French is taught from nursery and Latin from year 6. The bespoke 'Learning qualities programme' encourages children to think more independently and take responsibility for their own learning (praised in an ISI school inspection). Classrooms are modern, bright and spacious; science labs are immaculate (including snakes!). Class sizes average 16-18. ICT provision is well planned, with an ICT suite providing a weekly lesson for all year groups. In the prep school every form has a full set of Chromebooks which are used on a regular basis in lessons and preps. Five SEN specialists help with (mild) learning difficulties and around 70 one-to-one sessions (including pre-prep) were timetabled when we visited. These are free, but school doesn't take children who need more than one session a week.

Traditional prep school sports for boys and girls, with matches on Wednesday and Saturday afternoons. First and second teams have an excellent sporting record in fixtures against other schools. School tells us it 'has addressed girls' sport' by drawing up C and D teams and organising more fixtures, and everyone gets on a team the majority of times. Pupils also compete in swimming, water polo, athletics, tennis, lacrosse and girls' tag rugby. School is a 'centre of excellence' for girls' cricket in Hampshire. Large gym and indoor 25m swimming pool sit side-by-side, with 25m traversing wall outside. Has several all-weather courts for tennis and netball, plus Astroturf for hockey and football. 'Sports day is fabulous.' Netball teams have had success at regional and national IAPS tournaments (with the U12 team recently winning the nationals) and individual footballers at national schools' level. Other pupils perform at county level in cricket, cross-country running, hockey, rugby and swimming. Court Cricket, invented at Twyford and played here for at least a century, is still in robust health at break times.

Outstanding art and DT departments, probably the best we've seen for quality of work. The standard of painting and ceramics is excellent and on display around the school. DT is also very good with some really imaginative work (high level of design) on show, eg insect 'hotel'.

Music block sits in unusual amphitheatre setting overlooking tennis courts. Bright, airy performance space upstairs with several practice rooms on lower floor; more pianos are dotted around elsewhere in the school. More than 80 per cent of children learn at least one instrument, including the less usual, eg harp, drums and bagpipes. Lessons are fixed for older children and rotate for younger ones. School is a centre for ABRSM and Trinity College music exams and many pupils pass these at higher grades. Three school choirs, including a show choir, school orchestra and various ensembles give occasional concerts. Drama is a weekly lesson for all taught by specialist teachers and more performance space in Mulberry Pavilion. Dance (ballet, modern and tap) is on offer as a lunch time club. Regular Shakespeare workshop for year 8 takes place after CE.

Apprenticeships (Saturday activities) are compulsory for all children from year 4. Activities become increasingly academic further up the school, and include ancient Greek, Arabic, critical thinking, debating, fencing, Mandarin, music theory, philosophy, photography and horse riding. Everyone chooses a different apprenticeship each term, and 'children often get their first choice.' Staff run weekday clubs after school, eg art, cookery, judo, water polo and yoga. Outdoor education programme, eg navigation, orienteering, shelter building and survival techniques, 'encourages children to solve practical and physical problems.' One residential course away for each year group every year; in school there is a treehouse complex with outdoor classroom and advanced adventure playground.

No longer offers full boarding, but can arrange for long-distance boarders to stay with local guardians on Saturday and Sunday nights (currently eight weekly boarders). Otherwise, most children board a few nights per week from year 6 in preparation for going away to senior school. Dorms for younger children; cosy two-man (or girl) cubicles for year 8s allow more privacy and the chance to room with a friend. We noted clean, well-appointed bathrooms, a comfortable common room and plenty of storage space for belongings. Weekly boarders have limited use of mobile phones (matron keeps phones at all other times). Parents full of praise for boarding houseparent, also head of sport.

Excellent meals are served cafeteria-style and atmosphere is informal; children can sit where they like (we didn't notice staff on each table). Perhaps (enviably) this isn't needed, as school works hard to instill a broad set of values in its pupils. Regular services in chapel throughout the term are reinforced by anti-bullying PSHE lessons and constant vigilance by boarding and teaching staff (often around in the evenings running clubs or supervising prep). Everyone belongs to one of four houses and is assigned a house tutor from year 6. End of term team feast for house with the highest house point scores; individual high scorers are 'sent up good' on Fridays for jelly babies from the head (a Twyford tradition). Still has a friendly atmosphere, although parents say times are now more formal. Nevertheless they add, 'It still feels like you're part of a big family with much involvement.'

Pre-prep is going from strength to strength. 'The nursery is outstanding.' Two classes in reception and year 1 grow to three in year 2, which is located in the recently built Forest Lodge. Nestling in the trees, Forest Lodge provides three spacious, bright and airy classrooms for year 2 – windows at child height is a nice touch. Children grouped for phonics and spelling ability; reading is taught both individually and in groups. French and music learned from an early age. Homework is limited to spelling, reading and topic work, eg Knights and Castles. 'It's a really full-on day.' Has small SEN room and ICT suite.

Lots of outdoor play; recent additions include a wooden covered outdoor classroom, giant Connect 4 games, a wooden train, outdoor musical instruments, a theatre stage and an outdoor adventure play area and biketrack.

All attend chapel services and use the pool and library. Puts on annual show for 'grandparents' week', where little ones can show off their music, ballet and ESB exam preparation. Clubs include gardening, hand bells, ukulele and recorder ensemble. Most go on to join prep school in year 3. Universal feeling from parents is that school is at capacity; would like to see new pupil numbers capped.

A relatively wide mix of families, but it's safe to assume that most are comfortably off. Two 100 per cent bursaries (means tested) for new children joining as weekly boarders in year 7; sibling discounts are limited to five per cent for third and subsequent children. Boys and girls are polite, confident and increasingly aspire to top schools. Old Twyfordians include Alexander Pope, Douglas Hurd, Hubert Parry, Mark Tully, Thomas Hughes and, more recently, The Apprentice winner Tom Pellereau. Very active Twyford Society keeps ex-pupils in touch.

Although well into the process of changing to a school with a much greater focus on academic success, Twyford is still a friendly school where parents enjoy being part of the 'family'. Will continue to send a good number of boys to Winchester College, but is clearly aiming just as high for girls and boys going on to other schools.

Upton Court Grammar School

Lascelles Road, Slough, Berkshire SL3 7PR

Ages 11–18 **Pupils** 1,028 **Sixth form** 280

01753 522892
www.uptoncourtgrammar.org.uk

Head of School: Since September 2017, Mark Pritchard BA (French studies) MA (comparative education). Previously a teacher here for nine years, working his way up to head of key stage 4, he left to become assistant principal of Ark Burlington Danes Academy, then interim principal of its primary school before returning to Upton Court as head. Has also been assistant principal of Upton Court Educational Trust.

Down-to-earth, mild-mannered and aimable, pupils say he is 'charismatic' and 'always around.' 'It's not like at other schools, where the headteacher is this distant, scary, authoritative figure – he's on the gate every morning and afternoon and the bus stop,' said one pupil, although another told us 'he's stricter than the last head.' Recent trainee teachers (this is a teacher training school) commented on how impressed they were that he eats in the canteen, freely chatting to pupils, many of whom he knows the names of. Teaches French – 'including all the marking, because it's important to keep a hand in.'

Most parents told us they have little or nothing to do with him, although one said, 'I've definitely noticed a change in rhetoric since he joined that recognises how putting a lot of pressure on children is not healthy. And I even heard him talking about mental health – a first for this school. So I hope it's more than lip service.'

Academic matters: Progress and attainment measures have put the school as top of the local area, including ahead of all other grammars, for the last three years. The school consistently achieves +1.0 for progress 8, which shows good value added. In 2018, 58 per cent graded A*-A/9-7 at GCSE and at A level, 57 per cent of entries were A*/B, 28 per cent A*/A. Encouragingly, pupils told us they get to pick subjects they enjoy, not the ones they'd told to do or offer the best job prospects, although some parents criticise that everyone has to do RE at GCSE. 'I think it's because it's low hanging fruit and bumps the grades up, but the consequence is that students are only allowed to do one other humanity and if they want to do an arts subject they have to drop that other humanity,' said one. Most pupils take 11 GCSEs, with maths and English achieving particularly good results (around a quarter get grade 9), while chemistry is another stand out subject. At A level – where three is the norm – a broad range of traditional subjects are on offer, with most pupils taking maths and at least one science. Impressively, the school collaborates with St Bernard's (Catholic grammar) across the road to offer subjects at both GCSE and A level that have less take up, such as classics.

IB no longer on offer, although school says it has 'retained some of the best bits', including EPQ, an enrichment course on the theory of knowledge and the CAS (creativity, action and service) programme, which gets pupils developing a new skill, doing something like fundraising or improving the community and helping in school or showing leadership (it's not uncommon to see clubs and extra classes run by sixth formers here). Head says it's all part of the school being 'keen to move away from the traditional grammar model of exams being the be-all-and-end-all – we value personal enrichment as much as academic aspirations.' Perhaps not all parents have been kept in the loop as one told us, 'The school is still very exam orientated, in my view. I would like there to be more education in the broader sense.'

Relatively little setting – maths from year 7 and English and sciences from year 9. French or Spanish from year 7 which is continued through to GCSE. Average class size of 26 up to GCSE (then smaller), with lots of praise for teachers, all of whom are subject specialists and 'many have doctorates,' said one wide-eyed pupil. 'They really get to know you, so they know what motivates you when it comes to learning and they know what path you want to go down and how to help you get there,' said another. But one parent told us this can be a double-edged sword: 'They expect the children to know where they are going in life and demonstrate that they are on the right path, which can be great for some children but scary for others who may not make those choices until much later.'

Support is, say pupils, both 'comprehensive and well organised', with back up ranging from topic clubs to surgeries and revision sessions (notionally voluntary but attendance strongly recommended and absences logged) to after-hours homework club. Everything is run either by subject teachers or, increasingly, by older pupils. In fact, initial one-to-one sessions for year 11s, run by sixth formers, were so successful that pupils can now book themselves an Oxbridge style one-to-one tutorial with fifth or sixth formers. 'My daughter told me if there's anything she doesn't understand in the lessons, there's always extra support on offer in one format or another,' one parent told us.

As with most grammars, relatively low numbers of SEN. Unusually for a selective school, though, this one opts for full immersion, with a warm, experienced team on hand to deliver the goods. Autism and dyslexia crop up with reasonable frequency, as do wheelchair users. 'The support is fantastic – they are God's gift to SEN,' one parent told us. 'They have been helpful and sympathetic and know when to step forward as well as when to step back, as well as providing assistance in terms of both personnel and equipment.' Another told us the SENCo office is seen as 'a place of comfort by my child – just how it should be.'

Games, options, the arts: Sporting talent is considerable. As well as individual successes (an 800m county champion and a student who plays for England in badminton among them), there is also a decent run of good team results, although the head was not able to reel off any examples when we met him (we later learned the year 8 and 9 boys' football teams have both remained unbeaten for the entire season and the year 8 girls' rounders team came second overall in the district). A small number also take sport/PE at GCSE. Annual sixth form sports day is a nice touch, featuring all the retro favourites, egg and spoon and sack race amongst them – brought back as a centenary celebrations special and so popular it has become an annual fixture. Yoga and mindfulness now on the sporting agenda 'in recognition of preparing pupils for the 21st century' and there is no shortage of less obvious sports such as rowing and rock climbing. Current facilities may not impress (although there's plenty of green space) but the new sports hall, four courts and multi-use games area currently under construction are likely to give opponents considerable pause for thought – due to be completed summer 2019. 'Both my children have loved sport here – the school attracts young, enthusiastic sports teachers who are just brilliant,' one parent told us.

Drama splendidly high profile, with lively lessons in new roomy drama studio often shared with St Bernard's. Popular at both GCSE and A level, with impressive results. Productions bring together the talent of the whole school (on and off stage) and are often written by drama teacher.

Music, says school, has whole calendar of events, ranging from battle of the bands to local concerts, often teaming up with drama. But there's only one orchestra and choir and relatively few have individual music lessons in school. And there's not much take up at GCSE or A level, although it remains on offer. Ditto for art. One parent told us, 'I think it's because the provision is limited. It's a vicious circle, I suppose – there isn't the take-up to offer the provision, but without the provision there never will be big take up.' Pupils, too, said they'd like to see the school make more of music.

We were surprised so many parents said there are 'no clubs to speak of,' but pupils explained most extracurricular takes place during the school day, including lunchtimes, on account of the school recognising that many travel long distances ('up to two hours,' say pupils) to school, 'so they need to get home once school is finished.' Everything from DofE to school newspaper and origami to coding is on offer, along with many student-led ones (one pupil we spoke to had just set up a medical ethics club which was attracting significant numbers). 'The most popular clubs are sport, though,' one pupil told us. Some noteworthy trips on offer, including to Google offices in California (computing trip) and Amsterdam (joint biology and art trip) to visit the Van Gogh museum and Body Worlds expo, plus annual ski trip and a month in Borneo volunteering – 'a kind of mini gap year in the holidays.'

Background and atmosphere: You can see Windsor Castle from the road, we were told – and what better metaphor for aiming high? Aspirations apart, it's been all change, several times over. Founded as a co-ed selective school in 1912, it split into separate boys' and girls' grammars in 1936, reforming as co-ed only in early 1980s on the current site, wheel coming full circle in 1993 when it regained its original name. Alumni, known since 1915 as Old Paludians (marsh, or slough in Latin) have had no such identity issues. Only downright loser is original school building, whose remains lie beneath Thames Valley University tower block.

A £25m refurb means the site has changed this learning environment beyond recognition. The original 1930s building now has plush oak flooring, modern white walls, roomy classrooms and 10 stunning science labs. In addition, there's a separate new block with specialist classrooms including drama studio, food tech (where we saw year 7s busy making fruit salads), DT room, computer rooms and vast canteen and sixth form centre (with three areas – one for group study work, one for private study and a mammoth common room – 'catering for every kind of learner,' pointed out one pupil). All spacious, light and airy. Towards the back of the site, there are older blocks for humanities. It was heads-down in almost every classroom we visited – 'you don't get low level disruption here – nobody would think to talk in class,' a pupil told us.

But while surroundings might be ultra-modern, what won't change is the old-school formality of staff titles. Male staff, conventionally enough, are 'sir' and females are 'ma'am' (to rhyme with 'harm'), which replaced 'miss', formerly in use, which was reviewed and found to be lacking gravitas. Applies to everyone – even we as visitors got our Judi Dench/Skyfall moment.

Food 'good', according to pupils, although queues can be long. We particularly liked the way that pupils are able to order giant celebration pizzas for friends' birthdays and the fact that pupils get to give input to the menus. As it's all prepared in house, the school now provides lunches for other local schools.

Pastoral care, well-being and discipline: Pupil support is commendably huge part of school's behind the scenes work and vital too given that pupils, who may have only IQs in common, come from backgrounds that range from well to do to anything but (including some who are the main carers for family members with debilitating physical or mental health issues). Team includes part-time counsellor, student welfare co-ordinator and there's access to an educational psychologist. Every child has a tutor who meets with them and their family at least once a year. 'We start with their aspirations, both academically and personally, and the tutor is the coach to help them reach that goal.' Though we wonder how many of those aspirations are of the parents, not the pupil, with school saying, 'It's not unusual for a year 7 to come in saying their family wants them to be a surgeon, and we're fine with that.'

No soft touch when it comes to boundaries, which are clear cut. No-nonsense approach extends to instant fine of litter pick if you're caught dropping rubbish; in-class bans on mobile use; and insistence on correct uniform (worn by all, sixth form changing blazer colour but little else). But it's not punitive, insist pupils. 'The teachers treat us like young adults – everything is done with respect not bossiness.' 'Behaviour is genuinely outstanding,' claims school. 'Pupils have high expectations of themselves.' No permanent exclusions in living memory; less than a handful of temporary ones, 'usually for poor choices.' Carefully managed process, involving the whole family and support with reintegration ensures 'zero repeat offences.' Goodness of all sorts is rewarded with house points leading to annual presentation of trophies, dominated by The Beast. So big it looks as if it could eat tiddler cups for breakfast, it's awarded for academic success, a (perhaps) not so subliminal message about what really matters in life.

Bullying dealt with seriously – 'we follow up with everybody involved.' But school prefers positive messages about being kind than promoting itself as an 'anti-bullying' school. Pupils we met said they couldn't 'imagine bullying as we are genuinely supportive of each other.'

Pupils and parents: Widening diversity of backgrounds, with nearly half Indian descent, followed by Sri Lankan Tamil and Pakistani; white British accounts for under seven per cent of intake. Considered a great cause for celebration, 'with no cliques,' say pupils, who are an incredibly cohesive group, with many cross-year friendships. We found them articulate, unassuming and grateful, underpinned with a rich vein of understated humour. It's the geography that defeats many parents, wide radius (home counties and London fringes) making socialising a near impossibility.

Entrance: Over 10 applicants per place, of which there are now 165 available in year 7. 'We are one of the strongest first choice schools in Slough – it's no longer enough to pass the 11+, you also need a high score,' says head. Families apply not just from surrounding boroughs, but up to two hours away. At least the tests, administered by Slough Consortium, take some of the pressure off pupils, who take just one batch of tests for four schools. Parents told us pupils are usually tutored in preparation.

If unsuccessful at 11+, school remains off limits until sixth form entry when everyone, including school's own year 11 pupils, apply for places (minimum of two grade 5s and four grade 6s required, in addition to which there are subject specific requirements, the majority of which are a grade 6 if the subject has been studied at GCSE or a grade 6 in facilitating subjects if not; further maths requires a grade 8 at GCSE; and there are separate entry requirements for combinations of science subjects). That said, occasional places do occasionally crop up (in year testing still applies), subject to waiting lists.

Exit: Some 20 per cent pupils leave after GCSEs, some to follow specialised courses, others because they want more freedom than school is prepared to offer. A few take up apprenticeships.

For those who stay on, popular universities including Kings, UCL, LSE, Southampton and Warwick. Two to Oxbridge in 2018 and four medics. Most to solid bread-and-butter subjects from accounting to civil engineering to pharmacy. The range, however, reflects school's admirable philosophy which trumps all. 'We encourage children to go to prestige universities but it's whatever is best for them.'

Remarks: An increasingly selective, highly aspirational school, with a strong academic focus. But there's less pressure than you might expect, particularly if your child knows the path they want to take in life before they join (a surprising number do). There's a good dose of non-academics too, although some parents would still like to see more.

Vinehall School

292

Mountfield, Robertsbridge, East Sussex TN32 5JL

Ages 2–13 **Pupils** 233 **Boarders** 30 full (from 7 years)

Fees: Day £9,555 – £17,817; Boarding £20,916 – £23,208 pa

01580 880413
www.vinehallschool.com

Headmaster: Since September 2017 Jonathan 'Joff' Powis, previously deputy head and head of geography at Papplewick. Geography degree from Leeds; also has a TEFL qualification and is an ISI boarding inspector. An all-rounder, his interests range from coaching rugby, cricket and football to directing school musicals and singing tenor in the school choir. He also plays the trumpet and piano, and counts skiing, sailing, canoeing and mountain-biking amongst his hobbies.

Entrance: There's an element of selection because all students are expected to take common entrance or the Cranbrook Grammar exam. Prospective pupils attend a taster day, and not all will be accepted. Those seeking places in year 3 upwards do a maths, English and verbal reasoning test. There are a small number of pupils with dyslexia and dyspraxia, but none with autism. This is more to do with geography than the school's attitude – the specialist Frewen College which caters for these conditions is just five miles away.

Exit: Most popular destinations in the independent sector are Eastbourne College, Tonbridge, Sevenoaks, King's Canterbury, Benenden, Battle Abbey and Bede's, but pupils go on to about 16 senior schools.

Remarks: If a pig could talk, should you eat it? Does a dog know it's a dog? These are lessons with which children here wrestle. Philosophy is big on the curriculum at Vinehall as a way of broadening education. 'Common entrance is quite prescriptive, it's rigorous and there's a great volume of knowledge required, but we're concerned that we teach children to jump through hoops. But do they think for themselves?' CE curriculum has been revised and STEM is now on the timetable for year 4 and above. A lunchtime philosophy club has now extended to lessons in critical thinking in years 7 and 8, and 'puzzle it out' sessions for the pre-prep. It's highly popular with parents and 'sold the school to me,' according to one. Others mention 'a lot of self-directed learning, which really lights the fire'.

Staff are also working hard on turning around the school's previous reputation as academically elitist – one mother admits that local talk almost put her off viewing the school. 'If they are a potential scholar they will get a scholarship, but we want every child to be happy. Not every child is going to get a scholarship, it's the minority, not the norm. Some schools put huge pressure on the children, they are driven by fear of not getting into the next school. We want to be academically excellent, but not for children to feel a failure if they find certain aspects difficult.'

The pre-prep comprises a nursery (from age 2) and kindergarten (from age 3) all housed under the same roof as reception to year 2 to enable easy transition. It's a modern, bright building with its own hall and library and a woodland play area.

One parent with children in both parts of the school feels that the pre-prep is more traditional. 'The two environments are very different, pre-prep is very formal and structured, and I'd like to see more freedom,' she said. But the school says there has been a continuation of new innovations in pre-prep teaching, including the use of iPads, a Mandarin club, and higher-order thinking skills sessions.

The prep is situated in a Victorian mansion built by banker Tilden Smith as his family home – the head's study has glorious views over 47 acres of school grounds and miles beyond. Corridors and staircases are lined with shields, each one representing a past pupil and his or her achievements.

There's a separate Millennium building – with subject classrooms arranged around a hub with a library at its centre; also a computer suite, science block, music building, and art, design and technology centre. Subject specific classrooms are used from year 5. Years 7 and 8 have a scholarship form and two mixed ability common entrance forms, with setting for maths.

Reporting back to parents is thorough. There's an 'industry card' each half-term, which reports on how hard a child is working only, with full reports at the end of term. A system called 'classroom monitor' breaks subjects into component parts so that parents and teachers can be better informed about specifics to work on – in maths it might say, for example, that a child is good at co-ordinates, but finds algebra difficult.

One third of the pupils receive some form of learning support, which can range from work on posture using Swiss balls, because it can help concentration, to one-to-one support in lessons.

'The calibre of staff in the prep is outstanding,' said a parent. And all the parents praise the prompt attention to any worries. 'I had an issue this morning, they emailed back half an hour later, and it was done and dusted in an hour,' said one.

Everyone studies drama, and productions are staged in a theatre which could grace a small town – it has all the professional equipment and a 250 seat auditorium.

Sports facilities include an indoor swimming pool and a nine hole golf course. School is now 'very sporty', say parents.There are rugby tours, and teams take part in the National Schools Indoor Rowing League. Girls' provision has been revitalised, and they're now winning more matches.

No more Saturday morning school for year 7 and 8s – a previous bugbear for some children and parents. Instead, there is an optional enrichment programme for years 3 to 8 – including sports, crafts, and subjects such as astronomy, media and philosophy.

School day now shortened – lessons finish at 4.30pm with optional activity programme including supervised prep (whoopee, say parents) until the school buses leave at 5.25pm.

The school attracts a number of international boarders (around 45 per cent). Full boarding is available from year 3, but junior boarders (years 3 to 6) have the option to board for four nights a week, while year 7 and 8 can opt for full or weekly boarding. There's also temporary boarding for occasional nights. 'I like it that they don't push boarding too much and you aren't deemed second class if you're not a boarder,' one mother commented.

Minibuses bring local children in from all points of the compass including Hastings, Eastbourne, Lamberhurst, Mayfield, Heathfield and Cranbrook. Some parents work in the City but there are also families who find it more of a financial struggle, and they say there is no snobbery. Those who have transferred from the state sector say it's been seamless and they've felt welcome.

W

Walhampton School

Walhampton, Lymington, Hampshire SO41 5ZG

Ages 2–13 **Pupils** 360 **Boarders** 20 full, 40 weekly/flexi (from 7 years) C of E

Fees: Day £9,000 – £17,625; Boarding + £7,125 pa

01590 613300
www.walhampton.com

Headmaster: Since 2012, Mr Titus Mills (Eton, University of East Anglia and Oxford). Has taught across the spectrum, latterly as head of The Paragon, an independent school in Bath, and prior to that as head of St George's International Junior school in Rome and deputy head of St Mark's C of E school in Lambeth. Named Titus after the family donkey. Married to Jemima, who is involved in many aspects of school life, from meeting parents to arts and crafts. They have three young sons at the school.

Head is charming, his ease of manner no doubt stemming from his Eton roots; he is also warm, penetrating, and very enthusiastic. Mr Mills relishes a challenge: he has turned around schools in the past, and has a remit to do something similar for Walhampton. Not that it was failing, but he is there to make it fly – 'he's brimming with positivity,' said a parent.

Since taking up his post, head has swept through the school like a brisk wind, removing all dusty elements and making significant changes to staff, uniform, even the school emblem (the sticking out tongue has been lopped off the stag). He works 'at the speed of light' said a happy parent, and will respond to an email request within half an hour with an action plan.

Entrance: Non selective. Tests for placing purposes.

Exit: To more than 20 senior schools. Canford and Bryanston most popular, followed by Sherborne, Marlborough and Radley.

Remarks: Walhampton is exceptionally lovely, with glorious buildings and grounds. But there's something more than that: a feeling that your favourite childhood fiction might come to life in this place. The prospectus dust jacket (no, we've never seen a dust jacket on one before either) is just like the map in the front of Swallows and Amazons – there's Portmere pond for sailing, Sandwalk pond for fishing; even a Curly Wurly mountain. For Enid Blyton lovers there's the Faraway Tree and a Wishing Seat. Beehives sit in a wildflower meadow and there are stables, camps and bluebell woods.

Thoughtfully arranged library – books reserved for years 7 and 8 on one side, so the librarian can see if a crafty year 3 nips across to pick a book that is not age appropriate, although 'We don't really do [books full of teenage] angst here.' Library sessions each week, but library evidently used at all times: a jigsaw is always on the go – a child stressed out by a lesson apparently calms down after five minutes with a jigsaw.

Walhampton's stately past is not completely diluted by its school present. Standing on the terrace during break, watching the children at play, it is extraordinary to think this is a school and not a home. The family feel is underscored by the fact that many teachers live on site with their families.

Children are a lively, happy bunch and properly young: they all play at break time, including the enormous 13 year old boys, who looked as though they should already be at a senior school, but raced around, twisting each other on a tree swing. There are the usual number of screens here, but children are equally likely to enthuse about an outside activity – riding, flags or the tremendously popular 'escape from Colditz': children have to escape from an area of the grounds, in the dark, and get up to the headmaster's study and ring the bell. Staff, equipped with miner's lamps as headgear, try to spot and stop them. 'Wet, windy and wild,' says the school mag, The Mercury. This is a school where they are not afraid to get dirty; or take risks.

Manners well to the fore: children leapt to their feet as we went around and held open doors, one small child moved out of our way, saying decidedly 'good evening,' (just after lunch). With much fanfare, Mr Mills introduced new comprehensible school rules so kids understand what they've done right and wrong. Beach huts in house colours collect stag tokens, handed out for behaviour, effort and achievement – very popular with kids who love posting their tokens. Each half term the school, pupils and teachers alike, aims to develop a particular learning characteristic – perseverance at the time of our visit: clearly taken very much to heart by the children, and the determined cross-country runner who came in last, but persevered to the end.

Children feel that their views are listened to: school council got the water fountains it requested and also managed to secure something more yummy than banana chips at break. Food much improved since regime chance and was delicious on the day of our visit.

Head's main focus has been on increasing academic standards, and for the first time in the school's history two boys were awarded academic scholarships to Winchester recently. Subjects are traditional (Latin is compulsory), but learning comes alive here: the Battle of Trafalgar takes place on one of the ponds, and ditches are currently doubling as trenches for WW2 enactments. History, understandably, is a tremendously popular subject. The head is keen to take learning outside as much as possible and as a result this was one of the most deserted schools we have ever toured. 'Mud is part of the curriculum,' said one member of staff. New outdoor classroom in the woods with firepit for winter warmth and canopy for summer shade. Class sizes range from 15-20.

In the pre-prep the little ones have wet weather red dungarees, coats and wellies and potter around happily with Ella and Daisy, the pre-prep hens. There's a outside area, Owl corner, with bushes to hide in, a wooden stag to climb on, and a rope to pull yourself up a steep slope.

Learning support provided across the spectrum. Although most fit mild to moderate categories, there are a few children here with severe dyslexia. Support charged as an extra, but 'not expensive,' said a parent. LSU provides 'exceptional support,' said parent of a child with dyslexia. 'No stigma,' and kids likely to help each other with difficulties. EAL support available.

Pupils know who to go to with problems and bullying is dealt with promptly. Parents feel that pastoral care here is very strong. 'The time and energy which goes into each child is remarkable,' said one. Most parents attend chapel on Friday nights – 'a lovely way to round off the week.' Kids say what they want to pray for – there's usually a rabbit or a finger shut in a car door (although the school is 'not deeply religious,' the mum added).

Head of sports sees works hard to engage children who say they don't enjoy sport – how about trying archery or golf? Great to see the girls learning rugby. Six Oppies (sailing boats to the rest of us) recently purchased. Riding is extremely popular-anyone for buzkashi? (a Mongolian game played with the stuffed hide of a goat). Even if it's not your turn to ride, you can always go down to the stable and fling your arms around a pony.

Well-equipped music rooms in new music block and over half of pupils learn an instrument. Pop bands – The Stags and The Does – as well as a selection of choirs and orchestra. Joseph was in its final rehearsals, and sounded good – a hefty show for a prep school.

There are around 20 full boarders, and up to 40 more flexi boarders – popular with busy parents For those who suddenly find themselves stuck in a late meeting, emergency boarding is a bargain.

Accommodation has been renovated and new handmade 'bespoke' bunks aim to 'create a dream bedroom where children feel relaxed and at home'. Things are kept very neat – posters are carefully framed – no bluetac and tatty edges. Nice little kitchens with cereals for any time and tempting hampers of healthy snacks. All kids come into school on Saturday for activities and boarders have special trips out on Sundays.

Parents are well heeled, lots of professionals and businesspeople. Apparently it used to be a school where grandparents paid the fees but this is no longer the case. Most pupils are from the surrounding area, including the Isle of Wight, but some also from London and overseas. Academic scholarships awarded to internal or external applicants from year 2 upward; sports scholarships of up to half fees from year 3 upwards aimed at those talented in a range of sporting disciplines who would not otherwise be able to afford to come to Walhampton.

Walthamstow Hall Junior

Linked with Walthamstow Hall Senior

Bradbourne Park Road, Sevenoaks, Kent TN13 3LD

Ages 3–11 **Pupils** 163

Fees: £11,775 – £14,850 pa

01732 453815
www.walthamstow-hall.co.uk

Headmistress: Since 2013, Diane Wood BSc. Educated at Manchester High School for Girls and the University of Durham, where she stayed on to complete PGCE in primary education after studying psychology. Also has certificate in education from Oxford Brookes University.

After teaching in state schools in Hampshire and Buckinghamshire, she moved to the independent sector, spending more than a decade in two GDST schools – Sheffield High School for Girls and then Sydenham High School in London where she was a senior teacher.

Stephanie Ferro is overall headmistress of both senior and junior schools.

Entrance: Non-selective. Most children join in the nursery and entrance is via an informal chat with the parents and a one hour taster session for the children to make sure they are ready to start school. Older girls attend a taster day when their English, maths and social skills are assessed.

Exit: About 30-40 per cent move on to the senior school each year but have to take the same entrance tests in maths and English as external applicants. Lots of discussion with parents about the next step and plenty of warning if it is thought their daughter won't pass into the senior school. Others to a variety of state and independent schools including Tonbridge Grammar, Weald of Kent Grammar and Kent College – girls are well prepared for all entrance exams including the Kent Test.

Remarks: Down a quiet road on the edge of Sevenoaks in a large, light and comfortable Edwardian house with many additions – all sympathetically done. Fresh paint and everything in good condition and an atmosphere of ordered calm and purpose. Lots of silverware displayed in the hall with cups for everything. Moved here from a house in the grounds of the senior school in 1992 and the short distance between the two means that the junior school has a separate identity but with all the benefits of a 'big sister' up the road. It uses some of the senior school facilities like The Ship Theatre and indoor pool but remains very much a self-contained unit with a different uniform and good facilities of its own including a large multi-purpose hall and a dining hall. Lots of outdoor space including the Dell with playhouses and bushes for making dens, a new wooden ship play structure, plus use of an adjoining sports field.

Girls are taught as individuals which means different abilities can be accommodated within one class with individual education programmes for the gifted and talented and anyone with SEN. They are set for English and mathematics from year 4. About 20-25 girls need some level of SEN support, mainly for mild Dyslexia and extra help with mathematics – two part-time teachers. Recent academic scholarships to the senior school, Sevenoaks, Benenden, Woldingham, Caterham and Kent College. Well equipped science labs with specialist science teacher. Emphasis on developing independent thinking and study skills and girls encouraged to think and find things out for themselves. Doing your best considered as important as being the best. Lots of cheerful art work about the place and three lessons a week with a specialist teacher from year 3. Own kiln for pottery and carpentry also offered. Many girls learn a musical instrument and everyone does class music right the way through the school. There are three choirs and a dedicated music centre.

Plenty of sport including pop-lacrosse, a gentler version of the game played in the senior school, also netball, tennis, rounders, cricket and athletics. Swimming particularly strong and a number of girls take part in national and county championships. Regular plays mean that all get a chance to perform – there are also gymnastics displays and class-led assemblies. Sixty or so lunchtime and after-school clubs include the usual music, art, dance and drama; chess is also particularly popular, with regular friendly matches arranged with other schools. Cookery club in the purpose-built mini-kitchen always oversubscribed.

Leadership roles taken seriously and each girl is given some responsibility – head girl, monitors, house captains, games captains or playing with the youngest children at break time. Year 6 girls run the library overseen by a librarian. Senior girls meet regularly with the head to discuss their responsibilities and carry out self-appraisals. Four houses, all named after female authors, with plenty of friendly competition in music, sport, swimming etc; each house chooses a charity to support.

A caring and nurturing school underpinned by Christian values, achievement is celebrated but house points are also awarded for effort and good manners. Parents have high expectations and are a supportive and happy bunch. Thriving parents association and each form has a social co-ordinator so all parents made to feel welcome.

Wraparound care now offered from 7.15 to 6pm.

Walthamstow Hall Senior

Linked with Walthamstow Hall Junior

Hollybush Lane, Sevenoaks, Kent TN13 3UL

Ages 11–18 **Pupils** 426 **Sixth form** 107

Fees: £20,070 pa

01732 451334
www.walthamstow-hall.co.uk

Headmistress: Since January 2018, Stephanie Ferro, most recently senior assistant head at Lady Eleanor Holles. Degree in ancient and modern history from Oxford, PGCE in classics and history from St Mary's Twickenham, and a masters in classics from UCL. A gap year as a youth worker in Essex after her Oxford degree inspired her to train as a teacher, a decision confirmed from her first lesson on teaching practice where she discovered the truth of the adage, 'Find a job you love and you will never work a day in your life.' She has taught in independent girls' schools for the past 25 years, with posts including head of sixth form at Tormead, deputy head pastoral at Wimbledon High and head of Redland High.

Academic matters: At GCSE in 2018, 71 per cent of entries graded A*-A/9-7. At A level/Pre-U, 40 per cent A*-A/D1-3; 72 per cent A*-B/M1-2. Girls are helped to develop 'smart' study habits so they can take part in all aspects of school life – music, sport, drama, art etc – and have an astonishing capacity for juggling time and taking things on. Curriculum and timetable very much set up for the girls and there is much discussion about teaching in the classroom and how to do it better. Girls take 17 subjects in first year including Latin, French and design technology. Creative textiles and a second foreign language added in second year. Most do RE GCSE early at end of year 10 with the majority achieving top marks. IGCSE in about 80 per cent of subjects and Cambridge Pre-U in economics, philosophy and theology and music. Particularly strong history department received Good Schools Guide Award for history teaching in the sixth form. Now offers the EPQ. Sciences taught separately from the beginning – top flight science teaching in modern labs part-funded by a grant from the Wolfson Foundation. Class sizes about 16 and not above 20 and much smaller in sixth form. Plenty of debate, discussion and interaction from early on – work in a team with teachers and lots of hands-on practical stuff. A 'stimulating, safe and challenging environment with high expectations for all,' according to one parent.

Most staff have been appointed within the last 10 years and there is a good range of ages and an increasing number of male teachers. A few staff flats on site for new young teachers. Five part-time teachers offer SEN support where required, mainly for mild dyslexics and maths support. Extra help in maths and English in small groups to year 7s.

In most cases girls can do the combination of subjects they want and 'twilight' GCSEs offered as extra subjects after school from 4.30-6pm for subjects that won't fit into the curriculum. Lots of help with UCAS forms from tutors and head of sixth form and sixth formers are taught in small seminar-type groups similar to university. Extra clinics to help children with homework and make sure everyone is doing as well as they can. All year 7 have to do cooking as part of PSHE and it is offered as an optional subject in upper sixth. Well-stocked and well-used library with panoramic views.

Games, options, the arts: Inter-house music and drama festivals and inter-house sport – all girls take part. All girls in years 7 to 9 do music, drama and art and about half take Trinity drama classes. Lots of plays every year and most girls involved in drama in some way, either on stage, backstage or with the music and lighting. Plenty of space for performances in The Ship Theatre and main hall as well as the new drama studio – drama is offered as an A level. According to one mother, 'Everyone is given a chance to get involved in a smaller and less pressured environment than many other local schools.'

Thriving art department, wonderful art and textiles rooms – both fine art and textiles can be taken at GCSE and A level and 3D design also offered. Music can be studied at Cambridge Pre-U in the sixth form and is a big part of school life under inspirational director of music.

Sport popular (new sports hall including gym and dance studio); many sixth formers continue with team games and there are a number of county netball and lacrosse players, and cross country runners. Swimming is particularly strong and at a high level. Girls usually find something they enjoy – gymnastics,squash and judo are options for those who do not like team games. Pilates and the fitness gym popular with the older girls. PE is offered as an A level.

Background and atmosphere: Affectionately and universally known as Wally Hall, it is one of the oldest girls' schools in the country. Founded in 1838 in Walthamstow as a school and home for the daughters of missionaries, it moved to its present arts and crafts building in Sevenoaks in 1882 – it was 'built on prayer with money raised from church collections', became the girls' grammar school under the direct grant system and is now a fully independent selective girls' school. Much building and refurbishment, mainly from fee income, in the last 10 years, most recently a new sixth form centre including extra science and technology areas plus IT hub. Many parents attracted by the fact that this is a small school although, as one observed, 'Girls do well here and get involved in everything, but a very ambitious girl might need a bigger environment'.

Pastoral care, well-being and discipline: School organised into three pastoral teams: sixth form, middle school (years 9-11) and lower school (years 7-8). There are six houses and this system means different year groups get to know each other. Competition between houses can get quite fierce (in the nicest possible way) eg sports competitions, inter-house performing arts festival, and each house chooses a charity to fundraise for. Members of the sixth form run the house events and organise rehearsals, costumes etc and all are expected to be leaders of some sort. Pastoral heads and form tutors provide guidance and mentor personal and academic well-being – girls review their own progress and set themselves targets and there is plenty of praise and recognition. There is good careers guidance and lots of time and care taken with UCAS forms and the school organises a programme of talks about university and beyond and also helps with work experience placements. Firm policies on bullying. Girls' views sought on whole school matters including food (which is extremely good) through school council and pupil/staff relations seem to be pretty good – they even invite their teachers to the leavers' ball. No Saturday school but girls often come in for matches, rehearsals, activities and Duke of Edinburgh. Assemblies three times a week, more than just a prayer and a hymn, and everyone expected to participate in religious education and regular collective worship (parents of other faiths may withdraw their children from these).

Pupils and parents: Broad mix of parents including high flying City types, local business people, medics, members of the clergy and youth workers. Mainly local English girls. When the school was set up it was serious about equipping girls to follow in their parents' footsteps and become missionaries; they needed to be adventurous, resourceful and brave and much of this spirit lives on in the present school. The school's emblem is a ship sailing on the high seas, and at the end of their time at Wally Hall the girls take part in a special 'setting sail service' when they hand over their prefects' badges to the year below. Girls tend to keep in touch and many old girls send their daughters here. 'Girls expect to do well and are not afraid to put themselves forward'; they tend to be grounded with a strong sense of purpose and of community and want to make a difference. Almost all girls in sixth form take part in voluntary service – nothing compulsory – many help with reading in local primary schools, working in charity shops and riding for the disabled and help out at the local old people's home (which was founded and is run by old girls). Girls not frightened to succeed in front of each other. The school works closely with parents and there is an active group that organises social events and raise funds for bursaries and 'frills'. Some indomitable campaigners amongst the old girls, who are often leaders in their field. Alumni include Beverley Hunt, professor of thrombosis and haemostasis at King's College, London and founder of the charity Life Blood, also playwright and triathlete; Janine Gibson, editor-in-chief of Buzzfeed; actor Victoria Boreham; Rowan Pelling, newspaper columnist and broadcaster.

Entrance: Entrance at 11+, 13+ and 16+. Not super selective. At 11+, interview with headmistress, head's report from the pupil's current school and written papers in maths and English in the autumn term a year before entry.

At 13+ interview with headmistress, head's report from the pupil's current school and candidates sit either general entrance papers (in maths, English and science) or academic scholarship papers (in maths, English, biology, chemistry, physics and another chosen subject).

Entry into sixth form via interview, school report and a minimum of seven GCSES at 9-6 with 9-7s in the subjects they wish to study.

Some 15-25 per cent of year 7s have come up from the junior school but have to pass the same test as everyone else. Otherwise from a range of local state primaries and prep schools. About 10 girls join sixth form each year from other local girls' independent schools and grammars, often because of the wide combination of subjects available. Occasional joiners into year 10 if things have not worked out at another school.

Exit: About 20 per cent leave after GCSE, some to co-ed boarding schools and some to the state sector. Around 10 per cent take a gap year, but most straight to university to study subjects including medicine, maths, modern foreign languages and various sciences. Exeter, Leeds, Westminster, Southampton and Bath popular, and around a couple each year to Oxbridge (two in 2018).

Money matters: About 10 per cent of girls on some sort of bursary. Various financial awards from the Founder's Bursary, which can cover nearly 100 per cent of fees, plus scholarships in drama, music, art, and sport worth up to 50 per cent of fees. Help also available for current parents in financial straits. Sibling discount offered.

Remarks: Thriving girls' day school in leafy Sevenoaks. Produces quietly confident young women with a 'can do' attitude and an adventurous spirit. The strong academic results are a 'happy by-product' of all this.

Watford Grammar School for Boys

Rickmansworth Road, Watford, Hertfordshire WD18 7JF

Ages 11–18 **Pupils** 1,372 **Sixth form** 380

01923 208900
www.watfordboys.org

Headteacher: Since 2016, Ian Cooksey MA (Oxon) MA (Lond) (40s). Read biological sciences at Oxford. A state sector stalwart, cut his teeth at stellar grammar Tiffin School, Kingston upon Thames, where he rose from biology teacher to assistant head. Moved as vice principal to Tomlinscote School, Frimley, before successfully taking King's International School, Camberley, out of special measures. His first headship was at top girls' grammar school, Dr Challoner's High, in Amersham where he spent four years before moving to WBGS.

Had big shoes to fill – his predecessor moved on to become regional schools commissioner – but reportedly became at home very quickly at WBGS, where he arrived to find 'an incredibly dedicated, passionate staff giving way above and beyond'. A linear thinker and communicator, says his key targets are threefold: to continue to aspire to academic excellence in a school he says has 'no weak links in teaching'; to ensure that every boy makes the most of the opportunities available to him (he describes the extracurricular programme as 'amazing') and to develop collaboration ('we're not an ivory tower and we mustn't behave like we are'). Focused on engaging more people in the development of the school – 'the more voices that can be heard, the better,' he says – and as such created an upweighted prefect team, each boy with responsibility for a different area of school life, with whom he meets weekly.

Calm, personable (although we did hear the big voice when boys needed to be told to stop talking during a fire drill) and completely at home in this most male of environments; parents say he's 'putting his own stamp on things.' Upping the ante on well-being and determined to create an environment that helps pupils prioritise skills that lead to success in life rather than just bag top exam results: 'we work hard to mitigate boys putting pressure on themselves', he says. Married with two children.

Academic matters: In words of head, school is 'unashamedly academic' and results bear this out. Results are on the up: in 2018, 94 per cent of cohort got 9-4 in both maths and English GCSE, with 60 per cent A*-A/9-7 grades. Stellar stuff considering only 25 per cent of the cohort is selected on academic ability. Head says highest value added is seen amongst the boys with the lowest attainment on entry who are 'dragged up by the cohort'. Trad curriculum sees boys trying one of two modern languages (French or German – the school chooses which) plus Latin in year 7, with at least one compulsory at GCSE; there's barely an ology in sight and the only 'studies' are religious and sports. GCSE options are chosen in year 8 with the syllabus starting in year 9. Top five sets take triple science. Head says there is a 'strong culture of maths,' describing results as 'extraordinary', with high numbers taking both maths and further maths at A level and external candidates attracted to the sixth form to ride these numerical coattails.

A levels equally strong, with 43 per cent graded A*/A in 2018 and 70 per cent A*/B. Results in languages and sciences particularly outstanding, as well as economics at A level. Parents cite history, politics and classics departments as 'fantastic'.

Setting approached sensibly with 30 pupils in maths sets 1 to 6, 20 in set 7 and just 8 in the bottom set. Exceptional SENCo, two full time specialist SEN teachers and an 'army' of LSAs support boys with additional needs, including a number with high functioning ASD (39 with EHC plans on the register at time of writing) although head is careful to point out that 'the low functioning tend not to thrive in this environment'. The word on the street told us before our visit that WBGS had the best SEN department in the area, but is it a victim, then, of its own reputation in this regard? 'To a degree yes,' says head. 'There is a limit to what we can do and parents should be aware of that before choosing us for our SEN provision.' Assurances that school does its very best to find best solutions for those for whom the pace is just too fast and parents say 'support comes in really early' for those who simply need to be put back on track.

Games, options, the arts: No less than 21 competitive sports grace the WBGS fixture calendar, which sees 90 teams a year compete in around 600 fixtures against local heavy hitters from the independent sector as well as local district schools. It's rugby, hockey and cricket – no football, although our nerves were put to the test crossing the playground at break for fear of flying balls (quieter souls needn't worry – the hall was also awash with boys catching up on their social media accounts), so all's not lost for die hard footballers. Pupils split into three sets according to sporting ability with gentler options, eg table tennis or rounders for the less keen or able and parents say that it really isn't an issue if sport isn't your thing – in fact, you can get through school doing the bare minimum if you choose. Block fixtures take place at weekends with over 10 most Saturdays, sometimes with up to half a year group out representing the school. Recently every year 7 child played a competitive fixture: 'We have the outlook of an independent school but are more sensitive and subtle with it,' says director of sport. Hockey and cricket particularly successful and plenty of minor sports like cross-country, badminton and basketball on offer. Increased focus on inter-house matches and an impressive tour programme – hockey teams recently to Holland and South Africa, rugby to Argentina and Chile and cricket to Barbados.

Pupils describe music as 'phenomenal', comparing concert standards with those of the nearby specialist music school The Purcell. Now that's fighting talk. Twenty places a year awarded for musical aptitude (not to be confused with achievement) so not unsurprisingly there are (mainly traditional) groups and ensembles galore, including a joint orchestra with the nearby Watford Grammar School for Girls. Fabulous music centre, The Muse, with its 22 practice rooms, 200 seat concert hall, recording studio and music tech suite is best we've seen in any state school and over 270 music lessons take place every week. Three concerts per term and the music competition, which attracts 200 entrants, is an annual highlight. Parents who previously didn't know their sons had a musical bone are blown away by the passion inspired in them by the music teaching staff and the speed at which they skip through the grades. Not much on the tour calendar but head assures us this is an area for development – another of which is drama, which seemed sadly lacking in a school so rich with musical talent and facilities. What there is tends to err on the side of dramatic rather than all singing and dancing and pupils told us they 'just about' manage to put on an annual school play and have 'recently resurrected' the junior play. Small numbers do, however, take drama at GCSE. Art, although a thriving department producing super quality work, fails to attract large numbers at GCSE or A level, although recent upgrades to the facility may boost numbers.

Buzzing extracurricular programme with many clubs run by sixth formers plus frequent external competitions in eg maths and science. DofE thrives, with around one quarter of year 10 cohort working towards the bronze award.

Background and atmosphere: Started life as the Watford Free School, founded in 1704 by Dame Elizabeth Fuller, which then split into two single sex schools in 1884 and were renamed grammar schools in 1903. Like its sister school, has all the charm and character of a traditional grammar school (was, in fact, used as the set of the History Boys film): parquet floors, art deco tiles, panelling, honours boards and immense sash windows abound (augmented by the usual necessary more modern and, sometimes, less attractive add-ons of various architectural styles). All classrooms in main building have been recently refurbished and, thanks to the neo-Georgian windows, are flooded with light. The galleried main hall also oozes tradition, the walls adorned with portraits in oils of former headmasters. Good disability access on ground floor and school has track record in catering for profoundly disabled pupils. The generously sized library is equipped with fleets of gleaming new computers and quiet study areas for lunch time and after-school revision. Impressive food tech and DT facilities – school boasts CAD suite, multiple laser cutters and 3D printers. Decent playing fields stretch to the rear of the school and there are more off site, plus a good sized Astro. From year 9, pupils allowed to spend break times in nearby Cassiobury Park. The cherry on top is the large, modern sixth form centre with its galleried work and socialising spaces. Major investment in stunning new (2017) STEM centre.

Feels like the very large school it is. Eight form entry makes for an awful lot of boys and to visitors it's a buzzing and, at times, boisterous atmosphere. That said, school doesn't have a particularly uniform or macho vibe and parents of newbies say that despite reservations about size of school it is 'amazing from the outset'. Boys come, of course, in all shapes and sizes but there's also a feeling that this applies to personality types too – pupils say that 'everyone has their group' and that they 'welcome newcomers like a big family'. Parents concur that 'everyone can be themselves'. Despite strong academics, parents tell us that 'teachers encourage but don't push', although one or two whispers that parental pressure was an issue compared with other schools. There's a little bit of female influence via strong relationship with girls' school (schools have a shared Foundation Trust) with collaborations for trips, productions and some lessons at A level, eg sociology, DT, computer science and Latin. Mutterings from boys, though, that they 'have to wait' for sixth form for official socials.

Pastoral care, well-being and discipline: Two assistant heads oversee all matters pastoral with pupils' form tutors – who stay with them throughout school career – first point of contact. Head says that well-being is 'an area for further development' – although pastoral care is currently seen as a strength of school by parent body and pupils are aware of focus on mental health support, next step is to encourage self-referral. One-to-one counselling now available in school via external organisation, Safe Space. Although not pressured, parents say 'boys don't have an easy ride' and are kept on their toes with a grade tracking system, delivered online to parents each half term, setting targets for the next. Good behaviour is rewarded with 'double ticks', appreciated even by the older boys, and particular successes in class can result in handwritten postcards sent home by the subject teacher. Just one parents' evening per year with little written feedback in between – parents say they'd like more.

Head 'focused on promoting desirable behaviour' and, thanks to the critical mass of pupils striving to do well, has little cause to impose serious sanctions, with the exception of a small handful of fixed-term exclusions each term. Permanent exclusions are rare. School 'very quick to respond' when alerted to friendship issues or unkindness, say parents: 'they're very accessible considering size of school,' said one.

Pupils and parents: Reflective of local area, cohort is highly multicultural and demographically diverse, with around 10 per cent on pupil premium and about 25 per cent with English as a second language. Those who get in on distance tend to live within about a kilometre of school, with those on specialist or academic places travelling to school on tube from eg Northwood, Pinner, Harrow or Wembley Park. OBs (known as Old Fullerians) include the late comedian Terry Scott and former children's laureate Michael Rosen as well as a host of high profile sportsmen, businessmen (Steve Easterbrook, global CEO of McDonalds and Paul Donovan, former CEO of Odeon Cinemas are both old boys), politicians and media figures.

Entrance: Heavily oversubscribed but if you're smart enough to figure out the complex entrance criteria, you might be in with a chance of a place. There are 224 places available in year 7 for a combination of those living in the right WD or HA postcodes (we're talking 100s of metres from school) plus those successful in winning one of the academic or musical aptitude places that together make up around 30 per cent of the cohort (these also allocated according to postcode). Siblings, including those with a sister at Watford Girls, given priority. Apply by June for an academic or musical aptitude place – tests take place in September of the year prior to entry. Minimum entry requirement of six 6s at GCSE to join sixth form.

Exit: Around a quarter leaves after GCSEs – some because they didn't reach the minimum grade requirement to enter sixth form, others for apprenticeships or vocational courses at West Herts College. Around 60 per cent to Russell Group universities and 12 to Oxbridge in 2018, plus two medics.

Solid careers provision makes good use of successful Old Fullerians who visit to talk about their field of business. Parent body also volunteers to speak on broad range of career options and professions at newly introduced lunch time sessions for sixth formers.

Money matters: Active fundraising efforts by parents' association to provide eg equipment for new STEM Centre. Boys throw themselves into a host of money-spinning schemes by form from mufti days, movie nights and dodgeball tournaments to the recent year 12 25-hour maths challenge to raise money for local charities as well as the school.

Remarks: A popular and purposeful semi selective school which, according to parents, not only ticks the academic, sporting and musical boxes but also 'turns out real gentlemen'.

Watford Grammar School for Girls

297

Lady's Close, Watford, Hertfordshire WD18 0AE

Ages 11–18 **Pupils** 1,344 **Sixth form** 410

01923 223403
www.watfordgrammarschoolforgirls.org.uk

Headteacher: Since April 2018, Sylvia Tai, previously deputy head and then acting head following the departure of previous head Clare Wagner, who now heads West London Free School. Geography degree from Liverpool and PGCE from Oxford; fellow of the Royal Geographical Society. She joined the school in 2007 as assistant head, becoming deputy head in 2014.

W

Previously taught at Mill Hill County High, St Albans Girls, Tring and schools in Botswana. She is interested in developing global awareness and has travelled widely, both with the school and independently, leading school expeditions to places such as Mozambique, Borneo and Nepal.

Academic matters: School unapologetic about its fast pace and openly urges prospective parents to 'choose carefully', although parents told us there is 'definitely give and take' once girls are in situ. When pressed about SEN, defers immediately to the ethos of treating the most rather than least able as having extra needs: 'we drive girls hard and never accept the minimum.' Girls across multiple year groups uniformly (and with pride) use the word 'challenging' when asked to describe their school. Whilst bright pupils clearly thrive in this environment, the least able may be less well suited. However, there is a learning enrichment department to help girls with learning difficulties; school says they are 'well supported by our SENCo, specialist SEN teachers and all class teachers' and that all make good progress. Links with the local FE college enable the least academic to choose vocational courses to suit them.

In 2018, 74 per cent of GCSEs were 9-7; at A level, 40 per cent A*/A and 72 per cent A*-B – impressive given school's broad intake. No rigid setting system – girls are loosely set in maths in year 7 and in languages for GCSE. High flyers take triple science GCSEs, often leading to A level.

Staff and pupils say that maths is huge strength of school ('we have the largest A level further maths cohort in the area') with RS, Latin and art also getting a firm thumbs up. Sciences and maths are most popular A level subjects, followed closely by history: 'they all want to be doctors'. Two languages (girls can choose from French, German, Spanish and Latin from year 8) taken up to – and at least one at – GCSE. Strugglers in year 8 assigned a sixth form 'buddy' to tutor them in subjects they find tricky – with relationships often lasting way beyond a year or two. Unusually, EPQ now on curriculum so sixth form girls are trained in the necessary skills and assigned a specific tutor to guide their project. When it comes to university applications, girls say they are advised well and 'constantly reminded' to get involved in extracurricular activities to boost their CV.

Games, options, the arts: Girls can't decide whether music or sport is top dog – but there's plenty of both and all to a high standard. It's a very urban school, so playing fields are simply adequate, but there's an indoor pool, hard tennis and netball courts, impressive fitness suite and dance studio, and a fishes and loaves style feeling that the powers that be are skilled in making very limited budgets go an awfully long way. A and B teams are fielded for frequent matches in all the major sports, competing against fellow state but also private schools – 'and we often win'. A few grumbles from parents that if you're not picked for the A team from the outset, that's it – no chance, hence no real motivation to improve. Loads of opportunities for sports enthusiasts from year 10 upwards to help coach their younger peers in anything from swimming to football – one year 10 girl took it upon herself to start a club for year 7 girls who hadn't made it into the netball team, typical of the get up and go ethos that oozes from every corner of the school. Sport 'a bit half hearted' at the top of the school according to some parents, though school says sixth formers now encouraged to take part in a range of sporting activities with senior sports teams and a fitness suite.

W

Having heard the senior orchestra in full swing, we concur with parents, who describe school music as 'first class'. There are choirs, orchestras and ensembles galore, music in assembly every day and over 350 girls taking peripatetic music lessons. Drama has been less prominent, but is about to be added to the curriculum at GCSE and A level. There are plenty of productions to involve budding thespians, some in conjunction with the boys' grammar school. New arts centre should boost creative endeavours.

All girls have to participate in at least three extracurricular activities, mainly taking place at lunchtimes, one of which must be musical and one sporting. Clubs range from Spanish cinema and astronomy to 'groovy gamers', yoga or flamenco – definitely something to suit all tastes.

Background and atmosphere: Founded in 1704 by Mrs Elizabeth Fuller, the school originally taught girls to read, knit and sew as well as recite the Church of England catechism. It's come a long way since then and has none of that girly feel, but despite its multicultural cohort and thoroughly urban vibe, retains strong sense of a traditional grammar school (undoubtedly why it was chosen as the set for the History Boys). Panelled walls, parquet flooring and Victorian sash windows create a scholarly atmosphere and walls are laden with examples of work and information. There's an undercurrent of energy running through the school and an industrious and vibrant atmosphere.

Modern additions are the Food Factory ('we wanted to create a Caffè Nero style environment') – a casual dining room where girls can get hot food or healthy wraps and sandwiches – and the Hyde House maths block, completed in record time by the previous head side-stepping an earlier government's lumbering Building Schools for the Future programme by raising her own funds and organising the design and build. A new sixth form centre including a café is due for completion by April 2018. The library is well stocked and functional. Computers are everywhere, with girls allowed to use these for private study at their leisure, and there's a gleaming fleet of state of the art iMacs for music tech. Year 7s are gently eased into the school, spending their first year based in Lady's Close – an absolutely delightful modernised villa with its own beautifully landscaped walled garden, a sanctuary from the hustle and bustle of the main school.

The pièce de résistance is a fabulous futuristic glass dome (2015), an inspirational multi-use research facility (with a bird's eye view of the Elton John stand at Watford Football Club) which aims to extend the learning opportunities of A level science students. Funded by the Wolfson Foundation, it 'aims to nurture and inspire female scientists with high esteem, practical confidence and exceptional subject knowledge.'

Pastoral care, well-being and discipline: 'No major problems' – 'the worst we get is a stampede to the canteen on chip day.' School is, however, strict on uniform and behaviour: 'what other schools would deem nothing, we get cross about.'

It's seen as 'cool' to work hard and effort is rewarded as much as attainment at the annual prize-giving. Pupils set their own personal targets each term, with staff setting them clear academic expectations. Plenty of opportunities for responsibility at top of school. Head girl and four deputies elected by senior team and there are prefects for all subjects, music and sport, giving lots of girls the chance to shine.

Pupils and parents: Diversity at its best. Girls from all races, faiths and socio-demographic backgrounds are here in one seemingly happy melting pot. We were struck by how supportive they were of one another and without exception they look you in the eye and speak with great pride of their school and all it offers. With the arrival of two new Jewish secondary schools in the area, cohort is increasingly Muslim, although parents say that 'for the most part' differences in race and religion don't hinder friendships. Families largely hard working, dual income and it can be 'a struggle' to get them along to social events, but the fabulous Christmas Fair raises around £15,000 annually.

Entrance: Only those living in the very closest WD or HA postcodes need apply. Of the 210 year 7 places up for grabs,

45 academic and 18 music places are offered to outstanding candidates, 60 per cent of which are allocated for those in the nearest Watford postcodes and 40 per cent to those in the 'rest of the admissions area'. Eighteen places are then offered to those who live nearest but don't have a specialist place. Siblings are prioritised, including those with a brother at the nearby Watford Boys' Grammar. After siblings, remainder of places offered by distance from school to home. Sign up in May of year 5 for the aptitude and academic tests which take place in the September of year 6.

At least 65 external sixth form places. Both internal and external applicants must get a minimum of 46 points from the best eight GCSEs (or equivalent) including at least a 5 in English and maths.

Exit: Just under 20 per cent depart after GCSEs. Some 90 per cent of sixth formers to university with a respectable crop to Oxbridge each year (six in 2018, plus 15 medics) and many to Russell Group. Apprenticeships also encouraged where appropriate. Expert UCAS advisor based in sixth form centre on hand to guide girls in the right direction, and pupils we spoke to offered very positive feedback regarding help with applications and personal statements. A Face the Future programme in year 12 sees girls go through dummy application process for work experience, jobs and university, offering invaluable experience in interview technique – 'we really learned how to sell ourselves,' said one of our guides.

Remarks: WGGS manages to take rough diamonds of all backgrounds and abilities and polish them to a high shine. 'Phenomenal staffing' brings out the best in the girls and with the school's ability to deliver a truly rounded experience, you can be confident that you could send your daughter here, stand back and watch her achieve.

Wellesley House

298

114 Ramsgate Road, Broadstairs, Kent CT10 2DG

Ages 7–13 (4–13 from September 2019) **Pupils** 110 **Boarders** 25 full, 30 weekly **C of E**

Fees: Day £12,231- £19,917 pa; Boarding £26,331 pa

01843 862991
www.wellesleyhouse.org

Headmaster: Since September 2017 Gavin Franklin, previously a housemaster at Wellington College. Sport degree from Durham; represented British Universities at cricket and went on to play for Staffordshire and Warwickshire. Spent five years at the Oval, as performance manager in charge of elite player development, becoming a level 4 cricket coach, before moving to Wellington as assistant director of sport and English teacher. His wife Claire is also a Durham graduate and a teacher with an interest in sport; they have two young sons.

Entrance: Children can join at any time from 7 upwards – many from local day schools join at this age, with major intakes in years 5 and 6 particularly for boarders. Occasionally children join for the last year but it can be difficult getting up to speed for common entrance. Non-selective but entry via interview and reports and examples of work from the child's current school. Would only test if there were concerns about learning support or that a child might not thrive.

Surprisingly large catchment area with many coming from west Kent and East Sussex. About 15-20 from London with an accompanied minibus to Battersea at half term and exeats. Scholarships and bursaries available. Discounts for army families.

Opening a pre-prep in September 2019.

Exit: To a huge range of senior schools all over the country with King's Canterbury the most popular, others to Harrow, Charterhouse, Eastbourne, Benenden, Downe House, St Edward's Oxford, Sutton Valence and Cranbrook – great trouble is taken to pick the right school for each child. Over a third have won scholarships in recent years. Children hardly ever leave at 11+ and the school does not offer coaching for the Kent Test.

Remarks: Wellesley was founded in 1869 in Ramsgate and moved to its current purpose-built site in 1898, a light and airy red-brick building which has been added to over the years and which is surrounded by flower beds and playing fields. It merged with St Peter's Court in 1969 and went co-ed in 1977. It does not have the rolling acres of some prep schools but everything is immaculate and every inch of the grounds is used – there is plenty of room for den-making, a pond, vegetable plots and even some igloos when it snows. The playing fields are divided by an elegant avenue of trees which has been colonised by a group of noisy, bright green parrots. Lots of refurbishment recently and the squash courts, shooting range and the indoor heated swimming pool and barbecue area are all looking like new. Sunny, comfortable, well-used library with lots of space to sit and read and where children can curl up with a book. Each year group has its own common room – recently redecorated thanks to the fundraising efforts of the Friends of Wellesley.

Photographs of children past and present line the corridors and four rolling news boards around the school show BBC headlines, birthday announcements, notices and photos of recent events.

Avert your eyes as you drive through the cabbage patches and retail parks of Thanet – it is worth it. Many parents drive miles to send their children here, passing other good prep schools en route. It is a school which embraces the whole family and where friends are made for life: 'My daughter's best friends are still the ones she made at Wellesley,' said one mother. Parents, too, make great friends here – many a mother has been known to weep copiously during the leavers' chapel service. Old Welleslians often end up sharing flats together and there are usually a couple of Wellesley weddings announced in the school magazine. A busy, happy school where there is great emphasis on fairness and giving everyone a chance. Academic success is highly valued but good manners, tolerance and consideration for others are equally important. At the annual prize giving each summer, there are not only prizes for academic and sporting achievements but also the headmaster's prize which can be for anything from attitude and effort to just being a thoroughly nice person.

Younger boys live in Boddington House which is joined on to the main school and where they do most of their lessons and are cared for by a housemaster and a team of matrons, which gives them a very gentle introduction to boarding. They move over to the main school aged 10 where they are equally well cared for in large, light, airy and extremely tidy dormitories.

The girls live at the Orchard, set in its own grounds and surrounded by apple trees on the far side of the playing fields. The Orchard is run by Mr Nichol, who teaches geography and is in charge of the Thanet weather station, and his very elegant and bubbly Spanish wife, Elena, and it is very much a home from home. There is only space for 43 girls so it feels like a large happy family and is always oversubscribed. Bright, light dorms, all named after Kentish apples, with an abundance of pink and teddy bears on all the beds. One mother who was reluctant to let her daughter board said, 'I cannot deprive my daughter of the Orchard experience, it's truly unique'.

The school motto is 'Open up a world of possibilities' and this is exactly what Wellesley does. 'Children get noticed in a smaller school and get opportunities they would not get elsewhere', says the school. Everyone has 'a chance to shine' and with so many activities on offer virtually everyone finds something they are good at. Everything from photography and art, board games and chess, boys' hockey and girls' football, judo, fencing, riding at the local riding school, archery, cooking, needlework for boys and girls, even scuba diving, with the 'shrimp' course taking place in the school swimming pool. Golf is popular – there is a putting green in the grounds and the lucky few are allowed to play at Royal St George's nearby – this can lead to a certain amount of envy amongst the parents.

The average class size of 12 means that the school can support children at both ends of the learning spectrum. Children streamed from year 5 and setted in maths and languages – French (taught by a native speaker) and Latin are taught as part of the curriculum and Spanish can be taught by private arrangement. Very bright children can be stretched and academic scholars are either taught in a separate, accelerated class for the last two years or within the top stream – depends on the number of scholars from year to year.

The children are 'pushed and stretched with full support, and the school has pushed our son to be the best that he can be,' said one happy mother. School is quick to spot problems and about 20 per cent have some sort of learning support – some children taught within the class and some withdrawn but lessons rotated so they do not fall behind in any subject; close liaison between learning support and class teachers. Will go the extra mile for children with bigger difficulties. In class EAL support available for those who need it.

The school has recently been awarded International School status by the British Council, which means that the curriculum should have an international dimension to encourage children to have a more global outlook. It is already twinned with a school in India.

'The school achieves things it shouldn't for its size,' and it certainly punches above its weight on the sports fields. School puts this down partly to the close bonds that develop in a small boarding community and partly to the support and encouragement from staff. They are frequent winners of the JET cricket and rounders national competitions, much to the envy and astonishment of much larger and apparently sportier schools, and are always represented at the annual national athletics championships in Birmingham. One girl has recently been selected for the England athletics squad and a boy for England cricket training. There is a long tradition of cricketing excellence and alumni include England captains Mann and Cowdrey as well as the Loudon brothers and Sam Northeast, plus three day eventers and Olympic medal winners William Fox-Pitt and Georgina Harland.

Music is part of the curriculum throughout the school with all year 3 learning the recorder and all year 4 the violin, and about 70 per cent continue with at least one instrument; they will find a teacher for any instrument – one child is currently learning the harp. There are instrumental groups and an orchestra and the choir sings in local churches and at weddings; a recent highlight was a trip to Venice to sing in St Mark's on Palm Sunday. Two school plays a year as well as smaller form productions at Christmas mean everyone has a chance to get up on stage. There are also poetry and musical recitals and children are prepared for the LAMDA exams.

Colourful artwork displayed all over the school with 'six of the best' selected to hang in the head's study. Masses of outings and trips; most year groups visit France and year 7 has an outdoor pursuits trip to the Lake District for an 'educational adventure'. Various charity fundraising events throughout the year from cake sales to sponsored swims and fancy dress days – when children can put their sewing skills to good use. Burns Night is celebrated each year with haggis and reeling and there is a programme of lectures from parents and visiting speakers.

Lots of traditional boarding school parents as well as local professional families and about 40 per cent of boarders come from overseas. Arrangements can be made for children of other faiths, but most are happy to attend chapel twice a week and the full choral service on Sundays. Children not overly sophisticated and do not grow up too quickly but are still self-assured, confident and comfortable talking to adults. Usually about 60 children in at weekends with plenty going on and outings planned – ice skating, clay pigeon shooting, bowling or just going to play on the beach. The top year is allowed 'down town' into Broadstairs on Sundays where they can spend their pocket money – a much looked forward to privilege and many opt to stay in for the weekends just for this.

The Friends of Wellesley House organises social events and fundraising activities including lunches for new parents, quiz nights, the bonfire night and other parties.

A small and extraordinarily caring prep school with traditional values which produces self-assured and considerate children who go on to schools all over the country.

Wellington College

Linked with Eagle House School

299

Duke's Ride, Crowthorne, Berkshire RG45 7PU

Ages 13–18 **Pupils** 1,040 **Sixth form** 455 **Boarders** 850 full **C of E**

Fees: Day £29,040 – £33,360 pa; Boarding £39,750 pa

01344 444013
www.wellingtoncollege.org.uk

Master: Since 2015, Julian Thomas BSc MBA FRSA (apparently 50s, though looks about 27). Read computer science at King's College, London – not a common headmagisterial start. Took a Cambridge PGCE (after a brief brush with banking), winning a half-blue in rugby league. Taught maths at St Dunstan's College and Forest School, co-authoring several text books. Thence, as director of studies, to Portsmouth Grammar and on to Hampton School as second master for four years during which he took an MBA in educational leadership (international). Prior to Wellington, was head of Caterham School for eight years doing great things. Engagingly, he tweets as @Welly_Master.

Instantly likeable. Relaxed, open, friendly and clearly capable, Mr Thomas relishes everything about the college. Pupils feel known and engaged with. 'He'll just stop us and say, "What do you think of this?" about some idea or other. He really wants to know what we think.' And, 'He knows stuff about you. He'll just ask, "How did it go?" It's amazing.' 'Exciting,' was the word Mr Thomas used most often to us. And we heard it often from parents and pupils too. Wellington grows greater and richer in his care.

Leaving in July 2019. Robin Dyer, second master, will hold the reins until a successor takes over.

Academic matters: A place in which learning matters. 'It's cool to do well there – it's embarrassing if you don't.' Offers both A levels and the IB – 47 per cent currently opting for the IB. A level results are impressive overall. Maths and economics by far the most popular options; history and Latin get impressive results. Minority subjects, eg some languages and art history, also outstanding though a less starry showing in eg English, business and photography. All A level students also take the EPQ. Overall, 63 per cent A*/A grades in 2018. IB diploma average of 39 in 2018.

Mainstream range of GCSE subjects; results in maths and all three sciences are excellent. Of the options, history, geography and Latin are especially popular – Latin with spectacular results; Spanish and Greek also sparkle. Good choice of languages (now including Russian) but German no more buoyant here than anywhere else, sadly. Alongside the core GCSE subjects (which include one ancient or modern language), everyone takes two or three electives from a range eg computer science, dance and photography. Year 10s also take a level 2 EPQ. Overall, 87 per cent A*-A/9-7 grades in 2018.

Julian Thomas no longer publishes examination results for national league tables. 'A school like Wellington has a duty to do what's right in education,' he says. 'The things that really matter can't be measured by league tables.' We agree. This approach is supported by eg Harkness tables – large oval seminar-style tables to facilitate sharing rather than imparting knowledge. And, as independent learners, the pupils do much of the preparation for lessons. Every kind of modern IT device and programme abounds but most designed, again, to allow for sharing learning.

Two-weekly cycle of lessons – each one hour long. Regular monitoring, reports and 'interims'. Staff:pupil ratio of just over 1:6 which is remarkably low, although actual class sizes are not smaller than average. Some parental grumbles about the high turnover of staff: 'They do go. They like to have Wellington on their cv and then they get promoted.' But many long-serving staff, very few of whom have lost the light in the eyes.

Everyone is assessed on entry for baseline skills. Remarkably high number of mild or other deficits picked up at this stage – sometimes coming as a surprise to parents. Good support for the 10 per cent of pupils on the SEN register. Emphasis here as throughout on independent learning. Help delivered individually or in groups. Some forego a second modern language for individual support and maybe take one or two fewer GCSEs. One-off subject help sessions abound.

Games, options, the arts: 'If I stayed here for twice as many years, I still wouldn't get round to trying everything,' is a cry we heard over and over. 'You have to sign up for everything you like the sound of in College Carnival [freshers' week to you and me] try it all out, then make a longlist, then a shortlist and then try and do what you really want to. But it's still difficult.. and there is class work too..'

Sports, clubs and enrichment activities galore and any teacher or pupil with an enthusiasm is encouraged to start a club of their own. So – a tea drinking club when we visited where the members. er, drink tea. And a ukelele orchestra was in full swing. 'And our concert band is the biggest in the country.' 'Service' is central to the ethos, providing numerous initiatives to work here and abroad with the less privileged or less physically/cognitively able. They walk the talk.

Rugby rules – this is a quintessential rugby school. However, girls' sports are now firmly on the agenda and the new arena is upping both the provision and the profile of girls' sports to more of a parity. Though rugby will still rule! The third form can take dance as a curriculum option. We saw a class of excellent textile work but, sadly, not a boy in sight. WTV is an institution and produces professional quality broadcasting. New performing arts centre whose auditorium seats 900+ is complemented by TV editing suite, recording studios, concert rooms etc. Drama and music pretty spectacular anyway. Visits by professional companies of the highest order too, especially for the occasional Welly Arts Fests. Art in many media, DT and general creativity busting out all over. Trips, exhibition, visitors – it's all just too much.

Boarding: Seventeen boarding houses – 'inhouses' close to the main building, and 'outhouses' nestling in the grounds, some with their own dining rooms – each with its own character, facilities, traditions, lore and argot and each seemingly inspiring loyalty and affection. Houses bar one are single sex. High standard of bathrooms, showers etc. Lots of honours boards – new and old. Feeling that the character of a house much depends on the character of the sixth form boarders in a given year – some being more inviting and less exclusive than others.

Saturdays are full school days with lessons in the mornings and sports in the afternoons but most go home after that until Sunday evening. Around 150-200 boarders in school most weekends – obviously mostly those with families abroad – and a full programme of activities is on offer if you want it. Wisely, overseas boarders are distributed between the houses so everyone meets everyone. Four weekends annually when everyone is required to stay in school. Occasional grouses about the disparity between the houses in terms of upkeep, facilities – and sofas. More water dispensers around the site would be popular and also the introduction of bikes on which to get around – even if only for the older students.

Careful and thorough induction and acclimatisation activities to help newbies settle in – and to support their jittery parents. Masterclasses give parents a chance to take on eg social media, teenage eating and coaching. Countless events offer parents opportunities to feel part of the wider Wellington community – embraced enthusiastically by many but, of course, not all.

Background and atmosphere: By top English public school standards Wellington, which opened in 1859, is an upstart newbie. It was built as a monument to the first Duke of Wellington (the vanquisher of Bonaparte) by a grateful nation and Queen Victoria laid the foundation stone. But it stands proudly with our most illustrious schools and you cannot ignore the pride, the history, the tradition and the splendour of the place. Third form history is largely based on the college's own past and the extensive archives are a rich resource.

Four hundred acres – around half of which are playing fields, lakes (five of them), forest and gardens – embrace the college's main building: a surprising (given the essential Englishness of the place) exercise in low-rise, Rococo-chateau-red-brick designed by John Shaw Jnr (Prince Albert's choice). Chapel designed by G Gilbert Scott. Rarely for a school chapel of this size and capacity, this one has a warmth and genuine consolatory ambience. 'It's one of the things you never forget,' a wise alumnus told us. 'Maybe because Wellington is so modern and progressive, we love the chapel because you can think over the college history and what it was like here before.' Numerous later buildings – mostly in red brick – are in sympathy, even the newest glassy additions. The Mandarin Centre – complete with gold Chinese dragons, lake, bridge and traditional gateway – comes as a bit of a surprise. Quads – especially the Combermere with terrific central huge bronze of The Iron Duke's horse, Copenhagen – are simply stunning and the upkeep of everywhere is impressive. The V & A is the hip modern café and meeting place.

The forest and lakes abut the centre. The darkness of the close-growing trees add a welcome touch of the less formal and structured and people do take themselves for walks there, especially when – as they will – closer relationships develop in the sixth form or when a breathing space and solitude are needed. But the school life provides little time for such things – even in the sixth, there are only 45 minutes of free time, between 9.00-9.45pm.

Orderly, friendly, purposeful and relaxed. An air of engagement, quiet busyness and enthusiasm pervades the place plus a sense of privilege – not entitlement – and a focus on learning of all kinds. Parents seem universally thrilled: 'They generate a culture where it's all about having a go – nothing is impossible – there's such a buzz about the place.' 'It wouldn't suit everyone – you need a lot of energy and independence,' Interestingly, the word 'whacky' crops up a lot – meant warmly and kindly.

Wellington is now at the heart of a major global and national educational business with a portfolio of schools, several in China, and two academies here. This informs aspects of life on the home front – partnerships and exchanges and there is Dukebox – an online sharing platform for the entire family of schools.

Pastoral care, well-being and discipline: Famous for it – well-being, mindfulness, restorative justice, coaching, leadership, counselling etc – they explore and practise it all. 'Our children – who are all so different – are equally happy,' said one parent. 'I'd give it 10 out of 10 on the pastoral side,' said another. Carefully structured pastoral care system – every teacher is also a tutor and attached to a boarding house. But self-discipline is the norm. A school with rewards and punishments but punishments are rare and exclusions far rarer. Repeated bullying will see you out but isolated episodes seen as an opportunity for learning. Virtually all staff have training in coaching and this, alongside the school's Basic Courtesies, Core Values, and Mr Thomas's Five 'I's – 'Inspired, Intellectual, Independent, Individual, Inclusive' – underpin the tangible moral purpose of the place. 'The Stiff Upper Lip is long gone,' we were told. Nonetheless, some of the most forbidding uniform rules we have encountered (especially for girls). 'I like them to look smart,' says The Master. Vast dining hall (former school hall?) with excellent menus on a four-weekly cycle. We snaffled a memorable flapjack.

Pupils and parents: Majority of UK pupils come from west London and the home counties. School's weekly boarding policy adds to its attraction in the south east. Around 13 per cent come from state and non-prep schools; around 12 per cent from overseas – from 41 countries at time of our visit. Around a third of pupils based overseas are British expats. Interestingly, a good proportion of the UK based boarders are from non-British or dual citizenship homes. A genuinely inclusive and cosmopolitan constituency and a feature that is fostered by its schools overseas. Very few overseas boarders need EAL support – but those that do get individual help for which the college does not charge. Parents feel welcome here – 'I've never felt I shouldn't be on site. They are brilliant at involving us.'

Entrance: Around 190 pupils enter year 9 – some 110 boys, 80 girls. Around 900 apply. All candidates sit the ISEB common pre-test in the autumn term of year 6. References from present schools also sought. Long-listed candidates visit the college in January/February for an assessment day – a mix of collaborative problem-solving activities plus interview. Offers made in March – for entry from 2021, will no longer be conditional on passing CE.

Around 25 boys and 20 girls join after GCSEs. Sixteen-plus candidates submit recent school reports and a personal statement about a year before entry. Applicants outnumber places 10 to one. Long-listed candidates attend an assessment day in November of year 11 and sit three papers in the subjects they mean to study in the sixth form, plus a maths skills test and an interview plus group discussion. References too, of course. At least 7s expected in all subjects, 8-9s in subjects to be pursued in the sixth. Internal pupils also expected to produce 6+ 7s but there is always 'leeway if they are good citizens'. Attention paid at all levels to characteristics such as independence, inclusivity, grit plus the college's Virtues.

Exit: Penny numbers leave after GCSEs. Good proportion of Oxbridge places – 18 in 2018, plus three medics. High numbers also to, especially, Bristol, Durham, Edinburgh, Bath and Exeter but school plans to expand the breadth of destinations and wants to provide 'tip-top advice on all options' – including the modern, high calibre, degree apprenticeships path. Also a good number to the US and Canada (18 in 2018) – Wellington has led the way in sending its leavers to good universities across the pond. Runs the best conferences on this as on many other subjects. Tremendous list of notable alumni includes: Christopher Ewart-Biggs, British ambassador assassinated by the IRA, current politicos Crispin Blunt, Michael Spicer and Edward Garnier; Harold Nicolson, numerous sports jocks including James Hunt and Max and Thom Evans; arts and entertainment types eg Robert Morley, Nikolai Tolstoy, Rory Bremner, Sebastian Faulks, Christopher Lee, Will Young and Elize du Toit; the Beeb's Peter Snow and Robin Oakley; practically the entire British military including 15 holders of the Victoria Cross and hosts of other worthies in many fields.

Money matters: The international schools help to fund the school's burgeoning bursary fund – scholarships no longer carry any financial benefit, with funds now routed into means-tested bursaries, worth up to 95 per cent of school fees. Some £1.7m and rising annually available. Prince Albert Bursary Fund offers life-changing bursaries up to full fees to entrants who would otherwise have no chance of such an education. Ten holders at time of our visit. Foundation supports the children of deceased military officers up to full fees. Scholarships at 13+ for academics and music – art, drama, dance, design engineering and sport now offered at the end of year 9 after a full year at Wellington. However, students are invited to participate in Inspire Days in these areas during year 8 as an initial stage in the scholarship process. At 16+, scholarships are awarded in all of these areas.

Remarks: Hard to imagine it done better. A site and campus to dream about. A school with mind, heart, guts and a constant fizz.

Westbourne House School

Shopwyke, Chichester, West Sussex PO20 2BH

Ages 3–13 **Pupils** 356 **Boarders** 4 full, 1 weekly, 64 flexi (from 7 years) **C of E**

Fees: Day £10,650 – £18,345; Boarding £16,875 – £24,585 pa

01243 782739
www.westbournehouse.org

Headmaster: Since 2011, Martin Barker (BEd Exeter), deputy since 2007, previously at Papplewick in Ascot. Married to Helen, with two children. Keen to equip pupils with a broad range of skills and open minds to cope with the unknown world to come, and says, 'it's not the super pushy school people say it is. We do our best in all areas to be as good as we can be, but inclusivity really matters'.

Parents like the headmaster, describing him as 'fair'; 'kind...follows through and listens'; and 'solid, reliable and trustworthy'. They say that their children 'respect him and have the right level of awe...they wouldn't mess with him'. The word 'scary' did come up when pupils described their headmaster, but also 'nice', one adding that as you get older you can 'sit next to him at lunch and talk to him like a normal person'. And year 6s weren't too scared to throw custard pies at him at the end of their school play.

Entrance: Non-selective. Prospective pupils attend a taster day.

Exit: Feeds a wide range of senior schools, sending significant numbers to Brighton College and its almost opposite, Seaford College, plus Hurstpierpoint, Lancing and Portsmouth Grammar. In 2018, 39 scholarships.

Remarks: 'There's grass!', said a parent, asked why they chose the school, and indeed the immediate impression is of an elegant house, and grounds which stretch in every direction, including a woodland playground (no, they can't climb trees). '[It's an] amazing environment with lovely energy', said another. 'The kids always run into school. All three of them love it.'

The headmaster likes pupils to 'have a go' and hopes that confidence will flow from doing so. Personal development interests him more than anything else, a parent commenting, 'building happy, confident children is their theme'.

There are activities of every sort, from debating (against parents) to music of all sorts, and 'amazing drama productions' in their splendid theatre. Each year has a play, and everyone takes part, the headmaster's wife commenting, 'if children are shy, [they] get so used to performing and taking part, [they] don't seem so'.

Westbourne is of hothouse repute, but it's not so one dimensional. Certainly, there's an atmosphere of determined concentration in lessons, and they 'do push for excellence and scholarships', says the head, 'but it's just as satisfying to bring on the non-academic child. We're pretty diverse, and keen to emphasise personal bests.' Parents will send their children here to get them into the big named public schools, but Westbourne House, to its great credit, is non-selective and 'a much more healthy community [for it]', says the head. Achievement matters, but effort also gets recognised, say pupils. There is no doubt that the culture here is one of working hard: a notice on a board says – 'work hard until you don't need to introduce yourself'.

School chosen by one parent because they were 'impressed by the special needs support...'. The Individual Needs Department supports around 20 per cent of pupils who have academic, emotional and/or behavioural problems, in one-to-one or small group sessions, and is chargeable only if parents ask for support, not if the school identifies the need.

'I try to get brilliant staff. The rest takes care of itself', says the head, and parents report 'more strength within teaching staff than ever'. There are extra sessions during reading prep at the end of the day for pupils who need extra help, and personal tutors for year 7 and 8 pupils. By the time pupils reach CE, they are, say parents, 'not daunted or nervous'. '[It's a] really clever machine...[they're] so ready for it'. Parents feel the school is 'well structured with...goals in every different area'; 'focused' was also a word which came up quite a lot, one saying it is 'driven, but also nurturing'. 'We want results...', said one parent firmly.

There's opportunity for down time in the art department, a relaxed loft space where the teacher encourages children to express what makes them individuals. Gaily coloured boats made from driftwood sail across the wall, and the picture of the week was pop art bearing the legend: 'women who seek equality with men lack ambition'.

Pre prep, from nursery to year 2, is housed in a separate building, with a magic-filled nursery. Someone was teaching Read Write inc phonics, as in many schools, but every part of this exceptional teacher was engaged in communication: she seemed to use her voice and whole body to illustrate the sounds, so you felt that there was a story behind each one – the 3 year olds and your reviewer were mesmerised. The reception classroom is as much outside as in, a group of boys dragging around mathematical shapes in full wet weather gear and determination. 'They need to be out, and that eases things for those who want to be in', said the teacher. Things are steadily more formal from year 1, and children are ready for the move to the big school by year 3.

Pupils say, 'everyone's really busy', and indeed these are some of the busiest children this reviewer has met, with lessons finishing at 4.55pm, followed by reading prep until 5.30pm, optional activities until 6.30pm, and Saturday school (except for twice termly 'leave outs'). Parents say, '[It] sets them up well for senior school. They organise themselves very young'.

Parents don't mind Saturday school, which consists of four lessons, chapel and matches; they like going to chapel, and like the Saturday picnics. Pupils don't like it, and have one wholehearted desire: to abandon Saturday school. 'Matches are OK, but lessons...', said a pupil in disgust. However, the school feels the breadth of experience and the depth of knowledge the children acquire during their time at Westbourne is a key factor in what they go on to achieve.

Patrols, the house system here, are 'one of the best aspects of the school,' said a parent, commenting on the happy mix between the years in each. A parent said, 'it's a warm caring school...got really nice atmosphere...kids are very caring to each other, and for younger children'.

Behavioural expectations are high; holding open a door is expected, say parents. Children say it's 'quite strict if you do something wrong', and one parent said her daughter was a scared about getting a 'note' for eating a biscuit in the changing room. But, parents say, 'it is weighed towards credits and they can be for anything...or having a smile...' Pupils are all aware of the process for reporting bullying, and say, 'it does get sorted out'. A parent said a problem was taken seriously, and both she and her child were happy it was properly dealt with.

This is, in the main, a listening school, although one member of pupil council said precisely, 'they listen, not necessarily implement'. But the monkeybars were the result of council suggestion, as was the easing of the no fleeces in school rule, it being persuasive when pupils said, 'if we can't wear fleeces, you need to turn the heating up'. Girls now also allowed to wear trousers and shorts, this traditional school taking an enlightened approach to this basic question of equality, comfort and choice for girls that other closed-minded schools would do well to heed.

Facilities are fabulous, and pupils play games every day. The standard of sports is very high, one parent saying, 'they won't necessarily make the top sets at senior school, but will make the A team at sport'. Teams here win most of the time, one parent even suggesting that it might be good for the A team to know what it feels like to lose. The vexed question of teams provokes much comment from pupils and parents, but the headmaster says, 'we pick the A team on merit, but the lower teams are rotated strictly...if the children don't play one week, they are included in the next fixture'. Parents describe their touchline behaviour as supportive, noisy, passionate – but respectful. 'Westbourne House has a reputation for cliquey, scary parents', said one. 'It's not fair. They are there, [but] there are lots of people. [It's a] very good community'.

'Boarding houses are so nice', said a pupil, 'like a real house', and indeed, there is a row of houses as if lifted from a nearby town, each complete with garden and slide. Older pupils sleep in these 'outhouses', while younger pupils board in the main house. Pupils like the fact you can submit a list of requests in the morning, asking for bread, butter and honey, and it is delivered in a basket to the house in the evening – 'like a stocking'. Boarding accommodation is light, comfortable and high spec.

Pupils love the activities, particularly in the summer – 'sometimes bouncy castles, slip and slide, and go karts', and the Boarders' Adventure Badge, where they learn survival techniques, including night navigation and outdoor cooking. Parents like the fact that children learn to be organised, and independent.

Pupils are enthusiastic about the food, which they say is 'really nice, particularly pudding', one pupil telling us seriously that, 'there are all the food groups...it's a healthy meal, and you can get seconds; but not of pudding'. Pupils eat 'crusts' at morning break; almost literally so, bagels with or without butter, but also fruit and carrot sticks.

The headmaster says it would not suit a child who does not want to get involved, and parents agree that the school is brilliant for a sporty child, or one into drama and music. 'Not so many children outside the standard deviation', said a parent. 'No weird kids,' he clarified.

Winchester College

College Street, Winchester, Hampshire SO23 9NA

Ages 13–18 **Pupils** 693 **Sixth form** 285 **Boarders** All full **C of E**

Fees: Boarding £39,912 pa

01962 621247
www.winchestercollege.org

Headman: Since 2016, Dr Timothy Hands, previously master of Magdalen College School. A state school pupil turned down by Cambridge ('I was told by the careers adviser at my grammar school that I wouldn't get to university at all'), he studied violin at the Guildhall before reading English at King's College, London, then went on to St Catherine's, Oxford, followed by Oriel, where he ended up as a lecturer. He became housemaster at King's Canterbury, then second master at Whitgift School, then head of Portsmouth Grammar. He comes from a long line of teachers, including both parents and an ancestor who was schoolmaster on HMS Victory. Likes sport and music – was co-leader of the London Schools Symphony Orchestra and conductor of the Oxford University chamber choir, Schola Cantorum. The author of several books about Victorian literature and teaches English A level.

Married to Jane, a solicitor who read classics at Oxford; two sons.

Academic matters: Winchester offers Cambridge Pre-U examinations as a replacement for A levels in all subjects, finding them more flexible and academically challenging. The school takes a dim view of A levels, especially in modern languages which have been 'vandalised' ('you can now take an A level in French without reading a book!'). Most pupils take three subjects, but some, mainly mathematicians, take four (or even five) Pre-U exams.

Results always outstanding (74 per cent at D1-3, the A*/A equivalent, in 2018), and the school continues to offer the shortest list of exam subjects of any reputable sixth form in England. Forget film studies and froth – here you will not find sociology, classical civilisation, politics, business studies, PE or psychology. Maths, chemistry, physics and economics the most popular Pre-U subjects, followed robustly by history and English lit. Philosophy and theology on a roll at the minute. No great cornucopia of GCSE choices either: all boys sit nine IGCSEs in two or three sciences, maths, English, Latin, French or German, plus other subjects which can include history, geography, music, art, design or more languages. In 2018, 92 per cent A*-A/9-7 grades at IGCSE.

'Div' is the unique and highly-prized complementary programme at the heart of the Winchester ethos. It aims to instill a knowledge and understanding of British, European and world history and culture and, as such, is a true, liberal education. 'The boys and dons love it. It's the one bit of this over-structured world in which they can pursue their own intellectual interests.' 'It means the staff have to be of the highest calibre so that they can lead this cross-subject, cross-cultural tutorial,' a parent explained. Average age of teachers has come down significantly in recent years, and is now a youthful 38.

Now fully embracing IT, with introduction of Firefly (learning platform) and Surface laptops for all. Offers learning support for around 100 boys, mainly for mild dyslexia, dyspraxia and information processing.

IT not cutting any edges, reflecting an institutional reserve about the digital world. Little, if any, work done on computers in a boy's first year (or two) here. Offers learning support for around 100 boys, mainly for mild dyslexia, dyspraxia and information processing.

Games, options, the arts: Sport is 'brilliantly flexible', a parent told us. Enthusiasts can play as much as they want. 'My son went from the 4th team at his prep school to the A team here', chuckled one mum. 'There's a great spirit in the school sport', another told us, 'very unpressurised.' 'If you are determined to do no games, it's possible' (refreshing, and probably unique, to hear this said in a British public school). But some sort of physical exercise ('ekker') is compulsory. Main sports are soccer (coach is ex-Southampton FC captain Jason Dodd), Winchester College football (read the rules) and cricket (huge here – the cricket coach also runs the Hampshire U16s) but these are supplemented by everything from aikido to water polo. Fabulous playing fields and sports facilities of all kinds. Recent national competition wins in fives, fencing and sailing.

Music very important, very strong and very classical. James Blunt, Genesis and Mumford and Sons may have attended public schools but they would not have been Wykehamists. Two-thirds of boys learn a musical instrument; many learn two or three, taught by a long list of specialist teachers. Pipe organ very strong here (one Winchester boy we know was making a tidy sum playing weddings while still in sixth form). Music school includes 50(!) practice rooms, a music tech classroom, recording studio and editing suite. Vast range of musical ensembles and performance opportunities – weekly Tuesday concert and many more throughout the year – many open to the public.

Art and drama lively and of quality, though they do not quite enjoy the accolade of music. CCF compulsory in year 10, after which it can be replaced with community service.

Boarding: All boys board. First year boys are generally in rooms of four to six. By IGCSEs they're in rooms of two or four. All sixth formers have single rooms, except the scholars. A boy's life here begins and ends with his house. Houses, while still more autonomous than at any other school in the UK, have been brought some distance into dreary conformity in this era of health and safety, school inspections and the like (school says: 'have greater consistency of practice than before'). There is now a lot more consistency of discipline, food (all meals are eaten in house) and day to day routine and less competition between houses (and housemasters). Current crop of housemasters praised by the parents we spoke to. Accommodation and food improving but still seen as of secondary importance, both to the school and to (British) parents.

Saturdays consist of lessons until lunch, then sport, then reading, then prep. Many boys go out after chapel on Sundays – to lunch at home or out with parents, and older ones can go into town. The school's inflexible attitude towards Sunday boarding is a source of contention for a few boys who have to pass up outside sports fixtures.

Background and atmosphere: Founded in the 14th century by William of Wykeham, Bishop of Winchester, Chancellor to Richard II, and the sage behind the school's motto: Manners makyth man. Began in 1387 with a warden, 10 fellows, two schoolmasters, three chaplains, 70 scholars and 16 quiristers – the Winchester version of choristers. The bishop also founded New College, Oxford, with which the college maintains strong links. The quiristers are now educated down the road at the Pilgrims' School but continue to board at Winchester College and sing in chapel. So this is a quiet land of flinty walls, leafy quads, a venerable chapel, many other buildings of ancient date and visible history (the school was used as Cosette's Paris convent in the film version of Les Mis). Later foundations, eg Eton College, seem like modern upstarts by comparison. Not that the college hasn't kept building and acquiring. There are 10 boarding houses in adjacent streets, and buildings for all major disciplines. The college has built a new museum in a converted stable to display its trove of treasures – paintings, porcelain, silver, scientific instruments, books etc.

The atmosphere is donnish – the masters are called dons here and the college has a language of its own (called Notions) for almost every aspect of daily life. The lack of girls, together with the school's academically elitist ethos, gives the boys the gift of unselfconsciousness rarely seen elsewhere. The school considered admitting girls under previous head – 'I started off thinking we'd do it', he remembered. In the end, they decided against: 'Girls dominate academically, especially in the lower years. To introduce that here would change the intellectual ethos of the school. What we do is distinctive – we do not have a wide ability range. It is the high quality of the boys' ability at the "bottom" that is key here.'

Surprisingly, the school has no formal relationship with Winchester Cathedral – who needs it when you've got such a superb school chapel (built 1392)? The cathedral is used for school choir concerts. 'It casts an ecclesiastical aura.' Has a 5+ year relationship with Midhurst Rother College (academy) and some pupils from the academy come to Winchester for a Saturday morning programme of classes.

Pastoral care, well-being and discipline: School rules cover 10 tightly spaced typed pages and make a terrifically good read. You will find a complex list of warnings about alcohol (depending whether wine, beer or spirits and where purchased) and learn that the possession of firearms or explosives is forbidden (with the exception of 'shotguns brought into school with parent permission'). Boys are also reminded not to wear 'T-shirts bearing slogans which are anagrammatical' (what harm is an anagram, we ask?). No hats. And before you ask, no earrings.

Mobiles allowed so long as they are 'inaudible and invisible'. School takes a hard line on drugs. Unusually, for a school of this vintage, there is no sixth form bar. Housemasters run most aspects of a boy's life – pastoral and academic – but serious matters end up with the head.

Pupils and parents: Some 87 per cent of boys come from the UK. All pupils speak English as it if were their first language; around 20 pupils are bilingual. Quite a lot of Hong Kong Chinese families – who tend to coalesce at the academic hothouses of this land. 'Russians haven't found us yet,' commented one of the admissions staff (more likely, they shun it because it's single sex). Boys come from a large assortment of preps mostly in the southern half of the UK, with Pilgrims' School, Horris Hill, Twyford, The Dragon, Summer Fields and Sussex House leading the field. The school does not break its back to court parents – neither current nor prospective: there is one rather sober open day each year.

Parents we spoke to were keen to emphasise that though boys must be clever and academic to be happy here, they need not be geeks: 'There's a view that Winchester boys are anaemic swots. There are some very studious individuals here – yes, but there are also normal, clever but lazy boys who like their sport and are not averse to sunshine.' Not the place for hovering parents – signing on here takes a leap of faith and the school is set in its ways ('clear about what it wants and expects,' says the school). List of well-known old boys is long, but curiously unexciting. Lots of politicians, academics, cricketers, journalists, pillars of The Establishment.. and Tim Brooke-Taylor.

Entrance: You'll need to be on your toes. The school asks parents to register their sons after they've turned 8 but 'well before the end of year 5'. No need for early registration for those attempting scholarships – winning an award carries with it the automatic right to a place. Admissions for Commoners are via the housemasters who see 25 to 30 sets of parents when the boys are 10-11, interview and test them (a short verbal and numerical reasoning test), get reports from existing schools and offer places to around half. A deposit is then requested and the place is firm, barring (rare) failure of the college's entrance exam which is taken two years later in May of the year of entry in all usual CE subjects (with Greek and German as additional options, but not Spanish). It helps to have an idea of which houses you are interested in – parents may arrange meetings with up to three housemasters. 'If parents are still unsettled after seeing three houses, this may not be the school for them', said the admissions department with customary directness.

Scholars and exhibitioners selected by exams in English, maths, science and a multiple choice 'general reasoning' test. Candidates must also choose three optional papers from among: Latin, French, Classical Greek/German/Spanish, history, geography, maths II or general paper II. Scholars live in College – a separate house pulsating with hyperactive brain cells. The life of a scholar here is not for all, and we know of families turning down an academic scholarship (especially now that they bring no automatic fee remission). A half dozen boys come fresh into the sixth form via exam and a minimum of six GCSE 9-7 grades (ie mainly A*s but the odd A won't rule you out).

Exit: In 2018, 36 to Oxbridge. The rest to a predictable spread of the best redbricks. Increasing numbers to a distinguished list of top North American universities eg Brown, Chicago, Columbia, Dartmouth, Duke, Georgetown, Harvard, MIT, Princeton, UNC, UPenn and Yale. Although the six grade 7s at GCSE for sixth form entrance is a low hurdle for most boys here, the college is said to be 'ruthless' (school says 'firm') about enforcing this rule. A handful of unfortunate boys receive 'the letter' each year.

Money matters: Since 2011, all scholarships – given for academic, musical and sporting ability – bring zero fee remittance. However means-tested bursaries can be awarded up to 100 per cent of the fee where necessary. Music scholars, of which there are 10 (usually grade 8 by age 13), receive free tuition on up to two instruments and singing; music exhibitioners (closer to grade 6) get free tuition on one instrument. NB Charges an inexplicable £500 'entrance fee' (in addition to a registration fee and deposit).

Remarks: A very special place for intellectually curious boys and their teachers. Unique.

Windlesham House School

302

Washington, Pulborough, West Sussex RH20 4AY

Ages 4–13 Pupils 324 Boarders 164 (from year 4) C of E

Fees: Day £8,985 – £23,058; Boarding £21,606 – £27,816 pa

01903 874700
www.windlesham.com

Headmaster: Since 2007, Richard Foster, head at Pembroke House School in Kenya, then at St Anselm's in Derbyshire for 14 years. Thoughtful, warm, much liked by parents and pupils. Incredibly busy wife Rachel is in charge of everything pastoral. Three grown up children. Windlesham is the most child centred school Mr Foster has ever taught at – though he is careful to point out (perhaps with the more conservative parents in mind) that 'children [here are] liberated – not liberal.'

Entrance: Non-selective. Academic assessment from year 1 upwards for setting purposes plus night's stay from year 3 upwards. Waiting list for many years. No scholarships, but means-tested bursaries available.

Exit: Pupils move on to over 35 different schools, including Hurstpierpoint, Bryanston, Marlborough, Oundle, Brighton, Cranleigh, Eton, Lancing, Sevenoaks and Wellington. Seventeen scholarships/exhibitions in 2018.

Remarks: Gorgeous grounds, movingly beautiful even on the miserable day of our visit, with the elegant Queen Anne house standing at the end of a long drive past a mixture of woods, playing fields and golf course. Game rambling around (they don't shoot it here – just clay pigeons). Beautiful entrance hall with roaring fire adds to the impression of arriving at a country house hotel; one specialising in modern art – it's everywhere, and extremely good.

Feels happy and free – described by one parent as a 'tree climbing education centre.' The amazing grounds are fully used by the children; one parent described how the matrons have to drag them in to bed during the summer months, and how kids are out playing golf and cricket before breakfast – 'kids have the freedom to be children' (children with a nine hole golf course).

Parents and children all comment on the strong community at Windlesham – 'it's an incredibly kind place' – which aims to be a family home away from home. No uniform promotes the homey feel, although the strict dress code prevents a grungy look. There's no label competition here – 'they ruin clothes at school, so don't send them in anything good,' said one parent wryly.

Huge amount of energy devoted to pastoral care. Many staff live on site: one parent said 'they never clock off'. One parent described the 'brilliant support' from the school after a family death – they have a 'genuine love of children [here].'

High level of responsibility and support shown between children. Peer listeners appointed from the top class, peer mediators in each year- described lavishly by one of our guides as 'unpaid spies', but a peer mediator calmly countered with an example of a love/hate triangle successfully resolved by her and her counterpart. Any help from adults? 'No, of course not – confidentiality,' she said in a shocked tones. For prep age children, they are astonishingly responsible and outward-looking. This is one of the school's aims, with the head's mantra firmly in mind – be kind, be kind, be kind. Any bullying nipped it in the bud early. 'There's not a great deal of it,' said a parent, whose daughter experienced bullying which was dealt very efficiently.

Huge emphasis on good manners here: children pay good heed to the head's warning – 'get your greeting in before I do.' Good evidence of this on our tour: all pupils held open doors, flattened themselves against walls as we passed and leapt up in classrooms.

Pupils can board from the age of 8 and around half are full boarders, 18 per cent from overseas. 'Boarding provision is exceptionally good,' said a mum, whose kids started as day pupils, and all ended up boarding at their request. Pupils agree – 'it's a sleepover that doesn't stop.' Homely girls' dorms, with posters, cushions, bears; spartan boys' fare, with coloured duvets the most cosy touch (despite the school's best efforts). 'It's the girls who need One Direction posters,' said one of our guides loftily. Girls also get bedside tables and lights – boys don't because of their tendency to play cricket in the dorms. Dormitory phones for good night calls to parents (time restricted to give everyone a chance).

Twelve is the biggest boys' dorm, six the smallest, nine-three for the girls. A little unfortunate that the girls' dorms are named after colours – 'azure,' 'saffron' etc – to suit their delicate natures? – whereas boys' dorms are sturdily named after senior schools – 'Wellington' et al. Unfortunate indeed, but no other whiff of sex discrimination here.

Bathroom facilities extremely clean, but not all that new. Nightly showers, although boarders can relax in a birthday bath. Each year has a comfy room, reduced to cheerful bedlam for the boys, ordered comfort for the girls.

Parents say school is just not the same for day pupils, who don't have the same access to activities or teachers as boarders. Boarding is particularly useful as work steps up in preparation for common entrance, parents say – early bird lessons start at 7.15am, and work ends at 6.30pm, so it's a long day for commuters.

Academically, parents and pupils are happy with most subjects, exceptionally so in English and science, but French is 'not that popular,' say the kids, and parents agree, citing a reliance on work sheets. School says it has taken on new teachers since our visit.

Another parent suggested maths is also a key subject that could be taught better, although the children we spoke to gave maths teachers a glowing report – 'if you listen carefully they're really funny – very sarcastic.' One teacher apparently tells stories of his life in mathematical fantasy (difficult to imagine how this might go...). The head says they are about to appoint an additional maths specialist – an acknowledgement this is an area with which some children struggle.

Rigorous reporting for parents: monthly progress report with attainment and effort, both child and parents get a copy, and a full report at the end of each term. Annual parents' evening (termly for juniors). 'Amazing level of communication,' say parents: written letters from kids every week, emails and phone calls. 'School responds promptly to any query, over and above what you would expect.' Another parent commented how welcome she felt at weekends – you can attend Saturday chapel, watch a play rehearsal or recital. '[You] never feel excluded as a parent – always welcomed.' Parental portal has live stream of events, also available for catch up, ideal for parents who aren't local.

Three computer rooms, one reserved specially for junior use. Dell laptops and iPads to book out, also available to assist those with mild learning difficulties (about 15 per cent of children here). Learning development unit with head and team of assistants. Bright, well-stocked library, open from before breakfast until bedtime, news with a Tory bent – Telegraph and Times, with the honourable exception of the i.

Feels quite hunting, shooting, fishing, but manages not to feel exclusive. Sports are the usual public school fare. Parents are delighted that sports kit left hanging around at school is returned washed and pristine. New sports hall and swimming pool get good use.

Most boarders are around at weekends (though it's possible to go home four weekends a term). Everyone's around on Saturdays: morning school, matches in the afternoon. Plenty of activities available – Capture the Flag is extremely popular at the moment; but also debates, mountain biking, gardening in the walled garden, shows and games – pupils can keep extremely busy if they want to (though some kids just want to live in the woods, and that's ok too.) All love cooking club – you have to run fast if you want to sign up.

All have drama lessons, three productions each year, everyone who auditions is included in some way. Own theatre – the Malden Family Theatre – with visiting productions every term. Some rumblings from parents who are a bit tired of seeing the super-duper children starring again. Music compulsory all the way, but popular even with those who are not musical because of the inspirational director. Over 80 per cent play an instrument. Vast array of music groups of all complexions, from Miremba to rock choir.

Early years housed separately at Little Windlesham (reception – year 2). Relaxed setting, emphasis on flow and play. Tapestry method of contacting parents, who receive a video stream of their children in class directly to their email at work, which parents love. Described by a parent as being 'part of [the] big school – but very gentle, with a lot of time [spent] in their special oasis.'

The head says Windlesham would suit most types of kids, providing they join in and have a go at things. One parent suggested it would not suit a child who needs to be totally organised by others; nor is it a place for shrinking violets; although conversations with shy pupils suggested they could find their feet and flourish here. One parent emphasised that those who want their children to be day pupils should avoid Windlesham – all kids here will want to board eventually.

Parents from the Foreign Office, business, Forces, professions, and lots of expats. Some 20 different nationalities in the school, around 12 per cent non British. Assesses language skills on entry, but will give special assistance to learn English as a foreign language. Some 50 per cent of kids local, 50 per cent from abroad or other parts of the country. Parents like the mix of children from different countries, and to a degree, backgrounds – a few means-tested bursaries and no judgement, say parents; although four wheel drive likely to be parent vehicle of choice.

Several parents of leavers said their children are homesick for Windlesham: the move from this caring environment to senior school can be quite tough; but as a parent said, no one would want Windlesham to be less fabulous.

Woldingham School

Marden Park, Woldingham, Surrey CR3 7YA

Ages 11–18 **Pupils** 544 **Sixth form** 160 **Boarders** 228 full, 56 flexi **RC**

Fees: Day £20,085 – £22,440; Boarding £33,570 – £36,540 pa

01883 349431
www.woldinghamschool.co.uk

Headmistress: Since 2016, Alex Hutchinson (40s) MA (Oxon), PGCE (Bristol); took on the headship after a year or so as deputy. Her first degree was in chemistry and she continues to teach once a week. Ever since her first post at Clifton College she has gained her experience in girls' schools. Head of science at St Mary's School, Ascot, she then moved north as head of sixth form at Central Newcastle High. Add to this her experience as head of sixth form at 'out and out London day school' Wimbledon High before joining Woldingham and she presents a very solid proposition in particular to the London parents looking to take their daughters out of the city.

Mrs Hutchinson believes in being 'comfortable and clear about who we are: we're very confident that we deliver an excellent education across all levels. Girls here are not just the academic stars but those who have different things to offer'. Still, she's convincing that a girl destined for A*s will achieve those just as well here as anywhere – 'we're never going to take the foot off the pedal in the classroom.'

We meet in her parent-friendly office with plump soft furnishings, beautiful full-length windows and student artwork. We find her to be very friendly, engaging, carefully prepared with an attractive delivery that could see her a broadcaster in another life. In common with many pupils, her mother attended the school. She lives within sight of her office with her husband, also a head of a local independent school, dog and cat. She plays hockey twice a week. Somewhere amongst the rose pergola walk and lawns there must be a veg patch too as she likes to grow her own. The students feel warmly towards her and love the fact that she lives 'just there' and find her accessible in other ways: 'she's not like one of those heads where you walk past and just smile'. Parents tell us: 'like a breath of fresh air, her enthusiasm for the school and the girls knows no bounds.' Another: 'fantastic, young, enthusiastic and very approachable.'

Academic matters: In 2018, 67 per cent A*-A/9-7 grades at GCSE. Highlights include Latin and all of the sciences, with consistently good results across English and maths. Meanwhile at A level, 61 per cent of grades were A*/A. Popular subjects include English literature, maths, biology and history whilst the artists in particular shine.

Girls are expected to study a language (not necessarily modern, could be Latin) to GCSE; Mandarin is a club. Most sixth formers take three A levels. Further specialism introduces A levels in textiles, psychology, media studies, government and politics and classical civilisation.

Oxbridge support starts in the lower sixth with girls assigned a teacher to support their applications one-to-one. There is no fear of being made to feel like a 'geek' for being good at something, say parents. Girls interact with their subjects outside of the grounds: a lower sixth student was joint winner of a recent Cambridge history prize, with successes also in 'teen tech' and poetry competitions.

Almost 25 per cent of staff have been working at the school for more than 10 years. A parent commented: 'The girls seem to relate well to both the male and female teachers. They respect them and feel that they can easily approach them if they need further explanation with a subject that they find tricky.' A girl we met thought: 'They are here to support you as a person, as you grow into yourself'. We watch an upper sixth economics class where the teacher sits inside the circle of desks giving detailed essay feedback.

Maximum class size is 22 up to GCSE then 14 in the sixth form. Lower sets have smaller numbers so that students can receive more support. One mother said: 'During the first three years they do not believe in setting pointless holiday homework, they believe the girls work hard enough during term time'. Hurrah.

An experienced learning enhancement department provides support for standard numbers of girls with SPLDs such as dyslexia but also small numbers with ADHD and autism spectrum disorder. All are screened on entry. The majority receive 'light touch' support, only a few receive direct support and a reduced curriculum.

There is a significant programme of carefully thought through support for girls with EAL needs. Unusually, some one-year GCSE students (usually girls from Spain and Mexico) are prepared for the Cambridge English ESOL examinations.

Games, options, the arts: Sports facilities are not lavish given the space – plans are afoot – and a parent's view that 'sport is average, but music and drama are outstanding' and artists in particular shine, does seem to fit with the picture of the school on view today, although there are some noticeable sporting successes, recently in hockey and netball. Main sports also include swimming, tennis and athletics, with aerobics, lacrosse, table tennis and squash added in higher up the school. There is a dance studio and an indoor tennis dome. The school is notable in supporting its elite athletes, currently including cross-country, skiing, lacrosse, modern pentathlon, carriage driving – enabling them to take part in term time without falling behind. No timetabled football but soccer club is popular and cricket is coming.

Slightly less than half the school has individual music lessons, including singing. Some stand out performers have places in national orchestras. Musicians gave two concerts on a tour of Prague recently.

The most recent ISI report commented on 'the quality of writing not as fluent as speaking, particularly in the sixth form' – which the head finds incomprehensible, given the number of poets and writers the school produces. We saw the work of one published poet, also an artist, in the stunning art studio, quite the biggest we've ever seen, allowing each upper sixth student to have their own 'nest'. Fascinating projects in progress include one from a student developing her own religion and researching curses and another who was building a 'city to the lost creativity of children' in wax. Naturally, several are heading to art school.

With Carey Mulligan a notable former pupil, it's not altogether surprising to find drama facilities of such a high standard: the 550 seat theatre is stunning, with a flexible stage and space for a full orchestra. Helping girls to settle into year 7, everyone takes part in a production, most recently Roald Dahl's The Twits and The Witches. Very professional-looking production posters from former years line the staircase. Higher up the school the number of shows is limited but there are opportunities to take part in backstage work. Drama available at GCSE and A level.

Pupils are far from just sequestered away in their valley. Computer science students have recently returned from a trip to Silicon Valley; year 11s and sixth formers spent four days in Berlin; year 9s visit the battlefields of Ypres and geography students enjoy an annual trip to Iceland. Eighty clubs on offer: Mandarin, archery, tap dancing, coding, dark room photography, rock-climbing and dissection caught our eye. Day girls are encouraged to stay for extracurricular activities but are free to go home from 4.30pm. Sports matches and supervised study with friends until 6.30pm. Transport is provided to facilitate this and many stay. On Saturday mornings, Saturday Active for year 7 to 10 boarders provides a range of activities.

Boarding: Year 7 and 8 boarders have a separate block, Marden. It's tidy but plain, plentifully kitted out with sofas. Décor-wise, if we had been told the over-50s lived here we would have believed it, but what does that matter when you have all of your friends here to crowd around I'm A Celebrity and share in the odd yoga class? The upper sixth block is next door and they've recently initiated a year 7 movie night so that the older girls don't seem in any ways remote or intimidating. Years 7, 8 and 9 share a room, from year 10 girls have their own, with sixth formers getting en-suites: compact, but modern, fresh and functional, perfect for studying. Boarders are free to go home at weekends from 4.30pm on Friday. There are often boarding house pets, whether that be elderly Doris or a new, highly anticipated puppy. Flexi-boarding on hand: simply sign up for one to two nights a week a term in advance.

Background and atmosphere: Founded in 1842 by the Society of the Sacred Heart, 100 or so years later at the end of the Second World War the school of 100 pupils moved to Woldingham from Roehampton. Main house is all highly decorative Victorian red-brick without and dark panelling within. Plainer 20th century additions and conversions form a courtyard and then a Millennium building smartly houses arts.

The grounds, complete with cattle, horses and the odd deer, extend to a staggering 700 acres, a secluded wooded valley on the edge of the North Downs. Along the two mile drive and you're likely to encounter only the odd rider. The school does feel quite isolated, even if in reality it is not. Sixth formers are allowed to take the train into London at weekends (with planning) and clearly relish the privilege.

It no doubt adds to the family feel that the girls we meet are emphatic about. When the head tells us about a year 7 pyjama day we imagine the whole school wearing pyjamas to lessons every day – who would know? As for snow days, we can't think of anywhere better. As the head says, 'we're good at relaxing – staff v girls "Would I lie to you?", pancake race, inter-house go-karting...' A mother confirmed: 'There is a charming sense of fun about the school – even amongst sixth formers if they think no-one is looking.'

Pastoral care, well-being and discipline: 'We are absolutely a Catholic school', says the head – just the odd statue and religious painting on view. One third of girls are Catholics, but almost more integral to the school are the values of the sacred heart: faith, intellect, community, personal growth and social justice – 'it's very tangible for us, it's how we make decisions,' says the head. Girls no longer wear uniform to mass on Sunday but all faiths attend, even if it is just for a moment of quiet reflection.

Day and boarding pupils are allocated to one of four houses and tutor groups are also arranged by house. The first Saturday of the autumn term is a house festival of dance, music and costume making.

The health centre is staffed by qualified nurses and a counsellor is available. With gender in the news we quiz the head on gendered vocabulary: 'I say "girls", but I would say that I'm aware of this every time I use it, which was perhaps not the case a year ago'. Each parent mentions the relative lack of pressure their daughters find here. Marden has an adventure playground and the head agrees girls may be able to 'stay younger for longer'.

Parents are all praise for the pastoral care: 'Excellent. If there is an issue the problem is dealt with kindness and discretion. Invaluable,' is typical. Little need for sanctions. Digital matters are the greatest challenge now, with posting something inappropriate online warranting an immediate suspension. In years 7 and 8 the school takes away devices, from year 9 girls are allowed to self-monitor, and boarders in years 7-10 hand in their devices at night. Sixth formers enjoy some uniform privileges such as their own suits, shirts and jumpers as well as taking on responsibilities as 'ribbons', one of the most charming traditions of the school, where they wear sashes and take on house or school leadership roles.

Pupils and parents: Who might the school suit? 'Not one stereotype of girl', says the head. Parents agree upon 'girls who respond to encouragement rather than pressure.' A predominance of west Londoners and those from nearby Surrey and Kent. More than 100 from overseas, predominantly from Hong Kong and China but comprising 30 nationalities. 'A complete mix of backgrounds, ethnicity and relative wealth, from the daughters of Russian oligarchs downwards but all part of the school community,' said a parent.

A perusal of old girl careers throws up a number of mumpreneurs as well as a varied clutch of famous names. Interior designers including Neisha Crosland, also Louise Mensch, Vivien Leigh and Clarissa Dickson-Wright. And Carey Mulligan. Old girls may get married in the school chapel and come in for business breakfasts to share their experiences.

Entrance: There are 60 places available at 11+, 30 at 13+ and 20 at 16+. Occasional places at 12 and 14+. Candidates for 13+ may apply in year 6 for deferred entry (same online test as for 11+) or in year 8 for standard entry. Assessment day includes an English writing paper, group interview and fun creative activity. The school is looking for pupils with interests beyond the academic, with reasonable adjustments for SEND. Sixth form candidates are examined in two of their chosen A level subjects and a general paper.

Exit: Around 20 per cent leaves after GCSEs, with places filled by incomers. An incredibly broad range of university courses, which speaks of inspiration well beyond the purely academic – quite a few budding criminologists, digital media specialists, vets, anthropologists, electrical engineers, land economists and art historians. Three medics in 2018; Bristol, Edinburgh, Birmingham, Durham, Cardiff and Exeter popular. Five off to the US in 2018 and one to Hong Kong.

Money matters: Not prodigiously well endowed so bursaries and scholarships unlikely to play a major role. Academic and co-curricular scholarships are offered at 11+, 13+ and sixth form, designed to recognise exceptional achievement, intellectual curiosity and persistence. Awards typically cover five to 20 per cent of day fees. No need to be stratospherically accomplished for music scholarships as potential also recognised. One scholarship to a local girl each year and two in science. Bursaries are intended for girls who demonstrate strong academic potential and where the financial circumstances of the family will make attending Woldingham impossible. Forty students are in receipt of a bursary, a few up to a life-changing 100 per cent of fees.

Remarks: Girls are sure to find a home from home in this Catholic school which welcomes all and promises fun, fabulous dramatic and artistic opportunties, strong academics and the chance to be young for a little longer.

Woodcote House School

Snows Ride, Windlesham, Surrey GU20 6PF

Ages 7–13 **Pupils** 107 **Boarders** 32 full, 35 flexi **C of E**

Fees: Day £17,850; Boarding £23,850 pa

01276 472115
www.woodcotehouseschool.co.uk

Headmaster: Since September 2016, David Paterson, brother of proprietor and ex-head Nick, and previously deputy head. Born and educated at Woodcote, he returned in 1992 with his young family after a career in the City. Joined as head of mathematics and became deputy head to his brother in 2000. Woodcote is a real family affair with Nick still teaching English and Spanish, and Nick's son Oliver teaching maths and Spanish.

Entrance: Places offered following internal assessment test in VR and NVR and interview with the headmaster. No linked schools or significant feeders. ('Wish there was a pre-prep,' said one mother). All quite laid back. Some boys will have been on a list since birth, others rock up mid-term somewhere along the line. Most families are from London and home counties. Boys may board from year 3. In essence, the school is looking for boys who will put something into the school. Will take the odd hard luck story, a boy who has been bullied elsewhere or got lost in a larger set up. Head has a 'conversation' with prospective pupils and their parents, and will suggest a chat with the SENCo if it seems appropriate – nothing more formal than that. 'We are not going to say, in effect, "you are not clever enough for our school", but you have to be robust enough to cope. We want boys who don't mind getting their knees dirty. I wouldn't say we don't want sissies or prissies, but we want boys who want to be boys.'

The Paterson family put up the equivalent of two sets of boarding fees as scholarships (introduced to mark school's 150th anniversary) and divide as they deem fit – five boys could get 20 per cent of the available cash, or two boys get the lot, or sometimes nobody gets anything – school does not give them away for the sake of it. Must spot a spark or talent, academic, musical or sporting – boys are invited to a taster day, during which they are assessed in the classroom and on the sports field.

Exit: At 13 to all the top-notch public schools, from Ampleforth to Winchester, with clutches of academic, music and all round scholarships won. Lots to Sherborne of late, plus of course Eton, Harrow, Wellington. Parents given lots of guidance on future schools – evidently a strength of this place. WH parents are not always chasing Eton and down the list schools. It's all about what is best for the child, and plenty of other factors are considered. 'So the list of schools WH boys go on to does not always reflect the actual academic achievement,' said one parent. And any leaver will not have heard the last of Woodcote. Legend has it that popular long-serving master Colin Holman – a modern day Mr Chips – has been known to drop a note to many of the boy's new senior school housemasters when he remembers a nugget of useful information about them, to the effect of 'If he's like this, try this'.

Remarks: Superb example of that dying breed – the thriving family-owned school. Idiosyncratic – you will either 'get' this school or you won't. Sceptics ask where the owls are kept, but its parents and boys are so glowing in their praise it's unreal. Feels like a proper country prep, although it's just 40 minutes from London. Combines top notch teaching with tons of outside activities so that the boys are both mentally and physically challenged every day. But also makes time for them to do their own thing, so they are happy and flourish. Nice balance of nurture and push.

Unapologetically focused on doing its own thing – even the unusual brown and yellow school uniform seems a manifestation of a school confident in its own skin. Several parents mentioned how their sons had blossomed at this school, developing their personalities and interests. 'We aim to turn out a young man with good manners who is well-rounded, honest, trustworthy and friendly.'

You will see at a glance that this school isn't splashing your cash on fancy facilities, though new theatre recently completed and there's been some updating of classrooms and dorms – the place is delightfully worn at the edges. It really does look as if 100 boys have the run of the place. There's a relaxed feel, plenty of rough and tumble, all part of its charm. Not precious, but quite a cocooned existence. Known to sort out an odd bod or two.

Set in its own 30 acres, including some attractive woods, the main building is Regency and hits you with a real sense of tradition and history – ask about 18th century highwayman, Captain Snow, when you visit. But school has been in its present incarnation since 1931 when it was bought by the Paterson family. Old boys would definitely recognise the place – and that's the idea. 'The Paterson family is very strong and not swayed by fashion. They know what they want to provide and are very good at doing it,' explained one parent. Healthy sprinkling of old boys have their sons here.

Pictures of former pupils line the walls, and many of them were clearly recalled by Paterson matriarch Angela (Nick's mother) when we bumped into her during our visit. And the main thoroughfare, Red Lane, is a literally well-trodden path of black and red tiling, pitted and undulated from the patter of boys' feet over the years. Then the dining hall, where whole school, pupils, staff, visitors, all eat together, is decorated by the honours board and pictures of school founders. As they sit chatting together boys are clearly in a stable, traditional environment and confident about talking to adults.

Lessons are relaxed, but industrious. None of the staff 'just teach', they all wear a number of other hats so the boys see their teachers all the time, as much outside the classroom as inside it. Hence no forced formality about the classroom setting, but all is most respectful – staff exude an air of relaxed authority. Still boys scramble to their feet when visitors enter the classroom and to walk through the grounds with a staff member is to be met with a cacophony of 'Morning sir, morning sir'. Very small class sizes, average 10, never more than 14 and just four in the scholarship class we visited – having fun with the Kubla Khan. Fairly holistic approach to teaching as staff tie in topics across subject areas, so that talk of battlefields in history will link to their locations in geography. Staff more like synchronised swimmers, rather than everyone ploughing up and down their own subject lane. Parents full of praise for an enthusiastic staff always pushing for excellence.

Long day (8.20am to 6.10pm) for day boys, furthest of whom travel around 20 miles to school. First thing every morning is prep – sensible move as boys are nice and fresh and aren't able to get help from parents. Not a whiff of an interactive whiteboard around the place and school is currently rather conflicted about the role of ICT – never a huge deal here, where teachers largely prefer projectors and coloured pens. 'Many schools will find their fancy ICT suites defunct as everyone clutches hand-held devices like iPads now.' (Not that school has those either.) 'ICT is certainly a subject in transition and we need to decide what stance we will take'.

Nothing state-of-the-art about other facilities either, though the boys we met described them as 'good' – 'we've got everything', said one. It's a bit scruffy and ramshackle in places, but not because nobody cares, rather it's just rather battered in places as a result of hundreds of boys kicking around the place – it's clearly a home from home for them.

Woodcote is able to accommodate some special needs and has a dedicated SENCo to handle boys on the autistic spectrum, dyslexia and EAL. About 20 boys (but a fifth of the school, remember) have some type of learning support, for which their parents pay extra. Languages taught are French and Spanish – a significant Spanish entourage among the pupils and Nick Paterson is a fluent Spanish speaker. A few boys from Thailand and Russia and some 15 per cent of Forces families, who particularly appreciate that the place is properly focused on boarding, so that weekends are busy and boys are far more than simply 'minded'. School keen to get the UK/overseas balance right – the latter about 20 per cent. Very good relationships between the boys themselves and then between themselves and their teachers. The overseas boys tend to spend exeats with their more local friends, leading to an informal exchange programme.

Years 3 and 4 are housed in a separate juniors' building to facilitate a slow integration into main school life. Lots of praise for junior head: 'She is so very kind to my sons,' said one mother. Similarly, year 8s are given a taste of teenage life when they spend a term during their final year living in Dominies House – within the grounds, but away from the main school and set up to give year 8s some preparation for their life to come at public school – not least a taste of going to and from school each day.

Parents struggle to put their finger on a stand-out subject – 'It's all fantastic', said one mother. 'Whatever the talent, they will bring it out' – but music and art mentioned several times. A Woodcote boy beat 13,000 entries to come second in The Sunday Telegraph/Saatchi Gallery prize. And if your son plays an instrument, however badly, he will perform – this place is big on performance opportunities. 'My heart was in my mouth as I saw my son approach the piano, knowing that he'd only been learning for a couple of weeks,' recalled one parent. Not much timetabled drama, but usually a production per term. Staff write the plays – they seem to enjoy it, though it's probably also a necessity to find parts for so many small boys.

The philosophy here is that it is good to be a big fish in this small pool. One mother with several boys at the school felt strongly that each of her sons had found an inner confidence at Woodcote. 'I don't mean they are cocky, in fact they are more polite now, but simply that they've all formed quite distinct personalities and developed a love of study that definitely wasn't there before'.

While things are rather cosy inside, outside the school the boys are spoiled for space, with 35 acres of grounds to run about in, and are encouraged to try out a huge range of outdoor activities. Boys are even kicking about on Rip Stiks during break. From the usual cricket, football and rugby, to the more unusual CCF, bushcraft and even clay pigeon shooting (for older boys) there is masses on offer. School takes its sport seriously and reckons to punch above its weight when taking on other (almost always larger) schools – has only lost 20 per cent of its fixtures over the last five years.

Keen on outdoor education, school considering a 'very small' smallholding, and an outdoor pizza oven is also on wish list. Shame more use not made of on site swimming pool – but boys seem too busy with other things to be very bothered about this.

And fears that a non-sporty boy might flounder in this place are apparently unfounded as more indoor types can make the teas and help the parents park their cars on match days. 'In fact my incredibly non-sporty son even got a few games with

W

has the feeling of a grand country house with wood panelling and a faint scent of beeswax polish.

Ten houses, some in the main house, some in the old farm buildings and the more modern ones dotted around the grounds. All have a common room for each year group, a small kitchen, a computer room and library. Recently opened sixth form social centre with café. The remarkable flying saucer shaped chapel designed by Francis Pollen and opened in 1974, with new pews designed by the Thomas Heatherwick Studios, is central to the school: whole school worship held once a week and a mass every Sunday.

About 60 per cent of the children are Catholic and 'there is quite a lot of religion', said a mother, 'but the ethos is very inclusive and the children accept it as part of the school. It makes them think of other people and that there is more to life than who has the best mobile phone.'

Younger pupils wear uniform, sixth form boys and girls a matching suit and academic staff wear gowns.

Very much a boarding school which takes day pupils, and despite there being more than 40 per cent day pupils, the headmaster is determined to keep it this way – the day pupils are involved in all aspects of school life and activities and have to attend Saturday morning lessons and play in matches if they are in a team. A network of school buses brings pupils from as far afield as Guildford and Tunbridge Wells.

Strong ethos of service and everyone expected to undertake some community work, culminating in Worth in the Community Day at the end of the summer term – anything from helping in primary schools, gardening for old people and work in local homeless hostel to drama productions and concerts in local care homes. Pupils encouraged to take on challenges and each year a small group attempts the cross-Channel swim; five have made it so far.

Pastoral care, well-being and discipline: 'Pupils are very well cared for here,' says the headmaster. 'We don't tolerate drugs, alcohol or bullying', and the school runs a programme of lectures and seminars on the dangers of drug and alcohol abuse. Every house has a houseparent and deputy, there are house-based tutor groups which meet at least twice a week and every house has a chaplain. The school is small enough for everyone to know each other, and tutors and houseparents know pupils well and spot problems early on – it is hard to slip through the net here. Counsellor in three days a week – busy but manageable. The chaplaincy sits at the centre of the school and has a mixed team of monks, teachers and young Catholics known as the Forerunners, plus a part time Anglican chaplain – each house is allocated a chaplain. 'The monks are very special; they are always around but quite low key,' said a pupil, 'and you can call in at the chaplaincy whenever you want – and they often have cake'. The chaplaincy promotes pilgrimage and service and organises trips to Lourdes, Camino de Santiago, and the Taize community in France during the holidays, and everyone is expected to go on a retreat. Annual trip to Worth Abbey's charitable outpost in Peru which runs children's homes in the Andes.

House and school prefects act as mentors to younger pupils. 'The seniors are so nice to the juniors and there is good mixing between year groups, especially through the societies,' said a parent. Everything you need to know can be found in the school magazine Worth Knowing; 'I could not resist the pun,' says the headmaster.

Pupils and parents: Most day children live within an hour of the school and boarders mostly from London and the home counties. About 20 per cent from abroad, mainly from Catholic countries of Europe and South America with a dozen or so from Asia. The school is improving integration between IB (mainly foreign) and A level students, who now have mixed tutorial groups. Quite a broad spectrum of parents but a large number of prosperous City workers, often with both parents commuting. Strong Catholic ethos, but families from many different religions who like the sense of community and responsibility to the wider world, and don't feel religion is being imposed on their children.

Active friends' group gives parents a sense of belonging: 'You can get as involved as you want – there are a lot of social events and the school is generous with its hospitality, which can lead to the development of a Worth Girth,' said one parent. The school likes to involve the whole family via annual parents' meetings and seminars and family mass as well as the parent portal. Although only about a third of the pupils are girls – 40 per cent in some years, and school plans to achieve this throughout – they more than make up for it in energy and ambition and 'keep the boys on their toes,' said a parent. We were pleased to hear that International Women's Day is celebrated.

Former pupils tend to stay in touch and the strong sense of being part of a community carries on afterwards – a blend of confidence and humility without the public school swagger. Well-known old Worthians include actor Robert Bathurst, art dealer Philip Mould, comedian/actor Harry Enfield, England rugby player Nick Walshe, racing driver Henry Surtees, after whom the pupils' café is named, and Tom Mitchell, who captained the silver medal winning GB rugby 7s team at Rio. As the girls come through, we expect to see their names up in lights as well.

Entrance: Pupils come from a range of local prep schools as well as Catholic prep schools in London. Most join in years 7 or 9 or for sixth form with a few places available in years 8 and 10. Eleven plus assessment tests at Worth in January year of entry – online English, maths and non-verbal reasoning – and informal interviews and small group tasks plus report from current school. Overseas pupils can sit the tests in their home country.

Thirteen plus entry via the common pre-test plus assessment day with informal interview and group tasks in the spring of year 7. Common entrance is for setting purposes only.

Some international pupils join in year 11 for one year pre-IB course leading on to full IB diploma in sixth form. About 25 join sixth form – reports, references and interviews plus at least six GCSEs at grade 6+.

Exit: Most popular universities are Bristol, Warwick, Manchester, King's College London, St Andrews and Edinburgh with a fairly predictable range of subjects: economics, history, geography, languages, philosophy and music being the most popular. One to Cambridge to study medicine in 2018. A handful to art and drama school each year. A small number to US universities – school can help with applications but pupils often get outside tuition for SATS exams. Happy to look at alternatives if pupils not keen on university. A handful leaves after GCSEs, usually to go to sixth form colleges.

Money matters: Academic, art, drama, music and sports scholarships offered, plus exhibitions. Max award of 40 per cent goes to the top scholar in each category and other scholars may receive 20-30 per cent – additional means-tested bursary can take this up to 50 per cent of fees. St Benedict's scholarship of up to 100 per cent of fees for local children from families who are in full communion with local church but can't afford fees – a child must be capable of achieving a scholarship in one of the categories.

Remarks: This school has everything going for it – beautiful setting and only 30 miles from London, good sport, music and art and improving academic performance, and an ambitious and energetic headmaster.

Wychwood School

74 Banbury Road, Oxford, Oxfordshire OX2 6JR

Ages 11–18 **Pupils** 120 **Sixth form** 25 **Boarders** 20 full, 15 weekly/occasional

Fees: Day £15,900; Boarding £21,300 – £24,900 pa

01865 557976
www.wychwoodschool.org

Headmistress: Since 2012, Mrs Andrea Johnson BSc (50s). Comes from a family of teachers and doctors and intended 'never to do either'. She read chemistry at Durham, did a PGCE 'because it might be useful' and unexpectedly fell in love with teaching. Formerly assistant head at Tudor Hall where she worked for 20 years, she is the first head of Wychwood not to be an old girl. Teaches chemistry to year 7 and 11. Married to a retired scientist, two adult children, at least one intends to continue the family tradition and is training to be a teacher.

Mrs Johnson is energetic, genuine and very friendly – her presence is reassuring, rather like a wise owl, and one feels she could cope with anything (parents tell us that she does). Just as well really, since that's what you need to be able to do when you run a small school. And as far as Mrs J is concerned, when it comes to education, small really is beautiful. She sees Wychwood as a place that can be responsive to the needs of the individual, to educate girls who 'want to think and achieve but would sink in the hurly burly of a bigger school.' The school gets its fair share of 'burn out' refugees from some of Oxfordshire's super-heated girls' independents, but is equally a positive choice for many families from the word go. 'We enable any child who comes here to get the best possible exam results.'

Parents we spoke to were extremely supportive of Mrs J and tell us that they welcome her sensitive moves towards modernisation and determination to raise the school's profile.

Academic matters: With only 120 pupils in total, results would benefit from micro, rather than macro analysis, but they're respectable: in 2018, 40 per cent A*-A/9-7 at GCSE and 49 per cent A*-B, 29 per cent A*/A at A level. Small class sizes mean teaching staff can give every girl individual attention and customise their approach. We watched year 8s getting to grips with evaluating historical sources and you could almost touch the intense concentration in the room. In fact quiet and studious pretty much sums up the atmosphere of Wychwood. A display of beautifully produced project work showed Jane Eyre's end of term report, as well as prospectuses and other material from Lowood (somewhere that definitely wouldn't make it into the Good Schools Guide).

In a smart and well-equipped lab we came across the head teaching year 7 chemistry and yet more rapt attention and eager answers. The biology lab was festooned with a long, pink papier mâché tube; 'That's a life-size model of the large intestine,' we were told. Length, not girth, we hope.

One thing we kept hearing about Wychwood was that 'teachers have time for you' and that 'they encourage us to follow our own interests'. The school will ('within reason') run a course for just one student; for instance, GCSE astronomy was taught for the benefit of a single stargazing girl. In the sixth form, some A level classes might just be two or three strong – more like the tutorial teaching that goes on at the university down the road. Individual tuition in particular subjects can also be arranged and in some cases girls may repeat a year.

Girls take maximum of nine-and-a-half GCSEs and different strengths and interests are accommodated: double or triple science; both Englishes or just English language; psychology; art, textiles and, unusually, photography. Most do French and Spanish, German offered privately, as are GCSEs in, for example, Chinese, Japanese, Persian, for native speakers. Exchange trips to Spain and France in alternate years. All do short courses in RS and ECDL in ICT. At A level most popular subjects are maths, the sciences, photography and history of art. BTECs in business, music, travel and tourism now offered as alternative to A levels in these subjects.

Games, options, the arts: Textiles, art and photography each enjoy their own light and modern studios in a converted stable block decorated with impressive examples of students' work. As one pupil commented, 'for our size we have so many resources.' It was in the textile studio that we had a sneak preview of the new uniform 'unshortenable' skirt, designed by the textiles teacher. If it's successful she should patent it and make her fortune, but since it doesn't feature something that padlocks it to below the knee we fear that girls will always find a way. Newish uniform design has not been received joyfully, but is it ever? In fact, as far as we could see, Wychwood pupils seemed rather modest in their skirt minimising aspirations, compared to other schools we've visited.

Few mutters that Mrs Johnson isn't as supportive of the arts as former heads have been. School says that girls may opt for more than one GCSE out of art, textiles and photography but since they only take nine-and-a-half in total they often only choose one. At A level girls can do all three if they so choose.

There's a school orchestra and choir, a chamber choir and music lessons are offered in any instrument – harp seems to be a favourite. House plays, written, designed and directed by the girls, are performed competitively; LAMDA exams popular. D of E up to gold offered and Model UN.

If your daughter is sports mad and keen to play for the winning side then, with heavy heart, we suggest you look elsewhere. On the plus side, as a parent pointed out, 'you always get picked for the team.' Not that Wychwood is a complete stranger to victory: our guide was still buzzing from a recent and unexpected rounders success. As the head says, 'Girls learn to lose with grace, but when they win ...' On-site facilities include tennis, basketball and badminton courts, and fitness suite (in a rather gloomy basement room). Nearby off-site are an athletics field, Astro, and more tennis courts. Main opponents are Oxford High and St Helen's; years 7 and 8 play against The Dragon. School does all it can to support girls competing at high levels (county and national) in particular sports by adapting individual timetables etc. Rather surprisingly we discovered that there is a Wychwood equestrian team. No sign of horses trotting down the Banbury Road, rather girls with their own steeds compete on behalf of the school. Recent 'uproar' when timetabled sport was reduced to an hour a week during GCSEs. Schools say that this was to accommodate girls doing 12 GCSEs at the time. Timetabled sport will increase once option choices are rationalised. Quite right too.

Until the 1960s swimming took place in the nearby River Cherwell. Girls used to cycle down to a muddy pool called (for reasons lost in history) the Rhea, where non-swimmers were initiated by being dragged through the water on the end of a pole. Punting was also on the curriculum. There are delightfully nostalgic accounts of the Rhea and its rather whiffy mud in the school's centenary history book. Today's Wychwood swimmers use the Kidlington pool, undoubtedly safer but much less to reminisce about in future years.

Boarding: About a third of pupils board, a fairly even split between full and weekly or flexi. Parents book flexi boarding (usually 1-3 nights per week) at the start of term but school can, and does, accommodate pupils at short notice. Day girls can stay after evening activities such as trips to London or the theatre – bunk beds (only for occasional boarders) add to the sleepover excitement. We were told that news of major road works caused a spike in boarding applications – even fairly local parents appreciate the benefits when gridlock threatens Oxford's already notorious traffic.

When we describe the boarding as 'homely' it's a compliment as well as a reality check. Years 7-9 have large first floor rooms – sash windows and high ceilings – with three to four beds in each. School says mixing the age group helps foster sisterly ethos; colourful curtains and duvets, bedside clutter and lots of family photos and posters add to the family feel. There's wardrobe and under bed storage but no desks – homework takes place elsewhere under supervision.

Sixth formers have characterful single study bedrooms, mostly up in the eaves. Rooms have names such as North Pole, Elysium and Valhalla – harking back to earlier and less centrally heated times. What would their former occupants think about today's duvets and power showers?

During the week there's a table plan for supper – another way of making sure everyone knows each other – but things are more relaxed at weekends. Girls can make themselves snacks – they just go down to the kitchen and ask for supplies. Activities include film nights, Oxford-based bowling, ice skating and trips to Port Meadow along with regular forays to Camden and Bicester Village for shopping. Boarders also take part in community activities – most recently litter picking for Oxclean (voluntary but apparently rather popular). There's a big trip once a year to somewhere like Thorpe Park that's funded by old girls – day pupils can go too but they have to pay.

Background and atmosphere: The school was founded by a Miss Lee and Miss Batty in 1897 and has always been on Oxford's busy Banbury Road. Miss Lee, the younger of the two, was a pioneer, obtaining a first-class degree in English at St Hugh's and going on to lecture and become vice principal. She funded the school from her earnings and continued to lecture in both Oxford and London. The school was named after Oxfordshire's Wychwood forest in 1918, having formerly been known unofficially as the Battery or Battery Lees, and a uniform of forest green was adopted. One of the early teachers, the redoubtable Miss Rendall, went on to found another Oxford school, Rye St Antony.

Today's Wychwood is still domestic in scale, the original brass plaque on the door (featured heavily in promotional literature) modestly announcing its presence in an area where a Latin primer, carefully launched, is bound to hit a venerable educational establishment. There's nothing flash here, no plate glass or modern architecture, but everything is well loved and cared for. Head of boarding is from the hotel industry – what a good idea – and facilities have been upgraded accordingly, although The Randolph it isn't. This was Mrs Johnson's first undertaking on arrival, strongly backed by the 'brilliant' governors, the chair of whom is a former pupil.

Pastoral care, well-being and discipline: Mrs Johnson says, 'a child can't learn if she is unhappy.' Parents say that pastoral care is outstanding: girls who need it are given time and space but this doesn't mean that the school can't be tough when called for. In a small community one person's actions can significantly affect all and Mrs Johnson will ask a girl to leave if she feels that the school can't accommodate her needs. As one parent put it, 'Yes, your daughter is an individual, but she is also part of a respectful community.' Some grumbles that pupils arriving at odd times eg half way through a term can make things a little disjointed.

Famously democratic, girls are genuinely involved in decision making – much to the horror of the Daily Mail in the 1960s (plus ça change ...). The founders' original forward-thinking structure of councillors and 'citizens' with voting rights, responsibilities and privileges still operates today (albeit with a few modern tweaks). As Mrs Johnson says, 'We're so small that everybody can be involved.'

Lower ground canteen is as nice as a lower ground canteen can be. Girls mostly complimentary about the food – favourites are the breakfasts and Friday fish and chips. There are, and have been since the school's foundation, buns at break time. Cook deserves honourable mention for skilfully adapting meals so that girls with eg dairy or gluten intolerance can eat the same as everyone else.

Some might discount a school such as Wychwood because of its small size, but consider the benefits: it's responsive, girls notice there's a play or event on down the road (this being Oxford it's more than likely) and arrangements can be made to go double quick. Parents are very involved, professionals including medics from the John Radcliffe come in to talk to pupils – this happens in other schools but it's more likely to be a lecture than a conversation. Parents told us that Wychwood was uncliquey and that foreign students integrated very well. One commented that it was very good preparation for work because you 'had to get along with everyone'.

All schools say that they nurture every child as an individual, but common sense tells us that this is easier to achieve in a school of 110 rather than an academic super tanker of 800 or more.

Pupils and parents: Used to be known as the 'Dons' school' but draws from a wider pool these days. Majority of local parents are Oxford professionals – lawyers, doctors etc. Girls we met were thoughtful, independent-minded – lacking the swagger of nearby sisters perhaps – and fiercely loyal to their school and its ways. Lots of summer-born girls, fair few refugees from schools that were too big and girls going through upheaval eg parents' divorce. And then there are girls who visited on an open day and 'fell in love' with Wychwood.

Former pupils include Margaret Casson, architect, designer and photographer; Joan Aiken, writer; Vicky Jewson, film maker; Rebecca Stockland, opera singer; Matilda Leyser, actress and aerialist; Izzie Lawrence, comedian; Honor Fell, microbiologist.

Entrance: Girls join at age 11 from local primaries/preps and there's another influx from preps at age 13. Prospective year 7s spend a day at the school and are tested in maths and English. External candidates for sixth form need minimum of six GCSEs at grades 9-4 with 9-7s in A level subjects. Places may be available in other years, subject to interview and assessment. Girls may now sit for year 9 place in years 6 and 7 (as well as in year 8).

Exit: Around 40-50 per cent leaves after GCSEs. This isn't a school that unthinkingly crams sixth formers onto the non-stop university express, although most girls do go on to further study. Occasional one to Oxbridge (none in 2018). Art and design at Oxford Brookes and elsewhere popular; other courses range from chemical engineering at Surrey to midwifery at Birmingham City to food and nutrition in Hong Kong. Girls have also gone on to be Norland nannies, Montessori educators, farriers and business entrepreneurs.

Money matters: Day fees on a par with local equivalents – OK, you're not getting the sports facilities but you are getting something pretty close to a customised education. Boarding comparatively good value. Academic, music and creative arts scholarships of approximately £1,200 pa available, as are means-tested bursaries.

Remarks: Charming pint-sized power house. Much-needed alternative to the academic overdrive of some other Oxford girls' independents (if it didn't exist someone would certainly have to invent it). A positive choice for many relieved families, one of whom described it as 'a jewel, we wouldn't want our daughter to be anywhere else.'

Wycombe Abbey

Abbey Way, High Wycombe, Buckinghamshire HP11 1PE

Ages 11–18 **Pupils** 631 **Sixth form** 192 **Boarders** 574 **C of E**

Fees: Day £29,205; Boarding £38,940 pa

01494 520381
www.wycombeabbey.com

Headmistress: Since 2013, Mrs Rhiannon Wilkinson MA MEd (50s). Previously principal at Harrogate Ladies' College, one of many curves in perfectly rounded career that includes five years at Haileybury as director of studies and two at Cheadle Hume School where was director of pastoral system. Married with children – husband, Donald is a retired headmaster.

Choice of profession early and unwavering, thanks to family clan of fulfilled teachers (has happy memories of washing out paint pots in mother's classroom). Started in large comprehensives in Devon and south Manchester, then (sensibly ignoring relative's confident predictions of 'career suicide') spent 11 years in Hong Kong and Brunei schools where managing international and affluent families honed parent-whispering skills. Only career downside – has lived in school accommodation since age of 27. 'Probably makes me a sad person.' (Not on evidence so far.)

Far more to the post than simply ensuring all that excellence in terms of popularity and superb results carries on ad infinitum, from righting genuine wrongs – 'would always be first to admit if we make a mistake' – to curbing 'me, me, me' excesses, nicely. 'You can't run any school for an individual,' she says.

Key is transparent admissions process, ensuring name and glittering prizes don't blind families to school values. 'Want parents to choose us because truly know us, not based on the name.' Spends every Tuesday with prospective parents – 45 minutes apiece – to get message across.

Staff love her and she's getting there with parents. 'A true educationalist who is clearly passionate about the school – maybe too passionate,' commented one. 'I don't think you can be too passionate because if you weren't you would lose your enthusiasm when you face some challenging times,' counters Mrs W.

Weekend 'meet the head' lunch programme under way to increase exposure, linked to match fixtures for maximum efficiency. Has also put in the time with pupils, from individual meetings in top years to throwing jolly party at house in grounds for all 65 first years. 'By end of first half term, knew everyone by name,' says parent.

Expert knowledge extends to on-site wildlife, from nesting red kites to badgers, deer and – her favourite – Stumpy the Canada goose, named for deformed wings, tenderly cared for by school with occasional Jammy Dodger as a treat.

Girls like what they've seen of her: has achieved finely judged balance that hovers somewhere between friendliness and formality, thought parent. 'She's super, so there for them, doesn't go round being all huggy or anything – they're scared of her in a nice way and the staff are also very behind her,' said mother.

Unlike predecessor, doesn't teach – yet – and is eyeing up the timetable (shame to waste that Oxford history degree). May have work cut out with building programme – two new boarding houses on site of disused swimming pool. Also starting, in a quiet way, to build public profile – was quoted in The Times talking about the ability of boarding to rescue children from otherwise pressurised existence. Looking at results with jaundiced eye this might seem a tad kettle and pot-like but no, she insists, school does amazingly well with all-embracing support rather than 'trot on Smudgy' crack of the whip. Pupils might feel cocooned; they won't feel driven.

Leaving in July 2019. Her successor will be Jo Duncan, currently head of the Royal High School, Bath. Studied English and theology at St Andrews, with the intention of working as a lawyer or teacher. After stints working in schools in Hungary and Romania during her university years she realised she felt 'very at home in the classroom' so opted to do a PGCE at Homerton College, Cambridge. First teaching post was at The Latymer School, where she taught RS for four years. Then moved to Benenden, where she spent seven years and 'fell in love with boarding and its community feel'; appointed to her first headship at Princess Helena College in Herts in her early 30s. Married to Murray, a London lawyer; they have a son and a daughter.

Academic matters: Easy to see results as inevitable consequence of admissions process – bright in, gleaming out. Results impeccable – 84 per cent of A levels and 95 per cent of GCSEs graded A*-A or 9-7 in 2018. 'Results are amazing,' said parent. 'Feels as if no barriers to what the girls could achieve.'

However, not quite the effort-free equation it might appear. Smaller numbers applying to come here means school has to spread admissions net just that bit wider than equivalent boys' schools – and it's how they manage the talent that's their forte. Whisper it softly, but sexism is still rife in education, thought parent. Boys get the very best, but for 'the girl it doesn't matter quite as much, so a school like [this] has not got such a huge pool of clever children to draw from.'

There's also the darling daughter factor, thinks Mrs Wilkinson, where doting parents can't quite bear to part from their girls. 'They are very precious, daddy's little princess, the friends of mothers and hard to let go.'

Everyone here is bright – with compulsory Latin and attempt at classical Greek for all, wouldn't cope here if they weren't, though don't overdose on GCSEs, with 10 or 11 the goal for most, one girl insistent on 13 talked down to more manageable 12. 'Great achievement is bringing up girls who are competent but don't shine and getting them to get the really top grades,' said parent.

Not a place where learning support is rushed off feet: though 54 (around 10 per cent) are identified as having special needs, for most this translates into academic support – aka learning enhancement – to plug previous curriculum gaps, particularly for overseas pupils. Just five have help with SpLD, a further five working with EAL specialist – and every pupil in the school needs to enjoy the challenge. 'My daughter's somewhere in the middle [which means] she has a lot to strive for and works harder,' thought mother.

Key is micro monitoring. No slightly below par result is given the benefit of the doubt, no progress chart left unplotted, communication between staff of the instant message variety. Parents, pupils and staff know exactly where every girl is in every subject (pre-GCSE tracking grades include three for A* – high, secure and low – alone). If anticipated trajectory shows any signs of premature wilting, the SWAT team is ready and waiting. 'The ones that would struggle, they just spend more time with them. Literally, the teacher's all over them,' said mother. 'Nobody's going to fail their grades by accident,' agreed another. Timetable underpins the message – Saturday kicks off with breakfast at 8.00am with lessons until 11.50am (detention, scheduled for 8.20am, isn't compulsory, we were pleased to hear).

Tests, predictably, are frequent but well managed and not done 'in a kind of heartrendingly tedious way,' thought parent. Inevitably, some girls find relentlessness of approach harder to bear than others, but transmogrified into gratitude when desired grades came in. 'There are times when you think "wish you would stop hounding me and accept standard" but it's worth it in the end,' said sixth former.

Parental comments acted on. Issue with one teacher relating to lesson pace 'sorted out instantly and school kept us informed on an almost daily basis [until] problem solved,' said parent. One teacher, total convert to boarding, felt it enabled tiny changes where girl 'not quite herself' to be picked up and sorted before could escalate. 'It's that swift response to a change in demeanour – remarkable, rewarding and very satisfying.'

Staff fabness is the norm, best teachers trending at top of charisma settings and 'adored' by pupils for effortless ability to take scenic route through the curriculum and 'teach round the subject, which I think is really important,' said mother. (Latest inspection report gushes agreement.)

Among many favourite subjects history teaching gets rave reviews, sharing joint honours with maths. 'School encourages you to do the subjects you love,' says pupil. 'Very foolish to take on two years in sixth form to study subjects you're not committed to,' agrees teacher.

Fairly brisk staff turnover inevitable consequence of recruiting top talent – no weights are going to hold back rise to greater things for long. Recent departure of fab director of studies to become head elsewhere par for the course. 'If you're recruiting at the top level, it's going to happen,' said parent, one of many who perceive this as price worth paying for quality teaching, while long stay figures (average age 46 with 76 staff members here for 10 years plus) do send reassuring message of stability. Only niggle is that some departures could occasionally be better timed, thought one. More quality staff accommodation – school lags behind others in this respect – would also help, feel staff and parents.

While care and attention that goes into creating the finished pupil hugely appreciated by parents, we heard more than once that aspects of culture had been a tad joy-free. 'There's a sense that growing up is a serious business,' said parent. 'We don't laugh at ourselves, we don't question ourselves that much. We know what we do, we're good at it, deal with it.'

Similarly, when rules are broken 'there's no knowing smiles, no "I've got to give you this penalty, please don't do it again but we're still friends",' said parent. 'It's "we really expect girls of your age to behave much better than this and it's not funny at all".' Occasionally po-faced? Possibly, thought staff. 'I think staff felt they needed permission to let hair down,' says head.

Staff confirm that fun, once the three letter word that dare not say its name, is now out and proud – mostly. Immediate muting of clearly very jolly (and refreshingly noisy) Latin lesson heard when this reviewer hove into view suggests not all teachers have got the message that head is, as one put it, 'in favour of jollity.'

Girls, though, stress noses are removed from grindstones on regular basis. Everyone works hard but there's 'lots of laughing and joking in the kitchen,' stressed sixth former. 'Not so serious that you shouldn't be scared to come here. We know how to have fun.'

Games, options, the arts: As with other high-achieving schools, everything you'd expect in the way of stunning stuff to play, perform or create is on show on a nearby pitch, platform or podium. Bashful won't get you places though, thought parent. 'If you're not going to do grab the opportunities, probably wouldn't suit.'

Caters for all sorts in innumerable venues, sweet-toothed first years to Cadbury's World, skiers to Whistler, budding sixth form medics to West Herts Hospital and female highflyers past and present regularly celebrated with events and talks – subsequent pupil write-ups, even by youngest, are little gems of well-observed journalism.

The 550 plus weekly instrumental lessons are also somehow fitted in, handful most years reaching diploma standard, substantial numbers hitting grades 7 and 8. Drama, equally ambitious, includes day of Shakespeare miniatures – Titus Andronicus (and others) each done and dusted in just 30 minutes.

Games widely enjoyed and lots of them, team sports 'formidable' with even tiniest slivers of talent encouraged to flourish. Teams don't straddle the alphabet – size means lacrosse, for example, only reaches C after the first year when 'have more teams so as not to make the girls feel left out.' Sure footed pretty much across the board, football, netball, tennis and squash teams among those whizzing up to quarter final stage and above in national tournaments, sailors recently taking part in world championships.

Not so sporty thrive, happy to trade games for other interests, school good at helping find inner something ('funasize' weekend activity option sounds fun, bootcamp possibly less so). Music, drama, or art, 'they'll find a way of making that come to you,' said parent.

Marvel of timetabling helps to avoid overloads – one third year had opted for piano, violin, ballet, riding and extra lacrosse. 'Very tailored. I don't know how they do it,' said parent. Sheer willpower and not letting sun set on unfinished work was pupil tip though can lead to lateish finish (10pm rare but not unheard of).

Only small bone of contention was desire to embrace the new rather than stick to tried, tested and trophy-ed – one parent thought rowing, recently introduced, could be made more of. Another, however, had nothing but praise for polo, also new to the school and thus far a galloping success.

Boarding: It's all or nothing full boarding (unless you're one of the very few day pupils). School operates non-negotiable 'closed' weekends (following hols, half terms and exeats). No choice over houses either – decision is made by school and that's that, though with posh lighting, carpet and paint upgrade programme, will be few complaints wherever you end up – fabbed-up bits of Daws Hill, for example, well worth a visit.

Oldest and youngest pupils have own houses. First years get chickens for extra homeliness, upper sixth ditch poultry for first taste of independence – wear own clothes, too (sensibly point out that as universities don't insist on work wear, why should they?). Can be heady experience – school occasionally has to coax those briefly high on prospect of unlimited toast making and TV watching back into more humdrum aspects of school life.

In between (years 2 to lower sixth) girls join one of 11 mixed-age houses (two new ones just opened), each with around 45 pupils. Older girls are enlisted as mother and granny substitutes, brilliant at 'been there, done that' advice, many issues resolved without recourse to adult intervention. Also compels older girls to keep conversation within age-appropriate limits, pointed out parent. It's rounded off with formality of timetabled slots with housemistresses and elected house prefect system (one housemistress uses two vote system, one for loyalty candidate, the other 'for one they'd really like to win – they're never wrong').

Add packed programme of evening and weekend activities, from shopping trips to ice skating and even, according to website, 'vegging out' (inverted commas – theirs – probably say it all) and parental approval pretty much universal.

Background and atmosphere: Entrance via one of High Wycombe's statement roundabouts makes countrified setting a particular pleasure. 'Abbey' is a misnomer (it's a nun-free zone, name for status purposes only) but from ecclesiastic trimmings in main building – an 18th century former mansion – to performing arts centre overlooking lake, with incredible number of performance areas (one handily combining grand piano and chaise longue for artistic swooning to music), school is very easy on the eye.

Founded 1896, school was 'new experiment' by pioneering Miss – later Dame – Frances Dove. One of Girton College's test batch of girl students and school's first headmistress, was every ounce a character, on-line portrait notable for fabulous, gravity-defying hair probably held up by principles alone.

Her aim – girls' education every bit as good as boys' through pursuit of excellence, development of talents, godliness and an understanding of the needs of others – remains top of the checklist. School's view is that even if her reaction to chicken nugget-making or 'baking with Mr Whiteley' sessions might be harder to call, Dame Frances would feel right at home with current ethos and achievements.

All happens on suitably inspirational site, originally belonging to Carringtons (current Lord Carrington is school enthusiast and regular visitor), enlarged by 1929 purchase of next door estate, Daws Hill, big enough to house a school all on its own, used for weddings and a good five minutes from main school by car (staff often drive, girls in its three boarding houses take compulsory scenic route). Has just got back World War II underground bunker, annexed after school was requisitioned as HQ for US Eighth Air Force – history department no doubt licking lips at potential for truly authentic lessons.

Little sign of world-weary London – and on and on – vibe here. Instead, children remain children – against the odds. Delightful Fairies event (you'll have to ask for details – we're sworn to secrecy) where magical beings turn every house into (tinsel) town one night in Christmas term, appears proof against teen cynicism.

Was it really healthy to put so much distance between pupils and real life, wondered one older girl, worried for health of contemporaries' souls. Definitely, think parents, who appear simply relieved that school's imposition of rules, including bans on make up and travelling unaccompanied on public transport until reach 16, keeps them off the hook. 'Might be a bit ridiculous but means girls feel safe and can be scruffy and dirty when it's appropriate,' said parent.

They also love their jargon. Prefects, unofficially, are 'mons' (once monitors); booters the temporary lockers where pre-lunch gubbins is stowed. (And, oh, the relief of seeing a bit of learning sprawl, with books, calculators and even the odd sock in contrast to pristine conditions elsewhere.)

There's Big School (actually the school hall – smell, instantly recognisable, of 'dust, old wood and overworked brains,' thought staff member) overlooked by bust of Frances Dove, grim as death, a martinet in marble, exiled from classrooms where was scaring the teachers (a joke, they said – though we wonder..)

Add Gym Courtyard (gym went years ago), four boarding Out Houses, inside the school grounds but 'you have to go out to them' – well, of course – and Long Corridor – the through route that thinks it's a communal room – and no wonder that even long-serving staff freely own up to being occasionally surprised by unfamiliar nooks and crannies.

Pastoral care, well-being and discipline: Housemistress as personality cult may be dead but continue to exert considerable beneficial influence, experts in even-handedness and clued-upness, matron and tutor completing house triumvirate. 'You get this impression, if something's happened in the morning, housemistress will know about it by lunchtime,' said parent.

Not always a breeze. Some girls won't get on with others in their house – and sophisticated urbanites vs the rest can make for occasional trouble. Staff antennae don't miss much, however, and one parent was pragmatic. Daughter has 'realised that she's just going to have to get on with it,' she said.

Pupils and parents: With school seen as nearest you'll get to girls' Eton equivalent in terms of ethos, location and facilities (impressive list of joint social events adds to sibling feel), it's often purchased as part of matching pair. Old girls are solidly brilliant type you'd expect (reality TV slebs aren't their thing, so far) and include Rt Hon Lady Justice Butler-Sloss, Baroness Howe, plus star journalist India Knight and actress Rachel Stirling.

You won't find idle rich featuring in the parental mix: hard-working, high-flying, well connected and dual income professionals dominate – as indeed they must to stump up hefty fees, though still find time to attend matches.

Some reservations about amounts of money sloshing about. 'Do worry that when many of her friends have their own Addison Lee account daughter might have a warped view of what is "normal",' said one mother. School asks for birthday celebrations to be limited to pizza or noodle bar excursions to avoid escalation of party politics.

'Don't want them to be in a privileged little bubble,' agrees head, while pointing out that anyone who can afford the fees unlikely to be on breadline. Fast growing bursary programme will help those who can't – new boarding houses will lead to gradual increase in numbers to 600. 'Thirty extra girls over seven years won't dilute product,' says head.

Girls may cover the gamut of characters, outer appearance occasionally au naturel as regards make up but sharing hefty degree of inner self-confidence (it's the quality most commented on by parents elsewhere) and appetite for success. 'Good with strong, silent type,' said one parent. Won't be squashed and there's 'healthy situation where girls help each other [but] if you're not the type that is striving to do well, you'll soon be left behind.'

Entrance: Potential pupils will 'like their notebooks and fluorescent pens – busy little bees who love finding out the way things fit together,' says head – which might help when it comes to working way through complex entrance procedures and deadlines. Register 18 months to two years in advance for 11+ and 13+ entry and at least 15 months ahead for sixth form hopefuls – minimum nine A and A*/9-7 GCSEs required. Pre-tests for all candidates.

Feeders include high profile preps in London and South East: Maltman's Green, Bute House, Francis Holland, Pembridge Hall, Glendower, Ken Prep and Garden House in year 7 (65 places – around 180 applicants). Godstowe and The Dragon at 13 (more competitive with 100 applicants for 25 places), separate exams for UK prep and overseas/senior school candidates). Around 25 per cent international pupils, Hong Kong, Malaysia and Nigeria most strongly represented. Thirty day places awarded to top performing locals.

Exit: Head's lightbulb moment was to stop post-16 exodus by giving fifth formers Through the Keyhole invite to previously, and pointlessly, top secret delights of upper sixth boarding house. While Westminster remains most desirable of alternative destinations (for some, lessons with b**s just too much of a lure) vast majority now stay on. With 28 Oxbridge places in 2018, six to Imperial and eight medics as well as Yale, Stanford and Cornell, why risk chances elsewhere, argues head?

Money matters: At five per cent off the fees, scholarships more gloss than dosh (hopefuls also need to invest six pounds in past papers); exhibitions worth £600 a year. Help for those in need via expanding bursary fund, donor generosity permitting.

Remarks: A classy, focused school, true to high-minded educational objectives of pioneering founder. Knows what it's about and makes year in, year out results look easy. Appreciative parents accept school for what it is and don't expect much in the way of radical change – except, that is, at Christmas, when the Fairies come to call. 'Encourages girls to dream big and shows them what is possible,' said one. 'We'd do it again in a heartbeat.'

Yateley Manor

51 Reading Road, Yateley, Hampshire GU46 7UQ

Ages 3–13 Pupils 400 C of E

Fees: £11,160 – £15,300 pa

01252 405500
www.yateleymanor.com

Headmaster: Since 2015, Robert Upton – an individual in the full bloom of his middle years. Astute, visionary and, as his staff observed 'a stickler', he deals with the complexity of headship with the sort of stylish professionalism that is bound to appeal equally to parents and children.

A graduate of the University of Greenwich, where he took a degree in estate management, completing a series of property management placements. Consequently, unlike many school leaders who have spent their lives in the bubble of academia, he has a grasp of the kind of futures that his pupils will encounter and that Yateley Manor parents live. He gradually came to the realisation that a teaching career made more appeal than dealing with mortar, and has gone on to acquire a breadth of experience of both the maintained and independent sectors that few of his contemporaries possess. After an opening six year spell in a primary school, during which he completed an MA in education, two primary headships in Sussex (the second of which saw him lift a school out of special measures within a year) were followed by a move to Bede's Prep in Eastbourne as director of studies, before his transfer to Yateley Manor. This, he proclaims is 'the best school I've worked in, because the staff are fantastic.'

He is only the third headmaster at Yateley Manor since the late 60s and has been shrewd enough to maintain the traditionalism of the head, who was in post for more than 40 years, whilst building rapidly upon the reforms instituted by his predecessor, who remained for six. And so, he has left his spacious and elegant study, that could feature in Homes and Gardens, largely untouched: bookshelves are wide, some filled with hardbacks from decades ago, furnishings are soft and tasteful. The tone is calm. But this all belies the modernist that the head is and the energy he displays.

Going against the widely held, and myopic belief, that it is best for a new head in his first year to stand back and just observe before implementing change, he has done what he brushes off as 'a fair amount'. This is to understate the difference he has made, especially in the technological sphere, where every member of staff, for example, has been given an iPad: not to prove that the school is somehow 'up to date' but because the head believes in both the power and the potential of interactivity. Unlike some schools who might make this investment and then let their teachers develop e-teaching and learning in their own way, he has introduced a programme of training, in conjunction with his staff development manager, which has ensured, as he says, that 'nothing has come as a shock.'

He has established a new website – a major advance on the former one – and, like many a head now, he blogs. His weekly articles are headed, rather like concept albums of yesteryear, with titles such as Giving Sleep the Blue Light and The Poison that is Stress.

Despite teaching one maths set he has still found time to develop ideas such as The Hub: a room in the heart of the school which is now a centre for parental coffee and chat. Above all, he wants to maintain and develop the strong family values that run, as he states, 'like a vein' through the school. To this end, parental ambassadors (two or three in each year group) have been appointed to define a social pattern and supply added strength to Yateley Manor's strapline that although it is 'your child' and 'their journey', it is 'our focus'.

Unsurprisingly he dismisses, with a wry shrug, the notion of any kind of term time work/life balance, although he is an early morning weekend cyclist, zipping on the lycra at 7am for his 40km surge. A large fundraising event, involving staff and parents, saw the completion of a cycle challenge from Yateley Manor to Paris in 24 hours. Very much a believer in the life truth that to stay balanced there must be movement, he leads his school with élan.

Entrance: Non-selective. Partly as a result, around 38 pupils from a roll of approximately 400 receive some form of learning support. This is provided by the head of LS and her team of four; assistance is given in class, in small groups and individually.

There are means-tested bursaries, typically giving financial assistance to one family in each year group (applications are assessed by an independent company). Parents benefit from the fact that the Yateley Manor fee is all-inclusive. There are no additional charges for lunch, snacks or residential trips.

Exit: Pupils progress to a wide range of senior schools: for example, Farnborough Hill, Salesian School, Reading Blue Coat, Lord Wandsworth College and RGS Guildford. Normally Yateley Manor's leavers would be expected to secure around 15 scholarships/awards. The school's academic reputation is therefore high, whilst the prefects whom we met at their regular Monday break time briefing with the head, could not have been more impressive.

Remarks: Yateley Manor sees itself at the forefront of curriculum development in the independent primary sector. This conviction is in great part rooted in its adoption of the Prep School Baccalaureate, a scheme that is designed to give pupils a more effective preparation for senior school life than the narrower pathway of common entrance or scholarship study. The PSB includes all core subjects but also incorporates a record of achievement in all other disciplines such as humanities, classics, art, design and sport. In addition, pupils are instructed in life skills which, for example, stress the significance of good communication and self review. As one of the four founder schools that began this scheme, the school is well used to hosting visiting teachers who wish to gain from Yateley Manor's experience. Seventeen schools now run the PSB.

For a school situated on the fringes of suburbia, it has a welcome degree of space and benefits from its design whereby both the nursery and the pre-prep are housed within the main building. On-site playing fields are well appointed and on the edge of the estate is a separate teaching block which used to house a state school. This has recently been purchased from the local authority. Located within it are an admirable suite of music and practice rooms, art & design centres and modern languages. There is a stand alone drama studio.

There are four choirs (recently the Senior Manor Singers sang mass in St Mark's Cathedral in Venice), an orchestra and numerous ensembles. The art and design is stunning; we especially liked the photographic projects and the collection of giant educational crisp packets with slogans such as Obesity Guaranteed emblazoned on their sides. French runs throughout the school and Spanish is taught in the senior years.

Drama features strongly: a recent play for years 5-8 was Olivia! which contrasts well with Shakespeare in a Week productions – recently Macbeth and A Midsummer Night's Dream. There is a comprehensive club and activities programme too, including Photography in Art, Quirkle Club, ballet and Masterchef. And then there is chess. Uniquely, in our experience, this has a designated room, the Ruy Lopez room, named after a 16th century Spanish chess playing priest. Boards are at the ready: the school's own chess YouTube channel has over 6,000 subscribers and has accumulated well over a million viewings.

In the drop zone, is the indoor swimming pool that might ideally be somewhat longer and the changing rooms which could do with more heating. Design plans are well advanced to replace them.

The trinity of pupils, staff and parents are notably enthusiastic about all that the school provides. Over our tasty beef curry at lunch, one senior girl stated that 'I want to stay to year 11 because I will miss my friends', whilst another gave approval to iPad based lessons which are 'quite cool' and to an assembly where the head tucked into a tin of dog food in order to explain that one shouldn't judge a book by its cover. Some teachers apparently 'really enjoy silence', whilst there are the normal jibes about 'loads of homework' in the final year.

The staff feel a great loyalty to the school, somehow finding the time to put on a biannual Christmas panto, and clearly feel intimately involved in its development. There is a daily staff briefing and parents receive rapid attention if they email in with problems. One senior member of the management team was especially complimentary about the innovative leadership of the school provided by headmaster and governors (profiles of the latter can be viewed on the website) who are 'always keen to move things forward'. Many schools trot out trite phrases which claim that 'pupils will be prepared to face the challenges of an ever-changing world'. At Yateley Manor this is not a pretence but a reality. The excellent school magazine is entitled Discovery.

Unsurprisingly, then, the school is popular with parents. They talk of its 'friendly, family feel' and that their sons and daughters are 'super comfortable in their own skins'. Kept very well informed by the weekly multi-paged newsletter, curiously titled Inamos (an acronym that will defeat even the most determined Googler but stands for In A Manor Of Speaking), they clearly feel that the school lives up to its promises. The FYMS – Friends of Yateley Manor School – is a well-established support group and organises quiz nights, termly discos and a biannual ball. A full coachload of parents goes on an annual Harrods shopping trip.

The Yateley Manor day can start with a full English breakfast at 8am, whilst prep supervision is available until 6.30pm, hence providing the sort of structure that working parents require. The plethora of activities that comprise the school's holiday clubs extends its appeal still further, as does the transport network which serves from, amongst many other places, Camberley, Farnborough, Hook and Odiham.

It is fitting therefore that the school's logo, which appears on every item of literature, the website and the coffee mugs, is a symbol of advancement: a ship. Some might see it as a Drake-ish galleon, but it is in abstract form, a clever combination which interlinks the past to the present. With a clear sighted head at the tiller, and his crew well ready to surf the educational waves on the horizon, there is not a better time to jump aboard.

Yehudi Menuhin School

Stoke d'Abernon, Cobham, Surrey KT11 3QQ

Ages 8-19 **Pupils** 85 **Sixth form** 28 **Boarders** 68 full, 4 weekly (from 9 years)

Fees: Day £41,811; Boarding £42,951 pa for those not on music and dance scheme

01932 864739
www.yehudimenuhinschool.co.uk

Head: Since January 2018, Kate Clanchy, previously senior master at Westminster School. Degree in modern and medieval languages from Cambridge, masters from the Institute of Education and an MBA. Initially head of marketing for a French water company; French teacher at Dulwich College, head of modern langs at JAGS, deputy head at St Paul's Girls before joining Westminster in 2013. She's also a governor of Oak Lodge School for pupils with hearing difficulties.

Academic matters: 'It's not the best, but it's OK,' was how one student described the academic provision. Results are certainly more than OK. In 2018, 67 per cent A*-A/9-7s at GCSE. A levels were 62 per cent at A*/A, 90 per cent A*-B. No-one is here for the academics, but that said, the ability profile here is above the national average, and students want to do well on all fronts.

Most students take seven GCSEs from a narrow range of subjects: music of course, then maths, English, single or double science, history and German, the school's main language because conservatoires in Germany and Austria are popular leavers' destinations here. Other languages are also taught when the need is there, and Russian, Japanese, Turkish, Mandarin have all been offered. At A level everyone takes music, and then chooses one or two further options from English, history, biology, chemistry, maths, further maths and German. No physics, because the low demand makes it hard to justify employing someone to teach it. 'That's a tricky one for us, and we'd love to be able to offer it.' Art taught throughout the school and some lovely work on show, but not usually taken as an examined subject. 'I wish there were more options,' was a concern voiced by one student and echoed by others. But the school's academic music programme, a longstanding jewel in the YMS crown, was highly praised by everyone. 'It's incredible!' 'Amazing!' 'Inspiring!' 'Harder than at Juilliard!' were typical comments.

Impossible to build year groups as such, because of very small numbers. Instead, learning is organised in four groups based on key stages. D group is made up of pupils in years 3-6, C group of those in years 7-9, B group years 10-11, and A group years 12-14. Classes are very small, and all students get a high degree of individual attention. No SEN teacher, but the school's few dyslexic pupils receive ongoing support from the regular staff and teaching assistants; one-to-one tutorials where necessary. Strong EAL support, with students who need it given regular lessons with dedicated EAL teacher. 'I couldn't speak English very well when I came,' one student told us, 'and the school has really helped me.'

Games, options, the arts: Music is, of course, the school's raison d'etre, and at least half of each day is devoted to it. Everyone has a daily practice target to meet, and it's perfectly usual for the older students to do four or more hours a day. Younger students do less and their practice sessions are supervised. Pupils receive two one-hour lessons per week on their principal instrument, and half an hour on their second study, and everyone learns composition. There are also courses in classical improvisation, choral singing, aural training and general music studies. The result is a landscape of really stellar music-making in which the students live and grow. The orchestra is stunning, and chamber music is wonderful. Huge programme of concerts, including twice-weekly ones at the school given in the beautiful Yehudi Menuhin Hall, all blond wood and gleaming Steinways, and dozens across the UK and abroad. The three pupils we saw in concert had excellent posture, were compellingly confident on the platform, and gave virtuoso performances of great beauty and taste.

Pupils have two hours of timetabled sport per week, chosen from a range of swimming (in the school's own indoor pool), football, PE, badminton, tennis, cross-country running and dance. Yoga is optional but encouraged, and an Alexander technique teacher is always available for those who want or need to see her. Annual football fixture with the Purcell School for Young Musicians in Hertfordshire. The latter usually win, it has to be said, perhaps because they number brass players and percussionists among them who tend to come up beefier.

Art is much-loved and drama has always flourished at the school: shows are staged in the Square Room, and a recent production of The Tempest was set quirkily in a boarding school. Plenty of trips to concerts, theatres, art galleries, museums, etc. DofE scheme.

Boarding: Boarding has been intrinsic to the school's ethos since its inception. The tiny number of 'day boarders' are in school from 8am until 6.30pm and are regarded as boarding pupils who sleep at home. The youngest students are weekly boarders and can go home at 4pm on Fridays. The rest stay on for Saturday morning school, after which they can go home if they choose, although many of them come from too far away for this to be possible.

The girls and the youngest boys live in Music House in quarters that we thought well-appointed and attractive. Students are grouped in 'pods' of broadly similar ages; same-age room mates can't be guaranteed because numbers are so small. Younger pupils share two or three to a room, older ones may get an ensuite to themselves. Pianos everywhere – Debussy's L'Isle Joyeuse drifted out dreamily from under the door of one room as we passed – and practice sessions are timetabled throughout the day. We'd heard reports of students practising themselves into a decline, but the house staff and students we spoke to denied this. 'We patrol the corridors and we do stop students over-practising,' said the housemistress, 'but they learn common sense.' 'It's very busy here during the day, and we want to sleep,' agreed a soignée young violinist.

The boys live in Harris House, which has a brand spanking new extension providing seven ensuite rooms and a kitchen for student use. Like Music House, it was clean, orderly, cosy and dotted with pianos. We liked the wall of clocks showing the current time in different countries around the world – 'We have pupils from every time-zone and it was a way of making them feel at home,' explained the housemaster.

As a rule, boarders have to be at least 9, but the school conceded that this wasn't rigid, and they have taken children as young as 8; we heard from one mother for whom this hadn't worked, possibly because children of that age are the exception here rather than the rule.

Background and atmosphere: Founded in 1963 by Yehudi Menuhin to give musically gifted children the chance to develop their potential to the full through a sympathetic curriculum, enhanced practice opportunities and superlative teaching in an immersive environment. Initially only for pianists, violinists and cellists, the portfolio has since been expanded to include double bass players and guitarists. The YMS approach has had its detractors and historically the school has known darker times, but some truly world-class musicians have come out of the place, although 'it's not the purpose of this school to produce lots of little Yehudi Menuhins'. Tiger mums please take note.

Beautiful Victorian mansion setting in Surrey village suggests peace and harmony. Once inside, the feel is a curious mix of very relaxed and rigidly controlling. There's no uniform, the dress code is informal, and staff and pupils are on first name terms. But as a seasoned schools' reviewer, it was clear to us as we went round that this school doesn't like criticism, or what it perceives as criticism, and that it keeps a tighter grip on the way its pupils make music than the other specialist music schools. Unlike Purcell, Chetham's and Wells students, those at YMS can't choose to continue on programmes at Saturday junior conservatoires, for instance (indeed, the school's Saturday morning programme would make this impossible.) The only exception is the double-bass players, whose teacher also teaches at RCM junior department. And despite a packed calendar of performance opportunities, the system by which pupils are chosen for the most sought-after of these is a closed one (at other music schools it's often done by audition), and several pupils told us that they felt consistently excluded. 'They choose the students who are a safe bet,' said one, a remark which had everyone nodding vigorously, and others said, surprisingly, that in the time they'd been at the school they'd had hardly any chance to perform chamber music. 'We have to give pupils the opportunities that are right for them,' was the school's response. 'If you have a high-profile concert, you have to put the people in who will pull it off. It's not always easy to be fair on paper.'

However, students were adamant that the atmosphere between them all was supportive, and not destructively competitive. 'There's actually not much competition; I've never felt it here,' was a comment that everyone agreed with, and their relish for the musical experience here was unstinting. 'It's the best you can get for the age we're at'; 'It really prepares you for music college'; 'They are such good teachers!'; 'My violin teacher is like a mother to me'; 'For practice, it's so much easier to be here, everything is so close' – etc.

No parents' association. School's reason for this is that parents come from too huge a radius for such a thing to work. Ex-parents told us that they had felt kept at arms' length, with one even telling us that they never felt welcome. But the only current parents to contact us wrote, 'Headteacher and indeed other teachers are approachable and welcoming even though they must be under pressure also.'

Pastoral care, well-being and discipline: Yehudi Menuhin believed in the importance of a homely, family atmosphere in his school, and we saw children playing contentedly in the school's leafy grounds, cheering on their friends in the lunchtime concert, and generally appearing happy and at ease. Students attested to the kindness of the staff. 'The school's been really patient with me,' said one, philosophically. 'When I first came, I wasn't a well-behaved child. Anywhere else would have asked me to leave.' In this small, artistically-driven community, the kind of misbehaviour most schools have to deal with is rare. Pupils have worked hard for their place here and want to keep it.

Staff to student ratio is low, and there are regular weekly meetings about pastoral issues. 'If someone's falling through the gaps, it's picked up,' affirmed housemaster. However, all the staff we spoke to put much emphasis on pupils 'self-managing': 'There's a lot of autonomy here'; 'They just get on with it'; 'They're surprisingly mature'; and we did wonder if this sometimes meant pupils were left to flounder. The school emphatically denied this – 'I have never taught in a school which discusses, and, yes, cares for pupils at this level'. The students themselves offered slightly ambiguous observations, such as 'We do a lot of our stuff on our own in this kind of school'; 'The older ones usually take care of the younger ones'; 'The boarding staff are doing the best job they can.' However, inspection reports have consistently rated the school's pastoral care as excellent, and the only parents to respond to our appeal for feedback wrote, 'Pastoral care is very important to us since we live far away but have been happy with the attention so far in that area.' We could not find any other parents of current students who wanted to talk to us, although we were contacted by parents whose experience of the school had been negative and who had taken their children away.

Pupils and parents: Just over half are from the UK (although this figure includes a few international families who have relocated so that their child can attend the school), the rest from overseas. Very broad range of backgrounds and nationalities makes for a truly cosmopolitan school community: students currently hail from the UK, Ireland, France, Germany, Switzerland, Spain, Poland, Bulgaria, Bosnia-Herzegovina, Serbia, Turkey, Morocco, Tunisia, China, Taiwan, South Korea, Singapore, Japan, Thailand, Brazil and Mexico. It's a musical hothouse and has its fair share of eccentrics, but it's impossible not to be won over by the results. The young people we met were all really lovely: articulate, thoughtful, intelligent, personable, good-mannered and good fun.

Alumni include Nigel Kennedy, Tasmin Little, Nicola Benedetti, Kathryn Stott, Melvyn Tan and Colin Carr.

Entrance: No set entry point. The process is long and thorough: preliminary audition, then main audition, then a three-day residential assessment during which they take part in all aspects of school life including instrumental lessons, academic lessons and boarding. Children have to be robust. A rejected recent candidate played incredibly but wasn't ready socially. Academic ability not important.

Students who join the school in the sixth form must stay on for year 14, continuing with their instrumental tuition plus academic music and possibly another AS. This could be seen as another example of the school's determination to control its end product, but the year 14 students we met were positive about the experience, and felt it to be of benefit to their musical development.

A child must join before their 17th birthday, but otherwise a student's age isn't taken into account and the year groups aren't even. School won't admit into year 11, but happy for students to repeat a year and go into year 10.

Exit: The overwhelming majority to music conservatoires around the world: at this rarefied level, they choose the teacher with whom they want to study and apply to the institution where that teacher is based. 2018 destinations included the Royal College of Music (three), the Royal Academy of Music, Conservatorium van Amsterdam, Julliard school New York and one off to study music at Cambridge. Occasionally a student wishing to pursue broader academic options will leave at 16.

Money matters: Inevitably one of the most expensive boarding schools in the country, given all the top-calibre specialist tuition, but hardly anyone pays full fees. Families who have been continually resident in the UK for at least two years receive means-tested funding from the government's Music and Dance Scheme. For those ineligible for the scheme, the school has its own bursary fund: it has a good endowment, and fundraising is ongoing. Where they can, they match what the Music and Dance Scheme would pay.

Remarks: This is as unusual a school experience as it's possible to get, and one that parents need to choose with their eyes wide open. Don't send your highly academic teen here and then complain that they can't do triple science. Don't put your 8-year-old here if you want them to have lots of friends the same age. Try not to send your child here in the secret hope that they'll be the next Fritz Kreisler. But if the music offered here is what your child wants with all their being, and you believe that they couldn't be as happy anywhere else as they could be here, go for it.

London

M25
M1
M4
BARNET
HARINGEY
HARROW
CAMDEN
HILLINGDON
BRENT
HAMPSTEAD
A
B
EALING
KENSINGTON
HOUNSLOW
RICHMOND
UPON THAMES
MERTON
KINGSTON
UPON THAMES
SUTTON

A
HAMPSTEAD
CHALK FARM

ENFIELD
WALTHAM FOREST
REDBRIDGE
HAVERING
HACKNEY
ISLINGTON
NEWHAM
TOWER HAMLETS
CITY
SOUTHWARK
GREENWICH
LAMBETH
LEWISHAM
BROMLEY
CROYDON
M11
M25
M20

B
PADDINGTON
KENSINGTON
KNIGHTSBRIDGE
BELGRAVIA
CHELSEA

Junior Schools
Senior Schools
Junior & Senior Schools

LONDON

The Academy School

3 Pilgrims Place, Rosslyn Hill, London NW3 1NG

Ages 6–13 **Pupils** 95

Fees: £19,470 pa

020 7435 6621
www.academyschoolhampstead.com

Principals: Garth Evans BA (late 50s) and Chloe Sandars LRAM Prof Cert FTCL (early 50s) founded the school in 1997. Garth, whose hoary appearance and wry sense of humour bears more than a passing resemblance to Bill Murray, was born and brought up in London. Educated at Westminster and Queen Mary University London, where he read English. Garth's sugar hair, large frame and intent look lend him an aura of wisdom and experience. He enjoys telling the tale of his great grandfather who was part of Scott's expedition to the Arctic. Married to Bee, who is responsible for admissions, teaches geography and is the school nurse. The couple divide their time between London and the south coast near where their (now grown up) children were educated at Sevenoaks.

Garth is charismatic, coming across as a maverick. He sees the big picture and values the important things in life. 'Education is about finding what's your thing, whether that's a maths thing or a guitar thing,' he says. 'The aim is to achieve excellence but dare to have fun while you're doing it.' Although he is the disciplinarian in this establishment, the children remark on his kindness and empathy as well as his intellectual rigour: 'He notices when you aren't happy and makes you feel better,' commented one 10 year old. He started his career teaching English and now teaches maths: 'much better to teach a subject which doesn't come naturally,' he twinkles. He has the older children doing trigonometry and going far beyond what is expected of them – the key thing here is not the grades and 'getting into' a particular school, but instilling a love of learning.

Garth and Chloe met while they were both teaching at Trevor-Roberts, and tutoring too. They decided there was a need for the kind of education The Academy so effectively provides and set up the school in 1997. Chloe, educated at Oxford High School, the Royal Academy of Music and Trinity College of Music, is engaging, thoughtful and thorough. She is passionate about teaching maths, which she does brilliantly, by all accounts, to years 5 and 6. 'It's vital to engage the girls, to make it interesting for them, to show the patterns and make the connections. Many girls switch off maths, and think that they're no good.' Married to Andrew, who left his job in the City to become part of the team, they have two daughters, both educated at St Paul's Girls'. Andrew, educated at Magdalen College School and Cambridge University, deals with the data and the detail (he prefers to describe it as 'the financial, management and regulatory aspects of the school'). He also teaches history. With Andrew's and Bee's support, Garth and Chloe have the time and space to to do the things they love, teaching, inspiring and nurturing the children. Each of the four individuals are key corners of this very stable leadership team.

Entrance: Entrance into year 2 (though very occasionally they will take someone, a sibling for example, who is in year 1, typically at the beginning of the summer term). This is essentially a school that begins at 6 and they need to be ready for specialist subject teaching from the word go. The school will entertain applications at any time from then on and is refreshingly welcoming and willing to see if they can make it work. Parents and children come in to meet the principals and the children will be assessed while spending some of the day with their peers. Do they fit in, can they keep up? 'We're happy to work with the very strong as well as the weak,' says Chloe; the important thing is to make sure it's the right fit. Maximum of 95 pupils in total (space is at a premium).

Exit: To a range of London day schools, hardly any to board. Deft management of parental expectation.'We are very transparent,' says Chloe. Parents sent not only the results of practice papers, but the papers themselves as well as the marks (without the names) of the other children in the class so that they can see where their child sits in relation to others. Most get their first choice of school; some go as far afield as Merchant Taylor's, Haberdasher's Aske's, St Paul's and Westminster, others to North London Collegiate, Channing, City of London, UCS, Highgate, Mill Hill, North Bridge House, Francis Holland or South Hampstead. Parents here tend to be sensible and listen to the advice of the experts who really do know where their children will thrive.

Remarks: An intimate, small co-ed Hampstead prep school, tucked into the grounds of a church off the lower end of chic Hampstead High Street, The Academy is not well known but most of those who discover it are delighted. Ofsted, in its recent inspection, was bowled over, awarding it an outstanding in every category, not an easy achievement these days. Chloe, referencing the report, smiles: 'Just because we are relaxed I wouldn't want people to think we are lax'.

Everyone is on first name terms, no 'Sir', or 'Miss' here. Rules are kept to a minimum. The uniform is a low key navy tracksuit, there is no ornate reception area filled with flowers, no grand office where parents can meet the principals in private to discuss their children. The fabric of the building, charming though it is, could definitely do with a lick of paint, yet the informality belies a rigour in the classroom that is less easy to perceive on a brief visit. Expectations here are high, there is an attitude of genuine scholarship, children are taught thoroughly and no one slips through the net. 'We know who the 10 weakest readers are and they will get extra individual reading every day,' says Chloe. The aim is to inspire the children. Subject specialist teachers from the start, who really know their subject, imbue their pupils with a love for their it. Parents remarked on how committed the staff are and how skilful at navigating between different abilities, particularly in the early years.

Not a school for a child with serious special needs, however, but they can cope and do an excellent job with pupils with mild dyslexia or dyspraxia. No specialist teaching but rather one-to-one work out of class. One part time SENCo sees only a handful of individuals on a regular basis. Behaviour here is good: 'The discipline is imaginative and creative rather than heavy handed,' commented one parent. 'They look for the positive all the time and treat the child as an individual – a complete person – which is enormously productive.'

Class sizes are small. The child-centred approach extends to making sure that an artificial date such as a birthday doesn't impede or impair progress. As they move up the school the pupils are set for maths and English, but this is done with a great deal of care and tact and there is plenty of movement between the sets. An absence of IT generally, whiteboards and computers particularly, is noticeable. Teaching here is old style, and effectively so.

Parents remark on how nurturing the school is but some expressed surprise at the amount of homework and the focus on academics. 'I thought it was relaxed,' said one mother, 'but actually they have very high expectations and the pace is fast'. This is tempered by a warmth and focused attention that is

A

unusual in most busy London preps. Not only do all the teachers know each child but Sally, a therapist, visits on a regular basis and spends time with individual children who need emotional support for whatever reason, whether for problems at home, difficult friendships at school, or a bereavement. There is a room full of paints and toys where the children can feel completely safe.

The chapel building lies at the heart of the school and is used for anything from whole school theatrical productions and concerts to lessons and even table tennis in break. 'We love curling up next to the radiators in there in the winter,' said one child. 'It's such a warm and comfortable space.' Classrooms occupy the rooms that line the edge of the chapel and when we visited, a class was being taught geography in one corner, while a younger class did classics in another. The central courtyard between the chapel and the main building is reminiscent of an Italian villa – elegant borders, small angular grassy lawns, wrought iron fences, tasteful paving and a few plants sown by the children for good measure. Tucked behind the main building down a narrow path, past the vicar's house, is the hall where they can run around playing team building games like dodgeball or capture the flag. At break time, out come the skipping ropes and hoops. Some heat their packed lunches (brought from home or ordered from the local organic café) in microwave ovens in rooms adjoining the hall and there is a comfortable room with sofas and chairs where children can read and talk.

With the exception of the lavatories, which you might be forgiven for expecting to find in a (grand) house rather than a school, the rooms are small. The library is not much larger than a box room; when we visited, books were scattered untidily on the floor and piled round the edges. However the children love coming in here, curling up on the piles of cuddly toys and choosing the books from the carefully compiled coloured, spotted index. Art takes place in several different rooms at the top of the school; we saw some Picasso influenced self portraits, a collage project based on Matisse and some papier mâché balloons as well as wire sculptures and an impressive array of random clay figures soon to be fired in the kiln.

It would be a mistake to judge the school too much on the premises, however, as they are just part of the picture. The school makes creative use of whole of London, whether it's regular hikes to the Heath for fresh air and exercise, walks to the Royal Free sports hall for team sports, or cultural trips to theatres and museums. Unusually, from the age of 10 the children can go to designated local cafés to buy their own lunch on a Friday.

The big annual event is the musical production. Most recently the whole school was involved in a production of Oliver! performed in the chapel. Every child is involved and 'for several weeks everything revolves about making it splendid, which it is,' observed a parent. Although there are not a lot of concerts, productions and whole school events, when there is one it tends to be exceptional. Music is popular, and of a high standard – Chloe's interest and talent are important influences. One enthusiastic pupil relayed how she loved making up a music poem using different sounds from household objects, whether with a water bottle, a table or a saucepan. The talent contest at the end of the year is another hugely successful whole school event. Everyone gets to shine, whether by dancing, gymnastics, reciting poetry or singing a song.

There are games – cricket, tennis, badminton, football, handball, table tennis and netball etc – every day, and a double games lesson every Thursday at the Royal Free Sports Hall. They have qualified sports coaches and play matches against other schools, but a parent observed that the number and quality of competitive matches is disappointing, feeling that sport here is more about getting exercise and having fun than anything else. School disagrees and says 'our children.. make very considerable progress in sport'.

When we visited the school had just celebrated its 20th birthday and it's come a long way since the tiny number of pupils it started with. It's still small: the numbers have consistently remained at around 90 for the past five years. This is how they mean to keep it – in a school this size, 'you can properly know every single child,' says Chloe. Shaped like a fish, the school tends to start small (in years 2-4), increases in number in the middle, creating a bulge between years 4 and 6, and then slims down again for the final two years when there tends to be very few girls and about 12 boys.

No organised, structured parents' meetings, PTA, class reps or coffee mornings and very few emails. The school is small enough for things to be conducted more fluidly and informally. If there is a problem the door is open for parents to come and discuss it and 'you can always call Garth on his mobile,' said one mother, 'as can my child if he is having a problem with his maths'. One parent expressed relief that she isn't bombarded by emails here as she has been by other schools, while another observed that it can appear disorganised when they are asked for their consent at the final hour for a rock climbing trip. Parents appreciate the regular updates on progress, together with lists to show where their child ranks in the class.

Parents here are an eclectic mix. Plenty of professionals, doctors, and lawyers as well as academics and scientists, most are local but some originate from all corners of the world, from Scandinavia to China. The one thing they all have in common is they want their children to be happy and to reach their potential. Reams of grateful letters when their children leave, demonstrating again the positive relationships that families form with the quadrumvirate. This all contributes to making The Academy, despite its focus on scholarship, far less of a pressure cooker than many schools of its kind in north London and beyond, though don't underestimate its earnest approach to the work they do.

ACS Hillingdon International School

Hillingdon Court, 108 Vine Lane, Hillingdon UB10 0BE

Ages 4–18 **Pupils** 580 **Sixth form** 100

Fees: £10,640 – £24,400 pa

01895 259771
www.acs-schools.com

Head of school: Since 2017, Martin Hall (50s), who hails from Aberdeen, studied economics and philosophy in Glasgow then to Worcester College of Education where he did his PGCE (secondary economics), working first at St Olave's Grammar school and then off to Tanzania for two years' voluntary service. 'It was very formative, it made me content with small things and realise that a good teacher can achieve wonderful things regardless of a school's facilities'. This tall, affable man still has an outdoor spirit and a desire to do good. He came back to the UK for more teaching jobs but then returned to Tanzania and there he met his wife. That was his first experience of IB teaching, to which he is now committed: 'more room for experiential learning'. After a further stint (six years) at the Inter-Community School of Zurich, he moved back to Tanganyika International School, overseeing two campuses and gaining a good head for business.

He was drawn to ACS Hillingdon because it allowed him to get back to the the UK, to be closer to teaching again, and he immediately liked the warmth of the school and the 'ambition and pluckiness' he felt that this small school has. Pupils are excited about him teaching economics – they 'are lucky to have him so involved, even though they like their other economics teacher'. He is aware of the challenges – a transient population, a lack of tradition, a need to provide a huge range of curricula for the pupils with so many different academic trajectories. However, his wide experience and open nature mean he may have solutions – building up a coherent curriculum and creating identity: 'learning is not just about communicating knowledge, it must be transformational'. After several changes of head and an acting head here, everyone very much hopes he does indeed have a vision and will stay to carry it through.

He has all three of his children at ACS and his wife teaches at a local primary school. Parents say they don't see him often – most contact is with the principals of high, middle or lower school. New high school principal September 2018, middle school principal in post since 2014, lower school principal in post for more than 20 years.

Academic matters: Non-selective and taking pupils at all times of the year from all different academic traditions means this school needs to be flexible and adaptable and have a good range of curricula to offer. The IB middle years programme has been dropped and the school now offers its own special blend of IB, British and American courses, with average IB points of 33 in 2018, though some high flyers who do very well.

Reception and year 1 have their own spacious bungalows and playground, and the linked indoor outdoor learning, teaching assistants and generous facilities make it a dreamy place for kids to be. 'Parents choose this over the local state schools in order to allow their children to learn through play – it matches a more international style of school where pupils don't start formal learning until after they are 6 years old'. Teachers and teaching assistants supported by specialist art, music and PE teachers.

Lower school continues the comfortable atmosphere, with a sofa in each classroom, groups of tables, teamwork, collaborative projects and thematic learning. EAL support extensive in these early years if needed, and highly differentiated reading schemes. iPads used regularly, with technology lessons ensuring they know how to upload video and recordings and photos of their work onto the intranet site to be shared with parents and saved at the end of the year in a digital file. Lower school pupils can then use their technological skills for creating, building and innovation and STEAM (science, technology, engineering, art and mathematics) integrated in all their learning. We have rarely seen so much opportunity for building and making – enough Lego, straws and cardboard to make tiny fingers itch. Native language enrichment ensures pupils keep up and develop their mother tongue, and they learn Spanish in lower school as well as having a language of the month so they are exposed to languages to match the different nationalities. Parents called the lower school 'phenomenal', with good structure and purposeful development.

Middle school pupils have homerooms where they meet and have lockers, but they move to specialist teaching rooms, gaining independence and study skills. Spanish and French for all in middle years. Choice of drama, dance or visual arts each term. And again, generous lashings of designing and using technology, including building robots, in all their learning – presentations, videoing, displaying, investigations and finding solutions. 'I wish my child could have more lessons with the technology teacher – she is fantastic and they learn so much'. The school has a Genius Bar that is available to resolve problems with devices – don't we all wish we had access to that!

Teachers expect pupils to question and learn from mistakes: no rote learning happening here. 'We teach them to be ready for things we don't even know will be in their futures'. Pupils were expected 'to ask yourselves what would you have done in that situation'. Pupils going on a school visit to Apple asked designers 'what was the worst mistake you ever made?' Realising it is from mistakes that come the most exciting developments. Parents are concerned that since abandoning the middle years programme, neither pupils nor teachers are clear of the curriculum. 'The middle years seems to have lost its way – my child doesn't have a clear idea of where they are or where they are going'. 'It is all very laid back and chilled, but that is not what I am wanting from a school'. Though in annual parent surveys, most say their children are challenged by the curriculum and some parents appreciated the flexibility of not having the MYP.

A new suite of science rooms with large light rooms dedicated to physics, chemistry and biology, with and space for experimenting. The success of the science labs can be seen in the students' extended project choices, with conference level posters of research: 'How does temperature affect the concentration of iron in fresh and frozen spinach?'; 'How do the different lengths of hydrocarbons affect the rate of combustion?'

Upper school involves more independent learning. Weekly sessions with university guidance counsellors in the first term to ensure they are on target with deadlines and that they have chosen pathways that will suit their education goals. 'My daughter enjoys the breadth the IB offers over the science A levels she would have taken in her old school'. Pupils have a choice of IB courses, American AP courses or High School Diploma courses, but they all have to be involved in CAS (creativity, activity and service). We met pupils who were following the IB diploma fully, some who were taking the odd IB course as part of acquiring the High School Diploma – plenty of choice and options to be busy and extended. Pupils seemed motivated and engaged: 'The IB course is really hard, and even though I have an unconditional place at university and don't need the grades, I owe it to myself to do as well as I can in the exams'.

Upper school students have a wood-panelled library worthy of an Oxford college, the middle school library provided a generous study space and chill out zone, and the lower school library had sofas and hidden corners to lose yourself in a book. Three full-time librarians make sure that despite the modern acceptance of iPads, technology and screens, all the pupils read and love books.

Most of the learning support is based around EAL and language acquisition together with supporting pupils' mother tongue languages. There is some dedicated learning support. The use of technology through the school does help to support different learning styles. Parents also liked the way that particular strengths were noted and pupils extended and challenged with extension work or put into advanced classes – especially in maths.

Games, options, the arts: Exceptional artworks in a huge range of media cover the walls, including photography displays, with a large number of pupils choosing art at IB and achieving well above average (last year 25 per cent of pupils achieved a grade 7 out of 7 in IB art). Four dedicated art teachers going above and beyond as we saw printing, graphics, modelling, painting, mosaics, collage, displays, oil, portraiture and in depth analysis. A pottery kiln is an added bonus – pupils were making plaster casts of their hands and using these to make sculptures based on Anthony Gormley's work – serious stuff, particularly for the lower school.

A

Film studies a relatively new IB course – very popular, with excellent sound, filming and editing suites as well as trips to nearby Pinewood Studios.

A large space dedicated to STEAM activities – science, technology, engineering, art and mathematics. Learning to work in teams, design and build experientially and practically develops problem solving skills. The technology room includes a student built 3D printer, alarms, pupil built robots, drones and devices worthy of the most technologically advanced homes.

Regular PE lessons take place within the school timetable (twice weekly) but it is the after-school sport that is extensive – sports fields 10 minutes away host a range of sports and competitions against other international schools both locally and abroad. 'There is an emphasis on participating, thanks to the encouragement and the general ethos of the school,' according to one dad. Swimming at a local pool. Specialist PE teachers ensure that the cabinet of trophies is well stocked with wins by the Hawks.

One parent said 'the sport culture is excellent, there is a balance between academic development and strong sport involvement. Sport is used as a positive balance to develop a rounded person'. 'We see sport as an integral part of our child's school life': even though it takes place after school, 'they come home less stressed and fitter than if they had not done the sport between school and homework'. Parents commented, however, on the few galas and matches with other schools. And one pupil complained about mixed sex football teams as numbers were too few for separate teams.

Music taught by specialist music teachers twice weekly from reception onwards, with middle and upper schools having use of a dedicated building, Harmony House, with individual practice rooms (plenty of peripatetic music teachers for individual lessons), music lesson rooms and generous suites of computers for composition work. 'I like it that they are able to extend their musical interest – my child is now part of a rock band'. A choir allows pupils to help complete their CAS requirement.

After-school activities included theatre, fencing, golf, cooking, eco club, street dance, kickboxing, zumba, track and field, chess and language enrichment. Older pupils involved in Duke of Edinburgh, National Honour Society and International Schools Theatre Association.

Background and atmosphere: Set amidst a leafy, residential suburb, is the 1855 grand country home of the Mills family with their 13 children. It became a convent in 1920 and was bought by the school in 1978. Listed building status means that the fine stucco work, high ceilings and elegant windows are lovingly maintained – and now used and enjoyed by pupils and staff. A glorious red room used for recitals overlooking immaculate lawns and manicured planting. Modern buildings have been added on – slightly incongruous, but very spacious and practical gyms, classrooms, canteen, with a brand new science floor on top. High school uses the older buildings, lower and middle school the more modern section and the youngest classes have their own bungalow and playground space next to the learning support Pavilions.

The grounds tennis courts, a multisport all-weather sports field, vegetable patch looked after by the eco club and parking for the 37 school buses at drop off and collection times. School playing fields a short bus ride away. Overall a great feeling of space – staff room enormous, wide corridors for pupils to move around, huge science labs, extra rooms for team working and studying, generous numbers of art rooms, meeting rooms, music rooms. A luxury to have so much space for learning and playing so close to London.

Parents felt that they had good access to teachers on the whole with three reports with narrative each year.

School lunches a flexible arrangement as pupils can decide each day whether they are eating school lunch or packed lunch (a fingerprint system avoids money being brought in). Large salad bar (special low salad bar for the tinies), good range of hot food, sandwiches and soups, and interesting menu from a different country each day. No pushing or shoving, things run smoothly and calmly and mealtimes chatty but not noisy.

Pastoral care, well-being and discipline: International pupil body very accommodating – parents grateful 'that we are family to each other' and that 'kids are kind'. Many parents mentioned the small size of the school as a positive: 'everyone knows each other' and 'teachers are really available for students and they know them well'. A 'positive peer group' and 'international mix of kids adds a real richness and creates a nice social network'.

'I haven't had to expel anyone – a short discussion with pupil and parents quite enough to right any wayward behaviour. And that is limited to some roughness in the playground or leaving premises without permission – never anything worse than that,' says the head. This is not a traditional or rigid school – kids set their own standards in the main and stick to them. There is a sense that pupils are reasoned with rather than told. And parents confirmed that they are emailed or phoned if there are any issues to avoid them escalating, though some noticed increasing amounts of 'mouthiness' going on in middle school years.

Pupils and parents: Some 70 per cent of pupils come to school on one for the 37 buses that either collect from homes or from collection points. Families around Gerrards Cross, Richmond, Chiswick and St John's Wood (known as little America). A growing number of local British families. 'Most of us have several passports and may not even have lived in the country our passport is from' – but some 35 per cent American, 17 per cent British, plus small numbers from 40 other countries.

Parents in banking, oil, film, increasingly military and diplomatic services. The school sees a change towards more 'local international families' – those that came for a short time on international placements but have stayed and are now very much local families.

Entrance: Admission at all times of the year after visits, references, school reports and questionnaires. Children accepted without English in lower school but higher up must be able to access curriculum. There is learning support department for mild learning differences. Some mobility difficulties can be accommodated but the old, listed building not suitable for wheelchairs.

Exit: Good career input – 'I have an internship this summer thanks to the school' and school counsellors help with university choices. University applications to UK based on Measurement of Academic Progress data obtained on all students, and internal tests. Increasing numbers are staying all the way through school 'we extended our stay in the UK so that our child can finish at ACS'. Exit to Bournemouth, Imperial, King's, SOAS, Birmingham, Warwick; or in the USA – Boston, Emerson, Florida State, Northeastern, Parsons, Syracuse. A peppering to other countries including Canada, Australia and the Netherlands.

Money matters: School fees do not include bussing service nor lunch nor learning support, but huge range of facilities and equipment an indication that the school is not cutting corners. Privately owned by a not-for-profit corporation with two sister schools in the UK and one in Doha. Becoming a charity so they can offer more financial assistance (scholarships previously only for two final years, but now financial awards from 20-100 per cent available at 11, 13 and 16).

Remarks: This school gives a well rounded education, humane and with priorities about the student's well-being rather than school's image. Not wildly competitive in any area, with the drive coming from the students rather than imposed. Music, sport and art balance the enquiry-led academic life of students in spacious and generous grounds with good facilities. 'We chose this school because it felt very relaxed and there was a happy buzz in the school with children laughing and talking,' say parents.

Alexandra Park School

Bidwell Gardens, London N11 2AZ

Ages 11–18 **Pupils** 1,560 **Sixth form** 471

020 8826 4880
www.alexandrapark.school

Headteacher: Since 2008, Michael McKenzie MSC PGCE (late 40s) – educated at a comprehensive in Birmingham, he read chemistry at Nottingham, followed by his teacher training at the Institute of Education. Head of year at William Ellis School in Camden which he cites as one of his 'most enjoyable times in education', then head of sixth form at LaSWAP and a brief stint at Parliament Hill School. Subsequently, deputy and associate head at Beal High School in Redbridge. Familiar and comfortable with Alexandra Park School's ethos before he applied, as the founding head had been his teaching mentor.

His reputation had preceded him and phrases such as 'the consummate PR man', 'fantastic salesman', 'smooth' were not an exaggeration. This head could sell sand to the Sahara – and it doesn't take Einstein to suss out how this once mediocre comprehensive has now become top of the league of schools in Haringey. The head says: 'If I am called a salesman, it's only because my commitment to the product – in this case education – is unequivocal.'

We finally meet (after trying to pin this head down for a while) and are greeted as if we were royalty – beaming smile, firm handshake and the exuberance of somebody who clearly delights in their job. Friendly and chatty – one could almost forget the purpose of our visit and drift into a non-relevant conversation. But be not fooled – this head is very much on the ball, and relishes the school's many achievements and outstanding students. He constantly finds his students 'very entertaining', and delights in meeting different kids every year. 'I have a student now. who is possibly one of the brightest I have ever come across. I am so excited to see how it pans out for that person..I am constantly motivated by bright pupils and those who want to challenge.'

He is a state school head through and through and says he could never be beguiled by the private sector. 'London has a very interesting education system. One of the strengths of this school is the mix. We still have pupils from as far afield as Tottenham from when school's catchment used to exceed five miles.' However, he is realistic that this diversity has changed over time, as the school's popularity has reduced the catchment to 0.7 miles – which by virtue of its location (pricey Muswell Hill), will invariably make it more socially homogeneous. 'I can't control that element, but it will be a long time before that happens. There is still a good mix at APS, which keeps the school a little bit sane.'

Described by parents as being 'very much on the ball'; we imagine this head doesn't allow himself much downtime. Married, no children.

Academic matters: The proud recipient of a World Class Schools award, which means that APS belongs to a pretty exclusive club of only 19 schools nationwide. The award is given to schools who 'equip students with knowledge, skills and confidence to thrive in a challenging international environment where those who succeed take risks and continually pursue improvement.' APS's motto is 'success for all' and the school pulls off the very tricky achievement of being a successful London comprehensive welcoming the full range of abilities and social spectrum. 'Unlike other schools round here, it doesn't pick and choose. It's very inclusive,' said one parent.

The intake may be all-encompassing but the academic values remain traditional. 'We don't play any games with the curriculum,' says the head, and the school is notably strong on core subjects. 2018 results at GCSE: 84 per cent got 9-4 in both English and maths, with 40 per cent of grades 9-7. Most pupils take 10, including all three sciences. Spanish, French and Mandarin standard languages with Turkish also an exam option for GCSE and A level. Classics also a popular option with more than 120 pupils studying this at GCSE and A level.

Has specialist status as a science and maths school and an international school. More than 200 students last year had the opportunity of studying in partner schools in France, Spain, South Africa and China. Mandarin on the curriculum here and is more than token – students can spend time on an immersion course in Beijing, with 57 studying the language pre-GCSE, a dozen or so in the sixth form, and APS is one of a select group of schools in the Mandarin Excellence Programmae.

Some setting from year 7, depending on the department head – so maths and science are setted, English is not. When students first arrive, they are split into 'Alex' and 'Park' – one lot doing Spanish, the other French. This has been the subject of much heated debate as students are no longer offered the choice. One disgruntled parent told us: 'My family live in Spain, so I was very keen for my daughter to learn Spanish, but she was put into French and there is no room for movement.' Latin and classical civilisation popular. Arts and media studies – unsurprisingly in this heartland of the media classes – are notably good so, to counterbalance the trend, has opted for a specialism in science and maths, with a dramatic upswing in results. Good vocational curriculum, with BTecs in sport, business, art, salon services and catering, some taught at the College of North East London. 'It means children who might have been less engaged have something positive and interesting to do, and those taking academic exams have the space to focus,' said one parent.

Popular sixth form – in 2018, a creditable 33 per cent A*/A grades and 65 per cent A*-B grades at A level; 32 subjects on offer – strongest include English, French, physics and 'a really happening' history department.

Strong gifted and talented programme – pupils take early exams in maths, statistics, astronomy and classics. Astronomy has become so popular that the subject caused much controversy last year as the school didn't anticipate how many students would want to do the course, and spaces were limited. One parent told us: 'When we heard that astronomy was being offered as a GCSE, we jumped at the chance – we're middle class after all, of course we'd want our kids to do an extra GCSE!' However, there were many disappointed students who didn't get onto the course at first, 'but credit to the school, they listened to parents and extended the provision', putting an additional astronomy class to cater for all 60 students.

Also notable SEN support under dynamic head of special needs, with additional support in year 7 for those who've not yet achieved the requisite level in maths and English. This school seems to succeed where other large comprehensives fail, in that the large bulk of students who fall in the middle are as well monitored as those at the extreme ends. One parent told us: 'My daughter was very middling in her primary school and didn't have much confidence in her abilities. However, she has really thrived at APS, and whenever I go to parent evenings, one would think my daughter was top in everything.' Another parent told us: 'My son was really floundering before he came here, but he has really blossomed. The teachers get him.'

A National Teaching School, indicating the importance the school places on appointing the best practitioners and ensuring they receive the latest training. The teachers have been particularly praised as being a young and enthusiastic cohort with infectious enthusiasm – although, as with all schools, 'you do get the odd one who makes you think, why are they still here – are they unsackable?' Such is their dedication to the job, that the school is open on Saturdays and Sundays for several weeks before exams, for students who feel they need an extra bit of support: 'This is all off the back of the teachers, and not because I ask them', Mr McKenzie assures us.

Games, options, the arts: Busy, busy, busy. Specialist music and drama with a media suite and dance on offer. The school has a vibrant and very well-resourced music department with large numbers of students choosing to study music at key stage 4 and 5 and also a range of vocational courses including music technology. Extensive extracurricular programme including three choirs, orchestra and jazz band and the department organises an annual concert tour to Europe. More than 250 students take music lessons; 25 peripatetic teachers. Every student is expected to study music and drama each week. Large scale productions of Oliver! and Grease have included around 60 pupils running the entire event, from on stage to backstage to front of house. The school also has an annual Shakespeare performance.

Art also popular, 'one of the reasons my daughter chose this school.' Lucky pupils can draw inspiration in the stunningly bright art studio overlooking the golf course, which the head says he's been trying to claim for years as his office, 'but the art team won't let me.' (We were particularly struck by a fantastic portrait of Barak Obama drawn by a GCSE student.) Energetic visual arts with A levels in photography, art and product design, plus a creative and media diploma for those wishing to work on large-scale projects. Also a wonderful facility for textiles and those wishing to do fashion design.

Though relatively limited on-site space for sport, games spill over into adjoining Dunsford Park and plenty of variety to suit all tastes. Basketball, football (West Ham's wonder youngster, Reece Oxford, is a recent ex-student), netball, rugby and cricket are main sports, but judo, aerobics, trampolining, tennis, badminton, wrestling and rugby also part of the offering. Online student newspaper. Eclectic range of after-school clubs includes astronomy, knitting, fashion, pursuit cycling and cheerleading.

Trips a big feature, with more than 120 throughout the year including student exchanges to China (for those studying Mandarin), geography in Iceland, French in the south of France, art in Madrid, politics in Washington and design in New York. Good careers advice with visits to universities and higher educational conferences.

Background and atmosphere: Local parents lobbied the local authority to create a new school in the area and APS was eventually founded in 1999 on the site of a former FE college. A relatively constricted site of five acres which feels more spacious due to the surrounding greenery of Muswell Hill golf course and Durnsford Park. The original mix of pleasant brick buildings, some from the 1950s, some from the 1980s, have been joined by a sleek modern extension (winner of a 2006 Civic Trust Award) and the sixth form centre. Extensive recent work has created a new humanities block, additional science labs, ICT suites and a media department.

Although visually impressive outdoor space was always a challenge, through clever remodelling of outdoor areas, the purchase of adjacent land and the use of the adjoining Durnsford Park, students now have a range of areas to eat lunch, play or just 'hang out'. This is particularly true for sixth form students who, although taught in the main school, now enjoy a separate social and study space and their own cafeteria. Mr McKenzie says: 'Now pupils don't wistfully look out onto all that beautiful green belt – they can actually benefit from it.'

Parents unanimous on the remarkably welcoming atmosphere: 'Everyone from the lady on the gate who checks uniform to the school receptionist makes you feel at home'. Even the police officer seeing kids onto after-school buses does it with a smile. Parents also enthuse about the school's multiculturalism and inclusiveness ('They really try to be for everybody') and genuine concern ('It's far more nurturing than some of the other local comprehensives'). But concern is not cosseting. Mr McKenzie is also a very visible presence and is on the gate most days: 'He is very chatty to us parents – sometimes a bit too chatty and I worry that my daughter and her friends will think I'm terribly un-cool hanging out with the head.'

Pastoral care, well-being and discipline: Traditional values apply. 'Kids need firm boundaries and it's important for the school to set them,' says the head. 'We expect them to be at school, on time, in uniform, ready to work.' Smart red and black kit is strictly enforced. 'There used to be a gang who wore their uniform in a special way and that's now all ended,' said one parent approvingly. Mr McKenzie also tries to clamp down on big clusters of students hanging around outside the local café at lunchtime, occupying the pavements. Not the school's best PR (although we have to say there are very few other places for them to go).

Behaviour in general is 'excellent' and school aims to keep it that way by instilling a sense of responsibility. 'We're training pupils to choose to do the right thing.' Misdemeanors are promptly and firmly dealt with – 'When my son got into a fight, there was absolutely no messing. They threw the rulebook at him'. Whilst Mr McKenzie considers himself to be fair, he is not one to pussyfoot around; 'This is definitely not a non-excluding school. If a child is making it difficult for other children to learn and we have exhausted all other options – we will exclude.'

'Other options' could include a trip to The Bridge, a prospect so mortifying that the mere mention is enough to make even the tardiest of students get their act together. One parent told us: 'My son is a bright child and generally well behaved, but has the potential to be swayed by peers. He was sent to The Bridge fairly early on, to deliver a message to a teacher. A stroke of genius'. According to that parent, the experience was enough to ensure that her son was 'never late or naughty in class again'. After further questions, it pans out that The Bridge is a fully staffed, self-contained base providing a wide range of interventions to those 'who present challenges in class.' One parent said: 'I imagine that children with a nervous disposition would probably be terrified.'

Drugs not a notable issue. 'It's bizarre,' says the head; 'at a previous school we had an incident every week. Here perhaps they're more savvy, more mature and are listening to our advice.' Weapons, too, had been conspicuously absent until just one recent incident in school – but the offender was promptly excluded.

Year 7 has its own 'transition manager', and one parent we spoke to, whose child had joined from neighbouring Rhodes Avenue, told us that 'there were a few opportunities during the summer term for new students to spend a day at APS and be taken around to orientate themselves.' Pupils remain in the same tutor groups for five years with a director of studies for each year. They're also supported by learning mentors and counsellors.

About 56 pupils with statements of special needs/EHC plans have mainly cognitive rather than behavioural difficulties and the school copes well with autism, Asperger's and Down's. One parent told us: 'I shopped around many schools before I chose APS for my son because of his very particular needs. I have to say, they have been amazing for him. If he was upset they would know about it. And nobody laughs at you here for being different.' The pupils we met were a lovely blend of savvy, street smart and witty ('the only thing that's missing at the school is a statue of me') – whilst polite and thoughtful. They shared one common notion – that they were all really happy to be there and felt listened to and looked after.

Communication between parents and school clearly a strong point – 'All my emails, however trivial, get answered promptly'. And various methods of positive re-enforcement are used: 'We often get phone calls home or postcards telling us how well our daughter is doing.' They also have a commendation system of silver, bronze and gold: 'Their rewards system is brilliant. It makes the pupils want to do well. '

Pupils and parents: Wide social spread, from the comfortable middle-class suburbs near the gates to some of the most deprived kids in the country – 'a high proportion on the cusp of social needs'. Middle classes tend to dominate the PTA, which runs endless jumble sales and bazaars and is strongly involved in the day-to-day running of the school, but the kids themselves mix well. Very supportive parents – 'Parents helped set it up and want to make it work'.

Entrance: Around 1,600 applications for 232 places. Usual priority to looked-after children, those with statements of special needs and siblings, then distance from the gates, which is now just under half a mile. The largest percentage (approx 20 per cent) from adjoining high-achieving primary Rhodes Avenue, as well as from Bounds Green, Our Lady of Muswell, Bowes, Coldfall, Coleridge, Hollickwood and Muswell Hill and another 30 or so local primaries.

Majority of existing pupils continue into sixth form of 340, with 70 or so joining from other local schools. External applicants for A levels should have at least five GCSEs at 9-4, with 6s in A level subject choice. (The head has been known to invite pre-A level students to his office, to lay out the pros of staying on at APS, if he gets a whiff that they may abandon ship for another local sixth form.)

Exit: Some 10-20 per cent leave after GCSEs. Around 60 per cent to Russell Group universities, including regular places at Oxbridge (five in 2018, and two medics). 'What is heartening is in the last three years these Oxbridge students have read a range of courses including English literature, law, history, maths, modern languages, music and natural sciences.' Other popular destinations include Cardiff, St George's, Manchester, Queen Mary's, UCL, Exeter, Leeds, Bristol, Warwick, King's College London and Birmingham.

Money matters: Training school and academy trust status bring in extra funding.

Remarks: A notably welcoming place for children (and adults) from across the borough. Not an academic pressure cooker but a school with high standards for all.

Alleyn's Junior School

A

Linked with Alleyn's School

Townley Road, London SE22 8SU

Ages 4–11 **Pupils** 242 **C of E**

Fees: £17,361 to £18,081 pa

020 8557 1519
www.alleyns.org.uk

Headmaster: Since 2015, Simon Severino (40s) MA (Oxon) PGCE. His degree subject was in geography and his first teaching job was at Culford Prep School, from there to Dulwich Prep London where he rose to deputy head, and then headmaster of St Andrew's Prep in Eastbourne.

When he arrived, although appreciative of the quality of the school, he was determined that there would be no resting on laurels and has instigated greater rigour in the classrooms appropriate for the 'bright cookies' the school attracts, and stimulated the co-curricular. There are now more clubs on offer, right down to the infants, more performance opportunities and more ways in which to express themselves. Friday mini lectures for children and parents have proved popular – guest journalists, authors and musicians so far. He has also worked hard to integrate with his parent body, introducing headmaster's coffee mornings. He likes the 'human scale' of this school, where no-one will get lost, and the fact that with the infants and juniors under one roof there is a community feel and 'Infants have their heroes and role models'.

Parents described him to us as 'a good listener, which enhances his leadership skills' and 'approachable, thoughtful, calm, gentle, yet authoritative.' We found him friendly and confident in his vision for the school, which he seems to have implemented at high speed, and open to anything that is fed back to him: 'we're happy to admit when we get things wrong'. He lives within a stone's throw of the school and his wife teaches at Dulwich Prep London. He has two children, a boy and a girl. Out of school he enjoys family time, being in the garden and his Arsenal football club season ticket.

He describes this as a school where children will be 'pushed and challenged, yes, but not a hothouse' and an aim is for children to leave 'comfortable on all stages', whether that be musical, sporting or academic. A fan of co-educational schooling, he feels it gives 'a greater spectrum of ways of being and a greater number of niches' in which to fit.

Entrance: There is one class with 18 or 20 places (half girls and half boys) at 4+. Parents become aware of their child competing for one of just nine or 10 places, with about 10 applicants for every place; many choose also apply elsewhere too with these odds. At 7+ there are 24 or 25 places, and a six-to-one chance of getting in. Nine plus is a more unusual entry point and competition for these four or so places is stiffest of all.

The school is quite clear that selection is for academic potential. Four plus assessments are based on EYFS curriculum, 7+ and 9+ are based around the requirements of the national curriculum. Pupils identified with SEN will be assessed by a member of the learning support department.

Children come from a range different schools and nurseries. There is a particular concentration from the wider local

A

Dulwich area but children come from all over south London – Blackheath to Beckenham to Clapham to just north of the Thames.

Exit: Year 6 pupils sit the same 11+ assessment as external candidates for Alleyn's Senior School, but it is simply used for benchmarking, the opportunity to gain academic scholarships and as a target to work towards as they have guaranteed places. Less than a handful exit to other senior schools, seemingly tempted by single sex schools such as JAGS, Dulwich College or the City of London schools. Six academic scholarships to junior school children in each of the past two years and a large number of sporting awards, along with music and art awards.

Remarks: The big news is that year 6 pupils no longer sit Sats. No more need to take so much time out of the timetable for any preparation, and with a guaranteed place at the senior school to progress to, the greatest pressure the children would seem to face here is on their initial entry. This frees up time for a year 6 diploma instead, which includes citizenship and life skills.

Class sizes rise gradually from 18-20 in reception to 22 in years 3 and 4 and 24 in years 5 and 6. As we tour the classrooms everything seems utterly spick and span, beautiful displays, activities set out on every table for forthcoming lessons; even the courtyard playground is laid out ready for break-time with dressing up clothes, crates for imaginative play, a box of hats, in addition to the pirate ship play equipment.

Meanwhile, the atmosphere in classrooms is fun and relaxed; all of the teachers take the time to talk to us, seeming to have an excellent rapport with their classes. Parents observe: 'small groups where children work at a similar pace work well' and a mother said of her daughter, 'Her confidence in maths has been nurtured in a way that has been a joy to see.'

The year 6 children we meet from are eager, polite and full of beans, quite delightful and terrifically proud of their school. There seems to be little about the school they don't know: even the fact that the school has a 'qualified nurse, not just a first-aider'. We particularly like the modesty of the school mascot, an elderly ceramic cat named Edward after the founder, who wears a tiny coloured ribbon around his neck according to which house has the most points.

French from from the start. The English coordinator has introduced a new, rigorous approach to grammar along with weekly DEAR sessions (Drop Everything and Read), which have gone down well with parents. There is now setting in maths from year 4. There's a refurbished ICT suite with a high pitched roof. The school appears particularly ambitious for science with a dedicated lab and a specialist teacher. Various years experience food tech at the senior school.

More than 20 out of a total of 59 staff have been at the school for more than 10 years. One parent said: 'They encourage the children to step outside their comfort zone and create a safe place to take a chance, experiment or to fail without fear of embarrassment or humiliation.' Another told us: 'The teachers are extremely approachable, down to earth, and there is a high level of communication with parents.' We met an enthusiastic full-time librarian, building displays around the curriculum. There are over 7,000 books in the library and of course dressing up for Book Week.

As if anticipating our disbelief, a parent stressed: 'There really is no exam pressure.' Holiday homework is occasionally given but it is usually optional. Parents are urged not to pressure children if they are too tired for homework at the end of the day – music to our ears. A parent who had just gone through the junior to senior step up felt that the school works hard to ensure a smooth transition.

There is a forest school in reception and around 50 school trips a year. Year 6 and the chamber choir visited a professional recording studio; citizenship was brought to life at Commonwealth Day celebrations at Westminster Abbey, where one pupil talked to Prince Harry and another received a wave from Theresa May. A recent ski trip was the school's first for a while. Year 5s go wild with a bushcraft trip and Isle of Wight watersports trip, and year 6 have long enjoyed a Normandy residential. What do our guides like the most about their school? 'Lots of responsibility' and 'all of the trips and going away'.

The school makes the most of the on-site sporting facilities shared with the senior school including the recently refurbished swimming pool, a sports hall, Astro and acres of playing fields. Sport is compulsory and a significant part of the co-curriculum. All children can play in teams from year 3 and there are sports tournaments for all in years 1 and 2. School has offered girls' cricket and football in the co-curriculum for many years, and these two sports are now in the formal curriculum.

There is a large, busy playground between the music block and the playing fields where the older children let off steam, plus some picnic benches in the shade for quieter moments and a small, wooden adventure playground.

The music school is housed in a block dating from 1899, with all children having at least two class music lessons a week and many having individual lessons too. This is an exceptionally musical school, due in no small part to the fact that all children in years 2, 3 and 4 are part of the 'strings scheme', learning the violin or cello, and all year 5 follow the 'brass and woodwind scheme' in curriculum time. No wallflowers: the whole class is in the year 6 choir. And as if this isn't enough, there are 15 different musical and ensemble clubs. In Roald Dahl's centenary year, the year 6 play was a version of James and the Giant Peach with a 1960s spin.

There are over 60 clubs each term taking place before school, at lunch time and after school until 4.30pm. Virtually all are without charge. Great for working parents: after-school care is provided for children up until 6.00pm for a reasonable price.

Red-brick and purpose built with its entrance towards the rear of the main school, the building was opened in 1992 by Terry Waite, CBE. Classrooms are bright and spacious on two floors. Parents describe the atmosphere as 'relaxed, informal', perhaps particularly in the infants, where the children wear sweatshirts rather than blazers and striped shirts or dresses, but we observed this throughout the school. The head feels the school is 'tolerant and accepting, understanding of differences' which means that children can 'feel comfortable being themselves'.

Teaching focuses around thoughtful 'learning dispositions': empathy, courage and self-belief, thoroughness and focus, responsibility, resilience, imagination and reflectiveness. One mother told us her daughter 'particularly enjoys engaging with the older children through the house system'; another said her child 'feels incredibly safe and nurtured at school'; another, 'the school celebrates that every individual is special and different. They are being taught to be kind to each other in the school as well as to the people outside of the school.'

Around 10 per cent of children with SEND including dyslexia, dyspraxia and processing difficulties. The head of learning support works with a learning support assistant and a speech and language therapist – support is included within the fees.

Children reflect a diverse London population – 20 per cent are bilingual. Parents describe each other as 'friendly, laid-back and unpretentious' and feel children who will get the most from the school are 'those who enjoy busy schedules'. Another described parents, like their children, wanting to get stuck in and involved in the community.

A

Alleyn's School

Linked with Alleyn's Junior School

Townley Road, London SE22 8SU

Ages 11–18 **Pupils** 1,012 **Sixth form** 302 **C of E**

Fees: £19,851 pa

020 8557 1500
www.alleyns.org.uk

Headmaster: Since 2010, Dr Gary Savage MA (Cantab) PhD FRSA (40s). Having studied history, he topped this off with a PhD on the French Revolution. With a CV comprising the best names in education – he was under master at Westminster School, master-in-college and head of history at Eton – some parents wondered whether he would introduce a fearsome new academic regime on arrival, but one immediately realises this would not be his style. Instead he set out to 'engage the community to have more academic confidence'. And how? 'Let them breathe more, set the tone and create opportunities.' To this end he has introduced the sixth form governors' research project prize; and, fittingly for an arts-loving head, the headmaster's review prize for years 9 and 10, where they write a critical review of a play, book or exhibition, hoping to inspire all 'to enjoy London critically'. His message to teachers has been to take their own enthusiasm and 'impassion kids, not just teach the syllabus'.

He grew up in Suffolk, attending his local state school, and still supports Ipswich Town football club. Married for 25 years; he and his wife, who works in TV, spend much of their down-time in Berlin. With an office decorated in Hague blue featuring a vibrant neon artwork from one of the pupils, we found him to be charming, passionate, energising and the most stylish head (spotted emerald green tie) we've yet to meet.

The parent view is equally impressed; the adjectives they find to describe him are 'dedicated, determined, approachable, hard-working'; 'caring and committed' and 'impressive, forward thinking, open-minded and inspirational'.

Academic matters: In 2018 at A level, 74 per cent of grades were A*/A; 92 per cent 9-7 at GCSE. Notably strong performances in A level French, art, art history, Greek, drama and philosophy.

There are six year 7 classes per year. Typically around 23 pupils per class rising to around 24 for year 9. Classes are smaller for GCSE courses in years 10 and 11. Upper School (sixth form) teaching sets vary from one to 14 depending on subjects.

The vibrancy of the science co-curricular dazzles, with a scientist and broadcaster, working as a scientist-in-residence, going into classes and curating a programme of Friday science lectures, not to mention the roof-top observatory, but we noticed A level biology and chemistry performing a notch below humanities subjects for the past three years. The head comments that science entrance to university is strong. Computing and DT are currently low points. At GCSE the sciences are far stronger. Maths is setted in years 8 and 9 with stunning IGCSE results.

The Alleyn's Learners' programme in years 7 to 11 aims to empower pupils to understand how they each learn so that they can utilise this as they progress to GCSE. It's all about 'developing life-long learners as well as well-rounded people,' says the head.

One period per fortnight for Spanish, German and French initially. Those choosing three creative subjects also study philosophy and history of art. Triple and double science depending on aptitude. The school is alert to what might be too much pressure. No early GCSEs in year 9 and no more than 10 subjects. One parent blessed with academic all-rounders said: 'possibly too light (if anything) on homework, rather than too heavy, but very acceptable workload.'

There are two pathways in the upper school – one to four A levels, the other three A levels plus an AS. Sixth formers may be tempted by choices including psychology, art history, classical civilisation, politics, informatics, Greek and drama and theatre studies. We hear of students finding their academic passions in which case hard work ceases to be a chore. Sixth formers are given the platform to succeed with university applications: a subject specialist to comb over personal statements, extension societies. They are encouraged to have opinions and learn to hold their own (and rise to our more left field questions with ease). A large cohort of Oxbridge applicants strengthens aspirations and builds success.

Over 100 academic and support staff members have been with the school for over 10 years. A parent told us: 'I believe the teaching staff are very skilled, the teaching is varied and interesting. The school manages to engender a very strong work ethic'. And pupils comment: 'People do work hard and to a high level; the quality of teaching means you never feel under-prepared.'

We have heard of the odd dyslexic child from the school heading elsewhere due to an increase in pace towards GCSE (although the school has no record of anyone leaving for this reason), but the school currently supports around 150 pupils with identified SEND and points out: 'We very carefully track the progress of our boys and girls with dyslexia, to ensure they receive the support they need, and they do very well indeed at both public exam points'. Classroom differentiation and six week courses in small groups focus on study support and some one-to-one is provided. A mother with two dyslexic children said: 'They have felt hugely supported and encouraged by staff and fellow pupils and are thriving.' A tiny minority with EAL needs.

Games, options, the arts: The school is situated in the midst of 30 acres of lush playing fields with the Shard and the City just a glimmer in the distance. Every pitch imaginable, plus a newly refurbished 25m pool. The school is proud of its sporting heritage and parents feel it is 'taken seriously, but enjoyable'. An extensive sporting co-curricular: almost 400 girls and boys attend football club. By the third week of term when we visited, 300 pupils had already represented the school at a match. A similar number play netball and hockey. Water polo makes more than a splash. As ever, some sports dominate and some feel their particular passion is sidelined. Teaching staff have known sporting success: the deputy head, a former GB hockey captain still coaching at national level, is typical. D of E and CCF are popular – one often sees pupils in camouflage conducting exercises on the sports fields.

Similarly, most art teachers are practising artists. The art studios on the top floor didn't show any stunning displays at the time of our visit, instead there was an appealing art college air with paint spattered easels and overalls in rows.

Some 550 individual music lessons per week, taught by 40 visiting music teachers. A significant number of grade 8+ musicians attending junior conservatoires on weekends. All manner of choirs including gospel, jazz and barbershop.

In years 7 and 8, pupils follow a carousel of two terms drama and one term dance. Students appreciate how lucky they are to have the Michael Croft Theatre, a wholly professional flexible space where lower, middle and upper schools put on a production each year. 'Music and drama are outstanding.

Lots of opportunities for a range of talent,' said a parent. House music competitions are hotly contested. Musical alumni include Dobrinka Tabakova (composer in residence BBC Symphony Orchestra), Benjamin Wallfisch (Oscar-nominated film composer), Florence Welch (of Florence and the Machine) and Jessie Ware.

Most clubs included in fees. The school buzzes until the final bell at 5.15pm when everyone is expected to be off site. Fantastic mentoring culture sees sixth formers instigating and leading clubs and societies, where they give talks in whatever their passion and career aspiration, such as law, politics and medicine.

Background and atmosphere: If the school seems both snazzy and contemporary 'part of a global 21st century' it is, but it's also one with a heritage – two years away from celebrating the 400th anniversary of the charitable foundation on which it stands. Traditional elements, such as the well-supported alumni society, thrive. Commitment to bursaries and playing a role in London Academy of Excellence, Tottenham, continue the community spirit of the founder. Buildings of every type dot the campus. A splendid, lofty, panelled Great Hall bears portraits of former headmasters and is used for assemblies. The Edward Alleyn building, red-brick and plenty of glass giving views of the playing fields, houses classrooms, a lecture theatre and a coffee shop sixth formers refer to as Costa. New state of the art lower school building is now home to years 7 and 8, with pupils and teachers raving about the open spaces and ambiance. Its versatile atrium has already proved its versatility with a year 8 architectural exhibition as well as a number of pupil and parent gatherings.

One parent talked of 'a unique energy I didn't feel in any of the other schools we considered'. Others feel the atmosphere is 'quite simply happy', 'and most important of all not obsessed with exams.' One family felt 'it is an overwhelmingly kind community where you are allowed to be yourself and to excel in your own way, without necessarily conforming to any norm.'

Pastoral care, well-being and discipline: The head's latest speech saw a recommitment to well-being, providing a safe environment in uncertain (political) times. He confirms his aim is for a 'holistic, kind, relaxed school at ease with itself'. Parents universally single out the pastoral care for praise: 'Unbelievably amazing!' said one. Another: 'My over-riding impression is that there is very little bullying, and kids (and young adults) are taught and encouraged to be respectful of one another.' This is repeated at every turn. The co-ed nature of the school means there are relationships between pupils, but everyone seems to take the environment totally in their stride as a preferred norm and there are always people to talk to: 'you never feel stranded', tutors 'have your back' they tell us.

Pupils and parents: Will you fit in? Families are often 'city people, third sector, journalists... Londoners,' says the head. Accordingly this is a cosmopolitan bunch: pupils speak over 30 different languages at home, with a tiny few overseas nationals. One parent ensured we're entirely in the picture regarding parents: 'decent, obviously quite posh'. Prepare to be part of a community – 'involved' crops up frequently.

What kind of child would be happy here, we ask parents? 'Curious, independent and confident – but it is also a great school for children who are less confident because the school culture is so kind and accepting,' is representative. Upper school students wear business attire; our female guide negotiating the stairs niftily in platform wedges approved of the degree of latitude given.

Entrance: By far the largest entry point is 11+ when there are 135 places on offer and over 700 applicants annually. Prospective 11+ pupils can now come along as part of the admissions process for an Experience Alleyn's afternoon, which is designed to offer a taste of life at the school with lessons in sport as well as academic classes. At exam time, candidates are assessed in English, maths and reasoning (verbal, non-verbal and spatial), and a confidential report is sought from the current school. Candidates who fare well are invited to return for a small group activity and one-to-one interview. Over 300 are interviewed and the school takes a balanced split from state and primary applicants and those with different aptitudes. Adjustments for demonstrable SEND.

One third of the intake is drawn from Alleyn's Junior School pupils who are all guaranteed a place. Pupils come from both preps and primaries, most very local, so Dulwich, Herne Hill, Streatham, Clapham and Wandsworth. But the huge Foundation coaches that line the road at pick up time shuttle children from far further afield including Bermondsey, Croydon, Beckenham, Chislehurst and Kensington and Chelsea.

Only 10 to 20 enter at 13+, with similar entry requirements. For the sixth form there are 15 to 20 places on offer; all candidates sit general papers that test their skills in critical writing, qualitative and quantitative reasoning regardless of their A level choices. The competition will be 100 strong.

Exit: Almost all to first or second choices of university. Most popular destinations recently: Bristol, Leeds Manchester, Durham, Cambridge, Oxford, Imperial, UCL, Edinburgh and Exeter. In 2018, 26 to Oxbridge, 11 medics and five took up places outside the UK.

Money matters: More transparency than we often see regarding the financial commitments involved for prospective parents: spelling out the cost of school lunches and sports gear. Most scholarships are worth around 25 per cent of fees for the academic, sporting and musical. Application fees are waived for any children receiving free school meals. All bursaries are means-tested, with a focus on fewer but larger bursaries. Some 84 pupils currently receive bursaries and 70 per cent of these are fully funded. There even may be help with uniform, travel and school trip costs.

Remarks: A vibrant, 21st century school built on solid values where excellent grades seem just part of a broader and deeper education towards confident young adulthood.

Allfarthing Primary School

6

St Ann's Crescent, London SW18 2LR

Ages 3–11 Pupils 406

020 8874 1301
www.allfarthing.wandsworth.sch.uk

Headteacher: Since January 2017, Tom Holmes, previously deputy head at St Mary's in Richmond. Has also worked at Honeywell and at a primary school in Surrey.

Strikes just the right balance between humility and authority and was an instant hit with the parents – no mean feat, given the turbulent journey they'd been through following the departure of the previous head, who'd reigned for 25 years. 'The school was very academic and had an amazing reputation, but she left and there followed a number of headships that either didn't work out or were temporary and which led to the school dropping from outstanding to good, with a feeling of discontent among the parents,' explained a parent. 'When Mr Holmes came in, it felt like a breath of fresh air – teachers looked happier, everyone saw the sense of direction that had been lacking and there was more focus on mindfulness and teamwork.' Another said, 'Sports and the arts have picked up pace dramatically since his arrival – a great way for children who aren't academic to find confidence.'

Many also love the fact that 'he greets every child by their name on the gate each morning.' Pupils call him 'kind,' 'always around and interested,' and 'strict when he needs to be, but always fair and never shouty.'

His first job was threefold: replace the high level of supply teachers with permanent recruits; up the ante on English and maths; and make some quick wins – introduce houses, year 6 mentoring, tighten up systems, be more visible etc. The remaining jobs, he says, have been slower burners – including ensuring the school meets every child's needs and expanding SEN provision. 'Essentially, I've shaken the bones of the place,' he says.

He is keen on sport eg touch rugby, cricket and cycling, and lives in Twickenham with his wife Kathryn and daughter Lottie.

Entrance: At 3+ into the nursery or 4+ into reception. Priority goes to siblings and then those living closest to the school. Attending the nursery does not guarantee a place in the infant department. Don't be put off the 400m catchment zone banded about every April – it's not as brutal as it seems, insists the head, with a zone of 1200m usually being the reality by September (mainly due to the transient nature of Wandsworth and parents opting for private schools instead). For occasional places in older age groups contact the school to check availability and put your name on their waiting list.

Exit: Something of a scattergun when it comes to secondaries, with no more than three or four to any one school – 'which is why I'm very keen to support parents to find the right school for their child, be it state or private,' says head, whose knowledge of local schools is 'impressive,' according to parents. Popular state choices are Burntwood, Ashcroft, Graveney, St Cecilia, ARK Academy and Bolingbroke Academy; odd one to Kingston or Surrey grammar schools. Around 30 per cent to independents, Emanuel, Whitgift (which starts at year 6, leading to an annual exodus of a handful of children at the end of every year 5 – 'always a shame,' according to remaining parents), Ibstock Place, Wimbledon High School, Trinity and Whitgift. Odd one to Lady Margaret's, KGS and Streatham & Clapham High School.

Remarks: Situated on rather a busy corner, the tall, 1920s building offers large, bright classrooms; eyes are immediately drawn to displays of children's work and art designed to capture imagination and interest. Reception and nursery classes have indoor and outdoor classrooms, ample resources laid out thoughtfully. Huge Astroturf area (which can be netted across to host two separate games), playground equipment, tennis tables, outdoor classroom (although children told us, 'it's not used that much, except in summer') and nature zone, with beds for the children to learn about growing food, composting and studying mini-beasts. Separate playground for younger ones (up to year 3) but they get to use the bigger (more exciting) one during lunchtimes. Large inner-city mix 'from high-earning bankers to very working class and loads of different ethnicities – fabulous diversity,' as one parent put it. Around 30 languages spoken; around a quarter on pupil premium.

Standards are high and monitoring and assessing of progress is meticulous across the age groups to ensure underachievement is picked up and addressed swiftly. School's results in maths are impressive. Ditto with English; lots of drama and speaking and listening activities are incorporated into the curriculum. Everyone learns Spanish from year 3. Parents report good traditional teaching with interesting history and geography projects alongside whizzy IT – all classes can access iPads, chrome books and trolleys of laptops. School very well in national assessments and has an above-average added value score. 'The teachers are amazing,' we heard more than once from parents – 'they're big classes, but they get to know which kids need extra support or challenges in every subject.' We saw children fully engaged in every classroom; not a yawn in sight. Homework at the talking end in lower years (less a case of 'talk to your child about Vikings' than 'Here's what we're going to be doing on Monday – can you help them prepare'). Plans in place for a homework club.

SEN support delivered inside the classroom for core lessons, plus small group or individual teaching when needed. 'The school has been instrumental in turning our two children with SEN around – one in particular needed lots of help and we didn't have to fight for any of it. It was recognised it was needed and they delivered, both on the academic and emotional side,' said one parent. Another told us, 'It was the school that recognised my child's problem. At first, I was in denial but they talked me through the process and the support they could offer, which has involved lots of one-to-one work but all the while never excluding him from the class. The patience they have is astounding as he's very active and needs a lot of attention.' Speech and occupational therapists visit the school as required. School has partnership with Place2Be to ensure strong mental health – pupils, staff and parents are involved, with the option for children to drop in anytime.

Two multi-purpose halls (and soon to be a third) provide space for PE, assemblies, dance, drama, art and lunches cooked on site in the recently refurbished kitchens (although the number of lunchboxes suggest it's not as popular as it could be). On site sports include lacrosse, football, hockey, cricket, gymnastics and tag rugby; older pupils walk to Southfields secondary school for swimming lessons. Sports days are held on the local common.

Music has rocketed in recent years and features highly on the daily curriculum; super purpose-built accommodation with a dedicated music teacher. Opportunity for all from year 4 to learn an instrument, with many achieving grade 6 before moving to secondary school. Each child chooses a string or wind instrument for group lessons in year 3. The chamber choir, guitar ensemble and wind ensemble all perform locally, sometimes with audiences in the hundreds. Encouraging setting for musical families, currently something of a rarity for a state primary. Children told us they'd like more drama – 'it's mainly an after-school club when you're older,' one said, although there are all the usual class assemblies and plays. Art on the up, with each class getting involved in an annual themed project, the results of which are displayed in reception.

Remarkably good Friends of Allfarthing Group raises money for all sorts of activities (including every class teacher having funds to spend on two workshops and one trip a year on top of what's already offered) and equipment through traditional and creative ways. Monthly book club lottery raises funds for the library and other book purchases. All tastes taken into consideration for before- and after-school clubs, which run daily, with parents and pupils suggesting some of the choices available. Wrap-around care offered onsite by an outside company from 7.30am to 6pm – again, well used. A few rumbles among parents about costs, compared to other local schools, but all grateful for the provision. Plenty of local trips and three residentials – one each for year 4 (one night), year 5 (two nights), year 6 (four nights).

Pupils – who we found polite, confident and articulate – are encouraged to voice their opinions through the school council and class reps, on school rules, sensible behaviour and other

A

issues that benefit everyone's participation and enjoyment. Behaviour kept in check, also thanks to the 'good to be green' system (warning cards lead to red cards for misdemeanours; three red cards leads to an after-school detention; 'less than 10 a year, though,' says head, and only one exclusion in last two years). Bullying minimal, report all – anti-bullying week is a big deal here and worry boxes in each classroom are well used. Praise as big (if not bigger) a focus as punishment, with house points and a mention in celebration assemblies considered high currency by pupils.

Overall a popular school with supportive parents, smiley, focused and engaging teaching staff and a terrific head who is working hard to continually improve and develop provision. As one parent put it, 'This is a school that really knows your child – no cut-and-paste jobs on the reports here.'

The American School in London

1 Waverley Place, London NW8 0NP

Ages 4–18 **Pupils** 1,350 **Sixth form** 240

Fees: £27,050 – £31,200 pa

020 7449 1220
www.asl.org

Head of school: Since 2017, Robin Appleby; has a degree in English from Dartmouth College as well as two masters degrees. She taught in the States (Ohio and then New York) before joining the American School of The Hague and stayed in international education as well as being a trustee on the Council of International Schools. The two previous heads at ASL had long tenures and she is rather hoping to do the same, though she is from a different mould to the last head and 'may bring a new style to the previous head, though it is early days,' according to parents.

She aspires to a progressive approach to learning and wants ASL to represent 'best practice in US' with the child at the centre of the process. She believes in 'learning by doing,' which very much fits with the long existing ethos and curriculum in the school, with emphasis on understanding concepts, not learning by rote or for exams. She was attracted to the 'sense of tradition at ASL..a highly functioning school'. She is hoping to increase diversity as well as 'make innovative changes that will help prepare pupils for future opportunities'. Robin fells her challenges include ensuring pupils get the best from technology without losing social skills, and developing their emotional quotient alongside their intelligence quotient.

She is accountable to a very active board (around 20 members) who 'are supportive of change but protective of ASL'. They are involved in strategy while she is left to manage the school 'democratically'. She also has an articulate parent body. Staff say that she is 'marvellous' and 'really intelligent' and parents told us 'she is receptive and doesn't hide in her office – we think she is going to get a lot of stuff done!'

Academic matters: Not only the brightest of pupils but also the most motivated come to ASL for an American education. 'Pupils here need to have passion,' according to students, 'and they can't be bystanders'. They 'need to be advocates for themselves with teachers'. Totally American curriculum with an emphasis on critical thinking, collaborative working, questioning and listening. Classes average 20 pupils. Parents told us that 'the instruction is outstanding'.

Lower school has specialist teachers and well equipped classrooms (though lower school playground needs some enhancing). Space to learn outside, both in plant filled courtyards and the playground and at the learning centre at the school's 21 acre playing fields in Canon's Park. Some phonics in youngest years but emphasis on 'word awareness' and use of 'whole language', with reading schemes, lots of experimenting and learning through play. By grade 1, iPads and technology integrated in learning, with document cameras in all classrooms and pupils being taught coding and touch typing. Spanish taught from the youngest classes. Team planning for mixed ability classes.

Each year group has a central hub, promoting camaraderie between classes. Huge lower school library has seating pods like sailors' bunk beds as well as soft floor cushions. Weekly library lessons particularly useful for project work. Science room with specialist teachers and parent volunteers allows for experiential learning. Colourful displays of work and motivational messages all around the school rather than neat, copied stories, which gives an indication of priorities – all about what they have understood, with plenty of discussion. 'They teach them to think and be inquisitive,' say parents. No homework is given in the lower school – through pupils are expected to read daily and seem to do projects on subjects that interest them. This 'home learning' has taken a while to be accepted, but parents on the whole appreciate the lack of pressure and believe that 'they take ownership of their own learning.'

Middle school starts in grade 5 (year 6). Laptops given to pupils in grades 7 and 8 and then in high school it is 'bring your own device'. Language learning expanded in middle school to choice of Spanish, French or Mandarin, but little in terms of maintaining mother tongue languages, though the library has foreign language books. Science rooms for each year group mean that experiments can be left out. The Make, Innovate, Learn Lab (MILL) does what it says on the tin – it is used for robotics, designing and making, and plans to 'revolutionise teaching and student learning at ASL by inspiring student to explore, innovate, collaborate, and to change the world'. An indication of the aspirational thinking that fills the school. No streaming but parents spoke of their pupils being extended and supported. Middle school pupils praised 'supportive teachers' and explained that 'they were slow at marking sometimes, but that is because they have a life too, you know'. They said 'ASL respects what you are comfortable doing and you are not pressured but encouraged'.

High school pupils an articulate and motivated lot – with good results to boot, SAT averages of upper 600 in critical reading, maths and writing, and 20 AP programs offered with 92 per cent scoring grade 3 (out of 5) or above in 2018. One parent said that 'high school is where things become more challenging and purposeful'. Enormous range of classes on offer each semester, from game design to macroeconomics, from Russian literature to computational circuits, from sport leadership to advanced dance performance. Languages taught as in middle school with the addition of Arabic. Separate biology, physics and chemistry labs. English taught round oval tables with discussion-based learning only (and each lesson is mapped to show how the discussion moved around and who spoke). Journalism encouraged with guest speakers and pupils producing the school magazine. (Impressive recent magazine dedicated to gun crime.) No external exams until AP in upper school, but progress mapped with grade level outcomes. Pupils told us that they have very full timetables as well as a big involvement in sport – they might get three or four hours homework if they are taking a large number of AP classes. 'Teachers stay behind school and are always available to help you – even if they are not your actual teacher.' They suggested that 'math has a good reputation, and social studies and history are good'.

The head believes that 'we have an ethical and moral responsibility to those who need support' and the learning support department tests and teaches pupils both in the classroom and out. Parents we spoke to were highly impressed with the support their children had – 'they gave her study skills she uses all the time' and 'they recognised a need and acted on it to support her'. Special mention by parents on the way the learning support department liaises well with both parents and teachers. Non-English speakers taken in up to grade 3.

Games, options, the arts: Drama has the advantage of professionally equipped theatre seating 450. Fairly full on productions at all ages. The theatre also used for concerts – everyone takes music, with youngest pupils learning recorder and then moving on to ukulele with an enthusiastic and experienced specialist music teacher, then in middle school each pupil gets given an instrument and music lessons as well as belonging to a choir. This appears to pay off because even in the high school, where music is a free choice, 120 pupils sing in the high school choir and go on music tours. Two jazz bands, ensembles, quartets, orchestras – plenty of opportunities for music making.

Specialist art rooms with pupils being creative in the widest sense – designing, engineering, building as well as painting, sculpting and drawing. Higher up the school, there is a photography lab and dark room, video classes, ceramics and kilns, textiles, banks of computers for design work, and a light filled art gallery to display work.

'The school is dominated by sport,' according to parents. It's an integral part of school life, running alongside and with at least equal importance to academics. Lower school has its own gym and own specialist PE teachers. Pupils excited by interestingly named 'spy training' (circuit training). Two full sized gyms, a fitness centre and sport rooms for middle and high school, with playing fields out at Canons Park, a half hour drive away. Wide range of sports during the year – boxing training, fitness suites, gymnastics, athletics, swimming, basketball and of course football. Tournaments against other international schools in London and abroad. 'We like it that our kids get to stay with families when they go on tournaments'. All the students get swimming lessons in school and can use the pool for training as well as competitions. Families can use the pool and the gym facilities outside school hours.

Endless clubs – 'we can create a club if we have an idea, we make an application for resources and get given a grant,' pupils told us. A board advertising large numbers of societies included Amnesty, autism awareness, robotics, South Asia, magic, creative writing, computer science, fitness, dance, textiles – the list of clubs worthy of a university freshers' week.

High school pupils expected to be involved in community projects too ('service learning'). Staff members (not just teachers) take groups to local homework clubs, care homes, community centres, gardening projects, community projects, where they help on a regular basis. 'It is the highlight of my week,' said one staff member.

Background and atmosphere: Started in 1951, it was originally designed with open learning areas, it has now adapted these to individual year classes. The theatre has been renovated and there's a new art building and fitness suite. Most recent developments continue to make this inner London school a veritable Tardis – there is a large swimming pool under the newly raised and improved playground. The school has a strong sense of identity and stability and pupils said they felt 'safe'. 'The security guard checks if I am getting a taxi and makes sure he knows who I am getting in the car with.' Not least thanks to the extensive security that surrounds a school with some very influential and/or wealthy parents – no access without an ID or appointment, with several guards and a bollarded entrance.

The hub of the school is the meeting area outside the theatre – used by parents, pupils and teachers. The canteen is large and spotlessly clean with a generous selection suiting all dietary requirements. Handy snack bar for eating outside meal times – useful for those staying on for practice or sport or activities. Pupils in grades 5 and 6 don't like the fact that some days they have assigned seating (but it 'helps avoid cliques and ensures new friendship groups can develop'). Parents considered that 'it is not a tidy or fussy school and it has a warm environment'. Not a formal atmosphere, but highly respectful (one of the school's core values – along with kindness, responsibility, integrity and the ability to act). 'Teachers truly care,' say parents. 'They feel they owe it to these children to find out what works for them.' Pupils said, 'there is an awesome social environment, but you have to get involved, you get your social group through common interests'.

Pastoral care, well-being and discipline: Emphasis on being emotionally articulate from very early on – 'ways we can show kindness' in kindergarten, and drawings of 'what is in my head' to encourage thinking about feelings. From an early age the pupils are taught conflict resolution. We saw two 7 year olds sitting outside a classroom discussing what had gone wrong in the playground – 'Did you even listen to me?' 'I heard you but I must have misunderstood you.' 'Well, now I am telling you again' – and then later we saw them working together in the PE lesson. Conflict resolved!

Middle year pupils told us, 'this is not a good school if you are rebellious (you go on behaviour report and if you get three of those you might be suspended)'. So a clear discipline policy understood by all. They told us 'counsellors are there to give emotional support if you need it'. They were completely unanimous in saying that 'we feel safe at school'. Many of the pupils are very well travelled and streetwise, but quite a mix in terms of life experience.

School counsellors, well-being classes; 'excellent orientation activities really helped me when we first started,' said pupils, and they in turn become student ambassadors. This school is used to helping at transition points. 'There is always a teacher to speak to,' according to pupils, 'or you can speak to your class representative to take it up in council meetings'. 'Everyone is very accepting here – people are all treated the same,' according to middle school pupils, though older pupils told us 'you have to be proactive here'.

School fees are among the highest in London and pupils are privileged to have a raft of highly motivated and professional teachers in a school with seemingly endless resources and excellent facilities. 'Families have good values and no sense of entitlement,' according to one parent – hard to believe it to be true of all families. 'This is an entitled group of young people, with hired limousines to the prom and branded trainers. I was not comfortable with the fancy cars and the party scene,' another parent said. Teachers are dedicated and motivated, with plenty of professional development training to keep their educational practice cutting edge. Teachers tend to stay and if they are prepared to work for demanding pupils and parents, then being in London in such an innovative, dynamic school surely has much to attract.

Pupils and parents: Articulate beyond their years, these pupils are constantly encouraged to 'speak out', and are expected to be involved at all stages. They are taught to explain their feelings – 'the social emotional side is encouraged,' according to parents – and 'to advocate for themselves to teachers and to others'. Active school council. Pupils here know that they can be heard and instigate change. Pupils say, 'you can't be a bystander, you have to speak out for what is right'. 'We think that integrity is important – you have to do the right thing'. Clearly the school's message about core values including respect, integrity and the courage to act (written large throughout the school) has been fully absorbed.

Parent evenings sometimes involve student-led portfolio conferences – showing the work they have done, which in the younger years can include videos and talking about their work. We didn't come across students who were arrogant or self-satisfied – 'you have to be accepting of other people,' students told us.

Parents are involved at every level – making cakes, helping teach science, attending sports matches, hosting visiting international students, volunteering in the library, fundraising and giving money. International Community Committee provides weekly activities to help parents bond and get to know London. All parents we spoke to mentioned the 'welcoming community' that exists at ASL.

Parents largely from the financial sector, though diplomats, journalists, entrepreneurs also represented. Not all American parents, plenty of 'third culture kids' with parents from different countries. The admissions page comes in nine different languages as there are applications from around the world. A few British pupils: 'I wanted a school that had a curriculum that was freer and not focused on one or two subjects,' one English pupil told us.

Entrance: The million dollar question – how to get in? 'We are looking for pupils with a passion, who like to learn and will thrive and be independent'. 'Parents have offered gifts to get their pupils in but they are not accepted.' Families of younger applicants will all be invited to visit: 'we need to know that we can work with the family, that we have common aspirations'. Higher up the school, applicants need to explain their motivation and interests and school reports will be scrutinised. More families are staying on (only a 10 per cent annual turnover) though even this can be difficult for pupils. 'My kids find the fact that staff and pupils often move quite difficult. Perhaps it is an inevitable downside of a school with an international community.' This is 'an academically challenging school' and pupils need to be able to keep up.

Exit: Most pupils go on to university in the USA including NYU, Northeastern, Middlebury, Georgetown, UCLA, University of Chicago, Duke, University of Pennsylvania, Tufts, Yale. Far fewer but increasing numbers – around 10 per cent – go to UK universities: King's College London, Goldsmiths, University College, Imperial and Bath. One each to Oxford and Cambridge in 2018. UCAS accepts students' AP, SAT/ACT and subject test results.

Money matters: A big priority is to increase diversity in this exclusive school. Parental giving is in the culture (and prominent on the website, where they say 'annual giving is a tradition') and there is an annual £4m fund for bursaries. School very proud of the fact that 12 per cent of pupils on some amount of financial aid. The financial stability and strength is evident in the buildings, extraordinary resources and the 'efficient, extremely professional administration'.

Remarks: The grande dame of international schools in London, it has plenty to be proud of and yet continues to expand and develop, both in terms of the buildings and educational methodology. The school encourages both inward looking questioning (how to plan and study, how to think through and achieve goals, what is your passion, what motivates you) and outward looking involvement in the world (conflict resolution, what we can offer to others, how to work and plan in a team, world issues). 'You cross that threshold and you enter little America' but it has huge resources and extraordinary facilities, and a dynamic learning atmosphere in a central London campus, so you can see why there is huge competition to get in and staff and families stay loyal.

Annemount School

18 Holne Chase, London N2 0QN

Ages 3–7 **Pupils** 100

Fees: £13,875 – £18,000 pa

020 8455 2132
www.annemount.co.uk

Head teacher: Since 1993, Geraldine Maidment BA MontDip. She followed a degree in German and art history from University College London with a stint at Sotheby's. Here, she realised she preferred people to objects. 'I'd taught children as a teenager, and loved the interaction. I realised that it was a vocation.' Started her career at Bassett House, then, when her own two daughters were tiny, launched Hilltop Nursery in a local church hall. In 1993, she bought Annemount, winning out against considerable competition. ('Mine wasn't the highest offer, but they felt I would continue the style of the school.') A two-year stint in the US with her late husband, an academic at the Open University, allowed her to take a masters in early childhood education at Denver University. A talented linguist (she speaks five languages), she's also a very 'outdoorsy person', who enjoys music, the theatre and cooking. Parents undoubtedly respect and trust her. 'She cares deeply about the children and wants their happiness above all.'

Entrance: Sensible to sign up early. The school tries to keep families together, but admissions are by observation, with each child invited to a play session to ensure they're 'suited to the programme we offer and would enjoy it.' Most enter nursery at rising 3 or reception, but children considered at any point.

Exit: Most sit 7+, though a few leave before ('There's no pressure about moving if that's part of the family's plans,' said one mother). At 7, to a broad sweep of north and central London schools. Popular co-ed options include Highgate, Belmont, Devonshire House and Northbridge House, with girls off to Channing, City of London, South Hampstead, Haberdashers' Aske's, boys to Haberdashers', UCS, Lyndhurst, St Paul's Juniors and St Anthony's. Head's office lined with individual files on each child and 'evidence-based' discussions about future schools start in year 1. 'Sometimes it's easy to fall in love with a school and lose sight of what is best for the child. We want children to be happy and shine, grow and mature into positive learners with good life skills.' Most parents respect the head's counsel: 'We knew she'd done this a million times before, so we completely trusted her.' Children are well prepared in a fun, relaxed way, with 7+ camps (in half terms and holidays) and 7+ clubs, and head has close links with the full range of schools, ensuring transition is as smooth as possible. Not the place for those who expect hothousing.

Remarks: The school follows the national curriculum, and numeracy and literacy (with one-to-one reading daily) are taught to the highest standards ('excellent,' say the inspectors) by an ample supply of well-qualified, empathetic staff. Parents particularly praise how well staff understand their pupils. 'They really get to know them academically, socially and emotionally,' said one. Another commented, 'When I go to parents' evening, I always feel teachers are describing my children, and what pleases me as much is that my children are happy and confident enough at school to behave in the same way as they do at home.'

Teaching equally successful at challenging the most able and supporting the struggling (though, perhaps, more of the former than the latter). The school has received an award from the National Association for Able Children in Education, and addresses ability largely through 'differentiation'. 'We look at who will benefit from being stretched and give them the opportunities to showcase their strengths. A singer or string player may be given performance opportunities, an able writer encouraged to enter competitions or discuss what they've been doing.' Those with difficulties are given equally seamless support, with a specialist learning support teacher, closely monitored assessment and a well-planned timetable of booster sessions worked out with teachers and, where necessary, external experts. Homework – 'manageable and achievable' – encourages independence, and parents are expected to play their part, giving children real money when shopping, measuring with them in the kitchen.

Plenty of specialist teaching, with French taught by a native speaker (in situ for 20 years), chess by a coach who supports the British junior team. Budding athletes and dancers are also aided by professional experts. Music is central, and singing given emphasis both in lessons and clubs (choir). Highly popular violin programme, with instruments passed down via the PTA. 'They like carrying the case; they think everyone plays,' says the head, who believes that learning enhances study skills and develops the academic.

Hugely popular clubs (athletics, cookery, adventure, football, science and art) from reception. 'For such a small school, the extracurricular is amazing,' said one mother, whose children participate most days. No breakfast or after-school club, however: 'It's a school, not day care,' says the head firmly. 'Umpteen school trips', too, near and far, ranging from a summer walk around the school's leafy surroundings to Verulamium (St Albans), which inspire activities such as learning Roman numerals.

Founded in 1936 as a gift to their former governess by some generous parents, the school has had only two heads (the first remained in situ till she died at the age of 93), and has something of the feel of a secret passed on from generation to generation. Housed in a low-rise private home, it makes the most of this domestic mood (with birthday teas, for example, in the head's study.) Located in leafy Hampstead Garden Suburb – 'marvellous to park and safe to walk around' – it has a large and beautifully maintained garden studded with rose bushes and apple trees. This, thoughtfully subdivided into a sensory garden, a vegetable plot (where pupils harvest their own potatoes) and a woodland garden (where children can pile up logs), acts as the school playground. More vigorous games like football – the school has its own team and strip – are played off site, while gym and swimming take place at Hendon Sports Centre. No dining hall and everyone brings their own lunch boxes.

'We make every child feel safe and loved,' says the head, who sees developing independence as a key part of her brief. 'I want pupils to greet and be greeted with a handshake, speak in full sentences, express gratitude through letter writing, and manage their belongings from an early stage.' Parents encouraged to support these goals and most are impressed by the results. 'Even my 4 year old knows there's show-and-tell and will remember to bring something.'

All pupils given responsibility, with a school council from reception debating such issues as how to improve the library and which charities to support. 'Travel ambassadors' encourage safe walking and 'rangers' ensure everything in the garden is 'ticketty boo'. All year 2s given a go as head boy and girl. Disciplinary problems are rare. 'I've never heard of any,' said one parent.

Families generally live within a four-mile radius of the school, spilling out from Hampstead Garden Suburb into West Hampstead, Highgate and Alexandra Park. Parents, from all round the world, are mainly professionals, with the rest in media, business and sport. Most choose Annemount because they share its values ('We agree with Mrs Maidment that children should play outdoors, have time to be bored, just be children,' said one parent), and virtually all delighted with the outcome. 'We feel our children have been nurtured and encouraged and are incredibly happy,' said mother. 'The real benefit is that they started off by loving school,' commented another. 'I give it five gold stars.'

Ark King Solomon Academy

9

Penfold Street, London NW1 6RX

Ages 3–18 **Pupils** 896 **Sixth form** 123

020 7563 6900
www.kingsolomonacademy.org

Principal: Since 2008, Max Haimendorf MA Oxon (30s). One of the first generation of super-bright heads to swop a City job for teaching. He graduated from St Hugh's College, Oxford, in biological sciences and joined the first cohort of Teach First. As part of his on-the-job training, taught science at Uxbridge High School, then worked as the scheme's PR. A period with management consultants, Oliver Wyman, clarified his career goals: 'Teaching seemed so different from the usual conveyor belt that takes Oxbridge graduates to the City,' he told The Guardian soon after his appointment – when still in his 20s – as the youngest head in England.

At King Solomon, he has taken the core problem ('the endemic issue of educational disadvantage') and addressed it with a Wyman-like mixture of 'creative enterprise and analytical rigour'. Still boyish in looks and enthusiasm, he is much admired by those in the sector. 'From the beginning, he was impossible to intimidate, full of integrity and had a "whatever it takes" and beyond approach to the care and outcome of pupils,' said one fan. Married to fellow Teach First evangelist Rebecca Cramer (co-founder of Reach Academy, Feltham).

Academic matters: The school's slogan is 'Climbing the Mountain to University' (an image perhaps more suggestive of blood, sweat and tears than joy in learning), and progress from base camp in 2007 has undoubtedly been exceptional. In 2018, 73 per cent of students got 9-4 in both English and maths, and 38 per cent of grades 9-7/A*-A, making it one of the top-performing state schools in the country. (And KSA doesn't do 'soft', so about half the pupils garner the full sweep of the EBacc, passing English, maths, science, a modern foreign language and a humanity.) A solid performance, too, at A level, with 65 per cent A*-B grades.

The approach to peak performance here is specific (and inspired by international example, such as the US Charter Schools). KSA keeps a tight control on numbers, never going beyond the 60 that start in reception, making its secondary school, at about 400, exceptionally small. A longer school day allows for deeper immersion, with English and maths the central plank of learning up to year 11. 'We believe that without mastery of English and mathematics, success in academic study beyond GCSEs is impossible,' says the head.

Many pupils start primary with well below average skills but make outstanding progress in literacy and numeracy in the early years, and the emphasis doesn't let up thereafter. Those in year 7 spend a chunky 12 hours a week studying English language and lit plus a further five hours reading (in and out of school). Pupils are expected to notch up 30 'ambitious' new words every term and timetabled book clubs encourage 'challenging' discussions about what is read. No dumbing down outside the classroom, with years 7 and 8 performing, designing and marketing their own unabridged Shakespeare production. Mathematicians, too, stretched both at school and in the public arena (with individuals and teams entering the UK Maths Challenge, Ark Maths Challenge, Times Tables Rock Stars Wrange and more).

A focus on the 3Rs, however, does not mean other subjects are neglected. In primary, two hours a week are devoted to science, expanded to four at GCSE, when a truly remarkable 75 per cent of students take triple science (a statistic to make many independent schools blush). Here again, a wide range of related extracurricular underpins the main menu (Curie-ous Club, Year 8 Science Fair, Dissection Club, Journal Review Club, Open Labs). French taught for a committed hour-and-a-half each week in primary and nearly all go on to take a GCSE in French or Spanish. Highly structured homework programme from year 7 helps embed it all.

The school has embraced the theory of 'cognitive overload', so the secondary curriculum is kept deliberately narrow and teaching style is traditional, with teacher-directed lessons and pupils spending a significant amount of time working in silence. All agree that teaching is outstanding (made so by weekly coaching on professional development). 'We tell our teachers we are going to help them become better teachers,' says the head. 'It means very talented people want to work with us.'

Post-GCSE only 16 subjects on offer though economics, politics, psychology and business studies are added to the range. The school only teaches A levels (plus one BTec in business studies), believing that 'these are the best preparation for university study'.

About 12 per cent on the SEN register and SEN well supported with three SENCos, on-site speech-and-language therapist, and regular tutorial sessions to help staff with teaching and learning strategies. Aid given both in and outside the classroom, including by Westminster-supplied specialists. Lift for those with mobility difficulties.

Games, options, the arts: Music is heavily embedded in the curriculum, taught for its 'cognitive benefits, moral, social and cultural understanding and potential to build effective teamwork' – plus, no doubt, its advantages on the well-honed UCAS form. All supplied with a cello, violin or viola from year 3 and taught to read music, with regular whole-class lessons and small-group instrumental sessions. Compulsory participation in the school orchestra, which is timetabled from year 7 to GCSE. Popular annual summer orchestra tour abroad for older pupils.

Elsewhere, extracurricular heavily entwined with curricular goals. After-school clubs focus on English (with all invited to participate in a year-long creative-writing programme), languages (including Latin), maths, music, and sport. Debating (entries in national competitions) enhances public-speaking and contributions to the school magazine – The King's Speech – train up potential broadsheet talent. Trips, too, are intended to stretch, so local outings to The Imperial War Museum, British Library, Houses of Parliament and LSE public lectures, and residential adventures include living on a farm, visiting Paris or camping – experiences which are, as the website points out, 'in many schools.. the privilege of those who parents can afford them'.

PE every week and offered as a BTec; other sports (girls' and boys' football, basketball, cricket, dance, martial arts, badminton, table tennis) available in after-school clubs, played in the spacious, well-maintained playground. School fields football and basketball teams, which compete in Westminster and Ark competitions, and are 'working towards' a netball and a rugby team. Art pursued earnestly (with skills tracked, targets set and 'key words embedded'). If creativity still manages to make it through, enthusiasts can develop 'new techniques' as part of the out-of-class enrichment programme.

Background and atmosphere: KSA is a leading light of the 35-strong chain of academies run by Ark (Absolute Return For Kids), a charitable trust founded by hedge-fund financiers intended to improve the life chances of children by creating high returns on philanthropic investment. The USP of Ark Schools, set up in 2004, is closing the achievement gap between children from disadvantaged and more affluent backgrounds and the charity aims to apply sound business disciplines to all its programmes, with a strong emphasis on target-setting, monitoring and evaluation.

King Solomon operates very much within the brand with all energies directed to the end game of making 'a university education something which is accessible, exciting and aspirational'. The curriculum is 'planned backwards' with that goal in view. Sights are constantly focussed by add-ons such as the Odysseus Project (in partnership with OxFizz), which provides free tutoring courtesy of volunteers from Slaughter and May, McKinsey, The Telegraph, Barclays, Accenture and the Cabinet Office. Societies for medics and Oxbridge offer specialist advice.

An all-through education is, of course, a key part of the strategy ('The disruptive effect of the transition from primary to secondary can often affect confidence, behaviour and academic attainment,' says the head), while the scale is critical. 'We create a community where there are no strangers and no pupil will be left behind.' The school as family is another leitmotif. But this is not simply an exercise in Victorian paternalism distancing children from undesirable influences beyond the school gates: the modern way is to solidify home-school links and educate the birth family, so the head pays a visit to welcome both parent and child into the community and mum and dad are encouraged to participate (including handy Positive Parenting workshops).

Built as Rutherford School for Boys in the late 1950s as part of London County Council's secondary school building programme. The Grade II* listed building with its distinctive roofline, Carrara-marbled foyer and varnished concrete and tiled surfaces was designed by Leonard Manasseh at a high point in the development of post-war school design.

Pastoral care, well-being and discipline: The disciplinary style is a further integral strand of the approach. Again, objectives are clear: 'We are responsible for teaching the children in our care how to work hard, and how to be good people.' The school aims, in Manichean fashion, 'to create a light and dark culture'. 'We make it normal, expected and visible that the majority of the group do the right thing.' Everything is explained ('We never ask children to do things.."because I said so") but after that 100 per cent compliance is expected.

Praise is an important part of the package, with daily 'shout outs' to identify who and what has been done well as well as class (to celebrate 'the successes of the team') and individual rewards ('to rejoice in personal choices, growth and successes'). Good behaviour is also rewarded financially (at least, notionally). An elaborate 'payslip' system gives pupils an (imaginary) sum for turning up. Those in credit at the end of the week are allowed to take part in Friday enrichment, while big earners win an annual bonus – attendance at a week-long residential course at a leading university.

Those – and, alas, there will always be sinners – who for whatever reason do not make the correct decision are given the chance 'to reflect on the choice they made and what different choice they can make in the future to achieve a better outcome'. To facilitate this, a 'follow-up conversation' with families is also sometimes necessary. Persistent offenders are taught in isolation.

Behaviour in immaculately-ordered classrooms is (perhaps unsurprisingly) impeccable, off-task chatting virtually unknown. Silence – gained by clapping out a quick rhythm – is also expected elsewhere, including in the corridors in years 7-9, with a (slightly) more liberal regime thereafter. Some have described the silence as 'disturbing', including one visiting head. Parents are, however, delighted with the outcome. 'The school has given my daughter a great start in life,' said one. 'Every day she becomes more confident.'

Pupils and parents: Surrounded by streets full of some of the sterner remnants of turn-of-the-century local authority housing, the school sits in one of London's most deprived wards and its intake reflects its locality, with 58 per cent on free school meals (the government measure of poverty), 75 per cent on pupil premium. Top 20 per cent in the country, too, for ethnic diversity, with over half speaking English as an additional language.

Entrance: Working along the lines of 'give me a child by the age of 7', King Solomon is very much intended to be an all-through school taking pupils from reception to Freshers' Fair. Non-denom and non-selective, after the usual specialist categories (including children of staff, where priority is given to those who teach subjects 'where there is a demonstrable skill shortage'), siblings and distance from the gates are given priority. More than three times oversubscribed at 4, with the furthest successful applicant living less than half a mile away. Don't hold your breath for a place in year 7: all year 6s transfer automatically at this point and the school does not expand (so no new openings at all last year). Sixth form, on the other hand, may have spots available. School also operates its own nursery, with 60 places on offer.

Exit: King's Solomon's raison d'etre is to guide first-generation university goers on the straight and narrow to higher education, a goal now being fully realised with ex-pupils off to study the full range of subject options (from chemical engineering and law to creative writing and psychology). At this point, most don't stray too far from home and London colleges are well represented (Queen Mary, SOAS, Royal Holloway, Goldsmiths, King's, LSE, Imperial), but more adventurous types are off to Warwick, Leeds, Reading, Kent and Sussex. Not huge numbers to Russell group as yet but, no doubt, it's only a matter of time. Offers specialist preparation for Oxbridge and medicine and the first student headed for Oxford in 2018 (history). Three have gained places on highly competitive degree level apprenticeships at leading employers, including Accenture and Bank of England.

Money matters: Being part of the Ark chain of academies brings considerable financial benefits, and after-school clubs (from £5 a term) and trips (including the annual music tour abroad) are heavily subsidised. Ark bursaries also available to underwrite university fees for high achievers.

Remarks: Teaching is inspirational and results significantly better than many schools in affluent suburbs. Some find the approach a bit 'cult-like', but who can argue with the outcome? 'What is being achieved at King Solomon is extraordinary,' remarked an observer. There's no doubt that KSA pupils are safe, happy, secure and also successful.

Arnold House School

1 Loudoun Road, London NW8 0LH

Ages 5–13 **Pupils** 270

Fees: £19,032 pa

020 7266 4840
www.arnoldhouse.co.uk

Headmaster: Since 2006, Vivian Thomas (50s). A user-friendly, down-to-earth chap with an easy warmth and an unscholarly taste in garish ties (red flowers and giant yellow fish on the day we visited). Makes a point of being accessible on school gate duty at least twice a week and is generally popular with parents. 'Relaxed, confident, intelligent, and understands how parents feel about their children,' said one. Educated at University College School, Hampstead, followed by St Luke's College, Exeter, where he studied PE and history. Had a trial for QPR aged 17 and dreamt of becoming a professional sportsman but, after failing to make the grade (at football, tennis and rugby), he turned his talents to education. Taught PE and maths at UCS, followed by a spell at an international school in Venezuela. He returned to London to become deputy head at Arnold House, then head of Keble Prep, Winchmore Hill. Married to Rowena, he is a man of varied interests, who 'struggles with golf', enjoys travelling and takes guitar lessons with 'a madman in Dollis Hill who used to play with Ginger Baker of Cream'.

Entrance: Application form (plus the usual fee) due before child's second birthday, followed by an open evening held in April/May approximately two and a half years before the intended entry date. Interested parents (roughly 180 families for 40 places) are then invited to meet the head for a 20 minute chat. As always, it is the parents who are being assessed as much as the child. Don't say, 'I need you to get my son into Westminster'. Do say, 'I'd like my child to be happy and enjoy an all-round education'. Prospective pupils then invited for an informal one-to-one assessment and places offered 15 months before entry date. 'I hate the idea that it'll be down to the little boy, that he might be "not good enough",' says the head. 'What I want to know is, will he be a nice little boy to teach? When you open a book, is he able to be engaged? Or is he climbing the walls, unruly and impolite? I don't want it to be a skills-based test, and I find it astonishing that there are tutoring agencies for 3 and 4 year olds.'

Main entry point is into year 1, with occasional ad-hoc places in other years. Younger siblings and sons of old boys looked on favourably. Partial and full means-tested bursaries are available in years 5, 6 and 7 to prepare boys – most likely from state primaries – for 13+ exams (and bursaries) to independent secondaries.

Exit: Strongly 13-plus focused school. A wide intake means a broad exit, but high fliers get into all the top schools, often with scholarships to boot. Two-thirds go on to London day schools, with the remainder heading off to boarding school. Strong links with City of London Boys, Mill Hill, St Paul's, UCS and Westminster. Boarders go to Eton, Harrow, Marlborough, Radley, Rugby, Tonbridge and Winchester amongst others. Over-ambitious parents are discouraged from entering their son for exams all over the place. 'After many years of headship I know the system inside out. I am very honest with parents. What may look like an opportunity to them is in reality a rejection letter on the mat. Granny's all keyed up, everyone is rooting for him, but I know it's just not going to happen. I'll say, "Your son is moving along quite happily; do you really want him to get that knock back?"'

Roughly 25 out of 30 boys get their first choice school; the remaining five or six take a bit longer. 'When boys are on the waiting list it's my job to turn that into an offer. We have excellent relations with schools, and that's when the prep school head really earns his corn.'

The school offers excellent results with less of the stressful, hothouse hysteria that so often accompanies the 13-plus experience. 'I offer places to parents who understand the Arnold House ethos,' says the head. 'They should want their son to join knitting club, cooking club, play music and sport, and not be getting anxious if he doesn't get three hours homework a night. We are here for bigger things than getting into a top academic senior school.'

Remarks: While some sniff that it is old fashioned, for others the traditional values of Arnold House are its strongest selling point. 'It's just like the perfect country prep school, but in London,' sighed one happy parent.

In the stressful, results-oriented atmosphere of the London prep school system, Arnold House is an artfully constructed oasis where boys can still be boys. Pupils are even encouraged to have snowball fights and inter-house conker competitions (safely supervised, of course). Admission is non-selective and the school frowns on hothousing, yet year after year leavers gain entry to the holy trinity of Eton, St Paul's and Westminster.

'These boys don't need to be pushed,' claims the head (rather airily). 'It's a question of 'nudging' and bringing a boy nicely, like a fine wine, to the point where he is ready.'

Arnold House was founded in 1905 with nine pupils by a Miss Hanson, who was keen to prove boys could be prepared for public school entrance by a woman. She was successful, and the school has now expanded to fill three adjoining houses in a quiet St John's Wood side street. The buildings lack any particular architectural pizzazz, but inside it feels spacious and well laid out, and is probably one of the cleanest schools we've visited. Even the boys' loos were sparkling, and instead of the usual dank, unloved urinals we found modern boutique-style plumbing with glossy lime green and red cubicles.

Entrance is into year 1, with 40 places split into two classes, though classes are smaller at the top of the school due to natural shrinkage. They are mixed up every couple of years to ensure academic parity and 'social refreshment'. Setting begins in year 4 for maths and English, with subjects taught by specialists from year 5. French from year 1, Latin from year 5, and ancient Greek is an option in year 7. No separate scholarship class, but boys with scholarship potential are identified at the end of year 7 and invited to join specialist lessons.

Lots of examples of creative, value-added education. Instead of the bog-standard year 8 battlefields trip, pupils spend time researching Arnold House old boys killed in WW1 before visiting France and finding their graves in the war cemeteries to pay their respects. An inspired way to bring history off the page. There is an embarrassment of before-school, after-school and break-time activities ranging from an 8am Quiz Club to Mad Scientist Club, Bug Club, darts, French Fun and Games plus all the usual sport, music and art activities.

Like many London schools has a shortage of outside space. There is an adequate playground, but boys must travel to the school's seven acre sports ground in Canons Park (35 minutes away) for games. The younger boys travel by coach, years 6, 7 and 8 by public transport as it's often quicker and the boys have more time on the pitches. ('You'd expect, with the fees we pay, that the boys wouldn't have to get there by tube', muttered one disgruntled parent.) Here there are workrooms, a theatre, tennis courts, pitches for football, cricket, hockey and rugby and full catering facilities. Older boys play team games twice a week, younger boys once a week, and there are additional PE and sports sessions at local leisure centres. A busy fixtures list for A, right down to G teams, means that even the most athletically-challenged pupil has an opportunity to represent the school.

The music department is outstanding and has many scholarships under its belt. Some 85 per cent of pupils learn at least one instrument and many learn two. Twenty different ensembles on offer, from flute group to jazz and African drums, with lots of opportunity to perform in concerts. Years 7 and 8 can use the whizzy i-music suite for production, recording and podcasting.

Art is taught to a high standard and doesn't get quietly sidelined as exams loom for older pupils. No need to feign enthusiasm when pupils arrive home clutching yet another art project. We saw wonderful Cubist self-portraits from year 3 and some very accomplished papier-mâché shells that any parent would be proud to put on display.

SEN support is excellent and, with a year of free one-to-one sessions before charges kick in, is more generous than at many comparable schools. One permanent SEN qualified staff member is supported by three visiting specialists for dyspraxia, speech and language and occupational therapy. Pupils who need extra help are identified in years 1 and 2 and either given classroom support by the six teaching assistants, or allotted one-to-one sessions as necessary. Dyslexia screening for every pupil in year 4 as a 'final trawl' to identify those with SEN needs, which can often mean brighter pupils in which dyslexic tendencies are masked.

So what type of child does Arnold House suit? 'My son has been blissfully happy, but there is a certain rough and tumble that goes with a boys' school, and I think if they are very fragile they might find it easier at a co-ed. They don't have to be uber-sporty though, there's drama, singing, art, something for everybody.'

'We take the boys as they are,' says the head. 'We have boys with IQs below 100 all the way up to 140. Once we take a boy on we're looking to be together as a team for eight years.' He admitted that, occasionally, if a boy looks like he is struggling by year 4 or 5, he will have a meeting with parents to decide 'whether or not this is looking like a good plan'.

Behaviour at the school is generally accepted to be good. 'We expect the boys to rise to a certain level of behaviour. I don't know if you can teach kindness, but you can certainly teach consideration,' says the head. There's the usual system of sanctions and rewards with Good Citizenship badges for 'being a good egg' and Industry badges for trying hard. Senior boys get ties for art, music, games and responsibility. 'I'm always pleased to hear how strict the school is,' said one parent. 'My son is well-behaved, but I occasionally hear of other boys being told off, and they are properly told off.'

Bullying is rare but, as in all schools, it happens. Usually nipped in the bud early by class teachers, but suspension has been used when necessary. 'In 7 years I've had only four situations where I've had to step in,' says the head. 'There isn't a parent I've met who thinks their son could actually be the bully, so it always has to be thoroughly investigated.' The head is very hot on cyberbullying. 'If a boy is being talked about in a derogatory way on Facebook on Sunday night, then it's going to cause problems at school on Monday morning. Even if it happens outside school, I will deal with it.' Only one parent we spoke to was unhappy, feeling that a situation had been dealt with 'too late'.

Parents are a mix of multinational successful professionals, with 50 per cent close enough to walk to school (should they ever choose to leave the 4x4 behind) and others coming from further afield (Notting Hill, Islington, Highgate). Reputed to be a friendly, sociable parent body, though the higher-than-average fees mean there's a lot of wealth sloshing around. 'There are a few amazingly flash cars, but also plenty of beat-up cars like ours. It's an easy, mixed group and I've seen no snobbishness whatsoever.' This is not the place for wags, trophy wives or school gate show-offs. 'It's definitely not a "women who lunch" school,' said one mother. 'All the mothers have, or have had, interesting careers. At my son's nursery I was the only working mum and had nothing in common with anyone, so I find the professional ethos here a relief.'

School lunches would definitely win a triple gold star from Jamie Oliver. A very jolly cook was making roast beef, Yorkshire pud, parsnips and broccoli on the day we visited, and the gravy was even made with a dash of wine.

The Arts Educational School (London)

Cone Ripman House, 14 Bath Road, London W4 1LY

Ages 11–18 **Pupils** 235 (180 girls, 55 boys) **Sixth form** 108

Fees: £15,390 – £16,990 pa

020 8987 6600
www.artsed.co.uk

Headmaster: Since 2012, Adrian Blake (40s) BEd MAPgDip NPQH. Trained as an actor and worked professionally before finding he liked education, and retraining. Started his career as lecturer in performing arts at North East Surrey College of Technology, followed by a spell as director of thinking and learning and advanced skills teacher at Greenshaw High School. Moved to Lambeth Academy to become assistant principal, then came to ArtsEd in 2009, initially as director of teaching and learning. This background may help explain his consummate ease with modern education and its jargon – unusual in a performing arts school head. A fast-talking enthusiast, who seems genuinely to know the names of every single ArtsEd pupil past and present. Still teaches 15 periods a week (extracurricular martial arts included), and greatly liked by parents and pupils alike. 'He is truly inspirational, and the children really respect him'; 'Very present in the lives of the students, and my son especially enjoys his lessons'; 'A very dynamic character whom the pupils love and want to impress,' parents told us. Married to a deputy head at a nearby state school.

Academic matters: Several of the pupils we spoke to said that they'd come to ArtsEd because they weren't excelling academically – 'I really just like acting, I'm just not into this academic stuff,' was a comment echoed by most. If so, they appear to have found the right school to help them find their academic feet. 'I'm enormously passionate about learning, and when you put creativity into leaning, everything is richer,' asserts head, and the figures support the claim. In 2018, 30 per cent 9-7 at GCSE, with 68 per cent of A level passes at A*-B and 39 per cent A*/A, and at least triple distinction for all BTecs. Creditable results for an academically non-selective school.

Maximum class size of 24, and students are taught a core of subjects that covers all the basics, including French and the humanities. At GCSE students take double science; it's rare for anyone to take triple science, although not unknown. One mother attested to the subject's overall popularity: 'My son loves the lunchtime science club, which is really igniting his passion for the subject.' Homework is, according to everyone, kept to reasonable levels, and the children are given at least two days to complete any assignment – an important piece of commonsense in a school where pupils have so many other claims on their time. 'Although there isn't as much homework as at other private schools, I'm confident that the teachers are gauging the pupils' needs well, and I feel my child is in safe hands,' wrote one parent. Others were equally positive about the academic provision overall. 'The staff are very inspiring. Since being at ArtsEd my daughter has become very keen to succeed in her academic studies – I've never seen her so determined to do well,' commented a grateful mother.

In the sixth form students choose A levels, or a mixture of BTec and A levels, and at this stage the options are almost entirely arts-based: dance, drama, art, music, film studies, etc. English, history, and French are there for the more academically minded, plus maths, which is, according to head, very popular. No science A levels offered: the sixth form is built according to demand. Sixth formers we spoke to praised the teaching and the high level of individual attention given. 'The teachers are one of the reasons I love it here – they give you so much time,' was a typical comment.

Full-time SENCo offers support to the 25 per cent of students with dyslexia and other SEN, and this provision was particularly highly praised by parents. A mother, whose son moved to ArtsEd for the sixth form after receiving inadequate support elsewhere, wrote, 'With the help of the excellent SENCo team, my son has thrived and achieved really good academic results in all his subjects. He is more confident in his academic ability now and feels understood and supported with his dyslexia.' New dedicated sixth form SENCo as well.

Games, options, the arts: Students in years 7 to 11 choose to specialise in either dance or drama (see Entrance), but everyone receives classes in both disciplines. The vocational and academic teaching is interspersed throughout the day, and the amount of time students are required to spend in school increases as they move up: younger students stay until 5.30pm doing vocational work two or three days a week, in the sixth form it's every day. This is no hardship to the students or their families – it's what they all joined for. Lively and busy programme of shows and presentations including two major productions a year, all of them resourced and rehearsed to an extremely high standard. 'It's such a professional environment,' a sixth former told us, 'and the work ethic you're taught to have is fantastic.' 'You come in each day and there's such a buzz that you just want to stay!' said another.

Extremely good facilities, some of them shared with 'the degrees', as the ArtsEd undergraduate students are known here. The amazing Andrew Lloyd Webber Foundation Theatre that hosts the school's major dance shows and concerts is at the heart of the school, along with several smaller studio performance spaces. The school can boast many successes in national initiatives such as the National Theatre's Connections and the Independent Schools Association Drama Festival. Students are encouraged to get involved with all aspects of production, and film is also increasingly popular, with regular access to the purpose-built film and TV studio.

Music is taught at all levels and lots of instrumental lessons available. One recent leaver went on to the Royal College of Music to study the oboe. When we visited, the school resonated to the rhythms of an African drumming class, complete with enthusiastic whoops and wails.

'Sporty kids wouldn't like it here,' was the unanimous opinion of the students we spoke to. The school has no outside facilities of its own but the students go off site for sports each week, and there are regular kickabouts at lunchtime. But no-one is here for the sport, of course, and with so much dancing going on, the children keep super-fit. Visual arts are also strong and creative, as the variety of work on the walls confirms.

ArtsEd isn't a stage school or an agency; the emphasis is firmly on academic success and vocational training, and it does not go out and seek professional performing work for its pupils. That said, professional directors and producers regularly come to the school looking for the right child for a particular role, and the head will always consider what he calls 'enhancing opportunities'. An ArtsEd year 8 pupil was appearing in Harry Potter and the Cursed Child when we visited and we met a young lad who'd enjoyed six months in Bugsy Malone. The industry likes ArtsEd youngsters, it seems. 'I know a high-level producer who won't consider stage school children any more, because they're prepared in a certain way – but he comes here!' remarked the head, with pardonable pride.

Background and atmosphere: ArtsEd grew out of the Cone Ripman School, founded in 1939 and itself the result of a merger between two previous dance schools. Originally located just off Oxford Street in Stratford Place, the outbreak of war forced a move to Tring in Hertfordshire where the school shared premises with the Rothschild Bank at Tring Park Mansion House. In 1941, the school was able to move back to Stratford Place, but kept its Tring premises as a second, boarding school. In 1947 both places were renamed The ArtsEducational School, to reflect Grace Cone's and Olive Ripman's commitment to a proper academic education for their young performers. Gradually the two schools diverged, and are now good friends but completely independent of one another (in 2009, to avoid confusion with its former partner, Tring changed its name to Tring Park School for the Performing Arts). ArtsEd moved to its present premises in a leafy part of Chiswick in 1989, renaming the building Cone Ripman House in honour of its founders. Cone Ripman House does nothing much for the eye on the outside, it has to be said, but has been extensively modernised and refurbished within and looks airy and streamlined.

The original Cone Ripman School was for girls only, and even today ArtsEd is still girl-heavy. This is almost always the case with performing arts schools, but seemed particularly so here, where only a quarter of students are boys. A sixth former admitted that she 'wished there were more boys', but the boys themselves were philosophical about it. 'It's a bit of a problem, but you make friends across the years,' observed a year 10 lad, equably.

Parents and students alike described this as a happy school. 'Everyone knows everyone, and everyone's so kind to each other'; 'It's a really nice atmosphere, it allows you to progress.' Parents concur: 'Our daughter has been at ArtsEd for two years and they have been the happiest school years of her life. ArtsEd is like a big family,' wrote one. Everyone praised the 'positive competitiveness' the school fosters, and insisted that no matter who got which part, 'we're in it together, we work as a team.' Chances to shine abound. 'If you audition for a part and you don't get it, you know there'll always be another opportunity,' a level-headed teenager told us. 'We offer developmental opportunities throughout the year,' confirmed the head, 'and parents will see their children do any number of things.' 'Watching your children in demonstrations of work is amazing; you can see them and their cohort growing in confidence,' agreed a parent. The young people we met were quiet, polite, respectful and proud of their school.

Has been awarded an Independent Schools Association Excellence Award in recognition of 'excellent academic standards, alongside specialist performing arts provision and record numbers of pupils achieving places at universities and conservatoires'.

Pastoral care, well-being and discipline: Students work hard to win their place here, and still harder once they arrive, so behaviour problems are rare. Occasionally there are the friendship group issues that you'll find at any school. However, everyone here knows the importance of getting on with each other, and staff work actively to promote harmony and healthiness, both physical and emotional. 'In my old school there was a lot of bullying, but everyone here gets along, and the teachers always talk to us if there's an incident,' said a year 7 girl. Parents agreed: 'Staff are kind and approachable and my child has great respect for them.' The head was adamant that there were no eating disorders in the school, and the canteen certainly seemed well-used and well-liked, selling a commendable variety of healthy and appetising dishes. A few sixth formers live too far away from the school to travel there daily from home, and instead lodge in nearby digs (this isn't allowed for younger students). The school isn't affiliated to any boarding provider, but helps students find host families, and has set up an 'away from home' group that meets every fortnight.

All students are assigned a staff mentor in year 10, and in year 11 the head personally meets all year 11 students to talk about future plans. The school prides itself on developing 'emotional resilience and bounce-back-ability' in its pupils. 'We really grow the understanding, and we enable them to do their best at auditions,' said the head. Parents valued this aspect of the school very highly. 'The school emphasises professionalism in preparing them for a demanding and sometimes brutal industry,' was one comment. 'ArtsEd students leave school very well prepared for the big wide world,' was another. 'You make connections here,' a sixth former reflected, 'and you're well-connected when you leave.'

Pupils and parents: Inevitably, many of the children come from families of film-makers, actors, writers and dancers, but not exclusively so, and the students we spoke to were adamant that 'you don't have to have a showbiz background to do well here'. Not much ethnic diversity when we looked round, perhaps reflecting perhaps the differing aspirations of London's various communities. Most of the children we spoke to were local, but the school recruits from a wide radius – one year 7 student travels up from Brighton each day, and we met a sixth former who'd relocated from Ireland.

ArtsEd alumni include, to name just a handful, Julie Andrews, Darcey Bussell, Martin Clunes, Nigel Havers, Bonnie Langford, Tuppence Middleton, Finn Jones – the list is impressively long.

Entrance: Twenty-four places at Y7, but school won't take full number if there aren't 24 good enough to take. Places do come up in other years: always worth checking. Entrance is by audition: students can try out for either the dance or drama pathway – or they can try for both, in which case the school will offer a place on the one they feel is best suited to the student. Written assessment in maths and English is simply to gauge academic progress: the school is academically non-selective. A number of additional places available at year 12. Similar entrance procedure, albeit more detailed and tougher: audition, workshops, interview.

School looks for 'potential... that real passion', but not for would-be stars. As head observed, 'I don't do divas. Everyone's talented here. Staff are talented. We're all here because we're passionate about the arts, about education, about training.'

Exit: Typically with this kind of school, a few leave after GCSEs, having decided to pursue other life choices, in particular to study science at A level, since it isn't offered in the sixth form here. ArtsEd students have successfully applied at this stage to schools such as Latymer Upper and Tiffin. At 18, around 80 per cent to an impressive array of prestigious conservatoires: RADA,

LAMDA, Royal Central School of Speech and Drama, English National Ballet School, London School of Contemporary Dance, Trinity Laban, etc. A number move upstairs to the highly regarded ArtsEducational degree schools in acting and musical theatre. Some pursue a career in film at places such as Bournemouth & Poole or the National Film & TV School. Others go abroad to institutions such as the Juilliard or the New York Film Academy. A few go into the industry immediately: a recently sixth form leaver went straight into playing the lead role in The Curious Incident of the Dog in the Night Time. A small number to university, mostly to read arts subjects.

Money matters: ArtsEd fees are remarkably reasonable given the high level of specialist tuition the students receive, and lower than those charged at many other independent schools in this part of London. For those who need help, the school offers means-tested bursaries of up to a third of the fees for students in years 7 to 11. In addition, eight full-fees scholarships are available in the sixth form. The school does not receive any government or local authority funding.

Remarks: A dynamic, purposeful, well-oiled institution where creative youngsters learn to work hard and achieve highly. 'With the school's expert guidance and support the transformation in my child has been remarkable,' said one mother, and another reported her daughter as saying, 'Mum, I don't think there's another school in the world that is as good and as fun as ArtsEd.'

Ashbourne Independent School

17 Old Court Place, London W8 4PL

Ages 14–19 **Pupils** 275 **Sixth form** 253

Fees: £24,750 – £26,250 pa

020 7937 3858
www.ashbournecollege.co.uk

Principal: Since 1981, Mike Kirby BApSc MSC (60s). Raised and educated in and around Toronto, his second degree in aerospace engineering and astrophysics. He became a maths teacher because he was 'entirely unsuited to the aerospace engineering profession' and still teaches once a week. An extremely tall, gently ironic man with a slightly lazy sounding Canadian drawl, but with a mind that is not remotely idle. No plans to hand over the reins entirely, as we speak, but has a plan for the succession in place if the mountains of electronic paper, needed by modern legislation, threaten to swamp the pleasure of running his school. His son, Lee, is already in place and is given the 'thumbs up' by parents, particularly in his handling of student interviews and the energy he brings.

Academic matters: Results are up there in the sector, with 49 per cent A*/A grades in 2018 and 75 per cent A*-B. GCSE results were 50 per cent A*-A/9-7.

GCSE students only account for some 10-15 per cent of the total roll-call but an increase of numbers is on the cards. The range of courses covers the core compulsory subjects plus computer science, graphic design and textiles. As in the rest of the school, the classes are tiny as Ashbourne guarantees that there will be less than 10 pupils in a class and they 'will only violate this policy in an emergency'. This rule means that Ashbourne could well be a GCSE slot for a student having trouble finding their feet in the ultra-competitive world of more conventional London schools, or for teenagers who might be happier in a more 'grown-up' environment.

The vast majority of A level students are here for two years, although they still offer one-year courses (for first time fluffers and very able students) and 18 month courses (a rare bird in London) which can be a life-saver for parents whose lives are suddenly disrupted and for international students who may be on a different timeline at home but want to join the English system to qualify for university entry here.

Strong maths and science departments (recently renovated labs) unsurprising for the brainchild of a maths teacher, but the school also has a proven A level track record and successful results in English, a wide range of language options, theatre studies and art. They are extremely flexible and will try to construct a timetable that allows for a more unusual course selection than is often available meaning some subjects only have two or three students in a class. Pupils say that this can lead to some fairly wacky timetabling and you can find yourself working every hour of the school day (9-6) for three days a week and theoretically putting your feet up the rest of the time. However, with mock exams every half term and reports four times a year on everything from grades to punctuality there's not much latitude given to slackers.

More teachers than is often the case tend to have done time in the outside world before turning to education (although all have professional and academic qualifications), with backgrounds ranging from the civil service to the wine trade. School has recently appointed a specialist teacher to help students on the 'dys' spectrum; however all successful applicants need to be able to keep up with only a moderate amount of help.

Probably partly because of the number of international students there is a steady demand for economics and finance courses, and carrying on the original theme there is a specialist engineering programme. Laying the groundwork for Oxbridge entrance and organising legal seminars for law school applicants and preparing them for LNAT tests are also a core part of their offering.

Games, options, the arts: An atmosphere and ethos that is more university than school and a site just off Kensington High Street makes it understandable that games are not timetabled and the students tend to be the initiators of any new sport. There is a very popular eight-a-side football club, the Ashbourne Allstars (a name chosen perhaps for its alliterative qualities rather than their goal scoring prowess) and students talk of how helpful the school is if they want to start any form of sporting club, down to finding a venue and providing the funds for equipment.

For the rare students with time on their hands they promote a series of clubs from tango and salsa to meditation and mindfulness, plus an astro particle physics club (seriously impressive). There's an annual visit to a European city but these are, on the whole, a fairly well-travelled bunch anyway.

The music department is an essential component, according to MK, as it 'makes the school round', and they offer scholarships to outstanding students. New practice rooms and all the computer techy stuff necessary for advanced music composition are attracting more students to a place where the synergy between music and maths comes naturally.

Drama (also with many scholarships on offer) is 'absolutely fantastic' according to one ex-student and they take full advantage of being a short bus ride from the theatrical Mecca of the West End. Drama students go to plays regularly and get the full greasepaint experience by producing, directing and acting in theatres hired by the school.

A top-floor studio with an additional textile space feels more like an art school than an art department and the standard of work is correspondingly high. The head reports that art and

A

drama numbers are steady but under pressure as they are not facilitating subjects for Russell Group universities.

Once a year, everyone becomes creative and produces the Ashbourne Revue (always oversubscribed), which showcases dance, drama, music and fashion (much helped by the quality of the textile department).

Background and atmosphere: It may have been in the same building for 27 years, but what started as one teacher in one room with two students aiming for better grades has grown into a school with nearly 300 students, and maths, science and economics A levels have been joined by 30 other options.

As one parent commented on the school exterior, 'how it looks is not its most impressive side'. Turning off the High Street, under the stern gaze of two armed officers protecting the back entrance of the Israeli embassy, you follow a steady trickle of casually dressed teenagers (definitely no dress code) heading in through a somewhat scruffy door and up some concrete stairs.

The vibe inside is relaxed modern office rather than school lobby, with the receptionist half-hidden by a bunch of flowers and a library where young people are working on computers or chatting: apparently, a warning shot is fired if the noise level disturbs the workers on the teachers' side of the glass wall. The simple classrooms are designed to suit the teaching method, more chairman and board members than teacher and pupils, with everyone sitting round one large table and plenty of spaces to work around the school when not in class. Decoration is minimal apart from Rothko prints (much appreciated by us) and posters advertising the existence of an LGBTQ club and various other societies.

Across the High St are the other two buildings, both on the same lines of functional classrooms and science laboratories, although the art room adds a splash of colour. The layout, constrained by its location, is not perfect, and a slightly wistful look comes into MK's eyes when he talks about the possibility of housing his school in a less bitty manner.

Pastoral care, well-being and discipline: The GCSE pupils are under more supervision but everyone has a personal tutor whom they see twice a week, and the school counters its outwardly laid back atmosphere by using a highly sophisticated electronic system which both teachers and parents can access. This not only keeps a close eye on each student's academic progress but also on basics like whether they actually turn up for lessons and hand in their work on time. One parent told us that when her normally dead punctual daughter turned up late 'they were on it in a flash, leaping into action and checking where she lived'. Some 10-20 per cent of the students live away from home, but the responsibility lies with the parents for finding suitable accommodation and ensuring their welfare, although the school will provide advice and hopes to flag up any potential problems through its tutorial system.

This is very much a half-way house between school and university and some of the usual problems can arise, as they do in all London schools. Drugs and alcohol are only too readily available and sometimes the principal has had to exercise his zero tolerance policy and show the offenders straight out the door. Parents support the 'very hard line' and feel that the message he gives is a massive deterrent for the students. We also observed that on the surface everyone appeared to be much more intent on passing their exams than being led astray by London's temptations.

Pupils and parents: MK expresses slight surprise that the ratio of UK to International students over the last 10 years has nearly been reversed to 65:35 from the exact opposite, although he doesn't feel that Brexit is playing a part.

Still some students needing improved grades for top universities, but these re-takers are less than 10 per cent currently with MK stating that they 'often are able to turn A/B students into confident As'. Most (about 70 per cent) of the English students come from private education and many from schools where they found it 'hard to cope and are looking for a different landscape'. The international cohort are truly global, but this is an environment where your English needs to be fluent as students are encouraged to speak English all the time, not just in school, where it is compulsory. As a result EAL classes (at no extra cost) have fewer takers now, although there are students of more than 40 nationalities.

Entrance: The school is 'picky' rather than selective, particularly for years 12 and 13, and is looking for at least a grade 4 average at GCSE. The process involves an academic assessment and an interview with either the principal or a senior member of staff. According to one pupil this was 'not scary', but another told us that he was turned down initially and had to work really hard to persuade them to take him (possibly more because of his attitude than his lack of qualifications).

Exit: Usually over 50 per cent to Russell Group universities with particularly popular destinations including UCL and King's College London. Three to Oxbridge in 2018 and one medic. Drama students tend to go to university rather than drama school but art students often go straight to art college, some without doing the initial foundation year.

Money matters: This level of teaching and class sizes never comes cheap in central London but to ease the pain Ashbourne offers some scholarships and bursarial help for exceptionally gifted drama, music, art and academic students.

Remarks: For a self-disciplined teenager, who wants to be treated like a grown up, learn to run their own life and concentrate on academics this could be just the answer. A parent backed this up saying that they 'treat them like adults but the boundaries are still there'.

Ashmole Academy

Cecil Road, London N14 5RJ

Ages 11–18 **Pupils** 1,530 **Sixth form** 311

020 8361 2703
www.ashmoleacademy.org

Head teacher: Since 1997, Derrick Brown MA MBA DipEd – degree subjects psychology and business. Formerly a scientist, but changed career when he realised it wasn't all about 'filling pretty liquids into tubes. It was actually quite isolating and I'm a people person.' He was advised at the time to become either a teacher or a prison governor. He opted for the former. Prior to headship at Ashmole, he was vice principal at Leigh City Technology College in Dartford and then senior deputy at Cranford School – both schools much the same size and diversity of Ashmole and in comparable outer London suburbs.

Early 60s, but 'nowhere near retiring.. I wouldn't know what to do with myself'. Quietly spoken, serious and tirelessly focused on getting things done, an outstandingly successful head. His drive and determination stem from his own 'not great' secondary school education which prompted him to challenge the state school system – in this case to turn a bog standard local comp into one with all the academic benefits of a private school education, without the fees. As he says: 'Why should only a privileged few have these opportunities? I want to make it available to all kids.'

Mr Brown vowed when he started at Ashmole to make an immediate impact on results: 'It was a fairly averagely performing school with not very high aspirations.' He took a hard look at the areas that were lacking and the following year results were already up by 10 per cent. 'I created partnerships with parents, worked on the discipline and talent scouted good teachers.' His 'football manager's mentality' of never being satisfied, and always finding something to improve on, has awarded Ashmole the title of 'super state school' according to the Evening Standard.

One gets the feeling that this head has little time or inclination for hobbies. With two grown up children of his own, any extracurricular activities he may pursue are of the more 'unusual' kind – which currently, he says, is revamping an old wreck he bought (we're presuming he means property). Although there's no resting on laurels for this head, he has already consolidated Ashmole's reputation as a provider of comprehensive education at its best.

Academic matters: This school hasn't been awarded the title of 'super state' for no reason. As the head says: 'Every subject excels here, no subject is weak.' Ofsted outstanding – it has managed to sustain many years of exceptionally high results. Strong value added. Entirely non-selective, so the results are impressive. Way ahead of the other non-selective schools in the area. 'There are no tricks here – all the students come from the local community.' Anyone can do well here, we were told – boys, girls, the less motivated, 'everyone exceeds their personal best.' Classes are setted in main subjects – 'mixed ability doesn't work except in certain areas', says the head.

In 2018, 87 per cent got grades 9-4 in both English and maths, 41 per cent 9-7 grades. A levels 30 per cent A*/A and 62 per cent A*-B grades. French is popular and there's a very strong exchange link with the twinned town of Le Raincy, a suburb just outside Paris. Spanish and German are also offered at GCSE and A level, but less popular.

Students are closely monitored and undergo assessments after every half term. The head says: 'If we see underperformance, we can intervene and work with the child individually to make them improve.' However, one parent we spoke to disagreed. 'Ashmole is a great school if you are the academic, studious type. However if, like my daughter, you don't fit the mould, you're going to have more of a struggle there.' Teachers are also closely monitored and parents feel that there is quite a high turnover, although the school says it is similar to most London schools. But if this is the case, it is not an unhealthy state of affairs anyway, according to the head. He says: 'A stable school with no turnover can be a recipe for complacency and disaster.'

A third of the school has English as an additional language – support in place to make sure they progress, either through extra help or (mostly) in-class intervention. Around a seventh have some kind of SEN – about one or two per cent with EHC plans. Learning support is located within its own area, providing adequate space that caters for all needs. The weakest 30 or so students drop languages after year 8, taking BTec business instead, although this varies every year. These students have extra help with the basics.

Able, gifted and talented pupils – those who have all round ability across the core subjects of English, maths and science (around one in four students at Ashmole) – have their own programme designed for them. This bespoke Ashmolean programme involves a variety of activities which 'encourage aspiration,' whether this be by visiting higher education institutes or learning through Firefly, the school's virtual learning environment. However, one unhappy parent called it an 'exclusive' club and a very 'rigid' system; 'most students who are on the programme come on it straight from primary school and there seems to be little movement.' She also said that much is made of the G&T students and the privileges offered to them, which makes the other students feel less worthy. Another parent disagreed, saying that her child has been 'on and off the programme many times according to her grades.'

Games, options, the arts: The opportunities are plentiful and the facilities wonderful. Huge floodlit Astroturf court, playing field, sports hall and separate studio for dance, aerobics and net sports, but no pool. Outdoor table tennis on offer, which proves to be a very popular lunchtime activity. Outstandingly successful in both boys' and girls' football; the boys' football team recently won the Barnet Cup and the girls' team reached the semi-final of the Middlesex Cup. Rugby also a biggie and the year 8 rugby team won the Barnet Saracens tournament recently. One parent told us: 'Even if your child is not the academic type, the sports on offer can give them the opportunity to shine.'

Much acclaimed music department. Amy Winehouse spent a few years here (although head, who was here at the same time, says: 'Amy left us quite early on to join the BRIT school'). Having a music specialism, they are able to employ the very latest technology. Music scholarships on offer to help those with talent develop their skills, and an increasing number of pupils take individual music lessons. A full range of extracurricular music programmes also on offer, including an orchestra, jazz band, chamber string group, junior string group, brass band, senior wind ensemble, Latin rock band, two choirs and show band for the annual school musical.

Drama popular – big, well-equipped studio and major musical production each year. Standards are high – recent 'fantastic' production of Hairspray. Impressive art studios and some astounding individual pieces of art. The school has its own radio station and two recording studios. Plenty of lunchtime and after-school clubs, including film club, debating societies, Mad for Books club, philosophy, homework clubs and numerous language clubs. Enrichment groups offer a choice of cultural, entrepreneurial and environmental activities. 'The options here are great,' a sixth former told us. 'We're bombarded with courses and clubs which enrich us as people.' He was not wrong.

Background and atmosphere: This is a different school, quite literally, from the Ashmole of yesteryear. It had survived in pretty dire conditions for years but, on his arrival in 1997, the head organised the sale of six acres of school land and began a visionary building programme with the proceeds. The design of the new buildings was the result of collaboration between the school, a very proactive parent committee and the architect. Rehoming happened in 2004 at a cost of £14m. The result is a bright and spacious, well-mapped-out building, 'which is easy to navigate,' one parent told us. All subjects grouped into their own sections and everything immaculately labelled. No chance of getting lost here. The only confusing things are the different coloured named staircases, like the 'orange staircase,' which in fact is blue. The head told us: 'When we designed the building we wanted to colour group it into sections so, for example, people could meet at the orange staircase, but this wasn't DDA compliant for partially sighted people, so everything has to be kept white and blue.' Lifts are also available for students with disabilities.

Large, wide corridors with beautiful wall displays, seriously impressive artwork and a convivial atmosphere. As we progressed from section to section we witnessed quiet classrooms (with the odd exception), with an atmosphere that encourages work and discourages messing around. 'We have a

B

policy at this school that lessons should be silent, unless they require a discussion. It helps to keep the class focused.' We also noticed a lot of reading going on – by individuals in the canteen and elsewhere. The head told us that he insists every student carries a book of their choice around with them. 'There is no such thing as doing nothing,' he said. 'One can always read.'

Set in 28 acres of land in quiet, residential Southgate, the outside of the school is none too shabby either, especially for a London comprehensive. Plenty of outdoor space. Remarkably free of litter and immaculately kept lawns, outdoor classroom and environmental area, fully equipped with wooden table and benches. So much excess land that Ashmole primary school opened on the premises in September 2016. 'There is such a lack of primary schools in the area, it makes sense,' says the head. We say: Start booking your kids in now.

The new sixth form block, kitted out with its own Starbucks, was opened in 2014. This was many years in the waiting, needed £1.3 million (raised through fundraising events and tightening of the old school purse strings), two contractors and various other obstacles. One student told us: 'It's so exciting, I'm just upset I'll only have one year to enjoy it.'

Pastoral care, well-being and discipline: Big on discipline. 'Not for the free spirit,' one mother told us. Strict adherence to their uniform code expected – no exceptions or students will be asked to go home and change. Lo and behold: if pupils are caught outside the school premises with a shirt hanging out, they will be seriously reprimanded, sometimes even face a detention. Mobiles, too, are strictly forbidden, except for the sixth form – confiscated immediately if found and, to add to the humiliation, parents have to go in to school and pick them up. While this has been a bone of contention with many of the parents, who like to get hold of their kids after school hours, others feel it is a good thing. 'If nothing else because there have been some phone thefts in the area, but muggers know not to bother with Ashmole kids as they never have phones on them,' one parent told us.

Zero tolerance of drugs, weapons and violence – on or off the premises. Much has been done to combat bullying, which has clearly been a problem at Ashmole in former years (as in many comprehensives of this size). CCTV cameras operate along main corridors 'to monitor any deviant behaviour that may occur' and when the new building was designed head specifically requested wide, open spaces free of 'little cul-de-sacs' where vulnerable students could be cornered. As Orwellian as this may sound, bullying is now virtually non-existent and parents are very grateful.

Disruptive or abusive pupils are sent to the individual learning room, where they are under supervision, have no contact with their friends and hate it. Two or three days there usually does the trick, but head will exclude for serious offences – roughly five permanent exclusions a year. 'We just can't let a disruptive child continue,' he says. 'They are given community service and various other deterrents, but if they are hell bent on being disruptive, they're out.' The result of this is a school in which pupils feel secure and comfortable and everyone knows the score.

Each key stage has its own learning mentors and key stage managers whom pupils know they can go to if they feel the need. Parents aren't so convinced. One parent we spoke to said: 'It's not always made clear who we should be speaking to, or emailing. I have left messages on several occasions and no one has responded. I think the communication between parents and year heads could be improved.' However, for the most part, parents and students we spoke to seemed extremely happy with the school. One sixth former told us: 'I've loved every minute of this school. The sixth form is like a big family, even for external students.'

A large amount of interaction between the year groups, encouraged by the cultural and charitable activities. Pupils feel they have friends in all years. Charity work plays a vital part in the general ethos of the school and every year students and staff raise thousands of pounds for a variety of good causes. Overall, the school has a general sense of self-discipline and a fostering of civilised behaviour.

Pupils and parents: Vast ethnic mix, as you'd expect from the Southgate area, though more Cypriots – Greek and Turkish – than anything else. Main religion is Christianity of all sorts, the second is Islam. Mostly working parents, but a supportive and hard working PTA makes big contribution to the school's development. Pupils are cheery, ambitious, focused and involved. Notable former students include: Amy Winehouse, former S Club 7 member Rachel Stevens, musician Stephen Sidwell, goalie Mark Bunn, Oscar winning producer Mark King, The Feeling lead vocalist Daniel Sells and Channel 5 tsar Sham Sandhu.

Entrance: More than 1,100 apply for the 232 places – of which siblings will take around 80. You'll get in if you have a sibling there, are a looked-after child or live very close – otherwise no chance. 'I wish I had bought on Cecil Road years ago. Houses must be worth a fortune now', one parent sighed. Up to 20 music aptitude places; these pupils, along with others who show talent, are placed on the music scholarship programme.

Exit: Some 50-60 per cent leave after GCSEs, mostly for vocational courses elsewhere. The rest need to get 6s in the subjects they wish to study for A levels to stay on in the sixth form; small fall-out after year 12. Around a third to a half of sixth formers to top universities; generally a few to Oxbridge (two in 2018, and four medics); others to places like Durham, Warwick, London universities, Nottingham, Leeds. Science, law and humanities are all popular.

Remarks: Slick, sensible and effective. Check out the housing market.

Bancroft's School

611 –627 High Road, Woodford Green, Essex IG8 0RF

Ages 7–18 Pupils 1,142 Sixth form 245 C of E

Fees: £14,751 – £18,123 pa

020 8505 4821
www.bancrofts.org

Head: Since 2016, Simon Marshall (early 50s). Formerly headmaster of the English College in Prague and, before that, deputy head academic at UCS Hampstead and, in an earlier incarnation, head of English at KCS Wimbledon. A very calm and incisive communicator who has the underlying confidence to deal in nuance. He believes he has taken over a school which is already performing at a very high level, and his attention seems divided equally between maintaining all that is good, and trying to help all constituencies within the school think of themselves and their ambitions perhaps a little more laterally. No academic slouch himself, having read classics at Cambridge, where he was also a choral exhibitioner and did a PGCE. Thence to Oxford, where he took a degree in English literature and then a MPhil in 18th century studies. A keen mountaineer and runner, he enjoys gardening, music and theatre. Married to Eleanor.

One parent, steeped in the ancien régime, described him as 'a great listener, sensitive to tradition, but definitely working in his ideas. He's greatly liked, and the way he is celebrating arts and humanities is just what Bancroft's needs.'

Head of prep since 2012 Joe Layburn MA, previously acting head. MA in German literature from University College London, followed by a 15-year career as an investigative journalist and TV reporter, primarily for Channel 4. Retrained as a teacher and joined Bancroft's Prep in 2004. A steady pair of hands, popular with staff, children and parents. Author of a trilogy of children's books. Married with three children; two were educated at Bancroft's from prep onwards and one at a special needs school. Keen on running, cycling and West Ham United.

Academic matters: Notable results across the board (in 2018, 69 per cent A*/A grades at A level). Many go on to study medicine or engineering at top universities. The head is emphatic about the hard work and deep commitment of staff, but places a big emphasis too on the work ethic of pupils. Maths and physics are stellar, and all the sciences excellent. Arts, languages and humanities results are, by any standard, very good. This slight asymmetry has less to do with teaching, about which all parties wax lyrical, than with the nature of the constituency: many families here are first generation users of independent schools, and there is an emphasis on traditional 'respectable' professions. One gets the sense the head may be keen gently to nudge pupils into believing there are more destinies for themselves than they might sometimes imagine. 'Bancroft's boys and girls have such heart and power,' he says, 'such creativity and imagination'.

The GCSE hit rate in 2018 was a whopping 85 per cent at A*-A/9-7. No obviously weak links but maths and science again at the heart of success. Perhaps rather fewer taking the more obviously creative subjects – art and music, for instance, or DT. Drama is now in the curriculum, but getting real momentum behind these is less about facilities (which are good) than about winning over sceptics. It all takes time. Modern languages have been the beneficiaries of this patient dedication. German, French and Spanish are all on offer from year 8; Russian becomes available in year 9 and Mandarin in the sixth form. A particular, enlightened feature is that subjects can be chosen not, as elsewhere, from 'blocks' but from the whole curriculum. Given that Bancroft's is not a rich school, and that staff are required to teach an average 31 periods per week, this flexibility is all the more impressive.

A terrific learning environment. The library, revamped with a stylish mezzanine floor beautifully integrated into the whole, is a proper scholarly resource – a place where pupils actually sit quietly and read. Given that library is all too often a euphemism for 'IT suite' these days, this delving among books redounds greatly to the credit of both staff and pupils. The latter evidently appreciate the librarians– 'they are fantastic – they get in anything you need'. The sixth form has a quiet study area and the Great Hall is used, amongst much else, for societies, debates and visiting speakers. IT everywhere – lots of rooms with new PCs, including a tiptop language lab.

Prep classrooms busy, not over-orderly and relaxed – we wanted to look at the displays, all of which seemed interesting and not as predictable as they so often are. We also approved some of the interesting work in progress, especially the lesson on moulds – 'We had to throw them away as they were beginning to smell,' was a rueful observation. Year 6 has critical thinking lessons – 'to expand our minds, to think out of the box, to widen our imagination,' we were told, earnestly. We were impressed by the sensible 'traffic light' system whereby pupils assess their grasp of what they have learnt and where they need help.

Learning support department screens all at 7+ and 11+. School has a dedicated SENCo and there are two part-timers in assistance. All new staff get some training in spotting those with learning difficulties but the head is mindful that all staff need encouragement to stay alert to those with learning difficulties: these will mostly be mild dyslexics and all will be given some kind of individual support – the precise nature of which depends on need, but may well involve one-to-one time. Lower sixth get help to 'develop individual learning skills'. 'They are wonderfully flexible over special needs,' said a parent.

Games, options, the arts: Sports are 'big' and well-resourced. Large playing fields on site plus vast sports hall with 25m pool. Five minutes' drive away is school's own West Grove with pitches, courts, tracks etc. Strong in all major sports – hockey, rugby, netball, cricket and tennis. Achievement to match – triumphs in netball, rugby and cricket as well as tours in these and hockey to, eg, Canada, Singapore/Malaysia, South Africa and Barbados. Historic complaints that sport is too elitist have become less strident but not disappeared: 'It's too often the same brilliant sportsmen getting the limelight,' said one parent. The school has taken these seriously and evolved B and C teams, along with soccer. There are practical constraints, not least finding the necessary facilities and fixtures with other schools. 'I know they're working on this,' said one parent, 'and not before time. It's our one grouse about the school.'

There is a serious wish on the part of the head that sport should reflect the values the school is trying to impart. 'We're properly proud of all the sporting success,' he says, 'but we want to create ways in which the best kind of team experience is genuinely attainable to all who seek it. Sport should offer all our pupils a medium through which they can cultivate the kinds of strength and conditioning which will sustain them throughout their lives.'

CCF is huge, very popular and enthusiastically pursued by those who surprise themselves by how much they get out of it, girls as well as boys – 'It's taught me how to get on with people I'd never mix with normally'; 'It's good that the sixth form help with it – you can have a bit of a laugh with them'. Thriving DofE. Over 200 pupils are involved in it with 30 taking gold – 'doing my gold was the hardest thing I've ever done,' said one girl, 'and the best'. Also a Sea Scout group with cubs and scouts.

Equally, steadily increased provision for arts across the school. Music and drama enthusiastic and popular – annual concert in Drapers' Hall the big annual event, with bands, solo performances and musical mix the main features. HM particularly enthused (moved, really) by the recent TAAL production – a pan-Asian body run by the Hindu, Muslim, Bhuddist and Sikh Society, but involving pupils of all ethnic groups – which embraced dance and music of all kinds. 'It was an explosion of energy and creativity,' he says, 'and it tells a big story'. Vast range of instruments studied, with eight classical concerts each year. Jazz, rock and other genres all celebrated in addition to the main and chamber orchestras. A suite of Apple Macs to support composition. Two big drama spaces – the Great Hall and a fine performing arts centre. A recent triumphant production of Les Misérables but also Amadeus and Sweeney Todd. All year 7s and 8s do drama as part of the curriculum, and there is house drama production as well. Productions at Edinburgh Fringe Festival.

Art, electronics and DT departments are buzzy spaces. Art is well-displayed and the studios are wonderful oases of light and space, as well as excellently equipped. Excellent outcomes for the seriously committed – one recent leaver having secured a spot at Central St Martins. Pupils are given considerable latitude to be creative in design. After a period of staff turnover, DT is becoming more embedded and there are hopes that it will soon be on offer for A level. Like so many schools, the cultural leap to move away from the old woodwork/metalwork shop mentality hasn't happened overnight, but the head sees an emerging synergy not merely between art, DT and electronics but extending to physics and the sciences, with big potential growth in product design.

Background and atmosphere: Founded in 1737 by the Drapers' Company on behalf of Francis Bancroft as a school for poor boys; moved to Woodford from Mile End in 1889 into the present large and imposing red-brick Victorian gothic revival building – clearly designed to impress, with serious scholarly credentials by architect, Sir Arthur Blomfield, also responsible for Selwyn College, Cambridge. This is one of his more benign and attractive buildings, with towers, crenellations and oriel windows, a splendid central quad and admirably generous corridors which, though originally intended for 200 boys, still feel spacious for today's quadrupled numbers. Twisty, brick staircases and leaded lights which grab eager 10 year olds immediately – 'I chose it because it was like Hogwarts'.

Large Great Hall – typical of date and type. Excellent Courtyard Building with colonnaded atrium and sitting area, dining room (all seniors eat together, although the sixth form can exercise the option to eat in their common room). The food gets good press, too, in contrast to the dismal recollections of one old boy now a parent ('I'm pretty jealous, actually'). Some 1960s add-ons but much better later additions (such as enormous multi-purpose sports hall) and adjoining buildings, eg vast head's house now used for admin and offices too, with head's garden open to everyone for quiet time and 'well-respected'. Nice new physics labs and modern language rooms and DT suite.

Integral chapel one of the best bits (complete with much-loved chaplain who is, says a parent, 'just extraordinary – you should hear what my children say about him. They leave chapel filled with fresh understanding about the need for mutual respect.') Each year group comes once weekly for an ecumenical service. Brass plaques to former heads and a vast stained glass east window set the tone for the services, which are inclusive in all ways, given the mix of pupils. Chapel also used for arts events – words and music etc, a classy extracurricular feature here.

Prep is in two conjoined, inviting-looking, modern red-brick buildings at the lower right hand side of the main school playing fields – two-storeyed and with big windows. Newish science, drama, music and DT rooms, a good-sized hall with flexible seating – lots of IT and new laptops. The library, recently refurbished, is well-stocked and a good mix of fact and fiction. Outside space good and super all-weather surface for littlies with monster chess set and apparatus – not surprisingly, 'Everyone loves coming out here'.

Parental tributes to general efficiency of school and its communications. Sense of order, purposeful activity and common sense all-pervasive.

Pastoral care, well-being and discipline: Unstinting and uniform praise for pastoral care is very rare, and yet this is what our enquiries to a range of parents and pupils revealed. Tributes to the teaching staff, overall friendliness, care and attention given to individuals pour from everyone and are a delight to hear: 'My teacher is amazing – he's given me extra lessons every week'; 'They'll help with anyone – not just the Oxbridge candidates'; 'The teacher gave my daughter as much time as she needed when she was struggling'.

Staff respond especially to the wholehearted and aspirational nature of their pupils, who are so laudably devoid of a sense of entitlement. The system which facilitates such praise is based around form tutors – usually of between 13 and 17 pupils. There are also houses for competitive purposes. With 200 plus pupils in each, the heads of house and their deputies have a formidable challenge in knowing their charges.

The teachers seem also to believe pupils are overwhelmingly biddable and friendly. 'Of course,' says the head, 'teenagers can make mistakes'. Like every other school, helping youngsters to make sensible use of IT is a preoccupation for teachers and parents, but as HM says, 'adults don't always find it easy either.' He is trying to encourage a pastoral style which can be more generally proactive and – it follows on – pupils find it easy and unthreatening to volunteer fears and anxieties.

Pupils and parents: From as far away as Potter's Bar, Winchmore Hill and Cheshunt, though most from between 10 and 20 minutes' drive away. Transport from local tube station to encourage pupils to look out of town towards green space for schooling. Vast ethnic and social intake – 'very well-handled by school,' say parents. Most parents first-time buyers who 'work very hard to pay fees'.

OB notables include Dennis Quilley, Sir Frederick Warner, Sir Neil McFarlane, Hari Kunzru, Adam Foulds, Yolanda Browne, Andrew Saul, Anita Anand, Lord Pannick QC, Samantha Spiro and Mike Lynch.

Entrance: At 7+ into the prep – oversubscribed by about three to one. Testing in English – reading and writing – and maths takes place on beanbags. Children seen (and offered doughnuts) in small groups with head and deputy – it's 'as informal and low key as possible'.

Some 60 pupils come up from the prep school to the senior school at 11. Around 500 apply for 65 additional places. 'It's nice to be wanted,' says the head, 'but we want to stay well away from complacency'. There are entrance tests in maths and English plus interviews – 'we need to fashion something more imaginative.' he says. 'We're working on it.' In practice around a third of those whose first choice is Bancroft's will get in. Umpteen feeders, though several from St Aubyn's, Loyola and Woodford Green Prep. Around a half from state primaries.

Candidates for the sixth form sit the school's own entrance exam in two proposed A level subjects, need six 7s at GCSE plus the usual references. Around 20 places at this level – very few (around 10 per cent) leave.

Exit: Around 90 per cent of the prep moves to the senior school. Around 10 per cent leaves after GCSEs. Twelve Oxbridge places in 2018; 17 medics, dentists and vets. Most popular current destinations Birmingham, Exeter and Nottingham followed by Bristol, King's College, Loughborough, Leeds and LSE. Others off to Amsterdam, Maryland, Milan and Toronto.

Money matters: Bancroft's has always sought to keep its fees low. There's been a hike recently which has led to some mutterings, but the HM says ruefully, 'It's always a dilemma. We don't want to change our identity, but we must be able to plan for the long term.' He feels some of the building projects of earlier times could have been better conceived had there been less of the short-termism which customarily happens when budgets are too tight.

Fifteen Drapers' scholarships offered annually at 11+ worth a quarter to a half of fees. No means-testing – based solely on performance at entrance exams. Also music scholarships worth half or quarter fees plus free tuition in one instrument. Several Francis Bancroft scholarship awards – means-tested but with a generous financial threshold, worth up to full fees, based on a sliding scale dependent on family income. Bancroft's Foundation set up in 2012 to mark 275th anniversary has already raised significant amounts to increase means-tested provision – enough to fund six Foundation scholars.

Remarks: An outstanding school – bright children, dedicated staff, and one of the most remarkable heads we've met. Given all its strengths, it deserves to be much more widely celebrated, although a deep part of its charm (and virtue) is that boastfulness and self-advertisement is off-limits. 'We can never repay what this school has done for our children,' said one parent. We wanted to shout it out from the rafters – this place is superb.

Beatrix Potter Primary School

Magdalen Road, London SW18 3ER

Ages 3–11 **Pupils** 426

020 8874 1482
www.beatrixpotterschool.com

Headteacher: Since 1988, Stephen Neale MA Dip Ed Tech Dip Ed. Growing older and wiser, he remains a popular hands-on head, described by parents as a real character, somewhat unconventional and very easy to get on with. Brave enough to make his own decisions and not a person to get tangled up in bureaucracy. Married to a Polish opera singer, with one grown-up son. His enthusiasm for travelling, links with other schools and exploring different cultures all over the globe influences many of the school's activities. Beatrix Potter has gained the British Council's Full International School's Award twice. A steam train enthusiast, Mr Neale also enjoys sailing and travelling.

Entrance: Admission to the school via the standard Wandsworth primary school admissions criteria. Looked after children and special needs pupils first, then those living closest to the school. Admission is usually oversubscribed, but if you are not lucky enough to get a place in reception, it's always worth calling the school for occasional places in the older age groups.

Exit: Pupils move onto a big mix of senior schools. Around 60 per cent to state sector: Burntwood, St Cecilia's, Southfields, Wilson's and Wallington Grammar. Forty per cent to independents, including Emanuel, Dulwich College, JAGS and Wimbledon High School.

Remarks: Good solid curriculum continues to be at the heart of this delightful primary school; all pupils are well grounded in literacy, numeracy and IT. Imaginative range of projects covering history, geography, sciences and international links are embedded into classroom work and the arts. Fab recent technology suite and equipment, where pupils can contact children all over the world via Skype and Facetime. These links often turn into fantastic foreign adventures for pupils, and have led to the school being asked to host a European Link Project. The caretaker's house has been redeveloped so the school can offer accommodation to pupils and their teachers visiting from abroad.

It's not a pushy school, but everyone gets to where they want to go. School produces parents' booklets packed with information on how to support your child at home and get involved in their education. The ethos is all about being a happy, balanced person who is able to move on to senior school well equipped to cope in new settings. Head runs advice sessions for parents to assist them in selecting the right senior schools. Children with SEN are well cared for by full-time SENCo and her assistant, who run a variety of small groups for children with different additional needs. School is eager to work with parents and other therapists to help children achieve to the best of their ability. Since the refurbishments, the building is now fully accessible for children with physical disabilities. Kids City runs on-site breakfast and after-school clubs.

Mr Neale and architects have worked hard over the last few years to redesign much of the school, and there are now two classes right through. Outdoor spaces have been improved with courtyard areas, picnic tables and three outdoor courts and there's a large new sports hall. Sports coaches are brought in from local clubs for lacrosse, cricket, tennis, tag rugby and football. Parents say the arts are developing well, particularly now the school has separate spaces for art, dance and drama. Another bonus of the expansion is the school offers freshly cooked lunches every day. Initially the expansion process caused quite a few wobbles and rumbles from some parents. However, everyone is now in agreement that the school is able to offer more to its pupils while still maintaining its long-term reputation for being a warm, friendly community school. PTA and school governors are all very active and fundraise substantial amounts of money for both the school and various charities. Past and present pupils have many fond memories of the school. Some can't stay away, returning to do their teaching practice or even joining the teaching staff permanently.

Belleville Primary School

Webbs Road, London SW11 6PR

Ages 3–11 **Pupils** 947

020 7228 6727
www.belleville-school.org.uk

Executive Headteacher: Since 2001, John Grove BEd MA (50s). A true local, born and educated in the borough; even his MA comes from Roehampton University on the far flung edge of Wandsworth and his previous job was head of West Hill Primary. Asked to take over this then struggling school, he used his immediately apparent mental energy and vision to change Belleville into a superstar amongst primaries, and his relaxed, calm exterior exudes confidence. His only sadness about his new role – he is now executive head of the multi-academy trust that includes three other schools – is that he now has less contact with the children and thus their parents, but this is belied by the ease with which the little ones interact with him and the number of parents who greet him on the street. Dedicated to discovering new and better ways to run his own schools, he covers the globe (from Finland to China), investigating educational methods that can be put into practice at Belleville.

Entrance: Consistently oversubscribed, the furthest offers by distance at the moment are under 500 metres for the school and just half that for the two nursery classes. Because the distance is measured from the Webbs Road site, this can mean that a child whose bedroom overlooks the Meteor street premises is unable to skip across the street to school. The long waiting list continues for all age groups as parents of children who find a place here tend to be reluctant to move. Admissions criteria follow Wandsworth Council's guidelines but a change has just been made to give places to the children of members of staff (all employees, not just teachers). Four form entry with

B

an additional bulge class in some year groups and a very high proportion (can be over 25 per cent) of siblings.

Exit: In 2018, as usual, the majority transferred to state secondaries, with Bolingbroke Academy (39 children) way out in front and about 10-15 per cent offered selected school places at the Sutton grammars and Graveney. Over 75 independent offers, including 10 scholarships, but ultimately only half this number moved on to independents, including major London players such as Alleyn's, Dulwich College, Emanuel and Streatham & Clapham High.

Remarks: Dominating the crest of the hill, reminding one of a mediaeval castle looking over its fiefdom (in this case the pushchair-filled Northcote Road), Belleville's Victorian brick building is a strong, confident presence. The wandering pigs, a noted nuisance to late 19th century residents, have long since gone, replaced by rows of well-tended, now extremely expensive, Edwardian houses.

A classic example of 19th century school design with three identical floors, allowing a steady upward progression from nursery at ground level to the heights of year 6, housed under the ornate beamed roof. Inside it's any colour as long as it's blue, but the building is far lighter than you'd expect (one of JG's improvements being to uncover the boarded-up windows) and the graphically designed, framed examples of school activities and pupils' work give the public spaces a much more cohesive feel than we normally see.

The head's first aim was to improve the standard of teaching by increased teacher training and support, and the goal of constant assessment and improvement remains his number one priority. It is blindingly obvious that he has hit the target, not only because of the exit results but also because his senior team have almost all been with him for over 10 years and new (about one third experienced, one third trained here and one third NQT) teachers increasingly stay put. The school is now a National Teaching School, which explains the emphasis they place on regular courses for their staff and, intelligently, they bring in all the newly qualified teachers they hire for three weeks of intensive courses in the term before they let them loose in the classroom.

JG has also invested time and effort in investigating and introducing far Eastern and, in particular, Singaporean maths teaching methods (Belleville is a Maths Hub), but the rest of the curriculum is no poor relation and children achieve strong results in all the core subjects. They are grouped by attainment for reading but are kept in mixed groups in other subjects, although they offer additional challenge and 'booster' classes outside school hours. Specialist teachers for PE, languages, art, music and ICT.

Local musicians, artists and actors are encouraged to come into the school part-time and we witnessed the enthusiasm of the year 6 Djembe drumming session although, due to the decibel level, we were pushed to distinguish the various compositions. According to the excellent website, they will also be designing a clay pot in art, inspired by Grayson Perry – should be colourful.

The inclusion director has a dedicated SEN team and a full-time learning mentor. At present there are approaching 100 children identified in house as needing additional support, with fewer than 10 having an EHCP. A bonus from the addition of the site on Meteor Street is that they now have a stair-free premises so that they can handle a wider range of physical needs. A very clear anti-bullying policy, particularly necessary in such a large school, as well as a straightforward Safeguarding Code of Conduct with a charming bee motif.

An amazing 37 different languages spoken by children of 22 nationalities, the French contingent numerically miles ahead (Brexit may alter this) with about a third of the pupils this year having English as an additional language. However, the diversity of their backgrounds was obviously not affecting the children that we met, who appeared completely at home in their blue surroundings, and the little ones were unabashed by the head and the stranger with him – in fact they cheerfully poked their heads round his open door and chattered about their day.

There could be a clue about JG's attachment to his beloved Chelsea FC in the blue strip (odd, that) worn by Belleville's football teams, proud of being borough champions. Cricket teams hold the same title, the year 5/6 gymnastics team are regular finalists at the London Youth Games and, judging by the cups in the cabinet, sport is taken seriously. All children take part in some sporting activity (unsurprisingly not such a large selection as at some of the local independents) for at least two hours a week from year 1 and there are after-school clubs for the seriously keen. It was a toss-up whether the teacher or the children were being more enthusiastic in a PE class we saw and the inter-house trophy is a wondrous, shiny creation.

Parents praise the mass of extracurricular clubs, finding breakfast and homework club particularly useful, but on offer as well is at least one club for each letter of the alphabet (barring Z), ranging from Arty Party to yoga dance, although these are subject to a charge (free sessions for children on free school meals). The PTA raises substantial sums, enough for minibuses (in the past) and 100 new iPads, about to be collected by a happy ICT teacher.

However, the most important new fact about Belleville is that it is growing. Now part of a multi-academy trust with Alton Primary, Churchfields Primary and the rather quirky Belleville Wix, where they teach the English curriculum to one third, half and half English/French to the second third and the remaining third belong to the French Lycée and follow the French curriculum in French – unlikely though it sounds, apparently it works.

There could be a danger that the Meteor site is seen as a second division version of Webbs Road, but we felt that it was simply the same message in a different package. In our opinion Belleville is a very professionally run and well-oiled machine doing its best to overcome the naturally corporate nature of such a large-scale organisation. JG has great faith in the logic of managing a sizeable group of schools, saying that 'if you can get it right for one child, it is simply doing the same thing for more of them'.

Belmont Mill Hill Preparatory School

Linked with Mill Hill School, Grimsdell Mill Hill Pre-Preparatory School

The Ridgeway, Mill Hill Village, London NW7 4ED

Ages 7–13 **Pupils** 522

Fees: £18,099 pa

020 8906 7270
www.millhill.org.uk/belmont

Head: Since 2015, Leon Roberts MA PGCE. Taught for four years in the state sector, moved to Keble Prep as head of history for the next four years then became deputy head (academic) of Belmont in 2004 before being promoted to senior deputy head (pastoral) in 2010 and finally taking on the headmaster's role. Married with three young daughters, including twins, he enjoys cricket (playing and coaching, both boys and girls), walking and watching Nordic Noir drama.

Down-to-earth, hands on and with an equally energetic style as the previous head, he approaches the job with the same consultative and open approach – he's building on a school which is in great shape (which he's been involved in creating) and adding his own mark.

Entrance: Automatic entry from pre-prep (Grimsdell) to prep (two-thirds of entry); a few (very rare) exceptions. For external candidates, 7+ and 11+ are the two main points of entry. Occasional places in other years. Heavily oversubscribed for external candidates; reading, creative writing and maths tests together with a reference from their previous school.

Exit: Some 95 per cent move on to Mill Hill School, although all have to sit the entrance exam (only for setting purposes). 'Children for whom Mill Hill is not the right school' leave at the end of year 6. Once in year 7, automatic place at Mill Hill at 13+ provided they don't mess up. A parent felt that going through to 13+ was a massive advantage. 'At 13 they are desperate to make the next jump and are confident to do it. They are not little 11 and 12 year olds floundering around.' Occasional transfers to boarding schools eg Harrow, Tonbridge and Stowe.

Remarks: Established in 1912, following the success of its senior school Mill Hill, Belmont Prep opened its gates with one student – Harold Pearse Soundy. A year later it had 12 pupils. Originally a boarding prep for boys, it has been a day school since the 80s and co-ed since 1995. The school is in an enviable location on Mill Hill's Ridgeway – set back from the road and flanked by large houses and beautiful greenery. Hard to believe that central London is so close. Harder still, after taking in the 35 acres of parkland and the panoramic views of the Totteridge Valley. Undoubtedly the school's selling point, the grounds and its facilities are impressive for a London-based prep school.

For a sporty child, this must be nirvana; seven rugby pitches, 10 football pitches, three cricket pitches, five cricket nets, five rounders pitches, two Astro mini hockey pitches, six Astro tennis courts, six netball courts, a fully equipped gymnasium and a small dance hall. Finally, a 1,500 metre woodland cross-country course known as The Oti (in memory of a former student who died of sickle cell anaemia). Pupils also have the use of the new 25 metre indoor swimming pool at Mill Hill School. As one parent told us, 'Forget this school if your child has absolutely no interest in sport; they'll be unhappy'.

Outdoor facilities also include a large wooden adventure playground, a variety of large games including a giant chessboard and a gardening area where pupils tend seasonal plants and flowers. We spotted a little recycling area only to learn that Belmont has been awarded the much coveted Eco-Schools Green Flag Award.

The original 18th century house acts as the main entrance to the school and houses the function rooms, main reception area, staff rooms and the head's office; a slight anti-climax after the spectacular exterior. Tastefully refurbished (with the original beautiful winding staircase) but several of the classrooms on the upper level seemed on the cramped side and lacking in imagination. The science labs (in the Cloister Block) and the gymnasium, particularly, struck us as archaic and in need of a refurb. That said, the Jubilee Hall, which accommodates most of the lower school classrooms, the dining/assembly hall and the head of lower school's office, is modern and airy.

The school has a slightly informal, genial vibe. Colourful and interesting displays of student work adorn the corridors, and the pupils we witnessed, whilst not particularly noisy, were 'spirited'. The latest ISI inspection spoke of pupils 'with confidence, whether in a classroom discussion, reading in an assembly or conversing with adults'. This was particularly evident amongst the school's council members – a bunch of 8 and over boys and girls who were bright, articulate and bounced off each other like the future spokespeople they may one day become. They were confident, polite and hard pushed to find anything negative to say about the school. One bemoaned the fact that lunch should be better organised, whilst another commented incredulously that 'we've been to play other schools that don't even have their own cricket grounds' – which made him feel very lucky.

A Belmont child is a busy one. School opens at 7.30am for optional breakfast and, from there on in, a cascade of activities barely allows for an oxygen intake. Fifty clubs are on offer during lunchtime and after school, so if elastic or kicking a ball ain't your thing – why not try ancient Greek? Or perhaps origami, Dead Poets Society (we presume without Robin Williams), jazz band, Belle Plates or Bollywood dance. Popular after-school activities include chamber choir and horse riding. Fabulous trips (including a history trip to Venice) are offered from year 6.

Academic results are well above national expectations. This, we are told, is achieved through 'excellent teaching' (ISI 2012), a broad curriculum that includes French from year 3 and Latin from year 6 and smallish class sizes. Teachers have annual performance reviews and their planning is monitored termly. No sluggards allowed here. A couple of parents we spoke to said that academia across the foundation has definitely been stepped up a notch over the past few years. One parent told us: 'Belmont was always more of a nurturing school, but the goalposts seem to be constantly changing and you feel like you are kept on your toes the whole time.' In school's view, 'High academic performance is our number one target'.

Sats abolished in favour of continuous assessments from year 3. No longer follows the CE curriculum because nearly everyone goes through to the senior school. Instead, teaches a Mill Hill curriculum which aims to give the same rigour as the CE version but tailored to enable pupils to delve deeper into subject topics.

Places at Mill Hill are not unconditional, but any early problems, academically or behaviourally, are usually flagged up whilst the child is at Grimsdell (the pre-prep), so there are 'rarely any surprises.' 'If we didn't feel a child could cope, we wouldn't allow them to progress to year 7.' The school has a small learning support department and is happy to accommodate children with mild cases of dyslexia and dyspraxia. Anything more severe, and 'we're not the school for them'. Small groups of gifted and talented children are arranged across the years, and most are prepared for the 11+ and 13+ scholarship awards.

Belmont is a Christian foundation based upon the principles of 'religious freedom'. Chapel services are obligatory, because if you start pulling pupils out, 'you lose the ability to say we can work together'. However, the school's pupils represent a wide range of faiths and cultures, so chapel services and assemblies are inter-denominational.

During our tour, we noticed the school undergoing building works – six new classrooms, two science labs and an impressive hall. Shortly after our visit, we discovered that Belmont, along with the other two schools in the Mill Hill foundation, was merging with the Mount School for girls (hmmm!). The merger came as a great shock to parents who were informed by email, with no prior warning. School insisted that it was not planning a permanent expansion; pupil numbers have increased by some 55 or so, and boy: girl ratio is now more even. The Mount building now houses The Mount, Mill Hill International school.

Belmont Primary School

B

18

Belmont Road, London W4 5UL

Ages 3-11 Pupils 470

020 8994 7677
www.belmontprimaryschool.org.uk

Head: Since September 2018, Elaine Lacey, previously deputy head at the Blue School in Isleworth.

Entrance: Preference given to siblings. Next in the pecking order are those who live within the Primary Admissions Area – 'catchment' to you and me. In recent years, even living in the catchment has not guaranteed a place at the school. Children in public care and those with medical/social needs come high up in the pecking order. After that – don't even try. Parents are known to rent property within the area just to qualify, and then..? More hope from year 2, however, as a steady trickle leaves to go to prep school/move out of London.

Exit: A decreasing half to Chiswick School, and a clutch to West London Free School and Hammersmith Academy as well as the usual numbers to Twyford, Lady Margaret, Gunnersbury and the Green School. The rest (about 20 per cent) to local independents, including Godolphin & Latymer, Notting Hill and Ealing High, Latymer Upper, Hampton, Ibstock Place. The occasional one to St Paul's Juniors at 8 as well as at 11. Lots of outside coaching during years 5 and 6 to prepare for independent school entrance exams. School asks for a financial contribution for the school reports required for entry into such schools.

Remarks: The reluctance of the previous head and staff to welcome us to look round this super, oversubscribed, well-funded state primary (or indeed respond to our messages) bemused us – especially considering that Belmont is one of the most successful and popular state primaries in West London, with seven applications for each place.

Pupils bubbled with enthusiasm and love for their school as they showed us round. An abundance of facilities – from musical instruments, playground equipment, books and materials to the brand new stage for dramatic performances. Results are excellent, showing much higher than expected progress between key stages 1 and 2 and with a quarter getting well above expected levels in year 6.

The school caters for an affluent corner of Chiswick and the catchment area is becoming ever tighter. Families from sumptuous houses in the Bedford Park area can no longer expect to get a place. Were it not for the council accommodation on the school's doorstep, you might not get the social mix one would expect in an inner London state primary school at all. Our first impression was that there was an unusually high proportion of white middle class kids; the head was keen to give precise statistics and told us that 52 per cent of Belmont's pupils are from minority ethnic groups (in this case Eastern Europe and a few affluent UK residents from say, Canada or Sweden). This ain't your typical London primary.

School is housed in a large, three-storey brick building that benefits from the high ceilings, large windows, well-proportioned rooms and wide corridors typical of Victorian buildings of its kind. A generous refurbishment programme has resulted in shiny polished floors and child-friendly primary and pastel walls – helping the building to fall firmly on the side of happy, modern school rather than gloomy Victorian institution.

Two classes at either end of each spacious floor, each one charmingly named after fruit – apples, pears, cherries. The main hall in the middle space between classrooms is used for play (reception and year 1 – lots of dressing up and imaginary play goes on here), assemblies (years 2 and 3 on the middle floor) and drama and gym (years 5 and 6 on the top floor). Yet more rooms house musical instruments galore (drum kits, pianos, flutes, various percussion), two well-stocked libraries, two ICT suites (the juniors have the luxury of one computer each, one between two for the infants) and dedicated SEN provision. Teaching up to the end of year 2 is mixed ability; setting in maths and English from year 3. Two sets, the higher slightly larger.

About 20 per cent of children identified as having special educational needs but a very small proportion of these have EHC plans. School has coped in the past with more severe special needs, but children must be able to climb stairs.

About a quarter of pupils don't have English as a first language (about 43 different first languages other than English recorded) but no marked difference in the performance of these children – credit to the school. Dedicated part-time EAL teacher as well as SEN coordinator with a team of teaching assistants. Those with EAL needs are seen individually or in small groups for as long as necessary. A reading recovery teacher sees individuals who, by year 1, are falling behind – with 'fantastic' results. When we visited, there had been a relatively high turnover of staff (we were assured that this is a result of career progression, maternity – no reflection on the school). Five male teachers – always a bonus. Years 3 to 6 have 40 minutes of French weekly. Everyone has two hours of physical activity a week.

All classes have class music lessons and learn singing with a specialist teacher. Many learn individually, too – often more than one instrument. Recorder is offered to the whole of year 3 and there is a choir. Swanky staging facilitates an annual production from year 6. Other year groups, sometimes working together, also put on shows each year. Photographs on display suggest a high level of dramatic productions, much supported by parents, many of whom are 'in the arts'.

Good sports provision. A school sports partnership linked to Chiswick School and an outsourced sports programme (football, netball and athletics) in addition to members of staff teaching sport. On Friday afternoons here there is 'enrichment time', when for 30 minutes children can choose from a wide variety of activities, from Glee Club to comic making. Strong after-school club provision. These include, as well as the sport and music, Big Bang Science and Doughlightful – a clay modelling activity.

The Belmont Home School Association – PTA to you and me – raises between £20,000 and £30,000 each year. This has helped make the playground ever more luxuriant, with designated spaces for quiet reflection, a wilderness garden, covered areas for performances with costume boxes, lots of bike sheds, a super climbing wall painted by parents and plenty of gardening boxes replete with flowers, herbs and plants.

The early years spill out beautifully into carefully designed outdoor play areas, secure from the rest of the large playground. The nursery is particularly spacious and attractive – three large rooms, own toilet facilities and a large kitchen area ('mummy sometimes comes in to help us cook', said an excited 3 year old) as well as access to the hall and library. Few chic little independent nurseries provide as much as this. Everyone eats in the school canteen and the number of pupils having cooked lunches delivered by the borough increases all the time. The rest bring their own.

Ofsted hasn't done a full report since 2007, when school was judged 'outstanding' (confirmed by an interim assessment in 2011). Staff are greatly aided by a posse of 'liberal middle class' parents only too eager to help in all areas of school life, including arranging fundraising events to enable disadvantaged pupils who might not otherwise be able to afford to take part in trips etc. They are aided, too, by an excellent governing body, as well as by a good relationship with her local authority. A very small number of exclusions in previous years, but none for some time. A proper and well-understood system of sanctions. Also an established homework system with extension work on the school website for those who want to push their offspring further.

Many parents commented that they were sometimes frustrated by the blank wall that meets their follow-up questions on their child's progress and results. 'Teachers can be cagey', remarked one parent, 'which makes me nervous. I might be surprised'. If you can cope with this and a certain complacency ('we don't need publicity', we were told at one point), then this is a no-brainer – an excellent state school with most of the advantages of an independent school but without the fees.

Blackheath High Junior School

Linked with Blackheath High School

Wemyss Road, London SE3 0TF

Ages 3–11 Pupils 374

Fees: £10,521 – £13,518 pa

020 8852 1537
www.blackheathhighschool.gdst.net

Head of juniors: Since 2012, Sarah Skevington (early 50s), LLB Sheffield PGCE, formerly head of the school's early years dept. She practised as a solicitor specialising in family law then retrained as a teacher. She has taught throughout the EYFS and key stages 1 and 2 at local state primaries including Brindishe Lee – 'outstanding' in every category – and Invicta, which she found both challenging and inspirational.

She went to school in Greenwich, at St Ursula's and has raised her family here. Her three grown-up children attended a co-ed school, but since teaching at a GDST school she really appreciates 'what single sex can do for girls', and as a working mother has 'sympathy for working parents'. In her spare time she likes walking in Greenwich Park and lots of trips to the cinema and theatre.

Mrs Skevington is calm, quietly spoken and welcoming. Her office is the home of Florence the labradoodle, who on the day of our visit had flopped silently beneath her desk, offering a tantalising glimpse of a grey furry foot. Children delight in walking Florence. A parent commented: 'Mrs Skevington is wonderful. She has grown into the role since taking it over and we are very happy with the direction the school is taking under her leadership. She is very good with the girls who really like her.' Another, 'She is professional, personable, level-headed, I could go on...'

She pays tribute to her incredibly hard-working staff, saying this is very much a Blackheath community school, 'it's culturally diverse and all the better for it'.

Entrance: By interview with parents and child. Whilst the child plays, the head is looking for parents who 'understand our offer', in other words are not super-pushy or those who might baulk at no formal homework in reception.

Now has two full-time nursery classes.

Exit: Most (some 60 per cent) move up to the senior school. If the head considers that it isn't the best place, will discuss with parents at an early point. Remainder mainly to day independents eg City of London Girls, Alleyns, JAGS and local grammars in Kent and Bexley, eg Townley and Newstead Woods. Others occasionally off to board.

Remarks: The junior school building is the original first GDST building. Inside is a beautiful Victorian school hall, brought up to date with the insertion of coloured panels into the large lantern skylight. On the sunny day of our visit the hall was full of bright colours, while children below practised their circus skills. A grand, double stone staircase sweeps down from the entrance to the classrooms on the ground floor. The walls feature quotes from inspiring women of our times: Maya Angelou, Anita Roddick and Deborah Meaden.

Classrooms are large, bright and airy, with one teacher and one teaching assistant in every class of 16 in nursery and around 48 girls in every other year group. Classes vary between excited exuberance at year 1 to quietly attentive year 5s. The library, recently rescued from an ill-judged make-over, has had its wonderful parquet flooring revealed, with new freewheeling bookcases in spring colours. Some girls are library prefects and make book recommendations. Playground in full swing at lunchtime was quite a sight, with girls busily making the most of all the different levels: there is climbing equipment, space to run around on hard surfaces, a sandpit in a separate area for the nursery, a maths hut, sensible sun canopy provided by the PTA, and even a small forest school, which the head admits is more concept than actual woodland.

Asked for an example of good teaching, the head cites lessons where year 5s designed an app, then linked up (virtually) with the nursery children, who tried out the app, giving instant feedback. 'Simple stuff done well,' says the head. She observed the head of English teaching girls about persuasive writing styles, saying the girls were hanging onto her every word, and later tried out their new skills writing to ask her to do away with homework.

A parent agreed her daughter is taught 'without feeling she is under pressure. Subjects are taught in an engaging, fun way which increases her enthusiasm to learn and do well.' Another liked the fact that 'the teachers use innovative ways to get concepts across – for example using a "money week" to make the concept of money and savings so much more exciting, and asking parents who work in the financial services sector to come into class'. The French teacher is the best of both worlds, a native French speaker, trained as a teacher in England. Currently there are iPads in group sets, but the school is working towards one for every pupil.

The junior school has 72 girls on the SEND register with needs such as mild speech and language difficulties, dyslexia, dyspraxia and other mild learning difficulties. Needs are catered for within the classroom through differentiation and TA support as well as small group and one-to-one withdrawal. The head says that dyslexia is on the rise. One parent who was appreciative of the school's support nonetheless found the part-time SENCo to be 'extremely stretched'.

Sport is set to have a change of pace with the appointment of another specialist PE teacher. To date, not the sportiest. Head and parents wish the school playing field was closer – it is a bus-ride away. To allow girls as long as possible on the field they have recently introduced a club prior to PE, so that parents drop girls off at the field. Dance is offered as part of the curriculum. Swimming is at the local pool.

Music flourishes under the 'talented and energetic' head of music: there are 150 music lessons currently timetabled each week for instrumental or vocal lessons – from beginner to grade 6. From the youngest performers in year 1 through to year 6, every year group entertains parents at an annual tea-time concert, and the juniors recently joined the seniors for a beautiful performance of Noyes Fludde at the Royal Naval College. Year 2 girls can have a generous 10 lessons for free on a new stringed instrument to really test whether they like it. The chamber choir is award-winning – four times in a row at the Beckenham Festival.

Girls recently displayed clay busts made in DT at Ranger's House owned by English Heritage in the good company of European masterpieces. We enjoyed the display of a recent holiday project where girls chose any piece of art to recreate photographically at home, with staff joining in too: super renditions of The Girl with A Pearl Earring, Frida Kahlo self-portraits, and our favourite: Mrs Skevington, the school caretaker and Florence posed as Mr and Mrs Andrews by Gainsborough.

A Stone Age workshop stopped just short of making fire in the school hall with two twigs, and seemed to be delivered by an actual cave man. The school makes the most of London, with girls popping out to explore the Cutty Sark, the front row at Wimbledon and further afield. Boasts over 50 clubs and must be one of the few junior schools with own radio station. A GDST alumna, Rachel Joyce, author of The Unlikely Pilgrimage of Harold Fry, adjudicated the annual poetry competition. 'They really do a wonderful job of including all the girls in class plays, assemblies, nativity plays,' said a parent. The hall is large with retractable raked seating so that everyone and their iPad can get a good view.

The co-curricular and extracurricular programme not universally popular with more than one parent who wished for more focus on academics. One said, 'I am not convinced the school is capturing the academic potential of all the children', and another, 'may not be a bad thing to ramp up the academics a notch.' The head says children are learning a great deal through structured play and that they don't drop everything for Sats, but nonetheless girls gain a plethora of level 5s, including girls who are more than mildly dyslexic and some level 6s, with girls exiting at 11 'ready for anywhere'.

Transitions are managed thoughtfully. Year 5s feel much more grown-up with the provision of lockers in their classrooms, as they begin to move around to specialist teachers. Year 6 pupils are made to feel special with a prize-giving and lunch with their parents before they head off to senior schools.

We agree with a parent who said, 'The school is friendly and welcoming – it feels like a family.' And everyone, but everyone, agreed on fabulous pastoral care, with one saying: '[It] is exemplary – the main reason we chose the school above others. Not only do the staff look out for the girls, they are encouraged to look after each other, and the buddy group system works well to encourage that. My daughter is thrilled that she can call some of the big girls her friends'.

Parents say the happy pupils we saw at lunchtime cannot wait to get to school in the morning. They might be described as 'bright and sparky, polite and well mannered, kind and empathetic. It's not for kids who want to be pushed, graded or constantly winning.' And as for self-portraits, a parent obliged: 'A nice mixture from different backgrounds and cultures who all want their daughters to enjoy learning.' One parent with a talent for slogan writing summed it up: 'Childhood is not a race and at BHH they enjoy the journey.'

Blackheath High School

Linked with Blackheath High Junior School

27 Vanbrugh Park, London SE3 7AG

Ages 11–18 **Pupils** 361 **Sixth form** 68

Fees: £16,494 pa

020 8853 2929
www.blackheathhighschool.gdst.net

Headteacher: Since 2014, Carol Chandler-Thompson BA (in history) and PGCE, both from Exeter (early 40s), formerly head of the Girls' School, North London Collegiate, Jeju, in the Republic of Korea. Prior to setting up NLCS in South Korea, she spent seven years as head of history and politics at NLCS. Before that, teacher of history and head of PSHE at Haberdashers' Aske's School for Girls, Elstree.

The move to Korea enabled her to continue to be part of NLCS with the remit of setting up a school from scratch. She was drawn to the GDST for its 'girls first' philosophy but also the sense of community where 'older girls don't feel too superior to talk to the younger ones'.

Youthful, open, highly articulate and full of energy for the transformations in hand, she lives in Woolwich with her partner, Emma, and although barely having time for sport these days (though something of a triathlete), she enjoys the downhill run home from Greenwich towards the river when possible, and being back in vibrant London after the monoculture of Korea. Having said that, she misses Asia and we met her just prior to a holiday in Sri Lanka.

It's never easy following a longstanding head – her predecessor, Mrs Laws, was head of Blackheath High for 14 years – but girls and parents alike quickly took to Mrs C-T. A parent said, 'She is approachable, energetic, personable and committed and will clearly blend her own ideas and purpose to good effect within the school as her influence evolves. She very quickly secured a place of affection and respect amongst the girls and staff.' A pupil: 'She's refreshing; different in such a good way'.

The ISI's verdict on the sixth form, 'good and sometimes excellent', is a somewhat lukewarm tribute amongst a sea of 'excellents' for all other aspects of the school. As well as reinvigorating staff and teaching, she is bringing her experiences from NLCS's highly successful sixth form. And whilst she's very happy for the school to be known for the strength of its pastoral care, she has focused on moving that reputation to highlight academics. Having heard her talk about her involvement in this year's 11+ selection process, we've rarely heard of such care and attention given to spotting potential beyond mere performance on the day.

Also on the agenda is raising the profile of sport. Never known as a sporty school – amusingly illustrated by girls in the playground sitting chatting either side of the nets on the table tennis tables – the head has appointed a new director of sport.

She aims to ensure no ceilings are put on the girls. 'Girls are stretched and pushed here but they don't succeed through the failure of others; it's about challenging themselves'. Whatever girls want to do, whether it's apply to Oxbridge or become a professional singer, the school will absolutely support them. The word 'aspiration' crops up a lot, and parents say, 'She was very quick to pick up areas which needed improvement and is addressing them eg widening the girls' aspirations... She is very thoughtful and passionate to further advance the school.'

Academic matters: In 2018, 59 per cent 9-7 at GCSE and 31 per cent A*/A (69 per cent A*-B) at A level; results don't dominate league tables or the GDST leader board, but the head says it's about value-added.

No surprises curriculum-wise. GCSE science starts in year 9. Excitingly, as befits the Greenwich location, a handful of the top physicists are invited to study astronomy GCSE, alongside similarly selected state school pupils. Most lessons taught in mixed ability groups apart from maths, set from year 7. Computing, not ICT, thankfully. School, and the whole GDST, is keen on STEM subjects and a recent look to the future event allowed girls to have their eyes opened by an engineer, a dentist and a computer programmer. Art and design flourishes and is as popular as the single sciences. Plenty of keen actors: drama is a likely choice.

Proud to be one of the first schools to offer Mandarin. All pupils take Latin from year 7 plus a choice of modern foreign languages from French, German, Spanish and Mandarin. Some leeway for girls with SpLDs. Carefully structured language trips and exchanges, gaining in adventurousness as girls go up the school, taking in Paris, Trier in Germany, Castellón in Spain. 'Exchange trips with a school in Germany from year 8 onwards fostered her interest in and ability with the language, as did the encouragement to do work experience in Germany in year 12,' said an approving parent.

Things get more varied at A level with the addition of economics/business, further maths, music technology, textiles, theatre studies, politics and psychology. Highest grades recently in art and design and English literature. Biology, chemistry, business and economics rather bring up the rear and none of the mathematicians reach the tip of the top.

A parent said, 'Every subject area has had at least one teacher who has been inspiring and is completely trusted by the girls'. Our guides went further, telling us how much they appreciated the excellent standard of teaching; they could only think of one instance when a maternity cover teacher had not been up to scratch, but they felt it was quickly dealt with, and convinced us they wouldn't hesitate to raise this with the head of year. Another parent said, 'As a result of the excellent and inspirational teaching, she has developed a passion for the subjects which she intends to study at university.'

Co-curricular flourishes: eco week saw year 6, from the junior school, and year 13 geographers working together to experience what life is like for slum dwellers. During the recent election, the politics society organised mock elections with some pretty impressive drop-in guests, including all of the local party candidates. The newly introduced Wollstonecraft Programme, far more vibrant and modern than it sounds, offers girls from years 7 to 11 a non-examined choice of courses including the creation of Girls' Hour for broadcast (think R4 Woman's Hour), creating and marketing apps, global perspectives and introduction to film analysis.

The clunkily titled Matrix of Knowledge course in year 11, subtitled A History of Western Civilisation in 23½ Lessons, prepares girls for entry into the sixth form and Russell Group applications – it develops critical thinking, research and debating skills and culminates in explorations of the riches of London such as The Wellcome Collection and Sir John Soane's Museum. Theory of Knowledge takes this further in the sixth form. And whilst the school isn't considering IB, other elements from this such as the extended project are in place. Originality is the order of the day: one girl even grew her own skirt. A parent added: 'The school offers an excellent series of TED lectures'. The librarian said she's just had her book budget increased and girls say the selection is well-chosen and they can also request anything they want.

Plenty of praise for the school's career preparation. Girls are encouraged to start thinking of their aptitudes and possible options for their future from around year 9. There are trips to inspire. Girls in years 9 and 10 were given a behind the scenes tour of Microsoft by interns, who had each fought off 60 others – let's hope they are being paid. Sixth formers make use of online help from Unifrog. A parent told us: 'My daughter received excellent advice, encouragement and support from the careers teacher regarding a work placement in year 11, and an opportunity in year 12 to shadow an undergraduate at a Russell Group university.' Another, 'The quality of the guidance and the fact that it is offered early ensures that the girls can build a very strong application, when the time comes, for places in further education.'

The head speaks warmly of the SENCo, currently studying for a masters, who initiated the 'pupil passport', where each girl records what works for them and their particular learning style in the classroom. The senior school has 56 students with a form of SEN, including dyslexia, dyscalculia and dyspraxia, and currently one child with a statement/EHC plan. Girls receive in-class and out-of-class support, which incorporates differentiation or small group or one-to-one support, depending on need. The head has also appointed a separate EAL co-ordinator.

Games, options, the arts: Despite its location close to the edge of Blackheath and more or less alongside Greenwich Park, the school's five acre sports field with a pavilion and an all-weather pitch is a short bus-ride away. Winter sports are netball, hockey and cross-country. Summer sports are rounders, athletics and tennis. Girls benefit from the wider GDST network for competitions as well as local tournaments. Girls try fencing, trampolining, gymnastics, table tennis, football and dance. The annual Iron House race sees 40 athletes from across the school, including staff, showing their stamina in Greenwich Park, including the gruelling near-vertical climb to the top. It's a breeding ground for competitive runners.

Girls with a love of the wider outdoors enjoy D of E – everyone does bronze, with just a hard-core few making it to gold. Also on offer is an international three week World Challenge – previous trips have been to Namibia, recently to Peru. The cost is steep but girls raise the money themselves, rather than digging into the bank of mum and dad. There are also taster sessions in canoeing, sailing and horse-riding, and girls get a chance to go on PGL adventures to challenge any fear of heights and brave the English weather.

The school makes the very most of its situation in Greenwich, recently putting on a stunning production, Noyes Fludde, at the Old Royal Naval College. The head of music, a former professional drummer, has shaken things up. There are over 200 music lessons a week and extracurricular is chock full of music: orchestra, chamber choirs, samba band, rock band, ukulele orchestra, glee club and a number of percussion ensembles. There are biannual international music tours, and many pupils study at junior conservatoires. Everyone arriving in year 7 can take part in a taster scheme where they have the opportunity to learn an instrument free of charge.

There are clubs timetabled for each year group from Viking and Anglo-Saxon club in year 7 to Iron Woman, self-defence, debating club, crochet collective – who meet in the outdoor classroom – and an F1 club. Any sixth former can start a society.

The theatre is a purpose-built performance space on campus, but pupils also put on plays at Greenwich Theatre. A parent enthused, 'The drama was outstanding...always thoroughly engaging and bursting with energy and enthusiasm.' A competitive audition recently resulted in the world premiere of

B

creepy Coraline: an ambitious adaptation scripted by the drama teacher. Plenty of rehearsal spaces and professional equipment.

High quality art is displayed around the school. We were lucky enough to see the GCSE and A level examination pieces, including dresses one might covet, much in demand for the end of school ball. The art teacher welcomes all into the studio, even if just to do their homework in inspiring surroundings.

Background and atmosphere: The first purpose-built GDST school, opened in 1880, it maintains the tradition of a thorough academic education for girls for highly competitive fees. The school is situated on one of Blackheath's fine Georgian streets, although now very busy with traffic. A tall, red-brick building with stone dressings, with the somewhat odd addition of a 1960s church, currently used as a dance studio. Developments include a new library, refurbished classrooms, science labs, art, DT and music facilities.

Parents enthuse about the school's warm atmosphere, saying: 'By the time my daughter reached the GCSE years, the teachers knew her as an individual rather than as a number'; 'very positive atmosphere, friendly, supportive, collaborative'; 'everyone is enthusiastic about learning and has an open mind to new ideas incorporating very well the different cultural backgrounds the girls are coming from.'

Old girls include talents in all areas, particularly the media, perhaps most notably: Mary Quant, Baroness Jay of Paddington, Labour politician, Helen Lederer, comedian, and Katie Stewart, cookery writer.

Pastoral care, well-being and discipline: The head has split the roles of deputy into academic deputy and pastoral deputy, and there is a new part-time school counsellor. Pupils who volunteer are given training in peer mentoring by Childline. Mentors are assigned a year group and available at lunchtime, before and after school. One we spoke to clearly enjoyed it.

Parents praise the emotional support given to the girls: 'The teachers frequently remind the girls of the importance of finding time for rest and relaxation in their busy schedule to safeguard their well-being in what will be a very challenging world.'

The head girl team takes the pressure off one individual and shares around the privilege. They clearly feel listened to and that this is their school. They've initiated eating with the lower school girls once a week, like kindly big sisters. The transition to year 7 is thoughtfully handled – new girls take part in a summer school, more for fun than anything else, with cake-making and a picnic in Greenwich Park, making sure no-one gets lost on day one.

Pupils and parents: Pupils come from a diverse range of backgrounds. Nearly one third are bilingual.

Who is this school for? Parents say: 'girls who do not fit into a stereotype but have their own thoughts and opinions'. The sixth formers we met seemed confident, sincere, happy and very mature: a delight. Without boys to impress, there were none of the false eyelashes or make-up we've seen at co-eds recently. Girls between lessons were exuberant, loud, even.

A mother with two daughters at the school enthused: 'My children are ready for anything; they have been prepared step by step from juniors onwards to become increasingly independent. They are totally trustworthy and sensible. They can cope with minor emergencies and they look after one another. They support one another emotionally and practically.'

The PTA is active and seem a relatively down to earth lot, organising car boot sales with bacon butties.

Parents feel in touch with the school. They receive grade cards or full reports twice a term with detailed information about a girl's progress, as well as strategies and suggestions for improvement. School days are long, cue a sigh of relief from working parents: pupils can arrive at 7.30am and stay until 6pm. There are also minibus routes ferrying girls from all across Greenwich, Rotherhithe and Lewisham.

Entrance: There are 60 places at the 11+ stage and most recently there were around 190 applications. No guaranteed place for junior school pupils, but all year 6 girls take the entrance exam in maths, English and non-verbal reasoning. Senior staff interviews all candidates. Best performing girls attend an academic scholarship interview with the head. Any SEN students with an ed psych report are granted extra time. The school has introduced a 13+ entry point with scholarships available for exceptional external candidates. Most girls fairly local but a few from as far away as Dartford and Chislehurst in Kent and Leyton, East London.

Into the sixth form, there are 60 places available, currently undersubscribed. The girls we met described lots of their peers being attracted elsewhere simply to try something new – and by 'boys'. You'll need a good range of GCSE results with 9-7s in the subjects that you wish to study, plus an excellent school reference.

Exit: Subjects from anthropology at Bristol and Aberdeen to zoology at Leeds. Between a third and a half leave post-GCSE. Around half of sixth formers to Russell Group destinations eg Warwick. None to Oxbridge in 2018. Few linguists. It's a very arty list of leavers, heading off for art foundations, even a famous shoe design course, but balanced with plenty of scientists, medics, a medical geneticist and dentist. These girls have found their passions and are not afraid to specialise.

Money matters: Scholarships and bursaries for girls entering years 7 and year 12 only. Scholarships based on entrance test results to a maximum value of 50 per cent of fees. In addition, scholarships are awarded for art, music and sport at 11+. A bursary of up to 100 per cent takes into account means, plus academic merit. There are a variety of sixth form scholarships including four provided by HSBC.

Remarks: The girls may not be super sporty, but they certainly seem super happy, comfortable in their own skin and a great recommendation for the school. One to watch under the dynamic head with academic ambition and transformative building works.

Bousfield Primary School

South Bolton Gardens, Old Brompton Road, London SW5 0DJ

Ages 3–11 **Pupils** 430

020 7373 6544
www.bousfieldprimaryschool.co.uk

Headteacher: Since 2014, Helen Swain BEd MA, deputy head for last eight years. Has been in teaching for 26 years and joined Bousfield as a year 6 teacher some 20 years ago.

Entrance: Due to cuts in funding there are now 60 part-time places in the nursery on offer, rather than the previous 30 full-time places. Two parallel classes from reception to year 6, each with 30 pupils. Applications for the nursery are done through the school; applications to the main school via local authority.

No automatic transfer from the nursery to the main school – parents must reapply. Children who are in care or have an EHC plan are considered first, followed by siblings and then proximity to school (currently approximately 0.5 mile and shrinking). Distance measured as the crow flies. Places do become available further up the school, due to high mobility rates of pupils, so worth persevering. Hugely oversubscribed. As one current parent put it: 'If you get offered a place here, you'd be mad to turn it down.'

Exit: Most popular secondary schools include Holland Park, Chelsea Academy, Lady Margaret's, Fulham Boys' School and St Thomas More. Over a third go on to independent senior schools, including Latymer Upper, City of London, The Harrodian, Putney High and Francis Holland. No special preparation given for those doing 11+ exams. School knows a large amount of tutoring probably goes on, but says pupils get plenty of exam practice anyway. Much parental advice and support given when it comes to choosing next school.

Remarks: Strikingly international, with 41 different first languages currently spoken at home. Sixty per cent have English as an additional language. After English, the most prominent languages are French and Arabic. School sees this cosmopolitan element as a real strength and the high level of harmony being something to celebrate. A significant number arrive with very limited English. It is 'sink or swim, but usually swim.' Much language teaching on offer, including Italian classes laid on by the Italian Consulate and French to all KS2 pupils. Bilingual pupils tend to outperform monolingual ones overall. Much coming and going due to large expat intake. Only about half the class in year 6 has been there from reception.

Superb academic results, particularly given the huge EAL contingent, though school always looking to 'up the ante.' English, maths and science Sats results well above national average. There are plans afoot to introduce some setting for maths and reading in year 6, though lack of space means separating children into groups is challenging. Pupils' progress is tracked carefully.

When we visited, children were beautifully behaved and fully engaged. A sense of calm pervades the school. Manners and presentation clearly high on the agenda. No uniform. Packed lunch or school lunch. Fruit given to the younger years.

One full-time teacher and one teaching assistant in each class, as well as extra support staff for pupils with statements and EAL pupils in the early stages of learning English. A great team of dedicated staff, who 'put the hours in.' Many loyal, long-serving teachers (20 members of staff have been there more than 10 years), as well as newer ones. A strong team – 'no prima donnas.'

Bright, vivid displays throughout the school. Some classrooms smallish; every iota of space used. School is a 1950s listed building, with courtyards and coloured panels, which makes expansion and development problematic. Beatrix Potter was born and brought up in a house on the site.

Arts are very strong in the school, though not at the expense of academics. Lots of music, dance and drama going on. School believes performance helps to build children's self-esteem. Pupils are offered a rich curriculum, full of workshops, plays and concerts. More than 90 learn a musical instrument. Guitar and strings ensembles, two choirs but no orchestra. Parents attend practice workshops, so they know what a good music practice at home should involve.

Plenty of sport – gym and games as well as after-school clubs offering tennis, football, cricket and even cheerleading. Swimming for years 3 and 4. Pupils take part in borough events (including athletics) in the summer term.

Quantity of homework has been reduced as parents were completing too much of the pupils' project work ('you can always spot the hand of a parent,' we were told) and copious amounts were being downloaded unthinkingly from the internet. Homework now more focused on the basics, with reading, spelling and maths given from early on.

Some children with EHC plans. More on the SEND register, receiving support of some kind. No specially trained teachers but school feels they have strategies and experience to help those in need. Has experience of pupils with Asperger's syndrome, autism, ADHD, emotional/behavioural difficulties and moderate/severe learning difficulties, as well as dyslexia, dyspraxia and hearing and visual impairment. School is not a centre of excellence for all of these – very occasionally pupils move to special schools, either when Bousfield can no longer adequately support them or when they move to secondary school. Staff say Bousfield is 'an inclusive school' that does its best to accommodate those with difficulties.

Strong parental involvement, with school questionnaires showing overwhelming parental support and high levels of satisfaction. Numerous opportunities for parents to attend curriculum workshops and 'book looks' (when they visit to look at children's books). Parents welcomed in at the beginning of the day.

Some wrap-around care available, albeit not all on-site. Breakfast club on offer and pupils can be escorted to a neighbouring school (with more provision) at the end of the day if required.

Bousfield has close connections with artist Quentin Blake, who attends prize-givings and pops in regularly. All leavers receive a prize at the final assembly and Blake says his spirits are raised as each leaver is celebrated. 'After the ceremony, I go away feeling that at this point in their lives perhaps they really have all won,' he adds.

A great sense of purpose permeates this thriving school, with pupils bright-eyed and focused, offered a lively, dynamic and interesting education. As one satisfied parent lamented: 'I just wish it could go on into secondary school.'

Brandlehow Primary School

Brandlehow Road, Putney, London SW15 2ED

Ages 3–11 **Pupils** 358

020 8874 5429
www.brandlehowschool.org.uk

Head: Since 2015, Ellie Loughnan (40s). She has been at the school for nearly two decades, arriving as a newly-qualified teacher and proceeding through the ranks to deputy head and SENCo before taking over as head. An outstanding communicator and team player, she's relentlessly positive, dealing with pupil behaviour ('I'm so proud', 'brilliant') and parental waywardness (such as taking over teachers' parking spaces) with equal upbeat grace. She's also a hugely capable administrator, managing the recent tricky downsizing of the school and building works with calm efficiency. Parents feel lucky to have her. 'Though it seems a bit of a cliché, she really does take time to find out what makes every child "succeed",' said one. 'She's great,' said another. Despite her undoubtedly heavy workload, she still makes time to run half marathons for charity, and is actively involved in the local junior football league.

B

Entrance: Unlike many London schools coping with the latest baby boom, Brandlehow has been reducing its yearly intake from 45 to 30, a decision intended to more accurately reflect the school's physical capacity. While ensuring a less cramped time for those already past the gates, not the best of news for those considering queuing outside. After the multitude of siblings who come first in line, newcomers will generally have to live within 75 metres, an increasingly costly option as the school itself has created something of a micro property boom. Tour mornings available for those wanting to look and yearn.

Exit: Leavers well prepared for what lies ahead from year 4. The immediate area is not packed with first-rate secondaries, but well-informed parents investigate selective options (Graveney, Ashcroft Technology Academy, Lady Margaret, Tiffin). Quite a number, too, opt for private (Putney High a popular local choice) or make the traditional leap to the country at this tricky juncture.

Remarks: One of the country's top performers in year 6 tests, with nearly every child reaching the government targets and progress at the top end of the improvement range in reading and maths. This, of course, is partly due to pupils' 'cultural capital' (with only the smallest percentage on free school meals), but equally down to its stimulating curriculum and 'relentless pursuit of excellence'. Teachers are well-trained and popular, lessons meticulously planned (says Ofsted) and aspirations high. Daily reading encouraged at home, weekly and bi-weekly homework (spelling, times tables, etc). Modern languages (French) from year 3. This is a carrot-not-stick sort of place and praise is lavishly sprinkled, with awards for in-school achievement ('handwriting heroes', 'world-class writing' and 'homework halos'), and a 'wall of wonderfulness' for those taking the initiative and doing 'incredible' work not set by the school. Pupils clearly respond well to the approach. 'My kids really enjoy school,' said one happy parent, reflecting a widespread thumbs up.

Those who struggle with specific difficulties are identified early and given appropriate support, overseen by a head who herself offers coaching in SEND and ADHD. Well-organised in-school offering, including specially trained teaching assistants, aided by external experts provided by the local authority.

Head regards parents as 'active partners in a child's education' and involves them closely, giving regular updates through Parentmail, detailed curriculum outlines online, and regular access to children's work through dedicated Book Look events, when children discuss what they've been doing in the run up to parents' evenings.

Sport an undoubted strength, and pupils split into four houses ensuring athletic prowess evenly spread for competition. Tennis, cricket, athletics, swimming (years 4-6), and Outdoor and Adventurous Activities all taught as part of the curriculum, plus plenty on offer in the playground (Astroturf pitch, table tennis, hopscotch, climbing frame, basketball net, gym equipment, etc) and in-school clubs (lacrosse, tag rugby, yoga, badminton). Competitive sports day held annually at Wimbledon Park track, with a trophy for 'sporting excellence' plus proper medals for those triumphing in everything from long jump to javelin. Dedicated PE uniform, in which pupils have proudly represented Wandsworth in the London Youth Games and fought their way to 10th place in London primary school rugby.

Music (timetabled once a week) and other arts strongly encouraged (with lively artwork throughout), and curriculum enriched by a multitude of free, teacher-led clubs (including coding, chess, Irish dancing, photography) before and after school, with paid options extending the range for budding linguists (Mandarin, Spanish, French) and musicians (violin). Plenty of trips, from a farm and aquarium to Barnes Literary Festival and Wandsworth Recyling Plant. Year also punctuated by exciting events, such as Book Week (with dressing up and guest poets), Rockstead concerts, and Science Week, where visitors recently helped pupils dissect a squid, learn first aid, and discover how to become a doctor.

Gardening a major focus (with classes named on a horticultural them – Maple, Sycamore, Holly, Lavender, etc). Not one but two gardens, incorporating a meadow, frog colony, pond, composting heap and miniature orchard, as well as raised beds. Green-fingered enthusiasts can also enjoy weekly gardening club, and regular family gardening sessions on weekends.

Safety, physical and emotional, a top priority, with staff posted at gates morning and evening, and reminders to parents to report back concerns. 'It's better for us to know about something that happens at school while children are still here,' says the head, suggesting parents advise kids not to wait to till they get home. Worry box in each classroom and all encouraged to be able to name three grown-ups they would feel happy to talk to if something bothered them. Practical measures taken, too, to address hardy perennials such as nits, with a hair-tied-up policy to fight the insect enemy. Strong international outlook, with former teacher posting regular updates about his cycling circumnavigation of the globe, letter links with partner school in Rwanda, and the school recently playing host to a dozen visiting Norwegian pupils.

Regular meet-and-greet coffee mornings allow parents to vent concerns (the divisive issue of cake, apparently, being one), which are all carefully responded to in writing by the head. Lunches, cooked daily on site by the school's award-winning chef, satisfies even the pickiest, with three hot options (honey-and-ginger stir-fried vegetables, fillet of cod provençale, recent plats du jour) plus salad bar. (This is a school where after-school snacks are generally confined to bananas and rice crackers.)

Though the school doesn't brag of it, its central core is a rare grade 2 listed building by Erno Goldfinger, one of only two Modern Movement primaries by the mid-century maestro. Built in the 50s of pre-fabricated concrete (and part destroyed a decade ago), it has since been surrounded by a flurry of cedar-clad classroom to accommodate increasing numbers. These low-rise buildings cluster round attractive, open and well-equipped grounds (picnic tables, Giant Connect), with quiet reading areas and dedicated sport pitch.

Parents generally well-spoken, well-qualified professionals, with dual-income families well catered for in before and after-school clubs (where there have been complaints about the sharp-elbowed booking up spaces, which then go unused). Half from a wide range of minority ethnic backgrounds (about a quarter speak English as an additional language, though few are beginners) and South Africans, North Americans and Australians find the can-do atmosphere particularly compatible. Busy PTA helps fundraise (Christmas Fair, children's disco, etc), reorganise the library and run the multitude of cake sales (so many, they have to be rotated).

Though not financially favoured by the local authority, the recent challenging climate has left the school relatively unscathed as parents give generously (a recent summer fair raised over £11,000), and head has been clever at finding additional revenue sources elsewhere (a Co-op scheme, for example, has aided library improvements). Whether money will become tighter now the school has downsized remains to be seen.

The BRIT School

60 The Crescent, Croydon, Surrey CR0 2HN

Ages 14–19 **Pupils** 1,293 (821 girls, 471 boys) **Sixth form** 920

020 8665 5242
www.brit.croydon.sch.uk

Principal: Since 2012, Stuart Worden BA MA GTP (40s). Previously school's director of theatre, though involvement stretches back, one way or another, almost to its foundation in 1991. Before that, was all over the place (literally, not metaphorically – he's highly organised) as, like so many of school's staff, has combined education, education, education with production, production, production. Though past isn't yet mythologised, may yet happen, given that when whistles through key moments of his career, 'the years change each time,' says affable minder.

First act of our (possibly world exclusive) version opens in Chichester, where the 'first and only' theatrical type in his family (brother, also in education, got there by more conventional means), he was taken on regular trips to the theatre – 'virtually at the end of my road' by 'lovely' mother. Was hooked, particularly by the language, leading to writing/producer roles with everyone from the National Theatre to the Royal Exchange Manchester, Playwrights' Co-operative and Working Title Films.

Teaching cropped up early on, too, with FE/HE posts on the film writing MA course at Sheffield University in 1990 as well as a spell as drama teacher at Lansdowne College in Kensington, reprised during two years at the Chichester College of Technology in 1991-1993.

May not look like conventional head (he's creative industries smart, down to intelligent glasses) but is meticulous when it comes to rock solid efficiency of school administration. His ethos is creativity within a framework, from the details (photographic ID for visitors, lessons that run to time or he'll want to know why) to the big things – buildings, new and refurbished, that are no architectural folly but really work.

Wants students to leave not just with creative potential on the way to being realised but equipped with hard-headed entrepreneurial nous to back it up (there's praise in literature for a student's massive on-line following).

His long term involvement in community arts – helped create Steam Industry, a theatre for all initiative – has also led to blossoming of school's outreach programme which is increasingly varied and demanding, though also, he stresses, 'purposeful and long term.' Virtuous circle, too, as those seeking to make career in the area can opt for community arts practice BTec qualification – developed by school and so far unique in the UK.

Pupils work with hospice patients, asylum seekers and rape victims and also act as talented big brothers and sisters to pupils in new, much-needed primary that Mr Worden helped get off the ground – projects naturally including a home-grown musical. BRIT Kids, for local 8-15 year olds, includes community classes and free performances at local Ashcroft Theatre, themed day for tinies, too.

He attracts huge praise from staff. 'He's professional, a good leader, very polite, expects high standards and is very positive,' thought one, speaking for everyone else.

Pupils, too, like his friendly, hands-on approach. 'When I needed help with recording for radio, he was like, "give me a minute and I'll do it",' said one. As a result, takes a while for everyone to work out who he is, particularly those whose previous experiences with authority figures were of a bruising nature. 'He doesn't give out a principal vibe,' said year 11 pupil who had only recently clocked who he was.

Older pupils, though, had no problems with identification. 'Love the way he comes round, sits with us and chats,' said sixth former. 'Not like any principal I've met,' reckoned another. 'He makes an effort to talk.'

Perk of job is 'daily' feedback about pupil success (during GSG visit, it was smash hit involvement in London Fashion Week). As to qualities required by prospective students, he's 'not sure' where talent features in the equation or passion, either, come to that. Instead, stresses importance of being 'nice and kind. Creativity and the arts need you to be open and then you should be willing to share your skill with others. I think that's a special quality.'

Is regularly asked whether school might extend to cover wider age range or sprout satellite versions in the regions. Likely to remain a one-off, he thinks, an 'extraordinary' place that does far more than equip pupils for careers. 'Parallel with that is the sense that the school goes to so many people and uses the arts to enrich their lives.'

Academic matters: Wouldn't be hard to see school as a giant performing arts centre with added classrooms. Not that 'straight' academic teachers would thank you for the description, or principal, come to that. ('Not a Fame Academy' a recurring leitmotif in literature). Staff are either traditional types who 'come here because they think it's the right school to teach at and want to be part of what we're doing here' or creative industry professionals who want to teach 'in a place that specialises in what I'm skilled at,' thought principal. No passengers: choreographers, film makers, playwrights, composers all welcomed but need to commit to training: on the job GTP programme is particularly popular.

Academic staples are bunched together, with sociology, humanities, science and musical theatre in East Wing (actually the main building of Old Grammar school – pay attention at the back). While inevitable focus on performance can make it seem as if you're never more than two minutes from a rehearsal, rooms are well-soundproofed to avoid stardust leakage into classes.

Staff work hard to harness pupils' energy, GCSE groups enjoying animated discussions on causes of youth crime in lively sociology lessons, maths teacher moving us along from fidgety class, distracted by visitor. 'This is a creative enterprise,' says young, happy-looking teacher. Once here, it's a hard place to leave. Teachers, like pupils, praised 'inspirational' atmosphere – latest arrivals include new head of costumes, fresh from Eastenders – and warmth that 'sucks you in'. Though no coloured hair (something of a pupil speciality, though 'they get over it after the first year'), they span the gamut from blouse and skirt to finest beard, bomber jacket 'n' red trainers combo.

Star quality tends to reside in BTec/UAL results. Full-on approach makes results extra impressive. In years 10 and 11, pupils take BTec level 2 diplomas (counting as four GCSEs) as well as following well-equipped and solidly taught GCSE classes in core subjects – some streamed, if ability range demands it, subjects broadly EBacc-themed. Given intake at year 10 – nerve-wracking standing start for any teacher – results are spectacularly good when it comes to performance-related topics such as dance and drama, and pretty respectable in the must-do areas, too. In 2018, 21 per cent 9-7 at GCSE; 94 per cent of students achieved a grade 4 or above in English and 80 per cent achieved a grade 4 or above in maths.

Inevitably, still greater pressure for sixth form, with UAL level 3 extended diploma, equivalent to three A levels (choice of broadcast and digital communication, community arts practice, dance, interactive media, music, musical theatre, technical

B

theatre, theatre and visual arts and design) the starting point with rich rewards. In 2018, 57 per cent D* (equivalent of A level A*) for BTec; 49 per cent A*-B and 26 per cent A*/A at A level.

Welcome flexibility allows teachers to devote whole days to some post-16 UAL modules. 'Means you really get to learn,' thought one, approvingly. Course options can lead to slight difficulties: not everyone, for example, is drawn to the sewing that's currently a must-do part of the visual arts and design and technical theatre arts courses – though discussions are currently under way on possibility of evolving a stitching-light option.

For those needing extra help – there's screening for all during May induction day – terrific SEN is a huge strength, generously accommodated, including cosy, cushioned area and Smartboard-equipped classroom – 'keeps sense of routine' – where struggling pupils (SpLD biggest need, also some ASD and ADHD) get parallel lessons at slower speed, multisensory approaches added 'until it works'. Most staff 'very supportive and recognise that approach builds self-esteem'. Doubters (and there are a small number) are won over by success stories, including pupil who went from U to A* in English GCSE.

Whatever the choice, it's a full-on commitment, eminently do-able for the already organised, efficiency step-change required for those who aren't, and a tough old regime for all which can come as shock to anyone expecting straight drudge for drama swap.

'Same as any old school but one where there's less time for academic subjects,' thought slightly jaded year 11 boy. Even with sensible timetable structuring separating academic and performing arts days, extra workload means 'you need to push yourself and get ready to learn.'

Games, options, the arts: Stuffed with opportunities for performance and just about everything that goes with it, arts naturally the main drain on space, from eight music rooms, all sound-proofed (plus innumerable additional rooms for individual lessons – drums, vocal, keyboard, bass all popular) to two theatres – one, Obi (as in benefactor Sir Maurice Oberstein rather than Kenobi) complete with two storey barn doors to make scenery shifts from adjoining scenic workshop easy peasy.

Textiles/costume design space in main building a pleasure to experience, too, recently remade with retractable door splitting teaching space, allowing GCSE students to spark off older pupils.

Hands-on stuff rules, however. Literally so in case of portable appliance test, pupils shinning impressively up ladders to check the lights. 'Need to understand what's dangerous,' said teacher (and a useful all-purpose teenage rule, too).

With students billed by specialism, (dancer x and musician y) in school literature and so much going on, can sometimes be hard to know where lessons end and the extracurricular begins. Even college awards nights become performances, most recent complete with Great Gatsby staging and X Factor style audience votes (which would brighten up more conventional speech days elsewhere no end).

Driving everything is all-round enthusiasm, fuelled by wide range of sixth form specialisms and staff contacts – brilliant, of course – with some interactive media students, for example, getting chance to work with Aardman studios.

Sixth former taking BTec in technical theatre had had a ball working on Tim Burton-inspired costumes for Hamlyn, put on in local theatre and one of 40 productions through the year ranging from Artaud and Brook to Brecht, Caryl Churchill and much in the way of full-blown Shakespeare, many others with words and scores written by the staff and/or pupils.

Traditional educational add ons far from absent, however. Duke of Edinburgh runs conventional course (though Jack Petchey awards – imaginatively awarded for academic rather than community service excellence in years 10 and 11 – do not). Sport isn't neglected either. School has own Olympian to its name, and while council has hung on to school's (small) sports field, necessitating relocation of sports day (and other fixtures) to nearby Norwood Lakes, the keen have school gym – somewhat battered but serviceable – for basketball (popular girls' team, which meets on Mondays, 'vicious', thought year 13 boys, admiringly).

Background and atmosphere: Patriotic acronym is down to British Record Industry Trust – great and good still feature on governors' list – whose funding and influence led to school's foundation in 1991 (after Mrs Thatcher, fearing creation of home for resting thesps, had been won round – or so the legend goes).

They're hugely proud of what they've created, says principal, and with good reason. Despite growth of vocational training colleges covering the 14-19 age range, school remains a one-off, the only free (prospectus uses capitals to emphasis) performing arts and technology school in the country, state funded but outside LA control.

Set within easy walk from Selhurst Station – not likely to become new Hoxton any time soon – school, though not an obvious looker from the outside, is full of thought, care and taste when it comes to the interiors. Inevitable tired corners mainly in vintage old school building (site originally housed Selhurst Grammar), one of three of varying styles and vintage. Newest, light and bright, is very plush indeed though smart rooms and corridors largely rule throughout the site, with plenty of tarting up (paint 'n' porthole doors even in otherwise non-refurbished areas, for example).

Feel is urban grit, rather than Surrey Downs (even feels like a long way to leafy South Croydon) with undeniable pressure on space. No pupil common rooms, for example (one year 11 girl had asked teacher to keep an eye on possessions during the day – gladly done, too) – immaculate carpeting in many corridors provides comfortable sitting space for the needy (speckly stone finish remains in original school building) with one student sitting by banked lockers busily sorting out vast pile of music.

Little in the way of school jargon, bar slightly confusing names. (Blue Block, though lovely, isn't blue). Main (and alias-free) building, built new for school's opening, has been substantially refreshed. Features include internal windows opening out on to corridors (principal's office too, at his request, providing a window on to the world), walls liberally decorated with high quality art (everything from Aboriginal-motifs to Banksy lookalike and delicate Japanese figures disporting themselves against parchment backdrop).

Academic year, too, is unusual with five eight-week terms, interspersed with fortnight breaks. Officially 'best supports delivery of the curriculum and ensures students return refreshed', though according to one teacher, production demands mean 'you'll often find students coming in over the holidays'.

With the exception of occasional overt whackiness – bins spray painted in wild array of colours following theatre teacher's guerrilla decoration initiative over the summer holidays – what dominates is sense of all-through professionalism.

And while absence of uniform, bells (and whistles, at least off stage) may not tend towards the norm, expectations certainly do, with teachers unlikely to indulge in too much time-drift as 'students will tell you when break is,' reckoned one.

Pastoral care, well-being and discipline: It's a busy old day; lights up 7am, not dimmed until 12 hours later. Though 'no-one will be here all that time,' says principal, some will operate in unconventional hours – drama and dance students, for example, warming up in the early hours before auditions or classes, studios booked up way in advance so pupils can edit their films.

Outstanding attendance, particularly at sixth form level, testament to commitment but also in stark contrast, in some cases, to pupils' unhappy educational experiences elsewhere. Several talked about feeling 'like outsiders' in other schools. Here, blend of rigour and tolerance seems to suit everyone. 'I felt I'd found people like me,' reckoned one sixth former.

'We think it's a good place to be looked after,' says principal, who is particularly proud of large scale speed meet and greet induction where grizzled year 11 veterans help newly arrived year 10s to settle in.

Body image can (predictably) be an issue, countered by strong message highlighting the glory of the individual, school stressing its more unconventional successes such as Adele to ensure that identikit size nothings aren't touted as the only aspiration worth pursuing.

On-site counsellors, presence discreetly advertised to students via form tutors, provide additional back up, while healthy eating (just about the only niggle otherwise superlative inspection report could find) is now a major school focus, with year 10 science pupils reporting on savoury snack fat content to year 13 dancers, canteen staff challenging pupils 'in a friendly way' if appear to be opting for unhealthy/minimalistic lunch (those on free school meals compelled to have healthy meal, though 'it's not about being a dictator but guiding and supporting,' thought staff member).

Staff enforce gentle discipline – students in library, verging on slight chattiness in quiet zone, were instantly quelled by (silent) entrance of smiley but no-nonsense librarians. Creativity within a framework something of a necessity, especially with school jam-packed, recent BTec additions adding another 200 to sixth form so 'as much as can take without bursting,' says school.

May be a timetable but there's 'no "you will do this number of hours" – it's their school,' says principal. Adds up to atmosphere that engenders sense of independence combined with professionalism – a lesson for the future, as with sixth form pupils given permission to leave lesson to conduct library research, but with return time and teacher expectations clearly outlined.

Pupil voice is heard loud and clear, too, in everything from 'almost daily' cake sales to fundraising for forthcoming productions to active student council which recently voted to ban environment-unfriendly disposable cups at lunchtime, 'commit to bringing in refillable bottles'. No wonder giant painted portrait of the blessed Jamie on wall of bigger canteen dispenses saint-like smile like a South American folk hero by way of inspiration.

Pupils and parents: Education should be accomplished without removing innocence along the way, thinks the principal. 'Friends assume it's going to be like Fame, but it's really down to earth,' felt sixth former, though performers in particular exhibit healthy dose of chutzpah and aren't backwards in coming forwards, adding in a couple of pirouettes and a solo on the way in. We enjoyed early morning dancing huddles outside (professional-looking gurning, too, in one case) – and tales of close harmony rivalry in the canteen.

Though unified by drive – 'at an ordinary school she'd be the leader of the pack, here, she's in a class with 30 of them,' reckoned mother of aspiring dancer – school community otherwise diverse. Families range from chimney sweeps to the loaded, many drawn from immediate area, which is 'socially complicated,' says principal, characterised by side-by-side pockets of affluence and deprivation – eligibility for free school meals is above the national average, and school also runs 'BRIT loves Selhurst' campaign, offering free tickets to locals.

Entrance: Not for everyone. One talented singer-songwriter had opted instead for Guildford ACM. 'They advertise it as once you go there, 75 per cent of your future career is done, but I know it's hard work.' Some find the place for themselves – press coverage is pretty much non-stop. One girl, now in sixth form, paid first visit to keep friend company and ended up the one with the place.

A minority very local (15 per cent from Croydon), though vast majority (75 per cent) from South London, remaining 10 per cent, selected on raw talent, not postcode, can come from anywhere in UK. (School stresses desire to avoid impossibly long journeys, somewhat spoiling effect with X-Factor winner Leona Lewis, quoted as describing two-hour round trip as 'so worth it'.)

Oversubscribed all the way through, less so for those entering in year 10, massively for sixth form. For 14 year olds seeking place in year 10, process less daunting, though useful to muster clear ideas on what pupils would gain from coming here.

Technical courses based on portfolios followed by workshops the norm. Inevitably stressful for would-be performers. 'She got recalled, she cried, she stuffed up in her first audition and thought "that's it" – but got in,' said parent who felt school wasn't looking for fully formed talent (there are rumours of already successful child stars being turned away) but 'something in kids that they can bring out – they don't necessarily want someone who's completely polished and finished and looking for it as a way into the next big thing'. A fair comment, thought school. 'It's about unlocking potential rather than a finished product.'

Exit: In a handful of cases, some year 11 pupils may not make the sixth form, most after discovering that love for performing arts has worn off. 'Might get to age 16 and think, I don't want to be a dancer – I want to do something else with my life,' says principal. 'They might just change and that's a good thing.'

At least 70 per cent, usually more, do carry on into sixth form, and almost everyone, even those who leave post-16, go on to further and higher education elsewhere – most recent extreme example swapping bright lights for animal husbandry.

Principal stresses proof that employability issues amongst the young can be triumphantly overcome. According to school survey, 70 per cent of past pupils end up working in creative industries. A few are household names but this is definitely not yardstick of measurement. All, says principal firmly, are superstars even if not household names because 'are the best box office manager or record label executive.'

School's well-designed vocational courses, with an eye and a half on the future, help speed the process along. Community-related courses, for example, lead to a virtuous circle, helping local bodies and in the process raising future trained community facilitators – a growing area for well-regarded HE courses such as Royal Central School of Speech and Drama's applied theatre and education BA degree. Others end up at RADA, Rose Bruford, Drama Centre, East 15, Bristol Old Vic, Guildhall and LAMDA, or head off to university – Leeds, York, Sheffield and Birmingham among them. One to Oxbridge in 2018.

Once through, you'll find their words, music, performance, directorial and backstage talents just about everywhere you look, from fashion shows to musicals, national theatre to community arts, in the UK and internationally.

Remarks: Vocational dazzler with some academic bright lights as well. An educational showstopper, and one you definitely won't want to walk out of half way through, which tempers sprinklings of stardust with lashings of nuts and bolts reality checks. That's what they say. We secretly think it's like collecting every school's coolest kids and putting them in one place. If we could set this review to music, we probably would.

B

Bromley High Junior School

Linked with Bromley High School

24

Blackbrook Lane, Bickley, Bromley, Kent BR1 2TW

Ages 4–11 **Pupils** 314

Fees: £13,782 pa

020 8781 7001
www.bromleyhigh.gdst.net

Head of junior school: Since 2012, Claire Dickerson BA (Anglia Ruskin University). Since arriving at the school 14 years ago, she has seen the school from all angles: beginning as a year 4 class teacher before moving to reception and then taking on the headship in 2012, at a particularly exciting time as the school moved to its own version of a creative curriculum. We found her to be focused, warm, open and an accomplished wearer of heels. Parents tell us: 'She is very approachable and we feel that we can have access to her whenever we need it'; another said, 'Our daughter was thrilled on her first day when Ms Dickerson was able to remember all their names and she takes a personal interest in each and every child.' Her outside interests are skiing, swimming and theatre. She lives locally and has two grown up children in their 20s.

Entrance: There are two forms of 20 pupils at 4+ and an additional eight girls join at 7+. The 4+ assessments are in the January prior to entry and 7+ assessments are held in the November of year 2. Most recently there were 80 applications at 4+ and 20 for the year 3 places. Thereafter a waiting list for occasional vacancies.

Exit: Around 70 per cent move on to the senior school. Around a quarter leave at 11+ to attend local grammar schools. The school is very clear that it is not a prep school and girls will not be prepared for external testing, leaving them free to explore a broad curriculum throughout years 5 and 6.

Remarks: The new curriculum has freed the teaching from Sats: instead the focus is the creative and cross-curricular, which the head feels has inspired the staff and 'sparked' the girls. Reception girls might be sculpting a mermaid, but they are learning about building 3D shapes and developing their research skills by investigating appropriate sea companions. Parents seem highly delighted with the imaginative approach to learning; one told us: 'The teaching throughout has been fantastic, varied, and full of different learning opportunities such as visitors and trips that have enhanced the curriculum'. One aim is to give each child the confidence to put forward their own ideas. Year 6 girls describe having 'talk partners' which change every three weeks, where they pair up to discuss topics, and that those who have finished their work will buddy up with a girl who might be stuck.

On polar fun day a real-life explorer shared tales of blubber and frostbite. Pupils dug up the grounds searching for archaeological artefacts on Roman day. We have seen plenty of Tudor houses built from cereal boxes and straw as part of the history curriculum, but never heard of them being set on fire to no doubt replicate the Great Fire. This seems to sum up the staff's ability to take things to the next level here.

The counterbalance to this is a careful teaching of the core subjects of reading, writing and maths. Maths is nearly always taught separately from the cross-curricular work. Handwriting is all joined up for most by the end of reception. A new system has been introduced for comprehensive academic tracking which, coupled with close home/school links, ensures that if a child does have a blip it can be talked about and supported. Homework escalates gradually, starting with some over the weekend in reception. There is a computing suite and years 5 and 6 each have an iPad which remains at school.

Literature is often at the heart of themes; World Book Day decorations adorn each classroom door, the library is well-stocked, houses are named after authors and the girls had recently enjoyed a visit from children's Laureate, Chris Riddell.

Girls like to come to the library at lunch times if they're in the middle of a particularly good book. Languages are taught to give girls a flavour of what they might go on to study: French throughout, then Spanish in year 3, German in year 4, Latin in year 5 and double French in year 6 culminating in a five day trip to France. Girls say they are ready for it, as they've 'been practising' with shorter trips such as the choir's weekend trip to Belgium where they visited a chocolate factory and also sang at the Menin Gate memorial at Ypres.

Girls benefit from being able to share all of the sports facilities of the senior school, such as the indoor pool, and are the current GDST gymnastics champions. They seem to try everything and are playing an increasing fixture list, including a few against boys' schools. A recent win against a local independent boys' school was particularly important says the head, not so much for the win, 'but knowing they can compete as equals'.

The music wing contains practice rooms and a high ceilinged performance space. Lots of individual musical tuition and girls learn the recorder in year 3. Wind and string ensembles and the chance to play with senior girls in the orchestra. The junior school is the reigning Bromley Festival schools' choir champion in its age group. A year 5 girl is currently playing Matilda in the West End. There are whole school drama productions twice a year. This summer it's the Mikado.

A tempting array of weekly clubs. Some sporting and musical, but also ballroom dancing, nature garden, chess club, circus skills, 'hot off the press' and our favourite: guinea-pig club.

The junior school building is tucked behind the senior school and a major re-development will be finished in 2020. Plain, brick-built, functional, some of the classes and the library have nice views across the tennis and netball courts to the woods of Jubilee Park. Plenty of playground space, mainly tarmac but the year groups are carefully divided: the reception children have a large weatherproof canopy and a pirate ship; there is a fake grass 'Teletubby' hill for the slightly older girls and plenty of space to run around for the Hawthorns, years 3 to 6. Making use of the grounds, the school has also adopted elements of the forest school outdoor learning.

The atmosphere is orderly but relaxed with children exuberant in PE and busy at playtime. Classrooms are large and utilitarian with meticulous displays. Girls were particularly neat in their uniforms of traditional summer dresses and grey wool blazers on the day of our visit. A parent: 'Every facet of the school seems to run like clockwork'. Confidence is most often mentioned by parents, with one telling us, 'Our youngest daughter is a completely different child since starting Bromley High. She has grown in confidence and has really thrived'.

Working parents may be delighted with the breakfast club, which runs from 7.30am. Additional fees for this and the after-school club. Had better hope that trains run on time, as late pick up fees are steep.

A large proportion of girls for whom English is an additional language, reflecting bilingual families. Just a few with a SEN. A part-time SENCo leads a team of eight teaching assistants who offer additional classroom support to any child needing a little more individual attention. One-on-one support is available where needed. Parents seem unanimous in the trust they place in the head and her staff and the 'nurturing' pastoral care to be found here.

Bromley High School

Linked with Bromley High Junior School

Blackbrook Lane, Bickley, Bromley, Kent BR1 2TW

Ages 11–18 **Pupils** 580 **Sixth form** 118

Fees: £17,091 pa

020 8781 7000
www.bromleyhigh.gdst.net

Headmistress: Since 2014, Angela Drew BA PGCE MBA (50s). She studied English literature in Durham and then spent a year working with mentally disabled adults before entering teaching. She is an ISI inspector. Previously deputy head (academic) of Epsom College. She was head of English and drama at The Mary Erskine School in Edinburgh and has taught at George Watson's, Whitgift and Prior Park College. She teaches AS thinking skills from Y10. Friendly and open, she wears her headship lightly. A hope and ambition for the girls is that they will not just be prepared for the modern world but lead it.

After the departure of her relatively short-lived predecessor, Mrs Drew's initial year must have been spent on something of a caffeine high as she hosted 30 coffee mornings with groups of parents. 'She is passionate and proud of the girls, supportive and comes to so many events during school time and outside school hours. I believe she promotes the importance of an all-rounder with particular focus on the academics,' said a mother. Another: 'I think the headteacher has come into a well-established and successful school and she has made her mark. She has shaken up the PE department and this has improved. She has employed extremely good teachers and bought in different teaching methods'.

Married with a daughter completing a masters degree at Oxford and a son studying history at Leeds, Mrs Drew enjoys reading and theatre and is a committed Evertonian. She lives nearby in rural Kent.

Academic matters: There has been a great curriculum shake-up in recent years, with most recent results not reflecting the wider choice of subjects available to GCSE students. As well as the expected core curriculum girls could choose dance, photography, classical civilisation, economics or additional maths. The sixth form offering adds in psychology, government and politics, business studies, plus a Pre-U in theology and philosophy. In 2018, 66 per cent A*-A/9-7 at GCSE; 32 per cent A*/A at A level.

In the sixth form classes do not exceed 14 pupils, some tuition groups are just a handful, and girls seem unfettered to pursue their own interests. Indeed this seems to be a strength of the school. Subjects don't have to be chosen with any timetabling restrictions and our sixth form guides described being encouraged to find their passions, no matter how slowly these emerge, whilst teachers offer guidance with a weather eye to careers and UCAS applications. Mrs Drew: 'we're very focused on where they're going, but they are free as to how they get there'. Triple science, literature and maths are the core (and the mathematicians really shine). For two consecutive years, upper sixth girls have gained the Salter's Award for the second highest chemistry A level mark in the UK.

The school isn't considering the IB but elements such as the extended project are on offer. Up to 16, few stray far from the more academic subjects: most take nine or 10, including several IGCSEs. Plenty of modern linguists, but curriculum changes have provoked a huge resurgence in classics – 39 girls were studying Latin in year 10 when we visited. When we queried whether Mandarin is on the horizon, Mrs Drew says she is 'tempted'. DT, but no food technology: a swing too far from gender stereotyping? Having seen the girls' impressive rainforest cakes in the geography bake off, perhaps there is little left to teach.

More than 20 teaching staff have been with the school for over 10 years. The school's latest ISI report declares teaching to be 'exceptional'. Praise for the teaching from parents ranges from the extremely appreciative to slight wistfulness from a couple who have come up from the all-singing-and-dancing junior school. A typically balanced report: 'There are some teachers who clearly go above and beyond to be approachable and encouraging and these members of staff are well liked and respected by the girls.' The head has appointed a new academic deputy, a former head of science at St Paul's Girls', who has encouraged independent learning and 'risky' lessons. Mrs Drew has also introduced external workshops led by graduates to cultivate good study habits for both pupils and parents.

Trips, masterclasses and competitions inspire free thinking beyond exercise books. Year 12s were recently boggled by a speech recognition lecture by a leading light at Google; sixth formers secured tickets to see Simon Russell-Beale perform their set text at the National Theatre; whilst GCSE artists took a study tour of Vermeer's Amsterdam; meanwhile year 11 biologists extracted the DNA from strawberries and the historians put Hitler on trial. Terry Waite was soon to take part in a cross-curricular 'brain day', discussing how he survived captivity.

The curriculum has switched from ICT to computer science, a new computer lab has been unveiled and GCSE and A level students joined 20,000 classrooms worldwide in two weeks of 'an hour of code'. Science labs are well-equipped and gradually being modernised. Meanwhile, girls have been proud winners of two Arkwright engineering scholarships. Serious contenders in the national Maths Challenges. Year 10s also recently won gold in the national Biology Challenge. A parent told us that the girls have so many public speaking opportunities it becomes 'second nature'. Those year 10s seem to be on fire, having also qualified for recent Oxford finals of the international youth debating championship.

Maths is set immediately on entry; science is set in year 9 and English from year 10. As always, parental thoughts on the amount of homework down to the individual child's stamina: some think it's a lot, particularly in the exam years, whilst some 'could actually do with a bit more' lower down the school. Holiday homework 'keeps things ticking over'.

Only a tiny number of girls receiving one-to-one support for identified learning differences as support is provided in lessons. Most girls with SEN have dyslexia but a few have dyspraxia or are high functioning ASD. No additional fees for learning support. Those capable of working up to three years beyond their chronological age are offered extension opportunities within the curriculum and via clubs, competitions and collaborations across the GDST, maths masterclasses and a STEM day.

Everyone does work experience in year 11 after GCSEs. The head recently took a group of year 10s – anyone who wanted to come – to meet an old girl at Cambridge. Teachers are said to be 'plugged in' to additional opportunities such as CV boosting competitions to enter. The GDST alumni network of 75,000 is invaluable for arranging work experience. Café Scientifique is a drop-in lecture series where girls are exposed to parents and old girls with inspiring careers and life experiences. And those prepping for Oxbridge have the benefit of the whole network of schools to form a cohort.

Games, options, the arts: Sport is compulsory for all girls up until the end of lower sixth. Upping the ante – bringing the fixture list and ambition in line with the 25 acres and facilities – was one of the head's first priorities. She has recruited a new director of sport, previously head of netball at Alleyn's, and a male hockey coach. The U16A hockey team was Kent county champion. Someone is keeping score as they tell us the hockey teams have played 123 fixtures in the last year celebrating over 300 goals. The Olympic size Astroturf is newly floodlit. Girls compete in netball, athletics, swimming, cross-country, rounders and are accomplished gymnasts. Increasing numbers getting to go on the bus, as the school fields A-D netball and rounders teams. Sixth formers are thrilled with the new gym, like a mini health club, for use with a buddy at lunch times or after school. Year 10s give zumba and aerobics a go. The school's indoor pool can also be used by girls' families one evening a week and Saturday mornings. Girls able to brave the British weather enjoy the bronze and silver Duke of Edinburgh challenges, compulsory in year 10, with a couple completing gold before reaching university.

More artists than musicians in terms of academic study, but a very musical (and all-Steinway) school. Music theory is taught to years 7-9. We met a lone A level student, studying music tech. The majority of girls learn a musical instrument or have vocal tuition. Last year the senior school music tour was to Prague. One parent suggested there would be more take up of instrumental lessons if girls did not miss important lesson time. Some 24 peripatetic music staff teach to grade 8 on 16 different instruments and over 60 per cent played their way to a merit or distinction last year. There is regular success at Bromley and Beckenham Music Festival and girls have performed at Southwark Cathedral, the Royal Festival Hall and enjoyed tours to Spain and Normandy with choirs and ensembles.

Each year sees dance and drama productions with students performing, singing, playing in orchestra, and lighting, choreographing and undertaking backstage skills. One has a starring role in EastEnders.

High quality art is displayed around the school. We squinted through the door at the appealing art studio with mezzanine level as exams were in progress. Several pupils have exhibited at the Turner Contemporary Gallery. The DT facilities are extensive and enthusiastically used with the usual laser cutter but also a 3D printer.

Lunch time is deliberately long. Clubs range from the cosy such as 'knit and natter' and card games, the sporty – rugby, horse-riding or squad training – to the stimulating: robotics, DT divas and TED talks club. Musicians might try jazz, percussion or chamber strings. We were assured girls do not spend their lunch hours cutting up cadavers but were intrigued to note the forensics club. Sixth formers are equally engaged running their own discussion group, most recently on the death penalty.

Background and atmosphere: The school opened in 1883, aiming to provide education for girls on a par with that of their brothers, and the first entrants described it as a bit like being in the army: there are photos of girls doing PE wearing ties. Originally in a Victorian building, the school relocated to its present site in 1981. The wooden honours boards line one of the modern corridors, their name in gold being something the girls still aspire to today.

The campus is spacious and green but with few mature trees to take the edge off the already plain buildings. The Parents' Association's most recent purchase has been sturdy wooden parasols to provide much-needed shade. Views come into their own from the upper floors – a science teacher jokingly referring to his lab as the penthouse. There is the large Crompton library – Richmal Crompton, the author of Just William, taught at the school – open until 5.30pm every day to facilitate homework. Sixth formers have their own large, light common room where they can eat their lunch, hang out on sofas and study in free periods. The dining hall is newly decorated in a zingy lime with lots of fruit and salad in evidence.

The grey and burgundy uniform here is particularly smart, with blazers on when not in lessons. The fashion seems to be for patent loafers with knee socks. Girls assured us that there isn't an 'it' bag culture. Sixth formers look smart and ready for anything in 'business attire', mostly jackets with skirts but they are free to express some individuality.

Girls burst out of lessons onto the wide carpeted corridors seeming relaxed. Asked to describe the school, a parent said, 'I feel there is pressure for the girls to succeed but above that I feel they push each girl individually to get the best out of them'; another, 'I feel the school is quite competitive – but very caring as most teachers know each girl individually and care for their welfare.' One of our guides said fondly of her time here since the age of 4: 'it's a really nice bubble'.

Pastoral care, well-being and discipline: Everyone we spoke to praised the school's pastoral care. 'I think the school provides excellent pastoral care. Teachers are involved and approachable and seem to work together,' said one. Parents universally expressed confidence in the school's ability to take care of any issues of bullying and felt that their daughters would be able to raise it. The school has one of the most thorough positive mental health policies we have seen, with a particular awareness of eating disorders, depression and self-harm as very live potential issues for students. There is a part-time student counsellor and 'big sister, little sister' pairs senior with younger girls.

Rules seem low key. Girls are allowed to wear 'discreet' make-up from year 9, earlier than many. Mobile phones to be kept in lockers away from lessons. From Mrs Drew's nonplussed response to our enquiry about any exclusions we gather that discipline is not something she has to worry about. Girls are engaging seriously with the current new wave of feminism and issues such as university rape culture. They have recently set up a LGBT club.

Pupils and parents: Although parents describe the school as 'mixed', it is not as culturally diverse as more central London schools with just over 10 per cent of girls speaking another language at home.

Mainly white British with a mix of other ethnicities including Chinese, German, Portuguese and Hindi. The majority of girls come from the local area of Orpington, Bromley, Beckenham and Dulwich via a direct train route, but a proportion of girls also travel in from rural Kent.

The commutes of working parents are well-supported with both a free breakfast club from 7.30am and a homework club after school until 5.30pm.

Entrance: Over 70 per cent of the junior school girls transfer to the senior school, the majority without an 11+ assessment, although some choose to sit the test. Places for outsiders are offered via testing in the January prior to entry in verbal and non-verbal reasoning and creative writing plus a short mathematics extension paper. We are told that competition is stiffening as pressure for places increases. Pupils with identified SEN are given 25 per cent more time.

Pupils join from a range of independent prep schools and state primaries including Breaside Prep, Blackheath Prep, Merton Court, St Christopher's, The Hall, Rosemead Prep, Oakfield Prep and St Olave's Prep. External applicants to the sixth form subject to GCSE entry requirements, school reference and interview.

Exit: Some 30 per cent leave at 16 to enter mainly co-ed sixth forms. Around half of A level leavers to Russell Group universities with LSE, UCL, Exeter, Bristol, Sheffield, Warwick, Bath and Nottingham amongst the favourite destinations; one to Cambridge (theology) in 2018.

Money matters: Bursaries and scholarships in penny numbers for girls entering at year 7 and the lower sixth only, including honorary scholarships and minor awards for artists' materials and music lessons. Academic scholarships based on entrance test results. Bursaries are available on entry to the senior school and offer up to full fees for the academically gifted who could not otherwise afford to attend. Parents should expect their finances to be scrutinised in detail on application and each year thereafter. Some sixth form scholarships for which candidates must prepare a written application.

Remarks: A selective school, offering a wonderful range of opportunities to widen horizons and develop new interests. Suits academically able girls with lots of drive.

Broomwood Hall

Linked with Northcote Lodge School

68-74 Nightingale Lane, London SW12 8NR

Ages Girls 4-13, boys 4-8 **Pupils** 662 (pre-preps 419, prep 243)

Fees: £16,125 – £19,785 pa

020 8682 8830
www.broomwood.co.uk

Principal: Lady Katharine Colquhoun BEd (50s). Has a rather regal manner but her vision has seen this school mushroom from humble beginnings to a thriving empire with over 600 pupils (as well as 200 boys at Northcote Lodge – the brother school down the road). 'She's remarkable,' one parent told us. 'Inflexible at times, and you have to toe the line with her, but she is seriously impressive.' Lady Colquhoun knows she has an able team behind her and believes the ability to delegate, which she learned as the eldest of five children, is her secret.

Lady Colquhoun has made the transition from headmistress to joint principal with her husband, Sir Malcolm. She still teaches literature to prep school girls, whilst he deals with administration and property. School has a board of directors which oversees both Broomwood Hall and Northcote Lodge.

Headmistress since 2001, Carole Jenkinson BSc PGCE (50s). Varied career, including time as ski rep, with stints at International Tribune in Paris and British Council. Started her teaching career at Northcote Lodge. Universally respected and admired by parents; everyone we spoke to described her in glowing terms. She exudes calm wisdom. Very knowledgeable about senior schools of every hue and spends a significant proportion of her time visiting potential schools up and down the country. Teaches maths to year 7 and verbal reasoning to year 4, so has a good grasp of each girl's abilities and character before recommending suitable senior schools. Now head of all three Broomwood Hall schools: two lower schools in Garrads Road and Ramsden Road, and the upper school in Nightingale Lane.

Entrance: Lower schools hugely oversubscribed, non-selective and located in the heart of Nappy Valley. For reception class, parents must register their child in advance on the provisional list and are invited to register formally and pay the £100 fee once they have visited. This is followed by a 'readiness assessment' around the child's third birthday, a year prior to entry.

School says it looks for a wide variety of characters rather than a type and aims to have a good spread of birth dates throughout the year, as well as a 50:50 mix of boys and girls. Forty reception places at Garrads Road and 80 at Ramsden Road. Priority to siblings.

A strict one-mile radius rule applies which ensures all children can walk, cycle or scoot to school. Head encourages parents to apply to several schools in the area, to avoid disappointment. Not a huge international contingent – still predominantly well-to-do British families with some Europeans and Americans.

Three forms per year in the prep, rising to four per year from year 7. Maximum 18 per class. Vast majority come up from lower schools. Those coming from elsewhere must register on the provisional list and provide a report from previous school. Parents have a tour and time with the headmistress, and prospective pupils spend a morning in the school where staff assess their academic ability in a classroom setting.

Girls in the prep come from as far afield as Fulham, Chelsea and Dulwich. A Fulham parent we spoke to felt that those who were not from the immediate area were made to feel like outsiders by parents – 'the Wandsworth brigade can be quite intimidating for non-locals as they stick together like glue.' The school itself bends over backwards to integrate the new recruits. Morning and evening minibus to Fulham and Chelsea. Places vacated by 11+ leavers are quickly snapped up.

Exit: Most lower school girls to the upper school and most boys transfer to Northcote Lodge. A few disappear at this stage to country preps (such as Cheam, Ludgrove and Cothill) and some opt for neighbouring day schools (Dulwich Prep, Dulwich College and King's Wimbledon among them).

Some 25-45 per cent leave at 11, mostly to south London day schools (eg JAGS, Alleyn's) or to boarding (eg Benenden, Downe House). More and more stay until 13 and then tend to head to co-ed boarding (eg Bradfield, Bryanston, Marlborough). Usually around 20 per cent of girls awarded scholarships.

Remarks: The Garrads Road site is an arts and crafts style Edwardian mansion. Large, pretty garden with lots to keep children occupied – hopscotch, vegetable patch, climbing frame, sandpit and outside classroom for reading on summer afternoons. Ramsden Road is on two sites – The Old Vicarage, a rambling, red-brick former parsonage, for the first two years and 50 Nightingale Lane, around the corner, for the next two years. Both feel homely, with tartan carpets throughout. The upper school, also in Nightingale Lane, boasts an amphitheatre where girls perform plays.

Schools have a relaxed, country feel; on the day we visited, pancake races were in full swing in the playground at Garrads Road and children and teachers were having a ball. Teachers engaging and inspiring; these are lively places to work. Good mix of long-serving and new staff, with some having chosen teaching as a second career. The parents we spoke to felt the lower schools give a solid academic grounding as well as a joyful start to school life.

Reading is of paramount importance and the libraries are well-stocked and well-used. School rewards hard work in all areas: copious numbers of cups awarded to pupils (including for good manners and friendship). Head believes children must learn that they will only win a cup when they have tried really hard and must learn to accept that they will not win every time.

B

Girls certainly keep their heads down in the upper school, although there is also great fun to be had along the way. Setting in English and maths throughout school. The upper school is ahead of the pack when it comes to technology. Girls bring in their own iPads and older girls learn computer coding (which they love).

Some 60 upper school pupils receive some form of SEND support. School feels able to support mild dyslexia and dyspraxia but wouldn't be the right place for anyone with severe difficulties. Currently 30 children with English as an additional language.

A very well-run, flourishing school that knows where it is heading. For those who want a modern education underpinned by traditional values, there is arguably nowhere better south of the river. Tea is served at the end of lessons, followed by compulsory supervised homework at school. Viewed as a godsend by busy parents, and children say they like being able to relax (save for rote learning) once they get home. Some parents, admittedly, would prefer homework to be done at home so they can keep a closer eye on their child's progress. Clubs, including flower arranging and glass painting, finish at 6pm.

Drama is a real strength; everyone is in two plays a year, one of which is biblical, 'so they know their Old and New Testament stories by the time they leave.' Flamboyant productions. Bright art and DT studios, complete with impressive equipment. Talented head of lower school music writes plays and composes scores for productions. Eighty per cent play a musical instrument. Four choirs.

Substantial amount of sport on the weekly timetable. Full-size hard tennis court in the Garrads Road garden used for PE. Cricket, football and rugby pitches 10 minutes away on foot. One parent we spoke to felt this is 'possibly not the right school for a really sporty child,' though others disagreed and said there were plenty of matches going on. Some pupils currently performing at pre-county level. 'We've definitely become a sportier school,' says head. Currently winning or drawing three-quarters of matches; school excels at cross-country and netball.

Principal believes old-fashioned values hold true and is keen on instilling good manners in her pupils. Children hold doors open for adults and look you in the eye when they talk to you. Girls are required to have a comb in their backpacks at all times; ear piercing strongly discouraged. Pastoral care is a great strength of the school. A trained counsellor is at the upper school regularly to help girls with eg potential eating disorders, exam phobia or bereavement.

Delicious food. Girls are encouraged to make conversation at meals and to hold their knives and forks correctly. Leiths has written a bespoke cookery course for Broomwood and all girls in year 7 have weekly cookery lessons. During the summer term pupils put on their aprons and cook a three-course meal for their parents. Always a great success and highly anticipated.

Good communication between schools and home. Lots of social events, including leavers' dinner – a swish black-tie affair for parents, pupils and teachers. Massive amounts of fundraising for a school it has built from scratch in Ethiopia. Parents are very supportive of the enterprise, though one or two grumbles about not enough money being given to local charities. Drop off and pick up times involve huge numbers of mothers, either in gym kit or walking the family labrador, though schools note that more and more mothers work. Some joint upper school ventures with Northcote Lodge (debates, clubs and field trips) – but one mother we spoke to felt that the girls and boys hardly mix and that this is a missed opportunity.

Schools turn out well-adjusted girls, fully prepared both academically and socially for the next stage. Parents emphasise what a great job it does in producing confident, happy and successful girls. As the school handbook firmly explains: 'We don't expect parents to become heavily involved in the minutiae of the learning process; we do expect you to leave your daughter's education to us and let us get on with it.' If you do that, your daughter will be in safe hands here.

Head acknowledges that parents are more demanding than a decade ago but understands 'that the significant financial output for school fees means they inevitably want to know they are getting value for money.' Welcoming, gentle schools full of delightful, cheerful, well-behaved children.

Bute House Preparatory School for Girls

Luxemburg Gardens, London W6 7EA

Ages 4–11 **Pupils** 310

Fees: £16,458 pa

020 7603 7381
www.butehouse.co.uk

Head: Since 2012, Helen Lowe (50s), BA Oxford Brookes, LGSM Guildhall School of Music and Drama. Married to Phil, whom she met at drama school. They have two grown up children. Having 'got acting out of my system' she started her teaching career in big Essex comprehensives, where she taught drama. She is verging on the evangelical about the profoundly positive benefits a background in drama can have – 'everyone should go to drama school because it's all about people and understanding other people's point of view'. She then went on to teach at primary schools in Richmond and became the literacy consultant for the whole of the borough. Her experience in the independent sector includes being a drama teacher at St Paul's Girls' in the 1990s, curriculum coordinator at Lady Eleanor Holles junior department and head of juniors at King's House in Richmond, where she taught for three years. Bute House is her first 'stand alone' headship, ending the 20 year tenure of the formidable Sallie Salvidant.

Bright and bubbly, Mrs Lowe likes to make an impact. Never one to be seen without her pink lipstick, snazzy glasses and white blonde hair well coiffed. Her confident manner ('I'm very bossy,' she admits with a twinkle) could be overbearing were it not delivered with such warmth and humour. Parents remark on her enthusiasm and ability to make changes without a fuss. Good changes, that few had even noticed were needed – a whole school Christmas celebration at a local church for example. 'I am a great communicator,' she says. Parents agree. She holds open house individual appointment sessions where parents can discuss any of their concerns about the school. She not only puts her point across impressively but listens too. What's more, the parents listen to her, even when it might be news they don't enjoy hearing – that their daughter won't suit a school they have set their hearts on, for example.

She knows the girls properly, and by the time the 11+ process kicks in, she is well-equipped to write their reports for senior schools and advise the parents on the best school for each one, having taught all girls in their second half of year 5 and first half of year 6. 'I have the best interests of the child at heart,' she avers. This may not always coincide with pleasing the parents but it doesn't faze her. When it comes to decisions about boarding school, however, she is sensitive to the fact that this is a decision that affects the whole family, not just the girl. A refreshingly modern and human touch from a prep school that sends a fair few to the top girls' boarding schools.

Entrance: There are two entrance points: reception – a one form entry where 22 places are allotted by ballot (after taking into account siblings, which could mean that the number is easily halved), and year 3, when girls are selected after sitting the 7+ exam (in the January of year 2). About 400 girls are entered into the ballot, two years before entrance, which is then scrupulously and rigorously drawn – by the chair of governors, with the head, the bursar, the school secretary and a lawyer in attendance. No question of rigging, and absolutely no point in ensuring that little Emily can recite her 10 times table.

For year 3, about 200 register for 38 places. Assessments in English, maths and non-verbal reasoning are carried out in a relaxed way along with various activities which focus on team work and social interaction. The girls are carefully observed by a number of teachers and Mrs Lowe said, 'hand on heart', they weren't just looking for the most academically able and – don't choke on your skinny flat white – they have turned down girls despite their marks being among the highest. They are looking for girls who respond well to learning, with a positive and enthusiastic attitude. This is a school determined to maintain its mixed ability, academically non-competitive ethos (this and the ballot were the two non-negotiables in her interview, Mrs Lowe tells us).

No sibling preference at 7+ assessment, but school 'looks very carefully at sisters'. Occasional places thereafter are competed for by test, and the school has a waiting list for each year. Girls come from the local boroughs and as far as Barnes, Ealing, Kew, Putney, Wimbledon and north London. Vast diversity of backgrounds; the US and Asian contingent is fairly significant and a number are bilingual in combinations of French/Mandarin/Italian/German, to name but a few.

Exit: Majority go to St Paul's, then Godolphin & Latymer and Francis Holland SW. Even if they don't go there, these are the schools to which most parents aspire. The rest either usually board (though none in 2018) – Wycombe Abbey, Downe House, St Swithun's favourites – or go to other all girls' day schools eg Putney High, Lady Eleanor Holles. Recently greater interest among parents in co-ed – Latymer Upper is becoming increasingly popular. Interestingly, around the same proportion of those who enter at 4+ as those who come at 7+ go on to the most academic schools. Bute girls trail scholarships: 36 in 2018. Nine in music.

Remarks: One can be forgiven for thinking that this is the prep school for St Paul's Girls' School; it used to be years ago, but hasn't been since the 1950s, and it's a dangerous mistake to make. Although Bute is lucky enough to share the St Paul's swimming pool and some games pitches, and is only a stone's throw away, it is an entirely separate and distinct institution. You may have won the jackpot to get your daughter in here, in that she will have a fabulous education during her early years, but you haven't been granted a stepping stone into the hallowed halls of St Paul's Girls. There are no friendly ears to be bent. Iris will have as great a chance of getting in there from any of the good London preps as she does from Bute House.

An outstanding prep school, Bute House manages to combine solid substance with flair and panache. There is lots going on: the academics are excellent despite – or probably because of – its non-competitive ethos, but this is one of the most passionately competitive about sports of any of the girls' day schools we have seen. In the classroom, however, there is no setting, streaming or ranking, and marking is all done by comment: 'That's what contributes to the girls being so good and kind to each other – and makes it such an amazingly warm, happy and friendly place,' comments Mrs Lowe.

Learning support is known as 'learning enrichment' here – SEN and G&T girls occasionally removed from their lesson in order that their learning be 'enriched'. The head of the learning enrichment department is a SEN specialist, as are the other members of staff who both support those girls needing extra help and extend the more able girls. Teachers from the LED work in class alongside class teachers as well as sometimes taking groups of girls out of the classroom. The teaching is clearly, for the most part, inspired, and this is true of the learning enrichment programme too. Fifty-two girls are on the LE register, many needing only minimal support. This support is free. Those who don't speak English at home have one weekly support session. Some see the SENCo on a one-to-one basis and some in small groups. Ninety on the G&T register. School says that any difficulties are diagnosed early and dealt with as soon as possible.

We detected some sensitivity around the issue of special needs. The school says that it 'makes it clear in its parents' contract that girls with specific learning difficulties who need a great deal of additional support may be encouraged to look for another school that can meet their needs better'. School is keen to point out, however, that a dynamic SEN teacher coupled with a change in priority and ethos from the top means that everyone here gets the attention they need. However, there does appear to be some tension between the non-competitive academic ethos and the fact that ultimately this is an academic school with parents who have academic aspirations. Mrs Lowe asserts that early identification of any issues should enable all the girls to achieve highly, and she is especially keen to ensure that every girl achieves to the best of her ability. She says she also looks carefully at the transition from year 2 to 3, since this can cause anxiety for parents who perceive that the new intake may well be more academically able, and the flood of new girls will result in their daughter becoming 'lost'. The strong non-competitive academic ethos comes as a shock to a lot of parents who are attracted to the idea of Bute House as a top prep school with a history of a relationship with St Paul's – often in competitive professions themselves, they find themselves feeling frustrated not knowing whether Molly is top of the class or not.

Any competitive instincts can find an outlet in the sports programme, however. Bute girls are known in the prep school world to be formidable netball players and there is a D team as well as an A so everyone should get a chance to play. Some mutterings among mothers that this is not the case – but we suspect that the kudos of playing in the A team is such that both daughter and parents aspire to that. Gymnastics is also very popular and of a high standard. Although gym squad, run by external coaches, is only for the most talented, school says that those not in the squad have plenty of opportunity to be involved in gymnastics. Excellent sports facilities, especially considering its inner urban site, with use of St Paul's pool next door, and swimming is strong – plenty of squads and galas so that everyone gets a chance. Mrs Lowe attributes the excellent team spirit among the girls to the lack of competition in the classroom.

An innovative head of drama has been injecting some exploratory imaginative work into the drama curriculum; the class we saw were all lying on the floor with their feet in their air waving their arms. Head of music also young and energetic – a benign 'Jack Black school of rock' type, he arranges lots of different groups, bands and orchestras ('smiley strings', 'string fever', 'jammy jazzers' to name a few). Girls have class music twice a week from reception through to year 6 and most learn at least one instrument, from the double bass through to the bassoon.

Rich curriculum – everyone does French from reception, Spanish from year 5 but no Latin at all. Specialist teaching from reception in drama, music, sport and art (and DT) as well as French. Specialist science teaching from year 4 and proper DT facilities – saws, work benches, as well as a well-equipped art room – first class and unusual in a London prep school.

Huge superbly-equipped science lab and lots of outside space – netball courts as well as playgrounds, comfortable sitting areas and plenty of greenery. Every floor has stairwell storage for laptops, which are available for the girls to use when needed. Excellent library, well-stocked, well-organised (there are two librarians) and most importantly well-used. Lots of music rooms for lessons and practice. All the girls do one drama performance once a year. The show at the end of year 6 is a highlight, with a recent production being Annie.

C

The Bute building itself is a surprise – a somewhat futuristic 1950s neo-greenhouse farrago with add-ons in pine, pink render, louvred glass and warm-toned brickwork in a quiet Victorian terraced street just off fashionable Brook Green, five minutes from the Hammersmith jungle. It has a splendid atrium with the reception and offices and big screens with the news of the day, timetable changes etc; even the day's birthdays – rather nice. One eye catching and charming tradition is the corridor outside the hall, the walls of which are covered by little ceramic tiles, each one made by a Bute pupil as a record of their time at the school. The school, thereafter, in the head's words, 'is a bit of a Tardis' and one is not prepared by the hotch-potch exterior for the spaciousness – of each classroom, the immense hall and outside space as well as of the airiness and uncluttered feel of the whole.

The classrooms are a feast. Reception is big and there is plenty of space for everyone at the little tables and around the many activities. Everything is beautifully laid out – pencils in pots, a discovery table with 'new life in spring' exhibits – most remarkable – a canopied and cushioned book corner and lots of lovely dressing-up stuff including some pretty cool shoes. All the children use the garden, complete with lots of climbing things and a real – not a bouncy – castle and sandpit. Reception children have their own times when they also use large wheely toys. This is perhaps the most colourful school we know – everywhere are displays, pictures and models – all bursting with vitality, wit and fun. Many rooms, including the hall, are flexible, and divisible into two. All classrooms have smartboards and, oh joy! – all are air-conditioned. The girls eat in one half of the hall and drool over the food. 'It's just the best'..'it's cooked to perfection!' Free cucumber and carrot wedges are served at break and there are water-fountains inside and outside school.

If your daughter is lucky enough to get a place here she will have stimulating and exciting time, making good friends and building excellent foundations for her future. Your aspirations and ambitions need to be tempered, however; the school she ends up going to next will be right for her, but it may not necessarily be the one you had in mind when you set out on this odyssey.

The Camden School for Girls

Sandall Road, London NW5 2DB

Ages 11–19 **Pupils** 1,000 **Sixth form** 450 (150 boys)

020 7485 3414
www.camdengirls.camden.sch.uk

Headteacher: Since 2010, Elizabeth Kitcatt BA MA (Institute of Education), previously deputy head here and English teacher ('I still do a tiny bit of that'). Completed her probationary year at Walworth School in Southwark in the mid 80s where typical leavers' destinations were professional boxing or market stalls ('I learned to teach English without ever turning my back on the class,' she told the Association of State Girls' Schools.) First taste of leadership at the Archbishop Michael Ramsay school nearby, before moving north of the river as head of English at Parliament Hill School, where she 'immediately loved the pervading optimism about girls' potential and the sense that it was OK to be a feminist'.

'Not a natural extrovert,' commented a longstanding parent, 'and I think isn't comfortable in public settings or interviews.' (Indeed, she refused to meet the Guide, and most of her open day speech detailed the intricacies of the entrance procedures.) 'But she is grappling pretty well with real constraints on the budget.'

'Businesslike, very committed to the school's success,' said another parent. 'My girls like her but don't feel they know her.'

Academic matters: Successful applicants generally feel they have won the golden ticket. 'The teaching has been really impressive,' said a parent whose daughter had attended a private junior school. 'We didn't take the decision [to move her to a state school] lightly but we have no regrets.' In 2018, 49 per cent of GCSE grades were A*-A/9-7 and 96 per cent of girls got 9-4 in both English and maths ('very important, because it gives them a firm foundation to move on'), putting it in the top two per cent of comprehensives for both attainment and progress. No pretence here that exam results don't matter: posters extolling the latest successes were conspicuous at the open morning. 'Our very optimistic motto is Onwards and Upwards,' says the head. 'Education for all is still at the heart of what we do.'

French and Spanish for everyone in the first term of year 7; they choose one to continue from the spring term onwards. Classics in year 8, with options to study Latin or classical civilisation in year 9. Classical Greek is a twilight option (its continuation amidst budget cuts enabled by crowdfunding amongst parents). More vocational offerings at KS4 include health and social care and hairdressing and beauty therapy.

The main school intake is selected only by banding to achieve a balanced ability range. Some setting for maths from year 7, science and languages from year 8. 'They can move up or down so they know there's something at stake,' said a parent. At KS4 there's a small English group for those who need extra help.

'Years 7 and 8 were challenging in some ways,' a parent commented, 'but one of the things that impressed me the most was how well they integrate them and maintain a strong atmosphere of academic success and girl power.' 'I never felt she was held back,' said another. 'On the contrary, they were pushing her hard. They find a way of encouraging people at different levels.' 'I'm impressed with the education my daughters are getting and pleasantly surprised with the level of academic enquiry,' said a mother.

The sixth form is the jewel in the crown, with entry requirements to match for both internal and external applicants (a minimum of several grade 6s at GCSE) and a large external intake of boys and girls, many from independent schools. A largely traditional academic subject offering with a definite popularity bias towards the humanities, English and history attracting large numbers, though a good take up for maths too. Most take three A levels, though high flyers with mostly 7+ grades at GCSE may take four. In 2018, 49 per cent A*/A and 78 per cent A*-B grades.

Detailed individual higher education and careers advice for sixth formers, including those applying post-A levels. 'I got so much help from the UCAS officer and teachers, including what books to read, even though I applied to Cambridge after I'd left,' said an ex-student.

Support for those with SEN may consist of individual help in class or small group withdrawal for eg help with literacy, numeracy or settling in to year 7. 'Get in touch with our SENCo,' said head at open day. 'She will consult on whether we can meet your daughter's needs. We're very welcoming to a wide range of SENs – we do our best to be inclusive.' There's a range of lunchtime homework clubs with teachers available to lend a hand to anyone who feels the need for extra support.

Very low staff turnover – 'It is important to me that they could have the same teacher in year 7 and year 10,' said the head – and all maths and science teachers have a degree in their specialism, which is by no means a given nowadays.

Games, options, the arts: Music has always been high profile here, bolstered by those who come in on music places at year 7 and year 12. 'The teachers are fantastic,' said a parent. 'I'm often in tears at concerts because it's so moving what these girls can do.' Two orchestras, three choirs, chamber groups and a wind band have performance opportunities throughout the year, ranging from a chamber concert to the choral society and orchestra performing works such as Brahms Requiem or Haydn's Creation.

Drama is rather less in the spotlight, available as an A level but not a GCSE option, with public performances largely confined to the annual sixth form play and end of year whole school musical ('really impressive,' a parent commented). However, 'They encourage performance and speaking out loud,' said a pupil. 'By the end of year 7 or 8 most of us are quite confident, even those who were very shy when they joined.'

Art 'brilliant', with 60 per cent A*/A at A level in 2018 and 32 off to study art related courses. Eclectic and intriguing work displayed through the school. 'They know how to help you improve in your own way,' said an ex-student. The art displays, in a parent view, 'are more interesting than those at Central St Martins.' Photography an A level option, and a twilight course in the main school. DT includes textiles and resistant materials.

Not historically a sporty school, but a parent reported it is much improved – 'they've realised that sport is important.' Netball court and gym on site, but most sport takes place at the Cantelowes sports ground just across the road, where there's a floodlit Astro and a skateboard park where year 7s have lessons. Trampolining, netball, handball and basketball are all on the curriculum and teams compete in borough-wide competitions ranging from football (with an Arsenal team coach) to rounders and dodgeball, for the coveted Camden Shield. Professional dance tuition for year 7s, who put together a performance piece for the Borough Showcase; school-wide CSG Dance Company is by audition. There's a cross country team and lots go running on Hampstead Heath with the Highgate Harriers. Sporty year 8s and 9s are invited to spend a long weekend in Devon climbing and abseiling, raft building, wading through bogs.

Other school trips range from year 7s to the British Museum to GCSE geographers off to Iceland, linguists to Madrid and musicians to Italy.

Particular opportunities to broaden horizons at the top of the school. Weekly sixth form assemblies host speakers on 'current and divisive issues'. Tempting sixth form masterclasses have included Tamsin Greig on Shakespeare's Twelfth Night, Robert Peston discussing Why Brexit, Why Trump?, John Mullen on Charles Dickens and Jonathan Freedland asking Can you be a liberal and a Zionist? Year 12s are offered enrichment classes which range from football to debating to the history of ideas. 'We discussed really interesting things,' enthused a student. 'Anything from Dante's Divine Comedy to Israel and Palestine.'

Background and atmosphere: Founded in 1871 by renowned educationalist and suffragist Frances Mary Buss in her mother's home in Camden Street, as an affordable alternative to her other school, North London Collegiate. NLCS moved from Sandall Road out to Edgware in 1938; the Camden site was bombed during the second world war, and it was 1956 before CSG moved into the rebuilt school. Once a grammar school, it turned comprehensive in the late 1970s.

Compact site off the busy Camden Road with a motley collection of buildings, from the high-ceilinged, large-windowed Victoriana through 50s red-brick and 60s concrete and glass to the most recent redevelopment, the light and bright extended foyer and dining room. Outside – amidst the separate sixth form centre, music cottage, netball court and gym – includes grassy areas with benches where, say pupils, 'we eat lunch with our friends'.

No uniform (writer Fiona Millar remembers voting to abolish the bottle green uniform soon after she joined the school in the late 60s), liberal and progressive ethos, with all students encouraged to be politically aware and engaged in community action and activities. Influential school council organises events such as Pink Day (breast cancer awareness), International Women's Day and charity fundraising. 'They really do want you to get involved,' commented a parent. 'People feel very connected with the school and define themselves in terms of it.'

C

Pastoral care, well-being and discipline: Transition for new year 7s aided by a team-building trip to an outdoor activities centre. They often keep the same form tutor and head of year through the main school so can build strong relationships with them. Parents generally feel the school is proactive on pastoral care. One, whose daughter had had friendship problems in the early years, commented, 'they were really onto it – they'd chatted to the girls and had suggestions for me on helping her move forward. I was really glad they were on top of that and kept me in touch with what was going on with my daughter.' A pupil commented: 'There are cliques, but people will always help you even if you wouldn't hang out together.'

Broad range of leadership opportunities: alongside a sixth form leadership team that includes a head girl and boy plus senior prefects, there's a main school (year 11) head girl and her deputies, with a 'quick chat and a Kitkat' on offer to anyone who would like advice from a fellow student. Undoubtedly, some to struggle with anorexia and self harming, others with exam pressure, which the school does its best to counter (school counsellor and therapist available). 'We had a meeting with the head of year whose message was don't stress out – keep doing your hobbies and going on trips,' said a year 11 parent. 'We left the meeting feeling so much better.' Sixth form head is 'superb – progressive, warm, nothing is too much trouble,' say parents, with an open door policy 'if there's any hint of a problem.' 'It gives you a freedom that most high achieving schools don't,' said a student, 'but there's a real backbone of support.'

Pupils and parents: The sixth form may be, as one parent said, 'more like a private school', but the main school is hugely diverse ethnically and socially, including many middle class families who did a tactical move to the area during the late primary school years, plus large numbers who speak eg Bengali, Greek or Somali at home (the school has a Bengali liaison colleague). Some 30 home languages and around 40 per cent disadvantage figure (pupils eligible for free school meals during the last six years). Parents see this mix as one of the great advantages of the school. 'It made her so comfortable with every sort of religion and background.' 'I like the variety of it – it's a microcosm of the world...She's learning about privileges and gratitude and that's one reason why we put her into this school.'

Benefits from supportive and high flying parent body, characterised by the local left-leaning media and political classes plus 'glittering alumnae'. They all add 'huge cultural capital' as speakers, mentors and fundraisers, with anyone from Alastair Campbell to Natalie Haynes to Caroline Criado Perez dropping in to give a talk. Camden girls – including sixth form boys – tend towards the cool, confident and indie, strongly opinionated and sure of their place in the world.

Parents say: 'Very good for independent minded, critical students...Possibly not a good school for the very shy, who might find it all too overwhelming.' 'I don't know anyone who didn't come up with a good group of friends.' 'An eclectic and interesting group of girls.'

C

'They go off to extraordinary things,' said a parent. Alumnae include Ellie Rowsell (lead singer/guitarist of Mercury Prize winning Wolf Alice), Emma Thompson, Georgia Gould (leader of Camden Council), Arabella Weir, Tamsin Greig, Julia Hobsbawn and Julia Donaldson.

Entrance: At 11, everyone sits an assessment test which places them in one of four bands – 28 admitted from each band. Preference within this to those with an EHC plan naming the school; then looked after children; then siblings; then those with exceptional medical or social need. Eight music places: three offered to those scoring highest in musical aptitude test; next 50 invited back for a five minute instrumental performance audition to compete for other five places ('we're after a certain amount of technical fluency but musicality is more important'). Distance the tie-break for the remaining places – generally rather less than half a mile. CSG is definitely a school which people move (or pretend to move) house for. If that's your plan, living within a few feet of the gates is your only sensible course of action.

In the sixth form, Camden goes co-ed, admitting a further 150-170 new pupils (from about 1,000 applicants), no more than half of whom can be boys. Once again siblings are given precedence (but only if the sibling is still at the school on the date the applicant starts). Other places are dependent on distance from the gates, whether there's space in their chosen subjects, academic references and GCSE grades, predicted and actual (documentary proof required). Grade 6s essential in at least five subjects, including maths and English language. At this point, a further 15 music places on offer to those who play 'an orchestral instrument to a high standard.'

Exit: Quite a number leave at 16, either because they don't make the grade or because they prefer a sixth form college, apprenticeship or employment. Vast majority of leavers at 18 to further or higher education, including 17 to Oxbridge in 2018, seven medics and a dentist. Sussex particularly popular, as are art colleges and music schools.

Money matters: Camden is a voluntary aided school and has to contribute 10 per cent to its building costs. Parents give generously and there is an annual fundraising appeal, with monthly donations from £10. Plenty of further fundraising activities, too, where celebrity watching is the order of the day.

Remarks: Pulls off the difficult job of being a hugely popular, high achieving, all ability comprehensive. Benefits from the support of a greater range of well known and inspiring alumnae than most independent schools. As a parent said, 'There's a very special ethos.'

Cameron House School

4 The Vale, London SW3 6AH

Ages 4–11 **Pupils** 119

Fees: £18,465 pa

020 7352 4040
www.cameronhouseschool.org

Headmistress: Since April 2018, Dina Mallett, previously head of Cumnor House School for Girls for two years. She spent eight years as deputy head of City of London Girls' Prep and nine years at Dulwich Prep London.

Entrance: All children are assessed at 3, so no need to rush to get your baby onto a list; register up till a year before entry. A popular school – over 200 applicants for 20 places and school acknowledges how difficult it is to choose – 'It's heartbreaking to reject anyone.' Ultimately they look to create a class with a balance of the confident and the shy and some happily in between. They work closely with nurseries and rely on their reports (children come from a wide range including Pippa Poppins, Paint Pots, and Miss Daisy's). Putting school down as a genuine first choice always helps.

Exit: A few boys at 7+ or 8+ to, eg, boarding or Catholic schools (Ludgrove, St Philip's), but school actively discourages year 3 leavers so fewer and fewer now. School has fine tuned the 'stepping stones' options for boys who want to do 13+ common entrance and sends them for two years at 11 to, eg, Newton Prep, Fulham Prep, Sussex House, Wetherby or the Hampshire School Chelsea. Lots of advice given to parents from year 5 onwards.

At 11 girls and boys go to a broad range of schools each year – current favourites include St Paul's, Godolphin & Latymer, Westminster Under, Wycombe Abbey, Francis Holland, City of London and Alleyn's. They nearly always get their first choice school, we're told (due in large part to school's determination that parents choose the school that suits their child, whatever they themselves might prefer). 'And they interview beautifully because they're so confident.'

Remarks: A tiny (one class per year of about 20), cosy, pretty school, but don't be misled into thinking it's just chocolate boxy – Cameron House is a serious player in getting children into sought-after London schools. Wide range of ability, but what all children have in common is that they are confident and very, very smiley.

They are given a lot of preparation in the final year. In year 6, class sizes shrink so everyone gets more attention, compulsory homework club gives all children an extra hour at school and removes the pressure from the parents. 'We shoulder the worry, and the last thing we want is to see 10 year olds being counselled for stress.' A lot of staff channelled into year 6, when they do group work, prepare for scholarships, have mock interviews and confidence-building workshops. The formula clearly works – they get results, but no-one could describe this as a hothouse.

Approximately 15 children are helped with mild to moderate SEN – dyspraxia, dyscalculia, dysgraphia etc. The school takes a holistic approach. Learning support is timetabled and structured with clear IEPs drawn up – parents pay extra. Programme for the gifted and talented run within the class. In addition a select few are invited to join the Discovery Club and Explorers Club. Cautious approach to the gifted and talented programme. Children are identified towards the end of year 1 – 'We wouldn't want to have to say, "You weren't gifted after all!"'

A town house with not a great deal of space, but the soft plush tartan carpet throughout the stairwell, lavatories with pretty wallpaper, water filters, attractive blue furnishings and every teacher referred to by their first names – without even a Miss or Mister attached – give the school a homely, uninstitutional feel.

Children have fun here, whether it's enjoying music, drama or sport, watching caterpillars transmorph into butterflies or playing giant magnetic chess in the playground (a good excuse to see the lovely Dina, to get the chess pieces). Even maths can be made to be an excuse to dress up and laugh – Bubbles the maths clown visited, the hall was filled with balloons and children came to school dressed as shapes. In Book Week everyone dresses up.

Nearly everyone plays an instrument or has singing lessons – the lessons happen in a little Wendy house type hut in the playground. Major dramatic productions – The Lion King, A Midsummer Night's Dream among them – take place in a closely guarded secret venue – 'Let's just say a theatre off Kensington High Street,' is as far as school will be drawn. 'We aim high' – list of impressive artistic accomplishments for such a small school includes getting to the final for young choir of the year at the Royal Festival Hall. They have an orchestra, string quartet and three choirs.

One of school's challenges has been to stop the boys leaving at 7+ or 8+ – signs of success. Although previous year 6 classes have had few boys, some none at all, when we visited there were an equal number of both sexes. 'Parents are starting to realise that they can get their boys into Westminster Under, St Paul's Juniors or Latymer at 11, and there are plenty of stepping stone options between 11 and 13.' Children are kept a lot more active here than at many similar schools. Games takes place three times a week – children can do cricket, football, hockey and netball as well as martial arts in the huge loft space at the Boudokwai centre. Lots of matches (most of which they lose, commented one parent) but the advantage of being a small school is everyone gets to have a go – it's not just the sporty types who do everything.

A lot of expat families, mainly from the US, Canada and Australia, reflecting the cosmopolitan area. We saw masses of glamorous long-haired mothers off to the gym after drop off. Lots of City types, but also more than the usual number of creatives – artists and actors, as well as doctors and art dealers. All parents are very involved and enjoy the open door policy of the school.

A charming school that will discover your child's strengths, nurture and support them.

Canbury School

Kingston Hill, Kingston, Surrey KT2 7LN

Ages 11–19 **Pupils** 56 (39 boys, 17 girls) **Sixth form** 7

Fees: £16,893 pa

020 8549 8622
www.canburyschool.co.uk

Headmistress: Since 2014, Louise Clancy BEd. Spent 11 years as deputy head of Greenacre School for Girls, Surrey. Has taught at some challenging comprehensives. Teaches GCSE art and design. Described by one parent as 'down to earth. She just loves the children.' Another said, 'Her office is in the middle of the school and she hears and see exactly what is going on. The children like the fact that she is accessible and often pop into her office for a chat. She's easy to talk to but everyone respects her.' Married to a retired policeman. Two grown up daughters; one works in theatre and one in commerce. Now a doting grandmother. Enjoys baking and cooking, which she finds therapeutic, and is a dab hand at portrait painting. Loves travelling, with a soft spot for Cyprus.

Relishes being head here. 'I wanted to be a head of a small school where I could know each child's name. I just fell in love with Canbury,' she confesses. Ambitious for her school. Very keen to improve the teaching and learning on offer – wants it to go from good to outstanding on her watch. Parents feel she has turned the school around and believe she is determined to transform it further still.

Academic matters: A mainstream co-ed independent school that is able to support pupils of all academic abilities, especially those with SEN. 'We have a reputation for working with teenagers who have needs but are not special needs teenagers. This makes us different,' explains head. Pupils generally take a maximum of nine GCSEs. Due to size of school, results vary greatly from year to year, depending upon cohort. In 2018, 73 per cent of pupils achieved grades 9-4 in maths and English; seven per cent of grades were A*-A/9-7. Science viewed as particularly strong, as are creative subjects.

'We are an independent school. We just do everything on a smaller scale.' School is good at targeting the differing needs of the individual pupils. Everything is done with the intention of making the curriculum as accessible to each pupil as possible. 'We personalise and adapt the curriculum, where we can. We teach to their strengths and we are continually reviewing the students' needs,' says head. Science lessons, for example, are practical-heavy as most pupils are kinaesthetic learners. School offers Spanish as it is considered more accessible than French. For those who struggle with foreign languages, there is also the option of taking a BTec qualification in travel and tourism. 'We don't want their confidence to plummet, so we offer an alternative where we can.'

One parent commented, 'The school is incredibly accommodating. They teach foundation and higher-level GCSEs at the same time, which must be a challenge'. Another parent said at times her son felt some lessons could be better, but overall most teaching was good. 'Spanish is excellent and maths clinic was a blessing. It meant my son could go over trickier topics again, often on an individual basis, which he found really helpful.' Maths is taught in mixed ability classes for first three years, then set thereafter.

Head explains, 'We do have a range of students with quite different needs. Some have no special needs at all but like being in a smaller school. They have looked at bigger schools and felt they were not for them'. Pupils have a variety of difficulties including slow processing, OCD, dyslexia, dyspraxia, autistic spectrum disorder and cerebral palsy. Others have health issues including transplant patients who need a gentler environment where they will not get knocked about in the corridors. Students with high anxiety and school refusers also come here to be nurtured. School does not take on children with behavioural problems. 'Our pupils are happy, and I won't take on new students who will disrupt our existing students. We do not accept children who are violent, and nor do we take children with complex needs as we are too small. No intimate care offered. We only take pupils if we feel we can meet their needs,' states head matter-of-factly. She explains, 'We have able children who can't always get it down on paper. They just need extra support and they do well academically here.'

Many pupils arrive in a vulnerable state with shattered confidence, for a variety of reasons. Head describes how 'some arrive broken and we make them whole again. When they leave, they are fully functioning, productive members of society.' Pupils are very accepting of each other's needs.

New sixth form since September 2018, offering a bespoke curriculum.

Games, options, the arts: Plenty of sport offered, with five hours a week in key stage 3 and three hours in key stage 4. Weekly swimming lessons for first couple of years. Kayaking on the Thames and rock climbing also on offer for the more adventurous. Swimming galas, cross-country championships and sports days aplenty. Highly competitive house sport. School also regularly participates in borough events and some pupils perform at national level. Mixed teams, often made up of boys and girls from different year groups. Where possible, Richmond Park used for games lessons as well as school's own playground, with a wonderfully bouncy surface.

Strong performing arts programme that mixes creativity with technology. Christmas entertainment is mostly student-led, where the teachers provide a skeleton of the production and pupils are expected to do everything else. Head convinced one of the many advantages of being a small school is that all pupils can take on a leading role. 'Everyone here gets the chance to be the star of the show!' she smiles.

Stunning artwork throughout school, including a huge mural of the headmistress. One girl proudly showed us her immaculate portfolio, bursting with striking images and thoughtful write-up. Photography very popular and school has own kiln. Students from nearby Kingston University come into Canbury to collaborate on projects with pupils.

Music taken seriously. Pupils were rehearsing enthusiastically for school concert on the day we visited, and parents feel the 'singing is beautiful at Canbury'. Head comments, 'We have extraordinary pupils doing extraordinary things.'

Clubs to suit all tastes including doodling, Minecraft, karate, yoga and nail varnish art (which acts as an informal communication club). Duke of Edinburgh award offered to silver level.

School bends over backwards to ensure all pupils get chance to go on annual overseas trip. 'No child is denied the experiences on offer.'

Background and atmosphere: Founded in 1982 by John Wyatt and housed in a large Edwardian villa on Kingston Hill. When founding headmaster retired in 1997, an educational charitable trust was set up, with a board of governors.

Maximum class size is 13. Currently many more boys than girls but ratio fluctuates. One parent admitted that 'at times, the small size of the school has been frustrating for my son. He would have liked a larger group from which to make friends. It can be limiting.' Up to two adults per classroom. Speech and language and occupational therapists come in regularly, as does a counsellor.

Buildings a little frayed around edges but renovations imminent. Massive ground floor refurbishment planned to include new reception and school hall, flooring and lighting. Rooms are mostly multi-functional. Facilities include a fully kitted-out science lab, ICT room overflowing with Apple Macs and a stairlift. Study Support Suite, housed in the attic, is an oasis of calm where pupils are supported on a one-to-one basis and in small groups. No school kitchen due to lack of space.

Pupils seem unconcerned by lack of space. On the day we visited, pupils were happily playing at break time in the playground with balls flying in all directions. Much laughter and ready smiles in the corridor. Children seemed genuinely delighted to be here. On spotting the head, pupils bounded up to her and could not wait to share with her how they had found their GCSE exams that morning.

Pastoral care, well-being and discipline: A supportive and caring environment. One parent told us, 'My son had missed a lot of school and had had a terrible time before he came here. He has blossomed at Canbury. He has done everything he should do at school, and more. They certainly know how to get the best out of the kids.'

School is hot on discipline and British values are upheld. Manners are important here. Uniform reintroduced by current head. Mobiles banned apart from at break times and lunch. Once a pupil caught with a cigarette was sent home immediately. Another who had shaved his head was made to stay at home until his hair had grown back. No tolerance for inappropriate use of internet. 'If behaviour is good, they learn,' believes head. The pupils we met were polite and friendly and clearly felt at ease with their teachers. Hands-on head who is quick to tell pupils to smarten up if shirts are hanging out or ties are at half-mast. When pupils need to cool off, members of staff take them for a walk in Richmond Park to clear their heads. 'We don't mollycoddle them,' says head. 'We treat them like all the other teenagers in the country but when they fall, we catch them.'

School is keen to praise its pupils at every opportunity. They are given responsibility with a prefect team headed by head boy and head girl. Success is recognised through house points and badges on school blazers. Headmistress's letter is the ultimate reward. Achievements are celebrated in assembly and prize-giving.

Pupils and parents: Most come from within a 10 mile radius, in particular from Barnes, Putney, Wandsworth, Kingston and Hampton as well as central London, but becoming increasingly local. A sprinkling from overseas. Head says parents are highly supportive and raise huge sums for the school. Current parents are teachers, barristers, solicitors, politicians as well as some media folk.

Parents generally feel they are kept in the loop via weekly newsletter, though one mother complained that parents were not informed early enough about a teacher leaving. Talks regularly put on for parents, including how to cope with teenage anxiety.

Entrance: Non-selective. Pupils come here from a wide number of feeder schools including Parsons Green Prep, Hurlingham School, Finton House and the Lycée. Main point of entry is year 7, though pupils accepted mid-year if there is space.

Prospective pupils join in classes for the day where teachers set 'a number of tasks to establish the student's current level of ability in a variety of subjects'. Online diagnostic assessments also demonstrate the way pupils learn and their potential. Behaviour and interaction with other students are also important in deciding whether school can offer the pupil a place. Sometimes further assessment days are needed before a decision can be made.

Most special needs are identified prior to pupils arriving here but further assessments are carried out in year 7 and extra support is then put in place. Head is very frank with parents from the off and personally shows all families around. She wants parents to be aware of what school can and cannot provide.

Exit: Roughly 80 per cent continue their education at sixth form, with others going on to apprenticeships, and a significant number progress to university. Pupils' destinations have included Blossom House, Carshalton Boys', Coombe Sixth Form, Esher College, More House in Frensham, MPW, Richmond College, Waldegrave and St John's Leatherhead; they can now stay on in the new sixth form. One parent felt the head has a good knowledge of suitable schools for her son and was supportive in helping find the right place for him. School tries hard to help pupils find relevant work experience and one pupil we spoke to was bubbling over with enthusiasm about her placement in a local primary school.

Money matters: Small number of bursaries up to a maximum of one-third reduction of fees available, to both current and prospective pupils.

Remarks: This school genuinely transforms lives. One parent commented, 'It has literally been a life saver for my son. They believed in him from the start. I can't speak highly enough of the school.' Another parent enthused, 'Canbury has allowed my son to be the man he should be.' Head says, 'We are the best kept secret in south west London, but the message is getting out. We're being talked about. We really are a school like no other.' School motto sums up school perfectly: 'Unique. Happy. Inclusive.' A remarkable place.

The Cardinal Vaughan Memorial School

89 Addison Road, London W14 8BZ

Ages 11–18 **Pupils** 964 **Sixth form** 357 (152 girls) **RC**

020 7603 8478
www.cvms.co.uk

Headmaster: Since 2011, Paul Stubbings MA. Educated at Worcester Grammar school and Durham University, where he read classics. His conversation is littered with his experiences of 'damascene' moments – his love of Latin and Greek, his vocational calling to become a teacher. One wonders (though he didn't say it) whether it was a similar enlightened moment that drove him to fight for the headship and steer the school away from the dangerous rocks of conflict between the Westminster diocese and a section of the governing board. He certainly stepped into the breach when horns were locked over a tussle between whether the school should be a 'pan London Catholic school' or whether priority should be given to local residents of the borough. He was promoted from deputy head, pastoral – aka the enforcer, and feared by many in the role. He refers to himself in that incarnation as 'the chief chastiser – good at scaring kids, but not nastily'. One former parent described him at this time as a sergeant major, famous for issuing multiple detentions as snowballs flew on one of those rare fun-filled winter days. A smooth negotiator is certainly not the role one would immediately assume for him, but since he has taken the reins the school has been running without much jolting, and both parents and staff are delighted. He is completely 'home grown', and has taught here in various roles since his teaching practice placement in 1988. He officially started as a classics teacher in 1989 and still teaches Latin to year 7.

Since morphing into the top man, he sees himself as more of an avuncular figure to the students and confesses that he misses the ongoing day-to-day bustle. However, he embraces having to articulate the direction of the school and describes his vision as the replication of qualities of Cardinal Vaughan himself – namely his energy and foresightedness, firmly rooted in a Catholic foundation. He regards the school as embodying the best of tradition and 'the old', whether is be the traditional hierarchy or the gowns the teachers still wear. 'The only times hierarchies don't work,' he says, 'is when they cease to be benevolent'. However, he acknowledges that change cannot be avoided: 'I have to row this school forward in order for it to stay the same'.

As we left his large modern study, he with a flourish of his gown, two boys were waiting outside whom he confided he was about to exclude. The lines here are straight and inflexible, and if you cross them you can be in no doubt of the consequences.

Academic matters: Consistently impressive results and school makes no bones about aiming for academic excellence in its comprehensive intake. Sunday Times continues to rate it as the highest attaining comprehensive school in the country. School has specialist status in mathematics and IT and computing is BIG here – computer science is now part of the curriculum – an innovation that puts paid to the any suspicion that the school might be stuck in the past. A level results 78 per cent A*-B grades, 51 per cent A*/A in 2018. Range of subjects offered not immense but includes economics, music tech, Latin, philosophy and sociology. It has to be said that the 'newer' subjects do not attract vast numbers. School also offers applied A level in business – Bs for most. Most popular – and successful – A level subjects are maths and Eng lit, both astonishingly good. GCSEs: again not a huge range of options – French and Spanish now the only modern langs, though Latin thrives and Greek is available at GCSE. Most popular subjects are engineering – a double qualification – French and ICT. Everyone takes RS. In 2018, 55 per cent 9-7 grades overall. And remember, this is a comprehensive school.

This degree of success is not achieved by having independent school sized classes. In the lower school class sizes are 28-30, though music, DT, art and IT groups have 20 pupils. At KS4, class sizes vary but core subjects are taught in groups of 25-30. Most sixth form classes are under 20. Girls and boys seem to achieve similarly though there are some mutterings about sixth formers being 'encouraged' to drop subjects rather than continuing to A level if it is felt they are unlikely to do well. Accolades abound – the Vaughan is in the top 20 of just about every league table, often near the top. It is regularly named 'top Catholic comp in the country' by those who have such plaudits to give away. Parents and pupils, for the most part, add to the encomia. No-one could eulogise the school's shiny new facilities – apart from all the IT stuff – or accommodation. The level of achievement here is down to the quality of the teaching and the staff and pupils' pride in the place. We heard of 'lovely teachers', the good monitoring of progress and much high praise, especially of the music dept. Bright pupils speak warmly of their 'inspiring' teachers – 'they are amazing – best in the business' – and they mean it.

All applicants are tested – to ensure that school takes across the ability range and to better enable banding once they arrive. School takes 'more than our fair share of children with an EHC plan' and it is a beacon of hope for those parents of children with significant difficulties, seeming, as it does, to offer real education in a compassionate community. Majority with SEN, though, are mild dyslexics and dyspraxics. Who goes where is decided, of course, by the LA but school is concerned about the sheer additional physical space taken by extra LSAs who accompany some of the children with more severe SEN. And this is understandable. Many rooms are small and rather poky and corridors are not spacious. Busy SENCo and others give in-class support but parents give mixed reports. One parent felt that her dyspraxic son's problems were picked up very late and that the support he was subsequently offered was barely adequate. Similar reports from others. School, however, tells us that such comments are 'vastly outweighed by parents delighted with our SEN arrangements'. School unashamed of its high octane essence. 'Here we have traditional, hothouse academic teaching. It can be a bit of a shock for those who come in from outside.' G&T pupils offered Greek – where else in the state system is this a growth area?

Games, options, the arts: Despite having to travel for 30 minutes on a bus (to Twickenham) for rugby and football, these sports are not only popular but also strong. Vaughan teams are not to be messed with and are widely respected by their competitors in West London. The first XI recently won the cup in the QPR league, the second XI, no slouches either, won the shield. Athletics and cricket in the summer. Fixtures on Saturday mornings, though if you get a detention you are in danger of being dropped from the team – no leeway there. There is also a gymnasium on site in the 1990s extension known as the Pellegrini building, painted in bright blues and turquoises;

the well-known 'boys at games' fragrance welcomed us as we observed a volleyball game. Rock climbing, basketball, table tennis also on offer. Girls in the sixth form can play netball, and some do rock climbing.

C

Several parents referred to a divide in the school between the 'sporty' and the 'musical' side. Music is certainly as keenly practised, respected and given an equal, if not even greater status as sport, and we were very impressed both with the sumptuous musical facilities and the array of opportunities for performance. When we visited there was great excitement as the head of music rushed in to show Mr Stubbings an article in the Financial Times about a carol composed by one of their 15 year olds and performed on Radio 3. Large practice rooms and smart rooms for performance. There are several grand pianos for simple practice, you understand, and a plethora of choirs from the elite Schola Cantorum – replete with claret-coloured cassocks and leather-bound hymn sheets, providing music for the school's liturgies – to the sixth form choir and the school choir. As well as a full orchestra, chamber orchestra and various trios, there is the hugely busy Big Band that performs in concerts and events all over London.

Various venues are used for concerts including the Albert Hall, Cadogan Hall, St John Smith Square and Westminster Cathedral. The Schola goes on regular tours outside the UK, including Italy – all the grandest places in Rome – plus Spain, Greece, Holland, Germany, the USA and France. The Schola now has its own Songschool – just like in a regular cathedral choir school – in which the choir rehearses; a real boon. Those with a talent for singing also get the opportunity to sing in operas at the Royal Opera House as well as the ENO; recent productions have included La Bohème, Die Zauberflote and Carmen. More light hearted musical productions take place in the summer – Guys and Dolls, Sweeney Todd, The Pyjama Game, to name a few. Other than the annual musical there is little drama to speak of – never a strength here and not an academic subject. School's original main building began life as a theatre and we wondered why so little use is made of it in this way – the stage and gallery are intact, if a little dog-eared. Good art: we liked what we saw of the ceramics, sculpture, mobiles, printing et al – lively creative stuff – and equally good DT: wood, metal and plastic work. Three workshops and lots of benches means there is plenty of room to work and create. Engineering and graphics popular at GCSE – this is where lots of that work takes place. Plenty of imaginative and rewarding extracurricular trips and visits – especially for the musicians; parents glow.

Background and atmosphere: The Vaughan is located in posh Holland Park – wide, quiet streets lined by well-appointed Victorian villas and mansion blocks. Shepherd's Bush, on the other side of the monster roundabout round the corner, is a world away, whereas Kensington High Street – about 15 minutes walk the other way – seems a natural neighbour. Founded in 1914, the school is a memorial to the third Archbishop of Westminster, Herbert, Cardinal Vaughan. It began life as an independent school with 29 pupils but became a grammar school in 1944 and a comprehensive in 1977. Girls were first admitted to the sixth form in 1980 and their presence is firmly established. They are not just a token presence, either – the ratio is 60 boys to 40 girls, which is significantly higher than their cousin school in the neighbouring borough. No chance of going co-ed throughout – simply no room. The original building – Addison Hall, which Mr Stubbings affectionately refers to as Hogwarts – was a musical theatre, but its exterior – possibly what attracted its purchasers – is more reminiscent of a Rinascimento palazzo in pink stone. It now boasts an entrance with highly-wrought grillwork in which the school's motto, Amare et Servire, and crest are displayed. The Old Building, as it is known, houses years 11-13. The New Building was built in the 1960s and much added to since then. It has an attractive exterior with a pretty little garden and an impressive reception area, which abuts the main hall – full of pupils on supervised private study when we visited – no 'free' periods here. DT and IT are housed in the Pellegrini Building, named after a former head. Some roomy places inside but the overall impression is of a rather cramped school with little space – especially outside – and many rather bleak areas.

Situated in these leafy, pricey avenues, you'd expect an upmarket local school population. But it isn't so. School takes from all over, some travel from as far as the northern reaches of Barnet, Harrow and Hillingdon, others from the furthest reaches of Southwark, Merton and Kingston. The only common denominator is a commitment to the Roman Catholic faith. Previous head was wearily, but pugnaciously, defensive of the charge of being socially or academically elitist. He wrote, 'people ask why our pupils' performance goes so far beyond national averages. After all, our top results at A level and at GCSE, over the last five years, have improved six times more than national results. Is it because, as some would like to believe, we "cherry pick" pupils from privileged backgrounds? I don't think so.' Mr Stubbings, too, is often accused of running an elitist school, with only some eight per cent of pupils on free school meals (against 21 per cent in the local authority as a whole). His retort? Selection is random.

The life of the school is imbued with its Roman Catholic inspiration. Everywhere are photographs of pontiffs, cathedrals and the school's own choir singing in various glorious cathedrals. Year groups go on retreats at Tyburn Convent and at Farm Street and the school day and week are punctuated by regular mass, confession, Benedictus, Angelus and so on – all lessons begin and end with the Sign of the Cross and some teachers have prayers in each of their lessons – to a degree rare even in RC schools. But there is also a spirit of enquiry. Vaughan pupils address seriously 'the Dawkins delusion', 'the problem of free will' and 'the just war theory'. Philosophy pupils attend Heythrop College for talks on philosophy of religion, epistemology and ethics, and theology pupils explore the history of Israel. The ethos is embraced and warmly defended by pupils when appropriate. They are aware of the privilege of being here and of the secular – and other – pressures that might have it otherwise. While most parents express great satisfaction with the school in general, we heard a few murmurs from those who are less than ecstatic. 'It's fine as long as all goes well'.. 'they're not brilliant at dealing with problems'.. 'they're not great at getting back to you' (school says, 'we pride ourselves on excellent communications with parents and prompt responses to their queries') and 'it's best for the really bright'. School warmly disputes this too. And most are truly grateful for what they receive.

Pastoral care, well-being and discipline: Discipline couldn't be much tighter. The boundaries are clear and few transgress. Immediate expulsion for 'supply' of drugs – sharing them with a friend; fixed term exclusion for possession. 'We don't have a drug problem in this school because they know the score,' asserts Mr Stubbings. The senior sixth former who was our guide was so concerned with punctuality that he didn't allow us to admire the work in the art room. The atmosphere is orderly and you could hear a pin drop walking through the corridors during lesson time, despite the open doors into the class rooms. Occasional bullying is 'firmly and speedily dealt with'. The occasional idiot caught smoking in the streets – sixth form pupils are allowed out of school in breaks – is punished. 'If they're in my uniform it'll be exclusion,' says Mr Stubbings. We saw lots of Vaughan pupils out and about and they definitely do not frighten the horses. 'Old-fashioned good manners' expected and, in general, displayed. Catholic ethos underpins everything and is palpable. Sex ed taught 'by the RS dept for the moral side and the science dept for the biological details'. Four houses – Campion, Fisher, Mayne and More.

Pupils and parents: Pupils come from a wide area covering most of London, some from as far away as Hertfordshire and Surrey. Around half are from ethnic minority groups. Some 30 per cent speak English as an additional language. Here the offspring of a few of the well-heeled 'old' RC families from Kensington learn alongside those of their Filipino, Portuguese or Spanish live-in domestic staff and the children of Irish immigrants from Wembley, in a context hard to find elsewhere. Parents very appreciative of parents' evenings when teachers come to find them rather than the usual ghastly queuing for a two minute slot with a glazed-eyed teacher. Notable former pupils include actors Richard Greene – Robin Hood in earlier days – and Roger Delgado, footballers Bernard Joy of Arsenal and Fulham and the last amateur to represent the England national football team, Paul Parker, Kevin Gallen of QPR and Eddie Newton, novelist Helen Oyeyemi and comedian Dominic Holland. Also WWII flying aces Donald Garland VC and Paddy Finucane DSO and recent Olympic rowing gold medallists Martin Cross and Gary Herbert. Many seem, however, to have careers in the City.

Entrance: Pupils come from over 50 schools. Around 830 apply for the 120 places at 11+. At sixth form, around four apply for every place. Most of the sixth form entrants will be girls – lots from Sacred Heart – and the entrance requirements at that stage are primarily academic, although they do have to have been baptised and a priest has to attest to mass attendance – 9-6s at GCSE in the subjects they will study in the sixth. School has long been (in)famous for the rigour of its admissions' criteria and stories abound of devoted little church-goers being rejected on account of imperfect catechism or knowledge of parables. 'Nonsense!' bellows school. Early baptism (within six months of birth), weekly attendance at mass, holy communion – all are taken for granted in applicants; no mention now of the 'family involvement' that was so contentious. Applicants split into three ability bands, 12 music places. School uses 'random allocator' for the 70 or so places that remain after priority places have been taken (Catholic children in care, siblings etc).

Exit: A regular mighty handful to Oxbridge (14 in 2018), all doing solid subjects at real colleges. Most of the rest to heavyweight universities to do heavyweight subjects – such as law at King's, maths at Imperial etc plus medics and vets – and a sensible fistful to eg sports psychology at Bournemouth. A notable number to architecture and engineering. Some 10 per cent leave after GCSEs – most to join other schools, a few to employment, another few to other RC colleges.

Money matters: School asks for a voluntary contribution for the Governors' Fund and the vast majority stumps up – some more, some less, but no-one comes after you if you don't. A few instrumental bursaries for sixth form entrants who must have reached at least grade 6 on an orchestral instrument.

Remarks: Some see the Vaughan as a 'quasi grammar school' and its cousin in Fulham as a 'quasi public school'. Whatever label you attach to it, our view is that it is the kind of school many parents in London are crying out out for but few, very few, ever find. A unique opportunity if you are lucky enough to qualify, however it won't suit all boys. Be sure your son is someone who responds to rigorous discipline and doesn't flake (or rebel) under stern authority.

Central Foundation Boys' School

32

C

Cowper Street, City Road, London EC2A 4SH

Ages 11–18 **Pupils** 780 **Sixth form** 176 (24 girls)

020 7253 3741
www.centralfoundationboys.co.uk

Head: Since 2010, Jamie Brownhill LLB (40s). Originally a lawyer, he worked as a construction litigator for city law firm Mayer Brown before training as a teacher at CFB in 2000. 'I wouldn't have gone to just any school,' he says. 'It was very much a sense of vocation and moral purpose that leads one from being a city lawyer to such a challenging environment.' And lucky for the school that he did make that choice – after just five years at the top he'd completely turned it around.

Extremely visionary and not one for small talk, he is prone to sounding as if he's permanently giving a speech, making big, sweeping statements ('One needs to have a vision and follow it through'; 'There's a recognition that a head has an incredible impact' etc), which make him an impressive orator. 'Even in the corridors, he has important words of wisdom,' one pupil told us. Parents talk about being 'blown away' by him. One said, 'Our older sons were educated privately and we looked round 15 schools for our youngest, including private, selective and comprehensives – but this one stood out head and shoulders above the rest, largely because of Brownhill. He sets the tone, the culture and the expectations within the school and we love his inclusiveness, his energy, drive and commitment.' Praise indeed. Another commented, 'We love the fact that he's from the outside world – it gives him a much broader perspective than heads who have spent their entire careers within education.'

Rare is the day that pupils don't have some contact with him – he greets them every morning, runs weekly whole-school assemblies, teaches history to the lower years and he's usually out and about during changeover and break times. His office even overlooks the playground. Staff say he has a finger in every pie (which one admitted can be as frustrating as it is helpful), but ultimately they agree it's enabled him to make the school what it is, with the systems he's brought in for the likes of behaviour and targeting being described as 'nothing short of brilliant.'

Academic matters: GCSE performance has put this school in the top 10 per cent of schools nationally for added value, while the sixth form results mean the school is in the top 15 per cent of KS5 providers in the country – very impressive for an inner city comprehensive with 65 per cent pupil premium (in fact, it was nearer 80 per cent when the head joined). In 2017, 87 per cent got 9-4 in both English and maths; and 34 per cent of grades were 9-7, with the strongest results in maths, English, science and computing.

French or Spanish from year 7, with after-school provision available in the other. After-school classes also available for Mandarin, Arabic and ancient Greek (all of which can also be done at GCSE), though few continue languages to A level. Setting in English, maths, science, languages, geography and history from year 7, with a reassuring amount of movability. Homework in abundance – building up from an hour in year 7 to two hours in year 11 – and woe betide any student who doesn't hand it in on time.

In 2017, 68 per cent A*-B grades at A level and impressive 43 per cent A*/A. Subject choices are largely traditional – sciences, maths, economics and computing most popular – but the school is part of the Islington Sixth Form Consortium, meaning there's the opportunity to study the likes of photography, psychology, media studies and a whole wealth of languages at one of the other member schools.

C

Head believes the school's success is largely down to maximum class sizes of 24, plus the major push on the fundamentals in year 7 and 8, which ensures literacy, maths and learning habits (how you revise; how you organise homework etc) are up to scratch, ready for GCSE learning (unlike at so many other schools, where the overt focus is on years 10 and 11). 'It seems to me that the importance of learning is at the heart of every single piece of communication with the boys,' one parent told us. Perhaps this explains why the boys we spoke to were not only enthused about their studies, but able to directly relate them to their futures.

Lessons, which are all taught by subject specialists (most of whom have firsts or 2:1s in their degrees), are well-planned and, according to students, engaging. 'If you don't respond well to a teacher's learning style, they'll adapt it for you,' one told us, whilst several pointed out that teachers are always available by email or after school to go over anything you don't understand.

Teachers say they are helped by the centralised system for dealing with behaviour (same-day detentions even for small transgressions), along with a painstaking focus on tracking and monitoring, which they say means they can get on with the job in hand. Very few teaching assistants – they tend to be used on a temporary basis for getting a child's behaviour sorted. There's a mixed diet of practical, interactive lessons and heads-down learning. Food tech, for example, always involves cooking, whereas in the maths and languages lessons we witnessed, it was very much a case of chalk and talk.

SEN provision – which covers the usual dyslexia, ASD etc – is almost exclusively classroom based (and helped by those small class sizes, as well as setting) and offers exceptional outcomes for students, evidenced by the results. 'I couldn't have asked for better help throughout my son's education,' said one mother, whose son is dyslexic. 'He's had the "Why me?" moments when he's had to work much harder, but the school keeps him positive, as well as making sure he has attainable goals and extra support and time where he needs it. Dyslexia has certainly never made him feel he can't achieve as much as anyone else.'

Games, options, the arts: Football and basketball are the top sports, with boys doing CFB proud when it comes to competing against other schools. Cricket is on the up and there's also fencing, boxing, martial arts, table tennis and gym workouts. Whilst the school is good at playing to the boys' strengths (hence winning all those high level competitions), the head is adamant that sport here is for all. 'There's no stereotypical male bravado around sport at this school. In short, you don't get the jocks,' said one parent. On-site facilities include an undercover Astroturf pitch, running track, a couple of gyms and two halls. Off-site, the boys do climbing, swimming and more. 'When a young person leaves here, they really know how to access the community's facilities,' says the head.

Music is integral to school life. Incredibly, every boy who wants to can borrow an instrument for the duration of his time at the school. We're not just talking recorders, but cellos, saxophones and clarinets. No wonder 150 students are heavily involved with the department. From 7.30am every day, there are rehearsals, whether for the three school choirs, orchestra, bands (including house band and concert band), string quartets, woodwind groups etc. The department's equipment is sophisticated and there's a 10-strong staff team, including two full-time music teachers. Expect to see a raised eyebrow if you use the word 'peripatetic' to describe the visiting teachers – this dedicated team say this is the only school in London they work in, where they are considered part of the school community – the result of which is that they are more than willing to put extra time in for the three main performances per year. Parents describe these performances as 'amazing.' 'We nearly all had tears in our eyes at the last one,' one parent told us. External opportunities range from singing in the Royal Albert Hall to providing the musical entertainment for local law firm functions. While many of the musical children are also academic, others aren't – and music gives them a great opportunity to excel.

A delightful art room is home to some serious artistic talent – much of it bold, brave and inspiring. Drama also thriving, with weekly lessons for years 7, 8 and 9 in the two-roomed, carpeted drama studio. There are three main performances per year, providing opportunities for both pupils in the lower and upper years. Debating strong; they were national schools Debate Mate champions recently and were third out 250 schools in a recent competition when we visited.

Day visits to all the usual museums and galleries that this school has on its doorstep, as well as French and Spanish trips (year 9, 10 and 11), an annual ski trip open to all and a rural activity trip for sixth formers. Extracurricular provision focuses on music and sport in the main, with other options ranging from cooking (particularly popular) to arts club and gaming to drama. The school takes full advantage of its location, with excellent links with the City.

Background and atmosphere: There could hardly be a more unlikely location for a school – smack in the middle of the City. Squeezed between, and overlooked by, law buildings and financial institutions, you walk in expecting it to be bursting at the seams. But this place is a Tardis, with a roomy outside courtyard (some of which is covered) and Astroturf pitch, along with ample classrooms of various sizes, break-out rooms, labs, halls, library, dining room, sixth form centre, art block, drama and more. The oldest parts date back 150 years and boast beautifully tiled walls and polished wood floors, albeit with a few areas that look in need of a lick of paint. 'The school even smells of tradition,' said one dad – and he's right.

The school originally opened in 1865 by Rev William Rogers (chaplain to Queen Victoria), who recognised the pressing need for more education in the City. Having initially used temporary buildings in Bath Street, the current purpose built school then opened in Cowper Street in 1869 and the Great Hall came four years later, by which time there were over 900 boys. Post-war, it became a grammar, then in 1975 the school returned to being a comprehensive, with various building works having taken place over the decades – the most significant of which is about to happen. 'The development project, which will cost between £30-£40 million, will involve a science block and a new reception, followed by a new arts centre, then a four court sports hall – along with some more general landscaping and renovation,' explains the head, who points out that the works will be staggered to ensure minimal disruption.

During lesson times, the school is so quiet that you could be forgiven for thinking the place is empty. It's another story at break times, though, when boys inevitably let off steam – and with everyone changing lessons or having breaks simultaneously, it can be loud. 'It's essential, in my view, to avoid interruptions, so when we learn, we all learn and when we move, we all move,' says the head.

Pastoral care, well-being and discipline: Eight form groups of 18 students per year, all with a tutor that stays with them as they rise up the school (with which every student is allocated regular tutorials). Meanwhile, directors of learning (heads of year) do a detailed analysis of each student each term, looking at issues such as attendance (including at after-school clubs), punctuality, learning and behaviour. Then there's a house system, which generates all the usual leadership opportunities and cross-year friendships. There are three student counsellors and a high level of engagement with CAMHS.

No word gets used more by the head than 'community' and it's this ethos, say students and their parents, that ultimately makes the school such a supportive environment – a place that students want to be. Some older students told us bullying used to be a real issue, but that this head's zero tolerance has helped – measures such as teachers in playgrounds and even bus stops and underground stations, mean there are no longer any hiding places. 'There are instances of bullying,' one boy told us, 'but teachers are good at sorting it out quickly.'

The glass cabinet in the reception area sets the tone for discipline. Displaying beautifully hand-written notes from the headteachers in the 1800s, outlining intricately detailed rules around issues such as not throwing paper and not pulling other boys' hats off, this isn't just a light-hearted look back to harsher times. The message remains crystal clear that boys must not misbehave, even slightly, or else they'll get short, sharp shock – notably an hour's detention. Talking in class, forgetting your PE kit, lacking focus, failing to hand in your homework – all these things will land you in deep water. No wonder Ofsted marked behaviour here as outstanding and we did not see a single boy failing to pay full attention in class. 'There is the odd time when a boy flares up and hits out,' the head told us when asked if there are ever more serious misdemeanours, but it's not like it once was, reflected by the drop from 190 exclusions per year before he joined to just 10 in the academic year we visited.

Boys are expected to dress immaculately both in and outside school. The messiest you'll see is an undone top button. 'I have a room with every piece of uniform in every size, so if a boy forgets something, they can borrow it,' says the head.

Unusually, sixth formers can do paid work in school eg working in the kitchen and doing lunchtime duties in the year 7 play area. 'We don't want the students working every hour at Sainsbury's to earn money, which would get in the way of their work. It means everyone wins,' says the head.

The student council is taken seriously and individual requests are often met too. 'One student in year 7 asked for there to be a skateboarding club and they set it up within a month,' one student told us.

Pupils and parents: There are 35 first languages spoken by students at this truly ethnically diverse school; it's English for 47 per cent of students, then Bengali (16 per cent). Nineteen per cent of students are white British, with other significant numbers being Bangladeshi, Somali, Turkish and Black Caribbean. Because of the banded entry system, some of these students come from neighbouring boroughs, as well as the whole of Islington. The students are a mixed bag socially too – both extremes of wealth and poverty, plus everything in between.

There's no PA, although parents are seen as key to enabling the boys' learning and there's almost 100 per cent attendance at the two annual parents' evenings and other talks and meetings. We found pupils to be articulate and enthusiastic, even in year 7, and there's already a huge sense of pride. Notable former pupils include Anthony Wedgwood Benn (before he became plain old Tony Benn), Kingsley Wood, Jacob Bronowski, Richard Seifert, Ronnie Scott, Martin Kemp, Trevor Nelson and Reggie Yates.

Entrance: More than 600 boys compete for the 180 places. All applicants take CATs (Cognitive Ability Tests), with students split into four ability cohorts. Within each of these cohorts, the boys closest to the school get in. All sixth form entrants must have 6s at GCSE in the subjects they want to study, including English and maths, as well as getting through a detailed interview. 'The way we see it, we have a short period of time to achieve a lot, so we need to know students have the right character and work ethic,' says the head. Attendance in sixth form is 98 per cent (compared to the average of 85-90 per cent for London) and the head intends to keep it that way. Usually, around 10 of the school's own applicants tend to get turned away, while around 25 new students come in (of whom 10-15 are female).

Exit: Around 60 per cent stay on to sixth form, those who don't have generally decided to study A levels elsewhere, including the private sector. Maths, engineering and computer science are among the most popular subjects chosen at university (although there is a huge breadth of subjects overall). Courses include biomedical sciences at UCL, psychology at Durham and law at Manchester.

Remarks: This extremely disciplined, well-ordered and highly academic, urban school runs a tight ship, giving boys who are prepared to toe the line a chance to leave with both excellent exam results and a genuine readiness for the modern world in terms of character, moral compass and work ethic. A hidden gem right in the heart of London, it is a school going from strength to strength and has the feel of a grammar, without the selection. 'It's a hugely well-kept secret, with many parents – including me – thinking, "Why don't all local boys apply?"' summed up one parent.

Channing Junior School

Linked with Channing School

1 Highgate High Street, London N6 5JR

Ages 4–11 **Pupils** 336

Fees: £17,610 pa

020 8342 9862
www.channing.co.uk

Head: Since September 2018, Dina Hamalis, previously academic director of Sarum Hall. Degree in education, specialising in English and history; spent five years at St Albans High Prep, moving to Highgate School (curriculum coordinator) then UCS pre-prep (SENCo, G&T and EAL coordinator) before joining Sarum Hall in 2011. She is an ISI inspector.

Entrance: Main entry at 4+. About 200 assessed (ie observed performing a range of 'nursery tasks') for 48 places (two classes of 24) in January before entry, then whittled down in a second round. 'We're looking for bright girls, who are interested, engaged and willing to have a go.' The school's increasing popularity means they're now first choice for most applicants. No 7+ entry; a smattering of vacancies higher up. Most families, however, are here for the duration.

Exit: The mode' is 'all-through', and the focus is to prepare girls well for the next stage, not for admissions elsewhere. ('We don't provide extra tutoring or practice papers'.) The assumption is that all girls will proceed to the senior school without further entrance testing. ('Not having to do the 11+ is a real advantage,' said one mother. 'It enables you to have a longer term view of education, which is very appealing.') In most years, a small handful leave for other schools. Some to board, some to the

C

state (including highly competitive selective schools, like Henrietta Barnett and St Michael's Catholic Grammar), one or two to other leading independents. Children who would really struggle at the senior school are also gently guided elsewhere. 'It isn't a question of having a bar that has to be met. We want girls to thrive. Some children find the academic pace a challenge and flourish nonetheless, but if a girl's self-confidence starts to dip, we help the family find the best alternative.'

Remarks: Set opposite its senior school, behind high walls and tall gates in Highgate's traffic-packed high street, the school's rather forbidding exterior belies the pleasures within. Located in what was once Fairseat, the fine Victorian mansion of the Waterlow family, the junior school moved into its current accommodation in 1926, retaining a generous slice of the original gardens (the remainder was donated to the community to become adjoining Waterlow Park). The expansive house (with far-reaching views) now contains large, light classrooms, a performing arts studio, music rooms, a practical room for science, and plenty of elbow room for all. The gardens, with their mature trees, also house an adventure playground while three new outdoor learning areas (mud kitchen, classroom and a pavilion) are used by every class. All in all, 'it gives them a freedom rarely found in London. They can go into the bushes and make dens and still feel totally safe.'

A fundamental aspect of the school's approach is its personalised attitude to the academic; all are taught to a high standard, but not all are taught in the same way. ('One of my daughters needs – and gets – much more support than the other,' said a parent.) Bright and breezy teaching moves at a brisk, imaginative pace. (We watched girls create a 'storm' using a variety of sounds, for example, for a lesson on weather.) Specialists in ICT, modern languages. Art, DT, PE, drama and music throughout. Innovative new Spanish language programme engages all pupils in 'Spanish language and culture'. French also added in year 3.

IT firmly embedded from the off, with a dedicated IT room lined with Apple Macs, and iPads used as 'learning tools'. 'Somehow they see them as something completely different from the tablets at home. Here they're used as dictionaries, for creativity and for research.'

Reasonably heavy homework load. ('My daughter couldn't manage more,' said the mother of a girl in year 5), but it's cool to work hard and parents, pupils and students all have high aspirations. 'The school manages a good balance between stretching them academically, while still nurturing them and treating them as individuals,' said one parent. 'I feel my daughter's pushed about the right amount,' said another.

Designated additional learning coordinator works with classroom teachers to put together appropriate learning plans. Children are sometimes withdrawn from lessons to work in a quieter space, but always follow the same work as their classmates. Gifted and talented also given additional stretch.

Attractive, well-used library with dedicated librarian, encouraging even the youngest to borrow, express opinions, and carry out research.

Music undoubtedly a strength, with enthusiastic head of music working closely with her equally energetic colleague in the senior school. Regular music lessons, plus plenty of opportunities to perform in music assemblies, orchestra, brass and wind bands, string quartet and choir. Wide range of individual music lessons, with vast majority taking classes in anything from saxophone to harp. (The school currently has four harpists.) Does its best to ensure girls find an instrument that 'fits their character' and lets parents borrow rather than buy in the early stages. Three girls recently invited to join the National Children's Orchestra, and usually several music awards to senior school. Art, with its own designated room, also vibrant.

Large sports hall on site (recently vacated by senior school, which now has its own), plus well-used netball and tennis courts. Swimming takes place elsewhere, and the school has its own playing field a brisk walk away, used for sports days and rounders matches. Pupils have competed at regional and national level in tennis, swimming and cross-country.

Has significantly boosted the extracurricular offering introducing in- and after-school clubs ranging from judo and gymnastics to fencing, ballet and chess (with one Grand-Master-in-the-making competing in the U11 World Chess Champions). Busy schedule of visits (eg Neasden Temple, Sky Studios, engineering workshop) and residential trips for older pupils.

Girls are well behaved – leaping to their feet to chorus 'Good afternoon' – but building confidence is as critical as good manners. 'My daughter used to be very shy,' said a parent, 'but performing in everything from music assemblies to poetry readings has made her much more self-assured.' The atmosphere is friendly and bustling, girls engaged and enthusiastic. 'My daughter loves the school,' said one mother. 'If we ever discuss moving, she says she doesn't want to leave. She has a wide variety of friends – the school's not cliquey at all.'

Channing used to be very much a local school, but the increased intake and improved academic reputation mean that, while there are still plenty of locals (some whose families have attended the school for generations), the pool now spreads out five miles, with plenty arriving from Islington and beyond. Families are also more international than before, though still largely made up of a solid core of affluent professionals. Active parents' association arranges regular events and last year also helped raise £17,000 or so for charity.

Channing School

Linked with Channing Junior School

Highgate, London N6 5HF

Ages 11–18 **Pupils** 597 **Sixth form** 130

Fees: £19,410 pa

020 8340 2328
www.channing.co.uk

Headmistress: Since 2005, Barbara Elliott, MA PGCE (60s). Mrs Elliott attended a girls' grammar school in Lancashire, then read French and Spanish at New Hall, Cambridge. Taught in both the independent and state sectors before arriving at Channing. Much liked by pupils and parents. Gets to know pupils well at the outset by inviting year 7s in for a chat. With experience of all-boys, all-girls and mixed schools, she remains a firm advocate of girls-only education. 'I've seen girls in co-educational schools sitting silently for years. Girls here are not without an interesting social life, but here they have the freedom to be themselves and try new things.' Like her pupils, there's nothing of the wallflower about Mrs Elliott, whose fashionable glasses and stripy tights signal her buoyant and breezy personality. Pomp and distance play no part in her regime (for example, she happily sat crossed legged for morning assembly in a charity swap with a junior pupil), and she runs the school with a light touch.With four adult sons, all now successfully established, she's an enthusiastic grandmother and dog-lover.

Academic matters: Channing is an academic school, but not one where academic achievement overrides all else. The intake here is slightly broader than at some of the local competition, and not every pupil will be cut out for straight A*/9s. ('Here, if a girl is outstanding at art, but not at maths, it's not the end of the world,' says the head. 'Some are exceptionally bright; others exceptional at something, but, naturally, not everything.') Every girl, however, should get the best she's capable of, and often significantly more than might be expected. ('Some achieve more than you'd have ever have thought possible.') At GCSE, most garner a pleasing string of 9-7s (84 per cent in 2018); at A levels, the dominant alphabet is again A*-A (62 per cent).

The sixth form is not huge – about 65 in each year – and nor is the subject range (19 on offer); the core is serious stuff and the conventional arts/science divide is roughly in balance, with biology and economics attracting similar numbers to history and English (though few physicists). Maths tops the popularity stakes; biology and politics take away the highest grades. Good spread of languages, with Spanish, French, German and Latin all on offer at GCSE and A level, plus Greek as a twilight GCSE subject. Adelante programme from reception upwards aims to produce girls fluent in Spanish and with a love of Hispanic culture.

The school prides itself on the quality of its teaching. ('Our teachers are experts in pedagogy,' says the head.) The Independent Schools inspectors found teaching 'excellent', and also waxed lyrical about the 'exceptional' quality of 'pupils' learning and achievement'. No doubt at all that value is added here – in every direction. Good take up, for example, of the research-directed Extended Project Qualification (EPQ). Technology, too, thoroughly embedded, with all girls issued with a school iPad 'to support research, investigation, creativity and communication'.

Special needs addressed by a qualified SENCo, called on to assist a range of difficulties, from profoundly deaf pupils to 30-or-so girls with mild visual impairment, dyslexia, or processing issues. 'We carry out appropriate assessment, but it's as much about helping teachers to adapt their teaching to meet individual needs.'

Games, options, the arts: Art and music both unusually strong. Art ('absolutely amazing,' said one pupil) is housed in roof-top studios with stunning views across London. Strong emphasis on drawing as the basis of it all, but art rooms are lined with Macs and scented by oil paint. Plenty achieve external glory, with recent prize winners in Young Art at the Royal College of Art. Student work also displayed (and sold!) at a north London gallery. Music, always strong, has undoubtedly been enhanced by the completion of the new music school, which has added 10 practice rooms, a technology room and a sound-proofed percussion studio. Record numbers now take external exams, including the first set of musical theatre awards (with 23 distinctions). Plenty of opportunity to perform in-house – annual and lunchtime concerts, plus informal recitals – and in formats that range from string quartets and guitar ensembles to a jazz band and contemporary music group. Recent finalists, too, in Voice Festival UK. Biannual international tours to eg Lisbon, Madrid, Vienna, Boston and Venice.

Limited running around space on site, so probably not a first-choice for those who live for goals and glory. Though 'we have county level sportswomen, and local netball clubs train here most evenings,' says the head. But if go-fight-win is not top of the agenda, keeping fit and healthy definitely is. PE compulsory throughout and newly refurbished multi-use games area plus sports hall make this a pleasure, with vastly improved opportunities for volleyball, badminton, cricket and dance, plus recent successes in cricket, tennis and football.

West End quality performing arts building recently completed and LAMDA classes very popular. Staggering range of school trips and activities, from history in Berlin and classics in Greece to a music tour to Madrid and regular theatre outings to the West End. Clubs follow prevailing interests and currently include feminist society, robotics, chemistry, classics, life drawing and creative writing.

C

Background and atmosphere: School housed in four tall and graceful Georgian buildings on Highgate Hill overlooking one of London's most beautiful and under-visited parks. Backing these, head has done a serious job of rearrangement, making the most of a relatively small site with the addition of a new complex (containing the music school, the gym and a sixth form centre). 'If you're investing in your daughter's education you expect 21st century facilities,' she says.

Established in 1885 by a Unitarian minister and two members of his congregation to educate the daughters of Unitarian ministers, the school's clientele has broadened, but it retains the founders' values of liberalism, democracy and religious tolerance. There's no prize-giving, for example, and the most valued award is a Conabor Badge, bestowed on 'girls of good character' (or, as one recipient phrased it, 'for being good'). 'Girls really aspire to be awarded this badge,' says the head. 'It's what most embodies the spirit of the school.'

Pupils are active and engaged, participating enthusiastically in both academic and extracurricular activities (15, for example, gained D of E gold recently, impressive numbers even for a much larger school). 'I've never worked in a school where the focus on advancement and learning is so great,' says the head. 'They all have a common purpose. They're very ambitious and focussed.'

Pastoral care, well-being and discipline: This is a calm and orderly place, but it has little to do with a system of tight rules and stern warnings. 'I'm not quite sure how the detention system works,' admits the head, who oversees 'a record of serious discipline' going back 13 years which takes up just two pages.

Strong emphasis on student leadership, with two officers in every form – 'they hunt in packs' – including two head girls. Older girls also apply to become 'school officers' with designated areas of responsibility. 'A lot of girls aspire to the leadership team,' says the head. 'They have real influence.' As well as 'advising constructively', year 12s set up and run clubs and have recently sat on a panel interviewing a teacher for a job. 'I hadn't done this before,' says the head, 'but they were so clear in their thinking, so mature and perceptive.' The code of behaviour is also co-written by the girls. 'We live together in this community.'

Head's priorities are 'integrity, independence, scholarship and altruism' – old fashioned virtues, adapted to a more complex modern setting. She acknowledges that the pressures on her students are greater than ever before – 'Not all girls sail through life without hitting stormy waters' – and the school works with parents all the way, helping minimise screen time and maximise mental and physical health. 'They believe in happy girls, rather than ones who are pushed,' said one mother.

Girls generally get on with minimal bullying and cliques. 'You know everyone here, you feel very comfortable and there is a real sense of joining together.' 'It's a very safe place,' said one parent. 'If your child is slightly quirky, you know they will still be fine.' However, we have had reports of recent less-than-sympathetic responses to teenage anxieties. Head appointed a counsellor on the advice of the sixth form.

Pupils and parents: Essentially a local school, so no fleets of coaches to far-flung locations. Most pupils walk or come by public transport, from a broad sweep round the gates. 'Mainly north and west, though we do get a few from east London.' Parents are cosmopolitan (South African, European, North

American, Asian), highly educated ('At careers fairs, if you shout, "Is there a doctor in the house?", there's a rush') and value education ('expectations are very high'). They're also 'tremendously supportive'. Pupils, quite often the daughters of old girls, are confident and motivated, thriving in this relatively small school.

Entrance: At 11, 300-400 sit the London 11+ Consortium exams for around 56 places, joining the 40 or so coming up from the junior school to form four forms of 24. ('Junior school pupils don't have to sit 11 plus – it's a dream ticket,' says the head.) Will in future consist of a cognitive ability test (rather than maths and English exams) with great emphasis on the interview. For sixth form entry, applicants are interviewed and expected to achieve nine or 10 9-7 grades at GCSEs, with a minimum of 7 in the subjects they intend to study. 'I can sometimes bend the rules for existing students as we know they have firm foundations,' says the head, 'but we'd turn away someone from outside who didn't have the grades.'

Exit: A few leave at 16 – to board, to co-ed, to local state schools. The rest depart two years later for serious subjects at predominantly Russell Group universities. Two to Oxbridge in 2018, then UCL, Nottingham, Leeds, Exeter, Bristol. About half go on to science-related degrees (with a good smattering of medics and vets). The head takes a personal interest in all applicants, interviewing each girl.

Money matters: Not a hugely rich school, but still does its bit, with five per cent of annual income devoted to bursaries, 'supporting families who hit hard times'. Academic scholarships at 11 worth 10 per cent off the fees, but music scholarships (grade 5 with merit minimum required) are particularly good, with up to 50 per cent discounts. In the sixth form, art, music and academic scholarships (of up to 50 per cent off tuition fees) on offer to existing students ('We want to recognise their talent and potential, not find them sloping off elsewhere') as well as external ones. Bursaries also available at this point.

Remarks: A cosy, vibrant, local school in a very attractive setting, with high academic standards, up-to-date facilities and happy, motivated girls.

The Charter School

Red Post Hill, London SE24 9JH

Ages 11–18 **Pupils** 1,211 **Sixth form** 311

020 7346 6600
www.charter.southwark.sch.uk

Head teacher: Since 2013, Christian Hicks (40s) grew up in West Norwood and was educated at nearby Dulwich College, then collected a BA in German studies and European literature at Bristol, an MA in English and American literature at Newcastle and an MA in effective learning at the Institute of Education.

Very likeable, open and seemingly far less ego-bound than some heads. Mr Hicks lives in Beckenham with his teacher wife and three young children – two boys and girl. Out of school he thrives on learning new things, recently taking up magic and completing the Yorkshire Three Peaks Challenge. What could be more useful in a demanding headship than a head for heights, stamina and the ability to pull rabbits out of a hat?

Despite his own alma mater, he is committed to the principle of comprehensive, inclusive education. Previously deputy head of Blackfen girls' school in Bexley and before that deputy head of the Royal Docks Community School in Newham. His move was not without ambition. The Charter School is never far from the dazzle of the spotlight, its every move noted and often written about in national newspapers by the influential parental and local body. The Charter School East Dulwich opened in September 2016.

Head jokes about his tough remit of improving on the already vastly improved academic standards. Has high expectations of his pupils, aims to challenge, inspire and be highly visible: he isn't too grand for break duty and is on the door with his headship team every morning and afternoon to greet, send off and confiscate any attempts to flaunt the uniform. He sees one of the most vital parts of his role as 'getting the right people on the bus' – the hiring and firing of an exceptional team of teachers.

Academic matters: Unfazed by the ending of modular assessment at GCSE, 84 per cent of pupils gained 9-4 in both English and maths in 2018. At A level, 67 per cent of grades were A*-B and 41 per cent A*/A.

Standard-ish curriculum at GCSE, including French, Spanish and Latin plus Mandarin for those with an aptitude for languages at year 7. The school has been teaching Mandarin with some success and finds it accessible for those with dyslexia. GCSE English results have soared, maths is solid, and sciences are strong. History and art and design are both popular and successful. Weak spots most recently media studies and RE.

Relatively few taking computer science, but the school is ahead of the curve in making the transition from ICT and is looking forward to pupils who have been coding at primary school joining in future years. A group of girls recently won a competition to design an app for a local business, whilst prizewinning games designers met the Duke of Cambridge at an enterprise event at BAFTA HQ.

A few less deskbound options such as catering, PE and performing arts and a handful of BTecs on offer – science, business, social care, engineering and ICT, with most success in business.

Head assured us that school will 'really push children who have been successful at primary school' – hence this school does well by the more able, with some 20 per cent of pupils generally achieving at least eight 9-7s. Stand-out performances include lashings of 8/9s, but we noticed the school proudly trumpets the achievements of pupils gaining three 3s if this means that they have achieved well and are on track for their next step.

Best-performing subjects most recently at A level are: further maths and maths, biology, chemistry, fine art, English literature, history and a few -ologies. Languages seem a complete turn-off. Head says school is not alone in this. Aiming for an all-round academics, school will run subject even with a single pupil if necessary. Equal numbers of girls taking maths and a strong showing in sciences too.

Twenty-one teachers have more than 10 years' service – hard to believe as they appear extremely youthful. As one parent noted, 'teachers are mostly young and cool.' In fact one was so young and cool that we witnessed the receptionist assuming he was a pupil. Head and parents point out the calibre of staff attracted here by the unusually leafy milieu for an inner city salary. Head is very clear about his expectations of staff: 'don't come here if you're not prepared to work hard for successful outcomes for the students.'

A thrilled father of three girls told us that 'science teaching at The Charter is fabulous; several staff have Oxbridge PhDs and the teaching is inspiring.' Others said: 'Our children are inspired by their teachers and are really motivated to learn' and 'the staff clearly work really hard and are extremely conscientious.' Average class size at key stage 4 is 20, with 30 the maximum and some as small as five for 'nurture groups.' In the sixth form the average is 18.

With regards to homework and pressure one parent said: 'There is a good balance of homework throughout the term and a very balanced approach to exams,' whilst another warned that 'it's very intensive.' Parents kept thoroughly in the loop. The school is quick to bring them in to discuss a student who is not attaining their individual target for each subject. Coasting is not permitted.

The school dazzles in its business and enterprise specialism, creating aspiration in thinking ahead to future careers – opening students' eyes to the wider world and maximising their situation in London is a real strength. The school has links with PwC, King and Woods Malleson, O2, King's College Hospital, the Worshipful Company of International Bankers, Shell UK and more than 100 business mentors.

One parent tells us that assistance given to her son included 'mock interviews, workshops on CV writing, presentation skills and financial awareness workshops.' The CEO of the Science Council recently spoke to year 10s about STEM careers and a doctor from King's College Hospital runs an annual seminar on applying to medical school. Students also sampled uni life at Lille, London South Bank and Brighton and large groups are taken to both Oxford and Cambridge to inspire.

Someone here is in possession of an amazingly A-list little black book – a truly top-notch class of the great and good drop in to inspire regularly. Imagine the thrill of a Romeo and Juliet masterclass with none other than Joseph Fiennes; Jo Brand speaking to celebrate International Women's Day; Professor Sir Michael Rutter talking about his latest research to psychology students; not to mention professional Bollywood dancers teaching the Samba. Nor are they short of invites: the day prior to our visit 30 pupils met Boris Johnson at City Hall at a reception to honour the contribution of African and Caribbean soldiers in the First World War.

Head emphasises the value of the growing D of E programme in fostering key learning aptitudes such as resilience. Around 300 day and residential trips every year, from Bletchley Park to Belgium, Berlin and Beijing. London theatres are made good use of with trips to the National, Unicorn and Young Vic this year. One parent said: 'The school also works closely with many charities and my son was lucky enough to take a charity trip to Kenya this summer.' The school is aware of hardship issues and helps with small bursaries where it can.

Quite high numbers of SEN: around 20 per cent of students across the school cope with varying degrees of learning difficulties, so everything from specific learning difficulties such as dyslexia or dyspraxia to physical disabilities, autistic spectrum disorder or ADHD. Large learning support team of 23 staff, including specialist SEN teachers, higher level teaching assistants and learning support assistants, support students in mainstream classes but may also be able to offer small group withdrawals, extra literacy and maths intervention sessions, touch-typing, handwriting and reading clubs and input from a range of external agencies.

Games, options, the arts: Sports are compulsory – and the only time girls and boys are taught separately. Footballers enjoy links with professional clubs such as Millwall and Fulham FC. Cricket and rugby are on the up: the MCC coach cricket and the RFU rugby. The coaching team includes national class coaches in table tennis and aquathon. Students recently started play basketball competitively and are now enjoying BMX at Burgess Park.

Successes across the board, with pupils competing regionally and nationally, particularly the girls: the school boasts a national champion in rowing; under 13 girls' cricket team recently won the Lady Taverners' competition at the Oval; year 8 girls' rugby recently placed sixth in London; year 7 girls' netball team won the Southwark league. Over 500 pupils take part in after-school sports club every week.

The school appears rather boxed in by the neighbouring houses and plentiful sports ground of the neighbouring girls' school, but pupils use a playing field a five-minute walk away. Indoor sports hall is large and there is an on-site floodlit netball court, ball-court and Astroturf.

More than 200 learn a variety of 20 different musical instruments up to grade 8, with some lessons significantly subsidised and many trying an instrument for the first time. Two choirs and a jazz band, which may be led by teachers or pupils. Past students have gained places at the Royal Academy of Music. A favourite alumni is rising star Kwabs – The Guardian calls him 'the new Seal' and he has a recording contract with a major record label.

All pupils study drama once a week in years 7, 8 and 9, enjoying purpose-built drama studios and a flexible theatre space. A highlight of the dramatic year is the whole school theatre performance – most recently Guys and Dolls – featuring staff alongside pupils. A parent said of the art: 'I have been delighted with the art department. I feel the teachers really care about what they teach.' London galleries are frequented and facilities include a kiln, dark room, screen printing and Mac suite.

Lunchtime and after-school clubs include young historians, tennis, handball, track cycling, music theory, ukulele, African drumming and study skills. Pupils sign up on a first come first served basis. Most are free, with a small charge for tennis and swimming clubs.

Background and atmosphere: Smaller than most city comprehensives, The Charter squeezes into a plot a few strides from North Dulwich station and at the heart of Herne Hill. Built on the site of the defunct William Penn School, it opened in 2000 following a concerted campaign from parents in an area dominated by independent schools, but without a good state option.

Savvy parents realise that they have something of a find on their doorstep, but some nervousness persists locally around the legacy of the failed school, and the head is aware school has to work hard to ensure that no one child lets down the reputation of the whole amongst the local community. Ofsted has rated it outstanding twice since 2006.

Most of the buildings were remodelled rather than replaced. It is light and functional but now looking more than a little frayed at the edges, both inside and out. We wondered how a shy year 7 moving here from one of the cosy local primaries might make the transition. The head told us: 'This is a family school, a local school. When children move here they are often joining siblings or friends' – a third of every year group has school siblings. And everywhere in the mornings and afternoons one sees little gaggles of Charter pupils walking to and fro. Each year 180 new pupils join, but the school very often operates in year groups, with assemblies for each year. Lunchtime arrangements – a mix of indoor and outdoor seating under-cover – with year 7s heading to lunch 10 minutes earlier to avoid being overwhelmed.

Prior to lessons we noticed some boisterous boys in the corridor, but once lessons had commenced the atmosphere was exceptionally quiet and calm, with each lesson we viewed in both arts and sciences equally industrious.

Parents talk of happy children who are able to be who they want to be here. When the head was writing his mission statement, pupils asked him to add 'happiness' because that is how they feel.

C

Pastoral care, well-being and discipline: The relatively relaxed school uniform – polo-shirts and pullovers mostly, so no ties and without the blazers of the other nearby state seniors – is deceiving as to the school's culture of high expectations. Given the issues of the school in its previous incarnation, the school set out to be something of an innovator in managing behaviour and is known for its no-nonsense attitude to discipline, which it balances with care. Behaviour officers, not in evidence on our visit, have a remit to swoop into any classroom to remove a student who has overstepped the mark. The head says that 'any pupil who is disrupting the learning of others will be in school until 5pm.'

More serious offences such as smoking will result in exclusion – gross misconducts are half what they were five years ago, although slightly up this year. The emphasis is on inclusion and working with pupils to find a way back to contributing positively. There is a whole raft of rewards including VIVO Miles – like air miles for good behaviour – extra school trips, presentations and a phone call to parents from the head or head of year.

Mobile phones are not allowed in school at all, except for sixth formers who must keep them out of sight. Any confiscated phones must be collected by a parent. No piercings other than one pair of ear studs; no hats, hoodies or outlandish hair colours.

Pupils should always have someone to talk to. There are strong relationships between staff and pupils, a tutor system, year 11 mentors for year 7s and a school counsellor. Even the staff get a buddy each.

Pupils and parents: A large part of the intake is from privileged Dulwich Village, Herne Hill and East Dulwich, but pupils encompass every kind of home life. More than 30 per cent of students are pupil premium students – the performance gap is significant but closing. On entrance, students demonstrate a wide range of ability but it is notable that by year 11, 56 per cent have risen to the two highest ability bands. A parent told us: 'This school is for children who want to learn, want to get somewhere in the world. It caters for all in that there is something for everyone.'

The school prides itself on its inclusivity and parents say it really 'celebrates diversity.' Forty-seven per cent of pupils describe themselves as white British, with black British African as the second largest group (11 per cent of pupils). Surprisingly few EAL students and whilst there are many bilingual pupils, 93 per cent have English as their first language.

Parents come from all walks of life. Very effective PTA has just bought a 16-seater minibus for inter-school sports matches.

Entrance: The hoo-ha over the school catchment area is in the past. Admissions criteria are looked after children, then siblings, then distance criteria using safest walking distance as a measure, which places the catchment currently at no more than 1,600 metres from the school. Parents in East Dulwich may want to get out their pedometers. No feeders as such but largest cohorts from Dulwich Hamlet Junior School, Dog Kennel Hill School, Heber and Goodrich local primaries.

The sixth form is more inclusive than many: pupils must have five 9-4 grades including maths and English, with a minimum grade for subjects of study which varies.

Applications for places stand at seven to one. Crowded annual open days – often 2,000 attendees – are held in September for year 7 and November for the sixth form.

Exit: Nearly all to university, art or music college. Remainder to start gap year, apprenticeship or work. Recent destinations include Bristol, Durham, Birmingham, Edinburgh, Imperial College London and Leeds. One to Oxbridge in 2018 and four to medical/vet school.

Many pursuing other dreams have exited to equally prestigious destinations, such as RADA, major London art colleges and the Royal College of Music. Two pupils recently gained sought-after City apprenticeships with KPMG and investment company M&G, whilst the Queen recently presented one girl with a Southwark Council scholarship to pay all her university tuition fees.

Remarks: A truly local comprehensive and for those on the doorstep it may be the stepping stone to very good things. Well connected, with increasingly impressive academic results driven by a talented staff promising much for children who want to work hard and those who have previously found opportunities thin on the ground. For parents wondering whether there is life beyond school fees we recommend joining the open day throng.

Charterhouse Square School

40 Charterhouse Square, London EC1M 6EA

Ages 3–11 **Pupils** 200

Fees: £17,040 pa

020 7600 3805
www.charterhousesquareschool.co.uk

Head: Since 2009, Caroline Lloyd (40s). BEd in geography from Exeter University (although her parents had wanted her to do a 'proper' degree). Her first job as an NQT was at Charterhouse Square School in 1994, straight after leaving university: 'I was young, determined and desperate to be a teacher.' Indeed Caroline (as she is known to staff and pupils), knew she wanted to teach from the age of 7 and 'used to line up my teddies, pretending they were in class.' However, she had a very specific idea of the kind of school where she wanted to teach and only five schools matched her criteria – Charterhouse Square being one of them.

During her 15 years at the school and prior to becoming head, Caroline experienced teaching in all year groups from nursery through to year 6. After leaving to start a family she returned six months later on a part-time basis as she 'missed teaching so much'. In 2008, the school was purchased by Cognita and the position of head was advertised. Caroline says: 'It was never my intention to become a head, but I was worried that someone new would come in and not see how special the school was' – so she applied for the post. After so many years at the school her application was seen as a natural progression by both parents and children. One parent told us: 'The school was good before with the previous head, but it's great now. The children have just blossomed under Caroline.' Another praised her for being such a consistently visible presence; 'She knows every pupil by name and is naturally great with children. The school just seems to run seamlessly.'

Tall, attractive and immaculately turned out, she could have been separated at birth from the Middleton sisters and would look quite at home sipping Pimm's at a polo match. Her boundless enthusiasm for both her job and life in general is infectious but don't be fooled, this head is no pushover and knows that some people might go so far as to call her a control freak: 'I'm on the school door every morning and most afternoons. I feel that if communication is strong, we can get things sorted before they escalate out of control.'

One can't imagine too many things getting out of control at this genteel school, which has had no permanent exclusions in its 25+ year history; the head concedes that her main challenge is 'managing over-aspiring parents.' She says: 'I've often had to remind parents that I'm actually on the side of the child, especially when they are being pushed too hard to get in to certain secondary schools.'

Entrance: Completely non-selective, entry is by lottery – unless you have a sibling who already attends. Twenty-six 3+ places offered each year and roughly 70 on the waiting list. No point planning the Caesarian or putting names down at birth, you can register up till the end of June the year before entry and a ballot is drawn on 1 July. Head says this comes as a shock for some parents: 'who have been used to pulling out a cheque book to buy their way in' and concedes that 'It can make me pretty unpopular.' Cheque book will, however, come in handy for £4,000 non-returnable deposit payable when accepting a place.

Exit: Most to high calibre selective London secondaries. Fierce competition for places at both (girls and boys) City of London schools and some pupils even pulled out early at age 7 or 10 by parents who think this will increase their chances of getting in. School says this is a shame and 'can be disruptive.' Other leavers to eg Channing, Francis Holland, Forest School, South Hampstead, North Bridge House and Queen's College.

Remarks: Charterhouse Square School is located on the south side of historic Charterhouse Square in Smithfield, central London. The square was built on what was the site of a 14th century Carthusian monastery (an almshouse and chapel remain) and also London's largest Black Death plague pit. The five-storey Victorian building occupied by the school, though smart enough, is easily missed among neighbouring offices and apartment blocks, but any lack of character, not to mention green space, is more than made up for by such a central location. This is a City school and parents know exactly what they're buying into when they make the decision to send their children here. One told us: 'I am able to drop my kids off on the way to work, which is one reason I chose this school. The other reason is that I noticed how happy and well-mannered the pupils were when they were out and about. I know some people think it looks more confined than other schools, but it works for us and my children are very happy here.'

Though it wouldn't suit those who like to plan ahead, most parents seem to welcome the diversity and 'range of abilities' that result from school's non-selective, lottery-based entrance procedure. It's an unusual independent school in other ways: there's no uniform and it's first name terms for all teachers, including the head. One parent told us: 'I love this school for being individual with very individual ideas.' Another said: 'Coming from a convent school background I was initially horrified about the idea of first name terms, but I have to say it works very well and makes the teachers far more approachable to the children, without diluting any respect.'

Head has worked hard to ensure that hers isn't a one size fits all school: 'When I came on board, early years was very formal and a bit of a hothouse. Drama was only every other week and there were no school trips. I think it's about broadening the curriculum so that we can make sure that all pupils can excel at something.' Parents wholeheartedly agree. Teaching described as 'exceptional' and 'instilling a love of learning.' Years 4 and 5 are taught together so that they have the same teacher for two years before the all-important year 6. They work on a two-year curriculum, with the exception of homework, and English and maths textbooks. They are also ability grouped. One parent told us, 'I'm not really sure how it works – but the kids seem to understand it, so that's the main thing.'

Designated SENCo provides one-to-one support and booster groups for children with SEN, which accounts for a handful of the school's intake. The nature of the school building (five flights of stairs) may make it unsuitable for pupils with physical disabilities.

Pastoral care is paramount and school employs a number of highly effective strategies to help pupils feel safe. Older pupils can make use of classroom 'feelings boxes' to share concerns privately with teachers, and the 'buddy' system supports new pupils. Every parent we spoke to raved about this: 'It's a great system as it makes new children feel less intimidated and older children rise to the responsibility of looking after the younger ones.'

Our tour started in the early years foundation stage classes, nursery and reception. Nursery was having its annual 'animal dress up day' and we were greeted by tigers, bears and monkeys plus a couple of unidentifiable but colourful animals. Sweet little add-on area designed for role play was effectively outside, but covered by a canopy and surrounded by a high wall. This, we were told, was to prevent anything landing on the tracks of Barbican station, something that carries a huge fine (on an hourly rate). Thankfully, this has not happened so far.

Small but well stocked library from where children are encouraged to take books home nightly, and a carpeted school hall with beautiful white piano and colourful wall display of ukuleles. Extracurricular activities such as judo and table tennis take place here and all children have the opportunity to learn a musical instrument. 'Informal' Spanish also offered in the early years. One parent said: 'I was amazed when we went on holiday to Spain last year, that my 5 year old daughter was able to communicate with a local in pidgin Spanish.'

Bright, neat, colourful classrooms were full of interested, happy and very polite children and the atmosphere of the school is extremely warm and friendly. Pupils who were leaving told us how they'll miss Charterhouse 'sooo much', especially the teachers. 'What I really like about the teachers is that they are all so friendly. Also, we are often asked to tick a box privately at the end of a lesson about whether we found the classes easy or difficult. If we are really struggling, we can sometimes get an extra private lesson.'

Despite the limitations of a tall and narrow building ('I often had to walk up five flights of stairs when I was pregnant,' the head told us), children don't seem to lack breathing space and fresh air. During the warmer months they spend their lunch break in the private Charterhouse Square gardens; when it's cold and wet they play in the school's 'jungle' downstairs. Organised sports take place nearby at Coram Fields or the Golden Lane Leisure Centre. Pupils do take part in inter-school sporting events, but no regular fixtures because of the issue of 'bussing children around.' One parent did say that this school is perhaps not the right option for the 'extremely sporty child', although another said that her two boys 'are extremely sporty and it meets their needs.' A highlight in the calendar is sports day: 'It's just such a joy, well handled and fun.'

No school meals prepared on site and no dining room because of limited space so until recently all pupils had to bring in a packed lunch. School has now organised for a company to bring in hot food in thermos containers, if the parents require. The head says: 'This system works very well and the advantage is that parents know what their children like and can order accordingly.' We are told the quality and choice is great, with meatballs, pasta, wraps, soups and stews on offer.

Lack of space may deter some, but Charterhouse Square is a wonderful option if you live and work in the City. This is a successful school and a happy environment in which pupils of varying abilities thrive and with comments such as: 'My child loves every day of her school life!' who could ask for more?

Chepstow House School

C

108a Lancaster Road, London W11 1QS

Ages 2–13 **Pupils** 318

Fees: £20,655 pa

020 7243 0243
www.chepstowhouseschool.co.uk

Headteacher: Since 2010, Angela Barr BA Ed (50s). Has been head since school started. Previously head of the lower school at Pembridge Hall, another Alpha Plus school. Studied geography and education at Christchurch College, Kent University and then taught in a state school in Essex before taking off and travelling around Africa for a year, with her husband Simon. 'I loved school and always wanted to be a teacher,' she says with passion.

Marked her 50th birthday celebration with another trip to Africa (Namibia) with her husband – this youthful, warm and attractive head is a spirited and independent character who lives for the moment and is all about the 'doing now.' Indeed, it's not often we come across a head who has zip-wired across the Thames to raise money for charity. One parent told us: 'She really is up for anything.' Another said: 'It was truly amazing and helped raise some much needed money towards the Evelina Trust at St Thomas's. It shows the sort of head she is.'

Teaching, she says, is her hobby – 'I love it so much it doesn't feel like a job' – and she is by all accounts a very hands on head who personally supports youngest pupils with their reading. 'I am a big believer in getting children reading,' she says. Also works hard to make sure her staff are teaching with all the different learning styles in mind – 'essential in a co-educational school.' Parents have told us she is on the front gate to greet pupils every single morning, and knows every child by name and even their siblings: 'It gives a really personal element to the school and helps the younger ones settle in.' 'Firm but fair' we are told, and whilst she is open to new ideas and welcomes feedback from parents, 'she also won't be led by them, however influential and high powered they are.'

Still ambitious for the school as 'it's still growing' and, more importantly, 2018 saw the first set of (very creditable) 11+ results.

Entrance: Non-selective, so it's a case of registration at or as soon as possible after birth (embryonic stages even better). Current cost £150 – non-refundable if you don't get a place. School allots five definite places a month, and tries to stagger them among children born at the beginning, middle and end of the month, so no advantage in booking your Caesarean for the first of September. Attempts are made to keep an even number of boys and girls and those who drop out are replaced like with like, as far as possible, from the waiting list. That way they don't get a surfeit of, say, boys born in August. Priority given to siblings. The school now includes Little Chepstow Nursery which can accommodate 40 children, all of whom will be guaranteed a place at the school if they have spent the full two years there. Chepstow House has expanded gradually to year 8, with entry points at 7, 8 and 11.

Exit: Pupils can now stay on until 13, with first year 6 leavers off to eg Francis Holland NW1, South Hampstead, St James Girls, St Paul's, City Boys, KCS Wimbledon. As a result most pupils now continue through, although there is a handful whose parents still opt for the 7+ to gain entrance to schools such as Wetherby, where competition is possibly less rife than at 11+. One parent told us: 'It's a shame Chepstow House doesn't go on until 18.' (We couldn't help feeling that there is no pleasing some.) Those staying on to 13 have applied for schools ranging from Eton to Canford to Wetherby Senior to Westminster.

Remarks: Born into the now well-established stable of Alpha Plus Group schools, this nearly fully matured school has much to live up to – no doubt in part due to the huge demand there is for good schools around the sophisticated area of Notting Hill. However, so far the school has risen to meet that demand with style. It moved to its stunning new home on Lancaster Road in 2014 (bang opposite its rival Notting Hill Prep), into a building formerly known as the Isaac Newton Centre. Tucked away from the hubbub of the Westway, the impressive black wrought gates are the only giveaway that there may be a school around. On entering what looks more like a portcullis than a gated entrance to a school, followed by a short walk through a tunnel, one arrives at the bright, glass-fronted reception.

Chepstow House is built all on one level..but what a level. The corridors are endless. With red carpet throughout, it feels more like a large, glamorous chalet, than any school we've been to. A very shiny and exquisitely maintained school, where even the teachers – blonde, long limbed, healthy – look as though they have stepped out of their own teachers' version of Tatler (we felt decidedly old and washed out). Children, too, look enchanting in their quaint red berets and jackets, girls in tartan pinafores, boys in red tank tops and grey shorts (some parents worry about their sons getting cold knees in the winter – although they can graduate to corduroy trousers from year 4 upwards).

It does feel very moneyed, but not pretentiously so, quite understated but with a few eye-catching facilities. We particularly liked the main hall (which also doubles up as the dining area and performance space) – and is designed with a semi-circular upper level, which parents can stand on and look down to watch their children perform. 'A bit Shakespearean', one parent said. Colourful mosaics of various animals adorn the walls, 'which most of the children have helped to make.' We were also struck by the imagination of many of the teachers, particularly in the gloriously colourful art room, with an assortment of interesting objects dangling from the ceiling or on the walls. The art teacher was enthusiastically describing her latest art project, which involved recyclables, at the time.

Another thing that caught our eye (and the first time we'd seen this in any school we've been to) was a very realistic looking fully clothed 'dead body' in the science lab, with an exact replica of a cordoned off area as a murder scene (even down to the windows with No Entry tape strips across). The science teacher – who clearly has a great sense of humour – told us that it was the pupils' job to find out how he died, by carrying out a series of forensic investigations. Genius and imaginative, we thought. The drama room, too, was an interesting space with the ceiling swathed in colourful Moroccan-style chiffon material. Much thought had gone into the aesthetics of the school, evidently.

Classes named after birds (get to year 6, and you make Eagle status). With a teacher and teaching assistant in each class the children get lots of support and attention. French and music start from reception. Three sets for maths in year 2 and lots of differentiation in the lower years. Maths Whizz, used from year 3, is a programme which individualises each child's maths programme 'to stop anyone falling through the net.'

Each child has the use of an iPad – technology skills are learned on the job as well as in a separate lesson devoted to IT. We saw children as young as 4 year using iPads in the nursery. Any learning difficulties are identified quickly, says head. School sets high standards for reading and writing, and tracks development and progress in-house with a reading test as well as SEN assessment. One parent told us that her child is severely dyslexic, and needs a lot of extra support: 'Chepstow House picked up on this really quickly and were really on top of it.' This was echoed by other parents in similar situations.

The sense of purpose is palpable. During our visit, children were focused and interested in their lessons. We were amazed by the quality of writing from children as young as year 1. Gone was the giant, looping, large-spaced scrawl we often see from 5 and 6 year olds, instead replaced by neat, legible writing kept between the lines. 'We spend a lot of time working on both their gross motor skills and fine motor skills. We even do magic spells with them, where they learn to pick up things with small tweezers.'

Music is vibrant and the pupils are introduced to a number of different genres. A number of pupils have violin, guitar or piano lessons taught by peripatetic teachers. Sport has also been taken up a notch since the school has grown and Chepstow competes successfully with other local independent schools. It's also very inclusive: there is an A and a B team for most fixtures, and everyone has the chance to compete. Sport is on site from reception to year 2 – from year 3 upwards they go off site for sports such as football, cricket and hockey as well as regular swimming and access to a climbing wall. 'I love the sport here; boys get to do netball and girls get to do football,' said one happy pupil. Lots of extracurricular, too, from fencing, dance and martial arts to Spanish, coding club and even skateboarding.

Ofsted was glowing in its report and the only minor thing criticism was the need for some sort of external covered area for pupils to play in all weathers. This has been addressed, and indeed the outside play areas are some of the nicest we've seen in a city school in terms of space and facilities. Lots to play with and play on, colourful and interesting and all beautifully maintained by the onsite manager and a couple of ex-parents who oversee the 'grow your own' area.

Parents from all over the globe – plenty of Americans, Australians and Canadians, a fair few from Scandinavia, Eastern Europe and Russia, as well as French and Italians. Attracts the less traditional English who prefer co-ed at this stage. Parents are in media, finance, law as well as in the arts. Head makes good use of the parents' experience. One parent arranged for someone from Sky News to give a talk in assembly while another organised expeditions to private art galleries hosted by another parent.

Parents are generally very supportive and enthusiastic. 'It's a tight ship – with high energy,' we were told. A very active parent committee, which managed to raise a gobsmacking £390,000 last year – through galas, fairs and produce selling (together with the head's zip-wire challenge). The school also ran a separate charity appeal for the partner school in Ethiopia, which raised enough money to build an children's home in the grounds: 'It was quite a year last year; I think it'll be a quieter one this year.'

Lots of smiling faces, both parents and children, when they arrive first thing. Kiss and Drop, as it is enchantingly called, is a system for parents who don't want to come into school and hang around until the official start time of 8.30am. Head welcomes everyone and is proud of school's open door policy. 'We are not hiding anything,' she says. Nor does she have to. These children are very lucky indeed to have such a focused and privileged start to their education.

Definitely one to watch if you live in or near this very oversubscribed area of London.

The Children's House School

C

King Henry's Walk, Islington, London N1 4PB

Ages 2–7 **Pupils** 113

Fees: £13,920 – £14,730 pa

020 7249 6273
www.childrenshouseschool.co.uk

Head: Since 2016, Kate Orange Cert Ed (Wellington, New Zealand College of Education) – 60s (not that you would know it) with an interesting background in education. After graduating in New Zealand and working for two years as a teacher there, she moved to the UK, cutting her British teeth working for the Thomas's School group in their first school near Sloane Square. However, after two years and with a yearning to work in France, she moved to a village school in Provence, which she says was the most incredible experience: 'I was a New Zealander and this was my first experience of living in a completely foreign environment.' With her schoolgirl French, she even managed to wow officials (from the Mitterrand government at the time), who were sent to the school to inspect this new foreign teacher: 'I became a national cause celebre'. She spent her spare time there acting with a Parisian theatre company, performing at the Avignon Festival. Her love affair with France has persisted.

When she returned to London three years later, she worked in knowledge management for a City law firm for four years. After having children, she taught at an Islington school for two years before moving to The Children's House as a class teacher. She took on the role of deputy head in 2005, taking over as head when the long-standing former headteacher retired. 'This school just has a lovely feel to it; it's very child centred, which in turn makes it very family centred', says Kate (as she is known to all, even the pupils). Indeed, during our visit, her office door burst open on two occasions with pupils desperately wanting to ask 'Kate' something. As one parent said, 'This school very much operates an open-door policy at all times. You can have a chat to Kate whenever you want, and you often see parents popping by her office in the morning. She's also very quick at responding to emails.' Another parent said: 'I've had both heads and they've both been great, but Kate has a real educational rigour to her and the school has a great academic focus without hammering it home.' Others talk about how dedicated she is and how she knows everything about every child in the school.

Married with two grown up children, one in law, one studying architecture, Kate is a classical music enthusiast and belongs to small group of people in southern France who facilitate concerts in Provence, where she tries to spend around three months of the year.

Entrance: Register for nursery as soon as possible after birth; nursery children are now guaranteed the offer of a place in reception (£100 registration fee and £2,000 deposit). Places are offered by date of registration and sibling priority. Most places in the pre-prep are filled from the nursery, but 'one or two' spaces might be available in reception, again based on date of registration. Consideration has been given to expansion, but finding suitable premises has been as issue.

Exit: A few leave at at 4 and 5. Twenty-eight children enter reception in two classes of 14, but numbers naturally reduce to a manageable 20 by year 2, 'although this number does vary from year to year – we don't like to turn anyone away who has come through the nursery.'

The vast majority of 4+ and 7+ leavers go to St Paul's Cathedral School, North Bridge House or The Cavendish with the occasional one to Channing, Highgate, Lyndhurst etc.

Remarks: Founded as a nursery in someone's front room in 1973, when 'there was little in the way of early years provision and nothing in the way of policies and procedures', the nursery is now a fully-formed school in central Islington, housed in a former Hindu Temple, the first of its kind in London: 'Hindu Saints still pilgrimage here, but not during term time', we are told. Situated a brisk 15 min walk from the pre-prep (although there is flexibility in pick-up times for parents with children on both sites). Two year olds upwards enjoy a rich and dynamic offering (including conversational Spanish, dance, yoga and art) taught by fully qualified teachers. 'It's a lovely, friendly place,' said one parent. 'They really care about each child.' At the nursery we were impressed by the large, bright and airy rooms with a plethora of activities to stimulate any child. Although there is no attached outdoor space, children are taken to a nearby garden three times a week and to soft play weekly. Hours increase from mornings only in the nursery to full days for pre-reception children.

The pre-prep came into being when a former parent spotted a school to let in the local newspaper. 'Our nursery parents always felt it was a pity that children had to move on at 4 and 5.' Now they can remain in the fold, housed in a petite and picturesque Victorian school building. The classrooms lead off a lovely sheltered playground. 'It's idyllic, like Enid Blyton,' said one parent.

Very much a 'child-led' school, 'We like them to work collaboratively, one child supporting another.' It's not a hothouse, but with the 7+ ever-present at the end of year 2, children are expected to do homework after school on most days (introduced gently in reception and year 1) and during the summer holidays before entering year 2. 'A fairly challenging environment', one parent said, but another added: 'Whilst they do take the 7+ very seriously, they do it without panicking parents.' However, as Kate says, 'being a small school, the teachers do get to know the children very well and are quietly assessing their progress on a daily basis. We can then cater for their individual needs and there is a lot of fluidity between ability groups.'

It is a very creative environment in which the arts – music, art and dance – are central to learning. Children might make shoebox interiors as a part of a home topic, create giant tetrahedron mobiles in maths, or paint and embroider textiles in a study of fabric-making. During our visit, the children had just been learning about the Jewish Festival of Succot and had created their very own Succah (a temporary wooden shelter) in the playground.

Specialist teachers extend the core. Spanish is taught from nursery onwards for one lesson a week, and ICT has a dedicated teacher and a full-class supply of laptops throughout. Singing and rhythm are taught by a music teacher, plus a weekly half-hour violin lesson with two professional violinists. 'We could have chosen any instrument, provided the children learned pitch, rhythm and musical notation. Most children play the violin very well by the end of year 2.'

The school prides itself on being very inclusive and an on-site SENCo addresses both minor and significant difficulties. Good support is given to those with English as an additional language, addressing the requirements of an increasing number of bilingual children.

The children are introduced to team games and specialist ball-skills teachers provide additional PE lessons in one of the two large adjoining church halls. Well-equipped playground. 'We have a lot of play resources and use them to extend children's learning with carefully planned activities' – a fabulous wooden pirate ship was a recent addition. Regular trips to nearby King Henry's Walk Garden provide the opportunity to observe seasonal changes and grow their own vegetables in the allotments.

Plenty of enrichment. 'The school is fantastic at making lovely things happen for the children,' said one parent. Each class has at least two visits a term, always educational and usually entertaining (storytellers, puppeteers, exotic animals, LSO concerts and an African drummer to name but a few) as well as numerous themed events. During our visit it was the annual Our Wonderful World Week. 'Everyone is invited to take part, from grandparents to aunts and uncles, to share something from their country of origin, which could be food, stories, music etc.'

After-school clubs twice weekly, and activities change termly – everything from sewing, fencing, chess, cookery, science, drumming to football skills could be on the agenda. Homework club 'helps parents and promotes a sense of independence in the child.' Lunchtime clubs include coding, games and puzzle club.

School uniform is minimal and practical (navy and white with specific school sweatshirts and fleeces). The school encourages healthy eating and children bring in lunchboxes, supplemented by a snack with fruit in the morning (provided by the school).

Traditional values of courtesy and consideration are central to the ethos. Kindness is rewarded here, and if you achieve 10 certificates, you get to choose half an hour's 'golden time' for the whole class: 'Being kind is paramount', said a mother.

Founded by parents, The Children's House remains a parent-driven operation, with active participation from its Parent Committee. All vote for the council of management, which administers the school. Unsurprisingly, the cosmopolitan families (Islington and Hackney media, lawyers, bankers and artisans) form a tight bond both with each other and the school, regularly arriving to read, organising the summer fair, quiz night etc. There is a genuine commitment to community links and charity fundraising. 'We couldn't do it without the parents, who are amazing.' One of the things parents like most about The Children's House is its home-away-from-home atmosphere, and 'being made to feel so welcome.' One parent told us: 'Literally, my only criticism of the school is that it doesn't go up to 11. It's such a shame to leave such a happy place.'

The school offers three fully-funded and some partially funded bursary places.

Christ Church Primary School Chelsea

1 Robinson Street, London SW3 4AA

Ages 4–11 **Pupils** 210 **C of E**

020 7352 5708
www.chchchelsea.rbkc.sch.uk

Head: Since 2009, Avis Hawkins, BSc NPQH (40s). Read psychology at Royal Holloway with a view to becoming an educational psychologist, but got the teaching bug while training at the Institute of Education. Started her career in a state primary in Lewisham, then opted for a struggling school for the challenge;

'That made me the teacher I am'. Appointed deputy at Christ Church in 2000 and was the natural choice to step into the role when previous head retired.

Attractive, energetic and disarmingly open, she has both children and parents on her side; 'So personable and friendly,' said one. Another added, 'Not the kind of head who just sits in their office', though with the white and grey Danish-look furniture, complete with functional teaching table – no leather sofas here – she might be tempted. 'Open door' policy taken literally; pupils appeared in her study and opened up drawers in her desk during our chat. Her wide smile only wanes when lamenting the tight budget. In response, she has created an enrichment assistant, who makes the most of local contacts, invited to talk to hand-picked groups of children. Recent visitors include a fashion designer, artists from the nearby Saatchi Gallery, and volunteers from the Chelsea Physic Garden. 'I am taking experience-based learning and applying it to the curriculum', she explains. Married with three children, two at the school, her hobbies range from food to DJ-ing. There is no doubt she leads by example.

Entrance: Vastly oversubscribed C of E school, with perennial waiting list. Priority given to siblings and families attending St Luke's or Christ Church, Chelsea; remaining places for other C of E families and locals. Takes from RBKC and Wandsworth, with a few from Hammersmith and Lambeth. Single class intake at reception, with occasional places further up the school. One parent told how 'wealthy families used to take them out at 7', but it appears they have now got wise, and none leave unless through relocation.

Exit: Increasing numbers, 30-50 per cent, to independents, including Godolphin & Latymer, Alleyn's, Dulwich, Westminster; lots bag bursaries and scholarships. Many to top London state schools: Lady Margaret, The Grey Coat Hospital and Chelsea Academy, plus Fulham Boys School. One parent felt more help could be given to parents with bursary and scholarship applications.

Remarks: Located in the hushed affluence of a terraced square, in an area of celebrated artists, writers and politicians, this charming Victorian school has an exterior that harks back to a bygone age, when Chelsea was no more than a collection of small parishes, and church, schoolroom and public house all clustered together on one corner. 'A village school in the heart of London' was how one parent described it and the charm lingers on, with lollipop cherry trees and a butcher's boy bike poised to deliver lunches to a nearby nursery. However, step inside and you have a Narnia experience: the interior has been redesigned to a spacious and functional plan, with chic grey walls, birch wood trimming and rows of navy pillars. Purpose-built in 2005, the main building on the north of Christchurch Street opens out to accommodate an internal playground for reception, with multi-coloured apparatus, as well as an open central stairwell and roomy classrooms for years 1-3. Behind doors we found a cookery room, art studio and ICT suite, as well as cosy beanbags in the reading room (emphatically 'not a library') and a multi-use hall with gym and dining tables. As one parent put it, 'Every nook and cranny has to be made useful'. Outside and across a wide pavement (or The Piazza) the older years occupy what was the infant school, opened in 1850 by the patron, Earl Cadogan, we are reminded on a stone plaque. Three classrooms here have a more studious feel, with individual desks facing whiteboards, but each has its own corner with plump cushions for bookworm breaks. Opposite stands Christ Church, a Victorian gothic parent building, visited on feast days and Fridays by the school, while at the fourth corner of this tiny crossroads is the playground, discreetly hidden behind a tall wall of ivy. The large play area has been landscaped to accommodate a sports pitch, gardening plots, a pergola and free play areas. 'I would like a bit more playtime,' sighed one child, and we were not surprised. Several parents commented how well maintained the buildings were, and one ventured, 'environment helps behaviour'. The charming neighbourhood is reminiscent of a scene from Mary Poppins; all it lacks is a dancing chimney sweep.

C

This is a school that claims to take a holistic approach to education, but still hits the spot academically. Class sizes are 30, with a 22:1 student to staff ratio, but with lots of small groups or half-class sessions at specialist subjects. The head assures us, 'if you're looking for a school at the top of the league tables, we're not the school for you', but it is hard not to be impressed by these children's achievements on paper. Numeracy and literacy is managed by the leadership team as a through-school experience, not split into key stages. Verbal reasoning and non-verbal reasoning are taken in year 6; 'We pay lip service to the 11+ exams,' says the head. 'Aspiration is important'. We witnessed a Friday afternoon English class hard at metaphor and metre. Inclusion is a watchword too, with several SEN children supported within each year group. A range of difficulties, from dyslexia to ASD, are managed by a dedicated department and visiting OT, SLT, nutritionist and school nurse. The head welcomes the differences: 'it makes everyone aware of social behaviours'.

Not surprisingly, the staff profile is 'very static'; several boast 10+ years of loyal service, so the head continually makes waves with professional training programmes. The school forms an alliance with four other local primaries, mutually inspecting and monitoring each other and offering suggestions. The head also has a knack of finding restless retirees and enlisting them into some extracurricular activity: a retired headmaster takes gardening, as a curriculum topic, directing the wheelbarrows, tending the chickens and watering the kale beds. Another ex-teacher runs cricket sessions in morning break, and several volunteers have become student teachers, and later join the staff. As one mum put it: 'They are very good at growing their own'.

There's a daring zing to the curriculum, or, as the head puts it, 'I am trying to make the curriculum wide enough and rich enough so children can find their talents beyond the three Rs'. This is evident in the music teaching: over 50 per cent of the school take up an instrument. Youngsters can pick up a ukulele, trumpet or drums, as well as the more usual options, funded for a term by the school. As an Artsmark school, there's an artist in residence in each year group, who encourages messy creativity in an upstairs studio. Year 1 recently completed a metal-bashing project, while the corridor was arrayed with giant paper planets. A recent leaver went on to star in the West End production of Matilda, a talent no doubt fostered in the ambitious Christmas and Easter shows; productions have included King Lear and Richard III (abridged). A specialist sports teacher co-ordinates team games in Battersea Park or in the Royal Hospital pitches nearby. There's room for football and netball on the hard court in the playground, dance for boys and girls in the hall, and swimming from year 2 at nearby Chelsea Sports Centre. A mass of after-school clubs include Mandarin, chess, judo, and knitting as well as a kayaking experience up river to Putney. One parent had to pinch herself when faced with the list of clubs, for fear she had confused it with the exclusive school up the road.

Christian values appear modestly within the school, as a poster on the doorway or mosaics of Biblical scenes on the walls. There is daily assembly, led by the head, or a celebratory one each Friday, known by the visiting vicars as 'The Oscars'. Here the children applaud each other's achievements and two Students of the Week are named from each year. Other incentives to good behaviour include an afternoon's golden time, sparingly reduced for poor behaviour. One parent said,

'They are all incredibly well behaved and respectful', and 'the last thing they would do is exclude a pupil'. The youngest children have a designated 'shepherd' from year 6 to sit with them at lunch. The system looks after the lambs but also instils a sense of responsibility in the older pupils. One mum worried that responsibility was not always shared evenly between the children: 'They could mix up responsible roles, like reading in church'.

Unlike many London prep schools, the pick up was not dominated by hooting 4x4s; instead, parents chatted outside in groups. The school's community spirit was evident; 'phenomenal at bringing everyone together. Very welcoming', thrilled one mum. Many meet up crossing the bridges from Battersea. One dad stressed the 'connectivity between teaching staff and parents'. There are parent workshops in maths and English, with crèche, to coach parents in helping with homework. Day to day queries are dealt with by phone or teacher meeting. More than one mum reported how they got an overnight response from the head and an invitation to meet the next day. Children are 'a mix of privilege and none', as the head put it, though all looked equally smart when dressed in the navy and cherry uniforms and stripy ties. Parents and offspring raved about the improved catering. The kitchen is literally a home-grown affair, using eggs and produce from the school's garden, cooked up into healthy meals by two mums, who have a background in catering, with a sprinkling of advice from the community nutritionist. One of the cooks even delivers carry-outs by bike to a nearby nursery. The result is an education in healthy eating and sustainability. According to the kids, it tastes good too, especially the pizza and apple crumble.

We agreed with the mum who said: 'I knew it was good, but I was surprised how good it was'. A diminutive state primary school, which rivals the local independents in the brainy stuff but which displays ingenuity and imagination in its broad curriculum. The resourceful head syncs her band of dedicated staff and parents to strike up a winning tune and lively, inquisitive children take up the chorus. Well, Chelsea is famous for its smart set.

City and Islington College

40

283 – 309 Goswell Road, London EC1V 7LA

Ages 16–19 **Pupils** 1,600

020 7700 9333
www.candi.ac.uk

Director: Since 2015, Peter Murray BA MA PCGE Oxon, late 50s, previously deputy director of sixth form. Read history at Kings College, London, before taking a masters in 19th century social history at Warwick. Drawn to teaching by an inspirational role model at school: 'If you've had a good experience, you think... I might enjoy that....and I did'. Cut his teeth in secondary schools in London and home counties, before moving to tertiary education in Richmond upon Thames College, arriving at Candi (as it is known) in 2000 to co-ordinate humanities, then as deputy for seven years. No stranger to the area, he grew up in Islington, supports the Gunners and saw his younger sister attend the college, operating under a previous name, in the 80s. 'She had a really different and a really good experience,' he muses.

A keen runner and 5-a-side football player, and at 5 o'clock on a Friday evening, showed no signs of slowing down. Although his monochrome office has a touch of the impersonal about it, he expounds vividly on the college achievements, is conversant with the myriad different A level courses and glows with pride at his students' individual successes; 'a lot of our students come from a background where they don't have networking opportunities... where there is not a lot of academic success'. Describes the college as 'schooly, but it's not a school, it's not a university...like university, with safety nets'. Views his appointment as head as 'evolution rather than revolution', aiming to continue the progress of his predecessor in forging contacts with business and industry. 'There's a lot of advantage to be gained from networking and in London we are in a very good position to do that...building students' confidence and knowledge and an understanding of the world of work, building their aspiration'.

Academic matters: A sixth form college for A levels, sheltering under broader academic umbrella of City and Islington College and Westminster Kingsway College, has the advantage of offering a wide range of subjects (over 34 on offer when we visited), delivered by A level specialist teachers, in a tailor-made environment for 16-18s. Class sizes are kept to around 20 (22 max) in the popular subjects, supported by over 140 staff and technical assistants; smaller numbers attend the more unusual options, electronics, dance, graphic communication, Turkish. One parent was impressed by the flexibility in the timetable: 'They've been very open minded about changing course'. Mainstream subjects like physics have seen a surge in popularity, boosted by the college's two female physics teachers, while the college has extensive technical back-up for a range of practical options including textiles, photography and media studies, whose students get to show final pieces at nearby Screen on the Green. In 2018, 30 per cent A*-B at A level. The head describes the student experience as academically rigorous. Around 60 students take the EPQ, which distinguishes independent learners and researchers. The staff are A level specialists, some with doctorates, some authors of school text books – and unanimously got the thumbs up from parents.

The head gives it straight from the shoulder about the Ofsted inspectors' tour. 'Overwhelmingly they were grade 1 lessons; I didn't have to hide anyone from them, there are no bad teachers here'. The management team he describes as 'fantastic' and 'sparky'; the parents' verdict: 'interconnects well as a team'. The head's mission to create links with industry and academia has a two-fold effect. Describing how aspiring medics get to sit alongside UCL students at the Royal Free Hospital, he commented, 'It is stimulating for the staff, and that comes back into the classroom'.

An inclusion co-ordinator supports a full range of special needs, from mild dyslexia to ASD, with one-to-one support in class or in separate smaller rooms, depending on the level of need. The user-friendly building, complete with lifts, accommodates physical disabilities too.

Games, options, the arts: Wednesday afternoons are for enrichment. Students who aren't lucky enough to be visiting the Supreme Court or meeting a Nobel Prize-winning astrophysicist can enjoy more earthly activities, including football, basketball, netball, boxercise and gym, co-ordinated by a sports youth worker, off site. There's an in-house dance troupe and theatre shows, including an annual talent show and a Christmas production, which take place in the drama studio or at Islington's Almeida Theatre. Students from both music and music tech courses join with others in a combo band, though numbers don't allow for a choir or orchestra. The walls of the corridors display lively posters for a wide choice of clubs: history club, talking religion, talking politics, geo-justice, robot club, as well as political debates about local elections and the London mayor. Teachers make the most of the graphic design students in promoting courses: 'Why learn a language?' asked one eye-catching poster and 'Congratulations on completing your coursework' cheered another message. Trips out include London museums and Tate Modern; residentials for geographers to Derbyshire, while the RS class gets to visit a Buddhist retreat in Scotland.

Background and atmosphere: In an area that Dickens refers to as where 'London began in earnest', the college site at Angel stands at a confluence of the metropolis's business and residential life. To the south and east it touches the City with its commercial and banking quarters, to the north it embraces the mixed residential areas of Highbury, Finsbury and Holloway and the buzzing shops and bars of Upper Street. The college's sparkling glass, steel and chrome structure catches the eye, with its grey themed interior and a city garden. Past the turnstiles and uniformed security checks, the visitor is greeted by a large canteen/hall/chilling area on the ground floor, labelled 'a thriving hub' by one mum. Beyond this is the library, with its purple and grey colour scheme, and shelves of journals. Many of the rooms are convertible to smaller meeting rooms, with soft dividers and screens; an adjacent IT suite houses computers as far as the eye can see.

A tour up the glass stairwell, with Barbara Hepworth-style holes, takes us to the classrooms and workshops above. Textiles, photography, and visual arts studios look out over the many cranes and offices of the cityscape, while film studies are found further along the corridor they call Media Street. Disappointingly little to see of the students' artwork in the designer building, and one mum felt the art and design department could be more inspiring. However, a room full of recording equipment run by dedicated techies provides support for the many and successful media students (alumni include singer, Paloma Faith; actor, David Oyelowo OBE; TV presenter, Reggie Yates; and news reporter, Symeon Brown). Humanities and languages classrooms have a floor to themselves, with seven science labs below; fully equipped with the latest kit and a flock of white coats and goggles; 'It seems to be very well resourced,' commented one parent. A vibrant hub on the first floor, full of upholstered chairs and scarlet beanbags, houses the careers advice centre.

A lone horse chestnut tree on a patch of green breaks up the austere landscape of the grounds (this is EC1 real estate) while an all-weather court on the roof of the science building next door allows for floodlit matches. Students can take a break between classes at brutalist picnic tables or work up an urban sweat at a game of garden ping pong.

Pastoral care, well-being and discipline: Dress is teen-casual and it's first name terms for teachers; 'that doesn't stop them calling you Sir for two years,' laughs the head. The relationship relies on mutual respect; 'we are trying to turn them into young adults,' he says and students we spoke to were aware of the journey. 'It's preparing me for life after', said one. The young adults recognised the school's high expectations: three warnings for misconduct or poor work, followed by a 'cause for concern' notice. One parent reported that the tutor had been quick to notice when her daughter's new-found freedom had gone too far, and called a meeting; 'we all three of us got her back on track'. No bullying, except the occasional modern menace of cyber-bullying. A more serious misdemeanour involves discussion with the parents. Serious alcohol or drugs issues are rare and accountable to a disciplinary panel; 'there's less goes on here than in my own sixth form of 90,' owns the head. A mum praised the pastoral tutor system, for 'quite closely monitoring' a particularly shy daughter. The college is conscious that its population is at a fragile stage of adolescence, so employs a full-time counsellor, alongside others including a mental health and well-being worker. 'As a society we are more enlightened,' explains the head. 'In the past people got on with it or sunk'.

Students with issues knew how to contact their tutor, and met with them every week in the normal way to discuss progress. They were in no doubt how to seek out help in applying for university from the full time careers officers; 'They are always telling us who to go to', said one. The higher education department offers advice on UCAS applications, explains personal statements, carries out interview practice using former members of staff and even helps plan gap years. They run a dazzling timetable of tutorials, eg applying for Oxbridge, medicine, teaching, nursing or apprenticeships, along with a range of informative talks ('STEM work experience for Girls' caught our eye) in addition to masterclasses in work-related skills such as online IT courses and young drivers' workshops. 'I talk to universities all the time,' says the head, which explains the respectable number of offers to competitive courses, though it was disappointing to find a capital-centric attitude in the students we met, who appear content to study close to home.

Pupils and parents: Starting afresh in a new sixth form, rather than staying at their secondary school, gives the students a real chance to reinvent themselves, and the ones we spoke to described a variety of reasons for choosing the college: 'it gives you more independence'; 'looking for somewhere you are doing things by yourself'; 'it's more diverse'; 'more subjects'; 'closest to home'. One parent commented about her daughter, 'She hadn't had a good experience, and had a lot of catching up to do with feeling good about learning...it's a place that gives inspiration to the students'. More girls than boys (60:40) and a typical urban cultural diversity: 'The ethnic mix is a real mix; 30 per cent Asian; 30 per cent Afro-Caribbean; 30 per cent white,' says the head, plus a few international students who 'want to have a London experience'. With huge numbers of students, the variety of ambition was also evident: the high achievers gain scholarships with banking or legal companies, others apply for vocational courses, while some are content to munch cookies in the canteen. 'The scale allows the range,' explains the head.

Parents commented on the study body as 'a mixed bag of individuals...from far and wide' and 'it's very diverse'. They meet the teachers at the annual parent evenings, or at individual sessions with the tutor or course leader, if requested. Surprisingly for such a large cohort, the parents all felt involved, and emails and phone calls were answered promptly. The school sends out a termly newsletter, though no-one we spoke to had read it.

Entrance: Five 4s needed at GCSE to study three A levels, higher grades required to take four subjects, and the college sets its own entrance test for maths. Applicants are encouraged to visit the open day in November and apply before the end of January. Oversubscribed, more than four applicants per place, but interviews 2,500 before making offers. A nucleus of students from Islington and Hackney, and has a partnership with three local schools: Elizabeth Garrett Anderson, Holloway and Islington Arts and Media, which have priority, although current cohort attended 200 different secondary schools. A taster day at the start of July is followed by registration at beginning of autumn term and a last opportunity to finalise courses. A handful of international students, who board with local families.

Exit: The head is rightly proud of his statistics: 70-80 per cent to university, one fifth to the Russell Group, a few to Oxbridge. Courses in 2018 included human, social and political sciences at Cambridge, fine arts at UAL, dentistry at King's College London and politics and economics at Exeter. Several students praised the dynamic careers advice service, which supervises applications.

Money matters: Centrally funded by Education Funding Agency; international students self-fund. Dedicated college advisor supports applications for a host of bursaries, sponsorships and additional expenses, including travel. Parents pay towards school trips.

C

Remarks: City and Islington College offers students a new beginning with a wealth of courses and great facilities. The students are encouraged to take advantage of their position in the heart of London to forge connections with the world of work and academia. Throw in supportive staff, a savvy head and a blessed central location at Angel and no wonder they are off to a flying start.

City of London School

Queen Victoria Street, London EC4V 3AL

Ages 10–18 **Pupils** 935 **Sixth form** 260

Fees: £17,901 pa

020 3680 6300
www.cityoflondonschool.org.uk

Head: Since January 2018, Alan Bird, previously deputy head at Brighton College, and responsible for much of the college's day-to-day management. He has also been head of sixth form there. First class degree in economics from Cambridge and a masters from LSE, where he was an Economic and Social Research Council scholar. Has also taught economics at his alma mater, RGS Guildford, and spent eight years as head of politics at Tonbridge. He is a pianist up to diploma standard and a proficient cellist and organist, a good skier, swimmer and squash player. He is very interested in politics, especially US politics.

Academic matters: Offers A levels – but a move to Pre-U is on the way, initially with biology, history, RS and modern languages. All in the sixth can opt to take the Extended Project Qualification in addition to three or four main subjects. School and is on the look-out for a replacement for the ECDL – something with programming built in, a cry we hear everywhere. Links with IT companies being developed to further upgrade the offering. No weak subjects or depts – results at A level and GCSE uniformly impressive. Columns of A*s, As, a few Bs and very little in the lower order columns (90 per cent A*-A/9-7 grades at I/GCSE and 68 per cent A*/As or equivalent at A level/Pre-U in 2018).

Maths much the most popular A level but modern languages hold up and Latin and Greek battle on. Mandarin compulsory in first two years and, seemingly, catching on here rather more than elsewhere. Links being forged with schools and organisations in China. Economics and drama the only concessions to the more 'modern' subjects – no psychology, business or other 'studies'. Lots of academic prizes eg recent successes in Olympiads, the prestigious Erasmus Essay Prize and the international Juvenes Translatores prize. 'My son's teachers have all been wonderful – especially in maths and the arts,' a parent enthused. A second felt, 'My sons are always stretched to be the best they can be but never pushed. They don't let you become so obsessed with work so you can't do other things. The teachers plainly want the best for each boy.' Another was concerned: 'There seems to be a drive to climb the league tables. We don't want that. It's not why we chose the school.' But school assures us there is no shift in the aims in that respect. Around 60 on the school's SEN register – mostly dyslexic or needing help with organisation. Not a prominent feature of the school's mix.

Good library – rather like a top notch public library in design and atmosphere but with 50,000 books, periodicals, CDs and PCs galore plus cases housing the more venerable volumes for show. Unique, in our experience, is the school bookshop – a real one. Super 'science lecture theatre' but memorable lectures seem to be on anything but science.

Games, options, the arts: Sports and arts praised unreservedly by parents despite the trek to the school's main sports centre at Eltham. 'They do fantastic things with them. The music tours are amazing.' More than half learn an instrument; many take LAMDA exams; much-praised joint productions with the girls' school in eg choral concerts with a choir of 200+. Music tech facilities of a high order. Lively drama – productions at all age levels. Smallish, pretty basic, studio theatre but excellent main, flexible 150-seater theatre would do credit to an upmarket fringe venue. Weekly school publication The Citizen produced by students. Four high-ceilinged art studios – all do art and music to year 9 – and much varied and vigorous portraiture on display. We enjoyed the ceramics – especially the satisfying crunch of some material or other underfoot. DT on the bottom floor also lively and fun and more DT and to a higher level (as yet no GCSE) on the cards, to boys' delight.

Football is main winter game and the school is a powerful presence in inter-school tournaments. Basketball, cricket, water polo, swimming and athletics all strong. Current National Water Polo champs and champs in London basketball and football tournaments – no narrow academic focus here. On-site huge sports hall, weights room and pool. Sizeable Astros marked out as pitches. Rest happens 25 minutes' away at sports clubs around the metropolis. Some 200+ on D of E Award programmes; CCF surprisingly lively for a city school but offering mouth-watering, subsidised opportunities – 'I did a powerboat course and got my licence from it,' said one young man.

Excellent range of trips and tours with a focus on educational value and enrichment rather than the extravagance one sees elsewhere. Good use made of London and its riches – a three-weekly trip to somewhere in the capital made by all year 9s. Good range of clubs with a bent towards to the literary and the philosophical – we like The Diaspora Club, The Comedy Society and Modern Language Society, in particular. Many have their own sizeable domains – we passed The Railway Society room – 'thousands of pounds worth of kit in there,' we learned. Debating is popular and lively as is Model United Nations. Lots of outreach and charity work done out of conviction more than duty. Overall impression is of a varied, creative and quirky programme with plenty for everyone from sports stars to unashamed geeks.

Background and atmosphere: A school with a long, complex and obscure history. Its original benefactor, John Carpenter, and his executor intended his legacy to be for 'the finding and bringing up of four poor men's children with meat, drink, apparel, learning at the schools, in the universities, etc, until they be preferred, and then others in their places for ever'. The school as we know it today was finally established four centuries later, in 1837, first just off Cheapside, moving, in 1883, to Blackfriars and finally, in 1986, to a purpose-built, magnificently-sited, establishment between the Thames and St Paul's Cathedral. While it can no longer claim the nobly charitable purpose intended by Carpenter, it retains a liberal, progressive ethos, not least in its determinedly ecumenical attitude to religion and its generous bursary scheme, and much is being done in 'outreach' – eg working with The City of London Corporation's academies, charitable ventures, multiple imaginative and beneficial links.

Wherever you are, great city buildings look in at you through many windows. And the river light is likewise inescapable. The building – which seemed over-warm and airless to us on a mild spring day – is wearing well. It's a little municipal – the signing, wide corridors and atria are reminiscent of an NHS hospital – but the whole is softened by relics from its previous home (we appreciated especially the row of Victorian leaded lights lining the dining room celebrating school luminaries), trophy cabinets, miles of red lockers – and the arts and crafts about the place. Displays stay up for rather too long, we gather, so that people stop looking. Extraordinary things like the fragment of a second century AD limestone Roman head of Mars found as part of an old riverside wall. Large 'concourse' used for events, adorned by plaques and statues to more school luminaries. Also, seemingly, hundreds of PCs everywhere. School houses are named for great figures in the school's history.

Pastoral care, well-being and discipline: Houses are 'important but not that important', we were told, ie sports, chess, intellectual competitions etc run on house lines but 'being in a different house never separates friends'. Sixth formers are grouped by shared subject teacher rather than houses. Every parent stressed how happy their son(s) were at the school. 'The boys in his class are so lovely – friendly, happy and always polite and nice to each other,' one told us, while a second said, 'It's a nurturing environment – they offer help, they set him up with a mentor and try to nip problems in the bud'. A third felt that the boys were 'very respectful of the teachers – it's a liberal ethos and it works'. And a fourth, 'The boys help each other in all kinds of ways'. Few discipline problems, though we heard one class giving a language assistant a bit of a rough time.

Pupils and parents: From all over London and the home counties. Mostly native English speakers, but a great diversity of home languages spoken including Chinese, Hindi, Russian and Tamil. Very few need EAL support. Brains the only common denominator – parents, who like the social mix in the school, are mostly professional, bright, urban and appreciative of broad and liberal educational values. 'They learn to respect everyone,' said one, 'and realise that not everyone can afford parties in limousines.' Formidable list of notable former pupils (known as Old Citizens) includes HH Asquith (PM 1908-16), Arthur Rackham, Ernest (Oh for the Wings of a Dove) Lough, Denis Norden, Julian Barnes, Daniel Radcliffe, Mike Brearley, Anthony Julius, Steven Isserlis, umpteen brainbox academics, legal eagles, cleverclogses of all sorts, among them three winners of the Nobel Prize.

Entrance: Highly selective. By competitive exam in English, maths and verbal reasoning in year 5 for 10+ (40-50 places for which around 160 apply), and year 6 for 11+ (60 places for which around 550 apply) and 13+ (40 places – ISEB pre-test at 10, followed by interviews and conditional offer based on CE – perhaps 350 apply) plus interview and report from current school. At 11+, two distinct competitions, with those after 100 per cent bursaries sifted by taking an online reasoning test in December. Around half of all entrants come from preps, the rest from state primaries. At 16, applicants are tested in their two top subjects – 20 available places for which 75 apply. The school courts the primary/prep sector early – admission in year 6 is unusual and they clearly steal a march on the rest.

Exit: Up to 15 leave after GCSEs, almost all to state sixth forms. All leavers go on to heavyweight subjects at good universities – around 15 per cent to Oxbridge annually (20 in 2018) and the rest to eg UCL, Bristol, Durham, Warwick, Edinburgh etc plus eight medics and five to the US (USC, Carnegie Mellon, Duke, Wesleyan and NYU).

Money matters: Around 10 per cent of current pupils on 100 per cent fee remission via 'sponsored awards' available at 11+ and 16+ for bright candidates whose family finances would not stretch to fee-paying school without assistance. All applicants sifted via reasoning tests. Gross parental income to be below £45,000. Around 30 academic scholarships available at all entry points, worth up to 25 per cent of fees. Candidates invited to a 'demanding interview for which no preparation is helpful'. Sports scholarships – good footballers especially welcome. Music scholarships and choral bursaries – these for those who become choristers at The Temple Church and The Chapel Royal.

Remarks: 'A very down-to-earth school,' asserted a parent and we agree. An inspiring yet grounded school with solid values, providing vision, opportunities and a wonderfully civilised start in life for its lucky students. A jewel in London's crown.

C

City of London School for Girls

Linked with City of London School for Girls – Prep

St Giles' Terrace, London EC2Y 8BB

Ages 11–18 **Pupils** 639 **Sixth form** 150

Fees: £18,384 pa

020 7847 5500
www.clsg.org.uk

Headmistress: Since 2014, Ena (pronounced Enna) Harrop BA MA MA MPhil PGCE (40s), a modern linguist, originally from Spain. Her previous incarnations include head of Spanish at Royal Russell and head of modern languages at Royal Grammar, Guildford. She joined City Girls as director of studies in 2010 and – unusually and remarkably – was appointed internally to the headship, clearly to the delight of the entire school. One of the most popular heads we have encountered.

You can, instantly, see why. She is the real deal. Formidably intelligent, chic, softly spoken, charming and beautifully articulate, her credo is the centrality of gender equality and the necessity of the modern world being gender-blind. And, as a head and the mother of three daughters, she lives the dream. Her (teacher) husband took her maternity leave when their last daughter was born. In the words of her pupils: 'She was – before she became head – a kind of figurehead.' 'The message of feminism she promotes in the school is so inspiring.' One admitted, 'I was scared when she came on our school trip but she was so relaxed it wasn't daunting at all'. And another, 'When she became head we just thought it'd be great to have more of her'. And every parent we spoke to concurred.

'Independent learning' is a phrase you meet a lot here and, again, the head – with her list of degrees – walks the talk. 'I feel tempted,' she told us, 'to take at least two A levels at this school – economics and art.. and then there's..' A very modern head; a recent assembly was on 'All you need to know about pregnancy and childbirth' and she refers to 'the nappy barrier' to women's achievement. Behind her desk sits a text: 'Feel the fear but still do it.' With Mrs Harrop as role model, a City student will leave as well-equipped to take on and challenge the world – while remaining her essential self – as any young woman could.

C

Off to head Crofton House School in Vancouver in July 2019. Her successor will be Jenny Brown, currently head of St Albans High School for Girls. English degree from Oxford; worked briefly in publishing before escaping to teach English at Cranleigh, followed by Highgate School, South Hampstead High, Channing and St Paul's Girls where she was director of senior school.

One half of the Good Schools Guide's first set of identical twin head teachers – her sister, Jane, is head at Wimbledon High ('it's lovely to be able to share ideas'). Lives in Highgate with playwright husband, Ben, and enjoys theatre, literature (muses 'who would I head towards first in Heaven – Shakespeare or Donne?') and a weekly swim in Hampstead Ponds. Writes poetry 'when creative space allows'. Two children.

Academic matters: Maths rules. As elsewhere with clever students, this has become the most popular – and successful – A level subject, and recent takers outnumbered the entire languages cohort. 'My girls are strategic,' explains EH, 'and they know that if they take a language they are less likely to get an A*/A than if they take maths'. The girls say: 'People really like maths – they see the use of it.' Other popular subjects – in an, admittedly, conservative range – are history, chemistry and English. Mandarin, after a very successful course to GCSE, now offered at Pre-U, and should markedly boost the number of language takers, which has increased anyway since EH took over.

Overall, A level results included a creditable 82 per cent at A*/A in 2018. GCSE results no less impressive with 95 per cent A*-A/9-7. However, although results are obviously a key factor in the school's success, the school itself puts the emphasis elsewhere – on, for example, independent learning and thinking. Lots of computers and library has a bank of borrowable laptops. Librarian seen as 'wonderful', though library itself, possibly, not the most impressive feature – we were bemused by some strange cataloguing and location of books and it felt a bit tired. Although a third of the pupils speak a language other than English at home, almost none need EAL help. Around 12 per cent with a mild SEN of some kind, all supported as needed on an 'as and when' basis but no-one with major learning difficulties here. School not easy for those with mobility difficulties.

Games, options, the arts: Art is, according to all, wonderful. We saw some terrific painting and the results at A level and GCSE are phenomenal. Good hall for display of work and three studios, all richly and messily busy – the colour and variety of the top floor a refreshing relief. DT taken by all years 7-9 in good sized studio with everything you'd expect, including inventive year 7 torches. Lots of music – individual, large and small groups, pursued with excellence and enthusiasm. Two good sized teaching rooms at top of the building plus numerous practice rooms. Drama in huge hall and Black Box Theatre at the top of the building. Well-designed literature for shows is evidence of classy production values throughout. Draughty outdoor theatre a splendidly imaginative recent innovation – a bit like a Greek theatre, only colder.

Games, remarkably, mostly take place on site – planners found flat spaces, inside and out, for two tennis courts, a large Astro pitch, various other spaces for a gym, 25 yard pool, table tennis and newish dance studio. Outside space overlooked by flats – the girls must get used to it. Non-selective approach to some teams gives all enthusiasts opportunities and it works. They do cross-country round the high level walkways. Many representatives in borough games and several notable individual successes on local and grander levels.

But perhaps the most exciting aspect of the extracurricular offering is London itself. 'There are all the galleries and museums – 'they are so easy to go to from here, you can get there in a double art lesson'. 'It's one of the reasons I came here,' typifies the response. Young Enterprise, likewise, outside speakers, visits, lectures at UCL, the Royal Institution etc, trips and tours – all add to the avid seizing of a rich variety of opportunities here.

Background and atmosphere: The original school began life in 1894. William Ward, who believed in giving girls a broad and liberal education with an emphasis on scholarship, left a third of his fortune – £20,000 – to the City of London Corporation for the foundation of a girls' school. Livery companies, banks and city firms continue to give financial support; the Corporation still administers this and the board of governors is appointed by the Court of Common Council. The Corporation has an education strategy and its portfolio of schools gives rise to mutually beneficial links between City Girls' and state primaries eg sixth form community service.

One of the more surprising school locations in the UK. Navigating the Barbican complex is notoriously tricky, but if you negotiate the grey concrete and glass mini-village to its heart, following brick-paved walkways, you will find the school. It sits between the ancient church of St Giles, Cripplegate (glass office blocks behind) and the Guildhall Conservatory, the Barbican arts venue and city flats with their valiant window boxes – with a large, flagged and lilied, ornamental pond between. Also surprising the eye and breaking up the harshness are the gallant trees and the improbable wodge of ancient London wall which squats defiantly opposite the school's main entrance.

The school opened here in 1969 – the first, pretty much, of the reincarnations of venerable educational institutions needing new and purpose-built homes. A bold conception and it wears well. The inside is as stark and work-full as Gradgrind could have wished, though lively displays and lots of big windows help relieve the Spartan architecture. Sixth form centre cleverly bolted on. You go in and out a lot – rain and shine – as you negotiate the five storeys. Good-sized dining hall and jolly good menu – Wok Theatre, Italian/Indian Fusion and Big Bowl Salad looked tempting.

Famously diverse mix of pupils and staff as befits the school's situation in the heart of the city. 'Diversity' is a word you hear a lot here, in numerous contexts. Not least the effect of coalescing people from so huge an area. Likewise, we heard 'exciting' a lot. The girls say, 'It's always busy here – but in a good way, and being in the Barbican is so exciting!' Pupils are bright-faced, smiley, articulate and confident – with no trace of arrogance. They have a sense of their responsibilities to the wider world alongside their own personal ambitions.

Pastoral care, well-being and discipline: Light but 'tightly run' discipline. 'The teachers really care that the girls are happy,' a parent told us, and 'they deal quickly with problems'. 'No-one gets thrown out if they haven't had loads of warnings first,' girls told us. 'They bring in parents. It's mostly just poor behaviour over a long period but it hardly ever happens.' And most pay tribute to the excellence of pastoral care and their 'lovely' teachers.

Pupils and parents: They come from a vast circumference around the city – Chigwell to the north east, Harrow to the north, Shepherd's Bush and Fulham to the west – even as far away as Cambridge. 'It's helped me become a lot more independent and the school gives us "travel buddies" when we join so that we can get used to the journey with someone experienced.' Parents say: 'The mix of girls is wonderful. They're not a flashy lot and they're not tarted-up either.'

Entrance: Numbers of applicants, as at other academically selective London schools, now hitting heights of absurdity and severely straining schools' resources, especially here, where physical space needed on assessment days is limited. School is no longer part of the London Consortium so sets own exams in English and maths and what is graphically described as 'an interview with teeth'. Twenty-five from own prep plus around 850 now applying for the 75 additional places at 11+. NB acceptances on a first-come-first-served basis, with offers withdrawn when the 75 places are filled (usually within days). Around 70 applicants for the 10-15 places at sixth form. Sixth form places conditional on school's own exams taken in potential A level subjects and on 9-7s at GCSE in all subjects.

Exit: Around 15-25 leave post-GCSE to board or go co-ed or to sixth form colleges. Early warning given if sixth form standards likely to be a problem. Some parental criticism of the less than gentle manner in which this has taken place in the past but the Harrop regime is softening the approach, and this has become a rare occurrence, though the criterion for staying – ie eight grade 7s at GCSE – remains in force.

Sixth form leavers are starry – 17 to Oxbridge in 2018, with 10 medics and one to Ivy League college; the London University colleges also take a good number. Great range of serious courses – nearly a third STEM and number of linguists now rising. Notable former pupils include Claire Rayner, Hermione Lee, Alison Weir, Elizabeth Emanuel, Romola Garai, Winklemans – Claudia and Sophie – and Daisy Christodoulou. Also Anna Blundy and Dido Armstrong, who both did their sixth forms at Westminster. They might not move now?

Money matters: Around 25 per cent on some kind of fee assistance. Bursaries from 25 per cent to 100 per cent. Unusually no academic scholarships, but music, drama and art scholarships of up to £1,500 a year at 11+ and 16+, and an 11+ sports scholarship.

Remarks: By any standards, a top school for girls, with an edge of excitement, modernity and realism. Makes the most of what it is, where it is. Said a parent: 'My daughter is incredibly happy there. She has blossomed. Her friends and the head are amazing. I've only ever heard good things.'

City of London School for Girls – Prep

Linked with City of London School for Girls

St Giles' Terrace, Barbican, London EC2Y 8BB

Ages 7–11 **Pupils** 93

Fees: £18,384 pa

020 7847 5500
www.clsg.org.uk

Headmistress: Since 2017, Rachel Hadfield, previously assistant head for curriculum at Foxfield Primary in Woolwich. Geography degree from Durham; has also been class teacher at Dalmain Primary in Lewisham.

Entrance: Twenty-four hotly contested places at 7+, sitting nationally standardised tests in English, maths and verbal reasoning plus some spelling and writing tests of the prep's own authorship. Register your daughter early to be sure of her being seen: the school assesses a maximum of 150 girls, and is always oversubscribed. Of those 150, the top 50 are called back for a further day's appraisal, during which they're examined in English, maths, science and DT – this last because it allows the girls to be observed in practical activities and working as a team. The 24 places are then offered to those 'with academic ability and the potential to become independent, happy learners.' Girls are seen in the November of the year preceding entry; closing date for accepting or declining offers is mid-February.

C

Exit: Parents take note: entry to the senior school is not automatic. By Easter of year 5, reserved places (ie places that are guaranteed) are offered only to those girls 'who continue to develop'. Any child who joined the school later than year 3 doesn't get one at all, and must sit for a place along with the external candidates. School insists that 'the vast majority go through'. Some parents' perceptions are different; see below. Destinations of those who do go elsewhere include St Paul's Girls', North London Collegiate, Francis Holland, Channing and Queen's College London. 'We've been hugely successful in placing girls at other schools. Schools like City Prep girls, and they don't get them that often.'

Remarks: Broad curriculum, with specialist teachers from the senior school coming in to teach music, art, DT, PE, Latin (years 5 and 6) and modern languages. The girls learn a different language each year: Spanish in year 3, French in year 4, German in year 5 and Mandarin in year 6. The idea is that the girls acquire an enthusiasm for languages which then helps them to choose the right ones when they go on to senior school, which is certainly commendable. It struck us as odd, however, that they only studied each language for a year before having to drop it and move onto the next one; a year 5 girl we spoke to admitted that she'd now forgotten the Spanish she'd learned in year 3.

As well as benefiting from the senior school teaching expertise, the excellent senior school facilities – swimming pool, sports hall, library, Astroturf, tennis courts – are also available, which doubtless explains why there's no difference in fees between the two (though prep fees do include lunch). Sports and gymnastics are strong, and music likewise, with the Y6s doing a Prep Opera every year. Impressive LAMDA results. There are also lots of residential trips which are perennially popular. Wide variety of clubs, and after-school care provides an opportunity for girls to do their homework as well as have fun. ('They have a register to make sure you don't wander off,' said one of our tour guides, earnestly.) Sixth formers from the senior school run clubs for the prep girls, which, says school, creates 'a big sister culture. They're great role models for the younger girls.'

Other than some worrying reports which we outline below, it took a long while for parental feedback to reach us about this school. Our first invitation was met with complete silence, and even a second appeal didn't yield very much. (This was in contrast to the parents of girls in the senior school, who were quick to tell us how happy they were.) Those who did eventually contact us agreed that the girls are worked hard but achieve highly. A couple remarked on the school's competitive nature: 'The girls are incredibly competitive, but also very supportive of each other, and have a strong sense of loyalty to their school,' said one. Another observed, 'If you're prepared to buy into the idea of City and have a daughter capable of swimming in its often competitive seas, it will be a worthwhile experience for her and for your family.' These parents emphasised that their daughters were enjoying their time at the prep, had made friends and embraced the opportunities on offer there.

However, some of these same parents expressed disquiet about the entry process to the senior school. 'The goalposts seem to have been moved,' said one couple, 'The message about not everyone getting reserved places is stronger now than it was when our daughter got in.' The same worried mother continued, 'Choosing to put a child through an entrance exam when they're 6 is not an easy decision; in our case we hoped to avoid the stress at 11+, which we now find we may not do. I suspect the feeling of rejection and the dent to self-confidence is higher if you don't get a reserved place from the prep and can't stay with your friends, than if you apply and fail as an external candidate.' School told us that an average of four girls leave City Prep's year 6 every year: two out of choice, and two who were 'advised to go elsewhere.' School figures show an average of three girls a year recently have not been given reserved places. This figure seems high to us, given both the stringent nature of the admissions process and the acknowledged high workload put upon the girls during their time here; and we did ask about this. 'Not all girls develop the same,' was the comment. 'Some go upwards and some go downwards; sometimes things happen in families to disturb girls.'

Parents and former parents are divided in their feelings about the school. On one side of the argument, accounts have been passed to us of recent City Prep girls whose confidence, and even health, had been so undermined by the school's approach that their parents voted with their feet and took them out. These parents write with angry eloquence about the school's 'complete lack of nurture and care' and claim that it 'values malleability and obedience over originality and sparky intellect.' They allege that there is poor support for special needs such as dyslexia, and that some of the teaching is sub-standard ('After we moved her, we discovered that she had been so poorly taught that she needed to relearn a year's worth of maths,' said one mother, and another mother reported an identical experience.)

The school insists that it works closely with parents, and that the girls' happiness is paramount. 'We love quirky individuals. We've got lots and lots of those. Girls are allowed to be themselves here.' And indeed, other parents told us that their daughters loved coming to school. One, whose child had excelled there academically, spoke of the school's 'really good pastoral side.' 'The prep is a nurturing and non-threatening environment,' said one mother whose child was now at CLSG senior, 'and I would have no hesitation in recommending it.'

Picking our way through such contradictory accounts was difficult. We can only conclude by suggesting that since entry to CLSG senior school isn't guaranteed, parents should think closely about whether City Prep is the right choice for their daughter or whether a prep school not linked to any senior school, but with a proven record of getting its leavers into the destination of their choice, might suit their family better. However, we hear encouraging reports of a loosening of tension under the new head.

School has plans to expand by opening a pre-prep – in what is currently a car park beneath the all-weather pitch.

Coldfall Primary School

Coldfall Avenue, London N10 1HS

Ages 3–11 **Pupils** 680

020 8883 0608
www.coldfall.haringey.sch.uk

Head teacher: Since 1996, Evelyn Davies (50s). Ms Davies is one of life's 'superheads', a woman who has taken a 'bog-standard' primary and transformed it into a star act with an 'outstanding' Ofsted, three-form entry and very happy parents. Most find her open-minded and approachable. 'I had an idea', commented one, 'and she immediately said "let's have a chat about it".' Hard working and well-organised, she gets things done. 'She's not ticking boxes, she really gets involved in the nitty gritty'. An active opponent of testing, testing, testing, she's even been to parliament to protest, winning the admiration of her local MP ('if I were the minister for education I would grab Evelyn Davies and put her as a key adviser. That way our children would be well educated in every sense of the word').

Entrance: Places given out using the standard local authority formula: children in local authority care, followed by special educational needs, siblings and distance from the gates. Recent expansion means a bit of leeway for those living a few streets away. Admission to full time nursery via the school.

Exit: A primary whose catchment fortunately straddles the borough's two highest flying comprehensives. The largest chunk of year 6 proceed to Fortismere, just next door. Sizeable (and growing) slice to Alexandra Park, down the road. Enviable success rate too, in grammar school entrance, then in dribbles to a wide range of local and distant establishments.

Remarks: This meticulously run school has everything going for it. Teaching here is enthusiastic and thorough, with staff constantly looking to improve performance. Academic standards are high and virtually every child reaches the government targets, many far exceeding them. Though the school has an 'unusually high' number of children with special needs, both those who struggle and those who excel are provided with plenty of booster classes. Not all parents, however, feel difficulties are necessarily dealt with sympathetically. 'Our son has considerable problems', said one, 'and we found the attitude very inflexible'. Behaviour is good and positive performance (particularly regular attendance) rewarded (classes compete enthusiastically for attendance teddies).

Facilities here can only be described as exceptional for a London primary. The original, large, low-lying Victorian schoolhouse, once a secondary school, has now been joined by a sleek, modern addition, providing extra classrooms and a new gym. Expansive grounds boast country-like playing fields, as well as two large and notably well-equipped playgrounds kitted out with basketball and netball nets, table-tennis tables and sheltered cabins. Pupils also benefit from the school's own allotments and nature trail, as well as access to nearby Coldfall Woods.

Sport played enthusiastically and successfully. Two hours of PE weekly overseen by a qualified sports coach and training approached with professional efficiency (gymnasts, for example, use flip cameras to study performance). Both boys and girls triumph in borough-wide competitions, boys winning recent golf and football championships, girls excelling in football and netball. Pupils also qualified for the London Youth Games.

Plenty of enrichment, in lessons and out, including chess (with championship-winning chess teams), French (taught by a native speaker), computer programming and cooking all part of the regular mix. Excellent range of clubs (including geology) and activities. Successful school choir has made appearances at the O2 and Barbican and one enthusiastic parent recently organised an entire week of dance with over 60 workshops and professionals imported from the West End. 'Things don't just happen here', said one mother. 'Everything is well planned and thought through'. Regular trips beyond the school gates include at least one visit to a museum, gallery and musical event for every pupil.

In the main (though not exclusively), parents are comfortably off Muswell Hill locals, so there's a good sprinkling of designer trainers in the playground, but this is low-key prosperity. Almost a third of pupils speak a language other than English at home. Both mothers and fathers (plenty of the latter at pick-up time) involved in making the school a success. 'All parents', said one enthusiast, 'are given an opportunity to contribute, not just non-working mums'. Many arrive at weekends to help with the gardening, and the thriving PTA organises summer and winter fairs, weekly coffee mornings, a Valentine disco, quiz night, fashion show and organic vegetable scheme. Sizeable sums are raised for playground, computer and PE equipment. 'There's a real feeling that everyone matters', said one mother. 'The kids are really blessed'.

Coleridge Primary School

Crouch End Hill, Hornsey, London N8 8DN

Ages 3–11 **Pupils** 912

020 8340 3173
www.coleridgeprimary.net

Head: Since 2014, Leon Cheouke BA PGCE (40s). After a first degree in community studies at Manchester and a PGCE at Goldsmiths University of London, Mr Cheouke arrived at Coleridge in 2000 and, apart from a year teaching in New Zealand, has been there ever since, working formerly as deputy to his long-serving and popular predecessor. Continuity and growth have his model. 'He said he wasn't going to change much and he hasn't,' said one parent. 'He's kept the best bits, really listened to what parents want and cares about all the children rather than statistics.' Keen on politics, Dr Who and vinyl.

Entrance: Coleridge is a very large school (120 each year enter four reception classes), but, sadly for aspiring parents, Crouch End is an ever-popular destination for family existence, and siblings tend to elbow newbies out of the way. Mumsnet types moan, too, about affluent applicants guying the system by renting nearby. The only advice is live as near as you can (ideally, within quarter of a mile).

Exit: The majority to a strong set of local comprehensives (Highgate Woods, Alexandra Park School, Fortismere), plus a handful to state selectives (Laytmer), independents and home schooling.

Remarks: Coleridge is a super primary – in both senses of the word (with 960 pupils, it's the size of many secondaries). Long one of the neighbourhood's most sought-after schools, in 2007 it expanded onto two sites, doubling the number of slots available. New arrivals now start in the original 1960s low-rise, before moving across the road to the bright, old-meets-modern addition in year 2. Parents originally worried the expansion might damage the close-knit feel, but agree the mood has been maintained. 'Because the school is on two sites, you feel you're dropping off somewhere quite small,' said one. Many feel, too, the scale equips pupils well for life afterwards.

Teaching an undoubted strength (maths, considered by Ofsted 'impressive'), with staff praised as 'bright, funny and incredibly enthusiastic'. 'The teachers are well tuned in with the children; they listen to them and treat them as individuals,' said one mother. Results excellent, with large numbers of year 6 pupils reaching well above standards expected for their age (some, it has been whispered, with the aid of tutoring). 'Standards are high, but they still make it fun,' said one mother. 'They're very aware of not putting too much pressure on the children.' Careful monitoring and target setting ensure the approach to each child is tweaked for maximum benefit. Progress equally successful for those with special educational needs or struggling on the foothills of English, who all make 'outstanding progress'.

Everything done to make the day exciting and interesting. Philosophy taught weekly to enhance critical thinking and pupils regularly involved in lively political debate (the environment, housing, teachers' salaries), while the school's de-luxe scale allows for a raft of specialists (two for art, one each for music, PE and Spanish). Homework (classified as 'home learning' and operating on a long-term timetable) is intended to develop research skills rather than become a domestic battleground. Two spacious libraries, with a dedicated librarian, are open to children in break and lunch.

The school holds the Arts Council's prestigious Artsmark Gold status for encouraging pupils to become involved with the arts, and the arts are, undoubtedly, a major strength. ('We've found that it's within the arts that children who may find the more academic areas of school life challenging are able to develop their "voice",' says the head). Art taught in a light, purpose-built studio and exhibitions held regularly, in school and out. Music excellent, with weekly singing assemblies and lively participation in choirs and competitions (Coleridge Royal Albert Hall choir, Crouch End Festival Choir, Sing Up competition). Dance and drama, too, made much of, with an annual whole-school play, dance classes (again with tailor-made space and links to The Royal Ballet), drama classes (with ties to the National Theatre) and numerous arts-related clubs held in lunch hours and before and after school. Parents love the approach. 'They do a lot of art and don't concentrate all the time on maths, English and science,' commented one. 'I moved here because I liked the creativity.'

Sports and games considered fundamental for healthy living and esprit de corps, as well as 'an integral part of the equal-opportunities practice' (so girls encouraged to play football, boys to dance). Gymnastics and games taught throughout, with older pupils learning netball, Kwik Cricket, athletics, tag rugby, tennis and football, some taught by specialist coaches. Swimming lessons at local pool. Frequent fixtures against other local primaries and sports day is a proper affair, with no dilly-dallying about all fair in love and sport, and school records recording 'x is the fastest at'.. ('The teachers decided to do this to challenge the children,' comments the head.) Outdoor education also delivered through regular attendance at forest school in nearby woods, where, as well as practical skills like putting up shelters, pupils develop teamwork and communication.

Huge range of after-school clubs (capoeira, meditation, fencing, drumming, photography, squash, art academy, tennis, school newspaper) and visiting talks (Highgate Woods feminist group – all former pupils – on gender equality, a Google employee to launch a technology competition). Also, privately-run breakfast and after-school clubs.

Crouch End is cool and media savvy – the school's Glastonbury-themed fête gives you a clue, as does a recent outing to The Guardian newspaper (where else?) – and while pupils come from the usual metropolitan multi-stranded ethnic range, the less advantaged are not unduly well represented. (Those in receipt of the pupil premium is 'below average', states Ofsted, a relative rarity in London.) 'Now that the school is bigger, there are more people from the flats and estates, and it's bit more ethnically diverse,' commented one parent. Children, however, tend to have names like Esme, Flora and Felix, Planet Organic features in after-school snacks, and prominent on the noticeboard is an ad announcing 'half cello for sale'. Parents, on the whole, comfortably off (£13,000, for example, raised at the summer fair), but also reasonably relaxed

C

and school is warm and friendly, with parental involvement a major part of the ethos - 'I love the community feel,' said one. Though some comments, too, about a small number of the 'vocal and opinionated' who the school attempts to keep at polite arms' length. Pastoral care an undoubted strength (with professional, confidential counselling offered on a one-to-one basis). 'Moving towards' a house structure. No uniform.

Pupils of all ages are confident and articulate (with year 6 recent victors in the Winston Churchill Public Speaking competition, beating off considerable prep school opposition) – and happy. 'My son has really thrived here. He was quite shy before he went but he has made a lot of progress socially and really loves school.'

Now, as always, the It school in the neighbourhood.

C

Colfe's School

Horn Park Lane, London SE12 8AW

Ages 3–18 Pupils 1,145 Sixth form 175 C of E

Fees: £12,663 – £16,929 pa

020 8852 2283
www.colfes.com

Headmaster: Since 2005, Richard Russell (50s), previously deputy warden of Forest School. Educated in Ireland and went on to read classics at Cambridge. He started his career as a Latin teacher; teaching initially attracted him as it would allow him to pursue his interest in archaeology and attend digs during the long summer holidays. Knows everybody and what they're up to, teaches Latin to year 7. He spent 15 years at Sevenoaks coordinating the IB programme; however, he has never thought it particularly suitable for Colfe's and is a great fan of A levels. A professional and pleasant person, say parents, easy to get on with and ambitious for his pupils. He lives in Blackheath with his wife, who works in the City. Nowadays holiday times see them heading for their house in Sicily, where they make their own olive oil.

Head of junior school: Since 2016, Catriona Macleod MSc. Worked at several London prep schools, becoming head of science and then deputy head at Streatham & Clapham junior school, head of juniors at Dunottar School, then head of junior school at Knightsbridge School. Has recently worked in a senior role at a free school in Hertfordshire.

Head of pre-prep since 2013 is Sarah Redman (50s) BEd. Mrs Redman was deputy head of the nursery and pre-prep school for some years before becoming head teacher. Parents comment on her warmth and friendliness, 'exactly the sort of person you can entrust your small child to'. Married to a fellow teacher, who is head of a local state primary, with three grown-up children, one of whom is an actress. She enjoys gardening, theatre, arts and crafts, the influence of which can be spotted around the pre-prep.

Academic matters: Well-planned academic curriculum in the junior school runs alongside inspirational sport and arts options. Six-year-olds upwards learn French and Spanish in alternating years. Mixed ability classes of around 18; each child is monitored regularly to check progress. Lively pupils perform well in both national and house competitions; particularly successful teams for maths and chess. 'A very caring school, where the teachers recognise every child as an individual.'

Exam results heading upwards most years – 61 per cent 9-7 at GCSE in 2018, with particularly strong showing in maths and science and 47 per cent A*/A, 78 per cent A*-B at A level. Maths, English and the sciences are popular closely followed by economics and history. Most take nine or 10 GCSEs including a language, choice of German, French, Spanish or Latin. Whole school aim is to make classes active and stimulating; everything is in place for high flyers who might be heading for Oxbridge but also for those who might need to go more gently. Setting for maths, sciences and languages. History and maths departments are particularly strong performers; provision for accelerated learning groups for additional maths qualifications. Sixth formers can take Extended Project Qualification. Students with mild specific learning difficulties are supported by specialist staff. The library is a well-used resource, with full-time librarian who also doubles up as head of careers, open until 6pm, during Easter holidays and to students on study leave. Outstanding advice and guidance on selecting courses and universities. The school recently ran a conference to introduce the option of going to university in the Netherlands.

Games, options, the arts: Arts and sports are strong all round, structured to suit all tastes and talents. 'Sport for all' policy means there is something for everyone, be it dance or being a member of one of the successful rugby teams. On-site facilities including a gym and 25m swimming pool, which hosts swimming galas, kayaking, water polo and lifesaving courses for year 10s. Additional large playing fields at Leathersellers' sports grounds a few minutes away by minibus on the Sidcup Road. Former Surrey and Kent opening batsman coaches cricket, and athletes often selected to represent Greenwich in the London School Championships. More or less everything on offer on the sporting front for juniors too, with lots of house competitions. Junior girls' netball team have been national prep school champions. CCF with its unique Army Air Corps unit popular, as is D of E, with many progressing to gold award.

Large art department includes printmaking equipment, a kiln for ceramics and a dark room. Parents comment on the energetic drama department; pupils encouraged to write and produce their own plays. LAMDA classes, stage management and technical theatre skills all on offer; impressive variety and number of productions. Up-to-date music rooms and individual soundproof practice studios; swing bands, orchestras, and choirs galore. Huge range of clubs and societies to join: particularly popular are maths, chess and debating along with many inter-house competitions, quizzes, drama, sports and concerts. Regular outings, theatre visits and trips abroad; sixth formers visit the Gambia annually to help build and maintain a school. Good participation in the arts, but relatively small numbers go on to take these subjects at A level, drama and media studies taking the lead over art, design and music.

Art is incorporated into much of the junior school curriculum and classrooms are bursting with interesting displays, models and sculptures. Specialist art teacher organises a big end of year exhibition. Musical education starts early with recorder in year 1 and ukulele in year 2. With around 80 per cent taking instrumental lessons, the school boasts choirs, orchestras, chamber groups, rock band and specialist brass programme. Creative drama, regular plays and lots of opportunities for performers in musical and dramatic assemblies. Dance workshops are popular and include everything and anything from flamenco to African dancing.

Background and atmosphere: Founded in 1652, to educate 'the poor boys of Blackheath' by the Rev Abraham Colfe of Lewisham. Later the school was left in the trust of the Leathersellers' Company, whose livery members make up a majority of today's governing body. Leathersellers have recently pledged an additional £1 million in bursaries. Was a state boys' grammar school for some years before opting to go independent in the 1970s rather than become a comprehensive school. Went fully co-ed in 1999. Strong links with six state schools, five local, one in the Gambia.

Corridors adorned with pupils' work and achievements; atmosphere is positive and busy with smartly dressed, friendly pupils and helpful staff. Bleak, utilitarian brick buildings softened by shrubs and trees; new Stewart building houses sixth form centre and Roebuck café.

Junior school in green and tranquil setting on the edge of the main school; new buildings are shooting up so the school can now accommodate three classes across the age groups.

Pastoral care, well-being and discipline: Pastoral care continues to be excellent and very much part of the school's ethos. Well-established house system in senior school; everyone attends regular house tutor meetings; years 8-11 are in vertical age groups, sixth formers and year 7s in separate groups. There are lots of opportunities for leadership and mentoring within the house system to help pupils develop maturity, gain confidence and a range of life skills. Frequent house activities and competitions ensure everybody is involved in the school community. School nurse and independent counsellor. Parents say home-school links are encouraged and the head of pastoral care is always available to speak with them. One commented that pastoral staff have done well in creating a supportive and caring atmosphere. Pupils seem thoughtful and considerate to others, older pupils particularly good at mentoring younger ones. 'A very caring school, where the teachers recognise every child as an individual.'

Pupils and parents: Mainly professional types from Blackheath, Lewisham, Lee and more recently other areas accessible via train links. Head is keen to recruit from as varied a pool as possible, so a lot of effort is made to encourage children from state primaries as well as independents to apply. Big old boys' and girls' society runs a number of activities and fundraising events. Everyone is invited to the annual service in memory of the founder Rev Colfe. A good all-rounder school producing an interesting range of pupils going into many different careers. Alumni list reflects the school's diverse range: Eric Ambler, author, Lord Vaizey, economist, Kenneth Grayson, first professor of theology at Bristol University, to name but a few; also actors, musicians, politicians and sportspeople.

Entrance: Most join juniors at 3+ or 4+ via information observation morning. Year 3 no longer a main point of entry; assessment for occasional places further up the school. At 11+ interview, reference from current school and exams in maths and English. Sixth formers are offered places on the basis of an interview, reference and predicted GCSE grades.

Exit: At 11+ about 80-90 per cent move into the senior school; a few opt for local state grammars. Around 10-20 per cent leaves at 16+ for sixth form colleges. At 18+ to huge a range of different universities (majority Russell Group), including two to Oxbridge and one medic in 2018.

Money matters: At 11+ and 16+ scholarships and means-tested bursaries are available for drama, art, sports, music and academics. Around 20 to 30 per cent of pupils receive some form of fee subsidy.

Remarks: Pleasant, relaxed atmosphere. Provides a high standard of education without being overly competitive. Its focus on individual successes and promoting a balanced approach to life and learning is not to be underestimated in today's hectic world.

Collège Français Bilingue de Londres

87 Holmes Road, London NW5 3AX

Ages 5–16 **Pupils** 673

Fees: £10,230 – £11,205 pa

020 7993 7400
www.cfbl.org.uk

Headteacher: Since 2011, François-Xavier Gabet (50s). He has degrees from University of Lille – in teaching French and French as a second language. Has taught in French schools in France, Saudi Arabia, USA and Australia and was a French language adviser to the US state of Louisiana. Set up the first bilingual French/English school in Melbourne (while also teaching at Monash University).

He was the ideal founding head for this newish London school and arrived a year before it opened – to plan every facet. Despite his traditional website photo, when we met him he was fashionably turned out in jeans, turtleneck jumper and blazer – looking more like a high-tech dot-com CEO on London's Silicon Roundabout than what one might expect of the head of a prestigious French school.

Steeped in the high standards associated with French educational tradition, he is refreshingly internationally-minded and aims to help his multilingual students recognise the advantages of being part of a global network of schools. While well aware of the rigorous demands of the French system, he asks teachers to be flexible, creative and generous in their approach. He cares about the school's relations with the local Kentish Town community (he does not want CFBL to be a 'French bubble') and works closely with the board (whom he describes as 'capable, professionally-accomplished and yet humble') to find ways to improve this full-to-capacity school.

Fit, energetic and quite the coolest head this Good Schools Guide editor has met, he is married with a daughter at university in Belgium and a son in secondary school.

Head of primary is David Gassian, and Cerian Maraviglia is the deputy head of primary.

Academic matters: The French primary model has two divisions – maternelle (reception and year 1) and primaire (years 2 to 6). At the junior section of the CFBL 50 per cent of children have French and English language instruction and 50 per cent follow the French national curriculum. Half the staff are UK qualified and half are French. The teachers are timetabled in such a way that when classes are being taught by French teachers, the English-speaking staff are freed up to support students whose English language skills need bolstering and to ensure that English literacy standards are of a high level.

There are two forms of 25 students each for the youngest classes, 30 per class from the age of 7+. Classes are of mixed ability but the combination of French and English teachers means that they are able to differentiate the curriculum. English and French as a foreign language taught up to four times per week. Other specialists include teachers of PE, music and ICT (interactive whiteboards in all classrooms), while the bilingual French librarian works closely with the teachers in developing the literacy scheme and creating class libraries.

The French secondary model has two divisions – collège (years 7 to 10) and lycée (years 11 to 13). CFBL offers the collège division, following on from the school's primary section. According to the new norms of the French educational system, all students in secondary school are taught English for five hours a week and begin a third language (German or Spanish) in year 11. They are also taught music, sport, IT and art in English.

Students (already working in French and English) have the option to join the international section of the DNB (Diplôme National du Brevet) where 45 per cent of the curriculum is taught in English, preparing them nicely for the new international diploma (DNBI). They are taught history and geography two hours a week in English. Of the 60 that took the exam and passed in 2018, 38 got very good and 14 good.

Parents have mixed views – some feel the bilingual programme gives their (French-speaking) children lots of good exposure and immersion in English while others say the level of English is not as challenging as they'd like and that it's essentially French with a few English classes. Bilingual school models are never straightforward, with different perceptions about what exactly they mean. IT is taught weekly – some parents would like to see a bit more, but concede that with the extra time already devoted to languages, this would be challenging.

The pupils work long hours (approximately 30 per week) – the additional English language means more hours than usual – so parents should be clear on this before they enrol their children. This is in addition to the homework load. The French educational system is regarded as one of the best in the world and academic standards are not an issue here. It's deciding if you want to do this with the added challenge of a bilingual or trilingual programme.

No specialist SEN support but class teachers are able to provide some support and there is a part-time educational psychologist too. Parents pay for diagnostic testing. A speech therapist is available.

Games, options, the arts: Though extracurricular activities don't traditionally loom large on the French educational landscape, they do make a great effort at CFBL. More sports on tap here than is the norm for French schools – the football team practises locally and took part in an international tournament. Netball is popular with girls. The school is working on launching a choir and developing interest in instrumental music activities. Sixième students (first year secondary) go on a residential trip with outdoor pursuits activities aimed at integrating new students and team building.

CFBL has an exchange programme with schools in Uruguay, Valence and Berlin for students studying Spanish or German, and strong links with a school in Spain. Mandarin club recently introduced. The head hopes that these experiences will help students and parents value the importance of learning languages and about other cultures.

Background and atmosphere: The Collège Français Bilingue de Londres was born out of a previous French ambassador's call for increased capacity to meet the growing demand for French education in London. With funding from the French government and from French companies (we're guessing banks and perhaps Eurostar, whose London base is conveniently nearby), who formed a charity to acquire the school property, the school's mission is to offer a French curriculum in a bilingual context to 700 students. The school was at one time known as L'Île aux Enfants and located in a nearby building that now houses La Petite École, a feeder primary school.

Housed in a Victorian school building in Kentish Town. The head is aware of the impact that the mass arrival of a French community in the heart of this traditionally working-class area of north London has had and is working to win over the hearts and minds of locals. Most families living in the area were attracted to the Victorian terraced properties and the 'gentrification' of the area is thought to be partly thanks to the school (as well, of course, as the long-standing local Camden School for Girls). Part of the neighbourhood charm offensive was the introduction of French language classes for the local community.

The school backs on to some picturesque residential streets, though it fronts onto a street that is less so, and a bit of planting and tidying of the outside pavements and garden patches would improve the first impression. Step inside, however, and it's another story. The refurbishment is brilliant, taking full advantage of the Victorian features, with high ceilings, large windows drawing in masses of light, brick and glazed tile walls and parquet wooden floors, while incorporating modern touches. The upper school library – with high ceilings and huge windows – is fully equipped with impressive French and English collections, loads of computers and armchairs. Cosy primary library in its own little building on the playground – most of the resources are French, although they are developing the English language collection.

A small portion of the central playground has been forfeited to create a bright and airy cafeteria. Lunches compulsory, with meat and fish served daily and vegetarian options available for those observing kosher or halal diets.

The school has recently acquired an outdoor space a five-minute walk away. This will feature a massive inflatable structure for sports and other activities and will be available to the local community too.

Part of the AEFE (Agency for Teaching of French Education Abroad), CFBL is one of an international network of schools directed by the French ministry of education. The school is managed by a 12-member board – six representing the companies that helped fund the acquisition of the building and six elected by the parents. Its goals are to provide continuity of education to the French expat community in London, but also to prepare students to go to the best French universities. In fact 80 per cent of students who graduate from the Lycée Charles de Gaulle head to British or US universities. The head feels that the internationally-minded, multilingual emphasis of the school serves to provide good preparation for these options later on.

Pastoral care, well-being and discipline: Parents are very pleased with the school, many jumping through hoops to secure places. A parent of a child with SEN described it as particularly caring and attentive to her child. Classes are smaller than most French schools – a maximum of 30 in a class, with a two or three form intake. Discipline is not a worry for parents – one parent speculated that the presence of more UK-trained teachers (there to deliver the bilingual programme) strengthens the pastoral care perspective of the teaching faculty (not always as high on the French teachers' radar). The school runs careers counselling through a jobs forum that parents help to organise. The school employs a full time nurse as well as a part time speech therapist and child psychologist.

Pupils and parents: The community is a blend of expat corporate types on international assignments and more permanent French families who have found themselves in London for other reasons, including entrepreneurs, local business owners and French nationals whose marriages have created bi-cultural families. Parents suggest that the socio-economic atmosphere at CFBL is less 'rarified' than one finds in the more salubrious environs of the Lycée Charles de Gaulle in South Ken. While some end up at CFBL by default (no room at the Lycée), others prefer this school. The size is another factor – even with its capacity of 700, it is much smaller than the Lycée. French families who find the Eurostar terminal at St Pancras convenient are increasingly moving into neighbourhoods that are handy for the train journey through the tunnel to France and for the school.

The community is about two-thirds French. Some parents feel the school is less international than they would like, while others who come from France find it very international by comparison. There is obviously an underlying French cultural and educational foundation, but it seems that with a school community consisting of many dual national families, they seek to honour all cultures and traditions. Parents are happy that the children integrate easily, although some say teachers don't make as much of this diversity as they might. A parents' association provides lots of volunteer opportunities for those who want to get involved.

Entrance: Due to the recent opening of new French schools in London, not as oversubscribed as previously. We hear that a maximum of 30 per cent of the places are allocated to children whose parents work for the consortium of French companies that helped to secure the school building. The list of partner companies is available for inspection if required.

Admissions priorities are: siblings (both primary and secondary), children from another official French school (local or abroad), including students following the CNED (the French distance-learning programme), then any miscellany of Francophones fortunate enough to get in. It seems there are some last minute surprises. The nearby La Petite École is a popular feeder, while others opt for local British independent schools while they wait for the coveted place at CFBL.

Exit: Some expat families move abroad and continue their education in the French system. Others, finding the fees an issue (though remarkably good value when compared to most London independent schools), enter local state schools. Students who are less confident about their French language skills may leave after quatrième to do GCSEs in the local British sector, although the English section at the Lycée Charles de Gaulle is an option for them. Most of the students head to the Lycée International Winston Churchill in Wembley to enter their baccalauréat programme.

Money matters: The fees at CFBL are reasonable by London independent school standards (although CFBL fees are marginally higher than the Lycée Charles de Gaulle). As a charity, school engages in some fundraising activity – such as its annual gala event.

Remarks: An interesting school that embodies all of the academic rigour associated with the French tradition, but with a strong emphasis on languages and English. A sparkling little gem in the heart of Kentish Town, it is a bilingual environment with a truly international mindset.

Collingham College

23 Collingham Gardens, London SW5 0HL

Ages 14–20 **Pupils** 200 **Sixth form** 170

Fees: £4,260 – £21,570 pa

020 7244 7414
www.collingham.co.uk

Principal: Since 2012, Dr Sally Powell, BA PGCE MPhil DPhil (Oxon). Degree in English literature from Royal Holloway, London. Masters and doctorate in Victorian literature. Teaches English literature A level for four hours a week and tends to take the fast track group. Still passionate about teaching. 'It would be a deal breaker for me if I had to come out of the classroom,' she states. Huge Brontë fan: 'If I can teach Wuthering Heights then I normally do.' Has been here for 15 years, previously as vice principal and deputy principal. Over 20 other members of staff have also been here more than a decade. 'I'm the new girl!' she jokes. Loves theatre and art. One teenage daughter who is destined to come here for her A levels. 'She would come here now if I would let her!' she says. Warm, enthusiastic and welcoming.

Parents like the fact that head knows every pupil by name as well as their background. They describe her as 'easy to talk to,' 'kind' and 'wonderful – she champions the children.' Nobody we spoke to had anything but praise for her.

James Allder BA is the deputy and teaches geography. Very knowledgeable about the school. They make a good team.

Academic matters: In 2018, 22 per cent of A level grades were A*/A and 58 per cent were A*/B; 22 per cent of I/GCSE grades were A*-A/9-7. A good mix of academic and vocational courses offered at A level with maths, business studies and economics currently popular. A staggering 25 subjects possible at GCSE, including Arabic, classical Greek and photography. Pupils generally take eight or nine GCSEs. Rare for pupils to come here to retake GCSEs – pupils tend to take them all here over the full two years, starting in year 10.

Pupils can either take A levels over two years or opt for the more intensive one-year course. For fluent French speakers, a dedicated A level class is arranged so they can complete the course at speed. No restrictions in terms of subject combinations, however unconventional. 'It is entirely bespoke.' Head feels that strongest departments currently are English, economics and chemistry but also singled out art as being extraordinary.

Revision A level and GCSE classes also offered at Easter (three weeks) and Christmas (three days), with intense practice of exam-style questions. Open to in-house and external pupils. Small groups guaranteed. Just the ticket if your offspring needs structured handholding in the exam run up. Head says it is a great way to recruit future pupils. Once they see what is on offer, many are keen to jump ship. Some 11+ and CE tuition also possible in the holidays and after school.

International students, though a tiny minority, have mandatory English classes for eight hours per week. All these students are prepared for IELTS test, a requirement for study at British universities. Many non-native speakers are timetabled to take classes in art, photography or PE in which they can work alongside fluent students and improve their language skills.

One of the college's main selling points is the small classes, with a maximum of nine pupils at GCSE and eight at A level. 'A luxurious way to learn and a luxurious way to teach,' says head. School bends over backwards to put on whatever class is requested, even if only one pupil is taking the subject, eg Japanese. Masses of individual attention. Mixed ability classes.

About 20 per cent currently has some form of SEN – overwhelmingly mild dyslexia, dyspraxia or slow processing. College has taken high functioning autistic students in the past but you have to be pretty independent to thrive here, so not the place for someone at the severe end of the spectrum. SENDCo offers learning support on individual basis. Weekly study skills workshops put on for all pupils with topics ranging from how to organise one's files to how to take notes and how to memorise material. Pupils also offered one-to-one support from teachers, at an extra cost, either for a short boost on tricky topics or longer-term help. For example, if you are dead keen to do economics but your maths is not quite up to scratch, you can have individual tuition with the economics teacher. Parents welcome this in-house support rather than having to find an external tutor.

Many teachers here are academics, often with doctorates, and love the intellectual life. 'That is what makes our A level teaching so very strong.' College shares some teachers with Imperial, a stone's throw away. Deputy explains that 'the flexibility of our timetable means some teachers are part time and many of them do something else as well as teaching here. Both art teachers, for example, are professional artists. That gives a real depth and breadth to their knowledge.' One parent we spoke to commented that most teachers are inspirational, though possibly not all.

Head is excited about the 'electus programme' which aims to stretch the most able. Bright sparks selected to take additional classes, go on visits and write a dissertation over the summer holidays, similar to the EPQ. Head is convinced there are more opportunities for able students here than at larger schools.

Games, options, the arts: Extracurricular provision limited. Pupils who are talented musicians or on the sports field tend to pursue these passions externally. 'By the time you are 16 or 17, you know what you are interested in. They are in London, so they can find a place where they can do whatever they want. We have students who are top end ballet dancers, tennis players, skiers or violinists and the school fits in around their lives and schedules. It is a different type of schooling,' explains head. One mother we spoke to felt many of the pupils here are not the sort who care much about making a sports team or school orchestra anyway. 'Collingham does not attract many of those types,' she said.

Two hours of sport per week for GCSE pupils, mostly football in Kensington Gardens, plus tennis and rounders. In the sixth form, students can choose between football and yoga. 'We play in a small inter-college football league but we are not particularly good,' confesses deputy. 'Definitely not a sporty school. Quite the opposite,' said one parent. Annual music concert is run by the students and includes varied performances from rap and computer-generated music to drama and poetry recitals.

High standard of art displayed on the walls around the school, despite the small size of the studio. Photography is popular and school has its own dark room. Parents feel able artists thrive here. No drama performances at all. 'Not the school for you if you are looking to take part in musicals like Seven Brides for Seven Brothers or Oklahoma!' jokes head.

Plenty of trips and outings arranged including to Houses of Parliament, law courts and recording studios. Residential trips to Paris, Amsterdam and Florence as well as ski-ing in the Alps and walking trips to Snowdonia for the more energetic. A level pupils and GCSE pupils come together for these, which helps to foster a feeling of community which could otherwise be lacking. Activities week includes a charity walk, art and drama workshops and work experience. Everyone must get involved in some capacity.

Background and atmosphere: : Founded in 1975 as Collingham Tutors. Based on two sites, half a mile apart, one for GCSE students and the other for A levels. GCSE pupils come over to use the two labs, the art studio and to study Spanish in particular. The building in Collingham Gardens was previously Gibbs' Prep School where Prince Edward was educated, and before that was a magnificent terraced home, with servants' quarters up at the top. Though the vast drawing room on the first floor has been transformed into a study room/exam hall, it has retained it grandeur

Pupils tend to get on well as a group. One parent we spoke to felt the distinct 'lack of nastiness and cliques' was refreshing. 'They are quite a sophisticated bunch, though.' A level pupils are free to come and go during the day, as long as they are back for their lessons. Supervised study periods between classes for first year of sixth form, so there is a little more structure and less to-ing and fro-ing than one might expect. GCSE students need to be in school all day other than lunchtime. Many eat at cafés in the 'French quarter' in South Ken, though it has been known for pupils to head to McDonald's. 'They are generally far too cool to bring in a packed lunch!' laughed one mother.

School is good at celebrating achievement. A board of 'high fliers' is in pride of place in the entrance hall with their photos, grades and university places for all to see. Acts as a spur to the current students to try to get themselves onto the board in due course.

Pastoral care, well-being and discipline: Excellent. Lots of individual care offered. Everyone has a personal tutor who regularly meets with them on a one-to-one basis to discuss both performance and well-being. Half-termly target setting and termly parent meetings. Given the size of the school, anyone who is struggling is picked up at lightning speed.

Zero tolerance of drugs, alcohol or bullying. On the day we visited, there was a group of pupils standing across the street, cigarettes in hands. Though not ideal, head would rather that staff can see what is going on and who is out there than have them skulking down back streets. College will not accept any behaviour that will disrupt classes, though this is rare. 'There is a university-like feel to the place and most students rise to that challenge.'

Some pupils who come here have had a fractured school history, possibly because parents have moved around or because they have experienced bullying. Some have just fallen under the radar in bigger, more conventional schools and crave a fresh start. There is certainly a band of more fragile students. One mother commented, 'It is wonderful there is a school like Collingham to scoop up these children who have lost their way elsewhere. Once they get here, they can finally breathe again.' Another said the school had been wonderful with their child's depression and never judged her. 'Everything at the school was fitted in around her recovery.' Small classes help with low self-esteem. In-house counsellor.

Small, manned café in basement, open from early morning to evening serving main meals and snacks. You could eat all your meals down there. 'Sometimes I do!' quips deputy. Those with eating disorders can be monitored in a subtle way by the lovely cook. 'As a community, we are quick to pick up on what is going on'. Everyone seems to be looking out for everyone here.

Very rare to be expelled. 'If a child is getting the tone wrong then we are there to support them. We help them to develop those social skills.' Deputy explains, 'We will give them a second chance but not necessarily a third, fourth of fifth chance..'

Pupils and parents: Over 95 per cent are UK students though the college is strikingly cosmopolitan with a diverse range of parental backgrounds. Ninety per cent of pupils speak English at home and five per cent speak French. Over half of pupils come from London and home counties day schools with another 20 per cent from British boarding schools.

Good communication between the school and parents. 'Much more than you would find in other schools,' states head. Parents feel they are kept fully informed and that anxieties and concerns are acted upon. Head believes parents discuss matters freely with the school partly because 'there is no long gravel drive to navigate. They come in off the pavement, straight into the hall and my office is just there.' Certainly not an intimidating school.

Notable former pupils include actress Minnie Driver, and assorted members of the Jagger clan.

Entrance: No open days. The vast majority comes through word of mouth. Every student is considered on a case by case basis. 'We spend well over an hour interviewing a pupil with their family. We really try to get to know the family dynamics. We want to know how supportive they are going to be – that is important to us'. School would never take a pupil who had been expelled from their previous school for drugs because 'the parents who are sending their children to Collingham are sending them here in good faith that we are policing and monitoring, as best we can, our students' behaviour'. Head admits it can be heart-breaking because they may have just made a silly mistake. 'They may be a delightful student from a delightful family but regrettably that is our policy'.

Normally, 10 new students join year 10 and 20 join year 11. Entry is also possible throughout the academic year. Normally around 60 students enter the school for the first year of sixth form, with year 13 entry taking on an additional 10 A level pupils and 20 one-year pupils.

Exit: Those who leave post-GCSE tend to go to state sixth forms. Some return within weeks, as they realise it can be better to be a big fish in a small pond.

Most sixth formers head to university, many inevitably to London. Bristol, Leeds and Oxford Brookes also currently popular. Pupils select a range of courses including engineering, history and English. Some opt for art foundation courses at eg Central St Martins.

Some parents think it is 'Oxbridge or nothing' and Collingham feels it is key to manage parents' expectations. Oxbridge preparation includes extension classes and help with entrance exams. One to Oxford in 2018; others to University of British Columbia (English), Isart Digital Montreal (game programming) and Peking University (pre-university programme).

Money matters: Fees depend upon numbers of subjects being taken, length of course and whether full or part time. 'We try to keep fees as manageable as possible and we offer multi payments.' High performing students from state sector are sometimes awarded a means-tested bursary, to a maximum 30 per cent reduction in fees.

Remarks: Head explains, 'We are the last, or one of the last, domestic-orientated sixth form colleges in London. The others are very international. We have carved out a niche for ourselves that we are jealously guarding.' Parents and pupils rave about the friendly, supportive environment here and feel cherished in this intimate environment.

Coloma Convent Girls' School

Upper Shirley Road, Croydon, Surrey CR9 5AS

Ages 11–18 **Pupils** 1,048 **Sixth form** 340 **RC**

020 8654 6228
www.coloma.croydon.sch.uk

Headteacher: Since 2017, Jackie Johnson, who joined the school in January 2016 as associate head. History and theology degree from Birmingham and a PGCE from St Mary's Twickenham; she has taught history and RE in a range of Catholic schools. Before joining the school she was executive principal of the Bishop Challoner Catholic Federation of Schools in east London, and has also been head of St Philomena's Catholic High. She is married to Phil and they have two grown up daughters. Interests range from walking and attending matches at Watford Football Club to Old Testament and liberation theology.

Advertising for a new head for September 2019.

Academic matters: Consistently one of top comprehensives in the country for results and progress, achieved through blend of top teaching, forensic (and largely behind the scenes) analysis and, school's secret ingredient, exceptional choice for pupils. Everyone, high achiever or otherwise, can opt for subjects that they enjoy and thus will excel at. 'I've got way too many favourite lessons,' enthused year 10 pupil.

GCSEs for all in English language and literature plus maths, science, RS, a language and humanity. But it's the options list that's a thing of beauty – offered within the timetable where possible (art and design, business and communication and DT) and as twilight club if not (PE and Spanish) with music featuring on both lists to ensure enthusiasts don't miss out because of a subject clash.

In 2018, 91 per cent achieved five GCSEs at 9-4 including English and maths, 43 per cent at 9-7. Immediate benefits obvious, breadth enabling vast majority to gain at least one grade 7. 'Even weakest can be strong in some subjects,' says school. Pupils agree. 'Made me realise that I could push myself and my capabilities here,' said one.

At A level, with 60 per cent of grades at A*/B (25 per cent A*-A) in 2018, more of the same, with girls listing their dream subject combination (30 to choose from) and school (assuming large enough group to make finances and logistics work), making it happen – timetabling a marvel of ingenuity. Many complete four A levels and a handful do five, everyone taking PE, PSHE and religious studies on top. Firm emphasis on facilitating subjects with several nods to wider range of interests including health and social care and DT. No BTecs – money the major factor, though in ideal world, would offer both. No IB either – current system felt to offer breadth and to spare, grateful medics recently coming back to extol joys of leavening sciences with arts or a language.

Minimal setting and none in year 7 – avoids any sense of being programmed for failure. 'Spend the first year sussing out where they need to develop,' said parent. Class sizes sound big – maximum of 30 for first three years, 24 in years 10 and 11 and 14 in the sixth form (17.5 pupil to teacher ratio overall) but often far smaller, stresses school.

No resting on laurels. Even quiz former pupils on what could be improved – uni-standard referencing techniques, for example, recently added to sixth form curriculum. Strong staff team of just under 80 includes half a dozen or so former pupils influenced by strong desire to 'return the favour', as a parent put it, devotion to duty likely to be stand-out quality in application letters. Morale is high with happy blend of newcomers and long termers (23 have been here for decade or more), school a pioneer of in-service training and keen to welcome in new ideas.

Organisation is straightforward. Teachers teach, senior management manage, helped by data crunched anyway you want it, courtesy of resident expert. No decline too small to pinpoint or too difficult to reverse. Masses of lesson observations, positive reviews – what worked well, what could have worked even better, deliberate avoidance of corporate blame game and focus on collaboration emphasised by titles – team leaders rather than heads of department.

Girls, similarly, encouraged to put in the effort – long-ish school day can end at 5.00pm or later – but never to feel that 'school is continuously holding them to account'. Take learning needs in their stride (just over 100 pupils with SEN, five statemented and 110 with EAL requirements), working with primary schools to ensure smooth transition and offering range of support that includes one-to-one and in-class help.

Results in calm, low-pressure atmosphere though 'plenty of organised noise,' says teacher. Trust in the school required – difficulties may not be raised until parents' evening, and one mother felt more feedback during the year would be useful. Overall, approach felt to be on the button. 'Some of daughter's friends at other schools are always stressing,' thought parent. 'Here, they prepare them gently.'

Games, options, the arts: 'Gives the children all the opportunities,' said parent. Every day jam-packed with total fulfilment for arty, active or both – helped by flourishing parents' association that's stumped up for new laser cutter for DT department (works wonders on wood) and refurbishment of two grand pianos (the two aren't connected). Community the focus for fundraising, 100-strong charity committee choosing different cause each year as well as supporting linked school in Uganda. Run special charities week featuring talent show and daily cake sales (carrot a dominant and healthy ingredient, stresses school) but not allowed to spill into vital learning time.

Pupils are expected to make the most of activities – school stresses impact on outcomes – and most stick to termly pledge to try something new, 70 sixth formers, for example, turning up for optional netball club. Those who don't tend to change their minds pronto – 'got a bit boring when everybody was leaving for a choir competition or a match and I was just sitting there,' said one.

Trips, likewise, ranging from French and German exchange trips to netball tours (South African recently), hone practical and socialising skills, while annual visit to Lourdes can be life-changing. And so what if it's budget rather than de luxe version? Twenty-five hour coach journey for year 9 Austrian ski trip was 'nearly the best part,' said pupil. Even year 7s pack in Disneyland excursion, teachers still smiling at midnight, despite coach's cargo of 'grumpy girls burned out with far too many sweets,' said parent.

While parents rate every area as 'exceptional', music is perhaps most exceptional of the lot, recently acquired specialist music status merely official acknowledgement of the fact. Think not just big but bumper-sized, with eight choral groups and 500-strong main choir (all year 7 pupils expected to sign up for practical demonstration of virtues of cooperation, regardless of singing ability). Also two orchestras, numerous bands including – amazingly – a six-strong harp ensemble and over 300 individual weekly music lessons (French horn, bassoon – even double bass to grade 8). While already run 40 events each year (schedule is described with heartfelt sincerity as 'hectic' – audition-only St Cecilia Singers' triumph in national choral competition one of many successes), 'to do' list constantly being extended, multi-school youth music festival latest to be added.

Just as busy and successful on other fronts. Out of school hours, high-energy clubs range from CCF (run with Royal Russell, local independent school) to D of E, though plenty of others – including chess and prayer clubs – of a more cerebral nature.

Sports also described as 'exceptional', say parents (no surprise there), from range (orienteering, kickboxing and handball all on the menu) to successes. Recent Croydon champions for cross-country, indoor cricket, table tennis, often moving on to success at county, regional level and sometimes national level. Lacrosse particularly noteworthy. School one of few (possibly only one) in state sector to offer it, yet regularly trounces independents like Brighton College.

Teamed with generous facilities (two gyms, all weather floodlit sports pitches, field and track in extensive grounds). If three 50-minute sessions for first two years (two in year 9 and one in years 10-12) aren't enough, umpteen ways of filling any spare gaps, like early morning fitness sessions for those who don't get their kicks (penalty or otherwise) from team sports. 'Stuff happens at lunchtime, before school, after school and at the weekend, I don't know how teachers have a family life, to be honest,' said parent.

Background and atmosphere: Everything derives from living the motto, 'labore est vocare', which is known and understood by all, each lesson starting with a prayer. Parents approve. 'It's a good grounding to think of others and have a bit of reflection, whatever your spiritual beliefs are,' thought one.

Upholds values of educationalist The Very Reverend Canon Van Crombrugghe, who founded the Congregation of the Daughters of Mary and Joseph in native Belgium in 1817 in premises owned by Count of Santa Coloma. Convent opened 1869 in Croydon, school followed two months later (with just one pupil), moving to current home (with rather more) in 1965. Links with order still close, sister ('young in spirit and delightful in every way') running repository. Josephite brothers, meanwhile, went on to found St George's College in Weybridge, relationship as cordial as distance between the schools will allow. Initially independent, school joined maintained sector as grammar, becoming a comprehensive in the 1970s and merging with sister school, St Anne's, which survived flying bombs (commemorated by touching stained glass panel in chapel entrance) but couldn't withstand vicissitudes of shifting educational policy.

Site is neat, tidy (beautifully clipped shrubbery lines attractive paths), survival of original Victorian buildings (coach house particularly pretty) and inevitable Portakabin presence offset by tactical use of trees. Giant specimen is framed dead centre, to magnificent effect, by picture window in vast, airy performing arts hall, one of many improvements and new builds that keep coming, courtesy of non-stop grant applications and budget-finessing. Others include an all-weather pitch, sixth form centre, after-school users radiating industry under its curved roof, as well as 50th anniversary Jubilee Building, home of 'brilliant' art and boasting eccentric but charming turret.

Some economising elsewhere, low tech computers lovingly maintained rather than cutting edge, lunches paid for with real money and non-flushing loos or wobbly chair legs logged by pupils and staff on paper slips. With funding for just one technician and small but dedicated maintenance team, staff and pupils expected to treat this like home from home only better (slightly exasperated note in staff loos impresses need to keep the bowls clean...).

Girls as spick and span as the premises, non-negotiable school uniform policy including compulsory white socks or tights for juniors (helps make them more visible to motorists). No makeup or body spray or 'unnatural hair colourings and letters home stress importance of retaining modesty, even on home clothes day. Goes down well with parents. 'Not appropriate to be flashing your cleavage when you're 15 and going on public transport,' said one.

Pastoral care, well-being and discipline: Structure ensures continuity, with form tutors normally unchanged through to GCSEs. Each year 7 and 8 form group also gets two sixth form prefects to help with settling in process. School stresses importance of self-motivation and personal responsibility, parents expected to ensure daughters' punctuality, arrange dentist appointments outside school hours and to avoid term time absences (requests need to be made at least a month in advance).

Sanctions and rewards as clearly worked out as you'd expect, commendations awarded for effort and attainment and teachers encouraged to 'catch pupils being good in order to find opportunities for praise and rewards.' Misconducts awarded for everything from using mobile phones in lessons (they're also banned on school trips) to failure to sign homework diaries. Escalation of reports; exclusion for most serious offences – though a vanishing rarity, with a strong emphasis on forgiveness. 'We all make mistakes and need to move on,' says school.

Friendship issues usually resolved, though long-term bullies would be asked to leave if didn't change their ways (and with serious incidents kept on file for six years, strong incentive for them to do so). Clearly works – almost unheard of for pupils to be asked to leave. Little details all taken care of, down to staff escorts out of school and on to local buses – 'don't have to do it but helps keep the girls safe'. 'Really lovely,' says parent, while bus drivers comment on courteous behaviour (witnessed first hand when they stopped this reviewer leaving vital bag behind).

And sensitive support extends also to parents who report that if family crisis strikes, will be contacted by dedicated pastoral head to see how they're coping and offer a sympathetic ear.

Pupils and parents: Bright, motivated pupils will do well – rebels or late sleepers may find it harder, though 'wrong sort of rebellion is tamed,' reckons member of staff. Important, stress parents, to be realistic about school's expectations. 'Have to be in at 8.10am and factor in your journey – if that's difficult for you then this is not the school for you,' said one.

Depth of religion, too, needs to be thought through. 'Can't lag it,' stresses mother. While sex education is offered according to government guidelines, you're left in no doubt as to school's stance, say parents (marriage first). School delights in happy integration of pupils who span range of backgrounds and circumstances and develop streetwise (but sensible) nonchalance, heading off to shops or homes in Bromley, Coulsdon and Crystal Palace on public transport. More affluent learn to appreciate good fortune along the way. Daughter 'realises what she has is pretty damn good,' said parent. Locals connected with the school – one in eight of women in Croydon, it estimates – feel the same way. 'I do as much as I can to support them,' said one former pupil.

Tend to live long and prosper – one recently made it to ripe old age of 107 and like pupils, have plenty of opportunities to be involved, from joining choir directed by retired head of music to helping organise events – usually plenty of volunteers and warm welcome for all. 'Can turn up and go to anything on your own – not cliquey at all,' said parent.

Entrance: Five form entry – total of 150 in year 7. Applications from families from other faiths (number 7 on admissions criteria) or none (number 8) in theory welcome, but vanishingly unlikely to translate into offer of a place given 700 applications each year and 450 or so Catholic families ahead of you in the queue, though school never takes popularity for granted. 'We welcome everybody.'

Early and whole-hearted commitment to Catholicism is required and attendance at mass, baptismal age and first communion will all need verification. Ever-shrinking home to school distance the tie breaker.

Around 30 per cent of sixth form from other schools, when faith criteria no longer apply. Minimum six GCSE passes at 4+ for mixed course (BTec/A level), increasing to eight grade 6/7s for four A levels. Need to be on your toes as school barely advertises the fact – prefers those already in the know.

Exit: Loses around 40 post GCSE to co-ed sixth forms, mostly those taking vocational subjects and a few with longest journey time opting for an easier commute. Over 90 per cent of leavers either to university or art foundation courses, 40 per cent Russell Group. All sciences well represented though wide range also includes English, psychology and law. One medic in 2018.

Good Oxbridge record with some pupils most years (one in 2018). Lead up to applications process predictably thorough with own, qualified careers advisor (a rarity), highly detailed website content and early planning – pupils in year 8 play interactive games that match interest with possible careers.

Money matters: Some funding for residential trips for parents on benefits.

Remarks: Awe-inspiring in every direction, bulging with extras despite limited funding. 'The school is like a clock tower: you need to make all the cogs work together,' said pupil. Swimming pool would do wonders for the mechanism. Caring hedge fund managers should apply direct to school.

Colville Primary School

Lonsdale Road, London W11 2DF

Ages 3–11 **Pupils** 430

020 7229 6540
www.colville.rbkc.sch.uk

Head: Since 2011, Jagdeep Birdi BA QTS (40s). Studied history, English and education at Lancaster, then headed for the Big Smoke, where he has since taught across five different London boroughs. For the 11 years before he joined Colville, he was deputy head at Ronald Ross, Wimbledon, then at Sir John Lillie, Fulham.

Despite the school leaping from its place in the bottom 200 schools in the country to one of the top 200 since he joined, he's not one to wax lyrical about vision, strategy and grand plans. In fact, this modest, mild-mannered man even struggled to answer our questions about what makes the school stand out, although you don't have to talk to him for long before his passion and dedication for both education and this school reveal themselves. It is this heartfelt, unaffected and laid-back attitude – in which aspiring for the best is seen as the most natural thing in the world – that staff say sums up his leadership style. He joins the children daily for lunch, as well as doing the meet and greet daily and both children and parents chat to him informally – he knows them all. 'His natural manner is to make us feel as if we're an important part of the school – that our views about the school matter as much as the teachers,' said one parent. Another told us, 'I don't think you could find a more accommodating head.'

His first-floor office – a Big Brother set-up, with floor-to-ceiling glass overlooking the key stage one area of the school – seems an unlikely choice for such an unassuming leader. Until, that is, staff explain that actually, it means they can see when he's free to talk to and, perhaps more crucially, it places him firmly at the heart of the school rather than being hidden away in some corner office.

Entrance: After the customary priority for looked-after children and those with special needs, siblings are next on the list. Then it's down to distance, which currently stretches to 0.45 miles, although this is rapidly shrinking, with over 200 applications for the 60 reception places. Even if families move to another part of London, they tend to stay, with some children coming from as far as Hackney and the far side of Barking. Cohort is truly ethnically diverse, with 46 languages spoken and no dominant group among them (even the most common language spoken apart from English only has 18 speakers). 'These children know how to acquire a language – that's a good thing,' says the head, adding that diversity is seen to enrich the school. Seventy per cent of pupils at the older end of the school are on free school meals, although that figure drops to just 10 per cent at the bottom end, telling you all you need to know about the change in reputation of the school.

Exit: The largest share – half the pupils – go to the local comprehensive of Holland Park, whilst around a quarter go to Kensington Aldridge Academy. The rest go to a wide range of comprehensives right across London, with a handful per year group now moving into the independent sector.

Remarks: 'Let's not beat around the bush – this school used to be appalling when my child, who is now in year 6, joined,' said one parent. 'Colville was the school that nobody really wanted for their child and the one that poor low-income families got lumbered with,' reported another from the same year group. But in the last five years, standards of attainment achieved by the school have shot up, with Colville having received two ministerial congratulations in the last two years alone – and the parents, particularly those of the older kids, can't believe their luck.

Teaching was poor, acknowledges the head, and the school wasn't in a good place. 'A number chose to leave during my first few months. Now we get top-notch teaching staff coming in and the teaching is rigorous, particularly in maths and English.' There are specialist teachers for computing, games, art, music and French, all of whom teach from reception upwards and every teacher we saw in action – bar none – was successfully engaging the children. There's a lot of them too (males as well as females), with some classrooms we visited having four teaching staff for 24 children. Most of the teaching assistants are graduates. These extra adults bods in classrooms also means there's more room for learning-through-doing. In fact, we didn't see one instance of chalk-and-talk during our visit.

Outside, there's a reasonably sized tarmacked playground that's tucked behind the fashionable Portobello Road and overlooked by high-rise flats and town houses. Playtime here does what it says on the tin here, with raucous children running around loudly and happily and making full use of the new plush, large wooden climbing structures. There's also a school garden and separate edible garden (with links to Wholefoods in Notting Hill). 'You don't get left out here because we have a playground buddy system,' one pupil told us. A school survey, completed just prior to our visit, found that 99 per cent of children felt the school is a respectful environment, where pupils are respected whatever their background.

Originally, the school opened in 1879 as Buckingham Terrace Primary, when six teachers – poor things – were charged with 550 pupils. During the WWII these pupils were evacuated and when they returned after the war in 1945, the school reopened as Colville Primary. The old laundry building (girls were taught laundry back in the day) has now been converted into a modern, welcoming space for reception, while another outdoor building is home to the nursery. The rest of the school is taught in the three-storey main building, where the (mainly) large classrooms boast high ceilings and where there are three school halls, one doubling up as the dining room known as Le Bistro (one pupil told us the one thing she'd change about the school is the food; that said, only 20 or so kids choose to bring in packed lunches).

The well-stocked, spacious library is welcoming, while the art studio/come food tech room is huge and light. 'I never thought my son would like art, but he loves it now,' said one parent, who praised the specialist art teacher's links with local galleries, including the Saatchi gallery. Music is taken seriously, with all children given the opportunity to play instruments, with a steady stream of six peripatetic teachers teaching in small groups and individually. There's a school choir (which has performed at the likes of the Royal Albert Hall) and orchestra. Truth be told, much of the school could do with a lick of paint, and it's never going to look state-of-the-art due to the age of the building, but the way the space is used is impressive and the £4.5 million refreshment has made some exciting changes.

Sport is fun and inclusive, with all the usual options, some of which are taught on site, while others, including swimming, involve a short walk to the local leisure centre. There are links with major local football clubs and Lord's cricket ground and dedicated coaches regularly visit to teach and enthuse the children. 'Sport is brilliant in comparison to other inner city schools,' one parent told us.

The school's motto, 'Inspiring success', is clearly not an empty phrase here, but something that they aspire to for every child. Part of this involves setting – in phonics and reading from October half-term in reception, and in maths from year 2 – while another area of focus for the school is SEN. With seven statemented children when we visited, and plenty with extra needs ranging from those on the dys spectrum to those who may not have quiet areas to study at home, the school has made sure it is a learning environment where individual support is prioritised and provided both inside and outside the classroom. Without really planning to, the school has also gained something of a reputation for specialising in hearing loss.

Behaviour is generally good, with a traffic light system helping to keep youngsters on the straight and narrow and privilege points to counter them, which can be redeemed for toys out of the special cupboard when they reach increments of 10. 'Ten points will buy you a nice little toy, but if you save up 30 or 40, you can get something like a Bop-it,' said one pupil excitedly.

There is before and after-school provision, plus a breakfast café which parents can come to and 42 before and after-school clubs from breakdancing to violin and ballet to gardening club. School trips a plenty to the capital's museums, Kew Gardens and Holland Park (the latter for forest school), while year 4s upwards get to go on residential trips. Community links are a strength, with children involved with everything from Jamie Oliver's (for cooking sessions) to Salvation Army (where the choir performs to the elderly).

We found this school refreshing, unpretentious, aspirational and spirited. It is also testament to the fact that, with the right leadership, a poor performing school can become a school of choice within a short space of time – not just for parents

Connaught House School

47 Connaught Square, London W2 2HL

Ages 4–11 **Pupils** 67 (42 girls, 25 boys)

Fees: £15,600 – £17,100 pa

020 7262 8830
www.connaughthouseschool.co.uk

Principal: Since 2017, Victoria Hampton (30s), who previously ran the early years part of the school and has taught here for several years. Started and run her own nursery in Oxfordshire, was deputy head of a nursery in Clapham and has a host of qualifications for teaching young children – Montessori diploma, early years foundation degree, Hornsby diploma (dyslexia). She has three young children of her own and loves being part of the fabric of the school. Gentle, with a mellifluous voice and perfect diction (which we suspect matches her handwriting); the children clearly love her as do the staff. She knows them all and is actively involved in observing and participating in lessons throughout the school. One change she has implemented is to bring the reception class (known at Junior One) up from the ground floor so that they can have plenty of space, free flowing between two large, high ceilinged rooms.

She is the daughter-in-law of previous joint principals Jacqueline and Frederick Hampton; Jacqueline's mother founded the school in 1952 with just six pupils. It is still an intimate, cosy, family-run school, refreshing in this age of private equity backed independent schools. 'We are a school first that happens to have to run as a business.' Phew – such schools do still exist.

Head since September 2017 is Ellie Grunewald MA UEL, BA (Liverpool) PGCE (Kingston), previously academic co-ordinator here.

Entrance: Sixteen reception places. 'Very gentle assessments' of 3-year-olds. Absolutely no preparation necessary. Priority to siblings and second and third generations. After that, proximity to school. 'The local community ethos is something we value very highly and would not like to lose.' Academic and music bursaries are available to those applying at 7 or 8.

Exit: All boys have previously left at 7 or 8, mostly to local prep schools such as Westminster Under School, Sussex House or Wetherby, the odd one going north to UCS junior school, but can now stay on till 11. The girls generally opt for London day schools – Francis Holland NW1 is currently the most popular, but many also to Godolphin & Latymer, City of London, More House, Latymer Upper, Queen's Gate and South Hampstead High. Boarders generally choose Wycombe Abbey or St Mary's, Ascot.

Remarks: There is no danger of the slightly old-fashioned, wonderfully personal and child-centred ethos of this tiny school changing. It has not expanded at all since it was first founded. It still occupies the same building, and is very small; you will know quite quickly if you love it or not, but if you don't, be careful not to write it off too soon. This is a rare little boutique in the increasingly branded, competitive world of London day schools and it offers a uniquely personal touch. Children enjoy lots of outdoor activities in nearby Hyde Park all the year round, including parachute games, obstacle races, rounders and football. Fencing, dance, and martial arts all take place at Little Venice Sports Centre. Tennis, football, hockey, basketball and the annual sports day happen at Paddington Recreation Ground. Swimming is at Queen Mother's Sports Centre in Victoria. There is sport every day of one kind or another. Although we heard some whispering from former parents – that the children didn't get to run around enough and there were insufficient sporting opportunities – we could see no evidence of this.

Plenty of music assemblies and lots of performances. Everyone takes part, and the large, high-ceilinged room in the middle of the building is a comfortable and intimate place to perform. We were treated to a mini concert, which included violin and recorder players as well as piano and singing – impromptu concerts of this kind are not unusual, we were told, and you can see how much confidence is imbued into these tiny performers as a result. The art room is a relatively dark, pokey room in the basement, but the quality of art that is produced defies the facilities. We saw small children beavering away at covering balloons in newspaper to create hot air balloons. We were shown wonderful wooden red buses and fire engines, built by the children, and split-pin dolls clothed in fabulous petite Victorian dresses and hats. Colourful displays adorned the walls, and bright Chinese lanterns and colourful fish were bobbing from almost every ceiling.

Plenty of drama; each junior form does its own play once a year (these have included the Gruffalo's Christmas and Charlie Cook's Favourite Book), and years 4, 5 and 6 have performed Sleeping Beauty. Drama productions and concerts take place at the Carisbrooke Hall down the road or the Steiner Theatre close to Baker Street. Annual carol concert in St John's Church, Hyde Park Crescent, which everyone is expected to attend. 'We would rather it were inclusive.'

Clubs are varied and numerous. They make a huge effort to ensure that everyone from years 2-6 tries everything. There is lots to try, from embroidery, pottery, board games and mini beasts to any kind of dance from country to zumba as well as chess and music. Recent trips have included the Globe Theatre, the Courtauld and the Tate Modern, the Celtic Harmony Camp, London Zoo and to the obvious museums – Science, Horniman and Transport.

You need not worry about little Freddie not getting enough attention either. There are only 16 pupils in a class – they try to keep an equal number of girls and boys in the early years (and, in future, higher up). Junior One (reception) has two teachers and a qualified teaching assistant. Forms 1, 2 and 3 have both a form teacher and qualified teaching assistant in each class. They pride themselves on recruiting excellent teachers with 'diverse interests'; there is a competitive fives player on the staff at the moment. It is relatively easy to pick up any learning difficulties, we were told. They have a few cases of children with glue ear who may need speech and language therapy. Specialist therapists, for, eg, dyslexia are brought in at parental expense but Victoria Hampton herself is a dyslexia therapist, and they prefer to keep as much support in school as possible. We were told that there is usually only one child in each year group who needs any kind of help at all. A high number of children speak English as a second language, and although they need a reasonably good grasp of English at assessment, because of the high level of teacher support (and a recently introduced EAL club) they usually progress very quickly.

All in all, a very special little school which is loved by parents and pupils alike, where the children feel challenged every day and their parents are constantly amazed by what they know. 'The closest you can get to home schooling,' declared one. If that sounds appealing, take a little trip to Marble Arch now.

Coombe Girls' School

Clarence Avenue, New Malden, Surrey KT3 3TU

Ages 11 –18 **Pupils** 1,322 **Sixth form** 272 (100 boys)

020 8942 1242
www.coombegirlsschool.org

Executive headteacher: Since 2011, Deborah Walls (40s). As executive principal of Coombe Secondary Schools Academy Trust, also has oversight of Coombe Boys' and Knollmead, formerly a failing primary school but now undoubtedly destined for far greater things. Her second time here – after teaching posts at Wallington High School for Girls and Langley Park, did stint in 1996 as head of languages, before being promoted to assistant head, moving back to Wallington as deputy head in 2003 and then closing in on Coombe again when was appointed in same role at boys' school. 'When you've worked [here] it becomes a part of you,' she says. 'It's more than just a job, it's part of your life.'

Discerning readers will also have clocked career focus on single sex schools which, yes, reflects Mrs Walls' strong belief that they're an educational essential. Means chance to find out who you are in safe environment, she believes. 'You can be yourself and let your individuality come out.'

Not that she wants anyone closed off from 'big world of opportunities,' as she puts it. Even before mixed sixth form, many co-curricular activities such as public speaking and ski trip are co-ed, while whole year groups of boys and girls have annual timetabled session themed according to age and interests – year 7s enjoy rocket making, year 8s self-awareness, while in years 9 and 10 there's more formal focus on options and higher education. It's diamond model light, the perfect scenario, thinks Mrs Walls. 'Gives the best of every world.'

Her family's talent for languages (grandmother, a teacher and languages expert, was a particular inspiration) meant career and specialism never in doubt, particularly when coupled with precocious ability to see flaws in the system (sussed, aged 11, the drawbacks of teaching languages in English). Enjoys travel, though helping own children achieve happiness and success are about as close as she comes to a hobby as, unsurprisingly, not much in the way of spare time pursuits.

Still manages to fit in some teaching but thoroughly enjoys organisational side of the role. Just as well as calls on time come thick and fast, from recent appointment as governor of King's College Wimbledon to beaming in advice to struggling schools, helped by colleagues. As Coombe is a national teaching school, also involved in growing new crops of teachers and bringing returners back into the fold. So many other requests to participate in kudos – and time – heavy research projects roll in that these days, writes risk analysis before making decision. No point spreading resources too thin, she says. 'We sit back and look at it from every angle first.'

While clearly a first class operator, also warm with great sense of humour but above all with burning desire to do her best for the girls, something that appears to permeate school consciousness. 'You may not hear much about her but know she has our interests at heart,' said one. They're also impressively confident in speaking their minds. When we asked year 9 pupil in her presence if she was enjoying producing complex-looking design for tote bag, we got a matter-of-fact 'no.' Sensitive to colleagues' needs, too. During tour, expertly bypassed trainee teacher in danger of losing the thread when confronted unexpectedly by head, assistant head and energetic note-taker.

Goals? With lots still to do, we're not sensing any appetite for a move elsewhere (though must be plenty who'd leap at the chance to recruit her). Parents value her strengths – 'Good combination of organisation, professionalism and approachability,' said one – and take her other commitments in their stride. While naturally delighted that appointment of new head at boys' school (former assistant head at Coombe Girls') now means Mrs Walls is here more often, parents have boundless confidence in school management's ability to cope when she's called away.

'Ideal person to lead the federation into its next stage of development,' was commendation from predecessor here. Professional and warm, she's supportive of other women attempting to get to the top and involved in local initiative for women leaders. We suspect that seeing her at work and clearly getting so much from demanding job is probably just as effective when comes to inspiring future generations of girls.

After major restructuring Andrew Platt, previously deputy head, took over as headteacher in September 2017.

Academic matters: School 'honoured' that remains hugely oversubscribed – and not hard to see why parents would be bonkers to bust a gut securing place anywhere else if successful here. If daughter has tried out (unsuccessfully) for nearby grammars – and many have – don't worry, stress parents. The bright flourish here, some reckon more so than they would have done in the febrile atmosphere of ultra-selective alternatives where can take full marks just to get noticed. In 2018, 23 per cent of A levels graded A*/A and 52 per cent at A*/B. At GCSE, 33 per cent 9-7 (84 per cent attained 9-4 in both maths and English).

Success founded on strong relationships between staff and pupils – confidence boosting a speciality. 'School has really built her up,' said parent of previously shy daughter. Staff feel well supported and, like parents and pupils, given regular slots where can raise difficulties and issues and know will be listened to. Asked if they ever go home, they laugh (but don't actually confirm that they do). Official school day, which runs 8.40am to 3.30pm with five 60-minute lessons, often extends into evening and weekend activities. School also unleavable in career terms, with 27 members of staff (average age 39) into their second decade or more. Newcomers or long-stayers, all exude palpable warmth down to smiley trio on duty to greet latecomers who run velvet glove rather than gauntlet, while row of clocks set to other time zones tells you how tardy you'd be in Buenos Aires.

Plenty of little touches – teacher (male) baking cake for GCSE geography pupils: 'Oh, Sir!' they shout, celebration breakfasts for good results, librarians who take no chances – up to year 8 'we read to girls and they read to us' – and offer full set of daily papers: The Times to tabloids. Above all it's a sense that girls are known and that teachers 'are rooting for them,' said mother.

Curriculum planned to nth degree – each subject served in parent handbook filleted into component parts with garnish of thoughtful enrichment activities, many of a useful nature (times tables tests for maths), others winningly desirable (geography trip to Paris for all year 7s). Some classes are set (maths in years 7 and 8 plus English in year 9), others in mixed ability groups (technology and languages), while science sometimes is and sometimes isn't, flexible approach dictated by range of each year group's ability and changing schemes of work.

Though there's extra stretch for gifted and talented, achievements in all their diversity are celebrated. Nitpickers might point to percentage of low achievers making expected progress in maths – currently it's just 32 per cent according to Dept for Education data. But given latest in series of letters from government, praising results, and stunningly high Progress 8 figures – numbers passing toughest GCSEs – any nits picked would be of microscopic dimensions.

For disadvantaged pupils (around a fifth) mostly a pretty positive picture, with half securing five or more GCSEs including maths and English. Low-ish numbers of pupils with SEN (currently 25, seven with statement or EHC plan), all supported in timetabled hours, with everything from teaching in lessons to room 41 – a dedicated haven for those struggling with sensory or emotional overload in or out of lessons. It's a rare pupil they can't cater for, SEN working closely with staff providing weekly briefing on needs and support. Similar system for EAL pupils including buddy system and catch up or slower paced lessons, though not needed by vast, linguistically competent majority.

Inevitably, families not above supplementing with tutors if pace of lessons leaves children behind. No criticism, says one, just normal for the area. 'A universal problem.' School feels shouldn't be necessary and points to numerous initiatives – tracking and lots of it, blips quickly picked up with extra catch up and revision sessions for anyone in danger of falling behind. 'Try to get the absolute best out of them,' thought parent and school reckoned to listen to parents and respond quickly, complaints limited particularly now anxiety over turnover of science teachers has slowed, department has no vacancies and (impressively) biologists, chemists and physicists are all teaching own subjects.

Post 16, there's a split screen approach, more academic subjects here, vocational at boys' school and 35 courses in total. Otherwise beamish Ofsted report had reined in lumens slightly – attendance and results were felt to be below par, some of brightest lured away by excellent fare on offer at outstanding local sixth form colleges.

School has responded by upping budget for careers and uni preparation and bringing in dashing new subjects including A level classics (follows success of Latin GCSE, taught out of hours with support from King's College School) plus government & politics and economics, each new addition somehow woven into the timetable by staff specialist (swears more fun than other hobbies – cryptic crosswords and fiendish sudoku).

Smaller but significant perks such as sixth form snack exclusives (panini, jacket potatoes and sausage rolls) and relaxed uniform code (we admired one girl's dazzling blue Doc Martens, just seen under sombre trousers and conventional shirt) have no doubt played part in improving results and pupil retention.

Games, options, the arts: In addition to all the curriculum must-haves, many wonderful-to-haves such as active Duke of Edinburgh. All this despite limited resources, felt to tail off only slightly in sixth form (dance would be popular addition to the menu, thought several pupils). Plenty lower down the school, though, with year 7s working on cross-curricular project, themed to 'my journey' which culminates in presentation to parents, as well as covering off everything from cultural diversity to healthy lifestyles, touch-typing and research skills.

It's all approached with dash and enthusiasm, visible also in enthusiastic art and DT, dresses cascading ruffles and crank handle wooden toys on display, walls brightened by everything from lavish, Rubens-style picture of woman's torso to accomplished year 9 self-portraits in chalks. Performing arts, felt by parents to have been a notch below par, now on the up again with revitalised productions, some at Rose Theatre in nearby Kingston, courtesy of new, dynamic head of music (peak beard, creative tie) and vibrant drama department.

Sports appropriately energetic, facilities – own grounds as well as impressively large sports hall – felt to give it the edge in comparison with many other more space-challenged secondaries nearby. Houses compete to speed run a mile round the grounds in aid of Sports Relief and teams frequently successful in outside events, year 7 football team achieving silver in borough event, trampolining a particular strength, one former pupil going on to become county coach.

Parents complimentary about achievements though wish lists would include extra coaching, funds permitting. 'It's not a level playing field,' said one with feeling, if not literal accuracy.

Background and atmosphere: Set in heart of New Malden, between lush Kingston Hill mansions and more workaday housing and on same compact site since foundation in 1955 as Coombe County Secondary School.

Original uniform, mustered for diamond anniversary celebrations, a smart affair, including woolly scarf and squashy felt hat. Though both have gone, other nostalgic touches remain, including original wooden bars in gym, space now repurposed as dance studio and occasional exam room.

Site is spotless, courtesy of maintenance team whose devotion extends to post-break litter-picking sessions. Plenty of greenery – year 7s have own grassy area and even the cut-down playing field, which could so easily be sea of mud, is a well-tended space, while small hedges, something of a planting favourite, brighten up odds and ends of space no end.

Niceness extends to other areas. Floral scent wafts from newer, far bigger sports hall. Particularly fragrant staff? 'Just what the cleaners use,' says teacher. And despite one parental comment that catering had suffered slight decline, range and quality looked impressive, all meals cooked from scratch by team in at 6.00am to add dainty finishing touches, no toasted sandwich minus its upmarket cardboard envelope or St Valentine's Day cake lacking an icing heart. And all served with sugar-free drinks and low prices (roast and a pud for £2).

Sixth form centre a building of two halves, one for quiet study (plenty of 'shushing' from supervising teacher if it isn't), common room on the other. Appears girl-heavy but boys magically appear at break time (just follow the sound of the football).

Rebuild of this and other less than gorgeous areas (flaking paint is pointed out by teacher with a certain relish) would be top of Mrs Walls' wish list. Pristine additions – geography recently rehomed while staff also have a posh room for best – show what can be achieved.

Pastoral care, well-being and discipline: New pupils eased in with visits to feeder primaries and summer school at end of year 6, including trips to London Zoo – website is big on reassurance, with relaxed pupils sharing tips. First day 'one of the best and scariest, felt was going to die but at the same time really excited.'

New or not, school makes no bones about expectations. With so much going on, likes pupils to get the full benefit of school life and stresses importance of punctuality, with sliding scale of detentions from 10 minutes with tutor after school for one offence to a one hour Friday session for five late arrivals – plus parent meeting. Request for term time absence unlikely to be considered, let alone granted, for anyone whose attendance drops below 98 per cent.

All other breaches (arriving in mufti, failing to stow outdoor coats in lockers, long, fake or varnished nails, using phones during school day) sanctions are strict and explicit, exclusion for 'defiance' the non-negotiable norm for persistent offenders followed by 'formal reintegration [where] your daughter's future will be discussed.' One to avoid, though, stresses school, it's only tiny minority who fail to obey the rules. Just as well, as there's now greater formality (compulsory blazers for all).

Plenty of support for families (we hope that 'talk to your teen' advice on website, containing conversation-igniting gems such as 'That looks interesting, what are you doing?' is as popular as it deserves to be). Parents accept need for rules with slight sigh (decision to ban popular black leather, lace up trainer derivative caused a bit of angst), girls similarly philosophical, hitching up skirts again as soon as doorstep length inspection completed.

Teachers approachable and reassuring – 'Ones you click with are a comfort, especially at exam time,' said sixth former – and tough issues addressed head on, from mental health issues and grooming to bullying (including advice on how to cope if child is bully rather than victim...). School has at least one eye fixed firmly on friendship issues, pupils so effectively mixed and matched on arrival that pretty much guaranteed you'll leave with different mates from the ones you arrived with. Pragmatic approach of 'getting everyone to sit down and talk it over rather than screaming at each other,' said pupil, generally felt to be key to resolving majority of difficulties.

Pupils and parents: By far best known former pupil is children's Jacqueline Wilson (now with a new building named after her); also Olympic athlete Anne Packer. Alumni association, only recently set up, promises to bring many more successful former pupils – plenty of creative and City types – back into the fold.

Regardless of background, packed with conscientious, hard-working sorts and notable for strong sense of community – tragic pupil death led to whole school rag week, everyone contributing, most popular event penalty shootout, sixth form boys doused with water if failed to save goals. 'What could be better?' said girl.

Entrance: From over 900 applicants, takes 210 in year 7, popularity inevitably resulting in a 'Honey, I shrunk the catchment area' issue (under two km in first round of offers), to school a source of mixed pride over popularity and sadness that so many who want to come here can't. Arrive from numerous primaries headed by Burlington Junior School, Christ Church C of E, Coombe Hill Junior School and King's Oak Primary.

Post-16, there's second chance at a place here, seven GCSEs with 6s or better in chosen A level subjects required. More places for girls – 210, compared with 100 boys – and priority for existing pupils, 40 per cent going to external candidates, who'll be vetted for academic potential and attitude to learning.

Exit: 'Aspire' programme offers Oxbridge taster events (with input from King's College School) and STEM-related courses, designed to ensure pupils get the rundown on full range of top careers and courses and don't settle for second best. In 2018, a quarter to Russell Group, one Oxbridge place and one medic. London unis – UCL, King's College and Queen Mary – regularly feature as most popular destinations, others to Bristol, Cardiff, Exeter, Leeds, Nottingham. Recent spread of subjects also includes law and modern languages.

Money matters: Asks for annual payment of £120 per family – voluntary, some families contributing more.

Remarks: Fabulous education, staff who can't tear themselves away and delighted parents. What's not to like? 'A pure comprehensive which is very rare and does what it does really well,' said mother. 'I wouldn't consider anywhere else because my daughter is so happy.'

Coombe Hill Junior School

Linked with Coombe Hill Infant School

Coombe Lane West, Kingston KT2 7DD

Ages 7–11 Pupils 420

020 8949 1743
www.coombehillj.kingston.sch.uk

Head of junior school: Since 2014, Mark Clutterbuck, previously deputy principal at Chessington Community College.

Entrance: Some 99 per cent of junior school entrants automatically from the infant school. Others all local, round the corner.

Exit: Majority of to local state schools, impressive number to the highly selective Kingston state grammars Tiffin Boys and Girls, more to Coombe Girls and Boys, others all over. With the improvement that has taken place in the current local state schools, very few pupils now move into the private system.

Remarks: A brilliant, buzzing, exciting state school more than ever holding its own against the many local private sector schools. Very much an upmarket area; the pupils are a huge ethnic mix from a variety of backgrounds, with parents who help, encourage and enjoy the multinational involvement.

We were taken round by some senior pupils eager to show us everything that was going on. We didn't miss a nook or a cranny and were suitably impressed. Everywhere was clean, bright and full of happy, thoroughly involved children. Classrooms overflowing with interesting displays. Technology everywhere. Parents told us 'excellent teaching', 'fantastic, exuberant teachers', 'great facilities' and 'really like the way they make learning fun and incorporate different subjects in one lesson'. We were delighted to see a good number of male teachers, two of whom are heads of year. Classrooms a bit squashed but that didn't appear to matter; flexibility is the name of the game. All mixed ability but the brightest separated into four groups for maths and literacy. We were told, 'the teaching is something special, a real collaboration between teacher and pupil, teacher and teacher, and pupil and pupil, they all help each other'. 'No cramming, the education is broad and full, they are taught to debate and to question and to discover for themselves'.

Lots of music, singing and playing different instruments. Private lessons available for those who want to learn a particular instrument. Everyone learns the recorder in year 4. Our guides proudly showed us the range available for them to try. Great art on display in the atrium and, when we were there, models of Andersen shelters – 'very difficult to make!' For a state primary, the sport is exceptional. A brand new games area provides for cricket, netball, basketball, football, rugby and other sports, some of which they play competitively against other schools. Not enough, some parents think, but it is a privilege not there for all primary school children, so they are lucky. And they have their own heated swimming pool – two sessions a week for each class. Added to that PE and dance form an important part of the curriculum.

Our guides led us proudly round their extensive grounds. Every class has an outdoor learning day once a year. As well as the usual play areas, there are wildlife areas, including a pond and a 'hotel' for insects, a vegetable garden – 'some we eat, some we sell' – and, really exciting, a pen for chickens whose eggs, of course, also get eaten.

Sympathetic SENCo who seems to really care for the children, making sure no needy child slips through the net. Several groups, run by learning support teachers, take pupils out of class where necessary, but never during a core subject. Non-stop records kept and a provision map for every child in the school. Those with behavioural problems get one-to-one support but they do try to make sure that they are given enough individual space. SENCo works closely with both the behavioural team and the class teachers, trying to tackle problems before they go too far. Says it's important to try and pre-empt difficult situations before they get out of hand. 'I really love my job'. Parents say, 'Children respected and nurtured. Bad behaviour not tolerated'. 'Quick to deal with problems'.

A large variety of after-school clubs which are extremely popular and introduce children to new skills and ideas. An hour a day, all taught by their regular teachers with a minimal charge to cover materials.

Mix of nationalities means cultural activities from all over. Most festivals are celebrated and any excuse for dressing up is grabbed. Knowledge of the world is part of the learning process – every child and every country is important. Music and art are an essential part of the school day. Parents rave about every aspect, haven't got a single criticism. Only worry, will they be able to maintain this high achievement level?

All in all, a tip-top school that has managed and absorbed the necessary expansion over the last few years and the broad ethnic diversity that is Greater London today.

Coombe Hill Infant School

Linked with Coombe Hill Junior School

Coombe Lane West, Kingston KT2 7DD

Ages 4–7 **Pupils** 300

020 8942 9481
www.coombehillinfants.com

Headteacher: Since 2013, Janet Berry. SENCo and senior assistant head for three years prior to taking over the headship. Has been at the school for 13 years, starting part time when her children were pupils and progressing through the ranks as they got older.

Entrance: Much sought after local school. The closer you live the better, although it may still prove difficult to get in. More than 550 first choice applications for 90 places; over half go to siblings. Admission policy strictly adhered to – medical or social needs get priority. Occasional bulge years add an extra class.

Exit: Almost without fail to the junior school next door. One or two to local independent schools, of which there are plenty.

Remarks: From the moment you walk into it, through the art gallery entrance, you realise that this is a lively school bursting with happy, interested children. A vast ethnic mix – about 60 per cent need some EAL support, mainly in class except in extreme cases. No attached nursery, so some children arrive speaking no English at all while others speak two or three different languages. The resulting mix is 'demanding but fascinating to work with.' All classes – five or more of up to 30 children in each age group – mixed ability. One full time teacher for each, plus a teacher's aide for at least half of the day and other extra staff who help wherever needed. All are highly trained and experienced, often current or ex-parents. 'The school has a really family feel,' we were told.

Fantastic semi open-plan layout, all on one floor, loads of natural light. Corridors of well-equipped classrooms, all with interactive whiteboards, computers and educational displays. Children's creations abound. Pupils enjoy themselves, eagerly joining in all activities. When we visited all of them were absorbed, participating and learning, and eager to show us what they were doing. Three excited year 2 pupils were delighted to take us round their school and point out their favourite places and activities.

Fantastic IT suite, good lending library with videos, games, reading and maths schemes. Great art on display everywhere.

One of the special things about this school (and the junior school next door) is the massive amount of outdoor space. Plenty of room to run, climb and explore. Children certainly make the most of it – log cabin for special projects and areas for planting and learning. Imaginations soar. Pupils have the use of a heated swimming pool (in the junior school's section of the shared open land) in the summer term. Each class has weekly sessions, weather permitting.

Mix of nationalities means cultural activities from all over. Most festivals are celebrated and any excuse for dressing up is grabbed. Knowledge of the world is part of the learning process – every child and every country is important. Music and art are an essential part of the school day.

Lots of after-school clubs that change termly. Sport, drama, music, art, computers and other themes – all good fun, all for a minimum charge.

This is a popular school and houses in the area are very sought after. They are very lucky, too, to have active, involved parents who raise a fortune and provide funds for the school's continuing excellence.

C

The Coopers' Company and Coborn School

St Mary's Lane, Upminster, Essex RM14 3HS

Ages 11–18 **Pupils** 1,386 **Sixth form** 450

01708 250500
www.cooperscoborn.org.uk

Acting Headteacher: Sue Hay is holding the reins. A historian, she joined the school in 2013 as deputy head in charge of teaching and learning, and has overall responsibility for academic standards.

Academic matters: There's an assumption that students will do well here ('It's built into their DNA that they will want to succeed') and they do, with the school consistently achieving near top GCSE results nationally, with 95 per cent getting 9-4 in both English and maths, 39 per cent 9-7 grades in 2018. They are especially strong in English language, English lit, mathematics and art and design, but pupils also do exceptionally well in RS, DT, textiles technology and music. The most popular GCSE choices are history, German, geography and sport/PE, and fair numbers also choose Spanish and French.

At sixth form, there's a wide curriculum of traditional subjects plus newer courses – media studies, psychology and politics. Popular choices are the sciences, especially biology ('We buck the national trend when it comes to STEM subjects a A level,' says head), business studies, history, maths and psychology. In 2018, 33 per cent A*/A grades, 67 per cent A*-B.

Spanish, French, German or Mandarin from year 7 (parents get to state a preference when they apply to the school), with a second language introduced in year 8, at which point Mandarin and German are also available. 'Modern languages are big strength of the school,' said one parent, reflecting the views of others. Pupils are setted for maths in year 7 and there's an element of setting in languages and sciences at GSCE. Homework considered an essential part of shaping pupils' academic experience, particularly in relation to independent learning and thinking skills.

Teachers renowned for going the extra mile both inside the classroom and out. 'No teacher gets an interview until they've taught a lesson which we find to be good or outstanding.' A fair amount of emailing goes on after hours, for which both students and parents are very grateful.

Despite high results, the school is always working on improving grades and has introduced Go 4 Schools, an online tracking programme, enabling parents and teachers to login at any time to monitor how the student is doing, with both individual and overall grades, target grades and how they can improve, enabling all three parties to monitor progress and make any necessary interventions to keep grades on track. 'It really helps cement the three way partnership between students, parents and teachers,' says school and parents agree. 'We have a good idea of both where our children are relative to where they need to be,' said one parent. The bottom 15 students in the year are provided with extra measures, as are the 15 at the top. SEN has a strong team of six staff members, mainly providing classroom-based help for children with issues ranging from dyslexia to autism, although less than one per cent of these have an EHC plan. 'For major SEN issues, other schools in the borough are better equipped.'

Although the school is very academic, we found it to be the antithesis of an exam factory, offering a broad and liberal education, with a major emphasis on extracurricular activities that all students are expected to get involved in. While PE accounts for the majority of the 142 clubs on offer, other subjects include music, drama, IT and all the academic subjects right through to beekeeping, chicken keeping and robot building. Many of the school teams enter national competitions – 94 of them the year we visited, reaching national finals in 33 of them and world finals in two. The debating team reached the finals at Oxford University.

Games, options, the arts: This is the number one co-ed state school for sport, if you take as the criteria the number of national level finals reached across all sports. Also regularly enters for international events, with the triathlon team having reached the world finals, coming second mixed team, the year we visited. Students took part in the opening ceremony of the 2012 Olympics and were also involved in the handover of the Olympic Flame for the Rio Olympics. Regular competitions against leading independent schools, especially in athletics, cross-country, badminton and swimming. Not surprisingly, the students we spoke to were deeply proud of the school's exceptional achievements and aptitude.

The rich curriculum ranges from circuit gym training to trampolining, cricket and netball to indoor rowing and PE remains compulsory throughout the school years, even at sixth form. Facilities, including a swimming pool, are impressive and sports trips are notable, including rugby tours to New Zealand and Australia, athletics training in Lanzarote and tennis training in Florida. 'The attention to detail in the coaching is second to none,' said one parent. 'Nobody is left out, with everyone given a chance to thrive,' said another.

Well-equipped art studios, with a studio offering individual cubicles for pupils who need a designated area in which to work. An 'open house' policy approach encourages independent work and, along with the clearly outstanding levels of work on display, creates a wonderful 'art school' atmosphere. Pupils consistently have work displayed in exhibitions around the country.

Drama standards are high, with two roomy practice areas, including a state-of-the-art renovated theatre, with retracted seating. Plenty of performances throughout the year, including one main annual performance – Singing in the Rain the year we visited.

Music also strong, with five school orchestras (including an all ability one), two choirs and regular ensembles and concerts. Expect brass band more than rock music 'as we like to keep things traditional,' says head. Around 180 students are taught instrumental lessons in school. Students take part in music festivals and competitions, as well as playing at significant events such as the Lord Mayor's Banquet, and at a more local level within school, for example during assemblies. The inclusive and supportive ethos of the school means you never get students saying, 'I don't think I'm good enough to play in front of my friends'.

Huge range of extracurricular choice, covering almost every conceivable area, from chess to fishing – many instigated and are run by pupils. 'The amount of opportunities is amazing – everyone tries something they never thought they would,' said one student. School trips are also big here, with around 40 domestic and 23 international ones every year. Besides the sport-based ones, there are language trips (year 8) and exchange trips (year 10) to support Spanish, German, Mandarin and French and other trips to explore interesting places such as Namibia and Botswana.

Background and atmosphere: A rich history dating back to 1536 when it was first established as a free school for boys. Its name came in 1552 when the Coopers' Company was asked to take over the running of the school. It was then located in Stepney, Tower Hamlets. In 1891, it joined foundations with the Coborn school for boys and girls and remained at sites at Mile End and Bow until it moved to Upminster in 1971. 'Our first students would have seen Shakespeare's plays.'

Now situated a good distance from the main road amid 25 acres of greenery, and home to a pond visited by ducks and geese, the school feels spacious, exceptionally neat and tidy and well cared for. And although some of the main school buildings from the 70s are looking tired, modernisation and development have seen new buildings regularly erected since the 80s, the latest being a sixth form block.

The school motto, Love as Brethren, appears quite literally in shining lights as you walk in the school and you won't find a student who doesn't believe it's central to school life here, with many using the hashtag

LasB when they sign off emails or post on social media. We found the atmosphere to be happy and thoughtful, with students displaying a healthy level of boisterousness during break times, but heads down during class.

Pastoral care, well-being and discipline: Students describe the school as being a 'protective cloak' and 'like a family,' with the young people looking out for each other and staff on hand to help with any issues students may have. The school buys into a student counselling service and clearly takes mental health issues seriously. A house system helps create vertical links, as well as the horizontal year groupings. Peer to peer mentoring, and around 150 sixth formers work with younger pupils.

Plenty of leadership opportunities, with a democratic process selecting school captains from year 12 pupils, who must apply for this prestigious position. The one boy and one girl selected hold office throughout their final year. School council plays a key role in the decision-making processes – including the appointment of senior staff. Pupils are given a sense of importance and are consulted on important developments. Reward system is fully utilised, including housepoints, certificates, postcards and phone calls home, letters from head and spotlight in assembly.

Not much room for making mistakes here, however, with zero tolerance of bad behaviour and very high expectations of conduct. These expectations, and the punishments for failing to adhere to them, are all outlined in both a contract that students have to sign before coming to the school, and a visually friendly charter. Staff are trained in them too, so that there is complete consistency, and parents are also expected to be on board. 'If students don't meet the standards, they can expect serious sanctions. We're quite happy to run Saturday detentions, for example, and would exclude.' Indeed, school had permanently excluded a student the week before our visit for intimidating behaviour towards a staff member, although these are rare. Talking when teaching, or not focusing in class, are considered as bad as writing on school walls. Other no-nos are mobile phones (except in sixth form), eating outside allocated areas and failing to adhere to uniform rules, with not a silly haircut or rolled up skirt in sight. But while it might all sound draconian, we found complete buy-in from parents and students. Bad behaviour here is simply 'uncool,' students told us, with one pointing out that the rules are so well embedded into school life that in reality, nobody really thinks of the school as that strict. Bullying rare because, according to students; 'mocking just isn't what we do here.'

Pupils and parents: Most students from aspirational families. Around 80 per cent white middle class, the rest of a mixture of ethnic minorities. Although it's a Christian school, there's an eclectic mix from all recognised world religions. Many parents are supportive of the school and help out at school events, with an active PA of about 30 members – good for a secondary state school. They arrange various fundraising events including a monthly sale of supermarket vouchers to parents and staff and they had just raised enough funds for a new minibus when we visited. We found pupils to be articulate, grounded, respectful and polite – traits for which they are known throughout the local community. They are very proud of their school, as well as extremely appreciative of having a place there. Everyone is welcoming – greeting visitors with smiles and hellos, saying thank you, holding doors open and even singing to themselves as they pass by.

Entrance: Unusually large number of feeder schools (around 100). Admissions rules and catchment area complicated due to the school's historic links to east London and wish to preserve the principles of the Coopers' Company and Coborn Educational Foundation.

Over 1,000 applications for just 180 places and a fair number go to appeal. Ten sport and nine music places, which hundreds apply for. All other applicants must be actively connected to one of the main world faiths. Some places for children of staff and former students; others by promixity; others to those who live in specific areas including Havering, Brentwood and Billericay.

Most stay on to the sixth form after GCSE. Around 50 places for students from outside but, again, massively popular with over 700 applications. Applicants need at least eight 9-4 grades to be considered for a place, to be sympathetic to the school's Christian character and be willing to uphold its 'Love as Brethren' ethos by giving time to serve the school. Oversubscription criteria prioritise looked after children, highest predicted grades and then availability in specific sets. 'Our sixth form is equivalent to a grammar school, in terms of offering traditional subject choices and the fact that we take the cream of the crop.'

Exit: Around half leave after GCSE for one of three reasons: to study a vocational course at college, to study different subject choices at other local schools or (a few) to take up an apprenticeship. Almost none leave to go into low-paid work. Around three-quarters of sixth formers to university, which is high for the area, of which a third go to Russell Group universities. Particularly popular are Warwick, Bristol, Durham, Birmingham, Bath, Exeter, Loughborough and Imperial. Four to Oxbridge in 2018.

School provides a range of opportunities to prepare for post school, including careers advice from year 9, conferences, workshops, competitions and special events at universities such as Nottingham and Cambridge. Many go on to study pure science subjects or vocational courses such as medicine, veterinary science and dentistry. Other popular subjects include psychology, economics, architecture, art history, journalism, politics and theatre design.

Money matters: The school allocates £10k to assist pupils that need help and also provides music and sports grants of up to £500 through a bursary system from The Coopers' Company and Coborn Educational Foundation.

Remarks: World class in the true sense of the word, this school is a dynamic, exciting place to learn, preparing students for successful lives. Dazzling reputation in the local community and largely responsible for increased house prices in the Upminster area. 'If you're not one of these things – academic, sporty or musical – it's probably not the school for you,' pointed out one parent, whilst students say you need to be willing to put in more time than regular school hours and more commitment than the bare minimum. 'There's no room for just plodding along here,' explained one. But for those that fit the mould, it's outstanding.

C

Croydon High School

Old Farleigh Road, South Croydon, Surrey CR2 8YB

Ages 3–18 **Pupils** 570 **Sixth form** 75

Fees: £9,840 – £16,656 pa

020 8260 7500
www.croydonhigh.gdst.net

Head: Since 2016, Emma Pattison BA (30s). Previously deputy head (academic) at St John's School, Leatherhead, preceded by spells at Guildford High School (four years as head of MFL for juniors and seniors) and Caterham (languages teacher and head of year 8). Experience in co-ed schools hasn't dimmed enthusiasm for single sex education. 'When you can tailor the curriculum for the kinds of things you know girls will enjoy, it's so exciting,' she says.

Though teaching runs in the family (mother and grandmother) it was only after a short spell as a management trainee that Mrs Pattison saw the light and changed careers. Describes first headship as wonderful 'in every way', from school culture ('sensational') to buzzy and engaging pupils – 'had the year 8s in yesterday for tea and cake and just laughed with them for half an hour.'

Staff also a thoughtful bunch, one giving Mrs P. something 'to help you spend time with your daughter' (approaching school age). Not, as we'd speculated, a cloning kit but a jar layered with pre-measured cookie ingredients. No doubt a parenting essential given the long hours she puts in. Piano practice (she started her degree in music before switching to languages) is already confined to weekends.

Makes it her business to know what's going on – and it shows. She has a little list based on parent concerns. While the precise contents were undivulged, it seemed identical to ours. High fliers are encouraged to aim for the stars, the keen to get their share of the sunlight. Unloved junior school lunches and moving up day (previously disorganised) have been transformed, while the substantial fee hike between junior and senior schools is being smoothed out. Girls feel she cares what they think, parents are favourably impressed by her know-how. 'Very on the ball,' said one.

Junior head: Since 2015 is Sophie Bradshaw BA (30s). Second time around – was head of KS2 here before a spell at Ardingly Prep – and is delighted to be back. Nor just an academic whizz – first class honours in primary education and maths – but RAF trained, original plan to fly helicopters scuppered by the realisation that only teaching would do. Family (who'd worked this out long ago) were unsurprised.

A different breed from predecessors who were brilliant with girls but 'a bit tweedy,' reckon parents. 'She means business,' said another, 'but in a way that convinces pupils they want to do it. They adore her.'

Academic matters: Focus, says head, is on selective but bespoke education. High teacher to pupil ratio (one to eight), small class sizes (average 17, maximum around 22 and often fewer, under a handful for A level) and solid support (drop-in or individually tailored in the senior school) all help. One pupil was taking maths, further maths and music plus a science for A level; another philosophy and ethics, drama and politics. GO (girls only) tagline (on careers-linked literature) reinforces the fact that anything is possible.

Numbers of younger teachers are growing. 'There's something of a generational shift,' says school. Maths staff get particular praise. Motivators for joining (and staying) include excellent facilities (labs in particular), though pupils' attitudes are the clincher. 'Can teach, don't have to be a policeman, love practising craft and seeing the penny drop,' said senior maths teacher.

Junior timetable synced with senior school, some specialist teaching from nursery, more added as pupils move up. Ambitious languages – Spanish (years 1, 2 and 3) German (year 4) and French (years 5 and 6) build up to Latin in top year. Also run creative thinking days (focus on problem-solving) and, for older juniors, philosophy.

Junior maths now transformed. New passport (also covers reading and writing) gives juniors (and parents) goals to achieve in their own time with a certificate at the end. 'Not just everyday sums, it's games – fun – such a good way of encouraging the kids to learn more,' said parent.

Pace, never sluggish (individual sciences from year 7, for example), 'kicks up a notch in year 9,' said a parent. Gentle insistence on organisational skills pays dividends, say parents. While there's tolerance if homework or a test missed, pupils must be proactive with (credible) explanations – and a lack of engagement is swiftly communicated to parents.

Good range of GCSEs and IGCSEs (constantly under review) includes options like computing and 3D design, spice provided by trips (for computing as well as more conventional subjects).

Most go on to three A levels (business studies a recent addition) plus extended essay, four if have the appetite and ability. Ditto those who prefer to channel spare energy into sport. 'Let them do what they want to do,' says head. Standalone AS subjects, like photography, also on offer. Approach translates into consistently good results. In 2018, over 50 per cent of GCSEs graded A*/9-8. At A level, nearly a third A*/A grades.

While 2014 inspection report was largely glowing, commented that independent learning didn't always come naturally to the school. Watching year 4 juniors working out how royal barber would go about shaving Henry VIII (very, very carefully), and year 8s embarking on effortless improv themed to Taming of the Shrew with a complete absence of self-consciousness, it was clear that things had changed. 'Not shy, not cynical – that's a girls' school,' says head. For able seniors, there's the GO-Beyond programme where teachers expand on off-curriculum topics – 'How to develop your very own language,' say, or 'Russia'. The really exceptional (rather than merely gifted) juniors have Altitudo programme, resulting in impressively mature work, such as an imagined (and completely credible) conversation between Decartes and Locke.

The message is that no career is impossible, reinforced by careers in the classroom event for juniors (bring a cryptanalyst to school) to Pathways Mentoring for sixth formers. While doctors and lawyers pop up regularly to enthuse and inspire, head was delighted that one of brightest and best sixth formers had heart set on agriculture college and a farming career. No point pushing Oxbridge when it won't suit, she says. 'Some get there and are miserable because they're not super academic though they are super bright.' Communications are very effective (email, Twitter – one account per department), quick responses at all times. 'Very reassuring and efficient,' says a parent.

School's size and philosophy means no middle ground to get lost in. Head of learning support works across the school and all pupils are automatically assessed for special provision (extra time/movement breaks) in public exams. Most pupils are highly able though support, for the 24 junior and 30 seniors with identified SEN, mild only (specific learning difficulties, autism, ADD/ADHD, sensory processing, visual impairment) is extensive and sensitively handled. Junior pupils, for example, often receive subtle in-class support rather than being singled out for lunchtime sessions. It's 'so girls don't feel self-conscious,' said mother.

Expectations are high, pupils thriving on challenge and with a prodigious work ethic. Homework is chunky but sensibly allocated, online and in planner, so no excuse for forgetting (one parent reckoned lure of the smartphone was significant factor in time management). 'Won't suit those who aren't prepared to work with their children,' stressed mother. Buy in and pupils will do well. 'Results are very good if you follow what they tell you to do,' said another parent.

Games, options, the arts: Keen, committed and talented can be on the go non-stop. 'Could join a zillion clubs,' said parent. Can lead to a few lunchtime clashes, though sensible catering ensures that no one goes hungry. Recent additions like rugby and football join existing lineup – handball to dodgeball, swimming to golf, with space and facilities inside (dance studio, fitness suite, impressive pool with tiny flotation jackets for nursery pupils) and out (netball courts, Astroturf and a new pavilion). Successes include biathlon (national), hockey and tumbling (regional), and swimming, netball and cross-country (local).

It all starts early, from participation in the whole school play (some year 5s share the stage with seniors – enjoyable for all) to free violin or lessons in year 3. It's in addition to the 150 individual lessons a week, from beginner to diploma level, and leads on to bigger things and sometimes huge ones (half a dozen or so double basses are lined up in the senior school music room).

Art, too, evolves from inclusive junior school displays representing every shade of talent to impressive senior school work (like the GCSE picture where painted legs meet fabric trainers with real laces). Even charity work goes way beyond cake sales. The goal is to produce girls, says head, with 'compassionate ambition'. Charities a case in point: pupils select preferred good causes and pitch their case for share of the funding. Results in enduring links with local groups, which include Women's Aid and knife crime reduction. Fundraising highlights included a fashion show, male models courtesy of local boys' school (one tastefully accessorising high end frock with a plaster cast following rugby injury).

One mother's perception is of school having to hold back the keenest and encourage them to keep at least two lunchtimes a week clear. Another felt a bit of gentle enticement for the less gregarious would be helpful. Head has already zoomed in on concerns. With dance club – raised by several parents – on the way, and more focus on the keen but non-virtuoso sporting and musical element, nobody should feel sidelined.

Background and atmosphere: Founded in 1874 and part of the Girls Day School Trust, school moved to current base in 1966. Boasts 20 hilly, attractive acres in south Croydon (with a natural amphitheatre in the dip), buildings wearing their architectural vintage (red brick and white fascias) with pride.

Uncompromising on the outside but inside one of the most efficient and welcoming schools we've ever come across – and that includes the parents, available just about instantly to extol the delights of this small scale haven for girls, and come to its defence (criticise at your peril). Nothing like the friendly reception – door holding, wonderful behaviour as matter of course – to convert prospective parents. 'Just felt right,' said one, who had instantly succumbed.

Junior block classrooms are generously proportioned suites. Star attraction is the 4D room with touch sensitive floor, soothing sounds and projected images – used to inspire stories (we could have stayed all day). There's one oddity – the weird, claustrophobic staircase (Mrs Pattison prefers 'quirky') leading to year 4. 'The girls love it.' (There is an alternative route.)

Otherwise, school is spacious and easy to navigate. Keep going and you should end up back where you started. Plenty of light, large halls en route. Main (school assemblies); huge and impressive (sport), attractively teamed with green chairs, light wood tables and colourful piles of fresh fruit (dining).

Refurbishment was underway when we visited, blue carpets replaced with businesslike grey with ivy leaf motif (which garlanded pupils at inaugural prize giving). In among the pristine modern science labs, one old era survivor (wooden benchtops and a faint aroma of long ago experiments) lingers on – for now at least.

Sixth formers' attractive area features small, round tables on one side (two girls working in squashed but companionable silence). On the other, waiting-room style blocks of expectant-looking chairs (it's occasionally co-opted for assemblies) and walls packed with quotes. 'It is never too late to decide what you might have been' (go to it, George Elliot).

Pastoral care, well-being and discipline: Strength of care felt to be exceptionally strong. One pupil cited teacher at another school turning away a pupil in difficulties. 'Said he had too much marking. That couldn't happen here.' Girls encouraged to look after each other (strong buddy scheme in place). 'Will assist so nobody feels all alone,' thought parent. Small size normally an advantage – only downside the small friendship pool. 'Can get tired of the same faces,' said a parent. Posters in junior school extol pupils to 'tell how you feel, tell a teacher, tell a friend' while effective house system (juniors and seniors have their own) has inner layer – smaller group of 15 'families'.

Staff (particularly in senior school) recognise mental health issues as big (and daunting) responsibility. Teachers with their own daughters there (fair few) felt school's efforts – peer listening, links to Young Minds and close dialogue between parents and staff – all help. 'No school will say it has no problems and would be lying if they did but staff and girls care and are looking out for you,' said one member of staff. Eating disorders – 'heart-wrenching,' says head – supported in whatever way is best – including staged return when pupil is ready.

Pupils and parents: Many current parents work, majority local, others from Caterham, Oxted and Dulwich. 'We are not just a local school,' stresses head. Minibuses are a useful addition to trains and trams – both a slight hike away. Around half from minority ethnic backgrounds – British, European, Pakistani, Indian, African, Caribbean, mixed background, Sri Lankan, Bangladeshi, Japanese, Chinese, Greek, Turkish and Asian – languages (Tamil, Farsi, Swahili among them) equally varied. EAL support provided where needed.

PTA's mission is to forge ever closer links between senior and junior parents. Not everyone is keen. Small element said to feel responsibility ends with setting up of fees on direct debit – but we'd suspect are a small and rapidly dwindling band given sense of purposeful accomplishment that dominates life here.

Alumni include obstetrician Wendy Savage, novelist and commentator Jill Tweedie and – best known of the lot – much missed cellist Jacqueline du Pré.

Entrance: Main entry points (juniors) are nursery, reception and year 3. In year 7, half the intake is from own juniors, half from over 20 local primaries and preps. Additional places in year 9 and sixth form, steady trickle in other years. Non-refundable registration fee, deposit on acceptance of place. Overseas applications welcomed, Chinese students in particular (accommodation/guardian must be arranged separately). Head impressively addresses them in – we assume – Mandarin on the website, where the final page of international section is also printed upside down (either layout glitch or appeal to Antipodean market).

Assessments at every stage. For nursery, 45 minutes of structured play (informal, can't be prepared for) under watchful eye of the head. Designed to ensure pace won't be a problem and 'don't turn many away,' says school. Five mornings from the off, full time attendance the goal for all.

Proportionately longer assessments further up the school. Reception – an hour in small groups – picture matching and sorting objects, co-operation and good use of spoken language. Seniors tested in maths, English (writing, reading, VR) plus interview and reference (approximate minimum score of 105 in year 7 but often much higher – some siblings may not make it). Limited sample papers – year 7 only available on line. At sixth form, external candidates will need minimum of six GCSE passes at grade 6, depending on A level choices.

Academic scholarships (year 7) based on entrance exam performance and interview. No percentages given but think small – it's all about the honour. School's juniors sit exams for awards, otherwise have automatic entry. Also art and design, drama, music (minimum grade 4 in at least one instrument but usually much higher) and sport.

Similar range in years 9 and sixth form, where also offers Jacqueline Du Pré scholarship (music) and – unusually – for year 13, Jenny Park Award (English and the arts). Additional awards in range of subjects.

Exit: Vast majority of juniors expected into year 7. From year 5, focus on how to achieve transition with additional support rather than giving notice to quit.

A few seniors depart post-16 (mostly to local co-eds). Rare for school to ask pupils to leave at the end of year 11 or year 12 – and won't happen without much prior discussion. 'Not about saying you're not welcome but asking if three A levels are the right profile,' says head. Unscheduled departures for other reasons very rare. Sixth form numbers will be boosted as numbers rise through the school – and three form year groups become the norm once more (2008 recession hit hard). University destinations in 2018 included history at Warwick, biochemical engineering at UCL, games design in Amsterdam and operatic studies at the Royal Academy of Music.

Money matters: Bursaries, some via GDST for years 7 and 9, two sponsored by HSBC for state school sixth form candidates, available. May be more help for deserving leavers.

Remarks: 'They're so happy there – and that's all I ever wanted, to have a lovely environment where they didn't feel threatened and teachers are more like their friends,' said junior parent.

Cumnor House School (Croydon)

Linked with Cumnor House School for Girls

C

168 Pampisford Road, South Croydon, Surrey CR2 6DA

Ages 4–13 **Pupils** 370

Fees: £11,145 – £13,380 pa

020 8645 2614
www.cumnorhouse.com

Headmaster: Since 2017, Daniel Cummings, previously head of the White House school in Balham and the school's fourth head in 18 months. BEd from Exeter; taught in Australian primary schools whilst on a year's travelling; helped to set up the Epsom and Ewell School Sport Partnership; taught at Merton primary schools before being joining the White House in 2013. His wife, Abigail, is also a teacher.

Entrance: Three form intake with 20 boys maximum in a class. Automatic entry from the school's Cumnor House Nursery, which parents told us they found a very attractive feature of the school. Otherwise, boys come in at 4+ for a taster day, which for most is nothing to worry about. Maths and English are checked to ascertain if the child will cope at Cumnor, but not formally assessed. Other entry points at 7+ and 11+. School aims to be as inclusive as possible, and all kinds of families pay the (very competitive) fees to send their boys here.

Exit: Given the school's non-academically-selective admissions process, Cumnor's exit record is truly remarkable. Students can be prepped for either 11+ or 13+ depending on parents' and boys' wishes, which, families affirm, the school is always careful to consult. Those who opt for 11+ are put in a dedicated class. Vast majority to Trinity or Whitgift, with Royal Russell, Caterham and Epsom College next in popularity. Such is the school's success that refugees who come to Cumnor at 11 often pass at 13 with scholarships into schools which turned them down two years previously. 'We've been in the game long enough to know what the senior schools are looking for.' And year on year, the results prove them right (57 scholarship offers, including quite a few for sport, in 2018).

Remarks: After years in the schools' reviewing business, we were nonetheless surprised by the fervour with which parents talked to us about Cumnor House. 'It's a lovely, brilliant school. I would recommend it to anyone and everyone!' cried one mother. 'The boys there are lovely young men, and the teachers are amazing, they always want to go the extra mile,' said another. 'It's been a really positive experience for our son,' said a third. 'We couldn't fault it.' 'No negatives, and nothing to regret. It's fantastic!' said a fourth. And this is just a sample.

Cumnor House is surely triumphant proof that single sex education from an early age can really work. If a How-I-Hope-My-Son-Will-Turn-Out contest existed, the boys we met here would all be candidates to win. Their manners are astonishingly good. Everywhere we were greeted with courteous smiles and handshakes; in one instance, even with a bow. Whilst they hurled themselves around the playgrounds at break-time, they were nonetheless well-behaved and considerate, both to each other and to us. 'You might want to walk quickly, 'cause it's raining,' urged one of our tour guides with anxious politeness.

Everywhere we saw evidence of lively and careful teaching, and the boys were vociferous about how much they enjoyed lessons. 'History is my favourite, because it's all about old things, and did you know that Henry VIII died because his bottom exploded on the toilet!' cried a year 2 lad enthusiastically. The older boys were more conservative in their praise, but no less warm. 'The teachers are very kind', 'They're inspirational!' 'Lessons are always fun', 'Because of my science teacher, I want to be a scientist,' we were told. Work on the walls was imaginative and of a consistently high standard. Strong SEN team supports boys in need of extra help; the school welcomes all learners, although the school acknowledged that boys with more than moderate learning difficulties would struggle at Cumnor, and we ourselves felt that this wouldn't be the right place for them.

Parents in search of flashy facilities might initially be nonplussed by Cumnor's honeycomb, let's-patch-on-another-annexe-here school campus. The main site used to be residential, and the impression is still of a large, rambling house full of staircases and inglenooks. Decor-wise, it would be fair to say that it lacks the feminine touch: somehow, despite the displays and children's books lining the walls, there isn't much colour in the place. Desks are endearingly old-fashioned, and occasionally downright scruffy. But honestly, who cares? The classrooms are all well-resourced, there's an excellent ICT suite, the boys radiate contentment and their achievements speak for themselves. And there's nothing scruffy about the sports facilities: the huge sports ground boasts £50k's worth of new cricket nets and a new clubhouse, the sports hall is adequate and the swimming pool block was warm, light and inviting, which may be why the reception teachers were all in the water with their young charges when we visited. Cumnor's swimming is very successful (the swim squad practises from 7am), and the school has won national as well as local competitions. Football, rugby, cricket and athletics are likewise strong, nurtured by a team of very dedicated PE teachers. Old boys include Mark Butcher, Alistair Brown, David Sales, Chris Robshaw and Elliot Daly.

For the non-sportsmen, however, there is plenty of other fare on offer. Music is flourishing, with over half the boys learning at least one musical instrument, and a pleasing variety of bands and ensembles to join. The school's choral singing is particularly impressive: previous fixtures include Salzburg Cathedral and the Barnardo's National Choir Competition (which they won). Drama is also lively, and the school puts on at least two productions a year. There are lots of clubs and societies, and the boys are encouraged to try new things. 'We don't want boys who are in at 8.30am and out at 3.30pm. We want them to take risks. We tell them, if you haven't auditioned for the school play, why not? If you aren't learning an instrument, why not?'

A few years ago Cumnor joined the Cognita schools group, thereby increasing its financial clout in a very competitive locality. The Lodge Schools on the other side of the Purley Way declined and fell during the financial crisis, whereupon Cognita bought up most of the site and asked Cumnor to open a girls' school (see our separate entry) and expand Cumnor House Nursery. Reception boys are also housed on this site in Woodcote Lane, and we wondered if that didn't provoke grumbles from parents dropping off more than one child. But no: the school runs a shuttle service between the two sites, and parents can choose to which one they deliver both sons and daughters, knowing that the school will safely ferry their children to where they need to be. (And this, frankly, is more than can be said for some of the parents; the thoroughfare outside the Pampisford Road site gets very exciting at drop-off time, as local residents will feelingly confirm.)

The Croydon area is multicultural, and one of Cumnor's greatest successes is the way that it takes a highly diverse group of boys – every colour and creed is represented on the school roll – and helps them all become polished and likeable English gentlemen, in the best possible sense of the phrase. It may not be the place for the kind of child who just isn't into school no matter how good it is; incurable mavericks would be exhausted by the ebullient enthusiasm and team spirit here. But make no mistake, this is boys' education at its best.

However, we and no doubt parents hope that the current head will bring stability and have a longer reign than his several recent predecessors.

Cumnor House School for Girls

Linked with Cumnor House School (Croydon)

58

1 Woodcote Lane, Purley, Surrey CR8 3HB

Ages 4–11 **Pupils** 180

Fees: £11,145 – £13,380 pa

020 8660 3445
www.cumnorhouse.com

Head: Since April 2018, Amanda McShane BA PGCE, previously deputy head and head of science at The Old Vicarage School in Richmond-upon-Thames. Music degree; started her career as a year 6 teacher at a Surrey state primary school, becoming head of science and head of music before moving to the independent sector.

Entrance: Families span range of cultures and backgrounds and, increasingly, a greater geographic area. Surrey and South West London (Tooting, Clapham and Streatham) feature increasingly as minibus network (shared with Cumnor House Boys' School) helps to widen the net.

Many pupils move up to reception from one of two co-ed Cumnor House nurseries – both officially affiliated to the boys' school; all nursery pupils automatically offered a place in reception as long as the school can meet their needs. External candidates register (after visiting – there are weekly tours and regular open days) and are accepted on a first come, first served basis. Welcome applications in other year groups when assess ('with a small "a",' says school) over half a day to 'ensure that this is the best school for them and that they will be happy here.'

Scholarships awarded to exceptional current pupils though school didn't want to put a percentage on it (mega honour and glory but low monetary value). Bursaries also for existing pupils if families fall on hard times.

Exit: Sixteen scholarships in 2018 – most academic, some music, one each for sport and drama – to schools including Croydon High, Caterham, Royal Russell, Old Palace, JAGS and Streatham and Clapham High.

Remarks: Site is approached through chi chi private estate, mini mansions fronted with pavements soused in gravel (man with a brush and pan busily sweeps up the excess). There's been a school on this six-acre, gently hilly site for 100 years (lion on small commemorative lawn marks former pupils killed in WW1). Went into decline after the 2008 crash and was acquired by Cognita in 2010, making it the newish kid on the block in comparison with boys' school.

It's blessed with generous playing fields, a multi-use games area (netball court with go-faster stripes for range of sports) and garden with raised beds (each year group tends its own). Assorted playgrounds are well used, while reception pupils, delightfully rounded up for lessons with clapping games and songs by older 'buddies', mainly stick to their own space, also an outdoor learning area.

Heart of the school buildings is a pretty Victorian villa with preserved period quirks and homely rather than glitzy ambience. Newer buildings off to the sides include an unobtrusive teaching block and sports hall that avoids common distribution ambience with blond wood flooring and red-painted beams.

Under new ownership, has become a highly regarded alternative to the area's other girls' junior schools. Several exist but are mostly linked to senior schools – fine for those sold on the ethos, less so if you fancy a punt at other schools, including the excellent state grammars in the area.

Here, anxious parents are soothed with the balm of reassurance that whatever senior school you have in mind, your child will be carefully prepped for it (three entrance exams generally suggested as the maximum). There are plenty of staff (a mix of ages and experience) on hand to help, a good teacher to pupil ratio (just one to nine full time equivalent) and small class sizes (average mid teens, maximum 20).

Small size means it feels like home, thought one pupil, who had felt diminished by numbers and lack of attention at previous school. 'Here, teachers will pick a girl who is calm and puts her hand up nicely. In my old school, they just picked the noisiest.' Wouldn't work here, with universally wonderful manners, notably 'the ones you see when they don't know you're looking'. We were greeted politely. 'I hope you have a good visit,' said one pupil, gravely. (We did.)

Parents, meanwhile, had nothing but praise for school's calm, confidence-inspiring approach. If pupils' appearance doesn't put their minds at rest (blazer plus natty headgear – beret with a boater in summer) staff know-how generally does the trick, on open days and beyond. 'They gave me a lot of information on exactly what I was looking for,' said a mother. 'Meticulous planning,' say school inspectors – and parents agree.

There's clarity about what's taught and when. Take 11+ preparation. While school stresses that ideally pupils should enjoy free time over the summer holidays – 'they need a respite' – parents can ask for practice papers at the end of year 5. 'You feel looked after,' said one. Sense of security filters down to pupils. 'There's not even one day my daughter's said, "I don't want to go to school",' agreed a parent.

It's a tribute to high quality teaching that sees pupils through all the basics (French currently the only MFL, Latin offered in top two years). There's no setting, teachers versed in excellent differentiation. No room for doubt as to how your daughter is doing, with annual VR/NVR, reasoning, numeracy, reading and spelling tests to monitor progress as well as annual academic exams and informal assessments. Clearly going well in a Lake Woebegone way. 'Nearly everyone got over average,' exulted a pupil of recent exams.

Inspectors (in 2014) had noted a few gaps in the recruitment process and governance. School has since upped the ante and every box is now ticked several times over. Pictures of school's safeguarding leads are much in evidence and assemblies stress, and stress again, the need to 'tell a grown up if you're sad' – pupils we met were impressively aware of this.

Looking after people is something everyone here does well, from lunches (cheerful chef, in at 6am to get homemade bread and biscuits on the go), to learning support. A small number of pupils (currently nine) have English as an additional language.

Just one has a diagnosed learning need but 10 or so more have some support from class teachers which, say parents, is sensitively handled. Similarly, misbehaviour is quickly dealt with and sanctions sensibly applied (may miss a favourite lesson, for example).

Having the boys' school nearby is a great asset but also – inevitably – a source of comparison (especially as fees are the same for both). Line up the clubs and girls have fewer – one parent pointed out that even if she wanted her daughter to do an after-school activity every day, it wasn't available for her year group. It's also a more ladylike offering (ballet, textiles, swimming, computers, book, gym, pottery, chess, art, drama and Bollywood) compared with boys (current affairs, drama, chess, Italian, classics, Mandarin, Russian, history, Spanish, science debating and computers).

While relative size and different leaving age (boys stay to year 8) accounts for this school's less resources (boys have two science labs to girls' one, for example), the feel is a tad unemancipated and appears to extend into timetabled lessons (girls do food tech and science; boys have physics, chemistry and biology from the off). The boy's school also wins on scholarships, regularly scoring far more relative to its size (especially for sport, but academic too).

'Boys are different, girls are different but we would like [girls] to have the opportunities,' said one parent. 'We don't want them to feel left out.'

Girls do have separate sciences, stresses school (a term for each), while clubs are affected by demand. Spanish was tried and only got a handful of takers while Mandarin came and went when teacher moved on.

Life skills training for both boys and girls is on the horizon, boys will soon be on their way over to enjoy food technology (they can already sign up for after-school care provision) and girls will have more access to boys' school activities. The goal is 'general parity' between the two schools. Clubs may not be identical but girls won't go short.

Sports widely felt by parents to have been on the underwhelming side here – while the U11A girl netballers had nine fixtures in a recent school year, for example, the U11A boy footballers had 32.

Visitors who, like us, noticed an absence of current awards in the cabinet shouldn't be alarmed – they were at the engravers 'to update our achievements,' explains the school.

Girls already do well in swimming galas (it's over to the boys' school to use the 'superb indoor heated swimming pool'). Tag rugby is available as a club, hockey now added to the list (so recently that at least one parent wasn't yet aware of this), all helped by recruitment of a third PE specialist who will ensure that there's more on offer for everyone (currently those not selected for the small number of teams can end up feeling left out).

Performing and visual arts, in contrast, are a star attraction. Girls reckoned there were around four productions a year (some with boys' school). Music is good, with an orchestra and choice of choirs, chamber (selective) and main (which isn't, though you get a separate badge on your blazer for both). Specialist teachers give 90-ish lessons a week, up to grade 5 or so, many of the keenest playing several instruments and very keen. As we toured the music room, group of four year 5 girls was arriving for first band practice, composing the music to go with their own lyrics.

Art consistently gets the top rating, thanks to 'amazing', department (of one) who presides over a room brimming with creative clutter inspiring works ranging from a collection of gold-painted papier-mâché athletes suspended from bicycle wheel to ceramic animals.

Currently a model of decorum, school is a gentle oasis that inspires trust – parents couldn't praise it highly enough. Add a bit more oomph to extracurricular and sporting options to ensure that girls don't feel second best to the boys up the road and it will be practically perfect.

DLD College London

199 Westminster Bridge Road, London SE1 7FX

Ages 14–20 **Pupils** 434 **Sixth form** 282 **Boarders** 223 full

Fees: £19,000 – £23,000 pa; Boarding – £35,500 to £47,000 pa

020 7935 8411
www.dldcollege.co.uk

Principal: Since January 2018, Irfan Latif BSc, previously head of Sexey's School in Somerset (40s). Read chemistry at King's College London followed by a PGCE. First teaching post was at Kidbrooke School in Greenwich, then taught at several independent schools, including Haberdashers' Aske's Boys, Whitgift and St Benedict's in Ealing, where he was head of chemistry and director of science. Before joining Sexey's he was deputy head at Bedford School. He and his teacher wife Jocelyn have two daughters.

Academic matters: College offers a two-year GCSE programme aimed at international students with intensive English tuition in the first term; a minority (usually those who are older or who have transferred from other schools where they started their GSCEs) do a one-year GCSE course. There's also a two year GCSE course increasingly popular with British students. Most take seven subjects, from a list of 12 options including the basics, plus French, religious studies, art, graphics and drama. Russian, Chinese, Spanish, Italian, German and Arabic are available via individual tuition. Commendable results from a mixed ability intake. In 2018, 14 per cent A*-A/9-7 grades.

A level students get a choice of 33 subjects, including music technology, photography, film and media studies, sociology, psychology and languages, in more or less any combination. Art, economics, religious studies and philosophy are consistently popular, alongside English and maths. In 2018, just under 60 per cent A*-B grades and 30 per cent A*/A. BTecs also available in media production and business.

Some students are disaffected when they arrive, but it's rare for them to be anti-education after a few weeks. 'Because of the small class sizes – on average, 12 – they get lots of individual feedback and huge amounts of encouragement, and most start making progress very quickly,' says the college, attributing their academic success to their focus on fitting the right course to the right student.

Parents can't praise the system enough. 'The small class sizes, and the extra attention that provides each child with, have been the absolute making of my daughter,' one parent told us. Another, who has had two children at DLD, said, 'DLD has a record of helping children who felt they weren't going to achieve anything in a regular school to really do well. There's something about the small class sizes, easy-going environment and quality of teaching that gives them a chance to break out of set patterns of underachieving and underperforming. It really shows, more than anywhere I've seen.'

The college can cope with a wide range of special needs, generally picking up several previously undiagnosed cases each year, including dyslexia, ADHD and autism. Thirty-four per cent SEN when we visited and those benefit from support with study and essay writing skills; individual help is also available at extra cost. 'Our SEN students get more or less the same level of results as the others, due to the amount of input from SEN department, which is run by a two-strong team. This extra help is critical.' Accredited by CReSTeD, whose most recent report speaks of it as a unique school.

Very bright students also well catered for, with parents confirming that their children feel stretched and challenged in a positive way. Others point to the personalised approach of monitoring, feedback and target setting ensuring that students continue maximising their full potential at all times.

Indeed, educational expectations are high for all, with patchy work not accepted by staff. 'We believe in helping students believe they can move up to the next level.' Many staff are from Oxbridge and some come from non-teaching backgrounds – the theatre, the City, the BBC. 'This means our tutors know exactly what employers really want from graduates and it also means they have great connections,' said one student. 'My music teacher, for instance, has invited in songwriters, a music lawyer and others to talk to us, as well as sending out our coursework from people in the industry to get feedback.'

Teachers only employed if they are accessible to students outside classes, with many not only being available on email, but on a live chat system. Students say they are treated as adults and for many of them, it's that mutual respect that gets them back on track with their education. The most recent ISI report states that students like being at the college and are very happy with the personal support that they receive.

Extended Project Qualification increasingly popular, with 12 students doing it when we visited, although college admits some drop off in first few weeks. 'It's a tough programme.'

Games, options, the arts: A level art and photography are two of the most popular and successful subjects here, and the artwork we saw on display in the large and well-equipped art rooms was striking, with a notable creative energy among the students while they were working. 'I can honestly say every photography lesson is fun,' said one student. LAMDA examinations on offer and the DLD youth theatre puts on two performances a year.

All GCSE students play curricular sport at local centres on Wednesday afternoons, including football, basketball, tennis, netball, dance, rock-climbing and aerobics. Sports clubs and matches after school too, including cricket and yoga. On-site sporting facilities include a swimming pool and gym in the basement. 'But although sport is accessible and enjoyed by many students, DLD is probably not the best place for your child if they're really, really sporty,' one parent told us.

Music popular, with facilities including a recording studio and various practice areas, all of which are soundproofed. There's a vocal group, ukulele group, recording studio club and 59 students do private music lessons, including classical and jazz piano tuition, rock guitar, pop singing, singing and drum kit.

Extracurricular offering has improved in recent years, including Duke of Edinburgh Award, EPQ, debating and art clubs. Located in the heart of Westminster, it's no wonder the school takes full advantage of the galleries, museums and theatres practically on its doorstep, with overseas trips to the likes of Barcelona and Paris.

Boarding: The new site includes over 220 student beds over 15 floors, with views over the Thames. The areas are gender split, with younger ones on the lower floors. Strict curfews in the week from 9.30-10.30pm and, which are extended on Fridays and Saturdays until 10.30-11.30pm (depending on age). All full boarders, although some do visit home during weekends and half term and the school is very flexible when it comes to students wanting to visit friends and families. Boarders will often arrange their own activities for the weekend, but there are always free activities going on in the boarding house, including movie nights, quiz nights, zumba, birthday parties etc, along with visits to local museums, galleries and places like Harry Potter World.

Mostly single rooms, of different shapes and sizes, all ensuite. Some twin rooms share a bathroom. These rooms have a partition between beds that can be extended along the whole length of the room if required. 'It's the twin ones that are the most popular,' a staff member told us. Rooms are hi-spec, contemporary and minimalist, with a clear wow factor. 'I love my room,' one student told us. 'And because it's soundproofed, I can be as loud as I want and study in peace regardless of how loud anyone else is.' Weekly inspections mean they are kept reasonably tidy, although lots of unmade beds when we visited. Light, airy and spacious communal kitchen on each floor, complete with comfortable seating areas, fridge, freezer, microwave, kettle and toaster, but no hob or oven, with students expected to eat main meals in the refectory. 'It's a really sociable area,' one student told us.

Pastoral care for boarders includes a strong team of house parents, who are fully residential, run by a director of boarding and his assistant – who in turn is overseen by the vice president of principal welfare.

Background and atmosphere: Now one of 16 schools and five colleges owned by the Alpha Plus Group, founded in 1931 to provide tutoring for Oxbridge and Colonial Service entrance exams. After World War II it began to specialise in A and O level teaching. In 2004 it moved from Notting Hill to light, airy, refurbished premises in Marylebone; in 2015 moved again, amalgamating with Abbey College in a new, purpose built site on Westminster Bridge Road.

On first sight, this shiny new building looks more like swanky corporate offices than any school, both outside and in, but a closer look reveals that education is very much at the heart of the design. A large open space – with huge projector screens on the wall, and which doubles up as a 350-seat performance area when required – forms the central atrium. Then the teaching and study areas – all arranged in colour co-ordinated zones so students can't get lost – sit around the edges. These facilities include six high-spec labs, a creative arts and media faculty, 40 tutorial rooms and an open plan library, study and ICT facilities.

Informal atmosphere, more akin to a college than a school, with staff and students on a first name basis and no uniform. But there's no room for slacking, with students engaged, inquisitive and busy both in the classes when we visited. 'Academically, it's tough, but people want to learn,' said one student. Helping students keep up is a vast array of break-out areas dotted around the different floors – some with individual booths for private study, whilst others have small or large tables for group study.

Active student council, which meets twice a month and organises plenty of charity events (breast cancer awareness day when we visited), as well as bringing about changes such the reintroduction of table football, although one parent told us she'd like to see 'more of a student voice overall.'

Fresh food available in the cashless refectory, which is reviewed by a food committee comprised of students and staff. Starbucks also on site. The day begins for students at 8.50am and finishes at 4.40pm, with enrichment extending that until around 6.30pm.

Pastoral care, well-being and discipline: Very strong pastoral system, which had recently been restructured when we visited, so that there are separate staff for pastoral and academic care. 'This is important because we do attract some needy students, including school phobics and SEN,' says college. 'There's no stigma if you need help,' said one student. 'Staff really care about you here,' said another. Parents we spoke to were very moved by what the school had achieved for their children pastorally. 'Staff are so kind and supportive that I'm welling up thinking about what they've done for my daughter,' one told us.

Electronic register is taken in every lesson and parents are texted or emailed if attendance becomes a problem. Each student has a weekly meeting with their personal tutor to talk about progress and future plans; three directors of studies and three directors of welfare work closely with the personal tutors. Expectations, rather than rules, are the norm here. 'My son kicked back about things like strict uniform and not being allowed to go out at lunchtime at his last school, and he's much happier here, where you're expected to turn up and do your work and be respectful, but without lots of petty rules and an authoritarian environment.'

Significant proportion of pupils smoke (nurse runs a stop smoking programme), but there's tough penalties for misusing drink and drugs – those under suspicion are sent for drugs tests, to general parental approval. Most students, even the most troubled ones, buckle down eventually, although occasionally things don't go to plan, with around two exclusions every academic year.

Sanctions include supervised study; also a system of verbal and written warnings based on employment law. Bullying is taken very seriously, although students told us the atmosphere is so relaxed and accepting that it's exceptionally rare. 'Nobody judges you here,' said one student.

Peer mentoring had around 60 students involved when we visited. 'It's improving my interpersonal skills,' said one student.

Pupils and parents: Students aged between 14-18 (with the odd exception up to 20), most of whom have come from private schools. Some have been ill; some have had mental health or other problems; some have found their previous school too rigid or too stressful. Others come from peripatetic diplomatic families. Some lack confidence and need to learn good working habits. Most thrive in the informal but structured atmosphere. Around 30 per cent from UK, with others mostly from Germany, Latvia, Ukraine, Malaysia, China, Burma, Vietnam, Italy, Kazakhstan and Russia. Little, if any, sense of community among parents, which one said is 'disappointing, but hardly surprising.'

Entrance: Everyone is interviewed and previous schools are asked for references and reports. Those going into the sixth form need a minimum of five grade 4s at GCSE; if they haven't passed maths or English they will need to retake these, alongside their A levels. No student who has been disruptive elsewhere is accepted without a discussion about the need for a change in behaviour. School is registered for 725 students, although only 500 when we visited. 'Our vision was always to open the new facility with 500 and build it up.'

Exit: Quite a few students move on after GCSEs – perhaps to state sixth form colleges – but more than half go through to the sixth form. Those aiming at Oxbridge (no places in 2018) are given an intensive course including lectures, seminars, mock interviews and individual tuition. Popular destinations include UCL, Goldsmith's, King's College, LSE, Imperial, Cass Business School and Bristol. Wide range of degree courses, with business studies, economics and specialist art areas being the most popular. Extra help also for potential vets, doctors and dentists, via a bespoke medical programme (one to medical school in 2018).

Money matters: Several scholarships available, worth 10-100 per cent of fees, on the basis on academic attainment, plus means-tested bursaries. 'We're fortunate to have free rein to be sympathetic to the individual.' Indeed, one local boy supported 100 per cent financially when we visited.

Remarks: This unique educational environment seems to capture all the best things about a college environment, combining them with the pastoral care and motivational structures that are more typical of school provision. All this takes place in small classes, with one-to-one help when required, in a state-of-the-art, purpose-built building in the heart of London, where students have the option to board on-site. The result is an informal atmosphere with an underlying structured regime where everyone is kept up to scratch. A fantastic place for the very bright, as well as re-motivating the disaffected, although not for young people who want a more traditional boarding school experience.

Drayton Manor High School

Drayton Bridge Road, London W7 1EU

Ages 11–19 **Pupils** 1,502 **Sixth form** 333

020 8357 1900
www.draytonmanorhighschool.co.uk

Head: Since 1994, Sir Pritpal Singh BSc MA FRSA. Educated at Highgate School, where he was a boarder; he has maintained close links with his alma mater. Read chemistry at London University. Deputy head at Cranford Community School, as well as head of science, head of chemistry and head of year group at several other comprehensive schools. Knighted for services to education in 2005 and has received the accolade of head teacher of the year.

A true visionary who has turned the school into the success it is today. No mere figurehead. Very visible around the school – he still greets pupils daily after 23 years in the job. Dedicated to his pupils and justifiably proud of his school. Parents and pupils see him as an excellent role model. Treats everyone with respect and dignity: 'We show that everyone is valuable. Subtle things, we need to live it out. You have to give of yourself, consistently'.

No longer at the chalk-face. 'Some heads feel that teaching is crucial to their stature. I loved teaching and was at ease in the classroom but feel that I have nothing to prove. It's better for me to walk around the school and drop into lessons, see lots of students in the lunch queue or at the bus stop. That way I get a better spread of contact.'

Calm, assured and with a warm sense of humour. 'He is very composed and that is reflected throughout the school. There is a sense of peace about the place, no matter when you visit and that comes from the top,' commented one parent.

Married with two grown-up sons, one of whom is an engineer, the other works in IT. Family is important to him. Loves sport and coached rugby for 14 years. Also enjoys listening to music, with a weakness for the Rolling Stones. A well-travelled man.

Relishes his job and considers himself fortunate. 'I could have been a pauper in India. I just happen to have been born into a family that valued education'.

Academic matters: In 2018, 23 per cent of grades were A*/A at A level, 53 per cent A*-B. At GCSE, 74 per cent got 9-4 in both English and maths; 19 per cent of grades 9-7. Has awards for exceptional GCSE results and letter of congratulation on EBacc results received from minister of state for school standards.

Thirty subjects offered at A level, including media studies, sociology and psychology. Popular A levels currently maths, biology, chemistry and history. Government and politics, as well as history, recognised nationally as superb departments. BTec qualification also offered in creative media and applied general qualifications in business. Wide choice of GCSE subjects including computing and economics.

Pupils can take between five and 12 GCSEs. Modern languages offered include Spanish, French and German, though no Mandarin nor Russian. One parent we spoke to wished that her daughter could have taken two modern languages at GCSE but not possible. On average, 35 pupils learn Latin in first year with around 20 pupils taking it for GCSE in year 10. 'The students love it; the parents love it and it adds something to the character of the school. It attracts good, interesting staff and it adds an extra dimension,' says head.

Average class size is 23; maximum 31. Five one-hour lessons a day. School recognises the benefits of setting by ability – English and maths from year 7 and science, French and Spanish from year 8. Head states, 'Differentiation is a strength – all our pupils are pushed, whether very able academically or not.' Awarded 'outstanding' in last Ofsted inspection.

EPQ is embraced here, with a broad range of subjects chosen by pupils ranging from bovine TB to Jane Austen. About one third of the year end up taking it. Head encourages the pupils to take it on if manageable: 'It's a conversation we have with the student and family.' Pupils were highly focused in the lessons we observed, whether being tested on GCSE biology modules or role-playing gritty scenarios in drama group. Head delights in the fact that 'they enjoy being challenged. They can listen for long periods of time. They can express their opinions with confidence'.

Over 300 pupils on the SEND register, well above the national average. School offers excellent provision for those with milder end of learning difficulties such as dyslexia, dyscalculia and autism and those with social, emotional and mental health difficulties. Staff are trained to deal with attachment and anxiety disorders as well as school phobias. Baseline assessment on arrival. Beautifully designed new inclusion centre. 'Probably the best facilities in the school for the students who need the most support,' explains head. 'They all arrive early as they love coming to this area.' Alternative curriculum in phonics, literacy and numeracy offered to those that need specialist support in the first few years. EAL pupils also withdrawn from class for extra help if needed.

School stretches the very brightest sparks too. Gifted and talented pupils might be given extra lessons or be sent off on a trip. One mother we spoke to commented that her clever son 'was very well supported and extended throughout.'

Homework club in library for those who struggle to concentrate at home. The pupils we spoke to did not find amount of homework too onerous, with one even shyly confessing that she enjoys it. Booster revision sessions laid on for A level and GCSE pupils after school, in holidays and at weekends, so no-one is left to flounder in exam season.

Teachers are ambitious for their pupils and are rated highly by the parents. 'You really feel at parents' evenings that the teachers know your child inside out.' Pupils feel most teachers are 'easy to talk to.' Over 20 members of staff have been at school for more than a decade but there is a healthy balance with plenty of youthful faces too. Head admits that recruitment of excellent staff 'can be challenging with teacher shortages' and it can be hard when a head of a faculty leaves but 'we are like a gyroscope. It takes a lot to knock us off our stride'.

Games, options, the arts: Wide array of sport offered from cricket to gymnastics and dance. Some pupils perform at national level as well as county level. School is regular winner of cups and tournaments across borough and new display cabinets are being built to house the abundant silverware. Netball, rugby and football particularly impressive. Excellent facilities. Everyone is encouraged to participate at some level, whether house dodgeball or more giddy heights.

The arts faculty is made up of art and design, drama, music and media subjects. Numerous choirs. Concerts galore, both formal and informal. Numerous opportunities to take part in musical events, from participating in national orchestra days to hearing musicians at Albert Hall. Currently 150 students learn an instrument. Head is ambitious to improve the music department. 'We want to be world class, with the best facilities,' he states. Excellent new art, design and technology studios too. Though some impressive work on show, including sensational portfolios, art is not a popular A level. School takes part in Shakespeare Schools Festival. Annual summer showcase is highlight of school year. 'The shows are sensational,' according to one parent.

Sixth form enrichment options include chess, debating and trampoline sessions. Pupils participate in National Citizen Service and fundraisers for children's charities. School promotes learning outside the classroom including ski and snowboard trips to Maine, homestay visits in France and residential stays in Devon.

Background and atmosphere: Opened as a grammar school in 1930, before becoming a comprehensive in 1973 and an academy in 2011. Still feels like a grammar school, with its stained-glass coats of arms in the library and its Latin motto Nec Aspera Terrent, meaning 'hardships do not deter us'. Sums up ethos of school.

Current head is only the fifth head in school's history and many of the buildings are named after his well-loved predecessors. Yellowing old school photos adorn the corridor, reflecting the changes in its history from genteel 1930s arrangements to hippy groupings from the 1970s.

An £8 million building programme, including a new humanities faculty, outstanding new library and refurbished science labs, has transformed the school. Beautiful central piazza, complete with immaculate topiary and a total absence of grime or litter make for stunning premises. Vivienne Westwood's striking Union Jack on a main corridor adds a dramatic punch to what could otherwise feel like a National Trust property.

Pupil successes are celebrated, whether at congratulatory breakfasts, coffees, lunches or a year 13 boat trip to Craven Cottage. Prizes awarded in all year groups for effort and progress, as well as for humour and good character, and for courage.

Pastoral care, well-being and discipline: Each year comprises 240 pupils, organised into nine tutor groups. Each pupil sees their tutor every day. 'I love my tutor,' smiled one boy. 'When I meet with heads of year, I expect to be told the key things that are going on in each year group. I've got my finger on the pulse, as have my deputies,' states head.

Discipline is important. Schools keeps rules to a minimum but expects them to be obeyed. Only sixth formers are allowed mobile phones and punishments for others in possession of them are no-nonsense. Third time caught with a mobile phone counts as defiance and can be met with an exclusion. 'Even for sixth formers, if they are caught doing anything iffy then the sanctions kick in. They respect that,' explains head. Strong policies in place regarding social media. 'Our values are clear on social media – it all comes down to good manners.' At risk of permanent exclusion for possession of drugs and offensive weapons. Four or five permanent exclusions annually. One mother summed it up: 'The kids respond to the discipline.

There is not much wriggle room!' Another parent said, 'The children know where they stand. They know the consequences for bad behaviour and the school carries through with these. No idle threats at Drayton.' One mother commented that some boys mess around in class but that generally there is zero tolerance of larking about. Head thinks it can be a relief for the pupils to have to comply with strict rules: 'They can blame me. It allows them to perform at a high level.' Over 95 per cent attendance rate.

Head believes a caring ethos is at the heart of the school. 'We insist on high standards. Being courteous and considerate comes before academic prowess. How we treat other people is the number one priority. That is our bedrock. It's the Drayton Manor way.' This sense of decency is expected not only in the classroom but between lessons, at break time and even at the bus stop. 'The whole continuum from home to school is important for us. It does not end at 3.30pm. They need to learn that this is their life now.'

Head recognises that it can be hard being a teenager. 'It's important they know there is more to life than just being popular. The children feel safe here and can develop their own personalities. They can express themselves without being made fun of.' The pupils in turn say they can trust the staff and feel that if they tell the teachers about any problems, they will make it better. 'Pastoral care is not just about having the structures in place but trying to work out what it feels like to be one of the students. We think a lot about it,' says head. One girl said the school had supported her incredibly well through a bereavement and another mother expressed her gratitude for the way Drayton had built up her daughter's shaky confidence. Very few suffer with depression, anorexia or self-harming.

Ninety-five per cent of food is home-made, including breakfast for early birds from 8am. Chef worked in a Michelin-star restaurant and certainly wowed us with delectable pastries. Lots of options, including halal, gluten-free, vegan and vegetarian, though one pupil told us 'it would be easy to get away with just eating a cookie every day for lunch as no-one checks'.

Pupils and parents: Socially mixed intake, from affluent professional families to the very deprived. Pupils head in from north and west Ealing and Hanwell. One third white British with many different ethnic minority groups. Sixty-five per cent EAL and over 50 different languages spoken at home. Parenting support classes offered. Above average number of pupils on free school meals.

Excellent home-school communication. Head genuinely likes meeting people and enjoys being around at events such as parents' evenings.

Old Draytonians include footballer Peter Crouch, BBC business editor Kamal Ahmed and Lord Justice of Appeal Sir Michael Fox.

Entrance: Non-selective. Successful court case means that children gain a place at Drayton Manor if it is the nearest school to their home. If you live a mile from the school but it remains the nearest school to home, then you will have priority over children who live half a mile away but have other schools from which to choose. Head explains, 'Roughly speaking unless you live 0.8 miles away or less, you won't get a place.' Massively oversubscribed, with roughly six applicants per place. Waiting list for all years. Generally, a grade 6 is needed at GCSE to pursue the subject in the sixth form, whether existing pupil or from outside. Fifty or more pupils join in year 12, to replace those who leave after GCSEs (they usually head for vocational courses elsewhere or employment).

Exit: Up to 50 per cent leave after GCSEs. Popular universities include Leeds, UCL, King's, Sussex and Brunel. Subjects range from international politics to mechanical engineering; 18 medics in 2018.

Interview practice for those applying to Oxbridge or for medicine, as well as shared careers workshops, at Highgate School. Oxbridge society prepares pupils for applications, including test practice. Two Oxbridge places in 2018. Head says pupils don't always know what they are capable of so encourages those who would never have considered university to believe that they can achieve it. He explains, 'This is a seven-year programme. You can't just turn it on in year 12. Students need to learn how to crack the code. They need to learn not to be intimidated by institutions.'

Money matters: Sixth form bursary. School uses its pupil premium to fund learning support, masterclasses, mentoring, Easter revision and some subsidising of school trips. Voluntary contribution of £10 per family per year.

Remarks: Head said, 'I think you can see why I have stayed so long. It is remarkable how the students have responded to my approach.' Certainly, the pupils we spoke to were thoroughly impressive: modest, polite, caring and articulate but with a developed sense of fun. An inspiring and exciting school that provides a truly outstanding education.

DUCKS Kindergarten and Infants School

Linked with Dulwich College, Dulwich College: The Junior School

87 College Road, London SE21 7HH

Ages 6m–7 **Pupils** 237 **C of E**

Fees: £13,365 – £15,720 pa

020 8693 1538
www.dulwich.org.uk/ducks

Head: Since September 2018, Miranda Norris, previously deputy head of Junior School, Dulwich College (Singapore). She has also been director of studies at Wetherby Prep, taught at the British International School in Jakarta, Indonesia and been deputy head of juniors at Dulwich College Suzhou.

Entrance: Into the kindergarten, six places for babies aged 6-18 months; 18 places for toddlers and up to 40 places for 'ducklings' of between 2 and 3 years. The infants' school comprises nursery from 3+ to year 2. There are usually five to 10 places available at the nursery, then 10 to 15 reception places, with places occasionally emerging higher up the school.

No assessment for entry into the kindergarten, but children entering at 3, 4, 5 and 6+ will have an assessment to ensure their learning is up to date and at a stage where they can take advantage of everything the school has to offer. Priority throughout is given to the children of college staff and DUCKS siblings. We imagine the younger members of the college staff could keep the baby room next to filled. Given the small size, keen parents will want to register early.

Exit: Girls and some boys exit to a wide range of destinations at the end of year 2, beginning locally with Alleyn's, JAPS, Sydenham High, Oakfield Prep and Rosemead, spreading to Streatham & Clapham High School and St Dunstan's College.

The majority of boys (around two-thirds) move on to the junior school. There have been grumbles about the numbers being offered places in the past. The school says that realistically the college may not be the right school for every child.

Remarks: The teaching staff is mostly female, some mothers with relatively young children themselves, hand-picked based on 'qualifications and enthusiasm'. Parents seem to feel this a place where children can be themselves free from pressure. One said, 'It has impressed me that the staff are willing to work individually with children at a pace suitable for that child in that subject.' Another told us, 'My daughter is not interested in academic subjects but the teachers have awakened an interest in learning in her.' One felt that the school enables children 'to develop at the speed that they require, unlike the hothousing that is encountered at some prep schools.' This means 7+ time won't be overly-pressured, which won't suit all.

Parents suggest that there is a good balance between the kind of learning through play where children are having so much fun they are oblivious to the learning and good, solid foundation skills teaching. 'Being taught how to count by jumping in puddles was a particular favourite of my sons,' said one mother. Another told us, 'My son rapidly caught up with his classmates in literacy skills, having moved to the UK from a country where phonics and literacy are started at a much older age.'

On our visit, the nursery children were busily and noisily involved in a variety of activities and play which only the trained eye would realise were carefully structured to deliver the early years curriculum – plenty of role play corners, freedom to go in and out, and excellent use made of glittery pasta. Their playground stretches up the grassy bank behind the school with forest school elements newly introduced at the top. Reception classrooms are large.

Head of the kindergarten says modestly that the school is not unique but doing what they do well. She cites her staff as following the children's interests in their teaching – she points out the artwork on the wall where a child has painted what he wanted rather than following the given theme, but it is still valued and appreciated. In the toddler room, decorated with a jungle theme when we visited, learning is very much child-initiated, with lots of sensory discovery.

No sightings of lunch, but pupils declared enthusiastically that the lunches are 'yummy' and 'tasty' – they are prepared on-site by DUCKS' own chef.

Achievements are celebrated in assembly, being invited to share a good piece of work with the head or with rewards including fruity tea. From year 1 the usual stickers, certificates, shields and trophies. Not a homework-free zone, but a parent said, 'just the right amount of homework and holiday work to keep the children ticking over.'

The school is committed to early identification of SEN – all pupils are carefully observed and assessed, if any SEN identified then they work with the parents to establish the best support for the child. There are nine children with identified needs currently. The school recently admitted its first pupil communicating with British Sign Language – children, parents and staff have all received training with a BSL instructor.

Aims for PE set realistically for the age group, looking to develop spatial awareness, love of physical activity and play as well as social skills. Rather boy oriented, tag rugby, football and cricket on offer, and everyone learns to swim. A parent explained: 'The PE teacher is one of a kind, immensely talented and patient. The children have sports three times a week as well as extracurricular sports clubs if they choose. My son has at least five hours of organised sport a week.' Everyone learns to swim in the college pool.

Music is taught by specialists and all of year 2 learns the recorder. 'The music teacher pulls together amazing productions given the young age of the children.' Very able children are able to join groups at the junior school.

After-school activities every day of the week run until 4.30pm at a cost of around £4 per session offering an appealing mix of down-time or, for those with the energy, 3D modelling, swimming, ballet, football, netball and more. When there is always so much to fit into every day, lunchtime clubs can be useful: 'I love that my daughter has had the opportunity to start ballet with her friends at lunchtime', says a mother. So, clubs seem to offer redress the balance of the traditionally 'male' sport on offer for the girls.

DUCKS is so tucked away in Sydenham – one almost has to be in the know to venture in search of it when making the rounds of nurseries and pre-preps. If you are coming from Dulwich Village, Herne Hill or East Dulwich, it lies beyond a local curiosity, the Dulwich estate's antique toll-gate, which makes the road south of the college impassable to all but those willing to pay a pound a time to pass. Excitedly, we enquired as to whether DUCKS parents are given a toll-gate pass – not even staff are privileged with such a thing. Parents soon get the hang of the loop around.

A mere infant in terms of the almost 400 year old college, DUCKS recently celebrated its 20th anniversary. One might imagine that the school occupies only the large Victorian house fronting the road, but this is home only for the younger children: a good thing, as the rooms are slightly gloomy.

The majority of the classrooms are actually situated in a wooden-clad building looking over the playing fields and onwards to stunning views of the City and the glittering Shard. It looks very much like a cricket pavilion, echoing the actual pavilion used by the school until it burnt down in 1997 – the silver lining being the opportunity to create something which worked just for them.

The peace and quiet of the setting is a rare and unusual treat for any London family, and lends itself to numerous environmental themes, lots of muddy fun and gives rise to the names of the classes, all of wild birds. At the rear of the school are several soft surface playgrounds, segregated for various age groups, so plenty of space for letting off steam with no shortage of ride-on toys and a veranda ensuring children can play outside even on wet days.

The word used repeatedly by parents to describe the atmosphere here is nurturing. Parents told us, 'It is supportive of shy children but equally has the space and facilities for children who have boundless energy' and 'although not fiercely competitive, it does expect the children to stretch themselves.'

Whatever rumours of previous discord between staff and management have made their way to us, there have been key new appointments, teachers spoke of their happiness working here and much may now be set to change.

No concerns voiced with regards to pastoral care. One parent said, 'Outstanding pastoral care, and the school is good at communicating any concerns about our children with their parents'. 'They discuss bad behaviour in circle time in what appears to be a very meaningful way for the children.' Years 1 and 2 are all buddies to lower school pupils, whilst senior boys from the college visit as part of their community service.

Something about the building suggests a place more akin to a nursery than a school, but parents surprised us, saying it would suit 'a child responsive to structure who is keen to learn' and 'those who prefer a more free and easy approach to learning would probably find things difficult.'

The school is proud of its pupils' cultural and linguistic backgrounds, celebrating them throughout the year. Currently 17 children in the kindergarten are at least bilingual and 29 children in the Infants' school are bi- or trilingual. Far fewer, just a handful, have EAL needs.

The school praises the parents, who embrace themes and initiatives keenly, even recently attempting to pry themselves from their phones and tablets for a 'screenless week'. One mother with an eye for telling detail said: 'This is not a school where working mothers and stay-at-home mothers compete, or where a parent can achieve kudos by the quality of party bags at their child's party.' Phew.

One summed it up with satisfaction: 'Outstanding. I have wanted for nothing.'

Dulwich College

Linked with DUCKS Kindergarten and Infants School, Dulwich College: The Junior School

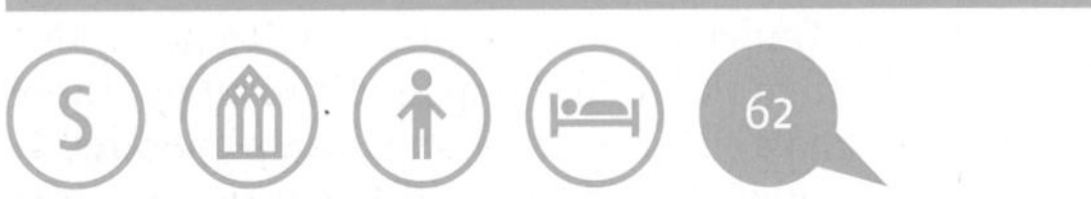

Dulwich Common, London SE21 7LD

Ages 11–18 **Pupils** 1,364 **Sixth form** 469 **Boarders** 130 full/weekly

Fees: Day £20,448; Boarding £40,017- £42,681 pa

020 8693 3601
www.dulwich.org.uk

Master: Since 2009, Dr Joseph (Joe) Spence BA PhD (50s), a graduate in modern history and politics; the Irish histories and literature of his postgrad line his study walls. Previously headmaster of Oakham School and for 10 years until 2002 held the prestigious position of master in college at Eton, housemaster to the King's scholars. His first decade at Dulwich College will coincide with the college's 400th anniversary.

Grammar school educated, he describes his career path as the 'story of accident', a happy one. Immensely warm and charming, putting one at ease, the embodiment of the oft repeated 'Dulwich boys can talk to anyone'. He brings a sense of fun to those around him, appearing to wear his responsibilities lightly.

Married to a lawyer, with two sons and daughter, he still finds time to write, recently penning a new libretto for a concert at King's College Cambridge. 'My duty is to make sure that every Alleynian leaves with something intellectual... a passion which will be with him for the rest of his life'. Parents unanimously declare him to be outstanding, enthusing: 'a good orator, a great listener'; 'a great presence and a motivational leader'.

His vision for the transformations in progress – physical and philosophical – start with 'get the classroom right, then everything else', but quickly go beyond with the desire to create a generation of original thinkers. You don't have to be a scientist or an artist here – instead the aim is: 'learning that is free from the syllabus' allowing boys to take risks in a dazzling programme of challenges, symposia, performances and adventures.

Academic matters: It's well known that improving the academics was top of the agenda. The college is now in the top eight per cent for value added nationally and the master is confident that the best is still to come. In 2018, 84 per cent of I/GCSE grades were A*-A/9-7. Plenty of A*s in sciences, English literature, maths, French and Spanish. At A level/Pre-U, 61 per cent A*/A, and (again including Pre-U) 88 per cent A*-B. Maths is most popular by far, followed by physics, history, economics and chemistry. High percentage of A*/As in physics, plus history of art, English, further maths, history and art. A levels remain as the core upper school offer but individual heads of subject have the flexibility to offer Pre-U.

Academic teaching is described by parents as solid lower down the college but inspirational higher up. Thirty-five per cent of teachers in residence for over 10 years. The master says candidly that now only a handful are perhaps not on message, and he won't see boys stuck with them, which chimes with parents, who say, 'very good standard of teaching, noticeable improvement' and 'incompetence would not be tolerated'. They also describe staff as 'hugely committed'; 'they understand a boy's potential'; 'they set the bar high academically' and 'the daily report system is excellent'.

The master drives innovation. A key recent appointment is the director of science, formerly at lauded Brighton College, plus two new deputy heads. Turning things on their head, 'flip' lessons might give boys homework first, then the boys come in and discuss how they found it, or mini-whiteboards may enable a teacher to see at a glance whether boys have 'got it'.

Curriculum is largely as one might expect; choosing options is quite complex. Languages have a particularly strong focus throughout. French, Spanish, Chinese and Latin are taught in the lower school, later on there is the addition of German, Italian and Greek. Appealing language trips. Exchanges take place too, but with boys considerately settled in host families in pairs.

The only setting is for maths. All pupils study separate sciences up to IGCSE and the college doesn't necessarily encourage the collection of an excessive number. Intellectual boys wishing to stretch themselves further between years 7 and 11 can enrol on the scholars' programme, described by one as 'the highlight of my week'.

Quirkier A level options include critical and contextual studies and ancient history. Liberal studies in the upper sixth in conjunction with the girls at JAGS allows boys to try something new: modern poetry, yoga, book-binding, Italian cinema and even ballroom dancing.

Also for sixth formers, the Dulwich Diploma, which looks to offer the depth of A level with the breadth of the IB: the three components comprise academic study, including an extended essay or research topic of their choice – recent examples Who Killed Sylvia Plath? and Is Medical Research the New Imperialism? Whilst all of this adds up to a very full plate, parents say there are 'high expectations with excellent support through study skills sessions' and 'it's pretty intensive in terms of workload but not too high pressure'.

A team of four well-qualified learning support teachers are shared with the junior school, and provide support to individual boys with a diagnosed learning difficulty – 20 per cent. Eight per cent of middle and upper school boys receive EAL support.

Games, options, the arts: In year 7, whilst skills are built and some sports tried for the first time, rugby, football, hockey and cricket are all compulsory. By year 8 choices emerge, one being dropping rugby for fencing. Tennis currently squeezed for space with only three courts. No single sport is compulsory in the middle school but a plethora of teams make it tempting to get involved – skiing, rowing, fives, squash, cross-country and basketball, to name but a few. Years 10 and 11 may try golf, rock-climbing, self-defence, taekwondo and rugby 7s, whilst upper school choices aim to involve boys in sport, perhaps officiating or coaching as well as trying gentlemanly pursuits such as croquet, horse-riding and sailing. Boys are able to use the superb facilities at nearby Herne Hill velodrome.

Seventy acres of playing fields recently reseeded, and rugby is the triumphant sport. Success, too, for the under 14s rowers, who are national champions and the school supplies four members of the under 15 GB water-polo team. Boys we had lunch with laughingly said the only thing they didn't like was swimming as there was no point trying to keep up with the Olympic swimmers and water-polo players.

'Arts, music and co-curricular are outstanding'. We arrived just in time to be treated to a sensitive rendition of W H Auden's Stop All of The Clocks as part of that day's house poetry competition. The school has a rich theatrical tradition, a flexible theatre space, Chewetel Ejiofor and Rupert Penry-Jones are OAs, makes the very most of the London theatre scene, and each year produces three drama festivals and 24 performance pieces.

This term's Dulwich Creative week was produced with all of the finesse and confidence of a national arts organisation gone guerrilla and saw art hijacks where every pupil – astonishingly even the babies in the kindergarten – produce a clay self-portrait, which then came together into one installation. A surreal note remains overlooking the cricket pitches, giant polyurethane mushrooms by international street artist Christian Nagel. Art and DT facilities are light and bright, and where we found some of the most exuberant classes in full flow.

Numbers learning instruments peak in the lower school at 45 per cent of boys falling to 25 per cent by the upper school. Standard of musicianship varies from enthusiastic beginners to boys who are leaders of section in the National Youth Orchestra or principals at Glyndebourne and the ENO. The music department is in the process of upgrading: there is a shiny new Mac suite for music technology, a new acoustic percussion suite, and small and large practice areas. Another funky new facility is the electric 'shed', fully sound-insulated, a great place to let rip with the electric guitar.

World class performances from a formidable debating team, who recently trounced the competition at the Oxford and Cambridge Unions. Where next for the boy currently ranked number one in the world?

Long lunch hours ensure even the senior boys feel they have time for a sophisticated list of clubs and societies, which continue after school. Poultry society boasts its own hens; whether they are ever eaten is set to be a college myth. Our curiosity was piqued as to what goes on at the Gentlemen's Club (no-one seemed to know); presumably no cigars.

The careers office has a 2,000 strong network of former parents and corporate contacts: a recent event invited 40 such to the Dulwich Picture Gallery. Boys were instructed to read up on everyone's biographies then were sent off to network fiercely.

Boarding: There are 130 boarders, two-thirds in the sixth form, majority from China and Hong Kong but also Eastern Europe. The boarding houses are on the campus, modernised period houses decorated with OA sporting team photos: quite basic in our view, small-ish rooms with less than luxurious en suite bathrooms, but unlikely to worry most boys intent on studying and playing hard surrounded by friends. Common rooms with large screen for movie nights, table football and all-important toasters.

Background and atmosphere: Founded in 1619 by the wealthy actor and businessman, Edward Alleyn. He set up and endowed the Foundation, which distributes its surplus profits to a group of schools including Dulwich College, JAGS and Alleyn's. The college moved to its present site in the 1870s. The main buildings are stunning Italianate red brick designed by the son of the architect of the Houses of Parliament.

Sitting amidst vast manicured pitches, the college is a gracious and intriguing south London landmark. Closer up, the collection of modern buildings forming a large part of the teaching spaces, particularly in the lower school, are plain and nothing more than functional, quite possibly a bit depressing. The buildings housing the upper school feel fresher – Ned's place looks like a commercial café, and there is a huge common room, whilst a second one was sacrificed to create a popular 'work room' with banks of computers. Ironically for a school that appears so stunning to the passer-by, it's the fabric of the school which could currently disappoint parents if not boys.

However, we donned hard hat and work boots to inspect the then almost complete Laboratory, costing over £21m, which is now open and should put the college's science offer ever more firmly on the map. Led by prestigious Grimshaw Architects – Cutty Sark, The Eden Project – It literally removes the divide between arts and sciences, including a 240 seat auditorium, as well as five IT suites and 18 glassy labs. The finishing touch, which may transform the feel of the college as much as anything, is the bright idea of removing the central car park, replacing it with landscaped recreational and thinking spaces.

The Dulwich College partnership schools overseas thrive, the latest in Yangon, Myanmar, but the master is clear that Dulwich is his absolute focus: he has delegated all but top level sign-off. Similarly, although he has championed outreach and partnership with a London academy group, a pie-chart of time devoted would see this account for only 10 per cent.

Sartorial traditions define the college – 'colours' blazers are boldly striped affairs awarded in recognition of achievement. 'Buy a big size,' advises the school captain – they will be de rigueur come OA reunions. You need a spotters' guide to identify old school ties, there are so many for every society and event. The master sees the Christmas fair attracting 3,000 local residents as a way to prove that the school isn't 'stuck up'. He is aware that the uniform gives off mixed messages, but wants the boys to wear it with pride and believes the school is and should be 'class, creed and colour-blind'.

School lunches seem due for a make-over, but boys won't starve. Students we spoke to in the lower school were amusing, boisterous; those higher up articulate, but not at all arrogant, and all with different interests. A regular visitor to the school said, 'The boys appear relaxed and happy, there's always plenty of banter and camaraderie in evidence'.

Pastoral care, well-being and discipline: A senior prefect told us he's a rarity, having been at the school all the way from year 1, but has relished meeting new boys – 'each intake year interests and friends shift' – and although the school is large, boys feel they know each other within their year. The transition points are handled thoughtfully, ensuring boys get to bond with each other, for instance on a Welsh adventure when joining the lower school.

Houses are named after great Englishmen, and wooden boards throughout the school see Drake, Spenser et al jostling for position – house competitions facilitate new friendships as well as much rivalry.

We were on the look-out for indifferent pastoral care, but found no evidence for it whatsoever, instead much praise. A parent – 'Boys know where they stand with the master, and whilst he's friendly and approachable, boys know he won't tolerate certain misdemeanours...hard line on bullying'. Another, 'He strikes the right note on being nurturing but also seeing that the boys get on with being independent'. 'A caring atmosphere which celebrates the individual,' said a parent of a child diagnosed with ASD. Gross misconducts such as possession of drugs or bullying would result in consideration for exclusion, whether fixed term or permanent, rather than an automatic exclusion.

Pupils and parents: The college is academically selective and socially inclusive, with a very culturally and ethnically diverse population, augmented by the boarders. Lots of multilingual children who might speak Chinese, Russian, Spanish or French at home. Boys mentioned pupil-led assemblies: recent topics include homosexuality and discrimination. The school captain said: 'There is no Dulwich way. You don't have to conform.'

A parent: 'It takes boys who are sporty, academic, musical, artistic and a mixture of all those things. If your child is gifted in one area, they will soar here. If they are a good all-rounder they will be encouraged to be a great all-rounder.' And it may come as a surprise to find that parents describe each other typically as 'a good bunch of mixed, non-stuffy parents', 'unsnobbish and not cliquey.'

Alumni include Chiwetel Ejiofor, Raymond Chandler, P G Wodehouse, Nigel Farage, Lionel Barber, Sir Ernest Shackleton.

Entrance: Not the ultra-elite intake of a few London schools, but still a top 15 per cent ability profile. At 11+, half of the 75 boys arrive from Dulwich College Junior School and half from a variety of local primary and prep schools including Hornsby House, Blackheath Prep, Rosemead, Dolphin School, Oakfield, Honeywell, Belleville, Corpus Christi, Dulwich Hamlet, St John's and St Clements. Parents are asked to send a letter from a registered professional regarding SEN needs to ensure appropriate assistance with the entrance exam. At 13 + the main feeders are Dulwich Prep London, Northcote Lodge and Fulham Prep. Non-refundable registration fee of £100 for Brits and £200 for overseas candidates.

A good number come from the immediate vicinity of Dulwich, but Foundation coaches brings pupils from as far away as Notting Hill, Canary Wharf, Wimbledon and Chislehurst.

Exit: Recent leavers to over 47 universities including Bristol, Durham, Edinburgh, Exeter, Imperial, KCL, LSE, UCL, Warwick and York; 26 securing their Oxford and Cambridge places and six going on to medical schools in 2018. Increasing focus on global destinations, particularly Ivy League.

Money matters: Nearly a third of boys have some financial assistance: two-thirds of these from scholarships (from a third of fees to 105 per cent), a third from bursaries (up to 100 per cent of fees). Dr Spence has stated his ambition for for college to provide financial support to up to 50 per cent of its pupils in year 7 and above. 'Superb value for money,' said one parent of three privately educated children. 'Quite simply, Dulwich College far outstrips the rest in terms of communication, professionalism and results'.

Perhaps most exciting of all in terms of evolution is the college returning to its early 20th century past in launching a New Dulwich Experiment, championed by the master, which will see up to 50 per cent of pupils coming from families who cannot afford to pay full fees, opening up admissions to some of the brightest pupils from all backgrounds. In some ways it is a protective measure against becoming a school for the global super-rich, and the master freely admits it is 'enlightened self-interest', but partly funded by OAs keen to give something back, it sits very well in this already socially enlightened place.

Remarks: A school with a long tradition, with all of the prestige that comes with it, but now with a thrilling new dynamism which is raising the academic ante in every way, creating glittering new learning spaces and delivering a stunning co-curricular vision. Far more inclusive than one might imagine, the new bursary scheme needs to be trumpeted far and wide to ensure the school is on the radar of the brightest from all backgrounds.

Dulwich College: The Junior School

Linked with Dulwich College, DUCKS Kindergarten and Infants School

Dulwich Common, London SE21 7LD

Ages 7–11 Pupils 221 C of E

Fees: £20,448 pa

020 8299 8432
www.dulwich.org.uk

Head: Since 2013, Dr Toby Griffiths (40s). Educated at Whitgift School and the University of Edinburgh; completed a masters in educational psychology and a doctorate in educational psychology at Oxford. Previously a six year stint as deputy headmaster at Lanesborough School in Guildford, where he was involved in the management and marketing of the school in a parent-facing role: a good precursor to being head. He has also taught at St Paul's Juniors, and eight years at The Dragon, where he was boarding housemaster and head of maths. Part of a teaching dynasty, his father taught at Whitgift for 38 years and his mother was a prep school head. He and his brother, also now a headmaster, were hockey blues together at Oxford. He considered teaching psychology, but from the moment he experienced the Dragon 'all bets were off' – he loves the junior school age group: 'their energy and enthusiasm, they seem so alive'.

Parents enthuse: 'He is approachable and responsive' and 'very much involved in every aspect of the college and knows the boys well'. Determined and no doubt extremely competitive: 'bring it on!' he said (with regards to a forthcoming school inspection).

The green spaces of Dulwich made moving to London easier. He lives nearby with his wife, Vicky, now working in the City. Their son is at the top of the junior school and daughter at nearby Sydenham High.

Entrance: Approximately 45 places available at age 7+, many taken by boys coming up from DUCKS, six to eight places in years 4 and 5. Register in the autumn preceding the desired year of entry. Assessments during January in maths, English, verbal and non-verbal reasoning. Not looking for perfection – understanding of differing educational experiences – but all round ability. Successful applicants invited for an interview and an activity morning; process now includes a taught element 'to see how boys react in a lesson situation and how well they learn something new'.

Dr Griffiths says the junior school has gone from being popular to very popular, with now over three applicants per place, and is increasingly seen as the 'start of the college'. Boys come from as far away as Greenwich, Orpington and Fulham, up to a 40 minute commute. The school lists an eclectic list of feeders at 7+ in addition to DUCKS: Herne Hill, Bertrum House, Broomwood Hall, The Villa Pre-Prep, River House Montessori and Babington House, though seemingly not many of the nearby state primaries.

Exit: Almost all (nearly 100 per cent) go on to the college. The head says that those who don't go on from the lower school are very rare, and only after extensive dialogue over several years regarding where they would thrive best, and then it is the parents' decision. We asked a parent if they felt their son was well-prepared for the next stage; they replied, 'absolutely. And if we didn't, we would feel comfortable raising any issues with the teachers and headmaster.'

Remarks: Once more sporty than academic, the balance has been redressed, and it is now much more of an all-round school. Dr Griffiths says, 'It had always been a through school, but at one time the boys from the junior school had taken their foot off the pedal whilst everyone else worked hard to get there [the college], so four to five years ago the bar was really raised to ensure primacy of the classroom'. It does mean that there is no need for exam pressure to dominate. Focus is on 'doing their best, not pass or fail'.

Big leap in scores of boys coming in recently. Teaching time has been increased by 40 minutes per day and all children now have two periods of French per week. No gripes about teaching reached our ears, quite the opposite: 'The boys seem fired up by what they learn. There has been a practical element to subjects which fires the imagination and creates interest.' Curriculum is taught by form tutors with specialist staff initially for French, art, DT, music and games, with additional specialists in later years.

Parents pretty united on homework, saying, 'We don't feel it is intensive at all. Obviously there is homework, but we feel that it is suited to our sons' capabilities. There is extension homework for those boys who are more academic and help for those who perhaps find it takes longer to grasp certain things.' No holiday homework – other than when preparing for the 11+ exam. 'Doesn't feel too pressured re exams or testing'.

Improved rewards system – commendation certificates, bronze, silver and gold, are presented in assembly. Reports for parents show effort and attainment, which is appreciated by parents who conclude, 'it will likely do much to encourage the children.' 'Very little pressure on the lead up to exams. In general, we haven't known when the boys are due to have any sort of assessment.

Surprisingly low levels of SEN. All children are screened for dyslexia on entry to year 3. Some may be referred for further testing and diagnosis. There are four full-time learning support teachers shared between the junior and senior schools. In the junior school, teachers work with individuals and small groups to provide extra support where needed, perhaps in terms of how their working memory affects spelling, organisation, numeracy, creative writing or comprehension. Less than two per cent receive EAL support, but many from multilingual families.

This is the time for experimentation. The headmaster tells us, 'We want boys to be and to try everything by the time they leave here – a rugby player, actor, musician, chess player, mathematician and writer'. Should not have to choose between a swimming gala and orchestra practice – the sporty head says he won't let fixtures take over.

'With 70 acres of fields there is no shortage of sport and it is all first class,' cried a delighted parent. All boys play rugby, football, hockey and cricket, everyone has the opportunity to play a competitive fixture, whether extra or intra school. Aim is for boys to represent the school in every sport – 'everyone gets to go on the coach and shake hands with the opposition', so far managed it for football. 'Our sons are not in the A or B teams for sports, but they always get to play matches and be involved in the sporting community'. Fitness should be a given with gymnastics, swimming, rackets and athletics in addition. Stars include a year 6 national breaststroke champion and several county representatives in cricket and chess. A highlight for many is the trip to the college's outdoor centre in the Brecon Beacons. Everyone performs in the year 3 and 6 plays. The recent Bugsy Malone performed in the Edward Alleyn Theatre looked enormous fun.

Music department seen as first rate. All the boys in the junior school learn a stringed instrument in year 3 and a wind instrument in year 4, and perform in two major productions. Some 40 per cent then have individual lessons. 'Our younger son has decided to have extra violin and guitar lessons and we are not a musical family,' said a surprised parent. There are opportunities to play in ensembles and orchestras and sing in the choir. Pupils benefit from the wider college co-curricular activities.

These boys are readers – the library has 8,000 books and a full-time enthusiastically chatty librarian who insists that books are not just for book week, that she never tells everyone to 'shhh!' and that 'life's too short to finish a book you're not enjoying'. Art projects line the walls, currently takes on Mark Rothko and work inspired by a trip to Tate Modern to study Henry Moore.

Just the swim squad and chamber group up and at it early. At lunchtime a couple of by invitation clubs such as madrigal and chapel choir, but also each year has choices such as karate, tennis, book club, chess, sewing and various music ensembles. After-school clubs have been extended (there are 95 in all) and now run until 5pm, with after-school care available until 6pm. Boys can do their prep in the homework club or try Russian, dance, cycling, magazine club or French aviation.

The location on the southerly edge of the college campus in a peaceful backwater just a stone's throw from the useful South Circular and station makes drop-offs and collections pleasant. The building itself is modern and handily adjacent to the lower school, with a pitched roof, wide corridors upstairs and quite spacious classrooms. Year 3s have their own playground.

We were impressed that year 6 boys were entrusted to lead us solo on our tour of the school, with only a little assistance from Dr Griffiths on time-keeping – not every school entrusts its pupils, of whatever age, to speak as they see fit with a visitor wielding a pen. It speaks volumes. Parents, too, speak of this level of trust between boys and teachers. One said of their son, 'He truly looks forward to being at school. He has had very supportive form teachers – strict, but fair, so there is an obvious level of trust.'

Boys seem to feel listened to and have seen their ideas put forward to the school council come to fruition, such as more play equipment for the playground.

A parent told us, 'This school excels in its pastoral care. We couldn't ask for better.' Others agree, 'They know the students very well and truly try to understand not just individual students, but the different dynamics amongst various groups of boys.' And in the case of a problem with peers raised with the school, 'The boys were supported, but given opportunities to address the issues themselves.' Teachers are seen as responsive – known to answer emails out of school hours.

Competitiveness abounds – house allegiances start here – but there is room for inclusiveness: all year 6 boys are prefects, rather than an elite group. And every year 6 child has a buddy in the lower years.

Parents say, 'The boys feel like they belong in the school and with each other.' And, 'The atmosphere is one of feeling included. It is not an exclusive school.' Parents themselves sound unpretentious and appealing, describing each other as 'friendly, relaxed, supportive of their children', 'from all walks of life', 'welcoming, fun, and interesting.'

As for the college as a whole, appearances can be deceptive and there is a rich social mix. Many say there is no type for whom the school particularly caters, 'it's tough to see what kind of child the school wouldn't be suitable for.' Several say: 'He can't wait to leave the house in the morning.'

A few academic scholarships at 10 per cent of the tuition fees, plus means-tested bursaries may be available for the very able whose families fulfil the financial criteria.

Dulwich Hamlet Junior School

D

Dulwich Village, London SE21 7AL

Ages 7–11 **Pupils** 390

020 7525 9188
www.dulwichhamlet.southwark.sch.uk

Head of school: Since 2016, Claire Purcell BEd (40s). Having gained her degree at what is now Southampton University and her first teaching post in a Hampshire school, Mrs Purcell headed to the Hamlet, rising from class teacher and senior manager with a music specialism, via deputy to the new post of head of school over the course of 20 years. Extremely modest, she is, however responsible, for the incredibly rich musical life of the school. One parent told us of her son punching the air when she was made head. We would have liked to spend more time with her but our visit coincided with year 6 Sats. She is devoted to music and family and we hear plays the recorder and sings wonderfully too. She has two young children.

Executive head since 2007 is Sonia Case BA PGCE (50s) who has no plans to retire. Since the school became part of a multi-academy trust, she has been executive headteacher of Dulwich Hamlet Junior School and The Belham Primary School, an exciting reinvention of a Victorian school in Peckham which she is building from the ground up. She has an office at the Hamlet, but currently splits her time, spending three days at the Belham, whilst this school continues to spin along like a well-trained top.

Mrs Case started life as an actress, including a role in the original series of Poldark, before moving into advertising and has worked in education for over 24 years. Prior to leading Dulwich Hamlet she taught at three state primaries in Bromley. Parents describe her to us as 'a driving force', 'dynamic', 'passionate' and she 'encourages readiness to learn by expectations of excellent behaviour'. We found her to be vibrant and full of fizz with a real passion for where the right style of teaching can make a difference to individual children. She has two daughters and two grandchildren.

Entrance: The main feeder school for Dulwich Hamlet is Dulwich Village Infants' School. No automatic entry from one school to the other. Unlike the infant school there is no faith stipulation governing admissions. The school is oversubscribed but not to the tune we had imagined from its local reputation, and there is always some movement on the waiting list after first offers are made. Stories of houses being rented nearby to get in persist, but a hard line is taken by the local authority and are perhaps more focused on the infants' school than here.

Other admissions come from local prep schools such as Ducks, JAPS and Herne Hill and some other local state schools.

Exit: The majority of children fall into the catchment for the nearby Charter School and head straight there, whilst a percentage of both boys and girls move into the independent sector, to Dulwich College, Alleyn's, St Dunstan's or Sydenham Girls' School. Some children attend schools further afield such as the Grey Coat Hospital school or grammars in Bromley and Kent. According to parents, those preparing for selective entry elsewhere sometimes use tutors, more for exam technique than academics.

Remarks: The school consistently ranks near the top of league tables with regards to academic attainment. Ofsted, declaring it outstanding in every category, has long since moved on to other more variable territories. It does well by children across the board, but also by high attainers.

Teachers have two surprising qualities; they are young and quite often male. Mrs Case delights that they are enthusiastic and fresh from training, full of the kind of multimedia experience and latest thinking that invigorates what she describes as a 'glittering curriculum'. We concur that it is pretty sparkly and ambitious. A parent told us about a year 6 English lesson which involved tightrope walking. We visited shortly after Shakespeare week, where each year took a different aspect of A Midsummer Night's Dream and created a film to be viewed by the whole school and parents. Students study for LAMDA exams. Stem week answered questions such as 'can you eat a candle?' and 'how do you get the fizz in pop?' Prospective parents should brace themselves for a particularly high number of dressing up days – Roman, Celt, Greek, Indian and Shakespeare. Drama often comes into lessons with role-playing techniques used. There are currently striking papier-mâché sculptures of Ted Hughes' Iron Man around the school and we saw year 5 pupils creating blueprints of wild flowers inspired by Victorian women artists employed by Kew Gardens. Displays within classrooms are 'learning walls' whilst those in the public spaces, on lovely felt boards, exhibit the children's work.

A couple of parents said to us that the teachers have 'all been so different but have continually excited and stimulated my children'; they are 'approachable and accessible' and 'most are imaginative in their teaching and enthuse the children'. Setting of children is minimal as Mrs Case points out that removing the brightest would disadvantage those who would benefit from a higher level of discussion, but there is setting for maths from year 3 to enable more teaching resources where needed.

Parents describe sport as having improved dramatically since the school has had access to neighbouring sports fields. There are also courts adjacent to the school in use most days for either netball or tennis with specialist coaches. At least half of the students in each year group have represented the school, participating in football or netball tournaments, and many attend sport clubs before or after school. The cricket team – girls as well as boys – won the British Land cricket trophy, playing the final at Lord's. Years 4 and 5 are strong swimmers, both having won their Southwark schools' swimming galas this year. A parent said of sport: 'the school balances a competitive spirit with inclusivity'. There is a minibus for away matches provided by the PTA. The cross-country team represents the school nationally.

The school excels in its musical provision. All children receive music lessons conducted by specialists, and then nearly three-quarters learn musical instruments up to grade 5 taught by peripatetic music tutors. Whatever the instrument, there's an ensemble for it – woodwind, brass, strings or guitars. Steel pans are very popular. The fusion ensemble developed an original composition, Londinium, which was presented with an award for innovation and performed at the Royal Albert Hall as part of the primary proms. There are two choirs, who have sung at The Scoop on the Southbank, the Young Voices Concert at the 02 and the Bromley Music Festival. Recorder playing is taken to a new level here, with an annual recorder festival featuring a workshop, performance from professionals and inter-school concert. We were lucky enough to hear the early music ensemble play at Dulwich Festival; the standard seemed so high they could provide the incidental music to Wolf Hall.

Parents are asked to make a voluntary contribution of less than £100 per annum to help fund the extracurricular, such as trips and specialist workshops.The school offers a wide variety of fun after-school clubs including cookery, knitting, magic, Lego robotics, yoga and clay, with some charges.

The school presents as a picture postcard Victorian school, with patterned brickwork and scalloped roof tiles, at the heart of picturesque Dulwich village, encircled by sunflowers in the summer, thrilling many a parent and passer-by with nostalgia. The school has had many incarnations, but the main building dates from 1897. On the sunny spring morning of our visit, the nearby village hall promoted a barn dance, whilst the petite row of shops sell ice-creams, children's shoes, beautifully curated art and school stationery: it's an idyllic slice of middle class 'village London'.

Through the gates it doesn't disappoint, in fact, the rear outlook looking across the Griffin Fields, unseen from the road, which the school leases for sports, is a hidden delight. Between the admin building and 'village building' housing the traditional high-windowed Victorian school hall is an Astroturf playground. There is free play, but also structured play at lunch time such as teacher-led football. We liked the Astroturf shady veranda of an attractive wooden classroom built with 'bulge' funding, for those wanting to escape the hurly-burly.

Space at the front of the school is newly transformed into a garden with raised vegetable patches, bug houses and composting and what will be a wild flower space for curriculum work. Lunches with an international menu can be eaten either in the refurbished dining hall or at circular picnic tables under a shady canopy in the playground. Above the dining hall are DT and food technology facilities which outclass those of several of the nearby prep schools. A couple of the celebrities familiar to everyone who lives locally were parents here and opened the transformed building. Year 5 participates annually in a project run by the Architectural Association. There is a large library and break-out space for year 5. And the whole school hall now boasts a sophisticated sound system paid for by the PTA. Given the school's focus on design and media, the ICT room uses Macs.

Pupils describe the school to us as 'fun and happy'. Despite the affluent catchment area, there is apparently more of a social mix than one might imagine. Certainly a wide range of languages is spoken within the school, from Urdu to Japanese and Hindi. A word which crops up several times from parents is 'inclusive'. The school has a full-time inclusion manager, and there is small room for one-to-one teaching. The school is also a Dyslexia Friendly School, though one parent mentioned being disappointed the school had not highlighted her child's dyslexia to her. Parents say that bullying is not unheard of but they trust the school to resolve such matters swiftly. They say: 'the general atmosphere seems to be caring' and 'they will go out of their way over the smallest issues to ensure every child is happy and included'.

The children of parents hopping onto the local trains and buses to commute are well provided for with a large dedicated classroom and qualified staff offering breakfast and after-school care. A parent described her peers to us as 'high powered with equally high expectations', which we are told is a fair portrait. Most seem grateful and appreciative, as one mother shared: 'I frequently find myself telling my kids I wish I could have gone to a school like theirs', whilst another concluded: 'quite simply a joyful experience'.

Dulwich Prep London

42 Alleyn Park, London SE21 8AT

Ages 3–13 **Pupils** 850 **Boarders** 20 flexi (from year 4) **C of E**

Fees: £13,074 – £19,314 pa

020 8670 3217
www.dulwichpreplondon.org

Headmaster: Since 2009, Michael Roulston MBE MEd (50s). Educated in Ulster, he is warm and friendly, zipping about and offering to 'play mother' with the Darjeeling on our visit. First impressions aside, one senses his combination of vision, drive and no nonsense was forged during his first headship in the 1980s at The Model School – an informally, religiously integrated school in Northern Ireland. His contribution to conflict resolution in the field of education was recognised by the BP Gulbenkian Citizenship Award in 1994. Married with three children.

After a stint in Japan as headmaster of The British School in Tokyo, earning him an MBE for services to education, he became head of Cranleigh Prep in Surrey. A man who clearly thrives on challenge and change, with his eye on the prizes – his and the boys. We see him as a definite 'on message' moderniser, sprucing up the old traditions, delivering a slickly presented school with a few fashionable nods – boules, allotments – without straying from his brief of happy parents and successful pupils at CE. Prior to our visit we had heard him described by parents as being 'rather like a successful CEO'. We found him to be business-like certainly, but not stiffly corporate.

He says of the school, 'It's fun, full of energy from the earliest years all the way though...every day you cannot but be inspired by what the boys do. They are valued, recognised and well-loved.'

Retiring in July 2019. His successor will be Louise Davidson. Degree in economics and social economic history; worked in banking, PR and marketing before postgrad teacher training at Cambridge. Her first post was teaching maths and science at King's Junior, Canterbury. Studied and taught special needs at Edinburgh University, became SENCo at a London school, leading to headships at state primary schools across the country and then Leader in Education roles.

'I am confident that I can hold my own in a 10k, play and coach football (including in goal), swim and teach swimming.' Keen on family travel and adventures. Her husband runs an international genocide prevention charity; three children, the youngest will join Dulwich Prep London.

Head of the pre-prep since 2011, an early years specialist, Mrs Ruth Burtonshaw BSc Phd PGCE Dip, dyslexia and learning.

Entrance: Admission is selective. Multiple points of entry but majority start in the nursery at 3+ (girls and boys), at 4+ (boys only) or at 7+ (boys only). Limited number of means-tested bursaries to new applicants in years 3 and 4, determined by academic assessment.

Exit: Don't think that entrance to DPL is a do-not-pass-go ticket straight to Dulwich College, but a large proportion of pupils do gain entrance. Recent leavers to 28 different schools, foremost Westminster, Alleyn's and Tonbridge. Conversation regarding choice of senior school starts as early as year 4 and headmaster claims that every boy achieves his first (guided) choice of destination. Good tally of academic, sport, art and all-rounder scholarships or exhibitions – lots to Dulwich College. Only two or three boys a year choose to leave at 11+.

Remarks: Founded as Dulwich College Prep School (DCPS) in 1885 but is completely independent from Dulwich College and is an educational trust with its own governing body; and now, to clear up the confusion, has a new name Dulwich Prep London (DPL). Situated in west Dulwich, a few minutes from the train station, the buildings, mostly fairly modern, crowd around the playground. Four distinct sections divide up the 800+ pupils, each with its own library and classrooms. It really works – 'the boys are quite protected from feeling lost in a huge place, and they're fully prepared for moving on,' said a parent.

The main curriculum is fairly traditional. French from year 1 and everyone tries their hand at Latin. Spanish offered as alternative to French. We found the lack of fashionable forward-thinking options such as Chinese or Russian surprising when even the local state primaries are giving them a go. Head says Mandarin was offered as a club, but there was little interest.

Setting in maths from year 4, extended to all examined subjects by year 7. This really works, with parents confirming there is sufficient flexibility for boys to move within the year to find the right level and to be encouraged by their ability in different subjects. Young, male teachers were particularly noticeable in the classes we visited, in amongst the boys or sitting on desks. Relations looked easy in lessons ranging from European history, via maths, to music technology. Energy fairly resounds and parents of pupils at the lower school, particularly, describe it as 'buzzing'. Homework is, as ever, controversial. One mother commented that whilst the boys love the varied topic work, parents find it 'never-ending' at weekends.

Almost 20 per cent are identified with a learning difference, mainly mild to moderate dyslexia. The head says that the school (highly-trained specialist staff) will do its best by all, but any with significant difficulties may be guided to a more specialist school such as Fairley House. We saw great learning integration in the older years with dyslexic boys using laptops alongside their peers; parents confirm that boys don't feel singled out in any way if they need extra help. Nonetheless, some comment with feeling on just how tough it can be and wish for a little more two-way communication with teachers.

Well-resourced sport, with fixtures both after school and on Saturdays. Seven full-time PE teachers, specialist coaching from year 4, more than 70 teams and achievements at national level, particularly in rugby and swimming. Every boy has an opportunity to play. Parents say coaching is less good at the lower levels, and whilst clubs offer exciting opportunities from rock-climbing to kayaking, 'alternatives to the obvious sporting options are very limited in the younger years.'

Drama features both an annual year 6 and upper school play. Year 7 classes have drama and each year 8 class is off timetable for two weeks to produce an original production. Art continues to year 8 with clearly inspiring teaching, new facilities and technologies. We were wowed by the boys' 3D acrylic sculpture, after Jackson Pollock, and the excitement in the room as they made sophisticated digital animations. Music is rich, appealing and widely pursued, with over 20 ensembles and choirs and concerts of every type at venues in and out of the school. Ninety per cent of the boys from year 2 upwards study an instrument, many reaching grade 8.

Clubs (only a few additional charges) and activities run at lunch-time for boys from years 1-4, but also 4-5 pm from year 5. Current options include Lego, Warhammer, movie-making, beekeeping, street dance, juggling, Greek and golf. Wide array of trips – no stone unturned on the London museum circuit; further afield during school holidays (often built into the fees) eg Pompeii and Normandy. All this plus a thought-provoking lecture series – recently featuring a holocaust survivor, notable writers, broadcasters and adventurers.

Parents from the nursery year to higher up the school all comment on the benefit of a single sex school where teachers are free to focus on knights, dinosaurs, bloody battles etc. If there's one thing this school seems to do brilliantly it's the ability to really 'get' boys and how they learn and put this into practice. There is wiggle time (dancing around between lessons), marble parties or even a pool table as a whole class reward – 'the motivation and excitement are huge.'

The school motto is 'one for all and all for one' and the houses are named after North American Indian tribes from Chippeway to Objiwas. The winning tribe raises their flag weekly up the pole in the playground and if this is all sounds incredibly macho, we hear the boys sometimes choose to sing ABBA as their victory song. Meanwhile others, who choose the calmer activities from book club to weaving and needlework, do so without fear of ridicule. Some parents transfer from a co-ed environment for exactly this reason.

While the head's emphasis on character and kindness rings true – right on cue we witnessed children relating a contemporary version of the Good Samaritan – a couple of parents commented that it can take a while to find your niche. 'If you're not good at sport, you're not popular in the playground.' This is a school which aims to develop 'resilience'. When asked which kinds of boys would be happiest here, parents suggested: 'a self-starter, bright and athletic' and 'you've got to be robust'.

No surprises that the majority of parents are highly affluent, most living within an expanding 10 mile radius of the school. However, we hear that there is a healthy mix from the scarily ambitious to the more laid back, so there is a good chance of finding like-minded souls.

School has one boarding house called (not so aptly in our opinion) Brightlands; this can accommodate 25 weekly or flexi-boarders from year 4. Rather a sombre looking house with a garden, next to the pre-prep. Recently redecorated, with a young and welcoming housemaster plus family, but we spied scary paint colours downstairs and 1950s style curtains in the dining hall and we wondered how this rated, as a home from home, compared to the boys' weekend surroundings. Definite fun, though, is one week a year when years 5, 6 and 7 stay from Sunday to Thursday; you can win the Tomahawk Award for life skills such as button-sewing and bed-making as well as trying a spell away from home.

The pre-prep early years department is a stunningly designed new-build – all wide open flowing spaces, blending indoor/outdoor. Classrooms give onto a huge covered sandpit for wet days and a splendidly green view of playing fields, woodland and the grounds of Dulwich Picture Gallery. Nothing locally compares to the rural feel of this setting, a great comfort for any parent who didn't expect to raise their children in one of the world's biggest cities.

Girls are the minority in the nursery but are carefully selected and more than hold their own. Parents of girls have little need for concern – except getting them in, applications are oversubscribed. Rainbow Club, staffed by regular teaching staff, offers care and activities pre and post school, from 8am to 4.45pm. The head assists in girls' applications to local private and state schools. Almost all the boys move up to the prep.

Dunraven School

94–98 Leigham Court Road, London SW16 2QB

Ages 4–18 **Pupils** 1,506 (229 in primary) **Sixth form** 215

020 8696 5600
www.dunraven.org.uk

Principal: Since 2003, David Boyle (40s), BA NPQH FRSA. Married with a young daughter. A north Londoner by birth, more than a decade at Dunraven has made him a thoroughly naturalised Streatham man, and proud of the success he's done so much to create. 'My main interest is work,' he explains (although he concedes a liking for literature and cinema), 'and alongside work, my family.' Under his energetic leadership, the school has achieved creditable results, and acquired a bewildering array of designations: National Teaching School status, High Performing Status, Beacon Status, Advanced Healthy School Status, Investors In People status – and on it goes. Along the way, It remains the most popular school in Lambeth with eight applicants for every place. Parents describe him as an excellent manager and highly effective communicator. The secret of his success? 'I love what I do,' he shrugs. 'And I like working with people who enjoy what they do.'

Head of secondary: Jessica West; head of primary is Michaela Christian, previously at Fairlawn Primary School in Lewisham.

Academic matters: Results are a testament, says head, to the commitment of 'a fantastically creative and hardworking staff team.' At GCSE in 2018, 24 per cent of grades were 9-7 and 70 per cent of pupils got 9-4 in both maths and English.

Expectations are high. 'We start from the premise that the children will do well, and might do even better than we think.' Younger pupils are kept aware of how well the older ones are doing, and the benchmark is set higher each year. 'We're aiming for "astounding",' says head, with a modest smile, and indeed school was rated outstanding by Ofsted in 2014.

The curriculum in key stages 3 and 4 is broad and balanced, thanks to what's called the Dunraven Baccalaureate: English, maths, science, humanities, languages, and all the arts, because 'the kind of learning opportunity you get through the arts is invaluable.' Other subjects are also offered, notably DT, ICT and PE/dance. Visiting teacher from Westminster comes in every week to teach Latin, which is proving a popular option at GCSE and A level, but we thought the language provision could have been broader. French and Spanish are offered, with the G&T students given the chance to do both; but there used to be Mandarin. The impressive sixth form, housed in its own new purpose-built centre, is the most successful in Lambeth, and offers a wide range of academic and vocational courses – A Levels, BTecs, GCE applied and the AQA baccalaureate. In 2018, 14 per cent A*/A grades at A level (45 per cent A*-B), somewhat down on the previous year. All Dunraven year 11s can apply to study there and most do, but places are sought after and are not guaranteed. Strong enrichment programme of activities, both on and off site, includes theatre and opera visits, excursions, exchanges, competitions, and residential trips abroad.

SEN provision is excellent and enlightened. The school has its own on-site speech therapist and parents were full of praise for the SENCo, who was described as 'fantastic', 'works like a Trojan', 'highly empathetic'. 'We felt that our child was properly supported throughout her time here,' was a typical remark. Hosts a specialist centre for children with speech, language and communication needs.

There were parental murmurs about their child being unable to study all his/her preferred subjects at GCSE due to timetabling issues (a problem not unique to Dunraven), but the majority of feedback was overwhelmingly positive. 'My child left with a love of all his subjects, based on great teaching,' was one comment. 'There is rigour in all that Dunraven does,' was another, and everyone we spoke to praised the 'constantly rising level of academic achievement.' The children agree: 'The teachers are good and you learn stuff,' said a cheerful year 7 boy, who'd been temporarily sent out for being cheeky. 'You make friends, you learn, every class is suited to you,' added a strikingly poised year 10 girl.

Games, options, the arts: You can do almost any sports here: in addition to football, rugby, cricket and basketball, there are opportunities for badminton, fencing, swimming, diving, the martial arts, boxercise, trampolining and ice-skating (using facilities at Crystal Palace). Engagement with games remains good throughout KS4. Drama, dance, art and photography are all popular, and the Soul Choir enlivens many a local church concert. Music is also strong, and the excellent Play It Live initiative, part-funded by the local authority, enables the children to work regularly with professional musicians.

Background and atmosphere: The school is approaching its 100th anniversary. Originally founded with a bequest from the Earl of Dunraven, it expanded onto its present site in 1960, moved into the Philippa Fawcett College in the 1970s, became grant-maintained in 1993 ('A very important decision for the school'), and became an academy in 2011. £25 million mixture of rebuild and refurb (under the last government's Building Schools for the Future initiative) now complete, including new sixth form centre. Some very inventive touches, including the use of recycled shipping containers for new buildings, which look incredibly smart and cost half of what was originally planned. Primary school opened with reception class in 2013 and will expand with a new class each year. School initially in temporary accommodation but moved into new buildings in summer 2014. The aim is provide a seamless progression from 4-18.

Smart blue and grey uniforms, own clothes for sixth form (with a requirement to be 'respectable'). Students work purposefully, and – during our visit, at least – an air of orderly quiet prevails. The pupils we met were polite and helpful. Even the malefactors hanging around outside the classroom who'd refused to go in, for reasons they were unable to articulate, knew what was expected of them. After chatting to us about how much they liked their school really – 'It's fun here...there are nice trips... a good after-school club, something to do every day' – they filed in equably to begin geography.

Pastoral care, well-being and discipline: Considering the size and diversity of this school community, we were impressed by how calm and purposeful the students were. The emphasis everywhere is on courtesy and consideration, and the pupils confirm this: 'The people are nice. The teachers are good and you learn stuff.' Parents praise the staff as 'incredibly supportive', and any bullying is dealt with swiftly and effectively with 'restorative justice' sessions and behaviour contracts. Very low turnover of staff tells its own successful story.

Pupils and parents: An inclusive, socially and ethnically mixed intake that reflects the diversity of the area.

Entrance: At primary level priority to looked after children, then siblings, then by distance (straight line home to school). NB applicants must complete Dunraven's online supplementary information form as well as applying through the LA. They will have an automatic right of entry to Dunraven Senior when they reach year 7. The head positively radiates excitement: 'This provision will eliminate the trauma of secondary transfer. Everyone will benefit. We'll be able to offer expertise and opportunities to enrich the primary experience, and their different pedagogical approach will increasingly influence us.' Heady times indeed.

D

Entrance tests put secondary applicants into one of five ability bands; the school, which is heavily oversubscribed, then takes 20 per cent from each band, allocating places in line with its (non-academically selective) admissions policy.

Exit: At 16, the majority (65 per cent) progress to Dunraven sixth form; a few move to local sixth form colleges, training etc. At 18, nearly all leavers go on to university, with an increasing number of top university successes every year, including Oxbridge (one in 2018, plus one medic), Bristol, Durham, Leeds, Manchester and Camberwell College of Arts. The rest take a gap year, or have a lead into work of some kind. Head says, 'The aim is to get to the end of Y13 with a real choice and a sense of control about your step.'

Money matters: EFA-funded academy since August 2011, and in receipt of many grants and awards in recognition of its academic success and work for the community.

Remarks: A dynamic, exciting, successful school community. Proof that you can have a comprehensive school that works for everybody.

Dwight School London

6 Friern Barnet Lane, London N11 3LX

Ages 2–18 Pupils 320 Sixth form 52

Fees: £4,590 – £21,990 pa

020 8920 0600
www.dwightlondon.org

Head of School: Since January 2016, Alison Cobbin BA Dip Ed MBA (50s). Brought up in Australia and qualified as an English and history teacher at Macquarie University in Sydney. Moved to London in 1995 with her husband and then three young daughters; after a career break, joined Dwight (then Woodside Park School) as, variously, English, games and theory of knowledge teacher, IB coordinator and upper school principal. Moved to a SE London independent school as pastoral deputy head before returning to Dwight as head of school: 'I came back because I had made a shortlist of all the things I wanted from a school, and when this job came up it ticked all the boxes.'

The boxes it ticked were: co-ed, not too big, International, non-selective, and most importantly did the IB. Alison says once you've been to a school which upholds the values of the IB, it's very hard to go back: 'The IB is built on such a different philosophy – its broad base is so different. It's more collaborative than the English education system and does more than just work towards getting into the best university.' To which Andy Atkinson (upper school principal) adds: 'The IB is not subject to government changes and grade inflation – you know that if a person achieved 40 out of a maximum 45 several years ago, that would still hold true many years later with the exception of the odd curriculum change.' We were sold.

The new leadership team of the upper school – Alison Cobbin and Andy Atkinson – have been called an exceptional team and inspiring to staff and pupils. One parent told us: 'Andy is a very strong character and has a real vision of what he wants to achieve. The profile of the school has definitely improved since they both came on board, as have the results.' Andy's international credentials are impressive. He was previously director of the two International Schools of London, and has taught extensively abroad. However, he says: 'There are not many IB schools like Dwight. It's a unique school in north London. Some of the kids are a little bit different, a little bit eccentric, and some are happy for the first time about coming to school.'

However, this is very much a leadership team of three. Lower school principal Matt Parkin BEd DipEd NPQH has been at the school since 2007. He has taught in the UK, USA and Indonesia and one could say has had a pretty colourful background in education. Following a seven year stint working in the state education sector in Devon, Matt was part of a start-up school in Houston, Texas. In the five years he was there he increased the school from 50-strong to 400. He was then offered a post to teach at 'one of the best schools in Asia' in Jakarta, Indonesia, which had an outdoor swimming pool, a theatre and a multimedia centre. As much of a draw as that was, Matt yearned for a school with an international outlook back home. 'There are not many of them around, and a job came up at Dwight, so I took it.'

Academic matters: Runs the IB programme at all levels. Year groups in lower school divided into two parallel classes with a maximum of 20 in each. Lots of child-inspired batiks, pottery and art help create a vibrant atmosphere. IB learner profile is displayed everywhere. IB primary years programme (IBPYP) well linked with the national curriculum, which keeps inspectorates happy and ensures children are well grounded with an international mindset. All lessons in each half of term based around one aspect of the curriculum. Specialist teachers for music, art, PE, French and EAL. Homework important and can be done at after-school club.

In 2018, average IB point score 30 (out of possible 45). One or two students each year opt to take a Dwight High School Diploma, earning IB course certificates rather than the full IB diploma. Average class size in upper school not normally more than 15, although we spoke to one pupil who had just three others in her geography class. 'It's great! Almost like one-to-one tuition.' Good results for IB middle years programme exams with several top students getting more than 60 points out of 70. One parent said the only downside of the IB from her point of view is that 'if you are weak in a certain area – such as maths or languages – you can't drop it, as you need to take one subject from each of the six subject groups.' However, there are choices within these.

Dwight also offers Pamoja Online courses which enable Dwight IB diploma students to take a wider range of courses while experiencing the kind of online learning that is increasingly common at university level. School says: 'These courses are fantastic. They are based in Oxford and provide a quality programme which is strictly monitored. There are over 50 different nationalities at Dwight and it's not always feasible to accommodate everyone, so these courses are a great online alternative. It is the equivalent of an IB course online.'

French is introduced in lower school, Spanish and Mandarin added as an option in upper school. Other languages considered on request at additional cost. (One Portuguese teacher does a lesson via Skype.) RE is not an IB subject, but world religion is. Photos throughout the school buildings depict many school trips, dramatic and music performances and community service activities, suggesting that a lot of learning is regularly extended out and about. After-school homework club for those who want extra help.

Through the QUEST programme (at extra cost) the school can accommodate a range of learning needs, with the support of specialist teachers. EAL (also at extra cost) regarded as essential for children who lack English proficiency – two to five lessons a week, one to one or in a small group depending on needs. A mother tongue programme is available for Japanese pupils – the second largest group in the school (about 10 per cent) and some other languages (no extra charge is made if four or more students are in the same group and level). IB diploma students must be completely fluent in English.

A dedicated SENCo for the roughly 14 per cent on the SEN register: 'Because of the nature of this school, we're not equipped to deal with many pupils with very diverse needs.' But parents do say that what they like about Dwight is that it suits a great variety of children. 'I wanted a school where all of my children would be well served'.

Teachers are international and IB-experienced. Over 60 per cent come from overseas: 'London is a bit of a destination for teachers. For those not from abroad, they look at their IB training as a fantastic experience.' Parents speak enthusiastically about the teaching staff and their willingness to help and respond quickly to any parent concerns. One pupil told us: 'The teachers here are great – you can talk them about anything, even after school.'

Games, options, the arts: Games obligatory once a week for each year group – the school has its own sports field 10 minutes away by minibus and uses other local sports facilities. They compete not only with local and national schools but also with international overseas schools. One pupil told us. 'I love the sports here, there are lots of options and the school is even planning a trip to Venice to play beach volleyball.' Parents say they like the variety of sports on offer – not only the traditional ones but a wider range: rugby, football, basketball, track and field, sailing, ice skating.

Lots of after-school clubs and extracurricular offerings. Strong music – about 15 per cent learn an individual instrument; there are rock, jazz and chamber groups. The choir has sung at London's 02 in Young Voices, and for some lucky pupils, the 'highlight of their life' was performing with the Dwight New York choir at Carnegie Hall. Other clubs include cartoon club, sewing club, origami and magical maths.

For the last period on Tuesdays, the pupils do mixed age group activities including community service projects. This helps to develop relationships across the ages, reinforcing the 'Dwight family' concept.

Lots of outings to concerts, theatres and galleries as well as trips home and abroad. Year 6 students spend a week at the Dwight School in New York, some year groups in upper school have their activity week in Normandy (practising the French that they have been learning since they were 3) and some of them go on exchange to the Dwight School in New York. Older students are developing a community service project in Nepal. They raise funds and students and staff travel there to do volunteer work. The arts dept has been to Vietnam to study music and dance; they have also visited Hollywood, India and Cuba.

Model United Nations conference is also popular. This year saw the school representing Saudi Arabia.

Background and atmosphere: The school was originally founded in 1972 by Dr Stephen Spahn, chancellor of the Dwight School in New York. Previously known as Woodside Park and North London International School, the school changed its name in a rebranding exercise to Dwight London School, to heighten awareness of its association with the Dwight family of schools that now has campuses in Seoul and Shanghai, with Dubai opening imminently. 'Dwight family' is a term used by staff and families alike. Dwight London has an advisory board of local parents and others who lend expertise and guidance and serve as a supportive sounding board for the principal in the strategic planning of the school.

The school is on four sites in two locations. Lower school is in Woodside Avenue. Kindergarten and reception based in their own little house, The Lodge, with its own garden for play. Part-time options are available and there's a wraparound care programme from 7.30am to 5pm for the lower school.

Years 2 to 5 in the main building here have good sized, light classrooms with washing lines displaying student work. Each child has own drawer for storage. Computers everywhere. Media resource centres, a small library collection; great gym, which doubles up as the dining hall. Healthy food served from the kitchens next to it (where meals for the kindergarten are also prepared). Photos of all the year 6 students displayed in the passage with their personal blogs. Good music room and lovely art room. Whilst we were there we saw some wonderful examples of art which had been selected for the Dwight Travelling Art Show – a yearly event where the top 20 chosen art pieces make their way around the different Dwight campuses of the world. Well-equipped library with Harry Potter translated into an assortment of languages.

A recent popular addition to the school is the Dwight radio station which is broadcast online: 'This is another way we feel pupils can demonstrate their learning, without it just being test test test.'

Year 6 has a separate eco-building with easy access to the specialist classrooms and playground; school has green flag eco-schools status. If we were being finickity, we would say that the interior could do with a bit of sprucing up – a new lick of paint. The red, white and blue colours of their motif (which is painted virtually everywhere), becomes a little bit wearing on the eye after a while.

Playground not huge but much use made of local park for cross-country runs and scientific experiments plus compulsory swimming once a week at a local pool. They also regularly use the school's own playing fields a short bus ride away.

The upper school is in the former Friern Barnet Boys' Grammar School and in nearby Jubilee Hall. The main building has recently been refurbished and is clean, bright and welcoming, making very good use of light throughout. The administrative offices and faculty room share the same corridors as the classrooms, which must strengthen the sense of community. Every wall is full of original and creative student art and photographs, and there are posters with quotes from Gandhi, Martin Luther King and Nelson Mandela, who we learned are the role models for the three upper school student houses.

The Jubilee Hall holds more classrooms, two science labs, the upper school library and a pleasant canteen open throughout. This looks out onto an outside playground where students engage in a bit of exercise during break or lunch, and a small world garden beyond with picnic tables and benches. The school admits that conditions are a little crowded, and they are on the lookout for new property in the area.

In recent years the Dwight community has collaborated to help families have a 'soft landing' when they arrive in London. A handy Welcome to London guide written and updated annually by the parents is found on the website with tips for families living in north London. Lots of welcome and goodbye rituals for students coming and going. There are also a variety of ways that rising year 6 students are supported as they move to the upper school. It's all part of the school's intention to give everyone a Dwight Hug. One parent told us: 'We were given a really warm welcome when we arrived and were immediately put in touch with the Parents' Association. The parent network at Dwight is fantastic.'

The individualised approach we heard so much about from parents was evident during our visit. We were shown around the school by an extremely theatrical and colourful student (who we definitely thought should be on TV) – and many others we spoke to were equally as quirky, interesting and slightly eccentric, with amazing back stories. Another seemed to be a science whizz who showed us her extraordinary end of M5 personal project (a culmination of their IB middle years) – and had created a working Enigma machine with morse coding etc.

E

Pastoral care, well-being and discipline: The IB philosophy and emphasis on tolerance and global understanding is reinforced everywhere in the school with big signs bearing the IB ethos (inquirers, reflective risk-takers, etc). Kids are divided into houses – Pioneers, Artists and Visionaries – and are awarded 'sparkies' (which refer to the IB philosophy of igniting the sparks of genius).

Kids seem happy, and although there is a uniform there are various options, so they can choose how casual or dressy they want to look. Parents love the small size of the school. 'It's a massive advantage. Everyone is known, everyone can shine and blossom.' One parent we spoke to who has home schooled her child for a while said that Dwight is the first school her son has been happy at: 'This school has literally been our saviour. I love the IB ethos in tailoring the work to your child's needs – it's so much more of a progressive approach.' The school recently introduced a vertical tutoring system, which encourages pupils to get to know other pupils from different year groups

Parents assure us that they were not aware of any incidents of bullying. With students from so many different cultures, school says it 'comes down hard on any form of bullying.' Drugs 'not an issue' either: 'the pupils that come here from abroad are often fairly naive and not part of that London culture.'

There is an LGBT community and a 'safe room' offered to those, who, for whatever reason, need to hang out alone for a while. 'For some pupils, this is the first time they have been able to express who they really are. This is often not the case in their home country.'

Door to door minibus service offered which collects pupils from as far afield as St John's Wood etc.

Pupils and parents: Dwight has a larger British student body than most other international schools in London (some 30 per cent), which seems to make it easier for international families to integrate into the local community. The impression from parents and from our visit is that there is relatively little sense of the 'expat bubble' in this international school. Long term families who joined the school in earlier incarnations (pre-IB) say they have been very pleased with the introduction of the full suite of IB programmes, and the interesting international experiences and friendships that Dwight's growing expat community brings. While they do see the turnover of families as a factor, many of these friendships endure and lead to exciting trips during the holidays to visit old friends who have moved on.

Entrance: Parents describe the school as 'selectively inclusive'. In all of our conversations (with parents and staff), no one emphasised 'academic results'. Though most enter in September, since the school serves expats, there are students entering throughout the year, from abroad and from local state schools. Interview and report from previous school only real requisites, as is a commitment and understanding of the IB programme. Interviews sometimes done via Skype.

Exit: About 75 per cent of lower school pupils move on to the upper school; some leave after the IBMYP, moving abroad or to sixth form colleges. University counselling programme in year 12, but it seems parents often start earlier, commenting they'd like to see a bit more attention to this area. Sixth formers mainly to university, a lot London based (eg King's, Goldsmiths, Westminster) with others to eg Scotland (Dundee and Aberdeen), to California and Waseda, Japan in 2018.

Money matters: Tuition is marginally less than other international schools in London. Extras include school trips and activities such as Model United Nations and some after-school activities. Good range of means-tested scholarships for families with an income of up to £120,000 pa (more if you have two or more children). These are awarded not for pure academic ability but for 'demonstrating the characteristics of the IB learner profile'. Also offers bursaries of between 25-50 per cent for children of visiting academics and NGOs. These are all available to current as well as new families.

Remarks: Dwight is a school where the education of the 'whole child' and the learning journey genuinely appear to be as important as exam results. A brave but rewarding choice for London born children ('none of my friends had heard of Dwight before', said one parent) – those looking for something a bit different and outside of the English curriculum. And a safe bet for International students who want the benefit of the IB in a more localised setting. The school does all it can to provide each student with opportunities to pursue their individual interests, all within the IB context. 'It's a kind school.'

East London Arts & Music

45 Maltings Close, Bromley By Bow, London E3 3TA

Ages 16–19 **Pupils** 300

0207 515 2159
www.elam.co.uk

Principal: Since the school opened in 2014, Charlie Kennard BA MA QTS (30s). Educated at Latymer Upper, read economics at Edinburgh, then went straight onto the Teach First programme. Taught for two years at Stuart Bathurst Catholic Secondary School in Wednesbury near Birmingham, working with some of the most economically disadvantaged children in the country; then joined the Teach First management team and subsequently became director of its sister organisation Teach for Malaysia. In 2012, happened to have a conversation with his brother Will, the platinum-selling musician of Chase & Status fame, decrying the lack of opportunities in the music business for young people from low-income families. ELAM opened two years later. No grass growing beneath Charlie's feet.

Youthful, fresh-faced, a child of the modern age and totally at ease with it, Charlie (all first names here) is also a man who genuinely believes in his students and works tirelessly to bring them on. A recent study found that 60 per cent of music chart acts had been educated at a private school compared with one per cent at the same point 20 years previously. He regards this as unfair and a waste of talent. 'Growing up, my brother and I were around professionals, whereas 60 per cent of the kids I was teaching in Walsall had neither parent working. Some of them were more talented musically than my brother – I've said this to him, and to his credit he didn't punch me in the face – but for them, succeeding in the creative industries was like a trip to the moon.' His mission is, quite simply, to put this right. 'We were impressed with the principal – his dedication and vision and ability to recruit great staff,' wrote a mother.

A popular and very active presence around the school – 'My boss is the students' – but also a calm, quiet individual who wears his commitment lightly and without the least zealotry. This is all the more remarkable given what he's achieved in such a short time: taking on the headship of this exceptional school at the age of 27, overseeing the construction of its state of the art premises on the site of a derelict warehouse, and leading it to its present success – it was rated outstanding in all areas by Ofsted in 2017. Sitting in his minimalist office, touched by his concern over our odd-looking cup of coffee from the school canteen and chatting comfortably, it took us a little time to realise we were in the presence of greatness. But we were.

Married to Victoria, a lawyer, with a baby daughter.

Academic matters: ELAM's ethos is straightforward: to enable young people to succeed in the creative industries through offering the right skills training plus access to high quality professional opportunities. 'There's often no straightforward route into the creative industries,' observes Charlie, 'so we're trying to create a clearer pathway, especially for those who can't afford to work unpaid until they get their foot in the door. It's vital not just to help students get their qualifications, but to get them started on the next step.'

The school originally offered music only, but now ELAM students can opt for one of three pathways: music, games design, or film and television production. Music trainees study for the BTec level 3 extended diploma in music. Games and film students study for the University of Arts London level 3 extended diploma in creative media production & technology. Both are equivalent to three A levels in UCAS tariff points and teaching time.

Having the different specialisms housed within the same school 'creates a great dynamism, and the trainees collaborate with each other.'

Everything taught here is underpinned by industry demand. 'The UK's creative sector is growing at a humungous rate. Music punches well above its weight in this country. Film and TV are going through the roof, not least because a high number of American productions are made here to take advantage of generous tax breaks. And there's a huge, huge industry demand for gaming skills.' From the outset, the school's approach has been to work with industry to define the curriculum. Universal Music UK was a founding partner and still offers 'unbelievably fantastic' support. Other partners include Decca, Lovebox, Virgin EMI, Abbey Road Studios, Lovebox, Polydor, Machinima Sboc – and more.

Trainees are worked hard from the off, and quickly come to relish the challenge of rising to professional level standards and deadlines. 'Before I came to ELAM I knew nothing about making games,' mused a year 12 student as he showed us an impressive virtual environment he'd created set in a submarine, 'but it's hands on here, you're thrown in at the deep end, it's about constant improvement. Coming here is one of the best things that's happened to me. It's amazing.' Teaching universally praised – 'They're brilliant professionals, they don't have to be teachers!' – but students were adamant that there was nothing relaxed about it. Meeting deadlines was hectic and often stressful, we were told, but they liked the professionalism of it. 'It's like you're an intern for a job.' 'They'll tell you if your work is rubbish. They're blunt with you and honest, and I think that's the best thing.' 'The learning here is quick, they don't mess around.'

Understandably, perhaps, some parents need to be convinced that the school is right for their child, particularly those whose offspring are academically successful and could have joined a more conventional sixth form; but once their child is here they appear to be very much won over. A parent of a student on the music pathway told us, 'The school does everything it can to provide the very best tuition, not just in music but in every discipline involved in the professional music industry. Above all, it teaches the importance of collaboration and the necessity of taking a collaborative approach. ELAM could not provide a better grounding for somebody looking to make music a career – whether as a performer or in other aspects of the industry.'

Maths and English are compulsory here, and an intrinsic part of the school's mission to enable young people to be industry ready. 'They have to be able to express themselves clearly and be comfortable with handling data – these days, the taste makers are the ones who can analyse trends'. Students who didn't achieve at least a 4 at GCSE must retake. School has a 100 per cent success rate for English resits; maths currently at 60 per cent. Those who have already passed these GCSEs when they arrive can opt to do either A level maths and/or English, or a level 3 qualification in quantitative reasoning plus the EPQ – both are equivalent to an AS. Principal is unapologetic about these aspects of the provision, but readily concedes that not all trainees have full enthusiasm for them, and some of the young people admitted as much. 'I had to resit my maths, and the work for English is killing me, I'm not gonna lie,' sighed one, 'but I enjoy that I get to do the music I want to do, and get to meet industry people.' And personal reluctance notwithstanding, all the trainees agreed that the school was right to insist on it. 'The stuff they teach us, whether you like it or not, it's relevant,' said one. 'A level maths is very applicable to game design,' said another, who came to ELAM with a full crop of top grades at GCSE. 'I have these small moments when I'm using the maths I'm learning in my gaming and it's really exciting.'

Designated SEND team offers one-to-one, group and in-class support to the small number of students – around five per cent – who need it.

Games, options, the arts: Every student is given a mentor from their chosen industry, and additionally all trainees do two weeks' work experience every year with some pretty awesome companies. Universal Music alone offers around 40 placements, and the list of others reads like a Who's Who of hip commercial creativity: Spotify, Apple, YouTube, etc. 'For our least able kids those two weeks are transformative,' says Charlie, and everyone we spoke to raved about this part of the provision. 'I got to go to Red Bull Music for my work experience!' cried a young singer. Trainees soon find the confidence to set up their own projects, and these seemed to be happening everywhere we looked. We came across five personable young men who proudly gave us their business cards for the music production company they'd set up and did a good pitch to us there and then. We checked out their website afterwards – alive and banging.

School is equipped with industry standard facilities including an amazing 440-seat theatre and any number of live music rooms, recording studios and computer suites. Wherever we went, trainees were getting together to rehearse songs, practise riffs, do a spot of sequencing, or just strum a guitar and unwind. 'Everyone's basically learning from each other in this school – it's musically multicultural,' said a talented young pianist who broke off from his drumkit practice to chat to us. Everyone on the music pathway has one-to-one tuition in at least one instrument, and music theory is also taught.

Extracurricular activities not confined to the set pathways: Love Of Literature week had many trainees producing poems and plays. Sports provision, however, is meagre and when we asked the trainees about it we were met with perplexed silence. 'There's a football match on the 10th,' one lad finally volunteered, sending everyone else into fits of giggles. 'We're terrible at all that,' admitted the principal. Trainees are educated in health and fitness issues, and yoga and dance teachers apparently come in from time to time, but no details about this were forthcoming. Given the amount of time the gaming trainees in particular spend in front of a screen, we were surprised at this deficiency.

Lots of music and media trips to large games and film expositions, workshops at places like the Royal Albert Hall. The school often gets invited to special events such as the Mercury Prize and the BAFTA Games Awards.

Background and atmosphere: Situated hard by the thunderingly noisy A12 and accessed from half-boarded up Bromley-by-Bow tube via a grim-looking subway, ELAM's surroundings can't be called pretty. But that, after all, is the point: the school was founded to help young people from low income backgrounds, particularly EastEnders, and the building itself stands tall and proud, clearly signed for all to see.

E

Once inside, ELAM gives out an aura of calm professionalism that is very engaging. Indeed, it doesn't feel like a school at all, but like a rather glitzy recording company with a more than usually young workforce. A small but pleasing display of pop art adorns the spacious entrance hall, trainees in casual clothes with headphones and creative hair styles move about with assurance and purpose, banter and music drifts down from above. All very civilised. No sixth form common room: staff and trainees alike meet in the canteen, so that staff can be seen having working conversations. 'You can't just tell someone what is not professional, you have to model it yourself,' insists principal, who wants ELAM to feel like a creative company rather than a school. Walls very bare at present, but high quality framed student art work is planned. Meanwhile, 'corrugated card round the edge of a noticeboard is not our vision'.

ELAM was supposed to be a two week summer project to 'enhance and inspire' creative youngsters in the area, but very quickly took on a powerful momentum of its own. Sir Nick Williams, former principal of the BRIT School and David Joseph, the CEO of Universal Music, urged that more was needed, for the sake of both students and the industry. 'The environmental factors of demand and supply said that we needed to create a school,' recalled Charlie, 'My brother and I almost wanted it not to take off so that we could go back to our lives, but it couldn't be stopped.' The school began life up the road in Stratford as the guest of School 21, housed in their sixth form block and admitting 75 students. In April 2017 it moved to its present quarters and September 2018 saw it at its full capacity of 300, highly regarded by the community, the industry and the DfE, and '10 times oversubscribed'. By any standards, an astonishing success story.

Pastoral care, well-being and discipline: 'We've been super-tight with discipline,' commented Charlie, and the behaviour we saw was exuberant but controlled and respectful. Many of ELAM's year 12 trainees are technically year 13s because of having dropped out of their first year of sixth form elsewhere; but once here, a lot of the students' previous issues seem to dissolve of their own accord. As one trainee put it, 'In secondary school, they tell you what to do. Here, you have a creative imagination and they support it.' Another confirmed, 'I hated secondary school, hated everything about it, but I want to be here. As soon as you walk in, everyone's welcoming, friendly, passionate about what they do. You get to meet other people who like what you like, so we get to build and grow together.' Teachers are, say parents, 'accessible and approachable.'

The school strives to instil professional values at all times, so punctuality and meeting homework deadlines are taught in that context, and are, according to parents, extremely effective. Likewise, dress code is relaxed but school is strict on anything too revealing, because it gives the wrong impression for work. Attendance is strictly monitored and any concerns are flagged up quickly. 'It is made clear to the trainees that opportunities such as good work placements have to be earned,' observed a parent, who rated the pastoral care as excellent. The catering looked mediocre when we visited, but the principal was already on it, with a new caterer appointed, and the school is looking into how this could also provide training opportunities for the students.

Perhaps the best endorsement for the school's approach comes from the trainees themselves, who take their role as creatives extremely seriously and are overjoyed to have landed at a school that does the same. 'If you're not serious, don't bother coming here,' was a comment from one year 12 lad that had everyone vigorously nodding. 'Never mind wasting your own time, you're gonna waste other people's time.' 'If you don't have passion, integrity and drive, you might as well not come here,' confirmed another trainee. The result is an atmosphere that is genuinely inspiring, according to parents. 'It is striking how students help each other and cheer on their peers at school concerts.'

Pupils and parents: A very heterogeneous cohort – some privately educated with a raft of top-grade GCSEs, some from the poorest council estates in Stratford with nothing, and 'everything in between'. Currently around 30 per cent of students on free school meals, but school is well aware of the increasing number of middle class families turning up at open evenings as the word spreads and will be 'aggressively recruiting from local comprehensives' to ensure diversity and balance.

Intake is from 22 London boroughs and beyond. A small number come from as far as eg Norwich, Wales and Newcastle. School is not registered as a boarding provider and therefore can't help with accommodation for the latter, but will put them in touch with other trainees who have done the same and who can recommend host families.

Entrance: Online application in which students' creativity and motivation is assessed. If the school is satisfied about these, applicants are invited to an assessment day. This includes a one-to-one interview and a problem-solving group activity with people they've never met before – the school here is looking for 'collaboration, integrity, communication.' Those applying to the music pathway must also do a performance. Once the day is finished, applicants are scored out of five, and only when it's identified the high scorers does the school look at their academic record and references.

Exit: Around 50 per cent to university or conservatoire: destinations have included Manchester, Newcastle, Goldsmith's, University of East London, Liverpool Institute of Performing Arts, BIMM, Leeds College of Music, the Academy of Contemporary Music. Most students on music or music-related courses. The remainder to a variety of apprenticeships or employment with companies such as BBC Radio 1 and 1xtra, Odd Child Music, PMR Records, Sony, Warner, Univeral Music, Apple and Spotify.

The school supports former trainees by allowing them access to ELAM rehearsal studios after they've left and by appointing some as ELAM 'ambassadors'. It also actively uses social media to promote the work of both current and former trainees. 'Our son feels that ELAM has provided him with an invaluable stepping stone towards his goal of being a professional performer,' wrote a grateful parent.

Occasionally students have dropped out owing to a misconception of what ELAM is about and the hard work and commitment that will be expected of them – we gathered that this had particularly applied to the Gaming pathway, perhaps unsurprisingly. School is therefore currently strengthening its initial assessment and induction process to ensure that all trainees thoroughly understand what's involved in 'turning the thing you like doing into the thing you do for work every day'.

Remarks: Hugely impressive, outward-looking, professional yet caring, and totally unique, this school really took our breath away. A godsend to any aspiring young creative lucky enough to come here, not least those who couldn't imagine how they would have fared anywhere else. Well on the way to becoming one of London education's hottest tickets. Apply early.

Eaton House Belgravia

Linked with Eaton House the Manor Boys' School, Eaton House the Manor Girls' School

3-5 Eaton Gate, Eaton Square, London SW1W 9BA

Ages 4-9 (becoming 4-11) **Pupils** 240

Fees: £17,850 – £20,700 pa

020 7924 6000
www.eatonhouseschools.com

Head: Since 2017, Huw May (late 40s) MAed, NPQH, Advanced Diploma Royal Welsh College of Music, BMus, previously head of Eaton House the Manor Pre-Prep. Earlier experience in headships include Sydenham Junior School, Roedean Junior School and St Aubyn's pre-prep. A professional singer for several years before taking up teaching, he is a trained ISI inspector.

Mr May lives over the school during the week, returning to his home in Sussex at weekends. Gardening, classic cars (MGs and older Mercedes) and walking his dog Harvey – boy-approved relaxations. He has quickly gained the respect and trust of parents who find him 'approachable' and 'a good listener'. They especially value the fact that he has 'the boys' well-being and interests at heart'. Ambitious for his school, shows vision and is full of enthusiasm for developing each boy's all-round potential, emotionally as well as academically. A parent commented: 'We really value the immersive approach to learning and the school's entrepreneurial spirit; for example, Mr May has set up a partnership with the Science Museum'.

Mr May's arrival, after a brief tenure by respected long term deputy Annabel Abbott, coincided with a change to school organisation plans (see below). He has speedily got a grip, emphasising individual learning plans for each boy, and the school seems as good as ever, with excellent results in his first year.

Entrance: Genuinely non-selective (but this is Belgravia). Main entry is at 4+ into kindergarten with, on average, 70 places. Places are allocated on a first come first served basis, with priority given to siblings, so it is important to put your name down early. Large deposit payable on accepting a place. There is no financial help on offer. For entry further up the school, the occasional places are subject to an assessment to see if the applicant will fit into the year group. Entry at 8+ is possible, now that the prep is open, but has yet to develop in any volume in its first year. Eaton House Schools Group is happy to let it develop at an organic rate.

Boys come from a wide range of Belgravia nurseries plus Victoria, Pimlico, Fulham and Battersea, with a few from as far away as the City. The majority of pupils have British or part-British nationality (60 per cent) with the remainder mostly European.

Exit: About 40 per cent leave at 7+, and most of the rest of them at 8+, a third of them to Westminster/St Paul's juniors, the rest to a mix of good junior schools (King's College Wimbledon, Dulwich), prep schools (Wetherby's, Sussex House, Westminster Cathedral Choir) and top boarding preps such as Summer Fields, Caldicott, The Dragon and Ludgrove. This would be an impressive record for a selective school, let alone one with EHB's broad intake; Mr May is clear and direct in advising parents on which schools they should aim for.

Eaton House Belgravia now, for the first time, offers options beyond 8+, with several from the pre-prep forming the first, select year 4. Pupils will be able to stay on for three years and then either take the 11+ entrance or spend the final two prep years at Eaton House the Manor south of the river, with others who are aiming for 13+ places at top boarding schools like Eton or Tonbridge (school bus provided for the 10-15 minute journey).

Remarks: Eaton House Belgravia is part of the Eaton House group of schools. The principal Hilary Harper and her husband took over Eaton House Belgravia in 1978 and developed the school into the group it is today. On retirement in the summer of 2016, she sold a majority stake in the group to private equity group Sovereign Capital, though her daughter, chief executive Luchie Cawood, has a significant stake and is thoroughly involved in the schools.

Parents who choose EHB want a traditional pre-prep (and, in future, prep) experience and the school delivers with a 3Rs curriculum, academic rigour and plenty of extras. In particular they value 'the excellent, nurturing male and female teaching staff who ensure they know their boys and care for them'. Classes are small with so far only informal sets for maths and English in years 2 and 3, so that the boys gain a full understanding in all maths and English topics.

EHB offers a very particular brand of boy-friendly teaching. Boys work hard in short bursts in the morning; in the afternoon games are followed by clubs and activities such as football, cookery, coding and Spanish. The extensive list of clubs changes regularly. They are supposed to enjoy the work and to have a riotous time in extras and 'run around after school and relax in supervised activities'. Some parents suggest that 'this would not be the right school for a slow developer, as the boys work at a fast pace and it becomes demanding in year 2 with plenty of homework.' Some teaching talk & chalk (albeit on interactive whiteboards these days), but much based on doing something physical, thinking through what you have done, and then applying it to a problem.

Individual provision ('differentiation') involves weekly consideration of how to support each child: all will at times be taken off into a side room for one-to-one. Not just academic/SEN support: there's Move Fit, run by physiotherapists for anyone who needs to improve coordination, and occupational therapy, for example handwriting and touch typing. In the kindergarten, Lego groups help develop social skills.

Communication between home and school is frequent and well-coordinated. The original plans to grow Eaton House Belgravia Prep organically on its south Kensington site changed in 2018 to expand Eaton House Belgravia pre-prep up to 11 years on its own site. The school is comprised of two immense, linked cream town houses on several levels. The basement houses the kitchen, dining rooms, staff room, some individual music lesson rooms and a well-used science lab where boys enthusiastically carry out experiments and make discoveries. On the ground floor there is a well-stocked, light library and classrooms. The top two floors of the No 3 building, previously administrative offices and living accommodation, have been been converted into classrooms, DT and art rooms for the new prep school.

Boys enjoy their art and we saw some house competition inventive illustrations for selected poems, as well as arresting year 1 wild west T shirts for a forthcoming fashion show. We spotted an attractive watercolour crab on our tour and evidence of interesting artwork in topic lessons throughout the school.

Mr May is clearly going to add zest to an already excellent musical provision (inter alia he has commissioned an opera for the school). Music takes place in the hall and is timetabled for all. Boys perform in fortnightly music assemblies and termly concerts and take part in competitions and charity events. Parents say that the head of music nurtures and encourages all ages to take up an instrument – drums, piano, singing, trumpet, guitar and violin all taught – with those who are fearful of performing offered strategies to gain self-confidence. The school has a dedicated ICT room, touch typing and coding are encouraged in the curriculum and classrooms have touch interactive boards and now tablets.

There is only one tiny outdoor space, but planning permission has been submitted for a sizeable outdoor learning centre. The fairly small hall/gymnasium is tightly packed when the whole school assembles. By necessity the days are very structured. The school council suggestion of Five a Day interruptions of five minute physical activities by desks is popular and beneficial. Boys are bussed to Hyde or Battersea Park every day to let off steam and play sports. Staff ensure boys are not taken out of sports and bemoan the time spent sitting in traffic. Swimming takes place at the Queen Mother's sports centre. Parents comment approvingly of the sport and 'the diverse clubs on offer including optional weekend activities, so there is lots to do'. A number of football clubs operate outside school hours. The boys enjoy their fixtures, stating that 'If we lose against the Manor, who are bigger than we are, we beat them at chess'.

Boys care about their food, and now this is freshly prepared on the premises, but some parents still believe there is further scope for improvement. The house system underpins all areas of the school and is very effective. It supports a culture of positive reinforcement regarding behaviour and respect, whilst enabling the boys to interact and enjoy the healthy competition on which they thrive. There is real engagement and an understanding of responsibility; 'Boys don't want to let their house down and captains write prayers for assembly'. Good manners are encouraged and one special feature we observed was the practice of one boy in every class shaking our hand, making eye contact and welcoming us to the class. The boys learn to make presentations and recite poetry confidently in public. 'I want them [the boys] to develop skills for life including adaptability, resilience, and determination and learn to listen and articulate their opinions confidently,' says Mr May.

The majority of pupils live within walking distance, with some international families and many parents working in the City as lawyers or bankers, and most are very ambitious for their sons. 'We don't mind taking a round boy in a square hole' and parents agree that the school happily accommodates boys 'with different personalities and backgrounds, providing a really good real experience'. School advises, 'EHB is probably not the right school for you if you want your son in bubblewrap' and parents agree that the boys 'are not coddled and must be able to cope with academic rigours'. All boys wear uniform shorts and long socks whatever the weather. The pace is fast and there is an expectation that everyone will join in and accept challenges; excellent preparation for the top academic prep schools they are aiming for. 'We are slightly quirky' and the school is not purpose-built or manicured but full of energetic, interesting boys. Boys and staff muck in and this works a treat, as the boys are clearly happy. Staff are always on hand to advise parents about a suitable choice of prep schools where their engaging personalities and good manners will be an asset.

Eaton House the Manor Boys' School

Linked with Eaton House Belgravia, Eaton House the Manor Girls' School

The Manor House, 58 Clapham Common Northside, London SW4 9RU

Ages 3–13 **Pupils** 510

Fees: £16,143 – £19,743 pa

020 7924 6000
www.eatonhouseschools.com

Head: Since 2016, Sarah Segrave (40s), who has a BA in education and history from Durham and an MA from the Institute of Education, and was previously head of the girls' school. She joined the Eaton House schools in 1993 as one of the founding teachers. She taught history, Latin and was housemistress at the prep, became head of the pre-prep then in 2010 head of the girls' school. It was difficult to leave the girls behind, but feeling that she 'lived and breathed Eaton House' and wanting someone who knew the schools to take on the role of prep head she stepped forward. The new role also combining the position of director of education for all four schools on the site was the final draw. She aims to move forward but hold onto the traditions of the school.

Married to Nick, with two children at the school, she lives in Earlsfield. Far from travelling in with her husband who looks after IT for the group of schools, she's more likely to have left the house at 5am. Parents describe her as 'professional yet very approachable' with which we concur, and hearing of her exceptionally long days, dedicated and extremely hard-working too. A parent observed, 'she's introduced a lot of positive changes'.

Pre-prep head since September 2017 is Nicola Borthwick, previously deputy head of the girls' school.

Nursery head since 2005, Mrs Roosha Sue.

Entrance: In the words of the head, 'entrance has sky-rocketed' and entry is now three forms throughout. Entrance to the pre-prep at 3+ is non-selective; simply register for a place as early as possible. Boys migrate from the pre-prep more or less automatically via continual assessment, although if the head feels the school isn't right for a boy families would be advised and this is the case for one or two each year. Entry at 8+ and 11+ into the prep is selective via testing in maths, English and verbal reasoning and by interview. External entrants should register no later than the autumn prior to entrance. There are three applicants for every place at 8+. Boys enter from both local state and independent schools.

Exit: Over the past seven years boys have headed to a list of 35 different schools, the most popular being Eton, Dulwich College, Harrow and Charterhouse, most at 13+, but an increasing few at 11+.

Remarks: About a third of the staff have been at the prep for over 10 years. The head describes them as the school's 'best asset and biggest strength, very passionate about what they do with incredibly high standards'. Parents tell us: 'very good teachers, inspiring yet demanding'; 'teachers ensure the subjects/topics are fully understood, taking extra time where necessary'; and 'great cohesion between subjects in the curriculum', citing a combined geography and art project involving a trip to the British Museum and a week's work about James and the Giant Peach involving art, reading, writing, sport and drama. There is an emphasis on boys as readers, supported by excellent reading lists and a rather old fashioned library which is soon to be refreshed.

In the first two years boys are taught by their class teacher; subsequently all subjects are taught by specialists and there is setting for English and maths. Reasoning in addition to the usual curriculum including Latin and French.

Prep class sizes average 16, maximum 18; hence some of the classrooms up under the roof are small rather than spacious. Boys were diligently working with the breeze wafting in from the common in every class we saw. Our guide was so enthusiastic that a Latin class was unmissable; he raced us up three flights of stairs moments before our departure. Science is taught in a charming old lab, where one could believe Faraday actually worked, and a sparkling new lab about to have its wrapper removed; we found a science teacher already in residence, thrilled by the pristine equipment. There is also a new DT lab complete with three 3D printers and a laser cutter. The art studio has the most stunning view of London's skyline towards the Thames, perhaps inspiring a wonderful scale paper model of London landmarks, our favourite a beautiful Greenwich Observatory.

This is a school with excellent academic outcomes, very good value added, ambitious parents and consequently a school of 'really high expectations'. The head has ensured that targets are set clearly and there is greater transparency, so that children and parents know how they are doing across all subjects. 'Good shows', to which we want to add the word 'jolly', are for excellent work. A smiley face outside the head's office shows the times when she is free for visits to share them. Exam weeks are dotted with sport. Parents speak of boys taking it in their stride and that 'homework is manageable,' particularly lower down the school. There are currently 16 children with SEN, mostly mild dyslexia and dyspraxia, for which they receive up to two one-to-one periods of support a week.

The head is currently rethinking the scholarship programme, for which boys are selected in year 7 and commences in year 8. We got the sense that conversations about destination schools with parents were tackled with diplomacy and frankness in equal measures to ensure everyone has a realistic choice without underselling themselves. Parents given insight but their choices are supported: such those who decide they would prefer their child to attend an ultra-academic school where a child will be in the bottom 10 per cent versus another school where he might gain an academic scholarship.

There is one hour of ICT a week, boys use Learn Pads and there are banks in classrooms as well as an ICT room. The head is looking at the most engaging and productive teaching methods to get the boys from A to B. She challenges her staff, saying: 'Has your lesson made a difference to a child today?' and continues to teach herself to see the children from different angles.

Sport is 'highly competitive,' say parents, with boys battling it out. Football, rugby and cricket are their major sports and hockey, cross-country, swimming, karate, tennis and athletics are minor sports, but more than one parent told us they'd like to see more fixtures, national tournaments and tours. The U12 footballers came fourth in English Schools FA Cup and there have been sports scholarships to Dulwich College, Bedales, Radley and Whitgift.

Two music lessons per week and weekly drama – two major productions per year. Some 70 per cent play instruments, beginners to grade 5. Staff get involved in the Battle of the Bands. 'The boys are encouraged to join the vocal ensemble and the choir,' said a parent.

There is an early morning room from 8.00am and a supervised homework class until 5.00pm without charges. In addition there are a great number of clubs that run before school, during the school day and after school such as DT, chess, running and Spanish.

The Eaton House group of schools, first founded in 1897 on Sloane Street, also includes a school in Belgravia. This is a large operation now, but the division into three schools with autonomous heads means that the staff know children really well.

We are used to the maze-like experience of schools that have adapted old buildings to suit over many years, but this school nonetheless could confuse a Minotaur. The children giggle sweetly at our disorientation and trip adeptly from one part of the school to the next.

Behind the period façade, the elegant Georgian house dating back to 1792 facing the green of Clapham Common and housing the boys' school has classrooms often high up in the rafters, lots of lino – more practical and less elegant than it appears, and behind this a functional quadrangle of classrooms forming the pre-prep. Then there's the new-build delights – the new science lab and two bright modern dining halls complete with eco-friendly exterior 'living wall' in the style of the new girls' prep building. At the time of our visit the builders had been in situ for a whole 10 years. The children have, of course, weathered it stoically, but everyone is looking forward to the scaffolding coming down and the playgrounds being reinstated.

The pre-prep classrooms are in a block formation, large and bright off wide lino-floored corridors, rather standard issue after one has seen the new buildings: boys must have a sense of graduating when they attain the staircases, views and quirks of the prep school classrooms. But we found the nursery teachers enjoying their very spacious purpose built classrooms with in-and-out spaces close to the dining hall.

One of the louder and more exuberant of schools we have visited at the start of the day and in the playgrounds: 'friendly and happy,' offered a parent commenting on the atmosphere. A pupil summed it up as a school: 'where teachers are encouraging and the children are kind'.

Revisiting pastoral care has been very high on the head's agenda – 'if children aren't happy they won't flourish.' She wanted to rethink what she saw as a bit of a feeling that 'boys will be boys being acceptable'. The school rules have been rewritten collaboratively with pupils; they previously made no mention of bullying. Assemblies are an important place for discussing PSHE-like topics, so now there are junior and senior assemblies pitched to the different age groups, a recent one tackling the topic of stress. Boys are asked if they know whom to go to for help and encouraged to talk to whomever they feel the most comfortable with at any time. Boys have also been introduced to the idea that this is a 'telling' school and talked about whistleblowing in society. A mother told us: 'The head of pastoral care is really wonderful'.

Parents from all walks of life, many dual nationalities – German, French, Spanish, American families and almost 40 children from overseas. Parents describe each other as 'relaxed, friendly, sociable and down-to-earth'. A mix of working and non-working mothers who make newcomers welcome.

No bursaries, but the school has been very supportive of families who have found themselves in financial difficulties during their prep career.

E

Eaton House the Manor Girls' School

Linked with Eaton House the Manor Boys' School, Eaton House Belgravia

E

58 Clapham Common Northside, London SW4 9RU

Ages 4–11 **Pupils** 260

Fees: £16,141 pa

020 7924 6000
www.eatonhouseschools.com

Head: Since 2016, Oliver Snowball (early 40s). BA (in English literature), MA (in theatre studies) and PGCE. Previously a teacher of English and drama at Tunbridge Wells Girls' Grammar School, then at various points head of drama and senior housemaster at Kent College Pembury. Most recently deputy head and interim head at Kent College Prep.

Energetic, immaculately turned out, friendly and engaging, with an almost paper-free glamorous (if hot on a summer's day) office/greenhouse, Mr Snowball seems to have hit the ground running with his vision for the school and is clearly engaged with contemporary educational debate. Firstly, he has introduced a focus around seven character traits that he feels will help children perform to the best of their ability. They include grit, optimism, empathy and trust. The head and teachers model the attributes and discuss them in assemblies. The challenge is to make the results tangible, but it is clearly working well with girls, jotting down on post-its when they have demonstrated attributes, and staff able to feedback evidence to parents. More creativity and thoughtful planning went into the Adventure Book – an A4 book which is a girl's own space to explore ideas just for herself without any right or wrong.

A parent who has seen a lot of change at the school told us she has generally been impressed with it all. Others say: 'I think that Mr Snowball sets a very warm, supportive and nurturing tone for the school. He also seems to be a genuinely kind person, with time for the girls as individuals.' Another mother agreed: 'He learnt my daughter's name and face very quickly and always congratulates her on good work she has done or outside achievements when he says good morning.'

He is married to Claire with two children and the family is enjoying the novelty of London, being 'resident tourists'. Without quite so much country air at his disposal he has inevitably found himself joining the local joggers around the common.

Entrance: Currently non-selective at aged 4; offers made around a year before entry, with sibling priority. Any later entrants are required to spend a day at the school during which they sit a maths and English assessment. Rows of scooters attest to the vast majority travelling from within a two to three mile radius, with many from the neighbouring streets.

Exit: Girls head to both a broad and notable mix of day and boarding senior schools, from Godolphin & Latymer, JAGS and Putney to Benenden, St Mary's Ascot and Woldingham.

Remarks: Standard curriculum. French not Spanish, as befits this corner of London perhaps, and Latin and critical thinking for the senior girls. Mr Snowball is pleased to see the children responding well to more 'curve-ball' open ended type questioning in lessons which will serve children well as the 11+ landscape potentially moves away from simply testing maths and English. His focus will be on improving independent thinking, creative and analytical skills, and whilst wanting to stretch the upper abilities will try to ensure the middle range are not forgotten. One mother shared her delight with the way academic learning alongside well-matched trips have inspired her daughter: 'This week she came home talking about the Roman walls around Londinium and London Bridge's timeline, and wanting to look up related topics in books or on maps.' Another parent: 'The trip to 10 Downing Street was amazing. Teachers are very enthusiastic, which rubs off.'

Parents believe the main emphasis of this school is on the academics and arrive looking for a top London exit. The head comments: 'We are an academically rigorous school; we are not a hothouse' (his office aside). Parents would seem to agree, but there is more talk of the pressures of homework – which begins in year 1 – than we often encounter, and the head says that he will be reviewing it at the end of his first year, given his belief in family and down-time. One parent: 'There is probably more homework than there needs to be at times but it's a good learning process.' Another: 'I would say quite a lot of homework, but not more than they can handle. My daughter does a lot of sport outside school, and the teacher is always prepared to let her complete homework the following evening if necessary. There is a certain amount of exam pressure, but we live in a very competitive area.'

There are a tiny number of children with identified SEN in the school currently – mainly dyslexia, mostly with mild tendencies, but one or two with mild dyspraxia and ADHD. One full-time and one part-time member of the learning support team offer one-to-one sessions, regular review meetings with parents and external specialists.

Of the 25 staff only three have been at the school for more than 10 years, with a couple of NQTs bringing the latest ideas into practice. All female except for the head of music. The head describes them as 'passionate and dynamic', 'incredibly impressed with their work ethic, the best I've seen at any school' and 'open-minded to new initiatives'. We created quite a stir by commenting on them, revealing the girls' knowledge of all of their neighbours' daily habits. Smart new science lab, and lovely charcoal drawings of characterful Vikings on one classroom wall. The art room is light and bright with lovely work in evidence of a cubism project, designs for Harry Potter book jackets and Giacometti sculptures tying in with the Tate exhibition.

This is a school of keen readers, but the library didn't do too well out of the rebuild: behind a closed door in the new basement, it's a tiny and, we felt, uninviting space with a modest collection of books to choose from. When we enquired as to whether girls would come here at lunchtime, they were understandably bemused.

Not, as yet, the most fiercely competitive sporting school. All girls have a PE, games and swimming session each week at the nearby Clapham leisure centre and everyone learns ballet. All girls from years 3 to 6 play netball, hockey and rounders or athletics in the summer. The new netball courts on Clapham Common are useful, but the girls can also make use of the huge new basement sports hall and gym for indoor football, hockey, fitness and netball. Recent sporting success from year 6 has boosted year 5's performances too. This year, the U11 netball team won the IAPS Smaller Schools tournament and the U9 A and B teams won their respective hockey tournaments involving a number of other London prep schools.

One parent told us: 'in my opinion, music and drama, although taught and appreciated with enthusiasm, get a little squeezed out.' The head (with his theatre studies background) agrees that there is room to develop. There is no head of drama – form teachers currently direct productions – but the school will introduce expertise from outside when needed. The girls we met were very much enjoying rehearsing Bugsy Malone. A parent suggested: 'I think the girls and boys could have a little more interaction, eg in drama.'

Everyone learns the recorder and over a third of girls currently learn piano, violin, flute, drums, guitar or voice, ranging from beginners up to grade 4. There are three choirs: the non-audition junior and senior choirs and Bel Canto by audition for potential soloists. There is also an orchestra and children perform in music assemblies and concerts.

A fun and sophisticated mix of clubs, running until 5pm, some with an intellectual bent such as Plato's Child, a mix of English and philosophy for year 5s, plus book-making, curiosity club, introduction to psychology and yoga. Some are joint with the boys next door and many with additional charges. There is also an early room club from 8.00-8.30am for parents in need of an early drop off.

The school seems to be perceived as very much 'traditional', but we'd add without being remotely stuffy. Mr Snowball can see why it has that reputation: there is the very distinctive green and red uniform of blazers and boaters, a sense of formality, he shakes hands with every child on the way in and the way out and there is the calendar of events from harvest festival to sports day. But as he's demonstrated, the school is as modern and fresh as the new buildings in terms of the contemporary educational thinking they engage with. These buildings, opened in 2008, are light, bright and full of unexpected views, green roofs and the odd living wall – a very pleasant space in which to learn.

This is very much a girls' school – 'There is a lovely feel of girl power about the place!' said a mother – but given the school's buildings and structure, with the boys' prep next door, it seems instead to have the atmosphere of one big family with brothers and sisters and family friends educated alongside each other, sometimes in adjacent classrooms. There is one combined residential trip with the boys in year 3.

When we asked parents about the school's feel, a typical response – whether talking about the girls' school or Eaton Manor as a whole – was: 'The school has a relaxed atmosphere, although most parents have a common goal to get their children into a top secondary school.' Every classroom we stepped into certainly seemed focused on the task in hand but also calm and relaxed, plenty of discussion in science and quiet pottering about in art. One mother observed 'It's 'pretty competitive' but also, 'She sees the school as her second home. She feels very comfortable with the other girls and teachers.' One parent got into the spirit of things in answer to our wondering about whom this school might suit: 'Bright, busy, friendly, kind, chatty, confident, open, ambitious girls, prepared to pack a lot of stuff in and work hard.'

Rules are straightforward: to be kind, be polite, be careful, be tidy and be smart. A parent said: 'The teachers are extremely kind but they are no-nonsense in my experience.' The house system has recently become 'more substantial'. Housemistresses will know the girls right through their life at the school. Girls in the upper years are 'big sisters' to the KGs (reception), which they seem to love. Year 6 girls feeling both nervous and excited about next step very much appreciate old girls coming back to talk to them about their senior schools.

Predominantly British with a few girls coming from families where one or both parents are western European, Asian or American. Approximately 10 per cent of girls are bilingual or trilingual. Only a couple of overseas nationals. A handful receive EAL support.

No bursaries or scholarships currently, but watch this space as scholarships are being introduced.

Eaton Square School

79 Eccleston Square, London SW1V 1PP

Ages 4–13 **Pupils** 387 **C of E**

Fees: £20,850 – £21,900 pa

02079 319 469
www.eatonsquareschool.com

E

Headmaster: Since 2010, Sebastian Hepher BEd (early 50s). Educated at Alleyn's and University of Greenwich. Began teaching career in state sector, at Hurstmere Boys' in Kent, followed by The London Nautical School. Joined Eaton House Pre-Prep in 1990, before being asked to lead Eaton House The Manor in 1993. Under his headship, the school grew from the initial embryonic phase to a thriving prep school. Married, with four children currently at four different schools, with the youngest here. Swims in his local lido every day of the year, come rain or shine. Avid reader of Russian literature. Warm and charismatic, with a good sense of humour. Every parent we spoke to described him in glowing terms. 'He is the reason people gravitate towards the school,' according to one mother. Teaches reasoning. Also oversees the new upper school in Mayfair.

Entrance: Main intake is at 4+ via assessment. The school runs several nurseries for children from 2 to 4 and these pupils are assessed by head of nurseries and head of pre-prep. They are given priority over other candidates and make up well over half the intake. 'It's not automatic but very rare not to accept a child from one of our nurseries,' explains head. Assessments, in November for external candidates, involve phonic and numerical activities, as well as colouring, cutting and talking to teachers. Between 100 and 150 external applications for 30 places. Sibling policy.

Occasional vacancies further up the school are quickly filled from the school's waiting list, after the child has successfully completed a series of online tests and spent a day at the school in a classroom setting.

Exit: Most girls leave at 11 and boys at 13. Very few girls stay on for the 13+, usually those heading for co-ed boarding. Pupils progress onto a wide range of senior schools, both boarding and day. Rare to send more than a couple of children to any one school in any given year, though the new Eaton Square Upper School may buck the trend. Recent leavers to Eton, Harrow, Charterhouse, City of London Boys, St Mary's Ascot, Beneden,, Latymer Upper, Allyen's, Dulwich College, Godolphin & Laymer, Francis Holland x 2, City of London Girls, Queens College.

Head starts dialogue about senior schools in year 5, often encouraging parents look at boarding too even if previously dismissed out of hand by international clientele. Head acknowledges that 'London schools are not the place for the average boy' and that some need to cast their net further. Numbers of boys heading to boarding has increased noticeably and is 'beginning to bubble for the girls.'

Remarks: Situated in three large town houses in the heart of Belgravia. Separate buildings for senior prep, junior prep and pre-prep. One parent likened the children to mountain goats, as they make their way up and down the steep stairs.

Founded in 1981. Recently became part of the Minerva Education Group. Teething problems have left some parents feeling a little raw. One mother we spoke to said, 'The transition to the new ownership has been pretty bumpy, especially as it coincided with an escalation in fees'. Head feels some parental perception has been inaccurate and that school fees have not actually increased more than usual. Indeed, the second year of ownership has seen a reduction to the usual increase. On the positive side, Minerva has enabled the school to buy a building on Piccadilly overlooking Green Park for its new senior school, Eaton Square Upper School, which will eventually go up to 16.

Current head is credited with having pulled the school up by its bootstraps academically. It has grown both in size and standing on his watch. One parent commented, 'It used to just be a sweet, local school before Mr Hepher took over. He is much more ambitious and has taken it to another level'. Pupils now follow a more academically rigorous and broader curriculum. Excellent language provision.

Head abhors the culture of tutoring and believes 'we need to educate parents.' He has addressed the matter of intense competition for senior places with intelligence and worries that increasing number of schools using pre-tests works against late developers. School prepares pupils well for senior school entry without being a hothouse.

Typically five reception classes and four year 1 classes. Class size fairly small, with a maximum of 16 up to year 5 and a maximum of 18 in final years. Currently only eight pupils in each year 8 class and 11 in year 7, giving plenty of scope for individual attention. Pupils are placed in sets for maths and English at start of year 2 but these are fluid, with 'plenty of room for manoeuvre'.

Parents feel pupils are well prepared for transition to senior school, partly because the curriculum is kept broad throughout. From the start, all pupils are encouraged to be articulate and confident citizens. Head believes that good manners are essential. Each class has its own official greeter who comes to the front, shakes hands firmly and welcomes visitors on behalf of the rest of the class. A charming touch.

Thriving pre-prep department. Vibrant, colourful classrooms where emphasis is on practical work, consolidated by written work. 'It's hands on, creative learning here.' Impressive writing on display up the stairs. Everything is beautifully presented, from the work crafted by the children to displays produced by teachers. Charming library area where children can be found earnestly recommending books to each other.

As school is non-selective, there is a huge ability range. Full-time SENCo, supported by highly experienced learning enrichment team. Approximately 30 pupils currently having SEN support (mostly dyslexia, dyspraxia and dyscalculia), either one-to-one or small group sessions. Two children with EHC plans. More able pupils extended through challenging extracurricular activities.

Pastoral care is well structured. Head worries about life being stressful for these children. 'We have a duty of care to shield children from excessive pressure which London and the system place on them. Parents who are anxious tend to pass that on to their children. I worry that we're causing a very anxious society. We want to make sure that children are happy when they are here.' Whole school comes together once a week for a reflective and celebratory reflective assembly at St Michael's Church, Chester Square. Charity is an important part of school life. Huge amounts raised by parents and children.

Teachers mostly in late 20s and early 30s; some 10 members of staff have been here a decade. One parent described them as being 'friendly, energetic and good at communicating with the parents. Just what you want'. 'We haven't had a bad teacher yet!' said another, whose children are currently in the middle of the school.

Sensational drama. Huge annual musical performed by year 5 and 6 children at Unicorn theatre in the West End. Professional theatre director hired for the occasion. Years 7 and 8 perform something more challenging such as a Greek play. Younger children perform on stage twice a year. Music also a central part of the school with over 100 pupils learning an instrument. Performances in abundance, from carol services to rock concerts. Art taught to a high standard. Extra scholarship classes offered to the most artistic; the standard of portfolios is considered exceptional.

Despite its lack of outside space, school takes sport very seriously and coaching is excellent. Mainstream sports all offered as well as ballet, climbing, fencing and kayaking on the Thames. Pupils compete strongly in prep school ski-ing championships, recently bringing back a clutch of gold medals. Legendary swimming squad currently on a four-year unbeaten streak. Unusually, pupils swim here from day one. Football also strong, with plenty of practice taking place in Battersea Park. All children make a team of some description. 'The problem is finding enough other schools who can field C and D teams,' laments head.

Extracurricular activity viewed as important. Sensational residential trips. Year 3 heads off to Sussex for a four-day adventure. Years 4 and 5 go on a ski-ing and cultural trip to France where pupils practise speaking the language in context and also have daily French lessons. Snowball fights with the teachers apparently one of the highlights. One mother was delighted that the children were made to 'carry their own skis and make their own beds.' A novel experience for some, apparently. Pupils in year 6 go on a classical tour of Rome and Naples. Year 7 spend a week at a château in Normandy. Post common entrance, year 8 head to Scotland to celebrate.

Pupil composition is predominantly expat. Americans, Australians, Italians, French, Spanish mostly, with a sprinkling from Germany, Russia and Asia. One mother observed that there had been 'a thick crust of oligarchs' children in the past, but not any more.' Currently 14 per cent of pupils require targeted EAL lessons, which are intended to 'help speed up the process of full inclusion in the classroom.' Rare for mothers to work. A sea of nannies at the school gate on the day we visited. Pupils mainly come from local area. School bus service in operation to and from west and south-west London for those who live further afield.

Parents are encouraged to become involved, from hearing children read to giving career talks. Strong sense of community here and very active PTA. 'When you go into the school, there is a smile on the staff's faces. It's not the sort of school where you drop your child at the door and never get to venture across the threshold,' explained one mother. Head feels parent body is caring and empathetic, 'Parents who come here are quite open, as they have often changed city and country themselves. You need to be outward looking to do that and this feeds into their children. It creates a lovely atmosphere.'

Heady mix of traditional British education with an international flavour. Children are happy here as they have the freedom to be themselves. Judging by stampede to get into the building at the start of the day, Eaton Square offers its pupils a joyful start in life.

École Jeannine Manuel

43–45 Bedford Square, Bloomsbury, London WC1B 3DN

Ages 3–15 **Pupils** 440

020 3829 5970
www.ecolejeanninemanuel.org.uk

Head: Since the school opened in 2015, Pauline Prévot (40s). Degree in biology and science education from Versailles and Saint Quentin University and a DESS, or masters, in computer science. Her first job was with École Jeannine Manuel in Paris where she taught for 12 years, joining the maths department then became science and maths lead, and head of computing. She developed a Jeannine Manuel maths curriculum that is about critical thinking and working maths out in an experimental and experiential manner, and was thrilled by the opportunity to move to the brand new site in London, which she loves. Her husband is the financial director at the school and her two children are pupils here and they live five minutes away. She is hoping to stay for some time to come. They are building a senior leadership team, but with the school so new and pupil numbers growing so quickly, staff will need to grow and settle. Parents said the head was approachable and accessible but they mostly speak to one of the separate heads of the junior or senior school. They said she was 'fantastic', 'deeply committed to teaching' and 'a passionate educator' and 'very animated when giving workshops to parents on the maths method'. The school has a strong board of trustees, including the dynamic and impressive head of the Paris schools, who comes over regularly, speaking at open days. Ms Prévot 'won us over completely and gave us confidence,' said one parent.

Academic matters: This is bilingual teaching done well – English pupils are challenged to raise their standard and French pupils not allowed to coast in French lessons, but are pushed to improve too. 'We chose this school because we wanted both languages and cultures taught and didn't want to lose one or the other. Our children were happy the moment they walked in and we were no longer paying for schools where our kids sat bored in French classes.' It follows the French national curriculum except for English, science and Mandarin, where it has developed its own.

EYFS includes a one form nursery, with space to play inside and outside, reasonably well equipped with dressing up and play areas and plenty of art, rest time with kids lying down after lunch with blankets from home and quiet music – a safe, calm environment. Reception and year 1 start basic phonics and lots of coordination work in preparation for writing, but this being the French system, reading and writing proper waits until they are in year 2, with EYFS given to memory, poetry learning, speech and physical coordination.

Junior school classes of up to 20 pupils, with teaching shared between a French native speaker and an English native speaking teacher. Day books show work in neat French handwriting, maths with cuisenaire blocks, writing marked at pupils' own levels – each one expected to challenge themselves from whatever level they start at. They start to learn reading and writing in French (fewer graphemes make it to learn to read and spell in than English) and once they have mastered French reading and writing, they can then start English in little groups, working at their own level until they are all bilingual. Parents said that by about 8 years old all the kids are fluent in both. Maths very practical 'and at a higher level than my nieces and nephews in English schools'. Joint sciences, plenty of humanities (no RE in the French system) taught by both French and English teachers, art, music.

'Children get a tailored education – each of my kids has been pushed and developed in different ways'. 'Teachers don't have kids comparing to each other, they need to show progress at their level and they are expected to be ambitious for themselves'. 'Grading is based on effort and achievement and they need to show improvement,' explained one junior school parent. There is a no homework policy until senior school, though junior pupils said they sometimes have to do reading or learn a poem. Older pupils not overwhelmed with the hour or so homework they are expected to do.

Senior school has pupils using lockers and moving between rooms, half the subjects in English and half in French. Only humanities taught in both French and English under a curriculum that shows historical events from two different perspectives. The battle of Waterloo seen from both the winners' and losers' point of view – pupils see how to question the source and look at cultural context. 'It allows pupils to think about what is truth and to question fake news'. All lessons include collaborative, participative working.

Interactive whiteboards allow group work done on iPads to be shared by the class in real time. We saw groups collecting references from a text and uploading it to a shared table of references so they could all learn from each other's research. English enhanced with outings to theatres, workshops and some challenging teaching. 'I was blown away by the depth of understanding and analysis my child showed when explaining a Jekyll and Hyde text.' A french student won an English playwriting competition run by National Theatre with hundreds of entrants. Total bilingualism noted by parents – 'they flip from one language to the other and you can't tell what is their mother tongue language'. 'There is an organic mixing of pupils and exchanges take place in both languages'. This is achieved by intensive language teaching in 'petit groupes' so that by the time they are 7 or 8 they are all at the same level; higher up the school, new pupils are given intense language support so they can integrate. Late joiners who have insufficient French to learn maths under the school curriculum can do maths IGCSE.

Maths gets special mention by parents who believe 'that it is at a higher level than comparative French or English schools'.

Extra tutoring or language learning takes place in years 7 and 8 during the 45 minute daily Drop Everything And Read (DEAR) period while most pupils lie out on giant cushions and read from the English or French reading list. This might also be the time when dyslexic pupils or those who need help from speech and language therapists get extra support without missing other lessons. No special needs teaching but parents said that 'this is not a one-size fits all curriculum, but there are customised classes to boost pupils. Because that is happening all the time, no-one notices the dyslexic child who has specialised activities, since they are all rotating and doing work at their own level'. The school won't take a pupil it is not equipped to support, but everyone is used to therapists coming in. Most classrooms are wheelchair accessible and school is happy to adapt room timetables if needed.

Parents mentioned appreciating the 'incredibly nuanced report cards that assess both effort and achievement and show that teachers know each child's strengths and weakness'. Well as teachers know their pupils, there are no external examinations until IB except for language exams, so pupils are tested with internal exams and results matched to École Jeannine Manuel in Paris and Lille to check for progress. Currently the small classes, motivated pupils and teachers, are showing better results even than the Paris pupils. IB qualifying school status applied for.

Games, options, the arts: Very little outdoor space – each balcony and terrace used to the utmost with little ones using climbing

E

blocks and playhouses, and older ones using the basketball nets. Longer playtimes involve donning wellington boots and going into Bedford Square, or older students to Coram Fields, with footballs and rackets. Junior kids do go out every day and there are big efforts to provide sport despite there being no playground; older pupils are allowed out at breaktime. They have a contract with the YMCA sports centre for gym and indoor courts, and with University College EnergyBase for more gym space and basketball as well as Coram's Fields for team sports. Some fixtures against other French schools, but pupils said that 'it wouldn't suit a child who was very sporty' and parents said, 'it allows them to explore different sports but won't make champions'. Having no homework in junior school allows them 'time to explore their own interests,' according to parents.

DofE provides opportunities for learning to map read, big hikes and volunteering, and they are making volunteering opportunities within school for the younger kids.

Art taught in classrooms (very fine Picasso portraits being done in year 3 the day we visited), and we saw critical thinking demonstrated as pupils explained and discussed the thinking behind a gilded shopping trolley artwork. Continuous opportunities to express ideas orally and to get used to public presentations.

No individual music lessons, but juniors can try out instruments in class, while senior pupils go up to music room to hear and learn to appreciate different types of music as well as playing and composing.

Talent show very inclusive and diverse – a Rubik's cube champion, yoyo tricks, a rap done by two students in both English and French – comparing Shakespeare and Molière. Not your everyday talent show from a London school.

Clubs at lunchtime and after school, for juniors while they wait for senior school to finish (eg drama, storytelling, fencing, chess, choir, parkour, arts and crafts) and for seniors (eg robotics, debating, gymnastics, choir, street dance, basketball).

Background and atmosphere: Jeannine Manuel spent some time in London during the war as part of the resistance and believed in the need to create understanding between nations, and the importance of language in learning about other people and their culture. To this end she opened a school and developed a pedagogy based on collaborative working and critical thinking. The Paris École Jeannine Manuel has 2,400 pupils and the Lille branch 800, and École Jeannine Manuel is now an education 'brand' with a reputation for high academic standards and exciting teaching that means it has long waiting lists. Jeannine Manuel's son Bernard, a passionate educationist, worked to ensure funds from the Fondation Jeannine Manuel were set aside to open a school in London as a tribute to his mother's love of London and to make bilingualism a reality.

Three very fine Georgian buildings built in 1770 by Robert Palmer (fine enough to be included in the architectural Open House weekends) have been joined sympathetically and are now both elegant and functional. They face Bedford Square and are next to the British Museum and a minute away from Tottenham Court Road station, so could hardly be more central London. The Bedford Square building has room for up to 500 pupils and another building in Russell Square, which will have space for a further couple of hundred pupils, is being renovated ready for senior years as they move up to IB.

High ceilinged, carpeted rooms, with fine stucco architraves, neat modern furniture and lockers for pupils. Two particularly large rooms with tables and benches that open out from wall storage allow all pupils to eat school lunches or packed lunches in several sittings. Lunch is very French – a protein, a vegetable and a carbohydrate, as much as they want to eat, but no choices and no hot dogs. Set lunchtimes means not only do they all eat the same food, but that they all eat it together. A proper shared mealtime.

Polite, calm atmosphere, youthful teachers and purposeful collaborative teaching methodology. We didn't see any pupils daydreaming – too much going on and classes too small for that.

Pastoral care, well-being and discipline: Pupils said that if they had any concerns or issues they could and would speak to teachers at any time, and believed it would be dealt with. A well-being curriculum carried out in all years may have something to do with this. None we spoke to said there was bullying or roughness, though some admitted to social issues between friends. One parent said, 'minor things are dealt with efficiently at school, by caring teachers, with little parental involvement'. 'Pupils were told to go away and think about it and come back to resolve the problem – which they did'. We were told that 'pastoral care is excellent' and 'there is a nurturing environment', but it would seem that it happens simply because of caring teachers rather than strict systems or policies. The school only goes up to 15 for the moment so no drug or smoking issues – yet.

Pupils and parents: Most of 185 pupils who joined in the first year they opened were Parisians who knew of the École Jeannine Manuel Paris reputation, as well as French families who hadn't been able to get into any of the other French schools in London. The current 440 pupils are from a much more mixed demographic – lots of third culture kids whose passports and backgrounds are very international. Lebanese, French Canadian, Hong Kong, Irish, increasing numbers of British families who, according to the school, are looking to 'maintain some European culture – the Brexit effect'. Parents are bankers, lawyers, doctors. Pupils were surprisingly unsophisticated for such a well travelled lot – worldly, travelled, educated, but no designer trainers to be seen. Parents we spoke to said kids were 'gentle', 'no bling', 'allowed to be kids'. Pupils move at 11 from other French junior schools or from British primary schools 'if they are looking for a small, centrally placed private school with an emphasis on critical thinking'. French pupils' parents want them to keep their French up and keep links to their roots when the French schools which are subsidised by the French government are full, or they may be seeking an alternative to schools that are totally French in language and pedagogical style. School buses go north to Swiss Cottage, west to Kensington and Shepherds Bush via Paddington and Marylebone, and to Fulham and Chelsea.

Entrance: Unlike the Paris branch, there are not (yet) long waiting lists for this school. One form nursery, then two classes per year. Selection of pupils very 'light touch' – a simple test of language and maths. Mostly they are looking for parental commitment to the school's ethos. 'You have to believe that the school will do the educating but they need the family to support their ethos.' 'It is an inversion of normal entry requirements,' said one parent. 'They interviewed us for over an hour, wanting to know about our backgrounds and education and aspirations. They hardly tested our child at all!' The joy of not having to sit through 7+ or 11+ entrance exams is enough to tempt many parents, one imagines, as well as the absence of working towards exams generally. Beginners in French accepted at all levels, beginners in English up to year 7.

Exit: Currently, leavers only when families move country; otherwise, pupils seem to be staying on and so the school is growing with them and creating ever more years until it has a sixth form. Since no sixth form yet, hard to know where these pupils will go to, though the École Jeannine Manuel in Paris sends three-quarters of its pupils to universities outside France, almost half to UK universities – and of those 90 per cent to Russell Group universities. If the school gets IB accreditation (currently only has candidature status) then it is certainly well equipped to do well in London too, with current cohort of determined, mature, well-educated pupils from aspirational families. No home tutoring goes on that we could find out about, little homework and little pressure, just a set of enquiring minds and high expectations. UK universities can look at the Brevet French exam results taken at 15, or the English lit and lang IGCSE, or foreign language exams taken to public exam level (DELE for Spanish, DAF for German, HSK for Mandarin).

Remarks: Ideal for a mixed heritage family where both French and English languages and cultures are of equal importance, and heaven for a child who wants to be encouraged to think and discuss and experiment rather than regurgitate facts. Not good if you need the reassurance of endless public exams and certainly no preparation for 11+, 13+ or GCSEs (except English lang and lit). Not a sporty school or a competitive school. Each child challenged to improve from their own baseline and they all seem to want to rise to the challenge, making the most of London, of each other and of themselves.

École Française Jacques Prévert

59 Brook Green, London W6 7BE

Ages 4-11 **Pupils** 260

Fees: £6,520 – £7,277 pa

020 7602 6871
www.ecoleprevert.org.uk

Director: Since 2016, Delphine Gentil, who was a head for 10 years in a country school in France before applying to the French authorities to be moved to Jacques Prevert. She is in London with her two children, who attend the Lycée Charles de Gaulle, and her husband commutes regularly from France. She is sporty and cycles and swims regularly. Cheerful, enthusiastic and clearly hardworking, she is thrilled to be in London and hopes to extend the minimum three year contract (maximum allowed by the French state is five years).

She is enamoured by the greater freedom she has in England regarding the curriculum, the budget choices and the collaborative work between London's French schools. More pastoral care, more awareness of the need to support pupils with SEN (her special area of interest) and improved English curriculum have been her particular input to the school in her short tenure. Excellent Ofsted report reflects her efforts. Parents say she is 'excellent' and 'respected by staff, parents and teachers', although some parents also bemoaned the turnover of heads imposed by the French department of education. Parents praised 'the great lengths she goes to, to make sure pupils acquire diverse experiences rather than just learning about things "the French way", including supporting teachers' projects such as going to the opera in Holland Park, going to the Hindu temple in London, getting out to see art and theatre, bringing in experts from other cultures'.

Entrance: Admission at all times of the year, not academically selective, priority given to children from French schools (either in France or abroad). French aptitude test if pupils are not from a French school and are over 6 years old, to ensure they will be able to access the curriculum, though children can join the infant section without knowing any French. Some 80 per cent French pupils and a few British, Turkish, Canadian etc. British families choose it if they live locally and want a reasonably priced small independent school (all the scooters parked up showed evidence of locally living pupils and a sustainable travel plan). Means-tested bursaries available to French citizens.

Exit: Pupils mostly expect to move on to the nearby French Lycée (which remains the parents' main choice with a number of pupils joining the International Section if their English is good enough – all applicants for IS got places recently). It used to be a feeder school to the Lycée, but a secondary school place there is no longer guaranteed. If not, then they might choose the newer Winston Churchill school in Wembley or other French schools. A couple each year to English schools – Francis Holland, for example – though parents aware that they will get little, if any, advice on transfers to to non-French schools.

Remarks: The school follows the French curriculum entirely; half staff brought in from the French authorities, so they are French 'fonctionnaires', and half the staff are locally employed. The head has managed to bring about some changes thanks to good resources – interactive whiteboards and updated classrooms to make the most of the small, awkwardly shaped rooms in the 'charming and historic' red-brick house facing Brook Green in Hammersmith. Parents appreciate the setting, 'leafy and facing the green and in a lovely part of London'. Two sets of stairs (one for going up and one for coming down), a tiny playground, canteen in the basement with good quality (mostly organic) food made from scratch on the premises. Lunch menu published weekly, though kids bring in packed lunch on Wednesday when they all have half day.

The school has been updating its IT provision – 70 new iPads to back up the small suite of computers in the well-stocked basement library. Enthusiastic French librarian brings in guest authors and teaches library skills. Pupils are encouraged to borrow from both the French and the English libraries. Emphasis on rote learning and neatness, with a strict French national curriculum to follow and emphasis on reading and writing only after year 2. Before then, plenty of work on fine and gross motor skills, language acquisition and memory. Specialist teachers for English and music.

Four hours a week of English work with English teachers, who follow an adapted curriculum with differentiated content and teaching according to pupils' level of English. If a pupil comes in with no French (one of the 20 per cent non French pupils, for example), they are given extra support in French. One parent told us that 'at the end of year show you can't hear their English accent or know whose mother tongue is English'. However, parents pointed out that this is French school, not a bilingual school, so all English teaching is a bonus. Pupils seem to reach a surprisingly high level of English thanks to some inspirational English teaching – quite a few pupils named English as their favourite subject (though science and lunch time followed closely on our straw poll). French parents said that English tends to be the main language in the playground (helped by playground assistants speaking English). That, together with PE and science often taught in English, helps their children acquire really fluent English and become truly bilingual; all of the pupils we spoke to slipped easily from one language to another. Parents and the head are aware of the 'challenge of a good level of English instruction in a French school'. The very much improved English teaching and newly developed English curriculum was raised by most of parents as being a real asset now, achieved by no longer requiring these English teachers to be bilingual and therefore having a greater choice of teachers. Parents said 'the quality of instruction is superb', giving as an example the fact that this small school had several pupils who came in the top one per cent of 30,000 French students in an international maths competition.

Lunch playtime either in the small playground or opposite in Brook Green, sports at local centre include swimming

E

as well as rock climbing, ice skating and rugby, alternating between years and terms. Littlest ones have gym in school hall. Dedicated music room and teacher who helps pull together end of year show and Christmas choral performance. Some art by class teachers enriched by visiting artists who help on projects and for inspiration. Thanks to increased interest in supporting diversity by the current head, there are pupils on a register with different levels of educational support – some with in school and in class differentiation and awareness, some with outside support, families frequently using French speech and language and other therapists. The odd pupil with a teaching assistant (paid for by parents). Building totally unsuitable for anyone who can't manage the many stairs.

E

The head is very keen to work on pupils' well-being, since she 'can see how pressurised both they and their parents are, living and working in London'. She has introduced workshops looking at mental health and self-esteem, and 'who they are as a group and how to behave in a group', with lectures and training by a psychotherapist who works with pupils, parents and teachers. Pupils are an enthusiastic bunch, wanting to share their love of the school – 'I love everything' repeated by several pupils we spoke to. If they had come from schools in France, they appreciated the art and music and sport, which don't happen much in France. If they had come from English schools, they liked the clear rules and purpose. Working parents also appreciate pre- and post-school care in morning club from 8am onwards ('my child just loves morning club,' said more than one parent) and after school in clubs and then daycare until 5pm.

In many families both parents work, but they are very involved in this close-knit school – either on the management committee or in the PTA, or as class representatives, meeting three times a year to discuss class issues. They help to run the many subsidised extracurricular clubs, taking pupils to outside school clubs, organising rotas and finding leaders to teach, for example, coding, football, karate, chess, zumba, art, cooking. The school management board appoints the local staff who are not appointed by the French government. Parents can see the head informally, as she is at the school gates each morning and evening, or by email or appointment. Head regularly meets with 13 other French curriculum schools in London and they share good practice and joint training.

Parents all mentioned the 'outstanding value for money' aspect of the school – 'much more reasonably priced than other London private schools, and one of the cheapest French schools in London too'. But they also all raised the fact that pupils 'feel looked after and loved, in an environment where they are safe and taken care of'.

EIFA International School

36 Portland Place, London W1B 1LS

Ages 2–16 **Pupils** 310

Fees: £18,150 – £22,500 pa

020 7637 5351
www.eifaschool.com

Executive Head: Since September 2018, co-founder Isabelle Faulkner, Quebec lawyer and English solicitor, has two children, one in university and the youngest finishing his IB diploma.

Head of school since September 2018 is Françoise Zurbach, who has been teacher, pedagogical counsellor, and head of school in France and London for more than 20 years. With a French father and English mother, she spent her first 10 years at an English school in Montreal, moving to France and continuing her education in the French system. She spent 20 years teaching in a small French primary school, moving to head Wix primary in London in 2013.

Academic matters: Nursery children in Little EIFA follow the EYFS, taught in French and English; therefore children learn literacy and reading at an earlier age than would be the case in a traditional French setting. Little EIFA offers flexible part-time hours. Primary students follow the French national curriculum using a bilingual French-English model. Each year group (two form entry in most years) has a Francophone (and French-qualified) teacher as well as a native-speaking English qualified teacher, who plan jointly and teach different parts of the programme in both languages, creating a completely bilingual learning environment for every year group.

In the senior school, years 7-9 continue with French curriculum (taught in both languages). In year 10 students may take the diplôme national du brevet as well as follow the IGCSE subjects now that the school has been authorised by Cambridge Exams and Edexcel (68 per cent A*-C/9-4 in 2018). Senior school staff bring solid international school experience and a good overall understanding of the various curricula – English national curriculum, international curricula and French programmes. School benchmarks student learning via French standardised tests and is inspected by both Ofsted and the IEN (Inspecteur de l'Education Nationale Française).

As the school has 'homologue' status with the French Education Ministry, French and English teachers must be qualified and hold recognised credentials. One parent of a very bright child was effusive about the way he is challenged academically. School engages specialist teachers for children with learning challenges for those who need additional support; there is no cost to the parents for this. Students who are not yet fluent in English or French may also be expected to take lessons with language teachers.

Games, options, the arts: More on offer than in a typical French school. After-school activities are offered by teachers with a special talent or interest, as well as external providers. A range of musical instruments and ensembles including rock bands; activities such as rugby, football, capoira (Brazilian martial arts), ballet, yoga, language clubs, IT coding; a few parents mentioned a creative writing course and one teenage boy refreshingly told us it is his favourite activity; homework club every day. Some parents see it as a way to extend their children's exposure to French or English. Year 2 pupils were very proud to be the winners of a recent European film competition for the animated movie they created.

Early morning drop-off and after-school care till 6pm are available for Little EIFA children; this is convenient for working parents, but also those whose older children may stay after school for club activities. Extracurricular activities incur additional fees but no one we spoke to grumbled about that: they were very happy with the range of activities on offer. There are opportunities to take part in sports competitions and tournaments with other French and international schools in London. Parents told us of a trip to Brussels where the students had a hand in crafting an EU law on the environment.

Background and atmosphere: The co-founders, plus their fellow investors who form the governing board, have had good support from the local Howard de Walden Estate – major landowners in London W1 – who were keen to see EIFA on the menu of international schools available to the local Marylebone gentry.

The combination of the strategic planning and foresight of the founders and this collaborative partnership with HdW Estates has enabled this school to secure two impressive buildings for their prep and senior schools. Originally conceived as a prep/primary school in 2013, but parents wanted their children to continue to be educated bilingually, and so a senior school opened and moved into its own premises in 2016.

Little EIFA and the prep school are in a large late Georgian building in Portland Place. Little EIFA is based in a well-organised maze of rooms in the basement level with enclosed outdoor space exclusively for the youngest children. On the ground floor are the reception children and the library, stocked with 5,000 books – half French, half English (on the day we visited full of relaxed but fully engaged children with their noses in books), in bright rooms with original period features such as lofty Wedgwood-blue painted ceilings decorated with crown moulding and fireplaces. Other primary classes perch higher up on top floors with large windows that brighten the rooms year round.

The senior school is a short walk away on quiet side street with a nicely refurbished building that contains bright classrooms fully equipped with all the requisites – science lab, study hub, an amazing large art studio with walls of windows on two sides, and an inviting canteen that serves as a multi-purpose space. This room features a huge painting of a London cityscape with silhouettes of children in the foreground, donated by a parent and painted by South American artist Walter Blanco as part of a school event. Children's work gets equal prominence, and there is also a collage of maps of all the countries the children come from featured on another wall. There is a clean, uncluttered feel despite the ample careful displays of student work and art. Daily recreation and breaks take place at nearby Regent's Park. Students use the library at the prep school or visit nearby Marylebone Library.

EIFA is an urban school; parents say that some families come expecting more, but what makes it all worthwhile is the positive EIFA school culture – that is the major draw for families we spoke to.

Pastoral care, well-being and discipline: Parents tell us that EIFA has a strong sense of community and this is part of the attraction. The diversity of families helps to create an ambiance where acceptance and respect are the norm. The school is young, and there is a definite 'pioneer spirit' among those families who joined in the early years and who speak with pride about what the school community has created. Communications are good and parents feel well informed and able to approach the school teachers or administration whenever needed. Senior and junior school parents describe the teachers as versatile, devoted, nurturing and impressive. The kids we saw in the classrooms, study hubs and library looked happy and were welcoming and at ease with their visitor. Some parents attribute the good behaviour to the school's small size. No uniforms except for PE and games classes. Active parents' association regarded as refreshing by many who find this parent engagement a welcome change from the norm at other French schools. It's also an important support that can help to integrate parents new to London. Meeting minutes and photos of activities are on the website.

Pupils and parents: The increasing number of French-medium schools on offer in London has enlarged parental choice; those selecting EIFA want what it says on the tin – an international school with a French bilingual programme. Over 40 nationalities; the French, Americans and Canadians are the main groups but there are many bicultural, bilingual families of mixed nationalities; some local residents, others expats. A few French families seeking the dream life in 'France's sixth city – London' (with perhaps one parent commuting to France for work). Though some of these families have returned to France, the school has not yet seen the impact of Brexit and continues to grow. In many respects a 'neighbourhood school' and many children walk or ride their scooters, but some travel longer distances – the school's outsourced school bus service covers to Highgate and Hampstead to the north, Notting Hill to the west, and Fulham to the south west. Parents do not seem to mind having play dates scattered across London.

Entrance: This young school, which has only recently opened a secondary department, does not yet have waiting lists for the senior school. It is currently relatively non-selective, with admission is based on completing a straightforward application form and providing school reports. Does not require fluency in English or French for entry up to year 8.

Exit: Parents say that some families who aspire to the French Bacc opt to move at 11 to the bilingual school in Kentish Town or one of the Lycées, and some, particularly those whose parents are not French speakers, transfer to British independent schools, but an increasing number of families are choosing to stay on for senior school as it introduces IGCSEs.

Money matters: International school prices are to be expected here. The school has needs-assessed financial aid. Low student-teacher ratio (6-1), and since extras such as English or French language support and special needs support are not extra, the fees are competitive with those of other international schools. Lunch is included in the school fees and is compulsory unless the child has dietary restrictions. It is prepared by outsourced caterers, and is tasty by all accounts (and our own sampling).

Remarks: This is a niche school with high aspirations that ticks the right boxes for families who appreciate a certain discipline associated with French education (we saw lots of immaculate handwriting), and the opportunity to acquire or maintain French language fluency, but who at the same time like the quirkiness of an international school that draws on global themes and topics to enhance the students' learning and world view. The principal was quick to say, 'EIFA is not a French school, it is a bilingual (French/English) international school.' The rich displays of African masks made in art classes, green Irish shamrocks to celebrate St Patrick's Day, student rehearsals for Wizard of Oz, beautifully written essays on Macbeth and even stir-fry chicken noodles for lunch serve to illustrate her point. Worth a look.

Eleanor Palmer Primary School

Lupton Street, London NW5 2JA

Ages 3–11 **Pupils** 239

020 7485 2155
www.eleanorpalmer.camden.sch.uk

Head: Since 2003, Kate Frood MA,OBE (50s). Knew she wanted to be a teacher from the age of 8 and started her career doing just that at nearby Fleet Primary in 1983. Aside from a four-year stint as a maths consultant to Islington Council, has taught in Camden ever since. Trained when child-centred learning (as opposed to testing) was the focus, and this has remained fundamental to her approach. In order 'to keep her hand in and share ideas', continues to teach year 6 maths. 'She really knows what kids can do and – more importantly – what they can't,' said a mother. 'She makes sure every child is well-prepared for secondary.' Liked and respected by parents. 'She's a brilliant head, incredibly good behind the scenes and incredibly forward thinking,' said one. 'Problems are dealt with before they turn into problems.' Awarded the OBE for 'services to education' in 2014. One daughter who attended Camden School for Girls.

Entrance: Hugely oversubscribed, with about eight applicants per place for a single reception class of 30. Proximity is key and there's been much tut-tutting about families renting to squeeze through the gates. (Camden now scrutinises applicants carefully, particularly looking for those who own or let another address locally.) Full-time Camden-funded nursery of 26, but bagging a place here does not guarantee admission into reception (children have been rejected in the past).

E

Exit: Pupils here tend to go on to local community secondaries, generally the cluster round Dartmouth Park – William Ellis, Acland Burghley and Parliament Hill – plus some to Camden School for Girls. A few, too, to selective state schools, and a further sprinkling to independents. By and large, however, this is a parent body committed to state schooling.

Remarks: Housed in a medley of low-built mid-20th-century buildings on a reasonably spacious, but very urban, site, the school has well-cared for and imaginatively used grounds, including an adventure playground and colourful entrance ornamented with art, fish, running water – and a prominent plaque declaring 'racism is unacceptable'.

Academically, the school falls firmly into the Outstanding category, with high standards in the core and a rich offering well beyond. Heavily committed to topic-based study, with themes such as World War 2 or Victorian childhood taught using imaginative links between history, geography, art and literacy. 'We see learning as an adventure,' says the head, an adventure explored through plenty out-of-school visits and and in-house contributions from storytellers, artists and experts.

The school has both a national reputation for maths teaching and a highly-praised literacy strategy. Children read daily for half an hour and end every afternoon with a class story. Great emphasis, too, placed on the best children's literature, with new titles added regularly and a handy booklet of recommendations. Year 5 studies and performs a Shakespeare play. French for all from year 3, taught by the classroom teacher. Homework (including daily reading and times tables) from the start, and ICT well embedded, with access to a myriad of laptops and iPads.

Eleanor Palmer is a 'teaching school' – one of just 350 in the country – teaching teachers how to teach. This, according to parents, can have both its upside and its down. 'It means,' said one mother, 'the staff are young and hugely energetic, willing to work after school and at weekends, but some are also pretty inexperienced.' Head, however, tends to restrict the rawest recruits to the younger years.

The ethos of the school has been shaped by the work of Carol Dweck – whose perspective is that effort and persistence are what really count. 'This teaches children to see mistakes and failures as positives and makes for a very energetic and inclusive culture,' says the head. So, no star charts, no ability sets; instead, each child is encouraged to achieve their personal best, with marking emphasising steps forward rather than what's gone wrong.

Special needs is led by the head, aided, in school, by support teachers and learning support assistants, and, out of it, by an educational psychologist and occupational therapist. Parents feel the SEN offering has improved in recent years. 'The head is very responsive and things like touch typing are now standard.'

Two hours of PE weekly, with a dedicated sports co-ordinator mentoring both those who struggle and those who excel, as well as arranging participation for all in out-of-school tournaments. Plenty of alternatives, too, to conventional team sports, with dance and skipping workshops, fencing and taekwondo sessions. The school is also 'very committed' to walking. Nearby Parliament Hill used for class activities and sports days.

Specialist music teacher visits twice weekly, overseeing a 'strings programme', which provides all pupils from the age of 8 with (free) group tuition by a specialist in violin or cello. Multiple opportunities to perform in concerts and musicals.

Head very much of the '50 things to do before' philosophy, and her objective is that all leavers should have completed a substantial tick list of activities, from growing their own vegetables to visiting a farm. Trips, trips, trips make the most of the wealth of galleries and museums a bus ride away, as well as of opportunities further afield (everyone gets four residential stays, ranging from camping in Epping Forest to a year 7 week at a Michael Morpurgo's Farm for City Children.)

As the leader of a 'multi-cultural community', the head has taken up the option to skip the daily act of Christian worship. Instead, the red-letter days of all the major religions are covered in assemblies and younger pupils are taught philosophy by trained philosophy teachers. The school is also a level 2 Unicef 'rights respecting' school, which entails listening to children's views and including them in such decisions as the fairness of team selection. Every class draws up a charter based on agreed rights, and then lists how adults and children will respect these. 'Once behaviour is seen in this way there is little need for rules,' says the head. Local councillors, politicians and lawyers, too, are invited in to teach pupils about their rights and responsibilities as citizens. Charity link to school in Sierra Leone.

Kentish Town is more affluent than formerly, particularly after a recent influx of French émigrés, and the popularity of the school means the sharp elbowed have gained ground in recent years, but you'll still find a good cross section of traditional locals and recent refugees alongside the organic set. About 20 per cent receive free school meals, a national average, but well below what might be expected for the location. As the head concedes, this can be a positive, as those from more affluent backgrounds provide 'a critical mass of high-achieving, motivated, liberal, middle class kids – so all my working class or refuge kids get caught up.' Parents, too, feel the balance works ('I think it still has that community school feeling,' said one) and are full of praise for its warm and nurturing atmosphere. 'Our children have been extremely happy here – and very well educated.'

The Ellen Wilkinson School for Girls

Queen's Drive, London W3 0HW

Ages 11–18 **Pupils** 1,350 **Sixth form** 270

020 8752 1525
www.ellenwilkinson.ealing.sch.uk

Headteacher: Since 2014, Rachel Kruger B Mus Ed, B Mus Hons, BSc (pure maths), MBA (late 40s). She arrived here in 2012 as deputy head, and taught maths and music. In 2013 she became acting head and took over as permanent head in March 2014.

Originally from Stellenbosch in South Africa, Ms Kruger studied Bloemhof Girls' High School in Stellenbosch. She has spent the last 15 years in schools in Ealing. Prior to starting at Ellen Wilkinson, she taught maths for 11 years at co-ed comprehensive Dormers Wells High School, and music at Uxbridge High School for two years before that. She now feels she has come full circle, relishing the atmosphere of this all girls' school. She is clear about the benefits of single sex education for girls. 'I love seeing the girls in year 7 playing hide and seek,' she says. 'I doubt you would find that in a mixed school.' The women in the senior leadership team all went to girls' schools.

Modelling behaviour and expectation for her pupils is key for Ms Kruger. You can immediately see why she is hugely popular with parents, staff and girls. Wreathed in smiles and generous with her warm greetings to everyone she passes, she exudes positive energy. 'Everyone respects her,' said our guide. 'The girls benefit from her warmth,' commented a dad. She combines a tough, focussed approach with the soft femininity of the floral print dress she was wearing when we met. Just being in her company makes one feel that anything is possible and nothing is too much of a problem. Open and relaxed in conversation, she is easy to talk to and parents warmly appreciate her approachability and her ability to listen and deal with things quickly and effectively. They describe her as 'a good leader' and 'effective manager'.

She clearly loves her job and puts her heart into it, is active in the head teachers' group among Ealing schools, and receives lots of support through mentoring from other female leaders, as well as giving support in return. She knows the girls, and unusually for a head of a busy secondary school, still finds the time to teach maths. A love of learning is one of her defining qualities. A trained opera singer, she is currently studying for a law degree. No plans to change career, however. 'I just want to keep learning,' she twinkles, 'and it has the added bonus of setting an example to the girls: they can see my disappointment if I don't do as well as I would like and they witness me striving to do better.' Parents remarked on her gutsiness in singing a solo at a winter concert – 'if the girls are expected to do this, so should I be.'

Academic matters: In 2018, 30 per cent of all GCSE grades were A*-A/9-7, and 71 per cent got 9-4 in both maths and English. English, sciences, languages (including Arabic and Latin) all strong. RE is a noticeably popular subject at which girls do well here. A specialist maths and science college since 2002, a healthy proportion of the girls take maths, biology and chemistry A level. Further maths, psychology and philosophy are recent additions to the A level choices. In 2018, 47 per cent A*-B and 23 per cent A*/A grades at A level. Several vocational options at level 2 and 3, including business studies, and health and social care. Suggestion in some quarters that sixth form is less stimulating and a few start to look elsewhere after GCSE. Lots of setting – maths and English from year 7, science and languages from year 8. Mandarin now offered as part of the curriculum from year 8. School runs maths and science taster sessions and master classes for feeder primary schools, with excited pupils trying out practical experiments in real science labs.

Food tech, product design as well as textiles offered at GCSE. The latter particularly popular. We saw examples of a project on headpieces in Alice in Wonderland. One year 11 pupil won an award with the London College of Fashion and went on to work with print designers in East London. Lots of extracurricular academic clubs, including Latin.

Busy careers library, particularly well used by years 9 and 11; 'we're giving support with careers a lot, but apprenticeships too,' says the careers officer.

A number of students need learning support and are taken out of class for one-to-one sessions. Those on EHC plans tend to be girls with a physical disability who need practical help. Lots of careful differentiation takes place in the classroom, we are assured, and careful monitoring as to who needs more support. 'We are gradually moving this support away from the just the SEND department and giving the support in the class room,' says Ms Kruger. One full time SENCo, one deputy and one EAL teacher. Higher level teaching assistants and several other teaching assistants in both SEND and EAL departments. Some 70 per cent of students speak English as a second language, supported by a strong EAL team and school, deservedly proud that the results of the EAL students are well above national averages. Value added scores strong, among the best in the borough.

Games, options, the arts: Frequent drama productions as well as concerts, jazz band and string quartet. All girls do drama in years 7 and 8 and a fair number continue to GCSE. The shiny polished Victorian main hall is used for annual theatrical productions as well as concerts and there is a good sized drama studio. A number of successful musicals are preformed each year, including Oliver!, Little Shop of Horrors and Les Misérables and they performed the Rocky Horror Picture Show at a local theatre. 'The standard is professional,' observed more than one parent. Music is a passion of Ms Kruger's, and she encourages lots of concerts throughout the year, the winter concert being a particular highlight, with other different kinds of opportunities for the girls to perform and develop a musical interest.

PE facilities have been transformed by the recent addition of a new sports hall. Successful basketball and netball teams; girls here also play football, run cross-country and our guide plays handball for Ealing. School enters teams for a number of competitions, tournaments and fixtures against other schools. Minor sports clubs too, including trampoline, badminton, and ultimate frisbee. They recently received funding from London Youth Rowing and were awarded Middlesex Education Provider of the Year for tennis. Lots of outdoor space, with grass and all weather hockey pitches as well as tennis and netball courts enabling the school to host a number of competitions across the borough. Ellen Wilkinson prides itself on being a 'sports leadership academy', one of very few schools in London to have this status and based on the fact that the school offers the Sports Leadership Award at both level 1 and 2. Perhaps more importantly, our guide confirmed that it's 'cool to be sporty'.

Three large and spacious art studios, bursting with industry and colour and situated around a green grassy area, are an inspiring place to explore different styles for budding creatives. Art GCSE results are good, and A level results, though less consistent, are solid.

Extracurricular clubs range from sporting and music to academic and learning support. However at lunch time girls can also choose to do a variety of activities from tapestry to debating and dominoes to eco learning. It's up to the girls how much they get involved.

Background and atmosphere: Named for the Mancunian Labour MP, Ellen Wilkinson, who led the Jarrow March in 1936 and became the first female Minister for Education in 1945, the school was founded in 1974 and is still the only all girls comprehensive school in Ealing. With nearly 1,400 pupils it is a large school.

First impressions as you arrive in the new foyer are of a thoroughly modern, state of the art school, with clean lines, minimal decoration, and monochrome appearance punctuated with bursts of colour – a fresh bowl of flowers strategically positioned, for example. The new building, which houses senior staff offices, administration and conference rooms, as well as the entrance hall, is replete with white stone floors, glass walls and Perspex chairs. The smell of fresh paint blends in with the scent of freshly cut flowers. The library – also recently finished – is designed in the same style, and on a clear winter's day, when the trees are bare, there is a clear line of vision from one building to the other.

In between, however, there is a hotch-potch of different styles: Victorian, polished wood floors and high ceilings, lined with gold leaf embossed honours boards, and a tranquil Japanese garden surrounded by 60s two storey blocks, where the girls can enjoy lunch in the warmer months.

The grounds feel extensive with a number of netball courts as well as 'the field' – a wonderful large green space, only spoilt, when we visited, by an unsightly amount of litter. School already onto this with plans to fence the field off. This is where the girls do athletics and can sit outside and eat lunch.

E

New girls in year 7 are given a map when they arrive and then packed off on a treasure hunt to acquaint themselves with the territory.

There is a distinct professionalism about everything here. A tightness. Things are done well. Crisp. Effective. Even the uniform has smartened up with crisp white shirts beneath their maroon v necks.

Pastoral care, well-being and discipline: An area that has vastly improved under Rachel Kruger's compassionate but firm leadership, confirmed by all the parents we spoke to. There was a lot of low level disruption that needed tackling. Part of this was to revamp the pastoral team, another to ask the students to write their own code of conduct. 'A strict but comfortable school, everyone is kept in order but we don't feel pressurised, we understand the rules are for our benefit', confided our guides. One parent commented on how swiftly a problem between a teacher and her daughter was resolved by the head of year. There are systems in place and they seem to work. Staff work hard with parents, and communication is improving, we were told. Fathers attend workshops on sex education, all parents now want to get involved.

'We help everyone to find their own way through acceptance; kindness is a big word here, ultimately it's their choice whether to do the right thing,' says Rachel Kruger. Politeness and good manners are essential requirements here. Swearing at a member of staff will result in exclusion. 'We will do everything we can, use as many resources as possible before permanently excluding,' assures Ms Kruger. Pastoral systems include peer mentoring – both internal and external – and the five star canteen with a focus on hygiene and health is part of the campaign against any kind of food disorders. Ms Kruger acknowledges the challenge of gender identity. 'They are legally women until they are 18,' she says firmly, 'and therefore can remain in EWS, but they get fantastic support' from Gendered Intelligence – a community based project that delivers educational programmes as well as offering advice and counselling. Ms Kruger puts safeguarding before everything, something that was reflected in the recent safeguarding audit, which was outstanding.

Pupils and parents: Most parents and daughters here made a conscious decision to choose Ellen Wilkinson above any other school. The odd pupil has chosen it because someone in her wider family has been here, many because it is a real community school with a local feel. Some teachers are former pupils. One parent said her daughter chose it 'because of the extracurricular clubs, diverse cultures and because it's sporty.' Most like the all girls atmosphere, but this is definitely not a religious school. One Muslim parent said her two priorities were that her daughter be 'happy and safe'; Ellen Wilkinson fits the bill.

A genuinely relatively balanced mix of cultures and religious groups with about 20 per cent white British, 30 per cent Asian, 20 per cent black and 20 per cent Arabic, others include Japanese (some choose this over the local Japanese school), Chinese, Polish and other European. Sixty-six different languages are spoken in the school. Although in some families the mother might speak very limited English (though the father's English is fluent), 'all groups integrate', affirmed everyone we spoke to; there are no cliques based on race.

They all share a common interest in developing the confidence and aspirations of all the girls. 'They will be the leaders of tomorrow', affirms Ms Kruger. Tolerant, broadminded, self aware and thoroughly 21st century, our guides looked slightly baffled at our questions about diversity. Girls here are proud of their school and have a strong sense of giving something back and contributing to society.

Entrance: Always oversubscribed, with over 500 applicants for 216 places. Priority given to looked-after children, siblings, children of teachers at the school and those with specific medical or social needs. Then distance to the school is the deciding factor – currently around 1.5 miles.

About 40 girls from other schools join the sixth form each year, with a baseline of 5+ 9-4 GCSE grades for A level courses, including 6s in their A level subjects. Those who don't make the grade can take two or three BTec courses.

Exit: The majority go on to university. Large numbers to the London colleges (UCL, Kings, Queen Mary's, SOAS and Goldsmith all popular destinations) to read a range of courses from biomedical science and chemical engineering to photography and Japanese. The maths and science specialism here is clearly effective, as most go on to study STEM related degrees. One off to study psychology at Cambridge in 2018, and two medics.

Around 40 per cent depart after GCSEs to sixth form colleges elsewhere (eg Harris Westminster, William Morris, St Dominic's in Harrow and Hammersmith Academy), a few to further education colleges.

Remarks: A school with history, substance and a wealth of experience that is more than keeping up with the times and has a refreshingly modern and progressive outlook. Under its current leadership, a warm wind blows through its wide corridors which, together with high expectations and standards, makes for a thoroughly healthy and successful institution.

Eltham College

Linked with Eltham College Junior School

Grove Park Road, London SE9 4QF

Ages 11–18 **Pupils** 679 **Sixth form** 228 (67 girls)

Fees: £17,775 pa

020 8857 1455
www.elthamcollege.london

Headmaster: Since 2014, Guy Sanderson MA (Oxon) PGCE (40s). Studied PPE and then modern history at Trinity College, Oxford. Having started out as a stockbroker in the City, he followed this with a stint at the UN High Commission for Refugees in Pakistan and Afghanistan before teaching at a series of academic independents – St Paul's, Whitgift, City of London Boys' School and Reigate Grammar, where he rose to head of sixth form and deputy head.

His office, newly decorated in tasteful grey with fresh flowers and framed photography of the boys in action, is a small sign of his modernising intent and ambition to make the school one of the country's best independent schools. However, it is important to him to be able to do this in his own time in his own way and not to be straitjacketed by targets. The parents we heard from seemed pleased the school is being given something of a shake-up. One confided: 'the new head is clearly very driven and personally career oriented. From my perspective this is no bad thing. If he does well it will mean that the school has done well.' And: 'Determined to improve the school's academic standing, modern in his approach... he knows the pupils and is interested in them individually.' 'He is not, however, afraid to say no and stand steadfast by his principles.'

In tune with this dynamic image, Mr Sanderson tweets encouragement to the far-flung corners of Elthamians' daily activities. Boys will find his door open at lunch times and he's delighted to find they drop in to suggest ideas for new clubs or initiatives. Year 7 boys are invited to his office on their birthday for a doughnut. In answer to our question as to whether there should be a head girl as well as head boy, he says that it is simply a case of the best person for the job and in the case of this year that means there is. With a wife who is a FTSE 100 headhunter it's a topic of debate.

Mr Sanderson has relocated from rural Sussex with his wife and three children. A keen skier and open water swimmer, for the past two summers he's swam the Bosphorus. The family lives in a house overlooking the playing fields, together with the chickens, but not the pigs, from Sussex.

Academic matters: In 2018, 82 per cent of grades were A*-A/7-9 at I/GCSE; 62 per cent A*/A at A level (90 per cent A*/B). Senior curriculum wise very trad but with a careful eye to future global employment prospects. More academic subjects have been added and the less academic such as sports studies removed. Timetabling isn't completed until each boy's preferences are accommodated.

Everyone does single sciences at IGCSE and the short-course RS. A Level additions are economics, psychology, government and politics, pure and further maths, unusually geology (a 30 year tradition) and recently introduced computing. Maths is the most popular A level and taken as an IGCSE. All those from the top sets taking maths early have consistently gained A* and mathematicians throughout the school regularly compete nationally. Years 8 and 9 have been finalists in UKMT for the past three years. There are very strong student numbers in economics: currently the second largest A level cohort. A glittering array of highlights from the science department. The physics department is recognised as a centre of excellence by the Institute of Physics with stellar grades; most recently a chemist was in receipt of the prestigious Roentgenium award; year 10s were also finalists in the Royal Society of Chemistry's challenge in Kent. The school regularly produces Arkwright scholars who go on to study engineering at the country's most desirable destinations. One Eltham geologist scored the highest geology A level mark in the country, losing a mere four marks.

French, German, Mandarin and Spanish are introduced gradually over the first three years with boys choosing a minimum of two. The head has appointed a new head of classics, introduced ancient Greek to complement Latin and says all language appointments will be either Oxbridge graduates and/or native speakers. Italian is available and Russian off timetable. Whilst French holds its own with several studying French alongside their chosen degree subject at university, German is the second most popular language. Of nine recent Mandarin GCSE passes, only one was a native speaker, though A level Mandarin is only available off timetable to native speakers.

Class sizes average 22 but with smaller teaching sets in all languages, maths, science and some creative subjects. A quarter of teaching staff have been at the school for over 10 years but the head says this is a changing picture. Keen to develop staff, he devolves leadership, empowering them to run with their own project ideas if it will benefit the school. One of our guides said of the teachers: 'They're all passionate about their subjects; lessons are very interactive'. The head tells us of a lesson he witnessed recently where the boys were studying glaciation using edible food stuffs. Parents are aware of teaching standards being consciously raised. For the most able, there is a new head of academic scholarship running a programme of debating, lectures from outside speakers and encouraging boys to prepare and deliver papers to their peers.

There is a full-time learning support teacher. All new pupils are screened on entry for possible difficulties. Around 10 per cent with identified SEN needs, the majority with dyslexia but a few with ADHD, ASD or communication issues. The school says that the majority of cases are quite 'mild' and most support is within lessons. A dyslexic pupil described the school as: 'Nice atmosphere. Positive, helpful teachers'.

Despite the hard-working atmosphere and desire to up the academic ante parents do not feel there is too much pressure – the extracurricular provides relief from academic work, year round rather than annual testing is a relief, with not too much holiday homework and sufficient time left within the year for revision.

Pupils are carefully prepared for university exits, including a new focus on US universities. A pathways programme ensures pupils are en route and prepared for possible careers, making use of the network of Eltham alumni for work experience placements.

Games, options, the arts: No doubt that almost everyone is sporty but that seems to be mostly by dint of encouragement and breadth of opportunity. Rugby is the school's big thing: England U16 champions for two consecutive years, winner of the U15 Kent 7s this year and 13 county players. Winners of U15 and U16 county cups in hockey and cricket. Players of international standing are in good company, with a couple representing England in fencing, a GB skier and three England internationals and last year's U13 England chess champion. Coaches are often national players but the head stresses to them that they must have an interest in teaching not just the elite but 'the grass roots'.

Plenty of opportunities to try new things such as climbing or sailing. For those with a lighter interest there are clubs and societies for table tennis, basketball and pilates. With regards to having a go, the school aims for all boys to represent the school in an activity. Glad to see the girls as well as boys have a tug-of-war in the annual house competition.

The school is proud of its musicians who achieve exceptionally well academically with the last few years, consistently delivering an Oxbridge place or two. Around 65 per cent of pupils learn an instrument. One parent told us: 'I was particularly touched to see my child play a string instrument in his first term as we are not a particularly musical family.' Choral singing is a high point. Ensembles, choirs and orchestras play across London. Recently parents were treated to performances at Ronnie Scott's, the Barbican, St John's Smith Square, the Royal Albert Hall and beneath the hull of the Cutty Sark.

This is the first school we've visited with its own art gallery. The Gerald Moore Gallery houses school and external exhibitions. The exhibitions assist students to achieve offers from top graphic design, fine art and architecture courses. All the art teachers and technicians are artists and pursue their own practices and an artist-in-residence has a studio within the department.

Drama is on the curriculum for all years 7 to 9 and is available at GCSE and A level. The drama department produces a major musical every year – recently Les Misérables with student-led orchestra. Students also directed, acted, managed and teched a production of Richard III. Those jaunting to Edinburgh for The Fringe were rewarded with 5* reviews in the national press for their performance of Sweeney Todd. Plenty of distinctions in LAMDA exams.

Clubs and societies often seem to be extending in tone but Dixieland band, 'magic: the gathering', slick sticks, run for fun, Fair Trade and Morris dancing caught our eye. Those looking forward to a far-flung expedition may need a head for heights with past destinations including Nepal and Borneo whilst students tackle D of E from bronze to gold.

Background and atmosphere: Originally founded as a boarding school for the sons of missionaries, boys attend chapel twice a week as part of a strong Christian tradition with caring for the community still an important part of the school's ethos. Since moving in 1912 to this elegant 18th century mansion with a columned entrance, surrounded by 70 acres of green fields, it has grown in size, stopped taking boarders and girls have been part of the sixth form since the 1970s. Despite the increase in size, boys and parents referred approvingly to the school so often as 'small' that we checked the pupil numbers. The atmosphere is peaceful but buzzy indoors and out; students engrossed in lessons or off to play sports with huge kitbags.

Apart from the elegance of Central Hall, now housing the humanities classrooms in style, with its beautiful wooden boards of Oxbridge scholars and charming sepia photographs of sports teams gone by, the school comprises a collection of blocks in various states of repair. The science block is so delightfully retro we expected to bump into the Enigma Machine at any moment. However, labs are being modernised and an imaginatively conceived £14m development project nearing completion is extending the sixth form centre out into the playing fields, mirroring the students' imminent transition to university, also providing new language classrooms, a new mathematics suite of classrooms and a well-being centre. The DT facilities comprise a series of large professional-looking workshops with a laser cutter, 3D printer and a CAD-cam suite. The library is large and well-resourced with books, journals or ebooks, with a separate sixth form area up a spiral staircase.

The school's most famous alumnus is Eric Liddell, the Olympic athlete who won gold in the 400m at the 1924 Paris Olympics, forever immortalised by Chariots of Fire, hence the namesake sports centre, which provides on-site indoor cricket nets, a 25 metre pool, dance studio and fitness suite. In addition £3.5m is earmarked to further develop the sports facilities including a new pavilion, second Astroturf and 4G rugby pitch.

We asked to meet a few sixth form girls, curious to hear about their experiences. Those joining from girls' schools spoke of wanting to find larger teaching groups for their A level subjects. Whilst all felt slightly nervous on arrival, they don't feel in a minority, as the numbers suggest. They spoke of finding the boys welcoming, the atmosphere competitive academically, offering them different points of view, but less 'cliquey' and more relaxed socially.

Will accept girls into year 7 (and year 3 in the junior school) from 2020, becoming co-educational throughout by 2024.

Pastoral care, well-being and discipline: The school as a whole receives glowing praise for its pastoral care, the front line being form tutors. One mother told us of the care and consideration her son received during a difficult time at home. Co-curricular clubs run pre- and post-school, whilst a breakfast club allows parents to dash for the commute. A careful and detailed anti-bullying policy and zero drug tolerance. Incidents are not unheard of but parents report that they are swiftly dealt with. A fairly strict, disciplined environment with quite a long list of sanctions available to teachers to keep efforts up to scratch academically.

The deputy head is the head of pastoral care. Parents universally praise pastoral care here, one going as far as to describe it as 'exceptional'. This is certainly one of the best resourced pastoral care teams we have encountered: two qualified nurses, a doctor, counsellor and two chaplains. Boys waved to the nurse during our tour. When we quizzed the head as to the school's consideration of the kind of mental health issues variously affecting girls and boys today he was engaged and had recently returned from a conference on the subject.

There is a recently appointed head of transition to ease in year 7s. Form tutors, the pastoral front line, are described as 'accessible and generally very quick to respond to any concerns' and now stay with boys for their lower school and then middle school years. Communication between school and home is felt to be excellent.

We raised the news stories still to be found on a Google search of the school concerning the conduct of two teachers. The incidents were before the current head's time and concerned activities outside of the school but have resulted in a review of safeguarding and DBS checking procedures for staff.

Pupils and parents: The majority of students come from within a five mile radius, taking in Blackheath, Greenwich, the Isle of Dogs and Surrey Quays but also south to Bromley, Chislehurst and Sidcup, Orpington, Farnborough and West Wickham. Far fewer with different languages spoken at home than we see in central London schools. A tiny few international students. Working parents are catered for: pupils could be in school from 8am purchasing breakfast in King George's Hall, whilst the library is open for after-school study until 5.30pm, not to mention myriad activities taking pupils until the end of the day, often with no extra cost. Parents were described to us as including 'multi-millionaires' and the 'down to earth'.

What kind of child would Eltham suit? Parents mention 'all-rounders' and 'bright, motivated, independent children who will rise to a challenge'. The head says there is no Eltham boy; it will simply appeal to those who want to make the most of opportunities.

Entrance: Academic standards are high and entrance is by selection based on academic merit and on an assessment of the pupil's likely positive contribution to the school. Everyone needs a good reference, and computer adaptive verbal and non-verbal reasoning is now a feature of testing at every stage. The majority of pupils come seamlessly through from the junior school and 40 to 50 external pupils join at 11+, with around five (including girls, from 2020) competing for every place. External candidates take entrance papers in English and maths. Those with SEN needs may be allocated additional time. New 11+ joiners hail mostly from local preps including: The Pointer School, Blackheath Prep, Breaside, Heath House and St Olave's but also Chislehurst C of E Primary. Only a few joining at 13+ but it is an increasingly competitive entry point. Candidates sit papers in English, maths and a modern foreign language or Latin.

External candidates to the sixth form take an exam and if successful are interviewed. In recent years girls have arrived from the local GDST schools and St Ursula's Convent, amongst others. Candidates sit papers in two subjects of their choice. Offers made are subject to a minimum of six 9-7 grades at GCSE including the four subjects of further study.

Exit: Almost all boys stay on to the sixth form. The trend has been for departing pupils to head for Exeter, York, Bristol, Warwick, Durham, Leeds, Southampton, Imperial and Loughborough, so one can be pretty confident of attaining Russell Group aspirations. Five to Oxbridge and seven medics in 2018.

Money matters: A generous number of scholarships on offer at each entry point, which could be for academic ability or music, sport, art and drama (16+ only) – the financial reward varying from the token to the quite substantial. Everyone sitting the entrance test will be considered for academic scholarships, with further requirements for music, art and sports scholars. Fewer than 10 per cent of pupils are in receipt of means-tested bursaries, which could range from a helping hand to 100 per cent of fees.

Remarks: With an energetic head on the case and money being spent in bringing the facilities up to scratch, it could be a wonderful place to find a niche and increasingly achieve great things: heading in a more academic direction than of late but still extremely sporty.

Eltham College Junior School

Linked with Eltham College

79

Mottingham Lane, London SE9 4RW

Ages 7–11 **Pupils** 229

Fees: £15,690 pa

020 8857 3457
www.elthamcollege.london

Master: Since 2010, Edmund Cavendish (50s) MA (Oxon) PGCE. Studied modern history at Queen's College, Oxford. Deputy head at the senior school for five years. Prior to this, he was head of history and then head of sixth form during 16 years at Ipswich School, following four years at Merchiston Castle School in Edinburgh. This junior school setting was new for Mr Cavendish, but he relishes the enthusiasm of the younger boys and feels his experience of the senior school – he still teaches the Oxbridge historians – is helpful in enabling him to bring the two schools together, very much a focus since the arrival of Mr Sanderson, the new head of the senior school. He dips in and out, ensuring he teaches something to each year so that he gets to know each boy. Another focus has been ensuring the stretching of the most able wherever their talents lie – this could be in the shape of elite coaching for the sporting or opening up the senior orchestras to junior musicians.

Parents say he is 'is a great champion of the traditions of the school' and 'I think the work he is doing on mental health is amazing and the implementations made mean a less stressful, more enjoyable schooling'. He lives close to the school, has been married for over 30 years and has two grown-up daughters, one working in Burma, the other for McKinsey, and two dogs that have as prominent billing in the framed photos in his office.

Entrance: Capped at 60 across three forms of 20 boys at 7+ entry and then rising to no more than 22 boys in a form for years 4-6. Candidates are assessed in maths and English, including an element of verbal reasoning and reading. Historically chances of getting in have been pretty good but applications are increasing. The same test subjects for entry at 8+, 9+ and 10+. Pupils mainly enter from local preps and pre-preps such as Babington House, Bickley Park, The Pointer School, Breaside and Colfe's. Open mornings in the autumn.

Will accept girls at 7+ in 2020, gradually becoming co-educational throughout.

Exit: Pupils from Eltham College Junior School are not required to sit the 11+ exam for the senior school and all but a dozen head there, often with scholarships. Those leaving do so mostly due to a change in family circumstance eg relocation, plus a few to the local grammar schools. The significant change is that boys from the junior school no longer sit an entrance test for the senior school. Other initiatives ease the year 7 transition and have built the all-through school feel: boys become familiar with the buildings, facilities and teachers.

Remarks: All of the usual curriculum subjects. As well as French, Mandarin is taught from year 3, which boys describe enthusiastically as 'fun, but hard sometimes'. Boys are set for maths throughout and for English comprehension from year 5. ICT rather than computing at the moment. Terms alternate between DT and art. There is a focus on developing cross-curricular thinking skills via 'philosophy for children' whilst following a growth mind-set approach of challenging every boy to believe intelligence isn't fixed but can be developed. Plenty of fun workshops and curricular trips to the London museums and galleries on the school's doorstep as well as short residentials further up the school. No doted-on school pets – the science lab terrapins have been replaced by giant African snails.

A slightly mixed picture from the few parents we hear from regarding teaching. One satisfied parent: 'I have been nothing but happy with the teaching' and another: 'All subjects are taught to a very high standard'. Whilst for another: 'The junior school could do with the shake-up currently refreshing the senior school'. It seems this is very much on the cards. The boys we meet who strike us as fairly free and easy with their views are wholehearted in their praise: 'The teachers are very kind; when you are feeling stressed they help you' and 'They want you to get the best marks possible'.

The parents we spoke to welcomed the fact that testing here does not feel intensive throughout. Mr Cavendish elaborates that teachers 'don't over-hype' tests and that a new system of monitoring enables the school to build up a picture of how each child is developing. At the end of each half-term boys receive a grade card with a mark for effort and attainment. In years 3 and 4 boys tell us 'everyone is mad about collecting merits'. By years 5 and 6 it's no longer 'cool' to collect them but boys nonetheless make use of the teachers' comments. A parent reported: 'Homework seems OK: in year 6 it's around 20 minutes each day. There are revision packs during the holidays which aren't compulsory'.

No doubt that almost everyone is sporty but that seems to be mostly by dint of encouragement and breadth of opportunity. The core sports on offer are rugby, football, hockey (on the up, reaching the regional under-11 finals) and cricket for two afternoons a week plus a brief gym or swim period. A mother sees the benefit of sports teaching by both male and female coaches. Boys are wowed by the coaches with national team experience. Competitive fixtures and galas, inter-house competitions plus clubs in which to try new things such as judo or basketball. Every effort is made to encourage boys of all abilities to don head-to-toe stripes and play for the school. This year every boy played rugby in at least one match fixture. There are plenty of individual successes too – one boy plays for Kent U11s cricket and three skiers were recently selected for the national training squad. The teaching of fencing must be good: we met one boy who tried fencing for the first time at a school open day and is now GB number two with highly ranked team mates to spar against. Boys also excel in chess competitions and LAMDA exams. One parent summed it up: 'The diversity of activities allows most children to find a niche that they can feel part of'.

E

Music is a significant part of the curriculum and 85 per cent of pupils have weekly individual lessons, currently up to grade 5 – the high uptake inspired by a project which enables all boys in years 3 and 4 to receive five weeks of free instrumental tuition. There are several choirs and ensembles and an annual music concert. Plenty to aspire to: trebles enjoyed singing alongside the seniors recently at the Barbican with the LSO. Years 3 and 4 perform an annual play or musical, as do years 5 and 6. As on our last visit, however, we hear consistent rumbles about the focus on a talented few: 'the chosen ones reappear very often across activities'.

A school for the sons of Victorian missionaries, with a house named after Dr Livingstone of 'I presume?' fame, the school relocated to its current site in 1912: a Victorian mansion with an uninspired modern wing extension. Inside, this provides for a high-ceilinged art room and a multi-sided hall with floor length windows overlooking the playing fields. The chic grey paint of the senior school make-over is yet to reach the outpost of the master's office but classrooms are being transformed from top to bottom into brighter spaces with the boys' approval. The small library – 'we love David Walliams' – now boasts coloured beanbags popular for hanging out or doodling on wet days. There are separate outside spaces allocated at breaktimes to the younger and older boys. Art displays could be improved in our opinion, but boys are justly proud of a wonderful mosaic of London they helped to design and make to celebrate the school's centenary. It seems like a family home that can afford to get bashed about a bit without anyone worrying about the soft furnishings. The high decibels at break time only add to the atmosphere.

A mother otherwise very happy with the school did tell us that she believed 'less confident children can sometimes be allowed to hide in the background'. There seems no doubt that it is a competitive place. At the same time, there is no need to conform: we hear that difference is accepted and quirkiness happily embraced – certainly borne out by the boys we met who seemed to listen to each other and respect individual talents. One thing that might unify boys here: we'd describe our tour guides as keen as mustard. Our overwhelming impression was of the boys' enthusiasm for their academic subjects. We raised an eyebrow at the idea of a Latin club at lunchtime, not a bit of it; two relived being caught out in a comprehension test by a tricky piece of grammar as if it was a narrowly missed sporting goal.

The school as a whole receives glowing praise for its pastoral care, the front line being form tutors. One mother told us of the care and consideration her son received during a difficult time at home. In line with national averages there are currently fewer than 20 pupils with any form of SEN, almost all of whom have dyslexia, a couple with ASD. Pupils are supported by individual lesson plans for in-class support and some booster classes. Boys tell us their friends with dyslexia value the support but inevitably don't like feeling different. Some 43 pupils are listed as EAL but most have adequate English, given the entrance requirements. Co-curricular clubs run pre- and post-school, whilst a breakfast club allows parents to dash for the commute. Boys were keen to tell us about their efforts at charity fundraising and seemed modestly unaware of how they'd been chosen for leadership opportunities. Boys talk about 'we' much of the time and clearly feel proud of their school.

Elthorne Park High School

Westlea Road, Hanwell, London W7 2AH

Ages 11–18 **Pupils** 1,100 **Sixth form** 200

020 8566 1166
www.ephs.ealing.sch.uk

Headteacher: Since 2012, Eliot Wong BSc PGCE Dip Ed NPQH (40s). Married with a school-age daughter, Mr Wong is a west Londoner through and through. Educated at St Peter's Primary school in Hammersmith and then Burlington Danes, he graduated with a first class degree in mathematics from King's College London before following his vocation in teaching (maths). He still finds the time to teach further maths to a class of about five who choose to do it ('it's the most enjoyable thing I do') as well as running revision classes for GCSE. Sixteen years of his career have been spent in schools in Ealing. Previously deputy head at Brentside High School, and before that assistant head at Cheam High School. He has also worked at Cardinal Wiseman (head of maths) and in Woking.

Thoughtful, determined and with a razor sharp logical mind, Mr Wong has achieved much improvement. Graphs depicting GCSE data are moving in a healthy northerly direction and the latest Ofsted inspection in 2015 graded the school as good (from a requires improvement in 2013) with the proviso that it only missed an outstanding because there were only two years of available results data. Far from being disheartened by missing out on an outstanding, Mr Wong sees this as an opportunity to innovate and change continually: 'once you achieve an outstanding, there is a risk of complacency,' Mr Wong smiles. An advocate of Jim Collins' hedgehog concept, Wong believes if you focus on doing one thing really well everything else will fall into place. In his view it's the teaching that you need to concentrate on. 'If you teach really well, behaviour improves and parents are happy.' He measures the quality of teaching in a number of different ways, including regularly observing lessons and checking exercise books.

A simple but effective change he has made is to the school's mission statement: from 'achieving in a learning community' to 'achieving excellence in a learning community.' He has introduced rigour, challenge and aspiration and observes that 'most staff have responded very positively'. A regular tweeter, he celebrates his students' achievements in the public sphere as well as making sure his school remains prominent not only on social media but also in the mind of the local authority, from which he has been effective in extracting funding (for the new £14m expansion, for example). He is proud of the liberal atmosphere that is immediately noticeable, but asserts that 'we are old fashioned in some senses – in that we work hard and show a positive and respectful attitude.' However, this is achieved not by 'imposing draconian measures' but through 'trust (and verification) and expectation'. That is the Elthorne way, he says, and applies as much to the staff as to the pupils.

Excellent teachers and motivated pupils are only two legs of the three-legged stool; another focus of his is parental involvement. He has introduced the 'text challenge', challenging parents to support their children with weekly texts about particular issues, in current affairs, for example. Mr Wong is deeply conscious of having to find ways to add value not only to aspirational families but also disadvantaged families. 'If you want to get the best out children you can't drag them, but you need to stimulate them with interesting, engaging lessons and the support of their parents.' This is the ACE formula – Achievement, Challenge, Excellence. It seems to be working.

Mr Wong is well respected by the pupils (they panic if they are on their phones when he appears in the playground), but parents speak of their frustration with his failure to respond to emails, and to complete references on time, and complain how difficult it is to get hold of him. An industrious, and thoughtful head, however (his office is decorated with hundreds of yellow post-it notes), he is highly committed and canny.

Academic matters: Huge improvement in results. In 2018, 78 per cent got 9-4 in both English and maths GCSE and 60 per cent got 9-5; at A level nearly a quarter of grades were A*/A, almost three-quarters A*-B. ALPS value added rates the sixth form as 'outstanding' for teaching and learning and results. Each year five or six pupils take further maths A level.

Elthorne Park is currently the top performing school in South Ealing and Hanwell (and has held this position for the third year running), and is in the top quintile of schools nationally in terms of GCSE attainment (including English, maths and two sciences). Out of over 5,000 non-selective, co-ed schools in the country Elthorne recently ranked 91st in performance tables, putting the school in the top two per cent.

Ofsted identified particularly imaginative teaching in modern languages with high standards of marking. Over half the year takes at least one language and French, Spanish and German all get a good smattering of 9-6 grades, Polish too. A foreign exchange is organised for each language and about 50 pupils go on a language exchange each year. Elthorne's modern language results are in the top five per cent of the country. Mr Wong says he will support anyone who wants to learn Latin (and ancient Greek) but a visiting teacher will have to come in specially or the pupil will have to go elsewhere.

The quality of teaching is closely observed and monitored. 'Book looks' at least half termly to check that marking is up to standard and each teacher is observed three times a year. Each year to GCSE has six classes with about 26 pupils in each. Setting in maths from year 7, English and science also broadly set as well as modern languages. Excellent DT department, offering separate exams in food technology, textiles, resistant materials and graphic products. Music, drama and theatre studies are strong, as well as all three sciences, particularly chemistry. All departments run 'intervention sessions' to support pupils who are falling behind.

Some 75 per cent of students have been taking Ebacc subjects for some time but 'I will no way force every student to do subjects that aren't suited them,' avers Mr Wong. BTec courses in media, business and health and social care also available as well as level 1 courses in eg motor vehicle maintenance and salon services. The ASDAN Award Scheme provides a course in basic skills, life skills and general knowledge for those students who wish to limit the number of GCSE courses they study.

Innovative style of teaching includes 'flip learning'. Students in the sixth form (and some classes lower down the school), given an iPad and required to research a subject before a lesson. The lesson can then be conducted in a more discursive way – students therefore learn to think, as well as to carry out independent research.

Enrichment lessons form part of the curriculum for years 7 to 9 – an effort to broaden the academic experience so that pupils are not confined to Ebacc subjects. They might study, eg, Japanese or film. Gifted and talented pupils can used it as a springboard to enhance their skills.

One parent observed reluctantly that there remains a culture of low expectation at Elthorne, however, citing as an example the practice of basing target grades at GCSE on earlier Sats results. Parents also commented on a lack of support with regard to A level choices and the university process. There is a lack of clear communication and flexibility about options, they say. This results in a few going elsewhere for sixth form when their inclination would have been to stay. School's response to this is that the senior leadership team now interviews every year 11 student and discusses the extracurricular guarantees made to every student, which range from travel abroad to gym membership and personalised help with Oxbridge applications. Communication when a child is not reaching targets, on the other hand, is very good, observed another parent. A subject teacher will send a text, and similarly if a child gets detention, the parents are sent a text.

The number of students with SEN is not high – less than 20 per cent – but a relatively high number of students (between two and three per cent) with statements/EHC plans. 'They are attracted to us as we are a nurturing school, and they are well supported,' says Mr Wong. The SENCo has a team of 10. Children are supported in class as much as possible with teaching assistants attached to subjects. EAL tuition takes place outside the classroom. One parent observed how little support you get if you are a middle class kid with dyslexia – we have heard that before. A £14m expansion project, the Additionally Resourced Provision for Special Needs, opened in 2017. This is a hub of activity working to support children with speech, language and communication problems and those with specific learning needs (SLCN – speech, language and communication needs). The new development also houses facilities for all the students, including a new hall and drama studio, a life skills room and two extra ICT suites.

Games, options, the arts: 'Expressive arts are at the heart of our community,' says Mr Wong. We were impressed with just how much goes on in here – in creative arts, drama, music and sport. Elthorne teams have excelled in the borough in various sports including cross-country, netball, basketball, rugby, football and cricket. Girls' sports are especially strong. The current year 11 girls' netball team has been unbeaten for the past four years and the U13 girls' football team is national champion. There are regular competitions and matches – inter-form and inter-school as well as regional. An annual sports day, which includes track and field athletics as well as softball, takes place at Perivale sports ground.

For budding thespians there is the opportunity to perform extracts from Shakespeare plays at the annual Shakespeare Festival. In addition there is an annual major whole school production, often a musical (recently they performed Grease). Students get involved with all aspects of the production – costumes, choreography, music, set and props. Decent drama studio where lessons and rehearsals take place. Performances happen in the hall.

Gifted musicians are identified and giving lots of opportunity to compete and perform. Numerous concerts and recitals plus a classical music competition and annual rock concert. Plenty of ensembles – brass and guitar as well as a chamber and whole school orchestra. Macs in music rooms where students are taught music composition. The popular summer festival and barbecue brings together performances and displays – art and DT as well as drama and music.

Lots of trips and activities including annual ski trip and Spanish, French and German exchanges (with a twin school), as well as geography field trips and visits to eg Oxford University and the theatre. Plenty of extracurricular opportunities such as public speaking competitions, D of E, bushcraft and PGL trips, the STEM challenge (EPHS were recently regional winners) and UK maths challenge. A plethora of clubs take place after school, from debating to film and volunteering in the community.

Background and atmosphere: Elthorne may be in Hanwell but it stands out from other schools of its kind because it's situated on the edge of the seven and a half acres of green space that is Elthorne Park. Children can spill into this area during lunch break (supervised), and the football pitches and sports areas are a tremendous additional resource. The main buildings are positioned around a central courtyard – a mixture of low, single storey, temporary, and two storey buildings as well as the shiny, modern sixth form centre. Eight modern, spacious and well-equipped science labs, a suite of specialist music rooms, a purpose built drama studio, four art studios with a dark room, graphics and kiln facilities. Specialist DT including food technology, textiles and resistant materials. Plenty of Macs available for use in graphics as well as in music. Large sports hall as well as separate school hall where lunch, assemblies and drama happens. Purpose built sixth form centre. A feeling of space – no cramped corridors and a comfortable well-resourced library.

Maroon uniform creates a somewhat dour impression and can be worn scruffily: 'they are not super strict about ties and tucking in shirts here,' said our guide with warm appreciation. This school is far from dour, however, but vibrant and buzzy. While Mr Wong clearly has a firm grip, the school has a relaxed feel; children are not deferential but their behaviour seems to fall on the right side of the line.

Pastoral care, well-being and discipline: Mr Wong describes the school as a healthy mix of old-fashioned and more relaxed values. While there is a finely tuned system of 'levelled' detentions (ranging between a 15 minute personal detention with a teacher to a head teacher detention on a Monday night) as well as a three strikes policy and a system of internal isolations, the key element is trust. This can't be imposed, says Wong, through draconian measures, but through example and respect. He talks about 'the Elthorne Way,' an expectation of high achievement and excellence through a healthy symbiotic relationship between staff and pupils. Students appear relaxed, but that doesn't mean they aren't polite and well behaved. Mr Wong works hard and expects those around him to work hard, both staff and pupils. 'I believe in hard work and striving for excellence,' he says, 'I don't believe in excuses.' Trust is key – but trust with verification. We will trust them, he says, but we will check on them. The students have a voice – the student council have regular breakfasts and lunches with staff and there is an annual student survey. They, too, are listened to and treated with respect. When it comes to drugs and weapons, however, the line is clear and inflexible.

Parents warmly supportive – and appreciative – of the school's approach to incidents that happen outside school hours, often with the local community. They step in quickly and with tact and understanding. Behaviour – according to most parents – is 'on the whole good'.

Pupils and parents: Just under 50 per cent of families here are white British. The rest split fairly equally between black, Asian and Eastern European. Some support for EAL but most have learnt good English at primary school. Local Ealing families who, on the whole, are keen their children do well and will work hard with the school to achieve this. Relatively low number of pupils are on free school meals (25 per cent compared with a national average of 28 per cent). Stable student population.

Entrance: About 1,000 apply each year for 240 places in year 7. The four main feeder primaries are Fielding, Oaklands, Little Ealing and St Mark's – perception among parents is that Fielding dominates. As the primaries expand, so there is greater pressure on places. Proximity to the school the main criterion (after the usual criteria have been taken into account – children in public care, exceptional medical or social circumstances etc). Catchment has shrunk from a 1.5 mile radius to a one mile radius. Parents want their children to come here and consider it to be outstanding – regardless of what Ofsted says. Siblings given priority. To get into the sixth form you need a minimum of five 9-4s including English and maths at GCSE with at least a 6 in chosen A level subjects.

Exit: Of the upper sixth approximately 75 per cent go on to university, with about a quarter of these to Russell Group. Brighter pupils attracted elsewhere for sixth form, observed one parent. 'No NEETs for the past three years!', says head proudly. Some 93 per cent stay in education post-GCSEs, around 50 per cent stay at Elthorne to study advanced courses in the sixth form – over 70 per cent of these study A levels, but all sixth formers study advanced (level 3) courses which may include BTecs. About 20 per cent each year go on to art school and one or two each year go to the BRIT school.

Money matters: A local authority funded, well-resourced school – reserves, we were told, are greater than five per cent. Lower than borough average spent on supply staff, large proportion of budget spent on teachers and education support staff. Almost double spent on learning resources and ICT compared with local and national averages.

Remarks: Value added – an often overlooked measure – is strong here: mid and high achievers will make significant progress, especially compared with their peers nationally. If you have a motivated child, keen to do well, this school won't hold him/her back but will inspire and work to meet that potential. A school with a genuine liberal arts and creative ethos. A precious gem in this age of emphasis on Ebacc subjects. Let's hope it will preserve its arty tradition as it consolidates the academics in the face of pressure from on high.

Emanuel School

Battersea Rise, London SW11 1HS

Ages 10–18 **Pupils** 930 **Sixth form** 200

Fees: £18,582 pa

020 8870 4171
www.emanuel.org.uk

Headmaster: Since 2017, Robert Milne previously deputy head (pastoral) at King's College Wimbledon, where he also taught English and coached a variety of sports. Started off teaching English at Oundle; after this he moved to King Edward's Birmingham as housemaster of a day house, before moving to Magdalen College School as head of English.

Academic matters: Both A level and GCSE grades have been steadily improving year on year. In 2018, 31 per cent of A level grades A*/A (83 per cent A*-B), and 64 per cent A*-A/9-7 at GCSE. Grades in chemistry and physics at GCSE are streets ahead of the rest. Strong results in maths but mathematicians sometimes outclassed by a huge cohort of historians who really shine at A level too. Politics and economics are also popular. Linguists in handfuls.

GCSE: all pupils study English, maths and one language from French, German, Latin and Spanish – French and Spanish are far more popular than German. Either double or single sciences; the decision on the final route is made during year 11. Pupils choose a further three subjects from a wide range: art, economics, classical civilisation, DT, drama/theatre studies, geography, history, RS, music and PE. Not complete freedom to choose. A levels add in business, further maths, politics and psychology. The majority of pupils are now expected to take three A levels and the EPQ.

Twenty-nine teachers have been at the school for more than 10 years. The most recent ISI report offered a host of 'excellent's when referring to both the teaching and attitudes of the pupils to learning, noting the good rapport between staff and students, though almost every parent we asked about the teaching staff began carefully with 'on the whole'. One said: 'There are some exceptional, inspiring teachers across the school who can transform a child's understanding.' Another: 'Overall, I would say the teaching is very good with some excellent examples thrown in'. Some offer praise without reservation: 'My wife and I are astonished by how much she loves the academic lessons too; we can't remember that school was this much fun when we were teenagers.' Interestingly innovative, the school has been keen to try the Harkness method where teaching is done in a small group, with a maximum 16 of students sitting around an oval table with tablets for instant online access: it's felt to encourage participation and the exchange of ideas.

A little more than average numbers with a learning difference, but a well-qualified head of learning support with two assistant practioners, both with qualifications in the support of dyslexia. The school does not screen all on entry, only if making 'poor progress'. Those with an ed psych report will have a 'learner profile' created to advise class teachers of learning preferences, some small group withdrawal. A few extras on offer such as an early morning spelling club and homework club every day of the week. Pupils talk of the value of touch-typing lessons and a Cogmed course, designed to help with working memory. Some 12 pupils currently have EAL assistance.

As befits the happy and relaxed atmosphere of the school, children don't seem to feel too intensively pressured. A typical report: 'Children seem to be prepared for exams without being over stressed.'

All departments seem plugged into national competitions. Year 10 students entered and were shortlisted for the Cambridge triple helix science writing competition. A DT student was recently awarded a prestigious Arkwright Scholarship. Maths students are regularly successful in both the UKMT Maths Challenge and the Hans Woyda competitions. Science students compete in the annual Science Olympiad, over half taking home a medal. Two students have won prizes in the Peterhouse essay competitions in recent years, both of whom were later awarded places at Cambridge. This is also a well-connected school which has no problem attracting an impressive line-up of speakers, such as Samira Ahmed, Sir Bob Geldof, Professor David Starkey, Alastair Darling and Lord Coe. Rowan Williams came to talk to the literary society about the Christian symbolism in the Narnia series. Sir Tim Berners-Lee, possibly the most famous OE, returned to the school.

A member of staff is responsible for Oxbridge applications and arranges university visits for all of year 10. Oxbridge candidates attend seminars held jointly across the Westminster schools group. Work experience begins in years 10 and 11. The sixth form makes use of OEs coming back to the school to give them advice on everything from surviving the first year at uni to spending a year in industry. There is an annual careers convention attended by more than 70 guests, working the parent body as much as former pupils.

Games, options, the arts: A parent told us: 'Emanuel does punch above its weight in sports for the size of the school. That is down to the encouragement the children get from the games staff.' Sport is a major feature of the school, with rugby followed by rowing the most popular. One parent said: 'If you don't like rugby you can have a problem'. Teams are kitted out in striking navy and gold stripes.

Facilities are extensive: apart from 12 acres of on-site games fields there is also access via a private gate to facilities on Wandsworth Common plus 14 further acres near Raynes Park. The sports hall includes a climbing wall. There is a large pool and a boathouse at Barnes for 75 boats. Rowing is historically the most successful sport at Emanuel with over 50 international and Olympic rowers in the record books and recent medals for girls and boys.

The school has also been awarded top 100 cricket schools status by The Cricketer Magazine; rugby teams successful. Plenty of netball and hockey stars too, locally and at county level. Some would like to see more done outside of these core sports: there are naturally fewer matches and opportunities outside of the major sports.

Some 300 individual instrumental lessons a week, of all grades with many reaching grade 8. Recently, two pupils gained places to attend the junior Guildhall School for Music and junior Royal Academy of Music. It is common for students to gain choral scholarships to Oxbridge colleges as well as win places at music colleges. A good rehearsal and concert space.

Drama is a highlight with many OEs entering careers within the field of drama, film and television. Recently one boy starred in Dickensian. Recently, the senior play was Brief Encounter; the junior play was The Lion, the Witch and the Wardrobe and the year 7s bonded over The Witches. A parent: 'I look forward to every concert or school production as it saves me a trip to the West End.' An enlarged theatre of around 100 seats was opened by Ralph Fiennes and Mike Leigh.

Passports at the ready – too many international trips, sports tours, departmental exchanges and adventures to mention covering what seems like the entire of Europe and further afield to India and the US. Over 40 clubs and societies: choir, computer club, drama club, technical drama club and Eton fives are all after school. Many others take place before school and at lunch time including one for Dr Who fans.

Background and atmosphere: A school with a history – founded in Westminster in 1594 by Lady Dacre. The school's magazine, Portcullis, has recently reached its 300th edition. Unusually, it was co-educational from the start with just 10 boys and 10 girls. The boys then moved to Wandsworth in 1883 to the current building, originally a Crimean war orphanage. The school became a voluntary aided grammar school in 1944 until it resumed its independent status in the 1970s. In 1995 it became co-educational once more. The school is growing and will continue to do so up until about 960 pupils. There is a courtyard in the middle of the main building dedicated to three Queen Elizabeths. The first on the throne at the foundation; the second who planted the central tree, Queen Elizabeth, The Queen Mother; the third her daughter who made a royal visit in 1994.

A smart new bridge provides access from Spencer Park, showcasing the school at its best angle – called the Memorial Bridge in memory of the Clapham Rail crash in 1988. The railway line provides only a gentle rumble of trains going past. Despite this, the school has the feel of a green oasis – the buildings' outlook onto the sports fields at the rear, particularly the outdoor café under the cricket nets, is very appealing on a sunny day. The library, at the heart of the old building, is remodelled to blend modernity with aspects of the school's heritage, including an archive area and 'family photo wall' of OEs. Large and well-stocked, with a spiral staircase and mezzanine, it lends out up to 500 books a week; teen fiction such as The Fault in Our Stars leads the way. This is a Christian school with Christian values and the chapel with stained glass windows remains on the first floor. Sixth formers have their own modern block with plenty of corners to hang out and a café akin to Starbucks.

The main building is impressive, but far more institutional and shabby inside than we expect – it even smells rather like a hospital. With new developments – a £10m humanities building including a film studio and a separate 'temple to maths' including a maths café, grand foyer and lecture theatre – suggest the fabric of the school is starting to match the head's ambition.

Parents report: 'Whenever you visit the school there is always a very happy atmosphere among the students and great camaraderie'; 'there has been an increase in the number of highly academic children at the school but I still feel that the school is not a pressure cooker'. Another: 'There is a definite atmosphere of letting everybody have a go at everything without judgement – it doesn't matter how good or bad you are'. 'It's fun and pretty cool,' added a student.

Pastoral care, well-being and discipline: A system of form tutors who see pupils every day combined with a house system and easy access to the head of year ensures that any problems that arise should be spotted and dealt with quickly. We hear they are quick to respond. Parents agree the school is supportive and caring. There are two chaplains, and a fully trained counsellor.

A detailed anti-bullying policy is in place, updated to include cyber-bullying, giving pupils, staff and parents clear guidelines as to what to do and a fairly long list of sanctions if pupils are not behaving with courtesy and co-operation. Every pupil carries a conduct card. Chocolate as a reward has been dropped for the sake of blood sugar levels. We hear one report of the school's rigorous discipline procedures seeming quite severe to newcomers. But there are also 'lots of parental talks to help support children.' Useful in a co-ed school, we're told by a parent: 'Their sex ed offering is similarly "full on", which I fully support'.

Pupils and parents: Coming from all over London and occasionally beyond as the school is within seven minutes' walk of the transport hub of Clapham Junction. Many parents work in the media or creative industries. The Fiennes family is connected with the school. The majority of pupils are white European in ethnicity, and reflecting the local area 26 pupils have French as their first language. Ten per cent are from overseas. Parents tell of us of making friends here, something that happens less at senior school. There is even a choir for mums and dads and socialising in the pub in Barnes whilst watching the rowing. They describe each other as 'committed and unpretentious'; 'friendly, mostly working parents'; 'down to earth and genuine.'

Entrance: Registration for entry from 2020 no longer capped. One of the few London senior schools offering the opportunity to avoid all of the hoopla and stress of 11+ with a 10+ entry point, it is apparently still as competitive to enter, as at 10+ there are only 40 in a year group rising to 130 in year 7.

At 10+ and 11+ there are papers in English, maths and verbal reasoning. At 13+ English, maths, science and a language. At 16+ an English essay and three subjects of the applicant's choice (in subjects they intend to study for A level) and a reasoning test. Pupils with SEN will be considered for extra time if appropriate.

Some 70 per cent enter from state primaries at Y6 and Y7, higher than we often see, but it is a wide community. Students come in from over 200 feeder schools such as Belleville, Fulham Prep, Honeywell, Hornsby House, Hurlingham, Maple Walk, Orchard House, Our Lady of Victories, Thomas' Clapham and Wimbledon Park. Biannual open days plus several week morning tours per term.

Exit: Some 15 per cent leave after GCSEs. Current popular university destinations are Exeter, Durham, Sussex and Essex, with long tail of others heading off to pursue everything from PPE to product design, both in the UK and abroad.

Money matters: A generous number of scholarships and bursaries and unusually lunch is included in the standard fees. One in five have a scholarship. Fifteen children currently received 100 per cent assisted places, which the head hopes to roll out to 20.

Remarks: One to keep a decided eye on as it makes its upwards progress. Something of a boarding school atmosphere – open seven days a week in a day school format.

Falkner House

19 Brechin Place, London SW7 4QB

Ages 3–11 Pupils 200

Fees: £9,780 – £19,080 pa

020 7373 4501
www.falknerhouse.co.uk

Headteacher: Since 2017, Flavia Rogers BA PGCE (30s). Educated here followed by St Paul's Girls' School, then studied history at Exeter University. First job at the Nightingale Bamford School in New York, then taught history at Kingston Grammar School. She has been here since 2008.

Falkner House is truly a family business in every sense; Mrs Rogers' grandmother, Flavia Nunes, was Falkner House's founding head, and she works alongside her mother, Anita Griggs (school principal) and sister Eleanor Dixon (head of Falkner House Boys). Mrs Rogers has three children, all of whom are at Falkner House, so she feels she has an unusual perspective of being both consumer and producer. 'Seeing things from the angle of a current parent is incredibly useful and means I have insight into what life is really like for children and families at the school. For example, do we really do what we say when we say we have very little homework in the lower school? How does this translate at home?' She has known her husband Sam since they met at St Paul's and they live across the road from here.

Mrs Griggs and Mrs Rogers are an exceptionally tight team. They spend a huge amount of time together (every weekend as well), clearly love what they do and love working together.

Entrance: Register within a year of birth. No automatic entry from the (co-ed) nursery. Some 160 girls compete for 24 reception places in an assessment that looks for 'focus, working memory and enthusiasm,' as well as more elusive qualities such as 'grit' and good manners.

'A child cannot be prepared and we don't assess whether or not they can read.' Many will inevitably be disappointed, but parents are let down as gently as possible. 'No selection system is perfect. We don't get false positives, but we sometimes get false negatives.'

Exit: The 'next step' is considered thoughtfully, with parents invited in for a planning meeting in year 5. The majority, now as always, to London's academic girls' schools (St Paul's, Latymer Upper, Godolphin & Latymer, City, Francis Holland

SW1, Queen's Gate, Putney High). A small number to board, with Wycombe Abbey, Cheltenham Ladies and St Mary's Ascot featuring strongly. Frequent academic, music and sporting scholarships.

Remarks: Flavia Nunes set up Falkner House in 1954 with the intention of providing girls with the same standard of academic excellence enjoyed by their brothers – by no means a given in those days – and the school continues to provide a broad and challenging education taught by a dedicated, energetic and innovative staff. 'They're the real stars,' says the head.

Reading is central to the offering. All younger girls are expected to read nightly at home and a love of words and books is encouraged by regular attendance at two libraries, essential reading lists and a weekly library lesson from year 3. Poetry is learned by heart and recited in class and competitions; recently launched own poetry anthology of verses 'every Falkner House child should know'. Girls become articulate and confident, both on the page and in conversation.

Beyond the three Rs, a rainbow of opportunity. French throughout, classics from year 3, Latin from year 5. Music is exceptionally strong and varied with plenty of performance (wind band, string group, choir, chamber music ensembles). Art room buzzing and history of art taught from reception, with regular outings to museums and galleries. Dance and drama included in the core curriculum, with regular outstanding class productions, and a popular after-school ballet club.

Technology here is not just for display on the timetable, but blazing a trail – a hardworking teacher has reinvented the year 5 and 6 curriculum to be delivered on iPads. Recently Apple named Falkner House one of six groundbreaking schools worldwide for its innovative approach.

Light approach to both homework and exams. The latter are introduced in year 4 as 'It's important for girls to learn to take both the test and the results in their stride; to learn their best is good enough and what we value is their effort over the result.' says the head.

This is a highly selective school and few have serious special educational needs. Mild difficulties, however, are addressed successfully by experienced staff and high flyers given regular extension work.

Despite a handkerchief playground, sport played competitively to a high level. Coaches ferry girls to Battersea, Kensington Gardens, Latchmere Leisure Centre and Chelsea and from year 3 the school fields A, B, and often C squads in netball, athletics, swimming, rounders and cross-country. 'It's a culture of "play the game within the spirit of the game",' says the head. 'We do not kill to win.' Win they do, however, producing recent swimming and fencing champions.

Fresh food cooked daily – and described as 'amazing' by our guides, with staff monitoring manners and a balanced diet. 'We've taken out all mention of healthy eating,' says the head. 'All children here eat healthy food, so why create more anxiety?'

The school is still located in the two spacious, multi-storeyed Victorian houses where it was founded and retains the echo of a post-war family home, with carpeted corridors and the head's office elegantly kitted out with antiques. Tradition, too, maintained with daily 'prayers' (Christian hymns and the Lord's Prayer) held in the delightful, parqueted assembly hall. Remembrance Day, carol service and the Queen's Jubilee accorded due dignity. 'The girls should understand the culture.'

Other traditional strands include both a house and prefect system. Head girl, deputy and prefects appointed for half term stints, so all get a go, while other routes to glory include sportsperson or artist of the week, eco monitor and badge girl (responsible for helping the teacher).

Head's mission is to endow pupils with self confidence, independence of mind, kindness and good manners, and girls clearly enjoy the process. 'It's fun,' said one. 'No-one is not friends,' said another. Top year girls are paired with those coming into reception, and this union of 'big and little sisters' means new arrivals are never left stranded. Precocity definitely discouraged (no nail varnish, no jewellery and only 'sensible' shoes).

The girls are strongly encouraged to be self-sufficient. 'I'd prefer parents not to come in and hang up the children's coats – children come to school to learn independence,' says the head, who is also firmly anti-PTA (school says it prefers to get to know each and every parent individually). Nevertheless, the home-school link is strong and parental involvement expected with homework and music practice. Parents regularly invited to attend events, from mini concerts to Father's Day breakfasts.

Families mainly within walking distance, then spreading out to Hammersmith, Chiswick, Fulham and the City. Highly qualified, often working in financial services and a mix of nationalities. Unsurprisingly, some can be a tad competitive, something the head keeps firmly in check. 'If someone rings up to demand why their daughter's not in the netball team, you just have to say, "I'm sorry you're cross, but let's try and be reasonable. There are other people better at netball".'

Given the location, families tend to be affluent. The website includes requests for housekeepers and year 6 parents are politely asked to plan family holidays 'to avoid jet lag before the 11+'. No formal bursaries or scholarships, but the school always helps out existing pupils in financial difficulties.

Opened a boys' prep for 4-11 year olds in Earls Court in 2017, plus a co-ed nursery.

Fine Arts College Hampstead

Centre Studios 41–43 Englands Lane, London NW3 4YD

Ages 13–19 **Pupils** 211 **Sixth form** 175

Fees: £21,690 pa

020 7586 0312
www.hampsteadfinearts.com

Principal: Candida Cave (50s). Elegant, quietly spoken, compassionate and creative, a lovely lady. Attended Ruskin School of Art, Oxford, then started teaching art and art history when a flatmate fell in love with an Italian racing driver and needed someone to take on her tutees. Quickly discovered she had a flair for teaching, and soon had 20 more students. Set up Fine Arts College as a part-time concern in 1978 with artist and co-founder Nicholas Cochrane in rented rooms at the YMCA in Great Russell Street; then in 1982 took the plunge and opened a full-time school in a house in Belsize Park. School moved to its present site in 2002.

Until very recently she was still actively involved in teaching at the school, and still teaches on study trips and lectures. Painting is her passion, and she has exhibited in various galleries in London and elsewhere. Also a keen theatre and concert goer. Married to Stephen, a historian and writer, she has a grown up son and daughter (the latter now head).

Attributes success of school to its founding ethos: 'We wanted to have the sort of college that we ourselves would have liked. We wanted a holistic education, where the arts were as important as academic subjects. We wanted a co-operative, self-motivated style of learning. And we wanted to know everyone's name.' Parents agree. 'I have nothing but praise for Candida, and the atmosphere she creates in the school is so positive,' commented one.

Her daughter, Emmy Schwieters, has been head of the college since 2019. Read English and history of art at Leeds, and worked in the hospitality industry before joining Fine Arts in 2003, taking on the roles of head of the history of art department and director of studies.

Academic matters: In 2018, 20 per cent A*/A and 50 per cent A*-B grades at A level. At GCSE 76 per cent A*-C/9-4 grades. Impressive results for a school that doesn't select on academic ability.

Biology and maths are offered at A level, but as you'd expect, the arts and humanities dominate, along with economics and business studies and an excellent range of languages (take-up for Italian is high). Teaching groups are small, allowing for a seminar-style delivery of the course. The approach relies for its success on students' chattiness and willingness to participate, but that's clearly not a problem here. We dropped in on a delightfully lively and sparky year 13 politics lesson where the students were all very ready to speak up, and the standard of contributions was informed and thoughtful. Nearly 30 subjects on offer to sixth formers, and it's possible to do entirely art-based options: we met a student who was revelling in being able to study fine art, graphic design, photography and fashion/textile design. 'My previous school could only offer me art. This is brilliant!' Most students still take four subjects and drop one after year 12. EPQ also available. School also offers a one year A level course, often taken by those who have done a year of the IB and decided it's not for them.

F

Since 1994 school has taken students into years 10 and 11 in response to parent demand. It provides both a conventional two-year and an intensive one-year GCSE course, the latter offering a lifeline to able students who have nonetheless struggled in more academically pressurised environments. In September 2018 the first year 9s joined the school: just one small cohort of 10 pupils when we visited. The lessons we saw were very quiet, reflecting perhaps the kind of children that at this age would prefer this eccentric and artsy little school, but pupils said they appreciated the very high level of individual attention they received and seemed glad to be here. At GCSE most students do eight or nine GCSEs, including three arts subjects and one science, biology, which is now taught in purpose built lab (rather than an ordinary classroom).

Drama is very popular and taught in the school's 'big space' – which, truthfully, isn't that big – and is extremely popular at all levels, and it's probably no coincidence that the school has as many successful performing alumni as artistic ones. Music and music technology taught in purpose built room that pulses with purpose. But naturally it's the art rooms that really impress. Light, peaceful, littered with classical busts, the creativity here wafts over you like a Mozart aria. Even the skeleton used for teaching purposes was in the throes of ecstasy instead of the normal demure pose. We paused to admire a sculpture of Laocoön fighting off the serpents that students were copying in order to produce a monochrome portrait, using tone rather than colour to create a 3D look. 'You can't do a bad drawing of it, really,' mused the officiating teacher, drifting over in paint-splattered smock, tea in hand. Small class of students bent over their work, completely absorbed, and we were much struck by the atmosphere of focused and calm artistry.

Big emphasis on classical antiquity and ancient history is such a pleasure to see. But the modern world is also very much in evidence throughout the curriculum. Excellent graphics classroom was full of punchy, inventive work by the students, and film studies and media also very successful. Photography is thriving here, and we were relieved to see the dark room still very much in use – 'For the students, it's not nostalgia, it's a new thing.' Textiles room an absolute treasure trove of fabrics, buttons and bows, inviting budding fashion creatives to dive right in.

We didn't get the chance to speak to anyone from the lower school, but the sixth formers here are clearly very happy. They relish the freedom to think and develop for themselves and the emphasis laid on a collaborative approach, describing the sixth form experience as a 'proper step between school and university'. 'You force yourself to do a lot of work – and you end up accomplishing more.' 'The creative range here is unparalleled.' 'If you aren't motivated to do work in your own time, you'll fall behind. But if you have that drive, they'll help you 100 per cent. In fact, they'll help you anyway.' 'We're expected to be creative and think differently. The teachers here are open to discussion and challenge, and they're always willing to stay behind and help you.'

SEN provision is strong, and students told us they felt very well supported here. 'The teachers are just great, and really helpful, and needing help isn't an issue here'. 'We try and support in the most subtle way possible,' says Candida, 'If a student has dyslexia, then their personal tutor will be a dyslexia specialist.' School keen to emphasise, however, that it isn't a special school and can't support one-to-one teaching throughout the curriculum.

Games, options, the arts: LAMDA extremely popular and successful, and each crop of exam results brings plenty of distinctions at grade 8. Peripatetic music lessons also available throughout the school – 'I can actually sing now!' said a grateful student after commencing singing lessons here. Lower school does a range of sports every week including team games such as football and netball, although the emphasis is on enjoyment and fitness rather than competitive fixtures. Yoga also offered. Frequent trips to exhibitions and to places of beauty and culture both at home and abroad, as well as to theatres and musical events. Students encouraged to initiate projects if they wish to, and there have been a number of charitable and fundraising events of this kind.

On the whole, though, young people here are engaged full time in what at other schools is usually peripheral – film, fashion, music, art, drama – so there isn't the demand for off-timetable activity that you'd find elsewhere. As one student put it, 'There aren't that many extracurricular subjects, because most people here want to focus on their A levels.' Those seeking a full-on, UCAS-form-busting programme of opportunities should look elsewhere; the students we spoke to here were happy with the balance.

Background and atmosphere: Once the school was a sixth form college almost exclusively offering specialist arts teaching. Over the decades it's evolved into a more general provider of non-selective education at 13+ with a particular emphasis on the visual arts. It is not, nor does it aim to be, the fine arts equivalent of a specialist music school, and students are not selected on their artistic ability.

Now in its 40th year, the school is spread over multiple sites, all within a few minutes' walk of each other. The main building in Englands Lane is a former Victorian dairy: still flanked on all sides by grey and beige brickwork, its interior is a honeycomb of small corridors and classrooms. The cobbled main courtyard is the first thing people see, and it really is rather special. Beautifully adorned with shrubs, trees, potted flowers and wooden benches, the impression on a summer's morning was one of shade and sunshine in a Tuscan village. The students make full use of it in the warmer months and say it's amazing. 'I fell in love with the school as soon as I saw it!'

Since 2015, the school has been owned by Dukes Education, which has enabled it to purchase a nearby former stables for turning into additional classrooms, but space remains an issue here. There's no library, for instance – students use local public libraries instead – and sixth formers would love a common room of their own. But these privations haven't made a dent in the atmosphere here, which is buzzy and cheerful. 'We use the local cafés instead, and that pushes us to be more sociable,' said one student. 'The feeling at Fine Arts College is always welcoming, and I'm really loving being here,' was another comment.

Pastoral care, well-being and discipline: Everyone is given a code of conduct to sign – which includes not making a mess, rather endearingly for an art school – so expectations are clear, but in the main there are few rules and no cause to break them. The school is run on mutual respect, and Candida Cave is proud of how well the students respond to this. 'We haven't had to exclude or suspend anyone for 10 years.' Those who arrive exhausted and discouraged from different school environments quickly find their feet. Parents and children alike told us that this was a kind and accepting place. 'Bullying is non-existent here.'

Teachers are addressed by their first names, and there's no uniform for any of the year groups. Dress code is casual, with the only requirement being that the students must be decently and inoffensively attired. Prettily-appliquéd sweaters and fashionably-motifed sweatshirts abound, and there's no shortage of pierced ears and noses. Nonetheless, anyone expecting to find the place a pushover will be quickly disabused. Students' progress, both academic and pastoral, is comprehensively tracked. Everyone has a personal tutor whom they see every week for at least an hour. There are fortnightly reports so students can see how well they're doing, and consistently low effort grades will swiftly result in interventions, including (for sixth formers) being made to drop a subject if they're clearly not trying at it. Anyone who is more than 10 minutes late for a lesson isn't allowed to join it until they've made the work up in a study space outside the classroom, 'so I'm never late!' commented a student; 'it's been really effective for me.' Said another, 'It's a good idea, because after all, it is distracting when people are late.'

The college will admit school refusers and home-schooled if it believes they would benefit from what it has to offer, but does so on a trial basis and tracks their progress particularly closely; no term's notice is required by the school from parents, but school also has the right to ask them to leave after half a term if it's patently not going to work.

No school lunches. Students bring their own, or eat at local cafes (some of whom offer a discount to FAC students) with parental permission, and Englands Lane is patrolled by staff members throughout lunch break. 'But quite a few celebrities' children go there, so the paparazzi can be out in force when the students are coming and going,' warned one mother. Students themselves unfazed by this, and just enjoy the independence. 'It's 100 per cent better than my last school – there's no ordering about, just freedom and an ethos of mutual respect.'

Pupils and parents: Mostly, but not exclusively, British students, drawn mainly from a local radius, but some coming from as far away as south London, Essex and Watford. Many are seeking an alternative to boarding, selectivity or just the conformity required at a large school. Parents are relieved and grateful that they've found the place. 'My child is really happy there, and enjoying life so much more.' Some international students, particularly post-GCSE.

Alumni include artist Robert Fry, actors Orlando Bloom and Helena Bonham-Carter, and guitarist and singer Johnny Borrell.

Entrance: Entry points at year 9, year 10 and year 12, and school admits around 12 annually to each of these year groups. Reference from current school is required, but no testing. All applicants are interviewed personally by Candida Cave for at least an hour; she looks for a sense that they've clicked with the school and what it has to offer – 'they have to want to be educated here.' If she's unsure, she'll ask another member of staff to interview them as well. School is happy to admit at any point in the academic year.

At 16+, school looks for a minimum of five GCSEs at grade 4 or above, but doesn't make the offer of a place contingent upon this. 'If they don't have maths or English GCSE they must take fewer A levels and get these done.'

Exit: About a third leaves after GCSEs. The remainder move on after A levels to a wide range of destinations, including LSE, UCL, King's College London, Edinburgh, the Courtauld Institute and Central St Martins. A trickle of Oxbridge successes, including one in 2018 (modern languages). The occasional overseas success eg Pratt Institute, New York. Popular courses include classics, English, history, philosophy, history of art, fine art, graphic design and photography.

Money matters: Each year either one 100 per cent scholarship or two 50 per cent scholarships to existing Fine Arts College students who demonstrate outstanding achievement in academic, artistic or musical fields of study, as well as exceptional commitment and exemplary behaviour. Limited number of bursaries available to students who have previously been educated in the state system who would not otherwise be able to afford private education.

Remarks: A haven of culture, creativity and kindness amidst the tumult of north London selective schools, and a route to success for those who have been disheartened hitherto. 'I've had a really good time here, and I'll be sad to leave,' said a year 13 girl, and of the boys added, 'It's a really nice community. I actually don't mind getting up in the mornings and going to school. And I've never said that before.'

F

Finton House School

171 Trinity Road, London SW17 7HL

Ages 4–11 **Pupils** 321

Fees: £15,378 – £15,588 pa

020 8682 0921
www.fintonhouse.org.uk

Headmaster: Since 2016, Ben Freeman BEd (design technology) PG Dip (educational leadership) (late 40s). Still very much 'the new kid on the block' (his own words), Mr Ben, as he is known here, is not just new to Finton House but new to Wandsworth and the buzzing metropolis of London. Previously head of Windermere Prep for eight years, a school that had already munched its way through two heads in quick succession before he arrived, he was brought in to rescue the situation having been teaching at Malsis Prep school in North Yorkshire (which no longer exists).

The fresh air of the English countryside runs through Ben Freeman's veins. Born and brought up in the Wirral, he was educated at Rossall School and then the University of West of England, Bristol. He cut his teeth teaching in a secondary state school in Bristol but was lured to Malsis to set up its DT department. By the time he left he was deputy head. Married to Sarah, who is training to be a teacher and ran the outdoor education at Windermere. She has three grown up children. The landscape of Ben Freeman's life so far has been one of natural beauty – sea, hills, lakes: it's no wonder that one of his passions is the outdoors. Walking and sailing as well as skiing are his means of relaxation and he is keen to instil in his pupils a love for everything outdoorsy. He regards his two main focuses here to be developing the technology so that the teachers are using cutting edge digital platforms in the class room, and making sure the children live a healthy life, a combination of plenty of exercise, practising mindfulness and well-being, eating healthily and limiting screen time.

Most parents are pleased with a more down to earth approach he brings to the school. He is the Gordon Brown to his predecessor's Tony Blair. 'He looks the children in the eye when he greets them in the morning,' said one mother, 'rather than looking over the top of their heads at the parents.' Some find him inscrutable. A troubleshooter in the past, there seems to be quite a bit for him to get on top of here too. A tricky period when the school lacked a proper head, issues with SEN provision, a lack of balance between boys and girls and the usual challenges of a very competitive field for the 11 plus transfer. Some parents suspect that he is out of his depth but he comes across as genuine and concerned to do the right thing for pupils and parents.

F

Entrance: Names down at birth if you want to be sure of a place. First come, first served, though siblings continue to be given preference. Even numbers of places offered to boys and girls (between 25 and 30 places for each in reception). Tours on request: those on a waiting list are offered week day open mornings, parents with a definite place are shown round individually and meet the head.

Occasional places do come up further up the school, especially in years 3 and 4 when some pupils move here from the state sector. A child attends the school for a taster morning and informal assessments.

Each year the school says it welcomes two or three children with special needs; they have to apply along with everyone else and places are offered on a first come, first served basis. When a child with SEN receives an offer, then the parents meet with the SENCo and head of special needs to ensure his/her needs can be met before the place is confirmed. Some state funding for children with an EHCP/statement.

Exit: Most leave at 11, though a (very) few boys still leave at 7 or 8 (occasionally to KCS but more often to board). At 11 they go to a range of south London schools, with Streatham and Clapham, Wimbledon High and JAGS currently the most popular destinations. Fairly high numbers choose to board at, eg, Benenden, many of those needing to bridge the gap before starting at 13 go to Northcote Lodge (for boys), Broomwood Hall (for girls) or boarding preps. A handful of scholarships (10 in 2018), several academic as well as art, music, sports and design technology. School prides itself on advising parents carefully so as to limit the number of applications to three schools only. 'The senior schools know the applications are genuine and our success rate is high,' affirms the head of academics.

Remarks: Tucked into a corner of a warren of narrow Wandsworth residential side streets, which, at 8.30 in the morning teem with 4x4 SUVs negotiating their right of way, Finton House is a cosy, intimate and smart little school. The playground is a sea of navy cord (girls in wide culottes, boys in cute shorts or long trousers), and blue and white crest emblazoned blazers. Overwhelmingly white middle class, 'Wasp like,' said one parent, this has long been the first choice of school for the established well-heeled English resident of Wandsworth. Traditional families that tended to move to the country after their decade in the smoke, and for whom the grinding competitiveness of the 11+ was never much of an issue, gave their children a nurturing, but solid foundation here. The school, which is non-selective, was regarded as unpressured and positively inclusive. There is a history of accepting children with a wide range of special educational needs: historically there has been a child in each class in every year with a statement or EHCP.

The character of the school is changing, however. Fewer families move to the country, more stay for the duration and will be negotiating the 11+ to one of the London secondaries. Always diverse in terms of ability, the school is becoming slightly more diverse socially, though the number of international families is still surprisingly few compared to other schools in the area. It is more common now for both parents to work (though one mother we spoke to remarked that there were very few nannies in the playground), and boys are more likely to stay until year 6 (although there were only five in the top year when we visited). School is actively working to keep the boys. One parent commented on the importance of inclusivity academically as this goes some way to making the school feel diverse. As the academics become more streamlined the school is starting to feel more homogenous. A dedicated parent body, with a system of class reps as well as committees for major events (helps to reduce cliquishness, we were told).

Many of the teachers (of whom the majority are women) have been here for well over a decade. Longevity of staff is seen as a strength by some, a weakness by others who regard some old timers as complacent and out of touch. A broad range of ability was evident in the class assembly in which some pupils were able to recite large tracts of memorised text beautifully, while others were reading their one line from a prompt. However all are rewarded for their effort, enthusiasm and interest with celebration certificates each week. Lots of singing – 'everyone sings at Finton' – whether it be the song for the celebration book – 'for working hard and being kind you have exercised your mind!' or singing Happy Birthday! to a classmate and the plethora of songs during assemblies.

Broad curriculum all the way through to year 6. Specialist DT (from year 1), art, music and computing teachers all the way through. Sport is taught by trained PE teachers from reception. Drama included as part of the curriculum and taught by class teachers and the English department. Seventy per cent of pupils play at least one instrument. Class music lesson and a recorder lesson from year 3. Plenty of groups and ensembles – everyone can have a go.

The ethos of being supportive and inclusive of children with special educational needs continues, though a number of parents feel this has been heavily diluted. The school has traditionally had a good relationship with Wandsworth council and will support a family trying to obtain an EHCP. Mixed reports about how the funding is managed, dissatisfaction in some quarters, primarily centred on poor communication. The deputy head oversees two SENCos, one of whom is responsible for learning support, the other for SEN. They are supported by five part-time specialist teaching assistants and in addition there is an occupational therapist and a speech and language therapist. Each class has a teaching assistant assigned to it, and a child with greater needs may have someone else in addition to this. Occupational therapy room complete with gym mats, beanbags and climbing ladders. Most classrooms have an amplification system so that all pupils can hear. Just under 40 per cent of children in each year group receive some form of additional support.

Three classes per year of about 20 between reception and year 4. Historically the numbers have dropped considerably in years 5 and 6 – fewer than 20 in each class, though numbers not as low in the final year now as they used to be. Occasional places at the top of the school unfortunately cannot be filled as the numbers are capped owing to planning restrictions.

Homework can be pretty intense, especially if your child struggles academically. One parent talked about the pressure of homework as early as year 1.

A healthy bursary fund set up in memory of much loved former head, Sally Walker, offers bursaries (four on 100 per cent, but there are 80 and 70 per cent bursaries too) for children arriving in years 2 and 3 (often from the state sector). School carefully manages their exit at secondary to enable the experience the child has benefitted from at Finton House to continue. Frequent fundraising extravaganzas are organised by the parents and wholehearted support of the governors means this is likely to continue to grow and be a great feature of the school. Nor do you 'have to be destitute' to apply for a bursary, says Mr Ben. Question mark as to how the bursary fund is going to be used with the decline in spaces in years 2 and 3.

The school is blessed with a spacious playground, complete with climbing frames, Astroturf, and Wendy houses. A separate, modern wing for reception, the Emma Thornton building, houses DT, cooking, science, music and learning support. Light and airy – even in the basement. DT feels vibrant and ambitious, the room filled with little wooden robots (a whole school project) when we visited as well as teaspoons fashioned into characters. Materials used are mainly wood and textiles; year 6 were making go-carts. Lovely smells of old fashioned carpentry workshops, and tools like saws, drills and glue guns adorn the place.

Wonderful art room at the top of the school in the eaves. Parents we spoke to praised the inspirational art teacher and we witnessed her in action – the children completely absorbed in colourful Indian art forms and the use of glitter. The year 6 project was concerned with drawing and printing bugs. Lovely circular seat where children can be invited to read, draw or just rest, as a reward. Busy library overflowing with books and children reading them when we visited (it didn't seem staged). iPad and laptop stations on each floor are used discriminatingly in the class room.

A flagpole flies the flag of the house with the most house points that week. There are inter-house competitions in cricket, football, netball and rugby as well as hockey, rounders and swimming. Sport takes place at Trinity fields and Tooting hard courts. Cupboards displaying a plethora of silverware, cups and shields line the basement. The music department is carpeted and warm (a good place to retreat to practise); lots of percussion instruments and, on our tour, singing filled the space. The five boys in year 6 (when we visited) double up with year 5 boys for team sports.

Lots of positions of responsibility for children at the top of the school. The head boy and head girl have to make speeches in front of the school, prefects regularly meet Mr Ben and are in charge of house points and there are several house captains as well as games captains and one swimming captain. Subject monitors – those who show a passion or talent for a particular subject – as well as three library monitors. Children remark on how much Mr Ben gets involved – whether it be cheering teams on at the swimming gala, greeting them in the playground, or commending them on individual pieces of work. Parents delighted with the prize day he introduced at the end of the academic year.

An excellent foundation for the all rounder but, despite the cosy size, don't expect it to be as 'fluffy round the edges' as it used to be.

Forest School

College Place, Snaresbrook, London E17 3PY

Ages 4–18 **Pupils** 1,364 **Sixth form** 279 **C of E**

Fees: £13,095 – £18,681 pa

020 8520 1744
www.forest.org.uk

Warden: Since 2016, Marcus Cliff Hodges (50s). An imposing man – looks tough and dynamic – but thoughtful, likeable and very easy to meet. A career schoolmaster in the very best sense of the word: an English degree from Cardiff plus a masters from the Institute of Education then teaching posts in Gstaad, followed by Bedford and the assistant headship at Latymer Upper. Hit the top spot (warden) at Forest after a spell as head of the boys' senior school and acting warden. No sense at all of his being overawed by the job – 'it's actually a very liberating experience' – and he is evidently devoted to a school he knows and understands intimately. A keen fisherman and mountaineer, he communicates calm dependability. Married with a teenage son (a pupil). 'Steeped in the place and a great appointment,' said one parent, adding, 'he's quite formal and old-fashioned in some ways. No bad thing.'

Academic matters: A highly efficient and effective feel to the teaching backed up by excellent results. In 2018, at A level, 50 per cent A*/A grades. At GCSE, 77 per cent of all grades were A*-A/9-7. Maths, science, English and history appear particularly strong. Less obvious drive to continue with modern languages – take-up at A level is slight. Masses of (trained) support for those with organisational difficulties and specific learning difficulties. The overall sense is of very capable and determined teachers plus a school packed to the gunnels with bright students and a few very high flyers. 'It's a high-achieving school,' said one parent, 'but not a hothouse. That's suited us. I really hope that it stays that way'.

Teaching was judged 'excellent' in the latest ISI report and there is no sign of anything less than ongoing commitment. 'My teachers really mind,' said one girl, 'and it makes such a difference to the way we all work'. The warden agrees: 'There is masses of good practice,' he says, 'but the real challenge is to make teaching and learning tailored around each individual pupil. Not to pander to them, but to empower them.' Forest has made a big play of 'learning characteristics' – independence and flexibility being two of them. Teachers use these to check on their charges' progress.

Professional but pragmatic attitudes to special educational needs: basic screening tests are given to all pupils on entry and parents are told immediately if extra support is needed. A learning support department with four qualified staff lead the drive to help, whether that means specialist lessons to pupils or advising subject teachers how to contribute. There are no pupils on EHC plans, but about 80 currently have IEPs.

The great singularity of Forest is its diamond structure. Between the ages of 4 and 7, the school is fully co-ed. Between 7 and the end of GCSEs, classes are single-sex. Eating, recreation, sport and most other activities all take place together – it's just that boys and girls learn separately. At sixth form, they revert to co-ed. 'We haven't retained it as an historical curiosity,' says the warden. 'We believe in it. We think it's best.' As it is a one-site school, he has a valid argument that the school falls in the co-ed camp.

Games, options, the arts: Sitting on 50 green acres on the edge of Epping Forest, sporty children are in clover. The facilities are astonishing – a sports centre on site and an Olympic swimming pool. Football, in the warden's words, 'is deep in the DNA of the school', but he believes that no one sport enjoys a monopoly of prestige. 'Having sufficient alternatives is critical if people aren't going to feel excluded,' he insists. The U15 footballers have recently been in the ISFA final, and hockey is making a strong comeback, with three U15 players (two girls and one boy) in the England squad. Girls' football is also booming and the school tries to cater to all tastes and talents, taking advantage of the Olympic velodrome, West Essex golf club and local rowing clubs. All pupils have to do four games or activity periods per week, right up to their last year. 'It's simple,' said one pupil, 'they want us to have something to think about as well as our work, otherwise, you can end up fretting.'

Very strong dance (musical theatre, street, ballet and tap) welds into performance. There's an annual multicultural music and dance spectacular – the so-called FUSION. Every house enters the annual house drama competition and the school theatre stages three major productions each year. The Michaelmas Play draws its cast from the whole school community. Recent productions include Oh What A Lovely War! and Dick Barton – Special Agent! They are rightly proud of old pupil Paapa Essiedu, who graduated from studying theatre studies here to playing Hamlet at Stratford. For the past five years at least one pupil per year has won a place at a musical conservatoire. Clear indications are appearing of the booming significance art, design and technology play in the life of the school and a new head of DT has recently signed up.

Background and atmosphere: Began life as a proprietary grammar school in 1834. Forest's founders included the Spode industrialist, William Copeland, and the governor of the Bank of England, William Cotton. It grew sufficiently rapidly to have sacrificed some 100 old boys in the Great War but the big growth came in the last century, with girls being admitted in 1981.

The campus feels more like a well-ordered village rather than an institution, despite the number of pupils – modern, dynamic youngsters with an eye on what's happening next but without the brittle, jarring quality of some metropolitan children. The way in which they wear their uniforms, and interact with their teachers and each other, backs up their positive view of the school. One parent said: 'All types of pupils and all kinds of achievement are celebrated. The teachers set the example and the older pupils take their lead from them, and it seeps all the way down the school'.

The school communicates a palpable ethos of teamwork and service. D of E and CCF are both massively popular, and being linked to the Royal Green Jackets augurs a commendable degree of toughness. Civic engagement is highly prized: there is a close link to Haven House, a local children's hospice. 'We're not going to solve its funding,' says the warden, 'but our ongoing involvement is about more than money'. New initiatives are constantly springing up, most recently with pupils helping run a youth club in Chelmsford for young people with mental health issues.

The vast selection of lunchtime and after-school clubs show that Forest embraces irony as well as all that is wholesome. Warhammer and chess clubs, well-known destinations for some who are less than extrovert or athletic, enjoy prominence, as do those for Manfood and cake decoration. Alongside the medicine, engineering and law societies, those of a less squeamish disposition may enjoy time spent at the dissection society.

Pastoral care, well-being and discipline: Discipline is low key, but the school does not shy away from addressing occasional poor behaviour. 'We have most of the usual teenage issues to confront but I believe the safeguarding here is outstanding and that the whole ethos of pastoral care is embraced by the staff,' says the warden.

Forest is, depending on how you look at it, two schools (or even three), albeit on one campus and sharing the same ethos and genus: there's the pre-prep, the prep and the senior school – the latter divided into lower and middle schools and sixth form. Each has its own head of section who oversees pupils' academic progress.

Pupils' own tutors and housemistresses and housemasters look after pastoral care. Houses exercise a big hold on pupil identity as well as holding considerable importance in terms of school competitions (note – not just sport but also including art, dance, drama and MasterChef). There's also a chaplain (and a very beautiful school chapel) and compulsory year group services each week. It has a very Church of England feel but the susceptibilities of those of other faiths are carefully considered when it comes to hymn selection. 'I'd actually prefer it to be completely secular,' said a parent, admitting that was 'a minority view'.

Pupils and parents: Buses bring in children every day from places as far afield as Epping, Docklands and Highbury, although many pupils make their own way to school using the excellent public transport links. Liaison with parents is taken seriously: in addition to termly written reports and an annual parents' evening, there is a yearly information evening in September. 'This way parents become clued-up rapidly about what we see as important over the next 12 months, and it gives them confidence and a good reason to work with us,' says the warden. Lots of other events as well – the parental conference programme includes talks on revision, drug awareness, IT – but there is no sense that this is a school which would ever allow an 'in-crowd' of parents to emerge, and is all the better for it.

Distinguished alumni cover all bases: H Tubb and WJ Cutbill were founding members of the Football Association, and Paralympian equestrian, Liz Stone won gold at Atlanta in 1996, whilst Ella Purnell and Nicola Walker are enjoying successful stage, TV and film careers. Less generally famous perhaps is squadron leader Geoffrey Wellum DFC, a renowned Battle of Britain spitfire pilot. He has credited Forest with giving him the spiritual support, courtesy of his time in chapel, to fight another day in the clouds.

Entrance: Selection for the pre-prep takes the form of a morning of low-key activities for which parents are asked – perhaps more in hope than expectation? – not to coach their children for the 32 places (16 boys and 16 girls). There are further entry points at 7+, at 11+ (the start of the senior school, at which point some 120 pupils are selected from at least 750 applicants) and 16+, where the school might well take in another 20 or 30 pupils, depending on availability.

Exit: Almost all the prep school pupils move into the senior school, unless families are relocating, and the same applies to the GCSE cohort. A few leave at this point, sometimes because of families relocating, and there will be a tiny contingent who decide it's not for them or who don't cut the mustard academically for the sixth form. This is a high-octane environment: two were awarded Cambridge places in 2018 and almost all leavers go on to Russell Group universities. Four medics in 2018, but the broad base of subjects studied at university testifies to the school's academic range and depth. One off to the Royal Northern College of Music and one to study liberal arts at UC Berkeley.

Money matters: There is a range of scholarships and exhibitions, for both academic and musical prowess, as well as bursarial assistance, depending on means.

Remarks: A powerhouse with a heart. The school has an immensely purposeful feel to it – no doubt influenced by the warden, but also by skilled and serious-minded teachers and parents.

Fortismere School

South Wing, Tetherdown, London N10 1NE

Ages 11–19 **Pupils** 1,771 **Sixth form** 427

020 8365 4400
www.fortismere.haringey.sch.uk

Co-heads: Since February 2018, Zoe Judge, previously director of sixth form and Jo Davey, previously deputy head, who had been interim co-heads since 2017.

Zoe Judge joined Fortismere in 2002 as a pastoral leader and a member of the English department, having begun her teaching career at a high-performing school in Barking and Dagenham. She was initially a head of year and has over the years taught English, media and film. In 2006 she joined the school leadership team as the assistant head with responsibility for key stage 3. In 2010 she became director of sixth form.

Jo Davey joined as a part-time consultant in 2013 while deputy head teacher at Blanche Neville School. She had previously worked in Camden schools as a history and politics teacher and as a school improvement consultant with responsibility for vulnerable groups.

Academic matters: A large proportion of bright, motivated pupils and also a greater than average number of pupils with SEN, with a relatively small mid range. In 2018, 76 per cent A*-B at A level, 42 per cent A*/A; at GCSE 42 per cent A*-A/9-7 and nearly 80 per cent got 5+ grade 9-4s including both maths and English.

Every subject previously set from year 7; this has been loosened but school still sets early for maths and science whilst English is taught in mixed ability classes. 'We trust the faculty heads on that but they must show that it works.' Relatively low class size of 24. Everyone learns French or Spanish in year 7 and promising linguists are offered Mandarin in year 8 (now a Pre-U in the sixth form). They are encouraged to take two languages to GCSE; around 80 per cent of pupils take at least one. The top 60 per cent are encouraged to take triple science GCSE.

Teaching standards mostly very high, with the odd exception, say parents. 'They expect of lot of the students – I think they push them very hard. They encourage and extend them, particularly with the personal projects in the sixth form.' Reporting system to parents has improved. 'They tell you what your child's target is, what level they're performing at now and whether that's okay. I've mostly found teachers very responsive when I've emailed them.'

The sixth form admissions criteria are 'closer to a grammar school', with at least five grade 6s at GCSE required for A level, and 7s for certain subjects eg maths. A small number of vocational options (five grade 4s at GCSEs required): music technology, ICT, business, media and sports science. School also teaches classical heritage and global perspectives Pre-U courses. Maths a very popular A level alongside history (teaching dubbed 'exceptional' by parents) and English. Respectable numbers pursuing biology and chemistry and – as one might expect in this liberal, intellectual area – philosophy, psychology, government & politics and sociology, though linguists disappointingly few.

'Amazing' preparation for Oxford, said a parent. 'It was all very low key, but there are several young Oxbridge graduates teaching at the school, and they ran workshops, put on seminars, did mock interviews and put pupils in touch with other students who'd been through the process recently. It was all there but it was up to the kids to push themselves that much further.'

With its large, segmented site and high pupil numbers, possibly not the most suitable school for children with learning difficulties, but many choose it nonetheless, 'and we do a very good job with them'. A relatively large proportion with EHC plans (mostly with autistic spectrum and behavioural issues) – these have their own teaching assistant. However, 'we try to keep away from TAs velcroed to children', and they are included in class work as far as possible with small group sessions to help them develop independent learning skills. Linc team helps those experiencing learning difficulties – temporary or permanent. The secondary department of the Blanche Neville School for deaf and hearing-impaired children – some joining in mainstream activities – occupies an impressive building on the site.

Games, options, the arts: Fabulous newish music block, with recording studios, composing and practice rooms plus multi-use performance spaces, mirrors the subject's importance here (though few A level takers). Symphony orchestra, big band and several choirs; community choirs and orchestras include parents as well as children; Saturday music school. 'We play a key role in the local community. We have always had a lot of hugely musical students – it comes with the parent body.'

Impressive displays of art and fabulous photography coursework on show during our visit, plus bright papier-mâché aliens and rats created by younger year groups. Photography a popular A level and one can see why. Drama also 'massive'. 'We're a very artsy school. It's our natural default setting.' 'Fantastic' production of Little Shop of Horrors included the actual plant from the West End show; sixth formers regularly take productions to the Edinburgh fringe and help with GCSE drama performances.

Sport has been bolstered by increased amounts of time in the upper years plus the introduction of Colleges, or houses, which run weekly inter-college competitions and encourage non A team players to get involved. However, parents report that it is possible for the less athletically inclined to avoid breaking into a sweat, and it is fair to say that reports of sports team triumphs do not feature largely in school newsletters. Sports hall, tennis/netball/basketball courts, acres of playing fields and 'very popular' table tennis tables.

Large range of trips includes 'brilliant and very well organised' week in Beijing for Mandarin speakers, exchange visits to France, Spain, Senegal and India ('though you do have to queue up at 7am with your cheque to get a place on the popular ones,' commented a parent), D of E, outdoor pursuits in the Brecon Beacons, ski trips, field trips and cultural visits. A steady stream of authors, scientists, politicians etc comes to give talks; librarian organises team of pupils to shadow Carnegie medal deliberations, reading and reviewing shortlisted books; teams enter debating competitions.

Background and atmosphere: Large site amidst leafy Muswell Hill Edwardiana has been the setting for a series of schools of all sorts, including private, grammar and comprehensive. Fortismere was formed in 1983 by the amalgamation of Creighton and Alexandra Park Schools (Alexandra Park School nearby is a separate entity). There remains a hotch-potch of buildings from its various incarnations. North and South

Wings linked by a quarter-mile pathway round the playing fields that can resemble a storm in the North Sea in inclement weather. Accommodation beginning to show its age but bright and cheerful. A multitude of noticeboards – with college news, photos of trips, information on clubs.

Very much a community comprehensive with a relaxed atmosphere (subject to 'behaviour for learning' sanctions), and pupils strolling around in jeans and tee shirts. 'Proudly non-uniform', though with a veto on revealing too much skin or underwear. 'It's part of the ethos for children to be able to express themselves,' said a parent.

Pastoral care, well-being and discipline: Good transition system, with year 6s spending three days at the school in the summer term getting to know the site and teachers. Operates vertical tutor system, with 18 pupils of different ages from the same college in each group replacing old form tutor system. All staff – including admin staff – are tutors, 'which enables us to have small groups, and also increases student respect for non-teaching staff'. Mixed reviews from parents and pupils, some enthusiastic whilst others feel that the system needs time to bed in and become a tradition, and that they would prefer to spend the time with their peers.

F

Student leadership team, which includes head boy and girl and their deputies, has a meeting with the head each Monday. 'It has already had a real impact. They really challenge us about why we do things, and it makes us think about structures.'

Previous head's introduction of zero tolerance for lateness and absenteeism shocked some families and delighted others, with one parent terming it 'draconian.' 'The behaviour here was good, but we thought it could be better. If you are disrupting the learning of others, that is not negotiable. Parents complain, but when we tell them their child is stopping other people learning, they find that hard to justify.' Refuses permission for holidays in term time: 'We get a lot of poorly relatives in far flung places towards the end of the Christmas and summer terms.' In response to pupils' requests for carrots as well as sticks, Positive Points system gives house points for helpfulness, participation, tidiness etc and is widely reported in the newsletters.

Pupils mostly very happy and have good relationships with staff, but some parents feel that the pastoral system is variable. Some teachers 'do resolve your issues,' said a parent, citing the 'novel and interesting solutions' to stress suggested by her daughter's college head. However, 'I had a very unsympathetic reaction from the school to a family death. I found their policies very inflexible.' 'They didn't seem to be sensitive to the needs of my younger daughter,' said another parent, whose children had joined from a different education system. 'I really didn't feel she got the support she needed, and I felt that no-one had an overview of the situation. I also had no response to a very carefully worded email about a pastoral issue that had upset her.'

Permanent exclusions rare, and usually for persistent defiance or repeated breaking of behaviour policies. Will swap recalcitrant pupils with other local schools. 'We're good at managed moves – they can be very effective.' Will also use outside providers such as local boxing and football academies for those who clearly need a different approach. 'We prefer to try something different before moving to permanent exclusion.' A parent commented: 'There are some wild and woolly kids, but they don't tend to disrupt classes.'

Works in collaboration with the mental health charity, Place2Be, to provide therapeutic counselling for students as needed.

Pupils and parents: Largely affluent, liberal, middle class families – artists and musicians, writers and actors – plus quite a few looked-after children. 'It is a very political school. We have to remember that parents don't just read the Guardian – quite likely they write for it too.' These are mostly cool kids, relaxed and confident, proud to be at Haringey's most popular comprehensive. 'My daughters' friends are lovely,' said a parent. 'They meet up to study and all help each other.' Ex-pupils include singers Michael Kiwanuka and Jess Glynne.

Entrance: Takes 270 pupils into year 7. Those with an EHC plan naming the school – and there are many of these – automatically get a place. Then priority to children in care, those with particular medical, social or emotional needs, and siblings, with the remainder by distance, usually less than half a mile.

About 110 outside students come into the sixth form, from state and independent schools. Requires 5+ 9-4 GCSEs for vocational A levels and 5+ 9-6s for academic A levels, with higher grades for certain subjects eg maths, from both internal and external students. Those who don't perform well in year 12 are liable to be directed elsewhere.

Exit: Small numbers (around 30 per cent) move on after GCSEs, generally for more vocational courses. Nearly all sixth form leavers to university: Sussex, Leeds, Manchester and Bristol the current favourites; 16 to Oxbridge or medical school in 2018. English, philosophy, psychology, maths, law, geography all popular.

Money matters: Very active parents' association, the FSA, which underwrote the refurbishment of the sixth form centre.

Remarks: A popular and high-achieving comprehensive that successfully includes those with difficulties as well as extending the most able. School's vision is to have 'an active mind, a finger on the pulse and a big heart.'

Fox Primary School

Kensington Place, London W8 7PP

Ages 4–11 **Pupils** 359

020 7727 7637
www.fox.rbkc.sch.uk

Executive head: Since 2006, Paul Cotter BA PGCE (40s), who is executive head of the federation of Fox Primary and Ashburnham Community School, Chelsea. Previously deputy head at Avondale Park Primary, North Kensington. As successful head of Fox, became acting head of Ashburnham, and oversaw the transformation of the smaller school at World's End. Sees the formal union of the two schools, both with multicultural populations but from different social spheres, as a positive; 'Fox has benefited from the whole experience. We've had to reflect upon our own practices'. Described as 'approachable' by the parents, and visible at the school door every day.

Head of school since 2013, Emma Madden BA (Cantab) MA (IoE); mid 30s. Like Paul Cotter, joined Fox from Avondale Park Primary in 2007, swiftly rose through the ranks of assistant, deputy, then associate head. Married with two children, husband works as an environmental campaigner. To call Ms Madden purposeful is an understatement, more like a human dynamo. She takes great pride in the school's training record, and is at the door every afternoon, keen, committed and capable; but don't expect a relaxing chat over coffee.

Entrance: LA managed, prioritising looked after children, exceptional need, siblings and children of staff. Then by random allocation within priority area, which extends from Chepstow Villas to Kensington High Street, from Kensington Palace Gardens to Holland Park, including more billionaires' basements than you can shake a stick at, and a small local authority housing estate. Some occasional places, but loyalty is encouraged; 'We only want people to come if they intend to stay,' says the head of school, with a nod at the 'state till 8' brigade.

Exit: Roughly half of all leavers go to Holland Park School, a few to Chelsea Academy. Others (with helping hand from a tutor) successful at top London day schools, including St Paul's Juniors, City of London Boys and Girls, Latymer Upper, Godolphin & Latymer. Parents say head makes no judgement about where the child goes, as long as it's the best fit.

Remarks: Perfection comes in small packages, and the teaching at Fox Primary is no exception. The small classes (two of 24 per year) and the impressive KS2 Sats results (around half reach level 5) have consistently put the school high in the league tables. The key to its success is training good staff, of which they are justifiably proud; 'It has huge respect for teaching as a profession,' a parent remarked. Emma Madden is unashamedly serious about the school's role as a training centre, providing professional development for two London boroughs as well as courses for newly qualified teachers and TAs. In addition the school is a maths hub for central and west London, sharing methods among teachers as far as Shanghai.

We were surprised to hear that, though energetic and youthful-looking, some staff had more than 10 years experience, and a few up to 20. The best of the newly qualifieds in training at the school are persuaded to join. 'There's a lot of support for young teachers', said a parent. 'I guess you want that fresh voice, but you want it to be quality'. The school has children with statements supported by the two special needs teachers, one a science specialist, but overall number of SEN children is lower than average. EAL proportions are high. One parent remarked how quickly the class teacher had noticed and dealt with her daughter's reading and maths difficulties. Support came in the form of small group work and individual attention; 'she's flying now,' commented the delighted mum.

Classrooms are high ceilinged, utilitarian design, with steel framed windows, many brightened up by pots of geraniums. The younger years enjoy the ground floor rooms, where round tables in primary colours, a carpeted reading corner and bunting brighten the space. They make the most of their direct access to the rear playground, where netball posts share the tarmac with raised vegetable beds. Upstairs, we met a class of older children, in quiet discussion at a large group table. Another group was colouring the Brazilian flag in a geography lesson, strains of gentle music in the background. We heard from one articulate boy that a parent had visited earlier to teach them some Portuguese in addition to the Spanish, taken in class. On the top floor a music activity had children, grouped in front of the whiteboard, following acoustic patterns by clapping out rhythms. A display of the SS Windrush emblazoned the white walls of the oldest children's room in celebration of black history month. The children we met were unpretentious yet confident, happily engrossed in their work. PE in the hall, involved youngsters shooting hoops in sensible royal blue T shirts and track suits. No uniform otherwise, though Hackett rugby shirts were all the rage.

Fox values are displayed around the school: collaboration, loving learning, independence, creativity. All children learn recorder in year 3, with individual instrument lessons offered further up the school. A school orchestra practises before lessons. Shows are big at Fox, with end of year productions carrying an ethical message (Charlie doesn't just find sweets in his chocolate factory but Fox's moral values too). 'They are really nice events,' said a parent, 'with a lot of real warmth towards the child who stands there'. Other children join the inter-schools' debating team. A makeshift studio in a classroom at the top of the school allows the specialist art technician space to do her thing. We saw satisfying slab pots and displays of paper cutting.

An experienced PE teacher, 'adored by the children' ensures every child in year 6 represents the school in an activity: football, tag-rugby, hockey and netball run alongside judo and athletics in local leagues. Table tennis is a big success, with an all-weather table in the playground, and involves ex-Fox students in national tournaments. With many working parents, clubs after school are popular, one parent told us; 'The day people sign up, parents are queuing into the street'.

Founded in 1842 by a doughty female philanthropist, Caroline Fox (curiously under-celebrated at the school, we thought), when modish Notting Hill was no more than muddy fields. Originally a charity school for the local labouring classes, Fox Primary moved to its present site behind the antique shops of Kensington Church Street in 1935. Since then, the utilitarian architecture has withstood a sea change of bohemian chic in the neighbourhood. Within the high walls surrounding the school, some of the noble intentions of the founder re-emerge in a save the planet philosophy. A children's eco committee rakes out compost, feeds the wormery and monitors rubbish, and has achieved the Green Flag award. Solar panels operate on the roof, while a water butt supplies the gardening teacher with rainwater to cultivate some tasty extras for lunch. The chickens have now given way to beekeeping and two hives produce Fox honey, which is sold for school funds. These city children are not just playing farms, they grow their own lunch and even supply produce for a local restaurant.

Lunches are cooked on site, with meat delivered by Lidgates butchers on three days; the rest of the time it's a meat-free menu. Some choose to bring packed lunches. 'Food's excellent,' said a parent. Favourite dishes included chicken and rice and yogurt fruit compote. Fox publishes its own cookbook, with toothsome photographs by one of the parents (not a turkey twizzler in sight). Trips out have included the Holland Park edible garden and London Wetland Centre, as well as the walkable South Kensington museums.

'We celebrate success a lot,' remarks Emma Madden, both among the four houses (named after species of fox: arctic, desert, silver, red) and at afternoon assembly, timetabled at 3pm, to keep the mornings free for the most concentrated tasks. Children are motivated in class by the chance of becoming 'Star/Speaker/Reader of the week' or by competitions, eg 'Who can invent the healthiest snack?' with a trip to a local café as a reward. Homework is regular but not excessive, numeracy once a week, reading and spelling daily. 'Behaviour is very, very good', remarks Emma Madden; 'children need to have clear expectations'. Parents' concerns are managed by face-to-face meetings with teachers in the playground each morning, or by email. Despite this, one mum felt notice of school decisions did not always get through. 'I know the information is there, but it's just letting the parents know...it's been a full time job keeping up with it all'. Parents' evenings twice a year bring opportunities to chat to the class teacher, as does the annual International evening, a festival of the multi-national flavour of the school.

The parents are a committed lot; 'Fox is fortunate as it is in an affluent area,' said one mum (very low numbers on free school meals). Despite the area being known for its cosmopolitan beau monde, the school's parents include a few past pupils as well as professionals from business, legal and arts spheres. Fundraising by the parents, through summer and winter fairs, aims to create benefits for children from all backgrounds – Caroline Fox would be proud.

For the fortunate who break through the oversubscribed entry lists and can breach the formidable railings outside, it is a rare find: a quality education with a broad curriculum, led by a staff with vision and commitment. As one mum said, 'It's a brilliant school and we are very, very lucky'.

Francis Holland Junior School, Sloane Square

Linked with Francis Holland School, Sloane Square

F

Graham Terrace, London SW1W 8JF

Ages 4–11 **Pupils** 165 **C of E**

Fees: £18,480 – £20,910 pa

020 7730 2971
www.fhs-sw1.org.uk

Head of juniors: Since 2015, Caroline Spencer-Kruger, previously deputy head.

Entrance: Assessments at 3. Some 150 girls tested in January for 24 places. School assesses 'girls' potential and readiness to learn.' School was horrified when a parent asked about tutoring for their 3-year old and advises, 'Parents need to read to their children, take them to the park and talk to them. That's the best preparation for these tests.' Places occasionally available further up the school and prospective pupils are then assessed in the classroom setting. Barely a spare seat in the house.

Exit: Fairly evenly split: one third to the senior school, one third to other London day schools and another third boarding. One parent remarked that she thought it would be 'a hard jump to go from Francis Holland Junior School to a large co-ed. Girls are protected here and can be quite gentle. I'm not sure they are always ready for the hurly burly of senior school.' Popular day destinations include St Paul's, Godolphin & Latymer, Latymer Upper, JAGS. Current boarding favourites are Wycombe Abbey, Downe House and Cheltenham Ladies'.

Remarks: A small, academic school, tucked away behind Sloane Square. One form per year of 24 maximum. Shares a site with senior school. 'Low pressure in the early years,' says school. Reception children have naps after lunch in first term when sleepy. From year 4 it hots up, with summer exams in maths, English and science from then on. No setting but plenty of differentiation. The consensus among parents we spoke to was that 'you need to be academically robust to cope here. There are so many projects and tests, and parents are expected to be able to support their offspring massively. It feels almost relentless at times.'

More academic than senior school: 'The girls here are clever and motivated,' said one parent. 'Strong foundations are laid but the girls work hard for it,' according to another. The standard of work on display was astonishingly high. The girls themselves feel that they are well prepared for the 11+, but 'we don't feel too much pressure.' Year 6 pupils kept working to proper timetables once 11+ exams are over; no coasting here. Teaching is superb and staff considered by the parents to be high quality. Teachers come over from senior school to teach PE, science, French (from 8) and some art. Well motivated staff. 'We're a strong team'.

Bright classrooms, inventive displays, beanbags and colour everywhere. Wonderful library, shared with senior school, and huge numbers of books at every turn.

Girls have beautiful manners and stand up with military discipline when adults enter the room. Highly articulate and fluent. Very keen to show their projects to us when we visited and tell us what they had learnt. Highly engaged in lessons, from early years upwards.

Plenty of time for fun, with highly-anticipated trips to Cornwall in year 6 and Canterbury in year 5. Sport is a real strength. Ballet taken seriously: compulsory in the first years, fabulous ballet studio. Highly anticipated Princess Margaret ballet competition every summer term – her daughter is an old girl. Lots of music and drama, including impressive end of year 6 musical. Girls take the initiative by providing the costumes, designing the posters and rehearsing on their own at break times. Great emphasis placed on creativity throughout the school. Junior choir from year 3 and a very select chamber choir for the most talented singers. Significant numbers learn instruments from year 1 onwards. 'Girls need time to be bored. They should not have every moment of their lives timetabled.' Wants them to discover what interests them for themselves. Plenty of clubs on offer including chess, speech and drama, pottery and French.

A very caring school in which older girls are expected to, and do, look after the younger ones. Year 6 pupils write and illustrate books for year 1 pupils. Lots of raising money for charity. All year 6 girls are prefects, though badges confiscated for poor behaviour.

Families are increasingly international. 'A bewildering number of languages spoken in the playground at pick up time,' according to one mother. Children come from nearby Westminster, Chelsea, Knightsbridge and Pimlico.

'A happy school,' is the consensus amongst parents. Bullying very rare. School feels girls are 'traditional and polite'. One pupil acknowledged, 'It will be the saddest day of my life when I leave Francis Holland to go to my next school.' School described as 'vibrant', and it was certainly buzzing on the day we visited. A real energy about the place. Francis Holland girls have a wonderfully stimulating start to life here, with devoted care and attention from outstanding teachers. No wonder there's a queue to come here.

Francis Holland School, Regent's Park

Clarence Gate, Ivor Place, London NW1 6XR

Ages 11–18 **Pupils** 500 **Sixth form** 127 **C of E**

Fees: £20,040 pa

020 7723 0176
www.fhs-nw1.org.uk

Head: Since 2016, Mr Charles Fillingham (early 40s). Urbane and very approachable, he exudes a calm pleasure in his role and the school. A modern linguist, with degrees from University of Wales, Bristol and King's London. His career has been spent between maintained schools and independent – he had a spell at The Grey Coat Hospital and was deputy at City of London School for boys. He commutes from Surrey each day and spends what free time he can rescue with his wife and two young children, 'though I try still to read French literature'. Like so many other heads, a marathon runner. His three deputies are women: 'They are all in position entirely on merit – but it also really matters for the girls to have outstanding female role models.' Much liked by parents who were particularly wowed by his deftness and approachability in an Q&A session led by pupils very early in his tenure: 'he was easy, natural, and played fair'.

Academic matters: Punching in many ways well above its weight. 2018 saw nearly 55 per cent of A level grades at A*/A, and 72 per cent of GCSEs A*-A/9-7s. Given the entrance is not nearly as academically selective as many, they're doing extremely well and across the full range of subjects. This wasn't always the case – a recent big hike in a couple of STEM subjects.

Mr Fillingham, not surprisingly, takes particular pleasure in the immense value-added over which the school presides. Many girls are outperforming their own expectations of themselves, and he's in no doubt why: 'Small classes, immensely hard-working and well-qualified teachers'. This sounds too good to be true, but parents back up the claims: 'totally committed teachers'; 'wonderful care when my daughter needed to work from home' etc. There's no arguing with results. There would be appear to be a slight tilt towards the arts and humanities in terms of subjects being studied, but two girls went off to Imperial recently, six to study medicine and another dentistry. These successes have elicited pride and pleasure from both staff and pupils.

Equally telling, the school seems not to suffer from the level of attrition which has led bright and ambitious girls to move to chic co-ed sixth forms after GCSEs, with some 80 per cent staying on. 'We don't begrudge a girl her deserved success when she wins a place at another school,' says Mr Fillingham equably. 'We will miss her and wish her well'.

The school's strengths in the classroom owe a good deal to unobtrusive but effective early intervention. There are three teachers dealing with pupils' special needs – often related to dyslexia and dyspraxia. 'All the girls who come here are pretty clever,' says the head, 'and so we ought to be able to help them manage these problems'. Although a number of girls don't speak English at home, the school has not had to make special provision for EAL. Modern languages are thriving in the school – everyone takes at least one for GCSE, and Mr Fillingham is now busily fundraising for the school to buy a house in France as a study centre.

This sensitive integration of pupils from a range of cultural backgrounds is part of the explanation for the school's academic success, which has undoubtedly been assisted by a high degree of staff retention. 'We're losing one member of staff after 42 years this summer,' says head, 'and will be the poorer for it'. He insists that his experience of older colleagues has been only positive and uplifting and that their diligence and enthusiasm has benefited staff as well as students.

Games, options, the arts: Despite being located a stone's throw from Baker Street, the school takes sport seriously – and it shows: the place abounds with buzzy girls who exude the kind of energy which comes from plenty of exercise. It may help that Regent's Park is just across the road, and this allows pupils to make full use of the fact that central London is still full of green spaces.

'The sport is good, but not desperately competitive,' said one parent, 'which has been great for my daughter. She has got into teams which, at certain other schools, wouldn't have happened. And that was great for her.' Tennis and rounders are both flourishing and the netball and hockey teams went on a tour to South Africa last year. Hockey takes place a five minute coach journey away at Paddington Recreation Ground and, for those of an equestrian bent, there are trips to the stables at Hyde Park. There's also a splendid swimming pool in the basement (the head has just extended opening hours) which perhaps explains the fact there is so much competitive swimming and water polo. The school also has a fitness suite and a gymnasium, and gymnastics is big news.

This is an intensely musical school. On our walk round the school we passed a brass ensemble and a string trio, and as well as three orchestras and Jazz group, there are also innumerable chamber groups and five choirs. Recent tours to Russia and the USA testify to music's popularity and another is now planned to China. The head is particularly pleased that the two Frances Holland schools (including the one in Sloane Square) recently shared a platform for a splendid concert, fruit of the work of both schools, to mark the founder's birthday. About two-thirds of the girls have instrumental or singing lessons – hence, the most recent big school production (The Sound of Music) seems to have a particular resonance. Photographs adorn the walls, and the memory is clearly fresh for all those lucky enough to participate or attend. Drama is also lively and very strong, with inter-form competitions for all years, and a dizzying array of short plays.

Masses of clubs ('and they actually meet,' said one parent): touring the school, it was easy to spot how easily and cheerfully engaged pupils seemed in all they were doing. The two art studios conveyed a special joie de vivre – lots of lunchtime and after-school activity goes on here as well – and pupils' work exhibits, in addition to drawing skills, plenty of exposure to different materials and textures.

'We have this mantra about being kind,' says Mr Fillingham, 'and it has to reflect a reality'. All sixth formers do volunteer work – sometimes at local primary schools or in local charity shops – and there is an annual Francis Holland Summer Camp in which pupils spend a residential week with other local children in the Westminster borough. Duke of Edinburgh Award is popular with many girls, and several continue it right through to gold. There's also music and reading with elderly people and with Swiss Cottage School, and a series of links with children's centres in Sri Lanka and Tanzania. A host of activities are also anchored around wider fundraising: the Help Fund raised £17,000 recently. 'There's a big spirit of giving back,' a parent said. 'It's made the school a much bigger deal in my eyes.'

Background and atmosphere: The school was founded by Rev Francis Holland in 1878 and endowed with an uplifting motto, taken from Psalm 144, 'That our daughters may be as the polished corner of the temple'. There's a definite patina of that ecclesiastical temper in the building into which it moved in 1915, although nowadays, of course, everything is bright and lively. Still, architecture tells a story and it maintains close links with St Cyprian's Church across the way and still holds many concerts and services there.

The school's pride in confident and ambitious education is palpable, and the most important way this manifests itself is in an atmosphere which is effervescent and unstoppably cheerful. We're not talking about manic high spirits, but something purposeful and upbeat.

The environment supports this – and, in addition to its ascetic advantages, the place looks intelligently cared for. There was no litter or graffiti (God forbid) and scarcely any mess, even in the sixth form common room. But everywhere buzzed and, while the place felt busy, we divined no sense of tension or crowding. Girls up to GCSE have a uniform – it's worn easily and properly, and the effect is reassuring rather than pompous. Sixth form girls dress 'as for their workplace' and seem to accept this without the need for too many standoffs. Rumours of gripes following a ban on wearing black trainers at school shows among some younger girls, but – in the words of the parent of an indignant daughter – 'that's all good growing-up stuff'.

'I think it's very telling,' another parent said, 'that the staff get along with each other so well. They work late; they turn up to watch plays and concerts; they compete at school quizzes. It's a community which functions.'

Pastoral care, well-being and discipline: There are thoughtful systems in place to harness the abundant goodwill one sees. Every girl has a form tutor who is themselves supported by a deputy, and any concerns are fed through to a head of year and to the pastoral deputy head. There are no houses – formal competition within the school tends to be inter-form. Like most schools which aren't too large, they capitalise on the strength that virtually every pupil is well known to several teachers, and anxieties and inconsistencies are usually quickly picked up. A counsellor also visits on three days a week to provide collateral support. There are a range of opportunities for pupils to shine, starting with a head girl and a small cohort of deputies, as well as a school council. One of the head's recent innovations has been arranging for senior girls to read routine announcements at assembly ('quite empowering, actually,' he reflected).

Parents welcome the clarity of the system and the commitment offered by staff as well. 'London girls can be quite feisty,' one parent reflected, 'and the school offers early and thoughtful engagement when there are problems.' Although there is a system of detentions in place (usually for lateness), the head is emphatic that the girls are sympathetic company and very reasonable. There have been no exclusions, temporary or otherwise, in recent times

Pupils and parents: Lots of communication with parents. There are six sets of reports a year, which sounds like overkill, but the head believes that 'calm, regular, communication serves everyone best', and there is also at least one parents' evening annually per year group. 'Very often, both parents do demanding jobs, so the feedback is essential,' he adds.

Frances Holland attracts what, if poorly managed, could be a challenging constituency of parents, in which the elite professions (lawyers and bankers in profusion) are generously represented. The head insists: 'We enjoy the loyalty of all, and we try to return it in willingly – and even-handedly.' And that loyalty seems to extend to one of the school's most famous alumna, Joan Collins.

Entrance: At year 7, some 600 girls apply for just 75 places. Prospective parents are encouraged to come to an open morning during their daughter's year 5 or at the start of year 6. The school tries hard to make the essentially heartless business of selection as humane as it can. As part of the London 11+ Consortium, the process now consists of a cognitive ability test (rather than maths and English exams) with great emphasis on the interview. At sixth form, candidates are tested in their probable A level subjects as well as interviewed. At this point, there are usually around 20 places and about six successful applicants.

Exit: Girls arrive from a whole range of feeders – 45 schools last year supplied 75 girls. Some two-thirds of the girls come from prep schools, the others from primaries or international schools abroad. Once they're in, Frances Holland sees it as an article of faith to stick by them, come what may, until A levels. In other words, indifferent performance at GCSE debars nobody from the sixth form: 'The gain in trust and goodwill outweighs any hit you may take in the league tables,' opines the head. Three to Cambridge in 2018, and nearly all the others to Russell Group universities, plus several off to study art or drama. 'The calibre of advice for those seeking entrance to US colleges is superb,' said one parent (though none off there this year): this is very often a source of grievance in independent schools, so – praise indeed.

Money matters: Fees are mid-range relative to London, and the school tries hard to ensure there are as few extras as possible. Special trips are billed separately, as are music, yoga and speech and drama lessons. A recent change has been to ensure no extra charge is made for books ('a useful discipline for all of us,' comments the head). Lunch, about which we received glowing opinions, is also part of the package. There are a good range of scholarships at 11+ and 16+ for academic, musical and artistic excellence. There are also a number of bursaries, depending on individual needs and circumstances.

Remarks: A distinguished school which communicates sanity, high standards and sterling example. Teachers and pupils talk easily in classrooms and in corridors – men and women alike – and seem to enjoy one another. Mr Fillingham evidently relishes his work: 'Frankly, I find the people with whom I work – staff, pupils and parents – easy to like and impossible not to admire.'

Francis Holland School, Sloane Square

Linked with Francis Holland Junior School, Sloane Square

90

39 Graham Terrace, London SW1W 8JF

Ages 11–18 **Pupils** 375 **Sixth form** 82 **C of E**

Fees: £20,910 pa

020 7730 2971
www.fhs-sw1.org.uk

Headmistress: Since 2012, Lucy Elphinstone MA PGCE MEd FRSA (50s). Educated at Barnstaple Grammar School, Devon, and Newnham College, Cambridge (English). Very varied career, including stints in publishing, catering, property and ghost-writing. Wide teaching experience from 3 to 18 years, and countless leadership roles including head of a pre-school, head of English at King's Taunton, director of studies in two prep schools, director of drama and resident tutor at Fettes College. Came here from Downe House where she was head of sixth form, senior leader and Oxbridge co-ordinator. Four highly successful adult children. Living in London for the first time since her 20s and loving the culture. Hobbies include ski-ing, watercolour painting, Scottish reeling and Victorian children's literature.

Keen to build up girls' resilience to help them deal with the challenges ahead, including multiple career changes. Wants pupils to be confident risk-takers. In her assembly on the day we visited, she encouraged girls to take on board Christopher Robin's advice to Winnie the Pooh: 'You are braver than you believe, stronger than you seem, and smarter than you think.' One parent described her as 'ambitious for the school and highly visionary'. Another claimed, 'She's shaken the school up. It was good before, but she has lifted our spirits.' Girls consider her to be 'a great role model.' Dynamic, vivacious and engaging.

Academic matters: In 2018, 41 per cent A*/A at A level; 80 per cent A*-B. Maths and English currently popular, with ever-increasing numbers taking science and economics. Compulsory Extended Project Qualification in sixth form, introduced by head to develop girls' research skills and to prepare them for the next stage. Photography, art and design and computing recently introduced at A level. Eighty-four per cent A*-A/9-7 at GCSE in 2018. Spanish, chemistry and history results impressive. Setting in English, science and maths by year 9.

Excellent reports about provision offered to pupils with special needs: 'no longer just lip service,' said one parent. All pupils screened for dyslexia on arrival. A handful of pupils have EAL requirements and are seen on a one-to-one basis by specialist staff. Extra support continues to sixth form.

Some teaching described as 'fantastic', but one parent we spoke to felt there were 'still some members of staff who need weeding out. They aren't inspiring the girls and aren't getting the results.' Approximately a third of staff has been there at least 10 years. Recent appointments, particularly of younger members of staff, seen as very positive. Staff feel 'empowered' by head.

Academic success is recognised with flamboyant prize-giving at nearby Cadogan Hall, with performances by talented dancers and musicians. The girls were hugely excited to see staff wearing their graduation gowns and 'felt proud' to be part of Francis Holland. A great success, introduced by head, who is clearly keen to celebrate success in all fields.

Two parallel classes throughout senior school. Classes start at 16 on average and rarely go above 20 in lower years, diminishing to six to eight in sixth form. Would split sixth form classes if they exceeded 10 pupils. From year 11, all girls have an academic mentor, so everyone is fully supported, and no one is left floundering. Girls genuinely feel that staff are keeping a close eye on them and that they are guided through university entrance 'incredibly well'.

Games, options, the arts: Sport now taken very seriously, at all levels, and is compulsory for all. Head believes, 'Sport is important as it teaches you that you can't always win, but you can pick yourself up and carry on'. Everyone is raving about recently appointed head of sport. Well-equipped gym and netball/tennis court on site. Outdoor sports in Battersea Park, including tennis, hockey, athletics and rounders. Top years can try Pilates, yoga, squash and boxercise as well as more traditional team sports. Most parents are delighted that fixtures are now arranged on Saturday mornings and the school wins most matches.

Music is flourishing. Nearly 60 per cent learn an instrument. Choirs, orchestras, chamber groups and jazz groups galore. Two choir tours to Europe each year. Head wants creative and enterprising pupils and girls recently set up own theatre company. Highly successful theatrical collaborations with boys from nearby Cardinal Vaughan School, with minimal adult input. Parents consider drama to be a real strength. Speech and drama v popular with many reaching top grades in exams.

Impressive selection of clubs including debating and philosophy, as well as animal club for younger girls. School has a renowned menagerie of animals, from gerbils and snakes to chinchillas, and younger girls get to take home animals for the weekend. Girls encouraged to become proficient in public speaking: debating club from year 6, and mock elections and English Speaking Union events arranged. Broad horizons and an informed awareness of current affairs expected.

Background and atmosphere: Sister school to Francis Holland Regent's Park: the schools share a governing body, staff training days and have the same ethos. Same site as junior school, in a Tardis-like building behind Sloane Square. Head aware that being in the same place from 4-18 years has its disadvantages and is keeping her eye out for property nearby. Beautiful interior decorating: stunning new entrance hall lifts morale on arrival and upper sixth common room seriously plush. New Centre for Creative Learning with rooftop garden, performing arts studio and ICT suite should aid school's vision of developing 'creativity, innovation and enterprise'.

School described as 'vibrant', and it was certainly buzzing on the day we visited. A real energy about the place. Francis Holland girls have a wonderfully stimulating start to life here, with devoted care and attention from outstanding teachers. No wonder there's a queue to come here.

Pastoral care, well-being and discipline: Described by parents as being 'nurturing'. Lower sixth and year 8 girls are paired with year 7 girls in Big Sister programme, to make sure they settle on arrival at the school. Head concerned that 'high performing parents have high expectations of their children.' Aware that girls can feel pressurised and a well-being programme, including mindfulness, has been set up to help girls to cope, when it all becomes too much. Head is a trained counsellor and pastoral care is high on the agenda.

Strong ethos of service fostered, whether fundraising for school in Uganda or organising tea parties for elderly in Battersea. Girls are expected to give something back.

Head would expel a girl for drug taking; those caught smoking pay money to a cancer charity, phone their parents from head's office and do community service within the school grounds. Won't tolerate unkindness or rudeness and girls we met were fantastically polite. Sixth formers allowed out for lunch but 'school food is delicious, so we prefer to stay at school for lunch and just go out for a coffee,' said one.

Pupils and parents: Happy, confident and charming girls who seem ready to take on the world. Well-heeled and polished with ready smiles. Couldn't wait to tell us how lucky they felt to be here. High octane, international families: mainly French, Spanish, Italian, Russian and American. 'A bewildering number of languages spoken in the playground at pick up time,' according to one mother. Majority live within a three-mile radius of school. Communication with parents now greatly improved with weekly e-newsletters and reports. 'We are delighted that we finally know what is going on,' said one.

Notable former pupils include Vanessa Mae, Sienna Miller, Cara Delevingne and Rose Tremain.

Entrance: At 11+, a cognitive ability test (rather than maths and English exams) with great emphasis on the interview. Part of the London 11+ Consortium. Some 500 girls sit for 50 places. Bar raised each year. At 13+, exams in English, maths, science and French. For sixth form, by entrance or scholarship exams in proposed A level subjects.

Exit: A trickle leaves after GCSE. Most sixth formers to university. Occasionally one or two Oxbridge places. As one girl put it, 'I have applied to Oxford, but it's just one of my choices. It's not made into a big deal here. My other choices are great too.' Art foundation courses also popular. Medicine, economics, history and psychology are favoured courses; Durham, Bristol and Exeter regular destinations. Increasing numbers to American universities, especially for liberal arts degrees, and not only those with a direct American link; others to Spain, France and Canada. Head of careers is a very successful recent appointment; she asks girls at beginning of sixth form, 'What is your dream?', and then helps them to chase it. Higher education fair organised by school. Girls well supported once they leave, throughout university and beyond if needed. Relations with alumnae now actively fostered.

Money matters: At 11, four academic scholarships, as well as music, art and drama scholarships. Bursaries at 11+, 14+ and four in sixth form. Daughters of clergy offered remission on a third of fees.

Remarks: This school is undergoing a transformation and the excitement is palpable. Expectations are high and challenges are being set, but the girls and staff know they have a strong leader and are following her willingly. 'An excellent appointment,' said one parent. 'We feel seriously lucky to have our girls here on Mrs Elphinstone's watch,' said another. Though small, this school is now punching above its weight. An exciting and exhilarating place to be.

Fulham School

200 Greyhound Road, London W14 9SD

Ages 4–14 **Pupils** 708

Fees: £16,869 – £18,729 pa

020 7386 2444
www.fulhamprep.co.uk

Headmaster: Since September 2018, Will le Fleming has been in overall charge of the senior, prep and pre-prep schools. He was previously deputy head and director of the senior school at St Paul's Girls' School. Educated at Eton and Cambridge, he is a teacher and writer whose work in education began with Historic Royal Palaces, managing a substantial programme of teaching for all ages from primary to A level. In 2009 he moved to St Paul's School where he was rapidly promoted to undermaster, a post including close involvement in admissions and liaison with prep schools.

Head of prep since September 2018 is Neil Lunnon, previously deputy head pastoral at Wellington College, where he spent 24 years. He also spent three years at Eagle House Prep as deputy head.

Head of the pre-prep is Di Steven Bed (late 40s). Educated at Glasgow University with PGCE from Dundee and an NPQH. Thoroughly professional and immaculately turned out, Ms Steven is imbued with the skills of guiding and bringing up young children for over 25 years. She has been at the school for over 13 years and took over from Jane Emmett at the pre-prep when Jane started the prep. With her lilting Scottish accent, spoken in soft, undulating tones, her clear boundaries and high expectations, she is a safe pair of hands and well equipped to oversee the 250 pupils in her care.

Academic matters: The quality of the teaching is good, though not necessarily uniform in style. Parents particularly praise the quality of teachers in years 1 and 2 and one mother of a boy enthused about the muscular male teaching in the top years of the prep, something that she felt was important for her son. A healthy mix of long term teachers as well as fresh blood. Year 3, the first year of the prep school, continues with class teacher based teaching, 'helping them to make the transition,' but specialist subject teaching is introduced in year 4. Children are divided into five sets for maths from year 4, Latin is introduced in year 5, and those further up the school have the option to do ancient Greek. Classrooms are spacious and numbers vary between 16 and 20 in each class. Between years 4 and 6 there are four to five classes in each year. Years 7 and 8 have three classes, mainly boys staying to take common entrance, but usually including one or two girls.

Parents appreciate being told exactly where their child stands in relation to the rest of the class, as well as receiving a report every term. 'It gives me a much more realistic sense of how my child is doing than I received at his previous school,' remarked one parent. The transparency extends to the advice given about senior schools; a comparison of pupils' scores in tests with the pass mark of a particular school helps to keep expectations realistic. As with many prep schools that continue to year 8 (and now beyond), the school attracts genuine specialists in their field and the rapport between staff and pupils is positive, we're told.

The broad church quality of FPS, and its inclusive approach, go some way to diminishing the 11+ pressure, as does the new senior school. However, school is also very conscious that within this the academic needs of each child have to be met. Has introduced a scholarship set at the top of the prep to stretch the brightest (when we visited they were celebrating academic scholarships to St Paul's, Hampton and Sherborne). Particularly proud of the Trivium, a general studies course that pulls in knowledge from different areas of the curriculum and involves, for example, pupils presenting to an audience on the French elections, big game hunting or African drumming. This is something that the whole prep school participates in, not just the brightest.

Currently 20 per cent of pupils need extra support – whether because they have been formally diagnosed with SEN (only mild dyslexia, dyspraxia catered for; no one here has an EHCP, although there are pupils here with ASD and ADHD), or 'just need a leg up – a helping hand with study skills etc' and don't necessarily need the help of the SENCo. One parent wondered whether she should be pushing more for support for her dyslexic so: 'They don't seem to be very on it,' she remarked. Full time SENCo has four staff in her team dealing with every need including EAL (the numbers of which are high here at around 40 per cent).

Games, options, the arts: The music 'is totally amazing,' said one mother; 'sometimes they can field two school orchestras who put on stunning, ambitious performances.' There are also plenty of choirs, a wind group, jazz group and brass group. Busy parents come in especially to support the orchestra. One mother was delighted that her son, who had shown no previous interest in music, was loving it here. Children excel at their individual instruments and the music room, where class lessons take place, is overflowing with bongo drums, xylophones and keyboards. Plenty of large drama productions: years 3 and 4 recently performed Robin Hood and Alice in Wonderland, year 6 Annie. The pupils also enthused about the teachers' annual Christmas production as well as the Christmas talent show that included a Trashion Show complete with clothes made out of rubbish and recycling.

Lots of sport, with an emphasis on team sports, and focus on the traditional – football, rugby, cricket, netball and rounders, with tennis, hockey, swimming and basketball too. Sports take place at the old WASPs ground in Acton, swimming at Fulham Pools. The size of the school, in the middle years at least, gives strength and depth and they hold their own in competitive matches against other schools (although one parent with children in the top two prep years commented how disappointed they were that matches had been thin on the ground). There are sports tours (a recent netball tour to Cardiff where they trained with the Celtic dragons), lots of medals and awards and a tangible sense of pride among both staff and pupils at their sporting achievements.

Art and DT are given generous time in the curriculum (each class doing a term of each and then rotating). The departments are bustling but, like so much here, efficiently organised and calm. We witnessed 10 year olds designing clay pots using Aztec art and saw some flamboyant portraits of kings and queens displayed in the corridor, painted and then decorated with fabrics and beads. In DT their construction skills 'were being challenged'. Years 6-8 get to use glue guns. 'We keep everything very organised so that the children can find things and become independent; they learn not to rely on the staff,' explained the head of DT. Plethora of after-school and lunch time clubs (chargeable), from magic club and newspaper club to fencing and gardening. Good use is made of the city, with regular trips to the Royal College of Music, the Natural History Museum and theatres as well as residential PGL trips for the older children. Our guides enthusiastically recounted stories of getting stuck on the mud slide on their recent trip to Wales.

Background and atmosphere: This was a very large prep school, and it's getting bigger as it expands into an all through school to 18. From small beginnings in 1996, with a few tinies in a scouts' hut near Putney Bridge, it's become a bustling hub of a school, now on three separate sites (the pre-prep is still located near Putney Bridge, senior school on its new site at Castle Court in Broomhouse Lane) with minibuses weaving their way between, and also ferrying children from all over west London, Wimbledon, Ealing, Kensington and Kensal Rise. A proper prep school that doesn't just cram for the notoriously narrow 11+, but teaches a broad curriculum, covers common entrance (and beyond) and prepares each child for life at senior school, it has been a remarkable success. So much so that the next phase in its development is to carry on through GCSE to A level. The plan is that it will grow incrementally but always remain small, relative to other senior schools, at fewer than 300 pupils in total between years 9 and 13.

The main building for the prep school (years 3-8) is a large Victorian building, complete with large paned windows, wide corridors and staircases, polished parquet floors and heavy iron radiators. Situated just behind Queen's Club in Barons Court, it is lucky enough to have plenty of outside space which is used for sport as well as play. A climbing wall, Astroturf pitches for football and cricket (played by both boys and girls) and even a red, old style telephone box tucked into a corner. In London a primary school with this much space is more likely to be state than independent and FPS (as it's known) certainly has the edge over its competitors in this respect, many of which are housed in cramped premises over several floors in town houses with barely any outside space at all.

Well-stocked library, books ordered neatly, with interesting displays, beanbags at one end, large oval tables at the other. The tidy spaciousness nurtures focus and concentration. The grand entrance hall, with smart chairs, mood lamps and magazines, is more reminiscent of a Harley Street waiting room than a busy prep school, as is head's super plush grand office, in the style of a chic boutique hotel suite.

Pastoral care, well-being and discipline: The simplicity of the ethos, governed as it is by the 'three Cs – courtesy, commitment and consideration', helps to keep children focused on what's important, without fuss and a weighty rule book list of dos and don'ts. Although there are more boys than girls, particularly in years 7 and 8, the school refreshingly appointed a head girl this year rather than a head boy. Senior schools, we were told, remark on the confidence of the FPS pupils – they don't have an air 'of being beaten down by life' – and this is something the school feels passionate about, preserving their childhood and sense of freedom for as long as possible.

Pupils and parents: Situated in a cosmopolitan corner of London, the demographic of the school reflects its local area. There are currently 29 different nationalities in the school, including an increasing number of Turks and large numbers of Europeans including Scandinavians, as well as Americans and Canadians. There is also a core group of British families here and the parental body is 'remarkably down to earth,' observes one teacher. 'You're unlikely to spot celebrities in the playground here, and most of our parents are allergic to anything flashy.' They generally adopt a 'sensible attitude,' and there are 'surprisingly few helicopter parents'. The number of scooters at the pre-prep, parked neatly in rows and (almost) in colour codes, is testament to how many make their way to school without harming the environment.

Entrance: The pre-prep is non-selective in reception, with 90 places offered on a first come first served basis (from date of registration). Priority and discount offered to siblings (there are normally between 25 and 50 siblings each year), and school will carefully consider both the balance between boys and girls and when their birthdays fall in the year. Five open mornings a year give everyone a chance to visit; parents who have registered are invited for an official tour with Ms Steven. After reception, occasional places can arise, but your child will be informally assessed, spending a morning at the school. Automatic transfer to the prep. Outside entry into the prep is by assessment and interview at 7+, 8+ and 11+, or occasional places in other year groups. Entry into year 9 in the new senior school consists of the ISEB pre-test in year 6 for external candidates – their purpose to make sure the candidate will be able to manage GCSEs. Some limited scholarships available for year 9 (academic, sport, art, music and drama).

Exit: Most of the pre-prep move on to the prep; children won't be prepared for the 7+ or 8+ and Ms Steven will tell you candidly but pleasantly if your child is not suited for say, St Paul's Juniors or Putney High junior. Despite this, between two and five children out of 90 do sit the exams each year. Some leave at the end of years 2 or 3 when often families move to 'the country'. Several boys a year move to boarding preps at 8, but most girls and more and more boys now leave at 11+ to a huge range of London day schools as well as a few girls' boarding schools. At 13+, it's mostly boys who have stayed on and are going to boarding schools, though the odd one is destined, (post pre-test in year 6), for eg Westminster, Hampton, St Paul's or KCS. School has a reputation for matching the right school to the child, rather than being swayed too much by fixation on brand or location. This may explain the breadth of destinations in terms of ethos, type of school and location and the fact that there are no large groups going to any one school. In the past pupils have gone to eg Hampton, Dulwich, Godolphin & Latymer, City of London, Putney High, Emanuel School, Francis Holland etc, or to board at Benenden, St Mary's Ascot, Harrow, Charterhouse Marlborough, Eton or Winchester. They can move up automatically to the new senior school. A clutch of scholarships each year, including academic ones to top academic schools.

Remarks: On the whole, the school receives resounding parental support. The positives include the swiftness and sensitivity of the school's response when things go 'wobbly', the pride their children take in their school, the breadth of the education, and the fact that the focus is on each child's individual needs and capability, rather than unrealistic expectations of the cohort as a whole. A large school, without doubt, but one which doesn't lose sight of the small detail. The four houses successfully nurture loyalty and cohesion, and teachers on the gate each morning greet everyone by name. However, dissenters question whether they can raise the academic game enough to ensure that sufficient pupils are meeting the ever-higher targets of London day schools. Although the senior school may go some way to reducing the pressure this, together with a determination to allow the children to enjoy their childhood for as long as possible, sheltered in the vibrant broad church that is FPS, is likely to be one of the new prep head's greatest challenges.

Garden House School

Turks Row, London SW3 4TW

Ages 3–11 **Pupils** 475

Fees: £17,700 – £22,800 pa

020 7730 1652
www.gardenhouseschool.co.uk

G

Principal: Since 1973, Jillian Oddy BA, who is also the owner. The structure at the top of the school appears quadrangular but in effect is a triangle topped by a circle – Jill Oddy.

Head of girls since 2017 is Annie Lee BA MA PGCE (50s). The newest piece of the equilateral triangle, she is a woman whose self-assurance is barely masked by her good manners and understated exterior. Her music degree led to teaching posts including Wimbledon High School and her last job as head of All Hallows in Somerset and she keeps her hand in playing piano in assembly. Parents feel that she has done a very good job in filling the small number of cracks and improving the staff training and consistency.

Head of boys since 2006 is Christian Warland BA (50s), Jill Oddy's son, who left his life as a lawyer to join the family firm but still appears, despite his easy exterior, slightly surprised to find himself a schoolmaster. However, he relaxes happily when with the children and immediately bent down to help a small boy struggling with his maths.

Head of early years since 2014 is Julia Adlard. Originally employed here in the mid-80s, she is a real pro, who effortlessly demonstrates her understanding of and fondness for small children, and also her knowledge of the skills they need when they move on from the cosy environment of the lower school.

Entrance: All 26 children tend to move up from the nursery and together with the automatic sibling entry policy this means that there are usually only 40-45 places available for external candidates. Most years there are three or four children applying for each space. Admission is by interview and they are looking for both children and parents who will fit into this family school. Occasional places later on due to families relocating.

Exit: Two-thirds of the boys leave at 8+, a handful to conventional boys' boarding schools such as Ludgrove and Summer Fields but most to London day schools eg Westminster Under School, WCCS, Sussex House and Wetherby Prep. The girls, almost all of whom stay until 11+, tend to head for various London day schools: Francis Holland SW1 number one at the moment – 10 girls went in 2018 – with Godolphin & Latymer and Queen's Gate also popular; or the conventional girls' boarding schools such as Downe House, Benenden and St Mary's Ascot (favourite choice over the last five years).

Remarks: Jillian Oddy took over the school from the refreshingly unqualified and charmingly named Margery de Brissac, ballet teacher to the offspring of political grandees including Winston Churchill. Margery started the school in 1950 and ran it until she handed over in 1973. Her legacy is obvious with lots of little girls at the barre, although we were told that there are no takers from amongst the boys when ballet stops being compulsory.

The school's home for the last 15 years has been a purpose-built building, bang in the middle of red-brick Sloanedom but with the architectural gem of the Royal Hospital literally round the corner. We walked into a particularly sweet atmosphere as it was Cake Day and the Bratby of John Betjeman (strong as it is) was eclipsed by tables loaded with a kaleidoscope of wildly decorated cupcakes. Fingers pointed proudly at their own creations and one small boy, beaming at us, whispered 'I just ate a volcano' – proof that even cupcakes can be woven into the curriculum.

The nursery lives on the other side of Sloane Square and is long on teachers (six) but definitely short on space with a tiny front yard (although they also share a playground with the school across the road), a wide passage and two classrooms all crammed into the back of Holy Trinity church, so maybe not suited to a very boisterous child. Not entirely cut off, they make the best of their limited area and do gym and ballet in the main school as well as attending assembly there once a week.

From reception upwards the classrooms are in Turks Row and the meshing of the lives of boys and girls (despite being taught in separate classes) seems to work beautifully. Streaming is kept to the minimum, hardly at all in the boys' school and only for maths in the girls'. The high ratio of teachers to children (1:5) means that they feel able to teach the cohorts together. Neither is technology ignored as there is a well-equipped ICT room and coding and computer programming are both taught, the school's comment being 'we are far more conscious of applied maths these days'.

No formality when we entered the classrooms but engaged, cheerful children heads down over their work or, in the case of the little ones, raptly listening to the day's story. The only exception was the classes who had been making Christmas biscuits and were rather endearingly, if inefficiently, trying to clear up the considerable mess before heading off for a swimming lesson. The leavers' destinations (three scholarships to Downe House last year) prove the success of the academic teaching, but 'we are, definitely, not a hothouse,' said CW.

Lower down the school individual phonics support is available, and later on, if any of the 'dys' or ASD families, are diagnosed they can provide one-to-one support as well as extension classes for the most academically able, but most SEN and EAL needs are handled in the classroom. Well aware of the dangers of the internet they 'put the fear of God' into the parents and make them sign up to a code of practice.

The art room is smaller than some but has a high ceiling above shelves crammed with crates, overflowing with props. The size of the space certainly fails to cramp the imagination of the head of art – in fact she regularly produces art scholars, who are encouraged by an invitation-only after-school club. Everyone has class music lessons with over 80 per cent learning an instrument, leading to plenty of opportunities to take part in concerts and the annual carol service. Drama is part of the weekly curriculum and they experience the real 'theatricals' with the summer show held at the Royal Court.

Sport is less of a problem to organise than some central London schools with the green spaces of Burton Court across the road, and all the traditional sports are on offer, but it is probably not the school for an intensely sporty child unless they show a bent for fencing, which all take from the age of 7. A staggering number of after-school clubs (extra charge) and sport and fitness clubs in the morning for the early birds.

High praise from parents about the handling of the choice and transition to senior school but, with the relatively narrow field of traditional schools, this may be a less daunting task than for some heads. Having said this, the parents here are a demanding lot with serious aspirations for their children, so finding the right spot for each child is a pressurised task. If you are a high achiever earning a substantial salary you expect your chosen school to deliver the goods – and they do.

There is a great deal to like about this school and we were particularly pleased to have an opportunity to talk to a group of teachers, one of whom shared our enthusiasm for introducing

Philosophy for Children (P4C). The only proviso would be that although they undoubtedly do an excellent job for all the very diverse (by nationality) children in their care, it might not be as easy for some parents to fit in if they were unfamiliar with the slightly rarefied world of the Chelsea/Belgravia borders.

Glebe Primary School

93

Sussex Road, Ickenham, Uxbridge UB10 8PH

Ages 3-11 **Pupils** 625

01895 462385
www.glebe.hillingdon.sch.uk

Headteacher: Since 2017, Melanie Penney MA (special education – hearing impairment) BA (theology, religious studies, drama) PGCE, previously assistant head and deputy head. Before that, at Pinner Park, Harrow. Never in any doubt about teaching being her vocation. Originally joined Glebe in 1999 as a SENCo and class teacher. 'In 2009 I was asked to cover the deputy head who went on long-term sick leave and when that post ended a year later, they wound up creating a position for me of assistant head. In January 2017, following a staffing restructure, I became deputy head. Six months later, I became headteacher – it's been quite a rollercoaster.' Headship was never the plan – 'I love being in the classroom, so I still teach RE to year 6s, but I got swept along with management and now I love it.' Trained as a specialist teacher of the deaf.

One of the warmest heads we've come across, and highly regarded by staff, parents and pupils, who call her 'aspirational' and 'not one to let things stand still, always looking for improvement.' 'Everything at this school is done with compassion and it all comes from her,' one parent told us. 'Everything – and I mean everything – starts with the child and she provides the consideration, kindness, familiarity and humour that stops there being a "them and us" feel,' reported another. She's out on the gates every morning and afternoon, 'always smiling and approachable and she doesn't shy away from parents speaking their mind.' Pupils like her open-door policy and her hot chocolate Fridays (when two 'beacons of outstanding behaviour' from each class get a hot invitation).

Lives in Berkshire with husband, Steve, and their son and daughter, both at secondary school.

Entrance: Looked after children and SEN get priority, then it's siblings and after that it comes down to distance. Catchment area shrunk a few years back as school grew more popular, with some pupils even transferring from schools that previously had a better reputation. But as school increased to three form entry, it's expanded again, with families now hailing as far as Slough, Hillingdon, Uxbridge and beyond, 'though few come further than three miles.' There's quite a bit of movement in the area (10 per cent of pupils come from military families stationed at the local RAF base and often only stay for two years; and high house prices force many families who look to move from renting to buying out of the area) so it's worth checking places further up, although when we visited there were waiting lists for years 2, 5 and 6.

Exit: One or two go to the independent sector and a few to local grammars, but the majority head to Vyners School in Ickenham (over half) or Douay Martyrs.

Remarks: Set in the deepest London suburbs (Ickenham tube is near the end of the Piccadilly and Metropolitan lines), the school moved into brand new two-storey L-shaped block in 2014 which now caters for three-form entry. Apart from one remaining prefab, which is used for before- and after-school care (provision by school from 7.45am and by an outside company until 6pm; waiting lists apply) and music lessons, everything takes place in this shiny new building, with red accents everywhere you look, including in the uniform – a nice reflection of the vibrancy of the school. Everywhere is clean, bright and airy, with wide corridors and break-out areas and colourful displays of pupils' work on the walls. Good, clear (again, red) signposting at every turn means there's no chance of getting lost. Highlights include the large hall that doubles up as canteen ('the food is really good,' pupils assured us) from the pupil-named Pegasus café and homely nurturing room 'where you can go when you feel sad,' as one pupil put it. Well-stocked, if rather disorganised, library. 'Disappointing that they didn't put in any dedicated rooms for the likes of art,' admits head. Ditto for science labs, we thought – one would have been lovely, even if it doubled up as a form room.

The school's go-getting motto is 'We can and we will!' and the strength of the academics do it justice. Sats results are above the national average and although a recent Ofsted report found that 'more able pupils have not always done as well as expected', the school is addressing this, mainly through setting. It starts in reception, with setting for phonics, then from year 2 in writing, from year 3 in maths and – depending on the cohort – in English from year 4: 'We realised those at the top needed pushing further, with things like greater depth of comprehension.' History and science are popular, showing 'it's not just a school hell bent on maths and English' (as one parent put it); French for all from year 3.

Teachers ('all of whom are effective, although one or two lack the warm touch,' says one parent) are encouraged to be constantly reflective, including via regular video observations which they go through with the head or one of the two deputy heads. Technology well integrated into lessons, with enough iPads for two classes to use at any one time and laptops aplenty. New outdoor classroom.

The caring ethos is another USP for this school. 'A happy child will learn' could just as easily be its slogan. There's a dedicated pastoral worker, who works not only with pupils but staff and parents. And there are plenty of leadership opportunities, with photos on the wall of the head boy, head girl and house captains, with other opportunities including prefects, mentors and buddies. 'Kindness is in the very bones of this school,' said one parent.

Around 10 per cent of children have SEN, 17 of whom had ECHPs when we visited. Described as 'taking a united approach,' the school works closely with both families and outside agencies and 'we look at the child, diagnosis or not.' The school is a regional centre for those with impaired hearing, with two specialist teachers of the deaf (one is the head) and places for nine hearing impaired children. Every classroom has a Soundfield system, amplifying the sound of the teacher's voice, and there is an inclusion office with a speech and language area and two teaching rooms. All of the children are on the roll of their mainstream class and school aims for them to be taught in class alongside their hearing peers, with support if necessary. 'This is an incredibly inclusive school,' one parent told us.

Sports include football, netball, cross-country, athletics, cricket, hockey and tag rugby, much of it delivered by a specialist sports coach. The school takes part in inter-school competitions, with a particularly strong girls' football team, unbeaten so far – 'unusual for us, believe me,' says the head, who has historically had to do a lot of talks on 'how it's all about the taking part.' 'But while we're gracious in defeat, we are getting more focused and really giving winning a go.' All pupils do the Daily Mile three times a week, come rain or shine.

All children get the chance to study a musical instrument. This starts in year 1 with African drumming, year 2 with recorders and year 3 with the ukulele. Keyboard and guitar also on offer for all, while peripatetic teachers offer paid-for lessons in violin, cello, clarinet and flute. Surprisingly, no school orchestra, but there is an annual music concert and a choir that works its socks off at Christmas time visiting local shopping centres and old folks' homes, as well as taking part in Young Voices at the O2. Drama does not feature in stand-alone lessons, but every year group performs at least once annually, in addition to class assemblies and the likes of performance poetry. 'All children get a chance to shine on stage,' one parent told us. Clubs range from gardening to Mandarin, plus all the usuals – 'and if we suggest a new club, the school usually listens and acts,' one parent told us.

G

Art is 'so more than just mixing paints', according to the school – they set regular ambitious goals such as self-portraits, 'then working back from that to ensure the pupils have the skills they need to achieve it within a set time period.' No get-out clause for less arty teachers; they're simply encouraged to learn from their colleagues or watch YouTube tutorials.

Behaviour mainly good, 'with small proportions of children who find it hard, predominantly due to SEN.' The school has 10 expectations widely displayed, plus a strong rewards system. Sanctions, where necessary, include removal of five minutes from golden time (free time on Friday afternoons) which can be earned back. Anything more serious involves missing playtime and writing letters of apology, with parents called in where necessary and around one temporary exclusion a year. Parents impressed with 'the way problems in friendship groups are taken seriously and dealt with sensitively' and the 'nuanced approach to preventing and dealing with bullying.' Staggered playtimes, friendship benches, trained year 6 play leaders, PSHE and regular assembles on kindness all help.

Families predominantly white British, reflecting the local area, with around 17 per cent Asian descent. Mainly middle-class, but less so as catchment expands, and mostly dual income. Thriving Friends of Glebe. Former pupils include TV presenter Sue Cook and London 2012 athlete Julia Bleasdale.

This is a school with a strong nurturing ethos and robust (but not pushy) academics. 'Children leave here not just reaching their potential, but as really nice people,' one parent told us. 'My daughter wanted to give Easter presents to 17 different members of staff, from teachers to dinner ladies and cleaners and to me that sums up Glebe as every single person who walks through the gates is valued.'

Glendower Prep School

87 Queen's Gate, London SW7 5JX

Ages 4–11 Pupils 238

Fees: £19,200 pa

020 7370 1927
www.glendowerprep.org

Headmistress: Since 2012, Sarah Knollys BA PGCE (50s), educated at Exeter (French and Italian) and Roehampton Universities. She came to Glendower following her previous success as founding head at Maple Walk, the pioneer New Model school which started 'out of a trunk' as she puts it, with two pupils, and had 150 by the time she left. Married to Christopher; they have two grown-up sons.

Her natural enthusiasm and warmth are engaging and, in a charming fashion, she quickly puts visitors to her elegant, oak-panelled study at ease, whether adult or child. Parents like the fact she is accessible and approachable. This is a head who knows her school, spends time shadowing all 14 classes and is prepared to spend time with every prospective parent. She teaches Latin to year 6 after their entrance examinations and helps out where she can, listening to readers in reception, or sharing squash and biscuits with year 6s to support them prior to their 11+ examinations. Monday breakfasts to celebrate up to six girls' achievements are, she tells us, 'one of the highlights of my week' and when we joined her, the girls were sparky, delightfully polite and self-assured. She writes in the weekly newsletter, responds promptly to parental emails and is there every morning to greet families.

Passionate about Glendower and especially the girls, she is proud of their enthusiasm for learning and ability to laugh at themselves, so refreshing. When we told her that the girls had wholeheartedly praised their teachers to us and loved the emphasis on learning and all the opportunities on offer, she was unashamedly touched. Her aim is to bring out the best in each and every girl and that is shared by her staff. She is justifiably proud of the school's pastoral care. Long-serving parents have liked her attention to the girls' well-being and welcome the introduction of small tutorial groups. Caring for others and kindness are key here and she has involved girls in the local community and in charity work both nearby and abroad.

Moving on in July 2019 to head Notting Hill Prep, but she has a strong leadership team in place who share her vision and parents we spoke to are confident that her legacy will continue.

Entrance: Thirty-six places at reception with girls coming from more than 20 different nurseries. No sibling priority. Informal, small group assessments – essentially to see if the girls interact well and can do the basics competently. English fluency matters. As one parent summed up overall, 'girls are expected to be engaged and interested in their learning'. Some bursaries available for needy local girls or those already in the school who fall on hard times. Unsuccessful applicants for 4+ entry and later applicants placed on a waiting list for consideration. Occasional places do occur with longer assessments to see how they cope and interact with their peers. Unlikely to offer after year 5.

Exit: Very impressive results reflect the school's established excellent academic profile with girls consistently moving on both to top boarding schools and, mostly, to prestigious day schools. Boarding includes Wycombe Abbey, St Mary's Ascot, Benenden, Heathfield. Day includes St Paul's Girls', Godolphin & Latymer, Latymer Upper, Francis Holland SW1, South Hampstead, Putney High. Catering for individual personalities and talents, Mrs Knollys and her team 'really know the children' and, taking account of individual personalities, have widened the range of schools in recent years, which makes excellent sense.

Remarks: Founded by two intrepid spinsters, Miss Edith Lloyd and Miss Maud Cornwell, in 1895, Glendower is a charitable trust, and has always been run as a not-for-profit organisation. A nostalgic relief as spanking new profit-making companies pop up throughout the city, establishing expensive schools to meet demand. The school colour purple is all-pervasive; from the helpful website, to the girls in their uniform, sporting natty purple berets, smart winter dresses with purple and white striped blouses, or summer purple and white checked dresses, to their purple bags, folders and playground benches. The year 3s we accompanied to a Shakespeare workshop at nearby Beit Hall looked smart in tailored, velvet -trimmed grey coats with matching tights and neat hairstyles sporting purple clips and ribbons. The school feels like a welcoming grand house with its well-stocked library and airy, panelled entrance hall, carpeted throughout with excellent displays on every staircase. Every classroom is light and well-equipped, sets of iPads regularly employed, with only the science laboratory below ground level. School will shortly gain additional space without increasing the pupil roll. This will provide a smarter entrance, make moving between the two buildings seamless, no longer involving considerable stair climbing, and more rooms will allow staff flexibility for teaching in more groups.

Class sizes of between 16 and 18 with one teacher/assistant to nine girls mean that they receive considerable attention and their strengths and weaknesses are known and acted upon. One parent commented, 'Teachers are engaged on an individual level. We can email them all if we have any worries and they will provide support and are prepared to put themselves out.' The parental portal is well-used and informative. 'They are constantly improving the IT interface with parents to support them.' Not a school for those with serious SENs but school will pick up and support those with mild difficulties and make individual learning plans for those who need them. Between five and 10 per cent of girls are on the SEN register without any stigma, just plenty of support including handwriting club during lunch break and touch-typing practice. Speech therapists and occupational therapists come into school for a few. Some, who have been diagnosed dyscalculaic, receive external support, at Emerson House for example. EFL is given in small groups or one-to-one to the few who need a little extra help.

Well-qualified teaching assistants, all with degrees in upper school, are given opportunities for professional development. We heard excellent French accents during our visit with specialist native speaker from reception upwards. Mandarin is on the curriculum for years 4 and 5 with girls often obtaining full marks in the ISEB tests. Parents are a real international mix, US, Chinese, European, so many girls are bilingual or trilingual, but mostly long-stayers with very little movement. Parents of occasional place pupils praise how well the girls treat newcomers and how welcoming other parents are, arranging coffee mornings and play dates. 'If parents want to be involved they can be but if not, this is accepted, not questioned'.

Specialist teaching in music, drama and PE from reception with most subjects specialist taught from year 4. Girls seem happy, love their school and all it has to offer. They commented, 'everyone is busy here, there's no lounging about'. They are responsive in lessons and we witnessed their enthusiasm for acting, playing a trumpet, carrying out experiments using microscopes and devising a board game employing algebraic substitutions. The Glendower '6 rs', (learning habits), including resilience and reflection, underpin everything. The broad curriculum is, parents agree, 'varied and fun' with a wide range of clubs, including football, spy, coding, Spanish, bridge, chess and magazine writing, along with music, art and, extremely popular, drama.

Inspirational speakers have included the local mayor, plus others who have climbed Mount Everest, explored the North Pole and rowed the Atlantic: great role models preparing them for a changing world. We witnessed a whole school initiative to ensure girls understood the importance of recycling and their responsibilities. Much care is taken to provide a post 11+ programme which includes Thames conservation and young enterprise projects, Latin, poetry reciting competitions and balloon debating competitions against other schools. Full advantage is taken of the school's location with trips to museums, galleries and theatres. The science department arranged to borrow moon rock samples to celebrate the 50th anniversary of the first landings on the moon, and one team recently came third in a national science championship. Girls' work has been exhibited at the National Gallery as part of its Take One Picture initiative.

Despite the lack of a sports field on site, Glendower has a reputation for sports with proud reports in the school magazine. It is a serious business; just take a look at the sport selection policy on the website. There are weekend netball workshops involving famous players, year 6s take part in local football tournaments and girls have won IAPS fencing, sailing and triathalon events. Mrs Knollys remarked, 'they enjoy sharing and celebrating one another's achievements'.

Music thrives. Around 90 per cent take music lessons, which can include singing (several choirs) and musical theatre. We attended orchestra practice with good trumpet, violin, flute and clarinet players, and there are brass, string and woodwind ensembles. Some are members of the National Youth Orchestra and National Youth Choir. Girls chatted to us about termly productions including year 3's silent movies and parents looked forward to the autumn harvest concert in the local church.

Plenty of leadership roles, from librarians to sports captains.

'They leave with a "can do" approach to life and are well balanced as the staff really care about their mental health just as much as their academic progress,' we were told. This is a happy school, keen not to be seen as a hothouse. 'It achieves a perfect balance between encouraging girls to do their best and reaching high academic standards whilst ensuring they feel supported and have opportunities so they grow up with good values,' said a parent Others agree: 'As parents we worry about the daunting examination system: Glendower makes it as soft and gentle as it can possibly be. It's all about the child, not what exit results look like on paper.'

G

Godolphin & Latymer

Iffley Road, London W6 0PG

Ages 11–18 **Pupils** 820 **Sixth form** 215

Fees: £21,615 pa

020 8741 1936
www.godolphinandlatymer.com

Head mistress: Since 2017, Dr Frances Ramsey, MA PGCE DPhil, 50s. Previously principal of Queen's College, London for eight years. Before that, 17 years at Westminster School where she was director of studies and academic deputy head from 1998 to 2003, when she became the school's first woman master of the Queen's Scholars. (Give it another few hundred years and the title could catch up, too.) A big cheese in the Girls' School Association and HMC (she prefers the more modest 'highly regarded'), she has two children, one at school, one at university.

Could, like husband, have spent life in academia but recognised that her interest in 'big ideas and movements' would be better served by school teaching. 'I did it and loved it.' Varied days inevitably dominated by meetings of one sort or another. Impressively, still manages to teach each of five year 7 forms for half a term, though 'do it mostly to get to know the girls.' It's important. 'Heads would be missing out if they didn't.'

Quiet, forceful, and an excellent role model for the girls – both super-brainy and poised without being disconcertingly super glam. Rated as nice, authentic. Pupils describe her as an 'approachable, positive authority' and 'normalised', and clearly feel at ease with her – no corridor double-takes when she goes walkabout.

Former pupils who remember the school in its pre-independent, grammar school days are resigned to, if not wholly comfortable with, today's glitz and gloss. Dr Ramsey, however, makes the strong case that the humanity of the old grammar school ethos has been retained – and pupils, and parents, tend to agree.

Goals? Head talks of boosting pupils' resilience and ability to flourish in a rapidly changing society. 'The school is in a really good place. When I talk about where we're going, it's about refinements rather than revolution.' Parents see her as stable force – not trying to change the school but enhance its many good points. 'They strive for high academic results...I think she is pushing that even further.'

G

Best bit of being a head? 'The opportunity to influence young people's lives and to give them the best possible platform to move into what's quite an uncertain world.' Parents don't dispute this. 'I am very glad about Dr Ramsey,' said one.

Academic matters: Results matter (of course) but are achieved with a minimum (if not an absence) of stress, something that often becomes apparent when families hear of the more competitive atmosphere that dominates elsewhere.

'Not high achievement at any cost,' says school. 'Want girls to be well-rounded – simply getting that set of top grades is not enough.' Best, though, to see that in context. Dr Ramsey tells of girls' ability to empathise with the very few who recently gained only As, rather than A*s in their chemistry GCSEs. 'In other schools this would have been devastating – but our girls realised that for them it was a real achievement.' This reviewer's B grade coughed politely and left the room.

We were welcomed in every lesson we went into where girls were tackling a variety of tasks with gusto and good manners. From making chocolate chip cookies in food technology (apologetic teacher stressed that this was last lesson treat – emphasis is almost exclusively on healthy eating) to year 10 class studying roles in Kindertransport play, or collaborating in a dear little two-person pod (roofed, though corridor location makes chances of sudden rainfall very slim), sense of mutual respect between teachers and pupils came across strongly.

It's reflected in parent feedback. No complaints about any subject areas, with classics singled out for particular praise. Tiniest of tiny suggestions in otherwise sparklingly clean bill of health from school inspection before last was incorporation of more IT. Now a certified Google Educator and Apple Regional Training Centre and also offers iPads for all, felt to be well used by all teachers (and reduces number of printed handouts).

Subjects spec has recently expanded to include Mandarin Chinese and computing from year 7 (both available as GCSE and A level). Many study additional maths in year 11. In 2018, 97 per cent of GCSE grades were A*/A or 7-9.

Choice of A levels or IB in the sixth form. IB remains very much the minority but a growing one. In 2018, its 21 candidates achieved average mark of 40 (well into the top achievers). Cohorts now top 30.

Of the remaining 80+ candidates taking A levels, 94 per cent of exams were A*/B and 73 per cent at A*/A in 2018. Almost universally blip free (bar single figure Ds or beyond in chemistry, physics and maths – often down, says school, to personal issues – 'personalised support for pupils who find the sixth form programme challenging,' says the school. Some parents do use tutors. Fine for short term goal, catching up if pupil was previously educated abroad, or to fill in a specific gap, says the school, which urges parents to come clean to avoid pedagogical clashes with school teachers. 'Nothing worse than tutor giving contradictory advice,' says Dr Ramsey.

Plenty of wraparound extras – subject-related clubs and societies with 'amazing' external speakers. School has educational partnership with recently opened 11-18 academy down the road in north Kensington – shared lessons so pupils there can access wider range of subjects. It's also Ogden Trust's hub school for physics in local state schools.

School's approach felt by parents to be sensible, grown up and intelligible. It's big on cooperation, helped by manageable classes and high teacher to pupil ratio (6.5:1). Inspectors praise teachers not just for knowing subjects inside out but understanding what makes the girls tick. Will stress that 30 minutes of maths homework means just that, whether work is finished or not. No endless striving for unreachable perfection.

Pupils take a very active part in the process, attending – and contributing – to all parent-teacher meetings from year 7, and self-evaluating themselves as learners so teachers know how best to help them. 'We have learner surveys twice a year and teachers do everything they can to find what techniques help you,' said pupil.

Continues as girls move up the school. 'Teachers are really good at tailoring how they teach lessons and how they format them,' said pupil. No shortage of fun, either. 'We got quite bored with writing in geography so we made a music video about deforestation, instead,' said middle school pupil. Homework challenging but do-able – and here, too, teachers will involve girls in timings and allocation.

'Encourage them to take responsibility and embrace challenge,' said parent. Starts small (organise eg own school bags and homework diaries, with minimal reminders to parents), takes in eg public speaking along the way. 'Get very comfortable with taking a risk and speaking in front of the class,' said parent.

Approach designed to help girls cope with difficulty. Everybody makes mistakes – school helps pupils to articulate difficulties and collaborate to resolve them. 'Will say what they feel is challenging...get a group together to work on it and focus on whatever is difficult,' said parent. 'We expect quite a lot of independence from the beginning but are there to support them if it goes wrong. It's not about sink or swim,' says school. 'We explicitly talk to the girls about learning to learn,' says Dr Ramsey. 'We don't assume here that if a teacher says "revise for a test" that pupils will know what is meant by that. Revising for a test is a complex thing and they need to know the best strategies to employ.'

While SEN resources are praised, pupils won't enjoy life here if constantly struggling to keep up. Just under 10 per cent of pupils have some kind of learning needs, says head, and while SEN team is 'very good at finding individual strategies, the need itself shouldn't be a barrier.'

Games, options, the arts: Even-handed approach to every aspect of school life that ensures that whatever your interests, you'll have the impetus and support to make the most of them. (Ensuring girls' enthusiastic participation is part of staff responsibilities, according to current job ads.)

Masses of activities on the timetable, loads out of it and if that's not enough, girls are encouraged to grow their own, many groups run by sixth form, some with staff moderators. We saw flyers for open platform club's next meeting – 'Are good people also capable of evil?' – as well as a call for musicians to audition for a mystery new band. One pupil was in the process of setting up a mixed netball tournament involving London children with SEN, for example.

Most do two to three activities a week (sport participation felt to decline in senior years where girls have multiple interests, or switch to fitness options such as strength and conditioning, and pilates). Generally compatible with academic demands because of understanding teachers who will redistribute homework. 'The fact that almost everyone can keep on top of their homework is really a testament to how well it's tailored,' said pupil. 'If you have a match, teachers will give you an extension.'

Music in profusion from instrumental groups to choirs, all supported by highly qualified peripatetic teachers teaching 600 individual lessons a week. If not to girls' tastes, welcome to set up own vocal groups.

DofE offered all the way to gold and school, understandably, broadcasts the good news about results at every possible opportunity. 'Lots of detail in head's speech about sporting achievements, silverware for hockey, cricket, musical and theatre performances,' said (very slightly jaded sounding) former pupil at recent reunion.

Mind you, hard to blame Dr Ramsey, with recent successes including cricket (county and London Youth Games championships for U13s), netball (U14s reached finals of national schools competition) and hockey (where U13 and U15s reached last 16 in independent schools hockey cup). Over 70 girls now row, crews recently gaining gold at national schools' regatta, two girls invited to GB trials. Football, felt by some to be slightly poorer cousin, is played weekly. Currently only enough kit for nine players. 'Not so good when playing 11-a-side,' pointed out supporter.

Otherwise praise that generally, it's play for everyone where possible, with every team granted some fixtures. Daughter – keen on hockey but not a top player – 'never felt excluded,' said parent.

Background and atmosphere: School is what you might call sector-curious, starting off as independent, becoming a maintained grammar school and moving back into the private sector in the 1970s, where it seems likely to stay. Celebrates its birthday in September (a surprise to more mature old girls, who remember it being 4 May, with a birthday song to go with it).

Make it through initial security vetting to reception and visitors will experience a green treasure of a site in highly urban Hammersmith (easy walk to tube and bus station) – its Victorian buildings with (small) gravel sweep, set in six acres, are bounded by roads on every side. It's also immaculate – we saw two lost pairs of trainers and a sports shirt placed neatly on a bench, awaiting collection,

Though panoramic vistas are inevitably limited, there's plenty of charm to be had. Even the less eye-delighting buildings (such as the new sports hall, a typical example of the genre, with fab features including climbing wall and fitness suite) don't loom over the others. Assorted pitches and courts to the rear have been converted to all-weather surfaces). Beautiful,' said parent. 'It all blends in.'

Real grass is confined to a couple of attractive little courtyard areas (girls bring out cushions on fine summer days from the library) and an ecology garden where ducks are hatched and then, we were told, 'retired'.

Even-handed allocation of facilities is in keeping with a school philosophy designed to ensure that girls feel free to follow their hearts as well as heads when picking the subjects – and activities – that most delight them. 'Really push the girls to open their minds,' said parent. 'Gives them the potential and support to explore whatever area they're interested in.' Spills over into school life: pupils have put on pressure for the school to become plastic free. 'Now have reusable cups in the dining hall though not quite enough of them yet,' said one.

Most subjects are treated with generosity (sciences each have their own floor, for example) though DT – currently offered up to GCSE – could do with a bit more space.

Highly proficient and beautiful art – a popular GCSE and A level choice – fills the corridors and staircases. All technically excellent and varied – from the vaguely hallucinogenic (vast drawing of corset from which crabs were emerging – as they do) above a notice declaring that 'we are not afraid to tackle scale,' to flamboyant knitted insects. Nice to see, however, that house notice boards (six, all named – no surprise – for inspirational women) are curated exclusively by the girls and refreshingly un-manicured.

Infectiously enthusiastic librarians (tracked us down later to ensure we'd got the gist of apparently unlimited online resources) open up early and close late (and would probably work 24/7 if they could). Two floors, one fiction (conversation allowed), one fact (with quiet, quieter and quietest areas). Books approximately arranged by age-appropriateness but decisions arrived at through guidance rather than overt censorship.

Star feature is acquisition of converted church. Previously grime-streaked and deteriorating, it's now a lush performing arts centre linked 'seamlessly' to the music department and its music tech and practice rooms.

Until the currently silent organ gets the multi-million-pound restoration it needs, main attraction is centre's magic floor. Literally a moveable feast, it goes up and down more often than those magnificent men in their flying machines, accommodating orchestra pits to whole school assemblies. The source of great corporate pride (frequently mentioned by staff, less so by girls) appears on own video (will be Vlogging next).

Pastoral care, well-being and discipline: Dr Ramsey's focus is on being 'respectful, courageous and remarkable.' School felt to be supportive when pupils have difficulties related to academic or other difficulties, including mental illness. Have two counsellors, two nurses and part time doctor.

'Really cared and were there,' said parent, of child who was struggling. Offer peer mentoring, buddy system between older girls and new pupils. (Sixth formers also direct year 7 Christmas play.)

Clear lines where it matters but school doesn't sweat the small stuff if it can be avoided.

School council's campaigning also means that girls can now wear up to three earrings (per ear) 'as long as not massive,' said pupil. Similarly, rules on uniform changed so now allowed to travel to and from the school in sports kit. However, staff are on duty before and after school to ensure that girls are correctly attired – wearing tracksuit bottoms, not skort, for example. (School takes this area very seriously. 'There are ... postural, physiological and safety issues to consider when purchasing school shoes...' says school uniform document.)

Not all pupils comply though reasons for rules are carefully explained, said parent. 'Although the girls find it annoying, you do eventually have to have that conversation.'

Some nice touches. We liked the positivity tree in main corridor garnished by fairy lights and cards, themed to 'What makes you smile?' 'Food', 'Having no homework,' 'Matt Smith' and 'Alice's dog,' among the suggestions.

Challenge Your Limits programme, designed to boost resilience and address fear of failure – which school describes as 'a very significant inhibitor to fulfilling potential' – by 'giving tools to overcome this fear and develop the confidence to pursue their individual hopes and aims.' Described as 'very successful' (though – unusually for school which is generally very good at evaluation – agrees that 'it's quite hard to measure resilience in a metric...').

Girls, who initially had their doubts, say it does have an effect. 'You hear the word "resilience "and everyone goes "here we go again," but it subconsciously goes in,' said one.

Two-way communications generally felt to be excellent. School receptive to feedback (good and bad). It's a 'don't be shy, let us know approach,' said parent. Only reported blip was where mega stress point – a recent A level results day – was felt by some parents not to be as well handled as it could have been, with (a very few) girls who had just missed out on first choice places not having staff support instantly on hand to remove and comfort.

All the parents we spoke to, however, felt were generally very pleased with school's approach. 'You're very carefully advised before, during and after,' said a parent. 'I think you would have a heads up about whether you should have a little bit of concern.' Dr Ramsey confirms this. 'We would ensure a pupil got an email at 8am saying that we understand you may be disappointed, and inviting her to come in to the school.'

Pupils and parents: Website can sound a tad unnerving for anyone who's not part of the London super smart set that appears to be organising get-togethers – including cookery sessions for parents. Crab ravioli tutorial, anyone?

The reality is a warm and welcoming cosmopolitan and multilingual community (if predominantly white British) that comes across from first contact. Highly active parents organise everything from weekly river walks (dogs welcome) to Ladies' Poker.

G

Current pupils who'd visited were instantly struck by tour guides who 'were enjoying showing people round. It was infectious,' said one. 'One tour guide was French, one was Chinese and it was so multicultural and supportive,' agreed another.

Friendly, gently humorous pupils seem notably happy with their lives here, setting high stock on the ability to be themselves. 'There's no stereotypical girl,' sayid one. 'We can have bookworms in our classes, people who are loud, people who are funny, people who are blatantly not funny. The school allows for any kind of girl. I think we're more carefree and relaxed than other schools.'

For the best time, thought pupils, it helps to be reasonably gregarious. 'There's a big social element to it, you're not going to have the best time if you just stick to your studies,' felt one.

Unlike other schools, sixth formers wear their own clothes and look entirely presentable without being OTT – no pressure to get up early to achieve a reality show level gloss. 'I think it's really positive that I get that extra sleep,' said senior pupil.

New year 7 parents are grouped with others from similar postcodes – makes those initial journeys in a lot less fraught – with events from gala fundraising nights to coffee mornings as well as evening drinks so working parents (especially fathers) aren't left out. 'We buddied up with two other families and it was just great,' said parent.

Results in lifelong friendships between parents and pupils. Even the few who leave at 16 are included in all reunions. Pupils go on to huge range of careers, from star-studded (singer/songwriter Sophie Ellis-Baxter) to academia (Baroness Susan Greenfield) and every profession going.

Entrance: Miss the 11+, when around 900 applicants sit for 110 places (five form entry) and that's normally it apart from a small sixth form intake.

Admissions process kept 'as fair as possible', says school, with a quarter of intake coming from state schools. Will offer extra time (with appropriate paperwork) for anyone with SEN but candidates expected to deliver the results. 'If not scoring up with the others when have had the extra time, might not be the right school,' says head.

Now part of London 11+ consortium which sets a 75-minute cognitive ability test (VR and NRV plus maths). Curiosity, thinking for yourself and ability to enjoy learning here all count – interview (for all) matters – though under review. If more than 900 candidates (and looks as if will be getting there soon) 'might have to look at it,' says registrar. Current school reference also taken into account. No sibling policy. At 16+ around 12-15 places available, very keenly competed for.

Exit: A few girls leave after GCSEs, some lured by leading co-ed sixth forms (eg Westminster), a very small number to study subjects – like psychology and DT – not on offer here. Normally good numbers to Oxbridge (15 in 2018), increasing offers from US unis (about 15 per cent); school felt to support and prepare very well.

Money matters: No academic scholarships but music (first year) and music and art (sixth form) available (up to 30 per cent of fees), with bursary top up. Otherwise, families can apply for means-tested bursaries (no number given, can vary year by year) either before entry or in cases of hardship once attending the school. Parents have to declare income and 'realisable assets'.

Remarks: Parent in earlier review felt that 'to have your daughter offered a place here is a real gift.' Nothing's changed. 'I count myself lucky that we wound up here. It's been absolutely fantastic,' said parent. 'My only wish is that it would be so nice if there was a school like it for boys.'

Grafton Primary School

Eburne Road, Holloway, London N7 6AR

Ages 3–11 Pupils 510

020 7272 3284
www.graftonschool.co.uk

Head: Since 1993, Mrs Nitsa Sergides OBE (awarded in 2012 for services to education), 60s. Qualified as a teacher in 1973, followed by 19 years of teaching at another local school. Became deputy head of Grafton Primary in 1991, and head two years later.

Cypriot born Nitsa (as everyone calls her) is the embodiment of Mediterranean warmth. Her pupils adore her, 'lovely to all of us, talks to us like family.' Her teachers are loyal (incredibly low turnover of staff) and parents marvel at her dedication: 'She's quite amazing, her enthusiasm never wanes and she genuinely wants the best for everybody.' 'She is truly exceptional. Apart from her incredibly nurturing side, she has a gift of being able to get hold of every resource going for the school.'

Nitsa came to the UK at the age of 13 with teaching firmly on her radar; 'I think I was 7 when I realised that's what I wanted to be.' Now in her third decade at Grafton School, she still wants to make a difference. 'I believe that children must be given every chance to succeed regardless of background or ethnicity. We try to create opportunities some pupils may not otherwise have.' This could be a yearly trip to the coast (which for some pupils is their first experience of the sea), or the chance to learn a musical instrument.

One of Nitsa's proudest achievements is that she hasn't had to exclude a child for 11 years, 'I always believe more in preventative measures rather than reactive measures.' She also believes that, given the correct guidance, inner-city schools can be as good as any: 'My three children are all products of Islington comprehensives. My son is now a neurosurgeon and both my daughters are barristers.' Married for 40 years to an engineer, 'my bouncing board', she loves visiting art galleries and museums and spending time with her grandchildren. Such is her infectious enthusiasm that we left her office grinning.

Entrance: Standard local authority criteria of siblings, proximity to school and children in care etc. Competition for places is fierce – most recently 354 applicants for 60 places. As word spreads about this school there is concern about wealthier parents buying property in now trendy Holloway to get their kids a place, with predictable consequences for Grafton's rich diversity.

Exit: Mixed bag on offer for secondary schools in the Islington area. Most go on to Acland Burghley (if they live close enough), Highbury Fields, Highbury Grove, Mount Carmel school for girls, St Mary Magdalene or others including Islington Arts school, Central Foundation Boys' School, Camden School for Girls, Highgate Wood, Parliament Hill and William Ellis. A few try for grammars like Latymer or Dame Alice Owen or independents such as City of London.

Remarks: A tricky one to find, Grafton Primary sits adjacent to the Holloway Road, off Seven Sisters Road, accessible by car via a tiny slip road. Most pupils walk to school thereby avoiding the perils of Holloway's one-way system.

We were expecting great things and we weren't disappointed. Rated outstanding by Ofsted for the past 10 years and awarded the title of Beacon School, Grafton defies its demographics. A staggering 55-60 per cent of its pupils would qualify for free school meals (although in Islington, these are fully funded for all pupils), 25 per cent of children have SEN, 12 per cent with statements. Grafton is genuinely inclusive – big on equal opps for pupils with disabilities and a vast ethnic mix. One pupil told us, 'I have friends from so many different cultures and we are like a big family.' We heard the word 'family' used frequently and there is definitely a sense of unity and loyalty as well as pride in this school.

Grafton has recently become a teaching school, meaning that it now trains teachers and support staff from other primaries. It is also one of only a few pioneering schools to have been chosen to introduce the CAME maths programme (Cognitive Acceleration through Mathematics Education), which promises to have a significant impact on both pupil and teacher development. Maths is already a very strong subject at Grafton. Up to 20 per cent of year 6 achieve a level 6 in maths Sats.

On entering, one is immediately struck by the spectacularly colourful lobby. Rarely have we seen so much artwork, sculpture, ceiling displays (including a wonderful tree of life installation which ran the length of the lobby and through the school's office). Grafton has partnerships with art professionals, a specialist art and design teacher and an artist in residence, believing that time given to creative subjects helps children achieve in other areas.

The interior of the school is charming, if a little cramped (could be because every inch of space is covered with student displays). The Victorian building is DDA compliant and has a lift for wheelchair users. A £3.5m refurb means all classrooms are now up to spec and there's a new sports hall and reception play area. Library is still a work in progress but promises to be a great space.

Outside is an oasis of calm – amazing, considering proximity to the very urban and not very pretty Seven Sisters Road. Grounds are fairly large for an inner-city school and in addition to the playground there is a quiet formal garden with benches for students to have lunch and read (undergoing a refurb during our visit) and a wildlife garden. This mini eco system with pond and bug hotel feels a million miles from the city. 'Many parents volunteer their time in the garden and elsewhere', we are told. At the end of the wildlife garden is a glass building that we thought was a greenhouse; it's actually the art room, a quirky space crammed with creative materials.

In the assembly hall we were treated to a music assembly in Swahili, just one of the 34 languages spoken here. On site translators assist parents from the three main non-English speaking groups – Somalian, Turkish and Bangladeshi, and the school told us, 'We do what we can to make parents from all sectors of society feel included.'

The pupils we met were a highly articulate bunch – happy, confident and engaging. They loved their school and the opportunities it offers. One told us, 'Julia Donaldson has visited the school and some Paralympians came to talk to us, which was amazing and inspiring.' Another said he loved the cricket and football 'and we've won many tournaments.' A few negative comments about the lunches (free of charge for all pupils) and we thought that some of the food did look pretty unappetising. It seems almost churlish to mention this when for some pupils it may be the only cooked meal they get in a day.

Parents and pupils generally seemed extremely happy with their school. One parent did mention that she would like more sporting activities within the school day as opposed to just afternoon clubs, although she added that the Grafton school day is such a busy one, she's not sure where they would fit it in. Another told us, 'The school is amazing at being proactive, especially with day trips. If they're not hopping on the bus to St Paul's Cathedral, visiting the zoo or going to art galleries and museums, they're doing a walking tour around London. That's the benefit of being so inner city with free bus travel.' The quality of teaching came in for particular praise. One mother told us, 'My older children go to private schools and I know that the teaching my youngest is getting here is better than they received at her age.' She also said that there is a very high ratio of staff to pupils – 1:6 in the first two years – again, as good, as if not better than at some independent schools.

Graveney School

97

Welham Road, London SW17 9BU

Ages 11–18 **Pupils** 2,035 **Sixth form** 720

020 8682 7000
www.graveney.org

Principal: Since 1989, Graham Stapleton MA (60s). Read history at Trinity College, Cambridge, and started teaching at the school 40 years ago when it was Battersea Grammar School. Married with two grown-up children, his hobbies include reading (20th century American novels and historical fiction) and listening to soul and jazz. He has the air of a history professor about him. No immediate plans to retire as he wants to stay and oversee the new Tooting Primary School. 'Fantastic and inspiring', declared one parent. 'He really cares about each and every student'.

Becoming CEO of the Graveney Trust, with a new head due to be appointed for September 2019.

Academic matters: School is regarded as one of the top 200 state schools in the country. Thirty-five subjects available at A level – English literature the most popular and film studies recently added to the list. In 2018, 62 per cent A*/B grades at A level, with 33 per cent A*/A; 91 per cent of pupils obtained 9-4 grades in both maths and English at GCSE, with 48 per cent A8-A/9-7 grades. Focus is on the academic subjects. Some 85 per cent of students take triple sciences. RE is a compulsory GCSE. All students study a foreign language – French, Spanish or German (with Latin and Mandarin available as twilight subjects – before or after school) – and many take one to GCSE.

Pupils are divided into ability bands as soon as they enter the school in year 7. They are banded largely by English scores and then set for maths from year 8 onwards. Extension programme for those nominated by teachers (includes PE, music and art as well as English, maths and science). Some concern from potential parents about what school is like for those who don't get into the top band (extension group), but anecdotes from current parents say that the next band (upper) is also very high achieving. 'Whichever band your child is in, the teachers will push them to achieve their best', said one mother. 'They seem to have a knack of finding out what motivates your child and then encouraging them'. There is movement between the bands so no need to panic if your child is not in the extension group. However, some parents complain about the high number of students in the extension classes – up to 33 in some cases.

Large number of students with special needs (55 with statements/EHC plans) – 'because we have such a good reputation', explains the principal. SENCo and various learning mentors look after these students.

Games, options, the arts: Everyone is encouraged to take part in team sport and play for their form or house. Sports include rugby, football, volleyball, netball, cricket, tennis, athletics and basketball. One parent complained that there is only one timetabled session of games per week but principal stresses that all students are encouraged to take part in one extracurricular sports club after school. Even PE classes are streamed, so students get chance to play with others of similar ability.

School puts a special emphasis on music. All children eligible for free school meals get free music tuition. Around 350 learn an instrument at school (taught by peripatetic teaching staff) and more learn outside school. Each year around five students are members of the London Schools Symphony Orchestra and some students go on to study music at university or music college. School orchestra has 40 students, and choir has 70. All encouraged to take part in a musical event or production. Over 200 sixth form students recently took part in a production of Singing in the Rain.

Background and atmosphere: School is spread out over two campuses so despite its size (around 2,000 students) it doesn't feel overcrowded. Formerly a teacher training college, the original Georgian building (now rather scruffy) houses the art department. Other buildings have been added on over the years. School was due for refurbishment before government budget cuts so now looks rather tired. However, new RIBA award winning sixth form block plus new classroom block now open.

When we visited at break time, students were orderly and well behaved. Pupils all stood up when principal entered class – emphasis on good old-fashioned manners. No lockers, so pupils have to carry everything round with them, complained one parent.

School meals fantastic – delicious food and good selection, though some grumbles about the lengths of the queues. Newish lavatories for boys and girls (replacing the 'rather ghastly' previous ones).

Pastoral care, well-being and discipline: Teachers really do seem to care about each and every student. When we visited we came across the head of art berating an A level student for not completing his coursework. Afterwards she confided, 'He'll get an A* but he needs to understand that he has to put in the work.' This attention to detail is followed through at all levels. We also met a year 11 student being mentored by the principal to ensure that he gains the all-important five A*-C grades at GCSE. 'Are you making sure your homework is handed in on time?' he enquired. 'Mostly', mumbled the student.

Pastoral care is very good and students with difficulties are mentored by students higher up the school who have been through the same experiences.

Pupils and parents: Parents include middle class arty types and a good cross-section of the local community. Pupils in the extension group (those selected by ability) travel from further afield whereas others live locally and walk to school. Pupils are proud to belong to the school. 'Now I'm at Graveney I believe I can do anything', a year 9 student told us proudly.

Alumni include Naga Munchetty, BBC newsreader, Amol Rajan, editor of The Independent and Kyle Sinckler, England rugby international and member of the 2017 British Lions squad.

Entrance: For year 7 entry all applicants take the Wandsworth year 6 test. This selects 25 per cent of places by ability (63 pupils out of 2,000 who sit the exam), with 75 per cent selected on proximity to school. Sibling policy now applies to all pupils, including ability places (although it does not guarantee a place in the extension group: pupils still have to take the test to see which class they go into).

Students need five GCSEs at 9-4 including maths and English to stay on into the sixth form. Most do and are joined by an extra 150 (over 1,000 apply for these open places). Sixth form popular with pupils from the private sector, especially from single-sex schools. 'I think they want a more culturally diverse environment', says the head, 'and of course at that age they want to meet the opposite sex'.

Exit: Up to 20 per cent leave after GCSEs, perhaps because they haven't achieved the crucial grades. Those with poor end of year 12 results are also advised to find alternative courses. Around half to Russell Group universities, including 10 to Oxbridge plus nine medics in 2018. Some to music, art or drama colleges.

Remarks: Pupils who manage to get in are assured of a top class education in a socially mixed environment. Local parents often turn down places at schools like Alleyn's and Dulwich if their children manage to get a place here.

The Green School for Girls

Busch Corner, London Road, Isleworth TW7 5BB

Ages 11–18 **Pupils** 900 **Sixth form** 100 **C of E**

020 8321 8080
www.thegreenschool.net

Executive Head: Since 2015, Sally Yarrow (late 40s) BMus PGCE, educated at Aylesbury High grammar School and Hull University before completing her PGCE at Goldsmiths. Started her career as a music teacher and music remains her passion in education. Previously deputy head at St Marylebone school, a consistently high performing all girls C of E secondary, she fits like a glove here but has nonetheless stepped out of her comfort zone, having been at St Marylebone for almost her entire career. 'I could have stayed there for the rest of my working life, I loved it and was very happy, but I was ready for a new challenge,' she confides. With two school age boys of her own, Mrs Yarrow is approachable, youthfully girlish and enthusiastic, and deeply principled. Very popular with parents and pupils who regard her as having made a real impact. One parent described her as shrewd with a definite presence. Many of the girls see her as stern and strict, 'which is no bad thing,' affirmed another parent. On a very local level, she introduced whole school assemblies in the capacious sports hall, a hugely popular fixture with the girls which gives the school a sense of unity and purpose. She is definite about her vision and expresses it without any fudge or waffle. Her expectations are high but her approach is entirely child centred. 'It is all about what's best for the pupils', she says. 'We are a fully comprehensive, inclusive and diverse school and I am very proud of that.'

Her title is now executive head of the Green School Trust and she oversees both the girls' school and the new Green School for Boys. Parents confident that Stephen Burns, previously deputy head, will be an effective head of school responsible for the day to day running of the Green School for Girls

Academic matters: Consistently impressive GCSE results. Sixty-nine per cent of pupils got 9-4 in both maths and English and 30 per cent of grades were A*-A/9-7 in 2018. History, maths English and religious studies perform particularly well with high numbers of 9-7s. Science is also getting stronger. A level subjects include art and design, film studies, sociology and psychology as well as BTec level 3 in health and social care. High numbers choose biology, psychology and religious studies at A level. Value added scores are good (Progress 8 is a positive 0.5, placing the school in the top three per cent of schools nationally) – pupils make good progress, a valuable indicator of good teaching and a well run school. Parents comment about their daughters in the lower sets being stretched just as hard as if they were in the top sets. High expectation runs through all the layers of the school. Number of pupils with English as an additional language is very high – there is the option to take a GCSE in a native language, or indeed any language in which a pupil excels, in year 9.

A level results do not match the impressive GCSE scores – 'yet,' Mrs Yarrow intervenes. 'We lose a few of the high achievers after GCSE, and the girls for whom English is not their first language find the challenges are greater at A level – but this is something we are very much working on at the moment,' she explains, adding 'there is a huge amount of support for sixth form provision.' In 2018, 46 per cent A*-B and 22 per cent A*/A grades. The school is part of a Hounslow sixth form consortium (others include Gunnersbury, Brentford, Gumley and Chiswick), so girls in the sixth form here can travel to other schools for certain lessons, which may include boys. Extended Project Qualification (EPQ) is popular and highly successful. It taps into all the skills and qualities that Mrs Yarrow is so determined to develop here, self-reliance, resilience, being able to think and stand on one's own two feet. An enrichment programme in the sixth form, 'broadening horizons', incorporates academic literacy, discussion and discourse. It is aimed at developing academic minds; their form tutors are known as 'coaches' and they coach them with their studies. Opportunities for stretching as sports leaders, in Young Enterprise and LAMDA. Sixth form mentors, or co-tutors, work with particular forms as part of their leadership development, and they assume positions of responsibility whether as prefect, head girl, or one of four deputy head girls or assistants (a mirroring of the schools' staff senior leadership team).

Additional support given to those who need in it in years 7, 8 and 9 in maths and English (known as the Bridge Group). There can be as many as 15 pupils taught in a lesson of their own by the very experienced SENCo as well as a teacher and learning support assistant. Girls are taken out of language lessons to attend these classes. Less than one per cent of students have a statement/EHCP.

Setting for maths from year 7, and from year 8 in English and science: 'This may change; there is a fairly broad range within the sets,' avers Mrs Yarrow, who is mindful to ensure that teaching in the lower sets doesn't create a false cap of attainment. Teaching methods, language used by staff and senior leaders' attitude all encourage the building of a growth mindset and resilience. 'This is one of our school priorities,' says Mrs Yarrow, 'along with the application of performance skills to all the subjects and to life.'

Games, options, the arts: Wide choice of sporting activities include rowing, netball and badminton. School participates in various borough competitions including the National Youth Rowing Competition. Plenty of facilities on or adjacent to the site – netball courts as well as rugby and football pitches. Tag rugby one of the main sports here. A large, modern and squeaky clean sports hall can accommodate volleyball, dodge ball, trampolining and self-defence as well as netball, basketball and badminton.

DT GCSE options are textiles and food technology, but no electronics or resistant materials. Eighteen sewing machines as well as three embroidery machines and two overlocker machines, but only one textiles teacher. If your daughter wants to do A level textiles she will currently have lessons at one of the other schools in the Hounslow consortium. Everyone does food technology in years 7 and 8. Art is a popular A level. We saw some impressive ceramics, a very tangible pineapple in particular.

Old hall used for fashion shows (a fundraiser) and drama productions. There is also a drama studio – where we witnessed a very noisy game known as 'the splat game' designed to warm up the acting genes. Lots of productions by all year groups. Annual school productions have recently included Archie Dobson's War, Much Ado About Nothing ('slightly adapted,' we're told) and The Ash Girl. The sixth form theatre company recently produced, performed and directed The Great Gatsby.

Since the arrival of Mrs Yarrow, a huge and healthy increase in numbers wanting to join choirs and bands. Music has had a heavy injection of hers. Girls describe it, with infectious enthusiasm, as 'a really fun subject'. Music technology popular; lots of fancy equipment – Apple Macs and keyboards, and we saw a year 10 class writing a rap song. Lots of practice rooms for the large numbers who play an instrument – many play more than one, and music permeated several mainstream lessons we saw.

Debating club also very popular – open to any year group and recently, we were told, they examined issues from gay marriage to stem cell research and thrashed out the question of whether Black History Month should be abolished.

Plenty of residential trips – especially in year 9 – to Spain and France as well as ski trips to Austria. Duke of Edinburgh awards, bronze (year 10), silver and gold.

Careers advice and support strong. School awarded level 3 Investors in Careers.

Background and atmosphere: Although this is a Church of England school with a Christian ethos, it is overwhelmingly multi-faith. About a third of pupils are from Muslim families. One parent explained that girls' schools are popular 'because girls won't lose the attention of their teachers to the boys, the discipline is good and they can choose science subjects without feeling overshadowed by the boys'.

A five form entry school, the Green School is on the large side but not vast. Swathes of green tartan stream into the welcoming café Sorrento opposite the school. Not shouty girls, but considerate and polite, and all different cultures and backgrounds seem to integrate well as they pile into their waffles before the start of school. They file in an orderly fashion into the vast sports hall for assembly, in time to the soothing classical music that bounces off the sporty walls, and the hall becomes a sea of green uniform.

A school steeped in history (it was originally founded in 1796), the main building is a handsome 1906 Edwardian brick and timber building situated on the busy junction at Busch Corner in Isleworth. This now houses the library and a performance hall (where the clock has always been wrong) as well as some classrooms. Linking them are long, wide corridors which smell of freshly polished wooden parquet floors. Gold leaf plated wooden merit boards from the 1950s line the walls, and cupboards stuffed with silver cups nestle in corners. A satisfyingly traditional smell of learning, scholarship and achievement. The library, despite its traditional feel, is buzzing with activity. This is where girls come to do their homework – both during and after school hours. Books here are well thumbed and there are plenty of computers.

The modern buildings are bright, filled with sunlight, with lots of space. Our guides particularly enjoyed lingering in the sociology classroom, a favourite subject here. The sixth form centre is civilised with attractive space to eat and talk as well as have meetings, perform plays and listen to talks. An area to chat and use mobiles is screened off from an area to work and use computers (we presume for work). The school canteen is comfortable, streaming with sunlight through the large windows when we visited. All the girls we met said the food was good. Many get in early to eat breakfast here at 7.30am.

The school is divided into five houses – named here after trees (Willow, Oaks, Beeches etc) for the purpose of competitions, whether sporting, academic, or other – there is an inter-house Christmas carol competition, for example.

Pastoral care, well-being and discipline: The pastoral care here is universally acclaimed. A number of parents described how much their daughters have grown in confidence here – whether as a result of performing in plays and assemblies, playing sport or being encouraged to question and challenge their teachers during lessons. While there is respect for the staff among the pupils, it works both ways, enabling the timid types, prone to being overly deferential, to emerge from their shells and speak up for themselves. The school motto, Let your light shine, seems to have genuine resonance.

The very congenial school chaplain is in school three times a week and she takes part in assemblies and services. By all accounts she plays a key pastoral role for students and staff alike.

There is a clear disciplinary procedure which appears to be appreciated by pupils, parents and staff. Final step after three warnings. If a girl needs to be removed from a lesson for being disruptive, she is sent to the Improvement Area. Curriculum parking is when a student is removed from a lesson and 'sent to an appropriate parking lot' to work. Detentions here are known as 'learning meetings'. 'You don't sit around doing nothing but discuss a solution.'

Naughty behaviour seems to boil down to disrupting lessons and occasional bullying behaviour. The girls we spoke to looked wide eyed when we asked about drugs. This is a school of predominately good girls. Any incidents of bullying are dealt with quickly through the year leader and heads of year. Response is speedy and effective. Girls seem quite confident that they would go to the teachers if they needed to.

Social media – as in all secondary schools at the moment – is causing the most sleepless nights for heads. Here mobile phones have to be stored in lockers during the school day and if they are found on a girl during a lesson they are confiscated. The strict policy is bearing fruit – fewer social media related incidents this year than in previous years. A more relaxed policy is adopted with sixth formers, however.

One girl, who said she never used to like school, now enjoys coming to school and said she 'feels safe'. Parents, too, are confident that any issues of bullying, social media abuse or self harming will be dealt with swiftly and effectively. One mother described how 'in tune' the school is with its community: there is a genuine understanding of and empathy with the issues that face teenage girls at this time.

Pupils and parents: An immensely diverse, multicultural C of E school. Many Muslim pupils, some Hindu, as well as devout Christians and some of no faith. Many parents are practising Christians but plenty are not. Pupils come from Brentford and Chiswick as well as Staines and Isleworth and a wide range of local and far flung primaries. Over 30 per cent of pupils are on pupil premium. One parent talked of it being a 'balanced community', families from all walks of life, earning a living in so many different ways, but what virtually all parents have in common is a shared belief in high standards. They are committed to supporting their daughters to reach their full potential.

Entrance: Parents are expected to be committed to the Christian ethos and give full support to the school. Girls are expected to attend Christian acts of worship and take part in the religious curriculum. A hundred of the 155 places are reserved for practising Christians, 30 places allocated to 'other world faiths' and 25 are community places. Priority to siblings (including brothers at the Green School for Boys) and those who live closest.

Sixth form admissions (boys as well as girls) according to predicted GCSE grades and proximity.

Worth making an in year application for an occasional place. As with all areas of London there is movement and there are often new arrivals in years other than years 7 and 12.

Exit: A challenge for Mrs Yarrow is to keep as many of high performers as she can for the sixth form and encourage them to appreciate its strengths. In 2018, 60 per cent left after GCSEs. After A level students go to a wide range of destinations to read an equally wide range of subjects. One off to Oxbridge in 2018 and one to study medicine; others to destinations ranging from LSE and UCL to the University of the Arts (film and TV studies). A small number to art foundation and five per cent take gap years, including apprenticeships or internships with eg the BBC.

Remarks: We agree that this is a genuinely outstanding state secondary. The high standard of pastoral care and the attention that's paid to each individual and their needs makes this a good fit for almost any girl, but especially those who are aspirational, hard working and committed to doing their best. A tolerant, diverse school with strong Christian values – of the very best kind. Those with sons too keep an eye out – the new Green School for Boys is one to watch.

Greenford High School

Lady Margaret Road, Southall, Middlesex UB1 2GU

Ages 11–19 **Pupils** 1,755 **Sixth form** 539

020 8578 9152
www.greenford.ealing.sch.uk

Headteacher: Since 2009, Mathew Cramer MA PGCE NPHQ (mid 50s), a north Londoner by birth and son of a commercial artist. Mr Cramer was educated at Highgate Wood Comprehensive and went onto read philosophy and literature at Sussex University followed by a masters at Warwick and a PGCE at King's College London. His career started with a brief spell in Hong Kong editing textbooks, since then he has spent his entire career teaching in west London. He came to Greenford to teach English in 1995;

prior to that he was at St Mark's Catholic school in Hounslow, where his wife is now head of media. Warm, understated with a beguiling, dry sense of humour, Mr Cramer is an experienced and extremely effective head. His office is reassuringly cluttered, with an eclectic mix of pictures on the walls, from ancient maps and Greek temples (his mother is Greek Cypriot) to Hokusai's 'Great Wave off Kanagawa' juxtaposed with boldly colourful paintings by his students.

Modest about the achievements in his 10 years at the helm here, Mr Cramer says the school was always successful, 'a very warm school built on positive relationships between staff and pupils. I've tried to establish a culture that is happy but aspirational,' he says. 'I try to give lifeless buildings an identity, find ways to demonstrate that learning is exciting and give school a sense of vibrancy.' Passionate about literacy, he focuses heavily on reading skills when they arrive. At this point only a third can read above the standard of their reading age, and a third are well below the standard. 'It's essential they can access text,' says Mr Cramer.

Thoughtful and sensitive, Mr Cramer is very much a people person. Parents describe him as 'gentle but firm. He enjoys a good debate.' He puts staff recruitment amongst his highest priorities – 'it's all about the staff,' he says; 'the results of employing the right person for a particular role are tangible and visible.'

The school is flying high and has been for some time, receiving a number of awards, including the Gold Award from Boris Johnson, awarded for the highest progress figures. Mr Cramer notes this with a healthy mixture of scepticism and pride, and is more concerned to tell us about his bugbears: 'litter drives me mad,' he says.

Leaving in July 2019.

Academic matters: A fully comprehensive, non-selective school, Greenford High has to cater for two extremes, without overlooking the middle tranche. It does an impressively good job. Japanese, GCSEs and A levels at one end of the spectrum, and a BTec in business and enterprise at the other. DT product design, fine art and photography as well as business and economics are all offered; science labs are well equipped, science teaching effective. The high expectations for academic students do not just include a university exit, Russell Group, perhaps or even Oxford and Cambridge, but Harvard and Princeton too. At the other end of the scale, some apprenticeships are harder to achieve than a university place. Some 500 students were competing for one apprenticeship with Honda; it was a Greenford boy who won it.

Years 7 and 8 now have nearly all lessons their own 'middle school' building, and pupils graduate formally from year 8 into year 9 – they get a 'degree' to show they are ready for the GCSE course that starts from year 9. The only test is their attitude to learning. Those that are not ready continue for longer in middle school. 'This solves a number of problems,' says Mr Cramer, 'not least it stops year 8 from being a fallow year.' Setting from year 7 in maths and English (about nine sets in total), science is setted later (moderate setting in yr 7; more refined at KS4). Every pupil takes RE GCSE at end of the year 9, 'a gateway GCSE', 80 per cent pass, a third achieve A*/A, and 'even if they don't do as well as they would have done had they waited until year 11, it will have motivated and challenged them,' says Mr Cramer. At the end of year 10 they all take a language GCSE (which they have started in year 7 and could include Spanish, French, German or Japanese), some take two languages, some take a community language – facilitated, but not taught, by the school. A study club after school for years 10 and 11 supports their organisation, revision and individual learning. Some classes have a mixed year group – eg years 9 and 10 are mixed as are years 10 and 11 – usually for options at GCSE.

GCSE results in 2018 impressive, 35 per cent 9-7, and 77 per cent got 9-4 in both English and maths – some of their best results ever, which placed the school in the top 200 nationally. At A level in 2018, 44 per cent A*-B grades (22 per cent A*/A). Key Stage 4 ALPs grade (measuring student progress against the national picture) was a level 2 – Outstanding. At A level, ALPs grade was a level 3 – Excellent; these scores have been consistently this high for the last 10 years.

Particularly strong GCSE results in business and economics (business handily appeals to both ends of the academic spectrum and Southall has one of the highest number of small businesses), all three sciences, computing, Japanese (though small numbers take it), German and history. Most popular subject at A level, by some margin, is maths, with pleasing results. Excellent results at A level too in media, film and TV studies (best results in the country), DT product design, physics and fine art.

Greenford used to be a language college and 60-70 per cent of students continue to take a modern language at GCSE. Japanese has always been strong – 'it's always about the personalities,' says Mr Cramer. 'We were lucky to have an outstanding Japanese teacher and we continue to attract excellent teachers'. They are proactive – whether it be inviting the wife of the Japanese prime minister to the school or beating Eton and other high achieving independent schools at the Nihongo Cup run by the Japanese embassy. The experience spills into pupils' later lives: one ex-pupil is now working for big business in Tokyo. With difficult decisions impending on funding, however, the fate of Japanese here lies in the balance.

School is consistently in the top five per cent of the country for progress, and while the SEN progress is still above average at +0.15, SEND pupils make lower progress compared with other pupils in the school. A fair number of pupils have support with their learning, but only a handful on EHC plans. Mr Cramer is visibly pained that these pupils make less progress than their mainstream peers despite the fact that they are still making more progress than the national average, and confirms that this is one of their targets.

The university style campus is not necessarily conducive to people with EHC plans – but the new block, in development, will have an ARP area to work with students who have different needs, and a capacity for 20 students.

Greenford High has pulling power, attracting high quality teachers. One of the physics teachers we met is possibly the only Somali female physics teacher in the country. The school has a partnership with Teach First, as well as with the Institute of Education, and trains 30 teachers a year – many stay on. Healthy mix of the long established, stable and experienced, some of whom form part of the senior leadership team, and the young and dynamic, bringing fresh ideas and fuelling the tangible vibrancy in the classroom.

Games, options, the arts: Sport is strong – as in other departments at Greenford, standards are high. An Olympic judge runs the gymnastics, an ex-England player coaches the basketball. Excellent facilities in relatively new building (funded by PFI). Well-equipped and well-used gym. Lots of space on site, including fleet of MUGAs as well as grass pitches (though notorious Ealing soil means they're waterlogged for much of the winter months, we were told with wry raise of the eyebrow). Football and netball strong (though there was an observation from one quarter that if you are not particularly keen you can end up not playing much sport at all). Both genders shine in gymnastics and trampolining. Boys and girls taught separately for PE.

Despite corrosive cuts, school manfully continues to offer excellent art, DT, textiles, cooking and photography (three art teachers have had to go as department has shrunk from five to two). Impressive display of design products – toys and automated hoovers. School is proud owner of a laser cutter as well as a 3D printer. All pupils do art in years 7 and 8, between 15 and 20 do GCSE, a few do fine art A level and about about 4-6 a year go on to art colleges. 'It is important that we don't forget those students,' says Mr Cramer.

School very supportive of Cadets, Scouts and Duke of Edinburgh Award. Some 150 trips a year, including to Lille, Berlin and Tokyo, to Cambridge, Oxford and Reading. Mixed year groups help to spread the cost – school helps as much as it can with funding. 'There is not a culture of the haves and have nots here, much to parents' relief,' pointed out one father. 'School is open to any initiative and will run with it, but the students need to be proactive,' commented a mother.

Music – very few take it to GCSE or A level (music tech only). However there have been successful barber shop quartets. Drumkit and guitars available for anyone who wants to have a go. 'As with so much of the approach at Greenford,' observed a parent, 'if the pupils show enthusiasm and drive, the school will support them and nurture any talent or interest.'

G

Drama is taken by everyone in years 7 and 8, and 20 or so continue to GCSE, though it is not available at A level. Small theatre where students put on comedy shows.

Background and atmosphere: Founded in 1939, Greenford started life as a typical suburban grammar school, surrounded by farmland. The original 1930s buildings still stand and now form part of a new block. The school has gone through a number of different personalities since then and is now a large comprehensive with 1,800 pupils, increasing to 2,100 with the new middle school building, which houses years 7 and 8 and provides a 'small school' within the school.

The school buzzes with an atmosphere of endeavour, echoing its motto 'learning to succeed'. Mr Cramer likens the modern university campus style of the site to Sussex and Warwick Universities. The new buildings, opened by David Miliband in 2008, are constructed out of various materials, painted in bright array of colours and named alphabetically after key people (A for Aristotle, B for Brunel, F for Fitzgerald – Ella, not Scott). Each building has vibrant murals painted up the stairs, along the corridors, in the entrance halls – penguin book covers, famous theatrical production posters and a Scrabble board, a surrealist portrait of 'the Greenford giraffe' outside Downing Street, a double Helix climbing the stairs, a large map of England with university sites pinned to it. 'We wanted to make the place feel vibrant, that learning is stimulating and fun,' says Mr Cramer, 'and the students appreciate it, they respect their environment, we have very little vandalism.' The campus is surrounded by irregular grassy mounds, referred to as 'Teletubby hills', contributing to the overall sense that this place is an oasis of opportunity in the middle of its suburban setting.

The main reception, as you enter the school, resembles a busy airport – lots of people coming and going, a sense of industry and purpose. High tech gates and lanyard creations, but amidst all that security the atmosphere is human, friendly and flexible.

The canteen is café style, with a mix of round and long tables and a little tuck shop. Post-16 accommodation includes a common room with table football and a large quiet area filled with computer stations to work and prepare for the next stage.

Pastoral care, well-being and discipline: Strong emphasis on an ethos of helping others – not reacting out of self-interest but for the good of the community and the good of others. Initiatives like hosting a dinner for senior citizens in the school hall – organised and run by post-16 pupils – helps to reaffirm these values. Assembly – taken in year groups, so each year gets together once a week – reflects on a range of issues from moral choices to healthy eating and child exploitation. Each assembly ends with an act of worship – relevant to all faiths.

Cyber issues addressed head on. System of cyber mentors contributes to an awareness and support system for any abuse of social media. School receives £50,000 each year from the John Lyons Foundation towards this. E-safety talks regularly attended by all students – 'as a result, social media bullying and related issues are not a major concern here,' assures head.

'This is not a detention bound school,' commented one parent, 'but there are rules and there are standards, and they are high ones. If you want to get the best out of the school you are expected to work with them.. You have to look smart, hand homework in on time, but these things are done by cooperation rather than the coercion.'

Behaviour, on the whole, is good. Teachers here earn respect and get it. There is genuine concern and care for the pupils, so that although good results are expected, it is the result that would be good for each individual. On the more contentious issues, we were assured that incidents of knives in school are rare and the school takes a sensitive approach to the government initiative Prevent. Issues relating to religious extremism are tackled by the head in assemblies and through outside speakers who come to give talks. Homophobia more of a prescient issue than gender fluidity.

Pupils and parents: A diverse mix of different cultures and nationalities, about 40 per cent Muslim. Despite the diversity, the community is well integrated. When Pakistan play India in the test match, we were told, the school comes alive with excitement and the fault lines are more visible. Only five per cent white British. Other white communities from Eastern Europe, predominately Polish. Others come from all over, from Eritrea to Afghanistan, a fair few from Somalia. Many are very aspirational. Turnout for parents' evenings is always high, observed one parent. Lots are keen for their children to excel at the sciences. The demographic has shifted slightly in the last 10 years – mainly with the decrease in numbers from the Sikh community – and the school has now started to attract families with very able children – families who in the past might have chosen to send them to grammar schools or choose independent schools.

One parent commented, 'kids here are not very privileged but become privileged from being at Greenford'. Pupils are politically aware, will hold mock elections during an election even if it coincides with exams, are flexible and ready to think on their feet.

Entrance: Most oversubscribed school in Ealing. Receives more applications than any other school. There were 1,667 applications for 300 yr 7 places for September 2018; 435 first choices, 426 second choices. Siblings given priority. 'This is a family school,' says Mr Cramer; 'a family could live in Slough and get a place at the school' (many do – as many Sikhs moved to Langley and Slough). 'We don't have a catchment.' However the next criterion is proximity to the school and most live within half a mile, though 10 per cent of pupils live further away.

Exit: Around a quarter leaves after GCSEs. One off to Oxford and one to Cambridge in 2018, plus six medics. Mr Cramer makes lots of trips to Oxbridge colleges to make himself, his school and his students known. Approximately 230 go on to university each year but there is also a lot of investment in apprenticeships. 'You have to be realistic,' affirms Mr Cramer, 'university is not for everyone but it does offer the chance to lead a different life'. The occasional place is won at top US universities, too. One former student is now studying at Harvard, another at Princeton.

Remarks: If you want a strong head with a big heart, a diverse community which shares a desire for a high standards and has high expectations, whether it be for results, or attention to well-being, and if you are lucky enough to fall within the criteria for getting into this hugely oversubscribed school, you need look no further. But this is a school that gives to those who give: the more you put in the more you get out. Slouchers beware.

The Grey Coat Hospital

Greycoat Place, London SW1P 2DY

Ages 11–18 **Pupils** 1,050 **Sixth form** 233 (20 boys) **C of E**

020 7969 1998
www.gch.org.uk

Headteacher: Since 2011, Siân Maddrell BA (40s). Educated at Surbiton High, followed by a degree in French at Durham. After gaining her PGCE at Oxford, she began her teaching career at Grey Coat in 1992, quickly becoming head of modern languages and one of the first advanced skills teachers in the country. Left Grey Coat in 2000 and later became the first vice principal of Pimlico Academy before returning as head.

Friendly, thoughtful, efficient and clearly devoted to her school. Takes great pride in her pupils and their achievements. Not above picking up stray litter in the playground.

'We want to enable girls to take charge of their learning, make decisions based on Christian values, live in the world as independent women and meet the challenges of the 21st century,' she told us. 'We just try to focus on our pupils. It's a very ambitious school and the students will tell you that the expectations and aspirations are really high for everybody. It's about empowering the pupils to do their best. We want girls to be confident enough to be able to seize every opportunity.'

Enjoys sport, theatre and travel – 'I'm very interested in other countries and cultures.' Married with two sons.

Academic matters: School is regularly rated outstanding by Ofsted. Recently received congratulatory letter from schools' minister praising pupils and staff for attainment and progress as one of the top 100 non-selective state schools in the country. Has also won local awards for the success and value-added progress of its disadvantaged pupils.

In 2018, 86 per cent got 9-4 in both English and maths, and nearly 50 per cent of GCSE grades were 9-7. Girls take between nine and 13 GCSEs. At A level, 68 per cent A*/B and 38 per cent A*/A grades. Good range of subjects on offer to GCSE, including Latin, business studies and computing. Pre-U offered in Latin, Greek and art history, all of which are taught at neighbouring Westminster School. 'The pupils love their lessons at Westminster,' the head told us. A level subjects include film studies and sociology as well as more traditional fare. Biology, chemistry, maths, English, history, psychology and religious studies currently very popular. EPQ is becoming increasingly fashionable.

Grey Coat is a specialist language college and has an outward-looking, global focus. 'We encourage an international outlook as well as strong grades,' says the head. 'It is important for our students to gain an understanding of other countries and cultures and to have an open and inclusive approach, as well as to develop their linguistic skills.' All students study Spanish and a second modern language (French or German). Many continue with two foreign languages to GCSE. Opportunities to study Mandarin and Japanese out of school hours. Japanese exchange offered to girls in year 10; other exchange trips to Germany and Spain.

International May Fair for younger pupils is an annual highlight. Students are encouraged to represent a country – through fashion, food, dance, ecology and culture. The competition is judged by staff and the prize, awarded to the most impressive tutor group, is a trip to Paris. School is excellent at offering incentives to pupils; girls are encouraged to be competitive. Pupils regularly win local and national science and maths competitions.

Grey Coat prides itself on being an inclusive school. SEND pupils make good progress academically and are fully involved in school life. All year 7 girls are screened for learning difficulties on entry to school. Small support groups for literacy, numeracy and social skills run at lunchtime for younger girls. Five per cent have a statement of special educational needs. Gifted and talented extension programmes in place for more able.

Average class size is 27, with a maximum of 30. No setting in year 7. Year 8 pupils set for English, maths, science and languages.

G

Games, options, the arts: Good level of participation in wide variety of sport. 'We are the Westminster sports champions in practically everything and we provide a rich variety of sports,' says the head. Opportunities for fencing, squash, indoor rowing and athletics as well as team sports. Currently Westminster netball champions. 'We've struggled a bit with athletics as we have to bus the pupils over to Battersea Park,' admits bursar. Massive sports hall at Regency Street site. Annual gym and dance display.

Creative subjects taken seriously. Excellent facilities in art and design; these remain very popular subjects and the quality of art displays is very high. 'The standard of art work is mind-blowing,' according to one parent. Music and drama both strong. Instrumental and singing lessons are subsidised by school's foundation. Good range of choirs, bands, string and jazz groups and orchestra. Several concerts every year. Successful gospel choir recently reached semi-finals of BBC's School Choir of the Year competition.

Roughly 15 pupils a year achieve D of E gold award. Good spread of clubs, including maths challenge, debating, football, trampolining and creative writing. External inspirational speakers come in regularly to motivate and encourage the girls. Workshops led by outsiders a regular feature of the education offered here. School takes part in BBC News School Report, enabling pupils to make their own news reports for a live audience. Students develop their journalistic skills and have a ball.

Lots of time for fun here too. Talent show at the end of the Easter term is eagerly anticipated while staff pantomime is apparently 'the best day' of the school year. 'It's absolutely hilarious watching the teachers,' said one pupil. Post-GCSE celebration for year 11s includes a fashion show of their textiles work.

Background and atmosphere: Originally founded for boys in 1698. In 1706, Queen Anne granted the Grey Coat Hospital Foundation a royal charter and her portrait hangs in pride of place in the Great Hall. Original wooden boards detailing the names and donations of 18th century benefactors line the stairs. In 1874 Grey Coat Hospital became a girls' school, under church management.

A C of E school. Head says, 'Christian values play a key part of Grey Coat.' Church services held each term either in Westminster Abbey or St Margaret's, including a July celebration to which new pupils (and their parents) are invited. 'It's a lovely event – beautifully done,' said a parent. Confirmation services take place at Westminster Abbey and school has its own chaplain.

School occupies two fabulous buildings in the heart of Westminster, huge quantity of traffic and people encircling it on the streets outside. Strikingly beautiful building in Greycoat Place, freshly painted and polished. Statuettes of Grey Coat boy and girl adorn the front façade of the school. Wonderful entrance hall, glistening with trophies and artwork. School celebrates the achievements of the girls at every opportunity.

Original building at Greycoat Place is used by the younger pupils (years 7 to 9) but lots of coming and going of pupils from one site to another. Fantastic new arts block includes swish drama studios where recent productions have included The Tempest and The Winter's Tale. 'Drama is a subject that is taken very seriously at Grey Coat and the performances are very professional,' we were told. Facilities hired out to National Youth Theatre in holidays.

Welcoming staff. Healthy female/male ratio and mix of long-servers and newly qualified teachers. 'A positive balance,' says the head. Variable staff turnover.

Symbiotic relationship with Westminster School. Grey Coats go there for lectures, some lessons and Oxbridge preparation, while graduate trainee teachers from Westminster come here to gain experience of teaching in a state school. 'It's wonderful for our students that they have these opportunities,' says the head.

Pastoral care, well-being and discipline: Pastoral care is a major strength of the school. 'Each girl is part of a tutor group family and a year group family, so each feels looked after here,' says the head. Strict code of conduct, but relatively few behavioural issues here. Older girls are given plenty of responsibility, with 40 prefects in final year. Girls can become ambassadors for their year group in years 9 and 11, having successfully explained at interview why they should be chosen. 'There is a strong sense of community here,' says the head. 'We have counsellors, student counsellors, and older students working with younger pupils. It's about creating a sense that we're all in this together.' It certainly seems to be working well. A learning mentor is on hand to help girls organise themselves if needed, as well as a drop-in school nurse.

Girls start off in smaller, lower school – helps them cope better with the progression to upper school. 'It's rare to hear of anyone being miserable here,' a parent told us. 'The school keeps a close eye on its pupils and intervenes quickly if things are going awry.'

Food thought to be 'very good, with lots of choice,' according to one pupil. Vast quantities of pizzas being eaten at break on the day we visited. Oyster card system in place so girls don't need to carry money and the canteen is open from breakfast onwards. School is confident that 'we'd know if a girl wasn't eating.'

Head is justifiably proud of the excellent attendance record of 98 per cent throughout the year – rating it the third highest in the UK. 'All our pupils came in when the recent tube strike was on,' says the head. Pupils with 100 per cent attendance and punctuality for a year get a trip to the theatre.

Pupils and parents: 'A real mix,' the head told us. Twenty-eight per cent of pupils eligible for pupil premium. Two-thirds from minority ethnic groups. A third whose first language is not English – more than 50 languages spoken at home, including Yoruba, Swahili, Spanish, French and Dutch.

Big inner-city blend of families, including daughters of politicians and education professionals. School recently hit the headlines with the news that prominent politicians are sending their daughters here. Old Greys include TV presenter Sarah Greene and Tamsin Dunwoody. Recent leaver is Ebony-Jewel Rainford-Brent, the first female black cricketer to play for the England team (she presented awards at a recent prize-giving). Many old girls remain loyal to the school and return to the annual school celebration service in Westminster Abbey each year.

Entrance: Huge catchment area from the dioceses of London and Southwark. Pupils travel from as far away as Essex and Kent and are rarely local. Total of 151 places offered in year 7. Fifteen language places (following an aptitude test which 450 sit); 88 C of E places; 28 other church places; 20 open places.

Priority given to looked-after children, then siblings, church attendance for church places and a distance tie-breaker. The comprehensive intake is placed into bands following an assessment test – 25 per cent places to band 1, 50 per cent places to band 2 and 25 per cent to band 3.

Open events for year 6 pupils in September and early October each year. Sixth form open events in November. Relatively little movement of pupils. 'We are a very stable population,' says the bursar. Once pupils are here, they tend to stay put, even if it means travelling long distances. In-year admissions are dealt with by the local authority. A few boys in sixth form, all 'charming,' according to one member of staff.

Exit: Around a third leaves after GCSEs, usually for schools closer to home or offering subjects not available here. Their places are taken by a fresh intake. Around 90 per cent go on to higher education. School encourages pupils to aim for top universities and some 40 per cent go to Russell Group universities as well as art colleges. Popular destinations include Oxbridge (five places in 2018), Exeter, St Andrews, Leeds, Durham, Nottingham, Bristol and Manchester, plus one off to a dance conservatoire in Italy in 2018. Popular subjects include medicine, sciences, maths, English, religious studies and classics.

Money matters: Parents' Guild raises money each year for both the school and charity. Recently paid for a beautiful stained-glass window by Michael Coles. Parents are asked to contribute a small amount of money on a monthly or annual basis.

Remarks: A sensational mix of high academic standards strongly supported by caring and devoted staff. No wonder they are prepared to travel for hours each day to be part of this buzzing school. The girls we met were charming, articulate, interesting and purposeful. Their pride in the school was striking. Not only are they ambitious and successful but they're also happy. On the day we visited, groups of girls were sitting cross-legged on the tarmac playground at break time, chatting and laughing as though they didn't have a care in the world.

Grimsdell Mill Hill Pre-Preparatory School

Linked with Mill Hill School, Belmont Mill Hill Preparatory School

Winterstoke House, Wills Grove, London NW7 1QR

Ages 3–7 **Pupils** 189

Fees: £6,852 – £14,895 pa

020 8959 6884
www.millhill.org.uk/grimsdell

Head: Since 2014, Kate Simon (40s). A current Grimsdell parent, Mrs Simon is no stranger to headship. Between 2002 and 2008 she was head of the junior school of the Royal School, Hampstead (now incorporated into North Bridge Senior) and from 2008 was head of Girls' Upper School at Garden House School in Chelsea.

Entrance: Heavily oversubscribed, due in part to it being non-selective at age 3 or 4. 'I don't feel comfortable with failing children at that age', says the head. Most pupils come from within a five mile radius and there is a 'multi-cultural mix.'

Exit: The majority of pupils continue on to Belmont school. However, if the school feels that a child won't cope there, discussions about alternatives take place from year 1. 'We have to be realistic', the school says.

Remarks: Unfortunate name for a very pretty school. On a beautiful autumnal day, Grimsdell was the antithesis of 'grim'. Situated on Mill Hill's Ridgeway, but accessed via a small and very lovely private road, the school occupies the rather grand Winterstoke House. Originally a vicarage for the vicar of St Paul's and sold to Mill Hill School in October 1923, Winterstoke House was purchased to become a school boarding house to host some 42 boys.

The school became Grimsdell in 1995 – a newcomer compared to the other two schools in the Foundation. The reason for its formation was largely due to a Mrs Grimsdell, widow of an Old Millhillian, who bequeathed a large part of her late husband's estate to Mill Hill School. Following a request from the school governors, Mrs Grimsdell agreed that the benefaction be applied to create a 'much required' pre-preparatory school, and Grimsdell opened its gates. The school is situated adjacent to Mill Hill School but has its own grounds – not quite on the scale of the other two schools, but more than adequate for a pre-prep school.

This is a cute, cosy school. Nothing grand and pretentious, despite the impression given by its exterior. We were seated in a colourful and bright reception area with a large aquarium to gaze at while we waited to meet the head. Familiar sounds of over-excited kids emanated from one or two of the classrooms (and we were particularly struck by one over-zealous music teacher doing something very strange with her arms!)

All classrooms were light, airy and well equipped – particularly the Sunshine Room, which even in its name suggests something warm and nurturing. This is where pupils who need it go for extra one-to-one learning support. Specialist on-site teachers in music, PE and French are on hand and 4 to 7-year-olds have weekly keyboard lessons with a music specialist. The swimming pool at Mill Hill School is a great addition to the PE curriculum. Pupils use the theatre at Mill Hill School for concerts and performances. Cursive handwriting is taught from the start and we were quite amazed with the standard of year 1 handwriting displayed on classroom walls.

As with Belmont and Mill Hill School, Grimsdell's selling point is undoubtedly its idyllic surroundings. Pupils not only have access to 120 acres of beautiful parkland at Mill Hill school with its sports pitches, swimming pool and woodland, but they have their own great adventure playground and science garden to enjoy. A firm believer in the great outdoors, Grimsdell has its own forest school. Each session has a theme and activities can range from mini-beast hunting to fire building and cooking outdoors. With a school that states boldly in its prospectus 'there is no such thing as bad weather, just bad clothing', you had better be sure your little darlings have a healthy interest in outdoor pursuits. Forget this school otherwise – indeed discount the other two schools in the Foundation while you are at it.

Parents appreciate the expertise of the large Foundation, and the lack of pressure to take exams for future schools. One parent told us, 'Grimsdell is a secure and nurturing stepping-stone, which is illustrated by my own excited and eager children.'

Gumley House School FCJ

St John's Road, Isleworth TW7 6XF

Ages 11–18 **Pupils** 1,072 **Sixth form** 170 (15 boys) **RC**

020 8568 8692
www.gumley.hounslow.sch.uk

Headteacher: Since 2016, Caroline Braggs BA PGCE MA NPQH (50s), previously deputy head. Read theology at Heythrop College, London University, gaining her PGCE at the Institute of Education and MA at University of Surrey. Has taught at three other Catholic schools before but is delighted to be the head here as 'Gumley is the place I want to be.'

When Idi Amin expelled all Asians from Uganda in 1972, Ms Braggs and her family packed their worldly possessions into two suitcases and ended up as refugees in Birmingham. She was just six at the time. Ms Braggs comes from a family of strong, practical women and her can-do attitude makes her a powerful role model. She believes that what this school does best is 'educating the whole person. Gumley empowers the students to take their place in society. It teaches them to pick themselves up and be resilient when faced with challenges in the outside world. We prepare them for the future, for a global and a changing world.' As a refugee, she knows first-hand that versatility and adaptability are vital when facing life's challenges.

Ms Braggs attends all school events with gusto, regularly staying late into the evening. Pupils appreciate her dependability and her friendliness. One girl commented, 'Everybody finds Ms Braggs very easy to talk to. She listens to what we say.'

Any smidgeon of spare time is spent at the theatre, travelling (frequently to Madeira) and relaxing with extended family. 'My nieces and godchildren are my life,' she beams.

Academic matters: Generally very decent results but not releasing GCSE or A level scores for 2018. Around 26 subjects offered at A level. Currently, English, maths, sociology and chemistry are popular sixth form choices. Part of a consortium with Gunnersbury and St Mark's, so those favouring less conventional subjects such as classical civilisation can study them at their sister schools. Conversely, their pupils venture over here for media studies and economics. Compulsory RE at GCSE. Parents feel that teaching is 'generally very good throughout', though one mother we spoke to felt homework 'could be more structured and meaningful.' The school disagrees with her view, telling us that 'our research and knowledge does not highlight homework as a general problem.'

Gumley has a language specialism. French, Italian, Spanish and Mandarin offered, as well as Latin for the most able. Annual language festival celebrates the diverse languages spoken by pupils. School also has partnerships with schools in Africa, China and India, reflecting its international make-up.

SEND provision considered to be excellent. Three fully qualified teachers and nine learning support assistants. Gumley can support the milder end of physical and learning difficulties, including ASD, dyslexia and speech and language needs. Everyone is screened for literacy levels at the start of year 7. Those requiring help are offered extra tuition, in-class support and reading clubs. Wheelchair access throughout.

Head feels pressure on staff is worse than ever, and that recruitment and retention of teachers is a problem here, as it is nationally. Pupils rate their teachers highly as 'they listen to us and care for us. They want us to do well.' One girl we spoke to praised her teachers' speedy responses to emails, often well into the evening. Many teachers go well beyond what is expected.

Chasing league tables is not Gumley's style. Head explains that 'academic excellence is of paramount importance, but in tandem with the development of a young person's mental and emotional well-being.' She elaborates, 'We do not lose sight of the person while aiming high academically. Education is not just about maths, science and so on. It's about making someone fully human and able to take their place in society.'

Games, options, the arts: Sporty pupils are not short of opportunities here. Athletics, cricket, football, badminton, netball, rounders, gym and dance all offered. Excellent sports facilities, including eight tennis courts, five netball courts, a gym and dance/drama studios. Well-used Astro pitch. Athletics at park across the road. Gumley has secured numerous titles within the borough and at the London Youth Games.

Music is an integral part of Gumley life. Keen singers and instrumentalists are spoilt for choice, with numerous choirs and ensembles. Christmas and summer concerts are described by parents as 'exciting' and 'impressive'. Music department encourages pupils to try out different genres of music, one day experimenting with edgy rhythms on the drum kit, the next day performing traditional choral music. Enthusiastic staff choir.

Energetic drama productions ranging from Shakespeare to West End-style musicals. Pupils become fully immersed in the productions, including watching professional adaptations as preparation. 'It's the whole caboodle with drama,' states head. High profile drama festival. Annual poetry festival involves pupils writing their own poems. Gumley boasts its own poet laureate. Local and national poets and artists are invited in for inspiration.

Annual art exhibition. One talented pupil won the Young Brit at Arts Award, beating off competition from over 2000 competitors. 'Our art is outstanding,' explains head, and the masterpieces adorning the walls support this. 'We are a school that allows exploration of all types of art,' she explains. A* grades at A level for all fine artists in 2018.

Impressive range of after-school clubs, all free of charge, including maths, STEM, eco, Latin, as well as 11 sports clubs, and music clubs including Gumley Glee. Trips abroad include annual language exchanges with schools in Europe and China; geographers head to Iceland; history and politics pupils to New York and Washington. Head joins the pilgrimage to Lourdes. For those looking to challenge themselves physically, there is skiing in Austria and a water sports week in France. Something to tempt all tastes.

School is good at encouraging the girls to think about careers from year 7 on, to look beyond the school gates and to be adventurous in their choices. Gumley also has a business and enterprise specialism and has developed close links with a range of businesses. Lots of industry workshops and work experience organised by school, including with British Airways, GSK and Merrill Lynch. Alumni, including bankers, engineers, scientists and film directors, give career talks to pupils. They give their time for free, hoping to egg on the next generation. The phrase goes 'once a Gumley girl, always a Gumley girl.'

Background and atmosphere: Founded in 1841 by Marie Madeleine D'Houet, an aristocrat in post-revolutionary France. Inspired by the spirit of Ignatius of Loyola, she established her own religious order – the Faithful Companions of Jesus (FCJ). In setting up Gumley, she hoped to empower local women. Part of a group of four schools in England under the trusteeship of the FCJ; the others are in the Wirral, Liverpool and London. School motto is Vive Ut Vivas ('Live that you may have life'). Head sees foundress as an inspirational figure as 'she did not put a ceiling on herself. I want the pupils to realise that the power to determine their path in life is in their hands.' The school still follows the guidelines laid down by Marie Madeleine, as the head explains. 'She always said to the sisters that they should never tell a child off publicly. Take them aside and do it quietly. Never speak to a child as though their feelings do not matter'. Head stresses that being gentle is not about being weak; her mantra is the same as the foundress': 'strong in action and gentle in manner'.

A Catholic school (now an academy) for girls with a handful of sixth form boys, who choose Gumley for specific subjects such as economics, government and politics, and media. Boys are fully integrated, including a deputy head boy. Some non-Catholics attend who join in fully with spiritual element of school. Head is certain that 'they enrich the community. Though they don't have to participate, they often want to.' Respect for different backgrounds and faiths is fundamental to the school. Head firmly believes that the two most important commandments are to love God and to love your neighbour, and that these should be seen in action around the school.

Education is based on gospel and FCJ values with a focus on excellence, companionship, dignity, gentleness, justice and hope. The pupils themselves feel Gumley 'teaches us to be virtuous and hopeful.' Bethany, the chapel in the grounds, can be used for quiet reflection throughout the day, and is particularly popular in exam season, given its location bang next to the exam hall. Also used for a weekly mass (school has its own chaplain). Retreats implemented across all year groups, so pupils have time for quiet reflection away from the hustle and bustle of school life.

Gumley pupils are keen on fundraising. Substantial sums raised for variety of charities, both high-profile and local, especially those supporting children, the elderly, homelessness and Catholics. Pupils venture out into the community, visiting hospitals and offering story-telling sessions to local primaries. 'We teach them to put faith into action, through the understanding of linking charity work with the curriculum,' explains head.

Spacious campus. The central Queen Anne house is set in 10 acres of pretty grounds. Lawns are punctuated with numerous picnic tables, which are well-populated in the summer term. A large canopy covering an outside eating area lends an attractive Mediterranean touch to this corner of Isleworth.

Pastoral care, well-being and discipline: Pupils, parents and teachers all rave about the outstanding pastoral care. 'We strive for pastoral excellence,' explains head. Team is made up of two pastoral managers, two on-site counsellors and a teacher responsible for inclusion. One person oversees the smooth transition from year 6 to 7, and parents are impressed by this 'great induction and inclusion programme'. All pupils are in a tutor group. School will not economise on pastoral care and pays for staff supervision 'so they do not take difficult issues home with them'. The well-being of the whole community is central here.

Pupils are taught how to protect themselves, particularly online, and to consider the implications of present action on their prospects. Gumley emphasises the importance of learning to communicate with people from every walk of life. The head believes that 'if you can communicate with all sorts of people, you will fly'.

Discipline taken seriously. Low truancy rates. Expulsions are rare, generally only for extreme behaviour. School does all it can to support those who are pushing the boundaries but sometimes a parting of the ways is inevitable. Forgiveness and reconciliation are part of the Gumley ethos. 'Girls and boys are not known by their failings,' says head. Success is celebrated, including through awards for achievement, progress, perseverance and contribution to school life.

Food considered to be fine and there is a choice on offer, though sizeable minority opts to bring in packed lunch from home. One parent we spoke to felt 'there could be healthier food options at the canteen'. Breakfast for early birds from 8am onwards.

Pupils and parents: School composition is predominantly Catholic. Wide mix of nationalities with over 65 languages spoken at home, notably Portuguese and Polish. Three or four pupils arrive per year with minimal English, and support is offered to those whose English is not up to scratch. Broad ethnic and social mix.

Parents feel communication from school is generally good. However, one mother commented that the school would benefit from 'a report system that better informs parents of students' grades and progress.' School says it is 'stumped' by this parental comment as monitoring reports are sent home every eight weeks.

Entrance: Open mornings and evenings in the autumn term for prospective pupils. Non-selective academically in year 7, when 210 are admitted. Governing body in charge of admissions. Catholics taken before other faiths; all families are expected to support the Catholic aims and ethos of the school. Priority given to siblings, children whose parents work at the school and those living closest.

Pupils entering the school in the sixth form need English and maths level 5 and three different subjects at a minimum of level 5, with at least 6 in A level subjects. No faith requirement for those arriving for the final two years.

Exit: Some depart after GCSEs, either to sample co-ed, or because they prefer vocational courses, or for geographical reasons. Of those who stay the overwhelming majority opts for university. Recent university courses range from engineering at Loughborough to Chinese studies at Sheffield to film and TV at Southampton Solent. Some choose art foundation courses. Others prefer apprenticeships, including in the civil service and in engineering, which often translate into real jobs on completion.

Money matters: Gumley asks for voluntary contributions to the school development fund. Recently money has been used to help cover the upgrade of the security system, keep text books up to date, build a new roof, replace windows and make improvements to the music suite.

Remarks: Head wants pupils to be the best they can be. 'It's not the career, it's not the job, it's who you are that matters.' Gumley pupils are well-equipped to face the challenges of the 21st century.

Haberdashers' Aske's Hatcham College

Pepys Road, London SE14 5SF

Ages 3–18 Pupils 1,840 Sixth form 356

020 7652 9510
www.haaf.org.uk

Principal: Since September 2018, Alex Williamson, previously headteacher of Rutlish School.

Head of primary phase since September 2015, Emily Gyimah, previously deputy head at Hatcham Temple Grove. Degree in primary education from Brunel; spent two years as a KS1/KS2 class teacher at Monson primary school and then taught for five years as a KS1 and literacy leader at Hatcham Temple Grove. She was then promoted to Haberdashers' Aske's Federation phonics consultant, a position she held for three successful years before returning to HTG in 2014 as deputy head.

Academic matters: On of the primary phase's unique selling points (the other is its music) is its German immersion programme, which pupils begin in year 1. According to the school, the children are taught for half a day, every day, in German, and staff with ability to speak German are actively recruited. It's had a big impact on the children's academic performance. 'Our phonics results went through the roof, because German is very phonic in the way it's spoken' with 'skilled and fluent German speakers coming up through the school ranks.' This is all excellent stuff, and we were thrilled to have 'Heads, shoulders, knees and toes' sung to us in German by a flaxen-haired child of 6 who could have stepped straight out of Hamlyn. Every primary parent we spoke to, however, told us a different story. 'My son's been doing it for two years now, and he can only tell me the nouns. He doesn't have any better grasp of German than if he'd been taught it in the usual way,' said one parent. Another said: 'It was sold to us as an German immersion programme, that they'd be taught in German every afternoon, but in reality, it's turned out to be a couple of afternoons a week and it's teaching things like colours and days of the week. It isn't immersion.' Even the most enthusiastic of school supporters said: 'I don't really know if they teach the German – just once in a while, maybe.' Quite a mismatch. School please note.

H

In 2018, 27 per cent A*-A/9-7 at GCSE, 52 per cent got 9-5 in both maths and English. At A level: 50 per cent A*-B, 25 per cent A*/A.

Parents are generally satisfied, with most reporting that academic standards are good. 'Homework is prolific,' said one parent, adding, 'but it's mostly well thought through, well explained and supports classwork.' One parent was unhappy, reporting that their very bright child was 'constantly bored during lessons' and that 'the curriculum, especially in science and maths, is very basic, and the teachers, with a few exceptions, are not willing to take pupils beyond it.' The school contests this: 'We have the experience to help G&T children to get on,' and the leavers' destinations are certainly good. And adds: 'We run The Brilliant Club for our academically able students. You join in year 9, and you're assigned a PhD student [from Goldsmith's over the road] and given a task to do.'

Wide range of languages – year 7s get to choose two from German, French, Spanish, Mandarin and Latin, and higher up the school there are opportunities to learn classical Greek. Sixth form courses are 'strongly academic' – no BTecs offered, only A levels; the IB was explored but rejected as not inclusive enough for HAHC students.

Our impression was that the academic performance is very creditable given the non-academically selective intake, and that the school is both enriched and held up to critical scrutiny by a highly articulate parent body who expect the best and give no quarter when they don't get it.

Games, options, the arts: The school has its own sports centre in Nunhead, and students can do cricket, basketball, volleyball, football, netball and rugby (when we visited, the rugby team were about to head off to play another Haberdashers' school in Monmouth). Sport plays an active part in the junior school curriculum, with basketball, athletics, swimming and football on offer and funding awarded for Saturday and after-school provision. School adroitly links this with academic achievement – 'you have to be in the reading group to be in Saturday football.' The Little Leaders Group offers leadership exercises for children who don't get out much at home. Plenty of trips: river walks, London Eye, museums, visits to the theatre, all helped by an active parent body. Good programme of drama, and children are encouraged to do public speaking in assemblies etc.

The primary phase music was uniformly praised. Class music begins in reception, everyone learns recorder in year 3, and in year 4 those who are progressing well – generally around half of the class – are invited to learn violin, cello or clarinet. 'It's the discipline and the dexterity; and it's much easier in year 4 than when you're an older child.' The lessons are free and all children are allowed to carry on in year 5 if they want to, which at least a third of the year group always do. Those who don't want to continue can still be involved with the junior choir, and the Haberdashers' Livery Company and Temple Grove Trust can award bursaries to parents whose children want to learn other musical instruments outside school. Lots of concerts and the choir busks in Lewisham Shopping Centre to raise money for the 999 Club.

The music in the senior school is astonishing. No other word for it. We see many schools which claim to have marvellous music, but they really do have it here. We sat, open-mouthed, through student performances of Soave il Vento from Cosi Fan Tutte (sung in Italian), Mozart's Divertimento No 1 scored for two clarinets and a bassoon, Bartok's Mikrokosmos on the piano – all of it delivered with exquisite taste, sensitivity, musicality and technique. Then, just as we were preparing to move on, the choir started a ravishing rendition of Lotti's Crucifixus and we sat back down again. 'It's like being at a professional concert,' said the vice principal, with pardonable pride.

Unusually for a state school, classical music takes centre stage here, but it's for the many, not the few. Virtually all the children learn at least one instrument, and the lessons are free. The school abounds with orchestras, chamber music and choirs of every kind, and there are jazz bands too. Parents were uniformly delighted with this aspect of the school. We heard comments like 'all the music groups are fantastic'; 'there are concerts all the year round, musicals and even a school opera'; 'the music staff teach with ambition, enthusiasm and humour, and my children love it' and 'HAHC is a vibrant place where you are encouraged to fulfil your artistic potential.' We heard a murmur that rock music doesn't get quite the same encouragement, and the school admitted that this might be so. But what is on offer is so amazing, that it's hard to grumble. HAHC choirs provide the music for City Hall's annual Remembrance service as well as carols for Southwark Cathedral. The Haberdashers Company regularly asks school to provide chamber ensembles for events. As the vice principal put it: 'A very good part of this school is that the students gain the cultural capital to function beyond it.'

On a different note, the CCF also flourishes at HAHC, attracting some 160 students, and with a Corps of Drums that is, according to a visiting instructor, 'better than Eton's.'

HAHC is proud of all aspects of its enrichment programme. The school is 'thronged' with students after lessons finish, says vice principal – but parental feedback we received about it was mixed (music excepted). A common complaint was that it was hard to get information about the various clubs and activities and that a number of initiatives, such as Artsmark and D of E, had unravelled due to poor organisation or lack of assessors. 'All a bit half-hearted,' was how one parent described the netball, and another said that her children felt that 'a huge opportunity is being missed in terms of sport.. things just don't get organised.' These concerns were at odds with the school's excellent facilities and range of provision offered. School robustly defended its record on Artsmark ('We've handed out the certificates in assembly') as well as on sport, and says that D of E is now thriving, with a coordinator in place and a plaque awarded by the Duke of Edinburgh recognising the its commitment. The students we spoke to seemed happy.

Everyone agrees that debating is strong. Sixth formers have started a tutoring cooperative, coaching students from lower down the school and getting paid for it too. In general, HAHC students seem to gain confidence and skills from what is an unusually broad and intellectually stimulating extracurricular programme.

Background and atmosphere: One of the Haberdashers' 'family' of schools, both state and independent, and one of three schools in the Haberdashers' Aske's Federation, the others being Knight's Academy in Bromley and Crayford Academy in Bexley.

The primary phase was originally Monson Primary School, which was failing. HAHC took it on in 2008 and turned it around in three years. It is now rated outstanding. The school was being extensively refurbished when in 2010 a builder managed to cause a fire that gutted the place. The primary children and staff camped on various floors before moving into the new building in 2015.

Hatcham itself is divided between three sites. Jerningham Road, built in 1889 as a girls' school, now houses years 7 to 9 and is a very pleasing old Victorian red-brick. The older students study at the Pepys Road site, a rather gruelling 15-minute walk up Telegraph Hill. Minibuses shuttle pupils and staff between the various school buildings, all of which appeared well kept, blending tradition (stained glass, honours boards) with bang-up-to-date innovation and décor; in the parts we were shown, at any rate. School is co-educational, but in years 7 to 11 teaching is in single-sex groups wherever possible.

School-home communication much criticised by parents and we ourselves found this a difficult school to make contact with. (New direct lines for each school may help: until recently, all calls to any of the Federation schools had to be routed through the Haberdashers' Aske's Federation office, a system which parents loathed.) School counters that it has a policy that all emails must be replied to within 48 hours, that its communication is 'pretty good and pretty effective' and that all parents receive a handbook at the start of each year. But acknowledges, 'these days there's a need for real-time information.'

Pastoral care, well-being and discipline: Behaviour at HAHC reflects the school's large and diverse intake, but is perfectly fine, and all pupils we spoke to reported feeling safe here. The uniform is smart and smartly worn.

Many people commented on the school's 'good and healthy' atmosphere. 'The children respect the staff and the staff are interested in the children themselves, what their interests are and what makes them tick,' said one mother. Another wrote: 'The atmosphere is friendly and good pastoral care is provided.' The young people we met were courteous, assured and proud of their school. 'It's very welcoming here; I've made a large group of friends,' said one. 'The music department is great at involving everyone'; 'there's a really nice community feel here and the older and younger students talk to each other' were typical comments. Parents report that SEN provision is much improved and HAHC is the borough's school of choice for wheelchair-bound students.

As we walked about the primary phase, this impressed us as a lively, happy and well-behaved community of children. There were a couple of dissenting voices, including one who claimed that if it hadn't been for the automatic entry to HAHC's hugely-oversubscribed secondary phase she would have moved her child to a different school. The majority of parents, however, told us they were very happy with both the academic standards and the pastoral care. 'My daughter loves it – she wants to go even when she's sick,' said one mother, and others agreed. Comments included: 'The teachers are always helpful'; 'well done to all the teachers keeping standards up during all the moving about'; 'the encouragement and welcome my daughter receives has made her time at the school a pleasure,' and, from a mother without much English, 'I think it's a good school, really, really good.'

Pupils and parents: Reflecting the area, this is a very diverse community both socially and culturally, with about 50 per cent of pupils coming from ethnic minorities. As one member of staff dryly observed, at the end of the school day equal numbers turn either right into the Telegraph Hill conservation area, where a five-bedroom house might go for £1.3m, or left towards New Cross and some of the worst social deprivation in London. A number of professional musicians send their children here for the music provision. The school appears genuinely to integrate all its various members successfully. Ofsted recently wrote: 'The promotion of racial harmony within the college's richly diverse community is exemplary.'

Entrance: Two form entry to primary school. Sixty places in reception, with four more available further up the school. Usual state school admissions criteria apply: looked after children, medical needs, siblings, proximity. Oversubscribed. About 25 children come up from the school's own nursery, but parents should be aware that a place at the nursery does not guarantee a place in reception.

Senior school massively oversubscribed, with at least 10 applications for every place. Some 64 pupils from primary phase year 6 have automatic entry. Ten per cent of places allocated on musical aptitude – these pupils are selected by aural test. Otherwise, standard local authority criteria apply: looked-after children, siblings, proximity etc. No longer uses banding. 'Admissions is a hot potato for this school,' admitted the vice principal. Appeals by parents are in excess of 100 each year, but be warned – the school's decisions are almost always upheld, 'because we're exceptionally compliant with the rules.'

About 60 to 100 sixth form places available to external students – no admissions tests, but a minimum of six 9-4 grades required at GCSE, the same as for internal students.

Exit: Almost all primary pupils transfer to HAHC secondary phase, to which they have automatic right of entry. After year 11 about half progress to the school's sixth form, the rest to a variety of post-16 provision. Some don't get the grades necessary to move up to year 12 at HAHC and go to other local schools and colleges; a tiny number opt for Dartford Grammar and the IB. Careers officer follows the progress of all leavers, and the school is proud of having had no NEETS (young people not in education, employment or training) for five years.

Up to 10 per cent of year 12s don't get the end of year exam grades required to move up to year 13. At 18, about 70 per cent to university, including some 30 per cent to Russell Group. In 2018, one student to Cambridge. Of the remainder, nearly a quarter take a gap year, often applying to university through HAHC once they've got their A levels.

Money matters: State-funded academy. Parents not asked to pay voluntary contributions, and vice principal looked astonished when we asked if they were. Unusual and generous provision of scholarships to the 10 per cent selected on musical aptitude – the school will partially fund them to train at the Saturday junior departments of the main London music colleges, the Royal Academy of Music, Royal College of Music, Guildhall and Trinity. In addition, instrumental lessons offered at HAHC are free to all students, regardless of ability or level.

Remarks: A large and flourishing comprehensive that's lifted above the crowd by its results and amazing music and attracts many aspirational families into the area. Plan early if you want your child to go.

Halcyon London International School

33 Seymour Place, London W1H 5AU

Ages 11–18 **Pupils** 159 **Sixth form** 50

Fees: £23,985 – £25,110 pa

020 7258 1169
www.halcyonschool.com

Director: Since 2015, Barry Mansfield (50s); studied history at Nottingham and did his PGCE at UEA (history and English). His first teaching job was in an international school in Athens, followed by Nairobi, then Dubai, becoming head of English and learning about IB schools. He worked in Sofia Antipolis in France, then Jeddah, where he set up the diploma programme, before teaching in Bern International School in Switzerland (and setting up the MYP) while simultaneously doing an MA (Open University) in educational leadership.

All that IB experience fits very firmly with his commitment to the ideology of students as active learners. He believes that learning has a social, interactive component with enquiry based, collaborative learning at the heart of Halcyon. He is 'quietly spoken and has a calming, steadying presence' and 'whilst he sets rules and guidelines, his is not a dictatorial role, which allows others to have a voice,' according to parents. 'He listens, thinks things through and comes up with a solution'; 'I have never met a head who listens like that'. An egalitarian who shares an open plan space with colleagues. He has one son who went through the IB programme.

Academic matters: Teachers are passionate about their subject, which they discuss with students and other staff. Middle years programme followed for first five years, which involves enquiry-based learning – as much of it student-led as possible. Pupils like the fact that there is plenty of independent work. Modern, neat, floodlit classrooms – we saw students working on their laptops on beanbags creating, researching and preparing for tests with other students. Subjects all taught within a global context and in a cross-curricular way to encourage what parents referred to as 'soft skills like public speaking, discussing and learning to bridge differences and work together'. This leads to the IB Personal Projects which they present to the community at the end of grade 10 (year 11). Huge numbers of oral presentations, videos, multimedia work in addition to essays. Very few text books as the school provides students and parents access to countless online curriculum resources.

The IB diploma range means they all do, for example, maths and a second language (Spanish, Mandarin or private tutoring of mother tongue languages). To further broaden the school's offerings, students explained that they could take online Pamoja courses in eg IT, psychology, economics, business management and film, with the support of the school coordinator. Second IB results in 2018 averaged a creditable 35 points, with the first medic and the first Ivy League placement.

Science in well-equipped labs. Interactivity means that students can share their research results with the class by airplaying to large screens in each classroom. Outdoor learning day an example of the creative teaching with all lessons happening in Hyde Park: students measured respiration for science and exercise; some used iPad apps to paint and others did pencil drawings of trees; others acted in a Shakespearean play or wrote poetry; some tested pollutants in the Serpentine.

Clear assessment criteria and feedback. Both pupils and parents spoke about the close monitoring and watching possible in small classes: 'kids get pushed, they don't get lost or coast; when they need more, they get more because the teachers are very good at differentiating'.

New SENCo because none in place when Ofsted visited (and judged the school outstanding in all categories). Whilst all the technology is helpful for a child with dyslexia, and the small classes and self-initiated work allow each pupil to go at their own pace, there is no specific support for SEN and the school will only take children with learning differences if they are sure they can match needs and can accommodate them within the classroom. No pupils with EHC plans.

Games, options, the arts: Art room displays oil pastels, 3D model making, sculpture and papier mâché masks, mosaics, installation art and fabric printing. Two enthusiastic specialist art teachers and a DT teacher extend the popularity of these subjects.

Music is a challenge in a small school but noise limitations overcome by using electronic instruments and headphones, and the music room has a good supply of electronic keyboards for composing and playing. Some bands – ensemble, contemporary band, small choir. Soloists get to play in assemblies and at graduation.

PE twice weekly compulsory up to grade 10 (year 11) then optional in the sixth form. Table tennis in school and some gymnastics and plenty of dance, otherwise swimming, football, basketball and other sports at local leisure centre or in Hyde Park. Too small for many team sports but has a running club, table tennis and football teams (mixed training, separate fixtures). So not the right school if you want competitive sports.

Plenty of drama in school with students acting, directing and stage managing.

A number of extracurricular activities are also generated by students themselves – eg Model United Nations conferences which students organise entirely, and they work hard to include students from local state schools as well as other private international schools, plus Global Issues Network, charity fairs, school trips, student driven assemblies. Emphasis on pupils taking responsibility and leadership roles as often as possible.

Grades 6-11 attend a one week residential team-building trip each September.

Work and achievements shared and celebrated in class and assemblies and on the school website.

Background and atmosphere: The school opened in 2013; buildings that are in part grand and old, as the landlord is the neighbouring synagogue, but renovated and extended to provide a number of state-of-the-art classrooms, art room and super hi-tech labs. Meeting room and large assembly hall. The location could hardly be more central, and pupils say they 'use London as a classroom'. Strong commitment to sustainability with a vegetarian canteen and a virtually paperless operation.

Pastoral care, well-being and discipline: Well-being coordinator runs mentoring system with some pupils trained in conflict resolution and mediating. The aim is to make pupils feel that they are 'recognised and have a voice'. Pupils all spoke of the amount of interaction they have with teachers, who 'know you really well and are almost like friends' and 'are interested in what I have to say'. The staff are there to 'advocate for students all the time'. The school uses 'guiding principles not rules'. Assemblies and discussions about bullying, but students from all over the world are very supportive of each other – and they laughed when we asked about stealing, which they couldn't imagine in their school: 'we respect each other and our possessions'. High security but pupils not mollycoddled: they may visit increasingly wider areas outside at lunchtimes as they go up the school.

Pupils and parents: About one third from US, and second largest number are British, with a good mix from other nationalities, so a real third culture kids atmosphere. Parents said they wanted an international rather than American environment, and liked the fact that kids learned so much from each other's different cultures and backgrounds. They also liked the central position – that is why they had moved to London, they said, to make the most of the city. Small year groups but pupils make friends through multi-age courses and activities in school, as well as outside clubs and from inter-school connections. Articulate and inquisitive pupils said school is 'welcoming and friendly, you speak to everyone – and students who leave come back to visit and join in'. Active involvement by parents – careers talks, cake baking, trips, twice-termly meetings of class reps with the head.

Entrance: 'Holistic approach to admissions' which involves parent and pupil interviews with admissions team and the head, two years' school reports and two teacher references for younger pupils, three of each for older pupils. They need an academic profile of average or above and good enough English to access the very full-on IB diploma. 'Families are as important to us as the students': they are looking for those who will engage and are not expecting a focus on scores and data, and who will 'embrace the digital learning style'. Pupils told us it works for pupils who are motivated and curious, and that the admissions team were 'interested in my education and me and not only in talking to and selling the school to my parents'.

Exit: Early days for the school still, but expectation is that up to half may go to university in the US, about a quarter to UK universities, and the rest to other countries (eg Australia, Canada, The Netherlands). Second class of graduates headed off to study eg medicine at Liverpool, international law at UCL, sports admin at Miami, politics and international relations at Manchester and computer science at Delft University of Technology. An experienced universities and careers counsellor on staff.

Money matters: An expensive option and no green fields or grand library buildings to show for it, but this is a charity and all the money is being invested back into the school as well as gradually repaying backers.Teachers are well paid and un-rushed, with the calm that comes from having time to do the job properly. Bottomless resources in terms of technology – laptops, iPads, large screens, video recording, electronic instruments etc. Spotlessly clean. Excellent administration so good, clear communication.

Remarks: Advanced, not only in terms of digital technology but also in attitude. The school focuses on the pupils and listens to them, making sure they are happy and learning at their own individual speed, with no pupil left behind or slipping. Well-being a priority, proactive and central to learning, which is rare in pressurised London. A friendly school that not only cares and supports but also energises pupils to strive, self-motivate and learn.

The Hall School

23 Crossfield Road, London NW3 4NU

Ages 4-13 Pupils 460 C of E

Fees: £18,795 – £19,365 pa

020 7722 1700
www.hallschool.co.uk

Headmaster: Since 2013, Christopher Godwin, previously head of Bedford Prep. Read geography at Loughborough, then masters in Middle Eastern studies at Durham. Joined Bedford in 1993 as second master and director of studies before taking over the headship four years later. With no experience of London schools, his post came as a surprise to some parents, although he quickly won hearts and minds with his keenness to maintain the ethos and values of the school, along with his gentle and unassuming nature and fresh pair of eyes. 'There's a track record of people taking this job who are greying and in their early 50s,' he laughs, 'but I hope I've brought a new energy to the school.' Parents and pupils praise his emphasis on 'positive psychology rather than rules, rules and more rules,' as one parent put it. 'There's a strong pastoral element to his thinking,' said another.

Sees the next phase as making the school even more responsive to 'the world we now live in', with a growing focus on preparing boys for what their next schools require and embedding ever more IT into an already technology-heavy curriculum. Known for being open and available to parents and a great team builder among staff. Often seen out and about in school and is not precious about his office, whose conference table is often used by boys themselves. Teaches current affairs to year 5s upwards, geography to year 8s and frequently reads stories in junior school. Heavily involved in the assessment of boys. Keen and active sportsman, particularly rugby – now as coach rather than player.

Entrance: This is the top north London boys' prep school for those looking towards the country's top academic secondary schools, so competition for entrance is hotter than hot, with applications restricted to those registering before their first birthday – and even so, the school is three times over-subscribed. At 3, parents are invited in to discuss whether a child will apply to enter at 4 or 5 (32 places at 4, 22 at 5). 'This can be down to issues such as birth date, speed of development, grasp of English if they come from a bilingual family and, of course, the parents have a say too,' says head, although he stresses that it all comes down to the individual boy, rather than any set guidelines. All applicants are tested in the same year – 4+ entrants in January for coming September, 5+ entrants in late April/May for the following September – for which parents have been known to tutor their offspring at as young as 3 (although the school says it frowns upon this).

Boys are assessed in groups of six. 'We are looking for a hunch about their potential, measurement of underlying intellect that they'll develop in the long term, as well as how interactive, sociable and curious they are and their ability to concentrate for appropriate lengths of time,' says head. 'It's very detailed, with lots of personal attention, so that we get boys who are right for the school and who we can take right through the school.' Inevitably, there wind up being strugglers and these boys are said to have been 'guided elsewhere', although school insists this is rare and it's clear that increasing effort is made to help every boy keep up. Favours siblings, but no guarantees and many haven't got places in recent years. Occasional places arise higher up the school, with a formal registration process for the waiting list. 'They do a good job of picking the right boys,' said one parent.

Exit: Most pupils to St Paul's, Westminster or Mill Hill, others to, for example, UCS. Sizeable minority to other mostly single sex boarding schools, such as Eton, though co-ed boarding schools becoming more popular (and increasingly encouraged by the school), including King's School Canterbury, Sevenoaks and Arundel.

In 2018, five scholarships to Westminster, one to St Paul's, one to Eton, two to UCS and a choral scholarship to King's Canterbury.

Exceptional guidance in secondary school choices. 'We encourage parents of boys in year 4 upwards to start looking widely. We don't leave it with a year to go,' says head. The match is made by a meticulously planned programme of assessments, which include annual verbal and non-verbal reasoning and day-to-day performance, and which are all tracked on a graph for each boy. Scholarship form in year 8 for those completing the demanding exams of Eton and Westminster, but not all scholarships derive from this form.

Remarks: Prep schools don't come more ambitious than this. Catering to the needs of boys who are intellectually curious, academic and highly motivated, this is a school that stretches them in every direction.

Two classes of 16 in reception, reshuffled to three of 18 in year 1. By year 8, four classes of 12 to 14, with a scholarship form and three fast common entrance forms. Staff are a broad age range, and have notable experience and enthusiasm. 'They're strict, but you can have a real joke with them too,' said one boy, and we certainly found humour abundant in the classrooms and corridors, with a refreshing ease of communication between pupils and staff.

Specialist French, science, music, sport and ICT more or less from the word go. Latin added in year 5, Greek in year 7 for scholarship candidates. Setting in core subjects from year 5 and Latin from year 6 – no stigma flor lower sets, say pupils. Three sciences, taught in a more combined way than in the past. ICT provision has long been outstanding, with digital learning embedded into just about every subject. Advanced coding and programming is praised, as is the collaborative work using shared computer files. No Sats but exams taken very seriously, with all subjects examined twice yearly in the upper forms. 'The teaching is so good that you actually don't need to revise for exams,' said one boy, 'although most of us do anyway.' Does well in national competitions, such as the Townsend Warner History Prize and national Maths Challenges.

The school itself is divided up, with junior school (reception to year 3), middle (years 4 and 5) and senior school (years 6-8) on separate sites all within a short walk of this upmarket residential area. Junior school is made up of two well-ordered Victorian buildings, with the head living in a flat above. Middle school is a 1970s building that was probably cutting-edge at the time, but could do with a rethink in terms of use of good space now. Senior school is the original red-brick school building, with lots of quirky design features, including split level classrooms, which make for a cosy learning environment.

Classrooms generally on the small side, especially in the middle school, but well-ordered, and many are innovatively designed (especially the history room, with its very own upstairs library and historically decorated walls). Even the DT room, where boys were making splurge guns ready for their production of Bugsy Malone when we visited, is carpeted. Lovely, bright art room, with separate pottery room. Wathen Hall, which is the main hall, feels a bit past its use-by date. Well-stocked, two-story, library. Stand-out common room, known as the Pit, with a focal snooker table and split level, contemporary and airy environment.

Like most north London preps, outside space is limited, although the junior school has a colourful and imaginative playground, while the older boys use one all-weather pitch, which school admits 'can get crowded' at playtimes. Sport, however, is prioritised, with £2m recently invested in the sports field at East Finchley, which the boys are transported to by coach two afternoons a week, and where they play football, rugby, hockey, cricket and tennis. Gymnastics and fencing in Wathen Hall. Every boy gets a chance to represent the school at some point in a team game (nine football teams) and the school is currently looking to extend its fixture list outside London. Some parents concerned that sport generally favours the best boys, however. 'If the boys aren't sporty, they're not really bothered with them,' said one. County and national representatives at chess, fencing, skiing and tennis. Annual skiing trips to France and biannual cricket tour of Sri Lanka. 'We competed against teams that got 1,000 runs in 10 games in the last tour. The quality of cricket was amazing,' said one boy.

H

Over 80 per cent of boys play an instrument (often three), with an army of peripatetic teachers. Plenty of encouragement to join the large orchestra, string quartets, jazz group and choir, all of which regularly win music awards. 'You get to sing in some amazing places if you're in the choir,' said one boy. Drama taken seriously, with boys of all ages encouraged to perform in plays, concerts, public speaking and most notably debating. Huge range of clubs, including cookery, Mandarin, model making, computer maths games etc. Lots of links with the local community – boys join forces with other schools to do everything from enrichment maths to drumming workshops, and boys are also encouraged to help out at the community centre 100 yards away.

School accommodates all the usual SENs, provided the underlying intellect is there. 'My son is dyslexic and the school just took it in their stride, which had a hugely positive effect on his confidence,' said one parent. Learning support department, which is run by a full-time staff member (BEd and certificate in dyslexia), brings in outside expertise where necessary. Only one statemented child when we visited.

A strong reputation persists that the focus on academics is at the cost of emotional support. But we heard convincing arguments from parents and pupils that problems are nipped in the bud, with good pastoral care from teachers, two matrons and the part-time school counsellor, who has links with the Tavistock Clinic. In consultation with parents, the school undertakes a pastoral review every three years. Far less bullying under the current head, say parents.

Expectations (many of which are dotted on posters around the school) favoured over rules, but boys say punishment can be inconsistent. 'You can wind up with a worse punishment for running to pass a boy a book in the corridor than being really rude,' said one.

This isn't the kind of school where every boy knows each other (not helped by the lack of single campus) but school encourages peer support and cross-year activities. Lively school council. Boys say the atmosphere is supportive and friendly.

Parents mostly high-flyers – bankers, media types, lawyers etc – many with extremely high aspirations for their boys. Mainly local, but some travel from Notting Hill, Holland Park and Islington. Some said to be cliquey, with very strong personalities; active PA.

This is a school that offers boys with high academic potential a dazzling start in life. Most leave not only with great academic results, but excellent general knowledge, huge intellectual curiosity and an appreciation of all things cultural. Myths abound that these are boffins that are hothoused, but in fact we found they are boys with a great sense of fun and who are highly motivated, genuinely enjoying being stretched. But boys who wind up struggling could feel left out in the drive to achieve.

Hampden Gurney CofE Primary School

13 Nutford Place, London W1H 5HA

Ages 3–11 **Pupils** 240 **C of E**

020 7641 4195
www.hampdengurneyschool.co.uk

Headteacher: Since 1997, Evelyn Chua (50s). Born in a small town in Malaysia, Mrs Chua came to England to do her A levels at boarding school, before proceeding to study piano at the Royal Academy of Music. After a postgraduate degree in music education in the US and a brief stint as a classroom teacher, she took on her first headship at Hampden Gurney, when it had the lowest attendance of any primary in Westminster. The school is now one of the borough's most oversubscribed, and Mrs Chua's super-head status been widely recognised both by parents ('She's like the leader of a ship, you can approach her with any problem') and her professional colleagues (she received a Teaching Awards' Leadership Trust Award for School Leadership). Strongly motivated by her faith, she's focussed, dedicated and slightly formidable. ('The children are not scared of her, but they don't want to go up to her office.') Married with two children, she sees the school as her second home. 'Everything about it has her stamp,' said one mother. 'She could easily rest on her laurels,' said another, 'but she doesn't, year after year after year.'

Entrance: Open mornings held in the autumn term. The school is affiliated to the High Anglican Church of the Annunciation in Bryanston Street near Marble Arch, and gives firm priority to long-term church-goers. (Alternatives venues for worship include St John's Hyde Park, St Mary's, Our Lady of the Rosary.) Hugely oversubscribed with 150+ applying for 30 places.

Exit: Outstanding advice and preparation given for secondary school transfer, with early information meetings in year 4 and one-to-one talks with the head further along the line. About 60 per cent to independents (Westminster, St Paul's, Highgate, UCS, City and Laytmer Upper), many on scholarships and bursaries. Also to top-flight faith schools (St Marylebone CofE, Grey Coat Hospital, the London Oratory and Twyford CofE). About 50 per cent of year 6 apply for scholarships and bursaries, aided by a team of support assistants in the lead up to exams: 'Because of the amount of pressure they're under they need mentoring,' says the head. Parents definitely see the benefit. 'The school is amazing at preparing them,' said one grateful mother. 'It was definitely one of my reasons for going there. You know your kids are going to be given a choice.'

Remarks: By any measure, Hampden Gurney is an 'outstanding' primary school, lauded not only by Ofsted, but by numerous external bodies (Primary School of the Year, Outstanding Progress Achievement, National Association for Able Children in Education Challenge Award). Teaching – it goes without saying – is a strength. 'The head recruits really well,' said one parent. 'She's brilliant at finding enthusiastic young teachers, who bring in new ideas, and the staff are very committed to getting the best out of children.' Early years comes in for particular praise. 'They manage to get everyone reading very quickly, while being very nurturing.'

Broad curriculum includes timetabled Spanish, creative writing and humanities. Two hours a week of science as a separate subject from year 1 (helped by a small roof garden with a pond and greenhouse, and regular outings to science attractions, such as the Science Museum). Computer suite with dedicated hour-long weekly lesson, plus whole class set of laptops. Well-stocked library – one of the best children's libraries in the borough – central to promoting enthusiasm for reading, and pupils test their writing skills in out-of-school challenges, such as the Sunday Times' Goosebumps story-writing competition.

All undergo a thorough-going programme of aspiration raising. 'We inspire the children because we accept that every child has got ability somewhere and can achieve,' says the head. Loads of positive reinforcement plus Building Learning Power programme to instil resilience, perseverance, concentration, and organisation. Infants given extra help through a buddy system which matches them with older pupils. 'It's someone away from class to whom the children can express themselves.' After-school clubs maintain the focus and set sights high. Design club, for example, is intended for 'future engineers, architects and artists,' while journalism club lays the ground for the next generation of Fleet Street's finest. The home-school relationship is critical to the mix, and parents meet teachers at the beginning of the year for a briefing on curriculum, expectations and homework (from year 1). 'There's quite a lot of homework and it's encouraged to be done,' said one mother approvingly.

Special educational needs well supported. Dedicated SENCo and learning mentor work closely with classroom teachers (who are given specialist training) and parents. Outside experts called upon when required. School celebrated, too, for its gifted and talented approach ('Our policy starts with the expectation that there are gifted and talented learners in every year group,' says the head). Early identification then monitored by a full-time specialist, who develops reasoning and creative thinking through after-school clubs, visits, masterclasses and summer schools (at St Paul's, City of London School for Girls and Oxford University). 'It's OK to be a geek,' said one parent. 'It may not be precisely cool to be clever, but you're not penalised by your peer group for wanting to do well.' Head works personally both with those who struggle and those who excel and all acknowledge her talent as a teacher. 'If you're not improving or not where she expects, she will focus on this. She cares deeply about the success of every child and can really inspire children.'

Arts taken seriously. In-class tuition in theory of music and composition (including electronic works), plus the chance to learn either ukulele or recorder. Weekly music club run by professional musicians and links with both the Royal Academy of Music and Royal College of Music for projects and workshops. Individual lessons in piano, saxophone, clarinet and violin at a reasonable cost. Children's choir performs at mass and elsewhere (the Royal Albert Hall, for example, with the BBC singers). Dedicated art teacher. Dance club, taught by qualified dance instructor. Despite its tight urban location, the school manages a good range of games (netball, basketball, tag rugby and football), athletics and gymnastics. Swimming from year 1 at nearby pool. Plenty of sports clubs (some run by year 6) during and after school, on site and in the nearby park. Some inter-school competition, where the school performs with credit ('They often win because the school teaches them not to give up; you can do it, you will succeed'), but, for the very sporty, out-of-school options may be required. Stimulating range of clubs (girls' football, musical theatre, chess, origami, cooking, martial arts) and trips, both local and more wide-ranging (year 6 residential trip to the rolling Surrey hills).

Established in 1863 in memory of the Reverend John Hampden Gurney, rector of St Mary's Bryanston Square, the school's ethos is still strongly High Anglican, with compulsory attendance at weekly sung eucharist. (Parents, too, invited into school for weekly prayer group.) Termly visit to the church in Bryanston Square and year 6s take positions of responsibility as servers at mass. Order and discipline underpin it all. Firm emphasis on attendance and punctuality. Escalating punishment system (warning, missing play time, time out, Mrs Chua), but these are well-behaved children. 'Everyone comments on it if you go out on a school trip. They sit there and listen and all ask questions,' said a parent. 'It's a joy.' Wide-ranging pastoral strategy. House system – with houses named for local heroes Alexander Fleming, John Wesley, Michael Faraday, Florence Nightingale – develops cross-year bonding, and gentle competition (with certificates for academic prowess and good behaviour). 'The house system encourages everyone to work as a team.' Motivational speakers (Colin Jackson, Cherie Blair) invited in to teach about rejection and reflection. Strong, too, on promoting British values with hands-on experience of democracy, through school council, mock elections, voted-upon school prefects (including head boy and girl) plus visits to parliament and local council. 'They're taught to ask thought-provoking questions about life,' said one father. Smart red-and-blue uniform, with separate PE kit.

If Hampden Gurney didn't stand out in so many other ways, it would still be distinguished by its building. Opened in 2002, it was described by the RIBA as 'innovative, bold and dynamic.' Admirers refer to it as 'the beehive', the less well-inclined 'the car park'. Whatever your perspective, it's a clever solution to a tight urban site, offering covered outside play playgrounds on each of its three floors, and identical plans for each age group to proceed from nursery at ground level to top-of-the-school and top of the world in year 6.

Parents, who mainly live close by, are a healthy mix of those who could afford to go private and the just-about-managing. Overall a fairly cosmopolitan lot, often European (Western and Eastern, so German, French, Russian, Polish), almost all practising Christians. ('If you really didn't believe in God it might be a problem,' said one mother.) Strong community feel. 'It's a small school and everyone knows everyone. We all see each other at church, in the park, on weekends.' Energetic PTA, which raises more than £20,000 a year 'for all the softer stuff' such as arts and music provision. Voluntary subsidy of £40 per pupil contributes to school maintenance.

Most parents are delighted with the school ('My children have enjoyed themselves from day 1. The school really makes learning fun'), praising its well-structured discipline and high aspirations ('There's pressure, but within reason; it's certainly not excessive'). That said, some acknowledge the approach might not be ideal for all. 'You have to be a well-disciplined child who likes learning. If you're a wonderfully creative, dreamy child, it might not be the right place for you.'

H

The Hampshire School, Chelsea

15 Manresa Road, London SW3 6NB

Ages 3–13 **Pupils** 300

Fees: £17,100 – £ 18,855 pa

020 7352 7077
www.thehampshireschoolchelsea.co.uk/

Headmistress: Since September 2018, Dr Pamela Edmonds BEd MEd EdD, previously head of St Cedd's School in Chelmsford. Over two decades in senior leadership roles in prep and all-through schools, in the UK, Singapore, Thailand, Japan and Spain, including teaching the IB in south east Asia. An ISI inspector, she has climbed Mount Fuji, enjoys sailing, squash, theatre and ballet.

Entrance: Entry points at age 3 into the nursery, age 4 into reception, age 5 into year 1 and age 8 into year 4 – informal interview and assessment, designed to put children and their families at ease. Small entry point into year 7, 'but we're quite selective at that age, because of needing to guide them to the right schools.' Occasional places in other year groups do sometimes come up – always worth enquiring.

Exit: To a wide range of destinations, mostly London day schools. Girls move on to places such as Francis Holland, More House, Queen's Gate, Emanuel, Latymer Upper, with occasional St Paul's Girls' and CLSG successes. Most leave at 11, but no pressure to do so and some opt to stay on until 13 because they like it here. (The school has forged sporting links to other schools with 'small clusters of girls' at this age, which we thought eminently sensible.) Boys leave mostly at 13, to the likes of Latymer Upper, City of London, Emanuel, Dulwich, Wetherby sometimes St Paul's, King's Wimbledon and Westminster. School is proud of its track record: 'No child here leaves without the school that's right for them.'

H

Remarks: Founded in Surrey as a dance school in 1928 by June Hampshire, mother of actress Susan. On moving to London in the 1930s the school became mainstream and for many years was seen as a very traditional prep. Since becoming part of the GEMS group in 2007, however, it has modernised considerably and now has a reputation for delivering sound up-to-date academics in an atmosphere of kindness and friendliness. Years 1 to 8 are accommodated in the main premises on Manresa Road, a wonderfully spacious grade II listed building; it used to be the Chelsea library and still has the same air of calm tranquility.

Sheltering beneath the architectural grandeur is some pretty impressive modern technology: a splendid science laboratory, one of the best we've seen in a central London prep; height-adjustable interactive whiteboards; individual computer desks in the classrooms; and an excellent ICT suite where we saw children hard at work designing a restaurant. None of this has come at the expense of tradition, however, and bookworms would adore the fabulous school library: cavernous, marble-columned, galleried, and home to thousands of books. We thought it looked a tad underused, but the forthcoming appointment of a librarian is set to change that.

The school hall is a great space for PE, concerts, plays, assemblies and dance – the Chelsea Ballet School visits every week. Lovely spacious classrooms, and a well-sized and equipped garden for the children to let off steam. Team games such as rugby are played off-site in Battersea Park, and the children go swimming at Chelsea and Fulham baths. Lifts throughout mean that children with physical disabilities can be accommodated.

Broad extracurricular provision ranges from judo, fencing, archery and rugby to cooking, computing, debating, ukulele – 'We're constantly seeking to add to our clubs,' affirmed head. Music provision is good and there are plans to get it better. Children can learn piano, cello, violin, etc, and take part in choir, and there are regular concerts plus the annual Summer Arts Festival. No orchestra yet, and drama is currently confined to class rather than whole school productions, although the imminent arrival of a second drama teacher will bring more opportunities in this area. Lots of trips, including annual week-long jolly for the older children to places at home and abroad. Parent body is dedicated and 'very proactive, very influential in supporting the family feeling of the school,' according to staff. Recent events organised by the PA include a Fathers' Day breakfast and a United Nations day where parents drew on their own variety of backgrounds to run stalls showcasing food from countries around the world.

We liked the pupil work that we saw on display, particularly the French, and this struck us as a school where children are free to flourish at their own pace. Teacher pupil ratio is 1:9, ensuring all students get the attention they need, and there's particularly strong SEN provision, both for those with diagnosed difficulties such as dyslexia and those assessed as gifted and talented. Full time SENCo is called head of enrichment, and is integral to the school. Speech and language therapist visits. EAL is well catered for in-house: much demand for this, since this is a school with an international intake, reflecting the locality. Both parents and children very contented with their choice: 'The school gives an excellent balance between holding the kids accountable for high academic standards and a well rounded extracurricular activity programme,' was one parent's verdict, and a pupil told us, 'I like everything I do here!'

Early years are housed a few streets away in Wetherby Place, in premises which felt rather small compared to the main school. However, teaching rooms are bright and airy, and classes are small: 13 max for nursery, 14 max for reception. We saw child-friendly, child-centred learning and positive reinforcement everywhere, and the standard of work on the walls was high. The little ones go over to the main school for lessons such as art and PE and to use the library and play areas, thus ensuring that they remain part of the wider school, and a shuttle bus means that parents can drop their children off at either site.

In both locations, we were impressed by the peaceful, happy atmosphere. The bottle green and grey uniform is smartly worn, and children move about with a sense of calm purpose. Kindness really does seem to be the way here, and everyone we spoke to agreed. 'The teachers never, ever shout,' was one comment; 'they're really sensitive to the needs of the children.' As a charming and articulate young leaver put it, 'I've loved this school. I would have stayed here until I was 18 if I could.' 'My daughter's been made really welcome here, and we couldn't be happier,' confirmed a father.

Perhaps not the go-to choice for those seeking non-stop high-octane buzz from dawn till dusk, but a successful and busy school for all that, offering a supportive and relaxed environment in which children can be themselves and achieve their potential without having to compromise their nicer nature.

Hampstead School

Westbere Road, London NW2 3RT

Ages 11–19 **Pupils** 1,244 **Sixth form** 239

020 7794 8133
www.hampsteadschool.org.uk

Headteacher: Since 2006, Mr Jacques Szemalikowski MA BSc PGCE NPQH CPhys MinstP FRSA (50s). This head needs no Red Bull! Positively explodes with energy, a dynamo. Five minutes in his company and you are left exhausted. 'I don't know anyone like him – I always think he must be thinking 10 different things as he's speaking,' one parent told us. 'And you know that if any of those 10 things need acting on, he'll do them

– probably today!' He joined to make a difference, and in his tenure as headmaster of Hampstead School, he has.

A graduate in astrophysics, and a teacher for 25 years before his first headship at The Warwick School, Redhill; parents also like the fact that he has four children of his own ('It means he really gets it'). Crystal clear on expectations – a misbehaving student can find themselves holed away for the day in the internal exclusion unit, 'our naughty step'. He makes no apologies for his rigorous approach to education, both for his students and staff members alike, and works hard to raise aspirations for every child: 'Our students have played football at Arsenal and spoken in the House of Lords – the message is always "You can do this too".'

Doesn't teach ('It's a luxury I can't afford – I'm too involved in sector improvement'), but is on the gate every morning and afternoon, plus all breaktimes, and does a daily hour-long walk round the school 'so I get to know every child and every teacher'.

Parents praise his selection of staff, who get enviable professional development training, although this can be a double-edged sword, with many staff securing promotional posts in other schools, leading to high staff turnover. That said, the calibre of new teachers is impressive; 'We have an excellent reputation, so we are lucky to get excellent applicants.' As for the school's awards and competition wins, no stone is left unturned when there's an opportunity to fix another framed certificate up on the foyer wall – 'We are proud of what we achieve here, but it's even better to have it externally validated,' head says.

Academic matters: Is not releasing any 2018 exam results – GCSE or A level. Does well for value added throughout the school and the sixth form is in the top five per cent of sixth forms in the UK for progress. Consider that nearly half the pupils are bilingual (63 different nationalities), five per cent are statemented and nearly 50 per cent are on pupil premium.

So what's their secret? For starters, students are tracked from the moment they arrive (well, the summer before, actually). They have individual charts and are monitored several times a year. As soon as a student starts to slip or is found not to be doing their best, staff put in interventions ranging from one-to-one support to subject clinics. For the gifted and talented (known here as 'high potential learners' due to the growth mindset), there's also the Brilliant Club, involving university students mentoring the school's brightest. Homework levels 'reasonably high' but 'fair' and 'not unmanageable,' report students, and there are opportunities for after-school homework sessions – great for those lacking a quiet study space at home or for the particularly dedicated.

Extra help available for those who arrive with little English – catch-up is rapid. For SEN, support is provided both in and outside the classroom. 'My son, who is statemented, is a completely different child, thanks to this school – when he left junior school, he was introverted and didn't have friends and had the reading age of a 9-year-old,' one parent told us. 'Now, he loves reading, is at the level he should be and has a really nice mix of friends. Between the SENCo, head of year and his form tutor, they've completely nurtured him and given him all the support he needs while never overwhelming him.'

Big emphasis on (and take-up of) science, with the option of triple rather than double science for students who attain at least a level 6 at the end of key stage 3. In the top 20 UK state schools for continuing into science A levels. Maths also strong; school is very involved in maths challenges, with students achieving above national average numbers of gold, silver and bronze certificates. The school offers free Saturday school maths masterclasses for gifted mathematicians from years 5 and 6 of local primary schools. Other popular subjects include English, media, psychology and economics. Virtually no subject is offered at GCSE level which can't be carried through to A level. Choice of 19 A levels and four BTecs, including catering and hospitality – with multiple exit points for flexibility.

French and Spanish from year 7, plus opportunities to learn community languages. Setting from year 7 in maths and science, but it's fluid and reviewed annually – 'for instance, we dropped setting in English altogether this year because we found results were stronger without setting.' PE qualifications taken by every key stage 4 student, and nutrition and food is no add-on either – 'We don't just teach our students how to cook, we teach them how to cater for kings and queens.'

Games, options, the arts: Fizzes with activity. Music is popular and heavy investment in this department has meant that each of the school's 1,300 students is offered the opportunity to learn a musical instrument. Around 100 students have periplectic music lessons and a large number get involved in musical activities, including senior or junior orchestra, guitar orchestra, a very popular jazz band, junior choir and many more.

Drama also strong, with great on-site replica fringe theatre, partnerships with the Hampstead Theatre, Royal Court and Tricycle all help to inspire and, as one student noted, 'we get the opportunity to do things like professional lighting too.' Performances most terms.

Art thriving, with photography particularly loved by students. Masses of outside partnerships to keep things fresh (and competitive) and – true to the school's aspirational ethos – they're not satisfied with their gold award from Arts Council of England and were currently trying for platinum when we visited.

Note these three subjects aren't just exam options and extracurricular – all key stage 3 pupils get one hour of each subject per week.

Sport is going from strength to strength since the addition of a new four-court sports hall, dance hall with sprung floor, fitness suite, multi-use Astrourf and basketball/netball courts, which join the existing on-site indoor pool. Limited playing fields, though, as you'd expect for a London school. Strongest sports are football, basketball, table tennis (there's a ping pong table practically everywhere you look outside), athletics and dance. Winning matters, with a stuffed-full trophy cabinet in the foyer, but the sporting ethos goes wider to ensure every student gets involved in exercise.

Buzzing extracurricular activity. The school's debating society and Model United Nations do well (the latter team has beaten Eton three times in finals). Less academic options include gardening (they have an allotment which grows produce for the catering department – rhubarb and beans when we visited), poetry, rugby, dance and aikido clubs, plus several music ensembles.

Background and atmosphere: Hampstead Schmampstead – this school is no more in Hampstead than Arsenal (FC) is in Arsenal. Situated in between colourful but definitely not posh Cricklewood, Kilburn and semi-posh West Hampstead, you can see the flag before you see the school. Red and emblazoned with the school logo, it waves proudly high above this impressive large red-brick building. The main building, formerly the old Haberdashers' Boys' school, was built in 1908 and promises great things, with banners everywhere: 'Best ever GCSE results', 'Read more, earn more, learn more', 'Leaders of tomorrow' and so on. 'They do it in American schools a lot because it reinforces key aspirations at all times,' explains head.

But though you still wouldn't know it at this point, the rest of the school is unrecognisable from even five years ago. Brand new, all-singing-all-dancing facilities to the tune of £18.5m mean that most of the previous archaic-looking classrooms have been replaced – think bright, light, carpeted modern rooms and particularly large and shiny science labs, with lovely wide squeaky-clean corridors to get from A to B. There's a refurbished and roomy library – 'there is nothing you can't access in here,' said our guide proudly, although the number of books isn't anything to write home about. Dining and outdoor recreation areas are also new, as is the large assembly hall and aforementioned sports facilities. A well-equipped ICT and catering block is home to industrial spec kitchens, completely with TVs for cooking demos – we half expected Jamie Oliver to jump out to present one of his programmes. And back in the main building, there's a good sixth form centre with huge common room overlooking the central atrium.

Wheelchair access throughout – the school is completely DDA compliant. There is a disability resource which can cater for up to seven students with complex needs, complete with washrooms. These students are fully integrated into mainstream lessons.

Students' pride in their school is evident in the total lack of graffiti, vandalism and litter.

We noticed how they spoke of their school in terms of 'we' and 'us', not 'them', and their sense of ownership in the school means they aren't afraid to speak out. So while in many other schools the best that student councils do is get new fountains brought in, students here recently helped bring about a complete overhaul of the whole detention and reward system and new in-house catering ('the food is all cooked onsite now and it's so good,' one student told us).

Commendable efforts to involve the outside world, with lots of local partnerships and charity work. Enrichment days three times a year – with recent examples including year 9 trip to the coast, year 7 maths puzzles with experts, and business studies students visiting Brent Cross for an Apprentice-style activity. The school culture involves loads of celebration and rewards for achievement and improvement.

Pastoral care, well-being and discipline: 'If punctuality and attendance ain't your bag, this ain't your school,' found our reviewer during our last visit, 'and we've tightened that up even more now,' the head told us this time round, with pupils informing us that turning up even one minute late now lands them in deep water. The senior management team, head included, are at the gates to greet pupils from 8.40am, after which sluggards have to report individually. (Early risers' club offered from 7.30am onwards.) And the head is so intolerant of absence during term time that he's become the go-to headteacher in England to discuss the matter on Radio 4. 'If a teacher prepares a scheme of work using their highly professional skills in a school that's hard to get into and you get an empty chair, that's not only a waste of public money, but it's disruptive,' he says. 'And if you feel you can make the work up, then what's the point in coming to school ever?' The only two exceptions, he says, are illness and two days a year for religious holidays.

Uniform was reintroduced under current headship – 'it puts everyone on a level playing field – essential in such a diverse school,' he says. Different ties denote whether or not a student has been trained in HABZ (Hampstead anti-bullying zone, a model that has since been rolled out across other schools), and any student feeling vulnerable can approach those who have one – extremely popular among students. Non-teaching heads of year are the go-to people pastorally, say students; ditto for parents. Counsellor also available and well-used. 'Mental health is high on our radar – we train staff in mental health first aid and at every level, we're about building relationships with students,' says head. Buddying, mentoring and restorative justice schemes all bolster pupils' sense of security.

'We're not a marching in silence in hallways kind of school,' students told us, 'but you know what the school rules are, why they're there and what happens if you don't follow them' – and the internal exclusion unit, agree all, is a good deterrent. Classes during our visit were well behaved for the most part, with the exception of the odd class joker and one particularly raucous languages class. 'They'll be kept behind for that,' our guide whispered as she shut the door. If a student is found in a corridor during lesson time, they can expect a staff member to stop and question them within seconds (as we saw for ourselves) – woe betide them if they don't have their book signed with permission from their teacher (even to go to the loo). Good level of security – brings to bear the stark reality that you are in an inner-city school.

Only one permanent exclusion in living memory, but around 50 temporary exclusions per year – 'broadly in line with national figures,' points out head, who says they are the result of 'a range of behaviours that contravene our expectations of conduct, plus always for any form of aggression and bullying.' All include a meeting with both child and parent and restorative justice intervention if necessary.

Pupils and parents: From barristers earning £2m a year in moneyed West Hampstead to recent refugees in temporary housing, the demographic is hugely diverse – all the more admirable when you consider how far the school has come. One pupil told us: 'There are no cliques according to how wealthy your family is or their ethnicity – everyone mixes.' Seventeen per cent is white British – the largest group. An appreciation of the diversity of the school is prevalent – Black History Month, Gay/Transgender Month, trips to Auschwitz etc, and we saw posters for a forthcoming Irish night (Cricklewood has many families from Irish descent), to name a few. No shying away from big celebrations around Christmas, Easter and Eid, as at some other diverse urban schools. Around 95 per cent attendance rate at parents' evening, but no PTA. Communications from school praised by parents – 'that goes for general information to conversations about your own child,' said one. We found the students – who come from Kilburn, West Hampstead, Willesden and Cricklewood (and further still if they've moved during their time at the school or enter at sixth form) – polite, chatty, comfortable in themselves and ambitious.

Former pupils include Sadie Frost, Rachel Yankey, ex-MP Julia Drown, Alec Bogdanovic, Jake Lensen, Tobias Hill, Zadie Smith.

Entrance: From up to 71 primary schools (no named feeders; totally non-selective), and covering three boroughs – Camden, Brent and Barnet (admissions managed by Camden) – the school is now oversubscribed in every year. A far cry from before Mr Szemalikowski's time, when the school had a 'terrible reputation,' according to local parents. Around 20-40 external applicants join in year 12 (and some in year 13 who are disillusioned with their current place of learning); entry requirements vary according to the level of course, but applicants should have at least a grade 6 at GCSE in the subject they want to pursue.

Exit: Around 70 per cent stay for sixth form, the remainder go to other sixth forms or colleges or enter employment (increasingly on apprenticeship schemes). Of those that stay, there is some drop out after year 12 (mainly due to the high number of one-year courses available) and around 70 per cent who leave after year 13 go to university, with an overwhelming lean towards maths and science based subjects, although many also into humanities, arts etc. Most to London universities (Kings, Imperial and UCL all popular) 'because they can't afford to move away.' But some go slightly further afield to the likes of Sussex, Herts and Surrey. Over 20 per cent to Russell Group.

Remarks: The head's energy and vision has turned this school around, while new facilities have given it a long-awaited facelift.

A melting pot of culture and diversity, with a whole host of activities to keep even the most apathetic child interested, we think this is what all urban comprehensive schools should look like. But although there is room to make mistakes here – the kind that any youngster might make on their journey into adulthood – it's not for the fainthearted. Large and imposing, with high expectations, you have to toe the line.

Hampton Court House (Junior School)

Linked with Hampton Court House (Senior School)

The Green, Hampton Court Road, East Molesey, Surrey KT8 9BS

Ages 3–11 **Pupils** 247

Fees: £13,665 – £18,027 pa

020 8943 0889
www.hamptoncourthouse.co.uk

Headmaster: Since 2001, Guy Holloway MA (Cantab), NPQH, known as 'Guy' to all, who is also head of the senior school.

Entrance: Into the nursery at 3, or year 1 at 5+, following an informal interview with child and parents. During visit child will be observed by the teaching staff for both academic and social behaviour, and will meet with the head of lower and early years. If applicable, a confidential report from the child's current school will be requested. Head wishes to ensure that parents are committed to the school's ethos and approach to learning. At 10, children are tested in English and maths. More selective in recent years, but potential is still considered carefully. With approximately 35 languages represented at the school, the majority of students have at least one British parent. School runs buses from Chelsea, Kingston and Richmond and pupils come from central and west London and surrounding parts of Surrey.

Exit: Despite being an all-through school, pupils are all prepared for 11 + and 13+ examinations and scholarships. Most – some 70 per cent – stay on, but some move to a very wide variety of destinations: Lady Eleanor Holles and Ibstock Place currently most popular. Not surprisingly there are also families returning abroad as work commitments dictate. Increasingly parents are choosing to keep their children at HCH senior school.

Remarks: Very special indeed is the opportunity for all children from early years to year 4 to receive a bilingual education in English and French with fluent French speakers, so all can become at least competent and develop good accents. From age 6, pupils can also follow the French curriculum for the Centre National d'Enseignment à Distance, which we saw in practice as a year 5 group successfully completed assigned writing tasks to time. Grammar is taken seriously, along with teaching accurate use of punctuation, as seen in pupils' books. All learn Latin from year 5 and Spanish is lively and enthusiastic. Language options include Mandarin. HCH is one of the leading prep schools for this in the UK. French is taught through other subjects (such as mathematics and humanities) and we saw year 1 pupils completing maths addition work happily asking questions in French and slipping back into English with ease. It all seemed perfectly natural and there was support from classmates as well as teachers.

Many nationalities are represented amongst staff and pupils and the curriculum reflects this, so children learn to appreciate and respect other cultures. We saw a year 5 English class tackling creative writing and were impressed by the articulate, confident responses to our questioning, whilst attentive year 6 pupils were appreciating Beowulf. Parents value the imaginative cross-curricular opportunities teachers take to make topics more meaningful eg Queen Victoria in history alongside Great Expectations in English. We saw year 2s, basing their designs on South American wildlife, making imaginative moulds in art, which would later be used to produce Fair Trade chocolates

As well as a concentration on the 3Rs, art, drama and music are seen as central to education here – hooray! Talented musicians are given every opportunity to perform and share in music-making, and more than 50 children have music lessons in school. IT is well provided for with a designated room full of Macs with big screens. All sports are taken by qualified sports teachers and everyone up to year 4 has weekly swimming sessions at Imber Court Pool, a short ride away. In addition, after-school tennis lessons are on offer with tennis specialists. Early years children have their own garden, and all can freely enjoy the wonderful space for outdoor play. There are trees to climb, grounds to explore including a sizeable pond, and the stunning house itself in beautiful countryside. One parent remarked, 'HCH is not an imposing, austere place: instead, very warm and welcoming. My child has had an amazing childhood at HCH. They read books and then play outside enacting them, letting their imaginations run freely'.

A French parent we spoke to was very impressed with communication and the fact that teachers are approachable, know pupils by name and show interest in the families attending. 'The school is small enough to defuse situations so difficulties can be resolved at an early stage.' School is flexible about keeping children down a year or bumping them up one in consultation with parents. This can work exceptionally well, especially in a case of mild bullying, exceptional aptitude or slowness, but it can pose a problem if the child is destined elsewhere.

SEN provision is considered 'outstanding' as far as Ofsted is concerned (praise for the IEPs), with a few requiring direct support for dyslexic traits and social and communication skills. There is specialist one-to-one EAL support.

The food is amazing. The chef also oversees all food at a Fulham free school and is a key player in the government's School Food Plan programme. We saw healthy, appetising food choices with plenty of seasonal options.

Freedom to run about in home clothes and be encouraged to gain a love of learning without the usual constraints can, in many cases, lead to happy, self-disciplined, motivated children. Nevertheless, some parents flee after a while and are not assured that the ethos works in practice or that all claims are realised. This is not the right school for those conservative parents who prefer a more conventional, pedagogical approach and obvious rigid hierarchical structures.

Hampton Court House (Senior School)

Linked with Hampton Court House (Junior School)

The Green, Hampton Court Road, East Molesey, Surrey KT8 9BS

Ages 11–18 **Pupils** 109 **Sixth form** 20

Fees: £18,027 – £19,506 pa

020 8614 0857
www.hamptoncourthouse.co.uk

H

Headmaster: Since 2001, Guy Holloway MA (Cantab) NPQH, known as 'Guy' to all. With his own Russian/German background, he is passionate about the importance of languages, both ancient and modern. He studied at King's College School, Wimbledon, before reading English at Peterhouse, Cambridge. He spent many years in Paris, first at the international PR firm, Burson-Marsteller, and then at the École Active Bilingue, where he was head of English in the section Britannique. For several years he was a volunteer with Save the Children UK, working with disadvantaged children. He is now patron of the children's charity Their Future Today, which supports abandoned and institutionalised children in Sri Lanka.

Part of the 1993 founding team which opened the Harrodian School, where he was director of studies, he is a co-founder of HCH. A committed educationalist, he lectures at the Institute of Education's London Centre for Leadership in Learning. He believes in giving pupils a global perspective so they have an appreciation of cultures and informed tolerance, partly borne out by the international flavour of his staff appointments, including a Spanish head of pastoral care and a German head of mathematics. He runs a weekly seminar – a comprehensive history of music course for all children in years 1 to 8 – and teaches cultural studies to years 10 and 11. He believes staff have a responsibility as role models, sharing the love of their subjects with their pupils. He acts on his beliefs, eg, he encourages all in the acquisition of vocabulary and shared his personal discovery, lustrum, in assembly on the day we visited.

Guy sees his future as 'married to HCH'. He champions creativity and is justifiably proud of the school's culture, which 'enables pupils to fulfil their passions' and nurtures individuals so that they develop quality relationships as a life skill. He is approachable and totally committed to the school's ethos: 'We believe in questioning our beliefs' and 'The primacy of the idea over the person'.

Alongside his fascination for psychology and learning, Guy has a diverse range of cultural and linguistic interests alongside languages, including foreign travel, literature, chess and concert-going, and he is an active member of the Rose Theatre Players. He enjoys directing films as well as plays (over 30) at HCH and recalled many ambitious productions to us with pride.

Academic matters: The study and celebration of languages and the arts are integral to HCH, which is a UNESCO associate school and the only school in the UK to be granted Institut Francais status by the French government for its commitment to French language and culture. In a liberal, civilised, relaxed, atmosphere where staff are addressed by first names, individuals are encouraged to pursue their passions to the full, whilst learning how to appreciate art, music and drama. The staffing reflects this, with native speakers and professional performers as role models; so important. Undoubtedly languages are a strength at HCH with high numbers of 9/8s at GCSE. Everyone takes at least one language to GCSE, with nearly a quarter studying French/Spanish in the first year of the sixth form.

In 2018, 85 per cent of all GCSEs at 9-7. HCH has gained the Good School Guide award for best performance in English independent schools by boys in both psychology and Spanish. This is not a result-driven academic school; instead, the head describes it as a 'shared intellectual environment'. Pupils are prepared for 13+ as well as GCSEs and now A levels. As one long-standing parent put it, 'Don't expect one of the local hothouses without uniform. You won't find the mechanistic, predictable, step by step approach for all at HCH, but instead a joy in the educational experience where pupils gain a rounded introduction to life, and where it's not just about passing exams'. Unavoidably, not all parents are convinced, and some question the fact that, despite degrees, teaching staff do not necessarily have teaching qualifications, whilst others praise their 'inspirational enthusiasm' and the attention and support given to each individual.Ofsted has judged that 'the mostly good or outstanding lessons enable pupils to make rapid progress' and recognised HCH as 'good and increasingly outstanding'.

The school is a lead school in the Network of Excellence in Computer Science, with an emphasis on programming. 'If a child needs to be extended and takes a subject a step further, this is acknowledged and encouraged'. Pupils do need to be motivated and exert self-discipline as this will not be imposed from above.

In 2015 HCH opened its gates to a newly-established sixth form led by experienced, traditionalist headmaster Tristram Jones-Parry MA (Oxon), previously head of Westminster and Emanuel, and teacher of mathematics. Guy explained that the decision was made initially to offer 'heavy duty A levels as well as psychology'. We caught the end of a physics lesson with a small, predominantly male group of the first cohort of sixth formers in one of three new specialist science laboratories. The sixth form has been in the spotlight with its novel late start. Lessons run from 1.30pm to 7.00pm and the school is linked with Oxford University research, promoting a later start for under 20s which aims to maximise the benefit of improved sleeping patterns. Sixth formers can stay on to enjoy a diverse range of speakers, as part of the Form Seven adult education programme involving topics such as Napoleon and the Battle of Borodino, women and enlightenment science, and 18th century French art history. Second A level results in 2018 saw 76 per cent A*-B, 51 per cent A*/A grades.

School is very accepting and inclusive of SENs. SEN department comprises a SENCo, who comes into school twice a week, plus three others: one maths specialist, one specialising in early intervention, and the other very experienced in dyslexia and dyspraxia. They work in small groups or one-to-one, as best suits the child. Seventeen per cent of pupils are on the SEN register – mostly mild to moderate dyslexia or dyscalculia, but school will support ADHD and dyspraxia. One parent commented how proud she had been of the way her daughter and friends had been deliberately protective and inclusive of a pupil with ADHD, and another commented on the positive approach staff showed, allowing the pupil to let off steam by running up and down the corridors when necessary.

Games, options, the arts: The arts and music are superb, with imaginative use made of music composition linked with filming and animations, and pupils winning prizes for artwork and photographs. Small classes mean staff all really know the pupils. Talents are recognised and promoted and the school is sufficiently small to be flexible, a great plus if your child carries out arduous sports or music practice or has to attend rehearsals outside school. Many do, including a current ballet pupil dancing at the Royal Opera House; others attend West End show rehearsals and music performances, and there is a genuine respect for the work ethic involved. As Guy comments, 'Our current national gymnasts complete hours of training a week, and that requires real commitment and dedication'. In the lunch break we heard a young Cambridge choral scholar master successfully putting the choir through its paces, practising a Rutter anthem in the Great Hall. More than 60 students have one-to-one music lessons in school.

There is a varied sports curriculum, with fixtures against local schools in football, netball, cricket and athletics with coaching in rugby VIIs and hockey too. Sixth formers can use a gym across the road if they wish. Each year group has one full sports afternoon a week and there are daily lunchtime clubs as well as after-school clubs in judo, archery, table tennis, football and athletics. The school grounds are extensive and include a netball and tennis court, football pitch and a smaller 5-a-side football pitch. Pupils enjoy running in Bushy Park and Hampton Court Green. One parent did suggest: 'There are lots of clubs but it would be good if they had some physical activity every day of the week, building exercise into their daily lives', although acknowledging that 'healthy eating is considered and the food is amazing'.

Background and atmosphere: Completed in 1757 by the Earl of Halifax, Hampton Court House was intended as an extravagant gift for his mistress Anna-Maria Donaldson and was designed by architect and astronomer Thomas Wright. He was responsible for special period features including a heart-shaped pond and enchanting shell-lined grotto with its painted blue ceiling with gilded wooden stars, and an octagonal ice-house now used for drumming practice. Set within nine acres, the beautiful Georgian mansion has a stunning entrance hall with columns, gallery, ceiling, fireplace, conservatory, winter garden with palms and dining room, all tastefully decorated and looking out at the vista of Bushy Park. After Mrs Donaldson's death the house passed through a succession of tenants and was sold to Marmaduke Blake Sampson in 1871. He was city correspondent to The Times and Argentine consul in London, and was responsible for adding the picture gallery. Much later it passed to the tea-planting Twinings, until in the 1980s, quite extraordinarily, it was a Save the Children home for refugee Vietnamese children.

Following considerable restoration and refurbishment of the house, the school started its life with a pre-prep and prep in 2001, expanding upwards until it opened its sixth form in 2015. The irregularity of the classrooms, along with the abundance of comfortable sofas and country house items of furniture, may seem quirky to those parents used to pristine, purpose-built establishments. Nevertheless, much thought has been given to light, and the ambiance is spacious; pupils are not as crammed in as they might be in some central London schools.

This school has a palpable atmosphere and culture of kindness. As one parent explained, 'HCH is a microcosm of society based on respect and developing useful, responsible citizens ready to take their place in the world.' Parents rightly value the warm welcome and friendships made at HCH with fellow pupils and staff. We noticed the relaxed way in which ages and genders mixed happily and naturally at lunch, moving about with ease, whilst parents are delighted at the way pupils support one another, enjoying activities such as camping, chess, or performing in concerts and plays.

Pastoral care, well-being and discipline: At HCH the belief in developing quality relationships is key, whilst reflecting and learning from one's mistakes in a community based on mutual respect. Guy explains, 'I may hold a door open for a pupil but expect a pupil to hold a door open for me'. First names are used throughout, but despite the non-uniform, each pupil has an almanack in which there is a clear code of conduct and dress. When we visited we were impressed by the pupils' smart appearance. Undoubtedly some individuals would not thrive in such a liberal, non-hierarchical setting, and Guy admits that it is important to match the individual to the right school and that some have left because of this. Parents often visit several times for reassurance, but tend to agree that 'The teachers know all the pupils, and because of the small nature of the school, they are often able to intervene and defuse situations'.

School actively promotes mindfulness, and nutritional advice and time management skills are included in a comprehensive well-being programme. In the past the head has expelled a boy over drugs, and is very aware of safety and security. He regularly chats with the gatekeeper, who can spot if a child is looking miserable or has a concern.

Pupils and parents: Pupils come from a 30 mile radius, with many from Kingston, Surbiton or Hampton, and there is a school minibus which collects from Chelsea, Richmond and Kingston. Not surprisingly, there are a number of international families including some French, who want their children to maintain levels of French 'whilst immersing themselves in English and English culture'. HCH attracts the unconventional, the liberal, the arty. As one parent summarised, 'we appreciate an all-through school where time is found to explore ideas and there is a conventional output but not process'.

Former pupils include environmental campaigner and filmmaker Ayrton Cable, winner of Diana Award and nominated for the International Children's Peace Prize for his work in Malawi; two international ice skaters; many young actors and actresses eg Rupert Sadler, Harriet Turnbull, Nell Tiger Free and Isabella Blake Thomas; not forgetting a heavy metal singer, Austin Dickinson.

Entrance: Main entry points at 11+ and 13+. Interview for candidate and parents plus maths and English tests. Parents are welcome to visit more than once as it is essential pupil and family believe in school's distinctive ethos and approach to education. New sixth form applicants need at least six grade 6s with 7s in subjects to be studied at A level.

Exit: Will prepare for 13+ exams and, unsurprisingly, incredibly diverse range of destinations, including lycées abroad, state schools, Eton, Wellington, Westminster, Bryanston, Kingston Grammar, Wimbledon High, Surbiton High, with some scholarships, although in recent years more are staying on. There is some turnover of children because families move abroad, but those remaining develop a widening circle of friends. Some 60 per cent leave after GCSEs.

Money matters: Up to three scholarships – academic, music, arts – each year, worth 10 per cent of fees maximum. All 11+ candidates are automatically entered.

Remarks: Ideal setting for individuals who can be trusted to be responsible and will thrive on civilised, relaxed values and learn from enthusiastic, approachable teachers who share their passions for their subjects. Several parents acknowledged, 'We visited three times before making up our minds because the school offers something different'. In recent years the school has become more selective, but the head, quite rightly, remains interested in individuals and what they have to offer. As one parent remarked, 'This is a place where it is ok to be different and ask questions, and not be considered a nuisance'.

Hampton Pre-Prep and Prep School

Linked with Hampton School

111

Gloucester Road, Hampton TW12 2UQ

Ages Boys 3-11, girls 3-7 **Pupils** 232 (6 girls)

Fees: £12,060 – £13,935 pa

020 8979 1844
www.hamptonprep.org.uk

H

Head: Since 2015, Tim Smith, BA, MBA (40s). Previously deputy head academic, The Hall School Hampstead, for five years, originally joining in 1994 as games and French teacher, becoming head of learning support and then head of middle school. Also deputy chair of governors in Camden state primary.

Full of the joys of spring. Actually, make that all seasons. 'I love coming into this wonderful place every day,' he exults on the website.

A linguist, he's arty (a regular at the Barbican; partner is head of exhibitions at the Royal Academy) but has only ever wanted to teach. 'Always wanted to play schools,' he says of childhood in New Zealand. Years of wrestling with nervy North Londoners haven't dimmed enthusiasm for career he describes as 'exciting, rewarding, engaging, motivating, joyful and hilarious.'

A shrewd operator, choice of SW London school with less toxic parental vibe – at least for now – compared with NW London is deliberate. Ditto prep finishing at 11 rather than traditional 13, as many senior schools up year 7 intake at the expense of common entrance places. Keen to avoid ivory tower complacency, an occupational hazard for preps, he thinks (state schools often do it better) and keep the innovations coming to improve quality of teaching – 'the light at the heart of school'.

His emphatic approach has come as a bit of a shock to parents though (largely) in a good way. 'Quirky,' was a description we heard more than once. 'Eloquent,' ditto. Felt to have made real effort to get to know pupils. 'Had the measure of our son quite quickly,' said mother. Excitement of the job? Like other heads, says no two days are the same (we're dying to find the first school where they are). Unlike them, explains how. Easy to forget you're dealing with children, he says, who 'do lots of extraordinary and enlightening and motivating things no matter how hard you try or how much you want them to ... go in a certain direction.'

Doesn't pull his punches, particularly when it comes to nervy parents who tell him they only 'want the best' for their child. Do they imagine teachers 'munching on breakfast of baby seals and endangered penguins [and thinking] "I can't wait to come into school and be mean to children?"' he wonders.

Short shrift also given to their fears that strengthened links with Hampton mean school door, as one expressed it, 'no longer open for all boys'. Stresses that nothing is set in stone, academic standards largely going to be determined by intake and any change will be gradual – with no wholesale notices to quit. 'Won't be gathering children up by their ankles, and flinging them into park because they're not clever enough.' A relief all round, then.

Entrance: In a crowded part of the world where limitless parental aspiration meets finite school places, school's willingness to go extra mile a real help for parents – one family wrestling with decision was given mobile number to call during hols for extra reassurance.

Main intake at age 3 into co-ed nursery (20-22 places) and into boys only prep in year 3, when between 14-17 places on offer depending on how many boys leave at end of year 2 (some lured away by well-regarded state primaries). Screen for learning needs in kindergarten, then it's assessments for reception, and years 1 and 2, plus reports. Entry to prep currently automatic-ish for existing pre-prep pupils. Others have tests plus interview with head and report from previous school.

Exit: Girls at end of year 2 to local all-through schools such as Surbiton, LEH, preps (Newland House, Twickenham Prep) and state sector.

In year 6, healthy numbers to St James Senior Boys' School, Claremont Fan Court, Halliford and St George's College Weybridge. Hampton School, however, biggest destination of the lot with just under half moving there. Assured places scheme available from year 2 to year 5 based on combination of assessments, teacher reports, exam results and in-depth discussions by admissions committee unsurprisingly a huge parental incentive. Other boys welcome to sit 11+ on equal footing with external candidates. Eight scholarships in 2018 (four for Hampton senior school).

Remarks: Relationship with big brother Hampton School wasn't exactly a secret even before change of name (from Denmead) in early 2016. Part of Hampton School Trust since 1999, founded in 1924 by one of English masters in own dining room after own son's left-handedness made him an educational pariah.

Pre-prep, just a hop, skip and jump away across pretty public park, is where it all starts. 'The jewel in the crown,' thought one parent. Housed in original school buildings with grassed front garden and miniature lych gate entrance, home-like feel and nurturing ethos makes it a popular standalone option for daughters as well as sons.

Long-serving pre-prep head, Mrs Murphy, gets star ratings from all for ability to get the best from pupils, effortlessly wrapping up fun and learning together with cross-curricular approach felt to be particularly successful (pirates covered by coordinates in maths, on board rules in English and top marauding destinations in geography). Lots of experienced teachers who make connections but ensure pupils 'make the vital links for themselves.'

Attractive two-storey building houses eight airy classrooms, brace of IT suites, art and music rooms and efficient-looking library, all under nature and neighbour friendly living roof, angled to blend in with residential surroundings.

Plenty of greenery courtesy of allotment with raised beds and that horticultural essential, a potting shed, part of revamped outside space that also includes playing fields (shaping up nicely on day of visit) and all-weather area. Back gate on to Carlisle Park provides extra overspill games space, senior school's 27 acres and theatre also coming in handy for large scale events.

Other changes are less root and branch than nip and tuck and made only where demonstrably better than what's gone before (we liked the lesson bell, lifted from French educational system and featuring mellifluous four-note leitmotif).

'What we do is based on substantiated, evidence-based, peer reviewed, professional practice,' says Mr Smith. 'We're not pulling mad ideas out of a hat.' (Harvard University, no less, called in to help with review of pastoral care). Far more emphasis on tracking – no doubting where your child is and what they're capable of achieving, while assessments are regular without being excessive and can't be prepared for (and don't get Mr Smith started on tutors – 'A racket'). Formal exams limited to maths and English, with verbal reasoning added to English and NVR to maths from year 4.

Team of 20 academic staff in the prep (around equal numbers of men and women), 12 in the pre-prep (all female) and just under 30 non-teaching staff, including three gap year students.

Two sets for maths and English from year 4, three in years 5 and 6. Will often double up on teachers to support and challenge (school's headline staff to pupil ratio of 1:18 doesn't reflect this) while three-strong learning support team (same again for pre-prep) help small numbers (around seven) with ADD, ADHD and mild SpLD. Their highlight is the 'ladder of success' – top rung winners who successfully complete daily tasks acknowledged in assembly with 'huge, noisy fuss...' and edible prize. Individual support for EAL pupils (around 35 across whole school) in pre-prep and in class in prep.

Curriculum 'shouldn't be a mile wide but only inch deep,' says Mr Smith, who also comes up with own three Rs – 'richness, relevance and rigour'. Thus subject list doesn't bulge with the outré or unusual – French is only language taught, for example – but concentrates on core range done well, and given more time. Mr Smith is also bumping up recruitment of subject specialists – like parents, feels currently too many generalists, particularly in top years.

With staff training and appraisals also being revamped, teachers 'go the extra mile,' says parent, encouraged to go exploring if lesson takes a different tack. Universal praise for English, boys learning to 'critique their own work and improve it,' says approving parent. Love of books reinforced all the way through –school will set reading as only holiday homework, for example.

Maths felt to be improving, online resources used increasingly to advantage. Results in all-through confidence – year 3 boys eager to explain division by four ('divide by two and by two again'), others in year 6 yomping through hinterlands of mean and mode. 'Teachers aren't going to blow you out of the window if you get it wrong,' reported one. 'Make teaching fun.'

Exam pressure – which pupils agreed could be tough – similarly well handled, focus on preparation without panic. Boys able to rattle off practical techniques that help. 'Make the point, use a quote and explain,' said one.

Ad hoc prizes (including sweets and – from one teacher – even more popular tennis balls) are popular incentives, though discipline felt by parents to be excellent – 'Only takes a look for boys to be quiet.' Masses of reinforcement, from weekly award of courtesy cup in prep to flowers, cloth and special pud for best behaved pre-prep lunchtime table. Easily understood golden rules for younger pupils, though slightly tortuous house point system for year 4 upwards (fine detail runs to several pages) is being revamped. 'Too complex,' agrees head.

Trips range from creative writing workshops to suitably bloodthirsty Saxons vs. Viking experience – firmly linked to curriculum, while clubs span debating to cooking, changing by season. Otherwise, sport's the big thing, with three sessions a week and easily the highlight for majority of pupils. Biggest stars can, thought one parent, get the 'c-leb' treatment (the eternal problem) though another praised numbers of teams (A to D for rugby and football) and regular swapsies so Bs get at least second dibs on training and attention. Means that while truly uninterested might struggle, anyone who's keen but with a modicum of talent is felt on the whole to have a good time. Results justify the effort with frequent successes, school handicapped only by size (some larger Richmond-based opponents can choose from bigger pool of talent).

Swimming has been major casualty of timetable rejigging, axed in the prep (though still offered for years 1 and 2). Not everyone's happy about this – 'focus is on football and rugby to the detriment of any other sport,' said parent, but Mr Smith isn't budging. 'We're not going to use valuable curriculum time to teach them to splash around in some grubby pool when parents can do that themselves on a Saturday.'

Art, however, has had a reprieve. Initially pared back and rotated in 10-week blocks with drama and DT, has regained weekly slot on the timetable after fears that talented weren't getting enough time to hone work to scholarship standard.

With around 60 prep and pre-prep pupils learning instruments (beginners to grade 5), a choir, orchestra and wind band and several scholarships in recent years, performing arts are good, think parents, though anticipate better things to come. 'Don't have enough children, scratching, blowing, tweeting and trumpeting,' agrees Mr Smith. Added space for more of everything – instruments, informal as well as class-based concerts plus whole school annual production all on the way, activity across the octave and decibel range should increase.

Parents very sociable, newcomers quickly brought into the fold. While the many working parents can inevitably end up missing out on coffee mornings, 'Always someone who'll scoop up your child.' Helped by before and after-school care – 7.45am start (8.00am in the pre-prep), 5.30pm finish – more activities after school would make life even easier, felt one parent.

Mr Smith stresses (and will probably have to keep on stressing) that ethos of school won't change 'simply because ... we apply tenets of the admissions policy ever more carefully as time goes by.' Some current parents have yet to be convinced. Prospective parents eye up growing numbers gaining places at Hampton and make up their own minds.

H

Hampton School

Linked with Hampton Pre-Prep and Prep School

Hanworth Road, Hampton TW12 3HD

Ages 11–18 **Pupils** 1,270 **Sixth form** 365

Fees: £20,055 pa

020 8979 5526
www.hamptonschool.org.uk

Headmaster: Since 2013, Kevin Knibbs MA (early 40s). Joined Hampton as deputy head in 2007. Previously history master, head of lower school and senior master at Bolton School Boys' Division. Educated at King Edward VI Grammar School, Chelmsford and read modern history at Oxford (gaining two football blues in the process). A career schoolmaster who still teaches history to youngest boys. 'I happen to run a big business, but that's not why I chose teaching in the first place,' he tells us. Not one to hog the limelight. At his happiest when talking about the boys, of whom he is fiercely proud.

Very visible head who can often be spotted at weekends on the touchline and towpath, supporting Hampton boys and chatting to parents. Friendly, approachable and generous spirited. 'I am lucky to lead a school that is on this trajectory and I want to keep it going. It's a privilege to be in this job. I love it. I hope that comes through.' It does.

His wife is one of the chemistry teachers. He has a weakness for off-piste ski-ing in Colorado.

Academic matters: Results going from strength to strength with record grades. At GCSE, 93 per cent A*-A/9-7 in 2018. Boys performed outstandingly well in the free-standing maths qualification with over 90 per cent scoring the top grade. Hamptonians also impress regularly in national competitions, including as winners of the UK Maths Trust challenge for two years running, and in winning essay and poetry prizes. In lower years, all boys study chemistry, biology and physics as separate subjects, computer programming and coding, at least one language out of French, German, Spanish, Russian or Mandarin, and Latin which is compulsory in years 7 and 8. Setting in maths and modern languages from third year.

At A level, 68 per cent A*/A grades in 2018. Currently physics, chemistry, history, philosophy, German and Mandarin (short course) offered at Pre-U. At A level, maths remains perennially popular with regularly 30 per cent taking further maths. As one teacher explained, 'maths is like a magnet for these boys.' High uptake of chemistry, physics and economics too. In sixth form, all boys follow an enrichment programme which includes six-week courses on topics including university life and finance, mindfulness and current affairs. School offers its own extended project qualification, with recent essays focusing on quantum gravity and the feasibility of time travel.

H

School is no slouch on the computer front, with eight different ICT suites and a new coding room. Boys bring in their own iPads and use them in every subject. School council currently hotly debating whether to replace text books with ebooks.

Around 185 pupils have some kind of SEN. Support tends to be small group intervention (currently around 40 such groups) with lunchtime drop in sessions popular, especially as exams loom. 'Some of our highest achieving boys are on our learning support register and that's how it should be,' states head. Forty pupils are classified as EAL, though none requires additional support.

Over a third of staff has been at school for more than a decade. Each year roughly 10 per cent leaves, so constant flow of fresh blood, including some sparky graduates who are grabbed straight out of university and are trained on the job. Head acknowledges that 'we are a springboard school and people want our staff. Any of my senior team could run their own school but I am clinging on to them.' Approximately 40 per cent female teachers. 'That's changed a lot. When the boys leave here they know exactly who is in charge,' smiles the head. Pupils feel their teachers are friendly. One of the younger boys explained, 'Homework got the better of me at the beginning. But if you email a teacher to say you are struggling with the work, they are more than happy to go through it the next day. You just need to give them the heads up.' All the lessons we observed were lively and led by dynamic teachers, many of whom have grammar school backgrounds themselves and like the down-to-earth ethos of the school.

Games, options, the arts: School is well-known for its excellent sports provision, with at least 17 different sports offered. Over 27 acres of playing fields so all facilities (bar the Millennium boathouse) are on site and head has been known to joke that he would move the Thames if he could so that it could flow closer to the school. All-weather 3G sports ground very well used, including at break time when swarms of boys congregate there and kick balls about with great gusto. 'It's good for morale and improves concentration in the classroom,' states head. One boy told us that 'my mum loves the 3G grass as I never come home muddy!' Another told us that he fell in love with Hampton the moment he saw the huge number of pitches stretching into the distance.

Sports practice mostly takes place at lunchtime to enable those travelling home by coach to participate. Boys can choose which sports they want to play and the school excels at most. As always, Hampton is competing at the highest levels in national schools' competitions and churning out some exceptional sportsmen. Deserves its reputation for being one of the top football, rugby and rowing schools in the country. No hockey offered which one parent found 'disappointing, as many boys would be keen to play it.' School stresses importance of participation for all, and multiple teams are fielded in all age groups. One mother we spoke to was not so sure, saying that 'in reality, there may be some who struggle to make a team.' Starry old boys include Olympic gold medallists Greg and Jonny Searle as well as Surrey and England all-rounder Zafar Ansari.

Head insists that school is not just for those who can perform brilliantly on the games pitches. 'There are many quiet, effective learners who find their own niche. We want to make sure that all boys get opportunities'. Boys agree that 'there is no hierarchy of worth. Being in the first XV is not seen as being any better than being in the Voices of Lions.' School has worked hard to encourage this view and head is adamant that that academic, musical and dramatic successes are now celebrated just as much as sporting triumphs.

With over 50 clubs on offer, including model aviators, debating, and photography, there does seem to be something for every taste. Over 200 boys take part in D of E scheme each year. Adventure Society, open to all years, offers a heady mix of kayaking, power-boating, orienteering and sea-cliff climbing. For the more sedentary, chess is thriving: five teams regularly represent the school. One pupil is currently national chess champion. Beekeeping society is the latest club on the list.

Performing arts have taken off in the last decade and serious resources have been funnelled towards both drama and music. The Hammond theatre seats 380 and boasts a hydraulic orchestral pit, hi-tech lighting and sound systems and, one pupil told us, watching plays here 'feels like being at the West End.' Well-equipped art/DT department, and some stunning artwork lines the corridors, though surprisingly few take these subjects at A level. School produces a steady stream of Arkwright engineering scholars.

Around 400 boys have music lessons, many on more than one instrument. Significant numbers attain grade 8. Two current pupils with diplomas. Plenty of performances from rock, jazz, keyboard to strings and boys have 23 music ensembles to choose from. Celebrated male voice choir, Voices of Lions, enjoys a high profile and performs at Edinburgh Fringe. The lively rendition of Drunken Sailor in school assembly was apparently 'legendary'. Nine Hampton musicians have received organ scholarships from Oxbridge in recent years.

Background and atmosphere: The school was set up over 450 years ago thanks to a bequest of property and land by local brewer and businessman, Robert Hammond. Formerly a grammar school (went independent in 1975). Not the most beautiful of schools, though the warmth and friendliness of both staff and pupils makes up for the lack of architectural splendour.

School is outward looking and has developed links in the local community and abroad. Boys help in local primary schools and put on a Christmas party for elderly locals. School provides a Latin class for GCSE pupils from local state schools. Also has an association with a safe haven in Malawi. Hampton is proud of being a 'beacon school' for Holocaust education and raises awareness of more recent genocides. Certainly not a school that just looks after its own.

Close ties with neighbouring girls' school The Lady Eleanor Holles School. Since the appointment of the current head there, there is 'an enhanced desire to work collaboratively, especially at sixth form level'. Schools already share much, including drama productions, language exchanges and Oxbridge interview preparation.

Pastoral care, well-being and discipline: School takes great care to integrate boys who arrive at 13 with the well-established 11+ cohort. Pupils are supported by a pastoral team, including their form tutor and head of year, as well as sixth form mentors, though one parent we spoke to said 'the lack of a house system and small tutor groups may mean that some boys may slip through the net, no matter what the school tells you.' Some reports of bullying in the early years, though parents felt this was generally stamped out quickly. Head runs a weekly pre-school drop-in for boys to approach him on any matter they wish and he meets with head boy and his deputies once a fortnight and jokes that 'they tell me how to run the school'. This head has his ear to the ground.

Head has helped establish Hampton as a national leader in mindfulness. 'We're one of the early pioneers of it,' he says proudly. Believes it is a useful tool for helping these boys deal with 'the ups and downs of teenage life in this high achieving setting.' Mindfulness, life issues and well-being/resilience taught for nine weeks as part of the curriculum in fourth year, followed by a top-up session before GCSE study leave begins. One pupil we spoke to admitted that 'it can be a struggle to balance everything as there is so much going on here, but mindfulness helps.' Head believes that it is no coincidence that since it has become a mainstream part of the school, 'the academic results have improved, and the school has become a kinder, gentler and calmer place'. Head adds, with a smile, 'If it's good enough for Jonny Wilkinson ...'

Pupils and parents: Diverse mix of boys. Many parents have state school backgrounds and choose it for its unpretentiousness. Increasing numbers of European parents whose sons are bi/trilingual. Many boys walk or cycle to school and older boys can drive, provided they park at a distance. Extensive coach network (run jointly with LEH) attracts families from all over west and south west London and Surrey. Coach journeys with girls apparently awash with witty banter.

Parents are very involved with the school, often helping with careers advice and fundraising. Head admits the parents can be demanding, but 'we're better off than some schools in that respect. We seem to attract families which do not tip over the fine line between aspirational and obsessional.'

Entrance: Highly selective. A 40 per cent increase in registration since 2011. Now more than six applicants per place. No sibling policy. Pupils generally enter the school at 11, 13 or 16. The 11+ route is normally for 125 boys; current batch from 75 different feeder schools (54 per cent of them joined from state primary schools, the remainder from preps which finish at end of year 6). At 13+ a further 65 boys enter the school, from about 25 different independent prep schools. Around 10-12 boys join in sixth form though few places up for grabs at this stage. At 11+, entry is via school's own entrance exam (maths, English and reasoning) plus interview and reference. For 13+ entry, boys must sit the pre-test at 11; from 2020 offers will not depend on common entrance scores. Entrance at sixth form is via personal statement, head teacher's report, written and online assessment and interview. Boys must also get a good clutch of GCSEs, with a minimum six 9-7 grades including English and maths. The staggered entry at 11 and 13 works well and one teacher made it clear that 'we're standing firm with the 13+.'

Head devotes hours to speaking to prospective parents and says he tries 'to be clear about our ethos to parents. The families we choose need to be on board. It has to be the right fit for their son.' Warns parents not to 'force the pace' but to aim to put their son in an environment where he will be happy. Looking for boys who are academically able, inquisitive and hard-working, but they also need heaps of stamina to keep up here. A willingness to join in and try new things is crucial. 'Along with appointing staff, it is the most important thing I do,' says head. He manages to make the selection process as personal as possible and sends out good luck cards to all 1,200 applicants before entrance exams. A characteristically thoughtful gesture.

Exit: School is keen to point out that 'we do not cull anyone post-GCSEs' and there is no minimum number of GCSEs that internal boys must gain to be allowed to stay into the sixth form. 'We do talk to parents and pupils openly, however, if a boy is struggling. They might choose to put in place a contingency plan.'

Up to 20 boys head for Oxbridge each year (14 in 2018) in a wide range of subjects. Head explains, 'We don't get obsessed about it. It is certainly not a case of Oxbridge or die'. Vast majority tends to head for Russell Group universities. Occasionally, boys venture to the Continent while others choose medical schools (seven medics in 2018, including one at Cambridge and one in Bulgaria), drama schools or conservatoires. Favoured universities include Warwick, Durham and Nottingham. A handful disappears off to Ivy League colleges in the US, often on sporting scholarships. Boys regularly return for career advice long after they leave.

Money matters: Fifty-six boys are on full bursaries and another 127 are on substantial bursaries. Plans afoot to provide more such places and this is a matter close to the head's heart. 'In terms of the school's future, to maintain our grounded feel, and with fees going up, we need to make sure that more bursaries are available. We do not have a big endowment so have to do it through fundraising.' Academic, all-rounder, art, choral and music scholarships carry a remission of up to 25 per cent of fees. 'If there are financial issues, we do try to help,' says head.

Remarks: Hampton is riding high. Though head is conscious that 'we can sometimes hide our light under a bushel here,' they would be justified in shouting their achievements from the rooftops. There is currently a real energy about the school and boys appeared to be genuinely happy.

One of the aims of the school is for Hamptonians to strive 'for personal success while supporting those around them.' If the boys who showed us around are anything to go by, they are accomplishing their goal admirably. Hampton is producing young men of integrity. No wonder the head is so proud of them.

Harris Westminster Sixth Form

Steel House, 11 Tothill Street, London SW1H 9LH

Ages 16–19 **Pupils** 600

020 3772 4555
www.harriswestminstersixthform.org.uk

Principal: Since 2014, when the school started, Mr James Handscombe MA (Harvard) BA (Oxon) mathematics PGCE NPQH (early 40s). Previously deputy head at Bexley grammar school, Mr Handscombe started his career in what was perhaps his most formative experience, as a maths teacher at Tonypandy comprehensive school in south Wales. Youthful, purposeful, wholly unaffected but intimidatingly intelligent, he is relishing running the innovative and above all scholarly sixth form he is leading here at HWSF. Married with two school age daughters, he met his wife as a student in Oxford. A truly vocational teacher, Mr Handscombe could have done almost anything with his brilliance and brains, but the children he teaches are the lucky beneficiaries of his calling. Educated at a comprehensive in Sheffield, he went on to achieve a top first in maths at Merton College Oxford followed by a masters at Harvard.

His students admire him as a 'well rounded intellectual'. He is 'not boring or plain but has real cross-curricular knowledge,' one told us. He confided to us that he likes to see himself as a polymath. A regular tweeter, his 140 characters tend to be about an array of subjects from U2 lyrics to mathematical juggling. He described to us, as well as to the world at large on the HWSF website, his insecurity and lack of confidence when he arrived as a very young man at two of the best and most prestigious universities in the world. However he concludes that 'it doesn't matter where you come from: the only thing that matters is how interesting you are to talk to.' The three nouns, ambition, perseverance and legacy, emblazoned across the HWSF website and elsewhere lie at the heart of his journey as well as those of his students. It is ambition that propelled him, perseverance that enabled him doggedly to pursue that difficult path, and finally produced the legacy that he is now bequeathing to his students and with which, he hopes, they in turn will imbue generations to come.

Academic matters: This is a highly academic school. It takes the brightest and best students from all over London and the suburbs. Its continuing association with Westminster School is influential in setting the tenor of scholarship and creating high expectations among the students. Its aim, it states, is 'to nurture a community of scholars'. Its A level subjects are the 'facilitating subjects', those most valued by the top universities. Most popular subject by some margin is maths. The department is very strong with high calibre teachers who excel in their field. French, Spanish and German offered as modern languages. Classics, history of art, drama and German are all taught at Westminster School. Music, art, politics and economics are also offered alongside the sciences and the humanities.

HWSF follows the Westminster School timetable as well as the curriculum, right down to Saturday morning lessons. 'A real shock' to many students (and teachers) when they first arrive, observes Mr Handscombe, but they start to enjoy the quieter commute on a Saturday and the opportunity to become immersed in their academic study. As at Westminster, students here have set exeats each term when school is closed on Saturday. 'The core of Westminster School is threaded all the way through HSWF,' says Mr Handscombe. 'There are links at every level.' Teachers share schemes of work, the senior teams meet regularly, they share the same chair of governors, the two heads meet regularly and there is lots of mentoring as well as lesson observations. The same 'loyal dissent' that has characterised intellectual debate and classroom discussion at Westminster for generations is being fostered in its sapling.

Teachers here are young, energetic, and ambitious for their pupils. 'Learning is amazing' is a phrase you hear frequently and it is written all over the place, even on the cushions in Mr Handscombe's study. All pupils take four A levels, some more. Although there are a few people with mild dyslexia, Asperger's etc, they are all high performers and have to be able to keep up. 'Provision for students with exceptional needs is via the Student Support coordinator and the Harris Federation SENCo,' says Mr Handscombe.

Results are strong. In 2018 – the third set of A level results – 47 per cent of grades were A*/A. Students take the more challenging Pre-U in a number of subjects including English literature, modern languages, Latin, art and design and art history. High percentages of students achieved a distinction in these subjects (in most subjects well over 50 per cent). 'Our students work hard at hard work,' says Mr Handscombe. The results are a by product of this, not the main end game.

Games, options, the arts: An idiosyncratic feature of extracurricular provision at HWSF is the Tuesday afternoon 'Lab' – a time for scholarly work, collaboration, one-to-one sessions with teachers, and an important building block on the path to entering the country's top universities. On the same afternoon 'Lab lectures' take place. Stimulating speakers at the top of their field come to the school to lecture, whether it be on human rights, politics, climate change or science. A select number of students are invited to principal's tea with them afterwards for the opportunity to network and discuss thoughts and ideas in a more intimate setting.

Cultural perspectives – courses not part of their A level study – form part of the timetable. For eight weeks students study three from a wide range of colourful and intellectually stimulating cross-curricular courses. These include beginners' Mandarin, business start ups, The Other in literature, gender trouble from Freud to Beyoncé and introduction to grand opera. Designed to widen cultural horizons, inform the debate and prepare for interview, the programme also helps with the schools' challenge 'to convince them that learning is amazing'.

Students also become members of a weekly subject society. A president is elected to run the society and to chair discussions and debates. In addition there is a wide range of extracurricular societies from the hugely popular Afro-Caribbean Society (ACS, which boasts over 100 members) and the Intersectional Feminist Society (the IFS, in which there are plenty of young men as well as women) to Diplomacy (a highly competitive and mind-bending board game).

All students are encouraged to play sport on Thursday afternoons ('it's part of our ethos to be fit and healthy,' says the website) at venues across London. Football and netball are co-ed, athletics buoyant. HWSF students are the reigning athletics champions in the borough of Westminster. They also do a wide range of minor sports from archery and fencing to trampolining and table tennis. Debating society and bridge club for those who would prefer not to do sport, but they are no less competitive.

Art is offered as a Pre-U and each year a few do go on to do foundation courses, to study fashion or history of art at eg the Courtauld, or to train as architects. The art room is on the seventh floor: bright, busy and creatively chaotic. Music, also on the top floor, is offered as an A level – a few take it each year – and there are individual music rooms and instruments (guitars, electric and acoustic, pianos and drum kit) for recreational purposes. Carols at Christmas, a spring concert at St Margaret's on Parliament Square, as well as a few informal performances each year, either in the classroom or in the hall on the ground floor.

The library, on the ground floor, is like a magnet. Well stocked with books (generously donated by the Wigoder family foundation) as well as with very hardworking and focused students, it is always busy. It opens at 7.30am and closes at 6.30pm, yet at the senate meeting we were fortunate enough to attend, one of the requests from the student body was that the library hours be extended.

Background and atmosphere: Founded in 2014 HWSF, as it is known, forms part of the Harris chain of academies, or MAT (multi-academy trust). The school building is essentially an office block spanning eight floors (good for fitness though you can qualify for a lift pass if you can prove a need for one). Grey, functional, clean lines, minimal decoration; if it weren't for the unmistakable buzz of young bright people you would think there was not much of an atmosphere. However, a stone's throw from St James's Park tube and a short walk from Westminster Abbey and the Houses of Parliament, you can't escape the sense of purpose and excitement of being in a historic part of London where things are made to happen.

Despite its relatively short history, tradition is important here, and we were lucky enough to be present at the leavers' ceremony for the upper sixth. It was held in the splendid Westminster Abbey, and the young students filed in below the flying buttresses, bright eyed and full of optimistic confidence to listen to the various speeches and thanks of their principal and heads of house. Humorous and erudite, the speeches reflected the intelligence and acuity of this cohort. James Handscombe's final words were significant: 'You are the brightest and the best and I hope you will remember that learning is amazing, and that one day some of you will become teachers.. give me a call if you do.' There is a barely veiled intention that some of the students will return one day and take on the mantle, whether by contributing financially or becoming part of the teaching team.

Assemblies are held in Westminster Abbey once a month, and in St Margaret's once a week. As part of the intention to create a sense of history and ethos in the school Mr Handscombe and his team, and the wider Harris MAT, have set out to instil longevity in the institution, a place that will have a dramatic and lasting impact on these young people's lives.

The main aim is that the students are taught to think for themselves and become the kind of students universities are looking for. So far the work is bearing fruit in terms of both the results they get and also how former students are faring at university. The school keeps in touch with its alumni and a key part of their work is to track their progress and development beyond their time here.

This is an institution that is not just run by the staff. The senate (student council), its president and two vice presidents (the proud wearers of yellow lanyards, setting them apart from the rest) also play a key role, as well as the house captains. Students and teachers are given equal weight in the voting process. The process is rigorous. Of the 40 who apply for membership, 20 will be interviewed and 10 appointed. The president we met could run for office, at a national level, tomorrow. Seriously impressive.

What is striking about the students here at HWSF is that their passion for learning and for scholarship is nakedly evident. Whereas their cool cousins at Westminster School might be paddling madly underneath but floating serenely on the surface, all the paddling is laid bare here, and proudly so.

Pastoral care, well-being and discipline: These are highly intelligent, high functioning young adults, who are knitted together by a shared thirst for scholarship and who are generally held in high esteem by their teachers. They respect themselves and the institution. They look smart (dress code is suits but there is some flexibility). Behaviour is generally good. 'The most common transgression is bunking off a lesson to do other work,' says Mr Handscombe. He hopes he will never have to permanently exclude anyone, and hasn't so far; 'it will be a sign that we've failed. The secret of behaviour management is to give them learning, intellectual stimulation. They know that they have to manage themselves, and if I have to step in, we've got a problem...it's a deal, we give them excellent teaching, stimulating assemblies and talks, and they work hard and behave well.'

Pupils and parents: Looking over the sea of 250 pupils in year 12, the immediate impression is the racial mix. No one culture, religion or skin colour dominates. For many, English is their second language and some need support with their English. Some 40 per cent of pupils are on pupil premium. They come from schools all over London and some from as far as Essex and Kingston, Bromley and Barnet. One of our stunningly intelligent and articulate guides said with complete poise, 'A lot of students go out to get their lunch; I always eat in the canteen though as I am pupil premium.'

The largest proportions currently come from Lewisham, Westminster and Croydon. No-one knows anyone else when they arrive, however. There are no large swathes of pupils from a particular school or area. What these pupils have in common is a love of learning and thirst for intellectual rigour. 'It's the scholarly engagement that is key to the melting pot,' says Handscombe, 'and we will fight to preserve that'. One pupil admitted, 'I didn't know what scholar meant before I came here.'

We often found it difficult to distinguish pupils from teachers. Many teachers are young, most pupils mature, confident, assertive but relaxed. Students here are polite, but not overly deferential. They look you in the eye and politely disagree.

Entrance: Students choose to be tested in the two favourite subjects that they want to study for A level. Some 80 per cent take maths exams. There is a mixture of translating and writing for languages, and essays in the humanities and English. Physics exams consist of standard science questions with a focus on problem solving. The content is relatively basic (year 10 standard) but the questions harder than GCSE standard. Promising candidates can choose the subject they would like to be interviewed in – 'We want to see how clever they are – we're interested in their teachability, enthusiasm, aptitude, speed of learning and ownership of learning,' says Mr Handscombe.

A maximum 650 are interviewed from (in the recent intake) over 1,500 applications for 300 places, with priority to those on pupil premium who reach the required standard.

Exit: To a wide range of universities, including Bristol, Manchester, Nottingham, UCL and Queen Mary. In the third batch of leavers, 18 students secured places at Oxbridge and one went off to Harvard. They choose a wide range of courses. Popular ones include economics, law, physics and biomedical sciences. Some seepage at the end of year 12, with around 10 per cent likely to trip over the requirement to achieve at least four Ds in end of year 12 exams.

Remarks: A melting pot of the brightest and best pupils from all over London. HWSF is a genuinely stimulating and scholarly environment in which to study. The end game isn't to get into top universities, though that is what most students do, but to instil a love of learning and breadth of knowledge that will serve these students well throughout their lives. Students feel fortunate to be there. The staff feel privileged to teach them. A stunning combination.

H

The Harrodian School

Lonsdale Road, London SW13 9QN

Ages 4–18 **Pupils** 1,015 **Sixth form** 170

Fees: £15,000 – £23,040 pa

020 8748 6117
www.harrodian.com

Headmaster: Since 1999, James Hooke BSc PGCE (geographer). Educated at nearby Hampton Grammar, followed by Leeds university. Began his career in the City but swiftly changed to teaching abroad at St John's School, Buenos Aires. From 1994 deputy head at The Harrodian, working alongside, legendary Peter Thomson, becoming head five years later. Youthful in appearance, he finds seeing young people progress under his watch extremely satisfying and is sad to see them go. This is a head who regularly takes lunch duties, checking queue hoppers, happily chatting with pupils over meals. He moves about the school with calm, purposeful authority, and is, above all, accessible and approachable.

One parent observed, 'Although there have been changes as the school has grown in size, the ethos remains the same at the heart of it, and that emanates from the head.' What is impressive is that in a school of some 1,000 pupils, the head knows them, taking pleasure in acknowledging their interests and achievements. Parents agree: 'Mr Hooke knows them all as personalities. He stands outside, on the pavement, or on the side of the pitch. Pupils feel connected and valued. He often praises them for things they do outside school and manages to be at everything'. Committed to the ongoing success of the school, he moves effortlessly from leading pre-prep assemblies, to a sixth form planning meeting, to selecting future pupils ('increasingly difficult as demand has grown,' he comments), to evening engagements such as a prefects' dinner in the City. For relaxation, this energetic man can be found on the ski slopes with the school trip or playing golf alongside pupils and parents. When we visited, he was about to participate in a weekend Surrey cycling event.

Mr Hooke has put in place a dynamic, experienced team of senior staff and looks after them, inspiring loyalty. Among them is the calm, capable, head of pre-prep, Lucy Horan, who has been in place since 2004. Her previous experience was in the state sector – Our Lady of Victories in Putney and deputy head at the Oratory in Chelsea. Jenny O'Neill became head of lower prep in 2015, herself mother of three Harrodians, so 'I really know the school and Harrodian-style first-hand,' and is determined to create 'an even stronger sense of team and community in the prep school'.

Sixth form thrives under stewardship of business-like David Behan, ex-City banker and Oxford geographer, who was appointed as head of economics, and who collaborates with senior colleagues to ensure university application guidance and careers advice is given and changes carefully engineered as new-style A levels work their way through.

Academic matters: 'This school caters for individuals and allows children to be themselves,' was the observation of more than one parent. A broad curriculum caters for different tastes. 'All take single sciences at GCSE', explained the head, 'to ensure they keep their options open'. Streaming in English, maths and languages. Bilingual pupils are expected to study two different languages and all benefit from being taught by wholly native speakers, as we observed. Latin and religious studies survive. No design technology but graphic design, photography, media and 3D design offered. Unnecessary pressure is avoided but pupils are made aware of the need to apply themselves in GCSEs since the AS has disappeared and these grades help to secure future university places. Pupils spoke of the Aspirational Universities Club which they had found helpful.

Standards continue to rise as entrance becomes more selective. An impressive 80 per cent A*-B at A level (49 per cent A*/A) in 2018 and 56 per cent 9-7 at GCSE. Nevertheless, Mr Behan stresses, 'there is room for the individual for whom three Cs could be a real achievement'. The school is not setting out to be all about examination results, but nowadays there are plenty of high achievements to celebrate.

The number of pupils with SEN (notably dyslexia, dyspraxia and dyscalculia) is small, with one or two per form, catered for both within class and with individual support from the experienced learning support department run by highly praised SENCo. Dedicated staff work alongside one another with individuals in a light, spacious, well-resourced room at the top of the building which, in days gone by, was the headmaster's geography classroom. Typically, a parent praised the provision and how her daughter wanted to go to sessions and had noticed the difference since she had received targeted support. In addition specialist one-to-one EAL tuition is provided for the few that need it.

ICT is well provided for with interactive whiteboards and dedicated spacious rooms although we did not see younger pupils with iPads or sets of laptops, and the staff commented that the emphasis remains on teacher/pupil oral interaction.

Games, options, the arts: Highly-qualified sports coaches use the latest recording equipment to improve players' techniques and PE A level is available. Smart dance studio accommodates dance, fencing and gym. Amazingly, for its location, there are 25 acres of playing fields, as well as two all-weather pitches, netball, basketball and tennis courts. On and off-site activities for sixth formers include gym and weight training, swimming, spinning, aerobics, body pump and pilates, as well as rowing. Sport is compulsory throughout, with three or four lessons per week out of 30 for sport/PE. The emphasis is on participating, enjoyment and representing the school, with the Harrodian regularly hosting tournaments, swimming galas and athletic meets. When we visited the U18 rugby had been almost unbeaten in a highly successful season, with U16 footballers reaching last year's ISFA final. The Ski Academy offers bespoke training in the UK and France for the squad which competes in the English School Ski Championships. The annual golf tournament is very popular and pupils appreciate the wide choices, and sixth formers enjoy a sports afternoon each Wednesday. Attractive heated pool in colonnaded courtyard is open from April to October. The vast array of fixture lists is impressive, catering for a range of abilities, although a few parents we spoke to did not find the amount of sport lived up to their expectations. But one parent explained her son was 'offered a place at Winchester and declined as he wished to remain at the Harrodian and play for the A football team'.

'Superb music,' was parental consensus, with compulsory lessons up to year 9 with music and music technology available at GCSE and A level. Over half the pupils receive individual tuition across a full range of instruments and singing from beginner to grade 8. We encountered one prep boy on his way to ukulele and a girl awaiting her grade 4 singing exam during our visit, outside the school's auditorium with its raked seating. All are involved in annual carol concerts at St Paul's Church, Hammersmith. Pupils enjoy annual Battle of the Bands, an X factor style competition for year 4 upwards. Harrodian rockers compete to participate in the Isle of Wight festival. A sixth former spoke enthusiastically of a choir trip to Athens, whilst younger pupils chatted to us animatedly about many other choir opportunities including cadets (boys), stilettos (girls), training choir, senior choice, chamber choir and the Sixteen. 'All are encouraged to perform in assemblies and so grow in confidence and anyone can audition for parts in productions,' parents informed us.

Artists are very well catered for. We watched seniors skilfully painting in oils and acrylics in one of the many attractive art rooms and admired fine displays. As one might expect in a school promoting creativity, diverse courses are on offer, leading to university places to read history of art and art and design. In response to a design and photography challenge, pupils were invited to create a First World War inspired design to stay in one of the senior courtyard buildings until the end of the centenary. Display cabinets in an entrance hall bulged with highly imaginative shoes created for a house art competition. Drama also flourishes and is very popular. Pupils perform at the Edinburgh Fringe and we met one talented individual who had completed her extended project qualification on set design. The school encourages public speaking and debating, which helps pupils to grow in confidence and puts the young at ease when conversing with visitors like us.

Background and atmosphere: In 1993 pioneering Sir Alford and Lady Houstoun-Boswall bought the then country club for Harrods employees with its 25 acres and sporting facilities, to realise their vision for a co-educational preparatory school where children could thrive in a civilised environment without unnecessary pressure. The school has grown from the original 65 pupils and 12 staff to nearly 1,000 pupils and an established sixth form.

The cream, well-proportioned building is beautifully pristine with its sweeping lawn and manicured neat lines. We saw discreet scaffolding camouflaging the latest sixth form building to provide further facilities. Gardens are immaculately maintained, courtyards, olive and magnolias tastefully placed. One could almost imagine oneself in the country, looking out at the 25 acres of playing fields with pitches galore and, across the road, separated by stylish railings, the magnificent view of the river Thames. The exterior is matched by the interior with its sweeping staircases, vast entrance hall and spacious, well-lit rooms.

Pupils and parents comment on 'the warm, friendly atmosphere which marks this school out'. There is an outstanding sense of a vibrant community and this comes from the top. Both exterior and interior promote civilised values, all magically removed from the traffic, noise and hurly burly of Hammersmith Broadway. No wonder some pupils do not see any need to move to board in the country. The institutional aspects of school have been skilfully replaced by synchronised clocks, so no bells, but carpeting and great attention to decoration.

The pre-prep is self-contained in bright, airy accommodation and a paved courtyard. The conservatory provides space for listening to readers and small group work opening onto Astroturf for all the year round play. The attractive French-style garden, complete with water feature, provides a tranquil setting. The prep school is cleverly arranged so that, although senior pupils work in rooms alongside, younger pupils are not intimidated. In fact the natural mixing of age groups is a pleasure to behold. Prefects organise year 4s to obtain sponsors for a charity Easter egg hunt, and science week takes place throughout the school, from a workshop in the hall to Cancer Research teachers in the senior laboratories setting challenges. The coffee shop is another splendid touch, welcoming parents and visitors in the mornings and providing a convivial space for sixth formers, as well as the many comfortable three piece suites we spotted about the place. Lunches are served in a spacious dining room. Some parents and a few pupils we spoke to criticised the quality of the food. 'Too much pasta,' voiced several. The sausage and mash was very popular when we visited. The libraries are an additional bonus, lined with books and with librarians to hand. We were pleased to note the acquisition of reading desks with lamps straight from the old British Library Reading Room, where seniors were studiously in silence. Again the community spirit prevails with annual events such as dads' reading morning for year 4 to 7 and the annual year 4 Night in the Library event.

Pastoral care, well-being and discipline: Pupils of all ages commented on 'the kind teachers' and 'the welcoming atmosphere'. Bullying they did not see as a problem because 'everyone is so kind to one another'. 'It's amazing – everywhere you go there is someone to talk to,' said one year 8 boy. Much has been put in place to promote this caring community including mentoring scheme. Senior school students are selected and trained to provide one-to-one mentoring of younger pupils who they meet with regularly. They also run inductions for newcomers. There is a student leadership programme which gives year 11 and sixth formers the opportunity to develop and apply for roles as subject sports or community leaders.

The school has introduced mindfulness and life coaching for staff and students. A school counsellor is available for drop in sessions for year 7 upwards on a self-referral system whilst younger pupils require consent from a parent. There are timetabled citizenship lessons for year 9 and circle time for younger pupils. A student council meets regularly.

A healthy balance of gender and age among staff reflects the school community and many desire to return. We encountered one ex-Harrodian gap student and another ex-family member appointed to the staff. A young teacher's mother had worked at The Harrodian and Mr Hooke's own children attended the school.

The house system, alongside swimming galas and sports events, sees a flourishing array of staff and pupils zealously throwing themselves into planning and meetings. Pupils appreciate the house bake off, pumpkin carving competition, drama, music and house quizzes. Parents like the fact that 'Kids organise assemblies and ensure all children perform in front of one another'.

Pupils were very clear about the range of punishments leading to detentions and their fairness. No uniform except in the pre-prep but there is a clear dress code carefully explained in the parent handbook, and implemented. Parents commented: 'Some might say The Harrodian is an easier, relaxed school where anything goes, but it is no laissez faire country club. Far from it: there is zero tolerance for drugs or bullying. The school acts on bullying swiftly and effectively when it does occur.' A few parents suggested there could be more effort and consistency over pupils' awareness of others and politeness when moving around the school. However, parents feel they can see a member of staff promptly if they have a concern, and approach the head informally, which they would not attempt at a more traditional school. The PTA chair explained 'the school has no out of bounds areas, which means pupils can be happy, and feel free to express themselves rather than intimidated'

Pupils and parents: Notable former pupils include actors Will Poulter, Robert Pattinson, George MacKay and Tom Sturridge and musician Will Heard. Parents increasingly include entrepreneurs, those involved in advertising and public relations alongside professional families and international businesspeople. There is a real sense of continuity, the PTA chair having been there since the school's foundation. Parents value the fact all of their children can spend their whole schooldays here.

Entrance: The catchment area includes Barnes, Mortlake, Putney, Sheen and Richmond, as one might expect, as well as stretching towards Ealing, Holland Park and Chelsea, with a few older pupils travelling from as far as Wandsworth or Battersea by train. Main admission points are at 4+, 8+,11+,13+ and 16+, with occasional places at other times. Non-selective reception places by informal assessment and date of registration. Siblings are given priority but not guaranteed a place. Admission to the prep and above involves exam and interview. There are a few places at 8+ for children from the Merlin School in Putney.

At 11+ there is a diverse range of applicants for some 25-28 places (exam and interview). At 13+, common entrance or school's assessment plus interview.

Sixth form entry requires six or more grade 6s at GCSE, at least 4s in English and mathematics, plus 9-7s in chosen A level subjects. Standards less stringent for internal applicants as external applicants sit mathematics and English examinations, plus interviews in prospective A level subjects (six or seven external places) and current school reference. As head remarks, '16+ applicants include those who have had enough of boarding, along with girls, in particular, who wish to escape from single sex London day schools'. Increasing numbers staying on after GCSE with new sixth form facilities.

Exit: A decreasing few at CE to trad boarding schools (Eton, Harrow, Charterhouse, Marlborough, Wellington etc) and single sex London day schools (St Paul's Girls', King's College School etc). Majority stay on for GCSEs now with just a few going elsewhere eg to boarding or tutorial colleges. University destinations varied, ditto subjects, though economics and business currently very popular. In 2018, three-quarters to UK universities (Bristol, Bath and Leeds all popular), five to Oxbridge and several off abroad to study in Canada, US and Switzerland.

Money matters: Fees are in line with local schools. No entrance scholarships and limited bursaries are reserved for the unexpected crisis. Limited academic awards for internal candidates at 13+ and 16+.

H

Remarks: Head emphasises 'The Harrodian is not an international school with high turnover of pupils: rather, pupils reflect London's exciting, vibrant international community'. In this civilised setting, a diverse, cosmopolitan community happily thrives. One parent of four commented, 'The school believes that if a child enjoys where they are, they are more willing to learn', and that has proven to be the case for her family. 'The school understands that every child is good at one thing and if you harness that, then there is a positive outlook'. Current parents believe it 'would not be the right choice for pushy parents or those who shy from informality and creativity'.

Harrow School

5 High Street, Harrow on the Hill HA1 3HP

Ages 13–18 **Pupils** 825 **Sixth form** 360 **Boarders** 825 full

Fees: £40,050 pa

020 8872 8007
www.harrowschool.org.uk

Head master: Since April 2019, Alastair Land MA (Cantab), (40s), previously head of Repton after three years as deputy head here. Educated at Manchester Grammar School and Trinity College, Cambridge (first class hons in natural sciences). He comes from a lineage of skilled horticulturalists who nurtured his early interest in science. A man with a vocation to serve, he seriously considered a career in the armed forces (and hasn't closed the door on one in the church), but above all he 'always knew he wanted to teach.' His first job gave him the opportunity to combine the two and he spent nine years at Eton as biology teacher and commanding officer of CCF. Thence to Winchester College where he was master in college and senior housemaster. Father of two young sons.

Academic matters: Teachers, parents and the boys themselves describe Harrow as an 'academic' school. Harrow's results don't appear in league tables – head says he's fed up with the 'one-dimensional snapshot' they deliver – but results are impressive. At A level in 2018, 64 per cent A*/A grades, nearly 88 per cent A*/B and 84 per cent A*/A at IGCSE. IGCSEs taken in English, French, German, Spanish, history, geography, maths, as well as biology, chemistry and physics. Drama and PE introduced at GCSE recently.

Thirty-one subjects on offer at A level – all the usual, plus business studies, government and politics, history of art, music technology, photography and theatre studies, with a range of languages. Maths is the most popular subject at A level, with nearly two-thirds taking it. Half the boys do four subjects at A level rather than the usual three (one boy recently did nine). Sixth form electives are a recent innovation for sixth form pupils – a chance for boys to experience university-style teaching in specialist areas and have increased from five to eight periods a fortnight, with boys taking three one-term courses – the last relating to their chosen university course. Cerebral subjects on offer include programming, the history of western art, the greats of European philosophy, psychoanalysis and its impact on European culture, conflict and creativity in creation, post-genocide Rwanda and financial mathematics. Now offers EPQ.

Dazzling array of languages on offer – French, German, Spanish, Italian, Russian, Turkish, Polish, Japanese, Arabic and Chinese. All three sciences are compulsory at IGCSE. School has its own observatory with three telescopes and astronomy offered as a GCSE. Timetabled reading periods and new seminar programme for years 10 and 11. At GCSE classes range between 14 and 20 pupils while at A level the average is eight and none are greater than 12.

Embracing technology: all new joiners asked to purchase a (subsidised) laptop to be used in all lessons.

School caters for mild dyspraxia and dyslexia. One-to-one help given off-timetable, at no additional cost. Dedicated band of teachers (or 'beaks' as they are known at Harrow) includes many writers of scholarly books. Women make up 19 per cent of staff.

Games, options, the arts: There's no doubt about it, Harrow is a very sporty school, with hordes of teams regularly trouncing their opponents. Sport played five afternoons a week, 32 sports on offer and director of sport encourages even the less enthusiastic to 'have a go' at something. Main sports are rugby, soccer, cricket and Harrow football. The latter is played with a pork-pie shaped ball which absorbs the wet and can be propelled by any part of the body. Even though it's played in the depths of winter and is a very muddy affair the boys love it and only wish more schools played it (Harrow is the only one). When we visited pupils were counting the days till their Harrow football match against an OH team. Last year lots of their fathers had played and there was even one grandfather in the side – 'but we were very careful with him.'

Vast expanse of playing fields, sports centre with indoor climbing wall, weights room, 25m pool and sports hall, courts for tennis, rackets and squash, nine-hole golf course and Olympic-sized running track. School boasts national champions in rackets, fencing, fives and judo, two boys playing rugby for England and number of cricketers playing at national and county level. The mother of a gifted sportsman was full of admiration for the way the school nurtured her son's sporting talent whilst keeping him focused on his academic studies and helping him achieve stellar grades. 'The school sees each boy as an individual and were very supportive and flexible,' she told us.

Head of music admits that when he arrived there was a perception among rival directors of music that Harrow was 'an old-fashioned school where little value was placed on music and the arts.' To his delight he found the reverse was true and there's a 'wealth of musical talent.' Half the boys learn musical instruments and 50 per cent of these achieve grade 8 or better by the time they leave. Practice sessions timetabled for younger boys. Loads of orchestras, choirs and strong tradition of singing. More than 100 concerts a year, with recent performances at the

Royal Albert Hall and Royal Festival Hall. Steady stream of boys to top universities and conservatoires to read music too.

Excellent Ryan Theatre seats 400 and is used for school and professional productions but annual Shakespeare productions take place in the beautiful arts and crafts Speech Room. A huge, wood-panelled half-moon, it boasts authentic Globe-style staging and seats the entire school. Wonderful art and, befittingly for a school where photography pioneer William Fox Talbot was a pupil, photography. DT, sculpture, art and photography now in a new state-of-the-art facility that also includes a new digital design suite. There's no lounging around with nothing to do at weekends either – scores of extracurricular activities to choose from, everything from the Alexander Society for boys interested in military history to the Turf Club for horse racing fans.

Boarding: All pupils board at Harrow. We visited two very different houses – Druries, which dates back to the 1790s and is a maze of charming nooks and crannies, and the ultra-modern Lyon's, or the Holiday Inn, as a few wags have nicknamed it. 'It's the best piece of real estate around here,' joked one boy, hugely appreciative of its light, airy, five-star rooms. 'There's room for us to move around and not cause too much havoc.'

Each house has common rooms, games rooms (kitted out with plasma TV, pool and table tennis tables), garden and 'yarder,' an area where boys can run off steam and kick a ball about. Two boys sharing is the norm in the first year but by year 11 (or even earlier) they get their own room, complete with desk, shelving, computer and, occasionally, en-suite shower. All pupils' names etched on wooden house boards, with head of house's name picked out in gold. Boys can make toast and heat up soup in their houses – 'and the more ambitious make Pot Noodles,' said one boy. We trust he was joking. Meals are eaten centrally and food gets a firm thumbs-up – from us too, if the lunch we had with sixth formers was anything to go by. Boys are allowed to go out for a meal with their parents on Sundays but there's no weekly or flexi-boarding. Two weekend exeats in the autumn and spring terms and one in the summer.

Background and atmosphere: Harrow is one of only four all-boys, full-boarding schools left in the UK (along with Eton, Winchester and Radley). Boys have been educated here since the 13th century, but the school was founded in 1572 under a royal charter granted to local farmer John Lyon by Elizabeth I (Lyon's, the newest boarding house, is named after him). The aim was for the school to provide free education for 30 local scholars, a number later increased to 40 by the governors. School sits in picturesque Harrow on the Hill, surrounded by 400 acres and with panoramic views across London – of it, yet remote from it, as we said last time. On a clear day you can see Canary Wharf from the head's study and it's just 25 minutes by tube to Green Park. Visitors to the undulating school site take note – flat shoes are a must.

School is steeped in tradition and history. The 17th century Old Schools contain the beautiful Fourth Form room, with names carved into every inch of panelling, from Byron to Robert Peel. It's also where Professor Flitwick's charm classes were shot in the first Harry Potter film (lots of tourists gazing admiringly when we visited). The stunning Vaughan Library, designed by architect Gilbert Scott (he also created London's St Pancras Station) has chess sets on tables and stays open late during exam periods. War Memorial Building commemorates the 633 OHs who died in the First World War. You can't help but be profoundly moved by the Alex Fitch Room, an Elizabethan wood panelled room with stained glass windows and a Cromwellian table, given by a grieving mother in honour of her 19-year-old son after he died in the First World War. She asked that it should be used for the purpose of boys meeting their mothers and that a light should always be left on over her son's portrait. Plaques and memorials commemorating quirky events are everywhere. Charles I rested here while preparing to surrender and little inclines have memorable names like Obadiah Slope, wittily named after Trollope's unctuous Barchester Towers character.

Harrow Songs are legendary. No Harrovian, either past or present, fails to mention the strength of feeling they engender and the lump in the throat they provoke. Songs have been an important part of the school since 1864, when the head of music wrote the first song, and they are considered to be 'a unifying force.' In November each year the whole school assembles in Speech Room in honour of its most famous alumni, Sir Winston Churchill, for the Churchill Songs. Like rival Eton, school has its own jargon. 'Skew' is a punishment, 'tosh' is a shower, 'tolley up' is permission to work late and so on.

Pastoral care, well-being and discipline: Pastoral care is meticulous, with highly structured system of resident housemasters, assistant housemasters and matrons. Harrow's 12 houses are integral to the school and boys are fiercely loyal to their own house. Some houses are regarded as stricter than others and parents we spoke to said it's important 'to pick and choose carefully.' One of the houses – West Acre – was recently the subject of an ITN documentary series, following the life of the school for a whole year. Housemasters in post for 12 years and as well as doing most of the admissions assessments each gives their house its character and reputation. They also work round the clock – 'at the beginning of every term I say to my wife "see you at the end of term",' one housemaster told us with a grin.

H

Harrow takes a pragmatic approach to technology and social media but the boys are so busy there isn't much time to sit around and play computer games. Pupils understand that bullying is 'completely unacceptable' and head says that it has plummeted, 'not down to zero, but pretty close.' School does a bullying survey every winter and housemasters, year group tutors, matrons, two school chaplains, health education tutors and school psychologist pick up on most things. Discipline is clear and firm but the place feels pretty relaxed, with boys knowing exactly where they stand. 'You are given freedom but if you abuse the freedom you would be punished,' one boy told us. Zero tolerance on drugs and use or supply in term-time or holidays means expulsion. Anyone found with spirits suspended and warned while smoking is handled through 'escalating sequence of sanctions imposed by housemasters.'

Smart uniform of dark blue jackets (bluers), grey flannels (greyers), white shirts and ties, plus, of course, Harrow's infamous boaters. Boys wear them or carry them and either love them or loathe them. They're allowed to write their names and draw pictures on the inner rim and spray them with varnish to protect them. Members of Philathletic Club (school's top sportsmen) get to wear bow ties. Sunday wear is black tailcoat and the whole kit and caboodle.

Pupils and parents: Pupils come from all over and school is proud of its 'broad and varied intake.' We said last time that it's the sort of place where a Yorkshire farmer's son will be sharing a room with the offspring of a City banker – and it still holds true. Between 10 and 15 per cent are progeny of OHs, while 20 per cent are from overseas (some expat, others from vast range of countries – 40 at last count). Twenty-five with EAL requirements. Most boys are C of E but there's a 'significant' RC community. Small numbers of all other main faiths or none.

The boys we met were engaging, appreciative of the fine education they get and very proud of their school. 'It doesn't give you a sense of entitlement, just a great responsibility to give something back,' one boy told us, while a sixth former who'd joined from a state school at 16 said that he'd been 'pushed and challenged' and that there was 'a lot more opportunity for debate' than at his previous school.

Parents reckon the school suits all-rounders who work hard and like sport. 'It's very disciplined and the boys are busy all the time so they have to be organised,' one mother said. 'There isn't any time to get up to any mischief and the boys are really tired by the end of term. There's a real camaraderie about the place and the boys make life-long friends. I can't fault it.' Another reckoned that even though it's 'strict,' any boy would thrive at Harrow, as long as they can cope with being in a large school where they won't necessarily be 'king pin.'

Long and distinguished list of former pupils – seven former prime ministers (including Sir Robert Peel, Lord Palmerston, Stanley Baldwin and Sir Winston Churchill), 19th century philanthropist Lord Shaftesbury ('a towering figure – we refer to him a lot,' says the head), Jawaharlal Nehru, King Hussein of Jordon, Lord Cardigan (who led the Charge of the Light Brigade), General Sir Peter de la Billière, plus countless other men of military renown (20 holders of the Victoria Cross and one George Cross holder). The arts and sciences are equally well represented, with a dazzling list of luminaries including Lord Byron, Richard Brinsley Sheridan, Anthony Trollope, Terence Rattigan, John Galsworthy, Cecil Beaton, Edward and William Fox, Richard Curtis, Benedict Cumberbatch and James Blunt, plus Crispin Odey (one of the UK's most successful hedge fund managers), Julian Metcalfe (founder of Pret à Manger), cricketer Nick Compton and Tim Bentinck (better known as David Archer).

Entrance: Very competitive. Around 600 apply for the 160 places on offer at 13. Prospective pupils supply school reference and sit pre-test in year 6; most are expected to be invited for assessment at the start of year 7, through tests and interviews. Offers are made – subject to CE or scholarship exams 18 months later. Sixty-five per cent expected at CE. 'Some weight' given to sons of OHs and boys' siblings – 'but brothers don't automatically get in,' said a parent. Boys arrive from more than 100 regular feeder schools. All-boys' boarding preps like Caldicott and Cothill top the pack but others from a myriad of co-ed and day schools.

Total of 24 new pupils a year into the 340-strong sixth form. Candidates need at least seven or eight 9-7s at GCSE but many will have straight 9/8s. Candidates write a CV, plus letter to the head explaining why they want to come to Harrow, and take tests in their proposed A level subjects. The best attend a day of interviews and assessments.

Exit: Very few leave after GCSEs and nearly all sixth formers off to university, with 19 boys off to Oxbridge in 2018, and one medic. Other top destinations include Exeter, Bristol, Edinburgh and UCL. US universities very popular, with students heading for eg Brown, NYU, Chicago, Stanford and Yale.

Money matters: School has given franchises to Harrow Beijing, Harrow Bangkok and Harrow Hong Kong, with a fourth likely to follow in the next few years. These are all successful enterprises carefully monitored by Harrow and also fund generous bursary schemes at home.

Wide range of scholarships and bursaries at 13 or 16. School offers means-tested bursaries of up to 100 per cent of fees to pupils who win a scholarship of any sort. Up to 30 scholarships a year for academic excellence, music, art or talent in a particular area (normally worth five per cent of fees). There are also Peter Beckwith scholarships for gifted and talented boys whose parents can't afford to send them to Harrow. Two awarded each year to boys aged between 10 and 13 – these can cover fees at a private school from the age of 11 and Harrow fees from 13.

Remarks: Parents looking for a top notch, blue chip, full boarding, all boys' school will be hard-pressed to beat Harrow. This is a school on top of its game.

H

Hawkesdown House

27 Edge Street, London W8 7PN

Ages 3-8 (gradually becoming 3-11) **Pupils** 130

Fees: £16,350 – £19,170 pa

020 7727 9090
www.hawkesdown.co.uk

Head: Since 2017, Jenny Mackay, BEd from Westminster College, Oxford. Previously deputy head of juniors at both Lady Eleanor Holles and Streatham and Clapham High. Has also taught at Dulwich College, Eaton Square and in Dubai. Teaches year 3 comprehension and drama.

The day after running the London Marathon, Mrs Mackay took up her role as head. She recalls rehearsing her speech to teachers as she pounded along the Thames. 'I had to take it fairly slowly on the stairs on my first day!' she jokes. Keen theatre-goer and bookworm. Has travelled extensively. Proactive head who enjoys networking and spreading the word about Hawkesdown. As one parent put it, 'By cold calling the heads of local preps, and inviting them in, she literally rebuilt the relationship between Hawkesdown and these schools.' Stands cheerily at the entrance every morning welcoming pupils and parents, aware that minor problems can often be nipped in the bud through a timely word at the door. Married.

Entrance: Names down as soon as possible after birth. Pupils can join at 3 in the nursery or 4 in reception. Occasional places thereafter. Parents invited into the school two years before starting, to meet head individually. Confirmed or waiting list places offered 12-18 months ahead of start date.

Nursery is capped at 16, but room for 20 in reception. 'We appreciate that many families may want their children to complete their own local nursery, and so we are happy to take them in reception too'. Sibling priority at every stage.

Gradually becoming co-ed and expanding up to 11: its first girls joined the nursery in 2018 and it will take girls into reception in 2019, with the first year 4 class in 2022.

Exit: Informal chats begin with parents at the end of year 1 to identify possible prep schools. Most boys currently leave at the end of year 3 though sizeable proportion leave after 7+. They head for a mix of boarding and day preps, with most favouring London. Westminster Cathedral Choir, Chepstow House, St Paul's Juniors, Thomas' Kensington, Westminster Under, Caldicott, Summer Fields, The Dragon and Papplewick all perennially popular.

Some boys sit for one or two schools at 7+ or four or five schools at 8+. 'When one leaves depends upon where one is heading. If parents have a clear future school in mind, this will dictate which year they want to sit exams'. From 2022, boys and girls will be ble to stay on to 11.

Remarks: Founded in 2001 as part of a group of schools that includes Devonshire House and Lyndhurst House. Named by its owner founders, Mrs F Loveridge and Mr M Loveridge, after Hawkesdown in Devon where there is an ancient fortress. The name chosen reflects the team spirit, hard work and sense of community of those who built it.

Currently a free-standing pre-prep. The big change on Mrs Mackay's watch is the beginning of the expansion of the school to year 6 and the introduction of girls, starting in nursery and filtering up to the top over time. Exciting times ahead. Mrs Mackay's calm professionalism will surely mean Hawkesdown takes it all in its stride. Parents are delighted she is at the helm for this regeneration. No major building modifications needed to house additional pupils. School will become one-form entry, with an occasional bulge year.

School went through a difficult patch when there was an interregnum with deputy head becoming acting head. Shrinkage in numbers enabled school to plan forward. One mother stated, 'It is definitely back on track'. Another commented that 'the school now has a sharpened sense of direction.'

Huge emphasis on literacy and numeracy from the off and many pupils read well by the age of 5. On several occasions, head stressed, 'we are not a hothouse, but we do get the best out of the children.' No setting as small classes allow differentiation and no child is under the radar.

Inspired teaching much in evidence on the day we visited and not a dreary worksheet in sight. Pupils were busy being explorers on a magic carpet in one class and pouring out gunk into measuring cylinders in another. Without exception, the boys were captivated. 'I want the children to have a very creative experience, so they look back on these years with happy memories,' states head.

Homework is equally imaginative, taking the form of a Take Away Menu, with starters, main courses and desserts that allow for various creative activities linked to the term's topic. Pupils complete a meal over the course of the term. The menu of tasks might include learning one's name in sign language, paint blind or create a Florence Nightingale lantern. 'It gives them a chance to choose and be more independent in their learning,' explains head.

Head not in favour of after-school tutoring. She wants her pupils to 'have a life. They need to work hard in school but then have down time, so they are refreshed for the next day. We need to think carefully about what we expose children to.' One parent admitted there is a smattering of tutoring but 'not that much. The parents put in the work, though!'

Experienced SENDCo, on-site four days a week. All pupils screened for dyslexia in year 2. School does what it can to help with physical disabilities but there is no lift and it is not the easiest school to navigate. Some seven boys currently receiving speech and language therapy and one boy weekly one-to-one sessions. EAL support offered.

Non-denom but with a Christian ethos. All newcomers are given a stylish teddy bear, named Jack. Jack is an acronym for school values: joy of learning, all in, confidence and independence, kindness and respect. Children are rewarded with stickers when they demonstrate JACK values. Gold stickers also given for tying ties or shoe laces independently and for demonstrating community spirit.

Pastoral care is a priority. School very aware of mental health issues and accepts that taking prep school entrance exams at the age of 7 or 8 can be hard. Masterclasses and workshops for parents to help alleviate pressure on their offspring. Head has noticed a reduction in families being hellbent on supremely academic schools for their sons at all costs. Mrs Mackay knows that 'if you put pressure on children they crumble, especially if they are getting it from home too.' No such thing as a typical Hawkesdown pupil: 'We have the loud, quiet, quirky, those who struggle to tuck in their shirts, those who want to save the world ... we are very much about the individual.'

Children have a say in running the school and boys recently requested to serve themselves at meals. Bedlam on days when rice and corn are served, but generally works well and children feel empowered. Not all child-led initiatives are approved and drinking hot tea at meals was firmly rejected. Hawkesdown pupils do not go hungry. Food includes a sandwich mid-afternoon. Sophisticated home-made vegetarian options include polenta cakes and asparagus tart; rice cakes for snacks.

Located on a pretty road off Kensington Church Street, next door to Fox Primary, so the street is awash with children first thing. Purpose built as a school. Fairly cramped premises with tiny outdoor courtyard but Kensington Gardens is used for daily 'huff and puff'. Not bad as a back garden. PE takes place in school hall, as well as nearby Holland Park. Football, cricket and tag rugby offered, as well as judo and fencing. Tournaments and matches galore. Everyone gets the chance to play in a team. Possibly not the right school for the uber-athletic. Chess taken seriously and is compulsory from year 2 upwards.

About 30 per cent currently learn either the piano or violin. Choir meets regularly and performs at the carol service, Notting Hill Christmas market, harvest festival and summer concert. Annual event singing to elderly at a local residential care home. Parents feel that 'art has taken off recently'. Collages aplenty.

After-school clubs mostly run by school staff, but with some outside agencies too. Internal clubs include art, storytelling, cooking, brain benders, board games and cricket. External clubs include chess, Chinese Dragons (Mandarin with some art thrown in) and Relax Kids (mindfulness and yoga). Sport, anything IT related, art and drama are always a hit, but all have respectable numbers attending. Many are free.

Mostly dual-income professional families. Majority British but with sizeable contingents from America, Europe and Russia. About 40 per cent of pupils are fluent in more than one language. Most live within walking distance, and tend to walk, scoot or cycle to school. Most are very involved, but school is not afraid to tell parents to be more visible if they have not been glimpsed for a while. They are encouraged to attend assemblies, concerts and matches, as well as annual prize giving, sports day and carol service, and attendance is very high. Parents and grandparents read to the children twice a term. Parents recently watched delightedly as their children sashayed down the catwalk in eco-friendly outfits, complete with compère.

No bursaries but head explains that 'if someone was struggling while already at the school, we would have a discussion and see what we could do. We are a family and people do go through hard times.' No sibling discounts.

Changes are afoot. The introduction of girls and the extension to year 6 mean that this school is positively buzzing. Hawkesdown nurtures its pupils, encourages fun but also achieves academic success. Happy memories guaranteed.

H

Haydon School

Wiltshire Lane, Eastcote, Pinner HA5 2LX

Ages 11–18 **Pupils** 1,864 **Sixth form** 436

020 8429 0005
www.haydonschool.com

Headteacher: Since 2011, Robert Jones (50s). Read economics at LSE (he had an amazing an passionate school economics teacher who really encouraged him), followed by his first teaching job at Holland Park School in 1990: 'I've always wanted to teach at a comprehensive school – and this was a big state comp. I think it's because I went to an all boys comprehensive in Stockport and was the first person out of my family to go to university.'

Five years later, he was offered the opportunity to teach at an international school in Hong Kong, where he spent the next four years: 'My wife and I are both teachers and both love travelling, so it made sense to grab this opportunity when it came. We were there for the handover of Hong Kong, so it was an exciting time.' On his return he moved to Haydon School as head of department in 1999 and quickly moved up the ranks to become assistant head, deputy head, then head: 'I've always been quite ambitious.'

Some 20 years at the school – Mr Jones can barely believe it himself. Thankfully he continues to be inspired by the changes he has been a part of during his tenure. The school has grown significantly and the size of the sixth form (up to 460 students) is 'a unique selling point.' 'With so many new free schools opening up in the area, there is much more competition – but having such a large sixth form means that we can offer a huge variety of subjects.' He still teaches economics to A level students (we get the feeling he has more of a connection with the older students and is certainly more visible to them).

A Reading Football Club season ticket holder – he still plays football and coaches Ascot United U13s (his younger son plays for the team; the other is grown up). Married to a drama teacher. Still tempted to travel again later on.

H

Academic matters: Offers a broad curriculum with more than 30 GCSE and four BTec options, plus a multitude of A level subjects. 'We want to offer as broad a curriculum as possible', explains the head.

Language provision is very good (some 90 per cent taking a language GCSE) – with students starting off with French and Italian or Spanish. Mandarin no longer offered, which saddens the head: 'We had to drop it as recruiting staff was a nightmare.'

In 2018, 74 per cent got 9-4 in both maths and English (28 per cent 9-7 grades); at A level, 45 per cent A*/B. Parents generally praise the quality of teaching, and in particular the revision lessons offered around exam time, plus the quick communication with many teachers via email as well as the odd phone call saying, 'your child has been terrific today.'

Students need six GCSEs at 9-4 (including maths and English) to study three A levels. Those who do not have a good pass in English or maths can retake these alongside.

One SENCo and a team of learning support assistants support around 20 or so pupils with an EHCP. There is also a special centre where students can be taught in small groups.

Parents like the fact that class sizes are around 25, but some would prefer more streaming. 'At present in year 7 there is streaming just for maths,' said one parent. 'I would like to see this extended to other key subjects such as English and science, as they do in other local schools'. The school does cater well for the very able student too, we are told, with some 15-20 high achieving pupils (HAPS) in each year group given extra opportunities and extension work. One parent told us: 'Both my children have been on the HAPS programme, and both have benefited from it.'

Games, options, the arts: 'Sports at Haydon has been brilliant for my child', one delighted parent told us. 'So much on offer here and great facilities. A brilliant head of PE, which helps.' There does seem to be something for everyone. Rugby a biggie here, so too are football, cricket, basketball (all for boys and girls) plus netball and indoor athletics. There is also an ultimate frisbee team in the sixth form. New sports hall helps facilitate this, as do the extensive grounds with several tennis courts and sports pitches. Successes at both local and county level: 'We have won the borough cricket tournament four years in a row,' one proud sixth former told us.

Strong media department too, and a significant number of pupils go off to study media at Bournemouth University. Thriving art department achieves excellent exam results. Art, textiles and photography available at A level. The art on display was some of the most impressive we've seen (including some by TV and radio presenter Fearne Cotton – a former alumna of the school). A great DT facility in the Wood's building, courses including resistant material workshops and graphic design, 'a nice break from heavy academia', one student told us.

School has two orchestras, jazz band, samba band and wide variety of other music groups. Two big concerts a year as well as annual musical – and Haydon's Got Talent is a big yearly event. Lots of extracurricular offered – everything from film, poetry and philosophy clubs, to tai boxing, trampolining and fitness clubs.

Plenty of opportunities to travel; Snowdonia in year 7, annual ski trip in year 9, watersports in the South of France – and a biennial 'life changing' sixth form expedition to a developing country – recently Uganda – for three weeks, for those who can raise £4,000 for the trip.

Background and atmosphere: School is situated on the edge of the Northwood Hills in Pinner, surrounded by spacious playing fields with the feeling of being almost in the country. Originally two grammar schools (St Mary's and St Nicholas) that merged in 1977, in a what is now one large, rather nondescript 1950s building joined together internally via various passageways and corridors – we were disorientated after five minutes. 'You get a very good induction tour when you first join and teachers spend a long time showing you around', one pupil told us. 'They expect you to get lost in the beginning', another said.

A stark difference between the old and the new, 'the start of the yellow part denotes the new', we were told. First off, the new sports hall, which was very impressive. Bright with underfloor heating and well equipped with foldaway trampolines and badminton nets – soundproofed, too. Also impressive was the fairly recent sixth form block, amongst the best we have seen and simply vast. On offer was a choice of cold and hot food (so good that staff choose to eat there), a colourful chill out area, a pool table, computer area and a couple of quiet study areas, all partly cased in a glass exterior. Worth joining the sixth form for, we thought.

School has also benefited from a £5 million art and design building and £2 million music and performing arts centre (three music rooms, drama studio and music mixing room, plus one-to-one teaching rooms). The head told us: 'We did get quite a large cash injection, but the problem is the money has now all dried up. We have to be far more enterprising about how we raise funds.' This includes letting out the site the weekends to everyone from the Italia Conti Theatre School to local cricket and football teams.

Pupils looked well turned out in their navy and black uniforms with different coloured ties for each year group. 'It means that teachers can quickly look into the classroom from the outside and see which year is being taught.' A typical comp made up of all shapes and sizes – the handful we spoke to were a bright bunch with strong opinions and no major complaints. All seemed very happy to be there. We were particularly impressed with the two extremely eloquent and engaging sixth formers who showed us around. We chatted politics (Brexit) amongst other things.

Pastoral care, well-being and discipline: Most significantly, a new 'relationship charter' has recently been introduced, with everything now geared towards positive reinforcement rather than punishment. One parent said: 'Before this, pupils got a C1 (a first warning) for forgetting a pen but also for throwing a chair, which seems a bit crazy. With this new method they are doing away with detentions and actually talking to the child – finding out why they are late. Did something happen at home?' So far so good we hear, and pupils and parents are responding well: 'I for one am really happy that my children go to a school that is pro-change', one parent told us.

Hayden school values are reinforced throughout the building: Excellence, Respect, Perseverance, Community, Kindness. 'The students get really angry if a child misbehaves, that's the sort of school it is', one parent told us.

The school also has a great relationship with the local police (Hillingdon), who sometimes drop by for spot checks, and all pupils are required to walk through a metal detection arch for knives etc, with sniffer dogs for drugs. 'It's a great un-warned deterrent,' we were told. Parents are happy with school's approach to behaviour. 'I have always found that a high level of discipline is maintained from the minute the children arrive at the school,' said one.

School also operates a positive reward system, which 'is a great motivator: my child strives to get good news notes, commendations and other rewards.' Meanwhile a year 8 student said: 'I really look forward to the awards assembly. It's a way of showing how hard we are working.'

Several exclusions a year, but only as a last resort. 'We really don't want to permanently exclude unless we really have to. We also use an offsite provision (Jubilee Academy) to work with these young people.'

The biggest change the head has seen during his 20 years of teaching is sadly, but not unsurprisingly, the rise in mental health issues: 'I do blame social media for this. Snapchat is every head's nightmare.' School has brought in extra professionals to help with mental well-being (for staff too) and there are two full time student counsellors on board.

Bullying dealt with quickly and effectively, according to the parents we spoke to.

Pupils and parents: 'Haydon has a really good reputation round here,' a student told us, 'and all my friends at other schools wish they were here.' What is really special, we are told, is how many former pupils stay in touch: 'Quite a lot of them go into finance, and it is great when they come back to visit and tell the existing pupils how they got to where they are', says the head.

The school offers both pupils and parents a chance to voice their opinions – parent voice group meets four times per year. Many professional parents at the school, but a real mix as reflects this area of London. Active PTA which raises money via curry nights and quizzes etc.

Entrance: Most students live within a mile or so of the school. Admissions criteria: children in public care, then siblings, then children living nearest to the school, then employees' children. A good percentage of students join in the sixth form because of the variety of subjects on offer.

Exit: Around 40 per cent of pupils leave after GCSEs – for college, other schools, apprenticeships or employment – and up to 10 per cent after year 12. Some 80 per cent of sixth formers to university, around 30 per cent to Russell Group universities (the largest percentage of any state school in the borough). One to Cambridge in 2018 (veterinary medicine) and one to study medicine at Oxford.

Remarks: A friendly comprehensive that really does cater for all, with strong vocational courses as well as the more traditional A levels – all taught to a high standard. 'I would have no hesitation recommending Haydon,' said one parent. 'I feel my children are lucky to attend the school.'

The Henrietta Barnett School

Central Square, London NW11 7BN

Ages 11–18 **Pupils** 774 **Sixth form** 269

020 8458 8999
www.hbschool.org.uk

Head: Since 2014, Del Cooke BSc MBA NPQH (50s), previously head of Sir William Perkins's School in Surrey. Maths graduate with MBA in educational management, her broad experience covers the comprehensive system, sixth form college, adult education and boarding at Cranleigh, where she was head of maths, housemistress and finally deputy head. Although relatively new, she is increasingly seen as the embodiment of HBS – smart, quick-witted, friendly and empathetic. 'The girls want to hang out with her. She is like them,' summed up one parent. We found her instantly likeable, not remotely intimidating and surprisingly low-key. Made no dramatic changes so far ('It's such a fantastic school, you'd have to be pretty pompous to come in and turn it upside down,' she says), but is known as a visible head, particularly interested in getting the girls' views on various aspects of the school, and is clearly keen to focus more heavily on celebrating individual achievements. No bad thing, point out some parents, who say the girls can be 'far too modest, and need reminding how amazing they are'. Has a passion for music, playing a number of instruments, including self-taught bassoon. Married with three sons.

H

Academic matters: Consistently top or very near the top of both the GCSE and A level league tables. In 2018, 95 per cent A*-A/9-7 at GCSE (including a record-breaking 82 per cent of grades at A*/9-8), 74 per cent A*/A at A level. Most do 11 GCSEs, three or four As. Results strong across all subjects at GCSE, with a bias towards maths and sciences at A level, which around three-quarters of pupils choose, although history and English also have a healthy representation. Languages prioritised, with French, German and Latin for all in year 7, plus Spanish for all in years 8 and 9. Plus an option of ancient Greek. No setting.

Myths about this school being an academic hothouse, where girls are worked like dogs, are prolific, and even the head was initially put off the job because she thought it would be so pressurised. 'I was resistant, assuming the girls would be working in a ridiculously intensive environment. But it's the girls who drive the pace of learning and if anything, the staff sometimes have to tell the girls to slow down!' says the head. Pupils and parents agree, with one saying her daughter had just been advised to 'take some time out of her revision schedule to do something more relaxing.' Girls are encouraged to be independent, albeit well-supported, learners from day one, with many setting up their own societies and visiting universities for extra lectures. During our visit, we saw one noticeboard with pages from HB Scientist, the sixth-form produced (and very professional looking) science magazine that is sold throughout the school, whilst plenty of posters around the school advertised forthcoming speakers that pupils have organised – Zadie Smith when we visited.

Competitive learning is frowned upon, making way for a supportive atmosphere and strong sense of co-operation, which everyone agrees is a huge aid to the girls excelling academically. Teachers could hardly be considered more dedicated, although many parents say more of them are needed. 'Every one of the teachers would be a good candidate for a head of department in a private school, earning 50-100 per cent more money, but they choose to stay here because of the quality of the school and the commitment of the girls, which makes them very, very special,' said one parent. Girls love the fact that many of the teachers have had (non-teaching) careers in their subjects, also praising the informal relationships they have with them and level of responsibility the girls are given. Homework is given if and when teachers feel it's required, rather than hours every evening for the sake of it.

Games, options, the arts: Historically sports not brilliant, although improved facilities – large multi-purpose Astroturf court for netball, hockey, football and volleyball – have helped, with the school increasingly winning at both a local and borough level and holding its own against some top private schools. Facilities also include a gym, a state-of-the-art fitness suite with a good range of exercise equipment and a variety of pitches available on the nearby Hampstead Heath extension. 'Sport is very much on the up,' insists the head and there's a long list of exercise alternatives, including zumba, fencing, tang soo do, yoga, fitness, indoor rowing, cricket, badminton and dance. Rugby and athletics are also increasingly popular. No swimming pool but occasional opportunities for swimmers to take part in school events.

H

Thriving music department, with a symphony orchestra that everyone agrees is a joy to listen to, especially at concerts in the nearby ambient St Jude's Church. There are other orchestras and plenty of choirs, along with all manner of bands, including swing and rock. All pupils study music in key stage 3 and many go on to GCSE. Plenty of private tuition in a wide range of instruments, including double bass, bassoon and French horn, and there is an organ scholarship. Great excitement about the music wing built in 2011. 'Previously, we were taught music in our classroom or temporary huts, so it's a major thing,' said one pupil, who showed us the well-stocked rehearsal room and studio, with several soundproofed practice rooms. The same wing is home to drama, another lively department with strong facilities, with recent performances including Hamlet (year 9s), a play about Henrietta Barnett (year 7s) and a school-wide Our Country's Good.

Mirroring this wing, on the other side of the main building, is the DT and art block. Downstairs, the spacious DT room is home to all kinds of interesting inventions, including a Batman-style wooden chair and scooter that changes colour when exposed to sunlight. Meanwhile, the upstairs art room is a fantastic space, with some seriously talented work on display across all media. The wrap-around balconies on both wings are both aesthetically pleasing and provide an outside space for students to work during the summer months.

Lots of extracurricular opportunities, including Mandarin, tobotics (year 8 team recently got through to world championships in USA), creative writing, philosophy society, LAMDA, and many pupil-led activities. For instance, sixth formers currently teach Japanese to younger ones, as well as running a current affairs club, with speakers (invited by pupils themselves) including Melissa Benn and Lucy Holmes.

School trips, through each subject department, take every year group out once a year, with recent examples including Iceland (geography) and Greece (classics). 'It was easily the best holiday I've ever been on, just unbelievably interesting and fun,' said one pupil who went on the latter. French and German exchanges and Spanish trip to Seville. When we visited, 65 students were getting ready to head to the Rhineland for a music tour. Lots of day trips, particularly to theatres, museums and art galleries. Enrichment week, held in the summer, provides an entire week of outings. Own field study centre in Dorset, which every pupil visits for one week during her early years at the school.

Background and atmosphere: Founded in 1911 by formidable social reformer Dame Henrietta Barnett, the school is housed in architecturally stunning Lutyens designed buildings in upmarket Hampstead Garden Suburb. Not unlike the kind of buildings you'd find at Harvard of Stanford, it's also a beautifully landscaped campus. Facilities top-notch, particularly the colour-coded science labs and new swanky new wings for art, DT, music and drama, plus newly refurbished and extended library. Floors are polished parquet, classrooms are light and airy and corridors are tastefully decorated with everything from a recent photography competition to huge science-inspired pictures. Dining hall, where food is praised, and all-day café for year 10 upwards. Parts of the interiors could do with a lick of paint. But overall facilities feel spacious, with excitable students loving their environment, including after school, when something is going on pretty much every evening.

Pastoral care, well-being and discipline: 'No bells, no detention, no rules – it's so relaxed that if you came to school in your pyjamas no one would bat an eyelid,' wrote Tatler in its 2015 review, words that are now a source of great pride (not to mention humour) in the school 'simply because they are so true,' explained one pupil. Even a mention of the word 'discipline' will get you a blank look among pupils ('Why would you play up?' one said, genuinely bemused), whilst any occasional quirkiness that's perhaps inevitable among such an academic bunch is accepted as normal and certainly never teased. 'A few weeks ago, a whole class came out of art with painted-on moustaches and top hats from drama – it was so HBS,' laughed one girl. But this is no St Trinian's. Far from it, the girls' behaviour is impeccable and they always do their best, as well as being delightful and friendly. 'If a girl did step out of line, the teacher would just have a chat, adult-to-adult,' says the head, who believes it's the fact that the girls are treated like adults – with all the respect and trust that goes with that – that accounts for the lack of need for rules.

Bullying a non-issue, whilst part-time counsellors are on hand to deal with any problems. Currently a big push on reducing the stigma of mental health issues, with several noticeboards pointing to relevant resources. Strong student council, which is particularly strong in recruitment and raised funds for the new library, plus lunch council.

Pupils and parents: Girls are extremely bright and eager to learn, as well as both interesting and interested. Clear team spirit, where girls in different years bond naturally as well as through schemes like the student-led 'vertical families.' 'Of course, you get friendship groups, but absolutely no cliques,' said one pupil. 'It's a real community where everyone knows you and supports you,' said another. The school has always had a wide catchment area, based as it was on the vision of providing education to bright girls regardless of their means, although since the arrival of league tables, some pupils come in too far for the head's liking. ('I do question whether it's a good thing for some to travel really long distances.') Those in London mostly walk, cycle or get the bus or tube (Golders Green). There's also a parent-organised bus service to cater for those who can't easily get there by public transport.

Great ethnic mix – about a fifth Indian and a fifth white British, the rest from a variety of backgrounds. 'The school is the multicultural, meritocratic face of Britain,' said one parent, proudly. PTA provides refreshments at events, along with the odd quiz night, but not as active as some, particularly for socialising. 'It's inevitable, with families coming from such a wide area and diverse backgrounds,' said one parent, which probably also explains why after-school social life is not as vibrant as elsewhere.

Entrance: It doesn't get more selective than this, with 2800+ applying for 100 places. Some families move house once they have a place; others travel for long distances. Verbal and numerical reasoning tests in September, then the top 300 are invited back for English and maths tests in October. Pupils come from 50-60 primaries. Priority to looked after children and up to 20 on pupil premium who have been ranked in the top 300.

For sixth form, approximately 600 apply for a further 55-60 places, with six grade 7s at GCSE minimum requirement, including 7s in intended A level subjects. Girls already in the school are also expected to achieve this requirement, although in reality most far exceed it.

Exit: Up to 10 per cent leave after GCSE, mostly to sixth form colleges. Twenty-four to Oxbridge in 2018. Lots of medics and dentists (36 medics, dentists and vets in 2018) and a good cross-section of all other subject areas. Team of sixth form tutors provide UCAS advice, including raising expectations of what can be achieved. Alumni include Sarah Solemani (actress and television script writer), Ros Altmann (previously pensions minister), Baroness Evans of Bowes Park (leader of the House of Lords and Lord Privy Seal) and Debbie Wiseman (composer).

Money matters: Regular fundraising via PTA, pupil-led initiatives and a parental support scheme to which many parents regularly donate.

Remarks: One of the top academic state schools in the country, yet also one of the most liberal and nurturing; it's hard to exaggerate the emotional buy-in from pupils. 'The school becomes part of your DNA in a profound way,' said one. 'I don't know what happens when you get inside those four walls, but it is genuinely unique and stays with you for life.' Producing friendly, fun and delightful girls who come out with academic results that quite literally make the world their oyster, it's no wonder that top universities and employers love it too. 'My only sadness is that I can't see how it will ever be this good again,' said one pupil. A gentle and inspiring education for extremely bright girls, in a fabulous setting.

Hereward House School

119

14 Strathray Gardens, London NW3 4NY

Ages 4–13 **Pupils** 172

Fees: £16,500 – £16,950 pa

020 7794 4820
www.herewardhouse.co.uk

Headmaster: Since 2014, Pascal Evans (40s), formerly at Westminster Under and Colet Court. Gentle, reflective, low-key – but do not be deceived: Mr Evans has a very supple mind (with a law degree from Oxford) and is a man of wide-ranging talents and interests – passionately interested in football, and a serious runner who still puts in some 40 miles a week. 'I like the thinking time,' he says. 'Most of the knottier problems can be untangled in the course of a longish run'. Married with a Japanese wife and two teenage daughters – both trilingual.

Entrance: Most boys arrive in the September following their 4th birthday. As one might expect of a relatively small school which lies in the heart of Belsize Park, it's heavily oversubscribed. But Mr Evans and his colleagues are emphatic that they want an entrance process which is humane, conducted according to a criteria that is rational and democratic. Parents need to try to get their sons' names down by 2, but the testing is very gentle and every effort is made to take siblings of existing pupils. The emphasis is to identify families who can share the school's values and ethos and enable them to work for the best interests of the child. 'As the boys grow older it's always reassuring if one spots a child who, say, loves music, or sport,' says the head, 'quite as much as a potential scholar. But we're also looking to see if we can help them to taste or become immersed in new experiences.'

Obviously, there are a lot of Hampstead children here, but the reach goes further than that – lots from Islington as well as others from central London. There's some busy school bussing, but lots of tube and bus rides, as well – inevitably – as journeying on foot and by car.

Exit: Destinations testify to the school's ability to cater handsomely for the upper as well as less lofty academic echelons. 'Unstinting time spent on individual children,' said a parent, 'and an equal commitment to the needs of different children are having a big impact on selection.' When pre-testing was introduced by many top senior schools, a range of good prep schools found some pupils unexpectedly short of offers. There were indications that Hereward House was, briefly, among them – but, if so, it certainly wised up very quickly. Locals UCS and Highgate most popular destinations in 2018, but also Westminster, Haileybury (scholarship), St Albans, Mill Hill and Brighton College (scholarship) – as head says, 'pastoral boarding at its best can be transformative for some boys'. This kind of 'catholicity' used to be typical of London prep schools, but vaulting parental ambition of the last two decades can all too easily leave children and parents feeling second best. It is much to the credit of Mr Evans and his staff that they want no part of that.

Remarks: One of the charms of Hereward House is that it is small enough to be intimate – people know one another. The youngest children are carefully nurtured in basic social skills and helped towards physical literacy. Music and games, play and art and drama are all given due emphasis. Of course, all the time this is going on they are receiving a careful grounding in the rudiments of reading and writing and numeracy, which serves as an excellent springboard for the time when they gradually gravitate away from the form teacher to subject specialists.

Because of the size, systems here can be low-key. There are fewer than 20 staff members, but they tend to be versatile as well as highly capable. Obviously, the need for expertise is understood: there are two permanent special needs teachers and extra assistants brought in as required. But the culture supports turning one's hand to come-what-may: the headmaster teaches a decent number of lessons and views marking prep, setting classes and carrying chairs up and downstairs as a natural and perfectly appropriate task. The supremely capable director of music is also head of classics. In a modest-sized school, everyone pitches into the drama – the majority of senior boys were heavily involved in the recent production of The Sound of Music. 'Staff here,' says the head admiringly, 'just knuckle down. I find their example continually reassuring and admirable.' In the words of one parent: 'The teaching my son is receiving is of the highest calibre – the delivery is sympathetic and often original, and the substance is challenging'.

The potential downside of 'smallness' of course, could be the lack of choice. The 2016 ISI report, while mainly very complimentary, did suggest that the extracurricular curriculum lacked an element of range as well as some ICT provision. The school has since invested heavily in both hardware and systems management, and the results are welcomed by all parties, although the school website feels mundane and clearly needs some love. Philosophy and Mandarin have also been introduced and new clubs have appeared – coding, Greek and LAMDA all have their own enthusiastic followers. 'He has more after-school clubs from which to choose than he can ever manage,' said a parent, 'and he comes home enthused'.

Above all, there is no trade-off in terms of quality. Because the school is on a relatively small site, there may be a patronising assumption on the part of bigger preps that their own standards are higher. Yet the academics and music at Hereward House are outstanding and the drama and the sport are excellent. Given the number of pupils, it doesn't field the endless numbers of teams of the bigger prep schools, but plays excellent football, cricket and cross-country and uses local facilities (whether it's Primrose Hill for the youngest children or Brondesbury Cricket Club for the older ones) to best advantage. Nor has it sacrificed choice – judo, basketball, hockey and tennis are among other sports played to a high standard. Results hold up well and – admittedly it's not yet a premier league sport – the school's five-a-side soccer players can hold up their heads with the very best.

The school's biennial music concert may not be held in a state-of-the-art 21st century acoustically-perfect concert hall in school grounds, but it's a powerful expression of school-wide dedication and there are ensembles concerts every term which draw in roughly half the school ('and there are many, many other boys doing excellent music in addition to these,' says the head.) 'Outstanding,' said one parent with a very musical child. 'How they bring off this range of talent and dedication in a small school defies all probability'. It's unsurprising, then, that Hereward House pupils have won top musical awards to Eton and Westminster in the past two years. There's also been a surge of popularity in recent times in chess, which is a lesson in forms 2 and 3. 'It's a great activity,' says the head, 'and a powerful education in its own right. I'm glad some of our boys are proving highly successful at it, but what I really value is that it's reaching out to all levels here.'

In the 2016 ISI report, inspectors raised an eyebrow at a system of governance. It isn't hard to see why: the founding head (and still proprietor) is chair of governors. Her grandson is the bursar, and the previous head (who departed at the end of 2014) sits on the governing body. And yet, like all quasi-family schools, the potential downsides are nullified when relationships between the key players are strong, and a former senior school head has recently become a governor. Mr Evans exudes calm and satisfaction, and demonstrably believes he has the latitude to function effectively while benefiting from the support of those who have known the school longest of all.

We saw impressively relaxed and happy staff and children, and this – given the constraints of space – suggests that every aspect of pupils' lives has been thoughtfully and effectively considered. 'In six years as a parent,' said one mother, 'there's never been a day when either of mine haven't wanted to go to school. I don't take that for granted.' There's also lots of good interaction with the local community, enacted through fundraising initiatives, fun runs, a carol service at the local church and links with the Simon Community for the homeless. Facilities are good (a lab had just been upgraded and the playground relaid when we came round) but there's an eye to what's practical and reasonable, rather than lavish – and therein lies a clue to the underlying ethos of the school. It wants its pupils to give their best in every area of school life and, perhaps above all, to find ways to be themselves while always behaving generously to others. To execute that vision, in the heart of one of the most affluent and challenging parental constituencies in the prep school world, demands clarity of vision and steadfastness of purpose. The head's low-key manner, and his gentle appreciation of his staff, pupils and parents, speaks not just well of him and of them, but also suggests the governors who appointed him know their school as well as their man.

H

Herne Hill School

The Old Vicarage, 127 Herne Hill, London SE24 9LY

Ages 2–7 **Pupils** 290

Fees: £6,225 – £14,955 pa

020 7274 6336
www.hernehillschool.co.uk

Headteacher: Since 2016, Ngaire Telford (pronounced Nyree) 50s, a lady who radiates positivity and affection. She originally trained and taught at secondary school level in New Zealand, but fell in love with early years teaching after coming to the UK and being posted to a primary school in the Old Kent Road as a supply teacher – a baptism that might have frightened off a lesser soul. Took a 10 year career break to have four children of her own, all of whom went to Herne Hill School, thereby introducing her to the place. After teaching reception here part time, she became head of early years in 2009, then deputy head, and took on the headship in 2016. 'It really is a dream job for me, because this is such a lovely place to work.' Married to Duncan, a management consultant.

Tall, slender, elegant, beautifully dressed and full of joie de vivre, she is the very embodiment of a fulfilled working mother. Parents love her. 'She is simply the most inspiring head teacher I have ever met,' wrote one. 'She knows every child by name, she knows all their little quirks and is genuinely interested in their well-being and that of their family.' 'Mrs Telford's leadership is brilliant,' wrote another. 'Leads by example with her warmth and commitment'. 'Calm, focused, fun and very glamorous! 'I don't know how she manages to run the school like a family but also with such rigour.'

Interests include running, singing, and early music, particularly Bach, which may account for her remarkable equanimity.

Entrance: First come first served, and early registration is advised. There are three entry points: kindergarten (2+), pre-reception (3+), and reception (4+). School takes up to 60 children into kindergarten, but won't have more than 40 in school in any one session. Total year group number in pre-reception and reception is capped at 70, so places at these entry points limited by numbers coming up from kindergarten. However, every year there are children who move on at 4+ to the Dulwich Triangle schools, so it's always worth applying.

Gentle and informal assessment process. School looks for self-esteem and confidence, the ability to engage with the teacher, and the child's listening and communication skills. For those applying to reception, it's a bonus if they can write their name, but 'not the end of the world if they can't.' Some sibling priority, but points are taken off for parents who took their first child out to start reception elsewhere.

Exit: About a third of pre-reception children leave for state schools such as Dulwich Hamlet, and independents such as JAPPS, DUCKS, etc. However, school does not prepare for 4+.

After year 2 everyone leaves, most to the six local independent schools that offer 7+ entry: Dulwich College Junior, JAPS, Alleyn's Junior, Sydenham High, Dulwich Prep London and Rosemead. Head meets with all parents individually to plan (and sometimes manage) expectations, and school's track record of success is long-established. 'Everyone gets a place somewhere, most get multiple offers. Choosing is the hardest part.'

Remarks: Housed in the former vicarage of St Paul's Church, Herne Hill School began life in 1976 as a nursery school when the vicar's wife couldn't find one she liked for her own children. It became a prep-prep 10 years later in response to parental requests, and now it's one of the most highly regarded providers of early years education in an area not short of same. The beautiful original red-brick mansion is still the hub of the school, but the garden has been developed into an excellent children's playground complete with Astroturf. Tasteful new buildings provide space for the school's growing needs and numbers: the Oak Building, built underground to avoid taking up playground space, contains a splendid all-purpose hall with bleacher seating, beautifully-resourced kindergarten rooms and the kitchen. Since 2002, school has been owned by Swiss businessman Dominik Magyar, who works closely with the head and has brought the buildings and resources to their present very high level.

Preparing children for 7+ entry is a major part of the school's raison d'être, but the curriculum here is imaginative and the approach is child-initiated. As head observes, 'Learning needs to be about doing what children love, and they won't be 6 and 7 again!' We loved the Talk For Writing unit, where children learnt ancient Greek letters whilst studying Theseus and the Minotaur, and the maths room that was a riot of colour and creativity. French taught by native speaker, and the children spoke with beautiful accents. 'Fantastic teaching staff!' was the verdict of every parent we spoke to, and the standard of work on the walls, both in accuracy and inventiveness, bore this out. 'Lessons are fun yet challenging, and I have nothing but praise for every teacher we have encountered,' wrote one mother; 'my daughter has adored each one and has come on in leaps and bounds.' A father added, 'Insanely good teachers – where do they get the energy?' Staff-pupil ratio of 1:6 ensures everyone gets the attention they need. The learning support coordinator has her own room, cheerful and well-equipped, and supports a range of needs such as dyslexia, AD, EAL with a variety of interventions including one-to-one sessions.

Unsmiling and unshaven after the demands of putting 70 children through their paces for the leavers' show dress rehearsal, the music director nonetheless directed a bravura performance from the piano, although the play itself struck us as something of a propaganda exercise – we were a little startled when all the children carolled 'We're learning through play!' Parents admit themselves completely entranced by it all. 'The school's music teaching must be about the best in the country judging from the Lloyd-Webber-esque quality of its productions – the amazing choral and wind instrument performances teased out of pupils is staggering,' enthused a parent.

Forest school sessions are given weekly to all children in pre-reception and above in the school's own rather magical woodland area at the back of the school. 'I'm an outdoors girl myself,' explained the head, 'and the learning you do outdoors is so important.' Woodwork recently added to the curriculum, taught by an early years specialist.

Wide-ranging and inclusive sports provision by dedicated sports teacher on and off site includes gymnastics, football, cricket, velodrome club and swimming at Crystal Palace. Outside lessons, there are lots of optional activities available including baking, art club, slime club and jigsaw club, but the children are equally welcome just to relax and play with friends. 'We're quite big on unstructured time here.' Regular trips to eg Kew Gardens, Godstone Farm, The Polka Theatre, Leeds Castle, Battersea Children's Zoo.

'Love, Care, Excellence' are the school's founding principles, and parents raved about the pastoral care. 'There is a real emphasis on nurturing each individual child and promoting kindness and respect for each other,' wrote a mother. 'The team there create a wonderful atmosphere for young children, whose childhood is extended somehow by experiencing school in such a supportive and friendly environment,' was another comment. Mindfulness and reflection actively promoted. Yoga is taught twice a term – 'the breathing exercises help get rid of the butterflies,' said a young performer we met before the dress rehearsal. All the year 2 children either sit on the school council or act as a playground buddy to younger pupils, and the Big Brothers and Sisters Club arranges for them to read and play with the little ones. 'We feel it's a very special school,' said a mother, 'founded with real love, and it genuinely nurtures very happy children.' The school is non-denominational, but children attend harvest, Easter and Christmas services at St Paul's Church in the grounds.

After a change in the catering provision, the lunches are now superb – the best we've ever eaten in an early years setting. Dishes are freshly prepared on site, beautifully presented and genuinely appetising – we liked the jerk chicken, carefully toned down to appeal to young palates but delicious nonetheless. Puddings are low on sugar but popular and nourishing – we enjoyed our compote with yogurt and granola. Parents, most of whom are hard-working professionals, are as grateful as the children, and make full use of the breakfast and after-school clubs, where children from reception to year 2 can stay until 6pm (4.45pm for the pre-schoolers). Most families live within walking distance, but some come from as far as Brixton, Crystal Palace, East Dulwich and Nunhead.

When choosing to bring their children here, parents have to factor in the need to send them elsewhere at 7. The school has made such a success of being a stand-alone pre-prep, however, that we're inclined to think Herne Hill has got it right and that it's all the other schools who've got it wrong. 'Sending our children here enabled us to look for the right school for them at the right time,' as one parent put it. In the words of another, 'Superb school, sublime class teachers, very happy kids. I wish I still went to school.'

Highgate Junior School

Linked with Highgate School

3 Bishopswood Road, London N6 4PL

Ages 3–11 **Pupils** 400

Fees: £18,165 – £19,230 pa

020 8340 9193
www.highgateschool.org.uk

Principal of junior school: Since 2002, Mark James (50s), BA theology Nottingham University, followed by a PGCE in English from the London Institute and an MA from King's College London. Grew up in Somerset where he worked for a term at Wellington School: 'I had far too much fun running around with the kids and decided then that this was what I wanted to do.' He started his career in the state sector – Tiffin Grammar in Kingston – followed by a decade at Dulwich College, prior to becoming deputy head at King's Wimbledon School junior school: 'It was there I made the transition from senior school to juniors, after my wife suggested I give it a try. I loved it.' This is the head who had the task of transforming Highgate boys' 7-13 prep into a modern mixed junior 7-11 junior school: 'When the

H

school took the decision to go co-ed with the ambition to be academic and selective it created a unique place in the market.'

Friendly, down to earth, all round nice guy – who certainly doesn't come across as being filled with a sense of his own importance, yet as principal of Highgate Junior School and head of admissions for the whole school, Mr James is THE guy to know for desperate parents vying for a place at the school. But he stands resolute and assures us that places at the school can only be obtained through a child's own merits and the Highgate assessment procedure: 'Parents can inevitably be disappointed if their child is not offered a place, especially if they already have a child in the school, but as I often say it has to be right for each child and the offer has to be justified based on the evidence we have'.

Popular with parents and pupils alike: 'firm but fair', 'approachable', open to ideas', 'knows all the pupils and parents', 'involved in everything.' He is an enthusiastic can-do character, with a boyish charm and sense of humour (as was evident from the large jellybean jar crammed to the brim in his office). Married to a teacher – they have two daughters both who have both gone through Highgate School. One parent told us: 'It helps that he's had kids who have gone all the way through the school, so he knows the score.'

H

Of his role at Highgate School, Mr James says: 'I feel very lucky that I like what I do – what's not to like?' We couldn't help feeling the same as we stepped out of his office into the splendour that is the newly built junior school.

Head of pre-prep since 2012, Diane Hecht DCE (50s). Previously deputy head of St Columba's Junior School in Kilmacolm, she came south as two of her grown-up children had settled in London and feels that she has found a wonderfully similar school in Highgate. 'The girls here wear exactly the same tartan skirts as at St Columba's – it was meant to be!' Warm, efficient and enthusiastic.

Entrance: Hugely oversubscribed – 350 try for the 36 places at 3+. Sane and lovely pre-prep head admits that assessing 2 year olds has to be on the arbitrary side, so do not be amazed if your astounding tot just doesn't astound on assessment day. Teachers observe them at play in groups, look for capacity to listen and follow instructions, general sociability – so don't make them learn their letters the night before. Moving to 4+ entry from 2021.

At 7+ your child will be up against around 300 others battling it out for 50/60 places. Assessments at this stage consist of a reading test and an English and maths paper. Approx two-thirds of candidates will be invited back for a 'fun and interactive lesson' and a practical lesson which could be anything from art to music or science and, based on the outcome of that, will be invited for an interview: 'We are looking for an active and engaged child – a spark that sets them apart.' Other things count (where you live, parental statement etc), but not massively, it has to be said. No sibling policy, but 'every sibling is guaranteed an interview.' As far as school connections or being an Old Cholmeleian go, no preferential treatment we are told: 'oh no, that doesn't exist anymore.' Definitely have a plan B.

Exit: Nearly all go from the pre-prep to the juniors and nearly all go from there to the senior school. 'If your child has got into the school you're going to try your utmost to make sure they stay.' Plenty of warning given to those unlikely to thrive in the higher stages. Pupils generally only leave for financial reasons.

Remarks: There are schools (and we've been to many many private schools) – and then there's the £25m Highgate Junior School, so brand spanking new at the time of our visit, the imported fossilised stone was still setting. Tucked into Bishopswood Road – one of the many prestigious roads that line the route from Highgate to Hampstead – this two year undertaking (financed by the judicious sale of former boarding houses) was a project of deep consideration. The powers that be were very aware that whilst it was important for the school to have some sort of artistic mark to it, they didn't want the space to look like a museum, 'but one which would have appeal and comfort for our younger pupils.'

On entering the building one is immediately drawn to a breathtaking feature wall in the reception area, which was the work of a specially commissioned artist. Portland fossilised stone provided the backdrop with a design which gently curves its way to the upper level. Reptiles and amphibians of various kinds are sculpted into the walls and at various points throughout the school, to encourage children to explore and discover different surfaces and textures as part of their learning exploration. We were also told that this was based on the Fibonacci principle of combining maths with biological settings. (At this point we nodded sagely, had no idea what was being said and felt very inadequate.)

Light, space and fluidity are the core elements of the design. Entering the bright circular atrium, you can observe the goings on all around on both levels. This feeling of transparency was very much key to the design, 'so that visitors can see great things going on..rather than relying on pretty corridors of prepared displays.' The school offers bright and spacious classrooms, science laboratories, specialist rooms for art, DT, ICT, drama and music. Our favourite bit was the 360 retractable seat hall for assemblies and concerts etc. All classrooms, on the upper level or lower level, open onto a wonderful outdoor space. Balconies at the top – enclosed garden areas on the lower level with reading pods. The outdoor space also includes a small amphitheatre, a literary garden and a wonderful adventure playground, all surrounded by the extensive Highgate playing fields. Simply idyllic.

However, as we know from experience, a beautiful building doth not a good school make, so this school had much to live up to. We were shown around by two lively and phenomenally bright pupils, one of whom will no doubt be the brains behind something quite wonderful in years to come. The only pupil we have met to date who was trying to explain the ergonomics of desk sizes in the class in relation to the seating. But he did this without any pretentiousness, or awareness of how quirky this might appear. As one parent told us, 'most Highgate kids are just regular kids, without an air of snootiness, or look at us – we're the rich kids. That's what makes it so special.' We had to agree: all the pupils we met were like any other – happy, spirited, at times noisy, curious and just very astute.

Hardly surprising when you consider what they have to do in order to get in at 7+ (if they don't come in via the pre-prep route). Once in, pupils can expect a challenging but fun time, 'the best' we are told. The day starts at 8.25am prompt and then it's full throttle into the learning day with the added injection of a smorgasbord of languages on offer. Unlike most other primary schools with 'only' French on the syllabus, Highgate Juniors can expect everything from French and German to Japanese, Gujarati and Russian, with the aim of instilling a love of languages, since they have no need to pass an entrance exam.

Teaching staff, who were praised by one parent as being 'beyond anything', struck us as being a particularly young and attractive bunch. A low turnover of staff and continuity throughout the school no doubt contributes to the school's success. Teachers are fairly heavily vetted and there is an open door policy for all classrooms, for regular observation: 'Each term we have roughly 30 observations, which are graded, and if they are not where we would hope they would be, we would need to do something to bring up their levels.' Fairly tough, some might say, but there are reputations to uphold.

Class sizes don't exceed 22, and are set from year 5 in maths. The school can cope with mild SEN, but because of its selective nature, numbers are quite small. Dedicated SENCo and part-time learning support person. School doesn't believe in much one-to-one; they adopt a more inclusive approach 'so that pupils don't miss out.'

Homework, we were told by both pupils and parents, was slightly on the heavy side. One parent told us: 'The workload can be a bit much at times, but my daughter doesn't struggle as she's used to it from pre-prep. I imagine if you come in at the 7+ stage, it might be more difficult.'

Academia aside, there is so much going on. 'Everyone has their chance to shine in the sun', says the head and sport is a biggie here. It would be difficult for it not to be with the phenomenal facilities on offer, both outdoors and at the Mallinson Sports Centre. Everyone gets the chance to play, we are told, and both juniors and seniors are known to do well in competitive sports.

Drama and music thrive. Many children take individual instrumental lessons and in addition to these, there is a school orchestra, and numerous ensembles. Drama is taught as a separate subject throughout the school, and there are termly drama productions within and across year groups. Active drama club.

Lots of extracurricular going on too. It's amazing that these young kids can cram it all in, but somehow they do. Robotics club, maths club, newspaper club, debating, Minecraft, Lego, creative literacy, chess and mosaic making are just a handful of what's on offer – not to mention the multitude of sports clubs (including water polo). Lunch time lectures are offered mainly by parents whose kids attend the school (and there is a veritable feast of who's who).

A very sociable school with 'a big heart', one parent told us. Tons of charitable events organised by the school's enthusiastic PTA. Indeed last year we were told they raised a staggering 50k for various charities, via the usual summer and Christmas fairs and school productions plus the less usual sales of teddy bears, friendship bracelets, umbrellas and pupil-designed cookbooks. Parents are in the main a prosperous bunch, but a couple of the parents we spoke to were not particularly high earners: they just decided to make their child's education a complete priority.

Pre-prep separately, delightfully (and permanently) housed. Starts at nursery – 18 morning or afternoon tots in lively spacious space both inside and out with smiley, lively teachers. Whole school theme of colour and light when we visited and lots of attractive work on show. Glorious herd of Elmer elephants made from plastic milk cartons and coloured paper. Lovely singing – the most in-tune bunch of rising 5s we've heard. An orderly, relaxed and friendly school. We saw much warm interaction between staff and small people and just wanted to stay and watch.

Highgate School

Linked with Highgate Junior School

122

North Road, London N6 4AY

Ages 11–18 **Pupils** 1,400 **Sixth form** 317

Fees: £20,970 pa

020 8347 3564
www.highgateschool.org.uk

Head: Since 2006, Adam Pettitt MA (40s). Oxford modern and medieval linguist. Taught French and German at Eton, Oundle and Abingdon and was second master at Norwich School, under Jim Hawkins, former head of Harrow – a formidable team. Has French wife and school-age children and is quite the most interesting, eloquent and thought-provoking head this veteran GSG reviewer has met in many a long school visit. Propelled by a sharply focused and incisively articulated moral and educational philosophy, Mr Pettitt is spare, brilliant and energetic. He must be an exacting – though supportive – man to work for. His pupils can only benefit from his firm commitment to outreach to schools and to those without their advantages, to placing an understanding of language at the heart of modern languages, and to educational values rather than exams and results. The results will follow where this approach leads. Parents are unstinting in their praise. The most inspiring head we've met in years.

Academic matters: Head has a refreshing disrespect for the bodies deserving of it: 'You choose the exam board on the basis that it will have the least distorting effect on the way you want to teach' – bingo! IGCSEs now in Englishes, sciences, langs and history and many subjects now opt for the Pre-U as an alternative to A levels. This can only enhance the nature and quality of learning. English and langs the first to head this way. Mr Pettitt the 'de facto head of MFL' at the time of our visit so langs getting the oxygen they needed and number of takers is sure to rise. Mandarin now through to sixth form; computer science a GCSE option. Maths much the most popular A level and, with further maths, has impressive results. Also strong are English, art, Latin, all sciences and RS. Tiny numbers take theatre studies, Greek, classics, music – school does not offer music tech nor other popular 'modern' subjects eg textiles, psychology and loses a few post-GCSE on that account. Number of subject options (24) felt by some to be a little limited, given the size of the sixth form, and some sixth formers would like more drama and art. However, good innovations include the 'knowledge curriculum' and 'critical method' courses. In 2018, 92 per cent A*-A/9-7 at GCSE and 75 per cent A*/A at A level/Pre-U. Lively, student-led conferences. Mr Pettitt takes all criticism on the chin and, given that over 70 per cent of the staff are his appointees, this – as everything else – is fast developing.

Head's inclusive approach is just that: 'The quality of the way you learn is critical and every child's experience is equally important. Every day is important – I am most interested in the way each one of us teaches and learns.' IBAC – Independence through Buzz, Aspiration and Collaboration – the new acronym around the place. So this is not the school that was, nor the one people think they know. The fabric – see below – is radically changing and the character equally so. This is encapsulated in the sane and sensitively individualised approach to SEN. The Victorian main building is not good for those with mobility problems though school says 'we will try to make it work by moving our routines and schedules as far as we can.' Director of learning support covers all three schools and is a renowned expert in autism. The support for all conditions and syndromes as they emerge is individual, tailored, supportive and 'concerned with management rather than labelling.' The very few with EAL needs are usually the very bright.

Games, options, the arts: Blessed with playing fields and space beyond the dreams of other London schools. If the educational philosophy and general zip in the place doesn't inspire you, the sporting facilities will. Girls' sport, some feel – school disputes – still catching up with boys'; football and netball still pre-eminent but plenty more on offer and played hard. Sports hall, pool, weights, Astroturfs, squash courts – it's all here. No country school could offer more.

Interior activities also privileged and currently being transformed by an enormous rolling building project that will add considerably to teaching space but also, it is hoped,

H

to an eventual sixth form and arts campus. Drama and music thrive – many productions, concerts of all kinds and tours; art a little undemonstrative at the time of our visit but some lively colourful work around. Mills Centre provides studio and gallery space. Cultural life better displayed in the admirable school publications – professional-looking periodicals on history, politics, science, theatre and thought written and produced by pupils. Terrific range of clubs (they include vinyl and philosophy, beekeeping, LGBT soc and feminist society), trips, exchanges and tours – extracurricular is praised by many but not fully taken advantage of by all. 'I used to feel that some pupils' cultural references were limited to Arsenal: great though that club is, I want them to see and know so much more,' comments the head, happy to stress to parents that while these opportunities are on offer it is up to pupils to take them up.

Lots of charitable and outreach activities for both staff and pupils – several staff now working at local state schools as part of community partnership work. This very much part of the Pettitt ethos – outreach is not a box ticking necessity here but an essential part of what it is to grow into a valuing and valuable person.

Background and atmosphere: A school with an up and down history. Founded as the Free Grammar School of Sir Roger Cholmeley, Knight at Highgate, in 1565 – former pupils still known as Old Cholmeleians. Became Highgate School in the late 19th century – and no longer free. The chapel, undergoing terrific refurb at time of our visit, 'complete brick by brick restoration, new roof, stained glass windows repaired and cleaned, apse painting restored etc; lighting and heating to render God's work less chilly and gloomy,' in Mr Pettitt's inimitable phrases – and main buildings are 19th century. Some impressive bits – old gothic central hall with Norman arches, leaded lights, wrought iron balcony and cantilevered ceiling and splendid new Sir Martin Gilbert library in old assembly hall. A real library which, unlike so many schools' learning resource centres, actually has books in it, alongside all its rows of PCs, and an atmosphere to encourage concentration and study.

By the 1960s, the school buildings (some considerably less felicitous), including boarding houses, were spread over the heart of Highgate Village – the premier north London suburb whose denizens refer to it as 'the village' and who are, understandably, rather smug about living there. Charter Building adds new subject rooms in a five-storey glass cube. All very high tech – interactive whiteboards and PCs everywhere. The whole site is now a mix of the new, light, glass-bound, airy and stylish, and the old, rather shabby, small passages and dark areas along which school operates a clever one-way system – but all likely to look a great deal smarter and more coherent in the next few years. Much tramping up and down the hill between the main buildings and the Mills Centre, playing fields etc, and each day sees orderly crocodiles with professional chaperones trailing along.

School suffered during the 70s and 80s and took time to recover its reputation. Girls joined the sixth form in 2004 and year 7 in 2006, and the whole school is now fully co-educational and fully rehabilitated. A Christian foundation and an inclusive one, with multi-faith assemblies and speakers from different religions on a weekly basis. House system – 12 houses – but no fanatical exclusive loyalty to these, rather a friendly rivalry in competitions etc and designed to encourage the mixing of year groups. 'It's a family school,' a parent told us. 'Not everyone is terrifically academic, though they really make the scholars work. They are very encouraging to everyone.'

Principal education sponsor of the London Academy of Excellence Tottenham, a new sixth form with Tottenham Hotspur as its business sponsor. This is the base for the Highgate Teaching Consultancy, offering specialist training in sixth form teaching which goes beyond exams.

Pastoral care, well-being and discipline: We saw only absorbed and concentrating classes with lively teaching. Discipline, as pupils gratefully pointed out, is not dependent on the whims of individual staff but 'whole school,' ie you know what is coming to you at every level should you transgress. Very little transgressing these days and we have seldom seen so few uniform infringements (has consulted on introducing gender neutral uniforms) – everyone is smart.

Small classes 'very well-monitored,' say parents. 'It's extremely well-run,' we were told. 'We are kept fully informed and have lots of email contact with staff,' another told us. 'The teaching staff are so enthusiastic and they really care about my children,' another enthused. Occasional loutishness clearly frowned on by majority of pupils, who are a civilised lot. 'We have sent all our children there – they're so different academically and in their characters – but all have been happy.'

Pupils and parents: From a wide area of north and more central London, though most live near, if not within walking distance. 'Not ruthlessly elitist,' as one parent put it but lots of City lawyers, accountants etc with clear idea of what they want from the school. Pupils are friendly, happy and articulate. Most seem proud to be at the school and keen not to jeopardise their futures. Notable OCs include Rt Hons Charles Clarke and Anthony Crosland, Michael Mansfield QC, Johnny Borrell of Razorlight, Ringo Starr's son Zak Starkey of Oasis and The Who, Orlando Weeks of The Maccabees and DJ Yoda, Phil Tufnell, Sir Clive Sinclair, Alex Comfort, Nigel Williams, Sir John Tavener, Barry Norman, Gerard Manley Hopkins and Sir John Betjeman. Doubtless, old girl Cholmeleians shortly to make their marks.

Entrance: Wildly oversubscribed at every stage – on a scale we see most commonly with the grammars. Six hundred apply at 11+ for the 90 places available when the junior school pupils have been accommodated. At 13+, only 6-8 places available; tests and interviews in autumn term of year 7. At 16+, some 120 for 30. At 11, around 60 per cent from state primaries and 40 per cent – mainly girls – from local preps. The tiny 13+ entry is mostly boys entering from the obvious preps – Arnold House, Devonshire House, The Hall, Keble etc.

Exit: Around a dozen, mostly boys, leave post GCSE to, mostly, Camden School for Girls, which has boys in the sixth. Around 90 per cent gain places at their first choice university – Bristol, UCL, Durham, Edinburgh and Leeds among most favoured; some now head to top US universities (six in 2018, plus two to Canada, two to Amsterdam and one to the Milan Institute of Fashion). Good numbers to Oxbridge each year – 32 places in 2018, plus six medics and two vets. Economics, English and languages are popular subject choices.

Money matters: Scholarships – music and academic – at all usual entry points and now purely honorary. 'Much kudos, but not just to the particularly brainy but to those who exemplify scholarship (persistence, creativity, setting own agenda, leading learning in the classroom, originality),' stresses head. Bursaries up to the value of 100 per cent fees available each year and most go to those who get all or most of that amount. School makes extensive efforts via primary school visits etc to reach those who need to know.

Remarks: A new school in all but site and name – co-ed, modern, delivering a first rate education to the lively minds and limbs lucky enough to get in.

Hill House International School

17 Hans Place, London SW1X 0EP

Ages 4–13 **Pupils** 656

Fees: £13,200 – £16,200 pa

020 7584 1331
www.hillhouseschool.co.uk

Principal: Since 2002, Richard Townend (early 70s) – organist, scholar, and son of the founder. The present head is calm, shrewd, gently impassioned by the vision of the school which he runs – and a wonderful foil for an egotistical and anxious world. The running of Hill House, while ultimately in his hands, is shared among his wife and two sons. His beliefs are refreshing simple: 'bring children up with plenty of love and affection, and an example which allows them to understand the boundaries by which we must all live'. To that, and an inspiring academic education, add lots of fresh air, games, skiing and mountaineering, swimming and music. The morning of our visit, he was taking a vast choir practice of over 90 children, preparatory to a school assembly held at St Columba's Church. That isn't how most heads operate today – more's the pity.

After some stinging criticisms from Ofsted in 2014, the school found itself forced to address a range of health and safety issues, and to oversee some structural shifts designed to safeguard academic progress. It is a mark of the head's quality that he believes much good resulted from the whole episode. It was also very telling that the Ofsted debacle was chiefly notable for provoking an outpouring of parental, pupil and old pupil love and faith.

Entrance: Prospective parents have to go on a tour of the place – there's no booking: you just show up at one of the advertised times (these happen four days a week). 'Hardly sounds very onerous,' says the head, 'but just occasionally you'll get someone who tries to avoid it. No tour, no place. Simple as that.' If you like the place, then you fill in an application form. There is a waiting list, but – given the fast-changing plans of young parents and the fact that many go abroad – vacancies often crop up. The school tries to sidestep entrance tests, especially for the youngest children. Mrs Townend, wife of the headmaster, is in charge of admissions. She and her team make it their job to be friendly and accessible. Now offers 8+ music and art scholarships.

Exit: Wide range of schools including boarding schools. Most pupils go on to London day schools: girls' destinations include Frances Holland SW1, Queen's Gate, JAGS, St Paul's, Putney High, More House. Boys to Dulwich College, Wetherby Senior, KCS, St Paul's, Dulwich, Westminster, inter alia. Boarding destinations include Stowe, Gordonstoun, Harrow, Abingdon, Benenden and Charterhouse.

Remarks: The youngest, aged 4 and 5, go to Small School to learn their rudiments – physical development, communication and language and social development. With lots of free play as well as structured lessons, the aim is to build up confidence and competence. They move from Flood Street to Pont Street when they are 5 or 6, and start to focus on English, handwriting, maths and reading, supplemented by supporting subjects as well as lots of music, drama and games. Then it's on to Cadogan Gardens and gradually learning to adapt to specialist subject teachers as well as the all-important form teacher. Aged 10 and 11, the girls and boys have separate classes, as they set about preparation for senior schools. Most girls leave at 11, while the great majority of boys stay to 13.

'The genius of Hill House,' said a parent, who is also an old pupil, 'is that they apply intelligence and thought to getting a child happy. Being happy means feeling reassured, not indulged. When they are surrounded by teachers who focus upon them with a fond and shrewd eye, they feel reassured. They can start to learn.'

There are three special needs teachers to support those with particular needs. The ethos of the school is to attend carefully to anything which may stand between a child and their ability to meet their potential, but also to guard against anxiety. 'Early intervention and calm management seems to level most things out very satisfactorily,' the head observes.

Staff reflect the school's commitment to diversity and cosmopolitanism – a spread of ages and backgrounds, but with a healthy quota of bright and fit young ones heralding from all over the word, as well as those from within London and the M25. This is a family school and, as presently constituted, nobody who isn't a Townend would appear able to climb to the very top of the tree. While this might work to demotivate a lesser teacher, the staff here palpably relish the wonderfully idiosyncratic extended family to which they, and everyone connected to the school, belong. The proof of that can be seen in the extraordinarily high rates of staff retention. The head's deep knowledge of his staff, and fond regard for them, is an eloquent advertisement for the school.

'Almost too much sport,' one parent said, 'except that it seems to embrace all pupils, and so the effect is everyone of them feels involved and wanted'. All pupils play sport at least once every day. Given that the school buildings are housed in the heart of Knightsbridge and Chelsea, this poses some logistical demands, but the sight of boys and girls in rust-coloured breeches is well-known to residents of SW3 and typically presages a visit to or from various indoor and outdoor grounds (Duke of York's, Battersea, Queen's Club – the list goes on for ever). Longer journeys are also made possible by a fleet of six minibuses, operated (as with everything else here) by in-house drivers. As well as all the usual rugby and netball, football, hockey and so forth, there are limitless opportunities for individual sports and a full complement of inter-school fixtures. A particular emphasis is placed on swimming – to which the late Colonel Townend, the school's founder, attached a passionate importance.

There is more art, music and drama than one can imagine. The head is a fine organist and, back in 1972, a fine two manual organ with mechanical action containing 456 pipes was especially commissioned for the school and installed in the music room in Hans Place. There is also a stock of over 300 orchestral instruments, which are loaned to boys and girls for the duration of their time at Hill House, and everyone gets a slice of the action. 'I've just watched my son play at Peter Jones,' said one parent, 'and my daughter at St Columba's Church. They're not prodigies, but they're thrilled to be involved. And so am I.' Among many other offerings, there is an annual Christmas musical as well as a regular dance and drama club. The school has three art galleries and children's work is displayed everywhere – all of it is framed. In a typical Hill House touch, the frames are bought at the local Habitat and knocked together expertly by the school's works department. The impression is terrific.

Hill House famously has an overseas annexe in Switzerland. Since 1960 this has been located at Glion, a mountain village over 700 metres above sea level looking out over Lake Geneva. The children are given an experience of a boarding school environment in the setting of a mountain village: there are geography CE project courses – and, of course, skiing.

The founder, Colonel Townend, opened the school in 1951 and was still in post in his 90s. His somewhat autocratic manner, the Knightsbridge address and the fact that the young Prince Charles arrived as a 7 year old newbie in 1956 have led many to assume that this is a school for toffs. That is quite unfair. Its vision has always been both forward-looking and international. It was among the very first of the so-called prep schools to welcome girls, its fees are a good deal lower than many local competitors, and its pupil constituency much broader socially than its elite addresses suggest. True, the place is superbly equipped, but it is also quite crowded, teeming with life. The children and staff are both industrious and relaxed. Both genders and all ethnic groups are fully represented at every level.

There is a series of handsome London houses – Hans Place is the site of the original school and this is where the headmaster and school offices are located, but there are other houses in Flood Street, Pont Street and Cadogan Gardens. Two idiosyncrasies seen in each are revealing: a discreet investment by the school in the latest chemical technology to ensure the loos are odour-free (an issue in some schools) and the fact that all the catering is done in-house by support staff who have mainly worked here for years and years. No agencies, no fuss and consistently terrific reports of school lunches. The day of our visit we passed chefs chopping mounds of fresh carrots alongside mountains of fresh fruit. That isn't typical fare in school kitchens, more's the pity.

The school has a huge local reputation – arguably one of the few fixed points in that restless, rootless world of Knightsbridge. It embraces the local community in the fullest sense, inviting local societies and residents' associations to concerts and plays and festivals, loaning its facilities at knock-down rates (or, where appropriate, free) and also doing a mass of fundraising for local children's charities.

The ethos of the school revolves around being tolerant, well-exercised, stimulated and kind, and contexts for nurturing each of these are embedded within every aspect of the school curriculum. There is a well worked-out chain of communication embracing form tutors, year and section heads, senior tutors and housemasters, all ultimately reporting to the pastoral deputy head (the only very senior figure in the school who is not a Townend) and finally the headmaster himself. 'What matters,' says the head, 'is that every child knows there is someone to whom they can confidently turn.' Anecdotal evidence suggests this is overwhelmingly true. 'The key to it all,' said a parent, 'is an atmosphere of great friendliness and patience, accompanied by an underlying structure and sensitive discipline.'

The school draws in families from south, west and east London – lots of children commute by bus and tube – as well as those who walk to school from various smart Knightsbridge or Chelsea squares. We detected none of those snobbish hierarchies which, in some schools, can make relationships toxic. Parents are welcomed as part of the school community from the first minute, and many are first-generation users of independent schools. All form tutors – the first port of call between parents and school – set aside 30 minutes before and after school when parents can go and see them. There are reports at the end of every term (a particularly full one every summer) and an annual parents' evening to discuss children's progress with individual subject teachers.

The uniform is conspicuous but no more costly than others, and a big effort is made to keep extras to a minimum. Individual music lessons and Friday clubs are charged as (inevitably) are the trips to Switzerland. Some bursary help is available 'in exceptional circumstances' – the school works especially hard to try to look after families which have encountered bereavement.

Hill House challenges many of the complacent assumptions of our age. The fact that it's in Knightsbridge and that the uniform is so conspicuous could mislead one easily into inferring the opposite of the truth. The reality is a superbly effective and brilliantly resourced school – one which operates in a glorious time-warp in its preference for doing everything within the family and among the extended family: no school in the country can enjoy such deep loyalty from its support staff, which says a lot. Children of any race or social background will be gathered up here and utterly integrated.

Just like any family business, there are inherent vulnerabilities – and we suspect it may have been that which nettled the inspectors. But the commitment of the Townends to the constituency they serve is massive and wholehearted, and the palpable love and loyalty of all its constituencies (including old pupils), let alone their various successes, says everything.

Holland Park School

Airlie Gardens, Campden Hill Road, London W8 7AF

Ages 11–18 **Pupils** 1,300 **Sixth form** 240

020 7908 1000
www.hollandparkschool.co.uk

Head: Since 2001, Colin Hall BA PGCE (mid 50s). Born and brought up in Durham, he was educated at Durham Wearside grammar school. He graduated with a history degree from Sheffield and went on to to do a PCGE at Cambridge. His career has been meteoric. Each employer recognised his hunger and determination, as well as fierce loyalty (a number of references are reproduced in the staff planner for the benefit of his aspiring teachers). He arrived here from Longford Community School in Hounslow, his first headship; prior to that he had senior positions at Cheney School in Oxford and King Edward VI Morpeth in Northumberland. He still manages to find the time to teach English, which is the subject he has chosen to teach since his first job at Thurston Community School (now College) in Suffolk (his greatest joy, he says, is reading, and he read Sons and Lovers when he was 10). There is a more than a touch of Napoleon about him. A dynamo of man, we have rarely met someone who combines a seemingly unlimited supply of tenacity, fastidious attention to detail, boundless energy, aspiration for both pupils and staff alike and a total and passionate commitment to his vocation.

We were invited (unusually) to attend a staff meeting in the morning. Teachers here are (mostly) younger than 35 and Mr Hall invests as much nurturing and guidance in them as he does the pupils. Marking is assiduously scrutinised, lessons observed, goals and targets set. A canny head, he is also excellent at working the money and the room. The great and the good make up the body known as 'the friends of Holland Park'. Prizes such as the 'pupil premium award' are swept up, Alan Bennett attends whole school events, HRH the Duchess of Kent (known here as Katharine Kent) has her own set of keys to the building.

Deeply aspirational; 'no child is outside of our grasp,' he insists, 'no child is without ambition'. It does not surprise us at all that Michael Gove, the former education secretary, asked to come and 'observe Colin Hall' (although Mr Hall, with a disarming humility, says it did surprise him). Nor does it surprise us that when you Google him, Colin Hall appears among an elite band of 'super heads'. What is more surprising is that despite his Napoleonic appearance, parents describe him as having a big heart, a sensitive and empathetic approach. He also has a reliance on and affection for his trusted loyal advisers, the senior leadership team, but most notably his right hand man, David Chappell, associate head ('everyone is some sort of head,' remarked one parent. There are five deputy heads and five assistant head teachers as well as an associate head).

Academic matters: This is, unquestionably, a good fit for a bright, motivated pupil who has a particular flair for the humanities and English. A rigorous banding is applied across all subjects from the start. Band 1 pupils are considered by staff at pupils to be the crème de la crème. These are the ones taken on day trips to universities, for example and are the participants at the glamorous Perfect Tense event in the summer term when star pupils, selected by staff for 'outstanding achievement', are celebrated at a black tie awards ceremony in Holland Park – attended by the 'friends' of the school as well as by parents and staff. One pupil we spoke to remarked that 'even those in the top of band 2 rarely get to go to Perfect Tense.' While this isn't necessarily true, school admits to the disparity in numbers – approximately 65 per cent of band 1 pupils compared with five per cent of band 4 pupils are likely to be celebrated at Perfect Tense. Pupils (and parents) are keen to move up a band if they can swing it.

All this contributes to personal drive and aspiration and the results speak for themselves. In 2018, 74 per cent of pupils got grades 9-4 in both English and maths at GCSE. At A level in 2018, 50 per cent of grades were A*/A. Not a wide range of A levels offered, but all 'proper subjects'. English and biology currently most popular at A levels. Fewer than 10 take Spanish and/or French. A tiny few do design or music.

Teachers here are thoroughly committed. They have to be or they wouldn't last. Parents talk of a high turnover of staff, particularly in the maths department, but Mr Hall holds on fast when he strikes gold with a talented teacher. Lots of opportunity for career development and promotion. English, humanities and art are all strong here and the staff, in those subjects, long serving. Class rooms could be mistaken for museums – ordered, uncluttered, tastefully decorated and minimal. Mr Hall's attention to detail spares no corner. Lesson plans are scrutinised, progress reports monitored and the delivery of lessons constantly observed and remarked upon. We were given copies of the lesson plans of every lesson we saw, as well as examples of marking. All extremely thorough and impressive. The lower bands have the advantage of the some of the best teaching. No-one is allowed to coast here. Parents particularly enthusiastic about geography, history and English teaching. 'They lit a spark in my son,' remarked one parent, 'with a combination of inspirational teaching and incentivising notes of encouragement from the head'. However, another parent deplored a 'boot camp approach' – evidenced by an inflexibility and greater concern for the results and statistics than what might be best for the individual.

A measure of staff commitment is the practice of opening the school on Saturday mornings as well as for one week during the holidays – for what are called 'interventions'. About 200 children will come in on a Saturday to benefit from extra support and teaching. There may well be sports fixtures and practices on Saturdays too. As many as 600 students have lessons over the the Easter holidays. Teachers aren't paid extra for this; their professionalism demands it of them. Parents are impressed by the thoroughness with which progress is tracked. 'If my son gets a lower result than expected, the teacher will ring me to discuss why this might have happened.'

Many pupils take GCSEs early (a practice that is unlikely to be able to continue under the present regime). By year 10 some have already taken four or five subjects including French, Latin, English literature, history and RS. A few parents regret this suggesting, that their children weren't allowed enough time to enjoy the subject and study in depth, cramming in a short time instead. Others feel disappointed that their child might have been able to achieve an 8/9 in a subject if they had taken it at the normal time. Pupils we spoke to bemoaned 'the exam culture', the constant pressure and the stress this can cause.

Not the school for a child with special educational needs, whether mild or severe, and by Mr Hall's own admission 'you have to be very sure you can meet them.' The school does have lifts, so can accommodate physical disabilities, and perhaps even a case of mild autism. There are a number of students here with 'emotional and behavioural difficulties', we were told. Full time SENCo but one parent remarked on the high turnover of people in this role. In class support provided wherever possible; occasionally a student may be withdrawn from class to be given extra support.

Games, options, the arts: Excellent sporting facilities – lots of outside space, Astro and tarmac for netball, tennis, football and cricket on the doorstep, as well as a spanking, shiny, well-equipped gym with basketball courts etc in the basement, not to mention the 25m competition swimming pool. One of our year 11 guides enthused about netball. Girls in the team are keen and committed and will turn up for practice at 6.30am on a freezing winter's morning. There are house matches every term and a house sports week. As well as rugby, football, cricket and netball, plenty of minor sports also offered, including lacrosse, badminton, table tennis, athletics and rowing, and there are netball and football tours as well as a ski trip.

However, parents agree that the uptake and quality of boys' sport is patchy. Football is popular and the school competes impressively against the local competition which includes Cardinal Vaughan, Burlington Danes, Chelsea Academy and Latymer Upper. Matches and practice sessions are timetabled on Saturdays. Rugby and cricket, on the other hand, have some way to go. Although two hours a week is allocated, most do little above and beyond this; 'My son is getting overweight and has no way of letting off steam,' complained one parent. Perhaps the work pressure is such that students are afraid of committing too much time to doing anything outside the classroom? Either that or, as one parent put it, 'the boys aren't being enticed to do more sport'. However, the school will support pupils' enterprising initiatives – setting up an American football club, for example. A cricket tour to Ampleforth College in Yorkshire caused a great flurry of excitement, but 'the standard is low and enthusiasm quick to wane,' observed one parent.

The major drama production of the year is performed not by pupils, but by staff. The leadership team puts on an annual Shakespeare play each Lent term, well attended by the whole school community; it is clearly a strong bonding experience. Photographs of performances adorn the walls, and particularly amusing characters (who can't act for bacon, confesses one of the leadership team wryly) are discussed for months afterwards. With the exception of an annual 'drama evening' in March where a wide range of age groups perform a selection of pieces – perhaps from the A level or GCSE syllabus – it would seem that there is little drama for the students, apart from what takes place in the classroom during a drama lesson, or when studying a play during English. Apart from the school hall, used primarily for assembly, there is nowhere to put on productions on site, and no mention of any attempt to borrow or lease any local theatres.

A small but impressive choir is growing in quality and stature, and is led by one of the talented deputy heads. We were impressed when we saw a number of double basses and guitars in a music practice room, owned by the school but available for pupils' use. Some pupils receive financial support from the school to play their chosen instrument. Lots of prizes for music. There is clearly very positive encouragement coming from the top (and it helps that Katharine Kent is a strong supporter of the arts, especially music). An orchestra gets cobbled together from pupils who play an instrument outside school, but there is little continuity. When we asked one pupil why there are not more musical groups, she replied tartly, 'probably because they can't make us do an exam in it.' School is part of the tri-borough music service (which includes Westminster, Kensington and Hammersmith); however, one parent talked of the music as taking place 'in fits and starts'. Peripatetic music teachers are not accommodated as there is huge resistance to any pupil missing an academic lesson to fit in an instrumental lesson.

One of the assistant head teachers runs the dance department, which is burgeoning. Two dance studios in the school, and several teachers; dance is a popular mainstream subject as well as after-school activity. We saw boys and girls, gawky and graceful, making shapes and loving it. When asked about drama productions, most parents we spoke to talked of dance performances.

The art department is exceptional – and pupils heavily rewarded with prizes and praise for creativity. Mr Chappell, the exceptional associate head, is currently steering a very talented group of students from year 10 through to the sixth form through A level art in the bohemian environment of Thorpe Lodge. A run-down and enchanting building, once inhabited by the governor of the Bank of England and with its own magical gardens, Thorpe Lodge is situated within the school gates and a stone's throw from the main building. Here, the art students are given free rein to express themselves, and so they do. Huge self-portraits in oil, spectacular installations and a plethora of other work was currently in progress when we visited. DT is well equipped with several laser printers as well as 3D printer. With the art scholarship students and a passionate teaching team, the school well deserves its reputation as an excellent choice for those with a creative bent.

Background and atmosphere: What you see now when you enter the shimmering glass building, replete with tasteful furniture, aesthetically pleasing fixtures and fittings, not to mention the delicate fragrance of Jo Malone candles, bears almost no resemblance to the 60s monolith that was Holland Park Comprehensive several years ago. Mr Hall and his leadership team (referred to by one parent, wryly, as the 'men in black': though there are two women on the team, the preponderence of young white men – who when we visited were wearing black gowns – give some weight to the analogy) have wrought a remarkable change. It neither looks nor, more importantly, smells like a school. Fresh flowers, designer furniture (Ercol tables and chairs even in the classrooms as well as the front hall and communal areas), no mess, no clutter, and above all no damage. Everything is immaculate. The staff room is tastefully adorned with simple two seater pale blue sofas and blue Smeg fridges, banks of daffodils decorated the assembly hall on our visit, thoughtfully framed posters, paintings, poems and catechisms adorn the freshly painted walls.

The building itself is all glass and (sun) shine. Every one of the 1,400 pupils is housed here. With the exception of A level art in Thorpe Lodge, all lessons and activities take place in this one building. Everything is open plan, from the library to the unisex WCs. It's not possible either to smoke in the lavatories, or curl up in a discreet corner with a book – the building is easy to police and its corridors regularly patrolled. There is nowhere to hide. We were standing on the 'bridge' during break and it was like observing an installation – a river of smartly dressed, well-behaved young men and women moving seamlessly and smoothly up and down stairs and along the wide spacious passageways.

Pastoral care, well-being and discipline: Hall and his henchman is a phrase that slips easily off the tongue – even if it is said with some irony. There is little scope for miscreants. The leadership team members are ever present and enforce good behaviour – from attire to skullduggery. The open design of the building ensures that no misdemeanour goes unnoticed. If you're sent out of the classroom for poor behaviour – it's like being sent into a goldfish bowl. Uniform, attendance and behaviour all strictly observed. How else would the delicate Ercol chairs and tables that adorn all the classrooms contain not one scratch or speck of flicked ink or graffiti? These young adults are taught to take care of their surroundings, of themselves and of others.

In conversation, Mr Hall defies this appearance of zero tolerance. 'The development of individual relationships is so much more important than casting things in black and white,' he insists. He proudly states that no-one has been permanently excluded for five years, while accepting that sometimes the last resort is the only option. Parents are involved as soon as their child is excluded from lessons. Punishments include doing serious work over a period of two to three days – no break or lunch with friends. Restorative justice is a firmly held belief here – and constructive discipline.

Students are rigorously monitored. If they are disorganised, late or disruptive, are they getting enough support from home? Tutor system is key in pastoral care structure. If there is a lack of motivation in the class room, are individual teachers doing enough to support and guide – are workbooks being marked quickly enough, for example?

Pupils and parents: The school has had a glamorous history since its founding in 1958. It was the school of choice for the liberal left in the 60s (Tony Benn and Roy Jenkins both chose to move their sons from Westminster and Winchester respectively to Holland Park), and with Angelica Huston among the alumni, the school had a decidedly cool reputation. Colin Hall has restored much of this glamour during his 15 (plus) years. Although one parent referred to a 'champagne socialist' element among the parent body, it's no longer the choice of just the trendy left. A number of high profile members of right wing political parties are attracted to the school's rigour and aspirational ethos, but the creative, media element is still strong.

Located in one of the most fashionable and expensive corners of London, its demographic is very different from many schools of its kind across the capital. But only because standards are high. Parents who once might have saved and scrimped to go private are celebrating the fact that their children can be educated to such a high standard, funded by their taxes alone. You will still find here the odd Etonian or Wykehamist who has chosen to return to London in the sixth form. The catchment is narrow (currently a half mile radius) but it's not impossible to get a place if you live further afield if you can get in on the art scholarship ticket. Pupils here are smart, focused and polite. Ofsted rated behaviour outstanding and we agree. They know how much devotion comes from the top down into their education and they respond to it.

Entrance: The catchment area is getting smaller by the year. Now you have to live within about half a mile of the school to have a chance of getting in. About 1,600 applicants for 240 places. Can be as many as 50 appeals, with only a tiny few successful ones. Banding tests take place in the autumn of year 6. Siblings get priority; 24 places (10 per cent) are reserved for the specialist 'art aptitude test', with distance no object – 'you could live in Glasgow and get a place'. Normally about 380 apply for these 24 places. Applicants aren't interviewed, nor do they need to provide a portfolio, just two drawings under exam conditions. There's an art aptitude waiting list as well as a main waiting list – possible to sit on both. Large numbers from local primaries but particularly Fox up the road. Growing numbers from the independent junior schools.

Entrance into the sixth form is tough. 'This is a very academic sixth form,' we were told – the high standard of the sixth form regarded as a role model to fuel the aspirations of students lower down the school. At least seven GCSEs graded 9-6 including English and maths. Minimum of 7s in the subjects you want to study. Priority will be given to pupils from Holland Park, otherwise proximity to school will be the decider between two equally competing candidates.

Exit: After GCSE very few NEETs – almost all who leave join colleges, apprenticeships or other sixth forms. One or two to the independent sector but mostly to Holland Park sixth form (about 50 per cent) or to other state sixth forms. After A levels, some 90 per cent to university. Around two-thirds to Russell Group universities, including six to Oxbridge in 2018. Quite a high number take a gap year. Most popular are the London University colleges – particularly UCL and King's. Students read a variety of courses from veterinary medicine, medicine, engineering and law, to English, classics, architecture and theology. A few go off to art college.

Money matters: Now an academy, but retaining its very close links with the Royal Borough of Kensington and Chelsea, it remains the area's flagship comprehensive school. Always well funded by the Royal Borough, this is now matched by funding from the Education Funding Agency. It has all the appearance of an exceptionally well-funded school, so we suspect Mr Hall is very clever at tapping any available and potential resources.

Remarks: Ofsted rates the school outstanding under every category – indeed 'beyond outstanding' in several, and the inspectors are superlative in their praise for the school. It would take a harsh critic to disagree. This is a sparkling environment and your child will emerge polished and bright if s/he is academically ambitious, prepared to toe the line and thrives under pressure. Comprehensive it may be, but it won't suit every child.

Holy Cross Preparatory School

George Road, Kingston, Surrey KT2 7NU

Ages 4–11 **Pupils** 290 **RC**

Fees: £12,996 pa

020 8942 0729
www.holycrossprepschool.co.uk

Headteacher: Since 2011, Sarah Hair BEd (40s). Joined the school in 2004; 'knows the school inside out,' say parents. She has spent time as a class teacher, maths and English coordinator at a previous school then director of learning at Holy Cross. Passionate about education and IT; she was one of the first teachers in the 80s to have a computer in her classroom. Teaches year 5 computing: amongst her many interests in new technologies is how IT can be used to support education today and in the future.

Married with three teenagers, one son and two daughters, she comes from a family of educationalists, a tradition she is keen to continue. Parents say she has a lively approach to school life and learning and they all appreciate her bright and cheerful personality.

Entrance: Non-selective at 4+; priority to siblings and Roman Catholics, although the school welcomes all faiths. Prospective pupils attend an introductory morning. At 7+ children are invited to visit for the day where they are assessed for their suitability for the school. Admissions staff are friendly and helpful, occasional places do arise and a waiting list is kept for interested families.

Exit: Girls move onto a wide variety of secondary schools with Kingston Grammar, Surbiton High and Wimbledon High often popular, and a few to boarding schools eg St Catherine's, Woldingham, Sevenoaks. A few to local state schools.

Remarks: Whilst Holy Cross is not overly selective it achieves excellent results for all pupils. Well planned and thoughtful curriculum ensures high standards, so giving pupils the chance to cherry pick when it comes to choosing a secondary school. Reasoning is part of the core curriculum from year 3. Maximum class size is 22 and all classes have fully trained, high-level assistant teachers. Fantastic grounding in maths, English and IT, say parents. Specially structured English scheme used across the age groups, with a big emphasis on developing good essay writing techniques mixed with lots of speaking and listening tasks. This starts early, with even the youngest members developing the confidence to be able to stand up and address their classmates on a number of topics and share any special skills they may have.

There are four separate small teaching rooms for pupils needing individual support from the SENCo, and EAL is available as required. Drama and IT are linked to other subjects, helping to keep learning relevant and to encourage creativity. Well-resourced art and design rooms where pupils can engage with all types of media, much of which is elegantly displayed around the school. Impressive collections of pottery; the girls also benefit from having DT days, enabling them to plan, design and complete their projects as a whole. Science room full of active little girls in their goggles, with interesting experiments taking place and a specially designed area for baking and cookery clubs.

The old coach house is now the IT suite where pupils build websites and learn programming skills. The school has designed its own app for communicating with parents, and parents can contact teachers at any time.

Music is a serious subject with a full-time teacher coordinating and 13 visiting teachers. Early years classes learn recorder, then in year 3 everyone learns a brass instrument. Pupils are taught to read and compose their own music, and many go on to do exceptionally well, joining national youth orchestras and choirs.

The huge outdoor spaces offer lots of different play areas and all sports take place on site. Ample courts, three rounders pitches and own athletics track. Sports facilities are also used by other schools, for community activities and charity events. Pupils are keen participants in Surrey schools sports tournaments. Younger children have their own outdoor classroom and garden where they grow vegetables, harvest them and then learn how to turn them into soup.

Lovely Victorian buildings nestle comfortably next to modern additions; the recent multi-function halls are cleverly built into the hillside so as not to lose any of the gardens. Unique setting for a school bordering London: eight glorious acres of well-tended grounds with views out to Epsom Downs, situated in a historical estate that once belonged to the crown and is now part of the pricey Coombe Estate. The house was once occupied by John Galsworthy, author of the Forsyte Saga; in 1971 the sisters of Holy Cross purchased the buildings for a school. Still retains many original features including beautiful stained-glass windows and a wood panelled library.

Warmth and the quality of relationships remain at the heart of the school and the well-established pastoral care system. Sister Ursula, the last remaining nun, has had a long influence on the school, teaching pottery and running the Welcome Room where parents and children come to drink her tasty cocoa and chat. New school council has recently evolved to give the girls a voice in the day-to-day running of the school and discuss the all-important issues of new play equipment and lunch menus. Girls are elected as officers, with each class providing two representatives; all very democratic. School council chooses charities to support, the girls run a number of enterprising fundraising events themselves, and they have an ongoing link with Build Africa. Parents are unanimous about the positive effects of the school's pastoral ethos. One parent told of the kindness shown to her daughter when she first arrived, making the transition to a new school so comfortable. Wednesdays are homework free to ensure that girls have time to visit friends and pursue outside interests.

A school that shines for its holistic, inclusive and caring approach mixed with academic rigour. Continues to be a fine example of 21st century education, and provides a wonderful start in life.

H

The Holy Cross School

25 Sandal Road, New Malden, Surrey KT3 5AR

Ages 11–18 **Pupils** 941 **Sixth form** 200 (federated with Richard Challoner) **RC**

020 8395 4225
www.holycross.kingston.sch.uk

Headteacher: Since 2001, Tom Gibson BSc Dip Ed MEd NPQH (40s). Could be government poster star for rejuvenating benefits of headship – radiates fulfillment and energy, though also a possible fringe benefit of lifelong interest in sport. While original career plans as pro after studying PE at Loughborough came to nought (dawning realisation that wasn't going to happen, he says, hit him 'later than my friends'), teaching career, fortunately for pupils in his care, proved thoroughly acceptable alternative. Pretty much inescapable, given that computer has invariably said 'yes' to the idea. 'Whenever I do psychometric tests, always come out as a teacher or social worker,' he says, though without any discernable regrets.

Has viewed education from every angle, as a parent (four children through university, wife an early years specialist), teacher (in variety of co-ed special residential as well as single sex mainstream schools) and an inspector (of 30 or so schools when was seconded to Ofsted eight years into headship). Message he took home (and presumably back to school again) from assorted experiences was that even in struggling schools there's 'always something that's fantastic.' Here, fantastic is the norm, thanks in part to determination to ensure that staff creativity is unfettered by micro management. If teachers are professionals, he says, shouldn't require 'somebody on top of you telling you how to do your job.' Staff are definitely accountable – but must be allowed autonomy to do the job.

As a result, he's reassuring but often background presence to parents, strong, visible and approachable senior management team – 'the people you go to,' felt one mother – mopping up most day-to-day issues. Very definitely hands-on when required, however. When GSG visited, had just come off phone to LEA to arrange help for vulnerable pupil. He also (somehow) packs in a spot of teaching, including RS, as well as supporting some year 11 girls on reduced timetable.

Regularly sits in on other lessons, marvelling at other teachers' talents and happy to be outshone. 'Am I the best teacher? No, because that's not what I'm doing every day, and we've got some fantastic people here.'

Takes governmental caprice in his stride. 'Here long enough to adhere to political landscape without being blown off course.' Funding is one current concern (dominates meetings with other heads), recruitment another, though train and promote your own policy does wonders for retention rates (last big outside appointment was over five years ago).

'Teaching's a lovely job but we all need to feel we're progressing,' he says. 'The challenge is to ensure you can reward teachers financially and keep their interest up.' Seems to work, with many teachers there till retirement, though some younger staff are lured away by out of London quality of life – and lower property prices.

Praises his 'bright, skilled, sophisticated' admin team of action-packed enablers. Wish list is their command (collaboratively speaking), funding nosed out, ways and means found to overcome officialdom (recently built sports hall's pitched roof, for example, makes it multipurpose and thus LEA-compliant).

Job, though not entirely stress free – 'Of course there are times you worry' – remains endlessly fulfilling. 'Privileged that people trust their daughters to us,' he says – and goal is to repay trust by finding ways for every girl to succeed.

Academic matters: Won't disappoint, offering high-achieving home from home that should satisfy even those robbed of grammar school place – and all on their doorstep. Results just what you'd hope for. Progress made between years 7-11 puts school in top five per cent nationally, GCSE results consistently good, congratulatory letters from top politicians par for the course. In 2018, 81 per cent got 9-4 in both English and maths with 43 per cent at 9-7. At A level in 2018, 31 per cent A*-A grades. Impressive 33 subjects in total (34 counting 'other') offered post-16, including creative writing, human biology and media. Plenty of BTecs, too (from health to performing arts in year 11 and early years, hospitality, IT and science in the sixth form).

But also proud to care, with an overt stress on welcome for girls from all shades of the ability spectrum, something that doesn't always seem to be the case in results-hungry establishments elsewhere. School shines when it comes to learning support. 'Brilliant,' thought parent with dyslexic daughter. 'Help has been amazing.' Safe haven, staffed by SEN team, is open before and after school as well as during the day, with easy chairs, games and jigsaws among measures designed to bring temporary relief to pupils sometimes overwhelmed by lives.

And though there's inevitable worry over performance of disadvantaged pupils (about 10 per cent of school numbers), support is extensive, ranging from financial (uniform to term time and holiday activities) to academic (extra teachers recruited to provide one-to-one support). Mr Gibson is 'just as excited to have child who struggled at primary as someone at top of the class,' and backs it up with quality resources. Lower sets are tiny and get some of brightest and best teachers, thought parents. 'Tend to do better in bottom set than in other schools,' thought one.

Formidable efforts go into working out who goes where, with CATs baseline testing in June for September's year 7 intake, classes ordered according to the results – parents sometimes slightly miffed in the process, but generally mollified by subsequent extensive reshuffling as lights start to emerge from bushels.

Most able take 11 GCSEs including triple science, substantial numbers achieving government's EBacc measurement. Impressive as with just four core subjects (RS, maths, English and science), high take up of options (including geography and history) is down to quality of teaching (even notoriously snide 'rate my teachers' website bursts with praise and stars).

Dynamic history team – 'phenomenal and inspiring' among the many five-star reviews. Head of department is 'brilliant – daughter loves it,' said parent (who, like others, found it hard to name anything she wasn't delighted with) – and mentors colleagues in need of turbocharged pupil-whispering skills.

Maths also strong through the school and set from year 7, English following in year 8. Sciences well-resourced (as you'd hope – this is school's official specialist area), biology and chemistry particularly so with five teachers apiece. Now pushing boat out for physics with recruitment of additional teachers. From also-ran girls' science subject, sixth form take up now moving into double figures (12 in current year 12), despite rival lure of psychology, currently single biggest A level subject.

Just-opened future technology learning room features banks of i-gorgeousness as well as natural daytime lighting, sizzling green chairs as well as licence to doodle (flip up tables double as whiteboards) and join clubs in electronics – leading to extra GCSE – and robotics. And if message about brilliance of science and technology careers for girls isn't clear, shortly to arrive 3D printer, next gizmo on the wish list, should be able to spell it out in a choice of colours and materials.

Well-established sixth form partnership with Richard Challoner (also Catholic, high achieving but with boys and co-ed sixth form) adds greater range of subjects (popular) and extra travel time between the sites (less so). 'You've got to get to know boys some time,' thought one pupil – it's just the five-minute minibus journey that's off-putting. 'Effort...' groaned sixth former, who like the others, much preferred the Richard Challoner pupils to come to them, avoiding 15-minute walk under A3 if minibus is full.

Games, options, the arts: If he could, Mr Gibson would get girls to trade online introspection for more sport. Though smaller size means slightly fewer games specialists than at larger schools (have three rather than five elsewhere), determination and creativity fills in plenty of gaps, from pupil self-starters organising 7.30am fitness sessions to PE-hating group sensibly offered civilised alternative of a walk in nearby Richmond Park.

Provides ballgirls for Wimbledon, PE at GCSE and A level, and pupils see themselves as a sporty bunch, egged on by enthusiastic staff and helped by attractive sports hall which avoids box-like appearance common to so many of its kind, though most games are played in Kingsmeadow, just a few minutes' drive away. Apart from a few more matches for the keen, parents praised expectations ('high') and teams ('strong'), particularly netball (regular fixtures against girls' schools in the area, including independents such as Surbiton High) and handball (recent Kingston and London champions), cricket and trampolining.

Trips many and varied (year 7 camping, year 9 battlefields, sports and language trips, including French exchange) to suit every subject and pocket – trip to Thailand no jaunt for the entitled, requiring pupils to fundraise before working with disadvantaged children there.

Performing arts similarly no Sunday stroll in the park (with or without George). We saw year 7s performing confidently against tension-creating (and intentional) background dissonance, good preparation for rigours of Sondheim's Into the Woods, next on the to-do list (whole school production every two years).

Held together by boundlessly energetic teacher – has to be as 'only one we've got,' said one girl – who organises range of events, from rock and pop festival to musical tour of Kingston town centre – and felt to be talent spotter par excellence. 'Helps you find your inner music,' said year 11 pupil and, having discovered it, channels it into choirs, bands and – for the very keen – music GCSE and performing arts BTec.

Art, taught in enticingly cluttered studio heaving with work, 3D flower springing out from painted background; rhinoceros depicted with surprising lightness of touch a thought-provoking treat for viewer. Popular at GCSE, taken by about third of year 11 pupils, with 10 or so carrying through to A level where can specialise in textiles, art and design and – increasingly popular – photography (a must-do, thought teacher, for anyone planning glittering career as celebrity vlogger).

Background and atmosphere: Smallest girls' senior school in the area, 'though may not feel like it compared with primaries,' says Mr Gibson, with 900 plus pupils rather than the several thousand elsewhere.

Fancifully minded might see school façade, original building protectively flanked by two more modern wings, as embodiment of nurturing qualities that have endured since foundation in 1931 by The Sisters of The Holy Cross. Contemporary black and white photograph shows original five pupils and a rocking horse posing together in eloquent depiction of family atmosphere. Love, respect and living life to full all qualities school espouses today – though without drowning in cosiness, stresses Mr Gibson.

Religious dimension ever present – a cross formed from coloured glass blocks in sixth form centre contrasts with older stained glass in entrance hall – and never apologetically. Catholicism remains defining part of school life, with RS taken at GCSE by all, and compulsory part of sixth form education. Annual retreats offered to pupils and extensive support for Catholic charities including day centre for the homeless in London and orphanage in Thailand.

Homely atmosphere assisted by compact site, tucked into residential road close to centre of New Malden. School does best with existing material, small courtyards squeezed in between buildings – one with long, curved, bright blue benches for break time conviviality – though some more spartan areas remain: dining hall's main decoration is rows of lockers lining the walls.

Upstairs, there's the promise of far better things to come. In addition to serving decent coffee and chocolate muffins (a not very well kept secret from rest of school), sixth form centre is riot of colourful brilliance, with neon sign and psychedelic, curvy sofa in eye-bending electric blue and purple.

Uniform, however, is big on homeliness. School's approach is that 'smart uniform means smart brains,' said approving mother. Only issue has been over sixth form blouses – plain only originally allowed, parents unhappy. Happy ending with rules now relaxed and (subtle) patterns allowed to all-round relief. 'A minefield,' says Mr Gibson, with feeling.

No changes planned elsewhere. Years 7 to 11 wear non-negotiable long, green kilt. Not loved, but pupils get used to them and though expensive, made from parent-pleasing quality fabric that lasts. Even better, they're impossible to roll up ('Hurrah,' thought several mothers), which could be factor in several other local schools' decisions to opt for something similar. Summer skirt an improvement for some, owing to paler pattern that makes them 'less visible,' thought one pupil. But though uniform is instantly recognisable, not a taunting hazard – pupils travel without fear on local buses.

Similar approval for school's strict beauty products policy. It's absent from younger faces (at least, those we saw) and limited to natural look among seniors ('no lipstick, eye liner or cat eyes,' said one). Sixth formers, in default business attire, free to apply ad libere though sense of restraint appeared to rule.

Pastoral care, well-being and discipline: School that doesn't stint on detail – new head girl's name already on honours board early in autumn term. 'Treat every individual in holistic way,' said parent. 'It's not just about the academic progress, you get sense that they really do care.'

Settling in process for new year 7s starts with visits to primary schools in summer term of final year and carries on into first term, starting two days earlier than rest of school with just sixth form for company and let out early for lunch in first fortnight. Initial swaddling, including 'non-stop' enquiries about how things are going from teachers who know girls' names 'instantly', can feel a bit excessive, think pupils – but parents are delighted. 'A bit old fashioned – you could feel you're mothered to death but it's a good fault to have,' said one.

Pupil complaints and comments passed up the chain via Student Leadership Team – 'Have a lot of responsibility' – and mood is protective, controlled and gently aspirational. Bullying not common, thought pupils. And if it happened 'school would deal with it,' said one with confidence. Awareness of consequences felt to be undoubtedly helpful in putting off anyone contemplating unkindness – with notable turn of speed when parents need to get in touch. 'You can pick up the phone and talk to the people you want to talk to straight away,' thought one mother.

'Some parents say you can't be caring and high achieving,' says Mr Gibson. 'I say you need to be caring to achieve.' Succeeds, even when faced with challenging behaviour, in keeping girls in school. Appointment of inclusion manager and area where distressed can be supported without affecting education of others helps keep exclusion levels 'minute'.

Mental health problems, many linked to plummeting self worth, a growing problem, not helped by 'enormous amounts of aspiration,' says Mr Gibson. 'Expectation that everything's going to be A* weighs down on people.' School does its bit and more, with mental health-themed assemblies, training for pupil ambassadors and emphasis on coping skills for all to deal with anxiety, as well as more informal support (one parent praised cups of tea and chats available on tap).

Still 'probably not enough,' thought head, whose one (mild) bugbear is tendency for school to be seen by outsiders as sum of nurturing qualities. May be 'sweet, caring and academic' (Mr G recounts qualities with air of one who's heard them many times before), but there's no absence of challenge – or innovation to meet it.

Pupils and parents: Religion the unifying element in school population that spans cultures, ethnicity and lifestyles, with around a fifth speaking English as an additional language and seven per cent receiving free school meals. Area covered extends from Hampton Court round to Chessington, Worcester Park and into South West London fringes (Morden, Mitcham and Wandsworth) as well as Kingston and Richmond, affluence rubbing shoulders with deprivation. Supportive PSA brings everyone together, while girls' friendships span the range. 'Daughter made such a huge variety of friends, from Roehampton council estates to [luxury homes] in North Kingston.'

Entrance: Securing one of the heavily oversubscribed 150 year 7 places a doddle as long as you meet the criteria (Catholic trumps all, with priority, after looked after Catholic children, given to regular – ideally weekly – and priest-endorsed attendance at mass) and remember to fill out the right forms (supplementary information as well as standard common application). One member of staff thought non-Catholics might stand slightly better chance applying for in-year place, but we'd suspect slightly forlorn hope in a school which attracts applicants from almost 50 different feeder schools.

Additional 15 sixth form places on offer for non-locals (but still Catholic). Not unknown for families to move nearer to boost chances of success.

'When you've found the right school, fight tooth and nail to get in,' says Mr Gibson, sensibly tempering this with need to check admissions criteria to work out whether tooth and nail sacrifice, however extensive, will be sufficient to do the trick.

School big on empathy – will call parents pronto if there's waiting list movement. 'When place came up, the admissions head phoned straight away, said parent. 'Said they knew how anxious we had been. They really care.'

Exit: Up to a third leave after GCSEs. Year 13 leavers head off in every direction – majority to university including one or two to Oxbridge or to study medicine most years (none in 2018); a few are now opting for apprenticeships. Small but steady reverse flow of old girls returning as staff members.

Remarks: School notable for happiness, sense of security and combination of talent boosting and strong moral purpose. 'Seven years ago, didn't want to come here. Seven years on, don't want to leave,' said current head girl. After just a few hours there, nor did we.

Holy Trinity & St Silas

Hartland Road, London NW1 8DE

Ages 4–11 Pupils 210 C of E

020 7267 0771
www.camden.schooljotter.com/holytrinitynw1

Head: Since 2013, Lorraine Dolan (40s) BEd and masters in education, both from the University of North London. Her first job as an NQT in 1996 was at Holy Trinity and St Silas; 'My plan was never to stay at the same school for long but to have an open mind.' However, when Annie Williams took over as head of the school in 2001, Ms Dolan, who respected her greatly, found it difficult to move on. Fourteen years later Ms Dolan started to get 'itchy feet', and when Annie Williams took a sabbatical Ms Dolan became acting deputy head and from there decided to move into leadership. She subsequently left Holy Trinity to take up the post as deputy head at St Paul's Catholic school in Wood Green. Although she says her time there was a 'great experience', she couldn't achieve what she wanted as a deputy head. When Ms Williams died in 2012, Ms Dolan had begun looking at headship and when the post was advertised, she applied, believing that she had the skills, understanding and experience to drive the school forward.

Tall, with waist-long fair hair, Ms Dolan looks on first impression like someone who might be in the world of media rather than a primary school head teacher. Although softly spoken and friendly, this ex-convent school girl is definitely no pushover and hides a steely determination. It is a prerequisite for this job. Any weaker souls would not survive the legacy of the former head teacher, who changed the fortunes of a not particularly good school to an 'exceptional school' (in the words of Ofsted) and was a woman who had edited the word 'compromise' from her vocabulary. Ms Dolan says, 'Annie was a force to be reckoned with.' Ms Dolan offers a more 'open door policy' than her predecessor and welcomes parent inclusion in the school. One pupil told us, 'she's very approachable and a great role model.'

She has been described by a parent as being 'very old school, in a good way.' She is very intent on bringing traditional values back into the school and has particularly clamped down on the school uniform, which was a bit hit and miss prior to her headship. As she points out, 'You either have a uniform policy or you don't; you can't have a bit of a uniform.' Another parent told us that Ms Dolan 'doesn't rest on the laurels of Ms Williams and wants to make her own mark. She is around most of the time and is often chatting to parents in the playground.'

Ms Dolan has a grown up son, whom she had in her early 20s, and who, she says, 'has been the making of me in many ways.' The product of Irish Catholic parents, Ms Dolan went to a convent school, where she says she was 'often challenging the system'. Her son forced her to be responsible, and although she wasn't thinking of a career in education at that time, was accepted onto a Montessori teaching course, 'which was perfect as I could take my son with me and leave him at the nursery'. Little did she suspect then where that first rung up the ladder would eventually lead. She and her long term partner are both members of a cycling club, and she also enjoys running: 'Keeping fit is a great outlet for stress.'

Entrance: After the customary priority for looked-after children, the primary admissions criterion is church attendance, either at The Most Holy Trinity Church across the road or at St Silas the Martyr in Kentish Town. Approx 60 per cent come via this route; the remaining 40 per cent of admissions are catchment based. When Ms Williams became head, the school was very much bottom of the parental-choice agenda, but the intake has altered and now gets more professional parents – particularly in creative and media related fields. Not too many, school hopes – 'we have a good social mix and want to keep it that way'. At the moment, remains a class and ethnic melting pot, with the largest minority being Bangladeshi.

Exit: Mainly to the local comprehensives – Haverstock, William Ellis, Parliament Hill, St Marylebone and Camden School for Girls – but school has also developed a relationship with The Hall, one of north London's leading prep schools, and some year 6 boys go there with bursaries before proceeding to leading London independent day schools.

Remarks: Housed in a typical Victorian schoolhouse, a meander from tourist-packed Camden Lock; one has to enter two heavy-duty doors to reach the main reception – the first to the playground and the second to the main building: 'We qualified for extra security', the head told us (part of their recent funding programme). However, once inside with its pristine, soothing interior, you'd never guess where you were – fresh flowers, polished parquet and a big red school bell are all from another era.

Teaching at the school is strong; a number of parents have pointed this out and cited a couple of exceptional teachers, one of whom – Kirsty Mccreadie, the current deputy head – held the school together after the previous head's departure and is described by parents as 'simply the most exceptional, passionate teacher – the cornerstone of the school'. Ms Dolan herself has been very successful in turning the maths results around – something she has been working hard to address. When she first came on board, results had been dipping, but her close monitoring seems to have worked – more or less everyone gets at least level 4 Sats, with around two-thirds now reaching level 5+.

The teaching staff are generally well qualified, with two MAs, one law degree, three teachers who speak fluent French (so French is taught convincingly from reception to year 2), and a couple of graduate teaching assistants who, according to Ms Dolan, arrived with 'passion and drive'. The excellent teaching is partly the legacy of Ms Williams, who had said: 'I'm very snobbish about teachers – they have to have been to a good university and to have travelled. It gives them a cultural understanding', and partly due to the current head who adds: 'All the teachers are clear about my expectations. It's not OK for one child to slip through the net.'

Despite the fact that the majority of pupils arrive at Holy Trinity with well below average attainment, the school is at the pinnacle of the league tables, with results in English in the top one per cent nationally. Literacy is taught for two hours a day, primarily through poetry and prose. This again, we are told, is largely down to another inspirational teacher – Luke Williams, a specialist drama teacher who teaches English and drama from reception to year 6, through the works of Shakespeare. Every year the school puts on a whole-school Shakespeare play, including every pupil and member of staff, and has now helped found a borough-wide Shakespeare festival with five neighbouring primaries. Hardly surprising then that, according to Ofsted: 'Pupils' empathy with the works of Shakespeare is quite remarkable'.

All the arts are fundamental to the curriculum. Music is central to the school and one parent told us that music largely formed her decision to send her daughter there: 'The school just feels amazing when you walk in. There is the sound of laughter and always someone playing the piano or another instrument.' Pupils can choose to join the jazz band or one of two choirs, or learn an instrument from a long list of specialist music teachers. However, drop-ins on any of the music groups have been abolished in favour of auditioning for them, as the head firmly believes, 'if you make that sort of commitment, you need to stick to it.'

Art is equally important, and despite limited square footage, has its own department; pupils' work is hung boldly throughout the building. Painting even spills out into the large urban playground (underneath the rattling of the Camden overground train), where one inner-city wall has been reborn as a rural, summer scene (with a 3D vegetable plot to extend the experience). We were particularly struck by an astonishing ceiling display in the upper school hall of famous London landmarks – the London Eye, St Paul's Cathedral etc, all made from papier mâché. The idea for this came from a walk around London with year 6 pupils, who were learning about architecture (from a parent architect) inspired by the imminent development works to the school. One parent told us: 'We're so lucky at this school, there is such a pool of talented and creative parents who can come in and share their skills.' Trips are very much part of the education. Visits to the theatre, opera, ballet and museums are planned on a regular basis.

Though about 40 per cent of pupils are not Anglicans, the Christian message is strong, with a thoroughly involved parish priest (Father Graham), regular church attendance and class mass held half termly. Grace is said before lunch. Lunch itself is entirely healthy, and mealtimes, too, are considered a development opportunity. Music is played and, on Fridays, tablecloths laid. A firm emphasis on good manners. The 'golden rules' dictate: don't talk with your mouth full; learn to use your knife and fork correctly. Rules elsewhere are equally clear cut. Attentive good behaviour is the norm, but for those who stray, the first offence means displacement to another class; further disruption means an encounter with the head.

Although standards may be firmly upheld, one parent complained that the pastoral care system is not great and there isn't much of a structure in place. However, the head says that whilst historically issues were not dealt with, she 'has worked very hard to get parents to trust that when they raise a concern about their child, whether emotional or academic, it will be dealt with and monitored.' The children are supported by the class teachers. They have weekly circle time sessions and are encouraged to share their concerns as well as develop their understanding about relationships with their peers.

The school takes a proactive approach to its parents, and offers core subject curriculum evenings to support parents with home learning. Parents respond with energetic fundraising – the PTA raises on average £4,000-£5,000 a year which goes towards buying new computers. Ms Williams herself was no ingénue when it came to fundraising and won considerable support from charities – a legacy continued after her death, with the Annie Williams Education Trust, set up by her husband, which has already received many donations.

Plans are currently under way to expand the school building and make it more accessible, the school being one of 10 schools in Camden identified as in need of updating. This will include a three storey extension at the side to house a new office, reception area and staff room and will allow the hall downstairs to be opened up into a large performance space. Classrooms will be increased in size (as they are rather on the snug side) and a lift will be installed, as this old Victorian building is currently unsuitable for anyone with a disability.

'Superb' is Ofsted's summary of the Holy Trinity and St Silas experience, and pupils agree: 'We love it here, we don't want to leave,' said one year 6 pupil. And a parent added: 'I just love the mixed demographic and the fact that everyone talks to everyone. I once saw David Miliband [a former parent], in the playground chatting to a mother in flip flops and pyjama bottoms, about the best pirate parties for boys.'

Honeywell Junior School

Linked with Honeywell Infant School

128

Honeywell Road, London SW11 6EF

Ages 7–11 **Pupils** 358

020 7223 5185
www.honeywellschools.org

Head of junior school: Since 2001, Mr Duncan Roberts BEd NPQH (50s). Previously deputy. Inspiring and popular head who is well respected by teachers, parents and pupils. Good sense of humour. Keen sportsman who enjoys swimming, football and playing water polo and instils in the children 'the importance of both winning and losing with dignity'. One parent described him as 'a born leader, but also a team player,' while another told us that 'he gets on with everybody.' Has two young children.

Entrance: Once through to the infant school, each child is allocated a place in the junior school, though still necessary to reapply via the borough. Places do become available further up the school, so it's worth persevering. Incredibly popular.

Exit: At 11, roughly half to the state sector, including Bolingbroke Academy, Graveney, Burntwood, Grey Coat, Tiffin and Lady Margaret's. Those going down independent route head for Alleyn's, Dulwich, Whitgift, JAGS, Emanuel, Wimbledon High, Streatham and Clapham High.

Much support and guidance given to parents when selecting a secondary school. Head knows that a lot of tutoring goes on at top of school and concedes that the right tutor can help with fine-tuning. As one parent told us, 'It can get pretty competitive around here at the start of year 6, though I think it's more the parents getting stressed than the children. The school manages to keep the kids pretty grounded, but it can be fairly tense at times.'

Remarks: School is situated in a prosperous, middle-class area and the intake mostly reflects this. Head observes that a good proportion are 'advantaged children.' Thirty pupils per class. Around 17 per cent have English as an additional language but bilingual children catch up quickly, with weekly sessions for those needing extra support.

Excellent Sats results, with some pupils gaining level 6 (head isn't complacent, though). The progress of each child in the school is monitored very closely and immediate action is taken if anyone is seen to be treading water. The current focus is on improving the standard of reading comprehension. Low turnover of staff. One assistant for each year group from year 3. French taught to all pupils. Well-resourced school and heavily involved in teacher training.

A total of 75 SEND children and support is given both inside and outside the classroom – in groups and individually. Playground can be a noisy affair in this large school. Lego club has been set up for quieter souls who find the hustle and bustle of break-time too much, as well as a cordoned off quieter zone, but some parents still feel 'it's a bit of a jungle out there.'

Sport is a major strength and is taken very seriously from year 3. Inter-house competitions recently introduced so 'everyone can take part' and house points hard fought for. Welcomed by parents, as some felt that previously only the sportiest were given the chance to play. School participates in every tournament going – often with great success. Huge number of trophies on display to prove it. Swimming from years 3 to 5. Not just predictable sports here – cross-country and orienteering offered, and lacrosse played at the highest level. Before and after-school clubs are very popular. All tastes catered for, including tennis, Mandarin, knitting and baking. Early morning running club on the nearby common for pupils, parents ('mostly mums') and teachers.

Gold Artsmark awarded to for high level of provision in the arts. Huge orchestra with 60 members, as well as string orchestra. Individual tuition on a variety of instruments (recorder, violin, flute, cello), with regular concerts and performances for parents. The head's attitude is 'now you've got your grade 1, let's all enjoy it.' Recorder compulsory for year 3. Two choirs, so something for everyone, including one dedicated to popular music (scores from West End musicals). School hires drama facilities for year 6 production involving all 90 children. Recent productions include Bugsy Malone and We will Rock You.

This is a school which makes the most of being in the capital – lots of trips, visiting speakers and workshops. Year 6 outdoor pursuits residential trip to the Isle of Wight is a high point in the final year.

Supportive, vociferous PTFA. Whether they're hearing readers, producing a snappy school magazine, fundraising or coming in to talk about their experiences, they're a force to be reckoned with. Excellent wrap-around care on offer, including holidays. Communication between parents and staff has improved recently with the sharing of teachers' email addresses.

School has strong links with the community and actively supports local charities. The importance of being a good citizen and of giving back to society – 'either in time, effort or finances' – is instilled in the pupils. Good manners are high on the agenda and behaviour is very good. Head stresses that school wants Honeywell pupils to be decent citizens, as well as achieving academically. No uniform (apart from PE kit), after lengthy consultation with the school community, and some pupils could do with smartening up.

A first-rate state primary that offers the lot. Produces independent, confident children ready to cope with the next stage. Old pupils are always coming back to visit. As one parent told us, 'My girls loved Honeywell. I genuinely believe that it gave them the best possible start.'

Honeywell Infant School

Linked with Honeywell Junior School

Honeywell Road, London SW11 6EF

Ages 3–7 **Pupils** 325

020 7228 6811
www.honeywellschools.org

Head teacher: Since 2004, Jane Neal BEd NPQH. Previously deputy head, she has been at the school for 23 years in total. Two children – one at secondary and one at Honeywell. Softly spoken and reflective. Proud of her school and devoted to those in her care. 'She's seen it all over the years and not much ruffles her feathers,' said another. Passionate about early years learning and keen on reading, walking, cooking and children's theatre.

Entrance: At 3 to nursery, although there's no automatic transfer to infant school at 4. Nursery offers 50 part time places, plus 14 full time places (39 maximum in a class). From reception, three parallel classes, with 30 per class. Usually one assistant per class from reception. A handful leaves at the end of nursery. All must reapply to get from nursery into reception. Criteria for offers to infant school – looked after children, siblings, those with exceptional medical or special need, proximity to the school (as the crow flies). Once through to the infant school, each child is allocated a place in the junior school, though still necessary to reapply via the borough.

Exit: All to junior school. Transfer over to juniors is generally smooth, thanks to system of reading partners (pupils) and induction sessions (parents). As one parent put it, 'There's just enough mixing of the two schools for the move to the big school to seem like a natural progression.'

Remarks: Infants on the same site as the juniors, though each has its own head, both of whom specialise in their own age group. Schools share a governing body, staff room and some facilities. Infants get to see the highlights of junior school but lead separate existence day to day. As the head says, 'we get the best of both worlds.'

A total of 40 SEN children offered group and individual support. A small number of children with statements. Nurturing environment, especially in the early years. Forensic attention to detail when assessing the needs of each child – the school isn't just paying lip-service to treating each child as an individual. Excellent results at each stage. Head is aware that the middle achievers deserve special consideration too, not just the high flyers and the ones who are struggling. School is currently focusing on how to make maths more 'girl friendly.'

Loads of outside space and vast amounts of equipment for the pupils. The head told us: 'The children can do all the things here that they can't do at home.' Pupils have their own playground as well as the shared playground garden, complete with tepees, toadstools, fairy-tale bridge and enchanted forest – inspiring, imaginative and the envy of other schools. All-weather surfacing means that it's now used come rain or shine. Staggered use, so each year group gets the chance to use it. Jolly ICT suite, just for infants, complete with jazzy multi-coloured keyboards.

Good manners are high on the agenda and behaviour is very good. Head stresses that school wants Honeywell pupils to be decent citizens, as well as achieving academically. No uniform, after lengthy consultation with the school community, and some pupils could do with smartening up.

A very welcoming school. Happy staff and happy children, who are having an exciting time. Bright classrooms, with huge windows and colourful displays at every turn. Learning is made fun at Honeywell. The school produces articulate, confident children who work independently from early on. One parent told us: 'Honeywell's strength is that there is a feeling of community about the school. Everybody is looking out for each other.' As ever, the school is hugely popular but isn't resting on its laurels. Children get off to a flying start here and parents are willing to move heaven and earth to get their offspring a place.

Hornsby House School

Hearnville Road, London SW12 8RS

Ages 4–11 **Pupils** 430

Fees: £14,280 – £15,345 pa

020 8673 7573
www.hornsbyhouse.org.uk

Headmaster: Since 2012, Edward Rees BA (40s). Previously deputy head at Dulwich College Junior School, also an ISI inspector for the past 10 years. He grew up in Hampshire and became a keen cricketer while attending Charterhouse, playing in the past for the MCC. Today he lives in south east London and is married with a son and a daughter. Parents say he is a sociable and hands on head, always willing to talk, and quick to respond to issues or concerns they may have. The school was founded in 1988 by educational psychologist Bevé Hornsby, best known for her pioneering work in the field of dyslexia.

Entrance: At 4+ into reception. Non-selective, places are offered on a first-come first-served basis from a waiting list, in order of the age of the child at the date of registration. Priority is given to siblings. Thereafter occasional places; prospective pupils sit assessment tests in English, maths and reasoning. Not as many places as there used to be at 8 as the majority of boys and girls stay though to 11+. At 8+, the school offers a few means-tested bursaries. Always worth applying for as it is not overwhelmed with applications.

Exit: At 11+ pupils move mostly to London day schools; around half of the girls to JAGS or Streatham & Clapham High whilst half of the boys go to Whitgift. Others to eg Alleyn's, Dulwich College, King's Wimbledon (via new 11+ entry), Emanuel, plus state schools Graveney and Tiffin. A few to boarding schools eg Benenden. In 2018, 34 academic scholarships plus awards for music, sport, art and all-rounders.

Remarks: Over the last decade, Hornsby House has earned itself a good local reputation for offering a lively all-round education to pupils of varying abilities. A wide and carefully planned curriculum runs through this inclusive school, enabling children to develop at their own pace. All subjects are taught to mixed ability classes, with setting in mathematics for older age groups. Modern foreign languages are taught via a range of exciting topics and projects, French for reception to year 4, then Spanish for years 5 and 6. Parents feel teachers provide plenty of back-up work when needed plus extension activities for the more able pupils. Full-time SENCo with part-time specialists can offer support to children with milder specific learning difficulties, either individually or through small group work. There is an additional charge for one-to-one specialist teaching. The buildings are wheelchair accessible and staff are always willing to work with speech and occupational therapists as necessary. The school prides itself on developing potential in sports and the arts as well as academics, alongside helping parents to choose the right secondary school for their child. Proof is in the pudding: around a third of pupils are offered awards for music, art, sport or academics each year.

Whole-hearted teaching team with bags of energy; good mix of male and female, predominantly youngish, although there are some long servers. High staff ratio: two deputies, subject specialists, and all year groups have assistant teachers; reception classes have two each. A number of gappers add bounce to the sports and arts staff team as well as working as playground and classroom assistants. Many of these popular jobs go to past pupils; the gap year mentor remembers most of them from when they were in reception themselves.

Fairly compact site, cleverly designed by architects: it boasts lovely, light modern classrooms which sit side by side with the original Edwardian buildings. Whiteboards have disappeared in favour of the latest interactive technologies, all looked after by full-time technicians. Computing is very much on the curriculum. Minecraft, a newish club, helps with coding skills; pupils also use visual programming software. Art, drama, music and science have their own specialist rooms and teachers. Abundant arts and crafts on offer; Hornsby has been rewarded for all its hard work in art, DT and drama with Artsmark Gold. Pupils commemorated the 25th anniversary of the school by designing and constructing a fabulous mosaic in conjunction with artist in residence Tamara Froud. Drama teacher supported by an assistant puts on a variety of productions throughout the year across the age groups so everyone gets a chance to perform. Much looked forward to annually are the major year 4 and 6 productions. Music provision has developed in leaps and bounds since our last visit: two open choirs, chamber choir by audition and a small orchestra. Music room packed with instruments, mouth organs to African drums; pupils also benefit from workshops run by visiting musicians. Everyone learns the recorder and ukulele in class and individual tuition is available on some 11 other instruments. Considering the facilities and staff enthusiasm, some parents feel the orchestra is not particularly well supported.

Despite a lack of on-site space, sport is one of the jewels in Hornsby's crown; pupils use all the local facilities and are taken on sports tours. Main sports football, hockey, rugby and netball; all have successful teams, some impressive winning streaks and are always striving to improve. Cricket for all in the summer, proving very popular with the girls: definitely a few old girls who say they wish it had been on the agenda in their day. Anyone with physical difficulties or injuries can join in at their own level with the help of one of the stalwart sport assistants. Large underground kitchens and dining hall, which doubles up as extra space for gymnastics and dance. Parents and children like the open kitchens and serving hatch; children can see food cooking and what they're eating. 'Absolutely yum,' said two little ones.

All is brought together by the school community's positive, can-do attitude, and the house system which sees children of all ages working together on different projects. There is also a good choice of lunchtime and after-school clubs. Year 3 upwards get the opportunity to go on residential trips around the UK and France. Most families live locally; many are part of the strong Parents' Association, with some going on to become school governors. Parents we spoke to all commented on the friendliness of the children and the pleasant character of the school. In the final year pupils work towards the leaver's qualification the Hornsby House Certificate. This involves achievements including taking on leadership roles, displaying resilience during the year 6 trip to a Scottish activity centre, taking part in a charity event and speaking confidently in public: an ideal finale to the junior school years.

Hugh Myddelton Primary School

Myddelton Street, London EC1R 1YJ

Ages 2–11 **Pupils** 482

020 7278 6075
www.hughmyddeltonschool.org.uk

Executive Head: Since 2013, Nathalie Parker, BMus (King's College, London), PGCE (Goldsmiths), BSc psychology (Birkbeck). After various posts in south London including deputy head at an all-through academy, glamorous, smoky-eyed Ms Parker (40s) arrived at what, unexpectedly for her, turned out to be a school in difficulties. 'Its Ofsted and data suggested it was a good school, so when it was immediately put on warning notice it came as a shock.' Even so, she took the challenge in her stride, turning around the culture of the school in a matter of months and recently earning from Ofsted the most outstanding of outstanding reports. Charming and persuasive, she is lavished with praise by inspectors and parents. 'Inspirational,' say the former; 'visionary,' chorused a parent. 'She's very good at team building and organising, and is completely non-ideological in the best possible sense. She's prepared to use what works.'

Head of school is Tim Barber, BA history (King's College, London), PGCE (Manchester). Now that Ms Parker is spreading her expertise across the local authority, Mr Barber is responsible for the school on a daily basis. After work at primaries in the north of England and north London, he started at Hugh Myddelton as a year 2 teacher in 2011, and has since done virtually every job going. 'It been quite fast moving,' he notes with understatement. Down-to-earth, friendly and enthusiastic, he's also immensely hard working and committed. 'The two make an extraordinarily dynamic duo,' commented a parent.

Entrance: After an understandable dip in applications, word of improvement has now spread and queues are starting to form. This is a community primary so, once the usual reserved categories have been addressed, siblings and distance from the gates are next in line.

Exit: Strenuous efforts are made to ensure every pupil finds the right secondary, whether that's at a local comp (City of London Academy, Highbury Fields), selective state (Dame Alice Owen's, Queen Elizabeth Barnet), or independent (Highgate, City of London boys and girls, Christ's Hospital). Eleven plus preparation given for entrance tests and interviews, and high flying year 5 girls encouraged to attend City of London School for Girls summer school.

Remarks: What's extraordinary about Hugh Myddelton is the rapidity of its progress from floundering to fantastic, moving from 'causing concern' to 'can't-say-a-word-against-it' in just three years. (Nowadays, it sits in the top three per cent of all schools in England for pupils' progress in reading, writing and maths, and most whizz comfortably beyond the national norm.) The formula for its success lies in excellent teaching, exceptional teamwork and a relentless focus on the needs of every child, starting with incoming 2 year olds, who are given a speech-and-language fillip to ensure they're reception ready. Reading taught as early as possible, through phonics, corridor walls decorated with common words, and a 'talk-for-writing' strategy (originally introduced for those on the foothills of English, now working well for all).

Teachers consult daily to ensure each child is receiving what they require, and subject-specialist teams work across the age groups. 'In the English team, for example, all the teachers will look at each book, identifying what's being done well, what's needed to improve.' The overall approach is 'keep up, not catch up', supported through tailored work and one-to-one tuition where necessary. Once reading, everyone is given challenging texts, and writing standards are truly impressive. Year 5 and 6 benefit from an additional teacher, bringing class numbers down to 18-20, ensuring everybody gets added focus in these critical final years.

Special needs particularly well supported, with two internal teachers, a speech-and-language specialist and Ms Parker's psychology-informed background. Teaching assistants given specific training, too, and external experts called on as needed. Those who arrive with little English well catered for ('When my daughter started, she was groping for words,' said one parent. 'Now she loves English.') as are the gifted and talented – the school works with The National Association for Able Children (NACE). 'They're completely aware of who the kids are and are very good at getting everyone to learn without making them feel like losers or driving them to distraction,' said one father. 'They stretch them, but never push them too far.' Homework is made fun with six-week topic-based projects, produced with teacher and parent help, and displayed in the dedicated 'homework gallery'.

Virtually every child reaches the government targets in national tests, but tests are certainly not the main objective of the education here and the curriculum is broad and stimulating ('exciting,' say the inspectors). All taught Spanish by a native speaker ('Though we're thinking of moving to Mandarin,' says the head). Expansive new science and technology room allows hands-on experience of everything from cooking to stargazing. Well stocked library is the venue for book club and a welcoming place for older pupils to listen to younger ones read. Technology well supported with a plethora of chrome books and iPads, but personal mobiles locked safely away every morning on arrival.

Ms Parker, a composer by training, came to the school with the brief of improving the arts and sport, and, alongside her multitude of other achievements, these goals have been fully realised. A music specialist now works with classroom teachers, all learn recorder in year 3, keyboard skills in year 5, and singing thrives with junior and senior choirs. Free clarinet and brass tuition put into practice in school band. Music made real, too, with visits to orchestras at the Barbican and Royal Festival Hall. The visual arts also well supported by Islington Arts Factory, and the school has partnered with neighbouring Sadler's Wells Theatre, bringing subsidised tickets and opportunities to perform.

Generous, well kept grounds, Astroturf pitch and well-equipped gym are all put to good use, with a specialist sports coach teaching hockey, tennis and multi-sports. Basketball and football on offer before school, and after-school clubs include karate, gymnastics and street dance. All interests catered for, however, with clubs for Gutsy Girls (to encourage female leadership), archaeology and debate (with pupils excelling in Debate Mate primary-school league.). Much-enjoyed forest school ('Forest school is number one,' said a pupil) takes place in Abney Park in Stoke Newington, developing appreciation of the natural world alongside confidence and independence. High aspirations fostered, too, by 'spotlight days', when pupils visit City University and talk to students about law, computer science, engineering and psychology. Breakfast and after-school club are a boon for working parents.

Named for Hugh Myddelton, royal jeweller to James 1, the school was originally founded in the 1850s, but moved to its current building – a mid-century gem by Julian Sofaer – in the 1960s. A dazzling new extension added in 2009 was opened by former pupil Cat Stevens. The composite provides a luminous and harmonious backdrop to the calm, well organised and purposeful atmosphere within. Classrooms and corridors are spacious and bright, outside space, blessed by an electronic noticeboard and covered picnic tables, an oasis of green in a gritty urban world.

Behaviour, once something of an issue, is now acknowledged by Ofsted to be 'impeccable'. 'Children won't accept poor behaviour,' says the head. 'They're horrified if someone doesn't open a door.' The 'manners curriculum' focuses on topics such as 'meeting and greeting' and 'how to disagree politely', within an overall culture where the dominant motif is praise rather than blame (with parents regularly alerted to the positive through electronic ClassDojo system).

Pupils given plenty of responsibility – on the school council, as head boy and girl, as anti-bullying champions (the school belongs to the Anti-Bullying Alliance and bullying is a rarity). The message: 'Be reflective, responsible and respectful' is also regularly addressed in assemblies, which explore big world issues (gun law, Brexit, equal pay, etc) in 'thought for the week'. 'I'm so impressed by their general knowledge,' said one mother; while another admired the empathy this instils. 'My 6-year-old son came home the other day and said "I'll get you some money from my money box because women don't earn as much men".' Community engagement also firmly emphasised, and pupils recently won a competition with the bright idea of exchanging their own technical expertise with gardening help from the elderly.

Though money, as always, is tight, the head has been clever at tapping in to local resources, such as The Worshipful Company of Water Conservators and Thames Water, who helped fund the science room, and Foyles, who contributed to the library. Nearby City University provides volunteer students for extra tuition.

About 60 per cent of pupils are in receipt free school meals, but local professionals are increasingly in evidence. What's more, parental attitudes throughout have changed. 'When we started,' says the head, 'there was a sense of apathy, even hostility, a real sense of them and us.' That's definitely a thing of the past. 'Everything about this school is fantastic,' exclaimed one parent. 'My kids complain when it's the holidays,' said another. A year 6 who's gone through the revolution agrees with both: 'It's now an exciting place to come to school.' Wide ethnic mix, with no dominant group, and kids mix well in school and out. 'The kids love each other and spend a lot of time together. There's a real sense of community.'

Hurlingham School

122 Putney Bridge Road, London SW15 2NQ

Ages 4–11 **Pupils** 326

Fees: £16,290 – £16,950 pa

020 8874 7186
www.hurlinghamschool.co.uk

H

Headmaster: Since 2010, Jonathan Brough BEd (Cantab) NPQH (40s), married to Harry, a high powered city lawyer. There really was no way out for JB, born with a double dose of the teaching gene. His father made a slight push to suggest an unlikely career as an air traffic controller and his mother, a home economics teacher, might have liked him to be a food technologist but teaching won the battle early on. Now, he has occasional thoughts of what might have been, brought on by Bake Off, but he is clearly extremely happy about the choice he made. Before arriving in Putney, he ran a selective single sex school (the City of London Girls' Prep) and says that he 'was extremely fortunate that the vacancy at Hurlingham came up at just the right time'.

Admitting to being a 'stereotypical bookworm', with a preference for new hardback novels, he's a bit of a theatrical groupie, having ventured onto the boards in his student days. However his first love is his school and this 'finger in every pie' head is totally involved in the nuts and bolts of his scholastic kingdom, either when rehanging a stray duffle coat on its peg or unconsciously revealing an in-depth understanding of a particular child and its parents. His declared wish to be at the cutting edge of all things educational and proving his point that 'a non-selective school can be just as good (if not better) for gifted and talented pupils than any selective institution' is a big hit with local parents.

Entrance: Into three forms at reception from a range of nurseries but first priority goes to siblings and children from the newly acquired Lion House nursery and pre-prep, now officially under the Hurlingham banner, and then to those living within 1.2km of the school. Non-selective.

Exit: Most popular destinations currently Surbiton High, Putney High, St John's Leatherhead and Kingston Grammar; also plenty of offers from eg Emanuel, Ibstock Place, Notre Dame, Streatham and Clapham, Whitgift. Sixteen scholarships in 2018. This is a fine achievement given the total lack of selection at entry.

Remarks: Only a few strokes away from the start of the Boat Race under Putney Bridge, the busy road outside explains the slightly bossy instructions about delivering and collecting your children. TfL should take lessons from this military-style operation that takes place twice a day in the semi-underground car park. Child in back seat clutching belongings on lap is swooped on by teacher and bundled into school whilst parent, with eye firmly on rear mirror, waits for the signal to move swiftly on.

The proximity of the river also accounts for why the four school houses are called Herons, Kingfishers, Mallards and Swans. Apparently, the somewhat eccentric founder of the school was glancing from her waterside window (the school overlooked the river at that time) and spotted the ornithologically unlikely sight (particularly in the case of the kingfisher) of all four birds dancing in the water. As the myth goes, she immediately commanded that the children should, henceforth, be divided into colonies of birds but, in reality, the names were chosen by previous pupils.

Above the basement garage are stacked three floors of classrooms, a large multi-purpose hall and some rather skimpy offices; the deputy head's quarters resembling an engine, rather than a ball, room. An out of scale ante-room with panoramic school photographs on the walls leads onto an L-shaped hall. Here, via another ruthless planning schedule, the space metamorphoses from assembly room to karate studio to food hall to theatre, all in one action-packed day. We were intrigued that the props to achieve this were kept in a miraculous cupboard, crammed with tables to eat off and even a stage to act on.

Across the marginally dreary passage, dividing the admin and school hall from the rest of the school, you enter another world: literally every inch of every surface is decorated in some form or other, transforming this potentially uninspiring building. We particularly enjoyed the doors, in years 1 and 2, turned into illustrated book covers. After a lengthy inspection, we decided that our favourites were Lost and Found by Oliver Jeffers decorated with a plump, red scarf-wearing penguin and Whatever Next by Jill Murphy, represented by a teddy bear peering out of a box sporting a bright green colander as a hat. The doorways also fulfilled an additional function of making you feel that you were literally inside the book the children were studying.

In reception, three light, bright classrooms all open onto a playground, filled in the afternoon with small people engaged in a variety of outwardly jolly activities concealing a definite learning plan devised by the smiley, supervising teachers. Above this apparently relaxed operation are stacked three more floors topped with a new Astroturf outside space. There is an orderly feel to this purpose-built place with extensive libraries on each floor, and the layout allows the school to divide easily into junior, middle and upper with a natural upward progression from year 1 to the more serious academic atmosphere of year 6 on the top floor.

Once inside the classrooms, three to a year throughout, the relatively young staff teach the same syllabus to all the pupils but adapted to each child's needs. There are no specific scholarship sets, only maths is setted from year 1 and English in the run up to 11+. Instead, the teachers rely on their knowledge of each individual to decide how much work they can handle. A parent remarked that her daughter was asked by her teacher, 'Do you ever learn your spelling words or do you just know them?' and on being told the latter was given an extra five, more challenging, words to learn every week. This attitude was echoed by another parent who praised the bespoke nature of the homework handed out and the fact that the teachers know the children 'very, very well'.

They seem to have found the secret recipe (maybe down to JB's flirtation with food technology) to getting the maximum out of each child without taking the fun out of learning, and parents talk of their children being 'massively enthusiastic about going to school'. JB teaches mainly extension classes, often in his own space, evoking the comment: 'it was really good, we went and had our lesson in his office'. As pupils move up the school they are given increasing responsibility over organising their days, a popular move amongst parents who feel that they start senior school ahead of some floundering contemporaries. Homework diaries have to be filled in and they find their own way from lesson to lesson, more steps towards the increasingly independent life ahead.

JB is meticulous over preparing pupils for the 11+ and exams for their next school, giving them computer tests as well as maths and English and then advising on three sets of choices, optimistic, realistic and back-up. A surprised mother even told us that her son was so well prepared that he 'loved the exams'. Once 11+ is out of the way additional time is given to Latin and computing, which led to one ex-pupil at her next, high-flying school being charged with explaining technical skills to her new classmates. No child has failed the OCR qualifications that everyone takes in both subjects, fairly amazing as these is often used to test 16 year olds and Hurlingham is a school of totally mixed abilities.

When we visited, an art teacher was busily cutting out glittery stars, the results of a competition to design Christmas decorations. The entries ranged from the wildly wacky and somewhat impractical to the more traditional, but the winner came from reception, proving that in festive design, imagination can trump technique. The walls featured large paintings of animals, one a particularly convincing horse, clearly the work of a pupil who had really 'got it' when it came to equines. Art squeezes into and onto every nook and cranny, including the ankle level window to the parking lot featuring, literally, hundreds of small, brightly painted pottery people. Music is also built into the life of the school with an 'inspiring' head of music who, despite his professional musical theatre background, makes a determined effort to include everyone in regular concerts, even if their finger work produces the odd rather squeaky note.

Music, art, drama and dance also feature in an after-school club (MADD) and we were secretly pleased to be told by JB that the ukulele was passe in Putney and that 'DooDs' (junior clarinet) and 'TooTs' (junior flute) were becoming all the rage. Unsurprisingly, the Christmas play from reception runs along the angels and animals route, but the rest take a hand in writing their own scripts. Books, presumably partly due to JB's addiction ('book club is a real treat for me'), play a huge part in the school with the head of English handing out free copies of books suggested by the pupils, and a discussion society that decided, with a bit of prodding, that it would be incorrect to read Finding Black Beauty without reading its inspiration first, however distressing you might find the fate of Ginger.

Very slightly divided parental opinions on sport, with one mother telling us that she thought that it was a pity that there were not more specialist sports available whilst another said they did a great job, particularly in being flexible over boys who are un-keen on rugby being allowed to play hockey with the girls and fielding mixed cricket teams in the summer. All commented that a real effort was made to make it enjoyable even if sport was not one of your major talents, and the head remarked that you could feel a frisson of excitement through the whole school when year 2 marched out for their first match.

Special needs provision is comprehensive, ranging from sending children home with reading games to making life easier for a severely disabled child. The dos and don'ts of school life are made very clear at Hurlingham with six golden rules, deliberately written to show both sides of the coin, an example being 'We are kind, helpful and polite. We do not hurt the feelings of others'. To back up this philosophy, various tools are used from traffic lights in the lower school to Excellence and Order books further up. Postcards and giant golden stars announce good deeds as well as hard work and we are very pleased to report that the Excellence book was nearly full and the Order book barely started.

The organisational skills of JB and the rest of the staff in shifting over 300 different children in an endless pattern of activity – 'no two days are the same and they are never bored' – is admirable in itself, but the dedication to helping all children scale their particular peak, both academically and socially, is truly impressive. This is a kaleidoscope of a school where the whirling patterns are constantly formed into happy, successful children.

Ibstock Place School

Clarence Lane, London SW15 5PY

Ages 4–18 **Pupils** 991 **Sixth form** 140

Fees: £16,290 – £20,880 pa

020 8876 9991
www.ibstockplaceschool.co.uk

Headmistress: Since 2000, Anna Sylvester-Johnson BA PGCE. Previously three years as head at Arts Educational School. A far cry from her first job, aged 22, at SW London comprehensive teaching disaffected pupils, there only because of rise in leaving age. 'Quite an eye-opener.' Followed by a two stints at Lycée Français Charles de Gaulle, separated by spell at Green School in Hounslow, where she was head of English.

Married to local GP, with two grown up children (both Cambridge grads), Mrs S-J, a formidable, charismatic presence with ramrod straight posture, is the reason why school has shot from laissez-faire offshoot of a teacher training college to oversubscribed and highly successful all-through school today (with just-added kudos of HMC membership).

Though parents don't see much of her, no complaints. With well-regarded management team mopping up day-to-day concerns, Mrs S-J is seen as the visionary seeing the school on to future glories.

Supportive and doesn't miss a thing, say staff. 'She trusts me to make the right judgement – am careful about not taking advantage'. Pupils value her good opinion. 'If she congratulates you, it's a big deal,' felt a sixth former.

Parents know their place. Mrs S-J is 'effective' with 'incredible' charm – but will not kowtow. 'Unlike a lot of heads, she has no glossy exterior towards people who she feels complain for the sake of complaining,' said parent.

Approach has its benefits. 'Children are judged on the basis of who they are as individuals, not what various competitive mothers may be trying to do,' said a parent.

That said, parents stress that this is not a school for bolshy families. 'We're just really grateful that the school's telling our child what they're good at,' said one.

Head of juniors since 2015 is Miss Marion MacDonald. Previously at Cottesmore School, Sussex where she helped set up the pre-prep department. Brought up as only girl in boys' boarding prep (where father taught) she headed for a career in the City only to embrace destiny two years later and enrol for teacher training. Started here in 2013 as a class teacher before promotion to current role. Still teaches (year 5 maths).

Highly rated. 'Always looks on the positive side and lets us off if about to get a conduct mark,' said a pupil (this Panglossian view wasn't shared by parents or Miss MacDonald herself...) 'Peppy and energetic', 'has finger on the pulse', 'warm,' say parents.

Has banned unhealthy snacks in the playground. Operates better than open door policy – 'If you have a question you can grab her as and when, which I do appreciate,' said parent.

Best bit of the job 'without a doubt' is the children. 'They make me laugh every day.' Proud of friendly atmosphere. 'I don't believe in respect based on fear. It's earned.'

Academic matters: Forget 'alternative' reputation. Results now are as mainstream as they come. In 2018, 84 per cent of GCSEs were graded A*-A/9-7; 46 per cent A*/A and 73 A*/B at A level.

While inspectors are besotted with school's liberal and humane approach (several mentions in the latest report), school stresses its 'fundamentally conservative' approach with focus on traditional academic subjects, 10 GCSEs the norm with mother language an occasional extra.

Lunchtime house maths quiz (questions in German and French – no native speakers or bilingual pupils allowed) – reinforced the message. If you want an easy academic option, this ain't it. Mixed ability groups in year 7 with subsequent setting for science, maths and English. Two hours of homework in year 7 rising to three-ish in sixth form. Subject support and free supervised homework club till 6pm help to colour in the gaps.

Firefly – online homework tracking from distribution to completion – is 'brilliant for disorganised children or parents with multiple offspring,' says parent. Not the place for more than mild SEN. About 100 have some learning needs, only 40 or so get formal support – a few touch-type, for example – and nobody has an EHCP. Similarly, while there are plenty of EAL pupils (some multilingual), only 10 have additional help with English.

Mind-expanding activities include senior school subject-related clubs ('Make' – takes things apart and rebuilds – and 'Why?' – your questions answered) and lots of debate, with Year 8 geographers attempting to solve famine in Somalia in UN-style committee meeting (English Speaking Board qualifications offered from prep school upwards).

School is in top five per cent for progress, assisted by low pupil to teacher ratios (one to nine in seniors and one to 10 in prep), plus zest to uncover pupils' strengths. 'My child has transformed into a completely different creature,' said parent.

After gentle start in the pre-prep, pace becomes brisker in year 5 with introduction of timetabled tests – 'cycle', in school parlance – in maths, English and reasoning, which give class places and clarify the likelihood of making the cut to senior school. (Parents are asked not to – and don't – share results). School felt to tackle this tricky topic with honesty. 'Handle it very sensitively,' said parent. Ditto support for the anxious or disorganised. 'My child is a worrier – they spotted that quite early and spent time reassuring her,' said prep parent. All achieved with quality teaching. Old cynics have been replaced by younger enthusiasts (many in 20s). 'Almost exclusively exceptional,' said one prep parent. 'Have to be strict but they help, they're open,' thought senior pupil.

Attention to detail extends to dog ends of the academic year. After 11+ exams, prep pupils get a fiver to start a mini business – home knitted pom poms a recent highlight – while year 11s (known here as PVIs – pre-sixth formers) return after GCSEs for a summer school with left field options (creating balsamic vinegar capsules in s molecular gastronomy session) and conventional ones (making a clay bust in a day). Can convert pupils to formerly unenvisaged subjects. 'Didn't know I would take further maths,' said sixth former whose idea of bliss was work experience on an oil rig. Others raved about Mandarin, sport and art.

Games, options, the arts: Just contemplating the range of activities is exhausting, so numerous (around 70 clubs each for prep and seniors) that they stretch out of the week and into Saturdays. Why go anywhere else? 'I'm cancelling family's gym membership,' said mother. At least one club a week the minimum – one prep pupil was up to five, and counting.

Helped by compact campus – getting from A to B doesn't involve a trawl through the alphabet – though one parent felt stronger communications – particularly for new bods – about where to collect children would be helpful.

Arts remains the school's big thing, with addition of new, better facilities to do them in. Dance (ballet, street etc – nothing wrong with musical theatre but needs good foundations first, says head) is timetabled in prep with clubs for all ages. Though sheds senior boys along the way, some hang in there – several at pro standard.

Same richness applies to drama. Budding thesps have quick change performance space (smaller back up in prep school) which transforms from seating to scenery in minutes. Even the green room – all glass, light and views – is stunning.

Around 400 learn at least one instrument (string scheme for all prep pupils), with boys-only ensembles (and positive discrimination to ensure gender balance in selective IPS singers).

Glitzy productions such as Cinderella. Also have ensemble in residence which performs pupils' GCSE compositions live – beats headphone and computer rendition any time).

Quality of art is stunning and relentlessly original, from prep school's pen and ink reimaginings of Rousseau's tiger that avoid listless copies seen elsewhere to sixth former's Pre-U work, a menacingly beautiful street scene with hurrying people interspersed by stitched outlines of ghostly others – a thought-provoking tribute to the 'disappeared'.

As to sport – it's 'out of this world, run very fairly and with great good humour,' said parent. Despite fluctuating interest and talent levels it's often very successful, helped by continuity – sports teachers work with both junior and senior pupils.

Traditional division of girl and boy sports is mutating into something more equal and interesting – girls' football already here; boys' hockey mooted (but surprisingly few takers so on the back burner for now), co-ed cricket and water polo highly successful.

School keeps a careful eye on anyone in danger of what it describes as 'choice anxiety', as well as offering tea (a bargain £2 for the full cake and sandwich experience). No wonder parents describe the choice as 'overwhelming,' but in a good way, they were keen to explain.

Background and atmosphere: Site of two halves, bisected by a road (instant Saturday detention for failure to cross by footbridge). To the left (facing Roehampton) there's the art 'hut', showing age, DT, sports hall and large sports field, all bordered by semi-public Roehampton university accommodation (pupil access strictly controlled). Needs something stiffer than white hydrangeas to transform, so school wisely doesn't attempt it. On the other side, it's beauty all the way. 'I don't remember my school being this nice,' said another visitor, staring up at the winding, intricately carved staircase. Nor us.

If leavers lack heightened aesthetic sensibilities, it won't be for want of trying. Mrs SJ's combines an eye for beauty with another for a bargain (binocular vision worth having) and is an auction regular (finds include the ancient font masking the hole where grab rail, demanded by health and safety, was briefly planted). Main building features a pitch perfect recreation of a de luxe Edwardian country house lifestyle (the Duchess of Sutherland, house's original owner, would feel she'd never been away) to the best of contemporary design. Cleaners regularly wash the light walls (impressively fingerprint free) and there's even talk of 'low level dusting.' Library bookshelves have ironwork frames built to the head's design, shelves made of extra-strong American white oak. Even reception pupils' sandpit is actually plastic beads – tens of thousands of them. Flow authentically but rubbish for sand castles.

Outside, even the smallest of spare spaces is densely planted (with occasional tactical use of artificial grass). Statement vases as well as statement wheelbarrows pep up paths and enhance armadillos (the curved music practice huts) with those signature white hydrangeas everywhere. Though slap bang in the centre of the site, pre prep (reception to year 1 – gentler transition through EYFS) and prep (years 2-6) have a school within a school, think parents. Smart, well-equipped classroom blocks, library, art and ICT space and mostly soft surface play areas (pupils keen for upgrade to remaining asphalt). Remaining homeopathic quantities of the old Froebel school (display of earnest looking 1960s toys) don't impinge.

Prep uniform (navy cords for boys, Liberty print dresses for girls) is both sweet and practical (if a bit wanting in a heatwave, said pupils). Youngest wear emerald green jackets – ensures maximum visibility during school visits – navy duffle coat for older pupils. Wellies essential, say parents. Children will spend plenty of time outside. Teachers, too, have their uniform – males, anyway, all in shades of grey (required, apparently). Well, you can't have anyone clashing with those lovely cream walls.

New refectory/backup performance space (due spring 2019) will replace current cramped conservatory. We're guessing it's unlikely to be a riot of primary colours...

Pastoral care, well-being and discipline: 'We're quite relaxed,' say sixth formers firmly, looking, well, quite relaxed. 'If you have a worry they will show you it's not the end of the world.' Parents agree. 'When I went around ... I saw incredibly happy confident pupils, at ease with themselves and each other who looked like they believed that the world was a good and exciting place,' said one.

It's a tribute to effective pastoral care headed by class teachers (for juniors), with vertical houses, each with academic and pastoral tutor, in senior school. No mollycoddling but 'they do look after us,' said one. Daily Pupil Notes record staff concerns. Effective, say parents, who rarely escalate issues to top level.

Little fazes staff. Transgender pupils are accepted without fuss, uniform policy is flexible (skirts and trousers could be worn by either girls or boys) and there's plenty of give and take ('teachers will always give your child a fair hearing if they think they've been unfairly treated,' said one mother). However, this isn't a place for boat rockers. Parents stress the importance of complying with school expectations, and advisability of paying close attention to home-school contract. Only two or three days a year when blazers aren't worn, for example (sustained scorchio levels only) and detentions are the rule for missing homework. Perks for seniors include arriving early for breakfast, though no common room till sixth form). Zero tolerance for mobile phones, which don't in any case work anywhere pupils might be tempted to use them (loos and library, for example).

While one parent thought there was a little latitude for 'charming' naughtiness – if countered by unimpeachable work ethic and creative talent – tolerance for the merely disruptive felt to be low to zero. 'You fall into line and work hard.' Parents of those who don't (though admittedly we didn't encounter any) would almost certainly have a very different experience. 'It's not that kind of school,' said mother. 'To me this is a smart school that wants to keep itself smart and you have to abide by the rules.' Generally works a treat. 'The most well-behaved children I've ever taught,' says a smart young gent who's off to induct prep pupils into the mysteries of coding. Parents agreed, and were surprised to hear of the small number of pupils we encountered who failed to hold doors for their headmistress. Agreed that uncharacteristic. 'Low blood sugar,' felt Mrs S-J. Only other question mark was over quality of school lunches, particularly for prep pupils. 'Not always appetising and it can sometimes be cold,' thought parent. (School stresses that 'catering team at IPS work extremely hard to get it right and most pupils are positively glowing about the quality of our lunches.') Otherwise, 'I don't believe there's anything that hasn't been handled well.'

Pupils and parents: Catchment typical for area with a blend of well to do with sprinkling of self-effacing celebrities – not an oxymoron as 'don't make a big deal but you know who they are,' said parent. More local than most and friendly, too. 'Pretty nice people,' said mother.

Bonding helped by dynamic PTA selling secondhand uniform and running Christmas fair so successful that upmarket commercial organisations (multi ply cashmere variety) compete to pay for a stand.

Thinking (and living) local definitely a good bet given location – 30 minutes' walk from Barnes Station or a five minute trip on the (free) shuttle bus fleet that runs from 7.30am before school and until 6.10pm afterwards. Otherwise, 'a really challenging place to drive to,' said parent, though drop off parking logistics are eased by pleasant staff member who deals with the hard of understanding with smiling determination.

Entrance: Non-selective in reception (not fair to assess this young, says school), pupils accepted on date of registration. Occasional places in other prep years.

At senior level, substantial competition and growth in selectivity. Two-stage exam process (look for national curriculum level 5 or scores of 105/110). Everyone interviewed (50 staff involved), so anyone with exceptional qualities to offer but an iffy exam performance doesn't lose out.

About 60 per cent of junior pupils go on to senior school but 'no safe passage,' says school – compete on equal basis with external candidates. Informally, parents reckon that school will try to admit pupils, especially siblings, if parents keen – but worth considering how much they'll enjoy the experience. 'Unless they're the child that's happy to bump along at the bottom, they're not going to have a fun time,' said one.

Exit: Once accepted, senior pupils are supported through to 16+. Minimum of a year's warning for those who may not make the cut to sixth form. 'You've got to be academically minded and it's silly to be in an environment where you're not going to feel happy,' says the head. Post 16, some leavers into sixth form colleges (Esher and Richmond) for less 'crunchy' subjects, others to eg Hurtwood House to specialise in drama.

Very occasional unscheduled exits. Just one for drugs in past decade, says school (making it unique in SW London), though head stresses that 'no one is marched through the door. A mistake has been made and therefore we must assist.' Help with rehoming as well as taking in the casualties from other schools. 'We have to understand that we were all children once,' says Mrs S-J.

Bristol a popular university destination, followed by Bath and Oxford Brookes. Several to universities in the USA and Europe; six Oxbridge offers in 2019. Languages popular, usually several to art foundation courses.

Money matters: Music award available at 11+. Music, drama and sports scholarships at 13+ (no longer at 11+). Academic, creative arts and sports scholarships at 16+. Bursaries means-tested here as everywhere.

Remarks: Striking combination of space, style and success has led to regular appearances on more SW London parents' long lists than ever before. To flourish here, reckoned sixth former, 'you need to be hardworking, ambitious, have to want to do well, be positive, extrovert and not afraid to have fun.' A yen to commune with the odd white hydrangea won't come amiss either.

Ilford County High School

Fremantle Road, Ilford, Essex IG6 2JB

Ages 11–18 **Pupils** 1,016 **Sixth form** 298

020 8551 6496
www.ichs.org.uk

Headteacher: Since 2015, Rebecca Drysdale BSc (40s), who joined the school in 2012 as deputy and then acting headteacher. It was whilst she was doing her degree in geography at Coventry Polytechnic (now Coventry University) that she first caught the teaching bug. 'I had spent a year doing the Marks & Spencer's management training course and immediately took to the personnel side of things. This, coupled with the fact that I loved working with young people, made me realise teaching would be a great career,' she explains. Did her PGCE at Reading, then worked her way up the ranks across two comprehensives and a secondary modern (Chalfont Community College, Bucks; Copleston High School, Ipswich; Charles Darwin School, Biggin Hill), followed by a 10-year stint as assistant headteacher at Edmonton County School.

'I can be scary when I need to be,' she says (and pupils concur), but so long as everyone toes the line, she has a jolly and genial demeanour, as well as being both earnest and refreshingly unassuming – the type you feel would roll her sleeves up and get stuck in whenever needed. Staff describe her as a 'true listener,' taking on board everyone's point of views, which means that when she does make changes, everyone tends to move forward together. Teaches a little, 'but not as much as I'd like,' although she regularly does lunch and break duty, and students we talked to were clearly impressed at how often she chats to them in the corridors.

Sees her role as 'helping what was already a very good school to evolve,' although her attitude should not be mistaken for a lack of vision. 'I want this school to be the best grammar in the area,' she told us. 'I'd like to see people buying houses to try and get their sons into this school. I want people to move to Redbridge to come here.'

Academic matters: In 2018, 66 per cent 9-7 grades at GCSE, with strongest results shown in the sciences and mathematics. Everyone learns French and Spanish in years 7 and 8 takes one language at GCSE, though few take two or continue languages to A level. No setting before GCSE and only then in maths, science and English. Besides maths and sciences, other popular GCSE subjects include geography, history and English, and every child has to take at least one creative GCSE in the likes of PE (particularly popular), art, music and technology. 'We call it EBacc Plus,' says the head, who believes it enhances UCAS forms no end.

At A level, popular subjects include the sciences, economics, mathematics, history and government and politics. Most stick to academic rather than creative subjects, although sixth form enrichment ensures all students continue learning the arts. In 2018, 32 per cent A*/A grades. Subject-based reviews help to monitor each subject and data tracking to monitor pupil progress helps spot and tackle underperformance; not that there is much of that here, according to parents. Maximum class sizes, at 30 (and 26 in the sixth form), are at the higher end. The school funding crisis means that it is increasing class sizes andhasn't offered MFLs at A level for several years, but has now joined up with Valentines High School to teach French and Spanish.

Teacher profile on the older side, reflecting the low staff turnover and long-term experience. All teach their degree subject and many are examiners. Where possible, teaching is practical. Expect plenty of pongs wandering through the science block, for example, where one class was dissecting fish and another had their Bunsen burners all going when we visited. Meanwhile, a history lesson on WWII involved a mock trial for Hitler. In fact, all classrooms we visited were lively, with bright, perceptive students clearly hungry for detail and knowledge. Disappointing to walk past two classrooms with teachers shouting at their class, but maybe that's the price you pay for encouraging such energetic debate. School works on a two-week timetable.

Two-thirds of pupils with EAL requirements plus 30 or so who need SEN support. When we visited, there were students with cerebral palsy, hearing difficulties (including one who was profoundly deaf and also has vision impairment), plus all the usual – dyslexia to autistic spectrum. Can and does cater for wheelchair users, although there are some struggles with the old building – this will be made easier when the new ones are up. 'If students are bright enough to study here, we'll find a way,' says head, who says individual support takes place both in and outside the classroom.

But parental views are mixed on the quality of SEN support. 'My son has a physical disability and we were initially told by people in the area that this might not be the best school for him, but they've been amazing at meeting his needs, whilst still academically challenging him,' said one enthusiastic parent. 'I've been particularly pleased at how they've built up his confidence. SEN support here is very nurturing and they regularly suggest things I've never even thought of.' But others reported that the school's SEND knowledge was lacking, and their child was not well supported. We'd recommend a thorough quiz of the SENCo in regards to your child's condition, and requesting a detailed outline of the support that will be given to him.

The creative curriculum is big here, with students taken off timetable for six per cent of the time in year 7 and four per cent of the time in year 8. Mainly involves students working in small groups to build habits of mind that will stand them in good stead beyond school – leading a team, being a team player, debating, time management, structuring a piece of work etc. We saw it in action during our visit, with year 10s having created a morning of educational activities for year 7s on World Book Day. 'These students devised the plan, worked out the detail, came to me to pitch it, then carried it through,' says the head, who is loathe to call them 'soft skills' for fear of depreciating their value. Other examples include students pretending their plane has crashed on a desert island (they work out how they will survive), commemorating National Holocaust Day and committing to learning a new skill (usually off the list of activities from the Duke of Edinburgh award which, by the way, is an option from year 9 upwards). A particular favourite for students is the project that involves them researching an area of London, then taking a fellow student on a guided tour. The preparation is impressive, with students writing to the likes of Downing Street to request going through the magic gates. By the end, students have learned skills including independent research, preparing engaging speeches, navigating a map and using the tube.

Games, options, the arts: Cricket and football are by far the strongest sports at this school, where on-site facilities are in no short supply. 'Cricket is the most popular and we're good at it; football is also popular, but we're not always quite so good at it,' smiled one pupil. Swimming and rugby also well-liked, whilst other options include basketball, badminton, table tennis, rowing, sailing and rock climbing. Duke of Edinburgh caters for those who prefer walking and expeditions to actual sports. 'The focus here is on fitness for life, not just elite players,' says head.

Oracy is new to the year 7 and 8 English/MFL curriculum and some work for LAMDA exams, but beyond that there's only student-led drama clubs – not great for aspiring thespians. Even whole school productions are rare, although you do get some smaller productions and boys enjoy the annual Speakout Challenge. Art is a different matter, with rich, bold and inspiring work on display – including drawings, paintings and sculpting. We also saw students working on some particularly impressive photography. 'Art is core to cross-curricular work here,' one pupil told us. DT also dynamic, with spirited pupils working hard.

Provision for music is also good. 'This is my absolute favourite department. There are so many chances to learn and perform and there's plenty of sophisticated equipment,' one pupil enthused as he walked us through it. All students study music in years 7, 8 and 9. Over 100 children also have extracurricular music lessons and some exceptional talent can be found here. Some lessons take place at the Redbridge Music School. Pupils have plenty of opportunity to develop their talents on piano, violin, cello, double bass, saxophone, drum, voice and more through orchestra, jazz ensemble, choirs and various bands. There are concerts and performances in London and abroad. But few pupils take art or music A level.

Extracurricular provision is largely sports-based and there's plenty of subject intervention to enable students to further and deepen knowledge in specific topics. Beyond that, there's a rich variety of clubs, groups and ensembles covering everything from astronomy to chess and gaming to debating club.

Day visits to all the usual galleries and museums (particularly for art) and fieldwork visits to the likes of Dover Castle, Epping Forest and the battlefields. Relatively thin on the ground when it comes to residential trips, however, with the exception of exchange trips (mainly to Spain, Germany and France), and sports trips have included Spain, USA and Caribbean in the past. But the school has strong partnerships with schools and colleges in Germany, Spain, Switzerland, Denmark and Iceland and has British Council International School status. 'A lot of our international work involves video conferencing,' explains the head, with examples including peer assessment with a school in Indonesia and a shared wildlife project with a school in Ghana.

Opportunities to volunteer are frequent, including sixth formers going into local primary schools to teach maths and modern foreign languages to small groups. A faith ambassadors scheme involves boys giving talks on what faith means to them (or not – one did a talk on atheism) and there's fundraising projects for local and national charities too.

Background and atmosphere: Founded in 1901 as Park High Grade School, the school was originally co-ed and located in Balfour Road. In 1929, the boys' school split, then moved to its present location in Fremantle Road in 1935. Although smack in the middle of a built-up residential area, the school has a secluded feel. And while the building itself is traditional (think sweeping oak stairwells, large wooden boards with lists of past notables and trophy display cabinets), the fabric of the school is undergoing dramatic change. Newly opened is a science block with 10 labs and six demonstration classrooms, a sixth-form centre, DT suite and more computer areas.

The school layout resembles a figure of eight, with two storeys of classrooms organised around the two adjacent squares, with green areas in the middle that pupils can use at break times. The layout makes it easy for new pupils to find their way around.

The atmosphere here is bustling, lively and purposeful. We'd like to have seen the school corridors livened up with more displays of student work, but where they do exist, they are imaginative and intelligent.

Pastoral care, well-being and discipline: 'You don't learn until you get stuck' is the ethos here, making for a supportive environment, which balances the healthy competition between the boys. Where possible, form tutors – who are generally responsible for pupil welfare and progress – stay with their class all the way up the school. Meanwhile, the vertical house system means all boys have a head of house looking out for them too. The system provides opportunity for the boys to develop stronger skills in leadership, mentorship and responsibility, plus opportunities to develop relationships across year groups, right to sixth form. A visiting counsellor is available; the school regularly accesses Redbridge services for young people; and there are all the usual talks on sex, drugs and rock 'n' roll through to forced marriages and knife crime. 'One charity came in to do a drama workshop on domestic violence and that was particularly powerful,' says the head.

Year 7s receive peer mentoring from trained older pupils in year 9, 10 and sixth form. 'They're a bit of a role model for the younger ones to look up to,' one pupil told us. For one pupil, who joined at sixth form, this was 'one of the things I liked when I came, people always willing to help'. Bullying nipped in the bud. 'My child was bullied, but when I contacted the teacher, he had it sorted out within two days and he took me through all the measures he'd taken,' said one parent.

Boys are generally well-behaved – reports describe the behaviour as 'outstanding' – which is no doubt helped by the clear warning system and strict rules, for example on uniform. 'But boys will be boys and they are naughty sometimes,' acknowledges the head. Indeed, there was an incident the day we visited. No permanent exclusions, although there had been 14 temporary ones half way through the academic year when we visited, mostly for fighting, saying mean things and bringing in banned substances.

Pupils and parents: Pupils come from a wide mix of ethnic backgrounds, with Asian (Indian, Pakistani and Tamil) the dominant group, then white British, white Eastern European and black African Caribbean. They all come from the borough of Redbridge and some surrounding areas. 'The local authority drew up the smallest circle they could to fully encompass Redbridge, which means you get a little bit of neighbouring boroughs in there too, most notably Waltham Forest and Essex,' explains the headteacher, who describes the school as one of the few grammars left that are true community schools. 'We want it to stay that way,' she says firmly.

Pupils range from bubbly, stumbling and oblivious year 7s making their way between lessons, to the year 11s who are articulate, mature, friendly and inquisitive. In fact, the older pupils who showed us round asked us almost as many questions as we asked them – both rare and refreshing.

There's no PA here, to the disappointment of some parents, but parents generally have good involvement in the school, with almost 100 per cent attendance at parents' evenings and relevant meetings – and parents say that communication is good. The school does have some anxiety about boys whose parents 'have unrealistic aspirations for them' – the 'You will be a doctor!' brigade. But staff try to ensure parents understand exactly what the career they have in mind for their son entails, and to hit home that there are other jobs out there. 'If a boy's real interest and passion is for humanities and not science, fine, as that it is where he will get real satisfaction and achievement.' Work is also done from early on to emphasise that it's about the education, not just the grades. 'The qualifications will get you to the doorway, but you need more than that to walk through it – character, resilience and so on,' says the head.

Notable former pupils include Raymond Baxter, TV personality (Tomorrow's World), Sir Trevor Brooking, footballer, and David Miller, deputy chief inspector of Air Accidents. Lots of presentation evenings hosted by alumni, including some of these big names.

Entrance: More than 1,100 boys in the borough of Redbridge and nearby compete for the 180 places available each year by sitting the 11+ examination. The test, which has recently changed to CEM (aimed to unearth the brightest children, not the most tutored), is administered by the borough. School manages its own admissions to the sixth form, with places offered only to boys with 9-6 in their chosen subjects, plus at least eight 6s across the best of their GSCE results. 'It sounds counter-intuitive, but the idea is to get breadth as well as depth,' explains the headteacher. All sixth form entrants also require grade 4 or over in English and maths. Parents of pupils who get into this school say their sense of relief is huge, which is unsurprising given that it is the only boys' grammar in the borough.

Exit: Almost all (some 80-90 per cent) stay on to sixth form. Medicine and engineering are the most popular subjects chosen at university, although others include economics, architecture, dentistry, law and physics. Majority choose to study in London at eg King's College and UCL, whilst others go to Russell Group universities across the UK. 'If they're brave enough to go outside London, they're brave enough to pick far and wide,' says the head. One off to medical school in 2018 (in Bulgaria); generally several optometrists, pharmacists and biomedics.

Remarks: This is a school that delivers a very high standard of academic teaching and much more besides, producing young men who seem genuinely well prepared for the wider world. It's not for the faint-hearted, with firm rules and high expectations, but there's a strong support system to back it all up, with a caring head and exceptionally experienced teaching staff. We found boys well-adjusted, happy and hungry to learn.

International School of London

139 Gunnersbury Avenue, London W3 8LG

Ages 3–18 **Pupils** 400 **Sixth form** 75

Fees: £19,000 – £26,300 pa

020 8992 5823
www.isllondon.org

Principal: Since September 2018, Richard Parker, who has been principal of ISL Surrey primary school since 2015, and was also co-principal of the London campus. Started working in a law firm in the City, which may have been the inevitable job choice for a Cambridge graduate in history, but he left law and went to the Institute of Education, London, trained as a secondary school teacher and taught at several state London schools before he and his wife moved to teach in international schools in Spain, Argentina, Hong Kong, Portugal and Brunei. Two children.

Academic matters: Early childhood classes start full time from 3 years old and parents said it was a blessing to have all children at the same school with the same school hours. Long days for little ones, but the option to have a rest in the afternoon helps. Not that there was much sleeping when we visited – children were busy eating and cleaning up and playing. Lots of equipment and adults meant children were cheerful and well occupied. A very well-designed play area just for the early years with plants, wooden toys and climbing benches and even a mini amphitheatre, where story telling and plays take place. Small classes and high teacher:pupil ratio. Parents confirmed that much of the learning takes place through play.

Primary class size varies from but is never more than 22 pupils, which together with the fact that we saw a classroom assistant or extra teacher in many of the classrooms means that the high teacher:pupil ratio continues up the school, and confirms what the pupils explained to us as 'lots of support and help whenever you need it'. Parents said that the longstanding head of primary knows every child by name and is very present and responsive. The school follows the Primary Years Programme, an international curriculum leading to the International Baccalureate. Learning is done in six week Units of Enquiry and the aim is for each topic to cover all subjects. Much of the learning is student interest based and interactive, with peer to peer teaching and debate. The aim is for pupils not only to acquire knowledge but to have conceptual understanding, gain skills and develop beliefs and attitudes which they can demonstrate through responsible action. This interdisciplinary learning seems to be appreciated by pupils, who told us that school was fun and they looked forward to coming to school, and parents, who appreciate that pupils 'learn how to learn' and that the school has a 'liberal' approach to education'. Several spoke about the advantages of 'a fully integrated curriculum'.

The end of the Primary Years Programme is celebrated at a grade 5 exhibition. Parents we spoke to felt that since the curriculum is fairly child led, the level is well matched and work is differentiated by ability – possible with such small classes. However, some suggested that native English speakers may not be overly stretched. The language programme is a distinguishing feature of the school. Regular teaching in their mother tongue as well as intensive English lessons ensure that that pupils maintain their own language while acquiring a second or third language. Parents said that every child showed real fluency within two years. This basic tenet of ISL maintains that children will learn a second language better if they maintain and develop their first language – any language learning enhances language development as well as being good for personal and educational development. We saw pupils in tiny groups or individually learning Swahili, Finnish, Arabic, Spanish or French, and the library has an impressive selection books in 18 different languages.

The Middle Years Programme does not feel very different from the primary years. Pupils, however, felt that there was more work and more independence required. The language programme continues alongside the MYP with its emphasis on global contexts and key concepts. The aim is to acquire skills to help with learning and life. There are self-initiated personal projects, work on laptops (given by the school or supported with bring your own device initiative) and an emphasis on independent reflective learning. One student said, 'It teaches you how to work and gives you explanations', and another said, 'You are graded on how you work things out, not on the result only, and teachers mark on your critical thinking'. Clearly the message on reflective teaching and learning has got through. Facilities are not extensive, but the school is well equipped. Two science labs, plenty of laptops, a large well-stocked current library which includes newspapers and magazines, interactive whiteboards, and endless language learning rooms. The mother tongue language programme and intensive EAL continue where needed in middle years.

The IB diploma programme is housed in a building some 10 minutes' walk from the rest of the school, and so it feels like a sixth form college with fingerprint entry registration and a spacious, bright common room overlooking the small courtyard garden. The library is at the top of the building in a quiet study zone with many students wearing headphones. Smaller classrooms cover the various IB subjects on offer – economics is very popular, as are maths and the sciences (biology perhaps even more than physics and chemistry). A huge, light art room. Languages, unsurprisingly, often taken at higher level IB as most students are multilingual. In 2018, average point score of 33, with two students getting 43 points. Eighty-four of students graduated with bilingual diplomas.

A grade 10 foundation class (15/16 year olds) particular to the school gives intensive English lessons and preparation for the IB curriculum. Students follow a range of subjects (English, maths, science, humanities, PE, mother tongue) and the course focuses on developing their academic English so that they can move successfully into post-16 education. Most stay on to take IB diploma at ISL.

Games, options, the arts: Extracurricular subjects and the arts have taken on new energy recently – one parent said it was unrecognisable now with the number of clubs and non-academic subjects being taught. A new music teacher who is proving very popular and dynamic has increased the music uptake and output – all grade 3 pupils take violin now, and grand primary and middle years musical theatre productions clearly a matter of great excitement and preparation. Similarly, a new middle years drama teacher seems to be a good influence, using the large bright space at the top of the main school.

For art, classes are divided into three and students do a rota of visual art and design technology with both hard and soft materials. Laser cutters and 3D printers, sewing machines and collage, mask making and woodwork. A lively hive of activity and creativity with much emphasis on the planning and design elements.

A real highlight of the school for the pupils is the 'makers' space' where student-led technological creations can take place – either as part of a lesson or in breaks and after-school clubs. Video recording and editing, creation of a 3D printer, video game design, innovations and machines of every sort. Dyson would be thrilled, as are the students, with the possibilities to make and create. Students said to us that the school makes you want to learn more but without making it feel like work. We certainly got a sense of learning through creating in that classroom.

Sports led by three person PE team – dance, hockey, basketball, volleyball, football. Swimming every year in junior school with kids bussed to Brentford Sports Centre. The school has a gym and playground but uses a nearby playing field for wider sports activities. A recently signed contract will see the school having access to newly built sports centre at nearby Gunnersbury Park. Sports rarely involves many inter-school competitions but some fixtures arranged with other international schools. Lots of time and clubs for tennis, yoga, basketball and football. Parents felt that kids get an excellent sports education despite paucity of on site sports facilities, partly because they are taught general skills – such as kicking or throwing – rather than a specific sport. More competitive children use local sports clubs.

Other after-school clubs clearly well used – Glee Club was one child's favourite for musical theatre; there's also eg journalism, badminton, chess, Lego robotics, global issues debating. Many clubs led by students from the diploma programme, presumably in order to gain points towards the IB and to fulfil the community or action side of the programme. DJ-ing taught by one student who proudly told us this had resulted in his club members getting their own equipment and setting up as part time DJs.

Background and atmosphere: An older red-brick building with modern additions on two sides forms a U-shaped school round the playground/school bus parking area. All pupils now come in through the main reception area (fingerprint entry system as well as more usual registration in class) and there is a flow to the school despite its many additions. It was bought in the 70s and was one of the first schools to offer all three IB programmes (PYP, MYP and DP). It is one of three schools owned by a Lebanese family who are still very involved, although there is an active board of governors too. Some links and support from the conglomerate of the schools, but this school is the largest and most established, with the heads reporting directly to the board and the proprietors. It is liberal in outlook, catering for an almost exclusively international student body. This makes it wonderfully international in outlook and values including a great openness to other cultures. It also makes it painful for pupils who stay longer and live through friends leaving regularly. This turnover is part of the reality of ISL though an effort is being made to appeal to more local families, and not a moment too soon, according to parents. There is an active alumni body and one of its aims is to ensure links between ex-students of all ages are maintained. The transitions programme supports families and students when friends leave as well as supporting families who are new to the school – with a good family mentoring system.

Door-to-door bus service is available but with growing London traffic problems school strongly recommends that families choose to live in neighbourhoods like Kew, Chiswick or Ealing.

Pastoral care, well-being and discipline: Part of being an international school means that all the students have something in common, and pupils told us that was why they all got on so well and there was never any bullying, stealing or behavioural problems – they said, 'we are all different and that makes us the same'. They mentioned talks about drugs, mental health, guidance, sexting use of the internet and alcohol, and parents felt that kids had a good education in ethics and values – words like empathy used from early years. No-one could remember incidences of discipline so we couldn't get examples of this – though a discipline policy available in writing.

Student council in evidence and clearly plenty of input from pupils and parents. Some parents felt that the school listened to parents too much – the school is very anxious to please, rather than having the confidence to state its position. But perhaps the active and eloquent parent teachers association is hard to ignore.

Learning support department consists of SENCo for both lower and upper schools who sees pupils regularly as well as coordinating speech and language therapy and outside professionals. Pupils frequently self refer to full-time counsellor, who also supports teachers and sometimes meets parents. Counsellor also gives talks on relationships and general health (though sex education left to the biology teachers).

Parents spoke of the a 'warm atmosphere' and in particular the 'smooth transition', with school praised for its warm welcome to the many new faces each year. Good relationships between different year groups enhanced by vertical integration – clubs, mentoring, joint drama and fundraising activities etc.

School lunches delicious and prepared in house, with limited choice. A continental school feel with everyone eating the same food together.

Pupils and parents: Large numbers of Italians, Japanese, Americans, Dutch, French and British represented in the pupil body – which is why some families choose it. Also popular is its location – mentioned by every parent we spoke to – near Kew, Chiswick and Ealing. All family friendly areas and good for parents working in town. Not much evidence of chauffeur driven pupils or security guards for little princes and princesses, despite fairly chunky fees. Some of the classes are small lower down the school so less choice of friends for some, but 'more of a community than a school' and 'like family'.

Regular transition workshops to support parents. 'Strong' parents' association organises cookery clubs, outings, welcoming and pairing up of established families with incoming families as well as having regular meetings with school to both support and offer suggestions – and parents say school 'listens to us and is open to implementing parental suggestions'

Entrance: A rolling admissions policy to match the needs of relocating families. Initial contact through admissions team who work hard to ensure that visits and questions and contact generally runs smoothly and easily, since 'parents are already stressed enough'. Interviews by Skype if needed and sight of current school reports. They don't expect kids to have fluent English, but do expect behaviour they can manage and learning needs they can support. Learning support for up to two hours if needed included in fees, and extra (for example individual classroom assistance) paid for by parents. Sensible experienced admissions staff keen to maintain non-selective mix at the school, including those with learning needs. Registered as Tier 4 sponsors for visas.

Exit: Over three-quarters stay in the UK to universities including SOAS, King's College London, Cardiff, Exeter. A smaller proportion of students move to universities outside the UK including ESSEC Business School, Paris, Vrije Universiteit Amsterdam and Sciences Po, Paris.

J

Money matters: Privately owned by the Lebanese family who started with this International School of London and now also run the International School of London in Surrey and one in Doha, Qatar. The Makarem family are still on the board, have weekly updates and visit regularly.

Fees are substantial and often paid by employers. No extra charges for the mother tongue language programme (as long as there are at least five students), learning support, day outings, most clubs, but extras include transport, lunches, intensive English, and 'capital development fee'. No bursaries.

Remarks: A perfect school for a child to get intensive English language learning whilst actively maintaining their mother tongue and ideal for families who want to remain near central London. This school seems to be changing and flourishing with new and better facilities and management, whilst having a solid background of experience in international teaching. We liked the international culture of the school and the calm, purposeful atmosphere.

James Allen's Girls' School (JAGS)

Linked with James Allen's Preparatory School (JAPS)

144 East Dulwich Grove, London SE22 8TE

Ages 11–18 **Pupils** 779 **Sixth form** 190 **C of E**

Fees: £17,991 pa

020 8693 1181
www.jags.org.uk

Headmistress: Since 2015, Sally Anne Huang MA MSc PGCE. Previously head of Kent College, Pembury. Educated at Bolton School for Girls and Lady Margaret Hall, Oxford where she read classics and English. PGCE from King's College, London. Taught English and classics at Sevenoaks, where she was also housemistress. Sixth form housemistress at Roedean before becoming deputy head, a post she held for four years.

Head thinks that 'what JAGS does best is prepare young women for the modern world. That's the most important thing we do. We encourage intellectual curiosity, a sense of responsibility and purpose. We want the girls to lead purposeful lives.'

Girls adore her and are charmed by her easy manner and approachability. Seen as a very positive role model. Her open-door policy means pupils regularly pop into her bright red study at break time, often just to stroke her three dogs and say hello. Teaches one lesson a week of classics to top year at the prep school, so knows many of the girls when they arrive. Also teaches philosophy to year 7 and civilisation to year 10. Knows impressive numbers of pupils by name.

Liked by parents too, who appreciate her warmth and energy. 'She has refocused the school,' said one. 'Mrs Huang is already very popular. It was a difficult job stepping into the gargantuan shoes of the previous head but she has injected modernity into the school,' said another. 'A breath of much needed fresh air!' commented another.

Lives next door so regularly nips over at weekends to catch up on work. Husband Alexis is Chinese but grew up in south east London. 'Multi-cultural, ethnic diversity is very close to my heart and so was a definite attraction of coming to JAGS,' she explains. Two teenage sons. Interested in children's literature and is particularly keen on Marcus Sedgwick's novels. Loves theatre of all kinds, especially immersive theatre and frequently heads to nearby Globe. In the holidays, she is at her happiest walking her beloved dogs in Wales, where she has her home. Though brought up outside Manchester, she 'wants to be Welsh' and is an avid Welsh rugby supporter.

Academic matters: Strong results at A level, with 76 per cent A*/A 2018. Maths, biology, chemistry, history and English literature particularly popular. At GCSE in 2018, 92 per cent awarded A*-A/9-7. Girls normally take 10 or 11 GCSEs.

English department is particularly strong. JAGS was top of national league tables in Pre-U last year thanks to English literature results. No mean feat. Other Pre-U subjects offered are history of art and history. School is otherwise sticking to A levels rather than opting for IB. Head explains that 'a lot of the girls at JAGS are specialists so they might be better served with A levels and Pre-U courses.' Modern foreign languages also well taught, with French, Spanish, Italian, Russian, Japanese and German offered. Two of these must be studied until end of year 9. Bilingual girls can take a foreign language GCSE early but otherwise pupils take all subjects at end of year 11.

Inspirational staff. Quality of teaching described as 'fantastic,' 'incredible' and 'superb' by parents. Some NQTs taken on most years but more than half the teachers have been here over a decade. Head explains that 'recruiting here is great, due to the reputation of the school.' Males are well represented, making up around 40 per cent of the teaching body. Head observes lessons on a regular basis so knows her staff well and has been hugely impressed by the standard of teaching here. She acknowledges that recent upheavals in education have been a pressure on the teachers and she is also frustrated by the 'maverick' marking of A levels.

When academic problems do arise, parents feel they are dealt with quickly and efficiently. Setting in maths and French from year 8, though sets are fluid with plenty of moving up and down as required. Surprisingly few take the EPQ but head hopes to encourage more to take it up in future years.

Historically class sizes have been large – reaching as many as 28 in the earlier years. Now, having moved to a five-form entry, the maximum class size is 25.

Small numbers with special needs. School can support girls with relatively mild dyslexia, dyspraxia, ADHD, limited sight and hearing. Two SENCos in the school. 'We don't have girls who need a lot of one-to-one attention here,' explains head. Girls must be able to keep up with the snappy pace so would not suit a pupil with profound difficulties, though adjustments are certainly made to support SEN pupils where possible.

Games, options, the arts: Music is high profile and taken very seriously. All the parents we spoke to raved about the exceptional quality of music. Gustav Holst was a music master here for 16 years and school's main hall is named after him. Orchestras, ensembles, choirs and bands galore. Huge new music centre includes classrooms, IT suites and performance areas. Large numbers learn an instrument and play to high levels. Girls regularly win places in national youth choir and national youth orchestra.

Masses of sport going on. Netball and athletics considered to be especially strong. School boasts its own pool which is well used, even on the cold December morning we visited. Twenty-two acres of grounds. Enviable amount of space for matches and practice. One mother we spoke to complained that the sports department tends to focus on the most able, 'often to the detriment of those who do not excel as much.' School, however, explains that girls who are less able on the sporting front can at least play for their house, so everyone does compete at some level. Another parent felt that the school should try to concentrate on personal fitness more for those who were unlikely to make teams and that the state-of-the-art gym seemed under-used. Extraordinary climbing wall to challenge all levels. Shares Dulwich College's boathouse, so increasing numbers taking up rowing.

Hugh amounts of collaboration with Dulwich drama department too. Middle school and senior school productions include a healthy mix of frothy musicals and more heavyweight plays, ranging from Grease and Thoroughly Modern Millie to Tristan and Isolde. Plays considered to be slick and high quality and the set we saw would have put the West End to shame. School encourages girls to get up on the stage as much as possible, including public speaking in assemblies, but for those less keen on the limelight there are plentiful opportunities behind the scenes too.

The three art rooms as well as printing room reflect the popularity of this art throughout the school. All girls are encouraged to take one creative subject at GCSE, with roughly half opting for art. Displays of art and DT work around the school, including radios and board games, reflect the high standards. TeenTech Consumer Innovation Award recently won by two girls for a cycling jacket, with lights on the shoulders to indicate the direction you are heading in, was rewarded with a ceremony at Buckingham Palace.

Plenty of trips abroad: history department heads to China, RE girls to Israel, others do voluntary work in Romania, and the netball team has played in Barcelona. The cap on costs of trips has been lifted under the current head, with bursary girls being supported by funding from the school. Ski trips have been reintroduced. Head's belief is that not all trips need to have academic clout, that there is an awful lot to be gained socially and culturally from travelling abroad on school trips.

Background and atmosphere: Founded in 1741, by James Allen, master of Dulwich College, making it the oldest girls' independent school in London. Part of a foundation (including Alleyn's and Dulwich College) set up by Elizabethan actor Edward Alleyn. Increasing collaboration with close neighbour Dulwich, from music productions to cookery classes. 'Mrs Huang is encouraging more integration with the boys, which is very popular, as you can imagine,' laughed one mother.

Ethnic and socio-economic diversity is a fundamental element of the school's ethos. One mother commented, 'In the past it has felt more like a grammar school than a fancy private school. The head seems to be smartening the place up but keeping the diverse student population, which is an important part of the school.' Girls accept and enjoy the variety of backgrounds here. 'We never judge each other on background or clothes. Not at all. We are very inclusive,' explained one of the pupils.

Christian foundation though the school wears it lightly, as there are many girls here of different faiths and none. Charitable work is viewed as important. 'Girls are encouraged to have a social conscience,' according to one father. The Saturday literacy scheme is a typical example: year 10 and 11 girls help children from local primary schools with their reading at the weekend. JAGS also arranges Latin classes at Charter School next door. 'This sense of giving back makes us different from many other similar independent girls' schools,' states head.

Outward looking school that is keen to be recognised on the national stage: Arkwright scholarships awarded annually to budding engineers, girls also excel at the junior and senior maths challenges as well as literary competitions. Inspiring range of outside speakers.

Pastoral care, well-being and discipline: A nurturing school. Current head has done lots to improve pastoral care and girls have an array of people to turn to when they hit bumps in the road: form tutors, heads of year, assistant heads, as well as senior girls. Informal 'sister groups' within the school. The house system means girls in different year groups work together. The girls feel there is always someone there for them.

Three school counsellors, including one from the local church and a CAMHS counsellor specialising in mental health, sixth form counsellor, youth worker and school chaplain. Head assumed there would be many girls with mental health issues given the high achieving nature of the school but has been struck by how few there are with difficulties. She explains, 'We are managing it, but it is definitely there. Teenagers are under increasing pressure.' Girls are good at looking out for each other here and assemblies on self-esteem and a 'happy being me' programme aim to address problems head on.

Bullying is rare, and girls are taught the importance of being kind from early on. The way the girls interact with each other is crucial and the school will come down like a ton of bricks on anyone who misuses social media. Bringing the school into disrepute at weekends not tolerated. A girl would be asked to leave 'if she was having a negative impact on other girls', though current head has not had to expel anyone yet.

Pupils and parents: Over 50 languages spoken at home. Though some pupils are from affluent backgrounds, there is a sizeable proportion of the squeezed middle that is working very hard to pay the fees. Parents are doctors, lawyers, teachers, journalists, hairdressers, bus drivers and students, as well as media folk. Most families are dual income.

Pupils come from far and wide, though majority from south east London. Handful from north of river and Kent. Coach service shared with Alleyn's and Dulwich means travel from long distances is manageable. One pupil we spoke to travels for three hours a day and she is not alone.

Good relationships between parents and teachers reported. Parents rave about the improved communication and love the fact that they can now email staff directly. Head has been delighted by how 'rational, liberal and educated' the parents are at JAGS and feels under less pressure from parents here than at any of her previous schools. 'I didn't expect that. Parents here have a great sense of proportion.'

Entrance: Main points of entry are 11+ and 16+. At 11, around 500 apply for 120 places. Pre-selection assessment mornings in the autumn term, where girls are observed in a one-to-one context as well as group situations. The day consists of puzzle-solving activities, taster lessons taught by head and online tests in verbal, non-verbal and numerical reasoning. 'We know after this assessment day that there are some girls who will not thrive at JAGS.' Candidates are informed before Christmas whether they are to be allowed to take the entrance exams in January, but majority are called back. Written tests in maths and English. Offers are made in mid-February. No sibling preference. Nearly 90 per cent of JAPS girls come straight up to senior school. They have automatic entry.

For occasional places in other years, candidates sit tests in mathematics, English and reasoning (non-verbal, verbal and numerical); 13+ and 14+ candidates sit an additional modern foreign language paper of 30 minutes (if they have a second language).

Places in the sixth form are dependent upon entrance exams based upon subjects to be studied at A Level, GCSE results, school reference and interviews with head and head of sixth form.

Exit: Around 15 leave after GCSEs, often heading for co-eds such as Westminster or KCS Wimbledon. Every year some girls return within the first weeks of the autumn term, having missed the supportive environment of JAGS. 'We are happy to take them back, though we might not be able to accommodate their subject choices at this stage,' states head. A few new girls come in at this stage to replace the leavers and head intends to recruit more.

Most A level leavers head for university though some choose one-year courses at the Royal Academy of Music. Others make a beeline for art foundation courses, particularly Kingston, Camberwell and Central St Martins. Popular university destinations include Durham, London, Edinburgh, Leeds and Bristol. Increasing numbers to Oxford and Cambridge recently – 14 in 2018. One parent commented that, in the past, girls have not always ended up at the top universities, but head is changing that. She is focusing on giving pupils the confidence to apply for elite universities. Girls choose a wide variety of courses from biomedical engineering to history of art, and medicine is a strength: seven medics in 2018.

Money matters: Art, music and sport scholarships available. At 11+ academic scholarships are worth up to £4,000 pa. Over 120 girls currently on some form of bursary, with over 50 on totally free places. A few 16+ scholarships of £1,000 awarded, based on GCSE results but girls keep it pretty quiet as bragging is frowned upon here.

Remarks: One father commented, 'JAGS is everything you would want from a school. Girls are genuinely happy. They are given the chance to be what they can be.' Another said, 'The head is taking the school onwards and upwards. It was great before, but Mrs Huang is changing things for the better.' JAGS produces articulate, ambitious, confident yet modest girls. Impressive on every front.

J

James Allen's Preparatory School (JAPS)

Linked with James Allen's Girls' School (JAGS)

East Dulwich Grove, London SE22 8TE

Ages 4–11 **Pupils** 300

Fees: £15,645 pa

020 8693 0374
www.jags.org.uk/prepschool

Headteacher: Since 2007, Finola Stack BA PGCE Mont Dip. Currently working towards an MA. Co-founded Finton House School in 1987, before moving on to Cameron House as head in 1994. ISI inspector. Revered by the girls. Highly articulate, Miss Stack goes to great lengths to express herself as unambiguously as possible. One parent described her manner as being 'quite restrained, which can seem chilly, though she is probably just being careful.' Parents describe her as 'kind' and 'sensitive,' and appreciate her professionalism. Finds time to boost those girls with low self-esteem. The consensus among parents seems to be that she is 'fair, reasonable and at pains to do her best for the girls and for the school...but she won't be bullied by parents'. Not a head that hides herself away in her study. 'Very visible,' commented one parent. Leads running club on Thursdays and regularly sports a tracksuit at galas and inter-house matches. Teaches RE. Three grown up sons. Her main interests are 'family, theatre and exercise.'

Head of pre-prep, JAPPS, is Liz Channon, previously deputy head of Sydenham High Junior School.

Entrance: Entry at 4+ and 7+ in December and January each year. Highly competitive at both stages. Over 100 apply for 36 places at 4+. Open morning in October and school tours offered on Wednesdays. Reception teachers carry out assessments for 4+ entry through varied pre-reading, writing and number activities. 'Nothing to worry about,' reported one parent. 'The girls think they are just playing.' Written report from nursery requested. 'We're looking for academic potential. We're not looking for a specific type of girl. We offer places to a wide cross-section of girls with different dispositions and from a wide cultural base too.' School does not recommend tutoring as it creates a false impression of child's ability. 'We're not looking for the facts they know. We're interested in their thinking process. It is spottable.'

Maths, English and reasoning papers sat by prospective 7+ candidates. If girls meet the academic criteria, they are invited back for a reading test and interview with head. Report from current school requested. No sibling policy at any stage. Ms Stack comments, 'I do feel bad that sometimes sisters aren't accepted but we are entirely transparent in this. If we start muddying the waters, people will become confused about what we're doing.' All occasional places filled in double quick time.

Exit: Around 90 per cent moves on to senior school (JAGS), often with academic, music and sport scholarships. Automatic entry to JAGS provided that girls are up to scratch in maths and English in years 5 and 6. If not suited to the highly academic environment of the senior school they are encouraged to look elsewhere. Head takes great care with those who are moving on: 'If a girl has received good support at home and at school but is still not making the progress we anticipated, and it looks as though she will struggle at the senior school, then I'll work with the family to find the right school for her. It's a sensitive process'. All JAPS girls heading for JAGS must sit the entry exam on same day and in same circumstances as external candidates, so they have access to scholarships and bursaries. 'This in line with us being transparent. It also helps the senior school to see the nature of the cohort they are getting,' explains head. Has introduced taster days in languages, sports, science, drama and DT for year 5s from other local schools who are considering the senior school.

Remarks: Prep-prep runs from 4-7 and is housed in a converted Edwardian mansion in Dulwich Village. Two parallel classes per year, with 18 per class, rising to 24 in middle school. 'A wonderful start on the educational journey,' remarked one parent. 'I can't criticise the school,' said another. 'It's a lovely, gentle, happy place,' said a third. Beautiful garden with immaculate lawn, pear trees, lavender and a summer house. Heaven on earth for children. Plenty of time is spent outside just being little girls, pottering about, playing and riding up and down the path on wheeled toys. Sensory garden includes a house for a hedgehog and instructions written by the girls on the gate to 'look out for thorns!' 'A 4 year old is a 4 year old, however bright. Emotionally they are still very young.' No one is forced to grow up too fast here. How refreshing.

Praise and encouragement readily given. Girls are rewarded with gold leaves which they place on the gold leaf tree. On the day we visited, the tree was weighed down with leaves. One leaf celebrated a girl's ability to concentrate well, another was awarded for impressive show and tell presentations.

Even from early days, girls are given responsibilities and are listened to. They are taught to analyse problems and find solutions for themselves. Pupils from key stage 1 onwards have a school council. Girls recently suggested a Fun Friday when they can let their hair down. Everywhere we looked at the pre-prep, the girls were busy but not frantic. One father summed the atmosphere up as being 'comfortably dynamic.' A winning combination.

No worksheet-driven teaching here. Girls are competitive and lively and there was a distinct buzz in the air on the day we visited. For bright, sparky girls, it's hard to imagine a more exciting environment. Possibly a little harder for those who are less academically whizzy. French teaching singled out by parents as being exceptional – French, PE and music lessons taught totally in French as part of the immersion programme. Accents apparently spot-on by the time they leave. Plenty of differentiation but not rigid setting anywhere.

Teaching considered very strong throughout. We hear reports of some outstanding teachers and certainly witnessed a couple on the day we visited, including a dedicated science teacher busy preparing equipment for the imminent solar eclipse. By year 5, all lessons are taught by specialist teachers.

This school is constantly looking to ways to improve what it delivers. Recently introduced reading sessions after lunch break to encourage girls to read more avidly. Makes the most of its links with the senior school. Older girls come over to help with projects and to give extra mathematical support to the very gifted as well to run language clubs.

Currently 17 on SEND register, mostly for dyslexia, dyscalculia and dyspraxia – no global learning difficulties here. Academic and pastoral support free of charge. Pastoral care taken seriously with a successful buddy system in place to reinforce this. Librarians also provide a sympathetic ear for pupils who want to share worries with a non-teacher. The girls feel well nurtured here.

Huge amount of extracurricular activities on offer as school 'wants to work out what engages a girl.' Clubs currently include sessions on climbing wall, portraiture, gardening and coding. Mostly free of charge. Shares sport facilities with JAGS, including swimming pool, pitches, courts and athletics track. Plenty of matches against other schools. Good variety of sport offered including football, hockey and rounders. Everyone makes a team and sport here is inclusive, C and D teams fielded when possible.

Head of music considered exceptional and utterly dedicated. Parents are transfixed by his enthusiastic conducting at carol concerts. Huge variety of instrumental lessons. Girls encouraged to perform as often as possible. Numerous choirs, ensembles, string and wind groups as well as orchestras. Community music centre planned. Parents report on the high standard of drama. Year 4 and year 6 put on annual productions, the latter performed in the senior school's theatre.

Impressive design technology and art department. On the day we visited, one class was trying to work out how thermoplastic is like chocolate. Girls were enthusiastic, engaged and enjoying themselves. Art studio jam-packed with animal masks, lino prints and still life drawings.

School makes good use of its London location. Further afield, year 2 heads for Lille for a day, year 4 to Swanage, year 5 to Cornwall on an outdoor pursuits adventure and year 6 to Paris. When classes are mixed up at the start of year 5, three days of bonding on a bushcraft course occur. Pretty primitive – no running water and the girls cook their own food. 'Some of our girls would never normally do something like that!' comments head.

Multi-ethnic families from all over central and south London send their girls here. Coaches dart back and forth to Alleyn's, Dulwich College and JAGS daily. Every class has bilingual children and EAL support given to those who need it. Extra French conversation classes for bilingual girls. 'Lots of smart mummies with multiple children dashing about on the school run. Some fairly glamorous types with shiny black 4x4s and sunglasses, as well as a smattering of tiger mothers,' commented one parent, though school feels this is an 'unrepresentative appraisal.' Increasing number of families where both parents work. After-school care on offer is activity-based rather than glorified babysitting.

Parents remark on the sense of community here and participate in the life of school. 'It's important that the girls see we're a community, with teachers and parents all working together,' says head. Parents fundraise for projects, such as for a pond in the sensory garden. Head feels majority of parents is supportive and positive about the school but alert to the fact that 'some parents have strong views.'

Though some locals claim this is an elitist school that produces sharp-elbowed girls, school feels this is not the case. Head believes that 'above all, it's important all children here should be challenged, engaged and learn to give back. Given the advantages they have had, they need to ask themselves what they can then do to benefit others'. This ethos runs throughout the school.

JAPS deserves its outstanding reputation. With its enviable facilities, energetic teaching and dedicated leadership, it's unrivalled in this part of town. These charming, articulate and happy girls seem ready to take on the world by the time they leave.

JCoSS

Castlewood Road, New Barnet, Hertfordshire EN4 9GE

Ages 11–18 **Pupils** 1,250 **Sixth form** 297 **Jewish**

020 8344 2220
www.jcoss.org

Headteacher: Since 2012, Patrick Moriarty MA Oxon MA (Ed) NPQH (early 50s.) Grew up in north London and attended Haberdashers' Aske's Boys School, before reading philosophy and theology at Oxford, then training as a teacher at King's College, London. Taught (RE and English) at Latymer in Edmonton, Bishop Stopford's School, Enfield, and Haberderdashers' Aske's School for Girls. Arrived at JCoSS in 2010 as deputy head. 'The opportunity of a new school was very exciting and I liked the fact that it was a faith school.' Despite his unlikely background ('I told them I wasn't Jewish and I was contemplating studying for the priesthood'), he started nine months before the school opened, helping 'finesse' the curriculum.

J

Breathtakingly energetic, genial and thoughtful, he has undoubtedly delivered on the promise of balancing an outstanding curriculum and outstanding pastoral care. Ofsted, pupils and parents agree on his manifold virtues. 'Exceptional,' say the school inspectors. 'The best head,' said a sixth former. 'He's done an amazing job,' agreed a parent. He's also recently received recognition at the Jewish Schools Award for his 'outstanding and inspirational leadership'. Married to a musician, his out-of-school hours involve heavy-duty family responsibilities (two stepchildren at degree stage and two primary age children). He's also curate of a church in Barnet. Perhaps unsurprisingly, little time left over to play the piano and organ.

Academic matters: High expectations of what would be achieved, and JCoSS's 2018 set of GCSE results certainly didn't disappoint, with 40 per cent 9-7 grades, immediately catapulting the school into the top 10 per cent nationally. At A level, 38 per cent of grades were A*-A (as good or better than many independents), and 67 per cent A*-B.

Largely academic curriculum with most students taking 11 or 12 GCSEs though 'set to reduce slightly in response to concerns about depth of learning and student well-being,' says school. Modern Hebrew compulsory in year 7 (alongside French). In year 8, students can opt out of Hebrew and consider Spanish or Latin. Twenty-eight subjects on offer at A level, including psychology, sociology and further maths. Good take up of religious studies, which achieves notably strong results, as do psychology, English and sociology. Six vocational courses, a mixture of BTecs and Cambridge Technicals in the sixth form (in health and social care, creative media, sport, IT and business). About 70 per cent of students do purely A levels, about 10 per cent purely vocational courses, others mix and match. 'Our aim is to break down the boundaries and get all our students successfully into university.' Energetic teachers, happy to go the extra mile, and teacher-pupil relations clearly strong. 'I feel my teachers are talented and charismatic,' said one student.

One of the distinguishing characteristics of JCoSS is the Jewish education. Students take six lessons a fortnight of Jewish education, five concentrating on Judaism, one on other faiths. 'The kids ask for it, and we feel part of being Jewish is loving your neighbour and understanding your neighbour's religion.' (At GCSE, the second faith studied is Islam.) Jewish education continues for all into the sixth form.

Provision for SEN commended by Ofsted as 'outstanding'. The school, after consultation with the local authority, decided to create a specialist autism unit, the PSRP, with seven places a year devoted to those on the autism spectrum who can access the national curriculum (regardless of faith). The aim is to integrate these students as far as possible into the mainstream. Some spend all their time with the rest; others about half. 'It's highly personalised,' says the head. 'It's a brilliant model because it allows the maximum flexibility and enables all students to recognise and celebrate difference.' One designated SEN teacher per year group in the PSRP, plus two or three learning support assistants, all with specialist training. Others with special needs (dyslexia, dyspraxia, etc) – about three or four a year – are also well catered for, with three SEN teachers and around 30 learning support assistants, given one-to-one support where necessary. 'Able and ambitious' programme enriches the core offering for those who excel in any area.

Games, options, the arts: Sport still relatively in its infancy and limited grounds mean it's unlikely to be a big priority in the immediate future. 'We need a wider range of sport,' said one student. Some all-weather pitches and a spacious well-equipped gym, plus a multi-gym. Some 150 external recent matches in netball, football and basketball, with pleasing results. Badminton and table tennis a particular strength (recent Barnet champions). Rugby offering improving with enthusiastic encouragement from the sixth form. Elite sports programmes (with Saracens rugby coaching, Brentford and Southend football trials). Broad range of after-school sports clubs include sports leadership, table tennis, trampolining and modern Israeli dance.

Large art department with enthusiastic participants. Keen musicians enjoy chamber choir, jazz band, orchestra, guitar surgery. Good range of community involvement and social action: Duke of Edinburgh, Amnesty International, primary school volunteering, Israel club.

Background and atmosphere: Traditionally, London has not had enough school places for Jewish families, and JCoSS was established to be a 'pluralist' Jewish secondary, where all who 'self-identified as Jewish' would be welcome. 'Religiously, we were doing something different,' says the head. 'Here, whether you're Orthodox, Masorti, Reform or Secular, we believe that's a valid expression of tradition.'

Pupils feel the approach works well. 'At other Jewish schools, you might get the feeling that one person's opinion is not as good as another's, but that's not true here,' said one sixth former. 'There are Jews from lots of different backgrounds, but I've never seen an example of bullying on the basis of people's beliefs,' said another. 'We might disagree about Israel's stance for example, but we would debate it.' 'Religion is not pushed,' said a parent. 'It's discussed philosophically.'

The school is inclusive and ecumenical, with a strong stress on inter-faith activities, including visits to temples and cathedrals. Though 99 per cent of pupils are Jewish, last summer, for example, a Ramadan tent was erected in the grounds, where Christians, Jews and Muslims formed a circle of faith.

A long time in the making, the school finally opened on a leafy site in east Barnet in 2010, with 150 pupils and 15 teachers. In 2012, a sixth form was introduced and it is now full to capacity.

Spacious (£48m) modern building, with wide corridors, large, light classrooms (more added in 2017) and excellent facilities. Calm and order reign throughout. Kosher food for all, with cool café for use of sixth formers, staff and visitors. Tight security on the gates.

Students generally mature and focussed ('During my son's GCSE year everyone really settled down,' said a mother. 'I was amazed how motivated they all were.') The head boy and girl actively involved in bringing about change – getting everyone to donate blood, inviting in speakers from universities, etc. Also generous with praise for fellow students ('He's amazing at art', 'She did a wonderful job,' are constant refrains.)

Pupils clearly enjoy the school. 'There's never been a day when my son has not been happy to go,' said one mother. 'When I asked him if he wanted to consider somewhere else for sixth form, he said, "Absolutely not".'

Pastoral care, well-being and discipline: The development of each student as a 'Mensch' – a person of integrity and honour – is the backbone of the school, and moral worth very much emphasised and rewarded (one prize, for example, for kindness, is voted on by students, another awarded for 20 hours volunteering).

Growing house system, with head boy and girl, plus deputies. 'Students put themselves forward, and are interviewed; it's a proper process,' says the head. Discipline is relaxed but clearly defined ('Chilled,' said one parent, 'but not laissez faire.'). 'It's generally a very inclusive and friendly place, good natured and human,' says the head, who has overseen a few fixed-term exclusions, but only one permanent exclusion.

Pupils and parents: From the highly observant to the not observant at all, with a reasonable sprinkling of mixed marriages. A good chunk live fairly locally, but pupils come from as far afield as St Albans and Essex, Harrow and Hackney. Many arrive by school coach, where firm bonds are formed. Parents are predominantly university-educated Jewish middle class, but a reasonable number are aided by the pupil premium and free school meals. All tend, however, to be focussed on similar goals. 'The great majority of our students intend to go to university and get professional jobs in the future, and think and act in that way,' says the head.

Entrance: Around 720 apply for year 7 places here, with about 400 putting it as their first or second choice. The school is mixed ability, but priority goes to Jewish children (proved by attendance at synagogue or involvement with Jewish education plus volunteering in the Jewish community). To cater for demand, school increased places from 180 to 210 in 2017, with possible permanent expansion. Admissions process also changing, with less priority for feeder schools. 'We wanted to ensure there is room for children whatever primary school they have come from.' Order of acceptance is now: looked after children; siblings; 18 places on distance; staff children; then, by random ballot. The school does not expand the sixth form, merely fills the gaps. Minimum six 6s at GCSE for those considering A levels; five 4s for the vocational route. Jewish applicants are again given priority.

Exit: About 20 per cent leave after GCSEs. Some because they don't make the required grades, others to sixth form colleges or independent schools. At 18, virtually all to university, about half to Russell Group universities (Nottingham, Leeds, Manchester particularly popular), with seven to Oxbridge or medical school in 2018.

Money matters: Parents are asked for a voluntary contribution to help underwrite unfunded Jewish education.

Remarks: A school with a clear vision, which, in six busy years, has grown from a hopeful acorn to an oak of excellence. An inclusive place producing excellent results and happy, involved pupils.

JFS

139

The Mall, Kenton, Harrow HA3 9TE

Ages 11–18 **Pupils** 2,000 **Sixth form** 500 **Jewish**

020 8206 3100
www.jfs.brent.sch.uk

Headteacher: Since June 2018, Rachel Fink, previously head of Hasmonean Girls School. A chemistry graduate from UCL, she has an MA in Jewish studies from King's College London and a teaching degree from Michlalah, Jerusalem College for Women, and is a former JFS head girl. She spent 10 years teaching science in high schools in Israel, is a graduate of Cambridge University's Co-Exist interfaith programme and has been a member of a Partnerships for Jewish Schools' working party on mental health. Her husband, Stuart, is also a teacher.

Academic matters: Consistently in the top one per cent nationally of non-selective schools, JFS continues to achieve pretty stunning results. In 2018, 49 per cent of A levels A*/A, 76 per cent A*-B. At GCSE, 51 per cent 9-7, although interestingly the percentage of entries at 9-4 was 91, suggesting perhaps that the school's intake is top-heavy at the high achieving end.

Teaching here universally praised. 'The school is incredible academically'; 'The teaching is amazing'; 'I feel I'm being really stretched, especially in maths'; 'The teachers praise you so much, they really notice your achievements,' said students, while parents added, 'The teachers for the most part are either good or wonderful'; 'Most of my son's teachers have been spectacular'; 'They really push pupils to achieve their potential'; 'The academic standards are excellent.' Strong uptake of the EPQ, and an ongoing and wholehearted commitment to A levels; only one BTec offered and there are no plans to introduce the IB.

Year 7 pupils set for English maths, Jewish studies, Hebrew and PE, but in mixed ability groups for other subjects. Excellent support for both high and low ability students, and a large and well-equipped SEN department supporting the latter. 'The support to my child has been fantastic – staff have bent over backwards to help him,' an appreciative parent told us. Ofsted commented in its most recent report that more need to be done to support those towards the bottom of the middle, some of whom don't make such rapid progress as their peers. Parents, however, told us that the school catered well for difference. 'My children are different in every way and the school's been brilliant with both of them.' 'The school has found a way to reward each of my children for what they do well.'

School is very well-equipped, with interactive boards in every classroom, and no fewer than 14 science labs. Indeed, science was praised as a particular strength of the school. 'The resources here are really good. The teachers are some of the best in the school, and they always get outstanding results,' said one young physicist, proudly. Annual science festival, and the department creates plenty of science leadership opportunities. One-year GCSE astronomy course available to sixth formers as an optional extra, and Science Support Club for years 7 to 11. We dropped in on the year 7 Math-a-Thon, a highly impressive but good-humoured event where you could have heard a pin drop as the competitors stepped up to the platform and got to work in an atmosphere of palpable excitement.

French offered to all year 7s and Spanish to all year 8s, along with Ivrit (modern Hebrew). However, modern languages came in for something of a battering from both pupils and parents – 'They aren't great, but this is no secret,' wrote one mother gloomily, and pupils we asked tended to concur, dismissing Ivrit in particular as 'the subject everyone intends to drop in year 10'. Whilst admitting that they'd had some trying staff shortages in recent times, school insists: 'We're fully staffed, and we've got some really cracking teachers in that department.' And at least one student agreed: 'I think the languages teachers have really helped me.'

History and politics are extremely popular here, and classical civilisation is a recent and successful innovation – 'a really good course,' according to students. Jewish studies widely regarded as excellent, and won universal praise for its intellectual breadth and inclusivity. 'It's been taught in a way that's allowed my son to challenge the material, rather than trying to indoctrinate him,' said one parent, and another confirmed, 'My children have felt comfortable to question the teachers, who have always responded well.'

Games, options, the arts: Impressive array of trophies on display reflects the opportunities and facilities for sport on offer: netball, football, badminton, basketball, trampolining, fitness, athletics, rounders – etc. When we visited, the school had just won the Middlesex Regional Cup for Football in year 12, and everyone we spoke to clearly enjoyed this part of the school's provision. Magnificent climbing wall very popular and much-used.

Superb artwork everywhere we looked, including some really huge canvasses – 'They're not short of ambition,' commented the head of art. Drama also flourishes on a big scale, staging musicals like Little Shop of Horrors, Guys and Dolls and Fiddler on the Roof alongside Shakespearean offerings such as Twelfth Night and Much Ado About Nothing. Music is high-quality, lively and wide-ranging – 'The music department is really friendly.' 'They adopt you as one of their children if you go to rehearsals,' according to pupils. Students can learn 'any and every instrument', and there are regular concerts as well as an annual music festival and the ever-popular staff recital.

Sixth form newspaper held in high regard, and student journalism is strong throughout the school. 'Someone who likes to write and have their voice heard can always do so here,' said an aspiring reporter. 'Loads' of student-run societies, including the sixth form medical society, which lays on talks by prestigious visiting speakers – professors Jane Dacre and Alan McGregor recently headed the bill.

Lots of excursions, and many parents praised the year 9 trip to Israel – 'Incredible' and 'the highlight of my child's year.' High take-up of gap years in Israel arranged by the school.

Background and atmosphere: Founded in 1732, moved to Bell Lane in London's East End in 1832, where at one time it had 4,000 children on its roil and was the biggest school in Europe. The site was bombed during the war, and in 1958 relocated to Camden. Expanding numbers, plus the need to upgrade school facilities, led to the move in 2002 to its present purpose-built home in Kenton. The new school building was designed to be light and airy, to have learning at its heart, and to have the synagogue placed where it would be the first thing visitors would see. The latter is certainly the jewel in the school's crown, with beautiful stained glass windows and a library and study area in the gallery. It's in constant use, both for services and Lunch and Learn sessions. Elsewhere the building is curvy and lightsome, with wide corridors and a progressive feel, although here and there carpets and paintwork were showing their age. Sixth form area is particularly inviting, with spacious and attractive study areas.

The school is divided into four houses named after leading lights in the Anglo-Jewish community (Angel, Brodetsky, Weizmann and Zangwill), and is orthodox in the sense that its denominational authority is the Chief Rabbi. However, it admits children from a wide variety of Jewish backgrounds, both practising and secular, including around 10 per cent from overseas. 'The school prepares you to mix with any background,' said a very likeable sixth former. 'It's great for getting you out of the Jewish bubble, and it's a great place to be secular as well as observant.' All faiths are represented on the staff, 60 per cent of whom are not Jewish.

We liked the liveliness and warmth of this school community. 'JFS is really good, really welcoming, and I settled in quickly,' said one student. 'You can have so many friends in all the different year groups, because there are so many activities,' said another. To us, as we moved round the school, the students seemed cordial, purposeful, orderly and well-turned-out, wearing their blue uniform with care (mostly); carrying themselves with confidence, and, we thought, joie de vivre.

Pastoral care, well-being and discipline: In 2014 parental complaints about some students' behaviour led to an unannounced visit by Ofsted and the lowering of JFS's status from outstanding to requires improvement. Something of a shock, one imagines, but the school rallied, and following a monitoring visit from Ofsted six months later, was judged to be 'taking effective action to tackle the areas requiring improvement' and acting 'professionally and resolutely'. Measures have included restructuring the senior leadership team, new appointments on the governing body, improved information gathering about attendance, introducing a clearer sanctions policy, and working with an independent school improvement adviser contracted by the school's local authority.

Has it worked? Well, the school is, if anything, more oversubscribed than it was before, and responses from parents and children were overwhelmingly favourable. 'We have always been struck by the excellent behaviour we've witnessed in the JFS students we met,' wrote one mother. 'In my opinion, the recent downgrading only demonstrated what a ridiculous body Ofsted is,' said another. In December 2016 the school was regraded as good in all areas except the 16-19 study programmes where it was graded outstanding.

'Everyone feels safe here,' was a typical student comment, and school says, 'We have a strong message to the students: bullying is not tolerated,' adding that recent surveys of parents indicated that 90 per cent of parents felt that bullying was dealt with effectively. That said, JFS is a big school, and a few people expressed concern to us that behaviours such as blanking and name-calling sometimes slipped under the radar. As one mother put it, 'The school deals with bullying very well once they're made aware that there's a problem.'

Pastoral care was very highly rated. 'There's so much support,' said a grateful year 7 child who admitted having taken a while to find her feet, and students throughout the school concurred. 'Any issues have been taken up when I raised them,' said one. 'The mentoring system is second to none', said another. Parents added, 'The staff are always easy to contact – I've only had trouble once in the past nine years getting a teacher to get back to me,' 'One of my children had some anxiety over exams and self-esteem issues. The school has been exceptional and extremely supportive over this.'

Everyone agreed that, despite the school's size, their child had felt noticed and encouraged. 'When choosing schools, we didn't want JFS because we felt it was too big,' wrote one parent, 'however, from the first day we could not have been more impressed. The transfer process from primary to secondary school was flawless, and both our children made friends quickly.'

Pupils and parents: A broad social mix of families, with about eight per cent on free school meals. Students are confident, articulate, 'sometimes audacious.'

Entrance: Heavily oversubscribed, with around 800 applications for 300 places at year 7. Check school's website for ladder of admissions criteria. Following the famous court of appeal ruling in 2009, students no longer have to have a Jewish mother, but families need to complete a certificate of religious practice. Around 35 external applicants are accepted to join the sixth form each year, on the basis of GCSE results and religious practice.

Exit: Around 10 per cent leave after GCSE to try something else. Of those who stay almost all go on to higher education, either directly or after a gap year. Some 70 per cent to Russell group universities in 2018, with eight to Oxbridge, plus two off to medical school and one vet. Usually a few each year to music conservatoires or drama schools. Gap year option arranged by the school to study in Israel is always popular, with some even doing a second gap year.

Remarks: Still the school of choice for Jewish families wanting the best education – both Jewish and otherwise – for their children. As one parent wrote, 'When my son received his place at JFS, my husband and I felt we'd won the golden ticket, and our feelings haven't changed.' As another put it, 'I can't imagine sending my children anywhere else.'

John Betts Primary School

140

Paddenswick Road, London W6 0UA

Ages 4–11 **Pupils** 240

020 8748 2465
www.johnbetts.lbhf.sch.uk

Headteacher: Since 2015, Jessica Mair BA QTS NPQH (late 30s). After a degree in drama and education at Roehampton University, earned her teaching colours at London primaries from World's End to the East End, before spending two years in Argentina, as deputy head of St Andrew's Scots School: 'It was a very good experience, to be immersed in a different culture and way of thinking'. More recently, deputy head at Queens' Manor Primary, where, as head of inclusion, she was responsible for its special needs unit. She describes herself as 'a change agent', which gave her the courage to take up the reins at John Betts after a popular predecessor's 26 year tenure.

Visibly competent and professional in manner, she reveals the secret of her success: 'If you find out what a child is good at and make sure they are happy and settled, they will fly and make progress', a philosophy she acknowledges that has been handed down from her own headteacher at Queenswood. She and her 'very strong leadership team' have introduced careful changes in the traditional workings of the school, swapping individual desks for work tables, updating the curriculum to reflect a contemporary urban population and starting up an orchestra. Parents appreciated the changes: 'she's modernised us a bit... new staff, new ways to attract the children'. 'Very impressive, very together,' said one mum; also impressively quick up and down the many school staircases. 'I think it's important that children run to school', she laughs, leading by example.

Entrance: Vastly oversubscribed. Places are allocated by London Borough of Hammersmith and Fulham criteria: priority to looked after children, SEN needs, siblings, then according to catchment area, which in some years is no further than one tenth of a mile.

Exit: Fewer children leave at KS2 than in the old days, as shrewd parents have become more appreciative of the 'bargain' of a John Betts education. At 11, half go to independent schools: Latymer Upper, St Paul's (girls and boys), Godolphin and Latymer, Frances Holland, Harrodian; half to state secondaries: West London Free School, Hammersmith Academy, Holland Park, Twyford C of E High School.

Remarks: Eight classes of 30 (one per school year with a 'bulge' year for a double class intake), with a teaching assistant to support each class teacher, as well as learning support staff, for SEN children. The national curriculum is taught in a topic-based approach over two years, so both years 3 and 4 may be studying the same topic, but with differentiated work, to challenge them at the appropriate time. 'Our children are very good at asking significant questions,' comments the head. There is a 'London school turnover' of staff, though some are of nearly 40 years standing.

The curriculum includes French from year 2, Italian from year 3 and students from nearby independent schools visit in the lunch hour with an introduction to Latin. A feast of extracurricular clubs complement the children's day: chess, coding; as well as yoga, netball, and skittleball. Drama club, we heard, is 'incredibly well attended'. Years 3 and 4 swim at nearby Latymer Upper School and a football team, coached by parents, plays in a local league. One mum described how her son left school with the sports prize, and credited his confidence to the school's ethos: 'I feel he can deal with anything'. There is a tuneful school choir and, since the recent introduction of individual instrument lessons, an orchestra.

John Betts, a Victorian physician and philanthropist, established the school in 1859 and it continues to operate as one of only two voluntary aided non-denominational schools in London. The founder's desk fills the head's office and his portrait on the wall oversees that his original vision continues, as a non-denominational school with Christian values. 'The values that are handed down at John Betts are still here,' a former parent told us. 'My son has been taught to be kind, and tolerant and independent'. Sitting on the edge of Ravenscourt Park, the building is sometimes mistaken for a church, with its stately gabled frontage and marble portico. The local area embraces both community housing and smart stucco villas of Ravenscourt Park, so there is a vibrant cross-section of locals, 'a good reflection of London,' commented the welcoming receptionist. A short bus ride down the road are the business hubs of Hammersmith and Shepherds Bush, but inside the school's sleek new lobby, you are greeted by an oasis of calm and orderliness. We were slightly bewildered by the labyrinthine layout of the school, the three buildings of contrasting age and style interconnecting with stairwells and walkways.

Downstairs the younger children enjoy a low level suite of modern rooms, and an ICT studio, with smoky picture windows, which open directly into the playground. A glass canopy shelters the children walking to and from the adjacent 1980s extension, which houses a year 5 class. As we peek in, groups of six children round work tables are chatting constructively about maths. An old school hand bell marks the boundary with the original Victorian school house with its raftered ceilings and gothic windows, where we find a multipurpose room for music, art and breakfast club as well as an interconnecting classroom for the two bulge classes. The lively displays of work hung from washing lines include rock cycles and ancient Greece, as well as a useful board of speech bubbles, encouraging the children to

J

pipe up confidently with their own ideas: 'I noticed that...' and 'I disagree because...'. The head explains, 'We encourage chat'.

Behind the school, the playground has been given a makeover, thanks to the generous PTA, with an all-sports pitch, climbing equipment, a huge Four-in-a-Row and painted chess boards. Summer sports day is held in the open spaces of Ravenscourt Park.

The hall converts to the dining room, with congenial round tables for lunch, cooked on site by a private catering company, and staff eat with children. Hot lunch is compulsory, to ensure the kitchen is viable, but judging by the aroma of the day's special, Moroccan chicken with apricots, with homemade bread and carrot cake as sides (vegetarian option too), it's quite a treat. Whole school assemblies use the hall every Friday, and British values are promoted, in the form of kindness, tolerance, resilience etc. 'We're not just responsible for preparing them for the next step, but preparing them for the rest of their lives', explains the head.

Good behaviour is encouraged with gold awards at assembly, and house points for the three houses, Eagle, Falcon, Hawk. Mindfulness and yoga encourage well-being among the students, and if these are too soporific, there's always Wakey Shakey in the playground. No reports of bullying – the school council explores both 'bullying' and 'victim' behaviour patterns, and the police visit to teach 'bystander awareness'. One mum reported, 'My daughter takes part in a little nurture group that is all about exploring emotions in a private space for children to talk'.

J

Teaching tailored to the individual is conspicuous round the school. One mum explained, 'They craft the lessons to engage everybody'. We visited a year 2 maths class, where the majority of the children were involved in a carpet time activity with the class teacher. Nearby a child with special needs was enjoying independent calculations at the computer, while a cluster of faster learners gathered around a table for extension work with the TA. The sense of industry and enthusiasm was contagious and we were pleased to see 'hands up' was still in favour here. 'They work really hard to differentiate and that takes a lot of work behind the scenes,' explained one parent. NHS therapists and SEN support workers visit the children with additional needs. 'Learning support might be for a more able child', explained the head. Despite this, one parent confided, 'tutoring does happen at the school'.

The staff got the popular vote from the children – 'my son just falls in love with each class teacher,' said one mum – and the 'family feel' of the school is upheld by having several ex-parents as employees; others run school clubs. Head takes advantage of the wealth of experience in the cosmopolitan community.

We heard about the 'very dynamic PTA' whose reps 'do a good job of keeping everyone up to date'. In addition, the head writes a newsletter each week, and there's a policy that all enquiries receive a response in 24 hours. Parents were aware they could have a quick chat to the class teacher after school, or make an appointment for a longer discussion. The head encourages face-to-face or telephone calls and has a firm view on emails: 'written word can be easily misinterpreted, clear communication is key'. Parents help on school trips, popularly to the Kensington museums, Imperial War Museum and even The Royal Opera House, and years 3 and 6 enjoy residentials.

Children looked smart in navy, white and grey uniforms with touches of green and yellow on their stripy ties. 'The school council is not just a name, they are given autonomy,' one mum reported. A head girl and head boy are elected, along with prefects, giving the older children an opportunity to write a job application and undertake an interview, the head explained. 'It gives them exposure to talking to adults and public speaking experience'.

Possibly the best bargain in education west of Notting Hill; local authority funded. Extras for school trips made up by parents.

Dr John Betts must look on with pride from his gilt-edged portrait in the old study to see how the school's original principles of curiosity and compassion are flourishing. Traditional and modern practices enrich the teaching, add to this mix a dynamic head, a lively modern curriculum and energetic parents, and – local fee-paying institutions beware – this school is a rattling success.

The John Lyon School

Middle Road, Harrow HA2 0HN

Ages 11–18 **Pupils** 600 **Sixth form** 170

Fees: £17,898 – £18,582 pa

020 8515 9400
www.johnlyon.org

Head: Since 2009, Katherine Haynes, BA MEd NPQH (40s). Attended Oxford High School for Girls ('No doubt, that's the reason I'm driven in the way I am'), before reading maths at Warwick, followed by an MEd. Then taught in the Midlands, becoming head of maths at Edgbaston High School, followed by Warwick School, where she first started out as a school inspector and took the professional training scheme for headship. Her appointment at John Lyon made her the first woman ever to head an HMC boys' day school, but she had no hesitation in taking up the challenge. 'I felt I could provide a different perspective and saw what was possible. I wanted to make it more academic and put it on the map.' Has acted decisively on this brief, expanding the academic and extracurricular offering and polishing the pastoral care. Parents undoubtedly appreciate her approach. 'She's vibrant and dynamic, with no airs and graces, no nonsense,' said one fan. In term time she 'lives and breathes' the school, and all praise her involvement with pupils ('She really has time for the boys') and their families ('We were so impressed she invited parents of new boys to dinner at her house'). Continues to work as a school inspector, and, in her limited free time, enjoys gardening and travelling.

Academic matters: Small class sizes (20-23 in years 7-9, 18-24 at GCSE, 10-16 at A level) mean that pupils are well known by staff. ('A good relationship with teachers helps with their work,' says the head.) Currently reducing GCSE numbers from 10 to nine, 'to give more scope to go beyond the curriculum'. IGCSEs in maths, English and all sciences ('The exams are harder, but they make the transition to A levels smoother'). Carousel of languages, with Mandarin taster in year 8 (including a successful exchange programme with Harrow's sister school in the Far East), Latin from year 8, classical Greek from year 10. Post-GCSE, the school remains happy with A levels, adding classical civilisation, psychology, government and politics, music technology, computer science and, soon DT, to the subject range. Also major emphasis on the EPQ, with an impressive 100 per cent achieving A*/A most years. Results overall very solid (63 per cent A*-A/9-7 at GCSE; 31 per A*/A at A level in 2018), a reflection of the effort to instil self-discipline, hard work and high expectations. Parents believe the school gets the balance just right. 'The grades are good, but you're not made to feel awful if you're not at the top of the league tables.'

About seven per cent of pupils receive some sort of learning support (typically for dyslexia), which is provided by two specialist teachers in the learning support department. Those with English as their second language – the school does its best to accommodate families relocating mid year – also aided by a qualified EAL teacher. Gifted-and-talented programme, too, for those in need of 'enrichment'.

Games, options, the arts: Though the school overlooks some of the playing fields of Harrow, its own expansive 25 green acres are a five minute minibus-ride away. These have recently been updated with a state-of-the art MUGA (multi-use games areas) pitch, providing excellent floodlit facilities for hockey and tennis alongside football and cricket (and archery). Pupils also have access to Harrow's nine-hole golf course, squash and tennis courts (clearly made good use of, since one boy recently gained a tennis scholarship to the US). On site, there's a gym, 25m pool and fitness suite, with sporting options including basketball, judo, and badminton.

Drama a popular choice at GCSE and A level, with aspiring thespians busily practising their lines outside the two well-used drama studios on our visit. Boys also mount productions at Harrow School's Ryan Theatre and have the opportunity to work with professional companies, including the Donmar Warehouse, the Lyric Hammersmith and the Royal Shakespeare Company. Music – praised by parents as 'phenomenal' – benefits from a purpose built recording studio.

A 'rounded' education given a firm emphasis, with a timetabled programme of 'skills-based' activities including everything from cooking to changing a tyre. Out-of-lessons options also extensive, with a particularly high take up of Duke of Edinburgh (an impressive 30 pupils successfully completed gold recently). CCF also on offer, as part of the Harrow School cadet force. Plenty of trips (football to Iceland, cricket to South Africa, joint ski trip with Harrow, Wellington and Dulwich) and societies, from computing to chess. 'It's a very broad ranging education,' commented one contented father.

Background and atmosphere: John Lyon School – established in 1876 to 'educate local boys' – forms part (along with Harrow School) of the John Lyon's Foundation, and sits a street away from Churchill's alma mater in leafy Harrow on the Hill. The two schools have a happy, but not smothering, relationship, with heads of departments meeting for lunch, boys enjoying use of each other's more covetable facilities.

One of the head's greatest achievements has been a 10-year plan to modernise the outdated buildings. First on the list was the introduction of a dining hall. 'I wanted somewhere the whole school could sit and chat.' Moving the library to a new location has provided an attractive central space, where staff and students can socialise over a hot or cold meal (though the food itself is perhaps not a highlight – 'It's OK,' said one boy politely). Other, much-appreciated, improvements include a sixth form centre, occupying the entire Victorian school house, which provides both learning and leisure space for older boys. Next on the agenda is a flagship STEAM (the sciences plus art) building where DT, computer science and maths will unite with art.

A rebrand is also in the pipeline, which, it is hoped, will put the school more prominently in the spotlight. 'People describe us as one of the best kept secrets in London,' says the head, who clearly now intends the secret to leak out. 'We want to bring across the vision of what we represent: heritage and innovation, creativity and resilience.' Other widely acknowledged USPs include 'the family atmosphere,' the 'friendliness' and the attractively small scale. 'It's not too big,' said one father. 'Everyone knows my son's name, from the registrar to the guy who sits on the front desk.' Some feel the rebrand is long overdue. 'The school doesn't beat its own drum enough; it's sometimes seen as an also ran, which it definitely shouldn't be.'

Pastoral care, well-being and discipline: Great praise for the care and attention boys receive, with parents united in the view that the school does its utmost to develop every inch of potential. 'My son is a bright child, but not A*, nor is he massively sporty, but John Lyon is a lovely, nurturing, comfy school, which gets the absolute best out of him.' Confidence building in the public arena very much part of the package. 'My son has really flourished here and is turning into a nice young man who is able to talk to anyone.'

Boys generally motivated and ambitious with little evidence of teenage rebellion. 'We promote a code of conduct rather than having endless rules, so it's usually possible to pull back before declaring "time's up",' says the head. Even so, if that code is broken, lines are firmly drawn.

Girl-free zone compensated for by good links with neighbouring schools, so debating with North London Collegiate and Northwood College, drama with Royal Masonic.

Pupils and parents: Primarily local, very cosmopolitan, with over 50 per cent from Asian families, whose children will often be the first in the family to go to university. 'They're aspirational and hardworking and want to do the best for their children,' says the head. Boys are positive, focussed and keen.

Alumni include Michael Bogdanov, theatre director, Timothy West, actor, Stephen Pollard, journalist and Alastair Fraser, cricketer.

Entrance: At 11, 75 per cent come from local primaries (about 200 apply for 80 places, with increasing numbers making John Lyon their first choice); English and maths exams plus group activity. At 13 (when three or four forms expand to five), all from local preps, with main feeders Durston House, St Martin's, Orley Farm; English, maths, French and science exams (no pre-tests). The school is academically selective, but here the term 'potential' is not just rhetoric. All applicants are interviewed by senior staff (at 13, all by the head), with the intention of snuffling out 'those happy to be busy, active and willing to push themselves'. Small intake into the sixth form, plus occasional mid-year admissions.

Exit: Some 30 per cent leaves post-GCSE for local sixth form colleges. Of the remainder, 70-80 per cent to their first choice of university, with significant numbers to leading London colleges (LSE and King's), then Russell Group (50 per cent) countrywide. Two to Oxbridge in 2018. University advice up-to-date and thoughtfully tailored to individual needs (including STEP classes for mathematicians). 'We're ambitious for boys and see what's possible,' says the dynamic head of university applications. High proportion to professional degrees in science (one medic in 2018), law, economics, architecture and finance.

Money matters: Good value. The John Lyon's Charity continues to help with means-tested bursaries.

Remarks: A small, thriving school, with historic links to Harrow School, which provides a well-rounded, well-grounded education in a welcoming atmosphere.

Keble Prep School

Wades Hill, London N21 1BG

Ages 4–13 **Pupils** 220

Fees: £11,970 – £15,240 pa

020 8360 3359
www.kebleprep.co.uk

Headmaster: Since 2017, Mark Mitchell (40s) BSc from Leeds University, followed by a PGCE at Kingston University. He started his career as a science teacher at Ardingly College in Hayward Heath: 'I always wanted to teach, particularly science, so when I was offered a post teaching science at A level, I grabbed it.' However his main passion was teaching years 7 and 8, so he moved on to King's House School in Richmond followed by Feltonfleet school in Cobham. It was around this time he had his first child and, space being an issue, moved to Cheshire to the Terra Nova School where he was head of science, followed by deputy head and finally head teacher. He was there for a total of 12 years. However, after separating from his wife, he moved back down south again to the job of head of Keble Prep. 'As soon as I came through the school gates it felt right.'

K

Tall, tanned and friendly, Mr Mitchell makes a good first impression. A northern lad from Yorkshire who was 'swayed' by the independent sector the first time he taught in a prep school: 'It was quite a big deal for me, I had no idea of the prep school world initially, having gone to a standard comprehensive in Hull, after but my first impressions of seeing the school and its grounds, there was no turning back.' On a more serious level he believes that there is much more freedom with the independent sector in terms of tweaking the curriculum and going outside the envelope a bit more, 'otherwise what's the point of calling it an independent school?' Plus, he says, 'children are children and they all come with their own issues whether they be in state or independent schools.

Parents so far have generally been positive about Mr Mitchell as new head teacher, and talk about how he has brought in fresh ideas to the school, which was slightly fraying around the edges. Recent changes have included a new maths programme, after-school activities for reception and year 1 and alterations to certain aspects of the curriculum. Plus he has done away with 'the random half days that were really difficult for working parents.' Some parents have said he is slightly less approachable than the previous head, 'but deals with issues straight away and effectively.' We get the impression that teachers are under more pressure than before with assessments every term.

Firm, too, on discipline: 'shaking hands, eye contact and opening doors will hopefully become ingrained.' But often, he says, the tightening up of standards comes from the boys themselves and is not led by him.

In any spare time, Mr Mitchell is a keen tennis player, cook and amateur baker – so much so that he has introduced a weekly cooking club for the boys run by a chef. He also enjoys reading and listening to music to unwind.

Leaving in July 2019.

Entrance: Register a couple of years before entry at 4 but pressure on places is not intense. For some parents this school is an informed choice and they want a small Independent school – for others they have no choice as they live in a 'grey area' of schools in Palmers Green and couldn't get a place at a state primary school.

The school is non-selective, but before pupils start reception parents come for a meeting and their sons are observed doing jigsaws and playing games. 'The key thing is to ascertain that we will be a good fit for the child.' Probably not the school for a boy with a very specific or global needs, who is unlikely to be accepted. Some new entrants from the state sector at 11.

Exit: A small exodus at 11 to high-achieving local grammar schools and comprehensives, but school hopes to attract parents who understand the benefits of a school that runs to 13. 'We believe in 13+.' One parent did say, however, that her only criticism of Keble is that 'it needs to decide whether it's an 11+ or 13+ school, as many senior schools are changing their admissions policy.' However, she added that this was part of a 'bigger picture.'

At 13+, Mill Hill and St Albans are historically the two most popular choices, but horizons are expanding – 'we are sending boys to Highgate, Haberdashers, City, UCS, Westminster, Haileybury and St Columba's'. Wherever pupils go, the school does its utmost to ensure the best match between boy and school – 'we know the boys very well and recommend on personality'. A handful switch to the state sector – Ashmole, Finchley Catholic High and Highlands are popular choices, as are The Latymer and Dame Alice Owen.

Remarks: Driving to this lone prep school in an affluent suburban area of north London, (along roads such as Broad Walk, which make Bishops Avenue look like social housing) – we expected great things, so first impressions were slightly underwhelming, especially as we entered through the back for parking purposes. However, the minute we were ushered into the school, that feeling began to dissipate which was credit to the friendly staff who gave us coffee and plied us with delicious Fortnum and Mason biscuits.

A small school, which hovers at around 200 boys in all, so class size is reflectively intimate, ranging from 12-15 in two parallel forms. In the early years the school follows the national curriculum, with add-ons such as French, which starts in year 3. The pace is accelerated and curriculum expanded as boys get older – 'we adapt it to the boys, easing into common entrance after 11'. Specialist teaching in music and PE in first two years, then further specialisation in art, ICT and French; by year 5, all subjects taught by specialists and switch to a senior school system where classes are split for English, maths, history, Latin etc.

Enthusiastic teaching and boy-friendly approach. 'We try to make it very hands on,' said one teacher. 'We make models and castles.' Parents praise staff highly. 'My son is motivated, interested and enthused. It's a great credit to the teachers,' said a mother. 'The teachers are incredibly encouraging,' said another. In the past, the school has been criticised for not necessarily stretching the brightest, but has spent time, effort and money rebalancing that equation. A director of studies now has a clear brief and the brightest are given differentiated teaching in class and one-to-one support out of it. Boys are setted in English and maths from year 5, with informal setting in science, French and humanities.

The philosophy, however, is very much 'each child is an individual' and the struggling are equally well guided, with the full range of SEN support which includes a full time dedicated SENCo and a team of three other assistants. Low percentage of SEN however, and whilst the school can deal fairly comfortably with dyslexia, dyspraxia, mild autism and Asperger's, they would advise a parent of a child with a more specific need to go through the state system as they just can't access the same level of support here. However, where possible, they will try and make reasonable adjustments. Parents say that the benefit of the small classes at Keble Prep is the individual attention their sons receive, and the safe and nurturing feel. As one parent told us: 'The teachers really know my child, and will flag up something immediately if there is an issue.'

This is a small site and facilities are relatively restricted but rebuild has brought more classroom space (although still fairly tight and a bit airless, which is something they are working on), a new science lab and an art room, allowing for relocation of the library, which had doubled as a music room. Limited space, too, for sports, although three new Astroturf courts have recently been put in, and a new playground area: 'The redevelopment of the reception playground splits the space into two areas to allow for free-flow indoor/outdoor play.'

Games, played twice a week, are taken seriously. Rugby, football, cricket and tennis are the main menu and a school minibus transports players to local and distant pitches. Rugby has put the school back on the prep school circuit, and more recently too has tennis – they recently won the first north London independent schools' tournament they have entered. Parents say that Mr Mitchell has really pushed sport at the school, and he says that he is trying to get a weekly fixture: 'I feel we punch above our weight with other schools but I would like to enter a few more national competitions.' Boys can also let off steam fairly regularly at nearby beautiful Grovelands Park, and the school is also looking into the option of a forest school.

Various lunch-time and after-school clubs on offer include puzzle club, movie club, cookery club and spy club as well as a common entrance drop-in club. Music has also been taken up several notches, with an assortment of orchestras, choirs and instruments on offer.

Has been going for 80 years and its aim now, as always, is to serve the local community, a community of small family businesses rather than City professionals. Many parents are first-time buyers. 'Our parents often want what they didn't have for themselves.' Many have Mediterranean roots (Turkish, Spanish, Greek, Italian, Cypriot) and a firm belief in family, and the school reflects those values with a strong family atmosphere. Active parents' association that puts on summer and Christmas fairs, welcome evenings, curry nights, quiz nights etc. They have managed to fund a school minibus, some IT equipment and contribute to some of the playground revamp.

Very much a traditional prep, it retains distinctive black and yellow blazers, formal good manners and neatly brushed hair (long hair is definitely frowned upon). We did feel a tad sorry for the younger boys in reception who looked so stiff in their neatly knotted ties on the floor playing with plastic farm animals. We felt they had the rest of their lives to be City bankers. When we mentioned this to Mr Mitchell, he replied that this was something he had been planning to look into for the younger years, 'although I am aware that changing uniform is a major step so needs careful planning'.

Pastoral care was more old school before Mr Mitchell became head, but he is very aware of concentrating not just on academia, but on producing grounded and well rounded individuals: 'We need to equip these boys with the right skill set for life and cultivate a culture that is supportive of them in sometimes dealing with failure.' For that reason he has introduced a new PSHE called Jigsaw which is built around mindfulness and reflection, which he hopes to instil into the boys. He has also put in worry boxes outside his office and around the school, where pupils can either jot down their concerns anonymously or ask to talk to someone about them.

A 'big brother, little brother' scheme matches older pupils with younger ones – evident and unaffected warmth stretching across the age divide. Pupil seem happy and well rounded, and as a final year pupil said: 'I love the school and I'm going to miss it when I leave'. Parents are equally positive. 'We chose it because it's very friendly and has a great identity that boys can relate to.' 'We love the school. It's a home from home. My son looks forward to going to school every day.' Keble is not a wealthy or notably well endowed place, but is undoubtedly a happy and safe haven, where all boys are treated with respect and respond in kind. A very secure place to start your school days.

Kensington Prep School

596 Fulham Road, London SW6 5PA

Ages 4–11 **Pupils** 295

Fees: £17,193 pa

020 7731 9300
www.kensingtonprep.gdst.net

Head: Since September 2018, Caroline Hulme-McKibbin BEd (Homerton College, Cambridge), previously principal since 2009 of The King's School Macclesfield Infants and Juniors. Degree from Homerton College, Cambridge. Taught in state primaries in Trafford then at King's Junior when co-education introduced; became academic head. After a career break to have family returned in 2003 as vice principal; 2005 head of Alderley Edge School for Girls' junior section. Husband a business consultant, two daughters. Interests include netball umpiring, theatre, reading. The previous head, Prudence Lynch, retired after 15 years.

Entrance: Girls come from 40 local nurseries and most live locally, many within walking distance. There are over 200 applicants for 44 places at 4+. Register any time up to September prior to entry the following September, with assessments in January. Girls are seen in groups of five or six and observed during play with every aspect graded. 'I couldn't care if they can recite the three times table. I want to know if they understand the threeness of things in another context.' An understanding of English is important: 'It's no good if they have no basic understanding of what is going on and what adults say to them'. At 7 + there are a very few places but it is always worth trying as occasional places do crop up. Siblings accepted provided they can cope, but this is not automatic.

Exit: School aware that most parents choose KP for its excellent results. 'Fewer are considering boarding schools and the majority want selective, academic girls' day schools.'

A record number of scholarships in 2018: 32 (17 academic, 14 music, one art). Favourite destination is Godolphin & Latymer followed by Putney High and Francis Holland SW1. St Swithun's and Wycombe Abbey are the most popular boarding destinations.

Parents we spoke to who had experienced the ruthless competitive examination process commented on how they have complete confidence in the school system, and how well prepared the girls are so that they feel very secure. One recalled that the girls did knitting on a Friday afternoon to keep them calm. The process is carefully managed with plenty of meetings in years 5 and 6 alongside an open door for advice from the head.

Remarks: Founded in 1873 in Kensington, it was the first school to be established by the Girls' Day School Trust and today the only stand-alone prep school in the group. In 1997 it moved to its present site, previously a secondary Marist convent in just over an acre of grounds. Clearly values belonging to the GDST, which provides expertise and financial support alongside independence. The trust cares about the ongoing professional development of its leaders and staff. 2016 saw the completion of a £2.7 million building project appropriately titled Creative Spaces for Growing Minds. We saw the multimedia recording studio, and the eco greenhouse which complements the outside garden and pond. We were delighted to see the girls thoroughly enjoying their spacious classrooms with breakout areas and retractable doors, as well as the improved specialist drama, art, science and IT suites and two new lifts making the school thoroughly accessible throughout.

We witnessed a year 2 geography project work on the hi tech 'explore floor'. A carousel of 10 minute activities meant groups of six learnt about the United Kingdom in a stimulating, exciting way. Some learnt to use directions accurately and programmed small robots, others learnt to recognise London landmarks, whilst others learnt the difference between physical and human features. The girls we spoke to 'love the freedom to do what you like in learning. The teachers make maths and science fun.' Perhaps that explains why they do so well, winning the GDST Maths Competition twice recently, and four year 6 girls qualified for the UK MT Maths Challenge designed for years 7 and 8.

The dining room looks inviting with its bright colour scheme, modern lighting and freshly cooked food on the premises, which we sampled and enjoyed. There are a few classrooms with traditional desks but all have plenty of light and space. Accomplished artwork decorates walls, many of which are crammed with questions and ongoing thinking by pupils, not often seen on a school tour. Self-directed, independent and collaborative ways to learn abound, and in such an academic environment, girls need to be robust and willing to participate if they are to thrive.

K

With two courts on site as well as nearby Fulham pools and King's House Sports Grounds for sports day, girls are given plenty of opportunities to play in fixtures. In truth the games department is eclipsed by the starry music department. Girls perform at Cadogan Hall and there are three choirs, four orchestras, chamber ensembles and a main orchestra with over 100 players. A biannual overseas music tour takes place to Europe, for example to Holland and Venice, with a planned visit to Budapest. An artist in residence works alongside the art teacher as well as providing clubs. There is no pottery but we saw accomplished models. There is an extensive club programme which includes football and trips galore.

The early years section is superbly resourced inside and outside with free flow. The girls we saw were fully engaged in a breadth of activities without realising they were being assessed by experienced staff. One parent shared how 'the girls hear about fairies or the Big Bad Wolf visiting, and in year 2 a fairy lives in the classroom and girls can write to her if they have a concern and receive a reply.' Parents love the fact their daughters are happy and have fun at school. A director of individualised learning and assistant learning support coordinator ensure pupils are given extra support at different levels where necessary. This may be small group support by a teaching assistant or teacher within or outside the classroom. A school counsellor is in school three days a week. The online communication system supports homework with iPads and a learning platform showing how mathematics has been taught in the lesson.

Parents we spoke to remarked, 'The school has a lovely community feeling and right from the start girls know how important it is to be kind and good.' This is a caring, not a cosy school where girls need to be willing to be challenged. Inspectors awarded the school the highest possible grades across the board in the latest report. They rated the quality of pupils' learning and achievements exceptional. This is not a school for the fainthearted, staff or pupils, but it is one where all share the excitement and creativity of learning. KP is the ideal school for a high flyer. The pace is fast and the girls are happy, have fun and are zippy.

Kew College

24-26 Cumberland Road, Kew, Richmond, Surrey TW9 3HQ

Ages 3-11 **Pupils** 296

Fees: £7,050 – £12,150 pa

020 8940 2039
www.kewcollege.com

Headmistress: Since 2013, Marianne Austin (60s). Read geography at Durham and then spent two years at Sheffield doing an MA in town planning before becoming a chartered accountant, working at the (then) Coopers and Lybrand. Initially fired to teach when her daughter began nursery here, she arrived at Kew College in 2002 and has never looked back. ('I love the school and believe completely in what we're trying to do'). Has taught in years 2, 4 and 6, became deputy head in 2010 and three years later took over the reins. Mrs Austin exudes calmness and warmth, and a determination to support and empower all constituencies including her staff, whose professionalism and commitment evidently help to inspire her own. 'We obviously want the children to feel secure and happy' she says, 'not least because we want to foster a culture which allows them to take risks. And that's a life skill for which the need will never go away.' Loves travel and skiing and spending time with her husband and daughter and with her family in Ireland.

Entrance: Children can start in the nursery aged 3 – there are two classes, one in the morning and one in the afternoon. Get their names down as early as possible – any time from birth. There's no examination or interview, though prospective parents are required, as a condition of entry, to attend an open morning to get a feel for the place. Priority is given to siblings, and to the sons and daughters of ex-pupils. Mrs Austin says this does not occasion resentment 'because it's transparent'. Clear belief that, so long as parents are invested, this is a school in which almost any child can thrive. 'My daughter came from the state sector,' said one parent. 'There are no airs and graces here, but terrific values.'

Exit: Everyone leaves at 11, many to the big hitters in West London, usually with good number of scholarships. Mostly day – boarding very seldom on the radar. In 2018, largest numbers of offers from Hampton, Ibstock Place, Kingston Grammar, Notting Hill and Ealing and Surbiton High, with plenty of scholarships – 16 academic, several sports and three music. Also conditional 13+ places at Eton, Harrow and Westminster.

Remarks: Warm-hearted and effervescent learning environment. Staff are guided by the national curriculum, but teaching and learning go way beyond. In the nursery and kindergarten years, a clear emphasis on social skills and physical literacy, but of also being gently led into reading, writing and elementary maths. By the time children move into the infant house in years

1 and 2, ICT and science have become more fully integrated, and the children are becoming exposed to more specialist subject teaching. French (emphasis on lots of lovely sounds) actually begins in nursery, and 'understanding the world' introduces younger children to what will later become science.

Reading is huge here. Right from the start reading at home is encouraged. From year I, a 10 minute spell of nightly homework is also expected and, by gentle incremental steps, this is increased as children get older. A very industrious feel to the place, but none of the anxiety of a hothouse. 'They help children to extend their ambition in every way,' said one parent, 'but without getting het up.' Particular praise for thorough marking – 'lots of red and green ink, full of attainable target-setting and constructive comments,' said parent. Learning support is sensitively managed, with a SENCo and assistant 'The specific needs of children change,' says the head. 'Sometimes it's just a bit of anxiety'. Other issues, such as dyslexia, need longer-term support. But all children, however much or little help they receive, are fully integrated into the life of the school. Occasionally there are those with more significant needs, and every attempt is made to support them.

The school is housed in two big Victorian houses – classic west London stuff. 'We've been lucky,' says head. 'The original buildings were gifted to us by our founder' – something which has allowed the fees to remain at a relatively modest level compared to some. Now a third big building just alongside is home to year 5 and 6 pupils and to the art department. A further consequence is the rehousing of the library – 'right at the heart of the school, as it should be', says Mrs Austin.

Although the present site is on the edge of being cramped – packed lunches on site are essential – there's no sense of crowding. Timetables have been carefully worked to minimise bodies having to jostle, and classrooms comfortably accommodate classes of never more than 20 children. There's no sense of claustrophobia – rather of light, of bustling creativity and of calm good relationships. At the back, just across the school playground is the Octagon – a purpose built block dating from about 2000 which houses younger pupils.

Masses of sport – football, rugby, netball and athletics especially, and plenty of swimming – with plenty of fixtures with other schools. 'It's lovely to win,' says the head, 'which, fortunately, they often do. Sometimes, of course, they don't – and that's education.' There aren't any rolling acres here, so there's a coach ride for everyone on a Tuesday and Thursday afternoon to sports grounds only five minutes away.

The school also hums with music (the Young Voices choir was practising when we arrived – a very joyful sound). A wind band, a strings group, a young voices choir, jazz band, and lots of beat and drumming, and masses of music technology. There's a special art day every couple of years with visits from the specialists at the V&A. Clubs, in and after school, have that same determined outreach – not only those with a digital and IT base, of course, but masses of dance and even one for Lego.

Pastoral care is taken very seriously. Every Monday, the head meets with staff and their first item of business is identifying pupils who present concerns. The school has identified a range of structures best calculated to serve the children's interests – a house system, of course (excellent for games) but also heads of year who liaise closely with form teachers to ensure a full and up-to-date flow of information and insight. Lots of outings, of course, and older children might take longer school trips – year 5 were at Hooke Court in Dorset during our visit. The school is evidently proud of its traditions as well as of its routines – Founder' Day each spring is a major jamboree, and allows pupils to come together with teachers and other friends of the school.

The policy of teachers of other years visiting all parts of the school frequently helps accustom young children to faces which might otherwise be unfamiliar. Before moving to a new class, there are 'transition' days to help acclimatise, and that extends to opportunities for parents to hear the reflections of parents with older children who've already made the journey. It's easy to spot the confidence which flows between the different constituencies here. The recessional at the end of each day eloquently combines pupil safety with a gentle exercise in toujours la politesse.

The wholeheartedness of the children (very apparent) is suggestive – they seem to have imbibed a confidence and optimism from other pupils and teachers and also, no doubt about it, from their families. This is a school in which the parents' investment – emotional, social and financial – reflects a deep commitment to education in the fullest sense. Parents are big fundraisers for the school (the school minibus and a massive investment in the library are recent examples). Mrs Austin is emphatic that the exchange of confidence and goodwill adds immeasurably to the potential of the school. 'Children all feel part of the bigger picture,' said one parent. 'I don't know quite how they do it, but it's exceptional. They think beyond themselves, and it spills over into everything.'

Kew Green Preparatory School

Layton House, Ferry Lane, Richmond TW9 3AF

Ages 4–11 **Pupils** 280

Fees: £17,571 pa

020 8948 5999
www.kgps.co.uk

Head: Since 2004, Jem Peck BSc (geography) PGCE (science) (both from Kingston University). Taught at St John's, Kingston for nine years, then moved out of education altogether for six years into the corporate world, where he focused on event production, marketing, PR and team-building. Gaining this wider perspective has been 'incredibly helpful' to his current role, he says, 'particularly for recruitment and driving the creative feel of the school.'

A very visible presence throughout the school, he teaches English and reasoning to year 6 and is often in and out of the classrooms. Enthusiastic yet calm, he gets down to the kids' level when talking to them. 'Unlike many heads in the private sector, he praises the children directly rather than turning his back on them to tell the parent,' one parent added. He has a door that's always open (except for the very occasional sensitive meeting) to his office – which, by the way, is both the most stylish and child-friendly we've ever seen for a head teacher, complete with sink-in sofa and swivel armchairs, matching navy furniture, open fire and more toys than many home playrooms have. 'Children know they can pop in whenever they want and they very often do, whether it's to have a jam on my guitar, discuss ideas to improve the school or just instead of going outside to play,' he says. During our visit, even kids that had recently left the school popped their heads in with big smiles. Does it interrupt his day? 'That is my day!' he laughs. 'Paperwork can be left.'

Parents, whom he greets every morning, tell us they also feel welcome to pop in any time. 'There's no need to email first – if you have a concern, you can talk to him, or indeed any of the other staff, that very day,' says one, although another told us, 'You can find yourself being pushed in a direction you don't

K

necessarily want to go when you talk to him. For instance, he's good at persuading you that things you think are important are actually not.'

When not in school, you'll usually find him at sister schools Ravenscourt Park (primary) and Kew House (senior). He lives in Surbiton, has a teenage son and is a keen musician.

Entrance: Entrance is non-selective, with applications accepted on a first-come-first-served basis. This means you'll need to get in quick, particularly as this heavily oversubscribed school (which has some 90-160 applications for every 40 places in reception) accepts registrations from birth. Eighteen months before children are due to start, the school gives the parents a call to check they're happy to continue their journey. An informal taster day helps the children settle in and every year group has two classes of 20, with an equal gender split where possible. Occasional places (mainly when pupils leave because their families relocate) become available higher up the school, for which the school asks to see a report from the current school.

Exit: Most popular by far in 2018 Kew House. Then Ibstock Place followed by St John's Leatherhead and Hampton; six scholarships.

Remarks: The story goes that Maria and Ted Gardener, owners of Ravenscourt Park Prep School (which was becoming increasingly oversubscribed) were walking along the Thames towpath in Kew, when they spotted a tall Georgian style building that they immediately fell in love with. 'Mrs Gardener was so keen to see more of it that she got on his shoulders to look over the wall,' says the head. A year later, in 2004, the school opened there.

K

Overlooking the River Thames at the back and Kew Green at the front, the location of this school is made all the more impressive by its neighbours – Kew Gardens – where pupils often drop by with teachers as part of their learning. By no means the largest of facilities, you won't get the likes of science labs or food tech areas here, but pupils get full use of these and other amenities at Kew House, the school's sister senior school.

In the basement is the staff room and the school hall, which doubles up as the dining room (and where the very popular food is made from scratch on site); the ground floor is home to the headteacher's office and admin rooms, as well as some classrooms; and the upper two floors house more classrooms (all well-resourced) and private study rooms, including for music lessons. All are spotless, welcoming and colourful, with masses of original artwork (not just paintings, but sculptures and textiles) adorning the walls and shelves, whilst the atmosphere is buzzy, both during and between classes. The single-storey building at the front of the school – again homely and packed with artwork – is the early years centre, whilst three innovative wooden, glass-fronted pods are used for music lessons and small group work for SEN. The playground at the back consists of a double tennis court and a smaller lower level, but fun-packed, outside play area.

The ethos, which aims to be the same as its two sister schools, is all about increasing self-esteem, encouraging children to be confident to ask questions and make mistakes without feeling intimidated – all with the overall aim of enabling them to flourish, not just as learners, but people. 'This is a school that's all about celebrating attitude and effort, not just what is actually achieved,' raved one parent. Parents like that the raison d'être is not getting bums on seats in the premiership senior schools, despite the fact that they do get many kids in there. 'The school gets that not every child is destined to wind up at the likes of St Paul's, whilst still managing to pave the way for the ones who are bright enough to get in without any need for extra tutoring,' says one.

Lessons are based on the national curriculum, but with added enrichment. Setting from year 3 in maths and English, although head says 'it's a flexible feast,' and there are subject specialist teachers for art, music, PE and French. French from reception upwards, with Spanish, German and Italian part of the 50 extracurricular clubs on offer per week. Other clubs include sports such as judo, modelling, cooking, digital photography, computer programming, touch typing, writing, film club, children's newspaper, just to name a few. Whilst many of these finish at 4.30pm, the school is open from as long as 8am-6pm for an extra fee (includes tea). Plenty of trips, including residentials.

There's extra (mainly classroom or small group based) provision for those requiring learning support (14 SEN when we visited, two of whom had EHC plans), particularly dyslexia, dyspraxia and autistic spectrum, via the progress centre, which is run by the school SENCo and three other staff members involved on a part-time basis. Specialist help, including speech and language therapy and OT, is brought in. 'If I could change anything, it would be making this a bigger department, with help put in place quicker, but what's amazing about this school and SEN is that issues are never brushed under the carpet or stigmatised, which has been my experience at other schools,' said one parent.

Weekly drama classes for all year groups, with plenty of chances to perform. Film-making is valued, especially in year 6. Meanwhile, the range of art opportunities is more akin to a secondary school, including fine art, pottery, ceramics, textiles, screen painting, Photoshop and more – with more than enough facilities to support it. Pupils' work has been exhibited at the likes of the National Gallery, Hampton Court Palace and Saatchi Gallery – testament to the artistic talent here.

Around two-thirds (190 when we visited) of pupils learn a musical instrument during the school day. 'You name an instrument and we'll teach it if a pupil wants to learn,' says the head. There are two choirs (upper and lower schools), a chamber choir (for which pupils audition), an orchestra and ensembles for guitar, strings and brass. Plus music assemblies. When we visited, year 4s were practising a song they'd written (lyrics and music) ready to perform later that week with a full orchestra.

Sports-wise, only tennis and netball takes place on the school grounds, while rugby, football, cricket, hockey, rounders and athletics are played on the green opposite. Other local facilities enable students to participate in gymnastics, dance, swimming, cross-country, fitness lessons, athletics and traditional team sports, for which there are specialist coaches. Years 3-6 take part in competitive fixtures with other local schools and the school hosts netball, football and rugby festivals.

Pastoral care is strong, helped by the high staff-to-pupil ratio and small class sizes, plus the fact that children are regularly reminded who they can talk to about any concerns. Discipline isn't a word you'll hear much as behaviour is excellent. The last half-hour of lesson time on a Friday is dedicated to 'reflection time,' which allows teachers to reflect on individual or group successes and resolve any conflicts or concerns so that children don't have to carry them over the weekend.

The majority of children live within a three-mile radius – mainly Kew, Chiswick, Richmond, Barnes and Hammersmith. Families are a broad mix of professions including media types, lawyers, bankers and quite a few celebs. Parents are encouraged to get involved in school life, often giving presentations on careers and interests, and there's a lively PA.

Probably not a school for go-getting parents that want their offspring to get top grades in everything, no matter what. Not that it lacks academic rigour, with some impressive pupil destinations proving that the school caters for the very bright. A school for introverts and extroverts alike, we found the atmosphere to be caring, spirited and creative.

Kew House School

6 Capital Interchange Way, London TW8 0EX

Ages 11–18 **Pupils** 525 **Sixth form** 160

Fees: £21,387 pa

020 8742 2038
www.kewhouseschool.com

Headmaster: Since 2013, Mark Hudson MEd (50s). Previously senior deputy head and director of technology at top performing Thomas Telford School – joined in 1996 as director of technology, becoming deputy head two years later and senior deputy head in 2006. Before this, head of design and technology at Bishop Fox's Community School in Taunton for 11 years, preceded by post as a DT teacher at St James's High School in Exeter, after a year in the same role at Kingsfield School in Bristol.

An 11+ 'failure' (made grammar school for sixth form), he's an articulate advocate for children at risk of being written off too early. Wants to offer 'the very best of contemporary educational practice' and overcome inertia that, he says, governs too much of what schools do. 'I'd rather children experienced education than having it inflicted on them.' Goal is to bring disenfranchised pupils in out of the cold. 'There are far too many out there,' he says.

He's co-written textbooks, been involved in A level curriculum design, enjoyed a spell as a teacher fellow at the Royal College of Arts and had a hand in the building of four new academies sponsored by Mercers' Livery Company which wowed school's owners, the Gardener Schools Group, prompting the job offer here. Clincher was the chance to build his own senior school from scratch.

It's a long way from childhood dream of being a dentist. 'I was quite enchanted by it. It's such a nice environment to work in, to meet people and make them feel better.' (Either had exceptional dentist or exceptional teeth.) Academic requirements put this out of reach, however, and instead he had an interim period studying town and country planning. So 'stultifyingly boring' that quit in third year, switched to a design-based degree and never looked back.

These days, doesn't teach regularly but likes to drop into DT lessons ('can't help myself') and wow pupils with technical skills (no coincidence that design department is next to his office).

Out of hours, he's a self-confessed petrolhead and drives 'a very nice' Jaguar. No doubt curbs temptation to talk shop at home (wife head of lower school at feeder prep; they have two grown up sons also in design and engineering-related careers). Also walks, swims and plays golf.

Felt to be down to earth. 'He was moving the mouse mats back into place in the IT room,' said approving parent on an open day visit. He also fitted some of the table top plug sockets in the sixth form centre, and very nice they look, too. (DIY, unsurprisingly, is another interest.)

Commands healthy levels of respect from parents. Personable deputies fulfil the good cop role, thought one. ('We swap,' says Mr Hudson, deadpan.) Felt by pupils to be more approachable than he looks. 'Can give off aura of being stern but that's necessary, it's in the job description,' said one. 'But he's very nice.'

With applications for year 7 at gratifyingly healthy levels and waiting lists in most pre-GCSE years in operation, he's concentrating on growing the sixth form. School currently operates full service of A levels, despite the financial pain of tiny classes (we saw two pupils rattling round in vast art room, same number again in food technology lesson, some other subjects in single numbers). However, expects numbers to increase over the next two years. In the meantime, 'I'm happy to offer personalised tuition,' he says.

Directors are so delighted with what he's achieved so far that they've named the new sixth form block after him. Though grateful, he fears it might create the wrong impression about his ego. Should be kept in check as long as his down-to-earth mother is around. 'Normally they wait till you've died, don't they?' she asked, when he broke the news...

Academic matters: School, until recently the back up choice at 11+, offers an alternative in competitive west London. Instead of super selectivity, takes students from across the ability range. 'Far more professionally satisfying to see a student come in with moderate or even limited academic prowess and see them grow into someone who can do really well.' Thus prize-giving only happens in the sixth form. 'Immensely divisive if go by results alone,' says head.

He's also less than keen on termly/annual reports and 'speed dating' parent-teacher events – don't flag problems quickly enough, he reckons. Instead reports – shown to pupils first – are sent out every half term and parents are invited (and expected) to comment and get in touch. Works for proactive parents – welcome to drop in at any point – and have own café. 'If there's an issue, you go in,' said one. Others – 'have to train them up,' says Mr Hudson – felt you could end up slightly disconnected from what's going on.

Average class size 22, far smaller in sixth form (maximum class size of 12) with pupil to staff ratio of around nine to one. Good choice of subjects at GCSE – options include computing, PE, food tech and four languages (including Latin). Start GCSE curriculum in year 9 – time to change option subjects if have made wrong choice.

More generous still with A levels – currently 25 including computer science and music technology, Latin, statistics, product design and business studies. Most take three subjects (plus EPQ) and occasionally four (one pupil also racing through art in a year). Most popular subjects maths, sciences, politics, economics.

Unwilling to release results of first set of A levels in 2018 'due to the stats not working in our favour because of so few candidates, even though the results were very good'. GCSE results in 2018 45 per cent A*-A/9-7 grades. Inspectors approve so far – no recommendations for improvement in ISI compliance report (early 2018).

Admissions policy stresses (as do we) that parents must support the school's educational approach particularly as applied to length of lessons. Most are 90 minutes, while art, design and food tech, CAD, games and science lessons are all three hours long, joined by some GCSE option subjects higher up the school. No question of going out on an educational limb, says Mr Hudson. Tried and tested elsewhere, including at Thomas Telford. Adds up to a day's extra teaching time each week (and means less homework).

Benefits are manifest, says school, from easier trip planning (no complex negotiations with other subject teachers over missed lessons) to reduced time in corridors. 'Keeps the school calm,' says Mr Hudson. 'In my experience, 90 per cent of all pastoral issues take place when children are moving around.' Classroom time is also more productive – normal 40-minute lesson can be substantially truncated by late arrivals and packing up time. Head not keen on shattering siren of school bells so there isn't one. No clocks in classrooms, either.

The teachers we talked to were enthusiasts. 'Love them,' said art teacher. 'Can get things done.' Food tech teacher, pointing to fab-looking deconstructed Pavlova, agreed – even enough time to make the tiny meringues on top.

Undoubtedly requires sustained razor-sharp teaching and planning to ensure that interest levels (staff as well as pupils) don't flag. Some parents query if this happens all the time. Others are full of praise. Supplementary tutoring takes place as elsewhere. If gives a short-term boost or catch up, Mr Hudson accepts the need – and invites tutors to work with the school – but shouldn't be a permanent prop.

Some pupils we talked to felt that longer lesson time took a while to get used to. 'When you first start, feels a bit weird,' said one pupil, but worth persevering as boosts concentration and can build better independent learning skills – particularly useful in the sixth form.

Pupils rate help from teachers – 'focused on the individual,' said one. With no staff room, teachers are easily found either in classrooms or the café and willingly – say pupils – give up time at breaks or after school, plus holiday revision days (compulsory) in all subjects, with after-school homework club staffed by different teacher each night. No sanctions for unfinished homework. Instead, teacher and pupil will sit down and work it through. 'They're here if you struggle,' said a pupil.

Approach felt to be particularly helpful for pupils with specific learning difficulties (generally mild to moderate) as ensures time and space for extensive differentiation. 'Would definitely think of sending dyslexic son here,' said prospective parents. Four-strong SEN team, some smaller group lessons but focus is on effective staff training and integrated support in lessons.

K

'Great thing about the SEN is that it's embedded in everything they teach,' said parent. School's excellent reputation for SEN puts off some prospective parents (watch the shutters come down during open days). It shouldn't, says school, which stresses relatively small numbers involved. While 130 or so have an ed psych report, only 55 currently receive extra support in their lessons. Around 10 per cent of pupils have previously been educated overseas but vast majority of these bilingual – just one currently supported as EAL pupil.

All requires and largely gets strong and generally young teaching team, most reckoned by parents to be in for the long haul. Staff turnover 'modest', says school. In total, nine staff departures since launch, with six out of the seven founding team still there. In rare cases where teachers don't fit in will move on fairly quickly, think parents.

School's proud boast is that never use supply teachers – pay own staff for cover instead, better for pupils. Curricula are all written by school's teachers, nothing shop bought. Not all homework is online but aim is to get more of it that way, making lost assignments a thing of the low tech past and ensuring that anyone who's missed school finds it easy to catch up.

Games, options, the arts: 'We don't have the rolling acres,' says Mr Hudson – a distinct understatement with just a couple of courts on site (though nicely screened with vegetation) used for informal footie sessions at break.

Not the place for athletics, think parents, though range, all within a 10-minute walk or bus ride, is extensive. Swimming and indoor sport happens closer still at local leisure centre next door. Rowing – growing fast – at picturesque Strand-on-the-Green riverside. Cricket, rugby and football all on local pitches with good complement of girls' teams. Some individual successes (year 9 Surrey netball development squad) and team wins (recent national table tennis champions in ISA competition).

Activities list also impressive – 90 or so in total, changed termly. D of E, with speedy sign up, now takes the most enthusiastic through to gold ('fastest accredited school,' reckons head).

Lots of outside speakers, including parents (politicians, engineers, actors) and trips, some curriculum-linked, many local (Kew Gardens, Wetlands in Barnes) others residential, ranging from survival skills in Cornwall to art appreciation in Rome (could work vice versa, too). Older pupils may travel much further afield – one sixth former off to Great Barrier Reef – extended project topic. Good works happen locally (supports autism unit in Chiswick primary) and further afield (building eco-bungalow in resource-poor village in Laos).

Art is exciting as well as impressive – highlights on view included stunning A level project, inspired by 1970s slogans and street protests with raw, powerful words and images reproduced on clothes pegged on a washing line. Year 9's contrasting workbooks featured technically adept delicate plant images. Currently in single (well-lit) room, a second home to the most dedicated, with handy balcony for spray painting. Additional room for A level work on department head's wish list.

Lively drama with plenty of productions (High Society the latest in list that includes Joseph, Little Shop of Horrors and Pygmalion) though sixth form currently feel they're less involved than years 7-11 (down to small numbers, not neglect). Now offered as A level and can study for LAMDA exams and pupils regularly (and successfully) enter local competitions and festivals.

Music coming along nicely – lots of Steinways round the place and plenty of ensembles, selective and otherwise and including parent and staff choir and joint concerts with Gardener prep schools. The very enthusiastic may be home late – head doesn't care for disrupting curriculum time so all individual music lessons (around 100, beginners to diploma standard, learn in school, 50 outside) happen between 4pm and 6pm three days a week.

Background and atmosphere: School's owners – the Gardener Schools Group – run two successful preps in the area, both relatively recent additions to the local educational scene. Opened in 2013, this is first (and so far only) senior school in the group. Maria Gardener cited by parents as reason for looking at KHS in the first place. 'She's a special needs teacher herself and gets it when so many other heads and owners don't,' said one. Some events (eg quiz night, occasional concert) bring prep and senior school parents together – creates nice atmosphere.

Setting takes a bit of getting used to. From the road, it's a quintessential red-brick office block, surrounded by heavy traffic and redevelopment. Inside, however, head has had a free hand (and what appears to be considerable budget) to design it as he sees fit, to excellent effect.

Space is effectively and even beautifully planned, as well as being conspicuously neat and tidy. It's super quiet, too (making crash of a couple of doors in need of soft close fittings particularly noticeable).

Areas, subjects and staircases zing through the entire colour spectrum (pupils must travel to end of the rainbow and back several times a day). Even the displays coordinate with the paintwork, striking aboriginal inspired designs in terracotta and burned yellows a perfect match with the paintwork while the dinky but well-equipped labs are primary coloured, ditto canteen which features one of the few clocks (Swiss railway).

Lighting is just as eye-catching. Newer, second block housing sixth form independent learning centre on the ground floor notable for massive lampshades in contrast with smaller clusters twinkling away in corners, all bringing illumination where it's needed. 'Like Soho House,' say parents. Other practicalities include densely packed row of power sockets at counter top height makes laptop charging a doddle. Younger years, who use upper floors for maths and languages, must admire from a distance.

Uniform, in contrast, surprisingly preppy – blue blazers, jumpers and shirts plus brown skirts or trousers – some girls pushing to wear either. Parents seemed generally happy. 'I like it, the kids don't,' said one. Freshman-style hoodie popular with all. Parents have no problem with absence of official kitbag but one wish list would include same colour shoes for all (currently black or navy for girls, brown deck shoes for boys), particularly at concerts when 'you really notice it.'

Other sensible touches include absence of lead weight backpacks. Only sixth formers have lockers. For other years, daily textbooks (normally no more than four) come in and go home in strong plastic folder (previous iteration, in cardboard, proved too flimsy for the job). Saves back pain, time and trouble. 'They don't get lost because they go in and out all day,' said parent.

Pastoral care, well-being and discipline: Vertical tutor groups mean siblings can be together (if want to). Same personal tutor ensures continuity and in-depth knowledge of pupils. Generally works well – as long as long as teachers don't leave and pupils like them, say parents, though possible for pupil to request change of personal tutor if the chemistry isn't there. Rare, say pupils, and would 'need a very good reason.' Could make request a bit Beadle and Oliver-ish – off-putting for all but the most robust souls.

Worth enlisting support of head boy and head girl, current duo (nominated by staff, final choice through pupil vote) busy working through lengthy wish list.

Sixth formers want to be allowed off the premises during 45-minute lunch break (can't be done in the time, says school). School food is a work in progress though vegetarian options have improved, thought one pupil, and sixth formers can now order appetising-looking sandwiches. Not cheap – 'most expensive croissants in west London,' thought a parent, though 75p is not unreasonable, counters school.

Sanctions are unambiguous – instant exit for drugs and alcohol, only possible leeway is student who owns up to having a problem, but no guarantees. Break school's strict phone policy (allowed in school only if switched off) and it will be left in reception for parents to collect (only happens once). Forget school tie and you have to borrow one of senior teacher's cast-offs (one girl unfazed by shiny, multi-pleated number).

Some nice touches – like name tags, worn by all pupils (school reminds them to turn over when on public transport) that mean year 7s are known to all and to each other. 'Unusual but inclusive,' said parent.

CCTV throughout the building also helps, say pupils, who felt that people are 'generally nice to one another.' Parents agree.

Smartphones the perennial out-of-school issue. Opt for Nokia retro phones, urgest head – with limited success, even with the nostalgic joy of playing Snake. School has upweighted resources here – onsite counsellor recently recruited – and parents feel school is getting to grips with cyberbullying. Rare that pupils asked to leave for bullying but would happen if behaviour consistently 'detrimental to others – important that parents realise you stand by your principles,' says Mr Hudson.

Pupils and parents: Families thought to be less anxious and more down to earth than at other schools – some very affluent, many dual income. 'Very normal, very relaxed,' thought one. 'Perhaps more comfortable because they're more experimental, so quite chilled.'

Pupils generally make own way to school. Drop offs possible but infra dig beyond initial newbie phase. Mostly families relatively local – Kew, Chiswick, Barnes, Putney, anywhere within reach of Kew Bridge station (overground) or Gunnersbury (District line – a 10 minute walk). Currently need to do bit of dogleg to dodge busy motorway feeder road – a worry to parents – though working with developers to make this safer. Some pupils bike to school (plenty of cycle paths) and helmets must be worn. 'When forgot, teacher was on my case immediately.' The canny (or 'lazy toads,' says Mr H) catch bus a single stop from Kew Bridge, dodging busy roads and saving their tired legs.

Entrance: Now over 450 registrations for 88 year 7 places (four classes of 22) from almost 90 prep and primary schools, including Avenue House, Heathfield House, John Betts, Kew Green Prep, Orchard House, Prospect House and Ravenscourt Park School. Very occasional places in other year groups (school currently completely full – except for sixth form).

Aim is for balanced cohort of 'inquisitive, intelligent students displaying a confident sense of identity and an original approach to learning, problem-solving and creativity'.

So while entrance exams (maths, literacy, but no reasoning) count, there's 'greater weighting' for reports, achievements and interests, and presentation on subject of choice. 'Currently lots on single use plastic – the Sir David Attenborough factor,' says head. 'And cakes. We like cakes.' Staff may also visit current school. Process ensures that bright and articulate who may struggle to express themselves on paper get a fair hearing.

Exit: Have tended to lose half a dozen or so after GCSEs, many to state sector, but it's being balanced by new intake. First leavers in 2018 off far and wide, with a couple to Loughborough, others to Oxford Brookes, Bath, Nottingham Trent, Liverpool, Chester, Reading, Birkbeck and St Mary's Twickenham.

Money matters: No scholarships, bursaries or even sibling discounts though most SEN support included in the fees. Everyone expected to eat at school. 'School does not provide facilities for packed lunches.' On the bright side, sixth form coffee machine which charges £1 for everything, even, according to pupils, hot water for own teabag, is to be supplemented with Quooker or similar in the near future. 'Was charged for short period but now [a] dispenser is in place,' says school.

Remarks: Inclusive, different and surprisingly beautiful. Essential to understand and commit to approach – especially those extra long lessons. Emphatically not the place for clockwatchers.

King Alfred School

Manor Wood, 149 North End Road, London NW11 7HY

Ages 4–18 Pupils 650 Sixth form 110

Fees: £16,074 – £19,377 pa

020 8457 5200
www.kingalfred.org.uk

Head: Since 2015, Robert Lobatto MA Oxon PGCE (on the cusp of 50s), previously head of Barnhill Community High in Hayes. Married with two school age children. Educated at the Haberdashers' Aske's boys' school in Hertfordshire before reading history at Oxford, Mr Lobatto is firmly rooted in north London and its culture. Prior to coming here he spent 25 years in state secondary schools, head of history at East Barnet school, head of humanities at Highbury Fields, deputy head at Lister

Community School in Plaistow and head (at only 40 years old) at Barnhill Community High School in Hayes. The one thing all his previous schools have in common is that they are 'big, urban and ethnically diverse', he says. At Barnhill 85 per cent of the school were from ethnic minority backgrounds, 60 per cent on free school meals.

His quiet and unassuming appearance belies a man of steel and purpose. While head at Barnhill he spent eight years setting up a multi academy trust, the Barnhill Partnership Trust, taking on and turning round a primary school in its wake. He brings a wealth of experience to his current role, and despite the stark difference in demographic, says that KAS is much more similar to his previous school than he anticipated. He left the state sector disillusioned with a diet of data and performance tables – the strap had been rubbing for too long on the same spot.

He finds the supportive parental body, the resources, the small class sizes and, above all, the genuinely child centred approach hugely refreshing. 'In the state sector we were making decisions for the school rather than for the children,' he observes. He enjoys being accountable to the governors (here known in Pullmanesque speak as Council rather than a governing board). His role here is less about admin, more about strategy. The strategy that he is particularly interested in developing is around learning – empowering the children to lead their own learning. While he believes in 'a rigorous academic education,' he says, 'real learning is about empowering the individual in the learning process.'

When challenged about what kind of child suits the liberal, relaxed ethos of the school, Robert muses, 'There genuinely is a place for everyone here as we are trying to bring out the best in each individual child. There is an alchemy about the place, they come out confident, well-balanced and articulate.' With the small numbers at King Alfred, you don't need 'heavy-handed behaviour management processes,' he suggests. He knows all the pupils, who he describes as 'delightful, easy to talk to and well behaved'. He still finds the time to teach history, which he enjoys and which gives him still greater insight into the pupils and the way the school operates. He relishes the strong ethos of working with the individual and says he is 'hugely experienced at dealing with complex behavioural issues'. There are certain goals to be achieved, however: moving forward the academics, particularly science, is one, working more with parents to help them support their children, as well as to provide inspiration to the school community, is another.

A thoughtful man, Robert Lobatto clearly commands a great deal of respect. From groundsmen to junior school pupils, everyone we passed was keen to catch his eye and receive a nod or smile of recognition.

Head of lower school: Since January 2018, Karen Thomas, previously head of Kowloon Junior School in Hong Kong, and before that vice principal and PYP coordinator at Peak School there.

Academic matters: Focus here is not on exams and results, though there is a definite desire to see the pupils progress, excel and above all reach their potential. No tests, though the school keen to point out that the children's progress is monitored carefully. Barely any homework in lower school until year 5, although children take home reading books from reception onwards. 'When homework hits big time in year 10 the pupils have a massive shock', observed one parent. Lots of projects and creative building of volcanoes and the Great Wall of China, for example, between the age of 8 and 13. Pupils learn very much at their own pace and no one is told that they 'should' be at a certain point. 'This is fine if you are in it for the long term,' commented a parent, 'but if you decide to move your child you are likely to find s/he is way behind.' Another parent expressed it more positively: 'Bright and motivated children will do as well at King Alfred as anywhere else, but pupils who might have been crushed elsewhere do better. You must be prepared for the long haul and be patient as educational achievement is a longer process here than in other more pressurised environments.'

Relationships between pupils and teachers noticeably more personal than in most other London schools. This can lay the foundation for inspiring and motivational learning, and it is this individual approach that is at the heart of the ethos of the school and filters into every corner of school life, including the classroom.

At GCSE in 2018, 57 per cent of grades were 9-7. At A level over 30 per cent A*/A grades. However a much better indicator that the school is doing something right is its value added score. Progress between GCSE and A level is among the top 10 per cent in the country – there is a broad spectrum of ability here yet the progress pupils make is impressive.

Deservedly known to be a school for the creative arts more than for science, popular A levels here include art and design, history, politics and English. At GCSE high numbers do art and design and photography, and a good number choose performing arts and music studies, including a BTec group. More do French than Spanish, very few choose to do Latin, and food tech is now an option. Most of the 9-8 crop at GCSE is in English literature and history.

Additional support is available for students with mild specific learning difficulties – individually, in groups or in class. The progress of each student is monitored throughout their time at the school. Teachers build up a picture of pupils' learning profiles and identify those who might require specific intervention.

Games, options, the arts: If you want fierce competitive sport and silverware displayed in shiny glass cabinets, look elsewhere. Matches are often mixed – in age, gender (and competence). A successful match is one which everyone enjoys. Children of all ages are out kicking a ball on the field at the heart of the school, some are climbing trees, others working in the forge.

Music has always been popular. Trendy boys play in bands (there is a popular after-school band club). Old school Alfredian teachers with long hair in ponytails inspire a number of pupils to perform in orchestras and ensembles. Large music tech room, complete with Macs, drums and cymbals, percussion keyboards and djembes. Plenty of space for drama, including a large theatre as well as a 'black box' studio. Years 7-9 performed Emil and the Detectives, years 10 and above in Chicago and Anything Goes. However considering the number of parents in the arts, particularly the performing arts, one parent commented that the school punches well below its weight. Another parent observed that the school does not dance to the obvious 'wow' factor. What makes Alfredians stand out is not the polish of their performance but the evident joy and collaboration they bring to their performances, and that all are encouraged to join in. While other schools at a choir competition may look impeccably groomed with perfect pitch, Alfredians will be seen in a colourful jumble, singing and clapping with gusto, supporting and encouraging each other, wreathed in grins. They are not a shambles, however – the lower school has won the Watford Music Festival first prize two years in a row, and the upper school reached the national school finals.

Industrious and inspirational art room – three rooms at the top of the building that overflows with ceramics, as well as charcoal drawings of leaves and plants.

In the senior school, years 7-11 required to make their choice of co-curricular activities from a wide range, from pottery to golf; sixth form options include screenwriting for films, emotional intelligence and Mandarin. Strong commitment to volunteering throughout, with pupils helping out at the local special school and raising significant sums for international causes (including building a school after the tsunami in Sri Lanka). Good careers advice (which kicks off in year 7) helps with GCSE and A level options and UCAS applications pre- and post-A level. As one might expect, green is high on the agenda – one of the first schools to introduce solar panels and recycling bins.

Everyone we spoke to talked glowingly of 'the village project' – a week in year 8 when all the pupils set up a camp in a corner of the grounds, plan their meals, cook them over a camp fire that they have built, plan the layout of their camp, and build where they will sleep. Adults take a background facilitating role so that the children can take control of their lives and manage the fundamentals they need to survive.

The Forge, managed by a female blacksmith, is another central feature of the curriculum that builds into the creative, hands-on craftsmanship that the school is so adept at instilling into its pupils. 'A wonderful outlet for those that are not so academic,' enthused one parent, who said how much the family enjoy building up a new iron poker selection around their fireplace. Children who have practical skills love being given a chance to shine at something so esoteric. The village project takes a mobile forge over to the camp to use during their week, an example of how King Alfred excels in integrating the curriculum and mixing up different opportunities that are offered here.

Background and atmosphere: Founded by parents in Hampstead in 1898, original aim was to provide an education based on what was best for the child and encourage learning for its own sake. Part of the progressive movement, KAS sees its kindred schools as Bedales in Hampshire and St Christopher in Letchworth. Moved to its current site, a leafy patch of north London opposite Golders Hill Park, in 1921, and has recently expanded, with a school building for the infants across the road from the main site at Ivy Wood, once the home of Anna Pavlova. The emphasis here is for little ones to be outdoors, doing craft, and tuning into nature. Attractive grounds with a mixture of periods and styles (new fitness studio, music and drama block, lovely arts and crafts dining hall) grouped around a central village-like common. Star attractions include a wooded amphitheatre, an arbour (Squirrel Hall), formed from the sheltering branches of two ancient chestnuts, and the farm, complete with chickens, rabbits, ducks and bees. This latter forms a key part of the outdoor education – not just a quaint accessory. Design technology here is of the old-fashioned carpentry kind, preserving creativity, and forms part of the hands-on creative ethos. Pupils start design from 4 years old.

The original ethos – liberal, progressive, egalitarian, child-centred – remains core to the school's values today. Parents and pupils agree that the needs of each child are foremost. 'They try to act holistically. They look at the individual and find out what makes them shine.' In many respects the school operates as a large extended family, without the rigid age divide found elsewhere. 'It's a really friendly school,' said one year 9. 'Older kids look out for younger ones and you'll see sixth formers play with year 7s.' Most children seem to enjoy their time here. 'They skip into school every day,' said one long-time parent. 'Even after the holidays, they can't wait to get back.'

New Fives Court lower school building includes auditorium, cutting-edge art technology room with kiln and multi-purpose room for food science, rural studies and general science. ICT suite, learning support area and lower school library upstairs. Dotted around the site are climbing frames, sandpits and a gypsy caravan – all wood and natural materials.

Smiling groundsmen (always a good sign), colourful array of children, a refreshing indication of individuality. Discreet and rather beautifully delicate wrought iron gates secure the entrance to this charming oasis, off the busy North End Road. Blink and you'd miss it. Staff here are all very informal – streaming in and out of the staff room in all manner of clothes, except for suits and ties. Pupils also scruffy, and sometimes it's hard to tell the difference between staff and sixth formers.

A small school, with a total of 650 pupils from reception through to the upper sixth and fewer than 50 children in each year group, together with small class sizes – between 16 and 17 – makes for an intimate school community. This is enhanced by the village green atmosphere. School provides a genuine opportunity to develop personal relationships with both teachers and the wider school community.

Pastoral care, well-being and discipline: King Alfred will always give your child a chance. The school's detractors comment on a lack of boundaries and leniency in the face of transgression. 'Show us a London school that doesn't have its fair share of drugs and alcohol felons,' counter its supporters.

Robert Lobatto is regarded by many as introducing some much needed tightening – automatic expulsion for bringing drugs into school or using them in school. Otherwise the approach is more about discussion, reasoning with the offender and educating them as to why they have crossed a line. There are policies of internal exclusion (taking children out of lessons) and external exclusion (removing them temporarily from school) but, as with everything here, time is taken to explain, educate and be as fair as possible. 'We would always give kids many chances and do a lot of work to support and educate children about social media – drawing clear lines.'

This is above all a nurturing school. More carrot than stick. No hierarchies, very few rules but bullies will be suspended. However, probably not the place for a child who needs strong structures. Four counsellors and strong system of peer mentoring. No uniform but pupils tend to be unkempt rather than outrageous.

Pupils and parents: A fair smattering of A list celebrities, but 'which independent school in London doesn't have that' is the refrain. Plenty of parents who hated their school days seize the opportunity to give their children a chance to develop as individuals in a low pressure environment. Lots are Old Alfredians themselves who relish being part of this supportive community once more. Pupils, mainly from the wealthier suburbs of north London (Hampstead, Golders Green, Highgate, Muswell Hill), are confident and articulate and expect to be given equal weight as adults. Difficult to say what kind of child suits as often it can be counterintuitive. Blue stockings are given the chance to be bold, free spirits aren't squashed. One thing is certain, the parents need to be involved and supportive to make it work. More than in any other school the relationship is triangular, and all corners need to support to create success.

Entrance: Not selective at 4 but put your child's name down at birth. Date of registration decides visit order and over 200 apply for 40 places in reception. Always some places in year 7 though not normally more than 10. One hundred and twenty normally apply. 'We are looking for people who will get a lot out of King Alfred and give a lot to the school – those who are a good fit for our culture,' says Robert. Children don't just sit a few tests in maths and English but will spend a day at the school, will be asked to do group work, be interviewed in a group and will be assessed in the round. Do they have something about them? Are they sparky, confident, creative? At sixth form minimum of five 6s at GCSE – but school very flexible and inclusive, and will enable pupils to choose combinations that are individualised.

Exit: About 20-30 per cent leave after GCSEs, some to Camden School for Girls or other state sixth forms, others to UCS, Highgate or Francis Holland, for example. After A level, Bristol, Manchester and University of East Anglia popular choices. A few each year to do art foundation courses at eg Kingston or City and

Guilds, and some to music colleges. Candidates choose to study a range of courses from business management (Sussex), industrial design (Brunel) and biomedical science (Kent) to English literature and film studies (UEA), history (Bristol), international relations (SOAS) and maths and philosophy (Leeds)

Money matters: Though not particularly well endowed, attempts to keep fees as stable as possible while keeping facilities up to date. No scholarships, a small number (about four) of means-tested bursaries in year 7 and sixth form.

Remarks: A wonderfully liberal education for the free spirits who balk at rigid structures and too much discipline, but KAS can also set free the souls of those children who have always been overly keen to conform. Not a school for parents obsessed with league table position, nor those who would prefer to delegate the education of their children completely. Success will depend on parents, child and school all rowing in the same direction.

King's College Junior School (Wimbledon)

Linked with King's College School (Wimbledon)

K

Southside, Wimbledon Common, London SW19 4TT

Ages 7–13 **Pupils** 435 **C of E**

Fees: £17,940 – £19,530 pa

020 8255 5335
www.kcs.org.uk

Headmaster: Since 2006, Dr Gerard Silverlock (60s). A senior history teacher who moved to prep schools after distinguished spells at Salesian College Farnborough, Millfield and Lord Wandsworth College. Took up headship of Aberdour Prep in 2002, then headhunted four years later for KCJS, where he's been ever since. No plans to move on or retire – enjoys the job too much. Married to Victoria, a modern languages teacher. They have two sons, both of whom went to KCJS, and two daughters.

Impresses at once as a kindly, scholarly man of sense, and this was universally confirmed by parents queueing up to give praise. 'An excellent head and visible presence'; 'Knows each boy and his parents by name'; 'Charismatic and extremely popular'; 'Clearly loves teaching the boys'; 'The school is very lucky to have him.'

Entrance: Competitive, and getting more so all the time – one mother regretted that 'given the struggle for places at London schools, more and more super bright boys are applying to KCJS and travelling from further afield, making it unattainable for some of those who are more local.' Head confirmed that parents come from as far afield as Esher, Oxshott and Cobham in one direction and Notting Hill and Chiswick in the other.

Around 250 apply for 54 places at 7+. English, maths and reasoning tests and all candidates are interviewed. A further 14 places at 8+, then six more at 9+ and another six at 10+. There is no longer any entry at 11+: boys wishing to join the school at this stage now apply to the senior school, which took its first year 7 cohort in 2016. School looks for 'boys who are bright, intellectually curious, nice young men – not perfect, but able to manage themselves.'

The school maintains a local pre-prep, Wimbledon Common Prep (Squirrels). 'It's not a secret that we own it,' Dr Silverlock observed, 'but we've never badged it, and it isn't selective so it can't be an exclusive feeder to us.' Boys apply from an ever-widening range of pre-preps and primary schools.

Financial assistance has largely gone, transferred across to senior school bursaries.

Exit: Almost all to the senior school via the King's transfer exam in year 8 (21 with scholarships in 2018). Boys have to get 65 per cent in their final set of exams, which are set and marked in the senior school. But the average mark the boys achieve in these exams is 80 per cent, so, in the head's words, 'they're not intended to trip anyone up.' Occasionally boys opt for boarding school instead: destinations have included Eton, Winchester, Harrow, Sevenoaks and King's Canterbury.

Remarks: Completely integrated into the senior school, sharing the same superb campus and facilities, but with a uniform and identity that's very much its own. Rushmere, where the year 3 and year 4 boys are taught in classes of 18, is a lovely old Georgian building, made up of beautifully ordered classrooms and a lunch hall especially for the younger ones. Priory is home to the boys in years 5-8, and has some impressive spaces: we really liked the library, with its 17,000 books, full time librarian and silent, respectful hush. Excellent programme of visiting authors has included Jeremy Strong and David Walliams. New music block, and sports hall/swimming pool on the way. 'The boys are lucky to enjoy such surroundings in a London school,' wrote a grateful parent.

Academic excellence is intrinsic to the school's ethos, and KCJS is home to some very high achievers, but every parent we spoke to praised the school's ability to educate and encourage the whole child. 'The teachers know how to get the best out of individuals'; 'Teaching is first class, and my son had handwriting support for a few terms, which helped him'; 'The school tries to encourage downtime as well'; 'Lessons are pitched just right for boys to pique their interest and curiosity and encourage further learning.' We were shown round by three very bright, articulate and charming young men, all of whom emphatically agreed. 'The teachers are always there to help you!' 'They're really supportive. It's not don't, it's always do!' Successful policy of no hands-up in lessons, introduced to encourage boys to be better listeners, and boys aren't always told the grade for their work (although it goes into the mark book), so that they'll read the teacher's comments more carefully.

SENCo has an open door policy, with boys able to come in any time and ask for help – although it's a rather different role at this school compared with most, because there are hardly any children here with learning difficulties. 'To be blunt, they wouldn't do well enough on the entrance exam,' as head put it. Some boys with dyspraxia, some on the autistic spectrum. But school puts a strong emphasis on them being able to cope with the day's challenges, so this isn't the place for those needing more than a mild level of support. Pupils are most likely to seek assistance with organising their time, or with specific revision tasks.

Sport, once seen as elitist by some parents, is now proudly inclusive and the school is committed to a Sport For All approach. Lots on offer: football, rugby, athletics, cricket, plus many more. 'All boys are encouraged in sport and play in matches whatever their ability – there is no stigma to being in the F or G team,' according to one mother. Fabulous programme of music, with many wonderful opportunities for boys to take part: six choirs, two orchestras and a plethora of ensembles covering everything from classical to Brazilian drumming. More than 400 boys learn musical instruments, and there are regular concerts, both formal and informal. Drama flourishing, and parents praised the 'hugely dedicated drama teacher' who always finds a part for everyone ('she's useless at auditioning because she can't say no,' observed the head, affectionately). Extremely broad and appealing programme of clubs and activities, everything from cookery to Warhammer. 'We have been constantly amazed over the years at the huge staff commitment to clubs and events,' wrote a parent. Another added, 'The only complaint here is that there is not enough time to enjoy all that is on offer.'

Who wouldn't like it here? 'Only those who might struggle with the work,' suggested our really delightful tour guides. Discipline was described as 'fair and firm', and parents showed themselves satisfied with the pastoral care by having no complaints to make about it. We were impressed by the friendly relations between older and younger boys and the lively and cheerful atmosphere, and the words that came up the most in parent feedback were 'kind' 'fun' 'happy' and 'outstanding'.

Overwhelming majority of pupils come from affluent, professional backgrounds, but it's very much a multinational school: 60 per cent of the boys have one or more parents who aren't British. A third speak more than one language at home, and across the school cohort 29 different languages are spoken. The result, as the head proudly observes, is a school that is very outward-looking. In addition to the plethora of foreign trips you'd expect, there are regular exchanges to schools in Japan and India, where the boys stay with local families, and the school is an active fundraiser for the Obera Schools charity in Kenya.

As one parent put it, 'Despite the focus on success, the boys all seem happy. Four years in, we could not be more pleased with our choice of prep school for our son.' A superb environment for bright, motivated boys.

King's College School (Wimbledon)

Linked with King's College Junior School (Wimbledon)

Southside, London SW19 4TT

Ages 11–18 **Pupils** 962 **Sixth form** 405 (103 girls)

Fees: £19,530 – £21,600 pa

020 8255 5300
www.kcs.org.uk

Headmaster: Since 2008, Andrew Halls MA (50s), previously head of Magdalen College School, Oxford, prior to which he was deputy at Trinity in Croydon and head of English at Bristol Grammar School. His father was head of a grammar school, but he himself came up through the comprehensive school route, something which has very much shaped him as an educator – 'I've always been keen to reduce the dislocation between the state and the independent sector.' Read English at Cambridge, where he achieved a double first, and went straight into teaching because he loved his subject and was (and still is) fascinated by education. Married to Veronique, a French teacher, with two grown up daughters. Interests include reading, theatre, running – and anything to do with schools. Regularly writes for the Sunday Times, and his opinions are sought by many other quality papers.

Arrived at KCS to find 'a really lovely school' but wanted to strengthen its position in London, feeling that it was occasionally overlooked. It is not overlooked now. It was never exactly a slouch, but parents agree that the focus on academic achievement has been extended under Mr Halls's leadership, and with it the school's profile – which is now stellar. Commonly bracketed in parents' minds these days with London's top selectives eg St Paul's, City of London, Westminster – no mean feat for a school out in the burbs.

Parents clearly appreciate all he has done for the school – 99 per cent of them described the school as well led in a recent survey – and value the open culture he's created, with one describing KCS 'a very healthy institution'. There was praise for his regular appearances on the touchline at Saturday sports fixtures and his 'frequent, informative and carefully prepared' communications. 'The head is doing a great job in leading the school, and is held in very high regard by the students, mainly due to his friendly nature in mixing and in speaking to so many of them, especially at lunch times.'

Academic matters: Between 2008 and 2013 this was an IB-only school, and the general consensus was that you couldn't be taught the programme better anywhere in the UK. Results continue to be extremely impressive: in 2018 pupils averaged 41 points out of 45 and five candidates gained the full 45 points. A levels reintroduced in 2013, and in 2018, 79 per cent A*/A. At GCSE – which here are mostly IGCSEs – 96 per cent of grades were A*-A/9-7 in 2018.

Curriculum is both deep and broad, allowing students to grow intellectually in every direction. English department breathed erudition, with truly inspiring quotations on display from Jane Austen, Milton and de Montaigne. Languages offered include French – compulsory until the sixth form – Spanish, Italian, German, Russian and Mandarin Chinese. At GCSE almost everyone takes further maths and triple science, the latter taught in a splendid new science block that devotes a floor to each science. Specialist sixth form lab allows for a more relaxed intellectual atmosphere, and experiments can be left in place. 'The science department is fantastic – one of the best, a real strength!' enthused a sixth former. Parents praised the 'exceptional' teaching. 'One member of staff in particular has gone way beyond his duty to encourage, inspire and give confidence to our son,' reported a satisfied father. 'KCS is a wonderful school where the teachers are very dedicated to each and every pupil,' wrote another. The articulate, poised and likeable students we spoke to confirmed that the school did not encourage a results culture – 'People bounce off each other, because they ask interesting questions. The teachers encourage it as much as they can, because so much teaching here is based around discussion.' 'The teachers always go beyond the syllabus,' were typical comments. Superb facilities for just about every subject. We loved the large, modern library, with its separate areas for 'silent' and 'quiet' study – then found that it was about to be redeveloped to give students even more space.

School has an excellent SEN policy which ticks all the boxes, and the Learning Enrichment department, as it's called here, offers support to the few students with mild learning needs who make it through the school gates. But this was one area where parents did express disquiet, claiming that their children had been viewed as a problem the school wasn't interested in solving, and hadn't received the help they'd needed. EAL support is reportedly strong. The school is in the process of appointing a new head of learning enrichment.

Games, options, the arts: 'Amazing! There's so much to say – where do I start?' cried one sixth former, when asked about the drama. Regular productions include big musicals such as West Side Story and Shakespeare's The Winter's Tale, staged in the main theatre, and more intimate and experimental works in the drama studio. The school also has a long track record of taking productions to the Edinburgh Festival Fringe. The sixth form drama scholars run a club for younger students, and the annual house play festival involves around 150 pupils each year.

Music is outstanding but inclusive, with orchestras and ensembles to cater for every level from jazz to chamber music, and a particularly strong choral tradition. Plenty of opportunities for pianists, too – concertos, concerts, masterclasses. New music block (including a concert hall seating 200) will up the ante still further. Visual art is of a very high standard, with some gratifyingly edgy and imaginative work on display – not least the female nude that seems to be obligatory fare in these schools full of clever boys.

Sport is extremely strong, with notable successes scored not only in staples such as rugby, cricket, football, athletics, hockey and netball, but in many more niche areas – fencing, fives, badminton, rowing, sailing, to name but a few. Loads on offer, and everyone encouraged to take part. Extensive playing fields at the rear of the school and a further 20 acres three miles away, and new sports hall and swimming pool (currently in what our guides described as the 'green tin can building') due for completion in 2019. Lively and varied programme of clubs and activities: debating, creative, writing, Greek, art drop in – no need for anyone to be bored.

Perhaps the jewel in the crown, however, are the Co-Curricular Fridays, which all pupils named as one of the highlights of their week. Every Friday afternoon around 350 students go to various 'stations' (the school is partnered with 27 state primary, secondary and special schools) to help out: hearing children read, teaching, generally helping out. Students can also opt to join the CCF – very popular here – or work on arts projects. The result is a school which, said one student, 'is genuinely a community-based school,' adding, 'I'm not just saying this because it sounds good – it really is.'

K

Background and atmosphere: Founded in 1829 as a junior branch of King's College London and originally housed in their basement. Moved to Wimbledon in 1897 in order to expand and compete with other London day schools that were relocating to the suburbs in quest of fresh air and playing fields. Junior school opened on the same site in 1912. Girls admitted to the sixth form in 2010, and the first year 7 cohort started at the senior school in 2016. Still retains ties with its illustrious forebear in the Strand, not least in the school colours.

Handsome Victorian red-brick building faces a secluded and tranquil part of Wimbledon Common – a lovely location for a school. The site is much bigger than at first appears, encompassing both modern and original styles in a pleasing architectural polyglot that charmingly reflects the KCS ethos of scholarship and innovation. Beautiful old Great Hall with organ and all the fittings rubs shoulders with wind turbines and solar panels, and attractive internationally-flavoured sculpture points the way to the much-loved multi-use games area. Even when full of noise and excitement, as the latter was when we visited, the school exudes civilised and cogitative calm. The fabulous sixth form centre, spacious and equipped with its own reading room and fair trade café, made us feel envious of all the confident, courteous young people relaxing therein.

Pastoral care, well-being and discipline: Those who join at 11 stay in the same form with the same tutor for the first two years. At 13, all boys are allocated a house, where they're under the care of a form teacher who registers them and a tutor who acts as their 'moral guardian'. Tutor groups, consisting of 12 students of different ages, meet twice weekly. Tutor system was described as 'excellent' by a father, who added 'it gives us a ready outlet if things occur which we need to discuss confidentially.' 'The tutors really fight for you!' affirmed one student.

The deputy head introduced an initiative called Kindness at King's, and it genuinely seems to have worked. Parents speak of 'a great sense of camaraderie among students,' commenting 'the pupils are truly nice kids', and time and again emphasised how happy their children were at the school. Pupils concur. 'One thing that's very present in the school is pastoral support,' said a sixth former, while a lower school boy exclaimed, 'Older students talk to you; you're not just a little boy on the side!' A slight feeling from the year 7s we met – the first such cohort to join the senior school – that they would like more interaction with the older boys, but this was qualified with 'When there's a year 8 it'll be better.'

Was it competitive, we asked? Much smiling at this, before a personable lad answered, 'There's what I would call a nice amount of competitiveness. We're all trying to push ourselves.' A sixth form girl added, 'The competition here is healthy. We arrive with the attitude that we want to be challenged.' All the girls praised the inclusivity of the sixth form and denied the school was in any way boysy – 'It really doesn't feel like that.' One said she'd applied to KCS because 'my sister raved about it – she looked forward to every single day.'

Discipline described by head as 'quite traditional and firm'. Pupils would be expelled for drugs, theft, systematic bullying, etc, although head was unable to remember the last time he'd had to do this. Students adamant that any bullying was 'quickly eliminated with quite a lot of severity.'

Pupils and parents: Pupils mostly from affluent backgrounds, some of them extremely so, but all of them from homes that greatly value education, and, according to head, where at least one parent has been to a very good university. 'The children are highly motivated, but they don't think cash is king, and their parents don't want them to live in a bubble.' Good ethnic diversity, and plenty of international families. Notable Old King's include Charles Dickens Jnr, Robert Graves, Alfred de Rothschild, Dante Gabriel Rossetti, Buster Mottram and Roy Plomley.

Entrance: Head is proud of having introduced year 7 entry point for the senior school – entirely justifiably, we think. The junior school still goes up to 13, but 44 11+ places are now available in what's known as the Lower School, and at least half of these are filled by boys from state primary schools. Some 350 applied for the first intake in 2016, a figure which is increasing year on year. At 13+, 80 boys come up from the junior school and join the lower school cohort, together with around 35 boys from other London preps. Hardly any space for boys at 16+, but 50 girls join at that point, some from local independents such as Wimbledon High or grammars such as Tiffin or Nonsuch, some from much further away – a recent sixth form girl came from Essex on a 100 per cent bursary, and is now doing well at Harvard.

At all stages the school is looking for applicants who share the love of learning here – 'We want students who have a willingness to enjoy what we teach, academic ability and humanity.' A sixth former told us cheerfully and without any conscious irony that 'the school is very good at selecting those who'll survive – I mean, enjoy and thrive here.'

Exit: Hardly any leave at 16+ – literally one or two. At 18+, a really glittering set of destinations. For the past five years some 25 per cent to Oxbridge (41 in 2018, plus 13 medics and two vets), the rest to Imperial, Durham, Bristol, and similar. Growing numbers to North American universities. Subjects chosen include English, history, languages, mathematics, sciences, economics and engineering – not that many lawyers, interestingly, because one imagines there must be a fair few among the parents.

Money matters: Not one of our cheaper schools, but up to 100 per cent bursary assistance at 11+, 13+ and 16+ for those who need it. Bursaries are rigorously means-tested, and the families visited at home. Scholarships offered at the same entry points for academic achievement, music and sport, with art and drama added for the older age groups, but these are mainly honorific and carry only a small financial value eg £1,500 reduction in the fees.

Remarks: Intellectually exhilarating yet principled, this is selective education at its very best. For those able to take advantage of what it has to offer, a real golden ticket.

King's House School

68 King's Road, Richmond, Surrey TW10 6ES

Ages 3–13 Pupils 420

Fees: £6,495 – £15,360 pa

020 8940 1878
www.kingshouseschool.org

Headmaster: Since 2011, Mark Turner BA PGCE NPQH (40s). Studied French and Spanish at Bristol before training at Sandhurst with six years in the army. After leaving, taught at Merchant Taylors' before joining Durston House, Ealing where he was deputy head for nine years. Married with four children, two of whom are at the school. Feels he is lucky to head such a good, friendly, and mainly local school. Says it has a strong sense of community and provides a broad education. Parents like the fact that he teaches French to year 4, thereby getting to know the senior boys, and say he's 'very approachable' and 'a classic boys' prep school headmaster'. Feel that he has made the school gentler. One of his aims is to unite the three sections of the school: at the moment they feel like separate entities. To that end, he spends more time in the junior section than his predecessor, which can't be a bad thing.

Entrance: From the term they turn 3, boys and girls at nursery level. Then reception, boys only, September after 4th birthday. No testing, places offered a year before entry in order of registration. Siblings take priority. A few more places at 7+ and 8+ subject to passing entrance test. Occasionally places occur at other times, each individually assessed. Mainly families from surrounding areas including Roehampton, Kingston and Barnes. Buses run from Chiswick and Putney.

Exit: A handful at 11+, trying to beat the rush, but the school does not give this much support. About two-thirds to boys' only London day schools at 13+ with Hampton, St Paul's and King's College Wimbledon all high on the list. Big range of boarding schools, with Epsom College, Charterhouse, Eton, Millfield and Winchester the recent favourites. Several scholarships, both music and academic, most years.

Remarks: On three sites in leafy Richmond. Seems a happy, hard-working school. We were taken round by two delightful, polite and enthusiastic senior boys under the eagle eye of the school's marketing manager – we were certainly given the spiel.

Large nursery building on two floors. Huge, bright rooms with different areas for learning and play. Plenty of constructive fun to be had by eager under-4s, both boys and girls. Parents love it – one even said 'flawless'. Two outdoor playgrounds, one for physical play, one for creative/imaginative play. They think of everything these days. Send your children here and your sons get automatic entry to the junior school. Your daughters? They seem mainly to head off to the Old Vicarage.

The junior school – reception to year 3 – is just across the road from the senior. Two reception classrooms on the ground floor have their own outdoor play areas where all is still reasonably relaxed. It may only be the beginning of learning but they are definitely being prepared for the next stage; homework starts straight away. Writing practice first, then, when they are ready, reading. Only 10 minutes at a time but it's still homework for 4 year olds.

The rest of this rather rambling house contains two year 1 classes and three each for years 2 and 3. Average class size about 20. All have a classroom assistant as well as a fully trained teacher. It is at this point that the serious learning begins. More work, less play. Classrooms are not enormous but they are bright and buzzing. All the boys appeared happy and attentive. Space is at a premium, the library fills in a corridor and a piano lesson seemed to be going on in a passageway. The IT room contained a lot of slightly restless boys learning computer basics. But, no worry, there is plenty of room for burning energy outside in the big playground which, cleverly, has a partially covered area. Parents full of praise for Mr Gower, head of juniors, who they say is extremely approachable and quick to answer emails. He's usually there to welcome boys in the morning. Also, we were told, all children love Nurse Jo who cures all their woes.

In year 4 they move across to the senior school where they can take advantage of some bang up-to-do date facilities, of which our guides were rightly proud, and the real pressure goes on. Initially all classes are mixed ability and, apart from those subjects needing special equipment, are classroom based. In year 5 they begin to build up towards the common entrance syllabus and are setted in English and maths. Two science labs; DT and art rooms; two computer rooms including a suite of Macs for composing and design; a music room; a theatre where, our young guides boasted, amazing productions are put on; and a well-equipped music room. Parents say 'music used to be one of their weaknesses but is now one of their greatest strengths'. These are lucky boys.

There's plenty of outdoor playing space as well, for organised and free play, that area having been completely revamped recently. Parents say it's a 'shame there's not wider extracurricular'; 'there could be more broader based after school clubs'. We got the feeling that the emphasis is mainly on the curriculum, with the pressure to succeed being the be all and end all. A 21st century London problem? Or just a lack of understanding that there is more to life than passing exams? The head comments: 'We believe the breadth and balance of our curriculum is a strength and is far from being too focused on the academic. We also feel that while some schools reduce art, DT, drama and ICT to carousel lessons, we still give them regular lesson time up to year 8.'

We didn't see the 35 acre sports ground as it is a coach ride away in Chiswick, but we have seen a DVD and it looks pretty impressive. Senior boys go there twice a week and junior boys once. Rugby, football and cricket all played competitively – 25 rugby, 34 football and 20 cricket teams. Wow! And they have silverware to prove their prowess (including Prep Schools Rugby Nationals U13 winners). Tennis, swimming and athletics also figure. Astroturf area within the senior school grounds and a well-equipped gymnasium ensure plenty of PE.

Inevitably, in a non-selective school, there is a wide variation in ability but, parents tell us, lots of help in the junior school who are 'quick to pick up struggling children and help them so they don't get left behind'. Continual monitoring; boys needing specific help are given it free of charge – 'we give them the building blocks' – being taken out of class for an hour at a time. Free, individualised education programmes provided.

Strict code of behaviour both in and out of the classroom, weekly PHSE sessions and a pupil teacher ratio of approximately 12:1 ensure that the majority of problems are caught quickly. House and tutor systems also provide continuous monitoring. Parents say, 'communication lines excellent and emails responded to quickly'; 'quick to pick up on problems and good at keeping on top of them'.

Communication certainly seems to be a great strength; no parent could say they are not kept fully up to date. From the headmaster's termly letter to the weekly school newsletters, everything is covered. Information on matches, charities and school trips, contributions from teachers, prizes and praises – it's all there. An active and busy school.

Kingsdale Foundation School

Alleyn Park, Dulwich, London SE21 8SQ

K

Ages 11–18 **Pupils** 1,560 **Sixth form** 200

020 8670 7575
www.kingsdalefoundationschool.org.uk

Head: Since 1998, Steve Morrison. He had previously been senior teacher and head of maths here in the 1980s.

Academic matters: Results are on an upwards trajectory, with around 80 per cent getting 5+ for both maths and English GCSE in 2018. Highest performing subjects usually maths, physics, chemistry, biology, computer science, Latin, textiles, food technology and statistics. At A level in 2018, 40 per cent A*/A, nearly two-thirds A*-B.

Although head is keen for the school to showcase its achievers, he says: 'we are not just interested in the children at the top end'. The school believes it does well by pupils across the board. Head says: 'We don't believe we've got it cracked, we believe we did not previously do enough because not every child achieved their potential'. The school is proud of its high performers in whatever arena – the boy who entered the school with little hope, whose mother died during his studies but who turned down the opportunity to train as a professional footballer to enter the sixth form when he achieved nine A*s and three As at GCSE. He is now at Columbia University with a soccer scholarship. Or the boy who got five A*s at A level and is now reading medicine at Oxford. There are several more on the same track right behind. It speaks of individual talent, but also teachers who are able to nurture that talent with the right support and inspiration.

A broad and traditional set of GCSE options to rival many, includes triple science, Latin, economics and psychology. 'No vocational short-cuts', says the head. Pupils have the opportunity to study two languages, or one, from year 7: a choice of French, Spanish, German and Latin, with other languages as clubs, such as Mandarin. We watched a small French class of only 12 students taking place in the library. Students study a condensed key stage 3 in science, so that they can spend three years on their GCSE courses. Science labs are light, bright and modern with both benches for group work and lecture style seating. It's also a hi-tech environment. Every child has access to an iPad for home and school use, subsidised by the school, as well as PCs, Apple Macs and laptops.

Staff ratio is one to 10. The head says: 'Pupils actually like the staff and staff actually like the pupils'. A parent said: 'A real strength of the school is the commitment of the teachers'. Our impression from talking to sixth formers is that for the motivated student the staff will be right behind them, as one girl said to us: 'all you have to do is ask'. Particularly in the approach to the summer examinations, the school is open seven days a week with evening revision classes, Saturday schools, Sunday schools and one-to-one sessions. As a pupil said: 'Kingsdale doesn't sleep and never leaves any pupil behind'. Ofsted in its latest inspection believed there is more to be done to challenge the most able pupils, with teachers required to provide more detailed feedback on pupils' work so that they can make progress.

Classes we observed were working quietly and diligently. When we enquired of a pupil about disruptive behaviour in the classroom she said: 'There was a lot to start with, but the teachers deal with it... it might make you laugh... but if you want to work you can'.

For nine successive years, it has been identified as a special school for inclusion. One mother said of her experience and that of her children: 'They've been treated like they have a voice. We've been listened to. It isn't a one size fits all school'. A mother of a child with both dyslexia and dyspraxia talked of receiving everything she asked for. The focus is on in-class support provided by teaching assistants rather than withdrawal. There is monitoring of reading ages and provision of reading clubs, touch-typing classes, hand-writing groups, and GSCE support groups. Learning mentors provide additional support across year groups. There is also a school nurse for medical matters.

The sixth form opened in 2010. Courses include a baccalaureate programme comprising A levels, one AS level and an EPQ, plus extracurricular including D of E, or straight A levels. Also on offer: an access to medicine course. Ambitions are nurtured with trips to Yale and Harvard as well as the UK's most prestigious universities.

Games, options, the arts: The school has little outside space, but there are some courts and pitches behind the main building. To the rear is the new sports hall, seemingly made of golden plywood. It contains courts for basketball, netball, volleyball, badminton and more, plus a mezzanine for dance classes: ballet, modern, hip-hop and jazz. On the wall are posters of inspirational Olympians and female sporting role models. With a dynamic female sports director, there are teams and fixtures for every sport and some sporting stars among them: one was recently signed for Manchester United, another represented England at the Commonwealth Games 3000m and gained a bronze medal; one is member of the team GB gymnastics squad and one coach is a former rugby U21 international player. There are 42 sports clubs on site and locally, including inline skating, yoga, tennis, American football, go-karting, archery, fencing and trampolining, fencing, BMX bikes and cycling at the Herne Hill velodrome.

Music is truly outstanding and adds a real vibrancy to the school. The head of music, at the school long before the current regime, is renowned for her ability to inspire and her ambition for the children who may not have picked up an instrument before coming here. Every year the school hosts the Dulwich Festival Youth Concert and steals the show from the massed independent school ensembles – most recently with a group xylophone rendition of an especially composed medley of Bond theme tunes. Ensembles for every instrument imaginable running at lunch times and after school, as well as steel pans, rock band, theory classes, jazz groups and chamber choir. The new music building is all curvy plywood and includes music practice rooms, teaching spaces and a recital hall with raked seating, plus a music tech suite. We heard a student's composition which sounded professional, akin to the latest pop release, and girls singing acoustically around a piano.

The art room displays accomplished textile GCSE projects, books rich with embroidered textiles and illustration. Within DT pupils study food and textiles technology and product design. A large, light DT lab with all of the usual workshop equipment, plus a laser cutter and CAD-CAM suite. The library seems rather gloomy, with dark blue carpet and a little low on books. The upper school library has computers that rise from desks.

There are lunch time clinics for students who need additional help or are struggling with homework and plenty of academic clubs. The school works hard to offer opportunities for exciting trips that are accessible for all. There are annual language department trips to Europe and some more far flung: a sixth former told us of a music trip to Brazil, working with young children – 'I've never done anything more amazing in my life'. The 'trips of a lifetime' programme subsidises trips to destinations such as Japan, Namibia, Brazil, the USA and the French Alps.

Background and atmosphere: A local authority school which was cause for concern by the late 1990s, it was completely reimagined to the tune of £30m under a new management team and with the involvement of a design and innovation consultancy which placed the design of the new school at the heart of change, becoming a foundation school in the process. The design won multiple awards, including Building of the Year from the Royal Fine Art Commission for its architects, and is now the most popular state senior school in Southwark and wears this badge with pride.

Situated south of Dulwich and Belair Parks, the school is located in a particularly leafy part of south east London. Its location on a residential street lined with multi-million pound homes, next door to Dulwich Prep London, makes for a calm outlook, surrounded by mature trees and safe-feeling journeys home via the buses on the South Circular or nearby West Dulwich overground station. There could be a bit of discomfort around a state school so surrounded by the plushest of independent education's finest – we get the feeling that there is only minimal sharing of facilities – but since the revamp and the climbing academic standards there is much to feel good about.

As you step through the sliding doors you find the most striking feature of the school: a huge, slightly humid central quadrangle, originally the school playground, now acres of green flooring enclosed with a glass roof – a central bed of tropical plants adding to the greenhouse effect. When it rains the noise on the roof is pleasantly loud. This futuristic central space is encircled by plywood banks of lockers on wheels designed to look like little houses, and most stunning of all a central 'egg' or pod, with fantastic acoustics and a steeply raked bank of seating for concerts and addresses. The usual dark school corridors have been cleverly done away with, instead wide, metal walkways encircle the quadrangle linking the classrooms on the first floor. Classrooms are light with brightly coloured walls. There is a freestanding lift linked to the walkways for wheelchair users. It's an exciting space. At lunchtime hot food is served here too, and there are tables outside. It's a versatile space that can be used for anything from art exhibitions to trampolining.

Pastoral care, well-being and discipline: A large school, but staff work to make it manageable, particularly for those joining year 7, with divisions between the upper and lower schools and induction days. There are buddies, junior and senior school prefects and a house system. Around a quarter of the student population is from disadvantaged backgrounds. Some 26 per cent of pupils speak English as an additional language. The uniforms, fairly smart black blazers and house ties, seem to be worn with a bit of a hastily assembled attitude, especially by the girls higher up the school – plenty of micro skirts with knee socks and half-mast ties. Ofsted was most complimentary about the behaviour of pupils in its most recent inspection, saying pupils 'show respect and courtesy to one another and to staff'. The pupils we talked to were polite and passionate about their school, appreciative of their teachers.

With discipline in mind, the school's very design is partly about transparency. Teachers can see what is going on everywhere, without anyone feeling monitored. However, a girl eager to leave no stone unturned on the tour of the school told us as we crossed the playground: 'There are fights. Not daily. You won't get into a fight if you're well behaved'. The head tells prospective parents there have been no exclusions for five years, but following a recent incident, where a pupil returned to the school after the end of the day resulting in a stabbing, the head suggested that the incident concerned an excluded pupil. Our enquiries amongst parents and pupils as to what has been changed with regards to safeguarding at the school in response to this incident did not yield any firm information.

Most parents we encountered seemed excited by the school as a prospect. With such a large school there are inevitably diverse reports once pupils are there. One grandmother told us how quickly her shy grandson settled into the school and made friends – when he wasn't very happy with the school lunches he felt able to talk to the school about it: even better, they responded with changes. An easy-going mother was nonetheless disappointed to feel after two years that the teachers didn't really know who her daughter was at parents' evening.

There was a certain freshness and honesty about the pupils at the open day we attended who told us: 'Kingsdale isn't perfect. Kingsdale admits its imperfections as a way to improve'; 'pupils are well-supported and grounded with room to make decisions for themselves'.

Pupils and parents: From all walks of life and backgrounds and from all across London. Many join in little bands from their local state primaries in East Dulwich, Herne Hill, Crystal Palace, Gypsy Hill and Forest Hill. But as there is unusually no distance criteria, students come from Clapham, Greenwich and beyond. We met a sixth former who had attended a local prep but after attending an open day and winning a music scholarship could think of no reason not to take up a place here instead. And the odd refugee from the uber-competitive selective schools that dominate the local scene. The head's invitation is for prospective parents to 'show up when you like: someone will show you around.

Entrance: Admissions to year 7 via the local authority common application form – simply place the school as high up the list of preferences as possible for a chance of a place and await National Offers Day. Most recently applications stood at 11 to one. Pupils sit a banding test, in non-verbal reasoning, prior to the allocation of places, so that the school has an academically mixed intake. Numbers in each band will vary from year to year, so there is no way of assessing chances of a place. There is a complicated system of admissions criteria in terms of how places will be allocated – so complicated, the maths teachers are assigned to try an explain it to bewildered parents at open days. Fifteen per cent of places to those with music or sports scholarships; then siblings, staff children, medical or social needs, with the rest of the places by random allocation within bands.

Internal and external sixth form applicants who want to study A levels must get at least six 9-6 grades at GCSE including English language and maths.

A parent going through the admissions and scholarship process commented she wasn't sure she'd want the school in charge of evacuating the Titanic as everything was slightly chaotic. With so many applicants to places the school is possibly rather overwhelmed by the process, but gets there in the end.

Exit: Around 50 per cent of students achieve places at Russell Group/other top universities; one to Oxford in 2018.

Money matters: Unusually for a state school, scholarships are available in music and sports at year 7 entrance. The awards comprise additional tuition and coaching, such as £1000 worth of instrumental lessons for music and a scholar's programme – the musicians might attend workshops with professional musicians and the sports scholars take vocational qualifications in sports leadership. No need to be already at a high grade of accomplishment on your chosen instrument and sports scholarships are simply looking for 'potential' – candidates will be assessed for component activities and team work. Sixth form scholarships are also available in maths, performing and expressive arts.

Remarks: For those able to stretch to the local independents, there may be more peace of mind, particularly for the most able and ambitious, elsewhere. For parents looking for a vibrant school with a growing academic capability and a uniquely inspiring daily environment, join the crowds heading this way.

K

Kingston Grammar School

London Road, Kingston, Surrey KT2 6PY

Ages 11–18 **Pupils** 830 **Sixth form** 222

Fees: £19,230 pa

020 8546 5875
www.kgs.org.uk

Head master: Since 2014, Stephen Lehec, previously head of Aylesbury Grammar School. He joined Aylesbury as deputy head from Maidstone Grammar in 2006, becoming head in 2008. He has a history and English degree from Southampton and a PGCE from Oxford. Softly spoken (for a head) and personable, he works from an office so lush that it wouldn't look out of place in an interiors magazine or, at any rate, a Heal's ad. Not that he spends all his time there, with pupils telling us he's 'so much more hands-on than the last head.' Teaches year 7 history (and was trying to find time to start teaching sixth formers too when we visited) and meets regularly with pupils across all years. 'I never want to be the kind of head to say, "Remind me who you are,"' he explains.

Meanwhile, staff praise his collaborative leadership style and his reshaping of the executive team that encourages more sharing and avoids anyone being able to say, 'That isn't my job.' Parents describe him as 'available', 'pragmatic' and 'open to suggestions'. 'There's no element of "Leave us to it, we know best",' one told us. Refuses to overpush academia at the expense of developing the whole child.

Lives locally with his wife and two daughters and is a keen football, cricket and tennis player, having coached teams up to county level – although the school itself remains his biggest passion. 'If you asked my wife what's my biggest interest outside of work, she'd say "work",' he laughs.

Academic matters: Strong results across the board – in 2018, 67 per cent A*/A grades and 93 per cent A*/B at A level/Pre-U; 85 per cent A*-A/9-7 grades at I/GCSE – although maths is the clear stand-out subject here. A whopping four maths choices alone at A level. 'We support people who want a bit of maths to supplement their qualifications right up to those wanting to study it at Cambridge,' says the head. For both GCSE and A level, other popular subjects include English lit, sciences (where there's a good gender split) and history, and the school also offers IGCSEs in maths, English, languages, and sciences. 'We're big on the facilitating subjects here,' explains the head, 'although lots of A level students also add on the likes of theatre studies, PE or politics.' Pre-U in economics and 70-80 per cent take up of EPQ – often with pupils revisiting areas they gave up for GCSE, such as Italian. Some pupils yearn for cookery, although they do get the opportunity to cook at home and bring in the fruits of their labour for assessment and tasting.

Language department – an uplifting environment, with bunting made from European flags hanging from the ceilings – currently musters 15 languages, with year 7 pupils choosing two options from French, German, Spanish and Italian, plus Latin. In addition, there are options to do taster courses in everything from Mandarin to Danish and Russian to Polish. By year 9, pupils can pick up other languages more formally, with all students studying at least one language for GCSE and many studying more. Greek taught in collaboration with Tiffin boys. IT very much embedded into learning, with plenty of IT breakout areas across the subjects, many in full use when we visited. A little setting in maths and PE from year 7, 'but it's more tiering than setting,' says the head.

A new timetable system of longer, 50-minute lessons, has gone down well and the teaching staff are widely praised by pupils for providing interesting lessons and extra help when required, including extension classes and one-to-one tutoring. Not that the pupils are expected to give up oodles of their time. 'Far from it, teachers are really understanding that we have busy lives,' one told us. 'There's no sense of underachievement or failure if pupils don't get top marks,' said one parent. 'The ethos is more about encouraging and enthusing pupils,' said another. Lots of professional development opportunities to help attract and retain the best teaching staff.

Learning support department helps those on the dys strata, mostly mild, a few moderate. Learner profile compiled for all children seen by educational psychologist or specialist teacher – school a great believer in constant monitoring and tracking to ensure progress. Lots of laptop users and open to those with aural/visual impairment – 'so long as they can cope with the site.' One parent, with a child who unexpectedly became partially sighted, told us the school has been 'magnificent.' 'It was bolt from the blue for us and for them when she got this curious genetic condition, but they quickly assessed what they'd need to do to support her and to ensure she didn't stand out.'

Games, options, the arts: Hockey, rowing and, most recently, cricket, are the three strongest sports here. The school has also boosted netball and football, once considered the poor relations. Good gender split (the school's best cricketers were female when we visited), with netball the only sport played only by one gender and even that is being redressed, with the school considering using handball as way of getting more boys into it. Other sports – of which there are 25 options by sixth form – range from spinning classes to sailing. Plenty of sporting accolades, with 20 international level girls and boys at the school, and five currently playing at international level. Traditionally, the school comes in the top five schools nationally for hockey and amongst one of the best co-ed schools for rowing in the country – particularly good for a co-ed school, where they only have half the potential numbers of single sex schools. Around 80 per cent take up among pupils for Saturday and after-school sports.

The unfortunately-named Cage (two onsite courts with soft surfaces) is well-loved by pupils, along with the school gym. And although some sport takes place on the Fairfield – a field across the road from the main site, which is also used by Tiffin and maintained by the Royal Borough of Kingston – most of it happens off-site at Ditton Field, a 22-acre facility a bus ride away. Other sporting venues used by the school include St Mary's University and Hampton Court for Real (Royal) Tennis. A few grumbles from parents that there isn't more sport on site, although they quickly catch themselves sounding spoilt – this is London, after all.

Music a source of huge pride and joy, although it's seen by some, including the head, to have historically spread itself too thin, with too big a range of functions, so watch out for some more honed evening performances in the future. Three orchestras (beginners, junior and senior), four choirs (first year, juniors, seniors and chamber – which had recently sang at the Vatican when we visited), along with plenty of quartets and quintets from guitar to saxophone. Excellent facilities and around 250 private music lessons a week, many of which take place in the colourful contemporary pods, located in a school courtyard. 'Music tech is amazing,' added one student. 'You get to actually produce music from the word go.'

Exceptional performing arts centre produces some very polished performances (they used proper airline seats on stage and filmed 500 minutes of scenes around London that were used for background for one recent performance). But then again, professional staff come from a theatre background and there are regular visiting actors (Samantha Bond's daughter Molly Hanson, a former KGS school captain herself, when we visited) helping with everything from LAMDA exams to drama school applications. 'My son has really found his feet, thanks to the drama here – his confidence has grown immeasurably,' one parent told us.

Art and DT also excellent – masses of workshop/studio space, and we drooled over brilliantly conceived and executed works of art, both 3D and paintings, much of which you'd pay good money to hang on your walls. Professional quality furniture made by GCSE class, perspex clocks and clever ceramics make you want to get your hands gummy.

Co-curricular opportunities – which range from knitting to foreign language film club and from philosophy to debating club – fill a 40-page booklet, with many parents saying this is what gives Kingston the edge. Most pupils do at least one a day, with one telling us, 'I set up a new club myself – the economics society.' School usually open from 7am, with last staff leaving as late as 10pm.

Masses of trips, with the school taking full advantage of all the theatres, galleries and cultural events the capital has to offer, along with national residential trips and international residentials to the likes of Iceland (geography), Rome (choir) and Gibraltar (netball) just in one half term, and many others such as South Africa (hockey), Sri Lanka (cricket), China (cultural exchange) Utah (skiing), New York (art and drama) every year or two. Plenty of languages exchanges every year. A hardship support fund seeks to assist those in need.

Background and atmosphere: Whatever you do, don't put the school's postcode in your satnav (which takes you to the back of the school, where there's no entrance) and even when you do find the front, be warned there's no parking on site (although, thankfully, there are good public transport links). But despite the metropolitan location that's a nightmare to get to, inside the school you quickly forget you're in the midst of Kingston's tarmac tangle, thanks to the relaxed, welcoming and buzzy environment.

The original building is an attractive, well-kept, old-fashioned looking grammar school, while newer, modern buildings provide plenty of bright, airy spaces to learn, with particularly impressive science labs. Good café for sixth form, with TV, stereo system, drinks and snacks (and always someone playing chess, apparently). Space isn't lavish here, by any means, though what they've got has been used wisely and it is less cramped than some of its central London peers. The next big project being planned is a multi-million three or four storey building to include new changing rooms, space for engineering and art studios, bigger dining facilities (currently quite tight), additional library space and galleries with a real wow-factor – with the school hoping to build by around 2019-20.

Pupils – who wear white shirts and grey uniforms in years 7 to 11 (business dress in the sixth form) – look cheerful, both in lessons and during breaks, when they spill out into the various outside areas, including Fairfield during summertime. Strong student voice, with recently reformed school forum changing the likes of the lunch queuing system through to mobile phone rules. Renewed catering means take-up among year 9s (when, traditionally, pupils have moved to packed lunches) is now 95 per cent and is still popular in the sixth form when students are allowed out of school for lunch if they wish. Good home/school IT links. Fabulous sixth form development offices – a one-stop shop for exams officer, careers advice, head of sixth form and more.

Pastoral care, well-being and discipline: 'It's ridiculously caring here,' says the head – a bold claim by anyone's standards, but pupils and parents concur. Good system of heads of year, form tutors and heads of house – 'they get to know you really well' – along with a robust buddy, prefect, mentoring and house system that encourage friendship across the years, and plenty of positions of leadership among pupils, including older ones mentoring younger ones. 'I always say that, "If we don't catch you in the wash, we'll get you in the rinse," because it really is the case that if anything is bothering anyone, we have enough systems in place both to notice and to help,' says the head. Bullying and stress minimal. 'They're quick to pick up problems and keep parents in touch. It's in the culture of the place,' said one parent.

Discipline scarcely an issue here, with non-verbal and verbal warnings, misconduct marks, summons to head of year and occasional after-school detentions generally all that's needed – although head has excluded pupils for a day or two occasionally, for the likes of foul language and misuse of mobile phones. 'We need to show we won't tolerate these things on the rare occasions they do happen,' he says.

Pupils and parents: Mostly from a three mile radius (although increasingly from Clapham and central London), so at least they probably know how to navigate Kingston's surreal road system. That said, over 95 per cent of pupils come by bus, train, bike or walk. From over 150 primaries – some 60 per cent from state schools. Parents are a mixture of the predictably wealthy types and those who bend over backwards to afford it. School encourages plenty of parental involvement and there's a thriving PA. We found the pupils quietly ambitious, grounded and confident.

Notable former pupils include Edward Gibbon (The Roman Empire one), RC Sherriff (of Journey's End fame) Michael Frayn, Jonathan Kenworthy, James Cracknell, Andy Sturgeon (imaginatively roped in to help with the reshaping of the school's landscape), 2012 Olympic gold medal rower Sophie Hosking, a founder of Not On The High Street Sophie Cornish, and Hotel Chocolat's Peter Harris, as well as Ian Fortune, who was awarded the Distinguished Flying Cross (RAF version of the VC).

Entrance: The main entry points are 11+ and 16+ with some spaces available for 13+ entry. There's also an option to sit a 10+ deferred entry examination in year 5 to secure a place in year 7 (for which over 200 sit the test for around 20 places offered). More or less equal number of boys and girls. Interview seen as important – the school looks for potential, not just academic achievement, and it also helps weed out the overly tutored. Even at interview stage, the school is blind to whether the pupil goes to a state or private school. 'Unless, that is, they turn up in their straw boater, which some do,' says the head, smiling. Around 1,000 sit the 11+ test, with 360 interviewed, from which up to 250 places are offered for the 125 or so places they could fill. 'We're well aware people have more than one iron in the fire,' says the head, with lots of parents deliberating over issues such as, 'Do I go for Tiffin, which is free, or Kingston Grammar for its reputation?' School works closely with the feeder schools – especially at 13+, so as to not to encourage unrealistic applications. For external 16+, entry involves sitting exams in the A level subjects opted for, followed by interviews. Some 20-30 external offers are made every year.

At year 7, five forms of 20-25 pupils, dropping to an average of 16-18 in GCSE groups and to single figures for A level groups. 'I'm not convinced smaller class sizes necessarily affect outcomes, because good teaching should work in any size class, but it does mean we get to know the pupils better,' says head.

Exit: Around 80 per cent stay on into sixth form, for which pupils need a 9-6 grade average in their GCSEs including grade 7s in their chosen or related subjects and 8 in maths. Post A levels, 98 per cent go to university, 10-15 per cent after a gap year, with over 70 per cent going to Russell Group universities and an annual sprinkling to Oxbridge – seven in 2018. 'We actually get quite a few pupils turning Oxbridge places down, for example to go to Royal Veterinary College or Imperial to study medicine,' says head (10 medics in 2018). Top destinations include Nottingham, Bristol, Birmingham, Exeter, Manchester, London, Warwick, Durham, Southampton, Leeds – and a few to art and drama colleges. Biggest range of courses you could imagine, with maths, science, history and humanities among the most popular.

Money matters: Scholarships typically worth 10 to 50 per cent of fees available at all entry points and awarded on results of tests for academic scholarships and application and assessment for art, drama, sport and music. Bursaries worth up to 100 per cent of fees also at all entry points and means-tested – with the school aiming to fill 5-10 per cent of places a year this way. Worth a serious look if you are local, clever and strapped.

Remarks: There's no shortage of good schools in this area, all with their particular highlights, but this stands out for being relaxed and friendly, with an underlying buzz that seems to get pupils willingly and happily doing their best. 'There's a kind of intimacy about it that makes it the kind of school you wish you'd been to,' said one parent, whilst every single pupil and parent we spoke to, bar none, raved about the fact that the school really understands each child and what makes them tick. We found the extracurricular offering also stands out. Indeed, the ethos is all about developing the whole person, not just getting them through academic exams. A school that really lives up to its motto, 'Work Well and Be Happy', this is a place that sets young people up for a fantastic future.

Knightsbridge School

67 Pont Street, London SW1X 0BD

Ages 3–13 Pupils 401

Fees: £19,500 – £20,700 pa

020 7590 9000
www.knightsbridgeschool.com

Principal and founder: Since the school opened in 2006, Magoo Giles (50ish), known universally and affectionately as Magoo. Married with two children, one in the school. Via Summer Fields, Eton, the Coldstream Guards and two years as personal equerry to the Queen, he spent six years as head of nearby Garden House Boys' School. If he wasn't a teacher from the off, he should have been – he exudes ebullience, dedication and high educational values. With the backing of 50 friends and family members, he got hold of the building on the corner of Lennox Gardens and Pont Street – formerly home of The Hellenic College – and began to create a dream come true. Magoo is energy, enthusiasm, loquacity and huge fun in pinstripes. He is not out to process children for any particular school but to ensure his school maintains the values, atmosphere and friendliness that make a sound learning environment for all. Parents praise his pastoral care for their children. His school was celebrating its 10th anniversary when we visited. Hard to believe it's not been a fixture for far longer.

Headteacher since 2015, Shona Colaço MA PGCE MSB CBiol (50s), previously head of science, director of studies and, finally, deputy head at Hampton Court House School; a biologist by training. Married and with two children, she has upped the profile of science in the school and has also developed leadership courses for her staff – which can, of course, lead to their leaving to lead elsewhere. 'I am as ambitious for my colleagues as for our pupils.' Parents approve: 'The school needed someone more academic'. If listening to Magoo is like being showered by freshly uncorked champagne, chatting with Shona is a reassuring glass of fine wine. She is calm, efficient, warm and experienced – and just as much fun as Magoo, only quieter. Their rooms adjoin, an open door between them, and you can't avoid thinking 'dream team' when you see – and hear – them working together. A wise and mature appointment for a fast-maturing school.

Entrance: Nursery is just for siblings and most entrants join at reception into which they take four classes with a maximum of 18 children in each. They close the lists at 200 applicants and Magoo sees all candidate parents and children – the child does activities with the head of early years while the grown-ups chat. Occasional places thereafter – younger candidates spend a day with their own age group and older ones sit tests and are interviewed. All is designed to ensure that children will fit in and involve themselves and that school and child will suit each other. Most from local nurseries eg Miss Daisy's, Tadpoles, Chelsea Pre-prep and Pippa Poppins.

Exit: Most girls leave at 11 and boys at 13; Queen's Gate currently the most popular at 11, then Francis Holland SW1 and Harrodian; Wetherby most popular 13+ destination, with the odd one or two to Prior's Field, Uppingham and St Paul's. Wise approach to children going to the best schools for them. This is not the school for you if you want your sprog spoon-fed for a school with a name you can brag about.

Remarks: On the corner of Pont Street and Lennox Gardens in a tall, six storey, once private, house complete with grand, limed oak staircase, back stairs, ballroom, erstwhile kitchens, spacious halls, interesting and large triangular corner rooms and lots of little rooms and passages. Few vestiges of the late lamented Hellenic College and its Grecian legacy can still be found about the place. An upmarket prep was the natural successor to its prior tenant and Knightsbridge School has quickly established itself as the natural school for its local constituency of sophisticated, moneyed and cosmopolitan residents. Despite its location, the road is extraordinarily quiet much of the day. The school encourages its families to walk to school, in the interests both of health and out of consideration for neighbours.

Quiet learning in every room. Every class has a teacher and an assistant. We have seldom seen such engaged children, at all levels. Bright, young (mostly female and blonde) staff – all smiles and energy. Curriculum trad and sensible, complemented by brand-new Macs and iPads and laptops with in-class charger units and all used with proper educational values rather than for their own sakes. We even spotted some books! Those on school's SEN register are supported in-class, in small groups and individually. Speech and language and occupational therapists come in as needed. Full time SENCo of whom warm reports. Tribute from one particularly grateful young dyslexic learner: 'Learning support changed everything for me. I don't go to ICT classes, I have one-to-one instead. I'd never have got to Harrow without her help.'

Much enthusiasm for many teachers eg 'he is brilliant!' Parents praise the care and attention given to their children. Rare and only gentle grouse from both parents and children is about a high turnover of staff – especially among the younger ones. To some extent this reflects the school's success in creating new leaders but, as one harder-nosed, parent observed, 'They all want Knightsbridge on their cv'. Also some wise and older staff, so youth and energy are balanced by experience and thoughtfulness. But the hope that a house tutor would stay with a child throughout its KS career seems unlikely to be fulfilled very often. Parental praise for academic support given to those who stay into year 8. Somewhat quieter praise for support given to those who take 11+ entrance tests. 'We need more help with English and maths and less other stuff when the exams are coming.' But this may express perennial parental anxiety more than anything else.

Art room on top floor with pitched ceilings and skylight. Art activities limited by space and resources but what we saw was imaginative and pleasing. Projects on eg 'fish' and 'looking out of the window'. No real DT though some textile work; 3D printer in Mac room. Though the (very well-cared-for) building has its airy spaces, on-site activity space is limited. 'We do miss having a playground.' One good gym in the basement is supplemented by the excellent and capacious facilities at St Columba's church opposite with its huge hall – used by the school for everything that needs real space. Otherwise, buses take children to local parks etc and no-one complains of a lack of exercise – despite the lack of space. Hot days make much of the place airless and stuffy, despite fans and windows.

Much of the ethos is encapsulated in and by the little KS book given to pupils. Its 96 pages include everything from The KS Code and Song ('You're on the winning team all the way at KS/You get the most from every day'); selective capital cities (no Brazil, Nigeria or Israel but Monaco?); rules of various games including poker; wives of Henry VIII; 12 famous women (one is Coco Chanel); famous speeches; 'thank you' in 24 languages; the periodic table; signs of the zodiac; instructions on how to tie a tie and some predictable hymns. It is quite wonderful, whisks us cheerily back to our grandparents' childhood and we will carry it everywhere.

Parents and children enthuse about the range and variety of activities and clubs on offer – impressive for a prep, especially a day prep. Lots of rewards (Supers) and some demerits (Subs) and a well-understood system for both. Trophies, cups and shields galore. House system which works vertically and horizontally and important for competition in sports, quizzes, arts etc. Effective tutor system clearly trusted by the pupils and especially in moments of anxiety or distress. Also Place2Be – recently won award – a counselling resource with its own room and handled with tact. Parental praise for the home-school communications which are frequent and close. Teachers in the junior school are Miss, Mrs or Mr plus First Name. On Magoo's door is, simply, Magoo. Food looked jolly good to us – especially scrumptious fruit bowls – but a few junior gourmets grumbled about lack of choice.

Most families live in Kensington, Chelsea, Belgravia. A few from such outbacks as Fulham and Battersea. Lots of Americans. But, at time of our visit, around 20 home languages spoken so an interestingly diverse constituency reflecting the neighbourhood. Smallish percentage of pupils need and get EAL help but the staff can muster several languages between them and induction of ESOL pupils is carefully handled. International families love the fact that so many are from overseas, 'so my children don't feel alien like they would in other preps – it's a real melting pot,' said one. Very lively and popular Parents' Association particularly valued by the recently arrived international families who make friends and quickly involve themselves. Five PA committees and a Knowledge Society which invites guest speakers for parental enlightenment, education and entertainment. Every parent we spoke to stressed how 'super-happy' their offspring were. Lots of involvement in local charities and eco initiatives – a palpable concern not to upset the neighbours – many of whom are current parents – clearly a priority.

KS Foundation – largely supported by parents – offers two 100 per cent bursaries annually for children in years 7-9. NB this is an important opportunity, especially for state primary leavers who want to go to senior schools which start at 13+. The commitment can extend to helping bursary-holders into senior schools which will offer continuing significant financial support. Otherwise, no fee assistance lower down the school unless in cases of dire, short-term need.

A lovable school with a warm and community feel that surprises in such a location. If you have no other reason, it's worth moving to Knightsbridge for.

La Sainte Union

Linked with LaSWAP Sixth Form Consortium

Highgate Road, London NW5 1RP

Ages 11–18 **Pupils** 1,085 **Sixth form** 198 (25 boys); part of LaSWAP consortium **RC**

020 7428 4600
www.lasainteunion.org.uk

Headteacher: Since 2017, Sophie Fegan, 40s. Frenchwoman Mrs Fegan (who retains a slight accent) began at the school teaching French in 2008. Since then, she's moved up the ranks from (popular) teacher, to head of year, then deputy head, so no radical changes expected now she's in the top spot. (Though consultations are taking place with girls on ways to improve the school – and tartan trousers could, one day, be an option.) Smartly suited, earnest, evidently devout, she sees the school's mission as promoting 'gospel values so that girls can go on to lead good Christian lives.'

Academic matters: The head is emphatic that this is a 'traditional school offering a traditional curriculum with "no short cuts"': 'We aim to nurture a love of learning, engaging with difficult things and exposing learners to high culture.' (So, year 9 study the work of Bertolt Brecht and Arthur Miller, as well as French poet Lamartine.) Teaching, too, on traditional lines (ie silent, orderly and attentive), with classrooms staffed by the bright-eyed, enthusiastic and energetic. ('Teachers are kind and they help you learn,' said one girl; 'We really trust the teachers,' said another.) Work appropriately challenging and fast paced (a forest of 12-year-old hands, for example, was raised to define the meaning of 'variegated'). GCSE results are strong (81 per cent got 9-4 in both English and maths in 2018; 29 per cent 9-7 grades), particularly in English; RS also noticeably (if, perhaps, unsurprisingly) buoyant. Inspectors, however, have voiced concerned about the relative weakness of science and maths, and, in 2017, under the new exam system, GCSE maths undoubtedly seemed a bit wavery, with nearly a third missing out on that critical grade 4. 'Maths took a dip,' admitted one teacher, 'but there's an action plan to rectify it.' Here, as elsewhere, the impression is very much that the school is on the case – and indeed in 2018, only 18 per cent didn't reach grade 4 in maths. Post-GCSE, membership of LaSWAP sixth form consortium allows a wide choice of courses (over 30 A levels, from further maths to film studies, plus numerous vocational qualifications) either on site or at one of the sister schools, and sixth formers are given very good support.

L

Pupils, many joining from Catholic primaries, typically start out strong and just get stronger. Testing carried out in year 7 to assess 'needs', then broad banding applied, but no setting. Instead, the school uses carefully considered 'strategies' to address the requirements of its wide ability range. 'We don't say: you're bright, you're not bright. We teach them how to get where they want through hard work and love of learning.' Progress, as the head notes, is 'phenomenal' (significantly above the national average). Those requiring additional assistance are quickly identified, monitored by a senior member of staff, dedicated SENDCo, learning support assistants and SEN governor, and aided by small classes for English and maths, literacy and numeracy catch-up groups, and external help where needed.

Facilities generally good and up to date but, at least in some subjects, a distinctly old-world mood prevails. In DT, for example, the priority is for girls to 'make sure they can make their own clothes', with the advice that the best preparation for starting at the school is knowing how to thread a sewing machine! (First efforts – a small dress – are then sent to an orphanage in Tanzania.)

Games, options, the arts: Impressive extracurricular, with a stimulating range of activities available before and after school and at lunchtime. (Everything from Afro culture to Manga, feminist committee to cheerleading, gardening to first aid.) All the arts flourish ('We want students to have access to cultural capital'), but music a notable strength with instrumental lessons in everything from violin to bassoon, and plenty of opportunity to put skills into practice (school orchestra, soul/jazz group, gospel choir, chapel choir, regular concerts, chapel music tour). Annual art competition, poetry workshops, cross-school drama production (most recently The Crucible) encourage creativity, plus good use made of what London has to offer, with the curriculum abandoned several times a year for outings to the National Gallery, etc. Trips further afield, both nationally (geography to the Lake District) and internationally (Spain). Sport well catered for with own courts and gym providing scope for basketball, netball, handball, athletics, rounders, trampolining and rugby (with one girl recently selected for Middlesex County). Girls compete regularly in Camden competitions (rounders, athletics, basketball), frequently emerging triumphant, particularly in basketball. School council (operating at all levels) gives pupils leadership opportunities, as does Duke of Edinburgh bronze. Mass participation (50 girls) in Jack Petchey 'Speak Out' develops public speaking and political awareness (as do visits from politicians). Outward-looking approach also evidenced by the recent acquisition of the British Council's International School Award.

Background and atmosphere: Founded in 1861 by the sisters of La Sainte Union, a French order of nuns, for much of its history LSU was an independent Catholic boarding school, before becoming an all-girls comprehensive in the 1970s. Boys have been admitted into the sixth form since 1995; LaSWAP consortium includes nearby schools William Ellis, Acland Burghley and Parliament Hill.

Located in the heart of affluent Dartmouth Park directly opposite Hampstead Heath, its convent background has left it with gracious period buildings and spacious grounds, including a beautiful, peaceful garden (plus orchard), hidden behind its elegant 19th-century frontage. This cloistered mood permeates the daily routine, with prayers held every morning (inspired by the school's motto, Each for All and All for God, emblazoned on a banner across the assembly hall), compulsory attendance at weekly mass in the school chapel (sixth form non-believers are allowed to sit in silent reflection), and about 10 per cent of lesson time up to GCSE devoted to RE (five per cent thereafter). Charity and social justice both highlighted, and energetic fundraising undertaken for the LSU Tanzania project, North London Citizens' Project, and various local and national causes, with pupils taking a leading role through the house system in deciding when and which charities to support. Regular cake sales and other activities raise significant sums.

Pastoral care, well-being and discipline: A safe and pleasant place to go to school, with attendance and behaviour both exemplary. Girls in tartan pleats and forest-green blazers are generally orderly and well brushed. 'When they enter and leave, they're appropriately dressed. Paying attention to the small details means other things are right as well.' Between 11 and 16, pupils kept on site during the school day, with a keen eye kept out for unhappiness or unkindness, particularly in year 7, when the school runs an effective mentoring scheme with year 10. 'It's the biggest change in their education other than going to university,' says a teacher. 'It's exciting and exhilarating, but it can also be exhausting and a bit daunting.' The home-school bond unusually strong. The online Firefly system documents progress and shares behaviour with parents, who are also aided by workshops on issues such as mental health. Discipline here means instilling good habits: 'We teach children to self-discipline and always know right and wrong. We talk with them and sort them out.' Punishment, when necessary, is quick and clean, with same-day detention, 'so they know they're forgiven and can start the next day afresh.' Plenty of leadership roles for senior students, who act as heads and deputy heads of houses (named for patron saints).

Pupils and parents: Over 90 per cent baptised Catholics, but culturally and socially diverse, united by an atmosphere of respect and cooperation. Pupils – quite often the daughters of old girls – are generally co-operative and industrious. 'There are a lot of studious girls who work hard and get good results,' said one mother. 'If your daughter is that kind of child, she should be able to find like-minded friends.' Parents choose the school for its safe environment and academic focus ('My parents were impressed by its academic success,' said one high achiever) and for the articulate and responsible girls it turns out.

Entrance: Oversubscribed with admissions criteria that don't admit much leeway on the faith front, so realistically only thoroughly practising Catholics need apply. That said, living next to the school gates is not essential, and girls come from north, south, east and west (though a reasonable number worship at Our Lady, Help of Christians, Kentish Town, St Joseph's, Highgate, and St Gabriel of our Lady of Sorrows, Archway). Siblings given priority and 18 places also awarded annually for musical aptitude, with tests held in November of year 6 and Catholics given priority. Faith criteria not applicable to sixth form entrance, when boys and non-believers may apply to LaSWAP, a four-school consortium formed when LSU unites with neighbouring comprehensives Parliament Hill, William Ellis and Acland Burghley.

Exit: Reasonably large exodus post-GCSE, with about half departing for other RC schools (such as Cardinal Vaughan and The London Oratory), or local FE colleges (City and Islington and Westminster Kingsway). At 18, everywhere and anywhere, with top performers proceeding to Russell Group (UCL, Bristol, King's, York) and other leading unis, the vocationally inclined to apprenticeships. One to Cambridge in 2018 (engineering).

Money matters: Not a rich school by any means either in terms of its students (about a third in receipt of pupil premium) or endowments, but no one seems to suffer the lack. Active Parents and Friends Association raises funds to subsidise school trips, buy computer equipment, and refurbish accommodation (such as the sixth form common room).

Remarks: A safe, calm and orderly place to go to school, with a strong spiritual core, providing a rich all-round education and producing industrious, articulate, responsible girls.

Lady Eleanor Holles Junior School

Linked with Lady Eleanor Holles School

Burlington House, 177 Uxbridge Road, Hampton Hill TW12 1BD

Ages 7–11 Pupils 196 C of E

Fees: £16,731 pa

020 8979 2173
www.lehs.org.uk

Head of Juniors: Since 2016, Paula Mortimer BEd (40s), previously head of St Christina's school in St John's Wood. A science specialist with a degree from Oxford, she has taught in preps and all-through schools, latterly as deputy and acting head of Channing Junior School. Also has experience as SEN coordinator. Still loves teaching. 'I have no plans whatsoever to stop spending time working with children in the classroom,' she says. A hands-on head, she is known for fostering honest, open relationships not only with staff, but with pupils and parents. Very committed to pastoral care. 'For me, a role as head is all about ensuring children are secure and happy first and foremost, as that's what makes them successful learners. They're two sides of the same coin.' Particularly keen to see children take risks in the classroom. 'That's how they learn.'

Head of whole school is Mrs Heather Hanbury (see senior school entry).

Entrance: School's own entrance tests in English and maths at 7+, and top performers invited back for an activity session. About 48 places, split across two forms. Only two girls trying for every place, but don't be fooled – the older they get, the faster the ride, so best for those who seem exceptionally bright and eager to learn. That said, they do take some borderline performers. 'Some show high potential, but have not had the fire in their belly if, for example, they've been at a pre-prep that just drills facts into them. We are looking for what girls are capable of, not what they've already achieved – along with a can-do attitude.' Pupils come from a combination of primaries and many from pre-preps like Athelstan House, Denmead and Jack and Jill.

Exit: Some 75-85 per cent move up to the senior department – the school insists that in any one year, usually only three or four girls do not progress due to not being academically able. Thankfully, no exam separating those who get in vs those that don't – instead, girls are assessed on the basis of their classroom work and school exams and offered a guaranteed place in year 5. The few who don't make the cut get lots of support and extra help to prepare for tests to other schools and they may still sit the LEH entrance exam if they wish. Those who want to try for a scholarship also sit the entrance exams, along with the outside applicants. Those who do get a place, but decide to go elsewhere, opt for Tiffin Girls, St Paul's Girls or Nonsuch, with others going to Kingston Grammar, Sir Williams Perkins, St James' Girls and St Catherine's.

Remarks: A warmer welcome to a school you will not find, thanks to the lovely receptionists – and this really sets the tone for this surprisingly informal school where girls thrive academically, and then some. Four or five thick, bound photo albums take up the entire coffee table in the reception area, packed with pictures of the girls at carol services, on school trips, doing drama productions etc – also giving a flavour of school life here, where enrichment and extracurricular is seen as important as the demanding class-room based learning. 'My daughter recently told me she's taken up chess – I knew nothing about it. Absolutely brilliant!' said one parent. When we visited, two whole classes were absent for enrichment purposes – one practising for a big drama production in the senior school and one on a visit to the BFI, all dressed in Roald Dahl-themed costumes, complete with face-paint.

The school building started life as an attractive old house, although build-ons over the years mean that outside it is less aesthetically pleasing. However, unlike preps elsewhere, it has fabulous outside space – real space. A super garden area with excellent climbing frames and other apparatus, courts and pitches, much of it, of course, shared with the senior school. Particularly valued by girls are the 'hedge homes' – little dens in the hedges abutting the brook separating the school from the grounds. The girls use pebbles for money and run these little domestic havens just as they would their brick and drainpipe equivalents.

Inside, everywhere is carpeted, which makes for quiet corridors and a civilised feel. A sense of purpose and attentiveness pervades, but it feels as if the girls are having real fun too – and their work is displayed in every corridor in witty, appealing and imaginative ways. Great cross-curricular approach too – if they learn about the ancient Greeks, they make Greek vases; if they learn about circuits, they design and make a working toy car. Arts and crafts and DT throughout are unusual and clever – girls showed us examples of 3D mazes they'd made, along with personally designed carry-bags, clever photography, moving toys and home-made slippers. Even the plastic plates they use at lunch (where food has mixed views from pupils, but mainly good) are each designed by a girl in the school. Particularly great excitement about the animated films the girls make, using their own clay and cut-out models, in year 5.

The wow-factor science lab is designed for interactive learning, with five hexagonal shaped high tables with Bunsen burners and plug sockets in the middle with six stools round each, plus state-of-the-art flatscreen Apple TV on the wall. 'We recently hatched chicks in an incubator,' girls told us. The library, though inviting and well-stocked, is small and barely adequate for this number of girls – which staff acknowledge. Good traditional hall for productions, assemblies and younger girls' gym, and they use the fabulous senior school theatre. Decent ICT suite.

Weekly music lessons take place in a good-sized dedicated room, while around three-quarters have private music lessons in the senior school. Junior choir (for years 5 and 6 – you have to audition), chorus (open to anyone), orchestra and string group (which has performed in Hampton Court). 'My daughter adores her trombone classes – they really enthuse her,' said one parent.

Drama is also much loved, as we saw for ourselves during a practice session in the senior school theatre. Big singing and acting voices for girls so small – a treat to watch. The school takes part in everything from poetry recitals to debating competitions to Shakespeare festivals. Superb sports (great preparation for the legendary sporting culture of the senior school) and girls are lucky to use many of the older girls' facilities. In winter, the focus is on swimming, netball and gymnastics and in summer, on swimming, rounders, athletics and some tennis.

Back in the classroom, there's very little setting, although girls are sometimes taught in smaller, mixed-ability groups if it's felt it will aid their learning. French and extracurricular Mandarin are offered as languages, although the languages model is being reviewed. Specialist teaching in science, music, PE and computing from year 3, with everything else taught by the form teacher – then specialist teaching for everything from year 5.

Academically, this school holds a reputation of being a hothouse, which clearly infuriates staff and parents alike. 'They are just little girls who have a growth mindset.' The 'growth mindset' is a phrase you hear a lot here – with the school avoiding words like 'bright' and 'intelligent' like the plague. Homework seems fair – 20 minutes a night up to year 5, then 40 minutes. 'The school understands that if you're a working parent, you might not have time to do hours of homework – I applaud that,' said one parent.

Mild SEN – although note it's not called that here, with them favouring LDD (learning difficulties and disabilities). Help just as likely to be for a spelling group that need short-term strategies as for anyone with dyslexia or dyscalculia, which means no stigma. Short-term bursts of intervention is the name of the game here, with a major focus on arming the girls with tools and techniques to keep up with the fast academic pace.

Pastoral care strong, with deputy head at the helm. They take a proactive approach, with lots of staff meetings to discuss, 'Did you think what X did was out of character?' 'Did you think X has been a bit distracted lately?' etc. and they discuss it with girls if appropriate – and indeed parents, who they aren't afraid of calling to ask if everything is all right. Likewise, parents feel welcome to call the school. Girls praise the strong system of buddies, including coach buddy, house buddies and peer mentors, who help people out in the playground if they're sad. Lots of leadership roles (science leaders, head girl, house captains etc) and there's a term of mindfulness teaching for year 5s.

Bullying minimal, due to zero tolerance attitude, anti-bullying assemblies, golden school rules, talks about making the right choices and – perhaps most innovatively – a contract that each girl signs every year. If they break the contract, the head shows them the document and their signature and they get a firm questioning session – girls consider this deeply shameful.

Misbehaviour negligible, with little need for discipline – forgetting homework and calling someone a bad name is the worst of it, for which you get a 'sanction,' three of which in a half term mean you have to stay in during a breaktime. 'You lose perspective of behavioural issues in a lovely school like this,' said previous head.

Trips to interesting places – including the National Archives at Kew to look at Victorian prison records (after which they 'used metaphors to write poems as if we'd been in prison') and the Globe theatre, plus residentials to Surrey (year 5) and France (year 6).

Parents not all super-rich, with many parents holding down a couple of jobs to pay the fees. Lively PA. Most families live within a half-hour radius and arrive either on foot, by car or via the super-efficient coach system that is shared with both the senior school and neighbouring Hampton School for boys. Juniors get a coach buddy to make the whole thing less daunting.

Overall, we found the girls to be conscientious and bubbly (the ones who showed us round didn't stop talking, such was their enthusiasm for seemingly every detail of the school) and happy learners. 'My child loves going to school,' is a phrase we heard time and time again – and we saw for ourselves the reassuring skips down the corridors and beaming smiles in the classrooms. 'Anything you'd change about the school?' is one of our common questions to parents, to which we twice got the answer, 'Only that I didn't get to go there myself.'

Lady Eleanor Holles School

Linked with Lady Eleanor Holles Junior School

Hanworth Road, Hampton TW12 3HF

Ages 11–18 **Pupils** 700 **Sixth form** 200

Fees: £20,196 pa

020 8979 1601
www.lehs.org.uk

Headmistress: Since 2014, Heather Hanbury, previously head of Wimbledon High. MA Edinburgh, MSc Cambridge in geography then land economy. Prior to teaching, she spent nine years working in various management consultancy roles in the City, then as a corporate fundraiser – 'real world' experience that both pupils and parents value. Moved into teaching because she was so frequently told she 'should' – 'but I initially resisted it because I don't like to do the expected,' she laughs. Eventually had a change of heart and took a PGCE with the express ambition of becoming a head. 'I always wanted to run things. I like making organisations efficient, effective and happy' – something that everyone agrees she's achieved, with bells on.

Began her teaching career at Blackheath High School in 1996, quickly rising through the ranks to head of sixth form, before moving on to Haberdashers' Aske's School for Girls, thence deputy head of Latymer Upper School. Teaches all year 7s for half a term each ('I get to know them, but more importantly, they get to know me – far better than helicoptering my way into sixth form teaching,' she insists). And although she does herself down when it comes to her teaching abilities ('I do the least damage,' she laughs), girls say she's actually very good. The only school where we've heard pupils describe their headteacher as 'very sweet,' they gush over her assemblies ('She recently did a fantastic one on friendship and talked all about the movie Mean Girls,' enthused one) and say she is 'involved,' 'interested' and 'approachable' – attending every event imaginable, even wearing sports kits to matches.

In school, she adorns glamorous suits (no staff member we met would have looked out of place at a wedding), hums with energy, has just the right amount of modesty (as is the LEH way), is quick to smile and laugh and is intent on injecting some fun into school life. Her office is among the nicest, largest and swankiest we've seen – if you replaced her desk with a bed, it could pass as a luxury boutique hotel room.

Lives with her husband in Hammersmith. Interests include bridge ('I'm not very good,' – there's that modesty again), cooking and theatre.

Academic matters: Few teach academia better and it's done via thrilling, not drilling. 'What's the point in boring them into submission?' says head – although she admits it's not always easy, particularly around GCSE learning, 'which can be very routine especially for bright, lively minds.' 'I really admire the school's ability to go sideways in any subject, bringing in current affairs or going cross-curricular, for instance,' said one parent. Meticulous record keeping for monitoring and targeting. Results outstanding – 92 per cent A*-A/9-7 at GCSE in 2018. Staff clearly delight in what they do and all teach their own degree subject. Pupils told us teachers are always available, with the staff room practically empty at lunchtimes, as teachers run clinics or answer pupil queries from their departments. Sixth formers increasingly help the younger ones ('It's easy for them to remember the bits people find tricky in years 8 and 9,' explains the head. 'And it's good for them too – there's nothing like teaching to help you learn yourself.') Traditional subjects taken at GCSE, with computer science being offered since 2017.

Committed to A levels, rather than the IB or Pre-U, with the academic offering upped via EPQ, plus an enrichment programme across every subject. 2018 saw 75 per cent A*-A grades (95 per cent A*/B). Good range of subjects, including classical civilization, psychology and economics, although maths and sciences remain the most popular. Sixth form feels quite a separate entity here – these older girls are revered and there are lots of sixth form only areas, including their smaller classrooms which cater for more tutorial style learning, in which there are no more than 12 girls in any one class.

Setting in maths during year 7, with groups reviewed annually. Languages include Latin, German and French from year 7, with the option of Spanish and ancient Greek added at GCSE (although French remains the most popular language at GCSE). The school has one of the biggest German A level cohorts in the country, and Spanish is growing. Girls quite competitive around their learning, although they are also quick to support and praise others' achievements, with lots of patting on backs and high fives. Some criticism from pupils about the timetable of nine x 35-minute lessons. 'By the time you've settled into a lesson, that only leaves half-an-hour – and you've got four of those before break,' said one.

Few with more than mild learning difficulties here, for whom SEN support is embedded into classes, with some one-to-ones where required – and it must work as they get the same results as everyone else. A good school to consider if you have mobility problems or are wheelchair-bound – flattish site, lifts and wide corridors, plus can-do approach – although we were surprised no girls in this situation when we visited.

Games, options, the arts: Legendary for sports and the facilities in this 23 acre plot are outstanding for a girls' day school, including three spectacular and very green lacrosse pitches (which many of the classrooms overlook – lovely, especially in summer); six outdoor courts; a massive modern sports hall; and indoor swimming pool (recently refurbished). At the front of the school are grass tennis courts and croquet lawn ('embarrassing, really, but rather fun!' laughs the head). Some parents choose the school on the strength of the sports alone. Lacrosse, not surprisingly, is the main winter game and played to win – which they do. Rowing also a speciality – a welcome rarity in a girls' school, for which boathouse facilities are shared with neighbouring Hampton School, and they also collect lots of silverware. 'It's great because if you don't like running around after a ball, you can sit in a boat instead – although many do both,' says the head. Other sports include gymnastics, netball, swimming, basketball, fencing, rounders, athletics, tennis and badminton. Some girls feel sport can be a bit elitist. 'You start out with A-E teams in year 7, but now we've got an A team and half a B team – if you're not in those, you don't get anywhere near as much attention,' one complained, although others disagreed. Sports tours to eg Barbados and America.

Artistic talent evident from the walls of the new art rooms and corridors – there were several pieces we'd have gladly hung in our own homes. Beautiful ceramics displayed in a glass cabinet. Lively textiles and photography.

Music exceptional – the Holles Singers reach the finals of the BBC Youth Choir annually. We lost count of how many other choirs there were – some for which girls audition, others open to all. Orchestras and ensembles galore, with bands ranging from rock and pop to jazz. 'Unbelievably, we even have a symphony orchestra!' smiles the head, wide-eyed. Sixty per cent of girls learn an instrument with a peripatetic teacher. Brass popular, with many budding saxophonists. Plenty of space for all this in the shiny purpose-built arts block (where the arts studios are also based), with wow-factor purpose-built theatre where we heard a girl practising a solo song for the annual musical when we visited; she was amazing. Drama outstanding, with each year group performing something annually. The two big set pieces are joint musicals with Hampton School (years 11 up) and the summer musical (for years 7 and 8). 'They are something else – so professional,' said one girl.

Extracurricular life is thriving, including lively debating society, model UN and lots of charity and community work, including going into local schools. D of E and CCF take-up good. Masses of day trips to museums, theatres etc, plus residential trips from year 7 upwards – language exchanges, ski trips and battlefields, among them. Greece and Italy (classics), Berlin (history) and Iceland (geography) are other examples.

Background and atmosphere: The school was established in 1710 under the will of Lady Eleanor Holles, daughter of John Holles, 2nd Earl of Clare. This makes it one of the oldest girls' schools in the country. It began life in the Cripplegate Ward of the City of London, then moved to other premises in the City till 1878, thence to Mare Street in Hackney (that building now houses the London College of Fashion). The current school, purpose-built and designed in the shape of an E, opened in 1937. Such a long history is scarcely uncommon in many of our great public schools but rare in girls' schools. A palpable pride underpins the place. The staffroom has seen many distinguished names.

They include Pauline Cox, former head of Tiffin Girls', Margaret Hustler, former head of Harrogate Ladies' College, Cynthia Hall, former head of Wycombe Abbey, and Frances King, former head of Roedean, who all taught here.

Very long, horizontal, featureless and functional, the two-storey main building doesn't delight the eye but then again, it doesn't offend either. Inside, the corridors are wide, the rooms are light and everywhere is well-kept. Some areas are somewhat hospital-like, with lengthy corridors and polished wood floors. Latest add-on – the arts, music and drama block – was finished in 2013 and also includes jazzy new refectory. Big main library is well-stocked. Fabulous DT room. Lots of innovation in the cookery room – we saw girls were making their own versions of Bakewell tart. Excellent sixth form centre features small teaching rooms. The sixth form library is notable – light and overlooking the pitches – and includes more mature books and careers and university materials, with neat tables for study and rows of PCs. Nice sixth-form café and common room too.

Girls are well turned out in grey uniforms and the sixth formers look fresh and neat in casual dress. A sense of order and high expectations pervades throughout. It's cool to be clever and cool to be sporty. Strong links with Hampton School – just across the playing fields – including in careers and university preparation and increasingly for extracurricular clubs. 'It almost feels co-ed without having the distraction of boys in the actual classroom – what could be better?' delighted one parent.

Pastoral care, well-being and discipline: Much praise for the pastoral care system – a clear structure and everyone knows who to go to. Teachers described as 'supportive mentors'. One parent whose daughter needed significant time off called the ongoing support from afar 'incredible.' No noteworthy sins of the drink/drugs/fags kind and minor bullying problems are dealt with swiftly. A culture of openness means that it's all right to tell someone if you're not happy. Good buddying system, plus a great cyber mentor system, which involves sixth formers being trained to go into classes without teachers to discuss any online problems. 'The training means they know when a line is crossed and they report it to us to intervene,' says the head. In fact, e-safety overall is taken very seriously here, with a dedicated e-safety officer. School counsellor available three days a week. Plenty of talks on how to cope, including around exam time, and school wants to increase its offering around specific mental health issues. 'I think we're at the point we were with bullying 10 years ago – in that it's time to bring it out of the closet and admit it's ok to have issues and deal with them. It's about de-stigmatising,' says the head. Despite the school's reputation of being highly pressurised and hothousing the pupils, it's the girls who seem to be the ones putting pressure on themselves. 'It's just the culture of the school,' one girl told us. House system is a big deal here – there are even inter-house jigsaw competitions. Girls like the inter-year friendships this leads to, although some girls told us cliques can be hard to penetrate.

Low-level misbehaviour, such as forgetting homework, leads to a 'pink slip.' Three of those in a half-term and you get a strongly worded letter. But it's more carrot than stick here, with rewards of sweets if you don't get any pink slips and a class pizza lunch if your class does particularly well in something eg charity work.

Who wouldn't this school suit? Girls who aren't prepared to try new things (this matters more than whether you're good at it) or who aren't willing to work hard, said the girls we met. Food much better than it used to be, girls told us. 'There's loads of choice too – you can grab a sandwich or have a full-on hot meal.'

Pupils and parents: Parents tend to be much like the pupils here – academically brilliant, with a go-getting attitude. Not all super-rich, with many parents holding down a couple of jobs to pay the fees, something that the school values as enriching the school community. 'There aren't as many very wealthy families as I thought there'd be when I joined,' says head. Lively PA, called The Friends, is open to both senior and junior school parents. Mainly white British, although younger years are more ethnically mixed, with the second biggest ethnic group being Asian. From a wide area – Ealing, Windsor, Woking, Wimbledon and Chiswick, and all points in between. Public transport links aren't great, but an impressive coach map shows the multitude of routes they cater for (joint with Hampton boys' school) at the beginning and end of the school day (some later to cater for girls who do clubs) and which 50 per cent of the girls utilise. The rest walk, cycle or dropped off. Lots of parents have boys at Hampton.

Notable old girls include Lynn Barber, Charlotte Attenborough, Carola Hicks, Annie Nightingale, Saskia Reeves, Jay Hunt and Gail (University Challenge) Trimble.

Entrance: Around a third of entrants come up from junior department. Of the remainder, about two-thirds come from the private and a third from the state sector – around 40 different schools in total. Private ones include Newland House, Twickenham Prep, The Study, Bute House, Holy Cross Prep, Kew College. Four to five applicants for each place. Tests in maths, English, non-verbal and verbal reasoning and a problem solving paper. Expect the unexpected in the interview. 'We can tell a mile off if we are hearing not the girl themselves, but their parent or tutor. I'm absolutely allergic to that,' says the head, wincing. 'I don't even care if they do something silly in the interview – at least it shows they're being themselves.'

School sets its own exams for sixth form applicants, who need a 7 in subjects they want to study – and, in fact, 9-7s in pretty much everything. 'The odd 6 here and there is ok, but we want girls who can leap in with the rest and move fast,' says the head. Reports from current schools also count, along with an interview.

Exit: The school loses around 10 per cent of girls at sixth form – most to other high-level, but (crucially) co-ed sixth forms. A few leave for financial reasons. Around 80 per cent to Russell Group universities. Destinations include Oxbridge (11 in 2018), Durham, Bristol, London, Exeter, Edinburgh, St Andrews and a few to Europe and USA (four in 2018). Mainly traditional degree subjects, with lots studying medicine (16 in 2018), English, history, sciences.

Money matters: Drive under way to increase the number and value of bursaries. Means-tested and reviewed annually. Academic scholarships worth up to 10 per cent of fees at 11+ and sixth form level. Music scholarships up to 10 per cent. At A level, academic, music, art, drama and sport scholarships available – each worth up to 10 per cent of fees. Music exhibitions worth up to 7.5 per cent – and that's at 11+ and A level.

Remarks: This is a school that bangs the drum very loudly about empowerment, constantly reminding girls they can do anything if they put their minds to it – and they excel in giving them the tools to achieve that. Not for the faint-hearted, the girls work hard – and we mean hard – but they play hard too. If your daughter has the potential to be a determined, committed learner with a can-do attitude, this could be her ticket to a highly successful future.

Lady Margaret School

Parsons Green, London SW6 4UN

Ages 11–18 **Pupils** 736 **Sixth form** 162 **C of E**

020 7736 7138
www.ladymargaret.lbhf.sch.uk

Headteacher: Since 2015, Elisabeth Stevenson MA PGCE, previously deputy head at Grey Coat Hospital. Degree in medieval history plus later, part time, degree in early modern European history at Birkbeck. Taught history at Rickmansworth School before moving to Grey Coat in 2000 as head of history, then assistant, then deputy head. An excellent training ground for Lady Margaret, with which it has much in common. Although only a year into her tenure when we visited, her leadership, innovations and smiley presence were palpable. Parents and girls seem enchanted by her – 'so involved and visible about the school'; 'she speaks so well'; 'look – her door is open, it always is – that speaks volumes' – and in fact, both doors into her room – to the atrium and to the garden – were wide open: she could hardly be more accessible. Entirely visible around the school, Ms Stevenson is completely invisible on the school website, even if you put her name in Search, which seems a shame.

A practising Anglican, she celebrates the 'Christian values' and the 'centrality of worship' to her school's ethos. 'It frames and shapes the day,' she told us. 'Every assembly begins with lighting a candle and ends with a prayer. And we say grace at the end of each school day.' But she will not rush to embrace the option of admitting 100 per cent of pupils on the basis of a shared faith: 'I think as a Church of England school we should serve everyone in our local community, not just the church community.' She has ideas and principles but is not dogmatic. 'I don't think education is something that happens to you. It's about engaging. Schooling should be characterised by kindness and engagement.' Girls concur: 'She runs a tight ship and is very organised but is so approachable!'

Academic matters: They are doing something right here. Despite a scrupulously banded intake, the results they produce defy any reasonable expectation. It must be all about aspiration and ambition. Psychology, Eng lit, maths and history the most popular A level options in a range that includes history of art and IT. Forty-three cent of grades were A*/A and 69 per cent were A*/B in 2018. Fine art – see below – and history the most successful but few subjects saw many grades below C. Everyone takes core GCSEs which here include RS. Equal numbers for French and Spanish – no other languages timetabled. Around three-quarters take all three sciences. Fifty-seven per cent of all grades were 9-7 in 2018 (88 per cent got 9-4 in both English and maths). RS, perhaps unsurprisingly, the stand-out success. We were interested in the approach here: 'Not all the RS teachers are from the Anglican tradition. They are very open to all religions and always willing to debate and discuss.' We toured the school and witnessed class after class of girls, head down or in earnest collaboration – evidence of the head's claims that 'girls don't have to be ashamed of working hard here.. they are ambitious and want to do well – even the naughty ones!'

Overwhelmingly positive approach. The school uses the WWW (What Went Well) remark and an EBI (Even Better If) comment on every piece of work. We think this a sound way of keeping teachers up to the mark quite as much as pupils. We enjoyed many features of work and evidence of thinking here eg the What Is Your Favourite Book display board and were intrigued by the choices: – lots of Roald Dahl (predictable), one Pride and Prejudice (estimable), one Ulysses (impressive, if implausible) and one 50 Shades of Grey (lamentable).

At the time of our visit, 10 girls had statements or EHC plans and a further 60 received some kind of SEN support. Level of support varies according to need eg differentiated work and resources, LSAs in lessons, withdrawal, small groups and in-class support where needed. SEN department runs homework club, reduced timetables and curriculum support sessions. Also external agencies provide eg additional therapies such as speech and language and drama. School would welcome anyone including those with mild ASD but the site prohibits entry to anyone with complex physical problems. Those who need EAL support also helped by the SEN dept and on a similar basis.

Games, options, the arts: Art is exceptional. It inhabits six separate studios and rooms including a designated oil painting room. We were delighted by some of the most interesting, careful and creative work in painting and drawing we've seen anywhere; large numbers of fine art A levels are awarded A*s. Lively textiles, food tech lab and a sizeable DT workshop testify to the emphasis placed on head and hand collaboration here. Annual fashion show and competition display girls' own handmade work. Music, likewise, is celebrated here – both in theory (fabulous ICT suite for music) and in practice – lots of lessons, practice rooms, four choirs, ensembles and enthusiasm. Dramatic productions staged with verve and hard work and with impressive results. Until now, drama has not been a 'subject'. However, girls who chafe at the lack of timetabled drama will chafe – and leave for other schools in pursuit of it – no longer. It's now possible to take a GCSE in drama – Ms Stevenson very clear about its usefulness on the timetable in terms of character development, team work and expressiveness.

Energetic sports include rowing at Fulham Reach, games at Eel Brook, five minutes' walk away, or at Barn Elms, by public transport. Tennis in Bishop Park. Lacrosse, badminton, cricket – no shortage of sporting opportunities whatever your thing. And successes, both individual and in teams, across the board. 'Very well-run' D of E programme. 'Fantastic' dance opportunities – street to ballet on offer and parents rave about the choreography and production standards – 'they rehearse so hard!' A sense of trying everything and having a go.

Background and atmosphere: Parsons Green is a purlieu on the eastern edge of Fulham, in this hip part of London. A three-bed house will set you back more than £1.5m. Facing the triangle of grass shaded by ancient plane and ash trees which is the actual Parsons Green, the school is housed in a row of attractive buildings from several eras. Parsons Green tube station is a convenient two minutes' walk away. The school has an interesting role in the history of women's education. Founded in 1841, Whitelands College was a teacher training college 'to produce a superior class of parochial schoolmistresses'. Whitelands College School followed a year later. In 1917, when the school was threatened with closure, the remarkable second mistress, Enid Moberly Bell, rescued it and reopened it as Lady Margaret later that year. (She also moonlighted as the vice-chair of the Lyceum Club for female artists and writers.) Her life-partner, Anne Lupton, financed the purchase of the school's second building, Elm House, and named the school after Margaret Beaufort, of whom Erasmus, no less, wrote on her tomb: 'Margaret, Countess of Richmond, mother of Henry VII, grandmother of Henry VIII, who donated funds for three monks of this abbey, a grammar school in Wimborne, a preacher in the whole of England, two lecturers in Scripture, one at Oxford, the other at Cambridge, where she also founded two colleges, one dedicated to Christ, and the other to St John, the Evangelist.' The school's transmogrifications since founding reflect the

L

changing times and mores – from a grammar, to a voluntary aided and now an academy.

The Christian backbone of the school is proudly proclaimed by the 12 foot wooden cross with the Tudor rose ingrained on it which leans against the wall of the most modern of the buildings – a plate glass and marble statement – at one end of the extensive frontage. The two main buildings are handsome Georgian townhouses which retain some elegant features of their former selves and a mass of small rooms, passages and staircases. The school – when you are in it – is far larger than you'd guess from the outside, having accrued buildings, outside space and assorted additions. Most of it is well-maintained and treated with respect. We saw no litter. The girls, too, are well-turned out in their black with red stripe uniform. We witnessed the head turning down the odd collar and a girl or two pulling down a shorter than average skirt on her approach. 'She has smartened us up,' we were told. Sixth formers wear home clothes and treat this privilege with respect.

Excellent – and one of the best-stocked we've seen – library, a little cramped but full of girls actually working, something we do not often encounter. Good study areas elsewhere including one 'informal' and one silent one in the sixth form centre. Excellent Busby Auditorium – a real lecture theatre seating 140 – used for talks, rehearsals, presentations etc. Good and tidy displays about the place. One large tarmac playground. School food not seen as irresistible. About half bring lunch from home, most sixth formers go out to get it. But with pasta and salad bars, hot choices and fruit pots, it looked OK to us.

Pastoral care, well-being and discipline: Well understood pastoral care system. Problems first to form tutor, then head of year. School counsellor around two days a week for support. But girls attest to 'happier' atmosphere under new regime and a new emphasis on self-esteem. 'The head wants us to develop into confident young women.' When girls get into trouble – and in rare cases of exclusion – it is because of persistent behavioural lapses rather than anything else. Social media abuse a persistent hazard here as everywhere. 'We have a very strong community feeling but we do have girls who behave badly on occasions. We deal with it very quickly,' explained the head – this view supported by both parents and girls. Pastoral care described as 'amazing' by parents and school is assiduous in home-school comms. 'We have the numbers of absolutely anyone we might need,' said a parent. Parents also feel involved – 'they do listen to concerns'.

Pupils and parents: About as diverse as it gets. Some from local, affluent families who also apply for the local independents. Many from far less privileged homes. Great mix of backgrounds. Some 18 per cent speak a language other than English at home – a relatively small proportion given the school's location. Very active PTA – lots of drinks dos and other events. A few parents feel a bit pressured to involve themselves and cough up for school appeals but they stress these are, of course, voluntary and some keep away though everyone we spoke to praised the school's sense of community.

Entrance: Banding via non-verbal reasoning test which tests maths and a piece of independent creative writing. Sixty-seven foundation places reserved for girls who regularly attend C of E services. Fifty-three open places reserved for girls of any other, or no, religion. Applications divided into three ability bands making six categories. For each category, distance measurements are then applied. No priority for those with SEN unless statement or EHC plan submitted naming Lady Margaret. First priority to looked after, or previously looked after, girls, then (up to a third of places to) siblings. In effect, in the year we visited, this meant: 17 girls admitted from each of foundation bands 1 and 3, and 33 from foundation band 2. In the open bands, 13 were admitted from bands 1 and 3 and 27 from band 2. There was no point in living more than 0.3 of a mile away if you applied for an open place, but some foundation entrants lived up to five miles away. Church-going essential for the latter – at least twice a month for previous three years. Hundreds apply for the 40-50 sixth form places – applicants, like existing pupils, need six 6s at GCSE and between 9-6 for individual A levels.

Exit: About three-quarters stay on after GCSEs. One of the most impressive leavers' lists we have seen from an academy. Two to Oxford in 2018 and, while Oxbridge isn't the measure of all things, it suggests the school has an ambition for its alumnae lacking elsewhere. Otherwise, a good spread of universities from the newbies to the redbricks and, again, a diverse mix of courses chosen – from IT through midwifery to anthropology. Two medics and 11 off to study art in 2018. Rather extraordinarily, everyone seems to leave for higher education. An interestingly diverse list of leavers over recent decades includes Diana Garnham, ex-chief executive of the Science Council, Nigella and Horatia Lawson, Lady Zoe Barclay, actresses Kelly Hunter, Joanne Adams and Jessie Burton, film director Mahalia Belo, upcoming soprano Louise Alder, Martha Fiennes – oh, and Janet Street-Porter.

Money matters: Parental contribution asked for and willingly donated in most cases.

Remarks: Outstanding school for an ambitious, motivated, outward-looking girl. The anxious faces of the parents handing in their applications for next year's places said it all.

Langley Park School for Boys

South Eden Park Road, Beckenham, Kent BR3 3BP

Ages 11–18 **Pupils** 1,738 **Sixth form** 645 (227 girls)

020 8639 4700
www.lpsb.org.uk

Headteacher: Since 2013, Steve Parsons (40s); has BA in history from King's College, MA in school effectiveness and improvement from the Institute of Education and the professional headship qualification, NPQH. He has lived nearby in Beckenham for many years with his wife Ruth, also a senior school headteacher, and could not quite believe the fortuitousness of the top job arising at Langley Park at just the moment he felt ready to take on a headship.

Having come straight from Dunraven School, the highly sought after south London co-educational state secondary in Streatham, where he spent seven years as deputy head, he would seem to be a very good fit. As Dunraven too underwent lengthy transition to new buildings, he is relieved to find himself in Langley Park's stunning new quarters post the spade-work. Prior to Dunraven he was assistant head at Crown Woods College.

The previous head was at the school for 15 years, and Mr Parsons is aware he has a lot to live up to, speaks highly of the past head's vision for the school and says it will be 'evolution, not revolution', confirmed by parents: 'the transition from the previous head seems to have been very smooth: we have not noticed any major changes'.

Parents told us: 'I find him inspiring and a great leader for the boys' and 'he seems a committed, positive and hardworking head'. We found him to be very approachable, focused, modest, extremely tall and not lacking in courage, not only in taking over from a much-loved predecessor but in resolutely describing himself as a fan of football – more armchair than playing these days – in a school where rugby is the sporting religion.

Academic matters: Good results given the non-selective intake. In 2018, 76 per cent of boys achieved 9-4 in GCSE English and maths, 15 per cent 9-7 grades. English language GCSE is so good the school is in the top five per cent of results nationally. At A level 28 per cent A*/A, 60 per cent A*-B in 2018.

Everyone can find their level, with the seven entry forms at 11+ divided into eight ability-based learning groups at key stage 3, 10 at key stage 4 for English and maths. There is definitely no resting on laurels in sight: the head has ambitions for academic improvement, introducing the new year 7s recently to Dr Carol Dweck's Growth Mindset, inspiring them to believe they can do better and that everyone has the potential for success, a philosophy which will be taken up by the whole school. He's also aware of the need to future-proof students by teaching flexibility and adaptability to meet a barely imagined future job market.

Curriculum wise, at GCSE there is science at every level – so triple or general science and three art and design choices. Some creative options rarely on offer elsewhere at 16+, such as film studies, media studies, drama and dance, point the way to this being an amazingly artistic school. The idea behind the Langley Baccalaureate, promoted by the school instead of the EBacc, is that pupils are encouraged to retain an arts or creative subject when they're making their exam choices.

Pupils are also advised to study a modern foreign language, but it is not compulsory. German is twice as popular as Spanish and even more popular than French – more by tradition than design. The school has no plans to switch the emphasis at the moment. Special status in maths and computing with links to other schools to offer masterclasses. And the school is one of the few state schools offering engineering.

Apart from English and maths, the three sciences, particularly biology, are the most popular A level choices. There are also higher education oriented subjects on offer such as law, philosophy, psychology, economics, politics and further refined arts subjects – fine art and music technology.

On our visit the staff room was buzzing with a vibrant mix of grey haired and younger teachers including several former pupils. More than 20 per cent have been at the school over 10 years.

Parents see staff as hard-working and committed, enthusing: 'teaching staff are inspirational, very knowledgeable about their subjects and keen to stretch the students', 'the teaching is inclusive and of a high quality,' and 'assessment and feedback is thorough.' There is particular praise for English teaching, and the inspired geography teacher with packed classes who uses angel cake to explain coastal erosion – delicious! Pupils give rave reviews, mentioning teachers plugged into the wider world, bringing the latest research back into the classroom, and nothing being too much trouble.

Several parents we spoke to were in agreement regarding the relative lack of intense pressure and level of homework – very little or no homework during holidays – from lower school to sixth form. Whilst this could be good news for some, one, not alone, says: 'We live in such competitive times and I personally think my boys could be pushed harder'. The head disagrees, believing many feel the pressure on their sons is quite high.

Sixth formers are entrusted with independent study, nine free periods a week, and have several light and airy spaces, plus the café, around the school to work in, only lightly supervised by teachers based in semicircular goldfish bowl-like hubs. Pupils see the advantage of having their teachers close to hand – they always know where to find them when they need help. Students we saw were working diligently and told us, 'If you say to others "I need to work" they respect that'. The library with full-time librarian is open every day until 7pm.

The sixth formers we met impressed us with their drive and focus – they were determined on their university applications; one to Cambridge – and saw the school as doing everything to prepare them for their final exams: 'We work backwards from the final exam from week one'. Parents have confidence in the school's preparation for the next stage. Students speak of help with UCAS forms by a specialist, and joining with pupils from other south London schools in preparation for Oxbridge assessments.

With more than 30 learning support staff – visible in every class we visited assisting pupils – the needs of those with learning differences, particularly those with autism, are exceptionally well catered for here, attracting more than the average numbers to the school. The Sunil Centre, the base for learning support activities, is a discrete part of the school with its own courtyard garden and even magazine. Some 76 pupils are currently offered support and specialist input. Much is done in the classroom through differentiated learning, but the Sunil centre also provides quiet, smaller spaces and a separate exam room.

Four per cent of students have EAL requirements. The second most prevalent home language, after English, is French, followed by Lithuanian.

Games, options, the arts: A very sporty school – seven pupils currently play at national levels in sports from cycling to squash. Almost the only 'old school' features of the modern building are the traditional wooden boards in reception honouring sporting heroes.

L

A minimum of two hours sport a week is compulsory until the sixth form, and each Saturday one quarter of every year group represents the school in matches. 'We play the best of the best: all the independents', says the sports director of the fixture list. He commands an accomplished coaching staff, including former national league coaches, and 27 of the entire school staff are involved in extracurricular sport too.

No football; rugby takes centre stage in every way, not least the newly-seeded pitch in front of both the main school and sports building. On our visit it was still being cossetted behind fences, tantalising our guide who wondered if he'd ever get to play on it. The trophy cabinets bulge with local and national trophies for rugby, hockey, cricket and athletics. In the spirit of inclusivity, parents would like to see more matches for the lower ranked teams. New million pound hockey pitch. The under 16s were recently national champions, the first state school to make it to the top.

The school has held the Artsmark gold award for well over 10 years. The art department flourishes at an exceptionally high standard. Five students were recently chosen to have their work displayed in The Mall galleries at a Royal Society of British Artists exhibition, with two students being honoured as RBA scholars, a first for the school. The department holds an annual summer show where A level final work is hung for friends' and families' enjoyment in a local church. For those wishing to pursue the subject, a former pupil fresh from the cool of Shoreditch had recently returned to inspire budding graphic designers. The sixth form magazine was recently the winner of three national awards.

The 600 seat performance hall, also the home of the Bromley Symphony Orchestra, is rarely out of use. Dance is exhilaratingly popular here. Recent collaborations saw the PE department taking to the stage, whilst pupils provided an inspired interpretation of a WW1 love story as part of the school's commemorations. The riches of London's dance scene are mined, such as during a recent trip to see Matthew Bourne's Swan Lake at Sadler's Wells. A level dance is a new option. One parent: 'Our boys are not particularly interested in dance or drama; however, our eldest recently took part in a short dance performance during a show and loved it.'

A busy music department with dedicated practice rooms, large teaching spaces and a technology suite. Around 400 pupils learn an instrument, either during school or through private lessons mostly facilitated through a link with the Bromley Youth Music Trust. A dozen or so have reached the pinnacle of grade 8 and beyond, with some students performing in the National Youth Orchestra, the London Schools Symphony Orchestra and the London Jazz Festival. There are Christmas and summer showcases, an annual music tour and gala concerts.

Several by invitation lunchtime and after-school music clubs such as wood and string quartets or, for something a bit different, cantabile, or Cuban band.

A society or club for most academic subjects each week plus a few extras such as Jaguar cars, GCSE dance, Christian union and scrum half clinic, which sounds as if it mends broken noses, but apparently is more about technique.

Enrichment really comes into its own in the sixth form, with everyone taking on a couple of new things as well as their A levels, which can be either a sport or arts subject. Most popular are rugby, football and table tennis, but almost a third of students are trying out Japanese, with others learning Dutch, counselling or taking part in the Duke of Edinburgh Award or a current affairs group, Think Tank. If performing arts is more their thing, students can experiment with dance, taiko drumming, creative composition or world music.

L

Background and atmosphere: The school has been through a number of metamorphoses in terms of buildings, names and indeed locations since its first incarnation in 1901: at one point a technical college, then a grammar school. Having settled on its current location in Eden Park, Beckenham, it eventually outgrew its buildings, leading to a huge development project to create the site we see today. Pupils moved in during 2012, whilst the old school was entirely demolished.

Appropriately enough, given the sporty nature of the school, on first sight the whole complex appears like a smart new sports centre with ample parking. The red-brick main building with curved roof and exterior walls appears hardly large enough to house over 1,600 pupils, but inside the design functions brilliantly, with large classrooms, mezzanine levels, spacious corridors hardly appearing to be corridors because of light from above and large break-out study areas for sixth formers.

Each of the lower years has its own small playground. During our visit, seagulls swooped down trying to snatch snacks from the boys – 'time to get the hawks out,' said a passing teacher, not joking, apparently.

Pupils in the lower school wear maroon blazers, graduating to less eye-catching black ones. Then sixth form boys may wear a suit of their choice and girls have recently adopted a jacket of their own choosing – all look very smart.

Perhaps it was our exuberant guides, but as we walked the school we felt palpable excitement and energy amidst hard work. Everyone is agreed on the inclusive ethos of the school. One parent told us, 'The school is competitive but it seems to us that every aspect is valued at the same level. This is great as the boys always seem to be able to feel proud of some achievement: receiving a good grade, being in a team for rugby, being identified for great effort in art, having the opportunity to dance on a stage, working on a science project.'

Works collaboratively with new multi-academy trust formed by Langley Park Girls, Hawes Down junior school and Hawes Down infant school. The Langley Park primary school opened in 2016.

Pastoral care, well-being and discipline: School rules are traditional – no earrings for boys. Pupils need a cycling proficiency certificate to bring a bicycle to school. Respect, calm and litter picking mandatory. Mobile phones are allowed for sixth formers, but must be handed in lower down the school. The head says that exclusion figures are 'very, very low' and that 98 per cent of parents recently surveyed were very happy with the pastoral care and discipline at the school.

Form tutors are the linchpin of pastoral care. Several parents mentioned talking to staff on behalf of their child, but also reported problems being swiftly dealt with to their satisfaction.

There is deliberately no separate sixth form building, so that the younger years have role models around the school. The appointment of prefects by the head is like a mini job application – those putting themselves forward must each gather four or five recommendations from teachers.

Some thought might be given to the external sixth form candidates, who seem forever after to go by the unfortunate label of 'externals'. Our two tour guides both bore the label resolutely, but thought it unlikely their fellow externals, or indeed girls, would ever be school captain.

Pupils and parents: Parents as well as pupils are proud to belong to the school. We're told 'the term Langley Boy is one that is highly regarded and proudly stated.'

One parent explained: 'The school attracts gifted boys and later girls for the sixth form, who work in an educational environment that expects a lot of them. This high expectation draws parents that would normally be looking at independent schools.'

By far the majority of pupils are white British, with other white, black Caribbean and black African larger ethnic groups. The head describes his pupils as: 'confident, hard-working, proud of their school, articulate, supportive and active.'

Who will thrive here? Clearly the sporty, arty and academic, but parents add: a child who is 'well mannered, respectful, takes pride in their school's reputation, is a team player and competitive'; 'this school will allow your child to achieve their academic dreams and to bring out talents they never knew they had.' We'd only add the school seems to support and nurture ambitions and interests wherever they lie.

Communication with parents has been a weak spot and parents still shared a few niggles with us, but the head cites recent surveys of parental satisfaction.

Entrance: There are 210 places annually at 11+. With applications at just under three to one, chances of getting in could be far worse, but you will need to live within one mile of the school. Local estate agents say many move nearby simply for the school, creating something of a squeeze on prices. There are 45 local feeder primaries, including Balgowan, Clare House, Hawes Down, Highfield, Marian Vian, Oaklodge, Pickhurst Junior and Unicorn.

It's far harder to get into the sixth form: most recently 850 candidates fought tooth and nail for 150 places. Girls from Langley Park Girls School next door are subject to the same admission criteria as others.

Exit: Some 80 per cent stay on to the sixth form, with those leaving mostly going on to do vocational qualifications. The same proportion then head to university, very slightly more girls than boys.

Recent destinations include Kent, Portsmouth, Brighton, Sussex and Bournemouth, with 25 per cent of those taking university places heading to Russell Group destinations such as Birmingham and Southampton. Six to Oxbridge in 2018. Most popular subjects seem to be English, history, law, accountancy, engineering, physics and business with quite a few medically related, plus some budding pharmacists and psychologists.

Remarks: An exceptional example of comprehensive education with a sporting and artistic offer to match many an independent in smart new facilities. Easier to enter at 11+ (boys) than battle into the sixth form with increased competition from all around – including girls.

Langley Park School for Girls

159

Hawksbrook Lane, Beckenham, Kent BR3 3BE

Ages 11–18 **Pupils** 1,581 **Sixth form** 388 (40 boys)

020 8663 4199
www.lpgs.bromley.sch.uk

Headteacher: Since September 2018, Katie Scott, previously head of Portslade Aldridge Community Academy in Brighton. Taught history at Haberdashers' Aske's Hatcham College, head of history at Cator Park School in Beckenham, assistant principal at Haberdashers' Aske's Knights Academy, then vice principal at Sir Robert Woodard Academy before joining Portslade in 2015.

Academic matters: The reason parents send their daughters here. 'It was the academic side that appealed,' said one, who moved house specifically to secure a place. Plenty to shout about, too, with 68 per cent getting 9-5 grades in both English and maths in 2018 and 28 per cent 9-7 grades. Progress 8 an impressive 0.57. Particularly high percentages in single subject GCSE sciences and fast track languages, both reserved for most able. Students now take fewer GCSEs 'to reflect the increase in rigour' of the new GCSE specifications and allow more teaching time for each, with staff encouraged to include problem-solving and risk-taking into lessons.

Good news continues in sixth form. While new vocational courses are being added to roster that currently includes business, travel, health and social care with aim of broadening appeal (almost the only 'could do better' in otherwise glowing inspection report), the emphasis is unapologetically skewed 'towards the more able students'. Results – 45 per cent A*/B, 21 per cent A*/A grades in 2018.

Success doesn't, however, come at expense of the 200 or so pupils with special needs, many speech and language related (about 20 have statements). Good-sized and centre stage learning support unit, home to two key workers under direction of deputy head with SEN background, is widely appreciated as a whole school safety valve offering help for anyone under pressure.

Add enthusiastic teachers, including one working her socks off to spark discussion on ethics of designer babies amongst slightly somnolent GCSE biology class, and the technology head extolling the wonders of the computer programmed laser saw that cuts anything (Goldfinger would be envious, though less fussed by its ability to add detailed floral motifs) and it sounds like roses all the way.

Well, up to a point, Lord Copper. There's the odd wilting bloom. Success in some small but perfectly formed subjects (GCSE music, growing fast, consistently secures 100 per cent 6s or higher) is balanced by occasional whole-subject wobble (applied science a case in point). And despite GCSE success in languages, one of school specialisms (others are technology and sport) numbers die away post-16, with totals for German, French and Spanish scarcely into double figures (reflection, sadly, of national malaise). It's not for want of trying, what with Mandarin and Latin both available as popular lunchtime and after-school clubs, and the 150 EAL students, many bilingual, able to take community languages as additional GCSE. Currently, advanced linguists who take French GCSE early follow a slightly waffly culture-related programme with some cake-making but little academic bite in year 11. School's plan to move them on to AS level work may help though, judging by less than encouraging results in other schools, it may not.

Then there's the little matter of boys' school next door which clocks near identical GCSE results to its neighbour – 'girls should do at least six per cent better,' says school – and is also seen as the place to go for sixth form sciences. Resulting mini brain drain especially in chemistry and physics is cause for concern but could soon be reversed with appointment of whizzy new head of science who comes with tried and tested Pied Piper-like A level recruitment skills. Shouldn't be rocket science – sixth formers who ignore hype and stay on for science are glad they did. 'Class sizes are very big in the boys' school – I knew the school and the teachers and the course seems to suit me,' said one.

School wants everyone, including staff, to up their game, crunching primary school data so hard you can almost hear it squeak in effort to identify budding talent from arrival in year 7 and laying down the law with clear minimum academic goals for pupils (with hope, of course, that these will be routinely exceeded). 'Boys are often deluded about their own potential, whereas girls tend to underestimate themselves.'

Games, options, the arts: Sport highly rated. 'Amazing,' said one pupil. Lots to do and places to do it in – large if slightly sombre sports hall and gym inside and five tennis courts and an all-weather pitch in addition to five acres of green space outside. Old girls include Ellen Gandy, 2012 Olympic 100m butterfly finalist, and with current pupils making literal waves in diving and even water polo, and figuratively in squash, could be first of many.

Favours the competitive (lots of wins for netball and hockey squads in local championships) so 'you need to push yourself,' said parent. Theoretically, however, something for everyone and if the timetabled sport doesn't do it for you there's probably a club that will, from yoga to fencing. 'They really shine. You name it and they'll have it,' said pupil.

Robust though sport is, tends to be swamped by performing arts, which have pirouetted across website and ousted match results from shared online notice board, replacing them with close-ups of recent and seemingly non-stop round of acclaimed productions. Frequent high-quality, whole-school collaborations between dance, drama and music include large cast versions of Annie and Alice in Wonderland, which have gone down a storm, while with around 300 students learning instruments, there's a decent range of ensembles, too, including 50-strong jazz orchestra which recently toured China.

Mini BRIT academy feel never stronger than with dance: tap and street offered, but classical ballet a particular strength, masterminded (and frequently choreographed) by three dance teachers whose remit covers everything from hit versions of Twilight and Beauty and the Beast to GCSE, A level and, coming soon, BTec courses complete with glamorous overseas revision courses, all apparently done without drawing breath. Indeed, a new dance studio was recently opened by Deborah Bull of King's College London. Motto, unsurprisingly, is 'anyone can dance,' though, as sixth form boys as yet unconvinced, male performers are currently imported from next door.

In addition to 'look at me' events, lots of looking after others, with pupils from year 9 onwards lending a hand at local primaries while year 12s, who have Wednesday afternoons free thanks to miracle of timetable coordination, can opt to fill them with voluntary work, often as part of thriving DofE programme, open to all though you'll only get the go ahead if you're doing 'what your predicted grades say you should be,' said one. You can't keep staff away either: science teacher – a 'bundle of energy' – awarded MBE for educational work in community.

Background and atmosphere: In its 90-year history (last 50 on current leafy site), school has had several Time Lord-like incarnations, beginning as a county girls' school, becoming a grammar in 1945, a comprehensive in the 1970s and achieving the full collector's set with academy status in 2011. Connections with the past haven't been sloughed off, however, with original society for old girls (known as Adremians) still going strong. There's also traditional, ultra-smart uniform much cooed over by outsiders, less so by current parents faced with dry-clean-only blue piped blazer and hard-to-press pleated tartan skirt. 'I get granny to iron it,' confessed one.

School design, mid-20th century standard issue, features two-storey main building with separate blocks for drama/sport, science (11 perfectly decent labs), sixth form and technology (newest and nicest of the lot with six well-equipped workshops), together roughly framing three sides of large and picnic table studded if slightly bleak courtyard (the main R&R outside area until student council secured leave to use 'head's own garden', a green and pleasant space round the corner). Effect is pleasant and unintimidating. New girls get maps and are quickly at home – in some schools you feel satellite tracking and emergency rations wouldn't come amiss.

Everyone now very nice about multi-million pound newly rebuilt boys' school (similar name, no relation). Wasn't always thus. A predecessor head fought plans all the way to Supreme Court and won what turned out to be pyrrhic victory as second application was nodded through shortly afterwards. Bridges now mended, cordial relationships re-established and girls offered use of new facilities, notably the hear-every-bat-squeak acoustically advanced auditorium – 'when boys aren't using it,' says school, without apparent irony. Big brother (though a benevolent one) rules.

Make do and mend philosophy only goes so far, however. An additional floor on top of sixth form building (including café and social facilities) has recently opened, likewise a new dance studio, and there is planning permission for new music block.

Surprisingly little sense of overcrowding, and there's even a whole school assembly once a term or thereabouts – though 'if it were all boys, there would be accidents,' says school. (One pupil confessed to eating outside 'even when it's raining' just to get away from it all). Children seem to move in mysterious ways (possibly by converting themselves to compressed data format at busy times, more likely by learning to keep elbows in when using corridors). It's particularly noticeable at break, when what should be a scrum for the food and drink somehow isn't.

Mood is welcoming, helped by delightful, off-beat art displays (ceramic artichokes on sticks, anyone?) partial door 'n' floor refurbishment (light wood/portholes combo gives vaguely Nordic/nautical feel depending on preference), and homely areas including large, book-lined library, well used in and out of school hours, which hosts termly themed parties complete with cakes to keep reading top of mind when 'other things step in,' says librarian, diplomatically.

Pastoral care, well-being and discipline: Four houses; Lambda (yellow), Kappa (blue), Sigma (red), and Gamma (green) – fortunately no Brave New World Epsilon – as much an admin tool as a motivational one, used for imposing a little organisational clarity on eight-form entry. It's two forms to a house (block booking, no arguments) and little sense of feverish competition 'except on sports day,' say girls.

Friendship issues inevitably the biggest problem cited by parents, especially lower down the school. 'They look so grown up,' said worried mother who mentioned daughter's need to apply defensive make-up following pressure to fit in. If there is a problem, overwhelming pupil consensus is that there's always somebody to talk to – 'even the canteen people are friendly,' said one. Staff are often very popular, with tears on departure, though 'a few scare me, and I'm the parent,' said one mother. Relationships improve the further up the school you go. 'Students do have problems with teachers – no school's perfect but mostly they're great and there if you want them,' added another. Discipline, though firm, is considered: if there's out of character bad behaviour, staff will 'try to find out where you're coming from first,' said year 11 pupil, with exclusion very much a last resort and help provided, wherever possible, in situ.

Officially, form tutors are first point of contact, often staying with same group for several years. Parents praise ease of communication – teachers are listed in pupil planners and there are individual email addresses for all, up to and including head. 'If you expect other members of staff to give out their contact details you should be willing to do the same thing.'

Highly effective school council, a model of its kind, 'lets teachers know what students are thinking, rather than what they assume they are,' said pupil, and gets things done – broken soap dispenser that had languished for weeks in one of toilets was 'fixed within days' after complaints. It's helped by involvement of sympathetic teacher who 'is on our side but is honest and will say if we're asking for outrageous things.' Youngest girls have as much of a voice as senior pupils and an equal chance of being chosen from full meeting to present ideas to head. 'You even hear what sixth form are doing,' said one.

Pupils and parents: Tight catchment area means many new pupils arrive with others they know. While behaviour is 'fairly standard for teenagers these days; you stop for 10 minutes to let them cross and nobody says thank you,' harrumphs slightly gloomy local, her experience seems exception rather than rule: on morning of our visit no sign of anything other than almost universal good manners. Lots of hands raised in salute to waiting cars as girls (boys, too – a symphony in blue and burgundy respectively) arrived in their hundreds.

In school, too, doors are routinely held open and there's general sense of courtesy towards others (helped, quite possibly, by numbers of teachers in corridors, though a benevolent rather than sentry-like presence).

Parents are necessarily local, many the hard-working exemplars praised by politicians of every hue. As a fair percentage commute to jobs in London, don't necessarily see much of each other, although with quite a few events (first class fireworks display, for example) 'opportunities to socialise are there if you want them,' said one.

Entrance: Large school, tiny catchment area (has shrunk to under a mile before now though normally hovers just over). Means that despite size of intake (240 places in year 7) it's routinely oversubscribed and there's always a waiting list. Pupils come from nine or so local primaries (Oak Lodge, Marian Vian, Highfield Junior, Pickhurst, Unicorn, Balgowan, Clare House, Hawes Down and St Mary's Catholic Primary) though feeders in name only as attendance is no guarantee of place and distance (barring standard priority given to looked after children, siblings and now some staff children) is king. Estate agents testify to school's popularity. Parents vote with their square feet. 'We specifically moved to get a place,' said one (though other more dubious practices aren't unknown either).

Three-quarters stay into sixth form, again oversubscribed (minimum of 10 places available to external candidates, usually more in practice) and, like majority of local schools, co-educational, though boys so thin on the ground (around 20 a year) that spotting them not unlike real life version of 'Where's Wally?' A level places dependent on securing minimum of seven GCSE passes (about 50 turned away at application stage) with minimum grade 6s in four including chosen A level subjects, 9-7s preferred for toughies like chemistry and teacher recommendations for languages. Anyone opting for performing arts will also need to pass audition.

Exit: A third or so who leave post-GCSE stay close, some moving to boys' school next door (with a few, who don't care for the size, moving back) while a very few opt for selective grammars like St Olave's and Newstead Wood or independent schools like Trinity School in neighbouring Croydon. A few head off to larger colleges to study work-related courses, though school keen to slow exodus of less academic – should have 'right to continue here even if not high flyers'.

No compromises when it comes to onwards academic journey. Almost all make it into higher education, nearly all first or second choice universities with Bristol, Leeds, Warwick, Southampton 'all popular,' says head of sixth form, and the most able encouraged to try for Oxbridge. Normally a couple of places each year (two in 2018) and three for medicine. Law, business and administration, biological sciences and creative arts and design (including music and drama) head the list of subject choices, with social services, maths and English not far behind and a light dusting of languages and engineering.

New careers academy 'will provide specific advice and guidance backed up with seminars, careers days, contact with employers and practice at interviews and skills'. School 'has been commended for its outstanding preparation of UCAS applications.'

Remarks: Short on square feet but, remarkably, feels as if has enough breathing space for everyone, helped by honest, intelligent leadership, enthusiastic staff and pupils who seem happy to be here and for the most part do well. A real breath of fresh air.

LaSWAP Sixth Form Consortium

Linked with Parliament Hill School, William Ellis School, La Sainte Union

William Ellis School, Highgate Road, London NW5 1RL

Ages 16–19 **Pupils** 1,000

020 7692 4157
www.laswap.camden.sch.uk

Director: Since 2013, Georgina Atkinson, BA in business and French from Kingston University and L'École Superieure in Montpellier. Did her PGCE at London University, followed by a period of working in schools with sixth forms, teaching business. Subsequently, she worked for 10 years as head of faculty at Saffron Walden County High School in Essex, and then moved on to become assistant principal of Long Road Sixth Form College in Cambridge, where she stayed for the next three years. 'I'm passionate about education, particularly sixth form education and helping students find the right course to match their skills.' Georgina is also an Ofsted inspector.

Working across four schools is complicated; however, Georgina meets weekly with the four school sixth form directors and termly with the heads of the four schools that make up the LaSWAP consortium, to plan strategic overviews. The role of headteacher of LaSWAP rotates termly amongst the four school heads.

Ensuring consistency across four large comprehensive sixth forms is no mean feat, especially when the well-being of roughly 1,000 students is in question – a job made all the trickier by LaSWAP's free flowing arrangement, whereby students could have lessons in any one of the four schools that make up the consortium (La Sainte Union, William Ellis, Acland Burghley and Parliament Hill). To help manage this transient system, Georgina has recently introduced a consortium-wide web based system called e-Tutor, which is available to every tutor in the four schools, and a way of keeping tabs on each student and updating records: 'One of the major benefits of LaSWAP for students is the diversity of such a large place and the fact that students can commute between four different buildings – but because of this, they do need to be monitored.'

Each school already has its own director of sixth form, so Georgina rotates between each school. New LaSWAP office is at the front of William Ellis School and Parliament Hill School.

Academic matters: These four comprehensives, geographically within a few hundred metres of each other, created an amalgamated sixth form to provide the widest possible subject variety and range of qualifications. Lucky sixth formers here have a choice of a remarkable 41 A levels, as well as BTecs, NVQs, a choice of six vocational subjects, the new 'flagship' post-16 advanced maths studies, and post-16 GCSEs (for those who need to gain a grade 4/5 in maths or English) About 80 per cent of students follow a purely academic course, the rest take vocational courses, but those who want to can mix and match. Generally around 40 per cent A*-B at A level but cagey about 2018 results. The consortium's strengths lie in the visual arts (with consistently outstanding results) and arts subjects, like RE, film and media studies and English. Languages tend to perform well, but not many students take them up.

With such a wide and varied intake of sixth form students, we can't help wondering how the recent government move of abolishing most AS levels in favour of linear A levels will impact on future results. Georgina isn't overly concerned – in fact she welcomes the opportunity for students to learn subjects in a bit more depth: 'Students will learn how to learn more deeply and apply this. At the moment, many students acquire the knowledge for the exam, have the exam and then forget it.'

Some criticism for not always taking into account the wide range of ability in this relatively unselective sixth form, but not all would agree – 'In my classes, some people have 10 grade 8s and others mainly 4s, but I haven't found that a problem,' said one boy. A LaSWAP student, we were told, is one who wants to pursue 'more than just academic excellence, with its broad and innovative curriculum.' Teaching (with over 200 'highly experienced' sixth form teachers) is enthusiastic, knowledgeable and well prepared. 'Teachers are good, inspiring and they listen to you', one student told us, but another one grumbled that 'they enforce too much discipline here.'

All students are allocated a base school, depending on the subjects they choose or where they took GCSEs, but most study on a number of sites. Some subjects are taught on all the sites, the more rarefied – music technology, textiles and dance, for example – on only one. Each student is given target grades on entry based on GCSE results and is carefully tracked thereafter, with good exam preparation and help with study skills, as well as thrice yearly reports. 'The communication with home is excellent,' said one parent. 'If my son has done something well they email me. Equally, if he's not doing his homework, they'll let me know.' The academic side is clearly complex, but well organised. 'I wanted to change one of my subjects early on,' said a student. 'I went to see the head of year and it was sorted by the end of lunch hour.'

Games, options, the arts: The extracurricular here is a significant part of what LaSWAP has to offer, being as varied and extensive as the academic range. The activities, which largely take place on Wednesday and Thursday afternoons, provide 35 options, from ballet and debating to theatrical make-up, DJ-ing and maths masterclasses. Off-site sports include sailing and climbing. The programme is not compulsory, but everyone is encouraged to have a go, regardless of previous knowledge or expertise.

Sport is a biggie here and students with an interest in sports coaching and working with young people can enrol on the sports education and training programme which consists of level 1, 2 and 3 qualifications. If successful, students can progress until they achieve the advanced level 3 diploma in sports development, which leads on to university and/or employment. This takes place at the nearby Talacre Community Sports Centre.

Students also benefit from a wide enrichment programme of visiting speakers and volunteering opportunities that 'stimulate debate and interest in current affairs and the wider community.'

Background and atmosphere: The four schools (La Sainte Union, an all-girls' Catholic school, William Ellis, an all-boys' former grammar school, Acland Burghley, a co-ed comprehensive, and Parliament Hill, an all-girls' comprehensive) decided to unite their sixth form offering nearly 40 years ago. Each school retains its distinctive ethos and students generally enjoy the change of pace. 'I really like the different atmosphere in each school,' said one. Students can enjoy the plush new common room that Acland Burghley has to offer – or the beautiful and serene gardens of La Sainte Union. However, the free-usage of all the various facilities that are not a student's base school has caused a bit of controversy with some students. One told us, 'I thought I'd be able to use the facilities of the other schools, but the reality is I would be asked to leave if I was in the common room of Acland Burghley after school, being a La Sainte Union pupil. It really is for lessons only.' The school says that this is because all students have to be monitored and safeguarded by their head of sixth form, which would be too difficult off site.

And surely even the most disgruntled of students can find somewhere to hang out during lunch times, as the location of these schools would be hard to match. Whilst Acland Burghley is a short walk from bustling Kentish Town with its plethora of restaurants, cafés and quirky shops, both William Ellis and Parliament Hill back onto Hampstead Heath.

Parliament Hill and William Ellis combine to form a joint co-ed sixth form, the other schools retain the pupils they take in at 11, and each has its own director of sixth form and heads of year.

One great plus of the model is the halfway house it offers between school and sixth-form college. 'My daughter originally wanted to leave and go to college,' said one mother, 'but once she'd started at LaSWAP, she found the teachers treated her with more respect and she was given much more responsibility for her assignments.' The advantage for students who opt for continuity is that they remain in familiar surroundings while meeting new people and conquering new horizons. 'In the earlier years, my daughter's friends were all local,' said one parent. 'In the sixth form, she suddenly had a whole new set of friends from all over London.' New students, however, don't feel excluded – 'I felt everybody was in the same position as I was,' said one. 'People had friends from their original school, but they didn't know anyone from the other schools.'

LaSWAP is careful about taking both existing students and recent arrivals to a more independent level of study, with a well-planned induction programme, including a thorough briefing on the outline of each course and relevant dates and department procedures. Students like the friendly, laid-back but organised approach and strong sense of community.

Pastoral care, well-being and discipline: All students register at their base school, where they take most of their lessons. Here they have a head of year and a tutor who monitors their work and well-being, with regular interviews to discuss problems and set appropriate targets. Also a confidential professional counselling service and regular PSHE, with outside speakers, group work and discussions. Georgina is also in the process of setting up a sixth form peer advising system around e-safety and well-being. 'Sadly, as we know, there is more self-harming these days, or at least more people are talking about it. We want to train willing sixth form students to signpost professional support services to their student peers around mental well-being and mindfulness.' Students are also offered the opportunity regularly to access the services of two dedicated higher education advisors.

When a student starts LaSWAP sixth form, they are given a detailed planner (which is a colourful diary-like book), which includes a mine of information. Everything from planning one's workload, to code of conduct and even evacuation points at the four schools. There is also a Who's Who list at each of the base sites including who is the child protection officer etc. (For this fantastic planner alone we thought it was worth enrolling at LaSWAP..)

Dress code is smart casual, and at enrolment the consortium will stress the importance of having at least five outfits which fit this description. However, Georgina says that they don't like to tell students exactly what to wear, but instead she suggests that 'perhaps they look at people who go to work – either from magazines or commuters – and get ideas from that, so as to prepare them for the eventual workplace.'

Pupils and parents: Students from a huge range of ethnic and social backgrounds apply from a vast swathe of north London. Despite the consortium's leafy surroundings on the eastern edge of Hampstead Heath, all four schools are inner-city comprehensives with a socio-economic intake reflective of the term. Generally, pupils are confident and mature and get on well.

Entrance: LaSWAP has some 1,000 pupils. The number has slightly declined over the past few years because of other closer to home schools across London who have opened sixth forms. New entrants make up approximately 40 per cent of year 12. The entrance procedure is intricate, and careful attention must be paid to every step and date. First step is to register interest online. Then, armed with a ticket and a parent, prospective candidates attend the open evening in November. Applications must be submitted by post or by hand in early December – those who miss the deadline are put on the waiting list. All applicants who meet the deadline are offered a meeting at LaSWAP in February or March to discuss subject choice and given offers conditional on GCSE grades. Those with offers are invited to attend the one-day taster sessions held before the start of the summer holidays, when summer assignments are set. Post GCSE results, further enrolment appointments and places are confirmed. Now asks for at least five grade 6s at GCSE (rather than grade 4s, as previously) to study A levels. Pathways other than A levels ensure that individual needs are met.

Exit: Destinations are 'outstanding', and LaSWAP has a significantly above national average success rates to university in general, and Russell Group specifically – the most popular choices are Sussex and London universities, but across a wide range of degree courses: eg international relations, marketing, philosophy, politics, economics and business. Virtually all of their level 2 vocational learners go on to advanced further education, apprenticeships or employment – a third returning to LaSWAP for advanced applied courses. Three to Oxbridge in 2018.

Remarks: A good compromise between school and a sixth form college, with an extraordinary range of subjects on offer. Tends to suit the motivated and the self starter, but not ideal for those who will be distracted by studying on a number of sites or who require the disciplined parameters of a school sixth form to function at their peak.

Latchmere School

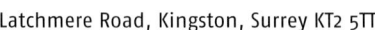

Latchmere Road, Kingston, Surrey KT2 5TT

Ages 3–11 **Pupils** 937

020 8546 7181
www.latchmereschool.org

Headteacher: Since 2008, Julie Ritchie, CertEd BPhilEd MSI SIP (Special) (50s). Previously at St Matthew's C of E Primary School, where she was shortlisted for head of the year award. Qualifications (bucket-loads of them) include degree in multi-sensory impairment, a souvenir of decade-long post in the 1990s as deputy headteacher at Dysart, a Surbiton-based special school.

Grew up in Grimsby, drawn to teaching from an early age – something of a family thing as a brother is also a head, though neither of her two grown up children has so far been bitten by the bug. Inspects for Ofsted, a heart-gladdening experience, though never fails to feel thrill of returning 'home' afterwards. Though she doesn't teach – she's at her desk by at 6.30am as it is, notching up 12-hour days – she's available to parents first and last thing and regularly consulted by staff too. 'I've got a lot of experience and they know that,' she says.

Gets to know pupils well – no mean feat given numbers – and parents are duly impressed. 'She made a point of saying how well my child had acquitted herself in a school production. I was quite taken aback as she is someone who could very easily be missed', comments one.

Smiley and effortlessly calm, head rarely raises her voice. 'This is a no-shouting school', she says, and indeed it's as quiet as they come. Short, sharp blasts of the school bell that periodically lash the air are the only sound to puncture the serenity (not to everyone's taste but necessary to minimise euphemistically termed 'time drift').

Makes no bones about need for exceptional staff to deliver the goods, tough old selection process identifying those who, like able pupils, enjoy being stretched and 'have the potential to be outstanding'. With many taking on load-bearing roles, they need to be. School's best practice managers, one to a year group, carry the can for quality of teaching and learning, and 'could be heads in their own right'. Within the next post or so, they often are. Numbers likely to be augmented as fast track trainees, appointed under government Schools Direct scheme, start to make their mark.

Professional to her fingertips, caring too, head sees parents as the ultimate experts. 'We know what the child presents in school but it's at home where they pour their hearts out. If we feel they're not functioning, parents are the ones who know'. Her biggest buzz comes from seeing 'children achieve what you wanted for them'. 'Pupils love her and have unbounded respect,' confirms a parent. And so they should.

Entrance: Very oversubscribed, with 500 applying for 120 reception places and not a hope for anyone living more than a kilometre away. Solid core of 'aspirational' parents, some Forces families (there's a nearby army base). All year round wraparound care a boon to working parents. Looked after children have precedence, siblings (up to 50 a year) get second dibs. Only exception is eight-pupil Topaz unit where pupils may come from further away.

Virtual school tour will, hopes head, ensure that non-starters are gently discouraged online rather that getting taste of paradise during a face to face visit, only to have it whisked away again when logistics are explained.

Exit: Majority to Grey Court School then the Kingston Academy. Some to local independents eg Hampton, Surbiton High, with scholarships. A very few to Tiffin grammars (rarity down to ever increasing levels of competition, so oversubscribed that place hunting has become an extreme sport).

Remarks: Author Jacqueline Wilson's primary (and much changed for the better, she reckoned, when she revisited). Opened in 1936, just in time for Second World War (nearby aircraft factory was regular bombing target). Infant school added a year later – dividing wall in place until reunification in 2007.

Large site with playgrounds generously bestowed means most year groups have a space they can call their own in addition to larger shared areas for infants and juniors. Substantial on-site asphalt legacy is greened up with trees and bushes, plus veg garden in small courtyard, together with reception-only delightful green run between knee-high rows of plants (like nursery, have own secure play area). Tactical introduction of soft surfaces underneath sturdy and attractive play equipment for older children also helps, while nearby shared playing fields are used for some clubs, junior games and sports day, now back to traditional competition-driven format and considered all the better for it.

Inside, plenty of space with large classrooms for all. Spares too, as though school is geared up for expansion to four-class entry, will take time to permeate every year group. Two schools into one means inevitable layout quirks, corridor-heavy design putting well-stocked library on the through route. Potential dinginess offset by lots of colour, particularly in nursery and reception areas where primary colours rule and some toilets have gone green (paint rather than eco flush). Assumes more monochrome hues as you go up through the school, though brightened with lots of little extras including giant paintbrushes strung across art room ceiling and boards, inside and out, crammed with enigmatic clay masks.

Reigning delight is flashy newish building housing year 6 classrooms upstairs, lunch/sports hall on ground floor. Also used for Monday morning whole school assemblies, smaller hall taking year groups two by two on other days, and notable for impressive red and blue light up buttons (disappointingly measure air quality rather than summoning International Rescue).

Though fab new buildings help, what really rocks parents' boats is success with non-standard issue pupils. 'Schools can all do the straightforward ones', reckoned one mother. 'What counts is how good they are with the off the peg kids'. Latchmere aims (learning, local community, laughter, loyalty, love and leadership) are oft recited, children 'accepted for who they are' and inclusion, very dear to head's heart, a big, well resourced, thing.

Despite leafy setting (Richmond Park within easy reach), pupil make up has a grittier, urban feel than you might expect, with challenges to match, including a few with difficult home lives and nearly one in five with English as a second language.

Staff, average age 40, around a third male (average pupil to teacher ratio of just over 21 to one) are expected to get on together, and get on they do. No coasting, either. Jaw-droppingly efficient systems still have enough give for teaching talent to flourish outside the box. One teaching assistant, a professional actor, has leave of absence to go on tour in term time, in return lending talents to sky's the limit school productions.

Mantra is constant improvement. 'Whatever we do, I ask staff how we can do it better next time', says head. 'And because they're bright, I only have to ask them once'. Accolades roll in, Artsmark award in head's sights adding to quiverful that already includes Sing Up and Sportsmark awards (both pure gold).

Most recent success is designation as Teaching School (an eat your heart out award bestowed only on the whizziest of establishments). Confers membership of six-strong alliance who pool ideas and resources, a boon when it comes, amongst other things, to pitching for extra funds.

Range of needs includes specific learning difficulties, speech and language and behavioural, emotional and social difficulties (BESD), while Topaz unit accommodates eight pupils with Asperger's, currently all KS2 but will extend to KS1, who join peers for some lessons, often with one-to-one support, but have separate base with own play area (small, nicely green, enclosed by no-nonsense fencing). Once identified (here, as elsewhere, some parents call in their own experts to speed up the diagnosis) support is unstinting, with nth degree differentiation in class taken as read. Pupil with memory and processing issues had checklist of stages to tick off on wipe clean board. 'Personalised it beautifully', thought mum.

Inspires 'very warm and fuzzy feelings' towards the school, said a parent, with size a plus point rather than drawback. Thirty-strong classes, bolstered with teaching assistant while nursery sessions (25 children in each) have two nursery nurses plus teacher. 'More people means more friends', felt a year 5 pupil, though in troubled times, 'there's a room you can go to if you're sad or lonely.' Felt, however, that some peer to peer disagreements are best resolved without teacher input. 'They can make it worse'.

Parents too, favour school over other highly regarded and smaller alternatives because of what one terms 'lack of prissiness'. Whereas artwork on display elsewhere was 'incredibly beautifully framed on the wall', only the best examples had made the final cut. Here, in contrast, it was 'messy, in a good way, with pictures from even the kids who couldn't draw'.

Resulting confidence is unmissable, pupils a winningly well-mannered bunch, helped to become so by oft-stressed emphasis on social skills. Lunch for reception children is part of the curriculum, with big teacher input, emphasis on eye contact and handshaking, stressed through the school, ensuring the conversational niceties are a (nicely) observed feature of school life. 'Are you having a lovely day?' head was recently asked by pupil. Impressively, words 'self-control' were all it took to calm large group of pupils: here, it's viewed as innate rather than a skill to be learned and children live up to expectations.

Equally true of trips (year 5s just back from up to the neck mud in Ashdown Forest) and school clubs (including astrophysics and Techo DJ, both catering for the starry-eyed). School stresses that 'only exemplary behaviour will be tolerated' and sanctions are well understood. 'We have a consequences list. If we're too out of control, we get sent to the head', said a pupil.

Much more, however, in the way of encouragement, explanation and reflection, from popular blue room, shoe-free, carpet rich and decorated with skyscapes, to peer mediation and circle time. Very youngest join the debate, too, with 'brilliant' nursery head encouraging exploration of moral dilemmas, in one instance through medium of glove puppets.

Parents are also expected to do their bit – recent newsletter noting rise in pupil absences the week before half term. With current 'outstanding' status at risk if attendance plummets, nudge psychology designed to keep families onside seems to be working, thinks head.

Pupils tackle everything with gusto. Top perks include later lunch sittings and joy of second helpings for top two years (Portuguese chef's creative ways with assorted healthy options much admired, though occasional pizza and hot dogs days remain top favourites).

Responsibility also enjoyed from the off. Nursery children check themselves in online ('no need to be afraid of technology', reassures prospectus), while covetable posts for year 5 and 6 pupils include monitor who hands out free break-time snacks baked on the premises. Lessons are regarded with equal enthusiasm, consistency a big strength with two deputy heads stepping into the breach to cover staff absences. Teachers' approval counts. 'Oh, no, they'll be so disappointed in me', said reception pupil after mother threatened to expose mild cheekiness at drop off.

Relationships are excellent. 'I love all the teachers,' said year 5 girl. 'They're really kind and make lessons fun'. Even more so now, following introduction of creative curriculum, many months in the making and all the school's own work. Substantial ring-bound master plan so full of fizzing ideas that it probably glows in the dark.

Core subjects taught by class teachers, topped up by specialists for art, some sport, music and French (rapid progress made courtesy of native speaker means 'pupils are probably bored out of their minds when they get to secondary school', thought insider). Resulting variety is relished – diplomatically. 'Nice to have a change; not that you ever get bored with your teacher', said year 5 pupil.

Spritely lessons big on group or paired activity. 'Means you can share ideas or ask if you don't understand', said pupil. Recent highlights include 'Victorian' maths (everything in imperial measurements, dunce's cap for wrong answers); hands-on science, year 5s adding bicarbonate of soda to vinegar and inflating balloons ('we weren't meant to shake it but we did, anyway',) and drama-packed history lesson, with army trenches improvised from desks and teacher 'shouting' commands (though we're sure it wasn't very loudly).

Buzz, frequently mentioned, could well be down to synapses sparking merrily away in the background as staff respond to latest gauntlet thrown down by the head. School has many laurels but you'll never find anyone resting on them. Instead, there's a ceaseless quest for improvement, anywhere and everywhere.

Some setting (maths from year 2), high achievers treated to once a week sessions in small groups, one-to-one support scooping up small numbers at risk of Sats underperformance. Though results aren't the highest in the local borough, pupil progress puts them almost at the very top. 'They may not always get it right first time, but they don't give up and keep on trying,' said a mum. Latest innovations include recruitment of weaker readers to mentor younger pupils, some improving by more than a complete Sats level in the process. School has also introduced pupil challenges to up the excitement factor, reception recently wowing head with enormous sheets of paper covered with 'the biggest numbers they could think of'.

But though competitive instincts once more considered acceptable, children know when to rein them in. Unsuccessful year 6 candidate in election for one of four team captain posts was gracious in defeat. 'I am delighted and he has my full support', he said. Politicians take note.

Fundraising clout is substantial. A jolly crowd, forging friendships that often endure well beyond the school, parents are big on purposeful socialising, coffee mornings and cake-making featuring heavily in weekly school newsletters. Have their own choir, adding to pupils' very well regarded three, plus orchestra (healthy numbers boosted by local authority-subsidised taster lessons). Take school duties extremely seriously, finding the wherewithal to equip Apple suite not once, but twice as new technology succeeds the old. Also fund and manage school's own swimming pool which 'wouldn't exist without them', said insider, in constant use from April to October. Children adore it, two even asking for donations towards running costs instead of birthday presents (surely a first).

Not the school for anyone in search of 00 gauge miniature education. This is a scaled up version that works, thanks to a head who expects non-stop excellence, staff who buy in to the challenge and pupils who benefit from constant quest to do everything that bit better every time. 'It's such a lottery', said one mum. 'You buy the house and hope for the best. I just couldn't believe my luck'.

Latymer Prep School

Linked with Latymer Upper School

162

36 Upper Mall, London W6 9TA

Ages 7–11 **Pupils** 170

Fees: £18,330 pa

020 7993 0061
www.latymerprep.org

Head: Since 2017, Andrea Rutterford, previously deputy head at Devonshire House prep in Hampstead. She has also headed year 3 and year 5 at Highgate Junior School.

Entrance: Highly selective, around 220 competing at 7+ for 38-40 places. Exam, after which 50 per cent invited back for science-related activities, team-building exercises and observation. The gender split is about 50/50. Two classes of 20 each year (occasionally 21). Families are mainly local, although the reach of the school has expanded in recent years to stretch as far as Kensington and Notting Hill.

Exit: Majority to the senior school, although transfer not automatic and all pupils required to sit the entrance exam. Does not prepare for other senior schools.

Remarks: Rivercourt House, an attractive 1800s villa overlooking the Thames, is the main building. Full of light, with an elegant staircase and plenty of original features and creaky floorboards, it has the feel of a well-to-do, kindly aunt's home. Next door, Latymer House accommodates more classrooms, food tech, cookery, IT and art – all very well equipped, with plenty of space. Both use walls and corridors to the max to display children's work. Even a window had lovely artwork draped across when we visited.

Opposite the rather limited outside space is an odd 1930s building, whose outside spiral staircase leads to the Seahorse Drama Studio, with a truly professional feel. Pupils also regularly parade down the underpass under the A4 to Latymer Upper to make use of facilities for sports, music and drama (recent productions including My Fair Lady, Toad of Toad Hall and Peter Pan). Prep school teachers do regular observations of year 7 teaching to get a feel for standards. All this, agree parents and pupils, makes the transfer into the upper school pretty seamless. 'They don't get scared because they're already familiar with it,' explained one parent.

Expect specialist teaching from day one, so whilst each class has its own form room, pupils go to subject-dedicated rooms to learn. Of particular note is the large, fantastically well-equipped art room at the top of the school, where pupils were busy painting clay pots they'd made, and a delightful, well-stocked library. Delicious baking aromas drifted out of the food tech room when we visited, whilst in the science lab, pupils could hardly have looked more animated.

The curriculum is future-orientated, with all learning Mandarin and Spanish, and technology is genuinely embedded throughout all subjects, with regular use of iPads in class, including art. This is not at the expense of more traditional learning, however. 'We want them to read and write before they can swipe,' says school.

Every child plays a musical instrument and half of them play two, for which one-to-one tuition is timetabled into the curriculum. Big on brass, with lots of children learning the French horn or trombone, whilst the cello also remains popular and there are two main choirs. Music tech also a focal point. 'I was certain my kids had no talent for music and I've been truly shocked what they've brought out in them,' said one parent.

The focus on sport that the upper school is noted for is seen as equally important here, with specialist sports coaches teaching both girls and boys rugby, football, netball, cricket, dance, rounders and – the particular strength of the school – swimming. New £14m new sports facility behind the 1930s building has revolutionised facilities. Sport is inclusive. 'Our aim is that every pupil leaves with one sport they like doing. That might not sound very ambitious, but actually girls often fall away from sport because they're not given the opportunity to find something they love. Not here.'

Over 20 school clubs, including zumba, film studies, The Latymerian (school magazine), chess, bridge, drama, coding, Warhammer and karate. Most are free, although a few bought-in ones, such as zumba, do charge. No after-school care, but the prep room remains open until 4.30pm. Plenty of day trips to places including V&A and Kensington Gardens, whilst residential trips include Norfolk (year 5) and Italy (year 6).

This isn't a school that believes in lots of rules. 'There's just a general expectation of respect and being nice,' said one pupil. And with the exception of some year 6s who have passed their 11+ swanking around a bit, it's all pretty low-key, with a genuine feeling of innocence. About the worst behaviour you'll see, say teachers, is children running to the next class, when they should walk.

As for bullying, it's hard to imagine here. 'Of course children sometimes fall out, and there are situations in which children lack empathy or fail to see the implications of what they've done. But there's very little deliberate unkindness. We think that's down to modelling by the staff and the fact that, for the children, the absolute worst thing for them is feeling they've disappointed us. They can't bear it.'

'You learn through trying,' is an unofficial mantra of the school, with the staff encouraging intellectual risk-taking. 'We are constantly reminding the children that the point when you're not quite sure is the point when you learn. Getting to the top therefore isn't the be-all-and-end-all and we encourage them to see that and value the moment when they're not quite sure.'

There are pupils with SEN, including dyslexia and Asperger's, and they've also had students who are registered blind or deaf. 'We delight in being open'; anyone with any kind of learning challenge is encouraged to make full use of the upper school's learning support department (now known as the academic mentoring department to remove stigma), which is run by three specialists. 'They offer unbelievable support,' said one parent.

There's a lively PA, which does all the usual fundraising and organising of school fêtes and social events, along with each class having a 'rep' and 'dep,' in close touch with the school. 'If there's ever an issue or misunderstanding, the rep and dep won't encourage parents to write saying, "We all think this or that". It's much more a case of them coming in informally and early to nip it in the bud.' Parents agree this works, and and value the relaxed, welcoming and open atmosphere.

We saw relaxed, engaged, happy and confident (but not precocious) children, who are clearly at home and keen to learn. 'You're encouraged to ask questions,' one pupil told us. 'In fact, if we are really interested in a particular area, that can drive the class in a new direction.' 'Teachers always tell us, it's our enthusiasm they want to build on,' explained another. For this reason, comment a couple of parents, it's probably not the best school for shrinking violets. 'I think a really quiet and withdrawn child might feel a bit lost here,' said one.

Unlike in the upper school, there is a house system, all named after birds. 'It gives a sense of healthy competition and gets them out of their year groups,' said one parent. There's also a school council, although it's not particularly active.

This is a charming prep that children genuinely adore. 'My child is often up at 7am fully dressed and asking when it's time to go,' said one parent, whilst another said, 'The children might not come out looking as neat as they went in, but you know they've had a really lovely time.' Despite the expectation on high academic achievement (which some parents say can be tiring), there's a big emphasis on a rounded education, and above all it's lots of fun, with warm relationships between staff and pupils. As one pupil summed up, 'this school is like one, big warm hug.'

The Latymer School

163

Haselbury Road, London N9 9TN

Ages 11–18 **Pupils** 1,369 **Sixth form** 439

020 8807 4037
www.latymer.co.uk

Headteacher: Since 2015, Maureen Cobbett BA (modern languages) followed by a PGCE from Liverpool University. Originally from Birmingham, she started out as a languages teacher in French and German – both subjects to GCSE standard and French to A level standard: 'Teachers are often inspired by that one teacher they had at school. For me it was a memorable French teacher.' Prior to her post at Latymer, Ms Cobbett was head at All Saints Catholic School in Nottinghamshire and in that time took it from an underachieving school to the 'most successful comprehensive in Nottinghamshire.' However after seven years in the post, she decided it was time to do something completely different and the right time to pursue her ambition of working and living in London: 'I wasn't initially aware of the post of head teacher at Latymer; it was my sister who lived in London who made me aware of the school. She told me about the conversations she had heard on the train from lovely, well-mannered children'.

Before meeting this head, we didn't quite know what to expect. Yes, Ms Cobbett is fairly businesslike by nature, very straighforward and definitely not concerned with winning us over – but during our meeting, we did witness a more affable and humorous side. Parents have clearly seen this side too. One told us: 'At this year's annual teachers' Christmas concert, she was there in the orchestra wearing a Christmas hat and playing the triangle.' And one pupil told us: 'She sometimes stops us in the corridor and tells us really bad jokes.' She is also popular with the teachers, we are told.

Since arriving at Latymer not all her changes have met with approval. Some parents were not happy by her immediate introduction of a stricter uniform policy. One parent told us: 'She definitely seems hung up on the uniform. It's fair enough if she wanted to change the jumper to a smarter one with a logo, but when she starts saying that girls have to wear tights, I don't think there needs to be that level of detail and it also gave the girls a little bit of choice'. However, a more satisfied parent said of her approach: 'I love what she's done with things like the school website. It's been updated and is much more professional now. Things just seem more organised'.

Whether or not she has divided opinion, one has to admire the daunting task of heading up one of London's most high achieving schools – not to mention in an uncertain financial climate. Ms Cobbett says: 'It's quite a depressing position to be in for most headteachers – they are facing funding being slashed and yet they are being asked to make standards rise. I don't see how the two go together.' That said, she remains passionate about education born out of the values instilled in her when she was a child: 'I come from a low income Irish family, but my mum was very keen for us all to have a good education. All five siblings and myself went to grammar schools.' She adds: 'I love what I do. I never considered anything other than teaching and I love being around young people. It makes you feel young.'

Ms Cobbett has two grown up daughters. 'I waited until they were older and doing their own thing before I moved, so I didn't have to uproot them too.' Any free time she allows herself is often spent doing sports or going to the cinema and theatre.

Academic matters: Excellent GCSE results, making it the top performing school in Enfield borough and within the top six per cent in London, with 84 per cent 9-7 grades in 2018. Pupils must choose a MFL from French or German in Y7 and they can then choose between French, German, Russian or Latin in Y8, 'languages to get into Oxbridge with', one parent jokingly told us.

Students study 10 GCSEs and the vast majority take the EBacc subjects. Geography is very popular as are the sciences. At sixth form, maths is the most popular subject and the school offers 'nothing apart from an ashamedly academic programme', so no vocational subjects. (Sociology has recently been scrapped due to funding cuts.) The majority stay on at sixth form – if they achieve at least six grade 7s at GCSE – but another 50 join from other schools. A level exam results for 2018 were 63 per cent A*/A, and 88 per cent A*/B grades.

Parents agree that the school is 'very good academically' and it certainly makes plenty of effort to award academic achievement across all years. Year 13s are awarded prizes in specialist subjects too, such as mechanics, statistics and government & politics. Pupils who do not gain a subject prize have the opportunity to be awarded either a Latymer Lodge or school prize for gaining a high aggregate at A level. There are also open awards for special achievements in spoken English, creative work, instrumental performance, music composition and fieldwork, as well as prizes for service to the community, thus there is plenty of motivation to strive and to win here.

Where pupils have a special learning need, they will find help through the learning support department which also arranges mentoring for younger students from sixth formers. EAL students are supported well and achieve equally well at GCSE and A level. One parent told us: 'At Latymer, SEN could be children who are super bright but actually need additional support for areas in social interaction which they may lack.'

It is important that academic success is supported by 'a life outside school' and students are encouraged to take part in the wide variety of activities on offer. Languages are supported by school journeys and exchanges through links with Russia, France and Germany; there have also been exchange visits with the Mwambisi school in Tanzania; other trips include geographers going to Iceland, classicists to Italy, artists to Barcelona, skiers to the French Alps, music to Austria, Belgium, Germany, the Czech Republic and scientists to Honduras and South Africa.

Games, options, the arts: More than 17 different sporting activities offered, which may come as a surprise to some, who know Latymer as a predominantly academic institution. One parent said: 'The school does have very good sporting facilities and outside grounds, and, whilst they may not do as well as other schools, the opportunities are there.' New long jump and athletics facilities 'but could do with an all weather pitch', one pupil told us. The school encourages active lifestyles and rewards pupils' enthusiasm for sport with a number of awards that recognise outstanding achievement both in and outside school. These include rugby (played very competitively), hockey, football (for girls and boys), netball, cross-country, rounders, tennis and cricket. One pupil proudly told us: 'We have some of the top runners in the county.' Students in years 7 and 9 have the opportunity to spend a week at Ysgol Latymer, the school's outdoor sports centre in Snowdonia, for activities such as hill walking, orienteering, climbing, abseiling and canoeing.

Music is extremely strong. Wonderful facilities – we counted approx 10 practice rooms and a couple of well-equipped studios. A quarter of the pupils learn a musical instrument at standards ranging from beginners to beyond grade 8. There are five orchestras (including reed and brass), a concert band and several choirs. They perform at school concerts and many are invited elsewhere, such as the National Festival for Music. 'The standard is amazing,' one parent told us, 'and what I really like is that the orchestras accept students of all abilities. It's not all about the top lot.'

Latymer had art specialism and so the subject has a strong presence outside the department, with astounding work on display around the school. Experts visit to do talks and run special workshops in oil painting and sculpture, and the department runs visits to the London Institute, Tate Modern and Tate Britain as well as European trips. As a result, examiners have commented on the good grasp pupils have of contemporary artists. Drama is supported by trips out plus the big theatre productions that take place at the school each year; a main school production in November (recently Anything Goes), a junior production in July, and the house drama competition every other year. Recent house drama offerings – one by each of the six houses – based on The Diary of Adrian Mole. One of the pupils directing it told us with a groan: 'We have to do everything – cast it, direct it and cram it all in during lunch times and after school..but it is fun.'

If Latymerians have any spare moment to breathe after all of this they can enjoy a rich range of extracurricular activities that shape life at the school; over 60 different clubs and teams run before, during and after school, and at weekends. Lunchtime clubs are run by the students themselves ('a bit like freshers' week'), which include a debating society, an Afro-Caribbean society, LBGT society, gardening, chess and more. There is a Young Enterprise group, an economics society and clubs whose sole purpose is to raise funds for less fortunate people, particularly supportive of local charities such as the food bank in Edmonton.

Background and atmosphere: Tradition creates the atmosphere at Latymer. It was established in nearby Church Street in 1624 at the direction of Edward Latymer, a City merchant, who bequeathed certain property to trustees on condition that they were to clothe and educate 'eight poore boies of Edmonton'. His, and the 'generosity of the many others since', are remembered each year on the school's Foundation Day. Pupils are proud of this tradition and seem enthusiastic about the events that keep it alive. The school's motto – Qui Patitur Vincit (Who Endures Wins) – aptly sums up its spirit, and is the title of the annual talk. The school moved to its present location in 1910.

Once we found the school all was pretty quiet in the snug waiting area, except for an ill student who was dealt with sympathetically and sent to medical. This episode added a more human side to a school whose academic reputation has become somewhat legendary. It is the first choice school for many north London parents with an extremely clever child.

Far from the dull, intellectual conformists we expected to meet, the students who showed us around were extremely well rounded individuals – one of whom was quite possibly the biggest character we've met at any school we've visited. She was extremely entertaining, exceedingly bright and full of praise for Latymer and her six years there. The other student, also very pleasant, had just been offered a conditional place at Cambridge. They both felt very 'lucky' to have spent their secondary school years here: 'Yes, there is pressure, but nothing we can't deal with and there is a lot of support offered.'

Built on three acres of land and flanked by 12 acres of playing fields, which separate the school from the main A10 road, Latymer looks deceptively small from the front; one parent felt that planting a few more trees would help the aesthetics. Walking into the school is like walking back in time. It doesn't seem as if much would've changed since 1910, which arguably adds to its charm. We have become accustomed to sterile foyers in many other schools: the one at Latymer is a modest and cosy affair with oak panelled doors and simple but exquisite charcoal drawings adorning the walls, all hand drawn by students. The lady on reception remarked: 'It's not fair is it? Not only are these kids ridiculously bright, but look how they draw!' We had to agree.

There are a number of outbuildings around the main one, added at various times over the school's life and capturing its spirit of progress: the Great Hall (1928), which seats over 1,000; the gymnasia and technical labs (1966); a performing arts centre (2000) and a sports/dining hall complex (2006). In 2010 the high-tech multi-purpose Seward Studio (performance space, auditorium, media studio, art gallery and drama theatre) was opened. The school also has a number of rooms dedicated to specialist teaching: 12 science laboratories, six fully-equipped technology rooms, and specialist ICT rooms with wireless networks. Also a very large, very well equipped library: 'I don't think there is anything I could need from a library that isn't here,' a student told us. Sixth formers now have a new modern common room equipped with a small café selling sandwiches and paninis etc (which is just as well, as the local eateries are pretty limited).

Pastoral care, well-being and discipline: The 186 pupils in each year are organised into six form groups, and each form group belongs to one of the six house groups. They remain in these groups throughout their school lives, meeting daily for registration and form periods, including, in the lower years, PSHE lessons delivered by the form tutor. Each year group also has a head of learning (first port of contact for parents concerned about progress) who, along with the deputy head of learning, also acts as mentor. House culture is strong. Each has a senior pupil to lead, democratically elected. Senior pupils organise activities which are used to inject a sense of comradeship and teamwork across all year groups, and to make new year 7s feel fully inducted into life at Latymer. They do this via sports tournaments and various competitions such as cake-making, drama and music.

Pupils are expected to abide by the school rules and the home-school agreement they signed with their parents on joining the school, but the school views 'self discipline resulting from wanting to learn' as a more important deterrent to poor behaviour. One parent did say that students who go to Latymer are already self-motivated: 'I doubt there are many behavioural issues, but that said, clearly students are under immense pressure. However there is quite a lot of support offered to them and the school never gives up on its pupils.' Support comes by way of two counsellors who regularly visit the school, and pupils can refer themselves; a head of year and an assistant head of year who would be the first port of call for a troubled student; and a mentoring system, where students from years 12 and 13 are trained to mentor the younger students. The school has also recently introduced into the curriculum one lesson a week dedicated to 'pastoral time' – issues ranging from drugs to bullying etc.

One parent said that 'while the academic side is challenging, it is not to the exclusion of everything else.' Another said she has 'always felt comfortable emailing teachers direct if I have a concern or question.'

Pupils and parents: Anyone and everyone who is 'very clever', though the school wisely lists acceptable postcodes in its admission criteria (and suggests that no-one should apply from further than an hour's journey). Roughly 65 per cent of the school's cohort are from ethnic minorities. Alumnae include Dame Eileen Atkins, actor, Simone Butler, bass player with Primal Scream, and Syed Kamall, currently Conservative MEP.

Entrance: Only those 'deemed capable of achieving the highest grades at GCSE are considered' at this highly oversubscribed, selective school. Selection is by the NVR test as well as literacy and numeracy. A parents said 'it used to be harder to get into', but around 2,000 typically apply for the 186 places, so many are still disappointed. Priority is given to looked-after children and those who live in designated postcode areas in the boroughs of Hackney, Islington, Waltham Forest, Haringey and Enfield. Offers also made to around 20 per cent of students who live in these areas and show 'exceptional musical talent and achievement' akin to grade 5. A further 20 places are awarded to those on pupil premium.

L

Around 50 external students join the sixth form. Pre-requisites including living in designed postcode areas, getting at least six grade 7s at GCSE, including for proposed A level subjects, plus entrance tests for those applying to study maths and/or/sciences.

Exit: Around 95 per cent go on to university or other forms of higher education in music and art. The school does not 'push Oxford or Cambridge though plenty apply, and plenty get offers' (18 places in 2018); 19 medics, two dentists and three vets. UCL, Bristol, Nottingham and other Russell Group universities are also popular destinations; courses include aerospace engineering, law, Chinese, Russian and Egyptology. Very few – one or two – leave to go straight into employment.

Money matters: Funding cuts affect Latymer as all other state schools. Parents have been asked to make voluntary yearly contributions. The school says: 'The response from parents has been very positive and they have been very generous. They don't want the school to suffer'. The school has also been appealing to the LOSA (Latymer Old Students Association) for donations.

Remarks: A peek back in time shows that some well-known former pupils like Baroness Claire Tyler (Chair of CAFCASS and president of the National Children's Bureau), footballer Johnny Haynes and Sir Bruce Forsyth CBE all did well here. Pupils clearly still do. This is a zealously traditional school with pupils who show a healthy balance between hard work and play. Ofsted has a similar attitude and in its last report described the school as outstanding.

Latymer Upper School

Linked with Latymer Prep School

237 King Street, London W6 9LR

Ages 11–19 **Pupils** 1,212 **Sixth form** 362

Fees: £20,130 pa

020 8629 2024
www.latymer-upper.org

Head: Since 2012, David Goodhew (MA Oxon), originally a local boy who has now moved 'back home', living 10 minutes down the road with his French wife, Céline, and two young sons. Read classics at Oxford and previously deputy head of Durham School. Spends at least one hour every day walking around the school – visits lessons for a few minutes, which both pupils and parents say sums up his 'hands-on approach' and 'openness to ideas for change'. Not stereotypical headmasterly, parents and pupils describe him as 'very approachable.'

Clearly, though, capable of stern decisiveness when needful. We were sad to hear of the departure in February 2018 of some pupils found to have been involved with cannabis. The school – in sacrificing, we understand, high-achieving pupils and this number of fees – clearly intends to send an unmistakable message to anyone tempted to offend in like manner.

Academic matters: Grades have been steadily improving over recent years. A levels in 2018 saw 70 per cent A*/A grades, with 91 per cent at A*-B. GCSEs were over 90 per cent A*-A/9-7.

Key aspects of the innovative curriculum include the Global Goals course in year 9 that critically examines the 17 sustainability targets set by the UN. This leads nicely into the UCAS-accredited World Perspectives, which has replaced the 11th GCSE in the middle school. Exploring global political issues, pupils love it and parents delight in their children 'watching more news' and 'talking about bigger issues at the dinner table.'

All year 7s learn Mandarin (carried on from the prep school, if they went) Spanish and all pupils expected to do a modern language at GCSE. IT has been ditched in favour or computing and coding and technology is genuinely embedded into all learning, with all pupils from year 10 upwards given an iPad. 'I do all my essays on it, plus I can do things like surveys,' said one pupil, while one upper sixth pupil has even designed a rowing app that is now used by the GB rowing team.

Majority of teachers hugely admired, with several references to them going the extra mile and being 'very imaginative in their teaching methods'. 'Staff really care, not just academically but in a pastoral way,' summed up one parent. 'I could frankly hug all of them,' said another. 'The teachers try and inspire you – there's no fobbing off of pupils' questions, ever,' remarked a pupil.

Careers and university advice is outstanding, thanks to a knowledgeable and dedicated team, including a careers specialist and international university admissions specialist. The latter post was brought in due to the recent surge in applications to American universities. 'Because of our rounded approach to education, it means our students are often drawn to the American university model of taking seriously areas like sport, music and drama, and the fact that you can delay specialisation,' explains the head.

Parents and pupils rave about the learning support department, which is now known as the 'academic mentoring department' (to remove stigma). Run by three specialist women who nobody seems to be able to praise more if they tried, pupils can visit for one-to-one sessions any time, whether they have severe dyslexia or just a piece of challenging homework, at no extra cost. The department's peer mentoring scheme is popular, whereby older pupils help younger ones, with benefits to both sides. 'If anything, the department could be bigger, though, as it's always full,' said one pupil, who added that on results day, this is where you'll find students running to give staff a hug. School reckons on around 10 per cent needing some kind of support, with just two statemented.

Games, options, the arts: Famed throughout the western (London) world for rowing (Henley, National Schools Regatta) and swimming (ESSA, Bath Cup, Otter Medley); these remain some of the school's strengths and are pursued with much enthusiasm and success. In the past a number of parents have complained that girls' sport has been taken less seriously than boys', but there's also notable accomplishment in for both in football, hockey and cricket (girl footballers coached by QPR trainers), plus netball and rugby, all of which are taught by professional coaches. Sport is also known for being inclusive, plenty of C, D and E teams, with enjoyment of sport valued as much as sporting prowess. One parent also points out how 'my son has been encouraged to try out sports he wouldn't normally opt for, which has been great for him.'

The impressive £14m sports centre (2016) – including swimming pool, sports hall and bouldering wall – enables a full programme of sports and fitness activities, including netball and cricket training before school and at lunchtimes whatever the weather, and there are now greater opportunities for teaching more sports simultaneously, as well as enabling classes in fencing, climbing, yoga and pilates. Sports grounds at Wood Lane used by the England rugby team for training.

All pupils take DT, art, music and drama to the end of year 9 and then choose, although we wonder how they decide. Art is outstanding, with talented and impressively free and imaginative artwork in just about every media, displayed everywhere from the head's office to the four good-sized studios. Similarly, DT is fantastically equipped, with an emphasis on creativity. One excited pupil passionately talked us through some of the machines: 'I once asked to build a stomp rocket powered table tennis ball dispenser for a project. I was allowed and it worked!' he added.

Performing arts also taken seriously, with a commendable theatre (plus other studios) and plenty of year group plays, plus an annual all-school one. Meanwhile, each week 800 individual instrumental lessons are taught by 40 visiting music teachers in air-conditioned, sound-proofed, purpose-built rooms. Group music lessons focus on getting children enthused with practical work, not simply focusing on theory. Singing takes place across several choirs through to grungy bands, and everything in between. Students even have their own record label, 32 Bit Recordings, with profits from releases going into the school bursary fund. 'The arts aren't considered an alternative to academia here,' said one pupil. 'There's room for people to excel in both.'

Astounding range of extracurriculars on offer, with over 100 clubs, as well as a good range of outside speaker. Trips, it seems, are organised to pretty much every corner of the earth, with the Horizon fund ensuring that no pupil is excluded for financial reasons. The annual 'activities week' causes much excitement, where students do anything from cycling coast-to-coast to building a shelter for teenage mums in Uganda. 'It all comes back to our rounded view of education,' says the head. 'Skills learned in leadership, resilience and teamwork matter every bit as much as academia.'

Background and atmosphere: Located on the banks of the Thames in west London, the grounds occupy a rectangular plot between the main entrance in King Street and the busy A4 into London, under which runs a cunning underpass, through which children parade to the prep school, sports centre, pool and Latymer boat house.

But if you didn't know better, you could be forgiven for thinking the school is a church, since your eye is immediately drawn to the huge stained glass windows of the gothic, red-brick main hall, which is nestled behind a long, low gothic arched wall. Dating from 1890, the hall now has several smart newer buildings surrounding it, most recently the striking glass-fronted library and science block, while the old car park has been transformed into a charming 'piazza', complete with giant outdoor chess set, which students describe as the hub of the school during nice weather and exam time.

Back in the main hall, expect portraits of old heads and war memorial tablets, along with brown glazed tiles on the walls and blue carpets on the floor, which very much set the mood throughout the old building, with its seemingly endless supply of nooks and crannies, hidden staircases and innovative linkages between buildings. 'Pupils can be here five years and still discover new areas,' said one pupil. Wooden lockers, which are dotted around the school, had just been replaced with metal ones when we visited ('so much nicer,' said a pupil), while the mezzanine areas of many classrooms give a nice warmth to many of the teaching areas.

In contrast, lots of light wood and huge windows feature in the newer buildings, the most exceptional of which is the science and library block. The ground-floor library is exemplary and one that many towns would be proud of – well-stocked, not just with books and DVDs but computers, with genuinely studious looking pupils. Meanwhile, the corridors of the three floors of science boast interactive periodical table, television with live newsflashes and even live lizards and fish (not together) behind glass, among other innovative features. 'We're just about to do a class on how much vitamin C exists in fruit drinks,' said one excitable teacher as we walked past one of the well-equipped labs. On top is a roof garden, weather station and observatory.

Other areas of note through the school include the huge dining room (now extended) and the well-used sixth form common room, with plentiful and colourful booths and sofas. Outside, expect inevitable queuing and log jams at changeover times, as a result of 1,400 students in limited space, but nobody seems to really mind.

Originally a boys' school, girls started coming in sixth form in the late 1990s, after which it became fully co-ed in 2004. Now 50/50 across every year group, with the head genuinely astounded that anyone could think single sex is preferable. Certainly, nobody could argue that uptake for maths and science among girls isn't strong here. Active school council, which recently put together an initiative for more recycling bins and voted against bringing in a house system.

Pastoral care, well-being and discipline: There was a perception in the 1980s (and, some argue, rather later) that the school was 'a bit rough,' admits the head. 'Not now. The behaviour is excellent.' Parents and pupils concur, putting it down to warm, mutually respectful rapport with staff, as well as pupils knowing exactly what's expected of them.

Head acknowledges that any school would be foolish to believe bullying is non-existent. What matters, he says, is what you do about it on the rare occasions it occurs. 'There's a big focus on encouraging pupils or parents to report it immediately, after which it's dealt with it quickly and sensibly,' concurred one parent. Despite some sixth form drink and drugs related expulsions some years back, the head says the zero tolerance to drink, smoking and drugs means it's not a problem now (and wasn't a big one then), which parents and pupils agree with.

Teachers genuinely interested in pupils' well-being, and although there's not huge interaction between the different year groups, pupils seem at ease with different ages.

Pupils and parents: Around 90 per cent from within a three-mile radius, who arrive by tube, bike or on foot. Diverse population for an independent school, which the school is clearly proud of. 'We attract a real mix from city investors, media types and academics living in leafy streets through to families on the White City estate, which is surely better than just those from a privileged bubble mixing with each other. What life lessons that does that teach you?' explains the head. Parents agree, describing the school as 'grounded'. 'Privileged, yes, but posh, no,' said one. Communication with parents – both via the school and the Parents' Guild – is considered good.

Incredible list of alumni, including Hugh Grant, Alan Rickman, Christopher Guard, Imogen Poots, Mel Smith, Gus Prew. Also Walter Legge and Raphael Wallfisch, and Pete Townsend's dad, who was expelled. Then there's Kulveer Ranger, Keith Vaz, George Walden, Joshua Rozenberg, Andrew Slaughter, Heston Blumenthal, Dr Hilary Jones and Lily Cole. 'If you're lucky, you get to meet one of them at a prize giving,' said one pupil.

Entrance: Of the 170 places available at 11+, 40 come from the school's own on-site prep. Of the remaining 130, 50 per cent come from local state primaries, with the other half coming from other preps. Some 1,200 candidates altogether. The entrance assessment consists of its own English and maths papers (no longer reasoning, with the aim of creating a more level playing field for the untutored), with successful candidates invited for interview. There's no 13+ entry.

L

At 16+, over 200 candidates for 30 places. Although attracting a high calibre at this age, entry for sixth form doesn't set a ridiculously high bar, with the school expecting minimum eight or nine GCSEs including maths and English, with 9-7 grades in the subjects they wish to study (or related subjects).

Exit: Careers and university advice considered second to none. Oxbridge (23 places in 2018), Bristol, Leeds, UCL, Edinburgh, Durham, Warwick, the US (13 places, plus five to Canada). Seven medics, one off to study music in Berlin, one to Milan and one to Leiden.

Money matters: Founder Edward Latymer, a wealthy puritan, pledged funds on his deathbed in 1624 to educate and feed 'eight poore boies'. So when the previous head came into post in 2002 and there were just seven free places (even less than Latymer's pledge) he took action.

The school has since raised over £13m specifically for the bursary programme, with around 175 pupils now on means-tested bursaries; the majority 75-100 per cent of fees. The school has just launched its most ambitious fundraising campaign in its history and the aim is for one in four students to receive bursarial support by 2024.

At 11+, academic scholarships (usually a one-off £1,000) and music scholarships (one of 40 per cent, others up to 20 per cent). Sixth form drama (40 per cent), music, art and sports scholarships (nominal amounts).

Remarks: Oodles of pupil pride about pretty much every aspect of the school, with only minor niggles from pupils and parents. 'If you're not academic, you'll struggle. But it's not just about the academia as there's this constant focus on being well-rounded,' said one pupil. If you're after a school that encourages academic curiosity and a real passion for life, this is it.

L'École Bilingue Élémentaire

St David's Welsh Church, St Mary's Terrace, London W2 1SJ

Ages 3–11 Pupils 120

Fees: £9,960 – £10,770 pa

0207 224 8427
www.lecolebilingue.com

Headteacher: Since its opening in 2004, Veronique Ferreira, who studied biochemistry at the University of Paris, and after obtaining her teaching licence in 1999 began her career as a primary school teacher in the suburbs of Paris, working with children with behavioural and academic difficulties. This gave her a lot of insights into the different learning styles of children, something that has shaped a lot of the teaching approach she has established at L'École Bilingue. Moving to London, she started in a French nursery school, but as parents continued to speak of their interest in a more bilingual programme, she pondered on how she might introduce a different sort of French primary school model in London. She focused on child development theories, looking at Canadian, UK (including EYFS) and French Breton bilingual educational models. Youthful yet wise beyond her years, her confidence is drawn from her solid foundation in pedagogical studies and the popularity of the school which was her brainchild. Her partner and the father of her daughter, Franck Laurans (head of administration), has provided the business knowledge needed to help her realise her vision for a school that is small, personalised and less rigid that the traditional French models where her students can 'find pleasure in learning'.

Entrance: L'École Bilingue is non-selective, but with only 15 places at the 3-year-old entry class, places are highly sought. Parents like the fact that, unlike other French schools, this is a transparent process. Priority is given to siblings (which can take up three-quarters of spaces), but after that it is first-come, first-served, so sign up early – from birth if you wish. (Nationality/passport are not a factor as in other French homologue schools.) Vacancies for children older than 3 are subject to space; worth a call but most classes are wait-listed, so as soon as someone leaves (and with many expats, children do leave) there is someone to fill the spot. Note that if you miss out on the first round you need to proactively let them know you remain interested.

Exit: The head meets parents individually to discuss the options, and some non-native French speakers may at this point opt for 11+ exams (a very few leave at age 7 or 8) and a move away from the French system. Recent examples include Francis Holland, City of London Girls' School and Holland Park. As the school is part of the AEFE agency for French education abroad, year 6 pupils have automatic access to French secondary schools such as the two Lycées (South Kensington and Wembley) or the Collège Français Bilingue in Kentish Town, which follows the bilingual mode, and the vast majority go on to one of these. While moving from L'École to the ginormous French Lycée is a big change, the Lycée tries to place two L'École students in the same year form group, so that helps a bit. The school has noted that French students repatriating to Paris often seek out bilingual schools there to keep their English language strong.

Remarks: The curriculum is bilingual French and English, and although the French curriculum model is predominant, the head says that she has looked in depth at other curricula, including the national curriculum, the IB primary years and the international primary curriculum, and drawn on elements of all these. Some subjects are taught in French (French, maths, history), some in English (science, English, geography) and some are taught in both languages simultaneously (arts, ICT, drama, music). Children move between English and French medium classrooms so that they are immersed in the relevant language for that part of the day.

Though a small school, the limited space is used to good effect and is immaculately tidy. The compact library is brimming with French and English children's books, a cheerful space where we saw some one-to-one learning taking place; walls lined with colourful boards neatly display creative work by students of all ages; we noticed some tailors' mannequins with student-designed fashions – part of a broader project including all the London French homologue schools in celebration of the centenary of the Lycée Charles de Gaulle. Some special needs support (French and English) available; some children with statements/EHC plans in the school receive individual support either in-class or on a withdrawal basis. Teachers (19 in total, average age early 30s) are a mixture of French and English, all suitably trained and qualified. Staff turnover is higher amongst the French teachers than the English as they may be here as accompanying spouses or may move on to other French medium schools in London or abroad.

By all accounts, the pupils are busy and engaged in a wide range of activities. They are especially proud to have been invited – by recommendation of the French education inspector – to participate in the French Parlement des Enfants (a sort of 'junior parliament'). This event has influenced some of the themes and topics that have been studied by pupils in all the year groups. Other academic extras sometimes include a French mathematics competition for French schools in the north of Europe. French assessments are given in year 3 and year 6 to measure attainment against French standards; the school is inspected by Ofsted as well as the IEN French Inspector for the northern European region.

Year 3 goes to Brighton for two nights, year 5 spends three days in East Sussex and year 6 goes to Brittany for a week. The music programme is strong and some children do extra Suzuki violin and piano. Parents sang the praises (no pun intended) of the innovative music teacher who had recently done a 'bilingual Beatles' unit. As with other London French schools, many of the extracurricular activities are organised by the parents' association, and parents run some of the clubs, which include fencing, dance, art, choir and football. There are no competitive sports on offer; they use the local sports centre – where many students do taekwondo after school; from year 2 they swim at Imperial College pool. There are two major shows – the annual Christmas carol service and an end-of-year show. We saw the former in final rehearsal – joyful voices,silver tinsel halos and red Santa hats.

Though the school is secular, the some of the ecclesiastical architectural features in the former Welsh church nestled in a quiet back street in Maida Vale have been put to effective use, making this a most unusual school building. An enclosed garden behind the school features a vegetable garden for pupils, an eco-pond (with resident creepy crawlies), and an area for messy hands-on learning with sand and water. There is an outdoor play area at the front of the school. A small multi-purpose hall is used for assemblies. Four-course lunches (optional) are prepared and served at school by cooks who know each child by name, chivvy those with picky palates to eat their vegetables and then report to parents on how many ate their carrots. Too much chatter is discouraged during lunches to encourage eating; an adult may read stories aloud instead.

There is a big emphasis on developing the 'soft skills' and the small size means that there is no anonymity in the school. Everyone contributes; everyone has a role to play. The appeal, parents say, is that at L'École they have found a near-perfect balance of strong (French) academic foundations in a very caring environment where everyone knows everyone. The intimacy of the school ensures that behaviour standards are high, and parents subtly suggest that the presence of several English teachers means that discipline is managed differently than in traditional French schools. Parents describe the children as 'kind' and very welcoming of new students. It's also highly inclusive. 'Birthday parties usually involve all of the siblings.'

Parents are big fans of this school, so much so that when they heard of the Good Schools Guide interest in meeting them, they organised a coffee morning (mostly mums, though one dad came) to share frankly their opinions about the school. The small size is an attraction – 'it's digestible for young children'. Another said, 'it's like comparing a mom and pop shop with B&Q'. One recent arrival accustomed to French schools voiced a concern that L'École may lack rigour; others from elsewhere in Europe and the US were delighted with the academic standards. Despite its small size, it appears that communication is patchy; some people seem to be in the know; others (particularly those new to the school) felt they were out of the loop. The school gate is definitely the place to find out what's happening. It seems that parents who are not fluent French speakers can find other parents willing to help and explain things.

Some 40 per cent of families are French (expat and local), 25 per cent are dual French/other nationals, 18 per cent are French/ British, and some eight per cent represent other nationalities (including French-speaking north Africans, Canadians and others). Some international families also speak Arabic, Spanish, Italian, etc. Most families live nearby and walk to school, though some are drawn from as far as Fulham, Kentish Town, South Kensington and Hampstead. Because of the school's South Kensington origins, a bus that comes from the Brompton Road area serves families who joined the school in the early days.

The school is owned by founders Franck Laurans and Veronique Ferreira. Parents like the fact that this couple, who 'live above the shop', are firmly at the helm; they feel they provide continuity and sustainable leadership that secures the school's future – at least for the time being. Some subsidies come from the French government for French national students,

Described by one parent as small, friendly 'village' school that draws on the best of French academics and English pastoral education, this bite-size school in the centre of London is worth a visit by parents who want something a bit different.

L

London Academy of Excellence

Broadway House, 322 High Street, Stratford, London E15 1AJ

Ages 16–18 **Pupils** 460

020 3301 1480
www.lae.ac.uk

Head Master: Since 2017, Scott Baker MA PGCE QTS. After reading history at Cambridge, he began his teaching career at Robert Clack School in Dagenham (the school he attended) in 1999. Has held senior leadership positions in a number of state schools including Sandringham School in St Albans and The Henrietta Barnett School in north west London. He is the school's third head since it was founded in 2012.

We met him in his modern, airy, white-with-splashes-of-colour first floor office – the decorative style is continued throughout this former 80s council office block that's located a minutes' walk from Stratford station. He was first in his school's 50-year history to have got to Cambridge, the first in his family to go to university at all, and the first state school appointee to head LAE. We found him unpretentious, razor-sharp and passionate about bright young sparks from all walks of life getting the educational chances they should. No wonder he calls this his 'dream job'. 'I remember reading about it opening in The Metro and thinking, "Crikey, that's a great idea – an Eton of the East End",' he said.

'He's warm, welcoming and highly intelligent,' one parent told us. Another said, 'He's dynamic, but there's no need to feel awe-struck around him as he's friendly and jovial.' Keeps a hand in at the coal face by teaching politics, leading (when the students aren't) weekly assemblies, having tea with all tutor groups and organising awards dinners, among other things. 'He's not like the headteacher in my last school, who you never saw – he's always around and really friendly,' said one student.

Academic matters: Not for the faint-hearted. All year 12s embark on four A levels although three-quarters drop one by year 13 ('it still gives you a competitive edge on your UCAS form,' insists school), chosen from 14 predominantly 'facilitating subjects' (what some might regard as 'proper subjects' or 'subjects favoured by the top universities'), including further maths, French and Spanish. Non-facilitating (but still strong) subjects such as government & politics, psychology and economics are also offered. Maths currently the most popular A level (70 per cent of year 12s take it) followed by sciences ('We are key providers for STEM, but not a STEM college because of our breadth'). Some students feel the humanities department gets a bit overshadowed by maths and sciences – 'It's a bit of a sticking point,' said one, 'the teachers are great, but they need more resources.' Growing numbers take modern languages, bucking the national trend, with additional languages offered outside the timetable (currently including Mandarin, Italian, Bengali, Arabic, Urdu and Japanese, but these vary year on year). Five specialist 'pathways' are specified under the curriculum (medicine, law, STEM, business, digital technologies), but students told us there is bespoke preparation for a career in any field, 'with second-to-none university application and careers advice'.

In its early days, the school was accused of kicking out students at the end of year 12 who failed to get high enough grades for entry to the most competitive universities. Head says 'the governors realised the admissions policy had flaws and no student can be asked to leave at the end of year 12 on the basis of their academic achievement.' Now 95 per cent progress successfully – something praised by Ofsted in their last inspection report. 'It's hard to fall behind here because of all the support,' one student told us, while another said, 'It's easy to switch subjects too' (eg there's a one-year politics A level in year 13). Impressive results – in 2018, 61 per cent A*/A, 90 per cent A*-B at A level, with LAE regularly ranked as one of the top sixth form colleges in the country and in the top one per cent for value added for the fourth year running.

All year 12s do a mini EPQ; a third progress onto the full EPQ, with stellar results. Exciting a thirst for learning and for academic endeavour is key here and the scholars' programme contributes incentive and prestige. Those with the top 50 scores for GCSE grades may be awarded Governors' scholarships or Merit scholarships – the prize being financial support for resources as well as more trips to Oxford and Cambridge.

Around 40 students are on the learning support register, although many don't have a diagnosed condition. Dedicated learning coach goes above and beyond the usual support and access arrangements with help in targeted areas. For example, some maths students are very able numerically but because more than half the students here have EAL, they may need help with academic literacy (increasingly required in the new maths A level). Results for those with SEN match those without and, in 2018, outmatched them by quite a margin. According to one student with a physical disability, the school is also 'excellent about mobility issues, including access to reliable lifts.'

School day is long – the library opens at 7.45am, lessons start at 8.30am, and if you take advantage (many do) of the optional subject clinics after regular classes, teaching doesn't finish until 6pm. Class sizes are capped at 25, with 22 for science (but most drop below 20 in year 13) and students get five hours teaching per week per A level; this, together with the extracurricular, leaves little or no downtime. 'But while there's lots to do, it doesn't feel crazy or over-pressured,' said one student. Teachers are all specialists in their field (a third have a doctorate; one biology teacher is a former doctor) and a passion for their subject make for lively, engaging lessons. Expect university-style lessons with lots of interaction – students here are taught to think, no doubt balm to admissions tutors' ears. Parents wonder at the levels of support given to their children by the teachers: from Saturday classes to making themselves available by email until 11pm ('not officially, of course,' says head). Reflecting the school's heavy focus on personal development, students also track their own progress (academic and extracurricular), taking part in a viva at the end of year 12, from which they can gain a diploma.

Although there's a more competitive landscape for academic sixth forms since the school's inception (key competitors are Brampton Manor Academy and Newham Collegiate Sixth Form Centre), LAE still regards itself as 'the strongest academic pathway to top universities for students in Newham, a claim born out by the performance tables which ranked us at the highest attaining school in Newham and the only one with an average grade of A.'

Games, options, the arts: Wednesday afternoons are dedicated to clubs and societies – 30 in total, some student led, including women in STEM, scrabble, chess, juggling, DofE, mindfulness & wellbeing, Japanese, photography, first aid, debating, Model United Nations. 'I've being doing parliamentary debating for the last two terms – it's so good,' said one student, while another told us she was setting up a new art club. A number of competitions organised against other schools. CCF now available.

On Tuesday afternoons, it's sport for all – with a huge choice of 25 from girls' and boys' football, rowing, sailing and pilates to basketball, climbing, canoeing, boxercise, volleyball, yoga and zumba. Games take place at venues including the Olympic Park, Redbridge Sports Centre, University of East London and Lee Valley. One student told us she chose LAE because 'the sport looked as good as the academics – I haven't been disappointed'. Growing number of fixtures, including against independent schools, with strong results for football and netball.

Historically, the arts have been thin on the ground, no doubt because they aren't offered as A levels. The appointment of a co-ordinator of music, drama and art has helped, with piano lessons now available, plus street dance, musical theatre, rock choir, improv society, among others – although sadly still no orchestra. However, music performances do take place during assemblies and there is a music room with a speaker system, microphone and guitars.

Trips kick off with a visit to Oxford University in the first week of year 12. 'It's a great idea because it raises the bar academically and is good for team building,' said a parent. All students visit Cambridge in year 13 and one other university of their choice. Students we met were buzzing about an upcoming sailing trip with Eton students, while other students go to Japan and Berlin. 'We proactively seek out opportunities for both day and residential trips, although we don't go in for the big USA type trips which need a huge lead in time for raising funds,' says head. All students do community outreach and charitable fundraising.

Background and atmosphere: Founded in 2012, LAE was the brainchild of Richard Cairns, head of Brighton College, and Joan Deslandes, head of Kingsford Community School in Newham. They met on a bus in Beijing and found they shared a passion for Mandarin (they both introduced compulsory teaching of Mandarin in their schools) as well as rigorous academic learning and a desire for social justice. Joan Deslandes needed somewhere to send her high fliers (Kingsford is an 11-16 school). Brighton College took two sixth formers each year from Kingsford, on full scholarships. These scholarships were funded by HSBC, which still continues to support the LAE today (HSBC also has input into the school's careers programme, including networking and mentoring). However, Joan Deslandes had another 40 high attainers at Kingsford, whose academic aspirations weren't being met. With the inspirational energy of these two first class educators, the early seeds of the LAE were sown. Most agree that Richard Cairns was a driving force in gaining a groundswell of support from the independent sector, one of the innovative features of LAE.

The first sixth form only free school, it has the benefit of strong links with the independent sector. Six 'partner schools' – Brighton College, Eton College, UCS, Highgate, Forest School and Caterham – share resources, knowledge, experience and contacts and also form the names of the six houses that the students are grouped into (as a student, you get the most direct involvement with the school your house is named after). There are also links with Francis Holland and Putney High schools. Support from these schools includes seconded teaching staff, shared INSET days, coaching and support, revision workshops, academic lectures, competitions and study days, Oxbridge admissions support (including mock interviews at the schools themselves), careers events and access to facilities (eg sport). Students told us of a debating day on educational injustice at Eton, complete with keynote speakers.

School is located on Stratford High Street – it's the yellow and glass building right in front of you as you walk out of Stratford station. Functional and businesslike, but the edge is taken off by the bright colours and idiosyncratic names (the large, tastefully decorated dining/study/common room area is called the agora), and walls throughout the building are adorned with wonderful large portraits of 'independent thinkers', from Coco Chanel and Elizabeth David to Srinivasa Ramanujan and Reverend William Buckland, saying profound things. All rooms are shiny, bright, light and airy; nothing feels run down. 'Shame there's no outside area – that's a real downside,' said one parent; a few students added they'd 'like more space inside, but it wouldn't have stopped me coming here'. School currently considering expanding, but not too much – the aim is 'to retain an independent school style of education.'

Pastoral care, well-being and discipline: The school's key values are excellence, kindness, respect, humility, independence and resilience and they underpin everything. High expectations around the everyday stuff – uniform, lanyards (zero tolerance on these not being worn), punctuality, not handing in homework. Parents are told if a child fails on any of these counts, although poor behaviour is rare; students are mature, proud of being at the school and highly motivated. One exclusion in the last two years. Mental health taken 'more seriously than it used to be', according to one parent, with a part-time counsellor, preventative workshops, relaxation room (set up by students) and talks with psychology students from Queen Mary University. Student-led networks include LGBT, mental health and feminism and gender equality.

Head of house, along with a team of five tutors in each house, is in charge of pastoral welfare. Each student's tutor is also responsible for their UCAS reference, PSHE and monitoring their academic progress; and this tutor is the first port of call for parents. Reports are issued at the end of each term, and parents also can meet the tutor and other teachers once a term – 'the ones we've met have a very clear picture of our son and focus entirely on what they can do to help him progress,' said one parent. Schools says they've had no reports of bullying; students agree – 'There aren't cliques here, everyone's in it together'.

Pupils and parents: Unusually high proportion of first and second generation immigrant families – particularly Asian and black. Fiercely aspirational parents (many of whom haven't been to university themselves) have a positive influence on the ambition of their children. Students are dressed smartly but, apart from the blue and gold ties, not uniformly.

The students we met, a mixture of year 12 and year 13, were the kind of people you would want to represent your country – model citizens. Thoughtful, articulate, mature, curious, polite and with an ease and confidence that belied the backgrounds of many of them. 'This school makes you confident,' one student told us. There is much competition for the prestigious leadership roles, especially house captain and prefect.

Entrance: Minimum of five 7s at GCSE with at least 6s in maths and English, plus subject specific requirements (7-9 in most subjects, 8-9 for further maths). School gets about 3,000 applicants and will interview about 1,500 for 240 places – according to their predicted grades. Half the places are given to students from Newham, other half could come from anywhere, with over 100 secondary feeders. 'It's perfectly normal not to know anyone when you start here,' a student told us. Those on free school meals given priority, provided they meet minimum criteria.

L

Exit: Impressive. Ninety-five per cent get an offer to a Russell Group university. School is pushing for more to apply outside London – a road trip to St Andrews, Edinburgh and Durham paid dividends and larger numbers are going to Durham, Bristol, Bath and Exeter than in the past; Warwick is particularly popular. Fifteen to Oxbridge in 2018 – a higher percentage than many top independent schools. Growing numbers to USA – one or two each year. STEM subjects popular; history and geography also well represented. About 30 will take a gap year and come back during that time for advice and interview practice. One parent told us, 'The guidance has been as good as if she's still there.'

Money matters: School still has the benefit of the HSBC funding that was a legacy of the Brighton scholars' funding. This is not a luxury, says school, but vital in a climate of continuing government cuts. Opportunities Fund provides financial support for trips and resources to those most in need, and the diligent few who are awarded scholarships also get financial help with resources and trips.

Remarks: This school provides a rigorous academic education to bright, aspirational students who are keen to seize the many opportunities on offer. Not only do students excel academically, they also develop confidence, resilience and ambitions that set them up for life well beyond university. An inspirational school for those willing to go the extra mile.

The London Oratory School

Seagrave Road, London SW6 1RX

Ages 7–18 **Pupils** 1,340 **Sixth form** 360 (80 girls) **RC**

020 7385 0102
www.london-oratory.org

Headmaster: Since January 2018, Daniel Wright MA, previously deputy head of St George's College Weybridge. History degree from Cambridge; began his teaching career at Gordon's School, moving to Godalming College in 2004 as head of history then director of faculty. Took up his post at St George's in 2015.

Junior housemaster, who runs the Junior House on a day to day basis, is Pheona Mackay. She is ex-RAF and feared by the parents, though loved by the boys. 'She obviously adores the boys,' said one parent, 'but I am a bit worried about approaching her.' Her attitude appears to be that the job of educating the boys is the school's, the less interference from parents the better.

Academic matters: Junior House boys are tested at the end of each term and reports are sent to parents, which detail their results, progress and targets. Otherwise, you get to meet your son's teachers only once a year. Some complain about poor communication lines between school and home, but say that on the whole they put up with this because they trust the school. 'You might not get to hear about a concert until two nights before,' remarked one parent. The school is totally integrated into the senior school – junior house boys even have lunch, as the senior boys do, in classrooms that become 'house rooms' at lunch time. However, there is little interaction with senior boys. Playtimes are organised so as not to coincide with the traffic of burly teenagers, and the whole of junior house has lunch at a different time from the senior boys.

Consistently impressive results at both GCSE and A level. School fiercely competitive with its notable rival – particularly regarding academic results. When considering A level scores school would like it be noted that they have a broader range of ability in their sixth form as their entry requirements are lower. What we like particularly is the range of subjects boys are choosing to take at both GCSE and at A level. Large numbers do maths and sciences – and a healthy helping of A*/9-8s in these subjects – but the humanities and languages are not neglected. History particularly popular, and double figures do art and DT each year. Heartening in an (almost entirely) boys' school to see this range, and we were particularly encouraged by a thriving German department. A level results in 2018 were 78 per cent A*-B and 45 per cent A*/A grades. At GCSE, 85 per cent of pupils got 9-4 in both maths and English; 47 per cent 9-7 grades. School will endeavour to facilitate any language if there is a demand, however low the numbers – Russian, Arabic, Chinese, Portuguese and Polish all offered and a good solid classics department encourages a number of people to take Latin and Greek GCSE. A few go on to A level.

Good results can partly be attributed to good and committed teaching, but must largely stem from an excellent work ethic that is drilled in from the start. Homework is rigorously monitored and it's a detention for repeated failure to produce it. Setting from year 9 and a number of GCSEs are taken in year 10. Sixth formers have to work together in a large room during study periods. No lounging around on comfy sofas here. A member of staff is ever present to monitor behaviour and we were conscious of our noisy footfall when we peeked in.

The less academically able are offered a sixth form course in advanced business – a hybrid of two A levels and an AS, leading to qualifications in business and computing, a practical alternative to a sixth form college course for those who can't bear to leave. Now offers the Extended Project Qualification. Classes felt by some to be too big – can be as many as 30 at GCSE; sixth form numbers are higher than elsewhere too. However, with 10 or so a year gaining places at Oxbridge, the Sutton Trust continues to rank it among the highest performing state schools in the country. Standards here are high and pupils strive to maintain those standards.

SENs catered for – attracts standard numbers of the usual spread of needs. Currently school estimates there are approximately 40 with EHC plans – a range of those on the autistic spectrum as well as some with emotional issues, social and/or communication issues. School can accommodate pupils with cerebral palsy. By all accounts the SENCo is 'magnificent' and there is an army of teaching assistants as well as learning support staff. In-class help along with withdrawal where appropriate. Murmurings of discontent in certain quarters – particularly parents who have sons with no identifiable special need, but may simply be dreamy or disorganised. 'Faulty communication lines and support is not swiftly forthcoming' are the central complaints. Wheelchair-friendly and SENs seen, in general, as just part of life.

Games, options, the arts: Junior House boys are committed and robust. The day starts early with an hour's choir practice from 8am, if you are in the Schola. All boys play two instruments – one orchestral, normally supported by the piano. For potential applicants, who must be of at least average academic ability, musical promise is the only criterion which counts here, once you have demonstrated your Catholic credentials – all the boys have musical potential. Not all boys are in the Schola – some just follow an instrumental course. The Schola sings every Saturday evening in the Brompton Oratory. Junior house boys play every instrument you can name, under the care of innumerable peripatetic teachers of high quality, and use all the senior school facilities. They tour, record and give stunning concerts. They work hard and play hard.

Not just music, sport too. Tag rugby is organised against other junior schools. They swim once a week in the school pool, and water polo is a popular after-school club. Plenty of other after-school clubs too – including Lego, programming and chess – but many boys are just too tired at the end of the school day. Art is vibrant and boys get to use the facilities of the senior school. They learn about eg da Vinci in lessons then put their learning into practical effect in the art room. Not a lot of drama, but plenty of musical productions – again, use of the senior school facilities greatly enhances the experience. This is true, too, of science. Science is taught in the senior school labs, and they get the benefit of having specialist teachers from an early age – not just the form teacher.

This is a big rugby school. If your son is a keen football player he will struggle to find much here apart from the house soccer competition. Rugby fixtures against a huge number of schools including the top public schools, many on a Saturday. Six teams in the first form alone, and more than 20 in total, so plenty of opportunities for everyone to have a go. Boys are bussed to Barn Elms in Barnes for training – a round trip of not much less than an hour.

Water polo also popular, with fixtures against other schools; hockey and cricket other main activities at present – all weather 4G playing field installed 2016; also a good, well-used, on-site 17m pool and gym. Also popular is DofE. CCF perhaps the biggest in any state school, both army and RAF – tours, camps and expeditions of all kinds. Lots of sixth involved in community work – helping at local schools and care homes, soup kitchens on Saturdays, the offices of a local charity etc.

A delightfully refreshing and modern attitude to educating boys: 'Arts are very important in a boys' school'; plans for a dance studio, which is in the pipeline. 'The boys will respond really well to dance classes.' That's right, says one parent, who remembers how much her son enjoyed knitting and crocheting while in the Junior House. Boys here will throw themselves into anything. The key thing is to make it fun.

Senior school music is also excellent, fuelled by those who come up from the Junior House, all of whom have exceptional aptitude. Some 600+ pupils learn at least one instrument. Bands, including the popular jazz group, choirs and orchestras thrive and are well-housed in the arts centre. The chamber choir recently went on a tour to Prague, and recorded their first CD with music sung on the tour. The Schola Cantorum is a choir of professional standard and considerable significance in the world of RC – and secular – music: three visits to Rome in as many months, including representing the Vatican in Al Gore's Live Earth initiative. They record for films and TV, were one of the main choirs at the mass for the beatification of Cardinal Newman on the Papal visit to Britain and are regarded with deserved respect. They sing at the weekly vigil mass at the Brompton Oratory. A recent performance of St John Passion was by all accounts breathtaking – but this is the norm here. Concerts take place at St John's Smith Square as well as the school theatre, and there are plenty of other choirs – these boys (and girls) want to sing. A recent highlight was the girls' choir performance at the Vigil Mass in Westminster Cathedral.

School's on-site arts centre is an impressive asset and includes stunning 300-seat galleried theatre in which full scale shows are mounted –a minimum of four performances each year, including one musical. When we visited, Sophocles' Antigone was in rehearsal – the sixth form play. Recent productions include Guys and Dolls, The Government Inspector and Henry V, as well as Joseph and his Technicolour Dreamcoat – performed by the junior boys. Good display spaces – a stimulating photo show by member of staff was good to see, along with a vast Paolozzi brutalist sculpture. Pupils go on to study art/art history and architecture at prestigious institutions. No photography or textiles on offer, though both are available in extracurricular clubs.

Lots of overseas trips in the holidays – foreign exchanges, cultural and historical visits. Rugby tours to far-flung places and singers and instrumental players performing far and wide.

Background and atmosphere: Founded in 1863 by the Oratorian Fathers, the school moved to its present site and buildings – in the lee of Chelsea FC's massive stadium – in the 1970s and has worn surprisingly well. Splendid extension and refurbishment of main teaching area recently completed – nominated for architectural award. A bright glass central atrium with pods of different sizes round the edge – for smaller groups and lessons away from the main central area, which is the school library. This is where sixth formers come during their free periods. There is calm peacefulness, no doubt enhanced by the Seven Virtues of Man, which are encapsulated in images and text in panels that climb to the glass roof at the top. Around the outer edges the Beatitudes are depicted. On ground level in the centre is a stunning modern statue of Mary with an adolescent Jesus, complete with apron and the tools of his carpentry trade. A welcome change from the Madonna and child, and so fitting in a school where mothers and sons are working out this next phase in their relationship.

This stunning new development is a modern and dynamic contrast to the old-fashioned class rooms for years 7 and 8, complete with the old style wooden desks, storage inside and inkwell on top. Everyone eats by house in their 'house rooms' (aka classrooms outside feeding times) with six separate serveries. An unusual system, but it seems to work. Some rooms and corridors, notably in the sixth form areas, are scruffy and lacking in soul, but with plans for landscape gardening afoot for the sixth form garden, as well as the creation of a quiet room for reflection and contemplation, it is apparent that there is always attention on improvement and change. We liked the brick courtyard, Chapel Courtyard, with its lead flashing. No football in break and at lunch time here. Health and safety has stopped that. The infrastructure has undergone a profound makeover since we last visited and the boys and staff reinforce an air of engagement and pride, a sense of collaborative energy and achievement.

The chapel, opened in 1992 by Basil Hume and dedicated to St Philip Neri and St Edward the Confessor, is simple in design and has a warm and gentle feel. Services here are intimate and spiritual – only room for one of the houses each day and for the young boys in Junior House; part of the Schola sings, eg, Faure Requiem. Beautiful. Major ceremonies held in the famous, huge, Italianate Oratory Church in South Kensington. The Catholic ethos underlies all aspects of the school but not obtrusively or obsessively – it is simply a given and central also to the plans to develop the community involvement of the school. Long-standing commitment to local primary schools and charities – such as SURF and the SVP soup kitchen – with sixth formers carrying out voluntary work and the music department involved in outreach programmes.

The Junior House really is tiny, with only 80 boys in all (20 in each of years 3-6) and can't really be regarded in a school in its own right. Parents talk of the shock arriving here after a state primary – 'This is not like a primary school. You entrust your children to the teachers here. You're not sure what goes on from the time you drop them at the gate,' said one parent. It is in a separate wing – situated, rather appropriately, in the heart of the music school – with four classrooms, a choir room and several practice rooms (as music is everything here), all recently refurbished. Old-fashioned classrooms, old-fashioned desks that lift up to contain a motley jumble of books and stationary. The music practice rooms adjoin and creakings of strings or blasting of brass form the background noise. It operates rather like a choir school, or an old fashioned prep school – only without the boarding. It is one of very few state choir schools.

Pastoral care, well-being and discipline: Discipline is tight – rules are strict and enforced strictly. Any mobile phones spotted on the premises will be confiscated and have to be collected by parents. The approach is 'compassionate', but zero tolerance for physical violence – automatic suspension for anyone who tries to sort a problem by 'raising a hand against someone else'.

House system – there are six houses with 200 pupils in each house – encourages friendships between the year groups and boys in the sixth can mentor those younger who need support over a subject or a problem. Parents mostly praise the staff for their pastoral care – especially the deputy heads – of whom one has been in the school for 20+ years since the start of her career and the other who is a past pupil of the school. However – as with the academics – a complaint we keep hearing is about communication channels and the prompt resolution of problems. There is a culture of deference among parents here, however, so it still takes some boldness to take a proactive step. The sixth form girls talk of close relationships across the two year groups – a benefit of having only 80 girls in total.

Shift in emphasis is taking time to seep through decades of rigorous and sometimes steely discipline. Aim is to see less 'reaction' and more proactivity, and that through charitable service programmes, and the self-reflection programme that goes with that, the young adults at the school will acquire a taste for 'goodness' and doing and being good. Part of this vision has been the establishment of the charitable foundation that is linked with the school.

Pupils and parents: From a vast geographical area, most London boroughs, inner and outer – some leave home before dawn breaks to come here. Over 50 languages spoken at home; serious Roman Catholicism the only – but unifying – common denominator. A higher number of professional families than in most inner London comprehensives, and the school still has a traditional public school air about it. Parents are warming to drive to involve them in all ways – social, educational and practical. Parents' groups for sports, music and food.

A lot of boys in Junior House have brothers in the senior school, and 'being such a small school, the parents tend to bond quite closely and stick together,' said one parent. The pace is fast and it's 'hard core,' said another. 'While there is a sense of exclusivity – the bar is so high to get in and you feel so lucky – these are very normal boys, not precious and geeky'. A wonderful start in life for your musical, resilient, self-motivated, Catholic little boy.

Reports in the main school are now termly and home-school contact far more a normal thing, though complaints persist of parents not being kept in touch. Children appreciate the knock-ons of greater parental involvement and find it supportive and helpful. The boys themselves are relaxed, friendly, ambitious and hard-working. Classes are head down and concentrating. We heard no raised voices, saw few inattentive faces. Pupils have a sense of pride in themselves and in the school which one would wish to see replicated everywhere. The only boy who wouldn't like it here, we were told, was someone who didn't want to involve himself.

Sixth form girls are no mere modern import designed to boost results. They date back to a link with a girls' school in the 19th century and were incorporated into the sixth in the 1950s after a merger. Their numbers are small but, says head, 'they add so much to the school'. It was good to see girls and boys out and about in the lunch hour clearly in relaxed friendship and at ease – no cattle market or points system here. Popular among politicians – Tony Blair and Nick Clegg both sent their sons here. Notable former pupils include Simon Callow, rugby union star Michael Swift and Hayley Atwell.

L

Entrance: Admits up to 20 boys at 7 into year 3, up to 10 of whom are choristers. All applicants tested for general academic ability and for music aptitude; potential choristers also tested for choral aptitude and suitability. Priority to practising Catholics who attend mass frequently, baptism before 6 months, siblings. All get automatic entry to the senior school.

Entrance to main school simpler than hitherto, but heart-sinking for anyone other than an assiduously practising Roman Catholic family. In fact, don't bother to apply unless you are a pillar of your local church and known to your priest, who will have to vouch for your bona fides – both pupil's and family's; early baptism essential. After long-running legal battle no longer includes 'Catholic service' – eg church flower arranging – as part of points system. Admission process involves completing the school's Supplementary Information Form and a local authority Common Application Form. Nine hundred plus apply for the 160 places. Junior House boys transfer automatically and parents praise the seamless transition. The current oversubscription criteria are based upon mass attendance, early baptism, siblings and attendance at the Oratory Primary School in Chelsea, with a ballot system as tie-break.

Sixth form also oversubscribed. Requirement is grade 6s in six GCSEs and at least a 4 in maths and English. This is the stated requirement, but parents we spoke to said the standard was in fact much higher. Beware the postman if your son looks like he won't make the standard expected at A level. A letter is likely to arrive during year 11 to warn that you need to find a place elsewhere. Forty places attract 200 applicants and, again, the RC credentials are what counts, plus 'expected performance at GCSE and suitability for an A level course which will be sought from each pupil's current school'. Girls join from Sacred Heart, Gumley, the Ursuline Convent and a few from Lady Margaret's.

Exit: All Junior House boys move up to the main school. Most (about 70 per cent) stay on after GCSEs; almost 400 in sixth form. Regularly win Oxbridge places (10 in 2018), covering the range of disciplines. Around half to Russell Group; four medics in 2018. Fairly equal spread of arts, sciences and practical subjects. Otherwise to good universities everywhere to read everything, with one off to the US in 2018. Refreshingly few silly subjects pursued – these pupils have been properly taught and sensibly advised.

Remarks: Much that is excellent and not just the obvious – the music, the academics, but also the attention given to spiritual and emotional development. An ideal choice for a son (or sixth form daughter) who toes the line. Approach with caution if you have a scatty child who balks at authority.

Lycée Français Charles de Gaulle

35 Cromwell Road, London SW7 2DG

Ages 3–19 Pupils 3,660 Sixth form 583

Fees: £5,726 – £11,980 pa

020 7584 6322
www.lyceefrancais.org.uk

Proviseur: Since September 2018 Didier Devilard, previously proviseur of the Lycée Victor Hugo in Toulouse.

Academic matters: Lycée Charles de Gaulle is the premier French school in Britain and one of the largest in the world. The raison d'être is to provide French education leading to the French baccalaureate, regarded by many as one of the most robust school-leaving qualifications there is. With many dual national French-English families enrolled, the Lycée also offers I/GCSE and A levels.

The French model is divided into: maternelle (reception and year 1), primaire (years 2-6), college (years 7-10) and lycée (years 11-13). In primaire and college, the school offers the French curriculum in French. From the final year of college (year 10) students either move over to the British section to do GCSEs and IGCSEs followed by A levels or continue through to the French baccalaureate. Parent perspectives on the Lycée vary significantly depending on their own cultural expectations of what constitutes a school education, but most parents seem to feel that overall the kids are well taught, learning lots, enjoying the challenge and loving the school's international community.

Primary class teachers do everything (including art and PE) while specialists teach IT and music. The quality of the art is down to the creativity of the teacher but we've heard of some great stuff with cross-curricular projects and older classes partnering with younger ones. Parents say there's 'frequent assessment and evaluation' so a struggling child is quickly identified. A primary parent with British school experience describes the French system as 'less flexible, but of high standard.' Class sizes are about 28, with an assistant in each class. Classroom arrangements are fairly traditional, with desks in rows, though we saw some more varied arrangements.

College is another story. Some students entering college come from schools where the entire enrolment is less than the year group they are joining. Students move around for different lessons in what one parent described as an 'anonymous teacher environment.' Students have advisers whom they see for maybe 30 minutes per week and there's no expectation of pastoral care on the adviser's part. They monitor pupils' progress through frequent assessment and parents are kept informed. The problem is that it's public knowledge, so if you are bottom of the heap everyone knows, which can take its toll on the self-esteem of less confident adolescents. The survivors – and there are plenty who thrive on the mounting pressure – develop strong independent skills and learn to manage their time and work successfully, attributes French parents expect to see.

The French curriculum is followed in the French section for the oldest students (confusingly called the 'lycée'). In year 12 there are three French baccalaureate pathways: economics and social science, literature and science, where the subjects studied vary as do the number of hours devoted to each. The word is that there is pressure from both school and parents to go down the prestigious science route. Because so many students are fluent in English, many do a GSCE in English within the French bacc stream.

The international version of the French baccalaureate follows the French bacc curriculum but has more courses in English and leads to the same official French bacc exams. (Not to be confused with the IB diploma.) Students join this programme in year 10; transfer from this programme into the British section is only available in year 12 and depends on availability of space. No 'bacc-light' – this programme reputedly demands an even heavier time commitment than the regular bacc.

The British section offers the GCSE/A level pathway. Students must be fluent enough in English to manage. Discipline is also an issue – nobody with a rap sheet gets in. Occasionally this route is apparently recommended for students who may not succeed with the French bacc.

Year 10 pupils do a wide range of about 10 courses, including French of course, but also a third language (pupils are spoilt for choice – Italian, Spanish, German, Arabic, Russian, Greek and Latin on offer). French IGCSE exams are compulsory, which pleases parents, though there seem to be some questions about timing with kids sitting exams too early.

In year 11 students generally drop one or two subjects as they get into their A level subjects. Parents rave about the maths, chemistry and physics, but suggest that those interested in the arts tend to look elsewhere (French education is not noted for intellectual autonomy or commitment to creativity, which are fairly fundamental for art). French and PE are compulsory throughout.

Deciding which route to choose – French bacc or British A levels – can be daunting. Those opting for the British tend to be dual nationals, non-French who joined the Lycée because their kids were in a French system and Anglophile French families setting down permanent roots in the UK.

The appeal of the French bacc is its strong global reputation, with its slavish commitment to developing intellectual rigour. But it's hard work, rigid, requires lots of memorisation and absorbing of new information. 'The French system crams knowledge into your brain – and we know the brain is a muscle that can be stretched,' said one French parent.

But some French students aiming for a UK university question the need to do the full-blown bacc when they can focus on more specialised A levels. Plus it's no secret that class sizes in the British section are smaller (about 12 compared to 28 to 30 for the French section) and the teaching style is more conducive to project work, class discussions and debates.

The French bacc classes, 'no wishy-washy child-centred approach,' are more traditional, 'cruelly elite' in a 'sink or swim' learning environment. 'Teachers instruct with minimal empathy. You listen and absorb the learning, which can be a challenge for students with strong personalities inclined to engage in debate and, God forbid, challenge the teacher.' Then there is the matter of 'loyalty to French heritage.' If they move to the British section some families lament the move away from the French educational tradition, even though it may be the right decision educationally. British section kids have more time for extracurricular activities. Places in the British section are competitive; with the Lycée full to capacity, expansion of this programme seems unlikely. But more French students are considering the advantages of the A level university pathway, so there are more applicants than spaces.

Ongoing discussion amongst parents about A level results. The small size of the A level cohort means there are limited courses offered and timetabling clashes can prevent kids from taking the courses they want, leading some frustrated families to change schools after GCSEs. It has also been suggested that some French parents whose children are in the British section have a hard time overcoming the 'pedagogical cultural divide' between the French and British systems; they simply don't understand the flexibility that British teachers have in delivering the curriculum.

The governance and management structure of the Lycée is naturally focused on the French curriculum. For a British deputy head, finding a way to sit within that institutional culture is undoubtedly a challenge. Although the policy of rotating the head makes sense for Lycées worldwide, it probably has an impact on attention to GCSEs, A levels etc in the British section. Each new head has to get up to speed with the whole (and for them, anomalous) British programme, along with all the other challenges of running such a large institution. It's a steep learning curve for even a top educationalist.

French bacc results are excellent, above the French national average. In 2018, 76 per cent of students got 'mention bien' or 'mention très bien' grades.

A levels are by comparison less impressive, with 53 per cent A*/A grades in 2018. French A level results could be more impressive, given the context, although the school points out that students only have three hours a week for French and take the exam a year earlier than other schools. Parents think this differential in results between the French bacc and A level has been taken on board by the school. At I/GCSE, 63 per cent A*-A/9-7 grades in 2018.

Although French nationality, language and heritage is the common denominator here, some kids are not completely fluent in French. It's full immersion, so if a child isn't capable of fully functioning in French by the age of 5, parents say they'll struggle when reading and writing begins. Others move their children out as they get older because parents lack sufficient French language to fully support them – unless they have a French-speaking nanny at home to sustain the French speaking day and supervise homework. English as a second language is taught from primary, with some setting for levels in consideration of the native speakers. In college, students are streamed for English. Other languages are available but no mother tongue instruction other than French and English.

For students with special needs, the educational psychologist and speech and language adviser recommends what sort of specialist might help manage the student's learning (dyslexia is not uncommon) but the school itself does not provide much support in-house. School has disabled access in all but one building but the logistics of the daily timetables and student movements mean that students with mobility challenges would struggle here.

Many teachers (average age early 40s) are civil servants, with professionalism and benefits for which French teachers are renowned. Forty-five per cent have been at the Lycée for more than 10 years.

Games, options, the arts: On Wednesdays, primary classes end early but extra activities like cooking, crafts, IT, sports and games are offered. Human Rights Club, Justice in the Heart and House of Students are student-led activities the British and French section students do together, but French section students have less time to devote to these.

Curriculum-related residential trips abroad include India, Berlin (history), Paris (Comédie Française), Greece (classics), Venice (Italian), New York (art), Moscow (Russian). Compulsory work experience programmes in years 10 or 11 are organised by parents.

A few hundred students do sports, many on Saturdays at the sports facility in Raynes Park, competing against London schools and schools abroad. There's a school sports day. Music is popular, with ensembles, orchestra or choir to choose from.

Background and atmosphere: School was founded to serve London's French population, but also to further France's 'mission civilisatrice' – making French culture and education available to the Brits. During the Second World War it became the home of the Free French and the head sits in the office once occupied by General de Gaulle, so the school's name has meaning. British section was created 60 years ago to offer the French programme in English, but the differences in the French bacc and A levels meant that a marriage was not practical, so the British section sits within the organisation as a 'stand alone'. Over the years the Lycée has spread and now occupies a city block across from the Natural History Museum. If approaching the area during pick-up you'll think you've alighted at the wrong end of the Eurostar.

L

Part of the AEFE (Agency for Teaching of French Education Abroad), the Lycée is one of more than 100 overseas schools directed by the Ministry of Education and is governed by a committee including the French ambassador and other diplomats. Heads are rotated, with posts lasting up to five years. British section is managed by Simon McNaught.

Facilities have been renovated to absorb increasing student numbers – a combination of interconnected new build and Victoriana and using lots of cheerful colours. Buildings open out at the back to play area shared by all ages. Parents say 'it looks confusing, but the kids figure it out in a day or two.' Primary is in a building shared by upper classes on the top floor. There's a large hall for dramatic and musical performances, music and art rooms; PE is outside in the central yard, at local sports facilities or own grounds in Raynes Park. The yard has large canopies with seating areas to provide all-weather cover; no indoor play area.

A large library mushrooms over several floors, separated into college and lycée sections. Classrooms have desks in traditional rows. Computers in the libraries, study rooms and computer lab, but not much evidence of technology inside the classrooms.

Lunch is served in a bright, clean cafeteria. Youngest have their own lunch room; lunch is compulsory unless there are extraordinary dietary needs. Varied three course menu looks just short of Cordon Bleu by usual school standards. Considering that the chef turns out more than 2,500 meals a day, the food looked and smelled very appealing; fish always on offer for those with kosher or halal preferences.

School also boasts an impressive medical centre, staffed with sympathetic nurses and a full-time doctor. Parents are happy with home-school communication, and it's easy to have a quick chat with the primary teacher at dismissal. The formal communication cycle is 'front loaded' with year-group parent events at the beginning of the year; after that it's up to parents to seek out the teachers – but they'll be in touch if there's a problem.

Pastoral care, well-being and discipline: With such an enormous student body, parents' reports are mixed. Some parents insist the kids 'don't get lost, are well looked after,' while others say that once in college 'students are a number and their teachers hardly know them.' The school tries to put students joining the college in classes with three designated friends to ease the culture shock of coping with the sheer scale of the Lycée. This is less a concern for rising Lycée primary students already familiar with the environment.

Playground attendants are a prominent French feature – supervisors keeping an eye on everyone. College students may leave campus provided they have parents' permission (most don't); in the top years most go out for lunch. A nifty school diary is issued to track home-school communication; the back cover has every student's photo, identification and timetable so anyone trying to slip out can be identified and sent back to class.

The children are cheerful and polite; primary teachers remind them about the importance of greeting people respectfully. No lockers – backpacks are stored here and there. No reports of any significant behaviour issues; everyone knows what is expected. If students fall short, they may be given more homework or required to attend school on Saturday. School psychologist offers counselling for students. Secondary school year group leaders have offices in their own sections of the school, with a secretary to manage the 300 or so kids in each level.

Parents warn that drop off and pick up can be stressful. By staggering start and finish times the school manages the flow of traffic pretty well under the circumstances. But parents need to be prepared for the possibly overwhelming feeling of chaos and confusion at the start.

Pupils and parents: The French connection is the common denominator. Vast majority are French nationals with at least one French parent, some dual nationals (eg British/French), a few British. Other nationalities include Canadian, American, Italian, Spanish, Lebanese, Moroccan and Russian. Many parents are in London on short-term assignments – diplomatic, financial services, media, industry. The generously subsidised fees (not available in the British section) widen the socio-economic net, attracting families who may not normally aspire to private education. Parents prefer this more realistic reflection of society to the rarefied atmosphere of economic privilege that they associate with many London independent schools.

Students come from all over – some with long commutes on public transport – but they feel it's worth it. In some cases the main wage-earner commutes to France or travels internationally but the family has chosen to stay in London in order to keep the kids at the Lycée.

The APL (parents' association) organises after-school activities, raises funds, supports the athletics programme and serves as a sounding board for issues of community interest. Some non-French speakers say it's difficult to become involved. Eclectic list of 'vieux garçons et filles' includes Jacqueline Bisset, the late Natasha Richardson, Gyles Brandreth, Lady Olga Maitland, Roland Joffé.

Entrance: Registration process begins around April of the entry year, with decisions sent in early May. Highly oversubscribed, entry is described as 'a nightmare, haphazard and chaotic.' Families normally apply to other schools as well; some start off elsewhere to await an offer. There's a priority list of criteria: children of French diplomats, siblings (in primary only), children from another official French school (locally or abroad), including students following the CNED (the French distance learning programme), then any miscellany of Francophones fortunate enough to get in.

Siblings trump everything else in primary so families bank on getting one tiny first foot in the door, knowing the others are pretty much a shoe-in. One French national tells us she put her children on the waiting list from the earliest time allowed. Her eldest was unsuccessful but a few days after the term began the younger one was offered a place, posing a dilemma for managing two-school runs simultaneously. When she explained this to the school, they somehow magicked up a space for the second child.

Best tip for locals is to transfer from one of the official AEFE Ecole Homologuée nursery schools such as École le Hérisson, L'École des Petits (Fulham) or La Petite École. Feeders for primaire entry include the annexe schools – Wix (Clapham), South Kensington, Ealing and Fulham. Year 7 feeders include École Jacques Prévert, L'École Bilingue, L'École des Petits and L'École de Battersea. For year 10 (British section) and year 11 (French section) it's the College Bilingue in Kentish Town (CFBL). Beware, though – not all schools with emphasis on French language are official AEFE schools, so check the Lycée's website if you're banking on this as your golden ticket. Families do move on so vacancies arise mid-year, but school always refers to the waiting list. According to one successful mother, 'this is the only hope for a local family wanting their child to go to the Lycée' and requires strategic planning of Napoleonic proportions.

No admissions testing and once a child is in, parents have no worries about future entrance exams such as 11+ or CE.

Exit: The Lycée prides itself on its careers department, with advisers specialising in UK, US and French universities. Careers counselling begins in year 11; a major careers forum involves experts and university reps from three continents. Some parents feel more coordination is required to rationalise the Lycée exams and Oxbridge and Russell Group entrance criteria, and more focus needed on writing UCAS personal statements.

Roughly one quarter go to French universities, with 10 per cent of bacc graduates gaining entry into the Grandes Écoles. British destinations include Oxbridge (four places in 2018), UCL, King's College London, Bristol, Warwick and Portsmouth.

Money matters: A 50 per cent AEFE subsidy (except for those in the British section) makes for bargain tuition by London standards. Some welfare grants and bursaries – and APL has been known to rally when a family falls on hard times.

Remarks: This is a huge institution yet parents say children are happy, well taught and love the cultural diversity. The waiting lists are testimony to the school's overall success. With the French and Francophile population growing daily, it seems that the entente cordial is alive and well in this petit coin of London.

The Lyceum School

6 Paul Street, London EC2A 4JH

Ages 3–11 **Pupils** 104

Fees: £16,185 pa

020 7247 1588
www.lyceumschool.co.uk

Headteacher: Since November 2018, Hilary Wyatt, previously head of Eaton Square Kensington (previously Hyde Park School), also owned by Dukes Education.

Entrance: There is no formal testing but the usual practice would be for the head to meet the child and their family to talk through everybody's hopes and ideas.

Exit: A very small year 6 dispersed to Alleyn's, Bromley High, Dame Alice Owen, North Bridge House, The Charter School and UCS in 2018. The school explicitly sets itself to teach to 11+ entry, although they will try to support and guide families who are looking to have their children prepared for 7+ and 10+. There are clear expectations that all pupils, bar the very youngest, will have a little homework, but care is taken to ensure that it leads on from what has being gone that day in school, and is never burdensome.

Remarks: The school began life in 1997. It communicates an unpretentious cheerfulness which is both attractive and impressive, and a strong sensitivity to performing and visual arts. Most of the teaching happens in the basement, which doesn't sound great – and, true, there's not much natural light. But the classrooms tumble over with happy children – a lot of quite concentration was apparent, and the teachers, many of whom have been appointed since the present head arrived, seemed calmly and gently immersed in the children and in what they were doing.

The doors open at 8am each weekday, and parents are welcome to be around until shortly before 9am – coming to assemblies, meeting teachers and so forth. Then it's school time and parents go off (many work in the City, of course, which makes dropping off and collection of children a great deal easier). There is no canteen, but packed lunches are outsourced to a local supplier ('more expense,' said one parent, otherwise a big admirer of the school). Children may provide their own packed lunch. School is finished by 4pm but there are after-school clubs until 5pm, generally managed by the teaching assistants. For some children, whose parents work late, there is a homework clubs until 5.45pm. It's a long day for a young child, but staff pace everything with a view to offering reassurance and, when the moment suggests itself, relaxation.

L

There's a lively and happy nursery department, with some pupils attending part time and some doing the full five days. 'We did a trial period,' said one parent, 'but very soon there was no doubt in anyone's mind. We'd picked a winner.' There's plenty of learning even here, but evidently gently calibrated to allow the children's days to be full of interest and excitement. By reception, there is more time and focus being given to the rudiments of reading and writing and counting, and the journey obviously picks up pace between years 1 and 6.

One singularity of The Lyceum is the emphasis it places on a topic approach – that is, picking up on a subject or theme which will allow the children to experience it through a host of media and disciplines. 'For me,' said a parent who has had two children go through the school, 'this way of learning has been decisive. It allows the children to get immersed and excited in a way which feels very natural and gives them all a reference point. It really impacts on their experience of school and of each other and spills over into home.' The aim is to stimulate and channel artistic and creative energies, and use these to help reinforce their excellence in traditional subject areas. The library is generously provisioned and clearly a favourite spot for many.

Pupils with special needs are able to draw off a specialist teacher who comes in several days each week. In addition to the qualified teachers, there is also a battery of teaching assistants, and full-time support staff in the nursery and reception years. The most recent two deputies have gone on to their own headships.

Theatre and music are at the heart of each pupil's experience. All children learn the recorder and most at least one or two instruments – and, of course, they sing. There is a full-time music teacher and a plethora of instrumental teachers. There's at least one big production each term and a big band, an orchestra and a chamber choir – impressive in a school of around 100 pupils, all of whom leave by the age of 11.

They are particularly proud of their summer term concert – the so-called 'summer pudding'. There are endless other concerts and performances besides: a Christmas concert at the Wesley Chapel, a chamber choir concert at St Giles. That's in addition to termly performances for most year groups, often tied in with the particular topics they've been studying during the term. Pictures adorn the walls – very expressive of the wonder of young children. All teachers share in the art, of course, but there is also an art leader to lend an overall coherence.

Both before and after school, clubs flourish: chess, dance of all kinds, French, Spanish, Latin, Chinese – the list goes on and on. There are also visiting speakers and the children seem completely unfazed by visitors and happy to engage with them. Twice a year every pupil from year 3 and year 4 goes away on week-long residentials, with years 5 and 6 going away three times a year. These are designed to extend academic learning (often that which features within pupils' topics), and also offer cultural, social and artistic enrichment. Most are in the UK, but recent year 6 destinations have included Paris, Amsterdam and Rome.

There's no escaping the fact that the school building is less than beautiful and there is no outdoor space. 'I'd worried about that,' admitted one parent, 'but I've come to realise that the children are out of doors and exercising a good deal.' One afternoon is spent each week at the Royal Artillery Ground, and they have started to play fixtures with other schools, including netball matches (for boys and girls). Football training is now under way at Finsbury Park, and they swim at the Golden Lane pool on Friday afternoons. One hour each afternoon, weather permitting, is spent on play in Bunhill Park. The school has fashioned an indoor playground for wet weather days. Links have opened up with local community groups – the chamber choir recently went along to sing to a group of local elderly people, and there's much energetic fundraising for good causes, also for elderly people and also for Great Ormond Street Hospital.

The ethos of the school is avowedly traditional, but mainly in the sense of celebrating ageless good manners – being mindful of others and of their feelings. There's no hint of stuffiness and, while it styles itself Christian, it embraces children of all faiths and of none. 'I find the children unusually empathic,' one mother told us. 'They're extraordinarily supportive of each other. Not my experience in other schools!'

Children wear a simple but appealing uniform – navy duffel coats are a nicely archaic touch, as are the girls' hats (felt in winter and a very smart boater in summer). They look confident and upbeat as they go about their days. At no point did we glean anyone taking on airs and graces – a great tribute to the school and its families.

As it is located in the middle of a transport hub, most pupils come to school each day by tube with their parents. Enough use a scooter for the school to create a scooter park in the indoor playground. Parents are made very welcome between 8am and 9am and many of them use that time to ensure they are in close contact with form teachers, who are the first port of call. There are also written reports twice a year and a two week slot at the end of each term during which parents can book to meet teachers for a full half hour. No parent's evenings as such.

A cosmopolitan feel – many Europeans and Asians – as befits somewhere in the financial heartland of London. Parents are industrious, unpretentious and seem very grounded. They want their children to have a happy and effective start to their schooling. With just over 100 pupils, the Lyceum has one form per year and, for the moment, seems happy to keep it that way. Fees are mid-range ('but the same as other schools with better facilities,' said one parent), and an effort is made to keep down extras. Nursery vouchers are also accepted.

This is a happy school, calmly and competently working on bringing out the very best in their youngsters, and laudably unprecious. The biggest potential drawback is the building, but it's had the effect of making everyone within the school work harder to ensure children enjoy all the benefits of outdoor space. 'This is real education,' said one parent. 'The children are happy and mindful of one another. It's not greedy, it's not pushy, and people care.' The smooth transition they make to next-stage schooling seems to bear all that out, and is a huge recommendation.

Moving to a new building in Worship Street in September 2019.

The Mall School

185 Hampton Road, Twickenham TW2 5NQ

Ages 4–13 (4–11 from 2020) **Pupils** 280

Fees: £12,240 – £13,767 pa

020 8977 2523
www.themallschool.org.uk

Headmaster: Since 2011, David Price BSc MA PGCE (50s), married with two children in their late teens. Brought up and educated in the Black Country, his first introduction to the western edge of London was Kingston University for his MA. After a spell as head of English at Latymer Prep he went down under to teach at Melbourne Grammar School. He says he felt a bit homesick there, so he returned to his 'pom' roots, moving on to be head of juniors and director of studies at The Mall, before becoming top dog.

Calm and understated, no fireworks, 'a mediator and negotiator', he inspires confidence that he knows exactly what the school is about and his role in its performance. Equally, the parents trust him to run a tight but friendly ship which will land their sons safely in their chosen academic port. Known to be behind his desk if needed, he also gets about a lot, often at the school gates talking to parents, invoking the comment that he uses these opportunities as 'a sounding board for new ideas'.

Entrance: The largest feeder for the first come, first served pre-prep is Jack and Jill Nursery, usefully sited on the green next door, but children also arrive from a variety of other nurseries or straight from the home version. Two forms move from pre-prep up to the main school but will now increase to three from year 3 onwards creating additional places at the existing entry point of 7+ and an occasional place at 8+. At these stages, potential pupils come to an assessment in maths and English during a day in the school where both sides have the chance to eye each other up.

Boys from a wide variety of backgrounds, often with two working parents, come here from all over west London, although one parent counted its proximity to their house as a huge plus. Despite tending to move on to similar schools, they can end up in very different lives, for instance Zac Goldsmith with his mayoral ambitions or the actor, Alex Pettyfer, who reverted to his schooldays by playing Tom Brown in a TV adaptation.

Exit: Until 2020, boys will be leaving at 11+ and 13+ so, during this period, a small percentage will still move on to leading boarding schools such as Eton or Harrow but the vast majority (increasingly more at 11+) head to local independent day schools, top of the list being Hampton followed by King's

College Wimbledon, Reed's, St George's Weybridge and Radnor House. Several boys to St Paul's each year and the occasional one to Westminster.

Remarks: The pre-prep, five minutes down the road from the prep school, has an exceptional, brand-new playground complete with a huge pirate ship and interactive games on the walls, imagination and energy equally well catered for. We badly wanted to play and boys have been known to cry on having to leave. It's small, and not so small, boy heaven. Incredibly tidy; even the smart red scooters have their own designated parking spaces inside neat white lines and a nice man was sweeping up the leaves that had dared to deface it.

Inside, the newly refurbished classrooms are equally colourful with interactive whiteboards, matching, bright plastic chairs and lots of lesson related photographs and images on the walls. We particularly liked the washing line strung with pages of handwriting on a pirate theme. 'He had a brown hat .... and no legs' was our favourite description of Captain Hook.

Juliet Tovey oversees it with a practised eye, having been involved in education all her career, teaching in a variety of state and private schools as well as working as a local authority maths consultant. Not much chance that she'll get caught on the hop as she runs 20 kms a week.

The two classes in reception and year 1 (maximum 18 per class) are each taught by a teacher and an assistant, the mornings being mainly for maths and English, the former prominently using the domino look-alike Numicon bricks. A reward system in each class allows all boys a daily start on the rainbow, with progress either to sunny uplands or downwards to a very unthreatening cloud. Apparently, they rarely stay in the rainy zone for long and can redeem themselves right up to the final bell.

Everyone has a hot lunch in the newly decorated basement where once a week there is a 'top table' for the four boys who have managed to avoid spag bol down their fronts and the temptation to talk with their mouths full. This innovation has worked extremely well and JT says it really does encourage good behaviour. Once the boys are fed, the afternoon is taken up with music and PE lessons and learning to swim in the pool at the main school.

One parent told us that JT had been 'fantastic over the transition from pre-prep to the big school' and the boys feel at home straight away because they are used to the feel of it, from coming swimming, on visits in year 1 and to Friday assemblies where they bravely march up to receive their commendations in front of the whole school, a sure sign of a confident small person.

The main school is nearing its 150th anniversary but has been on this slightly squeezed site since 1922, the only major interruption a fire in 1960 that wiped out all the buildings except the stable block. Possibly not a disaster, because they were able to rebuild and now have managed to cram in a 130 seater theatre, music rooms, an art studio, a DT workshop and science labs. Outside space is strictly limited but there are playgrounds, an outdoor classroom with ponds and a veggie patch, which had so impressed one leaver that he announced in the school magazine that he 'would like to become a naturalist'. There is also an indoor swimming pool, excellent for little ones as it only has a fraction of the normal chlorine levels and the temperature is more like a warm bath than an arctic lake.

The high academic standards are definitely a prime reason why parents enrol their children here: 'we wouldn't have put our boys in the school if we didn't think they could keep up with the pace'. Classes are an average of 17 (no more than 20) and will continue at this size after the top two years have been phased out. Form teachers and tutors (from year 4), about a third of whom have taught here for more than 10 years, closely monitor progress. Enthusiastic praise for the teaching – 'the academics are extraordinary' – is handed out all round, but French taught in French by Frenchwomen, 'part of the DNA of the school,' says DP, probably scores highest, swiftly followed by every other subject on the curriculum. A new science teacher has raised standards in her subject to the level that year 5 and 6 gained third place in the National Inter-School Science Quiz championship. IT which, admitted DP, had been 'a little on the back foot', has been sharpened up with speedier Wifi, more computers and an IT whizz permanently on hand to crack any problems.

The concentration in the classrooms is palpable, whether it be year 8s pouring over history textbooks or year 3s filing the edges off acrylic heart keyrings. That 'students step up to the challenge', as one parent stated, is clear when you look at the number of scholarships, including 21 to Hampton and nine to St Paul's over the last six years.

Tackled on the subject of SEND provision, JT talks about the benefit of enrolling boys at reception because they can start evaluation from day one and identify any potential problems before they move up. Once in the main school, there is regular appraisal and a supported English class in years 4 to 6, taught by the SENCo; at the moment about 12 per cent of all pupils need additional support including a tiny number of EAL boys.

The new head of sport has hit the spot with both students and parents as he has brought in 'a certain level of organisation' which both felt was somewhat lacking, in particular when it came to uniforms and matches. Swimming is the big thing here, they are borough champs and amongst the top five junior schools in the country. Field sports, rugby, football and cricket are played in Bushy Park, luckily only a stone's throw away, and although this is not known as a sporty school there is a concerted effort to find an opportunity for every boy to represent the school in some form of team.

Parents talk happily – 'big, big plus' – of the extracurricular activities that take place after school and allow them to do a late pick-up (until 6pm), with one mother informing us that she had been told off by her son for arriving early. Kiddy Cook aims at catching future masterchefs whilst tennis and chess clubs are full to bursting right up the school. Although the judo master is a 'tough guy', he obviously holds no fear for the boys as his judo clubs are hugely popular.

Arty boys are successfully encouraged with three year 8 boys winning scholarships to senior schools recently. Almost three-quarters of the boys play a musical instrument and they hold a Summer Prom and inter-house music competitions as well as training junior and senior choirs. Budding thespians are well catered for in the new theatre and it was smiley faces all round when we asked boys about their acting experiences at school.

Pastorally, the overall consensus is that the 'children are happy, due to the teachers and staff, who are patient and untiring' and have a motherly approach to new boys, who are given an older buddy to run to, which goes down well with parents. The proof of the pudding came from three separate parents remarking that one of the main reasons that they had chosen the school was because they wanted their sons to turn out like the boys who had shown them round. Most parents felt the rewards system employed (points on a credit card) was an incentive to behave as well as succeed but there was a comment that the criteria on awards were not explained clearly enough. We tackled DP over this and, encouragingly, he said that he would address the subject at the coffee mornings he holds with parents.

The resolution that DP and the governors have made to close the top two years will bring about a sea change and we listened carefully to parental reaction. The dust has settled and the general consensus appears to be that the move will prove to have been an intelligent, forward thinking response to the increase in entries at 11+ by local senior schools. However, the way that it was handled led someone to say that 'it was a shock we could have done without'. In our opinion, this considered decision to alter the shape of the school will not affect either its ethos or its efficiency.

Apart from the all singing and dancing pre-prep playground this is an unflashy, sensible, feet on the ground school. They concentrate on what they do best, giving boys a superior academic grounding in a safe environment and preparing them to succeed in senior schools.

Mander Portman Woodward (MPW)

90–92 Queen's Gate, London SW7 5AB

Ages 14–19 Pupils 651 Sixth form 598

Fees: £28,578 – £30,678 pa

020 7835 1355
www.mpw.ac.uk

Principal: Since 2016, John Southworth, previously a vice principal. Engineering degree from Leicester and MSc in defence technology from the Cranfield Institute of Technology. Has been a major in the army, director of co-curriculum at The Perse, principal of Lansdowne College and vice principal of MPW since 2014.

M

His army background (20 years) is evident in his no-nonsense, plain-speaking manner – and his cutting to the chase is valued by parents, most of whom don't want the hard sell but to know whether he'll take their child and how they're doing once there. 'You always know exactly where you're at with him and he never lies, unlike at the well-known public school my daughter went to, where they always said she was amazing at everything when she clearly wasn't,' said one. Others praise him for his 'rapport with young people' and his 'academic intellect, but without being conceited, pompous or arrogant in any way.' Doesn't teach ('no chance, I'd be doing students a disservice as I have so much on') but students confirmed his claim that he's both visible and approachable. Doesn't claim to know every student, although don't let on to the students (who describe him as 'friendly' and 'funny') as they think he does – 'he often stops us by name and remembers our subjects and interests,' said one.

Was preparing to move from Cambridge to Hove with his wife Clare and their black lab, Poppy, when we visited. They have two grown-up sons, one a paramedic, the other at university. Loves walking and is a keen sea fisherman and golfer 'to a pretty reasonably standard.' Fine wine also a passion.

Academic matters: Once well-known for being a 'crammer,' helping students with short-term goals such as exam retakes or Oxbridge entrance, today MPW cringes at the word – although students told us 'there's still some of that, with the one-year A level and GCSE courses and short retake courses.' But there's no doubt it's changed and MPW is now also a thriving sixth form college, with 65-70 per cent taking two-year A level courses (typically three subjects); and recently, there has also been an increase in students taking two-year GCSE courses (typically eight topics maximum) from year 10.

What marks it out is the range and flexibility of options on offer, with 27 GCSE subjects and 45 A levels, in any combination (and some do one or two GCSEs alongside starting their A levels). At GCSE, there's psychology, economics and business along with all the more usual suspects, while at A level offerings include nine modern languages, statistics, ancient Greek, Latin, geology and more art options than you can shake a stick at. A long day (9am-5pm for GCSEs; 6pm for A levels – although students can leave once lessons are over) and 36 classrooms allow a timetable that suits almost all. 'It's incredibly tailored – I honestly don't know how they do it,' a parent told us. Parents say the stand-alone one-year A level programme is great for aspiring medics moving from arts to science or those with weak results wanting to try their hand at something new; and the one-year GCSE is especially appreciated by those recovering from ill health or recently arrived in the UK. Results overall are strong (for A level, 35 per cent A*-A, 66 A*-B in 2018; for GCSE, 51 per cent A*-A/7-9), particularly in light of the wide-ranging intake, and a hefty dollop of star performers deliver top grades. Value added a key strength.

Without doubt, an exam-oriented place, with a persistent spotlight on the syllabus and exam technique honed by regular timed tests and ample supplies of homework – 'plus a very comprehensive coursebook for every course that's followed to the T,' say students – but it's clearly far more than an exam factory. 'We have some interesting debates around history since my daughter started here – instead of the usual teenage grunting, she shows real care for her subjects,' one parent told us. All pupils get close attention in classes never larger than nine and teaching staff – nearly all of whom have masters degrees and are public examiners and many of whom have published text books – are well-qualified. 'You're never embarrassed to ask a question that might seem obvious and teachers are always willing to give up an extra half-hour with a surgery or one-to-one if you haven't understood something,' one student told us. Walking around the college, there's more a feeling of tutorials than traditional school classes.

EPQ available for all two-year A level students. University of London International Foundation Programme, developed and assessed by LSE for overseas applicants looking to UK universities without the requisite qualifications, also on offer. And because 'accounting A level hasn't been popular' MPW is also trialling the Association of Accounting Technicians (AAT) level 3 advanced diploma in accounting as a more practical alternative – successful graduates achieve professional status as AAT bookkeepers.

Between 20-25 per cent of students have some form of special educational need, mostly dyslexia or dyspraxia and a few on the autistic spectrum, albeit at the milder end – 'the main thing is they can access the curriculum,' says head; if college can't help, they won't beat around the bush. There's still plenty of opportunity to take resits and for students that have planned a gap year but suddenly find themselves without the grades they'd hoped for, 'there is room for negotiation at interview, so they can still do maybe a ski season or couple of months travel in Thailand. But we provide them with the risks involved and expect them to catch up whatever they miss.'

Games, options, the arts: Stand-out art, with university-feel studios for ceramics, textiles, graphic design and photography. A levels available in all those subjects, plus general art. 'We love our art here,' enthuses head, whose modern office displays some of the students' prized work that has appeared in the Saatchi Gallery (other impressive artwork to be found throughout the rest of the college). On the longer-term wish list, he says, is to open a separate nearby art school. Music taught as GCSE and A level, but not enough space for orchestras or ensembles. 'You have to take the attitude of, "that's fine, we'll do our music out of school",' said one parent. Drama is available at GSCE and theatre studies at A level, with a nearby drama studio (above a pub) used regularly.

Sport compulsory on Wednesday afternoons for GCSE students, optional thereafter with Wednesday afternoon alternatives for A level students including debating, drama (leading to an annual Christmas performance), beginners' guitar, Mandarin, Spanish and Italian for travel, college magazine, widely attended lecture series, among others. Or you can just opt out and take the time off, which was the preferred option for most of the students we met. 'It's another reason students like MPW – many don't want to be stuck on a sports field in the middle of winter catching a ball or holding a stick,' says head.

For those that do sport, a fleet of coaches delivers students to a range of venues ('when it's not cancelled,' grumbled one parent). Well-qualified coaching staff in rugby, football and tennis and the head personally runs the golf lessons. Cricket nets at Lords used regularly. Rugby popular and successful, with matches against leading independents like Dulwich College and Epsom. Football, too, has an enthusiastic following. Those allergic to team sports can enjoy tennis, dance and yoga, and all students have free access to a local gym. But, say parents, quality of sport offering 'still doesn't come close to what's offered in schools.' Extracurricular on the up, with all the usual add-ons – student council, Duke of Edinburgh (bronze taken by all year 10s) and Bank of England Interest Rate Challenge. Students make full use of local museums and theatres with regular trips – 'and some of us just go there to study,' said one student. Tiny basement canteen provides food, although it looked pretty uninspiring to us – no wonder local eateries are a big draw.

Background and atmosphere: Founded in 1973 by three Cambridge graduates who hoped to apply the best bits of the Cambridge tutorial system to a school, providing more choice and less tradition. Now part of the MPW group, with branches in Cambridge and Birmingham, the London HQ is housed in a series of three adjoining high-ceilinged, sympathetically-decorated, stucco-fronted Victorian buildings in South Kensington. Be prepared to keep fit – they're all four storeys high (five including basements). Each one is identical, with labs, for instance, on the same floor of each, which, as one student told us, 'makes it easier to navigate, but going to the wrong one will cost you a lot of steps so believe me, you only make that mistake once.'

No scruffy corners anywhere, computers everywhere (some folding into desks) and excellent, light and airy facilities for the myriad of subjects on offer, including fully-equipped media suites, computing and film rooms, art studios galore, new drama studio, and six science labs. Smart reception areas, deep-pile red carpets throughout and whopping £10,000 spent on fresh flowers annually – 'we want it to feel special.' It couldn't, in other words, feel less like a traditional inner city – or any, for that matter – school, though we couldn't help notice the squeeze as students move around between lessons. It doesn't seem to bother them, though – 'more space would be amazing, but the trade off is being located where we are,' shrugged one.

Co-ed throughout, the vibe is grown-up, academically disciplined, but socially relaxed – no uniform and teachers are called by their first names. 'I like to think of it as a conduit between school and university,' says head. Students have a strong sense of community, with – they say – 'no cliques or bullying; it's just not like that.'

Pastoral care, well-being and discipline: Every parent we spoke to, without exception, praised the director of studies system. Each student has one, who acts as the pivot of their personal and academic life. They get to know the student's strengths and weaknesses, help them manage the workload and deal with other aspects of daily life, as well as being the main point of contact for parents (who, by the way, don't get parents' evenings but do get half-termly reports). 'My son worships the ground his director of studies walks on – she gets what drives him and works with that in a non-patronising way.' 'My daughter's director of studies phones or emails me if she wasn't herself in class to ask if everything is ok – that's outstanding service.' And so on. 'If students feel happy and safe, everything else slots into place,' says head. Counsellor also available.

A level students are only required to attend college for actual lessons; ditto with GCSE students, but only with their parents' permission – otherwise, they are supervised between classes and given timetabled library sessions. Behavioural management 'not really an issue,' says head, as boundaries and rules are clear – you have to attend, to behave and to be on time; failure in any one area leads to being 'on report' and 'they don't like that,' says head. Parents very much kept in the loop – 'you never get any surprises as they let you know the moment there are any problems,' said one. A couple of temporary expulsions a year, usually due to lack of work ethic which can rub off on others; and one permanent in the year we visited. Zero tolerance for drugs, with regular random drug testing. Freshers' week type activities help integrate newcomers.

Pupils and parents: We found students mature, sincere, comfortable in their own skin and supportive of each other – 'that's what makes them zing,' says head. At A level, incomers are those looking for greater freedom and informality, or for A level combinations or subjects not offered at their current school. Significant number of refugees from leading independent schools, day and boarding, plus the usual international clientele (which is capped at 30 per cent, but nearer 25 per cent when we visited – mostly Chinese and Russian, but from 60 countries in total). One parent grumbled, 'My child ended up in a class with only Chinese kids, and a Chinese teacher, and because their learning style is different it was geared towards them,' but most happy with the diversity. Families are, in the main, wealthy (you have to be to afford the fees) – everything from Russian oligarchs and celebs down to those whose grandparents and aunts cough up.

M

Entrance: Non-selective, though applicants must complete a maths and English assessment and most have good middling GCSE grades (three 7s, three 6s, a couple of 4-5s). 'But we don't lay down any particular entry requirement other than needing a positive academic and behavioural reference from their previous school.' If the student isn't keen to go to MPW, doesn't have commitment to their subjects and doesn't understand that 'the price of freedom is behaving like an adult,' forget it. Nor will they consider any student who has been involved in bullying or drugs. All students are interviewed by the head or senior member of staff.

Most GCSE students stay on for A level, even if they arrive with other plans – 'it's not unusual to have 50 per cent predicted to leave and it only winds up being 25 per cent,' says head. 'Once you get hooked into the MPW way, no other school seems very appealing,' said one student. Some join in the second year of A levels after a hiccup elsewhere.

Exit: Around a third leaves after GCSEs. Some 95 per cent of A level leavers to university, most to leading universities (particularly in London – Imperial, Kings, UCL, and LSE all popular). Four to Oxbridge and 12 medics in 2018. About 30 per cent annually to professional degrees (medicine, dentistry, veterinary medicine, science and law) and high numbers, too, to leading art colleges. Business finance also a popular course. Specialist preparation for Oxbridge, medics, lawyers, etc; experts also available for uni preparation in America and Europe.

Money matters: 'It's expensive, really expensive,' said one parent; others concur. But all consider MPW good value for money, albeit with some moans and groans about added extras

– 'I've been told we need extra tuition in one subject and I think they should provide it rather than me being expected to pay for top-ups,' said one parent. Around 20 scholarships a year, with 'very rigorous exams – the top mark we've ever had is 67 per cent.' Plus a 100 per cent scholarship a year for the best at English literature. For those planning 'worthwhile' travel in a gap years or holiday, there are also travel scholarships worth up to a £1,000. No bursaries 'because if you can't afford the fees, then a bursary may not be enough.'

Remarks: For those that don't suit (or who want a change from) more traditional schooling, this more liberal and very snazzy urban college is both positive and professionally run, with strong teaching, small class sizes, huge flexibility and outstanding pastoral care.

Maple Walk School

62a Crownhill Road, London NW10 4EB

Ages 4–11 **Pupils** 195

Fees: £10,047 pa

020 8963 3890
www.maplewalkschool.co.uk

Headmistress: Since 2012, Sarah Gillam, BEd from Homerton College, Cambridge. Originally Dorset born, but started her career at Lyndhurst House Prep school in Hampstead. She left education for a while to 'gain some experience in the professional world' but came back to education as she missed teaching and the children. Her 30 year career includes two middle school headships and one head of junior science. Prior to her role as head of Maple Walk, Ms Gillam worked for six years at the now defunct White House Prep school in Wokingham (although during her tenure, it was an outstanding prep school, she says). She was attracted to the post of head at Maple Walk 'because of its wonderful history and story' and because she felt it was a school with great potential.

Warm and likeable (she was very concerned that we should have nice biscuits with our coffee), slightly distracted but perhaps it was nerves, so keen was she to impress. However, the parents we spoke to praised her ambition for turning 'a small villagey school' into a 'proper prep school'. One parent told us: 'Ms Gillam takes very seriously the reality of living in London and has worked hard to make sure the pupils are well placed and prepared to take exams for secondary school. She has done this with a more rigorous curriculum.'

Ms Gillam herself says that she has been very keen to work on the process of transforming this school – already an amazing galleon – into a tighter ship with more rigorous applications and monitoring of crew. She has worked at strengthening the senior leadership team and now has an excellent range of advisors. Also an ISI team inspector, Ms Gillam says this can be a great resource for the school as she gets so many ideas from other schools as well as being able to confer with specialists 'who are at the top of their game.' She still teaches RE from year 3 upwards for one lesson a week.

Described as a very visible head who is always wandering around the school, is very approachable, open to ideas and someone who 'patently cares about her job.' She has an open door policy and as one parent said, 'is probably quite frustrated that more people don't walk through it more often.' Ms Gillam has three grown up daughters, one of whom is also training to be a teacher: 'If you have this as a vocation, it is something I would always encourage.' Any free time she has, she enjoys cooking, travelling and spending time with her family.

Entrance: Some 200 applicants for 20 places per form. Siblings get preference, then in order of registration – waiting lists for several years ahead. The advice given is 'get them on the list as soon as possible.' For spaces higher up the school, the head meets the parents and the child has a trial day in the relevant class, 'to check that they will fit in socially and academically'.

Exit: To a wide variety of schools, including Aldenham, City of London, Emanuel, Queen's College, John Lyon, North Bridge House, Wetherby Prep and St James Senior Girls in the private sector, and St Marylebone, Hampstead School and Twyford Cof E School in the state sector. A fair percentage generally awarded art scholarships at Holland Park School.

Remarks: The New Model School Company (NMS) was set up by Civitas (but is now an independent entity) when research identified a gap in the market for a low-cost chain of not-for-profit independent primary schools. Maple Walk was the first NMS school, starting in a rented room in a sports centre off Ladbroke Grove in 2004 with one teacher, two pupils and school materials stored in a trunk. A year later the fledgling school of a dozen pupils moved to the upper floor of a church hall off Kensal Road. In 2009 the school – by now with classes up to year 4 – moved to its own purpose-built premises in Harlesden, which have impeccable ecological credentials: a sedum roof, solar panels, a ground source heat pump, plus a no-car travel plan.

Although the school has had a reputation for being a no frills, low-fee-paying school and a decent alternative for the independent sector, parents we spoke to felt that it was now time to redress this reputation because, as one parent told us, 'it punches above its weight.' Another parent said: 'They do far more than you would expect from a school of this size and have really upped their game.' The general consensus seems to be that it delivers a great education and is a school which pushes each individual to strive. Indeed it made a recent Telegraph's top Ten Value Prep Schools: 'Excellent value for money', one parent said.

The education is traditional, with reading taught by phonics, French taught from reception, history taught chronologically and Latin taught in year 6. Maths is set from as early as year 1, but there is movement between sets. The school says: 'We recognise that within each class there are pupils of widely differing mathematical aptitudes and we aim to provide suitable learning opportunities for each of them.' The school follows the increasingly popular Singapore maths scheme, although this is 'often supplemented by other resources.' English is not set, but there is differentiation within the classroom for the more able and also for those who need more assistance. One parent told us: 'One of the perks of a school of this size is the small classes and that each class has a teacher and teaching assistant, so you know your child will get a lot of individual attention.'

The teaching was praised by parents and pupils alike: 'They have really nice teachers who know the children well.' 'Teachers are absolutely on it.' The head's after-school secondary transfer club introduces exam techniques to older children, and the year 6 class teacher 'is very experienced at secondary transfers'. 'They do their absolute best to make sure they are well prepared,' said a parent. Certainly parents are happy. 'They seem to be getting a very good grounding,' said one.

The school can cope with mild SEN – 'we don't assess children coming into reception, but we do ask parents to be honest and transparent and we may talk to their nursery if we have any concerns'. One-to-one literacy and numeracy assistance at extra cost; some children get speech and language support outside school.

Sport has very much been an area of focus for the school, with a 'competitive but inclusive policy.' Whilst onsite sport facilities are pretty basic, the school has the use of nearby Roundwood Park for tag rugby, hockey, football and netball etc. For the particularly keen, an early morning (7.30am) cross-country run is offered to both pupils and their parents. We were told of an inspirational PE teacher who encourages even the most uninterested of children to give competitive sports a try, even at the cost of sacrificing a win for the school. One parent said: 'My son is not great at cricket, but this teacher put together a team of all the least talented cricket players in the school to encourage them to have a go at a competitive game against another school. They loved it.'

An emphasis on children becoming confident public performers: the annual Craigmyle poetry competition (named for the charitable trust that paid for the new site and building works) involves everyone from reception upwards reciting a poem by heart, and there are public speaking competitions, music concerts and drama performances. 'The children are very confident,' said a parent. 'They have nice manners, they can talk to adults, they look you in the eye.'

This is a busy, busy school. Lots going on to excite and motivate – indeed their most recent Independent Schools Inspectorate report praises the range of extracurricular activities. This includes photography, art portfolio club, Spanish, chess, dance, puzzle club, drama and football.

The curriculum is further enriched by a wide range of educational visits for all year groups, whether it's mud-larking on the Thames or visiting the Imperial War Museum. There is the year 5 residential trip, which has included a bushcraft trip where students are taught basic survival skills, and the annual year 6 week-long residential camp – which could be staying at a château in France or a PGL adventure course on the Isle of Wight. One pupil told us: 'I really like the variety of things on offer here. There's lots of great stuff to do, but it's also quite academic.'

The school copes well with its limited premises. 'Of course that would be the one thing I'd change about the school if I could, but without physically moving the school, there's not much you can do', said one parent. But the outdoor space still manages to squeeze in playgrounds for infants and for juniors – with a climbing frame, football/netball court with climbing wall (also funded by the PTA, Friends of Maple Walk). There are interesting-looking outdoor 'pods' for music classes with peripatetic teachers. The gardening club grows vegetables in tiered beds and a butterfly/bee-friendly area is in concept. The children learn to swim at a local pool and try out a different sport each half term.

The active PTA has raised funds from auctions, casino nights and summer fairs to name but a few, for part-time specialist dance and sports teachers, and parents have donated computers, including a suite of Netbooks that travel round different classrooms. The school has a broadly Christian ethos, with some religious assemblies and nativity plays, but all faiths are welcome and Jewish and Muslim parents come in to talk about their religions.

Despite the low fees, it is still very much a white, middle class demographic – albeit mostly journalists, artists and musicians rather than bankers and lawyers. A much larger percentage of families now live locally (previously the majority from Queens Park and Willesden Green) and the fact that it is so predominantly white and middle class probably represents how the area has changed. But as the school says, 'it doesn't stop us hoping and trying to attract a more diverse demographic.'

Parents cite the 'village school' atmosphere as one of their main reasons for choosing Maple Walk. 'There's a nice, cosy, community feel,' said one. 'I liked the fact that it is small, pioneering and affordable,' said another. 'It's a really vibrant, eclectic community.' Parents emphasise how happy their children are – 'mine will look back and feel they've been part of something really special and exciting'.

Marymount International School

George Road, Kingston, Surrey KT2 7PE

Ages 11–18 **Pupils** 255 **Sixth form** 90 **Boarders** 85 full, 14 weekly
RC

Fees: Day £23,775; Boarding £38,705 – £40,425 pa

020 8949 0571
www.marymountlondon.com

Headmistress: Since 2017, Meg Frazier, previously head of upper school at the Stone Ridge School of the Sacred Heart for girls, Washington DC (one of 147 Sacred Heart schools in 30 countries). History degree from Dartmouth College, has over 25 years of teaching and admin experience in the Washington area in the Jesuit and Sacred Heart networks of US and international schools, plus worked with international boarders at Georgetown Prep in Maryland. Describes herself as an avid gardener and reader, a rusty golfer and a life-long sailor who enjoys cooking and travel. She and her husband have three children, one daughter studying in London and two sons, both seniors in US colleges.

M

Academic matters: Marymount is a Catholic secondary girls school offering the IB middle years programme (MYP) and IB to an international community. The first (1979) girls' school in the UK to take up the IB in Britain, Marymount's grade 6-10 curriculum is built on solid institutional foundations. In 2018 pupils scored an average of 36 points, with 27 per cent earning 40+ and 42 per cent awarded bilingual diplomas.

No resting on laurels; they've been reviewing the MYP to align it with IGCSE content, ensuring all topics are covered in the MYP context by end of grade 9. School wants parents to be assured of MYP rigour: the priority is to be learning-driven, not taught to the test. Range of IB subjects and results is excellent. Lots of sciences, 'and we do lots of field trips', say the girls. The school is offering a relatively new IB course, environmental systems and societies, which satisfies either the IB science or IB humanities requirement. 'My sister likes geography and science so it's perfect for her.' Marymount's MYP covers the broad spectrum of disciplines, with the interesting addition of philosophy to introduce the girls to 'the language of philosophy' before they embark on theory of knowledge at diploma level. Fab Lab (fabrication laboratory) full of computer controlled tools that can make 'almost anything' is used to teach computer programming, coding, robotics and design, and aiming to stimulating creativity across the arts and sciences. As would be expected, religious education is also a key part of the MYP.

School prides itself on the wide range of languages offered. Extra mother tongue support in German and French in grades 6-8 dependent on enrolment. Parents warn that languages are sometimes subject to demand and in a small school it's not always possible to satisfy all requests for second language. It seems that there are mixed messages here and prospective parents are advised to discuss this at the early stages to clarify.

The school does its best to support girls in working out alternative options – as one pupil explained, 'a friend who speaks Thai is taking IB Thai mother tongue; she's self-taught with the help of a tutor'.

The school is wireless throughout; iPads now in grades 6-9 and move up the grades as pupils progress; girls were excited to show off the first new Mac TVs, and there are more to come. The library has undergone a complete refurbishment – it has 9,000 volumes and membership of London Library enhances the collection.

Classes never more than 16 and many, particularly at diploma level, only four to six, fewer still for languages. Some classrooms are designed with small seminar-style groups in mind.

The teaching faculty is an international bunch, average age 40s. Pupil-teacher ratio is six to one and all staff seem to know most of the girls, affirming parent comments about supportive and nurturing environment with a caring individualised approach. Low turnover and enough long-termers to provide a cohesive core. Plenty of support staff and school nurse on site.

Mild/moderate learning difficulties and other issues managed collaboratively by the learning resource coordinator, teachers, parents and students themselves. Lots of individualised support throughout the school and the girls themselves were quick to talk about peer tutoring offered during free periods or after school.

The enrichment programme for able students has about 40 on the register. These students are invited to apply to programmes sponsored by Ivy Leagues (Stanford, Yale, Princeton, Johns Hopkins) and top tier UK universities. Additional provision includes extracurricular activities as well as resources which are made available to students for independent study and wider reading.

Games, options, the arts: Mix of competitive and non-competitive sporting activities available for all grades on and off site. If the school does not offer a particular sport they will help connect with local teams. Marymount is part of the International School Sports Association and they have produced an impressive record of results in soccer, badminton and tennis at championship tournaments hosted by member schools in different parts of Europe. One pupil training with the Chelsea Ladies' development squad and several play with the Richmond Volleyball Club. When girls were asked why they chose Marymount, one replied that she came for the sport and when you hear that one of their football trainers is with Chelsea, no prizes for guessing which team Marymount girls support.

Musicians have plenty of opportunities to play in ensembles and chamber groups. About 20 per cent take private instrumental or singing lessons; school boasts a 100 per cent pass rate in grade exams. Entry to the choir is by audition and choristers participate in school concerts and annual tours to European cities, performing in major churches and cathedrals. Teachers encourage girls to perform in local festivals and competitions.

Drama is inclusive and the entire community builds up to a major production each year. Keen thespians can participate in ISTA (International School Theatre Association) festivals and when we visited girls were buzzing about their weekend ISTA trip to Stratford upon Avon. LAMDA examinations offered. Visual arts seem focused on painting and photography – the girls tell us that the art teacher is an inspiring photographer. Framed art by generations of pupils displayed throughout the school. Fab Lab includes a range of 3D printers, laser cutters and other digitally driven tools.

Consensus is that the most fun of all is the 'international day', when everyone shares their culture and cuisine.'The Japanese do the best, and the [boarding] girls are already planning even though it's still months away'. Zumbathon – a fundraising activity involving the whole community beeping and bopping, swinging and swaying to music – was also highly popular and yielded no casualties.

As a Catholic IB school, community service involves everyone at Marymount. Middle schoolers do environmental projects that include cleaning along the bank of the Thames. Older girls volunteer in local activities including soup kitchens and schools and further afield join other RHSM students in projects working with children in places such as Zambia. All students take part in the spiritual life of the school and attend an annual retreat. Girls of all faiths come to Marymount and this provides opportunities for students to learn about other beliefs and traditions; care is taken to ensure that everyone feels comfortable at mass and prayer. We visited on a Hindu feast day and the girls said they had started the day with a Hindu prayer; Muslim girls wear their headscarves with confidence.

Boarding: Almost one third of the pupils board and there are four halls, each with its own duo of houseparents. Boarding rooms (some bunk beds) have recently been refurbished (2016) and facilities are clean and pretty tidy. Boarding areas are kept locked during the school day unless a girl has a reason to be back in her room. Oldest boarders have the spacious shared bedrooms above and the remaining nuns living in a wing just off their hall. Sisters no longer teach but are very much part of the fabric of the school, occasionally eating or sharing cocoa and study evenings with the girls.

The school's proximity to Heathrow is an attraction for boarding parents; the girls say that the school's proximity to London is the attraction for them. The lure of London aside, boarders enjoy theatre and music trips as well as days out to the seaside (Brighton) and theme parks such as Longleat. There's plenty going on inside school too, including dance and music workshops and opportunities to explore and develop one's faith. Worth mentioning here that the school also takes weekly boarders from local (ie London) families and it is sometimes possible to arrange short-term boarding for day girls whose parents travel.

Clear procedures allow boarders off-campus freedoms to visit friends and family while ensuring their safety. One guardian who has long looked after boarders during half-term breaks told us that some older girls feel the school is too strict. She helps them, and their far-off parents who hear the grumbles, appreciate that the school is being cautious and not unreasonable. Two exclusions in the last three years of boarders who, after several warnings, broke the rules about leaving campus.

Background and atmosphere: Established in Kingston in 1955 by 10 nuns from the Religious of the Sacred Heart of Mary (RSHM), sent by the Eastern American Province. Mid-19th century French founder of RSHM aspired to provide charity for all classes through schools, homes and orphanages that worked interactively across socio-economic barriers. Schools opened in France, Ireland, Portugal, England, the US and later Latin America and the rest of the world. The first sisters who came to Kingston started a 'year abroad' programme for US university women, then a school offering the US secondary school curriculum. Early 70s saw the arrival of Sister Anne Marie Hill, a determined Irish mover-and-shaker, well known in international education circles and now executive director of the network of schools. She introduced the IB, making the school more relevant to its growing international student body and reflecting RSHM's original ethos. During the noughties Marymount had a series of heads as RSHM grappled with transition to lay leadership and during that time the board of governors was created.

School works closely with the other Marymount partners under Sister Anne Marie's guidance, meeting every six to eight weeks to discuss areas such as strategic planning and communication. Increasingly involvement with the international network of RSHM schools – 19 worldwide – is now bringing more opportunities to the pupils.

The school is based in an affluent part of Surrey occupying a large Edwardian house plus various more recent additions connected by walkways. Elegant grounds with lawns, manicured flowerbeds and sculpted hedges. 'The teddy bear topiary sold me', said one dad, 'How can you not love a school that has teddy bear topiary?' (We presume he had already consulted the GSG about minor details such as teaching and pastoral care.) Main house, with original wood panelling and stained glass, is head office and reception. The nuns are loved by the girls and parents appreciate their presence. Small school chapel is used by boarders and local community alike.

Modern blocks house multi-purpose classrooms, the newly refurbished library and university and careers counselling rooms. Another block has the gym (floor replaced recently), music rooms and auditorium for assemblies, all-school mass, drama. Yet another has more dorms, new dining hall with a 'chef's theatre' – and, school tells us, much improved food from new catering company – classrooms, infirmary, student lounges. A new quasi-Scandinavian wooden structure houses more small tutorial rooms just right for the many language classes and designed with IB language examination conditions in mind. Most of the buildings surround the garden and have big windows that bring the outdoors in and give a refreshing sense of space and light.

Pastoral care, well-being and discipline: Spiritual values underpin the ethos of Marymount, rooted in the mission of the RSHM, 'that all may have life'. These values are made explicit on the website: even the most casual browser will see them on every page, running alongside photos. School welcomes girls from all faiths but we think it might not be a comfortable environment for the girl who has none. Plenty of support available at the school: academic, social, emotional and personal; more expertise called upon if necessary.

Parents' Association hosts a welcome back family barbecue during the first weekend of the school year when boarding parents are there dropping off daughters so they are able to meet day families. One parent said the school went out of its way, allowing their daughter to board temporarily so she could start at the beginning of the year, before the family transfer to London took place. Another described how the teachers made an effort to encourage her daughter to join the orchestra for a big performance, even though her late arrival meant she had missed several rehearsals.

Pupils and parents: Marymount girls are internationally diverse, cheerful, articulate, academically motivated, quietly confident and as a bunch, quite enchanting. More aspirational than ambitious, they love their school and really enjoy having peers from all over the world. They look out for each other, especially new ones, and although one day girl said she wished there were more ways to get closer to the boarders, everyone, including day parents, feels that the day girls and boarders are pretty integrated.

The girls are reflective about the realities of being in a single-sex environment. They feel they are able to focus more on learning, but they would like to find a partner boys' school and the student council has made some moves in this direction. Trouble is that 'all the boys' (schools) seem to be taken', but they have not given up. 'When adolescent girls become interested in boys, it can be frustrating to see how much they measure themselves against the approval of the boys in the group. Without that distraction they can develop as intellectually rigorous learners; they are their own people.'

The families that choose the school value the ethos of school, its Catholicism and internationalism, but are equally attracted to the IB. There are 40 nationalities in the school, British representing just over half. Other significant groups are German, Spanish, Japanese, Chinese, US, Australian, Korean and Italian. The numbers within these groups are balanced very carefully to facilitate integration. The school bus service extends into London to Sloane Square and more routes are under consideration.

Parents' Association organises events including outings for parents which are appreciated by newly-arrived expats.

Entrance: Local families are urged to attend one of the open days. Inbound expats on 'look-see' trips to London may book appointments. Girls' admissions based on availability and a review of school reports and teacher references plus interview. English language fluency is required with exceptions made for younger students for whom English is a second language. Most classes have waiting lists so best to apply a year in advance, though there is some turnover so you could be lucky.

Local feeder schools include Holy Cross, The Study, Fulham Prep, St Agatha's, The Grove, The Old Vicarage, The German School (Deutsche Schule London), Garden House, Unicorn School, Cameron House, Ursuline School. Day girls come from most SW London postcodes including Richmond, Wimbledon, Putney, Chelsea, South Kensington.

Exit: Most head to university and the chart we saw on the college counsellor's wall listing every 12th grader's destinations confirms that they are applying to many countries. Counsellor stays in close contact with parents, especially boarder parents, about each girl's plan and the process they must follow depending on the country of their destination. PSAT and SATS also offered.

In 2018, students off to Oxford, Imperial College, Warwick, Edinburgh, Bristol and Barnard College in the USA, plus Japan, Europe, and Canada.

Money matters: School has no endowment so financial stability is maintained by tuition and fundraising initiatives. 'Being an international school and in the current economic climate, we need to be sure we are guarded and forward looking – we can't rest on our laurels.' The PA also fundraises for activities that support the school and pupils.

Scholarships (academic, art, music, drama, sport, community service) for grade 6 and 8 students. Some offered for grades 10, 11 and 12. Some financial aid available for means-tested students. About 20 per cent of the pupils benefit from this.

Remarks: Successfully serves a niche market of internationally-minded families seeking a girls' school with a Catholic ethos. In the words of one parent, 'We've been over-the-top-happy. The school provides excellent support and people from all over the world fit in and are welcome there.'

M

Merchant Taylors' School

Linked with Merchant Taylors' Prep

Sandy Lodge, Northwood HA6 2HT

Ages 11–18 **Pupils** 890 **Sixth form** 280 **C of E**

Fees: £20,698 pa

01923 845514
www.mtsn.org.uk

Head master: Since 2013, Simon Everson MA PGCE, educated at Solihull School and Cambridge (English) before completing a masters in philosophy at Nottingham. Latterly head at Skinners' School in Tunbridge Wells. Was adamant that very few schools would tempt him away but couldn't resist the lure to MTS, where he took over 'a school with wonderful tradition, but one that's vibrant and relevant now.' Still 'loves the classroom' and 'borrows classes' when time allows. Moved immediately upon appointment to reintroduce significant financial benefits to scholars, with scholarships for the brightest and most able across the board now worth at least 10 per cent of fees: 'We are determined to seek out excellence and reward it.' Enjoys walking, bird watching and Scotland and is a qualified apiarist (beekeeper). An electric guitar sits tucked in the corner of his office – 'I wanted to put myself in the boys' shoes and remember how it feels to struggle to learn something new,' he says. Businesslike and sincere. Married to Ginny, a psychotherapist.

Academic matters: A school populated by an intellectually curious and highly motivated cohort. Academic rigour – and ultimately success – is par for the course here but head is clear that they do not want to create a monoculture: 'We reject the philosophy of moulding children into specific types.' Boys inspired by staff who, in head's words, are 'fiercely intelligent – no school is better than the quality of its staff', and are striking to visitors either for their youth, energy and enthusiasm or wit, wisdom and worldliness. Humour and empathy pervade the classrooms, evident as much in the way staff speak to the boys as the quirky touches around the buildings – we've never seen fairy lights or a Ferrari flag in a biology lab in any other school.

Traditional curriculum – and, although one parent said that academically 'it's not for the faint hearted,' school adamant that it's 'not merely a conveyor belt to top results'. 'Exam results are a given,' says school; 'it's about what else they leave with.' Boys take IGCSEs in majority of subjects with consistently outstanding results: 86 per cent A*-A/9-7 in 2018, with 71 per cent of A levels graded A*/A and 93 per cent A*-B. Flexible setting in maths and science from year 7, with some 'banding' in English literature from year 9. 'We tend to separate out the boys who read; the ones who can handle Chaucer and Shakespeare with no problem'. Top half takes maths IGCSE in year 10, with one third also taking French a year early. It's French and Latin in the languages department in years 7 and 8 with the addition of German, Spanish or Greek in year 9, all available at A level. Around 60 per cent take the EPQ. Maths, economics and the sciences top choices at A level with around half the number opting for humanities and English but with no less stellar results. Small numbers for languages – although school still timetables minority subjects such as Greek even for lone students.

Learning support (mild dyslexia, dyscalculia some ASD) viewed in the same way as educating the most able children: 'they just need a slightly different educational experience to everyone else,' although school also quick to point out that even those with individual needs 'must be able to keep up with the pace here,' and there's strictly no withdrawal from classes. ESL students must be instantly able to access curriculum as are fully immersed from day one. Can accommodate pupils with mobility problems, including wheelchairs.

School really shows its mettle in university application process and careers advice, an area which head says has reached 'Rolls Royce quality.' Parents describe the UCAS application process as 'incredibly well organised', with each sixth former assigned to the head of department of their chosen subject who acts as advisor and referee. Personal references from tutors are the cherry on top of the holistic application process. Boys encouraged to begin thinking about future careers early with a World of Work day in year 11, plus a joint careers conference with the girls of nearby St Helen's School. OMTs highly visible as mentors to current pupils, who are encouraged to use active database of over 600 old boys willing to offer work experience, and allowed time out of school to pursue such opportunities.

Games, options, the arts: Sport seen as a hugely important part of the MTS ethos, with sportsmanship and camaraderie as high on the agenda as winning. Part of the strong community feel comes from the whole school, including 80 per cent of the teaching staff, heading out to the (spectacular) sports fields together twice a week. Rugby, hockey and cricket are major sports and although there are varying degrees of success in the former (there was almost a hint of pride in the boy who self-effacingly told us he was in the 'least successful rugby A team on school record'), hockey and cricket are flying increasingly high, and the fixture list grows annually to encompass more top schools. School boasts over 60 county and five national sportsmen and the U17 cricket team were recently crowned national champions. This in no small part due to dedicated directors for each major sport, as well as regular visiting coaches. Sport for all – every boy competes for the school as often as is feasible with as much celebration when the 'Super E' rugby team (unbeaten) brings home a victory as the more elite squads.

With over 20 minor sports, boys have no excuse not to find something they love. One or two grumbles about lack of footie until sixth form, but that doesn't stop boys having a good kick around the quad at break times, and school provides goalposts for the purpose. World class facilities include all the usual suspects plus all weather hockey pitches ('better than the Olympic ones,' one keen player assured us), heated indoor pool, athletics track, lakes for sailing and kayaking, squash and fives courts, an assault course and fencing salle.

Endless opportunities to get stuck in outside of the classroom and sports field at lunch times and after school. Every sport imaginable, from sub aqua to cycling, has a society and there's chess, bridge and stamp club for those more inclined towards brain sports. Boys can flex their journalistic muscles by contributing to one of six school magazines or try their hand at societies ranging from dissection society to debating, most of these included in fees. Music and drama 'amazingly active,' says head, with ensembles and choirs galore, including Dixieland, Merchants of Groove and swing band in addition to a host of more traditional offerings. Two major theatrical productions each year in the Great Hall, in addition to smaller endeavours and a fiercely fought house drama competition. Parents rave about quality of productions. CCF (one of the largest in the UK) in conjunction with St Helen's, and DofE schemes offer super opportunities to follow outdoor pursuits and take part in trips to eg Morocco, Canada or Nepal. Huge sense of collective pride in relation to outstanding work with Phab, with funds raised throughout the year and an annual residential care week staffed by senior pupils, who consider it a great honour to be selected to take part.

Excellent standard of art and DT, which has 'outstanding' teaching, according to parents – MTS has a produced higher number of Arkwright Scholars than any other school since the scheme began in the 1990s. Atmosphere surprisingly relaxed and no sign of the macho testosterone culture that's endemic in so many boys' schools. 'We achieve results by inspiring boys,' says head. Enrichment programme for most able scholars 'turns seamlessly' into Oxbridge preparation.

Rugby and hockey tours to South Africa and Australia and cricket to Barbados. Years 7 and 8 classics trip to Naples, geography to Iceland and history to Istanbul. Eleven language trips each year and six language exchange programmes across year groups.

Background and atmosphere: Founded in the City of London in 1561 by the Worshipful Company of Merchants, then the largest school in the country. Relocated in 1933 to its current location

– a 250 acre site comprising a core of listed art deco buildings plus a host of sympathetically incorporated modern additions set before endless playing fields leading down to a lake. Visitors greeted by exquisite formal gardens and a handsome fascia. School lacks dreaming spires and turrets but gives an immediate sense of purposefulness and solid endeavour.

'Civilised' a word that comes up again and again, along with a sense of a truly cohesive community spirit. Older boys mentor the younger, the whole school eats together (no exceptions, no packed lunches) and assembles together – 'invaluable', says head. 'We are a corporate body not a disparate group'. There's also a great sense of the traditional juxtaposed with gleaming new facilities – a feeling that a boy who has walked the corridors of MTS would not be remotely overwhelmed walking into an Oxford or Cambridge college for the first time.

Pastoral care, well-being and discipline: Discipline 'almost always low profile due to our hugely positive culture,' says school. Boys are not 'spiky' or 'entitled', transgressions rare and bullying almost non-existent ('I couldn't believe how much friendlier it was than my prep school', said one happy boy). Vertical tutor system praised almost unanimously by parents and boys. For the most part, parents described tutors as 'almost part of the family', and many keep in contact with former tutees way beyond the A level years. Thriving house system facilitates yet more cross-fertilisation for friendships and opportunities for boys to shine in competitions, with weekly house assemblies covering topics from 'the art of small talk' and 'how to tie a bow tie'. Plenty of chances for responsibility at the top of the school. Head boy voted in by 50 per cent student vote, supported by 10 elected monitors and a JCR of a further 30 boys. School run on Christian ethos, with services held in chapel and all faiths welcome, but there's also a Muslim prayer room and societies for all main faiths.

Pupils and parents: 'What makes a Merchant Taylors' boy?' we asked. 'Well, we don't really do posh,' came the smiling reply. Our opinion: smart, charming, self-effacing and diverse. Not a hooray Henry in sight, but a group of boys wearing their school tie with humility and an awareness of privilege rather than entitlement. Fun to sit with (yes, even year 10s) in the dining room and totally at ease with adult company. Minds of staff and pupils alike on higher things than the minutiae of shiny shoes and tidy haircuts obsessed over at so many schools. Head says school is 'always hanging on the coat tails of the pupils' enthusiasm', and keenly supports pupil-led initiatives. Perhaps because around a quarter of boys receive some level of financial assistance, social awareness is a key factor in their all-round pleasantness – 'It just wouldn't be the done thing to crow about wealth or status,' said one parent. 'Many families make huge sacrifices to send their sons here.' School concurs: 'Those from affluent backgrounds wear their wealth lightly'.

A school where three worlds don't so much collide as mesh. A hybrid London/country school with appeal to local, north and west London and Herts/Bucks families. The London crowd loves the spacious campus, laid back feel and multitude of sporting options on offer, and those from the shires enjoy the slightly edgier, more worldly feel than they find in schools closer to home. Reflective of local area, around 40 per cent British-Asian, a large Jewish contingent and all other main faiths represented. Wonderfully inclusive – 'there's zero tolerance of racism or homophobia,' boys told us – and although firm friendships are formed on the tube trains and coaches that transport boys in, all reported that new friends are constantly made through tutor groups, forms which are mixed up each year, subject choices (from year 12 forms are grouped according to A level choices) and activities.

Parents maintain close contact with school, attending events and committees in droves. Head reported around 200 attendees at one of his recent termly parent forums. In turn, school has unique relationship with many OMTs well beyond the A level years, with tutors speaking with deep fondness of past tutees' achievements. Actor and alumnus Riz Ahmed chose MT as the backdrop for one his first movies and Grammy Award winning OMT band Nero (the lead singer read philosophy at Oxford, incidentally) recently returned as the surprise act at leavers' ball. Other famous alumni include Nobel prize-winning medic Sir John Sulston, Lord Coggan (former Archbishop of Canterbury), Sir Alan Duncan and Boris Karloff, as well as a host of others from the worlds of politics, business, sport, the military and the arts.

Entrance: Selective with two main intakes at 11+ and 13+. At 11+ around 380 boys (roughly two-thirds from state primaries) apply for 60 places. At this point, applicants tested in maths, English and a general paper with those delivering the goods on paper invited back for a one-to-one interview ('they always leave with a smile on their face,' says school).

A further 100 places available at 13+ with fewer applicants for each place but larger hurdles to clear: boys hoping for entry in 2021 or before are interviewed first in May/June of year 7 (registration by end of February) on strength of prep head's report with high flyers offered 'unconditional' places at that point in the expectation that the exam will present no problems. Those offered a 'conditional' place after interview will need to pass every paper in the CE-style exam in January (English, maths, science, humanities, MFL and optional Latin).

Potential entrants from 2022 onwards will face an entirely new process. Applications will need to be made by June of year 5, followed by an interview in the autumn of year 6. Conditional offers are made shortly after, subject to performance in examinations in January of year 6 (English, maths and a general paper). Those who accept a place will then take 'setting examinations' in almost all subjects in January of year 8. Candidates will no longer be able to try again at 13+ if not successful at 11+.

School clear that parents tutoring boys heavily for the exam 'are not doing them any favours – we're looking for intellectual curiosity, a passion for something, reasoning skills and ways in which boys can make a wider contribution to the school.'

At 16+ exams in four A level subjects; offer confirmations depend on GCSE results.

Up to 40 or 50 feeders at 11+, with preps including Radlett Prep, Manor Lodge, Buckingham College, Reddiford and Gayhurst. At 13+ large numbers from Merchant Taylors' Prep, St John's, Durston House and St Martin's, plus a few each from The Beacon, Davenies, Orley Farm, York House and St Anthony's, amongst others.

Exit: Very little fall out after GCSE. Eighteen to Oxbridge in 2018 with vast majority of remainder to top universities. London colleges feature highly (particularly Imperial, LSE and UCL) as do Birmingham, Bristol, Durham, Nottingham and Warwick. Strong numbers to read medicine (five in 2018), economics and engineering but diversity across the board from sports science to English, humanities, law and the occasional one choosing film or drama school over university offers, or heading to university overseas (one to Toronto in 2018).

Money matters: School prides itself on staying true to the ethos on which it was founded – to offer an excellent all-round education to boys from all walks of life and offer financial aid to those who would most benefit – these days, around 200 boys at any one time. Academic scholarships awarded to boys who perform particularly well in the entrance papers, with scholars benefiting from an enrichment programme. Up to five major academic scholarships at both 11+ and 13+ worth at least 10 per cent of fees. Also sport, art, drama, DT, music and all-rounder scholarships.

Remarks: A rare breed – a London school with a country feel. Sitting coolly around the top of the league tables, seemingly without trying too hard, a testament to teachers who inspire without applying undue pressure. Not the most obvious choice for macho rugby types, or for the parent hoping for their son to leave school with a public school swagger, but for those looking for an environment that actively encourages boys to 'lean in to difficult questions', get involved in enriching activities outside of the classroom, and that values the quirky and erudite, look no further.

Merchant Taylors' Prep

Linked with Merchant Taylors' School

175

Moor Farm, Sandy Lodge Road, Rickmansworth, Hertfordshire WD3 1LW

Ages 3–13 **Pupils** 362

Fees: £15,245 – £16,000 pa

01923 825 648
www.mtpn.org.uk

M

Head: Since 2015, Dr Karen McNerney BSc PGCE MSc EdD; biochemistry degree from Newcastle and PGCE in primary teaching from Swansea. Also has a masters in educational leadership and doctorate in early years education. Taught in prep schools in north London and Hertfordshire before joining Northwood Prep (now Merchant Taylors' Prep) in 2001. Teaching a vocation ('I think my parents would say I was always destined to be a teacher as I had two younger brothers that I bossed to an inch of their lives,' she laughs) and still teaches PSHE and library sessions.

Fortuitously began her headship the same day as the announcement that the school would change from Northwood Prep to Merchant Taylors' Prep, which won instant cheers all round as it means boys no longer have to take the 13+ to get into Merchant Taylors'. Not that she needed to win any brownie points as 'she was already popular as head of juniors,' says one parent. Softly spoken and surprisingly reserved, she's a world away from the bombastic stereotype of a north London prep head – but make no mistake about her leadership skills, with parents telling us, 'She really listens'; I find her approach modern for a prep school'; 'She's more creative in her thinking than other heads I've come across.' Pupils assured she's 'very much part of daily school life' although woe betide any who wind up in her (surprisingly no-frills) office as 'they only really come in here if they've done something very bad,' she says. Lives below said office with her husband and when you can tear her away ('it's such a privilege living here among all these millionaire houses in lovely Moor Park'), she loves her holidays.

Entrance: Selective. Vast majority join from hugely oversubscribed nursery located in former boarding house at neighbouring Merchant Taylors' School. Assessment at 3+ looks for 'teachability and sociability,' according to head. A few further places up for grabs at 4+ and 7+. No further formal intakes, with ad hoc in-year applications dealt with on a case by case basis, but newcomers will need to be up to scratch. No sibling policy, 'but if it comes down to choosing a younger sibling or new family, I'll always pick the sibling,' says head. Class sizes capped at 20.

Exit: As the prep school of Merchant Taylors', the vast majority of pupils progress to the senior school, several with scholarships. But transition isn't automatic, and a few are guided elsewhere, with conversations starting in year 5 if school thinks they won't pass muster. A few also to Habs and John Lyon, Aldenham, City of London School, St Albans, Mill Hill, Berkhamsted, Harrow, Westminster and Eton. Small numbers peel off at 11+ to local selective grammars, although less so now as boys get their offer to Merchant Taylors' in year 6 'so they don't feel they have to take the gamble with a grammar,' says head. Lots of support around senior school applications and scholarships – 10 offered by Merchant Taylors' and one by Norwich School in 2018. No plans to discontinue years 7 and 8, even though Merchant Taylors' starts at year 7 – 'it's a quirk, but one that works, thanks to lots of collaboration between the two schools,' says head.

Remarks: Be careful not to miss the discreet entrance as you find yourself gawping at the bling real estate on the Moor Park Estate, amongst which the school nestles. Originally a farm, a super spacious campus littered with grade II listed buildings lies behind the gates, steeped in history and providing boys with a village-like environment. Acres of fields provide sports pitches ('it was the acreage that really made it stand out for us against other local preps,' said one parent) and the overall impression is of a school that does nothing by halves.

No shabby corners at all, with highlights including spectacular oak panelled dining room, new art and DT studio and a dazzling modern theatre – easily the best in the area. Classrooms housing quiet, studious students are bright and well organised throughout, with cheery examples of boys' work adorning the walls and well-equipped outdoor play areas for all year groups (ping pong games galore during break times). Pre-prep very much part of overall school. Delightful new eco garden and two well-equipped science labs, although our guides told us, 'there's definitely more theory than practicals.'

Despite the school's Christian ethos, at least 80 per cent of cohort from ethnic groups (mostly Indian) reflecting the local area. There are so many medical families that it's often joked they could probably staff a hospital with the parents, plus many in the financial services sector, but also some 'from two-up-two-downs in Watford who are spending all their money on school fees,' says head. More families from further afield than ever, some as far as Potters Bar, Wembley, Barnet and Swiss Cottage. Working parents grateful for the school being open from 7.45am until 6pm and there's no shortage of after-school clubs.

Academically, standards are high but there's plenty of support and 'they make learning fun,' say pupils. 'The teachers bring subjects alive and make it about debate and opinions, not just facts – one was particularly inspirational in getting my son interested in history,' one parent told us. French from nursery with Latin from year 3. Greek taught in years 7 and 8. Setting from year 1 for maths and from year 3 for English. Maths taught to the progressive Singapore Maths curriculum from nursery onwards, with outstanding outcomes (and yet you still see parents at the local Kumon centre and signing up to the local tutor agencies, but that's north London for you). It can be no coincidence, we suspect, that the head, who is known for having her finger on the pulse, has reduced homework levels in favour of more 'enrichment,' 'whether that's piano practice, cubs, riding your bike or finding out more about a subject you loved that day.'

Full-time SENDCo gets the thumbs up from parents, although needs are very much at mild to moderate end. 'They've been utterly brilliant – I could never have believed my son would be where he is when we stared off on this journey,' one parent told us. Speech and language therapists and OTs brought in as required.

Strong emphasis on broadening the spectrum to avoid one-dimensional academic output evident in areas such as drama, music and the arts. 'The drama is phenomenal,' we heard time and time again, while we practically had to drag our pupil guides away from the snazzy foyer to the even snazzier theatre while they waxed lyrical about recent plays. All boys in year 7 take a LAMDA speech and drama course (with a plethora of merits and distinctions to show at the end of it) to ensure top notch communication skills for those all-important school interviews.

Music very much part of the bread and butter of school life, even more so since they merged with Merchant Taylors' – including greater collaboration with older boys, more challenging repertoire (think Mozart's Requiem for boys in the choir) and joint concerts (recently in Birmingham). The merger means greater availability of peripatetic teachers too, utilised by some 50 per cent of the cohort – 'we had one boy wanting to learn the bassoon and we were able to get a teacher,' says head. 'While most preps have a smallish music department, this one is outstanding,' a parent told us. Lovely new art facilities, although boys told us they'd like more art, and even here we found silent pupils with heads down.

Sport a bone of contention for some parents, with the not-unusual-for-prep-schools grumbles that sport isn't as competitive as it could be (school points out the first team for rugby was unbeaten in 2017 and the hockey teams are largely unbeaten, while competitive cricket is also strong, with U11s winning the country championship) and that 'it's always about the same boys.' 'I'd like to see more fixtures for the C and D teams and more celebration of those wins,' one said. But, then again, some parents we spoke to would gladly ditch contact sports altogether for fear of potential injuries – 'more individual sports, please,' said one.

Boys – whom we found self-assured beyond their years – clearly feel well cared for pastorally, with vertical tutor groups from years 5 to 8 enabling older boys to support younger ones, and we've never seen so many badges adoring blazer lapels, commending everything from house merits to achievements in chess or science clubs. Head of well-being ensures balanced approach to academia – perhaps partly to counter high expectations at home – with curriculum devised accordingly. Impeccable behaviour throughout – boys told us they get 'minutes' for minor misdemeanours (time out of their allocated fun time) and 'nobody wants that.' Anything more serious and you lose a house point. As for strictness levels, boys told us, 'Obviously you like some teachers more than others, but they're all fair even if it doesn't feel like it at the time.' One boy told us he'd experienced bullying, but that 'when I told a teacher, it was sorted immediately.'

Not a school for more liberal parents who 'just want their kids to be happy'. But the typical 'ambitious' north London parent should be more than delighted with this very driven school, with its ultra-calm atmosphere and resolutely focused boys. But these parents will need to buy into the wider extracurricular package too, which we think provides the perfect tonic to the school's more scholarly pursuits.

Merlin School

4 Carlton Drive, London SW15 2BZ

Ages 4–8 **Pupils** 210, 80 per cent boys

Fees: £14,550 pa

020 8788 2769
www.merlinschool.net

Headmistress: Since 2003, Kate Prest BA Music/Ed PGCE (Oxford Brookes), formerly head of pre-prep at The Harrodian. Welcoming, personable, caring, with tremendous enthusiasm, Mrs Prest (late 40s) teaches music to all and knows every child by name. She champions creative thinking and teamwork in a school, which parents agree is 'like a big family, where all are made to feel welcome and are well looked after'. Apart from the head, her PA and a long-serving member, staff are known by Christian names. Mrs Prest is proud of the Merlin spirit of 'have a go', which underpins confidence-building, and parents agree confidence is a hallmark of Merlin pupils. Mother of three, children attended the school, with husband in the City and no plans to move on, Mrs Prest thoroughly understands London pressures, the intense competition and high expectations. As one parent commented, 'Mrs Prest and Science Sue hold the tide in this highly competitive environment. She reminds us children are only children once and their childhood is precious. It is important not to get sucked into the madness'. Mrs Prest moves energetically in and out of classes without interrupting activities, and pupils are respectful but not intimidated by her, enjoying her encouragement and praise. Parents value her realistic advice and are full of praise for her open door policy and emphasis on verbal communication, which works well in this relatively small school.

Entrance: Early viewing is advisable for this very popular, non-selective school. Prospective parents attend a half-termly open afternoon or fortnightly tour on a week day morning. Offers are made in order of date of registration – priority given to siblings. Occasionally places occur higher up the school. Children come from local nurseries: Putney, Fulham, Barnes, Southfields and Wimbledon.

Exit: Some leave at age 7, remainder at 8. Destinations are various and widespread, with a number moving on to The Harrodian at 8 where they are interviewed in November rather than examined in January. Other popular destinations include Bute House, Putney High, King's College Junior School, St Paul's Juniors, Shrewsbury House, Feltonfleet, Latymer Prep, King's House, Prospect House, Rokeby and the occasional boarding school.

Remarks: Established in 1986 by Sir Alford Houstoun-Boswall, chair of governors and proprietor of both The Merlin and The Harrodian School in Barnes. Merlin is a well-maintained, converted Victorian house with large, high-ceilinged, light classrooms packed with colourful displays, and the original ballroom serving as the main hall. Four reception classes are 'at the heart of the school,' says Mrs Prest, close to her office and the front door but with timed access to the outside play area. Carpeted stairs abound leading up to the year 1s, specialist ICT room where all years have weekly lesson, and down to dining room, science room and music room in the basement. On the far side of the spacious Astroturf playground are purpose-built year 2 classrooms and, under cover, great resources for zoned play including dressing up and a bench where children can read or be quiet.

Small mixed ability classes (averaging 17). Significantly more boys than girls but parents we spoke to had not found this to be a concern. Mrs Prest explained how children are mixed up and start their day with 'quickies', working independently on literacy and numeracy skills, and are team taught and moved about in their sets. Teachers really know the pupils well with setting from second term of reception for phonics and mathematics; English and maths sets for years 1, 2 and 3 support the tailored teaching. We watched eager year 2 pupils carrying out a mathematical investigation using circles to identify right angles in their classrooms. In all the lessons we saw engaged, focused pupils, happy to explain their reasoning. Traditional skills include times tables and handwriting with specialists for French, science, computing, drama, games, art and music. Cross-curricular topics are carefully planned and head explained the importance of 'seeing and doing, not just being told'. In choosing the Merlin, parents spoke of how they were attracted to the 'energy and the stimulating teaching environment'. Pupils are proud of their school. They described their teachers as 'fair, they make lessons fun'; some mentioned year 3s dissecting sheep organs and handling bones in science. Interactive boards visible in upper school with emphasis away from iPads and technology as so much is readily accessible outside school, and head wants her teachers in front of children.

All pupils benefit from the specialist art room. Creativity abounds with ambitious drama and musical productions which feature original scripts and music. Successes are celebrated in the school half-termly magazine. Extracurricular activities such as sport, chess, yoga and sewing are very popular but do not begin until year 2. Performing is encouraged with choir involvement in local festivals and Mrs Prest ensures all pupils learn to understand music terminology, read and create their own music, playing the recorder or glockenspiel. At the time of our visit, 40 were learning a musical instrument, with individual violin or piano lessons rotated in school hours.

M

The Merlin Code is understood and any silliness picked up and dealt with quickly. Our visit coincided with a windy, wet day but the pupils' behaviour was exemplary, as inspectors also found. Kindness is encouraged. Playground buddies were named in assembly and there is a bus stop in the playground for anyone feeling lonely. Sport with experienced sports master is inclusive with one weekly indoor PE session, one outdoor session and one off-site games session. Pupils enjoy their lessons in football, netball, hockey, cricket and rugby with fixtures for older pupils. The in house nutritionist ensures a high standard of catering and puddings are a great hit.

Qualified, caring head of SEN with her team ensure support is quickly put in place and early dyslexia screening for the youngest and full screening if suspected in older children is available. Regular staff meetings identify any possible problem ahead and the school provides those children who experience learning difficulties such as dyslexia and dyspraxia with additional one-to-one reading, small literacy and maths support groups. Specialist one-to-one sessions are organised at an additional cost. Other support groups include social skills and EAL club. Parents are made to feel welcome; we saw some listening to readers, all are invited so that they can see class assemblies and plays and the two parent reps organise fundraising events for charities. They agree that this would not be the right school if you want acres of playing fields and masses of sport, or drilling for examinations. Some working parents might be put off by the school hours with school finishing at lunch time on Fridays and 4.30pm finish after clubs for the upper school.

Just as inspectors judged the school to be 'outstanding ' in all aspects in a recent inspection, so parents are delighted with this warm school with its emphasis on allowing children to have access to a stimulating, creative environment where they do exceedingly well and have fun. As one parent remarked, 'The Merlin is aspirational and taps into each individual child'. Another added, 'They give pupils lots of confidence, spotting opportunities and putting them their way'. The first head chose the school name with its distinctive wizard hat logo prior to tales of Harry Potter. Over the years this has become more embedded and developed and there is a sense of magic about the school and what it achieves

Michaela Community School

North End Road, Wembley, London HA9 0UU

Ages 11–19 **Pupils** 600

020 8795 3183
www.mcsbrent.co.uk

Headmistress: Founder and head since the school started in 2014, the vibrant and dramatic Katharine Birbalsingh MA Oxon NPQH (40s). A graduate of New College Oxford (French and philosophy), she did her teacher training at the Institute of Education. Previously deputy head of a South London state secondary, she spent all her years since university teaching in inner London state secondary schools, working her way through the usual channels. She has come a long way since her ground-breaking speech to the Tory party conference in 2010. Condemning the state of an education system that 'kept poor children poor' to roaring applause, Ms Birbalsingh, in her 30s at the time, looked startled at how well her speech was being received. Naïve politically, and not even a Tory, the accolade took her by surprise but she found herself without a job immediately afterwards.

She is clearly loving being in charge of this ground-breaking school ('I always planned on being a head,' she confides), and being able to fashion it according to her principles and beliefs. 'It's like being the conductor of an orchestra, but it's very important that it still works without me,' she insists. That is the beauty of systems and attention to detail. Passionate about social mobility and empowerment through knowledge, she and her team have created, in Michaela, a finely tuned collection of instruments that play beautifully in time and in sync. 'The systems here are tight and will only get tighter the more the school fills up and the older children influence and educate the younger ones.'

'When they arrive in year 7 quite a lot is about damage control,' she says. 'Some don't know their times tables, their reading is limited..we need to start teaching them the right habits for learning... we also have to help some of the parents to step up... However we don't do anything that's a waste of time – I don't believe in targets, they waste time... Every decision we make is whether it's right for the kids, not whether it's right for Ofsted.' Parents warm to her straightforward approach. She sticks to her boundaries and is uncompromising about what she believes to be right. They also notice her respect for her staff and others around her, and how much she herself is respected.

Confident, articulate, determined, driven and very brave, Ms Birbalsingh is an inspirational role model for both the boys and girls at her school and they feel very fortunate to have her.

Academic matters: Despite there being no GCSE or A level results yet (first GCSEs in summer 2019, sixth form opens in September 2019) to give testimony to the academic success of pupils here, it is already clear that the progress they are making and the standards they achieve are remarkable. The tools are teaching from the front, silence in the classroom (until called upon to speak), repeated memorisation of facts leading to deep retention of knowledge, regular self-quizzing, testing and open competition, as well as a challenging curriculum. Everyone does all the same subjects – English, maths, French, humanities, science, music and art. A pupil who is struggling may be allowed to take a reduced number of GCSEs; most will take eight though the bright ones will do nine, having done RS early in year 10. Pupils have two group music lessons and two art lessons a week. The library is stacked to the gunwhales (just under 4,000 books) in the grey, functional office-style bookcases, with classical literature, contemporary literature, predominately fiction and plenty of poetry and plays. There are class readers, Friday readers and Group readers. By year 9 all pupils will have read seven Shakespeare plays (including Macbeth, Julius Caesar and Othello) – the full versions, in the original. They will have memorised huge chunks of them and studied characterisation, plot device, pathos and humour. Reading is given great emphasis: the 'academically gifted' read over 100 classics from Homer to Orwell from the quality-controlled library. In English and maths as a whole the school's tests show pupils making double the expected level of progress.

Not all teachers at Michaela have a teaching qualification, something the school is proud of as it feels they are not all moulded from the same clay, but all are graduates from top universities including Oxbridge and Russell Group. They are motivated and enthusiastic. Ms Birbalsingh understands the pressure points on the profession only too well, so in her (or 'their' school, she prefers – 'this is very much a collaborative effort') there is no detailed marking, and box ticking exercises are limited to a minimum. Teachers are needed to supervise on staircases during 'transition', when the pupils march quickly in silence between lessons: if they were marking each essay in minute detail they wouldn't have time for this. Staff read all essays and make comments, but give detailed feedback to a class as a whole so everyone can share understanding of where the strengths and weaknesses lie. No pupil is spared. They are told exactly where they rank among their peers, and are praised for their performance in detail about what they did right, just as they are chastised about where they have fallen short – not enough focus in class, overlooking the opportunity to catch up in support lessons after school, not being diligent enough while self-quizzing. Teachers relish the opportunity actually to teach, impart knowledge, wisdom and learning. The job here is not about classroom control. These classrooms and corridors and dining rooms are strictly controlled at all times. Teachers are respected as being the ones whose age, wisdom and experience give them a natural authority. 'This', says Ms Birbalsingh, 'allows the children to be children, and they feel safe knowing where the boundaries are and understanding the consequences if they cross those boundaries.'

The plan for A level is that the most rigorous academic subjects will be prioritised – maths, further maths, physics, chemistry, biology, English literature, French, art, music, theology and philosophy, but Ms Birbalsingh is busily visiting outstanding sixth forms to learn about what works best – she and her team will fashion the sixth form just as they created years 7-11, with meticulous attention to detail and a fundamental belief in the acquisition of knowledge imparted from specialist teachers who love their subject.

Expectations are unashamedly high. Oxbridge and other top Russell Group universities are all within reach for many and the year 9 students are being taught to appreciate that already. One year 9 girl said that she 'isn't focusing on Oxbridge' as she wants to go the LSE. Pupils are streamed in four sets but there is fluidity between the sets and they are not referred to in front of the pupils. Oxbridge hopefuls can be found even in the lower half of the year group. One girl who arrived from the Sudan started in the bottom half of the year group; now, two years later, she is in the top..'but we never say "bright" or "able", only "are you working hard?" We celebrate the pupils who spend the most time on their homework – here there is no "bottom set mentality",' avers Ms Birbalsingh. Ms Birbalsingh has been busy networking at Oxford and Cambridge colleges, preparing a strategy, paving a path.

SEN is not a comfortable acronym at Michaela. Labels are seen as damaging. They would prefer to focus on the effort involved. 'Weakest pupils need more rigour, more focus and more practice,' asserts Katie Ashford, one of the deputy heads and an English teacher. Ms Birbalsingh accepts that some students need extra support – they have put on an extra lesson for those who 'are so far behind' in maths for example, but the focus is on each child.

Several parents remarked on their sons' appetite for homework. One year 9 boy works for two-and-a-half hours each evening. The incentives are there – they love to earn their merits, and as they start to see the fruits of their labour in their improved scores, a virtuous cycle is set in motion.

The teachers are wholeheartedly supportive of the regime at Michaela. You only have to read their book Battle Hymn of the Tiger Teachers – the Michaela Way to get a sense of their dedication, and total commitment to the ethos and practice here. Ms Birbalsingh almost purrs when questioned about the quality of her teachers: 'We have the best,' she affirms, citing their quality of life as part of her pulling power. Parents and pupils we spoke to agree.

Games, options, the arts: The art room here is disciplined, with as clear lines and boundaries as you find everywhere else in the school. Lots of charcoal and pencil drawings adorn the walls ('it's so difficult to find an art teacher who knows how to draw these days,' observes Ms Birbalsingh). Tasteful artwork – and carefully displayed, detailed portraits on the walls of each floor of eg Mandela, Boris Johnson and David Cameron. Clear simple lines – minimalist. Not fussy. Not messy.

Sport takes place one afternoon a week in a sports centre round the corner. Just football and dodgeball – not a lot of choice – but they get exercise and the opportunity to play matches against other schools as well as the chance to shine if sport is their thing. There are table tennis tables in the yard as well as basketball hoops – a chance to let off steam and be competitive between lessons. Apart from performing excerpts in class from the Shakespeare plays they are studying – eg Julius Caesar – not a lot of drama. 'We don't have the facilities – this is not what we are about,' is the explanation.

There is a focus, however, on a co-curricular programme that stretches the academic and cerebral. Visitors' programme includes talks, starting from year 7, from speakers ranging from hedge fund managers to barristers and politicians: recent examples include Boris Johnson, Nick Gibb, David Lammy MP and journalist turned teacher Lucy Kellaway. A rhetoric programme from year 9 paves the path towards Oxbridge applications. A scholars' programme will be run with the Brilliant Club from year 10 to challenge pupils with independent research projects and essays.

Every pupil will go on two trips a year, to the Natural History Museum, the British Museum, the National Gallery, the Globe Theatre and Cambridge University. Extracurricular clubs include films (pupils watch six classic films a year including Frankenstein, Romeo and Juliet and The Imitation Game), Future Leaders (pupil prefects are selected to lead conversations at family lunch), Lizard Point (stretching online quizzes of locations and regions) and competitions (Times Table Rockstars,

Poetry Declamation, Dates and Capitals). For the more athletic child there is football, table tennis and basketball and those with an interest in music can do chamber choir and flute choir.

Background and atmosphere: Founded by Katharine Birbalsingh in September 2014 as a free school 'with a private school ethos', the school makes an initially forbidding impression. An office block in the heart of a very industrial part of Wembley (the tube trains roll regularly past the dining room windows). Huge iron gates and a security system more fitting of a high security prison need to be negotiated before you enter the reception area.

Once inside the austere grey walls, the remarkable thing is that there is complete silence. Even in the reception and waiting area, the silence is broken only by the occasional whirr of a photocopier and the whispered exchanges behind the desk. On arrival all guests are presented with a list of rules – including 'Do not talk in normal voices in the corridors – only a whisper please!' 'Do not demonstrate disbelief to pupils when they say they like their school', and 'Do talk to the pupils at lunch and at break.'

As you tread carefully through the corridors you observe children at their desks in rows, arms folded on the desk except when they are eagerly throwing up their hands or writing carefully in their books. In the class room there is plenty of interaction. Teachers lead from the front but lessons are delivered not like a lecture but as a series of questions and answers. Feedback from the front (no marking policy – marking can waste too much teaching and supervising time).

'Transition' – when the children move between classrooms at the end of a lesson – is astonishing to witness. Like clockwork the system slips into place. Teachers station themselves at key points of the staircases and the end of the corridors. Children move at a rapid pace without running or talking. There are smiles and nods of hello – this isn't a prison, after all – but the focus is on supreme efficiency. Every moment of learning time counts and movement between classes can be a drain on these precious minutes. Here at Michaela there is a determination among staff, shared by pupils (remarkably), not to waste this valuable learning time. Once in the classroom, every pupil knows their role, and books, piled at the correct place on the window sill, are retrieved and distributed quickly and quietly down the line. By the time the teacher commands 'Go!' – dot on time – they are ready to begin the lesson. Merits and demerits are distributed as an acknowledgement of this performance.

'Family lunch' is another unique feature of the school, and key to the school motto 'Work hard and be kind.' It begins with the whole school chanting a poem in time. We heard Coleridge's Kubla Khan. Everyone eats the same food, vegetarian menus carefully chosen to suit all faiths and eating requirements. Hot, freshly cooked food but no canteen. Food is served by the children on individual tables of six. Each child is given a role and they all know exactly what they are doing, whether it's pouring the water, dishing out the food or clearing up. During the course of lunch each table will discuss a topic that has already been chosen by the teacher in charge – 'Does what you're taught at Michaela affect your behaviour outside school?', for example. Once the food is eaten it is time to record 'appreciations'. Individual pupils stand up and declare their thanks to the 150 pupils, guests and teachers present, for anything they like, from the care their history teacher took to giving feedback on an essay, to the help his mother gave him in getting him to school that day. The audience applauds, with two sharp claps, merits are awarded for effective articulate speaking, a demerit for any suggestion of ridicule or lack of respect.

At break, lunch, mid-morning and afternoon, children spill out into 'the yard', or as one pupil, remarked, 'it's essentially a disused car park', but it serves its purpose – fresh(ish) air, table tennis tables, football, basketball, a chance to let off steam and above all a chance to talk. This is where friendships are formed and ideas – other than classroom ideas – can be exchanged. Pupils clearly value it a lot, as part of the system of punishment includes being 'banned from the yard'. Apart from during lunch – which is formally structured with general group conversations rather than private individual conversations – this is the chance they have to talk to each other properly.

Pastoral care, well-being and discipline: Everyone in year 7 attends behaviour bootcamp a week before the start of the new school year in September. This is when the system – of detention, merits/demerits, how to manage 'transition', how to walk fast but in silence through the corridors, how family lunch works, which way to walk past your chair when leaving the classroom, how to address a teacher or any other adult, and what attitude to bring with you to Michaela – is carefully, systematically taught, reinforced and embedded. It is an invaluable week for teachers too, new ones especially. By the time term starts everyone understands the systems and can row together. One of our guides ('a girl who struggles academically,' we were later told) was articulate and polite to the nth degree, and proudly told us there was no bullying in the school. There are barely any moments to bully. The reasons pupils don't run in the corridor is that there would be an opportunity to knock into someone, for a fight to brew; for the same reason they walk in a particular direction around their chairs, and cross their arms on top of the table, to avoid surreptitious shoving, a sneaky peak at a mobile phone or anything else that may lead to demerit or detention, but ultimately being someone you don't really want to be.

Unashamedly strict, this is a 'no excuses' school. The discipline is centred on a system of merits and demerits – six detentions and you are in isolation, three demerits have you removed from a lesson. Detention is used regularly but intentionally. The time is not wasted. Each pupil is fully occupied with self-quizzing while they are in detention, and some even start to appreciate the progress they can make while being punished.

Kindness is as much a part of the ethos as achievement. Children are taught to understand that the strict regime is for their own benefit. Family lunch and appreciations, as well as everyone working to serve and clear the food, all contribute to an ethos of gratitude, kindness and empathy.

Parents need to support this approach, and it's often they who find it more of a challenge than their children. Faced with the prospect that a mobile phone would not be returned until the end of the half term, after a child had been caught using it in school, the parents have the choice of accepting it or finding another school.

Pupils and parents: Extremely diverse, pupils here come from a number of different cultures and are of different faiths, but no one dominates. Some walk to school, most take buses from all over London, but mainly from the north west, a few take the tube to Wembley Park and walk across the road to the school. One thing they do have in common, however, is that these are not pupils from highly privileged backgrounds. Half the pupils are eligible for pupil premium. Parents are told that they need to be prepared – 'Michaela', they are told at open evenings, 'will be like the personal trainer in fitness regime and that is what you are signing up to.' The occasional child leaves – not because they can't take the strain, but more often because their parents can't. However the majority of parents, pleased that their children are being taught to such high standards and that behaviour is excellent, are fully supportive of the firm line taken by the school.

Entrance: There are 120 places in year 7. Priority given to siblings, but otherwise the main criterion is a lottery system for people living within a five mile radius of the school. As word spreads, and the school becomes increasingly oversubscribed, proximity to the school will become ever more essential.

Application is through Brent Council, and for an occasional place, ring the council to get placed on the waiting list.

Exit: If Ms Birbalsingh's vision is realised, expect a number of pupils to go to top UK universities, including Oxbridge. The first set of results for year 11 will be in 2019 (though some took RS in 2018), for the upper sixth in 2021.

Remarks: A challenging and rigorous academic education with high expectations for every pupil. For the right child this is a truly extraordinary and superlative school. Not for the faint hearted, the cynical or the fragile. Strict, but with a warm heart beating below the surface, Michaela creates a safe, but stimulating environment, and the chance to fly.

Miles Coverdale Primary School

Coverdale Road, Shepherds Bush, London W12 8JJ

Ages 3–11 **Pupils** 241

020 8743 5847
www.milescoverdaleprimary.co.uk

Headteacher: Since 2008, Taranum Baig BEd with French, NPQH. Has studied at the Sorbonne. Previously acting head and deputy head of Dairy Meadow Primary, Ealing and acting deputy head at Stanhope Primary, Greenford. About to become an Ofsted inspector. Born in India and moved to London as a child. Conscientious and hard-working, though encourages staff not to stay too late at school, so they can get a healthy work/life balance. Gentle sense of humour Enjoys travel and tennis in her spare time. Married. No children. Head says her vision for the school is best summed up by a quotation of Martin Luther King, 'Intelligence plus character – that is the goal of true education.' Head adds, 'irrespective of background.'

Entrance: At 3 into the nursery. Admissions to the nursery are managed by the school office, but from reception to year 6 they are handled by LA, Hammersmith and Fulham. A place at nursery does not guarantee a place in reception. Heavily oversubscribed. Roughly 130 applicants apply for 25 places in nursery; 130 applicants for 30 places in reception. One form entry.

Exit: Pupils go on to Fulham Cross, Phoenix High School, Hammersmith Academy and Ark Burlington Danes Academy. Some move to schools out of the borough.

Remarks: School is named after Miles Coverdale, who in the 16th century produced the first complete printed translation of the Bible into English. Today, the school accepts all faiths. School has gone from strength to strength on current head's watch. She puts this down to high expectations of pupils and staff 'knowing the data' (school keeps a close eye on anyone falling behind), quality of teaching and an excellent team of governors. 'A combination of delivery and accountability,' explains head.

Housed in a vast red-brick, Victorian building in the busy heart of Shepherd's Bush. A mixed, multi-cultural area which is reflected in the ethnic diversity of the pupils. Largest contingent is West African, followed by white British/other. Sixty-six per cent do not have English as a first language. Languages spoken at home include Somali, Arabic and a variety of Eastern European tongues. Thirty-one per cent of pupils eligible for free school meals. Head acknowledges that some pupils come from unsettled backgrounds, so 'we can give them the stability they sometimes lack at home.' A very inclusive school.

Rated outstanding by Ofsted and placed in the top 100 schools nationally over last three years. Academically, each year group performs well above national average. Head confident that pupils can begin with low attainment levels but will have excellent results under their belts by the time they leave. 'We maximise potential.' Children fully engaged in their lessons and teachers full of energy on the day we visited. School works hard to narrow the gap between higher and lower attainers. Booster classes given to year 6 before Sats to make sure everyone performs well. A handful achieves a remarkable level 6 in maths and in grammar, spelling and punctuation before leaving. School has been awarded a gold club award for 'succeeding against the odds in improving pupils' aspirations and achievements.' Head is delighted that she has been made a National Leader of Education and the school has been designated a National Support School, in recognition of the continued school improvement work with other schools at local, national and international levels. A real feather in her cap.

Currently nearly 30 children with statements of special educational need. Early targeted support is the order of the day here, with maths and reading intervention groups for those falling behind. Specialist unit offers speech and language classes for children with language impairment (the only one of its kind in the borough). Pupils here are very much part of the mainstream school. These classes provide support for 20 pupils, between the ages of 3 and 7, in two classes of 10. Wide variety of difficulties catered for, from those who are unable to produce speech sounds to others who find it challenging to recall words. Most pupils then transfer to their local mainstream school at 7 or, if still in need of on-going help, stay at Miles Coverdale where they receive additional support. Full-time speech and language therapist. Children must have a statement before being accepted. A counsellor visits twice weekly to help with children with social and behavioural problems.

Strikingly attractive, bright and colourful school. Most classrooms are huge, often two rooms knocked into one. Food technology room where all pupils are given the opportunity to cook; large ICT suite. New library is wonderful: comfy sofas, bright murals of book characters and inventive furniture, all of which underline the emphasis on reading within the school. Even the most reluctant readers must be enchanted. Lots of small rooms dotted around the place for one-to-one support or small group sessions. Two playgrounds, one for each key stage, with plenty of equipment and a quiet area 'which doesn't get used very often!' Separate outside play area for reception pupils, complete with sandpits and water tables.

Staff consists of a mix of long servers of more than 20 years and more newly qualified. Low teacher turnover. Head keen on constant training of staff. 'We see ourselves as a learning community. We all need to keep learning. Every member of staff needs to keep developing to have an impact.' High pupil/teacher ratio, with two or more assistants per class of 30. High morale among the dedicated staff. One parent felt 'the teachers are close to the parents. They're welcoming and friendly. If you have an issue, they are happy to discuss it. They don't tell you to arrange a meeting and come back another time.' A teacher we spoke to happily gives up his free time to take pupils to events at weekends, such as chess tournaments.

Music is a strength of the school. Music co-ordinator encourages the children to join musical events going on out of school. 'I keep my eyes open for those with that something extra, then I push them on. I even go to the auditions with the parents'. Dynamic department which uses IT to great effect. Choirs put on performances for elderly in local nursing homes. Drama is also strong. Plays include an annual Black History performance as well as Christmas and year 6 productions. Poetry recitals, debates and presentations also encouraged. Numerous outings and trips for all age groups including to Royal Opera House, Lyric Theatre as well as frequent workshops including with English National Ballet and maths magicians. Children are exposed to a variety of enriching experiences from Shakespeare to street dance. Head says, 'The reason for us arranging these activities is that the core of the children here doesn't have access to this sort of experience otherwise. I want them to be introduced to the multi-cultural aspects of British-ness, to British values.' A hugely busy extracurricular timetable on offer here.

The school participates in inter-school sport tournaments but a lack of silverware reflects the dearth of recent victories. Coaches come in from nearby QPR football club. Fencing and football popular and cricket also offered in the summer.

Extended school day available to help working parents with a breakfast club and a nearby after-school play centre, meaning children can do a 10-hour day. Pupils able to attend up to three clubs a week and all are free; current clubs include karate, basketball and dance. Homework club. A popular five-week summer school is led by teachers and support staff and includes maths and literacy lessons as well as plenty of fun 'for those children who don't get away on holiday all summer.' Head very aware that many families struggle to cope, and the school does all it can to give the pupils a chance to enjoy life as well as excel academically.

High parental satisfaction. Those we spoke to were very supportive of the school and felt there were plenty of chances to get involved. A number of the parents work here as support staff. One mother said she was happy to 'let the school get on with it' as she felt 'it takes good care of the boys and girls.' School reaches out to parents and adult classes are held within the school buildings during the day, including English, computer-literacy, sewing and bike-riding. One mother we spoke to had experienced seven other schools before coming here and she believed that this one was head and shoulders above the rest.

M

Outward looking school which is very involved in local community. Teachers work with numerous outside agencies and school provides placements for work experience, teacher training and volunteering. Now has much higher profile within the community and is seen in a positive light by neighbours. Christmas and summer fêtes sponsored by local businesses.

Head says, 'We are what we are. We're successful. The results speak for themselves'. Year 1's mission statement sums up the ethos of the school: to 'respect each other, sing out loud, smile often and work hard.' Head has certainly transformed this school from one which had 'a poor attitude and negative feel' to one that is firing on all cylinders. Seriously impressive on every level.

Mill Hill County High School

Worcester Crescent, London NW7 4LL

Ages 11–19 **Pupils** 1,740 **Sixth form** 452

0844 477 2424
www.mhchs.org.uk

Headteacher: Since 2004, Geoffrey Thompson MA MBA (Ed) FCMI (50s). Formerly head of Duchess's Community High School in Alnwick, Northumberland. Educated at Campbell College, Belfast, then at St Catharine's College, Cambridge, where he read music. Started his teaching career at Langley Park School for Boys in Bromley, where he worked for 18 years, before moving to Norfolk as deputy head, then on to Northumberland. Though Mill Hill County has always been a school with high standards, his time in charge has improved it significantly. 'Having a vision and a blueprint is not my way,' he says. 'You have a set of principles and good judgement, you make decisions with other people and the place grows organically.'

A dapper soul, whose own tie is always immaculately knotted, he has a dry sense of humour and a delightfully precise command of the English language. Married to a teacher (who also works in the school), he has two daughters and a son. Out of hours, he enjoys reading, particularly modern history, travelling and music.

Leaving in July 2019.

Academic matters: One of the country's highest performing comprehensives. With nearly 60 per cent A*-B grades at A level in 2018, and 42 per cent 9-7 at GCSE, this is a school which believes in an academic focus – 68 per cent of pupils gained 9-5 in both English and maths. Apart from a handful of vocational qualifications in ICT and media, the curriculum is traditional, with a good range of modern languages (Spanish, French, German, Latin) and a quarter of pupils taking all three sciences at GCSE. In the sixth form – the largest in the borough – the 33 subjects on offer include sociology, psychology, economics and dance. Maths and science, however, are the most popular options (with 10 groups for maths).

Teaching strong throughout (with regular awards for science, geography and maths) and most subjects provide plenty of enrichment. In English, for example, there are Shakespeare and poetry workshops, in DT, direct links with industry. An undoubted strength of the school is the focused attention it offers for all. 'Every child is taught to their own individual abilities,' commented one parent. For those at the top of the spectrum, there are two members of staff to encourage A level students to aim for A*s and Russell Group universities, while those who struggle to make the 9-4 benchmark at GCSE are offered a one-year course in which to resit. At this juncture, too, the school participates in a Barnet-wide scheme which sandwiches vocational college training with English, maths and employment skills. Largest number of SEN pupils in Barnet with a department reflective of their very varied needs (including provision for blind children). A raft of teaching assistants provides in-class aid and specialist staff oversee classes and support students beyond. 'It's quite an operation,' says the head.

Games, options, the arts: The school prides itself on its extracurricular offering, but there's little doubt that music is the jewel in the crown. 'There are few local schools that can hold a candle to us,' says the head with legitimate pride. He himself rehearses all year 7s to appear in the Christmas concert and from time to time plays the piano at assembly or a duet alongside a visiting professional. Standards throughout are exceptionally high. Recently, for the fourth year in a row, the orchestra performed a joint concert with the Royal Philharmonic ('you have to be quite good for the RPO to come and play with you,' says the head). Meanwhile the school band featured alongside that of the Royal Air Force at the Watford Colosseum. Regular lunchtime concerts, major concerts twice a term, large-scale musical in the Easter term, plus an annual European tour for concert and jazz bands. A full range of other sounds, including gospel, African drum and steel drum. Boys participate as enthusiastically as girls – 'unheard of,' says the head – and one talented former pupil performs regularly at Ronnie Scott's.

In sport too, the school has become a 'force to be reckoned with,' particularly in boys' football and girls' netball. Basketball and rugby also on offer and table tennis played enthusiastically by all. Excellent facilities for sport include a range of pitches, three playgrounds, gym, sports hall and in summer, six-lane track and three tennis courts. Art thriving, with a weekly art club and life drawing workshop run by the Royal Academy for A level pupils. Numerous guest speakers and in-demand trips (languages to Barcelona and Normandy, politics to the US, annual ski trip) to inspire and raise aspirations. Good range of clubs run early morning and after school (which can be difficult for those who live at a distance), plus D of E, World Challenge and CCF (shared with nearby independent Mill Hill School).

Background and atmosphere: Originally opened in 1931 as Orange Hill Boys' Grammar School, which then combined with matching girls' grammar in the 1970s. Merged again with Moat Mount School in 1984 to create Mill Hill County High School. The school, fringed by a good expanse of playing fields and forest, now sits on a hilly site with panoramic London views. There, however, the picturesque ends, with well-used buildings crammed together in an intricate hotchpotch to accommodate more students than ever. 'It is overcrowded,' said one parent. 'They're the victims of their own success.' Older parts of the fabric include some fairly basic portakabins (which house dance and drama), but recent additions have provided modern labs, a sixth form centre, computer suites, seven new classrooms and an air-conditioned assembly hall.

The lack of elbow room doesn't seem to detract from the upbeat mood, with friendly and positive staff (on the day the Guide visited a member of the office team was ringing up a local primary school to ensure a forgotten jumper was returned to its owner) and parents praise the general sense of well-being. 'The school is very good at communicating,' said one. 'They keep us informed and I have the email addresses of all my child's teachers.' Another was grateful for the empathy shown at a difficult time. 'They were understanding and supportive when we had family problems.'

Not the easiest school to get to. No tube nearby, which contributes to the mood of semi-rural calm but can be difficult for those wanting to arrive early or stay late for clubs or games. Mill Hill became an academy in 2011, but still works closely with Barnet Council, particularly in its responsibilities for Oak Hill, a successful facility for 32 emotionally and behaviourally disturbed children, four and a half miles away.

Pastoral care, well-being and discipline: One of the first things parents tend to mention is the uniform policy. 'They're very strict on uniform,' said one. 'Everyone looks very smart.' The head sees uniform as a means of setting the expectation bar. 'We're very clear about what we say and insist that what we say is done. We aren't repressive, but you'd be unlikely to see anyone with their shirt tails not tucked in or their ties not tied.'

The head also spends one lesson a week making surprise visits to a range of classrooms. 'That way, you see what's happening. You chat to the children, look at their books. It's a co-operative relationship, but you could potentially see those same children in another context behaving badly.' The insistent focus on behaviour, attitude and good manners undoubtedly pays off. 'Most people who come across our students have positive things to say.'

Pupils and parents: About half the school's intake comes from the leafy and prosperous suburb of Mill Hill, with its high concentration of professionals and business families, but the intake is certainly not uniform. 'There are quite a lot of deprived children and the ethnic mix is huge,' says the head. It includes significant numbers of families who originate from the Indian sub-continent, Asia and Africa. Only a few, however, 'don't speak excellent English.'

Entrance: Mill Hill has entrance criteria guaranteed to drive north London parents into a neurotic frenzy, with 243 places at 11 sliced up into small print sub-sections. Lucky locals can benefit from one of the 90 guaranteed 'geography' places. But distance from the gates is frighteningly close (rather less than a mile). Siblings, too, are ensured a desk. After that children of members of the teaching staff (who have been working at the school for a minimum of two years). If there are 60 remaining places they are then awarded on aptitude and are split into: 24 for technology, 24 for music and 12 for dance. Technology is tested in two stages – a reasoning test in the summer term of year 5 whittles down about 1,500 to 240, the second round (in abstract reasoning and maths) held in September cherry-picks the rest ('it's harder than getting into Oxford,' jokes the head). Music equally competitive, with up to 400 auditioning, in two sections: listening and performance. 'You can, however, play a snappy piece on the classroom xylophone and come out higher than a carefully coached grade 4 violinist.' Dance candidates are selected by audition.

The large (and heavily oversubscribed) sixth form admits a further 40 to 60 pupils out of 600 applicants, with minimum entry requirements of six grade 6s at GCSE, including English and maths. Those wishing to study science and maths need 7+s in their chosen subjects though, and most come garlanded with a string of 9-7s.

Exit: No-one is ever asked to leave (except for disciplinary matters), but a fair few (27 per cent in 2018) move on after GCSE to local sixth form colleges, independent and grammar schools. Some 50 per cent Russell Group (one of highest representations of any comprehensive in the UK) with four to Oxbridge and four medics in 2018. Quite a number to drama and art-related degrees. A consistent trickle to the US.

Money matters: The transformation to academy status has released additional funds and these are now being used for building projects. Otherwise not rich, but not poor either.

Remarks: A cheerful, well-run school producing highly motivated, high achieving students. Exceptional music.

Mill Hill School

Linked with Belmont Mill Hill Preparatory School, Grimsdell Mill Hill Pre-Preparatory School

180

The Ridgeway, Mill Hill Village, London NW7 1QS

Ages 13–18 **Pupils** 675 **Sixth form** 259 **Boarders** 63 full, 39 weekly

Fees: Day £21,141 pa; Boarding £28,524 – £33,717 pa

020 8959 1176
www.millhill.org.uk

Head: Since December 2018, Jane Sanchez, previously principal deputy and then acting head. She joined the school in 2003.

Founding head of The Mount, Mill Hill International School since 2014 is Sarah Bellotti BEd (50s). Mrs Bellotti is steeped in international education, having spent 20 years teaching English in international schools in Rome and, latterly, nine years as the director of King's, Ely's International Study Centre. It has to be a dream job, this – a beautifully reimagined and refurbished school dedicated entirely to educating able children from overseas in English subjects via intensive language support to enable them to gain places at good English boarding schools – and down the road from and sharing the facilities of the main school. And she fits the bill. Intense and intensely committed to the task: 'I passionately believe in the international community – we celebrate internationalism here' – she exudes focused excitement and a determination to realise the considerable potential here. She spent her first year 'going across the world' spreading the word and recruiting pupils. At the time of our visit, there were 66, including, interestingly, 10 day pupils who find in the flexible curriculum etc something to suit their individual circumstances. Her new school is perfectly placed and equipped to make a real impact on this market.

Academic matters: Pretty trad curriculum though some interesting novelties eg an IGCSE in further pure maths and A levels in computer science and psychology, not found everywhere. Popular A levels are English, business studies and maths – maths being the stand-out success story in terms of results here. Results, otherwise, are a spread. Not vast numbers of A*s and a range from A-C across the board (in 2018, 39 per cent A*/A grades). Popular GCSE options are geography, history, RS and French. Best results in all three sciences, art, Latin and statistics – latter popular and successful but replaced by further pure maths (see above) under exam reform. In 2018, 57 per cent A*-A/9-7 grades overall.

Lots of changes under the previous head's regime include an Innovation Hub – a room where techie things can be tried out. If the DT workshops and the work we saw there is anything to go by (eg stunning sliding work station) great things will emerge. Another innovation is three-weekly progress reports – 'Before, if you were really good or really bad everyone knew but no-one really noticed the in-betweeners. Now you are monitored and have targets. It is more pressure but it's helpful.' And, of course, to counter the pressure, they now have 'mindfulness' and drop-in, stress-reducing activities like colouring. It had to happen. There are masses of catch-up classes, clinics and individual support. It's all there for the taking – though some sense among parents that the extent of what's on offer isn't always made clear – 'If we'd realised, we wouldn't have had a tutor. It was there in school for us all along.'

Good trad Piper Library – impressively full shelves though some stock needs updating and the bookshelves unaccountably not labelled. Good stock of periodicals. F/t UCAS teacher can be found in sixth form centre – 'She's brilliant'.

Interestingly, 20 per cent of the school's population is on the SEN register and we were told over and again how supportive the school is of eg dyslexics. Previous head immediately enhanced the staffing and provision in general and the effects are obvious. 'Some of them are slow developers but they can be absolutely the children we want and do well by.' Support is given by individual and small-group lessons which are timetabled not to cut across pupils' other periods, following and reinforcing aspects of the main curriculum and teaching study and organisational skills. Learning support assistants intervene in mainstream academic lessons to support particular pupils or groups. School mainly caters for pupils with mild to moderate specific learning difficulties but also accommodates some statemented pupils eg those with impaired hearing.

The majority at The Mount comes for the one-year IGSCE course, though you can stay for anything from one term to two years. No IB. Small classes with a maximum of 12 pupils. It takes children from 13-17. All teachers have EAL qualifications/experience. Flexible courses depending on the level of English you arrive with. Pre-A level programme. We met several students on our visits – clearly a happy, stimulated and cohesive group who were enjoying a first class education.

Games, options, the arts: Long and pioneering tradition in the arts. We remember coming for an arts festival some 30 years ago and the vitality we met then has only grown.

Famously sporty and, while having fun, sports are taken seriously here – girls' sports, seemingly, as much as boys'. 'We have fields and fields and fields,' pupils enthused. Partnership with Middlesex University provides high level support for elite athletes. Good to see extension activities with sports scholars – with specialist staff to help them build and challenge themselves. Remarkable number of representatives in local and country teams across a range of sports – netball, cross-country, cricket, golf and – new to us – bouldering. Lots of teams in eg rugby and hockey so not restricted to the real jocks. School magazine reports – written with an honesty rare in such publications – attest to the earnest approach and a capacity for self-appraisal we seldom see. However, some feeling among the pupils that there was, notwithstanding, a lack of ambition and acceptance of below par performances when a bit more get-go might tilt the balance.

'You don't have to be sporty,' said one parent; 'there's so much else to get involved in.' Exceptional music dept and no lack of ambition in its vast repertoire and the 230 concerts and services annually for which it provides the ensembles, choirs, soloists etc. 'The standard varies from professional to er, well.. but they are so inclusive – everyone feels they can have a go.' House music and house drama on alternate years involve – intensely – just about everyone, as does the music competition. Patrick Troughton Theatre (capacity 150+), a rigged stage in The Large ie main hall, and a spacious drama studio with seating for a small audience. We were impressed by the range of art media: 'They encourage you to try everything,' a non-artsy sixth former enthused. We loved the variety in what we saw – no production line stuff. Impressive range of activities on offer. 'There is masses to do,' and lists and lists of clubs, outings and trips bear witness to that.

The Mount could accommodate three times the present number – it is spacious, superlatively kitted out; no expense has been spared. While some facilities are shared with the main school, there is little lacking here – own DT studio, plenty of outside space. The only shared teacher is one of the PE dept. Excellent range of weekend activities, again, shared with the main school.

Boarding: Boarders make up a fifth of the school population and most are full boarders, based overseas. They come from around 15 countries from China to Spain. However, only a third of them need EAL support, which is given individually and in groups when needed. Small number of UK-based weekly boarders. Boarding is set to grow here and not just for overseas pupils. The market for weekly boarding in the London of busy working parents is buoyant and Mill Hill is beautifully placed to supply it. Vertically-aged houses; all but one are mixed. Good bonding activities for newbies. Enticing and varied list of compulsory weekend activities includes outings eg theatre and music trips, catch-up and revision classes, sports, clubs and interest groups – lots of choice. Day pupils come in for much of it. Boarding isn't state of the art – no en-suites here yet – but most are in two-bedders of reasonable sizes and all year 13 boarders in singles. Good games rooms.

When we visited The Mount there were, among its 66 pupils, 24 home languages spoken. School will not take more than 25 per cent from any one country. Boarding takes place in the main school and The Mount's boarders are fully integrated.

Background and atmosphere: Founded by nonconformist merchants and ministers in 1807 in the then village of Mill Hill, safely located away from 'dangers both physical and moral, awaiting youth while passing through the streets of a large, crowded and corrupt city'. It's not just safe but high

– ought to be called Mill Hill-on-the-Hill – and looks over the northern suburbs much as a more famous, boys only, school on a neighbouring hill does, only from a different angle. In many ways. A rare thing, a boarding school of this size – 120 acres – so close to the national hub and unique, now, in offering, as it does, coeducation from 3-18 with an inbuilt international school integral to its offering. In parkland with some glorious trees which still date from the planting of a former resident, the botanist Peter Collinson, the main building – colonnaded and with tall windows – makes a confident statement. Inside are some splendid rooms and many walls are lined with huge oil paintings of school worthies – again, this is a school which had, from its inception, no modest aims. Democracy rules here and even the grandest meeting room – The Crick – is open to bookings from pupils for meetings and discussions.

Countless additional buildings – many attractive, some functional – and dating from all eras. Walkways, staircases abound – 'You get used to stairs here'. We loved the rustic vernacular Winterstoke Library and were desperate to know what is housed in its little tower; we loved the McClure Music School (1912) redolent of an innocent age, and we loved the Favell Building (2007) – which houses humanities and the top floor of which is hung with huge flags from everywhere. An attractive chapel (1896) by Basil Champneys, architect of many notable scholastic buildings. The chapel – though obviously of Christian origins – is now very much an ecumenical hub, and actively celebrates all faiths and their key festivals. We visited over Harvest Festival but missed Rosh Hashanah, the week before, and heard about the preparations for Diwali on the week following. One of our guides explained about Ramadan and the difficulties of fasting. The chapel was decorated by self-portraits of the new year 9s who explain to the gathered classes why they depicted themselves as they had – an excellent way to start to get known and know others.

Away from the main corridor and atrium, some areas are pretty old-school Spartan and need painting or a general refurb. Others are mint and sparkling.

Strong and popular house system and here, unlike in many other schools, houses you belong to are actually physical houses – or, at least, parts of buildings. They are defined by a house colour scheme – you can't miss it in upper areas of the main building where the overhead light is retina-bendingly harsh. Parents praise the heads of houses: 'They deal with everything and they always phone you back'.

New sixth form centre is making staying on more attractive and the revamp is upping the profile and quality of what Mill Hill sixth form has to offer in general.

Outstanding food – we can't remember seeing – or scenting – better. The home-made cookies made us want to curl up and stay for the day.

The Mount – formerly The Mount Girls' School – has been beautifully refurbished. It has lovely grounds, good-sized classrooms and a happy collaborative atmosphere. The pupils – from everywhere – mix well with each other and the boarders they share houses with in the main school.

Pastoral care, well-being and discipline: Universal praise for pastoral care – both when you need it and when you only need to know it's there eg on arrival in the sixth form. 'It was so welcoming!' 'It's not a school where people act up much,' we were told, 'and if you do hit trouble it doesn't define the rest of your time in the school. They try to help you and find out why.' Very rare chuck-outs, mainly for drugs and nothing recent. House structure is the bedrock of the overall care and support and much praise for house staff in general.

Pupils and parents: Boys vastly outnumber girls, especially in the sixth form. This is true in pretty much all co-eds but is markedly noticeable here, partly due to the number of local, first rate, girls' schools. However, again, school is working on redressing this and, in any case, girls, evidently don't feel outnumbered and no-one complains that provision for them is second class. We did note an activity called 'programming for girls' and wondered.. Parents praise the inclusiveness – 'My three are all completely different and the school is brilliant for all of them'. Most day pupils live locally and are the, mostly, comfortably-off, ethnically mixed, professional families you'd expect in this prosperous part of north west London. 7 Active Parents' Association – clearly very popular.

Most Mount students based abroad but it could also be an option for recently relocated families, for local or other UK pupils whose education has, for any reason, been interrupted eg by sports prowess, filming, illness etc because of the flexibility and the intensive courses it offers.

Entrance: At 13+, 80 come up each year from linked prep Belmont, which means 70 places available for outsiders. However, places now offered in years 6 and 7 at Belmont – the prep school is expanding, particularly in hopes of attracting girls. Entry to the senior school from Belmont is not competitive so well worth investigating. Computer-based pre-testing in year 6 for external 13+ Mill Hill applicants in reading comprehension, verbal, non-verbal and numerical reasoning plus group activities and interview. Places also available via year 8 exams in maths, English, science, French and Latin (if learned) plus interview and report; 14+ places tested similarly.

At 16+, 22+ places available and candidates need at least two 7s and three 6s at GCSE.

Exit: Uncompromising chucking out post-GCSEs of those who didn't make the grade stopped by previous head on arrival. At least two 7s and three 6s expected but there is flexibility – as there should be – for those who otherwise make a strong contribution to school life. We find this so heartening – not every school should be trying only to cater for the super-bright. Most of us aren't. Post-A level, one of the most impressively diverse list of leavers' destinations – in terms both of course and university – that we've seen. This suggests a real focus on developing the individual and not turning out an identikit product – we like this. Three off to Cambridge in 2018 (history, engineering and human, social and political science); others off to study eg jewellery and silversmithing, digital film production, anthropology and international business with languages.

The list of notable Mill Hill alumni is equally multi-lateral: actors Jasper Britton, Patrick Troughton (Dr Who mk 2), Harry Melling (Dudley Dursley); Richard Dimbleby and Simon Jenkins; Francis Crick, Norman Hartnell, Bob Marshall-Andrews, Tanika Gupta and Dennis Thatcher.

Around 50 per cent from The Mount move to Mill Hill main school after, usually, a year. Some stay at The Mount for years 10 and 11. The rest to, mostly, other boarding schools better suited to their needs.

Money matters: More than 10 per cent of pupils receive some level of fee assistance and some few are on 100 per cent fee remission. Scholarships in academics, sports, arts all worth 10 per cent of fees – but bursaries available which can contribute, in a few cases, up to 100 per cent of the remainder. Three 100 per cent sixth form bursaries. Hardship fund may see you through short-term liquidity problems. 'Thorough' and regular means-testing, of course. Numerous smaller awards bring kudos and Mars Bar money. Some interesting one-offs eg The Grinton award – a senior school scholarship for a girl boarder who wants to study art and The Donald Hall award for someone who wants to take sixth form science.

Remarks: 'This school is a place where you can express yourself and do anything,' we were told. Spot on. Set to regain its pre-eminence in this part of the world, wider still and wider.

Montpelier Primary School

Montpelier Road, Ealing, London W5 2QT

Ages 4–11 **Pupils** 682

020 8997 5855
www.montpelierschool.net

Headteacher: Since 2003, Am Rai (40s). BA in sociology, Birmingham Poly, MA in educational management and administration at University of London, Institute of Education. Married, two children. Very experienced head who had already worked in seven London state primaries prior to his arrival at Montpelier. He had been twice seconded to rescue failing schools, and you can see why. He is a man of very clear vision and sound, liberal educational principles. He is highly articulate, straightforward and frank in conversation. In two hours' conversation, we were wearied by no jargon, no pseudo-academic parroting, no political posturing – so refreshing. There is no disguising Mr Rai's confidence and his ambition – both personal and, more overtly, for his pupils. The results are there for all to see. Montpelier's most recent Ofsted – with only two days' notice – achieved a full house of grade 1s, and school is now a National Support School, helping others to improve. The results top the borough's and top most other boroughs too. The children are stimulated, creative, challenged, smiley and rewarded. A very good head.

M

Entrance: Oversubscribed at all levels but high turnover among local international community means that occasional places at all stages are not uncommon. All managed by Ealing LA and, if you have no special circumstances, you need to live up close and purposeful if you are to get in. And families increasingly swap their large homes in less well provided for bits of the borough for flats round the corner from this school.

Exit: Some leave for local preps at end of year 4. Of the remainder, around 30 per cent go to the local hotshot comprehensive – Drayton Manor HS. Around 15 per cent to Ellen Wilkinson HS – the local girls' comprehensive. The rest either to local RC or CE high schools or to the local independents – Notting Hill and Ealing, St Benedict's, St Augustine's. Increasingly, some to the Tiffins, to Bucks, Berks or Middlesex grammars, to St Paul's Boys' or Girls', Latymer Upper or John Lyon, and some parents even move house after their bright buttons gain places there or at eg Henrietta Barnett. No disaster schools in the area – another good reason for coming here.

Remarks: Sited on a corner of two quiet, tree-lined roads and adjoining a pretty park. The surrounding streets are similarly well-appointed, orderly and solidly middle class – this is suburban bliss, though the North Circular grinds along only a couple of hundred yards away. The nearest schools are all independent and, not surprisingly, they are the chosen destinations for a sizeable minority of Montpelier leavers.

Three connected school buildings, and only one – due for renovation – makes the heart sink. The latest is a clever extension housing reception and admin. Infants and reception on ground floor – makes sense. Four playgrounds with good play equipment though not over-provided with soft flooring. Reception classes have integral loos, so no tots trailing down corridors. No overheated classrooms here – though we visited on a dull January morning – and no class feels over full, despite 30 in each and staff. Windows have replaced doors wherever possible – school has a light and open feel. Reception in large classroom with a teacher, a nursery nurse, a student teacher and a teaching assistant. Corner with fresh fruit and drinks available all day for whoever feels inclined. Some 40 per cent bring food from home but the school lunch menu – outside caterers – looked varied and appetising.

Infants' classes full of quiet, concentrated activity – seven or eight things going on in each room: water, measuring, building, weighing, word work, writing etc. Every class has a whiteboard and IT used imaginatively round the school – connecting people and activities and joining things up. Learning legacy boards provide testimony to what has been learned during the term. Monitoring and appraisal embedded into everything – each child has her own targets for the core skills and a list of 'I Can' statements to keep parents abreast of what has been mastered and what still needs to be done. This complemented by the clever use of iPads by teachers who photograph work and load it onto a parents' portal so that latest work can be admired at home. Now a National Teaching School, with the head and several teachers giving support to other schools on teaching and leadership.

Lots of imaginative cross-curricular learning: displays everywhere are evidence of lively thinking and teaching. Year 2 work on portraits looked at what portraits can teach us rather than being merely an excuse to draw ourselves. Super project on Medusa – each child had made a Wanted poster with clever text – and another class displayed illustrations of The Lady of Shalott with sensitive use of quotes. Oxford Reading Tree used throughout with built-in encouragement for parental participation and each child has weekly guided reading session to build comprehension skills rather than just skimming speed. A good hall/gym, a nice little library – properly used for lending and reading – two IT suites, art room, and every class has an art week in which they can drop everything else and experience sustained and concentrated work on a project of their own. Unusually strong music – 150+ learn an instrument in or after school – and school provides child care for siblings until 5.00pm to facilitate music activities. Everyone has an afternoon of sport weekly. Not much but better than many.

Remarkable amount of support given to those who need extra help with eg language, writing task or maths. We saw one-to-one sessions and numerous small groups in all available spaces. Also, for those with an SEN to whom – until recent changes in government SEN provision, at least – school has given exemplary support. And organised time made to equip those who arrive with no English with key words and skills. As socially diverse as any school in the capital. Around 55 per cent speak a language other than English at home – huge range of languages and cultures – among which highest proportions from the Middle East and Japan, then India and various bits of Europe. Families include a lot of 'corporate nomads' ie those with three or five year contracts who may be relocated anywhere on the globe. After-school language (French, Spanish, Arabic, Mandarin) and many other clubs.

The first thing that strikes you on an ordinary school day is how quiet it is and how class after class of 30 diverse children work absorbedly and happily together. In this large, highly organised school – and it is a large primary by any standards – children look relaxed and secure and, even amongst the smallest, there is a sense that school is about learning. Few behavioural problems – jumped on smartly when they occur. Head 'will exclude if a child is spoiling the lives of other children', but no-one excluded for bullying in eight years prior to our visit.

Parental talk of 'the warm community feeling', express gratitude that 'the children are looked after well and are happy,' and pay tribute to the truly multicultural ethos – 'all faiths and beliefs are celebrated'. Very active PTA and lots of community activities eg annual international food fair and remarkably effective fundraising summer fête.

Most staff – many are young – highly praised. Head is seen as dynamic and approachable by some and by others as remote and over-protective of his staff. No-one, however, wishes they had sent their children elsewhere, and none would dispute that he has made a stunning success of a school which, before, had been content to be good enough. 'We judge things by the happiness of our children,' asserts head wisely.

More House School (London)

182

22-24 Pont Street, London SW1X 0AA

Ages 11-18 **Pupils** 206 **Sixth form** 33 **RC**

Fees: £19,650 pa

020 7235 2855
www.morehouse.org.uk

Co-heads: Since 2014, Amanda Leach, previously deputy head here for eight years. BSc in sports science from Liverpool and PGCE from Exeter. Has taught at Cranbrook School, Kent, and Uffculme School in Devon. Spent a year teaching EFL in Rome. Joined More House in 1998 as a science teacher and has also taught ICT and PE here. 'Why would I want to leave here? I love it so much,' she enthuses. Married with two daughters; husband is director of sport at Bedales. 'I love being outdoors with my family. My kids are into gymnastics. We are not allowed to sit still for very long at home!' Described by one parent as being 'approachable and down to earth, though we don't see much of her.' Another said, 'I love Mrs Leach. She is breathing new life into the place. She has lots of energy and is a total delight.' Enthusiastic, effervescent and warm. Can be seen cycling to school from Putney every morning and girls wave to her along the Kings Road as she races past. A breath of fresh air.

Since 2017, Michael Keeley BMus. After studying music at Goldsmith's College he completed his teacher training at Birmingham University. In 1990, he became assistant director of music at the Godolphin School in Salisbury, then on to More House as director of music in 1993, promoted to deputy head in 2014 and then co-head. He continues to sing at St Paul's Cathedral as much as his teaching commitments will allow.

Academic matters: Wide range of academic ability. As one parent put it, 'There are less intellectually confident girls here who are nurtured, but there are also some very clever girls, whose parents have chosen the school because it is Catholic.' Core subjects taken in year 7 alongside Latin, history of art, dance, music and drama. All girls take two modern foreign languages and those that are bilingual can take that GCSE early. Maths, science and modern languages taught in ability sets. Religious studies compulsory for GCSE and many choose to continue with it at A level. Heads favour the philosophy and ethics course as it 'encourages girls to question their spirituality.' Pupils take eight to 11 GCSEs. Twenty-nine per cent 9-7 in 2018.

French currently popular at A level, though subjects wax and wane, depending upon the cohort. School happy to have only one or two pupils taking a subject at A level and class sizes seldom above four. Polish, Russian and Arabic all fell into this category recently, with no take up for physics or chemistry. Timetable built around what girls want to do and school tries to be flexible. Twenty-six different subjects currently taught at A level. In 2018, 33 per cent A*/B and 18 per cent A*/A grades. Extended Project Qualification taken by lower sixth.

Ms Leach has tightened up on academic rigour, making some significant changes since her appointment. Templates now printed in exercise books to ensure that feedback from teachers is detailed and effective and that there is constant dialogue between staff and pupils. School is also getting better at monitoring girls, with assessment points five times a year to ensure those not making enough progress are quickly identified. Colour-coded boards in staff room help teachers to see when a pupil is falling behind in subjects other than their own and gives a more holistic view of each girl's overall progress. Staff appraisals take place more regularly and twilight sessions help ensure staff are on board with changes being implemented.

Excellent provision for girls with specific learning difficulties. The department comprises a full-time SENCo, speech and language therapist and a part-time ESOL teacher. EAL girls have extra English support until it is up to scratch. School can support girls with dyslexia, dyscalculia and dyspraxia; currently one or two per year group have quite severe difficulties. About 25-30 girls currently receiving one-to-one support, with others having help with maths and English in small booster groups. Some girls stop support lessons around year 9 and then come back to having support nearer to GCSEs. 'It is flexible. Girls can dip in and out, depending upon their need.' All subjects offer weekly intervention classes for year 11 and above, from October through to start of exams. One parent feels that 'girls have to flag up their need for support themselves, but once the school is aware of it, provision is made pretty quickly'.

Gifted and talented programme for the brightest pupils. 'The top end is identified within three or four weeks of being here. A learning mentor then sits down with them and asks them whether they are being challenged in each subject'. Extension work might include Italian classes for able linguists. School explains, 'It's not just a case of giving them an extra worksheet. It's more undercover than that, but we know who has a special talent or ability. We take notice, but they don't feel pressurised.' Scholars and gifted pupils are invited to join More's Household, which offers lunchtime talks, given by internal and external speakers.

Games, options, the arts: Creative and performing arts at the heart of the school. Deserves its artistic reputation and currently boasts a textiles specialist, a painter and a mixed-media artist. Weekly, after-school life-drawing classes put on for sixth formers. Numerous visits arranged to London galleries.

Three-quarters of girls have individual music lessons. All year 7 girls play an instrument (brass, string or woodwind), bought through PTA fundraising. Strong choral tradition. In the last concert, 130 girls sang alongside staff, parents and alumnae. Annual international music tour. All musical tastes and talents catered for, from chamber choirs to karaoke and geek club, which involves hand-bell ringing for the Christmas concert. 'The music is exceptional. All-inclusive. You don't have to be talented to be allowed to perform,' according to one parent.

Drama is another strength of the school. Sold-out drama productions of As You Like It and Grimm's Fairy Tales. Biannual play and musical which run on a carousel system. Musical is staged in a professional theatre. If a smaller production is put on one year then a junior production is also staged so that as many girls as possible can perform. 'Everyone is given a chance.'

'PE is being taken much more seriously than in the past,' according to one delighted parent, and sports department is well led. New PE kit has made a world of difference and hoodies without pockets mean that girls are more likely to catch the rounders ball. For the first three years, all girls participate in netball, rounders, hockey, athletics and dance as well as a healthy active lifestyle programme. Years 10-11 may also do circuit training, fitness classes, spinning and climbing and sixth formers take part in boot camp. Two girls recently selected to represent borough in London Youth Games netball team. Teachers run the London marathon and raise significant amounts for charity in the process. 'The great thing about sport at More House is that everyone participates,' commented one parent. As heads explain, 'We are competing against bigger schools. Sometimes we win, sometimes we lose, but all girls get the chance to play in a team.'

Plenty of early morning and lunch time clubs, such as a thriving debating club, as well as play-dough modelling and knitting for those who prefer something more sedate. 'We want the girls to keep their childhood as long as possible. We also offer flower pressing. We don't want girls to bypass that lovely age.' Touch-typing compulsory for all in year 7. Most clubs are run by sixth formers and year 11 girls; some are run by professionals. Enviable overseas trips to Europe as well as skiing in America. Year 8 trip to France is a highlight, involving canoeing and camping overnight. Those that cannot afford the trips are subsidised, and alternative trips are also organised in London. 'Always lots going on here. That's why I am such a fan of the school,' said one satisfied parent.

Background and atmosphere: Founded in 1953 by canonesses of St Augustine. Since 1971, the school has been under lay management. Named after Sir Thomas More, the Tudor theologian.

M

In the heart of Knightsbridge, though not as glamorous as its location might suggest. Described by one parent as being 'essentially two houses in Pont Street with minimal outside space. Pretty scruffy and quite dark.' Much of the school was looking distinctly tired when we visited, but all has been transformed: classrooms ripped out, new furniture installed and redecorating throughout. One delighted mother told us, they have 'been busy tidying up the place, decorating where it was needed and making it more aesthetically pleasing.'

Heads determined that the school should 'not be a pressure cooker. We're not waiting for that top to blow off.' This is a very nurturing environment in which girls are constantly encouraged. One mother commented, 'At parents' evening, the teachers always highlight the girls' strengths and are keen to build on these, rather than just dwelling on what they can't do. It boosts the girls' confidence.' Very small classes which do not change from year 7 to GCSEs. 'That's my one gripe about the school. It would be good for everybody if the classes were mixed up regularly,' said one mother. Almost all classes have no more than 16 girls up till GCSE. Sixth form classes range from one pupil to 10 (but mostly much fewer). Family feel to school and all age groups mix well together, partly due to flourishing house system.

Pastoral care, well-being and discipline: Catholic heritage and ethos strong, with many crucifixes on display around the school. Currently 40 per cent Catholic, though there are girls of all faiths and none. School has its own chapel and the chaplain takes mass once a week. Girls are prepared for confirmation. 'Catholicism is quite a big deal here,' said one parent. 'We get the balance right between Catholic and non-Catholic,' believes Ms Leach. 'It's part of our foundation, to respect each other and to be kind. I'm not a Catholic, though I went to a convent school and then on to a missionary school, so faith is very much part of me.' Spiritual growth fostered here. Girls also raise decent sums for charity and this is seen an important part of their education.

Parents cite the pastoral care as being a main strength of the school, and those we spoke to felt that issues were dealt with efficiently and effectively. Heads keen that girls should develop a sense of perspective, and they are frequently reminded that 'It's not failure you should worry about. It's how you pick yourselves up. I don't paint a perfect image of myself. We all have ups and downs. It's my duty to help the girls through their difficulties.' Ms Leach stands at the door each morning as the girls file past. She can usually spot when something is amiss with a pupil. Layers of support in place, including tutors, and all 'minis' (year 7s) have a 'big sister' in sixth form. Because it is such a small school, eating disorders and emotional difficulties are spotted quickly. Hard for pupils to hide under the radar here.

Excellent relationships between staff and pupils. Girls see their teachers as approachable. As one parent put it, 'The teachers know the girls so well, that's the beauty of a small school.' Occasional short-term suspensions for rudeness to a member of staff but school is not overly quick to punish girls. 'If a girl has messed up, she's going to get an earful from her parents. I tend to ask them what they'd do differently next time.' Saturday detentions recently introduced for persistent offenders.

Pupils and parents: Roughly 70 per cent British. International contingent from all over, including Spain, France, China, Russia, America and Middle East. 'A mixed bag. Some with lots of money, who are driven in and out by chauffeurs, and others who are struggling. Quite diverse, with a good percentage of different cultures,' according to one mother. Girls travel from all over London.

Parents mostly professional. 'I don't think I have the most demanding parents in London. That's a reflection of the girls who are here. These parents want the best for their daughters. They are not idealistic in terms of what their daughters are capable of. They are realistic and know we're going to do the best job we can for them.' Parents feel the communication is good: 'We are kept fully informed, both with the good and bad. We are kept in the loop.'

Entrance: One open day only but private tours throughout year. Part of London 11+ Consortium. The entrance process now consists of a cognitive ability test (rather than maths and English exams) with great emphasis on the interview. This is pivotal in many ways. Head always tells girls that they will be able to answer all the questions as they are about themselves, so no need to be nervous. Increasing numbers of applicants every year but lists are closed once 150 have registered. Normally 32 places available (two forms of 16) though some bulge years of 48 (three forms). Girls are either offered a definite place or put on the wait-list. Very few turned down completely and when they are it is 'because they are not More House material as they are off the scale at either end. I can't support the very lowest ability or very highest ability, given the cohort I've got. I don't want one girl on her own at the top. If a girl can't be challenged intellectually by peers here, she's better off elsewhere. It would be great for my results to take them on, but I won't do it,' explains Ms Leach. Occasional vacancies further up the school are filled quickly. Three or four join in sixth form. School is looking for potential as much as performance at each stage. 'I want to find the golden nugget that's hidden somewhere in a girl. I want to watch them blossom.'

Exit: About 60 per cent stay on for sixth form. 'The ones who leave are those who are too cool for school. I'd rather have the ones who want to be here.' Some depart for co-ed establishments or go to local sixth form colleges. Post A level, many go to art college. Others head to universities all over: Queen Mary's, Exeter, Reading, Nottingham and Kent popular in 2018, with one off to the British Institute of Modern Music. Subjects include maths, criminology, psychology and classics. One parent felt the school 'isn't striving to get everyone into university. That's not what they are about. They try to support the girl in finding out what is best for them.' Even if a girl is deemed to be Oxbridge material, there is no pressure on her to apply if it's not the right course for her. Usually one girl to Oxbridge every couple of years though none recently. School is now focusing on more careers advice for girls and is aware that it should tap into the expertise of its alumnae more.

Money matters: School offers academic scholarships and exhibitions as well as creative and performing arts scholarships to year 7 and lower sixth. Entry bursaries for those starting the school in year 7, as well as special governors' bursaries offered in response to a particular set of circumstances. Normally only awarded to girls who are already at the school and in examination years.

Remarks: If your daughter needs a large, competitive school with plenty of space, this is probably not the place for her. But, as one satisfied customer put it, 'If you're after an all-girls, Catholic school in central London, this is a great choice. It's not for everyone, but if your daughter wants a small, happy and supportive school, this couldn't be better. If I had my time over, I'd send my daughter here again like a shot'. School is aware that many parents do not know about More House yet, but that 'word is getting out as we're getting better and better.' The way things are moving, this school is not going to remain a secret for much longer.

Mossbourne Community Academy

100 Downs Park Road, London E5 8JY

Ages 11–18 **Pupils** 1,322 **Sixth form** 289

020 8525 5200
www.mca.mossbourne.org

Principal: Since 2012, Peter Hughes BA (30s), who took over when founding principal Sir Michael Wilshaw left to lead Ofsted. 'They were big shoes to fill,' he admits, and although some parents say he's less inspirational and personable than his predecessor, he hasn't disappointed and is known for being both exacting and reflective. An Australian, he came to Mossbourne as part of the Future Leaders programme, which identifies, supports and trains potential head teachers. Has taught at Pimlico and Highgate Wood, and was an advanced skills teacher. Gained his BA in education (secondary mathematics) from Charles Sturt University, Australia.

Big on marginal gains, many of the changes he's made are peripheral, including introducing a lottery system to replace the pure distance criteria ('I wanted to stop parents trying to buy their way into the school by moving nearby') and offering an additional 10 per cent of year 9 places to those with the potential to become elite rowers. 'Originally we did this in year 12, but if we're going to complete against private schools, we need to train them at the same age they do,' he explains.

About as far from the stereotype of a headteacher as you can imagine, he is young and hip, with a shiny black office that wouldn't look out of place in a trendy media company. Mostly, though, he's elsewhere in the school ('I learned from my predecessor that you can't know a school from behind a desk') or offsite as he is CEO of the Mossbourne Federation, now overseeing Mossbourne Community Academy, new Mossbourne Victoria Park Academy (secondary school), Mossbourne Parkside Academy (primary school) and the new Mossbourne Riverside Academy (also primary) in Queen Elizabeth Olympic Park.

Living in Canary Wharf, he is an early riser, often seen out running at 6am with the rowers.

Academic matters: Exceptional results: in 2018, 70 per cent of pupils got 9-5 in both maths and English at GCSE. At A level, 40 per cent of grades were A*/A, 90 per cent A*-C. Not only are these some of the best state school results in the capital, they are also all the more extraordinary when you consider that some of the pupils arrive in year 7 hardly able to read. That said, Hackney is experiencing a rise in the quality of students leaving its primary (and secondary, for that matter) schools, making Mossbourne a less steep learning curve for students than it once was.

School has remained in the top one per cent in the country for value added ever since it opened, a feat the head puts down to several factors. First, they've created an environment with a 'can do' attitude, where it's cool to learn. Second, there are exceptionally strong structures in place, with a strict uniform policy, ferocious discipline and meticulous monitoring with weekly target setting. The 'personalised learning agenda' is certainly not just government jargon at this school. Third, young and eager teaching staff provide top quality teaching, helped by great facilities. 'Three things are expected of the teaching staff here – giving high quality feedback; providing nurture and care; and being accountable for their results. The rest is up to them,' says the head. Although some teachers are inevitably better than others, they generally do whatever it takes to help kids grasp the subject and are nearly always prepared to go the extra mile, say parents. 'Whatever support you need, they'll give it,' said one.

The banded intake is set on entry in all the main curriculum subjects (English, maths, science, humanities, ICT and modern languages), with significantly smaller class sizes for lower sets and considerable movement between sets. Music, drama, dance, PE, art and design technology are not setted. Three modern languages on offer at GCSE – French, German, Spanish – as part of the core curriculum, and students also have the opportunity to take public exams in Turkish (large take-up), Latin (significant take-up), Bengali, Swedish, Italian. 'We meet the requirements of parents,' says the head, 'so if they speak a certain language at home, but want their son or daughter to learn it in a more formalised way here, we can accommodate that.'

Traditional academic sixth form, offering around 25 A level subjects, the most popular of which are maths (around two-thirds take this), English (around half choose this), history, psychology and the three sciences. Also on offer are Latin and classical civilisation, plus creative options such as music, art and drama.

Plenty of computers throughout, many built into the modern white desks – technology is embedded into learning here. Homework is set in abundance, but a 4.20pm finish for all means students can spend the last period of the school day either doing homework, preparation for the next lesson or revision – especially good for students lacking a quiet space to work at home. This period can also be used for some of the 30 activities on offer – from bicycle maintenance to table tennis and from journalism to debating club – although only if the student commits to doing their homework later on those days. Saturday morning school not compulsory, but provides a safe place to do weekend activities such as the City explorers' club, revision lessons, Mandarin and other optional classes (including English for non-native speakers) and, of course, sports.

M

Outstanding autistic spectrum disorder provision via its own well-resourced teaching centre and well-qualified specialists. 'We take three children per year under this provision, which continues in sixth form and beyond, through the transition into college or work,' says the head. 'Everyone is fully integrated into mainstream school life here.' Parents are impressed. 'The help they've given my son around his dyslexia has changed his life. He went from struggling to write a paragraph in year 7 to writing reams of pages within months, and his growing confidence led to him moving up his sets too,' said one parent.

Games, options, the arts: Sports include football, netball, basketball, cricket and 'best in Hackney' for athletics. Rowing is big and continues growing, with links to the London Youth Rowing and London Regatta Centre, opposite City airport – originally a training centre for the Olympics and still a world-class training facility for the school's rowers, of whom the elite may train 12 times a week. Rowing is part of the PE timetable in years 7-9; recent medals at British championships and European and world indoor event. Impressive sports facilities include a full size sports hall and rowing gym, while all grass sports take place on Hackney Downs. Latest on the building agenda is a performance pavilion, a dedicated space designed by Rogers Stirk Harbour + Partners, where students can train on-site for rowing, as well as providing extra sensory provision for the school's autistic intake and enhancing the school's already notable music provision.

Music is a specialism, with over 250 pupils having subsidised instrumental lessons. Junior and senior choirs and bands, along with an orchestra, all perform in regular concerts and performances. Music scholars programme enables selected students to perform in public at the likes of the Jazz Café and Tower of London, and these students are also expected to share their learning back at school to help develop other students. 'My children had never done music before Mossbourne and I now have a leading guitar playing, violin playing child,' one parent told us.

Drama practice mainly takes place in the modern and well-equipped auditorium and lecture theatres, culminating in regular performances and an annual whole-school production, with recent examples including Charlie and the Chocolate Factory, Romeo and Juliet and Little Shop of Horrors.

Plenty of examples of skilled and creative artwork showcasing strong artistic talent across fine art, clay, screen-printing and more. A dedicated A level art studio means students never have to compromise on space and time to work. 'I always think art is one of the unsung successes of Mossbourne,' one student told us.

Trips to Edinburgh, Belgium, the Isle of Wight, language trips to Spain and Germany; Spanish play, poetry competition, debating, links with London College of Fashion. Lots of careers advice. 'My son talks about his future a lot – he has high aspirations,' said one parent.

Background and atmosphere: Founded on the site of Hackney Downs School, once a successful local grammar school, whose alumnae include Sir Michael Caine and Harold Pinter. By the 1990s, however, it had become notorious as 'the worst in Britain' and was eventually demolished. Mossbourne was rebuilt on the same site, a tricky triangle bounded on two sides by railway lines. Founding principal Sir Michael Wilshaw worked alongside architects, Richard Rogers and Partners, to design a school (costing £32.5 million) which met his requirements. Now one of the largest wooden structures in England (known locally for looking like an IKEA, not least because it's huge and blue on the outside), it was created in a V shape, which holds in its arms a welcoming triangular social area, complete with tables and benches, basketball areas, table tennis tables etc.

Wilshaw believed that pupils need to be kept under constant observation, so the head's office and the classrooms all overlook the grounds. No corridors – hidey-holes for bullying – and no staffroom, since Wilshaw felt teachers need to be involved at break times and after school, when most trouble occurs. Inside (where the IKEA comparison still feels apt, such is the emphasis on modern, innovative and fresh interiors) the triple-height space is light and airy and learning takes place in 'learning areas,' which are split into themes of sport, history, music etc – including one specifically for year 7s, whose transition is a major area of focus. Glittering new sixth form centre.

In each glass-walled classroom – all of which have an open door policy – all students begin lessons by reciting the Mossbourne reflection: 'Throughout this lesson I aspire to maintain an inquiring mind, a calm disposition and an attentive ear, so that in this class and in all classes I can fulfil my true potential'. Sure enough, the students we saw did look attentive and interested.

Active school council and peer mentoring scheme for core subjects. Prefects in year 13. No house system. Pupils we spoke to were articulate, polite and delightful – oozing pride about their school. We were also wowed by the set-up here. It's bright, contemporary and spotless, with superb facilities and seemingly endless examples of attention to detail, including language booths and a huge amount of space for private study.

Pastoral care, well-being and discipline: Woe betide students who don't toe the line here, with staff giving out detentions for things like keeping a watch on during PE, untidy uniform and being more than 10 seconds late when the morning whistle goes at 8.40am. 'We work on the principle that if you sweat the small stuff, the big stuff takes care of itself,' says the head. 'Nothing ever escalates into anything more serious,' agreed one student. 'The most serious offence I've ever seen here is talking in class.'

Among parents, it tends to be the middle-class liberals who struggle, with some thinking teachers can be overzealous. There was also a feeling among some parents we spoke to that new teachers are particularly extreme. 'There's a joke that new teachers here don't smile until Christmas,' one told us. 'My son got a detention for writing his homework on the wrong page – I mean, come on,' said another. But most approve, saying the heavy-handedness has made their child very driven.

No physical contact between students is allowed ('If a boy has his arm around a girl, how do we know it's not making her uncomfortable, but she's too embarrassed to say, for example?' explains head) and no more than six people in a single group in the playground. Staff always on hand, with stairwells manned between lessons and students monitored after school.

Pre-GCSE pupils wear smart grey and red school blazers and neatly knotted ties, sixth formers graduate to business-like suits and skirts (at or below the knee). Mobiles banned and students not allowed to enter shops on their way home or loiter outside the gates in groups. Racism a non-issue, and the same can be said for truancy, with a 96 per cent attendance rate.

Pastoral care exceptional. Everything is geared towards students feeling safe and comfortable so they are ready to learn, with as much access as they need to school counsellors, who come in as and when they're required (the school works with a private company), plus plenty of senior teaching staff (including the deputy head) whose sole responsibility outside teaching is pastoral care. Few personal problems go unnoticed, whether self-harm or being picked on. At the first sign, parents are invited to come and speak to the staff, with two dedicated meeting rooms available. 'We very much believe parents are our partners and are fundamental to the success of the school,' says head. Bullying extremely rare and when discovered, it's dealt with swiftly and seriously. 'My daughter told me about a boy who came out in year 8 and there was no nastiness about it at all, with everyone being really accepting – that would have been unheard of in Hackney in the past,' one parent told us.

Pupils and parents: A large percentage of the intake comes from the adjacent Pembury estate, an urban sprawl which tends to hit the headlines for its shootings and drugs rather than its high educational aspirations. Two-thirds of pupils are from minority ethnic groups (many Turkish Kurds), two-fifths speak English as a second language, 50 per cent are on free school meals. But also a fair number of clued-up, middle-class parents – the kind who used to go private or bus their children out of the borough – who fight from a great distance to get their children the superb education the school offers.

Entrance: Some 1,500 apply for the 216 places, making it one of the country's most oversubscribed schools. The head is looking for a balanced intake: 'We want a comprehensive – we don't want a secondary modern'. Applicants sit cognitive ability tests to divide into four equal ability bands. Fifty per cent of places in each band are given to those who live within the inner zone (up to 1km from the gates); 30 per cent of places go to those in the middle zone (1-2km) and 20 per cent to those in the outer zone (2-3km). Priority is given to looked after children, those with a child protection plan, siblings, those with medical needs and children of staff. Further places by lottery, which head says prevents parents from buying their way into the school by moving into a property nearby, although some parents say the inevitable consequence of the gentrification of Hackney is that this feels less of a community school than in the past. Offers an additional 10 per cent of year 9 places to those with the potential to become elite rowers (zoning does not apply to this group).

The lower sixth form has 200 places. Applicants must meet the demanding criteria of seven 9-4 GCSEs including English and maths, with priority given to pupils already at the school – around 100 of whom generally secure places. All candidates, including those already at the school, must also meet the subject specific entrance criteria in their chosen A level subjects. Whilst successful external candidates used to come mostly from other Hackney comprehensives, they are increasingly applying from further afield, utilising the quick and easy train route from Liverpool Street.

Exit: Those who leave at GSCE leave mainly do so to do vocational qualifications or go straight into work. After sixth form, 90 per cent to universities, nearly half of those to Russell Group universities (a wide mix). Seven to Oxbridge in 2018. Broad array of subjects studied, including music, maths, physics, engineering, law, communications; five medics/dentists in 2018. Remaining 10 per cent mainly into apprenticeships, with around 4-10 students taking a gap year.

Money matters: Money not a problem at this well-resourced school – everything from the buildings to the technology is of the highest standard and whatever the head wants to get done he has the means to achieve.

Remarks: If ever there was a school proving that the right ethos, leadership and sufficient resources can provide not just a good education – but a great one – in the most deprived of areas, this is it. Everything about it is geared around the concept of passive supervision and students feeling safe, nurtured and ultimately ready to learn. This, together with the combination of high quality teaching, excellent facilities and strong discipline and pastoral care, means it's hardly any wonder that results are outstanding and that parents fight hard to get their kids in.

Muswell Hill Primary School

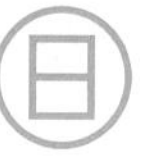

Muswell Hill, London N10 3ST

Ages 4–11 **Pupils** 420

020 8444 8488
www.muswellhillprimary.co.uk

Head: Since September 2018, Mandi Howells, previously deputy head of Carlton Primary School, where she taught since 1996.

Entrance: One of the most heavily oversubscribed primaries in the borough (approaching 600 applicants for 60 places). Having a sibling already at the school or living nearby are the two quickest ways through the gates, but 'near' means very, less than a quarter of mile if you want a realistic chance.

Exit: The school sits midway between two of north London's best comprehensives, so why consider anywhere else is the general parental view. Most leavers proceed to Fortismere, a few to Alexandra Park. A trickle, 'for those who live in funny roads', to independents, plus a few to various sought-after nearby grammar schools.

Remarks: Its last full Ofsted (2006) deemed this an outstanding primary, and there's little evidence this view should change. Results in year 6 remain rock solid. Teachers are a happy mix of experience and enthusiasm; most are in their 30s, with a healthy sprinkling of men. 'We're very happy with the teachers,' said one parent. 'They're very approachable and supportive.' The new management structure (giving responsibility for a number of year groups to three assistant heads) means classroom time is always in the hands of a qualified teacher (and parents have 'a point of contact' for concerns, gripes, etc).

Children eased gently into school life with parents allowed to stay in the early days. Good support for the basics, too, with an informative 'phonics workshop' for those unfamiliar with the jargon. French from year 3 (but 'only a little'). Good ICT, with plenty of coding. Science skills developed beyond the curriculum with final year pupils introduced to secondary school methods with classes at Fortismere. Philosophy, reasoning and 'reflection' from reception. Regular homework, with daily reading, weekly maths and spelling, plus 'the odd project'. Comprehensive special needs strategy overseen by a SENCo, aided by learning support assistants in each class and out-of-school specialists when required.

The visual arts important here – 'There's a lot of focus on art,' said one parent. As well as the standard fare, there's an arts week, art award, and involvement with a 'working' artist. School orchestra and choir (both provided in after-school clubs).

Sport 'huge'. Netball, rugby, dance, cricket, gymnastics, basketball, athletics and hockey all on offer, with external specialists honing skills to a high standard and plenty in the way of inter-school competition ('The trophy cabinet's not big enough for the trophies we've received,' says the head). But, if winning is the aim, the attitude remains inclusive. 'Football Friday' fields eight teams and eight groups of supporters (plus appropriate team shirts) and regs require three girls from each team to be on the pitch at all times. Good range of well-organised after-school clubs, from cheerleading and chess, to cooking and capoeira. (Paid for) before- and after-school clubs extend the school day for working parents.

Formed by the merger of an infant and junior school in 2000, the school now occupies an army camp of 60s low-rise buildings. Located on the site of what was once Muswell Hill Railway Station, there's lavish outside space, with an attractive, well-equipped playground for the youngest, good-sized courts and extensive running-around space (dotted with picnic tables) for their elders, plus a delightful wooded area and wildlife garden.

'Joy, discovery and diversity' are the defining themes of schooldays here, and parents agree that this is 'a really nurturing' place. Reasonably relaxed in a north London way, so no uniform. ('It's quite liberal, but I like that,' said one mum). Generally 'millennial' in approach, so clothes recycling point on site and pupils encouraged to walk to school. Broad cross-section of ethnicity and income, but the prevailing mood solidly middle class. ('It would be lovely to go for ice cream; let's find a date.') Fundraising, too, tends to reflect the area, with a concert of Vivaldi's Four Seasons a recent moneyspinner.

Generally a friendly, upbeat place, with parents bonding in the active PTA, which raises funds through a multitude of events, from quiz evenings and cake sales to fairs and fireworks night. Also active gardening and nature groups involved in 'site development'. 'It's a very nice community and I've made some very good friends.'

Produces articulate, confident children, who enjoy their time at school. 'My son looks forward to school every day.'

Newham Collegiate Sixth Form Centre

326 Barking Road, London E6 2BB

Ages 16–18 **Pupils** 503

020 3373 5000
www.thencs.co.uk

N

Principal: Since 2014, when the school opened, Mouhssin Ismail (late 30s), former City banking and finance lawyer at Norton Rose Fulbright and one-time Essex cricketer. Nobody can have any reason to question Mr Ismail's deep seriousness and intensity of purpose. Very much admired and liked by all constituencies – 'there are many explanations for the school's success,' said one parent, 'but Mr Ismail is at the heart of each of them'.

Previously assistant headteacher at Seven Kings High School, with a reputation as an outstanding economics teacher (as he still is), Mr Ismail is conscious that much of his own story has resonance for his pupils: 'I am a local boy, from an ethnic minority. My parents were devoted to my interests, but they had little formal education. But they provided me with example, and they taught me the value of hard work.' He is married with a boy and girl – parenting and cricket-coaching with his young family soaks up most of his spare time.

He clearly relishes the job, but in a thoughtful and believable way. 'We've started on a journey and, yes, it's exciting. But it's still early days.' His key ambitions for the school are academic: 'We'd like 75 per cent A* and A grades, 35 places at Oxbridge annually – because, without this kind of success, too many of our kids just won't have the choices and chances'. But he is also clear that the school has an equal duty to try to make sense of the elite universities and workplaces to which he wants his pupils to aspire. 'So building up cultural and social capital to support them in their ambitions is as important and, believe me, we take it seriously'.

Academic matters: This is a selective school, but virtually all of the pupils have been at non-selective state secondaries before they arrive, and the results are staggeringly good. In 2018, their third ever A level cohort scored 90 per cent A*-B and 99 per cent A*-C, trumping many of the local grammar and independent schools.

Unlike so many schools, state and independent, NCS is taking no shortcuts to get this kind of success. The A level curriculum in the core is pretty much confined to facilitating subjects recommended by leading universities: maths, further maths, English literature, economics, geography, history, psychology, religious studies, government & politics, chemistry, physics and biology are all offered. The glaring omission is the absence of foreign languages, ancient or modern. 'There just isn't the demand,' says the head, 'and we can't make it financially viable'.

Prejudice might suggest that this is a maths and science factory, but that isn't the case: 'our humanities results are also outstanding,' head explains, 'especially history and English'. In a school of some 500 pupils, overwhelmingly from ethnic minority backgrounds, this challenges many complacent assumptions. The staff (39 of them, two-thirds Oxbridge-educated themselves) are teaching right to the top end, and clearly to great effect.

How do they do it, one asks? Selection clearly plays a large part in this, and so too does academic intensity. Classes start at 8.30am five days a week, and the whole infrastructure – iPads for all, study periods instead of free periods – is unapologetically geared towards high achievement. Almost uniquely in our experience, private study periods live up to their name – the sense is that serious study is being undertaken in silence by everyone there. There's also homework, of course but, as one girl suggested, 'It's sensible homework – it ties in what we've been doing, or what we're about to do – and it's about making us think.' One parent acknowledged that there was a lot of work, but added, 'I think it's up to parents ultimately, not schools, to try to ensure our children don't get overwhelmed. If we need to restore the balance, we should do that. The school is already playing its part.'

Another assumption might be that this makes for an examination sweatshop. That would be grossly to underplay the much richer vision of education which underpins the place. Classes end at 3pm, and the extra time this frees up allows for a massive enrichment programme, drawing off the school's super-curriculum. There are visiting lecturers (Ed Milliband, Lord Mervyn King and Professor Lord Robert Winston among many others) and pupils team up with PhD students at UCL with whom the school is partnered. There are also myriad networks with business and industry, and a range of non-examined cultural and academic courses – living testimony to the extent to which the school is embracing a tradition of liberal humanism. 'Our pupils, for all kinds of reasons, can quickly feel strangers anywhere outside London,' the head acknowledges. 'To prepare them for university and beyond, they need a great deal more than A levels'.

Special needs are acknowledged to the extent that those pupils who have been diagnosed as qualifying for extra time in exams may receive it, but there is no in-house specialist to supplement teaching. 'Very few pupils are involved,' explains the head, 'and our staff are always happy to put in any extra effort required.'

Games, options, the arts: The school encourages sport, but there is no specific provision for it within the timetable. The East Ham Leisure Centre is literally next door, and the fact that Friday school finishes at 2pm is an inducement for some students to go next door for a workout. The school also supports students taking Duke of Edinburgh Award, and there are music and drama societies. It has had huge success in debating, with one pupil recognised for being the first state school student to be judged Best Individual Speaker in the Eton Debating Competition.

But there just aren't the resources – human, material and, above all, time – to enable its pupils to experience drama, music and sport in the ways available to those from top independent schools. On the other hand, the school is committed to facilitating these experiences – through links with partner schools, and local initiatives. In the same spirit, it supports volunteering and outreach programmes.

The school is acutely aware that it needs to help its students to confront and understand much of the world in a way which is often taken for granted by independent school pupils. 'Being in London makes that a whole lot more possible,' says the head. Trips to theatres and museums, galleries and other landmarks, easily otherwise overlooked, are an integral part of every student's experience.

The school has facilitated an all-expenses paid work placement in Abu Dhabi with leading international law firm White & Case LLP and overseas visits to Kyoto, Japan to engage in science workshops with eminent Japanese scientists as well annual trips to Washington and New York, where students have visited the White House, Pentagon, UN headquarters and Columbia University. There is a real sense that the school is replicating many of the outstanding features of a private school education, providing its students with opportunities that would not necessarily be available in a normal state school.

Background and atmosphere: Having started life in 2014, working in partnership with Newham Council, NCS is – and feels – like a local school. Of course, it's made distinct by being selective, and also by occupying a splendid grade11* listed building in East Ham. At the start of 2018, it became one of the flagship schools of the City of London Academies Trust – assuring it, amongst much else, of access to a centre of wealth and influence.

The atmosphere which results is also distinct: it's utterly metropolitan, for one thing – no rolling acres here and only yards away from the bustle of east London – and multiracial and multi-ethnic.

When we visited the students were calm, friendly and articulate – very focused in class, but never robotic. There was lots of relaxed interchange between teachers and students, and plenty of smiles but, underneath it all, it was impossible not to recognise the deep ambition of everyone there. There's a school uniform, enforced strictly, with students looking immaculate and professional at all times, worn not so much with pride (that may well be true) but with the same sort of calm pragmatism which characterised the whole place. They are busy young men and women and, in pursuit of their ambition: striking an attitude about uniform, or indeed about many of the things which exercise some more peach-fed youngsters, would seem rather frivolous here.

Pastoral care, well-being and discipline: Given that competition for places at NCS is intense, with approximately 3,000 applications being received for 300 places (driven by pupils as much as by parents), and that it is a day school, discipline is hardly an issue. 'Our parents value education highly,' says the head, 'and that's a cast of mind which they communicate to their children. The school benefits from that greatly. Of course, just like any group of 16-18 year olds, issues surface, but bad behaviour isn't one of them.' Managing work pressure, social media and the claims of competing friends may each occasionally call for help. So may no longer being at the top of the class – as so many were in their old schools.

Pupils see their tutors three times each week for 20 minutes – 'long enough for the basis of good relationships to be built up'. The head insists he and all his colleagues operate an open-door policy and pupils are insistent that this really happens. 'If I need help,' said one boy, 'I know that any of my teachers will be there to help at once.' Unlike many other schools, pupils are free to email teachers on work-related questions. 'It makes all the difference,' said one girl, 'and they reply so quickly.' A particular innovation are the weekly Ignite sessions – an hour each week – based around the ambition of nurturing good 'habits of mind' and dispositions.

The values which abound feel humane and collegial. 'When one of my friends got into Cambridge,' said one girl, 'the whole school was happy.'

Pupils and parents: NCS styles itself as a local school. Most pupils come from modest backgrounds – very often they are the sons and daughters of first generation Asians in Britain, who are ambitious for their children to have opportunities not open to them. They have the dynamism of achievers, and also the tolerance one associates with those living in a global city. As one girl put it: 'We're not usually rich, but we're not all deprived either. My parents went to university, which is a bit unusual, but not very.' One parent suggested that the creed of mutual respect and tolerance is a shock to a small minority of pupils, especially those whose earlier education hasn't prepared them for it. 'I believe this is happening,' he said, 'but it takes time'. Head insists he finds the parents 'invested in the school in ways which are helpful, and a pleasure to work with.'

Entrance: Entry comes mainly from the nine 'partner' schools in Newham – most are 11-16 academies. There are a small number of students from Tower Hamlets, Tottenham and Waltham Forest, and few may have to commute for up to an hour. 'We're quite determined that this will remain a school that serves Newham and students from east London, not least because of the work demands we make,' head insists. Despite applications from some independent school pupils, the trickle of middle class intake will not become a torrent. Selection criteria is rigorously academic – you have to get a 56 points from your top eight GCSEs (including English and maths) and then score between 7 and 9 in subjects being studied at A level (or 6 in some related subjects).

One parent admitted she'd been 'sceptical' about the school when her daughter first applied. 'But as soon as she arrived, my doubts started to fade. The teachers are so engaged. They really want to understand each pupil, and take a great interest in parents as well. Very different from what I was used to.'

Exit: The statistics make the scope of this school's ambitions perfectly clear. Some 95 per cent of 2018 leavers went to Russell Group universities. Ten students went off to Oxford and Cambridge, with 20 medics/dentists. Three got offers to join KPMG or PwC. These are stats which will leave many independent school heads and parents slavering.

A lot of time and care is expended on helping prepare pupils to make UCAS applications, to excel at interview and – in every way – to outperform the expectations that might otherwise be made of them on the basis of their postcodes.

The sting in the tail is that pupils have to perform at all points to continue to year 13.

Remarks: If NCS continues to deliver in the way in which it has begun, it will be the standard bearer for a whole new generation of schools. There are two irreducibles here: the enthusiasm and hard work of the pupils, and the way they are storming every educational citadel that confronts them. Of course, there is a concentration of talent – both of teachers and students – but that's just the start. The secret seems to owe much to unapologetically high expectations and a huge investment of time and care. That and bright children, no doubt.

The absence of rolling acres will put off some middle-class punters, of course, but they are hardly the target audience. It's a humane and imaginative society, as well as an academic powerhouse: a combination which should make a great many fee-paying schools sit up and take notice. For us, this is the real deal.

Newland House School

32–34 Waldegrave Park, Twickenham TW1 4TQ

Ages 3–13 **Pupils** 425

Fees: £11,544 – £12,918 pa

020 8865 1305
www.newlandhouse.net

Headmaster: Since 2010, David Alexander BMus Dip NCOS (50s). Previously head of Norland Place School and Haddon Dene School. Warm, welcoming and with a good sense of humour. Very kind and doesn't have a bad word to say about anybody. Justifiably proud of his charges. 'Our 13-year-old boys are a delight, as are our 11-year-old girls. I'm very proud to know any of them. I like what the school has done for them.' Parents say, 'What you see is what you get. Pupils and parents respect him but he knows how to laugh too.' Believes one of his main jobs is to steer parents towards the right school for their child: he wants his pupils to be at the top of their game at their senior schools. The children adore him because he's such fun: he is currently keen for the school to buy a boat which can act as a floating classroom on the Thames. Holds a commercial flying licence and commands a reserve RAF squadron at weekends. Mr Alexander selects the head boy and head girl by deciding which pupils he would most like to have lunch with.

N

Moving on in July 2019. His successor will be Christopher Skelton, currently deputy head at Newland Prep in London; has also been deputy at Dulwich College Junior School.

Entrance: All change, with new term time only nursery in own building (was former pre-prep), and 7+ entry phased out. Now has 50 per cent more spaces in reception following recent pre-prep expansion into brand new premises on main school site. Nursery places offered on first come first served basis – but only to families who have been offered a reception place. Often oversubscribed – best register your child as soon as possible after birth. At 4+ entry is on a first-come, first-served basis, with siblings given priority. Sixty places available at this stage and a waiting list in operation.

Academic and music bursaries available – up to 50 per cent of fees, negotiated on a yearly basis. Ten per cent discount for third sibling when all are in school together.

Exit: Predominantly to private day schools, occasional boarding, with Surbiton High, Sir William Perkins's, Reed's School and St James School heading recent destination lists. Hampton, King's College School and Kingston Grammar regularly feature. Girls leave at 11 and boys at 13. Girls can stay on to 13, but don't. 'It would be a leap of faith,' says head. Consistently high number of academic, sports, music and all-rounder scholarships. Head puts this down to outstanding teaching and the fact that the children are in a happy environment and so want to learn.

Remarks: Pre-prep is run by the approachable and calm Tracey Chong. All-female staff ('by coincidence') give it a homely air. Its brand building, right next door to the main school unites the two parts of the school and means additional places in reception. 'The teachers at the pre-prep are lovely and smiley and it rubs off on the children,' said one parent.

Classes at the prep are mixed ability, maximum 20 children. Lessons are lively and fast-paced with specialist teachers for PE, art, music and ICT from the start. Separate sciences taught from year 4. Children set for English, French and maths from year 5. Days are long, especially for those who start with the full cooked breakfast on offer at 7.30am.

Once the girls leave at the end of year 6, the boys are placed in two mixed ability classes and one small scholarship set; vacancies left by girls are not filled. Greek on offer to potential scholars. Parents love the fact that children get so much individual attention at the top of the school. 'A real strength,' said one. Children are well prepared for 11+, 13+ and scholarships. As the head puts it: 'We are a preparatory school. It's our job to prepare them for the exams for entry to their next schools.' Parents report that a massive amount of coaching goes on in the final years, of which the head is critical. 'It's not necessary. We are all fighting a coaching culture but people get sucked into it.' Head gives out CE results to boys as they sit around a camp fire on the year 8 trip to Wales. 'A lovely touch, and the boys never forget it. It's a gesture typical of the school,' said one parent.

Classrooms are spacious and light, with traditional wooden desks arranged in neat rows. Impressive ICT suite, tablets about to be introduced but head keen this shouldn't be a gimmick. The school enters a huge number of national and international competitions with frequent success. Recently won three World Maths Day trophies, out of a total of five awarded to UK schools. DT department is the envy of other schools and recently assembled a car for the Shell Eco-Marathon that achieved a mileage of 1,000 miles per gallon. Currently a group of senior boys is investigating the effect of tyre pressure on the environment and presentations have been made to MPs.

Plenty of choirs for each year group, new pop choir for year 7/8 boys is thriving. Several hundred individual instrumental and singing lessons take place every week. Lots of bands, ensembles and orchestras. Children have taken part in performances at the Kingston Music Festival and concerts at the Barbican with the London Symphony Orchestra.

Art clubs include weekend activities where parents can become involved. Local artists exhibit and sell their work in the reception area and include a couple of inexpensive pieces so that children can buy a picture if it catches their eye.

Sport is a real strength of the school. Boys play rugby, football and cricket; girls play netball, rounders and hockey. Swimming, cross-country and athletics also on offer and even more sport possible through numerous after-school clubs, including golf at neighbouring club. Main playing fields are five minutes away by minibus; two multi-purpose, all-weather courts and four cricket nets on site. Lots of tournaments and matches mean everyone gets the chance to compete.

Full-time head of SEN. Head believes 'a good learning support culture enhances what you do'. Provision for mild dyslexia, dyspraxia and dyscalculia, though not the place to send a child with severe difficulties.

Many long-serving staff. Head did away with 'teaching' and 'non-teaching' labels when he arrived. 'We're all teaching the children in different ways,' he says. One satisfied parent commented that staff were 'prepared to go the extra mile for the children.' Two gap year students help with sport and a French assistant teaches conversational French.

Parents are typically hard-working professionals. 'The school reflects the local community and lots of the children arrive at school on foot or by scooter,' says head of pre-prep. Active PTA raises substantial funds, half money raised goes to charity, the other half to the school – recently paid for a climbing wall. Activity-based wraparound club from 7.30am to 6pm.

A competitive, purposeful and demanding school which has retained old fashioned values (the pupils call the head 'Sir' and scramble to their feet when an adult enters the room). Pupils are challenged on all fronts and, as one parent put it, 'By the time the children reach year 5, they are under pressure to perform. It's not a soft school but, for the right child, there simply isn't anywhere better in the area.' One mother felt that 'it's not for the retiring child. I think they'd get trampled underfoot.' The head disagrees and feels the school caters for all personalities and abilities as there is so much on offer and so many chances to shine.

Newstead Wood School

187

Avebury Road, Orpington, Kent BR6 9SA

Ages 11–18 **Pupils** 1,065 **Sixth form** 267 (including boys)

01689 853626
www.newsteadwood.co.uk

Head: Since September 2018, Alan Blount, previously a deputy head here. A graduate of both Exeter (biology and education) and Canterbury Christ Church (masters in leadership and management in education) universities, he taught science at Oxted School and Carshalton Boys Sports College before joining Newstead Wood in 2014.

Academic matters: Not so much an academic hothouse as the sort of place where if you don't work reasonably hard you're the odd one out. School places great emphasis on staff and pupils 'co-constructing' the learning experience and on staff leadership and development – they should be critical questioners and facilitate, rather than direct, learning. An active school parliament and there are both subject and house captains who feed into decision making and who support fellow learners. In addition to termly reports and annual parent teacher meetings, the pastoral team maintains home-school dialogue.

Building learning and thinking skills starts early; problem solving permeates the curriculum. The extended project in the sixth form is designed to promote independent study and breadth of learning. Exam results are consistently impressive, with popular subjects being biology, chemistry, maths, English lit, economics, history and psychology. In 2018, 83 per cent 9-7 grades at GCSE. A level results no less creditable: 67 per cent A*-B grades and 37 per cent A*/A grades.

Strong enrichment programme – the usual timetable is effectively suspended for three weeks each year. KS4 students follow an elective option where they choose to study additional non-examined options, or devote time to volunteering or elite sport. Also a designated gifted and talented lead school – these pupils aren't noticeably singled out for special treatment but staff ensure lots to stimulate and push them. Dyspraxic and dyslexic pupils' coping strategies often uncovered during GCSEs. Individual education plans then agreed between pupils, parents and staff to overcome any difficulties with the support of pastoral and SEN team.

Games, options, the arts: 'Whatever they do, they do well,' said one parent and the evidence seems to support this. Good performances in hockey, netball and gymnastics and, though the school has no pool, it tops the results tables in national and county swimming events. Older girls help the youngsters.

The year 7 and 8 vocal ensemble was conceived and is run by sixth formers, one of several choirs and orchestras which perform regularly. Music is a real strength and taken seriously and at tempo here (better make sure you rehearse!); Vox CC, its senior choir, has performed at the Royal Albert Hall and in Prague. Drama is popular; 20+ student societies in anything from debating, politics, history, the environment, medicine to law, all run by year 12 pupils. Leadership and participation is very much what this school is all about and it's rare to find a sixth former who doesn't voluntarily take on extra responsibilities. For others, too, judging by the somewhat overwhelming stream of calendar reminders on the electronic board in reception, little excuse to be idle. Lots of after-school and lunchtime activities, as well as positions as sports ambassadors, Arkwright scholars to promote engineering in schools, language teaching in local primary schools, maths and debating competitions, Dragon's Den workshops and charity events – plenty going on.

Background and atmosphere: Set in a quiet residential area, has wonderful views across the playing fields towards the Downs, but the school buildings, though quite spacious, are unremarkable and jumbled – the 1950s, when it was established, not perhaps the best architectural era. Inside, the walls are brightened with artwork and benefit from the recent redecoration organised by the school's parent-run PET team. Various additions and upgrades; already has wonderful indoor tennis courts open to the public.

Pastoral care, well-being and discipline: Ongoing and slightly half-hearted battles regarding sixth form dress code but in the school's view it's churlish to make too big a fuss when most students behave and perform well. Students are generally not interested in acting beyond their years and the school encourages them to assess for themselves what's appropriate in different circumstances. More commonly issues arise through poor organisation or conflicting priorities, typical amongst bright, enthusiastic pupils.

As long as you are willing to work with the school, issues are normally swiftly resolved in liaison with staff and parents, the emphasis being very much on motivation rather than chastisement. Parents cite examples of a generally good response to concerns voiced, whether individual (friendship) or more general. The school is also alert to mixed expectations relating to academic and home life. In such cases, a counsellor and support teacher are available to provide guidance and support. A strong PSHE programme, which, eg, incorporates financial literacy, in which pupils can gain accreditation. Careers guidance is exceptional (a new Lifetime Achievement Award from Investors in Careers sits alongside their Gold Award). Abundant advice on university applications and longer term career planning. A well-stocked library provides a place to work outside of the classroom or a place for quiet contemplation.

Occasional incidents of bullying are addressed, with the girls themselves tending to side with the victim. Informal vertical contact is encouraged through extracurricular clubs and older pupils acting as mentors. The travel buddy scheme is a nice example, combining as it does environmental targets to reduce car use with accompanying year 7 pupils on public transport their first few weeks. Occasionally girls are to be seen eating and smoking outside the school grounds, but few complaints from local businesses and residents, who seem grateful to have such a well-thought of school in their midst – 'we'd all like our kids to go there'.

Pupils and parents: Said one parent, 'If they're really not up to and up for it, they won't enjoy it' – ie you need to be self-motivated rather than coached to get here. From a range of socio-economic and ethnic backgrounds. 'They stand out for being bright, self-confident and just getting on with it,' said one business regularly offering work experience to pupils from local schools. Both the Providing Excellence Together (PET) and the PA are active and effective, holding a variety of social and fundraising events over the year, as well as organising regular fairs through its careers sub-committee. Notable former pupils include Gemma Chan, Christine Hancock, Emma Johnson (clarinettist who came back to hold a masterclass at the school), Josie Long and Kim Medcalf.

Entrance: Most from local state primary schools. For year 7, entrance tests in verbal and non-verbal reasoning in September. Standards high, but the test experience 'more friendly' than for other local schools. Around 650-700 applications for 160 places. Preference to those who live within nine miles, then children of staff. When, very occasionally, places come available further up the school, those on the waiting list are invited to take an age-appropriate test and the highest scorers offered a place. Additional places are available for sixth form entry – including boys. A minimum of eight GCSE grades 9-6.

Exit: Those entering at 11 are expected to stay the course until 18 and only a few leave at 16, mostly to pursue specialist studies, eg performing arts or media studies. Five to Oxbridge in 2018 and five to vet/medical school. Rest to Russell Group -Southampton, London, Warwick, Exeter, Bristol, Nottingham, Durham, Manchester among popular destinations.

Money matters: Dedicated and enthusiastic PET and PA raise £30,000 to £50,000 annually, which funds the artists in residence each year and extra teaching resources. A covenant scheme and continuous fundraising events and activities to support the ongoing developments. Girls raise money for charities during house charity week.

Remarks: Capable and committed girls do really well here, most setting out on their future studies and careers well-qualified and equipped for the challenges ahead.

N

Newton Prep

149 Battersea Park Road, London SW8 4BX

Ages 3–13 Pupils 652

Fees: £8,940 – £18,930 pa

020 7720 4091
www.newtonprepschool.co.uk

Headmistress: Since 2013, Alison Fleming BA MA (Ed) PGCE (40s), a grammar school girl and theology graduate. Previously head of Dulwich College Junior School for four years, and before that deputy head at Highgate Junior School. A team inspector for the ISI and a governor of a local school. And, far more importantly, an ace head.

Forthright, articulate, warm and confident, Mrs Fleming inherited a large prep in good heart, good nick and with a massive new-build. She spent her first year listening, looking, learning and thinking. And now, subtly but decisively, change (all for the good, as far as we can judge) is happening. Her aims are to maintain the school's 'academically ambitious' ethos while developing its parental involvement and community links. In these aspirations, she appears to carry her own eclectic and inclusive school community with her. But there is far more of sound educational value afoot too.

Warm praise, especially from seasoned parents who have been part of the school under the last three regimes and who particularly value the increased headmagisterial presence around the school. 'She is always smiling and approachable,' we were told. 'She is independent-minded and has lots of ideas,' another enthused. A third said, 'She is fabulous. Really enthusiastic and has a really good combination of strength, warmth, leadership and vision.'

Entrance: Oversubscribed at all stage. Nursery application process, by 'playdate', ensures an even balance of i) boys and girls and ii) of autumn, spring and summer birthdays. There's a waiting list and those who don't get in can reapply for reception. Sibling policy.

Informal assessment the autumn term before entry into reception. 'A gentle process'. Staff observe the children to see how they relate to adults, their peers and the world around them. Year 1 or 2 candidates spend a day in class and take tests in reading, English and maths. Admission at year 3 and above by competitive testing. Any applicant for year 3 is considered for a scholarship (currently worth £250 per term) or a place backed up by a means-tested, top-up bursary. A surprising amount of financial help available. Most of those admitted at nursery or reception move smoothly up but this isn't guaranteed.

Exit: Leavers' lists are encouraging largely because there is clearly no stereotyped Newton product and they go to a wide spread of schools at both 11 and 13. Good range of scholarships – art, sports, dance and academic – won too (11 in 2018). Year 6s to eg Alleyn's and JAGS (current top choices), Emanuel, Dulwich College, City of London Girls, Sevenoaks, St Paul's Girls and the local GDSTs. Year 8s to similar plus impressive boarding schools (Wycombe Abbey, Wellington, Eton, Harrow, Bedales), Westminster and KCS. New role on the senior management team for a deputy head with responsibility for senior school transfer – a rare, if not unique position amongst prep schools. Watch the others scampering to follow suit.

Remarks: This part of London is not generally appealing. To find an enormous, sought-after prep school housed, partly in an Edwardian block of debatable attractiveness and partly in impressive and extensive new build, is unexpected. However, one only has to enter via the wall and tree lined esplanade to be transported into a very different and disarming world.

First impressions are formed by the children. They are happy, confident, relaxed, articulate, polite and eager to share their school with a visitor. Second impressions come from the place itself. From nursery, through lower school and up to the subject-specific classrooms and studios of the top two years, each learning area is well-structured, full of colourful, stimulating and thoughtful displays and staffed by smiley, interesting teachers. We longed to linger – the language rooms ('souriez et entrez!') invite learning, the art rooms are full of creativity, the science labs and IT suites are sleek and the library is simply the best we've seen in a prep anywhere. Worth lingering especially here – exceptionally well-stocked, each child's reading is guided and encouraged and the children find that they have everything they need for research. A real understanding here that books can provide complementary riches, in so many ways, to the internet – which is equally well-used. Sofas, carpets, beanbags and cushions and hundreds of lovely books. Learning and inventiveness hums. We ventured into the RS room and were instantly involved in a fascinating discussion about the compatibility or complementarity of religion and science.

The old building, seamlessly now melded to the new, is old school standard eg green and brown tiles, sensible corridors, parquet. The new build is high, broad, confident with big spaces of the kind you'd expect from a sizeable and prosperous high school. The newest bits are breathtaking for a prep. A splendid auditorium and equally impressive, acoustically perfect, recital hall. Many senior schools would drool. Vast airy dining room with seriously inviting food, eaten by all. Scooter and bike park: 'they really encourage us to bike or walk to school – you get a special badge for it'. Sports hall, gym and other spaces for muscle stretching. Two art studios full of lovely stuff. We liked especially the monster sculptures – custom-built in some cases ('our librarian really wants a dragon to hang in the library'), the earth-colour tribal shields, the batik, the ceramics, the marionettes.

Outside space is equally enviable – there is so much of it. A huge all-weather pitch and various other good-sized safe-surface areas, well-equipped and colourful – for the different age groups. So sports thrive and, as parents crow, 'it's not exclusive – they have a C team and everyone has a chance'. Most delightful is the 'garden' – tucked away between car park and road but a rus in urbe idyll once you're in, with shady leafy nooks, fruit trees, plots and beds, all well used by keen gardeners and for lessons of all sorts.

Around eight per cent have some sort of SEN – vast majority mild dyslexia, small numbers with eg ADHD or some speech and language delay in early years. Support is given either on an individual or small group basis by the director of learning development or by teaching assistants in classrooms, but head acknowledges that there is work to be done on the SEN side, which will be welcome to parents current and future. Music, under sparky head of dept, also rising to match the stunning new facilities. We anticipate the Newton's impressive lists of art scholarships might well be matched by music similar in coming years.

About 20 to a class except for two nursery classes of 24. Pupils from all over south west and central London; locals walk or scoot to school. All speak good English though around 50 (nine per cent) are bilingual eg French, Spanish, Italian, Urdu, Arabic, Russian spoken at home. Small group EAL sessions for those who need them.

Best is the creative and collaborative ethos and the sense of community. Inclusiveness is key, as parents testify – 'my children are totally different characters and it's been great for all of them' – and eccentricity is relished. There is little of the preciousness and snobbery one can sometimes encounter in other preps, and the pupils feel part of something bigger than themselves. As they told us: 'Our teachers are so approachable. You can always ask for help'. 'You're not babied by the teachers.' 'There's no fear between the year groups. Year 3s often come and chat to us in year 8.'

A parent summed it up, 'We're going to be really sad to leave.'

Nonsuch High School for Girls

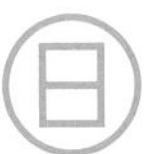

Ewell Road, Cheam, Sutton, Surrey SM3 8AB

Ages 11–18 **Pupils** 1,310 **Sixth form** 370

020 8394 1308
www.nonsuchschool.org

Headteacher: Since 2016, Amy Cavilla BA (40s), following what school terms 'interim leadership structure' after the abrupt departure of predecessor.

Educated at Godolphin & Latymer, MFL degree at Leeds, previously taught at Tiffin Girls (there for 12 years). Comes with fully formed love of girls only education and sympathy with the ideals of grammar schools. Smart, chic (sporting dashing asymmetrical hem to meet parents), she has two school age daughters. Impressive at open days, combining nice, motherly way with young visitors with hands on reassurance for nervy parents. 'Personally showed a group of parents around which doesn't usually happen,' said one. 'Have only heard good things about her,' agreed another.

Brings promise of a steadier hand at the tiller (reinforced by federation with Wallington High School for Girls). School has been getting through its heads faster than is healthy (anything but 'strong and stable'). But with results and added value rising again (not that they've ever been exactly bad), things are on the up.

Just as well. While grammar school parents tend not to mince their words, those at this school have been dishing them up whole, plain and unvarnished (even if polysyllabic). We've heard of one child not taking up a place in year 7 and some off the record grumbling by some members of staff (it's not always been the happiest place to work, some feel).

But that was then. Now there's Ms Cavilla, exuding air of calm control, staff rallying behind her and a new sense of optimism. She appears to be winning pupils over in small incremental steps. 'She's lovely,' said one. 'There's been a general improvement [since she came].' 'The school is neater,' we were told.

Academic matters: Results excellent. In 2018, 83 per cent of GCSEs were 9-7. At A level, 58 per cent of grades were A*/A and 80 per cent A*/B. Cynics might exercise 'so what' muscle but head – rightly – stresses government Progress 8 score. Between end of primary school and year 11, school adds three-quarters of grade to each girl's GCSE results. It's impressive, putting school in top two per cent nationally, no mean feat given that it's recruiting the best of raw talent in any case and is up against other super-duper selective establishments.

Current government comparison table – based on progress – puts it two places above Tiffin; no other similar school within 75 miles does it better. 'Can't fault it for the grades,' said parent. Ofsted rating of good (reaffirmed January 2017) no doubt frustrating – biggest question mark is over exceptionally able sixth formers, felt not to be sufficiently challenged. Where they get it really right, results are amazing – school accounts for a tenth of all GCSE and A level classical Greek entries nationally. Also praise for improved value added in A level physics, chemistry, biology and mathematics.

Currently economics, geography and English literature felt to lag behind and school needs to deliver more of the good stuff – additional top grades at A level 'should be even higher given starting points,' says Ofsted. No doubt something head will have in her sights for the future. In the meantime, parents stress school's focus on preparation and results. 'They're fantastic, pushing and pushing and monitoring the children, and obviously want them to obtain A*s and As all the way through,' said one.

Not big on SEN, with 'zero per cent' of pupils in receipt of an EHCP and low numbers generally, despite detailed policy. Where learning needs exist (and it's generally in their milder forms), we were told by one parent that girls' drive to succeed can mask difficulties so effectively that their SEN may not be identified while they're here.

The other bugbear (confusingly also the elephant in the room) is how much success is down to tutoring – up to three-quarters of all pupils, according to one parent, some having extra tuition five days a week. Ms Cavilla is not keen and says so. 'Vehemently put out that they don't want extra tutors but want them to have trust in the teachers – I thought that was very positive,' said one. Chances of making a difference are another question altogether.

Most girls take 10 or 10.5 GCSEs (RS short course) then study three A levels – though a substantial chunk, often the Oxbridge hopefuls, opt for four or more (one sixth former was studying maths, further maths, physics, chemistry and economics).

Though no prizes for guessing the big hitter subjects (maths has own corridor; science has two and 11 labs), school is also working hard to convey horses for courses message with girls encouraged to do subjects that appeal. Inspiring teaching very often does the rest: girls who take drama as a fourth A level subject, originally intending to drop it at the end of their first sixth form year, very often carry it through.

Impressively, niche subjects, axed elsewhere, are still on the books here, even when classes are diminutive – two for A level computing, for example. GCSE options (20 to choose from) include Latin, product design and modern foreign languages (girls can opt for triple science or triple languages). Highlight is astronomy. Impressive telescope ensures close examination of the stars they're reaching for and inspiration, we assume, for planet based house names.

Pupils praise the number of trips (previously few and far between, say parents, now impressive for languages and history), quality of the homework ('fun and exciting,' said year 7) and the teaching, gentle at the start but moving to a more dynamic, questioning approach further up the school. While pupils have their likes and dislikes, most staff felt to be hitting the spot. 'She's been thrilled with her teachers – she was whooping when she got her timetable,' said sixth form parent.

Corridors feature hard-hitting questions – asking pupils to consider evidence base for treating HIV with garlic, for example, as well as displays of the 'Did you know?' variety

(marking birth of famous scientists, for example). Plus the occasional glimpse into behind the scenes conversations – like the open letter from year 11 pupils thanking staff for 'doing the demanding (and probably underpaid) job of looking after us all day.'

N

Of the stand out subjects, history department much name-checked for 'passionate' staff team who encourage creativity. Papier-mâché hill fort is one of many enjoyable displays, while a drawing of Mona Lisa and cardboard Renaissance rooftop structures, created by year 7 pupils, form scene setting introduction to the 15th century. We can't speak for Leonardo da Vinci but they certainly impressed us.

Learning enjoyment is helped by free choice – no GCSE option blocks, no need to sacrifice a favourite subject. Pick what you want and the school will (somehow) make it work. Similar richness at A level, with extra support for those aspiring to Oxbridge or med school. But stress that it's not all about the results. 'Teachers say that exams are important but not the most important thing you'll ever do,' said pupil.

Teachers clearly happy – 'I don't count the hours, I love it here,' says one. Long stayers (up to two decades or more) are common and there are few vacancies even in the trickier subjects with, for example, all sciences taught by a full complement of specialists.

Games, options, the arts: Academics could so easily reign. But even though skiing is described 'an educational trip' to prospective parents, head is pushing benefits of being well-rounded rather than merely single minded. And though additional push is sometimes needed – school insisting that pupils leave the building in summer to ensure that the keen 'don't just sit in the library and work' – plenty of fun to be had.

No shortage of things to do once enticed out of the classroom, with normal big sports block including not just the usual cavernous hall but also dedicated classroom that confers useful prestige to GCSE and A level sports and PE studies classes can sometimes be viewed as a slightly dusty subject).

In addition to highly successful land-based sport (recent National Schools Championships finalists for badminton, borough winners in rounders, London netball champions, plus football, hockey, athletics, volleyball) – school has access to taa-daa quality swimming pool, built and managed by private firm (open to the public at evenings and weekends, though girls and paying customers have own entrances). Shame it lacks raked seating (means no galas and it's positively crying out for bunting and some noisy cheering), though 'we're not complaining,' says teacher. Lots of individual successes (archery and judo among them) and impressive creativity elsewhere – recent gym and dance display themed to 'A night at the movies' featured everything from Mission Impossible to Mary Poppins.

Activities, many after school and at lunchtime, include work with local community (get togethers for senior citizens with pupil-organised entertainment and cake); clubs (gardening visibly translates into quality shrubbery round the pond); sports tours and events. Mega highlight is 'ball girling' (school's description) for Queen's Club Aegon Championships. 'We arrived [...] saw each other in the beautiful kit for the first time [...] set off at 7:30am and sang songs all the way,' says newsletter account. DofE bronze, silver and gold (now back after gap caused by staffing issues and increasingly popular – mass recruitment in year 9 with 170 currently signed up) plus CCF offer plentiful heavy duty yomping (including popular overnight camping trip sustained by army issue rations).

Drama and music both busy and varied with many choirs and bands and 300 or so pupils learning an instrument (lots of violinists) in school, some reaching diploma level. Visual arts impressively accomplished and popular, judging by pupils' high levels of enthusiasm, quality work dotted around the school. Art room with high ceilings and wide windows spills over with colour and interest, from year 7 drawings of portraits of backs of heads (pigtails so detailed that every hair appears to have been accounted for) to attractive wire sculptures.

Background and atmosphere: While no opportunity to reinforce girls' stature and potential is missed (recent production – Blue Stockings – focused on first Oxbridge women students....) there does seem to be an inordinate amount of baking. We'd hope that boys' grammars also pride themselves on exquisite looking cakes topped with mathematical symbol as part of Pi week – but have our doubts.

Cake making aside, school, founded 1938, has stuck consistently to its principles of aspirational education for girls, aiming for 'excellence in all aspects of its work,' says website. Since 2015, federated with Wallington High School for Girls through Nonsuch and Wallington Education Trust (making the featureless acronym NWET). Jane Burton (previously headteacher of Wallington Girls) is the CEO, though all schools have 'own headteacher and unique identity,' says Ms Cavilla. Pooled resources add extra clout to eg careers advice and Oxbridge preparation.

Site is next to (and originally part of) Nonsuch Park, once home to eponymous palace, long gone, built by Henry VIII and intended to be so dazzling that none such could compare – hence the name. No-nonsense layout (arranged round one very pretty quad – complete with beautiful, plant fringed little pond and one rather more workaday one) has been recently enhanced with two new buildings beloved by everyone bar art team (blocks out good chunk of natural light). One is home to performing arts. The other houses vast, smart sixth form centre; heads of department, behind glass, like supervisors in very upmarket zoo, overlook the café and work and play areas (lots of cosy corners – as well as joltingly lime green chairs). Sparkling new and well-resourced library suffers from slight textbook overload – pupils arrive as keen readers though GCSE word load 'sucks some of the fun out it,' admitted one older pupil. Combines popular fiction (reassuringly well-thumbed Jacqueline Wilsons) with

seating in (more) eye-popping hues – lime, turquoise and navy (reduces chances of falling into a gentle doze).

Pastoral care, well-being and discipline: It's not always felt like the happiest place, and arriving with plenty of natural resilience remains a definite advantage, say parents. 'There wasn't a lot of encouragement or praise,' said parent whose child bailed out after GCSEs. Disquieting rumours of bullying also persist. However, school is clearly doing its best to introduce more underpinning in the form of resilience and conflict resolution training. The new head is felt to be making effective changes, and visible kindness of staff (one searching out pupil to tell her that missing item had been found) seems to suggest that prevailing wind is now more temperate than previous Arctic blast.

Happiness may not always be top of mind (cover page of sixth form prospectus is the only one to feature photograph of jolly, shiny, folder-wielding girls – the remaining 50 are text only). But 'if they're not happy, they won't thrive,' says member of the pastoral care team. House system is initially form-based to ensure instant bonding and competition with hotly contested sports and music (including annual Battle of the Bands). Loyalties tend to 'diminish up the years,' said older pupil, and are shaken up altogether with new classes in year 10. End of year winning teams scores reckoned in the thousands in year 7 and hundreds by year 10.

As elsewhere, other underlying worry is of pupils driving themselves too hard, also identified by Ofsted as needing extra attention. Balance is inevitably a hard one to strike. Even year 7 pupils stress that organisation 'is up to you' – teachers won't issue reminders so essential to 'write things down and tick off subjects' – and there's an assumed ability to cope. You will be guided (diagnostic board in chemistry corridor lists symptoms to help pupils work out when they need support) but not led.

Regular assemblies (year and school) 'generally convey a moral message', LGBT society is flourishing, while head has introduced peer mentoring in addition to the many academic clinics designed to unravel knots (of understanding, organisation or just worry). Nurturing now unmissably big, and includes pastoral care team (with own room) and pupil mentors. School has removed obvious stress points – recently doing away with homework over the summer holidays for younger year groups (persuading parents not to fill in the gaps themselves is, we'd suspect, an ongoing battle).

Pupils and parents: Car driving parents don't do much for community relations, blocking neighbouring streets and taking a devil may care approach to three point turns. 'Park across drives and refuse to move,' said enraged local. Similar cavalier attitude to parking in the turning space at the school, said insider. 'School has given up and just lets them do it.'

While chutzpah may be a unifying factor, there's diversity in every other direction including alumni – best known are cyclist Jo Rowsell, singer Katie Melua, journalist Christina Lamb and historian Suzannah Lipscomb.

School takes from 100 feeders, catchment is wide and new pupils will often arrive knowing no one. School makes much of support for less affluent families – around six per cent – who qualify for pupil premium and, impressively, make more progress than pupils overall; major expenditure is in study support. For those who can afford it, creative PTA has neatly combined pain of regular contributions to swell coffers with a raffle – donate £5 a month for potential prize of £500 – and also organises regular events.

Entrance: Realistically, need to be comfortably within top 10 per cent of ability range. 'Otherwise may not be happy,' says head, who also emphasises manageable commute, so that trade off for gaining a place isn't death of social life. She urges perusal of bus and train routes in advance: 'Girls should be able to travel here easily'. Would that put parents off? We very much doubt it.

Candidates sit qualifying selection test (register between May and August, conglomerate test with other local grammars) and if successful, take second test (shared with Wallington) in maths and English in autumn term (other schools operate different second tier tests). Possible to sit abroad if current school confirms that will take place under exam conditions.

Normally around 40 external pupils join the sixth form. Need average score of 49 based on best eight GCSE/IGCSE subjects.

Exit: Depending on who you talk to, numbers leaving post-16 have been higher than you'd expect, with Glyn's co-ed sixth form proving particularly popular.

Impressive range of higher education destinations, though not university fixated – one student recently offered hotly contested Sky Sports apprenticeship. Normally good numbers to Oxbridge (eight in 2018) and to study medicine, dentistry and veterinary science (22 in 2018).

Remarks: In the past, we had the sense of a school that felt a little inward looking, reflected in beautiful but tiny canvases on display, minutely examining window frames or ironwork railings. With school illuminated by radiance of academic success, let's hope that Ms Cavilla can continue adding a much-needed dollop of warmth to the picture.

Norland Place School

162–166 Holland Park Avenue, London W11 4UH

Ages Girls 4–11, boys 4–8 **Pupils** 235

Fees: £16,104 – £18,072 pa

020 7603 9103
www.norlandplace.com

N

Headmaster: Since 2002, Patrick Mattar LRAM MA (early 50s). Degrees in music and education management and administration. Educated in Solihull. Came here in 1989, as head of music, straight from the Royal Academy of Music. This was followed by six years at Wetherby, first as director of music then deputy head. Returned here as headmaster in 2002. Married with two teenage sons and laughs that 'parenting does not get any easier!' Wife is director of lower school at Sussex House.

Music is his passion. Performs piano recitals at charity concerts, auctioned off by school. Parents rave about his talent. He admits that practising 'takes up a lot of time but I enjoy it.' A keen cyclist.

Softly spoken, with an infectious laugh. Parents find him approachable, compassionate and hard working. 'A superb head who has given great stability to the school,' enthused one mother. Another commented that 'the school is jolly lucky to have him'.

Entrance: Non-selective at 4 (48 places at this stage, half boys, half girls). Names down as soon as possible after birth; ideally the form will be dropped off at the school on the way home from the maternity ward. Each month, four definite places are allocated to two boys and two girls, on a first-come, first-served basis, so it helps it your child is born in the first half of the month. Other children placed on waiting list. Head jokes, 'Have your child in December or January when everyone else is too busy thinking about Christmas to register!' Siblings must still register but get wait list priority and school has 'not yet failed to get a sibling in.' Head sees all parents who have places in reception to explain the ethos of school. He considers it important that parents share his philosophy. Head explains, 'We are non-selective, but we are very much part of the London academic environment, so parents need to be aware that their child must be able keep up with the pace'. Nursery heads' advice is invaluable about whether a child would suit the school and vice versa.

Exit: At 8, boys disperse to a range of schools including Wetherby, Sussex House and St Paul's Juniors. A few head to country boarding preps, such as Caldicott. Girls' destinations, at 11, include Francis Holland (NW1 and SW1), Godolphin & Latymer and Queen's College, with a sprinkling to boarding (eg Wycombe Abbey, Downe House). A couple of academic and music scholarships every year.

Head is aware that he is 'operating within a tighter academic belt' and that increased competition for London day places is a reality. School still gets similar numbers into same schools as it always has, 'though perhaps they need to work a little harder across the board to get there,' he smiles. Some parents complain about too much homework in the final years. Head is conscious of the 11+ pressure but also notes that 'it's incredible how motivated, rather than battle weary, the children are by year 6. Many of the girls are switched on by the whole process and enjoy it.'

Head believes that 'if a child is struggling here, you have to be very careful about where you send them next. Sometimes boarding can accommodate a richer variety of pupils than London day schools.' Gives as much advice as parents want on the next stage but states 'it's always up to the parents at the end of the day.'

N

Remarks: Founded in 1876. Situated in the heart of noisy Holland Park Avenue in three large town houses, connected by steep stairs and narrow corridors. Not the most spacious of schools but good use is made of the two smallish playgrounds decorated with murals and climbing wall, so children have the chance to let off steam regularly.

Mainly local families from Notting Hill, Holland Park and Shepherd's Bush. Most walk or come by scooter. Mainly professional families, many of whom are second and third generation Norlanders. Predominantly British, though with significant numbers of bilingual Europeans. Fifty-five currently have EAL requirements, catered for through classroom differentiation and a year one EAL club. Alumnae include George Osborne, Rosalind Franklin and Arthur Bliss.

The school is structured around the fact that the boys scatter at 8 and the girls at 11. For the first three years, pupils are taught in two parallel (but age differentiated) co-ed classes. In year 3, the girls and boys are separated so boys can focus on 8+ exams while girls head down the 11+ route. Effectively, school becomes single sex from start of year 3, though spelling remains co-ed and some mixed classes are re-introduced once the boys' exams are over. Up to 24 per class, down to fewer than 20 in the one remaining class in the final years. We spoke to one parent who wished the school also offered 7+ preparation, but no imminent plans for this.

Lessons are exciting. Inspired science teaching with emphasis on experiments. Recently, year 4 girls have been busy imagining they were water particles. Latin taught by head, post-exams in year 6. He also teaches reasoning to years 3-6 – 'A great way for me to get to know the children.'

Wide range of academic ability. 'As we're non-selective, we don't have a certain type of child. We love the variety we get.' Setting is fluid and discrete. School favours plenty of differentiation from the start (parents consider the most able to be well stretched and the weaker ones are effectively supported). From year 2, maths and English are divided by ability into separate classes and split lessons continue up to year 6. 'In effect, we are streaming pupils, though not for all lessons. What we are aiming for is very small group teaching.' It works well. Children do not fall by the wayside here, as they can do in larger establishments.

All children are screened for dyslexia at the start of year 2. Twelve currently have mild specific learning difficulties. School does its best to support those who are struggling but concedes the building lay-out is not ideal for those with physical disabilities. Visiting speech and language therapist. Some have one-to-one (at extra cost) or small group support. Mr Mattar himself has undergone medical training to support a current pupil who requires extra physical help, reflecting the school's consistently caring approach.

No laptops or other devices brought in from home. Small ICT room where computer skills are taught in half classes. Other than researching, homework is not done on the computer. 'Parents support this – they are quite a traditional parent body.' Head is mindful of the fact that senior schools are old-fashioned in terms of entrance exam requirements (cursive handwriting, decent spelling, accurate punctuation and grammar). 'If that changes, we'll change what we do in school too,' he states categorically.

From year 2 upwards, the whole of Thursday afternoon is dedicated to games. Twice weekly PE lessons also taught in the playground or hall, with an emphasis on acquisition of skills. Football and cricket for boys; netball and rounders for girls; swimming for years 2 and 3; tennis, touch rugby and rock climbing. Years 3-6 participate in matches and tournaments with neighbouring schools. Though most children make a team at some point, head thinks it is important that children learn to cope with the harsh reality of team selection. 'It teaches them to persevere and prepares them for disappointment at senior school. We are encouraging, though, and get them to keep trying.' Some parents complain about insufficient sport, especially at the top end of the school, though most believe this has been partly addressed through the wide variety of clubs offered, including 'netball shoot off' and 'catch it' clubs.

Plentiful opportunities for pupils to play music together, from string and woodwind ensembles to recorder and guitar groups. Superb ABRSM results, from grades 1-6. Recently, over a quarter gained distinction. Large music room, chock-full of instruments. Copious choirs. The chance of selection is high – 'that's the strength of a small school. Some are disappointed but that's life,' states head.

Art plays a strong part in the school. Large, airy art room. On the day we visited, there were stacks of clay on every surface and an assortment of mini creatures ready for the kiln. Children can try their hands at a rich variety of art, from weaving to screen-printing T-shirts.

Abundant opportunities for pupils to take to the stage. Children here learn to conquer any fear of public speaking early on and giving each child confidence is an aim of the school. A flamboyant musical in year 3 marks the boys' last year in style, as does the large-scale performance put on by departing year 6 girls.

Parents feel that issues such as bullying are stamped out quickly and effectively. All pupils play together in the playground; 'very inclusive,' according to one parent. Everyone (including head, teachers and pupils), looks after everyone else. Without exception, the teachers we met were bubbly and enthusiastic.

Refreshingly, Norland is not afraid to celebrate individual achievements at weekly assemblies and termly prize-giving. Each Friday there is a 'sports person', 'musician' and 'art duck' of the week. Three head girls selected, one per term, in the final year. Ample opportunities for leadership.

Parents are welcomed into the school and volunteers run library sessions. Head comments, 'The community of the school is a huge thing'. Lots of like-minded families who become close and go off on holiday together. Seemingly, a cohesive group of relatively unpushy parents. Emphasis on fundraising and children are expected to do their bit for charity, including getting their hands dirty. Head feels it is important for them to experience giving back, not just to be aware of it.

Very traditional school (from the berets and boaters to the emphasis on good manners and fair play) but combined with a forward-looking approach. On the day we visited, the school was awash with happy, sparky children who appeared to be thriving in this caring environment. According to one parent, 'the great thing about Norland is that it doesn't dim the flame of learning' through excessive exam focus. No wonder there is a stampede from the maternity ward.

North Bridge House Preparatory School

Linked with North Bridge House Pre-Prep School

1 Gloucester Avenue, London NW1 7AB

Ages 7–13 **Pupils** 465

Fees: £18,195 pa

020 7267 6266
www.northbridgehouse.com/prep

Headteacher: Since January 2019, James Stenning, previously head of sixth form and deputy head academic at North Bridge House Canonbury. Educated at a prep school in Kenya then Downside school, with an economics degree from Swansea, a PGCE and a masters in education leadership from Buckingham. Began his career teaching economics at St Olave's grammar, thence head of economics and head of extracurricular at Highgate (where economics became one of the most popular A levels, and he was heavily involved in DofE and outdoor education). Joined NBH Canonbury in 2014. Married to Tom, a group account director for an advertising agency. Very keen runner, often taking part in marathons in far flung corners of the globe such as North Korea, Sierra Leone and Nairobi.

Entrance: Entrance into year 3; most move seamlessly from the pre-prep but around 20 places remain for external applicants. Assessments in English, maths and reasoning taken in the January of year 2. Open mornings held throughout the year. Occasional places arise throughout the school so always worth a call.

Exit: Practically all aim for London day schools (the odd one each year may board at eg, Downe House, Sevenoaks or Haileybury), with Channing, South Hampstead, Francis Holland and Immanuel College most popular currently amongst girls, Mill Hill and City of London amongst boys. All girls leave at the end of year 6 (although they no longer have to, they do still leave). Most boys stay until the end of year 8. Some parents of boys who leave at the end of year 6 expressed concern that their sons didn't get the required support – 'school not geared up to boys leaving at 11'.

Remarks: Situated on the corner of Gloucester Avenue where Primrose Hill meets Camden Town, North Bridge House Prep School is a big and busy school on a big and busy road. Cramped outside but spacious inside, but there are plans afoot to renovate the playground to make it 'a more green and friendly space'. School compensates by sending the children to Regent's Park, a five minute walk away, where they can kick a ball and let off steam. A feature of all Cognita schools, security is thorough, tight and unforgiving. Everyone is vetted at the door, lanyards flow from reception. The timing of our visit was not long after the terrorist attack on Westminster Bridge, so with year 8 boys going out on daily trips in central London (part of the post common entrance curriculum) security issues were very high on the agenda. There are regular security drills and all the staff given guidance on how to talk the children about these issues. Everyone here is conscious of the importance of balancing safety with the need to take risks, but acknowledge that it is not an easy balance to strike in this climate.

The school has moved into its 80th decade, and it's over 30 years that it has been on this site, and nearly 15 years since it was bought by Cognita. Now under the leadership of corporate dynamo, Chris Jansen, Cognita has had a chequered history. Signs suggest this is soon to change, though change in education is slower than the pace of change Jansen is used to achieving. North Bridge House Prep has always been one of the more successful schools in its stable, but the streamlining, management, sharing of resources and marketing is clear for all to see. Data, tracking the performance of pupils and staff, is an important tool and is used very effectively here. The SIMS system paints a profile of the whole child. The staff are in control and parents feel safe and assured that their child is not lost in the system. There is mutual support and sharing of resources between the heads across the Cognita schools, particularly all four North Bridge House schools.

High praise from parents for the quality of teachers, particularly class teachers. While many said the school feels a bit like a machine – in a good way – they all said that the class teachers brought a very personal feel. SEN support is given primarily in the classroom. However there is flexibility, and occasionally your child may be given one-to-one lessons at the expense of a language if necessary. Range of conditions from ADHD and autism to dyscalculia and dyspraxia. Strong SEN team, says school, and concurred by parents, and it would only turn away a child it felt it couldn't support. There is a 'well-being officer' as well as a school counsellor (available at additional cost).

Children study both French and Spanish as well as Latin from year 6 and some take up ancient Greek. Academics are solid, sometimes inspiring. Ofsted says outstanding. Setted for maths from year 5. Girls and boys are also taught separately from year 6, the intention to prepare them more thoroughly for their respective exams. In years 7 and 8 there is a top, scholarship, stream and three other classes. Technology woven into the curriculum; there are laptops and iPads available on each corridor for use in any lesson. Two imaginatively decorated science labs with planets hanging from the ceiling, and molecule diagrams. Classrooms are high ceilinged, spacious and well equipped. Corridors wide with highly polished floors and well kept carpets.

Lots of co-curricular. Music, drama and sport all thrive here. Plenty of informal concerts in the local church as well as the large summer and Christmas concerts. You don't have to be a maestro to perform. Art room at the top of the school among the roof beams. An inspiring space and we saw cubist self-portraits inspired by Braque. Each child is given an art sketchbook that they use all year. Year 8s were out and about on a street art tour of Brick Lane. Drama productions take place in the 'chapel' (lunch and talks also happen here). Everyone gets involved; recent productions include Matilda and Canterbury Tales. Lots of adventurous trips – PGL and bushcraft, as well as to France, China and Morocco, and post common entrance sailing for year 8 after their intensive trips around London. Football and cricket for the boys, netball and rounders for the girls. Good use is made of Regent's Park and the Astro at Talacre sports centre in Kentish Town. Sports day is a huge event: around 350 parents and spectators attend the event at the Saracens sports ground in Barnet Copthall. There is a lot of focus on chess, taught by external specialists, and the pupils win competitions – national as well as local and within the school. A number of talks from outside speakers – engineers, journalists, army officers and others (parent contacts come in useful here and school recently started an alumni network). Topics range from the building of the channel tunnel to recycling and international affairs. Disappointing library, surprising in a school with such a strong focus on learning.

Discipline is strong. System of house points (four houses, Guinevere, Merlin etc) encourages children to try harder and behave well. From year 6 they can get demerits as well as merits. Lots of positions of responsibility from head boy and girl (though a slight mismatch here as girls are in year 6 and boys in year 8), to heads of houses and sports captains. All traditional prep school stuff that provides the glue and grit that make the system work. Parents a real mixture of busy professionals (in a high proportion of families both parents are working hard), mostly English and based in north London but there are some European nationals, and other overseas parents from further afield – US, Canada, China and Japan. Lots are in the media and the arts, and and there is a smattering of celebrities and a number of first time buyers. With little playground space to congregate in it can take time to find your milieu but most do and speak warmly of their fellow parents.

A large, bustling, well-oiled machine of a school that – almost always – matches expectations. Children here are busy, happy and safe. A good choice for your all rounder who isn't likely to get fazed and is ready to seize the many opportunities on offer.

North Bridge House Pre-Prep School

Linked with North Bridge House Preparatory School

8 Netherhall Gardens, London NW3 5RR

Ages 2y 9m–7 **Pupils** 190

Fees: £14,385 – 17,430 pa

020 7267 6266
www.northbridgehouse.com/nursery-pre-prep-hampstead

Head: Since 2015, Christine McLelland BEd (40s). Previously deputy head at St Nicholas Prep in Kensington (also a Cognita school), and before that worked in the state sector in both secondary and primary schools. She has been a class teacher for all year groups from reception to year 6 and held various senior leadership positions. Married to a teacher, an early years Leader, Mrs McLelland particularly enjoys teaching ICT and maths, the latter because she didn't enjoy it at school and is determined that it should be taught better now. Like many heads we meet she loved school and is proud to report that 98 per cent of her pupils say maths and problem-solving are their favourite subjects. She doesn't teach as much as she would like to now, but can teach anything and does what she can: 'its good for the soul, there are some children who always cheer you up. Spending time with the children is the highlight of my day.'

Started here as interim head in July 2015, following her predecessor's brief tenure and early departure for 'sad personal reasons'. The ship needed steadying. An SIS report in February 2016 identified a number of problems, particularly with the quality of the teaching. Inspectors nonetheless described Mrs McLelland's leadership as 'determined and effective, she is an excellent communicator who takes decisive action.' Parents describe her as 'smart, confident with good communication and marketing skills.' 'She complements Brodie Bibby in the prep very well,' one parent observed. 'Takes a bit of warming up. A bit defensive,' said another, 'but she came in at a tough time on the back of a worrying SIS inspection report and very weak leadership from the previous head.' McLelland describes herself as 'stubborn by nature, I enjoy turning a challenge into a motivation.' We would agree but might add 'with a manner that is a touch brittle'. However, when we met her she seemed to be feeling on the back foot and we were impressed by her fighting spirit. The conclusions of the inspectors 'did not come as a shock,' she asserted and 'a huge amount of work has been done since.'

Full of praise and gratitude for the support and expertise given to her by the Cognita management, Christine McLelland is a woman who isn't afraid to ask for help and seems to work well as part of a larger organisation. We noted that once or twice her vocabulary drifted away from the language of education as she started to refer to 'the product' and 'if you've got a good product the rest of it looks after itself.' Not words that fall naturally from her lips and we detect the influence of private equity backed management. Perhaps not surprisingly there was a high turnover of staff soon after she took over – 'some had a problem with planning lessons,' she says candidly, 'and were just recycling.' Fresh blood has been easy to recruit, however. Many come from the state sector like McLelland herself and she is proud of her high performing team. She loves the children here: 'they are very, very normal,' she says, 'not snobbish or rude but polite, kind and generous.'

Entrance: Children automatically filter through to the pre-prep from the nursery school at the age of 5, so fewer external places at this stage. Applicants are invited in to meet the headteacher – who heads both the nursery and pre-prep schools – prior to admission and places are allocated according to gender and date of birth, with priority given to siblings and children of past pupils.

Exit: Approximately 75 per cent move seamlessly to the prep school into year 3. Close liaison with the head of prep to ensure the transition is as smooth as possible.

Some still take the 7+ to eg UCS, South Hampstead, Highgate, North London Collegiate, Haberdashers, Belmont, Devonshire House or Westminster Under. The school is focused on journey for your child from 2-18 so while it will respect parents' wishes, you would be naïve to rely on your child getting into a competitive school from here at 7 without external support. Lots of tutoring in years 1 and 2, say parents, an unsurprising consequence but something that is nonetheless bemoaned by both the prep and the pre-prep.

Remarks: The pre-prep (years 1 and 2) is housed in a five-storey red-brick Victorian building in a leafy Hampstead cul de sac. The nursery (nursery, pre-reception and reception) is round the corner in Fitzjohn's Avenue in a similar building with big open spaces for play, exploration and exercise.

This is the base camp of the North Bridge House group of co-ed schools which are scattered around north London. The prep, a 7-13 (years 3-8) school, is in Camden Town, and there are two senior schools, one in Hampstead and the other in Canonbury, Islington. In theory your child could put down roots here and continue seamlessly through the NBH schools to 18, however to find a pupil who has been all the way through from the start continues to be rare.

Some of the infrastructure of the pre-prep in Fitzjohn Avenue seems to be a little tired and worn, from the broken tap in the visitor's lavatory to the uninspiring, sparse and functional head's office. A stark contrast to the classrooms, which were bursting with decoration, displays and colour when we visited. Wide staircases and corridors with high ceilings and large, well-proportioned classrooms create a sense of space and room to grow.

Fresh air and exercise is important here; pupils play outside at least twice a day. Wonderful space with an Astroturf playground, complete with slides and climbing frame, and chicken coop at the back. Pupils queue up to take responsibility for collecting the eggs and feeding the chickens – even during the holidays. Fresh food is prepared on site and eaten in a wood cabin in the playground which doubles up as a dining and assembly room.

Specialist teachers in music, art, PE and games. Music is a strength and time is made for performances, lessons and groups. The whole school learns percussion, singing and composition, peripatetic teachers also teach guitar, violin and piano, and lessons can continue into the prep. Plenty of opportunities to perform in assemblies as well as in one of the big shows per term (recently Charlie and the Chocolate Factory). LAMDA classes also popular.

Art is particularly impressive, and the lack of designated art room does not appear to have an adverse effect. Each class in the school annually produces a particular themed canvas, in the style of William Morris for example, which parents can then bid for in a private auction. An art exhibition is held at the end of each year and we were lucky enough to see this in the final stages of preparation. A rich collection of work influenced by Monet's water lilies, Kandinsky and sketches of corgi dogs reminiscent of Hockney's sausage dogs, reflect the topic Kings and Queens.

One hour of dedicated IT each week but otherwise use of computers and technology is embedded in the curriculum. These 21st century children are already deft in the art of managing a device and mini iPads and laptops are used across the school.

Safeguarding is an absolute priority in all Cognita schools and the pre-prep is no exception. Rigorous vetting and checking at the door for all visitors, who are issued with a set of rules and banned from using their mobile phones. We were even accompanied to the WC. Strong pastoral care: tabs are kept on the welfare of the children, assisted by a worry box in each in classroom into which the children can place slips and then follow up with the head of pastoral care. An effective system that is used and not just there for show, which is often the case. We saw it in action.

Children split into 10 classes (five in year 2, five in year 1), named after trees (Katsura, Beech, Hazel), one of the many innovations from Mrs McLelland: a move to trees from the birds creates more of an impression of growth, development and strength and can be less easily misinterpreted. Children now mixed into separate house groups too for sport and music competitions etc. Co-ed and inclusive, the school is nonetheless boy heavy. 'There is more competition from other girls' schools in the area,' observed one parent. Many move at the end of nursery to other schools, but on the whole parents are supportive of the school.

Majority of families live in the Hampstead area, within two miles of the school. Some with strong connections to the school – they may be alumni themselves or have other relatives who started their school days here. Eclectic mix of nationalities, with 27 languages spoken. Mix of educated professionals – fair few bankers and lawyers, as well as GPs, PR executives etc. Plenty of working mothers. Fewer big name celebrities than at similar schools.

Provision for EAL support is disappointing, we were told by more than one parent. Surprising for a school which proclaims to be all-inclusive and non-selective and which attracts a number of applicants from non-English speaking families. 'Best to make sure your daughter's level of English is secure before she arrives,' warned one parent. However, school assures us that EAL support for children is provided by learning support assistants across the school and insists that children with little or no English make progress and can catch up with their English speaking peers.

We received similarly confused reports about SEN provision. There are two full time SENCos and Mrs McLelland assured us that they wouldn't turn down a child with specific language difficulty or because of their English; 'we would look at their attention and ability to focus', she says. Yet parents we spoke to warned that school can only really support mild special needs. There were no children with ASD on the school roll when we visited. This is clearly an area that is benefiting from Mrs McLelland's eagle attention, however. A follow up report from SIS in November 2017 observed that pupils identified as having SEN and disabilities, including those with an EHC plan, make good progress because of very good provision and their needs are met 'with great sensitivity and care'. Pupils with EAL make very good progress because they receive 'very effective support.'

Mrs McLelland has been firmly focused on the academic side of things. In 2018 the pupils' attainment in maths put the school in the top five per cent in the country. Mrs McLelland attributes this in large part to excellent teaching from staff who are at the top of their game. CPD and sharing of best practice is high on her agenda. The improvement is acknowledged by the Inspectors. SIS, in November 2017, marked the quality of education as 'good' – a step up from their report in 2016, but probably not good enough for Mrs McLelland, her bosses at Cognita nor the parents. Leadership, management and governance also still fall short of an outstanding grade. We are not usually ones to pay overmuch attention to inspection reports, but Cognita has had a chequered history, is keen to raise standards and, we feel, needs to be called to account.

On the plus side, there has been a gear change in recent months: 'expectations have changed,' says Ms McLelland. Plenty of good, full time teachers with six or seven years behind them, including a relatively high number of male teachers, and we don't often see that for this age group. A native speaker teaches French.

Lots of attention is paid to encouraging the children to achieve academically. A ceremony, full of pomp and mortar boards, is held to celebrate the reception class graduation to year 1. An even grander one for the end of year 2, complete with 'graduation day' prizes, video montage and speeches.

Heartening ethos of 'giving back' – different charities are supported each year. Chosen by the children and the parents, these have included Diabetes UK and Little Village Camden, provides clothing and equipment for disadvantaged women and families.

A school with heart, although it is not always easy to feel the beat of it, on account of its impersonal systems and sometimes mechanical, rather than personal, communication. Schools that are a part of a large commercial organisation can often fall foul of the personal touch, but this suggestion is vehemently denied by the school. They have found just the right person in Chrstine McLelland to marry these contradictions and we are confident that as she continues to find her stride the school can only get stronger.

North Ealing Primary School

Pitshanger Lane, Ealing, London W5 1RP

Ages 3–11 **Pupils** 714

020 8997 2653
www.northealingprimary.org

Head: Since 2014, Sally Flowers, previously deputy head. She joined the school as assistant head in 2011. Prior to that, she was an educational consultant for nine years and before that she taught in mainly London schools. Did a BA in anthropology and history at Kent, her PGCE at Sussex and an educational psychology degree via Open University. Particularly loved consultancy ('I love training people') but now happier being settled and making a difference in just one school.

And making a difference, she is. This head is on fire. Not afraid of taking risks, she is exacting yet laid back, forthright yet friendly and is all about the children. No ego whatsoever. 'If the children are happy and know their rights, they can learn,' she says. Parents like that's she's 'a local mum' (she has three children), describing her as 'visible,' 'positive' and 'a very strong leader.' 'She's been seriously challenged by recent funding cuts, but she knows exactly what the school needs and works within her constraints to get it,' said one. Pupils say she's 'firm' but 'fun.'

N

Entrance: Looked after children get priority, then siblings and after that it's distance. Larger intake now due to three form entry but pupils still need to live within a mile of the school to get a place (no official catchment, admissions by distance as the crow flies). Like all Ealing schools, there's high mobility so there are often places further up the school, albeit with some waiting lists.

Exit: A massive spread. Usually most to Brentside High, others to Drayton Manor, Ellen Wilkinson, Twyford, Cardinal Wiseman and increasingly Ada Lovelace. 'Lack of places at secondary schools is a historical problem,' says head, 'but at least it's made slightly better by the opening of Ada Lovelace.' A handful each year to grammar schools, mainly Tiffin (boys and girls) and Henrietta Barnet, but some further afield. Depending on the cohort, around a third go private – St Paul's, St Augustine's, Latymer, St Benedict's, Notting Hill and Ealing and John Lyon.

Remarks: Pitshanger (the name of the main road on which the school is located) is considered a village all of its own with a tight-knit and diverse community and this primary school is at its heart. Ask anyone in the local area (most of whom seem to be pushing a buggy) where it is and chances are they'll know – a good job as it's pretty well hidden. And woe betide you if make the mistake, as we did, of trying to enter via the back entrance as the school will make you zigzag all the way through the residential streets to the front, a good five minute walk.

Once inside, the community feel is palpable, with down-to-earth staff and pupils and lots of laughter. Nobody stands on ceremony here. In fact, nobody really notices you as there's so much going on – a year 6 flash mob suddenly burst into spontaneous dance at breaktime during our visit, while every classroom and hall, along with many of the corridors, was buzzing with activity during lesson time. 'Bend the knees!' for dancing in the school hall. 'Hands in the air!' for singing in the dedicated music room. 'Well done – that's a long word!' for guided reading in a corridor. 'Who's ready for a hands-on experiment?' for science. You get the picture.

Nobody denies the move to three form entry hasn't been challenging – the school was originally built for one class per year group. At times, it can feel like it's bursting at the seams, but the head has utilised every inch – even the lower staff room is now a shared teaching space. It's by no means chaotic, however – this school is immaculate, with a clear sense of order everywhere you turn.

The school is divided into three main areas. Nursery, reception and years 3 and 4 are housed in a lovely bright and airy modern building at the back of the school site. Years 1 and 2 take up the slightly older, but still bright, building in the centre of the school. And years 5 and 6 are in the old part of the school – an 100-year-old Victorian building. Classes here are more cramped but corridor candy on the walls (eg Van Gogh, Spanish vocab) make them feel welcoming and warm.

Outside, children are also separated at playtime: nursery, reception and year 1 all have their own separate playgrounds. Years 2, 3 and 4 have the back playground and years 5 and 6 are at the front. We saw tiny-tots planting flowers in the planting area, a World War II bomb shelter that's been turned into a sensory garden and the school has its own garden which backs on to Pitshanger park.

Academically sound across the board. Our guides told us maths is 'easily the best subject – we love the quizzes.' 'Maths here is fun,' says head. Setting in this subject only, from year 3. Meanwhile, for English, there's a highly structured phonics programme and a big push on reading for life. Shame the library isn't more inspiring, but there's a nice touch on each classroom door – book cover images of both what the children and teacher are currently reading. Science (picked up in last Ofsted report as an area for development) is now on the up, with a more enquiry based approach, including with hands-on experiments in everything from magnesium to light. Spanish taught from year 1, along with a Latin club for children from year 5 (exemplifying strong links with local private schools, whereby their pupils come in to volunteer). Unusually, philosophy lessons for all. Dedicated teachers get good CPD, but as with most primary schools it's a shame there aren't more males.

SEN hovers at around 10 per cent – higher than other local schools, with an excellent reputation in this area. Particularly significant numbers of children with ASD. Plenty of praise from parents about the interventions that range from SENCos working closely with class teachers to pupil passports for vulnerable children. Sixty languages spoken among pupils, with school finding every opportunity possible to celebrate their growing diversity. 'Nobody feels left out here,' pupils told us.

'It's mega' says head about the clubs, with a list of privately run and teacher led classes that would give any posh prep school a run for its money. 'It's almost busier after school than during school.' Coding, debating, film club, hockey, golf, netball and tag rugby are among the favourites.

This is a creative school, with art embedded into lessons, especially in the younger years, and dedicated weekly music lessons for all. Peripatetic teachers cover a range of instruments including flute, violin, guitar and recorder. Three choirs (including choral), two orchestras and a singing club for younger ones, with plenty of opportunities to perform locally. Parents told us drama is less in the limelight than it once was, but it's still a core part of English lessons and there are all the usual end of year plays.

Sports are high profile, with a glass cabinet bulging with cups in the school reception, although head admits they 'don't win as much as we used to when we were two form entry.' Unfazed, she is more keen on embedding a positive sporting attitude than winning everything. All the usual suspects, plus the likes of basketball and dance. If there isn't enough room on the school site, the local Pitshanger Park is used.

This is a Place2Be school, meaning that this children's mental health charity provides school-based support and training to improve emotional well-being. Everyone raves about the counsellor – 'I go whenever I feel sad about anything and they make me feel better every time,' one girl told us – and with four additional volunteer counsellors, no pupil needs to miss out, although those with a critical need get priority over pupils who self-refer, and for parents there's a 'huge waiting list.' 'It's a powerful and fabulous service – we're very lucky,' a parent told us. Pupils have a strong voice here and the school has a Rights Respecting Schools silver award from UNICEF (they are currently working towards gold). Behaviour well managed through praise more than sanctions. 'Is it strict?' we asked our guides. 'Firm but fair,' was the response.

Two-thirds of pupils have the hot dinners which are cooked on site, the rest have packed lunches. The school has a healthy eating policy – no sweets or chocolates are allowed in children's lunch boxes and classes who eat the healthiest get prizes.

All parents must attend parents' evening – 'if they don't turn up, we relentlessly ask them to come.' Active PTA, although one parent told us 'I think they could do more.' Former pupils include Peter Crouch and Honor Blackman.

A friendly and positive school that's an integral part of the local community. Children are grounded, curious and happy and they achieve excellent results. 'I just wish they ran a secondary school too,' said one parent.

North London Collegiate Junior School

Linked with North London Collegiate School

Canons, Canons Drive, Edgware HA8 7RJ

Ages 4–11 **Pupils** 312

Fees: £16,923 pa

020 8952 1276
www.nlcs.org.uk

Head of junior school: Since 2003, Jo Newman BEd (50s). An old girl of North London, Mrs Newman read geography and education at Homerton College, Cambridge. After leaving, she dabbled briefly with the idea of retail – 'I love people and I think I would have been equally happy in a number of jobs' – before starting her teaching career at Haberdashers' Aske's Boys' Prep. Deputy head of the NLCS First School, then moved briefly to Spain for her husband's work. On her return, spent three years as head of Channing Junior School. Warm, can-do sort of person, excellent at team building (her last three directors of studies have moved on to headships elsewhere) and involving others. Cares passionately about education (part of a recent sabbatical was spent visiting schools in New York) and those in her charge. 'She knows every girl well,' said one mother, 'and really fights for their happiness.' Married to an accountant, with two adult daughters (both of whom attended the school), she spends off-duty moments cooking, visiting the theatre and walking.

Entrance: Some 250 try for 40 places at 4. A first edit looking for good, basic 'pre-school' skills eg handling a pencil reduces numbers to 90. A second evaluates 'learning, listening and following': 'they look at pictures, play games, engage in conversation.' Reading and writing definitely not required. 'They will not be asked,' says the head firmly. Children assessed carefully in relation to those very close in age. Much time spent working with nurseries to encourage applications. An early refusal does not mean don't ask again. 'We try to get across to parents that, if a child is not ready at 4, please bring them back at 7.' At that point, a further 8-10 places, with about 127 applicants, again assessed in two rounds. 'We want to know what they can do, not what they can't; we'd rather they spelt "enormous" wrong than "big" right.' Occasional other places.

Exit: Virtually all to the senior school (90 to 95 per cent). 'We're aiming to provide an all-through education and the expectation is that girls will move up to the senior school.' All sit the entrance test: 'Our research shows that it gives them confidence that they're as good as those coming from outside.' For one or two this might not be the right route, and parents are advised well in advance. 'The art is to make the right decision for each girl.' Some girls leave to board, a trickle to leading state schools, such as Henrietta Barnett and Watford Grammar School for Girls, but no cramming for entrance tests. 'We prepare them for secondary education not for 11+,' says the head. 'Our aim is to instil a love of learning and a breadth of opportunity.'

Remarks: NLCS is, as it always has been, an unashamedly academic school, whose aim is 'to enable girls to recognise academic excellence and realise that it's attainable'. This is achieved through outstanding teaching and a holistic approach to learning, not by hot competition. Here the goal is always 'personal best' rather than 'beat your neighbour'.

National curriculum followed throughout, but work often goes well beyond and around it – in years 2 and 3, for example, girls learn to play chess. Classes throughout primarily taught by a form teacher, though specialist subject teaching introduced early on. Senior school staff ease final year girls into their prospective home. A medley of foreign languages on offer (Spanish in year 3, German in year 4, Mandarin in year 5, French in year 6) as an introduction to the senior school range.

'Learning habits' (flexibility of mind, empathy, collaboration, resilience, reflectiveness, good judgement, self-assurance, curiosity, focus, risk-taking, persistence, initiative, originality) introduced early and made explicit. Year 6 guides on our trip were fully genned up on the terminology, pointing out their 6-year-old peers in full creative flow – 'we're making pop-up sea creatures,' said one year 1. 'It's very creative and very fun,' glossed an older girl.

Homework from the off, with reading and spelling in reception and year 1. Older girls get about 40 minutes. 'It's not all work, work, work,' said one. 'You don't feel scared or embarrassed if you can't finish.'

Two school libraries, clearly much-loved habitats. Golden Book Oscars awarded for best author, etc, with teachers striding the literary red carpet dressed as Voldemort or other fictional stars. Prominently displayed list of 50 Books to Read Before You

Leave Junior School ('I've read 47,' confided one year 6), with 'more mature' literature for the eldest.

Special needs carefully monitored. 'We look out for obvious signs in assessment,' says the head. 'We're very attuned to early identification.' Strong in-school support, led by a SENCo, for those with dyspraxia, etc. 'Every case has a conference.' The site itself works well for those facing physical challenges, and the school has, when required, incorporated additional aids, such as a hearing loop.

Extracurricular – 'the hidden curriculum' – is very much the bedrock of an NLCS education, whatever your age or stage, and girls here are active and energetic participants, whether in the latest theatrical production or music competition. A multitude of after-school clubs (with late transport on offer) range from cookery to bridge, and many sign up for three or four activities a week.

Drama important, with an annual play for each year group and a major year 6 extravaganza. 'It feels like a professional play,' said one, 'with costumes and make up'. Over 90 per cent learn one or more musical instruments, with plenty of performance opportunities – two all-comers' choirs, plus an auditioned year 5/6/7 choir competing on the international stage. Games three time a week, plus swimming lessons, plus after-school sports club, plus school teams. 'Squads are very exciting,' said one girl (and perform well against other schools).

Like its senior counterpart, the junior school was founded by the formidable Frances Mary Buss, one of the Victorian era's most dynamic crusaders for women's education. The school originated in Camden Town, but, in 1929, purchased Canons, the former home of the Duke of Chandos. The First School (reception to year 2) opened in 1993. Today, the junior school is housed in its own building, in two separate parts. One for the First School with its own hall, library, adventure playground and playhouse; the other for years 3-6 with a science lab, ICT suite and art studio. Girls also make use of the large, leafy grounds, senior school's excellent sports facilities (including pool) and dining hall.

N

Older girls are poised, purposeful and articulate. An encounter with representatives of the junior school council demonstrated school democracy in action. Their aim: 'to improve the school'; their achievements: the introduction of an adventure playground, a bird feeder, a poetry competition (complete with cup) and a raffle (with the prize of shadowing the head for a day). Sadly, a motion to supply sushi at lunch fell by the wayside.

Classroom teachers take responsibility for pastoral care, with a not-many-rules policy that stems from the founder. Discipline not really a significant issue. 'No one gets in trouble,' said one girl. 'If we do something wrong, we apologise'. Occasionally, there might be 'a warning' for 'saying a rude word', even more rarely parents are notified and the miscreant misses break.

More problematic issues dealt with sensitively, aided by a school counsellor and good communication with parents. 'We don't want little problems to become big problems,' says the head. She herself is very involved, with an 'open-door' policy. Parents kept well informed, with a regular curriculum newsletter and home-school diary. 'Today x lost a tooth,' read one, the tooth itself carefully enclosed. Plenty of information evenings – 'parents can be anxious, and we want to make them feel comfortable.' Parents themselves very proactive: 'All you have to do is mention an exhibition and they trot off to the museum.'

The school runs an extensive coach service importing girls from a large swathe of north and west London and Hertfordshire. Families – from all over the world – often have both parents working (so supervised breakfast and after-school care a godsend.)

A stimulating education, provided in an idyllic setting, producing articulate, confident, enthusiastic girls.

North London Collegiate School

Linked with North London Collegiate Junior School

Canons, Canons Drive, Edgware HA8 7RJ

Ages 11–18 **Pupils** 783 **Sixth form** 233

Fees: £20,028 pa

020 8952 0912
www.nlcs.org.uk

Headmistress: Since January 2018, Sarah Clark MA (40s), previously head of The Queen's School, Chester. Read history and classics at Newnham College, Cambridge. Has also been deputy head at Wellingborough School in Northamptonshire. Married to a history lecturer, with two teenage children. Avid supporter of Chelsea FC and loves to cycle, paint and write fiction. Active and breezy, she speaks exuberantly about working in single sex education. 'Girls can really be who they want to be. They don't hold back because they don't feel they need to be cool in the same way they would if there were boys around.' We hear she has been extremely hands on and immersed in school life from day one.

Academic matters: North London provides an unashamedly ambitious, academic education, consistently sitting in the top five schools nationally in terms of its exams results. In the sixth form, it is one of the rare London schools to offer both the IB and a mixture of A levels and Pre-Us. Virtually all pupils do outstandingly well in all exams. (In 2018, 85 per cent of A levels were graded A* or A; average IB score a disappointing 37, from a cohort of only seven girls. Superhuman outcome at I/GCSE, with 97 per cent A*-A/9-7.) The school puts this down primarily to the quality of the teaching: 'We don't teach to the test, we work well beyond it.' Parents agree teaching is 'inspirational'. 'The staff remain stable but are never allowed to get stale.' Girls are expected to (and do) work very hard, with plenty of homework from the off. 'You work as hard as you need to or want to,' said one recent arrival. Research skills are carefully nurtured and girls learn how to address their workload in a disciplined and organised manner.

Post-GCSE, English, history, physics and maths are notably popular. ('No gender bias! Hurrah!' commented one parent.) Modern languages (six on offer including Mandarin, Russian and Italian) and classics are unusually strong, with Latin for all in years 7-9. Traditionally, many took five AS levels, with many keeping a balance of arts and science, but the new A level regime has reduced this to four, with any slack addressed by 'an independent research essay'. Parents praise the school's flexibility in meeting individual interests, particularly in the sixth form. 'There's no pick-one-from-column-A procedure,' said one father. 'They don't mind if only one girl opts for a subject. They're willing to give one-to-one teaching if necessary.' Girls are free to choose what really interests them. 'They'll only query something if they feel a girl is being pushed by her parents or considering a subject which would put her out of contention for certain degrees.' Equally, however, they won't micro-manage any downside once choices have been made. 'No one told us our daughter wasn't very good at history and much better at English, which she was doing as a fifth AS level. We had to fight for her to be allowed to change.'

About 40 pupils have some kind of learning support. All receive an 'individual education plan', with students seen by a SENCo without losing lesson time. Despite its extensive and complex site, the school is also happy to cope with physical disabilities – 'as long as the pupil can communicate and access the curriculum' – working with parents to ensure the right support is in place.

Games, options, the arts: You could never be bored here, though you might end up exhausted. Every possible interest is catered for, from philosophy to animal welfare. Last year, pupils had a choice of 40 clubs and societies, 30 overseas trips and 30 concerts and productions. Actors to the Edinburgh Fringe, musical groups to Tuscany, and eager proto-journalists produced enough journals and publications (50 this year) to stock a newsagent, on topics as diverse as economics to Ebola – not to forget the cutting edge Wintour, named after celebrated old girl Anna Wintour, editor of American Vogue. 'We feel it's the extracurricular involvement which helps produce the academic success. There's something for everyone, something to capture the imagination.' Activities for senior girls take place after school, those for younger ones in the lunch hour. Finding time can still prove a problem. 'Sometimes it's hard to fit it all in,' said a year 8 girl. 'You have to decide.' No doubt, all part of the learning process.

Lacrosse is the dominant sport, though plenty of choice, too, for those not unduly captivated by fresh air and outdoor competition, with a fitness suite, trampolining and dance in a smart new dance 'space'. Well-used and buzzing art department, packed with enthusiasts and a range of high-quality work.

Extensive range of enrichment activities (Duke of Edinburgh, Model United Nations, debating, Young Enterprise) help develop public-speaking skills and an appreciation of the world elsewhere. The school has a strong international perspective and offers exchange programmes with schools in the USA, Australia and Germany. In 2011, North London opened an overseas campus in South Korea, NLCS Jeju, and students have the opportunity to visit the campus and do internships here, with NLCS Dubai new in 2017. Charity also firmly emphasised, including raising money for and teaching at a school in Zambia and visiting a local school for severely disabled children.

Background and atmosphere: Founded in Camden Town in1850 by the formidable Frances Mary Buss, a highly effective crusader in the cause of education for women. (She also established Camden School for Girls, with whom North London continues to share a Founder's Day.) The school bought its current spacious, 30-acre semi-rural site in 1929 to use as a sports ground, and relocated here fully in 1940. The estate formerly belonged to the 1st Duke of Chandos and, during his time, Handel was composer in residence. The central core of the building is a country house of 1760, now joined by a multitude of varied later additions. Pupils appreciate their attractive surroundings. 'It's so beautiful,' said one. 'When I first came here, I was blown away by the grounds.'

The atmosphere is calm, orderly, and purposeful, and most find it an enjoyable place to be. A recent arrival from the junior school, when asked if she'd thought about alternatives, said, 'I stayed here, because I couldn't see a fault with the school.' Some parents, however, find it quite protective (a good thing or bad, depending on your perspective).

Though the school is academic and fast-paced, it's not pushy. There are no academic rankings or prizes below the sixth form, for example. That said, a girl who doesn't tick along at the same speed could be less content. 'The academic stuff is just baseline,' said one parent. 'They're expected to get involved in clubs, societies, music, sport and community service.' Some also feel that a girl who needs plenty of validation or isn't super confident may occasionally feel swamped. 'I do know people who have pulled their daughter out, though it's usually more about the parents wanting their girls to be top in everything, which is just not going to happen at NLCS.'

Long list of illustrious old girls includes: Judith Weir, Stella Gibbons, Susie Orbach, Marie Stopes, Stevie Smith, Myfanwy Piper, Dame Helen Gardner, Gillian Tett.

Pastoral care, well-being and discipline: Girls here are generally industrious and motivated and heavyweight disciplinary issues are rare. The general approach can be summarized as: 'give girls plenty of freedom, make them engaged and feel valued'; purpose and focus will then follow. It undoubtedly seems to work, and even the youngest here appear remarkably poised and mature.

This is very much an education preparing girls for life as well as exams. The school feels that single-sex education gives them the freedom and security to experiment and develop confidence. Career aspirations are set high and reinforced with photographs of high-flying former pupils ornamenting the corridor walls. 'Our old girls often work in environments of domineering boys from public schools and hold their own. The school helps give them the courage to do that.' An active alumnae office furthers access to a valuable network. Student voice here is important and heard, with a school council and elected prefects – 'the Big 6' – who play a significant role.

Brown and blue uniform for younger girls, sixth formers can do their own things (big shawls this year's 'look'). Most appear stylish and smart, with few fashion extremes.

Pupils and parents: Mainly cosmopolitan, ambitious, middle-class professionals, many of whom run their own business or work in financial services. Girls come from every conceivable ethnic background (over 50 languages spoken at home), but an increasing number of Europeans (French, Dutch, Russian) and Americans, as well as the traditional high percentage of Asian and Jewish families. An extensive coach service, with long arms stretching out north, south, east and west, makes this a far from 'local' school. 'The girls reflect the demographic of London,' said one mother.

Entrance: At 11, 65 places for external applicants (joining 40 or so coming up from the junior school). Apply between June and November of the year before entry, with exams in English and maths in January of the year of entry. About 600 apply, with about 200 interviewed. 'We're looking for teachability and girls who will thrive and flourish with the pace of life here. We want flair and interests, a decent vocabulary and logical ability.' Excellent at establishing whether these qualities exist. 'The interview process is very good,' said one parent. 'It's rare for someone to slip in who isn't suited.' About 20 extra places available at sixth form. Apply between July and November of the year before entry, with tests in four subjects. Occasional places awarded throughout to fill any vacancies, when those already registered will sit appropriate exams.

Exit: Once girls are in, the expectation is that 'we see them all the way through'. A handful move on after GCSE to co-ed or state schools (but a few find the grass greener elsewhere). No-one asked to leave on the basis of exam results. 'They do not cull,' said one mother. 'Even if a girl is struggling, they'll do everything they can to keep her if she is happy.' Almost all get into their first-choice university, with 25 to Oxbridge in 2018 (seven Oxford and 18 Cambridge), 13 medics, two dentists and a vet and virtually all to top universities, including in the US (seven in 2018).

Money matters: North London has always prided itself on being affordable and accessible and offers plenty in the way of scholarships and bursaries. Academic scholarships (of up to 50 per cent of the fees) are awarded on the basis of performance in the entrance exams at 11 and 16. Music scholarships at 11 (girls must pass the entrance exam as well as the audition in which grade 5 is generally the expected minimum). Means-tested bursaries (reviewed annually) range from 10-100 per cent of fees and can be awarded in conjunction with scholarships. Bursary funding is partially underwritten by the South Korean franchise, and the school is looking for other projects to further extend these opportunities.

Remarks: An outstanding school for the girl who is quick and hard working and enjoys being busy and involved. Probably not the ideal place for those who might feel the pressure to be 'top' in an environment where everyone is.

North Primary School

Meadow Road, Southall UB1 2JE

Ages 4–11 **Pupils** 420

020 8571 7749
www.northprimary.co.uk

Headteacher: Since 2015, Nicola Forster BA NPQH PGDip (mid 40s). With a personal pedigree from the best Ealing schools, Ms Forster took a degree in geography and education at Roehampton, before beginning work in the first (of eight) London primary schools. She was promoted from acting head at Hathaway Primary to head at Ryefield Primary, Uxbridge, before joining North Primary, following its troubled spell making headlines over the solar eclipse. Inspired to teach by her mother's example, 'I learnt from an early age how you could influence children's lives through teaching,' she is at ease in her trainers and sportswear ('I'll put on a dress for the town hall!') despite having just run four times round the neighbouring sports fields with the children for Sports Relief.

N

Parents showed guarded respect; 'It's still early days; we all look at results,' said one, who had had experience of four successive heads at the school, but they applauded her candour: 'Her door is open, which parents do like'. Children approached her with ease in the corridor, addressing her formally as 'Mrs Forster' but responding familiarly, 'Yeah, cool!' Divorced with two teenage girls at the local secondary school, she is a keen runner. She has already introduced a new assessment system for the children and plans a shift of emphasis in the curriculum; 'We have very high attainment in literacy and numeracy; I'd like to increase the range'. She has refurbished some of the buildings, including a stylish makeover in a Victorian classroom to create a colourful office for herself and her deputy. She applauds her school's participation in the national evaluation scheme, Challenge Partners: 'it's really helpful to hear other people's points of view, to help us tighten our systems'. We forecast that, barring rare astronomical incidents, she is on course for a successful run.

Entrance: London borough of Ealing admissions criteria. Many come via the outstanding children's centre next door, Grove House. Catchment area includes the residential area west of Hanwell and north of Uxbridge Road. Oversubscribed.

Exit: Most to local secondaries: Villiers, Dormers Wells and Greenford High school are popular choices. Some go to selective state schools: Tiffin, Upton Court.

Remarks: Astoundingly high Sats results have earned this school its reputation. The head attributes much of it to the expertise of the staff and good resourcing; the parents put it down to commitment of the community. Two form entry with 30 children to a class, supervised by one teacher and a teaching assistant. Despite 98 per cent EAL – 22 different tongues, mainly Indian languages, but some Somali and eastern European – the teaching is in English, and the school is proud of its EAL lead status. There is some EAL support for the 30 per cent who arrive without any English, and bilingual staff throughout the school and offices. Lower than average numbers of SEN, nurtured in individual sessions or small groups in a corner of the hall. One mum was dissatisfied with the SEN support: 'My child has had one-to-one; it has sometimes been a bit tricky'.

The classes are named after flowers (Cornflower, Poppy etc) after the school's address in Meadow Road. No hedgerows now; the school is in one of London's more economically deprived suburbs, with twice the national average on free school meals. Drawing from an area between Hanwell and Heathrow airport, home to a large Asian community, Southall is famed for its productive and hard-working ethos. 'There are very high expectations from parents and teachers,' says the head. A dad acknowledged the pressure this puts on the staff: 'We've had an up and down period in the last few years...recently some teachers left', but he reassured us, 'teachers do get along with the pupils; the pupils are encouraged to achieve'. The head describes the staff as a real blend of ages and genders, some home grown, some from overseas.

A single storey brick and slate schoolroom, with ornamental weather vane, is what remains of the village school. Adjoining is a Victorian arts and crafts extension, while additional low-level classrooms from the 1970s spread out into the playground at the rear. 'The premises need a revamp,' said one parent, but the high ceilings and corridors lined with pegs, lend an air of trusty tradition to the building. The reception and year 1 classes on the ground floor enjoy direct access to the playground, where there is an outdoor classroom, as well as giant number square and Snakes and Ladders. Indoors, classes are peppered with scarlet tables and chairs, with carpet-time nooks. Upstairs year 2 was studying the Great Fire, with a flame-ridden dolls' house in Pudding Lane.

Gym frame and ropes for PE are installed in the first floor hall, used for assemblies, as well as whole school gatherings once a week. A modern dining hall connects the old and new buildings and serves a halal menu twice a week (fish and chips with Eve's pudding on the day we visited). Beyond is a corridor resplendent with children's work (design your own Greek urn was our favourite), with a full library at one end. We peeked into a discrete sensory room, for SEN time, and an ICT room, hiding 30 computers inside tip-up desks. The upper floor classrooms are a delightful mix of modern and traditional: whiteboards displaying familiar columns of spellings and fractions, while high-ceilinged rooms are ventilated by the original telescopic winder poles. Lively year 6 classes were in session when we visited, discussing the construction of pyramids, while a pair of young boffins at higher-level learning tasks, were cracking a secret code.

Visitors are greeted at the door by a colourful montage of art, reflecting the diversity of the school, with a collage of religious symbols served up on paper plates, and an appliqué wallhanging of local landmarks, from the famous Southall water tower to shops selling Asian sweets. In the reception class exotic instruments lay ready to play at one of the many school celebrations: Eid, Easter, Diwali, Holi, Chinese new year; 'It's one big party,' laughs the head. Some take the form of shows for the parents, such as The Elves and the Shoemaker or the traditional nativity play, with contributions from their own Bollywood dance troupe. There's a diverse choice of sports, too, football, cricket, netball and golf, as well as an American football club after school. Sports day is held at the local Spikes Bridge Park. Plentiful after-schools clubs include the three Rs: reading, rugby and recorder.

Mindfulness, from year 4, prevents the myriad amusements causing sensory overload. The deputy head keeps a model brain on his desk to teach the children the mechanics of de-stressing; 'It helps them deal with test situations,' says the head, and 'The stressed child would have a specific adult to link to'. Parents were satisfied there were no serious issues with bullying: 'In the main...it's a misunderstanding more than anything serious,' said one dad, and 'The kids are all respectful to the adults'. Communication with parents was felt to be good; 'there is a system', which includes face-to-face chats with the head or class teacher; 'Morning and night, someone is on the gate,' reassured the head. Emails to the office produce a quick response; 'School is good at getting back to you,' said one mum. There is a strong parent council – 'Which helps the standards...where some parents have issues, but don't know how to voice them,' said a governor – as well as a student council. Other school trips include the Kensington museums, the RAF museum and a residential to Surrey for the older ones, while the youngest children's outings include learning to make and post a mother's day card at the post office.

Dressed in their scarlet jumpers and white polo shirts, the children we saw were both relaxed and purposeful as they prepared for a trip to the local sports field. As one dad said, 'The kids feel safe and respected and enjoy going to school'. A strong PTA funds extras, such as new playground equipment, via quiz nights, a ladies' night and the lavish Mela, or summer fête, a cornucopia of sweets. The head was astonished at the generosity of the participants. One parent said, 'Parents are quite involved and do a lot to make sure their children do well... A lot of parents bounce ideas off each other; it's an Asian thing'. Some parents are former pupils. The head is quick to recognise the parental input: 'Children are very focused, families are very supportive; families are ambitious...the parents are like private school parents'.

A fusion of traditional and progressive values makes this school special, from code-breaking science lessons to Bollywood spectaculars, from Gulab Jamun to fish and chips. The community support is palpable and the academic success skilfully orchestrated by the head and watchful governing body, who make the most of the rich diversity among the children. North Primary is clearly a rising star in Ealing's firmament.

Northcote Lodge School

Linked with Broomwood Hall

26 Bolingbroke Grove, London SW11 6EL

Ages 8–13 **Pupils** 260

Fees: £19,785 pa

020 8682 8888
www.northcotelodge.com

Headmaster: Since January 2019, Clive Smith-Langridge, previously head of Packwood Haugh. Limbered up for the role by spending 16 years in marketing before switching to boarding schools (was previously deputy head at Walhampton). Brings essential savvy plus the experience of having captained a Chile cricket XI vs Brazil. Married to Sally; two daughters.

Entrance: At 8. At least 80 per cent from Broomwood Hall Lower School, the sibling school round the corner. The others mostly local, although school minibuses bring in some from across the river. Potential candidates must register for the main list some 20 months before date of entry although late registrations will be considered for the 'headmaster's list'. This is reserved for boys who show exceptional talent in art, academics, sport, design or music and who might be expected to enter for a scholarship at a senior school.

Parents and families attend an open day and meet the headmaster. A year before entry it's assessment time. A couple of hours at the school include tests in English, maths, verbal reasoning and ball skills, an interview with the head and some carefully observed playtime, including a snack. If your son is offered a place, you have to pay a deposit of £2,750, which is refundable when he leaves the school. They feel this encourages only those really serious about the school. There are no bursaries or scholarships.

Exit: Nearly all at 13, with around three-quarters to boarding school eg Harrow, Eton, Tonbridge, Sherborne, Bradfield, Marlborough or Wellington. The rest to London day schools, with vast majority to Dulwich College, others to eg Whitgift or Emanuel.

Remarks: Many are thrilled to be spared the 'pressure pot' felt to be all around in this part of south west London; this is very much the school's aim. This makes some anxious that the school is not as rigorous academically as it could be, feelings the school is aware of and feels aren't accurate. One parent told us: 'The teaching is inspirational; they have really developed an inquiring mind as opposed to a child who is learning for learning's sake.'

Until the final years, all homework (prep) is done at school and there are reports of happier home lives for it. There is a relaxed attitude to exams and revision: 'They appear to actively discourage any revision over the holidays, particularly in the younger years, and are very much of the view that holidays are to relax in,' a parent surmised.

About 20 per cent of pupils are monitored for an SEN and 10 to 15 per cent receive learning support, predominantly for dyspraxia, dyslexia, dyscalculia or dysgraphia, but the school says it is not the place for more severe learning difficulties. All boys are fluent in English and there are no EAL requirements. There is a full-time head of learning support and two part-time specialists; regarding one-to-one support, 'there's no stigma – it's just like a trumpet lesson'.

Sport takes place on Wandsworth Common, opposite the school, and is more at the forefront than in previous years, but we notice the lack of on-site sports facilities is still on parents' minds whether they are consoling themselves that they do just as well as other schools with more lavish facilities, or wondering why the fees can't fund it.

All boys play matches in the major sports and teams are competitive against much bigger schools. One mother said the school is 'very hot on ensuring good sportsmanship'. Plenty of minor sports such as golf, shooting, table tennis and running and there has been strong cross-country success. Karate is a big thing here: all boys learn and there are currently 24 black belts in karate club. With no pool, swimming has been rather overlooked, but a swimming squad is emerging. One parent felt that 'grass roots athletics gets little attention'. The school is proud of the recent Welsh rugby tour. The school says: 'Every boy who wanted to go, did, and we had 76 per cent of the year group on tour'. Latest cricket tour to South Africa. Sportsmen drop in to inspire and coach, most recently Ben Cohen, Ben Loosemore and Martin Brockman.

Over 60 per cent of the boys play an instrument, regularly taking ABRSM grades and sitting music scholarships for senior schools. Drama is on the up, resulting recently in a handful of drama scholarships to Whitgift, Harrow and Emanuel. Recent dramatic productions include Grease, The Wizard of Oz and West Side Story. Every year boys take LAMDA exams, recently with 72 distinctions.

Plenty of international trips: year 7s voyage to the Château de la Baudanniére; the year 8s to Normandy and the year 3 science and geography trip is to the South of France. There is an annual ski trip to Italy, plus outdoor pursuits and PGL. After-school clubs from the sporting to art, cooking and coding four days a week. There are termly costs for clubs that might be inclusive in other preps. This is clearly a civilised enclave: the bridge club has a waiting list.

Founded in 1993 with just 14 pupils and two teachers for traditional Broomwood Hall boarding families who preferred to send their sons to a London day prep than a boarding prep at 8 years old. The original founders, Sir Malcolm and Lady Colquhoun, remain as principals of Broomwood Hall and Northcote Lodge. Scottish notes – tartan ties, St Andrew's Day celebrations with bagpipes – nod to the Colquhoun's Loch Lomond forbears. Parents describe boys feeling part of a family, a community and proud to do so.

Housed in a pretty Dutch-style Victorian main house set back from the road, the school entry is flight of steps into a hallway with fresh flowers, plump carpets and oil paintings of the former headmasters. Boys wear tweedy jackets, soft blue shirts and look like miniature gentlemen, but frayed cuffs and stubborn mud stains speak of rough and tumble rather than any concerns over dry-cleaning. A teacher quips that the tweed jackets are 'standard issue' as he hangs his up. Year 4 classrooms are all in a row on the glass-roofed Shell corridor. Our guide told us: 'It's a big step up coming here, most people get nervous, but after two days I loved it! It's a family school, all children mix, it's nothing to worry about'.

N

'Caring' is the word that crops up most often from parents when describing the atmosphere of the school: 'friendly, inclusive, caring and focused,' elaborated one. When we enquire whether houses are fiercely competitive as we have seen elsewhere the boys are slightly baffled. Parents tell us: 'There is a competitive spirit but it is one with a great comraderie'. Such is the gentleness of the boys on the whole that the school is sure they will be 'less street-wise' than their peers when arriving at boarding school, and is addressing this in the weeks following common entrance, but feels 'it's a reasonable price to pay'.

We have never been quite so wowed by beautiful and relaxed good manners as we were on this visit. Not only did the boys unfailingly hold doors open for us and each other, but spontaneously congratulated each other on recent triumphs up and down year groups, and every boy who crossed our path said 'Hello' warmly. 'Discipline and manners are paramount, which we love,' said a mother.

With so many busy, working or indeed separated parents as a part of modern life, for some boys 'stability is school,' and it sets out to provide it. Once upon a time boys paraded so many reward badges, they decorated not just their lapels but right around the back of their collars. These have gone, replaced by a simpler award for the best performance relative to peers in a week, which now seem worth winning. Some instances of bullying find their way to us, but in each instance parents report it was swiftly dealt with. The boys we spoke to genuinely seemed to regard bullying as something they learnt about but had not experienced.

Most boys live locally but there are minibuses from Fulham and Chelsea. The stats show a homogenous, white British group less racially mixed than one would usually see in a London school. When we asked parents to describe their peers they told us: 'fantastic, friendly and really good fun... but the demographic of the school is very narrow'. Social shorthands abound: 'largely old money, a lot of red jeans but friendly and caring'; 'supportive mums who aren't alpha parents' and 'typical nappy valley'.

'Who might this school suit?' we asked parents: 'A child who will flourish given a supportive environment. A child who enjoys team sports and is sociable'. And, perhaps the most in tune with what we saw in action: 'a very happy school where the boys seem to buzz around enjoying their childhood.' School concludes: 'Northcote can cope with quirkiness and variety; we are failing if we only fit a particular type of boy'.

Northwood College for Girls

Linked with Northwood College Junior School for Girls

Maxwell Road, Northwood HA6 2YE

Ages 11–19 **Pupils** 502 **Sixth form** 100

Fees: £17,403 – £17,508 pa

01923 825446
www.northwoodcollege.co.uk

Head mistress: Since September 2018, Zara Hubble (very youthful looking 40s), previously head of Northwood College junior school. Educated at Westonbirt School and City of London Girls, after which she took a Montessori nursery teaching course then a BEd specialising in KS2 at Southbank University. Cut teeth at St Hilda's in Bushey before joining Heathfield, where she taught year 6 and ultimately became head of year 7. Moved to Northwood as part of merger with Heathfield in 2014, becoming head in 2015. Likeable, calm and poised, with two daughters at university. Keen skier and book lover.

Academic matters: In the ferociously academic context of this corner of North London, school is by no means at the top of the pile when it comes to results – but neither does it either pretend or want to be. Value added is the name of the game and head is delighted to be in top four per cent nationally in relation to this, if not topping academic league tables. Broad-ish church intake, coupled with ethos encouraging every girl to outperform her potential, means that academic superstars can coexist happily alongside their more pedestrian peers, with neither group feeling undue pressure. School more interested in 'building a portfolio of skills relevant to each girl' than cracking the Oxbridge whip – 'girls need a raft of skills beyond the academic. Soft skills can mean the difference between success and failure.' Listen up, neighbouring hothouses.

It's compulsory Spanish in years 7 to 9 in the languages department (not popular with everyone), with French or German as an option. Mandarin on offer from year 9. Classrooms we visited were formal in format – old school even: girls in rows facing the front and lecture style lessons. That said, lessons were interactive (think periodic table bingo) and when questioned in class, the girls we saw were incredibly articulate, confident and considered in their answers. Parents cite RS and English teaching as 'really impressive' and results bear this out, with the former producing 'ridiculously high' grades at GCSE and A level.

Girls take nine or 10 GCSEs from a traditional curriculum with compulsory language and three sciences, plus options including art, classical civilisation, drama, Latin and Greek, home economics, RE and textiles. IGCSEs now taken in some subjects, at the discretion of each departmental head. In 2018, 70 per cent of GCSEs scored A*-A/9-7. Similarly broad choice of A level options, although disappointingly low uptake of the more 'artsy' options – including English, history and languages – reflecting parent demographic aspiring to careers in the sciences for their daughters. 'Our families value STEM subjects,' says school. 'It can be a challenge to persuade them otherwise...but it's one we're happy to grapple with.' After sciences, psychology and RE most popular A level choices. Very respectable A level results in 2018, with 77 per cent A*/B grades and 50 per cent A*/A.

Because large number of girls move through from junior school, any SEN usually identified years before arrival in senior school, with seamless transition a major benefit for girls requiring support. Most mild SENs managed in lessons, with only occasional withdrawals. School supportive of girls pursuing interests or sports to a high level outside of school and will adjust timetable to accommodate if possible. Bespoke programmes occasionally put in place, for example to help girls be more outgoing.

Independent thinking is school's raison d'etre – even, according to the girls we spoke to, above and beyond sport, music or drama. Girls formally taught thinking skills from nursery upwards with a full-time cognitive development director to ensure consistency of message and integration across all parts of the curriculum. Even the youngest in the school evangelise the benefits of eg looking at problem solving from different perspectives – 'teachers don't spoon feed us' and 'we're taught how to learn from our mistakes', we were informed. School is pioneering in its approach and is working towards Thinking Schools International status.

University application process universally praised by parents and girls. Dedicated full time careers and UCAS advisor delivers 'loads of one-to-one advice,' say parents, plus programme to provide every opportunity for girls to build CV. Teachers described by all as 'really supportive', offering extra classes in preparation for eg medical exams. Visiting advisors are frequent fixtures, eg mock university interviews with admissions staff from Imperial College or staff at nearby Merchant Taylors' and endless internship opportunities both through school portal and GDST – one sixth former we lunched with was spending her summer interning at Nomura thanks to the latter, with another looking forward to her work experience in Beijing via the same route.

Games, options, the arts: Doesn't boast the most gleaming array of facilities we've ever seen and the field is tiny, but for what is essentially a London school, it's as well equipped as it needs to be. Stand out facility is the 25m pool – with everyone swimming all year round and weekly lessons for years 7 to 9. Sports hall has a new climbing wall used both in PE lessons and by clubs. Gym also attractive and well equipped, apparently well used at lunch times by older girls. PE and games compulsory to year 11. Tons of extracurricular sports on offer to suit all tastes – hockey, karate, basketball, you name it. Try as we might, we couldn't get the girls we met to extol the virtues of school's sporting prowess and, with just three compulsory games sessions per fortnight on offer, we wondered whether school was perhaps not the most obvious choice for super sporty types. Parents reassured us, however, that cohort includes a number of outstanding gymnasts, swimmers and even a British team triathlete – we stand corrected, but worth investigating further if your daughter is sports mad. The overall message for sport was: 'it's about right'.

Performing arts centre looks newer than it is and includes an excellent drama studio, recital hall with a sprung floor plus well kitted out music tech room and a plethora of instruments from steel drums up. Plenty of opportunities for budding thespians to throw themselves into productions, most recently Narnia for the lower school, and although there's no space for such performances to take place in a grand theatre, the assembly hall does the job. Parents describe music as 'absolutely fantastic' – for all tastes and levels – from a 50 strong orchestra that plays 'everything' from classical to pop, to jazz bands and chamber choir. There's hours of fun to be had leafing through the booklet detailing all the extracurricular activities on offer with something for everyone – from the active to the cerebral.

Background and atmosphere: Founded in 1878 in Endsleigh Gardens, Bloomsbury, with around 25 boarders and a handful of day girls. Headmistress Miss Buchan-Smith, concerned about the unsavoury influence of the Euston area on her girls, moved the school to its current site in Northwood in 1893. The current front building – red-brick late arts and crafts with leaded lights – was opened for 20 boarders and just two day girls. The Briary, next door, accommodated little boys, and although they are long gone, school pays tribute to those who went on to fight and fall in the two great wars with an annual wreath laying at Ypres.

Joined Girls' Day School Trust (GDST) in 2013 as a precursor to joining with Heathfield School (75 per cent of their girls made the move to Northwood), already a member of the Trust, the following September. Head reports that the governors thought 'long and hard' before taking up the rare offer of membership and all are delighted that belonging has not changed the culture of the school at all, 'merely provided a plethora of opportunities that a standalone school doesn't have'. Northwood girls now benefit from participation in GDST music and sport competitions, eligibility for travel scholarships, participation in conferences on eg Oxbridge application, as well as access to an alumni network numbering some 75,000 members, bringing a healthy pool of work experience and internships from which to fish. Staff also benefit from additional training and development opportunities, which bears obvious fruit in the classroom.

Beyond the main building and with notable exceptions (the quaint William Morris-esque, parquet floored reception area and quirky, characterful library) the site wouldn't win any beauty contests and space is at a premium, but the combination of disparate buildings somehow hang together nicely in their urban setting to create a cosy atmosphere – and all aspects are highly functional. The homely sixth form common room buzzes with chatter. Most striking to visitors is the calm – almost serene – atmosphere that pervades the school. Smiling faces are everywhere to be seen and parents and girls report nothing but kindly and supportive behaviour between girls.

Pastoral care, well-being and discipline: Minor transgressions only in the main and these, mainly tiny bumps in the road to adolescence, reportedly dealt with 'brilliantly and sensitively' according to parents who were full of praise for the pastoral side of Northwood life. Reports of girls experiencing 'the grass is always greener' effect and returning within weeks of departure, particularly for other sixth forms. 'There's just something about Northwood,' said one mother: 'everybody knows everyone'. 'Incredibly strong' house system plays into this, with fiercely fought competitions ('the life blood of the school', according to one pupil) in anything and everything, the highlight being the house music competition in which every girl participates. Bullying is a 'no go zone', say pupils. Older girls pick up concerns of their younger peers and head reports 'very few' eating disorders or instances of self harm – highly commendable in an academic girls' school – 'we don't value aggressiveness'. What about lost sheep? 'We grab hold of concerns early and work in partnership with parents.' Indeed, parents appreciate this approach and seize opportunities to attend school for talks on subjects such as social media and cyber bullying.

Pupils and parents: Majority from British Asian backgrounds although all cultures and religions represented (there's a multi-faith prayer room for free use by girls as and when) and a more sensible and earnest cohort you'd be hard pushed to find. No reports of cliques, with the majority of non-Asian parents relishing the opportunity for their daughters to 'stay younger a little bit longer' due to the positive influence of other cultures. Wide reaching coach routes transport girls from Ealing, Edgware, Kenton, Gerrards Cross and Radlett. Proximity to Northwood station on the Metropolitan line gives easy access from both directions.

Entrance: Girls joining senior school from other prep or junior schools take the London 11+ Consortium cognitive ability test, with great emphasis on the interview. Another 20 or so join for A levels, with places conditional on GCSE results plus online test and interview. Occasional places in other year groups so worth a call if you're moving into the area.

Exit: Almost all stay on for A levels with vast majority moving on to Russell Group or new universities. Just one to Oxbridge in 2018 (English and French); this explained by school's demographic with hard working, dual income families often not wanting daughters to move away for uni – hence many take places up at London colleges or others within commutable distance. Generally several medics.

Money matters: A few means-tested bursaries – up to full fees for particularly deserving cases. Scholarships for academics, art, music and sport.

N

Remarks: If neighbouring options are too academic, too large or too aggressive, Northwood is (in the words of Goldilocks) just right. Unfettered access to a world of opportunities in a supportive and purposeful culture await. In the words of one parent: 'girls come out happy, healthy and rounded'. What more could you want?

Northwood College Junior School for Girls

Linked with Northwood College for Girls

Maxwell Road, Northwood HA6 2YE

Ages 3–11 Pupils 400

Fees: £11,280 – £14,700 pa

01923 825446
www.northwoodcollege.co.uk

Head: Since January 2019, Mark Maddocks, previously deputy head and head of upper school at Notting Hill Prep. Classics degree from Oxford; has been head of classics at Orley Farm and Arnold House.

Entrance: Oversubscribed for entry at 3+ and 4+ with around three applicants for every place. Gently selective with nursery and reception places offered after observation in play. Head meets all parents: 'we're looking for children who are ready for school.' Up to 10 new places at 7+, when applicants are assessed in maths, English and reasoning and by interview.

Exit: Almost all to senior school at 11+ with a small handful taking up state grammar places most years.

Remarks: Three purpose built buildings on same site and a handy hop, skip and jump from senior school – handy when girls reach year 6 and start to take a few lessons with their soon-to-be secondary teachers. Delightful Bluebelle House is home to early years girls – designed with a wonderful playground, outdoor explorer area (minibeast heaven), masses of IT and spacious, airy and inspiring classrooms where girls learn Spanish via action songs, yoga and ballet from age 3. Three reception classes of up to 20 girls also enjoy this space with life skills such as resilience already high on the educational agenda. Lessons we observed were engaging and interactive and girls highly articulate. Years 1 and 2 in Vincent House, with junior school housing years 3 to 6 – both immaculate, modern houses, with every available space proudly adorned with colourful art and meticulous handwritten work. Benefits from sharing facilities including swimming pool, sports hall and science block with senior school.

Not a negative word to be heard from parents – 'they've really brought our daughter out of herself – we love the inclusive atmosphere', raved one and indeed girls are nurtured rather than pushed and, happily, few are denied the right to move into the senior school. Majority from British Asian backgrounds although all cultures and religions represented (there's a multi-faith prayer room for free use by girls as and when) and a more sensible and earnest cohort you'd be hard pushed to find. Thinking skills – pioneered by the whole school from nursery through to year 13 – taken very seriously by all with pupils able to explain the purpose of De Bono thinking hats with enthusiasm and clarity. All girls screened for SEN in year 4 and supported in small groups either within or outside the classroom. Around 30 girls receive EAL help.

Despite parents admitting that 'the academic is the most important thing,' school works hard to ensure balance with a dazzling array of extracurricular clubs which take place either at lunch time or after school. Something for everyone, with all major sports represented, ballet, martial arts, masses of opportunities for musicians to do their thing and everything else from outdoor explorers and gardening to newspaper club. 'Really extraordinary' major stage production each year – recently The Wizard of Oz – with the whole of year 6 participating and many behind the scenes roles up for grabs for lower year groups. Super catering, with lunches (included in fees) freshly prepared on site and all girls from reception up eating together in dining room. Hot suppers also available (charged as extra) up to 6.00pm and there's a breakfast club from 7.45am – great for working parents.

We spoke to parents who had wanted their girls to have the option of moving to other secondaries at 11+ and won places at – in some cases – arguably more high flying schools. Invariably, none wanted to leave, thanks in no small part to the clever balance of nurture and academic rigour they enjoyed at Northwood. Definitely one for the list if you want an all-through, rounded education – not to mention avoiding the 11+ frenzy...

Notting Hill and Ealing High Junior School

Linked with Notting Hill and Ealing High School

26 St Stephen's Road, London W13 8HH

Ages 4–11 **Pupils** 300

Fees: £14,313 pa

020 8799 8484
www.nhehs.gdst.net/junior-school

Head: Since 2013, Silvana Silva BEd (50s). She arrived at the school as a year 4 class teacher in 1989 and has stayed ever since. Deputy head for 11 years before taking the top job. A north Londoner by background, she attended St Michael's Catholic Grammar School in North Finchley and did her degree at Roehampton University. She always wanted to teach and previously taught at primary schools in west London. 'But as soon as I walked in here in 1989 I thought, this is for me,' she says. 'Everything has always been new and exciting.'

A positive, energetic and sympathetic head, she is very proud that the school was named as the Sunday Times independent prep school of the year in 2018. Much liked by pupils and parents. 'We offer academic excellence in a happy and relaxed environment,' she says. 'The girls have to be happy and they are our number one priority. Pastoral care is paramount for us.'

She still teaches both reception classes once a week and says it's the best part of her job. 'It's really important to get to know all the girls and their personalities,' she says. 'They are full of life and joy and love telling me about their day.

Married (her husband works for John Lewis), with one son who is doing his PhD at UCL. She's a great believer in 'healthy mind, healthy body' and in her spare time enjoys going to the gym, theatre and spending time with her family.

Entrance: The two main entry points are 4+ and 7+. At 4+, 100 applicants try for 40 places – two reception classes of 20 each. The girls are observed in groups of three or four doing 'nursery style activities' (playing, interacting and talking to junior school teachers). No formal reading or writing required. At 7+, 30 to 40 apply for an additional eight year 3 places. Girls are tested in maths, writing and verbal reasoning. Girls who do well in the test are invited back for a short, informal interview and a tour. The school is full but places occasionally come up in other years (mainly due to families relocating).

Exit: Virtually all progress to the senior school at the end of year 6. Confirmed, unconditional offers of places for the senior school are made in the spring term of year 5. The juniors still take the senior school entrance test with outside applicants though – so they can be considered for scholarships on an even footing. A few leave at 11 for other senior schools (such at St Paul's Girls', Godolphin & Latymer and Lady Eleanor Holles) but the assumption is that once they join the junior school they're here for the duration.

Remarks: The national curriculum is watched but certainly not slavishly followed. Girls do key stage 2 Sats – the head says teachers find them useful to track the girls' progress. 'It's all very low key,' she adds. 'There is a bit of preparation but no angst about them. It's just part and parcel of what we do.' Teachers focus on developing literacy and numeracy, with daily lessons in each subject. The school is rightfully proud of its integrated curriculum, introduced eight years ago. Designed 'to give meaning to humanities subjects', each year group from year 1 to year 6 is given a theme (anything from pirates to the First World War). When we visited year 6 pupils were studying the geography of the First World War battlefields and having philosophical discussions about what is worth fighting for.

Most subjects are taught by class teachers but science is led by a dynamic former research scientist from King's College London. She teaches girls from year 1 and enthuses them about the subject from the start – everything from snail races to learning how to purify water. 'We need to get girls passionate about science from a young age,' she says. Computing (lots of coding) and Mandarin are taught from year 1 onwards. French and German are offered as after-school clubs. Other clubs run at lunchtime and after school include computing, sewing, animation, art, touch typing and yoga.

Sensible levels of homework. Reception pupils get reading every evening, year 1s take spellings home and year 2s and up have homework – once a week in year 2, four nights a week in year 5 and every night in year 6 (but only for 30 minutes). Every so often homework is suspended and girls take part in an 'open homework' project – subjects range from hopes and dreams to heroines (choices included Mother Theresa, Rosa Parks and Malala Yousafzai; one girl nominated her granny). Girls have two PE lessons a week (gym, dance, netball, cricket), with weekly swimming from reception through to year 4.

The school is academically selective so while some have learning support for dyslexia and dyscalculia they must be able to cope with the pace of the curriculum. Support given one-to-one or in small groups. Strong links with the senior school. Girls from years 7 and 10 come and read to their junior counterparts, year 12s run a Minimus Club for year 4 girls and many pop in to say hello to their former teachers. Music, led by a former professional opera singer, is a tour de force. Girls take instrumental lessons from year 3 and there's an 80-piece orchestra. Plenty of opportunities to perform in concerts, bands and choirs too.

The junior school is located in a well-kept Victorian villa on a quiet residential road. It's on the same site as the senior school, with a green Astroturf, playground and south-facing garden at the back. Whole school assemblies are held twice a week in the junior hall but the junior girls also use the senior school's impressive hall and indoor swimming pool. The girls, in jaunty navy and red uniforms, walk across to the senior dining room for lunch. They all belong to one of four teams which compete for an annual team cup. Great emphasis placed on self-esteem, confidence and being happy at school and as girls progress through the school they take on responsibilities such as acting as 'playground pals' to younger pupils and elected reps on the school council.

Most pupils live relatively nearby. The majority have two working parents (lots of doctors, lawyers and media types) and the school runs a breakfast club from 7.30am and an after-school club till 6pm, both run by staff rather than an outside agency.

An academically excellent school that nurtures its pupils and helps them to develop into happy, confident girls. The head says that it's vital that the girls are happy – and they really are.

Notting Hill and Ealing High School

Linked with Notting Hill and Ealing High Junior School

2 Cleveland Road, London W13 8AX

Ages 11–18 **Pupils** 600 **Sixth form** 155

Fees: £18,561 pa

020 8799 8400
www.nhehs.gdst.net

Head: Since 2017, Matthew Shoults MA (40s). Educated at King's College School, Wimbledon, then read classics at Worcester College, Oxford. Spent two years on the civil service's graduate fast track scheme before deciding he wanted to be a teacher. After doing a PGCE at Cambridge he taught classics at King's, his old school, for four years. Moved to North London Collegiate School as head of classics, becoming deputy head and then senior deputy. After 12 years there he was appointed to the top job at Notting Hill and Ealing High School.

The first male head in the school's 145-year history, he was struck from the start by its warmth and friendliness. During his first visit one girl told him: 'It's a school of conversations,' while another said: 'The teachers trust and believe in us.' 'Yes, it's academic,' he says, 'but it's a happy place to be. It's our job to nurture the girls – and nurture their ambitions. It's incredibly easy to progress here.' Parents are impressed by his energy and dynamism and like the fact that he's very visible around the school. 'He's bringing in new ideas and is really good for the school,' one told us. Another said that the girls respected him and found him 'down-to-earth and easy to talk to'. Head has launched a drive to get as many pupils as possible involved in public speaking. We attended morning assembly during our visit and after notices about the forthcoming inter-house maths challenge and an appeal for clothes and toiletries for refugees, a group of engaging sixth form girls led a presentation about how languages affect the way we think. The head encourages pupils to come up with new ideas – girls often put their heads round his door and say 'I've had an idea'. Recent suggestions, both implemented, saw the launch of a dissection society and an origami club.

N

Head sees all year 11s as they decide their A level choices and all year 13s before they leave. He teaches public speaking and debating to all year 7 pupils so he can get to know them, will teach Greek to sixth formers next year and already spends time helping girls with their university applications. He often describes people as 'a good egg' and was amused when sixth formers presented him with an egg box labelled 'a pack of good eggs'. Inside were six decorated eggs, one depicting the head. In his spare time he plays the violin, sings, does cryptic crosswords and 'spoils' his three godchildren. He's also a third of the way through climbing Scotland's 282 Munros.

Academic matters: Results are impressive – 92 per cent A*/A/9-7 at GCSE in 2018 and 65 per cent A*/A, 93 per cent A*-B at A level Most popular A level subjects tend to be maths, biology and chemistry but arts and sciences are equally represented. Girls can take virtually any combination of subjects (luckily the assistant timetabler used to be a railway timetabler) and even if only one or two girls want to do an A level subject the school will run it. Most take three or four subjects at A level (25 subjects to choose from, including history of art, economics, psychology and politics) and 10 or 11 at GCSE. EPQ is growing in popularity for sixth formers and year 12 students take a variety of enrichment courses, choosing from an eclectic list of topics, from medieval art to the psychology of happiness.

Languages are strong here. All study Mandarin in years 7 and 8, plus either French, German or Spanish. Most take two languages at GCSE. Excellent take-up of Mandarin at GCSE and two-thirds A* grades in 2018. There's also a biennial trip to China. Latin is taught from year 8, with classical Greek offered from year 10. Class sizes of around 24, with maths the only subject set (from year 8). 'We want to create a sense that they aren't competing against each other,' says the head. 'It's how they are doing themselves that's important.'

Two dedicated learning support staff offer extra help where needed. Parents say the academic side of the school is 'very solid' and praise the way it helps new year 7s transition to senior school life. 'They want to them to settle in their friendship groups and develop their confidence before the work ramps up,' said one mother.

Games, options, the arts: Sport is important (at the time of our visit the new director of sport had been shortlisted for the London's sports teacher of the year award). The site is compact but clever architects have managed to fit a lot into the space. New four-court sports hall is impressive, as are the Astroturfs and 25-metre indoor pool. Sixth formers can train as life guards. The new extension to the school has added a stunning rooftop dance studio and fitness gym, with views across the school. All pupils take part in sport, from mainstream sports like netball, hockey, tennis and athletics to activities like cross-country, trampolining, running, badminton, cricket, football, zumba, yoga and kickboxing. Many notable local and national successes, including winning the year 7 Middlesex cricket tournament and reaching the national finals in under-14 netball.

Music is a real strength of the school. A multitude of individual music lessons and plenty of opportunities to play in orchestras and ensembles and sing in choirs. Recent choral tours to Barcelona, Florence and Croatia. Less experienced musicians get the chance to build their confidence by performing in atrium concerts. Parents say drama is 'fantastic' (there's a studio space as well as the main hall). School play every year, with girls designing the sets, lighting and costumes as well as performing and directing. Art department is vibrant and exciting, boasting three purpose-built studios kitted out with everything from digital scanners to a printing press. Several girls a year head to do art foundation and architecture courses.

Vast range of extracurricular clubs, many of them student led. Work experience is compulsory in year 11 and most girls find their own placements. On the day of our visit an enterprising sixth former was busy organising a fashion show at the school and had fixed for a national newspaper fashion editor and a representative from a well-known sports brand to attend.

Background and atmosphere: The oldest school in the Girls' Day School Trust (GDST) portfolio, Notting Hill and Ealing High School was founded in Notting Hill in 1873 and moved to leafy Ealing in 1930. The site has been transformed in recent years – a dazzling reworking of the central core of the school retained the school's period façade and a sleek glass extension has been added at the rear, with a spacious library, ultra-modern assembly hall, music recital hall, recording studio and sports hall. The extension looks out over a tree-lined courtyard with lots of benches to sit on during the summer months. Parents like the school's size. 'It's like Goldilocks,' said one. 'Neither too hot nor too cold. Neither too big nor too small.'

Sixth formers enthuse about their sixth form centre, a former children's home a five-minute walk away from the main site and equipped with six classrooms, common room, gym and café serving sandwiches, jacket potatoes, pasta, tea and coffee. Sixth form classes are small, girls don't have to wear uniform (no midriffs and no strappy tops) and they can go home in the afternoon if they don't have lessons. 'The sixth form girls like the fact that they get the support and outward-facing perspective but we aren't cocooning them,' says the head. Parents agree. One told us that her daughter had thrived in the sixth form. 'The environment is very nurturing but they are treated as adults too,' she said. Head of the sixth form reminds the girls of the importance of maintaining a healthy work-life balance – 'the vast majority are very sensible,' she says. Plenty of opportunities for leadership roles. Contenders for the role of head girl have to write a letter of application, make a speech and have an interview. All sixth formers are school reps and there's also a six-strong head girl team (including a sports captain).

Strong emphasis on helping others – girls of all ages raise money for chosen charities by running cake sales, nearly new sales, games and raffles. Strong links with the local community, including a Saturday morning Mandarin club for primary school children and a netball tournament for nearby primary schools run by year 10 girls.

Pastoral care, well-being and discipline: This is a school where pastoral care is prioritised as much as academic drive. When the head arrived he was struck by how 'joined-up' the pastoral care is. It's overseen by senior deputy head (pastoral) and staff work closely with parents. Heads of year meet form tutors every week to problem-solve and discuss any concerns. Girls can also talk to the school nurse and counsellor.

New year 7s are well supported via the big sister scheme (year 12s act as big sisters to them, offering help when they need it). Other activities include a picnic with year 8s and the chance to write a letter to their future selves, expressing their hopes and ambitions. Much to their delight, they receive it back in year 11.

All the girls we met were enthusiastic about being in an all-girls' school. 'It's far more relaxed without boys,' one told us. Parents say that issues and concerns are handled well – 'in a very thoughtful and individualised way'. In years 7 to 11 girls have to put their mobile phones in lockers when they arrive at school – 'if they are spotted with their phone we have a word with them,' says the head.

Pupils and parents: The pupils we met were enthusiastic, outgoing and full of charm. One parent told us that the girls were six months behind their central London counterparts when it came to social life and teenage parties– 'and we are very grateful for that,' she added. Girls predominantly come from Ealing, Chiswick, Hammersmith, Harrow, Notting Hill, Richmond and Kew. Travel links are good and 70 per cent travel in by public transport –tube, train and bus (the bus from Ealing Broadway stops right outside the school). They are a very grounded group of girls – 'in touch with reality,' says the head. Most parents work (lots of doctors, lawyers and media types).

Distinguished alumnae include historian Bettany Hughes, Labour MP Rupa Huq, stand-up comic Pippa Evans, London Grammar singer Hannah Reid and 2018 GDST alumna of the year Nirupa Murugaesu, the clinical lead for molecular oncology at Genomics England.

Entrance: Very oversubscribed but doesn't give out application numbers – 'because we don't want to put parents off'. Around 45 girls move up from the junior school each year, with another 50 coming from local primaries and preps. The school is a member of the London 11+ Consortium and entry now consists of a 75-minute cognitive ability test incorporating verbal, non-verbal and maths questions. All applicants to the senior school have a one-to-one interview. 'We are looking for girls with an inquiring nature,' says the head. 'We don't have a type. One of the fundamental aims of the school is for them to be themselves.'

Six or seven girls join the sixth form from other schools. Assessment is via a single paper consisting of a short essay on a subject of topical interest or news event, plus interviews with subject teachers and head of sixth form.

Exit: A handful leave after GCSEs, usually for co-ed independents and state schools. Some decide to head back within a few weeks and the school accommodates them if it can. Virtually all go straight to university (very few gap years), majority to Russell Group with five to Oxbridge and seven medics in 2018. Recent exceptions include one girl who got a highly-prized BBC apprenticeship and another who opted to train as a pilot at L3 Aviation Academy. One or two a year head to US universities (head thinks numbers will grow).

Money matters: The GDST has been providing high-quality academic education at a reasonable cost for nearly 150 years and Notting Hill and Ealing High does exactly that. Academic scholarships worth up to 50 per cent of the fees and music scholarships worth 10 per cent of the fees are available for year 7s. For those entering the sixth form there are academic, art music, sport and drama scholarships worth five to 10 per cent of the fees. Means-tested bursaries available too (scholarships can be supplemented by these).

Remarks: A forward-looking school that provides a stimulating education in a friendly and nurturing environment. Academic achievements are excellent and these energetic, exuberant girls are definitely a force to be reckoned with.

Notting Hill Preparatory School

N

95 Lancaster Road, London W11 1QQ

Ages 4–13 **Pupils** 370

Fees: £19,800 pa

020 7221 0727
www.nottinghillprep.com

Headmistress: Since 2003, Jane Cameron BEd (50s), three grown-up children. She was persuaded by the parents at Acorn Nursery not to retire or abandon her 'babies' to the vagaries of other schools but start her own prep so that their children could continue to benefit from her huge enthusiasm for education. Here is a woman who would love to stop the clock, not because she isn't entirely happy in her own skin (she clearly is) but because she loves every aspect of her job – children, staff and parents. One new boy in reception, in a case of mistaken identity, proudly announced to his mother 'we had assemberlee with David Cameron and she was very nice'; however, Jane Cameron (as she is universally called) would certainly have a poll rating way above that of any politician in this corner of north Kensington.

Retiring in July 2019. Her successor will be Sarah Knollys BA PGCE (40s), currently head of Glendower Prep. Educated at Exeter (a degree in French and Italian) and Roehampton Universities.

Started teaching career as SEN assistant at Finton House; rose from form teacher to maths co-ordinator, SCITT mentor, key stage 2 manager, senior management team and school governor at Allfarthing, a busy state school in Wandsworth; founding head, Maple Walk School, London (2005-2012). Married to Christopher; they have two teenage sons.

Bright and bubbly, Mrs Knollys exudes warmth and is highly accessible. She is the kind of person who rolls up her sleeves and gets on with it, whether it be teaching netball, transforming school lunches or wearing her slippersocks round the school on Red Nose day and dressing up in something crazy on Fun Friday. She gets things done – as can be seen from a previous job at Maple Walk, the pioneer New Model school which started 'out of a trunk' as she puts it, with two pupils, and had 150 pupils by the time she left. She has been on the Notting Hill Prep governing body for the past year, so has an insider's view of the school.

Entrance: Luck or an elder sibling has to be on your side to get into NHP as approximately seven names go into the scrupulously fair ballot for every place. One parent, whose offspring squeaked in, said it was a great relief as it is 'definitely the right place for us'. Siblings are always accepted and although it is not automatic for children from the Acorn Nursery (still attached to the school) to get in, it is certainly no disadvantage. Recently moved to three form entry but demand still far exceeds supply.

Exit: Almost all move on to independent secondary schools with the occasional leaver to Holland Park or Cardinal Vaughan. The usual suspects at 11+ are day schools such as Latymer Upper, Godolphin & Latymer, City of London, Francis Holland and at 13+ St Paul's, Westminster, City of London, UCS, Harrodian. Several to co-ed and boys' boarding schools, including Eton, Wellington, Rugby and recently Bradfield, with a few girls plumping for boarding at Benenden and Downe House. If any of the 'secure, cushion or stretch schools' turns down one of her pupils she banishes any sense of failure by saying that it's just the same as a restaurant telling you 'we'd love to fit you in but we just don't have enough tables'.

Remarks: Turn left at the bottom of Portobello (still an unlikely mix of market stalls, genuine and fake French bakeries, shops selling incense and Poundland), and you find yourself in the less exotic Lancaster Road. A typical Victorian schoolhouse, overshadowed by the rather solemn Serbian Church next door, houses the lower school, with years 3 to 6 filling a purpose-built (2011) building on the other side of the road. Yards away, round the colourful corner of Ladbroke Grove, they have squeezed a brand new block for years 7 and 8, also including massive spaces for music and art. The architectural styles are something of a hotch-potch and the outside space is not exactly state of the art although, to their credit, they have managed to squeeze in the unlikely duo of hens and an adventure playground. The only drawback: it takes smart timetabling to avoid children having to be endlessly escorted from A to B.

JC's determination to maintain her original ethos is immediately apparent on meeting everyone, from the very small people sitting on the floor, right up to the confident, friendly, amusing, only just children like the head boy and girl. This is a Thinking School and the evidence is everywhere, with hands shooting up when asked which habit was being studied this week. We sat in on a fascinating year 6 philosophy for children (P4C) class and wanted to vote ourselves when it came to choosing the question for discussion; in fact we would have paid big money to stay and listen to the intelligent arguments raised.

Seven academic and one art scholarship awarded to the 2018 leavers show that the system works and there is no need for parents to worry that philosophy is going to stop their children learning the basic building blocks. The ethos of the school is easily absorbed, particularly that learning how to learn is, at this stage, more important than anything else. Not a school that believes in offering a huge language choice (no Mandarin here): French all the way up, together with Latin from year 5 and Greek (optional) in years 7 and 8. Apart from the four founding teachers, there are another 15 who have been here for more than 10 years, but the average age is only 35 and the head says they lose very few, unless they are Antipodean, with quite a high percentage returning to the fold later in life.

The lower school head of SEN (who has been here since the school opened) is an articulate enthusiast for early intervention, and the children being given extra help responded happily to questions. One parent told us that when her son was diagnosed with ADHD 'they were really wonderful at supporting him', and we were convinced that the large SEN department was well on top of any problems.

Music is huge at NHP; there are several choirs, including a chamber choir which you have to audition for, as well as ones for the less sonorous. In fact being unable to sing is not considered an option here and you are encouraged to play an instrument even if 'you can't play for toffee'.

The vast new art room (plenty of room for the next Anish Kapoor) should give the subject much more visibility. Reception and year 1 take to the stage at Christmas with a sometimes slightly unorthodox nativity play which, last year, featured an angel joined on her way to Bethlehem by sundry others including cowboys/girls and footballers. Year 8s are given the task of writing and staging their own play in a week, whilst years 3 and 6 produce plays in the spring and summer terms.

Differing opinions on the amount of sport available, from both parents and pupils, some claiming that it was a bit light on the ground – 'they could definitely do more' – and others saying that 'they were brilliant getting him into sport'. At the moment the girls are confined to hockey as a team game, but apparently some are petitioning to play rugby with the boys. Not surprisingly for a Thinking School they have been told to go ahead, provided they can get enough mates to sign up. All in all, we felt that the consensus from the pupils was that they weren't missing out and there were plenty of after-school opportunities if you wanted to do more, including martial arts in year 1 and Boxclever higher up. 'There really is something to interest every type of child,' said one parent about non-sporting alternatives, including chess and coding.

Outwardly, NHP may appear a laid back school but discipline is key albeit, hopefully, self-imposed. Messing around lands you with an orange card and 'culpas' are handed out for more serious or repeated offences. These can involve a spell of community service or a detention at break-time, luckily a rare occurrence. The modern terror of online bullying plus the perils of the internet are areas that the head is extremely aware of, running talks for parents as well as strict monitoring throughout the school.

On asking Jane Cameron what she was proudest of, she answered, 'This may sound fluffy, but it is having created a community where everyone is happy'. Not a bit fluffy in our view, this judgement backed by a pupil telling us, with a huge smile, that coming here was 'the best decision she'd ever made'. Loud applause from parents, which carries weight, as this a collection of sophisticated, worldly individuals used to having their voices heard.

Nower Hill High School

George V Avenue, Pinner HA5 5RP

Ages 11–18 **Pupils** 1,881 **Sixth form** 383

020 8863 0877
www.nowerhill.org.uk

Head: Since 2012, Chris Livesey, BA from London in modern history. A Cheshire lad, who moved to London for his degree, continued his studies there (PGCE) and never went back: 'My first teaching job was at a comprehensive school in Wembley, and then I became deputy head at Nower High, where I stayed for the next 15 years before becoming head. I've basically had two long services in two schools.' Although he is loathe to admit that he must have been the natural choice to succeed the much respected former head teacher, we think few would've expected otherwise. One parent told us: 'Mr Livesey was always a well-respected deputy head and classics teacher and was always very visible.' Mr Livesey says that when he was offered the role of head teacher, he was 'extremely flattered to be entrusted with such a role at such a school' and wants to ensure that he gives the role his utmost level of commitment and hard work.

At 50+ years old, Mr Livesey manages to successfully combine a friendly and youthful demeanour with a straight up, very headmasterly, no-nonsense approach. One parent commented that 'children really like him, but when he walks in the room there is complete silence.' He loved his own schooling and as a result remains passionate about education. 'I went to an independent school in Cheshire – school was fantastic.' This head doesn't strike us as someone who will ever take his job for granted; quite the contrary – he enthuses about his loyal and committed staff, 'a very strong team of senior leaders, teachers and support staff', the lovely pupils and the general vibe of the place: 'You only have to look at the school's history to see that since it first opened its doors in 1929, the school has only ever had seven head teachers.' Heads, it seems, are at Nower Hill for the long haul.

He insists on a clean and tidy school. One parent told us: 'Mr Livesey is forever picking up litter and he never asks anyone to do it for him.' And his presence has been noted by many: 'He is always on the school gates and walking around the school. He is transparent in a good way. He doesn't hide how he feels about where he wants the school to be.' Punctuality is very important to him, and he himself has something of a daily commute from Richmond where he lives with his wife (an assistant head teacher in Richmond) and their three children.

Retiring in July 2019.

Academic matters: This Ofsted outstanding school is well known in the area for its academic standards. One local parent told us: 'Nower Hill has always had a good reputation, now it has an excellent one.' Part of its success could be down to its class sizes of 25 pupils, spread across 12 forms in a year group, part of it could be down to the dedicated teachers 'who always have their lines of communication open to parents' to the point where one parent told us: 'I feel a bit sorry for the teachers. They work so hard during the day and then call or email us back straight away if we have a query.' Ofsted said: 'The leadership of teaching and learning is exceptional.' And the head added that part of the school's success is that 'we pride ourselves on working hard for all learners.'

In 2018, 75 per cent of students got 9-4 in both English and maths; 29 per cent 9-7 grades. At A level, 64 per cent of all grades were at A*-B, with 33 per cent at A or A*. 'For a not particularly competitive school, they still get the results,' one parent told us. Another said, 'The school does very well at stretching bright children, whilst at the same time providing a round education for everyone.'

The curriculum is wide and varied with 24 optional subjects offered at GCSE level (Mandarin offered as an extracurricular language), with more able students being offered the opportunity to learn ancient Greek and astronomy. An enthusiastic parent told us: 'The options in year 8 are fantastic. Students start their GCSE course in year 9 and they are given a chance to chop and change a bit for the first term and decide if it is the right course for them.'

Each student has been given their own tablet, which they can take home and use for homework. Quite extraordinary in a school of 1,900 pupils and clearly highlights the school's priorities in terms funding. One parent told us: 'It's things like this that make this school so progressive.' The head is quick to point out that this is an educational tool only and that students don't have access to Facebook or Twitter: 'Everything they need has been put on there for them.'

Parents have also welcomed an online app called Show my Homework where students, parents and carers can access homework details and retrieve and submit work online. Students also have their own personal portfolio where they can store all their electronic documents, allowing access to them in or out of school. It is part of the school's Managed Learning Environment (MLE) for which Nower Hill won the award for secondary schools.

Excellent facilities for students with disabilities, including ramps, improved corridor lighting, lifts, handrails on steps, widened doorways for wheelchair access and yellow lines to assist visually impaired students. Roughly 13 per cent of the school intake is registered with an SEN. For those students, a well-supported inclusion staff team is on hand to offer extra support, including a SENCo, qualified SEN teachers, Inclusion manager, behaviour manager, mentor and counsellor. There is also extra support for maths and English

Games, options, the arts: The school has a very long tradition of strength in the arts subjects, which was evident as we walked round. Astoundingly good self-portraits from GCSE students were on display as well as an interesting montage of student-designed film posters. Several of Nower Hill's art students have had their work displayed in local art galleries, national exhibitions and at the Mall Galleries. Many continue their art studies post A level, at well-respected art colleges. Photography also strong.

Drama is popular and taken up in fair abundance. Big scale biannual musicals, which have included The Lion King and Oliver! Watford drama winners recently. The dance department offers a wide range of extracurricular dance activities including contemporary dance, tap, ballet, Bollywood, street dance and modern. There are many performance opportunities available both in and out of school; school productions, a dance showcase, summer extravaganza and a performance at the Royal Albert Hall.

Musical students have a choice of a dozen ensemble music groups and orchestras to take part in, including a soul band, and school hosts concerts several times a year. Some 400 pupils have peripatetic music classes, and groups include everything from steel pan ensemble to African drumming to a full 51 piece school orchestra. Well-equipped recording studios. One pupil told us: 'This school really caters well in all departments and has something for everyone.'

Sports play a big part in the school and there is a wide range of activities. The faculty prides itself on 'giving very generously of its time'. Sports include netball, basketball, handball, rugby, trampolining and indoor athletics. All clubs are fully inclusive. School athletes compete at borough, county and national level with 'considerable success.' Sporting facilities include a 3G Astroturf pitch, two tiered grass playing fields, six tennis courts, six netball courts a multi-purpose sports hall, fitness suite and gymnasium.

Aspiration is definitely a buzz word at Nower High, and an Aspire programme is run on Wednesday and Thursday lunchtimes for Y12 and Y13. This programme helps to develop 'interview, thinking and critical analysis skills, provides personal feedback and mentoring' to ensure students have the best possible chance at future employment. Training is also offered to become mentors for younger students and give older students the opportunity to run lower school science, sports and dance clubs as well as a variety of other leadership roles.

This school really puts a big 'C' in charity. It doesn't do things to tick boxes, or to excite an over-zealous PTA. Pupils seem to be charitable to the core. When we were there, a dedicated area of the school hall had been given over to black bags, full of clothes and toys for Syrian refugees: 'We like to instill charitable values in children of a young age.' School fundraising events have included a leavers' ball, pizza and quiz event and charity sports fixtures against staff. There is also the opportunity for sixth formers to work voluntarily in an orphanage in Romania as well as with elderly people in the local community. Events are planned throughout the year to raise money for their chosen charity – St Marcellin's Children's Village in Zimbabwe.

Background and atmosphere: Formerly Headstone Council School, this red-brick building on Pinner Road first opened its doors in 1929. The school's purpose was to educate 292 5-14 year olds with an average class size of 50. The school soon expanded to meet the ever-growing number of children resident in rapidly expanding north Harrow and Pinner. Its steady expansion has withstood many a hitch including the Second World War, when many of its male teachers were called up for military service and the playing field was dug up for trenches and air raid shelters.

Redevelopment work continued throughout the 60s and 70s (when the school became Nower Hill) – continuing throughout the 90s, which saw the start of a £2.75 million development programme, including a new 13 classroom block and the Gristwood Centre, housing music, dance and drama studios, a fitness suite and the sports hall. The school added a sixth form in 2006, which a few years later moved into its £4 million sixth form extension. The site was further enhanced in 2010 by the addition of a block of five science labs and a new English teaching block hosting 13 classrooms. This is one big site.

As a result, the site is a bit of a hotch-potch of buildings, none of them particularly pretty, but functional and purposeful and very much in keeping with large comprehensives. Plus, as every parents knows, schools are much more than bricks and mortar – and this school is so much more. The pupils who showed us around were extremely articulate, warm, kind and very proud of their school. Big mix culturally and harmonious atmosphere. Room after room was explained with equal enthusiasm (even the less aesthetically pleasing ones), and each montage on colourful walls was discussed in detail – especially those of past school trips. We were taken through a labyrinth of corridors and would've lost our bearings many a time if it weren't for our guides. There were a few nice touches we spotted on our tour, most notably the 'ancient' Greek columns outside the classics department (homage, possibly, to the head, who is partial to a bit of classics).

Other things worth mentioning include the spacious library, well-equipped with books and computers, and six different outlets for food and snacks, including a cold canteen for grab-and-go pastas and salads and a hot canteen. However, one parent did say that the downside of such a large school is the difficulty in accommodating everyone: 'My son finds school dinners all a bit stressful and too much of an effort to have something hot. There are just too many other kids and often nowhere to sit. I think they should stagger it more.' Sixth formers have now been offered the incentive of a £1 coffee and cookie in the common room, instead of traipsing to the local café and wasting valuable time.

Pastoral care, well-being and discipline: Discipline is 'bang on', one parent told us: 'For a school with this many children, you really don't hear of many incidents like bullying etc, and if there are, they are dealt with quickly and appropriately.' By all accounts Mr Livesey is a truly dedicated head, and he expects the same of his staff, where the well-being of his pupils are concerned. One parent told us: 'The teachers always walk out with the kids at the end of the day and often accompany them to the local shops. That way the shop keepers are always reassured that a grown up is with them.' Another said, 'You never ever see any Nower Hill pupils lighting up outside the school gates or nearby, like at other schools. The students here are very aware that they are representatives of the school and they wear their uniform proudly.'

Uniform is a very smart navy affair, with the odd splash of varying colours on the v-neck pullovers denoting the year group. All blazers have the school's crest with the motto 'service not self' emblazoned on it. Although strict on uniform, Mr Livesey does display a softer side, especially when questioned about the assortment of hair colour that passed us by (most noticeably green), on our tour of the school: 'I won't argue with a child about their hair. It's a very happy environment here and that's the main thing.'

In a school of this size, we wondered how feasible it is to oversee the well-being of all students and to prevent the more vulnerable ones from slipping through the cracks: 'We work very hard at keeping a large school, a small school', says the head. And indeed Nower Hill does seem to have a pretty robust infrastructure. There is a full-time attendance officer who works with parents around punctuality and is there to pick up on any possible issues. There are two co-ordinators for every year group and a well-staffed student support team. There are also two peer mentors for new students allocated to each class.

One parent told us: 'This school's motto should be above and beyond. They really do go the extra mile here. The lines of communication are always open if you need to speak to a teacher, and somebody always gets back to you pretty promptly.' Another told us how the school bent over backwards to help facilitate her daughter's studies after a long period absent due to ill health: 'Home tutoring was arranged for my daughter as soon as we needed it and the tutor was very impressed with the excellent support material provided to her from the school.'

Mr Livesey recently reintroduced a new house system to reflect the core values of the school. These six houses have been named after influential people who, together, inspire millions around the globe: Gandhi, King, Shabazz, Franklin, Bannister and Nightingale. The school sees the qualities of being well mannered, articulate, well behaved, hard working, smart and kind as part of the DNA, and reminders are displayed throughout the school. Ofsted said in the last report that: 'Student' behaviour is excellent..the school provides an orderly, welcoming environment entirely conducive to learning.'

The reintroduction of the house system has been welcomed by pupils. One told us, 'It's more fun and you become loyal to your house. It also promotes a healthy competition between the houses on things like sports days.'

As with any school, particularly of this size, disruptive pupils will always be an issue. However, Mr Livesey says that permanent exclusions are below the national average: 'We have very high expectations here. Any poor student behaviour is dealt with in a clear and consistent manner' through what the school calls its

Ladder of Consequences. This includes an inclusion centre for students temporarily excluded from lessons, which is equipped with computers and other educational resources.

Pupils and parents: Pupils and parents pretty much reflect the general demographic of the local area of Pinner and north Harrow. Roughly 30 per cent white British, nearly half Asian and the rest a mixture of other ethnicities. Parents are largely professionals, pupils aspirational.

Entrance: Hugely oversubscribed. Approx 1,400 applications are submitted each year group for 324 places. Waiting list system is operated by the local authority. School catchment is roughly a mile, and you'll get in if you have a sibling or a looked after child. However, one unhappy parent told us: 'My only real gripe with the school is that the sibling policy stops at GCSE, so if you have a bigger age gap between your children, there is no guarantee at all that they will get in.'

Exit: Around 40 per cent leave after GCSEs, mostly to do vocational courses elsewhere. Nearly all sixth form students go on to university, with the rest choosing a gap year, an apprenticeship or employment. Quite a few medics and dentists each year; usually a couple to Oxbridge (one in 2018). Oxbridge admissions preparation with academic mentors who have themselves been to Oxford or Cambridge. Popular destinations also include elite art colleges and music conservatoires.

Remarks: If you live in the north Harrow area and are within catchment of this school, applying for it is a bit of a no-brainer.

Old Palace of John Whitgift School

Linked with Old Palace Preparatory

Old Palace Road, Croydon, Surrey CR0 1AX

Ages 10–18 **Pupils** 490 **Sixth form** 100

Fees: £13,947 – £15,366 pa

020 8688 2027
www.oldpalace.croydon.sch.uk

Headmistress: Since 2011, Carol Jewell (60s), MA PGCE Dip Ed NPQH CSMB. Proceeded by a brief spell as acting head and a longish one as deputy, a role she took on in 2005 having originally joined the school as director of music in 1997. Before that, assorted teaching roles in a London sixth form college, a Banbury comprehensive and then (after a spell in Wales) at top-rated St George's School in Edinburgh.

Every inch the perfect head for this school imbued with its rich history, she says: 'I'm a traditionalist, all about good manners and courtesy'. But left behind by the times she is not. Having considered every educational philosophy or buzz word one might care to mention, she has her own take on it and how it might be relevant to the girls of this very particular community: 'We're about more than resilience here – if girls can be confident and enthusiastic, then they will be employable, people will want to work with them. As they walk out of the gate after their A levels I want to know they have a distinguished sense of social responsibility, of who they are and what they stand for'.

She interviews each and every prospective pupil to make sure in part that parents understand what is on offer here. Charmingly frank, she will also tell them what will and won't work for the school and if there's anything 'we're going to fall out about.' 'We don't do divas, we roll up our sleeves' – none more so than Mrs Jewell, who has personally introduced container gardens and benches – to break up spaces which were little more than thoroughfares or forgotten corners. Thoughtful, original, experimental, she's found that little touches such as a table with china and plants in an entrance hall will steady girls who might otherwise ricochet around.

The impression we get is that Mrs Jewell is up to some alchemy here. Meeting very many parents focused on grades and a career in the professions for their offspring, she is delighted with the school's excellent across the board ISI report but stresses, 'we're not just about excellent academic credentials but a broader values based education.' Her wish is to ensure 'girls have a quiet sense of self-belief and adaptability' – this is what will help them to succeed in a future we cannot yet envisage.

She welcomes us into her traditionally furnished office overlooking the medieval garden on a bitterly cold day before Christmas – she has cleverly taken to wearing not one but two tweedy jackets on top of each other to survive. Edinburgh is her home town, but she doesn't have a trace of her accent. Long-time resident of Croydon, which she says has been 'very kind to us' and where she has been 'blissfully happy'. She has two children, a boy and girl, both now grown up and working.

Parents say she's 'an inspiration, fiercely protective of her girls. A big reason we all chose the school.' 'A graceful, smart, elegant, educated, inspirational lady!' said one and we very much concur. 'Very caring, values each child for their own merits, approachable, kind, strong role model, good leader,' said another. She currently teaches year 7 Latin and is greeted with fondness wherever she treads – a computer science class, thinking she has dropped in to be their supply teacher on our visit, cheer.

Head retiring summer 2019.

Academic matters: The curriculum in year 7 begins with standard fare with the inclusion of Latin and French or Spanish. By year 10 keen scientists and stargazers may also take up GCSE astronomy, whilst if Latin is going well, why not add in a GCSE in classical Greek? Mandarin is offered as part of a club after school.

In 2018, 73 per cent A*-A/9-7 at GCSE/IGCSE with the strongest performances in maths, English language and biology. Ten subjects is the most common, some may opt for fewer if it makes sense for them. French is by far the most popular language taken to GCSE with native speakers able to notch up another.

At A level in the same year, 52 per cent of grades were A*/A, with the mathematicians outstripping all comers in terms of top grades and something new – psychology – proving both popular and engaging with plenty of As. A healthy list of choices including classical Greek, drama and theatre studies and government and politics.

Eighty or so teaching staff. Has recently appointed a new assistant head with responsibility for maths and numeracy across the school. Teachers 'very dedicated, always go the extra mile – they're all running clinics in the lunch hour if a girl wants extra help...but, girls have to do the running and come and ask for that help,' says the head.

A year 7 father observed of the teaching he has encountered: 'high standards across all subjects but also accessible introductions to new topics.' Another parent: 'Teaching is of a very high standard. It is clear from the marking by staff that they are diligent and alive to a pupil's abilities. Homework reflects that the pupils are expected to think laterally and expand their knowledge themselves.'

There are exams twice a year, which girls mostly take in their stride in preparation for GCSEs to come. A year 7 mother sent this message to prospective parents: 'not as intensive as I had been led to believe from the school's reputation.' The 'palace group' is for gifted and talented – offering individual mentoring and encouragement to undertake projects outside of the curriculum. There is a series of lunchtime lectures – recent topics on the art of conducting, what we owe to the Athenians and the ethics of Shakespeare.

Sixth formers are ably prepped for law and medical school applications as well as UCAS, and enrichment offers the university friendly experience of an EPQ, current affairs, financial awareness, science and ethics, food and nutrition and community service.

Pupils with SEND and EAL needs achieve success in line with their peers when it comes to exams. A parent with a hearing impaired daughter described gratefully how 'every teacher has made accommodations for her to maximise her learning and yet in such a discreet way that she has never felt singled out.'

Games, options, the arts: With the site the very anathema of green space or lush sporting facilities, this is something for prospective parents to take on the chin. The school does have its own 25m swimming pool, the use of Trinity's Astroturf for hockey and girls travel to playing fields by minibuses, a great recent addition to the school. The sporting ethos is inclusive, with the head looking to 'beef it up so that we can play more fixtures'. To that end a new director of sport has been appointed. Currently girls play rounders, hockey and football and take part in cross-country, athletics and dance. Fencing and trampolining have just been introduced. A parent commented: 'My daughter has taken part in lots of swimming competitions and I feel the standard of instruction she has received has been great.' Plenty of excellent sportswomen amongst the pupils – some participants in the London Youth Games, the water polo team took part in the English Schools' championships and contains a national player. Sporting clubs at lunch and after school include tennis, rounders, water-polo, fencing, indoor athletics and swim squad.

'Music is both high quality and inclusive – a real stand out,' a delighted mother enthused, with highly accomplished staff, no doubt hand-picked by the musical head. As one might expect, the choir regularly performs evensong at Croydon Minster as well as the country's finest cathedrals – St Paul's, Winchester and Salisbury and St Mark's Basilica in Venice. Take your seats (and bring warm coats or sneaky hot water bottles for some spaces) to hear regular recitals and concerts from choirs, orchestra, chamber groups, polyphonic choir, brass group, wind and piano chamber music, recorders and a school speciality – the steel pans. Pupils perform at local Beckenham music festival and are involved in productions such as a recent ambitious Tchaikovsky's Eugene Onegin.

Over 120 clubs. Parents talk of girls struggling to fit in all of the clubs, activities, performances and shows they want to be involved with. Hip-hop dance, critical thinking, anatomy club, mindfulness, Italian film, ceramics and more jostle for attention – good to see both an embroidery club and feminist society sharing a timetable.

Background and atmosphere: Who would have thought that the Archbishop of Canterbury summered in Croydon? But for centuries, he did just that when journeying from Lambeth, and occasionally hosted the royal court here in the oldest part of the school, adjacent to ancient Croydon Minster. Later, when the commoners drew too close, the archbishops removed themselves and the building suffered the indignity of becoming a linen printers, bleachers and laundry. By 1899 the Sisters of the Church were given the building by the Duke of Newcastle and founded the school. Archbishop John Whitgift, with the approval of Queen Elizabeth I, built almshouses and a school for the poor here in 1596, which became the charitable Whitgift Foundation now funding the Whitgift and Trinity schools.

One needs a certain amount of determination to reach the school amidst flyovers, terraces, ring-roads and tramlines: it's an urban mash up that makes stepping inside the school walls a huge relief. Once inside the grade I listed old palace offers wonderful spaces such as a beautiful chapel and a great hall with the finest hammered ceiling in southern England. We had to admit to some disappointment on finding little trace of majesty in Queen Elizabeth's bedroom – now a classroom – but the head feels that for the girls 'she takes her place in history.' A beautifully crafted modern building in red brick with stone mullions and cloisters provides ample teaching space and labs. Then, over the road there is the technology annexe housing art studio, DT, music rehearsal spaces in a light and bright environment and a large modern dining room where everyone eats together. On the top floors there's a professional dance studio, theatre rehearsal room and a sixth form common room where girls relax.

A mother described the school's atmosphere as 'caring, and whilst wanting to maximise achievement in every girl, does not do so in a strict competitive environment but a nurturing one that works to each girl's strengths.'

Pastoral care, well-being and discipline: There is a Church of England framework to the school: all Christian festivals are celebrated with no opt out. Lots of praise for the pastoral care: 'excellent pastoral care – both processes and, more importantly, people who genuinely care' being typical. Few seem to have had any encounters with the anti-bullying measures, but one mother told us: 'I have had one occasion to speak to the school about low level bullying and they handled this brilliantly.'

The four pillars or central beliefs of the school – service, courage, emotional intelligence, learning – are delivered through the house system. Girls in sixth form take assemblies – 'it works best when girls hear from their own age group,' says the head. The ability of pupils across year groups to work together as a whole is singled out for praise by the ISI. Lots of charity work in evidence in the community and further afield – playing with children in a local hospice and befriending the elderly in a local care home.

Pupils and parents: 'Mixed: an ethnic, racial and faith mix,' says Mrs Jewell, 'open-hearted, not angels!' Very definitely a helicopter-free, unpushy parental set.

Entrance: Somewhat awkwardly, the prep school finishes at year 5 with pupils completing year 6 within the senior school (together with some new entrants from outside) and sitting the 11+ alongside external candidates; and although 90 per cent of girls are offered places, they are not guaranteed. It's also a chance to gain scholarships and the head's award, which recognises high performance in either English or maths. A few peel off to grammar schools. External candidates arrive from a wide slew of primaries. Good transport links, motivated parents and an extensive network of school minibuses bring the school within reach of, for instance, Sutton, Wandsworth, Bromley and Herne Hill.

Despite the lengthy list of assessment topics – English, maths, reasoning, social interaction, parental support, general knowledge and creativity (assessed through maybe looking at a piece of art or talking about their work) – the competition for places is only very mild compared with more fashionable London boroughs.

Any child with an ed psych's report is allocated extra time. This is one of the few schools to state openly that they are looking for 'parental support'. We presume exceptions made for self-starters succeeding so far without it.

Exit: An impressive list of university destinations. Over 60 per cent to Russell Group, three medics and one to Oxbridge in 2018. Rather than straightforwardly academic subjects, as is something of an understandable trend these days and also perhaps reflective of a hard-working parental community, choices seem mindful of career directions, with a predominance of -ologies – criminology, psychology, marine biology – or, for instance, modern languages together with business.

Money matters: Around 45 per cent of pupils are assisted by some kind of bursary from the extraordinarily wealthy £5m Whitgift foundation – one of the largest in the UK – providing up to 95 per cent fee remittance. As a guide household income would need to be below £70k to apply. There is also a long list of scholarships and exhibitions (for year 12) which are not means-tested and are offered depending on performance in the entrance tests.

Remarks: A sense of history and her place in it awaits girls at Old Palace. The passionate head is one of kind and knows whom the school will suit. Step inside for a transformative academic education.

Old Palace Preparatory

Linked with Old Palace of John Whitgift School

2, Melville Avenue, South Croydon, Surrey CR2 7YN

Ages 1–10 **Pupils** 170 (40 boys in nursery) **C of E**

Fees: £11,316 – £11,823 pa

020 8686 7347
www.oldpalace.croydon.sch.uk

Head of preparatory: Since 2015, Tim Horton MA FRCO, degree in music from Jesus College, Cambridge. Previously at The Hall, Hampstead, but has also taught at Abbots Bromley School and Birkdale School, Sheffield. This is his first headship. He was attracted by the diversity of this community in particular but being part of the charitable Whitgift Foundation was important too – he says: 'it's much easier to teach values if you practise what you preach,' and there is a certain freedom here too: 'you don't have to put all of your focus on the bottom right hand corner of the budget sheet'.

Mr Horton radiates warmth, amiability and impeccable politeness, slipping in and out of teacher mode in classrooms at ease with every child whom we encountered and name-perfect. His two youngest children, a boy and girl, clearly delight in attending his school, even if it's not always easy to remember when he's in headmaster mode. Hard to believe, but his family also includes two older children, another boy and girl – having teens and toddlers at the same time raised a few eyebrows, but typically he says that it worked surprisingly well.

He felt this school 'had a huge amount to offer but was not outward facing enough.' That's all about to change, with new signage just the beginning. He'd like to collaborate with parents, to increase their sense of ownership of the school and for the school to be 'more actively proud'. With so much space to hand, there is clearly room for expansion. However, Mr Horton says the prep 'is going to grow gradually, otherwise we might lose the character of the school, the family atmosphere.'

Parents told us: 'He is a lovely, personable headmaster, who always takes the time to speak to the parents either at the door in the morning or in a private meeting.' One enthused: 'He has only been at the school for two years but quickly became part of the fabric of the school and I couldn't imagine it without him.' He is seen to have placed a particular emphasis on 'kind behaviour and good manners.'

Those who have chosen the whole school for their daughters, inspired by Mrs Jewell, head of the senior school, will not be disappointed to find that she is a presence here too, often attending pre-school and prep activities. As a mother noted approvingly: 'The leadership is second to none – it sets the tone here and everything that is a success at this school flows from this.'

Head of nursery is Jacqui Hines NNEB (40s), two teenage girls, one a gold medal gymnast. Feisty, fast talking with a supportive, calm deputy – 'I run around like a loon. She's the yin to my yang' – and runs a tight-knit team of 35 full and part-timers. Started as second in command, promoted to current post, three months in. Can't imagine doing anything else. 'Children are so lovely and innocent and speak their mind. Whatever you're pouring into them, you're shaping their lives'.

Entrance: For 4+, assessments are held in the reception classrooms covering language and social skills, maths, physical and creative skills as well as understanding of the world. Parents are also required to attend an interview with the head of the prep or deputy. We've previously described the intake as 'oversubscribed', but with two applicants for each place it's something of a breeze compared with schools even a fraction closer to central London. A fair few newcomers join the prep in other years and are quickly absorbed, with firm friendships quickly established, say pupils.

At 7+, pupils are assessed through written testing as well as an interview with the head. Choral scholarships available at this point. Pupils with any SEN needs will be supported during the assessment process and the possible provision within the school discussed with the head.

Exit: For girls at the nursery, assumption (by parents and school) is that they'll go on into Old Palace reception. Though their passage there isn't automatic (there's an assessment), in practice 'all our girls get places,' says head of nursery. Boys tend to stay in the independent sector, with Cumnor House and Elmhurst the most popular destinations, Park Hill Infants for those going on to state schools.

Year 6 is part of the senior school, on a different site, and everyone moves up automatically. They all take the 11+ there and some 70 per cent stay on for year 7 and above (though this is not guaranteed), many with scholarships, while others move on to local grammar schools.

Remarks: The average classroom size is 18 and maximum is 22. This is an academic school. The aim is for year 5s to be working a year ahead of expectations, with no need for Sats prep. The most able are stretched in the classroom with extension built into every lesson, and all children have individual targets. No homework in reception, just under two hours per week in years 1 and 2, building to just under three hours by year 5.

An 'excellent mix of child-initiated and adult-led activities,' says the ISI, which notably judged the school's early years foundation stage to be 'outstanding'. Much evidence of fun, hands-on learning and cross-curricular project work higher up. Year 3 built a 'ring of fire': impressive erupting volcano models, including one made of chocolate rice crispies. DT and computing are included. French from reception and a modern foreign languages 'experience' designed to fill a few cultural gaps on the way.

Fourteen staff have been with the school for more than 10 years and are described by the incoming head as as a strong team who pull together. Parents talk in glowing terms: 'The teaching staff are always so supportive of the children. They never say they cannot do something. Instead they encourage and support them to achieve their goals.' A mother with two daughters at the school told us: 'Not only are they technically brilliant, but they have an amazing ability to inspire the girls to learn. Both girls seemed to just 'get' reading, but that was absolutely down to the skill of the teachers and the fantastic teaching assistants. I can't fault them.' Mr Horton's daughter is so enthused she now colours everything purple and green (the school uniform colours).

Quite low profile provision regarding SEN. The learning support co-ordinator is based at the senior school. Any pupils with a SEN, such as dyslexia, have an individual student action plan outlining differentiation needed within the classroom, but no one-to-one support. Those with more complex learning difficulties and an EHCP would have one-to-one (subject to funding). Progress is regularly reviewed. Only one pupil with EAL needs currently. Pupils may attend extra English lessons and are provided with extra work allowing them to catch up with English and key vocabulary in different subjects.

There are plenty of sports fixtures for girls from year 3 upwards, and the ethos is inclusive – everyone has a chance to compete. There is at least one session of PE per week and older pupils have a sessions of games too. No minibus scrambling, with a large playing field and playgrounds doubling up for tennis and netball right here. Everyone has a swimming lesson each week at the senior school pool. Dance is taught by a specialist. There is a squad and a club for every sport. Not so many glittering sporting achievements; when we asked we were told about the year 3 and 4 borough cross-country championships gold medal.

Music flourishes, with a good range of free taster sessions in year 3 and many learning instruments, excellent facilities (a big, terraced room, piled high with xylophones and five practice rooms dotted round the place) and a decent range of groups, instrumental and vocal, headed by the audition-only junior polyphonic, which performs with seniors in Croydon Minster. We arrive during a rehearsal for the Christmas concert by years 3, 4 and 5. Nothing short of joyful and exuberant. Mr Horton feels it exemplifies the spirit of the school – 'we're not a typical girls' school – it's quite a robust environment' – which far from being a metaphor for needing to be quite resilient to survive, here seems to mean girls throw themselves into everything with gusto. Modelled by staff, too, who last Christmas surprised pupils with a performance on the steel pans whilst wearing reindeer antlers.

Bridge, ballet, orchestra, swim squad, Spanish, rounders and much more all on offer as pre- and post-school clubs.

Now situated within the former Croham Hurst senior school, the buildings are quite a ramshackle collection, some more nondescript than others, connected by covered walkways. Once inside everywhere smells clean, is warm, calm and bright. Classrooms are large with massive picture windows. We encounter children quietly digging in soil for rocks and creatures during a biology lesson and totally engaged in learning how to work out the value of an acute angle by thinking in terms of pizza in maths. A new science lab is intended to give science a bit of a lift within the school and the prep works closely with the senior school with regards to STEM subjects. An attractive library is well stocked with books and used for the accelerated reading programme.

Does Mr Horton's day finish in time for Homes Under the Hammer, we wonder? He has the developer's eye for potential and a north London teacher's amazement at all of this space – three large halls suitable for indoor sports, rehearsals, assemblies and gymnastics, even spare classrooms which can be set up for break-out activities, such as a jungle complete with soundtrack and lighting for book week. During the holidays he found a two bedroom flat and a set of changing rooms he didn't know existed.

A mother of two told us: 'Both of our children absolutely love the school, and my son is always so thrilled when he asks if it's a pre-school day and we say yes!' Another with children higher up the school said: 'The school is so warm and caring; however, there is a positive undertone of competitiveness. Healthy competition is encouraged in a caring atmosphere.'

Pupils eat in houses. Year 5 girls enjoy the responsibility of mentoring reception children – this begins with an introductory letter over the holidays and is a long term commitment rather than something that fades after the first day. As top dogs, without a year 6, they acquire the trappings of seniority early: all can be prefects and get to sit on benches not the floor during assembly.

The majority of pupils have English as their home language, with a couple of handfuls of overseas nationals, currently from China, India, Mauritius, Nigeria and Taiwan. Almost everyone mentions the diversity of the children and families here in an appreciative way.

Very well set up for working parents (most). Open from 7.30am with a free breakfast club, then an after-school club runs until 6pm. No need to panic during school holidays either, as a third party provides a full-time holiday club for a reasonable fee.

Children can attend the nursery from the age of 1 upwards. Open 51 weeks of the year, with a waiting list (though most are eventually accommodated). For the baby room, early registration essential. 'We get women phoning us the day the baby's born.' Mobility is prerequisite for the toddler room (most start aged 12 to 15 months); freedom from nappies, or close, for kinder room (around 2). Some children do full 7.30am to 6pm days from the start, others attend just a few mornings or afternoons a week.

Rooms are fairly plain and, dare we say, a little uninspiring, but well equipped, huge and full of light with above average staff to child ratios – plenty of glitter and dressing up corners. Those under 3 experience a curriculum focused on developing personal, physical and communication skills. Pre-schoolers aged 3 to 4 are sensitively divided into half yearly age groupings, progressing to the 'transition' class where they are readied for reception with an increasing amount of teacher-led activities and subject-based learning, graduating to pinafores and striped shirts and mixing with older children in the playground.

Orley Farm School

South Hill Avenue, Harrow, Middlesex HA1 3NU

Ages 4–13 **Pupils** 496

Fees: £14,160 – £16,335 pa

020 8869 7600
www.orleyfarm.harrow.sch.uk

Headmaster: Since 2013, Tim Calvey (40s), formerly school's deputy head and art teacher. Hailing from a teaching dynasty, grew up in Zimbabwe in the boarding house run by his father. Passionate about sport and art, got his teaching degree at Christ Church University before cutting his teeth at Northbourne Park School in Kent under an inspirational head 'who pushed all the boundaries,' then landing at Eagle House (Wellington College's prep) around the same time as Anthony Seldon took the helm at the senior school – spending a six year period there that 'shaped him.' In true Seldon style, impassioned by well-being and development – 'we have to find ways to release the pressure children are under.' A challenge indeed in this most competitive of postcodes.

Shades of Gareth Malone – sharp, quirky dress sense, warm charisma, palpable energy and a real human touch. Parents uniformly comment on how informal he is compared to other local prep heads. Happily donned Willy Wonka costume at behest of parent committee at recent Christmas Fair. Pupils describe him as 'effervescent' (well done that child's English teacher), 'enthusiastic' and 'funny' – the first head we have met known to wear Iron Man cufflinks. Rarely have we seen a head teacher so naturally connect with even his youngest charges, all of whom chat away to him merrily. Feels 'huge duty of care' to bright children and warns destination obsessed parents that it's about the journey and that Orley Farm is 'not for them if they just want their child tutored – we don't want to be defined by either the name of the school or our grades.'

Lives on school grounds with wife Rachel, who teaches RS and science at the school, and his three children – all of whom have attended Orley Farm.

Entrance: Vast majority enter at 4+ with places oversubscribed by about three to one. Children are observed participating in a carousel of activities and head is clear: 'don't bother tutoring your 4 year old' – school is looking for 'sparky children' and doesn't expect them to read or write. Around 20 places come up for year 7 when many girls, and a few boys, leave for 11+ schools. Short shrift given if potential parents are looking for prep merely as springboard to top schools. 'Have I put parents off with this attitude?' muses head. 'Probably.'

Exit: Huge breadth of destination schools with an impressive number to top academic schools (St Paul's, Westminster, Merchant Taylors', Habs, North London Collegiate, City of London and Godolphin & Latymer), as well as Hampton, John Lyon, Aldenham, Northwood College and Notting Hill and Ealing. A small handful each year to boarding schools.

Remarks: Occupies a Tardis-like plot fronted by a Victorian school building, tucked into a leafy residential area. Having just finished an £11 million refurb programme, school boasts smart classrooms and facilities galore (barely a tatty corner in sight), plus not only the shiniest dining room for miles around but also a state of the art library designed to inspire the most reluctant of readers. Delightful grounds sprawl behind the main school building, providing space for all manner of activities – as well as the Orley Farm chickens (the box of freshly laid eggs we were given on departure, rather than the usual piles of self-promoting literature, could almost be a metaphor for how this school differs from others). Main playing fields amounting to some 40 acres are over the road, plus separate gym and sports hall, pool and Astroturf.

A holistic vibe in evidence at every turn. Recent introduction of the Creative Curriculum in pre-prep much welcomed by parents who feel it 'brings topics alive' for the school's youngest pupils, to the extent that they want to do more under their own steam when they get home. The Edge programme, which sees children participate in experiences from planning – then following unaccompanied – a route into central London on public transport to fixing a bicycle puncture or spending time with local elderly people, demonstrates that school is not just paying lip service to developing EQ as well as IQ. There is, however, a question mark over how unanimous parents are in supporting this approach – definite rumblings in evidence from those who would like school to fall into line with local academic hothouses and reports of parents demanding homework for their 5 and 6 year olds (then setting it themselves when not forthcoming). This is explicable by school's demographic, typified by its geography. Around 70 per cent of families are Asian, with the vast majority dual income professionals, 'incredibly committed to education,' according to head. Many Harrow School and some John Lyon staff in parent cohort. Pupils, thankfully, come over as carefree, likeable and down to earth – head 'can't stand arrogance.' Teachers reportedly 'go the extra mile' and pre-prep parents are delighted with recent appointments of young staff.

Curriculum broad, with majority of girls heading for 11+ and boys for 13+ exit. French and Latin in the languages department, with a taste of Greek at the top of the school. Gentle setting from summer term of year 2 and children are class taught for most subjects until year 5. Classes maxed at 21, often with smaller numbers in English and maths sets. Head says 'academic life is a given – we go a long way beyond what's expected.' Staff ratios are 'absurd,' he says, with a full time classroom assistant in every class up to year 4. Full-time SENCo plus some part-timers to assist those with additional needs. Around 30 children currently supported with anything ranging from organisational skills to mild dyslexia, with withdrawal avoided wherever possible. Open to taking children with greater needs, recently profound deafness, as long as they are able to successfully access curriculum.

DT and art in strong evidence, both with impressive studios. Head still teaches art – his lessons greeted with enthusiastic fist pumps from pupils. Drama on curriculum to year 8; dynamic teacher who has breathed life into performances. Music, though, is the jewel in Orley Farm's crown, with choirs and ensembles galore ranging from the Fab Fives which sing 'funky' hits to the chamber choir which tackles three part harmonies with reported aplomb. Compulsory recorder for all in year 2 and over 90 per cent of all pupils learn a peripatetic instrument. Unsurprisingly, given facilities, sport high on agenda with 'strong' rugby and netball, a non-compulsory Saturday morning sports academy and A to E teams fielded whenever opposing schools are big enough to match their numbers. A few grumbles from parents that school could do more to develop those with less talent, but overall sports universally praised.

Four houses encourage 'healthy competition' amongst pupils and children are given positions of responsibility right from reception. We love the playground traffic light system used for solving disputes – no teachers involved, just worldly wise year 3 pupils to mediate spats. Each class has a form tutor as well as form teacher to monitor pastoral well-being. Psychodynamic counsellor on staff two days each week, with children able to self-refer for help with concerns related or totally unrelated to school (fears, phobias, stress). Extracurricular activities, known as 'hobbies', not as broad or varied as at some schools but solid, with all the usual suspects. Wonderful, annual Expeditions Week which takes everyone from year 4 up all over the place from mountaineering in Wales to 'total immersion' in a French château. Best of all, it's included in the fees.

Going places under fabulous head. If you're looking for a school to drive your child hard towards academic superstardom and a ticket to a top academic secondary, Orley Farm probably isn't for you. If, however, you want them to skip joyously into school every day, have time to play when they come home – and quite possibly land one of those coveted top school places on the grounds of their roundedness, likeability and passion for learning – get your name on the list and cross fingers and toes (tutoring won't work).

Our Lady of Victories Primary School

1 Clarendon Drive, London SW15 1AW

Ages 4–11 **Pupils** 210 **RC**

020 8788 7957
www.ourladyofvictories.wandsworth.sch.uk

Headteacher: Since 2011, Deirdre McDonald BA PGCE NQPH (40s). After studying English at university, Mrs McDonald worked in publishing, then decided to train as a teacher. She has a long association with the school – she was a governor and taught year 6 for eight years before becoming deputy head and more recently head. Her own children are now at university but attended Our Lady of Victories. Forward thinking and inclusive – parents say she is a caring and committed head who's available to all families as and when they need her assistance. Her background in publishing and interest in literature and language has inspired and influenced many school activities. Definitely an artsy type, she enjoys cinema, theatre, reading and travel.

Leaving in July 2019.

Entrance: Priority to Catholics in all categories; siblings only get preference if parents still regular worshippers. Ballot allocation decides places in inevitable event of oversubscription. Places sometimes come up in the older age groups (usually due to families moving away from London), so it's worth contacting the school for occasional vacancies.

Exit: At 11+, just over half of pupils move to popular Catholic secondary schools such as Cardinal Vaughan, The London Oratory, Sacred Heart, Ursuline High School, Wimbledon College, Gumley House. The rest go to local independents (Emanuel, Ibstock Place, Latymer, Hampton) or to Catholic boarding schools (Worth, The Oratory School, Reading and the IBVM convents).

O

Remarks: A first-rate primary school tucked into the residential streets of Putney, in the parish of Our Lady of Pity and St Simon Stock. Originally run by the Sisters of the Poor Servants of the Mother of God, the school was handed over to the Diocese of Southwark in 1978. Housed in the former convent (there are several modern extensions), its compact site is well kept and decorated with an array of colourful artwork by the children.

School is exceptionally well accomplished in all areas. The majority of children achieve level 5 by year 6, with everyone's progress assessed each half term. A well-balanced curriculum is delivered throughout and children achieve particularly well in maths and English. French classes from year 1. The school has won silver and gold awards in junior maths challenges. Creative writing is strong and pupils do variety of science, history and geography projects each term. Older children practise verbal and non-verbal reasoning for the Wandsworth 11+ tests and are taught how to write timed essays.

The school has strong links with the parish – it celebrates a number of religious festivals and the local priest visits the school regularly. At holy communion, children process from school to church, a day rounded off with a visit to the ice cream van. The choir sings in the church and at local care centres. Music, led by a dedicated music teacher, is very strong. Lots of music lessons in school, concerts and the school's recorder group and choir attends annual Music for Youth festival. Pupils take part in the National Theatre's Primary Programme (workshops held in school and theatre visits), alongside trips to concerts and the ballet.

Impressive PE programme offers a range of sporting activities at Dover House Road playing fields and swimming at the nearby Putney Leisure Centre pool. Good range of clubs includes fencing, zumba and Latin. SENCo and visiting speech and occupational therapists supervise learning support. Head is keen to ensure awareness of SEN throughout the school. Regular in-house training days and some teachers attend training courses run by a school specialising in specific learning difficulties and differences.

Lots of fundraising for charity organised by the school and parents, with many of the events run by the children themselves.

Palmers Green High School

104 Hoppers Road, London N21 3LJ

Ages 3–16 **Pupils** 260

Fees: £11,130 – £15,930 pa

020 8886 1135
www.pghs.co.uk

Headmistress: Since 2017, Wendy Kempster (50s) BSc PGCE. Originally from North Wales, Mrs Kempster studied maths at Reading University, where she went on to do her PGCE. Taught in Reading and Bristol, before moving north and taking time out when her children were young. Previously deputy head of Loughborough High, and assistant head and head of maths at Nottingham Girls' High. Attracted to PGHS because of the opportunity to know every girl: 'You can't do that in a school of 600 or 700.' Trained as an ISI inspector and an accredited advanced skills teacher, she's also been a school governor for over 15 years. Married to a fellow educator, she has three grown sons (all qualified or soon-to-be qualified as doctors). Enjoys singing, running, cycling, swimming, tennis – and mountains. 'I'm a country girl at heart, and every holiday I'm off to the mountains in the Lake District.' Down to earth and experienced, she appears to be keeping PGHS on a firm course and leading it to new heights.

Academic matters: The Sunday Times recently ranked Palmers Green in the top five small independent schools (though it has frequently hit the no 1 spot), and, its 2018 GCSE results bore out this accolade, with 79 per cent of I/GCSEs marked A*-A/9-7. Single class of about 25 in each year group ensures all girls get plenty of attention, and most make 'exceptional' progress at every stage from reception to GCSE. Parents particularly welcome specialist subject teaching (in art, DT, ICT, drama, PE and music) more-or-less from the get-go, with junior pupils sharing senior-school facilities.

Girls currently sit a mix of GCSEs and IGCSEs, depending on which exams the schools feels will best prepare them for A levels, and perform particularly well in maths, modern languages and all three sciences (where they are encouraged to reach high with lots of in-class and external enrichment, including visits from engineers and the RAF). Plenty of extra help, too, in a wide range of academic 'sugeries'.

French introduced in year 3, and year 5s enjoy a taster of Latin, German and Russian. French and Spanish on offer at IGCSE (with the option to take one or both).

Teaching, by well-qualified staff, strong throughout. 'Everything is very well managed,' said one mother. 'Pupils are happy and enjoy what they're doing in class. The teachers are nice, too, friendly and experienced.'

Learning difficulties tend to be mild, primarily dyslexia and a small number of autistic spectrum disorders. Support given in lessons ('Every member of staff has a teaching strategy to help girls,' says the head. 'We make sure the provision is not nebulous') with external specialists introduced as required. Extra classes before and after school and one-to-one tuition also available (sometimes at an extra charge). New push to stretch the able, gifted and talented.

Games, options, the arts: Not much in the way of outside space (a decent-sized yard, and an attractive early years playground) and limited numbers mean putting B and C teams together can be a challenge, so possibly not the best home for the super sporty. That said, as the head notes, 'The advantage of a small school is that everyone gets a chance to play in a team', and the school runs competitive teams in several sports, including netball and cross-country. All study gymnastics and dance on a half-term rota in the school hall, with outdoor games (netball, football, rounders, tennis and athletics) and swimming at grounds a short coach journey away. In addition, years 10 and 11 travel enjoy the facilities of a nearby leisure centre for trampolining, basketball, volleyball, aerobics, spinning and circuits. Wide range of sports clubs (netball, gym, fitness, yoga, rounders, tennis, football, athletics), too, and support given to those who wish to pursue a talent (such as ice skating) outside of school.

Artwork impressive, taught by a dynamic head of art, and girls pushed to achieve in everything from monoprinting to experimental work. About half take GCSE art, and many inspired to develop skills further in after-school art club. Recently refurbished and well-equipped music room. Timetabled instrumental lessons (clarinet, saxophone, flute, piano, singing, violin and viola, plus other options if requested). Girls given plenty of opportunity to perform in junior and senior school orchestras, four choirs, instrumental groups (recorder, violin, and woodwind) and a rock band club. A highlight of the calendar is the (highly competitive) annual house choral competition. Drama a popular GCSE option and junior school (including all year 6) star in annual play. DT has its own workshop with excellent facilities (3D printers, CAD etc), where girls in the junior school are taught in half-class groups, making everything from toy cars to fairground attractions.

Over 80 weekly clubs (before and after school and at lunch-time), including book club, debating (with inter-house competitions), ICT, literary society, film skool (sic), LAMDA exams and knitting. Most take D of E bronze. Lively range of visits (Science Museum, Downing Street, The Guardian), and visitors (Onatti Spanish Theatre, author talks, professional parental insight from parents who are dentists, doctors etc), plus residential trips (skiing in Italy, year 5 to Flatford Mill, year 7 bonding at PGL). 'The school provides a really rounded education,' said one parent. Well-stocked recently refurbished library offers an inviting place to read and study. Strong careers programme from the start of senior school. 'Because girls move on in the sixth form, we have to focus on this much earlier than other schools,' says the head, and all expected to undertake work experience in year 11.

Lunch, freshly cooked on site, is seasonal, farm-assured and free range, and includes a vegetarian option and sandwiches.

Background and atmosphere: Founded in 1905, by Miss Alice Hum, with just 12 pupils, by 1918 the school had expanded to 300 and moved to its present site. New classrooms and a dining hall added in the 60s and 90s, and the Elizabeth Smith Hall more recently to provide an additional venue for assemblies, workshops and exams. Despite its age, the school seems bright, modern and well kept, and the compact site makes it girl-friendly and intimate. Purpose-built PGHS nursery housed in its own building about a mile away.

The school's values are rooted in Miss Hum's Quaker beliefs – 'By Love Serve One Another' – and a recent survey of student opinion found an unusually harmonious and caring atmosphere. ('The girls comfort you with kindness and help you if you are stuck,' said one.) Girls, educated here for a long stretch, consider it a home away from home ('PGHS is like a second family to me,' said one year 6), and make regular return visits even after they've moved on. 'They love coming back,' says the head. 'They've been here longer than anywhere else and know they'll always be a Palmers Green girl.'

Today, the school is very much multi-faith (though traditional hymn books still in use, and carol service held annually in St John's Church, Palmers Green), but making a contribution remains important. PGHS shares adventures (such as the loan of Moon Rocks from NASA and study skills days) with local primaries.

PGHS is one of the last remaining girls'-only independent secondary schools in the area and head is a firm advocate of what single-sex can offer, giving girls the confidence to be themselves and achieve. ('When I was at school, they used to say, why do you want to do maths? That's not a girls' subject.')

Former pupils include Palmers Green legend, poet Stevie Smith, and actress Dame Flora Robson; more recently, telly stars Kathryn and Megan Prescott, award-winning poet Imani Shola, Lucy Collins, the first female naval submariner, and prima ballerina Marion Tait.

Pastoral care, well-being and discipline: The school's small scale means there's little danger of problems getting overlooked. 'We know everyone and there's no place to hide physically or emotionally,' says the head. 'Staff quickly spot if a girl who is normally happy is looking unhappy and pass on their comments straight away.' Teachers operate an open-door policy and pupils feel comfortable asking for help. ('I know I can trust any teacher with my problems, however small,' said one girl in the senior school.) House system creates bonds across the year groups ('Unlike bigger schools, you'll often find year 10s playing with year 7s, just as you would in a family,' says the head) and senior pupils mentor younger groups and take up roles of responsibility as head girl, house captains, prefects, etc. Junior pupils also take on roles of responsibility, while the culture of 'active citizenship' means girls are canvassed on decisions, such as the choice of caterers or the new school uniform (smart navy blazer and pink shirt for seniors, blue pinafores and summer boaters for juniors).

Behaviour tends to the excellent. 'We have only very minor disciplinary problems,' says the head, 'and I haven't run a single detention since I arrived.' Mental health, on the other hand, high on her agenda. 'It has become a growing issue because of social media. We don't allow devices in school, which at least gives girls six or seven hours each day contact free.'

Parents comment favourably on the 'nurturing' environment and 'old-fashioned values' (girls, for example, leap to their feet when visitors enter a classroom).

Pupils and parents: Parents, from a broad mix of cultures and backgrounds, are not super rich; mostly hardworking professionals, who have similar aspirations for their daughters.

Entrance: Selective, but not quite as intimidatingly so as some other north London options. Many join in nursery, but further official entry points at 4, 7 and 11, plus occasional places elsewhere. Younger applicants are sifted on the basis of 'ability and aptitude'; at 11, tests in English, maths, and reasoning, followed by interviews for those who perform well. All current junior pupils sit 11+ alongside outsiders, but almost all proceed seamlessly to the senior school. 'Only very occasionally do we suggest to a parent that they consider another school,' says the head. Some preference given to siblings, but entry not automatic. 'We don't want a child to be out of their depth or unhappy.'

Exit: PGHS sees itself very much as an all-through nursery-16 school. 'We view it as a journey,' says the head, 'and we're very candid that, as a through school, we don't offer specific preparation for 11+.' Nonetheless, teaching and curriculum mean girls are very well prepared and some do move on at this stage, when parents are often looking for selective state options (Latymer, Dame Alice Owen's, Henrietta Barnett, etc). In year 11, girls carefully advised and guided in their choice of sixth form, when again, they tend to favour the state (Woodhouse College particularly fashionable at the moment among the usual spectrum eg St Michael's RC, Fortismere, Ashmole), but independents (North London Collegiate, Highgate, Aldenham, City of London, St Alban's High School for Girls, Haileybury, Haberdashers' Girls) also well represented.

Money matters: Fees definitely on the good-value side. Scholarships at 11 to current pupils and incomers. Limited number of bursaries of up to 100 per cent, plus music awards (minimum grade 4 required), which fund lessons on one or two instruments.

Remarks: A small, friendly and nurturing school, providing a rounded education, with old fashioned values, and an excellent academic record that prepares girls extremely well to move on at sixth form.

Parliament Hill School

P

Linked with LaSWAP Sixth Form Consortium

Highgate Road, London NW5 1RL

Ages 11–19 **Pupils** 1,150 **Sixth form** 250 (550 in joint sixth form with William Ellis, part of LaSWAP)

020 7485 7077
www.parliamenthill.camden.sch.uk

Headteacher: Since 2017, Sarah Creasey, previously deputy head and associate head here. She started teaching at a single sex school in Wimbledon, then spent time at Hampstead School before moving to Preston Manor, where she spent 10 years, as head of English and then assistant head. She joined Parliament Hill in 2011.

Academic matters: A huge ability range here, with lots of bright girls and also plenty in need of extra support, whether educational or emotional. Accordingly, the school offers a range of options. Everyone studies for a core of GCSE subjects which includes maths, English, core science, RE, and short courses in PE and citizenship. They can add on more GCSE subjects, or choose a vocational BTec from a range that includes business, art and design, ICT and health and social care, or go for a young apprenticeship. Most of the latter two options are taught elsewhere in Camden. Everyone is allocated to either French or Spanish classes for the first three years, and can start the other language in year 9; about a third take a modern language GCSE. Other popular options at KS4 include additional AS maths and triple science; ICT AS and photography GCSE are taught after school as twilight classes.

In 2018, 80 per cent of girls got 9-4 in both English and maths at GCSE; 36 per cent of grades were 9-7. English has been very strong, maths and science historically rather weaker. However, maths now taught in ability sets from the second term in year 7, and the curriculum has been redesigned substantially. Girls arrive at the school with, on average, much higher verbal than non-verbal aptitude scores – 'but as a technology college we focus on building up their confidence and aptitude in maths and science'. The science department has appointed some very highly qualified teachers over the last few years. Triple science courses very popular, with excellent results. 'They're very good at assessing strengths and weaknesses,' said a parent, 'and throwing lots of energy at weaknesses.'

Downgraded in 2013 from its 'outstanding' status to 'good' by Ofsted, under the new harsher regime, citing the gap in achievement between poorer students and the rest. The school says it was based on 'historical examinations results' and not teaching. Indeed, Inspectors were able to identify many successful features of teaching and learning. Homework and marking – aspects formerly raised by parents as sometimes inconsistent – were areas that Ofsted pointed out as having had 'key improvement'.

Although there has been little fallout since this report from either parents or pupils, school is determined to win back their outstanding status: 'We will continue as a school community to strive for better things...and to be regarded in the wider educational world as a leading school and professional centre of excellence.'

SEN provision has been 'transformed', with an assistant head leading the the way on SEN and inclusion. Few state schools feel that they have sufficient funds to provide all the help every child needs, but 'we feel we've made substantial progress'. The Extra Mile project targets underachieving year 10 girls, who are mostly from white low-income families. The school is also a Potential Plus Partner School which aims to identify 'high learning potential students' by using a programme called Maurice B, which uses cognitive tests to help identify Oxbridge students.

Joint sixth form with next-door William Ellis School, with co-ed tutor groups. It is also part of LaSWAP, which includes La Sainte Union and Acland Burghley schools too, and has over 1,500 students. Each school teaches the core sixth form subjects, but students visit other schools in the group for more minority subjects eg film studies and further maths. The ability range encompasses those aspiring to read medicine at Cambridge and those working for an introductory BTec diploma in health and social care, with appropriate entry requirements. A scheme in conjunction with La Sainte Union targets very able scientists, who study together and take part in organised work experience and masterclasses. English is the most popular A level subject at Parliament Hill, with psychology second. At A level in 2018, 42 per cent A*-B and 19 per cent A*/A.

Games, options, the arts: This is a very physical school and indeed the reason that many pupils choose it above others. Its stunning location almost begs one to be outdoors. Students have the opportunity to experience a wide variety of activities in physical education and the curriculum alone includes dance, swimming, gymnastics, tennis, rounders, cricket, athletics, fitness, invasion games and trampolining. A year 7 student can expect to participate in a minimum of two hours of PE every week as well as learn to swim at nearby Swiss Cottage baths. This doesn't include the extracurricular sporting activities: table tennis, badminton, dodgeball, football, cheerleading and various dance activities.

Dance is the real hot favourite at Parli Hill and one pupil told us that she chose the school because it was one of the few schools in the area that offers dance at GCSE level. Dance at the school comes in many varieties including PHS Dance Elite, contemporary dance and street dance, and there are many opportunities to compete for the coveted Camden Shield by entering any one of the numerous dance competitions, including Rock Challenge and Camden schools' dance festival. (Parliament Hill actually won the National Rock Challenge a few years ago and delighted students were asked to perform at Disneyland Paris.) School also hosts an annual Sweet Summer Dance Show.

Furthermore, year 10 students are offered the opportunity to work towards either a dance leaders level 1 award or a sports leaders level 1 award. Both are designed 'to teach leadership qualities and give students an opportunity to gain experience in leading sports sessions for their feeder primary schools.' Sports teams play successful matches against other Camden schools. School has two tennis/netball courts at the front of the school and a grassy area at the back where the football teams practise, plus a rather ageing hall for gym and badminton with a fitness suite. (New multi-purpose sports centre is part of the school's rebuild programme.)

Everyone takes DT GCSE, with a choice of four options. The single storey DT block was built to an environmentally-friendly design with a green roof, and forms the fourth side of a grassy courtyard, twisting up to meet the original Edwardian building. On another corner of the building is the performing arts block, clad in green glass, which provides music rooms and the dance and drama studios. The top floor corridors are lined with expressive, colourful and imaginative GCSE and A level photography and artwork, and textile designs hang in the stairwells. 'The art department really struck me', one pupil told us when she was looking at secondary schools. (Pretty good photography studio space too.)

Music popular here too and many girls have instrumental lessons and can choose from a variety of musical groups to join including orchestra, rock band, flute group, jazz, string and brass ensembles, or sing in the choir. Those on free school meals get free music lessons. One big annual musical a year (recently Fame) and one main play. Drama also popular and pupils have a large and fairly new drama studio in which to rehearse.

A breakfast club every morning at 8am and plenty more activities ranging from Italian and drama clubs to creative writing and documentary making. They visit museums, theatres and galleries, travel to China and go on physics trips to Switzerland. D of E very popular, as is debating – many students have competed passionately in the Urban Debating League and the Debate Mate Cup.

Background and atmosphere: Opened in 1906, has an idyllic site on the edge of Hampstead Heath. Plenty of grassy space, including a sculpture park and kick-around area. Buildings range from solid Edwardiana to the 21st century award-winning DT and performing arts blocks. Is at last in receipt of £25 million, paid for by Camden Community Development Programme, which is funding a new maths, English and science block, a multi-purpose sports centre and a dedicated sixth form building – due for completion in 2019. Money is also going towards renovating the existing main Edwardian building (which was very tired in places when we did our tour, especially the loos, which could do with a major spruce up).

Harmonious atmosphere. Despite the huge range of pupils, both ethnically and socially, girls tend to get on well together, with few reports of bullying. Recently one of six in the country to win a Diamond quality mark for cultural diversity. 'Very much a community school', one parent told us – and very 'inclusive.' Bright and engaging students – one who travels from as far as Covent Garden because of the school's reputation: 'I started this school in year 8 as I wasn't very happy at my last school, and heard about Parliament Hill. I was particularly attracted by its location and outdoor space as well as the bright classrooms..I settled in pretty much immediately and everyone was so friendly.' And a parent added: 'The good thing about a school of this size is that almost everyone is going to find another like minded person to hang out with.'

Definitely a sense of personality at the school and of girls who know their minds: 'a lively atmosphere,' as one parent described it. Posters reinforcing 'female power' are dotted around the school – most noticeably near the sports hall. 'Female empowerment is very much part of the ethos at Parliament Hill. Girls here have a real sense of themselves as individuals. These are girls who will make a difference to the lives of other people.'

Pastoral care, well-being and discipline: Many vulnerable pupils here, including refugees and those with learning difficulties, who get 'excellent' support, says Ofsted. Liaises with its feeder primary school to identify girls likely to be in need of extra help with making the transition to senior school: 'Our transition is acknowledged to be excellent and supportive – we work very closely with families.' School also works with outside agencies that provide therapy or counselling to those in need, with a designated key worker in school. It also runs many programmes to motivate disaffected pupils, stretch the aspirations of bright girls and ensure everyone gets a chance to broaden their horizons. One parent told us: 'The school works very hard at narrowing the gap between disadvantaged and non-disadvantaged pupils.'

Assertive classroom management keeps most lessons running without disruptions (although we did pass some slightly rowdier ones on our tour). Big on some areas of discipline like punctuality, attendance and school attire – no uniform, but the rule is 'no gaps, no straps, no shorts' and students will be ticked off if they don't adhere to this. 'It's a problem in the summer,' one student grumbled. Older girls are allowed to go out onto Hampstead Heath at lunchtimes, together with pupils from nearby schools, William Ellis and La Sainte Union, and locals have complained about litter problems. 'We're very concerned. The girls regard the Heath as very special to them, and we're doing work on social responsibility to educate them that it's for everyone in the community'.

Pastoral care is very good, report parents. 'I've always felt they know my daughter very well,' said one. 'They school has contacted me whenever they've had concerns, and they've dealt with any problems quickly and well.' Ofsted remarked how: 'Students speak of the school being an extended family where they feel safe and supported at all times.'

Pupils and parents: 'Amazingly diverse' student population speaks some 50 different languages at home, though few are at early stages of learning English. Over 200 refugees. Nearly half of the girls are on free school meals, but also good support from some local middle-class families. OGs include actress Katrin Cartlidge, BBC journalist Laura Trevelyan, Lola Young, Baroness Young of Hornsey and Emma Hayes, manager of Chelsea Football Club Women.

Entrance: Takes 180 girls into year 7, with admissions organised through the local authority. Priority for particular SENs, siblings, children in care and those with exceptional social needs. Then by distance – generally within a mile and a half. Those joining LaSWAP sixth form to do A levels must have at least eight GCSE passes including three 4 and two 6 grades; various vocational courses available for those with lower grades. Increasingly becoming the school of choice for parents living in the area and not (as was the case historically), second choice to Camden School for Girls.

Exit: Between two-thirds and three-quarters of pupils move on to joint sixth form with William Ellis school, part of LaSWAP sixth form consortium. Some join other sixth forms, eg Camden School for Girls or Woodhouse College, others go to colleges such as City and Islington or Westminster Kingsway to do vocational courses.

Around a quarter to Russell Group universities; 2018 courses ranged from biomedical science at King's College London to Japanese studies at Manchester to international relations and economics at SOAS.

Remarks: Popular girls' comprehensive in idyllic situation on the borders of Hampstead Heath, with a diverse but harmonious student population. Aesthetically tired, but much needed cash injection in the process of changing that.

Parsons Green Prep School

1 Fulham Park Road, London SW6 4LJ

Ages 4–11 **Pupils** 200

Fees: £16,857 – £18,201 pa

020 7371 9009
www.parsonsgreenprep.co.uk

Headmaster: Since January 2018, Tim Cannell (50s), formerly head at The Prebendal School in Chichester, who joined PGP in 2017 to cover Helen Stavert's maternity leave and has been appointed permanent head. Educated at Chigwell School and Davies College, followed by University of Winchester (formerly known as King Alfred's College). Read theology and has a masters degree in education management. Taught maths and RS in several prep schools – Bialla International School, Papua New Guinea, and Eagle House and Moor Park in the UK – where he was variously day master, housemaster and director of studies. A keen cricketer, he also enjoys playing squash and listening to music. Member of IAPS and CSA; has two grown-up children, both Cambridge graduates.

Tim's hobbies and interests include walking and being outdoors, gardening, watching and taking part in sport, exploring new restaurants and renovating an old barn.

Mrs Lucinda Waring (40s) is the founding principal (since 2001) and majority shareholder. Originally trained at St Nicholas' Montessori College in Knightsbridge, she founded her first nurseries at the age of 26. Naturally inspiring some envy amongst her high-flying parent body, she aims to remain firmly 'back office' but has stepped up recently to aid the transition of the new head. The school is very much her vision – to create a school where children could thrive without undue pressure; she is on top of every detail and the children know and greet her throughout the school. She is married with one child.

Entrance: Parents can register from birth (£150 registration fee). Once on the waiting list, entrance into reception via pre-entry checks, including a full academic report from current educational setting. Entry into year 1 upwards by school report and morning activity session. Easy-going families preferred. Sibling policy: 10 per cent off for siblings.

The maximum number entering reception is 44, with almost twice this number on the current waiting list. Pupils enter from Fulham nurseries in the main. Occasional places in year 1 upwards (with references and assessment). A deposit of £2,000 per family to secure the place.

Exit: Preparations for exit at 11 plus are thorough and commence from year 4. Perhaps there is little the school can do to alleviate the inevitable pressure parents and children feel, but one parent said, 'Children need to be confident enough to be able to think: yes, I can do it! That's what this school gives them'. Staff insist they will speak up in the face of ambitious parents to try and ensure that children will move on to schools where they will above all be happy. Recent destinations range from St Paul's Girls' School, Godolphin & Latymer, City of London Boys', Dulwich College and King's College Wimbledon to More House, Portland Place, Arts Educational, Kew House, Francis Holland (Sloane Square), Harrodian, Queensgate, Benenden and Lady Margaret.

Remarks: The school has undergone a name change, becoming Parsons Green Prep (previously Eridge House). Despite the marketing-friendly name change, and ambitious air of the principal, there are no plans to expand the school: 200 pupils would be the absolute maximum.

The school was founded in 2001 in a formerly derelict Victorian villa in an enviable location and with that rare thing, some outside space behind a high garden wall, offering privacy and enough room to run around. The original building was restored and modern additions blended, offering new classrooms and the large assembly hall used for everything from staging productions to PE. The end result is a smart blend of light, modern-seeming classrooms large and small, wide enough corridors with spick and span displays and lots of stairs. Come August and with class sizes finalised, the staff may be busily swapping rooms so that each class is accommodated in the best possible space.

The playground is Astroturfed throughout, with just enough room for football, tennis and netball, and a good in and out space for the early years, with wooden play equipment and smaller quiet area with outdoor chess tables. Very physical older children may need more space, not that it will be easy to find in central London. The stockpile of micro-scooters racked on the playground walls points to pupils mostly living nearby.

The school sets out to provide a creative curriculum, but is well ahead of the curve at primary level in putting STEM subjects at the heart of the maths curriculum, following three years of careful training and planning. Every class has a STEM lesson once a week and there's a new engineering after-school club.

Parents say: 'Reading in the early years is extremely well taught'. Maths and English are taught in small ability groups. One of the numeracy tools has been effectively adopted from Montessori methods. The Mac suite has been upgraded and there is improved wireless technology around the school. Years 5 and 6 have their own individual android tablets with keyboards.

We were impressed by the individual targets on each child's work in every lesson. Teaching aims to take pupils from their learning comfort zone, where they might be engaged but not excited, to their learning challenge zone where they are encouraged to take risks. The school is currently increasing its expertise in stretching the able, gifted and talented. We found children eager to talk to us in every classroom we visited, either explaining clearly what they were working on, or coming unprompted to share their work.

Parents praise cross-curricular topic work, saying 'subjects are really brought to life', such as the year 6 challenge to design a theme park, using mathematical knowledge to design the rides and calculate their profits, whilst utilising art and creative writing to design the posters. Humanities teaching seems fun, too. Science day saw staff joined by a team from the Science Museum – children made gigantic bubbles, launched rockets and made goop.

French is taught weekly throughout the school with a specialist French programme, which continues after school, for those children who are already fluent French speakers. The occasional pupil exits to the Lycée.

Two assemblies per week. Christmas concert not a carol service. When we visited in October, they were looking forward to going crazy on Christmas decorations.

A third of the 36 staff has been at the school for more than 10 years. We have rarely heard so much praise for teaching assistants: in the main extremely youthful, so they have sufficient energy to keep up with their charges. 'Right people in the right places,' says principal and 'no staff who get stale'. Parents say: 'often young and enthusiastic about teaching'; 'lovely teachers allow children to be children'; 'willing to try a multitude of different ways to captivate children'.

Teachers are addressed (by everyone – parents, other staff) as Miss or Mr plus first name, so eg Miss Lucinda, which we found a bit Beatrix Potter-ish, but the principal says, correctly, 'it's friendlier for the children'.

Most parents are content with 'sensible homework', none during school holidays until key stage 2, and there is a dedicated homework session at school. Children are deliberately not overloaded. Trips could be to the local community supermarket or fire station, but also make the most of London from Fulham football club on the doorstep to Pudding Lane. From year 3 residential trips begin with camping and a French day trip.

Seven per cent of pupils have EAL needs. The school seems to have fewer than average number of children with learning differences, but a SENCo in place to ensure their needs are met.

Parents universally describe children who love going to school and 'can't wait to get in at the gate'. We can report beaming smiles and diligent application in every class we visited, and parents agree, describing the school as 'a happy place to learn'; 'intimate, caring, quietly competitive' and 'children do not feel any pressure at all and yet are making good progress'.

Some gripes about sport persist: 'No way near enough sport,' said one parent and another added, 'Not enough boys in year 3 to field a football team'. However, sport is evolving: now offers tennis throughout the year with new tennis coaches, and a coach from Chelsea FC runs three after-school clubs each week. Year 2 upwards play football, tag rugby, cricket, netball, rounders and have weekly swimming lessons. The school has recently joined the Independent Schools Association, which means more sporting competitions. The usual summer sports day and swimming gala. The upper school makes use of Hurlingham Park.

Children are taught guitar, piano, violin and now drum lessons – singing and guitar most popular. There's an orchestra and a choir.

'The summer performance is always excellent,' said a parent. Most recently A Midsummer Night's Dream and The Wind in the Willows. 'Would like more drama opportunities,' said another. A few entries for the LAMDA drama exams with several distinctions.

Chess is huge here, deliberately encouraged to develop logical thinking. Greatly improved clubs, say parents. Those now on offer pre- and post-school or at lunchtime encompass the fun and fashionable, including photography, fencing, orchestra, Mandarin, soccer, chess, baking, sewing, ukulele, running and study skills. Hot lunches and after-school clubs cost extra.

The school is very clear about the standards expected of the children, and parents see pastoral care as a real strength of the school: 'My child had been unhappy at a different school, but has thrived here'; 'I really like the atmosphere: it is very caring but with high standards of behaviour'; 'bullying isn't tolerated and the staff has been quick to act' and 'not much gets by the staff'. The new buddy benches in the playground have been a big hit, too.

Frequent mentions by parents of this school being well suited to a child who might be quite shy initially: 'a sensitive soul ' or 'young in year or late developers'. But parents with more than more child here, the majority, report it suiting all sorts of temperaments and abilities: 'outgoing children can shine'. A teacher believes it works well for 'bright children who are not afraid to take risks and who want to learn'.

Parents are without doubt a smart, city crowd: 'Friendly, international and professional with lots of dual-working parents,' said one. Many agree on a friendly welcome from other parents. Every other parent describes the school community as 'international' but the principal says this is more perception than actuality. Parent volunteers do everything and anything from weekend hospitality for the science lab chicks, to designing the logos for the houses, to being part of the eco committee growing and harvesting crops in the school garden.

Any parents with low-flying or tiger-ish tendencies, this may well not be the school for you. Those who are searching for somewhere to nurture and inspire happy, confident children – look no further.

Pembridge Hall School

18 Pembridge Square, London W2 4EH

Ages 4–11 **Pupils** 430

Fees: £22,242 pa

020 7229 0121
www.pembridgehall.co.uk

P

Headmaster: Since 2012, Henry Keighley-Elstub BA PGCE (40s), previously deputy head at Wetherby Prep. Educated at Eton and Leeds University, where he read classical civilization. He has taught history at Ludgrove, Cothill and Chesham Prep, where he was head of department and also senior master. As well as this being his first headship, it is also his first experience of an all girls' school, and one that finishes at 11 years rather than 13. 'I was worried about that at first,' he admits, 'but now I barely notice, and communicating with an 11-year-old girl is equivalent to talking to a 13-year-old boy.' Married to Sarah who works at IBM ('I have no idea what she does', he confides. 'Perhaps she's a spy.') They have a young daughter.

Mr Keighley-Elstub, slight of build, has an immediately warm, engaging and enthusiastic personality that makes even the stiffest person unfurl. His conversation is littered with verbs and adjectives like 'skip along' and 'groovy'. His upbeat, chipper approach is directed at everyone. As well as the girls, the parents and the teachers it embraces the peripatetic music staff, games staff and the odd visitor. Despite being an Old

Etonian with an unusually complicated name both to spell and pronounce (think 'Keithly'), Mr Keighley-Elstub is remarkably down to earth. He attributes this to his Northern pedigree (his father was a Yorkshireman but practised as a GP in Wimbledon where Mr Keighley-Elstub grew up). His family used to turn up at Eton in a clapped out old VW, but 'that wasn't remotely embarrassing,' he avers. 'Eton's not smart at all. The greatest compliment anyone could pay me,' he continues, 'is to turn up to meet me in jeans.' If he weren't so refreshingly open you wouldn't guess it – he looks immaculate in his well-cut suit and playfully shrieks when he discovers the odd crisp on the floor in a classroom.

He loves music – his wife is a violinist and he has recently formed a staff choir. He is also an enthusiastic sportsman (running is his thing) and he is determined that the girls here start winning some matches for a change. He champions all departments – art, music, sport and drama – equally and works to get them all to enjoy working together rather than being at loggerheads, as happens so often. He is relishing the challenges of his first headship and is not unaware of the benefits of running a school that is part of the Alpha Plus group. He talks of the wealth of resources available to him, from legal to financial as well as the supportive but 'hands off' nature of the governing body. Although ambitious with lots of energy, he is clearly here to stay for some time – 'I couldn't leave while there is still so much to do,' he says. 'I want to transform a good school into an outstanding one'.

Entrance: Names down at birth – 'but realistically that means within two weeks of birth,' says head. He is keen to dispel the myth that you need to plan a Caesarean and father needs to put the form through the letter box as the baby arrives. It absolutely makes no difference at all on what day of the month your child is born. They divide the months into thirds and take an equal number from each third. Non-refundable registration fee (currently £150) does not guarantee you a tour of the school. Personal tours with the head offered as soon as you are off the waiting list and offered a place (something Mr Keighley-Elstub has recently introduced – prior to his arrival tours with a member of staff offered at deposit decision time – close to starting). The competitive market (for children more than the schools) and wealthy catchment of West London means that parents don't blink at paying these sort of sums without even being given the chance to see the school before making a decision. The alternative to long waiting lists is a selection process at 3, and that would mean 'we may miss the wild wacky ones that add colour to the place,' says Mr Keighley-Elstub. Nevertheless, close liaison with feeder nurseries (he mentioned The Acorn, Rolfe's, Strawberry Fields, Minors and Ladbroke Square) to make sure girls will manage.

Exit: Plenty of scholarships, academic, sporting as well as musical and artistic, each year (14 academic, music and art scholarships and exhibitions in 2018, the majority to Francis Holland NW1) and fine boards in the upper school hall to commemorate them.

Most popular day destinations in 2018 were Francis Holland NW1, Godolphin & Latymer and St Paul's Girls. Most popular boarding destinations were Downe House, St Mary's Ascot and Wycombe Abbey. Plus a large contingent going to Bute House at 7+ in 2018.

Remarks: Situated in a particularly leafy, white stucco square in Notting Hill Gate, the lower school is in a tall building a minute's walk from an identical building containing the upper school. In between is Wetherby pre-prep – the boys' equivalent – and also owned by the Alpha Plus group. In the basement of number 10 (the upper school) is Minors Nursery – another Alpha Plus establishment: no wonder such direct communication about the character and ability of the girls can be made.

Round the corner in St Petersburg Place is the splendid St Matthew's Church where whole school assemblies take place each week. We joined a river of red blazered and straw boatered girls as they walked immaculately to the church. An overwhelmingly white collection of girls for such a multicultural part of London; they are international – American, Russian, European as well – but only about 10 out of 400 girls receive EAL help. Mr Keighley-Elstub described the ethos as 'lightly Anglican' but a very English education, which seemed to be requirement of even the most foreign of families.

Girls here are well spoken, eager to please and confident. Lots of awards and prizes and opportunities to speak publicly and take responsibility to build that confidence. We were particularly impressed with an astonishing game designed by a 10-year-old girl out of a cardboard box, which intricately displayed the planets and included chance and question cards which she had devised herself. She then explained through a microphone how to play the game to an audience of about 450 people in the church, including parents as well as teachers and children.

Classrooms spacious, bright and airy with wonderful high ceilings and tall windows. Lovely wide corridors and staircases that seem to go up and up for ever. Lush red carpet (to match the uniform?) in the lower school, upper school mirrors the lower school but in blue. We saw some very impressive still life work in the very studio-like space at the top of the school, which had brilliant ceiling windows, creating an excellent space to be creative. Well-equipped science labs in the basement with a good old-fashioned full-sized skeleton in the corner. Super space in the basement for drama and productions with a wealth of colourful and imaginative costumes and hats. All years get a chance to perform: year 5s do a Shakespearean medley, year 6s do their annual play in the local Tabernacle Theatre. Both buildings have large halls which double as dining rooms at lunch time. Wide choice of healthy cooked lunches and imaginative fruit (watermelon and pineapple – not just your regular apples and bananas). How refreshing not to see children eating packed lunches at their desks.

Healthy number of male teachers and the arrival of Mr Keighley-Elstub has seen barely any staff turnover at all. He feels proud of having injected renewed energy and purpose into the place and acknowledges that when he arrived there was a lot of reassurance to be done. Parents were rattled and there was a lack of direction. Those we spoke to referred to a terrible lack of communication. Many considered moving their daughters but remarkably few did, explaining that the pastoral care remained excellent throughout and they didn't want to uproot a happy child. Emphasis is now on communication – particularly with parents; improvement and consolidation of the academics; and improvement of sport.

Girls are starting to win netball matches now – and we were proudly told of how they beat Glendower recently. Netball and hockey played in nearby Avondale Park and Holland Park, athletics at the Linford Christie stadium in Wood Lane and swimming at the Porchester Baths. Plenty of inter-house matches so that everyone can have a go. Tennis as a club rather than a school sport, and rounders possibly on its way out. 'I don't see the point of it,' says Mr Keighley Elstub. 'It's rather a poor man's cricket'. He is very open to the idea of introducing football and cricket for the girls but so far there doesn't seem to be the demand. Several outside spaces in both buildings for fresh air between lessons and 'unless there's the threat of a tornado out they go,' says head, who can't understand why the girls had been treated with such velvet gloves in the past, with the mere threat of rain resulting in their reading inside.

Three classes of 20 in each year. Setting only in maths from year 3. Serious preparation for the 11 plus starts in year 5 but the groundwork is now being laid much earlier. Mr Keighley–Elstub teaches years 5 and 6 so he can give well informed advice about senior schools. He is not afraid to tell a parent if they are being overly ambitious academically but will look at the whole child and advise which is the most appropriate school on that basis. Vast majority of parents here are in finance – though the odd one is glamorously famous, you wouldn't describe this as a trendy school. Mr Keighley-Elstub famously put a stop to the cashmere scarves as part of the school uniform and supplied by a parent: this isn't the image he wants to nurture.

Large, busy, and traditional with a dynamic head, Pembridge Hall can only get better and better and could be an excellent choice for your enthusiastic daughter.

Portland Place School

56-58 Portland Place, London W1B 1NJ

Ages 10-18 (10-16 from 2020) **Pupils** 290 **Sixth form** 51

Fees: £21,030 pa

020 7307 8700
www.portland-place.co.uk

Head: Since 2017, David Bradbury, previously deputy head of South Hampstead High. BSc in physics, MSc and PGCE, all from Keele, plus an MA in education from the Open University. Physics co-ordinator at Bangkok Patana School for a number of years; taught at Chase Terrace High and Newcastle-under-Lyme College; head of physics at Nicholas Chamberlaine School and assistant head at Alleyne's High School. Hobbies and interests include archery, cookery, cryptic crosswords, film, literature and music, as well as hill-walking and board games.

Academic matters: A broader band of ability than in most of the fiercely competitive London day schools – something the school takes pride in and, together with its small class sizes, sees as a 'unique selling point.' Only 12 in a class in year 6, an average of 15 in years 7 to 11 (we saw several smaller ones) and smaller still in the sixth form means that attention can be given to each child – you can be sure that there will be both stretching and confidence building. A godsend for the discerning parent who can see through the merry-go-round nature of 11+ and wants to ensure their child is educated rather than exam-processed. Hence the increasing demand for places lower down the school; there is now one class in year 6. Piles on the value added – 'We're always near the top of the value added tables' is the boast.

No Latin or Greek at GCSE ('there isn't the demand from our parents,' we were told). Economics, computing, sport studies and media are offered, along with the traditional subjects. All pupils take at least one of French, Italian or Spanish; not much enthusiasm for taking up a second modern language. If your daughter speaks Italian at home, she is encouraged to do Spanish as her GCSE option. If you want your child to take a GCSE in, for example, Arabic, the school will facilitate it within the timetable, but the onus of paying and finding the teacher is on you.

At GCSE, 26 per cent A*-A/9-7 in 2018. The value added shows at A level, where the results are more impressive, most being in the B-D bracket, with a decent sprinkling of As (65 per cent A*-C, 10 per cent A*/A in 2018). We saw small tutor groups of as few as five – notably these were in science subjects. Clever ones, with offers from Oxbridge as well other Russell Group universities. Arts subjects tend to be busier (up to 15 in a group). However, sixth form is closing in 2020. Library manned by full-time librarian and a nice place to sit and read. Lots of fiction, used for competitions, book club and quiet study. As an academic resource it is risible (school prefers 'needs developing' and reminds us that the individual heads of departments keep library resources in their offices). Good IT suites and resources for the popular media and film options.

Setting in maths, science and English from year 7. Plenty of movement between sets, we were assured. Sizeable number of mild dyslexics but no additional support in lessons apart from general support from class teacher. Staunch policy of no withdrawals from classes (except once weekly for children who have EAL). School employs four specialist learning support teachers who will arrange to see children outside lesson time in groups of two or three to devise strategies to help them access the mainstream curriculum. No screening on admission. However SENCo oversees general provision and monitoring – 80 to 90 children perceived as having some kind of mild learning disability or difficulty and some have IEPs. Most with more than the mildest difficulties seek support outside school. Inside school, the attitude is healthy – 'I'm not treated as if dyslexia is a crime, unlike at my last school,' we were told. Two of the three buildings have lifts but school will be helpful if someone breaks a leg and move lessons to the ground floor.

Games, options, the arts: Well known for sporting prowess despite there being virtually no facilities on site. Pupils are bussed or walk everywhere – mostly to Regent's Park, with pitches and courts of all kinds, Seymour Place for swimming – and the results and achievements, given the conditions, are impressive. Years 7 to 9 have sport timetabled four times a week (one of the advantages of no canteen and shorter lunch breaks: time can be reallocated to sport). Football and netball tours of Barbados, swimming teams win competitions (Westminster champions five years in a row), masses of medals in cross-country and local honours in athletics and team sports. Pervasive pride in school sports, helped, no doubt, by classy Olympians on staff. However most really keen sportsmen and women do their serious sport outside school – girls' football a particular highpoint. Sport now compulsory to year 12 – one afternoon a week minimum of netball or football.

Music and drama similarly 'massive.' Music mostly means pop and jazz (we saw lots of ukulele enthusiasts). There are also a few violinists and woodwinders amongst the jazz pianists, guitarists, drummers and bassists who predominate, but eclectic range of music taken seriously. We were shown round by a budding actor in year 10 who enthused about the opportunities he has been given to develop his talent. Wholehearted, whole school productions annually – West Side Story, Singing in the Rain, The Producers and Annie are recent offerings; not on site as no suitable space but venues include the RADA studios in WC1. Upper school recently performed a resoundingly successful Richard III – which was then a sell-out at the Edinburgh Fringe. Lower school (up to year 9) recently performed Skellig as their annual production. Good-sized on-site drama studio can accommodate smaller productions (we were impressed with the assortment of costumes and props).

Art in the lower school is lively and inventive. We saw ink portraits in the style of Peter Howson, as well as pop art-style Creme Eggs. Fewer than 10 do art A level – facilities limited, though there is a textiles room and school excels in photography. DT similarly energetic – resistant materials, pewter casting, CAD and CAM, though all in rather small and poky rooms in basement. Lots of extracurricular stuff – when we visited a stress management workshop was being delivered to all GCSE students. Trips galore – we have seldom seen such a full programme. Much use made of London's galleries, museums and exhibitions, plus the nearby wider world and the opportunities it offers for field, sporting and other educational exercises, both here and abroad.

Background and atmosphere: This is a young school, founded only 20 or so years ago by the visionary head of science at St Paul's Girls', Richard Walker. His aim was to create a smaller independent co-ed senior school that wasn't super selective. Part of the Alpha Plus group, it forms one of their 18 UK schools and colleges, bringing the advantages of the economies of scale. Portland Place – the road – is a broad, straight thoroughfare in the heart of Regency London, two minutes from Oxford Circus to the south, two minutes to Regent's Park to the north. It is lined by august embassies (China, Kenya, Poland, Portugal) and the HQs of royal and learned institutions (architects, physicists, radiologists, anaesthetists). The main school building – Portland Place – identifies itself with a modest brass plate and is elegantly splendid. It is rare for us to compliment a school on its decor but a pleasure to do so here. Eye-catching blue carpet up and down the stairs (not just on the ground floor for show as elsewhere), magnificent ceilings, cornices, columns, capitals and fireplaces: nowhere more so than in the old ballroom, rescued from its carapace of false ceiling and fluorescent tubes and very much in use. All in tip-top nick. This building houses the lower years, the hall (used for gym and dance) and the top floors (formerly the servants' quarters) which accommodate music and languages.

A second building in Great Portland Street, five minutes away, houses the upper years and has a breathtaking eyeball-to-eyeball view of the BT Tower, seemingly within grabbing distance. Harford House, also in Great Portland Street and with a facade resembling that of a corporate HQ, is home to art, drama and science. It's a logistical nightmare – five or seven storeys to be up and down all day, three buildings – and it all has to be timetabled, supervised and navigated. We suppose everyone to be very fit – a real bonus for children who need lots of movement and exercise if they are to perform well mentally.

No school kitchen. Pupils bring packed lunches or order in from local cafés (which deliver dozens of paninis etc in little brown carriers). Years 10 and 11 and the sixth hang out in the many cafés in or around Great Portland Street and just love the privilege of this kind of freedom.

Pastoral care, well-being and discipline: Definitely an informal feel to the place. Although pupils are not quite on first name terms with teachers, one can sense an equality in the relationships not seen in more traditional establishments. Good use of sixth form mentors for years 7 and 8 – really fosters inter-age group understanding and friendships, especially helpful in so small a school. Solidly structured pastoral care hierarchy picks up and deals with problems, but there's a pervasive sense of everyone looking out for everyone else. People seem to know each other's little brothers and sisters here. Parents praise the home-school communications and especially the termly parents' evenings. 'The teachers are mostly young and energetic,' enthused a parent, 'and you really get to know them.'

P

Pupils and parents: More boys than girls (about 60:40 in lower years) – simply because there are so many more girls' and co-ed schools in London. Mixed, as befits its location – trad, moneyed, independent education veterans alongside newbies and newcomers from here, there and everywhere, blended with those who couldn't get into the 'academic' schools and for whom PP has been a jolly lucky find. From the whole urban sprawl – no longer just the north and west but around 30 per cent from east and south too. Mostly UK born and based but also from pretty much the rest of the globe, solar system and beyond, in a great undivided family. Brains? Yes, though common denominator more palpably pleasure, pride and enthusiasm for the place.

Entrance: There is a 10+ as well as an 11+ intake – partly to steal a march on the competition and partly to meet the needs of those who dread the 11+ circus and will do anything to avoid it (wise move). 'Informal tests' in English and maths with deputy/head of year. Year 7 has tests in English and maths and a chat with a teacher. For places at 12+, 13+ and 14+, same format plus additional test in science. School keen to dispel image that it's the go-to place for a child on the dys-strata. Child has to be able to cope and pupils who can't will be turned down. They come, at 11, from a large number of schools – state and independent. Sixth form is closing in 2020 and there is no longer a year 12 intake.

Exit: Wide range of post-A level destinations and courses, including sports and exercise science, mechanical engineering and forensic investigations at the newer universities. The odd one to study music and to art college; London, Exeter, Southampton, Liverpool universities popular. About 30 per cent leave after GCSE (mostly to non-fee paying sixth form colleges).

Money matters: No scholarships or bursaries offered at any point.

Remarks: Small, nurturing and refreshingly relaxed. A haven of creativity in the pushy academically competitive world of London day schools. A place for engaged, lively, normal kids – privileged, yes, but Sloanes, no. Becoming ever more popular as more and more people discover it. The challenge will be to maintain its ethos of 'broader academic intake' in the face of increasing demand.

Prendergast School

Adelaide Avenue, Brockley, London SE4 1LE

Ages 11–18 **Pupils** 827 **Sixth form** 218 (106 boys)

020 8690 3710
www.prendergast-school.com

Head teacher: Since 2016, Paula Ledger. Read history at Goldsmiths, master's at Kings' College and spent time early in her career briefly in the independent sector and in Japan, before moving into maintained schools, becoming latterly deputy head of one of the Harris academies. Very approachable, and manages to communicate that she is quietly confident.

Having inherited a school which won 'outstanding' in every category in its most recent Ofsted Inspection (that was in 2013), Ms Ledger might be seen as having an easy ride, but she is calmly ambitious for the school. She has a big passion for girls' education in general, and for raising their numeracy in particular – 'hating maths has been such a feature of so many girls' memories of school for so many years,' she says. 'I want us to take our part in changing that.' Wins much praise from parents for safeguarding academic standards and 'for being consistently approachable'.

A mother of school age children, Ms Ledger identifies herself strongly as a parent living in the local area, and is evidently driven by the determination to work on behalf of it.

Academic matters: A level results in 2018 somewhat down on previous years: 17 per cent of grades were either A* or A, and 35 per cent were B or better. A level curriculum is broadly based with the opportunity to take BTecs in a number of cases. At GCSE, 39 per cent of grades were 9-7. Prendergast is one of the top 10 per cent non-selective schools for attainment in the country. 'One big plus,' said a parent who has seen several children through the school, 'is the consistency of good results. Pupils and parents have learned to rely upon the school to play its part.' Another parent said her child had never found her feet at primary school, but thrived at Prendergast. 'I think the school freed her up. She's loved the challenge and loved the diversity.'

Games, options, the arts: Very strong arts – textiles especially, and it is telling how prominent these feature in the school's online promotional video.

A huge music profile. 'Any pupil can learn almost any instrument at school', the head insists, 'and many take up the chance'. There are different choirs – a gospel choir and an a capella group among them. Year 7 has a music lesson en masse once every week, which (given the timetable constraints under which all schools labour) says a great deal about the scale of investment in the subject the school believes appropriate. There are music assemblies once a fortnight and plenty of touring for those in choirs and orchestras – one recently to Belgium – as well as an annual array of concerts (one open air), a big one at Christmas as well as an annual Founders' Day Concert.

A musical is performed annually, but there are lots of smaller productions, mainly under the aegis of drama GCSE which has become popular and successful. Plans are afoot to introduce it at A level. 'We place a huge importance on making drama accessible,' says the head. 'One big plus of musicals is the number of people who can be involved on or off stage.'

Games are taken seriously, but the provision is not what you'd get in most independent schools. There's one lesson a week for games lower down the school. Depending on the time of year, rugby, netball, football, rounders, cricket and athletics are offered. There are some matches, but a crowded fixture list against other schools is not a big part of the school psyche. 'We have no reluctance to encourage individual sports,' adds the head. With the Olympic velodrome so near, competitive cycling is unsurprisingly popular. The Duke of Edinburgh Award has acquired a significant profile, with some 25-30 pupils each year going for bronze and silver awards, and some achieving gold. Sport melds seamlessly into opportunities for self-expression.

There are lunchtime and after-school clubs every day: music ensembles, gospel choir, rugby, netball, handball, cheerleading and homework clubs – the list goes on. 'My children have just soaked this up,' a parent said. 'The variety proves that the school really values people's differences. Choir for some, games for some. And Star Trek for others.'

Background and atmosphere: Prendergast is just one of a cluster of local schools whose foundation was a result of philanthropy. It enjoys a close relationship with the Leathersellers, a livery company, which continues to invest in the school in a range of ways. Perhaps the most conspicuous of these is support for gap year students to spend months in the school working as mentors. 'They're not teachers,' the head explains, 'but they are fantastic role models, and add greatly to the quality of the experience of school for so many of our children'. The Leathersellers offer scholarships and also help underwrite some of the expense of higher education in some deserving cases, and use their access to the City to help pupils enjoy some of its advantages and glamour. The Sir John Staples Society hosts regular talks – David Blunkett was a recent visitor ('a lovely man, but his dog put his muddy paws on my new shoes,' according to one attender) – and the school is invited each year to the Lord Mayor's Parade. 'These may sound old hat to some,' says the head, 'but to us these occasions can mean the world'.

Pupils look unobtrusively tidy and are happy to be around school. There's a distinct lift in most steps. There's a uniform up to GCSE, but not in sixth form. One father said that his son and daughters ensure that evening meals are never dull. 'They're opinionated and very interested in the world at large, and also the local area. I think we owe the credit for that to the school. It's a big gift they've given.'

Pastoral care, well-being and discipline: We drew a strong sense of confidence from among pupils. They believe they are lucky to be in a school that is high achieving – the concept of 'excellence' and 'outstanding' are very real to them. There is also the sense that the teachers 'really care' – this thought was projected particularly strongly from a group of 13 year old girls, not always an age group which is indulgent. Pupils insist that there is very little unpleasantness among themselves but that, when it does happen, it is acted upon at once. 'That's what the teachers do, and it's what the pupils want.'

Pupils and parents: Annual parents' meetings for each year group with all subject teachers, and a termly report in addition. One parent emphasised how ready teachers are to set up individual meetings with parents if there are difficulties or anxieties which need more immediate attention.

Entrance: Ten per cent of places are for music scholars, via a series of aural tests designed to measure potential, rather than favour pupils who have already learned to sight read, or taken grade exams. The other 90 per cent of places are allocated on the basis of how far applicants live from the school gates.

Exit: One medic, no Oxbridge in 2018. Others have left to study eg engineering at Imperial. 'Our top flyers include some from challenging backgrounds, including looked-after pupils,' says the head, rightly proud. Strong anecdotal sense that the sixth form is especially talented at creative subjects and languages. The school has exceptional success at getting pupils to art schools (the top ones – Central St Martins, Slade etc). Textiles is very strong and pupils have won several British Fashion Week awards.

Money matters: Support given to some students in the sixth form – 50 bursaries given this year. Three Leathersellers' Federation bursaries awarded each year to students about to go to university, comprising £700 towards each year of study.

Remarks: A remarkable school, doing remarkable work. Among its greatest virtues are its close identification with the local area – in socioeconomic terms, a very mixed area, but not of the kind which usually makes headlines. The school embodies a calm pride in itself. One parent said her daughter had told her after a recent prize giving, 'I'll always be a Prendergast girl.' Her mother added: 'Pretty good, I thought.' So do we.

Prospect House School

75 Putney Hill, London SW15 3NT

Ages 3–11 **Pupils** 320

Fees: £17,700 – £18,450 pa

020 8780 0456
www.prospecths.org.uk

Head: Since 2017, Michael Hodge BPrimEd (Rhodes), previously deputy head (since 2004). Montessori trained. Taught in London state system for eight 'wonderful' years. Either he, or a senior member of staff, greets pupils by name every morning at the front door. No longer teaches maths, which he misses, but always popping into lessons, where he invariably gets involved. When the headship came up, he saw it as an irresistible opportunity to 'take the school further.' Highly ambitious for the school. Repeatedly states that 'the children are the most important thing.' Knows close collaboration between parents, staff and pupils is fundamental to a child's success. A team player, who is well supported by strong senior management team. Greatly adored by parents and pupils alike.

South African, but after more than two decades here, his accent is almost imperceptible, though apparently resurfaces whenever the Springboks are playing. Keen cyclist and enjoys high-intensity gym classes. A dab hand at DIY. A born extrovert, full of good cheer.

Entrance: Non-selective co-ed. First come, first served. Open events two or three times a year, but bespoke tours also offered. One September intake only. School prefers children to start in nursery at 3, when there are two classes of 16. Nursery pupils need to commit to staying for two years minimum, starting with at least five mornings a week, rising to three full days or more by the summer term. All nursery children are visited in their own homes prior to arrival, followed by induction morning in summer term. Can start in reception, but only eight to 10 more places at this stage. In reception, years 1 and 2 there are 20 per class, rising to 22 thereafter. For occasional places, tests in maths, English and spelling. Must have visited school before offered a place. Sibling priority throughout.

Exit: The 11+ exam is the one part of the job that head dislikes as 'every year it becomes more and more competitive'. Pupils are now heading to schools further down the A3 than before. Vast majority to day schools. Perennial favourites include King's College, Latymer Upper, Putney High, Hampton, Kingston Grammar, St John's Leatherhead, Ibstock, Kew House, Surbiton High. 'If you're looking to leave at 7+ then this is not the school for you,' states head. 'At 11+, we support parents in choosing a school where their child will thrive.' Head speaks honestly to parents, giving them three years of data on their child.

Remarks: One of three schools in House Schools Group, along with Bassett House and Orchard House. Each has retained its distinct character but some sharing of ICT support and joint insets.

Housed in two large, former family homes. Began as a nursery in 1960s. In 2013, early years up to year 2 moved into separate site up the road, which boasts a stunning garden, complete with climbing frame, hedgehog house and place for fairies to flutter. Years 3-6 in original building. Two sites but very much one school. Both buildings possess bright, colourful classrooms with eye-catching displays.

Two mixed ability parallel classes throughout school, which are shuffled annually. School adopts different learning styles including Montessori elements for younger pupils. French from nursery, Latin from year 5 and Mandarin post-11+. From year 3, three ability sets for maths and English.

High expectations for all. Academics are taken seriously, but learning is fun, with one class enjoying a Mad Hatter's Tea Party after studying Alice in Wonderland and lots of dressing up as Anglo-Saxons and Tudors. 'If children aren't enjoying their primary schooling then we are failing them, as life is tough enough later on,' believes head. No heavy emphasis on testing, but pupils are well prepared for 11+ when it arrives. Despite its south-west London location, definitely not a hothouse.

Everything carefully thought out, with what is best for the children at the heart of all decisions. Range of reading schemes in key stage 1 to avoid comparisons with others and to 'stop them getting hung up on one scheme'. Nursery pupils swap classrooms with parallel class regularly so they can all enjoy each other's resources. Fantastic displays in nursery, including a life-size gingerbread house. Paradise for little ones. Head of lower school, the very approachable Mrs Hudson, warmly welcomes new recruits to the Prospect 'family'.

'We do not want our children to be tutored', head tells us, though he knows it goes on. He believes tutoring is wrong if used to get a child into a school to which they are not suited.

Seven academic scholarships in 2018; regular music and sports scholarships. No scholars board despite all regular scholarships bagged. Head comments, 'What does it say to a child who isn't on the scholars' board? We're not that type of school.' Cups and prizes awarded, for traditional subjects as well as for endeavour and citizenship. 'Everybody is catered for and we celebrate that.'

Head understands that each child is different and is proud that school is targeting pupils' needs better. Approximately 45 pupils with some sort of SEND. Supports pupils with mild dyslexia, dyscalculia and dyspraxia. Children in key stage 1 requiring help with reading, phonics, fine motor skills and speech are supported in focused grouped teaching; further up the school it is maths and English. Support ranges from small group work to tackle specific areas through to longer term individual support. 'When children go for extra lessons, it is just seen as a part of their learning, not as a separate entity,' says head.

Most able academically are stretched through differentiation, extension activities such as algebra and participation in external events. Talented musician currently getting one-t-one input from head of music. School is good at encouraging children to think for themselves, question, investigate and apply what they learn. No one is allowed to rest on their laurels.

Family feel. Lots of community spirit. 'The children are polite and well-behaved, but they are not robots without any personality,' says head of lower school. Pupils do genuinely love it here and the ones we met were bright eyed and bushy tailed. One chap told us, 'The only bad thing about this school is that it ends. I wish it was my secondary school too.' Another piped up, 'The teachers are kind and friendly. They're also funny!'

Excellent, open communication with parents, from ad hoc emails to daily phone calls if needed. Parents are encouraged to come in and talk through problems and school responds speedily to their concerns. Message books go back and forth daily, so everyone kept in loop. Staff have a daily briefing to share information on pupils so know who to keep a close eye on. Children not defined by past demeanours – 'we build on the positive.' The consequences for bad behaviour tend to be mild, such as missing 10 minutes of break. 'Not a big deal,' commented one child.

Parents feel staff are approachable, dedicated and know their offspring well. Healthy ratio of male to female teachers. No supply teachers – if a teacher is absent then other in-house teachers step in. Specialist teachers for maths, English, IT, French, music, PE, art and Latin.

Mr Hodge wants to be the kind of head that staff want to work for. He believes professional development of staff is vital and encourages an open discussion about their teaching, rather than critical appraisals. Wants them to be constantly improving their teaching as well building up their CVs, even if it means they move elsewhere as a result.

IT provision considered excellent and well-integrated into curriculum. Laptops, iPads (all years 5 and 6 have their own) and MacBooks everywhere. Homework apps. Head knows screen time can be used negatively so care is taken 'to educate them in how to use their devices properly.' Inevitably, some parents feel there is too much time spent in front of screens.

PE lessons take place at all-weather pitch on-site and gym is in hall. Pupils also use local sports facilities. Head wishes he had sprawling playing fields but knows this is the nature of inner-city schools. Sport offered includes football, netball, hockey, cricket, athletics, rounders, gym, tennis, swimming and dance. Judo, fencing and running clubs offered too. Sports day for all. Good number of matches for everyone but tournaments only for the most able. 'We do well. Football is especially strong,' states head. He expects the pupils to throw themselves into their sports and to give their best. 'You play to win. It matters, but it must not over-ride the enjoyment of the sport,' explains head. A few parental grumbles about sport. One commented, 'It's not exactly a sporty school.' School disagrees strongly, saying 'there is a huge amount of sport both in curriculum time and after school'. Another felt the school needed to expand the sports department, and another lamented the lack of time dedicated to swimming.

Legendary director of music. Over 200 individual music lessons a week, with a diverse range of instruments though not drums. Large orchestra. Numerous ensembles: strings, woodwind, brass. Annual musicals and concerts galore. Glorious singing in evidence on the day we visited.

Two identical productions of Peter Pan were staged recently, with different casts, so everyone could have a reasonable part. Typical of Prospect House – it wants everyone to have the chance to shine in their own way. All-singing, all dancing musicals are order of the day here: Mary Poppins, Sound of Music, Oliver! and Bugsy Malone.

Vibrant art department. One art co-ordinator per key stage. Dedicated art room in upper school, complete with kiln. No exhibitions, partly as head is 'sick of asking parents to spend more money to buy their child's artwork.' Puppets being made on the day we visited, with puppet show planned. Year 6 hugely excited about clock-making in DT.

Clubs include coding, yoga, chess, puzzles, football and calligraphy. Cookery perennially popular. Weekly homework club, where children take it in turns to bring tasty morsels from home to share with the rest of the gang. Reasoning club at the top end to help with 11+ preparation. All clubs are charged for. One mother welcomed the fact that clubs are now 'crunchier' and 'more academically focused than before.'

Residential trips for all of key stage 2, starting with two nights, rising to five days for top year. Destinations include Suffolk, Dorset and northern France. Day trips to perennial favourites: National History Museum, Hampton Court and Kew Gardens. Visits to local church to ask Vicar Ben questions about Christianity. Post 11+ programme is both fun and interesting, including a Bake-Off competition with prizes for cakes with best texture and taste, as well as sessions at the Globe, as part of a Shakespeare project.

Each site has own kitchen which provide freshly-cooked meals. Parents are delighted that packed lunches are no longer needed. Some choice at lunch 'but not masses as it encourages children to be picky eaters.' The youngest pupils were having a very jolly time at lunch on the day we visited, with plenty of chatter and empty plates all round. Smiley chef whose specialities include child-friendly dishes, including mild curry, Spanish chicken and pasta.

Mostly local professional families. Many children are bilingual, including Japanese, Spanish, Swedish and Dutch. Most become fluent very rapidly though some need support with English idioms and inference. Increasingly, dual income. No wraparound care offered which can be tricky for these working parents. 'We're working on this.' Thriving parents' association which organises Christmas fair, school discos and uniform sales.

Means-tested scholarships available for 7+ for those coming from state education. Family income must be less than £50,000. No sibling discounts.

A school that allows children to enjoy being children. Mr Hodge states, 'I want them to be happy. If they are happy, they will succeed.' He is achieving his ambition. This must be one of the most joyful schools in London.

Putney High Junior School

Linked with Putney High School

35 Putney Hill, London SW15 6BH

Ages 4–11 **Pupils** 320

Fees: £15,636 pa

020 8788 6523
www.putneyhigh.gdst.net

Head: Since 2017, Pippa Page-Roberts, previously director of innovation and learning at Kensington Prep. She began her teaching career at Rowdown Primary School, Croydon, before moving to Kingswood Prep in Bath, and has also been head of junior English at the Harrodian. Her other roles at Kensington Prep – where she spent 10 years – have been director of studies and head of English.

Entrance: Selective at 4+ and 7+. No sibling policy. About 130 apply for 44 places in reception. The girls come in for an assessment that lasts over an hour. Each one is seen on a one-to-one basis and every member of staff is involved in assessing. Parents are present but not interviewed. They take girls who are born throughout the year, so a proper mix of autumn, spring and summer birthdays. At 7, the assessments last up to three hours. Girls sit papers in English, maths and non-verbal reasoning. Classes increase from 22 to 24 in year 3, so a minimum of four places at 7+. Most families are local – within a two mile radius.

Exit: On average between 85-90 per cent continue into the senior school. A few choose boarding. St Swithun's recently popular 'but it largely depends on the family and their own connections with boarding,' says school. A few prefer to go to co-ed schools – Latymer Upper is popular, and very occasionally some go to Ibstock. A fair few move to St Paul's, Godolphin & Latymer or Lady Eleanor Holles, or choose to move to a state school, eg Lady Margaret in Parsons Green.

School assesses each year and from year 4 they start to get a feel for who might not be up to the academic standard of the senior school. The process is carefully managed through year 5 and 'no one ends up without a good school'. Senior school taster days are organised for the year 5s, mixing with the year 7s. All girls moving onto the senior school have to sit the exam and interview, but there are 'lots of opportunities for scholarships – academic, music and sport'.

Remarks: Situated on the same site as the senior school, Putney High Junior is definitely part of the whole rather than a stand-alone school. Not only are the facilities shared – the design technology workshop as well as the performing arts centre, sports hall, outdoor courts and very attractive cafeteria – but girls in the junior school also get the benefit of specialist teachers and co-curricular clubs – particularly art and ceramics. Part of the broader Girls' Day School Trust, the school also benefits from the advantages of being part of a well-established and specialist group of schools.

Emphasis here is firmly on academics. Structure is key, but there is a nurturing ethos, and 'waspish behaviour among the girls is nipped in the bud,' observed one mother. A noticeable softening in the atmosphere since our last visit. Staff and parents alike are much more smiley, open and approachable, we were told. Mrs Archibald, the very effective deputy head, frequently comes up in discussion with parents. She is head of pastoral care and music and the first port of call if there is a problem. There is a little post box, the Secret Safe, where girls can post any anxieties confidentially. This is checked on a regular basis and, by all accounts, those anxieties rapidly resolved. The buddy system, which involves year 6 girls pairing up with girls in reception as their Guardian Angels, contributes to the cosy atmosphere.

Relatively large class sizes (22 until year 3 when classes increase to 24), two classes in each year are taught in bright, spacious classrooms. Much of the old Victorian building was looking tired and in need of love and a lick of paint when we visited, but bright, confident girls wreathed in smiles and purple more than made up for the flaky state of the building. French is taught from reception, Spanish from year 5, philosophy and ethics from year 3. iPads encased in school colour – purple – used from year 4 onwards. 'A mixed blessing,' remarked one mother, although the girls clearly enjoyed presenting a project, having researched the material using the iPad as their main tool. There are also a number of laptops kept in storage outside the library for general use.

A learning support department is gradually starting to emerge; although school insists there has been one for the past few years, it appears to be still in a somewhat nascent state. Only one dedicated member of staff. She works from the Panda Room (parent and daughter room) and sees about 17 girls on a one-to-one basis, with more girls supported around the school in their classes. Some of these have specific – mild – learning difficulties, some simply require a boost in confidence.

Apart from the academics, music and the outside speakers who come and talk to the girls are regarded by parents as the main strengths of the school. A compulsory choir for years 5 and 6 – 'very good for the girls,' agreed the parents – as well as the more elite Small Choir. Lots of musical activities, groups, an orchestra – everyone grade 1 and above welcome. Orchestra in residence culminated with a concert to celebrate Putney High's 125th anniversary in 2018; successor is an orator in residence, aiming to encourage all girls to find their voice and speak up. Not much creativity in the classroom, observed one parent – 'I now pay extra for my daughter to do an extracurricular creative club.' Increase in intellectually-challenging clubs eg coding, engineering, current affairs, debating, problem solving. Thirty per cent of extracurricular clubs are charged for.

Junior school playground now transformed, with areas for pupils to challenge themselves and enjoy different types of play, from imaginative to physical. Pupils have helped to design an environmentally-friendly, 'natural' space. 'We want girls to take risks and challenge themselves because we want them to be bold, unafraid of trying new things, as well as to develop their curiosity and love of learning.'

A mixture of families – some from across the river, others from the other direction as far as Kingston and New Malden, but largely from the local environs in the junior school. A broad range of nationalities: a number of Asian families as well as the usual international mix of US, European and Scandinavian. Parents are hard-working professionals who want the best for their daughters and most step up at school events like the Autumn Fair, for example.

If you're looking for the 'wow factor' then look elsewhere. However if you want your daughter to have a solid start to her school career then this is a good bet. A safe but not sparkling choice for your bright, conformist daughter.

Putney High School

Linked with Putney High Junior School

35 Putney Hill, London SW15 6BH

Ages 11–18 **Pupils** 705 **Sixth form** 180

Fees: £18,900 pa

020 8788 4886
www.putneyhigh.gdst.net

Headmistress: Since 2015, Suzie Longstaff BA MA PGCE (late 40s), following a year as acting head and a previous six years as head of sixth. Mrs Longstaff read economics at Durham, did her PGCE at Homerton and gained an MA in education from Bath in 2015. She started her career at Shiplake teaching maths and ICT, then to Kingston Grammar as head of ICT and asst head of sixth. She joined Putney in 2009. It may be dawning on you that both her universities and all three schools are on – or virtually on – rivers and rivers all need rowers. Mrs Longstaff was Olympic cox for Team GB's women's VIII at Atlanta 1996 (her steering being described by one commentator as 'aggressive') and she has been captain of the Thames Rowing Club.

We found her warm, sparkly (on a very hot day), utterly charming, full of zest and fun and not remotely aggressive in her current role. Parents concur: 'She's brilliant.' 'She makes very good connections with both parents and girls.' 'A breath of fresh air.' 'Everyone likes her – she's open to change and very positive – and she comes to everything.' The girls echo this, describing her repeatedly as, above all, 'open' – and pay tribute to how she has made the school more relaxed. 'She walks around all the time, asking girls how they are.' We heard no dissenting voice. Mrs Longstaff is the mother of young twins who attend the school.

Internal appointments to headships are rare, can make waves and lead to choppy waters but Putney now has a keen eye on the course ahead and a steady hand on the tiller, steering with the lightest of touches.

Academic matters: Most popular and successful A level subjects are maths, biology and English Lit. A wide range of options given this is not a huge school – economics and psychology are popular. In 2018, 69 per cent A*/A grades and 93 per cent A*-B. GCSE results are terrific – as you'd expect: 92 per cent 9-7 in 2018.

Innovative bilingual programme offered to native speakers of Mandarin, Spanish, French and German ie the languages taught in school. Greek, Arabic and Italian now on the timetable. Few takers of languages at A level in recent years but this now set to change as head is sticking her oar in to the somewhat becalmed waters and stirring them up with energy and commitment. 'I'd like to offer Russian too,' she says. There are now three German teachers – surely unique in a school of this size – and some truly exciting trips eg the Spanish-takers to Costa Rica – to promote these vital subjects. A school making a specialism of modern foreign languages has long been needed and Putney is set to assume the role.

Much enthusiasm for the teachers and their teaching 'style'. 'They discuss rather than teach so you want to join in,' we were told. Also for the school's flexibility when it comes to options at GCSE and A level. 'People are doing the weirdest combinations

– you're allowed to do whatever you like.' 'Our daughters were not at all keen on homework but they have been inspired and now they really want to do it,' we heard, 'and even in the subjects they're not keen on!' Much praise for the very new head of careers – 'I talk to her every day,' one sixth former told us – and school has a strong offering in this area, organising a careers fair and making links with useful alumnae.

Lots of extracurricular stimulation in the form of high calibre outside speakers (Henry Marsh, AC Grayling for a start), inspirational trips and PIE – the Putney Ideas Exchange. We always like anything which celebrates ideas and this is genuinely exploratory, open-minded and, to some extent, pupil-led. Brilliant new interactive installation on the periodic table got even this science-phobe excited.

Average of 24 girls in years 7-9 classes, down to 15 for the GCSE years and around seven in the sixth form. Under three per cent have EAL needs -supported where needed. One sixth have some kind of SEN and the school has an unusually open approach. They will move classes to suit able girls with major physical disabilities if that enables them to attend and they welcome those who may need a full time LSA if that opens the curriculum to them. Mrs Longstaff's approach is, 'Great! How can we help?' and this is not just talk but borne out by the girls they have in school. Well staffed Learning Enrichment dept encompasses SEN.

Games, options, the arts: Rowing. Within a year of Mrs Longstaff's appointment, the school acquired the lease to a boathouse close to Putney bridge and now more than 125 rowers from years 8 to 13, backed by enthusiastic parents (and a pretty keen head), power up and down the Thames. But you don't have to do it, though everyone's eyes widen at the thrust given to sports since Mrs Longstaff took her seat. Unlike at many schools, here everyone gets a chance – lots of teams and a deliberate policy to delay team selection to ensure fairness for all. Some 85 per cent of them, we are told, represent the school in something that involves moving. Almost too much for some people. Some feeling that the sports staff now have too much power and girls' involvement elsewhere can suffer in a school where so much is on offer and there is so much eagerness to involve oneself in everything. Astro on site and smallish tarmacs but a few coach moments away are the main pitches and playing fields used by the school. Dance is big. Netball and lacrosse thrive and many other games and sports are on offer – acrobatics to zumba. And they win – masses. Top team GDST athletics recently.

Exceptional music, led inspirationally and with great success and financial investment – £30,000 recently spent on upgrading nine pianos, acquiring a baby harp and a new mobile recording studio when we visited. The head – prior to her rowing days – was herself a music scholar and, therefore is in sympathy with the needs of school music, as remarkably few are. Chamber groups win major competitions, girls leave with eg Oxbridge organ scholarships, and 'for several, grade 8 is a distant memory'. But lots of groups, choirs, ensembles of all kinds and our visit to the music centre with its many practice rooms was a not-particularly-well-sound-proofed joy. Drama similarly popular. Nice little studio theatre with battery of new lanterns and a good hall for shows. Also a delightful outdoor stage on the 'staff lawn' on which a junior production of Alice in Wonderland had just taken place – teacups lining the rim of the stage. 'We have theatre productions and concerts every two seconds,' one girl told us, quite seriously.

Impressive DT – 'someone made a really cool woven hedgehog home!' – and art: the catalogue of the sixth form art display which we just missed bore witness to genuinely original and skilful work in many media. Textiles – compulsory for half of each of the first three years – also big, popular and, at best, producing professional quality and highly desirable artefacts. 'There was this wonderful ballgown and someone made a leather jacket – very Alexander McQueen.' Not too much on display when we visited – not a lot of space for it – but also 'people do like to take things home'. Of course! School has all the mod cons – eg laser and 3D printers – as you'd expect – and use them with imagination and subtlety.

Latest resident, an orator (following on from orchestra, writer and entrepreneur in residence), tasked with encouraging all pupils to find their voice and communicate effectively via timetabled sessions and clubs.

Background and atmosphere: A Girls' Day School Trust (GDST) school. This one began life in 1893 – one of the latest of the many schools belonging to this venerable and highly respected organisation and, thus, relatively young, though celebrated its 125th anniversary in 2018 with, inter alia, a concert and a photograph exhibition of portraits of notable alumnae. The Trust itself celebrated its 140th anniversary in 2012 and, although each school is largely autonomous and free-standing, the features and advantages of belonging to this unique family of schools should not be overlooked – not least the attention now paid to attracting the right girls for its bursarial provision and the many opportunities now to compete against girls from sister schools in many activities.

Putney is on a compact site but clever use of space and imaginative building produces many surprises – among them the excellent sixth form centre opened by Jenny Beaven (one of its most celebrated old girls) in 2012. Study area, sixth form diner (open all day), internet cafe, outdoor balconies, huge sitting room, fitness room – few boarding schools offer more. This is an excellent resource and must be playing a major part in the school's growing success in retaining post-GCSE pupils.

Despite its relative smallness, nowhere feels cramped. Refurbished classrooms are light, pleasant spaces. All is orderly and well-maintained. Good, air-conditioned modern library with small stock in key subjects but a fast system of ordering books. Two small lawns, an excellent canteen with food everyone likes. 'I'm a vegetarian and I love it.' 'I'm seriously picky and it's great for me.' We would have been happy to stay to lunch.

Pastoral care, well-being and discipline: Parents and pupils enthuse about the new relaxed feel and the easier relationships developing both between staff and girls but also between girls in different years – fostered, in part, by a new house system. Parents tell us of their daughters' growth in confidence and the great care and attention to detail taken by the teaching staff. 'They are very good at dealing with pupils as individuals,' we heard from several and this concurs with Mrs Longstaff's emphasis on 'individualised care'. Some sense among a few that not all staff have yet adapted to this change in culture – also, that some girls shy away from the school's 'open' take on matters to do with mental health and 'mindfulness' – but the structure and the understanding is there, if not yet fully embraced by all. 'What we need,' agrees Mrs Longstaff, 'is people opening up and engaging in a conversation.'

The staff structure is supported by a counsellor and a buddy system – year 10 girls pairing with newbies and backed up by year 11 Big Sisters – adds yet a further layer of help if needed. Discipline itself is rarely an issue – a real sense of friendliness, looking out for each other and kindness is palpable.

This is a 'busy' school – girls, parents and head repeatedly stress this. So much on offer and very little time to do it all in a day school day. But this has to be ambitious and right though it may not be easy for everyone to go with the flow. But the sense is that swimming against the tide won't work. Haul yourself onto the bank and look for the lifeguard. She'll be there.

Pupils and parents: Around 40 different home languages spoken as befits this diverse and cosmopolitan area. Most girls are white and middle class but this disguises a wider range of backgrounds and home cultures than is immediately apparent. 'Not as flashy and full of girls hopping out of 4x4s as some schools,' we were told and we agree. A down-to-earth, real world school. Parent-home connections very much fostered by Mrs Longstaff, who regularly meets representatives from the Parents' Support Association which works to pick up parental concerns or suggestions and act on them. Parents an appreciative, sensible bunch – most families living within half an hour or so, though some rather further. As one admitted, 'It's a schlep to get here but it's worth it.'

Entrance: Vastly oversubscribed in the junior school (see separate entry.) Almost all junior school pupils move into the senior school. Some 650 external applicants for the 64 places at 11+ – the number of applicants at this level has doubled in the three years prior to our visit. They come from a vast number of preps and primaries. Exams in English and maths. Around 15 new girls come in at sixth form. They will need at least three at 8/9 at GCSE, three more at 7 and at least six at 6 including English and maths. Higher requirements for subjects to be taken at A level in some cases.

Exit: Some 90 per cent and rising now stay into the sixth form. Some go after GCSEs to eg boarding, mixed or IB schools but the number of leavers is falling – rightly. 'Quite a few left in my year and several came back, we heard.' The head doesn't bully the girls about this but 'I know ours is the best sixth form in London,' she says, endearingly. Thence to an impressive range of courses and places. Three Oxbridge places plus two medics in 2018. Bristol, Edinburgh, Exeter and KCL also consistently popular and a good spread of subjects taken. A few now each year to US colleges, often to take courses in liberal arts. Several OG notables including Jenny Beavan – Oscar winning costume designer and 2016 GDST alumna of the year, Camilla Cavendish, Olly Grender, Nicola Hicks, Sandie Okoro, Ursula Owen, Olivia Poulet, Edina Ronay, Elizabeth Symons, Melanie Phillips, Sophie Raworth, Pippa Greenwood, Jemima Rooper, Madeleine Wickham (novelist Sophie Kinsella), Anita Corbin (who took the portrait photos for the 125th anniversary exhibition). And mostly a thoroughly worthwhile, sensible and unpretentious bunch of women.

Money matters: GDST scholarships in academic, music and sports at 11+. Academic worth up to 50 per cent of fees. Sixth form scholarships in art, academics, sports, music, drama and design. Unique travel and science scholarship open only to internal candidates. The GDST now has a substantial bursary pot and this money is not always used up each year. If your daughter is bright or talented but the full fees are beyond your means it's well worth looking into it. NB Bursaries are means-tested annually.

Remarks: A good all-round school with an enthusiastic staff and a top quality head. 'Openness' now palpable in the faces and relationships and working its way through the school. Putney is no longer the also-ran of the London GDST schools. Under Mrs Longstaff, we feel, this school has caught the tide and is beginning to set the pace.

Q

Queen Elizabeth's Girls' School

High Street, Barnet, Hertfordshire EN5 5RR

Ages 11–18 **Pupils** 1,015 **Sixth form** 128

020 8449 2984
www.qegschool.org.uk

Headteacher: Since 2015, Violet Walker BSc (UCL), MA (Brunel), NPQH (50s). When Mrs Walker arrived as head at QE Girls, she must have felt she was returning home. Not only did she attend the school as a pupil in the 70s, she spent time here as part of her training as a maths teacher in the early 2000s. Before qualifying as a teacher, however, she had a pursued a number of other routes, qualifying and practising as both an accountant and a psychotherapist. Once launched in the profession, she rose rapidly, working as assistant head at Park High School, Harrow, and, most recently, as deputy head of Northolt High School for Girls (which she helped move on from special measures). Clearly seen as a 'safe pair of hands', her aim at QE Girls has been 'to marry the sense of tradition and what might be thought the old-fashioned values of my days with the very best of the latest in education.' This ambition has already been realised in a calm and competent fashion, and, since her arrival, the school's seen a rapid turn round of its academic fortunes. Both parents and pupils acknowledge her impact. 'The head seems a lot more in control,' said one mother. 'She really has her finger on the pulse,' commented another. A firm believer in what girls'-only education can offer, she acts as a coach for Women in Leadership, and her ambitions are 'for QE to be recognised as an outstanding school' and 'for girls to love school'.

Academic matters: In 2014, the school experienced a major shock when standards at this traditional high-flyer were called into question by Ofsted. Since then, a new head and a new Ofsted inspection have indicated the road to recovery is fully underway, with excellent recent results. At GCSE in 2018, 36 per cent of grades 9-7; at A level 25 per cent A*-A, 55 per cent A*-B. QE Girls is also now officially recognised as providing outstanding 'value added', with progress as well as achievement far above average. Teaching weaknesses (particularly of the most disadvantaged) have been resolved, with a raft of new appointments and energetic monitoring.

Girls enter year 7 from a wide range of local primaries and are quickly melded into a cohesive seven forms of 25-26. All study a largely academic curriculum, with most taking GCSEs in English, maths, science, at least one modern foreign language, history or geography plus an expressive art or technology subject. (They also study IT, RE, PE, PSHE.) Some career-oriented options, too, such as business studies and BTec in health and social care.

Teachers (including quite a few men) are enthusiastic, professional and popular. 'The teachers are really nice and you always feel comfortable going to ask for help' was a refrain heard repeatedly from girls across the age range.

Maths taught in sets from year 7 and maths and science (which came in for particularly criticism in 2014) are definitely on the up, with Ofsted praising the improvement for the middle ground. Not all parents, however, are entirely convinced by the transition arrangements. 'There has been a high turnover of maths teachers,' said one. 'My daughter finds that quite difficult as every teacher has a particular way of explaining things. Sometimes, she's just given worksheets and left to do them.' Science taught in a range of well-equipped labs, but no pressure to take all three (biology, physics, chemistry) to GCSE. 'You can go on to do medicine or science with double award,' said one teacher, 'so we generally only encourage those who really like science to do three.'

All start Spanish in year 7 and top-set linguists take up French in year 8 (with the option to continue with two languages to GCSE). Official praise for English, humanities and drama at GCSE, and DT gets the thumbs up from pupils – with girls enjoying the wide-ranging subject matter, which includes food ('I've just learnt how to cook a quiche,' said one enthusiast, 'and I'm going home to make another tonight'), metalwork, textiles and woodwork. Girls seem to flourish in what is often considered masculine terrain, and, according to a teacher who has taught in both single sex and co-ed schools, comfortably take on tasks they might have shied away from elsewhere.

Widening range of post-GCSE options (26), including business studies, DT, drama, media studies, music tech, further maths, psychology, philosophy, government and politics, photography and sociology. Also now offers a BTec in health and social care. The Extended Project Qualification (EPQ), which universities welcome for the way it fosters research skills, has also been widely embraced, with most of those taking it gaining A*-A. Sixth form class sizes are small (often under 10) and girls get close personal supervision from a 'pastoral mentor', a specialist in one of their chosen subjects. Good careers and university advice (including for Oxbridge and international options, though currently not many heading in these directions.)

Well-resourced facilities for SEN with dedicated space and well-targeted support overseen by a SENCo and senior learning mentor. 'My daughter was struggling in English and I found the school very pro-active,' said one mother. 'They identified her problem and gave her extra help, which not only improved her work but boosted her confidence.'

Games, options, the arts: Extracurricular as well as curricular drama highly popular, with girls auditioning enthusiastically for speaking parts or stage management roles in the annual production (recently Peter Pan). Art and textiles demonstrate imagination and skill, and broad range of in-lunch and after-school clubs provide additional opportunities for sports fans (netball, boot camp, hockey, yoga, football), budding intellectuals (Reading the Classics, Scrabble) and creatives (LAMDA, jazz band, fashion show club and film club). ' I have decided to work in film,' announced one year 9, who'd recently launched her debut work. Excellent facilities for sport, with large on-site pool and gym, eight tennis courts and ample grounds for running around (or simply lounging). Teams and individuals compete at borough and county level, performing particularly well in athletics. Variety of choirs, orchestra and bands (jazz, drumming, guitar, etc). Good range of trips and visits (PE to the Alps, English to Copenhagen, modern foreign languages to Spain) and all take part in an enrichment programme and work experience in year 12. Well-stocked library staffed by knowledgeable librarians. (Popular Accelerated Reader Scheme encourages reading more and reading more broadly.) Confidence also boosted by participation in the Jack Petchey's Speak Out Challenge.

Background and atmosphere: QE Girls traces its roots back to Elizabeth 1, when Robert Dudley, Earl of Leicester, requested a charter for 'the education, bringing up and instruction' of boys, and – at a future date – a school for girls. The boys' school was founded in 1573, the girls had to wait until 1888, when a small school of just 40 girls was eventually opened. Once a grammar school, the school went comprehensive in 1973.

One of the oldest girls' state schools in the country, it still enjoys the county council-funded building of 1909, but this has now been joined by a myriad of later additions (many erected in the 60s), plus general updating, replacing (after a fire), and extending to adapt to increasing numbers and new requirements. Very good facilities include an array of well-equipped science labs, technology rooms, drama studio, sixth form common room, spacious dining hall (with attractive views, outdoor snack bar and the latest thumbprint technology for cashless payment). The beautiful and extensive gardens are also a definite asset. Sixth formers have their own common room and silent study centre in the library.

Pastoral care, well-being and discipline: The school's stated goals are: to produce confident, independent, self-disciplined and considerate young women in an atmosphere that is calm, careful and purposeful, and they seem to be well on the way to delivering this outcome. In general, pupils are keen, articulate and poised. Though there will always be the odd disruptive force (and the odd exclusion), in general girls are well behaved and well mannered. 'I watch them going in and coming out,' said one parent. 'They always seem very well behaved, with teachers standing by to make sure they are.' Guidelines on behaviour are now firmer ('It's much stricter than it used to be,' commented one girl) but certainly not draconian. 'They let parents know if there's an issue, but they're not heavy handed about it.' Girls seem to enjoy the school very much and have excellent relationships with each other and teachers. For many parents – and girls – the fact that it is single sex is also a definite plus. 'No annoying boys, ' said one pupil succinctly.

Plenty of leadership roles in the sixth form (head girl, two deputies, designated senior prefects for student council, charity, sport, library, sustainability). Sixth formers also mentor younger girls, running clubs, supporting in lessons and acting as reading mentors, which provides a strong sense of cohesion across the school. The head is also a firm believer in preparing girls for the world of work, and as well as her own involvement with Women of the Future Ambassadors programme, ensures pupils have the opportunity to attend networking events with high-achieving women.

Pupils and parents: QE Girls sits in a leafy, primarily middle-class commuter suburb, and its intake is a fair reflection of its surroundings (though it also addresses the needs of a large nearby estate). This is north London, of course, so a rich ethnic mix, with school and parents celebrating diversity. 'For me, one of its main attractions is that there are people from all walks of life,' said one mother. Parents generally attentive and involved, with an energetic PTA organising a regular calendar of quiz nights, raffles, etc. Former pupils include Jane Duncan, president of the RIBA, singer Phildel, actress Stephanie Beacham and writer Anne Thwaite.

Entrance: A non-selective comprehensive, oversubscribed by about three to one at 11, when 180 girls are admitted using Barnet's 'community' criteria (looked-after children, then siblings, then distance from the gates). Very much a local school, many parents choose it because of its 'walkability', though transport links are also excellent with the tube just a minute away. Sixth-form admits a maximum of 25 new students depending on subject availability (and a GCSE point average of 5.5).

Exit: About half of those who enter at 11 proceed to the sixth form, often declaring how comfortable and happy they feel at the school. At that point, the rest tend to float off to co-ed comps and sixth-form colleges (Fortismere, Barnet College, etc). Virtually all those who remain gain entry to their first or second choice university. About a third to Russell Group, the rest to the full spectrum of higher education. (Popular destinations include: King's London, Brunel, Essex, Bristol, Leeds, University of Hertfordshire.)

Encouragingly broad range of subject choice, too, from aerospace engineering, marine biology and mechanical engineering, to economics, law, graphic design and optometry. One medic and one vet in 2018. A few to high-level apprenticeships.

Money matters: Funds from the original endowment still benefit the school, providing financial aid for those who could not otherwise afford it to participate in activities and support for small capital projects (such as the 2016 Upper Courtyard redevelopment). PTA-raised funds (£10 a month is politely suggested) contribute to desirable extras like school minibuses, picnic areas in the grounds and ICT equipment.

Remarks: A relaxed, safe and friendly place, now with a firm hand on the tiller and rocketing results.

Queen Elizabeth's School, Barnet

Queen's Road, Barnet, Hertfordshire EN5 4DQ

Ages 11–18 **Pupils** 1,235 **Sixth form** 310

020 8441 4646
www.qebarnet.co.uk

Headmaster: Since 2011, Neil Enright MA (Oxon) MBA NPQH FRSA (40). Educated at St John's College, Oxford, and has worked here since 2002, rising to become head of department (humanities – a geographer), head of year, deputy head. MBA in 2010 from the University of London Institute of Education, which focused on aspects of leadership, management and systems of effective learning.

Gives a knuckle-crunching handshake and oozes authority, but is cordial, jovial and empathetic. Pupils admit they sit or stand up that bit straighter when he's around, 'but more because we want to impress him than assuming we'll be told off.' Tellingly, one of the first things he did was put a huge glass window between his (more company boardroom than headmasterly) office and the corridor, with pupils encouraged to drop in with any concerns. Although not a timetabled teacher ('the demands of my job don't allow it'), he takes geography lessons across all year groups when he can.

Q

Converses easily with the boys, always eats in the dining hall at lunchtimes, attends every school event and has even been known to hang around at the bus stop after school to chat. Runs a very tight ship, with a well distributed leadership model. Areas of focus include driving innovation in the classroom and pastoral care.

Academic matters: Consistently top of the academic league tables, rivalling most schools, independent or state, in its exam results. Baseline assessment in year 7, then setting in all subjects (including sport), with half-termly tests thereafter. Testing very much part of the modus operandi. Many parents put off applying for fear of the stress (one parent told us she took her son out because 'the pressure was just too much'), but the school has heaps of motivational mechanisms in place, including personal tutors, who they see twice a day in groups, as well as having a one-to-one sessions every half term. Coaching and mentoring (including peer mentoring) also the norm. 'I arrived with good grades, but was a bit of a slacker, and the school soon sorted me out,' one pupil told us. Others talk about being 'carried along with the collective will to learn.' It also helps that hard grafting is admired, said another parent. 'In a lot of schools, you get teased for trying, but nobody's called a geek here. In fact, they somehow turn it around so that the boys look up to each other and respect others for trying hard in something, whether it's their subject or not.'

In 2018, 91 per cent 9-7 grades. Languages popular, with all pupils taking French, German and Latin from year 7 and continuing one modern language (at least) at GCSE, with Mandarin, Spanish and ancient Greek offered as extras. First school to become 100 per cent EBacc. A level choices are decided by tests in years 10 and 11 designed 'to tease out' aptitude. 'We don't rate GSCE results as a good enough indicator,' explains head. Seventy per cent of boys do four A levels, most get four A*/A grades (83 per cent of grades were A*/A in 2018); only a handful don't take maths, two-thirds take at least one science, many do a mix. No fluffy options whatsoever.

Strong teaching, with good gender balance, in every department. 'They go well beyond the syllabus and really care about you enjoying the subject and doing well,' said one pupil, with boys particularly enthusiastic about geography and history. 'Every lesson aims to push these boys up to their ceiling, which is made easier when there's such a narrow ability range,' says head. Boys say healthy competition pervades the classroom as much as the sports field, but there's plenty of group work, with many classes we visited organised with desks in clusters rather than in neat rows. Class sizes around 30, dropping to 15 at A level. Lots of homework (one and a half hours in year 7, one hour per subject per night at A level). Technology embedded in lessons, but not much use of tablets.

Enrichment throughout, with boys regularly taken off curriculum, and extra-long lunch breaks allowing for the myriad of clubs that also run before and after school (favourites include public speaking, karate and sports). Some clubs pupil-led, including an impressive politics one, with recent guest speakers including Vince Cable and Alistair Campbell. An expectation to do the Extended Project Qualification, with subjects ranging from photography to ancient history. Big push on symposia with high-performing girls' schools, including Henrietta Barnett, St Albans High School and North London Collegiate. 'Whilst there are huge benefits to boys learning in an all-male environment, boys also need to be able to work with young women,' says head.

Special needs at this school tends to be on the gifted-and-talented end of the spectrum, although school can accommodate mild autism, Asperger's and dyslexia and every department runs subject-specific clinics to support the struggling and challenge the most able. 'Because difference tends to be celebrated at this school, and the learning is so tailored anyway, our son's special needs have really been a non-issue in terms of his education,' said one parent.

Games, options, the arts: Rugby by far the strongest sport, with all participating in year 7. Fixtures list includes all major independent schools in the region. England under-16 head coach coaches the rugby squad and the school fields up to D teams on a regular basis. Rugby 7s has also been running since 1976, with school playing against 64 others, including Eton. Swimming, Eton fives, tennis, badminton, basketball, cross-country and fencing also popular. Plenty of county and national representation in bridge, chess and water polo. Eight-lane swimming pool, all-weather tennis courts, multi-gym and plenty of neatly trimmed green fields for team sports. But it's no big deal not to have sporting prowess in the obvious options, say students. 'I didn't like any of them, but have found I really do like tennis and swimming,' said one old boy.

Music department boasts three full-time music teachers, 17 peripatetic teachers and a music suite where boys can study A level music technology with all the latest recording equipment. Particularly strong orchestra and choir, both of which are open to all, plus chamber choir and ensembles, including Indian music, which boys run themselves.

Notable visual arts facilities, all open-plan, light and airy, with exceptional examples of mostly abstract work displayed throughout the school, including some choice pieces adoring the head's smart office. DT boasts all the latest equipment, with one pupil designing and making his own drone when we visited. Generally an academic attitude towards art, with many pupils interested in pursuing architecture.

Whole school drama performances take place in Shirley Hall, which has a decent sized stage and 400 drop-down seats (otherwise flat against wall when the hall is used for low-impact sports). New spacious food technology facility.

Name a country and there's probably been a trip there. Recent rugby tour to Sri Lanka, geography trips to Iceland, Switzerland and Sicily, music tours all over Europe, plus well-established language exchanges to Germany and France and set trips to battlefields, among others. Head keen that it's not always the same boys benefiting, either due to cost or ability.

Background and atmosphere: Plenty of visual reminders around the school that it was founded in 1573 by Robert, Earl of Leicester, with a charter from Elizabeth I. Rebuilt in 1932 by Hertfordshire County Council in a noble civic style with terrazzo flooring, parquet and panelling, all kept in spotless condition. Still well-endowed with land held in perpetuity and its own Foundation Trustees, QE went comprehensive in the '60s, reverted to grant-maintained status in 1989 and became a grammar school once more in 1994.

Atmosphere is ordered, focused and positive and even at break times, there's no casual loitering. At lunchtime, for example, boys wolf down their lunch so they can fit in football or other activities before attending a lunchtime club. Meanwhile, in class, boys are absorbed and single-minded. You'll find no low-level disruption here.

Leadership responsibilities from year 11, when own suits are allowed. Ninety prefects voted for by staff and students, monitor lunch (fresh food produced daily), playgrounds and classrooms. School captain and house captains appointed from on high. Student voice heard through pupil conferences. Boys also involved in appointing new staff by attending a class, then giving feedback.

A 15-year estate strategy means there are always plans in place around buildings. Among the newest additions is a spacious new library, with 100 computer terminals and 15,000 books when we visited. 'When other school librarians tell me they struggle attracting pupils in their library, I'm amazed,' the librarian told us. 'Ours is so popular that we practically have to fend them off at lunchtimes.'

Café 1573 provides a Starbucks-like environment for sixth formers, whilst other years frequent the dining hall, a modern space also with its own branding and colour scheme. School even has its own (cashless) shop, selling everything from uniforms (much lower cost than in shops) to pens, with all profits ploughed back into the school.

'Pupil progression' (broader and less vocational than careers advice) embedded throughout, whilst loyal old boys come back to chat to sixth formers about university and subject choice. Some act as Oxbridge buddies for the next generation. Big programme of volunteering, with all sixth formers expected to do 40 hours over the school year (although most do much more), including working in libraries, charity shops, hospices, charity shops and even supporting the local MP's surgery.

Pastoral care, well-being and discipline: Pastoral care mainly from form teachers, and a real strength of the school's provision. Motivation comes from a plethora of rewards and praise, including house points, certificates, merit stickers (for younger boys), congratulatory emails and postcards sent home to parents, showcasing of achievements on the website and 'good notes' in the diary which must be signed off by parents (there are 'bad notes' too for offences such as persistent failure to meet deadlines, but these are far less frequent). Plenty of silverware prominently displayed to remind pupils of the school's achievements.

No real misbehaviour to speak of – pupils have good manners, wear their uniform well, and do their work when asked. Head puts it down to clear expectations, a strong sense of discipline that feels natural rather than forced, and rewards. 'Not the kind of school for boys who don't like taking orders or challenging the system,' said one parent. Indeed, there are fixed-term exclusions for persistent 'failure to carry out school protocols' or misbehaving in lessons and head says he would expel a boy on the spot for offences including violence aimed at staff, consciously creating racial disharmony or bringing drugs into school, although no boy has been expelled in his time. 'We make absolutely no exceptions and that message is very clear,' he says.

Pupils and parents: Contrary to popular opinion, this school is not full of middle-class families. Ofsted noted it's the national average in terms of deprivation, with quite a few boys in receipt of pupil premium. 'We take great pride in the fact that the school is a complete meritocracy,' says head. 'There is absolutely no other means of gaining admission than doing well in the test for maths and English.' Over 80 per cent of boys come from ethnic minorities, predominantly Asian. Around half speak English as a second language, although they're advanced bilingual learners and generally only need help with areas like idiom and inference, which the school happily provides. Many of the boys who make it to Oxbridge are the first generation in their family to go to university, and in recent years one was a refugee from Rwanda. Majority travel from London borough of Barnet, although there are boys from all over north west London and the surrounding home counties, who are served by good public transport links and a nine-strong coach system facilitated by the school. Pupils are quietly confident, grounded, polite and exude intelligence.

Parents are considered as key partners of the school, regularly communicated with via pupils' diaries, live reporting on the website and emails. 'I've never experienced a parents' association like it,' adds head of Friends of Queen Elizabeth, with parents doing everything from providing work experience and mock interviews to giving lectures, supporting concerts and fundraising. 'The annual Founders' Day Fete raises up to £25,000 and has parents taking the day off work the Friday before to help prepare,' says head, although a couple of parents told us it's 'unfortunately the same old faces that tend to help.'

Entrance: More than 2,300 boys apply for 180 places. Tests in September (register between May and mid-July), which although tough are made as comfortable as possible, with year 9s present to put applicants at ease, 'including playing hangman'. Boys told whether or not they have met the 'standard required' before they have to make their choice of schools, so they have nothing to lose by taking the test. NB Meeting the 'standard required' does not guarantee a place. Pupils come from around 90 primary schools, but the ability range is narrow, with most in the top 10 per cent nationally. Occasional vacancies between years 7 and 10, offered to those on the waiting list. No sixth form entry for external candidates. 'I see this as a seven-year education,' says head, who adds that he's seen too many schools that take external sixth formers essentially run as two separate schools. Automatic transfer to sixth form for nearly all students, although pupils have to be recommended for individual subjects.

Exit: Up to 10 per cent of boys leave after GCSE. Reasons include not making the grade; preferring a mixed sixth form; hankering after a more relaxed environment; looking for subjects the school doesn't teach, such as law and psychology; or winning scholarships to independent schools (although that's rare – most families pick this school over the private sector). Almost all who stay go on to top Russell Group universities, notably Nottingham, Imperial, UCL and Warwick. In 2018, 28 to Oxbridge, and 19 off to study medicine, plus one veterinary medicine. Other typical subjects include economics, law and engineering. First-rate UCAS guidance provided to all boys.

Money matters: You wouldn't know it, walking around the school, but there's minimal state aid, with head saying he gets less money than many local comps. Gaps are filled with a voluntary £60 a month contribution from parents, funds from the Foundation and donations from parents, old boys and friends.

Remarks: A remarkable school that offers the top 10 per cent of learners from a diversity of backgrounds an exceptional and rounded education that even private schools struggle to compete with. Not for boys who may want to challenge the status quo, nor for the non-competitive. But for those who thrive in a highly ordered, hard grafting environment with an underlying sense of competition across all subjects, this is a great school that consistently turns out responsible young men with unbounded opportunities to succeed at university and their chosen careers beyond.

The Queen's CofE Primary School

Cumberland Road, Kew, Richmond, Surrey TW9 3HJ

Ages 4–11 **Pupils** 417 **C of E**

Q

020 8940 3580
www.queens.richmond.sch.uk

Headteacher: Since 2011, Katie Bentham (30s). Trained at Bishop Grosseteste College in Lincoln, part of the University of Hull. Began her career in London, at St Mary Magdalene C of E Primary in Westminster and Newbury Park Primary in Redbridge, where she also gained a masters in science education. Relocated to Scotland for her next job at Westfield Primary in Cumbernauld, then back to London and Marshgate Primary in Richmond, where she was the SENCo and part of senior management. Queen's is her first headship, and she was parachuted in after what appears to have been a bit of a hiccup with the previous incumbent. Our impression is of a pleasant and energetic lady who is working with a steely determination that has recently been rewarded with a coveted Ofsted Outstanding. The parents we spoke to hadn't met her in person, but, said one mother, 'The children feel they know her, and when they're at home they even refer to her as Katie!' (Head adamant that this doesn't happen in school.) 'Not afraid to make changes,' was one parent's verdict. 'Miss Bentham's great!' pupils confirmed to us, eagerly.

Entrance: Two-form entry, so 60 reception places each year. Usual admissions criteria: looked after children, medical needs, siblings. Thereafter, at least one parent must be a 'committed and regular worshipper' at one of the three Kew Anglican churches (St Anne's, St Philip & All Saints', St Luke's); after that, it's down to proximity. Rather convoluted – if in doubt, contact the school office. School is oversubscribed, but not dishearteningly so. Also worth applying further up, as much of the Kew community is professional and mobile, and occasional places do become available.

Exit: As you'd expect in this locality, a high number of private and grammar school places every year: Latymer Upper, Hampton, Lady Eleanor Holles, Tiffin, Kingston. Popular non-selective state school destinations include Christ's, Waldegrave, Sir Richard Reynolds and Richmond Park Academy. As with other state primaries, school doesn't prepare for 11 plus, and parents report that a fair degree of private tutoring goes on in the upper year groups. The children, however, were inclined to attribute their success to the school. 'It's really, really helped me get into the school I'm into,' said one engaging year 6 lad, who could have passed for Benedict Cumberbatch in his young days.

Remarks: Queen's is sited a stone's-throw from Kew village, which inevitably accounts for some of the school's character. As far as we could tell, this was a London-accent-free zone, and all the pupils we met were chirpy, well-spoken, well-mannered and quite delightful. We suspect that there isn't huge social diversity, and we saw very little cultural diversity as we looked round the lunch time crowds. (School says that it has above the national average number of pupils from ethnic minority groups.) But that said, the school works tirelessly to give the best school experience possible to its students, and clearly succeeds. Parents were incredibly warm in their praise, with the school's kind and friendly ethos mentioned again and again: 'A very positive culture of caring'; 'My two children love it there, they go happily every day'; 'The outstanding thing has been the care from all the staff'; 'The great strengths of the school are the atmosphere and the teachers, who are of a high quality and very dedicated'; 'A very friendly, inclusive environment'; 'Gentle and positive'; 'All the staff care about every child'. The children unanimously confirmed this. 'Is it friendly here?' we asked as we moved about the school, and group after group gave us an instant and emphatic 'YES!'

The Anglican faith is central to the school's ethos, and plays a greater part here than we've seen in any other C of E primary school. Fathers Nigel and Peter from St Anne's and St Luke's take assemblies every week, there's a Passion Play every year complete with crucifixion scene, and attendance at church services is regular and frequent: when we visited, for instance, the whole school had just returned from Ascension Day service. Even competitions can be devotional in nature, with the winning entries in the Easter Crosses competition making a colourful display on the school's website. But there was nothing dour about any of it, and the children impressed us with their cheerful and confident benevolence towards life, the universe and everything. There was also a happy awareness of other faiths, and visits to a synagogue and a mosque had been followed up with some lovely work.

The standard of writing and maths that we saw was very high, and Queen's academic record is sterling: most children here achieve well above the national average, with a number of them successfully taking the level 6 tests (a pass at level 6 is expected of the average 14-year-old). Robust systems of monitoring are in place to make sure that children's performance is being tracked. One parent criticised the 'large and ill-defined projects' set for homework and felt that the school didn't do enough to push the children to do as well as they possibly could; whilst another, conversely, felt that the school put too much emphasis on getting the children to perform 'excessively' well in their Sats. The majority, however, said they were contented with the academic provision. 'Very good academic results achieved without extra pressure on the students', and 'an excellent academic environment' were typical comments. There are bang-up-to-date interactive whiteboards in every classroom, an attractive library and excellent, well-thumbed resources. SEN provision was 'not in the best place when I joined' according to the head, but both she and the SENCo have worked hard to bring it up to scratch, and we liked what we saw of the provision in this area.

Popular breakfast and after-school clubs are welcomed by working parents, and there's a lively programme of extracurricular activities, with music being a particular strength. Despite its small size, the school fields two orchestras and two choirs, and a wide variety of instrumental lessons are offered. 'The concerts are brilliant!' enthused one parent. 'Every time you go into school your hear children singing or playing music!' Views on the sports provision were a little cooler, with many parents and pupils (boys in particular) wishing there were more, but everyone agreed that it was getting better, with a large new Astroturf, and there was much praise for a recent cricket tournament. The head insists that the amount of sport at Queen's has 'dramatically increased' over the past year, and two swimming trophies in her office bore testimony to sports being 'one of our vision priorities.'

Queen's is the only school in the country to change its name according to the gender of the reigning monarch – it was The King's School until 1953 – and is held in warm regard locally. A recent alumni evening was well attended and produced some misty-eyed comments in the visitors' book. But there's no question of things standing still. These are clearly exciting times for a school that has much to be proud of.

Queen's College London

Linked with Queen's College Prep School

43-49 Harley Street, London W1G 8BT

Ages 11-18 **Pupils** 380 **Sixth form** 97 **C of E**

Fees: £19,125 pa

020 7291 7000
www.qcl.org.uk

Principal: Since 2017, Richard Tillett (40s), former deputy head at Harrogate Ladies' College. Degree in modern languages and history from Cambridge. Driven by altruism from a young age, says he knew from the get go the City or corporate life wasn't for him, so eschewed the milk round corporates and joined the health service training scheme, specialising in mental health. Disillusioned by bureaucracy, gained his PGCE from Sussex and hasn't looked back. Taught history and politics at King Edward VI Grammar and was housemaster and history teacher at The Leys before joining Harrogate Ladies' in 2010 as head of sixth form.

Wife and daughter remain in North Yorkshire from where he commutes weekly. So what drew him to QCL from so far afield for his first headship? 'Just a brilliant fit', he says. 'I was struck by its extraordinary history and values – it's a school where the default position is to be kind'. Says pastoral care is 'absolutely the most important thing', and parents concur that this key cornerstone of Queen's hasn't wavered on his watch. Fans of former head (even the 'sexist' ones hoping for another strong female role model) have not been disappointed with his arrival, describing him in a flurry of superlatives: 'amazing', 'fantastic' and 'such a character'. Keeps his hand in teaching A level politics and has seized his predecessor's baton of believing that 'girls are able to do anything'. Had to manoeuvre his way through some awkward and unpleasant situations with some troublesome junior pupils early in his tenure, a situation that resulted in a handful of departures, but parents on the inside tell us 'things were dealt with pretty quickly' and the ship has stabilised now. Has made some major positive strides in changing sixth form curriculum to bring it in line with his vision: 'to prepare Queen's girls for the uncertainty of the future.' This on top of a whole school assembly to kick off every week and the introduction of a new house system. Next up will be to face the challenge of stabilising a formerly high staff turnover – we'll watch with interest. Mastermind specialist subject would be either Russian history (he's a Russian speaker) or Arsenal FC. Avid follower of football and cricket, cellist and lover of travel, good food and hill walking.

Academic matters: Not top of the academic heap in the London girls' day school scene but on the up and now giving local rivals Channing, South Hampstead High and Francis Holland a real run for their money – matching or outperforming them on results day. 'Academics are now largely where we want them to be', says head; 2018 saw school achieve its best ever results, with 57 per cent A*/A at A level and 89 per cent A*-B. Head has axed girls taking a fourth or half A level (apart from in exceptional cases or for those taking further maths) in favour of a standard three A levels plus EPQ for all. Broad range of subjects at A level, with 'totally flexible' timetabling making unusual combinations possible. English takes the popularity prize followed closely by history and religious studies, all with top results. Sciences and further maths less so, particularly physics, and stellar grades less prevalent in these departments. Languages also niche at A level despite strong provision in KS3 with Mandarin, Spanish, French and Italian all offered in year 7. Top Latin set introduced to ancient Greek in year 9 – also available at GCSE with a small take up.

Don't expect your year 7 daughter to be thrust into an academic frenzy on arrival – those at the top of their prep school might find themselves freewheeling at first. The approach is 'softly softly', say parents, with academic focus gently ramping up as girls progress through the school. Ten GCSEs is the default, with respectable results: 42 per cent graded A*/9-8 in 2018 and 71 per cent A*-A/9-7. Girls now take the robust IGCSE in almost all academic subjects (exceptions are Latin, RS and Italian), with no obvious areas of weakness. Computing GCSE newly introduced. 'Results are going up precisely because we are not a robotic exam factory,' says head, and girls concur, reporting the secret of their most recent exam success (aside from the 'unstuffy' teachers who are 'very generous' with their time) as 'being there for each other'. Parents 'not surprised' by good results pouring out of 'an environment with such a tremendous amount of respect that makes girls feel so comfortable.'

Three form entry into year 7 with a maximum of 22 per form makes for an intimate feel where 'all staff know who your child is'. We heard mutters, but only from one or two parents, about a 'lack of focus' on reading. Newly appointed director of teaching and learning now facilitates good practice and innovation amongst teaching staff. New Firefly platform not only allows staff to set online homework but also provides access to class materials and enrichment activities for pupils as well as showcasing best examples of work.

One 'talented' SENCo in situ and there are some 65 girls with diagnosed SpLD on the register as well as another 25 or so with undiagnosed needs. Approach to support is absolutely 'can do' and 'totally inclusive' with minimal withdrawal from classes – never from curriculum subjects. Most is included in fees and there's a collaborative approach with the pastoral team. School has experience dealing with dyslexia, dyspraxia and dyscalculia plus ADHD / ADD, visual impairment and anxiety disorders; 'girls who might be isolated in other schools are not, here'. Some of site is wheelchair accessible and, if necessary, timetabling would be managed to cater for pupils with mobility issues. No EAL students at the time of our visit but we were assured it was all doable.

Games, options, the arts: With its central London location, tiny (albeit charming) outdoor courtyard and subterranean gymnasium, we wondered whether Queen's could possibly be a good fit for super sporty girls. Parents of girls in upper years say 'definitely not', but since the recent appointment of a 'wonderful' new head of sport and the decision to stop marching girls to substandard facilities in Regents Park and instead transport them by 'nice warm coach' to the all singing, all dancing Paddington Rec, we think it's worth a second look. Thanks to access to these facilities, hockey and athletics are now available, as well as netball, football (coached by a former pro), tag rugby, lacrosse and cricket, played at nearby Lord's; school assures us that new pupils are 'assured an amazing sporting experience'. PE teachers run clubs almost every evening and there are fixtures aplenty for those that want them, with A and B teams plus a development squad for all sports – although success depends on the year group ('it's work in progress', says school). Sixth formers now have compulsory games sessions with broader options and are able to use the gym at Paddington. Their Wednesday afternoons are spent either taking part in work experience or charity initiatives in the local community.

Dance, on curriculum in years 7 to 9, has been 'revolutionised' by 'amazing' new hires who are inspiring girls with Fosse, African and tap in addition to more traditional dance forms. The annual dance show is 'on another level', say parents. Swimming takes place at Marshall Street Leisure Centre. On curriculum to year 9 and available at both GCSE and A level, with good take up at both levels, drama also 'massively ramped up' following arrival of another new, buzzy departmental head. Tons of opportunities to perform: at the time of our visit productions in rehearsal included Jane Eyre, Cinderella (panto version) and various pieces for the approaching house drama competition. There's also an academic drama showcase each year, up to 40 girls taking the Trinity Board certificates, a plethora of lunch time clubs to cater for thespian inclinations plus chances to collaborate with boys' schools on their dramatic endeavours – recently The History Boys with Harrow and Frankenstein with Wetherby. Music also flying high and yes, you guessed it, there's a super new director of music (with a passion for jazz) at the helm. Ensembles and choirs galore perform everything from classical and jazz to pop at the major concerts at the end of each term and informal half termly performances. School orchestra comprises pupils from grade 3 to diploma level, with sixth formers happily presiding over rehearsals if needed. School is well connected to both Wigmore Hall and the Royal Albert Hall to see professionals at work and there are applications most years to both the Royal Academy and Royal College of Music. Carols take place at All Souls Church in Langham Place, jazz musicians join their male counterparts as part of Harrow's big hand and there are plans to stage a collaborative performance with the Royal Philharmonic Orchestra at Cadogan Hall to celebrate QCL's 170th anniversary.

Background and atmosphere: Founded in 1848 and given a royal charter in 1853, the first institution in Great Britain to give academic qualifications to girls. Still on its original site spanning four elegant, well-proportioned Georgian houses – and so discreet you barely notice it amongst the neighbouring smart doctors' consulting rooms – it has been altered through the years to provide a well-equipped, modern learning environment whilst maintaining its historic charm. The William Morris wallpaper decorating the ground floor corridor – tastefully toning in with the teal sweater worn by girls in 'the school' (years 7-9) – together with the high ceilings, large windows and sweeping staircases, speaks volumes about the school's style. A warren of charming nooks, crannies and staircases hang all the facilities together; charming oak panelled libraries with light streaming in cater for different age groups and we loved the 'fish bowl' IT suite with its incongruously futuristic feel. Classrooms not the largest or most modern we've seen and the labs could certainly do with a face lift (although the lessons we observed were lively, interactive and looked huge fun), but they all do the job adequately. The multi- purpose school hall ticks all the boxes with its smart lighting rig, and an unexpected delight is the beautiful, modern sixth form centre – a largely glazed roof extension – reached via a lift that whisks the eldest girls up to a serene sanctuary of their own.

The overall vibe is one of intimacy and acceptance and although it no longer has the 'wild west' vibe of its past, there's definitely more than a sniff of freedom. Pupils of all age groups smile and greet one another in the hallways, there's certainly no feeling of social boundaries hampered by hierarchy and 'community' is a word that comes up time and again in conversations, the oldest girls saying that they are seeking out the same feeling in their university destination choices. Individuality is a theme too; the uniform – although under scrutiny by new head who is keen to keep things smart(ish) – is pretty casual; girls in years 10 and 11 (junior college) wear school white shirt and blue jumper but can choose their own bottom half (apparently brightly coloured and patterned trousers are in, black leggings are out). Sixth formers are free to wear their own clothes, and fashion statements such as blue or pink hair are allowed and not unusual; 'girls are allowed to be eccentric', say parents. Different sexualities and gender identities are embraced and supported. Parents say there's 'quite a feminist' culture – 'it's all about finding out what you're into and encouraging it'.

Pastoral care, well-being and discipline: Pastoral care a key strength of school, parents uniformly telling us it's 'really kind' and 'feels like a family'. Pupils love the 'cosiness' and 'old fashioned nature' of the school, with many telling us it was love at first sight when they walked through the doors on their first visit and describing it as 'relaxed' and 'non-judgemental'. Year heads and form tutors oversee the development of each girl with a head of section above them to step in on major issues as required. 'Staff talk to each other and join the dots,' parents told us. New school counsellor available by appointment one day a week. Disciplinary issues seem to be few and far between – perhaps because of the relatively relaxed vibe, there's no need to push boundaries with silly transgressions.

'Big sister, little sister' scheme has been enhanced to add a 'middle sister' so the younger party doesn't feel bereft when the eldest leaves the school. Years 10 and 11 are trained to mentor younger girls in relation to responsible internet use: 'they're the experts', says school. Pupils feel very well supported and the ethos is very much about helping them overcome mistakes within a safe environment. Even bullying is dealt with in the most humane way possible – despite zero tolerance policy, we were told that 'a happy child doesn't bully, so we give them support too'. New house system seems to be a good addition (although head admits it hasn't all been plain sailing) and girls, although initially reluctant to throw themselves into house events and competitions, admit to enjoying them all. Years 7 to 9 hand phones in when they arrive at school in the morning.

Pupils and parents: Tiger mums move along please – Queen's parents describe their girls as 'happy go lucky...perhaps that's why they do well'. Head says parents 'trust us to get on with it', although parents say school does like them to be involved, not that they need much enticing into school, with information meetings generally turning into jolly social occasions. We are assured that 'wealthy, spoilt girls are few and far between' these days and we felt no sense of entitlement amongst the sincere, ambitious and personable young women we met on our visit. 'Really varied' parent body according to head – plenty in academia as well as the creative industries and almost never flashy. Reflective of modern central London, many have international backgrounds and although the majority were born in the UK, around 40 different languages are spoken at home. Majority from quite nearby – Notting Hill, Belsize Park and St John's Wood – although we also met girls from as far afield as Harrow and Hackney. With such excellent transport links the majority travel to and from school by tube. Former pupils include Amber Rudd and Emma Freud; 'Queen's girls are interesting people', say parents.

Entrance: No automatic entrance from Queen's College Prep but a good percentage come from there. Otherwise over 40 different feeder schools, with up to a quarter from local state primaries. Mainly into year 7 via the London 11+ Consortium (formerly the North London Girls' Schools Consortium). Now a bespoke cognitive ability test (maths, VR and NVR), an 'imaginative interview experience' to explore candidates' skills, aptitudes and intellectual acuity and a common reference form for prep schools to detail wider contextual information on attitudes and character as well as academic performance. Some 500 applicants for 60 places. Unusually, everyone is interviewed before the exam. 'We like to form a picture of the child without seeing her test results.' Genuinely selective and looking for someone who is going to enjoy getting involved and seize the opportunities available. A handful join into sixth form; requirements are minimum of grades 6 or 7 in chosen A level subjects (although some subjects have own criteria) plus minimum grade 5 in maths and English and reference from current school.

Exit: Some 30 per cent leave after GCSEs, mostly to board or move into the state system. It isn't usual for girls to be asked to leave if GCSEs aren't up to scratch but school doesn't offer 'soft options' at A level so occasionally pupils do depart for this reason. Post A level leavers to a range of universities and colleges to read a vast array of subjects, from the trad academics to business related degrees in fashion or music. Russell Group universities feature heavily in the leavers' list, along with new universities, arts colleges and some overseas (there is a dedicated international university counsellor). In 2018, two to Oxbridge (education; theology and religion), two medics and one to Berklee, USA.

Money matters: Several means-tested bursaries available at 11+ and 16+, funded by the Old Queen's bursary trust fund – around 15 full and eight partial bursaries at the time of our visit. Academic, music and art scholarships, for up to 25 per cent of fees, for both internal and external candidates.

Remarks: Head is possibly the first we've met who claims to have drawn career inspiration from lavatory graffiti (albeit at Cambridge): 'work hard and be nice to people', it said, and to us that sums up Queen's. Proof that you don't have to be in a pressure cooker to get good results; solid academics, the arts, sport and tip top pastoral: 'it's all here for the taking', say parents. Dynamic new head and staff are moving things up a notch – we hope they all stay put. One to watch.

Queen's College Prep School

Linked with Queen's College London

61 Portland Place, London W1B 1QP

Ages 4–11 **Pupils** 225 **C of E**

Fees: £16,515 – £17,835 pa

020 7291 0660
www.qcps.org.uk

Headmistress: Since 2016, Emma Webb (40s) married to an ex-RAF officer with two children at school in Cheltenham. She read sociology and social policy at Royal Holloway whilst also working for British Airways, so more time at the grindstone than in the pub. After qualifying as a teacher and a spell in the state system and Davenies Prep, she followed her high flying husband to Saudi Arabia, where she spent 10 years, latterly as deputy head of primary at the huge, cutting edge British International School in Riyadh. A great tech fan, she is busy transforming the school systems from paper to screen and incentivising both staff and children. According to parents she has 'ironed out some of the idiosyncrasies' but 'maintained all of the best bits'.

Entrance: More put down at birth now for two classes in reception and although there is no active sibling policy, the head is confident that younger girls naturally follow their elders. The few occasional places higher up the school, almost all due to globe-trotting parents, are in high demand. This is a genuinely international school with parents who come from, literally, all over the world. A large percentage of parents work in the professions. Most of the girls live nearby, or at least north of Oxford Street, but a few come from Kensington or the City.

Exit: The head says that her ethos is to prepare girls for all schools and that she is direct with parents about the right school for their child. 'We advise parents on the school that we feel is best for their daughter rather than our results table.' She is also a fan of boarding and in the past girls have gone to Downe House, St Mary's Ascot and Wycombe Abbey, although none in 2018. In the main, parents either choose the usual London academic (often single sex) senior schools such as City of London, Godolphin & Latymer, South Hampstead or North London Collegiate or opt for the slightly less intense environment of Francis Holland (Regent's Park), Queen's Gate or Queen's College itself. The leavers win a fair number of scholarships, mostly to FHRP or Queen's College.

Remarks: Past the pointy hat of All Soul's Langham Place and the sexy art deco glamour of the BBC, you turn the corner into more sedate Portland Place, framing the distant trees of Regent's Park. Here, QCPS has some unlikely neighbours, including the decidedly odd couple of the People's Republic of China embassy and the openly hedonistic Quintessentially concierge company.

The hall is covered in imaginative artwork and you are immediately aware that you are in a busy school, even if some of the years are out on trips. The layout, spread over two original houses, is slightly confusing to an outsider as they are not joined on every floor but girls, scurrying purposefully, prove that it is no worry to them. The 19th century houses were designed for entertaining so the ceilings are high and the windows are large, at least until you reach the attic, but even there the seductively colourful and popular art room and the classrooms for year 6 are bright and airy. The dining room in the basement does strike chords of the 'downstairs' element of Upstairs, Downstairs but the classroom at the back escapes any gloom by opening onto an interior garden.

The tour de force is the brand spanking new STEM lab, paid for by parents, full of exciting labelled drawers and bins for pipettes and goggles as well as a row of startlingly clean, white lab coats embellished with the green school logo. Any budding scientist would have a field day in here and the head's enthusiasm suggests that she would love to join them, given half a chance.

The school was described by a parent as 'not a sausage factory', but EW is still keen to ensure that the academic standards attained by the girls gives them the widest choice of secondary education. She is particularly keen on maths and the sciences taking an equal place in the curriculum, along with the subjects more traditionally taught to girls: 'I want to encourage them to build bridges in ballet shoes', a comment that was endorsed by 'I waxed lyrical about the maths provision to my husband'. The sciences are condensed into two and a half of the three terms yearly higher up the school, allowing the pupils time to conduct an experimental project (not 100 per cent successful in the case of the irrigation of the vertical gardens on show).

Her enthusiasm for STEM has not allowed EW to neglect other subjects, with English teaching being praised as well as the introduction of Mandarin, Spanish and Italian as extracurricular options alongside French. The fact that none of the teaching staff left at the end of her first year is proof that they are all happy with the new hierarchies that she has established and certainly, on our visit, there was nothing but smiley faces. She has appointed a 'fab head of learning support' and believes that this is 'one of the highest impact hires' that she has made; parents would agree with her. Staff appear to handle the challenge of teaching a child with no English on arrival (provided it is at the lower end of the school) with absolutely no fuss and great success.

A major play for the creative arts is made at QCPS and Miss Rosy's Dance Academy plays a large part, with grateful London parents, casting around to entertain their children, remarking on how brilliant it is that she also runs holiday classes. The music department under the roof is noisy and enthusiastic, led by a teacher whom one parent described as 'magnificent' and, as he is South African, there is even the chance to play his native marimbas. As well as the slightly unconventional percussion-playing opportunities, there are the more usual events such as the Harvest Festival and nativity plays (a camel-based offering last year) in All Souls church, and annual musicals.

One of the head's targets is to increase the sports provision, in particular competitive sports – 'the single best change EW has made'. She has appointed a new head of sport and the offering is going to be widened to include current favourites such as cricket, now that scoring a century at Lords is open to all. Unfortunately, all inner London schools suffer from having little outside space and QCPS is no exception, the girls having to walk to the gardens at the end of the street to let off steam outside on non-sporting days.

At the beginning of the day an Early Birds breakfast club helps out over-stretched parents and after school ends, teachers run a variety of additional activities. External help is also summoned and your daughter can choose from a selection including coding, cooking, gardening, sign language and yoga. The food is alone in being given a low rating, despite a new catering manager and an attempt to move away from 'nursery food'.

EW is very much a new broom, which goes down well with current parents, one of them saying that 'the school has a more modern, professional feel' and that it is aiming to be 'a platinum brand in a competitive market'. This sounds as if the school's charm might be at risk, but we were persuaded that the head is simply trying to make it fit with the aspirations of modern London families.

Queen's Gate Junior School

Linked with Queen's Gate School

125-126 Queen's Gate, London SW7 5LE

Ages 4–11 **Pupils** 146

Fees: £18,510 pa

020 7761 0303
www.queensgate.org.uk

Director of the junior school: Since 2017, James Denchfield, previously head of lower school at Queen's Gate Senior. English and history degree from Goldsmiths College and PGCE from the Institute of Education. Taught English at schools in London and Norfolk before joining Queen's Gate Senior in 2009. The following year he became head of English, and has since progressed to head of remove then head of lower school. Has also worked with the North London Girls' Schools' Consortium (now the London 11+ Consortium), including helping to set the English paper.

His daughter was a pupil here; he also has a young son. He lives in south-west Hertfordshire, where he enjoys walking and bird watching.

Entrance: Around 100 applicants for each of the 23 places at reception. One 7+ competitive academic scholarship worth a third of the annual fees. Assessment morning with groups of 8-10 children given tasks and observed by the headmistress and other staff.

Exit: Around 90 per cent to the senior school. Rest to a range of good London schools and a few to boarding.

Remarks: A few doors down from the senior school and an equally discreet entrance belies the warmth, fun and productive activity that goes on here. Up to 23 tots in the first two years – each in a good sized room with teacher and two teaching assistants. Happy, absorbed children are relaxed and busy in rooms that are stimulating without being frantic. Some older classes quite noisy with a buzz of activity but everywhere, even the art room, is orderly and purposeful. Quiet, sustained work for the oldest girls, who would change nothing about the school save its lack of outdoors, and really like their friends. Rooms light and recently refurbished – and at a sensible temperature. Good sized hall – like the senior school, the old salon in grand architectural style. Good-sized library, well-used with a real, 'very hard-working' librarian shared with big sister school. Lots of multi-purpose spaces and facilities. Good IT suite.

Lots of music – choirs and an orchestra. Very lively art; we encountered Dragolina, an immense dragon being constructed for the coming Chinese New Year – and were glad to see good old-fashioned crayon work. Tastes of French, Spanish, German, Italian and Latin as the girls progress through the school. Fun, but some parents query the purpose: 'they really don't know any French at all when they go into the senior school'. Teaching of eg science done by senior school staff. By bus to sports facilities all over the place – ensures plenty of indoor and outdoor sports. Lots of lovely after-school clubs three days of the week – 'So hard to choose, Mummy!'

Parents happy. 'It's traditional, though things are livening up. It really suits my daughter.' Staff now mostly young and pretty international. We warmed to the sight of children spontaneously hugging their teachers (probably illegal!) A safe, cosy and well-structured start for your precious daughter. And once she's there, you could really forget about her education for the next 14 years and trust them to give her all she needs.

Queen's Gate School

Linked with Queen's Gate Junior School

133 Queen's Gate, London SW7 5LE

Ages 11–18 **Pupils** 410 **Sixth form** 100

Fees: £20,550 pa

020 7589 3587
www.queensgate.org.uk

Principal: Since 2006, Rosalynd Kamaryc BA MSc PGCE (50s). Petite, chic and with a lovely soft Irish voice, Mrs Kamaryc immediately comes across as the warm, calm and practical person to whom you'd want to entrust your precious daughter. A mathematician who still teaches – in her case, the bottom GCSE set. 'I just love teaching,' she says, and 'counts it a privilege to walk the school' once a day.

Mrs Kamaryc has an impressive pedigree, this being her second headship. She began teaching in Scotland and spent 10 years as head of Wykeham House School, Fareham – via Forest School and Woodbridge School. Parents enthuse: 'She gives terrific support to the girls,' we were told. 'She's extremely capable, a very safe pair of hands with a very clear vision for the school.' 'Very approachable though can seem a little shy.' Her catwalk walk at a school fashion show wowed everyone. 'She commands respect but she can kick up her heels too. She's fun.'

Academic matters: 'It punches above its weight academically,' one parent told us and the results bear this out. French, English, maths, art and geography shine brightly. Tiny sets at A level – often ones and twos – a rare privilege and at half the cost of the top tutorial companies. They will run an A level course with one pupil and don't ditch the subject – or its teacher – if it has no takers in a given year. Art and maths have biggest numbers. If a subject has more than seven takers they split the group. Some depts seen as better than others. 'English and history are very strong; art is amazing,' we heard repeatedly and 'though the teachers are all lovely, their actual teaching isn't always great – a little dull and uncreative sometimes.' But A level results are remarkable these days, 55 per cent A*/A, 79 per cent A*/B in 2018.

Good range of I/GCSE subjects for so small a school. Ancient history and classical civilisation, Latin and Greek, computing recently introduced and lots of modern languages, including Mandarin, available – and not just for native speakers. Good results in English, geography, French, drama, art – but no weaklings here (80 per cent A*-A/9-7 in 2018). 'We chose it,' said a parent, echoed by more, 'because it is not obsessed by exam results.' 'It's not a hoop-jumping school.'

School has 1.5 staff on learning support team – much praised. 'Incredible support for my daughter's mild dyslexia. Possibly not for much else,' thought a parent, and this is borne out by the head.

Games, options, the arts: Parents glow and when you make it to the loftily-situated art dept you understand why. The main studio entrance is festooned with trompe l'oeil blue velvet curtains and abutted by a display of white paper insects; inside is a huge range of work, all demonstrating boldness, creativity and imagination. 'We do some gruesome stuff,' chortled the dynamic and experimental head of art as we gaped at the 'urban zombies', the girl under a blanket of fresh minced steak and various startling depictions of blood and vomit. It was reassuring to turn to the multicoloured shoes on every step of the staircase, the cardboard relief masks, the fun, wit, skill of it all. DT even more surprising; facilities include a laser cutter, 3D printer and vacuum former. Products we saw included acrylic pencil and iPad holders and electronic dice. We warmed to a girl (flatteringly, given our age) mistaking us for a potential parent, who insisted on telling us: 'If someone wanted to do product design, they really mustn't go anywhere else.' Art and DT results from here are outstanding.

'Our drama teacher is so dedicated and lovely.' We interrupted a rehearsal of Darkwood Manor – a bit of Gothic horror written by the girls, gory in their white and cicatriced faces, blood and masks. No theatre, though a small semi-studio – 'we don't need a 100 seater theatre,' claimed a proud parent. Good music room with lovely Broadwood grand and reassuring number of real instruments plus modern keyboards with headphones. Many learn instruments and school music is lively and popular.

Sports regarded as much improved during Mrs Kamaryc's tenure, though almost all involves bussing hither and yon. 'We don't mind, it's not an issue,' parents feel, though some pupils we spoke to yearned for playing fields and pitches. It probably isn't ideal for your jumping bean, though on offer now are rowing, squash, fencing among others and girls love it all. 'We have 95 clubs,' we were told and a buzz of jolly fun activities and try-outs pervades the place. Some little sorrow that not everyone joins in with all this opportunity as fully they might.

Background and atmosphere: Queen's Gate is a smart, elegant road in anyone's book. You walk past this school and back again without knowing it's there, so discreet is its little brass nameplate. 'It's a fantastic location,' gush Kensington mummies, 'just like a house.' And so it is – three houses, in fact, knocked together and inside – apart from the fabulous cornices, ceiling roses etc, it's yer actual rabbit warren. 'Yes,' nods a wise mummy, 'but good teaching can take place in a tent.' We lost count of the number of floors and semi-floors above the basement (ICT, lab, lockers and gym and still somehow redolent of the butler's clipped footfalls and scurrying maids). Some upper floor corridors are so narrow that we fear future generations of Tubby Tillies may get stuck. Not that we saw any such here, of course.

Main entrance hall embellished with wall-mounted bell, a set of gongs, a digital clock, fire extinguisher, staff pigeonholes, a vintage radiator, a vitrine bulging with silver trophies and a venerable wooden post box we couldn't open. All this somehow seemed to sum up the whole. Wonderful main hall confected from the two adjoining salons from the houses' glory days – newish wooden floor and matching brass chandeliers. No playground, just a couple of tiny roof gardens for the younger years. Otherwise, breaks are taken in classrooms – and these, on, admittedly, a dark January day, were some of the most overheated we have encountered. Pupils and staff were busily fanning themselves as the rude bell shattered the silence and doors opened. 'It does get very hot,' a youngster confided, 'and sometimes it gets very cold.' Black (for pupils and staff) and white (for pupils) dining rooms, wonderfully elegant and decidedly different. Food reckoned to be good – around half bring in their own. Some come for breakfasts which sounded more than worth sliding out of bed and down the road for.

Main library is a beautiful room with splendid polished oak tables and equally venerable stock in many cases (nothing wrong with that) and a lovely place to work. Sixth form has surprisingly spacious common rooms with sofas. Also a kitchen and a work room, but work decidedly not happening when we peeked in.

No uniform, most dressed perfectly sensibly though this feature of the school clearly stresses a few. 'Some girls bring in ridiculous designer bags,' one mum kvetched, but no-one looked especially coutured to us – though perhaps we are not the best judges. Certainly a divisive issue for some – though not exactly on an 'in/out of the EU?' scale.

Pastoral care, well-being and discipline: Everyone praises the pastoral care. 'They are very good at sorting out individuals,' one father told us. 'My daughter is very happy there.' Another praised the good relations between the girls, fostered by the staff and the care taken to build inter-year relationships. A third described the amount of extra time and effort put in by the teaching staff. A fourth said: 'My daughter feels there is always a teacher to chat to if she has a problem' – and so on. Each term has a 'pastoral day' and a trip to France in year 7 is 'brilliant for bonding us'. Very little sense of serious disciplinary problems being on anyone's radar.

Pupils and parents: Head stresses: 'We're a very English school with an international community. Many of our parents came here from overseas as students – and stayed. We are a Christian foundation but we celebrate all faiths and cultures.' Evidence was the great excitement – and splendid dragon – we witnessed in preparation for the Chinese new year. Largest number of overseas nationals probably Italian, followed by French, Spanish, US, Aussies, Qataris and a few Russians. Much-loved by its old girls, many of whom are current parents; good supportive parents' group. Only, but repeated, gripe is that 'communications are not great' – a surprise to the school but something they are addressing.

Notable OGs include HRH the Duchess of Cornwall, various Redgraves, Sieffs, Guinnesses, Amanda de Souza, Jane Martineau, Nigella Lawson, Lucinda Lambton, Tracey Boyd, Aurelia Cecil, Trinny Woodall and Imogen Poots. Former head of MI5 Eliza Manningham Buller used to be on the staff.

R

Entrance: Around six applicants per place at 11+. Part of the London 11+ Consortium. Assessment process now consists of a 75 minute cognitive ability test (rather than maths and English exams) with great emphasis on the interview. Waiting list for all years, but occasional places occur (maths and English tests plus interview) so worth a phone call. A few in at year 12 but 'we are very selective' and six 9-7s at GCSE are a requirement. Head meets all prospective parents before anyone is tested on anything.

Exit: Almost all stay to A level. Of the 10 per cent or so who try pastures co-ed, boarding or state, some scuttle back tout de suite. Head says that she encourages them to 'be brave and look elsewhere' at this stage. You'd be brave – or rash – to move from so small and nurturing a community to a place where no-one knows a thing about you. Year 13 leavers go to a wonderfully eclectic bunch of good universities around the globe, with several off to the US (two places in 2018). Oxbridge is not uncommon (one place in 2018), solid Russell Group for most but around a quarter much further afield. Art, art history and classics more common than science, though two medics in 2018.

Money matters: All 11+ entrants are automatic scholarship candidates and 25 per cent fee remission offered to high flyers. Art, drama, music and sports scholarships also available – apply on registering. Similar 25 per cent remission available to sixth applicants. Means-tested bursaries too, but no point in applying until a place is offered.

Remarks: A lovely school for lovely girls in a classy and sophisticated milieu. Tiny classes, delightful teachers, charming friends with a faint St Trinian's spicy edge. Not for you if you want gritty urban reality – except, perhaps, in the art room.

Radnor House School

Pope's Villa, Cross Deep, Twickenham TW1 4QG

Ages 9–18 **Pupils** 420 **Sixth form** 81 (59 boys, 22 girls)

Fees: £15,900 – £19,350 pa

020 8891 6264
www.radnor-twickenham.org

Head: Since January 2018, Darryl Wideman, previously head of Silcoates School in Yorkshire and with 25 years of experience in independent education, including nine years at Silcoates. He has an Oxford degree in ancient and modern history, and still teaches history to a range of age groups, including A level; he has also been deputy head at Ratcliffe College and taught at Millfield and Fettes.

Previous head Rosie Gill is now a non-executive director and works closely with the senior leadership team.

Academic matters: The school is taking its academic mission extremely seriously – but equally its commitment to the wider well-being of all its pupils and their families. Once you're in, they want you to stay and to work hard – and that, in practice, is what happens. The results tell a good story: 65 per cent of A level grades in 2018 were A*-B and 32 per cent at A*/A. At GCSE, 49 per cent of grades were 9-7, and at least as important was that the grades were earned from success across a broad spread of mainly traditional subjects, with many GCSE pupils taking two modern languages and Latin. The school doesn't want to be narrowly selective, but it emphatically wants pupils who may not believe themselves academically exceptional to achieve more highly than they (or their parents) might have believed possible.

'I can't praise the teaching too highly,' said parent. 'However clichéd it sounds, the teaching my children are receiving is directed towards them, and I really believe others feel the same.' Another added: 'We didn't want my son tutored within an inch of his life, and that's not necessary at Radnor. He's working hard, he's thoroughly stimulated. And the place feels personal.' The slight gender imbalance among pupils is ironing out nicely now, although boys still in the majority 60-40.

The school is emphatic that the effervescence and ambition of the pupils owes much to the calibre of the teaching staff. A lot of care goes into both recruitment and retention and the turnover is modest – 'you need a bit of change, but continuity is critical, especially if the quality is high'. There are strong suggestions everywhere that this is a happy ship into whose vision staff subscribe wholeheartedly. Despite the nationwide moans of a paucity of teachers in maths and sciences, school has always had a strong field from which to make a selection. All appointments are qualified teachers.

There are two SENDCos – one, dealing with children up to year 8, who advises the classroom teachers in strategies required to help pupils needing learning support. The other, working with older students, has a particular responsibility to ensure that such pupils are adequately prepared for public examinations, with consideration awarded in line with statutory allowances. The informal brief of both extends, of course, very much further – 'like any other teacher, they have to win hearts and minds'. The interests of the small number of children with mild learning support needs within the school are strongly championed by all constituencies.

Games, options, the arts: This is a school which likes its pupils to be active – but, equally, aims to get them to buy into this by friendly example. Football, rugby and cricket dominate boys' sport, and netball, hockey and rounders the girls'. But the school doesn't welcome gender stereotyping. Over 100 boys and girls are now rowing, and mixed football and mixed hockey are not merely popular but being taken very seriously. It's also part of the school credo that everybody represents the school in at least one sport once a year, come what may – an ambition made possible because there are always two teams for each major sport within a year group. There are no games fields on site, but the University of St Mary's, Twickenham, with all those lush playing fields, is only five minutes away by minibus. So nobody is going short of green spaces.

At the time of our visit, the school was busily preparing for its forthcoming production of Oliver! – to be performed at the St Mary's University theatre. It has good drama and music rehearsal spaces in house, each of which is much used for the biannual house music and drama concerts. The latter is a focal point in every Radnor House pupil's life, since the democratising ethos embraces the arts vigorously and ensures these events are truly school-wide. There are some hints that the impact of the arts (and of after-school clubs) doesn't hit home everywhere: 'There's still some way to go,' said one parent, 'before the great majority of pupils are really buying into what's on offer'.

Background and atmosphere: Radnor House is a very recent addition to the tough and competitive environment of senior independent schools. It was the brainchild of David Paton (a former head of sixth form at the Harrodian) who was head between 2011 when it opened and 2016. He retains the post of executive principal. In theory, it sounds a fraught arrangement; in practice, it seems to work excellently with Mr Paton spending a day a week here 'really to exchange news and share thinking'. There is also a heavy-duty advisory panel of governors including the former heads of Alleyns and Hampton.

The school is housed in a handsome mid-19th century neo-Tudor fantasy, which was once the site of the home of the poet Alexander Pope – hence its name (Pope's Villa). There's a delicate and thoughtful balance which has been struck in its redevelopment: the reception areas (with a splendid glass atrium in reception) are of graceful proportions, and the back of the mansion overlooks the river. The combination of grass, water and sky reminds any visitor at a stroke that, whatever else, there is nothing humdrum here. There are lots of small staircases and moderate sized rooms, rather than great ballrooms, all piled high with IT, children's artwork and recent photographs of pupils in their various endeavours. The uniform is worn easily, comfortably – and the atmosphere is the opposite of starchy. Children (of all ages) meet adults' eyes and engage willingly and warmly, but there's no sense of their being ingratiating. A visit to the sixth form common room lunch break gave us a snapshot into something completely authentic and reassuring: low-buzz comfortable chat, interspersed by bits of work and people plugged into their phones. There is a sense that the children know they are enjoying many advantages in life, but are busy, capable and unpretentious – and draw much inspiration from their teachers who clearly are cut from the same cloth.

The school is rightly proud that 'our community engagement goes a lot further than fundraising'. All projects wherever possible focus on 'personal engagement in the cause of social transformation' eg the annual Make a Difference Day in which every member of the school, staff and pupils, takes a full working day out to make some kind of civic contribution.

Pastoral care, well-being and discipline: Pastoral care is based around form groups – of 20 pupils – with a form tutor, and year groups of 60 under a year head. These are the proactive pastoral figures, and two members of the senior leadership team are there 'to guide, enthuse and, where necessary, to be reactive'. The house system has just been relaunched, mainly for sport and social purposes, but with sixth form pupils acting as heads of houses in an effort to lend kudos and foment useful initiatives. The deputy head (pastoral) fronts most of the bigger pastoral issues, but there is an underlying commitment to transparency and accessibility which the school believes embraces all the staff. 'We see parents a great deal, because it's critical. We enjoy it, we value it, and we hope they do as well.' There have been no recent exclusions – the usual challenges of children aged 9-18, especially those associated with IT, are ones the school recognises, but it finds that a gentle guide on the tiller is usually all that is required.

Pupils and parents: Half termly 'assessment' reports give all parents a terse overview of recent progress and levels of effort. In addition to these, there is a full written report for all years and two meetings a year between individual parents and teachers. Other meetings are arranged as and when the need arises, with all the staff, including the head, always being willing to find time to accommodate requests for face to face discussions.

Three school buses help draw in children from the school's impressively wide catchment – one goes to Chelsea, one to Ealing and the third to Wimbledon. Socially and ethnically, there is a real mix here and many parents are first-time consumers of independent schools. The pupils radiate enthusiasm rather than entitlement.

Entrance: The main point of entry for juniors is now year 5 (as the classes for years 3 and 4 have been phased out – a sign of the school's growing popularity). Children sit an English and a maths test and, if admitted, will be part of a cohort of 20 when they arrive. A further 40 places become available at the start of year 7, selection for which is decided via the 11 plus. There's also a sixth form intake: you need to put in an application in the autumn of year 11, and get ready to sit a range of interviews as well as taking the Yellis computer adaptive test. The underlying rationale is clear – its entry policy is sensible and humane. It becomes more obviously organised around academic testing the further up the school you go, but never to the exclusion of everything else. Siblings are prioritised, but only to the extent that they can fit in comfortably.

Exit: Around a third leaves after GCSEs. Brighton, Reading and Exeter currently popular sixth form destinations. No Oxbridge yet – 'but that's only a matter of time, and also only one of many ambitions we have for our wonderful pupils'. Some interest is being shown by pupils and parents in European and American universities – one off to the US to study liberal arts in 2018 – applications for which are being finessed by a dedicated member of staff. 'There is a trade-off, I suppose,' said one parent, 'between results and values. At Radnor House, I am confident they can achieve the first, and I'm certain they are achieving the second.'

Money matters: Lunch is charged separately, as are school trips, though a big effort is made to keep costs down. The fees aren't out of line with competitor schools, and the ethos of the school has the low-key quality which accompanies an underlying confidence. Some bursary help is available 'in exceptional circumstances' but this is part of the school's development has perhaps some way yet to go. Uniform is smart but not showy or expensive.

Remarks: Radnor House works hugely hard but has a sense of its underlying values and of the direction it wishes to follow – and these both mark it out as a credible and confident player in the independent school world. The atmosphere is calm as well as energetic, and the head and her colleagues communicate values which are humane and imaginative. It is now poised to become a school of first choice and thoroughly deserving of all the good fortune which comes its way.

Ravenscourt Park Preparatory School

16 Ravenscourt Avenue, London W6 0SL

Ages 4–11 Pupils 415

Fees: £17,571 pa

020 8846 9153
www.rpps.co.uk

Head: Since 2015, Carl Howes MA (Cantab) natural sciences, PGCE St Luke's Exeter, previously deputy head at St Paul's Juniors, following head of maths and second master at King's House School, Richmond. His wife is a primary teacher; son, 20s, and teenage daughter. First RPPS head to come from outside, Mr Howes is committed to the school's ethos: 'I very much appreciated the thriving, happy community I inherited.' Seen most days in the playground, smartly attired, welcoming all; parents we spoke to describe him as 'highly approachable', 'a good listener, quiet but straight talking'. Mr Howes comments, 'I enjoy the connection with the children and as a head you have to make an effort': he clearly does, as prior to our visit, he accompanied year 5's Devon residential trip. He takes assemblies, debating club, teaches year 4 and 5 mathematics sets, some sport to younger pupils. He has introduced Headmaster's Awards which acknowledge pupils' effort and attitude. Pupils describe him as 'kind, generous with his time, turning up at weekend tournaments'. 'He's a perfect adult: he understands children and what they find interesting and funny'. We found him charming, measured in approach, with a fascination for educational matters, coupled with intelligent discernment to ensure RPPS equips pupils for, as he puts it, 'the challenges of an unknown world'.

Two terms into his tenure, inspectors judged RPPS 'excellent in all areas'. He appreciates staff are 'forward-looking' and 'responsive' adding, 'I am not a micro-manager'. Parents we spoke to recognise his ' light touch' which 'empowers the teachers', whilst upholding high expectations and 'sifting out what really matters'. To relax, Mr Howes cycles to work, runs five kilometres on Saturdays and plays the saxophone. When asked about his future ambitions, he has no wish to lead an empire, enjoying the holistic education and size of RPPS.

Entrance: Register on child's first birthday, not before, for one of 60 non-selective reception places allotted by ballot with siblings prioritised. Later applicants join waiting list with a few occasional places arising each year when families relocate. All are expected to stay until the end of year 6 in gender balanced classes of 20.

Exit: Popular day school destinations include: Latymer Upper, Kew House, Notting Hill and Ealing High and Godolphin & Latymer. Mr Howes has good relationships with senior schools and can advise accordingly. The school caters for a range of ability with impressive results, including 12 to 15 scholarships every year. 'If I could, I would like to abolish 11+,' summed up one parent, disenchanted with the process but pleased with how RPPS strives to address the stresses and strains, whilst others agreed how extremely well the teachers and headmaster know each child's ability and personality.

Remarks: Maria and Ted Gardener, former teachers, founded the school in 1991. With the additional Gardener Building in 2011, the school consists of four separate buildings on one site, close to Ravenscourt Park where most PE and games lessons take place. Some parents are nostalgic about when the school was smaller, believing the parent body was more cohesive, but acknowledge more families have benefited and are pleased 'it has kept its heart'. Part of the Gardener School Group Ltd with Kew House and Kew Green Prep, RPPS benefits from shared resources, expertise and fixtures. Some parents we spoke to talked about it being a business, especially the fact that 'the fees go up every year at the higher end'. Others bemoan the lack of bursary places, which they believe 'makes the school less diverse, to its detriment'.

The homely Old Vicarage building houses early years and year 1 in well-equipped classrooms with outside play area for supervised groups. Spacious science lab ensures pupils can carry out experiments. They are encouraged to solve problems and create models; we saw a sophisticated Galileo-inspired pendulum. Some parents criticised half termly homework projects as too demanding and questioned whether models were produced by other competitive parents. Homework and costume provision for theme days can cause difficulties for working parents but the 8.00am–6.00pm school day and after-school clubs are much appreciated. Children appear relaxed and enthusiastic, politely greeting us with 'good morning' in every class, and readily explained what they were doing. They were clearly absorbed in the task at hand, from year 5s in an English class reflecting on the plight of refugees, to year 1s explaining how to access and record work on their PCs in the IT suite. All classrooms have interactive whiteboards and iPads are used throughout. Pupils enjoy fun ways of learning to do computer coding, creating animations, games and stories collaboratively, and all are made aware of e-safety.

Fantastic facilities include a light, spacious art room with kiln. We saw high quality art work in different media on display, including a recreation of a Van Gogh-inspired painting made by classes using coloured curled card. Parents value the creativity on offer but some wish 'more of the artwork could come home'. Overlooking the playground, conveniently situated on the ground floor, is the excellent library. Librarians ensure it is accessible in break times and we saw pupils thoroughly enjoying the wide range of materials on offer. There is an attractive dining room where tasty, fresh food is prepared, monitored by a food committee including some parents.

All buildings contain cheerful rooms for learning support or small group work. The SEND register is reviewed after standardised assessments termly during pupil progress meetings and 25 were on the register when we visited. The department is well regarded. Parents find the SENCo and her team 'really responsive' and praise the school as being 'inclusive'. 'They cope very well with pupils with pre-identified minor learning difficulties.' There are withdrawal lessons and provision made in the classroom to cater for individual learning difficulties at no extra charge.

Staff are energetic and dedicated. As one parent explained, 'They tick all the boxes', and best of all, 'they really know their pupils'. Pupils describe RPPS as 'a friendly community' where 'everyone is made to feel the same, equally valued' and teachers as 'encouraging', 'very fair' and 'kind'. We saw Mr Howes in a new guise joining colleagues in street dancing at an assembly. This was part of the school's commitment to growth mindsets, an educational strategy introduced to encourage pupils to make mistakes and develop resilience, so they will try something new and persevere. Year 2s had no problem explaining this approach to us with a helpful visual chart in their classroom A two year cycle of values is shared in assemblies including intellectual humility, respect and tolerance, part of the school's holistic ethos.

Parents unanimously endorsed the staff's open door policy, which ensures prompt responses to their concerns whether small or great, and agreed they are never made 'to feel a nuisance'. Communication is 'excellent', ranging from website with parent portal and Parkside newsletter to weekly 'onthefridgedoor' which encapsulates the week's events and pupil achievements. Parents commented on 'the solid system' for pastoral care with clear guidelines. Pupils we spoke to happily explained 'reminder notes' alongside the RPPS Code of Conduct. 'There is always someone to share your concerns with and plenty of opportunities for responsibility.'

At KS1, boys and girls have games lessons together; at KS2, the boys do football, rugby and cricket while girls do netball, hockey and rounders. Regular fixtures and 18 sports-related clubs are on offer. Recently, the girls' netball team qualified for the IAPS finals and year 5 had its first football and netball tour to Jersey. 'Music is fantastic,' parents agree and approximately 230 individual instrumental lessons take place in school weekly with 15 peripatetic teachers. All praised the wide variety on offer: three choirs, two orchestras, music theory club, chamber music ensembles, rock bands, an a cappella singing group and recorder, guitar and brass ensembles. Children can take graded examinations in school and many are involved in outside orchestras. A recent year 6 pupil achieved grade 8 with distinction in the violin. Specialist facilities include a 160 seat performance hall with sound and lighting, music suite and teaching rooms.

RPPS follows a full primary curriculum, making use of specialist subject teachers and classroom assistants. Parents believe the pace is 'spot on' with increased homework and more emphasis on English and mathematics from the summer term in year 5. Parents praise the life skills RPPS develops, and how staff encourage pupils' independence, dealing with homework and 'organisational skills like packing for a residential trip, which sets them up for senior school so well'. After the examinations, children enjoy themed topics and a diverse range of activities, home and away. Year 6s we chatted to were very excited about their forthcoming production and there is an annual ski trip to Austria as well as a biennial music tour, recently to Tuscany. The curriculum is enhanced by theme weeks and staff take advantage of nearby galleries, theatres and exhibitions as well as parents sharing their interesting careers.

French is taught throughout with Spanish as one of the many extracurricular clubs.

This popular school caters for families with children of different needs and abilities, most living within two miles. The pupil body reflects the area, most being of British origin and a quarter from European backgrounds, often bilingual. Parents in varied professions, including marketing, law and banking. 'You can get involved as much or as little as you like,' they told us. Many participate, attending concerts, listening to readers or involved in the Parents' Association of Friends.

Parents agree the school 'is nurturing, inclusive, welcoming and truly caters for all-rounders', unlike schools 'with greater emphasis on the academics where pupils need to be more robust and confident'. Not the right school for parents obsessed with their children obtaining top grades in everything or those seeking a traditional, highly competitive environment. Even teams are colour coded rather than A, B, C, D, emphasising participation and lack of labelling. With mixed ability there is a balanced atmosphere which does not stop the very able from flying, but does mean all are encouraged. As one parent remarked, 'RPPS is a really fun, positive and nurturing environment for the kids, who become so confident and happy about their place in life'. Others said, 'This dynamic school caters for all sorts, any character; that is one of its strengths'. The 11+ preparation is a 'well-oiled machine' with 'loads of opportunities for different characters to learn and flourish', as recent results demonstrate.

Reach Academy Feltham

53–55 High Street, Feltham, Middlesex TW13 4AB

Ages 4–19 **Pupils** 780 **Sixth form** 50

020 8893 1099
www.reachacademyfeltham.com

Headteacher: Since September 2018, Beck Owen, previously associate headteacher. She was a founding teacher at Reach, becoming head of English and then deputy head. English degree from Cardiff and a masters in education leadership; previously taught in Birmingham. In 2018 she has been part of the Getting Ahead London programme, which has been supporting leaders into headteacher roles.

Executive headteacher: Ed Vainker MA (30s), previously principal since 2012. Following experiences as Teach First trainee in inner city schools and exposure to US Charter School movement, burning desire to set up school to right wrongs was born. His Eureka moment came in the US (he'd won an educational scholarship), when saw Waiting for Superman at cinema (got time wrong – was supposed to be Social Network but didn't want to waste babysitter) and stayed up all night, committing educational vision to paper. Serendipity was the clincher: a mutual friend introduced him to Rebecca Cramer, school's co-founder and previously secondary head, now director of education (third co-founder, Jon McIntosh, remains a governor but doesn't have active teaching role).

The first in family to go to university (Bristol, geography) and a fellow Teach Firster, Rebecca shared Ed's sense of injustice over dismal prospects for bright but disadvantaged pupils who ended up with middling exam results, education and careers instead of the stellar opportunities they deserved.

The solution? A school where the partnership with parents wasn't just about education but everything from aspirations to parenting skills and diet. It needed to take the very young (makes Jesuits look like beginners) and stay small so teachers could get to know children, and their families, inside out. Families short on decent life chances were to be the prime beneficiaries. Feltham, only five miles from Hampton Court Palace but an awful lot grittier (government's latest deprivation index puts it in bottom third of areas for education) was the ideal location, particularly given authority's commitment to building new homes and schools for fast-growing population.

First pupils (reception and year 7) arrived in 2012 and a new primary and senior year has been added on each September since, making a full house in 2018.

Rebecca and Ed are idealistic but clear-sighted, offering practical help where needed (including carpeting bare floors in one family's flat) but never letting poverty become an excuse for low achievement. They're hugely impressive. Rebecca is praised for pastoral and psychological expertise while Ed's the systems and strategy man with a brilliant little black book stuffed with useful contacts and a virtuoso approach to getting what he wants from normally intractable public bodies ('pre-schmoozing' was mentioned).

Both have understanding partners and young children – 'was planning to have a school dog but got a baby instead,' says Rebecca, whose just crawling son was a cheery addition to the morning meet and greet squad on day of visit.

Job could take over their lives but they work hard to ensure it doesn't and swear blind that a 5.30pm getaway is the norm, 'plus, of course, some email checking once the children are in bed,' says Rebecca. Personable and charming, though with the essential steely edge where necessary, they also have the ability to make others feel at ease. One parent, distraught when child launched into a tantrum at a get-to-know-you session, was instantly put at her ease by Rebecca. 'She came over and spoke to me like a human being and made me feel so relaxed.' Staff think they're pretty fab, too. 'Rebecca stays so calm, I've never seen her fazed or annoyed. She's always in control,' says one.

That said, children have a healthy respect for her. 'She's very much like "this is how it's going to be",' said one.

Now first stage one has been accomplished, it's on to phase two – a second school that will take pupils even earlier – pre-conception, if they get their way – and 'hopefully' bring together NCT (currently nearest branches are in well-heeled Chiswick and Teddington), local GPs, midwives and just about everybody who can ensure that parents get proper support from the very beginning.

Ed and Rebecca now envisage training up a brace of successors – and indeed one is now headteacher – who share their ideals but are happy to take on a going concern rather than a blank page while they work on further expansion. 'Would they be younger?' we asked. 'We are young,' say Ed and Rebecca, indignantly.

Academic matters: Social justice is the driver, goal transformational education ensuring that every able child gets top results. They've demanded, to some initial consternation, as big a proportion of families from disadvantaged backgrounds as possible.

Second impressive GCSE results in 2018 saw 31 per cent 9-7 grades, with 84 per cent getting 9-4 in both English and maths. School is already notching up the laurel wreaths, first all-through free school to garner an outstanding grade from inspectors and with good results (eg in year 1 phonics test) that put it way ahead of national averages. The acid test will come in 2021 when first year 11s home grown from reception sit GCSEs. The current year 4s are already working at same level as year 7 pupils – so it's looking good.

'We take an A at A level and work backwards,' says literature...'They expect great things for all of us,' agreed year 11 pupil. Only exceptions a couple of pupils who wouldn't cope with GCSEs, based here but taking vocational courses at other local colleges.

Crack team of teachers is key. Highly qualified and occasionally shoeless ('helps them feel grounded,' we were told), they're also known by their first names (means 'have power but don't feel bigger,' thought one pupil) and have no discernable 'off' button, replying to texts from early morning to late at night and over the hols.

'Seem to be there because they want to be there,' thought another. The few who don't self-select into new employment fairly quickly, but with 17 who've been here since the school first opened, most are clearly keepers.

Ark Schools group helps with training and all teachers, several former TAs among them, have a mentor and weekly observations. Though ethnically less diverse than pupils, it's not the whole story as a fair few also have first hand experience of achieving against the odds.

Curriculum is very much the school's own. Unsurprisingly, little quarter is given in lessons, from year 10s deep in semantic (and battle) fields as they analyse war poetry to year 2s dissecting Edgar Allen Poe's The Raven by way of a Hallowe'en treat.

There's role play to develop confidence for reception pupils and the involvement of senior school subject specialists (science, French) from year 3 onwards. Lesson length varies according to subject, little and often for languages but longer sessions (up to two hours for seniors) in literacy and numeracy, which dominate curriculum. Competence in both areas is a non-negotiable that's well understood by parents. 'If you want to go off and be a carpenter or something like that, there's no good learning that at school if your maths isn't brilliant,' said one.

Everyone is expected to take between eight and 10 GCSEs with art, music and MFL among the options – most bases covered though don't offer DT. Sixth formers (first entrants joined in September 2017) have choice of 18 A levels and two BTecs, plus electives (astronomy to photography – potential starter for extended essay project) and linked studies such as research techniques.

With pupils speaking 55 languages between them and English an additional language for 40 per cent, support network has to be robust – and it is, with before school catch up lessons and small group work for those needing a slightly slower pace.

Don't shirk from SEN and school is impressively dyslexia friendly (white backgrounds routinely replaced with pastel shades – far easier to read), while new resources are being added (sensory room is on the way). Stress, however, that while school is small, class sizes aren't – it's 30 or so up to end of year 11 – so wouldn't be the right environment for child in need of extensive small group or one-to-one support.

That said, parents confirm that the school won't give up on pupils with additional needs without a fight. Under a handful so far have moved on to more specialist environments and it's brilliant with those it can support. Rebecca's prizewinning account of school life for bright, autistic boy resulted in trip to education conference in Bulgaria where his speech on need for greater understanding of SEN, he told us, had audience in tears.

Games, options, the arts: Sense of togetherness permeates everything, from play featuring wisecracking teacher and pupil compere duo to school trips – six a year for primary pupils, with overnight stays from year 3, while all secondary pupils get a residential week in a university (Bath for year 7, York year 8 and Cambridge year 10) – 'a huge thing and a non-negotiable,' says Ed. Year 9s, meanwhile, work on Sports Leader UK and D of E qualifications (aim for silver in year 11). 'All part of making everyone part of the family,' said parent.

R

Smart thinking sees work experience happening in autumn half term to beat the post-GCSE rush. One year 11 boy encountered slebs on his – 'Dom Joly,' he breathed in star-struck tones, though not everyone's as happy. 'Rubbish,' said a girl, who had less fulfilling time with another firm.

Around 100 children learn a musical instrument in school (fair few enthusiastic beginners aiming for grade 4 in time for GCSEs) and even reception children, including the very shy, have acquired the confidence to perform in public within weeks of joining.

Art is also taking off, specialist teacher now installed, room uncommonly neat and restrained but filling up nicely with glittery stage sets ready to go for forthcoming production of Annie when we visited and some interesting individual work including year 9 pupils' rather beautiful Romero Britto-inspired designs.

Opening of second Reach Academy in 2019 or 2020, on a bigger site, should mean more outside space all round. In the meantime, sporting successes are coming (senior girls' football, cross-country and shot putt) while colossus of a sports hall also goes some way to compensate, as does its rooftop Astroturf (with views of glorious sunsets views over Feltham) – though one parent felt it could be used a bit more often.

SEN support extends to after-school clubs – yoga 'very good for those with dyspraxia,' says head of sport. They're popular with parents, with football, table tennis and trampolining all generally oversubscribed

Learning outside the classroom is a big feature, like so much here, plugging social as well as educational gap. Down on the farm that's a gated hop skip and jump from the playground, Nigel the farmer supplies and vets the livestock: beady-eyed chickens, hoping for seconds of mealworms (top favourites) have plenty of star quality but are comprehensively outshone by the two pigs. Pupils can volunteer to be young farmers and learn responsibility by working here after school.

Meat and eggs are sold to the parents who can also sample other edibles (spices, rhubarb and tomatoes and even a batch of home-made chutney), and there's also a virtuous circle, with pigs (sensibly not named) fed spare break time fruit (unlimited for all) though government diktats consign most other leftovers to landfill.

Adjoining forest school may be more of a coppice but gets non-stop multi-purpose use – tents, mini-beast hotel, and balancing wire slung between two trees. And though compact (you can definitely see the wood for the trees), it's an oasis to many of the parents who help out here. 'Like a day out – felt that wasn't in Feltham at all,' said one.

Background and atmosphere: No bureaucracy-heavy place, this. It feels fleet of foot – even on the 'phone. 'We'd rather deal with you ourselves,' says friendly receptionist, who offers to sort out the visit direct with the then principal (none of this transferring your call to umpteen other extensions, all with a voicemail on the end).

School's small is beautiful ethos makes it a rarity not just in its home borough of Hounslow but just about anywhere in Greater London. It achieved star status early on, seemingly the must-see educational destination of choice for range of ambitious politicians. Year 11s we spoke to had previously been quizzed by David Cameron (school was final official engagement before his post-Brexit resignation). Others who've dropped in include Lord Adonis, Boris Johnston and Michael Gove (though we bet we were the only ones to be offered school pud – complete with bowl – as a goody bag present).

Area, though not picturesque, is brilliantly connected for trains, automobiles (and of course many, many planes) though some parents prefer to collect, on foot if necessary, rather than letting even secondary-age children walk back on their own.

Inside, however, the school, designed from scratch by founders, is a well-thought out and attractive oasis of calm, from the separate primary and secondary meet and greet areas and playgrounds to the move to unisex toilets ('the boys' smelled and the girls spent hours looking in the mirror,' says Rebecca).

Life centres round five phases, each with its assistant head, made up of one or more year groups in own area consisting of classrooms off a multi-purpose central space (nursery, in own single long room, the only exception). Unless location is key (science, music and art) it's the teachers who move. 'None of this 100 kids rushing through the corridors to get to a lesson,' said parent.

Plenty, as you'd expect, on the wish list. New library needs more books; embryonic music tech room more tech. Donations come from a range of sources – Teach First, for example, was persuaded to part with some old sofas – ideal for the new sixth form centre (first occupants in 2017) which also boasts rooftop terrace and well-stocked fitness suite – but Ed and Rebecca are cautious about hitting the well-wishers' list too often. State education 'isn't really badly funded,' they reckon.

Pastoral care, well-being and discipline: There's a strong family feel here, starting at the gates (primary pupils enter to left, seniors to right), with handshake for all at start and end of the day 'without fail,' said parent. 'It feels lovely.' Inspirational quotes (JK Rowling, Ghandi, Martin Luther King) are juxtaposed with posters for Childline, and school is under no illusions as to some families' home life. For some, just getting children to school is an achievement, we were told by grounded family support worker. 'They deal with every angle of their upbringing,' said mother. 'Not just education but their social needs, too.' Practical support includes organising visits to the job centre, optician and food bank or – in one case – taking the children to feed the ducks at local pond to give parents a break.

Some pupils arrive so far behind their peers that may never achieve as much as they should, though progress can be dramatic – one primary school boy sitting quietly at the table to eat his lunch 'would have found it impossible when he first arrived,' we were told. Food really matters. For some children it's their first encounter not just with healthy diet but also with the social rituals of mealtimes. So there's food mindfulness in primary (distraction-free silence during first mouthfuls) to minimal choice menu, family service with older pupils serving younger ones, no packed lunches and home visits for serial non-eaters. Several new parents, initially nervous about fussy offspring, quickly reassured. One H2O refuser blossomed when was offered school's 'magic water for big boys.'

Elsewhere, children are guided towards the right decision by impressively low key but authoritative staff. 'Don't need to shout and scream, just clap their hands and everyone stops,' said parent. Incentives include payslips for good work and behaviour – exchangeable for golden time (primary) and activities (senior pupils). 'You get a lot of messages coming home telling you to congratulate your child when they've done really well,' said parent. Nothing flabby about two-step sanctions, however. First time senior school trangressors talk through reasons for poor behaviour while serial (or serious) offenders sit on their own in lessons and at break for a day, decision to readmit to polite society decided by class vote and communicated by buddy.

Parents, too, shoulder their share of responsibility. If a phone goes off in a lesson, will be called in to remove offending item and confirm they understand why. Similarly, late arrivals get automatic 30 minute detention, 'bad traffic' excuse a non-starter. 'Would need to have affected every car in the whole area,' says Rebecca, implacably. Tough love it may be, but after the initial shock, every parent we spoke to understood why it was necessary and appreciated the active encouragement to join in school life. All have open invitation to have lunch or, if worried about child's progress, sit in on lesson. 'Very open – there's nothing to hide,' said one.

Pupils and parents: One of several rumours we heard was of places awarded to wealthy parents identifiable by posh cars at drop off and pick up time. We diligently scoured the Tesco and Aldi car parks opposite at 8.00am and can report a pronounced absence of luxury marques.

Instead, there's a diverse community. Was 80 per cent ethnic minorities when first opened though there are now more pupils from lower income white families. Embryonic PTA, busily organising Christmas Fair when we visited, is doing best to create parent community – one mother, frozen out by the clique in previous, middle-class dominated primary, was full of praise.

Entrance: The school stresses – and stresses again – that its admissions procedure is completely transparent – if different to anyone else's. It doesn't stop suspicion creeping in, down to the long odds – over 1,000 families recently applied for the 120 reception and year 7 places (something that rivals even grammar school admissions) – that condemn majority to disappointment. Doesn't stop them trying (two parents turned up on day of visit to plead their case) – and second school can't come soon enough.

After looked after children come nursery pupils qualifying for early years pupil premium, followed by exceptional medical and social needs, siblings, others qualifying for pupil premium, staff children and those living within admissions area (chosen by electronic ballot). Transition process is painstaking, particularly when it comes to identifying those with learning needs. 'We'll go in and make sure it's identified early,' says Rebecca.

Main feeder schools are Victoria Junior School and Oak Hill Academy, geographical area covering Feltham, Southville, Bedfont, Hanworth and Hounslow (though early adopters include those from slightly further afield).

At the start, school was canvassing for pupils – and how. 'Rebecca came to our house and did an amazing presentation,' said one parent. Those who took a leap of faith and got in early thank their lucky stars. Neighbours who didn't and are on the waiting list (which does move, but at glacial speeds), wish they'd done the same. In the meantime, the rumour mill is whizzing round at speed while school does its best to highlight transparency.

It's currently having to repeat the process for sixth formers as applications are slightly thin on the ground for early intakes – sheer newness means not yet a destination school for high achievers. We'd strongly recommend taking a look.

R

Exit: There's some relocation – including visa expiry. Some departures at end of year 11 (about half so far) as school sets the bar high for sixth form admissions – six 6s minimum, 7s required to study toughest subjects (eg maths, sciences, languages, history). Similar number of 9-4 grades will see you on to a BTec.

For those moving on, options range from The Heathland School in Hounslow to Springwest Academy and St Paul's Catholic School in Sunbury. One parent felt school should do more to help with search. Don't hold your breath or expect much in way of handholding – school expects parents to do their homework and research alternatives. 'We don't spoonfeed,' says Rebecca.

Money matters: Sixth form bursaries for everyone on free school meals. As and when hardship bursaries also available – no pupil will miss a school trip because of lack of money.

Remarks: 'It seems too good to be true,' said parent. 'We kept saying "what's the catch?" There is no catch.'

Reay Primary School

Hackford Road, London SW9 0EN

Ages 3–11 **Pupils** 248

020 7735 2978
www.reay.lambeth.sch.uk

Headteacher: Since 2014, Caroline Andrews BEd from Sheffield Hallam (early 40s). Taught at Chaucer Junior from 1996-2000, then at Wix Primary where she became ICT leader, followed by deputy then co-head. Established the first state French/English bilingual school along with French Lycée. Made head here in 2014. Hails from Nottingham. Husband works in TV. Has a young son at another school as she feels 'it wouldn't be fair for him to come here, with me as head.' Most of her spare time is spent socialising with family and friends. Travels to far-flung destinations as often as possible. Keen gardener and enjoys cooking, which she finds therapeutic. Parents are big fans. 'Down-to-earth,' according to one. 'She's brought a new lease of life to the school,' said another. Welcoming and friendly.

Entrance: School, rather than Lambeth, is now responsible for own admissions, so children in nursery are more likely to gain a place in reception than was the case previously, 'though there is still no guarantee as we have 30 places in reception and 40 in nursery.' Waiting list in operation for occasional places further up the school. 'When pupils leave, we can now move more quickly to fill the place,' says head. Oversubscribed: roughly six applicants per place.

Exit: Small minority goes down the fee-paying route, and those that do usually favour Alleyn's or Dulwich College. Popular state destinations include Graveney, Lambeth Academy and London Nautical. 'We invite secondary schools to come and talk to parents at the end of year 5, and then again before parents need to make the final decision in year 6,' explains head. After-school tutoring delivered by class teachers if requested, prior to 11+ exams. 'We do have a discussion with parents if we think the school they want is not right for their child, though. We don't want the children to be put under excessive pressure. They are well-supported and well-extended here anyway, so most would get places without tutoring in any case,' believes head.

Remarks: Three-quarters of pupils come from ethnic minority groups. Half speak English as an additional language. 'Though for very few is this a barrier to their learning. It's more of an asset,' states head. Nearly 50 per cent are eligible for pupil premium funding, much higher than national average. Most live less than 400 metres away. 'We have a hugely mixed intake. Some are from the high-rise blocks opposite and others live in million pound properties,' comments head. Very high attendance rate.

Housed in a purpose-built, high ceilinged Victorian building in the heart of Lambeth. A surprisingly peaceful oasis in this ultra-urban location. Great sense of space throughout. Huge double classrooms abound with plenty of room for breakout activities. Recently converted library with doors opening onto a courtyard where year 6 pupils can be found reclining on beanbags, devouring books on sunny afternoons. Separate playgrounds for different year groups, complete with a climbing wall and quiet area.

Head is confident that pupils' varying needs are identified quickly and that children do not fall through the net – 'that's the beauty of a one form entry school.' All classrooms have at least one additional adult on hand.

Learning is fun here and pupils were all full of beans on the day we visited. Much learning is done through project work, from nursery upwards. Shakespeare was being studied when we visited and one pupil was writing painstakingly with a quill pen and ink. Homework involves reading, spelling and times tables until year 5. 'Then,' says head, 'we up the ante, with past papers and test preparation. We believe that the children are so busy at school and are offered so many extracurricular activities that homework doesn't add much before that, especially in homes where English is not the first language.' French offered from nursery onwards, though soon to be replaced by Spanish. Close links with the Lycée in Clapham where Reay pupils have penpals.

Pastoral care is a definite strength. 'We take mental well-being very seriously,' says head. School places great emphasis on outdoor learning in its beautiful nature garden, which includes a parent-built greenhouse, a tree-house, a pond for frogs and a bug hotel. Bluebells and blossom were in abundance on the day we visited, making it appear totally magical. One area is set aside for digging and another for making mud pies. Each class grows fruit and vegetables, including strawberries, tomatoes and lettuce. 'The garden is an area where children can get dirty and appreciate nature. Some children otherwise do not get an opportunity to play outside in this way,' explains head. She believes this area helps those who struggle to communicate, as some find it easier when busy in the garden. Weekly mentoring sessions also put on by local charity to help pupils build their social and emotional skills through activities and sport. One parent we spoke to said, 'Everybody looks out for each other here. The bigger kids look out for the smaller kids. The children nurture each other as much as the teachers do!' One parent mentioned an incident of bullying but was full of praise for the speed with which the school stepped in.

School can support a range of special needs, particularly emotional, behavioural and social difficulties. Thirty-nine on special needs register and five currently have an Education, Health and Care plan. Most classrooms are on ground floor so easy accessibility for those with physical disabilities. Learning mentor offers one-to-one support for those who are need it, either socially or academically. She also supports families and makes home visits if required. Extra language assistance given to those who do not have English as their first language. Dyslexia screening available from year 2 onwards, as and when required rather than as a whole year group. Plenty of workshops for gifted and talented pupils and extra maths sessions laid on by local secondary schools. Art therapist and speech and language therapist regularly visit.

'We try to broaden their horizons through art, music and drama,' comments head. Gold Artsmark awarded in recognition of rich arts opportunities here. 'Children like the freedom of art and we want them to enjoy it. We value it as teachers,' explains head. Music is also an important part of life at Reay. Year 3 pupils learn recorder, year 4 the ukulele and year 5 has a class orchestra, with pupils playing instruments ranging from violins and double bass to saxophones. Some subsidised individual music lessons offered in top two years. Performances put on for parents, including at the Albert Hall. No choir at the moment though head stresses 'we have a lot of singing so the whole school feels like a choir.' Annual nativity play led by year 2 and a pantomime by year 6.

School has an all-weather sports pitch where children play cricket, netball, football and hockey. All year groups swim from year 2 onwards. Running club takes place in a nearby park. Pupils compete in local tournaments and participate in cricket schemes at the Oval. Extra sport laid on before, during and after the school day including yoga in French and basketball in Spanish. 'We have lots of space both outdoors and in the studio for sport and dance. We are very lucky,' says head. One parent we spoke to, however, felt that 'sport is challenge. I wish they did more. I feel like my son could certainly do with more of a run around than he gets.' Good range of after-school clubs from cooking and coding to street dance, run by a mixture of outside providers and in-house staff.

Wraparound care offered before and after school, so pupils can be looked after for over 10 hours a day. Breakfast club from 7.30am, with toast and cereal galore. 'Lots of us on the staff are working parents so we appreciate the need for a longer day,' says head. Reay pupils can also enjoy holiday provision at a neighbouring school.

Pungent aroma of fish and chips emanating from the dining room on the day we visited. Children have a choice of salads as well as fresh fruit and vegetables. Some take in packed lunches. Herbs grown in the school garden are used in the stuffing at Christmas lunch. Head hopes more of their garden produce can make its way onto the children's plates.

Trips aplenty to theatres, parks and sports venues. Residential trips for year 4 to Kent (along with pupils from other local schools) and year 6 spends four nights in France. Parents pay, but school subsidises trips as does the PTA. Whole school ventures merrily, in a long line of coaches, to a Sussex beach every summer term. 'We take picnics and it's absolutely lovely, though exhausting. Parents come too,' enthuses head.

A family-orientated school. Specialist sessions organised for parents on topics including how to support their children with speech development. Many parents volunteer at the school. Some give talks to older children about careers. 'Most parents are very supportive. We have an open-door policy and encourage parents to come in and sort out problems promptly. It makes life a lot easier,' explains head. She also stands at the gate every morning and afternoon so parents can bend her ear about any issues then. Active PTA that puts on regular events, including summer and winter fairs and a school disco. Communication with parents has improved recently.

A very friendly school, where kindness and good manners are considered important. 'We place an emphasis on the joy of childhood here. We want the children to work hard but also to enjoy their time at Reay,' says head. 'The children are proud of their school and we are very proud of them.' A happy, caring environment.

Redcliffe School

47 Redcliffe Gardens, London SW10 9JH

Ages 3–11 **Pupils** 145

Fees: £17,730 pa

020 7352 9247
www.redcliffeschool.com

Headmistress: Since 2017, Sarah Lemmon (40s). SL is so happy in her work that she leaves her husband and son (an ex-Redcliffe pupil) outside Bath and commutes to London every week. Raised in Co Wicklow until she was 17, she has spent all her post-school life in London, not because it is the dull filling in a green sandwich but because she genuinely loves the city. Once graduated from Froebel College, she tested her natural instinct to become a teacher by doing a stint in the outside world but is clearly delighted that she made the choice to switch to education. She started teaching here 12 years ago and has climbed the ladder to the top, via the headship of the pre-prep, a cv that makes parents comfortable that she knows the school from the bottom up and, judging by their comments, certain that she is doing a great job.

Entrance: Approximately three children put down per nursery place but there is a lot of natural attrition due to some London parents' habit of applying piecemeal to keep their options open. It's a first come, first served, non-selective school with a front of the queue policy for siblings and the registrar says that she 'can't think of a time when there has been a problem with this'. All children are assessed for entry to the main school via a gently selective process and for the occasional places available further up. The vast majority of children in the nursery move up to reception, although a few go abroad or to the local Ofsted 'outstanding' primary.

Exit: Redcliffe is becoming co-ed throughout but boys have tended to transfer at 7+ or 8+ to conventional preps – Sussex House, Wetherby Prep or St Philip's – with the occasional parent choosing the country boarding option. The trend for senior London schools to take boys at 11+ is increasing but, just in case, the head is already sounding out schools like Thomas's Battersea and Eaton House, who will take in boys aiming at 13+ schools. She also brings in senior heads at an annual event for parents. Girls at 11+ mainly join the old favourite London day schools but the excellent results allow them to aim at the schools for high achievers such as Godolphin & Latymer, JAGS, City of London Girls and Putney High. An impressive proportion of academic scholarships, considering the size of the school, with the odd one for sport or music.

Remarks: The pre-prep hides in what was once an undercroft, below an uninspiring example of ecclesiastical architecture. It is now a surprisingly light and airy space, with a multi-purpose hall on one side and a cheerful passage leading to the nursery and classrooms for reception and year 1. The nursery is much praised by parents, one knowledgeable mother commenting that not only had they managed to persuade her son to sit on the carpet quietly for 'a decent length of time' but also that he came home burbling about the fun projects and activities that had filled his day. Meals, quite often a trying time at this stage for both small and large people, are no problem here as apparently the food is 'brilliant', and a parent told us that her candidate for the 'world's fussiest eater' wolfed it all down.

The pre-prep is not just about play, judging from some extremely neat writing and maths displayed on the walls, with an obvious emphasis on building confidence as well as academic skills. The most quoted example is how they successfully encourage every child (from reception onwards) to take turns at presenting work in assembly. We were told by parents that in some cases 'this was a minor miracle', persuading an acutely shy child to happily stand up in front of 150 people and start talking. SL, who believes in making sure that you never ask children to do what you would not do yourself, makes sure that the teachers lead the way by all taking assembly themselves.

The main school lives behind the modest facade of a late Victorian building on a London artery. This was originally the home of the school's founder, Lady Daphne Edwards, about whom little is known except that she left her house plus enough cash for a charitable trust, enabling the school to flourish and reach its 70th birthday. The trust funds have been well looked after and SL says that they have the wherewithal for expanding their space to match their co-ed ambitions, aiming to grow the school gradually from one to two forms.

With only 100 children, the common hustle and bustle of most junior schools feels muted and the housekeeping, despite the challenge of a cageful of fluffy chicks, is well on top of the dust bunnies. The sense of calm is apparent all the way up from the semi-basement, with its hall, tiny Maurice Sendak kitchen squeezed into the corner and classroom at the back, to the attic with its new, purpose-built music rooms and cosy staff room under the eaves. Children move about with purposeful expressions and an obvious certainty about their next destination, so this is definitely a well-orchestrated operation, although rather charmingly relaxed on the surface.

Despite this cool, rather than hothouse, atmosphere Redcliffe children leave with the full academic package: they may not have been offered the exotic curriculum options available in the larger local preps but they have no trouble in passing the 7+, 8+ and 11+ and succeeding in the ferocious competition for places at demanding senior schools. Naturally, there is some concern that the different requirements for boys (online pre-tests) will mean some additions to the current curriculum, but as English, maths, verbal and non-verbal reasoning are already on the timetable, SL believes that she is on top of this. They will certainly all be well-taught at maths as the teacher of years 5 and 6 is apparently 'amazing'.

Unable to take children with anything beyond mild dyslexia; there used to be murmurings that the SEN provision was possibly a little stretched and problems were not picked up fast enough, but the evidence is that this has changed. SL and her new SENCo are much more aware of where help may be needed, and the genuine family atmosphere of the school is a huge advantage.

Knowing that she is going to have older boys in her charge, one of SL's new initiatives is to increase the opportunity for the children to enjoy sport. Friday afternoons are for games in the form of optional clubs, rather than lessons, and an extended school day on Friday will allow them to ramp up the sporting provision. The new sports facility is only a few hops, skips and jumps away and there are beaming faces at the mention of the summer sports day. Redcliffe might not be the perfect spot for a football fiend looking for the rough and tumble of team games but, having said this, they have a potential international swimmer in their ranks, so an awareness of sporting potential is certainly there.

London parents are looking beyond academics, even in a tiny school, and pupils can join clubs for budding artists or chefs, practise for a parliamentary career in debating or aim at LAMDA exams. Trying to ensure that her charges do not lead too cloistered a life, the head casts a termly fly into the parental talent pool and lands a willing soul to talk to them about the world outside, as well as posting a weekly blog herself.

Enthusiastic comments on the standard of pastoral care from parents – 'it's like leaving your child with a relation rather than a babysitter' – and from older girls, who appreciate the new flowery summer frocks – 'I might even wear it after I've left' – show that the new head is sensitive about making changes. She is well aware that finding the correct balance between remaining a small traditional London prep school and being a forward thinking modern co-ed establishment is no easy task. We left feeling confident that she would crack it.

Rhodes Avenue Primary School

Rhodes Avenue, London N22 7UT

Ages 3–11 **Pupils** 690

020 8888 2859
www.rhodes.haringey.sch.uk

Headteacher: Since 2015 Adrian Hall BEd (30s). Gained his degree in primary education from Leeds University, then worked as a reception teacher at Castleton Primary School, after which he moved up the ranks to his first headship at Churchfield Primary School in Enfield, a post he had for eight years. During this time – in which he worked in a wide range of schools, some in deprived areas – he earned himself an NLE (National Leader in Education) in recognition of his work in supporting not only pupils but also teachers and leaders.

Instantly likeable, he is warm and laid back – a high-fives-in-the-corridor kind of head who wants children to feel comfortable in his presence. 'He's the best head teacher in the world,' one child told us, with others describing him as 'kind,' 'funny' and 'really nice.' 'They hero worship him – and he's a brilliant teacher,' said one parent – indeed he teaches year 4s once a week. But make no mistake – he is also highly efficient and savvy about all things educational, and the policies he's brought in around discipline and punctuality have been unanimously welcomed. 'He improved an already brilliant school – that's no mean feat,' one parent told us. Meets and greets daily – 'within a week of arriving, he knew every child's name and he always chats to us. What's more, if you put forward an idea, he's on the case. He's an incredible man,' said one parent.

Loves swimming and rafting and exploring London and the world with his family. 'My son is fearless so we spend many a weekend at theme parks.'

Entrance: Admission by means of the local authority criteria – which means that, in order of priority, it's looked after children and SEN, then siblings and after that, living as near as possible. With four applications for every place, this generally means within a quarter of a mile. Local estate agents are big fans – the success of the school, and its neighbouring comprehensive, has had a significant impact on local property prices.

Exit: The school backs directly on to Alexandra Park, one of the borough's best secondaries, and over half of pupils proceed there. Others to Fortismere and Latymer, with the remainder attending a wide range of schools including JFS, the Compton School, Greek School of London, Channing and Dame Alice Owen's.

Remarks: Undoubtedly helped by the fact that most families live within feet of the gates, this is a school with a true community feel – a vibe that parents say it has managed to retain despite moving to three-form entry of 90. And if ever there was an argument that schools benefit from great architects, this is it – the interiors meld the original 1930s building with the more recent extensions to create bright, light and modern learning spaces that are a joy to spend time in. The wide, carpeted corridors of the main split-level building are so much more than mere walkways, with private music lessons, art exhibitions etc going on throughout. The classrooms are big and airy, with huge windows – and the spongy-carpeted library is, for many children, their 'favourite place.' The art studio is well stocked; ICT suite is up-to-date; and there are two school halls – one purely for PE, while the other is also used for assemblies, lunch and performances. Nursery (now full time) and reception are housed in a separate single story building, also with nice, bright classrooms. Outside, there are separate soft-ground playgrounds for different age groups. And the chickens – a relatively recent addition that give a nod to the school site's origins as a farm – are extremely popular with the children.

Children are taught mainly by class teachers, with specialist teachers enhancing areas such as French, art and PE. Parents praise the themed approach to learning – with each year group studying a single topic every half term, with a cross-curricular approach thereon eg year 5's theme was Pole to Pole, when we visited – the history aspect speaks for itself, while in geography they learned about global warming and in English, they explored Shackleton's poems etc. 'You really get to see these themes come to life in the class assemblies,' said one parent. Teaching staff – a good mix of the experienced and young – are fun. In every classroom we saw, there was a feeling of merriment, creativity, learning through doing and of getting things done with a smile and a light touch. It clearly works – the school consistently dominates the local authority league tables, with reading progress in the top 20 per cent of schools in the country, and writing and maths in the top five per cent. Ofsted can barely think of a word of criticism. Sats results are outstanding, with the majority reaching the highest levels. Though the pupils tend to be of above average ability on entry, everyone we spoke to agrees the school goes above and beyond. French taught from year 2 and 'parlez-vous' is supplemented with fun activities like a French breakfast, croissants included. Setting in years 5 and 6 for maths and English. All teachers are trained in forest school.

Academic progress is charted minutely and parents kept well informed, with three parents' evenings and three reports a year. Strong support, too, for the struggling. 'My son has a special literacy person and she's fantastic,' said one parent. An 'inclusion leader' leads SEND, with a separate SEND lead in the early years centre – both cater for not only mild and moderate, but more severe, including pre-verbal and wheelchair using children. Their creative, child-focused support both in and outside the classroom has earned the school an Inclusion Quality Mark. 'My son has a specialist care team because of his needs and they were very impressed by how far the school was prepared to go to ensure he reached his full potential. It's just incredible,' a parent told us, while another said, 'Unlike other schools, they start with the child and adapt the school to them – rather than telling you how you have to fit in.'

Sport, music, art and drama are as high up the agenda as the three Rs. In sport, there's been a push on inclusivity. 'We want every child to be able to compete, so we've introduced a squad system for football, for example, whereby 30 children get to compete, instead of the six children in the top team in the old system,' says the head. 'It's working – sport here is much more about participation than it used to be,' a parent said, although school still keen to bring home the silverware. Netball, gymnastics, athletics and rugby are at the core, plus basketball, boating, golf and handball. Onsite facilities include the two sports halls and outside cage for netball and football, and they use public parkland just behind the school. Good links with the local tennis club, and year 4s upwards go swimming at a local public pool.

Drama regularly seeps into English lessons, and there are two extracurricular acting clubs, plus a whole-school Christmas production and class assemblies. Art is popular – sculpting and printing as common as traditional art. 'We had to make a fish out of a trash can recently – I thought it would be rubbish, but it was amazing,' one child told us.

Music permeates the culture here – we saw lots of instrumental lessons in action. There's an orchestra, chamber choir, school choir and boy band – all of which publicly perform – and children sing at the local tube station to raise money for charity at Christmas. Some year groups learn instruments as a whole, with past examples including cello, clarinet, recorder, drums and violin.

Extracurricular clubs include all the usual suspects, plus the likes of street dance, coding, meditation, sewing, chess, pottery and drama. Lots of competitions entered and usually won. Breakfast club from 7.50am and after-school play centre on site 3.30-6pm, plus holiday clubs. Trips and workshops are all related to the current topic, as well as two activity-based residentials – year 5 to Wales for a weekend and year 6 to Lincolnshire for a week.

This is a nurturing school, with a strong pastoral system that includes a school counsellor (one day a week) and art therapy sessions available from the specialist art teacher. Parents, too, can get support and guidance on issues like bedtime routines and healthy eating. Huge buy-in for the no-uniform policy which, says head, 'helps children feel comfortable and that they can really be themselves.' Plenty of praise for encouraging good behaviour – 'stickers go a long way.' Children who don't follow the 'golden rules' are given 'refection' and if that doesn't work, parents are called in. Bullying rare. Less than a handful of temporary exclusions, if any, each year. Student voice is big – the student council voted to bring in vegetable growing areas, among other things. Mixed views on the food. 'It's horrible,' more than one child told us.

Parents – a sociable and supportive bunch – are increasingly prosperous and professional, although around six per cent of pupils are on free school meals. Those with interesting jobs come in to share their expertise. Around half are white British; rest mainly other white backgrounds and Asian.

This is a friendly, upbeat and innovative local school with a fabulous learning environment, where pupils have fun, get excited about learning and have lots of opportunities around responsibility.

Richard Challoner School

Manor Drive North, New Malden, Surrey KT3 5PE

Ages 11–18 **Pupils** 1,020 **Sixth form** 260 (28 girls); federated with Holy Cross **RC**

020 8330 5947
www.richardchalloner.com

Head: Since 2015, Sean Maher BA (40s). Previously deputy head, rising through the ranks after being offered first post here four weeks into teacher training in 2001. Leadership skills amply demonstrated during secondment to Catholic secondary in Kent, transforming it in just under 18 months from 'requires improvement' to 'good' by upping expectations, improving discipline and putting classroom walls back in. 'Anyone could have done it,' he says modestly. Award of Kent Headteacher of the Year suggests anyone probably couldn't.

A local boy, combined studies at Emanuel and St Mary's Twickenham (studying English and history) with helping out in family bakery in Raynes Park (nothing like removing freshly baked loaves at end of night shift for sense of fulfillment, he says).

Little ruffles his feathers bar increasing amount of time spent on plugging growing holes in funding – every minute not spent helping pupils is a minute wasted. Tidiness also a major preoccupation, all senior teachers issued with own litter pickers. As badges of office go, not glitzy (sadly, there's no short but moving presentation ceremony either) but important, sending unambiguous message about standards and expectations.

While convention matters – uniform code for sixth formers specifying 'conservative' haircuts unlikely to change – Mr Maher also promotes the 'right sort' of Jesuitical rebelliousness – standing up against the prevailing wisdom rather than 'pointless' defiance. 'Boys need to be able to articulate their views – and unfortunately in society there is so much they need to stand against at the moment,' he says.

Devout, kind and focused on the pupils, he's a popular choice. 'Has best interests of everyone at heart,' says mother. No surprise that would-be staff will be asked if they really love children. 'Can tell straight away if they're really very awkward with the question.'

Impressive without being intimidating – 'Serious,' thought junior pupil – though older ones appreciate deadpan humour that's not far beneath the surface – and recently sang to whole school in assembly to demonstrate virtues of risk taking. 'He's down with the kids,' reckoned senior pupil – though Mr Maher isn't convinced.

Above all, a force to be reckoned with. His son, starting at the school soon, plans to 'come and have a cuddle if gets into trouble,' says Mr Maher. 'I said, "Son, if that's what you think, you've underestimated me".' We suspect that's unlikely to be the case for very long.

Academic matters: 'You won't see one child not engaged with their learning,' says head. Naturally we put this to the test during tour – and he's right. From year 7 French class on a virtual shopping trip – 'Un grand sac de Doritos Chilli 'eatwave s'il vous plaît' – to year 8 boys' thoughts on constructing a balanced argument in English – 'Always talk through problems; don't keep it in,' there's minimal fidgeting or disengagement.

Even class of year 10 maths pupils, all blazer-clad and diligently working through mind-expanding algebra in boiling hot classroom, and year 11 pupils who have gone straight from first GCSE (RS) to revision session (physics), are impressively focused if a tad goggle-eyed – there's no study leave here, just a collapsed timetable to keep everyone on task.

All contributes to cracking results. In 2018, 86 per cent of pupils achieved 9-4 in GCSE maths and English, 34 per cent of grades at 9-7; 28 per cent of A levels awarded A*/A and 54 per pent A*-B. Success down to inspired teaching delivered with dedication and plenty of innovation. Younger pupils now have own iPads (top years who have missed out as not here long enough to pay them off are philosophical about greater good) and even insets, last one involving staff treasure hunt, sound fun.

Teaching team is bursting with young talent, with plenty of senior teachers barely in 30s and now heads-in-waiting, some former pupils who were taught by 50 or so veterans who've been here for a decade or more. Old or novice, sense of pride in their work visible in corridor after corridor crammed with pristine displays – we particularly liked the Poetree, with poems nestled among painted branches and the swathes of playing cards in the maths corridor, each with probability problem.

Energy courses through the place – head is a strong believer in keeping boys busy and the pace is correspondingly brisk. Despite DT's demotion from core subject to option in line with government requirements, most boys still take 10 GCSEs, down from 11 (slimmed down to six for some SEN pupils). Reduction a possible relief given one former pupil's comment about ease of overdosing on arts or sport activities 'and then realising you've got an exam in a month...'

Most subjects are set from year 7 with two innovative transition classes in core subjects helping first years who hadn't hit Sats targets bridge gap between primary and senior school.

'Some present with big challenges,' says teacher, who's using colour-coded activities (red for independent learning, yellow for group work) to 'teach boys to learn.'

Everyone gets together for other subjects including DT (freeflow rooms, 3D printer and fab projects including programmable robotic cars). Well-resourced food technology, hospitality and catering a big hit with year 10 pupils, particularly top set types who find relaxation in creation of immaculate macaroons, sushi and crostini.

Range continues at sixth form level with 28 A levels and five BTecs, some high demand subjects (maths, history, geography and psychology currently top list of favourites) offered both here and at partnered girls' school, Holy Cross, others split between the two – timetable immensely complex to sort but currently working well, minibus plying between the two sites 'and easy to catch as long as you organise yourself,' said pupil. No plans for combined sixth form – with almost 500 pupils across two schools, semi-detached existence works better.

Generously proportioned and resourced learning resource centre, open on Saturday mornings and in holidays, provides a shelter for anyone having a rough time. Determined librarian's mission is to ensure that everyone reads – books must be carried at all times – while staff post current title on their classroom doors – maths teacher was deep in Candide; head tucking into The Jesuit Guide to Almost Everything, a recent gift from a colleague.

High expectations extend to SEN pupils – 76 pupils in much-admired ASD unit which takes LA-referred pupils (all statemented or with EHC plan) plus 12 in years 7-11 with social, emotional and mental health needs who get imaginative support – life skills programme recently boosted with acquisition of aquarium and (very popular) pet guinea pig. Focus is on inclusion with help from 26 learning support assistants. 'The philosophy is very much "we want you in the classroom",' says Mr Maher.

Current SEN team praised by a parent for 'exemplary knowledge of needs' and commitment to pupils. 'Chilled out, calm and very good at working out what students' individual needs are,' thought dyslexic pupil – extends to letting sixth formers taking three rather than two years to complete courses. 'If you can't do it one way, you can do it another,' supportive teacher tells parents. Building on expertise with new MLD unit for 16-19 year olds.

First class communication helps hold the whole thing together. 'Every teacher knows what's going on,' said parent. There's plenty of support, from timetabled revision classes to informal chats over coffee, particularly relished by sixth formers. 'Get on so well, wasn't that teacher and pupil divide,' said recent leaver. And humour is always on tap. 'Aah, isn't he lovely,' says wording under pic of puppy outside science lab. 'He's a guide dog for the blind and if you don't wear safety spectacles, you might need one...'.

Games, options, the arts: Not the right place for staff in search of quiet life and 4pm finish, warns school. With many charity-linked events – rough sleep event in school grounds raised over £7,000 – extracurricular programme spilling over into weekends and evenings, trips (rugby tour of South Africa) and clubs including art, video and media as well as vibrant house system with 40 events – house music competitions demand original composition as well as normal solo and group acts, rewarding extra commitment with bonus points – not surprising that potential staff recruits are asked what can bring to the party.

Best to arrive at interview with at least one extra talent and be prepared to offer it freely (there's no extra pay). 'Do it because of the impact it has on the children,' says Mr Maher. Recent sports award event a case in point, with staff (and some partners) organizing sit down evening meal for 180 winners and their teachers, reflecting considerable achievements.

Head is delighted with considerable sporting achievements, particularly in football where teams regularly reach final eight or better at national and district level, though would love to see rugby doing even better especially given permanent underdog status against largesse of independent school resourcing.

Pupils, bar desire for a swimming pool – likely to remain on wish list for foreseeable future – had few complaints and instead were eloquent about the way that whatever their interest, school's encouragement had helped them discover it – and find themselves. 'If it hadn't been for here, wouldn't be playing at county level,' said sixth former.

Arts equally popular, teaching highly rated, dynamic music teacher leading erudite GCSE discussion on monophony, performing arts BTec recently added to the mix.

Impressive facilities include imaginatively revamped St Bede's building include airy first floor multi-purpose hall, while bright dance studio (head's ambition is to give it official standing on the curriculum) is good enough to be hired out to private firm who no doubt relish its up to the mark light wood finish and mirrored wall as much as the pupils.

There's big performance space (large theatre) and gem of a drama studio, once the gym – its transformation into flexible, well curated black-ceilinged space with roll on, roll off seating, a professional lighting rig and teeny but impressive sound and lighting box yet another brainchild of previous head, who also managed to carve out funding and space from a corridor for tiny recording studio which is, courtesy of acoustic tiles, very nearly soundproof. Together provide worthwhile settings for ambitious plays and musicals that range from Shakespeare to home grown, one production each year touring in Hungary. 'A massive inspiration,' said past pupil.

Sunny art room, rather empty on day of visit, contrasted with sombre but highly accomplished monochrome tableaux on display, screaming mouths skewered with 3D spears. 'It's linked to fear and inability to express yourself,' said jolly teacher. Not a problem that afflicts many of the pupils here, judging by popular debating society propositions that range from pros and cons of immigration ('fiery,' says diplomatic member of staff) to 'Is feminism still relevant?' (Yes).

Background and atmosphere: Catholicism at its best though you don't have to share Mr Maher's beliefs to get the most from it. Chapel is of modest dimensions, though removable partition ensures that the growing numbers attending weekly mass (chaplain is parish priest and a school governor) can be catered for though 'knows his boys – never takes more than 20 minutes,' says the head.

Tangible manifestations of faith are numerous but not relentless – our favourite was Eric Gill-like Madonna and child in entrance to new block – an alternative design for school's foundation, finally realised on 50th anniversary, marked by bussing whole school to Westminster Cathedral on double-deckers for a special ceremony.

Once undersubscribed and so rough that 'story was you had to nail salt and pepper pots to the table,' says staff member, school has changed markedly though perceptions, particularly among the smarter Wimbledon Village set, have been a bit slower to catch up.

Their loss. The immediate surroundings may not be SW19-friendly, but even the most aesthetically sniffy will enjoy beautiful greenery of the ancient Hogsmill River that runs beside playing fields, as well as astonishing transformation of school itself. With curved roofs, plenty of wood-cladding and even mellow(ish) brickwork school presents unified face to the world, avoiding normal piecemeal additions so often derived on a one thing after another basis. Even the little details like repainting all the external window frames grey make a huge difference.

Inside, many of the long corridors running length of main teaching blocks have been transformed with glass panels, smart blinds and bright white paint. Outside there's a 3G pitch (superior artificial surface that can take conventional football boots) and athletics track – pupils allowed on grass only in late summer, mingling – happily enough – on the tarmac for rest of year.

It's masterpiece of nifty financial footwork by previous head ('genius in finding and stretching money – turned school from 1950s dilapidation to one fit for 21st century,' says head). No wonder even backroom bean counters are jolly – a rare sight indeed.

Even yet-to-be-transformed areas with Crittall windows, grey-flecked lino and thick brown tiled windowsills, are so well-maintained that have a rather desirable vintage look, though once head's money-charming skills are fully realised (and there's no chance they won't be), will doubtless get the necessary upgrades.

Pupil areas have been given similar TLC, with sixth form combined social and study area and bistro a particularly desirable perk. Though occasionally used for special events, normally out of bounds for lower school pupils who can only yearn over passing trolleys packed with seniors only fizzy drinks (as can buy up the road, no point in not offering) as well as bacon, sausage and croissants for break (all cooked in-house). Chips (girls) and southern fried chicken 'n' cheese baguette (boys) the top 16+ faves though, judging by prodigious quantities of food enthusiastically put away by lower school pupils and numerous lunchtime choices (including pasta, paninis and a veggie option) nobody appears to be suffering.

Pastoral care, well-being and discipline: 'It's like a family business,' says Mr Maher who (though not by way of proof) reports boys in lessons occasionally addressing him as 'mum'. Literally so, as many teachers don't just come in singles but often in pairs and occasionally in sets. We ran out of the times we were introduced to one teacher and told that partner or a sibling (they even do a nice line in twins) also worked here.

Winner in what would be cracking Top Trumps game is the Maher clan. Mrs M senior works in the café (and unfortunately wasn't in on day of visit as we were dying to have critique of son's leadership style), Mrs M junior, his wife, is a chemistry teacher, brother taught geography here and son is a potential pupil.

As in best run families, school discipline is achieved effectively with minimum of fuss, down to 'passive supervision' – staff always there but presence is low-key, issues often resolved through informal chats with favourite teacher.

Head speeds departing pupils on their way at end of day (no doubt fitting in a final litter check) while other staff patrol local shops. Even former pupils don't escape (one 30-something pillar of community told off for poor parking, reported distinctly gleeful wife).

R

'Very calm here,' said recent leaver, who felt that while would always be some naughty boys ('Don't let them tell you there aren't' – they didn't) response would be speedy and compassionate. Having witnessed the barely discernible fall-out from just one incident – pupil briefly and calmly removed from classroom after melt-down – we can only agree. Response to inevitable unkindness is similarly 'fantastic,' said parent.

'If you focus on the small things, you very rarely get to the big things, so we focus on the small things unrelentingly, shirt tails, top buttons, sensible hair cuts,' says Mr Maher. Rules are strictly enforced with sensible concessions. 'I abhor locked rooms,' he says – and they aren't, well-stocked fitness suite (like dance suite rented out after hours) the only exception – a health and safety rather than trust issue.

There's authorised queue-jumping for autistic pupils otherwise overwhelmed by lunchtime noise, younger boys using the outside entrance, year 11s, swelled by privilege of age, allowed to arrive via the hall, biometrics guaranteeing speed service for all.

Deliberate litter dropping was, unsurprisingly, taken very seriously, punishment – donning high vis jacket and doing a whole-school clear up – very definitely matching the crime.

Above all, success celebrated where and whenever it crops up. Basketball star blushingly praised for efforts is told by Mr M that 'will make a fuss in assembly,' while there's tea and cakes with the head for frequent 'above and beyond' award winners ('go to Waitrose the night before and clear the shelves,' he says) successes recorded on honours board (updatable paper rather than carved on wood). Senior teachers dispense the beverages, boys serve the food. 'A nice touch,' said parent. 'Do praise effort.'

Pupils and parents: Most illustrious former pupil is probably Spiderman actor Tom Holland. Others into professions (law) or sport – including Britain's first wheelchair referee.

Family feel is pervasive, with 16 or so girls joining modestly co-ed sixth form (plus 30 or so who come over from Holy Cross) instantly slotting in, praised by head for sparkiness and openness to change. Can be harder for routine-loving boys joining in year 12, thought school insider – nobody's fault, just down to intensity of bonds formed in earlier years.

Entrance: With hefty oversubscription and around four applicants for each of 150 year 7 places, essential to be realistic. 'Effectively if you're not a practising Catholic and you're not in one of our feeder schools [Corpus Christi, Our Lady Immaculate, Sacred Heart, New Malden, St Agatha's, St Cecilia's, St Clement's and St Joseph's, Kingston], it's going to be very hard,' says Mr Maher.

Strength of faith matters (weekly church attendance is one of entrance criteria). Then it's down to home address (living in two local deaneries helps) and distance to school gates.

Post 16, minimum of 10 external candidates accepted including small numbers of girls, permanent members of the school's own sixth form. All faith criteria as before, most courses requiring grade 6 or better in related GCSE.

Exit: In 2018, 30 per cent left after GCSEs. Majority of year 13 leavers move on to higher education with many gaining places at Russell Group universities. Birmingham, Warwick, Nottingham, Portsmouth and Kent all popular destinations. Often several to Oxbridge (three in 2018, plus one medic). Just under a fifth carry on in further education and programmes, remainder opting for apprenticeships including Civil Service fast track and BBC broadcast engineering.

Remarks: Faith-inspired, purposeful leadership and energetic teaching deliver first rate education that's big on family feel and hot on detail. Inveterate litterbugs might struggle.

Robert Clack School

Gosfield Road, Dagenham, Essex RM8 1JU

Ages 11–18 **Pupils** 2,070 **Sixth form** 456

020 8270 4200
www.robertclack.co.uk

Headteacher: Since 2018, Russell Taylor BSc, previously senior deputy. He grew up in Dagenham, is a former pupil here, gained a first class degree in economics at Queen Mary and trained as a teacher at the Institute of Education. He joined Robert Clack, his fourth teaching post, in 2002. 'I didn't come back with the intention of being the head,' he says, as if he somehow surprised himself, but nevertheless rose through the ranks and became acting head in 2017 following the departure of his predecessor due to ill health.

Trim, neat, spirited and uninhibited, he is proud of his working-class roots and has a noticeable rapport with the pupils, with whom he spends a great deal of time, both teaching (economics to year 13s the year we visited) and spending much of his time 'doing the rounds' of the school. 'It means I have to do a lot of the paperwork side of things out of hours, but I don't mind as the most important thing to me is modelling the values of the school and building relationships,' he says. Is unfazed by the fact that it's spread over two sites (soon to be three) 'because I get the chance to walk between them – again relationship building, but this time with the local community.' Parents say he's 'got a way about him: 'You can see he's in awe of the school, which is what most of us feel like, to be honest,' one told us.

Lives locally with his family; his nieces and nephew attend the school. His two big passions are being with his family and dog walking. Was a torchbearer at the London 2012 Olympic Games for being a positive role model in the school and local area and uniting the community with a £50,000 fundraising campaign to support a student with osteosarcoma.

Academic matters: Results are way above the national standard for a school with such a big, and expanding, cohort: in 2018, 67 per cent of pupils got 9-4 in both maths and English GCSE, with 18 per cent of grades A*-A/9-7. At A level, 53 per cent A*-B and 23 per cent A*/A grades. Used to be a specialist science college and science, maths and computing results still stand out – no mean feat in such a strongly working-class school. Pupils say the English department is also exceptional. French and Spanish from year 7, with pupils strongly encouraged to take one language at GCSE, while those who speak another language at home often take a GCSE in that too. Psychology and sociology popular GCSEs, as is the plethora of vocational options available at this level, including construction (in the impressive sponsored £30k onsite teaching area, where pupils can learn everything from bricklaying to plastering and painting), beauty therapy (in the wow-factor onsite beauty school where we'd have gladly become guinea pigs for a massage ourselves) and food and hospitality. A joy to see when so many schools are cutting back their vocational provision to focus on league tables.

The ability range is massive, from those aiming at A*s to those who joined the school with a reading age of 5 or 6. Setting in every subject in years 7 to 9, then in core subjects of English, maths and science. Pupils told us 'there's no stigma about being in a lower set – it usually just means you learn in a more visual way' and there's auditing to ensure fluidity between sets. Subject clinics and revision sessions are available throughout the year, including during some weekends and every Easter holidays; parents say it reflects 'the amazing commitment of teachers,' around 16 per cent of whom attended the school themselves. 'Honestly, the teachers are so supportive and that's not just academically but emotionally too – they really want you to do well,' a pupil told us.

Learning support and mentor rooms also enable children can come to catch up on literacy and numeracy – perhaps because they've been off sick or they're upset because of family problems and can't cope amongst their peers. Pupils also value the 'Robert Clack good lesson' template, which involves explaining to pupils the objective, interactive content and process of every lesson – 'you know what to expect every time you sit down in a classroom and the goals you're supposed to have reached,' said one. Homework levels on the high side, but nobody seems to mind and student planners are regularly checked by staff to ensure academic balance between pupils. Current focus on identifying and working with specific groups that are less aspirational than others, 'for example, the disaffected white British,' says head.

SENs – which includes the whole gamut from mild dyslexia and ADHD to pupils with Asperger's, hearing and sight problems and cerebral palsy – all get plenty of support as required. We heard from one family how a girl had 'improved so much that she can now spell better than me, despite having an EHC plan.' School praised for tailoring support 'in a very personalised and caring way' and pupils reeled off long list of modifications to chairs, desks and learning equipment in their smart new year 7 block.

The sixth form is part of the North East Consortium with two other local schools, offering more than 40 courses at different levels. Many sixth formers are the first in their families to stay in education post-16. No minimum entry requirements, as courses range from a certificate in motor vehicle servicing to further maths, though students who want to take A levels must have at least five grade 4s at GCSE. 'We don't set the benchmark too high because we want to give these children a chance.' Maths and sciences are the most popular A level courses, followed closely by English, history, economics and media studies. Vocational options in business, IT, food and nutrition and sport popular, as is beauty therapy – 'we give everyone the opportunity to be successful here'.

Games, options, the arts: Rare is the comp where pupils say nobody really hates sports, everyone feels there are enough teams and they get frequent wins at high level. 'If there isn't room for someone who is interested in a sport in an existing team, they either get to be a sub or a new C or D team is created if there's enough of them,' a pupil said, with all the ones we met raving about how much they enjoy sport 'because there's something for everyone'. And they bring home the silver too. They have been 23 years borough champions in athletics and recently came third nationally. Rugby also a strength for both girls and boys ('getting in the Essex finals used to be a big deal, now it's normal'), with a rugby academy attracting talented players to the sixth form. Football, netball, cross-country all do well and individual pupils have competed nationally in a range of sports, their team shirts displayed proudly alongside photos and trophies throughout the school.

A sizeable leisure centre includes a sports hall and fitness suite, open to the local community outside school hours, and there's a new sports hall on the lower school site. Tennis and netball courts galore and no shortage of pitches, including Astroturf. 'Teachers give up a lot of their spare time to sport – the children see this and it makes them have even more respect for them,' said one parent. Another told us, 'The fact that my son gets up every Saturday morning to do rugby means he gets to know a lot of the kids in other schools – the school encourages that mingling and I really believe it stops youth on youth crime in the local area because they wind up recognising each other when they see each other in town.'

Boys', girls' and mixed school choirs go from strength to strength (we heard them in an assembly – mesmerising), including entering national song competitions and hosting musical exhibitions. Ex-pupil Sandy Shaw gets stuck in enthusing pupils when she can, including attending concerts where she has been known to throw out a tune or two herself. Impressive school orchestra and jazz group perform at Christmas and summer concerts. Individual instrumental lessons are free (although we were disappointed that none of the pupils we met had taken this up) and whole year groups learn the likes of piano (two to a keyboard – year 7), ukulele (year 8) etc. There are regular whole school performances combining music, art and drama – such as Coram Boy and the

Lion, the Witch and Wardrobe. 'My daughter was very shy when she joined the school, now she sings on the stage at Christmas – and it's all down to the music teacher using the arts to bring her out of herself,' one parent told us.

School says they see art as vital, including as an extracurricular subject, and there's some lovely artwork displayed around the school, with spacious facilities for both this and DT, both of which have reasonable take-up at GCSE. But pupils we met unanimously cited art as the weakest department, saying it is less engaging and accessible than other subjects 'and it's always the same people do well.' Good food tech facilities and plenty of opportunities to make culinary delights; one year 7 pupil we met was itching to get the theory out of the way and get their pinny on.

School trips include a French exchange, sixth form politics and history visits to Washington and New York and sports trips to Canada, Barbados, Germany and South Africa. Cultural visits to Italy and Spain; expedition visits to Egypt and Latin America. Residentials to Isle of Wight and day trips to France, among others. School sees these as critical to children's development, with regular fundraising ensuring nobody misses out on the whole-class trips (although there was some irritation among pupils we met about how many inevitably miss out on the expensive extracurricular ones).

Background and atmosphere: The school is named after local legend Robert Clack, who was mayor from 1940 to 1942 and a champion for social justice. 'He was a passionate advocate for the people of Dagenham and the values he stood for – mutual respect, compassion, discipline, high expectations and aspirations, and hard work – permeate the ethos of our school,' says head. For decades, the school was considered excellent, and after a major blip in the mid-90s (kids riding bikes down corridors and even smoking in classrooms), it was brought back to its former glory in the late 1990s.

The lower school site opened in 1935, the upper school buildings, half a mile away, in 1955. A third site, for years 7-11, opens in 2020. With 360 in each year group, it is currently one of the largest schools in the borough and when it reaches full capacity of 4,000 it will be one of the largest in Britain.

It is one of the most deprived areas in the country, with the tower blocks of the Becontree Estate – one of the largest in England – casting a shadow over the playground. Yet this is one of the most ordered, neatest schools we've come across. Building works and acquisition of new land has helped eradicate pinch points and highlights include the uber modern year 7 block, zen beauty salon, good science block and stand-out sports facilities. No shortage of computers, but very few lockers, which bothers some parents. 'It's not ideal to have to keep a heavy bag with you all day,' said one.

R

We saw attentive pupils in every lesson we observed, looking impeccably neat in blazers and ties with plenty of pupil buy-in ('uniforms are great for equality and it's good to be smart,' said one). Pupils are also proud of their badges, reflecting the school's emphasis on praise and leadership responsibilities – we saw awards given out in assembly for 'citizen of the week' and for reading one million words. Racism issues minimal ('the worst we get is occasional silly comments,' says head), with students mixing in genuinely diverse groups outside classes. Active school council made up of 300 pupils.

A breakfast and homework club – along with masses of extracurricular clubs in everything from cheerleading to astronomy and sports to debating – mean school is open from 7am to 6pm. Outside in the community there's little trouble, with Robert Clack kids known locally for being respectful and well-behaved – a far cry from days of old. Food could be improved, pupils told us, and some parents told us about the 'very long queues' which can make 'getting something to eat at lunchtime quite hard.'

Pastoral care, well-being and discipline: School has one of the most consistent behaviour policies we've come across – pupils don't even say some teachers are stricter than others. Every positive action gets a reward and every negative action is followed with a consequence – and every student knows it. Praise includes colours for sport, music and performing arts; awards during assemblies; notes home to parents; and trips to the likes of Thorpe Park. Meanwhile, the non-negotiable, tiered sanction system includes lunchtime detention, new Friday after-school detention and temporary exclusion that takes place on-site rather than sending pupils home. Lateness – even by a minute – is not tolerated and there's a blanket ban on mobile phones ('social media is such an addiction and distraction'). All the big stuff – gangs, knife crime, drugs – non-issues for the most part because 'we take such a hard line that it just doesn't enter the school threshold'. One permanent exclusion in the year before our visit.

School adamant that unless children feel both safe and happy, they can't learn, with pastoral care mainly coming from teachers and school counsellors, plus an increasing emphasis on mental health. Bullying rare, which pupils put down to CCTV throughout the school and an ethos of students of looking after each other, with many friendships are formed outside their year groups (mostly through clubs).

Pupils and parents: Families largely from the surrounding estates, where there are some severe poverty issues, with many coming from several generations of unemployment – though proximity to the school puts a premium on the prices of the few houses for sale in the area. School largely reflects the fast-changing demographic, with around 35 per cent white working-class; 35 per cent Afro-Caribbean; 15 per cent Asian (mainly Bangladeshi); and the rest mixed race. We found pupils delightful – polite, resilient, articulate and hard-working. And although they are typically from underachieving backgrounds, most parents are very much on board with the school – we couldn't find a single one that wasn't thoroughly supportive. The school employs a parental adviser who visits families under stress and helps with advice and support regarding housing, clothing and food allowances. Head currently considering a scheme whereby parents who have experience around issues such as discipline, routines and study skills would help other parents struggling in these areas.

Entrance: Some 1,600 applications for the 360 places in year 7, with pupils coming from around 40 feeder schools, so pupils often arrive knowing nobody. Looked-after children get priority, as do those with special educational needs, then by distance from the upper school site – generally within just one kilometre. Around 30 pupils from other schools join the sixth form.

Exit: About 80 per cent of pupils move up to the sixth form. Nearly all A level pupils to university, around 30 per cent Russell Group. Usually a couple to Oxbridge (two in 2018, one of these to study medicine, plus seven other medics, and one off to the US with a scholarship). A handful to UCL, Queen Mary's and Royal Holloway, with other high-profile universities also featuring regularly among destinations. Some 70 per cent study maths and sciences, with the remaining 30 per cent covering virtually every subject going. The remaining sixth formers go straight into work (many on apprenticeships), with significant numbers moving into the City. Plenty of careers advice and help with UCAS applications, and the school has high value partnerships with the likes of The Worshipful Company of Chartered Surveyors, The Prince's Teaching Institute, Teach First and Business in the Community, all of which provide pupils with work experience or routes into careers, as well as promoting the work of the school. Successful and expanding network of alumni, who help pupils with everything from work experience to networking.

Remarks: We love this true comprehensive in one of the most deprived areas of the country. All roads here lead back to high expectations and aspirations and it's all done in a context of mutual respect and compassion, albeit unashamedly strict. Staff, parents, pupils and even many of those in the local community that don't have kids attending the school seem to be bursting with pride about it. And despite the fast expansion of pupil numbers, it's managing to hold onto the values it holds so dear. No wonder parents and pupils consider a successful application a golden ticket.

The Roche School

11 Frogmore, London SW18 1HW

Ages 2.5–11 **Pupils** 323

Fees: £11,475 – £14,970 pa

020 8877 0823
www.therocheschool.com

Principal: Since 2010, Vania Adams (50s). Another example of the educational gene with both her siblings university lecturers, she worked in broadcasting and publishing but decided to swap the office for the classroom. She still teaches 11+ English and loves 'getting stuck in' but also 'pops into' classes to spread her love of reading. She is also heavily involved in the annual production for the Shakespeare Schools Foundation, a major feature in the school's calendar. A warm, articulate, approachable woman with whom her pupils are totally at ease, this is definitely a carrot not stick headmistress.

She has taken over from the founders Carmen and James Roche but their influence and involvement, both in the governance of the school and the day to day (Dr Roche was helping one of the pupils when we visited), is still very apparent. According to parents the school is 'more organised and professional since VA's arrival but she has not changed its spirit.'

Entrance: The majority into nursery (24 children) here or their other nursery Keswick House (up to 50 children) or else into reception. There is a waiting list at 2 for both nurseries and the system is first come, first served but you can't jump the gun by a pre-natal move. Three reception classes with siblings automatically offered places. They are able to manage the full range of learning difficulties, provided that the child will be able to cope within the school's framework, and also EAL children if they are confident that they will catch up with their year group. The odd place on offer higher up the school, often attracting children who have not flourished elsewhere, as the head is very sympathetic to those who may have been the victims of an academic 'chuck out' policy and regards it as a challenge – result, a great success rate at 11+. A very flexible approach to bursaries, particularly for those already in the school, and there is a special pot so that no child misses out on a school trip or expedition.

Exit: The Leaver's List can feature dozens of schools, explains the head, as they aim to ensure a good range of offers. In 2018, Emanuel, Streatham & Clapham High School, King's College Wimbledon and Wimbledon High were amongst those top of the list but there was a particularly wide range, from Eton to local grammar schools. A satisfactory number of scholarships including four to Dulwich College. VA says that she makes a huge effort to 'manage parental expectations', starting in year 4, 'encouraging parents to trust us'.

Remarks: In a tiny corner of London off the Wandsworth end of Putney Bridge Road and close to the river, you might easily miss the unassuming white façade with its discreet plaque. This is definitely not one for the parent who wants to expound on the glamorous outside facilities of their child's prep school but, once inside, an Aladdin's cave of educational possibilities opens up. Undoubtedly a small cave, but every inch has been used, including a booth for a front office that only functions because of the tangible goodwill of the people working there. All possible display spaces are commandeered for colourful mobiles, crammed notice boards and words of wisdom.

The nursery, housed looking onto a modest playground, contains puzzlers who look up politely and pirates who are too engrossed in their adventures to notice a strange visitor. One tidy tot puts away her toy on a shelf whilst a cheerful boy digs messily for treasure in a fake blue sea, all encouraged by smiley, qualified staff. Forest school is also part of the curriculum, taking place in Wimbledon Park or occasionally in more rural Richmond Park where one small, wise person pointed out to the teacher that the mushrooms were 'yellow, so they're probably poisonous'.

Once up the stairs (no barrier for one small girl moving up from nursery to reception: 'I'm going to do this on my own'), you find yourself in what is palpably the heart of the school. This is a space dominated by a library (complete with two librarians, albeit stuffed into a very small corner) and surrounded by classrooms with eight to 10 pupils in each, all heavily involved in either maths or English. The numbers are small because they group them in these subjects from year 1 although it is a flexible system and pupils move up and down regularly to make sure that the pace is correct for each child and extra support is available if necessary. The library is well stuffed with classics and modern authors, unsurprisingly, as reading is a 'big thing' with reading diaries, voluntary Book Club and even participation with 10 other schools in Battle of the Books.

The top floor holds the multi-purpose hall and, although a non-denominational school, we were treated to the whole of year 6's rendition of Leonard Cohen's Hallelujah (complete with majorly enthusiastic synchronised waving), nearly reducing one not particularly religious GSG hack to tears but which, on a more positive note, had been the winner at the Woldingham Choir festival. The room also metamorphoses into the dining hall, served by a miniscule kitchen, a source of worry to one pupil who wished that chef had more room to work in. Year 6 lives up here too, engaged on our visit in a Philosophy for Children class on religion; lower down the school P4C is incorporated into topics in history, geography and RE.

To expand the space available they lease a building just down the road which now holds year 5, a surprisingly large art room, two music rooms and an extremely popular (high on the list of 'best things' when we asked) gym run by a physically imposing, newly promoted head of games. In an ideal world, the head would like this building to belong to the school and she is in talks about the possibilities of expansion, not that she wants more pupils, simply more room for them to occupy. However, as one parent remarked, 'although it is rather cramped and chaotic with children charging around, there must be a system as it all works'.

Games have been moved up a rung recently and parents notice that there have been improvements in both standards and the quality of the teaching, with netball fielding particularly successful teams and an original initiative making sport gender free (girls can choose rugby and boys netball if they so wish).

Sport meets charity with Run For Us in Wandsworth Park which all take part in, including the head, who would normally prefer a good book or an exciting new play. Extracurricular clubs also feature sport as well as everything from carpentry to cooking to chess, which has a huge fan club.

It was a very nasty surprise to all concerned when the school was downgraded by Ofsted. Parents were uniformly 'astonished and shocked' and it would appear that the inspector was more than somewhat unprofessional in her approach, only squeezing in minutes observing lessons. Nevertheless, VA accepts that there were some areas where improvement could be made and has brought forward the appointing of new legal and financial governors and a new early years co-ordinator. The rebuttal to the findings has to be the high regard in which parents (nearly 80 wrote testimonials for Ofsted after the event) hold the school and the three-fold increase in the sign up for places in 2019.

We simply wish that schools like this, where children hug the headmistress and the more academic move on to starry academic senior schools, had been around when we were young. The Roche Approach (Respect, Open-mindedness, Compassion, Humour and Effort), which might sound a tad jingoistic elsewhere, seems to be working beautifully.

Rokeby School

George Road, Kingston, Surrey KT2 7PB

Ages 3–13 Pupils 390

Fees: £13,911 – £17,322 pa

020 8942 2247
www.rokebyschool.co.uk

Headmaster: Since 2007, Jason Peck BHEd NPQH. Joined school in 1996 as a year 4 and science teacher, becoming deputy head in 2004. Has seen one son through the school and has one still there – 'it means I see things from both sides,' he says.

Initially keen to train as a vet, only to realise during work experience that he was thoroughly squeamish. Absence of James Herriot moments led him instead to a spell travelling and running own business, arriving at Kingston University in mid-20s better versed in ways of world, he feels, than some younger out of the egg fellow students. First and only previous post was in tough middle school in Merton.

R

Personable, open and with a good sense of humour, he operates from his tucked-away corner office, which boys told us they visit strictly 'by appointment only,' although they did say they see plenty of him during the school day, with year 5s getting an extra dose as he teaches them science ('It helps me to really get to know the boys, which in turn helps with finding the right senior school'). Dresses up for World Book Day and charity days. 'He's nice,' was the most we could get out of the boys, although parents (especially of boys in the lower school) were more loquacious. 'The ethos of Mr Peck, which is totally child centric, cascades through the whole school to all members of staff,' said one, while a star-struck mother gushed, 'Without wanting to sound like a ridiculous schoolgirl, I'm totally in awe of him – he's so human and real, constantly developing and growing the school.' One parent felt that higher up the school Mr Peck was less visible and his vision for the school less clear, but school points out that he attends everything, helps out with the morning drop off system, defines his vision and direction for the school at the annual speech day and provides updates in termly newsletters.

Any spare time, he says, is spent writing his first novel. 'Well, someone's got to fill JK Rowling's shoes,' he laughs.

Entrance: Catchment tends towards Wimbledon and Putney more than Kingston and up into Teddington/Richmond, although that's starting to change. Many parents live practically on the doorstep, lapping up the added convenience of next door Holy Cross, a similarly high-performing prep for the sisters.

Parents perceive the school as becoming increasingly selective, but school insists that 'while there is a level of selection, it's very low key.' So-called discovery morning that takes place in autumn term the year before entry into reception is, according to the school, 'an opportunity for a two-sided discussion to work out if we are the right place for their son, definitely not a pure assessment. You can't test at 2 – just not possible.' A few leave at end of year 2 to go either to King's College Junior or St Paul's Juniors, with those at the top of knee-deep waiting lists soon filling the spaces.

Exit: Every year group heads off to between 12-18 schools, with most popular destinations including King's, St Paul's, Hampton, Epsom College, Reed's and St John's, with a few (sometimes more) to Eton and one or two most years to Charterhouse, Cranleigh and Whitgift. Every year, one or two boys leave earlier because they are not keeping up academically – 'we are very transparent, so if we have concerns whether a boy can thrive here, we let them know as early as year 1,' says head.

Remarks: Sandwiched between two other similarly grand-homes-turned-schools, Rokeby is reached via private roads with barrier-only entry (for which school issues passes to non-residents). As with so many schools, the reception area, reached by the original front door, gives a flavour of what's in store – in this case, a homely, friendly vibe and impeccable manners.

The original solid Victorian building, with its (in places warren-like) carpeted corridors and classrooms of varying sizes, is home to year 4s upwards ('the point at which the level of work starts to really ramp up,' said one boy), with younger ones taught in newer (2013) purpose-built lower school, complete with gorgeous performing arts theatre where we saw littl'uns practising for their nativity play. Head admits the school could do with a couple of extra classrooms ('not because we are short on them, but for greater flexibility') and a new hall in the main building which, we clocked, can surely not have changed since the 1980s. But overall, facilities are excellent, including huge touchscreen boards, three whizzy science labs ('there are lots of practicals,' say boys), assorted music rooms (tuneful solos from windows – standard here is high) and fabulous corridor and classroom displays (some of them floor to ceiling) among the highlights. Cosy upper school library has brightly coloured chairs, well stocked shelves and a cheery librarian, but the rows of desks all facing forwards have the disappointing effect of making it feel like yet another classroom. Outside space is limited but maximised, with various beautifully-equipped playgrounds, courts, smallish Astroturf and year 8 common room (a log cabin).

Parents told us Rokeby is 'not right for families who want to take a more relaxed approach for their son's education'. 'It's no hothouse, but you do need to be able to keep up with the academic rigour,' elaborated one. Most schools we visit brag about personalised learning, but Rokeby aims to take it to the next level, assessing and monitoring to the hilt, taking into account every boy's strengths, interests and individual needs when devising their learning plans. 'It's not just about the teachers' awareness of different learner types – auditory, visual and kinaesthetic etc; we hone in at a much more micro level,' claims school. 'Very quickly, the school observed our son's talents and interests and has sought to develop them with stretching classroom work but also opportunities outside of school, such as a history discovery day at a senior school,' confirmed one parent.

Lots of staff enthusiasm, including much-admired DT teacher (all kicks off with ball mazes in year 3, progressing to robot wars and even design-led working speakers in year 8), charismatic drama specialist ('we do loads of the backstage stuff like lighting too,' said one boy) and history teacher ('who actually brings the past to life'). Latin a bit of a Marmite subject – 'it dominates compared to history and English,' groaned one boy. Two form entry up until year 2, then pupils are split into three forms for year 3. Art and sports, drama and music taught by specialist subjects from the off, DT specialist from year 3 then all from year 5. Setting in maths and English from year 5 (the year 'when everything is about maths and English,' admits school) and in French and science from year 6. French is taught from year 2 and Mandarin from year 3.

SEN department has one full-time and two part-time staff members who 'mainly guide teachers how to support boys to manage in their lessons, rather than taking them out of the classroom'. Parents generally satisfied ('any learning support needs are picked up very quickly with an array of specialists at hand to help the boys navigate through,' said one) although another told us her son struggled with a teacher 'who seemed to think [his SEN] was his lack of attitude and effort,' but head of year subsequently 'put in place a whole support system for him which worked brilliantly.' On the welfare side, boys can see the ELSA (emotional literacy support assistant), which helps them with things like anxiety (but they can't self-refer), and there's also mindfulness on the menu for most boys, plus a counsellor who's called in when needed. Boys describe it as a 'caring' school. Bullying at a minimum, they say, 'because there is so much work in place to prevent it.' No suspensions for two years.

Short, sharp shocks, aka tiered detention system, manage any poor behaviour but boys told us you can get through the whole school without one if you play your cards right. Lots of recognition and rewards – not just verbal praise, but certificates, awards etc. Manners so flawless that Rokeby boys are renowned for their politeness – but the boys we met from the upper school seemed so focused on their etiquette and saying the right thing that at times we felt we wondered if we were getting a rather wooden version of their real selves. Even standing with arms straight, hands gripping over each other, seems to be a uniform stance here. The moments they let their guard down, however, were a joy – earnest boys, but with added playfulness and candour.

Sport a major feature of school life, with a similar level of tracking that you'd expect in academic teaching. Plenty of success in cricket, football and rugby (main sports), with athletics on the rise. County and national success at skiing, county success at cross-country. School recently introduced a more able sports programme to develop their elite. Boys said they'd like more PE – 'by the time you've changed clothing, there doesn't feel much time left,' said one. But plenty of extracurricular opportunities, from karate to tennis, with other clubs covering everything from LAMDA and debating. Boys are encouraged not to do too many at lunchtimes, however, 'because they need a break.' Trips galore – both days out such as Latin to Bath and residentials abroad eg annual football tour to Holland.

Music boasts the usual school orchestra and various ensembles, with superb choirs – junior, senior, chamber and training, including an emphasis on making sure boys whose voices are breaking don't bail out of singing too soon. Lovely art studio, with boys' favourite projects including African sunsets (lower school) and Animal Farm trophy heads (year 8s).

Families – a socially active bunch – range from 'the extremely wealthy' to to dual income families who give their all to afford the fees – although breakfast club (from 7.30am) and homework club (until 5.45pm) surprisingly undersubscribed. Though school has its own transport, including minibuses and coach, the school's biggest challenge remains transport. 'Parents know they have to get stuck on a busy road at 8am if they drive here,' says head.

Could so easily be swamped by pressure and riven with nerves. And that's just the parents. But while results give it undeniable cachet as a prep whose top leavers continue to have the entrée to some of south west London's most sought after senior schools, this school is about so much more than getting hard results. We found the boys engaged with everything the school has to offer, and extremely proud of it.

Rosemead Preparatory School

70 Thurlow Park Road, West Dulwich, London SE21 8HZ

Ages 3–11 **Pupils** 350

Fees: £6,738 – £12,690 pa

020 8670 5865
www.rosemeadprepschool.org.uk

Headmaster: Since 2017, Philip Soutar BEd, previously headmaster of St Wystan's School in Derbyshire, and before that deputy head at Ackworth Junior School. Degree from Exeter; main subject areas are science, PE (he's a golfer) and drama (interests include musical theatre and amateur dramatics), and has taught in junior and senior schools. Married to Lisa, a primary music specialist at Dulwich Prep London; they have two children.

Head of the pre-prep since 2005, Mary-Elizabeth Everitt BEd Goldsmiths College (40s). She started in the state sector, before teaching for 14 years at Dulwich Prep London. Friendly and quietly spoken, she is focused and clearly made of steely stuff.

Entrance: Describes itself as 'mixed ability'. Children may enter the nursery during the term of their 3rd birthday; at 4+ into reception or at 7+ into year 3. Whilst the nursery is almost fully subscribed, there are sometimes a few places available at the prep. Assessments begin the November prior to entry, with a 45-minute play session for the nursery or reception entry and language and maths exercises for years 1-6.

Means-tested bursary scheme with no limit on numbers. No scholarships. Maximum class size is 22 in the pre-prep and 20 in the prep. No strict sibling policy, but will be taken into account. Unless your family is of Von Trapp proportions, the discount for four or more siblings is unlikely to assist you.

Exit: Pupils exit at 11+, with the school aiming to leave choices 'wide open'. We sense determined parents, as children make three applications on average, for which they are prepared with one-on-one interviews as well as practice papers. St Dunstan's much the most popular destination currently (21 places in 2018, nine with scholarships), then Sydenham High, Emanuel and Royal Russell. Others to Dulwich College, Trinity and Alleyn's. A recent rise in both places offered and a higher ratio of awards, particularly academic, art and sport (26 overall in 2018).

Remarks: A traditional curriculum ticks all boxes, but there is modernising afoot, which is going down well. The school cites updating the texts used in English, and in maths a new online tutor sets tasks at an appropriate level for each child, 30 minutes in class and 30 minutes at home each week, with parents able to dip in any time online to see how they are doing.

A carefully thought through decision to switch from the traditional French to the more globally relevant Spanish has been pretty universally accepted and lessons have been doubled to twice a week. Spanish commences in the pre-prep with singing, stories and movement. History, geography and science have also been overhauled. Recent ICT facilities include class sets of Chromebooks and interactive screens. Humanities are supported by a wide array of trips, and highlights of the year are cross-curricular theme days and celebrations.

Reporting now looks at core skills such as concentration and organisation skills, as well as subject-specific scoring, all of which can be far more useful than a paragraph of commentary.

Some 18 per cent of staff in place for more than 10 years. Not a high turnover, but there is now one male teacher per year group at the prep. Reports from some parents are not spotless – but others impress upon us the warm atmosphere between staff and pupils.

With three classes per year in the prep, the class groupings sometimes change after year 3, once teachers have been able to assess how children work together. This can be a tad unpopular, as it isn't necessarily about friendship groups. However, classes are fixed by year 5. Setting for maths from year 3.

The anti-bullying policy has been carefully reviewed, with a buddy scheme throughout the school and year 6 visiting to read to the younger ones, and sharing special assemblies such as that for Chinese New Year.

Learning support, termed enrichment, has six staff, two of them full time, with one-to-one support for just under 10 per cent of the school. Very small number with EAL.

The fenced playground, high up above the street, is the venue for learning a variety of ball skills. Years 1 to 6 have a weekly PE lesson, a swimming lesson and a full games afternoon. There are two male PE teachers, and a female director of PE. With children taken to nearby Dulwich sports club and Rosendale playing fields for football, hockey, netball, rugby, tennis, cricket and athletics and making use of Crystal Palace's national training facilities for swimming from year 3, one parent commented, 'It's a small school with minimum on-site sports facilities, but they seem to offer a lot and children don't know or care that the sports grounds aren't owned by the school.' Rosemead regularly has children taking part at the ISA finals, both as individuals and in teams, and recently competed at national level in football.

R

Parents say, 'Children work hard, concentrate and give of their best.' And our visit backs this up. The atmosphere was calm and industrious, perhaps particularly due to year 6 exams looming.

How high pressure is it? A parent who has had three children through the school reported: 'I think Rosemead gets the balance right – one of the reasons we chose it... the amount of homework is about right, more than your average state primary, but not as much as some of the more high pressure private schools in the area.'

Parents commented to us in no uncertain terms that art has been a real weak spot in the past, but we visited the large, recently dedicated art studio and saw the specialist teacher in action – a highly talented former assistant from the pre-prep praised by staff and parents. The school now employs a local artist to take groups for sketching and painting, and pupils have been awarded large numbers of art scholarships to senior schools in the last few years.

The prep has more than its fair share of violinists, as all year 1 at the pre-prep learn violin in groups. Some 150 children have individual instrumental tuition, with several reaching grade 5 by year 6. There is a large school orchestra and two school choirs; ensemble clubs for cello, brass, strings and recorder; and an 'electric fusion band' which plays at the annual Dulwich Festival. A musical highlight is the major concert at the end of the spring term. One parent commented on the 'superb Christmas carol service in local church... very impressive'.

Clubs – morning, lunch-time and after-school – offer mainly sporty and musical options, with a good show of language clubs for Spanish, French and Russian. Increasingly, this is a school for working parents and the school is well set up to offer a full day from 8am to 6pm.

Recently completed year 6 classrooms, together with a new library, bigger dining hall and ICT suites, stood out. Meanwhile, at the time of our visit, downstairs everything looked a bit shabby and utilitarian.

What will hold the school together as well as the head are the parents. Already established as an independent school for 70 years, in 1975 a group of parents took over the managing of the school and it became a limited company with an all-parent management team. It is now a non-profit making charitable trust.

Notable and somewhat off-putting is the location on the edge of Dulwich – a bit of a no-man's land on the traffic-heavy South Circular road – however, we did note that once inside we could not hear the traffic and the location between two overground stations is convenient for commuting quickly into town. The prep was actually a rehearsal space for the Old Vic theatre, hence the school hall resembling a proper theatre complete with fixed stage.

Two-thirds of families live close by, often walking to school; the rest come from all over south London, some from as far as Bromley and Elephant and Castle. This is a school for active parents who want to get involved – fundraising isn't just for external charitable projects but for valuable extras around the school. Talking of active, a team of Rosemead mothers recently rowed the Channel.

The school reports being bowled over by the response to their appeals for help: turning a piece of waste ground into a sunny little allotment for the pre-prep over the weekend, or creating a rota of volunteer librarians for the new prep library. All of which builds a real sense of community. Parents are a mixed and reportedly friendly crowd – we certainly saw gaggles lingering post drop-off – but particularly evidenced by the Easter family ski trip, which is not just for pupils but unusually everyone: parents, siblings, grandparents, old boys and girls and their families too.

The pretty purple uniforms are a delight, but the stand-out feature of the pre-prep is the charming church building, sympathetically developed to create high ceilinged classrooms, with beautiful arches and bits of stained glass – a lovely space in which to work.

The pre-prep has assistants in every class and high staff ratios in the nursery. School commences in earnest at reception with some parents wishing for a greater emphasis on play: 'hardly any toys in the classroom, much like year 1'. Reception is very different in feel to the boisterous fun we saw in the nursery, but the head points out the gentle start with just 20 minutes of phonics a day compared with an hour in year 1.

It seems to be different things to different families – the pre-prep's church building brings back fond memories for some parents of what a first school should be like; more pragmatically, it could well be a port in a storm when faced with the ultra-competitive local options at 4+.

Royal Russell School

    235

Coombe Lane, Croydon, Surrey CR9 5BX

Ages 3–18 **Pupils** 1,076 **Sixth form** 222 **Boarders** 147 full, 7 weekly (from 11 years)

Fees: Day £11,160 – £18,480; Boarding £36,525 pa

020 8657 4433
www.royalrussell.co.uk

Headmaster: Since 2011, Chris Hutchinson BMet. Second headship – first was at Newcastle School for Boys, which he joined in 2007. 'Teaching is in the blood,' he says. Opted for metallurgy degree but decided against engineering career. Worked for family owned and run school in Wales for two years, followed by formal teacher training at Cambridge and posts in top schools, starting with Clifton in 1990 where he met wife Alex – also a scientist. ('Some unfortunate Cliftonites were taught a lot of Hutchinson chemistry and physics.') Left as head of physics, moving to Wellington in 2000 in same role where was also a boarding housemaster.

Had completed full cycle (years 9 to 13) at Newcastle School for Boys when post here came up. Was encouraged to apply and felt instantly at home, compatible ethos of 'getting to know people well, giving them an individual opportunity to shine and supporting, rather than pushing them, on their journey' the clincher. He fits in a bit of energetic teaching and has advanced child recognition skills. 'Knows them – every one,' said staff member in full on Tiny Tim mode. Pupils equally chuffed. 'So, so good – really engages,' said one. 'Makes the effort to get to know you,'

Mrs Hutchinson has secured matching role at Woldingham (minimal rivalry for same pupils – so far, only one has moved between the two schools). Mr Hutchinson's hobbies include singing, gardening, Herefordshire, old Land Rovers and exercising his pets: dog Bosey (who spent considerable part of the interview curled up in his master's chair) and Linus the cat. Reflective, funny and kind, Mr Hutchinson is a major attraction for parents. Staff ditto. 'I took the job because of him,' said one, who praised mastery of details – 'Reports broken locks, picks up the rubbish' (he does, too – only gave up on stray banana skin on walk round because of its advanced stage of decomposition). 'Nothing is too trivial.' On day of visit, had just written 71 congratulatory notes to cast and backstage team of school production.

Headmaster of Royal Russell Junior School since 2009 is James Thompson BA QTS. Previously at Ardingly College Prep School and before that at Kingswood Prep in Bath, both with linked senior schools. Dream was to be a professional sportsman, but opted for teacher training (with PE specialisation) after coaching at own prep in Kent and loving it. If he needs a second opinion, family is riddled with teachers. Viv, his wife, is head of a Notting Hill nursery school. Two daughters, both here – and doing best to hide whenever papa hove into view, to giggles from friends – no doubt provide instant feedback as required. Mr Thompson remains big on sport (cricket, hockey, golf, skiing), even writing anon column on umpiring for The Telegraph. Parents see him as genial, good at dealing with tricky types and (in the nicest possible way) typecast for the role. 'Prep school head through and through,' said one, approvingly. Approach distinctly dad-like (and all the better for it). 'Don't want to mollycoddle – better to learn the consequences,' he said, as year 5s enthusiastically wielded fret saws to make moving wooden toys. He's 'very kind, prefers being in PE kit, hates suits and wears pink trousers and odd socks,' say pupils.

Leaving in July 2019. His successor will be John Evans, currently senior deputy head at Haberdashers' Aske's School. Studied English and education at Cambridge; has taught English at Dulwich Prep London. Married with two children.

Junior and senor school reviews, previously separate are now combined, with blessing of the school. Reinforces sense of togetherness that emanates from the top.

Academic matters: Known as a gentler alternative to more selective schools in the area, though 'we do get the brightest students,' says school. Now positioning itself as 'the family school of choice in south London' (plays better than Croydon, 'a sell too far' for gentrified sunny uplands of Nappy Valley, Wandsworth and Balham).

Entry requirements may not have shifted but winds of change are definitely well above zephyr level, starting with results. In 2018, 36 per cent of A level grades were A*/A (65 per cent A*-B) and 50 per cent of GCSE grades 9-7, while government-issued value added table recently put school right at the top of the country.

Messrs Hutchinson and Thompson have trimmed, rather than hacked, their staff teams, felt by parents to be stronger, if a work in progress. 'You'll hear some rumblings and grumblings in the car park and it's usually about staff,' said one. Thirty, average age close to 40, have completed first decade (one cheery and popular geography teacher on way to notching up ruby anniversary). For seniors, maximum class size is 24, average 18 to year 9, 15 for GCSE years and just eight for sixth form. Junior class average is 17 (parents make feelings known if numbers pass 20 in busy year).

New generation of vibrant staff newcomers love it here. One raved about mentoring ('have grown as a person'). Energy exemplified by new junior school librarian who has created oasis of great charm with imaginative use of lighting – Chinese lanterns, netting studded with fairy lights, even reading by torchlight sessions.

Despite school togetherness, juniors have own staff temperamentally suited to this age group. Combines specialists (music, computing, French, Spanish, sport and science) from nursery upwards with dedicated class teachers. Continuity and security means pupils 'retain their childhood for as long as they can,' says Mr T. 'System works,' agreed parent. 'Always somebody to hear you out and help you.'

In senior school, star subjects include A level biology, as popular with boys as girls. History, though, is the chart-topper, converting the marginally interested into passionately keen. Differentiation is a key part of the process, teachers praised for willingness to explain a topic in limitless different ways until it clicked ('and if that doesn't work, will ask someone else to explain it to you'). While 10 GCSEs is the norm, will adjust if necessary, provide after-school sessions and generally do what it takes. 'Always there to help,' said pupil. Nurturing qualities appreciated by parents – 'you won't get that in some [other] schools,' said one. International pupils similarly feel exceptionally well looked after. Though English isn't mother tongue for around 20 per cent, who can arrive with large gaps in learning, expectation is that all will take GCSEs and A levels. Support is flexible, generally at no extra cost and often yields rapid results. One new international sixth form boarder was delighted to have passed GCSE maths in first term. Junior school support similar, with one pupil attending local centre part time.

School's reputation for SEN remains undimmed. Currently, two senior students have EHCPs and between 14 to 20 per cent have ILPs. Have coped with 'very' autistic pupil, ADHD, and specific learning difficulties. Support includes additional literacy and numeracy sessions, assigned teachers who work with pupils in and out of lessons, though with just one full time member of staff in the senior school, there's a limit to the numbers they can help.

Parents also praised efforts with very able. 'School invests in children that need more time either because they're slightly behind or ahead – they have different programmes and challenges,' said mother of junior school pupil.

Games, options, the arts: 'All the space a child could need to run, jump and cartwheel,' says juniors' prospectus, with 110 acres well used by all, from nursery school pupils walking the 1.3 km cross country circuit (in a morning) to boarders taking it at a rather faster pace 'for fun' (takes all sorts). Bar an all-weather surface that, frustratingly, needs duvet day if there's a hard frost, facilities and options are top notch, including new pavilion (not picturesque but home to host of extras including gym and physio suite), and two swimming pools.

Little, indeed, that isn't offered, to parental (and inspectorial) approval. 'Everything is there so children don't need to spend lots of time away from education by driving to swimming,' said one. Sports successes could go up a notch or two, think some, though limited by smaller pool of talent to draw on, compared with single sex schools. Rugby, notable by absence, heads the parents' wishlist (and likely to remain there), hockey felt to get fair share of resources and then some. Overall, though, 'win more than we lose,' thought a pupil, results pages revealing impressive football success (teams reach semi-finals of London and national contests) but mixed fortunes elsewhere.

Junior school activities range from numerous informal concerts (music is timetabled from nursery) to residential trips from year 3 and over 40 activities (pupils pack in up to five a week), including coding club, swim squad and media club (filming and editing).

Same again for seniors – one year 10 pupil involved in choir, extra sport, Mandarin and popular CCF (night exercises more of a draw than drilling). Model United Nations vast – school hosts annual international conference and gamely lends other local schools placards for their own events.

Bar slight glumness from senior school pupil analysing recent production rather than doing it ('Interesting work?' we asked. 'Not particularly,' was the response) enthusiasm for the arts abounds. No wonder, given trips (West End to New York for thesps) and lavish facilities including auditorium in performing arts centre, the base for regular productions (Importance of being Earnest, Wind in the Willows). Pianists among the 200 or so musicians have new Bechsteins – I live in this practice room,' said one – with concerts in venues including the Royal Albert Hall for those who do make it outside.

Boarding: Most of the 147 full boarders in the senior school stay on for weekends and must attend at least three activities (fireworks and go-karting among them) a term. Other perks include after school exploration of fleshpots of Croydon and exclusive access to swish-looking coffee machine in dining hall. Homesickness still strikes but 'keep talking' was advice from one boarder, and will pass. For anything more serious, school has medical centre staffed round the clock.

Girl boarders have one house that backs onto junior school (Queen's – think revenge end of social housing). Boys do better with two (Oxford and Cambridge, now in two wings under one roof), all with day pupils too. Further six houses for day pupils only; flexi-boarding so day pupils can stay on for extra sport or rehearsals. Rooms and bathrooms are generally tidy and pleasant and happy, trusting atmosphere prevails with personal possessions left out, not locked away.

Though British boarders are substantially outnumbered by Chinese (majority in sixth form) and other nationalities including Russia, Armenia, Bulgaria and Ukraine, school, unlike many others, ensures that everyone mixes in multi-national social groups. Horizons are impressively expanded for all pupils, with boarders enjoying tea with local families. Website features overseas students (Bogdan from Romania and Yizhou from China among others) extolling the virtues of the school in their mother tongues.

Background and atmosphere: Ten minutes by tram from East Croydon, green and pleasant site, complete with own deer herd, offers antidote to crowded London senior schools. Originally a charity, founded by City of London clerks to support a colleague's orphaned children in 1850s. Grew into a school named for its first president, former PM Lord John Russell. Moved from New Cross to Purley in 1866, acquired this site in 1924. Sir Aston Webb – best known for Buckingham Palace façade, responsible for regal design. Added Royal to mark 1953 coronation and in 1961 became co-ed on single site. Upped numbers of fee payers in the 1970s to avoid closure (previous philanthropic desire to educate pupils FOC laudable but ruinous). Since then, has gone from strength to strength.

Buildings mainly very easy on the eye (and being attended to where they're not). Oldest is group of 1850s cottages with octagonal tower. Grander elsewhere including mirror image staircases that face each other across flashier of two quads, joining original building and later additions.

'Top of agenda was to turn this into a single school journey,' say heads. So junior school pupils get to know senior school early, using theatre, chapel and swimming pool and, from year 3 up, have lunch in the blue, vaulted dining hall (featured in TV hit show The Durrells). Plenty of space for traditional library and 'practical' block – DT room filled with sound of merry hammering as year 7s enjoy high volume metal beating. And despite lack of riches, site is smart, ditto pupils in recently revamped uniform that's high on practicality (largely washable) and low on crested shirts.

Similar neatness round the grounds (bar pair of school bags languishing, Hansel and Gretel-like, in undergrowth). Even food ingredients painstakingly handwritten on blackboard. Salad Nicoise contents – 'fish, sulphites and egg' – helps those with allergies. 'Learn how to manage them,' said parent. Thirsty have choice of squash in every conceivable flavor. (Milk, also offered, is 'not that popular,' thought pupils).

Pastoral care, well-being and discipline: A happy place. 'It's a punishment to keep son off school,' said junior school mother. 'My child absolutely loves it,' agreed another. Teachers supportive if families hit difficult patch. 'Will go above and beyond,' said parent. Pupils similarly complimentary. 'Does take time to settle in but you do feel welcome,' said one. Tutor groups help new pupils settle into school with older senior school pupils providing informal help to younger. Chaplain another source of support, chapel open all day for anytime prayers.

Heart of multi-layered friendship groups is strong house system (juniors have their own) which promotes cohesion and competition – usually at healthy rather than arms race levels. Add forms and streamed subject groups and 'you can have social groups that extend through the school – it takes some getting to grips with,' said parent.

Around one senior school pupil a year withdrawn or asked to leave (normal issues...) but it's sensitively handled, Mr Hutchinson often asking 'headmaster mates' to take a pupil who has lost their way. It's then, he reckons, that you discover just how much of an educator you are. 'They make awful decisions but shouldn't be punished for the rest of their lives.'

Most focus is on rewards for the triers. Even the prefects, who told us they can impose detentions, (head says otherwise) never do ('though we might remind everyone that we can,' said one).

Pupils and parents: Slightly more boys, many locals among day pupils (80 per cent from Croydon), rest from south London and into Surrey and Kent borders, lots of diversity, cultural and financial. 'Pretty much all walks of life,' said junior parent. 'And when you're doing reading at night, books aren't just about pink skinned children, which is great.'

Junior and senior parents tend to tread separate paths and organise own events. It's a homogenous mix – cars ranging from second hand to luxury marque, some parents dwelling in marble halls, others scraping school fees together. Wraparound care offered to Increasing numbers of working couples. Not flash, thought parent. 'Have quite a wide breadth of people there, and I think that gives it a nice atmosphere.'

Only mystery is where leavers end up. Not into the limelight, at least so far. 'We have a great many success stories, but nobody famous,' says school.

Entrance: Increasingly popular and currently at capacity in every year group. Undaunting entrance process. 'Very gentle' says school. Junior school entrants arrive the September after third birthday, are observed in small groups (no interview or formal test). 'We're looking to see if on track with development, communications and ability to interact.' More formal assessments further up the school – all joining in years 3 to 6 must be senior school shoe-ins.

Around 90 per cent go on to the senior school, some guaranteed places in years 4 and 5; they sit exams only if want to be considered for awards, often scooping the top scholarships, though there's no favouritism, stresses school.

For senior school, main entry point is year 7. External candidates sit entrance exams in maths, English and VR. Minimum score around 105, average of 111 and 128 minimum for scholarship candidates. Further 20 places in year 9. Varying numbers in year 12 – no entrance exam, with places based on GCSE performance.

Current popularity means school could probably nudge up selectivity a notch – but won't. 'Have niche in market,' says school, 'and we want to preserve it – we've just upped the quality of what we're doing.'

Exit: Loses a few juniors to local grammars and other independents such as Alleyn's and Caterham. Seniors tend to stay on post-GCSE. Many to London unis; others to study eg economics at Loughborough, aerospace engineering at Swansea, fashion and textile design at Southampton.

Money matters: No endowment to speak of but prudent management and fundraising keeps things ticking over nicely. Offers scholarships (academic, sport, music and drama) and bursaries of to 100 per cent (income shouldn't exceed £40,000).

Remarks: Think fab site, rising results, unified and inspirational leadership (and the odd deer) and get on that tram.

The Russell Primary School

Petersham Road, Richmond, Surrey TW10 7AH

Ages 3–11 **Pupils** 271

020 8940 1446
www.russell.richmond.sch.uk

Headteacher: Since 2011, Samantha Leir, previously deputy at the school. Her first teaching job was at Russell in 1994. From there she went to work for the local authority as a lead literacy teacher. Returned to Russell as deputy in 2003. 'She's always been a huge part of the school,' said one parent.

Two sons who both attend schools in Surrey. Grew up in Wales, the only girl with four brothers, so rugby is a big part of her life. Supports the Ospreys (Swansea). Her sons and husband also play rugby. She enjoys reading, cooking and swimming.

Entrance: Currently one form entry. For nursery places apply direct to nursery and for school through local authority.

Exit: Most go on to Grey Court in Ham, a couple to local grammars (Tiffin Girls' and Tiffin School), a handful to independent or church schools (Christ's, The Green School, Gumley), or to Waldegrave School for Girls if they live in Twickenham.

Remarks: Originally two schools (Petersham and Orchard Junior) built in the 1950s, they joined together to form the Russell School in 1980. Set in four acres of grounds and new buildings recently completed, but unfortunately outside areas – including wildlife garden, orchard and playground – currently mud and rubble. Hot school dinners are cooked fresh on the premises.

Now shares a site and expertise with Strathmore special school, though the schools are run separately.

There are gifted and talented groups for maths and writing. A Battle of the Books competition is available for gifted readers in year 2 and year 4.

Music is important here. A specialist music teacher is at the school for half of the week. She is also responsible for the school choir and orchestra. Children can learn recorder, flute, guitar, violin and even the harp. There are trips to the Royal Festival Hall and each year the school takes part in the O2 Young Voices competition. 'My son was so proud to be representing the school at the 02 centre,' explained one parent.

Drama is also strong, and as well as a big Christmas production and a year 6 performance (last year it was based around the theme of Pompeii), there is a talent show for the whole school.

A recent appointment is the deputy head, who leads sport at the school. Lunchtime and after-school clubs include gymnastics, athletics, basketball, football, netball, judo and golf, as well as chess, Spanish and art. A private company (Fit for Sport) runs a breakfast club from 7.45am to 8.30am, and after-school care from 3.15pm to 6.00pm, both at extra cost.

Parents are drawn from across the social spectrum. Some children live in the huge mansions on Petersham Road while others are drawn from the council estate over towards Ham. The PTA organises social events and parents are encouraged to come into school for special assemblies. 'Since Mrs Leir took over we feel much more welcome at the school,' said one parent.

It feels like a village school and it's amazing to have such space on the outskirts of London. If you can turn a blind eye to the state of the grounds you'll feel very smug that your children have a place here.

Sacred Heart High School (Hammersmith)

212 Hammersmith Road, London W6 7DG

Ages 11–18 **Pupils** 1,021 **Sixth form** 300 **RC**

020 8748 7600
www.sacredhearthigh.org.uk

Headteacher: Since 2014, Marian Doyle MA NPQH (50s). Previously deputy head since 1997. Before that, she taught English and RE at Haggerston School, Hackney, Phoenix High School, Hammersmith and latterly Holland Park School, Notting Hill Gate. A world away from the previous head (a deeply traditional woman who reigned for 23 years with what girls describe as a combination of awe and fear), Doyle is softer around the edges and fresher in her outlook. Not only does she look more modern (she wore fabulous killer heels when we met her), but the school itself feels more alive, with walls now adorned with colourful canvases of the girls at work and many inspirational quotes. School systems (from admin through to bullying policies) have also had an overhaul, thanks to the head's key vision of the school being run seamlessly. A parent herself, she is big on boundaries and 'tough love', but is also approachable and smiley, and is regularly seen around the school, popping into lessons and talking to the girls at break times. 'She is very keen to make sure that we like it here,' said one girl.

Academic matters: Impressive results, by anyone's standards. In 2018, 51 per cent 9-7 grades at GCSE; 54 per cent got 5+ 9-5s including both English and maths. Sixth form opened in 2013; in 2018, 32 per cent A*/A and 58 per cent A*-B grades at A level.

Maths the strongest subject, followed by English. RE, history and geography also stand out. In terms of languages, Spanish and French are on offer, and a group of around 15 girls are put forward for Latin GCSE, which they study at St Paul's. Science highly promoted, with 60 per cent doing science and maths post-16.

Each year group has five form groups, with setting across all subjects from year 7 into five or six groups, depending on the subject, with plenty of flexibility to move about as necessary. Class sizes vary, with many as large as 35.

Expectation for all pupils to do at least two after-school clubs (which they call enrichment), which has been accommodated by changes to the school day (which now comprises five 60 minute lessons and finishes at 3.05pm) and an expectation that staff stay longer to run these clubs on Tuesdays and Wednesdays. Outside facilitators brought in too. Subjects include all the usual suspects such as choir, sport, maths challenge, science clubs, drama etc as well as more unusual offerings including yoga and gardening.

S

One full-time staff member (qualified teacher, as well as a dyslexic specialist; has the national SENCo leadership award) is responsible for SEN, although no special unit. She puts in place three tiered levels of support – firstly, qualified teachers' support in mainstream, with the aim that specialist subject teachers can support in their areas of expertise; second (if necessary) additional support before and after school; finally (again if necessary) involvement of school counsellor or outside services, such as speech and language and occupational therapy. Difficulties catered for include dyslexia and other needs that are physical, such as hearing loss or severe long-term conditions, communication and language difficulties, ADD, ADHD. School also claims there are some serious mental health concerns. School reckoned there were 65 in total with SEN when we visited, five of whom are statemented/with EHC plan. Very rarely, if a child's needs cannot be fully met, the school works closely with parents and the local authority to find alternatives. Help for gifted and talented through a range of enrichment and additional opportunities.

'The help my daughter has received for her dyslexia has been second to none, including trying out a range of different techniques, and the communication with us has been excellent too,' said one parent. 'Her self-confidence has rocketed and she's doing really well in exams.'

School is designated as a national teaching school, leading the West London Teaching School Alliance, which means working closely with 28 other primary and secondary schools in west London to improve standards of teaching and share best practice on issues including initial teacher training, professional development, research and development, succession planning and mentoring. Head says it's her vision for the school to become known for its drive for excellence. 'I put the same level of effort into training and development for the staff as I do teaching the girls, because I believe the two are inextricably linked,' she says.

Although the teaching staff we saw were a pretty glum-looking lot (particularly unwelcoming when we went near their classrooms), girls are clearly impressed with their level of commitment. 'Lessons are really engaging,' said one. 'They make sure nobody gets missed,' added another. Indeed, girls are regularly reminded of a quote from one of the founders: 'For the sake of one child, I would have founded the society,' after which they're told, 'You are the one child.'

Games, options, the arts: For a small inner-city site, they certainly pack in the sports facilities, all of which are utilised to the max, with the girls doing at least two hours of PE per week and with the option of PE as both a GCSE and A level subject. In addition to the two tennis/netball courts (which double up as rounders pitches), there's a gym and activity studio for the likes of dance, pilates and yoga. The new £8m sports and science block is home to a massive sports hall that can facilitate three teaching groups simultaneously. 'It's four times the size of our gym,' enthused one girl. Also new is a running track and outdoor gym of the ilk you see in parks, all of which means the long-standing link with Hammersmith and Fulham Health and Fitness Centre will start to diminish. Rowing, softball, basketball and volleyball on offer, along with all the usual suspects, and after-school clubs include street dance, yoga, cheerleading, fencing, trampolining and football, among others. Plenty of inter-house sports competitions, the highlight of which is the annual sports day held at St Paul's fields (originally owned by Sacred Heart but sadly they sold it off years ago), and the school has increasing success in the borough in hockey, rounders, netball and athletics.

No shortage of peripatetic teachers for musical instruments including piano, flute, trombone, drums etc. There are junior and senior choirs, various ensembles, and the girls talk highly of the general music classes, as well as about the annual Battle of the Bands. 'Music is really good fun here,' one girl told us. We particularly like the random pianos in the corridors, all of which girls say get played regularly for practice, making for a lovely ambience when walking through the corridors.

Links to various theatres, including the Donmar, and the drama school LAMDA, give a flavour of how seriously drama is taken here, with annual all-school productions such as Hairspray and Annie. Art and DT studios are spacious, with state-of-the-art equipment and some extremely talented artwork produced by the girls. No cookery on offer when we visited, but this is being reexamined.

Background and atmosphere: The school, or 'convent of the Sacred Heart,' is built on a site steeped in Catholic history dating back to the early 17th century. During its 330 year history, four different orders of nuns have taught here. Today's Tudor-style, red-brick buildings were built in the late 19th century and there's no shortage of religious reminders inside, notably the huge, austere-looking religious murals all the way along the wide, spacious corridors of the cloisters, as well as the chapel, which doubles up as the main school hall. 'We have daily morning prayers,' said one girl, 'but apart from that, the presence of Catholicism in our everyday life is through the school's ethos and values.' 'The school provides a good moral compass, but there's no hard-line religion,' agreed a parent, who added that there's a sensible and modern approach to sex education too, within the context of the Catholic Church teaching.

In 1948 the convent school was reorganised as a secondary grammar school, continuing as a grammar school until 1976, when it received its first comprehensive intake. The school then took on academy status in 2012.

Most pupils use the entrance on Bute Gardens, whilst sixth form and visitors use the main entrance on Hammersmith Road, where you'll be greeted by a single receptionist behind an oak veneer desk and a couple of rows of cream leather chairs. The hum of traffic is loud, but it doesn't take many more steps into the school to feel as if you're in an oasis of calm – not at all what you'd expect from an inner-city comp. Even during class switch-over times, when the extra-wide corridors are packed with animated girls, it somehow manages to avoid the feeling of chaos that many other schools have (probably helped by the very strictly policed one-way walking system).

A steep stone staircase leads down to the converted basement, which forms the buzzy social space and café for sixth formers. The rest of the girls eat in the dining room which, head admits, 'could be more funky' and where the 'food is 'ok.' Those who have packed lunch eat at temporary tables that are laid out daily in the wide corridors.

Asked what they'd improve, girls told us they could do with more quiet study space, especially in sixth form. 'We are allowed to use the library,' said one, 'but it's not ideal.' Indeed, when we visited, the library was being used by an entire class and was by no means quiet, although in fairness it is two-story, with doors shutting out such sound on the top level. Well-stocked and imaginatively designed, it is also very light and inviting. Classrooms are bog-standard, with stand-out facilities for drama and music. Great excitement about the new science block, which should transform this current provision beyond recognition.

Girls encouraged to be proactive, rather than spoon fed, with lots of emphasis on them doing things, rather than talking about things. When we visited, a group of girls had gone to Mexico to rebuild houses for those in poverty. A further group of six girls went to Lourdes with the Handicapped Children Pilgrimage Trust. Impressive amounts of charitable work overall, including £10,500 raised for a sister school in Kenya for disabled children via activities including sponging teachers, making teachers eat chilli, sponsored walks and rowing the distance of the Channel in the gym. School is also part of a worldwide network of schools in 45 countries which creates opportunities such as a head girls' meet up to discuss leadership ideas and pupil exchanges across different countries.

Plenty of school trips to universities, BBC, Houses of Parliament, businesses including JP Morgan and all the usual museums and art galleries. Residential trips largely music-related, including to places such as Austria and Paris, whilst whole school European ski trips take place each year.

Strong student voice, with elected student members having requested that the science garden become more appealing, as well as having offered responses to the school's Equality Plan.

Pastoral care, well-being and discipline: Although current head is considered 'less scary and strict' than her predecessor, she is equally dedicated to high standards, pointing out that your daughter will be in detention if she arrives even five seconds after the bell goes. 'The point is that in professional life, if you had a meeting at 10am, you wouldn't arrive just after 10am,' she explains. 'We also want a calm start to the day.' It clearly works – there are few detentions in reality, with the girls we talked to never having been late in their entire six years. Other zero-tolerance aspects of school life include school uniform (especially length of skirts) and good behaviour, although pastoral care is highly praised here, with all the parents we talked to calling it 'very nurturing and caring.' Pupils are frequently reminded they can talk to form teachers, non-teaching pastoral support managers, the chaplain or two full-time school counsellors. In addition, there are strong links with Child and Adolescent Mental Health Services (CAMHS) and the charity Mind. 'One of my daughters went off the rails and had some counselling, which promptly nipped it in the bud,' said one parent. Head is by no means resting on her laurels, though. 'Like most schools,' she says, 'we have seen an increase in mental health issues and are very aware we need to talk about it in a more real and open way.' Peer mentoring scheme between year 7s and year 11s encourages cross-year relationships and older girls to take a leadership role.

Pupils and parents: This is top of the state school list for many families, not only in west London, but as far as Islington (with Tony Blair's daughter being the obvious example). Although it's non-selective and fully comprehensive, the majority of families are middle-class and with English as a first language. That said, there is genuine poverty among some of the girls, with head reporting that this is increasingly the case. 'We have 14 per cent identified as having free school meals and many others with an income only just above the threshold where parents struggle to make ends meet,' she says.

Strong PA and links between parents generally. 'It's unusually sociable among parents for an inner-city comprehensive, with lots of mums' nights out, quiz nights and family-focused activities,' said one parent. Good communications between school and parents, although some parents think the annual parents' evening, which falls in the summer term, is far too late in the academic year.

Entrance: Parents keep an extremely beady eye on the admissions policy of this heavily oversubscribed school, and many are unswerving in their commitment to find some way for their daughter to become one of the approximately 198 pupils to enter year 7. But you'll need to start early, as all girls need to have been baptised before they were 6 months old (although we did to talk to one parent who did it slightly later due to illness in the family) and to have attended one of 11 feeder schools, all named on the website. If you meet all the criteria, you won't need to sweat so much about how close you are to the school. Be warned that siblings don't automatically gain entry and are sometimes turned away. Separate admissions procedures for girls with an SEN statement/EHC plan. Parents praise the transition from primary school. Up to places for 40 external applicants to sixth form, for which you'll need eight 9-4s at GCSE, including subject-specific requirements.

Exit: Clear expectation to remain at the school to do A levels, and the majority do so. Others commonly go onto Cardinal Vaughan or The London Oratory, with a handful going into the independent sector, including UCS, St Benedict's and Latymer

Upper. 2018 leavers off to do courses ranging from aeronautical engineering at Imperial to anthropology at Exeter to fashion communication at Condé Nast College.

Remarks: An exceptional and relatively small inner-city state school that provides girls who are prepared to behave impeccably with a traditional education and sense of community that will set them up for life.

St Anthony's Preparatory School

90 Fitzjohn's Avenue, London NW3 6NP

Ages 4–13 **Pupils** 304 **RC**

Fees: £19,005 – £19,425 pa

020 7431 1066
www.stanthonysprep.org.uk

Headmaster: Since 2010, Paul Keyte (early 50s). Educated at Bloxham and then read philosophy and theology at Oriel, Oxford, where he got a first. Says he rather fell into teaching but 'loved it, and so stayed': after spells at Dulwich and KCS Wimbledon, he was director of studies at Winchester and deputy head at both Highgate and South Hampstead.

A warm-mannered and, as befits a philosopher, a reflective man. Evidently deeply thoughtful about the nature of the school, its potential strengths and pitfalls, and tries hard to interpret the school's Catholic mission to a multi-ethnic and metropolitan constituency. Although his own teaching background is rooted in senior schools, his pride in the school, and affection for pupils and staff, is palpable.

A pragmatist, when the need arises: 'Schools face ever more outside scrutiny. We have to embrace change and feel easy about accountability – but without losing what's special'. St Anthony's has always been a touch quirky – teachers always known by their first names, and music and drama given strong prominence within the curriculum. But, as Mr Keyte makes clear, parents tend to enjoy school idiosyncrasies only to the extent that they don't get in the way of children's happiness and well-being, and the ability to get to an appropriate senior school.

Plenty of action to back up his words: major refurbishment of the plant over the past eight years and, although it is split-site, both parts are now brimming over with fresh paint, ever-changing (and enticing) wall-displays of pupils' work, smart-screens in every classroom – and a huge drive forward in the range and quality of sport: 'children need to be fit and resilient,' he says. 'Life throws a lot at them, very early on.' He has even discreetly overseen the introduction of a dress code for staff – done with a light touch. 'Not rocket science, is it? We have to lead by example.'

Entrance: For the past few years, main entry point has been at reception, where there is now a two form entry. Boys come from about 25 different feeder nurseries: Catholic pupils have typically been at either St Mary's down the road or St Christina's in St John's Wood. Although the school is keen to maintain a strong constituency of Catholic pupils, everyone has to go through the assessment procedure. 'Given that most of the children are only 3 or 4,' explains the head, 'we try to make it feel like a play day as far as possible, and to identify those most likely to respond to our style of teaching and learning'. Occasional spots for boys coming in at other times, but the general rule is to take a tour and then, as early as possible, register.

S

Exit: Leavers' destinations showcase how adept the school has become at nurturing a whole range of interests and appetites: predictably, a broad sweep of London destinations, especially Westminster, St Paul's, CLSB, Highgate, UCS and Mill Hill. But there's been a surge in popularity for Merchant Taylors' and Habs, and for the Catholic London Oratory and Cardinal Vaughan. Some boarding schools are also becoming popular with St Anthony's families – Eton, Winchester, Harrow, Sevenoaks and Tonbridge have all featured strongly in recent years. For Catholic parents especially, so also have Stonyhurst and Worth.

Like so many London prep schools, St Anthony's has had to adapt to a ruthless and rapidly changing world in which many pupils are under pressure to join junior departments of their senior schools aged 11, rather than hold off until 13. For many pupils, years 5 and 6 leading up to the 11+ is the time of maximum pressure. 'The heyday of common entrance feels quite distant at times,' says the head. 'But for those staying all the way, we make sure these last two years are the most enriched: to release the full academic potential of youngsters, and spice it up with the individuality which St Anthony's has always sought to foster.'

Remarks: Taking children mainly at reception, the aim is to offer at once a broad and balanced curriculum. 'English and maths open up a whole world of learning,' says the head, 'and we want our pupils exploring all of it.' Science and ICT are there right at the start, but from year 1 there is French and Mandarin as well as everything else one would expect – history and geography, art and DT. Religious studies is also taught – but with an eye and an ear for pupils of all faiths and of none.

By the time pupils are 10 and have moved to the senior school, everybody studies Latin and there are after-school opportunities to do ancient Greek and Arabic as well. There's a specially equipped classroom for DT, as well as lashings of art, music and drama. 'We don't want any part in the reductionism in the curriculum one sometimes hears about,' says the head. 'Creativity is at the heart of the school.' There are also a host of out-of-school hobby and discussion groups – philosophy and chess among them alongside the arts. 'My son has been given masses of opportunity in which to find his voice,' said one parent. Another added: 'The staff have a genuine love of learning, and are superb at communicating it.'

Because testing, in all its iterations, has become such a big feature of life for prep school children from the age of 10 or 11, St Anthony's deploys a range of tests (such as CAT4, PIPS and MiDYis) to acclimatise pupils. 'They are useful visitors,' says the head, 'but life here is dictated, first and last, by what we believe to be enriching in its own right. Dedicated Study Skills department – one full time teacher and one part time, and two of the TAs have special training. There are regular diagnostic assessments to identify anyone needing extra input.

All qualified teachers at St Anthony's – from the half dozen or so who have been there for over 20 years to the young Turks. Five TAs have recently studied for their PGCEs while working full time at the school. 'They are astonishingly dedicated,' says the head, 'and many are already academically highly qualified.' One parent, whose son had won a scholarship to a famous school, said what he liked most was that his son had felt 'inspired, rather than under pressure'.

Limited play areas (it is in the middle of Hampstead, after all), although it does have its own rather splendid swimming pool ('Thank God,' said one parent). Normal games see pupils take a 10 minute coach ride to Brondesbury playing fields.

'There's the odd day when traffic is a nightmare,' said a father. 'But they do well at getting them out at break and into the fresh air.' Since we last visited, a quiet revolution has taken place in the profile of sport, perhaps not unconnected with the appointment of outstanding sports teachers. Recent pupils include a boy who went on to captain the first XV at a major rugby-playing senior school, and two members of the Lawn Tennis Association. The main staples are football, rugby and hockey in winter and cricket and athletics in summer, but efforts are made to offer reasonable choice. Cross-country is enjoying a surge of popularity: 15 teachers ran a half marathon recently and another is an elite marathon runner. 'This level of commitment', says the head, 'rather rubs off on the pupils.'

The school is explicit that it wants all pupils physically literate, and there are competitive fixtures with other schools from year 4. 'They have to be fit enough to cope with life's assorted pressures,' says the head. Inevitably, 'some have to learn they are not always the best in the pack, but the idea is that everyone who wants to represent the school at sport can do so.' There is a clear underlying message here – for parents as much as for children: emotional resilience is all-important, and teamwork and games can, or should be, a significant part of the learning.

As always, masses of drama, music and art, with regular visits to museums, theatres and galleries. One of the head's early moves was to triple the number of music lessons, and the fact that the school also acquired a grand piano and built a new music studio left no doubt that he and the governors were dead set on protecting the school's reputation as a bastion of the creative arts. There's a full orchestra and a jazz orchestra, and the head of music allegedly claimed that every boy who finished his time at St Anthony's could take grade 5 theory in music – quite an achievement, if true.

Plays are performed annually – every pupil takes part in a play for their year group each Christmas and summer, and there are myriad further opportunities for performance – in designated school assemblies and so forth. There's also a major Shakespeare production every year – the most recent ('a triumph,' said one parent) was Macbeth. Art is every bit as strong – a raft of student work has recently been gracing the Saatchi Gallery, and the walls of the school are filled with pupils' latest creative output.

Founded in Victorian times, the school moved from Eastbourne to Hampstead in 1952, and was a family affair until recently – indeed, the present bursar is one of the founding family. It has long enjoyed the reputation for being ever-so-slightly alternative. 'Terms like "wacky" and "bohemian" fall too easily from the lips,' chuckled Mr Keyte. 'Schools always spawn myths, and one myth is that it always used to be wackier than it is now – now being 30 years ago, 10 years ago, or here today.' One parent said, 'The place fosters individuality, but they also foster awareness of others. My sons' friends at the school were all lovely kids.'

In fact, there is strong continuity: it's less academically assertive than some of its competitors, and continues to invest huge time, as well as significant resources, in its arts and mixed curriculum. What is gently shifting is the extent to which it can compete, on all fronts, with the best. The plant is hugely impressive, there is a long waiting list and the staff are evidently completely committed. Taken over by Alpha Plus in 2009. 'They've offered massive support – moral and material,' says the head, 'and through the links they offer to other schools. In academic, pastoral and administrative terms, we are part of a powerful shared network of understanding and best practice.'

Good local community links and endeavour, and energetic and impassioned fundraising. A particular charity to which the school has attached itself – Mary's Meals – seeks to provide food for the neediest children all over the world, and pupils raised over £58,000 for the key school charities recently. 'Not bad,' says the head, 'and it came from the heart, I assure you.'

The prevailing atmosphere is of calm – children always generate a degree of noise, but the motif is jolly rather than manic, and there was a laudable absence of rush around the classrooms and in the school canteen (the food is widely regarded as excellent). It may be a boys' school, but it is blessedly short of that testy laddishness which serves to exclude rather than embrace. There is also a strong and experienced senior leadership team – of whom the bursar, head of junior school and academic deputy head are all women.

High ceilings and shrewdly-adapted Victorian buildings have managed to foster a sense of space and light. A school for all-comers, all types, and for all seasons. The sense of children at ease around the place is emphasised by the way they wear their uniform – a green and grey affair, which sits comfortably on them. The effect is to suggest an identity, and it's easy to see it's worn with pride – but, mercifully, without swagger. A big emphasis on kindness and tolerance. We heard teachers talking to classes and individual pupils, quite unaware that anyone was around, and the tenor was consistently one of calm benevolence. The payoff is obvious – the children seem remarkably patient and tolerant of one another. Very strong sense that the care of the children is anchored by affection and good sense.

A high-powered staff room – Oxbridge and doctorates all over the place – but school culture fosters collegiality among staff, and old hands willingly share best practice with newbies. Form tutors are the first point of contact for parents, and share concerns with senior teachers as well as with the pastoral deputy head. Stout denials from all parties that parents are anything other than strongly supportive. 'We aim at prevention,' said one long-serving teacher. 'We encourage anyone – child or parent – to tell us if they're worried or doubtful about something. It breeds trust, and it usually means stuff gets sorted out before it gets difficult.' It seems to work too – the headmaster has, in all his years here, invoked the sanction of detention precisely twice.

Reports get sent home twice a year, and there are two annual parents' evenings, as well as a lot of informal meetings. 'We aim to be around,' says the head. 'A lot of goodwill is built up, and a great deal of information exchanged, simply by teachers being around – not least at the school gates.'

Pupil constituency is noticeably more European than many other schools of its kind – hardly surprising given that St Anthony's is the only all-boys Catholic prep school in north London, and hence a favoured destination for the many Spanish, French and Italian who live around here. It also won a string of 'outstanding' commendations in its recent diocesan inspection, which helped to cement its credentials with this particular parent body. On the other hand, it's also a mainstream Hampstead prep school, with lots of parents drawn from the professions, the media and the City. Some remarkable old alumni – David Suchet and Antony Gormley among the older generation; a more recent luminary is Jack Steadman of the indie band Bombay Bicycle Club.

A very likeable school. Conscious of its individuality, but not in thrall to it. 'A nice balance of informality and old school,' said a parent. Smack in the middle of north London, it is championing values more abiding than merely those of fame and fortune. It achieves considerable success, but not by stepping over the bodies of others. As the head says: 'Working in a school isn't just for the glamour and the good times. The test of vocation comes when it's difficult.' The affection with which St Anthony's is viewed by parents and staff seems to suggest they, like the pupils, are only too glad to have bought into this wisdom.

St Augustine's Priory

Hillcrest Road, Ealing, London W5 2JL

Ages 3–18 Pupils 464 Sixth form 39 RC

Fees: £11,709 – £15,693 pa

020 8997 2022
www.sapriory.com

Head: Since 2012, Sarah Raffray BA (English and Latin, Manchester) MA (literature and modernity, Salford), 40s. With a career, seemingly, purpose-built for this post, Mrs Raffray is universally praised. She inherited a school with a venerable tradition but a recent, prolonged and very public upheaval accompanied by a mass exodus. It is a tribute to her energetic, frank and warm approach that the school is in such good heart and that it merits this, its first inclusion in The Guide. She knew what she was doing when she came here – 'I almost didn't apply but I had an "if not you, who?" moment and I absolutely believe in Catholic education, with a 21st century resonance. Unless you encourage people to sit still, go deeper and challenge things, everything becomes superficial.' School received an 'outstanding in all areas' diocesan inspection in 2016.

From St Mary's, Shaftesbury, where she'd been deputy head, Mrs Raffray had previously taught at St Mary's, Cambridge (head of sixth form) and St Bede's, Manchester. All good Roman Catholic schools and providing solid experience for taking on St Augustine's – less well-known than her earlier schools but, under her aegis, this is set to change – and not just in the locality. Not least among her achievements is the unity and community she plainly fosters – her parents tell us: 'she has recruited many really outstanding, teachers'; 'she is a figurehead with real presence'; 'a dedicated leader'; 'she walks the playground – it's good to see the boss of the shop at the door and she's not afraid to deal with difficult things..all her changes are good – she now needs to be even more ambitious'.

No fear of failing in that department. Lots of new initiatives and a wholesale upgrading of staff. Ten-year master-plan for capital development has commenced and will include a new hall, sports and drama facilities.

Head is relaxed, easy to talk to and very open. 'I can't bear the idea of a "safe" sixth form – we need to look after people but we need to be edgy too.. We're not afraid to say we got it wrong but we're learning all the time... ' One of the best appointments we have seen for years.

S

Academic matters: Small classes. A pervasive air of orderliness and atmosphere of quiet study. Pupils pay tribute to the outstanding teaching, especially of many newer appointees – 'they are real experts in their subjects,' enthuse parents. Range of subjects respectable but not huge – as you'd expect from a small school. IGCSEs now taken in all sciences, modern languages and English. Russian on offer, as well as Spanish and French. Ambition shown in the arrival of additional maths on the GCSE curriculum. Very good results in, especially, art, English and Latin GCSEs, biology and physics IGCSEs. In all, 66 per cent A*-A/9-7 grades in 2018. A level results suffer from too many post-GCSE leavers but that is changing. A very encouraging 40 per cent A*/A grades in total in 2018, with the retention of academic high-flyers in the current sixth seeing changes here. Far fewer leavers than previously but more still needing to be done. Girls would like thinking skills or critical thinking lessons. But the sixth form, newly relaunched, is ripe for expansion – with its new centre, enrichment programme and extended school day – and we are confident that, given another year or two and the school's reputation growing as it must, they will be turning girls away.

Good learning support from f/t SENCo plus f/t learning support/literacy teacher and much p/t help from subject staff and a dyscalculia expert. Parents of dyslexics appreciative of the support their daughters receive – 'my daughter outperformed all expectations and will now get a great crop of A levels – we never dreamed it'd be possible'. EAL also supported. School flexible over GCSE subjects when SEN hinders achievement – 'They let my daughter stop French – which she was never going to get. So sensible!' And all parents we spoke to praised the value added to their daughters' academic aspirations by the culture of the school.

Secured links with the French Embassy and Sorbonne in London, thereby officially becoming bilingual hub. Offers bespoke French intensive learning to a hand-picked few.

Some sense that the extra-bright could be stretched more but this, too, is on the way with a new Oxbridge group – open to all aspirants – from year 10 up. Also, blow-up pics of successful former pupils around the place, pour encourager.. Despite improving academics, this school is not striving to be another league-table topper and quite right too.

Games, options, the arts: With sports fields like nothing we have seen elsewhere in London, St Augustine's is uniquely privileged. And they're not just extensive but quite beautiful. Good new Astro used for team sports and athletics. Unsurprisingly, PE is a GCSE and A level subject. Much praise for new head of sport and team – 'a new energy,' said a parent. Hockey, netball and lacrosse on offer plus fitness and taekwondo. Matches played with enthusiasm. DofE is popular and girls rave about their trips eg skiing in Switzerland and Bulgaria, geography trips to eg Iceland and to Morocco where they helped build a girls' boarding school.

We were impressed, again, by the enthusiasm displayed in the art and photographic studios – much experimentation, colour and free expression in textiles, paint and modelling. Pupil art well-displayed in every corridor. Lots of musical activities too – choirs and ensembles and all backed, now, by tip-top equipment – IT etc – and super large music room. Carol concert held in nearby Ealing Abbey. School badly needs an all-purpose hall (and will, eventually, get one) but drama and music thrive notwithstanding and the chapel lends its own peculiar magic to events. Much success in eg Young Enterprise, Youth Speaks, Youth Games, maths challenges and various writing competitions and a sense of striving for achievable goals.

Background and atmosphere: The school was founded in 1634 by Mother Lettice Mary Tredway CRL (1595 –1677) a canoness regular and abbess who, together with Miles Pinkney (Father Carré), founded a monastery for the English members of her Order in Paris. A pension for English ladies and a school were attached to the new monastery, of which Tredway was abbess till 1675, when illness compelled her to resign. The priory survived, along with the school attached to it, until the French Revolution, when the English canonesses were forced to flee. They returned home, where they were able to live out their life as a religious community. Eventually the community established itself as St Augustine's Priory in Ealing and the school has occupied its rather wonderful and surprising present site since 1915.

It's tucked into a corner off the North Circular as it rises to meet the A40, yards from the unlovely Hanger Lane Gyratory System – as the monster roundabout is grandiosely named. From the front, the school looks a hotch-potch of brick and pebbledash buildings of no particular distinction. However, surprises await. From the back of the building, the view over 13 acres of fields to the spread of the capital is astonishing. There are gardens, an apple orchard, a prayer garden, a farm with micro pigs, sheep and chickens, an allotment, many mature and beautiful trees and the whole thing is an oasis. You don't hear the traffic, you just relax into this beautiful space. Many of the school rooms look over this – most notably, the exceptionally well-appointed sixth form common room and the art studio at the top of the building. The rear of the building also surprises – its monastic principles clear in the pastiche Norman windows, the row of windows on the floor above which would have been those of the nuns – now gone – and the simple cruciform architecture – more obvious when you walk the school itself.

'It feels like the countryside,' as a parent said. It also feels like a village community – lots of old girls and staff send their daughters here. Junior school occupies building at one end of the site – with its own meadow and nursery playground. Little demarcation between the junior and senior schools – seen as a plus by some while others feel there should be more of a 'step up' up at 11. Junior school itself is lovely – lively, imaginative activities with some pleasing mess (we hate sanitised nurseries) and happy, occupied children. Very orderly classrooms for older children and an air of productive purpose throughout.

We have seldom visited a school with so powerful a sense of commitment amongst its community. It's small – too small for a few – but the girls know each other and the strengthening of houses and inter-year activities are helping. Lovely features like the new outside theatre, the willow tunnels constructed by 'amazingly inventive groundsman' and a feeling that 'anyone who comes up with a good idea gets encouragement and, if need be, funding'. Lack of a proper school hall felt by everyone, but 10-year development plan now commencing should sort this as well as provide other much-needed facilities. All classrooms have names of saints or worthies – Thomas Aquinas houses science, St Cecilia music etc. Tuck shop and two refectories – modern, bright and with 'excellent' food. Whole school now bristles with new PCs.

Much of the interior is nondescript, though all is in good order – clean and spruce. But the chapel – even to heathens like your reviewer – is a source of pleasure. With balcony, vaulted roof, splendid marble columns and altar, and white walls, this Douai-inspired centre of the school life induces reflection and calm. Monday assemblies and three-weekly mass for each year held here. Little Muslim prayer room, but that this is a Roman Catholic school is inescapable. Life-sized statues of saints, crucifixes, pictures and pious posters and messages are everywhere, yet under half the school population is RC and not all those are practising. However, RC values underpin the school's teaching and the girls we spoke to were comfortable with the ethos, and felt the ethos of community and equality will stay with them when they leave. No-one felt oppressed by it.

Pastoral care, well-being and discipline: Very few problems. Some legacy of past difficulties persists but, as with everything here, a sense that Mrs Raffray and her team are on top of it and there is little left to do. 'We have changed our bullying policy. There are clear sanctions.' Impressive newish deputy has pastoral role among others. Universal praise for pastoral care and equipping the girls for the wider world: 'The school allows them to stay as children in an environment which wants them to grow up too early,' a parent told us. 'There are lots of leadership programmes and a growing sense of boldness and confidence.' 'Our daughters are very happy.' Big sister/little sister buddying between sixth form and year 7 newbies. Before and after-school care.

Pupils and parents: Roman Catholics (around 40 per cent of school's population) from Ealing and surrounds. Further 20 per cent are other Christians. Culturally and ethnically diverse, as you'd expect in this part of London – lots of Asians and mixed race families. Strong community holds all together. Middle class, professional families. Mostly from local primaries. School runs a minibus from Chiswick. No identikit pupil. Says head, 'The school has a tradition of accommodating girls who want to be different.' We met nothing but relaxed, articulate, smiley girls. Most famous old girl: actor and writer Phoebe Waller-Bridge.

Entrance: Ealing is well-served by good local state primaries – many of them RC. Nursery and reception places available but waiting lists now in years 3 and 4. Few places in years 5 and 6. At 11+, 60+ apply for c12 places via exam and interview. Places available for year 12. However, all this is set to change. This school is now a player and, notwithstanding the good local state provision, the school's site and, now, its academics and inclusive culture – along with the outstanding pastoral care and community feel – will drive custom. Get in quick.

Exit: Latterly a sizeable exit post-GCSE to state RC heavyweights, and local co-eds. That is set to change. All 18+s to higher education, mostly to good universities eg LSE, Warwick, Edinburgh and even Toronto, to read proper subjects. No Oxbridge in recent years but we met some impressive current candidates and would confidently predict success.

Money matters: Fees appreciably lower than those of local competitors. Worthwhile discounts for siblings. Academic/sports/music awards at 11+. Academic awards at 16+. All worth 10-20 per cent discount on fees. Bursaries for existing students in case of need.

Remarks: We came away with a bottle of their home-grown and pressed apple juice, and much more you couldn't bottle. This could be the school for which the cliché A Hidden Gem was invented, but we don't expect it to remain hidden for much longer under such inspirational leadership.

St Benedict's School

54 Eaton Rise, London W5 2ES

Ages 3–18 **Pupils** 1,076 (718 boys, 358 girls) **Sixth form** 218 **RC**

Fees: £12,990 – £16,845 pa

020 8862 2254
www.stbenedicts.org.uk

S

Headmaster: Since 2016, Andrew Johnson (50s), married to Dawn with two sons at university. Educated at Skinners' School in Tunbridge Wells; read modern languages at Bristol and then went straight into teaching. His degree landed him head of the subject at Winchester and then took him north, first to Birkdale School in Sheffield and then on to the top job at Stonyhurst, where he introduced the IB and embedded coeducation.

His arrival here was announced as 'a real coup' by the governors and he is definitely on a mission to try and make the world sit up and notice this school. An easy, tidy man with a controlled sense of humour, who despite describing himself as 'not an office worker' obviously has impressive management skills. He has brought in an infusion of new blood at the top, including a new deputy head, deputy head academic and bursar, and is confident that he can mesh the new with the old as far as staffing goes. Determined to get to know the pupils as well as the teachers, he tries to observe three lessons a week and cheer on as many of his vast array of rugby teams as possible.

Head of junior school: Since 2005, Rob Simmons BA MEd (40s), married with children and grandchildren. Schooled at St Benedict's; after a history degree and time abroad on voluntary service he returned to his alma mater, landing up with headship of the junior school. A trim, dapper dresser, he is not shy about his passion for aviation, planes neatly arranged on shelves and a favourite paperback, starring a Second World War aviation hero, tucked in amongst the history books. He has started Hot Chocolate (and marshmallows!) Friday for one pupil from each class who has ticked all the right boxes during the week.

Academic matters: Nursery, rescued from its Nissan hut island in the playground, is now housed in the junior school with an experienced head – 'I just love the little ones' – in charge. A full curriculum, including art, drama, music and computing alongside traditional subjects, is taught from reception onwards and in keeping with AJ's new approach to academics higher up, they have recently introduced setting in maths and English from year 5. The new building has been designed with early years children in mind and there are cosy break-out spaces (including a ribbon bedecked 'rainbow' room) and a full-time SENCo who operates on both a group and one-to-one level.

AJ's conscious decision to raise the game academically – 'we want to give a greater sense of zip to academic life' – has already paid off with a much improved set of GCSE figures in 2018, 66 per cent 9-7. He states that it will be a slower process, maybe up to five years, to make the same sort of progress at A level, but results in 2018 were respectable with 41 per cent A*/A and 73 per cent A*-B. He now monitors the school's ranking against other independents rather than all schools, and has introduced more frequent testing, so that 'we can be straightforward about a pupil's ability'. He has also expanded the tutorial system so that all pupils from year 7 onwards have access to two form tutors.

After three years of studying a wide range of subjects, including the option of Chinese in year 7, everybody aims at a minimum of nine GCSEs. Once in the sixth form most take three A levels with 40 per cent doing an EPQ in the lower sixth on subjects as diverse as phage therapy (how to crack treating viruses) and the moral stance of Woodrow Wilson. Students' wide variety of answers on particular academic strengths implied that they were confident about the teaching across the board. A source of pride to all was the pupil who beat entrants from nine other European countries to win the Youth Debating Competition in Budapest, a project well outside their normal comfort zone.

Some eight per cent of pupils receive SEN support from a full-time SENCo, operating alongside a new counsellor, whose brief is to listen to any problems that are brought to her by pupils or parents.

Games, options, the arts: Nursery and reception do PE including dance, but from the age of 7 serious sport begins. Girls play hockey in the autumn and netball in spring, boys play rugby for two terms and both head to the cricket pitches in the summer. Rugby tops the bill with twice weekly fixtures, international tours and the chance to be part of a London Irish training scheme. Not to be left out, girls play tag rugby, but the emphasis is on netball and hockey and they have recently fielded teams who have successfully toured abroad. Everyone is encouraged, according to one parent, and there is a large indoor sports hall with an impressive array of fitness machines and a full complement of professional staff to help would-be stars develop. Fencing is very strong; add in athletics, football, cross-country, rounders, swimming, badminton, basketball, volley ball and jiu-jitsu and you can see why the sporting side of the school often pops up when talking to parents, one naming its 'sporty' side the reason for choosing it.

Extracurricular offerings in the junior school range from the head's aviation club, which has proved so absorbing that one ex-member is now in the RAF, to the more grounded chess, gymnastics, ballet, sewing and drama. Regular trips to museums and theatres and in years 5 and 6 residential outings to the Lake District for the great outdoors and to Normandy to learn about baguettes and butter. Older pupils are given over 60 options to widen their horizons, lots of DofE awards and charity work but also a massive music offering from rock groups to close-harmony singing. The cadet force is popular and the less regimented can choose from arts, drama, dance, languages, science and extra sport.

Music is a common strand from little ones singing in their nativity play past the juniors who all learn the violin in year 3 to the near professional spring and summer concerts by senior pupils. There is a busy, buzzy art room at the top of the junior building full of enthusiastic children and imaginative mobiles, and in the senior school there is a new art, design and technology department. We were particularly impressed by a papier-mâché tour de force, posing as a futuristic chair, and students showcase their work with two major art shows each year.

Drama is not timetabled in the junior school, although nativity and form plays are an annual event, but once in year 7 – 'we have a wealth of acting talent' – it takes regular billing. The middle school recently put on Lord of the Flies whilst the seniors staged West Side Story and Amadeus.

Background and atmosphere: Nearly 400 years after the Reformation, the Benedictine monks of Downside decided it was time to expand from rural Somerset to suburban London. Initially known as Ealing Priory School, the school opened in 1902 with three boys and five pounds in the kitty, was given its current name in 1948 and has been fully co-educational since 2008.

The architectural chimera lying on the summit of a gentle slope above Ealing Broadway is composed of solid Edwardian villas, rather dreary brick buildings and a lot of tarmac all sandwiched between unlikely golden doors and the 1900s abbey; fortunately, the slightly weary creature is in the midst of a massive refurbishment.

They've already finished a building for the sixth form with art studios above, a small chapel featuring primary coloured windows, designed by a pupil, and an entirely revamped junior school in a modern Scandinavian style which ticks all the right eco boxes. Inside they've brightened up the reception area and the main school hall and plans are in the pipeline to revamp the elderly classrooms. Parents' reactions are positive, one saying that the school was 'a bit tatty', but now looks 'much fresher'. AJ would like to build a performing arts centre in the medium term and there is even talk of planting an avenue of trees once the builders have finally departed – a decidedly good idea as leafy, green trees would definitely improve the present overall monochrome effect.

Pastoral care, well-being and discipline: Rules are here to be obeyed and AJ is not shy of suspending pupils for a few days if they consistently break them or insist on remaining academically lazy, but hopes that this can almost always be avoided by close monitoring of each pupil's academic and social progress.

Cheerful 'worry' boxes are spread round the junior school and in the senior school there are quiet rooms and the new chapel (complete with chaplain) as well as the counsellor who is always on site.

The recent conviction of a priest, ex-middle school head, for sexually assaulting pupils in the 70s and 80s, plus the departure in 2015 of the deputy head, following his arrest over indecent images (not involving any St Benedict's children), have resulted in extremely thorough measures to safeguard pupils. There is both internal and external monitoring of the internet and the last ISI inspection was passed with flying colours. Parents remark that the school is very hot on e-dangers and the modern pressures put on pupils via social media and selfies. In our opinion St Benedict's is aware of the mistakes of the past and has moved on.

Some 55 per cent of the pupils are Catholic, the remaining 45 per cent from other faiths or with no faith. The school is no longer marketed solely as a Catholic institution, but talking to students made us very aware that the Benedictine ethos is still omnipresent. The visits to Lourdes, charity fundraising, weekly mass in the abbey and the voluntary service carried out by all members of the lower sixth plus the attitude of pupils to staff and to one another, remind you that this is a school that takes faith and social behaviour seriously.

Pupils and parents: A large number of dual income parents who work extremely hard in order to pay the below average fees charged here. In western London school terminology, St Benedict's is counted as middle of the road compared to some of its flashier rivals, but all parents that we talked to felt that it provided good value for money, very good pastoral care and that the new leadership team was pushing the academic standards to a higher level.

At the younger end of the school the children are almost all very local, but higher up the catchment area spreads significantly, and they now run regular transport from Hammersmith, Harrow and Richmond. The children who showed us round the lower school were smiley, charming and confident and all the older pupils were polite and articulate, if not appearing quite as sophisticated as some of their inner London contemporaries – not necessarily a bad thing.

Alumni include Julian Clary, Peter Ackroyd and the poet/songwriter Labi Siffre as well as a sprinkling of politicians (in particular Chris Patten) and rugby players.

Entrance: Entrance at 3 is non-selective; at 4 it is more formal, with children observed doing tasks in a classroom. For entry at 7 or above children are asked to do tests in maths, English and verbal reasoning as well as an assessment.

At 11+ pupils from the junior school compete in the same exam as external candidates from local state primaries and preps, for the 120 places available. There are occasional spaces at 13+ and in the sixth form but the bar is on the rise with increasing numbers applying.

Exit: Some 70 per cent of juniors move up to the senior school, and around 85 per cent continue to the sixth form. Leavers head to universities from Aston and Bangor to Warwick and York. One to Oxford (philosophy and theology) plus one medic in 2018.

Money matters: Academic, music and sports scholarships, worth up to 50 per cent of the fees, available at 11+ and sixth form for internal and external candidates. Bursaries available in the senior school are strictly means tested, but 'once a child is in, if a parent falls on hard times, we will do our best to help them'.

Remarks: The 'granular scrutiny' that the ambitious headmaster is applying to all things academic and pastoral is already bearing fruit, and this school is definitely on an upward curve scholastically. If you then take into account all the new buildings and refurbishment programmes, this could soon become better known amongst the schools to the west of the city.

St Charles Catholic Sixth Form College

74 St Charles Square, London W10 6EY

Ages 16–19 **Pupils** 1,200 **RC**

020 8968 7755
www.stcharles.ac.uk

Principal: Since 2015, Elaine Taylor BA MA PGCE. BA in history and sociology from Queen Mary's and MA from Institute of Education. Joined the college in 2009 as vice principal. Previously at St Francis Xavier College in Clapham, where she was assistant principal. Has also held positions of head of sociology, psychology and politics. 'Teaching was the only job I ever wanted to do, though I never thought I would be a principal!' she confesses. Married with two grown-up sons. Strong Irish roots and nips back to Ireland at the drop of a hat. Tries to switch off at weekend by walking and gentle exercise. Family is her priority at weekends and during holidays. An approachable, friendly and welcoming head. Well-respected by parents.

Academic matters: College offers a variety of courses at levels 1, 2 and 3. Pupils can take A levels or vocational qualifications or a combination of both at level 3. Hasn't released 2018 A level results, but usually around a quarter at A*-B. School offers three levels of study – advanced (A levels and vocational level 3), intermediate (GCSEs and BTec level 2) and foundation (BTec level 1 and functional skills in English and maths). Two per cent of pupils make up level 1. Ms Taylor explains, 'Level 1 students are those who have done very badly in their GCSEs at their old school, or students who have not been in the country very long and need to develop their numeracy and literacy skills.' Level 2 pupil numbers have grown to 150. 'They are usually students who have not done very well in their GCSEs either, but not atrociously, gaining mostly 4 and 3s'. Limited numbers of GCSEs offered and level 2 pupils tend to take maths and English GCSEs, alongside level 2 BTec programme. In recent years, the proportion of A level students has been declining in favour of those choosing the BTec route. Nearly 30 different A levels offered, including ICT, Italian and photography; newly introduced BTecs include media and music. 'We might cultivate the combined pathway a little more,' explains head, 'as it gives pupils greater flexibility'. Possible to start at level 1 and move on up to level 2 then 3. 'Some stay with us for four years and end up at university. We support them along the way.'

Around 40 level 3 pupils take the EPQ. Ms Taylor is very enthusiastic about this qualification: 'We are trying to develop it, as nearly all our students take three rather than four A levels now, and the EPQ will be a good differentiating tool when applying to universities. They all start off enthusiastically but a 6,000-word dissertation can be quite hard work!' Subjects range from whether the African elephant can survive to debates on the influence of gender on crime.

Well-resourced learning support centre, providing support for 10 per cent of pupils. College currently has 4.5 learning support teachers and three learning assistants who support the small number of pupils with EHC plans. One parent raved about the support her SEN son received: 'They really understood him and worked with his strengths.' Her son was given an individual tour of the school before arrival, so he would not have to deal with the hurly-burly of the regular show-round. Roughly 130 pupils qualify as having some sort of SEN, ranging from those who just need a bit of extra help with structuring essays to those who require a full-time assistant in every lesson. A fair number with dyslexia, Asperger's and autism. Help given to those who have English as an additional language but pupils need to be able to fully access the curriculum.

Over 30 teachers have been here for more than a decade, and a sizeable number were pupils here themselves. Ms Taylor feels that pressure on staff has become worse than ever and she is saddened that tighter budgets have led to staff cuts. Every member of staff is now up to their full complement of teaching and staff development has been curtailed.

Games, options, the arts: 'We don't force students to do enrichment but we really try to encourage them to do so,' states Ms Taylor. Basketball team has recently won the national finals. 'We are like the Leicester football team: we came from nothing and won the trophy,' beams head. Successful at football too. Fully equipped fitness gym is well-used, including female-only afternoon. Indoor and outdoor multi-function sports area allows some sport to take place on site but footballers trek to Westway to practise.

College has own dance and theatre studio. Drama is offered at A level and performing arts at BTec. Annual musical, open to all. Considered to be a highlight of the year. No students play instruments at school, no orchestra and no choirs. Not the place for your child if they are desperate to be part of a music ensembles. Art is very popular, with notably strong department.

College is outward-looking. Other enrichment opportunities include pupils teaching computer skills to local senior citizens one afternoon a week – so popular, there is a waiting list. Others work for charities or Young Enterprise and help with regeneration of local area. Regular outside speakers range from chief executives from Mastercard to religious leaders of all faiths. Lots of work experience organised.

Trips tend to be subject-related, including a cultural trip to New York every year for psychology and sociology students; a geography trip to Sicily where pupils visit Mount Etna; travel and tourism trips to Lanzarote. Getting harder to subsidise pupils who cannot afford it. Lots of visits closer to home, including to theatres and art galleries.

Background and atmosphere: Just off Ladbroke Grove. Tucked between a Catholic church, a Catholic girls' secondary, the Catholic Children's Society and a convent. Named after St Charles Borromeo, 16th century Italian archbishop who believed in the redeeming power of education. Founded by Cardinal Basil Hume in 1990.

Accepts all faiths and none but Catholic ethos pervades, though in terms of numbers only about 35 per cent Catholic, 30 per cent other Christians and 22 per cent currently Muslim. Compulsory RE programme, comprising one hour lesson a week. Ms Taylor explains, 'It is important to have a general religion programme. It is an opportunity for students to mix with students of other religions, to discuss a range of issues and to hear what others believe. It's good preparation for the world outside.'

Very inclusive, defined by Catholic values, with Christ at its centre. An explicitly Christian set of values from the Gospels, with a focus on inclusivity and service to others. A banner above the entrance proclaims, 'Show mercy to others as God shows mercy to you.' Voluntary mass every Friday and a daily morning prayer. Christmas and Easter services. On-site chapel. Annual trip to Lourdes to help the sick, organised by the full-time chaplain who also acts as an unofficial counsellor. Pupils find him approachable and he can often be spotted deep in a game of chess with one or other of them. One parent assured us that religion was 'not overwhelming'.

Pastoral care, well-being and discipline: Everyone is in a tutor group which meets daily, under one of the pastoral managers. 'This daily contact just keeps them on track,' explains head. External counsellors visit the school weekly. Even though this is a sixth form college, many school-like structures are in place. Ex-pupils say how much they miss the pastoral care once they go to university.

Zero tolerance of any form of physical violence or drug related incidents, both within the college grounds or in the vicinity. Immediate expulsion for these offences with suspension for lesser transgressions. 'Discipline is a headache,' according to one mother, though probably no more so than in some other London schools. Security guards at the gate are strict about checking for ID and no-one allowed in without it. Giving your ID card to another student results in suspension for three days. Pupils initially surprised how strict the college is, but head believes that 'the safety of the students is the most important thing. Some have challenging lives outside and it is part of the mission to encourage them to take the right path'. Knife tunnels erected sporadically, in liaison with police, so pupils 'know that we are monitoring them.' If pupils are late to lessons then they are not allowed in. One mother divulged that her son was worried he would be bullied as 'it's a rough place, but the college handled his needs well.' Principal disagrees that the college is rough, telling us 'this is simply not the case.'

Head believes the issues that pupils face are becoming more complex. She explains, 'We have many students who have mental health issues. More and more young people are coming to us who are already in the CAHMS [Child and Adolescent Mental Health services] system.' There have been incidents with suicidal pupils in the past. 'This often occurs on a Friday, with the thought of the weekend ahead.' Others have suffered historical abuse. Social media often the source of arguments. 'The exam competition is worse now – everything has to be an A. We put so much pressure on the young,' worries head. College is often a haven for those with complicated domestic lives and Ms Taylor believes it is her job to provide stability for those who are troubled.

Pupils and parents: Diverse, international set of pupils who come from 165 different schools. Pupils trek in from far and wide. Wide ethnic mix, with African students making up the majority. Over 40 per cent are on free school meals; most from low-income backgrounds. Lots of siblings and cousins. 'People hear about us very much through word of mouth.'

Parents are kept in the loop regarding their child's attendance, punctuality and behaviour via the parent portal and communication with tutors and pastoral managers. Two parents' evenings a year, so most feel as though they know what is going on.

Entrance: College is non-selective and places are offered based on a successful interview and reference from previous school. School interviews over 2,000 students a year. Priority given to disabled and looked after children, followed by pupils from Catholic partner secondary schools, then Catholic students from other secondary schools and finally non-Catholics. In reality, not many are turned down, but acceptance is dependent upon reference and interview. Ms Taylor states: 'We want to recruit as many students as possible, though there has to be some integrity about who we take.' Some start but do not last long – about 100 students are lost during the year. Prepared to take some from pupil referral units, in line with its inclusive policy, 'though we won't take them all.' If a pupil's reference is poor in terms of attendance or punctuality then unlikely they would be accepted.

For A level route, minimum six GCSEs at 9-4, including English language. Minimum five GCSEs at 4 or above for level 3 BTec vocational study. For intermediate route, four grade 3s or above at GCSE. Foundation level is suitable for pupils with GCSEs below grade 3.

Exit: Of the level 3 pupils, about 85 per cent go on to university. Some to Russell Group, with London a firm favourite, as students can save money by living at home. Increasing numbers are deferring as they are not sure that they can afford it, and others not even applying as they are put off by student debt. Popular subjects include business, sociology, psychology, Arabic studies and international relations. Just a trickle chooses history or English.

Many opt for art foundation courses and college has good links with Central St Martins. Others head for the London College of Fashion. One artistic past pupil is currently using his considerable creative skills in a tattoo parlour.

Some proceed straight to the world of work, particularly into retail, with increasing numbers opting for apprenticeships in business, IT or administration.

Money matters: Bursary payments made to nearly 40 per cent of pupils – grants for those in financial hardship studying full time. All charged a one-off resources fee when they start, to cover costs such as photocopying.

Remarks: Principal states, 'We want every student, no matter what their starting point to do the best they can. Everyone these days is measured by their exam results but education is so much more. We are trying to do something a little bit different to others. We take on students that sometimes need a second chance, because sometimes life does not go according to plan'. For those prepared to play by the rules, this college can and does turn lives around.

St Christopher's School

32 Belsize Lane, London NW3 5AE

Ages 4–11 Pupils 240

Fees: £14,700 pa

020 7435 1521
www.stchristophers.london

Head: Since January 2018, Emma Crawford-Nash MA BEd (Cantab), mid 40s, previously head of the prep department of Manchester High School for Girls. She got the top exam results in her year at Cambridge and a distinction in her MA. She has been teaching since 1995, specialising in English and the performing arts, and has also worked at Haberdashers' Aske's School for Girls, St Paul's Cathedral School and Nottingham Girls' High School, where she was deputy head of the junior school. Passionate about helping girls to do and be anything they want, she's also interested in theatre, music, dance, running and girls' education in developing countries.

Entrance: St Christopher's is one of London's highest-achieving academic prep schools, with results at 11 the envy of many of its neighbours. This, however, is a school which selects primarily on ability. Part of the selection procedure is standardised tests, so summer birthdays don't lose out. 'It is not an academic assessment. We observe how they play together and how they interact with other children.' The school operates a split entry and although all are assessed at the same time, girls with September to February birthdays will generally join in reception, whilst March to August birthdays join in year 1. Tests dates and results are co-ordinated with other leading selective north London prep schools. Early registration is essential (as near birth as possible) for those already resident in London. Entry lists are closed at about 300 to be assessed for 38 available places. The school, however, is always willing to be flexible for those who've just arrived. Siblings are given an automatic offer, unless it is considered 'they will not flourish'. Not flourishing, however, is fairly loosely interpreted. 'If you have two clever daughters and the third is not as bright, some parents think she'll upset the exit poll, but that's not the way we work.' Parents confirm that year groups cover a (relatively) wide spread of ability. Occasional vacancies after entry. One 100 per cent means-tested scholarship available per annum and other support available as necessary.

Exit: 'We're fortunate in London that there are so many great schools, and we are proud of the achievement of all our girls. There's no scholarship board here. We don't want to make some pupils feel instantly diminished.' That said, this is generally a school of bright sparks and ambitious parents and the majority proceed to the highest performing London day schools. St Paul's Girls' School, North London Collegiate and South Hampstead top the list, with City of London School for Girls, Channing and Highgate close behind. Quite a number of scholarships amongst them. A handful to high-performing state secondaries eg Henrietta Barnett.

Remarks: St Christopher's was founded in 1883 by two local literary lesbians, but established in its current form in 1950 by the writer Rosemary Manning. It became a charitable trust in the 1970s. Housed in a large Victorian family house (with modern additions) in fashionable Belsize Park, this is a top-flight prep school for top-flight north London parents and the ethos and atmosphere are reflective of that. The education the pupils receive here is thoughtful and exciting. It concentrates on the fundamentals, but only after the fundamentals have been carefully considered. 'We have to ask the question "what are we educating children for?" It's a world we know nothing about, a world very different from our own.' The school has carefully analysed the impact of technology. 'The girls think technologically and it can be much more difficult to get them to listen to a story and concentrate.' The issue is addressed by concentrated focus on the task of reading and understanding and girls read aloud every day from reception to year 3 and regularly thereafter. 'If you can't read, you can't do maths.' No concessions are made when it comes to literature ('We don't use abridged texts') and Dickens and Lewis Carroll are digested in the original. An excellent library underlines the school's priorities.

Much of the timetable follows the national curriculum ('It would be foolish not to – there are some very interesting things – but we cut away the trivia. We don't reject it, we tweak it') and the approach is based on 'child-initiated learning' with pupils taught to question and take responsibility for what they learn. Work is then tailored to the needs of each pupil, with maths books, for example, customised to the age and stage. (Though those in need of learning support are in the minority – mainly younger siblings – parents consider this tailoring, too, to be strong.) Spanish ('one of the most widely spoken languages in the world') is taught throughout, Latin from year 5 and French as a club from year 3. Specialist subject teaching from year 4, with drama added to the curricular mix, joined by history of art in year 5. Flexibility of mind is encouraged by the inclusion of chess. ('It's a brilliant thinking exercise.')

Hard-working, well-qualified staff, particularly in the final two years. 'I cannot imagine better teachers than the maths and

English teachers in years 5 and 6,' said one parent. 'They are really transformative.'

Despite the school's outstanding scholarship record, there is no scholarship class and no setting, except in maths in the final two years. Nor is this a school that crams for exams; preparation lasts just one term, when practice papers are given weekly. 'They're not missing core subjects from year 5, they still have time for all the extracurricular, they're not pressured and processed.' The approach here is enriching and the school believes there is as much value in creativity as in the core subjects.

Music is generally considered strong and enthusiastic, with two music classes plus a singing class each week. What's learnt here is put into practice with a junior orchestra, a wind group, a string group, piano club, junior and senior choirs and a chamber choir. This is media-land, too, and there is also a thriving film club, where girls learn to make their own. Cultural outings are very much part of the offering, with regular visits to theatres and museums and a young writers' workshop.

Sport is perhaps less important than it might be elsewhere (some parents complain that unless you're in a team, this can be a rather neglected area). Netball court and gym on site and regular matches against other schools in netball and rounders. Short tennis is also taught in the summer term and senior girls play lacrosse. Swimming lessons only in year 3 at nearby Swiss Cottage baths, sports day held at Hampstead Cricket Club. Though the outdoor space here is not unduly extensive, it is used very effectively, with an outdoor classroom, an Alice Garden and a science-themed garden. 'Children today have a very boring existence, chauffeured here and there, and we wanted to create an environment where they were allowed to be imaginative.' Indeed, the thread that runs throughout St Christopher's is that a good education is stimulating, interesting and exciting. The extracurricular is therefore addressed as energetically, with everything from public speaking to self-defence and Indian dance and, while there may be a Florence Nightingale workshop, the message that banking is as worthwhile a career for girls as nursing is instilled with visits to the Bank of England and a mock Dragons' Den. All staff are required to run two clubs a year and the offering is extensive.

Four houses, Brontë, Nightingale, North and Pankhurst, provide the basis for inter-house competition. The school has a strong family feel, sheltered and relaxed. There are no school rules ('We just ask for respect in the classroom and for them to be polite to teachers.') Good behaviour is instilled by discussion. ('Why did you do that? How do you imagine that would look?') Occasionally parents feel that emotional difficulties are not picked up as quickly as they might be. ('If you mention a problem, they take it seriously, but it's not always spotted,' said one.) Assembly every Friday is non-denominational. School meals exclude pork, shellfish, ham and nuts in order to cater for all. The facilities here have been brought thoroughly up to date, too, with a smart extension providing additional classrooms and impressive IT. The uniform of green Aertex shirts and blue trousers is practical and durable.

Over a third of pupils live within walking distance and the rest travel from affluent nearby postcodes like St John's Wood, Maida Vale, Islington and Highgate. Parents are often intellectual, professional, international and Jewish – and occasionally celebrities. 'They are interesting and incredibly well-informed. They are very involved and desperately keen to support their children's education.' ('Sometimes too keenly involved,' remarked one father. 'There are a lot of non-working mothers who once had high-powered careers and are now directing their energies on their children.') Occasionally expectations have to be gently adjusted.

A high-octane education producing confident, well-informed and articulate girls. 'The nice thing about St Christopher's is that it provides an excellent education without trying to breed a master race,' said one happy customer.

S

St David's School

23/25 Woodcote Valley Road, Purley, Surrey CR8 3AL

Ages 3–11 Pupils 150 C of E

Fees: £9,900 – £10,650 pa

020 8660 0723
www.stdavidsschool.co.uk

Head: Since 2011, Cressida Mardell (40s) BA PGCE, a classicist. Before joining St David's in 2007 she was a senior teacher at St Christopher's School, Epsom. Parents appreciate her positive approach, hard work and sound judgement, alongside a jolly personality and a good sense of humour. She lives locally and enjoys holidaying in France and walking with her two lively Border collie rescue dogs.

Entrance: Most join the nursery at 3+ (18 places); another four places in reception. Non-selective at this stage; occasional places in year 1 upwards subject to 'satisfactory assessment'.

Exit: Most popular destinations at 11+: Croydon High, Wallington County Grammar, Whitgift, Riddlesdown, Trinity, St Philomena's, Royal Russell, Wilsons, Caterham.

Remarks: Mixed ability school, which skilfully blends academic excellence alongside a good range of musical, creative and sporting opportunities.

Founded in 1912 with just five pupils, by Welsh (hence school's name) sisters Margery and Mary Talfourd Jones. The school has thrived through the decades and today's multicultural clientèle is still proud of its founders' Welsh connections. Pupils join in the Eisteddfod Festival and fly the flag on St David's Day.

Dedicated class teachers run maths and English lessons mostly in the mornings and then teach specialist subjects in the afternoons. There is an ICT room and a room for arts, science and technology; pupils often split for these subjects so class sizes are around 10, optimising opportunities for individual attention and development. French is taught throughout the school and year 6s learn Latin. Specialist teacher visits three days a week to assist children with any special educational needs. Additional support is provided in small groups, one-to-one or in class at no extra charge. ESOL can be arranged.

Very busy music department has a gifted and talented choir, brass ensemble, string ensemble and rhythm group. Most pupils play at least one instrument; older pupils are introduced to filming and music composition with the occasional commission, most recently a jingle for Halfords. Some great achievements on the sporting front; St David's has its own large playing fields a few minutes' walk from the school building complete with new all-purpose facility including Astro football pitch and tennis courts. Gymnastics is particularly strong; the school has won the ISA competition on several occasions. Swimming is another area where pupils excel, with eight children being selected to train as divers at Crystal Palace for the Olympics programme.

Parents felt clubs had been rather limited; this is now an expanding area, and the aim is now to offer a much wider choice of activities, after-school and at lunchtimes. Chess team have made it into Champion League finals for primary schools and the maths team recently came third in the Sutton Maths

Challenge. After-school care (at extra cost) is provided by the Jancett Nursery Group until 6.30pm.

Refreshingly, St David's has retained its independence and remains a small charity with a non-selective intake, so far avoiding being swept up by one of the large education businesses. Very successful results at 11 into the local grammar and independent schools, especially considering the non-selective intake and inclusive approach. Terrific value for money.

St Dominic's Sixth Form College

244

Mount Park Avenue, Harrow on the Hill HA1 3HX

Ages 16–19 **Pupils** 1,234 **RC**

020 8422 8084
www.stdoms.ac.uk

Principal: Since 2013, Andrew Parkin (40s). Studied music at Durham and Cambridge and started his professional career in London at The St Marylebone Girls' School. Went on to be deputy head at Sion Manning Girls' School in Kensington and then St Augustine's High School in Westminster. 'For 18 years, I worked in fairly tough comprehensives, which probably explains why the hottest topics for me are teaching, learning, attainment, consistency and attendance and punctuality,' he says. 'But I love the way that here, we get to combine these with informalities such as addressing each other on first name terms, as well as a greater emphasis on independent learning – the result of which is fantastic preparation for university.'

Not someone to hide away in his office, he greets students on the gate, observes lessons, teaches general RE (and occasionally some music) and regularly chats to students and staff. 'I'm not really a number cruncher – I don't believe that is what headships are about.' Clearly passionate about his role ('I absolutely love it! I feel I've got the most perfect job, with happy students that work their very hard, and no discipline issues'), he is also a keen member of several committees in the wider sector. Among the key changes he's brought to the college are a strong emphasis on teaching and learning, more peer observations, a hands-on leadership team and embedding IT into learning. Students don't have a bad word to say about him. 'He seems to know everybody's name,' said one. 'He's so approachable and easy going.' Parents similarly keen: 'He is absolutely fabulous – a supportive leader who's not afraid to get his hands dirty, rather than being just a figurehead.'

Both interested and interesting, he is keen amateur musician and is chairman of the BBC Symphony Chorus.

Academic matters: Some 29 subjects available in more-or-less any combination. Maths, history, the three sciences, economics and psychology are the most popular A level subjects – with strongest results in maths, chemistry, biology, history and economics (in terms of attainment) and history, classics, languages, music and art (in terms of value-added). In 2018, 32 per cent A*/A and 62 per cent A*-B grades.

Option to change subjects in the first week or two if you really loathe geography or have just developed a passionate interest in Italian. Currently, students can take four subjects in year 12, dropping down to three in year 13, enabling them to keep options open. Offers level 3 BTec national and extended diplomas, ideally suited to those who don't like the sound of lots of final exams, which can be combined with one (extended course) or two (national course) A levels. 'BTecs are often undersold, but they afford our less academic students an opportunity to achieve highly and go onto the likes of York, Nottingham and London universities. The business studies one has validity and is taught well here,' claims the principal. College has also brought in a core maths programme, which enables students to keep up with maths without taking the full A level.

Class sizes range from 2-25 and teaching is largely discussion-based. 'The teachers' subject knowledge is phenomenal – some have two degrees,' one told us. 'Teachers here are so inspirational and really passionate about what they teach,' said another, although be warned they are very hot on homework, being 'very strict on both completion and deadlines.' Professional development for teachers is a strength, with all having spent time in London schools. 'It's been great for them to see what life is like elsewhere – it's got them to reflect on their own practice and raise the bar,' explains the principal.

Good for those with physical disabilities – we met one wheelchair user, who couldn't praise the college highly enough. 'There's not one area I can't access,' she said. Students with hearing or visual impairments are equally impressed. Very few students with SEN, though. Support for them is 50 per cent classroom support, while the other half takes place in the Study Plus area, which other students access for anything from revision workshops to small project groups – all of which helps to prevent any stigma. 'Our son has Asperger's and the college has been brilliant – really going out of their way to help him on his terms and he got far better results than we thought he would,' one parent told us.

Offers the EPQ. 'They have a free choice of subject, but it makes sense to relate it to a subject they may do at university, and gives something to talk about at interview.' Large numbers of aspiring medics, so the college runs a programme of BMAT preparation and mock interviews. Excellent university and careers advice; has been awarded the Investors in Careers mark and has a designated HE and careers advisor. 'We're realistic and honest, and allow no poverty of aspiration.'

Effort and achievement grades given every six weeks. 'Our monitoring is much more frequent than they have time to do in schools. All our staff are focused on the sixth form – not on settling in year 7s or helping year 9s choose GCSE subjects, or indeed behavioural issues.'

Games, options, the arts: State-of-the-art sports hall includes a multigym and hall for badminton, table tennis and five-a-side football, with its use juggled between A level PE students and general recreation. Sport is not compulsory, but the hall 'has increased motivation and attendance. We've been pleasantly surprised that participation rates have been very high.' Indeed, the principal encourages all students to utilise the multigym, which is open from 7.30am-5.30pm. Outdoor space includes a five-a-side football/netball court and a football field set among beautiful woodland. There's at least one team for each of football, rugby, tennis, basketball, table tennis and netball – 'Football trials are particularly popular, with around 100 students applying for just 11 places,' one student told us. They do well in local leagues, and some competitions further afield, particularly for football and badminton. There's a cycling club and golf club, plus opportunities for cheerleading and street dance for those less competitively inclined.

Music is part of everyday life – we heard the practising for the annual bands' performances when we visited. Decent numbers (around 25) do A level, while seven peripatetic teachers cover individual teaching of instruments including piano, flute, strings, guitar and drums. Choir and orchestra both popular and good, with termly concerts providing opportunities to perform. Department comprises of teaching space, recording

S

studio and rehearsal rooms, and there's a newly installed electric organ in the chapel, that is used by keyboard players. 'I've been known to pop in to play it for half-an-hour myself,' admits the principal.

Top floor art studios could be bigger and better, but they do the job and are reassuringly cluttered with colourful resources and some very talented work. Three teachers cover art, art history and DT, and the sophisticated artwork and fashion creations are exhibited in the chapel annually, with several students each year going on to art and design courses. Drama studio is ok, but any lack of cutting edge practice areas doesn't put off keen thespians, who put on an annual musical production, plus various productions throughout the year. Great excitement about the devised pieces being showcased annually in the so-called 'shack' – a covered outside space for which the college hires in tiered seating. 'With the sounds of nature and the London hum in the background, and the sheer talent of the students, it's all highly dramatic,' says the principal, recalling that one performance required a pig's head having to be ordered from the butcher, then kept under health and safety conditions.

Volunteering and fundraising are important parts of the ethos. 'Charity efforts spring up out of nowhere.' Students do sponsored walks and sleep outs, work in soup kitchens, volunteer on a Catholic farm, join a pilgrimage to Lourdes. 'There's a philosophy of respecting other people and helping the wider community.'

Long list of day trips and residentials. 'London is used to the max – theatres, museums, concerts, Houses of Parliament and so on.' Among the regular overseas trips are Great Wall of China (general trip, open to all), Washington DC (history and politics students) – and there's an annual exchange with a school in New Jersey. Other recent trips have included music trip to New York, art trip to Rome, general trip to Venice and classics trip to Athens. Extracurricular activities not obligatory, but widely taken up – including everything from flower arranging to sports. Guest speakers regularly invited in – including The Spectator's editor Fraser Nelson, Sir Bernard Hogan Howe, Mark Damazer and Phillip Coggan.

Background and atmosphere: Opened in 1978 in what had been St Dominic's Independent Grammar School for Girls, run by Dominican nuns. Sits on a hill above a leafy, gated estate of substantial houses with large gardens that could have strayed from the Chilterns, and amazing views across London – as far as the City and Canary Wharf on a clear day. By the entrance to the 28-acre site is the chapel, a peaceful and atmospheric building with lovely stained glass, 'the heart of the college'. Assemblies (each year group gets four a year, which are supplemented by the principal's Sunday night emails on a theme for the week, such as 'What is truth?') and introductory talks take place here, as well as morning masses, and Muslim students use a side room for prayer. Four large blocks make up the key teaching areas – Hume (humanities), Catherine (maths, English, languages), Aquinas (sciences) and Siena (sports hall and psychology).

S

The most recently developed facility is the remodelled library – among the nicest we've seen, in which the £1m investment paid for a bright, airy space, with multicoloured seats and two glass-dominated mezzanine areas, with masses of study space and computers. 'It's well staffed and equipped – we love it,' one student told us. Indeed, it's generally packed until closing time at 4.30pm.

No common room ('We don't need one – we're not a school,' says principal), with students gathering instead in the spacious canteen, library and the Shack, where an all-day coffee kiosk augments the canteen offerings.

Faith is a major part of the deal here, with the principal big on the Dominican tradition – with links with its sisters and brothers all around the country. Mass is held every week, tutor groups take it in turns to choose readings, everyone studies RE. 'We want our students to develop on an academic, personal and spiritual level. We want them to critically examine their faith, to mix with people from other faiths and hear why it is important to them. It makes a tremendous difference to what we can offer and how they develop in later life,' says principal.

About 60 per cent of the staff is Catholic, but all buy into the ethos. Prayers are said each morning and each tutor period. 'It is a moment for thinking outside oneself – a lovely sharing moment.' Very good relationships amongst staff and between staff and pupils and overall, there's a real buzz around campus – the atmosphere is relaxed, informal, yet hardworking.

Pastoral care, well-being and discipline: Any student problems tend to be ironed out by teachers or the college counsellor, the latter whose hourly slots over two days a week are always packed out. 'If I could afford it, I'd have her here five days,' say the principal. One parent whose family had suffered trauma were particularly impressed by the pastoral offering. 'They could not have done more for my son.' Mental health issues, particularly anxiety, on the up, reports the college – but that's no different to what any other head tells us. In the main, things tick over pretty smoothly here – and students were aghast when we asked them if there was any bullying. 'Unlike a lot of sixth form colleges, where you get cliques, this one has a really warm and friendly atmosphere,' said one. Strong student voice – changing everything from more loo rolls in the toilets and better air-con to helping organise events like the annual talent show and cultural day.

Electronic registration for every lesson means that everyone is accounted for: the pastoral team phones parent and student if the student is not in by 10am. If lateness becomes a regular occurrence, homework is late, a student shows lack of effort, or takes unauthorized absence, then they're put on warning. If they still don't pull their socks up, they are asked to attend supervised learning and teaching (detention basically – although they won't call it that). 'It's an opportunity for students who haven't worked hard enough that week to do so,' says the principal, although not many students wind up actually having to attend one. If there's still no improvement, parents are called in – again, it's very few students overall. Zero tolerance for drugs or violence, but no problems with either for many years – in fact, no temporary exclusions whatsoever in current principal's reign.

Pupils and parents: About 40 per cent Catholic, most of the rest Hindu or Muslim. Homogeneous in that all take their religious faith seriously, with the exception of one or two atheists (but no zealous ones, unsurprisingly). 'All students are serious about academic life – you need to be motivated and have a certain level of intelligence to get on here,' one student told us – indeed, the college offers virtually no vocational courses. And as there is a high level of competition for places, those who get in feel a great sense of gratitude. 'I feel really lucky to be here,' is something of a mantra.

White British is certainly not the majority here. 'Harrow is one of the most diverse boroughs in the area, and we are reflective of that,' says principal. Good mix in terms of class too – with many students the first in their families to aspire to university. Parents are nearly all highly supportive, with 97 per cent attendance at the annual parents' evening – doubtless helped by the fact that parents can drop in anytime between 9am-7.30pm and the principal stipulates that they do so. 'I insist every young person has someone to represent them because it's my experience that when young men and women get to 16, many parents take a back seat, and that's not what we want here.'

Entrance: About 40 per cent from its two partner schools, Salvatorian College and Sacred Heart Language College – the rest from over 100 other feeder schools, stretching as far as 1.5 hours travel away. 'I know someone who comes in from Kent,' one student told us, while one from Enfield told us it takes her 'an hour-and-10-minutes travelling one way – and that's on a good day.' 'Most of our students live in Harrow, but if you looked at a heat map of London, we'd have dots representing students' homes all over it, and I think that's great,' says the principal. 'At 16, people are old enough to make decisions and if they recognise excellence and are prepared to make an effort to get out of bed for it, then I'm all for it.'

Students from the main two feeder schools are guaranteed a place, providing they get at least five 9-4 GCSE grades including English language. All other applicants must get at least seven 9-4s and meet the individual subject requirements. These range from a 4 in English for religious studies to an 7 in maths for further maths. Priority to Catholics, then other practising Christians, then other faiths and no faith. Applicants must acknowledge their commitment to the religious values of the school in writing. Conditional offers are made in March and are based on academic references, including predicted grades. Any remaining places offered based on subjects with spaces and highest GCSE average score. Some spaces also become available after the first year. 'Many parents round here work abroad, so there's quite a lot of movement in the area,' explains the principal.

Exit: Around 90 per cent to higher education. London universities are very popular, as are Nottingham, Southampton and Warwick. Law and medical/biomedical subjects tend to top the tables. Fewer Oxbridge applicants than one might expect given the calibre of students (eight places in 2018, including two lawyers and a medic), largely because so many are prospective medics (15 in 2018).

Money matters: Free if you're under 19. Excellent and enlightened system of bursaries for students and staff to fund specific projects and trips.

Remarks: Greatly sought-after college in pleasant leafy location with high academic standards and a strong Catholic ethos of care for each other. 'A lovely place to work and study,' say staff and students.

St Dunstan's College

Linked with St Dunstan's College Junior School

Stanstead Road, London SE6 4TY

Ages 11-18 **Pupils** 603 **Sixth form** 133 **C of E**

Fees: £17,196 pa

020 8516 7200
www.stdunstans.org.uk

Headmaster: Since 2014, Nicholas Hewlett BSc PGCE (30s): the youngest head we've yet to meet, but youth becomes him. He's still bouncing with excitement after two challenging years in post. After a brief spell in the City, he headed to King's College London to study geography, followed by a PGCE at the Institute of Education. Landing his first teaching job at Dulwich College, within three years he moved to Magdalen College School Oxford, as head of geography becoming housemaster, contingent commander of the CCF and director of the annual arts festival.

We were somewhat startled to hear a wish from a mother to hear him sing until we encountered his CV. Performing as a tenor soloist throughout his 20s, he also sang at one time as a lay clerk for New College Oxford. In 2011, he was part of the team that helped to lead a flagship school on the island of Jeju, South Korea, under the banner of North London Collegiate School. He credits being a part of transition and the brilliant leadership and mentoring at these schools for his confidence to lead the reinvention here.

The aim is to create one college rather than two quite separate schools and invigorate academic ambition, which he likens to 'tightening the plumbing of this incredible, beautiful building' whilst retaining the inclusive, diverse ethos of the school – a cornerstone of which is the introduction of a revitalised extracurricular offer named the Forder Programme, inspired by a pioneering early head who took boys on adventures all over London. Mr Hewlett lives in Croydon where he grew up and his interests include travel, literature, cooking and antique maps such as the beautiful one adorning his office.

We heard nothing but boundless enthusiasm in return from parents: 'He is ambitious for the college and very driven to secure its success, which is laudable. He is not afraid of change and he has conviction'; 'He is approachable, friendly and clearly driven. He also has a wonderfully eloquent turn of phrase.' Our sixth form tour guide appreciated greater transparency, more student voice and one-to-one drop-ins.

Academic matters: In 2018, 54 per cent A*/A and 72 per cent A*-B at A level and 60 per cent 9-7 at GCSE. Mr Hewlett's been on nothing short of a mission, observing lessons, mentoring and training staff with potential, doing significant pruning elsewhere, appointing a deputy head academic with experience of both Westminster school and the state sector, and students have had to raise their game too. Pupils are now innovatively graded on 'learning characteristics' such as 'engagement' or 'organisation' instead of simply the hard to measure 'effort' as well attainment.

On the ground, a student told us of 'an influx of better teachers'. The head says that his team is now in place and it's a matter of embedding. Parents speak of a change of pace: 'We are very happy that our children are aiming higher than before. It certainly isn't too intense.' Another, 'I have been impressed by the energy and enthusiasm displayed by all the teaching staff'. Naturally, there is still work to do. One parent also praised the teaching but said: 'Class discipline is less good, with a high level of ambient noise irritating for the more engaged students.' Whilst a mother said: 'It may benefit from developing a more competitive atmosphere for the more able students.'

The head likes the principles of the IB but also the rigour of A levels, so has decided to drop the IB in favour of the college's own diploma. This will consist of A levels combined with 100 hours of co-curricular and a global perspectives pre-U short course taken in the first term of year 12.

Everything you'd expect at GCSE in terms of curriculum choices, including Latin, and the languages taught are French and Spanish, German is offered, but no Mandarin. PE for those not wanting to be completely confined to a desk. Beyond the compulsories, Spanish and history are the most popular currently. Barely a handful of Latin students. More artists than musicians. Mathematicians, single scientists and historians perform well. Things get a little more varied at A level with the addition of drama and theatre, economics, and business studies. Most popular sixth form subjects last year were maths, physics, geography and art and design, with the most A* by far for the mathematicians. Plenty of artists, but no drama or music students at this higher level. Teachers are free to choose whichever exam board best suits their cohort. Class sizes are a maximum of 25 until GCSE, then 15 in the sixth form.

All of the parents we spoke to said that they don't feel their children are unduly pressured: 'The school has a policy of not setting homework during the holidays. A project is set for any children who would like to do something, but it is entirely voluntary'.

The school has always had above average numbers of SEN pupils. This continues: 95 students have learning support needs, 70 per cent of these with dyslexia. Learning support is for mild needs only, and only as far as this can be accommodated in class (no one-to-one provided).

Some 15 per cent of the senior college are registered with EAL needs. There is an EAL co-ordinator and students are supported in class and through withdrawal. In years 10 and 11 some EAL students can study for the GCSE in English as a second language.

Plenty of trips, workshops, competitions, adventures and fun drop-ins. Actor Adrian Lester gave the drama students four weekly workshops; English students make the most of London theatres, recently feasting on The Curious Incident of the Dog in the Nighttime, A View from the Bridge and Othello, and year 12 and 13 mathematicians returned with a slew of medals from the UK Maths Challenge.

Games, options, the arts: It's all here in terms of sports facilities including a swimming pool, cardio gym and weights, with more currently being brought up to scratch at the Jubliee sports ground. Sports are compulsory. The core are rugby, football, hockey, netball, cricket and swimming. Some individual successes: a couple of boys play for their county cricket team. A parent: 'My son throws himself into all sporting activities...it has been an enormous boost to his confidence and self-esteem that his commitment and achievements have been recognized'. In contrast another said: 'The children have felt under-prepared for their matches.' Help is at hand, with a new director of sport who isn't just focused on the elite or fixture results, but wanting every child to 'reach their physical potential'.

Some 200 students learn an instrument, from grade 1 to diploma level. A sizeable uptake, but by no means the most musical school we've visited. A mother told us: 'The gifted musicians are few in number and there are few opportunities for chamber music or innovative use of the talent pool'. However, plenty to thrill the ears in a rich timetable of recitals and concerts – some in beautiful London churches. The musical head believes the musical life of the school is very good. The St Paul's Symphonia recently joined school musicians in a festival concert.

Seriously impressive art lines the corridors, particularly the self-portraits. Large, light and popular DT workshops, including a separate space for sixth formers to work on their projects. A 3D printer and laser cutter. Students feel drama has taken a step up and there are 'lots of opportunities' with the appointment of a new head of drama; there are now three or four productions a year. The lower school recently relished putting on Bugsy Malone complete with splurge guns. A cross-discipline Gothic Evening included everything from gentle electrocution – the science dept – to one teacher reprising Kate Bush's version of Wuthering Heights. The drama studio looks very professional, all black, framed with lighting rigs, complete with sound desk. The inaugural St Dunstan's Arts Festival show-cases the school's music, drama, art and dance for the fee-paying public.

The Forder programme provides 100 activities a week, is compulsory and runs every lunch-time, but still with space for a lunch break. Pupils must try something creative, active and as a service. Sixth formers as part of the St Dunstan's diploma must lead, must do something new and must commit for a term. It gives students plenty to write about come university reference time. Sixth formers also gain leadership opportunities taking activities into the junior school.

Debaters find their voice in national and international competitions. We were shown rooms of shiny Apples and Dells – pupils will leave school with the versatility of understanding both. CCF offers army and navy experiences. D of E challenges run up to gold. A selection of fun-looking co-curricular – after-school, before or at lunch times: Mexican art and craft club, French culture club, Amnesty, Hans Woyda, draw and print drop-in, swing dance and fashion appreciation caught our eye – some additional charges for specialist sports classes such as judo.

We rarely mention food in our reviews. When we entered the incongruous, modern dining hall, which has a Pringle shaped roof and our guide claimed 'they are the best school lunches in London' we expected hyperbole. Behold – towers of jewelled couscous displayed in tagines, the freshest of baby-leaf salads, home-made soups in terracotta bowls, bread baked every morning to Paul Hollywood standard and eight varieties of seeds in copper buckets.

Background and atmosphere: The school foundation has its origins in the parish of St Dunstan's-in-the-East, established on St Dunstan's Hill in the City, the location of one of five schools ordained by the Archbishop of Canterbury and Bishop of London in 1446. By 1865 it was agreed to relocate the school to parish land elsewhere, where there could be playing fields and to be accessible by rail. The school was duly opened in its present location next to Catford Bridge in 1888. The school maintains its links with St Dunstan's-in-the-East, more commonly known as All Hallows by the Tower, and students take part in services and ceremonies such as the wonderfully curious 'beating the bounds'.

This relocation for more green space seems incongruous now as one approaches the school from the ever-congested stretch of the south circular between Forest Hill and Catford. The school shelters behind its red-brick gates next to DIY sheds, a railway station and inner city grot somewhat at odds with the pictures of children walking along a tree-lined grassy grove (the playing field presumably) on the website.

Inside, the red 'Hogwarts' building is at once impressive and in places shabbily homely. High ceilinged, metro-tiled corridors, lots of staircases with wooden handrails – no sliding – and a galleried Great Hall with stained glass windows, organ pipes and a multi-media desk for productions. Classrooms for year groups tend to cluster together, giving students a home base and possibly adding to the 'small' school feel. Sixth formers have their own shadowy domain which includes a large boarding school-style common room with sofas, snooker tables, study spaces and hot food from the dining room.

The already large and well-equipped library has almost doubled in size, retaining the wooden panelling, but introducing two soundproof modern pods with a teaching capacity of six for tutorials, adding a flexible lecture theatre and incorporating learning support and enrichment. The librarian inducts all year 7s into the resources available for their studies, which include 6,000 e-books. Interns from London universities will become subject mentors, helping with research skills or providing careers inspiration.

We observed a happy and relaxed atmosphere. One parent told us: 'our daughter describes the school as busy, lively, noisy and feels confident, with many friends. Our son describes the school as friendly, very informative and very sporty and active with lots of good trips.' 'Down to earth, practical, energised and caring' seems to sum it up.

Pastoral care, well-being and discipline: A parent confided: 'the pastoral care for the children has always been and continues to be excellent', but the head wants no room for complacency and so has appointed a new deputy head pastoral. There are four houses named after the first headmasters. Uniform rules are fairly stringent and students look smart. No mobiles on during the day. No beards in the sixth form. And ties at the conventional length: hear, hear. Hoodies are specifically forbidden, perhaps in case of inner city associations.

Pupils and parents: Pupils come from the immediate but also extensive south east London neighbourhood stretching across Lewisham to Greenwich, from the west such as Dulwich and further south to Bromley and Croydon. Fleets of coaches but also independent train travel.

The school welcomes international students and the numbers of Chinese students in the sixth form are visible; we wondered at integration when a student was unsure where they lived during term. A new head of inclusion and enrichment might consider issues like this alongside the remit to create a school that 'teaches to individuality'. In the future, international students will not comprise more than 10 per cent of the student body.

The community is one of hard-working families, many of whom are first-time buyers: 'down to earth, friendly and approachable,' said one mother of her peers. Creative types will find themselves in good company too. Old Dunstonians are musicians, politicians, businesspeople, sportspeople and scientists. Professor Sir Martin Evans, Nobel Prize winner for genetics, the very Rev Dr John Hall, Dean of Westminster and Lord Grade of Yarmouth, former chairman of the BBC and ITV, are among them.

Entrance: Whilst once upon a time the school was struggling for numbers, that is no longer the case. Year 7 is full and applications are up by 40 per cent. We believe this still makes it a gentle option compared with many. The head would love to lead on something truly radical with regards to 11+ entrance testing; year 7 applicants are currently tested in English, maths, verbal reasoning and abstract reasoning. Successful candidates are invited to return for an interview with a teacher and to meet either head or deputy head. No need for any nerves regarding parental interviews: it's simply time for a frank chat about the particular quirks of St Dunstan's offer and vision for the future. Testing takes place in January the year prior to entry. Unusually, there is an 11+ preparation scheme in place (for a fee), preparing candidates from all schools for the exams across three Saturdays. Far more entering from the local state primaries than is often the case – pupils come from Lewisham and Dulwich primaries, but also Heath House Prep, Oakfield Prep, Rosemead Prep and the Pointer School.

A small group of 13 or so enter at 13+, after taking English, maths and verbal reasoning papers. Prospective sixth formers are also required to sit papers in English, maths and verbal reasoning. Same interview process and references but the offer is conditional to the GCSE grades.

Exit: Most exit to university, with around 60 per cent to Russell Group. An interestingly diverse list of subjects being taken up for further study as befits the curricular offer here, recent range included biomedical science, design engineering, architecture, film practice, chemical engineering and neuroscience.

Money matters: There are academic, music, drama, art and design and sporting scholarships available at 11+ and academic and musical scholarships at 16+. Pupils who perform well in the entrance tests may be invited for an academic scholarship interview.

Potential scholars for the co-curricular awards must jump through a variety of hoops from one minute monologues (drama) to a colour study in oil pastels (art). Bursaries are generous and could run up to 100 per cent of fees for the right candidates. Family incomes will need to be modest but by no means breadline to be considered.

Remarks: In the next few years those pupils and parents taking up places are betting on potential. As the head says: 'we're not the finished article'. This location has to be a bit of a stumbling block but we expect parents looking for an effective and inspiring coeducational experience in south London to find themselves sorely tempted.

St Dunstan's College Junior School

Linked with St Dunstan's College

246

Stanstead Road, London SE6 4TY

Ages 3–11 **Pupils** 265 **C of E**

Fees: £10,131 – £16,269 pa

020 8516 7225
www.stdunstans.org.uk

Head: Since 2015, Paul Cozens BA (40s). Degree in education studies with music and French from Exeter. Describes himself and the head of the senior school as a Venn diagram with a 50 per cent overlap of core values. He brings much to the party, including music and mindfulness. Previously deputy of St Paul's Cathedral School, his first posts were at South Hampstead High junior dept and the Beacon School before being appointed as director of studies at Newton Prep. He is an ISI inspector.

Parents enthuse: 'He is dynamic, interested, brave... he is open-minded and interested in new ideas'; 'he manages to uphold the college's traditions while keeping up with the current times'; 'just right for the age group – visible, involved, friendly and approachable towards the children yet also minded to get the very best from them he can.' Our guides were somewhat amazed: 'He's friendly: not what you think a headmaster will be like!'

Entrance: For 3+ nursery places, informal assessment and interview with parents. At 4+, small group assessments with tasks such as listening to a story and discussing shapes and colours. At 7+, assessment includes brief English and maths papers followed by drama and science activities.

Exit: Whilst most children move to the senior school, around 20 per cent historically head to local state and grammar schools.

Remarks: Children and parents very appreciative of the teaching: an 11 year old reported: 'It is great to be able to work with fantastic teachers who are able to explain things in a way that you can understand.' A parent: 'I have always been impressed by how quickly each new teacher gains an understanding of our child'. Another: 'The teachers in the pre-prep were absolutely brilliant at devising lesson plans that engaged very young children, expanded their minds...and made learning absolutely fun.'

Despite these bright spots, Mr Cozens found plenty of scope for improvement. A new focus on a joined up subject leadership from nursery to sixth form benefits the junior and senior school curricula. Year 6 pupils moving on to the senior school find Mr Cozens teaching some ICT in year 7. Maths is taught creatively and memorably: designed a shopping centre whilst learning about area; creating and drinking 'mocktails' to understand units of measurement. Spanish is taught from nursery to year 1, French in years 2 and 3 and French, German and Spanish in years 4, 5 and 6. Latin is offered by way of co-curricular 'classics'. Mandarin is taught as a club. The maximum size of classes is 20.

Testing is more in the style of continuous assessments – children take it in their stride. Homework is deliberately light with little or nothing in the holidays. Some choose the school because of a relative lack of pressure, one parent feeling it 'would suit a child who thrives in a less competitive academic environment.' Those who need stretching are thought of too, however: the most able in years 5 and 6 have English and maths lessons with year 7 from time to time. We hear some year 6 children did feel under pressure, however, come the run up to the 11+ entrance testing.

All of the usual core sports take place on the extensive fields to the rear of the school – great to see the girls doing everything, even rugby. There's a newish head of sport who is redressing the balance: more time on skills, less time on matches. Some individual stars with a couple of county players.

A functional music block, with delightful sounds emanating; ensembles for everything, plus chapel choir, chamber music, big band and rock band. Music scholars perform at St John's Smith Square. As the children rise through the school dramatic opportunities grow in ambition. Pupils performed in a Shakespeare festival at Greenwich Theatre. One delighted parent said of her son: 'He went from preferring to be backstage when he first arrived to taking a central part in his year 6 school production.'

Given this inner city locale, the residential trips with an outdoorsy focus are a particular high. Junior school children take part in the college's Forder programme of extracurricular activities three times a week. Clubs could be music ensembles or opportunities to try new things such as debating or animation but also simply down-time pursuits like knitting and yoga.

Part Victorian red-brick, part Portakabin and part wooden 60s block. A whole new junior school building is in the pipeline, and architects have been appointed. In our opinion it can't come too soon, though with plenty of play equipment, a good art space, large ICT suite and bright, well-organised, clean classrooms pupils seem oblivious.

Children struck us as happy and relaxed. We witnessed reception boogying to Move It, Move It, year 2s in quiet concentration and those on the move holding doors open for each other politely. Parents say: 'It is a place where every parent feels comfortable leaving their child knowing that they will be looked after, they will be happy and they will prosper'; there is 'a huge emphasis on making them stand tall, but also stride out into the world with questions to ask 'and 'most importantly, the children are given lots of opportunities to be children, to do fun things and enjoy their lives at school.'

S

Pets lend a family atmosphere. We met Fluffy 'the slightly evil hamster' and children eagerly awaited Marley the rescue rabbit. Come lunch time they troop to the senior school dining hall for a lunch which bears no resemblance to 'school dinners'. Extraordinarily fresh.

Parents speak highly of pastoral care; as one said: 'My daughter is able to discuss problems or concerns very easily with her form teacher. My son is so at ease in the school environment he feels totally happy with any member of staff.' Younger children can approach house captains as well as form teachers, and 'worry boxes' are a starting point. Years 1 to 4 have reading buddies. On a year 4 DT day each child created a pop-up book for their buddy based on the younger child's interests. Head aims that children should 'understand the notion of being competitive, but realise that if you work hard and well together that will reap rewards'.

The mother of a dyslexic daughter told us: 'She loves her teachers, she feels very safe and nurtured there' and that when extra help was needed the classroom teachers more than rose to the challenge (no one-to-one help so for mild needs only). Overall, parents feel: 'It's a caring school and children know each other by name over their year groups.' Any bullying 'is stopped very quickly and sorted out.'

A parent provided a pen portrait of peers: 'usually hardworking dual income families drawn from a range of communities'.

Before and after school care. 'Very welcoming' events organised by the PTA, called the Family Society.

St Elizabeth's Catholic Primary School

Queen's Road, Richmond, Surrey TW10 6HN

Ages 3–11 **Pupils** 298 **RC**

020 8940 3015
www.st-elizabeths.richmond.sch.uk

Headteacher: Since 2014, Jane Hines BA (40s), after 10 years as deputy head and six as a class teacher here. Before that was based in Bristol, where had completed a classics degree before moving into teaching. Loved the subject but, coming from a family of dedicated, fulfilled teachers, no other career exerted the same pull. News of appointment greeted with delight by parents, who already knew her as voice of kindly calm authority and (correctly) anticipated more of the same. 'Very calm and quiet, a real listener – have never seen her anything other than totally serene,' said parent.

But it's not just about maintaining the status quo. Mrs Hines is as dynamic (supported by strong leadership team) as they come. 'Very receptive to ideas,' said approving parent (we suspect she gets to do a lot of listening). In a short space of time, has brought in specialist teachers (a rarity in any cash-strapped school), transformed the site and ensured everyone buys into the process.

Happy and united staff – revitalizing mix of long stayers and recent arrivals – are with her all the way, recruitment pinpoint sharp (though very high standards mean that a few don't make it past probationary period). 'Want this to be a place where staff can innovate and try things out,' says Mrs Hines. Remains 'the best job in the world,' she says. If she has one (small) regret, it's that she isn't currently doing more teaching. Though won't take on a full time commitment as 'Tend to be called away for meetings,' she does plan to teach one or two lessons a week. 'Important to have that connection with the children.'

Entrance: Despite priority for demonstrably committed Catholic families from four local parishes, there's hope if you're not. A bulge class, added every three years, greatly improves changes of success for applicants from other religions (Eastern Orthodox followed by other branches of Christianity) or even none. 'We welcome applications from everybody,' stresses Mrs Hines.

Exit: Top Catholic senior schools for most. Vast majority to highly rated newcomer, Sir Richard Reynolds, others to Gunnersbury, Sacred Heart Convent, Cardinal Vaughan and The London Oratory School. Some girls to Waldegrave and handful of pupils each year to independents such as Putney High and Hampton (use of tutors not unknown).

Remarks: Even in high-achieving Richmond, St Elizabeth's would be having a bad year if its leavers didn't exceed borough averages. Nearly all year 6 pupils achieve at least level 4s in reading, writing and maths. While not, of course, the only reason parents choose the school, knowledge that in addition to a loving, Catholic ethos in cosy, small-scale environment, child is going to end up with a first class education does wonders for peace of mind.

Cynics might wonder whether given the location – lush lower slopes of Richmond Hill – and motivated parents, school simply can't go wrong. But success is never a given. Even here, there's considerable variation in family backgrounds. Over half the pupils now speak at least one other language, some arriving with very limited English, initially lured into the language by talking about their interests.

Success for all comes about through focus on the individual. 'Don't rely on any one tool,' says Mrs Hines. Throughout, rewards are based on how hard you try, not how clever you are. 'Teachers don't just care about our marks – they care that we're happy,' says year 6 pupil. Staff in complete agreement. 'Tests do not lead our judgement,' stresses senior teacher.

Writers' wall, changed every half term, features stories that are a personal best for their authors, not just the same old top talents. 'It's the pupils we're proudest of,' says teacher. Similar spirit – rewarding effort rather than straight brain power – prevails elsewhere. When all the children who had represented the school in sport were asked to stand up in assembly, 'was almost everyone,' reports a parent. 'Not always the same sporty kids doing stuff.'

For older children there's a big push on community involvement as role models for reception pupils. Year 6 chaplains develop entire assemblies for them from scratch – prayers, story and activity, while play leaders teach them to take turns at break. 'Look after them as though their own brothers and sisters,' said mother. 'It's a lovely thing for them to appreciate everybody.' Fun, agreed year 6 pupil – 'though they can be a bit wriggly.'

It all helps towards gaining coveted Governor's Awards – mini D of E scheme with desirable badges awarded for service, skills and growing independence – vast list ranges from leading a school club to locating 20 countries of the world and cooking a healthy meal. Everyone – with support from school – gets bronze, extra keen go for silver and gold.

Less than secret ingredient in success is teaching staff, most women (the perennial issue of the missing men in primary school teaching) who are 'unbelievable,' said a parent. 'Exhausted at the end of term but they're still smiling.' Add dedication – 'All work well beyond their hours,' said mother – and with happy, united team working to high standards, most parents had a virtually blank wishlist. A few start with initial reservations about how the many teachers with own children here balance dual roles – but not for long. 'It adds to their commitment – and if someone goes out socially with teacher who is a friend, would always put their professional hat on,' said one parent.

Even staff job shares are a model of effective communications, full-time TAs – one per year group in reception to year 2 – who stay with the class all week providing valuable sense of continuity. 'Don't know how they coordinate it but they don't miss a thing,' says parent. Skill, love of teaching and ability to construct active, exciting lessons undoubtedly help, though the basics are never forgotten, evening sessions for parents – starting with maths – showing how building blocks are put in place between reception and year 6. Must be working as while literacy is popular – 'Can let your imagination go wild with stories,' said year 6 pupil – most children rated maths as top subject. 'Fun learning new things – teachers help you through hard questions but don't tell you the answer.' Whatever the subject, clearly enjoy themselves, from year 2 pupils' pictures themed to 'Sky in the pie,' to a bit of creative headscratching as year 3s produced self-portraits for their reports, instantly switching from productive conversation to joining in with teacher's song, marking end of the lesson.

While those needing a bit of extra support or stretch will have separate group sessions, school doesn't go in for setting – not good for confidence. Instead, success is down to differentiation – highly effective because all children are known inside out to every teacher: no unknown unknowns here. Learning needs taken in school's stride – won't turn anyone away and if can't support a pupil themselves (and with excellent training for TAs that includes support for dyslexia and speech and language development, there's plenty they can) will look outside, often involving Richmond's highly rated Achieving for Children team. On day of visit, upbeat play therapist had just finished a session in the school's bright, cheerful library, a comforting space to work through difficulties. 'Can let go of their feelings here.'

School food was only aspect of life that some parents felt could do with some (minor) tweaking. Constantly under review, says school, with pupils pre-ordering so last in the queue don't miss out on best sellers (pizza a favourite), everything cooked from fresh and a salad bar recently added. Staff vote with their cutlery sets (around half have school lunches) and Mrs Hines and deputy both (other commitments permitting) eat with the children every day, 'which shows how good it is,' they point out. On day of visit, absence of mess and cleared plates suggested was going down a treat with the pupils too.

With academics ticking over nicely, the most welcome development (mentioned by every parent we spoke to) has been loan of specialist teachers (music, sports and – coming soon – French) from St Richard Reynolds. Provides non-teaching time cover for other staff, a bit of smart planning that keeps costs down.

Parents are pinching themselves in disbelief over speed of change, with weekly class music lessons for all coupled with accomplished school productions – polished lunchtime rehearsal of Bugsy Malone under way when we visited, impressive dance movements accompanied by talented young saxophonist, reception diners, knives and forks poised between plate and mouth, a gratifyingly awestruck audience. With new instruments to try, samba drums a popular addition, and excitement of having some of work recorded, difference is tangible. 'I notice a big change in their enthusiasm,' says parent of previously less than keen child who now arrives home singing new songs.

Whizzy head of sport has revitalized what was previously slightly low key area, at school four days a week, in first thing and often on days off as well, and spending every waking hour dreaming up new and exciting things to do, report parents. Includes setting up swimming squad and running extra sessions to help prepare for matches. 'Lives and breathes sport and has a passion that's spreading through the school,' says Mrs Hines. Now has suitably aspirational space with Astroturf courts on junior playground – and school can host fixtures at home rather than borrowing space from Christ's, neighbourly C of E secondary school just down the road.

All happens on a compact site where 'every spit of space is used,' says staff member. Cleverly done, corridors minimal, monoblocks of colour creating sense of calm so stimulation comes from the teaching rather than the paintwork (riots of colour very much last year's pedagogy...). It's especially notable in bright, pristine reception classrooms, slightly separate from rest of school, opening onto cheerful, well designed freeflow playground, natural wood fence and climbing frame a nod to Richmond Park which runs just the other side of the back fence.

Energy carries straight on into myriad activities before and after school – and at lunchtime, with even reception having a go (though wouldn't do more than one a week). 'Tons and tons,' said mother, including big band, breakfast club, cookery, art, Lego club and DT. Parents, too, are immersed in life of the school, commitment extending well beyond fairs and cake sales to arranging for external speakers to come in and give talks.

'School has a lovely feel to it,' said parent, 'and Mrs Hines has taken it on and beyond where it was before. Our children there are so lucky.'

St George's CofE Primary School

Corunna Road, Battersea, London SW8 4JS

Ages 3–11 **Pupils** 236 **C of E**

020 7622 1870
www.st-georges.wandsworth.sch.uk

Headteacher: Since 2015, Sarah Collymore (mid 30s); BA in primary education from Northumbria University. Went straight into teaching at 21 at a school local to her in Newcastle, but then decided to come to London with a friend and never looked back: 'We visited at Easter to view some schools – St George's being one of them. I rocked up one day and 12 years later, I'm still here.' Hired initially as a teacher in early years, at the same time as her predecessor Janet Hilary (former head) – this irrepressible duo took the school from special measures and on the verge of closure to Ofsted outstanding.

A Geordie lass who oozes warmth and likeability – the kind-natured, sincere head that every school should have. Dedication for 'her' children is tangible, and she is clearly popular with both parents and pupils alike – a few of whom came up to her in the playground whilst we were there to congratulate her on her new post as head. If one great head was going to leave, she was the only other person for the job and the only one with enough experience to drive the school forward. And this is where she plans to stay: 'If you have the will and desire to serve a community that is where you stay. There is no question that my work is where what I do will make a difference.'

Mrs Collymore has been described as 'an outstanding teacher' in all the phases of primary education she has worked – from early years through to key stage 2, then to deputy head prior to becoming head. One parent told us: 'I feel very confident in Mrs Collymore's ability to lead the school.' Married with one stepdaughter (her husband runs an exclusion unit in a large secondary comprehensive), she laughed when asked what she does in her 'spare' time.

The passion and pure dogged determination that former head Janet Hilary put into the school cannot be overlooked. She clearly left an indelible mark on both the pupils and parents who we spoke to. One parent told us: 'I chose this school because I was aware of Mrs Hilary's work before becoming head of St George's, and I knew how she worked. Her skill was that she pulled parents and teachers together.' However, after 12 years in the post, Mrs Hilary felt it was time to move on and embrace other challenges. She was appointed executive principle for Floreat Wandsworth and Floreat Brentford, 'an opportunity I couldn't turn down.' But she did very much plan to stay in touch with St George's and maintain a close partnership with Mrs Collymore: 'We are the No 1 Ladies' Leadership Team after all!'

Entrance: After the customary priority for looked-after children, 50 per cent of the school places are offered for church attendance, mostly from the local St George's Church, although some have come from further afield. One parent told us she travels in from Brixton. 'I wanted my child to go to this school, so I drive him there every day.' The remaining half of the school's intake are siblings followed by distance, although alarmingly we were told that being on the same road doesn't guarantee a place: 'Because there are so many tall blocks, some of those residents won't get a place.' Cohort is predominantly eastern European/Russian, Caribbean, West African, South Asian, and an increasing proportion of South American pupils. A large majority comes from single parent families: 'Diversity is very healthy for us. It enriches us all.'

Exit: The largest share goes to the local comprehensive St Cecilia's CE, followed by St John Bosco RC, a new voluntary aided college. Other local comprehensives include Ark Putney Academy, Southfields Academy and Lambeth Academy. If you have a girl, Lady Margaret – 'virtually impossible to get in to' – as well as Grey Coat Hospital ('if it's good enough for the [ex-] prime minister..') are the schools of choice. One parent did say that she worries about the lack of decent secondary school education in the area, 'but try not to worry about it yet.' However, the head remains positive about the regeneration of the area and the new demographic buying into these properties. She says: 'I believe that in two years we'll have a secondary school of choice on the patch.' Recently, for the first time in the school's history, one of their students was awarded a scholarship to Dulwich College, and has since become something of a legend in the school – a source of huge aspiration for the other pupils. The head told us: 'Nothing can come close to the feeling you get when a child from the Patmore Estate in south London tells you that they are going to Dulwich College and will study to become a heart surgeon.'

Remarks: Set amidst the Patmore and the Savona estates in Battersea, dwarfed by the numerous regeneration projects in the area (most notably Battersea Power Station and Nine Elms construction, which is right next door) and tucked away at the end of a residential street, this small one form primary school could be easily overlooked. Indeed we almost walked past it, which would've been a shame, as this wholly unpretentious school is quite a hidden gem.

Over the past four years, standards of attainment achieved by the school have been among the highest in the country, and its progress measures puts it in the top five per cent of schools. This year alone the school received two ministerial congratulations: for the phonics results (100 per cent) and for being one of the highest achieving schools in the country in terms of attainment and progress.

For any primary school this would be a major achievement, but for a school where the proportion of pupils eligible for free school meals is well above average, and nearly 60 per cent of the intake comes from homes where English is not a first language (32 languages spoken at the school), the sheer ambition cannot be underestimated.

The school's motto, 'The best we can be', is not a useless platitude, but something that they really aspire to for every child. As the head told us, 'We teach our children dignity and respect and teach them to come to school ready to learn'. No time is wasted in helping and encouraging children who speak other languages at home to begin to speak standard English; 'language is our bedrock because of where the different parents come from.' In reception, children are 'spellbound during phonic sessions by the teacher's funny hat, the silly songs they sing to keep them all on task and by the praise they are constantly given for their hard work. Phonics lessons are consequently a joy, and filled with giggling, gleeful responses' – Ofsted.

Teaching generally very impressive and children we saw were well behaved and enthralled in what they were being taught. Innovative use of teaching staff to create small, focused teaching groups in years 5 and 6 has been highly successful, and means that no pupil is left behind, and all are able enjoy high levels of challenge in English and maths. Each class has one teacher and one designated teaching assistant, in order to free up one of them to give individual help to any struggling pupils. 'It's important to spend time with a pupil if they don't get it, before they become disengaged.' Fairly high turnover of staff because of promotion elsewhere. 'Being a one form entry, it is hard to promote staff at St George's, but as we're diligent with our funding, we never have a shortfall.'

Those with special educational needs progress exceptionally well because the assessment and understanding of their needs is finely tuned. Former head said: 'I find it difficult to believe that when I started here, apparently 72 per cent of pupils had special needs. Now there are 12 per cent. I believe too often children are labelled as special needs if they are underachieving.'

Statistics and academia aside, the first thing that struck us on entering the school was how very serene it was. Nobody spoke in loud voices and staff almost glided to their various destinations – we could virtually hear a pin drop outside the classrooms we visited. Evidently, much thought has been given into making this school a calm, inviting and safe haven for pupils – the antithesis to many of their lives. The small, but stunningly immaculate and colourful garden which acts as a centrepiece for the school ('there are around 15 goldfinches in the gardens and we grow our own rhubarb and strawberries') offers pupils the opportunity to sit and read or reflect – and the dinner hall has been designed to overlook these gardens. This is all part of the Calm School Code ethos, which everyone is expected to adhere to.

The second thing that struck us (as we too glided from classroom to classroom on account of the very shiny floors) was how immaculate the classrooms were and how pupils demonstrated such pride in all aspects of their schooling, from their beautifully laminated workbooks (with some exceptional examples of joined up handwriting from the lower year groups), to their pristinely turned out selves in their smart navy uniforms with tied back or braided hair. As one parent said, 'The school is pretty strict on uniform, but that is because they don't want anyone to stick out.'

Very little wall space seems to be taken up by specific topic work but instead by an assortment of learning aids – phonics, maths, famous quotes, charts etc. One wall was virtually made up of aspirational charts. Pupils can belong to the 144 Club (children need to know all their times tables up to 12 and recall them quickly), the 20-20 Club for years 1, 2 and 3 etc etc. Perhaps the most prestigious of all of these is the Superstar award. It is the responsibility of each class team to encourage as many children as possible to become Superstars. All classrooms must have the 'HAPPY' chart (an acronym for homework, attitude, punctuality, participation, yourself)) on display and must demonstrate all aspects of HAPPY to receive their badge. Teachers are responsible for talking to parents about how they can support with any of these areas. At the end of each term the children who have been awarded their Superstar badge receive a reward. Autumn term – Christmas movie at the local cinema. Spring term – party and disco. Summer term – trip to Chessington.

Aspiration seeps through the very foundations of this school, from the extremely well stocked and well looked after library to weekly maths assemblies (where certificates are awarded to pupils who have completed maths challenges) – through to enrichment days at local independent schools such as Newton Prep, where years 4 and 5 get to use the facilities and are taught art, music, sport, science etc by specialist teachers. Some lucky pupils have enjoyed a trip to nearby Chelsea Football Club where strong links have been forged, whilst others sat in amongst the musicians of the Orchestra Vitae. One parent told us: 'Credit to the leadership team at this school for encouraging our children so much that they want to achieve, and then achieve more.'

Breakfast club on offer from 8.15am and after-school care offered until 6pm. A wide range of after-school clubs including dance, cooking, zumba, football, karate, tennis, choir and gardening. Participation in sporting competitions including athletics, cricket, golf, netball and basketball, and swimming lessons offered from year 4.

This is a proactive school in every conceivable way – no opportunity is left untapped. Instead of being bah humbug about the extensive building work in the area, the school has seized the opportunity to work with the architects, designers and builders on the Nine Elms Regeneration Project – and even managed to secure a substantial donation from its developers for a brand new all-weather sports pitch and art classroom.

If this wasn't enough, the school has set up a programme of motivational speakers for the older children and thus far the likes of Baroness Scotland, Sir William Atkinson and broadcaster Julie Etchingham have all come to speak at St George's. The head says: 'We want our pupils to have ambition and aspiration and this programme really helps them to think about careers and life choices.' Generous donations and sponsorship have also provided many rich opportunities for the pupils, including seaside trips (many pupils never having been to the seaside), theatre trips and funding for the new school uniform.

Unspoilt and wonderfully refreshing, the pupils we spoke to talked of becoming chartered accountants, vets, footballers and comedians. What came through were spirited, happy children with big personalities and a real sense of ambition. One particular pupil who was touchingly wise beyond his years, just seemingly so grateful for being at this school: 'I just wish there was a St George's secondary school for us to go to.'

St Helen's School

Eastbury Road, Northwood HA6 3AS

Ages 3–18 **Pupils** 1,162 **Sixth form** 146

Fees: £13,841 – £17,448 pa

01923 843210
www.sthelens.london

Headmistress: Since 2011, Dr Mary Short BA PGCE PhD (50s) – did her PhD, in the politics of budget-setting in the 1920s, at Cambridge. Has taught undergraduates at Cambridge and pupils at independent schools including St Paul's Girls, City of London School and Haberdashers' Aske's Girls (deputy head). At St Helen's, she has upped the academic performance, partly by making the school more selective, but also by curriculum reviews, consistency of aims, better monitoring of performance, peer review of teachers, that sort of thing. But a league table obsessive she is not and parents say she's made her changes through evolution, not revolution. 'I think my main

S

contribution so far is making sure St Helen's understands what it is,' she says. 'In the past, the school knew what it wasn't, but wasn't sure what it did stand for. I'd say we're now firmly on the map as having academic ambition, but with very strong co-curricular.'

Our first impressions were of someone overprotective of her school and her girls; she later showed herself to be cordial, unpretentious and an impressive strategist. Parents describe her as 'businesslike.' 'She always makes time for you and is good at keeping parents informed, including through her blog which isn't some Ra Ra Ra newsletter, but a "here's what we're doing well and here's what we are trying to improve",' said one. But although she told us she has a very visible presence throughout the school, some juniors told us 'we don't see her very often.'

She has teaching in her blood and is married to a fellow teacher, with whom she lives in north London. Apart from history, likes walking, gardening and travel.

Retiring in July 2019.

Academic matters: Not the top of the highly competitive north London academic tree, but no slouch. No visitor to the school is likely to leave without hearing the word 'ambitious' repeatedly. 'They want you to aim high, but there's not masses of pressure,' one girl told us. Think carrots not sticks, stretch not push, although gets crisper as they get older of course. 'We want independent thinkers and I always say it's the quality of the questions you ask in class that matter more than anything,' says head, although one parent told us 'you get the impression that it's the compliant, hard-working girls they really want.'

In 2018, 52 per cent A*/A at A level; 79 per cent 9-7 at GCSE. Most girls take nine or 10 GCSEs, including a language, at least one humanity and a practical subject such as drama or DT. Reasonably even spread of success across subjects at GCSE, including maths and sciences. In sixth form, most take three A levels plus either an AS or EPQ. Popular subjects at this level are the sciences, maths, economics and history, with maths results particularly strong. Physics as ever with girls the slightly weaker relation, but school working hard on this and take-up is growing – the Heath Robinson Club is popular and interest in engineering is strong. Students are able to complement their A level programme with the St Helen's Portfolio, which comprises additional qualifications such as the European Computer Driving Licence; continue with languages they have studied to GCSE or acquire additional languages or study further mathematics; also recognises CCF, D of E, other clubs and societies. Girls rave about the Wednesday lecture series and university preparation courses.

French from year 1; then in year 7, girls choose two out of four languages – French, German, Spanish and Mandarin, as well as learning Latin; at GCSE, Italian and Japanese are additional options. No setting in prep, except two 'broad bands in maths from year 4.' In seniors, setting from year 7 in maths and at GCSE stage for sciences. But more 'differentiation in learning needs' and 'child initiated learning' than previously, says school. Lots of male teachers, lots of teachers who have had other professional lives before or even during teaching and a growing number of teachers who teach across both juniors and seniors, although fewer subject specialists teaching in prep than we expected. 'I encourage the teachers to use their own personal styles so the girls respond to their different personalities,' says head; inevitably pupils like some more than others. Parents praise the 'inspired teaching' in prep – plenty of competitions, incentives and outdoor learning. Homework starts in nursery with practising a sound a week, building up incrementally to around 40 minutes a day by year 6 and 60 minutes plus for seniors.

S

Thoroughly sympathetic to SEN, from the headmistress down. All pupils are screened annually from year 3 to year 11 to help spot any potential educational difficulties. Individual needs department with three staff provides support to pupils from age 7 both inside and outside the classroom. School can and does support autistic spectrum difficulties, mild dyslexia and dyspraxia, mild speech difficulties and children with hearing impairments. Support, but not separate teaching, for those who have English as an additional language. Some 350+ children currently identified as gifted and talented and supported with 'differentiated work schemes and activities.' 'I've got nothing but praise for SEN provision; we haven't had to push the school at any point,' one parent told us.

Games, options, the arts: Don't be fooled by St Helen's sedate hedges, modest perimeter walls and close proximity to Northwood town centre. So vast are playing fields, floodlit courts and pitches extending in all directions that you soon realise that most of this end of Northwood is St Helen's. Superb sports complex, including large indoor pool; new all-weather pitch. Lacrosse, netball, football, tennis, athletics, badminton, rounders, rugby and cricket all popular and many other games and activities available including pilates, aerobics, climbing and trampolining. County level for lacrosse, badminton and netball and national representation by individuals at swimming, gym, cycling, tennis and rugby. Supports those who excel (and need time off for national teams), but some parents feel girls at the less sporty end miss out: 'It's not sport for all here, with an elitist attitude to teams, and my daughter has no interest in fitness or sports now as a result.' All do ballet, PE, music and speech and drama as part of the prep school curriculum.

Art, DT and drama housed in the June Leader building, named after school's outstanding, and aptly named, head of 20 years (1966-1986). Art, having gone through a bit of a wobble, is now on the up with girls knuckling down to theory and individual skills when we visited. 'Art has a more academic feel now – no longer just a place to hang out,' says head. DT bubbling and well taught if not as jazzily equipped as some (though there is CAD and two 3D printers). Dance and drama (some joint with Merchant Taylors') much enjoyed, especially in the context of the annual House Arts festival – and again, there's popular take-up academically, with drama run as both a GCSE and A level. Plenty of performances, with recent examples including the prep school production of Matilda ('which made me weep,' says head), a musical written by the English teacher and performed by the middle school, and Kiss Me Kate! by the upper school. The Centre (multi-purpose space converted from old gym) also used for the performing arts and sport.

'Music has been great for years, but still gets even better year on year,' a parent told us, with numerous orchestras, choirs (the main one tours annually) and bands, again with much teaming up with Merchant Taylor's. 'Our jazz band played at their summer jazz night – it was wonderful,' says head. Around 250 girls do individual music lessons with peripatetic teachers. Plenty of varied opportunities for performing in school – new music centre – and the wider community, including regular concerts at St John's, Smith Square, London.

Collaboration with Merchant Taylors' also in CCF. D of E and Young Enterprise popular too. Visits from profs, writers and theatre companies. Co-curricular is bursting from every nook and cranny of the school, much of it student-led ('I've started up a foreign fiction book club for students and staff,' one girl told us), with hundreds of things for pupils to try and, when they latch on to one, the school will find ways of allowing it to be taken further. Particular successes in debating, maths and physics Olympiads, technology competitions. Lots of trips – Galapagos, Venice, Lake Tahoe, Ypres, Berlin, British Museum, galleries.

Background and atmosphere: Founded at the end of the 19th century with a vision of education for the whole child, which it still holds dear. A spacious school, trim and imaginative grounds. Dark green uniform up to 16; freedom in the sixth (including jeans). Plenty of recently completed developments eg Little Gables playground for pre-prep; junior school building with solar panels and green roof bringing all of key stage 2 into an exceptionally colourful, spacious and imaginative space; new reception with glass corridor; new computer science labs; swish new dining room with fabulous food. Longworthe, one of the former boarding houses, is now used for before and after-school care in which pupils with busy parents can spend a long day – breakfast and tea included and quiet places for prep and recreation. 'The school provides very long hours of childcare for those who want it – you see girls as young as 3 left from early in the morning until quite late in the afternoon,' said one parent. Nicely decorated new sixth form block (much studiousness observed). Hard to think of any facilities the pupils could want for.

A culturally diverse school, with strong Indian, Tamil and Jewish (a strong JSoc and well-established links with the local synagogue) contingents, and reassuring lack of cliques. Notable absence of the unhealthily thin.

We were repeatedly assured the prep is an integral part of the whole and although they share many of the facilities of the senior school (sports, dining room, music), several girls and parents told us 'they feel like three very separate schools – it's a shame there aren't more links.' The nursery, Little Gables, and key stage 1, Gables, are in converted houses on site, each with own playground, while key stage 2s are in the stunning new purpose-built building, already noted. Happy atmosphere, bright uniform, civilised loos and teachers who call their charges 'ladies' while managing not to make the girls too precious. It is natural for girls here to stay the course – now from 3 to 18 – and continue to feel that it's all in the family. Oodles of gushing about it all from the girls. 'I would lay down my life for St Helens,' said one girl, who didn't appear to be joking.

Pastoral care, well-being and discipline: 'Even by the first parents' evening, I felt they 100 per cent knew my daughter – right down to the things that make her tick or anxious,' one parent told us. Indeed, pastoral care here starts with individual teachers, who are expected to notice and to care how the girls are, and to react supportively and promptly to any sign of trouble. As a result, while teachers talk of all the usual friendship problems, the girls shrug them off and prefects do not see dealing with social ills as a significant part of their remit. Relationships within houses, year groups and tutor groups all seem close, giving girls a variety of communities to turn to. Healthy awareness of issues such as self-harm and eating disorders and a part-time counsellor and clinical psychologist visit each week. 'My daughter gets very stressed about exams and they've been spot on in dealing with it – the pastoral lead at the school goes well beyond the call of duty,' said one parent.

Staff/student relationships palpably amiable. 'If I bumped into a teacher here and now, I'd probably wind up chatting to them for about five minutes – they're all so lovely,' said one sixth former. 'There are no doors closed here,' insisted another.

High expectations and clear boundaries, but it doesn't feel overly strict. 'These girls are conservative and from aspirational families in strong communities – we have very few behavioural problems,' says head. Warnings for forgetting PE kit, handing in homework late etc, but most girls go through their entire school life without a detention. Inner London problems kept at bay. Certainly no drugs incidents, or indeed temporary exclusions, in living memory. The occasional foolish misdemeanour is dealt with individually but 'sanely. It's never public, it's not about humiliation – ever.' You're allowed to slip here.

Pupils and parents: Northwood is affluent, with lots of large detached houses. But girls come from much wider area – good coach service covers Beaconsfield, Elstree, Barnet, Amersham, Ealing, Hemel Hempstead and points between. Others get the train and some – thanks to better car parking – are dropped off. The circle on the map gets smaller for juniors, though, and smaller still for nursery 'where girls are very local.'

Resilient, personable and chatty girls. But while other heads encourage us to talk to their pupils without staff within earshot, visitor protocol here meant that junior girls came with an entourage of sixth formers and teaching staff (which inevitably meant no girl said she'd 'change a single thing'); the rules are the same for parents coming for individual visits during the school day, so visit on a working open morning if you want the low-down from the girls themselves.

Parents sociable, with thriving PTA. Old girls' network huge and devoted. St Helen's inspires great loyalty. Alumnae include Patricia Hodge, a great supporter, Vanessa Lawrence (United Nations), Lady Lowry, Luisa Baldini, Penny Marshall, Paula Nickolds (CEO John Lewis) and Maria Djurkovic.

Entrance: First point of entry is at 3 or 4 by observation and interview. At 7 by tests in English and maths and interview. School part of London 11+ Consortium which shares tests at 11- now a single cognitive ability test, plus interview; around 460 apply (around half each from state and independent sector) for approximately 100 places (sometimes more places are available due to bulge years) – not too terrifying as lots apply elsewhere too but school is increasingly candidates' first choice. Junior school girls have to sit the exam too, and up to 10 or so don't make the transition, either because they because they aren't academic enough ('in which case, we'd have conversations well before year 6,' says head) or they choose a competitor school. Just under half of the senior school places are filled by junior school girls. Occasional places available throughout the school. Interview and reference from current school as important as scores.

'Aim is to explore potential and to ensure that girls will be able to take full advantage of the curriculum and wider opportunities the school has to offer,' says the school. As ever true but never spelt out, parents should remember that they are on show too.

Between five and 10 join at sixth form. You need 7+ GCSEs at 6+ including good grades in the subjects relevant to the A level choices – 7s in sciences and maths; sometimes lower in humanities.

Exit: Much praise for the smooth transition from nursery to the juniors and from juniors to seniors. Around 15-20 per cent leave post-GCSE, most to co-ed or local state schools. All sixth formers to higher education. Three-quarters to Russell Group universities (London, Bath, Leeds, Warwick, Birmingham are popular). About a third science-related: strong bias to medical, biological and engineering courses, with a high proportion of dentistry and medical offers. Handful to Oxbridge annually (four in 2018); some parents feel the head makes too much of this ('It's always being mentioned'). Futures department, just off the sixth form study area, considered by the girls to be top notch.

Money matters: Currently supporting around 60 girls on means-tested bursaries (around 20 of those are on 100 per cent bursaries). These bursaries awarded annually either to girls whose parents could not otherwise meet fees or to girls whose families are experiencing temporary difficulties. Range of scholarships also available.

Remarks: By no means soaring the top of the league tables, but plenty of ambition for its pupils, academically and otherwise, with a strong underlying ethos of opportunity, progression and support. Girls are so devoted to, and sentimental about, the school that you wonder if they're all sent on a PR course upon joining. All in all, an inspired educational offering with superb and spacious facilities and where there's pace but without the relentless pressure of some of its key competitors.

St James Preparatory School

Linked with St James Senior Girls' School, St James Senior Boys' School

Earsby Street, London W14 8SH

Ages 4–11 **Pupils** 246

Fees: £16,425 – £17,910 pa

020 7348 1793
www.stjamesprep.org.uk

Headmistress: Since 2009, Catherine Thomlinson, BA in English and history from Roehampton. A St James' disciple to her fingers' ends, having spent almost all of her teaching career here after being educated at sister school, St Vedast (brief spell in South Africa before coming back to the fold). Two children, boy and girl, both of whom attended St James, including the senior schools.

A thoroughly lovely woman who radiates kindness, humanity and good humour, she is not above regularly serving up the veg at lunch ('a lovely thing to do because I don't have to think') and covering lessons when needed. When parents told us prior to our visit, 'She's adorable, I would take her everywhere with me,' 'She is divine and constantly pushing boundaries' and 'I literally love her', we wondered if gushing about the head is part of the T&Cs of having a child at the school – but actually, you have to meet her to realise she's one of a kind. When our confusion about her deskless and computer-less office became obvious, she explained, 'I think desks can create a barrier' so it's tastefully decorated with plush sofas and an oval dining table instead, making it among the most communal and friendly we've seen.

Despite her lifelong loyalty to the St James traditions, Mrs Thomlinson isn't afraid to modernise, most recently rebranding the school as a prep, including an all-new nursery. 'We wanted every door to be opened for pupils when they leave, whatever path they take.'

S

Entrance: Now from age 2, thanks to new nursery. From age 4, there's no assessment as such, but a meeting with parents while children get a taster of reception, plus a report from child's nursery where applicable. School looks for 'children and families who value what we value.' Children of alumni and siblings have priority. Places higher up the school often available, and children who apply aged 7+ take assessments in reading, writing and mathematics to ensure they can keep up.

Exit: Fewer than in the past move onto St James Senior Girls (located on the same site, with some shared facilities) and St James Senior Boys (now out in Ashford – comprehensive coach service provided by St James Schools), but it's still the majority, fluctuating between 60-70 per cent. Other school destinations include Merchant Taylors', Latymer Upper, Ibstock Place, Emanuel, St Mary's Ascot, Queen's Gate, Aldenham and Hampton. Since becoming a standalone prep (as opposed to the junior school of the girls' and boys' senior schools), there is greater emphasis on 11+ and recommendations for secondary schools.

Remarks: 'Isn't that the hippie school where they learn Sanskrit and only eat vegetarian food?' If St James parents had a pound for every time they heard that, they'd probably get a hefty chunk off their school fees. At least the public perception gets two out of three for accuracy – 'it's the hippie bit that's wrong,' insist most parents, although one did say, 'It all comes down to your definition of hippiedom, I suppose – there's certainly a lot that's unconventional and spiritual about this school.' Every lesson begins and ends with a 'moment of stillness' to 'give you that sense of ease and reflection', for example, and the school teaches a Socratic method of dialogue and questioning, with the children taught to develop open-ended questions and to debate as a class ('No putting-down of others' opinions is allowed,' says head firmly). Even the school's origins are alternative – it was founded by the School of Economic Science, seen by some as a cult, although the school has no associations with the organisation now.

The result is an unusual and admirable little school that's pervaded by an air of gentle wisdom and where their ethos of generosity, mutual respect and 'being the best human beings we can be' isn't just a case of paying lip-service to try to get the punters in – it permeates everything. While other schools introduced mindfulness as an add-on in recent years, St James practically invented the concept. Parents love the school and children love it more.

The school nestles quietly within residential streets, the outside resembling a monastery, with its high walls and expanse of sheer red brick, but the tableau through the security gate isn't in the least forbidding. Children play cheerfully in a pretty, cloistered courtyard (they also have a larger playground, complete with edible garden), while the preponderance of surrounding glass gives a modern, clean balance to the Victorian charm of the original building. 'The peacefulness and calmness of the school are tangible,' parents told us in advance of our visit, so we were surprised to arrive to loud screams (of delight) from a reception gym class. But that's the thing about St James – the overall atmosphere of serenity is not at the expense of vibrancy and good old-fashioned childish excitement. And it is this combo that wins most parents over as soon as they step foot inside. 'We looked at every school in this part of London but as soon as I did the tour here I knew it was right, there's something about the energy,' summed up one.

The 'pause', as it's known, at the start and end of lessons, 'gives you a chance to be still and turn any stress you might have into a little ball you can literally throw away,' according to one year 6 child, whose demeanour was composed beyond her years, while a younger one said, 'it calms me down after break or a more lively lesson if I'm still pumped up.' When thinking about secondary schools, one parent told us, children can find other schools totally chaotic initially, while another said that it can sometimes feel that other children are far more streetwise, 'like they're in the fast-lane while mine live in the moment – I like that, but that's not for all families.'

All the children, even the little ones, learn Sanskrit, in accordance with the school's belief that the Eastern philosophies have much to teach us – children love it because 'it feels special that only we learn it' and parents because 'it's a beautiful language, they even get to sing it.' St James describes itself as 'multi-religious', and philosophy itself is a very important part of the curriculum.

Academic performance is stronger than ever since becoming a prep, with verbal and non-verbal reasoning a focus from year 3 and interventions in English and maths from year 4, then setting in English and maths in years 5 and 6. Standards are high

– all the more impressive, given that the school's intake is not academically selective. But it's the way it's taught that stands out, say parents – 'unlike a lot of preps round here that cram children with facts, they get children thinking independently,' said one. 'The curriculum is structured in such a way that it ensures the children are nurturing both sides of their brain all the time,' said another. Teachers, who do increasing amounts of tracking and monitoring of each pupil, embody what the school professes to be, with a recent influx of younger teachers, 'which has given a breath of fresh air to the school,' according to one parent. St James's policy of teaching boys and girls separately, then bringing them together for social activities, gets mixed views from parents and children, but newbies are in luck – the school is now trialling co-ed teaching in every subject for the 2018 reception cohort (so far, so good) and the houses are also now mixed.

SEN provision is good. 'One of my children is dyslexic and they flagged it up as early as in year 2 and supported her all the way through,' said one parent, although a few mentioned that 'until recently, there was a feeling of parents having to forge their way with SEN – I'm glad it's moved on.' Thirty-three EAL children when we visited, but most are fluent so don't need support. We applaud the emphasis on using Shakespeare as a teaching resource at all levels, more so than in any other school we've visited, complete with annual Shakespeare festival. 'I couldn't believe it the other day when my son, who's in reception, was quoting Shakespeare's Winter Poem word for word at breakfast,' said one parent.

All children are involved in at least one performance (though no whole-school ones here) and a poetry recital every year. Music is everywhere, with 80 children taking instrumental lessons and there are regular concerts, often featuring the school's orchestra, as well as weekly music lessons and daily singing in assembly – repertoire by Mozart, Purcell and Vivaldi is popular. Year 6 girls belted out a carol in Latin for us so beautifully it made the hairs on our neck stand on end. The attractive art room is jam-packed with astonishingly good work – everything from silk screen to kiln work to print making. Big on fine arts, cross-curricular (some lovely year 2 Roman ceramics on show and a gasp-worthy model of WW1 trenches from year 6s) and turning their 2D work into a 3D equivalent.

Games or sport for all on most days be it gym, swimming or handball (they do particularly well at this), and the upper juniors (years 3-6) go off-site once a week to Barn Elms to hone their skills at netball, rugby, cricket, athletics, cross-country and the like. Lots of inter-school competitions – two boys we met were rushing off to a big rugby match. Swimming is held in nearby Fulham Pools – some success at national level among the pupils.

There's forest school and oodles of trips to Minstead Study Centre in the New Forest, plus a varied programme of outings closer to home, the usual London fare. Excellent range of clubs includes yoga, robotics and coding, chess, karate, young engineers, cookery, model-making, archery and fencing. Wraparound care now includes drop-off from 7.45am (free), ready for registration at 8.15am, and until 6pm (for an extra fee) after school. Use of ICT has increased, although actual ICT lessons are still for year 5 and 6 only; some parents would like it to be sooner.

Pastorally as good as it gets. 'Kindness is underrated,' believes head. 'Children need to feel special and loved. These are difficult words in a school but if children feel their teachers have totally got their back, the sky's the limit.'

Food here is vegetarian, so that all the children can eat together, and is included in the fees. 'I love everything,' more than one child told us, gobbling happily. We certainly went back for seconds and were not surprised to hear Jamie Oliver once held up the school as a shining star when it comes to school dinners.

This school impressed us as such a kind and enlightened medium in which to culture young minds, that we occasionally had to remind ourselves that this was a school we'd stepped into and not a Botticelli painting. It was almost a relief to hear one boy admit to talking too much in class and meet a teacher who was clearly knackered from her morning's work. But these tiny wrinkles only served to throw into greater focus the sweetness and calm of this remarkable community. Not a school for budding Piers Morgans, we suspect. But who cares?

St James Senior Girls' School

Linked with St James Senior Boys' School, St James Preparatory School

Earsby Street, London W14 8SH

Ages 11–18 **Pupils** 267 **Sixth form** 55

Fees: £20,100 pa

020 7348 1777
www.stjamesschools.co.uk/seniorgirls

Headmistress: Since 2014, Sarah Labram BA (40s). A classicist with a degree from King's College London, she is totally imbued with the St James ethos: a former pupil and head girl, whose two daughters were both educated at the junior and senior schools. She joined St James in 1996 as a classics teacher and has risen through the ranks to become head of department and then deputy head.

Hands-on, with a winning combo of directness, warmth and enviable serenity, she is often out and about around the school and clearly knows her pupils well, chatting easily with them in the corridors. Has an open-door policy, with pupils popping in to say anything from 'It's my birthday, would you like a piece of cake?' to 'Can you sign our permission slip to stay in at lunchtime to practice dance as nobody else is around?' 'She's definitely not a head that you only see for bad or serious stuff,' said one pupil. But, they add, she commands respect. 'I was late for assembly the other day, and I won't be doing it again,' said one. Parents praise her responsiveness, kindness and efforts to involve them by inviting them to give talks (a dad had come into talk about climbing Everest when we visited), try out the school food, hear updates about the school and present their own views. That said, her introduction of the three new roles of head of lower, middle and upper school means any parental concerns are usually dealt with lower down the food chain.

S

Teaches Greek to year 9s. 'Teaching is what I love and classics is my passion – I'm not giving that up!' she says. It also means she understands what's expected of other teachers, she says, while the 'inevitable informal chats in the classroom give me an insider's view of pupil needs too.' Lives in south east London and hobbies include theatre, classical music and walking.

Academic matters: Girls take the IGCSE in the three sciences for greater rigour. At GCSE, 69 per cent A*-A/9-7 grades in 2018. Stunning success in art, biology, classics and physics, and at least respectable everywhere else. At A level the subject options include drama and theatre, Spanish, psychology and history of art. In 2018, 81 per cent of A level entries were graded A*-B (55 per cent A*/A). Results creditable in most subjects – few grades below B – and art, economics, French, and physics particularly impressive. EPQ popular.

As with the boys' school, philosophy and spirituality are a major part of school life. Yes, girls are expected to work hard (we saw heads down in every classroom we visited) but every lesson is underpinned by the kind of big questions and ideas that form the cornerstone of all western and eastern wisdom traditions – but without being tied to the dogma of one. The result? Girls are encouraged to get the magic, awe and wonder of each subject – the wow-factor in addition to good, solid teaching. Plus, we found the girls could link pretty much everything – be it Latin, English or those knotty teenage issues like body image and social media – to guiding philosophical principles. There's also a big push on mindfulness, meditation and quiet time (five minutes at the start of the day and after lunch). 'I love the way they create space for inner reflection and how the school is so confident and unapologetic that this is their offering,' said one parent. 'If you don't buy into meditation or mindfulness, it probably isn't the school for you,' said another.

Sanskrit is continued for those who join from the prep school (introductory course offered to those joining in year 7) and available as an option at GCSE and A level. At least one a year chooses to study it at university. 'It's great for grammar,' says the head, 'as well as for the philosophy and culture that surrounds it. Plus, it marks you out as interesting and it's well respected.' In addition to Sanskrit, French and Latin from year 7; and Spanish (for those who don't carry on Sanskrit) and classical Greek (for the most able linguists) from year 8. Setting in English and maths from year 7; Latin and French from year 8; and science from year 9. Lots of homework, monitoring and targeting, with girls all initially tested in year 7, from which they are ranked (although they're not told where they sit).

SEN mainly at the milder end. Support mainly classroom based, with some one-to-ones and small group work taking place outside the classroom. 'Dyslexic girls often find Latin particularly hard, so we'll do small group work on study skills instead for year 8s, for example,' says head. 'The scaffolding they've put around my daughter has been amazing – it feels like they really care about getting her the best outcome,' said one parent. Strong gifted and talented provision. ICT not embedded as much as in some schools, though there's a decent ICT suite.

Heavy on careers advice, with girls given opportunities for 'tastes of reality' all the way through – much of which is embedded into lessons – with advice at every stage, which become increasingly intensive from year 9 up.

Games, options, the arts: This is a compact inner city school, so anything involving running takes place at the Chiswick playing grounds or Barn Elms multi-sports facility, both a coach ride away. On site, they cram in netball, aerobics, gymnastics, health-related fitness and dance etc and off site lacrosse, netball, athletics, rounders and tennis are the main sports. Does well in regionals and nationals for lacrosse (two Wales and one Scotland under-19 for lacrosse when we visited), along with some successes in cross country and netball. 'There's a drive to improve variety,' says the head, pointing to the recent introduction of football, table tennis, karate, cross country running and gymnastics – although this is mostly after school, to the disappointment of some pupils we spoke to. 'I wish there were more sports and more space,' more than one told us, and it was disappointing to find that some had reached sixth form having not been enthused by any sport. 'Sport is the one downside here,' some parents agreed. They have their own adventure club – the St James Challengers – and D of E. No swimming.

Artwork is exceptional – much of it professionally framed throughout the school. Visiting instructors add to the core curriculum. Now offers 3D design technology. Singing is huge – every Wednesday and Thursday, the pupils get together to sing and we lost count of how many times the summer concert was mentioned. Orchestras, choirs, ensembles galore – for which practice is before school or at lunchtime – and 75 were taking individual music lessons from peripatetic teachers when we visited. Drama popular and lively, with a new drama studio providing a great dedicated space that can be fully blackened out. School takes part in the Shakespeare Schools Festival. Years 7-9 and 10-13 alternate in doing a play or musical every year (the older ones teaming up with the boys' school – with other joint events including the summer concert, leadership days and dinner and dances for the sixth-formers.)

Small, but much used, cookery room, with year 7s taught the wider role of food in societies and how it can nurture relationships (eg they cook lunch for elderly folk from local old people's homes).

All the usual day trips you'd expect in the heart of London – theatre, ballet, museums, London Zoo, Bletchley Park etc – plus plenty of residentials, to the likes of Isle of Wight, Devon and further afield to the battlefields and Greece. Community service trips to places like Calcutta and South Africa, where the girls get involved in housing street children. Occasional overseas trips for choirs and sports teams etc.

A varied extracurricular offering – everything from politics club to computer science and Italian to arts. Minerva Society popular – after-school talks, including the likes of politician Natalie Bennett. 'I've been blown away not only by the quality of people these girls get – and it's they who organise the speakers – but by the quality of the questioning from the girls,' said one parent.

Background and atmosphere: Founded, along with its sibling junior school and senior boys' school, in 1975 by the School of Economic Science (SES) (see our online review of the senior boys' school for background and history), at which time the school was based in Queen's Gate, later moving to Notting Hill Gate and then, in 2001, to its current location in a leafy residential West London street. Located down a quiet road, within sight of Olympia, the main gate leads into an attractive courtyard, which forms the centre of the whole school, in which the junior and senior schools co-exist happily.

It would be unfair to say this three-storey school is bursting at the seams, but there isn't a great deal of elbow room, with compact (but very light and airy) classrooms – which probably look smaller than they are due to the clunky, traditional wooden desks, all facing forward for chalk-and-talk type teaching during our visit, although we were assured there's plenty of interactive teaching too. Recent improvements include a new sixth form centre, library and a fourth science lab. Good-sized and well-equipped music room. Big and airy school hall, plus gym and a refectory, all sitting on top of one another. Overall, the buildings are well cared for – lots of white-painted corridors, blue carpets, good wall displays and useful noticeboards. Outside space is limited, though care has been taken to provide little trellised alcoves for quiet chat around the tarmac playground, complete with climbing wall, and there's also the courtyard.

The food is vegetarian and the tables are laid invitingly – hot home-cooked food plus fresh fruit, salad, bread and cheese. Girls love it or hate it (older ones are more enthused). We loved it.

Girls seem down-to-earth, happy and supportive of one another, many draping their arms around each other as they walk from classroom to classroom. 'I can't think of a girl here that you wouldn't describe as nice,' one pupil told us. Plenty of room for difference, with no feeling that there's a St James 'type'. 'My daughter was terribly shy, but now speaks publicly, is head of house and organises outside speakers for the school. I'd never have thought it possible. She has blossomed as an individual, thanks to this school,' one parent told us. Girls aren't overly sophisticated, but not too sheltered either. Academically, hard-working, conscientious and reflective. The sixth form have privileges – no uniform, going out at lunchtimes etc.

Pastoral care, well-being and discipline: Highly praised, with the form teacher – who moves up the school with the class where possible – at the heart of pastoral care. And if you can't talk to your teacher (which all girls told us they could), then there are plenty of buddies and mentors. All the spiritual and philosophical emphasis mentioned earlier also helps guard against the usual teenage problems. No school counsellor, but there is a trained well-being coach. Bullying rare. 'Girls are sometimes unkind, but it's usually down to thoughtlessness and we deal with that quickly when we need to,' says the head. Pupils concur. Plenty of assemblies on everything from LGBT to mental health. House system taken seriously – with girls all wearing their house T shirts on Fridays and alternating in eating in the staff dining room.

Misbehaviour, when it happens, is low-level – chatting in lessons, failing to hand in homework on time, untidy uniform etc is about as bad as it gets, for which you get 'a slip'. Three slips in one half term lead to a detention and three of those leads to an extended detention, which basically means community service and reflection. 'At that point, you'd want to be looking at the root cause,' explains the head. We met several sixth formers who'd never had a single detention. Only one temporary exclusion, and no permanent ones, under current headship. No school council when we visited (suggestions box instead), but it was about to be implemented.

Who wouldn't fit in? Girls who don't appreciate quiet time. 'There's lots of wriggling and squiggling at first – that's normal, but then they get so used to it that it becomes completely normal, then by year 12 and 13 they are such advocates,' says the head. We found she was spot on. 'I'm so passionate about the value of meditation,' said one sixth former. Also not a school for the highly competitive. 'You don't measure yourself against other people here,' one pupil told us.

Pupils and parents: Mixed as befits its west London location. Around half white British; a fifth from Asian backgrounds (many of whom are attracted by the influence of the eastern philosophies); and the rest a huge mix including Chinese, black Caribbean and Eastern European. English as a second language a non-issue as even they speak English well. A tiny minority of the staff are members of SES, some are ex-pupils, but the vast majority of pupils are now from families who have no direct connection whatsoever. When we mentioned SES to the pupils we met, they shrugged their shoulders. 'We know it was relevant to the founding of the school, but it's just not part of our school life now,' said one. Some pupils travel significant distances, mainly from the west, with some taking at least an hour on public transport, though most pupils are more local. A growing contingent from the north west pocket of London eg Willesden and Hampstead. Parents range from the relatively wealthy to those who save every penny to send their daughter here. Lots of dual income families. Quite a few old girls' children come here. Lively PA, called The Friends, with all the usual quiz nights and stalls at sports day etc. One parent was disappointed by the lack of class reps. Former pupils include actors Emily Watson and Sasha Behar and novelist Laura Wilson.

Entrance: St James Junior girls move seamlessly through – NB now at year 7 rather than year 6. The rest come from preps and state primaries – around half from each. Main prep feeders are Pembridge Hall, Orchard House, Chiswick and Bedford Park, Glendower, Ravenscourt Park Prep, St Nicholas Prep, The Falcons School, Bute House, Garden House, Kew Green Prep, Thomas' Battersea and Thomas' Kensington. Some also from St Mary Abbots, Barnes, Belmont and Fox primary schools. Around 200 apply for around 25 places (the other 25 taken by juniors). School is part of the London 11+ Consortium which sets a cognitive ability test (maths, verbal and non-verbal reasoning) and has a common reference form. 'An imaginative interview experience, which explores skills, aptitutes and intellectual acuity of the candidates.'

There's the odd space available in most higher years. Entry criteria for sixth formers is at least five GCSEs at 9-5 including at least a 7 in the subjects chosen.

Exit: Up to 40 per cent leave after GCSEs – all for good, healthy reasons: some to co-eds, some to schools that offer alternative A levels or courses, often to state schools, occasionally to board or to nearer home. Some gap years. Around 70 per cent to Russell Group universities, with popular destinations including Cardiff, Bristol, Exeter, Durham, York, Queen Mary London, UCL and SOAS – and increasingly, East Anglia. One to Cambridge in 2018. Science or medicine related courses popular (one medic in 2018), the rest choose across a vast range – art (three off to Camberwell College of Arts in 2018) through to zoology and everything in between. Many pursue careers in which they contribute to the community, notably teachers, medics, nurses and working for charities.

Money matters: The school operates a means-tested bursary scheme. All current and future parents may apply. Future parents need to be registered with the school. This is not a rich school so don't look for masses of help.

Remarks: This small school is 'like a family', according to the pupils we met, and we got that impression too. Girls are supportive of one another and this, coupled with the emphasis on spirituality and philosophy, makes it a school that provides so much more than the academic rigour, which is a given. They take the view that it's no good being a straight A* student academically, if morally you are a C student. No wonder the school turns out such generous-spirited, honourable, sharp young women who know not only how to reach their full potential, but who have grown up understanding how to use that potential to the advantage of wider society. A gem for ethically minded families.

St James's Catholic Primary School

260 Stanley Road, Twickenham TW2 5NP

Ages 3–11 **Pupils** 683 **RC**

020 8898 4670
www.st-james.richmond.sch.uk

Headteacher: Since 2016, Louise Yarnell (30s) married to a teacher (not at St James's), with two small daughters (also not at St James's). LY told us, slightly ruefully, that there was no room at the inn due to the school not operating a 'children of teachers' policy. She arrived here from St Norbert's in Lincolnshire, which she had speedily transformed into an Ofsted outstanding school but then had to wait six years for a visit from the awarding powers. Her accent immediately gives away her origins from a part of the UK across the water, but she is now happily ensconced back in her husband's territory on the edge of west London, where she also went to college.

A bit cagey and slightly wary of us at first, she is clearly not only on top of the job but also proud of her school, so much so that she handed us a pre-written review, which was a very kind thought but we do like to write it ourselves. She invariably calls the children 'sweetheart' and some children definitely respond, one not-so-small girl flinging her arms round her as we walked round. There were mixed comments about her visibility around the school, but one parent remarked, 'she's very visible if you're late at the gate', and she came in for praise for her communication skills: 'The talk she gave at the carol service was a wonderful way to end the term'.

Entrance: At 3, 52 places in the nursery, almost 100 per cent moving up to reception. Parents say that they would be 'mad not to' and the remainder of the three form entry is filled from the four local Catholic parishes (priority is given to practising Catholics). The school is heavily oversubscribed and although the local birth rate is falling there are still too many children for the available chairs. The only hope of a spot further up the school is if the removal vans are ordered and parents have to, reluctantly, move their child to another school.

Exit: Parents who want their children to continue being educated in a Catholic environment tend to opt for St Richard Reynolds Catholic High School in Twickenham. Up to a quarter of the children move on to independent senior schools, such as Hampton and Tiffin, but almost always in the same segment of outer London. Apparently, the school tends not to make direct recommendations on the next step with parents mainly doing the research themselves.

Remarks: With a site tucked down a cul-de-sac next to a golf club and opposite a tidy housing estate, an outsider would need to see the school hoarding to be sure they had arrived in the right place. Past the gates and in through the door is a smallish reception space furnished with 'outstanding' Ofsted citations and a plaster Madonna, her mantle toning happily with the emerald sofa cushions beside her. Immediately, you realise that this is a school not shy about proclaiming the importance of its faith and the attendant ethos.

Off the hall is the nursery where small people were stuffing woollen balls – masquerading as buns – into a play oven or experimenting with manoeuvring a motley selection of chickens and black labradors over a grassy hillock on a computer screen. Outside, others were exploring the current topic of the Arctic by enthusiastically shovelling fake snow over miniature walruses and seals but ignoring the polar bear lying on his plastic back.

Past a screen featuring the four parish saints, together with their priests, the main school lies through double doors, surmounted by a plaque announcing that the block was opened by the Princess Royal. A long corridor, classroom doors interspersed with coat pegs and panels filled by pupils' work, provides the main artery and contains the lower years, with a floor above providing a home for the older children. There is an IT room, separate spaces where individual teaching can take place and an inviting library, complete with a librarian and a Narnia cupboard marked Book Shop. No secret world but plenty of books, provided by parents, which children can buy in instalments, but unlike the real world they can't take them home until they're fully paid up.

On the way to the playground outside is the George Tancred Centre for children with moderate autism, staffed by a team of six. It was nearly empty on our visit, proving the head's assertion that 'they are extremely successful at integrating them into the mainstream' to be correct. This was backed up by a parent saying that her son considered a child from the GTC as part of his class, even though she only came to some of the lessons. The teachers and assistants are all qualified and one small boy was certainly proud of his baking skills and made a good stab at pronouncing focaccia.

In contrast to the unremarkable façade, the back of the school is a glorious surprise with acres of grassy pitches and a newish PE building. Excellent use is made of this green paradise or muddy field (depending on the season), with children having at least two hours of games a week plus after-school clubs. They are borough champions in several sports ranging from swimming to tag rugby and even scooped a bronze medal in athletics at the London Youth Games, pretty good for a school where a class teacher is in charge of PE. In tune with their beliefs, there is even a contemplative spot furnished with benches and a gigantic pair of hands in prayer, sculpted by a parent.

Sats are consistently outstanding with French mentioned by all parents as brilliantly taught, partly due to the specialist French teacher who catches them very young. The approach is so successful that one parent told us she was 'blown away' that her 9 year old already spoke better French than her father, who was apparently somewhat put out. In addition, to help the child with a linguistic bent, the school runs after-hours clubs in Latin, Polish and Mandarin. The work ethic is very strong, encouraged not only at school but also by a sizeable chunk of homework every evening and it is definitely a source of pride if your house wins the annual cup with points handed out for homework, manners and attendance as well as academic success.

Music is major here and LY's first appointment, a hugely enthusiastic and friendly music mistress, proudly showed us her shelf of brand new, yellow ukuleles. Parents affirm that she is 'fantastic' and has made music great fun: 'it's more mainstream now'. The weekly music lessons can be topped up by extracurricular music technology clubs, recorder groups and private music lessons and there are several choirs.

As you might expect from a Catholic institution, 'manners maketh man' in this school and the children leaped to hold open doors and answer questions politely. LY says that she cannot remember having a child sent to her for 'making a wrong choice' in her time in charge, and she has never had to face the unpleasant task of calling in a parent over their child's behaviour. We felt that we would also have minded out Ps and Qs when she hove into sight and that her plan to introduce a 'habit of mind passport' for the exceptionally well-behaved might be a bit daunting for some.

The cerebral side is also encouraged by the accreditation of the school as a Thinking School in 2016. This strategy, based on Edward de Bono's Thinking Hats, puts controlled thinking at the core of the curriculum from day one. In practical terms this means more theme-based teaching with a new topic each half of the term, a change that children approve of, saying that it 'makes school more exciting'.

Large numbers of parents lend a hand, although the increase in numbers of working mothers means that there are fewer these days to help the mainly young (about two-thirds of the staff) teachers. There was zero evidence of this change causing a problem and the school gave the impression of running like clockwork, obviously partially due to the capable hands of the head. A larger staff turnover than one might expect but LY explains this by pointing out the cost of local housing, a serious problem for anyone on a state school wage.

The increase in working parents has led the school to organise a Breakfast Club and a Stay and Play scheme, which allow supervision from 7.30am to 5.30pm when necessary. Some of the only negative comments were around school meals: most of the children bring in packed lunches and there was not much enthusiasm for the food, particularly if you were not a meat eater.

The fairly affluent, middle class parents (miniscule percentage on free school meals) muck in by raising money (about £30k annually), used to buy anything from pianos to iPads, or by contributing worldly knowledge to help with assemblies. LY even persuaded one exciting father, who works for Virgin Galactic, to come and give a careers talk on building spaceships to an open-mouthed, goggle-eyed audience. Again as you would expect, charity fundraising is taken seriously with a different charity each week in advent and lent and pupils are in the thick of it.

A successful, orderly school believing firmly in putting children on the right path, not only in terms of academic achievement but also in their knowledge of themselves and their attitude to others, but might not suit those with a rebellious streak.

St Margaret's School (London)

18 Kidderpore Gardens, London NW3 7SR

Ages 4–16 **Pupils** 166 **C of E**

Fees: £12,591 – £14,589 pa

020 7435 2439
www.st-margarets.co.uk

Principal: Since 2008, Mark Webster BSc (early 50s). Educated at Highgate School and University College London (where he read psychology), PGCE at Cambridge. Spent 15 years at the Royal School, Hampstead (first in primary, then IT, psychology and maths, before becoming deputy and acting head). Never planned to become a teacher – 'If you'd asked me early on what job I wanted to do, I'd have said teaching was 999th out of 1000'. A chance encounter changed his mind. 'I was working in publishing, when I met someone who said their job in teaching was fantastic. I'd never met anyone who felt that way about work.' Now equally enthusiastic about his chosen profession, Mr Webster continues to be hands on in his approach and still teaches mathematics.

We were initially struck by Mr Webster's bold shirt of candy coloured stripes, which belies his very calm manner. He is not extrovert by any means (as his shirt may imply), but is calm, thoughtful and extremely warm and friendly. He takes the time to consider our questions, and responds diplomatically and graciously. Parents unanimously agree that he is a 'brilliant head teacher and a real leader.' During our meeting there are a number of students who pop into the head's office for a variety of reasons ranging from charity fundraising questions to other Christmas related issues. Clearly students feel he is very approachable, and whilst he does operate an open door policy like some other heads, unlike other heads, students actually take him up on this.

He says one of the benefits of working in a small school is that 'I have the privilege of knowing every student.' He enjoys the proximity and seeing the children grow up: 'You feel you can make a significant difference.' Unlike, he says, a much larger school, where perhaps you don't have the hands-on input: 'I can sleep well at night as I know I've done my very best.' Fundamental to his approach is the view that education is about instilling a sense of curiosity – 'Qualifications are a passport to the next stage, but if you remain curious you will never be bored'.

He himself retains a passionate interest in art, history and reading. Also plays football for Highgate Old Boys. A tactful, sympathetic enthusiast, Webster is a good fit for this family-like school. Possibly slightly unusual to have a male head teacher in an all girls school, but that doesn't seem to bother the parents. 'He is wonderful, we are so very lucky.' Married to a teacher; they have two young sons.

Academic matters: St Margaret's recently topped the Sunday Times Small Schools league table. When you consider that in 2018, 68 per cent of GCSEs were graded 9-7, it's not surprising, especially as the school is relatively non-selective and the ability range always includes the very able and those with more modest aspirations. One parent told us: 'I was a bit worried as I do have a very academic daughter and I thought she might not reach her full potential, but the luxury of a school this size is that teachers can cater for each individual in a mixed ability class.'

GCSE options include Spanish, French, art ('which is amazing,' one student told us), psychology and drama alongside the compulsory subjects. All girls are required to take the science trilogy (taught in a compact, but efficient lab) and the vast majority go on to do at least one science A level. A modern language is compulsory.

Setting introduced when necessary but, with limited space, teaching is usually differentiated rather than physically separated. Extremely low turnover of staff (the French teacher has been there for 25 years) – 'I've only had to write one reference in eight years', the head told us. This is largely because most departments are very small 'so teachers can actually make the role their own and achieve what they actually came into the profession to achieve.' This consistency can only be a good thing for the well-being and academic progress of the students.

School does cater for pupils with mild SEN, but 'we don't have the depth of resources for learning support that a larger school would have,' says the head. Two SENCo support plus a couple of teachers trained in dyslexia and dyscalculia, but the main support comes from classroom teachers. All abilities equally well catered for – 'We aren't results-driven and we try to exhaust every avenue'.

Games, options, the arts: The head's view is that education is a 'can-do', 'must try' matter, and is inspired by the celebrated art historian Sir Ernst Gombrich's attitude: 'You don't have to like it, but it's important to understand why other people do. We compel them to try lots of things. They may moan, but we make them give it a go'. Drama is taken seriously. Shakespeare is now a biggie here. 'Our drama teacher has a big pedigree in Shakespeare.' From year 7, pupils have a non-Shakespeare year where they are encouraged to devise their own pieces to perform. The head says: 'We want to encourage them to devise their own roles by exploring situations.' Other productions have included Matilda and Wind in the Willows. Music, too, is important with a variety of traditional and less traditional extra-lesson options – anyone who wants to can join the ukulele club: 'It's a very egalitarian and upbeat instrument.' A number of choirs, plus a junior school orchestra. At least half of girls have private instrument lessons at the school. Art immensely popular, with excellent results at GCSE: two studios, one reasonably spacious, the other definitely petite. Dance popular too.

Outside space is relatively restricted, with a largish garden transformed into an Astroturf playground. A local hall is used for gym and the school now has a sports area for netball, tennis and other sports two minutes' walk away. Minibus takes girls to Hampstead Heath for rounders or running, to Hendon Leisure Centre for aerobics, rock climbing and badminton and the Welsh Harp for rowing. Inter-house and inter-school matches from year 4 upwards. In David and Goliath mode, the school is unafraid to compete with much larger north London schools like Channing, despite the fact that 'We often lose'. One parent told us: 'For the super sporty, this school may not be your first choice'

Plenty of extracurricular going on: street dance, choir, theatre, cookery, cheerleading, philosophy, orchestra, chess, tennis and origami. Trips local and international, from walks on Hampstead Heath to Tuscany and Iceland.

An unusual incentive which the head introduced is '125' (a tribute to the school's 125 anniversary), which provides pupils with a list of activities to attempt before they leave the school: 'To complement the academic, performing and sporting curriculum we offer, the girls undertake activities throughout the year as part of the school's Skills Grid. The range includes the practical, the cultural and the altruistic: everything from touch typing, learning a magic trick or "doing something nice for someone who can do nothing in return".'

Background and atmosphere: Founded in 1884 and one of the oldest schools in Hampstead – it moved to its present site in a quiet, suburban Hampstead road in 1943. A large, elegant red-brick house accommodates 155+ girls and the head says, 'The house element has become a pivotal cornerstone of how I think about the school. Everything emanates from it being a house – the relationships, the attitudes etc. We've spent quite a lot of money on knocking down a lot of walls.' We believe he meant that both literally and metaphorically.

Fairly recent building work has completely altered the layout of the ground and lower ground floors to incorporate a new school hall. The idea was also to open up the ground floor as much as possible to give the house a much more open plan feel, thereby creating more light and space. Everything is transparent – even the head's office. The school has also added a pretty roof terrace to encourage reading and quiet study for the upper years.

On entering the building we were treated to the melodic voices of a few girls doing choir practice. We watched for a few minutes entranced. It all added to the warm and cosy atmosphere of the St Margaret's experience (it helped that it was nearly Christmas at the time of our visit). We were struck by how deceptively big the school seems on the inside. Yes, there are areas which are exceedingly tight and narrow, and would definitely not suit any physically impaired student, but the floors upwards seemed endless and the corridors often led into quaint hidden areas. Although classrooms were snug, they were adequate for the number of students in each class (no more than 20). None of the students we met or chatted to seemed particularly fazed about the spatial issue. As one parent said, 'they don't know any better, as some have been here since infants and go all the way through.'

We were charmed by the lovely reading area for the juniors and the loft-style library. It definitely felt as if we had entered a bygone era – not a conventional school by any means (think the Brontës). This, it seems, is what some parents most love about the school. One told us: 'Both the head and the school are very unusual in education and sadly part of a dying breed – not caught up in the madness of it all, but eminently sensible.'

The girls who showed us around were happy, polite and totally unpretentious. We were taken aback by one student who openly admitted she had had 'difficulties' in some areas, but unlike other schools she had been to, everyone at St Margaret's was 'friendly and caring.' (Again, another of the school's many charms is that it didn't select one of its obvious 'stars' to show us around the school and do the whole PR number.)

Senior and junior schools both occupy the same building and have the same head, with different uniforms but little separation between them. Uniforms are smart – red and white in the junior school, black and white in the senior. The uniform was changed a few years back for the seniors as they didn't like it. Girls are listened to here. There are two 'agony aunts' (senior students) available at all times for confidential chats, and a school council. One pupil told us: 'We voted for a tuck shop at the school council and now we have one. We can choose what is sold.' The school has three houses and pupils of all ages work together to raise funds for charities of their own choice and compete at sports.

The small, friendly and homely atmosphere 'allows the girls to achieve whatever they can – but in a safe, non-confrontational environment', said one parent.

Pastoral care, well-being and discipline: Discipline not a significant issue. Though head insists this is not the garden of Eden, disciplinary issues tend to be confined to infringements of uniform – 'We can live with earrings if there's no drink or drugs'. Bullying – 'We get a case every year' – is dealt with promptly. Detentions, it seems, are an alien notion: 'we haven't needed to give one since 2011.' One parent who is a teacher herself working in an inner city school told us: 'I have to laugh sometimes when my daughter comes home and says "OMG! One of the girls threw a pen in class".' Girls generally very well behaved and extremely supportive of one another – 'an extended family', one said.' Another told us: 'My daughter went through a very difficult time one year because of social media. I was alerted to this by her form tutor, who in turn had found out from three of her close friends, who were very concerned. She was closely monitored and supported throughout and got through it.'

Parents, too, tend to be very supportive; they are known to choose the school for its caring environment: 'You get ups and downs with some of the girls, but if you ever get a problem it's dealt with straight away,' said one. Most parents feel one of the school's greatest strengths is its pastoral side, allowing girls to fulfil their potential and know exactly who they are. One parent told us: 'This school allows every girl to flourish. It formed my daughter into the happy, caring girl she is today.' Another told us: 'What struck me about this school when I first looked around, and what still remains true five years later, is that the girls all seem to have that wonderful, quiet confidence. Not that brash sense of entitlement that some wealthy kids can have.'

The school has its own head of pastoral care but also relies on a school counsellor when needed and proactively encourages bonding with a variety of trips. 'The girls mix across the years and are often close to girls in the year above and below,' said a parent.

Pupils and parents: Nice, well-behaved, confident girls from a cosmopolitan range of backgrounds reflecting the school's north London location – a large chunk of second generation French and Italians. A fair number come from within walking distance, then in an arc stretching from Wembley to Islington (school minibus on offer for those who require it). Very much a family school in every sense – 45 per cent of pupils are sisters or relatives of current or ex-pupils. 'A lot of people like the sense of support and nurturing.' The school rarely advertises and most newcomers hear about it by word of mouth and favourable newspaper coverage. The internet has slightly altered the traditional intake, as it is accessible worldwide. One parent told us: 'What I like most about the parents who send their girls to St Margaret's is that they defy the Daily Mail stereotype of bling parents.' Daphne du Maurier was a pupil.

Entrance: 'Loosely selective.' From reception to year 2 assessment involves girls coming in for the morning and working with the class teacher. A handful of places offered from year 3 upwards and potential candidates take a standard set of English and maths assessments. Guaranteed transition from within at 11. 'Once we've made the commitment, unless there are particular special needs we can't support, we stick to it.' Now part of the London 11+ Consortium and external candidates take its cognitive ability test. They do operate a basic sibling policy: 'We're not über selective, but we have rejected siblings if we don't feel the school is right for them.'

Exit: About 75 per cent of junior school girls stay on to the senior school, though a small number move to more selective senior schools such as Henrietta Barnett or South Hampstead High School. There's no intention of opening a sixth form, despite parental requests: 'One of the things about being a small school is that you are aware of the things you can't offer, in terms of space and subjects, which is why we will never have a sixth form.' However by then most parents agree it is time to 'move on.'

Notably successful with applications at 16. Most popular choices at that point are local co-ed sixth forms such as UCS and Highgate, more selective schools such as Henrietta Barnett, and similar atmosphere girls' schools such as Channing. A reasonable number goes to the state sector – Woodhouse College is particularly popular. Good guidance on offer at both 11 and 16 – 'It's really important to make an informed choice. Not every school will suit every girl and they are used to being supported here'. School also works with them on interview practice and personal statements. One parent told us: 'Prior to looking around a few schools, I was advised to by Mr Webster to look out for things which would never have otherwise occurred to me – like to not be swayed by all the high tech stuff.' St Margaret's girls generally get their first-choice sixth form.

Money matters: Not an expensive school by any means, though a number of girls receive bursaries to cover all or part of their school fees: 'A reasonable proportion on some sort of financial help.'

Remarks: A gentle, nurturing school with a strong and secure family atmosphere providing a stimulating, tailor-made education. 'A little gem,' to quote one parent, though possibly not the ideal venue for the child who needs plenty of space to run around or one who requires the challenge of a big stage.

St Mary Magdalene Academy Primary School

Linked with St Mary Magdalene Academy

Liverpool Road, London N7 8PG

Ages 4–11 **Pupils** 210 **C of E**

020 7697 0123
www.smmacademy.org

Headteacher: Since 2016, Ruth Luzmore (30s), has brought enthusiasm, warmth, appreciation and energy to this small primary school. Memories of a very happy primary education led her to teaching. She studied in the evenings at Birkbeck College for a degree in politics, philosophy and history whilst earning a living in the daytime. She has continued working days and studying evenings since, gaining a masters in leadership at the Institute of Education whilst working as deputy head in another Islington primary school and now, as head of St Mary Magdalene Academy (SMMA) Primary, she is working towards a PhD in enquiry-based professional development. She says, 'it is good to have a life outside the job, which otherwise can be all-consuming'.

Her commitment to working hard and the importance of education for social change can be seen – involving teachers with an active senior leadership team, engaging parents through the parent-teacher association, good email and newsletter communications. The school also gives a voice to pupils, who say 'teachers listen to you' and 'you can talk to Ms Luzmore or teachers about any issues'. Teachers 'are open to change and we are evolving policy together'. Many of the TAs have been at SMMA for years – some taught parents of current pupils – and their monitoring in the playground means that 'the care continues from the classroom into the playground and they can be aware of pupils' issues'. 'I like being part of the academy group because it means I run a small, friendly school but can look outwards too, to the senior school.'

Entrance: Priority to children in care, then children who regularly attend one of the three local churches – St Mary Magdalene, St Luke's or St David's – then residents of Islington who attend another church, then siblings (some years as many as half the reception class is made up of siblings), then distance from the school (has been as local as within 0.3 of a mile). Heavily oversubscribed.

Exit: Almost all go on to the secondary school of SMMA, though a few to Dame Alice Owen, Highbury Fields, City of London boys and girls.

Remarks: Having a previous literacy coordinator as head ensures literacy is a backbone of the school: 'they need to leave not only reading but enjoying reading for pleasure'. Phonics taught formally (Sounds Write system) but then a wide range of strategies – topic based, class readers, buddy reading, reading road maps – to lead pupils through age-appropriate books. Writing in evidence on the walls and in neatly marked homework with the emphasis on self-expression. 'Enough homework to please parents but not so much kids spend all the weekend working,' according to one parent.

Maths coordinator makes sure that whilst they cover the national curriculum, maths is included in topics and in practical ways (eg visiting fruit snack bar run by sixth formers, raising money for charity – 'generating money is empowering for the children and helps them to realise money needs to be earned'). No setting in maths – 'we don't want to put limits on anyone's ability'; extra tutoring groups by deputy head extend or support pupils. Booster classes after school which, according to pupils, are 'really fun and help with your learning'. Pupils said, 'there are different levels of work and you can choose your challenge'.

Mandarin or Spanish taught from reception. Child-led, topic based learning leads to 'intellectual conversations around themes, so that the year 6 conflict module started with Middle Ages and battles and moved right on to Trump and Kim Jong Un'. Parents said that 'kids become obsessed with the theme for six or seven weeks; we prepare it during the holidays, discuss it over meal times – they are always thinking about it. It gives them a chance to really get into a subject in depth'. Year 1s were learning about people's jobs – a lovely set of dressing up clothes and equipment for role play. Pupils said, 'teachers are not too strict, they give us chances, listen to us and are fair'.

Good results at KS2, above national average in all subjects. However, it is the ability to discuss and articulate ideas that makes this school shine – pupils are used to developing ideas and backing them up. After Sats in year 6, pupils create an 'exhibition where they present a poster with their opinions and collected thoughts which they explain to visiting parents and teachers – a sort of conference' (PhD students in the making?). Topics have included 'How terrorism affects society', 'How do we work for political honesty' and 'The influence of government on health care around the world'. Mentor teachers work to support these mini presentations.

Music taught by inspirational and dedicated teacher – 'the four-part harmony 'put goosebumps on my skin, it was so impressive'. Peripatetic music teachers for some 10 different instruments. Pupils enthusiastic about the music, acting and dance. And they, plus parents and teachers, all look forward to the annual Shakespeare production involving the whole school acting and dancing the play.

One afternoon PE per week with specialist teachers ('really good,' according to pupils we spoke to). Also specialist are the language teachers and the dance teacher, who comes in for at least a term each year to help prepare for Shakespeare production. Swimming in years 3 and 4. Recent win at the London Schools Football Championship particularly impressive for a one form entry school and a cause of great delight. Girls' football well coached, according to pupils. The fact that there are a good number of male staff ensures regular break-time football practice. Playground spacious – pitch, table tennis, outside learning area, outside toilets etc, but money currently being raised to improve the amenities and make more use of flat roofs outside classrooms. Reception shares really well-equipped Astroturf playground with neighbouring Islington nursery.

School lunches cooked on the premises and eaten from china plates in older years. 'Younger years get to the salad bar so there is less left for us,' bemoaned older pupils, who also said 'you have to eat vegetables, which makes you get used to healthy eating, but we wish older children could get seconds'. 'Bring a parent to lunch' scheme allows parents to see lunch at school and parents say school is receptive to feedback.

Pastoral care a highlight thanks to the full-time school chaplain. American by birth, upbeat, leopard-print wearing and totally involved in the school and the pupils. She runs one of the mid-morning assemblies and helps ensure that Christian knowledge and ethos is embedded in the school. One pupil said, 'We don't just talk about values, we use them too'. They said that 'problems are sorted out straight away and you can talk to teachers about every issue, even things at home'. 'We learn about bullying and are trained as mini-mentors.' There are 'worry boxes' in the classroom for anonymous concerns.

SEN supported by academy SENCo, and several pupils had individual TAs. 'We have helped a few pupils acquire an EHC plan' and there are some 20 on the SEN register for medical or educational needs, though 'if I had a child with additional needs I wouldn't probably send them to SMMA,' said a parent, unsure if there is sufficient extra support. Pupil premium used in part to pay for extra helper in reception: 'We focus on reception because if we invest lower down the pupils have a solid knowledge to carry up the school, so we aren't trying to catch up in year 6'.

The school shares a governing body with the senior school. Parents very involved – invited to help with trips, raising money, running clubs, attending Friday coffee morning, at the welcome BBQ and the inclusive and community spirited Christmas fair. 'We are raising money for the school but we want everything to be as affordable as possible for everyone'.

Our opinion: everyone knows everyone in this small, friendly school with different year groups playing together and parents who are involved. A really solid, well-planned education with plenty of extracurricular clubs and activities. Creates articulate, thinking pupils who have been encouraged to engage in, and have meaningful conversations about, all their learning.

S

St Mary Magdalene Academy

Linked with St Mary Magdalene Academy Primary School

Liverpool Road, London N7 8PG

Ages 11–18 **Pupils** 1,110 **Sixth form** 220 **C of E**

020 7697 0123
www.smmacademy.org

Head: Since 2012, Vicky Linsley (late 40s): she joined the school as deputy head in 2008 and credit must go to her for the transformation of this school to a highly oversubscribed 'extremely well run' school with fantastic results. Vicky Linsley was a scholarship child who went to do history at Nottingham and then to Oxford for a masters degree and her teaching qualification.

Youthful, energetic and pragmatic, pupils call her 'inspiring' and 'really, really nice'. Very present around the school, she is generous with her praise of pupils and her pride in the school. An eloquent speaker, which helps her to build partnerships with businesses (Deloitte, Virgin Trains, local businesses). Teachers find her 'approachable, she always has five minutes for us, even for small matters'. She has nurtured many and entrusted them with responsibilities, maintaining a surprisingly stable staff body – no staffing vacancies when we visited and, unusually for any school, no shortage of maths or science teachers. She is an Ofsted inspector 'an opportunity to learn what works and what doesn't and bringing about change' – and works as a consultant with schools looking to improve.

Academic matters: The school has no qualms about saying that it has 'a clear focus on academic achievement' and it works to develop 'globally-minded citizens who are happy and successful'. For financial reasons it has stopped teaching the IB, but the IB ethos has strongly influenced the curriculum and teaching – encouraging independent and team learning, keeping timetables very full and having the equivalent of creativity, activity and service through the Inspire Programme.

The results have been rising and are impressive for a primarily non-selective school – 27 per cent of GCSE results were 9-7 in 2018, and 80 per cent of pupils got 9-4 in both maths and English. The sciences are especially strong with almost all pupils getting grades 9-6. Also strong emphasis on languages, resulting in 100 per cent top marks in Mandarin, with Spanish and French also successful. Religious studies (unsurprisingly for this church school) get excellent results. At A level, 35 per cent A*/A and 65 per cent A*-B grades in 2018. 'Good results thanks to a really excellent work ethos built up over time in the school' and 'not stressful thanks to three year GCSE programme and the school culture'.

Some streaming in lessons from year 7. The pupils who have got into the school on the language aptitude test are expected to take Mandarin enrichment classes as well as a European language taken by other pupils; those who join the Mandarin Excellence Programme have four hours Mandarin each week. The school has an extra three full-time Mandarin teachers from China, who also teach Chinese culture.

Year 9 pupils start their GCSE curriculum and class size drops to 25: 'having three years gives us time to teach more than just the content of the curriculum' and also allows for more outings in year 10, helping to 'raise aspirations and give a sense of purpose for exams'. 'We aim to give a broad and balanced curriculum so kids really enjoy learning, and they want to learn more because we have more time for content'. Generous selection of subjects, but core subjects given priority. Pupils said that 'teachers have our interests at heart and know what we like' and 'teachers care about you'. And parents raved about the youthful vitality, energy and enthusiasm of teaching staff.

Library used for English lessons and weekly library lessons and for book clubs after school; the school is clearly almost as busy before and after school hours as during. Parents say the school has 'nailed the curriculum and ensures the kids get the results they want'. Certainly, no one dreaming or looking out of windows when we visited.

Sixth form of 120 pupils per year completely selective by GCSE results, and once in, get a very full timetable of lessons, extracurricular activities, exercise and a real commitment to enrichment, with many collaborative projects – encouraging leadership and entrepreneurship. Pupils appreciated 'plenty of choice at A levels, but if you reconsider your subjects, you can change – the timetable seems to work for you to be able to take any subject combination you want'. 'Our teachers are organised and knowledgeable and enthusiastic.' 'They make it applicable to real life and raise ethical questions, not just teaching to get grades,' according to sixth form students. 'They get us involved; lessons are really interactive'. Maximum of 15 pupils per A level class. Not a huge amount of dedicated space for sixth form. Full time graduates supervise study areas, help with essays and 'keep work going generally'. This type of subtle mentoring works to raise expectation and graduates are also available to help with UCAS forms and encourage the idea of going to university. Every student in sixth form taken to visit a university (some now lucky enough to go first class on train with a parent or friend thanks to a partnership with Virgin Rail).

Special needs supported by SENCo with ASD specialism and part-time dyslexia specialist; all pupils screened before joining school. Some 13 pupils in school with EHCPs, and 70 accessing support in or outside school. Those who just need an extra bit of help can have tutoring sessions with maths and English graduates in the main hall. Parents say 'they don't give up on anyone' and that thanks to target tracking they are 'on it like a car bonnet if they slip'.

Games, options, the arts: School is open from 7.30am when children can be found in the chess club, martial arts training, extra lessons, or just coming in for £1 breakfast. The day often ends late, so plenty of time for clubs before, during and after school. Games in huge soundproofed state-of-the-art gym – no whistles or shouting needed to get classes playing team sports (basketball, hockey, dance, trampoline, cricket, badminton) for weekly two hours PE. Astroturf on the roof for football and sport and Finsbury Park for athletics. This is an urban environment and so the playground is not large, however, a mad keen footballer we met said that he gets to play 'all the time' – and has plenty of matches against other schools too. Girls' teams encouraged and included – no sense that anyone is second class here. Recognition for effort or achievement for sportspeople given at weekly assembly.

Arts rooms aplenty – sixth formers have own studio so are able to leave artwork out. Textile, pottery, art and tech GCSEs enhanced by equipment like 3D printers and laser cutters. You don't have to be doing tech GCSE to be involved in Formula E club, building an electric car and then racing it at Goodwood racing track. Proper, spacious cooking facilities for both food tech and popular after-school clubs and enrichment programme. Music a growing part of school life, partly thanks to MiSST (Music in Secondary School Trust), with every new pupil being lent an orchestral instrument and having small group lessons, as well as individual music lessons ('excellent peripatetic teachers,' according to some parents) for those who continue with their instrument. So 300 music lessons timetabled in somehow as well as orchestra, rock band, string groups and then the annual huge musical – 'a semi-professional experience for the kids with lighting, costumes, musicians.' 'My shy child just came out of herself through the school musical production'. For some 20 pupils the highlight of their year is going to a music residential to Radley School.

Inspire programme includes masterclasses (talks by Jeremy Corbyn and Nick Robinson recently, and the Grayson Perry talk was a sellout), workshops (Deloitte Consulting sent their chef to give classes, the RSC brought in a group to work on Hamlet) and City trips – not only to offices but also to British Film Institute and theatre outings (local Almeida theatre generous with free tickets to SMMA). Pupils join competitions and get onto programmes such as STEM courses, Oxford Girls' Maths Conference and Women in Leadership conferences, and to go for visits or internships at City firms they have partnerships with – RBS, Cushman Wakefield, Société Générale, UBS.

Students every year from China, Indonesia, Korea and even Kazakhstan attend school for a term as part of 'global citizenship', which is a founding principle of the academy. Once the students leave, friendship and global citizenship encouraged as pupils become email penpals. 'With the job market changing so fast, we prepare our children to have flexibility, interests, skills and ideas, rather than just careers'.

Background and atmosphere: This is a London Diocese sponsored school and the motto (James 3:13) 'show by a good life that your works are done by gentleness born of wisdom' sets the tone. A sense of kindness and action and learning emanates. RIBA awards for this purpose built school which one parent called a 'Tardis, a building that flows nicely and does not feel cramped'. Built around a closed atrium with all classes looking inwards to the central library and chapel built on stilts over the canteen. Windows onto the corridors, open study areas and flow of the building give a feeling of transparency and openness. Pale wood, excellent acoustic management, curved edges, large windows, glass-topped atrium all help to soften the edges of an otherwise totally urban and closed in school off a fairly main road. Pupils said 'there are no hidden corners or blind spots', 'we are really safe here'. We were struck by the calm and quiet in such a vibrant and active school – there are no bells in between lessons and playtime is managed well with room for activities in the playground without impeding each other.

Early establishment of ground rules about behaviour and study skills ('the SMMA way'). 'They have to learn to self regulate – we have 1,300 pupils and they need to learn about manners and being polite'. Christian ethos with teachers and pupils treating each other with respect (everyone on first name terms). Engaged and open-minded students listened and spoke kindly of each other when we met them. Teachers don't interrupt each other or the pupils. Mealtimes are a pleasantly calm and orderly event with pupils and teachers sharing food, space and conversation. The canteen is in the centre of the school, like a kitchen being the heart of the home, busy and used (from breakfast club to after-school snacks via the feeding of the 1,300 at lunchtime) and spotlessly clean. Pupils called food 'healthy and tasty' but of course raved about Friday chips.

Pastoral care, well-being and discipline: Spiritual, moral, social and cultural education embedded in the school through curriculum lessons as well as assemblies and activities and in form time. Full-time chaplain for guidance and support. 'Reverend April is my son's favourite person in the school because she is such a kind, generous presence, comes to cheer at basketball matches, and may well be the heart of the school in her eyrie in the centrally placed chapel.' A part-time psychotherapist (appointment by self-referral or suggested by staff). Pupils said there was 'no bullying, but if you see something you can go straight to a teacher or report it anonymously on school website anti-bullying page'. Teachers spoke of restorative justice meetings – how would you feel, how would the other person be feeling. The need to be 'kind' is the leading principle.

Tutors work with 'Guardian Groups' of pupils in the same house but across all year groups. 'It means we know older pupils and they tell us how to do things and we say hello to them round school'. It also means the older ones look out for the younger ones. The 'academy guardian' acts as first port of call for any issues as the group meets each day. The system seems to create a 'close and small community and allows us to get to know them really well and they trust us,' say the guardians. Pupils also said they liked having the same pastoral group throughout their school life because it 'is like my family away from home'.

The deputy head for expectations and standards, meets heads of year, the SENCo and chaplain every fortnight to ensure pupil well-being. They work on the premise of 'what would a good parent do?' in all dealings with pupils and he leads assemblies about humanity, compassion and expectations in order to ensure happy, and therefore successful, children.

Discipline from detentions set by teacher, heads of year and if necessary involvement of parents. 'Certainty of consequence more important than severity of consequences' – so pupils not intimidated or fearful. Parents appreciate the fact that they get phone calls not only if there is a problem but also if there is something to celebrate when their child has excelled.

Pupils and parents: The school is mostly non-selective and reflects the diversity of the area well. 'We chose it over an independent school because there is no sense of entitlement here, and our child has really polite, kind friendships with kids he would never have met at a north London independent school'. Around half on free school meals and eight looked after pupils. Parents told us that the school has high expectations and everyone is expected to comply – strict uniform policy evident, tight punctuality enforced, and serious work ethic encouraged. The curriculum guide given at the beginning of each year includes 'practical ways to reinforce your child's learning', 'how you can help' and 'resources for pupils and parents to support learning'. Learning is clearly expected to be a whole family endeavour. Parents said that they felt listened to – suggestions by staff, pupils or parents are heard and responded to positively.

Entrance: Of the 210 places in year 7, 30 come from SMMA primary school, then preference to children in care and siblings of pupils in the school. Ten per cent selective on language aptitude (400 children sat for those 18 places recently). Remaining places are 30 per cent Islington Church of England primary school pupils (catchment area around one mile) and 70 per cent on distance from school (currently about a half a mile from the school). A further 18 admitted in year 9 via language aptitude test. At sixth form, top third stay on to create half of the selective sixth form (no automatic transfer), which has 120 pupils in each of the two years. Usual entry requirement is at least seven GCSEs at 4+ including English and maths, with 6+ in proposed A level subjects – 7 for maths and 8 for further maths.

S

Exit: The 60 per cent or so that leave after GCSEs go to eg Woodhouse, Camden Girls or City and Islington College. But 'why would I go somewhere less good than here just to have a change?' Some 40 per cent of sixth formers go to Russell Group universities and a few abroad (McGill, Science Po). Three medics in 2018. Sixth formers get work experience with one of the partnership firms together with exposure to other worlds through the masterclasses and visits, as well as a paid for visit to a university, which all helps with personal statements for university applications.

Remarks: A shining example of an excellent school. Parents and pupils are aware that they have picked the golden ticket if they can get an education here – the results are evidence of top quality teaching, and pupil's involvement and happiness are enhanced by the wide enrichment programme, whilst the pastoral care provides a tight safety net. If you want a top notch inclusive comprehensive education, this is the place to go.

The St Marylebone C of E School

64 Marylebone High Street, London W1U 5BA

Ages 11–18 **Pupils** 1,116 **Sixth form** 330 (around 80 boys) **C of E**

020 7935 4704
www.stmarylebone.school

Headteacher: Since 2014, Kathryn Pugh MA (Cantab) PGCE NPQH (mid 30s). A Cambridge graduate with first class honours in English, she joined St Marylebone in 2005 as an English teacher and learning co-ordinator, and was promoted to assistant head in 2008, before succeeding the long-serving and legendary Elizabeth Phillips OBE. This is only the second school she has worked at. She arrived here after cutting her teeth (as she puts it) at Riddlesdown Collegiate, a large co-ed comprehensive in Surrey, where she taught English and drama. Straight after leaving Cambridge she spent four years working in business and media, and then in theatre and communication for 18 months in Malawi, as well as for the Teacher Support Network, an educational charity.

Tall and willowy, Ms Pugh looks more like a Chanel model than headmistress. She cycles to work each day and is described by her pupils as 'inspirational', 'accessible', and 'empathetic'. We were regaled with tales of her contorting herself into yogic positions during English lessons as well as her passionate encouragement of 'complete randomness in lessons'. Said to be a fruitarian, she is described as looking strikingly beautiful in her red cape, while standing in the midst of girls in green cartwheeling and cavorting. She 'mucks in – not afraid to get her hands dirty during the fairs'; and 'She's so dynamic,' enthused one parent, 'everyone wants to do their best for her, both her pupils and her staff...the school is lucky that it has so many years of someone so ambitious and committed.'

We spoke to her surrounded by her senior management team. This is a woman who clearly prefers to see herself as prima inter pares. Her predecessor was a great delegator, and responsibility continues to be very much shared. She wants to talk about the school and its achievements and defer to her colleagues. She is deeply uncomfortable when the questions focus on her. Appreciative of a strong and supportive team, Ms Pugh is doing sterling work channelling the goodwill of both her staff and a diverse parent body.

Academic matters: Results are excellent. At A level, 71 per cent A*-B with 37 per cent A*/A in 2018. School keen to point out that girls who take further maths and chemistry perform brilliantly. While English, maths, art and politics are the most popular subjects, school does have 10 STEM ambassadors, and offers two sixth form maths/ICT scholarships to students likely to go on to study STEM subjects at university. Psychology, sociology and economics among the options – the first much the favourite, with a spread of results. German now phased out in favour of Spanish. High take-up; French and Spanish students achieved excellent results with a high percentage of top grades – a great improvement since our last visit. Supervised study periods during year 12 help the less-disciplined with their homework. Relatively good teacher:pupil ratio, with setting from the start, and school invests in retaining good staff. Our student guides were keen to tell us how many of their teachers had doctorates and were specialists in their fields.

Offers a good choice of subject options – 'an amazing variety,' enthused one parent. A future skills award and child development have replaced health and social care; dance, Latin and business studies canter alongside the front runners at GCSE and all are in the ribbons. In 2018, 72 per cent got 9-4 in both maths and English with some outstanding performances (45 per cent 9-7 grades). RS results are knock-out and the curriculum is praised for its earnest inclusiveness. The Englishes are good, so are the single sciences. One full class takes triple science each year, though most take the double award. Maths more than respectable. School does, after all, have a maths and computing specialism as well as performing arts. All students study both French and Spanish in key stage 3 and over 75 per cent take at least one language at GCSE. Art, geography and history strong and popular. School has policy of taking some subjects – ICT, RS – early to excellent effect.

Gifted and talented programme now called Aspiration and Challenge, with the idea of achieving excellence for everyone. High Achievers' programme for those with high academic ability; Scholarship programmes those talented at dance, music or drama. Two SENCos, a full-time SEN teacher, learning support assistants and specialist centres for students with learning difficulties. It is a centre of excellence for severe emotional and behavioural difficulties. Can provide for moderate physical difficulties too. EAL is an important area also (about half of the cohort speaks a language other than English at home) and this department plays a vibrant part in celebrating cultural diversity.

Games, options, the arts: It has a performing arts specialism – with 14 places awarded to those talented in dance, drama or music. It is perhaps not surprising, then, that sport has a lower profile. That is not to say that there are not opportunities available, and there are a surprising number of athletically ambitious girls. Our guide was a pentathlete, excelling at high jump, long jump, shot put, 800 metres and hurdles, participating in clubs both in and out of school. Cross-country is also popular. Grey Coat Hospital School is the big rival at netball; they also play Portland Place and Holland Park. Plenty of inter-house sports competitions too (five houses across the year groups – Hardwick, Dickens, Barrett, Nightingale and Wesley). Annual sports day at Willesden Green. Other sports on offer include football, trampolining, rugby and tennis as well as the D of E awards scheme. They have managed to fit an underground sports hall into this already over-filled space and have a seven metre climbing wall. Sport very much available even if not always enthusiastically taken up.

Dance, drama and music are outstanding and production values are high. 'The girls take huge pride in their performances,' we were told, 'even if not everyone can take part. It is inspirational.' The inspiration is further fuelled by the innovative and outstanding three storey building that incorporates the visual and performing arts space, with dance studio and gym in the basement. This makes a huge difference – not least to the amount of space it frees for other curricular activities. In all respects the arts reign here. You can make everything from jewellery to ceramics and print your own photos. Up-to-date laser cutters in the well-equipped DT workshops. Graphics also well regarded. Debating, dance and musical performance of all kinds thrive. Scholars' concert happens in the Wigmore Hall; some musicals, eg sixth form production of Chicago, performed at the Rudolf Steiner Theatre; whole school production of Grease in the old-fashioned, polished-wood-smelling school hall.

Some disagreement among parents as to whether there is an opportunity for everyone to get involved in these productions and performances. Grumblings in some quarters that only the best are given roles – and here, there are a lot of girls considered to be glittering. So your aspiring Milly who doesn't quite make the grade may well end up sitting on the sidelines for much of her school years. School quick to point out that over 150 pupils across the school took part in whole school production at Christmas. We, like Ofsted, were impressed with range of other co-curricular activities which don't necessarily require high-confidence performance skills: book clubs, green committee, Young Entrepreneurs, Fair Trade group etc. However, opportunities like GCSE photography work in the highly professional Metro Studios only available to the three or four girls whose applications to take the course are considered sufficiently impressive. This is the reality of a state-funded school, but it must be trying for the also-rans and would-bes.

Background and atmosphere: Tucked between Princess Grace Hospital and Marylebone High Street and close to the teeming runway that is the Marylebone Road, the school is a leafy, contained oasis of calm and purpose. St Marylebone Parish Church is a focus point and contributes to the peacefulness. This is where assemblies and concerts happen as well as religious services. A closely-knit jungle of buildings from red-brick Victorian, complete with heavily green gloss painted corridors, to modern glass and concrete are packed onto this one compact site. Further down the High Street on Blandford Street is the sixth form building, which is modern, purpose-built, and feels more like a tiny university campus than a school.

Five forms per year, and with only 750 in the main school with up to 330 in the sixth form, St Marylebone is a relatively small inner London comprehensive – and this shows. As intimate as it can be, spread over two sites, it is an unintimidating place, with plenty of smiles and polite greetings between staff and pupils as well as between the pupils themselves. No space for lockers, so girls have to learn to be adept at carting their lives around with them and being organised about what they need for each lesson. Lunch is eaten in form rooms, though year 10 examinees and upwards are mercifully allowed out to settle in the numerous cafés round about at lunchtime. Sixth formers have their own canteen in Blandford Street.

Pastoral care, well-being and discipline: Pastoral care is very strong, affirm several parents. As well as there being systems of support in place among the staff and pupils, there is a strong mentoring facility between the older and younger pupils. This is an intense time of life for any teenager, but one senses that in this school the experience can perhaps become more intense than elsewhere. School says that the intensity is 'offset by a very caring community feeling which identifies and helps deal with problems' – and denies that this is a school of 'precious princesses'. Maybe it is part of the performing arts culture.

Girls, on the whole, very supportive of each other, though there is a lot of competition and this has to be managed. Behaviour is good. Cases of bullying rare, we were told. A smell of smoke doesn't linger in lavatories here, and a zero tolerance approach means that your child may well end up with detention just from talking in class. The bar is high, girls feel lucky to be here and want to behave well. Parents commend the fluid communication lines whenever a problem arrives. Lots of positive feedback when a struggling girl starts to perform well, as well as the more obvious commending of high performance. Much appreciated are the proper, old-fashioned termly reports which don't just parrot at you what the class has done but actually talk about your own daughter. Good, realistic and collaborative target-setting also works.

Pupils and parents: Broad social mix, made up of the heady variety of backgrounds and cultures that you would expect in an inner London comprehensive. Much more middle class than many of its kind, however, because this is the golden apple if you are after an excellent education for your creative daughter who also likes to perform. A higher proportion than usual of parents are actors, barristers, artists and, yes, even bankers, than you would find at just any ordinary central London comprehensive, many of whom have been privately educated themselves.

The gritty detail is there are approximately 65 per cent from ethnic minority backgrounds and from 90 different countries. Over 50 per cent of pupils are bilingual. More than 60 languages spoken at home. Sixty per cent C of E members; the largest second religious group is Muslim. School clearly tries hard to integrate the social mix – has an annual World Culture Day among many other initiatives – and attracts fierce loyalty. Girls travel some distances to get here – from as far as Hackney in the east to Ealing and Shepherds Bush in the west, Kilburn, Kentish Town and Islington in the north as well as Wandsworth and Southwark in the south.

Entrance: As maddeningly oversubscribed as you would expect – something like 1,000 applicants for 168 places. Looked after children and those with statements have priority. Sixty per cent C of E places, 40 per cent 'open', with distance the only criterion. Fourteen places annually given to those with outstanding aptitude in an aspect of performing arts (music, choral, dance or drama). Applicants divided into four ability bands with equal numbers accepted from each band. Tie breaker of how near to the school you live. In the sixth, 330 places – priority to existing students, though they have to fulfil requirements (minimum of five 9-6 GCSEs, with at least grade 5 in maths and English). Boys are taken into the sixth and, again, more apply than there are places for. Performing arts and maths/ICT scholarships for sixth formers. School receives five applications a week for occasional places.

Exit: Up to 40 per cent leaves after GCSE and goes to further education colleges, the independents, eg Latymer Upper, or other state schools, eg Camden, largely for a greater range of A level subjects or more vocational courses. Most stay, though entrance to the school's own sixth form is not a given, even for their own. Sixth form leavers to good universities and a range of courses; seven to Oxford and Cambridge in 2018. A few each year to read music. Students go on to study a decent mix of arts and science subjects, from biomedicine at Edinburgh to Spanish and Hispanic studies at Bristol to criminology at Manchester. A few each year to read music, usually several to art foundation, dance foundation and drama school – immediately or after a gap year.

Money matters: National funding programmes largely cut so bidding for extra money from various sources takes up a lot of time. The result, however, is a school that is well-staffed and well-equipped, if not to lavish private school standards.

Remarks: If your daughter is outgoing, confident and creative this is an excellent choice. St Marylebone is an exceptional school. It has the benefits of the moral ethos of a Church of England school but is ethnically diverse and serves many different communities. With a bright young head at the helm, its future looks as rosy as its history.

S

St Mary's School, Hampstead

47 Fitzjohn's Avenue, London NW3 6PG

Ages Girls 2–11, boys 2–5 **Pupils** 300 (15 boys) **RC**

Fees: £14,745 pa

020 7435 1868
www.stmh.co.uk

Headmistress: Since 2016, Harriet Connor-Earl BA (RE – from Brighton). In her late 30s, she is young for a head teacher – but definitely not green. She has been in the teaching profession for many years, starting off her career at a state secondary school in Haywards Heath before a stint in New York teaching at St Columbia Elementary School: 'I taught grade 8, but a lot of the expectation was teaching to test, so you couldn't be creative.' She still enjoyed it and benefited from the experience. When she came back to the UK, she worked for two years at Chapter School for Girls in Kent, followed by four years at Warden Park School. Subsequently she became director of studies and boarding housemistress at Ardingly College Prep School, Sussex, before being offered the post of head at St Mary's: 'The minute I walked in the chapel, I fell in love with it and the school..and the girls were the kindest and happiest I'd ever met.'

Children, she says 'are wonderful and curious and the best bit about humans.' She simply loves working with them and her career in teaching was preordained, from when she used to line up her teddies in her pretend classroom to having a mum and two aunts who are all teachers. We liked this head almost instantly (the aroma of the warm pain au chocolates and coffee we were offered did nothing to change our mind). With her wonderfully posh name, Mrs Connor-Earl is all the things you would hope the head of a cosy independent girls' school to be – understated and elegant, straight up but with a twinkle or two. Her girls would probably like to be her one day, and the parents would secretly like to be her mate.

She didn't have an easy task, following in the footsteps of her much respected predecessor. One parent told us: 'I loved Ms Rawlinson so much I was determined not to like Ms Connor-Earl, but actually that changed pretty quickly.' Most parents agree that Ms Connor-Earl is a lovely, approachable and welcoming head with bags of energy and a tough job of putting her mark on a school where some parents don't like change. One parent said: 'She has injected fresh ideas into a slightly tired school, which although well regarded for its pastoral side, was less so for its academic achievements. She now runs a much tighter ship and her enthusiasm and experience have brought about positive changes.'

A committed Catholic, she is married and has one son. Enjoys family skiing holidays, cooking and renovating her house in Brittany. She has successfully completed the 110km London to Brighton cycle challenge and raised over £3,000 for charity.

Entrance: All year groups are oversubscribed and prospective parents are encouraged to register as early as possible. Non-selective academically. Places go first to siblings, then to Catholics. Family-orientated ethos means that other faiths and cultures are also warmly welcomed. Nursery arrangements are particularly parent friendly. Children are admitted from 2 years 9 months and can stay to lunch or all afternoon with minimum notice. Boys make up a third of nursery entrants. A few further places for girls often become available in year 3. Some full bursaries available.

Exit: Plenty of offers from leading academic secondary schools, with several scholarships. Large numbers to South Hampstead and Channing, followed by Francis Holland NW1 and Highgate. Others to eg City of London, Queen's College, North London Collegiate and St Paul's Girls, or to state grammar schools (St Michael's, Henrietta Barnett) or boarding (Queenswood, St Mary's Ascot). Secondary school advice is a strength, starting with individual parent meetings in year 5. 'Parents trust us and listen to what we recommend', says the school. Boys leave by the age of 6, many to neighbouring Catholic prep, St Anthony's, others to Devonshire House, UCS, Hereward House, Habs, Highgate or The Hall.

Remarks: Founded in 1871 by the Congregation of Jesus, the school moved in 1926 to its present site, a spacious turn-of-the century building with polished mosaic floors and vast country-like gardens. Against this gracious period backdrop, facilities are thoroughly up to date, with a super new science lab, a large, bright assembly hall and a well-stocked library. Significant recent investment in IT: new iPads and laptops in every classroom and MacBooks in the music department to help pupils create digital music.

In 1992, when there were too few teaching nuns to manage the school, a charitable trust was formed to continue the good work under lay management.

A non-selective school, it still manages to pull off high-flying results at 11. Teaching (as described in their most recent ISI report) is 'excellent' – sharp, lively and very pupil focused: 'The teacher worked out my daughter in three minutes', said one parent, and 'communication with the staff is excellent', said another. Results are achieved by encouragement and risk taking, rather than a hothousing ethos. The head says: 'I don't believe that children should be assessed at 3 and 4 years old, and I also won't choose one girl from a family and not her sibling. Yes, it means I won't have 32 girls going to St Paul's, but I will have 32 girls going to the right school for them.'

The head has introduced an assessment programme, with pupils monitored from year 1 so they get used to the process and gain the experience: 'By the time they get to year 6, they are used to exams and we can pretty much safely say what they will achieve academically.' She has also introduced the four Rs into the school's ethos (Risk taking, Resilience, Respect, Reflection). One parent told us: 'Mrs Connor-Earl encourages girls to take risks and leave their comfort zone. They are rewarded for challenging themselves and making mistakes, to help them achieve more academic progress and build their self confidence.'

The brightest are stretched through a curriculum enriched with plenty of arts-related activities and sport. 'We wanted to make teaching more relevant and incorporate risk taking and thinking independently.' Interesting extra work for those who need stretching (lunch-time puzzle club, for example, is a big hit). Fluid ability grouping throughout, then setting in maths and English in year 6 in the run up to 11 plus.

Excellent support is available, with one full-time SENCo and various special needs teachers – depending on cohort – providing help in class and out of it (in lovely, bright teaching spaces). 'We would never turn anyone away. We try and cater as much as we can for all children – we assess them on a case by case basis.' One parent told us: 'You really feel they care about every single girl.'

Strong sport (new Astroturf) with a double court for netball and a well-equipped gym. All the usual team games: rounders, netball, hockey, football, plus swimming at Swiss Cottage baths (for years 3 to 6) and athletics in Regent's Park. Gymnastics particularly popular, with pupils competing at regional and national level. High achievement too in music and excellent dance and drama (including an all-encompassing production in year 6).

Heaps of extracurricular going on with everything from spy club, illustration, knitting, origami, gardening, cooking, yoga, various music clubs and chess etc to a wealth of languages including Mandarin, Latin and Spanish. We particularly loved the idea of year 5 book club with the head herself in her lovely, tranquil office accompanied by freshly baked cookies (it sounds so wonderfully Enid Blyton; we hope it's accompanied by lashings of ginger beer).

An after-school club until 6pm every day supports working families, with emergency places bookable on the same day. It includes a quiet area where children can complete their homework or read with a teacher.

Plenty of trips too. For year 4s it's their first residential trip with a night away, for year 5s an activity week in Devon and for year 6s there is a trip to the Alps post-exams and a trip to France to meet penpals and make croissants. Little ones go to a safari park or the seaside. Ex-pupils are also invited back once a year to enjoy a pizza and DVD night with the year 6s. Cake concerts are popular, with gluten-free brownies on offer. One year 6 pupil told us, 'There's a lot to like here and I'll be completely upset to leave.'

Boys are well integrated and given appropriate scope in the Big Boys' Club, where they play football and let off steam on imaginary motorbikes. 'It lets them be boys in this all-girls environment,' said one mother.

Very much a Catholic school, with about 70 per cent Catholic families. 'I think one of the most wonderful things about it is that the Catholic ethos permeates every aspect of the children's life', said one parent. Those who wish can be prepared for first holy communion by much-loved Father Chris on his twice-weekly visits to the school chapel. Pupils take part in mass and study Catholic Christianity. 'Many of our parents have had a Catholic education themselves and want that for their children' – but even those who haven't feel included. 'As a non-Catholic', said one parent, 'I was quite concerned at the outset, but Father Chris is so lovely and gives such interesting talks. They really teach the children how to be good and loving members of the community.'

Pupils are smiley and notably well behaved. They have a certain girlish innocence which is often so sadly lacking in today's techno age. Our two lovely guides giggled conspiratorially when we asked if they ever had the need to confess anything to Father Chris, to which one replied: 'Well, I did once borrow my brother's toy without asking and so did confess.' Everything here is geared towards doing things 'the St Mary's way'; those who slip up are gently reminded of 'expectations'. 'We want pupils to do their best.' Most pupils adore the school ('my daughter can't wait to get back after the holidays') and parents are equally appreciative: 'I can't say a bad word about this place. I have had three daughters come through this school, and I almost want another one just so she can come here.'

Mostly professional families from Hampstead and the surrounding areas, with a wide range of backgrounds (Europe, the US, Asia and the Far East). About half speak at least one other language at home (with good in-school support for newcomers on the foothills of English). Very welcoming parents, we are told, 'which can be unusual, especially in the London private school bubble. But here they are grounded and down to earth.' Despite its Hampstead location, this is a fairly understated place and, unusually for a prep school, offers a number of full bursaries.

St Michael's CofE Primary School

North Road, London N6 4BG

Ages 3–11 Pupils 450 C of E

020 8340 7441
www.stmichaelsn6.com

Head teacher: Since 2013, Geraldine Gallagher (40s), BEd Liverpool University. Was NQT in a 'semi-rural' primary school with a mixed catchment, then went inner city to work in a primary school in Hackney, an experience she called 'very good although challenging at times.' She left after a year to teach at St John Evangelist School in Islington where she worked her way up to becoming deputy head. Sixteen years later she was ready to embrace the demands of becoming a head and saw the post advertised for St Michael's CofE: 'I grew up in Islington so had heard of the school and it had always had a pretty good reputation, so decided to go for it.'

Focused, 'I've wanted to be a teacher since I was 14', grounded, and knows the score. Ms Gallagher was only too aware that this was not an easy school to take on, with its prominent milieu of extremely hands-on parents (a positive in many ways but could arguably marginalise the power of a new head). She says: 'In the main the parents here are very supportive, but like most people if things go out of kilter, they will let you know.' However, judging by the feedback we've had, she need not worry. One parent told us that Ms Gallagher has already turned things around for the better in so many ways since starting: 'Parents now know where they stand with her and with the school as she has clear rules and guidelines.' Another said: 'She is a fantastic head. Before she came there was a lot of discontent and the school was in quite a bit of turmoil. The school was operating on the ethos of an old head and it became a situation of us and them between parents and teachers. Ms Gallagher has brought consistency to the school and moved it forward.'

With three of her own children at the school, this head undoubtedly has a vested interest in its success, both academically and pastorally. As one parent pointed out, 'The ethos here is very much that you get out what you put in.' Married for 14 years, any extracurricular time that Ms Gallagher has is spent with her family on days out and the odd swim or two.

Entrance: Heavily oversubscribed at nursery and reception. Around 70 apply for 52 nursery places and 100 for the 60 reception places, which are allocated on a points system, 14 points being the maximum. (Four points for church attendance at St Michael's Church, three for living in N6. Thereafter, local Christians, siblings, other faiths.) Christianity very much part of the ethos. Open days every term and, if a vacancy is available, parents are welcome to look round. Places do arise, particularly in the higher years when some pupils leave for the private sector.

Exit: On the border of three boroughs – Haringey, Islington and Camden – St Michael's sends its leavers to as many as 30 secondary schools. About half to independent schools (many with scholarships), particularly Highgate, with which the school has a close association, and City of London, but also Channing, UCS, Westminster, North London Collegiate, Haberdashers' Aske's and South Hampstead, plus top grammars Henrietta Barnett, Latymer, St Michael's Catholic Girls and Queen Elizabeth School. A considerable chunk each year to Fortismere School, the popular local comprehensive in Muswell Hill.

Remarks: One of north London's most sought-after primary schools, St Michael's has high academic standards and a high proportion of pupils who reach well beyond the government's expectations at 7 and 11. This partly reflects the intake (largely middle class Highgate), but is also due to strong teaching – recently boosted by an overhaul of the teaching structure. 'Much more academic,' one parent told us; another said, 'The school is now back on track and on its way to becoming very successful again.'

The shift in the teaching structure came about following a period of upheaval at the time when Ms Gallagher was appointed head over two years ago. She says, 'I don't believe in old style leadership and pointing the finger. I knew the school had been though a difficult time, but I believe in working together to achieve the best teaching model.' This included bringing in several new members of staff and making some of the existing ones non-teaching heads of phases, which freed them up to oversee the efficient running of the year groups. While some parents were initially resistant, others feel their children are really reaping the rewards. One told us: 'There is a huge difference in what my son gets for homework to what my older daughter got at that age. It was a bit haphazard before, now it's more structured – not hothousing, just wanting each child to reach their potential.'

This is a school that doesn't rest on its laurels – which it probably could do quite comfortably by virtue of its catchment. A dedicated teacher/parent partnership ensures that even the least engaged child will derive something because of the constantly stimulating and original methods of teaching. Pupils still enthuse a year later about how 'a spaceship landed in their grounds', which they were allowed to explore – after which they were encouraged to write a story about the experience. This was courtesy of some very innovative parents, who together with the English leader spent hours creating the spaceship, and Troy, the 'legendary' school manager, who ran into each classroom shouting that a spaceship had landed, amidst loud noises and flashing lights.

This year saw a campervan book bus parked in the grounds to encourage pupils to go in and read during break times (a cool spin on the old mobile library). Other stimulating learning tools include a charming open reading shed in the grounds funded by parents, a play pod with an assortment of recycled goods to encourage imaginative play and an allotment run by parent volunteers. We also loved the idea of a 'kindness wall', which we spotted in a couple of the classrooms, and which, we are told by one pupil, 'encourages us to write nice things about each other.' The pupils we chatted to were an astute bunch, happy and friendly. We even got treated to one spectacular card trick by a pupil who said he loved the school because the teachers 'let me do magic.' Another pupil told us that as a Muslim he liked how a Christian school 'embraces other cultures.'

Parents are an unusually energetic bunch – the school's Parents' Association (SMSA) is possibly the most committed we have come across. Last year alone they raised an astonishing £61,000, through events such as a bonfire night, battle of the bands, fun run and, the pièce de résistance, the annual parents' pantomime. This, we are told, can rival anything seen in the West End and is the highlight of the school calendar. One parent told us: 'What makes this school so special is the dedication of parents. Because we are a church school with no extra funding we can only get the extras we want if we raise the money ourselves. It does create a lovely community atmosphere, but forget it if you want a school where you can just drop your kids off and not get involved.' For a recent production of Dick Whittington, it was not unusual to see parents rehearsing or building sets until midnight, on top of the jobs they do during the day. Luckily for the school, parents include actors, musicians and set designers.

Excellent drama, with two or three plays annually, plus a nativity play and annual summer concert. A good range of sport – gymnastics, football, tag rugby, tennis, cricket, netball and basketball – taught in lesson time. Swimming, taught in years 5 and 6, is particularly strong.

Fantastic and varied extracurricular programme provides a wonderful resource for working parents. Breakfast clubs start as early as 7.45am and for the particularly energetic early bird fencing and gymnastics are offered. The quieter soul can indulge in a bit of Latin or creative writing, and an early morning maths club is also offered for 'invited pupils.' After-school activities include football, netball, dance, drama (led by the school's celebrated drama teacher, Bob Williams CBE), orchestra, French, chess and fortnightly film club (pupils have won several awards for film reviewing as part of the National Film Club).

Charity a big part of the school's ethos. On the day we visited parents were arriving with hampers to distribute to the local community and a bus-load of senior citizens arrived for their annual Christmas party. At this much anticipated event, year 6s dress up as waiters and waitresses to serve food and give out individually handmade cards and wrapped presents.

Good SEN department. Specific programmes designed for pupils who are classified as SEN or statemented (roughly 16 per cent), and access to regular sessions with art, occupational, and speech and language therapists. Each classroom has an adjoining intervention room for those who need extra help with maths, English etc.

The school is a couple of hundred yards down from pretty Highgate village – barely visible from the road, but as you approach the main gates the beauty of this building and its grounds can be appreciated. Founded in the mid-19th century as a school to train young locals to go into service, by 1852 it was on its current three-and-a-half acre site with the intention of not only providing an academic education, but also cultivating the spacious grounds as a farm. The green fields and listed Victorian buildings have since been joined by a block built in the 1970s, two large, well-equipped playgrounds and a large, new all-weather court. Both building and grounds are extensive and it is easy to lose one's bearings. The only gripe we heard from parents was about improving the concrete play area. One parent told us: 'I appreciate it is all about funding, and it's definitely better than it was previously, when it looked like a camp site, but there has been just talk for a long time.'

St Michael's Catholic Grammar School

Nether Street, London N12 7NJ

Ages 11–18 **Pupils** 734 **Sixth form** 296 (35 boys) **RC**

020 8446 2256
www.st-michaels.barnet.sch.uk

Headmaster: Since 2017, Michael Stimpson BSc MSc MA MA PGCE NPQH (40s), previously head of St Bernard's Catholic Grammar in Berkshire. Degree in natural science and teaching certificate from Durham; went straight into teaching physics and much later completed his masters in astrophysics part-time through Queen Mary, University of London. He also holds two masters degrees in educational management (one in Catholic school leadership). Has spent most of his time in selective and Catholic schools, including a spell as head of sixth form at St Michael's. Keen on the role of extracurricular education – and of the Duke of Edinburgh's Award in particular, for which he has given up many weekends. He is married with three children and enjoys literature; walks in the wild bits of Britain and listening to the music of Westminster Cathedral Choir. He is a fellow of the Royal Astronomical Society.

Academic matters: St Michael's has won numerous awards (including Sunday Times State Secondary School of the Year) for providing an outstanding education and is now one of the country's leading secondary schools, always sitting within the top 20 grammar schools (often in the top 10) nationally at A level, usually in the top five at GCSE. 2018 saw 91 per cent A*-B grades, 62 per cent A*/As at A level. At GCSE, 81 per cent 9-7. Teaching is undoubtedly a strength ('There are very clever teachers who provide very good teaching,' said one parent) and the school works hard to maximize both pupils' and parents' aspirations. 'We give a great deal of time to thinking about it,' says the head.

All the girls accepted here are bright, but St Michael's still offers significant added value, with a packed, fast-paced curriculum ('You need to enjoy academic work and want to find out about things'). Almost all take 11 GCSEs, including a large compulsory core, which includes English, maths, history and/or geography, RS, a science (about a third take all three) and a modern foreign language (large numbers take two). Language offering particularly vibrant, with French, German, Spanish, Latin and Italian all on the timetable, and Japanese and Mandarin offered outside it. Italian and Spanish particularly popular A levels (as well as psychology, RS and maths). Sixth form has its own building ('St Michael's is really two schools, with two distinct regimes, a girls'-only school in years 7-11, and a co-ed sixth form college'). Only small numbers with special needs, but strugglers are provided with generous support. Homework is pushed hard. 'If you're ill you have to catch up on what you've missed,' said one mother.

Games, options, the arts: No playing fields and only a handful of courts, so team games not a forte (no hockey, for example), but a spacious new-ish sports hall (the largest school gym in Barnet) is used to the full to deliver high standard athletics, netball, volleyball, gymnastics, table tennis and badminton. Professional basketball and netball coaches bring out the best in nascent stars and the school is successful at local and regional level in a number of sports. The top performing school in the borough's inter-sports competitions for girls.

Academic music is excellent, with dedicated practice rooms and a recording suite, though the school is pushing for higher standards of extracurricular involvement. 'Lots of girls participate in choir and orchestra, but I would like us to have greater opportunities for high quality performance.' Large, well-equipped art and DT studio (offering material technology, food technology and graphics) with plenty of enthusiastic participants.

Good range of clubs (mainly in the lunch hour rather than after school as many pupils live far away) and trips (including skiing, modern languages and faith-centred activities, such as retreats and a visit to Lourdes).

Background and atmosphere: Founded by the Congregation of the Sisters of the Poor Child Jesus in 1908 as a prep school in the grounds of its convent. In 1958, a girls' grammar school was launched to share the site, and eventually the prep school was closed to allow the grammar school to expand.

Still quite a compact school housed in a motley collection of periods and styles. The Grange, which now accommodates the sixth form, was once a 19th century private house, and has the elegant proportions reflective of this history. The main school was built in the 1950s and comes with large windows and bright views. Modernisation is a constant theme (and drain on finances), but recent additions include an air-conditioned multi-media suite and sixth form study centre. Classrooms remain a mix of old and new, but all are equipped with interactive whiteboards. Attractive gardens, once the convent orchard, are graced by a monkey puzzle tree, large redwood and shrine to the Virgin Mary.

The school, which is voluntary aided, is conducted by its governing body as part of the Catholic church and the Catholic ethos remains fundamental. Prayers are said daily and every pupil attends a weekly religious assembly, as well as mass on feast days. But this is contemporary Catholicism. 'They go to mass, but they don't expect them to be cleaning the vestry floors,' said one parent. Attractive chapel with superior stained glass windows by Patrick Reyntiens, a master craftsman whose work also features in Liverpool and Coventry cathedrals. Girls put their faith into practice with charity work, helping in the community and giving food to homeless. Generally, the atmosphere is kind, warm and supportive. 'Academically, they push them to their limits, but they do look after them,' said one parent.'There's a very nice feeling to the school.' 'No one gets lost,' said another. 'It feels very safe.'

The school is currently undergoing a major refurb, which is expected to take just under two years to complete. Part of the main building (a four-storey teaching block housing the library, computer rooms, art, and some rooms for science, history and geography) will be replaced over 2018/19. During the building work, lessons will be moved to 'high-quality temporary accommodation' on-site and by January 2020 the new building should be completed and ready for use. This venture will 'replace a tired 1950s building with a new, more spacious and modern building.'

Pastoral care, well-being and discipline: The primary aim here is the formation of responsible and committed Catholic citizens. 'We try to create a relaxed and happy atmosphere, but we expect high standards of behaviour, self-discipline and responsibility.' Those from bohemian families are advised to think carefully about their choice. Even those who aren't acknowledge that the regime is firm. 'There is very strong discipline, which can irritate the girls,' said a parent. 'They will stamp on anything – possibly too hard.'

The pre-GCSE years have a slightly old-fashioned air. 'There's no talk of drugs,' said one mother. 'They do go to parties, but there's no big modern teenage culture.' Girls leap to attention if the head is spotted in the corridor and pupil pressure as much as teacher pressure patrols the classroom. 'My daughter said to me in astonishment, "a new girl in the school keeps answering the teacher back. Nobody will be friends with her. We like our teachers. They're on our side; we're on theirs".'

In the pre-GCSE years, uniform strictly enforced, with purple skirts at the knee or close to it, no jewellery or make-up. In the sixth form, mufti is permitted and the dress code becomes 'decency'.

Pupils remain accountable for what happens outside the gates if in uniform. Few problems, however. 'Most people who come here are impressed by the behaviour and friendliness of the pupils.'

Pupils and parents: Cradle Catholics from all over London and the world, with increasing numbers of Eastern Europeans, particularly Poles. Not as skewed to the professional middle classes as some other grammar schools, with more new immigrants (33 per cent do not speak English as their first language at home).

Entrance: Not perhaps as tricky to get into academically as some of the other North London grammar schools (some 390 apply for 96 places), simply because of its single-sex faith criteria. That said, the Catholic hurdle is not for slackers. Applicants at 11 plus must provide proof of first holy communion and at least one parent must also be a Catholic with a written reference from their parish priest stating they attend mass on Sunday with the applicant. There is no catchment ('you can come from Sheffield if you want') but only girls who meet the religious criteria are allowed to sit the admissions tests (in verbal and non-verbal reasoning, English and maths). Sixth form applicants are not required to be Catholic (about 20 per cent come from other faiths) but 'must subscribe to the Catholic ethos'. At this stage, there are a further 60 places (open to boys and girls with at least six GCSE passes at 9-7, with at least a 7 in the subjects they wish to study and no lower than a 6 in English and maths). Boys in this relatively large sixth form remain in the minority, with about 20 a year. 'The boys have to be quite brave,' said one parent.

Exit: Roughly 20 per cent of girls leave post-GCSE, to nearby sixth form colleges, like Woodhouse, or larger co-ed selective schools. Most sixth formers go on to the older universities. In 2018, 12 to Oxbridge (including one vet to Cambridge), plus another vet and two medics. Nottingham, Warwick and Birmingham popular followed by Durham, King's College, UCL, Loughborough and Bristol.

Money matters: St Michael's is a voluntary-aided school and parents are expected to contribute towards the cost of the buildings and facilities. 'The school would fall down otherwise.' An annual contribution of £275 a year is asked for and 90 per cent of parents contribute something. 'We don't go chasing the other 10 per cent.'

Remarks: A happy school, with firm discipline, high expectations and outstanding results.

St Olave's Grammar School

Goddington Lane, Orpington, Kent BR6 9SH

Ages 11–18 **Pupils** 1,050 **Sixth form** 480 (168 girls) **C of E**

01689 820101
www.saintolaves.net

Headmaster: Since September 2018, Andrew Rees, previously assistant and acting head. A chemist, he had been holding the fort since the resignation of Aydin Önaç. The school hit the headlines in 2017 as parents threatened legal action when their children were told to leave after failing to get three Bs at AS level.

Academic matters: By any measure, St Olave's results are top-notch. In 2018, 87 per cent of GCSE results were at 9-7, with maths particularly strong. At A level, 72 per cent of grades were at A*/A and 94 per cent were at A*-B. 'We have the very highest aspirations for all our students, and that translates into having the highest expectations. It's a given at St Olave's.' Parents

S

and boys alike describe the staff as 'dedicated', 'professional' and 'enthusiastic'. Students are encouraged to go well beyond the demands of the syllabus. 'There's a focus here on going further than the curriculum, on exploring and expanding your knowledge,' said a very personable sixth form girl. Boys from years 7-11 confirmed that the teachers were 'really good at spotting where you might need help.' 'St Olave's promotes independent learning, it has done from the beginning,' reported a satisfied parent. 'Our son can structure his own time without needing any input from us.' 'The academic rigour of lessons is great: our son is challenged, and he has the opportunity to share his ideas in a supportive atmosphere,' said another. 'High-achieving in a relaxed learning environment,' said a third. 'Our approach can be summed up in one word: scholarship,' affirmed the previous head. Although those parents whose children had been denied entry to year 13 because their year 12 summer exam results weren't deemed good enough – a practice condemned in a damning recent independent report – might sum up the Olave's approach in two words: 'weeding out'.

Very broad curriculum, encompassing everything you'd expect, and a few things you wouldn't: we were particularly pleased to see the new food technology room, and to hear that cookery was a popular part of the lower school curriculum. Lots of emphasis on computing, and robotics has taken off in a big way. Latin is compulsory in year 7, and Greek, Japanese and Mandarin are all offered as extracurricular options, but a recent decision to axe (school prefers the phrase 'phase out') Spanish and drama from the curriculum has ruffled the waters somewhat. The previous head urged us not to dwell on the matter, but parents and pupils alike told us they were disappointed about it (or, in the words of one, 'annoyed and angry'). We put these concerns to the previous head, who responded that the school had had to cut its cloth because of forthcoming government cuts, 'and we just haven't the numbers to fill a GCSE set.' According to the website, both subjects were popular and successful, so this struck us as a little odd.

School has now moved to a three-year KS4, so that students will choose their GCSEs in year 8 and begin their courses in year 9. At sixth form level, the school remains wholly committed to A levels (as opposed to the IB or Cambridge Pre-U). 'We prefer the depth,' said the director of studies, 'and complemented by a vibrant extracurricular provision, they suit our students best.'

Games, options, the arts: There can't be many state schools where rugby and Eton fives are the main sports. Fives is hugely popular, with many boys playing it every day ('It's quick and easy, and you can play it in your uniform!') – and they recently trounced many public schools to emerge national champions in three age groups. The school's rugby teams regularly win success at both local and national level (1st XV reached final of NatWest Bowl competition). Cricket is also big here – the school toured recently to South Africa. Broad range of other sports, including tennis, hockey, football (1st XI winners of North Kent U18 league), swimming, basketball, squash, badminton and athletics.

The arts are also strong. 'The jazz band is terrific,' said one parent, remembering a recent concert in Croydon's Fairfield Halls. Lots of choral singing, with all tastes catered for – 'I sing in six choirs!' one boy told us, proudly – and the school supplies all the choristers for the Queen's Chapel of the Savoy (one of them recently won BBC Radio 2's Chorister of the Year). Children can learn almost any instrument here, including the organ in the school hall, and take their skills into the school's many orchestras and bands. We're pleased to report that drama is also strong. A few years ago, there was just one annual production, and that was for sixth formers; now there are plenty for everyone, several of them directed by the students themselves. Lots of wonderfully cerebral stuff going on in clubs: we saw a superb English version of a German children's classic, translated and published by the students themselves, plus erudite student-produced journals for the law society, the history society, the medics' society, and more. Boys report being made to feel welcome in all the activities they tried. Ambitious and enticing programme of trips and excursions: in recent months, students have had the opportunity to visit Iceland, New York, Paris, Greece, South America, central Africa – the list goes on.

Background and atmosphere: Originally located in Tooley Street, Southwark, St Olave's received its royal charter in 1571: display cases in the corridors show treasures from its archive collection, and watercolours show the school at its various stages. It moved to its present spacious site, complete with beautiful modern chapel, in leafy Orpington in 1968, in quest of more space and its own playing fields – also, perhaps, to get away from the threat of being turned comprehensive. Long and proud history of being academically selective, with which the previous head was completely in tune: 'I believe this country neglects its brightest youngsters at its peril. They are the wealth creators and the job creators of the future. I spent 22 years in the comprehensive sector and I remain dedicated to its aims, but I'm also completely committed to giving these students the education they deserve.'

And yet, with all that was going on, and every reason for the Olave's air to be full of buzz and liveliness, we can only comment on what we found, which was a curious guardedness whenever we hove into view, not least in a reluctance to let us talk to the students without a member of SMT present; although, on our pressing the matter, they did agree. All staff, from the previous head downwards, reacted with surprise and displeasure when we passed on parental criticisms (perhaps, like some other high-achieving and oversubscribed schools, they don't often hear them), and a couple of the older staff simply refused to talk to us, actually getting up and walking away when we tried to ask them questions. One parent, whose son was doing very well at St Olave's, described the school as 'incredibly defensive', to which the previous head's response was, 'We don't have anything to be defensive about!' Others, however, have described a very different experience. 'On the few occasions I have needed to contact staff by email, their response has been prompt and helpful,' wrote one mother. 'Our sons have been incredibly happy at the school and we cannot fault it,' wrote another. We will watch with interest developments under the new head.

Pastoral care, well-being and discipline: Mixed responses from parents, with some praising the school's 'very caring ethos', and others saying that bullying issues took too long to be resolved. Strong prefect system ensures older boys take responsibility for leading and mentoring the younger ones, and highly selective intake plays its part in developing the very strong work ethic apparent in lessons. 'It's almost unheard of for behaviour to be poor here,' said the previous head.

Pupils and parents: From all over the borough and beyond; nearly 50 per cent from ethnic minorities. Less diverse socially, with only two per cent of students on free school meals. Extremely supportive and active parents' association, which works tirelessly to raise funds for equipment, facilities and travel opportunities.

Entrance: Roughly 1,100 boys apply for 124 places, and an additional four places are offered to choral scholars who must pass the same stringent entrance tests.

New admissions policy for entry into year 7. First stage is logic, maths and English test in September. Those who pass invited to sit second stage English and maths test later in the autumn. First and second stage marks combined to give final score and the first 124 applicants in rank order offered places.

Around 500 boys and girls apply each year for the 110 sixth form places on offer to students from other schools. Grade point requirement for sixth form entry for internal as well as external candidates has been upped to 64 from best nine subjects (nothing lower than 6 is counted). Those external candidates whose predicted grades meet these requirements will be asked to take written tests in their four chosen A level subjects.

Exit: At 16, the great majority to St Olave's sixth form, although between four and eight per cent of Y11 students don't get the grades needed and have to leave. Those failing to get three Bs in Y12 have also been eased out in order to keep results high, but in 2017 some threatened legal action and the school backed down and agreed to readmit them. At 18, everyone goes to university: majority to Russell Group destinations; 26 to Oxbridge and 33 medics in 2017.

Money matters: State-funded grammar school, supported by Bromley education authority and the Diocese of Rochester. Parents invited to pay around £500 pa in voluntary contributions to help pay for faciltiies, etc.

Remarks: For the bright, motivated boy who is prepared to knuckle down, St Olave's is an excellent fit. As one parent put it, 'Very good, very impressive, very supportive. And we haven't had to pay for it.'

St Paul's Juniors

Linked with St Paul's School

Lonsdale Road, London SW13 9JT

Ages 7–13 **Pupils** 458 **C of E**

Fees: £20,010 pa

020 8748 3461
www.stpaulsschool.org.uk

S

Headmistress: Since 2016, Maxine Shaw (late 40s). Warm and calmly informal, Mrs Shaw strikes a very reassuring presence in one of the most highly powered prep schools in the country. She has plenty of experience as well, having been head of a pre-prep for one of the Harpur Trust schools in Bedford and, more recently, at a prep in Limpsfield. 'I've enjoyed them all' she says, 'and this is as good as it gets'.

First female head of the school and winning much praise for calm management and coherent values, although one or two mutterings that emphasis on good manners and considerate behaviour might compromise academic edge. 'I'm with her every time', said one admiring parent, 'but you can never please everyone.'

Three children, the eldest at university. 'Between school and family,' she says good-naturedly, 'I find my time is pretty well taken-up.'

Entrance: Inevitably, a very oversubscribed school. The main entry points are 7+ where 54 boys are admitted (from around 350 applicants) and 8+ when another 18 boys join (around 260 applicants). They sit tests in English, maths and reasoning. No past papers. Those who don't make the cut at 7+ are able to reapply at 8+ and feedback is given to parents following the 7+ exams to help them decide whether to try again. Another tranche of boys, usually those who have been at state primary schools, arrive at 11+ (over 400 applicants for 36 places). They take the ISEB online pre-test at St Paul's and, if successful, are invited back to sit written examinations in English and maths. There is also a short interview.

Exit: 2018's leavers' cohort saw one boy off to Eton but the other 103 all went to St Paul's.

Remarks: A school in which almost anything seems possible. Head suggests that a child here is a bit like 'an octopus on zip wire – two legs are needed at all points to take proper care of academic matters – but that still leaves a further six'. She evidently identifies the school as both an originator and a facilitator of opportunity of all kinds. It is a broad and generous vision and, given the preoccupations of some of the parental constituency, even a bold one. But all the resources, moral and material, seem to be here and, the more it is fulfilled, the more children of all kinds will flourish here.

This isn't an archetypical prep school: it began life in West Kensington in 1881 and then relocated, along with St Paul's, to its present site in Barnes in 1968. Physically and psychically, it's part of St Paul's, one of the great senior schools in the UK, something which provokes looking outwards. The site is enormous but, thanks to the massive redevelopment of recent years, there is aesthetic style and beauty around the place. Also lots of green spaces, including a new Forest School area for use by the youngest two years, part of school's enhanced outdoor curriculum, and – just a stone's throw away – the Thames.

That bigness, and the historical hinterland, both impact on the atmosphere. 'There's a lot of laughter,' says the head, 'and much of it in the classroom'. She says this with understandable approval: academic and wider learning here is something approached in the context of sociability and confidence. Both traits were reflected in all the children we met.

Very determined efforts by the school to widen access. There are several 100 per cent bursaries but, as the head ruefully acknowledges, 'sometimes that isn't enough'. Resources are needed to ensure that all pupils are equally able to access the full range of provision – trips which cost extra and so forth. 'We do our best on that,' says head, 'but it's not only about money. It's about giving confidence and reassurance in subtler ways than cash. And, well, we do our best there too.'

Brimming confidence and high aspiration can breed complacency, and the school tries hard to subvert this. 'We talk a good deal with the children about privilege and responsibility,' says the head – but she also acknowledges that example is the most important part of education. She smiles at the memory of old-style philanthropy in many schools (collecting food for harvest festivals and so forth). 'Now our pupils don't just deliver food to food banks,' she says, 'they stack shelves'. The school council selects a charity, to which fundraising efforts will then be directed. Likewise, when pupils visit The Fish Centre, a local project for the elderly, they don't just perform, but mix. 'A lot of board games,' says the head fondly. There are links with local schools for shared sport, and plans are afoot to extend this outreach in the context of music.

School buses run by St Paul's senior school, as well as some organised by junior parents. Typically two parents' evenings annually for each age group: one focused on pastoral matters, and one reporting on academic progress. Three or four mini-reports with effort and attainment grades are sent home each year, and there is one detailed full report. St Paul's parents are typically not short of ambition and drive, as well as many being affluent. Head finds them 'hugely supportive' and 'usefully involved'. Clear sense that the present head relishes and respects the milieu from which most of her pupils come, but – in looking for best practice – may not necessarily confine herself to it.

The great singularity of the school is that it doesn't do common entrance because virtually everyone goes off to St Paul's senior: 'Gaining admission to the senior school is not a given,' reminds the head, 'they have to perform.' St Paul's is one of the great academic schools in the UK and is determined to keep it that way.

Still, Mrs Shaw is not weeping crocodile tears about not being constrained by CE. She doesn't use the word 'shackled' but one senses this is what she and some of her prep school head colleagues feel. 'It's an examination which still makes a big play around rote learning,' she says. 'Of course there's a place for that, but not too much, and not too often. Our pupils are given the chance to fashion skills of synthesis and analysis,' she says, 'and I know which I prefer.'

Some 55 teaching staff in the school – of whom all are professionally qualified and plenty of high-fliers. Many are long-established: the longest-serving teacher, at the school for 31 years, is retiring shortly. Men and women share equally in positions of responsibility, and there is plenty of young blood as well. Head evidently relishes the mixture of youth and experience: 'I know every academic school says this, but we really don't function as a hothouse – there's none of this business of having accelerated pupils two years ahead of their peers. We want children to enjoy the present moment.'

SEN provision relatively low key, as one might expect of a highly selective school, but there is a teacher is on site four days a week and kept busy, mainly helping those with dyslexia and dyspraxia.

Youngest pupils, aged 7 or 8, are taught mainly by their own form tutors, but gradually gravitate to specialist teachers. Form tutors are the adult axis of young pupils' lives at school, although a buddy system makes for an easy interaction between older and younger boys. Aged 9, boys are mixed into new forms which will take them through to the end of their key stage 2 education, although the curriculum is a good deal broader – engineering, classical civilisation and Latin all playing a part. At 11, boys embark on their key stage 3 education – with ancient Greek now part of the mix for all upper thirds (year 8).

As one might expect, lots of the very best. The combination of overwhelmingly bright and confident pupils translates well into life beyond the classroom. Occasionally, a few pupils may need to take a coach to playing fields in Barnes, but only if the school pitches are waterlogged: the school shares in all the superb facilities of St Paul's senior.

The main sporting focus is rugby in autumn, football in spring and cricket in summer. Teams are very successful on the strongest sporting circuits in the London area. There's also masses of choice, especially as the boys get older – tennis and swimming squads in every year group and, later on, rugby 7s, athletics and cross-country, and also badminton, water polo and fencing. Two afternoons of games each week for most pupils: top talent inevitably is carefully nurtured, but the school firmly adheres to a sport for all philosophy and with over 200 rugby, 150 football and 140 cricket fixtures each year, the proof is there that competitive sport is open to all. 'The breadth,' said a father, 'is awesome. When I think back to my own days at prep school, I don't know whether to laugh or cry. My son, and every son, really does have the chance to be, and to find, himself.'

For all the gung-ho and joyousness of mainstream team sports, the school is perfectly well aware that, for many pupils, there is no special merit in continuing them indefinitely. A multi-sports programme is offered to pupils in their last year at school: head says this 'is widely appreciated and actually brings some boys much more into sport.'

Music is equally high-powered. The super-talented have all the opportunity to develop individual prowess, but there are orchestras (two full ones) and ensembles in abundance. Recent musicals – Scrooge and Oliver! – were notable as much as anything else for drawing off the whole range of age and experience within the school. Junior choir fields some 80 boys who sing at morning services, carol services and school concerts, and there is a Junior Recital Choir of 30 boys which sings at special functions and outside concerts.

Tremendous art and drama, with big lunch time clubs in both. Big (and regularly-changing) displays of pupils' work are all around the school. As well as timetabled lessons, boys can also take part in cross-curricular drama workshops, provided by London's first-rate Theatre in Education groups. Plenty of theatre visits to the nearby the Orange Tree in Richmond and the Lyric in Hammersmith as well as the West End. After-school drama includes a Technical Theatre Club – perfect for those who love learning about light, sound and set design. Four large scale productions annually, with frequent extras added in. Drama productions include Ivan the Fool, Arabian Nights, The Emperor's New Suit, The Witches and Around the World in 80 Days. Also an annual talent show.

Clubs galore: bridge, chess, classics, coding, cookery – the list is endless. Pupil choice is a big feature of the lunch time clubs. 'The boys choose their own,' the head explains, 'and we take big steps to ensure the choices really reflect their own interests rather than those of teachers or parents. It's enormously empowering.' One recent addition, launched at the initiative of a pupil enthusiast, has been Magic Club which performed ('with great panache') before an audience of prep school heads.

Also many trips, some in term time which are included in the school fees: outdoor adventure and teambuilding camps, and a week-long residential field trip in the Lake District. Holiday destinations can be more exotic: recent ones include NASA's Kennedy Space Center in Florida, Silicon Valley, volcanoes and geysers in Iceland, and cricket in Barbados.

There's a pastoral team led by the deputy head who works closely with the heads of year, each liaising with form tutors, who are the first point of contact for parents. One deft touch is that each form room houses a 'pupil welfare box', allowing pupils an effective and private way of raising a concern. All pupils belong to one of four houses, encouraging contact across forms and year. There is also a cross-year buddy system, especially aimed to give reassurance to younger pupils when they first arrive at the school.

Busyness – that curse of early 21st children of ambitious parents – seems carefully managed here. Head perceives less stress than at many other schools, 'but also more support'. She is particularly struck by the effectiveness of pastoral care, which she ascribes partly to deft systems, but also to the time invested. 'There is a weekly meeting of pastoral leaders,' she says, 'which considers, minutely, any pupil causing concern. Look: it's a school, and sometimes there are worries. But we aren't sitting on our hands.'

All pupils have their own iPads for use in all subjects, but experienced IT staff and strong firewalls ensure that this is a safe and wholly constructive addition to young learners. Not many disciplinary anxieties – 'what little emerges is typically the product of overexcitement and inexperience,' says the head. 'The children tend to have a good framework of reference. If, exceptionally, they find they are in a detention, they usually understand why they are there.' There have been no recent exclusions. One parent admitted to having been 'frankly uneasy' about taking up the place her son was offered. 'I feared hothousing and macho competitiveness,' she said, 'and I couldn't have been more wrong. There is great intelligence and humanity.'

St Paul's Cathedral School

    262

2 New Change, London EC4M 9AD

Ages 4–13 Pupils 246 Boarders 28 (boy choristers)

Fees: £14,031– £15,105 pa; Boarding choristers £8,736 pa

020 7248 5156
www.spcslondon.com

Headmaster: Since 2016, Simon Larter-Evans, previously head of boarding, housemaster and head of English at the Yehudi Menuhin School. He studied ballet at the Rambert Academy, then spent four years as principal dancer, performing in the UK and abroad. After 15 years working in commercial management, publishing and IT industries, he gained a first class degree as a mature student in English literature, drama, theatre and performance from the University of Surrey, and a PGCE from the Institute of Education. He has been a teacher of English and head of year 9 at St Edward's School, Oxford, and a teacher of English and drama at Pangbourne College. He is married to Dawn, a director at Accenture, and they live 'over the shop' in a house within the school.

Friendly and approachable, he has quickly won over the SPCS community. 'He has a great manner with both parents, teachers and staff,' wrote one parent. 'Really lovely!' enthused another. 'Open to new ideas,' was another comment. A general feeling that the school, already good, can only get better with him at the helm. Interests include photography, gardening, cooking, cycling and writing. His study is lined with an erudite collection of books, and he is currently doing a PhD on psychological development in young musicians and dancers.

Entrance: Register early – school is massively oversubscribed. Single form entry of 20 in reception. First list is closed at 70, then reserve list of 40. After that, the school keeps names and addresses but doesn't charge a registration fee. Informal style assessment – number games, drawing pictures, telling stories, etc. Staff look for children who are able and who will get on well within the school. Preference is given to siblings as long as they're able to access the curriculum.

Year 3 entry of a further 12 pupils. School doesn't follow any kind of formal 7+ assessment programme, but children are tested in English and maths 'just to see where they are.' A few join at year 7, as others leave and places become available.

S

Choristers (boys only) can join at any time, including mid-year, but are unlikely to be accepted after year 5. The school takes around six per year. Auditions are held by Andrew Carwood, director of music at St Paul's Cathedral, who looks for a desire for music, an innate openness of the voice, and the ability to hold a tune.

New buildings planned which will enable two form entry to reception from 2020.

Exit: Diverse destinations, reflecting the intake: St Paul's, Westminster, Forest, City of London Boys' and Girls', Alleyn's, North Bridge House, Portland Place, Queen's College, Channing, Highgate.

Majority of girls leave after year 6 for London day schools. The few who stay on go to mixed schools with a 13+ entry eg City of London Freemen's. Excellent track record of scholarships, both academic and specialist. Choristers do very well, often winning music awards to top senior schools eg Eton, Winchester, King's Canterbury, Uppingham.

Remarks: The Choir School dates from around 1123, when eight boys in need of alms were provided with a home and education in return for singing the Cathedral Office. It wasn't a particularly child-friendly place, however, and by the early 19th century the stipend paid for the boys' upkeep was so inadequate that they were usually dismissed to roam the streets once service was over. Victorian philanthropist Maria Hackett, shocked by their predicament, campaigned tirelessly for 60 years to get them something better, and the present school was eventually founded in 1874 in Carter Lane. Threatened with demolition in the 1960s, it moved to its present brutalist modernist site in New Change. Originally for choristers only, it became a day school in the 1980s, and co-ed in the 1990s. The swimming pool that once occupied the basement is now the English department; needs must.

It is, to modern sensibilities, a very ugly building, but it's a truly lovely place to go to school, sheltering under the lofty and awe-inspiring splendour of St Paul's Cathedral, and flanked by St Paul's Cross, with its inscription that recalls 'such scenes of good and evil as make up human affairs'. The original roll of eight pupils has grown to 250, spanning reception to year 8.

Not a school for those seeking flashy facilities. Major building works are planned during the summer break in 2019 which will improve and expand both residential and teaching spaces, plus enable important outreach work. For now, however, the building remains a homely rabbit-warren of rooms, many of them low-ceilinged and endearingly scuffed. Pupils allude happily to the 'garden', the school's outdoor space, but it isn't very green, and the school's biggest space isn't that big. On the other hand, weekly assembly is held in the Quire of the cathedral itself, affectionately referred to as 'the school chapel', and how many schools can say that? Tell Out Your Soul was sung full-throatedly by children clustered four to a hymn book – not enough to go round, rather charmingly, in this most august of settings. Worship was friendly and child-centred but still assembly as we used to love it: a good sing, a bit of pi-jaw, a few notices, then off to the strains of the organ. Except that it's the St Paul's Grand Organ, and visiting tourists were agape.

They teach the International Primary Curriculum here; both head and staff like its theme-based approach. They're certainly doing something right. Everywhere we looked, we saw children who were confident, articulate, comfortable with wider learning. In a year 7 English lesson students had come up with their own scholarly questions about Shakespeare that they wanted to research: 'Did he copy work from Christopher Marlowe?' 'What was the political landscape when he was writing?' 'Who did Shakespeare take inspiration from?' and, bluntly, 'Are any of his plays not considered to be any good?' Year 5 maths lesson invited similarly independent thinking: children worked in pairs to 'mark' each other's (anonymous) mistakes on a recent exam paper, and embraced the task with relish, although the gleeful written comments may not have been quite what the teacher had in mind – 'What do you think you're doing?' 'You haven't put the units in, you idiot!' and, more generously, 'Don't forget to wright [sic] the answer.' The only modern language taught is French, but the children also do Latin, and Greek is offered for those who stay on to year 7. Pleasant and well-stocked library is used enthusiatically by the whole school. After a morning on the go teachers are still cordial and full of vim, and the standard of work on display is extremely high – we loved the year 3 postcards from Ariadne to Theseus, complaining about being dumped on a desert island. Science taught in dedicated science lab.

Full time qualified SENCo delivers integrated learning support in lessons, aided by team of assistants. School is able to cater for mild dyslexia, dyspraxia, etc. and doesn't see it as a barrier. At the other end of the spectrum, however, several parents contacted us to express concern about the teaching lacking stretch and challenge for the most able pupils, particularly in the middle years. 'They do differentiate in most lessons but they don't really challenge the most able with extension activities,' wrote one who seemed to speak for several. 'There are several gifted children in both maths and English for whom this is the case, and those parents are quite frustrated.' School strongly contests this. 'Extension materials are available in classrooms, and children are directed to them, or can elect to do them. The puzzle wall outside the maths room contains sums which are fiendishly difficult. But it it's true that we are not a hothouse, and we work hard not to make school a misery.'

Sport described as 'very inclusive and energetic' by parents, and boys and girls are equally encouraged to play all sports. Team games are played in nearby Coram Fields and Victoria Park, and the school has its own training playground on site. Swimming down the road in the pool at City of London boys.

Drama is 'inspirational, exciting and contemporary,' according to one parent, and recent shows have included Dr Jekyll and Mr Hyde performed by the year 8s and A Midsummer Night's Dream by the year 5s. Lots of clubs after school, and trips to all sorts of museums and galleries, both in London and further afield – the year 3 camping trip in Essex was 'the most fun ever,' according to pupils.

However, the stand-out activity, as you'd expect, is music, described by a mother as 'Superb! Very uplifting and of a fantastic standard.' Twenty visiting teachers deliver 450 individual music lessons weekly. Senior and junior orchestra, three choirs and an abundance of ensembles including early music group. Outstanding ABRSM exam results, with merits and distinctions at grade 8 common – all the more remarkable given that no child here is older than 13. Music-making here is inclusive – 'It is the norm to sing in a choir or play instruments,' confirmed one mother – but raised above the ordinary by the choristers, whose musicality pervades the entire school community.

Choristers' cathedral life happens before and after school, but their day school life is the same as the other children's. 'The school does a fabulous job of keeping the choristers integrated into the wider school,' wrote a grateful mother, 'but also manages to build a close sense of community and support amongst the boys.' For those who can cut it (for senior choristers, autumn term finishes at 4pm on Christmas Day), the musical training is unrivalled. 'I think the whole chorister experience is rather magical and has probably fundamentally changed my son's life and attitude to life for the better,' marvelled a parent. 'It has given him a love of music, a real sense of confidence, calm and an ability to slow down and relax.' 'It's busy, but in the best way, and it's become such a big part of my life,' confirmed a year 7 treble, before delivering a stunning rendition of Take O Take Those Lips Away that left us open-mouthed with admiration.

There are usually around 30 choristers and they all have to board. (They can also be of any faith – the school has no issue with this.) Boarding house is a little sparse, but welcoming: L-shaped common room offers books, board games, DVDs, sofas, a Wii, and the ever-popular Lego and K-Nex. Bedrooms were, we thought, rather cramped by modern standards, with up to eight boys to a room, but new accommodation is planned for 2020. Run by a mix of male and female staff. 'The boarding team are responsive and have endless patience for worried or slightly disorganised parents. The communication is very good and open,' wrote one mother. Parents can visit them in the evenings to help with homework, etc. There's time off on Saturday afternoons and boys can also go home on Sunday night, 'which really helps, because obviously we miss him!' according to a parent.

Behaviour is lively but generally impeccable throughout the school. House points system not unlike Hogwarts, with points won and lost for your house through good or bad behaviour. 'The sanction of removing house points is extraordinarily potent here,' remarked the head, and detentions are rare. Achievement and good behaviour rewarded through commendations, gold certificates, etc.

SPCS families are professionals from all walks of life – 'comfortable, but not super-rich,' according to school, which aims to keep its fees as low as possible. A few bursaries, funded directly out of fee income and limited to children in year 3 and above. The only scholarships available are for choristers, whose education is paid for by the cathedral. Strong international contingent – at least a dozen languages spoken here. A SPCS mother wrote, 'The school tends to attract interesting families from a wide mix of backgrounds.' Alumni include England cricket captain Alastair Cooke, Walter de la Mare, Charles Groves and Simon Russell Beale.

This is a kind, nurturing, but exciting place to learn and to grow up. 'Overall, it is a fantastic school. Caring, and academic without being too pushy,' was one parent's verdict. 'I'm delighted my children have been educated there. It's been a special time in their lives and they've all benefited from it in different ways.'

St Paul's Girls' School

263

Brook Green, London W6 7BS

Ages 11–18 **Pupils** 746 **Sixth form** 221

Fees: £24,891 – £26,760 pa

020 7603 2288
www.spgs.org

High mistress: Since 2017, Oxford historian Sarah Fletcher MA PGCE NPQH (50s). A lady who doesn't shrink from a challenge: she was previously head of City of London School, the first woman to captain that ship in its august history. Other posts have included Wycombe Abbey, St George's Montreux, Habs Girls' ('I loved the intellectual buzz there'), Lawrence Sheriff Boys' Grammar and Kingston Grammar, where she had her first headship. Relishes scholarship and her credentials for promoting independent learning are impressive: she was involved with the development and launch of the Pre-U and the EPQ.

Attended King Alfred's School in Wantage, where she was in the first mixed comprehensive cohort of what had been a boys' grammar. It wasn't an easy ride. 'The majority of my peers were not academically minded,' she reflects. 'They cleared out a broom cupboard for me to sit my Oxford entrance exams, and the good luck card said Mind The Drips.' She did her PGCE at Exeter in history with a subsidiary in special needs.

Parents are nervous of changes she has made so far eg in the senior management, which by September 2018 had only three people remaining from the previous team, but admire her energy, drive and 'light managerial touch'. 'She certainly is more approachable and down-to-earth than we've been used to,' was one mother's verdict.

Married with two grown up sons. Her interests are music – she plays clarinet in the school's concert band – and theatre. Having arrived at the top job in girls' independent education, she has no wish to move on. 'I love it, I really love it here – I feel as if I've come home.'

Academic matters: A roller coaster of cerebral activity, where the stellar exam results are a by-product of the joyful intellectual leaping and diving that make up the days here. Sixty per cent A*s and 90 per cent A*/A grades at A level and Pre-U in 2018; 99 per cent A*-A/9-7 at I/GCSE.

'You very much go beyond the syllabus,' the head girl told us. 'The entire cohort is exceptional, and the teaching really stretches them,' confirmed a mother. 'It's less about the facts and much more about analysis, thinking and going beyond the boundaries.' Parents full of praise for the way that intellectual stimulation extends to all parts of the curriculum. 'I have never met a child so enthused about Latin as my daughter!' 'My daughter thought she was a scientist. Now she loves the arts.' Lessons here are teacher-led but 'all the teachers are interesting people in their own right' so the results are great fun. We dropped in on a zestful English lesson where year 7s were lapping up Twelfth Night under the guidance of a cheerful young prof with a knack for making scholarship exciting. Questions from the girls poured in, and were handled with kindly energy and superb subject knowledge. Lessons we saw with older year groups were relaxed and seminar-like.

Wide-ranging curriculum is still quite traditional, and we loved the emphasis on languages. On arriving in year 7 the girls do Latin and have a course on Introduction to Languages. They then start whichever modern language their languages teacher specialises in. In year 8 they choose two further modern languages and continue with Latin, which remains compulsory until they start their GCSEs. In year 10 they can opt to do Greek. A feature of SPGS is the number of school-directed courses where the school itself is the awarding body, validated by an external examining board. Art, art history, music and drama are all taught this way and have enjoyed a great deal of success. 'Our qualifications are taken very seriously by universities, and they give the girls more freedom to follow what fascinates them.' Similarly, there's no EPQ here: long before it was introduced, Paulinas took the school's own Senior Scholarship programme, which involves writing an essay on 'anything you like – it's about pursuing a scholarly interest'. Our tour guide was doing hers on personalised medicine.

Despite the A level reforms, girls here still take four subjects and drop one at the end of year 12, which here is called the VII. The Pre-U is taught in some subjects eg English lit, French, history of art, but there are no plans to introduce the IB. 'There's no distinction here between hard and soft subjects,' claims head proudly. Nonetheless, she would like to introduce more engineering, and is looking at how to improve the provision of computer studies. DT is taught as part of the art curriculum, and our impression as we walked about was that the arts, humanities and languages still rule the waves here. It may be no coincidence that none of the high mistresses to date have had a degree in science.

S

Full time learning support coordinator handles the small number of girls with eg dyslexia and organisational issues, but this is a school where girls with even mild difficulties can find themselves bumping along the bottom. We spoke to one parent who took her dyslexic daughter away after hearing her observe sadly that she was never going to be top of the class in anything. But the school works to create as stress-free an atmosphere as possible around academic attainment. Work is rarely graded, and there are few internal academic competitions to pit the girls against each other. 'There's very little for them to compete about, and hand on heart, my daughter has never experienced any meanness from the other girls,' said one mother. Another wrote, 'Her teachers have been absolutely superb, unbeatable, and there's a tremendous respect for real intellectual curiosity and academia rather than exam results.'

Games, options, the arts: The art rooms frame the main hall, and in a very literal sense therefore are central to the school and its ethos. Artwork of an astonishing standard and creativity is everywhere. We lost count of the number of pieces that amazed us, but a Chagall-inspired painting and a wonderful leaf sculpture particularly stayed in the memory. We loved the year 8 art class making 'hybrids' – joining two or three animals together in clay sculptures, like something from a medieval bestiary. School still has its own dark room; we're always overjoyed to see these surviving in this digital age.

The music has been deservedly famous since Gustav Holst took up his post as director of music here in 1905. The music department was built in 1913 under his direction and a beautiful stained glass ceiling panel celebrates his suite The Planets. The Singing Hall has a lovely acoustic and holds about 250: orchestras rehearse here, and we saw a lively group composition session in progress. An exquisite harp concerto was being rehearsed when we visited, but the school also stages musicals eg Grease, Les Misérables, The Sound Of Music, often in collaboration with the boys' school. The Endangered Musical Instruments Fair is held every year in the Great Hall, and girls are offered free taster sessions offered on the ones that have caught their fancy – saxophone, bassoon, viola, etc. Wonderful range of ensembles, some inclusive, some by audition only, that play to an extremely high standard.

Drama, once something of an also-ran, is now strong and diverse, and taught in its own well-equipped black box theatre. Recent productions include an all-girls' Lord Of The Flies. Students have lots of opportunities to get involved – one sixth former set up a club for set design – although murmurs persist that it isn't as inclusive as it could be.

Lacrosse continues to be the main sport, but netball is also extremely popular – the school had to create an H team recently because so many girls signed up for it. School aims for and achieves excellence in sports as you'd expect, with students frequently picked to play at county level, but there are plenty of opportunities for everyone to get involved for fun. Other offerings include fencing, basketball, rowing, cross-country, swimming, gym club, kick boxing – the list goes on. Dance is offered as part of the PE provision.

Huge numbers of trips abroad, including an exchange with the National Cathedral School in Washington DC, language trips to Sienna, Montpelier and the like, history trips to Paris and Dublin, and so forth. 'We're mindful of not offering too many expensive trips,' observed the school's director of communications, 'but girls on bursaries can apply for up to 100 per cent assistance.'

Wide-ranging and enticing range of clubs on offer – dissecting, medieval society, art history, IT workshop – and the girls are always encouraged to run their own: we loved the secondhand clothes shop, Re-Store, set up by students to raise money for local charities. With so many activities to choose from, some girls can feel a little overwhelmed, especially as they move up through the school and choirs, sports, productions, etc become more selective. 'One of my very few gripes about the school is that there's so much to do, but nobody pushes the girls very much,' was one comment. 'Extracurricular activities are abundant and inclusive of all abilities in the younger years, less so in the senior school,' wrote another.

Background and atmosphere: Founded in 1904 to complement the boys' school after the latter had been around some 400 years, St Paul's Girls' quickly climbed the academic heights and is now widely regarded as the parthenon of girls' selective independent education in England. The building, designed by Gerald Horsley, is a handsome but imposing red-brick in the Queen Anne Revival architectural style. When we arrived the great wooden doors were shut and, on our ringing the bell, swung silently open without any accompanying words of welcome, adding to the school's air of slightly forbidding quietude. Indeed, for a community that prizes intellectual freedom, our visit had a curiously constrained feel to it. We were given no opportunity to speak to any students other than the head girl and deputy head girl, and were watched warily wherever we went, leaving us with an impression that the school's busy schedule left little room (or wish) for visitors. However, the lovely traditional old entrance hall, affectionately known as The Marble, soon warmed up at break times as girls poured out of lessons to chat and recharge their batteries. 'The atmosphere is one of considerable freedom – few rules and much humour,' observed a grateful parent.

From the outside, SPGS nestles cosily in amongst what must be some of the best kept residential streets in London, quirkily suggestive of the school itself in their individuality and mix of classic charm and modern innovation. Inside, it's much bigger than it looks. New building, built over some former netball courts, offers superb accommodation for the senior school, including lounge areas, work stations, quiet study areas and some inviting seminar rooms.

From many windows, the view of exquisitely pretty back gardens in the surrounding houses gives a feeling of peace and normality amidst the scintillating academics, and as we walked away at 4pm we were touched to see a young Paulina buying an ice cream from the Tonibell van that had pulled up outside the school.

Pastoral care, well-being and discipline: Since the 1960s, no uniform, as befits a free and open-minded culture. Girls are trusted to dress sensibly, and they usually do. 'When I go to other schools, it's weird to see everyone looking the same,' commented one of our tour guides. Amazing canteen (it served as an air raid shelter during the war), decorated with photo exhibition of SPGS history, and the food was simply awesome – we had one of the best school lunches we'd ever been offered, and the girls we saw ate with gusto. Girls can arrive from 8am for breakfast, and must be here by 8.30am. Day finishes at 4pm, and long lunch break gives lots of time for clubs and societies. After school, girls are generally off site by 6pm.

Endearingly, some year 7 girls were given detentions for gatecrashing a senior school lecture, but otherwise there are few sanctions. 'Generally, we can deal with most things by talking. There are very few rules, so it's hard to break them.' Small tutor groups ensure the staff get to know the girls well. School denies the presence of drugs, eating disorders and self-harming, but several parents we spoke to were adamant that they can be found here, inevitably perhaps at such a selective school where some of the girls will be very highly-strung.

The school hit the headlines in November 2017, when an email from the drama department to Old Paulinas, soliciting stories of sexual abuse for a documentary-style drama inspired by the MeToo campaign, drew a furious response and resulted in a teacher resigning. The parents we spoke to, however, had nothing but praise for how Mrs Fletcher had handled the crisis, and emphasised how happy they were with the pastoral care provided. 'Both my daughters have been happy throughout their time at the school, and felt fully supported by the staff; the pastoral care was exemplary.' 'The pastoral care has been very good and the girls aren't stressed – my daughter has made some lovely friends.' 'I wish I had known before my daughter started at SPGS that all the rumours were untrue. I haven't seen any bitchiness, competitiveness, or a single eating disorder.'

Communication between school and parents is 'prompt, reliable and efficient', according to several sources.

Pupils and parents: Intake is 'increasingly international'. Many girls here speak more than one language and we heard a number of north Atlantic accents as we moved around the school. Families of Paulinas are typically highly-educated, professional, successful and very supportive of the school, giving generously of their time, money, expertise and connections. Parents' Guild works to raise funds, but has no input into the running of the school.

School is quite 'stratified', claimed one parent, 'between the cool girls and the geeks, but you can be who you want there and everyone mixes with everyone else.' Glittering roll of alumni includes Celia Johnson, Rosalind Franklin, Victoria Coren Mitchell, Imogen Stubbs, Clemency Burton-Hill and Harriet Harman.

Entrance: At 11+, up to 110 places in 5 classes, with a maximum of 22 per class. Pre-test taken in the autumn term of year 6 weeds out those who'll never make it. Those who pass sit a further test in January, designed to reveal how much girls really think: maths, English and a paper on problem-solving. Those who do well are invited for interview. School is looking for girls who can 'reason, articulate and show quality of thought.' Largest single cohort is from Bute House, which regularly sends up to 20 girls here; the rest from a wide range of preps and primaries across London and beyond. Applicants for any occasional places that arise higher up the school are subject to the same stringent assessment procedures and should already be studying at least two modern languages.

At 16+, about 20 join each year. Applicants are tested on their A level subjects and invited to interview if they do well.

Not a particularly local intake, but parents have to declare on the application form how their daughter will travel to school, and for years 7-11 the journey cannot be longer than an hour.

Exit: A handful leaves after GCSEs to try co-ed or boarding, but the great majority stay on and gain places at top-flight universities at home and abroad. Around half go to Oxbridge (47 in 2018). The rest mostly to Durham, Edinburgh, Bristol and the London colleges. Increasing numbers to Yale and Harvard; Europe is also becoming popular, with girls recently going to Berlin and Munich.

Money matters: One of the nation's most expensive day schools, but about 15 per cent of girls are on bursaries of between 85 and 100 per cent. School is working to increase access to these and to become 'as needs blind as possible'.

Remarks: For very bright, academically minded, hard-working, grounded and motivated girls, this is the best start in life imaginable. As one mother typically put it, 'For both my daughters it has been a truly wonderful experience and one that they feel lucky to have had.'

St Paul's School

Linked with St Paul's Juniors

S

Lonsdale Road, London SW13 9JT

Ages 13–18 **Pupils** 953 **Sixth form** 400 **Boarders** 35

Fees: Day £25,032; Boarding £37,611 pa

020 8748 9162
www.stpaulsschool.org.uk

High Master: Since 2011, Professor Mark Bailey (50s). Career has included both academia and education: former head of

The Grammar School at Leeds, he has also been a fellow at Cambridge and at All Souls, and professor of late medieval history at the University of East Anglia, with whom he continues to be involved. Found time to be a rugby international (1984 to 1990) and is now president of the Cambridge University Rugby Club. A thoroughly engaging, astute, relaxed and kindly man, the complete reverse of what one might expect of the high master of such a venerable institution as St Paul's. We meet many head teachers who are fonder of their school than of the pupils in it. Professor Bailey, extremely clever himself, still cherishes the achievements of others. A people-person through and through, who likes 'reading, walking and the wines of the Rhone Valley'. Talks with a refreshing lack of jargon. Married to an HR consultant, and with a teenage son and daughter.

Self-imposed mandate on coming to St Paul's was 'Not to meddle with what this school does outstandingly well; leadership of exceptional institutions is as much about stewardship as change.' That said, he is skilfully overseeing a vast programme of refurbishment that is transforming the 1960s site into a school for the 21st century, and steering both school and students towards greater meritocracy and social responsibility.

Academic matters: The St Paul's recipe for academic stardom remains the same: cream off the very brightest, recruit the very best, light the blue touch paper and stand clear. The resulting sparks illuminate the sky. As one boy put it, 'The real pleasure about being here is going off-piste academically.' Another said, 'The quality of the teaching is beyond compare. It really pushes you further.' Parents agree. 'The teachers are brilliant at their subjects'; 'They're highly skilled at imparting their knowledge'; 'The teaching is simply superb'. A recent inspection report summed it up: 'The effectiveness of questioning in lessons, both from pupils and teachers, is outstanding.'

Broad and challenging curriculum includes ancient history, engineering and technology, and an excellent range of languages, Italian, Russian and Greek among them. Exam success is seen as a by-product of the boys' broader intellectual development; in 2018, 84 per cent of A levels/Pre-Us were A*/A or equivalent, whilst 96 per cent of GCSEs were A*-A/9-7. Amazing science building offers 18 laboratories, but such is the subject's popularity that, according to staff, 'space is still tight'. Beautiful library, silent and inviting, and facilities everywhere are excellent, although we were amused to see far fewer interactive whiteboards in the classrooms than we'd seen in a state primary school the week before. Interactivity here is still verbal and cerebral perhaps, rather than fibre-optical. Huzza! But we applauded the really intelligent decision to install air-conditioning in all teaching rooms, ensuring that minds stay alert in the muggiest of weather. (How many times have we seen pupils wilting in the heat of south-facing temporary classrooms?) Specialist support is given to those few students identified as having special needs, but this isn't the place for anything more than mild cases.

S

There are no plans to introduce the IB, which the high master describes as 'enforced breadth'. Various subjects eg modern languages and philosophy and theology now Pre-U. A levels now nearly all linear; boys take three or four (five if they take two maths) and can add EPQ.

You can feel the thinking going on here. Academically, a very special place.

Games, options, the arts: Superb facilities include six rugby pitches, six football pitches, five cricket pitches, swimming pool, courts for rackets, squash and fives, and its own boathouse stuffed with sophisticated rowing craft. The students wax lyrical about the sport on offer here – 'Sport for me has been the highlight here'; 'There is so much!'; 'It's a big part of my life at St Paul's'; 'Most of my friends have been the ones I play sport with' – and we saw dozens of boys throwing themselves about the playing fields in organised and impromptu games of just about everything.

Music and drama are both extremely strong; concerts are held in the world-class Wathen Hall, and new Samuel Pepys Theatre was recently opened. Art is taught in a magnificent suite of rooms, and the engineering and technology room is surely every young boy's dream. Clubs cater for every taste, although oddly enough we didn't see any, despite having arrived at lunchtime; even the four lads we finally came across in the 3D art room turned out to be revising their French ('I don't know why they're doing it here,' mused the art teacher). But the student-produced magazines we read were testament to the vibrancy of this community of thinkers: page after page of exceptionally mature, sparkily written articles on cinema, sport, current events, modern architecture; a real treasure trove of ideas.

Boarding: St Paul's is a day school – one of only two to be included in the Clarendon Commission's 'nine great public schools of England' – but it does have a very small community of boarders as well, a quarter of them from overseas, who seem to exist to justify the superb round-the-clock catering which all the boys, day and boarding alike, can access if they need to. Boarding facilities have been recently upgraded, and the boarding provision was praised in a recent ISI report. Study bedrooms, common room and TV room, music practice rooms and computer suite. At least two hours' prep a night followed by supervised activities eg music or sport keep boys busy during the week. Many boarders go home at weekends, often after Saturday morning sports matches.

Background and atmosphere: Founded in 1509 by Dean John Colet, and moved four times before arriving in 1968 at its present riverside home in leafy (and very wealthy) suburbia. A £77 million ongoing redevelopment has transformed much of the site. Visitors now are presented with an exceptionally elegant, blond, modern school campus; an architectural version of the Paulines we met, really, and with the same air of informality and purpose.

Having survived the Great Plague, the Fire of London, the Civil War and the 20th century, St Paul's can afford to relax and enjoy its own success. 'Academic rigour and loose ties' was how one parent described St Paul's today, and this was echoed by the high master: 'It has the feel of an über-grammar school. It's more like a university than any other school I've known.'

It's cool to be clever here, and so, inevitably, there is peer pressure to do well. This is mostly positive, say boys and parents, and drives everyone on, although one parent added, 'If you were at the bottom of the class, SPS would be a horrible place.' But high master denies this emphatically: 'More time than ever has been put into teaching underachieving boys and providing better support.' And another parent observed, 'The bottom of this particular pile still represents an extremely high level of achievement.' We saw boys working with good humoured focus for an eccentric and witty geographer who was padding around in Muppet-motif socks, interspersing teaching points with cheerful insults which the boys lapped up and batted back, in time-honoured boys' school way. (But there was a detailed scheme of work on the board that accorded with modern practice, demonstrating that old and new styles of education can be blended successfully.)

Indeed, SPS remains an extremely masculine community, where the testosterone coming out of the circuit gym knocks you over at 20 paces; and perhaps this shows most in the school's being unaware of just how masculine it is. The surmaster insisted that there was much 'mutuality' between the boys' school and the girls' school, but this was flatly contradicted by the Paulines we spoke to, and by one mother who felt that the school could do much more in this regard. We were ourselves surprised to find a large-scale female nude looking breastily down on us as we ascended the art department stairs, and more surprised to find another one as we went down a different way. There were no male nudes on display, and we couldn't help wondering why, out of all the subject matter that might have been on show, the school had chosen these particular canvasses. There are 'no plans whatsoever to admit girls at any stage of the school; no parents, boys or staff have ever suggested it' (high master). Which, if they want to go all Rubens-y about the stairwells, may be a good thing. But the Paulines we met were very personable young men, and the same mother who wanted more contact with SPGS also affirmed, 'Paulines are lovely, decent boys, really articulate, fun, clever and very nice.'

Pastoral care, well-being and discipline: Vertical tutoring system, ie mixing the ages of form groups so that younger and older boys are together. The concept is simple: boys will listen to their peers sooner than their parents, so utilise the more experienced boys for pastoral care and to lead extracurricular activities. It's been in place for over 10 years, and is clearly popular. As one parent commented, 'From the moment they arrive, the 13 year olds meet boys in every other year and get a sense of what they might do.' Tutors stay with the boys throughout their time at the school, and, says school, often become family friends – the advisability of which the school may be reviewing, in the light of recent events (see below). The nature of this hand-picked community means that bad behaviour is rare: 'There's an intuitive understanding of where the boundaries are,' says high master. 'I've never seen any evidence of bullying here,' was a typical student comment, and surmaster concurs: 'We have very, very few boys that would do what could be called bullying more than once, and if they do, we apply school sanctions quickly.'

Pupils and parents: One of the most expensive day schools in the UK, and compared with similar institutions, financial support for poorer families is small but increasing – see Money matters. The result is a community which is highly diverse religiously and culturally, but not socially. Parents mostly ambitious and successful professionals with sons to match, hard-working and free-thinking. Old boys list reads like a Who's Who of Influential Britons: a sample includes John Milton, Samuel Pepys, Field Marshal Montgomery, Isaiah Berlin, Oliver Sacks, George Osborne, Rory Kinnear – and Nicholas Parsons.

Entrance: State educated parents who are starry-eyed for their children but don't know the entrance procedure should start reading it now. SPS takes about 180 13-year-old boys each year, but it's impossible to go there directly from a state school. The 13+ candidates apply either from St Paul's Juniors, whose 80-90 boys nearly all go on to the senior school, or from any other prep school – usually those in the London area. St Paul's Juniors has its own admission procedures at 7+, 8+ and 11+; see our separate entry, and don't leave it any later than September of your child's year 6 (be grateful: it used to be year 5). Prospective Paulines sit an online common entrance pre-test at their prep school, on the strength of which about 350 are invited for interview. The school then makes conditional offers: boys have to get at least 70 per cent at common entrance. Entry from 2021 onwards will not depend on passing the CE but on 'continued good conduct and academic progress at their existing prep school, including an unreserved reference of support from their school in year 8.' The school is looking for 'intellectual curiosity and embracing of novelty'. About 20 more boys also join in the sixth form, which at SPS is called the Eighth.

Exit: Somewhat tardy with its sixth form leavers' destinations ('many pupils take a GAP year and apply to university after taking their A Levels'), but we imagine 2018 will be similar to these from 2017: 68 Oxbridge places, the rest to Bristol, Durham, Imperial, Edinburgh, UCL and other top universities. An increasing number (31 in 2017) obtained places at US universities such as Harvard, Yale and Princeton. Most popular courses: economics, engineering, geography, history and medicine.

Money matters: Scholarships are honorifics only – £60 pa and a silver fish in memory of John Colet. However, a more generous means-tested bursary scheme now on offer with support for families with an income of up to £120k(!) subject to doing well in the entrance tests. Some remission for families who send three or more children to the school.

Remarks: For very bright, confident, motivated boys who like to think for themselves, St Paul's provides a truly unrivalled education. A unique start in life.

St Peter's Eaton Square

265

Lower Belgrave Street, London SW1W 0NL

Ages 3–11 Pupils 308 C of E

020 7641 4230
www.stpeaton.org.uk

Head: Since 2016, Miles Ridley BA PGCE (late 50s). A degree in English and drama from Essex launched him into a career on the boards as an actor. Ten years on, married and with a family, he took a teaching certificate at Goldsmiths and began at a Lewisham primary school, moving quickly from class teacher to senior leader and SENCo. After 10 years he applied for SENCo in a secondary school more for the experience of the application than anything, and found himself heading a department of 25 teachers and assistants within the very large SEN dept. Further training as a teacher of hearing-impaired children led eventually to a position as SEN consultant for Westminster. He joined St Peter's as assistant head and took on the headship when the previous incumbent was headhunted elsewhere.

A quietly urbane man with owlish glasses, he arrived fresh from an editorial meeting with the pupil magazine sub-editors. Married to a lawyer, with two grown up children, committed to the school's Christian values and not above making the tea himself, from a handy kitchenette in the corner of his otherwise minimalist office. 'I'm a bit old school and like the idea of nurturing well-rounded young citizens..I want to know their moral education has been well supported.' He has made a start already by condensing the behaviour policy into four principles: everything you do must contribute to yours and everyone's learning, be polite, kind and safe; 'It fits into everything we do, more than I dreamt of,' he says. Popular with parents, who greet him each morning in the playground, and approachable to children, he has made a name for himself in introducing the school magazine and transforming the school's SEN support. 'He has been really supportive; any problem, we go straight to him,' said a mum. A child's verdict, 'He's kind of laid back but doesn't let us chat very much. He has rules'.

Entrance: Admission by Westminster LA criteria: priority given to looked after children, those baptised at St Peter's Eaton Square church, those who attend the affiliated church and then other C of E churches. Most of the 10 children from their own nursery gain a place, but have to apply. Oversubscribed three to one, until top years, when some filter off to local prep schools. Catchment area is mostly Westminster, but some from Lambeth and Wandsworth

Exit: About 50 per cent go to state secondaries. Most recently: Holyport College, Chestnut Grove, Lady Margaret School, Marylebone Boys' School and Notre Dame Roman Catholic Girls' School. Some success with independent day schools, including Latymer Upper, Queen's College and City of London School, with one or two applying to board at eg Pilgrims ('not without tutoring,' one parent murmured). Exit at age 7 or 8 discouraged.

Remarks: Academically up with the front-runners, with well above national average results in Sats. Parents praised the maths teaching, which adopts the Shanghai Approach, learned from visiting Chinese teachers. Literacy was also mentioned: 'My son started off uninterested in reading and is now one of the best in the class'. We saw formal grammar being taught in year 2, while junior cruciverbalists were compiling their own word-search. Latin is taught from year 3. Class sizes are kept at 25 with two classes per year group, except at the top of the school, due to (mostly) boys leaving early.

The class teacher is often supported by a TA and year 6s volunteer to read to younger children. London turnover of staff (or, as one child put it, 'Teachers leave very often'). We heard about Science Day, when students become science detectives; 'We made slime with borax and PVA glue and food colouring'. No homework policy though we heard replacing traditional homework with school supported Home Learning had upset some parents. SENCo supports some with learning difficulties, Down's, ASD and complex needs; 'we would never say, "no",' remarks the head. One mum of a girl with cerebral palsy described a general readiness among staff to manage her medical needs and frequent out-patient appointments. 'They treat her like a normal child. They administer medication at lunchtime and have never complained'.

Music is abundant across all years and from year 4 in the form of group violin lessons. 'There's lots of research about how learning a musical instrument gives you extra brainpower,' says the head. One mum criticised the lack of variety of instrument teaching: 'They made things so hard for the peripatetic teachers that they all quit...it was interfering with core subjects'. All children participate in singing and drama, performing in house singing competitions, at the church and local concerts, including in Victoria Station and Trafalgar Square at Christmas. Nativity plays for infants, and year 6 leavers raise the roof in a full production, the likes of Pirates of the Currybean; 'they are spectacular,' commented a teacher. Proximity to the West End shows enables easy access to museums and theatres on school trips.

S

Artwork was prolific; we particularly liked the pop art self-portraits and models of revolving stages, inspired by a visit to Cirque de Soleil. A termly magazine, SPARK, sponsored by an international publisher, showcases the children's activities in glossy magazine form, as well as providing a platform for aspiring writers and advice from young agony aunts. No sports fields; only a tiny green soft surface playground and basement hall, used by a specialist PE coach. The youngest children take yoga, while others start the day with Shake and Wake dance moves. Sports day takes place in Battersea Park and year 6s walk to Hyde Park for outdoor pursuits. Swimming at the nearby Queen Mother sports centre, from year 2. Parents run an after-school football club in Battersea Park. One mum lamented the lack of space for sports: 'shame there isn't more space to run and get energy out of themselves'. Year 6 enjoys a residential at Sayers Croft, which introduces caving, pond dipping and orienteering – all without screen time; 'it was really easy', said one boy.

A Christian school, in ethos, with regular visits to the high C of E Romanesque church in Eaton Square. Christian values are visible, from the motto 'Together, we will realise the potential God has given us', to daily hymns at assembly. The Saint Peter's Way code of conduct, with its four simple principles, is familiar to each child. 'It works', says the head, 'I have had emails from the public praising the children's behaviour'. As for bullying, 'we teach the child to understand the difference between teasing and bullying'. We saw charts of traffic light warnings in each class and incentives in the form of house points. A celebration assembly rewards good conduct with 'star of the week' and the four houses (named after the gospels) compete for house points. One mum commented it was 'very Hogwartish' and reported that the thrill of winning the house competition was so great there was no need to supply a prize.

Founded in 1815 by the parish of St Peter's at the east end of Eaton Square, the school started in Eccleston Place, before moving to its present site in Lower Belgrave Street, 'practically in Victoria Station,' laughed one mum. A Victorian red-brick frontage, with imposing square tower and large round windows, squeezed between office buildings and mansion flats, with original front-yard style playground, all within earshot of the London-Brighton line. Teaching space is chiselled out of every available corner, from the attic storey, where high ceilings give a gothic feel, down to the basement nursery. Red painted doors outside and spidery fire escapes lead to blue doors and creamy paintwork inside, with original artwork by Axel Sheffler on the walls. Fortunately, our guides knew where they were going, as we were quickly disorientated by the internal layout, recently redesigned, with plenty of small tuition areas.

The older years occupy the top floor, with banners of spelling words draped across the ceiling and an international map woven into the rug. Two-person desks facing the front in year 6, while further down the school we saw four to six children to a work table and in the youngest classes the bright picture carpets were used for group times. Most rooms have a touchscreen board ('like a massive iPad', suggested the children). A separate computing suite with desktops and an iPad chariot provide enough computers for a whole class. If you stare closely in the reception class you will glimpse the pet snails. The kitchens on the ground floor serve up lunch on long tables in the adjacent hall; jolly, illustrated menus announce a diet of school favourites, as well as Meat Free Monday. Lasagne and chocolate cake were voted tops.

As one parent put it, 'the playground is the thing you notice more than anything' due to the restricted size, lack of climbing equipment, and, when crammed with whooping children, the intense noise. Another parent mitigated, 'it's so not a reason not to send your child there'. The children, however, don't appear fazed by the lack of outside space. Our guides personified the St Peter's Way dictum, in being kind, polite, and articulate. 'The children always show you round,' said one mum. 'What better advert can you have?' We agreed. They led the way in trim blue and yellow uniform, complete with stripy ties. 'I would rather wear my own clothes, but I can understand why there is a school uniform', said one. Another informed us the clothes were available to buy at 'John Lewis slash Peter Jones'.

Parents, we heard, were 'driven, aspirational with a disproportionate number of barristers, lawyers etc, to whom standards are important...a real cross-section of that part of London'. A school council ensures the children have their say too. Many families walk or use the bus or tube to school; the head is on a mission to reduce idlers in four by fours at the school gate.

The new PTA has a talent for fundraising; recent initiatives include a Burns night supper. There are clubs before, during and after school, including breakfast, debating, drawing, yoga and French. Parents are satisfied with communication, via the 'very nice reception staff', who filter emails 'to stop the teachers from being harassed'. 'I've never had an issue in almost 10 years with teacher access,' said one mum. One small boy said, 'Mr Ridley is happy if children go to him, unless his sign is up'.

A top scoring school which provides an all-round education with a Christian soul. Ethical values underpin the direction and modern teaching methods provide a firm grounding for the school's metropolitan population. As one parent put it, 'it offers what a private school might be without the price tag'. Good things come in small parcels.

St Philip's School

266

6 Wetherby Place, London SW7 4NE

Ages 7–13 **Pupils** 105 **RC**

Fees: £16,200 pa

020 7373 3944
www.stphilipschool.co.uk

Headmaster: Since 2016, Alexander Wulffen-Thomas BA PGCE (30s). The suit, tie and polished shoes are neat, tidy and conservative but the first impression is that he might be happier outside (runs up the stairs at speed). Born in the wilds of West Yorkshire, one away from the tail end of a large family, brought up in Cheshire and schooled at St Ambrose Prep, St Ambrose College and then Stonyhurst. Read Russian – 'it's a country with a soul' – at Durham, then used his languages to find a job in the City. Left in his late 20s as it involved too much time in front of a computer screen dealing with dreary problems such as money laundering regulations and went to work at Westminster Cathedral Choir School, initially in an Evelyn Waugh-type role as a teaching all-rounder of history and games. Obviously more successful than the original as he landed the post of deputy head and then applied for the job at St Philip's, seeing it as a natural progression for someone with Catholic values and a leaning towards traditional teaching.

Married to Olivia; one dog – attends the school; no children as yet.

Entrance: The main intakes are at 7 (approximately 10 boys) and at 8 (another 10 boys). Usually three to four applicants for each place and mainly from local pre-prep and state schools as most of the boys live nearby. They are oversubscribed but make their choices based on teacher's impressions as well as academic potential; this is definitely not a hothouse school and they take in boys with minor learning difficulties as long as they can cope with the mainstream curriculum and routines. St Philip's does not hide the importance of its religious roots and the majority of boys are from Catholic families, often children or relations of previous pupils. However, the school is also catholic with a small c and about 10 per cent of the boys follow different faiths. When we asked some Catholic pupils whether this was ever awkward they responded convincingly in the negative, although possibly with a hint that the others might be missing out.

Exit: A minnow compared to some of its competitors in London, St Philip's rightly holds its head up high in the academic stakes, although its new leader is emphatic that this is not a 'show-off school and the pupils' work does the talking'. Parents are helped to make the choice of 'where next' by an excellent app produced by the head, and most boys move on to their first-choice school. Most popular destinations currently Wetherby Senior, Ampleforth, Dulwich College and Portland Place.

Remarks: Housed in a tall red-brick building in South Kensington, the only advertisement is a charming plaque depicting a very blue St Philip Neri, and you could easily miss the word underneath announcing that it is a school. The spiritual aspect remains very important and assembly in the morning tends to be RE with sporting analysis sandwiched between the opening prayer and the collect for the day (presumably when their horse was in training it also included prayers for the creature's chances in the 2.30 at Kempton).

It is a logistical triumph that they fit 100+ boys into this space, but it may help the pupils to organise themselves as there is literally no room for discarded items of clothing or belongings. On a hot day, the blazers hung neatly on the back of chairs and the old-fashioned desks were bare, lids firmly down. We did look inside a few, with the head's permission, but nevertheless feeling rather guilty due to the Keep Out notice in one, and found the usual variety of orderliness but absolutely no sign of any illicit items. Outside, there is a communal garden, which ticks the fresh air box but results in sighs from all concerned as it comes with major drawbacks, such as a noise cap, which is not ideal for small boys wanting to let off steam.

An individual school from day one; not many of its rivals can boast having owned a racehorse or having had a headmaster who doubled up teaching the boys with acting as chauffeur at the beginning and end of the day. Mr Tibbits – the name in itself a joy – started the school as the result of a complaint by a priest at the Brompton Oratory about the sad lack of education for Catholics in the neighbourhood. He was an exceptional teacher but may have been helped by fortifying himself for the task with a glass of sherry before lunch and a glass of red wine with the cheese whilst the boys unhappily chewed their way through Spam and mash, followed by blancmange. Nowadays, this miserable experience – no-one was allowed to leave until the last plate was clean – has been superseded by packed lunches, but the very mildly eccentric atmosphere remains. Only two more headmasters bridged the gap between his death in 1967 and Alexander Wulffen-Thomas's arrival in 2016, and maybe for this reason the 21st century is slightly less in evidence than at some of its rivals.

A high proportion of the teachers have been here for a long time but there is young blood, the head intends to move from one to two 'gappies' next year and there's a new multi-talented deputy head. Parents and children speak very highly of the teachers, not only about their competence but also about their kindness, one small boy taking a great deal of trouble to explain – vocally and by mime – how one teacher gave you a minus mark but was 'really kind' whilst she was doing it. They believe in ensuring that the basic building blocks are carefully laid and regularly checked, with daily spelling and twice weekly maths tests in lower forms, and also encourage learning by heart through poetry competitions. Higher in the school all the teaching is praised but maths and Latin are exceptionally strong, and science may well benefit further when they are able to provide the intended new lab. There are 'no mountains of homework', but parents are relaxed and confident that their boys will do well.

Art is hugely popular, taught in a surprisingly bright and airy basement with one parent saying that her 'totally talentless' child kept returning with 'frankly miraculous' objects. Not afraid of the big time, pupils are entered in Royal College of Art competitions and 12 students had their work displayed in recently. Music is an intrinsic part of life, from playing the piano at assembly to singing in the Schola, and all pupils are encouraged to play an instrument or sing, with up to half of them performing at the school concert.

Sport is important; possibly to compensate for the lack of space back at base, they have invested in acres of well-manicured games fields in Barnes where the whole school decamps on two afternoons a week, leading to boys having 'smiling faces when you pick them up after a games day'. Despite their tiny numbers they field teams that are not frightened of taking on larger boys from much larger schools and quite often succeed in beating them. Swimming is a weekly lesson and the boys have recently organised squash teams who play in tournaments at Queen's club. Most importantly, neither the boys or their parents seem worried that they will be at a disadvantage on the games pitch when they move on. On a daily basis, table tennis is played in the garden with a staggering number of boys whizzing round the table at any one time, and logically they are bound to turn out a champion at some point.

Homework clubs take place every day with some of the choices being languages, judo, art and fencing, but Airfix was definitely the favoured option of both one very enthusiastic boy and the head. There is no impression that this is a 'strict' school but the boys jump to their feet when the head walks into a class with a crisp 'Morning, Sir' and shake your hand, looking you straight in the eye. One parent, on being asked how they dealt with the inevitable small boy playing up, said that whilst discipline was not obvious, there were 'no hiding places; it's a tiny school in a tiny place'. When asked, the head told us that this was an advantage as every member of staff knew every child, which meant you could spot trouble and deal with it even before the boy was aware of it himself.

Lots of expeditions and a school skiing trip every year. On asking one boy whether he had learnt the history of Canterbury Cathedral at school before the impending visit, he replied 'Well, it would be silly if we hadn't,' then 'St Thomas a Becket' accompanied by an excellent 'being stabbed' routine.

The SENCo is a form teacher who co-ordinates any help needed and specialists are called in from outside when parents and teachers have planned a course of action, one parent confirming that they 'get it' when you have a child who might have social problems.

The fees are low by London prep school standards, partly because of the no frills approach – boys bring their own packed lunches – and partly because they have not invested in a shiny new look. Current parents seem very laid back about this, feeling that the whole nature of the school might change if it presented a more polished exterior, a sentiment echoed by the head's wish to keep this as a 'discreet school that speaks for itself'. A bursary fund can accommodate discounts up to 100 per cent of the fees, with an independent financial auditor assessing all applications.

At somewhere both as small and individual as this it could be easy to overestimate the importance of the teaching staff, but St Philip would be proud of this lot and the boys they turn out – shiny haloes all round.

S

St Saviour's CofE Primary School

Shirland Road, Maida Vale, London W9 2JD

Ages 3–11 Pupils 240 C of E

020 7641 6414
www.stsavioursprimary.co.uk

Headteacher: Since 1994, Lindsey Woodford, BA in education from London University. A warm, humorous, approachable woman with none of the lofty airs that waft around some heads. 'She's fun and she's ballsy, but she's strict. It's a winning combination.' Happy to muck in, she even joined a team of parents in a sponsored swim to raise £12k to Astroturf the playground. 'I don't know many other headteachers who'd don a wetsuit and swim 3.5km in the Thames. She's pretty game.' Her office, far from being a scary place, is crammed with 100-200 soft toys which have colonised every available surface. She is ably assisted by Ripley, her border terrier, who is adored by the children. Pupils who have done well (or are perhaps just feeling a bit glum) are occasionally awarded Ripley Time, which means being allowed to sit in her office for a supervised stroking session.

In her spare time Ms Woodford enjoys embroidery, crime novels, antiques and baking. We can vouch for her excellent homemade biscuits (gooey peanut butter flavour the day we visited). Very much hands on – small children approach her for a hug as we walk through the playground (and you can't fake that). Previously deputy head at St Michael's in Highgate, following stints at schools in Bucks, Brent, Haringey and Ealing, so oodles of experience. A local girl, she was born at nearby St Mary's Hospital and attended Parliament Hill School in north London. She is married to the contractor who created the nursery in 2000. The ultimate accolade comes from a grateful mother. 'I'm proud of how my daughters have turned out and I feel they have been formed by Ms Woodford as much as they have by me. I owe her a lot.'

Entrance: Heavily oversubscribed one form entry school. Over 90 applicants for nursery and 140 for 30 reception places. Nursery is mornings only, though afternoons are available for a fee. No catchment area; pupils come from as far afield as Camden, Kentish Town, Kensal Rise and Harlesden. After the customary preference given to looked-after children, admission boils down to enthusiastic worship at one of two affiliated churches, St Saviour's and St Mary on Paddington Green. This means 'at least three Sundays every month for at least a year before application'. Prospective parents might want to reconsider that sneaky lie-in every fourth Sunday, as admission is uncompromisingly awarded to the 'most frequent worshippers'. And don't even think of slacking off once you've got your foot in the door as progress from nursery to reception depends on continued regular worship – a rule that is enforced. 'We hate to lose children but it does happen,' admits the head.

Admission for siblings languishes way down at no 8 on the list of criteria, though occasional places in later years are well worth applying for as later places are awarded 'on need'.

Exit: Pupils progress to a wide variety of schools. Favourite state schools include Greycoats, St Marylebone and Twyford High School, plus Paddington Academy, Holland Park and St George's. The head is also very open to the independent sector ('We love a good badge') with pupils winning places at Highgate,

St Paul's Girls', Latymer Upper, City of London, UCS, Merchant Taylors', Channing plus boarding schools like Christ's Hospital and Wycombe Abbey. It's enough to turn an expensive prep school head green with envy.

'For the last two years we've got a child into St Paul's Juniors at 11 plus. We're very proud of that.'

Secondary transfer meeting in September where both state and independent school admissions are explained and various bursaries and scholarship options discussed. 'It's never too early to come and talk to me.' Parents who are considering the independent sector are given advice from year 2 onwards, plus suggestions for specific tutors. Ms Woodford is brutally honest about a child's chances of success. 'I don't mind where children go on to as long as it's the right school for that child'.

Remarks: Nestling in a quiet side street amongst the tall wedding cake mansions of Maida Vale, this Ofsted outstanding state primary has won more awards than you can shake a stick at. But, despite the wealthy area, this is no middle class ghetto school.

'It's truly comprehensive,' said one parent. 'You've got people who live in million pound houses and families who live in local authority housing by the canal. Everybody just gets on with it and befriends each other.'

Broad international mix with 35 languages spoken (the largest groups being white British, followed by Eritrean and other African). A tranche of bankers, diplomats and media types alongside a large number of low income families just above the free meals threshold. Twenty-four children on free school meals (approx 10 per cent) when we visited, though the number waxes and wanes. Winner of Mayor's Gold Club Award for succeeding against the odds in improving pupils' achievements. 'It doesn't matter to us that we get a badge for it, what matters is our free school meal pupils do at least as well, if not better, than other pupils. We buck the trend,' says the head.

The socially and culturally diverse mix makes the school's outstanding results all the more impressive. Over 60 per cent of pupils regularly achieve level 5 in Sats, and they are top of the Westminster league table for pupils achieving level 6 (expected level for 14 year olds). 'They really encourage each child to discover something they can excel in, whether it's art, English, maths or anything else,' said one happy parent. 'It's not just about sitting exams, it's about becoming a well rounded, caring, bright little person who wants to learn.'

Our immediate first impressions were that St Saviour's is an exceptionally smiley school. We got eye contact and a friendly grin from pupils and adults alike as we waited in reception, and the smiles kept on coming throughout our tour. In an age when so many children look down and mumble when addressed by an adult, the confidence of these pupils shines out. Clearly, the social graces are given the same importance at this state primary as they are in the private sector.

Bog-standard Victorian school building, but preferable to the cramped conditions so often seen in converted premises used by some London independents. Here the classrooms are large and light-drenched with walls of vast windows. Trad architecture could feel forbidding in dark stairwells, but they've done their best to create a bright, cosy and well cared-for learning space. Walls covered in excellent artwork. Comfortable sofas, toys and a multi-sensory room in the early years section. Pupil loos are clean and colourful (no smells) and only one wet tissue apologetically stuck to the ceiling.

Separate junior and senior playgrounds. Outside space is limited, typical of most inner city primaries, but they've made the most of what could have been a rather dank concrete area. Good range of outdoor toys including space hoppers, a climbing wall and some rather grand-looking trees in pots. Small side garden growing potatoes, rhubarb and herbs and we even spotted the head's mum who had popped in to tend the plants. Truly a family-oriented school.

Setting starts in reception, with four groups per class. Some groups might have just two pupils, while others are much larger, depending on the needs of each individual year group. Teaching assistants work with higher ability as well as lower ability pupils. 'We focus on what each child needs.' Weekly Spanish lessons from reception onwards with a linguist Star of the Week award.

Regular pupil progress meetings to identify and keep track of underperforming pupils. Each child on the SEN register has a target sheet so progress can be tracked in lessons and support groups, and to ensure no child slips through the net. A qualified SEN specialist working part time is ably supported by battalions of TAs trained in many different types of strategies and interventions. Success of the school's support safety net self-evident in outstanding results for all pupils, regardless of background. 'I have a dyslexic daughter and they are very clever with their thinking,' said one mother. 'If you can't learn your times tables they'll come up with another way to teach them to you. They teach each individual child, rather than sticking to a formula.'

Provision in sports and the arts is a huge strength at St Saviour's. Thriving PTA holds monthly fundraisers to generate over £65k a year, most of which is used to fund three specialist teachers for art, music and sport. This means, in addition to the standard PE hour with class teachers, all pupils have a weekly session with a professional sports coach. There are also dance lessons with a West End choreographer, covering fun stuff like Bollywood, musicals and Strictly Come Dancing. Then there's swimming in year 4, cycle training in year 5 and the year 6 pupils do a course of horse riding lessons in Hyde Park. Opportunities to try tennis, golf, cricket and tag-rugby and to compete in teams against other schools.

Art is taken seriously here and is of a high standard. The PTA-funded artist in residence works with each year group on a project relating to subjects they are studying in class, for example year 3 pupils made a giant sarcophagus when they were studying the Egyptians. We saw excellent William Morris designs done by year 5 while studying the Victorians, screen prints of the Tudors by year 4, and some awesome studies of real fish done by gifted and talented pupils. Pupils identified as G&T in art are given additional opportunities to work on projects with visiting artists (such as designing the 3D climbing wall), plus there are regular drama and music workshops run by outside experts.

For working parents there's an (oversubscribed) wrap-around care scheme running up to 6pm and a two week summer holiday camp. All staff members (including the headteacher) are responsible for an extracurricular club running from 3.30-4.30pm. Pupils can choose from horticulture, ICT, arts and crafts, media, football, website, cooking, construction, choir and many other options. More innovatively, there's a coding club, and coding is also taught as part of the curriculum in years 3 and 4. 'Coding is a big buzz in education at the moment and we're right at the forefront of that,' says Ms Woodford.

What sets St Saviour's apart is the head's boundless enthusiasm and creativity. 'What we do here is we don't say no. We consider all ideas and are willing to try new things'. STEAMco was a concept some parents had seen at a festival. It's now an annual day when lessons are suspended and every corner of the school is given over to different creative activities such 3D printing, learning the ukulele, an apothecary's garden, dance, sculpture, making furniture out of newspaper, launching home-made rockets, cooking and much more. Pupils are free to browse at will – some try everything, others stick with one experience all day. Year 6 pupils built an electric goblin eco-car designed to spark an interest in engineering, which they subsequently raced at Goodwood. Then there's

Maths Week. Every class pitches a business idea to Ms Woodford and she decides whether to 'lend' them £20. The class must turn a profit and pay her back, plus one per cent interest, by the end of the week. Business pitches mostly involve making and selling various sweets and cakes but pupils have fun and grasp the idea of profit, loss and interest.

Pastoral provision is outstanding. Each child selects two staff 'listening partners' that they can talk to about any fears or worries. Some staff members are chosen by 20 children, others just a handful, but even the catering staff and site manager have their listenees. Then there is a Buddy System in which each year 6 pupil is paired up with a reception 'buddy'. The buddies read and play together, go on trips and can be invited to tea by the respective parents. There is a daytime 'sleepover' where pupils bring a pillow, toy and sleeping bag and lie in the art room reading stories to each other.

Few behavioural problems. A general policy of positive behavioural reinforcement, high expectations and aspiration seems to work well. Much ado is made of the Star of The Week system, with postcards sent home, a mention in the newsletter and announcements at school. Four houses (named after planets) and team points awarded for a variety of endeavours. 'The school is strict and that's what I love about it. They will not tolerate any bullying and they don't like cliques either. Pupils are encouraged to be friends with everyone, so nobody is left out,' said a satisfied parent.

St Vincent de Paul RC Primary School

Morpeth Terrace, London SW1P 1EP

Ages 3–11 **Pupils** 250 **RC**

020 7641 5990
www.svpcatholicprimary.org

Head: Since 2015, Nathaniel Scott-Cree BA (early 40s). Teaching degree from Roehampton Institute of Higher Education, followed by a masters in Catholic school leadership from St Mary's Twickenham. Originally from the Surrey/Sussex borders, his first job was at St Osmund's School in Barnes, followed by a complete contrast in locality – Brixton – where he taught for six years at Corpus Christi School. He says: 'It was a very well run school. Parents moved to put children in there.' He left to become deputy head at St Vincent's Primary School in Marylebone, where he stayed for the next six years before being offered this headship. He has always taught in Catholic schools, which he says is his 'personal preference', and is 'very committed to them.'

Mr Scott-Cree is young in terms of head teachers: 'not the youngest,' he says, but he clearly has a wise head on his youthful shoulders plus bucket-loads of dry wit. His straightforward, honest and no spin approach instantly endears him to us. It was his dad who initially suggested teaching to him as being a 'good option' and he also felt committed to doing a job which makes a difference: 'I wanted to help improve children's chances in life and I believe that to be through education.'

His commitment to the job is evident in the changes he's brought to the school: the new house system; tighter security (more about those later); changes to the syllabus; better communication between the school and parents – and he's even teaching himself Latin in order to teach it to his students. He says: 'When I started here I decided to continue with Latin and run with it. I now teach two lessons a week in Latin for years 4 and 5.' He is liked and respected by both pupils and parents, who tell us 'he's really blended in well with the school.'

Married to a deputy headteacher at another school, Mr-Scott-Cree has three children of his own, and although he wouldn't dissuade any of them from a path of education ('if they believe it to be their true vocation etc etc'), he would point out the difficulty of teaching nowadays and all the bureaucracy around it: 'I probably wouldn't cut the mustard if I was entering the profession now,' he says drily. We beg to differ. Any spare time he has he mostly enjoys 'doing nothing', he says jokingly, but other than that he enjoys reading, listening to music and watching a good film.

Entrance: Always oversubscribed. Nursery children are not guaranteed entry into the main school at 4+. Priority given to practising Roman Catholics, with distance from the school used as a tiebreaker. First priority goes to looked after Catholic children, then baptised, practising siblings, then baptised Catholics. A waiting list is kept for occasional places.

Exit: Most pupils get their first choice secondary school. For most girls it is Greycoats (if it's good enough for the former Prime Minister's daughter..); other popular choices for boys and girls include Sacred Heart, London Oratory, Cardinal Vaughan and St Thomas More as well as independents including Westminster Cathedral Choir School.

Remarks: School was founded in 1859 by the Sisters of Charity of St Vincent de Paul to enable them to work with the poor of Westminster. Moved to current premises in the shadows of Westminster Cathedral, conveniently next door to St Paul's bookshop, in 1974. For a young and impressionable soul eager to soak up all London has to offer, fewer locations could beat this school in the heart of London.

It is hardly surprising that pupils come from a wide variety of countries and backgrounds. Around three-quarters speak English as an additional language. Indeed most of the parents we spoke to, although fluent in English, spoke it as a second language. Many parents choose the school for its diversity, but mainly for its strong Catholic ethos. One parent told us: 'As Roman Catholics ourselves, this school has a great reputation locally for its strong ethos of upholding values, discipline and academia, but also being a loving and caring environment.'

This is a Catholic school foremost and whilst pupils are taught to understand other faiths and cultures (Judaism and Islam weeks etc) there is a strong Christian ethos to adhere to. The head says: 'The behaviour at SVP is outstanding, but it is naive to say that incidents don't happen from time to time. However we do instil in pupils to love one another as I love you.' Chaplain Father Brian leads assembly ever Wednesday, and there is a collective worship every morning. One parent told us: 'I have sat in assembly for one hour and nobody moves. They are so engrossed and well behaved.' Good behaviour, thinking of others and cooperation goes without saying.

Pupils are monitored regularly to assess their progress and there are plenty of parents' evenings, giving everyone the opportunity to discuss their children. Parents comment on how approachable the head is and that you can pop by his office without an appointment. Mr Scott-Cree has also introduced a small letterbox outside his office, where pupils can write down any concerns they may have either anonymously or as something they wish to share (and confessionals with Father Brian are also offered).

When we entered the school at the start of our tour, we were immediately stuck by the double-door entry and security systems put in place. Sadly quite pertinent in light of the recent

Westminster attack, which happened a week after our visit and only a few minutes away. The head says: 'At the end of the day, I'm responsible for these pupils if something goes wrong. Where we are located there are a few unsavoury characters around, and whilst I don't want the school to be a prison, I want it to be as safe as possible.' And one parent added: 'Before Mr Scott-Cree was head, you could just walk in, which is incredible really if you think about it. I feel so much happier now that it's more secure and I feel my child is safer.'

Fairly compact site – outdoor space has been redeveloped to create three separate play areas for nursery children, infants and juniors. Cleverly designed, with lots of greenery and modern play equipment. Plus who could tire of seeing the majestic gothic structure of the neighbouring Westminster Cathedral, which almost borders the playground? Pupils also use the playgrounds and local facilities for team sports and have a dedicated sports coach for all PE lessons. Inside, school is light, modern and well designed but has the very nostalgic feel of a primary school from yesteryear. Peaceful chapel is very much at the heart of this friendly and well-disciplined school.

Large, multi-purpose hall where children practise for termly concerts and plays and musical performances. School is part of the Westminster Cathedral Choir School outreach programme and the choir performs at Westminster Cathedral as well as singing regularly at family masses. Well-stocked music room with an impressive selection of instruments – from glockenspiels to bongo drums. All have singing and music lessons, provided by a dedicated music teacher. Pupils talk excitedly about how they are encouraged to create their own music. Small charge is made for individual lessons on a wide range of instruments. (No formal library, but that is up for discussion: 'it's a space issue.')

Alongside the national curriculum, pupils benefit from being taught Spanish from the age of 7 (a good chunk of Spanish speakers already at the school). Latin is introduced in year 4. Academic results are exceptional. Staff have high expectations and have created a good learning ethos. The SENCo coordinates additional needs and runs a Units of Sound online literacy development programme for dyslexics.

Polite, engaging and kind pupils were what we witnessed during our time at the school (lots of opening doors for us). It struck us how unspoilt many of these children were: 'I went to Wagamama for the first time,' said one excited 9 year old (as part of a food workshop which included a trip to the restaurant). Other trips have included London Zoo, Legoland and various museum outings. Years 5 and 6 do trips to forest schools and Sayers Croft outdoor centre.

Sports quite big on the agenda and the school has fared admirably (given its size and on-site facilities) at football, swimming and athletics, 'and we have even been to the Olympic Copper Box Arena', one proud pupil told us. Sports now all the more competitive since Mr Scott-Cree introduced the new house system named after saints: St Theresa, St Joseph, St Francis and St Bernadette. One parent said: 'The introduction of the house system has added a healthy competitiveness to the school. My daughter is now desperate to earn house points.'

Yearly nativity plays are performed actually in Westminster Cathedral, with full costumes and music. (We'd be hard pushed to imagine anything more spiritual.) There are two other occasions in the year when they join the parish of Westminster Cathedral for mass. We are told that some parents choose this school for this reason. Sixth formers from neighbouring Westminster School work as volunteers, acting as classroom assistants and helping to run school clubs. ICT room doubles up as a cinema for film club.

Not a place for those who wish to sit on their laurels. Energetic PTA meets regularly to discuss the organisation of numerous fundraising events for the school. Each family is asked to make a small annual contribution towards the maintenance and building fund – for the benefit of the present community and to ensure continuation for future generations. Pupils are active fundraisers and run regular charity events. The school also works with Mission Together, a charity that encourages children to care about mission through prayer, learning and fundraising.

School was downgraded by Ofsted in 2015 to 'requires improvement', but was upgraded again in 2016 to 'good'. The head says, 'The issues that had affected the school have been addressed and lots of support has been put in place to get it back on track.' However, he adds that the report was limited in its judgment to one particular area, which can have a big impact. However, parents praise the school to the rafters and pupils say they look forward to going to school. One parent added that 'SVP starts with the assumption that there's something great about you and let's work on that.'

Sarum Hall School

269

15 Eton Avenue, London NW3 3EL

Ages 3–11 **Pupils** 184 C of E

Fees: £14,025 – £15,180 pa

020 7794 2261
www.sarumhallschool.co.uk

Headmistress: Since 2008, Christine Smith BA Cert Ed RSH (SpLD) (50s). Previously at Lochinver Prep in Potter's Bar, where she is now governor. Originally taught home economics and textiles at Edmonton County School, which she left to bring up her two daughters. Subsequently returned to teach deaf children, later becoming director of studies at Lochinver and setting up their learning support unit. When her children left home, she wanted a new challenge and 'fell in love' with Sarum Hall the moment she visited. Believes she's known for being kind, fair, calm, trustworthy, experienced and well connected in the educational world and, on the whole, parents agree, adding that she's 'lovely', 'nice,' 'always smiling' and a 'great listener.' 'Whether it's staff, food or sports day, if you have something to suggest, she'll seriously consider it,' said one parent. Mostly office bound, although she does greet the girls, teaches SRE, and dines with them, daily, along with all the usual lesson observations, assemblies etc. Not a captain that socialises with her crew, we feel, although the head points out that she has an open door policy and provides a long list of ways she supports her staff including organising end of term meals out. Married to an actuary, with interests including tai chi, cooking, theatre and martial arts (she spent time in Beijing learning about swords).

Leaving in July 2019. Her successor will be Victoria Savage, currently deputy head at Newland House School. BMus (Edinburgh), PGDip (Royal College of Music), PGCE (Buckingham).

Entrance: Main intake in September after 3rd birthday. Parents are advised to register their child as soon after birth as possible (non-refundable fee of £100), visit the school on a working day two years before said child is due to start and then confirm their continued interest in writing. Non-selective, although priority given to siblings and children and grandchildren of former pupils (of whom there are many). The rest of the 23-24 nursery places are based on the head's decision. 'I meet with all parents and am looking for those who understand that the arts, and indeed play, are as important as academic learning for children's development,' she says, although presumably that's all of them, unless they failed to research the school before applying. It's all a bit vague for our liking; we feel that fitting in probably plays a vital part.

Exit: Almost all to their first choice of school at 11: Channing, City Girls, Francis Holland, Godolphin & Latymer, Highgate, Immanuel, North London Collegiate, South Hampstead, St Helen's and St Paul's. Unusually for a north London prep, a fair number go on to board too, at the likes of Cheltenham, Queenswood and Wycombe Abbey. Recommendations as to the next school very much the head's own, for which she uses her 'first-hand knowledge of the girls, together with the teachers' recommendations, results, tracking data, and my knowledge of the families, which the teachers are not always privy to.'

Remarks: Nestling among the opulent period homes of this leafy north London street is a contemporary, RIBA-lauded, purpose-built building, with no fewer than three secured doors to get inside the learning environment ('Safeguarding means a lot to our girls' parents'). Inside the building, which was completed in 1995 (although the school itself dates back to 1928), the combination of high design standards, light oak floors, high ceilings, masses of natural light and (recently) air conditioning makes for a welcoming, airy space in which to work, move about and play. White walls are tastefully decorated with displays of the girls' work from across the curriculum but it's the pink (there's lots of it) that really sets the mood of the school, which parents repeatedly refer to as turning out 'very well-mannered young ladies.'

New national curriculum forms the cornerstone of learning, but without the dreaded Sats and with embellishment of other subjects, including French from reception, Mandarin in years 4 and 5 and Spanish for one term in year 6. Specialist subject teaching in music, IT and French from nursery, science from year 3, English, maths and humanities in years 5 and 6. Some setting in maths. Big emphasis on cross-curricular teaching, with girls preparing for a performance of Frozen when we visited, having made the characters (art), in preparation to perform the play (drama) in French (languages). Great attention to tailored learning, with plenty of classroom assistance and additional work, for instance, for those sitting boarding school entrance exams. Great preparation for 11+, according to parents.

Music, art and drama all thriving, with pleasant learning spaces. Majority of girls study one or more instruments after year 2, with plenty of opportunity to perform in assemblies, recital evenings and frequent concerts. Junior and senior choirs, open to everyone. 'My daughter does 8 music-related things a week including choir, music theory, music lessons and two instruments,' lauds one parent.

Drama performances generally involve double year groups, and English Speaking Board exams (and LAMDA if requested) are available to build up communication skills. Fabulous high-ceilinged studio art room, with girls studying sculpture, textiles, woodwork and more. New food studio where all pupils learn to cook healthy meals. Plenty of outings to exhibitions, including the Royal Academy, with which the school has close links.

IT suite organised in round tables. Well-equipped science lab, with a teacher having introduced sustainability in a big way to the school. Sunlit, well-stocked and welcoming library, with visits from authors, such as Helen Peters and James Mayhew. Nursery and reception areas nurturing, including an (again pink) indoor wigwam and freeflow outdoor space on the balcony, with two stylish 'SH' embossed canopies to keep the sun off young skin. Plenty of mingling with older girls, thanks to buddying and monitor opportunities, along with a shared play time once every half term.

Outdoor space had been recently refurbished when we visited. It's not big, but is exceptionally well-planned, with a new two-storey playhouse and colourful beach-huts, where you can do anything from arts and crafts to borrowing sports equipment. Surrounding this and the adjacent sports court are wormeries, raised beds and an environmental pond, allowing children grow vegetables and herbs and do gardening club, all of which have helped the school achieve Green Flag status. Pupil voice much improved in recent years. Big on charitable fundraising.

Daily sport (netball, hockey, rounders, soccer, cricket and tennis) takes place on the court or in the assembly hall, which doubles as a gym for both dance and gymnastics, and triples as a theatre. Swimming once more part of the curriculum, at nearby Swiss Cottage Baths from year 4. Cross-country at Primrose Hill. Annual sports day becoming more competitive, after parents complained it was too gentle.

Breakfast club from 7.30am, and homework club until 4.30pm, included at no extra cost. Over 40 after-school clubs (photography, chess and draughts, yoga, board games among them), also included in the fees, unless outside staff need to be brought in. Outings to London museums and galleries. Residential trips to Norfolk for year 5 and a château in France for year 6.

The girls themselves 'aren't the most savvy and streetwise,' as one parent put it – but they seem to like it that way. 'It can make the transition to senior school a bigger deal, but having nice, polite girls is a good trade-off,' said one. Behavioural problems minimal.

Great food (all clean plates when we visited and we cleared our own too) prepared daily on site and served on long tables with pastel spotty tablecloths, where staff eat with girls (after grace has been said).

Parents and pupils reasonably multicultural, but mainly affluent, white, middle-class. Plenty of bankers, lawyers and barristers. Many girls have brothers at The Hall or Arnold House (and head tries to coordinate term dates). Bursary fund, which is means-tested. One girl on it when we visited, with another about to join. Many of the governors have a connection to the school and have been there for many years, with (unusually) no set system of election or removal.

Learning support unit has one dedicated member of staff (trained to RSA level 7) who comes in four days a week. Copes with mild dyslexia, dyspraxia (five children in total when we visited) and the 'gifted and talented' at no extra cost. Support is mainly in the large dedicated room, but some classroom assistance too. Two deaf children when we visited ('The school has been incredible with meeting her additional needs and going the extra mile,' said the parent of one) and one child with a visual impairment had just been offered a place. But while school is well laid out for wheelchair access, no child who uses one has ever attended. Won't take children with serious behavioural difficulties, although never had to turn anyone away or asked a child to leave. Outside help brought in for speech and language when required. School nurse recently brought in, who doubles up as school counsellor. 'Both my kids were flagged as needing extra help,' said one parent. 'The school kept me informed, we had meetings and they made innovative suggestions, all of which has meant the children are now on the right path. I can't fault it.'

This is a small, intimate, highly structured and extremely traditional girls' prep in a stunning modern setting that gets children of a broad range of ability to reach their full potential, without too much pressure. Its emphasis on the arts and play, alongside academic learning, means it's not for the tiger parent and its preciousness, emphasis on authority and very high expectations around manners means it's probably not for the non-conformist child either.

Servite RC Primary School

252 Fulham Road, London SW10 9NA

Ages 3–11 **Pupils** 240 RC

020 7352 2588
www.serviteprimaryschool.co.uk

Executive head teacher: Since 2002, Kathleen Williams BEd NPQH (40s). Has spent all her teaching career in borough of Kensington and Chelsea. Previously deputy head of St Mary's Primary, Ladbroke Grove. Married with a young child, who (she hopes) will soon be a pupil here. 'I couldn't think of my son going anywhere else. I want him to have the grounded education which Servite provides,' she says. Loves theatre, opera and all things musical. Friendly, capable and calm; an experienced pair of hands. Servite works in partnership with less serene local schools, to help raise standards and strengthen leadership. Head is ably supported by associate head teacher, Claude Gauci, who takes over the reins when she is out nurturing other schools. They make a robust team. Head admits that teaching is a demanding profession, but 'we're lucky. It's a privilege to be part of this happy school.'

Entrance: At 3 to nursery but a separate application is required for entry into reception. If they don't meet the strict criteria, then nursery children don't make it through to reception. Oversubscribed: approximately 60-80 apply for 30 places in nursery and 170-200 vie for 30 places in reception. Ever-decreasing catchment area (currently about half a mile). Pupils come predominantly from World's End estate and Earls Court. Priority given to baptised, practising Catholics who worship next door at Our Lady of Dolours. Occasional places further up school, though pretty rare due to low pupil mobility. V few non-Catholics. School currently at full capacity with 30 pupils per class.

Exit: Not a feeder for one particular school. Vast majority go to local Catholic state schools, including Cardinal Vaughan, Sacred Heart, St Thomas More and London Oratory, as well as a handful each year to Chelsea Academy. One or two go down the independent path, usually to Queen's Gate on bursaries. No special preparation given for 11+ and school seems to have escaped fanatical tutoring which goes on elsewhere in final years. A breath of fresh air.

Remarks: This successful school is tucked away behind an unprepossessing façade on the Fulham Road, opposite Chelsea and Westminster Hospital. Surprisingly spacious once inside with large, light classrooms and three playgrounds for different year groups (the one for the smallest children particularly colourful and welcoming). Impressively large hall which transforms into a dining room, gym and theatre and boasts sophisticated lighting and sound equipment.

Head believes Servite offers a broad education, which encourages self-confidence and independence. Children are well prepared for life at secondary school by the time they leave. 'Servite gave my daughter the firm foundations on which to build,' said one grateful parent. Parents value the close association with the church that backs onto the playground. Pupils visit on holy days and every week one class celebrates mass there. Only three school rules – follow instructions; use kind and helpful words; keep hands, feet and objects to yourself. Pupils seemed to be adhering to these when we visited, though last rule appeared hardest to uphold.

Significant proportion of male teachers now. Staff consists of dedicated long-servers whose average age is 40. Appear devoted to the school and appreciate its family feel. 'They go the extra mile,' says head, 'and attend events at weekends such as school family mass with parents. No matter where the teachers live, they come to these events and the parents really appreciate it.' New teachers aren't taken on if they won't make a strong commitment to the school, beyond the classroom basics. Palpably strong relationships between teachers, parents and pupils. 'We have an open-door policy,' says head, 'but within a structure. Not mayhem! Boundaries are set in a respectful way and issues are dealt with quickly.' One parent said, 'The school is professional but understanding'. Problems tend not to fester for too long.

Academic standard has been raised and school now boasts impressive results. Able children are extended through creative writing groups and extra maths support. Some bright sparks achieve high levels in maths. Links fostered with Imperial College and Royal Institution to extend knowledge and develop scientific understanding. Spanish, music, dance and art taught by specialist teachers. Daily homework from the beginning. Project work given to older children to encourage effective time management and independent learning. School has pupils with a range of special needs, including autism, cerebral palsy and moderate specific learning difficulties. Behaviour support, learning support and pupil referral units offer considerable help to those in need. Currently five children with EHC plans.

School reflects the international, mixed community in which it finds itself. Head comments that many pupils come from 'poor, working families, where parents are often in domestic service.' Many families struggling but tend not to be on benefits. One in five pupils is entitled to free school meals. Roughly 60 per cent has English as a second language. Many pupils hail from Philippines, South America, East Africa and Western Europe. Main languages spoken at home are Spanish and Tagalog. Extra language support catered for through small targeted group work and some one-to-one support on offer. Parents happy with speedy progress made by those with limited English on arrival. 'Now you wouldn't know which ones were behind with English when they started,' commented one.

Fantastic, flexible wrap-around care on offer but school admits it's hard to sustain at a competitive price. Includes breakfast at start of day as well as tea, activities and opportunities to do homework at the end of the day. Children can be looked after from 8am-6pm. Parents aware they are lucky and are the envy of other schools nearby which don't have extended care on-site.

Impressive range of sport that is offered as taster sessions. Netball, football, athletics and swimming taught either on site, in Battersea Park or Chelsea baths. Dance and gym compulsory. A wide assortment of clubs including taekwondo, yoga, zumba and street dance. Football, drama and cooking currently very popular. Parents pay for these. Good use made of the local community and has strong links with neighbouring Chelsea Football Club. School participates in Educate through Sport initiative and an English reading programme offered by the club. Paul Canoville, first black player for Chelsea, regularly visits the school as part of its programme to promote positive attitudes towards racial diversity.

Excellent use made of its central London location. 'You name it, we've been there!' says associate head. From designing apparatus for Cirque du Soleil acrobats to jump over in the Albert Hall to PGL visits to Weymouth, the pupils have fun here. Parents pay for school trips, but school helps those who are genuinely struggling to meet the cost. School payment plan in operation and parents encouraged to save for trips on a weekly basis.

Impressive art, drama and music. Annual art show to which parents are invited. Fantastic, carved Viking longboats on display and amusing portraits done by pupils of the staff line the stairs. Christmas nativity put on by youngest children and year 5 performs The Passion at Easter. Two nights in July are devoted to a musical production, generally led by year 6 leavers, and about which parents rave. Years 1-6 learn a class instrument, including ocarina, violin and ukulele. Currently 75 taking one-to-one lessons in piano, violin or guitar.

Effective communication between school and parents via weekly newsletter. Parent council discusses initiatives such as school meals and uniform. Money raised by PTA tends to be spent on travel expenses for school trips, restocking library and equipment for playground.

School lives by its motto: 'Learning to love and loving to learn.' Family feel to the place. Children skip in each morning, excited about the day ahead. On the day we visited, ambulance sirens blared incessantly on the road outside while the children danced around merrily in the playground, totally oblivious to the noise and fumes engulfing them.

Above all, a welcoming school. No wonder head won't be considering anywhere else for her son.

Seven Kings School

Ley Street, Ilford, Essex IG2 7BT

Ages 4–18 **Pupils** 1,783 (360 in the primary school) **Sixth form** 523

020 8554 8935
www.sevenkings.school

Head: Since 2017, Jane Waters, previously head of secondary. She joined the school in 2007.

Kate Beaumont is head of the primary school, which opened in 2015.

Academic matters: If achieving top grades is your priority for your kids, then you have very little to fret about at Seven Kings. Despite its 'very average' intake, Seven Kings seems to sail effortlessly to the top of the league tables. Eighty-two per cent of GCSE candidates in 2018 achieved 9-4 in both English and maths; 37 per cent of grades were 9-7. The hugely oversubscribed sixth form produced respectable results – 47 per cent A*/B grades and 18 per cent A*/A.

S

This is a school that starts with outcomes required, then finds the best means to achieving them. 'This is no exam factory, but we do know the syllabus and the exam requirements, and we also know the kind of teaching that works.' Pupils concur that the teaching is both vibrant and innovative, with faces in classrooms looking hungry to learn when we visited. 'Teachers here bring subjects alive,' one pupil told us. 'There's constant encouragement to probe the teachers because they want everyone to grasp the subject really well,' said another, who added that even if you email a teacher at 8pm, you often get a reply. High expectations for teachers, who are expected to enthuse children at every opportunity (they must engage with at least six students when on 20 minute break duty, for instance). 'Someone once said, "You just do what it says on the tin when it comes to teaching," and it's one of the best complements we've had.'

Monitoring, tracking and a 'can-do' culture also contribute to academic success. 'You won't find a pupil we haven't spoken to in the past three weeks about their learning'; every student receives two formal one-to-one interviews about their academic progress per year, in addition to many more informal ones. Pupils praise the marking system that means they've given comments, rather than grades. 'Understanding what you've done well and what you can do to improve is more helpful than just a mark,' explained one. Also popular is the 'passport' that all kids in KS3 get. 'The children get visas to add in for good work, eventually being made a "scholar"'; school encourages a strong triangular relationship between students, teachers and parents to ensure that everyone is on board with learning outcomes in a well-communicated way.

English, maths and science by far the strongest subjects, with learning for science very practical (one of the labs is university-level), meaning that bangs and smells are part of the fabric of school life, with around 50 experiments going on a day. 'Students rave about science here'; school is a recognised centre of excellence in this subject, with some staff sitting on the boards of top science organisations.

Three languages on offer – French, Spanish and Mandarin – with well over two-thirds of the students studying at least one language at GCSE. Setting only in maths 'because all the evidence shows that setting doesn't work and puts a ceiling on young people's achievement,' says the head of secondary school. 'Research on boys in second sets, for example, shows that they are much more likely to move to the third set than the first set.' Plenty of academic after-school clubs, as well as after-hours opportunities providing support with homework and coursework. Plus other clubs for sport, arts, dance, radio, Amnesty International, Model UN, chess, model airplanes, astronomy, film and more.

Eighty per cent stay onto sixth form, where students get to choose from 22 A levels, of which science and maths are the most popular. One pupil, who moved from another school into the sixth form, told us, 'Teachers here give you a step-by-step guide to research, writing essays and getting through exams, whereas at my previous school, you're just expected to get on with it yourself.'

Seven Kings has a national reputation as a centre of excellence for disabled children. There is a specially adapted entrance and well-equipped medical centre, plus the classrooms are accessible by wheelchair. 'We are unbelievably inclusive, which brings such a richness to the school.' In addition, there's a well-staffed highly-skilled SEN department (23 per cent SEN when we visited, with 54 with EHC plans), providing exemplary provision. 'If we can get it right with vulnerable children, we can get it right with all of them'; they cater for the usual range of special educational needs.

Games, options, the arts: Two hours a week of PE, with very few complaints from pupils. Football, cricket, netball, rugby, long-distance running and athletics all core to the curriculum, with notable successes in cricket, football and long-distance running. Judo and fencing recently added to the growing list of sports. Facilities include an Astroturf pitch, front field, sports hall and gym, along with table tennis tables dotted throughout the outside areas.

Music highly valued, with spacious and well-equipped practice areas. Years 7 and 8 are on a scheme whereby the whole class learns a particular instrument together, with past examples including recorder, clarinet and trumpet. There's a school orchestra, jazz band, ensembles (including strings), as well as student led bands. Staff are employed to teach guitar and drums, as well as 35 lessons a week with peripatetic music teachers.

Plenty on offer for aspiring performers, including an extra period for drama in year 7 and 8 and all students in year 8 expected to take part in story telling to parents. 'We think it's is a great way of developing confidence and oral skills.'

KS4s put on an annual community play, focusing on issues relevant to them, with examples including the riots and refugees. Meanwhile KS3s perform monologues, as well as group productions. West End theatre groups regularly invited into school to do workshops, with students also being invited on trips to theatre performances, and there are whole school performances annually too.

School day trips to museums and galleries, as well as residentials to the likes of Berlin (history), Barcelona (art and culture), Vesuvius (geography) and Japan (science).

Background and atmosphere: The school started life as girls' grammar in the 1930s, and some remaining original features give a feel of the inter-war years, with an expansive spread of low rise brick buildings and a Betjemanesque assembly hall ideal for listening to the clock ticking away the exam minutes. Modern additions include the lecture theatre, glass entrance hall and shiny new science labs. Stand-out facilities include the spacious and well-used library; the DT facilities with impressive window displays of students' work; the well-resourced sixth form private study areas; and the sixth form common room, a great space with youthful wall art. Lots of colourful displays of students' work throughout the school, including huge canvases of artistic portraits. Inside the tall-windowed classrooms, the focus is on learning.

This is a place where the school motto is more than some inaccessible Latin phrase that nobody can pronounce. '"Friendship, excellence, opportunity" are what we're all about on every level,' says the school, with pupils and parents agreeing wholeheartedly. Mutual respect is also more than a hollow phrase, with students allowed in their classroom at all times, including break ('it's their school, so their classroom') and students overwhelmingly report that they feel valued by teachers. 'The head thanked the parents for giving them such great students at a recent event – and that pretty much sums up the attitude towards the kids here,' one parent told us.

You'll find no shortage of leadership opportunities and student voice, with a vast array of headship roles for students, as well as plenty of pupil involvement in everything from designing the new primary school and its uniform to observing and feeding back on lessons and providing ideas to improve learning. You'll even find students on the school gate to monitor lateness 'because there's nothing like having to explain to your peers why you're not on time,' says the head of secondary. Peer mentoring also popular. We found the older students confident and articulate, although the school says a lot of work goes into achieving that. 'Many come in quite passive and quiet, but our mantra is that a quiet student isn't a good learner,' says the deputy head. Innovative courses and workshops help, including a day of circus skills in year 7 (which takes pupils out of their comfort zone and reminds them that if you put your mind to it, you can often do things you never thought you could) and a teambuilding day in year 12. Staff get similar treatment. 'For example, we got new staff to do The Big Paint, which reminds them about how it feels doing something new – like the kids have to every day – and helps develop empathy,' explains the head of secondary.

Pastoral care, well-being and discipline: Seven Kings serves a neighbourhood that has social problems and deprivation typical of many parts of urban London. But despite its relatively stark surrounding streets – and the fact that many students come from difficult backgrounds – the school itself is an oasis of purposeful calm. Discipline is assumed, corridors are quiet, classes orderly. That's not to say there's no bad behaviour. 'We have 1,500 hormonal kids. Of course we have discipline problems.' Most are nipped in the bud, though, thanks to clear expectations and sanctions (mostly detentions), with exclusions kept to a minimum. 'What helps the most is that we can get it right with each child because we know them on an individual basis,' says the head of secondary school. 'For example, this week, a boy was misbehaving and when we looked into the cause, it turned out he didn't feel he was achieving success in class. Once we dealt with that, the problem stopped,' she says. The point is, she continues, that children often don't have the skills to navigate their way through what is a very complex world to grow up in 'and we never forget that when we're dealing with these young people.'

No wonder pastoral care and well-being are high on the agenda of every member of staff at this school, with particular attention from form tutors, year leaders, staff mentors and the full-time student counsellor. The school also buys in counselling support from outside agency Here and Now as and when required, as well as offering yoga and meditation sessions and occasional 'drop down days,' when the timetable is collapsed to focus on issues such as how to revise and stress management. 'In year 10, my daughter suffered from clinical depression. Her grades dropped and she didn't want to be in school. But the school pulled out all the stops to help her and she's now thriving at LSE,' one parent told us.

Bullying happens, but is rare. 'I experienced it in year 7,' one student told us, 'but the teachers took it really seriously and managed to stop it.' Pupils value diversity here – ethnically and in terms of disability, among other things – which students say helps in promoting a culture that values difference. No-one from years 7-11 let off-site at breaks or lunchtimes. Lots of talks around drugs, drinking and smoking, sex, eating disorders and cyberbullying.

Pupils and parents: This is a neighbourhood comprehensive, with students mainly living within a one-mile radius (some years, it's just half a mile) and coming from around 40 feeder schools (although most come from just four of these). More than three-quarters come from Indian, Pakistani or Bangladeshi backgrounds and 19 per cent are on free school meals. In the main, parents are very involved in their children's education – something that is very much encouraged, with curriculum evenings, a 'test the temperature' evening (parents' evening early in the term), as well as breakfasts with the senior leadership team. Parents even get the opportunity to be taught a lesson to see how it feels, followed by help from staff in how best to support their child's learning ('for example, we encourage parents to say, "Tell me something about your day" rather than just "How was your day?" which is a closed question,' explains the head of secondary school). 'By the Christmas holidays in year 7, parents really know what we're all about.' Parents aren't, however, a cake-baking, raffle-holding crowd and, to the disappointment of some parents we spoke to, there is no PTA. The kids themselves work hard and, and on the whole, behave well. 'They are bright and ambitious and absolutely gorgeous.'

Entrance: Over 2,000 local candidates apply for the 180 year 7 places, with a waiting list well into the hundreds. As it's completely non-selective, children in the looked after system/ those with a statement/EHC plan are prioritised (following the admissions code), followed by siblings, after which it's down to distance. Around 80 per cent go through to the sixth form, with around 2,000 applying for the remaining 140 places. Successful applicants need six 4s or above at GCSE, with 6s in their chosen A level subjects (7 for science and maths).

The Seven Kings Primary School opened in 2015 with 120 reception children. The impressive looking new-build forms part of the new all-through school which will grow by 120 places a year.

Exit: Out of 180 students, some 60 per cent go on to sixth form. The rest leave after GCSEs, mostly to do vocational qualifications, other courses, apprenticeships or go straight into jobs. Of those who leave after sixth form, 95 per cent go to university – about a third of those to Russell Group, including York, Birmingham, Leeds, Nottingham, Bristol, Bath, Cardiff. LSE, Imperial and Kings. Around half choose science degrees, with three medical students in 2018, plus one to Oxbridge. The rest go to other good universities ('Some choose not to go to a Russell Group') or destinations such as internships in the City. The remaining five per cent who don't go to university either take a gap year or go into apprenticeships (one had just gone into Louis Vuitton when we visited), art college or straight into the jobs including in the City.

No shortage of help with UCAS applications, and careers advice is embedded into the curriculum from year 7, with lots of work experience and enrichment. 'Opportunities that look good on your CV or university application aren't just encouraged – they are really promoted,' said one student

Remarks: This is a school with high aspirations, and the academic rigour can be tough because of the pursuit of excellence. But the results prove it's achievable, with a wide range of strategies ensuring that every student is pushed to reach their full potential. But there's fun to be had here too, with students clearly enjoying school life. Particularly notable is how respected they feel by the teaching staff, which clearly contributes to the good behavioural record. Parents who send their offspring here can be confident they will reach or exceed expectations, as well as coming out well-rounded and ready for university and/or a decent career.

Sheen Mount Primary School

West Temple Sheen, London SW14 7RT

Ages 4–11 **Pupils** 559

020 8876 8394
www.sheenmount.richmond.sch.uk

Headteacher: Since 2009, Ian Hutchings BSc PGCE NPQH (40s), married with two daughters. A boy from Bournemouth, he studied geography at St Mary's, Twickenham followed up with a PGCE and then launched straight into the world of primary education, where he has happily remained. He is very much at his ease here, having arrived as deputy head and then landing the top job. Coming across as a serious and dedicated man, an outsider might find his sense of humour more apparent on paper than in conversation. However, although dry, it is certainly there and his knowledge of and confidence in the school comes across in spades, whatever the medium.

S

He works very closely with his deputy, Maria O'Brien, and although they face opposite directions in the small shared office, they are definitely heading along the same path when it comes to running the school. Their agreement on aims and implementation is obviously built on mutual trust, particularly necessary at the moment as IH is also helping out at a school in another borough. This is an unsurprising decision as his belief in state primary education is deep-seated and his energy is immediately noticeable. Computing is what makes his eyes light up and he manages to fit a teaching slot into his schedule, saying, 'I love to see the children working with IT .... I learn so much from them.'

Entrance: You may need to live within spitting distance of the school as the catchment area is tiny, normally less than 500m. There is now three form entry at reception but the demand is such that you probably need to live within walking distance of the school, although they do take in the odd Richmond refugee. The increased intake has not resulted in more room for new arrivals as the larger number of siblings take up the extra places. Places further up the school are as rare as hens' teeth and usually only occur when a family moves from the area.

Exit: Slightly fewer takers than previously for the independent secondary sector, now down from 60 per cent to 50 per cent, partly due to the usual villains of less cash and the ever rising bar of the top London public schools ('10 years ago most of our children could get into any school;). However it could also be down to IH's enthusiasm for the local state schools, Grey Court in Ham, Christ's in Richmond and, in particular, Richmond Park Academy, which has a new head and is 'definitely on the up' as well as being just down the road. IH does not allow his enthusiasm for the state sector to stop him from maintaining close contact with a very wide range of independents and children end up in schools all over London (up to 20 different destinations in any one year), but always with a contingent heading to Hampton, Ibstock and Kingston Grammar.

Remarks: Walking down the path, on a grey winter's day, past a slightly tatty banner advertising Activity Camps, our hearts immediately lifted on spying a customised pink scooter with an equally pink pony's head attached. This is a friendly, outwardly relaxed encampment in a tidy, prosperous-looking corner of west London, which also contains a shiny gastropub and an architecturally undistinguished church. Parents move here specifically because of the school and some have known wailing friends to move out when their children have failed to get a coveted place. The functional buildings, including a new separate reception block with its own fenced off space, sit comfortably on their generous corner site and there is plenty of room for letting off steam outside. The expansion two years ago, 'a brilliant piece of juggling, despite the building chaos,' according to one parent, has allowed for a more logical arrangement of year groups as well as a cheerful room, housing a full-time inclusion leader for those in need of extra help or simply a bit of TLC.

IH says that he 'inherited a very well run school with tried and tested methods' but there's been no complacency on his part, and the systems that he has introduced, in particular the Learning Book (of which more shortly), ensure that every child's progress is constantly monitored. From the word go when a child is accepted, visits, play sessions and trial days take place, followed by a huge amount of time and attention to detail spent in composing the three teception classes, a task that would make a cabinet reshuffle seem a piece of cake.

When we visited, a reception class of rabbits (the others are dormice or squirrels) were busily stuffing small, shiny objects into tennis balls and were only too happy to discuss their methodology whilst others were counting pencils, the concentration visible. The nature theme for classes ends at year 2, somewhat of a relief for the head – 'I don't think I could cope with 19 animals' – but the children keep in the same carefully constructed forms all the way up the school.

At the start of year 1 the Learning Book, in which they do all their written work apart from maths, provides the framework for progress and also ticks the green box, eliminating paper wastage. Explained by IH, who modestly said he'd nicked the idea, as being a way of easily keeping an eye not only on marked work but also on handwriting improvement and that bane of most small children's lives, 'tidiness'.

In every classroom all the way up the school the hands (and in one case a crutch) shot up for the chance to be chosen to present their book to the head. The waving crutch – 'careful you don't bash anyone' – and the small girl, bright red with excitement ('don't forget to breathe, you might explode') were dealt with by a real pro, who appears to walk the narrow line between commanding respect and showing humorous, detached affection with the ease of a tightrope artist. 'His lightness of touch is amazing,' was one parental quote. Parents talk about their children thriving beyond expectation due to the 'brilliant', teachers with children coming home bursting to tell their mothers that 'guess what, he's going to give us free extra help in lunch time' or 'maths is not really like a lesson, it's such fun'. Regular feedback like this makes it hardly surprising that the Sats scores are consistently above the borough and national average.

Sheen Mount doesn't just say that it is a fully inclusive school but practices what it preaches, judging by the beaming faces of the children with special needs, ranging from mild dyslexia to Down's Syndrome. 'All children are treated exactly the same,' said the mother of a SEN child and thoughtful touches like a special session at the Christmas grotto and extra swimming help provide real reassurance. The staff also practise their well-honed integrating skills on a number of, technically, EAL children who have spent the first part of their lives abroad, although it's often not too serious a problem as many have had their Ps and Qs polished by the English half of a dual nationality marriage.

A fairly new, dedicated head of PE has made a 'tremendous difference' and after-school clubs for football, goalkeeping and badminton are all popular, although they may not be quite as keen as the mums' football team who recently came back from a tournament clasping medals, one sporty mum describing it as a 'world cup winning moment'. Top of the pops in internal clubs at the moment are Coding, 'taken by me,' said a grinning IH, and choir, both of which require parents to be at the keyboard the moment the opportunity goes live to sign up. External providers stretch the options offering Mandarin, Technokids, dance and a Kids' Guide to Money and Finance, maybe useful when suggesting to your parent what to do with the money saved by sending you to Sheen Mount. No dedicated art room but school plays and masses of additional music (40 per cent of children learn an instrument or singing) provided by Richmond Music Trust.

Away from the classroom, happy faces in the dining room (sausages and mash top choice for both children and teachers) and a minimal number of packed lunches show that a major effort to up the standard of the food has paid off despite the additional problems of providing for a challenging number of allergies. Considerable thought is taken over much anticipated trips, outings and a year 3 sleepover – 'it was magical – are all pronounced a big hit by parents.

IH does also spend serious brain-time on communication, possibly as an excuse to indulge his love of IT. It has definitely paid off because there is a really clear website and a weekly newsletter which has won plaudits from several parents. They all agreed that he was both visible and easily approachable if you wanted to talk and that if you couldn't see him, Mrs O'Brien was always there to listen. It's busy two way traffic here because this is a very hands-on school as far as parents are concerned, finding lots of money for extras but also mucking in with everything from swimming coaching to building the Christmas grotto.

There could be an argument that it is relatively easy to run a state primary sitting on the edge of Richmond Park, where the parents take such an active interest and raise bundles of cash, but it would be unfair to take anything away from this shining example of a junior school, brimful of eager small faces soaking up their lessons.

Shrewsbury House School

107 Ditton Road, Surbiton, Surrey KT6 6RL

Ages 7–13 **Pupils** 330 **C of E**

Fees: £18,675 pa

020 8399 3066
www.shrewsburyhouse.net

Headmaster: Since 2010, Kevin Doble BA (law and political sciences), PGCE (40s). Educated at St John's College, Jo'burg and has a postgrad degree in management. Previously second master and acting head at Edge Grove prep and before that head of English at Newlands School and Vinehall prep. This is his first experience of a day school, although he likens it to 'a boarding school with no beds' because of the breadth of opportunities on offer.

Eloquent, witty, driven and evidently relishes the vitality of the school day. Boys treat him like a celebrity – 'he's amazing,' 'inspiring,' 'kind,' 'really funny,' 'a great listener' and 'the best storyteller' were among the accolades we heard; 'not at all stuck up like the last headmaster I had,' added one. And with no prompting, these boys reeled off at least one anecdote to back up each claim – one told us about his ghost stories that have them spellbound; another about his stimulating lessons (he teaches year 5 English). 'He has the well-being of every single boy at the heart of everything he does – that's his starting point, and everything else follows,' said one parent, with others calling him 'passionate,' 'dedicated' and – for one mother – 'a big pull for why we chose the school.' Referring to the pupils 'these little guys,' this is not a head you'll ever see give an answer of 'because we say so' – although pupils did tell us they'd like to see the school council have more meetings and more say overall.

At the gates morning and night and out on the touchline as often as possible. 'You don't have to attend the same drama performance on both evenings,' joked staff with him recently. When he can be lured inside, he directs operations from his large but homely office that's packed with books, art, sports memorabilia, and big, comfy leather sofas.

A guest umpire for school and county hockey, he lists his recreations as sport, drama, children's literature, opera, painting and drawing. Keen traveller, enjoys going out for meals and generally 'recharging' during weekends and holidays.

Entrance: At 7, there are 62 places available, with around four applications for each one. Currently receiving requests to register children at birth. Most come from pre-preps, including its own Shrewsbury House Pre-Prep and The Rowans Pre-Prep (now part of the Shrewsbury House Trust), Wimbledon Common Prep, Park Hill, Lion House School and The Merlin. Around 10 per cent (down from 25 per cent a few years ago) come from the state system. Used to be a very local school, but catchment area has doubled in recent years, with 70 per cent of pupils now bussed in from over five miles away – many from Putney and Fulham.

'We say to parents that if you think this is the sort of culture you'd like for your son, and we think he will be able to thrive here and access the curriculum and wider opportunities, then it's almost certainly the right school.' But you won't get away completely scot-free on the assessment front – while registration is on a first-come-first-served basis, all offers are conditional and dependent on a one-day test ('to check our culture really is right,' insists head) in the autumn before anticipated entry. Those who apply too late for a conditional place are put on the waiting list and may be moved onto the 'headmaster's list' (about eight places are kept back for this) for an assessment, but again it doesn't guarantee a place. The school should be your first choice (current school heads are consulted). Occasional places available higher up the school. Some bursaries available

Exit: Very few leave at 11; most stay until 13, when they progress to some 15 senior schools, including King's College School (Wimbledon), St Paul's, St John's (Leatherhead), Westminster, Hampton School, Epsom College, Wellington, Charterhouse, Tonbridge and The Royal Grammar School (Guildford). A few go to Eton and Harrow. Parents say the head is 'very knowledgeable' when he discusses future schools for their sons, starting in year 5. 'He knows each boy and each school incredibly well, so he makes finding the right school a breeze – it's impressive,' said one parent. 'He won't sell you a fake ticket – he will absolutely tell you which school is right, having done all the leg work himself,' confirmed another.

School tracks boys after they leave – 'we want to know exactly what happens to them, even where they go to university, and what they study, as well as what clubs and societies they join, as it tells us a huge amount about the notion of engagement,' says head.

Remarks: Located on a quiet road in an upmarket residential area of Surbiton, the school is one of the UK's oldest preps, having celebrated its 150th anniversary in 2015. Based around a Victorian house, but with additional purpose-built classrooms and impressive facilities all on a six-acre site (including a huge all-weather pitch and a further seven acres at Almshouse Lane), they've recently had the green light for a further £15m of building works to include new dining hall and performance centre, among other things.

It's all home to a first-class prep, where academic rigour is balanced by an equally strong offering in arts and sport. But parents must be as committed as their sons. 'It's not a drop-off-and-get-on-with-it kind of school – you're expected to be at all the matches, attend the events and talk to the school at length about the next school, as well as encouraging your son to take up every possible opportunity and work extremely hard,' one parent told us. Add to the academic and extensive extracurricular offering a packed sporting programme, rehearsals, performances, charity initiatives, competitions and trips and you'll get the picture – these are busy boys and devoted parents.

Intellectually, boys need to be above average to cope here, despite the school taking a range of abilities, say parents. Homework is 30 minutes to one hour plus per night, right from the beginning. But – surprisingly, perhaps – the boys take it all in their stride.

S

A broad-based, eclectic curriculum is delivered by a talented teaching team. We saw plenty of lively lessons in practice, albeit a few yawns too. A French lesson, taught by a native speaker, with boys vying for an opportunity to speak, is typical. Similarly, lots of fun and experiments in science. Some great subject-specific classrooms, including one of the best history rooms we've seen – a modern museum with the teacher's own collection of helmets and weapons secured to the wall. Library also impressive – welcoming and cosy, with over 6,000 books, and lots of magazines and newspapers on display. 'We love it,' our guide said, telling us all about the reading buddy scheme.

Average class size is around 16, with an eight-to-one pupil-teacher ratio overall, with classes getting smaller as boys move up the school and into sets (setting in English and maths from year 4, French from year 5). Streaming from year 6, with up to a third of boys showing the most aptitude studying the same syllabus but at a faster pace (and setting still in place for the remaining two-thirds). Scholarship streaming from year 7, which can include the additional language of ancient Greek. Everyone studies Latin from year 5.

Less than 10 per cent of boys have a learning difficulty, with classroom-based help the only provision on offer. 'If a boy needs help outside the classroom, this isn't the school for them as we don't want them to miss out on the broader curriculum,' says head.

The school has an outstanding local reputation for sport – for many parents, this is their deciding factor. Main sports are football, rugby, cricket and hockey, with other activities including basketball, tennis, shooting, rowing (for the senior boys) and chess. And while many of the boys participate at regional or national level, the school gives equal weight to 'not quite there yet,' with boys regularly changing teams during their time here. 'Everyone gets top-notch coaching – with friendships formed across every team,' said one parent. This, coupled with the huge pride the boys have in representing their school, undoubtedly gives them the edge – they have a 70 per cent win rate across the board.

Music another stand-out subject, with the majority of boys taking instrumental or singing lessons, and there are 25 different musical groups (many open to all), with jazz and brass band especially popular. As with sport, 'boys are encouraged to beat out eight bars on the drum even if they've only had three lessons,' said one parent. Meanwhile, an annual summer soirée gives the top performers a chance to shine. Light-filled art studio is a hub of creativity, as is DT, with both regularly used in a cross-curricular way rather than mere add-ons. Drama not as good as it could be, say parents, but with a performing arts centre in the pipeline, there is optimism. LAMDA on offer and all boys do English Speaking Board exams. All the extracurricular you could shake a stick at – including rifle-shooting, judo, fencing, model making (Spitfires) and Nerf wars and (most popular of all) cookery. Post-common entrance exams, boys also have a go at sewing, ironing and first aid.

Not exactly strict, but clear expectations around behaviour – pupils write the school's code of conduct. Kindness features at the top, which boys told us 'keeps bullying to a minimum' (and is dealt with 'that very day' when it does happen, say pupils). Manners noteworthy, with no boy getting away with slacking, slouching or scruffiness. Pastorally outstanding, say parents, with one boy telling us, 'I've lived in three different countries and this is the school I settled in quickest – by a long shot.' Diversity is celebrated, say pupils – 'we are like one big family, really.'

A high achieving, purposeful all-round school, which is more inclusive than a first glance might suggest. A prep, in the truest sense of the word, where boys thrive by being a big fish in a small pond. But it's not for the faint-hearted.

Sir John Cass Redcoat School

Stepney Way, London E1 0RH

Ages 11–19 **Pupils** 1,440 **Sixth form** 435 **C of E**

020 7790 6712
www.sjcr.net

Headteacher: Since 2016, Paul Woods BA PGCE (40s). Originally from Enniskillen in Northern Ireland, he studied French and politics at Kingston University and did his teacher training at the University of North London. Previously head of Bishop Stopford's C of E School in Enfield. Lives in North London, where he began his career as a French and Spanish teacher, moving up the ranks to deputy head, after which he moved to Barking 'because I wanted to work in a more challenging location.' Later moved into his first headship at Bishop Stopford where, in his first week, the school was told by Ofsted that it 'required improvement' and he set to work getting it up to a 'good' status two years (to the day) later.

Students say his office door is always open 'except for meetings,' which encourages an informal drop-in approach. 'And he's nearly always in the corridors at class changeover and break times, when any one of us can chat to him – and we really do,' said one. With his easy, gregarious, one-of-us manner, it's easy to believe. 'This is a social institution, so what would be the point in sitting in an ivory tower or diarising everything?' he asks, adding that most things students talk to him about take all of 30 seconds. 'Then the issue is off their mind and they can get on with their studies.' Parents, in the main, have little to do with him. 'There's always someone to help you as a parent at the school – it's just not usually the head,' commented one, although there are obvious exceptions.

Teaches French (to year 10 the year we visited), while back in his office he is clearly a man with a plan, listing a lot of exciting proposals for the school from ensuring closer links between the different levels of leadership to a greater focus on the whole child – all with an infectious enthusiasm. 'One of my plans is a cultural entitlement programme because I want to be able to say to every single student, "You can expect this number of theatre trips, this number of day trips and this number of clubs to join".'

Academic matters: Consistently near the top of the value-added tables and has three times been ranked the most improved school in the country. Most students come in with lower than average achievement, but in 2018, 69 per cent got 9-4 in both English and maths at GCSE, with 25 per cent A*-A/9-7 grades – good results in RE (all students take this), English, maths and science. Students come from over 50 primaries (most feeling like the cat that got the cream when they get a place), but many have difficult home lives. 'Our first focus is on behaviour, on creating a climate for learning. Then we engage them with exciting teaching.'

Indeed, Ofsted's latest report (outstanding), in November 2015, talks of 'high quality and energetic teaching' – something the students also rave about. 'You're never bored and teachers give their all to make sure you both keep up and that you're kept enthused – they have very high aspirations for us,' said one. Monitoring of student progress is meticulous, with school targeting those who need extra help in a range of ways, from one-to-one help to subject clinics for small groups. 'I'm a big fan of their marking system too – there's always such detailed feedback,' one parent told us.

Setting for maths, English, science and RE from year 7, but with plenty of scope to move up or down according to individual needs. As a specialist language college, it is perhaps surprising that students only study one language for the first three years (it used to be two) from a choice of French, Spanish and Bengali, continuing at least one to GCSE. That said, many take more, with a wide choice of languages in twilight classes (for parents as well as pupils) including in Arabic, Japanese, Korean, Mandarin, Italian and Turkish – and many pupils take a GCSE in their own native language in KS4. Many go on French or Spanish exchanges and there are many international links and partnerships which have involved students visiting Poland, Italy and the Czech Republic.

There are vocational as well as academic courses at KS4, for example in food tech and business studies. In fact, there's an impressive emphasis on business and enterprise here, including strong links with Canary Wharf and City firms, with some offering work placements, scholarships to cover university fees and jobs after graduation to talented students. Sixth form business studies students can have mentoring from business partners, visits and seminars, lectures and summer internships.

The large sixth form, with some 500 pupils, has its own centre, including a library, IT suite, common rooms and a popular café. But students say this can be a double-edged sword ('Great for sixth formers to essentially get their own school, but we rarely see them,' explained one student), so is something the head is addressing. A level subjects offered alongside a variety of vocational courses and GCSE retakes – with most popular and successful subjects including maths, science and English, with wide take-up for psychology, RE and sociology too. In 2018, 17 per cent A*/A, 50 per cent A*-B grades. Many students come in from elsewhere to join those moving up, and quite a few have relatively low qualifications. Some start with intermediate level courses then move up to higher levels en route to university.

Around 10 per cent of pupils have SEN and the school has a large learning support team dedicated to supporting them. Learning mentors and assistants work through teachers and directly with pupils, helping to track their progress and ensure they know what they need to do to improve – and there are regular extension and catch-up classes. 'They're really good on SEN – I couldn't fault it,' one parent told us. Gifted and talented students are also identified for extra support.

Teachers seem to be as keen to work here as young people are to study here, with large numbers of applications for most teaching posts. 'We are high profile and attract high quality applicants,' explains head, pointing out that he just recruited a new physics teacher, with a first class degree. 'It's unheard of in London,' he says, as if still incredulous at his find, adding that many past students come back to teach – 'something we're extremely proud of.'

Games, options, the arts: Among the most successful schools in Tower Hamlets when it comes to competitive sports – 'a tremendous achievement when you look at the limitations of the site,' says head – and we agree. Indeed, outside sports facilities consist of a less than a handful of courts that double up as the playground – and although there's an indoor swimming pool (everyone learns to swim by the end of their first term), it's pretty shoddy, as is the indoor fitness suite currently housed in a portacabin. Decent sports hall, however, while the likes of running and football take place at offsite at nearby Spider Park (which has tracks and Astroturf) and annual sports day is at Mile End Stadium. Table tennis, boxing and fencing are also on the agenda. 'They try to get you enthused about some kind of exercise, although it doesn't work for everyone,' one student told us, and parents agree.

Visual arts no great shakes, but drama is hugely popular (including at A level – a joy to see), with a particularly dedicated and popular head of department, who ensures GCSE students get access to at least four operas and/or musicals, which they use to reflect on their own work. Actors regularly perform at The Half Moon Theatre – and we were impressed how drama is used to address certain pastoral themes that come up in school, with students writing and performing plays on these subjects.

Lively (and noticeably experimental, when we visited) music department, with over 100 students in every year group having individual music lessons. The steel band has played at the Albert Hall, the Mansion House and for the Lord Mayor's Show, and have won various awards. There's also a gospel choir, orchestra and various string ensembles.

Clubs are mainly focused on sports, but there's also Equality Group ('which deals with everything from homophobia to sexism' – Ian McKellen having recently been invited to the school to talk on LGBT issues when we visited), Amnesty

International, Whitechapel Mission, plus charity club, debating club and Christian and Muslim unions, among others. Student-led clubs are disappointingly thin on the ground, but head plans to address this. Residentials have historically not taken place during term-time, but again this is set to change – with access to The Hampshire Cass Mountain Centre in Wales making whole year group residentials a possibility.

Background and atmosphere: Formed in 1964 by the governing body of Red Coat School (established in 1714 for boys born within Mile End Old Town) and the governors of the Sir John Cass Foundation (a charity set up in 1710 by Sir John Cass for poor children in the East End of London). The school is owned by the Foundation, one of London's oldest educational charities, and Founder's Day in St Botolph-without-Aldgate church is one of the highlights of the school year. Its present site dates from 1965 and has been refurbished over the years since to include up-to-date science labs and learning centres stocked with computers – as well as an attractive glass-fronted main building. Classrooms vary in both age and size and while most are light and airy, some were exceptionally hot on the summer's day we visited (to be fair, school is trying to secure aircon – 'it's all a matter of funding'). Although it's in the middle of the East End, the school boasts a deceptively rural-seeming setting with a city farm opposite, a park next door and the school church and its tranquil graveyard beyond.

The library is open before and after school and on Saturday mornings, with learning mentors around to help. 'Many students have no computer at home, nor quiet space in which to do homework.' The great hall with stage and balcony doubles as a lecture theatre and can accommodate large (although sadly not quite the whole school) assemblies. 'These are important for setting the behaviour tone for the school.' Uniform is traditional, including a blazer, and while sixth formers wear their own clothes, they are expected to dress smartly. Although this is a C of E school, around 90 per cent of students are Muslims and two multi-faith rooms (one male; one female) cater for both. Cashless cafeteria serves hot food, while cold food is served from a hatch on the playground; sixth formers have their own indoor café. 'Food is good here, although we're pleased the head is on the case about getting more variety,' one student told us.

An orderly atmosphere pervades, with a high level of attentiveness during lessons. But kids will be kids and, refreshingly, that's allowed too – apparent in the corridors between lessons, albeit with classical background music and a strict one-way system (and certain routes for certain year groups) encouraging an overall sense of calm.

Pastoral care, well-being and discipline: The emphasis on security is palpable, with tall black, alarmed fences surrounding the school and quite a rigmarole to go through when arriving as a visitor at reception, along with CCTV cameras throughout the school and staff checking on destinations of those wandering the corridors between lessons – all of which, say staff and students, discourage vandalism and help students feel protected. Equally noticeable (many visitors comment on it) is the mutual respect. 'First of all we make them feel secure and safe, then we start to cultivate respect for all,' explains head, who describes the school as 'strict but not punitive.' Students concur, saying many of them go through school without a detention (most are given for lateness or failure to hand in homework). Students praise the fact that they (and their parents) are each assigned a named adult, whom they can approach about any personal problems – 'and heads of year are very approachable too.' There's also one full-time qualified counsellor.

Head insists that 'the high standards and quality of teaching, along with the consistent approach by staff' are relevant pastorally too. 'It means everyone is focused on why they're here and is the reason I believe we have to do very little firefighting pastorally.' 'The children are happy here,' concludes one parent. 'They know what's expected of them and they get down to work.' A lively school council makes regular suggestions for change – all the usual issues, including getting more playground equipment.

By all accounts, very little racial tension and very few exclusions – with only one temporary (and no permanent) exclusions in the last three years. Drugs very rarely a problem; carrying weapons even less so – both prolific problems in the local area. 'We do very occasionally have some challenging behaviour, but it does not threaten the learning environment. We try hard not to exclude if we can possibly avoid it.'

Pupils and parents: About two-thirds of the students are Bangladeshi, the rest from a variety of ethnic minorities, including many Somali refugees. Around 70 per cent receive free school meals. Although there's no formal parents' association, parents are mostly very supportive of the school and its high expectations for their children. Good communications between school and parents – 'I've always had quick responses from them,' said one. Students form strong peer groups. 'There's a very strong ethos of care for one another,' said a parent.

Entrance: Some 1,200 applicants for 208 places. Everyone is placed in one of four ability bands, assessed by the standard Tower Hamlets numeracy and literacy tests in year 5, with equal numbers of places offered from each band. This is a C of E school, so it does allocate a minority of places to committed Christians, with 40 places going to worshippers in a recognised Christian church, with looked-after children, social and medical needs, living in one of the listed parishes and then siblings in order of priority. The other 152 places have a similar priority order, but 20 are offered to first-born children. Families in the area tend to be large and siblings would otherwise monopolise the intake. Distance from the school is the tie-break. Sixteen places (four per band) are also allocated to those who score highest in the school's language aptitude test.

The sixth form is also highly oversubscribed, with over 1,000 applicants for 300 outside places. Most A level courses require five or more 9-4 grades at GCSE including English and maths, with some higher stipulations eg grade 8 in maths for maths or further maths A level (whereas with other subjects, including English, they'll consider a grade 6). But those with lesser qualifications can take lower level courses, and the majority of pupils from year 11 go through to the sixth form.

Exit: Up to half of students leave after GCSEs – usually to another sixth form or straight into a job. A quarter leave after year 12. And of those who go through to year 13, almost all go on to university, while others go into apprenticeships, voluntary work or employment. Of those who go down the university route, around 40 per cent go to Russell Group universities, the vast majority (for social and cultural reasons) choosing London universities, with Kings, UCL, Imperial and Queen Mary proving particularly popular. Has had several successful Oxbridge candidates (one to Cambridge in 2018, plus two medics). While there's quite a range of courses studied, these do tend to be heavily dominated by sciences and maths.

Remarks: A beacon of excellence in one of the most deprived areas of the capital (and indeed the country), which takes in students with low levels of attainment and sends most of them off to university where they get laudable results. If your child is prepared to behave well and knuckle down to work, the expert teaching and high aspirations here will almost certainly see their grades go from strength to strength (and that goes for those who enter from one of the higher bands too).

Sir John Cass's Foundation Primary School

St James's Passage, 27 Duke's Place, London EC3A 5DE

Ages 3m–11 **Pupils** 247 C of E

020 7283 1147
www.sirjohncassprimary.org

Headteacher: Since September 2018, Alex Allan, previously deputy head, head of the school's Children's Centre and SENCo.

Entrance: The only state school in the Square Mile, Sir John Cass is one form entry. Historically, about 100 apply for the 30 places on offer, with priority given to those who worship regularly at St Botolph's, Aldgate. Desk space decided thereafter by a mixture of church attendance and distance from the gates. The school also runs The Cass Child and Family Centre, an attached children's centre with full provision from 3 months.

Exit: To a wide range of secondary schools, north, south, east and west, notably to City of London's sponsored academies (where City-dwellers gain some preference), selective state schools, and leading faith schools across London. One or two annually to the independent sector. (Has recently started working with City of London School for Girls to help prepare pupils for 11+ testing, and supports children to apply for scholarship and bursary entry at City and other fee-paying schools).

Remarks: Sir John Cass traces its roots back to the school established by the alderman of that name in the churchyard of St Botolph's by Aldgate in 1710. The current gracious grade II* listed building – described by Pevsner as 'neo-Baroque-neo-Hampton Court' – dates from 1908. It formerly housed a secondary school, with all the benefits that implies, including broad corridors, large classrooms and a generous assembly hall. Its listing also relates to its 'boardroom', a glorious panelled reconstruction of a merchant's home dating from 1669, with a plaster ceiling and 17th century hand-painted panels, where lucky members of the student council enjoy regular meetings. 'It's quite a big building,' said a parent, 'but it still has a very intimate, personal quality. It really feels like a family, not corporate in any way.' As well as recent and on-going refurbishment, there are plans for a £5m extension and modernisation, and local building works will ultimately give the school access to a leafy square.

Academically, Sir John Cass has long been recognized as one of the country's best primary schools. Despite the fact that many of its pupils come in with well below average attainment, virtually every child here reaches the expected government benchmark and an exceptionally high proportion soar well beyond it. Success for all is guaranteed through excellent, experienced teaching and, often, by high levels of staffing, which enables children to be taught in small groups when small groups are most needed. (Two teachers, for example, work with reception and year 6.) 'The teachers are incredible,' said one parent. 'They give lots of extra support for whatever kids require.'

Huge emphasis is put on reading from the outset. ('We're less about children catching up than getting it right from the start.') Each classroom has a designated quiet space for private study, and pupils get plenty of extra support, both from City volunteers, who come in to hear children read, and parents, who are encouraged to make nightly reading as customary as tooth brushing. Good, well-stocked library, with full-time library coordinator, and year 6s are furnished with take-home Kindles to embed the literary habit. Regular – but not crippling – amounts of homework. Years 4,5 and 6 use laptops in class, but this is not a place which believes that technology is always the answer. 'Four year olds need to interact with each other and the natural environment'; no whiteboards in the nursery classroom.

A fully qualified native speaker teaches French. (The class we visited seemed encouragingly well beyond bonjour and merci.) Art, too, now has a refurbished studio and expert teaching three days a week, with several nascent Picassos reaching the finals of a recent Diocese of London art competition.

Music a celebrated strength, with a long-established Strings Programme giving all children in years 4-6 a weekly music class and a smaller group session to concentrate on technique. Performance developed further at Christmas and summer concerts, and star performers (who often achieve grades 4/5) invited to study at specialist music colleges and play at the Guildhall. Outstanding choir, under legendary choirmaster, has also made plenty of public appearances (including on the Queen's Christmas speech). African drumming and dancing recently introduced in year 2. Performing arts group meets twice weekly to study drumming, dance, drama and vocal techniques, all taught by specialists. 'Performance makes pupils more confident and articulate,' says school.

Sport goes well beyond the statutory minimum, with a recently recruited sports coach developing skills in rugby, hockey and multi-sport in the expansive school gym as well as swimming at several local pools. Unsurprisingly, Sir John Cass generally represents the City of London in inter-borough competitions for tag rugby, cross-country and swimming.

A significant proportion of children here receive the pupil premium and/or come from families whose native language is not English, and additional needs are taken seriously. The attached nursery is very much seen as the foothills of primary, with children encouraged to get muddy and explore materials. Special needs lead is aided by number of teaching assistants specialising in English as an additional language. A Tavistock-trained counsellor also attends weekly.

Lavish menu of trips, both in London (Buckingham Palace, Natural History Museum, Regent's Park) and beyond, which 'help pin down history and geography'. Out-of-London jaunts include a week-long stay at the Hampshire and Cass Centre in the beautiful Brecon Beacons, and a country-town mouse exchange to Caunton Dean Hole in Nottinghamshire, where urbanites can get up close to cows, fresh air and pond dipping. Lunch-hour and after-school clubs include chess and Lego, football and art, as well as inexpensive breakfast and after-school care.

Behaviour throughout is exemplary, with classrooms quiet, orderly and attentive (misdemeanours generally confined to coats not hung up properly on pegs). 'All the children get along. There are no dominant groups, no cliques.' One tiny child came up and gave the head a big hug, another waved as we entered the classroom.

As a voluntary aided Christian foundation, the school has a strong, traditional Christian focus, with a bible corner in each classroom, Christian assemblies and regular church attendance. Whatever their views, parents welcome the faith structure. 'My family are not religious, but I really value the fact that my kids learn about religion with children of all backgrounds,' said one mother.

School lunch eaten by virtually all with appetising food cooked daily on site and crudités laid out (and consumed) on all tables. City Gardeners work with pupils on a well-tended roof garden, so children can eat what they have grown, and a project with Leiths cookery school ensures everyone leaves with a repertoire of 12 dishes in their personal recipe book.

About 30 per cent of families are City residents, the rest are from adjoining boroughs. Though number on free school meals has diminished as more professional families move into the City, the school remains unusually diverse. The school has worked hard on developing the PTA, bringing everyone together. 'The school really represents London,' said one mother. 'It's very open-minded, very inclusive. For me, it's like a dream.'

Sir William Burrough Primary School

Salmon Lane, London E14 7PQ

Ages 3–11 **Pupils** 379

020 7987 2147
www.sirwilliamburrough.net

Headteacher: Since 1995 Avril Newman (60s) BEd, first class honours from Goldmith's, who has spent her whole teaching career in Tower Hamlets. A national leader of education, a JP and has been honoured with a Freedom of the City award. She cited her greatest achievement as integrating rigorous attention to academic standards with high emotional intelligence; qualities she noted 'don't always go together' but, in this case, are evidently modelled from the top. A warm, positive and articulate woman whose delicate stature belies a strong and dynamic force. She believes that every child should aspire to the highest possible standards in reading, writing and maths regardless of social or cultural background; the testimony of which lies in the reputation and success of the school and the low turnover of staff. One parent remarked: 'She is amazing, she really listens', and another described her as 'very accessible' and 'very good at dealing with a problem'.

She has an open door policy, literally (during our visit the lively community toddler group was in full swing just outside her office), and encourages parents to come in and talk face to face with her about any problem. Communication between the school and parents includes monthly Cup of Tea Mornings, described by one parent as 'Avril meetings', providing a forum where parents make suggestions for inmprovements. A lover of theatre, books and travel, she is married with two grown-up children.

S

Entrance: A highly oversubscribed school in a highly populated area means that the appetite for places is fierce: recently 180 applications for the 45 places on offer in reception. Customary priority is given to looked-after children, siblings then proximity – and last year you needed to live very close indeed (within 260m). The recent changes to the welfare system have resulted in some local families moving away so places in the later years do crop up.

Exit: Mostly a spread of local secondary schools with the occasional child attending an out of borough independent or grammar.

Remarks: In a densely urban area with the entrance tucked up a dreary back street, there is something quite magical about stepping through the gate into the friendly and colourful atmosphere. For a Victorian building spanning three floors, it is surprisingly light and airy with windows open and homely curtains billowing against a soft breeze. Children's artwork adorns all surfaces, proudly including some deft pencil drawings depicting, as one articulate boy observed, 'sociality in the city', as well as a net suspended from a classroom ceiling decorated with sumptuous rainforest paintings; a project complimented by a trip to Kew Gardens, one of many trips to take full advantage of the city's resources.

The classrooms are roomy and colourful, all with interactive whiteboards, and the library is calm and attractive. Unusually for a state primary, there is a dedicated and fully-equipped computer room backed up by widespread use of iPads. The recently refurbished reception classrooms are calm and comfortable with integrated toilets and a separate outdoor play space. The indoor gyms are a bit on the small side but there are two of them, and a series of outdoor spaces surrounds the school building, including a dedicated 'dance space' where children can dance to music outdoors during lunchtime; two multi-sport pitches; a netted cricket area; and a vast array of play equipment including a trampoline. When we visited, during playtime all children were busy climbing, skipping, playing table football or foraging in the wooded area making 'camps'. An advantage of reigning for over 20 years, Mrs Newman has overseen the planting and maturing of the lush trees that encircle the playground, adding an abundance of green to this urban oasis.

Sats-wise, some 95 per cent of pupils achieve at least the expected standard in the three Rs, well above the national average, and recently 29 per cent reached a higher standard. A National Support School, SWB is amongst the 200 top performing primary schools and in the top eight per cent for the progress of all children, regardless of background, the hard data testimony to the school's academic approach. All children, apart from those with particular special needs, have learnt to read and write (in cursive!) by the end of reception, when they partake in a graduation ceremony complete with mortar boards and gowns. Once the basics are established, the Accelerated Reader and Accelerated Maths schemes kick in: online, personalised programmes which motivate through quizzes, prizes and international competitions. Families are able to win what amounts to a small library between them once they have read a million words: 'our way of ensuring children have books at home'. Other incentives include a maths Olympics, where children win rosettes for knowing their times tables, and a spelling bee.

All this takes place in the mornings, with the afternoons dedicated to the creative, experiential learning of the International Primary Curriculum (IPC). Sir William Burrough was one of the first primary schools in the country to introduce the IPC, which adopts a global perspective alongside a thematic, topic-based approach to learning. In a project on the Romans, children traced each other's bodies to create a life-size collage and went on to act out The Battle of Marathon. The children make their own movies and animations using iPads and, if the plot demands it, a green screen.

An energetic and effective use of partnerships brings in professional coaching in fencing, judo, rugby, hockey and handball alongside reading, number and chess partners from City firms. A recently established link with the Worshipful Company of Musicians complements the already lively musical culture in the school, including a 60-strong choir and a ukulele ensemble. They even have a choreographer-in-residence who ensures that every child in the school gets moving, appreciated particularly by one parent who felt that 'dance is fantastic' at the school. After-school clubs include film and animation, Spanish, sailing and debating. Years 3 to 5 build up their independence on residential trips offering challenge and outdoor adventure. Year 5s and 6s get to learn Latin. There is a breakfast club from 8.30am and a teatime club that runs until

4.30pm, facilities that were much appreciated by many of the working parents we met.

The school's You Can Do It programme 'keeps levels of confidence and resilience high, and is deeply woven into relationships of respect, tolerance, kindness and courtesy'. We saw this in action as children held open doors, enquired about the welfare of others and remarked that 'we all comfort each other'. There is an emphasis on continual practice and one pupil commented that 'if you are unsure, there is always a teacher next to you'. A caring infrastructure is evident throughout: there is a room dedicated to part-time and summer-born reception children and year 6s were helped to feel calm before their Sats through afternoon yoga sessions. There is also a system of peer support via year 6 school monitors, who look out for the younger children, and year 4s, who help the reception classes learn to read.

All SEN support is offered in the classroom by teachers and TAs 'in the moment of learning' rather than in separate sessions or groups. This is a genuinely inclusive school with an expansive cultural mix. A small majority of pupils are from Bangladeshi heritage, others are of Somalian, Eastern European, Chinese and white British backgrounds. Some 75 per cent of pupils speak English as an additional language, though most are London-born and speak English when they arrive: the school's mastery of words proclaimed by repeatedly finishing as runners up in the English Speaking Union's Pan London Debating Tournament. Parents describe it as 'like a family', 'creative, friendly, inclusive' and one pupil commented 'they accept everybody who comes here'. When faced with the question of what the school might be able to do better, the pupils understandably struggled: 'I would change the sausages into hot dogs' and 'get a bigger trampoline' were about it.

Over her 20+ years as headteacher, Avril Newman has been inspired by the words of John Tomsett: 'A truly great school grows like an oak tree over many years'. Under the talented and passionate guidance of its head, Sir William Burrough has matured well like the trees in the playground. A happy, inclusive and high-achieving urban primary.

Snaresbrook Preparatory School

75 Woodford Road, South Woodford, London E18 2EA

Ages 3–11 **Pupils** 155

Fees: £9,147 – £12,235 pa

020 8989 2394
www.snaresbrookprep.org

Head: Since September 2018, Ralph Dalton BEd, previously senior deputy head pastoral at Woodford Green Prep. Worked in legal and recruitment services for 10 years before taking a PGCE. After working in various primary schools, he joined Woodford Green Prep in 2009, working as class teacher, subject coordinator, assistant head and senior deputy head.

Entrance: Most come in at nursery and go though to year 6. There is a low key family interview with the head. Places higher up subject to a family interview and in-class assessment. Pupils come from various nurseries in the local area, from Canary Wharf and Stratford out to Epping, Woodford Green, Romford and Loughton, and beyond.

Exit: Bancroft's, Braeside, Chigwell and Forest most popular local destinations, alongside City of London schools and St Edmund's Ware. Others to local grammar schools Woodford County High and Ilford County High.

Remarks: Small size and family atmosphere mean pupils settle in quickly. 'You don't have to be scared to talk to a year 6 because everyone knows each other,' a pupil said. One parent said that during her son's first year at the school he has 'waved to and greeted any older pupil we met in the street. And the bigger kids have invariably waved back.'

The main school is set in a 1930s Victorian house and was managed by the same family for 50 years. Its small, quaint classrooms are close together and the corridors are dainty, but it is an intimate rather than cramped feel. The nursery and reception are housed in a separate, purpose-built building overlooking a small playground, with the hall and a multi-purpose library room on the other side of the playground. Beyond that is a covered sensory garden, designed and constructed by an architect governor. The children grow plants here, and experiment with different climates and seasons. There is a huge blackboard where they chalk to their heart's content and above it a huge, colourful mural painted by year 6s.

The governors are very much involved in everyday school life, often to be seen popping in and out. They helped to extend the hall to create more storage space, they have helped decorate the staff room and to build the new canopied decking area outside the nursery so pupils can enjoy year round outdoor play free of leaves and rain. 'They are very sensitive to the needs of the staff and children.'

Single form entry, with class sizes of roughly 24 in the infants and 18 in the juniors, and plenty of classroom assistants. 'It is mixed ability here. What is exciting is seeing children who didn't come in as high fliers leave having made massive progress.' Most extra support for those with learning difficulties is provided in class, with a part-time specialist available as required.

French from nursery, optional German and Spanish, year 6s learn Latin and also embark on self-directed projects. Lots of investment in IT. We saw year 5s listening to a live commentary on an Arsenal v Southampton match and learning how to extract key information from a database to write up their news reports.

The school adventure service challenge is 'like a mini Duke of Edinburgh... we do camping, rowing, bird watching, cooking and it's lots of fun,' say pupils. Years 4 and 5 were excited about the annual trip to France where they visit a chocolate factory in Boulogne (they like this better than the snail farm). Whilst in France they spend time with penfriends and complete a shopping task in French, although some confess they have found ways around this: 'Luckily the lady that was serving us knew English'. Year 5 has a history trip to York and year 6 an end of year trip to Shropshire.

Before and after-school clubs include the usual range of sports plus country and maypole dancing, scooter club, creative writing, art club and knitting. Popular sports are football and netball, and considering how small the school is, they do well: 'Once we played in a tournament and there were two Snaresbrook teams in the football play-off and they ended up playing each other,' a pupil said with pride. There are no fields here so pupils take a minibus to Redbridge Sports Centre and Ashton playing fields.

One parent commented: 'I feel the school works hard to optimise the use of space available.' At breaktimes a daily games timetable saves the tiny playground from being dominated by football (football still an option at lunchtime when playtimes are staggered) and the children can try out a different game each day. 'Our games teacher came up with the idea,' said a pupil. It was inspired by Olympics sports such as handball and basketball. Most of the children take part and girls and boys play together. Other activities are on offer, too – they can read, do art, play table tennis.

When we visited, years 1 and 2 were in the hall preparing for a dress rehearsal of Rise and Shine. 'All have a part to play in the production,' said their teacher. The school tries to offer a taste of a wide range of drama and music, and each class gets a chance to perform. 'Lots of parents come to see the productions whether they have children in that year group or not.' Around 20 per cent of children learn to play the recorder, violin or flute.

House system gives everyone a chance to shine in different areas. 'Browns usually win on sports day, blues dominate swimming, yellows are good at choir singing and pancake races,' a pupil told us, 'so we each have our fair share of glory'. The many charitable and fundraising activities include readathons, movie nights to raise funds for Redbridge Night Shelter, sports events for the NSPCC and Great Ormond Street and harvest collections for the British Red Cross. Year 4 girls created a magazine, 'packed with quizzes, gossip and pictures. They made £61 by selling it to everyone'.

Pupils help inside school too. A year 6 pupil said of the nursery: 'We come in our free time and help the children and teachers with projects. It's also fun for us as this was our room when we were in the nursery.' It invokes a sense of service: 'This morning I was holding the door for a parent and I heard one of the year 4s say, "Dad, when I'm in year 6 I will be able to hold the door, I will say good morning to everyone".'

Support is good, say parents, with teachers always willing to discuss and address problems. Plenty of incentives and rewards for doing well, including Good Marks assemblies and commendation awards. The merit board includes an award to teachers for 'making a good start on the return after holidays'.

A new system of online live reports, with up-to-date comments from teachers that parents can access at any time, has replaced yearly written reports. The plan is to produce a detailed picture of how each child learns and how they are progressing.

Very active parents' association – '40 donations for the bake sale the other day', said a member – with an impressive participation rate considering that many, if not most, families have two working parents. Hotly-contested annual pancake race involves children, staff and parents.

South Hampstead High Junior School

Linked with South Hampstead High School

S

5 Netherhall Gardens, London NW3 5RN

Ages 4–11 **Pupils** 265

Fees: £15,327 pa

020 7794 7198
www.shhs.gdst.net/junior-school

Headmistress of junior school: Since 2013, Gabrielle Solti BA PGCE (40s), previously head of Notting Hill and Ealing Junior School for 10 years. A local: she attended SHHS junior school herself, taught at Trevor-Roberts and was deputy head of Primrose Hill Primary before taking the Notting Hill and Ealing job. Born into a musical family (her late father, Sir Georg Solti, was once described by the Telegraph as 'the most distinguished conductor alive'), she studied history at Oxford, interned at the European Commission (where she met her husband), then worked at Nestlé in France and the UK before taking a teacher training course at the Institute of Education. Says she is 'passionate about pedagogy – that's what we're here for. We're evolving how we tailor education for girls and get them involved in learning.' A hit with parents, who see their daughters blossoming under her liberal regime. Two children, one at SHHS.

Leaving in July 2019 to head the primary school of The Grammar School at Leeds.

Entrance: Application forms available to download during a two week period in the September two years before entry into reception; school assesses all those who apply within this period. Some 250 apply for the 24 reception places and around 130 apply for 24 more places in year 3 (applications close in the November of the year before entry).

Reception assessment is play-based, in the November prior to entry, in similar age groups of 12-13 girls with four or five staff observing and interacting. Mrs Solti sees all applicants herself. 'We're looking for signs that they will benefit from the academic education we have to offer – for their ability to notice, examine, explain.' A hundred of the 250 return in January in smaller groups when the school 'looks for a range of personality types' and aims at a balanced year group. No barrier against those with summer birthdays – 'we expect a little less of them'.

Year 3 applicants are tested in maths, English and non-verbal reasoning, with high performers invited back for interview and small group activities. At this point 'we are looking at what they can do', but hoping to see past tutoring to potential, and 'the small group assessments are the most useful in making final judgements.'

Inevitably the assessments are not an exact science, and though nearly all of those accepted do, indeed, thrive, the school is aware that there are plenty more suitable candidates than they have room for in both age groups.

Exit: Virtually all to the senior school, round the corner. Diminishing numbers don't make the move up. 'My job is to assess them properly and help them achieve what they need,' says the head. 'If a child works hard we can usually get them to the right standard.' Occasional leavers to eg Henrietta Barnett.

Remarks: Happily, staff do not have to cram their charges through the 11+ and thus can oversee an education outside of the box. The head introduced the concept of the Growth Mindset ('I can do it...' proclaim posters in each classroom), to encourage girls to take risks, challenge themselves and learn from mistakes. 'Self-assessment – what did I do well and what do I need to improve? – can counteract girls' tendency to be "people pleasers".'

She is at one with the senior school head in believing that resilience is one of the most important qualities schools can inculcate in girls. Pupils are encouraged to speak up – they have 'talk partners' with whom to share ideas in class, they perform in assembly from the youngest years, talk about their work, debate, recite poetry, perform in plays. By year 6 even the most naturally reticent are confident enough to show parents around the school.

Our extremely self-assured and chatty guides showed us how topic work encompasses a range of subjects. Reception children were painting pictures of jungles to decorate their role play area. We saw pictures of the year 2 (Raging Rivers) trip to the River and Rowing Museum; we viewed year 5's Chinese pottery vases, dropped in on their Mandarin class and heard about their impromptu trip to Liverpool to see the Terracotta Army exhibition – 'you have to grab these opportunities,' says the head. Year 4s sculpt Viking chessmen and have a residential trip to York ('really, really fun'). Year 6s were enthused by their visit to France (which took in a chocolate factory and a goat farm).

Our guides were keen to tell us about Open Homework. 'You're given a word and you can do anything with it, from art to baking'....'I made a board game'....'I made 100 paper aeroplanes'...'I painted a picture.' We liked the display board showing a reasoned discussion on whether girls would prefer to live in London or in a village in Africa.

Parents approve of the SHHS emphasis on inspirational and powerful women, which begins in the junior school. Year 5s learn about the Suffragettes (a then staff member spent time in Holloway prison), about Rebel Girls and significant Women Through Time. 'It makes the curriculum meaningful to them.'

No setting or grades in the junior school. 'We focus on what they did well and how they can improve.' A few have dyslexia, dyspraxia or are on the autism spectrum, but 'all are academically able. They may need support at different stages and in different ways, and we want to get in quickly with help. We have a wonderful SENCo.'

Sport rapidly improving, and girls use the senior school sports hall and playing fields as well as their own games area. They now play football alongside netball – hurray – and are jettisoning rounders for cricket. Year 5 were off to Sydenham High when we visited to be coached by an England cricketer. Even the youngest ran a mile for Sports Relief recently. Cross-country, yoga, fencing and dance all popular. Year 5s and 6s compete against other schools, with A-D teams, and PE clubs are open to all. 'We want them to love sport and enjoy being physical.'

Plenty of inter-GDST school competitions. Displayed in the entrance hall we saw awards for cross-country and quiz competitions, and for young choir of the year. The relatively recent house system – with houses named after Bronte, Curie, Parks and Pavlova – provides more gentle opportunities to compete.

There's a good musical grounding with all year 1s learning the violin or cello and all year 2s playing the recorder, and orchestras, ensembles and choirs for those who would like to progress further. Drama performances start early and year 4s were away at the senior school rehearsing for their production of Pirates of the Currybean when we visited. We heard about workshops on architecture and dance, robots and forensic science.

A big party celebrated the 60th anniversary of the junior school's move from Waterlow House on the senior school site to its own red-brick building round the corner in Netherhall Gardens in 1957. Pupils also dressed up in 50s clothes and listened to guests talk about their junior school days in that era – 'we heard about the great smog and how hard it was to get to school'.

This building now houses reception to year 4, plus the science lab (home to skeletons Bob and Bob Junior, where 'we do lots of experiments, so we can see what happens, not just hear about it') plus the art room full of clay sculptures. There's a bright and comfortable library where classes spend half an hour a week ('Really nice. You get to sit and read!') and there are 'star reads' suggested for each year group by previous years. A second building across the road, purchased in 1993 to cope with increasing numbers, houses classrooms for years 5 and 6 plus the music room, another library and the DT room.

Outside space is limited at both sites but reception has its own outdoor classroom with Wendy house, and a row of scooters indicated how many local girls get to school. They also manage to fit in a mini sports pitch and playgrounds with climbing frames. 'At the co-ed school where I used to teach the playground was full of boys kicking a football in the middle whilst girls played little games round the edges,' says the head. 'Here at least half of our girls can be seen running up and noisily at play time. There's space to run, jump, climb and throw balls.'

A creative and liberal start to education where girls are encouraged to speak out and challenge themselves inside and outside the classroom.

South Hampstead High School

Linked with South Hampstead High Junior School

3 Maresfield Gardens, London NW3 5SS

Ages 11–18 **Pupils** 673 **Sixth form** 163

Fees: £18,654 pa

020 7435 2899
www.shhs.gdst.net

Headmistress: Since 2017, Vicky Bingham (40), previously deputy head at Guildford High. Educated at the European School in Brussels – her father worked for the EU; classics MA from Oxford; PGCE in classics from Cambridge. Started her career teaching classics at Guildford High; off to St Catherine's Bramley as head of classics, before returning to Guildford as deputy head in 2010. 'I didn't always want to teach, but during my final year at Oxford I realised that by the time I retired I wanted to have filled my head with something worthwhile and I felt that teaching classics is important to humanity.' She 'fell into' working at girls' schools and has found them 'unpretentious, unstuffy, moving with the times.' With an international upbringing, she feels at home amidst the cosmopolitan buzz of SHHS. 'In many families at least one parent comes from overseas.'

We found her energetic, enthusiastic, full of ideas. Sees developing resilience as a vital part of girls' education, via a well-rounded, holistic curriculum. 'The more activities there are outside the classroom, the more chances they have to shine in something.' Very keen on debating and public speaking: 'I won an international public speaking event that gave me confidence and I want the girls to have that chance.' Also passionate about improving school's sporting offering, of which more later.

A big thumbs up from parents and pupils, who have experienced a rapid turnover of heads over the past few years, and fervently hope she is here for the long term. 'She's very focused on the girls,' said a father. 'I'm a big fan,' said another. 'The girls respect her, she's on their wavelength, she's a big hit at the school.'

A keen walker (with her dog, Max), she took up running at 34 and was first lady in her first race. 'Sport wasn't valued at my own school and I felt it was a waste of my 20s that I hadn't realised I was good at this.' She has gone public with her views on the British values curriculum ('somewhat jingoistic') and tutoring ('it robs children of the critical ability to surmount problems themselves'). The day we visited she hit headlines for her criticism of women who insist on micro-managing the domestic sphere as well as holding down demanding jobs. 'What kind of blueprint are some of us providing for our daughters by infantilising men?'

Her daughter is at the junior school here.

Academic matters: Results at GCSE hard to beat; in 2018, 89 per cent at A*-A/9-7. A levels 67 per cent A*/A, 88 per cent A*-B in 2018. Good showing in languages – everyone studies one MFL in year 7 plus Latin (a choice of French, Spanish, German and Mandarin) and two in year 8, taking at least one to GCSE – and a fair few continue to A level. Maths taken by about two-thirds of sixth formers with impressive results; psychology, history and economics all popular; generally good numbers taking science A level, though physics less popular (the department, we were told, has 'now stabilised', and indeed a physics teacher was shortlisted for a global £3m 'world's best teacher' prize).

Everyone studies four subjects in year 12, many dropping to three in year 13: some parents voiced a feeling that taking three subjects throughout would lead to less stress and more time for enrichment. The first term in year 12 sees a Friday afternoon Great Ideas course which is a springboard to an EPQ (increasing take up with strong results), and students are encouraged to enter for national essay writing competitions, Olympiads, engineering scholarships etc with some great successes. The Futures Programme, preparing for life beyond school, taps into the GDST Alumnae Network of over 75,000 members. Journalists, vets, psychiatrists, charity executives come back to talk about their work. In the younger years, the new This is Me project encourages girls to talk proudly about themselves and their achievements in an interview-style situation.

'I want us to do more than chase exam results and prizes,' says head, who believes that they get results 'without an insane amount of pressure.' 'I thought it might be hothousy and too pushy, but it really hasn't been,' said a parent. General agreement that any hothouse atmosphere is created by ambitious families rather than by the school.

Universal praise for staff. 'They're well supported by very able teachers.' 'When my daughter struggled with maths, the teacher went to endless trouble to help her understand it. And they're all like that.'

The SEN department here is not rushed off its feet, but there's always a proportion of pupils with specific needs such as dyslexia or dyspraxia, some of which don't come to light until the sixth form. 'Because they're so bright they tend to be able to work with strategies we give them.' Support given unstintingly: one-to-one when needed, but most within lessons. 'A good lesson for a dyslexic child is a good lesson for everyone.' Laptops provided to all those that need them.

Games, options, the arts: Historically, South Hampstead 'has never been a sporty school,' say students, and indeed many parents we talked to cited sport as the weakest link. However, head – who 'sees sport as a cornerstone of pastoral life', said a colleague – is overseeing a transformation. 'Playing as part of a team gives you a sense of pride,' she says, and there are now A-E netball teams in year 7, with increased competition feeding gradually up the school. Lots more competitive matches against other schools and over 20 sports now available thanks to recently expanded PE dept from athletics and badminton to yoga and zumba. Two netball teams recently reached the Middlesex finals, football is increasingly popular, with external coaching, and they have dropped rounders in favour of cricket as a key summer sport with coaching from ex-England players. Years 7-9 now get a full afternoon a week at the four acre sports ground, a 10 minute walk away, as well as PE lessons in the new sports hall deep in the bowels of the reconstructed school building. Sixth formers talked enthusiastically of the 'very competitive' staff v students netball match.

S

Music a strong point with numerous opportunities at all levels ('My daughter is a fairly average player but has plenty of chances to perform'), ambitious concerts and recitals large and small. And amongst the lunchtime and teatime recitals, choral and orchestral concerts, a ukulele ensemble, the Big Band and jazz groups provide a jaunty air, with the summer Jazz Night a showcase for saxophonists and their ilk.

Art as popular as at most highly academic schools where many parents push their daughters towards more 'academic' subjects. Small but perfectly formed A level groups produce some impressive work in 'relaxing and enjoyable' top floor sixth form art and sculpture rooms. Visits to local galleries and far-flung exhibitions: Vienna, Kyoto, New York. DT product design available to A level but take-up tends to be bijou at this level.

Recent production of Made in Dagenham – based on the 1968 sewing machinists' strike for equal pay at the Ford factory in Dagenham – 'very impressive' and there are plenty of musicals and classical plays, recently Euripides' Trojan Women. However, drama's not generally amongst the high flying subjects at GCSE, few take theatre studies at A level and we heard about some thespians moving to sixth forms elsewhere for this reason. Plenty of opportunities to speak up, though, with debating increasingly popular and compulsory public speaking competitions from years 7-10.

Huge range of speakers drop in, from Dame Stella Rimmington, Olympic hockey players and Angela Saini (Inferior: How Science got Women Wrong) to Michael Gove (who apparently provoked intense questioning on Brexit). Those invited by year 13s have included Laura Bates (founder of the Everyday Sexism Project).

Clubs for cheerleaders and comedians, Shakespeare and Dr Who devotees, fashionistas and philosophers. FemSoc discusses problems with the patriarchy; Womanities Soc examines the less-than-well-behaved women who have shaped history, created art or literature; the popular LGBTQ+ discussion group is now known as PRIDE. DofE hugely popular: 'nearly all my daughter's group seem to be doing it'.

Background and atmosphere: Opened in 1876 as St John's Wood High School at Swiss Cottage with 27 pupils, changing its name to South Hampstead High in 1887 and moving to a purpose built site in Maresfield Gardens with 300 pupils. And there it stayed, in the same red-brick building with the odd acquisition or two: Waterlow House, bought in 1921, originally home to the junior school, and rebuilt in 1988; and Oakwood, bought in 1991 as the new sixth form centre.

In 2014, after a major £35m reconstruction, the 600 pupils moved back from temporary premises on the Lymington Road sports ground to the multi-storey glass and red-brick home, full of light and air, that rises from an underground sports hall to a rooftop garden, with panoramic views of north London from its upper floors.

The walls are alive with murals and artwork, including the abstract Hampstead Mural panels by the late Gillian Ayres, commissioned in 1957 for the school's then dining room, now joined by five new paintings donated by the artist to celebrate the new building, and which form the school's modern art collection.

Waterlow Hall, lined with honours boards, is the site for assemblies and performances. Currently it is underwhelming from an acoustic point of view and fundraising is underway to transform it into a worthy setting for concerts, plays and speakers.

Oakwood House, the sixth form's own, is more reminiscent of wood panelled grammar school of yore. Sixth formers love the rooftop garden and ground floor grassy area with picnic tables and Mira Cinnamon statue. They have an agreeably informal common room with slouchy sofas and table football and, with staffs' rooms nearby, the head of sixth form is 'very available'.

The previous head, perhaps with the aim of giving the school a more pronounced individual identity, commissioned a variety of blue and yellow penguins with water bottles on their backs, carrying the message of water conservation, which dot the school. The girls, somewhat bemused, have taken the name Penguin for their own magazine, 'the voice of satire and quirkiness'. The current head is 'keen to tap into new traditions' and has turned end of year assemblies into a celebration of the life of the school. 'I cry every time we sing the school song,' said a sixth former unapologetically.

A tradition of celebrating girls' education and empowerment, with a suffrage week of events to mark the centenary of women gaining the vote. 'You learn early on about the value of women,' said a sixth former. 'Virtually all the girls here would say they're a feminist.' 'A good place for a girl to learn – not too precious,' added a parent.

Pastoral care, well-being and discipline: The usual pastoral scaffolding, including one-to-one chats with a tutor on a regular basis, also features a life coach and a counsellor. The counsellor, a child psychotherapist, 'makes herself approachable by coming into assemblies,' and even girls without specific problems go along for a chat and a biscuit, said a parent. 'She's brilliant. They've nailed it.' The life coach is there to help on a practical level – 'perhaps with specific things a girl would like to change about her behaviour. Some have recurring themes and we encourage them to think about what would work better.' 'My daughter finds her very useful,' said a parent. 'If you are struggling academically, she reorganises your life,' said a sixth former (which sounds fabulous; can we all have one?). 'There will always be a teacher you can speak to,' she added, mentioning how much care she had seen a teacher take with a pupil who became upset in her class.

As a highly selective all girls' school, South Hampstead might seem a likely candidate for widespread anorexia and the like, but no-one we spoke to – parents, girls or staff – felt it was a pressing issue. 'They keep a good watch on the girls,' said a parent. A deputy head confirmed: 'We keep a close eye if we think anything is emerging that suggests an eating disorder. We do have the usual gamut of teenage issues, but the girls are very supportive of each other – they will come and tell us if they feel someone needs help.' Staff are well aware of the dangers of modern communication modes. 'We're constantly talking about screen time, the pitfalls of Instagram reality, of trying to have a thick skin in relation to social media.'

'My daughter struggled socially when she first joined,' said a parent, 'and they were really onto it, very supportive.' Girls agree: 'There's a very warm atmosphere here. Very nurturing.'

This is liberal Hampstead, where being right on and tolerant is more or less a given. So how would the school cope with transgender issues? 'Fundamentally, we are proud to be a girls' school,' says the head. 'But if one of our pupils transitioned we would make kind, considerate, sensitive adjustments to make it possible for them to stay. We're ready for it. Our uniform includes trousers and could easily be unisex.'

Pupils and parents: Characterised by members of the north London liberal intelligentsia, with a good ethnic mix. The bulk of the intake from Camden and the surrounding boroughs, including many international families, with increasing applicants from further west. South Hampstead girls are 'diligent but flexible and creative about their thinking,' says head. They are 'great social campaigners – they like things with edge.' Parents are 'really supportive, like to have an open dialogue, like to give advice; they like us to be honest and transparent'.

Notable old girls include Helena Bonham-Carter (who opened the new school building), Lynne Featherstone MP, Suzy Klein, Angela Lansbury, Joanna McGregor, Rabbi Julia Neuberger, the late Lynsey de Paul, Fay Weldon, Olivia Williams, Naomi Alderman.

Entrance: Nearly all junior school girls (around 46) move up to the senior school without taking the entrance exam. They are joined by some 55 girls from approaching 600 applicants from outside, about 20 per cent from state primary schools.

The 11+ assessment for entry now consists of a 75 minute cognitive ability test (rather than maths and English exams) with great emphasis on the interview. The intention is to make the tests as tutor-proof as possible and to cut down on the prep school culture of 'endless practice papers'. An aim of the interview is to find 'children who can think for themselves when they encounter academic obstacles'. 'No silver bullet but we are doing something address the problems' of the advantages given to the tutored and prepped under the current system. Forty per cent increase in applicants recently.

At 16+ by exams in three A level subjects plus general paper, interview and predicted GCSE grades.

Exit: Between 15-20 per cent leave after GCSEs. A few to state sixth forms such as Camden School for Girls and Marylebone, and a few more to join their brothers at UCS up the road or to Westminster, one or two off to board. Sixth form leavers off to study eg art history at UCL, business and sustainable global development at Warwick, geography at Nottingham and linguistics at Cambridge. A good handful now to US universities (four in 2018) and to Oxbridge (six in 2018). Several medics (three in 2018).

Money matters: Academic and music scholarships of up to 50 per cent of fees, plus means-tested bursaries of up to 100 per cent, available at 11+ and 16+.

Remarks: A busy, buzzy school regaining its pre-eminence in north west London under an energetic head who is determined to empower her pupils. Said a satisfied parent: 'They really do care about the girls and giving them a broad education.'

Streatham & Clapham High School

42 Abbotswood Road, London SW16 1AW

Ages 3–18 **Pupils** 710 **Sixth form** 80

Fees: £13,692 – £19,743 pa

020 8677 8400
www.schs.gdst.net

Head master: Since 2012, Dr Millan Sachania MA (Cantab) MPhil PhD (40s). Former comprehensive student who gained a double first and a doctorate in musicology at Cambridge and then stayed on as a music tutor for five years before acquiring a PGCE at Kingston University. After stints as head of music at a girls' school in Windsor and deputy head at Immanual College in Bushey, was delighted to accept this post. 'Are you married?' we asked. 'Yes, to my piano'.

Parents praise his 'phenomenal attention to detail'. One told us he was 'not an obvious choice, but perfect', while another reckoned 'we are lucky to have him'. Other parental comments include 'definitely an individual', 'quirky', 'incomparable' and 'probably just what we needed but not everyone's cup of tea'. The girls seem to love him – 'even though he uses words we've never heard before'. Has a 'rescued' Bechstein grand piano in his study, which they are definitely allowed to tinker on.

Dr Sachania is amazed by the energy of both the school and the girls, which he feels derives from their cultural diversity. Impressed with their intelligence and really wants them to broaden their horizons and achieve beyond their potential 'across the width of endeavour'. Says he has an holistic approach and doesn't believe that pupils should obsess about being competitive with each other. He wants each girl to find her own forte and achieve her own personal best.

Has shortened lessons – 'shorter equals sharper and if necessary lessons can become double'. The sixth form, which is in a separate building, now has its own popular café area while a small lecture theatre is used for a variety of activities, from musical recitals to the once-a-week head master's lecture period.

Head of prep since 2015, Thomas Mylne (40s), previously deputy head of the Gatehouse School in east London. BA from the University of Brighton and PGCE from the Institute of Education; he has also taught at an east London primary school and been deputy head (curriculum) at Wimbledon High Junior School. Interests include cinema, travel, music and cycling; he is married (his wife works in publishing) with two daughters.

Academic matters: Junior girls happy, relaxed and proud to show us their work and talk about what they were doing. Good learning support. All children assessed on arrival at junior school, targets set each term and parents involved early if problems arise. Head meets all teachers once a term to ascertain that children have reached the expected levels.

'The school has really pulled its socks up' – that's the view of one parent we talked to. It offers a broad curriculum covering all the core subjects, and a wide variety of co-curricular activities to ensure pupils can learn and discover in depth. In 2018, 32 per cent A*/A at A level (70 per cent A*/B), and 66 per cent A*-A/9-7 at I/GCSE.

Setting in maths, sciences, modern languages and, occasionally, English. Class sizes are maximum of 26, many groups in the sixth form in single figures. All staff friendly and enthusiastic – average age early 40s. About a quarter have been at the school for more than 10 years. A selection of 12 non-core GCSE subjects on offer plus ancient Greek and astronomy. Head sees each year 11 girl individually with her parents to discuss A level choices.

One of the first things the head did was to introduce Kinza, a compulsory enrichment programme offering a range of over 30 topics which the girls study one afternoon each week in the Michaelmas and Lent terms. Staff run courses in subjects they don't teach (including forensic science, beekeeping and Arabic) and mixed age groups work together. Head says the course is 'emblematic of my educational philosophy', aiming to create 'civilised human beings equipped with a philosophy for living'.

Bubbly and enthusiastic head of learning support in school three-and-a-half days each week. School has inclusive policy, as long as girl passes entrance test. Some children have individual teaching assistants who produce strategies to help them deal with problems. Otherwise school provides help in small groups for 20 minutes once a fortnight from year 7 to year 9, and before school, after school or at lunchtime for years 10 and 11. One-to-one help has to be resourced externally.

Games, options, the arts: Surprising to find a school in a leafy London suburb with its own sports grounds and an enormous, all singing, all dancing sports hall, plus a dance studio and fitness centre. Plenty of cups to indicate sporting success. Football, hockey, tennis, athletics and lots of indoor sports. National gymnastic champions recently and notable successes in acrobatics, fencing, tennis and netball. The only criticisms from parents are that the school 'needs to offer more for C teams to improve their skills' and 'the sports department needs better organisation and more staff'. Needless to say, this is being addressed. One mother told us: 'The school is truly inclusive – my non-sporty child loves sport'.

Music strong (as you would expect with a musically talented head master), with lessons compulsory up to GCSE. Several choirs, orchestras and ensembles. Roomful of keyboards specifically for compositions. Parents say art facilities are 'brilliant' and we were impressed too. Large art room, smaller one specifically for the sixth form and separate pottery room with its own kiln. Drama also right up to standard; new creative arts building under construction. When we visited the whole school was involved in A Midsummer Night's Dream, with non-performers making costumes and painting scenery.

D of E taken pretty seriously – girls go trekking in Morocco's Atlas Mountains and have reached base camp of Everest.

Background and atmosphere: School was founded as Brixton Hill High School for Girls in 1887 and was one of the earliest GDST schools. It later became Streatham Hill High School, housed in the building now occupied by the junior school; senior school moved into current premises, previously occupied by Battersea Grammar School, in 1993. Now a spacious, well-equipped school, with recent additions of sixth form floor (popular sixth form café), stunning new dining hall and wildflower meadow roof at Abbotswood Road. The four-and-a-half acres of ground they stand in are miraculous in this busy area of London.

Junior school's unattractive building (school reports major refurbishments, including a new, 'very attractive oriel window') belies exceptionally light, large classrooms and happy atmosphere inside. Enormous sports hall, where girls can play hockey, and excellent outdoor area with adventure playground and enough space for rounders and tennis, guarantee plenty of fun, games and team training.

We were shown round by enthusiastic, confident girls who led us from the well-equipped nursery (with own outdoor play area) to busy reception classes and virtually every corner of the school. 'Do you want to see the loos?' they chirped. Huge library contains vast range of books and specific reading lists for each year. We also spotted shoes created out of recycled material and models of school areas (our guides proudly pointed out their own creations). Light art room with terrific views over London – 'whenever we do art, we know we're going to do something really messy', said our guides. 'It's such fun'. Science room was locked (health and safety) but they showed us well-equipped computer room and music room. Interactive white boards and computers in all classrooms.

Pupils' general feeling is that this is a happy, focused school. Parents say the support given to pupils is second to none and are adamant that it's 'not a hothouse'. Comments included 'there's no excessive pressure', 'they are allowed to be individuals and gain confidence', 'they mix across the year groups and get to know each other better that way'. One told us: 'At parents' evenings, they really do seem to know and understand our two very different daughters'. Another, with an exceptionally bright daughter, said that the way classes are divided, sometimes by ability, sometimes mixed, works a treat. 'My daughter is never bored', she said. 'The expectations of each girl are relevant to the goals she has been set'.

Pastoral care, well-being and discipline: Deputy head mistress is in overall charge of pastoral care and has a system for identifying problems early. Parents say communication is exceptional – emails are answered immediately and problems dealt with sympathetically. A parent told us of 'some unpleasantness... handled and dealt with properly and quickly'. Another talked about 'problematic disorder' in a particular class, which was 'completely sorted out by the head of department within a week'.

House system ensures girls work together as teams across year groups. Each form has a representative on the school council, alongside a form captain, so ample chances to raise problems. PHSCE programme deals with topics such as relationships, moral issues and citizenship in a sensitive and informed way. Sixth form mentor teams are invaluable – girls often prefer to talk to them rather than a member of staff.

Junior school parents told us: 'Communications are very good. All the staff are positive and professional.' The only thing they felt could be improved was sport. There's always something.

Pupils and parents: Mainly from the surrounding areas of south London and from variety of backgrounds – moneyed professional classes and entrepreneurs to local shopkeepers. Typical GDST range of ethnic and racial diversity.

Around 85 per cent arrive from the junior school. Parents of girls from state primaries said they liked the smaller size classes. Ex-pupils include June Whitfield, Angela Carter, broadcasters Maryam and Nazanine Moshiri, soprano Elizabeth Llewellyn and V&A curator Susannah Brown.

Entrance: Children can join co-ed nursery at 3 or reception at 4 via informal assessments. Further intake at 7+ via tests in maths, English and verbal reasoning. Written report from previous school also needed at this stage.

Eleven plus and 13+ places by interview and maths and English tests, plus science at 13+. Those coming up from the junior school have to pass a test in year 5 and also sit the 11+ exam. At 16+ minimum of six GCSEs required, with 9-7 grades in A level subjects, letter from previous head and interview with head master and sixth form head.

Exit: Around 90 per cent from the prep to the senior school subject to assessments. Some leave at 16 for local comps, sixth form colleges or boarding but around 60 per cent – and rising – stay on. Around same proportion usually head for Russell Group universities. Dedicated coordinator supports Oxbridge hopefuls.

Money matters: Typical GDST school fees, so more reasonable than elsewhere. Several non-means-tested academic scholarships available and number of means-tested, subject based bursaries at 11+ and 16+. All curriculum-related non-residential trips included in fees.

Remarks: Streatham & Clapham High is on the up. Take one energetic head master, add a good handful of enthusiasm, pep up the curriculum, add ambition and belief, introduce Kinza, tune a grand piano and – eureka – numbers rise. It would certainly appear that something is working. There is now a consistent waiting list for places and numbers staying on for A levels have rocketed from 36 per cent to over 60 per cent. As one parent told us, 'The head master is having an amazing effect'.

The Study Preparatory School

281

Wilberforce House, Camp Road, London SW19 4UN

Ages 4–11 **Pupils** 320

Fees: £13,650 pa

020 8947 6969
www.thestudyprep.co.uk

Headmistress: Since 2011, Susan Pepper MA PGCE NPQH (50s). Attended Godolphin & Latymer, then read modern history at Somerville College, Oxford. Did a brief spell as trainee manager for Nationwide, but quickly realised education was her métier. After finishing her PGCE, she taught History at Seaford Head School and St Paul's Girls', then moved to Francis Holland Sloane Square as head of history. It was clearly a happy move, because she stayed for another 20 years, becoming in turn head of sixth form and deputy head.

Made the crossover to primary years education when the headship at The Study Prep came up, and loves everything about it. The feeling is mutual. 'Very good, very thorough, so straightforward,' say parents. 'An excellent headmistress, very approachable'; 'She's done amazing things for the school'; 'Her door is always open and she has always given her time and advice when we needed it'; 'Always interested in the girls' achievements both in and out of school'; 'Her focus is the girls, and she really does know them.'

Runs the debating club, and remains an inspirational history teacher – 'My daughter loved her lessons and history is still her favourite subject.' Married to a draughtsman, with one grown up son. Interests include horses – 'The love of my life!' – and reading. A self-confessed crossword puzzle fanatic.

Entrance: At 4+, automatic sibling entry, thereafter by ballot. Around 120 apply for up to 48 places. School is completely non-selective at this stage, and doesn't ask to meet any of the applicants. 'We never know who we're going to get,' observed the head of the pre-prep, proudly. 'We're genuinely all-round.' Applicants for any occasional places that might arise for years 1 and 2 are given an informal taster day while the teachers observe them.

Usually a handful of places at end of year 2, and school assesses for these: papers in maths, English and reasoning, plus informal interview. Same procedure for any available places in the upper year groups, although school doesn't usually admit into years 5 and 6.

Bursaries available from Y3.

Exit: At 7+, a handful of leavers because of selective 7+ entrance point at neighbouring schools. School doesn't prepare children for this, but doesn't block it either.

At 11+ to a whole range of impressive schools: The Lady Eleanor Holles, Wimbledon High, Putney High, Surbiton High, Sutton High, Kingston Grammar, St John's Leatherhead, Epsom College, Notre Dame, Guildford High – etc. Occasional St Paul's Girls' successes. A very small number each year to board at eg Roedean, Benenden, St Mary's Ascot, but not many – parents here are generally in favour of the day school ethos.

Impressive number of scholarships – 39 awarded in 2018, an all-time record for the school, and testament to its nurturing of the girls' abilities on all fronts.

Remarks: The school is spread across two sites, both of them exquisite. In the heart of Wimbledon Village, years 4, 5 and 6 are in Spencer House, purpose built as a school back in 1905 when the original head, Miss Sidford, felt the need of something bigger than her own front room for her burgeoning student roll. Ten minutes' walk away, Wilberforce House, acquired in 1992, is home to the first four year groups, and occupies a truly magical position on Wimbledon Common's west side. Around 60 per cent of the intake is from SW19, giving The Study the feeling of a village school, although plenty come from further away – Wandsworth, Putney, Southfields, Raynes Park, even Fulham. After school care now offered until 6.30pm, to huge relief of working parents.

Classrooms are immaculate, well-equipped and inviting, with interactive whiteboards and all the fixings. Charmingly old-fashioned wooden desks with lift-up lids for the older girls ('The girls adore them!'). Small but newly revamped libraries, dotted with children sprawling luxuriously on scatter cushions, attest to the importance of books here. Specialist ICT teacher has bank of laptops and tablets at her disposal in addition to work stations in every classroom. Delightfully refurbished outdoor play areas. Exciting plans for Wilberforce House site prove that school isn't content to stand still.

Maths and English setted from year 3, an approach which parents welcome, saying it has enabled their daughters to be appropriately stretched and challenged. It certainly seems successful, judging from the high quality of the work we saw. Lessons are lively but focused, and the girls remain impeccably well-behaved. There are at least two members of staff for each class, a teacher and an assistant, ensuring that pupils get the attention they need.

For geography, history, science, etc the school recently adopted what it calls the Creative Curriculum, whereby all the subjects are taught under the umbrella of a particular theme each term. Thus the year 1 pupils had just finished beautiful portfolios on Out of Africa, for which the work included designing a ladder to help a visiting toy monkey down from the top shelf in the classroom, while the year 3s worked on some delightful Creative Recycling projects after the mysterious appearance of Stig's Dump in the school garden.

We were struck by how creative the teachers were, never mind the students – colourful and intriguing lessons seem to pour joyfully out of every classroom and wonderful displays are everywhere. 'We got letters in hieroglyphs when we were doing ancient Egyptians and we decoded them!' remembered one child fondly, and 'They make the lessons such fun!' was a comment we heard from every girl we spoke to. Excellent facilities for science, and school has increased the amount of practical work the girls do. 'Previously there was a very strong concentration on biology and it was all too facts-based. Now it's much more practical and hands-on.' French taught from reception – we listened to some year 4 girls chirrup away in delightful French accents. Spanish taught from year 6.

Homework kept to manageable levels for the younger ones, with about half an hour per night being standard. Big hike from year 3 to year 4, however, and again from year 4 to year 5, and a few parents told us they thought it could be excessive, particularly once the 11+ exams were over – 'The girls could be given a bit more time to relax,' was a typical and rueful comment. Others wished that there could be less poster and project based homework, with one adding that hours spent on this had impacted her daughter's enjoyment of certain subjects. A year 6 child told us, however, 'I don't mind all the homework, because you have to prepare for senior school.'

Full-time SENCo plus team of part-timers oversees provision for those with additional needs, mostly dyslexia and dyspraxia. Because girls are accepted unseen into reception, school occasionally has to work with parents to find an alternative school for children with more than moderate needs that can't be supported adequately here.

S

Extracurricular provision seen as one of the great strengths of the school. 'My daughter would participate in everything if she could, and she pretty much manages to!' wrote one mother. Wide-ranging sports provision includes netball, cricket, hockey, offered at school's own sports grounds at Beverley Meads, plus swimming at Wimbledon baths. 'I've been struck by how many more sporting opportunities my daughter has had at The Study than she will have at the senior schools we looked round!' commented a parent, sadly.

Drama and music both 'outstanding', according to parents, taught by specialists with 'limitless energy'. Girls can learn virtually any instrument and eagerly participate in choirs, orchestra, jazz, etc. 'I credit the school with discovering and nurturing our daughter's love for music,' was one parent's verdict. Regular productions are ambitious and hugely popular, ranging from The Wizard Of Oz to Macbeth, and LAMDA offered from year 4. An astonishing array of clubs encompasses fencing, yoga, horse & pony, chess, street dance, martial arts, music theory, touch typing – the older the girls, the bigger the choice.

Unending succession of trips – the Polka Theatre, British Museum and Hastings were some of the most recent when we visited. We thought the visual arts really exceptional. Under the guidance of remarkably expert, knowledgable teaching, pupils here produce work that is sophisticated and imaginative.

'I have nothing but good things to say about the pastoral care at The Study,' wrote a mother, and every parent said the same. A different value is taught each month – respect, kindness, generosity, resilience, etc. – and the older girls all take part in peer mentoring the younger ones. 'It's great fun!' said a year 6 pupil, 'and sometimes it's easier to talk to another pupil than a teacher when something's bothering you.' Much praise for the EQ Prep, a programme whereby counselling and support for both children and staff are embedded into the running of the school. The result seems to be a particularly happy community. The girls are chatty, lively, courteous to others and contented. 'We don't have many arguments, but the teachers sort things out really well if we do.' 'Everyone is really friendly here, and everyone makes you feel welcome.' We were also impressed at how, despite hailing from what has to be one of the most affluent areas in London, the girls didn't seem remotely materialistic: told to choose a treat for coming top in a recent house competition, they asked if they could sit on chairs during assembly. The widely-praised head of Spencer House attributes much of this to the school's non-selective ethos. 'You get the range of abilities and talents and passions, and the girls learn to support each other.'

The flip side of being such a kind and happy place is that staff can get out of practice in dealing with issues on the rare occasions when they do arise. Whispers reached us regarding a year group with some over-dominant personalities who, a number of parents claimed, hadn't been satisfactorily dealt with. There was also a perception that the school could be firmer with strong-willed parents who try to push their own child's interests ahead of everyone else's. ('Should be stronger with these parents, although they are very scary!' was how one mother put it.) School surprised and disappointed to learn of these comments, and responded: 'The school has robust policies and procedures for dealing with any pastoral issues that arise and the staff are well trained and experienced in implementing them.' And we must add that, despite these wrinkles, everyone who contacted us was unanimous in recommending the school, including the ones who had the above-mentioned concerns. 'Our daughter has been extremely happy at The Study and is sad to be leaving.' 'She has really loved her time there, and wishes that there was a Study Senior!'

We really liked this school, with its joyfully creative and caring workforce, and thought it conclusive proof that all-girls education from an early age can be simply brilliant. The children here struck us as articulate, loved, personable, relaxed, comfortable with themselves and others, and above all, completely and superlatively themselves. And that, surely, is what real girl power is all about

Surbiton High Boys' Preparatory School

Linked with Surbiton High School, Surbiton High Girls' Preparatory School

Charles Burney House, 143 Maple Road, Surbiton, Surrey KT6 4BB

Ages 4–11 **Pupils** 208

Fees: £10,857 – £13,974 pa

020 8390 6640
www.surbitonhigh.com

Headteacher: Since 2015, Sally Ralph BEd (50s), educated at a Gloucestershire grammar where she was head girl, followed by University of Bath. Mrs Ralph moved to London in the 1990s, teaching at Feltonfleet and Rowan Prep before becoming head of St David's in Ashford. She took up the headship of the boys' preparatory school after five years as acting head and deputy head of both the girls' and boys' junior schools. Parents, pupils and colleagues tell us she is a gifted mathematics teacher as well as a dynamic leader of young men. She remains active in the classroom, working with all age groups on a weekly basis and as the maths specialist. She has a passion for gymnastics and has had a liaison role between school and the British Gymnastics Association. A keen follower of many sports, who enjoys reading and trips to the theatre, she has two grown-up children.

Entrance: At 4+ informal assessment days are held in November each year for 40 reception places; also occasional places in other age groups. Assessments involve spending part or all of a day, depending on age, with the relevant year group and completing informal assessments in maths and English.

Exit: At 11+ regular academic, music, drama or sports scholarships (16 in 2018). Most go to local independent schools eg Reeds, Hampton, Kingston Grammar, Royal Grammar Guildford and Claremont Fan Court.

Remarks: A growing reputation for inspirational teaching. In the early years, pupils are taught mostly by their class teachers, with subject specialist teachers for modern foreign languages, sports and music throughout the school. Class sizes are between 18 and 22; each one has team teachers so boys can be taught in ability groups. Year 3 upwards sees the introduction of specialist teachers for all subjects.

Mathematics continues to strengthen across the age groups. The curriculum is developed and updated on a continuous basis, lots of themed projects run to link subjects together. 'Did you know you share 50 per cent of your genes with bananas?' remarked one little lad, who was busy making a DNA model in the science and art room. English and drama are embedded across the curriculum; spending the day as a Tudor child provides the stimulus for all sorts of history, arts and literacy activities.

The school is noted for being particularly good at helping children develop listening and speaking skills. Enthusiastic speakers read and write their own poetry, others join the debating club or the school council. French from reception, later on Spanish and Mandarin are added, delivered by The Dragons of Europe; boys work towards CE level 1. Popular annual event is the French musical breakfast; parents enjoy the choir while year 6s don bow ties and act as waiters serving coffee and croissants. Classrooms and corridors are bursting with displays of both academic and artistic work, demonstrating that there is plenty of imaginative teaching going on.

All subject knowledge is broadened through the use of the latest technology. Year 3s upwards all have their own iPad while younger boys can access school iPads. Focus groups, Friday drop ins and maths clinics are available to all pupils wanting to catch up or extend their work. Learning support staff are on hand to assist with a variety of mild SpLDs, touch typing is delivered through a club, and EAL is arranged as required. There are lunchtime clubs, academic, creative and active to choose from, breakfast club opens at 7.30am and there's an after-school club, which working parents find very useful.

Having bought a second building adjacent to the main school, the boys' prep is in the first phase of a long-awaited expansion. The school now has space for two classes in each year group. Reception and years 1-3 are based at the refurbished Charles Burney House, while years 4 to 6 remain at the original site in Elmers Avenue. Both buildings are large Victorian houses with small but well-equipped playgrounds. Boys benefit from a fabulous 39 acres of sports grounds in nearby Hinchley Wood, which includes tennis/netball courts, all weather hockey pitch, rugby/football pitches and a pavilion. Adjacent to the sports ground in is a lovely wooded area which allows numerous opportunities for adventure and learning outside the classroom, from pond dipping and observing wildlife in their natural habitats to family camping weekends.

Sport is a great strength throughout the three Surbiton schools. The physical education programme covers skills and techniques required for basketball, hockey, gymnastics, athletics and tennis. The main school sports are football, rugby and cricket. An extensive fixture list ensures all boys get the opportunity to represent the school in competitive matches. PE display cupboard shelves teem with awards and trophies.

Music continues to be high profile; the school arranges visiting instrumentalists and tuition for any instrument is available. In year 3, everyone gets the opportunity to learn a stringed instrument, the following year a brass instrument. Lovely music room brimming with instruments; boys have an impressive choice of choirs and ensembles to join. All the boys get the opportunity each year to be in musical and dramatic productions and assemblies.

Parents feel older boys are well prepared for 11+ exams and looked after all round in a calm and sensible way. Each boy is allocated a mentor to help with practice interviews and any queries. Mrs Ralph guides parents through the process of choosing the right senior school for their son. Parents are unanimous in commenting on the success at 11+, due to how well the school manages everyone's expectations.

A child-orientated school full of learning opportunities, where cheerful and articulate boys are also allowed to have fun and encouraged to be kind and thoughtful, with opportunities to link up with the girls' prep.

Surbiton High Girls' Preparatory School

Linked with Surbiton High School, Surbiton High Boys' Preparatory School

95-97 Surbiton Road, Kingston, Surrey KT1 2HW

Ages 4-11 **Pupils** 308

Fees: £10,857 – £13,974 pa

020 8439 1309
www.surbitonhigh.com

Head: Since 2015, Clemmie Stewart BA English literature and education (30s). Educated at Bedales and Winchester University, she has taught in both the independent and state sectors. Her teaching career started at Farleigh Prep, followed by several years at Talavera Junior School in Aldershot. In 2014 she joined Surbiton High as director of teaching and learning and was appointed headteacher the following year, after proving herself to be an outstanding English teacher. A go ahead and enthusiastic personality; parents we spoke to feel she is an asset to the school and will continue to steer the girls in all the right directions. She is always smiling, say her charges, which makes us feel happy. Talented all-rounder herself, Miss Stewart was a music scholar at Bedales and a horsewoman with success in the show jumping world. A country girl at heart, she loves travelling and exploring during the holidays, during term time she enjoys running and walking her dogs. She is a fan of many sports including Formula 1 and football, and an avid reader, and has a particular interest in how children's education advances continually.

Entrance: At 4+ girls are invited to attend informal child-friendly assessment mornings. Grouped by seasonal birthdays, autumn, spring, summer, this ensures each child is assessed with others of similar age and developmental stage. Several members of staff observe prospective candidates doing simple tasks based on stories and nursery activities. Two form entry. Occasional places may be available in other year groups. Assessments involve spending part or all of a day, depending on age, with the relevant year group and completing informal assessments in maths and English.

S

Exit: At 11+ around 80 per cent of girls progress through to the senior school; regular scholarships are awarded for music, drama, art, sports and academics (in 2018, there were five scholarships to the senior school). One or two go to local grammars or a boarding school. Occasional parent still moans about girls being not prepared for other schools, however majority of parents feel why go through the stress, when you have one of the best senior schools in the area at your fingertips? Occasionally a pupil can be advised in year 5 that they might fare better in a less selective school.

Remarks: Bubbling with activities, academic, sporting and creative, the school grows from strength to strength. Ms Stewart favours an innovative approach alongside traditional teaching, which she feels enables pupils to exceed their targets and make outstanding progress. Lovely bright interlinking reception classes with their own small play area. Early years provision was highly praised in recent ISI inspection; parents agree; pupils are given an excellent grounding in language, literacy and mathematics. Form teachers cover all subjects until year 2, subject specialists, including maths and English teachers, are introduced from year 3, adding breadth across the curriculum. Inspiring co-curricular links connect subjects effortlessly: a chocolate workshop leads to a fair trade geography project, African dancing and story writing. The possibilities are endless, exciting stuff and always something to look forward to, girls tell us.

In addition to stand-alone lessons, drama is embedded into class teaching through creative role-play, history in action days, and storytelling, helping to develop a range of communication skills. Imaginative art and DT displayed in classrooms and corridors, pupils are exposed to a variety of media. Older pupils can use senior school facilities and are taught by some of the senior art specialists. Three languages are offered, Spanish from reception, French is added in year 2 and Mandarin in years 4 and 5. Pupils are continuously monitored; targets are set to check progress and ensure no one slips under the radar.

School prides itself on encouraging children to become active learners with a big focus on language skills and decision making. IT strategy is always advancing with each pupil having an iPad, some lessons have gone digital, and girls are definitely tech savvy, say parents. Lots of praise from the parents for teaching staff, who are good mix of youth and experience and considered an inspirational bunch. Our guides were eloquent, proud of their school and keen to explain everything from their art and science projects to learning to skip when they were younger.

SEN, termed as learning enrichment, provides specific support to individuals with mild SpLDs, usually dyspraxia and dyslexia. Pupils are cared for on an individual basis, via one-to-one sessions or enrichment groups. Gifted and talented activities run to extend knowledge and, if appropriate, some girls are offered scholarship training. EAL is arranged as required; the school has quite a few families from Korea and South Asia.

Music continues to flourish; everyone learns to play a string and a brass instrument, with a good number of pupils having individual tuition on more than one instrument. Dedicated and well-resourced room for music theory and pupils get the chance to try their hand at composition. Host of choirs, ensembles and orchestras, with plenty of opportunities for solo performances; girls and boys often join forces on choir trips, musical and dramatic productions. Good selection of outings, residential trips and visitors are arranged for many interests. Around 70 clubs, world explorers, newspapers, jewellery making and dance to mention a few; there are also breakfast and after-school clubs.

Parent-teacher partnerships are well developed; majority of parents feel the school communicates with them effectively in traditional ways and more recently via social media. Pastoral care has a positive and family feel to it and school is always keen to develop social interaction; mixed age groups sit together for lunch, and reception class all have a year 6 buddy. Everyone is allocated to one of the four houses and encouraged to voice their opinions and ideas through the school council. Parents and pupils are active fundraisers for the school and charities; mufti day with an ice pop sale is a firm favourite for fundraising, girls tell us.

Sport has come on in leaps and bounds since our last visit; this part of the curriculum is given equal importance as academics. As with many inner-city schools, on site space is fairly tight. Known as LOC, 'learning outside the classroom' mostly takes place at their 39 acres of sports grounds and woodland close by in Hinchley Wood. A specially designed physical education programme teaches the skills needed for netball, hockey, rounders, tennis and gymnastics. In addition to this they also cover athletics, health-related fitness and team building. Netball team is extremely successful; girls start to compete in year 3 U8s, regularly reaching the finals of the national netball tournament. Boys' and girls' preps participate in mixed athletics and netball events; netball team recently came fifth in the London Youth Games, while the athletics squad came third in Kingston borough finals. Girls can also join the ski club, which uses the local dry ski slopes and competes regularly. Adjacent to the sports ground is a woodland area, offering further opportunities for outdoor pursuits and eco-projects, planting vegetables, discovering wildlife and camping trips; the prospects are plentiful.

A single sex school with co-educational opportunities as the boys' and girls' preparatory schools often link together. A happy, vibrant school for inquisitive and active girls. Unstuffy atmosphere but traditional ethos that fit comfortably with modern teaching and an innovative outlook.

Surbiton High School

Linked with Surbiton High Girls' Preparatory School, Surbiton High Boys' Preparatory School

13–15 Surbiton Crescent, Kingston, Surrey KT1 2JT

Ages 11–18 **Pupils** 1,044 **Sixth form** 217

Fees: £17,142 pa

020 8439 1309
www.surbitonhigh.com

Principal: Since January 2018, Rebecca Glover, previously head of Hull Collegiate School. Educated at Rishworth School and Leeds Beckett University; taught at Broxbourne School, Roundwood Park, Hymers College in Hull and Tadcaster Grammar (deputy head) before joining Hull Collegiate. Runs marathons, including London and New York; has led a team of divers off the Great Barrier Reef, in Maui and in Fiji; has climbed Mt Kilimanjaro; and represented GB in gymnastics.

Academic matters: Results are climbing steadily with everyone aiming high. Fifty-one per cent of A level grades A*-A in 2018, with 87 per cent at A*-B. At GCSE, 78 per cent of grades were 9-7. Maths results usually very good with large numbers taking further maths getting A*/A. Class sizes are large-ish at 24, sets for maths, languages and practical subjects are smaller. Teaching is vigorous and interesting, so pupils need to be on the ball. Year 7s kick off with learning the all-important, often forgotten skills of note taking and how to organise themselves and their bags; easier than it was, with modern technology. 'Teachers want us to become independent and active learners as soon as we can,' explain pupils. Classes we observed had a good multisensory element with pupils looking eager and engaged. Stringent monitoring of all pupils; no one is allowed to fall by the wayside. Weekly drop-in clinics, maths and English for all, other clinics are mainly for supporting GCSE and A level students. Everyone studies at least two languages: core languages are French, German and Spanish, but girls can also opt for Mandarin, Italian, Latin and Greek through to A level.

Technology is everywhere: an assistant principal for digital strategy arrived a couple of years ago, so progress in this area has been speedy. The latest technology is used to enhance lessons; everyone has an iPad, but don't worry, social media blocked, so no distractions during class time. Staff and pupils are trained to use personal organisers; iPads, digital archives and learning spaces are available to every department. Comfortable ICT suite set up in semicircular tiers so everyone can see the board easily; girls commented on the staff's sterling research work to find the best software for them.

Bustling library is an active resource centre, with reading clubs, creative writing workshops and external speakers to boost interests, alongside books, magazines and DVDs in different languages. English department runs a literary society, which meets weekly for tea and topical discussions on books, film and theatre. To inspire and teach the girls all aspects of writing there is a writer in residence. He collaborates with teachers to run artistic projects, helps prepare students for national competitions and has launched a student laureate programme for creative writing.

SEND learning enrichment staff run study skills groups and support pupils with mild dyslexic and dyspraxic type difficulties. Touch-typing classes are taught by an outside provider. Korean mentor and translator and two part-time EAL teachers work with girls whose first language is not English and prepare them for IELTS or similar exams. Gifted and talented programme offers a good range of co-curricular activities and extension tasks, special classes and mentors for scholars and Oxbridge preparation. School is keen to emphasise these classes are about offering equality of challenge to the most able pupils.

Sixth formers are well prepared for university life with lectures and special visitors to encourage them to look widely at the choice of courses available to them. Again, the school takes an all-round approach to pupils' futures; a leadership coach provides guidance and training for interview technique, public speaking, commercial awareness, careers, and preparing personal statements and workplace application forms. Young Enterprise gives the sixth formers an opportunity to try establishing their own businesses, designing products to sell and distribute in competition with other schools. The entrepreneur in residence works with pupils to help develop key work and life skills for business. The school is aware that while technology is changing rapidly, the skills for successful living do not, and takes seriously the responsibility to provide opportunities for pupils to develop their leadership and entrepreneurial skills.

Games, options, the arts: Now a paradise for sporty types; 'sport for all' is coupled with the pursuit of excellence: the aim is to provide the best for everyone whatever their ability. The school has 39 acres of grounds nearby in Hinchley Wood, an immense asset for a town school. 'Super 6 Sports' are netball, hockey, rowing, skiing, gymnastics and tennis, each with their own head and coaches. Fitness centre for aerobics, zumba, other sporting choices including golf, athletics, badminton and riding. Former BBC rowing club boathouse has recently been snapped up by United Learning, and an experienced team of coaches trains rowers from novices to national eventers. Riding club takes place in Cobham at the Silvermere centre. More competent and competition riders, some of whom have qualified for national championships, can join the equestrian team. Surbiton High has the largest and most successful school ski club in the UK; young skiers use a local artificial slope with extra sessions at the Snowdome. Each sport has its own head, professional coaches and mentors to manage events and arrange exciting annual tours all over the world. It goes without saying, girls are hugely successful locally, regionally and internationally; currently seven pupils are trialling or competing for GB. Surbiton Advanced Sport, known as SAS, is a specially designed programme for elite sports performers to help them balance academic work with a high level of training and competition.

Art department was preparing for an exhibition at the time of our visit to show off the talents of creative pupils. Impressive displays of large oil canvases, textiles, DT, photography and ceramics in well-resourced open plan studio with its own printing presses, kiln, dark room, computer suite and art library. Everyone can get involved in drama; masses of productions to ensure everyone gets the chance to perform. If singing or acting is not your thing, you can try stage management, set design, props or costume making. Year 9s write and perform plays for the house drama week; girls also perform at the National Theatre and an annual Shakespeare Festival. Energetic and inspiring head of music has developed the department beyond recognition, according to customers. From jazz to chamber music there is a full range of orchestras, bands, choirs and ensembles to join for differing abilities. 'I can't believe the great choices my sister and her friends have,' lamented an old girl. Music and drama are now thought to be thriving departments, which often collaborate, resulting in some stunning performances both in school and at the local theatre. Despite this, take-up at A level of these subjects is quite low. Clubs and societies offer something for everyone; there are around 70 to choose from, as well as the popular D of E and outings at home and abroad.

Background and atmosphere: The school is part of the United Learning Group, an independent Christian educational charity which runs and sponsors several independent schools and academies. Surbiton High now owns an entire block of buildings; the two most recent acquisitions are a large Victorian building which houses the junior section of the boys' prep school and Mary Bennett House, a modern building that has been developed into nine new classrooms and a large, flexible learning and event space. In the centre of these buildings are multi-sport courts and a grassed area for recreation, fundraising events, a performance space, and home to the school chickens, cared for by the chicken club girls.

Despite it being quite a large school, everyone comments on the friendly atmosphere. Voluntary work in the local community continues to flourish, with the hospital visiting scheme and the Friendship Hour: elderly residents are visited or invited to school events, summer and Christmas parties.

Pastoral care, well-being and discipline: High praise for pastoral care. When talking to one prospective family visiting with their (generally) sweet 11 year old, school staff assured them that 'we'll still like her when she is 15!' 'And they do,' says that mother; 'the pastoral care is really very good.' Most parents report an immediate and effective response to any issues. Generally a well-behaved bunch – largely complying with the zero tolerance policy on drugs, drink and cigarettes. Smokers hauled before head even if they were caught out of school hours and uniform. School nurse on site, doctor available weekly. Good induction routines for year 7s, followed up with 'big sister' mentoring programme. Healthy culture of 'telling' about problems and school quick to support anyone in difficulty and any of their friends who may have been involved. Not a bitch-fest – girls say their classmates are supportive of them. Parents pleased that school somehow manages to keep cliques and queen bees under control.

S

Pupils and parents: Predominantly busy, hardworking UK families, many of whom travel into the city for business. The clientele generally reflects the local population. Over the last few years the school has been attracting girls from slightly further afield due to good transport links; mainline train station approximate 10 minutes' walk away. Local community also includes a growing number of international families, particularly from south east Asia and Korea, who are well represented at the school. Many parents are involved in the PTA raising funds for the school and charities. One mother, a relative newcomer, told us that what impressed her most was how welcome new parents felt when attending fundraising and social events. Alumni: Mollie King singer and songwriter, Chemmy Alcott, Olympic skier, Nicky Morgan MP.

Entrance: At 11+, most prep school girls move directly onto the senior school. New entrants can try out the school on an Experience Morning before taking assessment tests in English, maths and, then for their interview write a personal statement and provide a report from their primary school. Not elitist, but parents say it has become more selective than it used to be, as its reputation grows. At 16+, some places for external candidates to join the sixth form via an interview, GCSE results with 9-7s in the subjects to be studied at A level and report from current school.

Exit: Just under a third leave after GCSEs, for local state sixth form college or perhaps boarding school. At 18+ around 80 per cent go to top universities (Birmingham, Newcastle, Durham and Exeter all popular). A record 10 to Oxbridge in 2018, plus three medics.

Money matters: Perceived by parents to offer good value for money. Help with fees is available through means tested United Learning and Church Foundation assisted places and bursaries for the daughters of clergy. Competitive scholarships are offered for academics, music, art, drama and sports at 11+ and 16+.

Remarks: An ambitious arena for driven girls ready to embrace life and all its challenges. Never a dull moment, owing to the school's growing reputation for offering outstanding provision across the board at a reasonable price. Recent ISI Inspection confirmed this, awarding the school excellent in all categories and exceptional for pupil achievement.

Sussex House School

68 Cadogan Square, London SW1X 0EA

Ages 8–13 Pupils 185 C of E

Fees: £20,745 pa

020 7584 1741
www.sussexhouseschool.co.uk

Headmaster: Since 1994, the engaging, cultured Nicholas Kaye MA ACP, Cambridge English graduate followed by music research (60s). Whilst deputy head here, following a brief spell at Asra Hawariat School in Addis Ababa, the opportunity arose to acquire the school from the Vernon Trust, which he seized with typical energy, creating an independent charitable trust. Sussex House has never looked back, going from strength to strength, achieving the recent accolade of Best Prep School award. Parents admire this 'erudite man' and the boys sum him up as 'diverse, really talented, passionate about music, poetry, architecture, and a playwright'. His study/Victorian parlour is crammed with bookshelves containing leather-bound volumes and novels by past Old Cadogans, an ornamental pianoforte and a cornucopia of porcelain, potted plants and objets d'art.

As one might expect in this very traditional institution, there are school photographs, house shields and embroidered banners made for the Jubilee and carried in procession on special occasions such as the annual All Souls' Day Requiem at St Mary Magdalene Church. Conducted by Mr Kaye, this was an uplifting service in which the Sussex House choristers sang exquisitely. All the parents we spoke to agreed Mr Kaye 'has an excellent rapport with the boys'. 'He sees the best in every child and gets the best out of every child.' One commented of his year 8 English lessons: 'The sessions are challenging, quite adult, like an Oxford tutorial'.

Entrance: At 8+, 36 pupils selected via English, maths and reasoning tests and interview. Strong English is a key requirement and there are no boys in the school with EAL requirements; however, it does cater for up to 23 boys on the SEN register who are given support without additional charge. Parents suggest, 'Not a school of mixed ability, although mild learning difficulties such as dyspraxia are dealt with'. Most live within a few miles of Cadogan Square. Regular feeders are Garden House, Eaton House and other central London pre-preps. There are no sibling discounts but bursaries up to full remission of fees in cases of genuine need.

Exit: Majority to Eton, then St Paul's, Westminster, Winchester and City of London.

Remarks: Mr Kaye chose the aspirational school motto 'Lead me to the rock that is higher than I' and, as he explains, 'This implies a journey which, unlike climbing Everest, is never complete'. Unusually for a day school, there is an Anglican school chaplain who leads important services in the local church which acts as the school chapel.

This is a distinctive, unashamedly academic school. After being greeted by gowned school marshal, Sergeant Khim Sherchan, formerly of the Gurkhas, we are ushered into a grand Norman Shaw arts and crafts town house with William Morris wallpaper and stunning fresh flower arrangements. Up the wide, ornate mahogany staircase is the ballroom, which provides a venue for daily assemblies, lessons around polished tables and tea time concerts. Spacious new science lab.

The music is stunning and every year concerts with a professional orchestra take place at the Cadogan Hall along with an annual musical at the Fortune Theatre. We heard a talented 9 year old play the violin with incredible skill and learnt he is also a valued member of the football team. One parent remarked, 'The school is small enough so that each boy finds a niche.' Creativity is an intrinsic part of life here, and why many parents choose it over other top prep schools. As a parent commented, 'The wonderful drama is performed in the West End, giving unparalleled opportunities for this age'. We saw some excellent architectural models in the making ready for the annual exhibition with the theme of Iconic Chelsea and boys told us they find their art classes inspiring.

They exercise in Battersea Park at least twice a week, and there are regular fixtures for A-D teams. The school day includes walks to Nicholls Hall for gym, fencing and music. The boys we chatted to would love to play rugby, but revel in football alongside options such as fencing, tennis, cricket, golf and swimming. Fencing is excellent here and the school magazine, The Cadogan, records many sporting achievements and activities, as well as superb poetry. However, break times are spent indoors, and parents who would prefer somewhere with outside space where boys can let off steam should look elsewhere.

All the boys we met commented on how the staff are prepared to give up their own time to help. The boys themselves are a superb advertisement for the school: intelligent, polite, lively, responsive and articulate. 'They are confident without being arrogant,' commented a parent, adding candidly, 'That is not to say that they are not sometimes boisterous, and need careful handling in this confined space.' The year 8s are prefects and wear gowns unless they fall from grace: a great incentive.

Average size of classes 18, with 12 in the top year when a scholarship group is formed. The curriculum is carefully tailored to suit the needs of those aiming at various different school examinations. Mr Kaye would love to have a six day week, 'but that is not possible', so much is packed in: orchestra practice and Greek before school, for example. As there is no dining room or kitchen, boys must bring packed lunches; 'not ideal,' state parents, but lunch time is a social occasion with the form teacher followed by numerous, popular clubs including architecture and discussion group. One ex-parent remarked on how 'well-rounded SH boys are', and that out of 250 boys at Eton in her son's year, three of the 12 chosen for the Eton debating competition were SH boys.

For those parents seeking a Summer Fields in central London, Sussex House fits the bill. Parents agree, 'It really does prepare boys for boarding at 13+ and gives them a wonderful, well-rounded platform'. It is not surprising that so many Old Cadogans hold the school with great affection. They include novelists Edward St Aubyn, Jason Goodwin and Richard Mason, along with actors Daniel Radcliffe, Jasper Britton, and Christopher and Jay Villiers, composer Michael Csanyi Wills, and many more recorded in the annual, very impressive magazine.

Sutton Grammar School

Manor Lane, Sutton, Surrey SM1 4AS

Ages 11–18 **Pupils** 935 **Sixth form** 287 (17 girls)

020 8642 3821
www.suttongrammar.sutton.sch.uk

Headmaster: Since 1990, Gordon Ironside MA PGCE (50s). Read physics at Cambridge, then taught maths at Alleyn's and Sutton Grammar before becoming deputy head in 1987. Married to a fellow teacher, he has three grown-up children who all attended Sutton grammar schools. One son continues what has become a bit of a family tradition and teaches in another local grammar school.

Affable, understated, hardworking and thoroughly dedicated to education all round. Staff love that he lets them get on with running their own departments – 'If I see it working, I don't intervene,' he says; 'He's hands-off, but supportive when needed,' they say. Teaches A level maths and GCSE RE – 'All senior leaders here teach. We are teachers first and foremost and managers second. Plus, if I understand the pressures teachers are under, I am better able to support them.' Younger pupils told us they don't have much to do with him; older ones call him 'approachable' and 'encouraging.' Parents believe the 'unaffected' atmosphere of the school and focus on 'just getting on with things' comes from him – 'he's great, but not one to shout about how brilliant either he or the school is,' said one parent. 'Perhaps not the most dynamic in personality, but works tirelessly behind the scenes to support his staff and pupils and always on hand for parents,' another told us.

Interests span across arts and sports and he enjoys the occasional round of golf – 'increasingly occasional,' he laughs. Involved in a lot of charity work; he is chairman of governors of the local hospital school.

Retiring in July 2019.

Academic matters: Highly selective and usually in the top 10 per cent of the highest achieving schools. Needless to say, it delivers mostly excellent results: in 2018, 81 per cent of exams were graded 9-7 at GCSE; 61 per cent A*/A at A level (84 per cent A*/B).

The secret to their success, it seems, are the teachers. 'Nobody lets you fall behind'; 'teachers regularly give up lunchtimes to help you' etc, say pupils. 'There's real enthusiasm for their subject – you see them getting really excited about it, even when they've worked there for years, and that really rubs off.' 'They don't necessarily stay on curriculum if we're really interested in a particular area – I love that.' Good mix of male and female, including in senior roles, most of them long serving; 'We only change one or two staff a year,' says head. Parents like the fact that they can email form tutors.

All three sciences and maths extremely strong. Plenty of large and light (though not all state-of-the-art) labs, greenhouse on the roof and pupils breed trout and salmon to release into the River Wandle. Seemingly infinite science-related project clubs and pupils regularly win the likes of UK Engineer of the Year and Intech science awards; one boy was listed as one of Time magazine's 30 most influential teenagers in the world for his science inventions, about which he's even done a TED talk. Sixth formers help to teach science in primary schools, while some local schools visit Sutton Grammar to experience working in a lab. Early work experience is arranged in hospitals for those considering careers in medicine.

Head is big on curricular (and extracurricular) breadth, so no need to fret about arts and humanities being shoved aside. 'The way I see it, everyone does everything for three years, then everyone specialises a little, but still keeping it nice and wide within their 11 GCSEs – or 12 if they're doing extra maths,' says head. 'I think it's what makes this school stand out from the grammars in the area,' one boy told us. Upshot is that all boys must do at least one 'doing, making or acting' GCSE such as PE or drama, plus all take RE, a humanity and a language. No classics, modern languages only – boys choose from French or German from year 7, then can add a second (including Spanish) from year 8. Setting in maths from year 9, with a bottom set for English in years 10 and 11 for those who need extra support. Homework built up incrementally, 'so there's never a time when you feel they're suddenly starting to pile it on,' said one pupil. Plenty of help with UCAS and careers, with all pupils seeing a dedicated careers advisor at least once in year 10 and again in year 12.

Citizenship taught from year 7 to 11 ('which means we can teach areas like democracy and politics, including radicalisation, not as a bolt-on but as integral,' says head) and enterprise from year 9 to 11 ('There's no point in our students doing these amazing inventions if they don't have the skills to sell them,' he says).

Commitment to breadth continues into sixth form, with options from the 23-strong A level menu including DT, drama, PE, photography and business studies and, impressively, there's a promise from the head not to cancel subjects that only get three or so takers. Most popular in terms of numbers are (you guessed it) maths and sciences, but history, geography and economics are also considered worthy pickings among pupils. Rigorous computer science skills are taught up to year 9, leading to good numbers choosing it at GCSE and A level – 'Some of our strongest maths students love the problem-solving aspect.'

SENCo oversees SEN provision throughout the school for those on statements, SpLDs, sensory impairments or high functioning ASD. When we visited, the school had more statements (eight) than two of the local comprehensives ('and certainly more than the other local state grammars'), which has meant no shortage of effort is put in to support students with additional needs – but neither the school nor parents claim it's perfect. 'We don't always deliver the goods, but we have a deserved reputation for caring,' says head, who stresses that pupils have to be able to cope and enjoy the fast moving and competitive environment. 'The provision has sometimes been excellent, other times not so good, but I'm not sure it would have been better anywhere else,' said one parent.

Games, options, the arts: If you're after lush green fields, plentiful courts and vast pitches, you'll be disappointed – 'It's always a bit of a worry on open evenings when you see some parents shocked at our tight little site,' admits head. But nobody really minds once they realise the students head off to a 27-acre sports ground 15 minutes away in Cheam for an afternoon of games every week. 'It's great, albeit a bit dated,' said one student about the grounds shared by old boys and Surrey football clubs; and back on the school site there's an onsite sports hall with gymnasium plus largish heated open-air swimming pool (admittedly not looking its best during our winter visit).

Probably not a school for the highly competitive who are dead set on thrashing other schools at everything on the sports field, but inclusivity is the name of the game here, with most boys are guaranteed to play in the A/B teams at some stage. And parents and pupils alike appreciate the way 'PE staff put so much effort in to finding activities students will really enjoy, whether that's badminton or table tennis.' Football is top sport in winter and athletics has replaced cricket's number one spot in summer. Cross-country (through local woods), basketball and gymnastics (in sports hall) also popular. Well established CCF (run with Nonsuch High) and D of E programmes.

Some imaginative art on display around the school, with option to take it at GCSE and A level. But it's not just art for art's sake – this school is a fine example of helping to transform STEM into STEAM by increasingly combining art and design with science, technology, engineering and maths, which those in industry claim is essential to meet economic needs in the 21st century. 'Product design is particularly popular,' one boy told us.

Chamber groups, orchestras and choirs engage in a range of musical pursuits, including a cappella singing. Tuition on any instrument of a boy's choice can be arranged, with the four practice rooms all in full use all the time. 'I wouldn't say it's a massively musical school, the kind where you hear music as you walk about, but the opportunities are definitely there if you want them,' says one pupil. 'I did not expect my son to be so musical and yet he wound up doing music at A level,' a parent told us.

Music and drama departments team up with Sutton High School for biannual musical production. Both schools and parents pull together to produce fabulous productions. Drama on the curriculum: a reasonable number of boys go on to take GCSE and A level theatre studies. LAMDA courses and exams on offer too. The old gym has been converted into one of two drama studios.

The push on extracurricular (as well as the canteen being open for breakfast) means things start to get busy most mornings from around 7.45am, with the last students heading off around 6pm; club list is huge with everything from board games to Young Enterprise club and from electronics to Rubik's cube club, plus all the usual range of sports. During the summer term there is an annual activities week. Trips include foreign travel (some students came up with the idea of a charity-focused trip to Malawi the year before we visited, which they persuaded staff to run – 'it was the best 15 days ever,' one pupil told us), adventure sports camps and a year 9 visit to the First World War battlefields. Some older pupils try their hand at teaching in local primary schools.

Background and atmosphere: Opened as Sutton County Grammar in 1899, charging fees of two pounds and 10 shillings per term. More or less everything you could want is on the compact site, with an eclectic mix of old and new buildings neatly surrounding the central tarmacked playground area. Latest additions include a two-storey maths block, sixth form centre, bigger dining room and extra science lab. 'The facilities have improved a lot over the last 20 years,' says head, although some boys feel it's a shame there aren't more outdoor areas. Light-filled library with dedicated librarians doubles up (as do many areas of the school) as private study areas for sixth formers, although shame not to see more books on the shelves.

Since 2017, sixth-form co-ed (17 girls currently). 'We're a boys' school and that isn't going to change, but we took the decision to take in girls principally because of funding issues and because being a little bit bigger helps all subjects to be more sustainable,' says head. The girls appear confident and everyone agrees they've 'helped sharpen things up.' 'And it's not as if the school is a stranger to girls – we've always had them around for CCF and they have historically been able to come and do single subjects as members of another school,' points out head.

Students from year 10 upwards are allowed to go off site during their breaks and lunch hour, 'though many stay as the food is so much better than it used to be,' a pupil told us. Sandwich bar in the playground (known as the Snack Shack) helps to relieve the lunchtime crush. Stylish but small canteen serves hot meals. Everything runs like clockwork in this traditional focused grammar school and pupils have a strong sense of pride in it.

Pastoral care, well-being and discipline: Fifth house recently added to existing four; besides the usual inter-house competitions, this system – along with year group tutors – forms the structural base for pupil welfare ie older pupils given responsibility to look after younger ones in same house. 'You feel the school really cares about you – you're not just a result on a spreadsheet,' one boy told us. Counsellor available one day a week, although some pupils we spoke to were not aware of this.

Pupils are taught to respect others and take responsibility for all aspects of the school and themselves. Everyone is expected to follow a strict but fair code on behaviour, hair and uniform. Faculty-run lunchtime detentions for more minor misdemeanours like forgetting homework ('some departments are much more lenient than others,' say pupils); Wednesday detention under deputy head with letter home to parents for more serious stuff like regular smaller offences or bigger ones such as swearing – 'but most never get one,' pupils told us. No permanent exclusions in recent years; around 10 temporary ones at most in any one year for anything from theft to violence.

'It's virtually non-existent,' says head re bullying; boys told us it does happen occasionally, 'but it's usually short lived and the usual things that people get bullied for in school – like being keen on studying – aren't picked on here,' said one.

Parents' information evenings and discussion groups run on a wide range of topics, often led by outside speakers. Parents are canvassed on subjects they'd like to know more about each term and pupils are welcome to attend too if they wish.

Pupils and parents: Parents mostly professionals from a wide mix of backgrounds – wealthy Surrey and south Londoners through to those from less affluent areas. Good transport links a boon for those further away. Around 60 per cent Asian (a lot more than the proportion in the local community, says head) now entering from year 7; the remaining 40 per cent dominated by white British and scatterings of other cultures including Korean and African Caribbean. Communications between school office and parents could be better, we were told – 'We get emails from the office and there are always mistakes, so you often get another three before the information is actually correct,' said one parent.

Boys are well-behaved, motivated and (with some exceptions of some surprisingly tongue-tied year 7s and 8s that we met) articulate. At least half come in expecting to become doctors (whether that comes from the parents or the boys, head says he's 'not too sure, but because we keep the boys on multiple tracks for longer than other schools, and push the extracurricular so hard, boys are easily able to change their pathway if they choose to').

The Suttonians have a very active old boys' network and a large number of them remain involved with the school. Famous alumni include Brian Paddick, Christopher Bigsby, David Bellamy and David Farrar.

Entrance: Places are highly sought after. Nearly 3,000 boys take the Sutton-wide selective eligibility test, which covers the five local grammar schools and involves English and maths multiple-choice questions. Register by mid-August. Around 1,000 get through to phase two, an exam set by the school with more open-ended questions, also in English and maths. Seventy-five of the places go to the highest scorers within a set postcode that 'doesn't go far beyond the Sutton boundary'; the other 65 are chosen purely on scores. PTA runs mock test days for around 2,000 children each year wanting to prepare for them. At 16+ around 40 competitive entry places are available for both girls and boys into the sixth form – successful applicants will need around three 9-8s and three 7s at GCSE.

Exit: Almost all to university, although the occasional pupil takes up a specialist apprenticeship in the workplace – 'we very much encourage this if it's right for the pupil,' says head. Nine to Oxbridge in 2018, seven studying medicine in the UK and in Europe with good numbers also opting for veterinary sciences. Others to a range of top universities, with London colleges, Southampton, Exeter, Bristol and Warwick all popular. Engineering currently the most dominant subject; law also becoming more popular.

Money matters: School asks parents to support the school financially – up to £50 a month, with around 80 per cent taking it up, 'although some pay more like a fiver a month.' 'I hated introducing it – I came here to teach, not to raise money, but the money flows in because parents value the breadth of what we offer,' says head. PTA raises around £80,000 each year for the benefit of pupils and for school developments.

Remarks: It's made clear to these bright boys (and now girls in sixth form) right from the off that the sky's the limit to what they can achieve, with some fantastic opportunities that reach well beyond the curriculum to ensure no potential in any area is missed. But what most impressed us was the way this all seems to happen in the most unassuming, down-to-earth way and without undue pressure. There's a smaller school vibe here, which has all the benefits of wraparound pastoral care, but it works hard to produce independent, mature thinkers. For many pupils – those who thrive on hard work and embrace intellectual experiences – it is a springboard to a very bright future.

Sutton High Junior School

Linked with Sutton High School

55 Cheam Road, Sutton, Surrey SM1 2AX

Ages 3–11 **Pupils** 260

Fees: £13,260 pa

020 8225 3072
www.suttonhigh.gdst.net

Head of junior school: Since 2015, Anne Musgrove BA QTS (40s). With a BA in education studies from the University of Warwick,

S

she has over 20 years' experience of teaching in both the independent and maintained sectors including a number of years in Australia. Formerly deputy head (academic) and acting head at Putney High Junior School, she joined Sutton High Junior School as deputy head in 2014 before promotion to head.

Gentle, smiley and softly-spoken, but don't be fooled – she is a strong leader with a single-minded passion for the school, 'working crazy hours' (as one parent puts it) to ensure the school continues on the accelerated academic journey she has set it on. 'The school had pockets of excellence, but I felt we needed to re-write the curriculum to get better scope and sequence overall. So we got in an educational consultant and have joined up the dots between subjects,' she says. Parents say the result is a 'more focused school academically, but without being the hot-house that many preps are around here.'

Girls clearly adore her, feeling able to pop into her cosy office (complete with beanbags – purple, as most things are in this school – for pupils to sit on) to discuss anything from friendship issues to a certificate they've gained outside school. 'She's super-kind,' one told us, beaming. Parents are impressed too. 'She's superb – I'm a massive fan,' is a typical comment. 'She knows all the girls by name and sometimes when I go to collect my daughter, I'll see her chatting to her in the playground, which is just wonderful.' 'She's totally engaged, as well as really listening to everything you say as a parent. In fact, she regularly asks parents for input,' says another.

Lives near Bushy Park, where she continues to pursue her interest in art and art history by visiting galleries and museums in the UK and overseas.

Entrance: Girls can join the nursery from their third birthday onwards and move on to reception at 4+. Younger children attend an informal play session before being offered a place; from 6+ girls sit assessment tests, run by the head. 'Because girls come from a range of different school experiences, it's their potential that we're looking for and we test them both verbally and non-verbally, as well as talking to them about their interests,' says the head, who adds that girls need to be able to adapt to a fast-paced curriculum, with different specialist teachers for subjects including French, PE and music – 'which, let's face it, doesn't suit all children.' For entry into other years (not unusual) phone the school to enquire about occasional places.

Exit: At 11+ around 80 per cent of the girls move to the senior school. Remainder go to co-eds or local grammar schools – the latter being Sutton High's hottest competition. Girls who are not suited to the senior school will have been advised (via an ongoing conversation) before year 5 to give them plenty of time to find an alternative.

S

Remarks: Set in the leafy suburb of Sutton – where more parents pay out on junior schools than senior ones (the good local grammars are free, after all) – this traditional school has long offered a broad and balanced curriculum, backed up with strong pastoral care. The difference under the current headship has been shifting up a gear academically, with a re-jigged curriculum and girls' progress now tracked in minute detail.

Nursery and reception have their own purpose-built building – an environment where they largely develop their own learning, with a focus on instilling basic literacy and numeracy skills through structured play while also developing independence and confidence. Moving up the school – where girls are taught in the main junior school building – English, maths and core skills become the focal points, peppered with plenty of music, drama and sport alongside traditional subjects. Setting for maths and English from year 4. French from nursery; Spanish from year 3, and Latin from year 6. Homework of around 30 minutes a day from year 3, moving up to around an hour for year 6. Subject specialists for PE, music and languages – and from year 6, DT, art, Latin and science. ICT embedded into learning, with all year 4 and 5 girls getting their own iPads.

Parents praise the way teachers (who include a few old girls and just one man when we visited) really get to know the pupils – 'which means they can really adapt to each girl's learning style,' as one parent puts it. 'I now know, for example, that my daughter is an auditory learner and how she best learns. The level of detail – which I know involves lots of behind-the-scenes meetings about every girl – is amazing.' Other parents compliment the way teachers develop a love of learning and natural curiosity in their young charges.

Parents are less impressed, however, with class sizes, which – although can be as small as 12 – have been known to exceed 25. 'I know they have more teaching staff to cater for larger classes but still, this number isn't so different from state schools,' says one.

School has a good reputation for identifying SEN (around seven per cent when we visited), with a part-time SEN co-ordinator who is entirely classroom-based. 'That is our philosophy – ensuring that SEN isn't seen as something separate to everyday learning,' says head – although we were concerned to hear from one parent who decided not to disclose her daughter's SEN, albeit very mild, to the school at all for fear of her child being 'stigmatised by other children.' Another parent told us, 'I'm not convinced this is the best school for someone with a behavioural issue like ADHD.'

Physically, the school is tidy and well maintained, with additions to the original two-storey Victorian building over the years. Notable facilities include a well-stocked library and impressive science lab. Colourful (although with an over-use of pinks and purples that borders on sickly) corridors lined with children's art, poetry and other achievements. Neat, amiable, highly confident and self-assured girls from a wide ethnic mix appear happy and involved in their work.

Plenty of curriculum-enhancing day trips, including the Globe Theatre, Kensington Palace, Hampton Court and – on the day we visited – Brighton beach for year 1s who were waiting excitedly in their pirate costumes. Residential trips start gently in year 4 with a two-day trip away, moving up to four days for year 5 and a week at PGL for year 6.

Drama is incorporated into the English curriculum and taught by class teachers. Dedicated music teacher works extremely hard and successfully, also linking with the curriculum ('For instance, we're currently doing songs with year 5 on recycling and the Tudors,' she told us), as well as producing two big concerts each year and regular musical assemblies. All pupils learn keyboard and recorder in class; individual tuition is available on any other instrument. Art offers equally wide-ranging opportunities, including everything for textiles to mosaics and sculptures to acrylic painting.

Sport is big, with a wide range of fixtures (one week of play followed by one week to review and consolidate), and plenty to get everyone else interested too. 'The PE teacher repeatedly encourages my daughter to put herself forward for things like a lifeguard course – they're not just there for the naturally sporty,' says one parent. The 25m indoor pool, large refurbished gym and modern dance studio are all shared with the senior school, while the juniors have three of their own hard courts and a small field as well.

Building on the pastoral care that comes as a natural result of teachers knowing the girls well, there's also a play buddies system, plus plenty of leadership roles. 'With my daughter, they put in so many little touches to help build her confidence,' gushes one parent.

As for discipline, it's more carrot than stick, with a lot of emphasis on 'golden rules' for the younger ones and 'right track' for older girls, which encourages them to do everything from being punctual to striving to do their best. And while there are 'consequences', they're all pretty gentle – reminders, warnings, time out and (worst case scenario) meeting with parents. 'If girls misbehave, there's generally a reason and it's our job to get to the bottom of that,' explains head. Occasional bullying is nipped in the bud.

High expectations around uniform staying neat (purple again). Food is excellent, with lots of choice – 'the best of all the schools I've worked in,' says head and we can concur it's very tasty.

A whopping 60 extracurricular clubs on offer include everything from gardening to chess and debating to street dance. And working parents will delight in 'Tops and Tails,' the on-site wraparound care facility from 7.30am-6.30pm down in the senior school, in addition to breakfast and homework clubs available at a reasonable hourly rate.

Parents hail from as far as Wimbledon, Southfields and Epsom, along with lots of local families, many of whom work in the City or run their own businesses. School's proximity to Sutton station means some take the train, dropping their offspring on the way to work, while others use the minibus or drive (with the usual niggles around parking – although head says you can easily park a few minutes' away and walk). No PTA, but they do have the Sutton High School Association (basically the same thing, but where the school takes over the logistics part of events like Burns Night celebrations and summer parties).

In summary, this is a small, pastorally-strong and evolving school with tailored learning and an increasingly academic focus that, thanks to the impressive wraparound care, may be particularly suited to working parents. 'This is a rare South London school that is ambitious and gets good results, but that is not pressured. It's one of the main reasons we moved to the area,' says one parent.

Sutton High School

Linked with Sutton High Junior School

55 Cheam Road, Sutton, Surrey SM1 2AX

Ages 11–18 **Pupils** 360 **Sixth form** 60

Fees: £17,043 pa

020 8642 0594
www.suttonhigh.gdst.net

Headmistress: Since 2012, Katharine Crouch BSc NPQH (50s). Biology degree from Leicester. Joined Sutton High School in 2003 and has held many roles including head of biology, head of pastoral and deputy head. Before that she worked at South Hampstead High and Tiffin Girls' school. Still teaches biology and PSHE when she can. 'Having a teaching role is important in keeping me rooted in what we are all here for,' she says. Girls say, 'It means we see her not just as a figurehead, but someone who really gets the day-to-day education bit.'

A jolly, convivial and candid woman who gives a warts-and-all version of school life ('Our Victorian buildings with character can present some challenges for teaching'; 'Our PTA was not a thriving place' etc), she makes a refreshing change from the rose-coloured-spectacled heads we so often see. And while lots of parents have little to do with her ('There's just no need when things tick along as smoothly as they do here,' said one parent), those that have had cause to see her describe her as 'approachable', 'forward-looking' and 'very on the ball.' 'She has a very loyal team of staff around her – that says a lot in itself,' said one. Possibly off the back of more general complaints we heard from parents that 'communications from the school have traditionally been poor,' she now invites parents to regular coffee mornings to offer input on issues like plans to refurbish the school hall.

Lives in Leatherhead with her husband and two dogs and spends much of her spare time walking them in the Surrey Hills. Has three grown-up children – two sons and a daughter.

Academic matters: While not as strong as some schools in the borough, there are solid results across the board in academics and the arts. In 2018, 55 per cent 9-7 at GCSE and 45 per cent A*/A at A level (80 per cent A*/B). At GCSE, best results in maths, biology, Latin, drama and DT, while at A level, maths, science, geography, art and DT are among those with the biggest wins. Setting in English, maths and science from year 7. Girls choose two foreign languages out of German, French and Spanish – first choice is guaranteed, although second is not. Latin also available from year 8.

Girls and parents alike praise teachers for 'going well beyond the call of duty' – with staff always available, including out of hours by email and running subject clinics where necessary. 'The lessons are very interactive too, with a good mixture of PowerPoint, games and debates,' one girl told us. No complaints about homework, which builds up from one hour a night max from year 7. 'You notice the difference in year 10,' pointed out one girl.

Specialist teacher for SEN, who (although not an educational psychologist) is qualified to test for dyslexia, among other things – 'great for those who are borderline SEN,' said one parent. One girl statemented when we visited, with around 10 per cent mild to moderate SEN. Most help is within the classroom setting, says head, with some one-to-ones also available. 'I've been impressed – they've helped my daughter enormously with her dyslexia,' a parent told us.

Enrichment programme for years 7 and 8 on Wednesday afternoons in second half of summer term. Girls work on a topic such as languages (options include Urdu, Greek or Mandarin), music (girls learn guitar, percussion or handbells), STEM (girls design and build their own model) or sport (fencing, trampolining options). Meanwhile, sixth formers' enrichment programme involves a mixture of speakers (on issues ranging from mental health to living with HIV), work experience and visits to places including parliament and a university library (to learn research skills). Good, practical help is also available as part of this, with all sixth formers taught about budgeting and money management, for example. Girls praise the careers advice, with careers office handily located in the library and biannual careers fair, which invites representatives from many companies into the school to pitch career paths and ideas to the girls.

Sixth formers also undertake the Extended Project Qualification to help prepare them for university – a fair whack of extra work alongside A levels, but generally considered a good thing to do. Friday afternoons are set aside for community service and fundraising activities.

Games, options, the arts: Stand-out facilities include large refurbished gym, modern dance studio and 25m indoor pool – all shared with junior school and open to pupils and their families at weekends and in the holidays. Plenty of tennis/netball courts also dotted around the grounds, although girls have to be taken by minibus to nearby Purley Leisure Centre for hockey and to David Weir Leisure Centre for athletics and annual sports day. Winter core sports are netball and hockey; and in summer, girls focus on tennis, rounders and athletics. For gym and swimming (both hugely popular), there are extracurricular clubs run by coaches and sporty girls compete in plenty of house and in local competitions (doing particularly well in county athletics and cross-country championships). But while the school reassured us sport is not just for the elite ('You're not made to feel irrelevant if you're not a really high achiever,' echoed one girl), a disappointingly high proportion of parents seem to dismiss their daughters as 'unsporty – so I couldn't really comment on sports provision.' At sixth form, sports offering expands to include the likes of bouldering, ultimate frisbee and badminton. Assortment of sports tours organised regularly to all parts of the globe.

The arts fare well across the school, particularly music, with dedicated music teachers, lots of practice rooms and music technology suite. Choirs include chamber (audition only), year 7/8 choir and mixed choir. Fine groups of young instrumentalists play in a range of ensembles and tuition can be arranged for any instrument. Consequently, there are some dynamic and well-thought-of orchestras. Largish hall for drama, which is a popular GSCE and there's always some A level take-up. No whole school production, but plenty of single and joint year ones, plus joint drama productions (and music concerts) with the boys of Sutton Grammar.

Full range of art and design offered up to A level, with options including painting, pottery, textiles, and resistant materials – with lots of wow-factor examples (reassuringly current) displayed throughout the school, some on vast canvases, although perhaps not as avant-garde as we've seen at some schools. Light and airy art rooms to work in, including one dedicated to textiles and a separate sixth form art room 'so the girls at this level have their own space to focus on larger pieces of work,' explains head.

Before- and after-school clubs offer further opportunities for sports and music, plus some less predictable offerings such as robotics, Christmas crafts and a creative STEM Club (where you make everything from bathbombs to ice cream). Most teachers run drop-in clinics to provide extra support for individuals and extension work. Residential trips a huge strength, with recent examples including year 8 trip to Dorset (annual), Iceland (geography) Geneva (science), Florence (art), Berlin (history), plus two annual ski trips and even (drum roll, please) Galapagos Islands every four years – just to name a few.

Background and atmosphere: Founded in 1884 with just a handful of pupils. Over the years, as pupil numbers have grown, neighbouring buildings have been purchased alongside a rolling building programme to keep pace with modern demands. Latest additions include the dance studio and extension to dining room ('It was a bit embarrassing before – not now!' says head – and we can vouch for the fact that it serves excellent food, with the fish pie we were served easily of dinner party standard). George's Café upstairs also available for more casual dining experiences for year 10s upwards (and all girls during break times). Sixth form centre is notable, with lovely modern spaces for work and play (including the fabulous top floor, appropriately named room The View with colourful couch and oodles of computers for focused work). Library is a decent size, including quiet and less quiet working areas – and to the girls' delight, not just books but DVDs to borrow too. 'You get them for three weeks, if you want,' a girl told us excitedly.

In the midst of all the buildings (which features the junior school on one side of the school and seniors on the other), well-maintained gardens and sports areas create a cloistered look, while inside the school is light and airy with neat noticeboards displaying useful information and some outstanding schoolwork. Busy pupils move round the site in an orderly way – but with a good sense of fun too. Girls have a good local reputation and the school is always interested in setting up community links, the most well-known being their work and artistic pursuits with Sutton Grammar.

Pastoral care, well-being and discipline: You'll be hard pushed to find a parent that doesn't reference the pastoral offering as the key strength of the school. 'Girls don't feel under pressure to be a certain way or certain type here and they're very supportive of each other,' said one. 'My daughter has been happy and confident right from joining aged 11 because of the way they have treated her, and the result has been that she's done really well academically,' said another – and that, really, sums up the philosophy of this school. 'We don't frown on competitiveness – for instance, we love our house competitions – but it doesn't seem to turn edgy,' says head, who says they very rarely come across classic problems such as eating disorders and self-harm. Approachable teachers, visiting counsellor (whom teachers are not afraid to refer girls to even for minor things), school nurse and clued-up head all help, believe parents and girls. 'I had one friend with some problems and the school got her back on track so quickly.' Also to the school's credit, all new entrants are allocated a buddy and form tutors and heads of year monitor academic progress, personal welfare and development with military precision. 'Leadership opportunities for the girls are in abundance,' added a parent – and student council helps compile the code of conduct in partnership with staff, giving everybody a chance to have their say. 'I like the way the school encourages girls to have a wide circle of friends. The attitude of "I've got my friends already, thanks," is wildly discouraged,' added another parent.

Detentions are the main sanction for misdemeanours ranging from late homework and messy uniform to inappropriate language, with a tiered system of short lunchtime detention, after school detention and (the most shameful) head's detention on a Friday afternoon. But most girls go through the school without one and head says bad behaviour 'just isn't an issue here,' with only one temporary exclusion in the last year. The school is even pretty relaxed about smartphones, with girls allowed them in lessons with permission – for example to take photos of the whiteboard instead of copying it all down, plus using the device for research where appropriate. Bullying rare. 'Girls can be bitches in any all-girls school – or any school, for that matter – but they seem to nip anything nasty in the bud here,' said one parent.

Pupils and parents: Good mix, socially and ethnically; lots of local business families and City types. Others travel from the edges of south west London and various parts of Surrey. School is conveniently located close to Sutton station so attracts a wide catchment, while school minibus services are available from Wimbledon, Southfields, Tadworth and Worcester Park. The Sutton High School Association (replacing the PTA that was going nowhere fast) means the parents get out of all the tedious logistical side of social and fundraising events, and just get to enjoy the fun bit. Old girls (reunions arranged twice a year) include Dora Black (Lady Russell), Susan Howatch, novelist, and Rt Hon Ruth Kelly, former Labour party politician.

Entrance: Around three applications for every place at year 7. Entrance by 11+ examination in maths, English and online maths, verbal and non-verbal reasoning tests plus an interview with a senior member of staff. At 16+ (when around 10 new girls join) entrance test consists of general papers, verbal reasoning and interview with the head of sixth form. At least eight GCSEs, grade A/7 or above in subjects chosen for A level.

Exit: Around 25 – 30 per cent leave at 16+, mostly to co-ed or grammar school sixth forms. 'The biggest reason given for girls leaving after GCSE is financial,' says the head. At 18+ more or less everybody goes to a wide variety of mostly top universities or art colleges, with currently popular choices including Leeds, Southampton, Exeter, Nottingham, Sheffield and the London unis. Science, maths and medicine courses for about half. Others to study history, languages and art, one gaining place on BBC Broadcast Engineering sponsored degree and apprenticeship. One to Oxbridge and three medics in 2018.

Money matters: Academic scholarships at 11+ and 16+ based on top performance in entrance or public exams. Other small scholarships awarded for art, music, drama and PE. Means-tested GDST bursaries are also available for up to 100 per cent fees.

Remarks: A small, friendly school suited to those who want a single sex education where girls don't get lost in a crowd. Pastorally, it is outstanding, with the school firm in its belief that if you ensure girls are happy and ready to learn then they will shine academically – which does indeed prove to be the case here.

Sydenham High School

15 & 19 Westwood Hill, London SE26 6BL

Ages 4–18 **Pupils** 630 **Sixth form** 60

Fees: £13,161 – £16,737 pa

020 8557 7000
www.sydenhamhighschool.gdst.net

Headmistress: Since 2017, Katharine Woodcock, previously senior deputy head at Queen's College. French and Russian degree from Bristol and PGCE from St Mary's College Twickenham. Has also taught at Oakham, where she became housemistress. She is married and has two children.

Head of Prep School: Since 2014, Claire Boyd, previously head of lower school and on the senior leadership team of Ravenscourt Park Prep. She has a politics degree from Royal Holloway College and a PGCE from Roehampton. Moving on in July 2019 to head Wimbledon High Junior.

Academic matters: French for all from 4, Latin is taught to the top two prep school years. Masterclasses at senior school for years 5 and 6 (most recently in maths, science, history and Spanish); sixth formers run clubs and activities. Prep school currently caters for range of mild SEN: dyspraxia, dyslexia, dyscalculia, Asperger's, autism, ADD, ADHD and EBD, but all must be able to manage the curriculum. Some specialist support available.

Of course the school has an eye to results and, given its broad intake, achieves well. In 2018, 67 per cent 9-7 at GCSE; 67 per cent A*-B (29 per cent A*/A) at A level. But it hasn't lost sight of the need to relieve the pressure and inject fun into, in particular, years 9-11.

Many activities designed to develop personal learning and thinking skills and break the routine. A parent attendee at the year 7 study skills workshop threw up her arms: 'Why oh why didn't schools teach me good habits so early on?' Year 12 has a busy schedule of outside speakers to help pupils make decisions about their future, plus a professional skills programme aiming to develop skills in eg networking, teamwork and problem solving. In younger years an annual off-timetable day encourages them to reflect on themselves as learners using anything from Dragon's Den workshops to mixed discussion groups.

Staff clearly recognise technology's potential to engage pupils. In its first year, the maths blog with lesson podcasts received over 37,000 hits in the run-up to GCSE, indicating the high standard of teaching in this area. Other web-based tools are available and staff welcome email contact, particularly during study leave and from parents with concerns. Pupils can take some GCSEs early to free up time for other interests and areas of study. Science is an area of strength – two year 10 and sixth form pupils recently won national awards and another sixth former a Nuffield bursary to study cancer treatments at King's College. Getting science GCSE out of the way in year 10 doesn't deter pupils from taking it up again in sixth form and beyond. Care is taken to highlight the relevance to different careers, leading to a high proportion taking science-based degree subjects. Their flying in the face of gender stereotyping is a source of great pride at the school.

As you move around the school, there's a real feeling that pupils and staff feed off each other's enthusiasm. The teacher looking on almost smugly, they positively fall over themselves to show off their geography presentations. The GDST network also provides a wider forum for experience and idea exchange, impressing many parents. 'Staff are endlessly inventive and flexible in meeting different pupils' needs.' It helps being relatively small. 'Many pupils leaving after GCSEs are surprised how much they miss being known to staff and the reassurance that familiarity provides,' said one parent and, as many others, identified it as a real asset which the school often doesn't do enough to promote. SEN pupils are well-catered for too. There is dyslexia screening and other testing in year 7 and the Learning Strategy Team provides by all accounts excellent tailored support with a clear focus on inclusivity. Says the head, 'We know girls don't want to feel different, and if printing exam papers on yellow paper helps some of them, then why not do it for all?'

Games, options, the arts: Stalwart and welcome efforts from newer staff to raise interest and standards in sports are reaping rewards. Regular netball and hockey clubs are well attended and successes against local schools are notching up. Rugby, football and cricket also have a keen following – they are not girly-girls. Trampolining is popular and, to encourage the less sporty, there is dance (very popular), fencing, golf and scuba diving. Rowing has become a major sporting interest at the school – 24 girls participate regularly from year 9 to year 13, training weekly at Dulwich College and on the river at Putney at weekends and competing in regattas. Even so, most parents agree that this is not the best place for the more competitive, 'never happier than when on a games pitch' girl. The separation by a short bus ride of the main school site from the major eight-acre sporting facilities is probably a deterrent, but also the distraction of other strong departments, most notably music and drama. However, recent initiative, the SydElite programme, gives monitoring, mentoring and workshop support to talented athletes balancing high level sport with academic and social life.

Supervised and informal music and drama rehearsals are very much in evidence around the school, with girls so absorbed that they barely seem to register your passing. Even those not opting to take exams get involved and opportunities abound. In addition to two junior and two senior drama productions each year; a variety of choirs and orchestras, ranging from wind, guitar, string and jazz, perform regularly with an expanded schedule of diverse concerts in the school's new 90-seater recital hall, complete with music technology department. A number of girls have auditioned successfully to appear in

West End shows and the school choir has performed at many prestigious venues, including the Royal Albert Hall. Standards are high, but above all girls seem to relish the freedom of being able to join up with friends and enjoy themselves. The slightly chaotic art room is overflowing with talent and more and more are going on to study art-related subjects at university. Usual range of extracurricular clubs, including D of E and some, such as ICT, maths and DT, designed to bolster academic progress. More unusual tastes – code-breaking, Japanese and fashion – are catered for too. Recent additions to enrichment activities include cookery for years 7 and 12 and first aid, photography and indoor rock climbing for year 12.

Background and atmosphere: The original Victorian buildings where the school opened in 1887 are across the road. In 1934 the school transferred to its current main building which is slightly set back and surrounded by a jumble of more recent additions, most prominently the music block and sports hall. While they provide welcome facilities they, and the sixth form block, rather detract from its overall elegance. Away from the busy road with buses struggling up the hill, you can imagine girls sunning themselves on the terrace overlooking the large Astroturf pitch bordered by mature trees. Inside, a relaxed, friendly and purposeful air with girls unselfconsciously running from one lesson to the next. 'So nice that they don't seem to feel the need to have the latest phone or bag.' Intimate feel in the sixth form block. 'Some felt uncomfortable being in a small independent girls' school but those of us left behind really appreciate it.'

Good facilities in prep school, new library and IT suite, classrooms brimming with lively displays. New playgrounds, additional classrooms and specialist science, art and ICT facilities were all recently added; more redevelopment in progress to improve appearances and movement between floors. Close links with senior school – head spends an afternoon a week in the prep school, takes assembly, which girls love and say is a very special time. Year 6 girls permitted to wear senior uniform.

Pastoral care, well-being and discipline: Parents praise staff for understanding girls' different character traits and identifying individual strengths, focusing on those in order to develop all-round confidence. Nice touches such as cards of congratulation posted home and the odd hug in the younger years. They also sense a 'spirit of sisterhood' and 'moral strength' amongst the girls, which prompts them to be mutually supportive and keep each other in line, generally without disciplinary measures from staff. The school prides itself on understanding girls; the needs of each year group are carefully considered and programmes developed to support them. A full-day of PSHCE each term often involves outside speakers and is designed to engage pupils fully. There is a clear underlying message. If they are to succeed, they must take the initiative and think for themselves.

Pupils and parents: Tends to attract creative parents – as well as some from established professions – of varied social, cultural and racial backgrounds who don't feel their girls would completely fit the mould elsewhere. They and staff tend to think of the girls as 'edgy, quirky and boundary-pushers' though they don't overtly appear so (little evidence of uniform rules being stretched). They want their uniqueness to be celebrated and for them to have the freedom to be themselves. For most it is a careful investment calculated to bring maximum return – many first time buyers. Old girls include actress Margaret Lockwood, Philippa Darbre (scientist), Sophie McKenzie (author), Sandy Powell (Oscar winning costume designer), Claire Bennett (fencing champion) and Winifred Gerin (writer) and Apprentice finalist businesswoman Bianca Miller.

Entrance: Informal entry assessment at 3+ – 'gives us an edge over some of our competitors who do formal assessment – children skip out of here, find experience enjoyable, even fun.' 'Weed out the stroppy and difficult' so hope it doesn't fall on a day when your child's in a bad mood.

Of around 200 applicants for senior school; 40-50 girls join the 40-plus coming up from the prep school. Most are from local preps and state primaries, although also from Wandsworth, Bromley and, since the opening of the East London overground, from north of the river. Many have brothers at Dulwich College. The head and senior teaching staff interview all girls, inviting them to talk about something they are proud of. They also take an entrance exam in English and maths in which they are expected to attain equivalent to level 4 or 5 in national curriculum KS2. Occasionally places come up in other year groups and the school is keen to expand its sixth form (currently there's capacity for 35 students in each of years 12 and 13). Overall there's been a drop in numbers in recent years, which the head attributes to the effects of the economic downturn and more boys' schools opening up to girls.

Exit: Around two-thirds to three-quarters of juniors to senior school. Rest to a range of schools, both state and private, including other GDST schools. Progression to senior school expected but not automatic. After GCSEs some feel they have outgrown the school. Cost-saving, convenience and co-education are also factors and about 35-40 per cent leave; some to go to local state schools or co-ed independents and some to board outside London. Of those who stay, occasional Oxbridge places (none in 2018) and others going to eg York, Warwick, King's College London, Manchester, Exeter.

Money matters: Art, drama, music and sports scholarships; new sixth form rowing scholarship. Means-tested bursaries include two full-fee sixth form bursaries for girls coming from state schools.

Remarks: The school doesn't have an instant wow factor but there's a palpable, almost defiant, energy running through the place. It seems to say, 'I will be who I want to be'. Girls emerge independent thinkers and confident communicators. All credit to the school that they become so in a happy, mostly settled environment.

Sylvia Young Theatre School

1 Nutford Place, London W1H 5YZ

Ages 10–16 **Pupils** 240 **Boarders** 25 (with host families)

Fees: £14,160 – £14,460 pa

020 7258 2330
www.syts.co.uk

Principal: Since 1981, Sylvia Young OBE (70s), founding principal and true trailblazer. An East End girl, she trained part-time as an actress at Mountview but realised that a performing career wasn't for her. Married, and working as a part-time librarian, when her daughters' primary school asked her to teach some holiday drama classes, and a star was born. In 1972 she started an evening school, enlisting friends from Mountview to help with the teaching and charging pupils 10p a class to cover the hire of the church hall. She started the full-time school in 1981, because all the part-time students kept asking for one.

Decades later, the school is one of the most highly-regarded names in arts education for under-18s, testament to its founder's revolutionary drive (rumour has it she can trace her ancestry back to Leon Trotsky), vision and simple humanity. 'I find it difficult to accept how well known the school's become,' she confided. Parents are more forthright in their praise. 'Sylvia is incredibly inspirational for the children, she is amazing with them,' wrote one. 'We have found Sylvia to be exceptionally supportive. Her culture runs right through the school and we have found it to be a strong and positive one,' said another. Given an OBE in 2005 for her services to the arts.

She and husband Norman still live in their flat on the top floor of the school building. Their two daughters, Alison, a theatrical agent who now works alongside her mother at the school, and Tony award-winning actress Frances Ruffelle, are both grown up and mothers themselves – pop singer Eliza Doolittle is one of the grandchildren.

Since 2005 MS Frances Chave BSc PGCE (50s) has been the academic and pastoral head. Ms Chave read maths at Exeter University, did her teacher training at Southampton, then taught at two large comprehensives (Cranford Community College and Feltham Community College), before helping to set up a third, Overton Grange School in Sutton, where she was deputy head. Came to SYTS because she wanted a change and the school wanted her hand on the academic tiller. Both provision and results have risen under her care, and she loves it here: 'It's a fabulous place!' she told us. 'Being in a school where every single student wants to be there is very special.' Valued by parents and students alike – 'Very welcoming and approachable; she encourages the parents to contact her ... always around the school and not locked away in her office,' was a typical comment. Not a performer herself, but loves theatre. Likes walking and cycling in her spare time.

Academic matters: At GCSE in 2018, a creditable 39 per cent of grades at A*-A/9-7. Not stellar, but very respectable given the school's totally non-academically selective intake. One parent expressed disquiet about the academic provision, claiming it was uneven, but the overwhelming majority were extremely positive. 'The standard of the education and the teachers' dedication to the children is second to none.' 'We have been impressed with the academic provision. The teachers mostly seem dedicated and fair.' 'Our experience has been that the academics are strong – they have an excellent set of teachers on the whole and they care, teach well and motivate the children.'

SYTS still adheres to the weekly curriculum model it first adopted out of necessity: three days of academic education followed by two days' vocational training. Housed in wonderfully spacious surroundings since 2010, there's no longer a need to push the desks back on Wednesday night and convert classrooms into studios, but, says Ms Chave, 'it really works. From Monday to Wednesday there's a complete focus on academics – it's quite a different atmosphere from the vocational days, and they're not always running off to get changed.' Students love it: 'It's good that they have the academics first, because then you're really ready to get going on the vocational side.' 'It's a really effective use of time, and you don't have to carry around so much.' 'The vocational days are the carrot they hold out to us, and it makes you work really hard on Monday, Tuesday and Wednesday.' A parent commented, 'An initial concern was that the three day/two day split could mean that the academic side could suffer, but this does not seem to be the case.'

Parents also praised the school's insistence that professional work shouldn't compromise the children's academic attainment. Every week the staff post online what needs to be completed and see that it's done, and when a child is absent longer-term eg on tour, SYTS staff liaise with the child's appointed tutors. One mother commented, 'My son has worked consistently over the past two years and has always had help keeping up with his academics, as the school takes this very seriously.' Another wrote proudly, 'My daughter is a working child and the school fully supports working children, but they do expect them to maintain their grades and work very hard.'

Pushed into three days, the curriculum is necessarily compact. For key stage 3 the core subjects English, maths and science are taught alongside the humanities, art, ICT and Spanish (the only language offered here). Music study is taught as part of the vocational curriculum. At key stage 4, students take eight or nine GCSEs: everyone does drama, English lang & lit, maths and double or triple science, plus two options from music, art, media studies, history and Spanish. As one student remarked, 'There are subjects we can't do. But the ones we do are really well taught.' The lessons we observed were professional and lively, delivered by cheerful, upbeat teachers with excellent communication skills. Students are vocal, attentive, diligent, very keen to get things right.

SENCo is in school on the academic days, aided by a SEN support teacher. The main needs here are mild to moderate dyslexia and some dyscalculia, and children are helped in class or with weekly individual sessions.

Games, options, the arts: Performing arts are, of course, the school's raison d'etre. Thursdays and Fridays are devoted to vocational training in acting, singing and dancing and everyone has to do all three. This was a huge plus for the young folks we spoke to: a boy who had previously attended another performing arts school switched to SYTS because 'at my last school you had to choose a pathway, either dance or drama, whereas I wanted to specialise in everything!' Lots of nodding at this.

Students are taught ballet, jazz, contemporary and tap; speech, characterisation, improvisation, stagecraft and audition technique; singing, aural awareness and technological awareness. The buzz in all these classes is palpable, and the students achieve great things, coached by top-notch industry professionals for whom they clearly have the utmost respect. 'The vocational training is amazing, second to none!' was a very typical comment. We saw the head of music – brusque, scary and taking no prisoners – coax an amazing performance of The Impossible Dream out of the year 10s. 'That should give me a tingle, I haven't had a tingle yet!' he admonished towards the end of verse 3, but we certainly got that tingle ourselves. 'Oh, he brings it out of you, I don't know how!' exclaimed a young alumnus who was also watching. 'He's so professional! I didn't have confidence in singing when I came here, and now I'm a singer. This school sets you up for a career in this industry.' Parents have regular opportunities to watch their child perform, and every December the children sing at the Actors' Church in Covent Garden. LAMDA exams taken by virtually everyone, and very high standards achieved. The Lab, an experimental drama club, meets after school and prepares plays for workshop performance.

Sylvia Young began her famous agency in the spare room of her house in 1972 armed with a scrap book of primary school portrait photos, with the aim of creating some extra performance opportunities for her young charges. A young advertising chap called Saatchi liked her style, and it went on from there. Today the agency is located on the ground floor of the school and manned by up to seven staff. All full time SYTS pupils are automatically members. At any point in the day children might be told they have an audition, whereat the school will chaperone them there and back. If successful, the agency deals with all the paperwork and licences. Some of the children become very successful indeed, playing principal roles in West End shows and on tour – one of our tour guides had just extended his contract as young Harry in Harry Potter and

The Cursed Child – and you might expect there to be an overly competitive atmosphere as a result, but there really doesn't seem to be. 'It's friendly competition!' insisted the students. 'When we come here we know it's going to be competitive; it's what we signed up for.' Students also learn a mature and resilient approach to the inevitable rejections. 'If they don't get a part, it's not them or their talent that's being rejected, it's that they're not what the director sees for that role,' insisted the principal. 'We teach them that NO stands for Next Opportunity.'

The year 6 pupils go swimming once a week, but otherwise there are no sports; the timetable doesn't allow for it, and the children keep super-fit with all that dance. Would the students like sports, we asked? 'No!' was the unanimous answer. Acrobatics offered as an extracurricular, but not much else: the children work hard both on and off the premises and it's not unknown for them to commute daily from eg Birmingham – so they're not looking to stay after school for the Philately Club.

Background and atmosphere: 'I was determined to call it a theatre school,' explained Sylvia Young, 'because I was from a drama background. At the time, the others were all called stage schools, and to me that meant little chorus girls with their hair in bunches.'

Initially housed in the Gainsford Club for amateur boxers in Drury Lane – now long gone, a casualty of the Covent Garden gentrification. The lease expired in 1983 and the school had to find new premises in a hurry, alighting on a derelict school in Rossmore Road, Marylebone. 'The building was full of dead pigeons,' Sylvia reminisced, 'so the staff and I went down to Church Street market to buy mops and buckets.' It was a happy move, however, and the school stayed there for 27 years, with each leaver inscribing their name on a brick in the attic walls – a lovely photo-montage in the school's current site shows all the bricks and reads like a Who's Who of British popular entertainment. In 2008, with the school's success continuing to grow, Sylvia put in an offer on a disused Church of Christ Scientist in Marble Arch – Ginger Rogers used to worship there – and here the school is now, housed in air-conditioned space and splendour following a two-year programme of gutting and total refurbishment. The school boasts 10 purpose-built studios, two computer rooms, two science labs, two art rooms, various academic classrooms, a library, and a large and airy canteen. There are even two small outdoor courtyards where students can let off a small amount of steam. School is proud of these central London rarities, but one rueful parent did comment, 'If I have a criticism, it is the lack of outside space in which to run around, especially on academic days,' adding, 'however, I do think that is a small price to pay for the extra benefits of SYTS.'

The school began all those years ago as a community initiative, and its priorities remain the nurturing of children and the family atmosphere, something which everyone we spoke to agreed was one of its best aspects. Students work hard, develop professionalism, make friends and are overjoyed to be here. 'I only have praise for SYTS and feel it was the best decision to send my son there,' wrote a parent. 'He can't wait to get there each day, and is the happiest he's ever been in a school.' 'The kids are immensely supportive of each other and very close,' commented another, 'and there is lots of fun and laughter.'

Pastoral care, well-being and discipline: School is 'very strict' about the everyday things – no chewing gum, neat appearance, punctuality, attendance. 'They HAVE to be respectful to each other and to teachers,' said Sylvia, forcefully. A parent wrote, 'One headmaster from a major public school told us that he always prefers to take ex-Sylvia pupils as they are so much better behaved than from any other school.'

Pupils are very presentable, smartly turned out in traditional red and black uniform on academic days, black movement clothes on vocational days. Refreshing emphasis on common sense, eg 'We got rid of the pink ballet shoes because it was so much kerfuffle changing.' Girls now wear black ballet shoes and can move from class to class in them. Hair is neatly tied back, even on academic days.

Children work to achieve a place here, and discipline problems of the mainstream kind are rare. Reprimands and detentions are usually all that's necessary, and there's a strong culture of rewarding academic achievement. The students we spoke to couldn't think of any recent episodes of bullying – in fact, they were clear that bullying was something they'd left behind at their previous schools – but insisted that staff were approachable and that they had confidence to speak out if anything arose. However, there was a consensus that a school counsellor would be welcome – 'I know that counsellors can't talk to other teachers, whereas here you're worried that what you've said might not be private,' was a comment that had everyone murmuring agreement.

Because children come from such a wide radius, some board with host families found by the school. SYTS is inspected as a boarding school and adheres to the national standards. 'We live overseas, and my daughter boards; she has been with the same family throughout her time at the school,' wrote the mother of a year 10 pupil. 'She is happy and well cared for there.' Some other students lodge with their own relatives or friends. For those living at home, journeys of at least an hour each way are common.

Pupils and parents: Children come from 'absolutely everywhere', some from affluent families, others from poorer backgrounds where the extended family is working to put them through the school. Girls outnumber the boys two to one, but the boys are unfazed – 'We've been doing the performing arts before coming here, and we're used to it.' 'And the boys here are really lovely!' cried a year 8 girl. Some pupils from showbiz backgrounds, but by no means all.

Everyone is united by a common love of performing. 'Our son has a wide and varied friendship group. They're all there for the same purpose, so there is a stronger bond between them,' said a father.

Alumni include Billie Piper, Keeley Hawes, Nicholas Hoult, Matt Di Angelo, Denise van Outen, Matt Willis, Rita Ora and Amy Winehouse.

Entrance: Around 350 apply each year – school takes between 30 and 40. One-form entry into year 6, two-form into year 7. Capacity for up to 26 in each class, but in practice the forms are rarely this big – 'We don't take children just to fill up places – they have to be good.' Thereafter students can join at any point other than year 11, although rarely at year 10 because GCSE preparation begins towards the end of year 9. Auditions are held throughout the year, and children can start mid-year if need be.

At all ages, applicants have to audition before a panel: they perform two acting pieces supplied by the school, plus a song and dance of the child's choice. 'We're looking for potential in at least one of the vocational areas,' said Sylvia, 'a student we feel we could train.' They also have to sit tests in maths and English, but these are diagnostic, and to check that a child can cope with doing in three days the academic study that other schools would do in five.

The school assesses progress regularly, but doesn't make a practice of assessing out. 'We wouldn't ask a student to leave if they're working to their best ability. We find that children develop at different times, and we know that all our students will leave us with a good level of attainment.'

Exit: No sixth form. At 16, around 50 per cent to dance schools – Bird's, Laine's, Urdang. Others to performing arts schools such as Tring Park, Arts Ed, ELAM, The Brit School, BIMM, LIPA. Some to independent sixth form colleges eg Hurtwood House, Ashbourne, often on full scholarships.

Not an obvious Russell Group route, but one student off to do A levels at Westminster School recently and another to Wimbledon High. 'I'm always thrilled when I hear of our students who've gone into law, medicine, forensic science...' remarked Sylvia with pardonable pride.

Money matters: Fees are extremely reasonable for an independent school in central London, remarkably so given all the top-quality specialist tuition students receive. Lots of children here on some form of financial assistance – equivalent of some £350k a year in bursaries. Children's agency earnings can be put towards the fees.

Remarks: Not a school simply for children who like to have fun on stage. Standards are extremely high, the discipline is exacting, the work hard and the hours long. Children need to have genuine talent, passion, and focus. 'If they don't have all this, then re-think!' advised several parents. But if they do, this is a fantastic school, combining sound academics with first-rate vocational training, and producing confident, happy, polished and likeable young people.

Tetherdown Primary School

Grand Avenue, London N10 3BP

Ages 4–11 Pupils 417

020 8883 3412
www.tetherdownschool.org

Headteacher: Since 2013, Tony Woodward BEd music (late 40s). Started off teaching on his home turf of Solihull, West Midlands, at a 'challenging' primary school where he became music and art co-ordinator. He came to London in 1997 to work as head of juniors at Rushy Meadow Primary School in Sutton, where he stayed for the next four years. Following this he became deputy head at nearby Robin Hood Junior School, and then moved on to become head teacher of another local school, Warren Mead Junior – prior to his headship at Tetherdown. His work in Surrey also saw him as a local leader in education, supporting leaders of struggling local schools and as an additional Ofsted inspector.

Primary schools are where this head has always wanted to be: 'It means I get to work with a whole range of ages from 4 to 11 year olds.' His parents were both road safety officers who went into schools to teach, so being around this as a young boy gave this head a taste of how teaching can really make a difference to children. Indeed, in the last few years since Mr Woodward took over the daunting mantle of one of north London's leading state primary schools, he has set about trying to make a difference to the school by introducing a lot more sport into the curriculum. One parent told us: 'Before Mr Woodward became head, the school was solely about academia and there was not much time factored in for anything else. '

Mr Woodward has since appointed a PE co-ordinator and a PE coach, and has set up a wide variety of sports clubs, both curricular and extracurricular, including football, netball, hockey, gymnastics and swimming. The school even won Haringey Sporting School of The Year recently and has won several trophies for football, tag rugby and cross-country. He is himself a keen sporting man (which is perhaps why it is so important for him) – trampolining was his specialty, and he came second in the European Championships at the height of his competitive career.

One parent praised the new rigour which Mr Woodward has imposed in his tenure at the school: 'There seems to be a lot more organisation around the admin side of the school and with regards to homework – which was getting a bit haphazard before he came on board.' Another said: 'Mr Woodward has a positive manner and a clear vision of how he wants things to be.'

This is a head whom we suspect quietly worms away behind the scenes rather than being a front of house guy. That's not to say his presence is not noted around the school (some say quite visible), but he doesn't come across as a massive PR man. He does the job he was employed to do, but don't expect a big sales pitch, or well rehearsed spiel. He likes to unwind by playing the piano and cooking.

Entrance: The school admits 60 pupils in reception, but there's still fierce competition to get in. In the past it was only siblings and those living feet from the gates who stood a chance, now at least an address in the same street might reasonably be expected to do the trick. (Needless to say property prices nearby have their own exotic micro-climate.) One family (we were told) was even in the process of building their own house virtually opposite the school to ensure entrance. Parents can view the school in the autumn term prior to entry, kids visit in the summer term before they start.

Exit: Lucky pupils whose parents bought wisely in the area are also pretty much guaranteed a smooth transition to one of the capital's best comprehensives. Smug parents, who've sorted it all by the age of 4, tend to assume their children will proceed to Fortismere, and the vast majority do go on here. The rest to North London grammar schools such as The Latymer or leading independents – including a fair chunk to Mill Hill School and Highgate and a few to Channing. ('This is Muswell Hill,' said one mother; 'parents tutor without hesitation.')

Remarks: Despite a recent Ofsted demotion from 'outstanding' to 'good', Tetherdown remains one of London's top performing primary schools. This is a school which regularly sits near the top of the local authority league tables and, even in an average year, over 50 per cent of pupils reach level 5 in English and maths. 'Teaching is consistently good, with some that is outstanding,' says Ofsted. Parents would agree, but there has been a high turnover of staff in recent years, which has been noticed and commented on by pupils. One told us: 'There were so many teachers and teaching assistants that came and went in year 4 – none of them seemed to last more than a few weeks, I'm not sure why'. However, the head is keen to point out that that was an exceptional year and not the norm (and the shortage was mainly down to maternity leave). 'There was a period of instability, but we are back on track and currently have a very stable staff team.'

One reason for its demotion by Ofsted was because 'a few high-attaining pupils are not always sufficiently challenged'. One parent told us: 'Tetherdown is a great local school if your child can just get on and do the work and doesn't need extra intervention in any way. However, if your child is particularly able or, conversely, has any special needs, it doesn't cater well for that.' However, another parent strongly disagreed: 'My child does require extra help and the school does have good SEN provisions – his needs were picked up on early on. But I would say that you do really do have to push for everything and communication is not as good as it could be.' Communication is something the school has been working on a great deal: 'We have an open door policy – parents are invited to feed in as well as receive feedback.'

With meticulous monitoring, more than a dollop of regular homework (one and half hours weekly up to year 3, then a whole lot more), and dedicated parents willing to supervise nightly reading from reception to year 6, you get some idea of how good results happen. The school follows the national curriculum but adds its own flourishes, with a good emphasis on making learning fun – whether this be tricky Tudor recipes, studying maths with the help of a visiting Maths Clown or sharpening up those multiplication tables in Beat the Parents at Mental Maths. 'The children have a lovely education,' said one parent. Pupils are rewarded by pyjama days and a system of rewards. Pupils are grouped, extended and supported according to ability. Recent requirement for the inclusion of modern language teaching is provided by French lessons from year 2, and the school is looking into the possibility of Mandarin.

Plenty of stretching and thinking in all directions, whether in an opera workshop or an after-school street dance club. Plenty of creative parents, too, who come in to share their expertise. All children learn to play the ocarina (Peruvian recorder) and individual instrumental tuition, subsidised by the local authority, is provided during the working day. Sport, which was previously the weakest link, is now more expansive and better equipped. In year 6, all children learn swimming and travel outside the school for specialist coaching. Breakfast club and plenty of lunchtime and after-school activities eg choir, drama, gymnastics and spy club. Regular school trips include an annual outing to the seaside for years 2 and 5, as well as visits to the British and Science Museums and trips to the local mosque.

Virtually all parents and pupils live within a few surrounding streets and the school has always offered an exceptionally tight-knit community. Expansion has marginally diluted the atmosphere, but has brought advantages. 'It used to be very much like a village school, where everyone knew each other and older pupils looked out for the younger ones,' said one mother with children at both ends of the spectrum. 'That was comforting, but sometimes your child didn't have a particularly wide choice of friends. Now there's plenty of scope.' Indeed, the school prides itself on having a 'wide mix of cultures, religions, backgrounds and languages.'

All classes are supported by exciting innovations in technology and children learn to communicate learning through a variety of platforms, including multi-media presentations, pupil-led video articles, iPad technology and even create their own apps.

The school has no uniform and rules are kept to a minimum. 'We have just three rules. Respect yourself, respect others and respect your environment. If you respect yourself you are going to work hard to become the best you can.' Parents admire the way these principles are implemented. Those demonstrating behavioural challenges are given the same support as those with academic problems – with intervention and targets. Children are encouraged to get involved: with the school council; with each other's welfare (by becoming play leaders and buddies); and with the broader community (for example, running a soup kitchen at harvest time). They are also lavished with praise. Regular Achievements Assemblies recognise work, effort and attitude. Anti-bullying is promoted throughout the school (as was evident by a large wall montage entirely devoted to bullying), because bullying has been an issue in the past. 'We take bullying very seriously, like any school, but we make children very aware about bullying, we liaise closely with the parents and we always use circle time and assemblies to make children aware.'

Tetherdown is located in North London's prosperous, professional Muswell Hill and the parent body is a mirror of the locality, with plenty of engaged parents who devote the same attention to reading rotas and library duty as they give to successful careers. However, one parent said that the school could do more to maximise the use of parents: 'There are many parents like me who are at home now, and have a variety of skills and could help more, but the school is not as proactive as it could be at utilising us more.' School maintains that parents are welcome 'to volunteer their time to share their expertise, support admin tasks and promote the school's high expectations', although they have found that parents are most often taking the opportunity to return to work.

Very active Parent School Association (PSA), which raised £25,000 last year and used the money to underwrite school trips, build a new woodland play area in the junior playground and contribute towards reading books and general resources. The head is very supportive of the PSA, which has been welcomed by parents. He says: 'Finance for the school is always one of our biggest challenges. This school is one of the lowest funded schools in Haringey because it is perceived as being in a wealthy area. What money we have, we invest in staff.'

Parents at the school are highly ambitious for their kids and for the school, 'some wanting a private school education from a state school.' One disgruntled parent told us: 'This used to be the school of choice in the area, but now according to our local newspaper, is the one you go for if you can't get into Coldfall, Muswell Hill or Rhodes Avenue.' We remain confident that it will resume that status again.

T

Thames Christian School

Wye Street, London SW11 2HB

Ages 11–16 **Pupils** 125

Fees: £15,780 pa

020 7228 3933
www.thameschristianschool.org.uk

Head: Since 2006, Dr Stephen Holsgrove PhD (50s); first class honours degree in civil engineering and a PhD in numerical analysis from Kingston University. Having worked in the IT sector for 20 years, he set up Thames Christian College in September 2000. His wife, Catherine, is registrar at the school.

Softly spoken, sincere but also something of a visionary, determined to shape a school in line with his beliefs, Dr Holsgrove's personal experience of school failing him up to the age of 16 has shaped his passion for educating children, and often helping them to find their way to opportunities they might otherwise have missed. Parents are grateful for Dr Holsgrove's dedication, indeed he laughs at our enquiry as to what he does outside of school. They say: 'He is very hands on and interacts well with the students.' 'Dedicated, approachable and passionate about education.' 'Caring and thoughtful, and his kindness follows down through the school.' 'Committed to getting the best out of every child whilst recognising possible challenges.'

On his horizon is the delivery of a brand new school building in 2020, part of a massive local regeneration project. As he shows us the plans we sense he can hardly wait. Innovatively designed, with multiple levels, courtyard spaces and improved location opposite the entrance to Clapham Junction, it will give him a new challenge with expanded pupil numbers – three classes in every year group, not two – and a sixth form.

Academic matters: Founded as a mixed ability school in contrast to the many independent seniors in south London; the ability profile is nonetheless slightly above the national average. GCSE results vary from year to year depending on the cohort, but in 2018, a highly creditable 77 per cent 9-4 grades with 34 per cent 9-7. Most pupils take nine GCSEs, some six, some 11.

We were impressed with the description of how the history teacher uses colour-coding in teaching how to structure an essay, which once grasped is transformative. Strongest performers right now: history, French, Spanish, music and art. Single sciences allow greater depth which suits many. More than the standard fare: additional maths and business studies too. No Mandarin, but can take native language GCSEs. One mother was delighted to find her son's potential for languages spotted, nurtured and quickly proving itself. Mathematicians take part in national competitions and those at the top of their game have benefited from masterclasses at King's College London School of Mathematics. Scientists get out and about too, taking part in the Royal Societies' Olympiads and challenges. Not simply an academic focus, but aims to produce good citizens who will contribute positively to society.

With an average of 14 in each class, classrooms are roomy, with windows high up or obscured by blinds ensuring focused learning in every class we visited. Trolleys of Chromebooks are wheeled in as needed. Several teachers struck us as young but very assured. The head is a supporter of Schools Direct – where teachers learn on the job rather than at university – saying that it enables the school to gain access to the brightest young teachers, he gets their commitment and finds them 'very capable'. Following Dr Holsgrove's lead, what really makes the staff stand out is their real world experience, chosen as role models – the computer science teacher is a former parent here with 20 years' industry experience: 'so geeky, the kids love him', says the head. The long-standing DT teacher whom we saw in action is an acclaimed designer and artist with public commissions to his name.

Seven members of staff have been at the school for more than 10 years and a further nine more than five years. Said a parent: 'I think the teaching staff are very diligent, inspiring and pupil focussed.' More than one parent commented that they were 'astounded' at parents' evenings by the level of understanding of their child teachers showed. They judged the amount of homework just right and said that holidays are holidays, with no burdensome projects.

Currently 30 per cent of pupils have identified special educational needs. Each pupil has personalised learning targets in each subject. Some benefit from additional one-to-one or help from a learning support assistant. The school's provision is recognised by CReSTeD, all staff have received in-house training on dyslexia-friendly practices and some staff have higher level SEN qualifications. There is also support for children with speech and language difficulties.

Inside the classrooms we observe a number of supportive methodologies in action: some children have hand-outs on coloured paper, there is a minimum of copying from the board, key words are underlined and all teachers use sans serif fonts for clarity. Seamless communication between staff: SEN colleagues have access via Google Drive to the detail of lessons so that they can be on the same page when discussing any problems with pupils. Just a few with EAL needs, who benefit from the same in-class and one-to-one support. A mother described her son as thriving: 'We put this down to the teachers taking the time to get to know the students and also to their teaching strategies'. Despite this level of support we are told that the majority of dyslexics here would be classed as mild to moderate. Some who migrate here were overlooked as the pace intensified in the early years at other local schools.

Games, options, the arts: The aim is for pupils to find sports they will love sufficiently to continue as adults and it's not lightweight: each week there's a two hourly morning session plus up to two full sporting afternoons. Those with an interest set up their own clubs. No sports on-site, but the high standard of local facilities and coaches bought in makes it a great experience: we're talking football pitches, athletics track, Astroturf, two sports halls, a gym and mirrored dance studio with a sprung floor. Pupils play matches and tournaments regionally and nationally. Successes in athletics. Several parents with daughters believe more should be done to encourage girls' participation in fixtures. Cross-country and volleyball draw the most, with hockey dominating netball. Thames footballers are champions. For the Americans, baseball as well as rounders.

Art is a highlight, most achieving 9-7, with wonderful drawing skills on show. Graphic communication is taught too at GCSE with great success – we saw an advertising campaign project for TfL which could have easily been mistaken for the labours of an ad agency. Pupils use Macs and the latest software. The head enthuses about the importance of creating something, getting beyond the blank page as a skill for life and instilling self-belief. Facilities include a kiln and laser cutter.

Music teacher formerly of the Tiffin Girls' School, and 20 pupils learn instruments up to grade 7. Variously termed 'the play' or 'an extravaganza' by parents, there is an annual whole school production and a medium sized rehearsal space. Recently: Smokey Joe's Café, a musical theatrical revue showcasing 39 pop standards at the Clapham Grand, with coaching from a professional singer and the school's musical theatre teacher. Concerts throughout the year. Pupils can take LAMDA exams.

Clubs sensibly take place on Friday afternoons. Sporting and creative choices include: life drawing, poetry, orchestra ensemble and 'Jesus & donuts', in other words the Christian Union. Homework club runs every day. Pupils regularly foray around London, with recent trips venues including both Tates, Greenwich Royal Observatory, the British Library, the Dickens Museum, the Globe Theatre and Southwark Cathedral. Meaningful and significant charity work and fundraising. Pupils have the opportunity to go on an annual trip to rural Tanzania to work with the charity, Go MAD.They help build goat sheds and water tanks to provide clean water for villagers. Enterprise is encouraged. Year 10 pupils recently took part in a competition to create a pop-up bookshop project. Biannual careers fair.

Background and atmosphere: The least auspicious entrance of any London school we have visited. A single storey box of a building, formerly a library and community centre, overshadowed by blocks of flats on every side, with few external windows and zero outside space. We left our car perched outside the front door expecting the wrath of a traffic warden at the least. However, once inside the doors, the warm welcome from staff and calm atmosphere of lessons underway began to soothe and enthuse us, and we left with a spring in our step, inspired.

Despite the name, whilst many teachers, parents and pupils have a Christian faith, the school simply reflects Christian values. Starting with just 12 pupils, it has now grown to a still petite 125. Parents single out the school's small size as a positive feature. The school proudly notes the next steps taken by its leavers, including PhDs, excellent A level results and awards such as that won by a pupil for his project making a replica anglepoise lamp at Central St Martins. A mother told us: 'My daughter looks forward to going to school and during a long break tends to miss both teachers and students. The children are inspired by past students who have gone on to be great achievers.' 'Every child is noticed and encouraged,' said a parent, and another explained how children are encouraged to 'step up', and how 'the size and structure enables it to be not too exhausting and not too noisy'. All of this tells of a sense of camaraderie and community which we're sure will survive and thrive even as the school expands again.

Pastoral care, well-being and discipline: Parents report that pupils are friendly across year groups and cannot praise pastoral care enough: 'pastoral care is excellent'; 'terrific – excellent communication and ethos of kindness throughout the school' and 'teachers are also very alert to students who are appear to be are disconnected or withdrawn'.

The school believes that emotional intelligence can be taught, and it is modelled by the teachers: 'we are what we do'. The deputy head, who leads on pastoral care, exudes calm thoughtfulness and says that pupils 'feel they can come and talk to us'. The school lives and breathes the fact that every pupil is different, and will help each child think through how to approach and take responsibility for their lives. There is less of a focus on punishment than on understanding the consequences of their choices. Children are rewarded for good behaviour with a points scheme, building towards fair trade chocolate bars. There is a clear code of practice on anti-bullying. Bullying is not unheard of, but parents note that incidents are swiftly and effectively dealt with. There is a school counsellor.

Pupils and parents: Parents describe their peers as friendly. Pupils broadly reflect professional families in the cosmopolitan, multi-ethnic communities of modern London, but a far broader range of family incomes here than elsewhere, with the majority of households not earning over £100k. Some 25 per cent are non-British, with the largest groups from the USA, France and New Zealand.

Entrance: Applications are in the autumn prior to the year of entry, with two applications per place currently. Entry is via an interview with a senior member of staff and a written test in English comprehension, writing and maths, but the head says: 'We don't turn away children because they can't do tests'. Adjustments for children with SEN. Sometimes a child might be taken on with an agreement to repeat year 7. No places for anyone with behavioural issues; looking for enthusiastic and dedicated learners.

Children enter from state primaries such as Belleville and Honeywell and mainstream or special preps such as Dolphin School, Hill House, Hurlingham, The Roche and The Dominie. The largest concentration of parents is in Wandsworth Town, Earlsfield, Southfields, Battersea and Clapham South, but also stretches to Dulwich, Streatham and north of the river.

Exit: To a mix of state and independent destinations after GCSEs including Ashcroft Academy, Graveney, Wallington Grammar, Harris Westminster and Grey Coat Hospital. As a creative school it's not a surprise to see a regular handful of leavers heading for the BRIT School.

T

Money matters: Good value fees with all extras included. Bursaries may be on offer for new entrants and also for families who have fallen into difficulties whilst at the school. Most families asked to contribute at least 50 per cent of fees, but some financial hardship bursaries available for 90 per cent of fees. Around five scholarships available per year on entry at year 7 worth up to 20 per cent of fees with no means-testing.

Remarks: If you are far-sighted enough to make it past the unpromising front door, this school offers the prize of meeting diverse learning needs brilliantly. With a new school building on the horizon, we suspect it will soon be more widely known.

Thomas Jones Primary School

St Mark's Road, London W11 1RQ

Ages 3–11 **Pupils** 235

020 7727 1423
www.thomasjonesschool.org

Head: Since 2001, Mr David Sellens OBE (for services to education), BA English, Goldsmiths (40s). Cut his teeth in teaching at New End Primary School in Hampstead, where he worked for five years as the youngest member of staff; 'I had a lot of energy, and the head at the time afforded me the luxury of opportunity.' His energy and enthusiasm swiftly saw him on the leadership team, at a time when the national curriculum was being implemented. However, feeling slightly constrained and wanting to do things his way, he started looking for a post where, he says, 'I could make a difference.' The role of deputy head came up at Ashburnham school and the young, enterprising Sellens, bursting with ideas, hotfooted it straight from artistic and aspirational Hampstead to a school south of the river in dire straits; 'I was suddenly thrust into an environment where results and aspirations were very low.' He and the new head, working closely together for sometimes up to 80 hour weeks, turned the school around over the next four years into Ofsted outstanding and awarded beacon status. Shortly afterwards, he was alerted to the fact that nearby Thomas Jones Primary School was on the verge of closure and, keen to become a head teacher, he applied for the post and promptly set about changing the fortunes of the school. Fourteen years on, he has exceeded the expectations of even the most optimistic.

In his second decade of tenure, Mr Sellens still appears like an enthusiastic and irrepressible newbie to the post. He is a hard man to pin down and his boundless energy sees him flit from one room to another, starting with the 8.45am meet and greet of all pupils and parents at the school gates; 'You'll like this,' he assures us; 'apologies if it gets a bit loud with the bell.' He describes his approach as radical rather than traditional. He teaches year 6 pupils English and says he doesn't pay 'too much attention' to the national curriculum. When asked if he sees himself as a bit of a maverick (after all, this is a head who walks into assembly eating a bowl of porridge and banana extolling the virtues of having a healthy breakfast, a head who ditches the traditional end of year musical, opting instead for Under Milk Wood), he says that although this comment has been levelled at him many times, he sees himself more as an individual who occasionally likes to 'buck the trend.'

Mr Sellens admits that he is 'incredibly fussy' about a lot of things. 'I'm fussy about [the state of] buildings, pupils' attire, their demeanour.' He also insists that pupils make eye contact with people and greet visitors with a handshake: 'He has meticulous attention to detail', one parent told us. This head is also big on homework – year 6 pupils can do up to two hours a night. Even with this 'bossy' approach, he says that he doesn't face much protest from pupils or parents, as there is a sense that 'it is being done for all the right reasons and the outcome is extremely strong.' One pupil said he was 'controlling – but in a good way.'

Brought up on the south coast, Mr Sellens says he was the typical story of an 'industrious' child from a humble background who won a place at grammar school and worked hard to better his situation. He always carried with him a strong sense of social justice which is what motivates him daily; 'I want to give every pupil the opportunity to shine, to look back and think they don't have regrets and it doesn't matter what they do, as long as they enjoy doing it.' When asked if he has any children of his own, he replies 'no', then pauses, has a think and says 'yes, 235 of them!'

Entrance: The catchment is so small for this one form primary school that you virtually have to live in the grounds to get in (we kid you not – one pupil who lives two doors away last year didn't qualify. Such was the outcry, she eventually managed to secure a place). The head says he is sometimes overwhelmed by the number of prospective parents, 'some with children who have yet to be born.' Distance from the school is now measured from the centre of the school outwards. (Mostly therefore to those in the nearby housing estate and their siblings).

Exit: Mainly to the local comprehensives – Holland Park or new Kensington Aldridge Academy; some try to gain bursaries or scholarships to independent schools. Last year, three children secured bursaries and scholarships to nearby Notting Hill Prep and further afield Christ's Hospital, West Sussex and King Edward's, Surrey.

Remarks: There are primary schools, and then there's Thomas Jones Primary school. Former secretary of state for education Michael Gove has waxed lyrical about this school on many occasions, claiming in one speech that it offers a better education than nearby £20,000+ pa prep school which taught the heirs to the throne. He said: 'There are state primary schools every bit as ambitious, as supportive, as exciting, as the smartest of private prep schools – like for example, Thomas Jones Primary in West London.'

Named after Thomas Jones of North Carolina – a passionate crusader against the evils of slavery in the early part of the 19th century – this state primary in the borough of Kensington and Chelsea (a short walk from bustling Ladbroke Grove) is as true to its ideological namesake as it is to his inspirational work. By any stretch of the imagination it is a major achievement for a primary school serving a deprived inner city area to secure a rolling five year average of over 99 per cent of children achieving level 4 and above in maths and English – about three-quarters achieving grade 5+ and a few achieving level 6 in maths (often top in the borough for both subjects). What makes Thomas Jones's achievement even more remarkable is that barely any pupils who sit the tests come from an indigenous English-speaking background, with one in three speaking Arabic as their first language. Moreover, 30 per cent of last year's cohort were on the SEN register.

Nowhere is London's diversity of culture or chasm of social inequality better highlighted than at this school. One side of the school (Lancaster Road) is flanked by grand period properties where a three bedroom maisonette can set you back a mere £2m. The other side (St Mark's Road entrance) is a stone's throw away from a large, austere housing estate, 'not fit for purpose' we are told, which accounts for roughly 70 per cent of the school's intake. More than half of the pupils live in difficult circumstances and are entitled to free school meals; some of them, we are told, 'don't own a desk and do their homework on an upturned tray or in the local library.' One parent we spoke to told us that the strength of the school is its diversity, 'and that it caters for all.'

There is nothing ordinary about this school – certainly not if one compares it to other inner city state primaries. The interior is so immaculate and shiny we could see our own reflection in the wooden parquet flooring and the walls looked as if they had been freshly painted; 'we keep them white so it's easy to match and cover any dirt marks.' When asked how they manage to keep a primary school of 230 children so unbelievably pristine, Mr Sellens tells us that the pupils demonstrate real pride in the school and often ask to be on the 'cleaning rota.' For a bog standard (architecturally speaking) 1970s prefab, as this school is from the outside, the inside came as quite a revelation. Light and bright 'to create an illusion of space', the open plan and organic design is quite remarkable both in terms of its functionality and aesthetics.

The artwork which adorned the walls had been carefully selected and beautifully displayed, and we were particularly struck by some stunningly creative models of castles made from toilet rolls and other household objects, displayed outside the year 3 classroom. We also liked a large, colourful mosaic of Elmer the elephant with a large caption reading 'It's good to be different.'

And then there are the candles! This most certainly was a first for us and we wondered whether this was part school and part holistic retreat. Large (glass-encased) scented candles, wafting scents of vanilla or lavender, flickered on teachers' desks in all classrooms bar the ones with the youngest pupils. The result was a calm, almost hypnotic ambience, 'the antithesis of what some students get at home,' the head told us. We even heard classical music (from Schindler's List) emanate from the year 6 classroom as they were in deep discussion about their current literature book. As Ofsted remarked, 'Immersion in the plays of Shakespeare and high quality literature, such as Lord of the Flies, has instilled in pupils a love of literature and has enabled them to reflect with confidence.'

No doubt the school's recruitment policy has played some part in its outstanding achievement. Many teachers are recruited straight from university and stay for a few years before moving on, possibly to jobs outside London where they can more easily afford a home. 'Some of them are very talented, they are enthusiastic and idealistic..they want to teach in this type of environment – even if sometimes they don't stop for very long.' It is now a teaching school and can train its own. Sellens attributes the quality of what is afforded to pupils to his skilled and deft team and especially the deputy Lindsay Johnson, who exudes gravitas and energy. She has worked at the school for 20 years and is, in Sellens' words, 'the lynchpin of the school's success.'

We were taken on a tour of the school by six well-mannered, extremely articulate and very lovely pupils of varying ages, who each in turn solemnly shook our hands, looked us directly in the eye and said 'welcome to Thomas Jones primary school.' This editor couldn't have felt more revered if she were the Duchess of Cambridge. Pupils were as pristinely turned out as the school they inhabited. Hairclips and bobbles matched their uniform and we were hard pushed to find a strand of anything out of place. The head told us it is extremely important to him that all students look exactly the same and 'exquisite in their uniform, so there is no way of telling their background.' Those from deprived backgrounds can get help with the cost of the uniform.

Future plans for the school include a beehive, which the school says is its modest way of contributing to the eco-system and 'teaching the pupils to care for something.' This will add to the existing mini outdoor nature reserve set amongst pretty, manicured gardens and (slightly sparse) play areas. Indeed, dare we say it, our one criticism of the school would be the lack of outdoor facilities (although we appreciate this is an inner city school) or much time given over to sports, which seems to be a criticism echoed by a couple of parents we spoke to. One told us: 'There's not much in the way of drama or sports at this school which is probably indicative of most state schools nowadays. Sadly, when schools are monitored so closely, something has to give.' However, netball, football and athletics teams, training after school, sometimes with professional coaches, have enjoyed significant successes in borough leagues in recent years.

Ofsted – which regularly rates the school as outstanding – has praised it for high aspirations: 'Year 6 pupils don white coats for science lessons and eagerly respond to the school's expectation that they are preparing for university.' We also noticed that pupils called their smart navy blue school bags their 'briefcases' and year 6 pupils are expected to pick up a daily newspaper, because as one former student told us, 'pupils need to experience language they don't normally use.' It is not unusual, according to Mr Sellens, to hear the children talking about going to university or becoming barristers or doctors when they leave school.

Everything about this school is aspirational. You won't find a 'home corner' filled with dolls, cookers or microwaves in the gorgeous and colourful nursery. Instead there is a medical corner filled with realistic medical apparatus and costumes. Similarly, we loved the weekly interchangeable corner in reception which encouraged playing various professional roles such as doctor or teacher. It has a gold healthy schools award and year 4 children were recently treated to a trip to a Jamie Oliver restaurant and have been learning how to make sushi wraps using healthy ingredients – and fish fingers and baked beans are banned from the school menu because 'we want to afford them food they wouldn't get at home.'

Thomas's Battersea

Linked with Thomas's Kensington, Thomas's Clapham, Thomas's Fulham

294

28-40 Battersea High Street, London SW11 3JB

Ages 4-13 **Pupils** 581 C of E

Fees: £14,235 – £20,868 pa

020 7978 0900
www.thomas-s.co.uk

Headmaster: Since 2017, Simon O' Malley (50s); MA English lang and lit from Aberdeen, followed by a PGCE in English with drama and games coaching at Westminster College, Oxford. Previously positions have taken him in and out of London and across the world: most recently at Wellesley House, Broadstairs where he was head for 12 years; initially The Banda School in Kenya, where he went for two years and returned after seven having met and married his wife Katy – they have always worked together; she is resident art teacher.

As impeccably immaculate as his school: we omitted to ask Mr O'Malley how he felt about his inclusion in Tatler's list of hottest headmasters. To our mind, a keen Roger Sterling, the silver-haired ad man of Mad Men, he credits his selection for this most sought after of jobs to his empathy with the cultural values of the school and perhaps his own sound-bitey vision for a school in perpetual growth mode – Better Never Stops. Sporty, he runs to and from school, has recently completed his first London marathon and enjoys golf and cricket. He has two grown up children.

Despite his taking over from the much-loved Ben Thomas, parents are on board and full of praise: 'he is approachable, intelligent and cares, a lot'. 'He seems to have time for everyone... one morning he will be at a music recital, the same afternoon at an away cricket match.' 'Very inspirational. I really feel he loves what he is doing.' Children smile his way and he congratulates achievement as we go.

Entrance: Sixty-three reception places. To avoid registration lists closing within weeks of birth the lists are now open between a child's first and second birthdays. Classes are selected with a balanced mix of births throughout the year and gender. A strong sibling policy reduces places for newcomers significantly. Children are invited to spend up to an hour taking part in small group activities observed by staff: they're looking for confidence to undertake tasks, follow simple instructions, language and social skills. The odd occasional place may arise higher up the school. There is a formal assessment during the Lent term for 11+ entrants, when 20 to 25 places become available. There are a few high value bursaries for pupils joining the school at a higher age.

Exit: A mix of London day schools and out of town notables with many opting for co-education. Over the past five years children have consistently gained places at St Paul's School, Eton College, Harrow, Wellington College, Westminster School, Marlborough College, Frances Holland, Dulwich College, Bryanston School, Downe House and many more, with a healthy number of scholarships across disciplines. In 2018, Bryanston, St Paul's and Harrow topped the list.

Remarks: A new enquiry-based curriculum is in the pipeline for the whole school aiming to set children up well for a lifetime as learners, whilst still meeting the ultimate hoopla of tests and scholarships. The theme of the week at the time of our visit was 'perseverance' and a mother reported as if on cue: 'my daughter is happy to make mistakes, learn from them and try again. She is not afraid to fail, because she is being taught that mistakes are a positive way to learn.'

Every subject is under an impressively rigorous continual review. A major focus is developing a new curriculum for the upper years as the landscape for 11+ and CE exits changes. Spanish joins the mix from year 7 with Mandarin for younger years. French remains, with advanced classes for the many native speakers. Outdoor learning, not forest school, but adventure based has proved a big hit with pupils and parents. As befits these digital natives the head is keen to stress the school's seamless integration of technology into every subject, whether it be use of 3D printing, programming drones, digital photography or iPads in years 4 and 7, giving children the discernment to use them well.

Maximum class size is 22 or 21 in reception. Classrooms are light, bright and spacious, more often than not full of hubbub and excitement on the day of our visit. Huge windows capture views of the city or towards the inner courtyard and sedum roof of the attractive dining hall. The older part of the school – tiled walls and concrete stairs – has been re-purposed for the creative arts, housing a pottery studio as well as large art room. Fabulous drama space with theatrical make-up closets. Large media suite and brilliantly child-friendly libraries with modular seating providing well-used reading nooks.

Given the locale and the scrabble for places, we were encouraged to hear from a parent: 'it doesn't feel like a hothouse' and 'for the junior years very little homework at all apart from reading a book'. More intense higher up: 'our 13 year old might have one and a half hours of homework and music practice of 30-45 minutes a night, and this may be after extra school activities.'

Around a third of the 110 teachers have been at the school for more than 10 years, but lots of youthful (mostly female) faces. A mother of two with experience all through the school reported: 'Some of the staff are exceptional, I am very happy with the teaching.'

Two full-time SEN staff in a dedicated large space with innovative pods, plus visiting specialists. Sixty children currently identified with SEN – more dyspraxia than dyslexia. A mother of a child with various undiagnosed learning differences on arrival told us: 'The school is incredibly supportive with revision help and timetabling for my son.' The son added: 'Without Thomas's I would be nowhere'.

An increasingly co-ed focus for sports provision. On the ground this means things like boys'and girls' cricket teams with any player eligible for the 1st XIs. Other main sports for boys are football, rugby and athletics, for girls netball and hockey, with everyone taking part in gymnastics and athletics. The odd Olympian dropping in. Also on offer: tennis, table-tennis league, golf, karate and fencing clubs. A thriving list of trad and on trend clubs – pottery, yoga, coding and girls' football.

A 'particularly strong' music dept hosts over 400 individual lessons a week. Choristers perform at the Cadogan Hall and Albert Hall. Ensembles of every kind: ukulele, rock, jazz and brass.

Spectacular drama full of West End wow: unsurprising once you know the Thomas's schools have their own technical dept staffed by industry professionals. This doesn't stop pupils behind the scenes applying stage make-up, creating posters, prop making. Ambitious productions of Macbeth, Cole Porter's Anything Goes, Disney's Mulan,and Beowulf for year 5 complete with huge monster puppets. An amazed parent commented: 'our shy-by-nature son now wants to be the lead in school plays'. Dance is an important part of the school too.

The zingy lime green used on everything from doors to walls in the new building helps, but the fizz definitely comes from within. 'Vibrant and bustling' are the descriptors we encounter most often from parents. 'Warm, sociable, fun, confident kids, kind, professional and highly organised,' another parent thought apt.

The Thomas's school motto, 'be kind', is written in stone, literally, above the door and the school leads the way with its pastoral care. A father reported: 'an overwhelming sense that they have this square and centre in everything they do.' A mother: 'very caring and very open...a teacher would call me directly just to say that my daughter was sad or upset about a certain thing so I could speak to her at home.'

Social and environmental responsibility is much in evidence, from this year's charitable support of a local community boxing club voted for by pupils, to an enormous pile of bags of clothing heading to good homes. A lovely art installation in a corridor features papier-mâché sea creatures entwined with single use plastics, and children go litter picking along the Thames. A stunning installation above a stairwell called A Shared Future, of suspended clothes found on a Greek beach belonging to refugees, has made political and social issues real for everyone here. A mother told us: 'the focus is on making the child a good person, not just an academic one'.

Rules are clear. The behaviour policy states a precise 6:1 ratio of positive to negative comments from teacher to pupil. Stars are so old hat: children receive 'golden unicorns' for notable behaviour or work. 'Reflection time' is a sanction for misbehaviour. An early adopter of mindfulness, pupils or parents may make use of the school counsellor. An extremely well thought through well-being policy aims to ensure no mental health issues go unnoticed and staff are well-informed on everything from FGM to radicalisation. As a parent confirmed: 'Thomas's keeps up and is always thinking ahead on how best to prepare the children for the world we live in today.'

Pupils travel from as far as Wimbledon and Barnes, Bayswater and Kennington. More than half are local. Large numbers of French and Italian but also Mandarin, Russian and Swedish speakers. Twenty-seven children receive some level of EAL support. Whilst many pupils are inevitably from extremely wealthy families, one mother shared: 'We live in a less privileged part of town and commute half an hour to the school. We have always felt 100 per cent accepted.' This note continues with others describing parents as 'friendly and non-pretentious'and 'within the school walls we're all equal.' One pupil in particular has brought global attention: Prince George. On a practical level this means extra security measures evident from the front door. Visitors have their phones placed in a locker. Parents, however, are simply issued with security passes, no-one has to sign a non-disclosure agreement and new parents and pupils are simply spoken to openly about expectations.

Thomas's Clapham

Linked with Thomas's Battersea, Thomas's Kensington, Thomas's Fulham

Broomwood Road, London SW11 6JZ

Ages 4–13 **Pupils** 650 **C of E**

Fees: £17,262 – £19,518 pa

020 7326 9300
www.thomas-s.co.uk

Headmaster: Since 2012, Philip Ward BEd (50s). One of the first heads appointed to the Thomas's group of London schools from outside of the Thomas family dynasty, in person Mr Ward is the very image of Hugh Bonneville as the Earl of Grantham. Perhaps it's his winning charm as head of the Clapham family, bonhomie, liberal sprinklings of the word 'chap', not to mention the labrador behind his desk. Any similarity ends there, however, as we found him to be a highly astute, strategically minded leader. Very persuasive; anyone wishing to challenge his point of view could need some determination not to be swept along with him.

Educated at Reigate Grammar School, he read history and PE at Exeter University, thence straight to Uppingham where he became director of PE and chair of the games committee, ascending through the ranks finally to headship of Feltonfleet prep in Surrey.

As he talks he often refers to 'we': part of a husband and wife teaching double-act. His wife Sue now teaches year 5 here. The move seems something of a surprise but they are enjoying being in London, able to nip into town for an evening. It also went down well with their two grown up children. Milly, the chocolate lab, comes to school every day and has been known to get lucky with the odd cupcake or two not meant for her. They like to get out to the Surrey Hills at the weekends for long walks if they can. During the week, there are a lot of late nights and missed dog walks.

We were impressed by Mr Ward's delightful manner with the children as we went around the school. He knew the name of every child we met. Some parents were sagely reserving judgement, but others were bursting with 'excellent!' already. One parent told us, 'The children love him' – we could see why.

Having taught at a senior school, he knows what's in store for children later in terms of pressure, and for now wants them to have fun, a childhood.

Entrance: The school advises that successful applicants register their children at birth; first 70 applicants from each third of the year put on main list for assessment with later applicants put on reserve lists. Pupils are selected at an informal assessment day at 3+, most recently seeing some 200 children for 80-ish places. And with no 7+ entrance, this is pretty much it. However, for entry from 2023 onwards, registration will open on 1 September three years beforehand ie when children are 1-2 years old.

This is a neighbourhood school in the main: children arrive from more than 30 different local nurseries. Those at the Thomas's kindergartens in Battersea and Pimlico are guaranteed an assessment, but not a place. Strong sibling priority, but no guarantees. Sibling discounts for up to four children. They look for children who will 'have a go' and are genuinely keen as well as sociable and co-operative within a group.

Very occasionally places available higher up the school. Fifteen to 20 Thomas's Fulham pupils move over to Clapham at 11+, their transition now given much greater care and consideration.

New-style show rounds every few weeks, for groups of six or eight prospective parents to meet the head and see the school – more intimate than previous hall talks, very deliberately sending out a new, more personal and welcoming message from the off.

Exit: The word from parents and pupils is that they have 'absolute confidence' in the school enabling them to reach their guided first choice. Around 20 leave at the end of year 6, 65 at the end of year 8, with some 65 per cent off to board in some shape or form. To many different schools. Recent popular London destinations include Alleyn's and Dulwich College plus James Allen's Girls' School, Wimbledon High, Whitgift, Trinity, King's College and Emmanuel; further afield Wellington College, Marlborough and Woldingham are among favourites. Two to Eton and 29 scholarships taken up in 2018.

Remarks: The school opened in 1993, and is housed in a huge four-storey Victorian red-brick, typical of many London schools of the time, this one formerly a girls' grammar school in the centre of prime, residential Clapham. Inside, shining maroon tiled corridors, very London tube like, multiply the children's voices at every change of lessons – it's reassuringly loud and exuberant. Reception classes are housed in groovy-looking pods with an in and out space – fun, but quite compact, and perhaps a bit warm in summer – with so much vibrant work hanging from the ceilings, it's like being inside a mobile.

The dining room needs some reinvention, currently high windows and too small, so that pupils eat in shifts. The food seemed no better than 'school dinner-ish' to our eyes, and it was Friday, but plenty of fried food as well as more healthy options. Large rear playground for breaks and games, with roped-off picnic tables for those who don't want to run around.

Specialist teaching introduced gradually up the school. Year 6 splits between those going for 11+ and 13+, with former getting much special preparation with past papers. Latter get exam technique and revision strategies in year 8, with a creative post-exam programme of extension subjects. The staff is a stable one, with 15 teachers having been at the school for more than 10 years. In his bid to make the school less autocratic, head introduced a new senior leadership team. Small changes have included greatly reduced homework and a less intimidating approach to school exams. Curriculum being revamped to include thematic inquiry based learning.

Parental praise for the teaching: 'Our children have enjoyed a multitude of inspirational teachers who go the extra mile'. 'Very supportive and nurturing whilst at the same time instilling the need for self-discipline and effort.' 'Apart from the French department, which needs a serious overhaul, the standard of teaching is superb. They manage to engage the children with original and inspiring teaching whilst also ensuring that the essential rote-learning/repetition aspects are in place.'

New director of computing and much investment in hardware. French is taught from day one by a native French speaker, but there is work to do for the new head of modern languages, who is expected to 'revitalise the department': indeed, a new approach emphasises international awareness alongside language learning. Latin from year 5, Mandarin now taught in year 4, Spanish a possibility in future.

Around 10 per cent of children have SEN, mainly dyslexia. Emphasis on differentiated learning and in-class support, but some withdrawal for one-to-one lessons. Strong learning support team assists some 150 pupils with a spread of learning differences, including a more able group. Refreshing for a London prep to be so proud of its efforts in this regard.

Great art facilities in a modern, light and bright separate block and an experienced newish head of art (formerly from Feltonfleet) is sensitively designing projects for each year group. Exciting to see a whole row of potter's wheels, and we were wowed by the impressive group of sculptures children had made by wrapping themselves in foil, inspired by Kader Attia's Ghost installation. Cookery a new addition. A film-maker in residence, a former head of art, is no doubt ensuring every moment is captured for the sharpening marketing act, as well as helping children to record and present multi-media projects across the curriculum. New DT specialist.

Sports fixtures list expanded with the aim of enabling everyone to play for a team. New sports ground on the edge of Wimbledon Common with pavilion and changing rooms. For the high achievers some glamorous tours such as South Africa too. Girls play netball, hockey, rounders and athletics. One parent told us: 'The head of sport gets the most amazing results out of the children, training and praising in just the right measure, and always there with a cuddle if they hurt themselves. The kids would throw themselves under a bus for her. The girls hold their own very well against schools with a far bigger pool of pupils and better facilities and the trophy cabinet is weighed down with the evidence of that.'

Boys play football, rugby and cricket. In part to keep the boys beyond 11, the head has beefed things up. We saw two current and former professional rugby players coaching the boys at the cricket nets, using an iPad to compare each boy's batting with that of a famous player. Further thoughts are hockey for the boys and lacrosse for the girls. Weekly swimming off site for years 1 to 4. Ballet part of the curriculum from reception – cue a class of tinies performing to parents and their iPhones on our visit. Mostly girls latterly; the boys who continue are often talented.

Performing arts are an outstanding feature – highlights have included a performance at the Albert Hall in celebration of childhood. A parent commented: 'There seems to be something on every week! It is quite astounding that children are so confident and unfazed by the opportunities to perform, either in sport or on the stage.'

Some 350 children have individual music lessons, currently beginner level to grade 8. A wide range of groups and ensembles, and frequent recitals, soirées and concerts. Those with gifted voices may be invited to sing in the chapel choir, whilst 'new voices' and senior choir provide opportunities for all to perform.

More than 60 before and after-school clubs include fencing, debating, golf, computer coding, newspaper publishing, running and Airfix modelling (run by the head).

Special days for everything, with plenty of outside expertise brought in to deliver workshops. 'Make a difference day' caught our eyes, with children heading off in mini task forces to spend time in genuinely helpful projects across the community, such as making decorations for their local hospice, visiting a Christian Aid centre and sending cards to sick children. Pupils seem to get out and about, get stuck in and see things for themselves. Woodland Adventure on Wimbledon Common is 'by far the most popular day of term'.

Strong focus on PSHE. A new Inspiring Living course is a philosophy of the school as well as a taught subject. A key component is a new focus on mindfulness (including new landscaped Mindfulness Place), and Mr Ward is at the forefront of the curve. 'We're going to do mindfulness together... more thinking time, more time for reflection,' he says with enthusiasm. We applaud him, but wonder how he will stop his mind spinning with ideas and objectives during his allotted four minutes.

Head and team have set out to reinvent school's pastoral care systems. The head has been known to drop external meetings and return from conferences to pick up immediately on anything that arises. A parent confirmed: 'They take issues such as bullying seriously and take measures to address it instantly.' Parents describe the atmosphere as 'Very caring, and competitive in the right way, ie set out to win, but it doesn't matter if you don't, as long as you try your best'; 'Positive, determined yet caring and fun' and 'nurturing'.

The head says, 'Every child wants a bit of metal on their shirt' and so there are now myriad opportunities to lead and take responsibility: as well as the usual heads of houses and games there are prefects for subjects or for eco and charities, even flag captains.

Parents are not first time buyers in the main: many boarding school educated, and an impressive bunch of achievers. One parent described them as 'vocal! Very involved in all levels of school life.'

Thomas's Fulham

Linked with Thomas's Battersea, Thomas's Kensington, Thomas's Clapham

Hugon Road, London SW6 3ES

Ages 4–11 **Pupils** 429

Fees: £13,770 – £20,016 pa

020 7751 8200
www.thomas-s.co.uk

Headmistress: Annette Dobson, 40s, opened the school in 2005. A slightly low key dresser with a laugh that reaches her eyes, one only has to look at her feet to see that snappy shoes and clear-headed dedication are not the sole preserve of Theresa May. Wanting to be a teacher from the get-go (maybe influenced by her mother's voice teaching in an adjacent classroom), she swam into the professional A stream by graduating from Homerton College, Cambridge. After a spell at North Bridge House, she crossed London to Thomas's Clapham, heading up the lower school, collecting a postgraduate degree and completing a study in phonics.

Thoroughly aware of the need to keep abreast of the numerous practical and technological changes in her world, she still keeps her feet firmly in the playground by maintaining a close, personal involvement with each child. On Monday mornings she stands by the door and shakes them all by the hand and, far more amazingly, remembers their names, a nice touch that illustrates the emphasis she puts on manners as well as her commitment to approaching her charges as individuals. Genuinely passionate about improving her school, she even spent her sabbatical visiting educational establishments around the world, although luckily she shows her human side by admitting to having eaten pretty well along the way.

Entrance: At 4, a non-academic assessment takes place in January for September entry. Eleven years of experience makes the head fairly certain about the kind of child that would or would not relish the opportunity of beginning their education here. She is tactful but clear that it is potential team players as well as bright individuals she is looking out for. There is a strong sibling policy (on average about half the slots go to siblings), which usually leaves a minimum of two children applying for each remaining place. Parents can feel very pressurised; one observer said that a 'parent was completely manic to get child in', but the process is fair with advance information for parents, and one child came out saying, 'I like this big school'. Places do become available further up the school, mainly due to the constant whirling merry-go-round that lands London parents anywhere from Manhattan to Moscow at the drop of a city chapeau. At this stage, children spend half a day at the school to make sure they will fit in and also need a letter from their previous school.

Exit: As you would expect from such a professional outfit, detailed practical information and knowledgeable help on the which, when and how of senior schools is handed out to help parents navigate this educational minefield. In 2018, roughly half the pupils moved to Thomas's Clapham or Battersea to prepare for the 13+. Others to a variety of schools, including King's College School, Putney High, Wycombe Abbey, Emanuel, Queen's Gate, St Mary's Calne, Whitgift.

Scholarships are won but head confirms that there are not many available at this stage, and this is not an academic hothouse, a point echoed by one parent who felt that a very clever child might not get as far here as in a more competitive environment. Parents seem pleased with the advice given on senior schools and the head's statement that they 'aim to work in tandem with parents to find the best fit for a pupil' is backed up by the results.

Remarks: This youngest outpost of Thomas's private empire has settled in a handsome Victorian school building, gazing out over the top of a smart new asphalt athletics field, at the green park beyond. Nineteenth century it may be, but with sparkling two-tone brick, huge windows and a tidy colour-coded interior, this is definitely not a modern version of Dotheboys Hall and there is absolutely no air of laissez-aller neglect: in fact the energy and enthusiasm of the school is almost instantly apparent.

With walls covered in pictures from an exceptionally imaginative art department housed in a large beamed outbuilding and neat, well-conceived timetables for music and games on the stairs, the atmosphere is vibrant. Happy, eager children look you straight in the eye and teachers appear to be enjoying themselves as much as their pupils. Judging by the cheerful munching of buns at break and excellent reports from the head girl, the food served on primary coloured plates (matching the house colours) keeps the energy levels up through a satisfyingly full school day.

Particular praise is handed out by parents of reception teachers, one commenting that her child coming into the school with zero skills did 'really well in her first year' and others saying that almost all the class are pretty independent, at least at the laces tying end of the scale, by the end of the year. All the way up reading is heavily encouraged, with pupils taking home a daily diary including a book page that parents have to sign off. A library complete with cheerful librarian is nestled under the roof. Maths is taught imaginatively, not just as learning numbers but as a link to other subjects, and science appears to be popular, apparently due to explosion experiments, luckily under control in two purpose-built labs. French is introduced in reception and croissants and conversation feature in a biennial French day in Fulham and a week's trip to France for year 6. History and geography are both taught with the emphasis on connections to the outside world, and with classics added in years 5 and 6, round out the rest of the curriculum. Like most schools with an ecumenical viewpoint, RE is taught from a moral guideline and historical angle.

The arts – particularly music and drama – form a central part of life, over half the children learn an instrument and nearly three-quarters sing in a choir. Very popular plays are put on in the school's own theatre by all year groups, and after-school or lunch time clubs encourage would-be gymnasts, thespians, musicians and ballet dancers to go further and take external exams, such as LAMDA and the Royal Ballet School. All children, including those whose idea of art is to splash a lot of paint about (actively encouraged last year by a gigantic Jackson Pollock themed bonanza) are able to learn the fun that can be had out of being creative.

Despite the practical problems of operating on a small campus set in bricked over West London, the head (a fresh air fiend) runs the full mile to bring the outdoors into the pupil's daily routine. Little ones do PE and ballet, in the lower school they have general games and later on they can pick from a wide offering of conventional single sex sports. Some take place in the park opposite, which is regularly filled with small people jauntily dressed in the school's red and blue uniform complete with stripey socks. Otherwise they walk or are bussed to nearby facilities, a necessary evil for London schools and which makes the head look longingly at the space available to her peers in the country. Despite the logistical problems, there is enthusiasm all round about games, both competitive and recreational, and particular pleasure when a team beats other schools in the group. Sporty children can choose further exposure by joining popular extracurricular clubs for gym or judo, golf or tennis, while swimming, sailing and kayaking are available if they want to get wet. Classroom themes regularly incorporate outside expeditions, both in London and further afield, often with the help of the Exploration Society to give them a more adventurous time away from the tarmac. Recently launched 'Thomas's Outdoors Programme', includes week-long visits in Lent term for year 5 and 6 children from all the schools to Thomas's Daheim, school's new 'mountain outpost' in Upper Austria.

Takes an early warning approach, starting in reception, to spotting any learning problems, which are jumped on quickly by full-time staff, backed up by specialist help from the outside. The head, who used to teach in this field, reckons that it is part of her job – 'we love off-piste children here, they are so often better at problem solving' – to help find the solution to each child's difficulties. Equally, she feels that tutors should only be employed to mend a particular gap in the wall rather than act as structural engineers, a policy which can be hard to get across in a city full of aspirational parents. Rules clearly exist but are wisely enough applied to make for few confrontations and the vice-head is on standby to have words with the inevitable, occasional small child trying it on. All the last year are encouraged to take a responsible role and show particular pride in overseeing the playground, although they sensibly admitted that they grabbed a teacher pretty quickly if anyone looked in need of first aid.

Twenty-first century technology connects parents, described as cosmopolitan, via a Twitter feed, and a newly updated portal allows them to follow their child's every move. Most of the content is popular (particularly the photographs), but one parent remarked that she preferred talking to the teacher rather than looking at her boy's exploits on an iPad. The head, however, convincingly counters this by saying that she will never allow face-to-face contact between teachers and parents to be lost. In another minor quibble a mother said that she was probably old fashioned but found receiving online reports irritating, as she likes to keep the real thing. An unsurprisingly lively PTA backs up the school and works its socks off to raise money for charity with the Bake Sale streaking home in the popularity stakes. Thomas's ethos to 'give not take' seems to have sunk in well as children often donate a book to the library to mark their birthdays and sometimes turn up with money for charity that they have raised off their own bat.

Promoting the Thomas's motto Be Kind quite so prominently might have backfired, but the evidence of the success of the strategy is everywhere. From the top ('fabulous, fantastic head') to the bottom (smiley children leaving the assessment clutching balloons), this is a school that really does succeed in doing what it says on the shiny tin.

T

Thomas's Kensington

Linked with Thomas's Battersea, Thomas's Clapham, Thomas's Fulham

17–19 Cottesmore Gardens, London W8 5PR

Ages 4–11 **Pupils** 377 **C of E**

Fees: £20,526 – £21,789 pa

020 7361 6500
www.thomas-s.co.uk

Headmistress: Since 2012, Jo Ebner BEd MA PG Dip Couns Cert FT NPQH (late 40s), previously head of the Royal School, Hampstead (now absorbed by North Bridge House and owned by Cognita); 'I got the school to a place where it was worth buying,' she says. Educated at North London Collegiate (where both her mother and her daughters were at school too) and Homerton, Cambridge, she also trained at the Tavistock Clinic as a school counsellor and completed her MA at the Institute of Education, London. Tall and statuesque, Miss Ebner has long brown, lustrous hair, is highly emotionally intelligent, with a self-deprecating sense of humour. She has three children – now in or approaching their 20s – and shares her comfortable office with her adoring golden retriever, Maddie.

Her first teaching job was at Primrose Hill primary school ('from the age of 7, I was determined to be a teacher,' she avers). She set up the first counselling service when she was at South Hampstead High School. She also taught at a primary school in Willesden and at the North West London Jewish Day school as well as a successful stint as deputy head of The Hall junior school in Hampstead. A deeply committed educationalist, she is heavily involved with the GSA (Girls' Schools Association), serves as a governor of several schools, including St Mary's Ascot, and has written several articles on parenting.

One of the first things Miss Ebner did here was to remove the position of lower school head. She is very much in charge of the whole school. While she operates an open door policy and parents praise her direct approach when dealing one to one, her reputation at the moment is that she can be distant, 'certainly not cuddly,' observed one, but 'very cheerful, involved and approachable,' said another. She teaches religious studies to year 2, and set up a mindfulness course for parents, staff and pupils – 'it is really helpful in the run up to exams,' she confides. She regards communication as being vital, 'the bottom line, as with any relationship, is that it's about trust.' A transparent approach will nip things in the bud so she makes herself available – parents can drop in to discuss any issues with her. However, she doesn't cosy up to them – avoiding the dinner party circuit so that she can remain objective about what is in the best interests of their children.

Passionate about investing in her staff and striving for the highest quality of teaching, whether through further professional development or promotion, she is regarded by parents as having made shrewd recruitments as well as keeping good teachers and teaching assistants who mature and develop under her leadership. Her teachers value her big picture approach to their futures and the encouragement she gives for them to seize opportunities. She set up a bespoke masters programme for all Thomas's staff, in conjunction with Roehampton University. At the time of our visit a few teachers doing this masters programme were enthusing about their research on, eg, the pros and cons of setting.

Entrance: Three classes of 20 (split 50:50 boys and girls), so in theory, 60 places at reception. However siblings take priority (though will only take siblings they think will thrive) so you should expect only about half that number of places. Over 100 tinies are interviewed the year before entrance. They are not looking for children who have been tutored and prepped but who are adaptable, willing to get stuck in and have plenty of initiative. The pace is fast here and your child is likely to have a number of different teachers during a typical day. Register at birth to be sure that you get on a list for assessment. Once the list reaches 180 it will close and your only chance will be a waiting list place, currently limited to 50 names. Occasional places rarely arise but there are formal assessments at 7+ and 8+, where school will consider applications from up to 10 children for each of years 3 and 4. School only ever offers a couple of places at this stage.

Exit: There is an option to continue to Thomas's Battersea from 11 to 13 and about a third choose to do this, mostly boys, and girls who are going down the boarding route – automatic transfer, subject to the head's recommendation. Some of these have been successful at the pre-test during year 6 and are armed with offers from top 13+ schools from King's Wimbledon and St Paul's to Eton and Winchester. Lots of help and preparation to ensure the transition is smooth, as despite being part of the Thomas's group, they are different schools with a different make up and transition isn't necessarily seamless. Battersea teachers come to the school to meet the children who are moving, and a number of events are organised to help with integration, from games in the park to cupcake decorating, as well as coffee mornings and drinks parties for the parents.

Otherwise a range of schools as one would expect as there is a broad range of ability here. Latymer Upper and Godolphin & Latymer currently very popular, followed by The American School, Francis Holland SW1, Queen's Gate and St Paul's boys and girls. A cluster of academic scholarships as well as the odd music and drama scholarship each year.

Miss Ebner makes it clear that the school does not prepare pupils for 7/8+. If you want your son to apply to St Paul's Juniors, Westminster Under etc, you're on your own – the school will not do any extra preparation. Boys do still occasionally leave at 7 or 8 to go to these schools – it's not impossible – but it is not something the school will actively encourage.

Remarks: A stimulating, creative but also nurturing school in a very fashionable corner of London, Thomas's Kensington has a cosmopolitan flavour to it without being flashy or ostentatious. Children here are privileged but not spoilt, and fizzing with energy that a highly dedicated team of teachers channels very successfully. Thomas's kids are exuberant, confident and very, very busy. Lots of drama perhaps contributes to their looking you in the eye and explaining things with an articulate awareness that belies their young age.

Situated on three sites in a leafy, salubrious triangle of elegant properties at the south west corner of Hyde Park, Thomas's Kensington was the first school in the Thomas's quadrumvirate (the others are Clapham, Battersea and Fulham). Founded by Joanna and David Thomas in the early '70s and the family members are still the proprietors. Their two sons, Ben and Tobyn, are heavily involved as joint principals. Joanna and David, who have a flat above the junior section of the school in Victoria Road, are still very present around the school. The involvement of such a charismatic family and their wholehearted dedication to the place gives it a distinctive, family feel. Joanna and David Thomas are highly respected among the parents who generously donate to the CAIRN trust, a charity they set up to educate children in Nepal.

All three buildings are elegant, spacious and well looked after. Reception children enter the junior section on Victoria Road thorough a little passageway and wooden gate into a secluded garden and play area. Lots of scooters and bikes parked inside the black wrought iron gates of the pale blue painted Georgian mansion. Most kids live close enough to walk and scoot so there is a refreshing lack of Chelsea tractors at drop off. Lots of fresh air for all; the little ones are split into small groups from each class at playtime and spill out into the little Astroturf courtyard between the reception classrooms. This is just one example of how the classes are mixed up here so that friendships can be refreshingly fluid betwixt classes. From year 1 they walk 10 minutes to Kensington Gardens for fresh air and exercise.

School is mixed ability – assessments for entry are not primarily focused on any kind of academic prowess. This, and the tendency to take siblings, makes for a broad range. Lots of focus on reading. Children are listened to four times a week and a 'mystery reader' regularly turns up at school. To one child's (and his father's) enormous delight one week the mystery reader was his grandfather reading via Skype from the USA. Any difficulties are picked up quickly by class teachers and any special educational need is coordinated by the SENCo and her team. Parents praise the school's responsiveness when support is required, and an occupational therapist as well as a speech and language therapist come regularly into school. A number of children go to the Kensington Dyslexia Teaching Centre (just around the corner). Controversially, school made the decision to teach mixed ability maths and English groups all through the school until year 5. The decision was made partly as a result of the masters research that one of the teachers is doing at Roehampton. The evidence apparently suggests that setting is not beneficial to either the less or the more able students. A number of parents of able mathematicians are not supportive, parents of children who are not at the top of the game are more open to the idea. School says the research is still ongoing. French is setted – some strong French speakers in the school. Spanish and German offered as after-school clubs (parents recently requested Italian, so this is to be introduced). Latin taster in year 4 and then taught as part of the curriculum in years 5 and 6.

The creative and performing arts and sport are all given a lot of emphasis here and the school positively hums with activity beyond the classroom. Thomas's children stand out as being sparky and articulate, and the extensive drama and dance provision must play some part in this. All children, girls and boys, do ballet during their lower school years. Chelsea Ballet comes to the school to teach pupils once a week. Each year group puts on a large-scale production in the theatre. We watched year 4's fabulous production of Aladdin – worthy of any professional production, complete with tiered seating and first class lighting as well as stunning costumes. Watched by parents, staff and pupils, but what was particularly noticeable was the warm support of fellow pupils, one year 6 boy spontaneously rising to his feet to make a congratulatory speech at the end of the show. Year 6 was due to perform Arabian Nights at Imperial College. Music also flourishes – everyone given a violin to learn in years 1 and 2. A number of groups and choirs to participate in, including a full orchestra and a chapel choir. Concerts are performed at the Cadogan Hall as well as on site. Lots of sporting fixtures – primarily against the other Thomas's schools, but others too, eg Fulham Prep. Main sports – netball, hockey and rounders for the girls, football and cricket for the boys, plus tennis for both in the summer term. Parents praise the inclusive approach – children are encouraged in music and athletics, for example, even though they might not be showing a particular talent.

Even more impressive than the wealth of opportunity within the school is how much energy is put into a community spirit and to giving something back. From the CAIRN charity – Joanna and David Thomas's baby – supporting children in schools in Nepal, to various outreach programmes in local state schools, children here are busy raising money or sharing resources and thereby instilling and being instilled with a sense of public responsibility, generosity and kindness. Independent-state school partnerships have been established eg providing and teaching Latin in local state schools, collaboration between orchestras and choirs, and whole school community days when children from each year group carry out various projects in the community from reading to local nurseries to art, drama and music productions. The TSF (Thomas's Schools Foundation) is focused on working with local state schools, to widen educational opportunity and to provide bursaries. Joanna and David, together with Ben and Tobyn, are all actively involved in leading the whole school community to support the Foundation.

A remarkably cohesive and vibrant school. Bubbly children that are nevertheless polite and well behaved; 'It can be noisy,' acknowleged one parent, 'but with laughter not screaming.' Privileged, yes, but spoilt, absolutely not. These children are developing a strong sense of social responsibility and couldn't be better prepared for the complex global environment they are growing up into.

The Tiffin Girls' School

T

Richmond Road, Kingston, Surrey KT2 5PL

Ages 11–18 **Pupils** 1,113 **Sixth form** 304

020 8546 0773
www.tiffingirls.org

Head teacher: Since 2016, Ian Keary BA NPQH. 40s. Previously head of school at highly rated Glyn, part of a multi academy trust in nearby Ewell, for three years, which he joined as deputy head in 2012. Reported to the overall executive head, the ideal way of developing leadership skills. Before that, eight years at Tiffin School (the boys' grammar, just down the road), four as assistant head.

Sporty (degree was in sports studies and English, gets vicarious fix these days as the father of two games and rowing mad sons), he's also warm, soft spoken and – as this reviewer can testify – generous with this time. He's proving a hit with parents and pupils, a tribute given that his appointment marks a definite change for school that's been used to heads of a different ilk – 'schoolmarmish,' as one mother put it.

Hands on, and how. Appears regularly in lessons, talks to pupils and even serves in the canteen. 'Doesn't want to seem too managerial,' said pupil. Teaches two IT lessons a week. Impressive given demands of the job and, he says, a good way of staying in touch with pupils and alleviating the admin-heavy side of his role (predictably puts in the hours wading through paperwork, much of it linked to applying for more money to improve the needier parts of the building).

Pastoral side appears to be big focus, feel parents – 'he really seems to care and that's true of a lot of the teachers as well,' thought one. His newsletters, balancing all aspects of school life, give a good insight into his leadership style. 'Everything gets equal mention,' said a parent who – like pupils – praised his unstinting attendance (close to 100 per cent) at school events. 'At every concert ... he's been there, get the impression that he supports everything round the school.' Also a good speaker, which plays well with highly articulate parents who put a premium on a nicely turned sentence.

He's thoroughly enjoying the job. Tolerant of new ideas if purpose and benefits are clearly presented by pupils (they will be); one of recent highlights was a tent in the foyer for rag week. That said, no plans for drastic changes – though office's previously pink walls are now white (similarly coloured chairs are on the wish list, pending spare cash).

He sees himself as a champion for young women – and a feminist. The goal is to ensure that pupils achieve don't just achieve academically (almost a given) but cope with setbacks, too. Ultimately it's 'about the passion and support that the staff show toward the girls [..] and giving them the belief that they can go out and make a difference in the world.' Given the number of activities they manage here – 'You'll start thinking they're my senior leadership team,' jokes Mr Keary (well, we think he was joking) – he's ensuring they get off to a wonderful start.

Academic matters: Let's not beat about the bush – fabulous results are the alpha and omega here and the reason school is so wildly oversubscribed. They're so used to success here that anything below a C doesn't actually appear on their results info (for GCSEs). Even Bs are relatively rare. Not that this is exactly headline grabbing news given that it's pretty much the same story year in, year out. In 2018, GCSE results were 95 per cent 9-7, ditto (or very close) in previous years. At A level, 92 per cent of grades were A*-B and 71 per cent A*/A. Eleven GCSEs the norm – seven compulsory (including three sciences and a foreign language); three options from impressive list that includes Latin, DT and drama. Most start with four A levels and drop one at the end of year 12, plus EPQ – some do extras out of school.

While competitive entrance exam guarantees fabulous brainpower, school's strength, say parents, is making sure teaching quality does more than merely take it for granted. Even Ofsted (which hasn't dropped in since 2009 – is this a record?) says that 'achievement is outstanding because the ... majority of pupils make the maximum progress possible...' Well spotted.

We saw lessons whose total silence reflected the sustained concentration demanded by the task. No fidgeting, just immersion so total that visitors can tiptoe in and out again, pretty much unnoticed. In happy contrast, wonderfully lively year 7 French class practising letter sounds at high volume (and with authentic sounding) Gallic intonation could be heard a corridor away.

Some inevitable variation in teaching quality, reckoned pupils, but teachers 'all have passion for subject' and don't stint when it comes to offering extra support. Curriculum, too, has been rejigged – where possible – around big, ambitious themes that give context and perspective from the lower school up. You don't just study Frankenstein but take in the whole gothic movement while you're about it, while Grapes of Wrath forms part of the larger canvas of the great American novel – an approach that doesn't solemnly add enrichment to the syllabus but makes it an integral part. Analytical skills, too, are developed early. Year 8 pupils, for example, complete mini EPQ using null hypothesis model (a concept that this reviewer, unlike the pupils, had to go home and look up). Topics – impact of Pakistani culture on London and Londoners and impact of ethical issues on British shoppers – impressively analysed.

While girls excel in every area, STEM subjects are particularly big. There's nothing they don't do, from Arkwright scholarships (win a steady number) to UCL lectures, with 13 labs of different vintages catering for demand – physics, in particular, a growth subject seen as stepping stone to engineering-related courses.

Some parents felt school should help more with extra preparation and mock interviews required for high pressure entrance exams. School disagrees. 'We will provide opportunities but we're not going to do it for you,' says head. It's all there for the taking, confirm pupils, if you have the gumption to ask for it. One successful med school applicant had worked with teachers and other pupils to hone interview technique. 'Wouldn't have succeeded without it.'

Only area of weakness identified by historic inspection was inconsistencies in prose writing, now a focus for teaching, reading encouraged with a welcoming library/LRC re-sited in former atrium overlooking playing field, fiction section as big as factual titles.

Given admissions process, geared to selecting those able to cope with fast-paced, whole class teaching (teacher to pupil ratio is 16.5), unsurprising that relatively few pupils – currently just seven – have identified SEN. Mostly specific learning difficulties (mild), one with high functioning autism, none with an EHCP. EAL figures, in contrast look high at over 35 per cent but in practice only a small number need support. 'Many pupils are two to three generations in, so it's not so much of an issue.'

Only downside was the reports of tutoring, not just for the entrance exams (rife) but throughout school careers, including rumoured Saturday classes that cover the school curriculum a week in advance. Perhaps inevitable? – 'Will be the girls who never go out at university and work all the time,' thought one mother. 'Parental prerogative,' says Mr Keary, with resignation.

Inevitably, you don't come to a school like this without sky high expectations – shared by teachers, rightly ambitious for their pupils – 'daughter feels that would be letting the school down if didn't get the top grades'. Encouraging, though, that school and pupils are aware and honest about the pressures – and sense and sensibility prevail wherever possible. Recently, did away with year 7 end of year exams and pupils were clear on advice to avoid working all hours – though can be their own worst enemies.

'All very well saying to very conscientious girls only spend 40 minutes [on homework], but she will spend two hours,' said one parent. 'Difference with boys is if boys do badly in a test it was a rubbish test, if girls do badly, they think it's them. It's this sense of them always having to do very well and creates a cycle,' said mother.

Trips help leaven the intensity of the learning experience, helping staff and girls see each other in more relaxed mode: 'let their hair down – good for everyone,' said parent. School is budget conscious (if can get there by public transport, they will) now notifying parents of costs further in advance. One parent felt trips had been slightly thin on the ground. Plentiful now, counters school, from year 9 battlefields trip to year 11 geographers off to Swanage.

Also enjoyed are shared activities with the boys' school, including the Tuesday programme, aimed at thinking beyond the normal timetable. 'More would be great,' thought parent.

Staff clearly like it here – unusually there were no vacancies, teaching or otherwise on the website. Only role on offer was that of governor – unpaid, still attracting many suitable applicants.

Games, options, the arts: The place to develop your feminist agenda, thought one parent, approvingly, particularly at sixth form level. 'School is very good at getting 16-year-olds to be political and vocal.' Debating here is flourishing, girls triumphing against some famous names and developing confidence and polish along the way.

All the big ticket activities like Duke of Edinburgh (bronze to gold medal) are on offer as well as clubs, some delightfully niche, set up by the girls – crochet, Scrabble and ukulele orchestra currently feature.

Girls do nothing by halves, from the cakes (featuring emojis and books) baked to celebrate the school's birthday, to year 9s' mini Young Enterprise scheme, importing and selling phone holders – making a cool £400 or so along the way. Also enter masses of competitions and events, from the arty (Kulturefest) to the digital (like Little Big Challenge, all about adding connectivity to everyday life). Pupils tend to sail through to the finals and very often win.

Sports – highly competitive (as you'd expect) with what parent describes as concentrated 'win, win, win,' approach – yield some good results, particularly at borough and county level. 'Girls who do it, do very well,' said parent. More encouragement for borderline enthusiasts would be good, felt another, echoed by some sixth formers who can drop all sport in their final year.

Art is sensational – GCSE works looks like A level, A level looks like degree show – we want it all. Much is on huge canvases – 'acts of bravery,' points out Mr K. Music, however, currently getting most parental applause, dynamic head of department felt to be taking performance of all sorts to new heights. Popular subject, with two GCSE classes, Pre-U rather than A level for sixth form, normally two to three going on to study at university, while many girls learn instruments – 200 individual lessons a week. The comments – 'Out of this world,' 'breathtaking,' 'of an incredible standard,' could have filled the entire review. Highlights many and various – from the ensembles to the recent 'very funny' production of Alice – with music written by pupil.

Background and atmosphere: All too easy to assume that fun has to be levered into the curriculum – a bolt on to the serious business of getting those results. Anything but. Painted towers of flower pots outside and mouthwatering display of knitted, ceramic and papier-mâché cakes in the foyer (theme: indulgence) are pointer for scope, variety and general excitement of life here.

Within minutes of arriving, we'd seen a catwalk rehearsal (pupils preparing to model their creations) and been treated to an astonishing and moving drama club improvisation themed to Frankenstein's monster with inarticulate howls (non-verbal unreasoning?) as well as laughter and tears. And this was just the lunchtime slot. School's well-named head of creativity (a smiling blur in the distance) must work round the clock.

Parents – and pupils – stressed time and time again that jollity is part and parcel of daily life. Take school birthday party celebration where everyone '...goes a bit bonkers, cheering and singing,' says mother. 'They seem to be allowed to have fun and be a bit silly and that's really important.'

It all happens on a stunning site, substantially rebuilt after fire, started by building workers, (not in school hours, fortunately). End result was creation of light, airy new wing.

The older side, too, is improving: sixth form centre with three areas – socialising, work plus light chat, and silent study (complete with immaculate kitchen – 'we tidied it specially' – for hot drinks and microwaveable treats).

Bar slightly overgrown bits (moss sculptures in small back quad agreed to be past their best), site is well managed, girls very respectful of surroundings, bags neatly stowed, dining hall impressively clean at the end of busy lunchtime session – tribute to recently revamped menu.

Pastoral care, well-being and discipline: 'School will say make sure you get an early night and eat properly – it's obvious, but at least they're trying,' said pupil. Similarly, mega award ceremonies reward more than academic success. 'My daughter didn't get a single prize – but said it's not an issue because people know they're getting the prizes for effort.'

It's necessary, given mindset of these conscientious girls where, said one parent, 'Fragility of their self-confidence is an issue' – never more so on A level results day when tiny number miss out on the grades and university place. 'We want them to get into clearing as soon as possible,' says Mr Keary. Instant identification and removal for tea and sympathy on top of current system ('see member of staff' online flag when pupil first logs on to get results) would be on at least one parent's wish list.

Impressively, have ditched year 7 exams. Other initiatives include timetabled pastoral hour each week, flourishing pupil-run LGBT society, mental health ambassadors and promotion of role models from every culture. Sixth formers we spoke to, passionate about importance of every pupil feeling happy within own skin, praised school's willingness to implement their ideas – latest, administered by full time pastoral care specialist, is stress bucket, full, on day of visit, of hundreds of tightly folded notes, each an anonymous worry all the better for being jettisoned.

House system felt to be focus for good-hearted but intense competition (one of the head girls, officially neutral, had 'accidentally cheered for old house...'). Brings everyone together – sixth formers very conscious of visibility to younger pupils.

Strenuous efforts by the school see impressive turn of speed when issues need resolving. 'Something occurred on social media, contacted school early one morning, within 20 minutes had call from tutor ... it was instant, so if you raise questions with them, they take it very seriously.'

Pupils and parents: Slight polarisation between socialite parents and those who take a back seat – paths usually set at the start of school life. The keen (via form reps) arrange year group meetings, meals out. 'It is sociable if you want it to be.'

We heard varying views on how well pupils got on – perhaps unsurprising in a large school. There were a couple of grumbles about monocultural friendship groups but most were frankly baffled by the idea. 'The girls mingle completely,' said one mother. 'Ethnic backgrounds don't make any difference.'

School keen to balance 'celebrity' and professional achievements of alumnae, who cover surprisingly large range. Creative element includes author Lynne Truss and writer Jan Etherington. Plenty of more conventional high flyers, from Grace Capel, human rights barrister, to award winning obstetrician Caroline Knight. Any other old girls cordially encouraged to contact alumnae organisation.

Entrance: At year 7, two-stage entry process, girls sitting maths and English tests in October, top scorers invited back for stage two in November. Priority for those qualifying for pupil premium funding and living within designated area made up of 47 postal districts – though these can change, (two were removed recently) – so do check the admissions criteria regularly. 'If you live outside the catchment area, don't expect to get a place here,' says school.

For sixth form, minimum entry is eight GCSEs, four at grade 7 or better and four at grade 6 or better. Almost no places at any other point.

Exit: Single figures post-GCSE do not make it into sixth form, a few choose to study elsewhere (mostly to co-eds). In 2018, 22 Oxbridge places and 21 medics.

Money matters: Discretionary sixth form bursary fund – three types of funding depending on need. Paid monthly to recipients and designed to fund textbooks, trips, specialist equipment for specific subjects, travel to school. Additional direct bursaries available from the government for students classified as vulnerable – for example, living in care.

Remarks: Expect to be challenged, encouraged and inspired – but not spoon-fed. Robust of mind will have a ball. Asked why she came here, one year 7 pupil told us that she hadn't been certain at first as though friend had told her it was a nice school 'she didn't support her answer.' Fortunately an open evening provided all the evidence she needed.

Tiffin School

299

Queen Elizabeth Road, Kingston, Surrey KT2 6RL

Ages 11–18 **Pupils** 1,213 **Sixth form** 382

020 8546 4638
www.tiffinschool.co.uk

Headteacher: Since 2015, Michael Gascoigne BA, 40s. Knows the school inside out – joined as history teacher after completing PGCE (Institute of Education) and training in some tough schools (think recreational chair-throwing). Subsequently became head of history here (1999), head of sixth form (2004) and deputy head (2009) – each promotion fortuitously happening just when was debating looking elsewhere (no coincidence, we suspect).

First generation in family to go to university, bursary to independent school firing career ambitions, though initially directed at policing or law. All changed when he took a temporary teaching post and thoroughly enjoyed it.

Humane, as articulate as his pupils (and that's a big compliment), he's a thoroughly likeable man who understands how boys tick and values his staff (he ensured teachers' room got much needed refurb ahead of other deserving projects).

It's no cinch. Constant pressure on budgets (spends a lot of time fundraising), and dealing with problems out of his control are the main downsides – as (occasionally) are the hours he puts in. Arrives at 7am and leaves whenever ('wife would say it's not early enough'). We'd suspect it's often close to 12 hour day, plus Saturday mornings.

All so far outweighed by the good parts, headed by relish for challenges ahead. 'No virtue in standing still,' he says – putting it into action with three million pound building programme and forging ahead with plans to ensure school becomes an ever more influential local presence through outreach and collaboration. 'A lovely guy, approachable, reassuring,' was one parent's verdict. Combines insider knowledge with at least one eye on future developments. 'No shoe-filler,' thought parent. 'Has his own ideas and agenda.'

Academic matters: Rich balance of subjects from year 7 based on fortnightly timetable. Slightly more English in first year, separate sciences from year 8 but, impressively, keep up art and music as well. Latin for all, also religion and philosophy and fortnightly session on 21st century life. Everyone takes separate sciences, one language and (unusually for non-religious school) religion and philosophy at GCSE plus three options ranging from humanities to Latin and Greek, PE, dance (a rarity anywhere, let alone in maintained sector) and DT.

In the sixth form, have retained AS courses as well as impressive breadth (choice of around 20 subjects – including those rarities, Latin and Greek), most pupils narrowing from four at AS to three A levels (maths, sciences and economics consistently popular) plus games session and non-examined enrichment course (with Tiffin Girls).

Class sizes (average of 30 to end of year 9 dropping to 24 in GCSE years and 16 in the sixth form) no barrier to exceptional results. In 2018, 80 per cent of GCSEs graded 9-7; 62 per cent A*/A at A level (86 per cent A*-B).

And not a question of taking the best, shoving on to academic conveyor belt and letting them off again at the other end (though with the prizes coming thick and fast, from Arkwright Scholarships to 99 boys gaining gold certificates in Junior Maths Olympiad or the Junior Kangaroo and year 13s winning the Student Investor Challenge – top out of 10,000 teams – they probably could). Progress 8, new government assessment tool, puts school in top five per cent for the value it adds between year 6 and year 11 – so complacency certainly isn't the order of the day.

Staff stability helps (20 on the books for at least 10 years – average age of teachers is 40 and 44 for all staff) – though recruitment as problematic here as anywhere else in London – property prices mean 'move out in droves'. Magic ingredient is school itself. 'There's an attachment that grows on you,' says Mr Gascoigne. Some churn is healthy – 'don't want all staff to be here for years and years,' but with most teachers leaving for senior posts elsewhere, controllable, so new staff can learn in an experienced department.

Subjects generally organised by corridor (and door colour – though with pea green for geography, dark green for physics and something between the two for biology, it pays to mug up on pantones). Doesn't take long to work out where you are, say pupils and in any case, there are plenty of clues, like the helmet ('Norman,' said tour guide, authoritatively) in history office and pickled lobster-like creature ('a crayfish – has flatter and wider tail') outside the science rooms, though guide voiced slight disapproval at location – 'out of place, should be biology when this is clearly chemistry.'

School catches boys in magic few years between arriving packed with enthusiasm and ideas and losing it to adolescent cynicism, says head. One boy arrived in sixth form with a fascination for fungi. 'Not the usual thing but we knew he'd love it here.' Helps to be proactive about trying new things, we were told by pupil, though come as you are and you'll be accepted. 'Here it's cool to care about knowledge,' agreed school insider. Certainly true of tour guides, thrilled to be here, erudite and delightfully tickled by oddities of school life – the mystery bricked up door 'to nowhere', the religion and philosophy office – 'strangely placed as the classroom is downstairs.'

Perhaps unsurprisingly, few pupils have statement of SEN – just 0.2 per cent, a tenth of the national average. That said, school caters for range of learning needs – though at 31, numbers are still low – ranging from hearing and sight problems to specific learning needs and Asperger's. Support comes via TA plus part-time additional needs literacy specialist who helps boys with dyslexia or organisational issues.

To teachers with the right approach (and parents struggled to find any without), they're a dream audience. Homework is 'about right,' thought pupil – neither excessive nor inflicted with a heavy hand. Instead, teachers will guide rather than lead, mention for example that there's a test coming up and leave the boys to make the connection.

Ability to suck up facts may be profound (it certainly impressed us) but these boys don't tolerate dull teaching. 'It might sound naughty,' said one (it doesn't, honest), 'but if I'm sitting in physics being lectured on the forces acting on a ball falling from the sky, I'm likely to be less interested than if I'm looking at a cross section of a cell' (they build their own from plaster of Paris and plasticine and they're awe-inspiring). Head agrees. 'It is not good enough to sit at the front and feed them facts. You need to know your subject, and to encourage them always to ask questions – that's how they learn.'

Games, options, the arts: Breathtaking. Just one issue of fortnightly head's newsletter (essential reading if you want a cross section of day-to-day life here) included the latest school trips (GCSE and A level art students to Venice, year 9 classics to Bath, year 7 to London Zoo), sporting success (cross-country) and performing arts, with 'particularly active' dancers doing their stuff at half time during the Four Nations rugby final at Olympic Park and working with the Royal Ballet and Ballet Rambert. Year 8s learn capoeira, a couldn't-be-better fusion of dance and martial arts. Pirouettes have never before packed such a punch.

Sign up for the choir and pupils could end up performing with world class orchestras – Mahler's third with the LSO, Stravinsky with the LPO and Tannha ser at the Royal Opera House in just the last few months, plus choir tours all over the place, as well as appearing on the Blankety Blank Christmas special hosted by David Walliams. They're not blasé, though can be tiring. 'Came back from Royal Opera House and fell asleep in my uniform,' said one veteran.

There's something to impress wherever your eye, or ear, falls, from art (surreal paper scissors and screwdrivers, mounted on clock mechanisms and ticking away the hours – message, if there is one, too deep for this reviewer), to rugby – 16 teams – almost a quarter of all pupils, who regularly give independent sides a drubbing – and rowing. Saunter through nearby Canbury Gardens of a Saturday and you'll often see boats waiting to be launched and some of the 100 boys involved warming up with a few laps by the bandstand – one of the few state schools to offer it at all, let alone on this scale.

Other sports – cricket (main summer sport), basketball, badminton, tennis, cross-country and athletics – are also available and to equally high standards.

Timetable helps, with music, drama and dance allocated six periods between them in year 7 – more if you add on games – and equal to science or maths. Means school 'can grab you early,' said parent, who'd seen son suddenly (and unexpectedly) blossom into a talented singer. 'Everyone's got something different to them,' said one.

Sometimes spark a new idea (one year 8 boy, initially reluctant to try dance, had already reached post-GCSE level; another had done 15 nights on stage at the Royal Opera House). But it's not just the conventional who flourish. 'If they want to learn the sitar or electric guitar or bongo drums then teachers let them,' said parent. 'The point is that they realise that the pleasure out of music is performance.' Top singers may end up as choral scholars but first year string players, scratchily delivering first orchestral performance, will get equal levels of applause.

'We encourage participation way beyond the lessons – school is not just about simply collecting the certificates,' says the head – and pupils praise resulting diversity. Trips are vital part of the process – and not just educationally. 'Playing pool in the evening changes things, you see boys in a different light,' says the head. And while missing lessons does create practical issues, school's view is that benefits outweigh need to catch up later.

In a day that stretches well beyond either end of official hours (dance rehearsals starting at 6.30am were the earliest we discovered – though choir, drama and sport require similar commitment) boys' ability to manage all their interests and academic work on top can be a worry to parents. Some, naturally organised, learn self-management early. But even the borderline chaotic somehow get through. 'My chronically disorganised son coped because he really wanted to do it,' said parent.

Background and atmosphere: Three cheers for Thomas and John Tiffin, brothers and wealthy Kingston brewers who between them left £150 in the 1630s to invest in the education of deserving boys. Canny investment in land by executor did their memories proud, though it wasn't until the late 19th century that eponymous school was finally opened (original site now home to local primary). They moved to current location in 1929, acquiring 30 acres of playing fields in Thames Ditton in 1948 (now owned by the old boys to kybosh any thoughts by rapacious governments of cashing it in for housing). Became voluntary aided, converted to academy in 2010 and are currently keeping close eye on opportunities created by potential expansion of grammar schools.

We don't doubt that J and T Tiffin would be chuffed with what their legacy has achieved. Behind the public persona of the horribly packed and inevitably anonymous open days is a warm, friendly school that's hard to leave. Many don't – or not for long. In quick succession we met retired deputy head, now back as a governor and unofficial archivist (school can trace every old boy since 1880) and former pupil, now a PE teacher here. 'Feels like home,' he said. 'I've even used my house key to try to get into the sports hall.'

Warmth extends to the admin team who keep cool while staying on top of copious amounts of lost property, from Tupperware packed with spectacles to the many missing bags – 'boys pick up the nearest one if worried about being late.' Jumpers ditto.

Pupils notice and respond. Helpful, caring teachers are 'best thing about the school,' said one, who had successfully mounted campaign to get a school corn snake (sadly on study leave – or serpentine equivalent – on day of visit). 'Wasn't dismissed as a silly idea.' Head finally gave blessing – once proper care plan had been presented and agreed.

From head's formal garden with sundial and homely bird feeders (lovingly tended by gardening parent) to cricket pitch, and MUGA surface which ...'is a pitch,' says head (amid in the swirl of jargon about multi-surfaces, G4s and suchlike, all you really need to know), site is greener and bigger than partial views from the three streets (and modern flats) that frame it would suggest. (Art rooms, appropriately, provide best panoramic view.)

T

Definitely has its architectural moments, from historic – attractive 18th century listed building housing classrooms, uniform shop and IT (marked by dainty china figurines) – to last century (1990s art and DT block). There's also cutting edge modernity in attractive two storey circular learning resource centre, bookcases radiating out from central desk and complete with spiral staircase inside (sixth form only) and sedum roof (outside).

Its twin has now emerged home to a stunning new dining hall, with five new classrooms and an IT suite up top, replacing the previous incarnation housed in a vintage Portakabin. Food is more than a match for the new surroundings: sweet and sour chicken and pasta with basilico sauce among the highlights.

Outside, careful design with smaller footprint will add more playground space and greater streetside appeal with glassed windows even offering reflections of the 14th century Lovekyn Chapel, the oldest building in town (though they don't own it – rather to their relief given the costs of upkeep). Means more streetside appeal for this distinctly average patch of Kingston – so a public benefit.

Though money is invariably tight (and tighter here than many assume), careful juggling ensures it goes where most needed. Yes, a few tatty staircases could do with a paint job but the displays are bang up-to-date, performance spaces are many and varied and even the gothic-windowed, red-curtained old style school hall also has thoroughly modern lighting rig. While Macs reign supreme in IT, spick and span food technology room stays well up to temperature and DT, still offered to A level (one of the only local schools to do so) remains beautifully dovetailed, nobody's complaining.

Pastoral care, well-being and discipline: School can't take on all the weight of world's anxieties, says Mr Gascoigne. Pressure to succeed – 'not unique to selective schools,' he points out – that flows down from management to teachers and pupils isn't helpful but can be overemphasised – and certainly the pupils we saw seemed notably uncrushed and extremely cheerful.

He sees social media demanding instant response, impossible to switch off, as a greater contributor to anxiety. School works with mental health worker who's in school for a day and a half each week and includes drop in system. 'We can't solve every mental health problem but can do best to help,' he says.

Merits for good work, contributions to lessons, attitude and helpful acts (in that order) more sparingly awarded after year 7. Lead to certificates, presented in assembly. Best of the lot is head's certificate (platinum) though it doesn't come along often. Dark face of the coin, demerits, treated with caution by teachers.

While will always be the odd behavioural issue and very occasional exclusion (for normal offences), it doesn't happen often. Most other difficulties (occasional missing laptop key) are caused by overdoing the joie de vivre that's inevitable consequence of considerable freedom. IT rooms, with prefect supervision, open at break, for example. 'Boys are not yet the finished product – will make mistakes, do things they shouldn't do. We're ultimately training them for independence and maturity in the real world,' says Mr Gascoigne.

There's much talk here of levels of happiness. Competition kicks in early – brilliant for bonding. Houses have recently increased from six to eight with rise in pupil numbers – one year 8 pupil, who'd moved as a result, initially very torn, though now wearing new tie with great pride – though form competitions, starting early in year 7, are also hard-fought. 'We sung [sic] our hearts and souls out,' writes first year pupil in newsletter of inter-form singing competition held within weeks of joining the school.

Pupils and parents: You find generations of local families who have come here, as well as fair share of celebrities, more tending towards performing arts and sport than straight brainbox, Nobel-winning fame as you might possibly expect.

Big hitters (literally in some cases) include sportsmen Alex Stewart (cricket) and Rob Henderson (rugby) as well as artist John Bratby and Jonny Lee Miller, an ex-husband of Angelina Jolie (probably happier being noted for starring role in Elementary). School is mounting major drive to round up alumni (especially the successful City types) and encourage them to do their bit for support.

Many current families need no urging. Joining the PTA is a good way to get in the swim and there are also subject-specific spin off groups fundraising for rugby, rowing and – probably the busiest of the lot – music. Each has own little community – 'Have got a whole load of new friends,' said one mother.

Main ethnic groups are white British, Indian and Asian. Area isn't immune from deprivation and school argues good case for looking beyond official government tally of disadvantaged pupils based on free school meals. If assessed based on other measures – postcodes, social class and levels of education (significant number of parents didn't go to uni, for example) – school's intake broader than it appears. Keen to broaden mix still further, in line with government thinking – possibly through changes to admissions policy. Definitely a case of watch this space.

Entrance: Entrance day could be a tourist attraction all on its own, Kingston streets packed with small boys and their parents queuing to get in. Same crowds turn up in Sutton and even Slough to try their luck at selective schools there, says head, so not as daunting as it looks.

Admissions now favour locals after considerable legal to-ing and fro-ing overturned previous cross-London (and further) free for all. Now there's an inner priority area of within 10km of the school and an outer priority area extending 14km to Kingston, Wimbledon, Thames Ditton, Surbiton, Richmond, Hounslow. Better all round, says head, shorter journey times ensuring that more can enjoy the before- and after-school activities.

Also more places – now 180 year 7 places (was 120 just a few years ago) allocated in two-stage admissions process, each consisting of English and maths assessments, weighted so as not to disadvantage younger candidates. Some occasional places in other years – new candidates only – those sitting but unsuccessful at 11+ can only try again for sixth form, when need (as do existing pupils) minimum five 7s and three 6s at GCSE with 9-7s in three desired A level subjects. Around a third of sixth form are new.

'Didn't think I'd get in,' said pupil remembering the agonising wait after merry round of entrance exams. One family was poised to accept independent school place, knowing that fees would be a struggle. 'Would have been the unluckiest boy in the school. Here, feel like the luckiest.'

Girls will be admitted to the sixth form from September 2019.

Exit: Vast majority to Russell Group and regular large contingent to Oxbridge (19 in 2018, plus 17 medics).

Money matters: Asks for voluntary donation – if possible £520 a year per child, to some a chunky sum. Understood that won't be affordable for everyone – pay what you can. Over the years, it's funded goodies including new labs and cricket nets – and there's also (discreet) help with uniform costs and school trips for those in need.

Remarks: Engage, inspire, excel, is the motto. It's more like a check list than an exhortation. Delivers 'well rounded, well read, normal human beings,' said a parent. 'It's an independent education provided by the state and we are very fortunate.'

Tower House Preparatory School

188 Sheen Lane, London SW14 8LF

Ages 4–13 **Pupils** 185

Fees: £13,089 – £14,838 pa

020 8876 3323
www.thsboys.org.uk

Headmaster: Since 2009, Greg Evans BSc MA PGCE. Was director of studies at Sussex House for five years and at Kings House Richmond for nine years before that. Early 50s. Genuinely loves his job and lives for the school. 'I always put the boys first. I keep their interests front and centre when making any decisions,' he explains. Wife is Icelandic, and they regularly escape to their place in Reykjavík. Teenage son and daughter. Self-confessed sports nut. Recently taken up spinning at the gym in an attempt to stay fit. Currently enjoying the challenge of learning the trumpet for first time. 'I am not an empire-builder, but I like to think I have improved the place.' Boys adore him; parents hold him in high esteem. An exceptionally dedicated head.

Entrance: Non-selective. First 18 to register are guaranteed a place. Siblings very rarely turned down – 'there would have to be something spectacularly wrong, as family is at the core of what we do.' Places generally fill up three years in advance with bulging waiting lists, so sensible to put names down as soon as possible. Not unknown for parents to check out the school before their son is born. Occasional places further up the school are snapped up quickly. 'We could probably almost double in size tomorrow, but we wouldn't be the same school. People come to us for a reason. We are the only single-sex, single-form boys' prep school in south west London and we are not giving up that niche on my watch!' states head.

Exit: St Paul's, The Harrodian and Epsom College currently the most popular destinations, with others off in ones and twos to eg Bradfield College, Charterhouse, Frensham Heights, Hampton School, Harrow. Head states, 'From a recent cohort of 20, I am very proud that boys went to 15 different schools. We make sure that the boys go to a school that is suitable for them. I tell parents very plainly to their faces that if I think they are trying to send their son to a school where they are going to be unhappy, that this will effectively be a mental scar on them all the way into adulthood.' Parents feel head knows their sons inside out and that he offers well-informed advice. Robust numbers of art, music, drama and sports scholarships. Vast majority stays through until 13; only a handful has left at 11 in the last few years.

Remarks: School is located on a residential street in East Sheen, on the edge of Richmond Park. No rolling acres but school is creative with space it does have. The façade is not beautiful, though the new build for reception pupils is a great improvement on the Victorian privies that it has replaced.

Warm, happy, family feel to the school, but it is nevertheless ambitious. One form entry with 18 in reception, roughly 20 per class thereafter. One mother commented that its small size was one of its selling points: 'Boys all know each other well and that gives them confidence.'

Junior and senior sections on same site, with plenty of interaction between the two. Older boys hear younger ones read and help them out at lunchtime. A healthy amount of hero worship goes on. Junior school considered to be gentle by parents, a place where little boys can be little boys. Every Friday morning reception boys head for the forest school where they build dens, climb trees and jump in muddy puddles. Some parents we spoke to felt that the transition from one part of the school to the other was hard: 'It's a big leap to go from such a nurturing junior school to a full-speed London prep at the end of year 3, but this has to happen at some stage.'

Emphasis on impeccable manners: boys are expected to shake their teacher's hand and look them in the eye as they say goodbye at the end of each day. Head wants them to look back on their prep school with a sense of pride. 'We send well rounded, polite but humble young men on to their next schools.'

House system is at the centre of the school. Boys are apparently more scared of getting a rocket from their head of house than the headmaster. 'They don't want to let the side down. We're a small school and it is very apparent if you stick your head above the parapet. We have a sense of collective responsibility here'. Community spirit is important. Pupils play music at local care homes, clear the river bank of weeds and regularly raise money for charity.

No academic scholarship class 'as it would be divisive and that goes against everything that we stand for.' If a child is sitting a scholarship, then teachers put on supplementary lessons as necessary. Though uncommon here, head believes that tutoring is a mistake: 'If your son needs to be tutored to the hilt to squeeze into a school then you're doing him a disservice and you are setting him up for a fall in the future'. Head aims to deliver a bespoke education, 'a Harley Street approach'.

Most able boys are well stretched, with setting in some subjects from year 3 onwards. According to one mother, the top set for Latin in year 8 certainly gallops along at a fair crack. One parent commented that 'if your son is clever, he will do very well at Tower House. The average boy finds it a little harder.' Another disagreed and felt that, given its non-selective intake, the school caters successfully for all abilities.

Reading is taken seriously and a reading wall records numbers of books read by each boy during the term. For the group of pupils who reads the most, a huge bag of sweets awaits. Library is enticing: jam-packed with adventure books and offset by jazzy mood lighting.

Currently 35 have some sort of mild special educational need, usually dyslexia. Small group booster sessions offered; 10 per cent receive individual support from full-time SENCo. Rare for a boy to need support throughout his time here.

Very successful on sports front. The envy of every other prep school in London with its access to the Bank of England's beautifully manicured sports grounds, just a stone's throw away. Excellent sports tuition from a host of specialist coaches. Head smiles, 'We've moved away from the enthusiastic history teacher coaching the first XI!' School is particularly strong at cricket, reflected in its eagerly-anticipated biennial sports tour to Barbados. All senior boys included, irrespective of sporting prowess. All boys from years 3 to 8 make a team of some sort. One father stated that 'Tower House can hold its own with the great names in the prep school landscape.'

'Art in every form is stretched and pushed here and it constantly amazes me. If you are creative you should come to us,' states head. Inspirational art teacher is supported by two talented artists in residence. Fantastic DT – boys keen to get out the saws, vices and hammers at every opportunity. Music is thriving too and 80 per cent learns an instrument. There is something for everyone on the music front including numerous choirs and ensembles.

Drama deservedly gets the headlines. Head beams when he talks about the drama here: 'I have the most gifted head of drama in the country. Boys will crawl over broken glass for him. He has ambitions for the boys which many other people wouldn't even consider. We see how far we can push it'. To date, Tower House is the only school, prep or senior, that has produced a full-length feature film which premiered in the West End. Head explains, 'We don't try to replicate that every year, though, as it would take over and we'd get a reputation for being a bunch of luvvies!' Head sees drama productions as being great team-building exercises as everyone can contribute, from the uber-confident thespian who delivers impassioned speeches to the lower-key boys who would rather focus on props or lighting. The current record is 91 boys involved in one performance. Here, as elsewhere, school lives by its motto of 'an opportunity for every boy'. Starry ex-pupils include comedian Jack Whitehall and actor Robert Pattinson.

Pastoral care is a priority. School has ring-fenced well-being and resilience sessions every half term. Boys are encouraged to de-stress regularly, whether through yoga classes, practising meditation or running before school in Richmond Park. 'We aim to give the boys the toolkit by which they can face the pressures of modern life'. Head has noticed outside pressures on the boys are increasing, not only academically but also on the co-curricular front, such as selection for sports teams and musical ensembles. 'Parents sometimes over-expect,' he laments.

Current clubs include debating, chess, touch-typing, sewing and maths games. One parent we spoke to felt that the clubs on offer could be more ambitious and less sport-centric.

School aims to make fees as all-inclusive as possible, so parents do not have to keep reaching for the cheque book throughout the term. Unlike many schools, learning support lessons, clubs and residential trips are not seen as extras. Full and part funded means-tested bursaries available from year 3.

Mostly professional families. Both parents tend to work. Excellent communication between school and home. Parents give talks to boys about their careers, in a variety of fields including medicine, law and journalism. Cosmopolitan mix, including significant numbers of Scandinavians and Spaniards at present. Head has introduced a grandparents' day and thinks it is important to involve them in their grandchildren's education, particularly as so many of them foot the fees.

A remarkably inclusive school that feels like a traditional boarding prep. One mother commented that 'it does what it says on the tin. It prepares them very well for senior school'. Another parent went further: 'The headmaster and his staff have one single objective – that of educating boys to the highest possible standard, whilst nurturing extracurricular talent, instilling courtesy and the highest moral values.' Undoubtedly, Tower House is thriving.

Trevor-Roberts School

55-57 Eton Avenue, London NW3 3ET

Ages 5-13 **Pupils** 180 **C of E**

Fees: £15,300 – £16,800 pa

020 7586 1444
www.trevor-robertsschool.co.uk

Headmaster: Since 1999, Simon Trevor-Roberts BA (50s). Son of the founder, Trevor-Roberts studied at Westminster School before reading English at Aberystwyth. In 1983, he joined his

T

father Christopher in the family firm, where he learnt his trade by example. (He has since been joined by his sister Amanda, who heads up the junior school.) Mild mannered and reflective, he has a very clear sense of what the school is about: 'We try to get children to enjoy the process of learning.' Continues to teach maths to the 13+ candidates, because he's found he, too, now has the knack of putting things across clearly. 'I shadowed my father for a long time and learnt how to do it by osmosis.' Parents find him immensely approachable and engaged. 'You always have complete access to the head and he knows all the kids incredibly well.' Married with two grown children, both of whom attended the school.

Entrance: Register as soon after birth as possible.School assesses the first 50 children on their list in the September prior to the calendar year in which they turn 5. 'We're not expecting any preparation, but we want to make sure it will be a happy transition,' says the registrar. 'We're looking for inquisitive children who want to learn. Getting that is more a dark art than a science.' The school generally tries to give priority to siblings, 'but only if it's the right school'. Often takes in one or two more in year 4, when the year group divides into two classes.

Exit: Girls mostly – though not exclusively – at 11, generally to Francis Holland, South Hampstead and other north London favourites. Most boys (and some girls) at 13, to regular placements including City of London, Eton, Harrow, Highgate, Latymer Upper, Merchant Taylors', UCS and Westminster. 'The head is very good at managing parental expectations,' said one former parent.

Remarks: This is a family-run school with a very distinctive ethos, deriving in large part from its origins. Founded by the current heads' father in the 1950s with just 14 boys, it was originally seen as a refuge for the 'unteachable'. 'My father had a reputation for taking those whom other schools had given up on and getting them through entrance exams to leading public schools,' says head.

Today, the school can take its pick of north London's brightest, but continues to select a mixed-ability (now co-educational) intake and provide a tailor-made education for all. 'They want every child to work to his or her potential and really do treat every child as an individual,' said one parent.

Children start in year 1 in a class grouped according to the calendar year of their birth. In year 4, this is rearranged to allow everyone to be in place for secondary school entrance. One class of 16-18 in the early years, two classes in years 4 to 6, then a single form again for the final two years. 'We like to move children around so they're not in the same group for eight years. It gives us the flexibility to allow those who require it a bit more time and accelerate those who need it.' Parents confirm this is skilfully managed. 'They're constantly readjusting their approach for different levels of learning, but not in a way that disturbs the children.'

Specialist subject teaching from the word go, with a classroom teacher for the core subjects, but music, history, geography, science and art all taught in their own space. 'It keeps the week fresh.'

Plenty of imaginative teaching by intelligent (including many Oxbridge), though not always qualified, staff. French from year 1, Latin from year 5, some Greek in year 8, Mandarin taught as a club. Special needs addressed by weekly sessions with the learning support coordinator and outside specialists.

Everyone staying for the final two years sits common entrance. 'We take it very seriously. Eleven plus is about flexible problem solving; by 13, it's more structure on the page.'

Very good at ensuring the basics are in place. 'Sometimes you have to be a bit tough. We insist that children use a pen rather than touch type. If you have to write an essay under exam conditions, you have to be able to discipline your thoughts.' No truck with overly formalised exam training. 'Non-verbal reasoning is not a subject,' he says crisply.

Formal homework from year 3, starting out with 20 minutes in English or maths ('It shows them how to work by themselves and for themselves'), up to two hours a night for the top forms. 'They do work very hard, but the atmosphere still manages to be reasonably relaxed,' said one mother.

Good relationships with staff are fundamental ('The teacher is not someone they're trying to hoodwink,' says the head), as is the view that effort should be lauded over achievement. 'Children are perfectly aware there's competition elsewhere, they don't need it reinforced. We want them to be in competition with themselves.'

Breadth well beyond the exam curriculum is given enormous emphasis. Outstanding music – 'We love music' – with a dynamic head, numerous ensembles (brass, jazz, string, woodwind, chamber choir, rock band) and much external participation (at the Royal Festival Hall, St John's Smith Square, etc). Twice weekly art lessons (one in year 7) in a bright art department at the top of school, with its own kiln. Extra art and DT on offer for enthusiasts on Wednesday afternoons.

Cultural values that have largely been submerged elsewhere – 'Everyone is encouraged to have a novel on the go' – with half an hour of silent reading daily after lunch. Poetry and drama matter and prove great confidence builders. 'My son almost died of nerves the first time he had to read out a poem,' said one mother, 'but now he loves drama and performing.' 'The plays are unbelievable,' said another.

Plenty of fresh air and exercise, with a good-sized, well-equipped playground, including popular table tennis, miniature railway and chicken coop ('the chickens are a great comfort to quieter, shyer children'). Primrose Hill, a few hundred yards from the door, enables twice weekly games. Definitely not a school, however, where 'go-fight-win' is on the agenda. 'Children love sport, but I don't want a First Eleven ethos, with the captain of games strutting around,' says the head. 'We do play matches against other schools, but everyone has a go.'

The senior school building, a fine example of arts and crafts, was the founder's own home and still offers delightful domestic interiors with William Morris wallpaper in the front hall and mid-century classic tables used instead of desks in the top forms. The juniors are housed in their own building with a separate dining room and science lab.

The atmosphere is civilised but structured ('It's a nice mix of the very strict and the nurturing and kind – teachers are always willing to talk things through'). Everyone has a hot lunch, served through an open hatch, 'so they can see where it is made.' Staff share the dining hall with pupils. 'Eating is socialising.' Food is freshly prepared on site using local produce.

Manners and uniform are both reasonably relaxed. Light blue polo shirt for younger children, dark blue for older ones. Trousers and skirts, 'something reasonable'. 'Jeans are fine, jeans hanging off the hips are not.'

Often the school of choice for the liberal, media intelligentsia (including some famous names), the type of parent who genuinely believes in the well-rounded education, not the rush to the top of the league tables. (Competition here, though it undoubtedly exists, tends to be on the level of how many operas your child has seen rather than where the family went skiing.) Mainly local, some from Notting Hill, Queen's Park, Islington. The head feels 'there's no typical child, but I've heard people say our children are very kind.'

Trinity Catholic High School

Mornington Road, Woodford Green, Essex IG8 0TP

Ages 11–18 **Pupils** 1,627 **Sixth form** 417 **RC**

020 8504 3419
www.fc.tchs.uk.net

Headteacher: Since 1981, Dr Paul Doherty OBE BA DPhil (Oxon) FRSA (70s). Middlesbrough born and bred, he originally studied for the priesthood at Ushaw College in Durham. After gaining a history degree at Liverpool University, he won a state scholarship to Exeter College, Oxford, where he met his wife with whom he had seven children. Having decided the academic world was not for him either, he became a secondary school teacher, working in Ascot, Newark and Crawley before being appointed as headmaster to Trinity.

'An inspiration' is the phrase you'll hear more than any other about this larger-than-life character and despite him being in his 70s, pupils, parents and staff alike seem terrified at the mere thought of him leaving. We found him solid and commanding, yet friendly and open-minded – a winning combo that helped lead him to getting an OBE in 2012 for services to education and that helped lead the school to gaining five consecutive outstanding reviews from Ofsted. Doesn't teach, but very much part of the furniture across both school sites, where he eats with pupils in the dining room, holds regular question-and-answer sessions and invites every child to see him on their birthday, presenting them with a card, sweets and £1 coin. 'He's always reminding us that we should treat every child here as our own,' one staff member told us. 'Perhaps not the most politically correct of heads, but I rather like that,' commented a parent, while others also praise the 'strong management team' he has around him.

Also a novelist and writer of non-fiction, with over 100 books to his name, some translated into 20 languages. Has written under various pseudonyms including CL Grace, Paul Harding, Michael Clynes, Ann Dukhas and Anna Apostolou – although he now writes only under his real name. His seven grown-up children were all educated at Trinity.

Academic matters: Setting in maths from year 7, but in no other subject. 'Mixed ability classes work,' insists the head – and they have the results to prove it, with 89 per cent of GCSE candidates getting 9-4 in both English and maths in 2018, and 34 per cent of grades at 9-7. Strong results across the board, particularly in the core subjects of English, maths and sciences, with pupils also doing exceptionally well in art, computer science, child development, English literature, dance, drama and food tech. Popular GCSE choices include history, computer science, languages and triple science.

T

At sixth form, 28 A levels are offered – mainly traditional subjects 'due to Russell Group demands' – although media studies, psychology and sociology also available, all with decent take-up. In 2018, 47 per cent A*-B and 21 cent A*/A grades, with strongest results in chemistry, French, Spanish, English language and literature.

Spanish and French from year 7, with Latin available in years 7 and 8 as a 'twilight course'. They don't hold back on homework which, perhaps inevitably, isn't to everyone's liking. 'I think they should give less in years 7 and 8 so that the children have more time to develop outside interests,' said one parent, while another commented, 'My child had to drop an A level due to the workload he was expected to get through at home.' Tracking of students is meticulously detailed and well communicated to both pupils and parents, and the school's monitoring and evaluation of this system is widely chronicled (including by Ofsted) as being second-to-none. 'We all know exactly where we should be in every subject – it's incredibly thorough,' one student told us. Meanwhile, a teacher said, 'It's very fluid so that we can raise standards where we need to and likewise, add in interventions where students aren't reaching their targets' – the likes of which include subject clinics and Saturday school.

The school's approach to SEN (110 on SEN register, including 30 EHC plans when we visited) is no less painstaking, with one parent praising the 'systematic approach to ensuring children get help both inside and outside the classroom – I couldn't fault it.' Adapting the curriculum is not uncommon – for example, so that a student can take six GCSEs instead of the more usual nine, with a bespoke curriculum and booster classes where needed. 'They've supported my daughter thoroughly without ever making a big deal of her special needs, and it's all coupled with clear expectations that she has to work as hard as she can. It's a great philosophy and has worked wonders for her.'

In short, a highly academic school – but an exam factory this is not, with several parents reporting that their multiple offspring's different academic levels were all catered for. 'One of my child found studying a breeze; the other really didn't, and the school managed both perfectly, finding their full potential but never making them feel over-pressured,' said one.

Games, options, the arts: All the usual suspects are on offer, including hockey, netball, football and rugby, and frequently wins competitions. Less traditional options include cycling (the school has bought in bikes), sailing (at Fairlop sailing lake), badminton and dance (to GCSE), and some parents told us the school was good at 'encouraging fitness – essential in the current climate.' Only a sports hall on site, however, with other facilities a 10 minute coach ride away; parents we spoke to either told us their children weren't interested in sport (telling in itself?) or that their very sporty child had been 'disappointed'.

The art suite – which includes three art studios, plus a smaller workroom – produces some striking artwork, which is displayed throughout the school. Visits to galleries often involve mixed year groups 'so they can learn from each other' and visiting artists are regularly invited to work in the workroom, with students observing them in small groups. This approach is extended to pupils too, with younger ones frequently invited to watch and critique older ones producing their masterpieces. Meanwhile, teachers are encouraged to inspire students through their particular area of specialism.

The focus on drama tends to be more academic than extracurricular, with no all-school productions. But there's plenty to shout about when it comes to value added, with very successful results at GCSE, although this attracts relatively small numbers, usually around 20 a year.

Parents itching to watch their little cherubs perform have more joy when it comes to music, however, with the Christmas carol concert and rock and pop concerts among the popular annual events. There are also plenty of one-off performances from the various school orchestras, choirs, ensembles and school bands – plus regular music festivals and competitions. Around 60 students from every year group from years 7 to 9 are taught instrumental lessons by a peripatetic teacher (some in groups), with numbers starting to trail off after that. The annual music tour, which involves a different European destination each year, is well attended. 'Trinity really feels like a musical school – you often see pupils performing, sometimes as a background at lunchtimes while you eat,' one pupil told us.

There's a comprehensive extracurricular timetable, resulting in many pupils staying on until 5pm at least a couple of times a week. Clubs focus on sport, music, IT and all the academic subjects right through to war gaming and chess (popular with the quieter pupils). This is a lead school in outdoor education, with a greater take-up of D of E (bronze, silver and gold) within the school than across the rest of Redbridge as a whole. At least one or two school trips every week to theatres, museums etc and some residentials too, including a recent ski trip to Austria, film and media studies visit to LA and regular teambuilding trips to Wales.

Background and atmosphere: The school is split between two sites, with the upper site (main site) on Mornington Road and the lower site on Sydney Road, a five to 10 minute walk away. The lower site (originally the local secondary modern school, St Paul's) is home to years 7, 8 and 9, while the upper site (originally Holy Family Convent School, the local girls' grammar – which merged with St Paul's in 1976) is home to year 10 upwards. 'It makes starting at this vast school much less daunting for year 7s,' one parent told us – pupils concur. That said, due to specialist facilities being split across the two sites (music is based in lower school, while most science labs are mainly in the upper school, for example), all pupils access both sites, with older ones often walking between them two or three times a day. 'We used to move the teachers around, but now we move the pupils – much better for fitness.'

The upper site is made up of nine buildings, dating between 150 and two years old: Trinity House, Keswick House, Rackham House, Monteluce House, Pelham House, Grainger House, St Joseph's House, Vincent House and Becket House – each home to a different subject area ranging from humanities to food tech. Meanwhile, the lower site is made up of a single 1960s building, with a remote science laboratory in the playground called the Padua Centre (named after St Anthony of Padua). 'This is where the snakes and geckos are kept – you can borrow these over the holidays,' a pupil told us excitedly.

Inside, much of the school looks tired and in need of a lick of paint, and everyone agrees they are limited by space – there's no dedicated canteen, for instance, and the library doesn't look anywhere near big enough for 1,750 pupils. 'The school was designed for six form entry – we're now eight form entry.' We felt it in the lower site during wet play, with every single pupil crammed in the corridors and main hall. That said, the facilities are good and some areas, such as common rooms, are surprisingly roomy, albeit unimaginatively designed with a sea of conference-style blue chairs and magnolia paint.

You will be in no doubt that your child is a Catholic school, with daily mass at 8.30am and prayers in the morning, at midday, at 3pm and before all meals. There's a chapel on both sites, plus a chaplain who puts a Catholic slant on any counsel provided to the pupils, while pictures of the pope adorn several noticeboards. But that doesn't mean pupils are spoon-fed religion – in fact, they are actively encouraged to question their faith. 'Some students wind up atheist and that's not seen as a problem – all views are welcomed,' one pupil told us. Overall, there's a culture of learning – when we visited, all classroom doors were firmly closed, all desks faced forward and all pupils looked engaged. Once the bell goes, though, there's all the noise and excitement you'd expect when hundreds of tweens and teens are able to let their hair down, if only for a few minutes between lessons.

Pastoral care, well-being and discipline: 'Firm but fair' is how most pupils and parents describe discipline here and it clearly does the job – pupils are well behaved and there have been no temporary or permanent exclusions for at least three years. 'All the students know the rules and that there are clear consequences if you break them,' explained a parent – notably detention (lunchtime or after school), community service (litter picking etc) or Saturday school, albeit with a warning system first. The most heinous crime, it seems, is distracting others in lessons, although pupils told us the school is also particularly hot on uniform and giving in homework on time. 'We have zero tolerance for lessons being interrupted – teachers are here to teach and pupils are here to learn,' the school told us – and a daily logbook is sent round to all classes so that teachers can record any misbehaviour, even if it's only a warning. 'It means teachers know they are well supported and students know the teachers talk to each other.'

Pastorally sound. 'Teachers are approachable, with most regularly reminding us that they are available if you are struggling either emotionally or practically,' said one pupil. In addition, each year group has a head and assistant head, who – together with the school chaplain – encourage any pupils to come and see them if they want to. There's also a big prevention strategy to help stop issues ranging from bullying to radicalisation becoming a problem in the first place. Plus, there's plenty of leadership and peer mentoring type opportunities, including a prefect system and Guardian Angels (whereby sixth formers look out for younger ones).

Excellent communications between school and parents all helps, say parents. 'There has never been a time when I haven't known what's going on with my child – they tell you when they're doing really well, when they're struggling and when they really play up,' one parent told us. 'When things go wrong, they get you involved quickly so they can resolve it and move on,' said another.

Pupils and parents: A great diversity of backgrounds and ethnicity, with 47 per cent minority ethnic (predominantly Black Caribbean), with the common denominator being – surprise, surprise – Catholicism (93 per cent). Although there's no PA, parents feel involved and there's almost full attendance at parents' evenings and a good turnout at events such as cheese and wine evening. We found pupils to be chatty, grounded, community minded and well-mannered, with a real pride for their school. Alumni include Tamzin Outwaite (EastEnders actress), Kele Okereke (musician), Matt Ward (record producer/songwriter), Gary Lucy (actor), Christine Ohuruogu MBE (Olympic, world and commonwealth athletics champion), Catherine Dalton, Dan Lawrence and Nicholas Browne (cricketers).

Entrance: The four main feeder primary schools are St Antony's Woodford, St Mary's Chingford, St John Fisher Loughton and Our Lady of Lourdes Wanstead – although pupils come from around 50 in total. Looked after children get priority, then it comes down to Catholicity and distance of Catholic primary school. Over 1,000 applications for the 240 places and many go to appeal, with long waiting lists further up the school.

Over three-quarters stay on to the sixth form after GCSE, for which the entrance criteria is 9-6s at GCSE for the subject they want to study. Around 50 more join from outside (depending on numbers staying on), although that figure has dipped recently as some local schools have introduced sixth forms. 'It's a shame as we could accommodate more than 50,' says school. Unlike the rest of the school, sixth formers don't have to be Catholic, but they must be willing to uphold the school's religious ethos.

Exit: Nearly a quarter leaves after GCSE – usually to study a vocational course at college or different subject choices at other local schools. A few do apprenticeships. Around 80 per cent of sixth formers to university, of whom approximately 45 per cent go to Russell Group universities. No particularly dominant universities or subjects – 'there's such a range, from law to technical theatre and they head off all over the country.' Around five medics a year. Three Oxbridge places in 2018. Pupils praise the university and careers advice service – 'There's nothing they can't help you with.'

Money matters: Parents are generous in their financial support, with a Gift Aid scheme in place for those who donate either via standing order or one off donation. Trinity holds funds to support those in need and parents/guardians are encouraged to contact the head if financial support is required. Strong links with local community groups also ensure that families are well supported.

Remarks: A strict, disciplined Catholic school with a strong pastoral system to ensure young people stay on the straight and narrow. This, together with the excellent teaching and monitoring, makes this a place where young people of all abilities thrive academically. Standards haven't slipped here in decades and it doesn't look like they're about to start any time soon.

Trinity School

Shirley Park, Croydon, Surrey CR9 7AT

Ages 10–18 **Pupils** 1,012 **Sixth form** 284 (78 girls)

Fees: £17,448 pa

020 8656 9541
www.trinity-school.org

Headmaster: Since 2016, Alasdair Kennedy (early 40s). He read engineering at Cambridge, but realised well before finals that what he really wanted was to teach maths and physics. Independent schools are woven deep into his DNA: his father was head of science at Fettes in Edinburgh. 'My early birthday parties were spent running around all-weather pitches,' he remembers. 'I loved that feeling that activity was going on all around me'. He did big stints at Rugby and Sevenoaks, before becoming head of physics at Dulwich, and latterly academic deputy there. He is married (his wife is in business) with three boys.

Despite the blue-chip schools which have made up so much of his life, he doesn't come across (nor does he seek to) as an obviously public school type. His manner is confident and engaged, but he communicates a strong sense that, whoever he is with, and wherever he may be, everyone is equally important in his eyes. 'The social elitism which coloured much of the public school tradition,' he says simply, 'is alien to me, and to my values. At Trinity, I believe we are bound up, wholeheartedly, in the pursuit of excellences of all kinds, but not in grandstanding.'

T

Academic matters: This is a selective school, but not preposterously so. The results, says the head, reflect 'plenty of hard work as well as natural talents'. At A level in 2018, 66 per cent A*/A (91 per cent A*-B) and at GCSE 88 per cent A*-A/9-7. A broad base of subjects with the accent, as on would expect, on traditional academic ones. Maths, English and history are very strong, and there is notably good biology. Modern languages seem a trifle subdued by comparison. The drive to STEM subjects impacts here as everywhere and, as the head acknowledges, other subjects feel the effect of that.

'Pupils are challenged academically,' said one parent with two children at the school. 'But they're enthused. The prospect of homework can lead them to huff and puff a bit, but that's normal. What's pretty consistent is that they're bowled over by all they are learning in the classroom.'

Special needs are taken seriously. 'It's entirely normal for boys in their early years to struggle with organisation,' says the head. 'We want to help them find ways to help themselves.' The school has a learning support team, which sees pupils, right through to sixth formers, on an individual basis. It also offers specialist help with maths and sciences for anyone struggling, and there are spelling clubs and unlimited assistance for anyone battling to get on top of exam techniques.

Games, options, the arts: 'The school's music is so good,' said one parent, 'that it defies any easy description'. Famous for the Trinity Boys' Choir, there are also superb opportunities for instrumentalists. Every new boy who does not already play a musical instrument is offered free lessons on an orchestral instrument of their choice and over half the boys in the school regularly take part in a musical activity. Ensembles include numerous orchestras, bands and chamber groups. Pupils participate in a dizzying array of national choirs and orchestras. The London Mozart Players coach the senior orchestra and Trinity Boys' Choir appears regularly at The Royal Opera House and at Glyndebourne. Recording studios, a 500-seat concert and no less than 26 Steinways help nurture the musical education of pupils of every level. 'So many schools alienate both top musicians and the apathetic,' said a parent. 'That isn't the case here.'

A fine reputation for sport: 'Participation is all,' said head. Some 65 per cent of pupils are in school teams so 'everyone who wants to represent the school can do so'. Trinity has worked hard and fast to integrate the new sixth form girls into its sports programmes. Boys do rugby in the autumn term, then hockey and switch to cricket in the summer; girls' hockey dominates the autumn term, followed by netball in spring and rounders in the summer. Tennis and athletics for both and there are any number of other choices: football, water polo, swimming, indoor hockey, rugby 7s, squash, golf, basketball – ad infinitum. The facilities are all on hand to support such choice, with two all-weather pitches, two sports halls, a climbing wall, a swimming pool and tennis and squash courts.

The DofE is flourishing, and there is a 150 strong CCF contingent, comprising both Trinity students and those from the local academy. Occasional mutterings can be heard that the pressure of sport and music can build up unduly in some pupils. 'To be fair,' commented a parent, who had felt their child had been overloaded, 'when the problem was aired, it was rapidly dealt with. It's inevitable, I guess.'

The vibrancy extends to drama and the arts. There is a dedicated theatre space, flexible enough to stage both large scale and studio productions, and junior and senior drama clubs perform both at school and across London. The school has close links with the National Youth Music Theatre and other theatre companies.

Background and atmosphere: Trinity is one of the Whitgift Foundation schools. It opened, in 1858, specifically designated the Poor School – an allusion to the economic circumstances of its pupils and not an aspersion on its talents. Moved to its present site in 1965, and while the facilities are stupendous, it is sometimes hard to find many kind things to say about institutional architecture of that period. But the buildings are beautifully maintained, if not aesthetically memorable – light, spacious and in every way perfect for all the very best kinds of learning.

The school has turned a potential drawback into an opportunity: the normality of the place has made it brilliantly successful in allowing it to pitch itself as, first and last, a local school. In socio-economic terms, Croydon and its hinterland is an area which veers between great suburban affluence and significant deprivation. 'There is no doubt,' AK says, 'that we are there for everyone', and there is close liaison with local state primary as well as independent prep schools. A strong sense of social awareness reaches beyond the locality, and the school has extensive links – including a feeding programme and placements for gap students – with a school in Malawi.

Their ambition has played off handsomely, not just in terms of demand for the school. Insofar as it's possible to generalise about 1,000 children and their teachers, they seem overwhelmingly appreciative of what the school does and is, and actively relieved that the school never tries to claim any social cachet. 'My mother was really relieved about that,' one girl said. 'I haven't found myself cut off from any of my old friends because of the new ones I've made here.' Men and women are both fully represented in senior positions in the school.

Pastoral care, well-being and discipline: Year heads take responsibility for each age group and the annual intake is small enough for them to deliver on their commitment to know each pupil personally. Up to GCSE, the forms have about 20 pupils, each overseen by a tutor, and these are the axis of the whole system, working closely with the pupils and the first point of contact with parents. In the sixth form, tutor groups have about a dozen students. Induction is carefully thought through: all new pupils and parents come to the school several times before the first day, and meet their form mentors. Every form in the younger years has a couple of sixth formers attached to it – 'much liked by all,' said one parent of a younger pupil.

Discipline is low-key, and relationships feel calm and cordial. Teenagers in any society can be unkind to each other, but both pupils and staff have confidence and this is quickly picked up. 'Having good structures is essential,' says one teacher, 'but it's even more important that it's seen, even by young pupils, as inherently wrong to pick on people.' Older pupils vociferously agreed. 'If you have a worry,' said one boy, 'there are so many teachers here who mind about that and are ready to help'. Of course, no school is immune to the complexities of the internet and the social challenges it may present. 'It nearly always comes down to helping people to identify moments of choice,' says the head 'and how to confront them. And that needs a culture of honest conversation – at home and school. We set out to do this.'

Uniform for all pupils up to GCSE. They look tidy, but not irritatingly scrubbed. Sixth formers have more freedom, 'so long as it's smart, coordinated and tailored,' says the head. 'It's not a big source of controversy,' he adds

Pupils and parents: Close links with parents are fostered, but in a usefully businesslike way. Grades are sent out every half term, recording progress and effort, and there are two parents' evenings annually, as well as a full school report. It's evident the school wants parents reassured (they are even given the chance to try out the school food, says the head, 'which they seem uniformly to find excellent').

The catchment stretches from Wimbledon in the west to Bromley and Beckenham in the east, with school buses easing the daily commute. Yet the feel is local. Parents are making the investment gladly, but also unsentimentally: the overwhelming sense is that they want their children to grow up into successful citizens, but not grasping ones, nor to indulge in airs and graces. 'That matters a great deal,' said one parent. 'We love opportunity and we hate entitlement. Just now, we can see our children living in gratitude.'

Entrance: About 40 per cent of pupils come from other independent schools, and 60 per cent from state primaries. Given the different constituencies, the school has entry points for boys aged 10, 11 and 13, as well as at sixth form for boys and girls. An entrance examination (centred around English, maths and verbal reasoning) is set to all applicants, who are also given an interview. At sixth form, in addition to the tests and interviews, all incoming pupils must have achieved at least six 7s at GCSE.

Exit: The overwhelming majority go on to Russell Group universities. There were 10 places for Trinity pupils at Oxbridge in 2018, five places for medicine and dentistry and one degree apprenticeship. Increasing numbers to US universities – Mr Kennedy commented: 'the best of them value the whole person, in a way which presents a closer alignment with our sense of education at Trinity than with the approach of some UK universities'.

Money matters: Fees are considerably lower here than at local rivals (eg Whitgift and Dulwich). Lunch and transport are extras, as are most music lessons and the bigger trips, but the school is conscious it doesn't want to price anyone out. One way and another, some 50 per cent of students are receiving some kind of financial support, and about half of these are on bursaries.

Remarks: There is a sense in which Trinity is a real standard-bearer: its students leave school with a respect and appetite for learning; its commitment to arts, music and sport seems to delight almost every pupil, and to reassure many parents who, often justifiably, worry that 21st century living involves no stimulus other than that achieved at the end of an iPhone. Its strong investment the local community helps to ensure that Trinity boys and girls leave the school emotionally intelligent and socially grounded. This is a school committed to practising the essence of good citizenship as well as to nurturing personal success.

Twickenham Preparatory School

Beveree, 43 High Street, Hampton TW12 2SA

Ages 4-13 Pupils 289

Fees: £11,055 – £11,970 pa

020 8979 6216
www.twickenhamprep.co.uk

Headmaster: Since 2005, David Malam BA Southampton (history), PGCE King Alfred's College, Winchester (50s). Clever and refreshingly candid. Like every other London prep head offering both the 11+ and 13+, he's reviewing the situation. No danger of losing Common Entrance, as long as leading senior schools (notably Hampton) retain 13+ entry. With better odds at 13+ than at 11+ and two extra prep years to enjoy – better than being bottom of the heap in a senior school – what's not to like, he says.

Dreamed of pro career in either football or chess and took both to a high level before studying history. Running a youth club made teacher training a natural step. Worked in schools on the south coast, followed by a year in a Christian school in Cyprus. Started here in 1995 as history and games teacher, before becoming senior teacher and then deputy head in 1997.

Though cites an impressive list of improvements, from mini amphitheatre to revamped grounds (including new sports surface) it's all outweighed by the staffing. Teachers must 'genuinely enjoy working with children and see teaching as a vocation, not a day job,' (all must run a club). Approach was clearly paying off, judging by feedback from parents and pupils. '[They] go the extra mile,' said one, praising willingness to travel to events nationwide 'and often abroad, too.'

He delights in pupil success (wears a tie in the school purple for celebration assembly), particularly in thinking skills and chess (one pupil recently won gold for Britain in the Mind Lab Olympics).

Though he has done his time here (four of his own children happily through the school, one remaining), appetite for the role, so far, remains undiminished.

Entrance: Non selective at 4+. Otherwise, occasional places only from reception onwards after assessments in English, maths and reasoning. Often take on a handful in year 6 to prepare for Common Entrance.

First dibs to staff children and siblings. Registered families sign acceptance form 18 months before start date. Deposit secures place – non-refundable if not taken up, deducted (with no interest) from final term's fees if it is.

Some pupils arrive at the school with undiagnosed needs, supported with, says head, 'best SEN in the area.' Parents rave about school's ability to identify barriers impeding progress –work with speech and language therapists and implement social communication programmes. 'Provision for children with dyslexia is outstanding,' said one.

Focus, however, is on pupils who will do well academically and not the right place for those who might struggle to access the curriculum. Where Common Entrance likely to be problematic, raised by school around year 5 though, if they want to stay, 'we would do our very best to keep them.'

Exit: Discussions about senior schools start in years 4 and 5. In 2018, three scholarships to St George's College Weybridge, Hampton School and Notre Dame. Hampton School (six pupils), Sir William Perkins School and Notre Dame (three pupils each) are most popular. LEH, Surbiton High, SWPS, St Catherine's (Twickenham) and Notre Dame feature among the girls-only destinations. Current most popular co-ed was St George's College. Others to Kingston Grammar and Radnor House.

Remarks: So good that last full ISI inspection dates from 2012. According to parents, all that was good then (just about everything) remains so. IT – only area with a (small) question mark – is being sorted with help from ever generous Parents' Committee.

Name is misleading – retained after outgrew Twickenham site in the early 1990s and moved to Hampton. Not that local punters are confused. Many come from Hampton and Teddington, others from Richmond and Twickenham, a few from Sunbury, Molesey, Walton and Thames Ditton.

T

Attracts maintained sector escapees who like school's reassuring normality. 'You don't forget where you've come from,' said one.

School's home is a pretty listed building. Modern additions including art and music block, complete with vibrant purple clock (also courtesy of parents) and matching railings. Colour also features in tasteful stripes down tracksuits, exercise in restraint that stops assembly resembling a storm at a lavender farm.

Multi-purpose hall features eye-catching wavy roof, sprung floor but variable acoustics. Older pupils must need keener hearing than ours to pick up more than the occasional word during otherwise delightfully inclusive whole-school assembly.

Open door at the back and the light, airy pre-prep kingdom is revealed. Freeflow rules outside with communal areas for all, while reception, year 1 and year 2 each have side-by-side plant-filled little gardens, with a secret leafy nature trail at the back, venue for (low) risk activities like building dens. Details-driven head of maintenance has fitted nest boxes round the pre-prep building (RSPCA occasionally called in to rescue stranded fledglings) and there's real grass over chilly perfection of artificial version (hurrah!), everywhere bar reception garden, where nature proved incompatible with over-enthusiastic scootering.

Pre-prep head Mrs Barnes, an English specialist, has been here for 15 plus years and exudes warmth. '[Pre-prep is] about being loved, nurtured, feeling secure and taking risks,' she says.

From year 2, testing pinwheels courtesy of teacher's hairdryer, to popular prep history teacher who performs own songs with jokes (terrible but the dates stick, say pupils), lessons are lively.

If displays were restrained in places (art room was a bit too neat and tidy for our liking though '20 minutes ago, it would have been at a peak of messiness,' tour guide assures us), opinions aren't. Pupils have views they're keen to air, given half a chance, from reception upwards. ('We always put a chatty child by the door to talk to visitors,' says Mrs Barnes).

Ask one child their favourite subject and you won't be allowed to leave until everyone else in the class has told you theirs, too. 'Mine is ICT, because it stands for Ice Cream Tasting,' said one impish year 4 pupil.

Considerable planning goes on behind the scenes. Pre-prep subject coordinators (specialists for music, sport, ICT) work with prep team on curriculum development to ensure seamless transition. The library is sensibly organised, with fiction and factual books in different rooms, work and play carefully separated, while do-able homework increases in upper years but so gradually you 'don't really notice,' thought pupil.

School's not very secret weapon throughout is emphasis on mind games with focus on problem solving, timetabled through the school and taught by specialists. Reception pupils might house different farm animals (where do you put the pigs if they won't talk to the sheep?); older pupils have more overt problem solving and strategy. There's even a week-long mind festival (think cerebral sports day – synapse and spoon race?).

Does wonders for exam technique – 'Helps your brain,' confirmed year 3 pupil –and boosts resilience. Just as well given the inevitable cloud on the horizon, those horribly stressful 11+ and 13+ entrance exams.

Generally, they're managed with kindness and sensitivity by the school and with grace and good humour by pupils. We did pick up a few worries at the top end of the school. 'How are you feeling about your exams?' we asked one senior boy. 'Fine... and that's the biggest lie I've ever told.'

But that's down to the system, not the school. Parents and pupils stressed (and re-stressed) the quality of staff. 'Kind and nice,' said a pupil (and umpteen mums and dads, often adding 'nurturing' by way of ringing the changes). Pressure to do well often comes from within. 'I wanted to repay my parents for the investment they've made in me,' said a scholarship winner, and clearly meant it.

Works because staff know pupils inside out (verging on over-cossetting, thought one senior pupil) with teaching and support tailored accordingly. Careful setting (maths plus small groups for English and French) avoids anyone feeling either singled out or sidelined.

Small details matter – one teacher writes end of week 'good news' note for each pupil. Rewards are all about doing better: credits and merit certificates to year 6; £5 Amazon vouchers for top years. 'Bet the teachers have never seen such good behaviour...' said year 6 girl of older boys. Demerits (for repeated transgressions – e.g. not handing in homework) are tactically used: 'Year 6s letting off steam after pre-tests is time to monitor everyone carefully,' says member of staff. Can result in 'sensible' detentions used, for example, to catch up with work.

Sense of being looked after is palpable. One of our guides has done 40 or so tours but insists that the 41st (ours) is a treat (we got bonus points for asking different questions). Even the fish in two tanks by the entrance – now approaching catch of the day size – seemed to exude contentment.

Rivalry does exist but is sensibly channelled. Would-be prep prefects nominate themselves, run hustings and incentivise the plebiscite with speeches and the odd song (sweets are banned). 'Odd maverick does get elected – and often surprisingly good,' says school. Otherwise, there's competition between the four houses, named for local notables. Each gets an assertive website write up, headed by surprising claim that David Garrick 'would be proud of some of our theatrical renditions of Boom-Chig-a-Boom in house assemblies.'

Presumably he'd also be impressed by the productions, mainly combining two year groups, younger as choir, older taking the main acting and singing parts, year 7 solo effort featuring cameo parts for staff. Sport was seen as less of a focus, reinforced by trophy cabinet. 'Three-quarters ... are for chess,' pointed out tour guide. Outdated, says Mr Malam, who reckons that sport is now on a par with other local schools and points to victories (winners of three football tournament in one term) as well as investment in good coaches and upping of fixtures.

Bar the normal girls vs boys anomalies (several girls we spoke to wouldn't mind a crack at football and cricket, though no boys were feeling the love for netball...) there's masses of choice. Curriculum supplemented by numerous after-school clubs (one athletics/chess enthusiast – clearly a born multi-tasker – sprints between the two to avoid timetable clash) and extensive charity work (pupils involved in selecting deserving causes), with long term support for Street Child African and school in Malawi.

Mind games almost essential to winkle out wish list items from these happy parents. For girls entering the school at out of the ordinary times, it can be hard to break into well-established friendship groups. 'Not the same for boys – they have football,' said one, gloomily – another argument for a girls' team?

Bar a few mild gripes about slightly variable lunches (hunger damped down by break time snacks, 'some the size of a three-course meal,' said a pupil) we'd rate this a must visit prep, which manages anxieties and aspirations of pupils (and parents) with aplomb and warmth.

Twyford Church of England High School

Twyford Crescent, London W3 9PP

Ages 11–18 **Pupils** 1,463 **Sixth form** 486 **C of E**

020 8752 0141
www.twyford.ealing.sch.uk

Executive head teacher: Since 2002, Dame Alice Hudson MA (Oxon). Educated at Slough Girls' High and Leighton Park, where she was the first ever head girl. Read English at St Hilda's Oxford. Taught at Central Foundation Boys' in Islington and Maria Fidelis, Camden. Deputy head at Brentside High School, Ealing before joining Twyford in 2000, where she was deputy and acting head before being appointed head. Made a Dame in 2017 for services to education but, with typical modesty, at the time said she was 'taking one for the team.' Married with four children, most of whom have been educated here. Committed Christian. Loves cooking and a keen cyclist. Dynamic and inspirational. A force of nature.

Associate headteacher since 2013 is Karen Barrie, previously deputy head. Degree in maths from Manchester and still teaches one lesson a week. Softly spoken with a gentle sense of humour. Lives and breathes the school, admitting that 'Twyford has been my children.' Described by Dame Alice as 'the most brilliant headteacher the school has ever had.'

Together they make a watertight team. Highly visible at school events. One mother noted, 'They are greatly respected but are approachable, chatty and open.'

Academic matters: Superb results. In 2018, at A level, 44 per cent of entries were A*/A, 74 per cent A*-B. At GCSE, 85 per cent of pupils got 9-4 in both maths and English and 45 per cent of grades were 9-7. Unsurprisingly for a faith school, all pupils take GCSE religious education one year early, with knock-out results. Most pupils take nine GCSEs in total, with a the most able managing 10. 'We are a high functioning academic school,' explains Dame Alice, and few would argue with her. Yet, aside from the stellar results, she also wants pupils to learn to love their subjects. It's not just about league tables.

A specialist language college. In key stage 3, half of the year group takes two languages and Latin is a core subject. Most pupils take either French, German or Spanish at GCSE, with a small proportion taking two. A minority takes Latin as an additional subject. French and Latin teachers train primary teachers in the borough in their subjects. Twyford is keen to share its expertise. Starry maths and science departments too. At GCSE, Twyford is in the top fifth percentile for progress in maths and science. Massive numbers take these at A level, some 30 of whom manage further maths too.

Strong sixth form, which has doubled in size from 250 to nearly 500. Twyford Additional Programme caters for around 50 high fliers each year who are likely to make Oxbridge or other top-notch universities, as well as those aiming to study dentistry, medicine or veterinary science. It 'aims to combine the extra skills and extended learning of the International Baccalaureate with the academic rigour and specialisation of A levels'. Focus is on developing thinking skills, presentation and honing interview techniques. Wide assortment of outside speakers wheeled in. Nearly all get A*/A for EPQ. Diverse range of essay subjects chosen including 'How far can humans travel in space?' and 'Was the English Civil War a '"War of Religion"?' One parent we spoke to said, 'The school expects the children to do well and never lets up on pushing them to be the best they can. There is a very, very high level of expectation and sometimes it can feel like a bit too much pressure. But it ultimately gets the results.' Another parent agreed: 'There is no escaping the fact that if you go to Twyford, you'll work hard.' No laziness tolerated, though setting from first years ensures not everyone has to proceed at a high-octane pace. Reports of huge piles of homework from year 8 onwards.

Less than five per cent of pupils in years 7-11 have an EHC plan, with a further four per cent on wider SEN register. The Alternative Resource Centre (known as ARC) has a specialism in supporting those on the autistic spectrum. A wonderfully quiet haven, especially compared to the deafening Uxbridge Road outside. Attachment disorder, anxiety and ADHD as well as dyslexia, dyscalculia and dyspraxia catered for. Those on the 'nurture programme' participate in about 85 per cent of mainstream lessons, but come to ARC for support in maths and English, on an individual and small group basis. They skip some language and humanity lessons, as well as singing, to attend these sessions. Support offered includes Lego therapy, homework and lunchtime clubs. A tranquil place for the vulnerable.

Pupils assessed four times a year, so school keeps a beady eye on performance. For those slipping through the net, swift action is taken to identify the cause of the decline. 'We quickly identify whether it is lack of effort, lack of support from home or poor behaviour,' we are told. Depending upon the cause, sessions are arranged with the school counsellor or behaviour consultant, parents are contacted, or pupils are pointed in the direction of booster groups or study clubs. All hands on deck to get the faltering up and running again. No-one is left to fall by the wayside.

Despite its academic successes, there is no chance of school resting on its laurels with Dame Alice in charge. She is constantly looking at what could be done better. 'We are deeply aspirational but averse to complacency. We are a self-evaluative organisation,' she tells us.

Strong core of committed teaching staff, with 85 per cent remaining static each year. When teachers do bolt, it is usually for positive reasons such as promotion elsewhere. Teacher recruitment can be challenging in some subjects, but head remains upbeat: 'We are perpetually appointing very good graduates.' Though some opt for in-house teacher training, others come armed with a PGCE. Plenty of non-Christian teachers but they must be 'in sympathy' with the Christian ethos of the school and be happy to participate in institutional worship. New teachers are nurtured here. As Ms Barrie explains, 'Our training and support for staff has to be as tight as it is for the students.'

Games, options, the arts: Certainly, no lack of extracurricular opportunities and head believes that 'the students have a richness of educational experience here'.

Twyford is a specialist music college, and parents consider the music department to be extraordinary. Currently over 20 ensembles, which have performed everywhere from BBC Songs of Praise (where the gospel choir was recent finalist in Choir of the Year) to St Paul's Cathedral. High spec music rooms, including recording studios, and professional-quality performance centre. Everything on offer including a traditional orchestra, laptop orchestra, brass collective and guitar and ukulele band. Pupils encouraged to perform internally and externally at every opportunity. 'The students don't just perform for themselves, they perform for others,' explains head. Fiercely-contested music competitions. Mammoth team of instrumental peripatetic teachers give lessons to more than 350 pupils each week. Drama department also firing on all cylinders. Whole-school musical productions (eg Grease, The King and I and Hairspray) staged at the end of the summer term. Lower school also puts on a Christmas show. Huge art department too, offering textiles, photography, computer-aided design, animation, print-making and clay.

Vast sports centre. Sports include rounders, netball, gymnastics, athletics, dance, football, cricket and hockey. Close links with professional coaches from QPR and WASPS, to develop most talented footballers and rugby players. Takes part in multiple local leagues and tournaments. An array of trophies stretching back to the 1980s reflects its sporting prowess. Twyford also competes regularly at county level cup fixtures for football, rugby and athletics. Girls' netball particularly starry, though one parent we spoke to claimed that 'sport for girls is not perfect. It is quite old-fashioned and what's offered to them isn't great. No girls' cricket or football or hockey.' For those less keen on kicking, throwing and hitting balls around, fencing, taekwondo and parkour await. Ominously-named The Cage is a fenced-off area for ball sports in the centre of the school. Though it resembles a prison compound, it is well-used and ideal for teenagers with surplus energy at break-time.

Plenty of chances for pupils to escape Acton. Trips punctuate the timetable. Language trips throughout Europe; cultural trips to Paris, Prague and Venice and sixth form historians visit St Petersburg. Active souls can ski or walk in the Alps. Closer to home, there are regular theatre and gallery trips. Parents pay for excursions, but a trip fund can be dipped into by those in need.

On top of their clutch of good grades, pupils are expected to add ballast to their CVs with work experience. Placements arranged everywhere from local primary schools and solicitors' offices to hospitals and local garages and even the Ritz kitchens. Some attend courses in hairdressing, childcare and carpentry, and others attend summer schools and workshops. Charity work also encouraged. 'We're big in the sixth form on what the students do outside of lessons,' explains Ms Barrie. Loafing around all summer would be heavily frowned upon.

Background and atmosphere: Twyford is part of a multi academy trust, along with William Perkin, the new Ada Lovelace and Ealing Fields, all in the same borough. 'We are stronger as a family than we were on our own. It has given us a competitive edge,' states Dame Alice. Much is shared between the schools in terms of front and back of house support, ranging from pastoral care, assessment and curriculum resources to finance and HR systems. Works brilliantly in terms of curriculum, as good lesson plans are shared on the intranet – particularly useful if one school has a weaker department. Not restrictive, however, and schools still have freedom to make own syllabus choices for themselves.

Twyford became a church school in 1981. School motto comes from St John's gospel, chapter 10 verse 10: 'I have come that you might have life, and have it to the full'. Pupils here are expected to live life to the full. This 10:10 ethos is shared by all the schools. Mostly Christian pupils, but all faiths represented. Two communions per year for each year group and the assembly we attended on epiphany was unequivocally religious. 'You need to know what you're getting into,' stated one parent.

The Elms, a grand Georgian building that houses reception, stands majestically at the heart of the school. Lawn in front is used by pupils to relax at break and lunch time. Jolly campus-style café serves hot food, with a canopy for those wanting a more Mediterranean experience. According to one mother, 'the real lack of variety on offer' at the café means her son is not alone in grabbing a meal deal at Tesco's instead.

Pastoral care, well-being and discipline: Pastoral support considered to be outstanding. Before each new cohort arrives, head of year 7 liaises with primary schools to ensure a smooth transition. Once here, year 7s have their own section of the school, as coming from a small primary to a whacking secondary presents its own challenges. Some older pupils are trained to become peer supporters to help with teething problems. One parent we spoke to commented that 'the nurturing side is strong and when my eldest had some wobbles in year 7 and in year 10, they couldn't have done more to support him. The school responds quickly to any problems and I have never felt fobbed off.' Chaplain comes in two days a week, one full-time counsellor. Seven tutor groups per year. Seven houses, named after cathedrals and abbeys: Truro, Wells, York, Fountains, Ripon, Durham and Canterbury. One mother we spoke to said that 'the school takes a lot of effort to make sure each child is prepared for the next stage in their education. In year 10, we had a one-to-one session with the head teacher to discuss our plans for A levels and university. They did this for every child in the year.'

Discipline has been tightened on Dame Alice's watch. You could hear a pin drop in assembly – not a single pupil was distracted or fidgety. Every pupil filed in past her, and each one was greeted warmly and reminded to stand up straight. Rules are strictly adhered to. Ms Barrie explains, 'We celebrate first. We reward positive behaviour and are not just punitive, but they need to understand the structure and rules.' Pupils left in no doubt about what is and is not acceptable, and one hapless boy who walked into assembly late when we visited was swiftly dispatched, with a late detention. Possession or supplying drugs, possession of an offensive weapon (including penknives), assaulting a member of staff or persistently disruptive behaviour lead to permanent exclusions. Pretty rare, though, and only a few each year are sent packing. Controversially, smartphones are banned, but 'dumb' phones (that only allow texts and calls) are allowed. Offending phones are confiscated until the end of term. 'The students know we might have to do a stop and search of their bags, if we have a good reason. If they are found with a smartphone, they know we'll confiscate it.' School not taken in by plaintive pleas of 'It's my Mum's phone and she must have dropped it in my bag by mistake this morning.' As one mother summed it up, 'The discipline if not for the faint-hearted. Zero tolerance for even minor things. You get a negative point for not having a rubber or talking in the corridor. But if you look behind the strictness you see a very kind heart, and senior management genuinely care about the children.' School runs efficiently but manages to retain the personal touch. Everyone knows where they are supposed to be at a given time and pupils scurry purposefully around the school towards their next destination. They do let off steam at certain points of the day, and break time can be pretty vibrant, but a sense of regimented order prevails most of the time.

Pupils and parents: Most hail from the Ealing area with large numbers from Brent, Harrow and Hillingdon and a few from Hounslow and Hammersmith & Fulham. Majority of parents are highly supportive and practically 100 per cent attendance rate at parents' meetings.

Around eight per cent of pupils in years 7-11 are eligible for free school meals. Just over half of the pupils are white, 31 per cent are black or mixed race. Christianity is the unifying factor. Fair amount of Polish spoken at home, as well as various other European languages and some Arabic. Not as multilingual in make-up as neighbouring schools.

Entrance: Oversubscribed. Some 190 places in year 7, with 150 foundation (Christian) places, 21 designated as world faith places and 19 music places. Details regarding length and frequency of attendance at church are pored over with a fine-tooth comb. As one mother reflected, 'Getting a place at Twyford is the hard bit. It's a full five years of nearly weekly attendance at church'. The music scholars' places have opened things up a bit. These places are offered to those with potential, as much as to those who have had money lavished on violin lessons from an early age.

A further 130-150 new pupils (out of 650 applicants) join the sixth form each year from elsewhere. Over 500 are interviewed, so a gargantuan exercise for the school. All applicants must 'be supportive of the aims, attitudes and values, expectations and commitment of this Church of England academy'. Minimum entry requirement is eight passes at GCSE at grade 5 or better, including maths and English. Each A level course has individual entry requirements, but generally a grade 6 or 7 in related GCSE courses is expected.

Exit: Around 60 per cent stay on into the sixth form. Those leaving post-GCSE tend to opt for local colleges offering more practical BTec courses.

Roughly 90 per cent of the sixth form heads for university, with about half to Russell Group. Birmingham, Manchester, King's, Leeds, UCL, Bristol, Kent and Sussex all currently popular. Thirteen to Oxbridge, 12 to medical courses in 2018. Science courses most popular, followed by liberal arts, maths-related and creative arts. Ten or so take art foundation courses. Only one per cent takes on apprenticeships, in areas such as accountancy and journalism.

Money matters: Bursaries available in sixth form for students from low income families.

Remarks: A heady mixture of energetic leadership, strict discipline and high expectations. Ideal for your driven child who is keen to throw themselves into what is on offer. Not the place for the rebellious or unmotivated. Parents are full of praise and they consider their offspring to be lucky. As one mother put it, 'Twyford pupils are inspired, challenged and happy. It sets them up for life'.

Unicorn School (Richmond)

238 Kew Road, Richmond, Surrey TW9 3JX

Ages 3–11 **Pupils** 172

Fees: £6,930 – £12,720 pa

020 8948 3926
www.unicornschool.org.uk

Headmaster: Since 2013, Kit Thompson BA (Oxford Brookes), PGCE (Roehampton) (late 40s), previously deputy head (academic) of Twyford in Hampshire where his wife teaches part-time. Initially a banker, he chose teaching early in his marriage becoming an NQT at The Unicorn, staying three years with English specialism. 'What attracted me back to the Unicorn was the school's distinctive ethos, a parent-owned family school and broad curriculum with its emphasis on creativity, laughter and learning.'

Commuting from Winchester, with a family Wimbledon bolthole when necessary, he enjoys the balance in his life. Three teenage daughters keep him busy and he relaxes by playing tennis, golf, or taking long walks with the family labrador. Holidays in Cornwall rather than exotic destinations and he has been known to accompany the biennial school ski trip.

Mr Thompson enjoys guiding the school forward, taking the articulate, highly-involved parents – some of them Old Unicorns – and grandparents with him, and has no immediate thoughts of moving on. Proud of the excellent inspection findings in his third year, he has made changes quietly but purposefully. The head's office has relocated from the top floor to beside reception and front door, making him very accessible; appreciated by staff and pupils alike.

Unchanged is his commitment to the school's ethos, which all newcomers, staff and parents, must buy into. Opening the front door at 8.20am, he enjoys welcoming all and seeing, as we witnessed, 'pupils smiling, relaxed but not disrespectful', just as they are when he takes lessons, break duties or assemblies. He knows the entire school community by name, as he told us. 'A great strength is the size of the school and the constant conversations.'

Entrance: Into nursery in September after child's third birthday with places offered from 18 months prior to entry, so parents say 'you almost have to put your name down at birth'. Siblings and children of past pupils are given priority. Arrival in other years involves assessment in English and, in juniors, maths. Single form entry throughout with maximum of 22. Slight movement at 7+ for variety of reasons, including relocation and occasional misfit between pupil and school. Up to 100 per cent means-tested bursaries available. One parent described how welcoming the school is, praising helpful office staff, and how 'teachers interviewed my child's bunny and Mr Thompson interviewed my daughter on a seesaw which completely put her at ease'.

Exit: Most popular destinations in 2018 were St James Boys, Hampton and Ibstock Place, and most head for London day schools. Some off boarding at eg Bedales, Downe House and Tudor Hall, others to state schools eg Grey Court, Tiffin Boys and Girls and the West London Free School. Head liaises with local schools and is an inspector with boarding and day experience. He believes, 'Everyone's got to trust. I hope and expect parents to trust us.' With the help of deputy and assistant head he offers guidance over future school choices with a range of options and parents feel supported throughout: 'He steps in when necessary.'

Remarks: Founded in 1970 by parents seeking an alternative to what they judged to be education without creative spark, The Unicorn is a registered charity and a limited company by guarantee with parents members whilst their children attend the school. Governors are board directors and since Mr Thompson's arrival, there are two co-chairs, one parent and one non-parent. Housed in an attractive, double fronted Victorian villa, the school benefits from being opposite Kew Gardens, close to Richmond Park. Games take place in Chiswick at Dukes Meadow and the University of Westminster playing fields, with swimming nearby at Pools on the Park.

Originally considered bohemian, not so now, the school has retained its special ethos – as current Old Unicorn parents we spoke to emphasised – of providing a child-centred education. 'A wonderful place to learn, creative and allowing for children's individuality'. Most pupils are local: from Kew, Richmond, East Sheen, Chiswick, Barnes, Twickenham, St Margaret's and Ham with some within walking distance. There is a healthy mix of Europeans and a steady flow from the Far East.

The curriculum includes specialist taught science, computing, music, creative arts, French and PE. Time is set aside every day for reflection and developing thinking skills: Brain Time in years 3 and 4, philosophy lessons for years 5 and 6. Classes divided into groups of 11 for many specialist subjects, maximising facilities, and excellent staff:pupil ratio. Parents explained, 'They gently ease the pupils towards 11+, putting the right focus on 11+ preparation without narrowing the curriculum'.

No formal EAL lessons, instead pupils are catered for in the classroom. School has identified about 25 pupils as having special educational needs but does not claim to cater for severe learning difficulties. One parent we spoke to with an older child identified on the autistic spectrum thought the school lacked experience dealing with this, but praised the head, 'who has bent over backwards to help', and the head of learning support, who has ensured staff have been given further training. Additional learning support is provided in pairs or small groups with some one-to-one expertly coordinated by well qualified staff. Parents pay for these lessons but they are subsidised by the school. Individuals are given differentiated work, and reading books are chosen with librarian's guidance. Touch typing is offered after school to develop keyboard skills.

Every Thursday afternoon year 3s upwards enjoy 12 or so extremely popular extracurricular clubs, mostly covered by fees with contributions for the priciest. Compulsory debating one term for year 5s, good preparation for interviews, and parents are actively involved. Some ferry pupils to Ham for riding, Slough for sailing, others lead cookery or gardening clubs. We saw enthusiastic potters, artists creating marbled eggs, others learning fencing. After-school clubs include La Jolie Ronde French, chess, karate, modern dance, musical theatre, choir, music theory and swimming, and end at 4.45pm. Juniors attend residential trips in Surrey, Cornwall and Cumbria.

This is not a manicured, purpose-built environment but a well-maintained, stimulating, setting with happy children engaged in learning, as we witnessed in a year 4 group mathematics session on problem-solving using an interactive board. Age groups are mixed: older pupils listen to younger pupils reading; year 6s travel with nursery pupils to swimming. Staff often team teach so there is plenty of communication about the children. Underpinning this is assessment data which includes emotional as well as academic information and signals to staff if a pupil is anxious or needs intervention promptly. Pupils describe their teachers as 'friendly and fair' and parents agree, 'they really know your child'. Inspectors judged teaching to be 'excellent, challenging pupils and fostering interest'. Parents of older pupils explained how their children were always busy, extended with differentiated work, including different text books, and setting in English and mathematics. Recent use of puzzles and riddles and reasoning for all has gone down well as school prepares for entrance examination shift. Many praised 'a bespoke education'. Parents seeking loads of formal testing, drilling and grading might well find this approach disconcerting.

Pupils are encouraged to be confident, as we saw in a polished year 4 assembly on Romans and Celts involving drama and music, revealing pupils' considerable knowledge of the topic. 'My child was a real ankle clinger when he arrived, and now he has become a public speaking competition winner and happily played his saxophone in front of hundreds of Cubs'. Weekly drama leads to school productions such as year 5's Macbeth and year 6's The Rocky Monster Show.

Elected school council representatives and head boy and head girl change termly. A house system has recently been introduced. Pupils like the competition and encouragement to gain house points. Staff ensure individual's strengths are recognised. As one parent applauded, 'it could be a certificate for being a smiley person or helpful in the playground, or for knowing all the dates of the kings and queens of England'. The assembly hall rainbow mural displays unicorns on distinct colour-coded paths (as each class is a rainbow colour, beginning with red and concluding with ultraviolet), for demonstrating the 14 Unicorn virtues. Recently behaviour has been a focus, with teachers and volunteers paying attention to the consistent application of the school's code of conduct.

The broad curriculum and creativity are fundamental. Musicians perform regularly. The Unicorn Singers have won competitions including gold in the junior vocal ensemble at the Richmond Festival, and reached the national finals of youth festivals. Three-quarters of the pupils learn an instrument.

Separated from the main building by the large playground is a coach house with spacious ground floor provision for early years, with walled garden and mud kitchen. We climbed the narrow staircase to a newly established spacious, light, well-equipped art room with its two specialist teachers. We admired a year 5 collage inspired by Holbein's Two French Ambassadors, part of their work on the Tudors. Witty and carefully executed, the left-hand figure sported the photographed head of Mr Thompson, and the right that of his deputy. Observant pupils had accurately reproduced the entrance hall's Victorian tiles, as well as the head's brown shoes and deputy's striking trainers. There is a kiln but no DT room, although puppets and models are made in organised workshops. Recently all classes drew on the theme of Kew Gardens, collaborating with animation artists to produce a short film. Unsurprisingly, the school has been awarded a gold Artsmark.

Kitchen on site: hot food was the only thing pupils suggested could be improved about their school, although parents seem happy with the menus.

Space is at a premium. The playground is made good use of with an Astroturf netball/football/running around area in one half and exciting play equipment in the other. This might deter parents who prefer more on-site games areas for their sporty offspring. Fixtures in netball, hockey, rounders and cricket for girls; football, hockey and cricket for boys. Recent successes in swimming, hockey, football and netball tournaments.

U

Involving parents throughout, The Unicorn is a welcoming, community, 'not a finishing school for primary pupils,' explained one parent, comparing it with other local schools. All agree 'it combines being nurturing with achieving high academic standards and creatively developing individual's strengths'. Parents who prefer to be distanced from school or whose primary focus is academic success with regular testing and regimentation may not find the ethos suits. 'Children are happy, not pushed in a certain direction', say parents, whilst articulate, relaxed pupils are full of praise for their teachers and school.

University College School

Linked with University College School Pre-Prep, University College School Junior Branch

Frognal, London NW3 6XH

Ages 11–18 **Pupils** 760 **Sixth form** 308 (90 girls)

Fees: £20,328 pa

020 7435 2215
www.ucs.org.uk

Headmaster: Since 2013, Mark Beard BSc MEd (early 40s), a chemist. Mr Beard came from Brighton College where he'd been deputy head with a period as acting head between the redoubtable Seldon and the remarkable Cairns – a good place to cut headmagisterial teeth. He is credited with this school's greatly increased number of Oxbridge entrants. He began his career at King Edward's School, Birmingham, where he is remembered as 'a jolly good chap', thence to St Paul's School, as head of chemistry. Mr Beard is married with two young children and enjoys squash, reading and ancient history.

He is energetic, open, likeable, relaxed and clear-sighted. He followed a loved and warmly respected head, Ken Durham, and big shoes can be hard to fill. However, 'I came in to be myself,' he asserted when we met. 'I set out my stall openly and clearly from the start' and whilst Mr Beard's appointment to this major school as a first headship was a considerable vote of confidence, he has more than filled his predecessor's shoes. He flustered some in the school community when, in his first term, he cracked down on aspects of this traditionally 'liberal' school – notably its somewhat relaxed attitude to uniform. 'I have been keen to explain..that liberal scholarship is not the same as liberal attitudes.. There is a school uniform and it is to be worn properly at formal occasions; you should be punctual to lessons, mind your manners and if you have homework, you do your homework.' Many parents applauded. 'Things needed tightening up,' one told us. 'I think he'll make it stricter, smarter and tidier – but within the ethos of the school,' thought another. He has broadened the curriculum throughout the school and has placed a stronger emphasis on community links with an expansive volunteering and outreach programme now in place. Parents and students recognise the changes they have witnessed. 'He's less overtly charismatic than Ken – more cautious and considered. He will be a very good influence.' Sixth formers concur: 'He'll do interesting things over time.' One thing that remains constant throughout is the 'soul' of the school. There is a buzz across the site. Students love to learn here and teachers love to teach here.

Academic matters: Mr Beard's charges have not let him down. Recent results have been some of the best in the school's history with 70 per cent of A levels/Pre-Us graded A*/A, 88 per cent A*-B in 2018. At GCSE, 88 per cent A*-A/9-7 grades. Impressive by any standards.

Far freer choice of GCSE and A level subjects than elsewhere including no blinkered – in our view – insistence on the holy trinity of sciences. Twenty plus A level options, with psychology recently added. Much teaching material tailor-made by school's own staff – that's proper teaching. Universal praise for the English dept. 'It's phenomenal,' drooled a parent. Very good languages dept and exchange system. Mandarin is growing seriously now and Italian is now an option in year 9 and beyond. School has switched to the Pre-U for languages, philosophy, DT and English. We approve. But teaching praised across the board. A sense of academic work being serious but also offering infinite opportunities for thought, exploration and discovery.

Parental approval of Mr Beard's instant moving of A level mocks from March to January. Much appreciation of staff dedication. 'They're always there if you need help. There's a young bunch of teachers and many run extra classes for those who need them,' we were told. There are also support mechanisms such as regular tracking and reporting back to parents, to help boys who need pushing.

All are screened in general literacy, numeracy and reasoning on entry. Mild SEN seen as no problem here. Two full-time and one part-time learning support specialists. Individual support either by withdrawal or classes before and after school – also for those with mild EAL needs.

Games, options, the arts: The school has traditionally focused on inclusivity over winning – an excellent principle. Regular Saturday fixtures for up to 18 teams including C and D teams and many extracurricular clubs/practices in eight key sports taking place before school, after school and lunchtimes. Under Beard, there is greater emphasis on performance. There is now an 'elite sportspersons' programme', additional soccer and cricket coaches, increased games options and other initiatives to allow pupils to reach their potential. Top sportsmen are given the opportunity to flourish: the 1st rugby XV won the Middlesex Cup in 2016 and 2017 and play their flagship matches at Allianz Park – home of Saracens. Recent results in several sports including some individual triumphs suggest that, indeed, a sport fuse is alive and kicking here. They have county/academy rugby players, hockey players and cricketers, England (ISFA) footballers, tennis players very high in the national rankings, international swimmers as well as individual rowers, sailors and fencers. £10,000,000 investment has improved the nearby 27 acre playing field site in West Hampstead, including building a brand new double pavilion.

'The music and drama are simply brilliant,' a parent enthused. Music has long been exceptional here and we noted the number and quality of ensembles eg the symphony orchestra, chamber orchestra, several chamber groups, umpteen bands of all kinds including jazz and swing and excellent choirs. Well-provided for. Many pupils take LAMDA exams to high levels. Students write and direct their own plays and performance values are high. Dance is now taught alongside drama in years 7 and 8 and two shows (one by year 12s and one by year 13s) are performed for a week at the Edinburgh Fringe Festival every year. DT and art are outstanding. Evident creativity, freedom and experimental ethos and the dept has more the air of an art college than a school. Many media, some wonderfully bizarre and arresting work and all good stimulating stuff.

Far more interesting sounding clubs and extracurricular activities than we meet in most schools. Friday afternoons are given over to sixth form enrichment with pupils choosing courses which broaden their appreciation of a subject they are considering studying at university. Applicants for medicine follow a tailor-made support programme throughout their time in sixth form. Pupils set up clubs to pursue their own interests so we found a medical ethics society, a law and justice society, an eco-friendly club and beekeeping among many others. We wanted to sign up to them all.

Far from being a crammer in atmosphere, independence in all things is key. 'If your kids are self-starters, motivated and organised there is so much on offer, but they have to make the effort to get it. They don't come after you,' an appreciative parent explained. 'There is so much on offer even for the less academic child,' said another.

Exceptional outreach activities include collaboration at all levels with several state schools and pupil volunteering.

Background and atmosphere: The main buildings, dating back to 1907, are solid and imposing but rest comfortably on the southern slopes of the Hampstead hill. An unusual history. Founded by the University of London and various interested liberal intellectuals in 1830, it was designed to give an education to boys from dissenting (ie not conformist C of E) families and, initially, had no form of communal worship – unique at the time. Also no corporal punishment and no boarding. Its earliest incarnation was in Gower Street, hence the designation of Old Gower for an alumnus. So, from the off, it was regarded as 'liberal', and the tradition has been proudly maintained. What does it mean? 'It means, "no rules just for rules' sake",' ventured one parent, and that's at least part of it. Another parent quoted a prep school head: 'It's a school for mavericks.' While we like this observation, we feel it's a bit off the mark and UCS suggests that, while the great majority of pupils are far from being mavericks, the school is inclusive and can certainly accommodate them. Perhaps best summed up by a veteran parent: 'It's a wonderful, liberal, free-thinking school – you can look however you want to look, whether whacky or entirely traditional. They are accommodating and accepting and they celebrate difference.' It also still means no RE or religious assembly and a spirit of tolerance and inclusiveness.

A terrible fire in 1978 destroyed the huge Great Hall but the rebuilt version is almost overwhelming in its size and gravitas – wood panelling, stucco ceiling, huge organ and brass chandeliers. All eat in the handsome panelled refectory – all refectory tables and forms – with a strangely monastic feel. Droolly enthusiasm for the school food. 'No-one complains here,' we were told, and the menu was about the most varied, tempting and creative we can remember.

Later buildings include the 2006 sports centre with excellent pool – also used by the local community; the sixth form centre with large and well-appointed common room, study areas – with and without PCs – and an excellent all-day café; the Lund theatre – a large and flexible space in which most productions happen and which is constantly in use; new state of the art library – 'a hub for innovative and creative teaching and learning'. Site now feeling a touch full (head prefers 'compact') although space still for super vegetable garden and beehives, three Astro pitches/courts and little green nooks for sitting and relaxing. Some smartening up going on hither and yon – a little paint and patching doing wonders as part of the rolling refurbishment programme, with the opening of the Kenneth Durham Social Sciences Centre and the construction of a Centre for Innovative Learning and Teaching. The emphasis here is not on every kind of here-today-obsolete-tomorrow IT gizmo but on rock solid teaching.

Girls arrived in the sixth form in 2008 to both trepidation and excitement from staff and boys. But it has worked, and not too much to the detriment of relationships between the school and its all-girl neighbours. 'The boys love the girls coming in the sixth form – it works very well,' one veteran parent assured us. 'They take very confident girls – the multi-tasking, vibrant, feisty ones – and they settle well.' The girls we spoke to bore this out, but they also paid tribute to the efforts made to integrate them before term and to help them quickly make friends once the year began.

Pastoral care, well-being and discipline: Houses are called 'demes' here and matter, but not too much. Praise for the Beard tightened-up regime. 'Some of the younger boys were getting lippy and needed reining in.' But equally, parents, pupils and OGs keen that the school's treasured 'liberalism' is maintained. 'It isn't a school for those who need a highly regulated, organised system,' explained a devotee. Another parent concurred, 'It's very friendly and informal. It's warm and family-like.' Much praise for the home-school communications. 'I have mobile numbers for all my son's teachers and they reply to emails almost before you've sent them.' Even warmer praise for the deme wardens: 'They are phenomenally good on the pastoral side.' Mr Beard has a light touch but a firm view. 'We want them to be the problem solvers of the future, not the problem causers. That's partly what a liberal education should be about.' Few discipline problems. Leavers reflect thoughtfully on their schooling: 'You learn to manage your time. They cultivate you into someone who can deal with a high level of intensity in your work. They build it up so that you don't really feel how much more deeply you are thinking. You become very independent and self-reliant in this school.'

Pupils and parents: From all over north and central London. Pupils are as diverse as the capital itself. They are articulate, thoughtful, independent. Parents are achievers, ambitious, cultured, moneyed – for the most part – and involved. 'Increasing numbers of middle class parents have to work hard to find the fees,' acknowledges Mr Beard.

Entrance: About two-thirds of 11-year-olds come from the junior branch in Holly Hill. They move up without needing to take an entrance exam. At 11+, 350+ boys, mostly from local primaries, try for 30 places. Exams in maths, English and reasoning in January. Around 40 per cent of applicants thereafter invited for interview.

At 13+, 300 boys apply for some 30 places – mainly from local preps, eg Arnold House, Devonshire House, The Hall, Hereward House, North Bridge House, St Anthony's and Trevor-Roberts, but also Notting Hill and Westminster Cathedral Choir School. Pre-test in year 6 in maths, English and reasoning. About 150 return for an activity morning and interview in the October of year 7. Offers conditional on performance at CE.

At 16+, some 200 apply for around 50 places. Most entrants at this stage are girls, but no actual quota – entry on merit. Girls come from eg City of London, Francis Holland, North London Collegiate, Channing, South Hampstead. Some from Highgate School. Also from St Marylebone School, Hampstead School and William Ellis. Selection via November assessment and about 50 per cent of applicants interviewed. Assessment is an objective test of thinking, reasoning and problem-solving. All offers conditional on GCSEs.

Exit: Everyone goes off to a good university to read a proper subject. London University is a favourite; many also to Durham, Manchester, Leeds, Bristol, Nottingham. Impressive numbers annually to Oxbridge (19 in 2018, with seven to the US, one Canada and one Australia, and five medics). The vast range of subjects they pursue is testament to the individuality fostered here.

Notable Old Gowers include: Tristram Hunt, actors Hugh Dennis, David McCallum and Bertie Carvel, journalists Ian Katz, Jonathan Freedland and Paul Dacre, Thomas Adès, members of Bombay Bicycle Club, Will Self, Justin Stebbing, Chris Bonington, Roger Bannister, John Barrett.

Money matters: Around £1m a year disbursed to pupils who would not otherwise be able to afford UCS. At the time of our visit, 52 pupils were on 100 per cent bursaries – one of the most generous provisions in the UK. Most of this funded by the letting of school facilities to the community, charitable work and donations. No academic scholarships but music schols worth up to 25 per cent.

Remarks: A very good school and set to rise even higher under energetic and confident head.

University College School Junior Branch

Linked with University College School, University College School Pre-Prep

308

11 Holly Hill, London NW3 6QN

Ages 7–11 Pupils 260

Fees: £18,789 pa

020 7435 3068
www.ucs.org.uk

Headmaster of Junior: Since 2014, Lewis Hayward MA Oxon MA ed management (OU) PCGE, a classicist (late 40s). An interesting former life – he began his teaching life in EFL in i) Nairobi and ii) Saudi. Thence to the relative quiet of Holmewood House and Highfield preps' classics depts until he left for Highgate School in 2009, where he became deputy principal. Efficient, professional and articulate, Mr Hayward is a modern head. He is voluble about the mega plans for refurb and new build which will bring up to date this charming school on its compact site, but he is also a man who greets every child by name and who knows not only the bricks and mortar but the concerns and qualities of his charges. 'Stretching without cramming' is his academic credo, and the parents we spoke to recognised this approach. 'He's slotted in very well,' said one parent who's known the place for years. 'He doesn't just say the right things but he works hard and is very approachable.' Another agreed, 'He wants to meet everyone's expectations.' A third told us, 'He had big boots to fill but all his changes seem good.' A sportsman, he runs nine miles daily as part of his commute from south London. He's in school by 6.30am to avoid the crowds and have quiet time. Energetic, focussed, clever – a good appointment for this special prep.

Entrance: Sixty boys are selected at 7+ from the 210-odd applicants. Two part assessment – i) a series of concentration and listening exercises and ii) a formal exam including comprehension, maths and NVR. Newbies join those who come up from the school's own pre-prep (from which entry is not automatic – they sit the same exam) or other local preps eg Hampstead Hill, Golders Hill, Mulberry House. NB sibling policy dictates that 'Having a sibling (current or former pupil) at the school does not confer automatic admission into the school. Siblings must go through the same process as all other applicants at their chosen point of entry. Siblings will not be admitted if we believe that they are unlikely to cope and thrive within the academic UCS environment or if we think that their admission in preference to another candidate would be unfair.'

Exit: Virtually all to the UCS senior school. Any who, by year 4, are not cutting it are supported with one-to-one, and those very few who clearly wouldn't thrive in the senior school are helped by the head to get in to gentler, more appropriate, schools elsewhere. Notable leavers include Sir Roger Bannister, Julian Lloyd Webber, Hugh Dennis, Ian Katz.

Remarks: In the heart of gorgeous Hampstead village, though you could live there for years and never know it was there. Purpose-built in 1928, the main house is functional rather than beautiful but still works well. Supplemented by a small science block and smaller arts block, the school covers pretty much all indoor needs on site plus a new outdoor terrace, with a recent sizeable rebuild and refurb.

Academic excellence is a given, and the children here are sponges who mop up everything intellectual, cultural, esoteric, thrown at them. Several long-serving and much loved staff give character, stability and stimulation. Recently, a UCS junior team reached the final of the Prep Schools' Science Quiz and they regularly star in the Primary Schools' Maths Challenge. Average class size 21. A few need EAL help and are supported by SENCo as are those with mild learning difficulties – all closely monitored.

Parents enthuse, but mostly about the quite extraordinary range of extracurricular activities on offer – we've not met anything quite like it at a cramped London prep before, and wonder how on earth they do it. Before-school activities include G&T clubs – open to all – in maths, English, coding, German, Mandarin etc. More at lunchtime and even more after school. 'More than I could have imagined,' beamed one mum, 'almost too many. My son wants to do all that's on offer but he simply can't.'

We watched several lessons and were struck by the diverse teaching methods employed by the much-praised staff. The French names for the parts of the body were being learned by groups of boys, sprawled on the floor, drawing jambes, poitrines, gorges etc. Boys in a drama class were wide-eyed and thoroughly engaged in an instant reaction game – no hanging back or bashfulness here. Self-discipline rather than rules, rule here – most classes were lively but controlled and we also saw several in which boys were silently reading, clearly lost in their own imaginary worlds.

Arts thrive – stunning theatre work on proper plays – The Dream and Private Peaceful most recently. Everyone in top three years gets involved. Serious music – an orchestra, two choirs – each 50+ strong, big band and numerous smaller instrumental ensembles – and everyone takes part in the big annual concert. Virtually everyone scrapes or blows something – 'We get 'em playing,' asserted impressive head of music. Very good art displays in corridors, though some few classrooms sporting boringly blank walls. Art block houses studio and DT room – classes split between the two. We loved the Japanese ceramic pots which boys had made and were decorating in authentic style as we watched. Laser cutter, 3D printer etc and we were impressed by the torches being designed via CAD and then made in the subterranean DT workshop. Best was the super cookery kitchen. Year 6 boys cook a three course meal for staff and parents and it all smelled gorgeous. Good-sized labs in science block, inhabited by enthusiastic boys plus a corn snake, tarantula, bearded dragon and some startling tropical fish. Good-sized library, well-used and sensible tracked reading scheme, punctuated by quizzes to monitor progress. Parents help with reading.

Although on site outside space is limited to little more than a rubberised playground (a small adventure trail is also planned), sports thrive. Outside table tennis and table football. School uses nearby fields plus sports facilities at the big brother school down the hill. Earlier complaints about few opportunities for those not in A or B teams seem to be being addressed now. Lots of trips – field studies to Norfolk; west country rugby tour; ski trip to Italy; football trip to Spain; art trip to Nice, Amsterdam or Barcelona and a year 4 field studies trip to Normandy.

Strong social network across this very diverse community. 'My son sees a lot of the other boys outside school.' Inside school, too, communication thrives – 'Every class has a council rep who can express grievances and they really do listen to them. The kids feel understood.' 'Older boys mentor the newbies so it's a bit like having an older brother in the school.' 'They just don't tolerate bad behaviour.' Parents stress the friendliness of the place: 'They were wonderfully supportive of me when we had difficulties and I was very emotional.' Consensus: 'It's a lovely, embracing and supportive school for boys from varying backgrounds, interests and personalities. My boys are all quite different but it was the right school for all of them.'

University College School Pre-Prep

Linked with University College School, University College School Junior Branch

36 College Crescent, London NW3 5LF

Ages 4–7 **Pupils** 100

Fees: £16,821 pa

020 7722 4433
www.ucs.org.uk

Headmistress: Since 2015, Zoe Dunn BEd PhD NPHQ (late 30s), an Eng lit specialist with an impressive pedigree and all in this neck of the woods. After four years at The Hall, down the road, Dr Dunn went to The Royal School – up the hill, and now taken over by North Bridge House Senior – first as deputy head and latterly as head of its junior school. After a sabbatical term on a Winston Churchill Travelling Fellowship, she founded and then led a local faith free school – The Rimon Jewish Free Primary School – down the far side of the hill for four terms. A brief maternity leave over, she took up the post here. She sparkles and charms. Clearly super-bright, she is also simply super and you want to find her children to benefit from her enthusiasm and energy. Herself a mother of a toddler (when we visited), she lives locally and engages her charges in lots of local affairs eg charities and arts activities. Keen on outdoor learning and forest school – 'so good for team-building' – she has also revived the house system. Parents are happy: 'She's very strong. All her changes are positive.. She understands the parent body.. She couldn't be more supportive when there are problems..She's pretty powerful but she's so approachable she somehow takes people with her.' One of three good recent appointments for this family of schools.

Entrance: Register (boys only for 4+ entry) up to a year before starting reception. Siblings get no preference – 'We have to maintain the academic standard of the school'. Occasional 5+ and 6+ places.

Exit: Though entry not automatic, most boys go on to the UCS Junior Branch, as the name-change to UCS Pre-Prep suggests. Some to eg St Paul's Juniors, Westminster Under. Girls to South Hampstead, City Girls, Channing. Both kinds to Belmont, The ASL, The Academy, Highgate, Heathside.

Remarks: Tucked away down College Crescent, you wouldn't know it was there, but the anonymous entrance conceals a surprisingly roomy little pre-prep and a bit of a gem. Now overlooked by the imposing brick and glass grandeur that is the newly reinvented and rebuilt South Hampstead High School, UCS Pre-Prep comes as a surprise. But, if you are keen on a 4-18 trajectory through one of London's best schools, this is where you can start. Once a co-ed pre-prep including nursery (whose previous domain is now an arts and science block), it has phased out 3 year olds and is phasing out girls. Class names all follow the bird theme (school was previously called the Phoenix) and are named Hummingbird, Barn Owl, Puffin etc.

Good use of a whole range of teaching and learning media throughout, including interactive whiteboards – often as 'input' at the start of a class to set in motion whatever learning activity is planned. Also iPads and netbooks, but Dr Dunn stresses the importance of traditional skills too. Learning support given in small groups or one-to-one for EAL (25 per cent of the children speak a language other than English at home, though only 10 per cent need support), SEND and as a booster for those showing gifted/talented tendencies.

Some 35 per cent of these tinies play an instrument (having lessons in school from 4 years old), and all children participate in the twice annual performances, such as Aladdin, which take place in the large theatre auditorium at UCS senior branch – very exciting for all. Specialist art teacher produces wonderfully imaginative work in these creative buds. And art room has a wall that can be endlessly painted and repainted – such a good idea. Selection of so few from so many clearly works.

Outside space is very limited but enthusiastically used, with playhouse and tunnel slide over safe surface flooring. School also has allotments and use of nearby fields and a surprisingly large gym at the top of the building. Also makes use of facilities – sporting and others – at big brother schools.

Families live in the NWs, some Ns and the odd W postcode. Sixteen home languages spoken at the time of our visit and all cultures celebrated when appropriate. School is linked to one in the high Himalayas and a teacher goes out each year carrying artwork from UCS Pre-Prep and brings back similar from a very different place. Parents seem universally happy despite hiccups like The Great Hot Lunch Controversy – resolved democratically, we gather (children bring their own lunches). Unstinting praise for the teachers: 'We're so lucky.' 'Phenomenal' ... 'Amazing.' Summed up by one parent: 'There was never a day when my children didn't want to go to school.'

Waldegrave School

Fifth Cross Road, Twickenham TW2 5LH

Ages 11–18 **Pupils** 1,349 **Sixth form** 303 (80 boys)

020 8894 3244
www.waldegrave.richmond.sch.uk

Headteacher: Since January 2019, Elizabeth Tongue, previously senior deputy head at Tolworth Girls' School.

Academic matters: Consistently achieves good results in English, maths and science GCSEs. French, history, art, drama,

RE always good too. The success rate in 9-4 grades is well above the regional and national average; 44 per cent of grades were 9-7 in 2018. Top of the Sunday Times Parent Power list for 11 to 16 schools for four years; now has a co-ed sixth form with 78 per cent A*-B, 43 per cent A*/A grades in 2018 A levels.

Quality of teaching is excellent. 'They're all so dedicated. I can't fault them,' said one parent. Achievements are recognised at assemblies throughout the year and at Celebration Afternoons at the end of the year. High academic standards are expected and some parents say that there is pressure on the students to get good grades. 'My daughter had to do French GSCE when she didn't want to do it as the teachers knew she would get a good grade.' But provision is made within the curriculum for all abilities, and modest acts such as helpfulness to the school or to others are duly acknowledged and rewarded.

Lessons are given in broad ability tutor groups initially, but setting for maths, science and languages occurs early on in the first years. In subsequent years, setting in other subjects if appropriate. All are entered for 6-10 GCSEs; some do up to 13 after discussion with parents and staff. Short course subjects such as ICT and PE well subscribed with good results.

Appointed as one of the first 100 Teaching Schools, and is also a National College for School Leaders National Support School. Designated area in an independent learning centre for gifted and talented girls and those with other special needs. Provides 'enhanced specialist teaching provision' for six girls with speech and languages difficulties/autism. With an incredible cultural diversity (43 different languages), EAL support is strong, even offering a lunchtime club for all age groups. On the subject of lunchtime, a great deal is compressed into a very short 35 minute break: careers advice, ICT, rehearsals for choirs and bands, puzzle club, homework clubs. Similarly, lots of before and after-school activities. A breakfast club at 8.00am every morning with badminton on offer at the same time for the more energetic. After school up until 4.00pm – choice is much more varied with a high take-up rate.

Games, options, the arts: Good range of sports offered – rounders, tennis, volleyball, athletics, rugby (with the Harlequins). Classes in the fitness suite, cricket, rowing (linked in with Walbrook Rowing Club) and table-tennis. Hidden from view from the road is a huge outdoor green area with tennis courts and marked-out running track. New sixth form block features four court sports hall.

School regularly wins regional netball leagues and was recently the Middlesex hockey champion. Also borough winners at netball and rounders. Running club is popular with 40 girls doing a 5k run twice a week with four teachers before school. One of the school's aims is to improve participation in sport. Gymnastics is strong – both a multi and traditional gym on site. A dance studio was funded through the National Lottery.

Extra opportunities include bridge, drama (big production every alternate year and an annual joint production with Hampton Boys' School), study skills, chess, art, music theory, ICT, choirs, rock bands and full orchestra. Art and music are both strengths. Year 7s all learn the recorder and in year 8 they get the chance to play the ukulele. When we visited we were blown away by the bird sculptures made in art lessons, inspired by their sister school in Madogo, Kenya.

After-school clubs include extra languages, eg Mandarin GCSE and there's even an astronomy club which parents can also attend. These cost extra but the pupil premium funds places for those who qualify.

Background and atmosphere: Original 1930s building has been added to over the years. Science labs are housed in newish block and brand new sixth form building opened in 2014, housing new sports hall and dining room. Outside play area transformed with money from the PTA with an outdoor theatre and landscaped surroundings. Food freshly cooked on site, and a biometric system for payment. Some girls take sandwiches. 'I don't want them having a slice of pizza and a muffin every day,' explained one parent. The girls themselves give this school a buzzy atmosphere. A former pupil remarked that 'all girls is a positive rather than a negative.'

Pastoral care, well-being and discipline: No real behavioural problems. First years are invited to spend a day in the school to find their way about and practise their journey to and fro – puts a stop to later excuses about buses being late. They also start the term a bit earlier before the older ones arrive. Prefects help out with the younger ones, organise charity events, welcome visitors and play an important leadership role in the school. Each tutor group elects a representative to attend the school council, which in turn represents the school at the Richmond School Student Council. All good training ground for debating and public speaking.

School is honest about bullying and admits that, like the poor, it is always with us. However, stringent efforts made to put an end to it. Girls, staff and parents exhorted to report any incident straight away and assured that something will be done.

Pupils and parents: Although the school has no religious affiliation, the majority of the pupils are Christian. More than 25 per cent are from an ethnic minority. All come from the surrounding borough of Richmond, which is known nationally for its high level of professional parents. A local parent declares it to be the sort of school where 'decent folk will be prepared to break all sorts of rules to get their daughters in.' Co-ed sixth form is making this school even more desirable.

Entrance: Fully comprehensive intake. It is the only all girls' state school in Richmond so is always oversubscribed. Despite clear and rigid guidelines about admissions policies there are always appeals. Priority to those with special needs and those in public care or who are deemed by the LA to have a particular need, to siblings, daughters of staff and those living in priority areas. Most girls will have attended local primary schools in the borough. Six places are available in total in the school for those with speech and language difficulties or those on the autistic spectrum – invariably very oversubscribed.

Forty out of the 280 places in the sixth form are for boys but majority of girls' places will be taken by Waldegrave students. Five 9-4 GCSE grades needed for entry, with 6s in the subjects to be studied at A level.

Exit: In the past students have gone to Richmond Sixth Form College, Esher College, Strodes College or to sixth forms of independent schools. This has changed as the oversubscribed co-ed sixth form enables around 50 per cent of girls to remain at the school to study for A levels. Seven to Oxbridge in 2018; one medic, one vet and one off to the US.

Remarks: A really buzzy school. 'It felt more dynamic than the other schools we visited,' said one parent. This school has so much going on that you're a lucky girl if you manage to get a place here. Now with the new sixth form you're even luckier.

Wallington County Grammar School

Croydon Road, Wallington, Surrey SM6 7PH

Ages 11–18 **Pupils** 1,095 **Sixth form** 350 (70 girls)

020 8647 2235
www.wcgs-sutton.co.uk

Head of school: Since 2016, Jamie Bean BA (30s). First degree in history and ancient history from the University of Nottingham. Unusually, he has worked his way up the school since joining in 2004 as teacher of history and classics, touching every step on the ladder from year leader to deputy on the way – pointing out there isn't a job in the senior leadership team he didn't try for size during colleagues' maternity leaves. He teaches a year 9 history class and a year 10 classics class, on which an appreciative parent commented: 'He teaches our son classics with tremendous verve and enthusiasm.' Having attained the ultimate accolade from Ofsted – 'outstanding' in all categories – in the school's 90th year, there is now space for him to focus on core values and his aim to make the school more outward facing, developing students' aspirations beyond top grades and necessarily a career in the professions.

Very tall and bearded, he lives in Tooting and cycles to school every day. During downtime he combines his love of photography and travel, bringing back inspiration for students. He doesn't remain aloof, within reason, doing an assembly on his own wedding last year. We find him to be refreshing, passionate about this school but unamused when we wonder whether his name has been a cross to bear in the teaching profession: 'no-one remembers Mr Bean,' he says dismissively to this not exactly ancient editor.

Parents tell us he is 'enthusiastic with a genuine love for the school. Always challenging the boys to strive for 100 per cent in all they do.' A mother added: 'My son says that he takes the pupils' opinions into account.'

Academic matters: In 2018, 53 per cent A*/A at A level; when we enquire as to where next with performance, does the school aspire to further leap up the league tables to bite at the ankles of the some of the south London independent big hitters, Mr Bean says firmly: 'we don't judge ourselves by A*/As,' focusing more on value added – the school is in the top one per cent nationally, which given the already highly selective in-take is impressive.

Pupils choose three or four A levels. Classics, art and design, philosophy, government and politics are added to the standard fare. A very strong showing in maths and further maths for top grades. Also performing well are economics, geography, history and Spanish. Relatively high numbers gaining less than a C in A level computer science since its introduction. Small numbers of linguists, after the popularity of French and Spanish lower down the school, and artists hugely outnumbered by scientists.

W

Sixth formers go off syllabus every Wednesday afternoon, allowing them to take up a sport, follow humanities programmes or attend popular guest lectures. Speakers have included a criminologist, members of government and leaders in companies such as Google.

In 2018, 64 per cent 9-7 at GCSE. Most opt for single sciences with plenty to celebrate results-wise. Plenty of science going on beyond the classroom too. One year 12 student, followed in the footsteps of other WCGS boys, in achieving the highest possible award in the Cambridge chemistry challenge in a field of 7,000. Year 12s also took part in a biology Olympiad and Imperial summer school to explore life sciences.

Two popular DT choices, unusually – electronic products and resistant materials, with large, meticulously organised, workshop-like labs. Drama included for creative performance types, plus business studies. Healthy numbers taking PE too. It's a surprise to see catering and hospitality on the curriculum, rarely encountered elsewhere, inspiring the odd chef and a food tech lab on the horizon. All other points of the compass straightforwardly academic. RS is compulsory. Almost everyone adds further maths to maths and does brilliantly with it.

Class sizes in some years compare well with the independents, averaging 25, a few up to 30. At A level the average is 18 and the largest 26. A 'deep thinking challenge' in every lesson stretches the most able and post marking students write their own 'purple pen response' as a further reflection on their work.

'Quite young, full of energy and ideas,' says the head of his staff. Twenty have been at the school for 10 years or more. Mr Bean says they are the reason pupils are passionate about their subjects, they know the students well, 'there's a lot of compassion and respect'. Confirmed by a pupil: 'they care a lot about each person, you're not just another potential A*.'

A parent added: 'The teaching is tailored towards identifying weaknesses and then looking to strengthen and improve those areas.' 'He finds the lessons interesting, engaging and challenging. He is encouraged to think deeply and to further research his subjects. He even finds the homework interesting!' said an amazed father.

There is 90 minutes of homework a day from year 7. As ever, some parents report this is as minimal and others a burden. One mother felt that it's tough on her year 9 son, who comes home has a brief snack and works on homework until 9pm most nights and then holiday homework too. Another pointed out: 'Students seem to be tested frequently and have a much greater workload than my younger son who attends a non-selective state school. There is, however, a much publicised support network throughout the school to help students who might need it.'

Sixth formers make use of large private study areas equipped with banks of computers for silent private study and make do with a corner of the dining room for break out moments, as they don't have a common room.

Some 70 students with varying identified needs including ASD, dyslexia and dyspraxia. Each student with SEN has a personalised IEP that is delivered in lessons. There's a dedicated SENCo and a learning support assistant. Mr Bean intends to 'increase opportunities and support for those who are struggling'.

A large proportion of boys, 45 per cent, has English as an additional language but none are in the early stages. There are reading and writing workshops in years 7 and 8 to ensure that all students have a solid foundation in English before starting their GCSEs.

Games, options, the arts: 'There's an opportunity every single day to do something off syllabus,' says the head, but the school is aiming to expand what they're doing with world class enrichment opportunities via an extended lunch time.

All students from years 7 to 11 have an hour and a half of games per week. Not compulsory in the sixth form. Biggest numbers playing rugby, some recently on tour to Canada – now sixth form girls too are fielding teams – then cricket and football, and pupils tell us that basketball is popular. We hear from parents that even those who have not played rugby at primary school can make it to the A team. A big table tennis contingent and plenty of outdoor tables in the playground. Two rugby pitches on site, a cricket square and an Astroturf cricket strip, plus nets. High praise from parents for the teaching ability and dedication of the sports teachers and coaches.

Seems rather quiet on the musical front, although the head tells us it's growing, and certainly there is a busy musical calendar and house music competitions. Less than 100 studying instrumental grades. Jazz and wind bands for all year groups and choirs in key stages. A delighted parent told us of her son's confidence being nurtured as he became engaged with the artistic life of the school: 'He is of a more introverted nature but still felt he could take part in two drama events.'

Good numbers doing D of E: 80 gaining bronze this year. Possibly the most famous work experience placement of recent times was a WGCS boy at Southern Rail – you may have heard him making headlines with his initiative when given the chance to man their Twitter feed during the much-loathed strikes. Sixth formers set up and run societies for the whole school. Rather a highbrow list, many with an academic focus, running until 5pm and all free of charge: notably film theory club, football discussion society and computational thinking society.

Background and atmosphere: The school was first founded in 1927, initially fee-paying, then became a grammar school in 1944. Plenty of keeping calm and carrying on during WW2 when bombs struck the building. In 1996 a new science block was opened by Sir Chris Woodhead, old boy.

From the moment we step inside, the building seems rather institutional; everything is durable – glittery concrete stairs, no frills. Classrooms are large, looking out onto wide corridors. Admittedly the day of our visit is bitterly cold and we need to hop between buildings on our tour, but there's not much charm in evidence and the most litter in and out that we've ever seen, not to mention abandoned bags in corridors and in the playground, as if someone suddenly shouted 'fire!' an hour earlier.

Absolutely not related to a lack of pride in their school, though, according to parents. The head suggests there is a family feel amongst staff and students, an example of this being the mandatory year 7 assault course, where the whole school turns out to cheer them on.

Pastoral care, well-being and discipline: Boys could be nervous on arrival in year 7, but this is taken care of with events prior to the school year as well as an extensive four day induction. 'Supportive' was the word most commonly used by parents to describe not only the pastoral care but the ethos of the school as a whole.

'We're building well-rounded individuals... the last thing we want to do is build well-behaved robots,' says Mr Bean. 'The high level of pastoral care is one of the school's greatest assets,' said a father. 'The older children are actively encouraged to act as role models for the younger boys and support them in house events.' Another shared: 'The relationship between staff and students is great, with no barriers or "them and us" mentality.' Not entirely spotless with regards to bullying: we did encounter one parent who had cause to speak to the school, but staff were swift to deal with concerns.

Plenty of traditions such as houses, privilege stripy ties and house competitions with cups donated by old Wally boys. Meanwhile, current hot topics regarding mental health and gender are very much on the head's radar and his approach is collaborative, inviting the school community to consider assumptions, for instance that boys and girls have different uniform rules in the sixth form, to find a way forward.

Pupils and parents: Most come from Croydon and Sutton but such is the draw of this school that bright sparks may commute long distances equipped with determination, railcards and parental enthusiasm for excellent free schooling.

It's not easy to see each other out of school, but they do. Some sixth formers drive in. As befits south London, it's a richly diverse community: most boys were born in the UK, but other countries of origin with significant numbers include India, Pakistan, Nigeria and Germany.

A mother relayed of her son: 'He absolutely loves the school. He feels that all his friends are a really good bunch of boys and are a good influence'. The sixth formers we meet are sincere, articulate and exclusively positive about their experiences, one about to head to his Oxbridge interview the following week. They feel the school isn't cliquey and advise getting involved.

Girls first joined the school sixth form in 2000.The girls we met felt welcomed by the boys from day one. Invited to accessorise with their own drawn-on moustaches for 'Movember', there's a determination to include. Perhaps in need of a domain of their own, however, they proudly show us their loos with provisions provided for each other and positive mantras on the mirrors.

You'll need to make space in your digital life for another WhatsApp group – Wallington parents seem more connected to their peers than is often the case. Parents spilled the beans on their peers, surprising us with their enthusiasm: 'Generally, very supportive and hands on,' thought a father. 'Genuinely lovely,' said another.

Entrance: Eleven plus tests take place in September, but register ahead in year 5. The school PTA lays on familiarisation tests, now big business, stretching over 10 days of nervous prospects. Papers consist of maths and English multiple choice based on the primary curriculum – no verbal or non-verbal reasoning. The competition is fierce, with seven applicants for every place, although since the Ofsted inspection the school anticipates even more of a crush. Gaining a pass mark in the 11+ enables one to list WGCS as a preference on the local authority application form, though not necessarily a place. Students with SEN may qualify for extra time or rest breaks. Up to 15 places for boys on free school meals and 15 for those in specific local postcodes, then children of staff working for the Folio Education Trust.

No longer has 13+ entry. For year 12 entry all external applicants (including girls) are asked to complete an application form from GCSE results day onwards. Three applicants for every place.

Exit: Seven to Oxbridge and 17 medics in 2018. Meanwhile very many other highly desirable destinations are solidly impressive with serious subject choices the norm. Healthy numbers of medics. Between 50 and 60 per cent to Russell Group universities. This might be higher except for a group heading off on gap years. Strong clusters to Birmingham, Nottingham and Durham. Economics, engineering, chemical engineering, biomedical sciences and chemistry in chunky numbers, but there's also space for philosophers, the odd ancient historian and a few architects.

Remarks: Don't expect frills for free. Places are fiercely contested at this south London grammar school for a reason – excellent teaching in a supportive atmosphere that sees the bright (everyone) go far. The young leadership know exactly what they're about and have the respect of the pupils.

Wallington High School for Girls

Woodcote Road, Wallington, Surrey SM6 0PH

Ages 11–18 **Pupils** 1,451 **Sixth form** 402

020 8647 2380
www.wallingtongirls.sutton.sch.uk

Headteacher: Since 2016, Richard Booth BSc. A former grammar school student, he gained a degree in economics from Hull and travelled extensively, living in Australia for a spell, before returning to Hull to train as a teacher. This is his first headship, having been deputy head at Townley Grammar School and assistant head at St Olave's Grammar School. He has two daughters, both now at secondary school.

Outwardly relaxed (and lacking the bone-crushing handshake that's customary among male grammar heads), but surprisingly reserved – not a single titbit offered about interests or passions. 'He doesn't give away much about himself, which is a shame because you want to see the man behind the headteacher,' one parent told us, while others said they felt 'unqualified' to comment on him because they 'don't know anything about him.' Among those closer to the school's inner circle, however, there's a strong feeling that he's 'quietly transformational.' 'He's absolutely brilliant and has made a real effort to put the girls at the heart of every piece of decision making, from bringing in sports they are interested in to ensuring not one girl slips through the net,' said one parent. Pupils told us he strikes a 'good balance between friendly and formal' and they all consider it 'a great honour' when he teaches them (currently year 13 economics). Particular praise for his 'heavy involvement in extracurricular'; currently running girls' rugby. The rest of the time, he says, 'I try to get out of my office whenever I can, but probably not as much as I should.'

Buck stops with previous Wallington head, Jane Burton, who is now CEO of the Nonsuch and Wallington Education Trust (NWET), widely seen as merger of the two grammars (the trust was consulting on a third school joining the mix when we visited). Both schools share a team of trustees, but retain own governing bodies, and although there was initial parental anxiety, that's all water under the bridge now. 'Bottom line is they're happy that the two schools still have their individual freedoms when it comes to vision and ethos,' explains head, who adds that the advantages of the trust were 'always a hard sell because they mainly exist behind the scenes – cost savings, sharing best practice and high-level teacher training, among them.'

Academic matters: As you'd expect, results terrific. In 2018, 73 per cent 9-7 at GCSE and 78 per cent A*-B and 54 per cent A*/A at A level. But while it's easy to see these results as the inevitable consequence of admissions process – clever in, clever out – head gets most animated when talking about the school's 'value added' scores, particularly how the most disadvantaged students now achieve in line with, or better than, other students (10 per cent are on pupil premium). Progress levels in sixth form particularly strong; 'there's been a real focus in the last few years to improve teaching and learning at this level, challenging and stretching the most able while still supporting those at the bottom,' says head.

School insists it's no exam factory, with any pressure coming from the girls themselves or their (often very aspirational) parents – 'we are certainly not a school constantly telling girls to do better than last year,' says head. Pupils concur – 'The school does everything it can to stop it, but you do see some girls getting stressed around exam times, especially those from quite pushy backgrounds,' said one.

Eleven GCSEs the norm, with all girls expected to take separate sciences, RS, a humanity (geography more popular than history) and one language (girls choose two from year 7 from French, German and Spanish, with school doing its best to accommodate preferences – roughly equal numbers for all three by GCSE). Strongest GCSE results found in maths, RS and English language, while the most popular of the non-core subjects are psychology and business studies (subjects are surprisingly wide-ranging here and also include GCSE rarities such as photography). At A level, a whopping 29 subjects are available, including media studies and DT four different ways. Maths, languages, biology, politics, philosophy and geography get the best results, while the A levels attracting the biggest numbers include maths, biology, chemistry, physics and psychology. All take at least three A levels and most do an EPQ, usually with great success. All credit to the school for encouraging them to get used to the format in year 10 when they have the option of doing the higher project – 'we are big on encouraging independent learning and enjoying learning for its own sake right from the off,' says head.

Setting only in maths from year 7. Otherwise, girls are taught in one of seven houses in years 7, 8 and 9; and although they are still registered in their house groups in years 10 and 11, they are mixed up into new teaching groups for some subjects 'partly to build up resilience to change.'

SEN not prevalent (32 girls when we visited – mainly dyslexia, dyspraxia and dyscalculia), but parents are pleased with the support provided. 'My daughter has dyslexia and the school has made a huge effort in the classroom to ensure she keeps up and she's triumphed brilliantly as a result,' said one.

Relatively small turnover of staff, according to school, although some parents 'disappointed with the number of supply teachers my daughter has had.' Permanent staff, however, praised for being 'very committed' and 'really caring about both their subjects and the girls themselves.' 'The teachers are really good at making sure you keep up – they don't let the brightest girls answer all the questions in class,' one pupil told us. 'You can go to them at break time, lunchtime or after school and know they'll give up their own time for you,' voiced another.' Disappointing to see many closed classroom doors during teaching time, though, and almost exclusive use of chalk and talk style teaching (with the exception of sciences, where we saw practicals galore), but girls assured us many of their lessons are interactive – 'sometimes, nearly the whole lesson is taken up with debate.' Five school days a year given over to enrichment, which include subject specific trips to the likes of Royal Observatory, Maritime Museum and London Zoo (residentials also on offer, such as geography field trips, while overseas trips include annual ski trip and netball tour to Barbados).

Games, options, the arts: Parents with girls in the A teams certainly have no complaints; 'the opportunities are vast and they really support them,' said one. Those with girls in a B (or lower) teams, however, aren't all so gleeful – 'they don't get anything like the same opportunities and I think that needs to be addressed,' said one. Fear not if your daughter isn't sporty at all – 'we're about finding your own passions, whatever they may be,' insists head, although no girls gets off the hook for the obligatory two hours of sports/PE lessons a week ('whatever the weather,' added one pupil, shuddering at the thought). Core sports are netball, football, rounders, cricket and athletics, the latter being the brightest shining star – 'we have been the borough champions for six years in a row – I remind pupils that's more times than Brazil has won the World Cup,' smiles the head. Dance and gym also prevalent in winter. Mammoth field, all-weather pitches (no Astroturf as yet, though four tennis and netball courts have been added to existing two) joined by magnificent sports hall, a yodeller's paradise, and mirrored dance studio.

Art (available at GCSE and A level) is strong, with manifestation of excellent quality displayed throughout the school, but why oh why lose all the natural light by pulling down huge dark blinds? As for drama (also available at GCSE and A level), the mere mention of it invites gush and fervour among pupils, who were itching to tell us all about recent performances including Sister Act, Hairspray and 39 Steps, and show off their new (second) drama studio, where they get involved in everything from directing to lighting. 'If you can't sing, though, it kind of rules you out from these big musicals – I'd like to see more house plays,' one parent told us.

Creativity also a feature of tech block – a real treasure trove of ideas, with fab A level creations including terrific lamp complete with fronds of LEDs and mood lighting, while younger girls were busy designing innovative underground spaces that would give the likes of London Underground a run for its money. No wonder so many become inspired, with around 10 students going onto study engineering related courses at university. Spreads the joy with lots of outreach to local primaries and enters many competitions like the Faraday Challenge.

We'd heard the school was strong on music vocals (recent finalist on TV The Voice is former school pupil) with five choirs, but hadn't expected to hear tens of year 11s singing (beautifully) in the corridor before their music lesson had even begun. Glee and 60-strong gospel choir both audition only (latter mostly seniors), junior and senior versions open to all. School orchestra and ensembles a plenty, plus impressively full looking timetables for peripatetic teachers. But pupils said they 'wish music lessons were as good as extracurricular music.'

Common sense approach to timing of the school day with earlier start and finish (8.25am to 2.50pm) and prompt close on Friday afternoons; packed programme of after-school clubs (all the predictable sports ones through to more unusual likes of yarn bombing) mainly Mondays to Thursdays only, ensuring that everyone (including hard-pressed teachers) can start weekends promptly and with clean conscience.

Background and atmosphere: Founded just over 125 years ago in 1888. About six minutes by bus from Wallington station, it's a fairly easy trek compared with boys' equivalents and presents unthreatening face to the world with mellow coloured brickwork, although the size is deceptive from the front.

Most recent additions include new snazzy library (open all hours – or a fair few of them), spacious sixth form common room (a mass of tables and purple chairs – impressive number of sixth formers actually working at them, not just chatting) and new silent-study area for sixth formers. Next on the facilities wishlist is expanding the canteen (a real bugbear of students – 'you can queue all lunchtime and never reach the front'; a pity, they say, as 'the food is actually pretty good'). Most of the rest of the school is a maze of warren-like corridors, brightened wherever possible with rows of pictures, and classrooms of varying sizes and with varying degrees of natural light.

Pastoral care, well-being and discipline: In addition to form tutor and head of year, those with problems have access to counsellor and ELSA (emotional literacy support assistant). 'And we do have problems – no more so than other schools, I'd guess, but there's no point in denying it,' reported one pupil candidly. But rather than ringing alarm bells, we admired the honesty, which seems to run through the veins of this school and which, according to the girls, helps keep discussions open and honest around everything from bullying to self-harm to eating disorders. Masses of posters, assemblies and PCHE lessons are devoted to mental health, along with Sharing is Caring campaign, which encourages girls who are worried about a friend to tell someone. Bullying, say girls, is mercifully rare and 'tends to mean friendships turning sour rather than anyone being purposefully targeted.'

'Not exactly strict – more firm but fair,' say pupils. 'And you always get warnings.' For most, that's enough to prevent the rule bending happening a second time – although a behaviour points system is in place, with anything from forgetting homework to talking in class potentially landing you in the (centralised) bad books and, eventually, in detention ('but these are rare and mostly for lates,' say pupils). Two temporary exclusions within the last two years; no permanent ones.

Pupils allowed to bring phones in and encouraged to use them for research in some lessons, as well as being allowed them for personal use in the 'phone zones' clearly marked throughout the school. 'Mobile technology isn't going to go away, so I see it as our job to educate them how to use it responsibly,' says head, who says it's caused very few problems.

Pupils and parents: No-nonsense, down-to-earth, lacking affectation, warm and bright. And that's just the parents. For pupils, add to this list hard-working, eager to learn and considerate. 'And they're all so different – one of my daughters is geeky, another sporty; everyone can fit in here,' reckoned mum. Everyone speaks their mind here too – no gushing for gushing's sake.

Around 80 per cent ethnic minorities, 'mostly Indian, after which there's quite large numbers of Tamil and black African students,' says head. No cliques, though – in fact the school is known for embracing cultural diversity (and won an award for it, too) with gusto, with events including cultural evenings with performances celebrating differences.

Entrance: Following early September deadline for applications, anything north of 2,500 hopefuls sit the SET test (the same test for all five grammars in Sutton) either here or at Nonsuch. The 900-1,000 who get through are then invited to sit the second stage test at Nonsuch and the 800 who survive this hear in sufficient time to include either this school or Nonsuch (or both) on CAF (common application form). But with only 210 year 7 places to fill at each school, many go away empty handed when formal offers are made in March.

Those who jump through both hoops successfully hail mainly from Sutton, with many from Croydon (rarely from the other side of Croydon, though), all across the borough into Surrey and a few as far into London as Tooting. 'Many girls the only ones from their primary school year and the most we'll see from any one primary school is five or six,' says head.

Cleverness, though essential, doesn't have to be extreme, is message. 'Girls who come with at least a level 5 in Sats would be of similar ability to pupils at the school,' says head, although he admits most are tutored to death regardless.

Exit: Loses around 5-10 per cent after GCSEs – either for more vocational courses or to go to co-ed schools. In 2018, 14 to Oxbridge and five medics. Over half of the remainder to Russell Group. Top destinations include Bristol, Birmingham, Southampton, St George's and Nottingham. Most popular courses are science, engineering, maths and economics.

Remarks: School speaks of warm, friendly and purposeful atmosphere. Yada, yada, we'd normally retort – another bland statement. But from the moment you walk in, this school has a sense of authenticity, enthusiasm and amiability that gives an impression of genuinely living its mission statement. And when parents or pupils criticise, it feels constructive never bitter, with a view to making a school they love even better. Though equally desirable, not all grammars are the same. We loved this one.

Walthamstow School for Girls

   313

Church Hill, Walthamstow, London E17 9RZ

Ages 11–16 **Pupils** 900

020 8509 9446
www.wsfg.waltham.sch.uk

Head: Since 2012, Meryl Davies BA (50s). Easy-going, enthusiastic and energised, she is prepared to go against the grain if it's in the best interests of the school – which staff, parents and students unanimously admire. Having studied French and linguistics at Sheffield University, she stayed on to do her PGCE as 'teaching was a long-time ambition.' Immediately attracted to some of the more radical teaching techniques of the 1980s and the more gritty comprehensives of inner London, she found the reality was quite an eye-opener, but one she nonetheless embraced, with one of her earlier jobs working on a London barge with school refusers to get them back into mainstream schooling. 'Working at the raw edge of education is an experience I think all teachers should have – you get to really understand what makes young people tick,' she says.

After moving on to Graveney School, Tooting, she moved up the ranks to assistant head, then took up a deputy headship in Elliott School, Putney, one of the biggest London comps at the time (where she was seconded briefly to take on a headship of a school on special measures). She then moved to Cator Park School for Girls, Bromley, before coming to Walthamstow in 2012. Disappointingly, results dropped a whopping 14 per cent after just a few months later, but it's widely acknowledged this was largely down to an earlier decision to get all year 11s to do a pilot course of double maths. Results are now the best the school has ever had. Seen by staff as an enabling, empowering leader, she regularly encourages others to front meetings. Teaches French to the lower school, runs a Monday surgery for parents and answers emails at weekends, seeing her job as 24/7.

Lives in South London with her partner and has three grown-up children.

Academic matters: Excellent results across the board, with the school consistently among the top performing non-selective schools in the country. 'There are no specialist subjects at this school – we aim to do well in everything,' explains head, although the school has a specialist status in maths and computing, which has done no harm to results in these areas. In 2018, 28 per cent of grades were A*-A/7-9 grades and 77 per cent of students gained grades 4-9 in both maths and English – some of the best results the school has ever had, which the head attributes to a combination of high expectations, inspirational teaching, regular monitoring and target setting and a broad approach to learning experiences.

No setting, except in maths from year 7. 'Historically, the school has never done it,' says head, 'and this works for us.' French or Spanish from year 7, with a taster in Urdu, and Latin also available at GCSE. At the end of year 8, students take part in the Languages Festival, a celebration of all languages spoken or studied in the school and the girls perform in a foreign language in front of their year. Latin offered as an additional language at GSCE.

Targeting and monitoring are huge, with personalisation of study plans meticulous in detail – one of the key reasons no student seems to get left behind. 'It's forensic,' smiles the head, who can talk at length at how girls are identified for different types and levels of help, depending on their individual needs and the way they learn. Peer mentoring is also a focus, with older pupils trained to work regularly with younger ones around student support.

A tour of the classrooms revealed engaged students contributing animatedly. Lessons, they say, are 'engaging,' 'interactive' and 'never dull.' 'Teachers want to see that everyone is on board and thriving in their subject,' said one student. The head points to the growing focus on sharing good techniques around teaching and learning, which she hopes will improve consistency of teaching methods across the school (something they've been criticised for in the past). Low staff turnover.

Phrases like 'That's not good enough' are not part of school life here, where the emphasis is on enabling and encouraging effort in much more positive ways. 'We pride ourselves on having a healthy atmosphere where we make people feel confident, not self-doubting.' The school motto, 'Neglect not the gift that is in thee,' resonates here, according to staff and students, who add that school is, in the main, fun.

School doesn't claim to stand out in terms of SEN, but around 15 per cent require SEN support and 25 per cent speak English as a second language. No wonder the language and learning department has a 16-strong team (some of whom are teaching staff), catering for the usual remit, including mobility problems (there's good wheelchair access here). 'I've been massively impressed by how much effort the department puts into my daughter's needs and how well they communicate with us about it,' one parent told us. 'The school is incredibly personalised and inclusive.'

Games, options, the arts: No shortage of sporting options – cricket, basketball, tag rugby, football, rock climbing, netball, trampolining, dance, self-defence and more – which mainly take place in the sports hall or so-called MUGA (multi-use games area), a large, hard-surfaced area of courts. Sadly, no school field, although there is some outside green space, including a landscaped woodland area, which is sometimes used for PE. The local YMCA, which is in easy walking distance, is used for swimming and fitness classes. Regular competitions against other schools, and some representation at regional level and occasionally national, with one former student having made the Olympic squad for volleyball, and another for athletics. School is also involved in the NEC Wheelchair Tennis Masters. 'Some other schools around here don't seem to value sport, but this one really gets that link between physical exercise and learning well in the classroom,' one parent told us.

Impressive art facilities, consisting of two main studios; students' creations in everything from ceramics to textiles and graphics to portrait work are exhibited throughout the school. 'We all have a great sense of pride when our artwork is displayed – there's a feeling of "I did that and my school appreciates it",' one student said. A particularly attractive year 8 Grayson Perry vase project, displayed in glass cabinets in one major corridor, caught our eye. Lots of cross-curricular projects, such as maths through art, plus plenty of visits to galleries and exhibitions. The school runs an annual exhibition of self-portraits by year 7s, which appears as part of the Walthamstow Arts Trail, attended by celebs and general public, and which raises money for their link school in Pakistan.

Drama popular and seen as a key part of increasing the girls' confidence and ability to speak out, with lots of performances by individual year groups and whole-school performances every other year, such as The Wizard of Oz. Strong links with the Unicorn Theatre in London Bridge. School also involved with Shakespeare Schools Festival.

Music department is understandably proud of their highly acclaimed steel pan bands, which regularly perform in public spaces, including the Royal Albert Hall. It's been a tradition at the school for decades, with a steel band ensemble in every year group, rehearsing every morning. There's an orchestra, choir, ensembles and bands, some student led. Four peripatetic teachers. The annual Modern Languages Festival involves each class in year 8 learning a song in the language they study and performing with their class in front of the entire year group. Dance is valued and seen as key to team-building.

Food tech is innovative, with plenty of competitions and links with outside organisations – ranging from an annual project with foodbanks, in which students learn to make dishes with very limited resources, right through to trips to fine dining restaurants in top hotels.

Extensive enrichment, including trips (eg black history month trips), workshops (eg in STEM, and also for young lawyers and for young doctors), events (eg Girls Can Crafting and Coding Event), entry to competitions (eg WSFG Cycle Planning Awards, Jack Petchey Speak Out Challenge) and links with other schools (eg primary schools are invited to the school for science days). The girls even run their own bank, through a longstanding link with MyBnk.

Extracurricular clubs include multimedia, origami, languages, sport, gardening, engineering and debating. 'Whilst these clubs are not compulsory, they are actively encouraged,' says the head. We attended a meeting of the International Club, where a group of students were busy planning all kinds of exciting initiatives, particularly schools they have strong links with overseas – including the Goodwill Secondary School in Roseau and Dominica and Ambore Read Foundation School, Ambore, Pakistan. Plenty of fundraising for the school in Ambore (over £15k to date), while teachers have travelled there to officially open the school and deliver lessons. A group has just returned after being the first volunteer 'teachers' at a school in Zanzibar. School also has live penpal links with schools in France and Spain and holds the British Council International School Award (for outstanding development of the international dimension in the curriculum).

Background and atmosphere: Main building – with the classic grade 2, red-brick grammar school look – was built in 1911, although the school itself dates back to 1890, when it was opened as a private school in West Avenue, which later moved to nearby Church Hill House. In 1911, the school was taken over by Essex County Council and in 1913 moved to its present site on land originally part of the Vicars Glebe. The school has since been enlarged in 1918, 1928, 1962, 1974 and 2010 and the resulting combination of new and old builds works seamlessly, with no need to even leave one building to enter the next. After a period in the late 20th century as a grammar school, then as a senior high school for 14-18 year-olds, in 1986 the school once again became a school for girls aged 11-16.

In the old part of the school, expect oodles of original features, from the parquet flooring and wall tiles to traditional radiators, with the oak panelled school hall forming the centrepiece. At the other end of the spectrum is the 2010 building, which includes the new Norris Hall, providing an impressive theatre-style auditorium. Spacious classrooms and labs boast masses of natural light, and there are some attractive break-out areas, including one with brightly coloured orange and black sofas, known by the girls as the Easyjet Lounge. A vast dining hall has mixed reviews of the food from students and the library is a good size. Everywhere – and we mean everywhere – is scrupulously clean and tidy.

Outside, the stand-out feature is the Greek Theatre, built in the 1920s and which has a circular arena with steps up to a stage on one side and pillared portico on the other. There's a reasonably sized green space surrounding the theatre, plus a rooftop area (to the 2010 building), accessible from ground level, with plenty of chairs and tables. Students also use the MUGA area at break times. Overall, there's a rural, village feel, even though they're only five minutes from the Victoria line. The only rude interruption to all this is the hideous end-of-lesson 'bell' that sounds like some kind of nuclear alert.

Breakfast is served from 8.00am and extracurricular activities run after school daily, with girls also given the opportunity to stay on to do work after school if, for example, they struggle with finding the space and quiet to do so at home.

Pastoral care, well-being and discipline: Pastoral care primarily comes from form tutors, and girls clearly feel safe and nurtured. Peer support is strong, and even without the formal mechanisms you get the feeling that students instinctively looking out for one another, especially lower down the school. There's a part-time counsellor, and emphasis on exploring issues that others school shy away from – from female genital mutilation to forced marriages. The school is Stonewall approved and multicultural events and projects ensure everyone's background feels valued. Transition for year 7s is notable, with a highly successful summer school giving a head-start on team-building. There's a mindfulness course for year 11s.

Strong student council and plenty of leadership opportunities, including interviewing staff. Although there are school rules, you're more likely to hear talk of rights and responsibilities, with girls very much feeling a sense of ownership in this school. 'We feel trusted,' said one girl.

Occasional bullying, although there are plenty of anti-bullying policies and the fact that this is a 'telling' school means students are quick to speak out not just about themselves, but any friends in trouble. 'Our staff are trained to notice signs,' adds the head, 'and when it happens, we involve parents quickly.' No permanent exclusions as long as anyone can remember, with fixed term exclusions well below the national average, usually given out for very rare instances of aggressive behaviour.

Pupils and parents: Multi-ethnic population, with students from over 50 countries – a great source of pride for the school, which celebrates this rich diversity in everything from assemblies to individual projects. Majority of students from Pakistani origin, followed by white (not just British), then black Caribbean and black African, with the fourth largest group being Indian. 'Mind you, this changes all the time,' points out the head. Girls seem confident, articulate, aspirational and optimistic. 'I could take any of my daughter's friends and they'd have a very clear idea of where they want to be in two or three years' time,' said a parent of a year 10 student.

Parents equally, if not more, aspirational, expecting a lot from their girls, with almost 100 per cent attendance at parents' evenings, consultations about subject options etc. Parents are also regularly invited to take part in questionnaires and parent forums and they are consulted about policy. No PTA, however, which is a disappointment to some parents.

Former pupils include Baroness Scotland, Jacqui Harper (BBC news) and Jeanette Kwakye (Olympic sprinter).

Entrance: Heavily oversubscribed, with some 700 applying for 180 year 7 places. Non-selective, the school follows the borough's entrance criteria, which favours girls in the looked after system/those with an EHC plan, followed by siblings, then it's down to distance. Those who get in mainly live less than a one mile radius. Occasional places further up the school when families move out of the area.

W

Exit: Vast majority of girls go on to sixth form college or local school sixth forms. 'They clammer to have our girls,' says head. The two main local colleges are Sir George Monoux Sixth Form College and Leyton Sixth Form college, whilst schools include Highams Park, Heathcote, City and Islington, Latymer, City of Westminster and Forest School. Most go on to study for A levels, with a heavy emphasis on sciences, whilst a few do BTecs. 'They are career savvy and know exactly what they want to study and why,' says head. Those after more specialist courses are prepared to travel, with some commuting up to a couple of hours every day.

Remarks: This is a relaxed and happy school, yet it's purposeful, vibrant and aspirational. The strong academic atmosphere, which is backed up by a great pastoral system, means there's no reason any girl should get left behind. We were particularly encouraged by the extent to which girls are encouraged to express themselves and to challenge stereotypes and indeed the status quo where appropriate. A true community school that believes passionately in the research that a single-sex environment empowers girls to realise their potential, this is a place that proves with the right teaching and school culture, anyone can thrive.

Westminster Cathedral Choir School

Ambrosden Avenue, London SW1P 1QH

Ages 4–13 **Pupils** 230 **Boarders** 24 full (choristers, from 8 years) **RC**

Fees: Day £16,350 – £18,582; Boarding choristers £9,747 pa

020 7798 9081
www.choirschool.com

Headmaster: Since 2007, Neil McLaughlan (40s). For a man with a truly Catholic background (large C), a Catholic boarding school and posts in all the obvious schools, including Stonyhurst, Worth and Downside (only Ampleforth missing), he is engagingly undoctrinaire and also extremely good company. On our last visit he told us that he hopes to be here 'for the duration' and there's no change here, in fact it would be hard to imagine the school without him, he does literally appear to be part of the fabric. Parents are equally convinced: 'he picks up on everything'; 'totally approachable'; 'understands my son'; in fact it's lucky that he loves living in London and is definitely not heading out the door any time soon. Prodded over any further ambitions for his hugely successful school, he admitted that only a lack of cash was stopping his dream of a senior branch of WCCS turning into a reality and we hope that help from above may solve this problem for him.

Entrance: A 'guinea pig set' started at the pre-prep last year and they will be able to take 30 boys at reception from September 2019. An assessment, described as 'very relaxed' by a parent, in groups for an hour to find out how they interact and respond. Entry at 7+ (16 places) and 8+ (12 places) is heavily oversubscribed with three to five boys trying for each place. Tests in maths, comprehension and composition, punctuation and spelling in the January before September entry.

Satisfying the Master of Music's accurate ear is only the first step for choristers who also have to make the same academic grades as the day boys.

Exit: Today's parents (almost all major players in the financial and legal world) set their sights on the internationally famous English public schools, with Eton firmly at the head of the boarding wish list and St Paul's, Westminster, Dulwich and City of London the main choices in London. All going to plan, 2019 will see five boys going to Eton, Winchester and Westminster and in 2020 up to eight headed for 'Etonia'. The choristers also tend to head in the same directions, nearly always with music scholarships.

Remarks: WCCS is as close to being a school inside a church as is physically possible: only a Westminster version of the Bridge of Sighs (thankfully, a happier outcome for its occupants) separates the school building from the cathedral's interior. In contrast to the solemnity of the surroundings, there is a wondrous space outside with an Astro pitch and running tracks as well as room for all the off-letting of steam that boys require.

Luckily, they found a building for the pre-prep just across the playground. Deeply suitable, having been home to Franciscans amongst its various incarnations, it is an architecturally surprising building, reminiscent of a galleon, with a rather sad St Francis serving as an off-centre figurehead. This unusual, one room deep, layout has been sensitively turned into a great teaching space, with light classrooms, a playground and a tempting covered porch for rainy days. The teaching is 'pacey' even at this level and the competition (using numbering fans) was fierce to be number one fan of tables. Music is already part of school life and one tiny violinist was spotted concentrating hard on his individual lesson.

The prep itself is unflamboyant inside (in contrast to the stripey brick exterior), the colour provided almost entirely by the cherry red of the boys' blazers and the occasional sparkly shoes of a female teacher. The corridors are lined with red and blue lockers, more than usual due to the number of instruments, and music stands replace works of art on the walls. Darth Vader appears, in poster form, offering an unlikely exhortation to earn points towards stars, described by our extremely articulate guide as 'an unlikely paradox'. These stars are serious stuff: they don't just stop at gold as in most other schools but also have an exalted platinum and diamond level – 'everyone gets gold but the others are quite hard'.

The top two floors are home to the chorister boarders and it's a pretty good sanctuary for such incredibly hard-working boys, who have to combine their full-on musical life (singing in the cathedral on a daily basis and honing their skills) with a packed academic timetable. The head says that their welfare is his 'biggest single headache' and that sometimes he has to tell them to take time out 'when they are bushed'. Anyway, the dorms, whilst not exciting and amazingly tidy, have a cosy feel and apparently the matrons and cleaning staff make sure that 'Teddy is on the right bed'. A big common room is equipped with pool and football tables and a chorister assured us that there was plenty to do at weekends – the most popular pastime being 'ripstiking' (a form of skateboarding) which looked extremely difficult when demonstrated and that was minus cassock..

The curriculum, 'begged, scraped and borrowed from every possible source', according to the head is 'not fogeyish in any way' despite its structured feel. There is obviously an extremely successful attempt to marry the 'grammar – logic – rhetoric' classical approach to a more modern, integrated way of learning. This is proper joined-up teaching and the combination of art/RE teacher who starts each RE lesson with a religious painting is typical of their modus operandi. Very little streaming is necessary because, as they explain, there is a narrow range of ability here, but there is a SENCo available to offer one-to-one or group sessions to anyone struggling, and also the odd boy with educational needs. However, it is made very clear that it is essential for everyone to be able to handle the speed of the teaching.

The art teacher explains that her life is made far easier by the fact that she has a large number of the most exciting galleries in the world on her doorstep, which eases the task of embedding art into the school's curriculum, and there is a kiln and a printing press to extend her creative options. Naturally, music is part of life here but not just for the choristers: one day boy told us that if you can hold a tune you can sing in non-chorister choirs and even perform outside the school. The choristers all play the piano and one other instrument, but the majority of boys also have individual music lessons and there are several orchestras of differing abilities (if all rather better than average).

The number of names signed up for football on the tidy notice board says it all and they have been winners of the Thomas's five-a-side tournament at both U10 and U13, but the size of the school makes it less sporty than some of its competitors (one boy wrinkled his nose when questioned on their cricketing prowess) – still, two sports scholarships last year (one to Winchester) is pretty impressive. Lots of alternatives to football on the clubs list with the boys responsible for suggesting magic, mad science and even British military fitness, all of which have takers.

WCCS families have changed over recent years and there is now a much higher percentage of Catholics amongst the day boys (up from 50 per cent to over 80) but there are Anglicans and several non-Christian families. We felt convinced by both parents and head that the spiritual element was an addition rather than a handicap and was not forced down the boys' throats: instead they got a buzz out of their connection to the cathedral and its faith.

Last time we wrote a review, we concluded by saying 'this is just about as near perfect as it gets' and we would endorse that sentiment today with only one caveat; this is now a school for seriously bright boys and it would be wrong for any parent to overestimate their son's academic ability when considering putting him up for the entrance exam.

Westminster School

Linked with Westminster Under School

17 Dean's Yard, London SW1P 3PB

Ages 13–18 **Pupils** 760 **Sixth form** 410 (137 girls) **Boarders** 188 (57 girls) **C of E**

Fees: Day: £27,174 pa; Boarding: £39,252 pa

020 7963 1003
www.westminster.org.uk

Head Master: Since 2014, Patrick Derham MA (50s). Previously head of Rugby School. Aged 12, he was sent to live and study on the naval training ship Arethusa, run by the children's charity Shaftesbury Homes to prepare young men for the navy. Two years later the ship was abruptly sold due to financial difficulties and, with a day's notice and little idea of what a public school was, he arrived at Pangbourne College on a bursary. He eventually became head of school and read history at Cambridge (first class degree), and feels 'my life was transformed by education.'

Taught at Cheam School and then Radley for '12 very happy years' before being advised by the warden there to go straight for a headship. Five years as head of Solihull were followed by 13 at Rugby, before landing the headship of 'the home of liberal education – the perfect culmination of my career.' His background ('my mum still lives in a council house in Scotland') has clearly been a powerful motivating force in his commitment to widening access to a good education. At Rugby, he set up the Arnold Foundation to provide bursaries for children who need the stability of a boarding education ('we didn't just cream off the brightest middle class kids'). He is a trustee of the Royal National Children's SpringBoard Foundation, a national charity modelled on the same lines, and involved with IntoUniversity, which gives disadvantaged children academic support and mentoring to raise their aspirations.

Very down to earth, personable, fantastic speaker, say Westminster parents. 'You feel like you can trust him'... 'He really cares about getting to know everyone'... 'Very responsive to comments'... 'My daughter thinks he's great'. Clearly no ivory tower head, he loves interaction with pupils and teaches A level history. Parents watching their sons compete in the recent National Schools Rowing Regatta were delighted to see him there cheering on the teams (they won the championship eights' title for the first time ever).

Married to Alison, a teacher, with two grown up children. Westminster seems to be in very steady, to say nothing of inspiring, hands.

Academic matters: With these very bright pupils, 'you can teach for the love of the subject and focus on the exam when need be,' says the head. 'It's a breath of fresh air,' said a parent. 'Intellectual risk taking is encouraged. They're never not challenged.' Many of the teachers are experts in their fields, encouraged to follow their interests. 'I cannot believe there is a more stimulating place to teach in the country,' said a teacher. 'It is so much more liberal than at my previous school,' said a sixth form student. 'It's not constrained by the syllabus – it's learning for the sake of learning. It really allows you to get a proper understanding outside the exam baselines.' Pupils tend to internalise that love of learning. 'They read and they question and they challenge,' says the head. 'In my first lesson one asked me, "Where is the evidence?" I'd never been asked that before.'

Everyone encouraged to include a practical subject like art, electronics, drama or music at GCSE. Huge range of languages includes Dutch, Arabic and Portuguese. Several parents commented that inspirational teachers had sparked their sons' interest in subjects they had previously hated. 'He'd always been a bit of a maths boy but now he is flying at English and languages too. They've understood how to teach in a way that suits him.'

Top exam results are, nonetheless, part of the package, with 97 per cent A*-A/9-7 at GCSE in 2018. At A level/Pre-U, the results were 88 per cent A*/A grades (95 per cent A*-B). New thinking skills course – designed as a more challenging alternative to critical thinking A level – introduces sixth formers to the elements of informal logic, and helps prepare for university entrance skills tests such as the Oxbridge Thinking Skills Assessment.

High academic ability is obviously a prerequisite, but study skills coordinator works with all those who need support for mild dyslexia, dyspraxia or Asperger's or just lack of organisation, helping them with the skills needed to cope with learning at different levels as they move up the school.

Links with local state schools Grey Coat Hospital and Harris Westminster Sixth Form – the latter sponsored by Westminster School – see sixth formers from these schools joining in German, Latin, art history and drama lessons. 'They've done a really good job at integrating us,' said a Westminster sixth former. 'I'm as good friends with students from outside as anyone else in the class.' Joint senior management meetings with Harris Westminster staff: 'We are going to learn from each other.'

Games, options, the arts: An almost overwhelming range of extracurricular opportunities. Societies often stem from the particular passions of both staff and students, ranging from feminist to secular to geography. English society may see Simon Russell Beale answering questions on playing King Lear at the National, whilst Piyush Goyal, national treasurer of the Indian Bharatiya Janata Party (BJP) party, tells the political society about Indian public affairs. 'I set up a society and had an ambassador from Panama come to talk,' said one student. 'Staff are really supportive when you want to set up new things.' Huge range of journalists and politicians, scientists and thinkers drop in to give talks; poet in residence inspires creativity. Trips everywhere: climbing in Cataluña, Beijing exchange, art history in Venice. Years 9-11 go off for a week's climbing, sailing, hill walking or camping at home or abroad.

'Phenomenal' music, with professional standard orchestral concerts at St John's Smith Square and the Barbican, carol service in Westminster Abbey, masterclasses, eminent musicians from Nicola Benedetti to Ian Bostridge giving evening concerts. One parent felt that 'unless you are excellent you won't get a look in,' whilst staff point out there are house concerts and ensembles for the less stratospherically talented. 'We like to think there is room for everyone.' Drama equally high performing – Guys and Dolls a recent sell-out but much cerebral fare too, plus house drama and GCSE/A level pieces – and again huge talent required to bag a role in the large scale school productions.

Art, too, 'wonderful', with much emphasis on traditional drawing and painting skills, life classes, film making facilities and a darkroom. Plus, of course, easy access to all of London's galleries and museums. 'My son had no artistic ambition when he arrived, but is now doing art A level. They have totally inspired him,' said one parent, whilst another commented: 'They let these academic boys be so creative – they feel free to explore.'

Sports – known as 'Station' – take place on Tuesday and Thursday afternoons, mostly on the enviably large playing fields in nearby St Vincent Square plus adjacent sports centre (in a previous life one of the Royal Horticultural Halls). In Westminster liberal fashion, no particular sport is compulsory, with a huge range of choices from sailing to judo to golf to girls' football. 'You wouldn't send a very sporty boy to Westminster,' thought a parent, who was grateful that her keen but not-particularly-athletic son had been in teams which he would have been unlikely to make at a more overtly sporty school. However, particularly successful at rowing (and was basking in the glow of recent success at National Schools' Regatta when we visited), fields nine football teams with 'at least respectable' results, and 'we do very well at niche sports such as rock climbing and fencing'. Often dominates the London School Cross-Country Championships and the Westminster Secondary Schools Swimming Gala, with pupils representing Westminster in the London Youth Games, and is successful at fives and real tennis. 'You are encouraged to try lots of things and find something you are passionate about,' said a student.

Volunteering taking on increasing importance with head's passion for outreach, with nearly all Westminsters teaching music or setting up debating societies in local primary schools, working on Hampstead Heath or learning sign language to communicate with deaf children. 'People are really involved and really making a difference,' said a student. 'Staff have the time, passion and faith in us to let us get on with things.' Phab week – where year 12 Westminster students host young people with physical and/or mental challenges, taking part in creative activities and seeing London together – is a 'life changing experience'. 'With privilege comes enormous responsibility to give back,' says the head.

Boarding: The last Anglican monastery in London now houses Purcell's, a girls' boarding and boys' day house with attached chapel. Five other boarding houses, all in or near Little Dean's Yard and all of which include some day pupils. Many rooms surprisingly spacious; younger boys in College, scholars' house, in dorms of up to eight, whilst upper years have their own rooms and those in between may share with one other. 'Because these are all old buildings, the room arrangements can be random, and sometimes we have to improvise.' All boarders are cared for in relaxed fashion by housemaster (male or female), some with own family; resident tutor and matron also on site. Breakfast and supper in College Hall, the medieval dining room of Westminster Abbey, which day pupils may also join.

The only full boarders are sixth formers, and Saturday evenings tend to be quiet, though school is increasing organised weekend activities, particularly for the 10 per cent or so of overseas sixth form boarders.

Boarders have supervised prep sessions, and there are evening activities in the sports and music centres after prep, but those after a full-on boarding experience jammed full of organised activities may want to look elsewhere. 'He likes it for the independence and to be with his mates,' said a boarder parent, whilst another said, 'It feels like a convenient b&b. Much better than having to pick him up at late after a rehearsal or lecture.' However, a sixth form boarder commented on the 'serious sense of community you can only get from living with others. The people in your own house become quite special to you.'

Background and atmosphere: Whilst some other great public schools overshadow their environs, Westminster is an integral but discreet part of central London, largely located in the walled precincts of the former medieval monastery of Westminster Abbey. Its main buildings surround the square of Little Dean's Yard, known as Yard, where pupils spill out after lessons to chat or kick a football or practise basketball. The Abbey, next door and with its own private entrance, serves as the school chapel, used for twice weekly services plus carol and other concerts.

Westminster had become a school by 1179, with pupils taught by monks of the Abbey at Westminster. It survived Henry VIII's dissolution of the monasteries in 1540 and has been in continuous existence since the 14th century, with Elizabeth I celebrated as the school's official founder.

'It is an incredibly tolerant and civilised atmosphere,' said a parent. 'Unlike other schools, they don't try to mould pupils into a particular product. They are quite laissez-faire.' Parents of quirky students are relieved to find a school that is very kind and accepting of eccentricities. 'If he was at any other school he'd be toast,' said one, 'Some schools can be so unforgiving: Westminster is the complete opposite.' Another reported that it has 'catered brilliantly' for each of her very different children. 'It's so wonderful to see these kids spark off each other.'

Has signed an agreement with Hong Kong education company HKMETG to set up six bilingual 3-18 schools in China by 2028, with 10 per cent of places free to less affluent families, and consultancy fees contributing to the Westminster bursary fund.

Pastoral care, well-being and discipline: Tutors attached to each house oversee the academic side, whilst housemasters look after all else. One parent felt that both have too many charges to know her son well. 'I feel his well-being is my responsibility, not the school's. I don't think anyone there knows him well in the round.' Others, however, described the pastoral care as 'exceptional', and a student said, 'I have always found the school really responsive. Your housemaster is always there and will take care of everything from not feeling well to having too much work.'

Pupils expected to be proactive, motivated and organised, with very full timetables but no compulsion to take part in organised activities. 'But anything you want to try, there's some way of doing it,' said a student.

Pupils and parents: 'Lots of people said I wouldn't like Westminster,' reports the head. 'They told me the pupils were arrogant, staff unmanageable, parents difficult. None of this is true.' Westminster families undoubtedly tend to be wealthy, intellectual, metropolitan, cosmopolitan and no doubt demanding, but most parents are extremely supportive of the school. 'It is very hard to withstand this full on praise and delight.' 'I am a real believer.' 'Fantastic on every front.' And from an initial sceptic: 'I am increasingly fond of it.'

Girls entering the sixth form report a much easier ride than they might have expected. 'I had heard rumours about the boys being awful and arrogant – but they weren't,' said one. 'Some would show off in lessons to begin with, but they calmed down pretty quickly.' 'I suspect they look for a certain confidence,' said another. 'If you were insecure you might find it intimidating.' 'It was quite a shock to the system at first,' said a third, 'but we can hold our own.'

'Westminster imbues in you a sense that it is fine to talk to anyone on equal terms,' said an ex-student. 'You have a real feeling of being special.'

Parents – nearly all are Londoners, with even boarders mostly coming from within the M25 – offered a cornucopia of outings to Dulwich Picture Gallery, tours of Westminster Abbey and the Houses of Parliament, plus quiz nights, drinks parties, concerts in the Abbey, and the opportunity to attend expert lectures with their children. 'Parents very friendly and there's a good sense of community and involvement,' said one.

Old Westminsters span the centuries and the professions: the massive list ranges from Ben Jonson, John Dryden, Robert Hooke, Lord Lucan, Kim Philby, AA Milne, John Gielgud, Tony Benn, Corin Redgrave, Helena Bonham-Carter and Imogen Stubbs to Dido and Mika.

Entrance: Register by the end of year 5 for 13+ entry (boys at state primary and other schools that finish at 11 may apply to Westminster Under School). Computer pre-tests in English, maths and reasoning in year 6; high performers who also have a good report from current school called for interview, which includes short maths and English tests. Those with conditional places sit either the Challenge scholarship exam or CE (pass mark 70 per cent) in year 8. Entry from 2021 onwards will not depend on passing the CE but on 'continued good conduct and academic progress at their existing prep school, including an unreserved reference of support from their school in year 8.'

For 16+ places, register between summer and October of the year before entry. Applicants – boys and girls – take exams in their four most likely A level subjects, and are interviewed.

Exit: Excellent and detailed preparation not only for Oxbridge but also for US colleges, with school trips to visit east coast universities. 'The school has been very supportive from an early age,' said a student, 'keeping us up to date with when to take subject tests and when to visit colleges.' Good preparation too for medicine, which is amongst the most popular degree subjects alongside liberal arts.

Up to half of sixth formers do, indeed, go to Oxbridge (61 in 2018, with 13 medics and others off to the US including Harvard, Yale, Stanford and Princeton), most of the rest to London universities, Edinburgh, Durham or Bristol.

Money matters: A number of means-tested bursaries of up to 100 per cent of fees available at 13+ and 16+; applicants must live in London. Bursaries also available at 11+; boys spend two years at the Under School before moving on automatically to the Great School. Eight Queen's Scholarships awarded at 13+; recipients must board, and the scholarship covers half the boarding fee. This can be topped up by a bursary in case of need. Five exhibitions at this level. Up to eight music scholarships at 13+ worth 10 per cent of day fee and four 16+ music scholarships, plus free instrumental tuition. Four 16+ Queen's Scholarships now available for girls.

Remarks: One ex-student commented that Old Westminsters of her acquaintance have gone into a far wider range of careers than those from other schools. 'They seem to be following their passion. Westminster instils a belief that you can do whatever you want to do.'

Westminster Tutors

86 Old Brompton Road, London SW7 3LQ

Ages 14-99 **Pupils** 45 **Sixth form** 40

Fees: £5,500 – £25,500 pa

020 7584 1288
www.westminstertutors.co.uk

Head: Since 2007, Virginia Maguire BA MA MLitt (40s). Moved on from her previous role as director of studies at David Game College (proprietors of Westminster Tutors) to running this tiny jewel in the crown of his group of tutorial colleges. She spent five years lecturing at a Thai university, 'learning that there are completely different ways of perceiving the world around us', which may account for her ease with the varied nationalities of the pupils in her charge. Her presence is notable in this educational microcosm, not just because of the proximity of her office but also because of the reaction of her charges. She may feel particularly at home because her mother was a pupil, but whatever the reason, she is obviously capable and respected. When not at her desk, she is a keen open water swimmer but 'definitely not of the Channel kind'.

Academic matters: There is a maximum capacity of 45 students of which, in any given year, there are likely to be about five doing GCSEs (including retakes), about 20 taking A levels and 15-20 doing A level retakes or Pre-U studies. Occasionally, they enrol people in their 20s who need to take different or extra qualifications for career or further study.

Occasionally the students are taught in a group (three maximum) if their target levels are the same, but almost all the teaching is one-to-one. They offer a wide range of subjects from classical Greek to physics and psychology and the head prides herself on being able to cater for obscure requests. For the more obvious subjects she has a pool of tutors and personally makes the match between pupil and teacher. One parent asked if the tutor could be changed if the relationship didn't work and believed it when she was told that it wouldn't be a problem, although luckily the situation never arose.

The school may be diminutive in terms of pupil numbers but in the quality of its staff it rates as a Titan. The teachers tend to be stars in their fields with a level of letters after their names that would make most of their profession blush. Head recruits mainly by word of mouth and from direct applications, mixing very high-powered people close to retirement or only wanting to work part-time with younger artists, musicians, writers and PhD candidates. The only rule is that they must have a 2:1 or first in their first degree; however this year, 40 per cent have Oxbridge degrees, 70 per cent masters and 35 per cent already have PhDs. The average period that they work here is three or four years but they often come back at different points in their careers.

Each student has an individual timetable and the system is immensely flexible, making it a logistics nightmare for the smiley, hugely competent college secretary, who has been struggling with spreadsheets for over 10 years. The students all praised the teaching and describe the tutors as being 'really on top of it' and one parent described it as 'brilliant across the board, all A*s'. Parents liked the 'old-fashioned, comprehensive reports that offer an accurate assessment with no false promises' and felt 'confident that we know where we are'. A pupil agreed that the report was fair and highlighted the areas where she needed to progress. One girl described a teacher as 'she knows what she's doing' (presumably a relief to her parents..) and other students talked about great personal attention such as being emailed in the holidays if they voiced a worry.

They efficiently combat the lure of Xbox and Netflix by constant communication with parents so that even potentially wayward students switch from sci-fi movies to science homework. GCSE pupils have homework diaries and if necessary A level students have study slots built into their timetables. The net result of this highly individual (in every sense) and carefully monitored approach is results – 36 per cent A*/As and 78 per cent A*-B grades at A level in 2018 – that exceed those of their competitors in the tutorial field and are impressive by any measure. Recently rated outstanding in all categories by Ofsted.

Games, options, the arts: Bearing in mind that the school is above a row of shops in central London with no outside space and that the 40 odd students are not all here on a daily basis, it will not come as a surprise that sports do not feature as a significant part of the curriculum. There is a circuit training session once a week but almost all other outdoor activities are organised by the parents or the children themselves, with a staff versus students bowling outing as the only competitive event that we found. When it comes to options and the arts, the school is much better placed as all art, music, English and humanities students have tutorial guides who often include lessons in the real world of art galleries, concerts and stage performances.

Background and atmosphere: Although it has the legal status of a school and has to abide by the same rules as its much larger competitors, the head is happy that there is not a 'schooly atmosphere'. This is hardly surprising given the nature and appearance of its founder. Miss Freeston inhabited a smoke-filled den in Victoria, giving the distinct impression that there might be a bed hidden under either the piles of books launching an attack on the ceiling or the ancient, smelly dogs on the hairy sofa. You might have thought she was just a parody of a mid-20th century female academic, particularly as she always wore a mid-calf, much sat in tweed skirt and layers of doubtful moth-eaten cardigans. However, you would have been foolish to underestimate her ability to understand people as well as texts. The exterior may have presented the unmistakable combination of erudition and dottiness, but under the holey woollens was a sensitive, thoughtful woman with a formidable understanding of bright, if lost, teenage girls. It was for this reason as much as her belief in the value of education that she started Westminster Tutors in 1934.

The school has kept the same ethos and atmosphere despite its move to South Kensington and the current building is still more of a rabbit warren than a conventional educational space. It might not impress parents or students looking for a polished, modern environment and it is not for teenagers needing wide open spaces. It is quite clear that the money goes on the staff and not on the classrooms: for instance, chemistry experiments take place in a galley kitchen. This slightly unusual classroom surprisingly passed an inspection from the A level boards with flying colours and without any culinary or chemical disasters. Orchids, a guitar and a chess set might not be what you expect in a tiny maths classroom but you probably would not expect a teacher who is also finishing a doctorate, either.

Pastoral care, well-being and discipline: The head appears to have Miss Freeston's understanding of the young but she is a thoroughly modern woman and the pastoral care is described by Ofsted as excellent in 'spiritual, moral, social and cultural' areas. A parent talked of the head as being 'good at keeping an eye' and several parents remarked on the quick response they received if they contacted the school. The only hard and fast rules are attendance and safety, both of which are seldom a problem. The head reserves the right not to enter students for exams but says that the threat has always been sufficient so far. The only odd rule that she is enforcing at the moment is banning them from sitting on the strange red sofa outside the café opposite, presumably due to the smokey nature of its usual occupants.

There is an elected head boy and head girl but they admit that their duties are mainly social, including that 'we have enough milk for tea'.

Pupils and parents: Over 50 per cent of the enrolments are by word of mouth, including a large number of alumni who want their children to have the same experience. A parent told us that they had chosen the school over similar options because the alternatives felt like 'crammers and were run on military lines'. He also said that he was 'happy coming into a place covered in modern art, and it just felt right'.

The intake tends to come from a mixture of top public schools and London state schools with a fair sprinkling from abroad as the transition can be handled more easily in an operation where teaching provision is adaptable. One student told us that it suited her better than her previous school because 'you can't just hide at the back'.

There is no obvious archetypal parent although most tend to be successful in their fields or professions. It can be an option for parents of fairly modest means as some pupils only need to attend for a year to get back on track or be helped into a top university.

Entrance: This is a totally non-selective school but the majority of the intake are above average academically. They may have found it difficult to succeed in the competitive world of a large, hothouse London day school or have come from another educational system. The head interviews parents and potential students and considers whether they would be suited to this very individual environment as well as their previous academic performance. They do not take students who have been expelled for serious breaches but are sympathetic to anyone who might have struggled to stay afloat in a larger pond.

Exit: The head tries to give very personalised university and career advice and is proud that she publishes the destinations in full rather than just choosing the highlights. In 2018, 71 per cent went to Russell Group or Ivy League universities, including one to Oxford. The majority of people choose the school because they want to make a successful transition from A levels to a top university but this is not always the case, and recently one student left to do a BTec in mechanical engineering and one to a retail apprenticeship because it was agreed that this was a better route for them. Parents agree that they are 'on the money' about university choices and come up with good suggestions to add to their children's ideas.

Money matters: Inevitably not a cheap option but compared to alternatives with larger classes it offers value for money.

Remarks: Students are shoehorned into tiny classrooms, reminiscent of the dormouse being stuffed into the teapot at the Mad Hatter's Tea Party and there is definitely an element of the unusual in the workings of this place but there is also an academic wizard at play here. The head may hanker after a swimming pool but the students lack for nothing in the level of teaching or encouragement in learning how to learn.

Westminster Under School

Linked with Westminster School

Adrian House, 27 Vincent Square, London SW1P 2NN

Ages 7–13 **Pupils** 280 C of E

Fees: £19,344 pa

020 7821 5788
www.westminsterunder.org.uk

Master: Since 2016, Mark O'Donnell, previously the head of St Martin's Ampleforth and also head of Alleyn's Junior School in south London. Educated at Stonyhurst and St Ignatius College, New South Wales, he has a masters in education from Harvard and a postgraduate diploma in education from Oxford. He is a Fellow of the Royal College of Arts, a Duke of Edinburgh assessor and an alpine ski leader. He is married with three sons.

Entrance: Academically selective (very) at 7, 8 and 11. Some successful applicants are merely 'well above the national average', about a third 'far above'. All candidates need to read fluently well beyond their chronological age and approach the unexpected logically and imaginatively. No obvious feeders, though all the usual central London pre-preps represented. At 11+, a reasonable chunk from state primaries, most of the rest from schools which end at year 6. (The school encourages entrants from 'those leaving at a natural point.') Twenty-two places at 7 (175 applying), a further 22 at 8 (175 applying), then 28 places at 11 (250 applying). At 11+, now uses computerised pre-tests in December before written exams for call-back candidates. About 40 invited at each stage for interview and further testing. 'We want to understand each child and decide if this is the right school for them.' What makes the fit? 'The school is about passion, enthusiasm, determination and a hunger for achievement. We're looking for boys who are independent, intellectual and individual. Everybody here loves learning.'

Exit: About 90 per cent go on to the senior school (including all those who come in at 11), with a good number of scholarships, but the school is equally happy to prepare for entrance and scholarships elsewhere. About 8-10 each year to Eton (often those with family connections), some with major scholarships. Generally a couple to Winchester, and sometimes a sprinkling to City, Dulwich, Alleyn's, etc.

Remarks: Academically top of the tree. Well-qualified staff (a number with PhDs) provides teaching that is mostly strong, lively and challenging. 'We're looking for boys who will think and problem solve. We want them to work things out, not be spoon-fed.' Most boys seem to relish the offering. 'I really like all my lessons,' said one. 'The teachers are very enthusiastic and if you have a problem they just want to help,' said another. However, the pressure to be high in the rankings comes as a shock to some.

Specialist teaching in all subjects from year 5. In English, boys are encouraged to 'develop their own voice'. Books are seminal, with even the smallest scouring the library shelves in their lunch hour. Reading lists updated termly and topped up with an in-house bookshop and regular swapshop. Weekly maths competitions hone skills both for lessons and the Intermediate and Senior Maths Challenge, where plenty achieve gold and beyond. Maths and science extension club. Programming from year 3. French throughout, taught by native speakers. Classical studies combined with Latin from year 5, stand-alone Latin from year 6, Greek in year 8. Annual Latin play competition. 'There's a real sense of intellectual endeavour,' said one parent.

Thorough monitoring, with internal exams November and June, plus mocks in the Lent term of year 8, as well as regular subject testing. Lots of rewards for achievement with cups and shields for virtually everything. 'They really ram home competition,' said one parent. Homework load significant at all levels. An hour a night in years 3-5, an hour and a half in years 7 and 8. Some parents have voiced the view that supportive homes are essential. The school says this shouldn't be necessary: 'We don't require parental support and you absolutely don't need a tutor. If you need a tutor, you shouldn't be at Westminster.' However, one parent commented that tutoring is 'rife'.

New arrivals at 11 – two forms of 12-14 boys – are given Saturday morning lessons from the moment they're accepted, then segregated for lessons (but not other activities) in year 7. 'We give them lots of attention, before dividing up the whole year group into scholarship and CE forms in year 8.' Those from state primaries can find the transition taxing. 'Catching up to common entrance in two years was difficult,' said one parent. 'There was an enormous amount of work and my son found it stressful.'

Few struggle in the conventional sense, but an experienced SENCo provides support with study skills, exam technique and organisation, arranging clinics where help from peer mentors is particularly productive. Plenty of 'enhancement', too, through debating, history of art etc.

Music of an exceptionally high standard (many boys with grade 8 and beyond and plenty of music scholarships to senior schools). Head of music (also musical director of National Youth Music Theatre) oversees over 500 lessons a week, an outstanding choir and biannual music trips.

Not everyone's idea of a sporty school, but the athletic ante has been raised recently with the addition of a number of well-qualified coaches. ('One boy attends the Chelsea football academy one day a week, but still manages his academic work.') For a central London prep, notably well-endowed with playing fields, and the expansive garden square opposite the front gates provides an ample supply of pitches and courts as well as an adventure playground. Games twice a week, with regular inter-house and inter-school tournaments in football, hockey, cricket, tennis and basketball. Recently-acquired sports hall just down the road (also able to accommodate mass gatherings of parents) offers further scope for indoor games, including judo, fencing, karate, wall climbing and nets.

Exciting theatrical tradition maintained by an 'inspirational' head of drama, with three productions annually (recent highlights include Lord of the Flies, School for Scandal) and a new performing arts centre. Art now housed in its own light and lovely double studio, with a self-contained art history library. Clubs every night (history, Mandarin, debating, etc). Chess (taught by a Grand Master) particularly popular, with 90 members and England players. Competitions galore, including hotly contested Scrabble tournament. (Some find the atmosphere slightly too competitive. 'They don't just have a Scrabble club or a chess club, they have a Scrabble competition or a chess competition.')

Plenty of external speakers and trips in London and further afield. (Recent adventures include classics to Sorrento, cricket to South Africa, geography to the Grand Canyon.) Philanthropy a core value. 'They learn to enjoy giving and love raising money for disadvantaged children.' (Parents and boys raised £45,000 last year, £18,000 in the popular Readathon.)

Founded in 1943 as a class of 17 boys located in the senior school, then decanted to Ecclestone Square, the school took up residence in its current spacious premises in Adrian House – a red-brick Victorian former hospital – in 1981. The Under School continues to share both governors and outlook with the senior school, allowing the same careful planning over future development. A large new building, directly opposite the existing school, opened in 2013, providing a lofty dining hall and indulgent stretches of well-equipped teaching space.

Discipline not an issue. 'You don't have to shout at Westminster; we encourage good behaviour through positive behaviour management and high expectations.' Certainly, one boy unbidden held open a door, all answered questions readily and politely. Immaculate uniform, perhaps, not a priority. In PSHE, 'they learn about emotional intelligence and empathy for others. We talk about life. We want them to be able to talk with us about anything and it will be OK.'

At 7 and 8, parents primarily prime-central-London (often City) high achievers. At 11+, more diverse, with pupils coming from as far afield as Dagenham and Guildford. Plenty of bilingual, multicultural homes. Parents tend to be proud (and occasionally pushy). Boys are extremely articulate (one 8 year old, asked how he'd cope with a broken arm, responded, 'I would just have to become ambidextrous') and can undoubtedly be boffiny ('Thus, you can see,' explained one 11 year old).

No scholarships, but a few means-tested bursaries of up to 100 per cent at 11 (which take the recipient through the senior school). 'Our philosophy is that the children who can come here should not be prevented from doing so for financial reasons.'

An exciting, demanding education for the intellectual, industrious child.

Wetherby Preparatory School

Linked with Wetherby School, Wetherby Senior School

48 Bryanston Square, London W1H 2EA

Ages 8–13 **Pupils** 360

Fees: £22,575 pa

020 7535 3520
www.wetherbyprep.co.uk

Head: Since 2008, Nick Baker BA PGCE (early 40s). A grammar school boy, he hails from Bucks, and was educated at Dr Challoner's and University College London, where he read geography, before qualifying as a teacher at Newcastle University. He has taught geography in a range of schools, including Holloway Boys comprehensive, head of year at Borehamwood, a former state middle school, and head of geography at Chesham Prep School (where he went as a boy, is now chair of governors, and which his two sons currently attend). He has taught at Wetherby Prep since it first started in 2004, initially as a senior master before becoming deputy head, and his brief continues to expand as he has also headed the new Wetherby Senior School since it opened in September 2015.

Tall, broad-shouldered and youthful, with a reassuring laugh that echoes from his belly, Nick Baker is hugely popular, with parents, pupils and staff as well as colleagues in the wider prep school world. A keen supporter of Watford Football Club, he celebrates their victories at whole prize-giving events as well as in his blog and emails, and even the many Chelsea supporters among the families here share in his delight and enthusiasm. Open and affable, his weekly newsletters in Wetherbuzz frequently include anecdotes about his two boys and what his family is getting up to. Hot on values and manners, one of the many 'challenges' he initiated is the Politeness Challenge. 'Much the best news is hearing that Wetherby boys are good house guests,' he says. Parents like the fact that he is so present, both around the school and at the many social events organised for teachers and parents, the Headmaster's Ball, or 'pub nights with dads', for example, as well as the Come Dine with Me event where teachers cook and wait on the parents. The adjectives that we heard most often were 'very professional', 'excellent communicator' and 'very driven and opinionated', but what is most apparent and consistent is that they trust him.

Entrance: At 8 into year 4 (when 200 sit for 40 places). Boys from the pre-prep have automatic entry. Everyone else (including from other Alpha Plus schools like Chepstow House, but apart from siblings who also enter automatically) sits papers in English and maths during an assessment day at the school and also takes part in group activities.

Exit: An impressive number to top academic schools, especially considering the range of ability in each year. In 2018, four to Eton, six to St Paul's, six to to Harrow, four to Westminster. Others to eg Winchester, City of London, Charterhouse and Wellington. Around a quarter to Wetherby Senior School (nine in 2018).

Remarks: Wetherby Prep, and its brother, pre-prep Wetherby School, are currently riding high and widely regarded by parents across London as the jewel in the Alpha Plus crown. Slick as a well-oiled machine, Wetherby delivers precisely what its parents demand: high quality teaching, a broad and extensive choice of activities and sports and exceptional communication. Many of the parents are bankers and Wetherby is the prep school equivalent of a well-resourced City institution. Boys here are polite (everyone stands up when you enter a room – 'our parents like that,' says Mr Baker) but sparkling and not squashed. One occasion which captures the spirit of the school is the prize-giving assembly which takes place every Friday in the Church of Annunciation behind Marble Arch. Parents and children cram into every corner and, after singing a hymn, prizes are distributed. These can be anything from the history prize to the prize for the best joke – let alone for sporting achievements (like running the marathon). Mr Baker conducts the whole occasion with warmth and humour. He clearly knows every child well and there is a lot of boyish banter. A cauldron of competitiveness, when house points are read out there are huge whoops and cheers. These boys really care if their house is ahead – especially if it's about the amount of food waste they are managing to avoid. We also witnessed a charming joy in their peers' achievements. The best kind of competitive spirit. We were most impressed when boys not only moved aside to let us sit down but also folded and cleared our chairs for us amid the chaos of cricket bats, violins, hockey sticks and trumpets at the close of proceedings.

Situated behind Marble Arch in leafy Bryanston Square, the Georgian building is grand and spacious. The signature red painted front door welcomes you into a smart, light, high ceilinged entrance hall, complete with wood panelled, gold leaf scholarship boards and lists of head boys, prefects and house captains of the school. Boys pile past heaving musical instruments and sports equipment, looking smart but tousled in cricket gear, grey and red blazers and caps. A sweeping staircase takes traffic up the several flights, a small back staircase channels them down. All the classrooms are large, light and airy, well-equipped and organised. The basement not only houses a couple of very well-equipped science labs, a fitness suite with rowing and running machines, and the dining room, but also a pet snake which boys can stand and stare at to while away any spare minutes in their busy day. Every boy has his own red locker – no need to lug every book and file around with him the whole time. School laptops seem to be littered at strategic points around the school and are available for anyone to use. There are also 20 desktop PCs in the library, which doubles up as an ICT suite where the boys learn coding, touch-typing and animation. School has recently expanded into a new building a short distance away in Manchester Street.

From year 4, boys are setted in maths and English and have specialist subject teachers; most other subjects are setted in year 6, when they also start Latin. Three classes per year, with about 20 in each class. With automatic entry for siblings and boys from Wetherby School, alongside selective entry for others, the school is mixed ability but, Mr Baker observes, 'the academic demographic gets stronger year by year. The average CAT score used to be 112 and is now 120.' Full-time SENCo, assisted by one other person, gives support to children with mild learning difficulties, including dyslexia, dyspraxia and mild autism. Support provided ranges from touch-typing to reading groups as well as one-to-one session in maths and literacy outside the classroom. Approximately 16 in the school are getting support at any one time. Lots of prizes and rewards including a meeting with the head – the Headmaster's Good Show – to commend outstanding work. One young 9 year old told us proudly that he was 'very good friends with Mr Baker' as a result of his regular chats with him.

Sport is strong and getting better and better each year, both in terms of what is offered, the facilities and the teams' performances against other schools. The Park Club, in Acton, is now their home ground, and although some parents complain of traffic and the length of time it gets to bus them there, most were very enthusiastic about the excellent facilities, the space and the fact that they no longer need to box and cox in various places around central London. Boys play rugby and football in the winter, athletics, tennis and cricket in the summer. Their annual sports day is a major fixture in the calendar. There are plenty of other sports on offer too – hockey (including roller hockey), horse riding, fencing, rowing, rock climbing and badminton. One gets the impression that when Mr Baker goes to his Alpha Plus governors to ask that the tap be turned on (to make provision for another club, for example), it will be done. Lots of popular 'fathers and staff' fixtures too, in cricket and football.

Parents enthuse about the 'excellent' music. 'Despite the fact that my son is sporty, his favourite club is choir,' observed one father. Dynamic head of music has a modern and innovative approach. Plenty of public performances, impromptu as well as more formal. Breakfast concerts happen twice a term, there is a junior and senior school recital and a band as well as an orchestra and a chamber choir. Art is well organised and cross-curricular. We saw lots of lino cuttings and Mac books in the art room as well as impressive pieces of work around the school. In DT they were building clocks, and there is a dark room for photography, but the 'backbone of the department is printing,' we were told. Drama could be better, Mr Baker acknowledges; some parents, more brutally, described it as 'almost non-existent.' They use the Rudolf Steiner theatre up the road for productions, 'but it's so difficult to get good drama teachers/ directors,' explains the head.

Parents here are slightly more diverse than those at the pre-prep. The numerous school buses run like clockwork and depart and arrive when they are meant to, enabling many parents to entrust their boys to the school transport, so they come from as far as Islington in the north east to Hammersmith in the west. Lots of well-heeled bankers and lawyers, and a smattering of celebrities – what would you expect in this part of London? – but a refreshing mixture of cultures and backgrounds. Nick Baker's openness and inclusivity – both in the weekly Wetherbuzz newsletters as well as in his public addresses – help to contribute to a real family and community feel. An outstanding school, polished and professional, and an excellent foundation for your all-rounder son.

Wetherby School

Linked with Wetherby Preparatory School, Wetherby Senior School

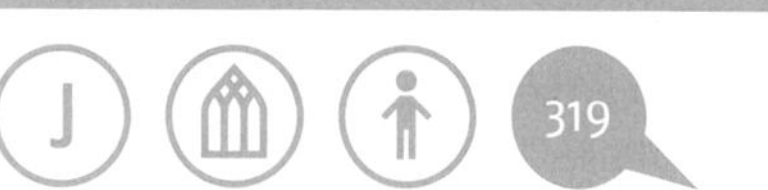

11 Pembridge Square, London W2 4ED

Ages 2–8 **Pupils** 345

Fees: £22,245 pa

020 7727 9581
www.wetherbyschool.co.uk

Head: Since 2009, Mark Snell BA PGCE (mid 40s). Educated at Eastbourne College, University of Westminster (a degree in business studies) and Brighton University, where he gained his teaching qualification. His first job was at Eaton House the Manor. Utterly down to earth, direct, no nonsense and unpretentious (although one parent observed that his 'oikishness verges on the pretentious given his background'). With his buzz cut hair style and his gruff manner, Mr Snell is so robust and hearty he could pass for the manager of a medium sized football club. He is also deeply committed and completely devoted to the boys and their needs. 'I enjoy life and don't give a stuff what anyone thinks of me,' he says. Most parents love him ('he still makes time to for me to discuss my son even though he's no longer at the school') though a few dissenters bemoan his encouragement of the alpha in these already uber alpha boys.

Deputy for two years before taking over as head, he is completely au fait with the ethos of the place and is hugely respected by his fellow Alpha Plus heads. ('Nick Baker is a great bloke,' he says. Nick Baker – head of Wetherby Prep – thinks the same of Mark Snell, though he put it slightly differently.) Previously head of maths at King's College Wimbledon, and prior to that he taught at Westminster Under where, he says, he really cut his teeth and learnt a lot of what he knows now ('though I'm thick as two short planks,' he repeatedly assured us). Despite his 'street' manner, he was born into prep school aristocracy and teaching is very much in the blood. He was brought up in a south coast prep school with his three siblings. His father inherited and ran Mowden School near Brighton (now a prep school to Lancing College), and the wider family are involved with Ludgrove Prep School (in Berkshire). His wife also teaches ('though she is much cleverer than me'). They have a son and a daughter, both school age.

His subject is maths, and though he kept telling us how dim he is, he had us stumped on more than one occasion as so many of his explanations were put in arithmetic form and he relishes statistics. Teaches maths to years 3 and 2, and loves it, he says. An added advantage is that he really knows each individual and can give informed advice on where next. 'If parents choose not to listen, that's fine,' he says; 'that's their prerogative, but I know the schools, understand the assessment data, and I know the boys.' Very accessible – to the boys especially, but to parents too. Many spoke of their complete confidence in him, his judgment, and his recruitment of teachers ('you feel confident that he will never employ a duff,' enthused one parent). A loyal Seagulls fan, his faux wood panelled study (a present from parents, along with most of the colourful decorations) has several Brighton and Hove flags and memorabilia and is brimming with evidence of his personality and the affection families past and present have for him.

Entrance: Non-selective. Register the month your baby is born, and ideally the day he is born. If you try to register any later than when your baby is 3 months old, you're too late. School gets approximately 35 applications a month – or about 360 a year for 88 places (four classes in each year group). Staggered entry by the month to avoid a preponderance of December (say) babies. You only get to see round the school if you are going to be offered a definite place. If you are on the waiting list there is still hope, but not a lot. Parents feel they have a golden ticket if their son gets a place here and are unlikely to turn it down for anything other than 'act of God'. Lots of international families and a number of children speak more than one language at home, but not much EAL support needed, as most arrive here fluent in English. No longer as local as it once was, parents prepared to travel far for the first class education they feel their son will get here.

Exit: High numbers to the most academic prep schools. In recent years as many as 40 per cent to Westminster Under, Sussex House and St Paul's Juniors. Increasing numbers, currently 45 per cent, to Wetherby Prep, where entrance is automatic and the standards are rising, so why go through the stress of exams? The other 15 per cent elsewhere – eg locally to King's College Junior School and Latymer Prep or to board at Summer Fields, Caldicott or The Dragon.

Remarks: The Wetherby brand is currently putting even Balenciaga in the shade. It is hard to find anyone, past, present or potential parent, who doesn't positively glow about the school. They single out the quality of the teaching – not only does Mr Snell recruit excellent teachers but he motivates them and makes them go the extra mile. Homework is 'innovative and thorough'. Communication with parents is 'exceptional', plus the 'school really understand boys and how to educate them.'

Lots of competitions and games inside the classroom as well as out. Learning here is fun, whether it's a project on the Romans or a fabulous end of year party, which incorporates an ice cream van and a bouncy castle. School is lucky enough to be able use the square opposite and the boys get lots of fresh air and exercise during breaks throughout the day. Reception and nursery children have their own outside playground, complete with springy tarmac and climbing wall, which is in constant use. On top of this they have several gym and swimming lessons (at Kensington Leisure Centre), as well as sport (in Hyde Park and Westway) in the afternoons. Lots of football and tag rugby in the winter, cricket in the summer. Plenty of fixtures against other schools, in swimming as well as field sports, and an annual sports day at the Wetherby sports grounds – at the Park Club in Acton. Dads' and boys' Saturday morning football is hugely popular, as are chess club, martial arts club, arts and crafts and drama. The choice of clubs is huge, from chess and cookery to Lego and French.

Plenty of music too – a choir in each of years 1, 2 and 3 as well as the wonderful Wetherby singers, created for those who couldn't make it into the choir but still love to sing. 'They make a terrible noise,' growled Mr Snell, 'but parents love it.' More than half the school learns an instrument – peripatetic teachers for guitar, violin and piano. There are instrumental concerts at the end of each term in St Matthew's church up the road as well as impromptu recitals in the hall. Drama part of the timetable as well as offered as a club. There is a performance at the end of each term, and the year 3s perform a major production (in recent years Peter Pan and The Jungle Book) at the Tabernacle Theatre.

Despite being non-selective the pace is fast here. Boys are expected to work hard right from the word go. We saw boys as young as 3 and 4 reading and writing (beautifully). Standards are high and everyone is aspirational – teachers, head and parents alike. Children who need support are usually identified early – good systems in place for spotting and diagnosing any difficulties. What is done about it next depends on the level of support required. At the more severe end – boys with moderate learning difficulties – many parents choose to take them to Emerson House in Shepherd's Bush to get that support. Others are taken out in groups for extra support – it could be the top, middle or bottom group in maths or English; others may have one-to-one support lessons. School employs one full-time and one other teacher who has half her timetable, dedicated to learning support.

There are 22 boys in each class, and they get lots of attention. Ratio of pupils to teacher (or teaching assistant) is high – more than one teaching assistant in every class room as well a lot of floating teachers. Lots of differentiation – and boys taught according to academic capability not according to syllabus. 'We teach them when they're ready to learn'. Only in the final year, year 3, are they grouped according to ability, in maths, English and reasoning. Relatively high number of male teachers (14) unusual for this age group. 'We can attract a different kind of teacher – Alpha Plus pays very well, especially at this level, and we rarely lose anyone to another school,' says Snell. Although they couldn't fault the education in the classroom, some parents boldly suggested that more attention could be paid to the importance of moral values. The idea of being 'nice' to each other, so focused on in girls' schools, is missing here, they said. These are alpha boys with alpha parents and, parents observe, there is a limited public spiritedness where writing cheques replaces baking cakes.

School is currently expanding up to 360 pupils. The new building in Pembridge Villas, once the site of Chepstow House, is already being used for reception and Little Wetherby (the nursery). New kid on the block is another pre-prep, Wetherby Kensington. Despite an increase in the number of places, we doubt there will be less pressure on them. A busy, successful, well-run, well-resourced school, full of happy, spirited boys. For as long as this formula remains the same Wetherby is likely to remain the brand parents want.

Wetherby Senior School

Linked with Wetherby Preparatory School, Wetherby School

100 Marylebone Lane, Marylebone, London W1U 2QU

Ages 11–18 **Pupils** 274 **Sixth form** 35

Fees: £23,970 pa

020 7535 3530
www.wetherbysenior.co.uk

Head: Since 2017, Seth Bolderow MSt BA, early 40s. Succeeded the much-loved Nick Baker who helped set up the school and ran it alongside the prep school for two years, but it was time to hand over the tiller to refocus on the prep school. Bolderow was regarded by some parents, who felt that they had bought into the 'Nick Baker ticket', with some suspicion initially. Formerly deputy head of Harrow International School in Hong Kong, Bolderow, whose name isn't the only thing that seems to have stepped out of a Thomas Hardy novel, hails from farming stock in Norfolk and was educated at Norwich school, and Exeter University where he studied classics. He was awarded a distinction for his Mst in Greek and Latin languages and literature at St Anne's College Oxford, and was sorely tempted by a life of academia. However, drawn to the camaraderie of the classroom and sports pitches, he commenced his teaching career at Blundell's, then Uppingham and King Edward's School Bath, before taking on head of sixth form at The John Lyon School and then making the move to the Far East with his girlfriend, soon to become wife. They have two young children. His proudest moment, he says, was delivering his son, less than a year old now, as there was a dearth of midwives at the time.

Full of appreciation for the wider network of support and expertise afforded by the Alpha Plus group (a common theme among heads of school groups, we find). The director of schools, Jenny Stephen and the recently appointed CEO Mark Hanley-Brown get a special mention, described as having 'education pedigree'. Bolderow's functional office is warmed by evidence of his passion. Piles of Classical Loebs and ancient Greek and Latin texts line the shelves. Quietly modest and understated, he is not one to play table tennis with the boys, as his predecessor was, and he keeps a respectable distance from the parents. While one wouldn't ascribe to him an urbane charm, he is authentic, a good listener and a man with a clear and defined purpose, and has won the admiration and respect of parents and boys alike.

Academic matters: First set of GCSE results in 2018, with 71 per cent A*-A/9-7 grades; internal data suggests pupils make very good progress, and systems in place to track progress constantly. 'For GCSE boys', says school, 'projected grades given to boys and parents after year 10 and 11 mocks are tracked against independent baseline data (MidYIS). Using Attainment 8 as an overall measure for each boy, we are adding 0.22 of a grade on average, with 29 per cent of cohort adding more than one grade.' Almost every parent we spoke to praised the quality of the teachers and how impressive both their subject knowledge is and their understanding of the ethos of the school and commitment to it. A blend of experienced and relatively newly qualified, an equal split of men and women, they are recruited from both sectors, state and independent, and while naturally differ in style manage to combine being unpretentious with a traditional approach. 'All of our teachers are really lively,' averred the boys we spoke to.

A traditional academic curriculum includes Latin with German, French and Spanish the choice of modern languages. Native speakers and those who show a particular aptitude will be invited to take the GCSE as early as year 8. Graphic design, no DT. Practical skills are taught, the use of laser cutters etc. An esoteric part of the curriculum is that every pupil to age 16 is taught philosophy and learning skills. The head of philosophy is keen to throw everything at them, from Plato and Aristotle to Kant and Hobbes. The aim, to create independent learners who can think for themselves – qualities top universities are crying out for. Boys setted for maths from year 7 and in English and science from year 9. There are five sets for science. Beginners' sets for German and Spanish in year 9. Class sizes are small, currently 16. Judicious and sensible use of sets and there is movement up as well as down. A healthy broad range of ability when we visited, but as the school fills up, and word spreads, we suspect intake likely to become more and more academic.

A specialist SENCo but no one-to-one support in the classroom. Needs of anyone with learning difficulties are met in the classroom through differentiation. A tiny few need EAL support (about 5/225). Lucid Exact Software used to screen boys once they're here to spot any difficulties, like dyslexia. School works closely with an dducational psychologist who is brought in when there's a problem. They avoid labelling as much as possible, but Mr Bolderow said that around 25 per cent of current pupils are on the SEND register. Whatever their needs, he says, they can all manage in class without individual support.

First sixth form intake in September 2018, most moving up from year 11, with a few places for external applicants. The sixth form will grow organically – from an initial 35 – as the larger year groups move up the school.

Games, options, the arts: Traditional sports, rugby, football, cricket, tennis and athletics, with lots of competitive fixtures. Two afternoons a week are timetabled for games and they play matches against leading London secondary day schools including Latymer Upper, Westminster and Kingston Grammar as well as the top two years of the prep schools. The downside, say a number of parents, is the one hour plus round coach trip to the sports ground, which is Trailfinders in Ealing. Some wonder how much time they actually get to play when so much time is taken up travelling. Nonetheless, the U15 football team had an impressive season, reaching the quarter final of the ESFA small schools cup. They are starting to punch above their weight.

The director of sport, an ex-Saracens rugby player and elite RFU referee, is highly praised by colleagues and parents. A 'fantastic sportsman, he is increasingly attracting sporty boys,' say some parents we spoke to. One parent was particularly impressed by his attitude to sport and exercise. It is not just about competition and fixtures, but laying down the foundations for a healthy lifestyle and contributing to a mental health. Year 10 boys are linked to gyms and can opt for boxing, spinning etc, and there are a range of minor sports offered from fencing to basketball. Even unenthusiastic sportsman have to do one afternoon of physical activity in the sixth form – other afternoons they can do work in the community or work experience.

Drama is vibrant and everyone gets a chance to be involved. Last year they did a 'promenade' production to great acclaim, as the actors moved round parts of the school performing. This year we witnessed the dress rehearsal for an edgy play set in a prison written by the head of drama. She fizzes with excitement as every head of drama should, and the boys respond positively. Some prefer to do backstage work, whether it be costumes and make-up or lighting and set design. Productions, small and large, throughout the school year, including a Christmas Cabaret. LAMDA very popular in years 7, 8 and 9 and the teacher is in school most days

'The head of music is an inspiration,' say the boys. A French horn player, he has a fleet of colourful plastic brass instruments and with his combination of music technology and practical playing gets all the boys involved. There are already a number of groups including a wind ensemble, brass group and rock school plus DJ Buster teaches them to DJ. While the school is still relatively youthful it is hard to get the strength in depth for a whole school orchestra, although there is a chamber orchestra which will expand to full orchestra as the school grows.

Art technician specialises in sculpture and this was evident in the displays. Much use is made of the kiln. We saw a variety of silkscreens, and while there is a separate art and graphic design teacher, there is much crossover in the work produced. Boys' artwork is prominently displayed in the headmaster's office and throughout the school, but there is also a lot of artwork that has not been done by the boys – perhaps to fill the space? A number of exhibitions during the school year; the younger boys exhibited their art and graphic design work at the Saatchi gallery.

Lots of trips: 'they are always off somewhere,' remarked one parent, to Croatia (geography), Barcelona (combined Spanish and football tour), Pompeii (classics) and closer to home. Located in the heart of London, they don't waste the opportunity to take advantage of the museums and theatres on their doorstep.

Activities take place at the end of each day and are built into the timetable. As well as 'academic catch up' clubs in every subject, they can choose from a range of activities, from bridge, to cinema, scientific illustration (an example of their innovative use of cross-curricular expertise) to boxercise.

Mr Bolderow is a governor at Queen's College and already the two schools are forming alliances, whether it be social, musical, Duke of Edinburgh awards or lectures. A relationship is also developing with Francis Holland Regent's Park, so there will be lots of opportunity to experience working alongside girls.

Background and atmosphere: The last link in the chain of the formidable Wetherby schools, owned and managed by the private equity backed Alpha Plus group, Wetherby Senior School caters for the oldest boys in the group but, founded in September 2015, is the youngest school. Alpha Plus have cleverly given all their Wetherby schools the signature colours – the red and grey, evident from moment you arrive at the brightly painted red front door, to the furnishings throughout the school, and the boys in their smart uniforms – and also through each school runs an ethos of traditional boys' education blended with a modern and global outlook.

The school opened in 2015 with 67 boys in years 7 and 9. There are now over 200 and the maximum number will be 600. 'The size is an essential part of our ethos,' explains Bolderow. 'We are big enough to be able to compete, have an orchestra, field a number of different team sports, but not so big as to lose the intimacy that we value so highly.' Expectations are high, but boys can be themselves and there is no particular 'Wetherby mould' that they feel they should fit into.

Set in the heart of central London, the main site is in a surprisingly quiet corner of Marylebone Lane, tucked behind the famous haberdashery shop with its colourful array of ribbons. A Victorian mansion block, it has the benefit of being a traditional building with soul, but high ceilings, large classrooms and a sense of space. A second, newly purchased, similar five storey building, Hannah House in Manchester Street, is largely the base for the junior years, and the centre for the new sixth formers in Marylebone Lane also has space for a gym in the basement. A flow of boys make the five minute walk between buildings, as the division of use is largely by department, but timetables are designed to minimise movement for the youngest boys. The new building has a large cafeteria, signature red benches and grey tables and staff eat with the students. Sixth formers can also have lunch and snacks throughout the day in their café in the sixth form centre in Marylebone Lane.

Pastoral care, well-being and discipline: One message we received very clearly from parents is that the care taken by all the staff and their sensitive approach to the boys' welfare is remarkable. Whether a response to a particular crisis, or the general awareness of the difficulties of being a teenager in the 21st century, the school takes it seriously and responds professionally but with compassion. They will not hesitate to bring in professional counsellors for support and one mother remarked how pleased she was that her son came home buzzing from a series of talks from 'the good lad initiative'. A group of cool young men promoting 'positive masculinity'.

Boys are split into horizontal groups within their year group, known as Tributaries or 'Tribs', and assigned a tutor, who not only sees them every morning for registration but also meets with them for an hour each week. The tutor, overseen by a head of section, is responsible for the welfare of the boys in their care as well as keeping an eye on their academic progress and behaviour. The system works well, was the unanimous verdict of the parents we spoke to, and the communication between tutor and parent is invaluable.

Mr Bolderow sees a different tutor group each Friday to talk about the school. They have about 20 minutes to ask questions and make suggestions. 'This is usually about the food,' admits Bolderow. The chef here (god forbid that you should refer to her as cook) used to work at Soho House and while the food is delicious, there was a plea from the boys to tone down the sophistication of the recipes, since when baked potatoes have been back on the menu. There is a busy school council which consists of representatives from each Trib, and which reports to school in assembly.

A tiny courtyard at the back of the Marylebone Lane building makes it possible for boys to play football, and they do; there are two common rooms here complete with table football, and a Nintendo Wii. A range of lunchtime activities at Hannah House, indoor and out, as well as time in the park. Most of the boys we saw in break were staring at their 'phones, disappointing but a reflection of the age. A number of parents we spoke to would welcome a more robust approach from the school on the use of mobile phones.

Only sixth formers allowed out to lunch. We happened to see a number of younger boys filing into a local tea shop at the end of the day and were impressed by their deportment in the bustling streets of Marylebone.

Pupils and parents: Wetherby Senior couldn't be more of a reflection of its central London location. Thoroughly multicultural, one parent might be Swiss, the other Swedish. Whilst the majority of the boys are long term residents of the UK, the school is a truly global environment with boys from all over Europe as well as Russia, the Middle East and the USA. Most come from London prep schools.

Boys we met and spoke to were refreshingly individual and polite. They look you in the eye, are confident but not arrogant. This is far from a macho culture. Boys here can be any kind of peg, and will still fit the hole.

Entrance: Academically selective at 11, 13 and 16. Tests in English and maths at 11, but school will also give equal weight to the reference from his current school and his performance at interview. For 13+ entrance all boys will sit the Common ISEB pre-test in year 6 together with an interview. Always worth checking for the occasional place. They are looking for boys who will contribute to school life and benefit from the rounded education.

Places available at 16 and an offer is made based on GCSE results.

Exit: At the time of going to press, no cohort has left the school, but all boys are prepared for university, and the expectation is that the most academic will go to the top US and UK universities. 'Staff are experienced in supporting applications to UK universities and the school will be working with US university specialists to support boys who are aiming to study further afield.'

Remarks: Wetherby Senior could not have arrived at a better time. Parents of boys will be flocking to its red door in this overheated education market in which it is particularly hard to find good senior schools for boys. If the school continues along the trajectory it has set for itself it will only become ever more popular. A marvellous education for the modern teenage boy.

Whitgift School

Haling Park, South Croydon, Surrey CR2 6YT

Ages 10–18 **Pupils** 1,475 **Sixth form** 363 **Boarders** 52 full, 54 weekly (from 13 years) **C of E**

Fees: Day £20,136 pa; Boarding £32,274 – £37,866 pa

020 8688 9222
www.whitgift.co.uk

Headmaster: Since 2017, Christopher Ramsey (50s). With two headships already under his belt (King's Taunton and Chester), Mr Ramsey could be described as a 'career head' in some ways, but he also enjoyed a successful career as a modern languages teacher at the Leys, Shrewsbury and Wellington. Arriving here, he has faced the formidable challenge of succeeding an exceptional and long-serving (26 years) head, Dr Christopher Barnett, but is full of calm praise for his predecessor. 'I was lucky: not merely did I take over an excellent school, but it was one which Dr Barnett had acclimatised to accept change as part of the inevitable drive towards excellence'.

With nearly 1,500 pupils and 200+ teaching staff, Mr Ramsey might look at a glance like the supreme technocrat, but he's personally approachable and low-key. 'A headmaster has a licence to be nosey,' he muses – he is certainly trying to be visible in all areas. 'He comes to lunch,' said one pupil, matter-of-fact. 'Often he says hello; sometimes he tells us to tuck in our shirts.' Married with three children (teens and early 20s), he still somehow tries to find some time to enjoy theatre and football – these days as a spectator.

Academic matters: A place rich in ability and steeped in high endeavour. All-out effort seems to be the default setting, and this is reflected amply in the results. In 2018, 74 per cent of all I/GCSE grades were at A*-A/9-7. The A*-B rate for A level was 83 per cent, 52 per cent A*/A. In the IB, boys achieved an average points total of 37.8 out of 45. 'Unlike some', said one parent, 'this school has really integrated IB into the life of the school.'

Delving below these very strong performances, it's possible to detect hints of the underlying academic culture. Competence and hard work abound: pupils and staff are ambitious for success and share in the prevailing ethos that academic attainment is a huge part of school life, but emphatically not the whole deal. Great care is taken of those needing learning support, with five specialist staff catering for them – at no extra cost in the normal way.

Those who join the Section Française follow the French Ministry of Education curriculum in French lessons, and must be more-or-less fluent French speakers.

'The work ethos is excellent,' says the head, 'and the school has for long tried to maximise its pupils' potential to deliver: good teaching, enough homework, proper marking – all that'. He is also clear that, by taking careful incremental steps, the school must encourage its pupils to become ever more independent learners. 'It's tantalising,' says the head; 'we all want them to have that independence. But, of course, that involves loosening the reins a bit. Naturally, that can feel scary. So, we'll just move at a sensible pace, learning as we go.'

It's hard to believe Whitgift won't confront the challenge with its customary energy and integrity – a description which applies as much to the staff as pupils. School is, famously, a nursery for future heads. About 15 are doing teacher training at any one time. 'The only downside,' says the head, 'is that they then get a promotion and leave us'. Mainly a young staff body, with 12 old pupils currently teaching.

Games, options, the arts: Big numbers have helped to make Whitgift a home of serious schoolboy sport, but competition and teamwork run right through the school's DNA. Teams have won more than 120 national titles in the past five years: stalwart rugby and football, hockey and cricket – with nearly 30 school teams fielded in each. Over 40 sports are available, including superb athletics, modern pentathlon, tennis and golf. The sports facilities are magnificent – top-of-the-range everything: fitness centre, squash courts, indoor Olympic swimming pool, indoor and outdoor pitches of every kind. Only rowers are forced to take a coach ride. 'We can offer many things,' head acknowledges, 'but not our own river'. Many boys represent their country in a wide variety of sports, or go on to top-level sporting careers.

This same thoroughness and ambition shapes the school's cultural life: breath-taking music, with a symphony orchestra and a concert orchestra. There's also the Whitgift Chamber Orchestra, an ensemble composed of both Whitgift pupils and other talented boys and girls from the London area, which performs regularly at major national venues alongside the Royal Philharmonic Orchestra. There are two big choirs: the Whitgift Chamber Choir and Minster Choristers. Orchestras and choirs tour internationally, and play at major venues, including the Royal Albert Hall, Royal Festival Hall and Cadogan Hall.

Cracking drama, and a lot of it. 'It's as good, at least, as its sport,' said one parent, whose children have experienced both. The main assembly hall converts to a tiered-seating theatre for major productions; there is also a separate performing arts centre and concert hall for smaller productions. Very democratic feel: opportunities for boys of all ages, with some productions confined to particular year groups. Informal links with film companies have seen Whitgift boys take leading roles in TV productions and the West End. Some boys are also members of the National Youth Theatre. Recent plays include The Government Inspector, The Lion, the Witch and the Wardrobe and Doctor Faustus. The school is currently sponsoring a boy in his last year to run his own theatre company. 'We try to make everything possible,' says the head, 'if that seems consistent with good sense'.

More than 80 clubs meet at different times during the week. As well as over 200 pupils engaged at any time in the Duke of Edinburgh Award, there is also a CCF with over 400 pupils in its ranks. Worth mentioning that two local state schools take part in this – a very natural way to achieve outreach. One recent trip involved boys spending a week at a marine commando training centre. Service culture runs deep within the school's DNA: there are currently 38 Old Whitgiftians serving in the army. The school also pioneered an exceptional (surely unique) exhibition Remembering 1916 – Life on the Western Front – a homage to the sacrifice of lives (of old pupils among others) made during the First World War, brilliantly showcasing its social sensitivity, historical skills and an acute awareness of its own past.

Boarding: Whitgift's decision to open a boarding house in 2013 was an eloquent statement of self-belief. Many established boarding schools have come to rely increasingly on overseas boarders to make their existing establishments viable, but Whitgift has catered for a versatile market – over 50 per cent of whom live in the UK. The house is superbly comfortable and well-equipped (top flight IT equipment, study areas, en-suite bathrooms and spacious, communal social areas with kitchen facilities), but feels a considerable social success as well. Full boarding for some (mainly from overseas) but also weekly boarding, which between them account for over 100 pupils, of whom about half stay over the weekends. There's also flexi-boarding for interested day pupils between 13 and 18. As well as the housemaster and tutors, there's also a head of boarding who represents boarders' interests within the school's senior leadership team.

A strong sense of identity and conviviality seem to have evolved over the past years in this fledgling boarding community. This has no doubt been helped by the school's determination to ensure that its facilities are made available for boarders out-of-hours, and to exploit the endless resources of London: the result has been to foment a palpable energy and excitement.

Background and atmosphere: Strong sense of a place at ease with itself. Great investment of time and energy from all constituencies for local causes – visits to primary schools, elderly and disadvantaged – as well as energetic fundraising. Pupils and staff communicate an aura of being glad to be here, but no grand public school airs and graces. 'That was what sold us,' said one father. 'We wanted our son to have a busy and fulfilling life, but the sense of entitlement one sees in some schools was completely alien.' Manners are easy, with evident fondness as well as respect for others. All staff we met emphasised the diversity of the intake – socially and ethnically: middle-class affluent children from the Surrey and Sussex borders, but plenty from south London who are anything but. Nearly 50 per cent of the children here are being financially supported.

Excellent concentration by pupils evident in each of the classes visited, but with a style of comfortable interaction that made it all believable. Head is currently two-thirds of the way through marathon one-to-one interviews with all teaching staff and says, 'one theme recurs, time and time again. I ask them "What should I change?" And they, virtually every time, say "don't change the kids".'

Pastoral care, well-being and discipline: Form tutors are the everyday go-to teacher, especially for the younger pupils. These feed concerns into heads of year who work alongside heads of upper and lower school. It's a tried and trusted structure, but what really seems to make it work is the calibre of pupil-staff relationships. Head is quick to praise his predecessor who was 'way ahead of the game in pastoral matters, and a big support of counselling, long before it was fashionable'. The school currently has three counsellors. All pupils are also members of a house which has come to be a vehicle for much more than just competitive sports. 'Increasingly,' says the head, 'it's a focus of all kinds of activity – plays, concerts and so forth – but also of identity.' One or two parents wondered out loud at the intensity of life. 'Mainly I'm delighted,' said one, 'but there is a cost: my children are pretty often exhausted.'

A conservative society – no doubt about that. Zero-tolerance on drugs and, the head adds, 'we make it perfectly clear that, 'when you're a member of Whitgift, you're a member seven days a week, 365 days a year. Boundaries are important at any time.' As he acknowledges, that tough line can risk 'the chop falls on someone more unlucky than anything else'. No recent exclusions, however. There is a 'headmaster's detention' on Saturdays for medium-serious infractions – something which, Mr Ramsey admits, with a twinkle in his eye, he is not called to supervise.

Pupils and parents: Full communication between home and school: termly reports, and at least one major parents' evening annually for each year group. In a school with a much broader socioeconomic constituency than some independent schools, the accessibility and approachability of staff is much valued.

Screeds of distinguished old pupils – Chris Cook, present editor of Newsnight, is a recent notable, and also Martin Jarvis and Derren Brown. Back in the day, Sir Bernard Crick and Lord Tedder also attended.

Entrance: Notwithstanding the huge numbers on the pupil roll, Whitgift is a highly selective school. Around 800 applicants at 11+ last year for the 180 places on offer. It evidently welcomes boys who are able, but likes them to be willing to contribute in a whole raft of activities. Entrance process inevitably emphasises the academic and the school is equally glad to receive pupils from independent or state schools. Main entry points are at 10+, 11+ and 13+ but a limited number of places are also available to boys at 12+ and 14+. The entrance examination concentrates on mathematics, English and verbal reasoning for younger applicants, while older ones sit papers in mathematics, English and science. Section Française applicants will also sit a test in French. Some overseas applicants may take EAL exams. If all goes well enough, they then come for an interview.

Prospective sixth form entrants need seven GCSE passes at grades 9-7 and sit the entrance examination in two of their subjects choices for A level or higher level IB.

Exit: There is no formal bar for getting into the sixth form for internal pupils; however, some do decide to move elsewhere at this point.

In 2018, five to Oxbridge and eight medics. Whitgift boys, once launched in life, often do exceptionally well – often far outstripping those pupils from schools with results even glitzier than theirs. Maths and chemistry results seem particularly strong, with a slight but perceptible bias among students towards STEM subjects – so often the default setting for ambitious pupils these days.

Money matters: The school allocates significant resources for means-tested bursaries. These are targeted at day pupils, but the school has made boarding awards available for boys of exceptional talent who might benefit from boarding. There are art/design/engineering and music and drama awards, as well as academic scholarships. Nearly 50 per cent of the students here are on some form of financial support – a consequence of generations of philanthropy and of the massive contribution of school luminaries and well-wishers.

Remarks: An outstanding school, through and through. Despite the peacocks parading on the lawn, nobody round here is preening. We happened to bump into a great throng of pupils at the local train station and were struck by their combination of energy, cheerfulness and calm courtesy. The head's confidence in them, the staff and parents is a good augury. Yet he is also alert to the irreducible truth that the school is massively privileged. 'We do need to keep helping them see the extent of the privilege they enjoy,' he admits. 'So that we help them become more automatic givers.'

William Ellis School

Linked with LaSWAP Sixth Form Consortium

Highgate Road, London NW5 1RN

Ages 11–18 **Pupils** 845 **Sixth form** 230; joint sixth form with Parliament Hill School, part of LaSWAP

020 7267 9346
www.williamellis.camden.sch.uk

Head: Since 2011, Sam White, chemistry graduate and previously deputy head of the London Oratory. Good news, say parents: 'He

W

has an exceptionally good manner with boys and parents.' 'The boys like and respect him.' 'Whenever I go in I see him chatting with a boy, and he seems to be genuinely interested in them.' A pupil concurred. 'He has been really keen to get to know us all. He is a good influence on us.'

He was appointed after the school had suffered a budget deficit, got through two heads in quick succession and been slated by Ofsted. A year into his tenure, Ofsted returned and pronounced the school 'good', quoting a teacher's remark that 'The headteacher is leading and pulling everyone here along.'

He felt that he was taking on 'a challenge, but manageable... it was a school that desperately wanted to improve'. His first job was tackling behaviour – 'we needed to re-establish clear boundaries' – and his first two years saw a high rate of temporary exclusions, which has now dropped significantly. He has also continued the work on improving the quality of teaching and, despite some initial staff turnover, maintained teacher morale and encouraged staff to work collaboratively to produce good schemes of work.

Camden is one of the few areas of the country where no schools have converted to academies, and the local secondary schools (which collaborate as a joint sixth form, LaSWAP) work closely together.

Academic matters: Huge ability range, with year 7 reading ages ranging from 8 to 17. In 2018, 63 per cent of pupils got 9-4 in both English and maths at GCSE, with 15 per cent 9-7 grades. Parents report that English, once a weak point, has been turned round by the 'very impressive' HoD; the school now teaches the IGCSE English language.

The school has a language specialism, and everyone starts French in year 7, with around half studying it to GCSE. School has links with the nearby Collège Français Bilingue de Londres. Most take up either Spanish or German in year 8 (offered in alternate years), but this is no longer compulsory, and some spend extra time on English fluency instead. Latin and Mandarin are taught in clubs, and fundraising enabled a recent sixth form Mandarin and geography trip to China.

Around a quarter of boys take single sciences to GCSE. Those with a more vocational bent can take OCR science, and choose from various other courses with a large coursework element such as business studies, travel and tourism, and ICT. Some spend a day a week in years 10 and 11 at Westminster Kingsway College studying eg catering, construction or motor mechanics. New food tech facilities open on site in 2019.

Fluid grouping rather than setting across the curriculum from year 8 (school hopes to group maths and science from year 7 in future) at the discretion of each faculty head. 'If a set of boys has a particular weakness in a subject we may put them together for a term, but there's plenty of movement.' Some parents would prefer more rigorous setting, but praise the willingness of staff to go the extra mile for boys at all levels. 'They will take time and a lot of patience with those who are bright but not pulling their finger out. I don't feel they are just settling for the easiest way of getting them through exams.'

Parents are mostly optimistic, though one complained about a lack of homework. 'We've found the teaching really good so far,' said another. 'My son is very happy here and seems to be doing well.' 'My son, who is very academic, is being well supported,' said another. 'I had severe reservations about some of the teaching during my son's early years here,' said a long-standing parent, 'but I don't now. I've never felt I had to get a tutor in.'

Teaching assistants are increasingly being trained to help with particular subjects, or with behavioural or language difficulties, rather than being velcroed to a particular child. The school uses some of its pupil premium funding (alongside sponsorship) on its City Year team of volunteers, who act as mentors, support teachers in class, run breakfast and homework clubs and supervise in the playground. The funding also helps with small group and one-to-one teaching, particularly in English, as well as counselling and interventions to improve attendance.

Joint sixth form with Parliament Hill School, which is part of the LaSWAP consortium that also includes La Sainte Union and Acland Burghley. This enables a wide range of courses including a choice of 41 A levels, as well as BTecs, NVQs, vocationally applied subjects and post-16 GCSEs. Students stay in their base school (which for William Ellis boys will be their own school or Parliament Hill) for the majority of lessons, but may go elsewhere for minority subjects. In 2018, 15 per cent A*/A and 42 per cent A*-B grades.

As well as working with Camden to provide one-to-one careers advice, school uses Future First, set up by old Elysians, to help it keep in touch with alumni and get them involved in giving careers advice, work experience and mentoring. It organises career sessions here and brings back old boys to talk about their work.

Games, options, the arts: A large trophy on the head's table when we visited is the house cup. Houses (named after local historic buildings: Lauderdale, Burgh, Willow, Keats and Fenton) are run by 'young, enthusiastic staff'. Pupils gain house points by competing at sports and taking part in talent shows, spelling bees, chess, model building, cake sales et al.

Year 7 and year 9 have a week camping at the school's field centre, The Mill, in Surrey. Boys also go on ski trips, language exchanges and field trips. 'The extracurricular activities have improved markedly over the past few years,' said a parent, citing her son's sessions at the Royal College of Music, playwriting with professionals, theatre and concert trips, Model UN.

Football and basketball are the most popular team sports, but rugby is up and coming – the RFU provides coaching and talented players are encouraged to join local clubs. The eight table tennis tables get enthusiastic use. Takes part in the annual Camden Shield boys' competition, which sees teams from six Camden secondary schools compete in football, table tennis, basketball, badminton, athletics and cricket. Pupils report that team sports peter out in the higher years: 'The teachers do try, but we tend to get a bit lazy in years 10 and 11.' The school has a newish sports hall, with facilities for PE and basketball and a multi-gym, and the playground doubles up as five-a-side football pitches. Sadly, the school cannot afford to hire the field next door, groomed for cricket when we visited, but it does play games on other parts of Parliament Hill Fields and uses the athletics track there. Clubs include cricket, running and trampoline.

Light top floor art rooms display impressive work; a sixth former was recently a finalist in the Camden Art Competition, and students have exhibited their work at the local Lauderdale House. Some parents find the music provision underwhelming, but there are choirs, ensembles and a range of concerts for all, from beginners to advanced musicians, often in conjunction with Parliament Hill School and La Sainte Union, which form a joint orchestra with WE. There are also workshops and masterclasses run by professional musicians. The head of music 'has been very supportive of my son writing and performing his own music,' said a parent, and a school group recently reached the finals of the Roundhouse Band Slam competition. School subsidises instrumental lessons for boys on free school meals.

Not a school that goes in for full-scale musicals, but has recently opened a new drama studio and there are many smaller drama performances, such as the recent drama club interpretations of the Ancient Mariner and Christmas Eve in the Trenches at the Winter Concert. Pupils work with outside organisations such as the Donmar Warehouse, and take part in the Shakespeare Schools Festival. 'They do it thoroughly and well,' said a parent.

Background and atmosphere: William Ellis was a public-spirited businessman who founded several schools in the mid-19th century, believing children should be taught 'useful' subjects such as science and to develop their reasoning faculties, rather than rote-learning religious tracts and ancient languages. William Ellis School, the only one of his schools that still exists, was founded in Gospel Oak in 1862 and recognised as a boy's secondary school in 1889. It moved to its present site, on the edge of Parliament Hill Fields, in 1937. Originally a grammar school, it turned comprehensive in 1978; the red-brick vine-clad buildings still have a grammar school feel. Brand new sixth form study centre.

'My son has had a very happy time here,' said a parent. 'He has a sense of belonging and pride in his school. It fosters a nice attitude and spirit in the boys – confident but not arrogant.'

Pastoral care, well-being and discipline: The head's tightening up on discipline and appointment of an effective head of pastoral care have helped to cut down on the low level disruption that once marred many lessons, and has made boys feel safer inside and out. 'They are much stricter on uniform than they used to be, and you no longer have to hack your way through a posse of boys smoking round the gate,' said a parent. Year 7 has its own quad, with table tennis and picnic tables. The year 7 head has links with most of the feeder primary schools, and boys are invited to summer school before they start.

One parent commented: 'The pastoral care is very good. A few years ago I went through a difficult divorce and they were brilliant at supporting my son.' Another said, 'Whenever I've emailed to ask questions, I've had an immediate and pleased reply. They are extremely responsive to an interested/meddling parent.'

Increasing emphasis on carrots rather than sticks, with boys earning house praise points for good work and good attitudes, from persistence to creativity. 'Relationships can be much more relaxed once ground rules are established,' says the head. Deep Learning Days, part of the PHSE curriculum, see timetables dropped for a day in favour of discussions on relationships, including peer pressure and bullying, careers and the world of work, with plenty of outside speakers. 'We try to make it circular – get the boys to present back to their peers what they have learned. Recently 25 year 9 boys did a play for the rest of the school.' One parent commented on her despondency at a lack of creativity in the PHSE teaching, but another said, 'They are very good at raising the boys' social and political awareness. They don't shy away from issues that can be sensitive, such as homophobia and religion.'

Pupils and parents: Huge ethnic mix, with less than a third of pupils from white British background, and others ranging from Irish to Turkish to Somalian. Wide social spread, from the large social housing estates of Gospel Oak to the multi-million pound houses of Dartmouth Park. 'There were cliques lower down the school, but in years 10 and 11 everyone hangs out together and we all get on,' said a pupil. 'The fact that the boys come from a huge range of backgrounds doesn't seem to matter one bit, which is a very impressive trick for a school to pull off,' said a parent. Old Elysians include Toby Young, Robert Elms, Sean French, Andrew Sachs and Len Deighton.

Entrance: Usual admissions criteria for 130 year 7 places: looked after children, medical and social need, siblings, up to 12 musical aptitude places, then by distance (usually up to about two miles). Generally around 300 outside places for LaSWAP sixth form consortium, with an intricate admissions system and a range of entry requirements for different levels of courses.

Exit: Most (65 per cent) to LaSWAP sixth form. Some go off to eg Camden School for Girls, Woodhouse College, St Marylebone, Fortismere or FE colleges. Around 20 per cent of LaSWAP leavers to Russell Group universities. Destinations in 2018 ranged from economics and Spanish at Reading to banking and finance at Middlesex to film practice at South Bank.

Money matters: Voluntary aided by the William Ellis and Birkbeck Schools Trust, but otherwise is as hard up as most other state schools.

Remarks: Small boys' comprehensive in idyllic situation on the borders of Hampstead Heath, now emerging rapidly from the doldrums under strong, popular and enthusiastic head. 'It can only get better and better,' said a satisfied parent.

William Tyndale Primary School

Upper Street, London, Middlesex N1 2GG

Ages 3–11 Pupils 450

020 7226 6803
www.williamtyndale-islington.co.uk

Head: Since 2005, Tanya Watson BMus NPQH (50s). She was raised in America (there's still a suspicion of an accent), then trained as a concert pianist at the Royal Academy of Music. While developing her performance career, she started taking pupils, and was so taken with teaching she decided to commit full time. Undoubtedly a good decision for William Tyndale, since, over the past decade or so, she's carefully nurtured this always popular primary into one of the borough's star attractions. Articulate, organised and capable, she's at the gates every day and is widely admired. 'She's a very strong leader and provides a real sense of order and reassurance,' said one parent. 'She's both very approachable and a little bit formidable,' said another. What parents particularly respect about her, however, is her commitment to extending beyond the expected. 'She's filled my children with confidence and given them opportunities I couldn't have anticipated.'

Entrance: Parent tours held twice a year by appointment through the school office. sixty reception places allocated via Islington Council. After the usual priority categories (including siblings and the children of long-serving staff), entrance is based on distance from the gates (adjudicated by a computerised mapping system). Needless to say, you have to live very, very close (within less than 0.2 miles). The school then operates a waiting list.

Exit: To well over 20 different schools. Popular local choices include Highbury Grove, Highbury Fields, City of London Academy and Stoke Newington, but a sprinkling across the northern reaches of the capital, including to Camden School for Girls and Mossbourne Community Academy. Last year, 14 (three with scholarships) to independents, including Highgate, City of London (boys and girls), and Forest.

Remarks: From the outside William Tyndale, which recently celebrated its centenary, seems a bit of a fortress, commanding the playground and lording it over the children below. Recent additions and a carefully modernised interior have softened the tone, with an inviting streamlined entrance, spic-and-span classrooms and up-to-date facilities (including plans for improved science space).

This is a school where the phrase 'every child matters' is definitely not empty rhetoric. Teachers take time to make detailed analysis of progress and, while standards are immutable, the approach to obtaining them is often tailor made. Results – for everyone – speak for themselves, with children, whatever their background, performing well above expected (and national) standards.

Literacy (undoubtedly a strength) is reinforced (and reinforced again) throughout the timetable. Classes named after famous children's authors (Morpurgo, Rosen, Dahl, etc) and class assemblies give plenty of opportunity to explore their namesakes. Lewis class, for example, not only delivered fascinating facts about the author of the Narnia books, but wrote its own wintry poems, did a snowflake dance, and used castles to discuss structures. Lots of learning poetry by heart, and older pupils take part in a school-wide poetry recital. Maths, too, made fun, with activities, such as the (prize-gaining) Multiplication Bee. Sky-high expectations for all, so timetabled Latin (with proper vocab tests, etc) from year 3 because the head believes 'it improves writing across the curriculum, helps pupils understand the nuts and bolts of English and provides a strong cultural base for their understanding of history.'

Other non-standard enrichment includes regular chess. 'The national curriculum can be a bit thin,' said one mother, 'but William Tyndale provides all the extra flourishes.' Dedicated librarian develops library skills. IT facilitated by iPads throughout. Recently relaunched homework strategy now targets individual needs. ('After consulting parents, the school stopped sending home those projects we all used to do. Now we get homework we know is right for our kids.') Outdoor classroom where all pupils work with the school's 'environmental educator', maintaining both a 'wildlife' and 'growing' garden (with fruit and veg contributed to school dinners).

SEND well supported – at both ends of the spectrum. Three specialists help with reading recovery ('Fantastic,' said a beneficiary) and other challenges. Extra tuition provided before school and during breaks so 'everyone has fair access'. One of the top performing schools in the country, too, for boosting the performance of disadvantaged pupils.

William Tyndale is a school where curricular and extracurricular do not operate in separate spheres. Art is 'exceptional', 'inspirational', 'really wonderful, chorused parents. The school has its own art block and artist in residence, and juniors study art for two hours a week and work with external arts organisations (Stamped Arts, Cubitt Artists) on large-scale projects, such as the chronological history of the school which lines the stairs. Pupils can also gain an Arts Award Explore qualification, by participating in arts activities (for example, the school's Film Club), attending arts events and keeping a portfolio. Understandably, the school has gained an Arts Council Artsmark Gold award.

Music, too, exceptionally strong, with weekly, specialist-taught music lessons in the dedicated music studio. Free recorder lessons for all in year 3, and Hackney Music Hub provides tutors in African dance and drumming in year 4 and samba in year 5. Instrumental lessons (recorder, flute, cello, brass, clarinet) also available. School orchestra plus two choirs (infant and juniors), with regular opportunities to perform in school (musical assemblies, shows, concerts) and outside (Pure Voice, Hackney Music Festival). School won a Sing Up gold award in 2016, and head undoubtedly brings her own expertise to bear. 'After a concert, she will pick out and discuss various themes,' said a parent.

Sport dynamic. Dance, gymnastics, cricket and rounders all on offer, with expert coaches imported for lessons and clubs. ('My daughter was taught by coaches from Arsenal, which she absolutely loved.') Swimming lessons at Highbury Pool. A rare primary school with a third-generation floodlit football pitch (available for hire to aid school's coffers), in constant use for lunch-hour sporting activities and inter-school competitions (mini Olympics, netball and football tournaments). Keen competitors in the Islington Primary School Football League (with both girls' and boys' teams highly successful), and in local hockey matches (with co-ed team), tag rugby and athletics tournaments.

Comprehensive programme of London visits (Geffrye Museum, Museum of London, Central Mosque etc), and extensive range of clubs (sports, music, creative writing, book club etc) with debating club notably strong. (Pupils recently won the London Primary Debate Mate Cup, confronting such knotty questions as: 'This house believes that people should break the law to save the environment', and 'This house believes that children should be paid for good exam results'.)

School is relaxed and informal, but not slack. No uniform and reasonably scruffy end-of-day look, but no question of come-as-you-please, so no jewellery, nail varnish or hair dye (to prevent jealousy). Masses of positive reinforcement for pupils (with awards for attendance and punctuality) and praise for parents (for making sure kids stay off playground equipment after school). Parents encouraged, too, to talk to teachers about concerns as they arise rather than bottle it all up until parents' evening. Draconian measures, however, for late pick up from (privately run) after-school club. (£20 fine, which increases by £1 a minute per child.) Atmosphere widely praised by all. 'It's a lovely community, very friendly, very disciplined,' said one father. 'It's very uncompetitive, and children are encouraged to help each other. I just don't worry about the children once they've gone in. I feel they're in very good hands.'

Parents a broad mix, so the expected chattering-class professionals (overheard in the playground: 'I forgot your smoothie, have you got a banana?'), but also 35 per cent on pupil premium, and wide ethnic range. Dads unusually well represented at after-school collection.

Parents here are well organised and generous. The William Tyndale Charitable Trust was set up to raise funds for school improvement, and has helped finance significant capital projects, including the new performance stage and sports pitch (£5,000), playground equipment (£10,000) and stairwell art project (£6,000). Regular money-raising events include the quiz night, summer fair and weekly cake sales.

Parents overwhelmingly delighted with William Tyndale. 'I feel so lucky. It's completely brilliant. I can't praise it highly en ough.'

Wilson's School

Mollison Drive, Wallington, Surrey SM6 9JW

Ages 11–18 **Pupils** 1,198 **Sixth form** 311

020 8773 2931
www.wilsonsschool.sutton.sch.uk

Head: Since 2014, Nathan Cole BA PGCE (30s), previously deputy head. Read history at Nottingham and was a postgrad at Cambridge. Began his teaching career at Saffron Walden County High and joined Wilson's in 2006, rising through the ranks to become deputy head in 2010. 'The school is in my blood. I love the bones of the place,' he says.

Born and bred in Yorkshire (where he was the first person in his family to go to university), his boyish looks and exuberance mean you could be forgiven for fleetingly mistaking him for one of the pupils. But rest assured your slip-up will be momentary – he is known for his authoritative strength of character and exacting standards. And it is this, combined with his sparky wit and playful banter, which has won him such great respect among the students. 'This school was great before he came along, but it's pretty much faultless now.' 'He's strict, but always fair and never stuffy.' Parents similarly gushing. 'A more committed, approachable and efficient headteacher you will not find.' 'He makes the boys feel they own the successes of this school, not him – and that generosity of spirit ripples through the whole school.'

The kind of head who is as at ease doing lunch duty as teaching PSHE to year 7s as tutoring sixth formers (all of which he does), he says, 'How can I put this? I'm not your stereotypical six foot two silver-haired grammar school head and I do not sit in an ivory tower.'

Lives a nine-minute (yes, it's that precise) drive away in Purley; he is a keen musician, 'fair-weather tennis player' and an expert on the history of Italian fascism. 'If I get the chance, I also enjoy eating in decent restaurants, although mostly it's the school canteen for me.'

Academic matters: One of a handful of grammars in the area, all high achieving, this one stands out for getting even better results than the others, as well as its supportive, 'we're-all-in-this-together' ethos, and as such makes for a friendly environment in which the innately clever child can thrive.

Boys achieve startlingly good results – in 2018, 85 per cent 9-7 grades at GCSE. Ten-and-a-half GCSEs are the norm – eight core, including separate sciences, while the half refers to the short RE course. Strongest results in maths (so many finish with A*s that it's practically de rigueur), English and languages, while the most popular non-core subjects include business, history and geography (also more musicians than the norm). Setting from year 9 in maths, sciences, English and all languages except Latin. But with the bottom sets still getting 9-8s, there's no real stigma about being in lower ones – and regular assessments ensure plenty of movement across sets. 'All that testing is quite a shock at first, but it's a good way of making you realise that natural talent alone doesn't cut it here – you need to work really hard too,' one boy told us. Homework heavy in year 7, drops in year 8, then picks up pace again in year 9, according to the boys. Languages start with French or German in year 7, with some boys picking up Spanish in year 9.

In sixth form, boys select four A levels from a modest menu of traditional subjects (not a whiff of photography, business studies, psychology etc), plus either a formal extended project qualification (EPQ) or an internally assessed project. Maths, daddy of the big hitter subjects here, is taken by all but a handful of sixth formers, with exceptional results, although surprisingly few (around 10) boys take it at degree (with most using it for degrees such as engineering or economics). Other particularly well-liked A levels include sciences and economics. Overall, 96 per cent A*-B (79 per cent A*/A) at A level in 2018.

Notable repartee between boys and teachers, while also respectful on both sides. 'The teachers are so into their subjects here,' one boy enthused. 'We came out of a maths lesson the other day, only to find that half-an-hour later the teacher emailed us excitedly about something she'd worked out that was relevant to the lesson.'

You could hear a pin drop in the corridors – despite the open doors of the classrooms – when we visited, with straight-backed, silent and captivated boys hanging onto every word of the animated teachers. 'Not all lessons are like this – they can be very interactive, especially the further you move up the school,' one of our tour guides assured us. Lots of extra help on offer, with regular review discussions and valued catch-up clubs in just about every subject, introduced originally for GCSE pupils but now, by popular demand, run from year 7 – often by a combined effort of sixth form and subject staff. Support also for those with learning difficulties, with some Asperger's and dyslexia cropping up now and then (seven statemented when we visited), although more than one boy told us, 'I don't know anyone with SEN,' with one adding, 'it isn't really a school for people educational problems.' Head, however, says, 'I think this is a good thing – that boys are not labelled as SEN.'

Games, options, the arts: Sport excels here, although it doesn't tend to be a deciding factor for parents. 'We'd choose this school every time even if they didn't own a tennis ball between them,' said one. Great outside facilities, certainly by south London standards (including 13 Astroturf courts and sizable fields – no time wasted on coaches here). Good range of sports, including less predictable offerings such as table tennis, rugby (a growth area) and climbing. Fixtures every weekend, in which the school does particularly well in football, cricket and badminton. And for the less or non sporty? 'We have some F teams,' said one boy. 'If you like football, but you don't excel at it, nobody cares,' said another. 'And if you don't like sports at all, that's also fine – people would just accept you might prefer, say, music or drama.' And with chess considered a sport here (hundreds play and succeed on the national stage), it's probably not something you're likely to hear anyway. Regular sports tours, mostly within Europe, with the odd exotic opportunity thrown in, such as cricket in Barbados. Some Olympic hopefuls in badminton.

Signs of artistic talent abound, with some inspired pieces on display in the snazzy exhibition area. But it's DT that really gets the artistic juices going here, not least because it's valued on 'serious' academic courses such as chemical engineering. Unusually, life drawing classes are taken from GCSE up (and very good the results are, too).

Music, meanwhile, is superb, with every year 7 boy learning an instrument with a peripatetic teacher. Upshot is a 150-piece wind band debuting at Christmas – with many boys developing a love of music they may not otherwise have had, plus lively membership among the various school orchestras and ensembles. 'Music has gone through an extraordinary transformation and the wonderful thing about it is that it's not just about producing excellent musicians, but seeing the boys stamp their feet with glee at the end of the concert because of their teamwork – and seeing the orchestra exploding in size,' one parent said. Choirs also popular, with an excellent barbershop including recent performances of Haydn's Nelson Mass and Mozart's Requiem.

You only have to mention the word 'drama' and boys' eyes light up, with everything from drama soirées to junior and senior productions providing opportunities not just in acting but in lighting, sound production, costume and set design etc (plus opportunities for keen musicians too). 'I stage managed our recent production of Midsummer Night's Dream and it was the best show I've ever been involved in,' said one student – one of many who took pains to tell us that no play is staid here, each given a modern twist. 'You should have seen us doing the set design – we even found an old unwanted bath chucked in a skip that we wound up using in the play.'

Extracurricular life is buzzing, with boys (especially in lower years) reeling off lists of all they do – not just in sports (although they dominate), but philosophy, chess, rocket clubs etc. Many are student-led, with past students having set up everything from Rubik's cube club to knitting club – 'to say some of the boys are quirky here would be an understatement,' says the head. Tip-top CCF (now one of the largest in the country in conjunction with a local girls' school – the military camouflage outfits were out in force when we visited) and D of E to gold award also on offer.

Background and atmosphere: Many grammars give the impression of being a throwback to the 1950s. This one doesn't – 'deliberately,' says school. Founded in the 17th century in Camberwell and, with the exception of a 38-year closure in the 19th century after a financial scandal, going strong ever since and celebrated its 400th anniversary in 2015. In 1975, lured by the space and local council's pro-grammar stance, it moved to its current premises, once part of Croydon Airport, and commemorated in nearby street names like Dakota Close and Hurricane Road.

While it's no looker from the outside – with square brown buildings set uncompromisingly in a large, plain playing field – the interiors aren't half bad. Corridors might be on the pre-loved side, but the classrooms, full of lovingly tended displays, more than make up for it. Science labs, too, slightly dishevelled from the outside, are a hive of well-resourced activity within.

No shortage of impressive large scale areas, either, including the traditional main hall – recently refurbished and a large sports hall and gym. But there are also more intimate and surprisingly luscious touches. The south canteen – as distinct from north canteen – (they don't go a bundle on fancy names; library has resolutely not morphed into a learning resource centre, for example) has cutting edge lighting, un-school-like black and orange walls and doubles as an attractive additional concert venue. Years 7-8 now have own new lower school with dining hall and classrooms, and there's also a mobile eatery for boys who want to wolf down something to eat then get onto the playing fields. Sixth form common room given a recent facelift.

Pupils whizz purposefully round the site, without so much as a skew-whiff tie in sight (instant black mark if they did).

Pastoral care, well-being and discipline: Motto is 'Non sibi sed omnibus' (not for oneself but for all) and boys, parents and staff wax lyrical about how it underpins every aspect of school life. 'Boys are so positive about each other's achievements – and so encouraging of each other even if they're not the best at something,' one parent told us. Approachable form tutors are first point of contact for pupils and parents, who stay with the same group for two to three years – 'very easy to talk to if you have any concern at all,' said a parent. Unusually, each form has two tutors throughout years 7-11, with pupils in years 9-11 registered and tutored in small groups of 15. First class transition arrangements, with year 7s taking precedence in the lunch queue during their first term.

As with any highly academic school, anxiety can be a problem. 'But they're good at pinpointing early onset symptoms and treating them quickly,' said one parent whose son became anxious – and there's a reassuring amount of talk among boys and staff (including head) around mental health awareness. Ditto with bullying, which boys say is 'extremely rare.' On-site counselling is available one day a week, plus occasional peer mentoring offered – and there's also a school nurse. 'One of the most important things for me is that boys feel able to be open about their feelings,' says head.

This is a strict school and they make no bones about what constitutes unacceptable behaviour, with the tiered detention system used widely ('You get more in the lower years so you learn your lessons early,' said one boy). But there's some wiggle room, with a warning system when it comes to things like late homework, for example, and even the penalty is a starter detention lasting 10 minutes. With plenty of chances to step back from the brink – and all school rules backed up with logical reasoning – pupils considered the system a fair one. No permanent exclusions in recent history, but a handful of temporary ones most years.

Mobile phones allowed only if they're switched off and locked away (and no photographic equipment allowed on phones for years 7/8), although some teachers may give permission to use them in some lessons – for instance for a dictionary in German lesson. Rules relaxed in the sixth form centre.

Pupils and parents: Pupils are an utter delight. Courteous, chatty and good-humoured (and – joy of joys – not entitled; 'I can't bear entitlement,' says head), they have an almost evangelical desire to draw you into their world and tell you about every aspect of the school. Families encompass every major culture and religion and, currently, speak 40 languages between them – a source of great pride for the school. As to parental involvement, there's a PA, which raises significant sums of money through its social events – 'but there's no pressure to get involved if it's not for you,' said a parent.

Alumni include actor Michael Caine, fashion designer John Galliano, opera singer Mark Stone, mountaineer Paul Deegan and aviator Sir Alan Cobham.

Entrance: Ignore the horror headlines of 10 applicants per place – the reality is more like four to one, with boys coming from around 75 feeder schools and no set catchment area ('although few travel more than 10/15 minutes to get here'). By law, there's no advantage in having a brother here (much to head's disappointment).

Two-stage entrance process, which you have to register for by mid-August. First, the selective eligibility test – the same for all Sutton schools, which involves English and maths multiple choice questions. 'All pretty average stuff,' says head. Those who are successful then invited to a second-stage (and notoriously harder – 'but not ridiculously hard') test, specific to the school, involving English and maths open-ended questions. 'There's no verbal or non-verbal reasoning because we know this is the bit you can coach children to succeed in.' For the same reason, doesn't make past papers available.

Total of 180 places offered in March to highest placed candidates and where there's a tie break, Sutton children have preference with distance to school the final deciding factor. None of the boys who get a place is told his mark, says head. 'I don't want boys to say, "I was in position X." I want them to come in seeing themselves as equals. Even the staff don't know the mark.'

No automatic entry into sixth form, with offers based on six 7s and individual criteria for subjects studied. Around 10-20 new boys join at this stage, most with at least six 9-8s.

Exit: Around 10 boys leave post-GCSE – for all the usual reasons such as relocation, wanting to join a co-ed or study a course this school doesn't offer (plus the odd one that doesn't meet the sixth form entrance criteria). As for the rest, it's top subjects and top universities (85 per cent Russell Group) in the main. In 2018, 26 to Oxbridge. Surrey, Nottingham, Imperial and Warwick among other popular destinations. Common subjects include medicine (17 in 2018), economics, dentistry and engineering – plus history and geography, albeit in smaller numbers. Head keen that boys don't feel forced own one single route, however – 'we had a boy doing a one-year apprenticeship at Jaguar, for example, which led to him doing his degree on the job.'

Remarks: Bright, clever and funny, and that's just the staff. Hard not to warm to a school where all the students do so well and with such grace. Boys here are hugely generous about other people's successes and learn to fly high without feeling they need to step over anyone else on the way – a valuable life lesson, if ever we saw one. Meanwhile, a wicked sense of humour ensures it remains a Pollyanna-free zone. A great place for boys who are effortlessly clever.

Wimbledon Chase Primary School

Merton Hall Road, London SW19 3QB

Ages 3–11 **Pupils** 630

020 8542 1413
www.wimbledonchaseschool.co.uk

Interim head: Deputy Keith Ellis is holding the fort whilst a new head is appointed.

Entrance: At 3+ to the nursery and 4+ into reception. Now expanded to three-form entry. Non-selective; applications must be made through Merton Council, usual admissions criteria. For occasional places in older age groups contact school or the council.

Exit: At 11+ majority to Ricards Lodge, Rutlish, Raynes Park, Ursuline or Wimbledon College. Others to Sutton Grammar, Nonsuch, Tiffin and Whitgift.

Remarks: Continues its long-held reputation for being one of Wimbledon's favourite choices for primary education. Very well thought of all round; academic expectations and achievements are high. Pupils are set by ability in maths from year 4. Stunning Starts, Marvellous Middles and Fabulous Finishes are how staff capture the children's imaginations and talents through the creative curriculum. Pupils are taught via many different media: lessons can include acting, music, dancing, art, design and technology. History and geography topics come alive through a variety of exciting activities. Everyone feels the positive impact and thrill of the creative curriculum; most notably these exciting projects have helped the children develop their writing skills. The arts make up an important part of the curriculum; full-time music teacher and specialist teachers for choir and orchestra also run brass groups, recorder club, drumming club and boomwackers percussion group. Teachers from Merton Music Foundation visit the school every day to give individual instrumental lessons. Musical evenings, assemblies, plays and concerts provide plenty of occasions for everybody to show off their performing skills.

Sizeable premises for a primary school, originally built as the girls' County Grammar in 1924. Playing fields, cricket pitch, tennis courts, a lovely wildlife area and gardens provide numerous outdoor and sporting opportunities. The children grow fruit, vegetables and flowers and are taught about which plants will attract particular birds and insects. Nursery and reception classes have their own specially-designed playgrounds attached to their classrooms, with new wing added to create space for expanded intake. Now space for 730 pupils. Stylishly-designed new building to accommodate classrooms, cookery room, specialist music rooms, an additional ICT suite, gymnasium and after-school care rooms. Some parents felt that the expansion and building would be disruptive for pupils, but now all appear to be in agreement that despite the odd hitch, the new space and facilities are an advantage for all.

W

Over 35 native languages are spoken by pupils; effective EAL programme; consequently nearly everyone does very well in Sats. Inclusion manager coordinates SEN, with two specialist teachers and a team of teaching assistants; also a visiting speech and language therapist and a play therapist. The school is fully wheelchair accessible and has a 16 place unit for children with speech, language and communication needs. Pupils attending the unit join with the main school in the afternoons for the creative curriculum, sports and music activities.

Exceptional range of clubs and activities. Friday film club run by a parent in conjunction with the British Film Institute has produced some successful young film critics. Far-reaching pastoral care; older pupils can train as peer mediators and playground buddies; any child feeling unhappy or needing to talk to an adult can post a note in the worry box. Parent support adviser is available to any parent who might wish to discuss their concerns. The Wrap Around Centre enables the school to offer a breakfast club, full-time nursery places and after-school care.

Parents are very much partners at Wimbledon Chase, assisting with hearing children read, clubs, general maintenance and the upkeep of the extensive grounds. Fundraising is also high on the strong PTA's agenda; dedicated parents' room, the nerve centre for meetings and a relaxing cuppa. Always keen to involve the wider community and improve their skills base: non-parent volunteers are welcome; a local volunteer has taken on responsibility for maintaining the wildlife garden.

An exceptional and innovative school and community with pupils, parents and staff all apparently delighted to play a part. Enthusiastic children bounce into school each morning eager to know what the day holds in store.

Wimbledon High Junior School

Linked with Wimbledon High School

Mansel Road,, London SW19 4AB

Ages 4–11 **Pupils** 330

Fees: £14,622 pa

020 8971 0902
www.wimbledonhigh.gdst.net

Head: Since 2003, Kate Mitchell BEd MA (50s). Formerly deputy head at Alleyn's Junior School, Ashville College Junior School, Harrogate and Stamford Junior School, Lincolnshire. Knows every girl and every parent. Parents say: 'easy to talk to, professional, approachable and dedicated'. Girls love her. Teaches verbal reasoning in preparation for 11+ and hears infant readers. Non-controversial.

Moving on in July 2019. Her successor will be Claire Boyd, currently head of Sydenham High Junior, and before that head of lower school and on the senior leadership team of Ravenscourt Park Prep. She has a politics degree from Royal Holloway College and a PGCE from Roehampton.

Entrance: Selective at 4+. Testing in November prior to entry. Specially designed, supposedly relaxing, activities in a nursery school environment. 'We're looking for potential, not what they already know.' If successful, a follow-up in January. More places available at 7+ when assessment covers English, maths and verbal reasoning, together with an interview that includes reading. Occasional places higher up. No sibling priority. Intake mainly from local Wimbledon and surrounds.

Exit: Most girls (around 80 per cent) move on to the senior school but take note, this is not guaranteed. Tests in year 4 identify those who may not make the grade and parents are pre-warned that their daughter 'could be better off in a senior school with a slightly slower pace'. This can also apply to less able siblings. All the rest offered senior places, some with academic or music scholarships.

Occasional moves to pastures new, often with a scholarship, recent destinations including St Paul's Girls' and Kingston Grammar. Some head for local grammars.

Remarks: A top school – a brilliant kick-off into the world of single-sex private education. Creative curriculum, ensures breadth and motivation, a desire to learn and discover. Based on literacy, tying in maths and linking in all other subjects in many different ways. Kate Mitchell says: 'Phenomenal! It really works.'

Our guides – happy, vivacious year 6s – obviously loved their school and were quick to show us everything that was going on. A library on every floor – 'we're at the top and ours is the best!' (Well, it did contain a large display of cups.) All children, from the youngest to the oldest, looked thoroughly involved in what they were doing and were keen to explain their activities to us. They grow up as they (literally) go up the school building.

We saw the youngest, at ground level, sitting on the floor or clustered round tables, listening to stories, gathered in small discussion groups, immersed in what they were doing: learning to learn. Easy access for outside play.

Upstairs, larger classes for the older children – average 24. Two years to each floor. Still a generally relaxed feeling of informality, outdoor clothes falling from their pegs in the corridors. Jolly-looking classrooms with plenty on the walls. Every child looked interested in what they were doing. Specialist labs for the older pupils. High tech equipment used but not excessively. IPads recently introduced into Y3 but school says not totally wedded to them yet. Homework for years 4, 5 and 6 periodically done online.

Nowhere is there a feeling of pressure, but these girls are definitely high achievers. Parents say: 'Girls are supported but not mollycoddled'; 'develop confidence as they go through'; 'well prepared for move to senior school'.

All children screened for SEN on entry and again in Y2. Approximately five per cent need extra help. Constant watch kept by the learning support coordinator who works with teachers to ensure all SEN pupils are accommodated in lesson plans – typically for barriers to learning such as dyslexia and dyspraxia. Progress tracked and peripatetic one-on-one help provided where needed. EAL not a problem despite the number of bilingual children in the school. Specialist coordinator/mentor for the gifted and talented.

Fantastic music, vocal and instrumental, a particular feature of the whole school. Plenty of opportunity to start early. Specialise in different instruments each year – percussion, recorder, keyboard, brass. Events, concerts, performances and regular musical shows. GDST Young Choir of the Year finalists recently; have sung at Queen Elizabeth Hall and the Royal Albert Hall. Musicals, concerts and plays put on in the ultra modern Rutherford Centre, which is much enjoyed by juniors and seniors alike.

Regular PE sessions in the gym and weekly swimming in the pool: amazing facilities for a relatively small school. Other sports played down the road on the site of the original All England Lawn Tennis Club. 'We set out to go there at a walk,' said a teacher, 'but after a while, we start to jog and then run there.'

What a pleasant surprise to find such a happy and purposeful school hidden away in a busy London suburb. On the whole the girls, and their parents, appear to appreciate it.

Wimbledon High School

Linked with Wimbledon High Junior School

Mansel Road, Wimbledon, London SW19 4AB

Ages 11–18 **Pupils** 640 **Sixth form** 170

Fees: £18,810 pa

020 8971 0900
www.wimbledonhigh.gdst.net

Headmistress: Since 2014, Jane Lunnon BA (Bristol) (40s). A North London Collegiate School alumna, read English at university and, after an initial career in marketing, decided she'd prefer to teach. Immediately found a job at Wellington College where 12 years saw her progressing to head of English and assistant director of studies. Then to Priors Field as head of sixth form and, later, deputy head. Returned to Wellington in 2010 as senior deputy to Anthony Seldon, who, she says, taught her to 'be ambitious in your aims'. She played a key role in the leadership team, working to increase the profile of girls in the school. Thence to Wimbledon High. She and her husband, who is still at Wellington, have two teenage children and live on the college premises.

Wedded to girls only education, Jane Lunnon is determined that 'academic excellence is underpinned by outstanding pastoral care within an engaging curriculum and equally stimulating co-curriculum'. She believes in the need to develop the girls' confidence and self-belief, combatting what she refers to as the 'intensity of self-effacement in women'. Says it's a real privilege to run a school so full of magic and alchemy with very bright girls and outstanding results. Believes in model leadership and that the girls should have 'the capacity to be secure and go out into the world with confidence'. Enthusiastic and talks non-stop – apparently very popular with parents. Warmly supported by the GDST, Jane Lunnon has exciting plans for development. What has been done already during her short tenure is mind-boggling.

One of only the GSG's second set of identical twin heads: her sister, Jenny Brown, took over as head of St Albans High in September 2014.

Academic matters: Without doubt an academic school. Testing starts at entrance level in the seniors and progression from the junior school is not automatic. Classes are bigger than many – up to 28 – but decrease when setting starts in year 9, averaging 22 for GCSE classes and fewer for A levels.

Senior school curriculum is broad and demanding. The 'gentle' years, before GCSE, introduce them to the joy of learning. They are encouraged to explore and challenge. Excellent support for all the core subjects but there is some feeling that optional subjects are assessed less frequently which, given that the girls are encouraged to cover a wide range, seems, to some, unfair. But, then, it depends on your feelings about assessment.. Some parents feel that they would like to see their daughters' course work assessments more often – 'it would be good to be more involved'.

Many GCSE subjects on offer and the last few years have seen a considerable shift to IGCSEs. Outstanding results. In 2018, 92 per cent A*-A/9-7 grades at GCSE and 70 per cent at A level (93 per cent A*/B). A double-edged sword this – some very bright girls are then tempted away by top schools with mixed sixth forms. However, there is also a steady stream coming in to the sixth from other schools, including some from the state system and rumour has it that some of the girls who leave WHS are not – as so often – completely happy with their moves.

Games, options, the arts: Not, historically, the sportiest of schools but that is changing. A fantastic swimming pool and large sports hall in the grounds, alongside great games facilities 10 minutes' walk away on the site of the old All England Lawn Tennis and Croquet Club. Parents say, 'it's a pity they don't swim regularly once a week'; nonetheless, they are rightly proud of their swimmers: national, county and regional prize winners; their hockey and netball teams who tour internationally every second year; their cricketers; and, recently, of their star rowers, one of whom came fourth in the National Junior Sculling Head. Skiing, taekwondo and fencing have also produced winners and there is an equestrian team waiting in the wings, an annual tennis tour to Portugal and a netball tour to Spain. So – a great range of sporting opportunities. Of course, they are also proud to ball-girl at the Wimbledon Tennis Championships every year. We met some of the Y7 sports enthusiasts and were impressed, not only with their achievements but also their confidence and ability to talk about them.

Very strong in music and drama. Fantastic music, vocal and instrumental, a particular feature of the whole school. Plenty of opportunity to start early. Musicals, concerts and plays put on in the ultra modern Rutherford Centre, which is much enjoyed by juniors and seniors alike. Some 80 per cent of senior school have individual music tuition and all of Y7 are members of the drama club. We were lucky enough to walk in on the senior chamber choir practising for a concert in St John's, Smith Square and, at the end of our visit, to hear some 'jamming' which included exceptional piano playing. Impressive. Several girls reach grade 8 in their choice of instrument and some work for diplomas, both classical and jazz. One Y13 girl was crowned GDST Musician of the Year in 2016.

Our guides proudly showed us the Rutherford Centre, a great facility for all the performing arts. Plays, musicals, plenty of dramatic opportunities for everyone – on and off stage. Sixth form drama students are now regulars at the Edinburgh Festival.

Clubs galore; the list is endless and imaginative: from art to biomedicine, debating to the Duke of Edinburgh (three golds in 2015), scribbling to engineering and many more. Also several trips and expeditions (including senior and junior World Challenges) organised each term, home and abroad. A busy, buzzy school where idling is not encouraged and plenty of time is given to co-curricular activities.

Background and atmosphere: This GDST school had its 135th birthday in 2015 and was top of the league table that year. A somewhat unexciting entrance to the building belies the buzz that you get as you walk round it. Stone staircases lead to bright corridors, windows onto the happy, busy atmosphere that emanates from both classrooms and laboratories. Girls look relaxed and involved. Rooms subject based. Teachers and parents, as well as students, can have coding lessons in the ultra-modern computer room. We gather a complete overhaul of the building is due complete with a lift with new STEAM facilities, new hall and sixth form centre top of the list.

Sixth form currently has its own house with relaxing and study areas, common room and café. The girls are allowed to wear their own clothes from the Easter of Y11 onwards, and 'have fun playing ridiculous games'. Relationships with teachers are easy and they are absolutely not spoon-fed. They say the lack of boys 'doesn't fuss us. In fact, it's probably less hassle'.

Pastoral care, well-being and discipline: All are screened on joining the senior school, whether they are juniors coming up or new entrants. Any anomalies are picked up and monitored and parents immediately involved. The school is very aware that capable and high achieving children can often mask their need for support and that the crunch point is at the beginning of Y10. All problems, however mild, are taken extremely seriously and teachers are constantly on the look out for signs of eating disorders etc. 'Learning to learn' lessons are wisely given in year 7.

G&T children are offered weekly enrichment afternoons in years 11, 12 and 13. The school is active in the London Challenge that enables talented girls from neighbouring (but less privileged) schools to participate in particular projects.

House system encourages a good mixing of age groups and, parents believe, increases confidence and crosses all boundaries. Masses of fundraising, either for the school or for special concerns and charities. Parents say: 'helps them learn about money'. Girls clearly look after and care for each other.

Pupils and parents: Not yummy mummies, more parents keen to get the best education possible for their daughters. Often both working. No school transport, so either live within walking distance (about half), or on a good public transport route. Some 22 per cent speak a language other than English at home. All keen to give their children a good, well-grounded education. A school that encourages individuals, so anyone could fit in. The majority have a good sense of community; a thriving Parents' Association.

Notable former pupils include: K M Peyton (author of Flambards series), Professor Lynn Reid (first woman to achieve rank of professor of experimental pathology in UK), Professor Marilyn Butler (first female rector of Exeter College), Michelle Paver (author of Chronicles of Ancient Darkness), Margaret Rutherford (actress) and Eboni Beckford Chambers (played netball for England).

Entrance: Selective at 11+: tests in VR and NVR for all candidates. Second stage for those who reach required standard is creative assessment day with group activities to assess problem solving and teamwork skills. An interview with the head may follow. Offers made at beginning of February.

At 16+: a taster day in May alongside girls in own Y10. In November, tests in verbal reasoning alongside up to four 20-30 minute written papers in the subjects they want to study at A level. Those wishing to study art, music or drama interviewed by head of department. All candidates interviewed by head and director of sixth form and take part in a short group discussion on a current media issue.

Exit: A few at leave at 16+. Of the remainder, together with those who join from other schools, a good handful to Oxbridge (nine in 2018) or London and the rest mainly to other Russell Group universities. Five medics in 2018. According to parents, the advice and guidance they are given about courses to follow and choice of university is second to none. Nearly all get to where they want to go.

Money matters: Academic and music scholarships on offer in Y7 – parents are disappointed that there are none for drama but there is a new sports scholarship. Many more offered at sixth form level in a wider range of subjects – academic, art, drama, music, sport. Perhaps this would be a good time to reward long stayers, who have been at the school all their lives, rather than mainly to tempt new entrants?

Remarks: Quite a school. It's extraordinary what has been packed into a relatively small space in the middle of a busy London suburb. First of all we were startled by a head who exudes enthusiasm and finds sitting silently impossible (though she does listen, too, and answers questions); secondly, we were taken round the school by some very chatty year 9 pupils whose fervour and ability to talk matched their head's. This school produces bright, open minded, self-motivated girls. Jane Lunnon has some major improvements in mind. An excellent school for girls who want to open their minds, co-operate and grab what is on offer.

Woodford County High School

High Road, Woodford Green, Essex IG8 9LA

Ages 11–18 **Pupils** 1,087 **Sixth form** 309

020 8504 0611
www.woodford.redbridge.sch.uk

Headteacher: Since 2010, Jo Pomeroy (mid 50s), MA in English language and literature (St Andrews), MEd (Open), NPQH. Spent two years in a comprehensive in rural Scotland before going to work in France for three years. It was at this high achieving international school that she became aware of 'what bright students are capable of if they are given enough challenge'. Back in the UK she spent another three years working in a comprehensive school with strong languages bias and at that point 'got interested in management, in getting into position where you could make a bigger change'. Sure enough, at her next appointment at a girls' grammar in Surrey, where she spent 16 years, she eventually became deputy head.

Students seem to be in awe of her. 'She has an open door policy and is really nice, but it's definitely next level on the respect side,' a sixth former told us; and a year 8 girl, whom she asked to tell us about the working music box she was creating in DT, exclaimed, 'How embarrassing – I can't believe she picked me!' Parents impressed with how 'she's always grateful for any help from parents', 'is always pushing boundaries to get the best for the girls' and 'even though she finds it hard, as do all heads, to recruit good teachers, she won't compromise, waiting months to get the right one if that's what it takes.' We found her surprisingly mellow, soon realising that's probably her secret weapon; quietly driven and thoroughly unflustered, she has a way of making grand plans for the school sound like it's all in a day's work. Keen 'for students always to be working just beyond what they are comfortable with', this high performing grammar is surely her nirvana.

Academic matters: Named London state school of the year 2019 by the Sunday Times, this school gets the best results in Redbridge. School maintains an outstanding record of achievement, with 81 per cent A*-A/9-7 grades at GCSE in 2018. Also strong on value added. All the more impressive when you consider that many of the students speak a different language at home, with over 40 languages spoken between these bilingual (and often multilingual) girls.

All teachers are subject specialists, whom girls say 'can't do enough for you.' 'The staff, from those in the office right up to the headteacher, really care about the girls and it's that – more than any targets or pressure – that I think helps them succeed,' said one parent. Peer support also helps – it's in the very bones of the school, with older students regularly mentoring younger ones. Literacy mentors, for example, provide targeted additional support for year 7s, and this 'sustained focus on academic literacy across the curriculum' has been highly successful; other students are accredited digital leaders. Homework levels reported to be 'manageable', with a growing amount of flipped learning in sixth form ('good preparation for uni,' say students).

Setting only in science and only at GCSE. 'We used to set in maths, but we found confidence levels are actually higher in mixed ability classes,' says head. Students take two languages from year 7 (French and either German or Latin), one of which must be taken at GCSE (girls do 10 in total). English, languages and science all strong here and girls take triple science GCSE 'unless there's a very good reason not to.' Lots of information and support provided to students and parents on choosing options.

In the sixth form, where roughly a quarter of students come from other schools, girls either take four A levels or, more usually, three plus the EPQ (other smaller research projects are also widely taken up in the younger years; and research is also a growing focus for teachers because, says head, 'educators should do research, it helps keep education dynamic'). Some subjects (eg Latin and music) only attract small numbers, but school ensures they remain on offer. In 2018, 79 per cent A*/B grades, 50 per cent A*/A at A level, with many going on to medical careers (girls' uptake of maths and science is exceptionally high). University preparation is second-to-none, with 'UCAS fortnight' in full swing when we visited.

'Not a huge number of SEN,' admits head. Two with EHCPs being processed when we visited. Most supported in the classroom – 'students don't like to be taken out of class; we focus more on sharing what works between SENCo and teachers.'

Games, options, the arts: Core sports are badminton (which we saw in action in the snazzy sports hall; girls regularly reach the UK badminton national finals), athletics, netball, rounders, gymnastics, cross country and dance – and girls can pursue multicultural dance options such as Bhangra, African and street dance. 'Honestly, there's more dance going on here than on a West End stage,' we were told. Outside, the school field and tennis courts are regularly utilised – not only for sports but a variety of co-curricular day activities (recently team puzzle challenge days, circus skills etc). One parent told us, 'My daughter has always hated sport, but three months at this school and she's taking up things like running in a big way.' Determined to avoid the predictable drop-out rate of older girls, a lot of thought goes into keeping up engagement, with the likes of boxercise and aerobics a staple part of PE. Sports leadership qualification offered in years 10 and 11.

DofE also available, although National Citizenship Service has taken over in popularity (taken in summer of year 11); in fact, take-up so big that David Cameron recently came to do a congratulatory talk on it to the girls. Sports also features highly as part of extracurricular, with other options ranging from self-defence to film making and from hairdressing to sign language, with students presiding over many of the clubs, as well as the many talks and charity events; and there is a society for everything – even to discuss current affairs. Parents are grateful for the breakfast club from 7.45am and homework club until 5pm. Sixth form enrichment programme includes dance, cookery, computing, art, sports and an extended period of voluntary service.

Art block regrettably tatty on the outside, but that doesn't seem to put the girls off, with the two roomy art studios something of a haven and open most evenings after school (plus, students on pupil premium can borrow equipment). Good connections with organisations such as RIBA and annual art exhibition curated by the students themselves. Visits galore to London galleries and museums, plus further afield from St Ives to Berlin, and The Royal Academy organises an annual life drawing session for A level students ('we warn everyone else to stay clear,' laughs head). Sewing machines in full use by sixth formers during our visit, apparently something of a rarity. DT (which makes up the third room in this block) increasingly popular.

Drama not a taught subject, although it does feature as part of English and extracurricular. The house drama competition is also a big deal – a half-hour musical written, composed, directed and performed by each house (Footloose, Moana, Grease and Mama Mia when we visited – with spectacular posters created by the girls, complete with flashing lights) and judged by outside experts. 'It's incredibly competitive,' says head.

When current head joined, she asked the then head of music if there was any possibility of a swing band. 'Not enough people play brass,' she was informed; now all year 8s learn a brass instrument and there's just about every kind of ensemble you can think of, plus a band and different choirs including folk group and staff choir. Individual instrumental and vocal lessons at all levels also on offer, although many girls do their learning outside of school. Girls also participate in the biennial Redbridge Choral Festival at the Royal Albert Hall. Winners of the Mayor of London Music Excellence Awards, this is a school that gets the balance spot on between being inclusive while also enabling top talent to really shine. 'The concerts are extraordinary,' a parent told us.

Expeditions to eg Ghana, Morocco, Indonesia, China, Cambodia and recently Belize and Guatemala,. Plus a list of topic-related trips as long as your arm. 'Most students go on at least one and they're amazing,' said one girl.

Background and atmosphere: Main, listed building dates from 1768 when it was built as the private family home of the Highams; later it became a military hospital, with wooden honours boards still displaying the names of some of the state registered nurses, including Ina Bucket (an inevitable source of hilarity for the girls). The school opened here in 1919, with every September birthday celebrated – one of the highlights of the year for the school, when they do a big parade with banners (banners are big here – all intricately sewn and displayed on walls), then a formal service, followed by 'lots of cake' and fun activities both on and off site. Such venerable features and rituals lend an atmosphere of tradition.

With its small upstairs classrooms, narrow stairwells and warren-like corridors, much of the main school building has an intimate, homely feel. Particularly welcoming library, once a bedroom, and which has one of the most progressive librarians we've come across, with regular video conferencing with other schools and universities as far away as New York; the pupils even watched a live operation just before we visited. That said, the ground floor corridor is home to larger, revamped and more modern looking classrooms, refurbished new food and nutrition rooms and – drum roll please – an Innovation Lab, of the likes we've never seen. Looking as though it's been plucked straight out of Silicon Valley, this vibrant, colourful, wow-factor room, complete with two robots and oodles of other hi-tech equipment including drones, is part of the creative technologies department used to harness computing in innovative ways. School also boasts large new Centenary Centre with science labs ('with telescopes and other tech equipment well beyond the reach of most schools'), computer facilities, airy classrooms, break-out and event areas and even an outdoor learning area on the roof, complete with greenhouse and astronomy dome. Outdoor Greek theatre also worth a mention – used for busking Fridays (girls eat lunch while pupils play instruments or sing) and annual Greek play.

Pastoral care, well-being and discipline: Peer support service run by older pupils seen as an integral part of pastoral set up here. 'It's a very supportive community – we look out for each other,' one girl told us. Plenty of other leadership opportunities. Terrifically active house system. For more serious issues, there are two part-time school counsellors and a welfare officer. Students told us they knew of no eating disorders, self-harm etc, but said that for some girls, 'the pressure can turn to stress if they're that way inclined.' School currently planning staff training to help students who suffer from panic attacks.

Behaviour, on the whole, excellent, with the consequence that students are trusted to do more student-led activities than might be the case at other schools. Temporary exclusions rare, with no more than two in any one year, 'usually due to misguided use of social media.' Pupils describe the school as 'strict, especially in the lower years'; head and senior colleagues, for example, take turns to be out on the gate every morning checking uniform – 'you see them tying their hair back when they reach the traffic island; they know the score.' Surprisingly, trousers only came to Woodford in its 99th year (as part of a consultation with students, which also resulted in the design of a new hijab).

There is a university success board to inspire the girls and former students are generous with their time, providing inspirational role models at careers events and prize givings, as well as getting involved in organising work experience and networking opportunities. Year 12s spend two hours a week in voluntary service, often working with children or elderly or disabled people. Students adept at applying for (often successfully) grants eg for 10 bikes so students can learn cycling proficiency.

Pupils and parents: Multi-ethnic population, with a significant Tamil and Indian population. Mainly middle-class professional families, but by no means exclusively, with pupil premium usually hovering around eight per cent. Catchment circle incorporates Redbridge and neighbouring boroughs, although some come from further afield in the sixth-form ('We do discuss distance with prospective students, though – we don't want them to spend too much time travelling,' says head). Most travel in by bus or tube 'although rather more than I would like get delivered to the door, which isn't good for the environment,' says head. Parents support the PFTA as an opportunity to solve many of the school's cash problems (£25,000 raised for the Innovation Lab; has previously funded a digital language lab, a minibus and external lighting).

Girls have an air of being confident, resilient and creative. Former pupils here include Lucy Kirkwood, playwright (RSC, National Theatre), Sarah Winman, best-selling novelist (When God was a Rabbit) and Peggy Reynolds, Radio 4 arts broadcaster.

Entrance: Massively oversubscribed for year 7 places, even though the school has expanded to six form entry (180 girls). CEM entrance tests, apparently tutor-proof, but head aware that many families now (as at other schools) see tutoring as part of the application process. 'We would obviously rather it wasn't that way – familiarity with the nature of the test is great, but tutoring is definitely not necessary and we applaud those brave enough not to put their children through that,' she says. Up to 10 per cent of places given to girls eligible for pupil premium who score above the pass mark. It is one of just three all-girls schools in the area (the other two are independent and Catholic). Common catchment area with boys' grammar school. Nearly all girls stay on to the sixth form, joined by 50 or so from other schools.

Exit: Around 10 per cent leave post-GCSE (although a few always try to return within weeks of sixth form starting, sadly not always successfully if places are taken). Nearly all that stay go to university, primarily Russell Group. Ten Oxbridge places in 2018. Other destinations include UCL, Queen Mary's, Kent, King's College London, LSE, Birmingham, Nottingham. While medicine, dentistry and optometry are always popular (17 medics in 2018), the school is also working hard to encourage students to study pure science, with increasing success; ditto with STEM and engineering. School is beginning to see girls going into computing and AI. Small numbers study classics and Latin; humanities also appear. Occasionally, girls go to American universities and school also encourages degree apprenticeships, with girls increasingly going down this route – for example in big financial firms.

Remarks: This is a highly selective school with a strong sense of community, second-to-none peer support and an enormous amount of pupil pride in the school. Coupled with the top-notch teaching, it's no wonder the academics – not to mention the extracurricular – go from strength to strength. Where other schools try and fail to marry tradition and innovation, this one seems to achieve it superbly and there's a heavy focus on female empowerment, with girls not only coming out with flying colours scholastically but gaining a good dose of confidence and leadership skills along the way.

Woodhouse College

Woodhouse Road, London N12 9EY

Ages 16–19 **Pupils** 1,364

020 8445 1210
www.woodhouse.ac.uk

Principal: Since 2013, John Rubinstein BSc (50s) – read maths at Sheffield University where he achieved a first class degree. It was during his PhD that he decided teaching was his vocation: 'Part of my duties as a postgrad was to teach undergraduates, which I really enjoyed, and I realised then that this was what I wanted to do.' His first teaching job was at a comprehensive in Manchester – prior to getting his first post in London. His third teaching job was at Woodhouse College in 1994 as a maths teacher. He stayed there for the next 10 years, only leaving when he was offered the post of deputy head at a school in Haringey. He came back to Woodhouse in 2008 as deputy head, and was promoted to principal five years later.

Originally from Yorkshire, this softly spoken head seems totally devoid of any of the salesman techniques often displayed by other heads. That's not to say he's not enthusiastic about the school or his pupils – he is clearly extremely proud of both – but no doubt he feels, as we do, that Woodhouse pretty much sells itself. Students and parents alike describe him as 'very approachable' and one student told us: 'Mr Rubinstein is always wandering around the learning zones and often spends ages with pupils helping them out. You can email him anytime and he always gets back to you.' Even after nearly 30 years in the teaching profession, maths is still his passion and he still teaches four maths lessons a week which equates to a full A level week: 'It keeps me in touch with students, with the experience of colleagues, but most of all because I love it.' He even taught his own daughter, who is an ex-Woodhouse student: 'I warned her that it might be slightly strange, but it worked out fine in the end.'

His wife is also a teacher and they have three children – two of whom attended Woodhouse and are now at university. Mr Rubinstein has many other strings to his bow – formerly an Ofsted Inspector for 15 years: 'I gave up a year ago as the workload was getting too much and I was fed up of staying in hotel rooms'; he also enjoys running and has taken part in many half marathons and 10k runs. 'I have done the Crouch End 10k run for 13 years in a row and now train some of my students.' Recently nominated the school caretaker for a CBE for 20 years of service to the school: 'He is the glue that keeps this community together.'

Academic matters: Woodhouse is one of the country's leading sixth form colleges, always in the top five nationally, usually in the top three. This is essentially an academic place, whose main focus is on A levels. In 2018, 35 per of grades were A*/A and 70 per cent A*-B.

Undoubtedly a key part of the success is enthusiastic, experienced and focused teaching. One parent told us: 'I can't say enough about the teaching at Woodhouse and how they inspire students. My son had no real intellectual curiosity before going there. Now all he wants to do is discuss the Russian revolution.' Another said, 'The teachers really seem to know our children individually and their particular traits.' The consensus seems to be that 'they're excellent at monitoring and keep their finger on the pulse.' Mr Rubinstein says that close monitoring of students is vital as some students choose the wrong subjects, and they are under so much more pressure than they used to be. 'If a student is underachieving, there will be a case conference and a discussion of perhaps reducing the amount of subjects they take. They will also be offered extra supervised study.'

Results are certainly not achieved by hothousing or editing. The principal welcomes the introduction of the new A level system, which returns to the old two year study programme with no exams until the end of the second year. He says that although results will change, 'we won't just be teaching towards an end of year exam. Pupils will be able to explore their subjects more deeply.'

A wide range of options on offer, with 27 subjects in almost any combination. Maths is the most popular A level choice (with 45 per cent taking it) and results are notably strong. One of London's largest providers of A level science, with many going on to science-related degrees. Four languages, including Italian, and an abundance of 'ologies', from sociology to music technology and the extended project also available. The EPQ is taken by over 100 students each year and yields high grades. One parent said that 'the fantastic selection of A levels, including classical civilization, really excited my daughter when she was looking at sixth forms, and this is what swung it for her.'

Though the majority at Woodhouse tend to favour professional courses at university, social science and arts-based studies are strong, with thriving theatre studies, economics, English literature and geography. 'Independent learning' is high on the agenda. 'We want students to prepare for lessons, so they can understand and interpret the information, using the teacher and their fellow students as a resource,' says the principal. Motivated students respond well to this approach. 'Teachers assume if you're interested in your subjects, you will want to read around them,' said one. 'They don't force you to work, but they'll give you the resources and make themselves available to you,' said another.

An enormous amount of help is offered to pupils with their UCAS forms, and extra workshops and weekly presentations are laid on nearer the deadline. A teacher is on hand every Tuesday after school to offer any extra help for university applications, and Mr Rubinstein is also very involved in the process and runs mock Oxbridge interviews.

All students have access to two learning mentors – one for humanities, the other science and maths – to sort out any day-to-day tangles. One full-time SENCo, plus one part-time specialist providing individual support for those with dyslexia and dyspraxia and a learning mentor to help with study skills. The buildings are 99 per cent adapted for those with physical disabilities.

Games, options, the arts: Woodhouse prides itself on providing 'a broad and civilising education' and all are expected to take part in at least two six-week courses of 'enrichment', the majority of which take place on Wednesdays afternoons, when there are no lessons. Most relish the opportunities to develop new skills in everything from observational drawing to street dance. Duke of Edinburgh and Amnesty International also on offer.

Art is strong and some of the pieces we saw on our tour were simply outstanding – something we honestly weren't expecting: 'Traditionally the more academic subjects are most popular here, and although art and drama are taken by smaller numbers, they are very successful. Several of our graduates go on to art colleges.'

Dance is also a strong curricular subject here and the college has two lovely, bright, mirrored dance studios. Sports facilities, too, are good, with a new sports hall and new floodlit 3G football pitch. Official team sports include football (girls' and boys'), netball and basketball, but individualists can also enjoy cross-country, squash, trampolining and kickboxing. 'If there isn't a club that you'd like to do,' said one student, 'the sports department are happy to try and set something up.'

Music, which was previously a 'neglected' subject, now has its own dedicated separate building outside, with a well-equipped practice room and a music studio, which works in conjunction with other Barnet schools, and offers lessons from peripatetic teachers.

Woodhouse students like to get involved and there's an active college council, which has recently helped introduce a daily loan system for netbooks. Plenty of outside speakers and activities including art trips, foreign exchanges, a ski trip and the opportunity to undertake voluntary work abroad. Debating has traditionally been strong at Woodhouse and the college takes part in the Model United Nations competition, which hosts around 40 different debates a year in various institutions, including Woodhouse.

Background and atmosphere: Located in a pleasant leafy suburb, Woodhouse began its educational life as Woodhouse Grammar School in 1925, but became one of the capital's rare sixth form colleges in the 1980s. Today all pupils are aged between 16 and 19 and all are studying A levels. With some 700 new pupils a year, the college is significantly larger than a traditional school sixth form, but smaller than a FE college.

The original stately Victorian façade (deriving from its former incarnation as the home of ornamental plasterer Thomas Collins) has now been joined by a motley timeline of newer buildings, leaving it today with well-equipped facilities. The bright, open plan Learning Zone is one of the most recent innovations, offering space to work in solitary silence as well as in small groups, and supervised open-access IT. In 2014 the college managed to raise two million pounds for a two-story, purpose built mathematics facility. 'Quite a lot of students here can't work in silence at home and don't have the facility to do the "hard hours",' says the principal. 'We wanted to create learners who can work on their own.'

To this former Woodhouse student, the college internally is barely recognisable as the Woodhouse of yesteryear. However, what still remains is the strong sense of individuality that Woodhouse was always renowned for – and is still clearly evident in the students we witnessed strolling around the grounds. All creeds, colours, dress codes, hair colour, piercings welcome (well, maybe piercings not 'welcome', but they're there). One student told us: 'I never feel we are judged on anything here. We know grades matter, but that's really it.' Another student told us: 'I've never been as happy as I am coming here. I used to loathe going to school, but now I'm worried about my time at Woodhouse going too quickly.'

The students we met were indeed a happy and likeable bunch. They all felt extremely independent and loved the free rein the college allows them. However, one student grumbled that she tends to go out for lunch in North Finchley High Road (a five minute walk), as the canteen is too small and can't often accommodate everyone – a sentiment echoed by a parent, who suggested that perhaps the lunch hour should be extended.

Values here are traditional. 'We believe in honesty, hard work, mutual respect and taking responsibility for your own learning.' The atmosphere is generally enthusiastic, as much for work as for play. 'Here it's cool to work, cool to be involved,' said one student. 'The atmosphere is incredible,' said another. 'There's a massive sense of community. There are always things happening.'

Pastoral care, well-being and discipline: Not every 16-year-old is ideally suited to the self-motivation required by an academic sixth form college, but here high expectations are supported by a well-thought-out tutorial system and plenty of individual guidance. Every student has their own tutor, 'My son sees a guy two or three times a week, whom he likes and respects,' said one mother. 'When he was having trouble at home, they really kept an eye on him.'

The principal is all too aware that students these days are under a lot more pressure than previously, 'and as a result are a lot more fragile and there is more self-harming.' For this reason, they invest time in what they offer pastorally, including a pastoral manager and a counselling service. One student told us: 'The pastoral care here is excellent. There's pretty much someone you can talk to 24/7, if you needed to.' Another said, they accommodate for everyone and there is even an LBGT community.'

The college sees itself as a bridge between school and university, and new students are eased into this more adult world with an induction day in the summer before they start. The enrichment programme helps aid new friendships beyond the classroom. 'Everyone makes friends ridiculously fast because there are so many people in the same position,' said one boy. However, one parent did say that her child found the transition from school to college 'socially quite daunting if you don't know anyone, as pupils are always rushing off to their different classes or study period – it's unlike school where you get to know your peers over time.'

Boundaries are firm and there's zero tolerance on punctuality. 'It's an issue they have to grasp,' says the head. 'If they're not making the effort, why should other students suffer?' However, unlike most sixth forms, there is no morning registration, instead pupils go straight to their class and their ID registers them when they swipe it at the entrance turnstiles. One pupil told us: 'I much prefer it this way. It means we can go straight to our lessons and not waste time.'

In lessons, students are attentive. 'If a teacher leaves the room, people get on with their work,' said one boy. We witnessed some of the most attentive and eager students we've come across, who were happy to talk with enthusiasm about what they were learning. There is definitely a strong work ethic that exists here. 'Issues found elsewhere are not even on the radar here,' notes the principal gratefully. Standard formula of oral and written warnings, with a code of conduct signed by all parents and pupils, but exclusion is a rarity. 'We have pupils from quite challenged backgrounds, but I have thrown out just one student,' says the principal. Parents agree that discipline is firm but reasonable. 'They run quite a tight ship, but it makes them responsible,' said one father. 'When my son's attendance was only 90 per cent, he had to see the senior tutor every week. As his attendance improved, he went less frequently.'

Pupils and parents: An eclectic mix – 'some nerdy kids, some cool kids, all sorts, colours and creeds.' The core is probably typical of the reasonably prosperous 'squeezed middle' of north London, but with a far higher ethnic intake than you'd assume from the location, and a far higher proportion of those who require some type of financial support.

Parents tend to be involved and supportive, students upbeat, mature, outgoing and energetic. They clearly enjoy the school – more than half volunteered on the annual open day held on a Saturday. 'They want to do well and they want to enjoy themselves,' says the principal. 'They're trying to get the balance right of working hard and having a good social life.' A parent agreed: 'My son is so happy. He really appreciates the fact that people are there because they want to learn, not because their parents are pushing them. Most students here are trying to better themselves and work really, really hard.' Past students include journalist Johann Hari, comedian Michael McIntyre and actress Naomie Harris.

Entrance: Priority is given to applicants from one local secondary school, Friern Barnet (although that accounts for roughly 20 places and they still have the same entry requirements). After that, it's predicted grades and/or interview. Competition is ferocious (about 4,500 apply for 700 places), particularly for in-demand subjects. 'We can afford to be choosy,' says the principal, 'but we're looking for a range.' All applicants with minimum predicted grade requirements (evaluated on a points system, with specific grades for individual subjects) are given a 20-30 minute interview (with optional parental accompaniment) in the February/March prior to entry. 'We're looking for maturity,' said one teacher. 'We want them to demonstrate that they are committed to A levels and really want to work, but we also want people who will get involved on a wider basis.' The interview is frequently of as much benefit to the student as to the college. 'We often spend it giving careers advice,' says the principal.

Travel time is also taken into consideration. Students come from as far afield as Highbury, but the school 'generally considers an hour and a quarter by bus the maximum desirable distance.' Applications available from the time of the open day in November until the closing deadline in January. All candidates require a confidential report from their current school and must be between 16 and 18 when starting at the college. The college operates a waiting list for the reshuffle that often takes place after results day in August.

Exit: Over 95 per cent to university – some 60 per cent to Russell Group universities, with the most popular destinations being London universities, Warwick, Kent, Manchester and Sussex. Most popular subject choices are economics, law, engineering, business and psychology. Fifteen to Oxbridge and and amazing 29 medics in 2018, plus one student off to the US on a full scholarship. Good advice about careers and courses, including a full time careers co-ordinator.

Money matters: Parents are asked for £100 contribution for the two-year stint, enabling the college to keep up to date with books and underwrite the enrichment programme and facilities (those who can't afford it, don't pay). A £50 refundable deposit also required for text books. The college has attempted to replace some money lost through EMA cuts with bursaries.

Remarks: An upbeat environment, with strong teaching and results. A firm stepping stone between school and university.

Wren Academy

Hilton Avenue, London N12 9HB

Ages 4–18 **Pupils** 1,288 **Sixth form** 254 **C of E**

020 8492 6000
www.wrenacademy.org

Principal: Since 2015, Gavin Smith (40s). He has a geography degree from University College London and a PGCE from the Institute of Education. He joined Wren Academy in 2008, having worked in various London secondary schools, and was part of the founding team responsible for the curriculum, assessment and enrichment programme. He is married with two young children.

Headteacher of the primary phase is Louisa Taylor.

Academic matters: This is a comprehensive, but the nature of the students in this leafy area means it is primarily an academic one. The biggest initial challenge was achieving a truly comprehensive intake: the previous school on the site had a very poor reputation and Barnet has a variety of popular state schools, including three grammars. However, within a short space of time Ofsted stated that 'the teaching at Wren is stunning', and this is not something you read very often. 'As well as maximising achievement – because children need that currency to move on – we teach learning skills and aptitudes. Children need the capacity to think for themselves. They are encouraged to seek out their own answers, to be flexible and take risks.' In 2018, 43 per cent 9-7 grades at GCSE. Sixth formers achieved 53 per cent A*-B, 30 per cent A*/A in their A level exams.

Parents are enthusiastic. 'The teachers are very wisely chosen.' 'They're great at finding and encouraging talents.' 'They really encourage them to aim high.' Newsletters all include brainteasers for parents and pupils to solve, and articles on ways of building learning power.

English, maths and science are taught in single sex classes. 'This gives us opportunities to stretch children in gender-specific ways. For example, in English boys can look at their powers of reflectiveness and empathy, whilst in girls' maths classes we can encourage them to take risks and concentrate on answering quickly. It helps to broaden their skill sets, and they enjoy it.' Research suggests that girls taught in single sex groups are more likely to continue with maths and science, and a good percentage of girls choose single science GCSEs.

The school sets for English, maths, science and foreign languages from part of the way through year 7. 'We like to get data of our own rather than relying on Sats results.' Everyone studies a language (generally French, though some take Japanese or Spanish) and most are expected to take it to GCSE. Regular language days involve a range of linguistic activities. GCSE courses start in year 9.

The specialism of design and the built environment enhances rather than dominates the curriculum, says the school. 'It influences our culture and our ways of thinking about tasks. We have a high emphasis on creativity, and each task has a creative phase, a planning phase and an evaluation phase. But we also have the opportunity to plan projects in architecture and civil engineering.'

Those who need extra help are identified at the beginning of year 7 and follow a six week key skills programme to help bring them up to speed. There are also after-school support groups that help with spelling and comprehension. Although some get one-to-one help from teaching assistants, 'the aim is for everyone to be unsupported in lessons eventually. We do what helps them to access the curriculum in the appropriate lesson.'

Games, options, the arts: The school week includes three extended days, with compulsory enrichment activities from 3-4pm. These range from samba band, Latin and knitting to debating. Staff and students learn together and either can win Excellent Learner of the Week awards.

Houses – named for Wren churches – give the main opportunities for sporting rivalry, but football, netball, basketball, badminton and athletics teams also take part in borough and regional competitions with increasing success. There's a sports hall, netball courts and a football pitch. Opponents have commented on Wren teams' good sportsmanship. Pupils can take sports GCSE or BTec, and enrichment options include rugby, trampolining and table tennis.

Art, design and technology very strong and creative – as one would expect in a school with a design specialism. Projects include designing sculptures of dream ice cream sundaes, creating a piece of artwork inspired by the River Thames and designing an Olympic stadium.

Music is keen – there's an orchestra, samba band, gospel choir, Indian drumming club – and increasing in quality as musicians move up the school and hone their skills. Drama also finding its feet; eagerly awaited annual school musical – eg Bugsy Malone and Hairspray. Wren's Got Talent showcases singers, magicians and musicians.

Background and atmosphere: Named for Sir Christopher Wren, designer of St Paul's Cathedral, which reflects its C of E status and specialism in design and the built environment. Opened in 2008 on the site of a failed school next door to Woodhouse College. Partly refurbished but mostly newly built, it has an open plan feel, with roof lights and large north windows, grey carpets and aluminium cladding. Steps leading down from the entrance hall to the library, 'the heart of the school', are lined by ledges where children can sit and chat, under treble-height rooflights, giving an amphitheatre-like atmosphere. There is a feeling of space and airiness throughout. Corridor walls are decorated with graphics of the footprint of St Paul's Cathedral, and with murals quoting inspiring biblical texts eg 'Be willing and available to provide support and guidance to others'.

The school is sponsored by the London Diocesan Board for Schools, hence its Christian character, and by Berkhamsted School, which provides some of the governors. The schools work together on areas such as curriculum development, Wren students go over to Berkhamsted for activities, including a year 7 residential retreat, and Berkhamsted sixth formers visited Wren to give their views on appointing a new head of sixth form. 'It's a partnership, and we hope that both schools will get an equal amount from it.'

Primary school on the same site adjacent to the existing school opened in 2015; it is growing one year at a time and will in 2022 become a complete all-through school.

Pastoral care, well-being and discipline: 'The teachers don't tolerate any bad behaviour,' say parents. 'It is a lovely, safe environment for learning'; and indeed the school had a supremely ordered feel during our visit. Three different breaks and lunchtimes help. So does the design of the building: staff and pupils share unisex toilets, and there is no staff room, so everyone socialises in the restaurant. 'It's a philosophy that when staff and students share the same space there is passive supervision, and students feel secure. They're encouraged to sit in here and chat – it's part of the curriculum.' 'Focus days' concentrate on matters ranging from sexual health to university choices.

Much emphasis on good manners and courtesy. Common sanctions include litter duty and community service. There's a Reflection Room for 'those who would benefit from time on their own'. Pupils have a high degree of autonomy, with plenty of opportunities to get involved in the way the school is run, from becoming prefects to interviewing potential teachers to taking part in curriculum reviews. 'In return, they generally play their part. There's a high level of buy-in.'

The chaplain, who plays a counsellor-like role, is generally considered a good egg. The only parental criticism is that some feel the school doesn't take their views on board. 'When you start a new school you have to put in place structures that will work. We opened with a very clear idea of what we wanted. We've always listened and explained to parents, but we haven't always amended our ways as a result.'

Pupils and parents: A diverse range, about 25 per cent white British, and characteristic of this leafy outer-London suburb; mostly 'ambitious people who want to do well'. Pupils have taken GCSEs in 13 different home languages. Active PTA which organises quiz nights and festivals, organises second hand uniform sales and has raised funds for the gazebo, which offers a shady outdoor place to socialise.

Entrance: Takes 60 into reception, and 184 into year 7. Priority to looked after children, medical/social need, siblings and children of staff. Half of remaining places community (by distance), half foundation (church-goers). Internal and external sixth form applicants need at least five grade 6s at GCSE including maths, English and the subjects they want to study at A level; prospective maths, further maths, science and French students need 7+ grades in these subjects. At least 25 external sixth form places.

Exit: Some 50 per cent leave post-GCSE. Courses include biomedicine, engineering, architecture, law and economics; universities include Exeter, Manchester, Sheffield and Queen Mary. Four to Oxbridge and one medic in 2018.

Remarks: This young school has already established a reputation for high teaching standards, courteous students and excellent enrichment activities. Likely to go from strength to strength.

Midlands and East England

Bedfordshire
Cambridgeshire
Derbyshire
Leicestershire
Lincolnshire
Norfolk
Northamptonshire
Nottinghamshire
Rutland
Staffordshire
Suffolk
Warwickshire
West Midlands

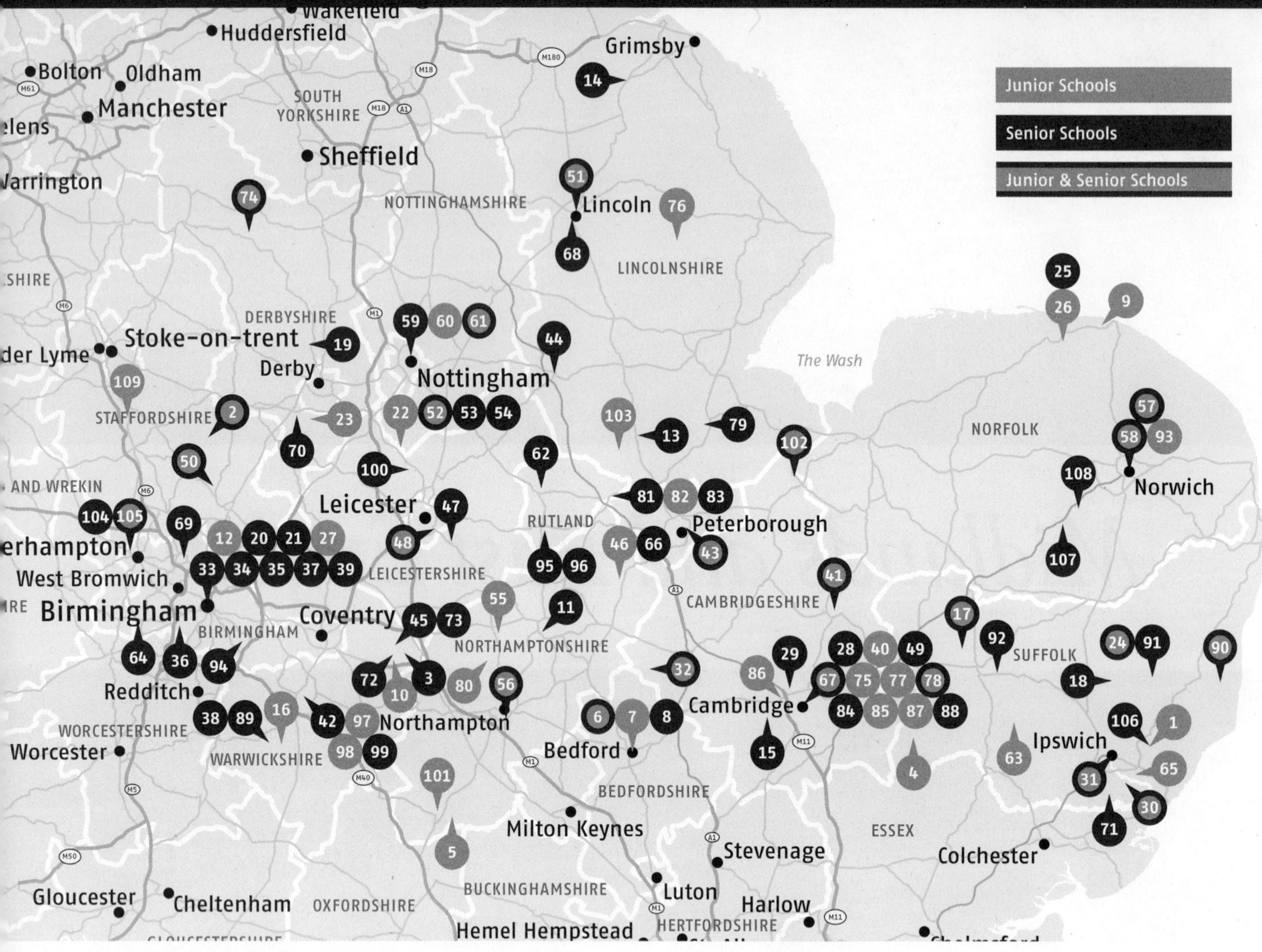

MIDLANDS & EAST ENGLAND

A

The Abbey

Linked with Woodbridge School

Church Street, Woodbridge, Suffolk IP12 1DS

Ages 4–11 **Pupils** 202 **C of E**

Fees: £9,741 – £13,473 pa

01394 382673
www.woodbridge.suffolk.sch.uk/prep-school

Head of The Abbey and Queen's House: Since September 2017, Nicola Mitchell, previously deputy head at Orley Farm. Has also taught at Edge Grove where she was, variously, head of geography, head of girls' games and director of studies. Three children, who have all joined The Abbey or Woodbridge School; she is keen on horse riding, swimming and skiing.

Entrance: About half of year 3 is made up from pupils progressing up from the pre-prep department, Queen's House, at 7; others join via test and interview from other local schools. Selective, but with scope for quite a range of ability; 'we are looking for those who can explore all that's on offer'. Places occasionally available in higher forms – always worth asking.

Exit: Vast majority (95 per cent) make the seamless transfer to Woodbridge, the senior school. A few go to state schools in the area – generally Farlingaye High. The parents of the occasional pupil that might struggle in the senior school will have been given advance warning, and advised to move elsewhere at 11. This is handled sensitively and is rare.

Remarks: This is a super school with many strengths and the widest and most varied curriculum possible. Main building is Tudor, lots of oak panelling, flagged floors, and even rumours of a ghost. Newer buildings for science, art and sport have been added, and the grounds are mature and delightful; 'this is a place for a sunlit childhood'. Pupils about the school are courteous, open doors and smile, but are intent on their own ploys and enjoyment. Small class sizes, around 20, gradually moving from class to subject based learning. Specialist teachers from the senior school teach science, languages and art to the higher forms. The Abbey language scheme gives all pupils a taste of four modern languages, Italian, Spanish, Mandarin, French, in consecutive years. Pupils at Queen's House pre-prep learn Spanish from 5.

The musical life of the school is outstanding. Free music lessons are available for pupils in year 3 for stringed instruments, with tuition in small groups, and as a result, a large number continue to play. The Abbey has four choirs, two string orchestras, and a variety of ensemble groups. Regular concerts and performances. Drama and dance also strong. Ballet and tap are taught throughout the school with the emphasis on fun and a chance to perform. The summer play, performed in the Seckford Theatre, is a highlight for the town as well as the school.

Sport is for all – everyone has the opportunity to play in a match. Main sports for boys are soccer, rugby, hockey and cricket; for girls, netball, hockey and rounders. Swimming and tennis for all throughout the year, plus athletics in the summer, and cross-country in the Michaelmas and Lent terms: not a place for couch potatoes.

Full-time SEN teacher gives support throughout the school. There is setting for maths from year 3 and for English in year 6. Communication with parents is taken very seriously. As well as the usual parents' consultations, staff are available on a day-to-day basis via telephone or email. This care of the children is at the heart of such a happy school. Chess, art, sport, music, academic and all round scholarships are available.

Abbots Bromley School

High Street, Abbots Bromley, Nr Rugeley, Staffordshire WS15 3BW

Ages 3–18 **Pupils** 272 (199 girls, 73 boys) **Sixth form** 61 **Boarders** 77 full, 9 weekly, 7 flexi (from 8 years) **C of E**

Fees: Day: £4,653 – £15,819; Boarding £17,550 – £29,721 pa

01283 840 232
www.abbotsbromleyschool.com

Principal: Since September 2018, Richard Udy BSc (geography, London University) PGCE (UEA), who took over after the abrupt departure of the previous principal. Previously head of the senior division since 2015, having arrived at the school in 2013. Before that he was at Finborough School. Since his arrival, he has placed a much-needed emphasis on ramping up the academic side of things, having realised immediately that many of the structures (or lack of) were not working. Cue major changes. Data tracking now happens on a monthly basis, every pupil is monitored and, where necessary, intervention strategies planned. A number of new staff have joined recently in key positions and, altogether, there is a new tone and upward direction.

Charismatic, down to earth with 'natural leader' written all over him, he really does seem primed to take the school to the next level academically. More than that, though, it is clear from the way he talks about various students, past and present – and indeed, the way he greets random students from both senior and junior – that he knows each and every one and, most importantly, he cares. There are many different types of heads – some are strategists, some born marketers – but not all display that sense of care and understanding which emanated from Mr Udy.

Having started out in the army and been heavily involved with training, Mr Udy says he felt a calling (which deepened after a stint in the City at Lloyd's of London) to go into teaching. Despite his pukka background (an army officer in the King's Royal Hussars for eight years), he comes across as both egalitarian and compassionate, which he puts down to having lived and worked with soldiers, 'which gives you a certain life philosophy. I understand people for who they are inside'. While training to be a teacher, he taught in some of the toughest 'failing' schools – 'far scarier than going into Northern Ireland in the army' – and even now he is able to talk about how some of those pupils overcame challenges. 'I witnessed wonderful students who struggled to get an education'.

The drive in his current role, he says, is identifying that intellectual spark, nurturing the academically inquisitive so as to 'light that candle' in each pupil.

Parents describe him as 'very approachable', that 'he transcends all age groups' and 'if there's a problem he will sort it out' (as well as more generic praise like 'amazing' and 'brilliant').

Junior head: Since 2015 is Wendy Gordon (BEd Liverpool), previously deputy head; experienced, calm and efficient.

It is a mark of her leadership style that the suggestions box outside her door is frequently acted upon and the school's 'have a go' ethos is encouraged via her 'have a go Gordon' initiative where she is challenged by pupils to learn something new: 'I drew the line at cartwheels,' she explains, 'but I did some gymnastics'.

Academic matters: In the pre-prep for 3-7 year olds the emphasis is on learning through discovery; heaps of outside experience in the grounds. The prep, years 3-6, has small class sizes (maximum of 18) and differentiated teaching. A broad curriculum prevails including science, history, geography, computing, languages, DT, music and swimming. One parent we spoke to, whose children had moved from elsewhere, said they came home 'fizzing about science, maths, dance...everything'. One child, who had previously been 'coasting' academically, was now 'excelling'.

The learning enrichment department (two staff in the prep) seems very clued up in tackling dyslexia-type issues and looks out for early signs, many of which are flushed out in cognitive tests, Mr Udy says. Around 25 per cent across the whole school need extra help, he adds; 'start early and the problem may vanish further up'.

Setting begins in year 6 and there are two streams in year 7 (for English, maths and science) with fluid movement between sets. One parent felt the quality of the maths and sciences teaching could be better. Another, however, whose daughter was again being taught by the same teachers who had taught her many years earlier, felt there was a vibrancy to the teaching and that longevity did not mean staleness.

Some classes in the senior school are fairly evenly split between the genders (although there are currently no boys in years 9-11, and they make up about a quarter of students throughout the school). Photography, sociology and politics available at A level; maths, geography, history, politics and sociology currently the most successful. Fairly even numbers of boys and girls take sciences.

Recent academic results are on the up. The 2018 results were their best yet: 43 per cent A*-A/9-7 at GCSE; 37 per cent A*/A at A level (47 per cent including equivalent in BTecs: BTec equine and BTec dance are popula)r.

Critical to greater academic success has been consistent pupil tracking and interventions (booster lessons) on any topic or exam technique. Students emphasised how collaborative the environment was in terms of helping each other. What's more, they said, in upper sixth you could drop in on a lower sixth lesson to get a recap on a topic.

The SEN provision seems pretty hot in the senior; one student we spoke to was glowing about the help she had received. That said, one parent felt there should be more targeted support for those children struggling with maths.

Games, options, the arts: There are two significant and rather wonderful offerings unique to the school. The first is the equestrian facility on site, with stables, indoor and outdoor arenas. Some highly experienced riders have their own horse with them and are permitted extracurricular time with their trusted steeds. Yet while there are some very talented riders who regularly win prizes, riding is open to anyone who fancies giving it a go.

The other is the Alkins School of Dance, offering dance and musical theatre courses. Around 45 students of the school's current intake choose the school for this reason. It was a delight to sneak a peek at 10 or so graceful ballet dancers performing to an extremely high standard along a wall of mirrors. A lot of students do these courses alongside A levels which might mean 20 hours dance per week and working till 8pm at night. Others might prefer to opt into 6-7 hours a week of dance for pleasure. One sixth form boy proudly told us he had started an all-male dance group. Very often 'it's about giving something a whirl', he said. A parent reiterated this when she said her daughter would never be a professional ballerina, but all her dance lessons were taken very seriously by teachers. 'It's very inclusive'.

Overall, a lovely aspect to the school is the timetabled enrichment sessions, where each term pupils select which clubs they would like to join – sports, craft, drama, photography, riding (the latter for those of 6+ only).

The junior schools has choirs and orchestras. The dance school means ballet, jazz and tap are also available (one parent said her 7 year old was doing about five hours of dance a week). LAMDA is on offer and there are lots of drama productions, ranging from the pre-prep nativity to the summer musical, recently Cinderella Rockafella and Robin Hood. Lots of responsibility given to years 5 and 6: they organise arts events and the Christmas bazaar with support from the staff.

At senior level, the enrichment sessions are a veritable banquet, with all manner of the usual sport options (including the more offbeat yoga, trampoline, zumba). There is also a fancy gym, lovely pool, sports hall, pitches. We are pleased to say girls' football is dominant.

As one would expect with a dance school within a school, performance opportunities abound, a vast array within of dance plus singing, music, drama. Music of all kinds is on offer and so many pianos, you almost trip over them (around 30? A teacher hazarded a guess). One parent said the school 'nurtures a child's creative side; that side of things is unbelievable'.

For those not inclined to perform, fantastically varied art and design options include everything from jewellery making to recycled art. Budding linguists can get stuck into Mandarin, Latin or Italian. Scientists may dip into forensic investigation, would-be authors into creative writing.

There are a decent amount of trips, some residential to London, France or Cornwall. Lots of competitions, such as The Big Bang for scientists. DofE is popular and there is a good array of clubs, such as the Perham society (alumna Dame Margery Perham was expert in British colonial history and the first woman to be a Reith lecturer) and the debating club, on top all of these enrichment sessions. The only slight note of caution from one parent was that in 'trying to help every pupil do everything they want to do', staff might be spreading themselves a bit too thinly.

Some lovely student-led initiatives, the summer soirée sounded supremely civilised, nicely dressed young people outside wafting around a grand piano. The annual commemoration day, where pupils dress up in traditional robes, was cited by one student as a treasured memory she will take with her.

The house system means lots of competitions; the house performing arts competition was a special favourite of students who felt they got 'to understand each other's talents better'. Mature stuff.

The weekly Guild lectures, dealing with topics like gap years or working in the biochemical industry, aim to prepare sixth formers for life beyond school. A wide range of ambitions: one girl was keen on biochemistry, a boy on maths and Harvard, another girl was pitching her sights on a career in dance.

As one of the sixth formers said to us, 'even if you have closed mind here, someone will open it up'.

Boarding: Separate boarding houses for girls and boys. Juniors can board from year 3 and each gets two free nights per term. 'My child loves the odd night boarding,' said one parent. 'It makes her feel independent'. Mix of ages, with younger pupils clustered together.

The girls' new head of boarding is a tour de force of vivacity and we can imagine the students feeling comfortable with her. In fact, one parent we spoke to felt her modern approach and dynamism – 'she is very on the ball about social media' – was very good for her daughter (even if her social media loving daughter didn't necessarily agree). Girls' boarding accommodation, the usual mish-mash of twinkly lights, lamps and colourful pics, seemed very cosy. Boys' boarding was a revelation: we expected a chaos of dirty sports kit, towels on the floor and stale deodorant, but it was the tidiest dorm we have ever seen. Beds made. No mess. Little personal touches (comfort toys or cushions on each bed). This oasis of calm and order was explained when we met one of the boarding masters who exuded human understanding and warmth but was also ex-army ('wherever you live, you make it feel like home'). One of the male students we spoke to explained how brilliant the master was at integrating new students and how well he understood what it was like to be away from home.

Lots going on during the evenings and at weekends: museums, Laser Quest or, as students told us, a simple fire pit and marshmallows were all it took to break the ice.

Sixth formers have individual bedrooms – desk, bed, all fine. Decent common rooms and kitchens and bathrooms.

Background and atmosphere: Set in the chocolate box village of Abbots Bromley, its two sites across the road from each other are rather delightful. A blend of buildings and eras, those dating from the 1700s co-existing with 60s charmless boxes. Stunning chapel.

The junior school is a riot of colour and imaginative displays, on anything from the Vikings to the writing style of Michael Foreman. School is setting up a small library. Art room the usual joy with all its projects simmering, from marble runs to circuits.

The senior school, it is fair to say, it is not the most whizz bang, high-falutin, glitziest school we have even seen. Yes, the science labs looked gleaming and everyone seemed to have the facilities they needed (across art, music, IT etc) but against a slightly shabby backdrop – 'old school' springs to mind. But here's the good news – we have rarely encountered students who radiated such pride in almost every crevice of the building, no matter how very ordinary it seemed to the un-tuned eyes of their visitors. Everything was cherished, displayed for our admiration and clearly very important to them – far more impressive than mere state of the art facilities. The school is clearly doing something very right to engender this sort of affection and sense of ownership amongst its students.

It has all the essentials, of course – decent library, some nice displays here and there on corridors, common room, study pods ...all used, a bit messy, comfy and loved. A working school, not a show home.

Pastoral care, well-being and discipline: Junior pastoral care is overseen by the form tutors. There are around 80 children in the junior school, so it is a nurturing environment. 'Every child you speak to is a happy child,' said one parent.

At senior level, there is a whole pastoral team. The students we met seemed supremely proud of their school and also very supportive of each other. Some had transferred from other schools, often state, or from other countries, and all spoke with enthusiasm (genuinely convincingly so) about the welcome they had received and how effortless it was to make new friends. 'They make it very easy for you to adapt', one said. None of the students felt behaviour or bullying were an issue but were quick to point out that as they were all in houses, all age ranges 'hang out together' and chat. It was not uncommon, they said, for younger students to confide in older students when they needed a bit of support, as it was often easier than making an initial approach to a teacher. Older students felt they understood when the matter should be escalated.

Lots of education about behaviour; a psychologist had recently given a lecture on all forms of bullying. There was lots of messaging around 'banter': how – unlike a certain TV channel – school should not be the home of 'witty banter', since it often masked something altogether more aggressive. Parents highlighted pastoral care as a big strength of the school; 'like a big family' was the echo.

The medical staff came in for praise – 'the pupils can ask anything and get an age-appropriate answer' – along with the chatty chaplain who regularly plonks himself down at breakfast for a chinwag.

Only sixth formers allowed phones, to attempt to offset social media influences, and teachers' eyes are, discreetly, always on girls and their eating habits during meal times. They eat in houses and manners are high on the list; no one leaves the table till the last person has finished.

Pupils and parents: The junior pupils we met bubbled happiness and pride. The senior pupils were lovely, chatty and down to earth. There was no sense of arrogance or entitlement.

Parents seem a candid, sensible bunch. All of them attested to the school being very good around communications and the prep school very accommodating to working parents.

The village may be chocolate box but the area around is not wealthy. Most families are dual income; fees often funded by several family members.

Entrance: Non-selective; school is looking for potential. Ninety per cent of juniors move on to the senior school; other senior school entrants come from abroad (every country imaginable) or local schools.

Exit: To a great diversity of courses across the UK: astronomy, engineering, law, fashion management and musical theatre. Several to Bristol in 2018. Oxbridge has not fared so well in recent years but this may be changing; one ex-student secured a place at Oxford to read biochemistry in 2018.

Remarks: A warm and friendly school where academic standards are on the rise and a vast array of extracurricular on offer, especially across performance and the arts. Dance and riding schools are wonderfully unusual features.

Ashlawn School

Ashlawn Road, Hillmorton, Rugby, Warwickshire CV22 5ET

Ages 11–18 **Pupils** 1,792 **Sixth form** 402

01788 573425
www.ashlawn.org.uk

Head: Since January 2018, Siobhan Evans, previously principal at Sir Jonathan North Community College in Leicester. Read sports science and English literature at the University of Stellenbosch in South Africa and did her PGCE before embarking on a year of world travel. While in the UK she was offered the opportunity to gain her British QTS at a residential school for students within the autistic spectrum. She is also a keen sports coach; having coached synchronised swimming and water polo teams, she now supports a local boys' rugby team as age group coordinator.

Academic matters: In 2018, 78 per cent of pupils got grade 4 or above in English and maths. At A level, 20 per cent A*/A, 51 per cent A*-B. Solid results for a school with a small selective element: 12 per cent of places via the 11+, another 10 per cent by language aptitude test. Not many choose two languages at GCSE, those that do study French and German. Pupils taught in sets with grammar (11+) contingent separate in top sets for first two years. Some MFL pupils taught with them. School actively promotes academic subjects over vocational but does offer BTecs in science, sport and health and social care.

Many young and enthusiastic teachers. We overheard (walls have ears) one teacher reprimanding a pupil – 'not good enough at all' – with the rest of the class obviously toeing the line. This was apparent on our tour. Lots of interaction between staff and pupils, and respect. Pupils there to learn, most want to please teachers and work hard. Good library being used as study area by some sixth form pupils. The dying tree in the corner was gasping for some water; do hope it got some.

Parents happy with academic progress and confident problems picked up quickly. Lots of revision sessions on offer, during the holidays as well. Parents able to access via Google classroom all child's grades, goals and homework etc so can keep a close eye on progress. Lots of learning mentors and encouragement for all. Parents happy, despite size of school, that no one slips through the net. Very dedicated deputy has introduced a reading development programme for years 7-9. All students, apart from grammar stream, partake. This helps pick up those year 7s who are struggling. Some 20/25 a year are specifically targeted, up to year 9 if necessary, meaning that none fall by the wayside. Deputy critical that reading not taught in secondary school, pilot proved very successful.

Sixth form making good use of new centre. Supervised study with all working hard and looking smart, boys in suits, girls in business wear. Psychology and sociology very popular at A level. Sadly very low numbers taking languages. Average sixth form lessons contain 16, maximum of 27, quite high but to be expected from such a large school. Average class size 26 in lower years, but up to 32 maximum.

SEN students well supported with an active Learning Development Department. All students assessed on entry for literacy and numeracy. Facilities for disabled with lifts and electric doors. Students usually taught in intensive small groups, in and out of lessons. One-to-one available if necessary, but unusual. EAL students, there aren't many, also come under the Learning Development Department.

Ashlawn is a teaching school and oversees teachers at five different schools in the county. Innovative and enthusiastic teaching is a result with lots of research and development, as well as support for young staff.

Games, options, the arts: Sport for all but we don't get the impression that it is a priority here. Only one team per year group for football, rugby, netball and hockey. Girls play cricket and rugby, but no teams, and no team for boys' hockey. A large variation of sport offered, including cheerleading at one point. Lots of indoor sports including table tennis, basket ball and trampolining. One of our guides was rather miffed that they had lost a gym and fitness suite to allow dining facilities to be expanded. But they do still have a large gym and plenty of outside space. Note the photos of alumni who have gone on to excel at sports. Lots of outside space and pitches. On the wishlist from a parent was an Astroturf and a hockey team for the boys, though they do have access to Astroturf at Rugby School just up the road. 'The PE staff are great at ferrying the teams around.' Parents spoke about keen staff identifying what sports children are interested in and trying to make them available. Wheelchair football for all proved popular, and the wider message about inclusion made apparent.

Music department quite large with lots of practice rooms being well used on our tour. Grease was the upcoming annual production when we visited with lots of rehearsals going on. We were very impressed with 'Danny's' practice performance. School orchestra and bands and choirs on offer, with lots of performances and recitals. Timetabled music lessons on offer, 135 pupils take them. Drama becoming less popular, particularly at A level, as well as music. Lots of impressive art on display. Lots of clubs and societies available, mainly after school, some during lunch time.

Plenty of school trips include much anticipated skiing.

Background and atmosphere: Situated on the edge of Rugby in a residential area, Ashlawn used to be two schools, housed on the same site: boys' and girls' schools with a 'strict line down the middle that no one could cross.' Amalgamated in the 1980s to make the huge school it now is, still on the same site. The small selective section of the school makes it very attractive to parents who also want an 'inclusive education' for their child.

We could not describe Ashlawn as an inspiring place architecturally, being very much 1980s utilitarian. Soviet bloc buildings spring to mind – it's bleak – but it serves its purpose and easily absorbs the large pupil numbers. Wide corridors provide ample space to encompass the masses at lesson changeovers. The sprawl of buildings means that five minutes are allowed between lessons for changing classrooms. Parts of the school are shabby and tired looking, but bear in mind this place gets hard wear. Very clean and tidy. Note the wind turbine producing electricity. All new buildings have solar panels.

School is open to opinions from parents, and listens. Plans underway to lengthen school day to enable more teaching time, and shorten lunch, but parent power put this on hold until dining facilities were improved. This has now been done and extended days being trialled.

Pastoral care, well-being and discipline: Parents spoke about a 'caring atmosphere' and how the 'pupils look out for each other.' Teachers aware of problems and quick to nip them in the bud, be it bullying or emotional problems. 'The school handles things well,' was the view of one parent, and all appeared to agree. Pupils stay in the same form from year 7-11, grammar and non-grammar contingent mixed. This means form becomes quite close knit. Our guides said they did not necessarily know everyone in their year by name, but certainly recognised them. Pastoral tutors, who are non-teaching staff for all year groups, and well used, also teaching enrichment subjects. Bullying dealt with when reported, and 'taken seriously'. An inclusion room for miscreants, who are taught separately and not allowed to socialise, helps avoid suspensions, which are rare. Behaviour consultants approached if need be. School counsellors not on site but plenty of pastoral mentors (similar to teaching assistants) who can be with a pupil all day if necessary.

Safeguarding taken extremely seriously, almost to the extreme. One of the few schools where our guide had to be accompanied by a teacher on their pupil-led tour of the school. And we have never been given a safeguarding leaflet and child protection booklet or been told not to record anything before. 'We stick to the letter of the law,' was said. In out view slightly pedantic and overzealous, but so be it. All pupils, up to year 11, hand in their phones at the beginning of the day and collect them at the end.

Pupils and parents: Pupils from all backgrounds. Parents supportive and involved and happy to voice opinions. Parents of grammar contingent opted for Ashlawn because it is 'inclusive' and wanted mixed education for their children. They don't necessarily agree with grammar schools per se but are happy to have the element in a comprehensive setting. Selective children come from a 10 mile radius, comprehensive more local. Pupils not particularly smart, but neat and tidy. Younger pupils wear burgundy sweatshirts and black skirts and trousers, year 9 and upwards in black. No blazers, but apparently sixth form boys enjoy wearing business suits. Girls can wear trousers, but we didn't notice many doing so. Pupils friendly and polite and happy to chat.

Entrance: Twelve per cent of places for top performers in the 11+ and a further 10 per cent are aptitude tested for modern foreign languages. School massively oversubscribed, 15 pupils for every place, despite there now being a 12 form intake in year 7.

About 30 per cent of year 12 is new to the school, coming mainly from partner schools in the town that don't have a sixth form. The odd one from single sex grammars in the town. Requirements depend on A level subjects.

Exit: Some 30 per cent leave after year 11, mainly for vocational courses at local colleges. The odd one to the single sex grammars in the town. Some 85 per cent goes to university. A few apprenticeships. The odd one straight to employment, gap years unusual, occasional Forces applicants.

Remarks: A school that is unashamedly academic and ambitious for its pupils. Its large numbers don't seem to put parents off, and pupils seem to thrive and are happy. Perhaps because of its size some elements of the school seem rather corporate and rigid, but who are we to argue? It obviously works for them.

Barnardiston Hall Preparatory School

Barnardiston Hall, Nr Haverhill, Suffolk CB9 7TG

Ages 6m–13 **Pupils** 212 **Boarders** 45 (from 6 years)

Fees: Day £8,040 – £13,395; Boarding £18,510 – £20,085 pa

01440 786316
www.barnardiston-hall.co.uk

Headmaster: Since 2017, Colonel Keith Boulter, Cambridge theology graduate and hockey blue (60s) and the owner of the school. Barnardiston is one of several schools and institutions run as a family business.

He was, in fact, headmaster several years ago, from 1990-2012, before stepping into the role of principal and passing the reins of day-to-day management over to the previous headmaster (Tim Dodgson who, while no longer head, remains at the school as a history teacher).

The Colonel has always been a force within the school, teaching mathematics, helping with games and choir work and followed everywhere by children, like the Pied Piper. He retains a certain bluff, military manner with great geniality and is greeted with wild enthusiasm and respect wherever he goes in the school. 'Who has camped in the garden with their teacher?' he asks. A forest of hands goes up. 'Who acted in the play? ' – hands up again (slightly different lot). 'Who wants more homework?' groans and shouts of 'Not me!' His early career in the Royal Army Educational Corps and, later, administering Gurkha schools, has helped shape the school's philosophy. Married, with a grown-up family, and lives in the grounds of Barnardiston. His daughter is head of the pre-prep department and his three grandchildren all attend the school.

Entrance: Non-selective. Pupils accepted at all stages through the school. A number come up from the nursery (six months-three years) to pre-prep. No formal exam but previous school reports are looked at and the children meet the head. Taster days are arranged for older children who attend classes, whilst particular needs are noted, and referrals/advice given to parents. The school has provision for educational support and few children are not accepted. Limited bursarial help for overseas pupils and siblings.

Exit: Most go on to a range of local independents at 13 – the Leys, Culford, the Perse, King's Ely, Framlingham, a sprinkling further afield. One or two leave at 11 for local state schools. Good guidance is given to parents. 'We suggest they visit three schools, two likely ones plus a wild card,' says the head. Pupils all get to where they want to go – a few scholarships each year.

Remarks: A country prep with a strong, slightly quirky character, very much the creation of its owner, Colonel Boulter. With a rural setting, agricultural rather than chocolate box picturesque, it has a splendid indifference to the customary marketing gloss. Boarders live in the main building, an Edwardian villa, alongside the headmaster and his family.

Subject teaching takes place in the converted stables which surround the courtyard, and the purpose built pre-prep department. A series of Portakabins are still in use, though no one appears bothered; in fact, the pupils see the strengths; as one pointed out in the 'temporary' science lab, 'We never have to worry about dropping liquids on the benches – they are so old!' The decorative theme throughout is inspired by the Colonel's travels including elephants and giraffes, displays from Tutankhamen's tomb, wooden carvings, ornamental ponds and, unexpectedly, two full suits of armour standing guard at the end of a passage.

Indoor sports and ballet take place in a marquee (heated), supposedly temporary but no plans to change this. School has a small theatre with raked seating and facilities for sound and lighting – 'We all learn to do it as well as act' – and productions are all-out efforts of the whole school rather than an elite group. Music, a particular interest of the Colonel, is well taught and popular; around 50 per cent learn an instrument.

No formal gardens or prefects' lawns here; the grounds resemble an adventure playground. Approached by a drive full of potholes ('We know the fees aren't wasted on tarmac,' said a parent, approvingly), skateboarding is allowed, as are tree climbing and den building, there is a miniature railway, a bouncy castle – all tastes catered for. Announcements are made over a PA system, known as the 'bing-bong', that operates all over the school; slightly disconcerting at first, rather like a tube station, but pupils like it and think it is sensible.

A lot of parents are commuters and chose the school 'because the pupils seem so happy and relaxed, very different from London schools,' said one. 'Mine have all made tons of friends and have a crack at anything going,' said another, though also warning that 'it's not a place for namby-pambys.' (We think that remark is directed more at parents than pupils.) Adventure and independence encouraged from the outset with form sleepovers. 'We camped with our teacher in the garden when I was 6!' said one pupil, and this spirit continues up the school. Orienteering very popular (Prep National Champions), camping expeditions, and all team sports played with gusto. Long-awaited Astroturf is now installed. Parents welcome the unfussy attitude but warn: 'If you like things just so and organised months in advance then it might not suit'.

Classes are small, average 14, and setting begins early in the key subjects. Latin and French from early on, though Latin is dropped in the top three years by some. Those who might struggle in other schools find areas where they can shine. 'The staff are brilliant at building confidence,' say parents, who approve of the less stressful approach. Educational learning support is provided in the special needs department (known as The Bridge). Needs range from an extra boost to cases at the mild end of the autism spectrum, dyslexia and dyspraxia. There is also EFL and support for gifted children. A few children have statements and are LEA funded but the school won't take pupils they cannot help.

Boarding facilities are on the top two floors of the main building. Though approached by a slightly depressing staircase, the facilities themselves are comfortable and homelike. Boys and girls occupy separate floors. Bedrooms, mostly four bedded, are light, well-decorated and some have en suite bathrooms. Rather posh bathrooms in fact – think department store loos – good lighting, warm and clean. Friendly matrons, who remain on duty until the younger boarders, at least, are in bed and asleep. Boys, who form some two-thirds of the boarders, also have a common room on their boarding floor with an enormous screen for weekend viewing. The girls have one in their bedroom but, I was assured, there is no signal so can only be used for DVD watching. Mobiles, for all pupils, are looked after by the school during the day and boarders are allowed to use them for only limited periods. 'Can be hard for some, at first, especially those from abroad, but we want them to join in real life here,' said the headmaster. Weekend outings to local towns/places of interest are arranged for those, largely from overseas, who stay in school. With notice, it is possible to remain through the half term holidays also. Occasional boarding is popular and encouraged towards the top end of the school, especially for those moving on to board at senior schools.

This is a tremendously jolly school where a sense of adventure is encouraged. Most pupils thrive and go on to do well at senior schools. 'We often hear of former pupils becoming prefects or house heads,' we were told. Perhaps not suitable for those with hearts set on scholarships to the top flight schools, but definitely worth looking at for those who appreciate a less stressful, unstuffy, purposeful atmosphere and a staff dedicated to the needs of its pupils.

Beachborough School

5

Westbury, Brackley, Northamptonshire NN13 5LB

Ages 2.5–13 **Pupils** 382 **Boarders** 5 weekly, 70 flexi (from year 3)

Fees: Day £10,728 – £16,845 pa; Boarding + £35 – £37 per night

01280 700071
www.beachborough.com

Headmaster: Since September 2018, Christian Pritchard, previously head of Ranby House, the prep school of Worksop College. Degree from University College of Ripon and York St John and a MA in education from Oxford Brookes. A keen musician with a background in computer science. He has also worked internationally as head of the British School in Amsterdam and head of the junior school at Taipei European School. He is married to Zoe and they have two daughters.

Entrance: Non-selective. An informal 'taster' day, with teacher-led assessments, gives the school some idea of a child's strengths and weaknesses; applicants for year 3 upwards assessed in English and maths. Some means-tested bursares.

Exit: Around half of year 8s leave with scholarships. Nearby Stowe and Bloxham most popular, with other destinations including Oxford High, Abingdon, Akeley Wood, Tudor Hall, Magdalen College School, Oundle, Millfield, Mount Kelly and Headington. A few leave at 11 for grammar schools eg Royal Latin.

Remarks: Set in an impressive rambling country mansion with a range of modern blocks surrounding it, the newest a huge sports hall that many senior schools would be proud of. Others include a very good sized school theatre, science block that usually has Bunsen burners in full swing, and a smart Boardroom Building, where children from nursery up to year 4 are based. There's also staff digs, where many of the 40-strong teaching staff live. All the classrooms are light, airy and inviting.

Whilst the reception areas have the typical 'smart hotel' look of many rural private schools, there's a refreshing emphasis on displaying children's artwork and practical touches like the fridge (albeit hidden behind tasteful built-in cupboards) by the front door so pupils can collect anything they've made in cookery lessons on their way home.

Total of 30 acres of lush countryside for pupils to enjoy – and they really do. We happened to visit on a sunny April day and at break time children were running and jumping all over the front lawn, but on rainy days they simply don boiler suits and wellies. School has a farm and sells its own sausages, and there are plenty of gardens dotted around, including the nursery sound garden and early years vegetable garden. Forest school means you'll often see pupils taking classes outside, and when we visited there was even a replica of a trench in one field. This formed part of the school's 'enrichment week', where teachers can focus all subjects on a single topic, in this case World War I.

Three sets for English, French, maths and science from year 3 upwards, subject specialists from year 5. Average class sizes of 14 to 18.

Not traditionally regarded as an academic school, it now prefers the description of 'happy, ambitious and challenging' – a combination that pupils and parents agree pretty much sum up the focus of the greater academic emphasis. So whilst year 1's computing lesson might focus on coding and older children can expect lectures from the likes of Professor Matt Jarvis from Oxford University on black holes, you'll also find display walls throughout the school celebrating the efforts of the less academically inclined.

Good provision for those requiring extra help (dyslexia, dyspraxia), via the learning support department. No charge is made for this – nor, incidentally, for tea and prep time after school; before- and after-school care; or most residential school trips, which include a year 2 trip to Amersham, whilst older year groups go to PGL, HMS Belfast, Spain, Paris and the Lake District. There's also a focus on gifted and talented via the school's able child programme. Self-assessment and peer-assessment are priorities and there's a big push to encourage children (especially the gifted and talented) to take greater intellectual risks.

Sport is central, with some pupils at regional or national level in sports such as trampolining and cricket. Every child is involved in team games and team photos displayed around the school are of the Cs, Ds and E too. Boys and girls play football and cricket, which one parent said reflects 'how Beachborough isn't a boys' prep school with girls, but a proper, genuine co-ed school,' where incidentally there is pretty much a 50/50 gender split in every year. Swimming club every week at Stowe School's pool, four miles away, and the newest sport in the school is triathlon, in which 30 children take part every Saturday.

Music is big here, with around two-thirds playing an instrument ranging from piano to bassoon. Year 1s and 2s get to try out the violin, recorder and percussion keyboard for 20 weeks before deciding if they want individual lessons. Two choirs, chamber choir and junior choir, for all year 3 and 4 children. Music tours to eg Bruges.

B

Each year group performs a play every year – a Christmas play for the younger ones, Shakespeare for year 8s, with other recent examples including Treasure Island and Pirates of the Curry Bean. Art – which is overseen by not just a head of art but professional artist – is imaginatively displayed throughout the school, and other activities include Young Enterprise, golf, Mad Science, tennis, archery, craft clubs and dance.

USPs include no Saturday school and a flexible approach to boarding. This includes up to four nights a week, and nearly half the children aged 7+ stay over at least once a week. This is no sleepover, though, with organised activities for boarders, a clear boarding school culture and all the strict rules you might expect, such as bedtime for oldest pupils at 9.15pm and silent reading before lights out. Dorms, which are located on top floor of main school building with girls' rooms on one side and boys' on the other, are well kept, welcoming and cheerful, with stunning wall art (Narnia for girls; war planes for boys). Long-serving school matron is based here.

Food is popular, with one pudding known as 'bird seed' (Rice Krispies coated in custard) easily the best loved course. Children eat calmly at long wooden tables, with teachers sitting at each end, and grace is said before and after each meal.

The code of conduct is clear, including 'being friendly is easy and it can make the world of difference' and 'always do your best, whatever the challenge.' By and large, the children seem to live by them, with pupils (and indeed parents) saying the school feels like one big family. Bad behaviour taken seriously, with a naughty bench for the younger children (although it's not called that), but the focus is on prevention and there's a new well-being programme. School says that whilst it's natural for children to fall out from time to time, they don't allow this to descend to bullying, which they put down to an anti-bullying policy, great pastoral care, a focus on rewards for friendly behaviour and the fact that little problems don't grow due to positive interventions. Parents and pupils agree. Active school council, which had just voted in increased choice in school meals when we visited.

The pupil body is almost exclusively white and, besides the 10-15 per cent Americans, almost all English. The majority of children are local, with some coming from Towcester, Bicester, Banbury and Milton Keynes. Parents mainly from farming industries, motor racing employees (Silverstone is round the corner) and hedge fund managers. Lots of family events, with the Beachborough Association putting on murder mystery evenings, coffee stops, quiz nights and an annual camp-out on the front lawn, for which tents were starting to appear when we visited.

This is a happy, nurturing school, set in beautiful surroundings. We found the children to be confident, polite and animated and completely lacking in arrogance. 'I've done things I'd never have thought of – like archery,' said one pupil. 'I love the fact that we're always celebrating people. I've learned that everyone is good at something,' said another.

Parents talk about the 'special atmosphere' and 'emphasis on inclusivity', as well as the 'individual attention that each child gets.' 'This place is a hidden jewel,' said one. 'The children are encouraged in whatever direction they want to go and the staff have a way of getting the best out of them.'

Bedford Girls' School

Cardington Road, Bedford, Bedfordshire MK42 0BX

Ages 7–18 **Pupils** 907 **Sixth form** 148

Fees: £9,438 – £13,263 pa

01234 361900
www.bedfordgirlsschool.co.uk

Headmistress: Since 2010, Jo MacKenzie BSc MSc (50s). Schooled in Australia, then read geography and economics at the University of Western Australia. Realised vocation aged 5 when gifted a blackboard which was promptly put to excellent use teaching pets, toys and her younger brother. 'Never considered any other career' (apart from – briefly – sweet shop owner). PGCE at London University's Institute of Education, followed by masters at Leicester University. Cut teeth at Bromley High and arrived in Bedford via stints at Blackheath High, Alleyn's School in Dulwich and Ipswich High. Appointed head of Dame Alice Harpur School in 2009 before being offered the chance to take the reins at the then newly created Bedford Girls' School.

Strongly in favour of IB and although GCSEs and A levels still represent the majority of public examinations at BGS is keen to drive IB ethos of creativity and independent thinking right through curriculum from year 3 upwards. Strong feminist views on vital role of school in giving girls a 'can do' attitude and says 'growth mindset is in the DNA of school – there's no gender stereotyping here'. Also heavily focused on giving pupils the attributes for success in the workplace rather than just to pass exams. 'What skills do 18-year olds need? Time management, working in teams, problem solving and creativity.'

'Forward thinking', say parents, and 'straight talking' with a simultaneously warm and businesslike manner. Still keeps her hand in in the classroom – observes lessons to 'get to know girls and what makes them tick'.

Head of junior school: Since 2012, Carolyn Howe, previously deputy head and acting head of pre-prep at James Allen's Prep School in London.

Academic matters: Just 20 per cent of sixth formers do the IB (head's target is 30 per cent) but its broad ethos of creative and independent thinking permeates learning right from get-go. Junior school recently introduced 'enhanced curriculum', with all subjects following a termly thematic thread (eg habitats or Aztecs), culminating in an independent research project and, for older girls, debate at end of term. Independent learning for juniors also encouraged, with fortnightly 'menu' of tasks within the topic to be completed in pupils' chosen order and at their own speed and iPads recently introduced for every pupil (kept in school, happily for parents) to develop research skills. In addition, there's a 'QED' (question, explore, discover) project to be completed every fortnight as homework. While on subject of homework – it's on the heavy side, with at least two subjects per night from year 3.

This approach to study ('we're always thinking about employability,' says head) carried – albeit to a lesser degree due to the restraints of GCSE curriculum – into senior school with strong focus on presentation and time management skills. Drama on curriculum from years 3 to 9 and available at GCSE and A level. Art and DT departments well equipped and vibrant, although it's a shame more artwork isn't displayed around school – it's rather stark in places.

Although head says school 'tries not to be too traditional', curriculum remains just that, with a solid array of all the usual suspects at both GCSE and A level. Spanish taught by native speaker from year 3 (exclusively, following decision that one language should be taught rather than two), with option of French or German in year 7, Latin introduced at end of year 7 and Greek available for 'serious classicists' at A level. Two classes of a maximum of 20 in year 3 grows to four classes in year 5, with pupils remaining mainly with class teacher for all core subjects (specialist taught for PE, dance, drama, music and Spanish) until year 6 when they start taking the short walk to the senior school for their science lessons.

Most take 10 GCSEs, with triple science and a language compulsory. Not the most academic of the area's independents (although parents say it's the head's vision to 'get school right up there') but results are more than solid and on an upward trajectory with 71 per cent of GCSEs graded A*-A/9-7 in 2018 and for sixth formers an IB point average of 37; doesn't reveal results for A levels. Value added 'quite extraordinary' according to head, who claims at least one grade is added across the board at GCSE and it was smiles all round from the sixth formers when we asked how well they were supported during university application time – all benefit from weekly one-to-one tutorials during years 12 and 13 and love the fact that they can give their personal statement to any – and as many – teachers as they like for feedback. Minor grumbles that uni applications don't go in as early as at some other schools though. Students say teachers are 'really supportive' and they appreciate lunchtime clinics to cover tricky areas as well as being able to email teachers direct, with replies generally flying back through the ether within minutes (similarly to parental missives). Around one third take EPQ. Numerous 'curriculum conversations' – evening or lunchtime events keeping parents informed of exactly what their child is learning and teaching methods – are much appreciated.

Around seven per cent of cohort (around 80 in senior school) receive SEN support. All levels of dyslexia accepted into school, provided they are of at least average intelligence and able to confidently access curriculum. Readers and scribes at exam time for most severe cases, although no classroom support in senior school and one-to-one support limited to 30 minutes fortnightly. Pupils with severe visual and hearing impairment and cerebral palsy cases currently on register, as well as a few with mild to moderate ADHD/ASD. Juniors needing additional support attend small early morning groups of around eight following referral by class teacher. TAs distributed where most needed rather than 'belonging' to specific classes but the jewel in the crown has to be Polo the reading dog, who visits daily – 'he doesn't judge and he doesn't criticise', says the head.

Games, options, the arts: When we asked what characteristic of the school most stood out for them, girls told us 'everything', but for us it was sport and music that really shone. Head concurs that school boasts a 'fantastic' PE department, offering an inclusive ethos (A to E teams fielded wherever possible for most major sports) and great depth. Good outdoor facilities on site (shared by junior and senior schools) and although the fields and grounds are nothing to write home about, there are a further six lacrosse pitches a short distance away at Cople Fields as well as the Harpur Trust boathouse on the nearby River Ouse opening up rowing as an increasingly popular option. Own pool means that junior girls swim every week and there's training by a former Olympic hopeful for more advanced groups. Fixtures introduced from year 4 and are pretty much weekly from year 5, with junior girls happily reporting that 'teams are rotated fairly – everyone gets a turn' and parents concurring that 'sport is for everyone'. But wave goodbye to lying in and lazy weekends if your offspring are especially sporty. Saturday matches are on the calendar right from year 4, with teams travelling far and wide to compete in tournaments and fixtures – one year 6 girls told us she'd had eight Saturday fixtures so far this term. PE in any guise compulsory right to year 13 but students can choose their options at the start of term from year 7 onwards and those less inclined towards dashing about in the cold after a ball of some description can opt for more serene pursuits such as yoga, badminton or trampolining.

Clubs galore. Juniors encouraged to 'dip in and out' as they please – 'we don't want to pigeonhole or limit them', says head. Seniors can create their own initiatives (oh, how we would have loved a cheese society when we were at school) and reins are often handed down through the year groups. Tons of house activity and competitions and sixth formers keep energy high with fundraisers and themed days – when we visited they were preparing for a Harry Potter day, complete with Triwizard Tournament set to take place in the common room. Own radio studio with year 10 students broadcasting shows, available to hear live on Wednesday mornings or to download from bespoke app. Young Enterprise, Model United Nations and Duke of Edinburgh all popular, as is CCF.

Smartly revamped music department is shared by juniors and seniors. More soundproofed practice rooms than we could count (good job as there are no less than 22 visiting peripatetic teachers, teaching everything from harp to drums), plus performance and recording studios. Five choirs (non-selective in junior school), plus plethora of orchestras and bands with something for everyone – even a fife club and a rock band run by two classically trained A level music students. Tons of opportunities to perform: every year group from 3 up stages an annual play in the junior school: year 5 delivers a WW2 tea party; new year 6 major production dovetails with an exhibition of work; years 7 and 12 put on a play together and there are two major productions every year, more ambitious now under newly appointed director of drama – recently Arabian Nights and an all-female production of Lord of the Flies. The house Glee competition, though, is where all comers can showcase their various performance skills with even the youngest girls taking to the stage to sing, dance or perform a puppet show and on occasion dancing dogs joining their owners in the spotlight.

Background and atmosphere: A mere spring chicken in its current guise, opening its doors to pupils from years 3 to 13 in 2012 as the result of a decision by Harpur Trust in 2009 to 'rationalise provision of education in Bedford'. This saw merger between Bedford High School for Girls and Dame Alice Harpur School, both with rich heritages dating back to 1882, to create Bedford Girls' School. Much coffee shop chitchat about who was the 'winner' of the merger ensued and the years immediately post-merger were rife with parental discontent surrounding the integration of two schools. Happily, that seems to be in the past ('just sour grapes,' said one former pupil turned parent) and the school appears to be sailing in calm waters now, with pupil cohort finally united in their ethos. 'We are absolutely fully integrated now', head assures. Hugely popular house system runs from year 3 up, with six houses named after inspirational women, each with their own Twitter and Instagram feeds to keep members engaged and enthused. House meetings take place every fortnight and a cup for the winner of the fiercely fought house point competition is presented each year.

School occupies an attractive collection of Victorian buildings on the edge of Bedford with architecturally eclectic additions to the senior school campus. Junior school uniformly bright, spacious and airy, set amongst delightful gardens, including new adventure trail (courtesy of PTA fundraising) and overall a lovely, nurturing feel – 'our girls seem to stay younger longer,' says head. Newly refurbished library – its super modern appeal juxtaposed with a beautifully maintained frescoed ceiling and floor to ceiling glass on two sides – forms fabulous centrepiece to the school building and sets the tone for this most pristine of learning environments (we almost found ourselves yearning to see a bit of tatty panelling or peeling wallpaper). Senior school similarly immaculate, having benefited from ongoing programme of summer refurbishments (most recently the drama department and dance studio) and another stunning library mirroring that of its younger sister, a popular 'hang out' for students at break and lunch times. Girls lower down the school can't wait to get their hands on the sixth form facilities – and it's not surprising. As well as the coolest professionally graffitied lockers we've ever seen, they've also got one of the largest common rooms, decked out in bright colours and squishy sofas; a study loft for quiet work and their own café serving coffee, sandwiches and hot food, more akin to an urban brasserie than a school caff. Sixth formers wear smart grey business suits and 12 are voted on to leadership group each year, including head girl, two deputies and house captains.

Pastoral care, well-being and discipline: Head says 'key to learning is relationships' and girls describe their bonds with teachers as 'very personal' and the cohort at large as a 'tight knit community – we do have anti-bullying ambassadors, but they're almost redundant'. Parents agree that any issues are 'nipped sensitively in the bud'.

Smooth transition to senior school a major selling point, with parents 'hugely impressed – anxiety just doesn't occur'. Form tutors are the first port of call in the event of any problem and girls keep the same tutor for years 10 and 11 to support them through GCSEs and another for sixth form. Few sanctions necessary – no suspensions or exclusions to report for some time; lunchtime detentions about as bad as it gets for all the usual misdemeanours. Diversity all in a day's work in terms of race, religion and sexuality – no major fanfare or fuss but just girls accepting and getting along with each other. Openly gay pupils 'no issue' according to head and there have been one or two transgender pupils pass happily through the school. These topics openly discussed with sixth form in PSHE lesson entitled 'the things they didn't teach you in sex ed'.

Pupils and parents: 'Normal girls from hardworking families' is how the head described students – and that's exactly what we found. Parents report a 'lovely balance' between all the benefits of a private education and the real world – 'girls are definitely not precious'. Students travel to school for up to an hour on a fleet of coaches from Herts, Northants, Beds and Milton Keynes, as well as on the train from St Albans – and increasingly from London, with parents anxious to escape the pressurecooker schools on their doorsteps. Strong local contingent remains, many with brothers at Bedford School, with whom BGS enjoys a close working relationship through linked curriculum activities in junior school and later CCF, concerts, choirs and occasional parent events.

Head speaks of the 'rich cultural environment' (between 30 to 40 per cent are from ethnic groups) but there's no sign of cliques. Long wraparound care benefits dual income families, with girls able to stay at school from 7.30am to 7pm for no additional charge (although it's worth noting that there's no provision for canteen food after school). New alumni mentoring scheme recently introduced and work on alumni database also underway to help students with work experience and career advice.

Entrance: Pupils join prep at 7 in equal numbers from pre-preps (Pilgrims and Polam School) and state primaries, with other main entry points in years 5, 7, 9 and 12. Although not oversubscribed or highly selective at any point, applicants should be 'above the average of 100 in baseline assessments', says head. Junior school assessment comprises writing, reading and maths plus a second round of art and science activities and group discussions.

Around half of the year 7 intake comes from junior school, who are guaranteed a place, and others from a broad range of primaries and preps far and wide. Up to 15 new girls join sixth form each year – they need five GCSEs at 9-6, with 6s or above for the subjects they want to take at A level. Applicants into year 7 tested in English, maths and VR and stay on for taster sessions in science plus interviews with headmistress and head of year.

Exit: Largish numbers (some 30 per cent per cent) leave after GCSE – mainly for co-ed, boarding or seeking out subjects not offered by BGS at A level. Majority to higher education, with small numbers either into the workforce or taking years out. About half to Russell Group universities; two to Oxbridge and three medics (one in Romania) in 2018, plus another off to Rotterdam. STEM leads the way, with about a third choosing this degree sector, followed closely by business or vocational related subjects, with a few off to degree apprenticeship courses.

Money matters: Good value. Fees comparatively reasonable and majority of clubs and activities (with the exception of peripatetic music lessons, LAMDA and extra dance) included. Only long term one-to-one SEN support charged as extra. No scholarships but generous bursary fund for senior school students, with currently around 100 girls receiving some level of financial assistance.

Remarks: A school where girls are valued whatever their interests or skills. Watch your daughter blossom and 'get the full-on experience' in this purposeful environment that thoroughly 'gets' girls. BGS, with its mixture of traditional and new values, has undergone a huge evolution but has now firmly established its own identity and, as one parent said, 'is really worth pushing the boat out for'.

Bedford Preparatory School

Linked with Bedford School

De Parys Avenue, Bedford, Bedfordshire MK40 2TU

Ages 7–13 **Pupils** 404 **Boarders** 16 full, 5 weekly, 3 flexi **C of E**

Fees: Day: £12,333 – £16,161; Boarding: £20,919 – £26,067 pa

01234 362216
www.bedfordschool.org.uk

Headmaster: Since 2013, Ian Silk (40s), previously deputy head of Bishops Stortford Junior School and former housemaster at Ardingly College. An English and drama specialist, brims with enthusiasm about all aspects of the school – most particularly the spectacular new theatre (2015) shared with the upper school and the town. Married to Sarah, with two sons both at the school – 'they are chalk and cheese,' he told us, 'but the school is brilliant for both of them.' Knows most boys by name – lots of heads do but this is a large prep – and has lunch with all new joiners in small groups.

Entrance: Mainly at 7+, 8+ and 11+. Not heavily oversubscribed but looking for the right fit, ability to keep up and fully participate in school life. 'At 7 some boys might not be there yet,' says head, 'but we encourage them to try again later.' Assessments in English, maths, NVR, creative writing, an in-school day – and that all-important report from current head. Large contingent from nearby pre-prep and fellow Harpur Trust member Pilgrims and around 30 per cent from local state schools. Buses from Luton, Milton Keynes and Hitchin broaden catchment.

Exit: Almost all (99 per cent) transfer to Bedford School with the odd exception departing for the state sector or, for international boarders, their mother country. No prep for CE or formal advice on other destination schools, but existing pupils sit the same test as external candidates for setting purposes. Parents report a seamless transition to upper school, with boys better prepared for workload than those joining from other preps.

Remarks: A boys' own paradise which simultaneously feels separate from and integral to the upper school and offers everything young boys could hope for, whatever their interests. In the space of one lunch time we watched boys hunting for creepy crawlies in bug hotels, singing with gusto in the junior choir, planing chess boards in the DT suite, creating games in the ICT suite, building sets for the school play, having a good old fashioned kick about – and of course, in time honoured tradition for a Friday, tucking into fish and chips in the school dining hall ('really good,' we were assured). Never a dull moment.

'Nicely contained' in a corner of the vast Bedford School campus, one of the main benefits of prep is that it enjoys unfettered access to the wealth of facilities of the upper school – as well as a fair few of its own. Classrooms ranging from the antiquated 'Inky' (incubator for fledgling Bedfordians) to more modern purpose-built additions sit around a central Astro play area where boys let off steam at break times. A separate adventure playground adds to the fun – although there's so much else going on, we're not sure when pupils would get the chance to use it. Classrooms feel cosy in comparison to the overwhelming sense of space elsewhere. Science labs are well-equipped and art and DT outstanding. Super work of exceptional quality, themed to ignite passionate creativity amongst the all-male cohort by their inspiring male head of art (who doubles up as games teacher), festoons the interiors. We loved the Viking shields crafted in DT and the fabulous gargoyle masks produced in year 8 art. Not a still life in sight.

It's rugby, hockey and cricket ('huge' according to head) on the sporting agenda, with a fully inclusive approach and school putting out as many as 18 competitive teams for fixtures, so everyone gets a ride on the bus and a post-match tea at least once a term, whatever their ability. Tons of music and drama to temper the testosterone. Hugely popular (and, crucially, non-selective) junior choir, plus chapel choir for years 5 and up, as well as instrumental lessons on curriculum for years 3 and 4. Great excitement on the dramatic front too, as all major performances now take place in what must be the most stunning school theatre in England – a £7 million structure built (thanks to a legacy donation) on the grounds of a neighbouring Moravian church – altar, stained glass and tablets sympathetically incorporated.

Dedicated SENCo with two supporting specialists and strong emphasis on training whole staff to support individual needs (mild dyslexia and dyspraxia; a few with mild Asperger's). Around 20 boys receiving support. Close communication with upper school a great strength: 'we hand parents and children over individually so nothing falls between the gaps,' SENCo assured. Strong ESOL team caters for overseas students.

Boarding in purpose-built Eagle House for up to 32 boys from year 3 and up, although most start after year 5 as either flexi, full or weekly boarders. A real home from home feel, thanks in no small part to super houseparent couple, as well as plenty of nicely furnished, comfy spaces with lots of personal touches for boys to hang out after school hours. Spacious dorms sleep between four and eight boys, who make them their own with pictures, posters and duvet covers from home. When prep's finished (supervised, in dedicated room for all bar the year 8s), there's a homely common room equipped with computers, a kitchen for snacking and a basement games room with table football and pool on offer. Where boys find the time to use these facilities, though, is anyone's guess, as there's also a full programme of after-school activities each day to take advantage of. Mobiles and other gadgets allowed but must be put on charge in the prep room overnight.

Around half the boarders overseas (from mainly Russia, China and Spain), good Forces quota as well, so there are plenty around at weekends once Saturday school (compulsory for all from year 6) and Sunday chapel are out of the way, to enjoy outings ranging from go karting or high ropes to bowling or the cinema, often followed by a takeaway or one of the housemaster's legendary barbecues.

'Zero tolerance' anti-bullying policy with clear protocol in place for inevitable – albeit rare – lapses. 'We show as much understanding to both sides as possible,' says housemaster. School counsellor available for boys to use for anything from home sickness to help with social skills.

All in all, a really super option for those looking for top notch day or boarding – as long as your sights are firmly set on an all-through education at Bedford. A kind, happy and successful school with the added bonus of a smooth transition to the thriving and successful upper school without the weighty stress of the 11+ or CE.

B

Bedford School

Linked with Bedford Preparatory School

De Parys Avenue, Bedford, Bedfordshire MK40 2TU

Ages 13–18 **Pupils** 717 **Sixth form** 278 **Boarders** 162 full, 76 weekly
C of E

Fees: Day £19,032; Boarding £31,125 – £32,190 pa

01234 362216
www.bedfordschool.org.uk

Head master: Since 2014, James Hodgson (40s), educated at Wellington College and Durham (classics) before being scooped up on the milk round by Ernst and Young and spending a couple of years as a trainee accountant. In his 20s, a cricketer hovering around the fringes of the professional game (and uninspired by the world of finance), he wrote to Cambridge on the off-chance of a late place on its PGCE course and turned up trumps, meaning he could pursue his long term ambition of running a boarding house as well as playing regular top class cricket, ultimately earning a blue.

Spent six years teaching in Sydney before joining Tonbridge School as boarding housemaster and director of admissions. Latterly senior deputy head of Magdalen College School, Oxford. Impressed on joining Bedford by the boys 'completely at ease' with the staff and each other – 'presenting awards in my first assembly, every single boy shook my hand, looked me in the eye, smiled and said thank you – quite something for a large group of teenagers,' he says. At peace with Bedford not quite hitting the dizzy academic heights of Magdalen but plans to up the ante a little 'for pastoral reasons – results are just a passport to the next level'. Passionate about boarding ('it develops the whole person') and ready to take on the challenge of keeping it thriving at Bedford. Parents feeling the effect of this already with the recent introduction of a full schedule of celebrations for leavers, including their own speech day followed by house events and a leavers' ball – 'a fitting end to a super education,' in the words of one.

Youthful, energetic and 'really personable,' according to parents – not just a safe pair of hands for parents to hand their sons to, but dynamic, likeable and inspiring. Accessible to pupils – has open door for a period each morning where pupils can come to discuss anything. Presence at matches and performances (with the occasional personal note of congratulations to performers afterwards) noted and appreciated by all. Married to Rachel, with four teenage children.

Academic matters: Solid academics, especially given broad church intake and large proportion who joined via the prep at 7+. 2018 saw 69 per cent of GCSEs graded A*-A/9-7; 37 per cent A*/A at A level and 71 per cent A*-B, with an average IB score of 35.

English and maths set from outset but rejigged along the way. Class sizes capped at 24, shrinking to a pleasing eight or nine for many A level subjects. All take 10 GCSEs, with around 30 per cent taking four full A levels in year 13 (mostly including further maths). Boys opt for either A levels or IB in sixth form. IB numbers 'a bit low' according to head with just over 15 per cent currently opting to take this route. School aims to boost numbers to around a third of the cohort.

Well thought out curriculum with separate sciences and all boys learning at least two languages; computing now taught to GCSE. Maths and sciences extremely popular options at A level as well as good take up in geography ('a very good department,' says head) and economics. German, Spanish, French and Latin on offer in the languages department, with Mandarin available as a twilight option, but rather low take up of these at A level. PPE an interesting offer in year 10 and parents praised standard of 'inspirational' RS teaching.

Boys with SEN (mainly mild dyslexia or dyscalculia) given bespoke care with the department tailoring help according to each boy's individual needs. Strong ESOL team caters for overseas students, who are offered extra English language sessions in place of another language and about half of them take IGCSE ESL instead of English.

Head acknowledges lack of strong articulation of sixth form – super facilities abound at Bedford yet no dedicated centre for years 12 and 13. Parents identified career support as an area in need of improvement – 'so much more that they could do'. The school's recent appointment of dedicated UCAS and careers specialist has raised the school's game in this area, which is demonstrated through the award of the highly regarded Career Mark (only seven other independent schools hold this award) and a Gold Education to Employment (E2E) award. UCAS application process highly praised, with parents barely needing to get involved in the process: 'exactly as it should be', although head hopes to up future Oxbridge numbers.

Games, options, the arts: Sport is the lifeblood of Bedford and although the list of recent accolades is too long to list (in all sports from rugby and cricket to swimming and golf), school maintains it's not just for the elite and says it offers all boys 'the same time on task' when it comes to training – the input and expertise from the directors of all major sports filtering down to even the lowliest of teams.

Are less gifted boys afforded the same kudos as the macho sporty crowd, we asked one sixth former? Apparently yes, since the introduction in recent years of colours for art, drama and academia in addition to sport – a welcome addition signified by a colourful array of scarves – and special striped blazers for those awarded cricket colours. Parents, too, concur that school 'absolutely allows boys to be all-rounders'. It's a rugby, hockey, cricket school – with strong rowing too (how many schools have their own boat house on a beautiful stretch of the river Ouse?) but plenty of other options to choose from: you name it and Bedford offers it, from archery or rifle shooting to pilates and fencing. National and international honours in all main sports plus golf and fencing, and boys have gone on to play for their universities and even their country in most sports played at Bedford, where the main challenge for staff is finding competitor schools strong enough to give them a good game.

Music of a 'fantastic calibre,' according to parents, with a super modern music centre – designed by award-winning architect Eric Parry and apparently positioned opposite the pavilion so that the director of music can keep one eye on the cricket scoreboard whilst conducting the school orchestra. Choirs, orchestras and bands a-plenty, a new music technology suite, gleaming new fleet of iMacs, a recording studio (Desert Island Disks with the head a recent highlight), rock room and inspirational recital hall – used for weekly performances by pupils and recitals from visiting professionals. Something for everyone and parents say even the most reluctant musician is inspired to join in. School's enthusiasm for making music illustrated by wild enthusiasm (parents and boys) for the annual house music, 'the best competition of the year,' by all accounts, which sounds like a cross between 20/20 cricket with boys, faces painted and fancy dressed, raucously chanting and cheering on their housemates, and young musician of the year ('as soon as the singing starts, everyone is silent,' explained our guide).

Possibly the most stunning theatre we've seen in any school, built on the site of a former Moravian Church, with original features sympathetically included to complement the modern architecture – all exposed brick and floor to ceiling glass. Shared with the town, and able to seat over 280, the theatre not only hosts school productions (recently Shakespeare's The Comedy of Errors by the prep and Henry V by the upper), often in conjunction with Bedford Girls' School, but also productions by visiting companies. A full-time technical director takes care of special effects and shows boys the ropes with lighting and scenery.

Outstanding work on show in the art and DT departments, with some mind-blowing projects on display in the year 13 workshop – no wonder so many move on to study engineering at university. History of art an extracurricular option.

A non-stop merry-go-round of extracurricular activities keeps boys busy outside of the classroom. Options range from public speaking to a very popular CCF in all three branches, run in conjunction with Bedford Girls'. Trips and tours galore for all manner of interests from sports tours to choir trips, academic excursions and – occasionally – just for fun.

Boarding: Six senior boarding houses – four on site and two just a short walk away – offer intimate and cosy homes from home for the boys who board here. Charming in that none are purpose built, the houses are adapted Victorian villas, each with its own character – all with a fraternity house feel. Described as 'an extension of the housemaster's home', the houses are bright and spacious, with reassuringly untidy dorms (we secretly approve – boys must feel at home to be quite so slovenly) and the kinds of communal spaces day boys would probably die for (Xboxes, pinball machines, pool tables, chess tables – you name it). In keeping with rest of the school, modern facilities are juxtaposed with traditional artefacts (shiny fleets of computers beneath panelled honours boards) and boys have the freedom to come and go during the course of the day. Masters describe the boys as 'like brothers', one commenting that 'there's nothing better than seeing a huge sixth former strolling to breakfast chatting to one of the year 9s'. Many boarders are former day boys fed up with the daily commute – parents love the fact that boys can 'grow with the school'. Over 65 per cent of boarders are there full time so plenty of buzz at weekends, with regular trips and outings as well as free run of sports facilities and time for valuable R&R. Compulsory Saturday school for all.

Background and atmosphere: Don't be put off if you approach Bedford from the M1 via a somewhat grotty suburban high street, at the end of which you catch first glimpse of the school like an oasis in the architectural desert. School takes great pains to remind us of 'the other half' of Bedford which lies behind it – smart rows of Victorian villas (two boarding houses among them) leading down to a beautiful river bank. The school itself has the feel of a university campus about it – the buildings, a delightful mix of old and new, surround the manicured playing fields. The main building is all turrets, spires and a bell tower, with a magnificent hall as the central point and classrooms on four levels.

Impossible to choose a stand-out feature or department as each and every addition to the school has been made with care and deliberation to fuse function and form effectively. From the professional-looking cricket pavilion to the super modern glazed music school (who could fail to be inspired in here?), stunning library full of gleaming new books – but with the antique ones carefully displayed – and the cottage-like art building, set in its own sculpture garden, the whole campus gives the aura of a school offering roundedness in the purest sense of the word. The word chapel doesn't quite do justice to the glorious building where weekly services are held – the school accommodated amongst panelled walls inscribed with war memorials of fallen OBs.

Sports facilities unsurprisingly top notch. Super weights room would give most private gyms a run for their money and there's a 25 metre swimming pool (reportedly 'rather chilly but nobody minds,' according to our guide). Recent refurb and renovation of tennis courts and cricket pavilion – opened by England captain and Old Bedfordian, Alastair Cook.

Pastoral care, well-being and discipline: Brotherly atmosphere helped twofold by small houses with a family feel and vertical tutor groups where boys can get to know others from all year groups, with the tutor being the first port of call in the event of a problem. Head describes school as 'a fantastic community,' with everyone pitching in to help with greater problems relating to mental health or general well-being should the need arise, and parents describe the way boys support each other through the inevitable occasional difficulty as 'magic to watch'. Teachers available to parents via email, with responses to queries and concerns flying back through the ether at great speed.

'Strong discipline makes a place happier', says head, and major transgressions are dealt with by the amusingly – and aptly – named vice master. Strict protocols followed in relation to serious misdemeanours with repeated conduct warnings leading to detentions. 'Absolutely no leniency' when it comes to dealing with drugs, either inside or out of school, says head. Timetable collapsed five times each year to focus on PSHCE with age appropriate focus on drugs, internet safety etc.

Pupils and parents: Parents say they have never met a Bedfordian they didn't like – their trademark being an ability to mix with all age groups with an easy, understated confidence. Many OBs in parent cohort, which is healthy mix of traditional types and first time buyers – lots of professionals commuting into London. Buses from Luton, Milton Keynes and Hitchin and easy access from Harpenden by train makes for a broad catchment, with the majority living within 40 miles of school and commuting for up to an hour. Just over 15 per cent overseas boys from 24 countries across Europe, Asia and Russia.

Entrance: Of the 140 boys who join year 9, about 60 per cent have moved up from the prep. Some 50 additional places for those coming from other preps (Aldwickbury, Beechwood Park, Kingshott, Lockers Park major feeders) and state schools. Optional ISEB pre-test in year 6 or 7 potentially leading to conditional offer, confirmed by school's own online entrance examination in year 8. A few extra places at 14+ then about 25 more into sixth form, when hopefuls will need six good GCSEs to go on to do A levels (at least 6s in the subjects to be studied; 7+ grades in maths and sciences). Not ferociously competitive for day boys but boarding places are at more of a premium.

Overseas pupils often offered places conditional to taking ESL, billed as an extra.

Exit: About 10 per cent head to pastures new post-GCSE. Good range of destination universities for those that stay on, with a handful to Oxbridge most years (two in 2018) and around two-thirds per cent to Russell Group – Birmingham, Durham, Exeter, Loughborough, Leeds and Nottingham feature heavily, with majority going on to study heavyweight academic subjects – lots of sciences and a few to medicine each year (eight medics in 2018, including one to Budapest). Others off to Berklee, USA, Mannheim, Germany, Denmark and Hong Kong. Small numbers opt for creative options or languages.

Money matters: Good clutch of scholarships and bursaries for entry into years 7, 9 and 12, with art recently added to the list and golf scholarships in conjunction with nearby Woburn Golf Club. Generous – up to 35 per cent of fees, non-means tested, up for grabs 'for boys with exceptional talent' – and buoyant reserves in the hardship fund. Just under 200 boys across the school currently hold awards, with around 10 per cent of these on 100 per cent.

Part of the Harpur Trust but financially independent and benefiting from an extremely active and benevolent OB network.

Remarks: A rare beast – an uncompromisingly single sex school offering flexible day and boarding options without losing its traditional public school appeal. Thriving and successful, with happy pupils and happy parents – a place where all boys can hit their personal best, whether it's on the sports field, in academia or in the arts. Understated confidence and purposefulness abounds. A school of established excellence ready to be taken to the next level by dynamic newish head. All in all, a really super option for those looking for top notch day or boarding – as long as your sights are firmly set on an all-through education at Bedford.

Beeston Hall School

West Runton, Cromer, Norfolk NR27 9NQ

Ages 4–13 **Pupils** 146 **Boarders** 44 (from year 3)

Fees: Day £8,850 – £18,270; Boarding £18,900 – £24,540 pa

01263 837324
www.beestonhall.co.uk

Headmaster: Since 2016, Fred de Falbe (50s). Eton (same vintage as D Cameron), followed by theology at Manchester. Was previously head of St Richard's, a boarding prep in Herefordshire that has since closed. His varied career has taken him into the film business, property management and a spell as a 'jackaroo' in Australia as well as eight years teaching in state

B

schools close to the family farm in North Devon, where, among other things, he carried out most of the maintenance work and raised Tamworth pigs. Was drawn back into full time teaching at Knightsbridge School, a popular day prep in London.

His style is exceedingly hands on – definitely not just a man in a suit, think parents. 'He's very visible around the school and pupils like that,' said one. Easy to talk to with understated charm, has already established good rapport with staff while pupils say he's interested in all of them, not just the stars. 'You don't have to be the best in something for him to talk to you,' said one.

Has strong views about the need to nurture confidence and self reliance. His advice to parents to 'give your child a broken Hoover to take apart and try and fix in the holidays' provoked media interest and he is happy to be associated with the idea of 'directed purposelessness'. Believes children should look forward to coming to school: 'Learning takes many forms and some of the best schooling is done when children are having fun.'

Is very pro 'the small country prep school where we all know each other,' and is not looking to expand the school greatly. His wife Juliet is immersed in everything going on at the school. A trained artist, she was able to fill in teaching art for half a term. Very much a partnership. Three children, now almost through school and at university stage.

Entrance: Non-selective. Numbers increase steadily throughout the school with year 8 the largest age group. Older pupils attend an informal assessment day. Can accommodate mild to moderate learning difficulties but all must be able to follow the curriculum. Not for those with behavioural problems.

A plethora of scholarships (up to 20 per cent of fees) offered for academic excellence, art, music, sport and general all-round ability for all ages plus some means-tested bursaries and help for parents who fall on hard times. Encouraged by former pupils, a drive to fund a greater number of bursaries is underway. The head is determined to encourage the widest possible access to the school. Sibling discounts on a sliding scale are available if two or more children are at the school at the same time.

Exit: Almost all stay to the end of year 8. Majority depart for out of county boarding schools – recently Ampleforth, Eton, Harrow, Oundle, Stowe, Tudor Hall and Uppingham. A clutch most years to Gresham's and one or two to Norwich School. Careful guidance is given and pupils all get where they want to go, many with awards.

Remarks: The school retains a strong boarding feel; many day pupils stay on into the evening for activities and supper (no extra charge). Very often the pupils themselves want to change. 'My son began as a day pupil, saw the fun and wanted to board – it was his decision,' said one mother. 'Mine both boarded and when family circumstances changed, we asked them if they would like to become day pupils – but they refused.'

Predominance of pupils from county boarding families who know what to expect and settle quickly. 'The atmosphere is so welcoming and friendly, lots to do,' said a parent. 'Older pupils look after younger ones, it is not hierarchical at all.' They make friends for life,' felt another. 'My daughter has done her gap year travel with old boys.' Lots stay in at weekends (30 is usual) and there are regular exeats at least once each side of half term. The recent introduction of flexi-boarding on designated nights is popular, though full boarding remains the choice of many, especially higher up the school. By year 8, virtually all are boarding full time. Parents chorus approval for the way pupils are prepared for senior schools. 'By the time my son left, he had developed the confidence to cope in a much bigger school.' Year 8s are integrated into the boarding houses with other years but have certain privileges (such as access to an all-important toaster). Mr de Falbe feels the opportunities to befriend and offer leadership to younger pupils in that final year stand pupils in good stead, besides promoting a strong community.

Children create a good impression. Respectful but 'at ease' relations with staff ('none of that giving them The Look', as one mother put it), unforced good manners – standing up for visitors and holding doors open for each other as well as adults. Mobile phones are not allowed in the school. Head feels pupils should be better occupied. 'We stick to the tried and tested phone box in the hall,' he says. Close supervision of computer use in the evenings and off duty; very aware of online risks and need to educate pupils. Traditional lunch (served at tables, grace is said, water jug passed round) for the whole school, including staff. 'We are improving the acoustics in the dining room – the noise is unbelievable, you can't hear yourself speak at times', says the head. Daily organised games and lots of off duty playtime punctuate the day. No prep before year 6 ('developing a good reading habit matters most,' says school) then it's 20 minutes a day, increasing in year 8, especially for scholarship hopefuls. Dog-friendly with several around and about in classrooms with their owners (staff) and spectating at matches. Humans (and no doubt dogs as well) are agreed on the benefits.

Idyllic setting, close to north Norfolk coast and nearby National Trust Felbrigg Estate. Sweeping lawns and a Regency house are the centre of a mixture of newer builds. Extensive sporting, music and art facilities. Everything spick and span with notices such as 'Please walk ON the grass' and, 'Why not hold the door for someone?' Walls crammed with details of daily happenings, pupils' work, art, photographs and achievements.

Small, mixed ability classes until year 4, when there's flexible setting for English, maths, science and languages. French starts in year 3, Latin from year 6 and Greek (for some) in years 7 and 8. The year 8 scholarship form gives intensive preparation for senior school awards, focusing on individual requirements rather than hothousing a group. Staff flag any problems straightaway via emails and parents are encouraged to have informal chats with them at pick up times, though effort grades are issued and more formal consultations can be arranged.

An educational support unit, based in an attractive suite of rooms, with excellent interactive displays and hard to resist games, is run by a sparkling and vivacious teacher who makes attending a session fun and even a privilege. 'We have drop-in sessions and parties and children really do see coming here as a treat.' Parents agree. 'My daughter only needed help for a year but kept on dropping in to see staff there as it was such a happy place,' said one. Roughly a quarter receive help of some sort, usually in English and maths.

A well designed and stocked library with wonderful squashy sofas to recline on is staffed throughout the day, including breaks and lunchtime. Pupils have timetabled library lessons for changing books and quiet reading. We visited on World Book Day, taken as seriously by staff as pupils, and were greeted by Captain Haddock (the head) plus the Gruffalo (DT master, helped by 'easy access to the materials,') as well as Matilda and Cruella de Vil – and not a single Disney princess to be seen. Art is taught in a barn style studio, mezzanine floor devoted to pupils' scholarship work, each with own desk and work area so they can come and go in their spare time and leave work in progress undisturbed. Music a school strength with 90 per cent of pupils learning an instrument in timetabled lessons, lots of space for rehearsal and practice and a host of choirs, bands, ensembles and plenty of performance experience. Focus on encouragement – all pupils join the junior choir, auditions only introduced in the higher forms.

School does all the usual team sports and one of the benefits of being a relatively small school is that 'everyone gets regular match play,' said a parent. Games every afternoon, played in 'spirit of enjoyment; competitiveness is important but should not be the last word,' says the head. Also sailing on the nearby

Broads (they have their own fleet of Toppers) and shooting instruction (prep league champions). Plenty of choice for after school and weekend activities: fencing, beach picnics, fashion shows, cookery club, trips to local attractions such as Bewilderwood, theme days as well as Beeston's got Talent, a well established contest, though highlight of the week for many pupils remains 'the visit of the ice-cream cart,' in summer.

A traditional, but not hidebound, country prep with vitality and warmth and a well deserved reputation for nurturing its friendly, confident pupils who are 'willing to give things a try,' said a parent. Solid grounding ensures they go on to make the most of their senior schools.

Bilton Grange School

Rugby Road, Dunchurch, Rugby, Warwickshire CV22 6QU

Ages 4–13 **Pupils** 289 **Boarders** 41 full, 15 weekly, 36 regular flexi (from 7 years)

Fees: Day £10,080 – £19,440; Boarding £24,570 – £26,490pa

01788 810217
www.biltongrange.co.uk

Headmaster: Since 2013, Alex Osiatynski. He has an impeccable background to understand the heritage of Bilton Grange. His own education was at Dulwich College and Oxford; he came to Bilton Grange from being director of music at Loughborough Endowed Schools, and has worked at Gresham's and the British School in the Netherlands. He is married to Freya and has two sons. Freya is a theatre design professional and her creative eye is visible in the imaginative decor around boarding areas and elsewhere. 'She is busy teaching professional theatre lighting skills to the children for the next school production rather than being the traditional tea pouring headmaster's wife,' Alex tells us. He is Polish by ancestry, and his family's close involvement in the Polish struggle for liberal democracy makes him acutely aware of the need to educate children in political global awareness – something in which he is clearly succeeding, judging by a group of older children who told us earnestly how important it was that every single person voted. He has overhauled communications with parents and this has been much appreciated. 'Boarding staff and academic staff get back to you so quickly and they often tell you things before you have had time to ask,' a parent told us. He is a head who is seen as having time for people, has high standards and is open and collaborative in style. He is generally considered to have driven a lot of change, some of it a bit rapid for a few parents, we gather, but Alex is now committed to those small steps that can take everyone along.

Entrance: Two or three form entry. Slightly more boys than girls (particularly amongst boarders) but it's not obvious looking round. Non-selective, though the school says they are looking for children who can access what is, in an age appropriate way, an academic curriculum. A number come in from London at 11+ for the final two years, to get the boarding experience or just to get away from the London hothouse. The school is very keen to offer means-tested bursaries and is working hard to forge partnerships to increase these. There is, as a result, a slightly wider social mix that you find in many country prep schools.

Exit: Parents felt very well advised by the school about appropriate choices at 13+. A few leave to go to grammar schools at 11 but mostly it's senior boarding – around half to Rugby but also Eton, Uppingham, Repton, Oundle, Bloxham and Stowe with a number of scholarships each year. As you might expect, the focus is on 13+ and the head is not keen on 11+. 'It puts a lot of pressure on children much too young', he says. 'They lose out on years of childhood'.

Remarks: Set in 90 acres of countryside and woods, the Pugin designed buildings stand as a symbol of stability, tradition and British cultural heritage. The children can't but be reassured and uplifted by the glorious wooden panelling and carvings of chapel, library and staircases, the huge windows, the period wallpaper sourced from the Houses of Parliament. Within this, modernity in the form of ongoing building development sits comfortably. Not all the 20th century builds are as stunning as the Victorian heart but buildings are being adapted and renovated.

Academically Bilton Grange does very well both by its high flyers and by those who are not going to get the big public school scholarships. A number of parents who have moved children out of the London pressure cooker told us that while Bilton Grange is less academically pushy than its London counterparts, it does get children to the best schools and even more importantly, it creates highly motivated and self-driven children who succeed well beyond 13+.

The school works positively with those who might be considered to have a mild learning difficulty. Small class sizes (around 12 to 16) allow for a lot of individual support within lessons and the increasing setting as they get older gives further tailoring to meet specific needs. Where difficulties are identified, specialist staff develop an individual learning plan which may involve a range of strategies – one-to-one sessions, in class support, Saturday literacy enrichment, for example. The school identifies high flyers who might be heading for senior school scholarships during year 7 and is about to look at year 6 as well. The children are offered various opportunities and teachers watch how they respond to the stretch and challenge. We visited as academic scholarship exams had finished, and one group was busy designing Bilton Grange's own Cluedo whilst another was making a trebuchet scaled up from some carefully worked out computer calculated designs. Others were writing policy papers for a forthcoming election in school to mirror the June general election manifestos.

While the curriculum is fairly traditional, the focus is on encouraging what the head calls 'flexible' learners. The school now teaches the three sciences together rather than separately with an emphasis on the applied aspect of science – the children had a talk from a Jaguar Land Rover designer recently and have been creating their own rocket-propelled cars. DT is a real strength. Even young children work on serious machinery and love it. The options and curriculum enrichment programme, which runs after school and on Saturdays, is extensive.

The school is also traditional in terms of its values and behavioural expectations. There is an emphasis on courtesy, respecting one another and the community but this in no way inhibits the children's enthusiasm, which is celebrated round every corner of the school. Parents, too, are expected to uphold the school values and the head has very little time for those who don't.

The school runs a lecture series for years 7 and 8, their parents and the wider community three or four times a year that aims to bring in leaders from a wide field to help the children become aware of the vast number of opportunities now available. There are other forms of outreach going on – one success is the Scout group, started and still run by the head. It is now the biggest in the district and gets together very regularly with other packs for scouting activities. School

B

welcomes parents in and considers their needs thoughtfully. This is regarded as a huge strength. There is a lounge area in a charming stone-slabbed Victorian conservatory for parents who are waiting to pick up a second child, or just want to chat or browse the senior school brochures, with a little play area for tinies. Talks that are regarded as important for parents to hear are videoed and sent to parents who can't make it. 'The school really understands working parents', one family told us.

Most don't start boarding until year 4. The school is very careful to try to ensure that boarders are emotionally ready for it – and indeed that their parents are. Some flexi-boarding is possible but by year 8 most are full boarders. There is deliberately gradual transition. Saturday mornings are optional for year 4s, with an exciting new programme called the BiG Saturday that should tempt many back before afternoon sports matches. By year 6, there are some Saturday lessons for everyone as well as the vibrant enrichment options. In years 7 and 8, everyone is in for academic morning lessons and games in the afternoon. If you are not actually in a match, you are in a training session.

We enjoyed the food, which caters for various special diets as well as provided keenly anticipated treats such as roasts and steaks. Matron is on the door to ensure plates contain a variety of colours. Boarding accommodation is refurbished on a rolling programme and the rooms, most of which house about six, are fresh and unregimented. Day children are very welcome to join boarders for prep and boarders are encouraged to invite their day friends in for the odd sleepover at weekends. Pastoral care is high on the school's priorities. The PSHE programme aims to tackle the issues that start to cause anxiety as the children head towards the teen age years. No-one was worried about bullying; yes, normal friendship ups and downs, but nothing the school isn't highly experienced at resolving.

Although it is a school where masses seems to be going on all the time, staff are conscious that children also need quiet times and these, too, are built into the day. Sports facilities are good and school encourages non-team sports (golf, clay pigeon shooting, zumba, trampolining) though the head also wants everyone to experience the community values playing in a team can bring. The children love the fact that they can do sport more or less every day and they like the fact girls play cricket. One family, whose children are clearly sporting stars, felt a bit more of the 'winning at all costs' drive wouldn't come amiss, but that was not a general view, most going along with the sport for all approach. In fact the school does do well in matches and the top players compete at county and, indeed, national level.

The grounds lend themselves to a vigorous relationship with the outside world. Some of this is formalised – a science garden, a gardening club – but probably more important is the tearing about outside that goes on around lessons. Drama thrives and much use is made of the theatre. 'Being able to participate in plays has really given my son the confidence he lacked before coming to Bilton Grange,' one father told us. The head is a musician by training and keen to develop music facilities. Lots of the children play instruments (about 80 per cent have individual music lessons each week) and there is a wide range – the harp as well as the mainstream orchestral instruments. There are many performance opportunities for the various ensembles and choirs, both in the school and outside.

Bilton Grange is unpretentious despite its splendid buildings. 'Not posh enough for some,' the head told us, with some pride. It has been co-educational for many years and there is none of the alpha male feel of some prep schools. It has a genuine child-centred core – children are not there just to fulfil parental expectations and not allowed to be mini-teenagers plugged full time into the cyber world – they are there to experience and enjoy childhood.

Bishop Stopford School

Headlands, Kettering, Northamptonshire NN15 6BJ

Ages 11–18 **Pupils** 1,552 **Sixth form** 468 **C of E**

01536 503503
www.bishopstopford.com

Head: Since May 2018, Jill Silverthorne. English degree, PGCE and MA from Leicester. From a Valleys family in South Wales, Jill grew up in the 80s when jobs were scarce and being disadvantaged was a way of life for her community. She always wanted to read English, and realised during her degree that she would rather like a career with literature at its heart. So teaching was a natural choice. She spent 10 happy years teaching mainly A level at a sixth form college in Rutland. 'I loved the excitement of being part of two of the most formative years of anyone's life.' She was promoted a number of times internally, then made the rather unusual move into secondary education. 'Most people seemed to want to go the other way, and my sixth form colleagues were shocked I was even contemplating the move'. But she hasn't regretted it at all. She joined Bishop in January 2001 as head of faculty, quickly promoted to assistant and then deputy head.

A Christian, she is attuned to the school's CofE values. She is delighted to be called 'headteacher' – 'What could be more satisfying,' she says, 'than being known as the leader of a team of amazing professionals in the career which is closest to my heart?'

Academic matters: In 2018, 91 per cent got 9-4 in both English and maths at GCSE, with 33 per cent of grades A*-A/9-7. At A level, 35 per cent A*/A, 65 per cent A*-B. Good, consistent results for a non-selective school. All pupils take RE at GCSE, most take one language, very few take two. 'They have lots of homework but have a strong work ethic instilled in them,' was one parent's view. 'They get results and have high expectations,' was another. English, maths, PE and sciences set in year 7 or 8, with sciences re-set in year 10. Nine maths sets in later years, so no slipping through the net. Teachers quick to contact parents if problems. 'My child's results slipped in maths; the teacher got in touch straight away. Subsequently moved down a set, which was handled extremely well, and results monitored afterwards. I was very happy with the outcome and to be kept so well informed.' All parents agreed that teachers knew pupils well. One parent would like more face-to-face meetings with teachers but agreed 'it was easy to get in touch via email and get a quick response.' Most parents had faith that their child would reach their potential at Bishop.

Whilst on our tour we listened to a keen discussion in year 7 geography about flooding, had a quick chat to year 10 maths students who were revising for a test, spent time with year 11 artists who were happy to show off their work and popped in to say hello to year 12 biology on our travels. All teachers were welcoming, as were pupils. We picked up a good vibe between staff and pupils. Interesting to note the 'corridor rules' prominently displayed throughout the school and many signs referring to the ethos of the school: 'faith, justice, responsibility, truth and compassion.' Walls clean and uncluttered, not a lot of artwork or, indeed, anything on display.

Sixth form housed in a separate modernish block with a large photo of staff and prefect team hanging on wall. Study contracts between pupils and school. If you are on target, and the leadership team agree, you do not have to be on site for free periods, a privilege quickly removed if standards drop. Intervention spoken about openly; they keep on top of this lot. Most pupils stay on site and study in the library or in supervised silent area; they even have security cameras to check behaviour. High expectations from staff, with a lot of onus put on pupils throughout the school. They rise to the challenge and seemed very dedicated. Head of sixth form spoken of highly by more than one parent. 'He's an inspirational teacher and a fabulous head of sixth form.' UCAS help mentioned by all sixth form parents and pupils. Close links with Uppingham School: interview prep and techniques worked on here. External careers person in school twice a week to offer another take on life. Common room rather utilitarian with no tea or coffee making facilities, but there is a sixth form coffee shop in the corner of the canteen that is well used.

Average class sizes are 27; many staff served for over 10 years. Learning support team proactive: 125 pupils identified, 33 with EHC plans. Lots of interaction with pupils and parents and teachers. Some 81 EAL pupils, but only two that need support from SEN.

Games, options, the arts: Sport for all and they're pretty successful with some pupils competing at county level. 'It's excellent for a state school,' said one parent. Lots of silver in the cabinet. PE classes set for different abilities. Lots of teams and practices; the less able but enthusiastic can join in. Enormous sports hall and enthusiastic staff who will embrace different sports if there is the demand. Football recently introduced for girls: 'at last,' said one of our guides, 'I've been campaigning for that for years.' International sports tours for girls and boys. Sixth formers have their own football league, seven a side, great for integration and camaraderie.

Music lessons popular with over 200 students having timetabled lessons. Lots of choirs, bands, orchestras: you name it, they've got it. Brass band regularly plays at Music for Youth Festival in Birmingham. Lots of drama productions, some pupil led, including shows at The Lighthouse Theatre.

Lots of school trips including skiing and battlefields as well as sports and subject led. Annual year 8 trip to the Scilly Isles spoken of with great fondness. 'The highlight of my school life,' said one pupil. DofE popular with high take up.

Background and atmosphere: Recently celebrating 50 year anniversary, the school sits not far from the centre of Kettering in a pleasant residential area. Architecturally it is what it is, a 1960s building that is functional rather than aesthetically pleasing. Modern extensions have been added but 'dreaming spires' can't be alluded to. No matter, it's a well run site, clean, tidy and fit for purpose, if rather stark and lacking in soul externally. But the inner soul gets lots of TLC. Plenty of outside space and good to see tables and benches for al fresco dining. Unusually for a modern state school, a chapel is on site, well used and welcoming and very much central to the school, physically and emotionally. One parent said the school has many fewer facilities than other schools in the town, but was not complaining: 'The teaching and care more than makes up for this.'

The school is founded on strong Christian beliefs and its five core values are displayed throughout the school. Faith, justice, responsibility, truth, compassion. Adhered to throughout a pupil's life at the school, and beyond. 'The school very much works to its core values, which is excellent,' was said by most parents. A thought for the week displayed throughout the school and daily act of worship for all pupils in years 7-11. Mindfulness also embraced.

Pupils wear unobtrusive black or blue sweatshirts, depending on age, and ties; many girls wear trousers. All look smart and tidy. Slightly boy heavy, mainly because of a girls' school in the town, but not to the detriment of the girls.

Pastoral care, well-being and discipline: Every parent spoke about the pastoral element of the school: 'it's excellent,' was said by all. All spoke about the social ethos of the school, and its kindness. All parents, whether of new year 7s or sixth formers, spoke about the school's reputation for pastoral care and said this reputation was a strong factor for picking the school. Pupils stay with the same form teacher from year 7-11 and it's unusual for staff to change so a strong, stable relationship is built between tutor and pupil. Flexibility for personality clashes between tutor and pupil factored in if necessary. One parent spoke about her daughter becoming unhappy in her form because of friendship issues. 'I spoke to the form tutor, met the head of year who got my daughter involved and she moved forms. They didn't just move her, they monitored her, counselled her and made sure she was not sucked back into the problems she had encountered. I was delighted how well it was handled and the outcome. They helped my daughter take control.' Another parent spoke about how well the school deals with new starters. 'Starting in year 7 was slightly daunting for my child, who knew no-one, but an excellent form teacher soon had them settled in, encouraging lunch time club attendance.' School well aware that pupils come from wide area and small primary schools. 'It is very much not sink or swim,' said one parent. The chaplain is available for counselling and many pupils use her. Outside counsellors available if need be and strong mentoring of pupils. They know their stuff and are well aware of problems that can beset teenagers. They also know who the vulnerable students are. Sixth form has even more support with a dedicated, non-teaching, well-being staff member employed.

Discipline also commended by parents. School vocal about this as well. 'Yes, bullying happens, but it is nipped in the bud quickly if the matter is raised with us. There are serious sanctions; we don't make idle threats.' Parents agreed with this statement. Disruptive pupils dealt with firmly. 'It's all down to good behaviour management,' says the head. 'Actions have consequences,' she continued, 'and if one person's actions are disrupting the learning of others, that is a cardinal sin.' The yellow and red card system is used in this case, but we get the impression that the red card is rarely needed. All parents agreed with the discipline standards and supported them. 'The school has clear expectations and all pupils, and parents, are aware of them.' Every parent said how happy their child was at school. 'They love it,' was often said.

Pupils and parents: All parents have bought into the ethos of the school and are extremely supportive. The faith element is very important to them. There are families of different faiths, as well as none at all, but all buy into the ethos. Pupils are from a wide area: Kettering, the surrounding villages and as far afield as Rutland and south Leicestershire. Parental paid for transport is laid on for certain routes. An added attraction is the school's proximity to the train station. Parents from a broad spectrum, including children of clergy. All are supportive; 'the best school in the town,' was said by all.

Pupils happy and friendly and proud of their school. Many second generation pupils, possibly a few third. A strong alumni network has been established. These ex-students keep in touch with each other, and the school.

Entrance: Entrance is on a faith based priority system. The school is oversubscribed in year 7. Pupils come from up to 50 primary schools, mainly from Northamptonshire and south Leicestershire. Sixth form entry is not faith based but academic. GCSE grades must be 4 and above. Those wanting to study maths at A level need an 7, 8-9 for further maths. Up to 70 join the sixth form, mainly from other schools in Kettering. Despite entry not being faith based, incomers need to embrace the ethos of the school. This is made clear before a place is offered.

B

Exit: Up to 30 per cent leave each year after GCSEs, mainly to vocational courses at local colleges. Local employers often approach the school with job opportunities. Apprenticeships actively embraced but the vast majority go on to university. Gap years quite popular. Two to Oxbridge and five medics (two in Budapest) in 2018.

Remarks: Classed as one of the top comprehensives in the country with an outstanding Ofsted; we can see why. Good, solidly consistent results speak for themselves, but this school has that little bit extra: the care, support and nurture it offers its students. Parents know this and fight to get their child in – it's incredible how many find their inner faith at times like this.

The Blue Coat School

Somerset Road, Edgbaston, Birmingham B17 0HR

Ages 2-11 **Pupils** 602 C of E

Fees: £8,268 – £12,714 pa

01214 106800
www.thebluecoatschool.com

Headmaster: Since 2016, Noel Neeson BEd (Glasgow) NPQH. It is never easy taking over from a long serving and much loved head, but Noel has managed to take staff, parents and children with him on a journey of discovery, renewal and challenge. Everyone tells us Noel puts children at the centre of everything. He aims to be the champion of the 'invisible' child and sees Blue Coat as a school that fights for every child, not just the very bright or very weak, but all. The changes he has introduced are all about what will make an even better experience for the children while building on the distinguished legacy of Blue Coat. He is a very visible presence around school – parents feel he uses every opportunity to meet and talk to them. His wife, Juliet, has also become a familiar and approachable figure. 'They are very much a team,' parents tell us.

Although clearly a Glaswegian through and through, most of Noel's teaching experience has been south of the border. He was a deputy in Kenilworth and a head in Leamington Spa – so knows the West Midlands pulse – before taking up his headship at St Peter's in Devon. After seven years there, he says he loves the multicultural feel of Birmingham and the cultural richness of the city. He sees Blue Coat's future as being at the forefront of educational initiatives. He is introducing cutting edge pedagogy and is keen to take the Blue Coat's strengths out into the community, putting links with both secondary and other primary schools high on his list of early priorities.

Entrance: This is a school that fills up so it is sensible to make enquiries early. The main entry points are into Buttons Nursery, the pre-prep or the prep at 7+ when a further form is introduced – from three to four forms in a year group. There may be places at other points so it is always worth trying. The admissions process gets more formal the older the child, and for the scholarships and assisted places is rigorous. There are up to six academic and music scholarships offered at 7+ to both internal and external candidates.

Exit: The vast majority stay till 11, though if staff feel a child would really struggle with the academic pace of the prep department, they will discuss other options with parents. Broadly speaking, families are wanting the Birmingham selective schools, and that is where very many go, with some scholarships every year to the independent ones. The King Edward state grammar schools are popular as are the two independent King Edward schools and Edgbaston High. Blue Coat has strong relationships with other schools as well and encourages parents to make sure they are looking widely to find the best fit for their child. Some go to eg Solihull, St George's, The Priory. In 2018, 15 scholarships/awards accepted.

Remarks: Founded in 1722, the school moved to its present purpose-built premises in the 1930s. Set in a spacious site between Edgbaston and Harborne, the buildings present a pleasingly harmonious and gracious facade. Many developments have been added over the years, including a large sports hall and swimming pool, but these are behind the lovely frontage.

The school is considered one of the strongest academically in the area. Academic progress is taken very seriously right from the beginning with quite a traditional approach to the curriculum, while utilising all the modern technology possible – Google Classroom, for example. A focus on cross-curricular themes helps to maximise the children's learning experience. The Great Fire of London was the theme when we visited, and it was encouraging to see how this was being picked up across the humanities and sciences in all sorts of creative ways. Each topic has a Wow Day built into the curriculum to add to the fun and stimulate thinking. Another current focus is on making the links between the pre-prep and prep departments stronger so that there is a growing sense that this is all one school in practice as well as theory.

There are assessments each term and the head has introduced a tighter tracking structure to streamline recording and reporting. There are high expectations in all subjects, not just English and maths – all subjects must be making a visible impact on children's learning. STEM subjects benefit from two science laboratories with lots of practical work going on and the STEM week project was very exciting, the children told us, with the launching of a helium balloon that could be tracked as it travelled.

Growth mindset is now well bedded into marking practice as well as in the informal setting of short term goals. Recognising effort is central to helping children develop a positive attitude to learning. The head is passionate about critical thinking, which threads through the curriculum.

The school is a Church of England foundation and while it welcomes children of all faiths and none, everyone is expected to attend the chapel services and participate fully in all aspects of the school. The traditional chapel services pass on to the children something of the English religious cultural heritage and parents of all faiths value it.

As with all good junior schools, Blue Coat encourages close involvement with parents. Friday chapel is a time for hearing the quality of the traditional church music, not only from the choir but the whole school. The chaplain's assemblies are highly interactive and entertaining. The one we attended involved sumo wrestlers (two disguised members of the senior leadership team) – ideal material for entertaining family discussions round the kitchen table, we thought.

Parents are largely aspirational professional and business people who are looking for an established co-educational school close to the city and the more affluent housing areas. Parents also value the holistic approach of the school, with its a focus on developing well rounded, confident children, alongside its strong reputation for getting children places at the selective grammar schools and into the prestigious King Edward's independent secondary schools, with scholarships won most years. Parents mention this rather sheepishly, but it is a huge selling point in the city.

Staff say that parents are very supportive, wanting to know how they can best aid their child's progress. Not by intensive examination coaching, is the message, with which we completely concur, nor by demanding the school sets more and more homework. Parents are encouraged to listen to children, talk with them about the world and its wonders, work on the social skills that come from lots of verbal interchanges.

Parents warmly applauded the school's support of children's learning needs. Small group tuition goes on from year 1, and a child who starts to struggle in one area is picked up very quickly, with intervention strategies introduced. These usually take the child out of class a few times a week on a short term basis. Intervention work in early years is normally done within the class using the teaching assistant. Each pre-prep class has its own teaching assistant.

Friday afternoons for year 5s and 6s are TED enrichment time – that's Thinking, Exploring, Doing. When we visited, the options included journalism, business enterprise, media mania, debating, young engineers, paper crafts. There is a forest school for the younger ones. There's plenty on offer outside the classroom for all ages. After lessons, children go to their houses, where they can play (wonderful!), do homework, go off to clubs.

Music has been very strong for many years. Huge numbers of the children have instrumental lessons and the quality of the singing, with an exceptional chapel choir, is very high. The school is now looking at how to take its music to the masses – recently the choir performed in York.

The art room is vibrant and heavily used outside lessons for art clubs. Practising artists visit and graphic designers visit to show the links between art and business.

Sport looks set to have a fresh drive, with the enthusiasm of the head. There is an increasing focus on teaching sport skills and techniques lower down the school. Sports facilities are excellent, with a modern sports hall, pool, grassed sports fields and new Astroturf pitch and cricket nets. Parents and children spoke warmly about occasions when the school puts out A, B, C, D and E teams.

There are two big drama productions each year – one for years 3 and 4 and one for year 6. These are highly anticipated and everyone in the year group is involved. The year 6 one is given very serious attention by both children and staff as it comes after all the secondary school entrance exams, with the consequent release of academic pressure.

Staff are seen as very approachable by both the children and parents. They turn emails round very quickly and at the pre-prep stage see parents on a daily basis. But it is more than just being efficient – staff are seen as pivotal in putting the individual child at the heart of a very tangible community. The house system, a legacy of the days when Blue Coat had boarders, forms a base for the children. They join one of the two girls' and two boys' houses when they enter the prep, and are given an older buddy, helping to nurture cross-year friendships. They can go to their house from 8am until school starts and do homework or play games there after school. The teaching house staff ensure that the houses are absolutely distinct from day-to-day school life.

Pastoral care is praised by parents and staff see it as pervading all aspects of their work. When unkind behaviour occurs, it is dealt with quickly and parents feel they are kept well informed. There is a behaviour policy or consequences pathway, but this is not a school that needs to take a heavy handed approach. The school is currently working on emotional logic and staff are being trained in how to help children move on emotionally, particularly at times of unhappiness. The children we met were confident, open and highly engaged in school life.

There are means-tested bursary places from 7, part of the school's original charitable mission. The school is keen to go out into disadvantaged communities in Birmingham actively looking for children who would benefit from this support. This will not, we imagine, be difficult. It is hard to think of a boy or girl who will not find something in this rich educational environment that will set them on a path of engagement, adventure and high aspiration.

B

Bourne Grammar School

South Road, Bourne, Lincolnshire PE10 9JE

Ages 11–18 **Pupils** 1,205 **Sixth form** 374

01778 422288
www.bourne-grammar.lincs.sch.uk

Head: Since 2005, Jonathan Maddox (late 40s). Educated through the then direct grant system in Hertfordshire and read maths at Oxford. Always knew he was going to teach – 'for me it's about passing it on, not changing the world.' Worked in private sector until took the job at Bourne. 'It was the largest school that I had applied for and was the highest achieving academically.'

He has big plans for the school, which is expanding rapidly. Not all parents support this expansion – 'no longer a local school for the area,' say some. Always very oversubscribed, but in recent years the catchment area has grown. 'Every pupil who achieves the 220 pass mark will be offered a place, and has been recently', he told us. 'Funding is tight, but I run a tight operation and have some very able governors, so we have been able to find the money for expansion.'

Head knows every pupil by name, no mean feat. He teaches year 7 citizenship and year 11 maths. Liked by pupils, well respected and described by one parent as 'incredibly hard working,' although another said he is 'not a people person.'

Academic matters: Unashamedly an academic hothouse. In 2018, 32 per cent A*-A/9-7 at GCSE and 37 per cent A*/A, 66 per cent A*-B grades at A level. Most children take 10 GCSEs in a wide range of subjects. Computing at A level was dropped, now reintroduced. Systems and control (a modern version of DT, 21st century electronics and manufacturing) rising in popularity, ably supported by rows of computers and a new systems and control block opened by the Duke of Edinburgh. Spanish taught to all for GCSE with good results. French and German also offered. Textiles, food tech and 'oily rag' DT recently dropped throughout the school. More 20 subjects to pick from at A level, including law. Sciences and maths most popular.

The lessons we observed showed hard working, well-mannered students. Parents talk about the fast pace of teaching, with those who can't keep up expected to catch up in their own time. Fine for the conscientious. This lot had their heads down and were getting on with it. Studious, busy and intense – so busy that time couldn't be taken from lessons to show us around. They are under pressure but many appear to thrive. Students are tested constantly. All know their targets, as do parents. If targets aren't attained, letters are sent home and privileges removed, particularly in the sixth form. 'Sub-standard work is not accepted and tests have to be resat if not up to par,' said one parent.

Learning support available for those who need it. Total of 91 students have SEN – in-lesson support arranged and one-to-one support available outside lessons.

Games, options, the arts: They're a competitive lot here when it comes to sport. Rugby, football, netball, cross-country running, cricket and athletics all have clubs and teams. 'The girls' PE teachers are excellent and incredibly dedicated,' said one parent, 'but the boys' teachers, even though excellent, I have to say I've been disappointed with, as the clubs and teams can be a bit hit and miss. I think this is because most of the male teachers have other roles within the school, so paperwork seems to take over at times.' Others disagree. The parent of a year 7 boy told us that 'sport is excellent,' while another said: 'Sport has greatly improved over the years.'

We didn't get the impression that it was sport for all, with teams for all abilities. But the keen are encouraged. Interestingly, individual stars get a mention in weekly bulletins, even those playing in teams.

Music and art well represented. About 10 per cent of students have extra music lessons timetabled on a rolling rota. Older students given preferential slots so as not to interfere with studies. Lots of bands, school orchestra and choirs at lunch times. Most clubs focus on sport and music, but Arabic for beginners and Christian Union also on offer. How well attended these are, we're not sure.

Artwork throughout the school (a dominant display in the entrance). Art A level fairly well supported, more so at GCSE. Now that textiles, food technology and DT have been dropped from the curriculum altogether it does raise the question about the more creative students moving elsewhere for sixth form. Drama has improved and 'the plays are very good – excellent in fact,' said a year 13 parent. Theatre studies and music studied up to A level, but few take music.

Lots of school trips, ranging from New York to local field expeditions.

Background and atmosphere: Founded in 1921, the school has been at its present site, on the edge of the small market town of Bourne in the Lincolnshire Fens, since the 1960s. Plenty of space but very utilitarian. Not a lot of soul in this place, but it isn't helped by the functional, block architecture. At lesson changeover corridors and staircases are crowded. A bit overwhelming for visitors and year 7s, but all very orderly. Disappointing to see rubbish lying about after breaks. Currently redeveloping and refurbing to make space for increased numbers.

School has always been mixed but boys wear black, girls green, and they look as if they are from two different schools. Nobody seems to know why, but it's tradition, so why change it? Sixth formers wear business suits.

Competition is rife here so it's not for the faint-hearted. Most pupils seem to cope well, though. The quieter, less able or diligent can fall by the wayside – we got the impression from a few parents that it was very much 'sink or swim.'

Sixth form block light and airy. A well-liked tutor on hand to offer advice and UCAS help. Upstairs area for quiet supervised study – some of it compulsory, particularly for those not making the grade. Concentrated, calm atmosphere, with an academic hum throughout. Sixth formers allowed into town at lunchtimes (unless privileges have been revoked) and have flexi-study afternoons at home.

Food available in the lunch hall and cafeteria area. Vending machines dotted about as well. 'I would like food to be served on plates rather than plastic trays,' one sixth former told us, 'but it's good and there's plenty of choice.' Pizza slices available daily, chips once a week. Pupils pay daily but parents can buy a squid card (top up card) which shows what their child is eating and spending and most do this. Some take a packed lunch. Outside seating available – good to see.

Pastoral care, well-being and discipline: We got the impression of a well-disciplined school and parents backed this up. Pupils well behaved in class and around the school. Most look smart, too. 'Bullying, if it happens, is stamped on quickly', said one parent. 'There were the odd tizzies in year 7 and 8, but these were sorted out very quickly and ever since my daughter has sailed through', said another. 'I like the fact that the child has the same tutor and form from year 7 to 11.'

Set structure of management team and teachers. 'They have a very odd system where you can only see four teachers on a parents' night as they are too busy,' a parent told us. 'This means that you only see the ones who teach subjects your child is struggling with and some you never meet at all – all rather negative.' Others disagree, saying that it's 'a good system.'

Some parents we spoke to said the school is 'excellent up to year 11' but thought it could perhaps ease up a bit in the sixth form and give the students more leeway. 'The teachers are excellent, though, and they really care,' said a year 13 parent, 'but I do feel that the school in general is too results driven and needs to be a bit more human at times.' Perhaps a bit more carrot and less stick.

Parents praise pastoral teachers. 'They know the children, understand them and speak to them like a parent would,' we were told. The odd gripe about pupils 'getting lost and sinking without trace', but teachers generally thought to be 'very proactive and inspiring.'

Pupils and parents: Pupils used to be from Bourne and the surrounding villages – quite a large area, given the rural nature of the county, and parents would move to improve the chances of their child getting a place. Pupils now coming from further afield because of the increased numbers. 'Sadly, it's no longer a local school and that spoils it,' more than one parent said.

Majority of parents are professionals and this trend is increasing as the catchment area widens and parents are prepared to let their children to travel rather than pay school fees. All parents aspirational for their children so mainly supportive and interested. The pupils we spoke to (they gave up their precious time at break) were pleasant, open and chatty.

Entrance: Pupils sit the 11+ in September in verbal and non-verbal reasoning. Higher up the school, youngsters take the 12+ or CAT test, subject to places being available. There aren't many, though. Sixth formers must achieve six GCSEs at grade 6 or above. English language must be grade 4 or above. Most pupils from local primary schools and the odd independent. They travel from Peterborough, Stamford, Market Deeping and further afield too.

Exit: Some 20-25 per cent leave after GCSEs, usually to other sixth forms or vocational courses at college. Most go to university (four to Oxbridge in 2018, plus three medics); Leeds and Nottingham currently popular. Subjects diverse, but many study STEM subjects. The odd one straight into employment or an apprenticeship, occasionally into the Forces. Increasing numbers taking gap years.

Remarks: Unashamedly academic and aiming higher – one of the top selective state schools in the county.

Caistor Grammar School

Church Street, Caistor, Lincolnshire LN7 6QJ

Ages 11–18 **Pupils** 686 **Sixth form** 182

01472 851250
www.caistorgrammar.com

Headteacher: Since January 2017, Alistair Hopkins (mid 40s). English language and literature MA from Oxford, followed by MEd education leadership from Buckingham. Started out as a journalist, editing the Cherwell at uni and winning a scholarship at The Times. Offered a job but wanted to go down the traditional journalist training route working on local papers; however, found he felt removed from the community as he progressed. After four years away from education, viewed it differently, and 'it seemed the natural thing to do, to teach, as you're part of the community working towards a common goal.' An interesting character, worked as a trainee vicar before uni, 'but it wasn't for me, as I wasn't mature enough then.' Has always worked in selective schools, in the private sector, 'which I sort of stumbled into.' This is his first headship and first state school. 'Caistor was the right school because of its size and heritage and I like selective schools as the pupils have a sense of purpose.' Had been trying to work his way back northwards since his first job at Bradford Grammar, but more than happy in Lincolnshire and plans to stay a long time, enjoying the friendliness of the locals. 'I've just slotted into the community; they have been very welcoming and want you to do well. I like Lincolnshire; it's a county that not many people know much about, as is this school. The students don't realise how good they are, I like their humility.'

A softly spoken and unassuming character, but very articulate, he is slowly finding his feet, and parents like him. A contrast to the previous incumbent who, we gather, was a big character and all parents alluded to this. Parents are getting to know him, 'he's always present at meetings and parents' evenings.' 'Very approachable and chatty,' said one parent. 'Not a huge personality but a steady hand on the tiller,' said another. 'He's making evolutionary changes rather than revolutionary and has everyone on board.' Parent-mail has been improved. Lockers now available for all pupils, a more modern approach being taken by the head including cashless catering. 'He's a breath of fresh air, younger, more approachable, he's made a great first impression.' The pupils like him, and he knows them all. A keen cyclist, walker and theatre-goer who spends time in Europe during the holidays.

Academic matters: In 2018, 56 per cent A*-A/9-7 at GCSE. At A level, 40 per cent A*-A, 67 per cent A*-B. Impressive results, but to be expected from a selective school. 'They never seem to be under any pressure,' was said by many parents, but all agreed pupils had high expectations and a great work ethic, instilled by the school. Maths the only subject set from year 8; modern languages – French and German – from year 10. About 15 a year do two languages. Latin on offer to A level. All do three sciences except the odd one doing the double award. 'It's an amazing place,' said one parent. 'I could not believe the change in my child and the step up they made academically. How did the school achieve that?'

Dedicated teachers praised for taking a calm approach. All parents spoke of the small school and teachers knowing, and teaching, every child in their first three years at the school. Sixth form mentoring of younger pupils effective. Lots of extra support including revision sessions. 'Academically, more than delighted with progress,' say parents. Parents and pupils all spoke of excellent support offered by staff, who are quick to respond to any queries. 'They are taught to be independent learners and to work things out for themselves, but help and support is there if they need it,' said one mother.

Subjects mainly split between buildings, with each one having a very different feel and look, ranging from the modern, which houses the physics labs and the biology department where we were shown plenty of skulls (and note the fish tank), to the architecturally beautiful and ancient, to the barely fit for purpose, but they make it work. Staff and pupils interact well in lessons. A large renovated chapel, used by all pupils for quiet study, also houses the library. One parent with a younger child was worried that the small size of sixth form might not allow for large enough classes for debate in certain subjects, but those with older children full of praise for staff and class sizes.

A prominent listed building mainly used by the sixth form, including common room and quiet study areas. Plenty of tea and coffee making facilities along with fridge and microwave. Notice the herb garden which is used for food tech lessons. The grand piano in the music department is well used. Pupils and parents talk about lots of help with UCAS in the sixth form, and plenty of encouragement. Plenty of support for SEN students: there aren't many of them but extra help on offer if needed. They're monitored and supported using a passport system. Average class size is 22, maximum of 34. Interesting to note that a significant number of staff are ex-pupils.

Games, options, the arts: The playing fields are a 10 minute run from the school and all pupils are expected to run there for lessons. A good way to keep them fit, we say. Sport is successful, albeit because of the size of the school there is usually just one team per year. Some parents complained about their child struggling to get into the team, others supportive of PE staff who rotate team members. No girls' cricket or football, yet. A sporty bunch with many playing at county level in diverse sports, including ice hockey and shooting. Mention must go to two ex-pupils, the Cliftons, famed for dancing on Strictly, who were both dancing competitively whilst at the school. Large gym used for assemblies as well as indoor sports. Fitness suite well used by older pupils. Lots of sports clubs on offer.

Creative subjects actively encouraged by the head, and popular. Sixth form artists have their own small studio, 'we are very lucky'; admire the view and the impressive work. Music and drama well supported with parents talking about 'excellent productions and the high quality of concerts.' They also mentioned, and appreciated, the extra efforts by staff to put on these events, many working across subjects. Lots of bands, choirs, music groups. Plenty of school trips including sports tours. DofE to gold.

Background and atmosphere: The school is just off the main square in the centre of Caistor, a small town in the Lincolnshire Wolds, down a very narrow street that leads to the church. Blink and you could miss it as the road frontage is tiny. Founded in 1631, originally as a boys' grammar school, it is still on the same site. The original school building, the tiny Old Hall, has an impressive front door that new year 7 pupils walk through on their first day. Our sixth form guides talked with great pride about this ceremony. At one point it was a boys' boarding school accommodating RAF children from the nearby bases, becoming co-ed in the 1950s. Boarding ceased in the 1990s. Dawn French was a notable pupil from this period. The attractive Georgian house, once the boarding house, now home to the sixth form, could be mistaken for a residential property. A Pandora's Box, the school is on a split level site that is not apparent from the entrance, and the size of the premises is surprising and well concealed. A mish-mash of ancient, utilitarian, modern and frankly barely fit for purpose all blends on the site with pretty gardens and tall trees. The New Hall is not aptly named. An old agricultural building with a corrugated roof, it used to house a swimming pool that has long been filled in. Exams are held here, as well as sports lessons; when it rains it must be noisy. The head has his eye on it for imminent demolition. But the mixture of Nissan huts, temporary classrooms (that have been there for years) and ancient and modern adds to the charm.

But the school isn't just a mish-mash of different buildings: step inside and you are certain of a warm welcome. Parents spoke about the 'family atmosphere and sense of community,' and 'the children have real pride in the place.' 'It just felt right, with a much warmer feel to it than larger schools we had visited.' We could feel this on our visit; everybody greeted each other, and us. The atmosphere was very laid back, relaxed and

C

welcoming, but there was a real sense of purpose. 'Common sense and courtesy,' said one of our guides when asked to describe pupils' qualities. Quite.

Pupils look smart in their uniform, black blazers, grey pleated skirts for the girls – or trousers – grey trousers for the boys. Girls wear striped shirts with no tie. 'I like the uniform, it's practical and smart and I like that girls don't wear ties. Ladies don't wear ties in later life so why should they wear them at school?' was one mother's take on it. Sixth form wear 'business suits, that have to be loose fitting,' said our guide. We get the impression that uniform policy is quite strict, no jewellery, nail varnish or make up for younger years, good. Interesting to see all sixth formers wearing lanyards for ID purposes. We can see why, must be hard to differentiate between staff and pupils, particularly as some sixth formers have beards. Please note Godfrey, the school cat. He takes pride of place by the fishpond, more in hope than anticipation, we feel.

Pastoral care, well-being and discipline: Every parent we spoke to praised the pastoral care. 'Strong friendships are made here, it's the sort of school where everyone knows each other, and looks out for each other,' was said more than once. Parents spoke about 'excellent pastoral care..They know the children, their foibles and personal circumstances and take care of them.' Head very aware of mental health. 'There is more to life than good grades. Service to the community, leadership and helping the younger years are equally important.' He's got a grip on it and aware pupils 'need to learn to fail.' Counsellors available if needed. Parents spoke of 'huge support' being offered when needed including the bedding down period when a new starter. A kindly eye appears to be kept, discreetly, on those that need extra support at times. Sixth formers train as counsellors and the new leadership team is very keen to promote 'diversity and acceptance.' Effective school council with requests for preparation for life skills for older years and tolerance training. Bullying stamped on immediately, but we got the impression that it wasn't a huge issue. Parents spoke about discipline being strong; 'I like that,' said one. 'The children know their boundaries and incidents are dealt with quickly.' The most telling comment came from one of our guides: 'We never feel that we are on our own. It's a small school and we feel safe and relaxed. Teachers take the time to get to know you.' Excellent.

Pupils and parents: Parents are supportive with not many 'pushy' ones. Most want children to be happy and have realistic, but high, expectations. Mainly Lincolnshire folk from a range of backgrounds; many children are second, or even third generation attendees. Mainly professionals from local area, quite a large farming contingency as well. All parents we spoke to were well aware of what the school has to offer and delighted their child is benefiting. Pupils come from a wide area, even from north of the Humber and Grimsby. Pupils friendly, open and engaging. They are obviously the cream of the crop academically but there is none of that 'academic arrogance' you can experience in certain grammar schools.

Entrance: Unusually, the school sets its own 11+ papers, differing slightly from the LA test in that it consists of only verbal reasoning. Pupils usually take the county's 11+ paper as well to give them the chance of getting into other local grammars if they do not get a place at Caistor. About 270 take the paper, 25 per cent from within catchment, 75 per cent without. A hundred places are offered. Students who live within catchment, a radius of 6.5 miles from head's office, have priority. Pupils rarely leave unless the family relocates, which is unusual. There is no sibling rule.

Up to 20 join in the sixth form; 50 apply for a place. Pupils come from local comprehensives, other grammars and the occasional private school. Applicants need a minimum of grade 4 in maths and English and grade 6 in four other GCSEs. There are no plans to expand numbers.

Exit: About 20-30 per cent leaves at the end of year 11, mainly to take A levels at local colleges; the school doesn't offer eg psychology or sociology. The odd one to private boarding school with a scholarship. The vast majority to university, nearly half Russell Group (one to Oxbridge and two medics in 2018), but apprenticeships becoming of more interest. Two or three each year to Harper Adams and Cirencester. A few gap years.

Remarks: Lincolnshire is a grammar school county so there is plenty of choice locally, but Caistor stands head and shoulders above the others, and parents and pupils know it, hence the clamour for places. A school that offers an all-round education, not just good grades. Able children are taught an excellent work ethic and independent thinking and are well set up for later life, nurtured and encouraged within a very tight, close-knit community. They are very fortunate.

Comberton Village College

West Street, Comberton, Cambridge, Cambridgeshire CB23 7DU

Ages 11–18 **Pupils** 1,807 **Sixth form** 466

01223 262503
www.combertonvc.org

Executive principal: Since 2001, Stephen Munday CBE MA PGCE (late 40s), a Cambridge economics graduate who still teaches economics to the high flyers in the sixth form. Goodness knows how he manages the time as he's a bit of a superman. He's executive principal of Comberton Village College, and chief executive of the Comberton Academy Trust that also incorporates Cambourne Village College, a recently established school in Cambridgeshire, Melbourn Village College and The Voyager Academy in Peterborough. He manages his time well and spends three days a week on average at Comberton. 'I'm totally in awe of him,' said one mother. 'He expects a lot from his staff and pupils and is duly rewarded.' He went in to teaching straight from Cambridge: 'there is a proper purpose to it.' Well liked and greatly respected, he towers over the school, figuratively and literally. 'He attends virtually everything and speaks very well,' said another parent. A regular church-goer and a keen follower of sport, he was awarded a CBE for services to education; we can see why.

Head of school is Peter Law, and Lorna Conroy is head of sixth form.

Academic matters: High achieving for a non-selective school. An impressive 43 per cent A*-A/9-7 grades at GCSE in 2018, and 87 per cent got 9-4 in both English and maths. At A level, 61 per cent of grades were A*-B and 29 per cent A*/A. 'They keep a close eye on them and let us know immediately if work isn't being handed in,' said one happy parent. All students study Spanish to GCSE, year 6s given a Spanish activity book before they join to give them a head start, and bright sparks (about five per cent of the year) are encouraged to take another language too. French and German also on offer, with Latin taught outside school hours. There were mutterings about extra language lessons after school which could be, whisper it, a disincentive.

'They know how to motivate year 11 boys,' said one parent, another added: 'Lots of after-school revision sessions; the teachers go the extra mile.' The bright are identified and encouraged, the less able equally helped along. 'What I like about the school is that they are flexible,' said another parent. 'If the pupil aims high and works hard, it's recognised and they are moved up a set; excellent.' Lots of vocational courses as well as academic. Lessons we observed involved plenty of interaction with teachers and pupils. Some seemed noisy, but controlled chaos was the order of the day. Odd to see one pupil in geography lolling with her legs across her friend, but if it works?

Impressive artwork and busy noticeboards; we admired all the pictures for the photography prize lined up outside the geography rooms. Given the International School Award for the fourth time. This global outlook links Comberton to schools in six countries, Europe and worldwide, offering chances for exchanges and visits. Room for 'disruptive and bad pupils' – happy to report was empty during our visit. The thriving sixth form bedded in well in new building with all mod cons.

A school open to all. SEND very well catered for with almost 20 per cent having some sort of extra support. A very inclusive, understanding environment for those with particular needs. Includes an Asperger's centre to cater for up to 40, many from outside the area, built to satisfy demand. Self-contained, well run and funded SEN department housed within main body of the school and run by well-respected staff. This offers sanctuary and calm for those that need it, either temporarily or permanently. Individual programmes set up for many; most join mainstream lessons where appropriate.

Games, options, the arts: They're a sporty lot. Plenty of teams and after-school practice, possibly more notable for enjoyment than success. Rock climbing wall in the gym. All the usual sports as well as less common such as dodgeball and handball. Disappointing to hear that only the boys are put into sets for PE lessons; what about the sporty girls? Lots of sports facilities including 3G Astroturf and the sports centre shared with the community including a heated open air pool. One of the gym areas could have done with a good hoover. MCC cricket hub for Cambridge. They're good at golf, too, and have chance to go off site for it, as well as rowing and leadership, where the older pupils coach primary school children. Sport viewed as 'inclusive and fun' by our ambassadors, who were looking forward to sports day. Endeavour awards as well as competitive prizes at this event. Sixth form includes various sports academies.

Dance, drama and performing arts well supported. Lots of after-school and lunch time clubs including orchestra, jazz, brass and Friday choir as well as dance in their impressive studio. Soundproof music practice rooms. End of term performances held in the new performance hall where visiting musicians hold recitals. Rehearsing for Les Misérables when we visited, all year groups involved. Odyssey performed recently and then taken to the Edinburgh Festival, where it got five star reviews. Successful debating team and well supported DofE going from strength to strength and now offered up to gold award.

Background and atmosphere: Founded in 1959 as a village college with 240 pupils, it's grown rapidly to accommodate the growing villages around Cambridge. It's never lost the community college ethos, with the wider community sharing many facilities, but is now a vast sprawling site on the edge of the village, still with plenty of room around it. Became an academy in 2011 and opened the sixth form at the same time. Functional rather than attractive, the older parts look tired compared to the light, airy modern areas. It's a vast place and could seem intimidating to a newbie coming from a small village school. Successful induction days help overcome this, with year 10 and 11 mentoring newcomers. There's no house system, but year groups are tight, with each designated a 'social area' at lunch time. 'We would like to have more covered space,' said a mole, 'and have campaigned for it, with some success.' Table football in the year 8 area, plenty of benches dotted about for al fresco dining. No complaints about the food, apart from lack of choice towards the end of the queue. Healthy eating encouraged and a new cashless system to try and speed things up as complaints made about lack of time.

Uniform is a rather dull grey polo shirt and sweatshirt, with year 11 wearing black, all a bit utilitarian. A strong school council that is well represented. Good to see that year 11 still has an important role in seniority despite the sixth form. No noses being pushed out of joint yet.

Pastoral care, well-being and discipline: Excellent, according to many, and well supported by parents. A large school that could be intimidating, but it doesn't appear to be a problem. They have strong anti-bullying policies that involve the pupils. 'There are a lot of us and sometimes there will be problems,' said one on-message ambassador. Perpetrator and victim are brought together on neutral ground for group discussions. They work hard to avoid punishment and problems are usually resolved without further action having to be taken. Pupils stay with the same form tutor from years 7-11. There are form reps, counsellors, mentors and teachers to turn to. 'They know their pupils well,' said one happy parent. 'We know who to turn to,' said one pupil. Pastoral care praised by many. 'It's a huge school but they are very supportive and notice if things are going wrong.' 'My daughter really struggled in year 7 and it got to the stage where she didn't want to go to school, she was so anxious, but once the school got involved she was transformed. Her head of year put her at ease and found her a mentor as well as a home support worker. I couldn't have asked for more and now she loves school.' 'They go that extra mile,' was heard more than once.

Pupils and parents: Bright, chatty, relaxed children who know they are lucky to be there. Majority of parents middle class, many Cambridge academics. But a strong mix including the less privileged, and all seem to slot together. Pupils and their parents appreciate the education they are getting.

Entrance: Surrounding villages south of Cambridge in the catchment take precedence after sibling rule. Lots of appeals due to population growth, and popularity of the school can make admission a nightmare. Numbers lower down the school being reduced as new school opened at Cambourne, within the same Trust, easing pressure of numbers. Entry into the sixth form requires minimum of five 6s including English and maths for those wanting to study A levels. They want serious sixth form students and all are interviewed.

Exit: Some two-thirds leave after year 11 to other local sixth form colleges to study A levels or take vocational courses. Sixth form becoming more popular each year. Pupils from other non-sixth form schools also joining, some from as far afield as Bedford. The odd one straight into work, two-thirds to university. Three to Oxbridge in 2018 and one medic; over a third to Russell Group universities.

Remarks: A huge school that serves the community well, and encompasses it. We can see why it's so popular; pupils relish it and parents want them there. The well supported, successful sixth form is the cherry on the cake.

C

The Croft Preparatory School

Alveston Hill, Loxley Road, Stratford upon Avon, Warwickshire CV37 7RL

Ages 3–11 **Pupils** 375

Fees: £7,962 – £12,213 pa

01789 293795
www.croftschool.co.uk

Headmaster: Since 2012, Marcus Cook BSc (sports science). Joined The Croft in 2002, from being director of sport at Arden Lawn. His career started with an initial spell as a teacher, before he did a stint as a professional rugby player in England and France. He came to The Croft as director of studies and became deputy before taking the top job. He gets The Croft through and through and is passionate about ensuring its continual development. The similarities between a rugby team and school life are something he finds illuminating for both. He tells us both are about learning to work with others and recognising complementary abilities in others. He has reorganised the management structures, aiming for consistency in the underlying strategy and ethos. He has created a faculty system which includes one for emotional and physical development that pulls the strong physical education side of the school into the work on growth of emotional intelligence. He wants children to value who they are and to this end, the school makes extensive use of 'Pack types', a psychometric-based card game about affirming different types of people and starting conversations about conflict resolution, living together and the dynamic make-up of teams. Parents see Marcus as a great role model for the boys and he is much loved by the children. Staff say he communicates very effectively with both adults and children who find him warm and approachable. Parents report he is very accessible. Marcus has two children, both of whom went to The Croft and are now at secondary schools.

Entrance: Children are admitted from 3 (a change from previously when they use to take 2-year-olds). Non-selective; applicants from 5 upwards have an induction day, with an informal assessment if thought necessary.

Exit: The school is proud of the fact that children go on to a wide range of schools, usually over 20 different schools each year out of a cohort of about 60. These include the selective independent schools in Warwick and Worcester, plus eg Bloxham, Bromsgrove, Sibford, Solihull, Princethorpe, Kingsley, Old Swinford Hospital. Parents report on the high quality of advice on offer for the 11+ transition. Children often win music or art scholarships.

Remarks: This is a proprietorial school, owned by the same family for about 30 years. They are very involved in the day to day running of the school. The governance is therefore slightly unusual with a board of directors and governing committee, but it appears to work absolutely in the best interests of the children. The school was founded in 1933 and moved to its present site, just outside Stratford-upon-Avon, in 1984. It used to be a farm, which provided plenty of space and delightful buildings to convert and develop. There are splendid views of the Warwickshire countryside all around. The old outbuildings enclose courtyard play spaces. Parents described the setting as 'amazing' and 'enchanting' and we would agree. Who would not want their child spending their childhood in this idyllic environment? The different spaces are used to offer progression. The children in one year are next door to the rooms where they will be working the following year so they become familiar with new spaces gradually. The buildings range from the cosy to the modern, with a number of large performance spaces, including a 600 seat theatre and modern sports hall with a sprung floor. All are beautifully maintained and well decorated. The proprietor of the school, Mrs Thornton, is a keen supporter of the arts and there are a number of wonderful outdoor murals, sculptures and wood carvings adding to the magical feel of the site.

The children are very appreciative of their environment and the forest school (two acres of gorgeous woodland with a lake) is a favourite. It is the traditional outdoor children's games they adore – tag, hide and seek. Hopscotch is marked out in play areas. There are vegetable beds where children learn to grow vegetables, which are then eaten for lunch. A large pig lounges in a pig pen for the children to watch in some awe. The school also has its own indoor swimming pool. Parents and children describe the facilities as outstanding and we would concur.

The school is accessible for those in Warwick, Banbury, Solihull and Evesham. While some are farming families, more are from business backgrounds. The headquarters of Jaguar Land Rover is seven miles away and some families have relocated from London, given the excellent road and rail links. The school is broadly non-selective though it recognises that a child has to be able to access the bulk of the curriculum in order to flourish there.

There are generally three forms per year group with a maximum of 20 children in a class. There is a full time SENCo and specialist SEN teachers and assistants, with a network of support in place to ensure children are reaching their age-appropriate potential. The ones who find academic work a breeze are encouraged to participate in the Challenge Club, which meets once a week for various enrichment activities. English and maths are set from year 2, but sets are very fluid. Parents are delighted with how quickly the school picks up on any slight learning hiccups and intervenes discreetly to ensure the children keep progressing.

There is a rich and slightly unusual extracurricular offering. While the school wants all children to experience team sports, the overarching principle is that children should be active and healthy and there is a variety of sports to encourage this as well as lots of outside play opportunities. There is a wonderful geology museum for example, to encourage the children's interest in rocks and fossils. Children return from holiday with samples to be identified. Skills are taught through clubs – the computer club is moving the children towards engineering skills and interests. There is a room devoted to a model train layout where children learn how to repair equipment, how to timetable and how to work together to prevent crashes. Parents and staff consider music to be exceptionally good. There are computers with the Sibelius programme so children can compose, and indeed they have produced some of the music for drama productions. The Hungarian Kodaly method is used to teach basics and voice. About 80 per cent of children learn an instrument and there is a range of groups in which they can perform, including a jazz band, string ensembles, choirs and an orchestra, which can have as many as 60 players. The programmes are described by parents as 'most ambitious', reflecting the high expectations and achievements.

The children love drama: the early years and pre-prep nativities as well as the year 6 show are much anticipated. The school uses its proximity to the theatre at Stratford to the full: RSC workshops and technical help enhance the school drama offering. The school puts emphasis on building confidence through performance, offering many opportunities.

Staff tell us that the school is increasingly outward looking, working on what it can take out to the community and how it can invite other schools to come into The Croft. There are sports tournaments for local state schools, Warwickshire cross-country competitions are hosted here and there is an evening netball club open to all. The children are encouraged to fundraise for local, national and international charities and The Croft supports a school in India.

Some pupils have physical disabilities, so the community understands differences and learns how everyone can live together supporting each other. The school understands that instilling good behaviour is an ongoing process with young children. They are encouraged to consider the impact of their behaviour on others and to think about why they have behaved in a certain way. There are positive and negative house points to help children realise that what they do affects others and every action has a reaction.

School lunch is run as a family service. Staff sit at small tables with a mixed age group and year 6s serve food to the younger ones. Lunch starts with a thanksgiving prayer. No school is all sweetness and light, though, and we hear that Mr Cook can be 'really strict' when he needs to be. Generally the approach is to intervene very early if children need guidance in terms of socially acceptable behaviour. Parents report this is usually in the form of a quiet word both to the child and to the parent to ensure parent and school are giving out the same message. The growing emphasis on emotional intelligence will undoubtedly impact positively on these children as they hit adolescence. Without making a great song and dance of it, the school wants to help with any emotional difficulties, and the parents are clearly used to sharing with the school any worries that occur at home as well as those that manifest themselves in school.

Communications between home and school have improved and the head has a reputation for listening to parents' concerns and taking action as soon as he can – not always quite soon enough for some parents, of course, but everyone acknowledged that the school really tries. This is a school that exudes stability and affluence without being showy. Increasingly both parents work, so children understand money doesn't grow on trees. It's a school where children can still be children in glorious surroundings. They are not 'precious or precocious,' one parent said, summing up our impressions. Academically, The Croft produces the goods but without relentless cramming. Parents reported over and over again that children are happy here, and that after all is what families want most.

Culford School

Culford, Bury St Edmunds, Suffolk IP28 6TX

Ages 3–18 **Pupils** 729 (338 in junior school) **Sixth form** 144 **Boarders** 221 full, 45 flexi (from 7 years)

Fees: Day £19,500; Boarding £29,985 pa

01284 385308
www.culford.co.uk

Headmaster: Since 2004, Julian Johnson-Munday (50s). MA in English at Leicester followed by MBA at Durham. Toyed with joining the advertising industry but ended up at Cranleigh, where he became hooked on teaching. Rose through the ranks to be a housemaster, 'the best job in the world,' headed to London (Mill Hill) but decided a small rural boarding school 'where I knew all the children' was for him. Very settled at Culford and well liked by parents and pupils. Accompanied everywhere by his two dogs, 'they slow the children down,' who are greeted with enthusiasm by pupils, parents and staff. 'He has a lovely way about him,' said one parent. 'Very paternalistic and knows the children.'

You can tell he did English: slightly dramatic, very witty, warm, possibly a bit of a luvvie, who we imagine enjoys his time 'on the stage' as head, but in the nicest way, with a self-deprecating sense of humour. Smartly turned out. Runs the school with great efficiency and warmth. 'He's completely aware of what is going on, but is happy to let his very efficient management team cope with the day to day minutiae,' was one parent's view. 'Pragmatic and takes difficult decisions at times, but deals with them with great empathy,' from another. Keeps in close contact with parents via email and social media. 'Very much on the ball,' was said more than once. All fourth form (they use the old fashioned descriptions of year groups here) pupils have tea with the head, and his dogs, who enjoy hoovering up crumbs.

Prep school head: Since 2008, Mike Schofield (50s). Studied history and sport at Bedford College; has been at Culford for 19 years, arriving as a housemaster from the state system. Still coaching local rugby teams and referees matches at Culford. Chatty and likable, knows all children well, again very paternalistic. 'Watching them perform on stage, it's like being a parent 22 times over.'

Academic matters: In 2018, 47 per cent A*-A/9-7 at GCSE; 22 per cent A*/A at A level, 45 per cent A*-B. Good results for a school that does not claim to be highly academic. BTecs recently introduced in sixth form; pupils can study these and A levels if appropriate. Spanish, French and Latin available at GCSE and A level, and taught in prep as well. Latin for the top set only in prep. All senior school pupils do one language, not many do two and unusual for all three to be taken. Maths is most popular subject at A level. Children set from year 5, gifted and talented spotted early and nurtured. No parent could fault academic progress and all spoke of being kept well informed of progress and problems. Extra help available if needed, and problems quickly spotted. IT well embraced. Old fashioned IT rooms have disappeared, it's all about laptops here, note the trolleys in the corner of classrooms loaded with laptops. Pupils encouraged to try all subjects, including art and DT, which proves popular further up the school. Good to see boys do textiles as well. Mention must go to the drones that are now being used in the grounds.

Excellent facilities including shared new science block, fabulous new £2.2 million library and refurbished art and DT blocks; alumni have proved generous benefactors. Sixth form centre with kitchen, used by groups quietly working. The new library is more popular for quiet study. Prep school has its own excellent library, well used with plenty of workshops and visiting authors. All seniors bring their own laptops.

A school full of energy. Happy children, relaxed teachers, all keeping busy and enjoying life, but don't be fooled, they are working hard. Saturday morning lessons for all in senior school. Senior school finishes at 5.30pm after clubs and sports practices, or prep for non-participants. Extended day runs to 9pm at no extra cost. Supervised prep and supper provided. Popular with many hard working parents as no dreaded homework to be done at home.

Small classes mean there's nowhere to hide, and teachers know pupils well. Parents appreciate this and most said it was one of the main reasons for choosing the school. 'You can see the rapport on parents' evenings and it's good to hear the banter between teachers and your child; this reassures us that all is well.' We can vouch for this from our tour of the school. Average class size in prep is 17, 20 in senior and 10-12 in sixth form. UCAS preparation exemplary with one-to-one help for all. 'Amazing advice offered including what to look for on open days,' said one parent.

No pupils with an EHCP but 55 on the list for extra help. 'Learning support is excellent, staff are supportive and reassuring.' 'They know what is needed. My child was supported throughout the school to A levels and got excellent results.' Lots of one-to-one teaching if needed, or two-to-one where suitable. Plenty of feedback for parents. EAL pupils also well supported. Mainly group lessons, but individual if needed. Lots of long-serving staff.

Games, options, the arts: Sport is king at this school, particularly tennis. Rated the best co-educational school in the country for tennis by the LTA, Culford attracts pupils from all over the world because of it. Elite athlete programmes on offer for tennis, golf, swimming and now football; these pupils have extra coaching and strength and conditioning classes, but never miss academic lessons. This lot are up with the lark and in the gym. Some 120 pupils play tennis all year round using the excellent facilities, including a four court championship standard indoor tennis centre. There are six grass, six hard and six Astro courts as well as numerous other pitches. Mention must go to golf as well, a new indoor studio with simulator and radar technology attracting golf scholars. More regular sports such as rugby, hockey and cricket (girls too) also extremely successful. Good to see there are teams for all, it's not just about the elite. Sports participation encouraged in the prep school; 'the unwilling are gently, but firmly encouraged,' says the head. This attitude prevails throughout the school. Large sports complex, lots of pitches and pavilions, excellent swimming pool, gym, studios – you name it, they've got it.

Music and drama also popular. Music centre in the beautiful old building, lots of rooms available for quiet practice. Many have individual singing and instrumental lessons. Loads of choirs, ensembles, orchestras and productions. 'Pupils are made to feel important whatever their role in the play,' said one parent. 'There are no divas; everyone's contribution is treated equally.' Loads of clubs and practices during lunch time and after school. Throughout the school are excellent works of art (new art department currently under construction). All pupils welcomed us with open arms, happy to chat and proud to show work.

DofE and CCF well supported. 'Children are brought out of themselves and encouraged to try things,' said one parent. 'The children are encouraged to take ownership of the opportunities they are offered.' Plenty of school trips for all including a freshers' week for lower sixth with a trip to the Peak District for team building. Sixth form life seems to be very sociable, lots of dinners in the magnificent main house, the Highland Ball and numerous other occasions. 'We get through lots of dresses,' said our guide.

Boarding: Boys' boarding full, girls' growing rapidly. Flexi-boarding popular throughout. Pupils staying three nights a week always have the same bed. Offers 10 nights a term, part boarding of three nights a week or full boarding. Parents appreciate that there is always a bed available if necessary.

There are two houses for boys and two for girls. Co-ed house for prep school. All houses mix day and boarding pupils so strong friendships develop throughout. Extended day option available: pupils stay until 7pm, popular with many parents.

Newly refurbished prep boarding has eight in a dorm, four bunk beds, with years 7 and 8 mixed together. Very neat with pupils bringing their own duvets. 'We change our sheets weekly and sort our washing out,' we were told. Pupils' dorms checked daily by prefects. 'We stand by our beds and are dismissed only when our space is tidy.' Phones taken away every night. Lots of outings and trips for boarders: roller skating, cinema etc, and they have the run of the grounds as well, though younger pupils have to stay within certain areas. Supervised prep for all boarders.

Senior boarding houses not quite as tidy, a bit shabby, but homely. The tidiness instilled in younger years seems to slip a little, but teenagers will be teenagers. Years 9-13 in together with upper sixth having their own rooms. Most younger pupils share, and there is one dormitory of 16 for the year 9s which is very popular. Plenty of facilities for tea and toast making, and comfy common rooms. Sixth form flexi boarding very popular as Paddy and Scott's Café opens on Friday night for sixth formers. Pizza and snacks served here, very popular for socialising. Some sixth form boarders have their own cars. School fairly relaxed about toing and froing; they sign in and out using an app. Very much a family atmosphere with houseparents having dogs, pupils keen to walk them – it covers their DofE service module. Mention must go to the resident parrot as well. Boarders encouraged to have day pupils to stay. Plenty of trips, which day pupils can also join; Alton Towers particularly popular, London shopping and buses run regularly to Bury St Edmunds, making excursions to local town popular and encouraged.

Background and atmosphere: Located not far from Bury St Edmunds, the school is situated in beautiful grounds, just shy of 500 acres. Entering through impressive gates you drive through the estate past a very pretty church, used by the school and very popular for marriages of alumni, before rounding a corner to an 16th century magnificent mansion house, previously owned by the Cadogan family. The new buildings flow well and blend in, with plenty of space around them. The prep school is in the old stable block, built around a quad with the library in the middle. The nursery is housed in a separate building, cleverly located nearest the main gates so parents coming and going aren't noticed. Parents, staff and locals seen walking their dogs in the grounds, which are so large that pupils are easily absorbed, as are the large sports pitches and buildings. The 'Culford bubble' that parents and staff talk about is suddenly apparent. Easy to forget there is an outside world whilst cocooned in this cornucopia of beauty. School well aware of this, as are pupils, who appreciate how lucky they are.

Founded on strong Methodist beliefs in 1881, the school is strong on moral values and there is much talk about the Culford Way. It is a relatively small school so a family atmosphere prevails; pupils and staff are friendly, jolly and welcoming. Everyone seems to know everyone. The school knows not just their pupils but the families as well. Pupils are smart with the senior girls in long, extremely long, skirts. 'They are brilliant,' said one of our guides; 'we can wear our pyjamas or tracksuit bottoms underneath when it's cold and no one knows!' Pupils encouraged to join in and try everything. 'Be the best person you can be each day,' is the prep head's mantra and it seems to work its way through both schools.

Pastoral care, well-being and discipline: Every parent we spoke to praised pastoral care. To be honest they raved about it. 'They pick up on problems – even at home – so quickly and are incredibly proactive,' said one parent. All spoke about the 'paternal' atmosphere and the sense of security the pupils, and parents, feel. House staff praised, and their dogs. Mental health problems quickly picked up on. School has focused on mental health for many years, 'long before it was flagged up,' says the head. Counsellors are well used, 'a good release valve.' Half of all staff are mental health first aiders, plans for every single member of staff to be trained.

Drugs have reared their ugly head in recent years and this is where the head comes into his own. 'Deals with problems empathetically, fairly but firmly,' was said by parents. Pupils and parents are kept well informed, nothing is swept under the carpet. Some miscreants leave, others given a second chance but have to agree to random drug tests. The head has had to have some fairly uncomfortable conversations with some worried parents. All parents spoke positively about discipline: 'They are tolerant to a certain extent but the children know where the line is drawn.'

Pupils and parents: A strong community of parents who are focused on a good all round education. These parents aren't just concentrating on exam results but on the development of well rounded individuals. Most parents are working hard to afford the fees and very grateful for flexibility school can offer with regards to boarding and late pick ups. Many second and third generation pupils, some even fifth. Most pupils live within an hour and a half from the school. Quite a large Forces contingent. Pupils happy and relaxed and do not show any signs of being under any undue pressure, but are obviously putting in the hard work. Mention must go to one of our charming guides, who had a disconcerting ability to walk backwards at full speed and hold a sensible conversation – we are convinced senior pupils practise this skill in the evening.

Entrance: Entry into nursery via taster sessions, pre-prep by day's assessment and taster session. Prep by entrance exam, entry to senior school automatic from prep, entrance exam if external student. Sixth form requires seven GCSEs including maths and English, grades 5+. Flexibility is key. Unusual for a sibling to be turned away if they don't make the grade; 'we are a family school.' Largeish intake at year 7, mainly from the state, and larger again in year 9 from local prep schools, including the Cambridge contingent.

Exit: Very, very unusual to have a pupil not make the grade for transfer to senior school. The odd one leaves to board elsewhere, usually following family tradition. About 30-40 per cent leaves after year 11, most to vocational courses or, again, to board elsewhere. Entry to sixth form denied if attitude doesn't fit. Two to Oxbridge in 2018 (maths and physics), three to the US on sports scholarships. Most go to university, the odd one into Forces or family business. Arts and dance courses quite popular. Interestingly, apprenticeships not on the horizon. Gap years quite popular.

Money matters: Academic scholarships and exhibitions available offering 25 per cent and 10 per cent off fees for years 7, 9 and 12. Sports and music awards. Discounts for siblings and discounts for Forces families.

Remarks: This small school, housed in beautiful surroundings, really is a family orientated place; note the dogs and pets making it home from home. Happy children and parents. The school takes much of the strain away from busy parents. The Culford Bubble could be a disadvantage, but pupils are well aware life exists outside the grounds. Its strengths are small class sizes, excellent pastoral care and tremendous facilities. Once a Culfordian, always a Culfordian, it would appear.

Debenham High School

Gracechurch Street, Debenham, Stowmarket, Suffolk IP14 6BL

Ages 11–16 **Pupils** 678 **C of E**

01728 860213
www.debenhamhigh.co.uk

Headteacher: Since 2012, Julia Upton BA PGCE. Read maths and computer science at Durham followed by postgraduate training at Cambridge. Previously head of maths, assistant head of sixth form and deputy head of King Edward VI Bury St Edmunds. Before that was head of maths at Denes school, Lowestoft and began her career at Stowmarket school. 'There was no plan to remain in Suffolk, it just worked out that way.' In her early 40s, she is a confident leader with a brisk, very friendly manner, and though extremely proud of pupils' academic achievements (Debenham recently come in the top 100 state schools at GCSE) she is just as proud of the school's happy and pastoral ethos, rooted in its Christian foundation. Believes the relatively small size of the school contributes to a sense of belonging and as an 11-16 school the focus can 'be entirely on the GCSE stage and the years leading to it'. She enjoys her job and thinks it 'important to keep on facing classes, teaching my subject,' generally to the older students. Liked, trusted and regarded as accessible by pupils and parents.

D

Academic matters: Eighty-eight per cent of pupils got 9-4 in both maths and English at GCSE in 2018 with 36 per cent of grades at A*-A/9-7. The top set takes maths a year early and goes on to do further maths in year 11. Sciences also strong; roughly 60 per cent are entered for the triple award and generally around 30-40 per cent of grades are A*/A. Good results in humanities too. Roughly 70 per cent take a language to GCSE, mostly French. Head is conscious of need to extend teaching of Spanish to lower forms (currently only taught in years 10 and 11) and increase the numbers at GCSE. 'We are working with our feeder schools to support the teaching of languages at the primary stage, as not all pupils arrive at 11 with a common grounding. It can be difficult to arrange in small village schools'.

There is good SEN support with one-to-one and group sessions and a small number follow courses leading to accreditation in social care and health studies. All follow a religious studies programme though only 10 or so take it at GCSE. About half take art or music GCSE. Parents speak warmly of the way pupils are encouraged to do their best: 'They are prepared well for exams but it's not the be-all and end-all'. 'The standard of teaching, on the whole, is very good'; 'good mix of well-established, loved figures, but a good turnover, very important'. A high proportion of the staff, roughly half, are part time, but the head views this positively, as it 'allows us to employ a wider range of teachers including for those subjects that only have a few takers, as is the case for textiles and other DT subjects'. There is a large, permanently staffed and well stocked library used for quiet work at lunchtimes as well as for timetabled lessons. With such a good grounding at GCSE, pupils go on to do very well at A levels in sixth forms elsewhere.

Games, options, the arts: The claim of 'sport for all' really does hold good as girls play cricket and football, 'rugby too, if they want,' as well as rounders and netball. Good sized playing field and all weather pitch plus sole day time use of the adjacent local sport and leisure centre. Regular fixtures against neighbouring state schools. Lots of clubs at lunchtimes and after school in the likes of dance, Pilates, archery and table tennis. The equestrian team has reached the national finals and there is also a ski team. Sport appears to be encouraged but not forced on pupils: 'You don't have to be mad on it,' said one parent (approvingly).

About a third learns a musical instrument and there are plenty of opportunities to perform in recitals, assemblies and concerts. 'We do a big play or musical every year using the pupils from the whole school,' as well as smaller productions of Shakespeare and other plays. Popular drama club run at lunchtimes though few take the subject at GCSE. About a quarter takes art and design; lots of work on display about the school. Pupils all encouraged to belong to clubs, 'partly to supplement the timetabled day but also to make friends outside their classes and year group, especially important in a school where many are bussed from some way off'. Year 7s must join at least two clubs in their first year at the school as part of successful integration. Involvement in charitable fund raising is encouraged and the five school houses run various challenges throughout the year.

Background and atmosphere: On the edge of a small, charming Suffolk market town, the school was founded in the 1960s to serve a small area but has grown steadily to its present size. Founded as a church school, it retains a strong connection with the town's church and clergy (including the bishop) are regular visitors; there are services in the parish church at Christmas and Easter. Though holding a strong Christian ethos, the head is clear that 'we are here as the catchment school and everyone is welcome whatever their religious faith, or none'. Parents are delighted with the friendly and family atmosphere. 'It is partly being on the smaller side, but even so, it is a big change from a village school of 60. They do everything to help year 7s settle in quickly'.

Buildings are mainly one storeyed and functional, no architectural gems here, with bits added on over the years. Lots of windowless corridors link classrooms and these, despite the efforts of the art department, can feel closed in, but classrooms have glorious views. Efforts have been made to plan sensible areas for lockers and places for pupils to gather in at break and lunchtimes. Praise for the food. 'Lots of us have lunch and they do snack things at break and the menu often changes'. The setting of the school is picturesque, but the slightly tired and rather litter strewn courtyard areas outside are planned for a revamp. Pupils are polite and friendly, moving around calmly at change of lessons with one way systems operating on staircases. Pupils' work, some of it highly detailed and informative, is displayed throughout the building and, 'it gives us something to read while we are waiting to be let into the classroom'.

Uniform is the usual trousers/skirt/polo shirt combo and is worn by everyone.

Pastoral care, well-being and discipline: Everyone loud in their praises. 'My son came from a tiny village school and only knew about six people but he settled straight away. They don't let cliques from primary school get a hold.' 'It has a warmth and friendliness; everyone feels they belong.' 'A family school.' The school holds transition days for pupils in the summer term before they start. These are subject based study days and are seen, primarily, as an opportunity for pupils to learn more about the school, meet their tutor and each other. The head of year 7 remains in position to maintain the close links with feeder primaries but tutors move up the school with their group. Older pupils, generally years 9 and 10, act as mentors for younger pupils. 'My son was a mentor and he took the responsibility really seriously.' An atmosphere of trust is created and pupils know who to go to if in difficulties, and the school recognises the importance of encouraging pupils' mental resilience. There is a pastoral support assistant and staff receive training on the importance of listening. Parents also are invited to workshops run on emotional and mental health run by psychologists. The local clergy are familiar figures and the school has a prayer space where pupils can leave reflections or prayers. Any discipline problems easily dealt with by staff who really know the children well.

Pupils and parents: Pupils are cheerful, motivated and, in the main, hard working. Predominantly middle class, managerial and professional, fewer than 15 per cent have free school meals and most have both parents working in nearby towns, though some come from longstanding local families with parents and grandparents educated at the school. Parents are aware of their great fortune in having such a high performing school on the doorstep. 'Why pay when the state school is so good?' said one mother. Why indeed? School/home communication is treated as a high priority as pupils often come from some distance and travel by bus, parents may not be able to have much regular contact with the school. Lots of parents' evenings covering year 9 option choices, careers and A level choices, future schools for sixth form, workshops on well-being, as well as the regular subject evenings. 'We get 95 per cent attendance,' says the head. 'Parents really support the school.'

Entrance: Those from within the catchment (radius of about 15 miles from the school, but check) with looked after children having the highest priority. If outside the area, siblings of those currently attending the school followed by those with a pastoral or other need.

Exit: Vast majority to nearby schools with sixth forms. Over 75 per cent go on to study three A levels followed by university, many to the Russell group and a clutch each year to Oxbridge.

Remarks: The small size and nurturing ethos have created an academically excellent school where pupils of all abilities do well, some outstandingly.

The Ecclesbourne School

Wirksworth Road, Duffield, Belper, Derbyshire DE56 4GS

Ages 11–18 **Pupils** 1,500

01332 840645
www.ecclesbourne.derbyshire.sch.uk

Head: Since 2011, James McNamara BA (history, Manchester University), who joined the school in 2003 and rapidly climbed the career ladder. While great teachers generally have an inconvenient habit of bouncing off to another school in search of promotion, Ecclesbourne's strategy of accelerated progression and development for teachers is all about conserving its gold reserves (school has only had four heads in its 60 year history). Retention is one reason, head suggests, for the school's great academic results and the latter is certainly a dominant draw for the majority of parents whose children are lucky enough to get a place.

The knot of factors which results in its extremely good crop of results, year on year, is hard to unpick. Aside from blood, sweat and tears, Mr McNamara quips, the primary reason is the culture, the spirit of achievement and success which imbues the school. Most heads say this sort of thing, but here the students concur. Pupils told us that 'messing about' in class was not considered 'cool'. It had, they said, been stamped out in their early years. The school is strict from the start; failure to have your planners signed off carries consequences (writing lines); you learn quickly and 'acclimatise'. Mr McNamara also points out that the sixth form students, the 'upper school', are embedded in the life of younger pupils as peer and subject mentors. From the start, younger pupils understand the end point to which they are aspiring. Being openly ambitious, he suggests, is an Ecclesbourne mindset. (We suspect there is probably another crucial factor in this mix: a body of parents whom one self-described as 'very ambitious for our children'.)

The head is also clear that to foster the desire to succeed academically, pupils need to experience success in other areas, including those out of their comfort zone: playing leads in school plays, sport, debating. It all feeds in, he says. He refers to the importance of the annual verse speaking competition where every child recites a poem to the class, the finalists performing in front of the whole school. Sure, the curriculum drops out when the school holds such events, he says, but it is a vital platform to appreciate eloquence and intellectual nimbleness and, crucially, to build confidence.

Mr McNamara is charismatic, with a relaxed air and a quiet sense of humour. 'He's always got lots of time for everyone', a parent said; 'he's friendly but the children respect him'. We joked about what might be termed his 'policy of marginal gains' with the school, but it probably isn't far from the truth. He has 'a continuous programme of development,' one parent said. He keeps evolving school facilities (sport, theatre), said another, keeping it on top of its game. He confesses he is always questioning what the school is doing and how. This might be simple, like wondering whether they introduce Shakespeare early enough, or reaching out to a new company for an apprenticeship. Right now, change is about bringing GCSE-style learning into year 9, he says. One thing this school does not do, is get comfy on its gold-plated laurels.

Academic matters: A broad curriculum runs from year 7, offering three languages (which they will run even with small numbers). All students study two languages and 70 per cent take one at GCSE. At A level, there are more diverse choices such as sociology.

In 2018, 25 per cent of GCSE grades were A*-A/9-7 (86 per cent of pupils got 9-4 in both in English and maths). Stashes of top grades in the three sciences, geography, maths and English. At A level, 32 per cent of grades were A*/A, beating many schools in the independent sector, with 59 per cent A*-B. Strongest subjects currently geography, English literature, history and maths; art and biology do pretty well too. Significant value-added, says head.

Setting in maths and English begins in year 7 (one parent described this as 'pseudo setting', suggesting it didn't quite go far enough), science in year 10. Lots of lessons are taught in mixed ability forms and one parent felt in the lower school the focus was about bringing on the less able children, which meant the very able didn't push themselves as hard as they might. The parent was quick to add this righted itself when the GCSE courses commenced, when everyone is 'pushed but not pressured'. As ever, it's horses for courses, though, as another parent felt his children, in the middle band, had been nicely stretched. Assessments and tracking are key.

Parents were very happy overall with the academics – and indeed why would they not be – but there was a hint that teachers could be reactive, rather than proactive. One parent whose son had been discouraged from choosing certain subjects based on his school exam results (he had been impeded by a health condition when he sat the exams) felt the school's initial response was a tad 'standardised', failing to look at the whole picture. The school reconsidered, she said, and reversed its thinking. There was a general consensus from parents that, as anywhere, 'some teachers do it fantastically, some don't', but parents said teachers 'were always there' for students. 'It's not a case of whether the teachers likes you, they help,' said one parent. 'They help all the children, all the time'. Another parent echoed this, saying the school had spotted her child needed motivating and had gone out of its way to pique his interest. 'They see the person behind it all; they are not just about achieving academic stats', she said.

Students seemed very happy with the quality of teaching; it was lovely to hear a sixth former declare his physics teacher was one of the best science teachers he had ever had, and praise the after-school classes. (One small, off-stage whisper, though: parents say widespread use of tutors is a contributory factor to success.)

Roughly the same numbers of girls and boys take science at A level. We asked the boys why they thought this was so at Ecclesbourne but not in other schools, where girls sometimes shied away from science subjects? Thankfully, they looked at us in a nonplussed 'why wouldn't girls excel at everything?' kind of way. On reflection, one clever sixth former put it down to having 'strong and inspiring female science teachers'. Good answer. Big tick.

The enhanced learning department provides extra support where needed. Head says the school invests more than is allowed for in the budget. The aim is for every child to be embedded in school life. The department is smack bang in the centre of the school and, pleasingly, the sixth formers we spoke to were incredibly respectful about it, saying lots of students (not just those with learning differences of any kind) might go if they needed a 'helping hand' early on in the school, and then maybe not need it again. Lessons are tailored to individual needs and taught either one-to-one or in small groups. Some children on the more severe end of the autistic spectrum are included in lessons where possible but also have their own projects going on, one being the 'egg project', selling fresh eggs each week. A nice bit of commerce.

Games, options, the arts: The house system (names inspired by famous men and women of Derbyshire) means lots of competitions: music, sport – a mini Olympics, even – chess, drama. The house captain writes the play, usually a variation on a classic with an Ecclesbourne twist, such as Macbeth the PE teacher.

Sport is very much encouraged: football (the girls were county champions in 2018), hockey, basketball, athletics, badminton, rugby, orienteering, dance. One parent grumbled faintly about the lack of sports fixtures, suggesting some success was parent-led. There is a sparkling new-ish sports hall (with fitness suite and dance studio), small playing fields on site (big enough for rounders and sports day) and bigger ones five minutes' walk away. There are also squash, equestrian and tennis teams, all using village facilities.

Some massive drama productions in the recently built theatre. Great enthusiasm about a recent West Side Story: 'one of the highlights of my school career', a pupil said. One parent told of his child's enthusiasm for stage management; 'they all find little niches'. The male student designers at a school fashion show were well supported and promoted.

Head flags up music as being particularly vibrant, with a whole array of bands and orchestras, playing at events such Derby Arts and in concerts and competitions eg Battle of the Bands, Stars in Your Eyes.

Pupils describe the trips as 'incredible'. They certainly have a nice steady stream of them, to eg the RSC at Stratford, the Technology Show, language exchanges, a UNESCO-related trip to Poland, a visit to a German Christmas market. Lots of projects, too: one sixth former cited the Lessons from Auschwitz project where students visited the camps followed by a two day seminar. Regular visiting speakers have included Patrick McLoughlin and Caroline Lucas.

Competitions such as the the Mock Trial in the local magistrates' court and The Big Bang. Crowded sixth form debating club. Plenty of after-school clubs from sport to history to textiles to Lego. Sixth form enrichment (introduction to Chinese, computer games design) and intellectual ideas courses (quantum physics, political systems, postmodernity). We thought it sounded wonderful, like an ongoing Hay festival.

Background and atmosphere: Established in 1957 as a grammar, the school has undergone a number of changes over the years to become the sprawling non-selective academy it is today. Head describes it as 'classic 50s build' but the number of modern add-ons, all organically in keeping, give the school a wonderfully modern, light and airy feel. At the time of our visit it was drumming up funding for a new science block.

Corridors have fantastic displays; impressive art department (paintings of human faces with feline features were arresting). English notices pleasingly packed a punch with Shakespeare plays prominent. A large Orwellian quote on the English classroom wall. The sum of parts feels vibrant, each corridor suggesting a great deal of effort has been invested. The library – head says the budget is huge – feels like the hub of the school. Lots of study areas for sixth form.

Pastoral care, well-being and discipline: Intake not particularly diverse but parents said that school is inclusive and celebrates individualism (whether gay, straight, footballing genius or arts fiend). 'There is an expectation that everyone can be themselves.' Some parents felt the school was not necessarily proactive about spotting problems, such as friendship issues, but they emphasised that once an issue was drawn to the school's attention, it was addressed very effectively. 'They do a really good job of making the children like school,' said a parent. Disruptive behaviour 'taken very seriously,' said the head, and we believed him.

On parent commented that her articulate but not high-flying child had been given a position of high responsibility, despite a potential backlash from parents of alpha children. 'They celebrate everyone, not just the high achievers,' said another parent.

Library opens early and closes late, creating a haven for new year 7s from small rural primaries, in particular. Only sixth formers are allowed phones. A strong curricular programme on aspects like social media starts early; head is aware of the 'immense pressures' it creates – the 'catnip of likes'. There is also an online 'safety centre'.

Pupils and parents: As one parent commented, Ecclesbourne parents tend to be 'very interested in education and keen to know all about homework'. Head avers that he welcomes their high expectations. They are also very supportive and proactive about raising funds.

There is one parents' evening for most years (extra ones in years 7, 10 and 12) and two written reports. We suspect there is a lot of parent-led chat in between, though.

The sixth formers who showed us round were eloquent, thoughtful, intelligent with a quick wit and no trace of arrogance. Yes, they would have been selected as cream of the crop ambassadors, but they were still very impressive. That said, lots of students are from the surrounding wealthy villages, mostly inhabited by professionals. As one parent succinctly put it, 'there is a bit of natural selection going on'.

Entrance: Now 240 year 7 places (an eight class intake). Some 500 applicants. A glance in an estate agent's window shows houses selling at a healthy price, boasting 'within catchment'. Parents were up front about deliberately moving into the catchment area and felt that this was 'a common story' and inevitably meant there was 'a premium to pay to get in'.

Yet, overall, the catchment area is fairly sprawling, encompassing rural areas and far flung villages, inner-city Derby, as well as the very well-heeled areas around the school. So it is a mixed demographic and, although social disadvantage and ethnic diversity are not common themes, there are some families with financial difficulties.

Exit: Around 75 per cent stay on to sixth form (90 per cent get the grades to stay on – broadly five good GCSEs – but might choose to go elsewhere, perhaps for more vocational offerings). Generally around a third to Russell Group universities including one or two to Oxbridge. Durham does well for Ecclesbourne students, too, but the doors of possibility are kept wide open all over the UK. Apprenticeships are top notch also and figure eg Bomabardier, Rolls Royce.

Remarks: A truly superb state school where the challenging extracurricular expands the mind and the consistently excellent academic results dazzle, turning out responsible, thoughtful and intelligent young people. You might have to 'buy into' catchment, however, to have any hope of attending.

Edgbaston High School for Girls

Westbourne Road, Edgbaston, Birmingham B15 3TS

Ages 11–18 **Pupils** 509 **Sixth form** 123

Fees: £12,774 pa

01214 545831
www.edgbastonhigh.co.uk/

Head: Since 2006, Dr Ruth Weeks BSc PhD. A Birmingham girl born and bred, she describes this part of her interesting and successful career as 'coming home', but with no disloyalty to her earlier jobs. A chemist by training – that's how she gained her PhD – she was about to begin academic research on muscles when the demands of her husband's career caused the family to move. In the course of her career she has been deputy head of Haberdashers' Monmouth School for Girls and head of Redland High (now Redmaids' High) in Bristol. So there's bags of experience here and a lot of intelligence.

A past GSG entry mentioned, with gentle irony we hope, the King Edward V1 consortium of schools as being the leaders in Birmingham education. Dr Weeks' response was vigorous, sharp and impressive. There was almost a suggestion of Elizabethan 'foul scorn'. 'We know what we are,' she said with asperity, 'and we know who we are.' The school is heavily oversubscribed but Dr Weeks and her SMT meet all the prospective pupils and their parents and visit them in their schools as well. The result is that right from the start of each girl's time at the school there is a warmth and understanding. The business of meeting so many parents and children – many times the number for whom there are spaces – is enormously time-consuming, but helps to spread a feeling of goodwill. It's also a shrewd move to keep in contact with local primary schools. Parents told us it was that personal touch that swung it for them and their daughters. Dr Weeks teaches chemistry to years 7 and 13, two significant years.

There is a whiff of the CEO amongst a number of modern heads; heads perhaps dominated by governors who see schools as businesses, and positions in league tables as proof of excellence. EHS does not feel like that, and a mention of the distressing frequency of schools getting rid of pupils who have failed to impress at GCSE and are therefore in danger of lowering A level league positions drew something approaching a snort from this elegant and intelligent head. 'Of course we don't,' she replied to our question. 'We have a job to do.' Actually, very few pupils fail to perform well at GCSE. Nonetheless, there is a caveat to all this. See Entrance.

It is said by some that before she arrived the school had become a trifle sleepy. Without being remotely bombastic or hectoring, Dr Weeks has injected new life into this distinguished school – the oldest independent school for girls in Birmingham. With wisdom and intelligence, concern for staff and pupils and an overall appreciation of the school's potential, together with a clear eye for what is needed and an infectious sense of humour, she has made the school more attractive to parents and increased the range and variety of what is now a broad and progressive curriculum as well as a stimulating extracurricular programme. It is a school for happiness, but not at the expense of academic endeavour and success. It might well be that the happiness that pervades is based on academic pride and pleasure.

Leaving in July 2019.

Academic matters: There is much rivalry over academic prowess and education amongst the many fine schools in Birmingham. Many parents with whom we spoke cited a school's position in the league tables as the clearest indication of academic thrust. That depends. Some schools home in on a limited number of subjects, with their sights fixed exclusively on league tables. Probably because the ratio of staff to pupils is very generous, EHS is able to offer a very wide range of subjects – 27 at GCSE, including classical Greek and Latin. In 2018, at GCSE, 62 per cent A*-A/7-9 grades. All that and a range of 30 subjects at A level (25 per cent A*/A grades and 56 per cent A*-B in 2018). It's a broad range, producing pupils with a wide cross-section of academic skills. Parents like the availability of choice, perceiving it as individual attention – smaller classes – and avoiding stereotypes. We witnessed some marvellous lessons with lively teachers who, rather than treat the pupils as if they were Strasbourg Geese, encouraged questioning and discussion and were rewarded by a lot of both. There is a palpable fizz in the classrooms. Fizz but no aggression.

Supporting this broad choice of examinable subjects is an extraordinary bank of extracurricular activities, always connected with matters academic. Thus the chess club is allied to mathematics; Lab Rats to science; Chinese calligraphy to art; knitting to textiles; creative writing club to English; Crest Awards to science; Mandarin for beginners etc. We gave up after counting after 30 options. No time is wasted: some sessions take place at lunch time, some after school.

Games, options, the arts: A recent building which has made a considerable difference is a wonderful performing arts centre called – for obvious reasons, when you see it – the Octagon. In itself it is a very attractive and versatile building and an ideal space for concerts, plays – senior and junior productions – assemblies, exams (aaargh), ballet and other activities. It was there that we were privileged to watch an unforgettable impromptu performance by the school's hula-hoop champion. A unique delight and rarely seen in schools of such calibre. There is masses of music and everyone seems to be involved in concerts of varying kinds. Art contributes much to the creative soul of the school. Three studios offer a variety of media including ceramics, printmaking and graphic design as well as traditional painting and drawing. Annual visits to Paris, Florence and Rome. As far as sport is concerned this school is pretty healthy: football, cricket, hockey, basketball, fencing, tennis, netball, rounders and cross-country are pursued with great enthusiasm. To have 14 acres of playing fields in this city school is very useful; to have a fitness suite is wonderful; to have a recently refurbished swimming pool – over 50 years old – is rare; and to have an all-weather pitch seems a real bonus. And it's nearly all happened since the school awoke under the perceptive wisdom of the Great Doctor.

Background and atmosphere: 'The aim of this institution is to afford to the girls of this important neighbourhood an education which shall be the best that this age can afford'. So said Miss Alice Cooper, the first head, in 1878. They are words that would be echoed nearly 150 years later. The founders were keen to make available a broad, liberal education and EHS has always been characterised by its non-denominational approach to teaching and learning, education rather than grade accumulation. A glance at the current list of governors confirms that the Quaker and Unitarian roots remain deeply embedded in the school. The atmosphere is friendly, warm and non-judgemental. Friday assemblies in the Octagon are spent silently listening to music; 'It's cool,' said one girl to us. Lots of charitable work. The reaction to our question about racial mix was a puzzled look. 'We're all happy,' was the answer. Silly question.

We had the doubtful privilege of reaching our destination via Five Ways roundabout. Thus it was already a pleasure and a relief to arrive at the handsome entrance. There we were greeted with warmth and courtesy in the car park by a groundsman. The warmth of our reception was constant, wherever we went. The atmosphere was palpable. Grounds staff, incidentally, are always very good indicators of what a school is really like.

An impressive array of new buildings has sprung up in the last few years. We visited the new, state-of-the-art sixth form area complete with comfortable chairs, books, improving magazines, tables to work at, facilities for making coffee and tea and a balcony terrace for dreaming. Why not? A marvellous room for discussing the great things of life and considerably superior to many universities. Five new specialist classrooms help accommodate all those subjects taught. The general study area has also been extended and significantly upgraded, to provide a wireless network, laptop computers and interactive white boards. All the gizmos. We visited the wonderful new library, which is now almost double its original size, with research and fiction sections as well as a fully equipped ICT suite.

Sparky teaching. Lively brains. But who remembers that 'education is what you remember when you've forgotten everything you were taught at school'? Wherever we went we were greeted with friendliness and courtesy and a welcome current of humour.

Pastoral care, well-being and discipline: This is a very friendly, happy school where teachers and pupils seem to get on well with each other with mutual respect and affection. Form tutors and individual subject teachers have a recognisable role to play but there are more layers than that. The arrival of new pupils aged 11+ does seem to bring out the kindness of the older girls. Time and time again girls told us how easy it was to settle down on arrival, not only because there is a mentoring system in place where sixth formers 'shadow' the younger, but because of the overall atmosphere.

Pupils and parents: Pupils come from all over Birmingham and beyond. Parents are a loyal bunch who are keen to do what they can to support a school for which they feel gratitude and fondness. There is an active and enthusiastic parents' association which has its own website.

OGs include Molly Dineen, film-maker; Lydia Hislop, journalist; Professor Sally Davies, chief medical officer at the Department of Health; Robyn Jones OBE, businesswoman; Philippa Lett, top model, and Kate Williams, author and TV historian. Plus Malala Yousafzai, girls' education activist and Nobel Peace Prize winner.

Entrance: Many join from the prep at 11, others from local primaries. Maths and English exams plus interview. Entry into the sixth form requires a minimum of six GCSEs at grades A*-B/9-6 (including English and maths), plus good grades in prospective A level subjects. Progression from year 11 at EHS into the sixth form and from the lower sixth to upper sixth is dependent in all cases upon sustained good progress and attitude.

Exit: Around 15 per cent leave after GCSEs. Huge variety of universities and subjects for those that stay on. Most years some Oxbridge places – one to Cambridge in 2018; one to University of Valencia in Spain; other popular destinations include Birmingham (lots), Nottingham, Aston, Exeter, Liverpool, Oxford Brooks and Manchester. A medic most years. A few gap years. Good, careful advice and help reported by parents and past pupils. Certainly no suggestion of pupils being compelled against their wishes.

Money matters: There are moves afoot, as with so many schools in Birmingham, to raise money to make the school more accessible to parents who need financial help. There are bursaries and scholarships available. Interested parents should not be embarrassed to ask.

Remarks: 'Rigour with kindness' is one summary we were given. Both words are appropriate. It's a wonderful school for the warmth and affection which pervades, along with academic toughness. The breadth does not hide the toughness: it succeeds not through a shapeless smudge but through wonderful, rigorous teaching and the right choice of subjects. It is attention to detail that makes the system work; that, and a shameless love of learning.

E

Elmhurst Ballet School

21

249 Bristol Road, Edgbaston, Birmingham B5 7UH

Ages 11–19 Pupils 190 (121 girls, 69 boys) Sixth form 58 Boarders 161 full

Fees: Day £18,936 – £19,626; Boarding £24,270 – £26,163 pa

0121 472 6655
www.elmhurstdance.co.uk

Principal: Since 2010, Jessica Wheeler BA NPQH (30s). There can't be many people in the world, never mind the UK, who combine professional dance experience with top notch educational management expertise. But Elmhurst has found it. Laban trained, she then became resident with the Laban dance company. Moved into teaching as freelance and guest teacher. Tough London comprehensive that employed her to teach dance spotted the charisma, energy and determination and she was fast-tracked to assistant headship before moving with a team of super fixers to work magic in one of the worst schools in London.

Aspirations since arriving at Elmhurst are to make it the dance school of choice in the UK and beyond. Her vision is a holistic one – to ensure talented dancers are also healthy and wise – and this is being realised through detailed, methodical planning, management and monitoring. She is stunning in every sense, and warm with it.

Brilliantly supported by artistic director Robert Parker, the driving force behind the increasingly world-class dance side of the school. He had a meteoric career through the Royal Ballet School, into the company and to Birmingham Royal Ballet as principal dancer. He knows the industry inside out and inspires huge respect in the young dancers. Coming from a Billy Elliot background, he is driven and self disciplined but also hugely charming, brimming with enthusiasm and cares passionately about the experience Elmhurst gives its young dancers. And he has collected a commercial pilot's licence along the way.

Academic matters: Given that admission is entirely done on dance potential, results are good and the principal and new deputy are determined to continue the upward trajectory for GCSE and A level results. In 2018, 51 per cent A*-A/9-7 grades at GCSE. At A level, 50 per cent of grades at A*/A in 2018, 65 per cent at A*/B. Academic staff are up against students who say all they want to do is dance, but while they might be guided by their hearts, they are surrounded by adults who know you can't dance for ever, however talented you are.

Principal and her team have brought in changes to ensure any dip in academic performance is picked up and acted upon swiftly. She is building a curriculum that will play to the strengths of young dancers who are increasingly getting their GCSE grades. Baseline testing for children coming in to allow individual target setting and tracking of progress year on year. Most importantly, there is now transparency for students and parents about where things are heading.

School is rightly proud of its serious A level programme – dance, music, art, English and maths are on offer – and hopes to introduce geography and biology. Most dance schools give up on academic side at 16 but there is a philosophical commitment here to the value of an academic training, heavily underpinned by the practical consideration that a student who is seriously injured at 17 or has simply grown a bit too tall must have alternatives to a dance career.

Classes are around 20 – smaller once options are chosen. A real strength, parents tell us. Some streaming for EAL students and English exams are very carefully chosen to meet the individual's best needs. Teachers all comment that the discipline and focus of the dance studio infuses academic lessons. The issue is sometimes getting the students to speak at all (they are so used to the silence of dance class). Teachers are very conscious that many of the students are kinaesthetic learners and match their teaching styles to maximise this.

Games, options, the arts: This a rigorous training for the most gifted and resilient. The artistic and dance side of the curriculum takes up about a third of the students' time up to 16. Then, as they head towards their three-year National Diploma in Professional Dance, it takes up two-thirds. Training is in classical ballet but there is also a strong emphasis on jazz, contemporary and other supporting dance styles. There is an assessing out process in year 9 and year 11, when students who have not developed as dancers as expected are asked to leave. Process is done as compassionately as possible and warning given in good time for families to find an alternative. About eight per cent of the cohort assessed out across these two key stages; however a percentage leave at the end of year 11 of their own accord to go to dance schools offering a different sixth form curriculum.

Recent major review of the programme drew on the views of the professional dance companies, ensuring students are prepared for the demands of the dance industry today. Increasing number and diversity of visiting artists, directors and choreographers, running workshops, masterclasses and lecturing to enrich the students' experience.

Partnership with Birmingham Royal Ballet (reason why Elmhurst moved to Edgbaston 10 years ago) is the icing on the cake for the artistic side of the school. It means getting top quality dance teachers is much easier than anywhere else outside London and students get the chance to perform regularly with the company. Even the youngest can audition for children's parts in productions like The Nutcracker. Also allows for easy professional exchanges.

Dancers simply don't do risky contact sports but Elmhurst is keen for them to try everything else and takes its responsibility for overall fitness very seriously. Attractive fitness suite has been created and staff and students are encouraged to use it, and there's a new multi-use games area. They also share sports facilities and coaches with a nearby mainstream school.

With no sports fields, there are no obvious spaces for younger children to run around but school's pretty, landscaped grounds give a sense of openness to the site.

Friday afternoons have been developed as an off-timetable fun time for learning new skills and offering enrichment and students love it. Sport, art and craft, academic clubs, drama, student-led choreography projects and yoga. Keen to showcase the students' talents outside dance, the school takes part in a host of national competitions – poetry and short story writing, for example, have seen recent successes.

Heart of the school is the excellent 250-seater theatre where the many performances take place, culminating in the outstanding end of year productions.

Boarding: Accommodation for the vast majority who board (just under nine per cent from overseas) is excellent, with many single and double rooms. When we visited the girls had set up their own beauty studio for pamper time with the help of a beauty-trained member of the house staff.

Sixth form accommodation has now moved into a purpose-built space nearer the main campus. This better links the sixth form experience and the rest of the school. Prior to this, one parent felt that when the children were younger they were in a very protected, small environment and then at 16 were suddenly launched into independent living. Students and parents commented on the recent increase in weekend activities, making the most of Birmingham, once Saturday classes have finished.

Background and atmosphere: The moment you walk into Elmhurst, you arrive in a huge dance studio, where there is invariably a class going on. From that point, you are in the ballet world. Students move around the corridors as though they are still on stage. They are graceful, hold themselves beautifully and even when they are chatting outside a maths classroom manage to group themselves as though in a corps de ballet. Most of the time they are either in dancewear or tracksuits in which they naturally look elegant and purposeful.

Staff comment on the maturity with which students relate to adults. Students we spoke to were articulate, able to express themselves confidently and had plenty to say. No bells and the atmosphere is calm and quiet. Something about the absolute dedication to a highly disciplined vocation infuses the whole place. Drive is there in academic as well as artistic classes. 'I have never been in classes with fewer discipline problems,' one teacher told us. 'The children succeed more than they would in other schools because all the time they are asking "how can I improve?" They do that in their ballet and they have that attitude to their GCSEs too.'

School's recently developed 'live, dance, learn' slogan captures the holistic approach to dance education. This is also underlined by 'the Elmhurst way', four statements posted all over the school to remind students and staff what it is all about – choose the right attitude, be there, make someone's day and have fun. We like the sentiments – they give an adventurous and humane dimension to the gruelling discipline of the ballet world.

Pastoral care, well-being and discipline: There has been a huge amount of heartbreak over the years about 'assessing out,' the process at the end of years 9 and 11 when students are told if they are good enough at dance to carry on. Elmhurst has done much soul searching as to how they can make this stressful time as bearable as possible for everyone concerned. They have introduced pre-assessment, which allows teachers to give early indication to both students and parents if things are not looking good. In some cases it can be turned around and every opportunity is given, but sometimes, no matter how much they work, it just can't. At least everyone knows sooner rather than later and the school support swings into action, looking for other alternatives (of which there actually are a lot). Pupils may not end up as Giselle at the Bolshoi but they could still have a career in the dance industry.

Overall, Elmhurst has moved way beyond the usual pastoral care. Students' health and well-being is at the core of everything and systems are in place that recognise the unique nature of vocational ballet training. Dedicated medical centre, with qualified nursing staff, on-site GP appointments, physiotherapy services, dance psychology, dance nutritionist, sports massage and chiropractor. New health and well-being centre aims at a holistic approach, fostering 'a closer working relationship between healthcare, artistic and boarding staff'.

The school is ahead of the game – linking with university researchers to ensure pre-emptive strategies are in place to keep the students dancing at their peak. More in the pipeline – working with international researchers to develop motivational programmes based on the psychology of success. Probably because of the emphasis on well-being, there are virtually no cases of anorexia. Principal told us that during her time at the school there have only been two diagnoses (both of which had positive outcomes) and that this is proportionately far fewer than at her last school (a large comprehensive).

The school holds student inset days, much like those for staff. Outside agencies come in to run workshops and talks on subjects like e-safety, cancer, injury prevention and choreography. Staff make every effort to ensure that parents have the same information to complete the circle and ensure maximum input for the students.

'The children are simply in love with what they are doing,' one houseparent told us in an attempt to explain the enthusiasm and buzz about the boarding experience.

Pupils and parents: Most are encouraged to apply by their ballet teachers and all are there because they want to dance. There is a real warmth in relations between staff and students and between the students themselves. One boy told us: 'I have finally got friends who have the same interests as me.' Everyone we spoke to stressed the very special people here and the friendships made. 'I have become a different person,' said one girl. 'I am independent and confident now that I am doing what I love.' Parents commented on the way the school by its very nature encouraged independence. 'Our son is noticeably more mature and independent that his contemporaries at other independent boarding schools,' observed one father.

Not surprisingly, parents are quite intense. They are acutely aware of both the dangers and the strengths of opting for a specialist vocational education at 11. A number choose the school because they can see that it tries very hard to keep the academic doors open.

Parents are more obviously desperate for their children to succeed than those in other schools (although given the limited employment opportunities with the world top ballet companies, they know that not many can). This gives an edge to how they relate to the school, and one or two thought some parents were reluctant sometimes to approach the school with criticisms. The last thing they want is for their child to be asked to leave. Those with children about to start auditioning for their first jobs were unsure if the school was doing enough to support them, although they recognised it did as much or more than other dance schools. A parent whose child had just had a minor injury wanted to see even more physiotherapy and counselling support. But even the most anxious parents agreed that their child couldn't be happier.

Former pupils (known as Old Elms) include actresses Helen Baxendale, Hayley Mills, Juliet Mills, Jenny Agutter and Joanna David, singer Sarah Brightman and ballet dancers Dame Merle Park, Diana Fox and Isabel McMeekan.

Entrance: Entrance is entirely on artistic merit. Auditions are held at various times in the year in the UK and overseas, although the overseas auditions are increasingly conducted via DVD submissions and then by Elmhurst staff travelling to host auditions overseas. Children will have had ballet lessons before they come and the school has links with some of the best local ballet teachers around the country. The school also runs its own associate classes for the under 11s in Birmingham, Sunderland, Manchester and Plymouth as outreach. Also visits some very challenged primary schools to talent spot. Students are reauditioned at the end of the third year (year 9) and fifth year (year 11) and places are either confirmed or not.

Exit: In 2018, 52 per cent left after GCSEs, though 90 per cent of these leavers go on to further dance training. More than 80 per cent of sixth form graduates enter dance related employment within six months of graduating – increasingly to join internationally prestigious companies. A graduate placement scheme has been introduce to allow students who don't gain immediate employment to stay at the school to sustain audition-ready fitness. The odd student for whom the idea of a ballet career has palled by the time they are 19 head to university. When we visited one had just got an offer from York to read English.

F

Money matters: Given that the fees include all the specialist ballet tuition, they are reasonable. Many UK families are able to take advantage of two government funded, means-tested, bursary/scholarship schemes: music and dance scheme (MDS) for those aged 11 to 16 and dance and drama awards (DaDa) for the sixth form. Awards are highly competitive but all credit to the government for ensuring highly talented children can get the specialist training they need, regardless of parental income.

Remarks: The only purpose-built ballet school in the country, this is the ballet school to watch. Elmhurst isn't afraid to look beyond the intense and sometimes claustrophobic ballet world. It challenges the conventional thinking that young dancers must be silent sponges soaking up the technical knowledge of their teachers. With the school's rising academic profile and development of pupil voice, the dancers coming out of Elmhurst are critical learners ready to take ownership of their own careers.

Elmhurst is not the Royal Ballet School and in that sense it has to fight really hard to prove itself. There are no laurels to rest on here. It reinvented itself when it moved to Birmingham and it has the drive and energy of a young institution hungry for success. The Royal Ballet School is still the first choice for the majority of families but Elmhurst is biting at its heels, offering something new and very special.

Fairfield Preparatory School

Linked with Loughborough High School, Loughborough Grammar School, Loughborough Amherst School

Leicester Road, Loughborough, Leicestershire LE11 2AE

Ages 3–11 Pupils 488

Fees: £10,203 – £10,656 pa

01509 215172
www.lsf.org/fairfield

Headmaster: Since 2013, Andrew Earnshaw, an effervescent mid 40s. Educated at Bacup and Rawtenstall Grammar School and Lancaster University. Has worked in both the state and independent sectors and also at The British School in Saudi Arabia. A deputy head at Beeston Rylands School before becoming headmaster of Nottingham High Junior School at the age of 34. Resembles an Anglicised version of Pep Guardiola and, like the Manchester City supremo, his organisation is at the top of the Premier League. A MAMIL (middle-aged man in lycra) who recently sizzled through a coast-to-coast ride, zooming through its 120 miles in eight hours. Humorous, perceptive, self-deprecating and with not a hint of the arrogance that some heads display, his popularity within the school with children, staff and parents is obvious. Like Guardiola he has invested his resources wisely: £8m has recently been pumped into a stunning development of the pre-prep department, which has created a swirl of interlinked buildings: clear evidence of his vision and style.

Some heads can struggle on their second headship as they adapt to new scenarios. Not Mr Earnshaw. He wants to be known as 'a head who says yes, rather than ... I'll think about it'. Consequently, this is an original community where staff are given the freedom to develop ideas for themselves: witness the fantastic forest school, created in a former wasteland at the edge of the playing fields, where pre-prep children can become mini celebrities in their jungle, as they learn to build a fire, cook, create dens and play plenty of hide and seek. In a school of such size (there are nearly 500 pupils on the roll) the head still appears to know every child by name, and to accompany him on a tour is a joy as both children and staff are genuinely pleased to see him. But this school combines the wisdom of the past with the freshness of the future. For example, boys still wear caps and girls wear straw boaters in the summer. Head wants his charges to look smart, so is often telling boys to tuck their shirts in. Everyone is stylish and polished .... and every child has use of an iPad to complement their learning. Academic standards are high. It is, as he says, 'cool to be clever'.

He must clearly survive on about three hours sleep a night – uniquely, in our experience, he both writes a card and rings up each parent to give a report on how each of the 70-odd new pupils has fared in their first week. Perhaps his most engaging and inspiring idea is his Wheel of Fortune. This gives children who have won 100 behaviour points for good conduct by the end of the academic year the opportunity to spin the giant wheel in assembly and win, for example, time off homework or a tea party with the deputy head. The most popular segment is 8, for, if the wheel stops there, the spinner is given eight wet sponges with which to splatter the headmaster at break-time in the playground.

His wife teaches here too and his two sons attend the school.

Entrance: Non-selective at 3+ into the nursery; entry to the pre-prep at 4+ depends on a judgement of a child's readiness for learning. From year 3 onwards tests are more formal with boys and girls sitting papers in English, maths and NVR. No scholarships or bursaries are available, although there is provision to support families if there is a sudden change in circumstances.

Exit: Nearly every child – at least 90 per cent – remains within The Loughborough Schools Foundation; girls progressing to Loughborough High School, boys to Loughborough Grammar School a few to Loughborough Amherst. A high proportion of academic scholarships at the Loughborough Schools are also won by Fairfield pupils. Scholarships have also recently been won at Oakham, Repton and King Edward's School, Birmingham. For the tiny minority of children who won't be academically fitted to the demands of the senior schools, this will become obvious by year 5 when Mr Earnshaw will start conversations with parents to identify the most sensible options at the end of year 6.

Remarks: On our tour with the head, the children were polite and bright. Everyone seemed genuinely pleased to see him and answer his questions and tell us about what they were studying.

When we asked one class what life was like at Fairfield, they responded with 'fun', 'great' and 'marvellous'.

Pupils are expected by the end of their time to have a reading age at least two years in advance of their chronological one – a flair boosted by the spacious and well-stocked library and a scheme that combines classics like Swallows and Amazons with the best new fiction, and ends with a quiz. French is introduced in the pre-prep with German, Spanish and now Italian in the more senior years. Some five per cent of pupils make use of the SEND provision, provided by a specialist team of teachers.

Competition is much encouraged. Boys and girls can enter for LAMDA examinations and we met a boy who had recently triumphed in a local Young Innovators' Challenge where he was tasked with designing a weight-bearing structure. And so he had knitted a bridge which withstood a 10kg weight. The clubs and activity programme takes place before school, at lunchtimes and after school. The variety is predictably vast, ranging from touch typing to first jazz, strategy games to dance. There are choirs and orchestras, netball, hockey and rugby clubs, a school council and even a harp ensemble. Music takes place in a splendid building shared with the senior schools. Fortnightly concerts are programmed whilst the string instrumental project for every child in year 2 safeguards the future. Dramatic productions every year for each of the year groups, recent epics being Aladdin and Joseph and the reception's version of Whoops-a-Daisy Angel.

Boys follow a termly pattern of rugby, football, cricket and athletics; girls compete in netball, hockey, rounders and athletics. Facilities are outstanding – the grass would grace Lord's or Wimbledon – and somehow the sporting staff still find time to organise and run the Loughborough Town Sports, held at Loughborough University, for over 40 local state primary schools.

As the school is a part of the Loughborough Schools Foundation, there is a natural long-term vision for families. Since Fairfield is independent within the Loughborough group, staff were closely involved in the planning of the new pre-prep building: one of the many highlights here being the custom-made carpet of inspiration embellished with key words.

The soul of Fairfield is in great part created by the fact that this is very much a family-based school. Many mothers and father have been educated here. Some 40 per cent of staff have their children in the school, along with the Earnshaws' two sons. Recently the head welcomed a child of a fourth-generation family.

It is unsurprising therefore that the Fairfield PTA is so well involved in the life of the school, providing, for example, the funds for the creation of the forest school and being at the core of the community. It is a very sociable body, organising beer & curry nights, a Christmas fair, golf competitions and trips to the pantomime. Parental literature is exemplary – a model of its kind.

But it is the people who make it fizz. A new member of staff spoke of 'the great, supportive team' who had helped her through her first weeks, and at lunch, as we savoured our lamb orzos, we found ourselves sitting with a year 4 boy. We asked him what his teachers were like. 'Kind and funny,' he replied. 'How?" we questioned. He munched away. 'Well, like at assembly Mr. Earnshaw told us how he became bald. It was because he tore his hair out to give it to a rhino who needed to grow a longer horn' (for those who don't know these things, apparently rhino horns are made out of hair). He munched some more and then came out with his last line. 'Teachers can be bit sulky when you don't do your homework.'

There is an ease, a positivity and an endeavour about it all. Wrap-around care is provided by specialist staff. Breakfast club begins at 7.45am. There are parents' information evenings (recently focused on anti-bullying and e-safety), and the head teaches handwriting to year 3. The inspectorate of 2016 had it right when they described it as 'excellent in every aspect'. Fairfield will appeal to most types of child.

As it obviously does to the parents. A new parent, after three weeks in the school, described both her and her boy's experience as 'fabulous'. According to another, 'children really enjoy it,' whilst a third remarked that 'the teachers are great,' citing the fact that if a child experiences personal problems then 'the pastoral care is excellent'.

So, if you are lucky enough, as a prospective parent, to live in the wide catchment area – buses run from Leicester, Nottingham, Derby and Melton – do put Fairfield on your visit-list.

Foremarke Hall (Repton Preparatory School)

Linked with Repton School

Milton, Derby DE65 6EJ

Ages 3–13 **Pupils** 453 **Boarders** 53 full (from year 3)

Fees: Day £9,240 – £19,860; Boarding £21,756 – £25,719 pa

01283 707100
www.foremarke.org.uk

Headmaster: Since September 2018, Robert Relton, previously principal of Repton Abu Dhabi, a day school for 3-11 year olds. Educated at the College of St Mark and St John, he is interested in PE and using IT in teaching. He spent 12 years at Ravenscourt Park Prep, as deputy head and head, before setting up and running Repton Abu Dhabi. His wife, Lola, is a consultant eye surgeon, and they have three young sons.

Entrance: This is essentially non-selective, although those who wish to enter from year 3 onwards will be given introductory papers to assess their abilities in English, maths and reasoning. The expectation and the reality is that children will progress to year 8, ultimately following either scholarship or common entrance systems of study. The learning enhancement department numbers four and works both in and out of the classroom, providing individualised and small-group guidance for those in need of assistance, especially in literacy and numeracy. There are up to 20 overseas students (all who have been assessed) and this international spread is encouragingly wide, students coming from Japan and Russia, Hong Kong, Spain and China. There is an EAL department to assist in their transition.

A range of scholarships and awards are available – for academic prowess at 7+ and for prowess and promise in music, sport and drama at 11+.

Exit: Being Repton's preparatory school, it is hardly a surprise that around 90 per cent of year 8 students advance to the senior school. Other popular schools, from a wide selection include Eton College, Harrow School, Shrewsbury School, Rugby School and Oundle School. Alumni include Georgie Twigg – a GB hockey gold medallist at Rio, the actor Tom Chambers, and England U21 footballer, Will Hughes.

Remarks: Shakespeare had it that 'all that glisters is not gold'. Foremarke's website is amongst the best we have seen; dazzling with high-quality photographs and text, a selection of enticing videos (one of which reminded us of an opening sequence to the Great British Bake-Off) and more menus than one would find in a chain of restaurants. Like many, it claims to be 'the leading prep school in the Midlands' (a phrase increasingly reminiscent of the 'best beer' Heineken advert) but does it live up to its promise?

Certainly, it makes a stunning start as, at the end of a long, well-tended, rhododendron-fringed drive, the Georgian hall comes into view, resembling part of a wing at Blenheim Palace. As we drew up, a gardener (hard to credit in early November) was cutting one of the perfect grass rectangles. Everything is immaculate. Sweeping steps herald the entrance to the front hall where sofas and log fires deepen the style. Home-made biscuits are served with coffee.

Throughout the school the facilities are impressive. Many join the pre-prep where play areas, consisting of a wooden adventure trail and a green area with tunnels and mounds that looks like something out of Tellytubby land, introduce the new building. The great majority of Foremarke's infrastructure is presented with similar polish.

The quad development, along with the adjacent Thomas Davies building, features rooms of a scope and flair that would in no way be out of place in a senior school, and, indeed, would be superior to many. Tremulous pupils, however, might not be too encouraged by the sign on the door of the history room which instructs entrants to 'abandon hope'.

The library will inspire, as will the theatre and the sports hall. The triple highlights, though, are the Charles Jennings music school (named after Handel's librettist) and the exceptional art studio and DT centre. We especially liked the pencil portraits in the former, while the latter is the pit-stop for four electric racing cars. These compete on circuits such as Goodwood and Rockingham, the school holding the course record at Aintree, on the track – adjacent to the Grand National fences – that used to host the British Grand Prix.

It is a truism that the most important factors in a school's success are the students and the staff, but the buildings and the beauty of the grounds at Foremarke all help to set the tone. Taste for the best of both the ancient and the modern is all-embracing.

This was also evident in our tour of the boarding houses. Full, weekly and flexible boarding options are available and around 40 students are in on weekends, cared for by the dozen members of staff who live on site. The girls' house, Nightingale, has a cottage-style feel to it and could have been decorated and furnished by a joint design team from Laura Ashley and Cath Kidston. There are two boys' boarding houses, Francis and Burdett. Francis' rooms take their names from their original function: hence there is the Gun Room and the Wine Cellar, the Still Room and the Butler's Pantry. As in Nightingale, the rooms are spacious and elegant.

Brand new dining room. The food is fantastic; as evidenced by our spectacular Thai curry. (Foremarke won the Tatler Award for the Best School Food a few years ago, whilst The Week magazine awarded a similar accolade).

At lunch, we talked with some girls from year 3 whose 'best things about the school' were flapjacks on Wednesdays and 'golden time' – 'where we can do drawing'. On the same table was a year 8 boy, hopeful of a place next year at Eton, who was of the outlandish opinion that Foremarke was 'the most rounded school in England'. We challenged him to detail his knowledge of all schools from Durham to Cornwall. He smiled, and without a touch of Trump-like arrogance, coolly explained that he could not imagine a better school, 'for all that it has done for me'.

And it is clearly not just because it prepares the way for students to enter some of the best senior schools. The extracurricular holy trinity of sport, music and drama sparkles. Girls play hockey, netball and rounders, boys football, hockey and cricket. A multiplicity of teams exists for sportists at every level and the school celebrates the Foremarke Football League which runs alongside the pattern of school fixtures. This year Barcelona (still without Messi) were the winners. There is sailing on the lake, athletics, fencing (a year 6 girl has recently won The IAPS national épée title), swimming, triathlon and even an equestrian team.

Music fills many pages in the Foremarke yearbook – The Preptonian – detailing the calendar of concerts, both in and out of school, and the excellence of orchestras, ensembles and choirs. The chamber choir sings at Remembrance Sunday at the National Arboretum in front of 5,000 people. This year's senior dramatic production was Twelfth Night. There are class plays too, and visits from the Young Film Academy and the Young Shakespeare Theatre Company.

Given this whirligig of opportunity, parents gush about the Foremarke brand of education. One Russian mother, for example, who had met the head in Moscow, had scoured England for a school that would be flexible enough to allow her daughter to develop her high class ice-skating. According to her, 'everything is superb'. Another reported that her family's transfer from Yorkshire had gone well because of 'the excellent academic experience and also the experience of life that Foremarke gives'. A third said that... 'Staff cannot be faulted. They take them way beyond the curriculum.' When asked about the lead up to year 8 examinations, the view was that 'they are very good at managing the pressure and making the hard decisions regarding common entrance and scholarship selection.' Parents kept well-informed by the school's weekly newsletter (the Foremarke Flyer), text-alerts working smoothly if triggered by late cancellations. We were left with the words .... 'Children have such fun. They're tired and they love it.'

And so, does Foremarke, founded in 1945, live up to its marketing promises after its first 70+ years? If it is affordable – fees might be too much of a stretch for many – our visit confirmed that the shimmering straplines are justified. It is, perhaps, an indication of the school's standing that, in the county of Derby's recently produced edition of Monopoly, Foremarke has been awarded a green square: rather appropriately, given its heritage, Regent Street. As all Monopolists know, the third green property is Bond Street; where jewelled gold glitters. There is plenty more to be discovered at Foremarke.

Framlingham College

College Road, Framlingham, Woodbridge, Suffolk IP13 9EY

Ages 2–18 **Pupils** 700 **Sixth form** 158 **Boarders** 90 full, 182 weekly, 321 flexi **C of E**

Fees: Day £8,736– £19,924; Boarding: Prep £36 – £39 per night. Senior full boarder £30,985 pa

01728 723789
www.framcollege.co.uk

Headmaster: Since 2009, Paul Taylor BA. Read history and politics at Exeter University. Formerly lower master (deputy head) at King's School, Canterbury, and before that director of sport at Tonbridge School. Very friendly, charming without overdoing it and a good listener. Aims to 'produce a decent, rounded human being who looks you in the eye' and believes the school's good performance should be better known outside East Anglia. Wife, Amanda, is secretary of the Framlingham Society and they have four children – two at university and two at Framlingham.

Retiring in July 2019. His successor will be Louise North, currently senior deputy head at Oakham School. French and Spanish degree from Durham University; began her teaching career at St Peter's School, York, and after stints as a boarding housemistress at both Glenalmond and Marlborough College, she joined Stonyhurst College as deputy head (upper school), taking up her current post in 2015. She is married to Dominic, a rare and fine books dealer, and they have two children who will be joining the college and prep school.

Head of prep: Since 2016, Matthew King. History degree from Nottingham; began his teaching career in Surrey before moving to Dorset, where he met his wife Emily while both were teaching at Dumpton School in Wimborne. Deputy head and then head of Pennthorpe School in Sussex, where he spent eight happy years before being appointed head here. He is a keen sportsman and writer who has taught subjects ranging from geography to drama and from cricket to ancient history.

Academic matters: Setting begins early for English and maths in the prep, and higher up for other subjects. French in pre-prep and Latin from year 7. Help for mild difficulties, notably dyslexia, but the curriculum is not geared for those who seriously struggle. Extension programmes are developed for 'exceptional students' (head prefers this to 'gifted and talented').

Performs well at both GCSE and A level, though not highly selective – strong commitment to pupils of varying ability. In 2018, 56 per cent of A levels were A*-B, 29 per cent A*/A. At GCSE, 33 per cent A*-A/9-7 grades. Some sixth formers take EPQ, with HPQ lower down. BTecs in music, sports, computer science and business studies.

SEN provision well established. Emphasis on supporting the pupils' needs – a register (updated termly) is kept to inform staff across the curriculum of any difficulties. Timetabled access to small group and individual tuition avoids pupil withdrawal from mainstream classes. All pupils must be capable of following the academic programmes at GCSE and A level. Provision for EAL also excellent – separate classes as well as individual tuition. Facilities well thought out, well designed and un-flashy. Exceptional library and design and technology building. Classes kept small, average size 12.

Games, options, the arts: Excellent provision for all sports. Artificial surfaces, new indoor pool and fitness centre (well used, especially by girls) – hosts many tournaments. Sport is important – all pupils take part competitively, whatever their level of ability. Music and drama popular too. New theatre/ performance studio and many pupils take drama options at GCSE and A level. Well attended regular public performances – pupils recently took The Importance of Being Earnest to the Edinburgh Fringe. Concerts held in local churches – Framlingham and Orford, as well as Ely Cathedral. Big takeup for DofE, with numbers reaching gold awards. Curriculum also supported by extraordinary plethora of clubs and activities.

Boarding: Prep school boarding is on the top two floors of the original building with spectacular views from every window, redecorated dormitories (mostly four to six beds) and common rooms – no twangy old sofas. Flexi-boarding very popular, and nearly every child from year 3 stays at least one night; 'The whole of year 7 and 8 seem to stay on Wednesday and Friday nights,' say pupils, partly no doubt, because there is Saturday morning school for these years.

Senior school boarding houses well planned and comfortable enough, though girls' quarters, unsurprisingly perhaps, are more home-like and with better decoration. Three houses for girls and four for boys. House competitions range from cross-country to crabbing. Pupils come and go with their own swipe card; most go home at weekends, unless from abroad.

Background and atmosphere: Founded in 1864 in memory of Prince Albert, Queen Victoria's husband (his statue takes pride of place at the front of the school). Senior school in imposing Victorian main building in stunning setting, perched on a hillside with a gorgeous view across the valley to 12th century Framlingham Castle. A variety of buildings added over time, none of them particularly distinguished, but well planned to make good use of beautiful and extensive grounds. Stupendous view of the castle from many perspectives (head has bagged dress circle view from his first floor study).

F

Prep school in idyllic setting down the Suffolk lanes. The original manor house has been rebuilt and remodelled as a memorial to former pupils killed both world wars. Remembrance is taken seriously and VC citations are proudly displayed in the panelled hall. This is a school for exploring and enjoying; massive oak staircases, terraces on which to play games or take off into the ravishing grounds. The country house atmosphere of the main building is complemented by a modern, multi-purpose hall used for concerts, assemblies and plays and well-designed buildings for DT and art, science and technology. Newish classroom block is reached via a covered passageway; spanking new dance and drama studio; new multi-use Fowler pavilion overlooking hockey pitch and cricket square.

Nursery and pre-prep occupy their own purpose built accommodation and play areas, but are very much part of the same site. Notice boards with details of after-school clubs, sport and music cover the walls, including one headed Celebration, and pupils proudly point out their names and faces.

A tone of respectful informality throughout. Pupils well-mannered and noticeably calm, even at lesson changes and in the dining hall at lunchtime.

Pastoral care, well-being and discipline: Policy of incorporating day pupils into boarding houses is now well established and a great success. Many pupils do 'occasional' boarding. A parent told us: 'I can email the housemaster directly if my daughter wants to board at short notice – on the same day, on occasion.' Anti-bullying posters dotted around school and any incidents picked up on quickly. 'The housemaster got to the bottom of the matter on the same day,' said one parent, 'and the boys are still together in the same house.'

Keeping sixth formers in the house system creates opportunities for leadership. As a relief from house responsibilities, sixth formers have their own common room and social areas – plans afoot to create a technologically sophisticated sixth form centre. The head rightly lauds excellent pastoral track record but emphasises that 'the family is more important. Schools can over-claim for themselves'.

Pupils and parents: Pupils are mainly drawn from middle class East Anglian families. In some cases, several generations have attended the school. A strong body from abroad, notably Germany and the Far East. Head sees the school as poised to appeal as much to the Oundle and Uppingham market as to its Norfolk and Suffolk constituency. Excellent reputation locally and no problems recruiting.

Pupils well-mannered and friendly, very at-ease in their school, 'Not precocious, but not scared of adults either,' is how the head puts it.

Entrance: For entry to the nursery and pre-prep, pupils are invited to spend a day (or morning) for an informal assessment; same for year 3 upwards but their day includes an entrance test.

Scholarships at 11+ for entrants to the senior school – academic, music and sport. At 13, pupils from the prep accepted 'on the nod' – assuming they can cope with the academic rigour of the college. CE and interview for everyone else, though tests in core subjects (English, maths and non-verbal reasoning) can be arranged for pupils from schools that don't do CE. The interview is key and head also takes prospective pupils' school reports seriously.

Significant numbers enter after GCSE, with places offered conditionally on the basis of an interview, school report and a minimum achievement of seven 5+ passes at GCSE/IGCSE or equivalent for those not following the British curriculum. Overseas candidates also sit tests in English and maths.

Exit: Everyone in the prep is prepared for common entrance. All but a handful transfer to the senior school (results help decide setting in year 9). Small number of leavers after GCSE. Almost all sixth formers go to university, with traditional universities well represented. Others go off to read anything from chemical engineering at Lancaster to equine management at the Royal Agricultural College to children's nursing at Kingston. The place of careers advice is stressed – head believes it should be seen as separate from the university application process. Parents rely on the school as an expert resource.

Money matters: A range of scholarships awarded for outstanding academic, musical, artistic and sporting excellence at 13+ and 16+. Further means-tested bursarial help is available as needed. Reductions for siblings and Forces families.

Remarks: A well run, unstressful school, with happy pupils and high levels of achievement in all areas.

Gresham's

Linked with Gresham's Prep School

Cromer Road, Holt, Norfolk NR25 6EA

Ages 13–18 **Pupils** 493 **Sixth form** 197 **Boarders** 290 full **C of E**

Fees: Day £24,420; Boarding £34,980 pa

01263 714614
www.greshams.com

Headmaster: Since 2014, Douglas Robb MA (Edinburgh) politics, MEd (Homerton, Cambridge), previously head of Oswestry School. A post-university spell of teaching in Zimbabwe and at Fettes College helped decide his career. Following a post teaching politics and economics at Loughborough grammar, he taught and was a housemaster at Oundle for 10 very happy years which 'totally persuaded me of the benefits of boarding.' Quite a commanding physical presence (a former rugby player), extremely quick-witted and entertaining, a live wire. 'He is confident enough to be able to listen to us and sometimes change his mind,' we were told by a pupil, and it is clear that he has 'picked up the vibe' of the school. He thinks 'it is dangerous to try and change a school; find one that's good and help make it the best. A school has a life of its own; I am a caretaker for a short time.' Believes the house system is central to the success of pupils learning and integrating well into school life. It can also help during the teenage years with 'opportunities for conversation and friendships, both amongst peers, but also with staff.' Has high expectations of his staff and spells out the commitment at interview; 'I pin them down, no woolly promises to help will do. This job is a vocation.' He is scornful of phrases such as 'work-life balance', believing that, in term time, successful teachers must be prepared to involve themselves far beyond the classroom itself, including meetings at odd times; 'Ten o'clock in the evening is not unheard of.' Is fortunate to be inheriting sound finances and is planning new boarding and music facilities and a sixth form centre. Is keen to continue raising academic standards – 'I never heard of a head wanting to lower them' – and to emphasise the central importance of boarding to the ethos of the school. Will accept pupils 'so long as they are prepared to work hard,' and their parents are realistic and in support.

Is married to Lucinda and they have three children (all at Gresham's). He is enjoying north Norfolk life, 'countryside, dogs, getting to know people.' Maintains keen interest in rugby, also golf, skiing and travel and 'proper holidays'

Academic matters: Class sizes between 12 and 20, and setting for most parts of the curriculum, mean pupils get focussed attention. Parents think the size of the school allows for pupils to develop at their own pace, though several also mentioned, not as a criticism, 'there is definitely more push; things are less easy-going than in the past.' Pupils generally take at least 10 GCSEs; 40 per cent at A*-A/9-7 in 2018. For the sixth form, there is the choice of A levels or the IB with between a quarter and a third taking the IB. The requirement for one of the six subjects studied to be a language puts off a lot and, as an exam, it is perceived as 'stiffer' than A levels. The previous head's attempt to enforce the IB for all by 2016 met with strong parental resistance, and was abandoned as a policy in favour of the status quo: all may, none must. The present head is clear, 'IB is an excellent exam and we encourage it, but it is not, and never will be, for everyone.' Creditable results across the board at A level with 29 per cent A*/A, 60 per cent A*-B grades in 2018. Solid IB results: average score of 34 points.

Around a fifth receive extra help with SEN, mostly dyslexia, dyscalculia, sensory impairments and poor self-esteem. The need for help appears greatest in year 9 and 10 and lessens as pupils progress through the school, perhaps finding their feet. The department is well staffed with full and part-time teachers, one devoted to teaching ESL, and help is offered individually and in small groups. Care is taken to ensure that individual difficulties are made known to subject staff. New entrants are screened to flag any problems early on and close relations nurtured with feed junior schools. Charged as an extra, but there is a termly cap on fees at £500.

Games, options, the arts: Outdoorsy lot who make the most of the facilities and seem to agree with the 'healthy mind, healthy body' outlook. All the usual team sports: rugby, hockey (for boys and girls), netball and cricket, with lots of match play for everyone and good coaching for those taking things seriously. School also hosts training camps, some residential, in cricket, rugby and hockey, in the holidays. Swimming is compulsory in the lower forms and an extra activity higher up. Weights room, rowing machines, yoga and cross-country running all popular. 'I often go for an early run; it is one of the reasons I like boarding,' we were told by one girl, and it is obviously not a place for those who prefer stewing indoors. The few who seriously dislike team games are treated humanely and allowed to do shooting (this is Norfolk), sailing, fencing, cycling and swimming higher up the school. Pitches, Astroturf and courts for tennis and squash galore, and a rifle range (members of the club have been junior ladies champion four years running, and several pupils have been selected to represent Britain in the U19 rifle team). D of E popular at all levels, with around 30 reaching gold each year; CCF and the BASC course (British Association for Shooting and Conservation) are options. New Outdoor Activity Centre includes a 250 metre zip wire, obstacle course, low and high ropes course and a 28 metre Bourdillon climbing tower named after Tom Bourdillon, one of England's greatest mountaineers and Gresham's alumnus.

The reputation of the school's drama department and facilities is renowned and the school has produced several professional actors, Olivia Colman (Broadchurch and Rev) most notable. With professional facilities (Auden theatre hosts touring companies as well as being used for several school productions each year – excellent sound and lighting systems, dressing rooms, proper auditorium, the lot), drama is a very popular extra activity: 'It was a reason to come here.' Parents loud in their praise: 'It is incredible what they can stage; lots of opportunities to develop a serious interest in stage management, lighting and sound as well as acting.' At least three major productions each year; it can be a real springboard for pupils who want to go on to study at drama school or university.

Music is equally valued – roughly half the school has timetabled instrumental tuition and there is a wide variety of choirs, ensembles, bands and orchestras. Despite a revamp for the Britten centenary in 2013, accommodation is under par and new facilities are a high priority on the head's building programme, which includes the new music school and sixth form centre.

Well-designed building devoted to art, textiles, and DT – splendid displays of pupils' work, excellent facilities and all manner of projects undertaken. Opportunities to use oil paints from the start, life drawing classes regularly held and artists in residence inject their own talents and energy into this thriving department. Superb exhibition space, lots to feast the eyes on – a really dynamic place to develop a talent. Art and design have their own rather eye-catching building in the prep too, with spectacular displays of pupils' work (including designs on backs of chairs) and every inducement for creativity. 'We do textiles, mosaics, woodwork, mess generally'.

Boarding: Strong boarding feel, but day pupils are well integrated having their own bed and/or desk, in their house, and though flexi-boarding is not actively encouraged, 'We happily accommodate pupils overnight on occasions when they are here late for rehearsals, performances or other school events.' Pupils do swap around quite a bit; choosing to board in the sixth form is popular; others, sometimes for financial reasons become day. Houses are comfortable, well lit and decorated with thought given to making things home-like, for example decent-sized kitchens that are actually used for cooking and eating in, rather than miserable little kitchenettes with a toaster and electric kettle, standing room only. Houseparents and matrons are always about, pupils return to their houses at break and lunch; bedrooms mostly shared between two or four.

The academic/pastoral divide is blurred; house staff teach their own subject alongside their pastoral duties. Lots stay in at weekends and there are plenty of organised activities though not what the head calls 'enforced jollity.' Houses sit together at their own tables in the revamped dining hall. The food 'has improved, we get more salads' (this from a girl) but we thought it still a bit on the stodgy side – room for improvement. Some houses have fruit always available, but not all, a source of some grievance, we discovered. Straightforward uniform; jacket and trousers for boys ('suits' in the sixth form), calf-length tartan kilts and new, light blue tweed jackets (rather chic) gradually replacing the old blazers. Coats hardly worn and if needed (one thinks of bracing North Sea breezes), 'We wear what we like so long as it's not too outrageous.' How sensible. Home clothes once the timetabled day is over and at the weekends.

Background and atmosphere: Founded originally as a grammar school (1555), rejuvenated in 1890s by George Howson, a headmaster with 'advanced' views in education. He introduced the teaching of sciences, abandoned corporal punishment and encouraged pacifist thinking – practically unheard of then. Set in over 170 acres of woodlands and extensive playing fields, school buildings extend on both sides of the old Cromer road leading out of Holt (pupils cross via a bridge) and are a mixture of styles and quality ranging from magnificent Edwardian and art deco halls and libraries with grand staircases, stained glass etc, through to more run of the mill classrooms, the innovative art and design block and the famous Auden theatre. Pupils get plenty of fresh air doing the brisk walk between lessons in different parts of the site. There is a well looked after air about the place and a programme of refurbishment of various houses is under way together with further planned developments.

G

Pastoral care, well-being and discipline: Nothing but praise from parents; 'My three boys all settled quickly and never felt out of things as day pupils,' was a remark we heard over again. The school focuses particularly on those not coming up from the prep school in year 9, and there is a 'buddy' system in place. 'Our son found it hard to begin with, but the school continued to support him; they were brilliant and he is really happy there now.' The small size of the school means staff and pupils all know each other and relationships are forged, which can help if there are difficulties at any stage. Good interaction between the different year groups and friendly, still respectful staff/pupil relations.

Apart from usual minor misdemeanours, a well behaved lot. There is a clear anti-bullying policy (lots of awareness notices on walls), counsellors and a school chaplain as well as matrons and house staff all keeping an eye out. Well understood rules on illegal drugs (zero tolerance), and alcohol: over 18s may drink ('enjoy a pint ' is the phrase used) either in the school's own bar or the Feathers in Holt; no PDA (public displays of affection), but few overstep the mark. The need for teenagers, sixth formers particularly, to handle stress is taken seriously with regular sessions on relaxation and quick intervention if a pupil is struggling. Sixth formers also choose their own tutors: 'they have to teach one of the subjects we are studying, it helps with university choices but of course liking comes into it too.'

Pupils and parents: Friendly pupils, unflustered and polite, with just the right amount of door-holding and rather less hair flicking and self-conscious teenage behaviour than usual. Unflashy, country school, 'It's a Barbour and boots place.' Day pupils are drawn from a large area of north Norfolk, many travelling for an hour each way; boarders from all over the country but predominantly East Anglia. Mostly farming, professional and business families with a sprinkling of county boarding families, plus lots from London – many choose the school for the contrast with the fiercely competitive schools in the Capital. Some move to Norfolk for this reason, both parents commuting, or one remaining in Norfolk during the week so children can be day pupils. About 20 per cent from overseas, mostly Europe.

Arts, sport, science and technology are all well represented amongst former pupils, who include Benjamin Britten, WH Auden, Sir Christopher Cockerell (inventor of the hovercraft), Sir James Dyson (vacuum cleaner), Tom and Ben Youngs (international rugby players), Lord Reith (first director-general of BBC), Prof Alan Hodgkin and Olivia Colman.

Entrance: Roughly 80 per cent of senior school have come up from the prep school, others from a mix of day and boarding preps, some from maintained sector. No common entrance; an assessment day is held for year 9 entrants in Lent term for following September. Tests in English and maths plus reports and references from current school. For sixth form, predicted grades (usually a minimum of A*/B in six subjects including those to be studied and minimum of C in English and maths) plus school report and interview.

Exit: A few to Oxbridge (two in 2018), sizeable numbers to London (Imperial, LSE, UCL) plus the other Russell Group universities. Wide range of subjects studied including a regular few to drama school and music colleges (Central St Martins, Guildhall). One to British Columbia and one to Groningen in 2017. Varying numbers (some 20 per cent) leave for pastures new after GCSE, usually in the maintained sector, plus the odd one for vocational work (gamekeeping a recent one). Head approves of pupils choosing vocational work and believes it reflects the diversity of the school.

Money matters: Thanks to a long association with the Worshipful Company of Fishmongers and its generous financial underpinning of the school's finances, a number of valuable scholarships and bursaries are on offer. Academic scholarships worth up to 50 per cent of fees offered for year 9 entry (can be topped up with a bursary, if financial need is demonstrated), drama, music, art and sport awards also offered, for up to 20 per cent. In the sixth form, scholarships are offered to those who do brilliantly at GCSE (if not already in receipt of an award) and help is forthcoming if families fall on hard times, at least to enable pupils to get through to the next public exam. Usual sibling discounts for three or more at one time.

Remarks: Well-established country boarding school with a deserved reputation for the encouragement of the arts, particularly music and drama. Its relatively small size and position make it a good choice for those looking for a broader educational experience within a school with a strong pastoral ethos. The twin paths of the IB and A levels will remain under the present head. Hard to think who would not thrive in this happy, well-run school.

Gresham's Prep School

Linked with Gresham's

Cromer Road, Holt, Norfolk NR25 6EY

Ages 2–13 **Pupils** 226 **Boarders** 45 (from 7 years) **C of E**

Fees: Day £10,050 – £18,090; Boarding £25,350 pa

01263 714600
www.greshams.com

Head: Since November 2018, Cathy Braithwaite BA(Ed) from Exeter, previously deputy head here. Taught in Staffordshire, Norfolk and Northern Ireland and was head of maths and director of teaching and learning St Francis School in Wiltshire for 10 years before joining Gresham's. She is married to Ollie and they have two sons and a black labrador, Isla.

Head of nursery and pre-prep since 2016 is Sarah Hollingsworth (30s), previously director of pastoral care at Oswestry School. She has had various early years and KS1 roles and is a trained ISI inspector.

Entrance: At all ages and stages from 3 (nursery and pre-prep), 7 and 11 in the prep school, although they will try to accommodate when possible at other times. Some year groups fill quickly, so first come first served. Accepts a fairly wide spectrum of ability, but admission is not a foregone conclusion. Informal assessment in the early forms, the same plus maths, English and verbal and non-verbal reasoning tests at 11. Pupils from the state sector often join for years 7 and 8 in preparation for the senior school.

Exit: Great majority, currently over 85 per cent, go through the school to year 8 and move up to the seniors. All take the 'exit' exam, those not likely to make the grade are warned in good time. Those wishing to go elsewhere at 13, and there are a few most years, are prepared individually for the entrance exams for eg Oundle, Royal Hospital and Millfield.

Remarks: On its own site, though only a brisk walk from the senior school, on the edge of Holt, North Norfolk's stylish market town. Uses certain senior school facilities such as sports pitches, swimming pool and theatre, but in the main it operates autonomously. Parents queue up to praise this relaxed and happy school where 'childhood still seems to last the right length of time'. One parent thought, 'My son came out of his shell here, he became a different boy'. A number of families have both Norfolk and London bases, but choose Gresham's for its 'less pressured atmosphere' over the more hothoused approaches in the Capital.

Common entrance teaching recently abandoned so greater flexibility in the curriculum. Excellent languages with the focus on fun and communication in the early years. French from year 6 with Spanish and Latin options from year 7. Other languages (eg German, Mandarin) can usually be accommodated on request. Science taught in designated labs, sometimes using the more sophisticated facilities of the senior school. There is mixed ability teaching up until year 4, then setting in most subjects, though 'these are flexible and pupils move up and down', with differentiated targets.

Educational support well-resourced, with five specially trained staff (two full-time) who are also class teachers. Caters for mild difficulties such as dyslexia and Asperger's, and emotional problems such as low self-esteem. About a quarter of pupils receive help, either in one-to-one tuition, small groups, or support in the classroom. Brilliant library, bursting with delectable titles, displays, opportunities to enter competitions and with an enthusiastic, full-time librarian. Open all day long (boarders can use it in the evening for project work), the atmosphere is quiet: 'we don't insist on a deathly silence, but purposeful reading does need peace and quiet'.

The performing arts, particularly music and drama, are very well taught both within the curriculum and as extra activities ('one of the reasons we chose the school'). Everyone sings in a choir in the lower forms, with auditions higher up for the senior and chapel choirs (runners up in the national Barnardo's Contest recently). Over two-thirds of pupils learn an instrument, some at the top grades, and there are many bands, ensemble groups and orchestras with frequent performances. Dance is on the curriculum in the lower forms and an extra activity later on. Drama is timetabled throughout the school; some larger productions are staged in the senior school Auden Theatre. Art and design have their own rather eye-catching building, with spectacular displays of pupils' work (including designs on backs of chairs) and every inducement for creativity. 'We do textiles, mosaics, woodwork, mess generally.' Loads of sport, all the usual team games with lots of fixtures, and though 'we understand not everyone is mad keen, but it's also important to have to keep going with something you wouldn't necessarily choose'. Shooting and kayaking available in years 7 and 8.

Mostly new buildings of one or two storeys set in the midst of extensive grounds, adventure play areas and piazzas; 'pupils have to play in sight of the gazebo'. OWLS is the new outdoor learning school with open-sided wooden classroom, spaces for campfires and an outdoor theatre, plus climbing tower, zipwire, obstacle and rope courses in the woods.

Separate boys' and girls' houses, each for 40 or 50 chidlren, in bedrooms of two to four. Exceptionally attractive and home-like decoration (strong Cath Kidston influence) and furnishings. Photographs of children enjoying themselves on every wall, bunting, posters; a mock-up of Giles Gilbert-Scott's classic telephone box houses the real telephone – no mobiles during the day or after bedtime. Houseparents and matrons always around, and pupils return to house at break and lunch.

Careful attention paid well-being and happiness. As well as the usual offers of counselling well displayed, there is a worry box to post in 'anything they want to discuss, however small it may seem'. Staff keep a weather eye, particularly in changing room areas, which are always supervised. In the un-canteeny dining room, pupils are helped to make good food choices, picking from colour-coded categories, green (vegetables), red (protein) and yellow (carbs). Early supper ('children are all starving by 5:30pm') which day pupils often stay for if doing activities, and cereal/toast and hot drinks in the houses before bed.

This is a happy, well-run prep that benefits from its connection to the senior school, but is definitely separate. Would suit most types but is not specially geared to prepare for common entrance or other highly competitive school entrance exams.

Hallfield School

48 Church Road, Edgbaston, Birmingham B15 3SJ

Ages 3m–11 **Pupils** 545 **C of E**

Fees: £9,792 – £13,020 pa

01214 541496
www.hallfieldschool.co.uk

Head: Since September 2018, Keith Morrow, previously head of The Elms, junior school to Trent College. BA in geography and education from Hull and postgrad education qualification from Bishop Grosseteste College; leadership experience at several state primary schools before joining The Elms. Has worked for Ofsted and the ISI, advised Cambridge Education and various governing bodies, co-ordinated maths, assessment and ICT and taught geography.

Entrance: This is a selective school with a current boy-girl ratio of 55:45, girls and boys being assessed for their suitability to learn from 2+ onwards, whilst more formalised tests in English, maths and reasoning are set for those who wish to enter from year 3 and above. A small number of means-tested bursaries.

Exit: As Disraeli observed, statistics can lie; but these ones don't, for the fact that Hallfield pupils won 19 scholarships to schools such as King Edward's School and King Edward's High in 2018, and achieved an 82 per cent pass rate for grammar school entry, constitutes the clearest evidence of the school's academic power.

Remarks: Unsurprisingly it all starts at the beginning and with the sense of a new belonging: the excitement sparked by the gift of a teddy bear (The Hallfield Bear) to all reception children.... And so, an unofficial competition starts as to where each bear can visit. We met one animated 4 year old who, having built some kind of rocket in the garden (assisted by his father), seemed convinced that his teddy had gone to the moon. The recent ISI report rates the school's EYFS provision as outstanding in all areas.

This surge of excellence continues as pupils make their transition to the more senior years. Given the 11+ aspirations of parents the academic pace is a strong one, but the pupils are comfortable with it and benefit hugely from recent reforms such as the half-hour of reading-time that takes place in the post-lunch period. SEND organisation and tuition – as recognised by this year's ISI inspection – is outstanding. The line between confidence and arrogance can be a thin one, especially for those academically blessed, but all those whom we met possessed the kind of humility and openness that would delight any parent. When they were asked to sum up their school in a single word the normal gushy ones such as 'fun' and 'amazing' featured. More revealing were the words 'changing' and 'trustworthy'.

If children have faith in the school's flair for change, then so do the teachers. Longer-serving staff talked with great warmth about the more concise and efficient systems of management and tuition techniques that have been put in place, whilst new staff stressed to us how friendly and supportive everyone had been. Thus, an atmosphere has been created where, they reported, their pupils 'don't want to go home'.

This is in great part due to the kaleidoscope of activity that the school provides. For a school so close to the centre of Birmingham, it is good to see that the playing fields are so extensive. This enables the school to run many teams in football, rugby and cricket for the boys (twice in the last three years the footballers have reached the national finals, played at St George's, England's headquarters) whilst the girls – known as The Vixens – form a similar number of teams for fixtures in hockey, netball and rounders. All children in the upper school take part in cross-country, gymnastics and swimming. Badminton is a special strength and nearly as many boys are in the dance club as girls. The school won the national championship in chess a few years ago.

Musically the pattern of quality is the same as specialist teachers lead choirs, orchestras and ensembles. Recently a senior girl won a place in the National Children's Choir and an Old Hallfieldian reached the last eight of X Factor as part of the girl-group Four of Diamonds. Drama, too, is spectacular; arguably the highlight is the Shakespeare Week for year 6 where the Young Shakespeare Company come in and take the children from base-camp to a performance-peak in five days: recently Hamlet and Romeo and Juliet.

Externally, links are strong – not only with other independent schools but also with local primaries. Hallfield runs holiday courses and masterclasses.

As with any school, not everything in the garden is lovely: not least as a result of the current badger-invasion which has created an explosion of muddy pyramids outside the head's study window. Soon, we hope, it could be sensible to amend the distinctly bizarre system of form nomenclature, which sees every new member of staff working under an irrelevant initial from a former master or mistress. A recent appointment took over the letter 'u'.

These, however, are tiny blemishes. On our visit parents lauded the school, stating that they were 'so delighted with the pastoral care' as 'everyone is treated as an individual'. Another said that her girls 'had thrived so much', whilst a mother in the pre-prep remembered that her son's 'tears at the start' had rapidly dried because 'all the staff are absolutely fantastic'.

All commented on the school's ultra-slick emails and texts. Electronic communication actually seems to work here, and everyone benefits as parents are kept up to date with what has happened and are sent reminders regarding future events.

Consequently, a kind of golden triangle has been drawn: one that combines children, staff and parents in a triple quest for excellence. Of late, alumni relations have been developed and the fact that an Old Hallfieldian is, by custom, invited back to address the school at speech day gives a completeness and a vision to it all. Last summer the first girl at the school, who joined in 1995, was the guest of honour.

The Hallfield Pen has the words A World-Class Education on it. That, perhaps, is for some international panel to judge, but this school, for all that it does, is very much one to consider.

Hills Road Sixth Form College

Hills Road, Cambridge CB2 8PE

Ages 16–19 **Pupils** 2,497

01223 247251
www.hillsroad.ac.uk

H

Principal: Since 2017, Jo Trump BA (40s); first in English from York and PGCE from Oxford. Made an early decision to opt for the post-16 sector, 'I discovered quickly where my strengths lay,' and held a variety of positions of increasing responsibility at Cirencester College, Peter Symonds College and Farnham Sixth Form College (now part of Guildford College), followed by a networking role for the S7 Consortium of Surrey Sixth Form Colleges. During her fast-paced career Jo found time to have a family and, for a period, worked part time at the Surrey Colleges. 'I never regretted slowing down for those years, and feel my overall perception and knowledge was developed by having the chance to stand back and get to know how the sector worked across several institutions'. Appointed deputy principal at Hills Road in 2009 before taking the reins as principal, a smooth transition as 'I was able to continue taking the college in the direction that I had helped define'.

Youthful and enthusiastic with an easy, approachable manner with staff and students, yet clearly very much in charge and with an incredible capacity for hard work. 'She is an excellent public speaker – really knows how to inspire the students and their parents yet remains warm and down to earth.' 'She is a parent and shares the same worries and concerns herself.' Relaxes at weekends 'with family, house, garden and several animals' in the country close to Cambridge.

Academic matters: Highly motivated, ambitious students are inspired and well supported by excellent teaching staff who are regularly available at lunchtime catch up clinics and at other times, if asked. The college makes plain at the selection stage and at induction days that this is not simply an exam factory, spoon-feeding to get results, but a place to learn the art of independent study and making the most of college life, as a grounding for university. 'It was made plain from the outset, work matters, and there is no time for faffing about,' said one parent. 'My sons learnt how to plan their work and about not leaving things to the last minute.' 'Mine found university was easy, they had been so well prepared,' a sentiment echoed by everyone we spoke to.

Broad range of subjects (over 40) but A level choices limited to three, plus compulsory EPQ. 'Keeping A levels to three means we can offer the combination of subjects that students really want.' Emphasis on the heavyweights; a mind-boggling 600+ take mathematics in each cohort, high take up for all sciences, history and English literature but languages (Latin included) and creative subjects do well too. Typically tutors guide students in their EPQ study. Recent projects have included making a film documentary, creating a replica of an Egyptian artefact and a mental health awareness scheme: 'Anything, so long as it is safe, ethical and not already examined'.

The study skills centre offers support including help for those struggling with the step up from GCSE to A level, essay writing, time management, dyslexia and ESL. 'Around a quarter of students use the centre at some point.' Attendance at timetabled lessons is compulsory but otherwise students are free to come and go, though many make use of the library (calm and studious), the many computer study areas and the zone for silent working or the Link, Hub or atrium, which allow 'collaborative working' between lessons.

Results at A level impressive with 72 per cent at A*/B, 41 per cent A*/A across the curriculum in 2018,and really outstanding in certain subjects including maths, further maths and the sciences with over 60 per cent A*/A. College regularly tops the league table for the highest achieving sixth form college, has been regularly shortlisted for the TES Sixth Form College of the Year and recently won the Sunday Times sixth form award. Students, perhaps coming from much smaller schools, revel in discovering that there are plenty of others like themselves and finding that 'hard work is cool'.

Games, options, the arts: All year 12s have a timetabled enrichment session each week, choosing from an incredible variety of options that include drama, ceramics, cheerleading, DofE plus a plethora of music and sports – all the usual team ones together with anything for which there is demand and support. Sport not compulsory, though 'everyone is encouraged to be physically active,' and, judging by packed cycle racks, many take this for granted in a cycling town like Cambridge. College has been represented at national level including the Olympics (hockey, goalball and triathlon) and regularly wins the Clifford Dixon trophy awarded to the college in the Eastern region successful across a range of different sports. Hockey, women's rugby, golf and tennis all top notch. Extensive playing fields, five indoor tennis courts, squash courts and a fitness suite.

Drama and dance flourish with many involved performing and staging productions in the college's professional Robinson theatre (gift from millionaire old boy). Technical training offered. Huge number of student-led clubs and societies, lunchtime discussion forums, speakers and debates on all manner of topics. The year 12 timetable is 'collapsed' for Social Action Week in June when, in groups of 10-12, students tackle a project challenge of their choice including such things as selling ice cream, sponsored walks, organising an art installation on Parker's Piece (famous Cambridge open space) and washing cars. Recent target of £10,000 was almost doubled. For musicians, not necessarily those studying the subject, great choice of choirs, ensembles (auditions for some), a jazz orchestra and other music groups. Regular concerts, formal and informal, make the most of local venues (King's College and Ely Cathedral being recent examples) as well as college facilities. A year 13 student is the current winner of the BBC Proms Inspire competition.

Background and atmosphere: On a well-developed site, close to the centre of Cambridge, the college takes every advantage of its situation. 'Education is the local industry and we make the most of the opportunities to hand.' The origins of the college lie in the Cambridgeshire boys' grammar school, whose building remains the centrepiece and a façade for the college. In 1974 it was reincarnated as a co-ed sixth form, growing rapidly from 600 to its present size. Close to the railway station, so accessible from as far away as King's Lynn, and has quite a feel of a university, the glossy brochures and prospectuses emphasising this. 'They are treated as adults who will make their own decisions, but the support scaffolding is still in place'. Few rules, no uniform and students are free to come and go outside their timetabled lessons but, as we noted, students are very self-motivated, and far from skedaddling when the bell goes are far more likely to head for the library.

A series of well-designed buildings are grouped around the open space known as the Quad. Not only is everything in a good state of repair but, considering the numbers of teenagers using the place, in mint condition: no litter, no graffiti and students who clearly respect the place. Skilful use of space means the size does not overwhelm and a fosters a sense of belonging. There are good directions to libraries, student support services and departments and students, 'settle in and find their way around very quickly.'

Pastoral care, well-being and discipline: The student services team have overall responsibility for attendance, students' well-being and counselling. The attractive and welcoming reception area, easy for students to approach, deals with day-to-day concerns and liaises with tutors. Students belong to a tutor group of around 25 and have timetabled lessons twice a week in year 12, divided between the tutorial programme and the EPQ. Tutors have several groups and though most continue to teach their subject, some tutor full time. Personal relationships clearly matter, but 'if you don't get on there are other options'. No registration first thing in the morning; 'Mine missed that, at first, they felt a bit rootless'. Instead teachers take attendance registers in lessons, keep weekly records kept and any quickly spot any backsliders, though there's very little of this as students are generally mature and motivated. Students can ask directly for counselling, whether for academic reasons or help with a personal matter. 'You do have to ask but they responded brilliantly when our son struggled at the start. He was offered support in a really positive way.' High praise on all sides for the Independent Learning Service; students can book in for individual sessions or simply to work in the designated quiet study area.

Pupils and parents: Mature, academically ambitious students; 'I wanted the company of people like me'. As all have chosen to come here there are very few troublemakers or slackers. Huge, undefined catchment that takes in most of East Anglia and beyond, with 'no-one being dropped off in a four-by-four'. Being on public transport for an hour and a half twice a day can be 'an experience after attending a local school, but they get used to it and the journey can be a social time'. The majority live in and around Cambridge and walk, cycle or catch a bus to the college. Students mostly transfer from local state 11-16 schools but a minority jump ship from nearby independents, students lured by the quasi-university atmosphere, parents by two fee-free years. 'Call me cynical', said a parent, 'but also possibly to take advantage of applying to Oxbridge from a state school'. This is Cambridge, so many parents are high academic achievers themselves and pretty savvy about the whole university application process. Students dress as they please and though being socially non-conformist is fine, adult behaviour is the norm, and those who struggle to fit in 'will be helped to look at other options', but this is rare.

The Students' Council is asked for its opinion on certain college matters and can raise concerns, but its interests are primarily social.

Entrance: No formal catchment, but 'As a rough guide we think a journey time of an hour by public transport is far enough'. Students need at least four GCSEs at 6 and four at 5 to include maths and English; the college is oversubscribed, so the 'at least' matters. Certain subjects, maths and sciences for example, require higher grades. Feeder schools asked for a reference together with predicted grades. 'We are looking for students who will make the most of all Hills Road offers.' Guidance meetings (informal interviews) are held in the February prior to GCSEs, and are offered to all comers, parents included, and the college then makes offers. An induction programme is held in early September.

Exit: Famed for high numbers to Oxbridge, generally 60-70 each year (55 in 2018), and majority to other top drawer universities, many to study medicine, law, mathematics or the sciences. Gap years taken by 20-30 per cent with quite a few making post-results applications. Students are given a lot of help deciding their future; 'the advice starts early, soon after arriving at the college'. No shortage of universities and employers keen to be represented at Hills Road degree and careers advice fairs. 'It's a buyer's market and Hills Road students do very well at university'. This year over 40 per cent of former students graduated with a first and over 94 per cent gained at least a 2:1. Many ascribe their success to the grounding they had at Hills Road: 'We weren't spoon-fed and it was a great stepping stone'.

Money matters: Financial affairs all in good order, often benefiting from generous bequests from successful (and generous) former students, the new theatre one such example. Grants available for day-to-day expenses.

Remarks: Provides outstanding education and experience for bright, highly self-motivated students. Successfully bridges school/university gap and presents the local high flying independents with more than a run for their money.

Impington Village College

New Road, Impington, Cambridge, Cambridgeshire CB24 9LX

Ages 11–19 **Pupils** 1,320 **Sixth form** 232

01223 200400
www.impington.cambs.sch.uk

Principal: Since 2016, Mr Ryan Kelsall, previously vice principal. Studied geography and sociology at Sheffield; has previously been head of upper school at St Bede's Inter Church School. Proud to head of one the few IB schools in the country, aiming to 'develop the young people in our care to be internationally minded global citizens who challenge preconceptions and celebrate difference'. Was a semi-professional footballer, also playing rugby, cricket and basketball at regional level; still plays for and coaches local teams, and chairs the successful Cambridge Cats Basketball Club. Enjoys spending time with his large family: two young children and their two older step siblings. Has also been boning up on languages since his brothers recently relocated to Spain and Portugal.

The former principal, Robert Campbell, is now executive principal of the growing academy trust.

Academic matters: A school with a split personality. Up to year 11 a good village college that attracts all sorts and abilities. In 2018, 37 per cent A*-A/9-7 grades at GCSE, with 74 per cent of pupils getting 9-4 in both maths and English. Outstanding results place it consistently amongst the top performing non-selective schools in the country. Most pupils take 10 GCSEs and do one language, though they can study two from year 7. Spanish, French, German, Japanese and Latin are all on offer, and star linguists are actively encouraged. Performing arts, music and dance all very popular, as well as sports and visual arts, including media. Courses also offered in catering, product design, photography and computer science. Some parental muttering about middle-of-the-roaders being overlooked, but nearly all progress well, including those identified as the More Able, who make up around 50 per cent of each cohort. They cater for a broad church up to age 16. Maximum class size up to 32.

And then we turn to the sixth form, housed in the old school gym, but you'd never know it. Unusually for a state school, the sixth form is international and has offered the IB for over 20 years. In 2018 the average point score was 34. BTec courses offered: computer science, media, sports and performing arts. Also a football scholarship programme with Histon Town Football Club. Some 40 per cent of sixth form do not have English as their first language, but lots of support offered and they come on in leaps and bounds. 'The international students really raise the game in the sixth form,' said one parent, 'and the locals follow accordingly, excellent.' 'The IB is ideal for the all rounder,' said another parent, 'and instils the discipline to study.'

A school open to all. Over a quarter have special needs including some in wheelchairs. The spacious Pavilion provides sanctuary for those that need it, with some individual lessons taught there as well. All attend mainstream lessons where appropriate. Lots of in-class support offered too. 'My son, who is on the autistic spectrum, receives 25 hours a week of support. He is never singled out but discreetly helped. They are very sensitive about striking a balance. Their door is always open to me as well; I couldn't ask for more.' 'They think outside the box,' said another parent.

Others comment: 'The school is very supportive, lots of extra help if needed.' 'There was lots of homework in year 7 but it seems to have dwindled off in the last few years, but they are doing well, so who am I to argue?'

All parents positive about communication with teachers, some a bit more critical about getting through on the phone and we have to agree with this. Homework timetable posted online; all information available for those who look.

Games, options, the arts: Lots of sports pitches and good facilities including an indoor pool and sports complex shared with the community. We were informed that the netball, rugby and football teams were doing well. Lots of sport available including oddities such as dodgeball. Plenty of teams including trampolining, and much after-school practice. Impington widely renowned for its drama, art and music. The performance school, a cross denomination of all the arts combined, actively supported by pupils throughout the school; Oliver! recently staged to rave reviews. Orchestras, choirs and rehearsals for numerous shows abound, and provide an opportunity for different age groups to mix. Dance studio well used by both sexes. Plenty of instruments studied to high grades and lots of practice rooms. DofE popular; many do bronze award. Plenty of school trips and a well-produced school magazine. Active social media. A wide range of enrichment opportunities on offer, including Impington Creativity, Activity and Service (iCAS) which is part of the college's timetabled provision and includes a huge range of subjects, from Portuguese, pottery and archaeology to peer mentoring, aikido and trampolining.

Background and atmosphere: On the edge of Cambridge, IVC celebrated its 75th anniversary in 2014. Having opened just before war broke out in September 1939, it is housed in a grade 1 Bauhaus designed building. Slightly austere and intimidating, but very much of its time. Inside, it comes into its own. Lots of curving corridors and light, airy parts with plenty of open spaces. The original building has sympathetic additions.

Our guides were keen to show us the science block including the plants and pond. They were very excited about the ducklings that had hatched and were hoping to show us some. Sadly, the next batch were still in incubation. Lots of artwork on display and busy noticeboards. We were even shown the isolation room for the not so obedient; happy to report it was empty.

Its ethos is very much of a community college. Open to all, with adult lessons held on site and a room for the community to use during the day. Nice to see a school sitting in the middle of the village for all to use. A flourishing house system at the heart of the main college, with a thriving Student Union led by a team of house captains. Aim is 'to create independent and internationally-minded students from the day they arrive' – whether local or from overseas.

A happy, busy, if messy place; the students seem very proud of their school. Students know their rights and fight for them. Uniform battles have prevailed, to the extent that one young man turned up in a skirt to protest that girls could wear them in summer but the boys could not wear shorts – we believe that he won his point. All students wear sweatshirts, year 11s in a different colour. They don't look particularly smart, but functional. Sixth formers wear their own clothes. Interesting to see some quirky characters: lots of different hair colours and lengths, and that's just the boys. 'We aren't draconian here. We have no ruling on hair. We don't make it an issue so it rather defeats the purpose; they quickly get bored with pink hair if there's no reaction.'

'The school is very inclusive and the pupils are very tolerant,' said a parent. 'They accept diversity and all are welcome, which is a fabulous ethos to have.' Another parent said, 'Despite its size they know everyone. I really appreciated that the teachers had pictures of all the new year 7s so got to know them quickly.'

Pastoral care, well-being and discipline: Pastoral care excellent. All parents very positive, particularly those with children using the Pavilion. 'I know if there are any problems someone will be in touch immediately,' was said by more than one parent. Teachers seem to know their pupils well; lots of mutual respect. The vertical house system is well-established, and encourages interaction between year groups. Tutor groups consist of around 18 students from years 7-11, each with a lead and co tutor, providing extensive support and attention for individuals.

Discipline has been improved in the last few years. Fewer complaints about 'disruption in the class and quieter ones being overlooked.' A strict disciplinary procedure in force; the college has not permanently excluded a student for over 10 years. 'My children are happy in the school and despite its size took to it really well,' was a frequent comment from parents. 'A happy place that involves the whole community,' said one.

Pupils and parents: Most main school pupils from feeder schools to the north of Cambridge, some from Cambridge itself. An eclectic mix of backgrounds. Parents range from academics and medics to the seriously underprivileged. All pupils seem to mix well and are tolerant of each others' foibles. Most parents have very high expectations, as do their children. The pupils we met were bright, chatty, confident individuals. Easy to talk to and proud of their school and all it stood for. Every parent we spoke to was very positive.

Some 45 per cent of sixth form students are international, hosted by local families. The majority are from Italy, Poland and Germany, with some from other parts of Europe and from further afield. All mix well, and the ones we spoke to were very impressive, adorned with nose rings and piercings and quite charming.

Entrance: At 11 from local primary schools. Appeals often succeed, hence the large class sizes. Those with special needs usually gain a place. In recent years has been increasingly oversubscribed.

Entry to the sixth form requires 5+ GCSEs at 4 grade or above including English and maths for A levels, grade 6+ for the IB.

Exit: Some 85 per cent leave after GCSEs, the vast majority to other local sixth forms to study A levels or vocational subjects. A handful into employment or apprenticeships, the odd NEET. The remainder are joined by local students and the international contingent. As expected, these leavers spread far and wide. The majority to university, many to European and American ones. One to Cambridge and three medics (two of these to Poland) in 2018; popular UK destinations Winchester, Anglia Ruskin, Bristol, Durham, East Anglia, Essex, Greenwich, Kent, Middlesex, Plymouth, Queen Mary's and Sussex. Others off to Wisconsin (soccer scholarship), Northern Arizona, Rome and Bologna. Subjects very varied but performing arts and drama seem popular choices with one to the Academy of Contemporary Music. A few straight to employment, over 10 per cent take gap years.

Remarks: A true village community college. It attracts some bright sparks but is very inclusive of the less able and the different. Good to see them all in it together. The international sixth form makes it a true ground breaker in the state system. A well run place that has true community spirit.

Ipswich High School

Woolverstone, Ipswich, Suffolk IP9 1AZ

Ages 3–18 **Pupils** 449 **Sixth form** 80 (5 boys)

Fees: £8,769 – £14,322 pa

01473 780201
www.ihseducation.co.uk

Head: Since 2013, Oona Carlin BSc, studied biochemistry at Imperial college, London. Previously deputy head at Putney High (GDST) and before that head of chemistry at the Royal Masonic School. Early 40s, elegant, but not over-polished, and approachable. Having a wide experience of different schools, including two years at the English school in Bogota, Columbia, she is convinced about the benefits of a girls' school, 'Leadership opportunities and a free unfettered choice of subjects,' plus of course all the benefits of belonging to the Girls' Day School Trust for networking purposes in the long term. Going down well with parents, 'Mustard – getting to know the place from top to bottom'; 'Has the right tone and approach and seems to have clear ideas of the school's direction.' Is unflustered by numbers leaving for pastures new after GCSE. 'It is a choice some make but we have so much to offer in the sixth form and those key months preparing for university entrance.' Wants to help girls find their strengths and play to them. A keen hockey player herself (plays for a local Ipswich side – sometimes against her own pupils) she has been known to cover a games lesson for an absent colleague; quite unusual. Has a down-to-earth attitude, 'Someone who will get things done'. Being with family and dog-walking are her main relaxations.

Junior school head: Since April 2019, Lisa Finch, who was previously heat of Stanway Fiveways Primary School in Colchester, Essex. She has a degree in drama and theatre, but is also interested in PE and numeracy, and is a qualified SENCo. She has substantial experience as a primary head. She and her husband Sean have two daughters, one at Ipswich High and the other at university.

The GDST has sold the school to Ipswich Education Ltd, part of the London & Oxford financial group, which has particular links to Chinese investors. The school is becoming co-educational, taking boys into the junior school and sixth form since September 2018.

Academic matters: There is an integrated curriculum in the junior school, though maths is taught separately with sets from year 4. Regular SEN review days; staff use a 'traffic light' system to identify difficulties as quickly as possible. Science, art and cookery taught in specialist classrooms in the senior school for year 6 to help the impending transfer.

In 2018, 64 per cent of GCSEs awarded at A*-A/9-7 and at A level a disappointing 12 per cent A*/A, 36 per cent A*-B. Mathematics and the sciences are all strong. Although the school is very aware of the pressure for top grades, it encourages a broader view of education, and subjects on offer include photography, astronomy, food science and Mandarin. All pupils study at least one foreign language at GCSE and Latin also has plenty of take-up. Setting for maths begins in year 7, though approach is flexible. 'Quite often a change of teacher is the key to understanding.' We agree. Half-termly effort grades and regular reports help to keep a focus and parents in the picture. All pupils are screened for learning difficulties on entry and any problems are picked up early and help offered, either one-to-one or in small groups. As a selective school, difficulties are generally mild dyslexia or problems with processing information. Sixth formers have study/tutor rooms at the top of Woolverstone hall, the main building, with spectacular views. 'We are so lucky to be at the top; the climb is a bit aerobic, but worth it.' Small teaching groups and plenty of guidance in the necessary study skills. There is a hard-working, but relaxed air, 'most of us get on with work without anyone saying anything.'

Games, options, the arts: All team sports played competitively and well, notably hockey. The recent Project Leapfrog, a GDST investigation into PE provision in all its schools, recommended that the school engage more outside coaches. This has been adopted; despite a bedrock of talent there was a need to develop skills and match technique. 'Things had got into a bit of a rut,' was a comment we heard from several. The head's personal interest is very welcome. Sports hall and swimming pool (also available to the public out of school hours), a dance studio and a fitness suite are available at the school. School aware that not all pupils enjoy team games and encourages plenty of alternatives, including yoga and pilates, horse riding (school has an equestrian team), sailing and fencing. Recognises that enjoying games or exercise generally may be a matter of confidence. The pupils all appreciate the spectacular grounds and the space for fun at breaks as well as for games.

Music and drama both strong. About half the school has individual instrumental/singing lessons and regular concerts are held at nearby Snape Maltings (Aldeburgh) as well as at school. There is a Young Musician of the Year contest alongside choirs, orchestra and ensembles. Diverse repertoire explored in orchestras and ensembles – something for everyone. Performs a musical and a play each year. The Hayworth theatre with flexible staging and raked seating holds 300. 'We did Bugsy Malone, my sister was Fat Sam!' said one girl, jumping with excitement at the memory. The theatre is well used for drama lessons and clubs as well as performances. Junior school multi-purpose, parquet floored hall, with stage used for regular performances in Friday assemblies, musicals, plays and a recent Strictly Come Dancing contest, has proved wildly popular. 'I did it with my sister, we did the Charleston and 20s stuff,' an enthusiastic pupil told us. Separate art, textiles and DT building. In year 7, 'We make clocks, egg holders, coat hangers and a soap dish,' the idea being to understand the materials involved and learn some necessary techniques. Food science is 'having a moment,' on the timetable for years 7-9 and available as an option thereafter. Several well-designed, home-like kitchens (sixth form has its own) within a separate building. Taking a creative subject at GCSE is, surprisingly, not compulsory.

Activities on offer after school for juniors as well as seniors include riding, cookery and knitting as well as the various music groups.

Boarding: With the announcement that the GDST is selling the school to Ipswich Education Ltd, part of the London & Oxford financial group, the school will develop boarding facilities, with the estimated completion of 2019. However, the head has assured that the school will remain a five-day-week school, giving the pupils a break at the weekend.

Background and atmosphere: Was one of the earliest Trust schools, founded in 1878 and transferred to its present site at Woolverstone Hall 25 years ago, though now transferred to Ipswich Education Ltd and going diamond model (single sex teaching for some subjects from years 5-11). Approaching the school along a tree-lined avenue surrounded by sheep is to feel a lift in spirits. 'It makes me feel pleased turning into the drive every morning', said one pupil, and the girls are all aware of their luck in enjoying such surroundings. Set in 84 acres of landscaped lawns, terraces and views towards the River Orwell, the hall itself, with pediments, urns and panelled drawing rooms, might easily double as the set for a period drama (or indeed, as a wedding venue – which it is). This is the hub of the school. Lunch is eaten in the orangery with seating on the terrace for sunny days and the Grab and Go bistro nearby for girls to get a quick snack, or lunch if they are short of time. The sixth form occupies the top floor (several flights, no lift and a reminder on the walls that in the past, servants, usually girls, carried buckets of coal and water up the very same stairs) with its own study areas, common room and well-equipped kitchen. A large separate teaching block, the sports hall, swimming pool and theatre are close by. Various outbuildings have been converted for art, DT and food science. The walk between the various buildings gives the chance for a breather and helps to foster contented pupils. Everything spick and span and well ordered.

The junior school is a bright, purpose-built, two-storey building sharing the spectacular grounds of the senior school. Recent sprucing up includes clapboarding the exterior – 'not sure I like it,' said a pupil. A bit reminiscent of Center Parcs, maybe. A well-stocked, redesigned library at the centre of the school, has flexible seating (look out for the sellotape chair) and play areas. Pre-prep and nursery have their own defined area of the building and separate playground. Decent sized and light classrooms, lots of work displayed and traditional desks – 'we are allowed to decorate the inside of the lids!'

Very stylish grey blazers with a grosgrain trim and grey skirts (cerise jackets in the juniors) give way to own clothes in the sixth form.

Pastoral care, well-being and discipline: Frequently cited as a strength by parents. 'Nothing is too insignificant for them to bother with'; 'some slight bullying was dealt with well – a lot went on quietly behind the scenes'. The policy of changing the form groupings at years 7, 8 and 9 is designed to help foster good social relations and help counter any tendency for cliques to form. 'Intense friendships can prevent girls mixing well. We usually have a few requests to stay with established friends, but most accept the benefits of a regular shake-up'. There is a seating plan for each lesson, also changed regularly, to reduce the anxiety of constantly wondering, 'Who shall I sit with?' It also helps teachers get to know pupils quickly. The houses, named after eminent women, are largely used for social, sporting and charity events. Year 7 pupils are all befriended by senior pupils. Good-tempered though respectful relations are the norm between staff and pupils. Few, if any, serious problems with behaviour.

Pupils and parents: Almost 70 per cent travel to school on designated coaches from the many pick-up points in a wide catchment, mostly Suffolk and north Essex. The journey is seen as part of school social life. Mostly professional/business and some farming families; many parents commute to London on certain days. The pupils are friendly and charming, easy to converse with but not overconfident. Good mixers.

Entrance: Informal assessment for those joining in reception (nursery is non-selective), informal tests in maths and English managed during a visit to the school thereafter. All pupils assessed for SEN. At 11, the majority come up from the junior department with another 30 from local state/independent schools. Entrance tests in English, maths and verbal reasoning, plus a report from current school. Juniors transferring also take the tests. For sixth form, at least five GCSEs at grade 6, 7 for maths.

Exit: Nearly all juniors move up to the senior school. Some two-thirds of the year group leave at the end of year 11 – some take advantage of the grammar schools operating just over the county border, others to sixth form colleges or local co-ed independents. A few choose boarding further afield. Post-A level destinations include University College Birmingham, Brunel, Canterbury Christchurch, Goldsmiths, Harper Adams, Royal Holloway, UCL, Plymouth.

Money matters: Academic, art, music, drama and sports scholarships are offered at 11, 13 and 16. Means-tested bursaries are also awarded for demonstrable need and academic merit, up to the value of full fees. Fee remission of up to 50 per cent for staff children.

Remarks: A thriving academic environment for girls – and, in the future, boys – who relish drama, music and sport in a glorious country setting. A day school with a boarding feel – and, in future, a boarding school.

Ipswich School

Henley Road, Ipswich, Suffolk IP1 3SG

Ages 3–18 **Pupils** 1,033 (246 in junior school) **Sixth form** 224 **Boarders** 46 full (from 11 years) **C of E**

Fees: Day £11,850 – £15,579; Boarding £24,402 – £30,171 pa

01473 408300
www.ipswich.school

Headmaster: Since 2010, Nicholas Weaver BA (30s). Read engineering at Jesus College, Cambridge. Previously deputy head (academic) at Portsmouth Grammar, and before that taught physics at the Leys School, Cambridge, the Royal Grammar School, Guildford, and Radley College. Urbane and apparently unrufflable, married with three children, all at Ipswich School. Committed to developing in his students 'the flexibility of mind to apply their knowledge to novel situations, using those high-level taxonomy skills which transfer across disciplines'. This has called for an intellectual approach to the Ipswich academic curriculum and wide-ranging co-curriculum.

'He is incredibly positive, dynamic, determined and clearly proud of the school and everything it stands for,' said a parent.

Head of Ipswich Prep head : Snce 2009, Amanda Childs BA QTS MA, Dip Ed (mid 40s). Was deputy head of Alleyn's Junior School and has taught at various UK independent schools plus in Bangkok. Married with two daughters, both through prep school. Forward-thinking and committed to maintaining a high staff-to-pupil ratio and teaching standards plus a jam-packed list of clubs. 'We have found the school to be very well run and organised under her leadership,' nods a parent.

Academic matters: Class teacher and three assistants provide for all of the learning areas in the EYFS curriculum. Introduced to Read Write Inc school literacy programme in the pre-school group and specialist teaching for PE and music, regular sessions with the school librarian. Lower prep (age 4 to 7) children have morning literacy and numeracy lessons in differentiated groups across each year group. In the afternoon they have the run of the interconnected year group classrooms for a choice of learning activities. Two parallel classes per year group, setting for English and maths from year 5 (until then up to six differentiated groups taught by qualified teachers). French from reception; recorder from year 2; specialist science, ICT, art and DT lessons from year 3. Language carousel – year 3 learn German, year 4 Russian, year 5 Spanish and year 6 revisit French – in preparation for senior school choices. Learning enhancement co-ordinator and team support learning differences, plus gifted and talented; specialists eg play therapist, speech and language, emotional well-being counsellors brought in if beneficial. 'Our son has had healthy competition in the things he excels in and encouragement in things he finds more challenging, without feeling overwhelmed,' said a parent. Oversubscribed at year 5 – smart parents move in earlier to get ahead of the game and take advantage of preferential transfer to senior school.

'We had a choice between sending our daughter to other independent schools and also a grammar school in Colchester but chose Ipswich,' said one clued-up parent, typical of many. Indeed, senior school leads the way in terms of exam results in the Ipswich area. 'People sometimes lazily categorise us a as a hothouse,' laments head. 'We are selective but there is huge value-added; the co-curriculum provides a wealth of opportunities for students' engagement.' In 2018, 65 per cent A*-A/9-7 grades at GCSE; A level results, 47 per cent A*/A grades. Speaks for itself.

Eight-lesson senior school day runs until 4.15pm on a two-week timetable. Paper and pen still in use but plenty of computer suites, Wifi throughout; laptops welcome but not essential other than for those with SEN (who have support outside the timetabled day and lunchtime drop-in sessions). Year 7s set after their first half term for maths – one set 1, two set 2s and three set 3s; 20 per set. Academic subjects including French or Spanish and philosophy, religion and ethics. In year 8 discrete lessons in chemistry, physics and biology, and Latin is introduced; year 9s begin Russian and DT and GCSE science courses. GCSE choices fairly unrestricted; revision sessions and subject clinics in the run-up to exams. All year 11s have a period of work experience. Four or more A levels (no IB here) for all – business studies, drama and theatre studies, economics, PE and psychology on top of the traditional academic, plus an option from new The Edge enrichment programme, eg politics, law, EPQ. Year 12 classes typically 10 to 15; smaller the following year. Growth mindset school, so Academic Excellence Programme rather than gifted and talented, with extension lessons a specialised seminar programme.

A wealth of advice on uni courses, higher level and degree apprenticeships, from heads of sixth form and careers office, with the help of Unifrog. Early UCAS applications encouraged – a noticeboard updated with uni offers received serves as an incentive.

Games, options, the arts: Most recent inspection report praised Ipswich as a school where it's 'ok to like rugby and poetry'. Indeed, 'our provision does not limit the students,' says head; students are encouraged to try as many new activities as possible. Our year 8 guide backed this up – 'I love the sports,' she said, 'but here you can do other things alongside. I had never done music before I came here but someone persuaded me to give it a go and now I really enjoy it.'

Lending library of instruments for young musicians in prep school and year 3s all learn a stringed instrument (provided). Director of music and assistant director teach two music lessons each week to every prep class. Sculpting, printing, painting, drawing, DT, home economics covered by art teacher from year 3 in a professional-style studio. PE taught by specialists – 30 or so year 2s were involved in hockey skills practice when we visited, led by two PE teachers and a gapper – enviable ratios. Co-curricular clubs include skiing at the local dry slope, horse-riding and fencing (extra charge) and in-school crafty, sporty, musical and hobbies.

Hockey and rugby are main senior school sports in autumn; netball and hockey in spring; cricket and athletics for all in summer. County champions in many disciplines, but also non-competitive teams for leisure players and a well-used, well-equipped gym. Sports hall has lines for indoor hockey and rounders as well as netball, basketball, badminton, volleyball etc. Courts for fives – national tournaments entered. Yoga studio. Acres of school playing fields nearby for lessons and training. A third of senior pupils take individual instrumental lessons; orchestras, including symphony, plus ensembles. Chapel choir sings evensong at St Paul's and tours regularly abroad (recently to New York). The annual Ipswich School Festival of Music attracts internationally-renowned musicians to school's Britten Faculty of Music concert hall. Productions and plays in own theatre all year round. Technicians busy backstage. Art impressive. DT compulsory in years 7 and 8 and a popular GCSE and A level option. The Edge enrichment programme develops life skills, accredited by the Institute of Leadership of Management (level 3). In addition weekly activity sessions from year 9 offer eg CCF (Army or RAF), voluntary work, journalism. Clubs from show choir to sub-aqua and drone. Debating strong; sixth formers have the Athenaeum programme, a lunchtime discussion forum for burning issues.

Curriculum-related trips – adventurous residential visit to Cumbria a highlight for year 8s, while similar in south Wales for year 12s also gives practical advice on teenage scrapes.

Boarding: School has just one boarding house, Westwood, which accommodates fewer than five per cent of students. A mix of full-boarding internationals and flexi-boarders who stay a few nights to suit family arrangements, club or training commitments. A short walk from the school along suburban streets, Westwood has a common room and kitchen and provides breakfast and dinner on weekdays and all meals at weekends. Equivalent of home at this otherwise day school – no popping to and fro during the school day. On Saturdays those not involved in school sports fixtures have organised activities laid on – trips to Norwich or Cambridge, marshalling and taking part in local parkrun, art and craft projects etc – and also plenty of free time to explore the town, or to stretch their legs in the boarding house grounds or on the Astro. School is oversubscribed for boarding and those who miss out are offered a homestay alternative.

Background and atmosphere: Only school mentioned by Shakespeare, in Henry VIII – 'Ipswich and Oxford, those twins of learning'. Founded much earlier but no-one knows when – an unpaid bill dated 1399 is the oldest piece of evidence. Henry VIII granted the first charter and school's coat of arms and motto, Semper Eadem (Always the Same), are those of Elizabeth I. School's poster boy for social mobility is Cardinal Wolsey, the butcher's son who went on to become the most powerful man in the country and re-founded the school in 1528 as The Cardinal's College. Plans fell with him, and the stone he intended to use to build the school in the 1500s was shipped off to build the palace at Whitehall. All that remains is a gate and the church which he had commandeered as the school chapel. Concept survived, however, and Ipswich School was established in the town centre before moving in 1852 to new buildings opposite Christchurch Park, which the senior school occupies to this day, with contemporary designed prep school building on own campus added in 2000.

Senior school is surprisingly spacious in a quiet, residential area, centring on the original Victorian edifice, but expanded with 20th century buildings, connected by a series of passages, steps and covered ways, all punctuated with well-kept horticulture. Facilities range from the functional (run-of-the-mill classrooms and corridors) to the fantastic (impressive library with windows by John Piper depicting the seasons, and built-in chapel with wonderful organ, played by local church organist if no organ student on roll). You never know what will be behind the next door. Art department is professional with huge DT area – woodwork, metals, plastics (including 3D printer) and textiles, and exhibition space. School's own Great School Theatre is open to the public too. Architecture of new music school reflects the school's Snape connection (annual concert there is a highlight) and offers superb acoustics, not to mention fabulous wall art of Benjamin Britten extract notated in stones carved with the names of benefactors. Clever and creative – very Ipswich. New sixth form centre with zones for relaxation and study.

Across the road, The Lodge nursery opened in January 2018 in a neighbouring house and now offers a comfortable and well-resourced setting for boys and girls from 3 months to 3 years 50 weeks per year, with the aim of moving most into the school's nursery class ('but no pressure').

Next door, Ipswich Prep campus has separate buildings for lower and upper prep. Corridors have lower prep classrooms on the right and resources on the left-hand side to aid navigation. Reception, years 1 and 2 classrooms adjoin each other, each fully glazed on one side and with a canopied outdoor area. Library and sizable hall for assemblies, music sessions, two weekly PE lessons and lunch (hot and salad options). Large playground, due for an upgrade, as well as an Astro area for games and PE.

Upper prep building strikingly modern, inspired by the maritime history of Ipswich – each floor a 'deck' – marvellous vista of Ipswich parks, museums, galleries, football stadium and even the Orwell Bridge from the 'top deck' viewing platform. 'All learning resources for our pupils,' says head. Hall and classrooms on the right side of cavernous for the numbers, all with large windows, underfloor heating and 'the best storage ever', according to one beaming teacher. Arts floor has generous spaces for art and music rooms and practice rooms for teaching 22 different instruments. ICT suite with computer for every child (information evenings make sure parents keep up); two classes' worth of iPads for upper and two for lower prep are based in the pleasant library.

School pavilion on senior campus overlooks immaculate on-site cricket square and three further sports sites for the use of Ipswichians of all ages a short walk away: Rushmere has three new hockey pitches (two in Olympic blue and pink colours, one green) and six netball/tennis courts, most floodlit; Notcutts has playing fields for rugby and football, pitches for cricket and rounders and a grass athletics track; and there is an Astro hockey pitch-cum-tennis court at school boarding house. Several local houses serve as accommodation for teachers.

Pastoral care, well-being and discipline: 'We do our very best to support children's well-being and are continuing to focus on it,' says prep head. 'That way they are better able to take advantage of the huge number of educational opportunities for them here.' Parents agree – 'I have a daughter who is confident, very hardworking and absolutely loves going to school,' said one. 'My wife and I like to take most of the credit, but there is no doubt that her work ethic, both academically, musically and in sport, can be traced back to the influence the school has had on her.'

Prep school lunchtime club offers respite for pupils who find social situations challenging. Matron always on hand. Lower prep 'golden person' is someone who has impressed with work, kindness or initiative; reward is sitting on a golden cushion for the week. 'Talking partners' scheme pairs children picked at random for the week – brings out the wallflowers. Newbies allocated a buddy to help with settling-in. Termly house captain and vice-captain positions applied for by year 6 pupils, voted in by their peers. House points awarded for good manners and friendship skills as well as work and self-organisation.

Home-school-pupil triangle robust at senior school. Every tutor opens channel of communication with parents within first two weeks of new term – usually a phone call. Support matrix of tutor, head of house, senior leadership team. Staff have half-termly 'care meetings' to co-ordinate approach to individuals. Matron and chaplain are central and even school office staff and estates team have a role – 'all eyes and ears that are valuable to the pastoral system,' says head.

Mental health first aid training for staff is ongoing. 'We have some high-functioning students who are very driven and the skills they need to learn can include not driving themselves too hard,' explains head. Regular reading weeks in the lower school – homework is suspended in favour of a good book.

Sanctions ladder, from yellow cards to detention. Exclusions for eg repeated offences, social media abuse, bullying, damage to property, violence. Drugs 'not a significant issue for this school,' says head, but recently wrote to parents 'to re-emphasise that it is not possible to be a drug user and a member of Ipswich School'. Firm, clear stance.

Pupils and parents: Ipswichians as a rule thoughtful and down-to-earth, thanks perhaps to the urban, real-world location and feet kept firmly on the ground at home. Fewer than five per cent international students – Hong Kong, China, some from Africa and Europe. Majority of seniors live within an hour, either side of the Suffolk-Ipswich border, and arrive by all modes of transport – trains, public and school buses, parent taxi, bike, on foot. Many from Colchester, served by three school bus routes. Sixth formers find on-road parking nearby.

Recent parent perceptions survey an 'eye-opener', according to head, delighted by the diversity of parents' values and backgrounds – local businesspeople, farmers and professionals, also London commuters. Impressive turnouts for school events and matches. New parent portal popular; parent forum has input on school matters.

List of notable alumni starts with Cardinal Wolsey and moves on to author and illustrator Edward Ardizzone, physicist Sir Charles Frank, Nobel Prize winner Sir Charles Scott Sherrington and writer Rider Haggard (King Solomon's Mines).

Entrance: Two settling-in sessions of 90 minutes for new arrivals to The Lodge nursery. In prep, main entry points are reception, year 3 and year 5. Nursery class has a maximum 24, which varies according to the time of year – intakes at Easter and September. Day, morning and afternoon sessions (including lunch), as well as early education funded sessions. Reception joiners assessed on interaction with other children, and one-on-one activity with teacher; English, maths and non-verbal reasoning tests for later joiners. Wide catchment, though half the pupils have a Colchester postcode.

Maximum 120 year 7 places; no more than 24 per class up to GCSE. Nearly half of year 7 intake from prep – entry on head's recommendation. Littlegarth in Colchester and St Margaret's in

Gosfield are big 11+ feeders; rest often arrive solo from village schools within an hour's travel. Entry by school's own entrance exam, plus a report from current school and a chat with the head. UKiset applications (online testing) for overseas admissions.

Additional 15 to 20 places made available in year 9. Holmwood House in Colchester and nearby Orwell Park provide 13+ entrants (Ipswich is 'scrupulous' about waiting to take those who visit earlier, emphasises head). Entry by school's own exam in March, or common entrance (dwindling number).

Entry to sixth form requires six GCSEs with at least 6s, preferably 7s, in chosen A level subjects, plus satisfactory chat with the head and report from current school.

Exit: Early offers in year 5 for most in prep school. They sit the same senior school entrance exam as external applicants, but a day earlier, and for benchmarking and scholarship purposes only. Discussions with parents well before if Ipswich School is not the best fit – 'designed to never be a shock,' says head – and options suggested, nearly always other independents. Vast majority move across the road, though inevitably a couple per year take up places at Colchester grammars.

Around a fifth leave after GCSEs for local sixth form colleges. Vast majority of those remaining head to university with a leaning towards traditional academic subjects at Russell Group establishments, particularly Exeter, Birmingham, Nottingham and London. Six to Oxbridge in 2018.

Money matters: Scholarships available at 11+ and 13+ – academic (Queen's) are worth up to 50 per cent of fees; music, art, sport, all-rounder, and Arkwright (for DT).

Means-tested bursaries available at 11, 13 and 16 'for pupils of high academic or all-round ability whose parents could not otherwise afford the school fees'. Head keen to coincide 500th anniversary of the Cardinal's College in 2028 with the launch of a new Wolsey Fund for transformational bursaries, working towards 'needs-blind' admission.

Remarks: Predominantly an academic day school, but with boarding school style commitment to the development of personal skills that will help take these able students a lot further than exam results alone.

Kimbolton School

Kimbolton, Huntingdon, Cambridgeshire PE28 0EA

Ages 4–18 **Pupils** 1,011 **Sixth form** 186 **Boarders** 49 full/flexi

Fees: Day £9,870 – £15,795; Boarding £24,705 – £26,280 pa

01480 860505
www.kimbolton.cambs.sch.uk/

Head: Since 2002, Jonathan Belbin (50s). History at Bristol followed by PGCE. Sporty so decided could combine sport and history by teaching. Spent a lot of time as sports coach. Joined independent sector by chance and never looked back. Moved around country expanding his roles before first headship at Kimbolton. 'I liked that Kimbolton was co-ed and boarding and I could see lots of potential.' Very well established and popular with parents, 'a bit of a shining light,' said one parent. 'He's interested in the kids,' was another take. All spoke of his high profile around the school and at matches and productions. 'He's very professional, not gushing or effusive, slightly distant from parents, but in a good way. I don't want a friend, but a professional, which is just what he is,' said one perceptive parent. 'He has good people skills,' was said by another. Has handled tricky situations well according to parents, 'dignified and straightforward, measured in his responses and manages the school well, in good times and bad.'

Has overseen many building projects and refurbishments, bringing facilities up to date over the years, the most recent being the new science and maths block opened in 2015. Numbers have expanded by 150 under his tenure. Still teaching PHSE and history to certain years so knows all the children. Profile high around prep school as well. Smartly turned out, youthful looking, friendly and welcoming. We got the impression of a head very much on the ball and comfortable and confident in his role. His children have all been educated at Kimbolton.

Head of prep since 2015, Philip Foley (50s). Studied education, so could spend more time playing sports, before spending a year in industry, then drawn back into teaching, 'the best decision ever.' Kimbolton is his fourth headship. Establishing himself well and knows all the children. 'He is making positive changes, slowly without upsetting anyone.' Parents like what they have seen of him and say he is very accessible, and always outside at the end of the day. Softly spoken and mild mannered, teaches years 2 and 4 so getting to know children well. Daughter joined sixth form on his arrival.

Academic matters: In 2018, 52 per cent A*-A/9-7 at GCSE, 52 per cent A*-A at A level, 80 per cent A*-B. Results have steadily increased over the last few years. Spanish and French available at GCSE and A level, taught from reception. Not many take two languages at GCSE, nine or 10 a year. Half the year group take all three sciences. Pupils taught in mixed ability groups apart from maths and languages. Maths is the most popular subject at A level; philosophy, religion and ethics now an A level option. All parents, throughout both schools, spoke of excellent academic progress and close contact with teachers. Academic problems picked up on quickly and help offered in both schools. Lots of subject workshops and drop ins available and popular with pupils. Prep pupils taught by class teacher until year 5 when subject taught and pressure ramped up, subtly, with more homework, getting them ready for senior school life. Maths set from year 3 onwards.

Excellent facilities throughout both schools, some – such as halls and sports – shared. Impressive new science block, please say hello to Colin the fish in one of the classrooms. Pupils working hard and more than happy to chat, pleased to show off their work. Very relaxed atmosphere between pupils and staff, but mutual respect apparent. Parents spoke of 'excellent teaching staff who know our children well and want them to succeed.' Most said, 'staff handled child well, knew them and brought the best out in them,' others spoke of their child 'flourishing.' One parent noted that 'the odd teacher appeared to be marking time and needed moving on,' but was sympathetic to the situation and said, 'these individuals are now a rarity here.' IT embraced, computing and programming taught to a high level and right up to date, so much so that our sixth form guides were slightly at a loss, we completely so. Excellent artwork on display in both schools. DT, textiles and cooking for all, in both schools. Sixth form offers 'life cooking skills' as an extracurricular course although home economics is no longer available as an A level.

Class sizes small, average of 17 in prep, 21 in senior with an average of seven in sixth form, so nowhere to hide, which is appreciated by parents. Some 40 pupils receive extra support throughout both schools, but only two are statemented. A handful of pupils bilingual, 18 on the EAL register. One-to-one available for learning and language support if necessary. UCAS support exemplary; staff appear to be very much on the ball. Sixth form common room in basement equipped with comfy chairs. Very much their own space, with large study rooms also available, and well used.

Games, options, the arts: As expected with two heads who are ex-sports teachers, games plays an important part at Kimbolton. 'We aim to get everyone out at least once a year representing the school,' said the prep head. Lots of silverware in the cabinets and lots of choice, bar rugby, which is not played. Football plays a major part, along with hockey for boys and girls. Prep girls are campaigning for football and cricket teams and head is open to the idea. Swimming on site with own pool and lots of pitches within the grounds. Lake where canoe practice takes place. Lots of teams for all levels. Plenty of sports clubs and after-school practices; 85 per cent of prep pupils stay after school. Most parents very complimentary about sport and facilities. All other parents spoke about the children being 'taught well and lots of choice.'

Music and drama popular and well represented. Lots of individual lessons, including over half of pupils in upper prep. Parents spoke of sensible way these lessons are timetabled, particularly in the senior school, so less academic do not miss essential teaching time. Dramatic productions spoken of highly in both schools. Lots of productions, choirs, orchestras, bands and after-school clubs. You name it, they have it.

CCF very popular with vast majority of pupils taking part from year 10 upwards. D of E also popular, up to gold. Lots of school trips, sporting and curricular.

K

Boarding: Boarding available from year 7. It's not a major part of the school, which is predominantly a day school with boarders making up about seven per cent of pupils. Boarders housed in two houses at each end of Kimbolton's High Street (it's not very long) and never the twain shall meet. Girls' house is full, boys' house has the odd space. Full and weekly boarding offered, flexi if space available. Some 45 per cent of boarders from overseas, others based just outside travelling distance, most within two hours. Quite a few children have parents in the Forces as the school is quite close to some RAF bases.

Parents impressed with boarding. 'The house is run really well and the weekly and flexi boarders are treated as full boarders, welcome to go on trips and excursions.' Parents spoke about children being kept well occupied, 'there is always a full term of events, booked in advance.' Parents of girls spoke about 'the mumsy chats' the staff have with their daughters. Curfews upheld and respected, older boarders given more independence. School happy for boarders to visit day pupils, with parental permission.

The two boarding houses are well equipped and modernised; tall boys will need to duck in certain rooms, with low ceilings and ancient buildings. Three in a room maximum, sixth form have own rooms. Communal common rooms for all age groups well used. We get the impression that because there are so few boarders they are a close knit, but welcoming, little unit. Lots of encouragement to participate in sports and extracurricular life. Supervised prep for younger years, older ones do it in their rooms at set times. They cook their own breakfast at weekends.

Background and atmosphere: Located in the small pretty village of Kimbolton, The Castle, originally an ancient castle and now a magnificent Georgian mansion, dominates the village sitting at the end of the High Street. Very little teaching actually takes place in The Castle, but admin and head housed magnificently, with sixth form in the basement. The prep school, at the other end of the village, an old red brick purpose built Victorian school house, was once the senior school. Originally a boys' grammar, dating back over 400 years, the school bought The Castle from the Duke of Manchester in the 1950s for a reputed £11,500, and a further 200 guineas for the magnificent paintings when the governors were offered them at the last minute – they had a quick whip round to raise the money. Since then the school has thrived and succeeded, reflecting rather sadly on the opposite fortunes of the Manchester family. The Castle housed Catherine of Aragon when she was exiled from London. She died in what is now the head's office and historians still pay an annual visit to pay homage. This is not as macabre as it sounds, but do note the secret panelled door into the head's office.

The prep school was opened in the 1950s, and became co-ed in the 70s. Both schools are accessible via a brisk walk through parkland. There's lots of space, 120 acres, to absorb pupils, who make the most of their magnificent surroundings.

Very much a family orientated school, and being relatively small, this atmosphere prevails with the school seeming to know parents well too. Pupils know each other, and the staff, well. Parents really appreciate this and, for many, was the reason they chose the school. 'My child isn't lost in large numbers,' was alluded to many times. A jolly, relaxed atmosphere prevails with a warm welcome for everyone. The distinctive purple, black and white striped blazers dominate, possibly an acquired taste, and not the easiest colour combination for everyone to look good in. Sixth formers wear black business suits. Purple dominates the school, it's their school colours and it's everywhere. Even the Christmas decorations are purple on the tree, matching the purple carpets et al. We're sure you get the picture. Food raised its ugly head with parents. It's raved about in the prep school, but standards slip when pupils move to The Castle.

Pastoral care, well-being and discipline: Every parent praised pastoral care. 'I don't know how they manage it,' said one parent who went on to praise the' kind, patient, supportive, caring teachers,' and believed this atmosphere is absorbed by the children, who behave in the same way. 'They pick up on problems quickly,' was said numerous times. Many parents spoke about the 'feel of the school' when they first visited, the friendliness of pupils and parents, and wanted that for their children. 'The children and parents are nice.' Friendship issues dealt with kindly and effectively. Counsellors available and well used.

Pastoral care and safeguarding so effective that the odd parent feels independence is being lost. But those with older children spoke about 'independence and more freedom in the sixth form.' Sixth formers a familiar sight in the High Street where they congregate at a popular coffee shop. Discipline at acceptable standards. 'They have high expectations which are usually met,' was said. Pupils in prep aware that if attitude unsuitable they will not be going up to The Castle. We are not aware of this happening in recent years so all appear to toe the line. Suspensions incredibly rare and low detention numbers. Pupils and parents happy that discipline is fair and appropriate. Lots of mentoring between pupils and effective school councils in both schools.

Pupils and parents: Most families rural dwellers from surrounding villages and small towns. Traditionally a farming and Forces school, this is now changing with many families moving from London whilst parents still work there. More families now coming from Cambridge's outskirts, so more medics and techy parents joining the fray. Most parents both working to pay fees and want a good value for money, all round education for their children, 'involved parents,' said the prep head.

Parents welcome flexibility school offers with boarding and late pick ups. Many children second, even third generation. Pupils happy and chatty and seem very relaxed, but ambitious and not fazed about leaving their rural idyll for urban sprawl; they are being well prepared.

Entrance: Pupils for reception assessed in small groups and teachers visit them at local nurseries to see that they are ready to learn. School happy to say no at this stage. Older children assessed and spend taster morning at school. No automatic transfer to senior school; all pupils take entrance exam. External candidates interviewed as well. Those from prep who won't make grade kindly weeded out in earlier years, but this is a rare occurrence.

Numbers double in senior school 1st year (year 7) with external pupils, 45 per cent, coming from up to 30 local primaries with a small intake in year 9. Senior school full, the odd place in prep. About 20 join the sixth form, virtually all from state schools, the odd one from independents. These pupils all interviewed by head and head of sixth form. Six GCSEs, grade B/6 or above needed including English and maths.

Exit: Nearly all prep pupils go on to senior school. In 2018 around 20 per cent left after GCSEs, mainly to vocational courses at local colleges, the odd one to board elsewhere in sixth form, again following family tradition. 'We don't cull,' said the head, 'they are good kids,' so those who want to go into sixth form usually do even if they don't make the grade, but must have the right attitude. Virtually all go to university, the odd one straight to employment, gap years minimal. Top destinations in 2018 were Newcastle, Leeds, UEA, Nottingham Trent, Reading and Birmingham. One medic and two dentists. One or two to Oxbridge most years. Apprenticeships not being embraced as yet, but school open to it.

Money matters: Scholarships available in senior school only, up to 20 per cent of fees, the vast majority academic, but the odd sports, leadership and arts available at 13+. The equivalent of six full means-tested awards at senior school per year group, usually given to 8-10 applicants, most subsidised by at least 80 per cent of fees.

Remarks: This small school, housed in beautiful surroundings, appears to be a well kept secret, much to some parents' bemusement. 'Why is it not more well known?' said by many. We get the impression that there's no need; the school is virtually full, has an excellent reputation locally and is providing a good all round education for local families wanting to use the private sector. Pupils can spend their whole education at Kimbolton enjoying the benefits of a happy environment, small class sizes and excellent pastoral care. Not flashy but classy. Those parents in the know appreciate that a Kimbolton education is money well spent. Shhhh.

King Edward VI Aston School

Frederick Road, Aston, Birmingham, West Midlands B6 6DJ

Ages 11–18 **Pupils** 915 **Sixth form** 275

0121 327 1130
www.keaston.bham.sch.uk

Head: Since 2004, Colin Parker (50s). History degree from Liverpool and higher degrees from Leicester and Warwick. Spent three years working in insurance before starting teaching in a large comprehensive and then moved to the selective sector. We were very impressed to see him in the play area at lunch time and the boys tell us that he is out there every day 'noticing things'. They regard him as approachable, down to earth, informed and caring about everybody; positive and with an incredibly clear vision for the school. Parents tell us he is out in the playground at the end of school too, and they also find him friendly and easy to talk to – 'he is a brilliant role model for younger teachers', one parent told us.

Colin describes Aston as having always been understated, and he himself is an attractive mixture of unassuming and dynamic. He avoids the ego-driven style of headship and puts the boys at the centre of everything. He treads a thoughtful path between his own, and historically the school's, firm Christian principles and the multi-faith world that is today's Birmingham. His sense of purpose is engagingly mixed with his sense of humour.

Colin is the most senior head in the King Edward's Foundation, an ancient and illustrious Birmingham institution. His experience and wisdom are keenly sought regionally and nationally. He is chair of governors of a primary school and governor at Aston University Engineering Academy. He is an accredited professional partner for newly appointed heads and on the Department for Education's Professional Conduct Panel. Married to Jo, a head of maths; they have three children.

Academic matters: Aston is academically selective and the strong results reflect that. At A level in 2018, 31 per cent of grades were at A*-A, 58 per cent A*-B. At GCSE, 56 per cent A*-A/9-7 grades. The science and mathematics results are exceptionally good and huge numbers opt for these subjects at A level. Reflecting patterns in other all boys schools, English and modern languages are not appealing to the same extent, though we were excited by the English department's initiative to explore the male identity and consider texts that examine what it means to be a modern man. A modern language at GCSE is now compulsory.

There are 120 boys in each year group in classes of 30. For optional subjects after year 9, group sizes are usually around 20-25. Unusually for an all boys school, a majority of the teachers are female and they reflect more fairly than many Birmingham schools the cultural make-up of the city. The deputy head and head of learning support are both female.

Over 10 per cent of the intake comes in with identified learning support needs, usually dyslexia or autistic spectrum. Support depends on the level of need and ranges from a teaching assistant with a boy most of the day to occasional meetings to help with organisation. This is all funded by the school. The school says it picks up quickly on any problems that haven't been identified at primary school and the appropriate support is there. For a highly selective school, we were impressed. The boys themselves spoke warmly of the willingness of teachers to give extra help at lunchtimes and the success of the student mentor programme. One boy who had joined the school at sixth form from a non-selective school told us how quickly the school had picked up on his lack of a strong work ethic and he is coasting no longer. There are strong induction programmes in place, not just for year 7s but also for those moving into the sixth form. One parent described induction as 'fantastic'. Parents also applauded the student mentoring scheme. 'I've been telling my son to do his homework as soon as he gets it, for years. But it is only since his sixth form mentor has said it that he has started to listen.'

Students spoke warmly of the support in place for university admissions both in terms of general UCAS advice but also help for those preparing for university entrance exams of one sort or another, including Oxbridge. Parents say that the information is very full but directed at the boys, not them.

There is at least a double lesson a week timetabled for enrichment activities, which are wide ranging and include volunteer work. In major exam years, there are sessions on stress management, yoga, mindfulness, aromatherapy. Some of these are supported financially by the parents' association.

Games, options, the arts: The school has been a lead in local sports partnerships for a number of years. For an inner city state school, facilities are excellent. Rugby is the big passion but plenty of boys relish their hockey, cricket and football. There are overseas rugby tours. By year 10, there are options for boys who don't like the conventional team sports. The boys assured us that the sports department is as interested in those who are not natural sportsmen as those who are. All the boys study fitness and health issues relating to sport.

There is a range of extracurricular activities including Amnesty International and all three Duke of Edinburgh Award levels. Houses compete in sporting and academic events – such as the house chess competition.

Music is high status. 'Sensational,' as described by one parent. The Big Band regularly tours in Europe. There are bands and ensemble groups for all levels. The head is determined that boys whose families do not have the background to support an interest in music at home will have that opportunity at the school. Indeed he believes that extracurricular activities are essential for providing the cultural capital that many homes cannot offer and he directs school money into ensuring the chances are there. Parents told us their sons find the opportunities inspirational.

House drama competitions are keenly contested, and a highlight of the drama year is the annual musical theatre production with the nearby King Edward V1 Handsworth girls' school.

Background and atmosphere: The architect of the 1883 school was JA Chatwin, who worked with Pugin and Barry on the Houses of Parliament, and the confidence and optimism of that founding period continues to pervade from the Chatwin bricks today. The school is squeezed into a site in the middle of one of the poorer areas of Birmingham that has always housed waves of immigrants. Today it is largely Asian working class, and the downside of having been on the same site since 1883 is a lack of space and a rather tatty immediate environment. There has been building going on since 1883, some of it very sensitively done, but there is a sense of a lot of people in a very small area. The school is hoping to expand onto some nearby wasteland, but the negotiations are taking a long time.

The boys are very conscious that they inhabit the oldest of the King Edward Foundation buildings and they are hugely proud of their history. There are old school photos adorning various walls as a reminder of the shared past, and a large memorial plaque with the many names of boys who died in the two World Wars. There are honours boards in the library, portraits of past headmasters, a rousing school song and carefully cherished archives. The boys are encouraged to understand that they are part of something bigger than themselves today and they all can add to the school's rich history.

The juxtaposition of that sense of the past that you find in many long-established independent schools and the ethnic make-up of the school today is thought-provoking, to say the least. Often described as the 'most Brummie' of the King Edward's schools, Aston has always reflected the changing nature of the local community. The school is majority Asian but there is a mixture of white, Afro-Caribbean, Chinese, Eastern European. It is less established middle class than the vast majority of UK grammar schools and its achievements are all the more remarkable because of that. The school has set out to attract families on free school meals, widening its social intake, and it is very successful in doing this.

Virtually everyone is involved in extracurricular activities and music lessons, so by the time the boys leave, the school has ensured that they have had many of the experiences that are part of the fabric of traditional British middle class life. There is a huge sense of motivation and focus about the school.

We were told by various groups about The Aston Man. This ideal was conjured up by a past senior teacher and is embedded in the consciousness of all the boys. The Aston Man is well rounded, sticks to his own moral values, is unique and stands out from the crowd. One boy, in Kipling-like terms, described The Aston Man as 'a young gentleman, gracious in defeat and respectful in victory'. His choice of language was used without a hint of irony, was spoken with considerable pride and was greeted with serious nods from the other surrounding boys.

Pastoral care, well-being and discipline: What is particularly striking about Aston is the way it has moved on from traditional stereotype of boys' schools. Perhaps it is the large number of women teachers, or the fluidity that the school has always needed to deal with the ever-changing Birmingham ethnic population.

To start with, we never heard anyone talk about 'boys', it is always 'students' or 'the young people'. The students spoke easily about emotional problems and explained the various formal and informal ways in which the school supported them through the difficult times they all experienced at some stage. Parents confirm that the school encourages the boys to talk to someone if they are not happy or don't feel safe. There is a school counsellor, a system of anonymous emailing to the safeguarding officer, a series of little podcasts that deal with teenage problems that the boys can access from anywhere without anyone being able to identify them, and student mentoring for personal problems, particularly strong through the house system with older boys supporting younger ones. One parent told us her son had used it because he was unsure of himself and lacking in confidence. No big problem, but the student mentor had been a great support. Parents spoke warmly of the speed with which the school reacts to any parental concerns. Staff can all be contacted via email and replies are prompt. All this is against a backdrop of a very thorough and thoughtful personal education programme.

The approach to discipline issues is absolutely clear. Behaviour that is against the values of the school is not tolerated and there is the usual range of sanctions. The school is not afraid to use fixed term exclusions for the more serious offenses such as stealing, or speaking unacceptably on the internet or in person. However, everyone told us that it is a very forgiving school and the approach to punishment is essentially redemptive, and seen by boys and teachers as a way of improving the individuals involved. Once the punishment is done, there really is a fresh start. Staff spoke of one of last year's vice school captains who had been excluded earlier on in his school career but developed over time to allow him to win one of the school's coveted student leadership positions. The head's view, which he shares with despairing parents, is that mistakes are far better made in school than outside. The school's main aim is to ensure that the boy is back on the path to becoming a good citizen, and parents see this. It is telling that there have been no appeals against fixed term exclusions.

Pupils and parents: Over half the sixth form comes from families where neither parent has a university education, but there are also a fair number of professional families, and those with a business background. Families largely come from north of the city centre – but it is not a school that draws exclusively from the leafy suburbs of Sutton Coldfield or Solihull. Possibly the large proportion of Asian families skews the career aspirations towards the medical professions and engineering. Families are very motivated to support the school. There is a strong Parents' Association and parents feel that the school actively encourages parents to be involved. The Parents' Association raises serious money each year by organising parking for Aston Villa matches.

The boys are a delight. Serious and earnest, deeply loyal to the school, they are aware of the privilege of being at a King

Edward's school. They appear to genuinely care for each other. They like being in a single sex environment and tell us they make lots of friends with girls at KE Handsworth through joint activities and on the Green Buses which bring lots of them to school. Teachers say the boys don't have to define themselves against girls and are more open talking about emotions than boys are in mixed groups.

Entrance: Although Aston doesn't demand the top marks in the Birmingham 11+ exams, don't be lulled into thinking it is anything other than highly competitive to win a place there. The numbers sitting the 11+ are eye watering and the relevant age group is expanding all the time in the Birmingham area. The criteria and technicalities of the entrance exam are clearly explained on the King Edward's Foundation website. A new criterion gives preference to pupil premium children. About 40 places are offered at 16+.

Exit: Very few leave after GCSEs. Of year 13 leavers, virtually all make a university application, mostly to Russell Group universities and other high tariff institutions such as Aston, Loughborough, Bath. Other popular university destinations include Birmingham, Warwick, Nottingham and the London universities. The most popular university courses are engineering, medicine, dentistry, economics, pharmacy and history. Two to Cambridge in 2018 and eight medics.

Remarks: Aston is a remarkable school by any standards and boys who get offered a place must be regarded as amongst the most fortunate in the West Midlands. It is a revelation, both in how education for boys can work to encourage gender intelligence and equality and also in how ethnic diversity can be tackled within the context of a traditional grammar school. Birmingham wrestles with the challenges of a multicultural city where a minority of the population does not want to integrate with aspects of British culture. Aston does not make heavy weather of this but goes steadily on its way promoting the values that have served the school and its boys superbly for many generations.

King Edward VI Camp Hill School for Boys

Vicarage Road, Kings Heath, Birmingham B14 7QJ

Ages 11–18 **Pupils** 1,204 **Sixth form** 303

0121 444 3188
www.camphillboys.bham.sch.uk

Headteacher: Since 2014, Martin Garrod MA (engineering) PGCE. Educated at Merchant Taylors' and Peterhouse Cambridge. Once upon a time a chartered engineer, switched to teaching in his 30s and served his apprenticeship in Bristol where, as a supply teacher, he enjoyed some experiences so frightful that they can only be said to have forged him. Beneath his unassuming, thoughtful and self-deprecating demeanour, you may be sure, there's tempered steel. Married to a Brummie, three children. Came to the city in '93. Taught at Handsworth Grammar, graduated to King Edward VI Aston as head of maths, moved to Camp Hill as deputy head in 2003 and was crowned head in 2014, a career-capping appointment and in our view a wise and excellent choice. No sense whatever that age has wearied him, a capacity for self-renewal every September being the salient attribute of the best teachers. He plainly loves what he does and loves being here. Drily humorous, humane, bombast-free and crystal clear when describing what his school is all about.

Keeps his hand in as a teacher by taking the top GCSE maths set and running the football. Applauded by parents and students for his omnipresence at school events of all sorts, including at weekends; one parent said, 'He's there morning, noon and night'. Leavens all this with a recreational mix of paragliding, rowing, reading and kicking back to an eclectic mix of popular classical and classic rock from the Stones through to Blondie.

Camp Hill Boys is famous throughout Brum, a city where parents sometimes talk about things other than schools, but rarely, for there is a gulf fixed between the best and the rest. To win a place at Camp Hill (or one of the other King Eds) is to win first prize in the lottery of life, and to attain that most parents would cheerfully saw off a limb. This is a school which routinely ranks among the top 15 state-funded purveyors of undergraduates to Oxbridge.

The school's standout feature is that it is fiendishly selective. It's a bit of a Bletchley Park for young people. Of the 1,000 or so who have the audacity to apply, just 120 win a place. Mr Garrod makes no apologies for this exclusivity ('not that I'm in any way anti non-selective schools') and defends it on two counts. First, all students are at a similar level, so teachers don't have to cope with a wide range of ability in any group. Second, 'able students surrounded by able students do better'. As a consequence, the school is able to recruit seriously bright teachers, many of them ex-Oxbridge, who love teaching their subject to bright lads, some of whom are even brighter than they are. Mr Garrod makes the recipe sound simple: 'These boys are bright; they'd be bright anywhere'. So they would, but, here's the thing, would they really do quite as well elsewhere? Stellar Attainment 8 and Progress 8 (value added) GCSE scores suggest not. Truly extraordinary (best in Brum) for a school with conventionally bright students who joined at a level that was already high. These figures also show that the school does very well by its less bright (or, as we would say, bright) students.

Camp Hill parents are the sort who want the best for their sons, and you'll find the usual tranche of classically pushy parents, many of whom want their son to be a doctor. We asked Mr Garrod if, in response to consumer demand, his school isn't just an exam factory. He responded equably that what concerns him is stopping boys from working too hard. He tells them, 'Trust us, we have long experience of drawing out the best from able pupils'. Instead, he urges them to make friends and throw themselves into sport and the many enrichment activities on offer, a range described by Ofsted in a rare departure from jargon as 'breathtaking'. His philosophy is 'Tighten up if you want them to be good, loosen up if you want them to be extraordinary.' With the entry exam behind them, he says, boys do best if they're given the opportunity to be extraordinary by doing lots, 'developing their creativity and exercising responsibility'. The Progress 8 score may be regarded as a measure of how well this is working. Full marks to Mr Garrod for making his case without once using the words 'holistic' or 'rounded'.

There's nothing new in this approach at Camp Hill. Which doesn't make Mr Garrod the continuity candidate by any means, but why tinker with something that works? The job of a head here is to fine-tune systems and ensure that the software (teachers and students) are busy, happy and fired up. This calls for humane rigour, and that's an arcane skill.

Academic matters: Standard grammar school curriculum. Maths and science strong, as you would expect, and most boys opt for these – 20+ a year go on to medical school. Humanities subjects are no also-rans, mind, and way above national averages. Some less sought-after A level subjects taught jointly with the girls' school next door, eg music and computing. Drama is taught at the girls' school, design & technology at the boys'. Superb teachers inside the classroom and out; they count themselves lucky to work here and amply repay the debt.

Every student must be able to access the curriculum so no special needs that require specialist support. Parents told us they like the regular academic reviews and feel their sons are, in the words of one, 'firmly on the radar'. Note: this is a school without teaching assistants (TAs), partly because there's no call and partly because, when they did employ some, the boys were often way ahead of them. Instead, sixth formers go into classes and support the younger boys. Intervention mostly to mend tangled handwriting and support boys on the ASD spectrum, of whom there are a number as there are in any school as bright as this. Entries to Oxbridge impacted by high proportion of applications to med school but normally number in the teens. A level results 2018: 89 per cent A*/B, 67 per cent A*/A. GCSE results: 81 per cent A*/A or 7-9. In the words of a parent, 'This is a school where it's acceptable to do well and be proud of it'.

Library not so much excellent as inspirational. Superb head librarian uses every ploy in the book to get boys reading, including events where authors, including former pupil, crime writer Mark Billingham, talk about their work. Pillars in the library display the most borrowed books in libraries around the world. Teachers display outside their classroom door the name of the book they are currently curling up with.

K

Games, options, the arts: Tons of sport including the seasonal big three, rugby, hockey and cricket. Also, eg, athletics, cross-country, swimming, tennis, badminton, basketball and squash – oh, and chess, whose exploits appear under Sport in the school mag. Acres of green space for all this and a very handsome swimming pool shared with the girls' school. Long tradition of teachers coaching boys alongside specialist sports staff. Proper annual sports day with, yes, a proper victor ludorum. Inter-school fixtures plus keenly fought inter-house matches. Hard for even the bookiest bookworms not to get caught up.

Strong and longstanding drama tradition established by much-loved former history teacher. Big annual productions for juniors and seniors, the latter together with the girls. Music terrific, fine studio, large ensemble room, suite of visiting instrumental teachers and more ensembles than you can shake a stick at – including tabla. Pretty much everything musical happens with the girls. At the top end, regular scholarships to Oxbridge and other top universities and music colleges; routine membership of the National Youth Orchestra. Art feels less developed but there's a growing number of extracurricular opportunities for those looking to nurture a talent alongside their academic programme.

Loads of clubs, some offshoots of academic departments, many started and run by the boys include choral soc, music tech, Christian Union, Islamic Society, French film club, Medsoc. Fledgling D of E by popular demand. Trips, of course, masses of trips all over the place including big annual visit to WW1 battlefields. Because everyone here is so brainy you have to smile when you learn that on a residential trip to an outdoor pursuits centre in Wales – sailing, climbing, fun stuff – 'half of us went off to search for creatures and insects in the water, while the other group went off to do some ... map reading and creating water flow charts'. Sensitive to the circumstances of pupil premium students, costs are held as low as possible. One parent noted that the top-end trips here aren't nearly as snazzy as those at some other state schools. Never mind the width, feel the quality.

Very good way to get the full flavour of everything that goes on here is to read back issues of the school mag, the Chronicle, online on the school's website. Most of it is written by the boys, and boy are they literate.

Background and atmosphere: Situated in the southern suburb of on-the-up King's Heath, birthplace of UB40, bang next door to bourgeois-bohemian Moseley, the school shares its campus with Camp Hill Girls. Buildings are typical grammar school, far from swanky, decoratively holding their own against 850-odd boys – a reminder, perhaps, of the facilities gap that has opened up with independent schools, raising the question, does it really actually make any difference? Fine old assembly hall with a ceremonial chair in which to enthrone the head on big occasions. Science labs refurbished impressively in 2016; new sixth form space 2018. Don't let that give you the idea that this is a rich school. It's not. It's comfortable, though. And we really like the board where people post thank-yous to those who have been kind to them.

Camp Hill Boys was founded in 1883 along with four other free grammar schools under the King Edward VI brand by the original and ancient King Edward's School, now independent. Today the consortium embraces nine schools in the city and is a multi-academy trust dedicated to exploding any idea that grammar schools are for middle class snoots by, since 2015, promoting social mobility to the free grammars with a requirement of 20-25 per cent entry by children who qualify for pupil premium. Are these children admitted with lower test scores? Yes. Does this discriminate against non-disadvantaged children with higher scores? No, the schools have got bigger in order to accommodate them. Budget cuts would have compelled them to admit more pupils anyway; the virtue of the decision to recruit these from amongst the poorest in the city is a matter for the politics of the beholder. In any case, Birmingham's free grammars have never been middle-class enclaves.

The scheme has bedded in well at Camp Hill. Pupil premium pupils attract greater funding and this is spent on a 10-hour programme to familiarise them with the test and support them thereafter. Some parents report that 'the disadvantaged kids work harder' and tell us that 'they fit in socially very well indeed' by which they mean that no one really notices.

The school is single sex, something that perhaps sits uneasily perhaps with some contemporary attitudes, together with the 2017 appeal court judgement that a nearby faith school which segregates boys and girls is in breach of the 2010 Equalities Act. The ruling applies only to co-ed schools and there are no plans to drop the policy at Camp Hill, nor is there any call. Clearly this affects the social climate which, as a pair of trackie bottoms dangling from a high window epitomised for us, is boyish. Prone to hilarity, if you prefer. Can be beastly to each other. Could go either way. Our only concern was to determine whether boys are kind to each other and our settled conclusion after vigorous investigation is that they are. One parent told of us of a good friend whose son is 'mildly autistic and no one has ever said anything mean or malicious to him'. Away from the (mildly exasperated) gaze of girls, these are unselfconscious chaps who greatly enjoy each other's company. One mum told us that she greatly appreciates the reduced risk of her sons falling into distracting relationships – 'friends with girls good, girlfriends, not yet, please'. Reflect on this, too: unhappy boys don't get great exam results. Boys and girls come together more in the sixth form where they have their own block and hang out in each other's common rooms, girls upstairs (tidy and clean), boys downstairs (table football and pool).

Pastoral care, well-being and discipline: Conventional pastoral systems. Parents report quick and effective response to problems. Thriving house system, massively competitive – 'the boys love their house competitions', the head told us. Big focus on teamwork. House festival every five years comprises every kind of contest down to sauerkraut-eating (ah, boys). Behavioural expectations are unyieldingly established in year 7, which is exactly the sort of boundary-marking boys like. 'They are respectful,' a parent told us, 'there's no cheek here.'

Maturing relationships with teachers mean that boys going through a bit of a phase find an advocate and guide. This is definitely a school where people look out for each other.

Pupils and parents: Pupils come from all over, some journeying for up to two hours. Every ethnicity under the sun and for around a quarter of students English is a second language. Birmingham is a notably diverse, colourblind city and we saw no signs of self-segregation. On the contrary. All social backgrounds represented and for everyone we spoke to this is a big positive; their sons make friendships across them all. We spoke to one parent who had budgeted for sending her sons to the fee-paying King Edward's School. Her eldest came to an open day here, loved it and instructed his little brother to follow in his footsteps.

Vibrant PTA known as the AFS (Association of Friends of the School). It raises over £30,000 a year for 'little extras' – classroom equipment, school magazine, extracurricular activities. Volunteers help out at school events and enjoy their own social activities.

Entrance: Entry by examination in verbal, numerical and non-verbal reasoning. Admission is in rank order of qualifying scores after allocation of places for looked after children, previously looked after children and those children who are eligible for the pupil premium. The process is pitilessly Darwinian and the papers are tutor-resistant. Expect the experience to be excruciatingly stressful for your entire family.

For sixth formers a degree of flexibility. At least a grade 7 at GCSE in subjects you intend to study at A level, though the school might consider one 6 in non-science, non-maths subjects.

Exit: Most to Russell Group universities including 14 to Oxbridge in 2018. In recent years an extraordinary number to medical school (29 in 2018). Degree apprenticeships – Jaguar Land Rover is just down the road and the big accountancy firms offer attractive options – are starting to pick up a few.

Remarks: Great teaching, superabundant extracurricular programme, first-class pastoral care. A simple formula but it's not often you see it done so well. A characterful, highly likeable school at the top of its game.

King Edward VI Camp Hill School for Girls

Vicarage Road, Kings Heath, Birmingham B14 7QJ

Ages 11–18 **Pupils** 1,070 **Sixth form** 323

01214 442150
www.kechg.org.uk

Head: Since 2012 and after nine years as deputy head, Linda Johnson. Previously spells at Yardley and Sutton Coldfield, 'but this is the place for me. I love it here.' Says she was surprised to be advised to apply for the headship, and even more surprised to be awarded it. The crown sits lightly. Parents and pupils alike speak of her approachability and friendliness, though 'she's no pushover,' said a father admiringly. She writes, 'the students who leave us should be feisty, caring, confident young women.' 'She's a superb role model,' a mother told us. 'Feisty, yes, and with a wonderful sense of humour, but she doesn't take her eye off the ball and is both dedicated and fun.' That word 'fun' cropped up frequently during our tour which was, in itself, a lot of fun. 'We're fond of irony, here.' Pomposity is as rare here as weeds on the centre court at Wimbledon. Popular with staff and pupils, Mrs Johnson enjoys teaching history and 'seeing the girls in another light.'

Academic matters: In view of the entrance system, exclusively and entirely via exams, it is not surprising that the academic standards of the school are very high. In 2018, 90 per cent A*-A/9-7 at GCSE, 47 per cent A*/A at A level. The most popular A level subjects are biology, chemistry and mathematics. What is initially surprising is that those three subjects also have mixed results: the reason, the head explained, is that many parents wish their daughters to study medically-related courses. The school often recommends alternative A level subjects but parents, ambitious for their daughters, insist. The result is that a few fail to achieve their chosen course and therefore need to pursue another subject at university. The pupils learn to contend with perceived failure, which is a useful lesson. However, it is worth emphasising that the grades are extremely good and achieved through intelligent pupils and some brilliant teaching.

Games, options, the arts: There are plenty of good facilities for those who enjoy games: tennis courts, swimming pool, hockey pitches, etc. The girls play with enjoyment and success. There's a rich and varied diet of extracurricular activities. Russian, Chinese, debating, lectures, orchestras, choirs, sports, mathematics club, art club, spelling bee, engineering society etc are all pursued with enthusiasm. What is clearly outstanding is the music, in its own purpose build block. The singing is excellent, and there are concerts all over the place; recently the chamber choir and strings group went to Slovenia. Lovely music echoing out as we walked through the school, inspirational teachers and happy pupils.

The drama is excellent. It has long been the head's wish to play the fairy godmother in the annual Christmas pantomime, with script written by a member of staff, but she has never progressed beyond the wicked witch. There are more serious dramatic performances too. It is one of the wonderful features of the school that they have time for so many extracurricular activities packed into an extraordinarily busy day and alongside pursuing high academic achievement. That is a credit to their energy and the dedication of the superb staff.

Many music and drama activities are shared with the adjoining boys' school.

Background and atmosphere: One of the six selective state grammar schools which belong to the foundation of the Schools of King Edward VI in Birmingham. The history of the school on the website offers a history of education for girls since its foundation in 1883. The school moved to its current site after the Second World War. As you walk around the delightful buildings you occasionally spot a stained glass window in memory of some excellent head mistress or event.

Later additions include new STEM building – an existing lab had top to toe refurbishment after pupils won 'design a lab' competition – and a new sixth form centre. The atmosphere is lively, friendly and purposeful. Pupils greet one with a delighful openness and friendliness and clearly the relationship between staff and pupils is very happy. We witnessed some astonishingly lively and inspirational teaching and, as one of the pupils we met said, 'There is always such a buzz and excited atmosphere. The teachers are brilliant and such fun.'

Pastoral care, well-being and discipline: The pupils are bright, the staff rejoice in this; the staff give generously of their time,

K

knowledge and enthusiasms and the pupils exult in that. There are inevitably cases when people fall beneath the general feeling of happiness, and there exists a system of support and advice, both from senior girls and members of staff. Different age groups breed different problems. Tutorials are held on a regular basis and individuals supported where necessary. 'It all works very well,' said a young girl to us.

Pupils and parents: It would be hard to say which is the ethnic minority in this wonderful school of mixed cultures and backgrounds. What is apparent from the moment you enter the school is the friendships and shared pleasures that different groups seem to enjoy effortlessly. We were told of the energetic and noisy debates that can dominate religious studies lessons. It all seems healthy and conducive to friendship and understanding. Parents appreciate the trouble that is taken with their daughters and those whom we spoke to were universally happy with what was going on in the school.

Entrance: There are 150 year 7 places. Entry is by examination in non-verbal and verbal reasoning and maths. The school now prioritises up to 20 per cent of children on pupil premium who have achieved the qualifying score, so the charity founded in 1552 is returning to its original purpose of helping less privileged children. Much liaison with local primary schools, and the latest admission criteria reflect this aim without lowering standards.

K

Exit: Vast majority – about 85 per cent – stay on to the sixth form. The most popular careers centre around medically related fields (19 places in 2018). Excellent advice about A level courses, career possibilities and requirements. Most pupils go on to good universities where they perform well; Birmingham, Manchester and Aston most popular recently. Four to Oxbridge in 2018.

Remarks: This is an extraordinarily good school. It demonstrates how it is possible to set high standards and to achieve them not through perfecting the technique of sitting exams, but as a result of talented teachers sharing their interests with intelligent pupils. It is absolutely not an exam hothouse. It is a school of great happiness and joy, celebrating intelligence and love of learning. Nothing stuffy, nothing pretentious, just love of excellence.

King Edward VI Five Ways School

Scotland Lane, Bartley Green, Birmingham B32 4BT

Ages 11–18 **Pupils** 1,302 (879 boys, 423 girls) **Sixth form** 401

01214 753535
www.kefw.org

Head: Since 2012, Yvonne Wilkinson BA PGCE NPQH. Read geography at Northumbria University. She was the first ever female deputy and acting head here during an interregnum before joining Holy Trinity School Worcester as head. Then on as head to Gateways School in Leeds, a girls only senior school where she was responsible for introducing boys (up to age 11) before being invited back to Five Ways to become the first female head.

Mrs Wilkinson is, in more ways than one, the Real Thing, and is leading the school to new heights and breadth. While it's impossible to believe her career is the result of ruthless greasy pole climbing or excessive restlessness, it seems that King Edward VI Five Ways was always her Holy Grail. If there was any restlessness, it is over now. No plans to move on and if there were, we are told, many staff and pupils would barricade her in.

Friendly and forthcoming towards pupils and staff (though on her own admission she cannot know everyone), those who do know her speak warmly of her friendliness, encouragement and lively sense of humour. She is articulate, thoughtful, witty and gutsy, when necessary – Yorkshire, but not the dour, monosyllabic kind. Listens generously; addresses the whole school regularly in assemblies and 'has interesting things to say,' one worldly senior pupil told us.

What she values most, she says, is the sense of warmth and friendliness that pervades the school. Ground staff, always a useful indicator of what schools are like, volunteered that to us and we felt it from the moment we walked in. All the King Edward schools are involved in visiting primary schools and establishing links to help widen the list of applicants. Even more effective is that primary school children visit Five Ways and attend classes prepared and run by sixth formers. We met a group preparing for a music class using rhythm and tone. The involvement, the thought, the care and the skill they showed in working out the best ways of making the lessons interesting and fun was wonderful to observe. 'We want to encourage children from all backgrounds. We have a vast catchment area. The only criteria for coming here is success with exams. Once they're here we want them to feel they can achieve anything worthwhile.'

Mrs Wilkinson is married to Robin, an award winning narrow boat designer and engineer. They have two children, both working towards careers in medicine.

Academic matters: The head is on record as saying that she's not really particularly keen on league tables but feels honour bound to shout with joy when the results are really good. Inevitably she does a lot of shouting, though time and time again we were assured by pupils and staff that 'this is not an exam factory.' We saw some wonderfully clear and challenging teaching and witnessed bright, motivated pupils who responded with genuine involvement.

'The curriculum is student led,' the head told us. 'We start with a blank page and see where the demand lies.' Some 28 subjects on offer at A level – all the regulars plus more niche choices such as philosophy, product design, geology and classical civilisation. Most popular were maths, chemistry and biology; the least popular Spanish, religious studies and Latin. At A level in 2018, 50 per cent A*/A grades (75 per cent A*-B). GCSE results impressive with 71 per cent A*-A/9-7.

Without diminishing the importance of the early stages of the school, it is the sixth form which seems to be the jewel in the crown. The sixth form prospectus is a work of art, and to be fair, there is a good story to tell: lots of subjects to choose from and a wonderful sixth form centre in which to draw breath, drink coffee, discuss the Great Things of life. The tutors and career guidance counsellors clearly do much to help and we were constantly told how helpful everyone had been. 'The induction is wonderful,' a parent told us. Many do the EPQ, and the ACE (Alternative Curriculum Education) programme is compulsory.

Games, options, the arts: The number of extracurricular activities supports the feeling that there is life beyond exams. The majority take place during the lunch hour and include fencing, DofE, chess, debating and no fewer than seven drama productions a year. And for those pupils who can't get enough of their academic subjects there are maths and biology workshops.

Excellent sporting facilities. A cricket pitch which could host county games and with a wide fixture list; a swimming pool with sound and lighting for aquarobics. (Please, no synchronised swimming.) Good rugby pitches, new artificial grass pitch, sports hall, tennis/netball courts and a climbing wall. Virtually everything you can think of. Sport is where house rivalry becomes most obvious and involved, there's inter-house rugby, football, netball, hockey, cricket and the notorious tug o' war. More of that later.

On the arts side there are drama and dance studios and music technology. We didn't see a great deal of art or music during our visit, although the facilities are in place, and we were told that about a tenth learn an instrument. Choir, orchestra, ensemble, samba and swing band practices must make for very harmonious lunch times.

Recent rugby tour to Canada and other sports tours to Italy, Barbados and Ireland. Lots of trips abroad. Eight recently, including Africa, India, China, New Zealand and Chicago. Five Ways; five continents.

Background and atmosphere: Originally sited on the Hagley Road at Five Ways, the school moved from its congested location in 1958 to current attractive 30-acre site in Bartley Green, seven miles to the south west of the city centre, bordering Bartley Reservoir and looking out to Frankley Beeches – even boasts own observatory. The only co-ed state grammar school in the West Midlands.

The grounds are immaculate – bravo, that delightful gardener – and the whole campus feels pleasantly contained and smartly arranged. Arriving at reception, and we did it more than once, is a delightful experience, not only because of the welcome given from behind the counter but also the smiling, friendly pupils.

Among the entertaining literature is a pamphlet entitled Five Ways in Figures. Rather fun, it's almost a spoof on the mania for statistics, but it tells you very succinctly a lot about the school: £40,596 was raised for charity and fees are £0! There are 1,300 library books, a 100 per cent exam pass rate and KEFW is working with 24 local primary schools. It claims to be one of the top five co-ed state grammar schools nationally. A veritable feast of stats.

Pastoral care, well-being and discipline: 'Firm and fair' was the response we received when we asked about discipline. That would seem a reasonable summary, judging by the behaviour of the pupils we saw, both collectively and individually. In groups they were friendly and helpful when accosted; on their own they were forthcoming and easy. Many told us how safe and happy the school felt. Parents seemed pleased with the arrangements and the trouble the school goes to help the unsettled, the anxious and the nervous.

Head believes in trusting people, hence BYOD (bring your own device). This vastly reduces time spent policing individual use of phones, tablets and laptops and, as Mrs Wilkinson says, wasting valuable hours and energy poking around suspiciously looking for what isn't there, instead of rejoicing in what is there.

One boy told us at some length how he felt responsible for the school in the sense that if he behaved badly – he wasn't specific – he would be weakening the structure of the school's society. 'The school is part of me as much as I am part of the school.' He had clearly given the matter a great deal of thought. He wasn't alone in that.

Pupils and parents: There are 60 different ethnic backgrounds in the school and pupils with 30 different home languages (so says Five Ways in Figures). About two-thirds boys. Parents we spoke to expressed pride and pleasure in having their children at the school. They come from a wide variety of backgrounds but feel that the melange works very well. So do the pupils with whom we chatted. Distances deter not: pupils come from all over Birmingham and 40 per cent beyond: Worcestershire and the Black Country.

Entrance: Very competitive. For entry at 11, 1,800 pupils chase 180 places. Priority for up to 20 per cent of places is given to those on pupil premium and looked after children, as long as they achieve a 'qualifying score', otherwise anonymous pupils accepted by strict order of scores. No interviews, no concessions for siblings or proximity to the school. One boy told us of the examination, 'I went in with a name and came out as a number.... But here I am.'

Sixth form applicants (including those from within the school) must apply formally. Minimum requirement is GCSE 9-7 in A level subjects plus at least grade 6 in English and maths. The school is hunting for new pupils and is shameless in its intentions. 'We welcome applications from students currently studying in other schools....We typically offer about 50 places to external applicants.'

Exit: About 20 per cent leaves after GCSEs, mostly those who failed to get the grades needed for sixth form. Almost all sixth form leavers go on to traditional universities. Eight to Oxbridge in 2018 and 23 medics. Birmingham, Leeds, Nottingham and Sheffield all popular destinations.

Remarks: KEFW is a cracking good school of its genre and, in terms of naked exam scores, out-punches many high profile independents. The pupils we met were universally articulate, natural and forthcoming. We returned the day after our visit to watch the inter-house tug of war. Here were the young academics, apparently taking the whole thing as seriously as experiments in the chemistry labs. To the untutored eye, both looked equally dangerous. But house rivalry, though fierce, was nothing to the tug of war – and war it was – between senior boys and teachers. Could that seriously academic member of staff, seen only the day before disseminating knowledge so interestingly and with such clarity, be the same man who was lying on his back, purple in the face and muttering eternal curses because his side had lost? Yes, this is an academic school, but that's by no means all. There's plenty of fun to be had too.

King Edward VI High School for Girls

Edgbaston Park Road, Birmingham B15 2UB

Ages 11–18 **Pupils** 602 **Sixth form** 152

Fees: £12,888 pa

01214 721834
www.kehs.org.uk

Principal: Since 2013, Ann Clark. Won a scholarship to Girton College, Cambridge, to read modern languages, specifically German, French and Spanish. Now teaches German A level, and French to half of the new girls. 'It's good to see how they're settling down socially and academically.' They, for their part, enjoy being taught by her. 'She's very approachable and clear headed,' seems the most common verdict. Attributes, incidentally, acknowledged by parents who like her a lot. She has more than 25 years' experience of teaching in state schools and university, and before becoming principal was deputy head of Heanor Gate Science College in Derbyshire.

Mrs Clark does not belong to the duchess style of head: she doesn't sweep along corridors scattering staff and pupils. There is a gentle elegance and grace about her, a quick and ready sense of humour combined with strong inner strength. Very experienced and wholly lacking in pomposity, she has two children of her own. She understands the ethos of the school and is building on it. Confesses to loving it all. Parents we spoke to were full of admiration.

Academic matters: One inspirational teacher – we didn't meet any who were not obviously passionate and fired up about teaching and, noticeably, not just their own subject – told us there were no cohorts, no clipped wings, no shaping and conscious moulding into a 'type'. What is required and encouraged is intellectual curiosity: 'creative living and critical thinking'. 'Trouthe schal delyvere' ('Truth will conquer'): those words of Chaucer appear above an entrance to the school. The great man would have been pleased, as was a recent inspector who wrote: 'The school has established a practice of probing enquiry and clear investigation in lessons, rather than delivery and acceptance. This has been welcomed by the pupils, who consequently participate eagerly and successfully.' This we can confirm and very refreshing it is.

'We take it all in our stride,' one girl told us without a trace of arrogance or smugness. The atmosphere, the energetic quest for knowledge and discovery is well summed up on the school's website: 'The ethos of the school is one whereby we want all girls to develop a love of learning and respect for the life of the intellect that will continue throughout their lives as well as achieving highly in public examinations.' In 2018, 76 per cent of A level grades were A*/A and 91 per cent A*/B. At GCSE in the same year 92 per cent of grades were A*-A/9-7. More important than any of this is the breadth: about 30 per cent of A level candidates do mixed arts and science subjects. The most popular subjects are maths, chemistry and biology followed by history and English. Good results; happy candidates. Everyone studies at least one language and linguists can now add either Italian or Greek ab initio. Years 9s can choose two creative subjects, and year 10 enrichment options range from engineering to food to sports leadership.

K

The academic facilities are excellent. There are seemingly hundreds of science labs, all impressively kitted out. Wonderful library where the librarian recommends, introduces and discusses with the girls what they have read. Pupils and staff blog tirelessly on a huge variety of subjects: uplifting blogs on how to keep happy; challenging blogs on matters of the intellect. One girl described the blogs as the beating heart of KEHS.

Games, options, the arts: A previous visitor remarked, 'this is one of the few schools where enrichment is genuinely as important as the academic'. In fact they feed on each other and the energy generated by both creates a powerful, tangible warmth. The cookery classes for third year pupils, for instance, combine the joys of creating delicious food with scientific considerations involving different herbs and spices, temperatures and mixtures. When we visited, discussions were ranging from developing countries to healthy living, from farming to supermarkets.

Art is extraordinarily good in the bright, open studios. Superb ceramics. Amazing drama, where we saw some wonderfully innovative work involving movement and dance, creativity and imagination, all run by a teacher whose energy and passion would have made a Catherine wheel seem like a jacket potato. KEHS has one of the finest concert halls of any school we have visited: the Ruddock Performing Arts Centre, shared with the boys of King Edward's School next door. Bags of music, with a tremendous variety of concerts, from smaller intimate lunch times to large, sweepingly impressive symphony concerts. Parents spoke of them with much enthusiasm, even if they didn't have a child of their own playing.

Sport is prolific with excellent results. Swimming, football, hockey, netball, badminton, fencing, tennis, indoor rowing, snorkelling, gymnastics, on and on goes the list. You name it, it's available and KEHS girls, as one pupil told us, are up for anything. Tours abroad, including a memorable and all-conquering trip to the Caribbean, are a joyous part of the overall experience.

Wonderfully bright and enthusiastic sports staff, genuinely involved in all round well-being. Moments of activity and physical involvement are balanced with moments of silence, of stillness, 'de-stressing': the effect spreads right through the school. The result is that everything – intellectual and academic activities, music and art, friendships and sporting rivalries – all seem to blend into one harmonious whole.

The sums of money raised for local and international charities, the different workshops run for local primary schools, the visits and the hostings all confirm the responsible and generous position of the school reaching out to its surrounding community.

Background and atmosphere: 'What a lot of schools were founded during the brief reign of Edward V1,' someone said to us the other day. It isn't quite like that – only King Edward's School for boys was founded by Edward VI – but there are eight schools of King Edward VI in Birmingham, six state and two, including this one, independent. All are part of the same foundation and all bursarial work is carried out jointly. The high school was founded in 1883; it followed King Edward's School to its present site next door, in fact adjoining, in 1940. Thus, as is often said, both schools have the best of both worlds. The campus is delightful: pleasing red-brick (but not the aggressive shade), with a dignified sense of space. The result is an atmosphere of happy, busy activity: intent but not too intense. Just as the girls felt they could take things in their stride, so the staff seemed happy to stride along with them. One mum told us of the excellent individual help girls could expect from their teachers, at almost any time. Most schools boast of the happy family atmosphere of their establishments. We heard no-one extolling happiness here. No need to: it just is.

Pastoral care, well-being and discipline: 'It's all built on trust', we were told. As a result there is no obvious hierarchy amongst the girls, no prefectorial system, no head girl. But there is an unobtrusive structure of which everyone is aware. It's based on an awareness of those around you, a shared endeavour and common sense. Girls who had recently arrived spoke appreciatively of the warmth of the welcome they had received and the friendliness of the older girls. Sixth form tutor groups are composed of a mixture of upper and lower sixth. This not only dilutes any stultifying sense of hierarchy, but makes it much easier for new sixth form girls to settle in. The sixth form council meets regularly with the director of sixth form to discuss any suggestions and ideas. When a new sixth form centre was being considered, there was much discussion about where it should go. In the end it was decided to adapt rooms within the main building so as to avoid any feeling of separateness or aloofness. Jolly nice it is, too. The cake looked delicious.

Pupils and parents: Wherever we went we were met with open friendliness, a willingness to chat and ready smiles. There were plenty of moments of quick and enjoyable repartee. They were amusing about the business of sharing buses and transport with the boys at King Edward's. Both groups come from a wide catchment area: Lichfield, Bromsgrove, Wolverhampton, Solihull etc. A healthy and delightfully friendly ethnic mixture ('we love arguing in religious studies'). Parents, mostly from professional backgrounds, feel involved and 'part of the community.'

Entrance: The examinations are particular to KEHS. At 11+, in October of year 6, three papers (two English, one maths) – no reasoning. Emphasis is on creativity and potential rather than what the candidate has been taught. Applicants might be faced with some creative writing or a poem to elucidate. Occasional places at 12+ and post-GCSE into the sixth form. Winning a place into the sixth form is, as with everything here, more than just a question of grades. There are exams in the relevant subjects, 'tough but fair' interviews and consideration of the previous school's report.

Exit: Very few leave after GCSEs. KEHS does not offload low performers and remains faithful to its commitment. The school's integrity is justly rewarded: very, very few drop below a C grade and most go on to a good spread of universities (Birmingham, King's College London, Durham, St Andrews, UCL currently popular), generous helpings of Oxbridge (15 in 2018) and medicine (12 medics and two dentists in 2018)), and thence to impressive jobs. One off to Savannah College of Art and Design, USA, with a scholarship. The variety of university subjects chosen (from fashion design to international relations) is impressive and a tribute to the school's help and advice, encouraging the girls to pursue their own particular passions.

Money matters: 'Currently almost a quarter of girls in the school receive some form of bursary support thanks to funding provided principally by the Foundation but also by alumnae through donations and bequests.' There are energetic and determined efforts to make the school increasingly accessible financially to a wider range of parents. This is proving successful.

Remarks: This is certainly a top academic school but it's more than that. It's a community where intellectual lessons are imbibed for life along with emotional and creative experiences; where disappointments are often confronted with courage and triumphs with modest pleasure. And lest this all sounds a bit earnest, it is worth emphasising that we were constantly made aware by lively, cheerful pupils – and staff – that for the most part life at KEHS, Birmingham is a lot of fun.

King Edward VI School (Stratford-upon-Avon)

Chapel Lane, Stratford-upon-Avon, Warwickshire CV37 6BE

Ages 11-18 **Pupils** 744 **Sixth form** 300 (130 girls)

01789 293351
www.kes.net

Headmaster: Since 2010, Bennet Carr BA FRGS (late 40s). Hails from Hertfordshire, took a degree in geography at QMC, and a PGCE at the Institute of Education, which sent him on a placement to a large inner city comprehensive school. 'I nearly didn't teach after that', he trembled, but fortunately summoned his sang-froid and joined The Bishop's Stortford High School, rising to assistant head, followed by St Olave's Grammar School in Kent, as an inspiring deputy. A fascinating tour guide to the historic buildings of King Edward VI School (known locally as KES), he declares, 'Inside I'm a historian, but I had a brilliant geography teacher at school', which prompts the recognition, 'The influence we (teachers) have is huge'.

He is knowledgeable about the school's heritage, 'Shakespeare is a global brand', and can indicate which portrait from the gallery was the model for Shakespeare's lampooned schoolmaster, Sir Hugh Evans, and identify the frescoes in the chapel whitewashed in the reformation by John Shakespeare, the Bard's father. In the Tudor schoolroom, he explains the meaning of 'sixth form' by indicating the sixth oak bench to be reached when the boys moved up the class. 'It's nice for parents to say their children go to Shakespeare's school,' he accepts, 'but I want it to be a brilliant school because the children have an outstanding experience here'.

Since his appointment at KES, Carr has increased the size of the school by nearly 200, introduced Mandarin as a compulsory modern language and improved the entrance chances for disadvantaged children. Married, with two daughters at local state schools, he is a wide-ranging conversationalist, a stickler for a smart uniform and high standards, 'My mantra is only the best will do'. From parents we heard, 'He has a magical ability to engage with people. He knows who you are and talks about things that are relevant to you at the drop of a hat' and 'He's very, very hands-on. He's more normal than most heads in his position'.

Academic matters: In 2018, at GCSE, 74 per cent A*-A/7-9 grades. At A level, 87 per cent A*/B grades and 63 per cent A*/A grades. Despite stellar results, the head cautions at our calling it a highly academic school: 'We are an academic school, but not an exam factory'. Arriving in the lower school (years 7 and 8) children join one of three classes of 30, while in middle school (KS4 over three years, 9-11), the class sizes reduce slightly according to subject. 'Our greatest strength is our small size', explains Carr. A parent added, 'literally, everybody knows everyone else's names'.

The younger children follow the national curriculum, with the addition of Mandarin, Latin and computer science. The head believes the introduction of Mandarin is a good preparation for the world beyond school. 'If you can speak English, Mandarin and Spanish, you can speak to virtually everyone in the world, one way or another'. At GCSE, all take triple science, with more unusual options including Latin, Greek and ancient history. The once obligatory RS GCSE has been replaced by a Higher Project Qualification option. Twenty-one A level choices for the co-ed sixth form include drama, psychology and PE. A parent told us, 'The school is brilliant at getting at talent and giving the kids the opportunity to make the most of it'. Another added, 'There's a very, very tight focus on academic performance'.

Small numbers of EAL children, although the head commented that the school is more ethnically diverse than the town. Nine per cent of students on the SEN register, with needs ranging from dyslexia to ADHD and Asperger's. Support is provided within the class, one-to-one and in small groups, with outside agencies engaged when required. SENCo's intervention praised by parents. 'She offered something way beyond what I expected in terms of flexibility,' said one parent. 'We've been overwhelmed with support'.

'There are a mix of young teachers and a number who have been here for donkey's years', one staff member told us. Unsurprisingly, we heard that there was no shortage of people applying. 'They are all experts in their area,' said the head. 'My job is to provide them with an environment in which they thrive'. In addition to the full timers, there are 15 visiting music teachers and a team of ex-pro sports coaches on the wider staff. One boy's verdict on his teacher, 'She's the cleverest person I've ever met in my life'.

Games, options, the arts: Huge photographs on the exterior walls of red-faced students scoring a try or captaining an eight down the river tell you it is a sporty school. The sixth form attracts athletic girls keen to play in one of the three netball teams, or try out for women's rugby. The head referees one of 13 rugby teams which play on Saturday, against a range of grammar and independent schools. As well as rugby, hockey, netball, athletics and cricket, boys and girls can choose from a range of healthy exertions including fencing and squash at the town's courts. They also share the town's boathouse and boast a Paralympic medallist old boy. Regular international sports tours.

Art was alive and kicking on the walls of the school, in the form of huge canvases, including one interactive portrait of a KES schoolboy which could be photoshopped in situ with a click of a telephone screen. As well as the art studio, where we witnessed a year 12 group studying Jenny Saville's style, we found a creative hut, full of attentive sixth formers quietly working, unsupervised, on their notebooks. 'The art department is absolutely superb', parents enthused.

Music is strong, possibly due to the free term's instrument tuition offered in year 7; 'lots of kids fell in love with it,' we heard from one boy. The introductory offer extends to giving boys a taste of ensemble playing. A wealth of orchestras and choirs (we were curious to hear King Eddie's Revival Big Band) and some children form their own ensembles. There are concerts in the chapel, including for Remembrance Day and a carol service. An annual celebration of Shakespeare's birthday was introduced by a Victorian predecessor, and students take pride of place: heading the town's procession (ambassadors and other dignitaries follow behind) and presenting a swan feather quill to the effigy of the Upstart Crow at Holy Trinity Church.

K

Shakespeare spent six years at the school, under a master educated at Merchant Taylor's school, Thomas Jenkins, who taught rhetoric and Latin, with a Welsh lilt, through the use of drama. The tradition persists today and the school nurtures its own troupe of boy players, Edward's Boys, who perform early modern plays with all-male casts, often in historic venues, such as Shakespeare's Globe and Middle Temple Hall. The master of revels is Perry Mills, deputy head (pastoral); 'he's very approachable and funny,' say parents. It has its own website, informs undergraduate English studies and records little-performed pieces, used by the BBC and university departments. 'They are the best tutor group in the school,' says the head. 'People fly in from all over the world to see them'.

Children are expected to take part in the broader opportunities on offer. Extracurricular activities are legion, with over 60 clubs to choose from, as well as sports and performance societies. 'There's more extracurricular in a week than in a whole term at other schools,' said one parent, though another pointed out that quite a few boys don't take part in many. We noticed Warhammer club, Leonardo club, robotics and LGBT Pride. Annual drama productions, described by one parent as 'Shakespeare with a twist'; another remarked, 'so much better than the RSC'. The school regularly takes a troupe to the Edinburgh Fringe.

Background and atmosphere: The Memorial Library contains the school archive, an emporium of memorabilia, musty blazers, sports trophies and documents about KES's long history. We learn that the school was established in 1295 by The Guild of the Holy Cross (hence the yellow cross insignia, which distinguishes it from other Edward VI schools). The boy king, Edward VI, suppressed the guild and granted its former property to the town, making the splendid Guildhall both the town council chamber (presided over by Shakespeare senior) and 'big school', a schoolroom on the upper floor. The boy poet would have sat on the blackened forms, under the hammer beam ceiling. The room still contains paired desks, covered in centuries of inky blots and engravings, and is used by the pupils each morning, open to the public as part of Stratford's tourist experience in the afternoons.

Shakespeare would have traversed the old courtyard to say prayers in the guild chapel, whose apocalyptic murals of devils falling into pits of sulphur are visible from where today's students sit each week for assembly. The old vicarage next door is now the head's house; the Pedagogue's House, a creaking, timber-beamed neighbour, contains the head's study and an adjacent almshouse, from 16th century, was the nation's first purpose built schoolroom. Odds Bodkins! It is hard not to be bowled over by all this living history. The children are tickled at being asked to pose in their uniform with tourists; 'It's really nice to study Shakespeare GCSE in a place that has a connection', said one boy. A mum confided, 'I think they get sick of it'.

But behind the stage-set beauty of the historic site buzzes a lively, modern school. Keeping the quadrangle design, the classrooms of the modern block open out to a central courtyard. Here we toured the sixth form common room: no-one was using the comfortable seating, though some worked in their private study room above, replete with computer stations. History, geography and philosophy have departments nearby. DT and design studios are on the ground floor of the nearby Fitzmaurice Building, while a shiny metal staircase led us into Dyson building and the strong science department. We stumbled in on a class of year 11 biologists in goggles, testing temperature change on the decay of fresh milk in bright pink test tubes. An invisible Ariel (aka biology teacher) had put on some classical music in the background to aid concentration. The newest building, with English and computing departments, is named after Richard Spender (alumnus 1930-1940). Climb up to meet the librarian, who takes suggestions from staff and students. 'They read a lot,' she said.

Despite being in the centre of the town, a stone's throw from the river and RSC theatres, the school does not feel cramped. We found students rehearsing in the purpose-built drama studio, devising an A level performance piece about dementia. The music department stretches to eight practice rooms with keyboards and a mixing studio, as well as a mountain of music cases in the instrument store. The students 'who speak the tongue that Shakespeare spake' also learn French, German, Spanish and Mandarin, in the language centre. We particularly liked the photos of baguettes on the door to the French department.

A large sports hall is used for PE and whole school events; rugby and cricket are played at an external site; no all weather pitches yet, but plans are afoot. We heard from one parent, 'the changing facilities are quite tired; could do with a lick of paint'. In a smaller gym, boys were perfecting rugby passes, with motivating slogans emblazoned on the walls. We particularly liked, 'Hard work beats talent, if talent doesn't work hard'. Loud music and perspiration pulsed from The Cave, a fitness suite where students can use the treadmill, exercise bike or lift weights in their free time or pop into the sixth form café next door for cold food, as an alternative to going into the town. The main school canteen offers a hot menu on a three week rota, including pasta, roast lunch, and a vegetarian option. 'There's scope for improvement there,' said a parent.

Pastoral care, well-being and discipline: Vertical tutor groups in four houses, integrating children from from years 8-13. Older students act as role models and mentors for younger ones, supervised by a group tutor. 'If you were experiencing anything like bullying that is the first place you would go to', we were told by a pupil. There's also an online forum, monitored by a member of staff, which allows students to post anonymous or named messages. 'You never get crowd control issues at KES,' a mum said. As to cyber-bullying, 'All schools are faced with a challenge', explained the head. 'We allow phones, but they are not permitted to use them in school time. We try and treat them like adults'.

The school's code of behaviour is made clear from the outset and students we met were aware of a range of sanctions in response to poor conduct: first a verbal warning, rising to detention in lunch time or, at worst, cry 'Havoc' and let slip the headmaster's Saturday detention. Parents were in favour, 'I've been delighted that it's quite strict...those rules are there for life later on'.

Pupils and parents: The students look smart in dark blue blazer, navy and gold jumper and gold stripy tie, denoting the wearer's house. 'Apparel oft proclaims the man,' writes Shakespeare or, as the head puts it, 'Uniform matters', and the students have obviously taken it to heart. 'It makes you very recognisable,' said one boy. 'It comes with a responsibility,' said a mum. Sixth formers wear dark suits, some with the colours tie, awarded for outstanding talent, leadership or success in extracurricular activities. Our guides were mature, polite and enthusiastic to be there. 'Everyone wants everyone else to do well', one girl told us. We were met by the Duty Boy at reception, a seat at the front desk taken by each junior boy, to get to know the comings and goings of the school and polish his interpersonal skills with visitors. Communication with parents, we learned, was 'very open' and 'they encourage people to raise issues'.

'Fundraising is a big deal,' one mum told us, with three parents' associations raising funds for arts, sports and more general needs like school trips. The arts fundraisers provide a bar at school concerts, to lubricate the intervals and subsidise future shows in the process; very civilised, we thought. Nascent friendships between parents blossom at the Saturday sports fixtures: 'they do lift shares and team up after school'.

Entrance: Warwickshire grammar schools selective entrance procedure, with competitive written exams, no interview. The head meets all new students before entry in September, and transition staff support year 7s. Catchment area covers a 16 mile radius, including Warwickshire, Oxfordshire, Worcestershire, Coventry and Solihull. A parent said, 'I don't think it's good for kids to be travelling; I'd rather the pass rate go down a bit than it be a magnet school. I wanted my son to have local friends in the town'. The 300 sixth form places, including 130 for girls, need 54 points at GCSE, for students applying from dozens of different schools. No catchment at this stage, just the commitment to take a full part in school life. Around 90 per cent of year 11s stay on to the sixth form.

Exit: Some 42 destination universities, including 16 to Oxbridge and 10 medics in 2018. Choices include Bristol, Durham, Edinburgh, York, Leeds, UCL and Exeter, also degree apprenticeships at Jaguar Land Rover. A popular careers adviser helps with applications.

Money matters: State funded grammar school. Annual voluntary donation of £365 per child (the pound-a-day-scheme) to cover non-academic extras. Leaving scholarships awarded to support university places.

Remarks: A rich pageant of English history provides the backdrop for Shakespeare's school. The inspired staff, led from the front by the head, tread the illustrious path of their forebears in teaching to dizzying standards, while today's happy breed of students enjoy a banquet of extracurricular opportunities and obtain first class places at university. So when Shakespeare wrote 'Thou has most treacherously corrupted the youth of the realm in erecting a grammar school' we think he must have had somewhere else in mind.

King Edward's School, Birmingham

Edgbaston Park Road, Birmingham B15 2UA

Ages 11–18 **Pupils** 874 **Sixth form** 226 **C of E**

Fees: £13,230 pa

01214 721672
www.kes.org.uk

Acting chief master: Keith Phillips, second master, is holding the fort following the resignation in August 2018 of previous head Dr Mark Fenton. Educated at the University of Birmingham (modern languages), has taught at King Edward's School for 31 years, 20 as deputy head. Keen rugby player, cricketer, cyclist and music-lover.

The new chief master from September 2019 – and the first female head in the school's 466 year history – will be Katy Ricks, currently head of Sevenoaks School. First class English degree from Oxford; spent three years here teaching English in the early part of her career. Has also taught at St Paul's Girls, St Edward's Oxford, Latymer Upper and Highgate (deputy head).

K

Academic matters: A seriously brainy school where like-minded boys spark off each other and achieve extraordinary things. That's as may be given the highly competitive selection process – these are, after all, some of the brightest boys in the UK's second city. But there's a pervasive culture of aspiration here and in general the boys set their own expectations of themselves as high as the school. Teaching is praised by both parents and students. One student told us, 'They want you to understand the subject, not just pass the exam'. KES is a comfortable berth for good teachers – where would you move to from here? – and some of them have been here for a long time.

The school ditched A levels in favour of the IB in 2012, the first school in the UK to do so in one fell swoop, at the time a breathtaking initiative leaving local schools muttering 'Are they nuts?' The rationale is that the IB is better suited to bright students, it develops independent thinking and calls for rigorous time management, all skills that one parent approvingly endorsed as 'right for the global marketplace'. Right for university, too. Parents also like the breadth required by IB: the same parent said, 'My son would have happily dropped a language if he'd been doing A levels'.

Unsurprisingly, maths and sciences are popular in a school where so many want to be doctors. Languages both ancient and modern are strong at IB and GCSE. Vocational considerations prevail at IB with economics coming through strongly and only small numbers opting for art, drama or music. Philosophy, though, has a fan club.

Results rival any school in the country. In 2018 at GCSE, 85 per cent A*-A/9-7 (65 per cent A*/9-8). IB results are equally impressive, with an average points score 37 and three KES students out of 146 worldwide got a perfect score of 45.

Special educational needs supported. Some dyslexia, dyspraxia and ASD, light to moderate, because you need to be able to keep up. Excellent learning support department also addresses self-esteem issues and offers emotional reinforcement one-to-one. This can be a pressured environment, the pressure often self-imposed, so there's keen awareness of the perils of self-harm and burnout. Especially efficacious is the mentoring support given by sixth formers. Inevitably, some boys, for all sorts of reasons, struggle. By way of balance, this is unquestionably a school where boys develop self-confidence. On the day of our visit, assembly was led by a 14 year-old.

Games, options, the arts: 'It's not all about exams,' says the school, and means it. These boys' brains ought to look after them well enough in the classroom; the important thing is that they learn also to make the most of themselves as people by finding out what else they can do – and can't, for there are valuable lessons in falling short. The head of sport told us, 'Most academically successful boys also tend to be the most engaged in broader activities'. If they can have fun at the same time, so much the better. Extracurricular activities are supposed to be fun.

So there's a busy sports programme together with great facilities (new £5 million sports centre for 2018 with sports hall, cardiovascular fitness room, multipurpose space, classroom and changing rooms). Gym open from 7am to 7pm. True to the school's good, old-fashioned grammar school traditions, sport is a big thing. The head of sport, an ex-professional front row forward, reeled off a list of staff who've represented England/GB. But, he was also at some pains to tell us, those who aren't sporty aren't made to endure freezing misery, they can choose from 22 'sporting activities' which include ultimate frisbee. He's a kind man and we believe him, noting only that everyone must take part in the annual inter-house cross-country run. The school fields 86 teams in 19 sports. Water polo is what they do best, but it's rugby that rouses the deepest passions. The fixture vs Bromsgrove has been contested since 1875, making it one of the oldest in the country. Rivalry with Solihull and Warwick go back almost as far. A non-sporty boy would do well to evince an interest. The head of sport is proud of the number of boys of South Asian heritage who get involved in contact sports.

The head of art acknowledges that it is a 'constant battle' to persuade boys and their parents of the value of art when they are focused on academic success and entry to high-earning professions. To mitigate this he stresses the value of creativity and self-expression: 'If they can't be artist practitioners then at least they can be thinkers'. One art lesson a week for all for the first three years. Gallery visits. Those who opt in at GCSE and IB have good studios and tuition. We saw some fine work.

Drama massively popular – the more so since it happens with the girls' high school next door. Big annual production a talking point for weeks after. Lunchtime club and Friday afternoon activity. Specialist techie team. The best are urged to audition for the National Youth Theatre, indicative of a professionalism of approach. Some of the students' devised work can deal with challenging social issues, eg gender transitioning. Given that many boys here come from socially conservative homes it is a tribute to them and the school that these productions are received with open-mindedness.

Music is the jewel in the crown. We all know what school music sounds like, we've all sat through school concerts and willed on heroic orchestral performances, squawks and parps and all. Well, the King Edward's Symphony Orchestra, comprising also girls from the high school, sounds, we can tell you, just like a real orchestra and we wish there was a video clip on the school's website to attest to it. This is unquestionably some of the best music-making in the country. Conventional wisdom holds that boys don't like singing, so your ears will prick up when we tell you there's a 170-strong boy voice choir. In addition to ensembles of all sorts there's also a composers' club. And a simply brilliant director of music.

The school's symphony orchestra sometimes plays the Birmingham Symphony Hall but the main performing space is the superb £11 million Ruddock Performing Arts centre, shared with the high school, the cost substantially borne by a grateful former pupil. Plays are performed here too, smaller productions in an integral black-box space.

Friday afternoons at KES are very sensibly given over to extracurricular activities. There are something like 50 clubs to choose from, many of them notably intellectual – philosophy, literature, politics, programming, debating. Unique to the school and deliciously nutty is the historical re-enactment group which gets to besiege castles around the country. There's outward bounding, community service and a popular cadet force. Oh, and trips, of course, masses of trips and expeditions. We especially like the year 7 camping trip to Staffordshire, a good bonding experience.

Background and atmosphere: In his Rotters' Club, author and former pupil Jonathan Coe has a character say, 'It is a disadvantage being located in Birmingham, which the rest of the country loathes, and with good reason'. To be sure, Brum is very much its own place which, given its culture of deadpan understatement, doesn't blow its own trumpet as loudly as it might. We found a much better valuation of this multicultural city by another former pupil addressed to today's pupils: 'You're at ease with diversity, you possess a cultural fluency and you are blessed with a groundedness, an extraordinary ordinariness that comes from being in a city like this. This social dexterity, this winning combination of humility and confidence, will stand you in very good stead.' Says it all.

Founded in 1552, moved to the leafy suburb of Edgbaston in 1936. Handsome red-brick buildings in, to coin a genre, grammar school Tudor, together with some good looking later buildings on a 50-acre site a stone's throw from the university. Classy. Associated with a multi-academy trust which incorporates seven voluntary-aided and two independent schools. Together, these schools constitute an expressway for the brightest boys and girls in the city, all of them committed to opening themselves up to the most disadvantaged and standing on its head any perception that grammar schools have been colonised by the middle classes.

Under the direct grant scheme (pre-1975), 80 per cent of boys at KES enjoyed free places and the school topped the league tables. After the abolition of the scheme the school declined. An audacious predecessor arrested this by raising money to fund free and assisted places. Those who, in the direct grant era, had enjoyed free places are now among the school's richest, most successful and most grateful alumni. As a result there's already £10 million in the bank. The target is £30 million, the goal needs-blind admission. Now 35 per cent of pupils have some financial support, 10 per cent have free places and the school is once again a league table topper. More than 70 per cent of are non-white British including sons of taxi drivers and restaurant workers. KES may well be the most socially and ethnically diverse independent school in the country. There'll be no slackening in its moral mission to educate the cleverest, not the richest.

That such a diversity of backgrounds and religions can rub along as happily as they do is both a marvellous thing and very much a Birmingham thing. We quizzed students and parents about this. 'The culture and ethos of the school is that everyone gets involved.' 'Everyone wants to be the best' but also 'community is important', 'All opinions are valid.' No stigma attaches to free places: 'Nobody notices and no one cares'. Here, it seems, shared goals and a traditional, meritocratic grammar school ethos bring everyone together in a spirit of common endeavour which supersedes differences. Also observable is a quality of gentleness. We sat in the dining hall at lunch and watched them interact. Really nice kids, really pleased to be here.

Pastoral care, well-being and discipline: We asked students about pastoral care. One spoke for all: 'Yes, they really do care about you'. Parents agree: 'I always feel there's someone I can talk to'. The mother of a boy who is rather a good tennis player said, 'The school cares about him and is very proud of him,' and is 'very supportive in helping him keep up with his work and outside tennis commitments'. The form tutor is the first formal port of call, but there is praise for the attentiveness of all teachers – they're quick to spot stress. There is also praise for the mentoring support given by sixth formers.

The social climate is, of course, inescapably boyish. This is mitigated by the presence of the high school next door and joint enterprises with the girls therein. Boys and parents are adamant that macho values do not prevail, rumbunctiousness is 'simply not cool' and the absence of girls does not engender social disability. For little boys, the first days in this big place full of huge boys are inevitably daunting but, they reassured us, they quickly discover they're among friends.

All boys are assigned to houses, which enjoy keen rivalry in a range of competitions. Scores are aggregated and the winner declared Cock House, a deliciously retro title. Boys love this sort of thing; they sing their bonkers school song with gusto.

Pupils and parents: Boys come from as far away as geographically viable – eg, Derby. Most from Birmingham and the Black Country. A good number also sit the exam for one or more of the free grammar schools – Camp Hill especially, the main academic rival. One parent with the luxury of choice told us, 'We were happy to pay because we could afford it and it's the right school for my son. We had no reservations and we have no regrets.' In this case it was the extracurricular activities wot swung it. Boys sometimes take a bit of good-natured ribbing for being posh, which of course they're absolutely not. A keen rugby player told us, 'Sure, and then we get out there on the pitch and beat them as usual'.

The school boasts some of the most distinguished alumni of any school in the country. Here's a small selection. Academics include a Fields Medallist, Richard Borcherds, and a brace of Nobel Prize scientists, John Vane and Maurice Wilkins. The cryptologist Hugh Alexander, Alan Turing's deputy at Bletchley Park, was here. Polymath Francis Galton left at 16 (in 1838) because he reckoned the curriculum was too narrow. Writers include JRR Tolkein, AE Housman, novelist Jonathan Coe, whose Rotters' Club includes a 1970s portrait of the school, and the crack cocaine of thriller writers, Lee Child. Pre-Raphaelite Ned Burne-Jones was here. As was Field-Marshal Slim. And Bill Oddie (capt of rugby). Politicos include Enoch Powell, David 'Two-Brains' Willetts and West Mids mayor Andy Street.

Entrance: Most at age 11, some at 13+. Own entrance exam in maths, English and verbal reasoning. Interviews for some. Whole experience designed to be 'as unstressful as possible', if stressful all the same. Some 30 from Blue Coat, Hallfield and West House. Smaller contingents from other independents. A good many in ones and twos from state primaries, and for them there's a get-to-know-you afternoon in the summer term. There's an evolved tutoring industry in Brum. To send a crammed struggler to KES may be reckoned child cruelty.

Exit: Most to university. In 2018, 17 to Oxbridge; 17 medics. Other popular destinations include Birmingham, Bristol, Leeds and Manchester. Fourteen per cent left after GCSE.

Money matters: Fees keenly competitive. Scholarships worth 5-50 per cent. Around £1 million spent on assisted places per year. Some boys sponsored by former pupils, reflecting the head's words to us about the 'massive engagement' of alumni who are 'passionate about the school'.

Remarks: Trad and trendsetting. A school with a great story to tell. Meritocratic, aspirational, socially inclusive and going places. Hard work, good fun.

King's College School (Cambridge)

West Road, Cambridge CB3 9DN

Ages 4–13 **Pupils** 404 **Boarders** 17 full (choristers), 12 weekly and 6 flexi (from 8 years) **C of E**

Fees: Day £12, 240 – £15,555; Weekly Boarding (boys) £24,210; Choristers £7,995 pa

01223 365814
www.kcs.cambs.sch.uk

Head: Since January 2018, Yvette Day, previously head of the Chorister School, Durham. She is also master over the choristers, in charge of the education and care of the boys who have sung in the college choir since the college's foundation by King Henry VI. Mrs Day was educated in South Africa and in England, holds an MMus degree in historical musicology from the University of London and more recently completed a law conversion course with the College of Law. Her husband, Andrew, is also a headteacher.

Entrance: Some children registered at birth, or before. All 4 year olds spend over an hour with the pre-prep department, so 'we can get the feel of the child.' Be warned, they're looking for bright bunnies. Siblings, past pupils and fellows of King's given priority. Parents also have a chat with the head. Entry at 7 after assessment. Chorister scholarships for up to five boys in year 4. Open to any boy in the world if he passes the audition, and many try. All choristers offered scholarships of up to two-thirds of fees or more, plus free piano lessons. Means-tested bursaries of up to 100 per cent at age 7, available for all. Children come from a wide commutable area, many from Suffolk and Hertfordshire, some boarders further afield. Many parents ex-Oxbridge, academics, medics, City people. Generally a good cross-section. All very ambitious and the driving force behind their offspring.

Exit: The occasional one at 11, but very unusual. No 'evictions'; they work hard, with the help of learning support, to keep them going, and then guide parents to make a 'sensible choice' for the next step. Only one has been 'moved on' in the last 18 years before age 11. At 13, over half to local independent schools in Cambridge, particularly The Perse and Leys. King's Ely, Oundle, Eton, Uppingham and Rugby all popular too. Every chorister offered a music scholarship. About a third of all leavers get scholarships, many music, some academic.

Remarks: Founded in the 15th century to educate the choristers, now housed on one site off a leafy road a brisk walk from King's College. The choristers are an iconic sight walking through the streets in a croc in their Etons and top hats heading for chapel. Primarily a day school with some 34 boarders, all boys, 24 of whom are choristers, the rest – some of whom flexi board – in the upper years. The choristers are an important part of the school, famous throughout the world, but are treated like any other pupils within lessons. But their life is different. Compulsory boarders from the age of 8 when they become full choristers, they attend six services a week at the chapel during the university term time, practice for an hour and half before school (in a purpose built acoustic room) and again in the evenings. Weekends during the university term means three more services. They travel the world touring and, of course, there is that carol service every Christmas Eve and the service on Christmas Day. It's a big commitment with many sacrifices made by the families, but very rewarding, and the boys thrive on it. Every care is taken to make sure they don't suffer academically or personally. 'My son, a chorister, has struggled at times with his work, but the support from the staff is excellent.' They still get to play in the teams but practice is out; there just isn't time. If a boy's voice breaks before he leaves he is still included and part of the set up.

These children are bright and teaching is excellent, with some well-loved, gregarious characters amongst the staff. The special needs department, one of the first to be set up in the country, is very proactive. 'The school contacted me very quickly when my daughter started to struggle with her maths. She was offered extra help immediately, which was excellent.' Lots of support available if needed. All parents commented on how well the staff knew their children. 'We like the school for its "ballsy" attitude,' was said by one parent, with many commenting on the relaxed, but focused atmosphere. Lots of new computers available. Plenty of artwork about, modern science labs and a very well equipped DT room. A large, stuffed library attended by a librarian who appears to be a school stalwart. Knows every child, loved by all. Every parent was happy with their child's progress and had confidence in the school. Pace increases further up the school with a scholarship class in year 8. 'They are realising my child's potential,' came up more than once.

Lots of after-school clubs, chess highly recommended, but music dominates. A fabulous music department, and that's excluding the angelic-looking choristers. Virtually every child plays an instrument, many two or more. Lots and lots of chamber groups, choirs, orchestras and quartets. If you can think of it, they've got it. A new organ in situ, played by many, and lots of acoustic rooms for practice, including the church-like room for the choristers.

Music aside, sport is playing an increasingly big part in school life. Many more top-notch staff employed, with more teams available and better results. New sports and cultural centre. 'Team selection can be a political minefield,' said one parent. 'I don't envy the staff but they handle it well.' The playing fields are at the front of the school, giving the impression of lots of open space – a bit of an illusion: every spare inch of the site is utilised.

A friendly, happy school, pastorally excellent. Bullying usually nipped in the bud very quickly. One father mentioned that an incident had been allowed to escalate before being 'handled excellently.' A mother praised the handling of manipulative children by the form teacher. 'He was sensitive, calm and firm.' 'The school's policy of keeping parents at arm's length and bringing the children together is the right one,' said one wise mother. A school counsellor available for all and the children are happy to consult. Older pupils mentor younger ones with a buddy system.

The boarding house is also on site. Functional, but immaculate with modern facilities. Bright, airy dorms, duvet covers brought from home, sheets changed by the boys. Housemaster (sic – a woman) praised and loved by all. An open door policy for the parents and homesickness dealt with kindly. Misdemeanours dealt with quickly. 'Punishment comprises chores, just like I would at home.' Tuck boxes brought out once a week with matron providing more on Saturday evenings. Dog walks on Sunday morning. Very much a family atmosphere, with parents included, as they often pop in mid week and, if local, walk the choristers back from chapel.

Bright purple blazers and sweatshirts make the children stand out. 'My son hates his sweatshirt so gets through a blazer a year.' Girls' summer dresses not popular with parents or pupils. Do note the purple carpet throughout the modernised buildings. Sartorial whimsy, perhaps?

All parents seem happy that the school is on one site and many mentioned of the 'family atmosphere.' Every parent we spoke to was delighted with the school and would strongly recommend it. We can see why; you can't help but feel the relaxed ambience. The children are bright and friendly, completely stress free and at ease with their teachers. But don't let that fool you. There is a rarefied atmosphere of intense learning – and you may get to hear some excellent singing as well.

King's Ely

Barton Road, Ely, Cambridgeshire CB7 4DB

Ages 1–18 **Pupils** 1,038 **Sixth form** 179 **Boarders** 196 full, 24 flexi (including King's Ely International) **C of E**

Fees: Day £15,531 – £21,459; Boarding £23,955 – £31,065 pa

01353 660707
www.kingsely.org

Principal: Since 2013, Sue Freestone GRSM Med LRAM ARCM (60s), who joined the school as head in 2004. She is again in charge of the senior school, after the brief tenure of Alex McGrath as head. Trained at the Royal Academy of Music and Bristol University. Was formerly head of Sibford School, and before that conductor and director of music at Colston Girls. Very energetic, approachable and unstuffy, with strongly held convictions and an expectation of high standards for herself, the staff and pupils.

Retiring in July 2019. Her successor will be John Attwater, currently head of King Edward's School Witley. Studied philosophy and politics at Oxford and trained as a teacher at York. Began his teaching career at Wells Cathedral School where he became head of religious studies and housemaster. Deputy head (co-curriculum) at Sevenoaks School, before moving to his current headship in 2010.

Head of senior school: Since September 2018, Jonathan Shaw, previously vice principal of Elizabeth College, Guernsey. History degree from Nottingham and MA in leadership from the Institute of Education. He is married to Katharine, also a teacher, and they have two children.

Head of the junior school: Since 2008, Richard Whymark BA (Ed) (40s). Previously head of Stonar Junior and before that head of boarding and deputy head of Salisbury Cathedral School. Has an engaging manner and a natural flair for communication – with pupils and parents alike. 'He is usually around at drop-off time', commented one parent.

Firmly believes a good head needs 'a strong voice and a reflective personality – no room for big egos'. Has an easy rapport with students and is clearly a respected presence – on hand to sort out spats. Art, travel and gardening are all interests but, clearly something of a romantic, his passion is for restoring Morris Minors. Has two children at King's and wife Joanna also teaches at the school.

Academic matters: Parents praise the emphasis on effort and progress in the junior school; certificates and prizes are awarded for these as much as for attainment. Both ends of ability spectrum well served, with support and extension classes available. 'Confidence is encouraged, but not cockiness', commented a mother. Tutor groups are reshuffled each year, to break up cliques and expand friendship groups. A buddy scheme operates throughout the junior school and problems are quickly dealt with. The top year groups use some of the senior school's facilities and are taught by specialist staff as a way of managing the transition from junior to senior. Setting in maths and English from year 3. Languages introduced early, with taster lessons in Japanese, Mandarin and Arabic. French, and Latin from year 7.

Though increasingly selective at 11 and 13, the bar is not quite so high as for certain of the Cambridge schools close by. Considering the reasonably wide ability range, the school is achieving very respectable and frequently glowing results. Pupils are setted for most of the core subjects; close attention is paid to individual progress, and though not an overly pushy school, 'drifting along with little effort will be spotted', a mother remarked. Twenty-four subjects offered at GCSE (42 per cent A*-A/9-7 in 2018) including single sciences, Latin and Greek. Religious and moral philosophy is compulsory. Twenty-seven subjects offered at A level with economics, mathematics and psychology all popular, and 47 per cent A*/A grades overall in 2018. Those with specific educational needs, such as dyslexia, are well accommodated. There is individual support available, together with a drop-in clinic, and a close eye is kept on subjects chosen at GCSE, with a flexible approach to certain subject choices allowed.

King's Ely Junior International offers 11-12 year olds intensive English language tuition alongside a wider range of subjects in preparation for 13+ senior school entry. King's Ely International prepares 14-16 year olds with sufficiently good English to take IGCSEs and be able to enter UK independent schools, including this one. The classrooms and boarding accommodation are separate, but the head is encouraging greater fraternisation with the main school: 'It can only benefit all pupils'.

Games, options, the arts: A strength of the school is what happens outside the mainstream academic timetable. Tremendous range of opportunities, from rowing at 6:30am to singing in cathedral services. Music predominates, with more than 50 per cent learning an instrument, and ensembles, choirs and orchestras galore. Junior school includes the 22 boy choristers, who alongside daily rehearsals, services and instrumental practice have a demanding schedule of recordings, concerts and broadcasts. The girls' cathedral choir operates from year 7. This is the first scheme of its kind in England, and is the inspiration of the present head, herself a professional musician. It will be interesting to see if the idea is taken up by many other co-educational schools connected with cathedrals. The choir sings regular cathedral services, as well as touring and performing elsewhere. The musical training given to these girls will prepare them for advanced study and choral scholarships at university. A new initiative is sixth form male choral scholarships.

Sport remains central and important, though perhaps 'not the be all and end all as at some schools,' said a parent. Besides regular hockey, rugby and so forth, there is an emphasis on the more recondite sports, especially rowing, which is taken very seriously. The school has its own boathouse, pupils keen enough to be up with the lark and even some Olympic potential.

The Ely Scheme (outdoor pursuits programme) runs compulsorily in year 9 and 10, and many continue. It includes kayaking, rock climbing and navigation, and pupils are encouraged to join either the climbing or kayaking club. The culmination is a major expedition, which could be traversing the Cuillin Ridge or the Picos de Europa, or climbing in the Alps or the Himalayas. Teaches self-reliance, responsibility and leadership skills. Many join DofE too.

The teaching facilities for art and design are impressive – as is the teaching. Eye-catching displays of recent work are quite outstanding and several pupils, thus encouraged, go on to study at prestige institutions, notably in fashion and design.

Boarding: Boarding houses are clean and comfortable, rather than deluxe. Boy choristers live in the Choir House during term time, Christmas and Easter holidays, with the housemaster and his family. When not practising or performing they are encouraged to play outside and the housemaster takes them on excursions during stayovers. The girl choristers have their own boarding house, complete with grand piano in the common room. They have weekend chorister duties about once a month, and stayovers – periods of intensive rehearsals and services – at the beginning or end of terms and half terms. There are eight boarding and day houses in all. The Old Palace (former residence of the Bishops of Ely) is now a sixth form centre, with boarding space for 26 girls.

Background and atmosphere: Occupies a sublime position adjacent to the cathedral, partly within the close itself, but largely in a sprawl of buildings (some medieval, others purpose-built) nearby. Glimpses of the cathedral, the Ship of the Fens, tantalise from many windows, notably from the head's office, in the Old Palace; hard for conversation to compete with the Romanesque masterpiece behind. The cathedral's presence is both seen and felt, but the school also has a close relationship with the town through a variety of initiatives with other schools and local organisations. Frequent road-crossing is managed by pupils safely and with aplomb – it is just part of school life. Other buildings include The Monks' Barn, which houses the dining room (think National Trust restaurant – food, if anything, even better), jolly atmosphere, staff eating with pupils. The library has been re-ordered, also within the ancient fabric, but retains a monastic feel.

The junior school occupies a site on the edge of the main school campus. Slightly bleak approach around the back of the senior school but the buildings themselves are well planned and designed. Attention is paid to the grouping of different classes, so years 3 and 4 (and so on up the school) are accommodated together, with their own suite of classrooms and play area. Youngest pupils cluster round a courtyard with a Tarzan trail for play time; years 7 and 8 slightly apart in their own building.

Pupils and parents feel they are listened to, and heard. The school council, a forum to discuss new ideas, is taken notice of by the powers-that-be.

Pastoral care, well-being and discipline: The Christian foundation of the school has a strong influence on the community. Rules are few, though strictly enforced, particularly for those boarding, but there is an atmosphere of trust. The head is very aware of the pressures on pupils and feels 'peer perception' can be 'the hardest nut to crack'. Emphasis on enjoyment as well as achieving.

Pupils and parents: Largely professional, business and farming families, drawn from surrounding Eastern counties; Kings Lynn and Cambridge both send cohorts (quick, easy train services). School believes 'it is in no-one's interest for pupils to travel more than half an hour each way'. Overseas contingent (about 12 per cent) including those in the King's International Study Centre. Past pupils include Alan Yentob, the tenor James Bowman and Olympian Goldie Sayers.

Entrance: Entry to King's Ely Acremont for ages 1 to 7 is by informal assessment and most progress up to the junior department; 7+ entry by diagnostic tests and informal interview. Screening for dyslexia and dyspraxia at entrance. Moderate difficulties can be accommodated but all pupils must be able to benefit from the full curriculum, with minimal extra support. Those applying as choristers (boys from year 2 and girls from year 7) must also pass the necessary voice trials.

Own exam at 11 to senior school and at 13+ to senior school, through a common entrance style exam (or common entrance itself). About 75 per cent of senior school entrants have come up from the junior school and the remainder from a mixture of local-ish schools, Framlingham Prep, South Lee and the Cambridge prep schools. Numbers well up and competition for places is increasing. Entry for the sixth form – minimum of six grade 9-5 passes at GCSE with at least 6s in chosen A level subjects.

Exit: Virtually all make the transition from junior to senior school at 13. The exam also decides setting for year 9. The occasional pupil not suited to the senior school is identified early and support given in finding another school in good time, but leaving is generally due to relocation. Up to 50 per cent of students leave after GCSEs, often for Hills Road or other sixth form colleges. Post A level, the majority leave for Russell Group universities to study a wide range of subjects, with a number going to colleges of art and design and performing arts courses.

Money matters: Boy choristers in the junior school get a 50 per cent fee remission, with 33 per cent scholarships in the senior school for those who remain in the school choir, and for girl choristers. The sixth form choral and organ scholarships (open to boys and girls) offer a 50 per cent fee reduction. Up to 10 per cent off for clergy. Generous dynamic discount in addition to CEA for Forces families. Bursaries for those in financial need.

Remarks: The school has an atmosphere of purposeful learning, and provides plenty of opportunities for all types to shine. A strong, happy school where the Christian ethos is taken seriously.

K

King's High School

Linked with Warwick Preparatory School, Warwick School, Warwick Junior School

Smith Street, Warwick, Warwickshire CV34 4HJ

Ages 11–18 **Pupils** 647 **Sixth form** 137

Fees: £12,975 pa

01926 494485
www.kingshighwarwick.co.uk

Headmaster: Since 2015, Richard Nicholson. The appointment of a male head to a girls' school can pose particular challenges, and challenge is probably the key to this appointment. Richard has set about challenging the stereotype criticisms of girls' schools as being staid, out of touch and narrowly focused on exam results. He is as passionate about empowering young women as any female head, and this radical dimension has inspired the school and wider community. With a background in girls' schools, director of music at St Catherine's, Bramley and then deputy at Lady Eleanor Holles School, he came to King's High well versed in what excellence in all girls' education looks like. He has since become the overarching head for Warwick Preparatory School and King's, within the Warwick Independent Schools Foundation (which includes Warwick School), and one of his successes is bringing these two schools much closer together.

He is a musician, and was an organ scholar at Pembroke College, Oxford. So far he is resisting joining local music groups, but doubts he can hold out for very much longer without indulging his passion for choral singing. A key priority at present is the impending move of the whole school from its present site to a new build, joining Warwick School and Warwick Prep school on a huge site at the edge of the town from 2019. But that is by no means all that is happening. Curriculum development, a new house system, pastoral progress and a huge drive on co-curricular opportunities are just a few of the areas that Richard has transformed. He is an inspirational figure for his staff, who have swung behind his agenda for change and high aspirations. 'He is dynamic and he listens to us', we heard from various teachers. 'He is brilliant', parents tell us.

Academic matters: There is a belief in a few quarters of the Warwickshire parent body that Kings' High is some sort of forcing shed for A grades. But that standard glib criticism of girls' schools that do very well academically is far from the case. Kings' High is carefully crafting a heady brew for the girls of absolutely top academic aspirations, endless opportunities to develop passions outside of the classroom and a focus on actions that will ground them in the real, inclusive world. There is no doubt Richard Nicholson has academic aspirations high on his agenda. He has appointed a director of educational innovation, a director of co-curricular activities and an academic deputy, who are all driving excitement about teaching and learning in a wonderfully holistic way. There is a researcher in residence who is working on all sorts of innovative ideas to share with colleagues. There is more digital tracking of girls' progress than formerly but staff tell us it is 'data for a purpose'.

The school is academically selective, but with considerable competition from excellent local grammar schools, it can't be highly so. The results are strong. At A level, 90 per cent A*-B, 63 per cent A*/A grades in 2018. At GCSE, 73 per cent 9-7s in 2018. Value added is very high both by maintained school and independent school standards, coming in the top 45 of both groups last year. Data shows the school adds nearly a full grade, comparing GCSE results with baseline tests in year 7. Ability sets for maths and languages from year 8. There is a small amount of joint teaching with Warwick School at A level, currently in German, drama and Latin. The sixth form is off academic lessons on Friday afternoons and can take a number of options, some joint with Warwick School, including Young Enterprise, BBC Young Reporter, French with business. This has now been extended to younger years with a huge range of options.

French, Spanish and German are the main modern foreign languages and Latin is also on offer. At a recent Language Showcase day, girls taught themselves enough Japanese to sing a song. There is a big push on engineering. It has been introduced to the curriculum in year 8 and Meteor – a programmable, humanoid NAO robot – is very popular. Around 40 per cent take maths A level. There are four or five forms in each year with class sizes of up to 24, with smaller groups at GCSE and in the sixth form. For girls who might struggle from time to time with academic work, the school has recently launched its Boost programme which brings together a range of academic support sessions, bespoke individual guidance, small group sessions and student mentoring. Parents with girls who are dyslexic spoke highly of the school's ability to spot problems quickly and implement an effective strategy. Girls who join the school at unorthodox points are given plenty of support. We found parents particularly keen on the student mentoring programme, where senior girls help those lower down the school with difficulties. Parents felt it was hugely beneficial for both the mentor and the mentee. While most of the Boost learning support offer is covered by school fees, bespoke one-to-one tuition and some small group mini-courses for KS3 students do come at an additional, though modest, cost. Girls say the support programme feels very non-judgmental, and also appreciate the online support websites the school recommends.

Games, options, the arts: Balance and extensive opportunity is the underlying ethos of this co-curricular side of the school, with a King's School Bacc qualification recognising a range of endeavours. The number of clubs and societies has greatly increased over the last year or two. They plan big at King's. The week before our visit there had been a Space Day with a range of high profile visiting speakers, special events and activities, including a rocket building challenge with a professional rocket engineer, with students from Warwick Prep and local schools invited. The day culminated in a dinner for staff and students with an award-winning physicist from Imperial College. This was followed later in the week by a live link up event with an astronaut on board the International Space Station – an event initiated and planned by a sixth former.

All of this was a part of a year-long school-wide space project with lecturers and events. Within Inspire, the academic enrichment programme, there are activities in most areas – Café Philo that focuses on PPE topics, the Lit and Phil Society, Café Scientifique, Ruth Court Mathematical Society, for example – all of which combine discussion with occasional inspirational world class speakers and events. The head and his team are developing the Landor Dining Society, with regular dinners hosting speakers.

Sport gets mixed reports. The negative comments from parents and girls were largely around limited facilities, and this is being addressed with the move to the new site. Nevertheless, the external sports results are very impressive – the school has been county champion in 11 different sports in recent years and the new director of sport intends to build on this. Professional hockey and netball coaches have been hired and there is a Talented Athletes' Programme, where girls get their own mentor to help them manage the sport/academics balance and train appropriately for them. Lots of different physical activities are on offer with a view to finding something that everyone can enjoy and will want to take with them beyond school. Unlike in their brother school, sixth formers can largely opt out of organised sport, which some parents disapprove of, wanting all the sixth form out playing hockey every week. Art is strong with much multi-media work on display around the school and the department has its own artist in residence.

There is much joint activity with Warwick School around music and drama and this will no doubt increase with the move to the new site. As well as the combined orchestras and plays there is also a number of all girls' performing arts events and groups, including opportunities through the newly established house system. Music is on the up – there are more groups, including a new jazz ensemble, and the girls are being encouraged to pursue individual interests. The new artistic director (music), also works at Warwick Prep and conducts the joint foundation symphony orchestra. There's a new Model UN group, D of E and CCF. The recent proliferation of clubs has provided increased leadership opportunities, girls attend National Council for Young Women meetings and report back, and debating is increasingly popular.

Background and atmosphere: You cannot think of the King's atmosphere without being influenced by its grade 2 listed buildings. These are both a unique blessing and something of an incubus. The possibilities for extending the site and making it fit for purpose in the 2020s have been taken as far as they possibly can, with every nook and cranny used to the full in the compact site, and hats off to the head who has continued investing in the site despite the imminent move – starting in 2019. Where there are now leaded windows and low oak beams, there will soon be glass and aluminum, open spaces and greenery. Of course this is wonderful but it will be with real sadness and regret that present and, particularly, past students say good-bye to the existing buildings. The sort of investment that the head has continued to make includes an Innovation Centre, which boasts desks and walls that can be used for scribbling down thoughts and inspirations. This, and the whole dynamic feel of the school with its can-do attitude, has meant the girls see their school as fleet of foot and poised to take advantage of every opportunity, whether ones suggested by the girls themselves or coming from outside. Both parents and girls note how swiftly the school responds to any concerns. When one group felt overwhelmed by homework, a temporary homework amnesty was speedily put in place.

Pastoral care, well-being and discipline: Pastoral care is regarded as a great strength, and whoever you talk to, there is a sense that every girl is known as an individual within the school. The head has set up a well-being working party so girls can feed in what they would find helpful in this area. Outside speakers address girls, staff and parents' forums on areas such as mental health. A mother and daughter befriending scheme allocates new year 7s a year 8 'sister' and a sixth form 'mother' to smooth their passage through the new school. Richard Nicholson introduced a house system and one of its advantages is increased links and friendships between the different year groups. There is a system of conduct and credit marks to encourage good behaviour and attitude to work. Conduct marks are given for minor misdemeanours and seem to be quite enough of a deterrent to stop anything escalating to the rarely given detention level. One mother reported her daughter had wept for hours on receiving her one and only conduct mark. When we asked the girls what were the worst crimes they could recall, the only thing they came up with was that someone had once smashed a window with a netball but, we were earnestly assured, she had certainly not meant to do it.

Pupils and parents: The girls are just lovely. What can you say? Who wouldn't want their daughters to be like this at 18? Confident but not arrogant; excited about their future but hugely loyal to their past; believing the world is theirs for moulding into something much fairer and better than has gone before; sure that they can do it, but knowing they will need support and networks and kindness and empathy to succeed.

Parents are deeply committed to the school. The majority seem to have professional, academic or business backgrounds, some travelling for their work rather than move their daughter to another school. There clearly is a significant range in family income backgrounds but parents say the school has a very egalitarian feel. There is an active parents' association.

Entrance: About a third of each year 7 intake comes from Warwick Prep. Overall girls come from up to 50 different primary schools each year, about half from state primaries and half from private schools. Foundation buses bring children in from a wide area. About 10 new girls enter the sixth form each year, places dependent on interview, school report and GCSE grades of at least 6 in all subjects plus 9-7 in A level choices.

Exit: Around a quarter leave after GCSEs (27 per cent in 2018). There is a big drive on preparation for university and beyond, with a full programme of careers talks and visits, using past pupils where ever possible. A Higher Education Evening includes representatives from a range of universities and there is careful and focused individually tailored work on UCAS applications and Oxbridge preparation. The range of universities to which girls go is wide as is the range of subjects. 2018 top 10 destinations: Bristol, Exeter, York, Durham, Leeds, Cambridge, Cardiff, Nottingham, King's College, London, Manchester. A handful go off to Oxbridge each year (two in 2018) but a new drive looks likely to change this. Far more A level scientists are applying for pure sciences and engineering than in the past, when they all went for medicine.

Money matters: There are scholarships and bursaries at 11+ and 16+ and the head – who was himself educated at an independent school through the government funded assisted places scheme – is passionate about widening access, so it may be the bursary pot will increase in the future. About a fifth of the pupils receive some form of financial assistance. Fees are about average for girls' schools in the Midlands.

Remarks: If anyone doubts that girls' schools are the catalyst for gradual but determined social revolution, they should come to King's High. At the heart of a relatively conservative area is this dynamic powerhouse for social change, unleashing on the quiet byways of Warwickshire the full force of young women who know what they want the world to look like and how to go about getting it there. There's a careful and not sensational development of confidence and leadership, a respect for serious academic thought and analysis that is not showy or judged by solely A*s. These mean that King's girls go out optimistic but realistic, determined to work towards making things better but emotionally intelligent in their sensitivity to the views of others. A winning combination. It will be fascinating to see how the move to the new site works. 'It is an increase in size', said one of the girls, 'but that means more space, not more people.' There is no doubt the schools will benefit from close proximity, and the new joint sixth form centre will be immensely popular. Will the very special atmosphere of King's High get diluted? We would be greatly surprised if anything could dilute that.

The King's (The Cathedral) School

Park Road, Peterborough, Cambridgeshire PE1 2UE

Ages 8–18 **Pupils** 1,187 **Sixth form** 347 **C of E**

01733 751541
www.kings.peterborough.sch.uk

Head: Since 2014, Darren Ayling (40s). An English graduate who was heading for an academic career before realising that he preferred the tuition work he was doing to fund his PhD. On job training within the independent sector followed. Deputy head at Ipswich School before joining King's for his first headship and first job in the state sector. 'I have always wanted to work at a cathedral school so jumped at the chance to come here.' Attends evensong on his way home every week. 'He has a hard act to follow,' came up more than once, the previous incumbent having been in situ for 20 years. 'He is always at the school gates at the end of the day and is very friendly,' said one mother. 'I liked the way he introduced himself to me and my son on an open day and shook his hand. He engages well with the children,' said another parent with three children at the school.

He has plans but is not rushing. 'I took over the school in a very strong position so need to maintain that. We are one of the best comprehensives in the country and I want us to be the best of all state schools. I would like to see the school more outward looking and receiving the national recognition it deserves.' He teaches the EPQ to sixth formers.

Academic matters: A creditable 49 per cent A*-A/9-7 at GCSE in 2018. Thirty-six per cent of A level grades A*/A, 64 per cent A*-B. Most pupils take 11 GCSEs; ICT has been removed from the core to allow for computing. Latin now available at GCSE; all pupils take French or German, many take both. Many take music up to GCSE – it is a cathedral school.

Pupils are setted for English, maths, languages and the sciences. Fabulous upgraded science blocks with all mod cons. The walls are wired up so energy usage can be checked. Monitors everywhere, all very high tech. A very proud teacher explained it all, but way beyond us. They all seem to understand it though, thankfully. Take note of the orrery in the gardens (a model of the solar system) – the physics teams' pride and joy. 'It's used to play football on too,' whispered an off-message mole. They even have a weather station, the first one at a school in Peterborough. Lots of talk of visitors from Singapore, China and the US to view it all.

'Loads of homework,' said one parent, 'but they just get on with it.' 'We know immediately if they are not doing their homework,' said another. Lots of talk of close contact with staff and immediate responses. 'My daughter felt she was being overlooked in some lessons and that her teachers didn't notice her. I spoke to the head of year about it and everything was dealt with very well, and solved almost immediately with them involving my daughter and how she could improve too.' Fun French lessons for the lower school. Hard at work in maths and English, very warm, stuffy classrooms, a bit of fresh air wouldn't go amiss. Impressive artwork on display, in reception area as well as around the school. Newly refurbished art room, bright and airy. Good to see DT and textiles work prominently displayed. 'There's good recognition at this school,' said another parent. 'They are quick to acknowledge achievement and make sure we know as well.' Nice sixth form block with vast common room and outside seating. Recently wired up for Wifi, television on the wall; 'We are allowed to watch it at break and love watching Wimbledon,' said one mole. A large, ornate library that covers two floors. 'One visitor asked us why we don't knock it down and build a swimming pool,' said one of our horrified guides.

Low numbers needing SEN support, but those that do are well catered for. 'I had doubts about sending my son, who has an EHCP, and have been really surprised about how well he is doing and how well supported he is,' said one happy parent. 'He is easily coping with the academic pressure and they have adapted to meet his needs.' Excellent.

Games, options, the arts: Plenty of sport played but mutterings from parents about 'cancelled games.' Lots of after-school practice and enthusiastic participation. 'My girls are desperate to play sports but there don't seem to be that many teams,' said one parent, but then adding, 'they take their kit every day and are always doing something, be it badminton, hockey, netball or in the gym; they love it.' All the usual sports including rugby, football, hockey and netball along with cricket, rounders, volleyball and trampolining. The playing fields are about a mile away, with the athletics track even further, so a quick trek across town at least once a week for lessons. Not to worry, it keeps them fit, gives them a bit of independence and teaches time management. 'We need to work out how long it will take us and if we can grab a snack before we go,' said one informer. Large, newly revamped gym with newish fitness suite overlooking it. House competitions hotly contested with enthusiastic captains encouraging participation. Sports day relished. 'Everyone gets points for competing,'

As to be expected from a cathedral school, music is important here. Choristers from the school, eight or nine from every year up to year 8, sing daily at the cathedral, and it's a big commitment. Evensong and early services including two on Sundays, plus all the Christian ceremonies. 'The choristers are like a family,' said one mother. 'The ethos of the choir and the discipline involved is a great leveller.' Choristers sing up to year 8 (at the behest of the cathedral, girls no longer continue as choristers throughout the school). 'I don't think the choristers receive enough acknowledgement from their peers,' says the head, 'something I wish to rectify, as their commitment is enormous.' Choirs, orchestras and bands abound, 17 extracurricular ones in total, with practices throughout the week. Many performances at the cathedral as well as at school. Almost 30 per cent of pupils have peripatetic instrumental and singing lessons. Large numbers reach grade 8. Mention must go to the organist who had just been offered an Oxbridge scholarship when we visited.

Drama productions enthusiastically talked about and supported. A new drama teacher spoken of with awe. Animal Farm as a musical a recent production. As You Like It, set in a circus, taken to Germany. Some productions run by sixth form for lower school. Other plays for the whole school to partake in. A newly refurbished hall with a new balcony section.

D of E well supported and lots of school trips, subject ones, including a geography trip to the Himalayas, as well as the usual ski trips and Auschwitz.

Background and atmosphere: One of only four state cathedral schools in the country. Founded in 1541 by Henry VIII with 12 students, it was originally housed in Peterborough Cathedral. Moved to its present location in the 1800s. An attractive building on a leafy street in a salubrious part of central Peterborough. Surrounded by houses, it is very discreetly sited and is hardly noticeable. The site is now full so no room for expansion, hence the sports fields being so distant, though a whizzy new multi media sixth form study room. Henry VIII still dominates the school, with a large portrait looking down on them in the dining room. Prefects wear flowing gowns so stand out from the masses. 'We wear full length ones on cathedral days, shorter ones for the rest of the time,' said one of our guides.

Every pupil has a swipe card that they use to access locked doors and buy lunch. Not to be lost, as access then denied. Amusing to see the year 8s locked out of the sports hall after they'd been on a run; not one of them had remembered their card. Our superior guides in their flowing robes talked to them about 'forward planning.' Nice to see these temples of wisdom fix the exuberant year 8s with a steely glare when they tried to barge through the door before us.

Healthy eating a priority here. 'Fish Friday is chip day,' said with a big grin. Food well liked, even though it does seem to be regularly on the agenda for the school council. Represented by two from each year, this august body gets results.

The pupils look smart in their burgundy blazers and striped blouses or ties. Some of the smartest we've seen, with echoes to its illustrious past. The school has gone from private, to grammar to comprehensive, introducing girls as recently as the 1970s. But don't be fooled, this is no ordinary bog standard comprehensive. It feels, and is run, like an independent, with its ancient history and links to the cathedral.

Pastoral care, well-being and discipline: The Christian ethos runs through this school from top to bottom. 'This is a faith school and a cathedral school, inclusive and tolerant with a mission to live life according to our faith,' says the head. 'They pray for family members in assembly and are excellent if anything goes wrong,' said one parent. Another said, 'They visited when a family member was in hospital,' and from another, 'They kept an eye on my daughter when my marriage broke up and were excellent.' Lots of mentoring of younger pupils by older ones. A very happy atmosphere, a genuinely caring place. 'My child loves it here,' was said more than once. 'Pastorally excellent,' said another happy parent. 'My son struggled as there were problems at home. They mentored him and turned his life around.' 'They see the children as individuals,' was another comment.

'I chose King's because of the discipline and structure and their excellent values,' was said by more than one parent. Discipline is hot, they don't stand for any nonsense and parents back this to the hilt. The pupils know where they stand and know the consequences.

Pupils and parents: Happy, relaxed children and equally happy parents. All are ambitious. Fair to say that the majority of parents would be classed as middle class professionals. Very few less privileged and a low percentage of other ethnic backgrounds, very unusual in Peterborough. 'We have a very supportive parent body,' says the head. 'All parents are ambitious for their children and fully back the school in all it does, which is excellent. Disciplinary matters are backed to the hilt by them.'

Entrance: Fifteen pupils into the tiny junior department in year 3, up to nine of which will be choristers. They all gain automatic entry to the senior school in year 7. Seventy-four year 7 applicants, and non-choristers in year 3, admitted on religious grounds. Children of worshipping members of the Church of England, or Methodists, confirmation of five years' worship required. Children of staff and then siblings next in line, then other faiths, then by distance. Twelve year 7 places offered on academic ability, three music scholarships. 'We have children from other faiths at the school as these parents also appreciate our ethos,' said the head. Many more applicants than places, particularly for the academic ones. Pupils come from a wide area, as far afield as Huntingdon, Leicestershire and Oakham, adding to the private school feel of the place.

Entry into the sixth form requires a minimum of seven GCSE passes with grade 6s in the subjects studied. But don't be fooled: this is the minimum required, but as it's so oversubscribed, accepted grades will be much higher. Sixth formers come from equally far afield, many from the private sector. No religious criteria at this stage.

Exit: Around a quarter leave after GCSEs, mainly to follow vocational courses. An extra 50 or so join the sixth form. Virtually all go to university, most to their first choice – many Russell Group. Five to Oxbridge in 2018, eight to study medicine. The occasional one to an apprenticeship, becoming more popular.

Remarks: A happy, nurturing school that is by far the best in Peterborough, and the parents know it and work hard to gain admission. Amazing how many families turn to religion at times like this, but who can blame them?

The King's School, Grantham

Brook Street, Grantham, Lincolnshire NG31 6RP

Ages 11–18 **Pupils** 1,119

01476 563180
www.kings.lincs.sch.uk

Head: Since September 2018, Simon Pickett BSC (physics), previously deputy head at William Farr School near Lincoln.

Academic matters: In 2018, over 50 per cent A*-B/9-7 at GCSE, nearly 30 per cent A*/A, 54 per cent A*-B at A level. French and German offered at GCSE; all boys study both subjects in year 7. Disappointing not to see Latin on offer. Take up of languages

K

at A level very low, but following general trend. Maths by far the most popular subject at A level, hotly followed by sciences. Humanities also popular. School well equipped with lots of computers. Very impressive artwork on display throughout. Lots of support on offer for the boys. Parents spoke of quick response to emails and being kept up to date with progress. 'The boys are under pressure, there's no doubt that league tables rule, here but they are well supported,' said one mother. SEN support available. Parents spoke of teachers getting in touch immediately if their son was struggling. Some parents mentioned excellent staff whilst others said they weren't 'a fan of every teacher.' It would appear some departments are better run than others. Most parents were happy school was getting the best out of their son. Lots of homework and high expectations, though one mother thought discipline about handing in homework on time is a bit lax in lower years. 'They need jumping on at a younger age, which will set them up well for later in the school.' The pressure is on academically but most boys seem to thrive.

Separate, modern sixth form area with canteen and more computers. There are links with KGGS girls' grammar school in certain subjects, but we didn't get the impression that huge numbers are involved.

Games, options, the arts: Despite the school being unashamedly academic, the boys are encouraged to broaden their horizons. Sport historically very successful. Waned in the last few years but bouncing back well. Lots of teams and practice sessions. Clubs for all; there was even talk of a netball club. One parent felt the late developers were often overlooked when it came to sport and struggled to catch up. Incredibly successful water polo team: the school has dominated the sport for years and produced many international players. Newish sports hall. The sports pitches are a short walk away.

Drama popular with a school production every year. Some years involves collaboration with KGGS round the corner; these have proved very popular, can't imagine why. Lots of music, bands galore with pupils and staff collaborating, ranging from soul bands to orchestra. A very impressive band performing at the open day. A third of boys have music lessons. The school is one of the leading music centres in the county. Interesting to note that school very supportive of outside interests when it comes to music and dance. Good to see.

DofE well supported to gold level and very active CCF force, though Navy are not represented. Lots of school trips, subject, sport and CCF related.

Background and atmosphere: Steeped in history, which can be traced back to 1329, the school has been on the same site, just off the town centre, since 1528. The boys were known as King's Scholars, Sir Isaac Newton being one of them. You can see his name carved in the wall of the original school building. William Cecil, the first Lord Burghley, chancellor to Elizabeth 1, was also an old boy. The school was small, under 100 boys, until the beginning of the 20th century. Since then it has grown rapidly and the architecture reflects this: a mish-mash of new, old and positively ancient. Built around a large playground, it has evolved over the years. Lots of wood panelling and magnificent fireplaces in the older parts, bright and airy in the more modern, with lots of Victorian additions too.

Beautiful, scented gardens are hidden behind the original school house, that now includes the headmaster's office. This sanctuary is inspiring and peaceful. The boys are treading the same path as some very eminent men. Historically associated with the Forces, particularly the RAF; service sons used to board up until the 1980s. Head very keen to point out the school has a 'sense of service' academically and socially and wants to give something back to the community.

Interesting to note that during the last few years the school's reputation has suffered in the town. Standards had dropped and comparisons by parents with the excellent girls' grammar were not favourable. This is now changing, but it has made the school slightly defensive and insular looking. Perhaps this is why the previous head wouldn't talk to us.

Pastoral care, well-being and discipline: The school is well aware of pressure the boys are under and teachers are quick to spot mental health issues. Interestingly, during the open day the previous head referred to mental health frequently. Parents impressed with pastoral care, 'much better than I expected,' said one mother. Any parental concerns about King's being highly pressured are quickly dissipated. 'They are not only results driven.' All parents said staff know the boys well. Bullying quickly quelled and problems nipped in the bud before they accelerate. 'A happy school,' was said by parents and we picked up on this during our visit. Interaction between staff and pupils is relaxed and friendly with lots of 'ma'ams' and 'sirs'.

Some parents were slightly disappointed with discipline, 'could be better at times, particularly when it comes to timekeeping and homework deadlines,' but all agreed that improvements have been made since the current head's arrival. These were niggles; all agreed that overall the boys are well behaved and well mannered.

Pupils and parents: Many boys second, third, or more generations to be attending the school. Catchment area recently expanded with no geographical restrictions on applications. This might affect the feel of the school in future years but, at the moment, very much a school for boys from Grantham and the surrounding areas. Parents have high expectations and ambitions for their offspring and are once again supportive.

Boys a happy, gregarious bunch. Sixth formers distinctive in their burgundy coloured blazers. Lower down the school boys wear black blazers. All well turned out.

Entrance: All boys take the 11+ as compiled by the Lincolnshire Consortium of Grammar Schools, featuring verbal and non-verbal reasoning. Some 185 take the test for 176 places. The school is virtually full, with the odd place higher up.

Up to 20 per cent of the sixth form, some 30 boys, is made up of newcomers. Boys need to obtain six GCSEs at grade 6 or above, including maths and English and 6s or above in the subjects they wish to study at A level. If they are oversubscribed, they will take those with the best results.

Exit: About a third leave after year 11, mainly to co-ed local colleges and schools. Vast majority to university but higher level apprenticeships being actively embraced. A handful to Forces, Harper Adams and Royal Agricultural University at Cirencester.

Remarks: A school that is unashamedly results driven. But not to the detriment of the boys, who are well adjusted and receiving a broad education. A few rocky years appear to be behind them and their reputation is once again deservedly high within the area. The school asks that we make it absolutely clear that the views expressed in the review are our own. Just so – here, and in all our reviews, we reflect the views of the parents that we have spoken to, and the results of our research, and reviews may not line up with the school's view of itself.

Lawrence Sheriff School

Clifton Road, Rugby, Warwickshire CV21 3AG

Ages 11–18 **Pupils** 929 **Sixth form** 329

01788 542074
www.lawrencesheriffschool.net

Headmaster: Since 1999, Dr Peter Kent (50s), who joined in 1997 as deputy head. Originally from Liverpool, studied English lit at Sheffield and then to Leicester to complete an MBA in educational leadership and a PhD in school culture. Title of thesis: 'Can you shape a school's culture?' Conclusion: 'Yes, but only in partnership with the students and parents.'

Previously head of English at Liverpool College, found himself comfortably ensconced in the independent system but wanted to work at a state grammar. Upon discovering Lawrence Sheriff (LSS), he was 'blown away', finding it 'very unusual, very distinctive.' As head, he sees his role as 'keeper of the culture', but clearly not happy to rest as a mere custodian, he declares himself driven by a 'power to innovate'. Gwen Temple is a strong second-in-command; there is a certain missionary zeal about their enthusiasm for the school, made clear as we chat over pizza and sandwiches in the sunny meeting room. But their appetite for success (unlike our appetite for the pizza) is clearly a healthy one.

Empowering underprivileged pupils is a priority for Dr Kent. He wants LSS to be the 'community grammar' for Rugby, and governors have drawn up their oversubscription criteria to allow priority admission status for those in receipt of the pupil premium.

Married with three children, two sons attended LSS. Although far from home and in kicking distance of the school that invented the odd-shaped ball, he remains a resolute Liverpool FC supporter.

Academic matters: In 2018, 61 per cent of GCSE grades were A*-A/9-7. At A level, 48 per cent A*-A grades, 72 per cent A*/B, a fairly impressive result for a less-selective sixth form.

A three-year key stage 4 enables students to take their exams early and allows greater flexibility for pupils and staff – all part of a wider ethos to provide a 'personalised' curriculum, tailored to the needs of the student. Central to this is the popular enrichment programme – not a dodgy science experiment, but a selection of additional half hour lessons scattered across the normal school timetable, where teachers get to teach something that they are passionate about. When we visited, choices ranged from astronomy to Sudoku, German film to knitting (yes, in a boys' school). Most students take an enrichment class for a term but some will stick with it for a whole year. Sixth form offers a BTec in engineering alongside A levels and EPQ.

A particular challenge for the school is the number of boys with disorders such as ADHD and Asperger's, more prevalent among those with exceptional talents in maths and computing – a specialism at the school. A group has been set up to help support students who find social situations difficult and the boys we met talked about some of the 'more socially introverted' students and how they benefit in particular from the vertical tutoring system.

Games, options, the arts: The school playing field is a good mile away from the actual school, but worth the walk, with five rugby pitches and an Astroturf field. Plenty of inter-school matches in eg rugby, hockey, football, cricket. Thanks to Sport England funding, the school is also a centre of excellence for table tennis. Several sports tours have been arranged in recent years, including trips to Barbados, South Africa, Uruguay and Chile. Most of the traditions that do exist at this largely informal school revolve around sport, and house rivalries run strong (houses Caldecott, Simpson, Tait, and Wheeler are named after former heads and benefactors).

It feels like a school with more sporty than arty tendencies, but on our visit we witnessed a gusto rehearsal of The Tempest in the impressive old Victorian mock-Tudor main hall, affectionately dubbed Big School and used for the majority of larger performances and concerts. Students from the nearby Rugby High girls' school collaborate on drama productions at sixth form. Orchestra, choir and jazz band.

Background and atmosphere: The origins of the school date back to 1567 when local benefactor Lawrence Sheriff left money for a school to serve local children. It moved to its present site in the 18th century, and became a grammar school in 1906. The school is now the selective boys' grammar for Rugby and the surrounding area, with the building owned and maintained by the governors, and running costs funded by the local authority. The school still receives an annual proportion of its funds from Rugby School as a legacy of the original bequest.

The site is an eclectic, rough and tumble mix of buildings-through-the-ages with many recent add-ons to cope with the expanding school population (the number of boys is now at around 900, up 50 per cent since 1990). Over £4m has been spent by the governors in recent years on new laboratories, workshops, studio space and a spacious sixth form centre with a huge common room, study area and separate canteen with part of the original Victorian section recently refurbed.

While it may not boast the gloss and grandeur of nearby Rugby School, the boys' pride in their school is clearly undimmed. Students must follow strict uniform rules: 'a smart uniform makes a smart person', said one year 10, pointing out that staff often refer to the boys as 'gentlemen'. 'So it's important that we feel like one', he explained.

A town centre location at the edge of a busy main road is accompanied by a rigorous security presence of ID checks and entry systems. Space does feel at a premium and green areas a bit lacking, but there is a bustle and banter in the corridors and playgrounds that all testify to a 'happy' place.

Now admits girls to the sixth form.

Pastoral care, well-being and discipline: 'Happiness' is an integral part of the school culture that Dr Kent and his colleagues have worked hard to promote. 'If students are happy, then learning is enjoyable,' explains Kent, who has introduced some pretty innovative measures in pursuit of such happiness. The school has a vertical tutor system where each house has eight tutor groups made up of students drawn from years 7-13. Tutors stay with students throughout their seven years in the school, thus ensuring continuity of pastoral support. It was controversial when introduced, but seems to work. Boys speak of 'strong bonds' and 'mutual respect' between year groups.

One of the stated aims of the vertical system is to reduce instances of bullying. While the school is emphatic that bullying is not an issue, one parent that GSG heard from did allege examples of physical violence among boys. An Ofsted inspection in 2013 was specifically tasked with examining such allegations but did not find any evidence of bullying and concluded that the school's safeguarding and bullying policies were 'very strong' and that the students 'were responsible and independent and had positive attitudes towards each other'. The students themselves also set up a committee to look at reports of bullying but disbanded it after six months when no evidence of any incidents could be found.

The school remains proud of its disciplinary record (no child has been permanently excluded in 30 years) and insists that academic achievement does not take precedence over student welfare. 'The results are brilliant but I'm more proud of the culture and the values we have created', says Kent. One parent we spoke to did refer to an 'exam factory' tendency at the school, but others pointed out that as a selective grammar, it is inevitably best suited to high academic achievers, who thrive in this environment.

Pupils and parents: Lawrence Sheriff boasts the oldest PTA in Britain – and has an entry in The Guinness Book of Records to prove it. But the committee is far from antiquated. With discos and curry nights a-plenty, the aim is clearly to put the 'fun' into fundraising. Parents are kept in the loop with a weekly newsletter and every year surveyed for feedback. Complaints about the absence of a cloakroom and lockers are a popular gripe, as is the walk to the sports field. One father of a year 9 boy took umbrage at 'mildly threatening' letters received regarding his son's absenteeism, blaming it on the importance placed by school league tables on attendance. But overall, parents had high praise for the school, with a number remarking on how they felt their input and involvement was 'valued'.

The boys who took us on our tour were, indeed, 'gentlemen'. Other than a few moans about long dinner queues and reluctant attendance at school choir practice, these were a group of boys proud of their school, brimming with self-belief but without a trace of arrogance.

Student population is majority white British, with around 20 per cent ethnic minority.

L

Entrance: Selective entry based on 11+. Year 7: 120 places with three boys competing for every place; some preference to those on pupil premium. Half of the places are secured for local children, with the rest from about a 10 mile radius, including Coventry and Birmingham (although one child did recently apply from Gateshead). Nearly half of the sixth form students (including girls since September 2018) join from other schools; entry requirements include GCSE points roughly equating to eight grade 6s, including at least 6 in English and 5 in maths; A level subjects require a 6 or higher at GCSE.

Exit: Around 95 per cent go on to university – mainly Russell Group, with four to Oxbridge in 2018, plus five medics; other popular destinations Bristol, Exeter, Edinburgh, Durham, Leeds, Liverpool, Manchester, Warwick. Despite the high university uptake, one boy insisted that there is no pressure from the school in this direction. 'If you don't want to go to uni but want to be an apprentice somewhere, that's fine – that's encouraged.' There is a tangible sense of equipping the boys for the 'real world'. Careers lessons start in year 8 with many boys drafting their first CV by the age of 13.

Money matters: No fees to pay, but the head is still very conscious of money as a potential barrier to entry and there are additional funds to help families with costs of uniform and school trips. As already mentioned, the school has also succeeded in changing the admission policy to favour those on the pupil premium.

Remarks: While poorer in pocket than its more famous public school cousin, Lawrence Sherriff can boast a wealth of ambition, drive and talent. Traditional in appearance and high-achieving on paper, it is a school striving – and succeeding – to be much more than a league-table topper.

Laxton Junior School

Linked with Oundle School

East Road, Oundle, Northamptonshire PE8 4BX

Ages 4–11 **Pupils** 263 **C of E**

Fees: £11,220 – £12,300 pa

01832 277275
www.laxtonjunior.org.uk

Head: Since September 2017, Sam Robertson, previously deputy head at the Modern English School Cairo. Degree from Cambridge, and a PGCE, in natural sciences and education. Newly married to Claire, also a teacher.

Entrance: Entry into reception is non-selective but the children have three visits to the school prior to starting so staff get to know them. Entry after that depends on previous school records. Assessment for the older pupils. Reasoning paper and maths and English tests for key stage 1, Saturday exam for older ones. 'There is no pass or fail as such, but it allows us to discuss the child's prior learning with the parents. We do not have a one size fits all approach here as all children are different.' Some are kindly advised the school is not for them, but not many. Means-tested bursaries available and a scholarship offering 10 per cent off fees for two years to a year 5 pupil. Spaces are available, but not many. Children come from a 25 mile radius of Oundle. 'Any further than that and we discourage them as it makes the day too long.' Broad mix of parents, some able to pay fees without noticing, others working hard to do so. A friendly bunch, very welcoming to all.

Exit: The main cohort, averaging around 75 per cent, to Oundle School as day pupils. But it's not a dead cert. Every child has to sit the entrance exam. Lots of advice and support given. Those not suited kindly steered towards a different route. The remaining 25 per cent to other local independents, mainly Stamford Endoweds and Oakham plus Kimbolton. The odd one to a boarding prep. Unusual for a child to leave the private sector. The occasional one leaves prior to year 6 to join local independents that have automatic transfer to the senior school. Eighteen scholarships/exhibitions in 2018 (academic, sports and music).

Remarks: Founded in 1973, Laxton Junior is part of the Oundle School network. Originally housed in one of their buildings, it moved to its present site in the picturesque town of Oundle in 2002 and doubled in size. The current well-designed modern building that flows well is light and airy with all mod cons. Great to see proper old fashioned style lift top desks in use, albeit modern ones. Lots of computers, a whole IT department, in fact. Our guides showed us the new 3D printer with great pride. Plenty of space inside and out and, despite being a modern building, not at all bland. Lots of posters and displays throughout, a lovely sunny book corner and well-used library.

The children are bright and cheerful, as are the staff. We were greeted with friendly smiles by all on our tour. Our guides were very entertaining and enthusiastic and more than happy to chat. 'We think it important that our children have good interpersonal skills and know how to greet an adult by looking them in the eye and giving a firm handshake.' And they did.

Teaching appears to be excellent, with extra support offered, free of charge, if needed. 'The school is totally proactive and offered extra help without any prompting. It's done quietly and effectively in free time so no lessons are missed. We are constantly updated about progress and couldn't ask for more,' said one happy mother. All parents commented on how well staff knew their children and motivated them. 'A fabulous all round education,' came up more than once. The lessons we observed showed happy, involved children. Fabulous reception area with lots of dressing up gear. 'Golden time' is free time for the infants on Friday afternoon, if they have earned it. Lots of good equipment including a touch table for number sorting. Our guide was very keen to help with this, as were we. But it wasn't needed: the young reception boy had it all under control and was more than keen to show us his prowess, which was excellent. Pity; we were dying to have a go.

Music is strong here. Fabulous large music room stuffed full of instruments. All year 2s learn either the violin or cello and most carry on with it. There are some 240 individual music lessons each week. Many children learn more than one instrument. Lots of ensembles, orchestras, groups and choirs. Amusing to see all the instruments piled up outside the music room.

Plenty of cups on display for sport. All the usual, as expected, including a girls' rugby team. One parent wanted to see more sport in year 2 rather than so much emphasis on music, but conceded that in the following years more time was allocated. The whole school swims once a week in Oundle's impressive pool. Lots of team photos on display and they are delightful, not the usual formal poses but full of fun. Plenty of outside space, including a lovely woodland garden with pond and bridges where time is spent searching for minibeasts. We were not successful in our search, unfortunately, but had lots of fun looking.

Plenty of after-school clubs including debating, gardening, chess and all the usual sports and drama. Also a very popular street dancing group. One parent who wanted to see some different clubs, 'perhaps a politics one,' was the only dissenting voice. Most said there was too much choice and restrictions had to be made. Lots of school trips, residential and day.

A friendly, happy, relaxed school. Pastorally excellent. The older children spend a lot of time with the younger ones, including walking them across the road at lunch time to the dining halls shared with Oundle School. Onsite dining facilities are on the wishlist, but the children seem to enjoy the walk in the middle of the day. Every parent very positive about the pastoral set up. 'The school cares, so much so that when my son first started and wasn't settled they allowed me to attend at playtime to observe that all was well. And it was.' Another parent commented, 'it's a lovely community.' Active school council with representatives from all years who have just introduced a 'friendship bench' in the playground. 'It's where you can go if you are feeling sad, lonely or cross. It's like a buddy bench. Sit there and someone will come and join you to make sure all is well,' one of our guides told us. 'We chose the school because of the pastoral care,' was a frequent comment.

The children look smart in their uniforms, white tartan pinafores or skirts for the girls and smart blazers for all. 'I would like them to wear caps,' was one mother's comment. A smallish school, but the size is what attracts many parents. 'It's family friendly and the children are lucky to be in such an environment. They promote independence and confidence as well as a good all round education.' As one mother succinctly put it, 'If there was anything bad about the school my children would be out of there.' Quite.

Leicester Grammar School Trust

London Road, Great Glen, Leicester LE8 9FL

Ages 10–19 **Pupils** 809 **Sixth form** 222 **C of E**

Fees: £13,029 pa

01162 591900
www.leicestergrammar.org.uk

Acting Heads: Deputy head (academic), Carl James, and deputy head (pastoral), Angela Ewington are holding the reins during the 2018-19 school year.

The new head from September 2019 will be John Watson, currently head of Bablake School in Coventry. Degree from Oxford in classics and modern languages, PGCE from Exeter and advanced certificate in educational management from Leicester. He has also taught at Sevenoaks School, Millfield School and Trinity School, Croydon.

Academic matters: This lot are high achievers. In 2018, 77 per cent A*-A/9-7 at GCSE and 46 per cent A*/A at A level, 78 per cent A*-B. Most pupils take 10 or more GCSEs. Chemistry is compulsory – most do all three sciences – as is one language. French, German, Spanish, Latin or Greek are the choices. DT well supported. Caterham provides a kit car to build each year. Last year's was driven round the grounds by the head. Twenty-four subjects offered in sixth form, mainly traditional academic ones, no 'soft' ones. Maths, further maths and the sciences are what this school is about. 'The children are stretched but not to breaking point,' said one parent. Another parent wasn't quite so happy: 'I would like to see the foot slightly less on the accelerator. They are driven very hard.' Another parent said, 'The school doesn't seem to be very flexible when it comes to changing sets, up rather than down.' 'Teaching is good, excellent in many subjects and support is there. But I do worry slightly that the child in the middle, neither flying or struggling, might get overlooked,' commented one parent. Many staff are old pupils.

The lessons we observed showed bright, engaged pupils, very keen to join in. Year 7 maths obviously inspired by their teacher, lots of arm raising and enthusiasm. Year 8 DT getting on with it, with very chatty, welcoming year 12s working hard on their own next door. Happy year 8s and teacher having fun cooking. Year 10s analysing Wilfred Owen poetry and keen to share the experience. The prep class sang to us in French. Sixth form classes varied from one-on-one in German to three studying philosophy. More in economics and labs. We liked the greenhouse just outside one of the labs, used for seedlings and cuttings during biology experiments. All focused. For such an academic hothouse there's a very relaxed, happy feel to the place.

Learning support available. One child with an EHC plan. Thirty-two with cognitive/literacy need, seven with physical needs and nine pupils with EAL, all fully supported. 'My child is dyslexic and was given extra English lessons rather than studying for a second language', said one parent. 'It was very well managed with no fuss and he achieved an A and A* in his GCSEs, which shocked and delighted us.'

Games, options, the arts: Sport becoming more of a focus and gaining momentum. Ex-internationals now on the staff and superb facilities on offer. Boys and girls playing at county level in hockey and cricket; netball, athletics, badminton, squash and golf too. Internationals in fencing, volleyball, orienteering, sailing and swimming. Others playing rugby for the county or for a local premiership academy. Overseas team tours in most sports. More than one team represented in most sports. 'The sports facilities are fantastic but I don't think they make the most of them, there only seems to be emphasis put on one rugby team per year, so it's a pity for the less able but equally keen players,' said one mother. The girls showing us around didn't agree, stating that 'there were lots of teams and practices.' Every parent commented on the 'fantastic facilities' that include numerous pitches, grass and Astroturf, lovely airy swimming pool, huge gym and a dance studio with mirrored walls. Oh, the joys of being in new premises.

Music and art very strong, particularly in the lower years. 'I specifically chose the school because of their strong music department,' said one mother. 'And if you play an instrument it's compulsory to be in some sort of band or group, which I think is excellent. It means that for a LGS pupil it is the norm. My daughter has made many friends, and in different age groups, as they are put in bands according to their ability.' 'Delighted to see boys in the choirs,' said another mother. Interesting that the music department is below the maths one. 'We get to hear lots of practising and notice improvement during the week', one sixth former told us. There are 28 bands, orchestras, choirs and groups that meet to rehearse weekly. Lots of opportunities to perform with monthly, termly and annual events. Also a music tour.

House singing and karaoke hotly contested, as is house drama. Yearly drama productions, rehearsals ongoing for school play The Exam. Last year it was Sweet Charity.

L

Lots of artwork on display, particularly in the art wing, and it's good. Many of the teachers successfully sell their own work, other work by local artists brought in and displayed. A pity interest drops off in the sixth form, but those that carry on get very small tutor groups.

Background and atmosphere: Founded in 1981 and originally located on the old grammar school site in the city centre. It opened with 94 pupils, but no sixth form. Ten years later it had 500 and a sixth form. There is also a junior school that opened in the early 90s on a separate site. Now both are together on the 75 acres at Great Glen. Long driveway conceals the school from the road. Large signs and flying flags announces its presence. All buildings are new, but can't be described as architecturally appealing, in our view. Functional rather than aesthetic. It feels like a mixture of a hospital and an airport, when you drive in. A one way system with parents seemingly dropping off on the move; no-one stops. Very efficient but slightly soulless. But what can you expect from such modern premises? The first thing you see when you walk through the sliding front doors is the large library. It's an academic school and they are drawing your attention to it. Inside is light and airy, lovely wide corridors so no overcrowding. Laid out simply and effectively. Still feels a bit like an airport though, but not unpleasant.

All very high tech. Fingerprint recognition is used for entry to the library and for lunch. 'Once my son saw that he was desperate to come.'

Pastoral care, well-being and discipline: Discipline not mentioned by any parent, which was interesting. Behaviour obviously not an issue. 'It's a kind school,' said one parent. 'The staff keep a close eye on the pupils and seem to know if something is wrong.' Another parent told us, 'I chose the school because they accept that not every child is sporty. They don't force them, but allow them to find their own niche. They are very much about including rather than excluding, and are very accepting of the quirky.' Another parent was more blunt: 'The geek or nerd will probably be safer there than anywhere else. They are very accepting of the oddball and eccentric and just seem to absorb them.'

All parents we spoke to were happy with the school.'Child focused' and 'children not frightened of the teachers'. 'Easy to get in touch with the school and emails answered promptly'. Lots of comments about problems being 'nipped in the bud' and 'dealt with quickly'. One parent did think the school had 'been caught on the back foot when it came to internet bullying, but quickly got itself up to speed and were keen to learn where they needed to step in'.

Student support run by the sixth formers, ably assisted by the school nurse. This is a counselling course that over 40 of the sixth formers take, with a class a week for eight weeks. They then use these skills for mentoring the younger years. The nurse also offers pastoral support. 'I was stressing about my AS levels last year and she was lovely and really calmed me down and helped me plan my time properly,' one of our guides told us.

Some parents felt rather isolated from the school, physically rather than emotionally. The vast site with its one way system and well planned traffic control doesn't encourage stopping for a chat. 'Because the school is away from the town centre it's not as social, for children or parents. They all seem to come home straight from school rather than socialise. A good thing in many ways, but not always', said one mother. There is a coffee shop on site that sixth formers can walk across to during the day, only to be used by staff, visitors and sixth formers during school hours. Apparently built at the request of the year 11s who were very miffed to be moving out of the town centre – where were they going to go on a 'date'? We suspect some parents are delighted with the move.

Pupils and parents: Pupils come from a wide area, but mainly from the city and environs. Pupils reflect the demography of Leicestershire, with 25 per cent of from Asian backgrounds. This percentage is slowly increasing. Parents forward-thinking, not bothered by tradition and mainly from professional backgrounds. Many connected to the hospitals and university in the city. 'We have parents with high aspirations for themselves and their children. The mix works. We adhere to the principals of Christianity but faith, race and gender aren't important. Everyone mixes well and parents are happy with the moral stance of the school.' The children we met were all very welcoming, friendly and engaging, more than happy to chat. 'Well rounded individuals, confident but not arrogant, such a good reflection on the school,' said a parent. 'I chose the school because it is forward looking, modern and multi-cultural, which reflects our society.'

Every parent we spoke to would happily recommend the school. 'I have three children at the school who are all very different. But all are happy and fit in well, which says a lot. If they're happy, I'm happy.'

Harry Ellis, England rugby international and British Lion, is an old boy now returned as a teacher.

Entrance: Entry at year 7 based on pre-assessment day plus an entrance exam covering maths, English and verbal reasoning. Some candidates interviewed. Over half come from Leicester Grammar Junior School. There is no automatic transfer; all sit the entrance exam. Another 20 or so come from the prep class that is a year 6 group taught within the senior school. These children come from local primaries and gain automatic entry to the senior school as they have already sat an entrance exam. The remaining children mainly come from surrounding state primaries.

Entry to the sixth form requires minimum two 7s at GCSE in chosen A level subjects and at least four 6s. All external candidates are interviewed. Some 20 or so join the sixth form each year, mainly from state comprehensives. Very occasionally one will come from nearby boarding schools.

Exit: Some 20 per cent leaves after GCSEs, mostly to the local sixth form college. Vast majority of pupils head to a Russell Group university; Leeds, Birmingham, Nottingham, Bristol, Leicester, Newcastle, Oxford Brookes and UCL currently popular. Six Oxbridge places in 2018. Almost 20 per cent each year study medicine or biomedical courses (seven medics and one vet in 2018); engineering and physics also popular. Gap years becoming more common.

Money matters: Discount offered for more than one child, five per cent for two, 7.5 per cent for three and 10 per cent for four. Means-tested bursaries available as well as academic, sporting, music and art scholarships.

Remarks: The new kid on the block is making its mark. Has more of a feel of a state city grammar than a private school. But forward-thinking parents who aren't interested in tradition, status and history are flocking to it. LGS offers very competitive fees, produces excellent results and the facilities are tremendous. Your child can complete all of their schooling here, as long as they make the grade. We think the competition will be sitting up and taking notice, and so they should be.

Leicester High School for Girls

454 London Road, Leicester LE2 2PP

Ages 3–18 **Pupils** 358 **Sixth form** 57 **C of E**

Fees: £8,985 – £12,195 pa

0116 270 5338
www.leicesterhigh.co.uk

Headmaster: Since 2013, Alan Whelpdale (50s). History degree, the first from his family to attend university. From Yorkshire and humble beginnings. 'I quickly realised that succeeding at school was my ticket out of Barnsley.' Decided to teach when helping sixth formers at a local school in his final year at uni. Stayed in Bangor to do his PGCE. Taught in the state sector, mixed and boys, before moving to a girls' grammar in London. 'I liked teaching the more able children as it was a challenge to really stretch them.' Left London for Durham High, then to Farnborough Hill before returning to Durham High as deputy head. Was acting head for three terms and they asked him to apply to be head twice. 'I turned it down as I loved teaching and didn't think the public role was for me.' Quickly realised he'd made a 'massive mistake' and being a head was the job for him. Leicester High is his first headship.

A practising Catholic who is married to the job. Passionate about teaching and education and puts the hours in because of it. 'Education can change lives, and I am living proof of it.' Chatty, intense and open, he is making great inroads at the school. Numbers were falling when he arrived. He's steadied the ship and intake is rising, as is the profile of the school. Described by parents as 'lovely,' 'brilliant' and 'he keeps in touch well.' All parents said how well he knew their daughters and how he was at every school event. High profile around the school. 'He genuinely wishes the girls well,' was one comment. 'He is open to ideas and doing an amazing job,' was said by more than one parent. 'It's because of him that the school is a success.'

Head of junior school: Since 2016 is Sarah Davies. Exeter joint honours graduate in English and primary education. Longest serving member of staff at over 20 years, and most recently head of year 6. 'She's brilliant,' was said by more than one parent. Previously, in the dim and distant past, worked at a state primary in Rugby. A warm and welcoming character who is happy to be able to keep tabs on her ex-pupils as they move across the playground to the senior school. Her two daughters are currently pupils at the senior school. 'Because she is a parent she sees things from both sides,' said one parent.

Academic matters: In 2018, 63 per cent A*-A/9-7 at GCSE; 79 per cent A*-B at A level, 46 per cent A*/A. Impressive results. Italian taught in year 6, along with Latin and Mandarin offered at junior level as well. French and Spanish introduced in year 7. A Latin club for senior girls. Maths is king at this school, with sciences hot on its heels. Further maths offered at GCSE with many takers. IGCSEs in this and five others – French, Spanish and the sciences – 'to stretch the girls.' Maths the only set subject, set for topic rather than whole subject so movement very fluid. Has increased results, and confidence in the subject, dramatically.

Some two-thirds of girls study both maths and chemistry at A level, with biology popular too. Humanities and languages often in classes of one or two because of low sixth form uptake. They are flexible with A level subjects: if they can timetable it a girl can take it. Photography A level introduced by request and lots of impressive artwork on display.

We were welcomed with open arms and chatted to by all, particularly the year 6 art class who couldn't wait to show us their work. Year 8s happily and enthusiastically dissecting a lung in biology lesson; we were happy to observe from a distance. Plenty of cross-curricular work going on; please note the artistic collage of the periodic table on display outside the labs. A very relaxed atmosphere throughout both schools: the girls were working hard and extremely focussed.

All parents from both schools spoke about how well their daughters were doing academically and how well supported they were. Girls get a good grounding in the junior school and quickly learn that 'it's cool to do well.' 'There is a brilliant chemistry between the girls and teachers,' was one parent's view. All parents said girls were happy to approach teachers if they felt they were struggling and got instant support and extra help. Strong mentoring with older girls helping younger, across both schools. Sixth formers go across to the junior school to hear younger girls read. 'I have great respect for all the teachers; they are doing a tremendous job with great enthusiasm.' Average class size 16, maximum of 24.

Not many girls have SEND but those that do offered extra support with no charge. Parents spoke highly of help offered. Four speak English as an additional language. Again support offered and rapid progress made.

Games, options, the arts: Don't be deceived by the apparent lack of facilities sports-wise. Gym on site also used as a school hall. Other facilities are a short walk away and well used, shared with Leicester University. Lots of silver in the cabinet. Strong gymnastic teams, county champions in badminton. Plenty of extracurricular sports clubs including a rugby club for the younger girls – head of sixth form is a keen player, apparently. Ballroom dancing also on offer, so a few budding Strictly starts in the making, possibly? Fun team photos on display throughout the junior school.

An enthusiastic music teacher is making great inroads. There's now an orchestra and several ensembles. Lots of choirs.

Drama and productions enthusiastically supported, aided by a newly opened drama studio. Performances at The Curve theatre. Fabulous drama workshops held by visiting dames including Janet Suzman and Glenda Jackson. Goodness knows how the head managed to persuade them, but he did. 'I asked,' he said.

DofE up to gold on offer, school trips galore. Lots of after-school clubs including homework clubs (at extra cost in the junior school).

Background and atmosphere: Known as LHS, the school has been educating girls for 100 years. Senior school housed in a large old Victorian building, amply extended, off a busy road fairly central to the city; it has been on this compact site for the last 85 years. Junior school on the same site is in bright building, bit of a rabbit warren in parts with lots of stairs but nice, airy, well decorated classrooms.

Parking is at a premium but there is plenty of outside space including a pond, outside seating and vegetable gardens that are tended by the girls. Vegetables are used in food tech lesson and for lunches. Please note the guinea pigs and rabbits; year 7s are in charge of them. The atmosphere is jolly, friendly and welcoming, from the man on the gate to the very friendly receptionist. 'A happy school,' was said by virtually every parent.

Very much a reflection of Leicester's ethnic diversity, a third of the girls are Hindu, another third Muslim. Immediately apparent that all mix well. 'Embrace and accept,' is the ethos of the school. Close ties within the community.

Pastoral care, well-being and discipline: 'Bullying is not a problem,' said the head emphatically. Backed up by parents. 'Any problems are quickly flagged up and dealt with quickly before they can escalate,' was said by many. The staff know the girls well, quickly pick up on any niggles and nip them in the bud. Because the school is so small there does seem to be a very tight knit community with the girls openly supporting each other and pleased about each other's achievements. One parent said, 'My daughter had friendship issues but the problems were solved very smoothly by the teachers. It was dealt with professionally and kindly.' Discipline not mentioned by any parent: they're obviously an obedient lot. Lots of mentoring between the years and sixth form girls can apply for a paid job looking after the younger girls in after-school clubs. 'I am confident that my daughter is safe and happy at school,' was a common theme among parents. Strong school council that appears to be listened to.

As well as being academically prepared for the outside world, sixth form girls are taught the practicalities. They have 'preparing for life' lessons including how to check your car tyres, change a wheel, first aid and how to change a light bulb – excellent. These girls are going to be invincible.

Pupils and parents: A strong community of parents, all very pro single sex education. City people, medics and academics, culturally and ethnically outward looking. Girls genuinely nice with no airs and graces, or pretensions, happy, confident, chatty, open and friendly. But all very ambitious for themselves and their peers. 'A happy child does well at school,' was said more than once by parents.

Entrance: Unashamedly looking for bright sparks but they have to fit the ethos of the school. All girls and parents are interviewed and it is made clear to parents that the school has a strong Christian foundation so all girls will be expected to celebrate this, including Christmas, and to attend church services, as well as other religious establishments. They are prepared to turn pupils away if they 'will not be happy at the school.' Verbal assessment for early years, written examinations for older girls. Automatic entry to senior school for girls in year 5. The odd one each year doesn't make the grade and is kindly guided elsewhere. Some 20 girls join from the state sector in year 7 to make two senior classes which are mixed between old and new girls. Entry to sixth form needs six 6s at GCSE with 7s in the subjects they wish to study.

Exit: Nearly all juniors move up to the senior school. Around a quarter leave after GCSEs, mainly into the state sector, a few to independent co-eds. Two to Cambridge in 2018 and six medics; popular destinations include Manchester, Nottingham, Birmingham and De Montfort.

Money matters: Scholarships, hotly contested, and means-tested bursaries available including a full scholarship in year 7 and a sixth form one for a girl from the state sector.

Remarks: A small but strong school that is developing a louder voice thanks to the head. Not an academic hothouse despite its results. Girls are independent, free thinkers. Feminists in the true sense of the word, they will tackle anything, be it academic or not, and expect to be equal. Long may this continue.

The Leys School

Linked with St Faith's

Trumpington Road, Cambridge CB2 7AD

Ages 11–18 **Pupils** 562 **Sixth form** 198 **Boarders** 250 full, 120 home

Fees: Day £15,900 – £22,035; Boarding £24,000 – £32,925 pa

01223 508904
www.theleys.net

Headmaster: Since 2014, Martin Priestley. Oxford PPE graduate. Claims to be an accidental teacher. Originally wanted to be a diplomat and applied to join MI6: 'I fancied being James Bond.' Whilst waiting for vetting to join the fast stream civil service, taught, and caught the bug. 'The civil service was not for me, too much use of the in and out tray.' Previously taught at Uppingham and was head of Warminster before joining The Leys. Attracted to the school because of its size, 'it's a big small school.' Knows every child. 'I was worried when the last head left as he was so good,' said one parent, 'but Mr Priestley has been very impressive, I like his style, he is very open.' 'He communicates with parents every week via the schools comm; we are very much kept in the loop.' Another parent said, 'He has changed a lot, modernised the school and is making good use of social media.' 'He is at every function and moves around the pitches talking to everyone during matches.' A German speaker who doesn't have a long commute, through the door from the hallway of his impressive looking headmaster's residence. We were privileged to meet Twiglet, his blind dog, obviously a regular in his office.

Academic matters: In 2018, 67 per cent A*-A/9-7 in GCSE, 43 per cent at A level. Impressive results that seem to be achieved without a pressure-cooker environment. Lots of clinics available for those needing extra support, most voluntarily seeking it. Parents kept well informed about academic progress. 'The children are taught to work hard and do their best; what more can you ask for?' French, German, Greek, Latin, Chinese and Spanish all offered at GCSE, many doing two languages. Pupils set in maths for all year groups and sciences from year 10. One parent would like to see more choice of subjects at A level. Most are covered but no politics or photography.

Excellent facilities, computers everywhere with iPads for each pupil. Very impressive art on display including pottery; lots of art rooms with fabulous smell of paint and oils. Sixth formers working on mezzanine floor. Fully equipped DT room including a whole computer suite. Beautiful large library, children encouraged to take books out, free reading periods up to year 9. Lessons we observed showed friendly staff and chatty children. A very relaxed atmosphere but don't be fooled, they were working hard. Noticeably less formal between teacher and student further up the school. Enjoyed listening to the discussions in A level theology; couldn't resist joining in – this lot were very harsh on drivers. Seemingly very young teacher who had the group eating out of his hand, but maybe we are getting old. School on Saturday, all day, for years 9-13, lessons as well as sport. They make good use of Cambridge; lots of chances to go to lectures and listen to eminent speakers.

Learning support lessons for some 50 pupils year 7-11, twice a week in small groups, sixth form weekly one-to-one lessons for 21. Around 16 other pupils monitored throughout the term to make sure their needs don't change. Good support offered and parents are pleased. 'My daughter was disengaged when it came to studying until the school spotted her dyslexia. They offered tremendous support, and still do. She is now completely focused.'

Some 15 per cent of pupils are from overseas, 35 different countries. Around 40 students have EAL requirements. These pupils have three English lessons a week and extra privately funded lessons available if required. Integration activities for all. Monitored throughout their time at the school to make sure language skills not holding them back academically. Many long serving staff, some living on site.

Games, options, the arts: This is a sporty school, renowned for it, with excellent facilities including all-weather pitches. Lots of teams for all year groups. Accepting of pupils who have outside sporting commitments and willing to offer extra support academically if needed. Interesting to see they have a girl in the cricket team; she's there on merit, excellent. Good to see that pupils play within their own age group whatever their abilities. 'It is good for them socially to be with their peers,' said one wise mother.

The school is very keen to emphasise that it is 'not just about sport.' And parents backed this up. 'Their plays are excellent, much better than some I've seen in Cambridge,' from one parent. Lots of drama clubs and productions throughout the year. An inspirational, enthusiastic drama teacher who pulls everyone along with her.

Music excellent, housed in its own school with a very proactive director. Eighteen music rooms including a recording studio and recital hall with excellent acoustics. Professional musicians perform at lunch times. Lots of music lessons, 200 a week. Many talented musicians including ex-choristers from the local prep schools. Loads of bands, choirs, orchestras and groups. Boarders often practise or jam in the evenings.

DofE compulsory in year 9 and 10. CCF from year 10; interesting that they don't have a RAF contingent, yet, but they do have a rifle range.

Many school trips to all over the world. Trekking in the Himalayas, three weeks in Southern Africa for biology recently. Numerous sports tours and subject trips.

Boarding: Pupils are split between 11 houses, including three day houses, and assemble there for registration and notices. The day houses have the same facilities as the boarding ones but without beds. School offers two sorts of boarding, full or home. Home boarding pupils stay at school until after prep and go home about 9pm. They are allocated a space within the house and are in all aspects boarders, except they don't spend the night. A popular option with many parents and pupils. Some 70 per cent board, with 50 per cent of pupils being full boarders and 20 per cent home boarders. Very much a family atmosphere, pupils on first name terms with staff and obviously very tight with each other. Sixth formers share light out duties and often pop in to chat to younger ones to make sure all is well.

Lots of house competitions. Year groups 9-13 housed together; sixth form have their own common room but often join younger age groups. One specific house for sixth form, mainly for new joiners. Lots of facilities including piano that is well used. Younger years share rooms, up to six in year 9, sixth form have their own rooms. Tea and toast-making facilities available, oven available for sixth form. Nice to see some of the dorms were messy. Clean, modern bathrooms, plenty of them. Matron described as a 'superstar' by our guide. Parents agree. 'It really is home from home and they do all they can to make sure everyone is happy,' said one parent. 'They are in a lovely environment and the housemistress really is a surrogate mum.' 'The younger girls have a "big sister" in the house that they choose and she will look out for them and help them settle in.' Prep supervised up to year 11; each pupil has their own desk in prep rooms. Phones and iPads taken away at night from younger years.

Lots of activities offered at weekends and evenings; they are kept busy. Sixth formers make the most of 'Cambridge boarding' and often head into town for dinner at the weekends, choosing to spend time in the city enjoying what it has to offer. Curfew of 10.30pm adhered to. Sixth formers also have a club with licensed bar. Pretty flexible approach to parties. If parents and host parents agree they are allowed to stay away overnight at weekends.

Background and atmosphere: Founded in 1875, The Leys is the only independent co-educational boarding and day school in Cambridge. Went co-ed in 1981. Situated on a 50 acre site a stone's throw from the centre of Cambridge. The buildings surround open playing fields so all feels very spacious. Lots of building undertaken over the years but fits in well with the original red-brick slightly gothic original ones that are beautiful inside and out. Founded by the Methodists, the school still has a strong sense of religious community with chapel services for all, whatever their denomination. Parent like the ethos. Note the original Wesley chapel, one of the earliest built, as a memorial to pupils killed in WW1,a perfect example of the arts and crafts movement. The school was evacuated to Scotland during WW2 with premises being requisitioned for a military hospital. Lots of talk of ghosts in the basement, but we didn't see any.

The big small school is an apt description. Large enough to be well supported and funded by generous benefactors, so offering excellent facilities and teaching, small enough to be intimate, with individuals recognised for who they are.

Pupils and staff lunch together, staff on a mezzanine floor, but many joining pupils. Delicious food we can vouch for. There was a quiet buzz within the dining hall: calm and orderly but relaxed.

Pastoral care, well-being and discipline: 'We are hostile to bullying,' says the head. Problems usually picked up quickly within the house, often resolved by pupils themselves. The house system is very effective with tutors and houseparents, as well as matron, getting to know the pupils well. They spend a lot of time together and quickly pick up if there are problems. Plenty of counselling services on offer if needed. 'There is a very strong community at The Leys,' said one parent. 'I was surprised and delighted at how well the teachers look after the pupils.'

Another parent said, 'Pastoral care is the school's biggest plus point. My child is so happy there and as they are happy they work hard.' 'My child has a voice and is listened to. Problems are dealt with sensitively and well.' It's not just academia here. 'They encourage the pupil to be the best they can be, and not just at studying.' Pupils are listened to. A new initiative is just being introduced by the pupils themselves offering a point of contact for those with race/gender/sexuality issues – very on trend.

Introduction to the school treated seriously. All year 9s invited to spend 24 hours at the school before they start in September, day pupils as well, a very effective method that our guide still spoke about. Lots of bonding sessions to create a community.

Discipline wasn't mentioned by any parent as it doesn't seem to be an issue. The head has had to exclude one pupil for drugs. 'We don't have a zero tolerance policy, but it's close to zero. I know teenagers dabble, but warnings are usually heeded. I'm a great believer in second chances, but not third.'

Pupils and parents: Parents are very much 'Cambridge' academics, entrepreneurs and medics and many more doing the London commute, hence the popularity of home boarding. Popular with Fen farmers as well. Many pupils second and third generation to attend the school. Most live within an hour, boarders as well, apart from the overseas contingent.

Pupils mostly well-rounded and self aware, friendly, welcoming and chatty. They can see there is more to life that just qualifications. A 60:40 mix of boys and girls. No obvious divide between boarders and day pupils.

L

Entrance: Every child is interviewed prior to the test. Year 7 intake of around 30, mainly from state primaries. The main cohort, about 70, joins year 9, mainly from local Cambridge prep schools. St Faith's is part of the foundation and a feeder school. Competitive entrance exam. Their own English and maths plus standardised verbal and spatial reasoning tests. Oversubscribed so they can take their pick.

Sixth form entry five 6s for current pupils. Same for new arrivals but 7-9s preferred. Between 25 and 30 join, mainly to board from day independents, the occasional state school pupil.

Exit: Some 25-30 leave after year 11, mainly to the excellent local state sixth form colleges. Very unusual to lose a pupil to another independent school. The occasional one doesn't meet GCSE hurdle, but again unusual. As expected most to university, RAU and Harper Adams represented by the farming contingent, others to eg LSE, Imperial, Newcastle, Reading, Exeter, Durham and Edinburgh. One off to the US in 2018.

Previous pupils have included tennis player Jamie Murray, a couple of rugby union stars, journalist/politician Martin Bell, the current King of Bahrain and a previous King of Tonga – an eclectic mix.

Money matters: The usual scholarships and bursaries. One full scholarship a year from the Wesley Foundation including all trips. The mindset behind this was so that no other pupil would know they were on a scholarship.

Remarks: A lovely place to study. You feel as though you are in the countryside but are minutes from the centre of the city of Cambridge so you get the best of both worlds. 'I don't begrudge a penny we have spent,' from one happy parent. Known locally as 'the friendly school,' we can see why, it is.

Lichfield Cathedral School

The Palace, The Close, Lichfield, Staffordshire WS13 7LH

Ages 3–18 Pupils 470 Sixth form 49 C of E

Fees: £5,295 – £13,815 pa

01543 306170
www.lichfieldcathedralschool.com

Head teacher: Since 2015, Sue Hannam. She already knew the school well, having arrived as deputy in 2009 and doing two stints as acting head before she finally took over. Sue studied at Innsbruck University and the College of Law and, following a degree in English language and literature at Birmingham, she taught in state schools and also qualified and worked as a solicitor, so LCS gained a wealth of educational and wider experience. She probably needs this experience, being the fourth head at LCS in five years.

Sue used to lecture in law at Reed College whilst in legal practice, and that legal ability to get quickly to the heart of a problem and sort it out has come in useful, with parents saying that over the last year there has been a sense of everything under firm control, and the school has rediscovered its sense of direction. 'She is a doer', said one parent. 'A fantastic asset', said another. She is dynamic, determined, thoughtful and much loved by staff and pupils. 'Sue is fantastic. She cares massively about the school and that cascades right down. She has the support of the whole staff', said one staff member.

Academic matters: LCS is non-selective and its intake around the national average of ability. Results at GCSE and A level are generally good considering that, with 38 per cent A*-A/9-7 at GCSE in 2018 and 52 per cent A*-B, 17 per cent A*/A at A level. Has introduced BTecs in criminology, applied law, business and sport and exercise science. Class sizes throughout the school are small – 16 to 20. There are learning support staff and teaching assistants in the junior school and learning support staff in the senior school who, parents tell us, pick up concerns quickly and set up six week intervention plans that are regularly reviewed. Sometimes intervention is shorter than that with the emphasis being on responding to individual needs as flexibly as possible. There is a robust tracking system in place all the way through the school and the head, with her deputy who has a background in state school leadership, has got lesson observations and more staff training in place. The two of them have introduced line management for middle leaders and department reviews, all contributing to the rapid pace of progress in the school.

The school structure allows for careful transition at the various stages. The nursery up to year 4 classes are housed at Longdon, a glorious rural setting, about four and a half miles away from the Cathedral Close on the edge of Lichfield. Then years 5 and 6 move up to the main site, but in their own hub. They start to share a few of the senior school facilities – the year 6s were very excited about using the science labs – and have some specialist academic staff, but they have their own space and there is a very strong, secure, nurturing feel about it. When they move to the senior school in year 7, the transition is very easy for them both socially and academically, with enough that is new for it to feel exciting.

For a small school, academic options are wide. Pupils can study French, German, Spanish and Latin. Option blocks are based on the pupils' free choice, and if the timetable can't manage a particular subject or combination, the school has run twilight sessions. The expressive and performing arts are very strong throughout the school up to A level.

Games, options, the arts: Music is a huge part of school life. For a small, non-academically selective school, the standard is unusually high. The choristers (boys only) have a demanding timetable and wonderful musical opportunities. There is no longer boarding so they now have to live within travelling distance of the cathedral for the early start. There is also a girls' cathedral choir which sings one evensong a week and combines with the boys on feast days. The school emphasises that it nurtures all musical ability, not just those who sing in the cathedral choir. There are 18 weekly rehearsing groups with various aspirational ensembles that allow pupils to move on in time to the senior ensembles.

The school is very keen to take its music to other schools and is part of a Music Share initiative which aims to improve singing provision in local schools and beyond. The music diary is full and varied, with a lot of performance opportunities, both within the school and cathedral and also out in the community, which the school sees as part of its wider mission. Just before our visit, the senior school had put on Offenbach's La Belle Hélène. The director of music is forging ever-closer links with the cathedral music team, which has oversight of life of the choristers, but he sees the school as a centre for musical excellence for far more than just the cathedral choirs, and believes that music should be something enjoyed and experienced by all.

Performing arts generally are very strong. There are drama clubs and performances going on all through the year and all through the school, in the school halls as well as other local venues. Particularly at the junior end, there is a big emphasis on getting everyone involved. Pupils can take English Speaking Board exams. Lots do and achieve highly.

The year 10 boys told us: 'We are not being big-headed but we are all quite good at sport. There are lots of competitive people in our year'. The school is very conscious that small schools on restricted sites have to work hard to make sport high profile and LCS is trying its best, and pupils told us sport is now really on the up. There are some sports facilities on site, a fundraising campaign is currently underway to build a new multi-use games area in the grounds, and great use is made of all the excellent local facilities – eg Lichfield hockey and cricket clubs. The sports department tries to put out as many teams as possible with the aim of getting every pupil playing in a school team a few times a term and encourages the gifted games players get involved with outside clubs as a way of beefing up what is on offer. They also encourage non-team sports – trampolining, orienteering, golf. At the juniors' Longdon site, male sports coaches have been employed to run lunchtime sports activities.

The Longdon site has lovely outdoor play areas and allows for a forest school. There are tracksuit days twice a week so there is no restriction on getting muddy. There are kitchens in the classroom for the younger ones and some of the curriculum is taught through cooking. There are regular cross-curricular, cross-school enrichment projects going on, some of which engage with the local business community, something the school is seeking to develop further. An etiquette week, sponsored by a local cutlery maker who provided each child at Longdon with a cutlery set while the school talked about the gracious art of entertainment, culminated in a pupil-organised tea party.

Background and atmosphere: Any school in the shadow of a cathedral has a very special feel about it. The children have Monday assemblies in the cathedral and use it for other special occasions. The Palace that houses offices, dining facilities and other functional rooms was the 17th century Bishop's Palace, a beautiful, classically-influenced stone building. 'We are its custodians', says the head.

There have been boy choristers educated here since the early 14th century. The prep school in the Close started in 1942, moving to its current location in 1953, and expanding ever since. Girls were admitted in 1974. The secondary school began to develop in 2004 and the sixth form opened in 2010. The school acquired another junior school at Longdon Green, moved year 4s and below out there, creating the additional space on the Close site for the expansion. Behind the Close frontage are more purpose-built classrooms, recreational and sports spaces. Expanding sixth form recently moved to a larger building within the Palace.

But the school does not just enjoy the cathedral atmosphere as a decorative add-on. The pupils are aware that they belong to something special and that the wonderful location brings with it responsibility. The year 10s (not a year group usually renowned for social conscience) talked to us about being in the public eye as they walk along the Close between buildings and coming to and from school. 'We have a responsibility towards all the tourists. We are part of the life of the Cathedral Close and tourists need to see how much we respect that', they told us.

For the head, it is the cathedral and all that means that differentiates the school. Part must be the music, of course, but she understands this in a much wider sense. There is a strong charity arm where the whole school regularly comes together to raise money and awareness of the needs of the wider society, but in fairness, a lot of independent schools see that as part of their mission. What is unique is the accredited ethical leadership programme that runs right from EYFS through to the sixth form. It gives validity to and recognition of a whole range of activities and behaviours throughout the school, building up layers of ethical understanding as a child gets older through practical day-to-day choices. It is a tangible way of saying to the pupils: we are about a lot more than exam results. We have the highest expectation of you to live in an ethical way in all you do and to understand what we expect of you as an adult in the outside world. 'This is what the world needs', says the head. It is excellent to see a cathedral school stepping up like this. It is a powerful justification for such schools, and the community is incredibly lucky to have found a head with this vision. It also has the potential to be a meaningful outreach for the cathedral with each generation of pupils. The cathedral can be seen as another support system for the pupils and then, as they leave the school, for their families and friends too. The ethical values cascade out.

Parents and pupils talk about the family feel of the school. Both sites are small enough for everyone to know everyone else. The pupils are very protective of each other. There are strong, positive relationships between pupils and staff and communication between staff and parents is highly praised. 'We all have the teachers' emails,' parents told us. 'If we raise a concern, the school is onto it straight away and gets back to us really quickly'.

Pastoral care, well-being and discipline: Parents say the standard of behaviour is high and any suggestion of deviation from this is stamped on immediately. They also like the fact that the school encourages pupils to resolve minor difficulties themselves, so they grow up feeling empowered and confident without always having to run to an adult. The school has high expectations of language use and the pupils rise to it. The worst things we heard about were 'girls being difficult – I certainly wouldn't call it bullying' or the occasional bad manners. Pupils say the teachers are 'quite strict' but that there is much mutual respect.

Because of the school's small size and its structure, there are many roles of responsibility for pupils and the aim is that all children have a leadership role. Because the year 4s are the top year group at Longdon, they take lots of responsibility that they wouldn't generally have until year 6. The children love it and really rise to the challenges. It is this stress on leadership that makes the new accredited ethical leadership course such a strong path for the school to cut.

There is a sense that excellent pastoral care must be at the heart of a school that defines one of its strengths as working with each child as an individual. Parents note that every member of staff, not just a form tutor, takes pastoral care as their responsibility, and there appears to be constant contact between teachers and parents when concerns are raised on either side. We thought this might get a bit much, but no-one at the school did. It is seen as part of the family atmosphere that is warmly embraced.

Pupils and parents: Pupils come from a wide area and now the school no longer offers boarding, some choristers are likely to have long journeys. There are a number of school minibuses that bring pupils in from areas not on a main rail or bus route. The train is a good option for older children, 10 minutes walk from the school and on a main line through Birmingham.

The Longdon pupils are engaging, bright and adore their school. A recent ISI inspector described the seniors as 'confident with lots of humility' and we would endorse that. Parents compared LCS pupils favourably with the aura of 'arrogance' they perceive in pupils going to the well-known selective West Midlands schools. The school is encouraging pupils to understand multiple intelligences, and they don't end up thinking that because they have an A*, they are the best. They understand they all have gifts to offer to a wider society.

L

Families live in Lichfield and around, with quite a number from the Sutton Coldfield area. This hidden gem of a school could be drawing from the populations around Stafford, Wolverhampton and Burton. Our impression is that there are a high number of families that are first time independent school users, who are attracted to the school because it does not conform to their prejudices about the fee-paying sector.

Entrance: The school is non-selective, except for the choristers, who are auditioned by the cathedral and school directors of music. Pre-school children are informally observed during a series of visits. Beyond this, entrance is dependent on assessment, interview and reports from the present school. The assessments are to ensure the school can support the pupil in a way that will ensure all of them flourish. Entry into the sixth form depends on GCSE results.

Exit: A few leave at 11 and some choristers at 13, with some (around 40 per cent) moving at 16 to colleges that offer a wider range of qualifications. Given the wide academic range in the sixth form, pupils go on to more diverse post-18 options than at many independent schools. Some go to good universities, and there are usually one or two off to read music, but the school is very clear that its role is to find out what is right for the individual and support that rather than feeling that everyone has to go off to university. One off to read medicine at Buckingham in 2018; many do vocational subjects such as business and management; Birmingham, Leeds, Loughborough, Reading, UWE and Liverpool currently popular. Apprenticeships and other forms of training on the job are encouraged. It is all about finding the inner passion and facilitating that.

Money matters: Fees are roughly what you would expect for a small school out of London. There are a number of scholarships, music of course, but also sport, art, drama and academic, plus a small number of means-tested bursaries. Learning support is not charged as an extra. Wrap-around care at both sites is at extra cost.

Remarks: The north of Birmingham destination for a musical child, particular one with singing talent. The West Midlands is a competitive area for secondary schools in particular, with very strong academic independent schools and free state grammar schools. LCS is a strong contender for families who don't want a highly charged academic powerhouse and exam factory but something with a very distinctive ethos.

Lincoln Minster School

The Prior Building, Upper Lindum Street, Lincoln LN2 5RW

Ages 2–18 **Pupils** 512 **Sixth form** 98 **Boarders** 66 (from year 3)

Fees: Day £11,931 – £13,632; Boarding £23,013 – £26,715 pa

01522 551300
www.lincolnminsterschool.co.uk

Principal: Since 2015 Mark Wallace (40s). A mathematician from Northern Ireland. Studied at Queen's Belfast. From a banking family and took the same path, working in offshore banking in Jersey before becoming disenchanted. Spent time working for Camp America and decided wanted to teach. Very sporty and an ex-international hockey player. Previously taught at Caterham and Kingston Grammar; this is his first headship. Wanted to be at a non-selective school 'so I can make a difference.' Very aware of need to increase profile of school and numbers. Approachable, friendly and competent and well aware of his remit. Popular with parents, 'a delightful young man', 'approachable,' said by all. 'He's ruffled a few feathers, but in a good way,' was another comment. All parents commented that he knew all of the children by name, and was very high profile within the school and starting to be within the city. 'He's keen to increase the school's profile and is putting himself out there to do so.' One parent called him a 'top bloke with a lovely way about him.' Works closely with heads of junior and pre-prep schools.

Prep and pre-prep head: Since 2012, Fiona Thomas (50s). A warm, welcoming lady with a great deal of Welsh charm. Originally from Cardiff, this is her third headship, the previous one being in Spain. A lady who inspires confidence and has managed the post-merger transition of both schools successfully.

Academic matters: In 2018, 37 per cent A*-A/9-7 grades at GCSE; 62 per cent A*-B at A level with 25 per cent A*/A. Solid results for a non-selective school. High flyers encouraged, less able nurtured. French, German and Spanish on offer at GCSE. One language for all, a few do two but, disappointingly, not many. iPads being rolled out for all. Plenty of computers available with up to date IT suites. Lessons we observed showed engaged pupils and articulate teachers. Pupils set in year 8 in most subjects. Excellent facilities, most of them modern. Parents kept up to date with academic progress and all commented that problems were picked up on quickly. Most spoke about the small classes being a huge selling point of the school. 'We are made aware of any academic problems quickly and support on offer immediately.' The school instils a good work ethic: 'They come home from school and get on with their homework with no fuss,' was said more than once. All parents commented on how well staff knew their child.

Pupils in the junior department usually getting extra support if needed so are able to keep up in senior years. Some 82

SEND pupils throughout the school. Individual learning plans after assessment; parents spoke highly of support offered. 'My daughter was struggling at one point, they spotted it, put her into support and she quickly caught up. We much appreciated it.' Support available in lessons for those that need it and staff aware of how to teach these pupils. Parents very much involved. EAL requirements for 28 pupils, mainly sixth form. A minimum of two hours help a week offered, more if required, particularly in year 11. One year pre-A level course, including GCSEs in key subjects, offered to international students.

Children get a good start here with lots of academic support and diligent, enthusiastic teachers pick up on any learning needs. The non-selection ethos means there's a broad spectrum of abilities, coped with well. Brand new IT suite and well stocked library. Languages taught from an early age by specialist teachers. Spanish in pre-prep, French from year 3, with a chance to sample the more exotic linked in with other subjects: Arabic, Mandarin and even a smattering of Welsh. Children taught as a class with separate subject teachers. Interesting to hear that pupils practise for 11+ papers, but Lincolnshire is a grammar school county.

Games, options, the arts: Sport rapidly improving, helped no doubt by enthusiastic support from the head who seems to have rejuvenated the department. All abilities encouraged to take part. Rugby and football for all, girls too. Rock climbing, judo, polo and squash all on offer. Squash team very successful. Lots of silver in cabinets: U15 girls tennis are regional champions, successful hockey teams and cross-country strong with one star ranked first U15 in the country. New sports hall a few years ago including a basketball court and indoor cricket.

Music very popular here; it is a choristers' school, supplying the cathedral with 25 of its 40 choristers (boys and girls in separate choirs, which sing at separate evensongs). Until recently all choristers at school here; now children from any school can audition. This is happily embraced by the head and some parents. 'It's good to see as there was a bit of them and us from some chorister parents,' said one. It's a big commitment. Practice starts before 8am for an hour every day with evensong beginning at 6.15pm. A long day, with late finishes every other evening. Choristers mostly join the choir in year 3; boys usually out by year 9, girls a little later. Choristers lead the way musically but many more pupils involved as well. Lots and lots of bands, orchestras and other choirs, very keenly supported. Lots of practice rooms including a drum room: drumming very popular, apparently.

Drama also popular. Lots of productions in junior and senior schools, some student-led, others include whole school. Modern theatre with sound and lighting box and new drama studio. Recording studio too. Art students support productions by creating backdrops and props. Excellent art facilities with fabulous views over the city; sixth form artists have their own work space.

Loads of after-school and lunch time clubs including strong debating club. Sports and music as well as homework club to enable later pick up for parents. DofE to gold and school trips far and wide.

Boarding: Boarding offered from year 3 but not many at this stage. Just over half of boarders are sixth formers, with 70 per cent of these from overseas (Brits are all weekly boarders, most living with an hour of the school), in three separate houses. Boarding facilities good. Pretty relaxed for the older children with school friends allowed to stay overnight. The Mount, for younger boarders up to year 8, includes most boarding choristers. Senior girls in Hillside, adjacent to the main school, with panoramic views. Senior boys in Eastgate, a large period house with massive gardens, also a stone's throw from the main school building. Easily accessible to the city. Close links with local hockey and rowing club, with boarders encouraged to join in. Gym nearby and weekend trips for overseas students. Use made of Forces links with trips to nearby bases and museums. Lots of social areas with tea and toast making facilities. Pupils eat at the main building. Supervised daily prep for all ages. Younger boarders do lots of baking and competitions. Maximum of three to a room, which are large and airy – and tidy. Older pupils, mainly sixth form, have their own rooms. Boys planning a garden, designing and planting it themselves. Chapel not compulsory on Sundays. Despite numerous nationalities and languages, a cohesive atmosphere prevails and freedoms do not appear to be abused.

Background and atmosphere: Formed in 1996 by the amalgamation of the Cathedral School for Boys, St Joseph's School for Girls and Stonefield House School. St Mary's Prep School merged with them in 2011 to become the junior school. Lincoln Minster is now the only private school in the city, housed on three separate central sites, a stone's throw from the cathedral. The main building, the senior school, is a combination of old and new. Aesthetically pleasing modern building, opened in 2002, which has blended well with the old, offering large church-like windows and sweeping, modern curves. Its curving corridors are particularly attractive. Sixth form housed in separate wing. Good facilities with comfy common room and eating area.

The junior school is a short walk away. On this site since 2014, an attractive old building with modern extensions, bright and airy, with a well-used outdoor classroom, sitting rather incongruously within a modern housing estate. It was once a city farm and school has large, leafy grounds and is well hidden from suburban sprawl. Each site has plenty of room around it with outside seating areas and large playgrounds. Pre-prep, up to year 2, on a separate site within a walled garden with the cathedral looming over the wall. Lots of space and play areas within a very secure setting, delightful surroundings.

Close links with the cathedral, not just the choristers, and ties are getting stronger, with work experience offers.

The pupils are easily spotted in their distinctive green, white and blue striped blazers, the junior girls wearing kilts – thankfully with a navy blazer; stripes and tartan would be a step too far. Sixth formers wear smart business suits and look the part. A friendly bunch.

Pastoral care, well-being and discipline: 'They know what they can get away with,' said one parent, 'and if they cross boundaries there is retribution.' All parents supported the school's stance on discipline. 'My child was given detention for something pretty innocuous. But they knew the rules, got caught, so fair enough.' Children excluded if necessary or given time out and taught in isolation – doesn't happen very often, but parents made aware of situation. 'What happens in school is dealt with by the school, which is as it should be,' said a parent. All parents commented on quick responses to emails and good communication from the school, including the head.

Pastoral care excellent, according to all parents, and the school prides itself on being nurturing. All the pupils are known to every member of staff and their development closely monitored. 'Problems dealt with confidentially and appropriately,' was said more than once. Niggles eased before they have chance to escalate. Support offered and coping strategies put in place for those struggling. Two counsellors and a school nurse available. 'We have a close rapport with our teachers,' said one of our rather earnest but delightful guides.

Pupils and parents: A strong community of parents. Professionals, medics, London workers, academics from the university and a strong contingent from farming and the RAF. All very supportive of the school. All we spoke to happy with their child's progress and would recommend the school. 'If my child is happy then I'm happy.'

Pupils chatty and friendly and willing to engage in conversation. Independent and well rounded and obviously very comfy and happy at their school. We got the impression of a very tightly knit community with firm friendships.

Entrance: All applicants and parents are interviewed; English and maths exams for 11+ and 13+ entry. Reports requested from previous school and prospective pupils offered a taster day prior to joining. Automatic entry to the senior school from junior. Many year 7 entrants from state primaries. Overseas boarders join for sixth form, after entrance exams. Sixth form entry subject to GCSE results: 'grades need to reflect their subject choices.'

Exit: About 15 per cent leave at the end of year 6, many to state grammar schools. School aware of this and does practice 11+ papers. In 2018, two-thirds left after GCSEs. One to Cambridge in 2018; others to eg Bath, Birmingham, Bishop Gosseteste, Ediinburgh, Harper Adams, Leeds Arts, Leeds College of Music, London South Bank.

Money matters: Fifty per cent scholarships for choristers whilst they are in the choir; other awards possible afterwards and some have music scholarships. Academic, sports and art awards also available, plus means-tested bursaries; discounts for siblings.

Remarks: We feel the school has rather sat on its laurels in recent years, having no private competition, but that is all changing with the current head. He is well aware of local competition from the grammars and an excellent academy in the city, and is working hard to raise the profile and standards. He's making inroads. The school prides itself on its pastoral care, has excellent facilities, gets solid results and, its real strength, has small class sizes.

L

Loughborough Amherst School

Linked with Loughborough Grammar School, Fairfield Preparatory School, Loughborough High School

Gray Street, Loughborough, Leicestershire LE11 2DZ

Ages 4–18 **Pupils** 208 **Sixth form** 40 **RC**

Fees: £9,816 – £12,189 pa

01509 263901
www.lsf.org/amherst

Head: Since 2016 Dr Julian Murphy (mid 40s). BA from Southampton, philosophy and politics; DPhil (Oxon) in the field of Islamic thought; MPhil (Middle Eastern studies), MSc (Birkbeck) in government and administration. Worked in politics for a few years as an assistant to an MP, numerous odd jobs in his 20s but his main intention was to be an academic and become a professor. By the time he had completed his doctorate, decided that academia was too solitary for him. Born a Catholic, but not a particularly devout one, found Catholicism again in his late 20s, 'as many people do, you could describe it as a dark night of the soul.' Turned to teaching, starting as an RE teacher at Woodbridge 'and fell in love with it.' Has always been in the private sector.

This is only his third school, and first headship. And he has got a challenge on his hands. School has been haemorrhaging numbers and he has been brought in to turn it around. 'They made no bones about it in my interview, but I liked the school and like a challenge. The school has a lovely ethos with happy kids. I'm confident it will work.' He has instigated dramatic staff changes, appreciated by parents. Previous poor management had allowed the school to drift aimlessly but Dr Murphy has grabbed it by the scruff of its neck and parents are noticing, and grateful. 'He's a really good leader, just what the school needed,' said every parent, whether they agreed with all his ideas, or not. 'Supportive, and he listens,' said one. All said he was approachable, like him and appreciate 'the new broom'.

Standards are already improving. He's not afraid to ruffle a few feathers and has done so dramatically by announcing that the senior school will start taking boys in September 2019 and has now changed its name to Loughborough Amherst School, after the first head of the school. A bundle of suppressed energy, nervy and enthusiastic, he will undoubtedly carry everyone with him; his great determination is apparent. A great debater, assertive and positive, he is having to work hard to convince some parents, particularly about the name change, but he's getting there. Teaches the occasional A level RE class and year 7 PHSE so knows all the girls. Two children of his own, a boy and girl, at the prep school.

Head of prep school: Since September 2018 is Izzy Winton. A practising Catholic, she comes from a deputy headship at a state primary. Very experienced in tracking and monitoring, she has been brought in to improve numbers and standards.

Academic matters: Twenty-six per cent A*-A/9-7 grades at GCSE in 2018. At A level, 21 per cent A*/A, 57 per cent A*-B. Maths taught in three sets in years 10 and 11 despite the smallness of the classes, 'but we have to do it,' says the head. English set if necessary but they play it by ear depending on year group. Sciences split into double and triple option with 40 per cent taking triple. French, Spanish and Latin all taught to GCSE, German being phased out. French and Latin taught in the prep. Most girls do one language at GCSE, but this is waived if they feel that is right for the individual pupil; few take one at A level.

The strength of the school is the small class sizes (the largest class we saw was 11 girls; sixth form average is five) and the lack of pressure. 'They know my child and the way they learn,' was said more than once. 'Focus is on effort rather than grades quite often,' said one. Senior school parents talk about teachers inspiring confidence in their daughters, so helping with learning. 'Good at giving everyone a chance,' said one perceptive mother. Teachers happy to be emailed by parents, and girls, with quick responses.

Youngest pupils taught in two year groups together because of dearth of numbers. Older junior numbers much higher and growing. Prep school small enough to have every child's photo on a board in class groups, a nice touch.

Many new parents chose the school because they liked the teachers and their methods. Parents have noticed improvement in the quality of staff, and are very pleased. All parents said teachers know their daughters well, 'and care.' Parents with older girls appreciate the almost individual tuition in some subjects, particularly at A level. There really is nowhere to hide in this school, but that can add pressure on certain girls.

Every lesson we observed was relaxed with plenty of discussions between pupils and teachers. We were met with welcoming smiles by all, staff and pupils alike, who were more than happy to chat.

Lots of support for sixth form girls including plenty of UCAS help. As there are only 20 or so in each year, individual attention for all. Nice touch to see last year's leavers and destinations on a board. Gives year 13s inspiration and aspiration.

Almost half of the pupils have some sort of SEN, and this is where the school's strength lies. The majority are being monitored, extra support for 20 and two have EHCPs. School is registered with CReSTeD as supporting pupils with dyslexia. It is renowned for taking children who have had a tough time emotionally. Lots and lots of extra support on offer academically and very close contact kept with parents and girls. 'My daughter has been given so much extra help academically and teachers understand that at times she needs to learn differently than in the traditional way.' 'Grades don't always matter, effort is definitely lauded and recognised.' Some extra lessons charged for, others not.

Games, options, the arts: They punch above their weight in netball and there's fierce competition with their neighbours Loughborough High a few minutes away, with whom they share facilities. Usually one team per year but years quite often juggled for a better mix of players. Sport being made more of a priority and extra staff being taken on to accommodate boys. 'I'm excited to see what the new teacher will introduce sports-wise; it can only be a good thing for the school,' said one parent. Plenty of sports clubs on offer. Boys in year 6 go to the grammar school for their sports lessons, historically a good way to familiarise them with the school where most would move on. Rounders popular and we had our heart in our mouth to see a match being played on the lawn in front of the convent surrounded on all sides by windows. We are quite sure this will not continue after September 2019. Head keen to be able to offer more choice of sports, teams and individual, and mixed football and cricket teams being considered. 'I'm determined that pupils will leave school having at least one sport that they enjoy and want to carry on with.'

Music excellent with many girls having individual lessons. Mention must go the impressive music school which is shared between the three Loughborough Endowed schools. Numerous bands, choirs and orchestras, mostly across the three schools.

CCF also across the three schools; we were proudly introduced to the first female leader of the RAF section. The occasional residential trip across all schools; DofE on offer. Plenty of school trips and tours including a recent netball tour to Dubai.

Background and atmosphere: Founded in 1850 by the Blessed Antonio Rosmini as a day school for the Catholic girls of Loughborough, the school is still on its original site. The convent, where many lessons are taught, is a beautiful building built around a quad with the nuns' garden as its inner sanctum. This is now used by the sixth form girls, who have their common room on the top floor of the convent. Girls were able to choose the décor; do note the very elegant chandelier, and nice to see balloons and ribbons to celebrate an 18th birthday. Our guides took great pride in showing us the mood lighting. Years 10 and 11 also have a common room within the convent, not quite so well decorated; note the hole in the floor with a warning sign, but the room is big enough to make it easily avoidable. The chapel is used for assemblies daily and can accommodate the whole school. Catholic ethos throughout and the spiritual life of the school is very much alive and kicking, and being actively embraced by the newish head. Each classroom has a crucifix and rooms in the convent are named after saints.

There is an air of tranquillity and serenity and all parents commented on 'the lovely atmosphere in the school.' And it's true, we felt it straight away, particularly in the convent. There is a slightly ghostly feel too in parts of the school that are hardly used because of the low numbers. The old verandah has a somewhat musty smell, but it does not detract from the atmosphere. It will be interesting to see if this changes in September 2019 with the influx of boys. Fences are being heightened and certain other changes being made to accommodate potentially more boisterous behaviour and kicked balls.

School joined the Loughborough Schools Foundation in 2015: it made sense as it shares the same large, leafy site as Loughborough Grammar, Loughborough High and Fairfield Prep. Since then, we get the impression that it has been grabbed by the scruff of its neck and been given a good shake with the new head implementing dramatic changes. Parents, and head, are slightly annoyed that the convent has the reputation for being the school 'for thick children.' An unfair misnomer it would appear, and head is working hard to change other parents' perceptions. It makes sense to become co-ed to allow boys as well as girls from Fairfield Prep to have access to a non-selective school where the pressure is less intense than in the other senior schools. 'It's only fair boys should have the same opportunity,' said one parent.

Junior school pupils looked smart in their berets and caps and their blazers with distinctive striped piping when we visited. One parent did comment on the shortness of some of the skirts, but head is well aware that waistbands are rolled up. Sixth form girls wear smart business suits in either black or navy.

Pastoral care, well-being and discipline: Pastoral care is one of the school's great strengths, acknowledged by every parent, and many talked about the nurturing environment, academic as well as pastoral. 'They know girls and how to handle them,' said by all. Many parents like the Catholic ethos, as do the girls, who enjoy the spiritual life of the school, whatever their background. Sixth form girls act as 'mothers' to year 7s and counsellors available on site. Being kind is very much part of the ethos and charity work actively encouraged. Some parents question whether boys will be handled as well as the girls pastorally, but new staff appointments are all from co-ed backgrounds, so provision is being made. Head very aware of mental health and educating parents accordingly. It was very obvious teachers know the girls well. One of our guides was celebrating her 18th birthday, and virtually every member of staff congratulated her. The benefits of a small school. One of the disadvantages was pointed out by one of our guides. 'Everyone gets involved in any disagreement, which isn't great.' Staff seem to be able to deal with this; as we said, they know the girls.

Interesting that discipline was a bugbear of every parent we spoke to: historically there didn't seem to be any. 'Discipline needs improving; the head has worked his magic in the senior school and now needs to instil it in the prep,' was one parent's comment. 'The new head is working on it and taking action.' 'The same names popped up every time for disruptive behaviour but this has now been sorted out.' Parents delighted with head's approach and fully supportive. There are now formal beginnings and endings to lessons where girls are expected to stand for the teacher. 'I think the girls quite like it and expect, and respect, boundaries,' says the head. And, of course, so will the boys.

Pupils and parents: Girls usually live within 30 minutes of the school. Parents mainly professionals and 'unpretentious with no airs and graces,' according to the head. Only 15 per cent are Catholic but all embrace the ethos of the school whatever their religion. Understandably some parents are very pro single sex education and are not happy with the imminent changes. Head has been able to persuade most about the benefits but accepts he might lose up to five per cent of families. Most parents are taking the view that they'll stay put 'as long as my daughter is happy.' Some have reservations about how boys will fit in, but are putting their trust in the head. Many parents are old girls themselves and unhappy to see the name change. 'It will be sad to see the convent go.'

Girls are a friendly, unpretentious bunch. Many are third, or more, generation. Kind and sensible, they are aware they have been fortunate to be taught in such an environment. The tranquil surroundings seems to influence the girls who appear to be very serene and untroubled: 'happy' is how we would describe them. These girls have high aspirations and are ambitious, good to see.

Entrance: The school is non-selective academically but head more than happy to say it is selective with regards to behaviour or if there is a special need they cannot cater for. Will happily turn away a pupil with a record, or evidence, of poor behaviour. Entry to the pre-prep by taster day; applicants for year 3-6 are also assessed during a day spent at the school. Pupils come from a wide range of primary schools. The highest intake comes in year 5, mainly from state primaries, with another influx in year 7 (via entrance assessments). Automatic entry from junior to senior school, unless behaviour criteria not met. At least five grade 4 GCSEs for entry to sixth form.

Exit: Most of the boys in the prep school head to Loughborough Grammar but now those that don't quite make the grade, or would benefit from a different teaching environment, can stay. The odd girl to Loughborough High but most stay on at the convent. A third leave after year 11, mainly to do vocational courses at the local college. Girls not suitable for A levels kindly guided elsewhere. The vast majority to university, eg Nottingham, Leicester, Newcastle, Manchester, Nottingham, Exeter. Gap years relatively popular, apprenticeships not mentioned.

Money matters: Some means-tested assisted scholarships awarded in years 7-10. New sixth form scholarship for applicants from state schools.

Remarks: Interesting times ahead, with the name change away from convent. Parents seem to be unsure whether to relish or resist, but we are quite certain that the school's ethos will prevail and the head's great determination will pull everyone along with him. He deserves to succeed: the school nurtures and encourages and in so doing brings out the best in the girls who achieve their best and, equally importantly, leave the school as well rounded individuals who are upstanding members of their community. And why shouldn't boys enjoy the same benefits?

Loughborough Grammar School

Linked with Loughborough High School, Fairfield Preparatory School, Loughborough Amherst School

Burton Walks, Loughborough, Leicestershire LE11 2DU

Ages 10–18 **Pupils** 977 **Sixth form** 300 **Boarders** 61 full, 2 weekly

Fees: Day £12,549; Boarding £28,752 pa

01509 233233
www.lesgrammar.org

Headmaster: Since 2016, Duncan Byrne (40s). Languages degree from Cambridge (choral scholar) followed by MEd from Buckingham. From a teaching family, 'so it was always in the back of my mind.' Didn't fancy being behind a desk all day; 'working with young people is unfailingly interesting and varied: there's always something unexpected, often humorous, that happens most days.' Very keen on single sex education for boys, 'they take more risks intellectually.' Encourages boys to contribute to local community, 'it makes them feel part of something and helps with well-being.' He's settling in well and making his mark. Parents like him, and we can see why: he's charming, affable and chatty. 'He's very easy to talk to,' was said more than once. Parents appreciate communications from him and follow his blog and social media posts. All say they like him and he feels very welcomed by community. Two boys, one at the school, another still in London, a chorister at Westminster Abbey. A musical family; head was attracted to Loughborough because of its music credentials. Lives on site in headmaster's house. Teaches languages to year 7s. Attends all home matches and has a high profile around the school.

Academic matters: In 2018, 65 per cent A*-A/9-7 at GCSE; 47 per cent A*/A at A level, 75 per cent A*-B. Excellent results but remember the school is fairly selective, though 'not as selective as you might expect,' says the head. French, German, Spanish, Latin and Greek all taught to A level. Head very keen for languages to flourish; 33 per cent of boys do two languages, 35 per cent study classics including Latin to GCSE. Maths is king, with around two-thirds studying it for A level. Sciences also very popular. Results have improved in the last few years with tracking of pupils becoming more effective. This means intervention is more prompt. 'Some boys are naturally lazy if they are not pushed,' says the head. Parents back this up, commenting on 'outstanding teachers who push the boys.' Parents kept well informed of progress. Lots of clinics for different subjects. Boys take advantage of these. 'They get lots of homework,' said one parent, who talked about the headmaster's blog explaining that the boys needed to do more at home. School well aware of boys and their foibles. All homework online so no excuses. iPads for all from year 8. The jury is out, with the head and parents unsure about the effectiveness of these as an educational tool. Half of the boys' work is handwritten so still lots of emphasis on 'old fashioned' skills.

The school is cleverly laid out with defined areas for each subject. Impressive library with spiral staircase in oldest part of the building. Chapel now used as a classroom, but small services still held here. Boys working hard and taking part in discussions in classes we viewed. Each science subject has its own block with impressive labs. Setting in maths. Lots of artwork on display. Mention must go to DT: a massive department, with state of the art equipment, run by a very enthusiastic teacher. Please note the electric racing car, built by the boys. The boys are taken driving round a local race track in the cars they have restored and built. Sports car being restored, and driven on sports day, funded by parents. Many more boys who are not studying DT join in with restoration work. The school has recent UK Young Engineer of the Year winners and many go on to engineering careers, including in motorsport. Some sixth form subjects are taught with the girls from Loughborough High: psychology, music, languages and politics.

Some 40 boys on the SEN register, one boy with an EHCP. Five per cent of these are seen every week by learning support at no extra charge, as yet. Around 120 boys are on the monitoring list. Diagnostic testing for all boys in year 7, 9 and 12. Class sizes average 16 in the main school, 10 in sixth form. EAL support is very good. There is an EAL co-ordinator who works four days a week helping the boarders, in particular, who are offered at least two hours a week support. Day boys can also use this service. Many boys, in line with the ethnic diversity in the area, speak a second language at home.

Games, options, the arts: Sport is compulsory right into the sixth form; 'it's good for them,' says the head, and boys are expected to participate and contribute. Rugby very popular and successful. Hockey, cricket and football also well supported, as are cross-country and athletics. Plenty of teams for all. Sport rotated and varied, so even the least sporty boy can find a niche. Excellent facilities a short minibus ride away at Quorn, their 70 acre site where most sports are played. On site are a swimming pool, large gym and cricket pitch. Parents happy that sports stars not favoured; 'they all muck in together,' said one parent. Another said their son 'didn't miss out by not being sporty.' One parent did complain about 'the amount of sports gear we have to buy. Do they really need at least two sets of shorts and so many different tops?'

Fabulous music school that is shared with the other schools in the Loughborough Schools Foundation. Please note the grand piano in one recital room; this is a Steinway School. Many boys have individual music lessons. As expected, music excellent and parents rave about the concerts and reviews, 'they have an amazing choir.' There are over 40 weekly ensembles. Plenty of orchestras, bands, choirs, most combined with the girls' schools in the foundation. Lots of instruments lying around the school during our tour. Drama and school plays talked about a lot by parents. 'They are well co-ordinated with lots of rehearsal time.'

Far too many clubs to mention but a nod must go to bridge and chess, and the slightly more unusual beekeeping. The head was very pleased to be presented with a jar of honey shortly after his arrival. CCF very well supported, joining forces with the girls. DofE popular and lots of school trips including trekking in Vietnam and plenty of sports tours. As one parent said, 'there is so much available, it's up to the boys to take advantage of these opportunities. They are pushed to try things, which is excellent.'

Boarding: Most boarders from year 9 upwards, nearly half sixth formers. Virtually all of them international, the vast majority from Hong Kong and China. LGS has been an international boarding school for 25 years. There are two boarding houses: Denton House for those up to year 11 and School House for sixth formers. Lots of cultural trips for the boys including visits to London, Oxford University and a pantomime at Christmas, as well as many more local trips to nearby matches. The boys are kept busy, encouraged to join the CCF and take part in the musical activities.

Very experienced housemasters know the boys well. 'The common room is the heart of the house,' said one; during the refurbishment he made sure that there was room to sit all 31 boys together. There is a house meeting every day at 6.30pm, even if it's only for five minutes. The newly refurbished dormitories house up to four boys; sixth formers usually in pairs. Each boy has his own desk. Very cleverly supervised, but allowing independence, doors are propped open between 6.30-8pm. Computers and phones allowed but Wifi use closely monitored, any misdeeds picked up immediately.

Sport compulsory three evenings a week, usually basketball, which is very popular. Boys allowed into town, which is a five minute walk away, in twos or more and out of school uniform. With all this activity it's easy to keep the computer nerd off his laptop. English language classes held in the house. Unlimited supply of hot water greatly appreciated by the boys. Note the chickens in the garden; boys enthusiastically collect eggs for breakfast.

Background and atmosphere: Established within the town since 1495, the school has been at its present site since 1852. A state grammar school until 1974. Sited just on the edge of Loughborough, a town not noted for its aesthetics, the school itself is something of an architectural revelation. Part of the Loughborough Schools Foundation which comprises four selective independent schools, Loughborough Grammar, Loughborough High School, Fairfield Prep and, since 2015, Loughborough Amherst. Loughborough Grammar shares a massive campus with the High School and Fairfield.

This handsome Victorian red-brick school is built around a quad. Modern extensions have blended in exceptionally well. As you enter under an arch, which is a memorial to fallen pupils, the school stretches out in front of you. Neatly mown grass, which only the upper sixth – and your guide – are allowed to walk on. Over the years the school has bought most of the Victorian and Edwardian houses on the opposite road so boys can roam safely in a traffic free environment. It is slightly confusing trying to find the main office; luckily a friendly sixth former took pity on us and guided us in the right direction. Very confusing, we imagine, for visitors. Upper sixth boys have their own car park – the privileges of being in your final year.

A large school, both in number of boys and space. Lots of grounds for boys to let off steam. A school of all creeds and colours, the boys all seem to rub along well together and the atmosphere is cohesive and cordial.

Pastoral care, well-being and discipline: The head was honest enough to say that in a school of this size bullying does exist but is dealt with rapidly. Backed up by a parent who talked of problems on the school bus 'that were dealt with effectively and fairly.' All parents were happy with discipline, many of them saying, 'the boys are not allowed to step out of line, standards are to be met.' Good. Heads of year play an important part in the boys' welfare and discipline. Parents spoke highly of them and said 'staff know my son.' Boys understand sanctions that are handed out and reasons for them.

School very attuned to mental health issues and is proactive and preventative. 'We want the boys to know and like who they are and learn to be good at being themselves.' Very keen to ensure boys have a balanced lifestyle, hence plenty of sport and music as well as studying. Certain parents need to have this balance explained, school happy to do this. Parents happy with pastoral offerings. 'The reverend and his team are always available if necessary.'

Pupils and parents: Boys travel from up to 25 miles away, covering Leicestershire, Nottinghamshire and Derbyshire. Busses from all areas. The school has a broad social and ethnic mix with a number of pupils speaking a second language at home. Families vary from old county families, where a pupil could be the fourth generation to study here, to university staff, academics, professionals, engineers, as per the area, and many medics. All parents want a broad independent education; interestingly, not many expressed a strong preference for boys only. Parents have high expectations and most are working hard to be able to afford the fees. Boys mix well and strong friendships are formed. Good to see that the geeky, quiet boy is as accepted as the rugby stars.

Entrance: Entry into year 6 is small, 17 places, and not publicised; mainly takes younger siblings. Most boys, 131, join in year 7, with a third coming from the affiliated prep school Fairfield, the rest from state primaries. Entrance exam; they are looking for bright sparks. A small number join in year 9. Another 25 or so join the sixth form, 10 overseas boarders, the rest from the state system, mainly to study maths and sciences. Five 6s at GCSE as an absolute minimum are needed for the sixth form, higher for certain subjects including maths, sciences and languages. Most new entrants have a fistful of 8-9s. School happy to turn a boy away if attitude and work ethic isn't right.

Exit: About 20 per cent leaves at the end of year 11, mostly to mixed colleges in the town. Virtually all go to university, 80 per cent to Sutton Trust Top 30 group. Sheffield, Birmingham, Durham, Cambridge, UCL, Nottingham and Warwick currently popular.Five to Oxbridge in 2018, eight medics and two dentists; many engineers, 'it's in the genes,' says the head.

Money matters: Scholarships – music and academic – and bursaries on offer of up to 105 per cent of fees.

Remarks: A large, traditional, urban boys' school offering a good, well rounded education. It's not just about grades, albeit these are an important part; these boys are turned out as grounded young men with a broad outlook on life. Fees are excellent value for money, deliberately kept low. The parents appreciate this.

Loughborough High School

Linked with Loughborough Grammar School, Fairfield Preparatory School, Loughborough Amherst School

Burton Walks, Loughborough, Leicestershire LE11 2DU

Ages 11–18 Pupils 576 Sixth form 150

Fees: £12,549 pa

01509 212348
www.lsf.org/high

L

Headmistress: Since April 2019, Dr Fiona Miles, previously senior deputy head at Haberdashers' Aske's School for Girls. English degree from Cambridge; she taught English at Habs' until her love of science took her to King's College London to study medicine. She then returned to teach at Habs', progressing through increasingly senior roles.

Academic matters: Loughborough High doesn't feel like an academic oven nor an intellectual boiler, more like a skilfully-used slow cooker. GCSE results 79 per cent A*-A/9-7 in 2018; A levels 79 per cent A*-B, 48 per cent A*/A, but that doesn't seem to be what this school is really about. There's palpable feeling of genuinely shared academic interests and concerns. We witnessed a fabulous teacher who described herself as being 'as nutty as a fruitcake' enthuse and encourage a group of sixth formers who were trying to decide what topics they wished to work on for their EPQ during the summer holidays. Music Therapy, The French Revolution and Literature, a fiendishly difficult sounding science investigation: 27 girls were volunteering to pursue their chosen topic over the summer holidays. They were liaising with teachers to act as personal tutors over the holidays. The decibel count was high and happy. These were not necessarily what Australians call Pointy Heads: they were girls of spirit and zest, girls who might, as one teacher put it, jump in puddles.

We heard girls talking about the wonderful help given in choosing universities and the right course; we heard teachers saying what fun it was to teach such lively and interested girls, 'though they can drive you mad'; we heard girls talking about the extra help teachers were prepared to give. 'Everyone realises how lucky we are to have so much support,' said a girl. In the splendid library we met a girl reading Plato's Symposium for pleasure and keen to discuss it, and another bursting to talk about Churchill and the Gold Standard; we saw some thrillingly exciting textile work. There was the faintest whiff of cordite and revolution amongst those artists who wanted to do more art and design but felt they were being prevented by the preponderance of maths and science. As might be expected, the facilities are excellent; the teaching superb.

Games, options, the arts: The recently refurbished Astroturf, a huge area, is shared with the boys – though not simultaneously. Hockey, netball, cross-country, tennis, athletics, rounders, soccer and cricket. Plenty of county players and more, though the delightful girls who showed us round said that they found the games too serious and just wanted to take exercise. So they went to the gym. Music is phenomenal. Housed in a superb modern building, it isn't, but it feels as if it is, the centre of the whole Loughborough complex. Inside there is a wonderful sense of activity and involvement orchestrated by the seemingly tireless music teachers. 'Music is what makes my daughter so happy at Loughborough,' a father told us. 'None of our family is musical but my daughter has taken to singing and loves it. It's been the making of her.' In fact there are 15 choirs, including a senior choir of a 120. Overall it is a thrilling place. Other extracurricular activities include DofE, in which over 70 girls are involved; debating, chess, bridge – the latter particularly popular. The girls we spoke to were thrilled that they are now allowed to join the CCF section. It is a sombre thought that one of the first women officers to be killed in Iraq was a former pupil.

Background and atmosphere: Founded in 1850 and one of the oldest girls' grammar schools in the country, it is now part of the Loughborough schools empire that includes the boys' grammar, Loughborough Amherst and Fairfield Prep, run by a central governing body. But, important this and fiercely protected, each of the schools on the very handsome campus is autonomous. Boys and girls do some lessons together – politics and psychology, for instance – and they share the music building, but overall they have separate identities with their own teaching blocks and accommodation. For those parents who cannot decide between single sex and co-education this might seem the perfect arrangement. As for the atmosphere, it is purposeful and friendly. Girls seem very much at home in the sensitively run set up and 'we are given the opportunities to air our views.' There is a wonderful variety of meals in the excellent dining room with cheerful, friendly kitchen staff contributing to the overall sense of well-being.

Pastoral care, well-being and discipline: Over and over again we heard comments about how friendly and helpful the staff are; how they are helpful not only with academic matters but with social and personal confusions. 'There's always someone to turn to,' seemed a subliminal refrain. There are anti-bullying guidelines in place but girls looked astonished at any suggestion they might need invoking. There is a genuinely warm and mutually shared feeling of interest and respect between staff and pupils.

Pupils and parents: Pupils come in from a 40 mile radius covering Leicestershire, Derbyshire and Nottinghamshire, and we have heard stories of families moving to be nearer the school. Parents we spoke to felt involved, consulted and considered. 'You can be sure of straight and honest feedback from staff at parents' evenings,' one father told us, 'none of that politically correct foggy stuff. What's more, the teachers really know the girls.' That certainly sounds refreshing.

Entrance: About 40 per cent of entries come from Fairfield, the Loughborough prep, the rest from local state and private junior schools. Intakes for year 7 are assessed in English, maths and non-verbal reasoning; the next three years in English, maths and reasoning. Entry into the sixth form is via GCSEs, reports and interviews. Typically 9-7 grades are required for those subjects to be taken at A level plus at least five grade 6s which must include maths, English and science. No wonder they get good A level results.

Exit: Up to a quarter leave after GCSEs for a variety of reasons: boarding, sixth form college or a subject which is not on offer at Loughborough. Girls told us that very few left because they were fed up. One to Oxbridge in 2018, plus seven medics, one dentist and two vets. Warwick, Leeds, Reading, Bristol, Cardiff, Newcastle and Liverpool currently popular. Much success with university places in a variety of subjects: sciences are popular, plus philosophy, politics, modern languages, classics, music and architecture.

Remarks: The best of both worlds with superb, inspirational teaching and alert, interested girls. Not a hothouse dedicated to clawing up league tables, expelling anyone who doesn't contribute to that, but rather a genuinely academic school where learning is prized and pursued with a measure of joy and satisfaction. A very happy school. A very good school.

Maidwell Hall

Maidwell, Northampton NN6 9JG

Ages 7-13 **Pupils** 118 **Boarders** 92 full

Fees: Day £17,505; Boarding £20,220 – £26,880 pa

01604 686234
www.maidwellhall.co.uk

Headmaster: Since 2001, Robert Lankester MA PGCE (50s). Educated at Charterhouse and Selwyn College, Cambridge, where he read history. Leapt into teaching after seven years in the City ('the best decision I ever made'). PGCE at Durham then 13 years at Uppingham, 10 as a housemaster. Exudes an air of calm confidence that pervades entire school and his charges (averaging around 127 in number) have acquired in spades his self-assured qualities as if by osmosis. Was responsible in 2010 for the introduction of girls, who are now fully established at around 40 per cent of the cohort.

Adored by parents who say he is 'incredibly all-seeing'. A teacher at heart, still teaches CE history and mingles with pupils at mealtimes. Lives on site with multi-talented wife, Carey ('a very special person,' say parents). With such idyllic rural surroundings, there's probably no need to escape to the country, but when the Lankesters do, it's to their home in Carmarthenshire, where they enjoy walking.

Entrance: Fifteen to 20 join school into year 4, with handfuls joining each year thereafter, resulting in numbers almost doubled at top of school. Small numbers of pupils join aged 7 and are taught with year 4, repeating the year. Very gently selective ('I can count on one hand the number of children we have turned away over the past 10 years,' says head), prospective pupils assessed in maths, spelling, reading and NVR, plus short interview.

Majority join from pre-preps or other prep schools and live within a 90-minute radius of school. Few London families. Forces 'significant'. Less than 10 per cent international.

Exit: Almost all stay until 13+, progressing to (mainly co-ed) public schools. Greatest numbers to Uppingham, followed by Stowe then Oundle. Boys in ones and twos most years to Eton and Harrow, a few more to Radley, with girls only very occasionally opting for single sex schools, eg Queen Margaret's, York or Roedean. Extremely rare exits at either 11+ or to day schools. Some scholarships, although head says, 'We don't push them. They can be a weight around your neck and ruin your last year of prep school. We'd rather good grades at CE than shaky scholarship results.'

Remarks: How many prep schools of such modest pupil numbers can boast such riches? Maidwell's gardens, rugby pitches, trout-stocked lake, six-hole golf course and 'wilderness' – where its pupils can climb trees ('only to three times our own height,' we were earnestly assured) and build dens to their heart's content – are framed by spectacular Northamptonshire countryside and farmland as far as the eye can see, the school instantly seducing visitors with its quaint Swallows and Amazons feel. A 17th century turreted hall is the main school building and boarding accommodation. To compare the fabric of Maidwell to other preps would be as to compare Sandringham to Beckingham Palace. Here you will find no trace of architect designed theatres or gleaming new boarding houses but a low-key wealth of facilities that's right in line with the lifestyle of the well-heeled parent cohort.

The overall vibe is wholesome, jolly and humane. No abrasive bells to signal the end of lessons or break: 'This is their term time home,' says head, 'and we try to make it feel as homely as possible.' Also: 'We have less a uniform and more a code of dress, allowing pupils to express their individuality'. The result is a charming array of corduroy trousers or culottes, a striped or checked shirt and tie of choice (boys and girl prefects only), topped off with a jacket tailored in pupils' own choice of tweed. Screen time almost non-existent, save the occasional sports match or the news for prefects. Phone calls home are made from one of a few good old-fashioned landlines situated in nooks around the school and the tradition of a compulsory weekly letter home to parents continues. Free time, or 'muckabout', is spent running around the vast grounds, taking part in one of the plethora of activities and sports on offer or – we were delighted to see – reading. Parents love that their children 'are not just getting an education, but a childhood too'. The 21st century has not bypassed Maidwell, though, and technology is very much alive and kicking in the classroom, with all pupils now taking a standard issue iPad to every lesson.

So, we asked, what kind of 8-year-old goes full boarding these days? Head very clear that Maidwell pupils are not 'sent away' from home as was often the case yesteryear. Boarding here is 'always a positive choice' and 'to be honest, the children clamour for it', he says. All have a 24 hour boarding trial in the summer prior to starting and, as far as we can make out, it's consistently a hit. About half of parents are 'old school', with the rest 'a lovely smattering of everybody else, but definitely not flash', we were reliably informed. Those we spoke to – most having had the debate about the benefits of weekly versus termly boarding – were keen advocates of the full boarding model, grateful that their children are not subject to the weekly upheaval of lengthy travels, the emotional switch between school and home life or constantly exhausted without a chance to fully recharge between Saturday tea time and Sunday evening.

Small class sizes of up to 15. All lessons taught by subject specialists, many of whom are trained secondary teachers, which 'enables us to be teaching at almost GCSE level by the time pupils leave', says head. Two streams in each year, with pupils set separately for maths. Trad curriculum (languages are French and Latin, with Greek for potential scholars taught outside of usual timetable). Parents of very academic children full of praise for teaching, with staff spending their break times to offer extra tuition to scholarship candidates around exam time. Exam technique covered in detail at frequent revision seminars in the run up to senior school exams and all CE pupils create revision plan with deputy head, with up to eight hours' extra independent study expected at key times: 'we make sure they are always in the right place at the right time', he says. High praise, too, from parents of the less academically stellar who, if necessary, are 'taken off quietly by the incredible learning support department', often resulting in pupils becoming 'unrecognisable' in their outcomes. Mild dyslexia, dyscalculia or dyspraxia all in a day's work 'but pupils do have to be mainstream', says head. Mild ASD (mainly undiagnosed) also fine but 'I dislike labels and won't allow them', says head. 'The structure of a boarding school plays to the favour of children who may have been told they have ADD or ADHD – we work with it as we would anything else'. Specialist EAL teacher supports international students, who are often withdrawn from French or Latin. We loved the vertical tutor system – there are no forms and pupils have the same tutor from the start of their school career to the end and meet weekly in groups of six to eight – 'it engenders a lack of hierarchy among the pupils', says head. Behaviour and manners a major strength of school: 'we are very strict, although pupils don't really realise it and parents comment on improvements after just a few weeks', says head. Mothers concur: 'if you want a well-mannered child, send them to Maidwell'.

On top of all the academic subjects, very strong art, led by the 'young, fizzy' head of department, and drama equally impressive. One 'massive' production every year, described by parents as 'brilliant – so slick and fresh.' About two-thirds take peripatetic music lessons in the somewhat makeshift music rooms. 'Not ideal, but it all just happens,' says head. Sport six days a week with 'everyone in the teams' and plenty of match day success. It's rugby, hockey and cricket for boys, and girls – whose sport is 'good now', thanks to new head of girls' games – play netball, hockey and rounders, albeit sometimes in mixed age groups to make up numbers. Great to see girls' football on offer as an activity – how about cricket next? Pupils jet away on fabulous sports tours (eg hockey to Barcelona, rugby to Dublin and cricket to Antigua). Weekly swimming in school's indoor pool, also used for free swims during activity time. Activities aplenty, with two compulsory during the generous 45 minute morning break and three in the evening each week.

N

Boys' dorms up a sweeping staircase off the main entrance hall and girls (who have to access their dorms via a different route in the evenings) on the charming attic floor above. Pupils allowed to board weekly during their first year – and can even choose to be a day pupil throughout their Maidwell career if they so wish – but very few do. Homely dorms sleep six to seven pupils. Dorm captains – top year pupils placed to keep an eye on their younger peers – in every room 'to make sure everyone's happy – and tidy.' Spectacular views across the grounds and surrounding countryside (beds in turrets most coveted) and the girls' rooms in particular, with their sloping ceilings, lending themselves to festooning with cheerful bunting. When we visited, pupils were buzzing in anticipation of the competition for most festive dorm decorations (whilst on the subject of Christmas, we are told that the carols round the tree, with the tradition of head boy/girl placing the star on top and youngest boarder a glass dove on a lower branch, followed by an 'amazing' Christmas lunch, are 'magical'). No boarding parents per se but head and his wife, a director of boarding, two matrons and three gappies live on site.

Whole school assembles each morning plus service in the church next door every Sunday, with plenty of parents in attendance. Meals all taken in quite the loveliest prep school dining room we've ever seen. Family style dining ('the food's amazing,' said pupils – and we can vouch for Friday fish and chips) served out by either a member of staff or, for the older ones, a pupil. Lunch fairly formal, with grace at the beginning and end announced by head's hand bell, and the tradition of a box of boiled sweets passed round to finish. At breakfast and supper pupils can sit amongst their friends or siblings in different year groups. Weekends in school are action packed, with Saturday morning lessons generally followed by a sports fixture and relaxed evenings in with pizza and movies. After church on Sundays, there are trips or friendly sports matches. As one parent told us, 'there really isn't time for homesickness'. House system in place with head boy/girl, house captains and fiercely fought competitions for absolutely everything.

Maidwell parents 'couldn't be more delighted' with their choice. Traditional in the most positive sense, parents describe as 'extraordinary' the extent to which staff know their children and love the fact that school allows its pupils to elongate their childhood, free from the pressures of social media and the internet, whilst packing a hefty academic punch and shimmying them smoothly into their next schools.

Northampton High School

Newport Pagnell Road, Hardingstone, Northampton NN4 6UU

Ages 2–19 **Pupils** 586 **Sixth form** 100

Fees: £9,750 – £14,331 pa

01604 765765
www.northamptonhigh.co.uk

Headmistress: Since 2015, Dr Helen Stringer (50s). History at Bristol followed by doctorate from Sussex and PGCE in London. Vast years' experience of teaching girls, most recently at Stephen Perse Foundation in Cambridge; this is her first headship. Knew she wanted to teach. Quickly realised she loved teaching girls: 'I'm passionate about opportunities for women and education opens doors for them.' Likens education to gardening, 'sow the seed and nurture.'

Small, softly spoken, and quietly unassuming, but a true leader with a deep passion and conviction. Parents ooze enthusiasm: 'My daughters would follow her through fire'; 'She's enthusiastic and generous; the school was lucky to find her.' Parents talked about the subtle changes she has made. 'She looks outwards, has got more involved with the community and raised the profile of the school.' 'She's a great leader and a fabulous head.' Parents describe her as 'friendly, approachable and inspirational.' We could see that. She's sees the broader picture, the empowerment of women and life after education. Holds tea parties: every girl will be invited to attend at least once a year, about six at a time, when they set their own agenda and chat about anything, be it dreams, politics or life. Still teaching year 9, 'I like to keep my hand in.' Very aware of the power of social media, and the downfalls, but embracing it.

Interim head of the junior school: Caroline Petryszak, who has extensive teaching experience at schools including Dr Challoner's High School in Buckinghamshire, St Mary's, Cambridge, and The Perse School for Girls (now The Stephen Perse Foundation).

Academic matters: In 2018, 53 per cent A*-A/9-7 at GCSE, 74 per cent A*-B at A level, 51 per cent A*/A. Plenty of languages on offer, French, German, Spanish, Latin and Greek, up to A level. Virtually all girls take one language, many two and the odd one three. Girls set from year 7. Parents kept up to date with academic progress and speak highly of 'inspirational teachers.' Lots of revision and drop in clubs, and huge support for girls. Pupils happy to approach staff for extra help. They get quick responses to emails; all said staff 'went the extra mile' in both schools and all said how well staff knew their daughters.

Lots of excellent facilities including libraries and IT areas. Lessons showed good interaction between girls and teachers. A very relaxed air, but focused, and importantly, happy. As the school is relatively modern, lay out is good with separate blocks for subjects. Parents appreciate the small class sizes, up to 20 in junior, 24 in lower senior, 20 in upper years and 15 in sixth form.

Junior school follows same ethos. Happy, perky girls. Our guides were an inspiration, full of fun and confidence but knew what they were about. Girls taught in class with subject teachers dipping in and out. They get a good start here, setting them up for the more academic teaching at the senior school.

Sixth form girls drift serenely around the school. Not overly smart in faux business suits but fit for purpose. They have a separate block with lots of quiet areas to study. Humanities and sciences equally distributed at A level – good to see. Lots of support for girls for UCAS; teachers obviously know girls very well and vice versa. University interview practice sessions on offer.

Not a huge number of SEN students, but well supported with individual education plans and parents very happy with outcome. One-to-one tuition if necessary, group tuition for most with all staff aware of needs. Some 59 pupils with EAL status but only 15 have extra support. Gifted and talented spotted young and nurtured.

Games, options, the arts: Huge sports complex offers something for everyone. Impressive, recently updated pavilion with fabulous viewing area and communal meeting place. Senior girls offered the usual, hockey, netball et al but also boxercise, yoga and spinning popular. Girls play football and if they ask for a sport they are given a chance to try it. Rugby was mooted so the local premiership team, Northampton Saints, was coerced to offer a masterclass. Rounders and volleyball teams as well. Plenty of silverware in the cupboard. They have a Paralympian swimmer and a county champion shooter. Sport encouraged in whatever form. All this competitiveness perhaps rubs off from the junior school – remember who the head is – and sport actively encouraged there, particularly ball team sports including cricket. Pity they don't have a basketball team. Lots of clubs and practices, and plenty of teams.

Excellent artwork on show with lots of choice, from sculpting to drawing to photography. We must mention the textiles work: not ordinary, run of the mill stuff but high fashion and high standards. Younger girls were making make up bags, having designed their own fabric first. Clever use of Photoshop and computing skills integrated here.

Music popular throughout the schools. Large music area and lots of practice rooms. Some 170+ girls have timetabled music lessons. Bands, choirs, orchestras galore, and well supported. Drama also popular with a large studio on site. Girls encouraged to use the lighting and behind scenes as well as act. A through school production annually, along with lots of other smaller scale performances throughout the year groups. As well as drama clubs there are others on offer such as knitting, engineering, debating – you name it, they've thought of it. 'There is too much choice,' said one mother; 'my girls want to do everything!'

Plenty of school trips including annual skiing. DofE to gold. Before and after-school clubs. Many parents drop off at 7.30am to catch the London train.

Background and atmosphere: Established in 1878, initially based in the middle of Northampton. In 1992 moved to the purpose built site in the village of Hardingstone on the outskirts of Northampton. Now being incorporated into the urban sprawl of the town, but not to the school's detriment and development can only mean more pupils. Despite being 25 years old the school site still looks new. Beautifully maintained and sensibly laid out, it flows well with large, bright classrooms and plenty of communal space. Based around two courtyards. 'You don't get lost because if you keep walking you end up back where you started,' said our guide. One courtyard used for seating, the other for experiments, along with a greenhouse. Everything is spacious and spread out. Junior school has its own science lab, art and food tech rooms and IT suite. A forest school for the juniors, numerous playgrounds, and a car park for sixth formers. Please note the spade taking pride of place in the boardroom. The Queen used this when she officially opened the new school and planted a tree. Sadly the tree did not fare as well as the preserved spade.

The dining area is central and shared by both schools. It was curry Thursday, poppadoms were piled high and all girls spoke of high culinary standards. And right outside is the nursery playground in a courtyard, which is at the heart of the school, so the youngsters take great delight in waving to the older girls. 'Once a High School girl, always a High School girl,' was said by girls and parents, and we can see why.

Pastoral care, well-being and discipline: The school is small so teachers know the girls well and parents spoke of excellent pastoral care, recently improved due to parental input. Girls have the same form tutor from years 7-11, 'they are super supportive,' having one-to-one tutorials and turning to them first in times of need. 'The girls are not aware how closely they are being monitored,' said the head. All teaching and non-teaching staff across both schools have teenage mental health training, and are quick to spot any problems. School well aware of pressures and problems that can develop. The girls now have 'life lessons,' including money/health/relationships/friendships; one parent said, 'My daughter complains about yet another PHSD lesson, but the message is getting across.' Even parents are involved, invited to 'living with teenagers' talks. Girls can email the counsellor direct.

One parent said, 'according to my daughters they could be stricter with some girls,' but they were very much an exception. 'The girls are encouraged to communicate with each other and work through problems,' said another parent; 'there is little interference from the school unless it is absolutely necessary, which is the way it should be. It means the girls feel empowered sorting themselves out, a good lesson for life.' It was made clear that the school closely monitors these situations.

A strong mentoring system. Year 11 girls mentor the year 6s so they have a familiar face to turn to when they join the senior school the following year. Seems to work well and the girls have fun at the same time. Girls are happy at school: 'they love being there,' said parents, who spoke about the girls being empowered – this word pops up a lot. School council powerful. Uniforms were changed at their request, sixth form common room upgraded and internal messaging rethought.

Girls taught to embrace and negotiate social media. 'The girls are building their own [LinkedIn] profiles so when they leave they are well on the way to being successful women,' said the head. They are also being taught social skills, how to work a room and join and leave conversations, excellent. Girls are encouraged to use their phones within lessons, albeit supervised, but phones are strictly banned at lunch time. 'We need to talk to each other,' said one of our guides. One parent not so keen on phone use: 'I wish they didn't use their phones at school, they are too much of a distraction.' But the head realises it's a sign of the times. As part of the GDST the school encourages the girls to network with other schools that are part of the Trust.

Pupils and parents: Girls come from a wide area, as far afield as Leicestershire, Warwickshire, Bedfordshire and Oxfordshire. An eclectic mix of parents and girls. Hard core of county set, many of which are second and third generation pupils. Town represented by a more diverse mix of medics, professionals, academics and London businesspeople. All mix well together. Parents very supportive and very pro single sex education. Many families making huge sacrifices to educate their daughters. Girls are bright, friendly and welcoming. The tight-nit community is very apparent. 'My daughter loves being there and has a tight group of friends,' said many parents. 'The heritage of the school and its reputation spoke for itself,' said one mother. 'I was meeting confident, yet humble, academically achieving girls and wanted that for my daughter.'

Entrance: From 2+ into the nursery, with priority places at the junior school – just over half take a place. No assessment for reception places; applicants for years 1-6 spend a day or morning at the school with their classmates and are assessed; school will say no if they do not feel it is right for a girl, despite having spaces.

More-or-less automatic entry to the senior school from year 6. The odd one or two don't make the grade, parents kept in the loop. Large influx of girls, up to 40, into year 7 from local preps and state schools. Up to 20 girls join in the sixth form, mainly from state but interestingly some from mixed independents. Five GCSEs at grade 6 or above to include maths and English with subject-specific grades for more academic subjects. Numbers have struggled in the junior school but are now growing, numbers stable in senior and increasing in sixth form.

Exit: Some 90 per cent move up to the senior school, the other 10 per cent to grammar schools out of county and the occasional boarder. Around 65 per cent retention at year 11, the 35 per cent leave for mixed state sixth forms or to board, the odd one kindly guided in a more vocational direction.

Virtually all girls go to university but apprenticeships being actively embraced with the GDST sourcing internships and work experience. Subjects studied show eclectic mix, mainly at Russell Groups. Five to Cambridge and eight medics in 2018; others to eg Birmingham, Durham, Exeter, Bristol, Leeds, Liverpool, Manchester, Warwick and York.

N

Money matters: Scholarships and bursaries offered through the GDST from year 7. Means-tested bursaries available as well as two HSBC scholarships of full fees to girls from the state sector.

Remarks: A small school becoming stronger thanks to the current head. Girls can spend the whole of their school years on one site, and many do. Offering much more than just an education, these girls are being set up for life. Empowered, well rounded young women who will be smashing glass ceilings as they make their way through life.

Norwich High School for Girls

Eaton Grove, 95 Newmarket Road, Norwich NR2 2HU

Ages 3–18 **Pupils** 607 **Sixth form** 100

Fees: £11,061 – £14,562 pa

01603 453265
www.norwichhigh.gdst.net

Headmistress: Since 2015, Kirsty von Malaisé MA (Cantab) PGCE (Roehampton university) (early 40s), previously deputy head at Putney High School. Trained as a musician at the Purcell School (was BBC Young Musician of the Year string finalist in 1990) and won a scholarship to the Guildhall, but chose instead to study English at Cambridge and to follow a vocation for teaching rather than performing professionally, though music continues to be central in her life. Head of English in two London state schools then at Francis Holland before moving to Putney High. Youthful appearance, has wit and warmth and an ability to go straight to the point.

Great believer in girls' education, 'we want to widen their horizons and arm them with the attitudes and ways of thinking that will help them navigate the world.' Has begun Inspiring Females, a programme of events each term including addresses and workshops led by local and national speakers on themes such as networking and building confidence. Wants girls to develop 'resilience and good habits of mind, the courage to take risks and not worry if things don't always work out'. Likes the direction the school was moving in under previous head and wants to continue to widen the opportunities offered for girls. Pleased reactions from parents who acknowledge the recent changes: 'They have really looked at themselves and the way the school is run'; 'Less stuffy', said more than one and 'We like the more open approach.' Away from school Mrs von Malaisé enjoys reading, 'non- fiction rather than fiction these days', music and in the holidays, mountain walking. She is married with a young son.

Headmaster of prep school: Since 2016 Nicholas Tiley-Nunn BA in primary education (30s). Educated at Woodbridge School, then studied for a degree in primary education at Christchurch, Canterbury before returning to the Abbey School Woodbridge for his first post. After a spell at Radnor House as assistant pastoral head, he returned to East Anglia to be deputy head of the Old School, Henstead alongside a developing career as an educational consultant in teaching maths and the publication of his first book, How to Teach Primary Mathematics. Also found time to marry Rachel, and their daughter is at the nursery. Wants the school to be an 'open place, welcoming to pupils and their families'.

Has incredible energy: besides running the prep department and being a member of the high school's senior management team, he continues to teach various age groups science, drama and games, runs weekly book clubs for years 3 and 6, meets and helps assess all potential pupils and continues with his writing career. 'Be bold, be brave, be beautiful' is (one of) the mantras in his drive to encourage confidence in the girls. 'Schools are great at mission statements but these don't mean much to 5-year olds.' Is very aware of pressures society places on girls and since girls' needs 'always come first here, they have the chance to learn from mistakes, to develop resilience and the confidence to know who they are, and that it is the small things that matter and can make the difference'. Parents very enthusiastic: 'He has made such a difference.' Pupils just as keen: 'He wants us to be ourselves – no identikit girls here!'

Academic matters: Consistently high levels of achievement across the board. In 2018, 56 per cent A*-A/9-7 at GCSE and 52 per cent A*/A at A level. Maths, English, the sciences and humanities particularly outstanding at GCSE. With rare exceptions, all girls take a foreign language up to GCSE – majority do French but German, Mandarin and Greek also on offer. Everyone in the senior school does Latin until year 9 with about 20 per cent taking it as an option at GCSE. Top maths set (currently 29, the largest) also take additional maths at GCSE. At A level, chemistry and maths lead the popularity stakes but, 'It's not a sausage machine for medical school, they are just as delighted with success in the arts,' said a parent. Maths, geography, Latin and art and languages also have exceptional results. Most take the EPQ.

'We are selective, but not super selective, we have quite a broad intake,' says Mrs von Malaisé and the prep headmaster agrees, 'There are very few girls who won't flourish and do well here.' Girls are encouraged to choose the options that really interest them, even if that means contortions with the timetable and at A level, even more so. 'Whether it is further maths, Greek or art we want the girls to follow their own path'. Success is thanks to 'the staff,' chorus pupils and parents. 'Always ready to give extra help'; 'Really went the extra mile to help my daughter when she was struggling at one stage'; 'Some outstanding subject teaching'.

The Inspiring Females programme is fully embedded in the school curriculum. The main aim of the programme is to inspire girls, educating them as to what is new in the world of careers as well as helping them access the traditional routes, and empowering them to make wise and confident decisions about their futures. Key to its ethos is presenting the authentic experiences of women at all stages of their careers and lives, through a variety of different events which are all shaped by the girls.

In the prep school girls are well supported in small classes (usually 15) and the idea that 'it is better to have a go and not quite manage it, than not to try at all,' says Mr Tiley-Nunn. Pupils are class taught throughout the prep with specialist subject teaching in music, games and modern languages from the start. The school has recently introduced mixed ability teaching in maths, which 'has been a game-changer in changing girls' perceptions of their own ability,' says Mrs von Malaisé.

Modest numbers require extra learning support – mostly mild dyslexia or other reading difficulties – usually dealt with in class in the prep, with some withdrawal for group or one-to-one help in the seniors. As all girls have their own iPads from year 5, 'it is easy to change background colours which helps some,' and subject staff are all kept well informed. Reading is 'the best habit any child can have,' says Nick Tiley-Nunn, who leads by example running a book club in his study which closely resembles an independent bookshop, with piles of enticing new books on every surface. Excellent libraries in both prep and senior schools, permanently staffed, open at lunchtimes and after school. There are also regular visits from nationally known authors and book clubs proliferate. 'Reading is cool,' say the girls.

Games, options, the arts: Outstanding sports provision on site including 25m pool (just refurbed), grass tennis courts, outdoor pitches and a sports hall. One whole afternoon a week is devoted to sport: 'It enables matches to take place and means we can cater for a far wider range of activities'. Girls excel – indeed are often the local and regional champions – at all the usual team games, netball, hockey, and tennis, and now cricket and football have been introduced to wild approval. 'Rounders seems a bit wet by comparison, though we like that too.' (They are currently the U11 champions.) Rowing, golf, sailing and riding are all on offer – girls travel in a fleet of minibuses to the Broads and the UEA, all close at hand. School has grasped that not everyone is games mad, so 'we can choose other things like zumba, golf and keep fit, especially in higher forms, but most of us still love team games'. School has produced several renowned athletes and Olympic champions in rowing, swimming and cycling. Games kit has undergone a transformation; 'It was still green knickers and aertex shirts when I arrived – I thought I had come to Malory Towers!' remarked a sixth former. The navy tracksuits with a discreet logo mean 'you can walk home through town and not get stared at,' said a local mother.

Thriving art department, DT and textiles also extremely popular. Great majority of girls choose at least one of these at GCSE and significant numbers continue with art to A level. 'It is just as encouraged as the more so-called academic subjects,' said a sixth former and several girls each year go on to study fine arts and design. Lovely high-ceilinged art studio. The annual summer fashion show with girls showing and modelling their creations is very popular. The theme this year, Domestic Bliss (in an ironic way, of course), a resounding success.

Drama is taught by specialist staff in many instances throughout the school and has a high take up at GCSE and A level. 'Super drama teachers, everyone can get involved – they are not just interested in the next Maggie Smith,' said a parent. Shakespeare, Greek drama and Restoration comedies regularly staged either in the main hall or the drama studio (there are plans for a dance and performance studio). Since appointing a head of performing arts two years ago there has been an expansion in the range of musical productions, as well as more serious drama, and means more girls are involved.

Music has a proud history and is taught by specialists throughout the prep and seniors. Many girls have individual instrumental tuition (lessons usually timetabled for lunch and break times) and revel in the opportunities to perform; few girls are not involved in one or other of the choirs, orchestras, jazz and concert bands or string ensembles (headmistress coaches) which mostly rehearse after school. 'It's quite a job to fit it all in, especially at Christmas and concert times,' said a parent. There is a winter arts festival, a major choral concert and carol service annually plus smaller recitals and concerts throughout the year. Despite this, only small numbers take music at GCSE and hardly any at A level.

DofE well supported with practically everyone doing the bronze award, and though numbers decline there is usually a strong cohort of at least 20 at gold level. Community involvement is encouraged from the start, carol singing at nearby old peoples' homes, the pantomimes performed at local schools by year 8s (organised by sixth formers) and various charity initiatives (the prep recently ran a Grow a Pound scheme to raise money for the local hospital, with puppy walking and sales of grown herbs some of the activities). There is a Stafford House (prep school) Brownie pack, 'wildly popular with a waiting list as long as your arm,' say staff.

Outdoor learning on a high: prep school girls are cultivating produce in a polytunnel, ready to sell as snacks in their shop, and senior girls are clearing Dingly-Dell to plant an apple orchard.

Background and atmosphere: Founded in 1875, the first of the GDST schools outside London. Occupies a desirable site on the Newmarket Road – the tree-lined main road into Norwich – centred on two mansions, Eaton Grove (seniors) and Stafford House (prep). A brisk 15-minute walk into the city centre means local school expeditions are easily arranged and many girls arrive on foot. Previously only glimpsed from the top deck of a bus, Eaton Grove can now be seen well from the road, its magnificent Regency façade a delight, thanks to an extensive pruning programme. 'We were rather hidden away,' says Mrs von Malaisé, who wants the school to be more visible. Stafford House is closer to the side road and very accessible for parents collecting.

Both main buildings have had extensions, mostly sympathetic, over the years and there is a sports complex, sixth form building and separate nursery called the Polliwiggles (Norfolk speak for tadpoles) mostly set around the Big Pitch, quadrangle style. Stafford House, though on the same site, has its own distinct area – surrounded by a playground and a forest school. Everything well cared for and scarcely any litter to be seen. There has been a serious programme of redecoration throughout.

At Eaton Grove, each classroom has a coloured wall eg green for geography, mostly polished wood floors and a traditional assembly hall with a stage and balcony. Excellent IT provision in The Hub and decent changing areas and loos – girls have their own lockers, usually in their tutor rooms. Cheerful hubbub at change of lessons, 'timed to give us a chance to get to wherever we are next – and a breather!' but no pushing or barging through doors.

Stafford House, the prep school, is on a (comparatively) smaller scale but offers similar surroundings, well-proportioned, airy classrooms, plenty of IT, a magnificent staircase and a good-sized hall. There are specialist art, science and music facilities and a transformed library with treehouse seating.

Lanchester House is home to the sixth form. Yet another converted mansion (though rather less aesthetically pleasing – blame fire regulations), it provides excellent study spaces – library, study booths for two or three, take your pick, common room, classrooms and a café; it even has a roof terrace.

Despite separate buildings, relationships at the school are strong and affectionate. Senior girls often visit Stafford House – sometimes for a reassuring chat, often to help with events, or (sixth formers) with reading. Old girls and parents return again and again for events and concerts and the bonds remain long after leaving. 'I was lucky to go there, I still have friends from Stafford House days' and 'You really learn how important friendship is' (this from an octogenarian); staff seem equally attached. The cathedral was packed for the funeral of a highly esteemed former headmistress (aged 98); easy to spot the many old girls – no one needed to look at the words for Bunyan's To be a Pilgrim – the school hymn.

Pastoral care, well-being and discipline: Beginning at the prep stage, girls are 'cherished and encouraged to discover who they are,' says the headmaster. 'We want the girls to think their own thoughts, not just go with the herd.' Parents say, 'They really care about the girls, staff are always ready to meet you and talk if there is a problem.' Not much slips through the net. Small classes mean staff know girls well and parents are encouraged to be involved. Moving up to the seniors is carefully managed with taster afternoons beforehand; chances for the new intake to mix with the 'home grown' girls and meet staff. A greatly beloved head of year 7 gives girls a strong start.

Traditional uniform – tartan kilts and navy blazers, patterned green frocks in the summer – worn up to sixth form, when girls can choose their own clothes. Compulsory school lunch until year 11, 'The food is pretty good, plenty of choices,' say girls, though we saw pupils with nothing but pasta on their plates. No prefects as such but sixth formers have leadership roles running clubs and societies and the Companies (houses) which girls belong to for sport, musical contests and other school events.

Form tutors travel up the school with their form. Heads of year deal with any day to day problems and girls all know someone they can go to if in difficulty. There is a school counsellor and a nurse who girls can see on their own initiative and lots do; 'She has a toaster and microwave in her room and you can eat your lunch in there and talk,' we were told. The Big Sister programme is another scheme to help girls have someone to turn to for help with 'friendship problems mostly,' said a sixth former. Form groups are swapped about at the end of year 8, the aim being to break up any developing cliques and give girls a chance to make new friends. This does cause a few grumbles from girls – 'I liked the form I was in already' – but most see the point of being mixed up. In the sixth form girls are in vertical forms so plenty of opportunity to make friends beyond subject sets and year groups. Negotiating adolescence, exams and the world beyond school are all subjects tackled in PSHE lessons and girls feel 'there is a general air of acceptance, it's alright to be who you are'. Staff know the girls well.

Pupils and parents: 'You can always tell a high school girl,' said a former parent and local businessman. 'They are intelligent and fun and not afraid to speak their minds.' 'Unsnobbish parents, anyone can fit in'; 'girls as bright as buttons but not too full of themselves' were comments from parents and former pupils. Several girls (past and present) spoke of the school 'helping me discover who I am – there were no barriers.' Girls and their parents often make friends for life, and significant numbers of pupils are daughters of old girls, though rather fewer than in times past. Families come from Norfolk and north Suffolk, the majority from within a 15-mile radius – lots by bus or train but school is well positioned for dropping off. Parents mostly local professional, academic, medical and business including some farming and a smattering of old 'county' families. More ethnically diverse than is typical for the area, though very few for whom English is their second language.

Former pupils include authors Nina Bawden, Jane Hissey, Stella Tillyard and Rafaella Barker, singer Elizabeth Watts and the actor Olivia Colman; also, several sportswomen such as Emma Pooley and Victoria Williamson (cycling) Sophie Hemming (rugby) and most celebrated of all: nurse Edith Cavell.

Entrance: Key entry points are 4+, 7+ and 11+, though places are usually available at other stages. Selection for reception and years 1 and 2 is through informal play and general assessment. For year 3 and above, prospective pupils spend a day at the school where they have an interview with the headmaster and do assessments in English, maths and reasoning. For the seniors (11+, 13+) pupils sit an entrance exam in the spring term in English, maths and reasoning and are interviewed in pairs, often by Mrs von Malaisé. Reports are requested from current schools.

Exit: At 11+ close to 100 per cent move up to the senior school. After GCSE around a quarter depart for pastures new – mostly local sixth form colleges, Norwich School, Wymondham College or, occasionally, boarding schools further afield. Post A level, most to good universities to read sensible subjects – eg law, medicine (a medic and a dentist in 2018), sciences generally, geography, English. Numbers to Oxbridge fluctuate, usually three or four, but six in 2018. Warwick, Edinburgh, York, Durham, Newcastle and Sheffield all popular and one off to Florida on a golf scholarship in 2018. Small group of gifted pupils depart for prestigious art, drama and music colleges each year. Plenty of guidance and advice about choices, including post A level after-sales service.

Money matters: The GDST keeps fees at relatively modest levels and the school is seen locally as 'good value for money'. Academic and music scholarships offered at 11+: art, music, drama academic and sports scholarships at 16 + and these can be topped up with bursaries, if necessary. Bursaries not confined to scholars but available generally on a means-tested basis. Around half the school receives help of some kind, full remission of fees on occasion but be prepared (rightly) for searching questions to decide eligibility. School lunches charged for separately but few other extras apart from individual instrumental lessons. The school runs a secondhand uniform shop.

Remarks: The lively, sympathetic atmosphere makes this an excellent choice for bright, energetic girls who want to enter fully into the life of the school and all it has to offer.

Norwich School

71a The Close, Norwich NR1 4DD

Ages 4–18 **Pupils** 1,152 **Sixth form** 342

Fees: £10,998 – £16,212 pa

01603 728449
www.norwich-school.org.uk

Head master: Since 2011, Steffan Griffiths (40s). Studied classics at Oxford and has an English degree from the OU. Taught at some high profile schools including Eton, Tonbridge and Magdalen College School. This is his first headship. A keen hockey player who was playing at a high level in his youth. From a family of teachers, the third generation, 'so it was a given, really.' Parents like him. 'He's very professional and high profile around the school.' Parents said he knew their child and was 'very approachable.' 'He's on the ball with regards to the children, and can communicate well with them at their level.' Smartly turned out, welcoming and with a fabulous office with views of The Close. Has updated and modernised a number of classrooms, overseen major refurbishment projects and is currently development of the new pre-prep department. Teaches general studies to year 9, 'so I know them all,' and classics at GCSE or A level. Has three children at the school and his wife is also a teacher.

Lower school head: Since 2007, John Ingham (40s). Maths and philosophy at Warwick. A Lancastrian, with the accent to prove it. His second headship. Oversaw the school becoming co-ed in 2008 and it is now 40 per cent girls; pre-prep department opened in September 2018. Parents really like him. 'He was not what I was expecting and is incredibly down to earth.' 'The pupils love him,' and 'I took a while to realise how good he is as a head, he's brilliant.' Sings in the choir, incredibly affable and chatty with all of the children. Initially wanted to be an officer in the army but 'found my vocation' with teaching.

Academic matters: In 2018, 71 per cent A*-A/9-7 at GCSE; 57 per cent A*/A at A level, 83 per cent A*-B. French, German and Spanish taught from prep, Latin added in senior school. Several take two languages at GCSE and most take triple science. Some streaming for maths, English and science. Students seem happy, enjoying lessons, and all feels very relaxed with friendly staff-pupil relationships. But don't be fooled, these children are working hard, and the results show it.

Note the brightly coloured doors in the prep school and the outside classrooms, including a well tended allotment. The newish science block near the headmaster's house has fingerprint entry and 12 labs, with chemistry taught on the top floor: 'they are the most likely to blow the roof off.' Subjects housed in different buildings in The Close, so lots of walking for senior pupils. Several IT suites and three libraries, one used for quiet study by the sixth form.

Parents happy with academic achievements and talk of 'very supportive teachers' in both schools. Teachers, many youngish, very welcoming and friendly. 'They are really good in the lower school and really up to date with their teaching,' said one happy parent. 'Teachers talk to my daughter as a real person, and that makes a difference. She feels that she counts and is relevant.' Parents talk about the school 'bringing out the best in their child.' 'My child just flew when they joined the school.' 'The children pick up the ethos of the school very quickly, they are taught to be independent and do a bit extra and it really works. There's no pressure but they work hard to achieve.' Parents appreciate low class sizes, average of 16 in the senior school, maximum of 24 in prep, much lower in sixth form.

Parents spoke about good communication from the school, with useful Parent Portal, though one said parents' evenings were rather chaotic and 'would like to see the year split so there was more time to talk to the teachers.'

SEN support in both schools, one-to-one if necessary, but usually small groups. Parents with SEN children talked of 'massive support' from staff. EAL negligible apart from new contingent of sixth formers, mainly from Hong Kong, who need minimal support.

Games, options, the arts: 'There is so much for them to do,' said one parent. Plenty of rugby, cricket and netball teams for all abilities across both schools, plus well-supported rowing teams, and lots of silver in the cabinets. 'There are lots and lots of teams and the communication from sports staff is tremendous.' 'Be they arty or sporty, the school encourages them and brings it out of them.' More than 100 clubs in prep, more in senior, and well supported by pupils who are encouraged to try everything. New dance studio, impressive sports hall and fitness suite.

Music plays a large part in this school. Sixteen of the junior boys are choristers, on 50 per cent bursaries, with great efforts made to keep them once their voices break. Huge commitment from these boys (and parents) with daily early morning practices and evensong performances several times a week; teachers keep a close eye and are flexible about homework if need be. Senior girls' choir sings evensong on days boys don't perform. Prep head makes sure choristers still get to play sports and are not separated from rest of school. 'The rugby team is full of choristers.' Some 50 per cent of pupils have individual music lessons; loads of bands, orchestras, choirs and a beautiful music room overlooking The Close.

Praise for 'impressive' senior drama productions. Lots of space in newly opened art studio, including photographic area, 2D and 3D rooms. Impressive work on display and a popular subject at A level. A young, enthusiastic 3D design teacher, and well-equipped textile room.

Sea cadets are the largest group in Norfolk. School trips range from a month in Borneo to a lower school outing to London where they stay on a boat 'and sleep in hammocks, which they love.'

Background and atmosphere: Founded as a boy's school in 1096, it is one of the oldest in the country. Housed within The Close, dominated by the cathedral, it appears to have taken over more and more buildings, including the original bishop's palace. Sixth form has quiet study area in the bishop's parlour; please note the portraits of previous heads. 'You get painted when you leave,' said our guide. They have a snooker table and table football in the junior common room, housed in part of the crypt. Plenty of outside space and attractive gardens. Whole school assemblies held daily in the cathedral. The only blot on an otherwise architectural dream is the incredibly ugly and shabby refectory building, and the food – quality and quantity – is the main parental gripe. Plans are afoot to improve on both.

As you walk under the arch into The Close, leaving the bustle of the centre of the city behind, all is calm. The school oozes contentment and serenity, despite plenty of pupils milling about; the ecclesiastical atmosphere seems to pervade. Everyone – from the excellent person who advises on parking to the receptionist and both heads – embraces all comers with an incredibly friendly welcome. 'We felt at home immediately,' said a parent, and the head: 'we offer a modern education in a glorious setting.' The alma mater of Horatio Nelson, the school ceased boarding in 1991 and became co-ed in 2008. Pupils are kept fit as there is a lot of walking between classrooms within The Close; we imagine this lot easily manage their 10,000 steps a day.

The lower school, including the new pre-prep, is at the other end of The Close, hidden away, housed in a modern building surrounded by playing fields and bordered by the river where the rowing takes place.

Pastoral care, well-being and discipline: Parents cited excellent pastoral care as a main reason for picking the school. School determined that no-one slips through the net; light spats dealt with quickly, problems nipped in the bud, robust procedures for dealing with bullying. 'The pupils know their boundaries and detentions are handed out if necessary,' said one parent. 'Problems are dealt with well.' Has recently introduced non-gender-specific uniform. Vertical houses help develop friendships across year groups. The school chaplain, senior tutor, school nurse and three counsellors all offer support. 'We work hard at it, and are good at it,' says the head. Parents agree.

Pupils and parents: Pupils come from far and wide across the county and north Suffolk. A third from within the city, the other two-thirds from as far afield as the coast. Many travel up to an hour each way; the station is a 10 minute walk. Many children are third generation or more to attend the school. Aspirational parents who buy into the 'iconic Norwich institution,' mainly professional with plenty of academics, medics and researchers. It was mufti day when we visited but the uniform of sorts was jeans and puffer jackets for all. Pupils friendly, welcoming and chatty. This is a happy school.

Entrance: Pre-prep candidates assessed for social and reasoning skills, 'and that the child will be a good fit.' From 7+, all sit some sort of written entrance exam plus interview. Almost automatic entry from lower school to senior. Some 30+ join the senior school at 11+, another 25 at 13+. Six 6s at GCSE needed for the sixth form, 7s in A level subjects. Head's discretion used for some who don't quite make the grade. Up to 40 join the sixth form from outside, around 15 from abroad, mainly from Hong Kong and China, who are housed with local families.

N

Exit: Very unusual for a lower school pupil not to make the grade for the senior school, 'none in the last five years,' says the head. Up to 10 leave after year 11, mainly for vocational courses in the city. Virtually all sixth formers to university, five to Oxbridge in 2018, plus six medics and three vets. Bath, Bristol, Durham, Edinburgh, Exeter, Manchester, Warwick, York and UCL all popular; one off to an art foundation course in Amsterdam. Apprenticeships not embraced as yet, but head working on parents to bring them round to the idea.

Money matters: Choristers receive 50 per cent bursaries. Means-tested bursaries, the occasional one up to 100 per cent, in the senior school. Subject, sports and music scholarships available.

Remarks: The school gets excellent results whilst appearing to apply very little pressure, and parents relish this. 'My child bloomed,' was said more than once. The calming atmosphere of The Close pervades with pupils seemingly achieving their goals serenely; underneath the surface there is lots of intense paddling, but not to anyone's detriment. A happy place where pupils and parents appreciate the 'iconic city institution.' It would appear that once a Norwich pupil, always an Old Norvicensian; the links remain strong.

Nottingham Girls' High School

Linked with Nottingham Girls' High Junior School

9 Arboretum Street, Nottingham NG1 4JB

Ages 11–18 Pupils 527 Sixth form 168

Fees: £13,581 pa

01159 417663
www.nottinghamgirlshigh.gdst.net

Head: Since April 2016, Julie Keller (30s). Heads of single sex schools seem to fall into two categories – those who stress their school's excellence with the single sex nature just being one of its characteristics and those who stress the excellence of the focused nature of the single sex education offer. Julie Keller is firmly in the latter camp. Not only is she passionate about single sex education but she has everyone in the school behind her vision. For Julie, only girls' schools have the expertise to ensure the best education for the next generation of female leaders. And with her as a role model, Nottingham Girls' High students should break every glass ceiling going.

Julie is a dynamo – fast talking, confident, absolutely on top of her game; she was deputy head at the school before taking on first the executive headship of the junior school and then the senior headship. She knows the Midlands well, having a degree from Leicester in economic and social history, and before she came to the Girls' High, had worked in a demanding mixed comprehensive in Nottinghamshire. She has a background in pastoral leadership but has also been head of history. Staff tell us she is inspiring, approachable and good fun to work with and they respect her honesty and integrity. They say that since she became head she is really looking at every aspect of the school to hone development plans and up the game.

Girls love her open door policy. She has a study right off a central corridor and has encouraged girls to put their heads round the door and share news. 'She knows all about us all', say the girls in awed tones. On our brief walk with her to the dining hall, she must have exchanged a few relevant words with every single girl she passed. Her priorities are to stretch and challenge the top end, to ensure teaching and learning is absolute top quality and make extracurricular and enrichment activities work better – all of which are moving rapidly in the right direction with the whole school clear about the aims and behind them.

Academic matters: The intake is selective and results are very strong. In 2018, 68 per cent 9-7/A*-A at GCSE and 53 per cent A*/A (82 per cent A*-B) at A level. Being part of the Girls' Day Schools Trust means the results are not only intensively dissected internally but also by the Trust as a whole, and the school consistently comes in the top few for value added calculations. Maths is outstanding but so are the humanities.

The head of educational support leads on learning difficulties, and parents whose daughters have had experience of this speak highly about it. Girls would not normally come out of lessons for this unless the decision has been taken leading up to GCSEs that they should take less than the standard 10 subjects. Programmes are individually tailored and there is no additional cost for this. Class sizes are up to 24 in the senior school and around 12 in the sixth form and it is expected that there will be sensitive differentiation within a lesson. Recent introduction of mentoring sessions, exam technique classes, subject coaches and peer mentors is resulting in a stronger support network for everyone.

Girls are identified for possible Oxbridge entrance in year 9 and well prepared from then on. Every girl is issued with an iPad and these are enthusiastically embraced by staff, girls and parents. Whether it is emails – 'We can just send a quick email to our teacher to explain why we are going to be late for a lesson' – or uploading text books and homework, or constant reference for research in lessons, these tablets are now seen as essential to maximising efficient progress for every girl. Girls email individual teachers with small queries about work and staff send much appreciated short emails to parents when someone has had a good day.

Games, options, the arts: The head has put excellence in sport, music and drama as a top priority. Sport in particular has not had the strongest reputation locally in the past. The head wants not just superb school performances but increasingly to see the girls succeed at national level. One of the first things she has done is to ensure that girls can continue with both sport and the performing arts so there are not the timetable clashes that can cause such frustration. Activities are now timetabled before school from 8.15am as well as at lunch times and after school. Girls can miss registration times for activities – 'You don't get excellence without giving it time', says the head. You need facilities too, with a spanking new 350 seater performing arts theatre completed in November 2016. Money has gone into sports as well with an upgraded Astroturf and new sports hall boasting a splendid climbing wall which even the reception class uses. 'We are building risk-taking and resilience all the way through,' the head of outdoor education told us. There are grass pitches offsite used for lacrosse and other games. Outdoor education has a major through-school emphasis. From fire-pit Fridays, where groups of girls take it in turns to cook lunch outside, playing instruments, singing and just enjoying being together, to climbing Kilimanjaro or the new climbing wall which sixth formers are encouraged to use in their non-teaching time, to joining the exploration society, where they build shelters and make fires, girls have every opportunity to develop confidence in their ability to relate to the physical world.

There is similar encouragement to engage with the wider society. Lots of charity work going on and the school won the lord lieutenant's award for voluntary service. They make videos to support local charitable causes, work on the national citizen service scheme as well as produce endless cakes for fundraising sales.

Background and atmosphere: Occupying several houses, in an increasingly gentrified Nottingham suburb, the school has capitalised on what is a relatively limited space to Tardis-like effect. The old sits next to the new creating a smart, imaginative yet unpretentious feel. Evidence of massive upgrading and modernising is everywhere – a new DT resistant materials suite, food lab, graphics studio, textiles and refurbished labs. The sixth formers have their own labs, art studio, library study area and sixth form building with common rooms and tutor spaces. Technology is everywhere with LED screens in useful public places announcing the myriad of events taking place. The dining room is light and modern with impressive food. Most city day schools are not offering chilli infused extra virgin olive oil to go with fresh salads. There was particularly delicious syrupy flap jacks too the day we visited.

The girls and staff all know they are in a modern, forward looking and confident 21st century school where there is an expectation that they will become tomorrow's leaders. The atmosphere is very aspirational and very individual. 'You can be the best you want to be here', say the girls. No gender stereotyping or any other sort of channelling of girls. Without labelling it as such, the school is giving the girls experiences of how to network, an area that research suggests lets women down at senior level. Here the girls learn about it through the buddying systems, mentoring, even drama competitions which the sixth form write and then work with the younger ones. Everything is about expanding who they know all the time. The Girls' Day School Trust is part of the networking. Girls say they get to know girls in other trust schools at trust sports rallies for example, and then continue to build the friendships online. The trust alumni events allow sixth formers to start forging those all-important professional connections.

Relations between girls and staff are conspicuously warm and relaxed, as indeed are the relationships between staff. 'We all get on and it's good fun', said staff members. The leadership team is relatively young, all at the top of their game and brilliant role models for young women. Well-being of the girls is high on the agenda but so is staff well-being. There is a sense of the spirit of good learning rather than the law – no-one sets homework if there is not a real point to it. 'We say to parents if the girls say they haven't got any homework tonight, then talk to them and go out and do other things.' We were pleased to hear that there is a determined attempt to fight the perfectionism that often dogs very bright girls. No-one has work sent back because it is messy. Girls feel listened to by the staff and therefore take ownership of school structures.

Pastoral care, well-being and discipline: Pastoral care is highly rated by all, in part because of the palpably strong relationship between girls and staff. There is a group of pastoral specialists who have lots of experience of year 7 and the sixth form. In years 8, 9, 10 and 11 the girls stay with the same tutor who gets to know their strengths and foibles in considerable detail. They can't swop out of a form just because they have fallen out with their best friends. 'We want to show the girls that you can rebuild relationships and sort out difficulties,' the head tells us. The school nurse is top quality and fully involved in the pastoral side as well as health. Families who had suffered emotional challenges couldn't speak highly enough of the whole staff's support.

The girls had considerable difficulty of thinking of any disciplinary breaches. The best they could come up with was being 'on report' for late homework. The head, however, says she is firm and will exclude for bullying and e-safety issues. But this is not a school where there is any sense that bad behaviour gets in the way of purposeful activity.

Pupils and parents: Articulate, lively, confident girls who know they are going places. Parents cover a fair cross section, both in ethnic and socio/economic terms. Many families with both parents working. Bursary support widens the range of families that come. Quite a number of families where mothers and grandmothers are old girls. Parents are buying into the school's aspirations and they support wherever they can. New formal parent groups are being trialled with parent reps. Excellent communications is high on the agenda and all the technology, which goes alongside traditional methods, is helping tremendously, though it is the strong motivation to make it all work on a personal level that tells.

Entrance: Unusually, there is no entrance exam for the girls in the junior school to enter year 7. Other girls sit papers in English, maths and verbal reasoning and there is an informal interview plus references from current school. The emphasis is on looking for potential.

At sixth form level, girls are invited to spend a day at the school, sample preferred A Level classes and have an informal interview. References are requested from the current school and conditional offers are made from December onwards.

Generally the school is looking for an average of grade Bs across eight GCSE subjects, including English and maths, with grade A in some subjects to be taken at A level.

Exit: Although more girls than the school was comfortable with left after year 11 in the first year the boys' school took girls into the sixth form, this tide seems to have been halted and the vast majority are now staying through to university. They go to a range of strong universities, a few each year to Oxbridge (five in 2018) but the school is 'not obsessed with it'. Medicine and engineering very popular (three medics in 2018) and other than that, a wide span of the disciplines. On the rare occasion something goes wrong on A level results day, parents say the school is spectacularly good at working with the family.

Money matters: As with other GDST schools, fees represent very good value for money. It is clearly not a school dripping money and endowments but on the other hand there is a style that money can't buy. About six per cent of income goes on means-tested bursaries.

Remarks: Many girls' schools would wilt under the news that the long established and renowned boys' school just along the street was starting to take girls into all year groups, but the Girls' High seems to relish the challenge. It has allowed them to celebrate their expertise in girls' education and there is no doubt everyone in the school sees their school as the one that is forward-thinking, energetic and innovative. There was more of an exodus than they would have liked in the first year but it has not taken the hit some thought it would and the novelty seems to have worn off. This is a first rate, 21 century offer with academic rigour but informal in feel, without establishment stuffiness. The new strapline is 'Be Extraordinary' and everyone believes they can.

N

Nottingham Girls' High Junior School

Linked with Nottingham Girls' High School

9 Arboretum Street, Nottingham NG1 4JB

Ages 4–11 Pupils 216

Fees: £10,419 pa

01159 417663
www.nottinghamgirlshigh.gdst.net

Headteacher: Since 2016, Laura Fowler (BA education), who arrived with a wealth of headship experience. She had been acting head at a state primary school in Essex and head of juniors for six years at Leicester High. She is absolutely on board with the aspirational vision of the whole school and incredibly quickly got to know all the girls. Being newish has allowed her to run meet-the-parents sessions where she is sharing her aim of strengthening relationships and wanting parents to fully engage with the school. Laura, who comes across as both wise and approachable, believes in getting in the classroom whenever she can and is doing some teaching in all year groups. Her staff and the girls love her open door policy.

Entrance: Girls spend half a day in the school being informally assessed. 'We want to see if they are going to be happy here', the head says. There are half termly sessions for 2/3 year olds – 'Tots have Fun' – where the school gets a chance to observe younger girls over time.

Exit: Most to senior school without formal assessment, but if the rigorous internal monitoring process suggestions someone may struggle with the pace of the senior school, this is discussed with parents in year 5.

Remarks: The old and new buildings that make up the junior school sit remarkably well together. One moment you are walking on a stunning Minton floor and then through to the Rainbow Room, a wonderful vibrant space that links two buildings. There is a lovely new library and ICT suite and a good size multipurpose hall.

Academically, there is a buzz about the school. There is much technology in evidence and the girls are confident users. As in the senior school, girls in years 5 and 6 have their own iPads and the girls in years 3 and 4 share class sets. The head and the staff tell us that there is constant reflection on excellent practice and that they are very conscious of modelling the behaviour they want the girls to develop. 'We show the girls that it is OK to cross things out – work doesn't have to be beautifully tidy to be exciting and interesting'. What an excellent approach to find in a girls' school. There is no obsessing about exams and assessments. Year 6 girls go away for a residential trip the week before the Sats. Teaching assistants work with class teachers where necessary. This can take the form of pre-teaching a topic, so girls go into lessons already confident. As in the senior school, staff benefit considerably from the broad GDST links with access to cutting edge teaching and learning research and professional training.

Music in the junior school is massive and virtually every girl plays an instrument. The concerts are wonderful, we were told by staff and parents, and there are lots of them, including tea concerts where every girl who is learning an instrument can play, regardless of level. It is this inclusiveness that parents love about the drama too. 'It is not all about over-rehearsing the stars,' one parent told us. 'There is the energy and naturalness you get when everyone is involved'. Outdoor spaces have been imaginatively used to create areas for each age group and a sense of woodland environs which is quite remarkable. There is an outdoor wooden amphitheatre and an outdoor learning area with low ropes and tyre swings which is regularly shared with local primary schools. As in the senior school, there is Firepit Friday when groups of girls spend their lunchtime in the outdoor education area, building a fire, cooking on it and doing campfire things. Much anticipated by all. There is a feel of adventure about the place – when we arrived, the reception class were in harnesses up and down the climbing wall.

Both staff and girls believe they belong to something very special. The head wants there to be a strong bond between every single girl, her family and the school. The school is working on lots of ways to show the parents they are part of something great. They are encouraged to come and watch a special lesson, to engage with the school on every level, attend IT seminars on safety and workshops on phonics and modern maths methods. Twitter is used very effectively and much appreciated by busy working parents. When girls are away on trips, staff send twitter photos to give the parents a glimpse into what is going on. New parents are phoned a few days into the start of term to check all is well.

There are lots of transition projects and joint activities with the senior school – for example, a year 6 and 7 hockey tour to Holland. The year 9s help with the junior sports day. A big sister, little sister buddy scheme operates between sixth formers and year 6s.

The head of the senior school, Julie Keller, spent the year before she took over as head running the junior school as well as doing her senior deputy head job. It has meant there is real synergy at every level between the junior and senior school. Julie says, 'I saw such a lot of excellent practice in the junior school that I have been able to share across the senior school'. Laura Fowler thinks it is wonderful having a senior head who loves the junior school through and through and really knows how it works. The girls value knowing the senior school head who still spends time there every week and the year 7s who got to know Julie so well last year are quite proprietorial about her now they have moved into the seniors.

The girls come across as happy and courteous and very excited by all the school offers. They couldn't tell us fast enough all the clubs they attended and the residential trips that were coming up during the year. Lessons, they say, are fun, and if they have difficulties teachers are really helpful. They are not nervous about talking to teachers if they are miserable either, although they clearly are also encouraged to believe everyone has a responsibility for everyone else's happiness. Teachers, we discover, are quite amazing and know that you are unhappy even when you haven't said so. The girls relish the many leadership opportunities they have as they go through the school and liked having their say at the school council. Best of all – you get to choose your own food at lunchtime.

The girls have picked up that they are in a very special place and relish the girls only environment. 'It is very calm here', one earnest 8 year old told us, and 'so we can try risky things whenever we want to.' The idea that girls can achieve at whatever they want is embedded early. The head says the girls have high expectations of themselves and learn quickly and deeply. 'It means we can do so much with them, take them out of school lots, go off timetable to explore practical skills and everyone still makes exceptional progress'.

Nottingham High School

Waverley Mount, Nottingham NG7 4ED

Ages 4–18 **Pupils** 1,052 (824 boys, 228 girls) **Sixth form** 237

Fees: £10,179 – £14,865 pa

01158 452232
www.nottinghamhigh.co.uk

Headmaster: Since 2007, Kevin Fear BA PGCE, educated at Douai and Southampton University. Head of history at King's Chester before joining Nottingham High in 2000 as senior teacher and then deputy head with academic and marketing responsibilities. In appearance reassuring and kindly, Kevin is fast talking and driven, an example of how staying in one school for some time can result in racing car pace, constantly pushing forward from a position of secure inside knowledge. He wants the High School to be unquestionably the top school in the region and his development plans include growing the school from the bottom up. Parents love Kevin's blogs and Twitter feeds. Pupils find him approachable and tell us that he attends 'everything'. His headmaster's lunches held weekly are seen as a practical manifestation of his desire to get to know each pupil and understand their concerns.

Head of infants and juniors: Since 2013, Clare Bruce MA PGCE. Educated at Hutchesons' Grammar School, Glasgow, read English at St Andrews. Spent two years in business. Head of Derby Grammar Junior School before moving to Nottingham High. Clare combines a professionalism with a warmth that endears her to both parents and children. Her comments on everyone's end of term reports are much valued by the children, as are her quotes of the week. A year 5 pupil reeled off the quote for the week we visited with considerable aplomb: ' If the world gives you a rainy day, jump in the puddles'. We liked it!

Academic matters: First and foremost, parents choose the school for its academic reputation. All subjects are achieving highly but the sciences, economics and maths stand out in terms of numbers doing very well and the pupils undoubtedly see these as a real strength, attracting girls particularly in the sixth form. In 2018, 64 per cent A*/A grades at A level and and 72 per cent A*-A/9-7 at GCSE. There is a good subject range, much as you would expect in an academically selective school. The school is using the longer run up to A levels to good effect – for example in the vibrant art department, the first term in the sixth form is spent exploring round the subject, not grinding through exam specifications. Three A levels is now the norm, and EPQ is big, with everyone doing the skills part of this to support future independent study, which in fact starts as early as KS2, where an hour a week is devoted to it.

In the infant and junior school, the selective nature of the intake means that the school doesn't have to focus exclusively on numeracy and literacy but can work on core skills in a wide range of other subjects. There are topic weeks: when we visited it was Explore week and the children were having great fun going out exploring Nottingham. The reception class has a maximum of 16 pupils. Class sizes in year 7 are around 20 to 24, getting smaller higher up the school. A culture of professional development for staff that means they are on a learning journey themselves, building the sense of the school as a complete learning community.

There is general agreement that IT could be further enhanced; parents like the app that enables them to see their child's homework. Pupils respond positively to the staff's high expectations. 'Teachers really push you, even if you are never going to get an A*,' we were told. The high performers are given regular extension tasks all through the school, often encouraging them to look at the bigger picture.

Two staff are dedicated to supporting a variety of learning needs. Pupils are screened on entry to the senior school and encouraged to disclose any learning difficulties before they take the admissions exam. Support may be in small group tuition or one-to-one. There is no extra charge for this. Pupils and staff say there is no stigma attached to needing support. In the infant and junior school, academic progress is tracked closely, parents are kept closely informed of any concerns and lots of support is put in place. There's a teaching assistant in every class in KS1, after which the learning support department might take over. If the school thinks a child would not be happy in the senior school, discussions with parents will start around year 4, but the aim is for everyone to move there.

Games, options, the arts: Sport is strong but 'we don't live or die by it,' says the head. The introduction of girls has widened the offer and as there are so few girls, lots get to play in teams that might not have done in an all girls' school. The juniors were delighted that they could choose which sport they wanted, so there's a junior girls' football team and mixed and girls' hockey teams. Some parents suggest there is still a bit too much emphasis on rugby for the boys at the senior school, and safety issues around rugby are clearly much more of an issue nationally than used to be the case, but the school places a great deal of emphasis on the safety of this sport. Some boys wish there were more sports options in games lessons lower down the senior school.

From year 9, pupils can choose between CCF, Scouts, involvement in the production team and a community action programme. We visited on a Monday, when those volunteering for the CCF wore their uniform all day. This, combined with the huge war memorial that dominates the magnificent frontage of the school, sends out a particular message which will appeal to some families. D of E is popular. There is much involvement right through the school in the very strong music department, with a lot of boys and girls alike wanting to sing in choirs. Students in years 10-13 can take part in the thriving Arts Society, which provides cut price tickets to local professional music and theatre productions. Plays and musicals in school are much appreciated by both those involved and audiences.

The co-curricular opportunities are wide. There is a Model United Nations and a degree of political awareness that makes the mock elections dynamic occasions. Perhaps this is the influence of alumni Ken Clarke and Ed Balls. Senior pupils are urging the school to become more eco-friendly and looking at plans for more recycling and sustainability generally. In the infant and junior school, the advent of girls has encouraged the staff to look afresh at what is on offer, and they are delighted to see lots of the boys joining the knitting club and pom-pom group as well as dance. Because the choice is so wide, a few senior school parents do worry about their children becoming overloaded and see them being pulled in too many directions. However, parents also liked the way that pupils could be involved in lots of areas and didn't have to commit to just sport or just music. There are masses of trips, including some adventurous ones overseas that often combine some form of community work. The pupil voice includes a suggestion box in the juniors and school council throughout. The school is keen to offer leadership opportunities wherever possible.

Background and atmosphere: Founded 1513 by Dame Agnes Mellers in memory of her husband. Originally situated in the Lace Market, moving to present site in 1868. It is very pleasing architecturally. The frontage is impressive and there have been some delightful modern extensions, including the sixth form centre and dining room, that are airy infills. The original Player school hall is oak ceilinged and can seat the whole school. A more modern hall allows for tiered seating and modern lighting equipment for the frequent drama productions. The pupils can soak in the Victorian gothic studious atmosphere of the libraries. The infants are currently in a Victorian villa across the road from the main school, which is something of a rabbit warren, though a homely, comfortable one. A spanking new junior school, which will open in 2018, will give the juniors and more of their own facilities while the infants will stay in their original building with its delightful outdoor continuous space areas.

N

The school is not in the most affluent area of Nottingham, but public transport links are excellent with a tram stop very close and school buses from far and wide.

The school started taking girls in 2014 and has admitted them throughout the school from 2016. There are currently 176 girls in the school as a whole. Nottingham High prepared very carefully for going co-education and has put considerable thought into the changes that might be necessary. What these changes have been are not that easy to pin down – though food and nutrition has been introduced (school assures us this is not just due to the advent of girls) and there are more dressing up activities and role play in the infant school. There have been more quiet spaces created, enjoyed by both girls and boys. The pupils say nothing much is different and certainly the boys and girls sound very comfortable with it all. Does it still feel like a boys' school? After all, there is only about two girls to every 10 boys at the moment. Well no, it doesn't feel like a traditional boys' school. The head says the reason it has been such a smooth transition is twofold – firstly it is a school that has had at its core a focus on the individual and now it carries on focusing on individual boys and girls. This is certainly a message that goes down well with parents and is reiterated by staff. The second reason is that Nottingham High has always been a superb school and not specifically a superb boys' school. Sixth formers said it works because everyone has a common vision of success, which we would confirm.

Pastoral care, well-being and discipline: The vertical tutor group system is seen as the highly successful foundation of pastoral as well as academic care. The aim is that pupils stay in the same group right through the school with the same tutor. Tutors keep in as close touch with families as necessary and are renowned for speedy phone calls and emails. If any unkindness is going on between pupils, tutors, who know their group so well over time, pick up on it quickly. The older ones in the tutor group are also ready listeners over pastoral concerns. There is a school counsellor as well as an outside counsellor. The PSHE programme is extensive and covers the usual areas, with a proactive approach that includes parental education on internet safety. The school prides itself on being very tolerant and open to diversity, which includes embracing the quirkiness of the pupil who doesn't conform to the usual stereotypes. There was a kindness and concern expressed by pupils and staff towards each other. The emphasis is on praise to reinforce good behaviours. Behaviour expectations are high and largely met. In terms of discipline measures, there is the usual tiered approach if work is not being done and a very occasional expulsion, but this does not loom large in any sense.

Pupils and parents: Communications with parents are a strength and an aspect the school is passionate about, constantly searching for ways to improve. The head makes effective use of social media. We found his tweets added a human dimension to the school. There are a lot of parents from the Nottingham hospitals and universities and the school probably reflects the aspirations of that group. The current 15 means-tested bursaries a year means there is a range of parental income and there are plenty of families who are pulling out all the financial stops to keep children here. You wouldn't mistake these pupils for those in the big London day schools. They are not particularly polished or alpha confident but nor are they arrogant or awkward. One young mother told us that when she went to university, she was struck by a group of students from Nottingham

High – super bright but very down to earth and comfortable in their own skins. She married one of them. There was an ease about the pupils we met and they are clearly proud of their school without taking anything for granted. The school is keen on outreach in the deprived areas of Nottingham, bringing in children for special days, working with teachers and giving the high school pupils the opportunity to understand more about the social needs of others.

Entrance: The school is selective all the way through. The bursaries are highly competitive and the whole school is selective, but the fee-paying places slightly less so. The entry process is about spotting potential at all levels, we were told, and it is not only the super bright who can get a place. For year 7, exams in English, maths and reasoning plus interview for all non junior school candidates. In the infant and junior school, admission is mainly at 4 but there may be spaces higher up. Children spend a few hours at the school and are given a series of activities which will reveal their potential to learn.

Exit: A few leave at the end of year 11, mainly to study vocational courses. Virtually everyone goes to strong universities, with sciences and engineering being consistently popular; 12 to Oxbridge in 2018 and 19 medics, dentists and vets. Sixth formers told us they were very well prepared not only to get through the UCAS process but also for navigating life once they are at university. We were pleased to learn that there is practical discussion about money and what might be feasible to earn while studying.

Money matters: Determined attempt to keep fees reasonable and necessary 'extras' such as uniform are deliberately kept simple. You can buy an ASDA blazer and stick on a Nottingham High badge. The school is working hard on building its development fund to provide more bursaries and keep fees down.

Remarks: The school is growing. The infant school started 10 years ago with one reception class and has now grown to three reception classes with a total of 47 pupils. There are families who are heaving a sigh of relief that male and female siblings can be offered a shared school experience in the Nottingham area. Though it is too early to comment of the full impact of co-education, early signs are hopeful. Achievements are celebrated both formally in assemblies, on notice boards etc and in smaller ways – the heads are very good at sending the appropriate and much valued thank you note. It is a school that fosters positive competition and is not afraid to draw attention to success, but also emphasises effort and the importance of striving for your best as an individual. There is a culture of hard work and achievement valued by everyone in the community. This is a school that is not standing still, where the staff are encouraged to keep looking at the experience of pupils and parents to make it the very best it can be.

Oakham School

Chapel Close, Market Place, Oakham, Rutland LE15 6DT

Ages 10–18 **Pupils** 1,044 **Sixth form** 392 **Boarders** 339 full, 219 flexi **C of E**

Fees: Day £16,905 – £20,535; Boarding £20,145 – £33,660 pa

01572 758758
www.oakham.rutland.sch.uk

Headmaster: Since 2009, Nigel Lashbrook (50s). Educated in one of the last grammar cohorts at King's Heath Boys' Technical School in Birmingham. Only pupil in his year to get into Oxford (Hertford College – chemistry plus lots of rugby), first in his family to go to university. Part of his final year at Oxford involved running some undergraduate classes; 'Have you thought about teaching?' he was asked (in a good way) so DPhil plans were changed to teacher training. 'I just loved it', he says.

His first post was Manchester Grammar School where he taught chemistry and coached cricket and rugby. After eight years he went from this academic day school to an academic boarding school, Tonbridge. At Tonbridge he was head of science and chemistry, a housemaster ('I finished being a housemaster just before the advent of email', he says with a smile), plus a term as acting head – good preparation for his next move, the headship of King's Bruton in Somerset.

Parents describe him as 'very friendly', 'affable' and 'approachable' and so he is, although that relaxed bonhomie belies the super-efficiency with which his school is run. We thought Oakham had a particularly collegiate air – Mr L is obviously extremely good at picking the right staff and delegating to their strengths. He's also forward thinking and alert to shifts in what Oakham parents want from their boarding school. At the time of our visit a new boarding package was being launched to replace the three nights a week 'day boarding'. There is now a five-night option (costing 95 per cent of the full boarding fee). Apparently it's something that families who live further away have been asking for.

He identifies parental attitudes as the biggest change he has seen during his career. While he feels that parents wanting to be more involved is a cause for celebration, 'the pressure of unrealistic expectations can be a great cause of anxiety for children. We work hard to get parents to see the bigger picture.' At Oakham, as elsewhere, the emphasis is on enabling children to become independent learners, to see 'fail' as 'first attempt in learning'. 'We want to unravel the cotton wool,' says the head.

Mr Lashbrook still manages to do 'a tiny bit of teaching' and as part of his commitment to lifelong learning plans to take diving lessons; 'the pupils like to see staff doing new things.' To this end Oakham supports staff who wish to undertake study for masters or PhDs (in education related subjects, of course).

He lives on site during term time but has a family house nearby from where he 'commutes' in the summer and Easter holidays (when Oakham's commercial directors 'sweat the assets', running high profile sports academies and other events). His wife is an economics and geography teacher – 'they make a great team', said a parent – and two of their three now adult children were educated at Oakham. Down time is for golf, cricket and the theatre. Is there anything he wishes he'd been able to do? 'Play the saxophone'.

Retiring in July 2019. His successor will be Henry Price, currently head of Wellington School in Somerset. Eton and Oxford (classics). A career teacher, first post at Sydney Grammar, Australia, next Sherborne, then Rugby for 13 years where, in addition to being head of classics and a housemaster, he was involved in all manner of extracurricular activities. Joined Wellington in 2014. Married, four young children.

Academic matters: In 2018, 37 per cent of A level/Pre-U grades were A*/A, 65 per cent A*-B, with 62 per cent A*-A/9-7 at GCSE (IGCSEs in core subjects). Double award science only (IGCSE), French, Spanish and German are the language options. Around a third of sixth formers take the IB and results are impressive: 2018 average of 35. Geography seems to be the most popular choice of A level, followed by maths, biology and economics. Two subjects – business and sports science – available as BTecs as well as A levels. We were a little surprised not to see more A*s at A level, especially given the very respectable number of leavers off to medical school and Oxbridge – proof of above and beyond teaching at all levels. 'Look at the bigger picture,' says a voice in our ear (it's the headmaster ...). We always do, and so do parents who choose Oakham for their children: 'We like the way they celebrate hard work as well as good grades,' said one.

We heard a great deal from Mr Lashbrook and his staff about the Oakham approach to teaching and learning. Words such as 'holistic' and 'enrichment' aren't just eduspeak here; lessons we observed were hands-on, pupils were working at their own pace and one felt that teachers saw them as individuals rather than a class. In the DT department (school has Design Mark) we came across a group getting to grips with ancient history in the form of early video games, telephones, cassette recorders and a BBC Micro. 'So what is a mix tape?' we heard one ask. Sigh. Introducing the IB middle years programme for 11-13 year olds: it 'encourages pupils to become creative, critical and reflective thinkers'.

The learning support department was settling in to new top floor premises when we visited – lots of technology but quiet, calm spaces too. Staff had chosen some wonderful pictures, all by 'our' pupils, we were told proudly. 'Mild' SEN – mainly dyslexia but also dyscalculia and dyspraxia – catered for via small group teaching, individual lessons (extra charge) or in-class support. Lots of study, organisation and revision support, all described by parents as 'brilliant'.

Senior academic mentor (formerly the formidable sounding 'master of scholars') is responsible for intellectual stretching of those with academic awards and Oxbridge candidates. We couldn't help feeling that this role (especially under its previous title) seemed a little un-Oakhamian. Not at all, we were told; the scholars' society is 'elitist but not exclusive', members aren't necessarily academic scholars: some have been talent-spotted by housemasters. After all, there are established pathways to extend and develop sporting, musical and artistic talents. Chosen pupils attend a seminar programme designed to play to particular specialisms and nurture 'genuine intellectual curiosity'. Whole school enrichment week in the autumn term is also designed to challenge and surprise all pupils. Most recent theme was the enticing sounding, 'rules and rebellion'.

The Smallbone library (named after a former head), is impressive, the foyer doubles as an exhibition space and was full of pupils' art work; it's also used for parent meetings. Upstairs, though, it is absolutely silent. Certainly no talking, no whispering and no headphones. 'Up here pupils can hear themselves think', the librarian told us (very, very quietly).

Games, options, the arts: A word to the wise: don't trot out the cliché 'sport for all' if you're visiting Oakham – unless you want to run five times round a rugby pitch and do 100 press ups as punishment. Director of sport actually shuddered at such a last century idea. The distinction is a bit lost on us because that seems to be what happens, even if the emphasis these days is on health and fitness as much as competition. Huge choice of over 30 sports, from sailing on nearby Rutland Water (Oakham's sailing coach devised and hosted the inaugural Water Quidditch World Cup) to polo (water and four-legged variety), and all take part, whether by competing or supporting. Outstanding facilities including 40 acres of grass pitches, two floodlit all-weather pitches, multi-purpose sports hall, squash and fives courts. The cricket square hosts county matches as well as school fixtures.

O

Over 100 pupils played in national finals in lots of different sports and the school will create 'pathways to foster individual talents, whatever they are.' Oakham's recent sporting honours are evenly spread between boys' and girls' teams with the girls' 1st X1 football team carrying off the Independent Schools Football Association trophy and the U15 rugby team reaching the NatWest Vase final. The 1st XI boys' hockey team came runners up in the U18 Hockey Schools Cup Final.

Drama and music are big news with countless opportunities to perform at all levels. The aim is to maximise participation as well as foster individual talents – at whole school plays, hymn practice or small in-house showcases to build the confidence of first timers. Over 300 pupils sing in school choirs and the chamber choir recently reached the finals of Songs of Praise School Choir of the Year. We were lucky enough to join an audience of townspeople and pupils at one of the weekly lunchtime concerts in All Saints Church. Young and old sat rapt in the pews, listening to virtuoso trumpet and oboe soloists give spellbinding performances. When asked, 'Why Oakham?' a prospective parent sitting nearby simply said, 'It's the music.'

Impressive numbers of top marks for art and DT at GCSE; specialist teachers in all disciplines including sculpture and textiles, visiting artists run workshops. The courtyard of four art studios was formerly the town prison and the new exhibition space was a workhouse – Oakham can truthfully say that its art takes no prisoners.. Wonderful sculpture studio where pupils can create in clay and mixed media on a large scale and even learn stone carving. Not huge numbers taking these subjects at Pre-U/A level but the results are excellent. Pupils regularly go on to top art schools and to study architecture.

New Exploring Learning camp for younger Oakhamians is a swashbuckling, Treasure Island-themed, problem-solving adventure in the countryside.

Boarding: Over half the pupils board and what with lessons on Saturday morning plus matches and other activities in the afternoon, day pupils probably feel as though they do as well. Parents of younger day pupils acknowledge this but say that the children like the chance to finish homework before they leave and enjoy time out in the common rooms. Quite a few local day pupils turn up for the Sunday goings on too. Food is praised by all – parents and children alike. All food is prepared in house and everyone eats together in the Barraclough. There doesn't seem to be any falling away of deliciousness as the day goes on – we heard no complaints about dreary boarders' suppers here. The homemade bread and soups, carvery nights and Sunday brunch came in for special praise.

One 'leave-out weekend' each half term. 'Transitional' boarding (two to five nights a week) is offered to lower school pupils (10-13 year olds) but the day boarding option of up to three nights a week for upper school pupils has been retired. 'It didn't meet the needs of families who live more than an hour's drive away,' we were told. Instead parents can opt for an up to five night a week package that comes in at 95 per cent of the full boarding fee.

Boys' and girls' middle school (age 13-17) boarding houses are on either side of a large playing field known as 'Donkey' (Doncaster Close). All upper sixth (known at Oakham as 'seventh form') pupils are based in two houses in Chapel Close, next to the market place. There are four lower school houses (two boarding) away from the main campus where younger children can enjoy their own space. Rooms that we saw were fairly standard issue – cabin beds with desks underneath, two or three to a room in the lower years, individual study bedrooms on the ground floor for the lower sixth. All the doors we looked behind in the boys' house featured, as ever, empty noticeboards, massive shoes and Lynx. Common areas are large and well maintained with the usual exhausted soft furnishings, big wooden bowls of apples ('we keep trying,' smiled the housemaster, indulgently resigned to choosing fruit on the basis of what makes the minimum mess if used as a missile), pool and table tennis tables. Year group integration fostered by lots of competitions and activities.

Youngest boarders do prep in the house library supervised by a member of staff or prefect until they're ready to work independently. Sensible rules about screens of all kinds, Wifi turned off at 10pm; youngest must hand in everything before bed. The term's programme of matches, activities, exam dates, UCAS deadlines and the like is up in an A3 frame near the entrance and makes exhausting reading. 'We like to do a lot,' said the housemaster, adding, 'This isn't babysitting, we put our heart and soul into boarding at Oakham.'

Background and atmosphere: Drive into the charming eponymous town (there's a butcher, baker and by the looks of things no shortage of artisan candle makers), past the Whipper-In hotel (Oakham is home to the Cottesmore, one of England's oldest hunts) and in the corner of the cobbled market place you will see Oakham School announced in fine wrought iron. Oakham and its near neighbour Uppingham were both set up as free grammar schools by Archdeacon Robert Johnston in 1584 to teach Latin, Greek and Hebrew to the sons of their respective towns. The two schools' fortunes and size waxed and waned over the next 300 years – as late as the end of the 19th century the original one room school house was still Oakham's only teaching premises.

The main site is a horseshoe of teaching and boarding accommodation and if there is a lack of fine or grand architecture then it is more than amply compensated for by the bright green fingers of a first-rate grounds team. If there were Good Schools Guide awards for best-kept school grounds then Oakham would certainly be on the podium. School is very proud of the courtyard garden with its grass-free lawn designed by near-neighbour Bunny Guinness. It's overlooked by the biology labs and no doubt the 30 varieties of native plants that make up the lawn provide a useful study in biodiversity.

Fair bit of Monopoly-style buying up of town sites – latest is a former pub which is soon to be reborn as a performing arts centre (plans 'moving forward'); the town's old police station is now a new medical and pastoral centre. Town and gown weave seamlessly in and out – one of the first lessons new pupils receive is about road safety, although we imagine that motorists are held up by pupils crossing, more often than the reverse. Our sixth form guides observed the school's road safety rules to the letter, despite absence of any traffic, we're pleased to report.

Sensible uniform of black crested blazers, white shirts, ties (boys only) and below the knee black and white kilts for the girls. All seems to be worn as intended: smartly and un-customised. Seventh formers sport the dreaded business dress – although apparently it's not dreaded at Oakham. 'We really look forward to wearing it,' our sixth form guide told us.

Pastoral care, well-being and discipline: Pastoral care was singled out for its high quality and 'generous scope' in most recent inspection report and we couldn't find anyone who disagreed. The parents we spoke to commented how observant teachers were – quick to spot and then get to the bottom of changes in mood or attitude. Like most things at Oakham the pastoral system is commendably well-organised and implemented with genuine interest and concern, not a whiff of weary lip-service to a box ticking set of 'guidelines'. The head of pastoral care told us how important it was that she and her fellow tutors teach: 'it keeps things real', she observed. Tutor groups are small and pupils keep the same tutor throughout their time in each section of the school. Boarding house matrons are all trained in youth mental health care and are 'eyes and ears' and girls often pass on concerns they may have about boys (who can find it harder to talk). Add to this a 'house family' and buddy system and every child should know plenty of adults or fellow pupils to whom they can turn if necessary. All pupils do a body and mind course that stresses the interdependence of mental and physical well-being. Respect, for oneself and others, plus very clear boundaries, govern relationships between pupils.

Pupils and parents: 'You get all walks of life here,' a parent told us. According to Mr Lashbrook the Oakham demographic is solid middle class, 'definitely not socially elite'. Pupils we met officially were clean cut and refreshingly uncynical (they always are) but those we saw from a distance didn't appear to have revolutionary tendencies either. Oakham probably isn't the place for determined bohemians or incipient Bolsheviks, but we've no doubt that the school would welcome them with a smile and find them plenty to do. Around 15 per cent from abroad – mostly Europe. Former pupils include Stuart Broad, Tom Fell, Josh Cobb (cricket); Alex Goode, Tom Croft, Matt Smith, Lewis Moody (Rugby); Crista Cullen (Olympic bronze, hockey, 2012, who opened the new hockey Astro); Matthew Macfadyen, Greg Hicks, Richard Hope, Lydia Rose Bewley (actors); Miles Jupp (actor/presenter); Thomas Hescott, Katie Mitchell OBE (directors); Phoebe Gormley, Sarah Curran (fashion/business).

Entrance: At age 10 and 11 from over 30 different preps and primary schools – exams in maths English and verbal reasoning. At 13+, pre-test in year 7 (online assessment plus discussion with deputy head or director of teaching); places subject to CE mark of 55 or over or school's own papers in English, maths, French and science. Around 50 new pupils enter the sixth form each year; they need a minimum of seven 6s at GCSE including the subjects they wish to study, plus satisfactory personal and academic references from previous school. All candidates are interviewed.

Exit: Some 10 per cent leaves after GCSEs. Around 70 per cent to Russell Group universities, good numbers to medical schools, others abroad. School employs a Yale Fellow who oversees preparation of candidates for US universities. Seven to Oxbridge in 2018; other popular destinations Leeds, Exeter, Nottingham, Nottingham Trent, Birmingham, Newcastle, Manchester, King's College London (KCL), York. Four off to the USA in 2018, plus one each to Canada, the Netherlands and the École Hôtelière de Lausanne. Oakham has been awarded the Career Mark for its excellence in careers guidance and several parents commented on how good the higher education, apprenticeship and careers support was.

Money matters: Comparatively good value, especially the boarding. Even more so if you consider that parents of day pupils are not charged for evening meals if their children have to stay late at school for activities. Wide variety of scholarships at 11+, 13+ and sixth form. Means-tested bursaries also offered, applications considered on individual basis. Ten per cent discount for Forces families.

Remarks: 'The Oakham of today started when we went fully co-ed in 1971,' the head told us and it's true that though the school is proud of its origins, four centuries of history are not its defining feature. This is a clear-eyed, energetic, forward-thinking school, aptly summed up by its motto, 'Et quasi cursors vitai lampada tradunt' ('And, like runners, they pass on the torch of life').

Old Buckenham Hall School

O

Brettenham Park, Ipswich, Suffolk IP7 7PH

Ages 3–13 **Pupils** 202 **Boarders** 16 full, 19 weekly, 54 flexi (from 7 years) **C of E**

Fees: Day £9,501 – £19,272; Boarding £16,521 – £25,110 pa

01449 740252
www.obh.co.uk

Headmaster: Since September 2018, David Griffiths, peviously head of Daneshill School near Reading and before that acting head of St John's-on-the-Hill. He and his wife Becky are used to working as a team: both have taught all age groups and whilst he was head of history at Haberdashers' Monmouth School for Girls, she was a teacher and head of house there. They have three young children.

Entrance: This is essentially non-selective. Taster days are available and children wishing to enter from year 3 onwards are assessed in English, reading and maths. Only if a child is exceptionally academically fragile will an offer of a place not be forthcoming. Bursarial assistance is available for military and clergy children whilst sibling discounts operate for parents with three children at the school.

Exit: Ultimately a major part of any parental verdict will depend on how pupils fare in final examinations. Most popular destinations in 2018 were Uppingham, Oundle, Oakham, Royal Hospital School and The Leys.

Remarks: Deeply embedded in the Suffolk countryside, a few miles from exotically-named villages such as Thorpe Morieux and Bradfield Combust, appears the splendid entrance to OBH. Lodge cottages frame the gates: an avenue of trees flanks the drive on which a pheasant sprints away to safety. The 80-acre estate opens up... Cambridge Blue flags edge the rugby pitches; red flags pin the greens of the golf course. The house, dating back to the mid-19th century, was the home of Sir Edward and Lady Warner until the former's death in 1955. Entering the building, we were struck not just by the gold lettered honours boards or the oak panelling, but by the fire that, even by mid-morning, had crackled its way through many a log. Sofas are voluminous; pupils bustle by on their way to lessons. A suit of armour stands in the corner.

OBH presents itself as a 24/7 school where, according to the sparkling registrar, 'The children rock around an old family house and are allowed to be children. They aren't treated as mini-adults.' The range of buildings and the way they have been adapted in, for example, the old stable complex is impressive and we especially liked the South Lawn with its well-tended pond (large enough to accommodate a platoon of ducks) and a variety of trees that formed Sir Henry's small arboretum. The children are encouraged to climb them. Whereas many schools would have corralled off this area as some kind of health & safety danger zone, OBH boys and girls are encouraged (in a phrase grudgingly authorised by some inspectors) to make their own 'dynamic risk assessments' and gauge things for themselves. Predictably, a lifebelt at the edge of the pond does not look like it has been used for years.

All classrooms, whether in the nursery, pre-prep or in the more senior areas of the main school, are spacious and stylish; not really a verdict that we could pass on the library, which is on the small side. However, the science complex is a highlight as it incorporates three laboratories. Also worth a look are the DT centre (take note here of the textiled scarves and the model catamarans), the performing arts centre and the suite of music practice rooms. The Britten Hall – opened in 2003 and named after one of the more famous alumni of the school – houses not just a selection of classrooms but also a major facility which doubles up as a gym and as a theatre. Assemblies are also held here, which, given the fizziness of the staff, are sure to be more inspiring than the dog-eared and broken-spined selection of hymn books on show.

OBH stresses the significance of outdoor education and runs a modular programme based on acquiring skills, such as 'how to make silver birch tea and super-glue' and 'the knots that you should know'. Then there are the physical challenges which build through each year until year 8 pupils are ready to deal with their 100-length swim and the Gold Survival Expedition. This lasts four days, recent locations being the Welsh Peaks and Northumberland.

Sport, music and drama are central to the school. Main sports are rugby, hockey, cricket and athletics for boys, and hockey, netball, athletics and cricket (increasingly popular) for girls. Swimming throughout the year. The spectrum of fixtures is impressive and every child represents OBH around six times each term. And there is so much more ... cross-country, golf, clay pigeon shooting. There is a cycle track in the woods. Musical opportunities are, if anything, still more striking. Four choirs, a jazz band, two samba bands and a string orchestra sing and play each week whilst dramatically recent productions include The Lion, The Witch and The Wardrobe and Mr Humbug sees The Light.

Learning support is coordinated by one of the two deputy heads – who switches more hats than a milliner as she is also director of studies and in charge of scholars – and takes place in the Learning Centre, situated in the heart of the school. LS caters for approximately 50 pupils out of a roll of around 200, including scholars who each follow an individually designed educational plan. Apart from the head of learning support, there are two full-time departmental staff who provide assistance in lessons, small groups and individually. A trio of external specialists are brought in if extra individual tuition is required.

There are exams three times a year and progress-tracking is clearly of a high quality. Class sizes are pegged at a maximum of 18; many are smaller.

There is a real enthusiasm for boarding, created partly through the fact that, along with a squadron of matrons, six members of staff live on site. The girls' house is characterised by a pinky fluffiness, hairdryers and posters which advise the reader to Keep Calm and Love your Pony. Dormitories, such as Pankhurst and Sharman, are arranged by year group. The boys' accommodation is similarly configured, although curiously the names of some of the original residents have been retained. Thus, boys could be assigned to Elizabeth, Isobel or Maud. Newish junior boarding house and more plans afoot. This will no doubt give a boost to the standard of some of the furniture and fittings which, although perfectly adequate, do not quite have the wow factor. Amongst the boarders are around a dozen children from overseas.

Staff are full of praise for the way in which OBH is developing. One recalled driving up on her first day and sensing 'that this is a very special place'. Appreciative of being kept informed via daily staff briefings, they express confidence that the school is sufficiently flexible to attract working parents. The number of staff children in the school gives a further spur to their attachment and involvement.

Children and parents become almost misty-eyed when they assess OBH. The former think that 'it's all so easy to settle here'. Teachers are 'absolutely amazing' and one boy commented, between mouthfuls of lunchtime crumble, that 'I know everyone' – unlike his previous experience in a Singaporean school where he was one of 3,000. On the debit side, the grass on the football pitch is 'too long' and supper, at 5.50pm, is 'way too early'.

Parents are similarly full of praise, for the overall 'slickness of everything'. They are kept superbly informed through a library of literature and the clarion call system which sends out electronic updates; 'the teachers cannot be faulted'. The Friends of OBH give a social appeal, organising bonfire nights, cake sales and lunches for new parents.

So, what could be better? The swimming pool could do with a roof. There could be a new sports hall; but our dominant impression is that OBH is very much on the rise. It makes much of its school colours – Oxbridge stripes of the sort that are found in Jack Wills shops. Less is made of the school's motto Spero – Latin for I Hope. Doctor Johnson had it that 'Hope is perhaps the chief happiness that life affords.' Much of it can be found at OBH – original, brave and, above all, happy.

Old Swinford Hospital

   64

Heath Lane, Stourbridge, West Midlands DY8 1QX

Ages 11–18 **Pupils** 622 **Sixth form** 242 (71 girls) **Boarders** 117 full, 172 weekly, 123 flexi **C of E**

Fees: Day free; Boarding: £5,850 – £11,700 pa

01384 817300
www.oshsch.com

Headmaster: Since 2014, Paul Kilbride, who came from Bethany School, Kent where he was deputy head. He had previously had experience in the state and independent sector, both day and boarding, selective and non-selective, single sex and mixed. His own education was at a British Army school in Germany from where he went on to Magdalen College, Oxford to read modern history. He exudes energy, charm and engagement. Totally committed to boarding, he loves the traditions of the ancient foundation at OSH. Parents and staff say he has taken on the challenge of pushing up academic standards with mounting success. He is regarded as excellent at leading the work on preparing young people for university, ensuring they have high aspirations and are very well supported. His engagement with all aspects of school life is legendary and he is seen as having brought a fresh vision of 21st century boarding into the school. The pupils, one parent told us, 'simply love him'. Paul is married to Emma, another Magdalen alumna, and they have three young sons.

Academic matters: The school is partially selective at year 7, with prospective boarders taking an aptitude assessment. GCSE results are strong – 35 per cent A*-A/9-7 grades in 2018, with 82 per cent getting 9-4 in both maths and English. At A level, 20 per cent A*/A grades and 52 per cent A*-B grades. These are a bit more variable year on year, but overall there is an improving picture. Although there are entrance requirements for sixth form, they are less demanding than many independent schools and sixth form colleges. The school takes in quite a number of pupils at sixth form level who may have been taught in a less effective way than the 'home grown' groups, and this, too, explains the variability of results here. Partly because of the range of academic ability in the sixth form, the school has recently introduced BTecs in sport and science, and vocational qualifications in business and ICT. The sciences, maths and psychology attract large numbers at A level and get impressive results. The school encourages the uptake of EPQ, which it sees as teaching pupils how to manage and test information for themselves.

Standardised assessments in years 7, 9 and 12 for baseline tracking. Learning support is provided through careful differentiation in class, some setting as the children move up through the school and a strong SEN department. Value added for those needing learning support is particularly high. Pupils do well, not by being forced or drilled but by increasingly cutting edge pedagogy. At the key stages, the teachers provide lots of extra help. Year 13 are encouraged to contact teachers when the teacher has free periods to clarify any last minute exam preparation. The head has introduced rigorous use of data, encouraged more timely interventions and tightened up punctuality to lessons by introducing sessional bells. He is generally considered to be excellent at holding staff to account.

This is a state school and like all others it is currently having to re-examine its budget. One or two less popular A level subjects will not feature on the curriculum next year and according to the head, everyone is 'rolling their sleeves up' to protect the front line teaching.

Games, options, the arts: Traditionally this has been a big rugby school, well able to hold its own with the large independent schools and won the NatWest Bowl in 2017. There is a variety of curricular sports. Rugby still is huge and a draw for a number of families, but now there is far more emphasis on broadening the offer both within sport and beyond. For those who try rugby and decide it is not for them, there are recreational sports groups, a multi-sports and a fitness programme. The sixth form girls play netball, join in cross-country, have fitness sessions and can opt for social walking. Music is 'phenomenal', we were told by parents and pupils. A number of orchestras, bands, ensembles and choirs perform in the school and in outside venues, including on music tours.

There are strong links exist between the school and the Birmingham Conservatoire. Drama productions are keenly anticipated and a dance competition is popular with boys and girls. There is CCF, DofE and opportunities for voluntary work in the local community for older pupils. The head has been encouraging more activities. Participation in co-curricular activities is high and carefully monitored by pastoral staff to ensure everyone is as involved as possible in the broader life of the school. There have been considerable attempts recently to ensure a realistic co-curricular timetable so all the opportunities for, say, year 8s, don't fall on the same day of the week. The school is responding to requests from pupils to introduce a coding and a STEM club, with others in the pipeline. For senior pupils, there are opportunities to coach junior teams and run clubs. Pupil requests are also increasingly shaping the Sunday activity programme, which includes go-karting, raft building and paintballing as well as museum visits. Some activities are charged as extras, though pupil premium money is used to ensure no one need be left out. The aim of the co-curricular programme is increasingly to prepare the pupils for a rich and rewarding life beyond school. A further manifestation of this aim is the eagerly anticipated enrichment week at the end of the summer term. The offer is huge here, reaching out to all interests, needs and pockets.

Boarding: There is an amazingly flexible boarding offer here. The school is highly committed to boarding but doesn't insist everyone is a full boarder from day one. House staff are aware of what a jump it is, particularly for younger boys and especially for those who come from small prep schools. Parents told us of boys who started off staying one night a week, then when they felt ready, increased it to two and three and then all week. We thoroughly commend this approach. Boarding allows time for all the extracurricular activities on offer. Families love the idea that everything is on site – no traipsing for hours to take different members of a family to different activities every evening and weekend. The head did away with Saturday lessons. Instead there is a full programme of activities and space for relaxation. The sports hall and music school are open in the evenings and at weekends. There are trips out every Sunday.

The head has also set up a year 13 boarding house, which is very popular and seen as a bridge between the tight structures of the rest of the school and the independence of university living. There are seven houses altogether and the ones we saw were were very well appointed, airy, light and looked loved. Parents and boys say that house staff pick up very quickly on any small unkindnesses that can occur in day to day living and deal with them before things have time to develop. Houses encourage the pupil voice in various ways and concerns can be raised anonymously. Each housemaster is well supported by a team of house tutors and matrons who are the human face of this corporate parenting. Induction is taken seriously. There are no academic lessons in the first week for year 7s: instead, a programme of activities aimed at bonding the group together. For the first half term, homework is a consolidation of year 6 work, aiming at getting everyone used to working in silence for an hour. There is an equally thoughtful induction for new sixth formers.

Background and atmosphere: Founded over 350 years ago, the school is a mixture of highly atmospheric historic buildings dating back to its foundation and very attractive modern additions. In some places the older exteriors have been preserved while the interiors have been completely renovated. The campus, considering that it is in the middle of a Midlands town, is unexpectedly spacious and green. The music school and sports hall are just adjacent to the main campus. Sports fields are situated both on and off site. The school is relatively small by secondary school standards and everyone said this contributed to a strong sense of community. It has a very stable staff but that includes a healthy age range. We sensed excellent relationships between staff and pupils. This is a school that exudes clarity of purpose. The pupils and staff know what they are there for, expectations are absolutely clear and there is a dynamic structured feel about all aspects of school life. The school does take children whose family backgrounds mean they are crying out for this approach, but everyone to whom we spoke responded positively to it.

Girls can join as day pupils in the sixth form and their number is capped at about 25 per cent of the year. Girls who come are clearly highly motivated and speak very positively about their experience. There is no doubt they are joining a boys' school, and some say that for the first few weeks the boys are quite territorial and socially awkward with them, but it soon settles down. The girls throw themselves into house competitions.

Pastoral care, well-being and discipline: The wide range of backgrounds and needs of the pupils make it essential that the pastoral care here is effective, and it is. Some boys are on carefully monitored welfare plans but all benefit from the considerable experience of the pastoral teams. The school tackles mental health issues on different levels. Some areas are covered through personal education sessions. Mindfulness is encouraged with the younger ones. There is peer mentoring. It promotes an online facility run by a cyber charity that offers confidential advice. There is a school counsellor. Pastoral care extends beyond the school. The head will intervene if he hears of unregulated pop-up or house parties. He is keen to work with parents, who are highly supportive of the school's efforts. The underlying ethos is that families matter and the school is very conscious that it is educating the next generation of parents. Parents see the school as standing for traditional family values, and while they love all the modern technology it embraces, the ethos of decency and respect for others is central to its continuing popularity. There is a traditional approach to discipline. Expectations are high, pupils are absolutely clear about the rules governing good behaviour and the consequences of someone falling short. There is a range of sanctions. Considerable thought is given to integrating boys back after a temporary suspension. The school has a zero tolerance policy on illegal drugs.

Pupils and parents: There is a genuine range of backgrounds. A number of families have dipped into the independent sector at junior school age or with other siblings, while there are also children who are sponsored to board through a charity because of home circumstances. In most families, both parents work. Although some children come from further afield, the majority live within an hour or two of the school. It is been a popular choice for Forces families. We spoke to parents who had specifically chosen OSH over independent schools because of the social diversity of the pupils. Parents regard communication between home and school as strong and appreciate the fact the school is always trying to improve it. A new communication in real time about sports fixtures has been much welcomed. One parent spoke appreciatively about how closely the school had involved her in decisions about the best ability set for her son to join.

Entrance: It may take you a bit of time to work your way through the terminology here. There various different options for year 7 entry. There are termly, or full, boarders. There are weekly boarders who can choose to go home on Fridays after prep. There are flexi-boarders who do everything a termly or weekly boarder does except routinely stay overnight – the only requirement is to stay over three or four nights a term. They can arrive for breakfast and leave after prep. Then there are day pupils who arrive in time for registration and finish after lessons. Application deadlines are different for various groups, so do check carefully. There is no entry testing for day pupils. Flexi-boarding pupils must take a sport, music or academic aptitude assessment. Boarders are assessed for suitability for boarding via an interview and school reference. Most join in year 7. A few join in year 9, but only as weekly or termly boarders. Sixth form offers are based on a minimum of seven GCSEs at 9-4, including maths and English (or an agreed equivalent for overseas candidates.) They recommend a grade 6 or higher in subjects to be studied at A level, with some subjects expecting 9-7s. Sixth form entrants come from state and independent schools.

Day and flexi-boarding places at 11+ are highly sought after – it is regarded as the best state day school in the area. It is worth noting, though, that not all co-curricular activities are available to day pupils, which is why families are keen to opt for the flexi-boarding option.

Exit: A relatively small number – perhaps a quarter – leave at the end of year 11 to go to sixth form colleges where there is a wider range of non-A level courses. Three medics, and a dentists in 2018, with one off to study biology at Tennessee and one pharmaceutical sciences at Utrecht. Popular UK universities range from Aberystwyth to Bristol to Sheffield. Quite a few get prestigious apprenticeships.

Money matters: If you are considering boarding, OSH represents amazing value for money and is well worth a visit. Tuition is free and parents just pay for the boarding side.

Remarks: Parents increasingly compare traditional independent Midlands boarding schools unfavourably with what OSH has to offer at a fraction of the cost, though also with decreasing resources. They like its diversity of family background. This has a very British feel compared with some other boarding schools. The historic buildings contribute to this, as does a real sense of continuity. The founding Foley family still have an interest in the school, with a family member having always sat on the governing body. OSH probably best suits those who are looking for a stimulating, rounded education that is not too academically or socially exclusive.

Orwell Park School

Nacton, Ipswich, Suffolk IP10 0ER

Ages 2–13 **Pupils** 307 **Boarders** 48 full (from 7 years)

Fees: Day £8,100 – £18,690; Boarding £21,621 – £26,001 pa

01473 659225
www.orwellpark.co.uk

Headmaster: Since 2011 Adrian Brown MA (Cantab) PGCE. Early 50s. Previously spent 20 years at Ipswich School where he taught French and German before being appointed deputy head (pastoral). He thinks, 'It has been invaluable, as a prep head, to have taught in senior schools. I know what they are looking for and expecting. Being "in the know" is something parents can depend on for guidance in choosing senior schools and entering for scholarships.' Wants all pupils to 'discover their strengths and develop skills that will stand them in good stead throughout life'. Believes in allowing pupils to experience the sometimes-uncomfortable feeling of 'not getting things right first time': 'We are becoming risk averse as a society and sometimes we learn best by our mistakes.' Strong advocate of collaborative learning and developing resilience and good communication skills, which are 'essential for life no matter what career path they follow'.

Continues to teach his own subject (French), usually in year 6, and remains a dedicated sportsman; he was a Cambridge blue and played professional cricket at county level (Essex). His wife, Nicole, also a trained teacher, concentrates on organising major events such as the Leavers' Ball and dealing with design and decoration throughout the school. Strong approval from parents for the way the head and his wife greet all pupils as they arrive at school in the morning. 'It is so welcoming for the children and makes it so easy, as a parent, to have a quick word'. They have three grown up children who have all flown the nest.

Entrance: Main entry points are at 4+ and 7+ but places continue to become available throughout. Year group sizes increase year on year. Nursery and pre-prep places are non-selective (taster mornings in class and a home visit). At 7+ and 11+ tests in maths, English and reasoning plus a report from current school and an interview. Not overly selective but as school only offers learning support for mild difficulties pupils must be able to follow the curriculum.

Exit: At 13+ post CE. Excellent track record for winning scholarships; usually over half the year 8 cohort win an award, some several, and to a range of senior schools throughout the country, including to the top drawer ones. No well-trodden path to favoured schools – fewer than five pupils go to the same school. Current popular destinations Framlingham College, Oundle and Uppingham.

Remarks: In a spectacular setting overlooking the River Orwell, it is difficult to picture more idyllic surroundings to grow and learn in; the splendid Blenheim Palace-style wrought iron gates open to reveal grounds of outstanding beauty with sweeping lawns, wisteria draped pergola, a ha-ha and the River Orwell glistening in the distance. A Georgian mansion, with significant additions (including an observatory) made by the Victorian philanthropist who then owned the estate, forms the core of the school. Many Downton Abbey features have been retained including the orangery (now used as an assembly hall), panelled walls, French windows and a roaring log fire in the entrance hall. Pupils revel in their surroundings and 'swimming in the pool and looking up at the trees', 'playing outside on summer evenings', and 'the view from the dormitories' were all mentioned as special; all seem aware of their good fortune. The recently built pre-prep department is a one storey building in its own grounds close by.

Stepping through French windows from the head's study (size of a small ballroom) onto the terrace is an ageless experience, but the school is thoroughly 21st century. 'We want to prepare pupils for the uncertainties ahead and a job market that we do not yet know'. A recently appointed head of digital strategy oversees the introduction of interactive panels in every classroom, the adoption of Firefly (virtual learning environment) and individual iPads. Use of mobile phones, however, is strictly limited to off duty times. Each day begins with a tutor period or assembly and a service is held in St Martin's church, close at hand, every week. Serious emphasis on academic attainment with pupils' individual strengths encouraged and targeted support where needed. In the middle school (years 3-5), pupils mainly class taught with specialists for music, DT, art and languages. Seniors (years 6-8) taught by subject staff and in sets according to potential. Classics continue to have status with Latin taught from year 6 and Greek, for scholars, in year 8. A notice on the classroom door says 'Mistakes welcome here!' and pupils confirm this, 'You learn best if you can say if you don't understand'. How true. French continues as main MFL.

Learning support is for all with a drop-in centre open all day and into the evening with plenty of help available, including typing courses, interactive revision sessions and assistance with speech and language development from trained therapists. 'They spotted that my son needed some help without me having to ask and ask,' we were told; and 'there is such an atmosphere of acceptance and support and no stigma attached to receiving extra help'. Those who require more formal support can be withdrawn for one-to-one help and this is charged as an extra. Communication with parents considered vital, as it is with any outside agencies involved such as educational psychologists. Real focus on study skills with pupils encouraged to take responsibility for their learning and personal organisation, particularly in years 7 and 8 as preparation for senior school.

Potential scholars are identified and streamed in year 7 and go on to form the 'scholars' group' in year 8. School well aware of risks in labelling pupils too early as gifted and talented and the enrichment programme laid on to nurture scholars is open to all pupils, parents and the wider community. This programme includes a series of 'Orangery lectures' given on a range of subjects plus scholarship preparation for music, art, sport and drama. Pupils take part in off-site initiatives such as the Uppingham skills day and the Gordonstoun challenge. Debating workshops, musical soirées, plays and careers talks all nourish and support pupils' motivation and widen their horizons. For the same reason a link has been developed with Mayo college in India with exchange visits to take place annually.

Performance culture well established in verse, singing and public speaking, usually as inter-house competitions or with other local independent schools. Grounds perfect for letting off steam at break and play times, the ha-ha providing a natural boundary. Den building in the spinneys and copses together with a genuine assault course in the woods provide plenty of opportunity to run free and exercise as well as more formal games provision of rugby, cricket and hockey. Girls all play cricket these days, there is a nine-hole golf course, squash and tennis courts, outdoor swimming pool and an equestrian and ski racing team. Art scholars have specially allotted areas for their work in the studio which they can continue with in spare time. Extracurricular activities include clay pigeon shooting and a stargazing club run from the school's own observatory.

The recent introduction of the OPS challenge, a sort of mini DofE with long hikes, camp-outs, bushcraft and outdoor pursuits holidays to Normandy in year 7 and the Ardèche post-CE provide opportunities for learning leadership skills – as well as enormous fun. Senior pupils are selected for the responsibilities of prefect, dorm captain, head boarder and house captains and the school has a head boy and a head girl, as well as two senior prefects.

Boarding increasingly popular, particularly in top two forms when it is seen as good preparation for senior school, but care is taken not to assume every child is on the path to boarding school. 'My son decided he did not want to board at senior school and we were supported fully in that decision.' Many begin with flexi-boarding, later becoming full boarders, even when they live close at hand to the school. 'I like being with friends and we have so much fun'. Dorms, for six to 10, have recently been updated to a high standard.

Oundle School

Linked with Laxton Junior School

Great Hall, New Street, Peterborough, Northamptonshire PE8 4GH

Ages 11–19 **Pupils** 1,114 **Sixth form** 371 **Boarders** 847 full **C of E**

Fees: Day £17,880 – £23,505; Boarding £27,885 – £36,690 pa

01832 277125
www.oundleschool.org.uk

O

Head: Since 2015, Sarah Kerr-Dineen MA (50s), previously warden of Forest School in London, is the first female head of Oundle. Seeing her name inscribed on the board outside the school's entrance hall, coming after 450 years' worth of (doubtless splendid) male heads, certainly gives one pause for thought. Mrs Kerr-Dineen was brought up in rural Sussex and educated entirely in the state sector. Both her parents were teachers and she describes herself as a bookish child, 'I read whatever was put in front of me.' After studying English at Cambridge, she went on to Oxford to begin research into the literary reception of the Elgin marbles for a DPhil. Marriage and children pressed pause on her studies (and we got the impression it definitely still is 'pause') and instead she took up a post at the Open University where she taught literature and was a tutor counsellor – despite having told her teacher parents she was never going to go into the family business. This was followed by part-time teaching at Kelly College, where she worked alongside her husband, a music teacher, and then it was back to Oxford where she spent two years at Oxford High and 13 years just down the road at St Edward's, teaching English, heading up a new girls' boarding house and finally becoming director of studies.

'I am basically a teacher,' says Mrs Kerr-Dineen; 'I will always teach.' And she does, as part of Oundle's recently introduced Trivium course for third formers (year 9s). 'We do the grammar, rhetoric, logic of cryptic crosswords, it's great fun.' So that's year 9 sorted out, but how does she get to know the rest of the 1,100 plus pupils? By going to as many events as possible, looking at photographs and 'working very hard to try and remember names'. The practice is paying off – several parents mentioned how impressed they'd been at her recall. Entertains the lower sixth to supper in her sublime 17th century house, Cobthorne, and eats with pupils in their boarding houses.

Mrs Kerr-Dineen, and other members of staff we spoke to, are keen to dispel the myth that Oundle is exclusively full of confident, high-achieving 'alpha' children and that it has a somewhat hard-line attitude to boarding. While we saw little evidence to support the former, there probably was some truth in the latter; cue moves to 'breathe more flexibility' into the system. From 2018 another exeat has been added to the long first half of the Lent term for all pupils: 'It's a dark corner of the year and a change of scene is necessary,' says the head. 'But,' she continues, 'apart from exeats, when we are in session, we are all here.' And if a child is tired, ill or just needs a break? There are no hard and fast rules, it's always about the individual and a 'conversation with the housemaster or mistress.'

Mrs Kerr-Dineen possesses both the breadth of experience and the cultural and intellectual heft that such a demanding and high-profile role requires, but without the excess of ego that could accompany it. Parents concur, while conceding that her appointment initially set off a 'bit of chuntering' among the 'more traditional types.' 'Her parent talks are excellent, she has a clear vision and has made good appointments.'

One of the head's first actions was to set up an anonymous telephone questionnaire for parents and she has, apparently, applied herself 'forensically' to the responses. 'She absolutely understands the importance of the individual in such a large school. There were one or two blurry lines when it came to pastoral care and she addressed these straight away.' One parent thought that in the past it might have been possible for a pupil to pass through Oundle 'unnoticed,' but that this 'definitely wouldn't happen now'.

One change noted by several parents is perhaps atmospheric, rather than material: 'We don't seem to hear so much about suspensions and expulsions now – not that there were loads before. There just seems to be a different mood when it comes to discipline.' 'School is listening more – to pupils and parents.' And, last but not least, 'It's terrific to have a female head, not to mention women in the school's other significant positions. They're great role models.'

Academic matters: A big school means a broadish intake at year 7 and 9, hence there's room for Cs and Ds, even the odd E, among the many As at GCSE and A level. Nor has school adopted the habit of kicking out GCSE underperformers. In 2018, 81 per cent A*-A/9-7 at I/GCSE and a pronounced dip to 58 per cent A*/A at A level/Pre-U (84 per cent A*-B). Most favoured A level subjects are maths, chemistry, history, biology, physics, English lit and geography – a healthy mix. And, hurrah, modern foreign languages are up there too, with great results and as many opting for French A level as economics, psychology and religious studies. Spanish and Latin aren't far behind. Music and drama are popular options at I/GCSE, but only a handful choose to continue with them to A level – although both are keenly pursued as extracurricular activities.

Oundle has a proud engineering heritage and, from what we saw, is determined to ensure the subject has an equally bright future. We are accustomed to the arms race of facilities in independent schools so it takes something very special to render us almost lost for words – but Oundle's Patrick Engineering Centre (design, engineering and technology), part of a newly completed STEM campus, did just that. We felt we'd walked out of a school and into a high-spec, high-tech light engineering company. Not only, we were told, does it have the largest footprint of any design and technology department in any school in the country, the equipment is so specialised there are probably businesses, and definitely universities (Imperial College London and Swansea University are partners), green-eyed with envy. Whatever next? We would not be surprised to hear that plans were underway for Oundle's own version of the large hadron collider.

Our notes became more and more phonetic as the head of design, engineering and technology proudly showed us one piece of kit after another (if you're interested a full list is on the school's website). 'We're the only school in the country that can 3D print in any material – elastomers, rigid plastics, clear resins, carbon fibre and titanium – pupils can even design their own materials.' He showed us a small model of himself, 'I was scanned and then printed in 3D!' Model racing vehicles made by Oundle's year 9 won first, second and third place, best engineered car and fastest vehicle at the regional finals of F1 in schools.

'It's not all about pressing buttons,' we were told. Pupils in the lower years start by learning 'artisan techniques' such as welding and use of traditional lathes – there's even a forge. The fact that the whole set up feels nothing like a school is deliberate, it's an environment in which pupils are 'challenged to develop their own creative problem-solving skills'. Around a quarter take DT for GCSE and half of those progress to study it at A level.

Science facilities are equally impressive and well equipped, if somewhat more recognisably 'school' than the Patrick Engineering Centre. We dropped in on a lower sixth class occupied with an extension work practical – making their own analgesics, 'They're putting into context what they've learnt on paper,' the teacher told us. EPQ students can set up and run their own experiments in dedicated project rooms.

STEM may be the school's showcase area, but those subjects which require little more than book and pen are taught to an equally high standard. The modern languages department is housed in the Adamson Centre, one of the older buildings. Seven languages including Russian, Arabic and Chinese, are offered as two or three-year courses up to GCSE level and all bar Arabic can be taken at A level. 'We're bucking the trend of language decline at A level,' the head of department told us, 'it's all down to inspirational teaching – what happens in the classroom is what makes pupils choose a language.' Extension opportunities for sixth formers include the school's Quadrivium (Quad) course. Like the third year Trivium course, Quad features rhetoric and public debate and challenges pupils to read widely and think laterally.

The pace is fast but support is there for those who need it – whether via Academic Voluntaries, weekly drop-in sessions for pupils who want one-to-one help with any aspect of their work, or from the educational support department. The department has six specialist staff who support pupils with (mild to moderate) SEND and EAL requirements. All pupils are screened for learning difficulties on arrival. Parents tell us that pupils are stretched and challenged, rather than pushed, 'they really want them to do well'. Nevertheless, Oundle probably isn't going to be first choice for a child who really struggles with organisation or needs significant support.

Games, options, the arts: Forget the STEM campus – that was last year, now it's all about the Sports MasterPlan. We hurried as fast as our note-taking allowed behind former England rugby player and now Oundle's visionary director of sport, Danny Grewcock. The existing facilities looked pretty good to us, but little do the swimming pool, athletics track and car park know that they are about to be flattened to make way for a new pool, sports centre and 'hospitality suite' overlooking the cricket pitch. This will also provide a much-needed whole school venue – none of the existing buildings is large enough.

Mr Grewcock wants to build on Oundle's undoubted sporting strengths in rugby, cricket, hockey, swimming and netball, develop rowing, and focus on other activities such as dance and cycling that may appeal to the ball shy. School has four floodlit Astros, masses of pitches, two boathouses and an indoor and outdoor shooting range. Developments seem to be a little tardy on the girls' sporting options front, with girls' cricket only introduced in 2017 and football and rugby still offered only as recreational activities. That's set to change under Mr Grewcock, whose focus is not only on competitive sport, but also on encouraging pupils to develop a life-long interest in physical well-being and challenging traditional gender stereotyping in sport.

Standing in beautifully tended gardens is the Yarrow Gallery, built in memory of Eric Yarrow, a former pupil who was killed at Ypres in 1915. It was originally a science and art museum but is now the school's exhibition space for both pupils' work and that of visiting artists. When we visited the gallery was exhibiting A level exam work of astonishing maturity and skill: intricate paper cuts, pen and ink drawings, light box work, collages and a surprising amount of sculpture – beautifully detailed portrait busts and some very lifelike iguanas basking on rocks. A level art and Pre-U art history are offered; emphasis is on fine art (drawing, painting, sculpture). No separate textiles or photography A levels but these can be pursued as part of the art A level.

Oundle has a great tradition of choral singing and everyone gets to participate, whether in one of the school's four choirs or at weekly congregational practice. Apparently, the thing is to ensure that Oundle's rendition of Jerusalem is louder than Uppingham's at matches. There are multiple orchestras, ensembles and chamber groups and any number of performance opportunities, from popular weekly lunchtime concerts in the town to playing at CCF ceremonies. School has not one, but four, organs and what started out as a small festival dedicated to that instrument has grown into the annual Oundle International Festival – a celebration of music, film and theatre organised by the Oundle Music Trust and enjoyed by the whole town. Compared to other areas the music department did look a tiny bit tired, but fear not, it is, we were told, next on the list for enhancement.

School plays are programmed alongside performances from national touring companies at the Stahl Theatre, converted from a former chapel in the town. The theatre has its own director, technical team and support staff who work with pupils to give them experience in all aspects of putting on plays in a professional setting. House plays are entirely run by pupils; houseparents are not involved at all – 'That's very Oundle,' said a parent.

Nearly half the pupils participate in CCF (army, Royal Navy and RAF). It's compulsory for all pupils in the fourth form (year 10) and many continue with it afterwards. For those who don't want to do drill on a Wednesday afternoon there's the community action programme, so successful and popular that the organisers have had to look considerably beyond Oundle – as far as Kettering, Corby and Peterborough – for worthy causes. Pupils work in special needs schools, supervise riding and rowing and help with primary school sports coaching and homework clubs. They can take part in environmental enterprises, work in local museums or even get involved in renovation projects at the Nene Valley Railway. We had a welcome sit down in the community action office – staff are genuinely proud of the difference pupils can make in the local community and the way in which they develop through their voluntary work.

On Tuesday and Thursday afternoons it's Vols time, with pupils choosing between reading, music commitments, academic surgeries and activities and societies. There are nearly 50 options including debating, climbing, design engineering and technology, or taking a turn running OSCAR, the school's radio station that broadcasts from its own studio in the music department. One pupil decided to make use of the facilities in the Patrick Centre to restore his family's 1940s bread van, a real labour of love.

Boarding: Oundle stands firm against the prevailing trend to dilute school boarding to a homeopathic version of its original self. There are no flexi, part-time or weekly options, it's either boarding or day. The resulting consensus makes for a very stable, cohesive community and all the boarders we spoke to – not just our 'official' guides – were genuinely positive and insightful about the choice they and their families had made. There are eight boys' houses and five girls' houses plus Laxton, a house for the 200 or so very local day pupils and Berrystead, a 'transitional' co-ed boarding house, for the 40 boarders in years 7 and 8. Day pupils in years 7 and 8 now enter a mixed junior day house adjacent to Berrystead. This move is designed to allow greater specialist provision for the youngest pupils, graduating their transition to the senior school and maximising opportunities for friendships between day and boarding pupils.

Like practically everything we saw at Oundle the houses, which are spread across the town, are spacious, well-resourced and very efficiently run. The head said that Oundle works because the house system subdivides it effectively into mini schools, and we saw this in action as we enjoyed a delicious lunch in Sanderson, one of the girls' houses. All meals are taken in house, giving staff frequent opportunities to check how pupils' days are going, pick up on any changes in mood or follow up quickly on anything that may have happened earlier. Each house has its own chef whose competencies are by no means exempt from the fierce inter-house competitive spirit. 'We lost our French chef – he went to another house. He was so good at puddings,' one of our lunch companions sighed. We felt it was our solemn duty to test the new chef's pudding skills and enjoyed every last morsel of scrumptious banoffee pie – not part of the standard French repertoire. 'Pupils are expected to eat what's on the menu', but they meet with the house chef every fortnight to help plan meals. Food in the boys' houses is, apparently, 'very different.'

Saturday is a full school day with lessons in the morning and sport in the afternoon until 5.30pm; Sunday is 'more relaxed', breakfast is optional (and can be eaten in pyjamas), although chapel isn't. Chapel services (Sunday plus two in the week) are on a rota because it's not large enough to hold the whole school. We asked boarders what happens for the rest of the Sunday: 'catching up with work' was one option, but going into a coffee shop in town for a 'full cooked breakfast, wearing chapel clothes' sounded like a better bet. Parents and grandparents can also visit for the day and will often scoop up friends whose parents live abroad and take them out for lunch too. International families like the fact there are no exeats and appreciate that a night away from school could be arranged if they happen to be in the country – on a case by case basis.

Rooms we saw were spacious and comfortable; accommodation varies between individual houses but usually it's small dorms of two or three in lower years and single rooms or bedsits for sixth formers. In Sanderson the head of house has her own bed sitting room, complete with stag's head on the wall. Of course each house is different, but that difference comes from its occupants as much as a predetermined identity. It's traditional for pupils to join the same house as a parent who attended, but apart from that the advice is to try and ignore 'reputations', consult the website and then visit a few before deciding.

Background and atmosphere: Oundle's earliest origins have been traced to the 15th century when it was a school serving the town's 29 guild houses. Officially it dates from 1556 when wealthy Oundle merchant, Lord Mayor of London and Master of the Worshipful Company of Grocers', Sir William Laxton, left some of his London properties to the Grocers' Company to endow his former school. Oundle's fortunes waxed and waned and waned again – beset both by poor choice of headmasters and wider troubles such as the civil war and the Great Fire of London (the latter destroyed many of the Grocers' properties, including those bequeathed by Laxton). The 19th century wasn't much better, with more sub-par headmasters and an outbreak of typhoid threatening the school's future until in 1892 the Grocers appointed complete outsider, Frederick Sanderson, as head. Sanderson was not only a scholarship boy from a poor family, for his time he was also an educational radical, believing that science, engineering and modern languages were as important as the classics. Despite initial resistance, his ideas about offering boys a wider education proved popular, not just at Oundle but throughout the public school system, and numbers increased. During the first world war Oundle deployed its scientific and engineering facilities as workshops, producing horseshoes and metal parts for shells and torpedoes – the tradition of 'workshop weeks' actually continued until the 1990s. Oundle went co-educational in 1990 and is now the third largest boarding school in the country.

The market town of Oundle and its eponymous school (or is that the other way round?) combine to make a large campus that is both public and private. The school's centre is a cluster of mainly late Victorian buildings (cloisters, great hall, chapel) and boarding houses, playing fields and teaching departments fan out from there. Townspeople enjoy the school's gardens, make use of its sports and leisure facilities and attend events and exhibitions; pupils and staff must dominate every aspect of the town in term time and are no doubt much missed by local businesses during the holidays. Pupils are on show as they move between houses and lessons – uniform (girls distinguished by their beloved long culottes) is worn by all, but some kind of unofficial consensus means bags are carried by none, so new pupils must learn quickly to negotiate some busy roads while balancing a pile of folders and books. A five-minute period of grace has now been introduced to allow for travel time between lessons.

Pastoral care, well-being and discipline: All of the above came in for unsolicited praise from parents. 'The houses are really well run, they're just the right size and the unit works brilliantly.' Tutors are pupils' and parents' main point of contact and the system was described to us as 'robust, in a good way'. That confidence notwithstanding, several told us that things can be tough at first for the youngest boarders, more so if they haven't come from a boarding prep, 'The size of the school is a bit daunting at first, but they soon find their group and community.' Day pupils are really well integrated and every effort is made to 'eliminate the difference.' Laxton, the day house, even has its own PTA (not usually found in boarding schools) and parents organise socials, second hand uniform sales and raise funds for travel bursaries.

Head was keen to talk about the importance of well-being and mental health, praising the structures that were already in place when she joined: 'It's something we all talk about a lot, everyone who works at the school has a role to play. In addition to house parents, tutors and prefects who are all alert to potential problems, we also have a dedicated suite of rooms where pupils can make an appointment or call in and talk safely and confidentially to a trained, independent listener.'

While many agree that the additional exeat was long overdue, we found little demand for additional exeats from older pupils, and definitely none from the parents we spoke to: 'It's much better than in one weekend and out the next, that can be unsettling,' and 'It's the best thing in the world, especially in the lower sixth. No parties – you're free to focus on work – my daughter loves it.' (We didn't get the daughter in question's take on this.)

We heard plenty of comments to the effect that Oundle is 'not a hand holding school' and the same applies to pupil relationships: hand holding or other PDA is a very serious disciplinary matter. A mother observed: 'It's not fast – boys and girls have pretty healthy relationships as friends, those girls don't take any nonsense'. School sets high standards and expects pupils to learn quickly, take responsibility and 'self regulate'. 'It's the implied contract of the place,' said another parent.

Pupils and parents: Consensus is that school is 'pretty good at picking the right pupils – and parents'. Pupils come from all over the country, about 20 per cent from abroad (full boarding makes it popular with expats). 'It's definitely not London-centric,' said one parent; another thought that while some families were wealthy, it wasn't a 'glossy' place; 'Lots of pupils have bursaries, but no one knows (or cares) who they are', they added. That was our impression too, we didn't see any pupils taking liberties with uniform, hair or make up. Even the sixth form girls we met hadn't fallen out of love with their culottes. 'We heard the new head might get rid of them' confided one, 'but it was just a rumour.' Phew. No mutterings about fundraising for high profile building projects either, 'They think very carefully about how they spend money – it's needs driven.' Governing body publishes a very readable annual review with key facts, figures (including income and expenditure) and 'objectives'. Top marks for transparency.

Old Oundelians (OOs) include writers Al Alvarez (poet), David Edgar (playwright) and Roderick Gordon (children's novelist), Bruce Dickinson (singer with Iron Maiden – do Google why he was expelled), Arthur Marshall, Sir Alan Budd, Sir Peter Scott and Professor Richard Dawkins, plus any number of engineers, industrialists, soldiers and public servants.

Entrance: Most join from prep schools: Witham Hall, Beeston Hall, Orwell Park, Old Buckenham Hall and Belhaven are the principal feeders. Modest but growing number from preps in the south east eg The Dragon, Summer Fields and Ludgrove. Parents are advised to plan ahead – entrance at 11+ and 13+ is very competitive. Trusty registrar makes it his business to ensure only those who will succeed are entered. Not many sixth form places going spare so bar is high. Minimum for entry is three As and three Bs at GCSE (or numerical equivalents), but successful external applicants will typically have all A*s and As.

Exit: Very few leave post-GCSE (seven per cent in 2018). University destinations are the usual Russell Group suspects – Newcastle, Bristol, Exeter, Durham, Warwick, Imperial, UCL. Mixed views on Oxbridge preparation, 'fantastic' say some, one or two thought it could be 'a bit' more proactive; 18 places in 2018. Increasing numbers to US universities. History, modern languages and engineering are the most popular degree choices.

Money matters: Boarding and day fees in line with similar schools. Wide and widening range of bursaries – around 30 per cent of pupils receive some fee remission, with the average bursary award just over 70 per cent of fees. Scholarships bring honour, but make little dent in the termly bill.

Remarks: 'Flying high', 'On top of its game', 'There's a real buzz.' Oundle has always been one of the UK's top-performing co-ed boarding schools, but parents sense a new energy about the place. We too were bowled over by this dynamic, innovative, forward-thinking school. Oundle challenges itself, as well as its pupils, to be prepared intellectually, personally and spiritually, for whatever the future holds.

The Perse School

Hills Road, Cambridge CB2 8QF

Ages 3–18 Pupils 1,602 Sixth form 355

Fees: £13,530 – £17,322 pa

01223 403800
www.perse.co.uk

Head: Since 2008, Edward Elliott (40s), who has been at the school since 1997. Educated at The Royal Grammar School, Worcester, then St Anne's College, Oxford, where he got a first in geography. Tried commerce (a graduate trainee at De La Rue) but quickly moved to teaching at the Whitgift School in Surrey. Married to Sue, a paediatrician, with two young daughters and a son. Certainly a finger very firmly on the pulse at The Perse as well as in the wider education community, though 'not swayed by current trends in education to make knee-jerk reactions,' surmised a parent.

Head of prep: Since 2014, James Piper BA PGCE (30s). Previously deputy head of Bilton Grange. Educated at S Anselm's and Repton. Read classics at Durham, PGCE from Pembroke College, Cambridge, and is completing a masters in educational leadership at the University of Buckingham. Started teaching career at Aysgarth, then spent 11 years at the Dragon School (was head of classics and housemaster of year 6 boys' full boarding house). Married, with three children. Outside interests include cricket and golf.

Head of pre-prep: Sarah Waddington, BSc MA PGCE.

Academic matters: Parents cannot speak too highly of the Perse Pelican Pre-Prep. Deserves its reputation as one of the hardest schools to get into for the best possible reasons. The Perse's trademark academic thoroughness starts here, even if the youngest pupils don't realise it. Children in the nursery (usually around 32) are encouraged to love learning and to ask questions, supported by happy, friendly staff.

School defines 'The Perse DNA' which is present in all stages. Of course the prep school is academic, with intellectual, fast-paced, sparkling learning, but there's also an emphasis on extracurricular activities – not just 'a school for bright nerds and geeks'. Sport, music, drama, outdoor pursuits... there's even rocketry at the prep to prepare pupils for the award-winning rocketry society at the Upper. New whizzy science department.

Brainpower is not thin on the ground in Cambridge and the Perse aims, and achieves, high academically to meet its market. Even given the genes, results are impressive across the board – 95 per cent A*-B and 84 per cent A*/A at A level/Pre-U in 2018. International A levels also offered. Three-quarters IGCSE and the other quarter GCSE, with 94 per cent of grades A*-A/9-7 in 2018. Heads of department have the freedom to choose the exam they feel offers the most rigour and currency. Results are of course stellar in maths and science, yet history, geography and languages are also among the popular sixth form options – a hint to the breadth of education on offer here. The Perse has developed its own course in engineering technology and makes innovative use of IT. 'Global studies' in year 7 offers a taster of a range of languages – Mandarin, Japanese, Arabic, Portuguese and Italian. All labs recently refitted to highest standard and computer science now lauded as 'the fourth science'. More than 60 students each year involved in the Higher Project Qualification (HPQ) – 'intellectually liberating' says head – and the sixth form equivalent, the EPQ, is also popular.

SEN provision is excellent, although head prefers the term 'learning maximisation'. All pupils are screened on entry, with the result that 120 pupils are supported, including those perhaps running at 80 per cent capacity who would not be spotted elsewhere. On-site SEN teacher plus liaison with educational psychologists, who all feed through to director of teaching in a concerted effort to work around the barriers. 'The school's reputation for only concentrating on high flyers is not borne out by the extra sessions, reviews and learning aids that have been provided for my child,' said a parent.

A few parental rumblings about the school's commitment to nurturing young teachers, some of whom don't come up to scratch straight away. The school points to its significant new teacher induction and continuous professional development programme, with mentoring from more experienced staff.

Games, options, the arts: Surprisingly for a day school, manages to keep two or three sessions a week for games and other extracurricular activities right through the school – 'almost too many to choose from,' say pupils. This is, in the main, a very popular policy and pupils relish the opportunities to develop sporting, musical or dramatic skills, and various adventurous options on offer – notably CCF (RAF only, unusually, and a popular choice for many girls). There's also the Perse Exploration Society, which runs trips in the UK for younger pupils, as far afield as Vietnam and the Himalayas for the eldest. A new option is the Wilderness Group offering further outdoor pursuits activities. Excellent sports hall block includes squash court, weights room and a large and well-appointed fitness suite; school employs a fitness coach who provides guidance and fitness programmes for students and staff. Much effort has gone in to providing a wide choice of opportunities for girls, who show their appreciation by their enthusiasm.

Art is rich and colourful, evidence of inspirational teaching, and includes ceramics and printing. Local artists exhibit in The Pelican Gallery within the teaching space. Impressive lecture theatre doubles as drama studio seating 180 – productions have really grown in recent years. New (very neat) music building – an extension to existing block – provides plenty of teaching/practice rooms, as well as space for larger ensembles and rehearsal hall to accommodate full-scale symphony orchestra with chorus. This doubles as a concert hall and is made available to the local community. About two-fifths learn at least one instrument and musical activities of all types flourish – baroque string ensembles, jazz, brass, wind and chamber groups, choirs and music technology. The school's musical excellence now seen by parents as a principal reason to apply and attracting correspondingly good budding musicians. New performing arts centre on upper school site. Most prep school pupils take part in three or four activities after school or at lunchtime very week.

Background and atmosphere: The school's history – nearly 400 years of it – is chequered and includes embezzlement in the 18th century, an assault on the head in the 19th and an incendiary bomb hitting it in 1941. Since 1960 it has occupied award-winning, purpose-built accommodation on a 28-acre site. Buildings are low, few higher than two storeys as is customary in this part of the world, but although not imposing; they are inviting and well integrated into the site. Hall doubles up as dining room, necessitating daily quick setting out and packing away of tables. Meals taken by staff and pupils together perhaps explaining the unusually orderly atmosphere. Two Astroturf pitches, very attractive, tree-lined playing fields, real feeling of space. A new outdoor pursuits centre and an additional full-size all weather pitch recently completed, with new sports pitches on 21 acres of land at Little Abington. Good careers room and resources in sixth form centre, which also has a well-used common room area, expanded to provide a separate work area.

Prep pupils have their own campus five minutes from the upper school and their own all-weather pitch (also used by upper school students).

Pastoral care, well-being and discipline: Pastoral care is taken seriously, with nurses on-site at both prep and upper schools, and there's a school counsellor and a pastoral safety net made up of tutors and heads of year. Interestingly, the house system was dusted off a few years ago to fill a gap in pupils' enthusiasm for extracurricular activities. Reintroduced as eight houses for pupils in years 7 to 11, leadership opportunities are appreciated by those lower down the school.

International links are being forged 'to prepare students for a world where employment will be global,' explains head. Exchanges to Spain, France and Germany as well as Sewickley, near Pittsburgh. Member of SAGE – Strategic Alliance of Global Educators – consortium of 10 schools from around the world (UK, US, Australia, Singapore, Hong Kong, China...) who share best practice and work together on a range of projects. Also involved in Christel House charitable foundation to establish first class schools in the most deprived areas of the world – Perse staff have been seconded to Bangalore and Cape Town.

Parents appreciate the school's meticulous planning and communication, making life easier particularly for those juggling several offspring – all information is provided well in advance and with great attention to detail. Emails from pupils and parents are responded to swiftly, 'even on a Sunday night,' marvelled a parent.

Although common sense prevails in all corners of the school and its operation, there is room here too for eccentrics, who only add to the increasing richness of Perse life.

Pupils and parents: A school for the 'intellectually curious,' says head, although fees prohibit mass takeover by bright children of poorly-paid Cambridge academics. Head is committed to ensuring that the school is a cosmopolitan meritocracy – a million pounds is spent on means-tested financial support for pupils aged 7 and over throughout the prep and upper, with more than 120 receiving fees assistance. There is indeed a real mix of backgrounds – rare in independent schools – which the school is certain contributes to the development of all pupils' emotional intelligence, preparing them well for life in the real world.

School ceased taking boarders in 1993, two years before girls arrived in the sixth form; it became fully coeducational in 2012, though still two-thirds boys. Most girls blossom here, with opportunities and resources few girls' schools can offer. Pupils are relaxed, unpretentious and natural – many come for the science but find they relish the sporting and artistic possibilities they discover. Majority live close by, though some from as far as Ely, Saffron Walden, Newmarket, Royston and elsewhere. Annually, a very few from abroad, under special guardianship scheme, seen as bringing new and refreshing dimension to school life. Distinguished list of alumni includes the late Sir Peter Hall, Rev Dr John Polkinghorne, the late David Tang, Dave Gilmour, Pete Atkin, Sir Mark Potter, Tess Howard (international hockey player).

Entrance: By assessment: 'observed play' for nursery (32 places) and reception (about eight places); entry into prep for external applicants (another 30 places) by the school's own entrance tests in English and maths and verbal reasoning, as well as an interview and report from the previous school.

Competition for places at The Perse Upper is not as fierce as the rumour would have it and pales into insignificance next to London's bunfight. At 11, roughly two and a half applicants for each place – 60 come up from the Perse Prep and another

50 from local juniors and preps. Sixty more are added at 13 (largely from King's College, St John's College, St Faith's). Entry is by tests in English and maths and verbal reasoning, as well as interview and report from the previous school. Also a short humanities video and questions exercise.

Entry to sixth form is by interview and a subject test for scholarships, with all offers conditional on GCSE performance – usually above 70 points required, with 9-7 in A level subjects. Most joiners come from local girls' independent schools (Stephen Perse, St Mary's) and the state sector.

Exit: Most – about 95 per cent – move from the prep to Perse Upper. Others to eg The Leys, Stephen Perse Foundation, King's Ely. Around 20 leave The Perse after GCSE, choosing Hills Road Sixth Form College in the main, but vast majority go on to The Perse's sixth form. Forty-nine to Oxbridge in 2018, rest to wide spread of other universities – three-quarters Russell Group eg Imperial, Bristol, UCL, Durham. Medicine hugely popular (18 places in 2018) as are English, history, law and natural sciences.

Money matters: Scholarships are mostly five per cent, occasionally 10 per cent. Determined to maintain its direct grant tradition and increase the amount of means-tested financial support available to bursary applicants. Recently spent over £1m on fees assistance for families who could not otherwise afford a Perse education. All sixth form applicants are now considered for an academic scholarship based on their performance in the entrance tests; they can then apply for a maximum of two other scholarships (art, drama, general, music and sport).

Remarks: A co-ed academic school and a 'cosmopolitan meritocracy' which prepares students well for the real world, not just intellectually but also emotionally.

The Priory Academy LSST

Cross O'Cliff Hill, Lincoln, Lincolnshire LN5 8PW

Ages 11–18 **Pupils** 1,875 **Sixth form** 520 **Boarders** 53 (in sixth form)

Fees: Day free; Boarding £12,300 pa

01522 889977
www.priorylsst.co.uk

Head: Since 2016, Jane Hopkinson (40s). Studied maths and chemistry at UEA in Norwich. Planned to be an accountant but work experience put her off. PGCE in maths found her returning to her roots to teach in a girls' grammar school in Grantham. Joined the academy in 2008, rising to deputy head here before headship at another school, returning here as head. Not very well known by parents but not expected to be in a school this size. 'I deal with the head of year. The head oversees the school rather than the pupils,' was one parent's take on it. 'She has a strong management team in place,' from another. All happy with plenty of online communication from head. Quietly spoken, effective and efficient, she strikes us as a lady who will 'get on with the job.'

Academic matters: In 2018, 82 per cent 9-4s in English and maths at GCSE, with 70 per cent of grades at 5+. Eighty per cent of grades were A*-C at A level, 30 per cent A*/A. Excellent results for a non-selective school albeit 10 per cent are admitted after an aptitude test. 'It's made very clear from day one that the children are here to learn,' said one parent. 'Guidelines are laid out before they start and are expected to be adhered to regarding homework and study,' said another. Gifted and talented spotted early on and nurtured, but not to the detriment of the less able. Children assessed every six weeks after each module and parents kept well informed. 'My children go to school every morning knowing what it expected of them, which is excellent,' said one parent.

Science popular throughout the school with a modern planetarium within the new science block inspiring budding scientists and capturing imaginations. Excellent facilities, including modern labs and separate ones just for the sixth form. Plethora of computers throughout the school including impressive IT area. DT room home to a robotic lab including a 3D computer. All year 7s study Latin for 13 weeks – excellent; also available up to GCSE. Many take two languages, all have to take one, for GCSE. Gifted and talented take triple science and many do two languages as well. Streaming from year 8 in sciences, maths and English.

The lessons we observed showed smart, engaged pupils with enthusiastic teachers. All pupils leapt to their feet when we entered the room, except for the sixth form. Pupils welcoming and chatty, lots of 'missing' and 'sirring'.

Maximum class sizes of 34 years 7-11, 26 in sixth form, but usually much smaller. About 10 per cent of each year has EAL requirements, higher for the boarders. Support available through learning support department and sixth form mentors. Every SEN student has a student profile explaining their needs and best way to support them in the classroom and at home. EHC plan students have designated learning support assistant working with them. All parents spoke highly of the LS department. And all parents said their child 'was reaching their potential.'

Games, options, the arts: Every conceivable facility when it comes to sports. Indoor 60m running track, outdoor all weather track and pitches; climbing wall, trampolines, gym, swimming pool, dance studios all housed in new sports centre. Lots of after-school sports practices and clubs, teams for all abilities. They even have their own spinning room alongside the fitness suite. Lots of silverware in the cabinet and certain individuals high achieving outside school as well.

Impressive music school, including recording studio. Loads of bands, orchestras and choirs, performing frequently. Lots of plays and productions, including whole school shows. Fabulous debating chamber used for cross year group debates et al. Sixth form still life art class concentrating hard and producing great work. Every GCSE and A level art student donates one piece from their portfolio to the school. Impressive gallery in large reception area.

DofE to gold and, unusually for a state school, active CCF with on site rifle range. Both well supported. Plenty of school trips, far and wide. One parent commented that not everyone got to do DofE because of large numbers and often 'names pulled out of a hat' when it came to school trips. 'It's frustrating, but I understand that it's difficult because of the size of the school. I suppose it's a lesson that you can't get everything you want,' was a parent's philosophical take on it.

Boarding: Boarding introduced for sixth form in 2012 and classed as outstanding in recent Ofsted report. Virtually all boarders from overseas, some expat. Around 50 per cent join the sixth form for a year only, a handful for a couple of terms, the remainder for the two years. Large drive now being made to attract more boarders, particularly Forces children. Newish head of boarding highly regarded by parents and pupils alike. Parents appreciate the boarding blog to keep up with goings on and talk of quick response to emails. Modern, purpose built boarding house with en suite facilities throughout. Very much like uni accommodation, and they are allowed a lot of independence. But all have to be on site to do 2.5 hours compulsory prep daily.

There is a 10pm roll call every night but apart from that they can come and go as they like. Allowed out until midnight at the weekend and head of boarding more than happy for them to stay with friends with parental permission. They can bake cakes and cook for themselves at weekends. Bake Off competition hotly contested, apparently. Plenty of trips at weekends; many don't take this up as Lincoln is a short walk away. Compulsory team-building trip at the beginning of autumn term. Head of boarding gently prises young men from computers if need be. Very flexible: one pupil has a weekend job, others attend evening clubs off site. School facilities, such as fitness suite, available for out of hours use. No restrictions on phones or social media within boarding house. A sensible rule as many have parents in different time zones. Despite numerous nationalities and languages a cohesive atmosphere prevails and freedoms not abused.

Background and atmosphere: Founded in 1992 on the site of an old girls' grammar school, and has grown dramatically. Now the largest school in Lincoln, if not the county. Housed on a massive site on one of the main roads into Lincoln. From the main road you only see the old, attractive, red-brick school house. But once within the grounds you realise how vast the site is. Pupils and staff walk miles during the day. 'We definitely manage our 10,000 steps,' said one guide. Walkways covered so no drowned rats during lesson changeovers. 'I would like to see the leaks repaired more quickly,' said another guide.

Large sixth form, over 500 pupils, housed in separate modern block, not far from the boarding house. All wear smart business suits and look the part. Most sixth form teaching done in this block. Large – no, massive – common room full of Chesterfield sofas and a TV broadcasting the news. Canteen for exclusive use, breakfast, lunch and snacks available. Amusing to see many students playing cards. Not quite a den of iniquity but possibly future poker players being hothoused here. Lots of computers and supervised free periods for year 12s in particular.

Government academy funding has paid for massive development including the planetarium, new sports centre, debating hall and sixth form, including boarding house. The whole school immaculate and well cared for. No sign of litter or detritus. Good to see one of our guides pick up the only sweet paper in sight. Plenty of open space including lots of water features, ponds, gardens and statues. Sad to see plaques in the memorial garden. Each year has its own garden for break times. They even have a chapel with underfloor heating, very popular at certain times of the year. A nice touch in the chapel – please note the labyrinth outside – is the 'blue book.' Each student signs it on their first day and 'signs out' on their last. Our guides were proud to show us their names and spoke with great pride about how it makes them feel they belong.

Pastoral care, well-being and discipline: Discipline is hot. 'Guidelines, rules and regulations are set out before they start and are expected to be adhered to,' said one parent, 'and they are.' Another parent told us, 'the whole class had to write a letter of apology to a teacher because of bad behaviour, even those not involved, and I fully support that.' Uniform deviancy also picked up on immediately. They don't stand for any nonsense and the pupils know and respect that.

There is no denying the school is large. Each year group is the size of a small school. But there don't seem to be any problems with new starters feeling lost or out of place. Induction days and bonding sessions are successful. Every year 7 goes on a team building trip to their facility in France during their first term. Heads of years and tutors appear to know their pupils well. Forms stay with the same tutor for many years.

Pastoral care complimented by all parents. Peer listening scheme with years 11-13 offering advice to younger years. They can talk live on the computer to these mentors about any problems. Counselling services on offer if needed. The atmosphere within the school is informal and relaxed despite, or because of, the strict discipline. Pupils know what is expected of them and act accordingly, with miscreants sorted out firmly, quickly and efficiently. There is an effective school council with its own budget. Latest purchase was mirrors for the girls' toilets. They also asked for, and got, more choice in the canteen.

Pupils and parents: Parents supportive and ambitious. Pupils come from a wide area, many from small rural primaries, and from all walks of life. Many Forces children from the nearby air bases. Pupils friendly, welcoming, happy and focused.

Entrance: Oversubscribed despite offering 240 year 7 places. Some 50+ feeder schools, each allocated at least two places. Pupils come from as far afield as Grantham to the south and Gainsborough to the north. Non-selective except for 10 per cent chosen by aptitute test in technology.

Entrance to sixth form 'open to all' but subject-specific for certain grades. Boarders interviewed by Skype. New sixth formers are mainly boarders.

Exit: Very few leave after GCSEs, between one and two per cent, usually for vocational courses at local colleges. The vast majority go on the university, with usually a few to Oxbridge. Apprenticeships becoming more popular and being embraced by the school. Very few take gap years and the odd one straight into employment.

Remarks: A school offering tremendous facilities and education. Very much the feel of an independent school with fantastic facilities and very enthusiastic teaching staff. Its reputation precedes it, and we can see why. As one parent said, 'please thank The Priory for its contribution to my son's education.' Quite.

Queen Mary's Grammar School

Sutton Road, Walsall, West Midlands WS1 2PG

Ages 11–18 **Pupils** 1,093 **Sixth form** 405 (105 girls)

01922 720696
www.qmgs.walsall.sch.uk

Principal: Since January 2018, Richard Langton MA PGCE NPQH, previously deputy head. Spent a year as head of school prior to formal appointment whilst his predecessor, Tim Swain, set up the Mercian Multi-Academy Trust, of which he is now CEO. Geography degree from Birmingham and a masters in geography in education from UCL. Was head of geography at Lawrence Sheriff School before joining QMGS in 2011.

A family man who has fully embraced the Queen Mary's community. His approach is to mix the traditional with modern life. From the ceremonious whole school assembly dressed in full traditional robes to active conversations about current issues: male suicide and equality. Open to ideas from staff and

Q

pupils alike, he has his finger firmly on the pulse when it comes to current issues.

Although not formally timetabled to teach, he does run EPQ classes, as well as helping with supervision and supply. He also teaches rugby, cricket and hockey.

Academic matters: In 2018, 67 per cent A*-A/9-7 at GCSE; at A level 70 per cent of grades were A*-B and 43 per cent A*/A (an impressive 32 students achieving A*/A grades in all of their subjects). Stem subjects remain the most popular option at A level. Some 70 per cent of sixth formers study maths A level and 94 per cent do at least one science. They are also expected to take a further academic option such as EPQ, further maths or study Massive Open Online Courses (MOOCs), plus volunteering roles and an extracurricular activity. The general idea is to turn out well-rounded individuals.

The legacy of the modern languages specialism for the school remains strong in the main school, with everyone taking at least one language GCSE, though few continue to A level. Mandarin is mandatory for all pupils in KS3 through the Confucius Institute, a well-respected programme with additional funding from China. There is also a Mandarin Excellence Programme for those who show promise. Mandarin is an option at GCSE and A level; few take the latter, though some do HSK (Chinese proficiency) tests.

Students seem genuine and hard-working in their approach to academia. Parents comment that they've never had to push their child to study or do homework: rather the impetus comes from the students, who are embraced in a driven culture. 'My son is so enthused by what he is doing. When he had a recent geography project he put in extra research, he was really excited.'

Staff are an experienced bunch and are true specialists in their subjects, think maths from Oxbridge. Staff numbers have increased as pupil numbers have risen from 700 to nearly 1,110 in recent years, and are set to grow further once the building work is completed. Staff turnover is low. Class numbers remain around 25 to 30 in lower school and 20 in sixth form. Pupils comment that teachers are really friendly and that the 'mentoring team is great for help'.

Levels of SEN remain low. Some support in class from teaching assistants and SEND support staff; also uses outside agencies. Catch up classes in English and maths available for those falling behind.

Old Marians showcase their specialities for pupils at the annual Futures Event. Year 12 and 13 have a 'next steps' conference with university and industry speakers in attendance as well as ex-pupils to talk through the university application process and careers ideas.

Games, options, the arts: They play cricket, rugby, hockey and tennis, do athletics and dabble with futsal, with first to third teams to give everyone a chance to compete. Girls' sport – mostly netball – is starting to pick up momentum; there are also classes such as boxercise. Good facilities: swimming pool, cricket pavilion, squash court, fitness suites and studio, large modern sports hall, tennis/netball courts, rifle range and extensive rugby pitches. An Astroturf is on the head's list – a big ask, but he places a high priority on sport. Corridors are adorned with press clippings of sporting successes, both inside and outside school.

All year 7 students learn a musical instrument, provided at no cost to parents through the Esmée Fairbairn foundation. Music concerts are professionally organised, featuring everything from jazz bands choirs, orchestra, string ensembles to electric guitar renditions of ACDC. Such is the quality that students were invited to take part in National Youth Orchestra of GB workshops. Take up for music GCSE is relevantly low – usually some 10 students per year; they don't offer A level music, though other schools in the same Trust do. No drama on the curriculum, though thespians can showcase their talent through productions of eg Romeo and Juliet.

Art and DT remain consistently popular with two GCSE groups currently running. New DT/art block (plus science labs and extended maths and English rooms) under construction. Industry links are promoted particularly in DT, with relations formed with the likes of JCB and Jaguar Landrover; regular Arkwright scholarships.

Enrichment activities include the Denison society (debating), creative writing club, chess club and MedSoc. Students say there are opportunities 'to do anything music and sports wise. It's a supportive atmosphere', with most taking a 'throw yourself in' approach. There's also a CCF; one Y11 parent said she had seen her shy son 'significantly grow in confidence due to the cadet force'.

Farchynys, the school's own outdoor Welsh centre near Snowdonia for the last 50 years, is used for year 7 inductions, history, geography field trips, modern language immersion courses.

Staff go that extra mile to organise trips and experiences – Canada for skiing, Himalayas, China, Borneo, geography trip to the USA – with pupils expected to raise their own funds. One parent joked that her son was away so much on school trips, 'we started to think he didn't like living at home!' Staff see immediate benefits. 'Going to our outdoor centre means we can draw on the experiences in class, both through what pupils have learned academically and through their developing skills of teamwork and resilience,' says one geography teacher.

House system popular with students, say parents. One remarked that her son was 'pleased as punch at the house speech day' and that 'it gave him great confidence.'

Background and atmosphere: Housed in a 1960s block but surrounded by green fields; you soon forget you are in the urban sprawl of Walsall. Building work apart, it is a calm yet bright environment. Its ethos is built on four pillars: academic in purpose, international in outlook, enterprising in spirit and generous in approach. Imposing wooden boards in the great hall show off the school's long history of awards, and historic traditions are highlighted. Under Langton's leadership the school balances formal traditions with a contemporary, holistic approach. Forward thinking includes Project Horizon – a cutting edge space probes project. Students won second place in the national Childnet film competition with their film on internet safety. Each subject department uses social media proactively, signposting students via twitter to current research and inspiring feeds.

In January 2018 the school joined four other local school to form the multi-academy Mercian Trust with four other local schools: Queen Mary's High School, Walsall (grammar school for girls), Aldridge (comprehensive), Shire Oak (comprehensive) and Walsall Studio School. A sixth school is in the pipeline. This partnership has opened doors: it's increased the choice of A level subjects, with students able to learn at other schools too, as well as sharing staff development. Two staff are on the acclaimed Chartered Teacher careers development programme.

A diverse school accommodating pupils from a wide range of religious, cultural and socio-economic backgrounds. It encourages competition but also addresses disappointment and defeat in eg sports matches.

Pastoral care, well-being and discipline: Any behaviour problems – though these tend to be low level and infrequent – are recorded, as 'it allows us to build up patterns,' says Langton. Older students steward and mentor younger ones. A bronze, silver and gold award system encourages an inclusive team spirit. Students are polite, and staff friendly; everyone knows everyone and there is an impressive atmosphere of courtesy. Behaviour overall seems exceptional; pupils have a sense of belonging and of privilege.

On the rare occasions when there have been minor problems parents have felt confident about the school's response, saying that students are encouraged to think through problems and that the school 'takes even minor problems seriously'. They praise the counselling services, saying they allow problems 'to be nipped in the bud'. One year 10 parent said her son 'benefited greatly for their fast-acting approach, stopping problems from spiralling.'

There are no elephants in the rooms at QMGS – mental health and well-being of pupils and staff alike are taken very seriously. Experts visit to give talks and workshops: the over-arching belief is in the power of talk. We were impressed by the humanity of staff in house assemblies, one sharing his own personal experience of post-traumatic stress in order to open up the conversation surrounding male suicide. Big topics are approached head on in order to develop the students' sensitivity, emotions and resilience. Staff go out of their way to break taboos; they invite role models such as LGBT speakers to 'break down barriers' and provide a safe space for discussion.

The school fully embraces fundraising for charities and indicatives such as Movember in aid of prostate cancer (think all male members of staff sporting moustaches). Crucially, they use the opportunities not just to fundraise but to open up big conversations with pupils addressing underlying messages. Parents reflect that the atmosphere is 'not just academic but safe and family led.'

Nurture groups such as the year 7 Doodles group housed in the art room give pupils the opportunity to find their own 'safe spaces' and reassurance at lunch times. Equally, staff liaise to ensure that these boys' well-being is prioritised. Breaks and lunchtimes are well organised affairs with prefects manning doors into the dinner hall.

Uniform is immaculate, including the sixth form, who are giving a little more independence with a different tie and choice of coloured pastel shirt.

Pupils and parents: There is no 'typical' QMGS pupil. Students come from a much wider range of backgrounds than at many grammar schools.

Students genuinely look happy to be a part of the QMGS community and are well respected by staff in return. Pupils say, 'it's not uncool to be hard working' here. There is a real sense of wanting to achieve, and support networks are strong. Students feel listened to and allowed to develop their own projects and ideas. Girls joining in sixth form maintain they have a positive experience and feel encouraged in their ambitions. In the sixth form common room girls and boys mixed easily, and girls were positive about their experiences saying that the boys had welcomed everyone in.

R

Parents are a supportive bunch; 90 per cent attendance rate for a recent parent's evening. Continual dialogue and feedback between home and school. The parent-led Queen Mary Association is particularly active in term of fundraising (they recently raised enough for a school minibus) as well as embedding a sense of community spirit. They organise events including fireworks, Burns night and a summer ball. Parents feel part of the school and say they are 'encouraged to contribute'.

Entrance: About 1,300 applicants sit the grammar school consortium entrance exam for one of the current 150 11+ places. Those on pupil premium get priority. Pupils come from as far afield as Birmingham and Derby, and from over 100 primary schools. Transition doesn't seem to be a problem, with parents commenting that 'it was well managed, with a summer project and assault course in the first week which helped to ease my son in.' Currently 20 per cent of pupils are on pupil premium and the head is keen to increase this. A firm believer in social mobility, Langton is doing outreach work with heads of schools in deprived areas to encourage their students to apply.

At 16+ there are some 500 applications from both existing and external students – around 100 of them girls – for 200 places. Pupils need to achieve a score of 54 GCSE points (minimum of 6 in maths and English and 7 in the subject they want to study at A level).

Exit: Some 15 per cent leaves after GCSEs for more vocational programmes. Four to Oxbridge in 2018. Strong UCAS support from staff and ex-students; recent medicine and medical insight day saw talks from professionals and a carousel of stations testing interview skills. No surprise that in 2018, 13 went off to study medicine. Some 70 per cent to Russell Group universities, most to study science or engineering.

Remarks: Model students who maintain a well-balanced approach to life – akin to the kind of maturity you would find at university level. An ethos of hard work balanced with a plethora of quality activities, opportunities and trips. QMGS is rich and fulfilling for both students and staff. A school with one foot in the past and the other in the future. Anything but dull – we didn't want to leave.

Repton School

Linked with Foremarke Hall (Repton Preparatory School)

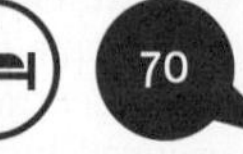

Repton, Derby DE65 6FH

Ages 13–18 **Pupils** 643 **Sixth form** 304 **Boarders** 434 full **C of E**

Fees: Day £26,493; Boarding £35,712 pa

01283 559222
www.repton.org.uk

Head: Since April 2019, Mark Semmence, previously head of Mount Kelly. An economist with degrees from Durham (BA and MBA), London (PGCE) and Warwick (MA), he taught at Ludgrove Prep, then worked in international sports marketing before returning to teaching, becoming assistant head at Rugby School. Played cricket for England Schools U19 and Durham University; a member of MCC Youth Cricket Committee. Married to Alison; they have two young daughters.

Academic matters: Repton sits securely among the top co-ed boarding schools for academic achievement, but we detect a little sharpening up, refining perhaps, on the teaching and learning front. English, government and politics, geography, art and maths appear to be the most popular A level choices and results in 2018 were 44 per cent A*/A, 77 per cent A*-B. Unusually there are more takers for music, French and even German A levels than for drama. We salute the recent solitary drama A level pupil, but wonder how they managed – lots of monologues perhaps? GCSE/IGCSE results in 2018: 66 per cent A*-A/9-7. Very small tail of D, E and even a few F grades, but vast majority of pupils are getting top marks across the board.

First stop on our itinerary was the Science Priory, a glass-fronted temple to – you guessed it – science. Laboratories, seminar rooms and lecture theatres with 3D projectors, all very high spec and high tech, more university than school and probably better appointed than some universities. We're not easily won over by technical wizardry but it's hard not to be impressed when an animated diagram of a human kidney appears inches from one's eye line. Each science has its own floor and there's even a bijou observatory on the roof – perfect for those dark Derbyshire skies. The building is full of natural light and the double height wall against the open staircases affords exhibition space for art students who like to paint a large canvas – we loved the huge dodo, wistfully regarding the busy, busy non-extinct species rushing up and down to lessons. In the top floor library we discovered the Repton village retirement group who come for tea and delights old and new such as bingo and IT support, provided by sixth formers as part of their community service.

Pupils are streamed on arrival and this is reviewed the same year after school exams, but there's sufficient flexibility for them to 'find their own level.' Lessons are 40 minutes long with an eminently sensible five-minute change over between to accommodate cross campus dashes. Learning support is either one-to-one or small groups; all pupils are tested on entry and there's effective liaison with teaching staff to monitor progress and implement strategies.

Pupils were falling over themselves to praise the dedication of teaching staff, especially the out of hours help available for GCSE and A level subjects during exam times. Parents agree, singling out 'brilliant' support for those applying to Oxbridge and US universities.

Games, options, the arts: 'Rugby's not big at Repton' we were told. You can play rugby here 'for enjoyment' but the oval ball finds itself in the unaccustomed category of a minority sport. On the plus side, an average player is likely to get first team matches. Repton is a hockey school (ditto football, cricket, tennis...). All pupils play hockey and can do so all year round on two floodlit water-based Astros, a sand-based Astro and indoor pitches. Facilities are so good that the GB men's squad trained here. Repton girls have won the national under 18 hockey finals a record 10 times in the last 12 years and boys were U16 and U18 national champions in 2015 and 2016. Repton's first football match was in 1878 and several boys have, more recently, gone on to play professionally for clubs such as Watford, Derby County and Sheffield Albion. School's 12 pitches are regarded with envy by visiting teams. Girls play in the Midlands league. Cricket too has a venerable history, Repton has produced 152 first class players and three England captains. On the day of our visit a prep schools cricket match was being hosted and diminutive figures were padding up ready to walk out onto the famous square (overlooked by a thatched pavilion) at the heart of the school. No complaints about teams lower down the alphabet being sidelined and no shortage of alternative options such as sailing, golf and riding.

CCF (army or RAF) has a distinguished history at Repton and is compulsory for all pupils in their first year. Attendance at week-long training camps during the Easter or summer holidays is also 'expected', as is parental support for these out of term activities. Those who choose not to carry on with CCF do either DofE or a school-run 'skills and service' activity. Interesting if worthy-sounding selection of co-curricular or subject based societies. Debating society is enjoying something of a roll, winning Nottingham University's schools' debating competition and reaching the national finals of the English Speaking Union's Mace competition recently.

Pupils' art is exhibited in the village gallery (former shop) and displayed all over the school. A level art is a popular choice and almost all candidates get A* or A; results for photography and textiles, though few, are similarly top notch. All teachers in the art department are practising artists and they and the two artists in residence have studios within the school. Textiles may not get many takers at A level but the standard of the work we saw during our visit and the enthusiastic and knowledgeable staff were inspiring. All pupils do at least a term of textiles and there are drop-in classes on Tuesdays and Thursdays for those who want to do an 'off timetable' GCSE in the subject. Whole school gets involved in the biannual fashion show, it's run by the sixth form and everything from outfits, models, marketing and social media to music and graphics is done entirely by pupils. The event is held in the 400 Hall where the stage can be extended to form a catwalk, it plays to 500 people over two nights and raises over £2,000 for charity.

The DT department offers an educative mix of traditional and modern: pupils can programme their designs for 3D printing or forge metal in the furnace. Head of DT proudly showed us lovingly maintained industrial standard lathes and milling machines supplied by local Midlands manufacturers.

'Opportunities for music are incredible' and the teaching is 'phenomenal,' we heard. Music is for all and house singing competitions are as keenly supported as diploma level soloists. Impressive programme of visiting musicians who give concerts and masterclasses – Julian Lloyd Webber recently judged the school's music competition – and plenty of opportunities for pupils to perform, whether at informal lunchtime concerts or main school events. Music school has pianos aplenty, including a harpsichord and a Steinway Grand Model D; 'It's wonderful to have the chance to play something so beautiful,' a pupil told us. School chapel is home to a 'magnificent' Harrison & Harrison organ. As elsewhere, very few take music A level, but school maintains good record of Oxbridge organ and choral scholarship awards.

1930s Hollywood swashbuckler Basil Rathbone first trod the boards at Repton and one imagines he'd be mighty impressed by the professional standard facilities enjoyed by today's actors. Drama is enthusiastically pursued at house, year group and whole school level and performance spaces include a black box studio and the 315 seater Auditorium Theatre. But alas, alack, the subject is only slightly more popular than German as a GCSE option and with barely a handful of takers at A level, the repertoire must be pretty limited.

Boarding: Ten boarding houses, six boys', four girls', are spread throughout campus and village. Girls' houses are newer and purpose built, rooms are smallish, as are windows. Boys do a bit better in terms of original features and historic atmosphere – rooms are larger, ceilings higher. B Block (Repton-speak for year 9 pupils) share three or four to a room; sixth formers get individual study bedrooms. In addition to houseparents, their families and pets, all houses have live-in matrons and a resident tutor. We found no inclination on school's part to persuade prospective parents that the houses are the same, but the reasons for a particular house's reputation are often more to do with practicality than glamour. For instance, the 'musical' house is the one closest to the music department, attracting musicians because it offers the least distance to travel to reach practice rooms. Parents recommend visiting at least four houses before selecting one and talking to any pupils you come across, not just the ones showing you round. Sound advice. Individual house profiles on the website are a useful starting point and some, but not all, have their own Twitter feed. Several parents told us they really enjoyed keeping up to the minute with house happenings via 140 characters.

All meals are taken in house – more and more unusual these days – which means that pupils are frequently back and forth, giving staff ample opportunities to observe how an individual's day is going. Teachers take their meals in different houses, as do visitors, and pupils become accustomed to entertaining whoever lands at their table. We ate a delicious lunch in School House (boys) and enjoyed hearing their observations on Repton life, some of which were lost to posterity amid the clatter and chatter of many boys refuelling for an afternoon of cricket and athletics.

Ten separate in-house catering operations, plus the same number of laundries, may be a bursar's nightmare, but pastorally and in terms of cohesion it's hard to beat. 'House is everything' was a phrase we heard again and again – not just from pupils but from parents too. A pupil told us: 'Boarding means you make really close friends, it also makes you behave more maturely – if there's a problem you have to sort it out. You can't be petty.' Competition between houses (in anything from singing to sudoku) is fierce but positive; it seems to create a kind of extra energy that propels all pupils along in its wake.

So, what about evenings and weekends? When lessons finish boarders can change into home clothes for supper and then it's prep and/or music practice (7-9pm). On Saturdays there are lessons in the morning, matches or other sporting activities in the afternoon and regular themed 'socials' in the evening. Socialising takes place in Grubber, pupils can have a Grubber account and buy snacks and drinks with a thumbprint. Sixth formers get together in the JCR. On Sundays after chapel pupils can either have a relaxed day, catch up with work or sign up for SLOPs (Sunday leisure options) – anything from shopping in Leicester to clay pigeon shooting or white-water rafting. Rehearsals for plays and concerts are also scheduled at the weekend. 'They keep them busy', a parent observed. Indeed they do. Each boarder has two privilege weekends per term, Saturday and Sunday nights that can be taken out of school by prior arrangement. Pupils may also go out of school on a Sunday after chapel to have lunch with parents, returning by 9pm.

Background and atmosphere: Repton was founded on the site of a 12th century Augustinian priory by bequest of Sir John Port in 1557. In return for their education pupils were obliged to pray for the Port family's souls – many parents today might consider this a much less painful form of recompense than school fees. The next 300 years saw acrimonious legal disputes, fluctuating pupil numbers and a general decline that was not reversed until the middle of the 19th century. Fragments of the original priory buildings remain, notably parts of the arch that marks the entrance to the school (moved to its current site in 1906) and a tower that was incorporated into the building that now houses the head's study and offices. The school started taking girls in the 1970s and was fully co-ed by 1991. Time and social change have not diluted school's Christian foundation: 'Repton is a Christian School and for all our values, not least Respect, our guide is the Scripture.' We hope values of respect and tolerance are similarly explicit in Dubai and Abu Dhabi where Repton has international avatars.

School and village merge harmoniously – the Spar shop must see a dramatic fall in its profits during the holidays, likewise the butcher who makes 'the best' sausage rolls. The 'Repton bubble' doesn't stop at the arch, there's an air of prosperity here, plenty of places for parents to take their children out for lunch at the weekend, and property prices are inflated by demand from both staff and parents who want to live close at hand. The Derbyshire address somehow makes Repton seem more remote than it is; as the school's website is keen to point out, London (Euston) is 75 minutes away (plus a taxi to the station).

R

Pastoral care, well-being and discipline: 'The teachers really know the children', or words to that effect, was what several parents told us. They describe pastoral care as 'completely joined up' so that, for example, if a pupil has a music exam or a national sporting trial, all members of staff know and will act accordingly. Because staff eat in different houses and at different tables every day they gain insight into all aspects of the pupils' academic, social and personal lives. 'You observe body language and can pick up on any tensions,' a teacher told us. The year groups are mixed at lunch which also fosters good relationships. A sixth form pupil who had joined from a state school ('for the maths and the hockey') told us, 'I worried about whether I'd fit in, but everyone accepted me straight away.' Universal praise for the way in which day pupils are integrated into houses, but be warned, the Repton 'day' doesn't finish until after prep at 9pm. It's also a long week, what with Saturday lessons and matches and even compulsory Sunday chapel for those who live near enough. Day parents tell us that traffic around Repton is pretty snarly in the mornings and recommend getting pupils in for breakfast at 8am to avoid the queues. No wonder it's common practice for parents of day pupils to buy or rent houses in or very near Repton village itself.

School currently being investigated by the Charity Commission for a number of safeguarding breaches.

Pupils and parents: Still very much a 'local' boarding school, majority of families from Midlands, Cheshire, Yorkshire, Lincolnshire, Lancashire; smallish contingent of international boarders. In addition to 152 first-class cricketers, many eminent military and clerical chaps and MPs both red and blue, former pupils include Roald Dahl and Jeremy Clarkson (neither of whom recall their time with affection), poet James Fenton, comedian Graeme Garden, novelist and screenwriter Christopher Isherwood, artist Anthony Gross and recent field hockey Olympic medallists Georgie Twigg and Ellie Watton.

Entrance: Around half join from Repton's nearby prep, Foremarke Hall; others from preps such as S Anselm's, Malsis, Orwell Park. Common Entrance pass of around 50 required. Some 30 or so pupils enter the sixth form, minimum five GCSEs at 6+ (7+s for chosen A level subjects).

Exit: Very few leave post-GCSE. Nearly all go on to Russell Group universities, one to Oxbridge in 2018, plus three medics. Growing numbers to top US universities (including Princeton and Stanford in 2018) – many with athletic scholarships for eg tennis, football and hockey.

Money matters: Range of scholarships and exhibitions – some titular only, some worth up to 20 per cent off fees. Fees broadly in line with similar schools. Considering six-day week and 9pm finish, day fees look like good value, but you may have to factor in the cost of a house in the village.

Remarks: This is a grounded, friendly school with high academic standards and secure moral values. It will hardly come as news to parents north of Watford, but whatever your child's strong suit – scholar, musician, artist, athlete or enthusiastic all-rounder – Repton could be just the right fit.

The Royal Hospital School

Holbrook, Ipswich, Suffolk IP9 2RX

Ages 11–18 **Pupils** 750 **Sixth form** 220 **Boarders** 334 full, 59 weekly, 27 flexi **C of E**

Fees: Day £15,690 – £17,490; Boarding £24,090 – £32,595 pa

01473 326200
www.royalhospitalschool.org

Headmaster: Since January 2016, Simon Lockyer, previously second master at Portsmouth Grammar and housemaster and head of department at Wellington College. Educated at

Blundell's School, Devon. Married with three children, all in the school. Affable and pin-sharp, parents describe him as 'approachable, positive, ambitious for the school – and no-nonsense'. He chose headship at RHS for its 'huge potential and the socio-economic diversity of the pupils, which is its strength'.

Academic matters: Head aims high academically and results are taking off. 'We're a comprehensive school in intake,' says head, who has brought greater academic focus to the curriculum and more subject choice. Pupils take nine or 10 GCSEs and in 2018 37 per cent were A*-A/9-7. Year 13s take three or four A levels as well as an academic elective subject or EPQ and, in 2018, a third were graded A* or A. Creditable, given the wide ability range – 20 per cent of pupils on roll have some requirement for in-class learning support or receive regular lessons provided by the learning support department and about one in eight pupils have EAL.

Plenty of scope for differentiation, thanks to the 'dynamic modern learning environment' – iPads all over and recognition as a beacon school for safe and effective digital learning. 'Impressive use of technology in lessons,' say parents. Real-world skills – including interviews, aptitude tests, CVs, personal statements, careers advice, mentoring, thinking skills, teamwork, computing and digital literacy, well-being and coping with stressful situations – are embedded throughout the curriculum from year 7. Newly introduced sixth form options are enterprise and entrepreneurship BTec (two A levels), sport BTec and sociology A level. 'Parents tell me they don't want a privileged and entitled education,' explains head. 'They want schooling that will prepare their children for the world.'

Games, options, the arts: 'The difference the school can make to children's characters – that's the real "value added",' says head and certainly the array of co-curriculars is impressive.

Not an elite sporting school, but an emphasis on variety. Three games afternoons a week with all the seasonal team sports represented and chances to taste 70-plus activities, from rock climbing on the school's own impressive indoor wall to squash, shooting and kickboxing. Gigantic sports hall (or gymnasium), indoor pool in another vast building and outdoors 96 acres of playing fields. Not to mention the Graham Napier Cricket Academy for girls and boys, golf course and bowls club. With such facilities on-site there's little need to travel, although several annual sports tours.

Unsurprisingly, given the school's heritage and Alton Water only a stone's skip away, sailing is a real strength and produces some elite performers. All year 7s receive a full week's instruction – 'we want to find ability among those who are not "dynastic" sailors,' says school's own director of sailing and water sports who teaches on RHS's fleet of 60 dinghies (from beginners' to Olympic classes), four Cornish shrimpers and four powerboats. Many achieve RYA qualifications, enter national and inter-school sailing competitions and have a recreation for life. Sailing scholars have individual tuition from RYA advanced instructors. Sailing trips to the Med and further afield every year.

Everyone recommended to take art, DT or music GCSE. Expansive art and design department with superb atrium exhibition space. Art and DT carousel offers a taster. Craft and design skills are encouraged and pupils work on projects outside class time. 'If you have a talent they push you to keep it on even if it's not one of your exam subjects,' said a pupil. Impressive investment in and commitment to music – John Rutter opened the superb music school and is patron of the school's annual concert programme, performed by home-grown and professional performers. Recitals hall has spectacular acoustics and two grand pianos, with 10 others in practice rooms, all Bechsteins and Faziolis. Aspiring organists perform on one of four organs, including a grade 2 organ that is a magnet for international performers. In fact, half of pupils learn one or more of a staggering variety of musical instruments (explains our bagpipe-playing guide).

Music compulsory for years 7 to 9 and a popular choice at GCSE and A level. Recording studio and Mac suite for music tech A level and also a club. Busy choir – charity gala concert, two choir concerts, scholars' concerts, as well as a tour to New York and annual performance at St Paul's Cathedral. Regular concerts and performances, besides chapel, for orchestras, ensembles and bands. A 60-strong marching band accompanies pupils' regular military-style parades, known as Divisions ('Divis' colloquially), which is open to all over grade 3 with drummers taught from scratch, including band marching skills – 'not the same as marching with the squad'. Band and guard tour every three years – previously to Canada; China and Dubai next. Members receive free music tuition in return for learning this tricky skill.

Clubs 4.15-6pm – 'technically you could do a different activity every lunchtime and every evening of the week'. Model UN, scuba diving club, Tycoon in Schools, yoga, golf and robotics club – choices for all tastes. DofE starts in year 9 and is compulsory for all. Overseas trips, excursions and tours are put on by academic departments, CCF and co-curricular activities. Four sections of CCF – royal marines, royal navy, army, royal air force – compulsory in years 9 and 10, but many continue. 'It's not a recruitment tool,' said a pupil, 'there's no pressure'. Parents endorse – 'Whilst our son may not go on to a career in the military, the skills he is learning through this are hugely important and transferable to the modern world.'

Divisions remain a cornerstone of RHS tradition and take place on special occasions, such as Remembrance Day, harvest festival, speech day etc. All pupils wear genuine naval uniform, with band and guards marked out by specific gaitors, and 'chiefs' (heads of school and prefects) with their own variations. Says head, 'It might look a little peculiar to watch at first, but no more than the Eton wall game, for example – Divisions are our equivalent. There is nothing more remarkable than watching 750 pupils, without a single member of staff, on the parade ground and taking an enormous pride in it.' Parents agree – 'Whether you are from a naval background or not, I believe most families embrace the school's heritage and Divisions.'

Boarding: 'Our house is our home,' said a boarder. Houses remain the hub of RHS life for all pupils, whether day or boarding. The house structure now better reflects family life, with a junior house for both girls and boys – boarding and day together – and two houses dedicated to ad hoc boarders. Sixth form house Nelson is very much a stepping stone to university – 'we gradually remove the scaffolding,' says housemaster. Programme of house refurbishment has seen the creation of open-plan sitting areas, snug TV rooms and spacious kitchens, at the same time retaining 1930s features – lighter and brighter.

Day starts and ends in the house with an early 'roll call', then a return at 'stand-easy' (break) for toast and fruit and to pick up books for next lessons from named pigeonholes. After 'mess' – sittings in the dining hall in house groups – another roll call in-house. Prep for the youngest pupils is done in after-school sessions in the main school buildings, but houses have work rooms for extra study. Free time has to wait until after 'stations' (house duties). 'You can slip into the routine quite easily – there's something quite comfortable about it,' said our guide.

Sixth form house now all single rooms, uni-style, with a shower 'cubi' between two, and kitchenettes and laundry areas for pupils to do their own 'civvie' washing in preparation for studenthood. Take pride in your appearance and look after your belongings to stay on the right side of housemaster, who conducts a routine room inspection – best floor rewarded with Krispy Kreme.

Twenty-six-bed medical centre has a full-time nurse and there's a school doctor and dentist (NHS), plus a counsellor who can be seen confidentially.

Background and atmosphere: Long and distinguished association with seafaring and the Navy sets the tone, although a conscious evolution – 'removal of the anchors,' in head's words – over the past 30 years has loosened some of the practical strictures and focused on applying the qualities and values of service life to 21st century education. The Royal Hospital School was founded in the early 18th century at Greenwich in what is now the National Maritime Museum, with a remit to educate boys in mathematics and navigation. A bequest from the estate at Holbrook and a generous endowment prompted a move in the 1930s to the current enviable location on the banks of the river Stour and overlooking Alton Water, and bespoke school buildings, replicating the Christopher Wren architecture of the school's original home.

RHS turned co-educational in 1991 and the first day pupils were admitted in 2006. Today 40+ per cent of pupils are girls and full and weekly boarders make up around 50 per cent to the total roll. School's parent charity, Greenwich Hospital, has invested an impressive £18 million in the site over the last decade but 'you would never build a school on this scale nowadays,' points out head. 'What we've got is really fit for purpose and is built to last. I'm not interested in vanity projects – you can spend a lot of money on design plans and consultations and I want every pound to go into creating the greatest impact on educational resources.' Indeed, there's no lack of ideas for the school and, thanks to the recently established development office, the funds to realise them are beginning to be forthcoming. 'We are in a fortunate position as so many alumni had a free education and feel really invested in the school,' beams head.

An ambitious programme of refurbishment is well underway, with most houses upgraded, along with the gym, dining hall and many classrooms. Next project is to create a learning hub in the centre of the school – library, careers, oracy and independent working space. Links are being forged beyond the campus, with business, industry and local universities, as well as maintaining the relationship with Greenwich Hospital and the navy. Says head, 'The school was built on a peninsular to be self-sufficient, even with its own water supply, but I am keen on "bursting the bubble" – we don't exist alone.'

Pastoral care, well-being and discipline: Nothing but praise for pastoral care from parents – 'school quickly understands students' strengths and areas for improvement and offers them opportunities to challenge and grow,' exuded one. Not a huge school – 750 in total – and house system creates worlds-within-worlds, where students say they feel safe and secure and well known as individuals by the adults responsible for their care. 'No one-size-fits-all approach,' noted a parent. Particular understanding of the challenges facing children of Forces families – 'there was a lot of moving about before I joined RHS,' said one such pupil, 'but now I have stability in my life and I feel the school deals with the difficulties really well'.

Saturday school, afternoon sports fixtures, clubs, Sunday Divis and chapel make for a busy life, but staff are on hand to help pupils to learn the skills of time management and to make sure day boys and girls don't miss out. Most boarding schools run on copious quantities of food and the RHS mess hall dishes up a daily full breakfast including granola and fruit compote, lunch with a 'theatre bar' special of the day (eg Szechuan chicken chow mein, potato or pasta dish), mess at 6pm serves up still more, followed by toast and supper snacks available in-house. Anyone still peckish can raid his or her tuck box.

Older students are encouraged to take responsibility. Six heads of school – two heads and four deputies – and around 28 prefects have duties in the mess hall, at Divis and around the school, and the mantle of role models. Sixth formers have the freedom to go out at weekends but often prefer to see what's going on at the in-house bar, which allows the odd drink and puts on themed party nights. All are aware of the school's position on banned substances (expulsion) and relationships (courting allowed outside lessons only). 'There is a clear line on bad behaviour and a consistent approach,' reported a parent, 'which is refreshing after our experience previously where it varied greatly.'

Pupils and parents: Growing local day population mixes with boarders from across the UK and the world (13 per cent of the roll from currently 21 countries). Still a high number of Forces families (10 per cent), with naval families supported by parent charity Greenwich Hospital. London is an hour away and school helps with lifts to the station, airport etc, and provides a 'blue box' repository for travelling pupils' belongings over the holidays. Most staff are East Anglian; 85 per cent live on site.

Head encourages parents to 'throw themselves in' as much as their children – a recent Remembrance Day service attracted 2,500 people and had to be run twice to accommodate them all – and houses host popular family social events. Parents address staff by first names and vice versa 'which gives a warm community feel and sense of mutual respect to the relationship we have with the school,' said a parent. 'A surprising informality, given the military connections...' Easy access to teaching and house staff either in person or via email and a useful parent forum sounding board gives feedback on recent or suggested initiatives. Social media is a constant link for parents further afield.

Entrance: The majority enter at 11 via entrance tests in maths, English and verbal reasoning. At 13+ another 30-40, respectable common entrance performance needed, and there is another influx in the sixth form. A reference from the current school is essential and all prospective pupils have an interview with the head.

Exit: Housemaster jokes 'in the past the RHS alumni organisation was called the royal navy' – over two centuries, 20,000 boys and girls have left the school and joined up but these days about 10 per cent of pupils head to Dartmouth or Sandhurst. 'The rest go on to a huge range of careers and individual pathways – it's a real cauldron-like fire spitting off in all different directions,' says head. Five in 2018 to Oxbridge and heavyweight universities eg Edinburgh, Durham, Bristol well represented. Significant numbers take a gap year, often for travel and following courses abroad.

Money matters: Complex range of awards and bursaries. School offers a limited number of academic, sporting, drama, music, art and sailing scholarships each year. The value of the award is at the discretion of the headmaster and can be topped up with a means-tested bursary. From five to 25 per cent discount for siblings. Forces families claiming the continuity of education allowance (CEA) are also eligible for discounted fees. Greenwich Hospital bursaries and discounts for the children of seafarers also available, depending on family income.

Remarks: A school unlike any other – modern interpretation of naval heritage suits a diverse intake of day pupils and boarders. Super sailing and music. Pastoral care paramount.

Rugby High School

Longrood Road, Rugby, Warwickshire CV22 7RE

Ages 11–18 **Pupils** 875 **Sixth form** 274 (6 boys)

01788 810518
www.rugbyhighschool.co.uk

Head: Since 2006, Charlotte Marten (early 60s). Studied English at Birmingham. Failed her 11+; fell into teaching by starting at a 'grotty tutorial college'; went to learn how to do it properly by doing her PGCE. First headship in Jersey, Rugby High is her second. Talks a lot about empowerment of women. Has taught in both state and private sector, always at selective schools. Parents have huge respect for her, and like her as well. 'She is hugely committed and passionate about the school.' 'She gives up a lot of time, is good fun and gets involved.' 'She's happy to laugh at herself.' All mentioned her high profile around the school and that she knows all of the girls. 'She gets stuck in,' we were told, 'to the extent that she will go bag packing at the local supermarket with the girls to help raise money for trips.' Capable, experienced and welcoming was the impression we got, and not fazed by many things. Keeps her hand in by teaching when extra help is needed. Latest project has been the introduction of boys to the sixth form in 2018.

Retiring in July 2019. Her successor will be Mark Grady, currently deputy head. PGCE in English and drama from Warwick, and an MA in acting from East 15. He was an English and drama teacher here before leaving to become head of department at Myton School in Warwick. He rejoined the school in 2014 as deputy head.

Academic matters: In 2018, at GCSE, 74 per cent A*-A/7-9 grades. At A level, 71 per cent A*/B grades and 44 per cent A*/A grades. Impressive results, but remember the school is highly selective. 'But it is not an exam factory,' said one parent. Some per cent of girls take two languages at GCSE; good to see that they are quite popular at A level. Many sixth form girls mentor year 10 and 11 girls, whilst year 10s mentor year 7 and 8. 'We had a letter suggesting my daughter would benefit from a subject mentor. It worked really well and her results improved quickly.' Parents talk of lots of support and encouragement from staff, with extra help in certain subjects offered immediately if necessary. 'My daughter is being stretched and quickly got used to being with some very high achievers.' Nearly 70 per cent of girls do all three sciences. Maths set from year 9.

Science block impressive; please note the vivarium, a rather grand word for a pond full of newts. They even have a slug club. Lessons we observed showed chatty girls and teachers, teaching noticeably much more relaxed in sixth form. Different table and desk layouts for different subjects, maths linear, discussion subjects such as politics and English set out in U shapes. Lots of UCAS support for sixth form. A couple of niggles regarding parents' evenings and 'some pushy parents taking up too much time,' par for the course for many schools, we find.

Small sixth form centre with quiet, supervised, study rooms, and a silent area with separate booths, so no distractions, open until 5pm. 'It's a great place to work,' said our guides. Sixth formers bring their own laptops. Maximum class size of 32, smaller in sixth form.

More than 60 SEN students. Interestingly, head says, 'we do it well, but could do better, and are always keen to learn from other schools.' She's mainly referring to emotional SEN needs. One-to-one teaching if necessary, interventions offering small group teaching to close gaps. EAL negligible despite girls speaking 32 different languages at home. Interesting to note that school employs a high number of part-time teachers. Head keen to encourage staff back on this basis, 'it's good for the girls to see that it is possible to combine the two, caring and a career.'

Games, options, the arts: New sports centre may change matters, but sport does not appear to play a huge part in this school. 'The school concentrates on academic achievements to the exclusion of sport,' was directly said, or alluded to, by many parents. Until recently facilities had not been improved since the 60s so on wet days sport didn't happen. Badminton, trampolining, netball, rounders, cricket and touch rugby now on offer. But teams are sparse, one team per year if you are lucky, and none for some sports. 'There aren't many PE staff and I can see the constraints, as the facilities were dire, the worst in Rugby. But the PE staff are committed, so they can now build on improving things.' No Astroturf, so very little hockey played, no fitness suite. Disappointing that sixth formers do not have PE lessons timetabled. But girls make the most of what is on offer. Students organised a Race for Life around the school playing fields and raised over £4000. Virtually everyone joined in, girls and staff too.

Music and drama well supported. Parents speak of excellent productions and lots of concerts and recitals. Plenty of music lessons in school. Lots of clubs on offer, many set up, and run, by sixth form girls. DofE to gold, plenty of trips, including skiing and World Challenge to Croatia and Costa Rica. Impressive artwork throughout the school and in head's office.

Background and atmosphere: On a jammed in site in the middle of a large 1970s residential sprawl on the edge of Rugby. Established in 1903, known as The Arnold High School and then located in the middle of Rugby, it has always been a girls' school. Relocated to its current site in the 1960s, renamed Rugby High. But don't let the rather drab exterior mislead you. Step inside and you are met with a lively buzz. The school hums with vibrancy and visitors pick up on this immediately. 'I love the feeling when you walk into the school, it's just lovely and happy with a real vibe, it's full of life.' 'There is a great sense of community here, very welcoming and happy.' We must agree. Many parents said they were happy to sacrifice lack of certain facilities and space because of this atmosphere.

Girls look smart in navy blazers and skirts or trousers. Uniform is gender neutral. Younger girls wear blue shirts, older, striped blue. All shirts must have top button done up, no ties. Uniform policy strict and no make up lower down (discreet for years 10 and 11) or nail varnish. 'You get sent to reception where they have nail varnish remover,' said our guide. Parents were very supportive. 'There are uniform checks and the girls are encouraged to be proud of their appearance and that they are representing the school.' 'It's all done in a positive way.' Sixth form girls have to look smart, and they do. The odd parent spoke about communication from the school not always being excellent. 'Parent mail can sometimes be a bit hit and miss; I'd like a bit more warning about events.' More than one parent alluded to 'IT wobbles'.

Pastoral care, well-being and discipline: Every parent spoke about excellent pastoral care which ties in with the sense of community. 'They encourage the girls to be independent minded and well rounded.' Friendship issues dealt with quickly and kindly. 'They have a clear policy about behaviour, and expectations are met,' said one parent. All spoke highly of pastoral care team. 'They've got the balance right, intervene when necessary and are prepared to listen.' Parents said the school knew their daughters well, and knew 'how to handle girls.'

Extra enrichment days include yoga for emotional well-being and social media awareness days. 'They've got it right,' said one parent. 'Life is competitive and they set the girls up well to deal with this.' More than one parent noted that 'happiness and self esteem are vital and the school has the balance right.' The head says, 'They need to leave school with more than a handful of A*s.' She actively encourages outside weekend interests such as sport and Saturday jobs, 'but not on both days,' said with a wry smile. Parents spoke about a very open, comfortable and supportive environment and said their daughters were happy to speak out because of this. Counsellors available if needed, pastoral staff well used. We got the impression they knew who the vulnerable girls were and kept a discreet, supportive eye on them. More pastoral training now being undertaken to recognise boys' foibles.

Discipline not really mentioned by parents; 'expectations are made clear and are met,' was the general consensus. Every parent said their daughter was happy at the school, 'they enjoy being there and are proud to be there.'

Pupils and parents: Parents very supportive and 'realistic' says the head, also very diverse, ethnically and financially. Virtually all very pro single sex, the odd one wanted a grammar education first and converted to single sex. Most like the size of the school, 'small enough to still have that family atmosphere.' Pupils come from a wide area, including east Warwickshire, parts of Leicestershire and Northamptonshire and over 50 primaries. Ethnically diverse, tight knit, friendly, focused, keen to learn and mix well. 'My daughter has made friends for life,' was said by more than one parent. Lots of second, third, or more, generation pupils. Quite a few of the staff are old girls.

Entrance: All girls have to pass the 11+. Priority given to those who qualify for pupil premiums, lower marks set for these girls, 'who come out very well at the other end of their school life,' says the head. Some 50 more pupils (boys and girls) join the sixth form, mainly from local state schools, the odd one from Rugby School. Five grade 6s – maths 7 – needed. School not quite full, the odd space in certain year groups due to family relocation.

Exit: About 10-15 per cent leaves at the end of year 11, most to study vocational courses at local colleges, the odd one to local independents. The vast majority to university, about half Russell Group, with seven to Oxbridge and three medics in 2018. Psychology, law, politics and international relations, economics, architecture and languages currently popular. Apprenticeships being slowly, but actively, embraced with girls taking places at Jaguar Land Rover the BBC and Deloitte. Gap years unusual.

Remarks: A tight knit community, large enough to offer plenty of choice but small enough to keep the family feel. A school fizzing with energy. It will be interesting to see how adding boys to the mix works out. These girls are getting a good all round education including excellent exam results but are also importantly taught that there is more to life than a handful of A*s. Good.

R

Rugby School

Lawrence Sheriff Street, Rugby, Warwickshire CV22 5EH

Ages 13–18 **Pupils** 802 **Sixth form** 367 **Boarders** 649 full **C of E**

Fees: Day £22,437; Boarding £35,760 pa

01788 556216
www.rugbyschool.co.uk

Headmaster: Since 2014, Peter Green MA PGCE (early 50s), previously head of Ardingly. Educated at St Joseph's College, Dumfries, then University of Edinburgh, where he read geography. Although he comes from a family of lawyers and judges he always wanted to be a teacher. Studied for Cert Ed in religious studies and PGCE at St Andrew's Foundation for Catholic Teacher Education (now part of the University of Glasgow). First job was at an inner-city comprehensive in the Gorbals. He taught at St Olave's Grammar in Orpington and then Strathallan before moving to Uppingham, where he was head of geography, a housemaster and introduced all-rounder scholarships. Spent five years as lay second master of Ampleforth, followed by seven years as head of Ardingly College, where numbers rose by a quarter under his watch.

A vastly experienced and engaging head (wearing fetching bright pink socks when we visited), he talks fast, sensibly and enthusiastically and is full of good tales and ideas. He says 'the whole person is the whole point of education at Rugby', and while this isn't a unique declaration for a head he believes Rugby is 'uniquely placed to make the claim.' Doesn't teach these days – 'I'd sack myself,' he jokes – but spends as much time as he can talking to pupils and staff and observing lessons. On the day we met he arrived hotfoot from discussing Lake District geomorphology with the youngest pupils in the school.

He's enjoying his job at Rugby – 'we have fantastic children here and it's a wonderful environment to work in,' he says. He finds the school's history a huge inspiration but emphasises that while Rugby is 'traditional,' it isn't 'traditionalist.' Delights in the fact that he's sitting in Dr Thomas Arnold's study – with a portrait of the great man, Arnold's own (surprisingly small) desk, a hidden key rack above the fireplace and the spiral staircase in the corner that pupils used if they wanted to talk to him privately.

The head says that Rugby is 'phenomenally strong' but is always looking for ways to improve – whether it's blended learning, flipped classrooms, character development, teaching tolerance and respect or engaging pupils in STEAM (science, technology, engineering, arts and maths) subjects. He's particularly proud of the fact that there isn't a Rugby type. 'The duckbilled platypus and the behemoth can be equally at home at Rugby School,' he says. Like his predecessor (Westminster head Patrick Derham), he wants Rugby to remain as inclusive as possible. The Arnold Foundation offers 100 per cent funded boarding places to pupils whose parents are unable to afford the fees and since 2003 well over 100 youngsters have benefited from the scheme.

Wife Brenda is an English and learning support teacher at Rugby. They have two children, a son who has finished university and a daughter still there. In his spare time he enjoys reading, opera and the opportunity 'to pray and be silent.'

Academic matters: Rugby has a tradition of innovation – it was, for instance, the first school in the country to teach science as part of the school curriculum in the 1850s – and this continues apace. The school offers the IGCSE in most subjects and A levels in 29 subjects (plus the Pre-U in physics, chemistry, biology and art and design). Around 50 students a year take the Extended Project Qualification (EPQ), which was developed at Rugby via a pilot qualification called Perspectives in Science and involves an extended piece of research on a topic they choose themselves.

In 2018, 60 per cent A*/A grades at A level/Pre-U. At GCSE, 86 per cent A*-A/9-7. 'The head is definitely on an academic mission,' a parent told us. French, German and Spanish offered at GCSE and A level, with exchange trips to Montpellier, Vienna, Madrid. Wonderful new language block, with 11 classrooms, two language labs and computers and software in every language. Sixth formers can study an ab initio language, such as Russian or Japanese. Pupils also write, edit and code their own online magazine, Page Polyglotte.

Most do three separate sciences at GCSE. The sciences are housed in an imaginatively refurbished Victorian building, with lecture theatre, seminar rooms and labs. Learning development department offers some support for those with mild difficulties or EAL, either one-to-one or in small groups. Enrichment programme for all pupils, with additional weekly sessions for academic scholars (140 currently). All pupils have their own laptops, supplied by school and charged to parents.

Teachers are skilled and experienced. Many pursue their own academic research and the school is producing its own document on approaches to teaching and learning at Rugby. School runs parallel sets (including two top sets) in English, maths and the sciences.

Games, options, the arts: Rugby has overseen a huge investment in sports facilities in recent years. It has the only listed gym in the world and, of course, the famous School Close, where William Webb Ellis first ran with the ball in 1823 and invented the game of rugby football. Members of the 1st XV are very proud to play on it, along with leading players and teams who visit from all over the world. More than 200 TV crews pitched up to film at Rugby ahead of the 2015 World Cup and the school featured in the opening ceremony (Prince Harry and Jonny Wilkinson had cameo roles in a video shot at the school). Immaculately maintained playing fields, with 13 rugby pitches and five cricket squares. Locals use school's three Astroturfs, tennis courts and 25-metre indoor pool.

Sports centre, with squash courts, polo pitches and fitness centre. Boys play rugby, hockey, soccer, cricket, tennis and athletics while girls' main sports are hockey, netball, tennis, rounders and athletics. Other sports include badminton, fives, rackets, basketball, fencing, gymnastics, tai chi, pilates, dance, aerobics, riding, polo, clay pigeon shooting, sailing and triathlon. One girl is the current under-19 British champion in wakeboarding. Huge number of sports tours – recent expeditions include hockey and netball to Australia and Singapore, rugby to Japan and Canada and cricket to Sri Lanka and Dubai.

Music department has more than 40 practice rooms, a recording studio and small concert hall. Music is magical, with masses of orchestras, choirs, ensembles and rock bands. Total of 600 music lessons a week. An impressive variety of drama productions at school's fully equipped theatre. Pupils stage a major school play and musical every year, plus a house drama season and annual arts festival. Art, design and photography flourishing and a third of sixth formers study related subjects at art school or university. Lewis Gallery, a light, airy space cleverly converted from old squash courts, runs programme of exhibitions by pupils and outside artists.

Boarding: Fifteen houses in total – eight for boys, seven for girls. Each boarding house has up to 60 pupils and the furthest is no more is than a 10-minute walk from the heart of the school. We visited soon after the school's annual pushcart race, hotly contested by all. The victorious house had a jaunty skull and crossbones flag fluttering from a top window.

Pupils eat breakfast, lunch and supper in their own houses – 'it encourages a real sense of community,' a parent told us. Food gets the thumbs up and there's plenty of it, including snacks in morning and afternoon breaks and in the evening. In a recent move, all but the sixth formers hand in their phones, tablets and laptops before bed each night. The new rule has brought a few grumbles from pupils, 'but nothing but parental support,' said a housemaster.

Houses are very wholesome. The boys' houses used to be less ritzy but are in the process of being upgraded. A house we visited boasted a cinema room, neat as a pin laundry, tuck shop (the 'stodge' in Rugby-speak) and individual studies for all. Each year group has their own common room and dorms vary from singles for sixth-formers to dorms of four to six for younger pupils. 'Your house is your home,' one boy declared.

Housemasters and housemistresses all live in (many with their own families) and see pupils as they come and go during the day. Youngest have to be back in houses by 9.30pm (lights out half an hour later), while sixth-formers return by 10.15pm (they don't have to be in their rooms till 11pm, though). Tutors are house-based and see their tutees formally at least twice a week, as well as when they're on duty.

Background and atmosphere: Founded as a grammar school in 1567 by Lawrence Sheriff, purveyor of spices to Elizabeth I. Moved to its present site in the centre of Rugby 200 years later. Home of the famous Dr Arnold and immortalised in Tom Brown's Schooldays. With its red-brick, Victorian schoolhouses the site feels rather like north Oxford. Pupils like being based in a town, close to shops and cafés. One told us: 'You get a sense of the real world. We aren't in a bubble.'

Glorious Victorian library, the Temple Reading Room, provides a quiet, inspiring place to work. Pupils attend chapel three mornings a week and on Sundays. Chapel – Thomas Arnold is buried beneath chancel steps – is majestic and awe-inspiring, with walls adorned with tablets in memory of famous Rugbeian writers like Lewis Carroll and Rupert Brooke. School chaplain describes the chapel as 'the base' of the school and pupils say it's a place where the whole school sings its heart out.

School went fully co-ed in 1993 and boy/girl ratio is now 55/45. All wear smart uniform for lessons. Girls sport distinctive ankle-length grey skirts, now redesigned so they can run in them. Girls say they really like their skirts – they suit everyone and you can wear woolly tights and leggings underneath to keep warm in winter, they told us. The only gripe from boys is that their tweed jackets get 'a bit smelly' in the rain. Prefects – or levée as they are known – wear different ties and gold buttons on dark blazers. Four buttons for heads of school (boy and girl), three for heads of house and two for school prefects – a simple and subtle way to work out exactly who's who.

The sixth form has impressive new Collingwood Centre, housed in a former Catholic secondary school on the edge of the site. Careers, economics, philosophy, business studies, art history, PE and politics departments are based there (politics classroom is set up as a mock House of Commons, even down to the green leather seats) and centre is used for studying, socialising and school events. There's also the Saturday evening Crescent Club, where sixth formers are allowed a maximum of two drinks (wine or beer) with food.

Pastoral care, well-being and discipline: School has put an enormous amount of time and effort into its pastoral care. It is also one of 10 schools across the UK chosen to work with the PSHE Association on the development of a new character curriculum, which aims to develop skills and attributes like motivation and resilience.

Each pupil is given a copy of the school's Guidelines for Life, which covers everything from its anti-bullying policy to relationships and where and when boys and girls can be in their free time. Policies on smoking, alcohol and drugs all clearly laid out. Expulsions are few and far between – two in the last five years. Public displays of affection (PDAs) between pupils banned – 'couples must behave in a way which would be appropriate if a member of staff were in the room,' says the school.

A host of opportunities for pupils to make sure their views are heard. 'Councils are huge here,' declared the head boy. He's right – there's a social council, music council, academic council, sports council and changes council. School is good at picking up on problems before they escalate. 'There are lots of people looking out for them,' a teacher told us. Cleaners spot things and chefs notice if a pupil hasn't eaten much at lunch.

Pupils and parents: Pupils come from all over, many from London, Oxford or locations within two hours' driving distance. Around 10 per cent international students. Parents are very supportive of the school. Many are sons and daughters of Rugby alumni and one described pupils as 'unpretentious, natural, spontaneous, courteous, tolerant and unstuffy.' Illustrious former pupils include Rupert Brooke (a girls' house is named after him), Lewis Carroll, Robert Hardy, Tom King, Salman Rushdie, AN Wilson and Anthony Horowitz. Not forgetting, of course, Harry Flashman and Tom Brown.

Entrance: No more 11+ admissions. Local children can sit exams in year 6 for deferred entry in year 9. Others sit aptitude pre-test and interview in year 7. CE pass mark is 55 per cent but average is higher. Boys and girls come from more than 300 feeder schools across the country, including The Dragon, Bilton Grange, Packwood Haugh and S Anselm's.

Around 40 new pupils (mostly girls, but some boys) join in the sixth form. UK candidates need at least three 7s and three 6s at GCSE. They sit sixth form entrance exams and have a house interview. Potential scholars are invited back at a later date for scholarship interviews. Keen competition for sixth form places.

Exit: Virtually all to university – around 94 per cent head to Russell Group universities most years. Bath, Bristol, Durham, Edinburgh, Leeds, Manchester, Newcastle and UCL are popular choices. Usually around 10 Oxbridge places a year (nine in 2018), with three others off to US/Canada. Gap years 'less fashionable' than previously and interest in US universities is growing.

Money matters: Complex range of bursaries and awards. School offers academic, music, drama, art, DT, computing and sport scholarships – it led the way in 2003 by limiting scholarships to 10 per cent of the school fees, although this can be augmented to 100 per cent if family need can be shown through a means test. Bursaries of up to 100 per cent of the fees, depending on parental means.

S

Remarks: This famous public school takes huge pride in its history and traditions – and quite right too – but it is genuinely innovative and forward thinking, especially when it comes to academic matters. Boarding houses have a real sense of community, pupils are welcoming and unpretentious and facilities are second to none.

S. Anselm's School

Stanedge Road, Bakewell, Derbyshire DE45 1DP

Ages 3–16 **Pupils** 238 **Boarders** 21 weekly, 19 flexi (years 3–8)

Fees: Day £10,950 – £19,500; Boarding £26,100 pa

01629 812734
www.sanselms.co.uk

Acting head: Lisa Donnelly, deputy head and head of pre-prep, is holding the fort after the departure of Peter Phillips.

James Mortimer BA (Oxon) PGCE MA is head of college.

Academic matters: Setting off a high-altitude balloon and tracking it from the comfort of a classroom is nothing new, but this is the kind of school that literally goes the extra mile, or hundred. S Anselmians think nothing of jumping in a minibus and driving four hours to Norfolk on an epic balloon chase while tracking the progress on laptops. Project based learning was introduced in collaboration with a Danish school and Harvard University several years ago and staff are now starting to see it embed. Software is up to date, think 3D printers, trials of VR, and their Lego Innovative Centre which showcases 3D inspired chess sets. When Griselda, a forest monster, terrorised the local woodland, pupils were so engrossed in using adjectives that they wanted to work through the dinner bell.

Projects have ranged from the prerequisite Roman V's Celt battle (two-day stopover and an actual catapult: no cardboard boxes here); giant plastic turtles, an ethical nod to the modern-day plastic problem; Tudor houses set on fire to allow pupils to experience the Great Fire of London (some cried); lessons in surgery with an actual pig's lung and a digestive system made out of Lego. The list is endless... anything goes in the name of learning. We tried to ignore the proudly displayed newspaper reports lacking in the fundamentals, with spelling mistakes in headlines, and pupils grappling with knives in cooking without basic chopping techniques. On the plus side pupils were self-reflective, one reasoning that she needed to take more risks in her work, another learning collaboration as part of a group.

College students – the 13-16 year olds – happily enthuse that there are 'loads of opportunities and good trips.' When we visited many were away: residential in Oxford, history trip in Hull, others at the Birmingham Symphony Hall. Those left behind were on task and mature. Small class size and mentorships help. Kinder class were head down and learning in a French lesson. Derwent completed group programming work showing the maturity of undergrads. Maths students were genuinely enthusiastic about their double lesson last thing on a Friday. Parents remark that it is 'a truly wonderful school' and that 'My boys look forward to going every morning and come home full of stories of what they have done that day.' First GCSE results in 2018 saw 21 per cent A*-A/9-7 grades.

The school is more than happy to accept children with special needs. This is backed up by a strong learning support department with dedicated spaces, three specialist teachers including speech, language and communication therapists and dyslexia experts, one-to-ones, group work and EAL support, as well as plentiful resources for specific needs such as specialised laptops. Additional charge for learning support lessons.

Games, options, the arts: No shying away from competition here: it's embraced at all levels, with the key being inclusion.

Children are divided into A, B and C teams with the As naturally playing more fixtures. 'We wipe the floor with other schools, despite our small size,' say PE staff. Pupils compete nationally in swimming and netball and have had an unbeaten season in rugby. The large range of sports from shooting to steeplechase, cricket for both girls and boys to the usual netball, hockey and tennis mean that players achieve at all levels including regional and county. Parents said the Astroturf pitch was 'a real bonus and all the children (and mums) are enjoying the hockey tuition' with families being invited in for weekly coaching. Smallish swimming pool.

Music is equally strong, boasting 15 peripatetic teachers and 15 ensembles: everything from rock bands to modern music and chapel choirs. The proof of pudding is in the listening – mesmerising sounds of music flood through open windows, showcasing the ability and dedication of pupils. The Hargreaves Hall auditorium offers a great performing space for all ages, with modern repertoires ranging from Fight Club monologues to full on productions of Around the World in 80 Days and Fantastic Mr Fox.

Art rooms are a hive of activity and include a ceramics studio plus specialist teacher, with textiles offered as a separate subject. When we visited, a local exhibition of art produced by the prep included hand crafted toys, product launches, metaphorical poems sewn and draped on a mannequin's skirt, the Cabinet of Curiosities containing ceramic fantasy creatures and even a bird's skull which the pre-prep discovered and donated. The whole exhibition – a work of art in itself.

After-school activities cover every taste. The rule is, if there isn't an activity with your name on, then there soon will be. Not a space is left unused here, with the gardens being the next big project – pupils have already started crafting grand designs.

Boarding: 'We have a pillow fight every Wednesday morning, so they can get it out of their system,' boasts the housemaster. Under his charming guise, the pupils gush boarding accolades with superlatives galore. There are no boarding facilities for college students (years 9 to 11). A few year 6-8 boarders are international pupils; in some cases, families have moved nearby so they can send siblings as day pupils.

One parent told us they live only four miles away, yet their son has chosen to board. Who can blame him when weekend activities range from watching live ice hockey matches and paintballing to water parks? Lots of staff are on site: no one wants to miss out on the fun. Older pupils earn the privilege to wonder down to Bakewell and spend a pound. 'It's a wonder what they come back with,' chuckles the housemaster.

Junior dorms have been spruced up with bright, but slightly garish and stereotypical wallpaper: flowers in the girls' dorm, and a world map (head's request) in the boys'. We did wonder why the girls only got daisies. Senior dorms are slightly worn looking, if not dull, and could do with a lick of paint. Bathroom facilities are modern and clean. None of which matters, really, because S Anselm's boarders are too busy making the most of their time, with prep, music, supper, sports, swimming and the Lego Innovative Studio to fit in; we are not even sure the TVs in the common rooms are used.

Background and atmosphere: The successful pre-prep and prep school expanded to open the college in 2015. There was a slight nervousness, but the college students are well supported in small groups, if they can tear themselves away from the packed schedule of scuba diving and hosted dinners to 'keep them busy in those teenage years'.

Locality – in the awe-inspiring Peak District – is massively important: 'It's everything about us and shapes us as a school.' Simple things like using Derbyshire oatcakes in their pancake day races, and studying iconic Derbytonians. Since most children live in the locality, it is easy for the school to integrate naturally into local life and a create a sense of community. Local state schools are invited periodically for sporting events, computer programming and science workshops.

There is so much going on here that it's not a case of ticking boxes, but more what boxes can we come up with next to tick off. Staff are positively buzzing with enthusiasm.

Pastoral care, well-being and discipline: There is the S Anselm's way based on common sense, sensible skirt lengths, no make-up, ensuring children remain children. We listened to the excited chattering of pupils and sampled Friday's fish in the cosy, sociable dining hall. Pupils went out of their way to help visitors and took delight in clearing away our things. Parents are confident their offspring are eating well, remarking, 'The boys tell me how good the school lunches are and my eldest loves the full English on a Saturday morning.'

Pupils are, on the whole, dressed smartly. The house system, based on four national heroes – Pitts, Churchill, Nelson and Wellington – is used at every opportunity to provide competition amongst pupils and staff of all ages, with the later exchanging friendly banter about a recent quiz night.

Staff are not afraid to address any issues head on – whether it's lesson time or not – with one teacher taking a pupil aside for a heart to heart when we were there. The on-site nurse personifies caring, showing a sprinkling of humour whilst looking after a senior pupil complete with sick bowl. Who wouldn't want this lady on hand in their hour of need?

Pupils and parents: Pre-prep pupils showed great honesty with their opinions: 'It's too easy, I did fractions last year, and I have to do them again this year.' Another, exasperated, 'We have to work until 5pm'. They don't. Pre-prep finishes at 3.20pm, with after-school clubs available. We found pupils enthusiastic and on task in class, barely glancing up. They were polite, courteous and relaxed. The Guide was not immune to the inevitable plethora of prepped answers by the older students, but found genuineness when probing. 'Good sport, no pressure.' 'Lots of opportunities and mix of everything.' 'Feels like a family' and 'really family-friendly environment.'

Staff use online learning journals in early years and reception to record pupils' progress for parents. While all agree it provides great communication, it ironically leaves staff with little to say on parents' evenings. Some can also get carried away with recording, as one teacher openly admitted she had conducted 38 observations on one child in nine weeks because 'they were achieving so many amazing things' and she just wanted to 'capture them for the parents.'

Lots on offer for parents, from quiz and curry nights to pet shows and the weekly Sunday supper where families can enjoy a delicious roast with all the trimmings.

Entrance: Most pupils join the non-selective nursery or pre-prep; prep school entry subject to an interview with the head and report from their previous school. New entrants to the college have an assessment and interview with the head and head of college. When one recent recruit instinctively opened the door for us, the deputy mused that students soon slot into the S Anselm's way of life.

Exit: Between a half and two-thirds move elsewhere at 13 – with some returning after experiencing new pastures. Phillips has a relaxed attitude to pupils exiting at 13+ – pleased when they gain their scholarships. It shows – all scholarship boards, from academic to sport and music, are up to date, and exit destinations include Shrewsbury, Oundle and Eton. First year 11 leavers to Shrewsbury, Gordonstoun, Sheffield High, Birkdale (with a scholarship) and a mixture of local sixth forms. The college is looking to expand into the centre of Bakewell, and it is likely to continue to grow.

Money matters: Academic, music, art and sports scholarships at 7+ and 13+. Some means-tested bursaries.

Remarks: S Anselm's tries to keep it real, true to the motto: Esse Quam Videri...to be and not to seem to be. The school embraces its Derbyshire roots, preparing students for modern life with traditional values. Individuality is key, and pupils leave with their characters intact, nurtured rather than remodelled. A juxtaposition of old and new, with a dash of good nature, humour and honesty that just seems to work.

St Faith's

Linked with The Leys School

Trumpington Road, Cambridge CB2 8AG

Ages 4–13 Pupils 540

Fees: £12,660 – £15,945 pa

01223 352073
www.stfaiths.co.uk

Headmaster: Since 2011, Nigel Helliwell (mid 50s). Studied maths and PE at Staffordshire teacher training college followed by a masters in curriculum studies from London University, which has influenced several curricular decisions at St Faith's. This is his third headship. A grammar school boy who first taught senior pupils. Planned to join the RAF as an officer but went to teacher training college on recommendation of his teachers. Changed to teaching prep school aged children as 'they are like sponges at this age. They learn more quickly and are more reactive.'

Softly spoken, quite intense, smartly turned out, kind and extremely focused. Parents and pupils like him. No, let's be honest, parents love him. 'I really like him,' was said in many different ways by every parent we spoke to. 'He's not showy. He took over well and has shown great initiative.' All parents said academic standards had risen since his arrival. His major changes have been curriculum based, introducing computing and engineering plus 50 minute lessons. 'He's not a yes man; he can handle pushy parents.' 'Not a people pleaser, but will listen.' All parents said he was approachable and very visible around the school, 'and the children love him, and he loves them.' We saw this when accompanying him around the school. All pupils greeted him, wherever they were, and he knew all of them. He personally delivers birthday cards to each child on their big day.

S

Entrance: Oversubscribed; they take registrations from birth onwards. Parents expected to visit school as part of application process. Be aware they want parents who will fit in with the ethos of the school. Priority given to children of Old Fidelians (10 per cent of pupils) those of staff at St Faith's and The Leys, and siblings. Head of pre-prep will visit nurseries to observe the child and discuss development. They are looking for potential but usually take 95 per cent of those on the list. Assessment for external entry from year 2. Around 40 sit exam for 15 year 3 places, with priority (but not automatic places) again given to siblings. Most pupils come from state system at this stage, and another six or seven start in year 7. Pupils come from a 25 mile radius of Cambridge. Parents made up of old Fidelians plus many more working at the universities and hospitals. More than 40 per cent of parents are employed within the engineering/computing/technology and science industries, reflecting the school's emphasis on STEAM subjects. This intake reflects Cambridge's cosmopolitan, international background with many pupils bilingual. Means-tested bursaries and scholarships available.

Exit: Around half of year 8 children go to The Leys where there are a guaranteed number of places on offer. These are not a shoe-in though, one or two children turned down each year. A further 20 per cent go off to board to eg Uppingham, Oakham, Oundle, Haileybury, Stowe, Felsted. The occasional child goes to one of the excellent Cambridge state schools. The remainder to other Cambridge independents eg The Perse Upper, The Leys. Some 15 per cent leave at the end of year 6, mainly due to parental anxiety about gaining a senior school place. Parents strongly advised to leave pupils at school until end of year 8, actively supported by most senior schools. Increasing numbers of scholarships.

Remarks: Founded in 1884 and housed ever since on a 12 acre site a stone's throw from the centre of Cambridge, with a further 20 acres of sports grounds minutes away, St Faith's offers a leafy, spacious oasis compared to many of the other prep schools in Cambridge. Plenty of space to park for parents, which is unheard of in the city, and lots of outside space for the children to play. Pre-prep children all had their wellies on at break time so were able to make the most of the grass even on a damp day. Please note the bands on trees marking how high they can climb; excellent to see tree climbing encouraged. The striking red, black and white striped blazers could be an acquired taste, but a perfect marketing tool. Matching red doors – thankfully not striped – and they even have a striking red-leafed maple holding pride of place in the playground. Whoever planted that had great vision. The school is very proud of its eco friendly credentials. New pre-prep classrooms built to passivhaus standards. Clouds suspended from the ceilings to lower noise and echo. Pupils encouraged to cycle to school and bikes serviced for free if they do so. A car share scheme is being introduced, actively supported by parents.

Pupils are set in all academic subjects from year 5. Parents very impressed with standards; 'It's an academic school where pupils are stretched.' All parents said 'they get the best out of the children, but with no pressure – encouraged, not pushed.' 'Children are taught good study skills.' Parents spoke about pressure being 'ramped up' in year 7 but again with no stress. 'They know when to use the carrot or the stick, and know the pupils well.' Extra lessons for scholarship pupils. 'There's lots of homework and comments from teachers.' All happy with way they communicate. No children with a formal EHC plan, but those with learning difficulties – some 50 of them – including dyslexia, dyspraxia and mild autism and ADHD, offered lots of extra help by the Discovery Zone, made up of five teachers. All children's records computerised with even the most trivial things noted. Subsequently school keeps a very close eye on them and picks problems up quickly. Many pupils take pre-test exams in year 6 to join senior schools in year 9.

Curriculum very much based on the future, a very forward-looking school. 'We need creative, flexible minds,' says the head. Engineering taught as a core subject to all pupils from year 3 (school won The Times Education Supplement Strategic Education Initiative prize in 2018). The children work in teams and their progress is impressive. Older pupils were making paddle boats when we visited and we were astounded by their skills. Younger children were learning how to cut and draw accurately using lasers. School very cleverly combines maths, sciences, DT and art skills for engineering, now in its brand new STEM hub. Computing also avant garde here. Head has made some very clever appointments. Heads of department have come from industry backgrounds, retraining as teachers, and this shows in attitude and knowledge. Also delighted to see that both engineering teachers are female. Please note the electric cars on display, built by the pupils during after-school clubs and a hovercraft is next – apt, as Sir Christopher Cockerell was an old boy.

New block offers lots of indoor space for experiments and large building projects. They even have an observatory and weather station. Lots of computer desks throughout the school. One day a term is spent completely IT free in all teaching, including no LED screens at front of classroom. All lessons we visited were upbeat and cheerful with pupils enthusiastic and engaged – staff too.

Spanish is the main language, taught from day one. Latin introduced in year 5, French in year 6, Mandarin and German in year 8. Music and drama popular. More than 30 ensembles on offer, and drama productions for each year group. 'There are some super productions,' was said by all parents.

Wide range of sports, including rowing. Head very keen (as he would be) and wants all abilities taught properly by qualified staff, 'then they will improve.' Teams for all, 'everyone gets a chance'; 20 acres of playing fields a five minute walk from school. Cricket for all, touch rugby for the less keen boys. Lots of silverware in the cupboard. One parent did say, 'it's difficult to break into the first team as there are firm favourites, but, to be fair, they are very successful.' Another commented on 'pushy parents demanding places, but happy that staff withstand this.'

Discipline and pastoral care spoken of very highly by all parents. 'We often don't hear about mild misdemeanors until well after the event, which is how it should be.' Another spoke of their child saying, 'we don't do that at St Faith's!' Parents said spats were dealt with quickly and kindly and coping methods for those struggling with friendship issues put in place. The odd suspension, one a year. 'We are a school based on Christian values,' says the head. 'Mistakes are made, punishments served and then we move on.' All year 8 pupils are made prefects. 'The slate is wiped clean and virtually all step up to the mark,' says the head. Plenty of buddy systems and close monitoring. Lots of after-school clubs and late pick ups on offer for busy parents. Popular breakfast club held every day, with parents and pupils eating together.

A joyous school: obvious as soon as you walk through the door. 'It's the pupils that make the place,' said one parent; 'we walked in and felt immediately welcomed by everyone. I wanted that for my children.' Children chatty and delighted to show you their work. Teachers equally welcoming. Good to see a high number of young male teachers, particularly in the prep. 'The school chose us,' and, 'they let my child be themselves.'

We enjoyed our chatty lunch with year 8s. Food was excellent so we have to disagree with one, and only one, parent's gripe about it. Chatty year 8s were happy but had one complaint: 'Tuck, which is a year 8 privilege, has been made healthy. We no longer get cookies and cakes but have healthy smoothies and fruit instead.' They were distinctly unimpressed.

Overall, a very impressive school. Plenty of space, an excellent innovative education but, most importantly, a joyous place to be.

St Hugh's School (Woodhall Spa)

Cromwell Avenue, Woodhall Spa, Lincolnshire LN10 6TQ

Ages 2–13 **Pupils** 174 **Boarders** 19 flexi (from year 3) **C of E**

Fees: Day £8,880 – £14,928; Boarding £18,750 pa

01526 352169
www.st-hughs.lincs.sch.uk

Headmaster: Since 2013, Chris Ward BEd, late 30s; first headship, previously deputy head of Worksop College Prep. He spent several years as director of music at St John's-on-the-Hill School in Monmouthshire, though now does some science teaching. Approachable, visible and welcoming to pupils and parents. A keen and competitive rugby player, spends Wednesday and Saturday afternoons refereeing matches or supporting from the pavilion, mingling with parents over a cup of tea.

Believes that St Hugh's is unique in Lincolnshire, as a stand alone co-educational prep school, providing all round care and catering for everyone. Is proud that 'when St Hugh's pupils leave they are able to stand on their own'. Parents feel that he has given the school 'a new lease of life' which they hope will continue.

Recognising the shift in the demands of modern parents for flexible boarding, he is transforming boarding under newly appointed houseparents and UK gappies to a more cosy, warm and family experience. Keen to build and strengthen the nursery provision to provide sustained growth in pupil numbers over the years and enhance the structure and shape of the school day.

Married to Angharad, who has traditional prep head's spouse's role, with three children, all pupils at the school.

Moving on in July 2019.

Entrance: Majority of the children rise through the ranks of the school's nursery and pre-prep with some recruitment in year 3 and 4. Prospective pupils spend a day at the school for assessment. Six minibuses bring children from wider areas.

Exit: Seventy-five per cent go on to independent senior schools in Lincolnshire and the A1 corridor, Uppingham, Oundle, Lincoln Minster, Repton, Stamford. Further afield Sedbergh and Barnard Castle. The remaining 25 per cent get places at local grammar schools, usually at 11 (some go at 13).

Remarks: Located in the attractive, former Victorian spa resort of Woodhall Spa, in the midst of what was RAF heartland, St Hugh's is situated in a leafy avenue of traditional, Edwardian villas. Founded by the Forbes family in 1925 as a boys' boarding school, loyalty to the school has been strong and successive generations of often farming families continue to be educated here. A charitable trust since 1962 and co-educational since 1981.

Whilst first impressions are of a modest establishment, once through the door the extent of the buildings and facilities become immediately apparent and the newly acquired playing field now allows the grounds to be described as extensive for a school of this size. New Astroturf; this addition to the functional yet well maintained sport hall and swimming pool provides sporting facility gold, particularly for the hockey players. An adventure playground and nature pond – increasing use of the natural environment, staff undertaking forest school training, part of a green school kitemark. Boarding facilities in the upper echelons of the main school house, well away from classrooms.

Nursery and pre-prep classrooms flow through a building across the playground from the older children. Bright, well resourced and full of colourful displays. Corridors adorned with interesting displays and children's work provide a sense of pride and commitment from staff. Good specialist facilities for science, music, art and DT with whiteboards in each classroom, a dedicated ICT suite and wireless connectivity throughout the school.

Scholarship success particularly in sports, music and arts, and the head plans to strengthen further the number of academic and all-rounder awards. In the early years foundation stage, the new department head has developed investigational skills in maths. Specialist French starts in nursery, increasing across subjects so that by year 5 all teaching is by specialists, with German and Latin introduced and setting for mathematics and science. Classes are grouped according to ability from year 5 with an average of 14 in a class. Whilst teaching broadly follows the national curriculum, there is a weekly session for senior pupils to enhance independent learning. Ten per cent SEN, mainly dyslexia and dyspraxia though several children with EHC plans. Personalised learning plans, good coordinated strategies between SENCo and teachers, with one-on-one support where required. Rated excellent for academic achievement and personal development in recent ISI report.

Sport rules the roost. Focus on traditional team sports and swimming, and everyone encouraged to play in a team. Good fixture list mainly against local independents but outlying location involves lengthy travelling times. It really is 'sport for all' – no one is left out. Hosts an annual netball tournament using boarding accommodation for teams from far afield.

Music flourishes with three-quarters of pupils from year 3 playing an instrument. Plenty of performance opportunities with termly concerts and musicals, and public recitals for the two choirs; two orchestras with seniors scaling symphonic heights; string and wind ensembles. Joint production with drama each year – recently the Wizard of Oz and Bugsy Malone – though plays, sketches and nativities, as well as assembly presentations, give lots of scope for budding luvvies. Elocution competitions too.

Expressive arts thrive in well equipped, dedicated rooms with specialist art, pottery and design technology workshops and weekly scholarship classes. Textiles and cookery are included throughout the curriculum.

St Hugh's pupils get out and about on numerous curriculum enriching visits and outings. Years 5 and 7 have residential French trips and year 8 has a week's outdoor pursuits experience. Biennial hockey and rugby tours to Dublin and South Africa.

Positive reinforcement is key to rewards and sanctions, with gold points accumulating for the benefit of the pupil and their house. Not just academic achievement: effort, good behaviour and citizenship are all equally recognised. We were wowed by the Wow board displaying individual exceptional achievements. When needed, clearly defined sanctions escalate through report cards to detentions. Parents feel very well informed about their children's progress through teacher emails and regular reports.

Pupils and staff are polite, friendly and welcoming; evidence of real rapport between teachers and pupils, anecdotal comments tinged with humour and respect; no doubt that every child is known well here. Citizenship prized – and awards presented at weekly assemblies. St Hugh's Award for actions above and beyond – recently presented to one of the house captains who went home for a night to bake a cake to cheer up a young house member who had sustained a complicated broken femur on the rugby pitch. Strong house structure (named for three previous heads) with sporting, general knowledge and arts competitions and fundraising activities. Peer mentors in years 7 and 8; worry boxes discretely placed for confidential concerns.

Attuned to changing needs (and a declining number of Forces children), the metamorphosis of boarding has seen children deciding to board occasionally. Everyone (children, teachers and parents) agrees that the food is 'fantastic', with plenty of choice. The place is absolutely spotless throughout.

Parents tell us that they 'love the wonderful family atmosphere' and that the children 'mix throughout the year groups and are very supportive and encouraging of each other'. One parent told us, 'I have seen older year groups, unprompted, clapping and encouraging the little ones as they walk through the dining hall to go to perform in a play, which gave them such a boost'.

St Hugh's turns out well rounded children who are polite and self confident. Happy children – and parents.

S

St John's College School

75 Grange Road, Cambridge, Cambridgeshire CB3 9AB

Ages 4–13 **Pupils** 477 **Boarders** 21 full, 15 weekly/flexi (from age 8) C of E

Fees: Day £11,625 – £15,330; Boarding £24,210; Choristers £8,070 pa

01223 353532
www.sjcs.co.uk

Headmaster: Since 2016, Neil Chippington MA (Cantab) FRCO (40s), previously head of St Paul's Cathedral School. Music scholar at Cranleigh, organ scholar at Cambridge, Fellow of the Royal College of Organists; music is certainly in his blood. Came to St Paul's from Winchester College, where he was a housemaster for eight years, and having himself been a quirister (chorister) at Winchester Cathedral. He is a keen cyclist and runner who regularly takes part in half marathons and triathlons, usually for charity, and recently completed a 280 mile three day cycle to raise money for Leukaemia Research. In addition, he has a strong interest in travelling and has over the years led school trips to a wide range of countries including Jordan, Iran and Turkey. He is married to Leisle, who is also a teacher, and they have two sons.

Entrance: Oversubscribed but not overly so. For entry at 4 the children are 'assessed' – using sequencing and other methods which, even at such a young age, show their potential – as are the parents. 'We want parents to have a feel for the place and we see what they want for their child. If we agree, we can work together.' Don't be complacent; children here are bright. At 7, assessments in English and maths and child is observed during half a day at the school. 'It's all about the child fitting in and coping.' Chorister bursaries for up to five scholars, all boys, at 8, of at least two-thirds of the fees. Means-tested bursaries for those who would particularly benefit. At 11+, potential music scholars welcomed as boarders, with scholarships available. Siblings take priority and then boy:girl ratio to keep the numbers even. Children come from a wide commutable area around Cambridge, or further afield for boarders. The majority of parents are academics, medics from Addenbrooke's or employed on the Silicon Fen,with a Newmarket contingent as well. Many work in the City. All parents very ambitious for their offspring, but nicely so and welcoming to newcomers.

Exit: The odd leaver at 11 but very unusual, usually heading to the state sector. No 'evictions', but occasionally, after much discussion and agreement, the occasional one will be moved on to 'somewhere they will be happier at.' Virtually all leave at 13. Lots of help with future schooling. 'They guide us away from making the wrong choice.' Over half of the year get scholarships/awards, academic as well as music. At least 50 per cent go to local private Cambridge schools, the rest off to board: many to The Leys, Perse Upper, King's Ely, St Mary's, Stephen Perse, Uppingham.

Remarks: The school is owned by St John's College and was originally set up in the 17th century to educate the choristers. Now housed on a leafy road in Cambridge opposite the college's playing fields, which they share, in three adjacent houses, recently redeveloped to include new outdoor woodland area on what was once the staff car park. On entering the main building the first thing you see are the choristers' gowns hanging in the hallway. They are very proud of the choristers, rightly so. They travel the world and are very talented. But once in the school they are just normal pupils. There are no 'stars' in this school so no cabinets full of trophies on display. They have them, but discreetly hidden in the dining room. The life of the chorister is slightly different to other pupils as they start practice at 7.30am, running through to the start of school at 9am, and again after school for a couple of hours. It's a massive commitment but handled well. The school ensures they don't suffer academically or personally.

A very tactile school. 'If a child needs a hug it gets one.' Many parents spoke of their children 'being allowed to be children and not to grow up too quickly.' 'They are imaginative and modern about learning,' said one parent. 'We are told very firmly to leave the education of our child to them and not to stress about exams. It works, the children are pushed, achieve highly but don't feel under pressure.' No exams until the penultimate year. Children taught to have enquiring minds and embrace learning. Mindfulness is taught to all, even the little ones, and stands them in good stead for future years. Hugely supported by parents. 'All of the teachers are of a similar mindset and embrace the concept and love the children. They wouldn't be here if that wasn't the case.'

Lots of after-school clubs, but not until year 3. Enrichment programme each Thursday afternoon for 9-13 year olds explores cross-curricular work across arts and sciences, plus My Mind programme, which includes tai chi for year 4. As expected, loads of music, not just for the choristers. The majority of the children learn an instrument, many two or more. Bands, choirs, quartets galore. All the usual sports teams, well supported. Drama very popular. Very impressive artwork framed and displayed throughout the school. A large, airy, newly refurbished art room where the older children can pop in and set to. 'All children can draw by the time they leave St John's,' the very enthusiastic art teacher told us. Timetables are flexible. Extra tuition offered, some at no extra cost, very quickly if needed. Individual needs department proactive. They are on top of the children academically and extra time allocated towards subjects for those aiming for certain scholarships.

A small contingent – including all choristers – boards. 'It means we can manage their time well rather than it being wasted travelling.' Larger numbers boarding higher up the school, many weekly, some flexi. Clean, bright, mixed boarding house. Lots of comfy sofas, snooker and table football. A large kitchen with huge table. 'Our parents can come and see us and have a cup of tea with us after services,' said one chorister. Very much an open door policy for parents. Strict rules within the house. No child can enter another dorm. No mobile phones in the boarding house and, very contentiously for our chatty guides, no tuck. 'They decided the choristers were getting too much sugar so cut tuck to twice a week and have now cut it out completely,' was the outraged comment. 'So when we go home we beg our parents for sweets.' There used to be accompanied visits to town with the older ones going in threes, 'as long as one of us was wearing a watch,' but these have now been stopped. 'They said all we did was buy sweets, but we only had £2 so what can they expect?' from our opinionated guide, 'and how do they expect us to manage money if they won't let us out to spend it?' All said with very good humour and a big smile. We feel our guides have a bright future ahead of them. Homesickness handled well. One pupil allowed to bring her rabbit last term. Lots of contact with parents, though not before bed, in private phone booths. 'Please note the phone number for Childline is listed on our contact lists pinned to the door.' This guide will go far. Dormitories clean and tidy. Bunk beds, six to a room max. Boarders change their own bed linen. Duvet covers brought from home. Houseparents loved by all, children and parents. 'I couldn't ask for more from them and the receptionist is magnificent.'

Uniform stands out with bright red blazers. 'The uniform is too expensive,' said one rather disgruntled parent, 'particularly the blazers.' The girls wear a rather dowdy summer dress, far too dull for the bright, exuberant characters donning them. 'Pastorally excellent,' was said by every parent. 'There are issues, usually girls and their friendships, but the school handles them sensitively and effectively.' The year 8s mentor the incoming year 5s.

Nearly every parent we spoke to felt 'we are very lucky to have our children at St John's.' We can see why. Certain schools have 'that feel', and this one does. It's a joyous place that's buzzing. Lessons are alive, the children are working hard, utterly engaged. And they are happy, exuberant, confident little people, from the youngest up. Children being children, nurtured through some tough, turbulent times, meeting adolescence with equilibrium and well set for future schooling. Long may it continue.

St Mary's School, Cambridge

Bateman Street, Cambridge, Cambridgeshire CB2 1LY

Ages 4–18 **Pupils** 639 **Sixth form** 93 **Boarders** 73 full, 4 weekly, 4 flexi (from 11 years) **RC**

Fees: Day £9,909 – £15,861; Boarding £26,286 – £32,562 pa

01223 353253
www.stmaryscambridge.co.uk

S

Headmistress: Since 2007, Charlotte Avery (40s). English degree Oxford, PGCE Cambridge. Taught in various schools, deputy head at Highgate where she oversaw the transition to co-ed. St Mary's is her first headship. One of triplets, all with Oxbridge degrees. A formidable intellect who is determined to get her point across. Dedicated to girls' education. Brisk and efficient but also kind and caring. Obviously stands no nonsense. Well liked and respected by parents. 'She can talk the hind leg off a donkey, but in the nicest way,' said one parent. 'She's brilliant, a whirlwind with great enthusiasm who carries everyone along with her.' Many parents spoke of her great vision and the 'huge changes she has made.' Others spoke of how she has promoted internally. 'A very nice person, tough and a great leader.' Very high profile and attends all school events. Interesting to note that she is an Anglican but head of a Catholic school.

Head of junior school: Since 2016 is Matthew O'Reilly. Read German and politics at Newcastle. Travelled the world teaching adults English for large businesses and interpreting. Returned to the UK to do his PGCE and started teaching in senior schools. Disliked this, so turned to juniors instead. St Mary's was his first job and he has worked his way up to head. Very well liked by all parents and settling into the role well. 'He is a young man with a quiet, calm, manner and great enthusiasm. I was delighted he was appointed head.'

Academic matters: In 2018, 63 per cent A*-A/9-7 at GCSE, and 46 per cent A*-A at A level. Impressive results from girls instilled with great self-belief and a strong work ethic. 'The girls work really hard but have great fun too,' said one parent. Lots of support for all, whatever their abilities. Parents kept well informed about academic progress and spoke about 'prompt responses' from teachers. Science and maths very strong with lots of science clubs. Fabulous new science hub, incredibly well equipped. Year 10s were working hard at an experiment and good to see large sixth form groups doing sciences. Spanish, French, German, Latin, Greek and Mandarin all offered at GCSE. Many girls do two languages, though small groups for A level languages.

Inspirational quotes throughout the school from renowned women. Good to see a noticeboard about exam week and preparing for them. 'Don't panic' was one piece of advice. 'A very proactive school,' was one parent's comment. Another parent said, 'How I wish I'd had teachers like that.' Lots of computer suites and iPads filtering through to all pupils. Certain social media sights blocked – good. Food tech offered at A level. A younger age group was cooking when we were visiting – some delicious smells wafted our way.

The junior school is a short walk away in Chaucer Road, in a lovely old house with lots of outside space. Girls taught here as per state system. One teacher for all subjects, but with specialist input throughout. Again lots of inspirational quotes, particularly from the founder, on the walls. 'They get a very good start here,' was said more than once. French for all and Mandarin taught to all but a few who have extra tuition when needed. All girls actively encouraged: 'You can do it,' is what a lot of parents said their daughters were being told.

Average class sizes of 20, smaller in the sixth form. Many teachers long serving. Learning support lessons for those that need it, about 100 SEN on the register, all with milder needs. 'My daughter needs extra support and time and the school couldn't have been more supportive helping her plan her work and revision as well as extra lessons.' Some 48 students have EAL classes, all in the senior school. Many more from overseas who no longer need this support.

Games, options, the arts: Quietly sporty and successful; cabinets full of silverware are testament to this. County cross-country runners, hockey players and netballers. Pitches situated a 10 minute minibus journey away. 'Sport for all and there are no sporting prima donnas,' said one parent. All talk about plenty of teams and 'masses of sports clubs.' Touch rugby and rowing on offer. Gymnastics popular. Sports rotated throughout the year so always something for everyone.

Drama very popular with lots of productions, clubs and workshops. Parents very enthusiastic about performances. Drama GCSE one of the most successful subjects; most gain top marks. LAMDA popular and encouraged for overseas students.

Art is big at St Mary's and it has a very strong reputation. The art school is situated next door to the main building. Sixth form art scholars' photos displayed in the reception area. Each sixth form student has their own space; we admired the quality of the work, ambitious and eye-catching. Impressive art on display throughout the school.

Orchestras, choirs, bands, ensembles galore, in both junior and senior schools. Our visit coincided with mass rehearsals at the junior school. Every room was full of performers practising. Music as a career actively encouraged.

Numerous sports tours and subject trips. DofE for all, up to gold award.

Boarding: The boarding community is international. Some 20 countries represented, with those from south east Asia being the largest cohort. Currently about half the boarders are in the sixth form, and virtually all from overseas. The majority are full boarders, though flexi boarding is offered. All boarders now housed in Mary Ward House a short walk from the school on Brooklands Avenue. Up to five younger girls in a room, with double rooms for years 10-12 and year 13s in single rooms.

Girls are encouraged to personalise their space and taught to do their own laundry. One father couldn't understand why boarders were allowed so much freedom – 'why do they need to go into town to buy sweets?' – but we suspect the boarders disagree with him. They are kept occupied with church on Sundays, optional, and plenty of trips to Alton Towers and the like. Parents keep in close contact and are happy their daughters are 'safe and supervised.'

Disappointing to hear from sixth form day girls that the new boarders don't mix socially with them. Lots of effort made to include them in sixth form socials but not many takers and very few attend the Leavers' Ball. Doesn't appear to be the case lower down the school: parents spoke of daughters going to stay with friends who are day girls.

Background and atmosphere: Now the only girls' school left in Cambridge. Founded by Mary Ward, an innovator of education for girls, St Mary's opened in 1898. Based on a strong Catholic ethos that is reflected throughout the school. All religions, and none, are welcomed and embraced, with the spiritual welfare of the girls being of paramount importance. There is a resident chaplain, a small chapel where services are regularly held, parents welcome to attend as well, and whole school services regularly. A strongly Christian school that believes that 'every girl is of equal value and has something to offer.' This belief permeates throughout junior and senior schools.

Outwardly the school is not particularly attractive. Squeezed into the centre of Cambridge along a large part of Bateman Street, the 70s façade is quite low key. But once inside the school it's another matter. Modern additions have been incorporated well, including new science hub opened by Dame Mary Archer in 2016, and it's interesting to tour the school going from ancient to modern: it adds character and works well.

The original building, once a residential house, is beautiful. Now home to the admin and head's office. The magnificent staircase and large bay windows looking out onto large gardens reflect back to another era. The gardens are well used with plenty of benches, an outside gym and table tennis table.

Sixth form housed in a separate building that used to be the junior school, across the road. Smaller classrooms for teaching, a dance studio, gym and showers; please note the hairdryers and straighteners. A beautiful building that has recently been refurbished. Comfy-looking common room, kitchen (we spotted the toast and Nutella), and outside space for dining. Interesting to see a sign up in the kitchen to say only English should be spoken. Impressive library with sixth form girls quietly working. Silent study rooms and less quiet ones, but all working hard in them. Good use made of Cambridge and all it has to offer.

The junior school reflects the senior school, with large gardens and an attractive, airy building. Pretty sensory garden and vegetable plots for each year. Both schools are very much 'girls' schools.' The empowerment of women, strong women, is a theme throughout. The girls seem to absorb this. Unaffected and naturally pretty. Very little make up worn and no strutting divas to behold – thank goodness.

Pastoral care, well-being and discipline: All parents praised the pastoral care. Very few bullying claims. Happiness and joy with strong moral values is their mantra and the girls take this on board. But girls will be girls, and the school knows it. Spats and sniping dealt with calmly and efficiently, usually with very little parental intervention. Parents spoke of a happy school with 'no queen bees or cliques.' A junior school mother said, 'some parents get too involved, collaring teachers at every opportunity. They are too protective to the detriment of others.' But that's junior schools for you. Most parents trust the school and know their daughters are 'safe and happy.' School knows how to deal with girls and their problems. A counsellor and female lay chaplain available if needed, and staff appear to know the girls well.

Instilling self-esteem and confidence is very much an ethos of the school and many parents spoke about it along with the Mary Ward philosophy that they have great belief in. 'My daughter was very shy when she started but they have brought her out of herself and her confidence now is amazing.'

Pupils and parents: Parents are very much 'Cambridge,' academics/medics/professionals. Many are old girls. All spoke about the values of the school and how important that was to them. About a third are Catholic. All very pro single sex education, even the mother who said, 'I was very anti single sex education initially, but St Mary's suited my daughter best and she's thrived.' Girls from a 30 mile radius around Cambridge with about 25 per cent from overseas.

The girls were interesting. Charming and unaffected in both schools. It was quite revealing to see the sixth formers, slightly scruffy, but not in a bad way, and minimal make up. As one mother said, 'they don't care what they look like as there's no-one to impress.' Amen to that.

Entrance: Entrance tests for all, even the reception children, who have a chat with a member of staff, count, write and sort shapes, 'to see if they will fit in.' Don't be fooled: they are looking for bright sparks. Skype interviews for those overseas. Most girls are interviewed. The senior school is oversubscribed and the junior school full from year 5. Automatic entry from the junior to senior school, with only one girl in the last five years weeded out in year 5. Quite a large intake at year 9 when girls arrive from the local prep and state schools, and from abroad to board.

Exit: Around 50-60 per cent leave each year after GCSEs, mostly to the excellent state sixth form colleges in Cambridge. The odd one to a co-ed independent, but quite unusual. Sometimes a girl is advised not to return for sixth form, but it's very unusual, and as far as we could tell entry to sixth form was automatic for current pupils as long as they have a clutch of good GCSEs.

Two to Oxbridge in 2018; London a very popular destination, reflecting the international profile of the girls. Sciences, medicine, vets and engineering very popular. The head is embracing apprenticeships and encouraging girls to explore this option.

Money matters: Scholarships up to the value of 20 per cent of the fees awarded and bursaries of up to 50 per cent available. Two Ogden Trust mathematics and physics scholarships open to lower sixth candidates from the state sector, means-tested and can be worth up to 95 per cent of day school fees.

Remarks: A girls' school offering a tremendous education to young women. Being instilled with the belief of the empowerment of women from such a young age, these girls will go far. There'll be no glass ceilings for this lot.

Spalding High School

Stonegate, Spalding, Lincolnshire PE11 2PJ

Ages 11–18 **Pupils** 975 **Sixth form** 240 (26 boys)

01775 722110
www.spaldinghigh.lincs.sch.uk

Head: Since 2014, Michele Anderson (40s). BEd in home economics from University of the South Bank in London, but has always taught geography. Her first headship. A Londoner who previously taught at selective and non-selective schools in south London and Kent, new to Lincolnshire. 'I was looking for a headship but was very particular about the school I wanted. As soon as I walked through the door here I knew, as "the feel" was just right,' she says. Finding her feet with plans for 'fine tuning and funding.' Parents are positive about the new incumbent. 'She's fantastic; she knows exactly what she wants and where she wants to take the school,' said one enthusiastic mother. 'I like her and she has integrated herself well, getting to know everyone,' said another. Getting her face known locally and forging links with other schools in the area. Still teaching geography to the year 8s and 9s, 'I love teaching and the worst thing about being a head is that I can't do more of it.' Well aware of teenage angst. 'In the upper academic ability groups stress and anxiety levels are much the same, whatever the gender. We laugh a lot and eat cake here, and it helps. I have never been to a school with so much cake.' Husband is a househusband, a great eye opener for the girls. 'I couldn't do it without him.' Daughter recently started here.

Academic matters: As expected for a selective grammar, results are good. In 2018, 46 per cent A*-A/9-7 at GCSE and 32 per cent A*/A at A level (58 per cent A*-B). 'We get lots of homework,' said one of our guides, 'but they teach us how to manage our time and motivate ourselves. We are pushed to work at the best of our ability.' 'They are pushed academically,' said one parent, 'but are well supported.' All parents report feedback from staff is very good. 'If there is a problem we are made aware of it.' Spanish, French, German and Latin – good to see at a state school – on offer at KS3 to GCSE with French or German (alternate years) and Spanish A level – lowish take up at A level, but growing. Most take the triple science GCSE. Sociology, sciences and psychology top A level subjects; law and criminology soon to be added. The lessons we observed showed diligent girls working hard; this lot have got their heads down and are getting on with it.

Class sizes are large, up to 30. The occasional boy in A level science groups – they get good results, hence their presence. Gifted and talented are spotted from year 7 onwards, meaning extra work and more challenges. IT lessons for all, year 8s building their own websites. A relief to poke our head in the computer rooms and experience a blast of cold air from the air conditioning. Some of the other classrooms were stifling and stuffy – outside temperatures much the same though, to be fair.

Sixth form has its own IT rooms, plenty of computers available. Tea and coffee making facilities in the roomy common room along with a microwave. A new tea urn is a recent purchase.

Number of pupils with EAL is 36 and rising, so more provision being made. Quite high for a rural area, but many Eastern Europeans have been settling and educating their children locally.

Very few pupils on SEND list but provision made, usually within the classroom. Individual or small group support available from specialist teachers if needed.

Games, options, the arts: The cabinets are stuffed full of silverware at this school. Quite a few girls playing sport to county standard, or higher. They have a budding golfer and a competitive riding team. All non-school sporting achievements are acknowledged and accommodated. 'My daughter is sometimes away playing at a tournament and the school staff are very understanding. They give her full academic support.' Lots of teams throughout the school, including chances for the less able, but enthusiastic, to play. Interesting to see that they play lacrosse, unusual for a state school. Also successful football and cricket teams. Plenty of pitches, including Astroturf. No swimming pool but impressive gym and fitness suite that is well used.

Plenty of girls learning musical instruments, tapering off in the upper years. Singing lessons very popular. Lots of clubs, sport and drama, as well as orchestras. Drama is a popular GCSE and A level subject. Whole school involved in productions of eg Oliver! The lower sixth runs clubs for younger girls including drama, pop choirs and orchestras. Winter and spring concerts held each year involving all year groups. Each subject has a club as well. All clubs are run at lunch times as after-school not successful because of the large area girls travel from. DofE offered at bronze and gold level and the school has recently become a licensed centre.

Art very popular with a thriving department that achieved gold Artsmark. Great to see the art rooms decorated by the girls from the gifted and talented group; they are given a free rein with the paints and their creativity. Tech block very well equipped with lots of girls' work on display. They have a lathe, laser and 3D printers, quite unusual for a girls' school – no sexism here, hurrah. Textile room impressive. More cake being made in the food tech rooms.

Background and atmosphere: Based at its present site for 50 years; the 60s architecture is not particularly inspiring. Go inside and it's another story altogether. The head's description of 'the feel of the place' is apparent straight away. We were greeted with smiles from the girls running a cake stall in reception for charity – yet more cake. The main building has lots of bright airy spaces. Large windows letting in lots of light. Some very narrow staircases and corridors but no sense of overcrowding. All very disciplined at lesson changeovers.

A school in the heart of the Fenland town of Spalding that has a strong sense of community, and is very much involved with it. A large school, that must seem vast to some of the girls coming from tiny village schools in the outlying rural areas. They're aware of this, and every girl is visited at her junior school prior to starting in year 7 – an admirable undertaking, as there are around 70 of them. Successful induction days help, and a summer school is now attended by virtually all newcomers. Friendly year 8 mentors on hand as well.

Plenty of outside spaces for al fresco dining dotted around the school. Just as well, as according to one mother: 'There just isn't enough room in the dining room for the girls to sit down and eat together, something that I think is important.' Food given high praise by our guides. Delightful to walk outside and pick up the scent of roses from the flower beds.

Uniform changed from short skirts to longer pleated ones. 'I would like to see the girls in blazers,' said one mother, 'but the pleated longer skirts are definitely an improvement.' Sixth formers wear their own clothes, but need to be smart.

A strong school council that appears to have influence. 'We campaigned for an extra study period and got it,' said a guide.

Pastoral care, well-being and discipline: All parents we spoke to praised the discipline. 'The girls know where they stand and what is expected of them,' was said more than once. 'They have a very strong mobile phone policy, that is adhered to strictly, excellent.' Pastoral staff are also teachers, a policy the head is very keen on. 'It means the pastoral staff know the girls well as they are with them in the classroom.' It appears effective. One parent told us, 'They quickly picked up an issue with my daughter and were in touch immediately.' Pastoral issues appear to be dealt with quickly and effectively. 'They know my daughter and the other girls well,' was said more than once.

The girls stay in the same form up to year 11 and are encouraged to socialise within that group. So much so that in year 7 they are not allowed to gather in other form rooms. 'It stops one room being completely overcrowded and makes us tighter with our own form,' said a mole. Sixth formers are encouraged to be mentors and have the Jackson Room, where younger girls are encouraged to go to discuss any worries. Training is given to the volunteers who seem to be able to alleviate most tensions. Good to see that the school is aware of mental health issues and 'girls' problems' in general.

Pupils and parents: The brightest girls in the area, from all backgrounds. Unusually for a grammar school, the vast majority of girls are not from privileged homes, reflecting the area itself. A small, but growing contingent from Eastern European and Asian backgrounds. Friendly, happy girls with high aspirations, matching their parents. Many girls are second or third generation in their family to be pupils.

Entrance: Lincolnshire 11+ selection test sat by all pupils. All those who attain the grade are usually accommodated, even though the school is slightly oversubscribed. Pupils come from a large area covering South Holland, out to Wisbech and Peterborough in Cambridgeshire, with over 70 feeder schools. Entry to the sixth form, which is growing, requires six GCSEs grades 9-4 including English and maths. Grade 6 or above in the subjects to be studied for A level. A growing number of transferees join every year, from the grammar school and other local schools in the town.

Exit: Some 75 per cent stay on to the sixth form, with those that leave mostly following vocational courses; a few to the local boys' grammar. The vast majority of sixth formers go to university, about 25 per cent to Russell Groups. Two medics in 2018. The odd apprenticeship or Forces. Very few gap years taken.

Remarks: A friendly, successful school that many aspire to, and parents relish. Often chosen over local private education on offer, and we can see why. The policy of eating lots of cake is obviously working.

Spratton Hall

Smith Street, Spratton, Northampton NN6 8HP

Ages 4–13 **Pupils** 376

Fees: £10,050 – £15,060 pa

01604 847292
www.sprattonhall.com

Head master: Since 2014, Simon Clarke BA (40s), who had been deputy (and pupil) at the school before taking over as head. Educated at Trent College and University of Surrey, he brought a wealth of experience when he returned to Spratton from excellent schools such as Gresham's and Millfield, where he was head of English and drama. A good deputy never upstages his head, so people may worry that a deputy taking over will not command centre stage effectively, but Simon's valuable experience as six years as deputy is much appreciated by everyone. He knows the children, parents and staff and hit the ground running. He understands the essential USPs of Spratton and is determined to build on them. He hasn't frightened the horses by imposing some grand new plan on everyone, but with considerable charm and diplomacy is moving the school forward to ensure its premier position in the region.

The already excellent pastoral care is enhanced by a magnificent kindness tree where children and staff add leaves to recognise acts of goodness and understanding. The already stunning academic rigour is enhanced by his emphasis on independent learning. Already at the forefront nationally in the use of IT, he runs very regular staff training to introduce everyone to get more advanced IT in the field of teaching and learning. He has a very strong senior leadership team round him. Parents love the fact that he meets and greets everyone as they come into school and when parents collect at the end of the day. 'It stops any small niggles building up,' he says. He has three children at the school and his wife is immersed in classroom life. He exudes a warmth and sharp intelligence (perhaps it is those piercing blue eyes) that gives confidence to the school community.

Entrance: Get your name down now! This is one of those schools that fills up from the maternity ward. Most children join in reception. There are occasional places higher up the school, as families leave the area. Children registered for reception visit the school on five occasions during the summer term before they start in September. They are observed and assessed by staff. If teachers have major concerns they are discussed at length with parents. Any year 1s and 2s will come in for a day and again be informally observed followed by an in-depth meeting with the family. Anyone wanting to join after that will take tests in reading, writing, spelling, maths and non-verbal reasoning.

Exit: The head talks to parents at the start of year 5 about future options and expects to meet with each family individually that year. Most go on to the big midlands' public schools, including Rugby, Oakham, Oundle, Uppingham, Stowe and Harrow. There are an impressive number of scholarships – academic but also sports, drama, music and DT. The head built up relations with these schools when he was deputy and is well positioned to advise parents on where is right for their child.

Remarks: Yes, it is a brilliant all round school, to which parents testify and children confirm by not being able to agree on what is best about Spratton, but it is also a school that is a big hitter nationally in a number of areas, perhaps most notably IT. This is deeply embedded. The school uses the tablets which all the older children have not just for word processing and research but for changing the very nature of teaching and learning. Children film their own science experiments to review at home. Teachers film their introduction to new topics and post on the school intranet. The staff training programme and rate of innovation is impressive.

Learning support is exceptional in its flexibility, rigour and inclusivity. There is no extra charge for it. If your child has been away from school for a week or two, or is just unwell and needs some intense work to catch up on, say, maths, the learning support kicks in. If a child has mild learning difficulties or dyslexia, there may be one-to-one sessions, or work in small groups when the team can see that is more helpful. Parents comment on the significant progress made by the children and how the fact you need some extra help from time to time is regarded as the norm for making the best progress you can, rather than something about which children and parents feel a bit embarrassed. Small class sizes (about 16 in a class) help, of course, as do the teaching assistants who are an integral part of the personalised learning agenda, and are as well informed as teachers about the learning needs of every child. Parents spoke admiringly of the quality of the teachers. The head of pre-prep, herself a totally committed and enthusiastic leader, says her first criterion for appointing teachers is that they must be inspirational, and we saw some of that.

Closely connected, and central to the success of the whole story, is the pastoral care. This is where the school's holistic view of the child is really lived out on a day by day basis. There are daily senior management team (SMT) meetings, to go through not only the smooth running of the day (of which more later) but the progress of individual children. 'We nip any problems in the bud', members of the SMT reiterated to us. Intervention is swift, effective and, parents tell us, discreet. The pastoral care and support staff have the reputation for sticking with a child who might be a bit quirky and not conform to everyone's idea of the perfect pupil. On the very few discipline problems that get beyond the forgetting-the-correct-equipment level, the school has a reputation for being firm but caring. In the prep department, classes are mixed up every year so the children get to know the whole year group well.

The house system is seen by staff as being key to the positive sense of community. As well as the usual competitions, children get house marks for pleasing behaviour and can lose marks for the reverse. These house totals are read out in assembly every week and when we visited, there was a palpable hush of anticipation and sitting forward on seats as the results were announced. The houses are also responsible for raising money and awareness of specific charities that the children choose. The house system allows for a number of significant positions of responsibility at the senior end of the school. The school is keen that year 8s do experience leadership, and even those who are not getting the coveted top positions have opportunities to take on other responsible roles.

Rarely do we come across a school where the parents are in complete awe of its efficiency. Usually there is the odd grumble that the school doesn't keep us informed about a minor change, but at Spratton, it is the parents who are worried about not quite coming up to scratch and letting everyone down by forgetting some date that has clearly been flagged up by the school. 'Highly professional' and 'superbly organized' are words parents come up with first when asked about the unique qualities of Spratton. 'Run like a commercial business,' said one, 'fiercely efficient'. It is an incredibly well-oiled machine as far as communications are concerned and very much appreciated.

On a more informal level, parents can have breakfast at school with their children when they drop them off, a boon for the busy family.

Everything else is in place, as one would expect. It is a broad curriculum, including French from year 1 and Latin from year 6. Cookery has recently been added to the design and technology curriculum and regularly comes top of the popularity stakes. One of the many male teachers delivers some of this, presenting a very encouraging role model for the boys. There is no doubt that in years 7 and 8, there is an emphasis on common entrance. Most parents want this, but one or two told us that others found it all 'a bit intense'. The pressure clearly builds up, but most felt it was carefully managed so as not to overwhelm. There is setting quite early and tests with revision are introduced soon to ensure everyone is exam ready in time. Even the 4 year olds have spellings to learn once a week.

There is a lot on offer on the extracurricular front. Sport is strong and the school does well competitively, particularly considering it is not huge. Cross-country is popular and successful. The aim is that every child will play in a team and it is certainly not just the A teams that get regular fixtures. Each team has its own coach. Arts are a strength. Most of the children take individual instrumental lessons, which feed into the high quality of the school music making. There is a drama production in the school theatre each year for every year group, as well as drama club productions. Artwork hangs all over the school – the aim is that every child should have at least two pieces on display at any one time. A recent term's theme of Alice in Wonderland produced some brilliant work in a range of media.

The original building exudes Georgian elegance and calm. Much of the teaching takes place in purpose built classrooms as the school has developed the site since it took over in 1951. The classrooms are bright, displays lively, there is a well-stocked library, drama space, music rooms, sports hall, theatre, three science labs and three IT suites. Everything you could possible expect in fact, except a swimming pool. The outdoor sports facilities are amazing and the higher fields have a wonderful view over the Northamptonshire countryside.

Senior schools say Spratton children are well-rounded, work hard and are fun. That is quite a big part of every parent's dream.

Stamford High School

Linked with Stamford School, Stamford Junior School

St Martin's, Stamford, Lincolnshire PE9 2LL

Ages 11–18 **Pupils** 606 **Sixth form** 182 **Boarders** 45 full, 15 weekly, 12 flexi **C of E**

Fees: Day £15,318; Boarding £21,552 – £28,446 pa

01780 484200
www.ses.lincs.sch.uk

Head: Since 2015, Mrs Vicky Buckman, 50s. The daughter and sister of heads, she grew up in the schoolhouse of a large urban grammar school in Cheshire which she later attended. Never planned to follow in their footsteps, but in her final year at Leeds University (BSc agricultural and animal sciences) she decided teaching was for her. Her first post was at Christ's Hospital in West Sussex where, at the age of 25, she became the youngest ever housemistress. 'It was a way of life and was great fun,' she says. 'I get how girls work. I got used to championing them.' In 2006 she moved to become deputy head of City of London Freeman's School. Has always worked in the independent sector.

Comes across as friendly, approachable and positive. One of her first jobs was to move her office 'from the back of beyond' to the ground floor so she could see what was going on. Teaches biology to year 8. 'I think it's important everyone sees the head teaching and writing reports,' she says. 'And it keeps my hand in.'

When Mrs Buckman started she asked pupils to give her time to get to grips with the role and explained that, initially, they might not see that much of her. The girls say she's now out and about – eating with them in the dining hall, attending concerts and supporting sports teams on the touchline. Clearly wants to be visible.

Every Wednesday from 8 to 8.30am she has Open Door when girls can go to her office and talk to her about anything on their mind. They seem to like this.

A trained ISI inspector, she is also a keen musician, gardener and swimmer and a qualified open water scuba diver. She believes in responsible risk-taking, something that particularly resonates with girls, she says.

Married to Stephen, a vicar; they have a son and daughter, both in their 20s, and a family cat called Borodin 'who is large, fluffy and ginger,' she says.

Mrs Buckman feels she has been very lucky getting the headship and we get the impression she is there for the long haul.The ISI inspected the school in the third week of the 2017 autumn term. At the time of writing she had seen a copy of the draft report. 'It was good and fair,' is all she will say at this stage.

Academic matters: The head believes if girls work hard, listen to advice and take advantage of all the opportunities anything is possible. 'I want them to be the best they can,' she says. It is certainly no academic pressure cooker. There is pressure and competition but girls we spoke to said this comes from each other rather than teachers. As one year 11 pupil said, 'The school pushes us to work hard but teachers also encourage us to take a step back before launching ourselves completely into revision. A lot of the pressure comes from ourselves because we want to do well. Our teachers are so passionate about their subjects and that rubs off on us so that we become passionate too.'

One pupil went as far as saying, 'They inspire me. I thought I wanted to become a lawyer but I'm now thinking of becoming a teacher.'

There's mutual respect here and you get the impression that although expectations are high the school has a friendly, caring environment where girls can ask for help and support if they need it. Class sizes around 20 with no more than 14 pupils for A level subjects. Teaching staff ratio of women to men is 50:50. The head's senior leadership team comprises mostly women.

Stamford High School forms part of Stamford Endowed Schools (SES,) which also includes Stamford Nursery and Junior Schools and Stamford School (boys). SES uses the diamond model which involves girls and boys being taught together in the junior school, separately in their senior schools then together again in the sixth form.

The girls seem to like this approach. As one younger pupil pointed out, 'It's nice having boys close by but good you don't have to see them all the time.' And a sixth former added, 'It's been the perfect mix for me. Having just girls around in senior school allowed me to grow up freely. In the sixth form it's felt like starting a new school and I've enjoyed mixing with the boys.'

The head believes more and more schools will follow Stamford's example: 'We became a diamond school in 2000 but we will always be true to the founding principle that we are a single sex school with a mixed sixth form. Girls thrive in lessons here in a way that they don't in a co-ed school. They ask questions, they are supportive of each other. Classes are more productive and teachers are teaching in one style to meet the needs of girls. Inevitably, in a co-ed school you tend to teach to the boys rather than the girls. The model works well because it offers the best of both worlds.'

Automatic entry from the junior school. Everyone else sits an entrance exam (non-verbal reasoning, maths and English). This means the ability range is quite broad. Most take 10 GCSEs including three sciences and a language; in 2018, 55 per cent of grades were A*-A/9-7. Rich choice of languages on offer: French or Spanish in year 7 then can add German or Russian in year 8. The brightest currently take French a year early then complete a short course in Spanish, although this is under review.

The five GCSEs at grade 6 boundary for progressing to the sixth form doesn't seem to be set in stone, according to some parents. We checked with the head who says each case is treated individually and there is flexibility. 'Ultimately we want our girls to achieve something for their efforts over two years,' she says. 'For some, a coursework approach may be better.'

Some 26 subjects offered at A level plus BTecs in sports science and business. Most study three A levels. Most popular and strongest performing subjects, with girls as well as boys, are biology, chemistry and maths. The joint sixth formers achieved 62 per cent A*-B, 35 per cent A*/A grades in 2018.

The school currently has no statemented pupils but has a watching brief on 195 girls who are on a learning needs list. These are pupils who have a below average score on a test that measures skills such as verbal reasoning, working speed and memory, mostly pupils with dyslexia. All teachers are aware of those pupils on the list and make adjustments in the classroom to meet learning needs. Extra lessons also available for those with English as an alternative language. No charge for special support although a nominal fee is added if a pupil gets extra help over lunchtime.

Many go on to Russell Group universities, but the head accepts that university isn't for everyone and says an increasing number are applying for apprenticeships, which she supports.

Games, options, the arts: Plenty of sport on offer including hockey, netball, cross-country, gymnastics, tennis, athletics, badminton and sailing (at nearby Rutland Water) with success at county, regional and national level. The U14 hockey team is currently county champions. We counted some 18 hockey teams and 24 netball teams so there seems lots of opportunity to have a go whatever your level, particularly lower down the school. For hockey, some age groups field three or four teams and at U12 there are five. Girls in the top teams are expected to commit to several training sessions a week and a match at the weekend, not unusual in the independent sector. As one parent pointed out, 'If you are sporty, a lot is expected of you.'

Fantastic facilities available – a £6.1m SES sports centre complete with all mod cons including fitness suite and 25m indoor pool. These are a 20-minute walk away at the boys' school – not ideal, but part and parcel of being a town centre school. Swimming available at the junior school's pool. Stamford High School does have its own on site sports hall, which has recently been updated to house a fitness suite.

Some 176 music lessons every week with plenty of concerts (string and band), choirs and ensembles. Dance productions too. A state-of-the-art performing arts centre at Stamford School is the venue for large scale productions, such as Grease, Les Misérables, and Hairspray. The High School has its own hall which has recently been refurbished with a portable stage and retractable seating so it can seat 600. More than 280 pupils take speech and drama and many are prepared for the LAMDA (London Academy) exams.

Regular visits to art galleries and exhibitions and recent overseas trips to Italy and Paris. No Saturday morning school but more than 80 voluntary activities offered such as bridge, golf and driving lessons for 16 year olds. Thriving CCF – this year's new recruits in the army section numbered 12 boys and 31 girls. Around 40 gold D of E awards each year. Girls encouraged to volunteer and get involved in the local community through charity work.

Boarding: This is a day school with about 10 per cent boarders. Around a quarter of these are from overseas and the school is actively recruiting with recent trips to mainland China, Russia, Ukraine, Thailand, the US and Nigeria. The rest are mostly local girls with parents in the Forces; Lincolnshire is home to several airbases.

Three boarding houses. We looked at Welland (11 to 16 years) – just around the corner from the school's main site and a 10-minute walk into town. It has a homely feel with two big TV rooms complete with large sofas and beanbags. Four or five students to a dorm with sixth formers sharing two to a room. Pupils also get the use of a fully fitted kitchen where they can make toast, bake cakes and even do their own laundry if they want to. There is a lovely large garden at the back. This is also home to two rabbits, which the girls help to look after.

Girls seem to enjoy a fair amount of freedom here. They are allowed to walk into town from year 7 at different times provided they are with another pupil. The houseparent is keen to encourage independence: girls can attend sleepovers or parties at the weekend with day girls provided parents give permission. The girls we spoke to loved boarding. One said if she didn't board she wouldn't do her prep – compulsory every night in the school library.

Boarders can opt for a three, four, five or seven night package. Around 22 girls stay on a Friday evening with 16 or fewer on site on a Saturday. A new service, aimed at busy London families, offers accompanied travel to and from King's Cross on Friday evenings and Monday mornings.

Background and atmosphere: Beautiful mellow limestone buildings, quirky narrow passages and stunning riverside views. What's not to like about Stamford? The SES schools sit at the heart of this picture postcard town with its 600 listed buildings (the TV adaptation of Middlemarch was filmed here). Stamford High School was founded in 1877 as part of the legacy left the schools in the Browne's Hospital Trust. It still occupies its original site on the south side of the River Welland.

The school entrance is not very obvious. We were so busy gazing up at the town's beautiful architecture that we missed it. But then we spotted a group of pupils who were obviously from SHS. The uniform is distinctive – navy blazer, long pleated below-the-knee navy skirt, white open shirt and black shoes (no heels). It sounds old fashioned but we liked it and, more importantly, the girls we saw love it. If they do have a gripe it's to do with tying their hair back, a rule the new head introduced. Parents support the head on this one, we believe.

Once inside the atmosphere is calm and orderly. Girls move about the corridors with a sense of purpose. No rushing around or shouting. On the walls hang pictures and short profiles of inspiring alumnae including Sarah Outen, the first woman to row solo across the Indian Ocean, and international Emmy award-winning actress Lucy Cohu.

Girls are friendly and come across as confident, cheerful and relaxed around their teachers. The ones we spoke to were certainly not snooty. A couple of spirited sixth formers were keen to take us on a tour, pointing out the newly-refurbished dining hall and home economics centre recently opened by former Bake Off judge Mary Berry.

They then showed us the new ideal classrooms, an initiative being rolled out as part of the head's drive to use the latest ideas and approaches in class. Interconnecting desks are covered in interactive whiteboards enabling pupils to write on their desks, save information and use digital technology to share it with the rest of the class.

Pastoral care, well-being and discipline: All girls have a form tutor who is a main point of contact for both pupils and parents. One pupil said, 'Everyone is so friendly and the teachers are so nice. If you have a problem you can go to anyone.' And a parent added, 'Pastoral care is very good. I contacted the school about an eating issue and the school was fantastic.'

Strict rules around the use of mobile phones. Years 7 to 9 must keep them in their lockers during the school day. Boarders have to hand in all devices 15 minutes before they go to bed. Some girls have tried to get round this by having several devices but the houseparent is one step ahead of them. Main sanction is being gated.

Pupils and parents: Mostly local families from a large catchment area and from all walks of life, thanks to range of bursaries available, with lots of military families who like a modern boarding option. For day girls an extensive network of bus routes from as far afield as Newark in the north to Peterborough in the south.

Some parents looked at the grammar school option but chose SES because they like the diamond model – particularly those with sons and daughters. One parent with a daughter in year 11 and a son at Stamford School said she loved the feel of the place when she looked round. 'It has a warmth about it. My daughter was very unhappy at her junior school. It was as though I had lost her, then when she started at Stamford High School I got her back. When my son and daughter come home after the first day of term they are so excited they can't stop talking. The schools are like one big happy family.'

One parent who had two daughters at the school said it suited both girls despite them having different strengths. 'My oldest is into science while my younger daughter is more into the arts and drama. But there are opportunities for both. The school is good all round.'

Another acknowledged her daughters had been very happy and had formed incredibly strong friendships. All said that given their time again they would still choose Stamford High School.

Entrance: Automatic entry from the junior school at 11. Entrance exam for outsiders and those after a scholarship.

Sixth form entrants (internal and external) schould have at least five GCSEs at grade 6.

S

Exit: Around 20-40 per cent leave after GCSEs. Nearly all sixth formers into higher education (many to Russell Group universities; two to Oxbridge and one medic in 2018) with a few to apprenticeships.

Money matters: Bursaries means-tested and up to full fees, scholarships worth between £500-£1,000 pa. Academic, music and sports scholarships available at 11+ and art, drama and all-rounder scholarships added at 13+. Similar number in the sixth form.

Remarks: Traditional atmosphere but with modern teaching methods turning out spirited, well-rounded, confident girls keen to get out there and test themselves. Former pupil Flight Lt Kirsty Moore, the first woman pilot in the Red Arrows, says, 'I arrived a shy, 11-year old and seven years later I felt ready to step out into the world and make it my own.' We think plenty more will feel inspired to do the same.

Stamford Junior School

Linked with Stamford School, Stamford High School

Kettering Road, Stamford, Lincolnshire PE9 2LR

Ages 2–11 **Pupils** 344 **Boarders** 7 full, 1 weekly (from 8 years) **C of E**

Fees: Day £9,414 – £12,102; Boarding £17,415 – £21,864 pa

01780 484400
www.ses.lincs.sch.uk

Head: Since 2012 Emma Smith (early 40s). Convent educated in Berkshire, early years BEd from Kingston University. From a Forces background, husband and sister still serving. Previously worked in the state sector in and around London. Bit of a baptism of fire at previous school. Hired as deputy head and within weeks made acting head due to a suspension. 'I had a very young staff [she was hardly Methuselah herself] with no leadership team. It was an intense experience that I enjoyed, but knew after two years I needed a change. My husband has family in Stamford, so I was delighted to get the job and go back to just teaching for a while.' Starting to get itchy feet when previous incumbent retired and was appointed head. Nice to see a rather glam head – black fingernails et al.

She's ambitious, with big plans that are coming to fruition. Reception classes have been moved into a newly converted stable block. A recent bespoke year 6 block. The school is getting larger, but with smaller class sizes, under her leadership. 'I think emotional intelligence is vital. If you are honest with children they respond well. And never underestimate them. They need to appreciate that they won't get on with everyone in life but need to treat people, particularly their contemporaries, with courtesy and respect. I want the children to bounce through the door in the morning, have an amazing day and then bounce back out again, full of what they've done. My aim is for them to learn to love learning and have a good work ethic.'

Parents are very supportive. 'She has great vision for the school and is making very positive changes,' said a year 5 parent. 'She ruffled a few feathers at first, but listens to people and has learnt to communicate with parents very effectively. Her handling of a very sad, horrible accident involving one of the pupils was exemplary. 'Parents were kept informed throughout, so avoiding any unnecessary speculation,' said a parent with two children at the school.

Entrance: First come first served into nursery and reception. A few places available higher up the school, via tests from age 7. Quite a large and growing junior school with most children coming from a 20 mile radius. Families attracted by the fact that you can almost certainly stay in the Endowed system until 18.

Exit: Some leave for other schools after nursery, but the majority go into reception. Automatic entry from year 6 into the senior schools means that from year 5 there's a sharp increase in numbers. A big chunk (some 47 per cent) go up to the senior schools, with the rest going to state sector or other independents. A couple each year are warned early that they might not cope with the senior schools. Handled sensitively.

Remarks: Part of Stamford Endowed Schools with its diamond structure. Co-ed in junior and sixth form, single sex 11-16. The junior school is situated just outside the historic town of Stamford. Feels very rural, on a very quiet, leafy, green site in a delightful setting with a very pretty playing field set in a dell. The recently converted stable block housing reception class adds to this, along with the recent nursery building. New-ish year 6 building awash with iPads etc. Lots of outside space, climbing frames and toys obviously well used. The classrooms spill into the outside space down here through large French windows, which were flung wide during our visit. Lots of newly-planted seedlings in the garden. All year 5s do nursery duty at lunch time and go down to help the toddlers. The main building is surrounded by pitches, grass and Astroturf. New learning garden and adventure area by the river. Fresh air seems to be king at this school. Windows are flung wide and the garden is inside with vases of flowers everywhere – all bright and cheerful.

Many parents relocating to Stamford from London, often returning to their roots, choose the school. The town was recently voted by The Sunday Times as the best place in England to live, and we can see why. A lot of pupils are second or third generation. 'We came from a state school in London and I was very worried about fitting in,' said one parent. 'We couldn't have been made more welcome, by the school, or other parents. I think it's a fabulous school. My children have gone from strength to strength and will try anything now, whereas they were very cautious before.'

All children learn musical instruments. Recorder for the early years, strings from year 2 (poor parents) and piano in year 5 and 6. Lots of clubs, ranging from chess to gardening, sewing, sports and orchestra, and there's even a left handed club. New clubs for year 6 include DR, science awards and gardening club, plus Saturday cookery and craft sessions. Artwork all over the place, and it's good. One of the teachers has her work displayed and on sale, great for the pupils to see.

Sport is thriving and open to all. School gymnasts were U11 Mixed Floor and Vault National Champions. Rugby, hockey, netball, tennis and swimming teams are doing well. 'The sport is tremendous, but I am disappointed that as a latecomer to the school my son has found it hard to break into some of the A teams, as there are "invitation only" squads for the best players,' said a parent. 'It is hard to improve and catch up if these squads are getting extra coaching. That said, both of my children are very happy and it's my only gripe'.

A lot of learning is through play in the early years. 'We came from overseas where a lot of emphasis was on academic success. I worried at first that the children didn't seem to be pushed hard enough. But I soon accepted that the softly, softly approach works well. My children have been transformed and are so much more relaxed and happy.' 'What I really like about the school is that it feels like a local school and very much part of the community,' another parent told us.

Spanish and French taught from year 3, Italian also available. They have a thumb scanner for the library; we enjoyed that. Every child reads for 15 minutes in class daily. Science week when we visited. Lots of excitement about making false blood for homework – from pupils and parents. ILIC – independent learning and intellectual curiosity – is a big ethos throughout all three schools, and they start them young, instilling a good, enthusiastic work ethic.

Special needs not overlooked. Some 63 have SEN status. SENCo teachers praised by parents. 'My child joined in year 3 and is on the autistic spectrum. The bedding in period took a while, but the school was very accommodating and listened to professional advice. My child has gone from strength to strength and is thriving'. Another mother said, 'My son is dyslexic and gets lot of support. Extra lessons, spelling groups and assistance are given if needed, but he is not made to feel different.'

Boarding starts in year 3. Most boarders are flexi or weekly, with handful of Forces children full time. Boarding house is a lovely, honey coloured stone building situated in the dell. Large garden with climbing frames, chickens and rabbits. We were welcomed by two slipper clad boarders who showed us every inch, chatting all the while. Definitely home from home; they even have jobs to do, with a rota. Nice and bright and airy. No phones upstairs, taken away at night, and no social networking. 'The children need to interact and be sociable, not glued to a phone,' the likeable housemistress told us. Homework supervised and lots of weekend trips: a forthcoming visit to the Natural History Museum involving a sleepover eagerly anticipated. Scruffy the dog is very much part of the boarding family.

There's a very strong parents' association that offers huge support to the school, providing funding for various trips and talks. They're listened to as well. The head is reducing class sizes because of parental pressure – mutual respect is the impression we got.

Parents didn't need to tell us that this is a happy school; we could see it for ourselves. Our delightful guides were proud, chatty and cheerful. Food is good, we were told, particularly the lasagne. Everywhere we went we were greeted with a cheery smile. A joyful place, offering a happy, positive start to education. A very good grounding to take to the increasingly impressive senior schools. Hard to see why you'd go elsewhere locally.

Stamford School

Linked with Stamford High School, Stamford Junior School

Southfields House, St Paul's Street, Stamford, Lincolnshire PE9 2BQ

Ages 11–18 **Pupils** 696 **Sixth form** 195 **Boarders** 43 full, 22 weekly, 22 flexi **C of E**

Fees: Day £15,318; Boarding £21,552 – £28,446 pa

01780 750300
www.ses.lincs.sch.uk

Head: Since 2016, Nick Gallop. A social and political sciences graduate from Durham, with an MSc in educational leadership and management; joined Stamford from the senior leadership team at Portsmouth Grammar School. He had been head of department at Wellington College after stints at Loughborough Grammar School and St Mary's, Walsall, so widely experienced. He knows what a good school looks like and seen how to manage change successfully.

The Stamford Endowed Schools diamond structure (co-ed junior school, single sex teaching from 11-16 then co-ed in sixth form) means Nick works closely with the two other heads and chief exec, Will Phelan, who was the popular former head of Stamford School. The governors did well keeping hold of Will and making an outstanding appointment in Nick. The boys say he is very open and friendly, 'not at all stuffy', and has really tried to get to know them. He is enjoying the contrasts with the south and finds the community welcoming, open and modest. One of his tasks has been to reflect to the school just how first rate it is. The boys are getting the best education they could get anywhere, he tells us.

He is lively and very articulate and boys and staff tell us he is a very good listener. He has the reputation for being reliable and trustworthy as well as flexible enough to respond to new challenges. Parents enjoy talking to him at social events and appreciate his Twitter feed and use of social media. He is busy making sure everyone understands the heritage of liberal educational thinking. He has encouraged a broadening of the year 7 and 8 curriculum, introducing The Challenge, a programme designed to embed cross-curricular skills.

He is articulating the values the school holds dear, defining what it means to be a good man in today's world. He wants the boys to be clear that kindness, respect and discipline are values that underpin everything at the school. He holds creativity to be a key 21st century skill, for the technologically savvy as well as for the artist and entrepreneur, and he is ensuring that the boys absorb all these elements through the opportunities Stamford offers. 'He is a forward looking head,' one parent told us.

Nick is a strong advocate, as you would expect, of the diamond model. It allows boys at an age when they could drift to organise events and take on formal caring roles such as mentoring, which in co-ed schools he has seen dominated by girls. Sport is a personal passion and he believes in the values of cooperation and belonging that team sports can bring. He is married to a teacher, has two daughters in the junior school and has been known to play the ukulele in a school rock concert.

Academic matters: Given a fairly broad academic ability range on entry, results are good. In 2018, 35 per cent A*/A and 62 per cent A*-B grades at A level in the joint sixth form with Stamford High, and at GCSE 55 per cent A*-A/9-7 grades. EPQ results strong, as are BTec sport level 3, though numbers here are small at the moment. They have also introduced a BTec in business studies. There is considerable flexibility around finding the right exam course for a particular cohort of boys – 'just because we have always done that one' won't wash here. French, German, Spanish and Russian are all available as well as Latin and get excellent results.

There is a serious focus on the intellectual hinterland around the curriculum. Developing intellectual curiosity as well as aspiration is important. Boys have set up a school blog to voice ideas on a range of academic matters. In the sixth form, an enrichment module extends the core three A level curriculum to include, for example, options of EPQ work, Microsoft accredited courses, sports leadership, an extra AS or even survival cooking. The 1532 Club offers serious academic enrichment outside the classroom. There are debates, talks by staff, boys, old boys and visitors aimed at introducing topics not necessarily in the curriculum. It can be used as another way of sharing the fascinating EPQ projects and adding to the preparation for university.

Every other Thursday afternoon, the whole school is off timetable. We happened to visit on a Thursday and enjoyed the amazing buzz. Year 7 were building a mechanical car and programming it for the climax of the afternoon, a race. Year 10 and 11 were asking questions in the middle school debating finals and year 9 were completely absorbed in a complicated trade game. It was a complete delight to observe these learning opportunities way outside of any exam curriculum.

There is a real thirst to draw on the intellectual world beyond school too. A group of sixth formers had just arrived back from a cutting edge science conference in Texas that had generated huge enthusiasm.

Everyone told us maths and sciences are strong and popular. The labs have all recently been refurbished, with space for practicals and for theoretical learning. There is a telescope and astronomy area. Some classrooms have walls are all covered in whiteboards and the tables to be written on.

Learning support is taken very seriously. Most learning support assistants work within classes and this has had a very positive impact on progress. The school is constantly reviewing data to determine when to set and who will succeed best where. There is some one-to-one learning support available, normally focussing on study skills. One EAL specialist. A parent with two mildly dyslexic sons spoke appreciatively of how the school kept her very well informed of just what interventions and progress were going on.

Boys, particularly those who have experience of other schools, comment on how excellent the teaching is and how teachers are 'always there for you'. There are occasional Saturday morning sessions as GCSEs loom. Teachers are happy to be emailed with an academic problem and respond very quickly.

Games, options, the arts: The head is rightly proud of the large numbers of boys who sing in the various choirs; over 100 year 7 and 8s make up a non-auditioned junior choir. There are lots of ensembles to cater for different levels and tastes including rock bands. We watched a rehearsal where musicians from the boys' and girls' schools played side by side with a Royal Marines Band to prepare for a joint town concert that evening. If it allowed the band leader to extol a music career in the Marines (no tuition fees, a degree, getting paid for playing your instrument), who can blame him?

All years 7 and 8 take performing arts subjects and there is a very healthy take up of drama and theatre studies at A level and GCSE. Drama is very popular and the staff – who teach across the boys' and girls' schools – are 'fantastic', according to parents and boys. SES remains one of the largest independent examination centres for LAMDA with around half getting distinction. Joint productions with the girls' school; rehearsals for Hairspray were in full swing when we visited. There is a big musical every three years and a number of smaller productions in between. House drama competitions ensure everyone is involved, even if not the next RSC star. There is a large performing arts centre with a theatre seating about 350 as well as smaller performance spaces.

Masses of sport goes on with the aim to encourage a life-long commitment to physicality, so there are options alongside the major sports, and the fitness suite is well used. 'It really is not just a rugby school', parents were keen to assure us, with fresh opportunities such as water polo. At the elite end, some boys are in national development squads and the teams do well in highly competitive fixture programmes. 'But if you have a pair of boots and want to play, you will be put in a team – the D, E and F teams have lots of matches too', we were told by both parents and staff. Once a year the whole school community takes part in the Burghley Run, a cross-country in the glorious near-by Burghley House grounds. A bonding experience, we are told, whether you love it or loathe it.

There is a thriving joint CCF (of three sections) with a contingent of about 350 cadets – one of the oldest and largest in the UK. DofE, also joint, is taken seriously here along with debating, astronomy club, robotics, dissection club, bush craft, chess – and on the list goes. The boys say there is no pressure to do things but they are clearly in tune with the school's message that there is something that everyone can feel passionate about. Parents like the fact that a boy doesn't have to be the best rugby player to be respected. 'They can have as quirky interests as they like,' one parent told us, 'and the others will just be very interested in them too'.

Community service features strongly. Boys help at a home for the elderly, reading and writing with visually impaired people. The staff believe it is this sort of exposure to the needs of the wider society that informs the boys' future careers just as much as their A level results.

Politics in the widest sense is a priority for the head. He encourages the boys to learn about and discuss current affairs and they are well informed and interested.

Boarding: The boarding side of the chool is relatively small and this creates, the boys say, a very close-knit community, though one that is thoroughly integrated with the rest of the school. Resident tutors and housemasters also teach, so there is always help at hand with homework. There are overseas boarders from a range of countries, but flexi-boarding – often taken advantage of by London families – is increasingly popular. Facilities are just right for boys and have recently been upgraded. We were particularly impressed by the very attractive large house kitchen where the boys all congregate after prep. There are billiards, snooker, computers, ping pong, lots of sport on Saturdays and trips to adventure parks, bowling, ice-skating, but also space to just be, for the boy who wants none of those things.

There are occasions when all the boarders across the SES schools get together. The Christmas formal meal for the seniors is one and Chinese New Year another. The boys are keen that these opportunities should increase and like the idea of building a whole school boarding identity.

Background and atmosphere: Stamford, the town, must be one of the most charming urban environments in the country, with its gracious Georgian principal streets and the river flowing through. The main school site is amazingly spacious and open considering that it is in the centre of the town. Other buildings are close by. This aids the sense that Stamford School is at the heart of Stamford itself, and the link is very important to everyone there. Some of the buildings date back to the original foundation in 1532, including a lovely chapel, and there are also modern buildings – some less attractive but serviceable, others pleasing. The boys like the fact they can stroll out into the town or do the 10 minute walk to the girls' school for some sixth form lessons.

The school also keeps close ties with old boys, quite a number of whom send their own children here. Old boys visit to share their career experiences and there's an overseas network that can be tapped into. Midnight mass on Christmas Eve in the school chapel attracts back old boys as well as staff, present pupils and a choir of 50. Old boys drop in whenever they are back in Stamford and there were a few helping with the Hairspray production.

The diamond structure is very popular. Sixth form boys said they all felt the benefits of the joint sixth form with the girls' school and increasing activities together. 'It gets a bit more serious in the sixth form, with the girls joining us,' some said, though a few told us 'they do talk a lot'. Younger boys said they would like more integration with the girls and with the juniors, but certainly don't want to have them there all the time.

There is a purposeful but relaxed atmosphere round the school. Parents say it is an environment where boys are respected for working hard and being clever. The boys we met were completely charming – open, modest, well grounded.

Pastoral care, well-being and discipline: The behaviour round school was excellent without being regimented. Boys say that most discipline issues are sorted out at an individual level with teachers spending time in one-to-one meetings. There are the usual grades of detentions, suspension and exit, but not much gets to the serious level. Boys can lose their scholarships if they don't pull their weight academically.

The assemblies in the old chapel take place in the middle of the day and boys say these are a welcome break in their busy day for quiet reflection on a broadly Christian theme. There are informal staff mentors when needed and overall we sensed a concerned, caring staff. Boys and parents clearly feel relationships are very positive.

The PSHE programme underpins the pastoral ethos. Boys felt it was relevant and forward looking, covering topics such as feminism and anorexia, as well as well-trodden internet safety topics.

Pupils and parents: It is usual in these reports to say how smart everyone looked. Well, the boys didn't, particularly – what they did look like was normal adolescent boys, which backs up the school's view that it is interested in individuals not production lines. Much more important than the odd shirt untucked was the obvious friendliness and openness of the boys. Parents comment on the healthy social mix in the school, though a few, who remember when the school could offer a lot of assisted places paid for by the local authority, are conscious that there are more well-heeled families than there used to be. Many parents are from business backgrounds, with quite a few working in London.

An extensive network of school buses brings children in from the surrounding areas – the farming villages but also Peterborough, Grantham, Newark, which widens the social mix. We talked to a number of parents who are both working to pay the fees.

Entrance: Main entrance at year 7, with papers including English and maths, and GL assessment reasoning tests for ability as well as attainment. 'It is only a snapshot', says the head. The school tries to look deeper into the profile of each applicant, weighing up their all round skills and the characteristics of determination and aspiration. About 40 per cent of boys come from the junior school, the rest from a mix of state and independent local schools.

For automatic entry into sixth form (year 12), at least five GCSE passes at grade 6 or better, including in the subjects to be studied at A level. Some 20 or 30 join from outside and they usually integrate quickly and well, a testament to the friendly atmosphere.

Although the school is oversubscribed and increasingly so, the raw score is not the only criteria – which is good news for boys who don't perform at their best in exams but would flourish in the Stamford environment. The school is interested in the aspirations of the family and whether they will buy into Stamford School values.

Exit: Some 20 per cent leave after GCSEs. About 90 per cent of sixth form leavers to university – all over the country and to read a wide range of subjects, including two to Oxbridge and one medic in 2018. Increasing interest is being shown in apprenticeship schemes and other high quality technical training options.

Money matters: This is a value for money school. Fees are very moderate for the independent sector in this part of the world, particularly on the boarding side. Scholarships and bursaries are available. About a fifth of all families receive some bursary support

Remarks: There are big hitters in the area and Stamford is well able to hold its own. Those much more expensive schools probably win out on the uniformity of excellent buildings and state-of-the-art facilities, but Stamford is determined to keep the school as accessible to as many as possible while not compromising the things that really matter in a boy's education. Parents were very aware of the richness of the opportunities and all saw the school as producing grounded individuals who can function in the real world. It is a gem of a school.

Stephen Perse Senior School

Linked with Dame Bradbury's School, Stephen Perse Junior School, Stephen Perse 6th Form College, Stephen Perse Pre-Prep (City), Stephen Perse Pre-Prep (Madingley)

Union Road, Cambridge, Cambridgeshire CB2 1HF

Ages 11–16 **Pupils** 538

Fees: £17,550 pa

01223 454700
www.stephenperse.com

Head: Since 2016, David Walker, late 30s. Graduated from Bristol with a first in physics and philosophy. Disillusioned by the experience of working in industry while a student, volunteered as a science teacher in a tough state school instead and ended up taking PGCE, against the advice of his colleagues. Two years of VSO in West Africa teaching maths and physics also developed his computer skills. Back in the UK, had a spell at Whitgift and then scaled the ranks during 10 years at Wellington College (their youngest housemaster).

This is his first headship – a clever appointment by the Stephen Perse Foundation of a fresh face to usher in a new era. Laid-back and likeable, a good line in banter with the kids, popular with parents and staff. Don't be fooled by the relaxed bonhomie – misses nothing. Married, with small son at SPF's Madingley Pre-Prep.

Principal is Tricia Kelleher, previously head of Perse School for Girls, now 'effectively chief executive' of the Stephen Perse Foundation of seven schools which is largely her brainchild. Today SPF offers a seamless learning journey for girls and boys aged 3 to 20 – 'it's about the schools supporting the learner rather the other way around, quite a pioneering model,' she says. 'Overall, we are a thinking school, an inclusive school with humanity, compassion and social responsibility; value added is more important than exam results.'

Academic matters: In 2018, a hugely impressive 81 per cent A*-A/9-7 at GCSEs. 'I rail against the word "academic",' says head. 'It only needs the addition of "hothouse" to be exactly what we are not. I prefer intellectual, but on top of that we're innovative, creative, collaborative, diverse..' All pupils (girls at the moment – first cohort of boys admitted in year 7 in September 2017, taught separately according to diamond model) take 10 GCSEs including at least one language (French, Spanish, German, Russian, Mandarin, Latin and Greek all on offer). 'They write the GCSE timetable around us so everyone gets what they want,' approved our guide. 'You can change right up to Christmas in year 10.' Most opt for separate sciences. Set for maths but nothing else – no need given the high levels of ability.

S

Every student issued with a school-owned iPad – 'we use them all the time,' shrug students. No more than 25 in a class, inclusive policy for those with dyslexia, Aspergers etc. We saw youthful teachers of all ages working alongside their students rather than directing from the front – despite the Cambridge brain drain, SPF attracts super-bright graduates who want to make real progress in education in an environment that gives them the scope to do so. In fact, the whole school screams collaboration, from the classroom walls covered in 'surprisingly expensive' write-on paint so whole classes can work out the next step between them, to the art room tables pushed together so everyone contributes to one enormous, creative surface. 'Lots of schools try to prepare pupils for a changing future but here we do material things that lead towards that, to develop the skills that make young people fit for success in the workplace,' says head.

Much thought behind the highly conducive design of the buildings and teaching areas, particularly in the sparkling new multi-floor extension, with its 'Scandi chic', clutter-free classrooms, all white walls and splashes of the school's famous teal emulsion. Not least the ICT suite, with a legion of Apple Macs arranged in concentric circles. Even the scrap of outdoor space remaining is given over to a basketball court and a picnic area – 'spark off each other,' the place seems to be saying. No wonder representatives from other schools ask to look around for inspiration.

Games, options, the arts: Huge new semi-basement sports hall and the only rooftop Astro pitch in Cambridge have revolutionised PE provision at the school. Playing fields shared with Gonville and Caius a 15-minute walk away for organised team game training and fixtures, but now basketball, badminton, volleyball and futsal among other activities make possible two weekly enrichment sessions, one of which must be a sport, and clubs before and after school and at lunchtime. Anglia Ruskin university students run sessions in return for use of the hall for their own training. Regular sports for boys are cricket and football, touch rugby and hockey; hockey and cricket for girls but an enormous range besides.

Two music classrooms and 'octagon' rehearsal space. 'I go to rock school after school so we use this whole space,' said one of our guides, looking forward to the forthcoming Battle of the Bands. Practice rooms for instrumentalists – unusual requests considered. Mixing desk used by popular drama tech and music tech clubs; student-run radio station studio produces weekly podcast. Guitars, drums and plenty of other instruments available for students to try out. Orchestras, choirs and a list of ensembles (including sax quartet), many student initiated.

Art housed in wonderful building down the street (used to be the sixth form), set out with sociable working spaces on the ground floor for years 7 to 9 and GCSE students who opt for fine art, digital art, textiles or sculpture. Upstairs, atelier-style areas for A level/IB students (based at Stephen Perse Foundation 6th Form 10 minutes away by bus) and exhibition space. Comprehensive DT workshop in main school building with areas for particular materials.

'Big show' every other year for year 10s to upper sixth – Bugsy Malone this year – and other drama productions give younger students a chance in the spotlight or behind the scenes throughout the year. Green room and impressive wardrobe of costumes, many run up by staff and students.

Years 10 and 11 enrichment sessions provide a sub-curriculum of thought-provoking, career-based and practical topics, for example psychopathology, debating and the production of Teal the school magazine; in addition, a staggering 140 clubs and activities (including DofE) to choose from each term, before and after school and at lunchtimes. Educational breadth is really shoehorned in.

Background and atmosphere: 'Visionary' is a word that crops up a lot here. In 1615 land for a Grammar Free Schoole was bequeathed by Dr Stephen Perse, a fellow of Gonville and Caius, who strongly believed that education should be a right rather than a privilege and accessible to all, regardless of means.

According to his wishes, The Perse School was founded for boys (now co-ed). In the spirit of the 19th century movement to educate women, in 1881 the Perse School for Girls opened on its current site on Union Street, a block bordered by residential streets on three sides and the University of

Cambridge department of chemistry on the fourth, and soon became known as one of the UK's most pioneering girls' schools (although initially, at least, there were boys in its kindergarten, including a young John Maynard Keynes). The school attracted even further renown as the inspiration for Cambridge-born writer and cartoonist Ronald Searle's St Trinian's books (published 1946 to 1952), about the japes of girls at a boarding school (original manuscripts are in the school's archives), though Searle has since admitted that other of the city's schoolgirls were also responsible.

After 126 years as Perse Girls, the school underwent a transformation and emerged in 2007 as the Stephen Perse Foundation with a fresh approach to the education of both girls and boys in Cambridge centring on a curriculum designed to encourage pupils to think independently, analytically, logically, creatively and imaginatively. This ethos runs through all of the seven schools that comprise the Foundation, on the 'diamond model' of co-education: while Stephen Perse Senior School educates girls and boys aged 11 to 16 on the same site but separately for the key academic subjects, Stephen Perse Junior School across the road and Dame Bradbury's in Saffron Walden cater for girls and boys aged 7 to 11 who are taught in mixed classes, as are the little ones aged 3 to 7 at Stephen Perse's City Pre-Prep (on the junior site) and the parallel Madingley Pre-Prep (on the city outskirts). At the top of the school, the genders are again reunited at Stephen Perse 6th Form, on its own self-contained site, 10 minutes from the senior school, and the recently acquired Cambridge Centre for Sixth Form Studies nearby, which offers a boarding education for students from the UK and abroad, aged 16 to 20.

The majority of the Foundation's facilities are at the senior school, but troops of children of all sizes from the various satellites have ready access to them and the educational resources being part of a larger organisation affords. The impressive visual arts centre, hall, library, music department and gymnasium are well used, not to mention the bright and flexible classrooms, basement sports hall, well-equipped ICT suite and rooftop Astro pitch of the brand new five-storey building, opened in September 2017 to coincide with the first intake of boys to year 7.

Though not flashy in the least, no expense has been spared on educational resources, with interactive whiteboards in every room, write-on walls in many and an iPad issued to every student, free of charge. Though precious little outdoor space remains on the site, the school owns its own playing fields 15 minutes' walk away at Latham Road, with all-weather pitches as well as a nature reserve and outdoor classroom, used for forest school lessons. With many of the administrative functions pooled, much effort and resource is focused on ensuring that the Foundation's ethos is lived and breathed in every corner, with regular training sessions for teaching staff and an extensive programme of cross-curricular and cross-school activities for Stephen Perse children, from correspondence between 3-year-olds in the parallel pre-school classes, to large-scale eco workshops for infants and opportunities for year 10s to mentor year 6s. 'We are not inspired by anyone else,' says principal. 'We are pioneering. The learner is at the centre of everything we do and we need to be dynamic to prepare our pupils to go out and make a difference in the dynamic world we live in; the moral purpose of education has never been so great.'

Pastoral care, well-being and discipline: Despite the growing size of the school, this remains a strength. 'We value the emotional and mental well-being of our pupils because if we do that they will thrive,' says principal. Indeed, there is a clear pastoral structure of form tutor and head of year, with counsellors on hand when need be. Few discipline issues, and a professional attitude pervades, even among the youngest. Teaching staff are pleasantly informal and classes chatty – the collaborative approach wouldn't work in silence.

Clearly a great fondness among the pupils for their school ('StevieP in common parlance') and a loyalty to each other, which has continued from the Perse Girls days. 'My mum came to the school,' says one of our guides, 'and although she doesn't like the new school colour, she says it still feels like the same school so she's happy I'm here.' What has perhaps moved on is the emphasis on health and fitness, thanks now to the sports hall and a much expanded rota of active clubs, and improved lunches in a dining hall designed to appeal to teenagers, all wood floors and white tables. Menu is on a three-week rotation with regular roasts and fish and chips, as well as daily options for pasta, jacket potato and salad. Breakfast club and late stay are also catered, as well as break-time snacks.

Pupils and parents: Pupils and parents reflect the city – global. Professionals, academics and high-flyers in the main, parents mainly work at the university, hospitals or tech firms, though some commute to London. High level of interest in their children's education and not afraid to ask the tricky questions. 'We have a great parent body here,' says head, 'very supportive. I try to embrace that relationship and make sure it's strong.' Informal information evenings for parents are well attended. 'They want to be educated on how we educate their children,' explains head. They also turn out in large numbers for arts and sport events. No formal parent forum though individual parents are welcome to air their views to the head any time.

Families mostly from Cambridge (witness the bulging bike racks) but many take advantage of the school bus shuttles from the park and ride car parks, and further afield from Newmarket and Ely. Station walkable. It will be interesting to see if the changes brought about by the Foundation (ie boys) will have an impact on the Perse girls' character; those we met remained the genuine type, enthused by learning, a touch earnest. Lower down the school, boys in a similar mould. We did detect a hint of spirit, though, that may have been lacking previously.

Notable alumnae a long list including racing driver and TV presenter Vicki Butler-Henderson, journalist and novelist Lucy Hawking, equestrienne and 2008 Olympic medal-winner Sharon Hunt, BBC diplomatic correspondent Bridget Kendall, author (of Wide Sargasso Sea) Jean Rhys, politician Angela Rumbold and author Meriol Trevor.

Entrance: Two-thirds from internal transfer (Stephen Perse Junior School and Dame Bradbury's) and the other third mainly from local state primaries. The entrance exam reflects the school – testing in English and maths with a collaborative challenge and interviews on top. Bright sparks wanted. Most join in year 7. The initial co-ed cohort 3:2 girls:boys, but school expects a more even ratio in future years, with considerable interest amongst parents of boys in the pipeline.

Exit: Slightly more than half leave after GCSEs for the high-achieving state sixth form down the road, but school anticipates that as co-ed takes hold, the pendulum will gradually swing in their favour and nearly all will continue through to Stephen Perse 6th Form, or the recently acquired Cambridge Centre for Sixth Form Studies, which offers a range of post-16 qualifications.

Money matters: Numerous scholarships and bursaries on offer, ranging from academic and sports to subject related.

Remarks: Intellectual and strategic vision has transformed this place into a model for 21st century independent schooling. Squeezing every drop of potential from its multiple sites, well-motivated staff and the offspring of surely some of the most intelligent parents in the world, the Stephen Perse Foundation represents a fresh approach to educating young people for their own benefit – and for the future.

Stephen Perse Junior School

Linked with Stephen Perse Senior School, Dame Bradbury's School, Stephen Perse Pre-Prep (City), Stephen Perse Pre-Prep (Madingley), Stephen Perse 6th Form College

St Eligius Street, Cambridge CB2 1HX

Ages 3-11 Pupils 299

Fees: £12,000 – £15,150 pa

01223 346140
www.stephenperse.com

Head of junior school: Since 2007, Katie Milne BEd (Cantab) education and geography. Originally from Dundee, soft burr. Joined the school in 1979 and was acting head twice before appointed head in 2007. Fair and kindly, firm when necessary, respected by pupils and parents, each of whom she makes it her business to get to know. 'She is everything a head teacher should be.. communicative, responsible, a leader, always present, and always approachable... her efficiency and caring should be a model for all head teachers,' enthused a parent. A geographer, but now teaches RS. Has deftly overseen the inclusion of boys as part of the Stephen Perse Foundation's move to the diamond structure of co-education. Works closely with head of pre-prep Sarah Holyoake and head of senior school David Walker. 'We're now working as a larger group of specialists across the 3-11 [pre-preps and junior] schools, so it's a creative learning journey for the staff as well as pupils,' says head. 'Everyone is excited about it.'

Principal is Tricia Kelleher, previously head of Perse School for Girls, now 'effectively chief executive' of the Stephen Perse Foundation of seven schools, which offers a seamless learning journey for girls and boys aged 3 to 20.

Entrance: Larger numbers in the twin Stephen Perse Pre-Preps (City and Madingley) with automatic transfer to the junior's year 3 mean just a handful of places remain for children from elsewhere (parents of newborns take note). Children who can't be accommodated may be offered a place at the Stephen Perse Foundation's Dame Bradbury's School in Saffron Walden. 'It's a Stephen Perse journey wherever you enter,' says head. Forty places in total in year 3 at Stephen Perse Junior; waiting list applies in other year groups – a few new joiners in year 4, and a couple more in years 5 and 6, for classes no larger than 22 ('our pedagogy is for active classes with plenty of space for children to spread out their learning,' says head). Pupils mainly from city and environs, school's own shuttle bus service serves park and ride car parks, and also Madingley Pre-Prep; no parking on-site to the chagrin of parents (this is Cambridge, however). No assessment for Stephen Perse Pre-Prep arrivals but others assessed in English and maths, with an informal interview. Bursaries available, means-tested annually.

S

Exit: Virtually all to the senior school with automatic entry; parents asked to opt out if not wanting a place so it can be offered elsewhere, such is the demand (fuelling Junior applications no doubt). Early and sensitive discussions with parents of children for whom the senior school is anticipated not to be a good fit. Transitiono eased by year 6 parent coffee mornings and tea parties with senior school head, while year 10 liaison committee members buddy with junior students and year 6 pupils have lunch at the senior school. Major induction day in late June prior to admission in September.

Remarks: Stephen Perse Foundation Junior School is one in a street of schools – not easy to spot from the outside. Inside is deceptively spacious thanks to economical use of the available space and calm ambience – wide corridors and restful décor (the Stephen Perse teal much in evidence in the carpet and feature walls, chiming with the uniform). Something of a maze with the middle on a slightly different level to the two sides, which makes for lots of stairs, and one wing the domain of City Pre-Prep, whose little pupils cross onto the junior side to use facilities. Library, complete with ingenious outdoor reading area, is open every break time and lunchtime. Cambridge graduate Ben Miller was a big hit when he visited to read from his first children's book. Good-sized hall transforms into dining room for lunch – 'puddings are better than the main course,' confide our guides, though their eyes light up at the memory of meatballs. High-ceilinged classrooms are uncluttered and large for the numbers, creative layouts designed to make best use of the space. Science lab 'feels very professional with all the proper gas taps,' said our young guide. Workshop for CDE (creative design engineering), which focuses on projects to be researched, devised, planned and executed from start to finish – the process more important than the outcome, though resulting snack bars and tree houses most impressive.

Critical thinking the key to a common skills-driven curriculum across the Foundation's 3-11 schools. No Tudors in year 5 and Victorians in year 6 here – more, explains head, 'what do we want a learner from year 1 to 6 to experience in terms of their historical understanding?' Maths is streamed in years 5 and 6. Lessons for discrete sciences – year 6s have science lessons in the Foundation's labs at the senior school site. French all through from pre-prep, Spanish from year 4, German and Mandarin have been introduced for year 6 in preparation for language choices at year 7. Children in years 3 to 6 use iPads for learning, through Google Classroom and a range of apps. 'Though we do still believe in handwriting, books and pencils,' says head. Children encouraged to record their thoughts or feelings in 'inside out books' – for their own benefit, but welcome to share with parents or form teacher. Said a parent, 'The teaching is excellent, not just because they inspire children to grow in all aspects of their development, but their attention to detail, innate intelligence and genuine caring for each child is very apparent.' SEN and EAL support largely within the classroom; places not offered to children whose needs cannot be met. Many pupils bi- and tri-lingual at home – recent European Day of Languages competition attracted entries for a recipe for happiness in a vast array including Greek and Mandarin. Annual Integrated Learning Week celebrates diversity – history, sustainability recently; parents speak and lead workshops, supported by teachers.

Broad sporting offer – rotation of fencing, tennis and gymnastics (swimming soon to be added) to give experience of individual sports alongside team sports – hockey, netball, cricket for girls; football, hockey, cricket for boys. Sport taught on four sites: sports hall, multi-use games area and rooftop Astro on the senior school site, five minutes' walk away; playing fields, Astros and pavilion at Latham Road, 10 minutes; further pitches at Gonville and Caius sports ground; university cricket club facility Fenners for indoor cricket in the winter; and a functional court for lunchtime netball practice and general activities on the junior school's own pocket handkerchief outdoor area. Tournaments with other preps, particularly since

IAPS membership (tenth in the UK for hockey). Most pupils learn a musical instrument and plenty of bands, orchestras and choirs as well as regular drama productions. Clubs – music, sport, languages, drama, mindfulness, art, design engineering etc – run by Stephen Perse staff but specialists for fencing, judo, chess and Mandarin (extra charge). Science clubs for years 4, 5 and 6 leading to intra-Foundation science competition in the spring; year 4 group recently won national CLEAPSS science competition.

The school's nature reserve is well used and years 3, 4 and 5 have outdoor learning along the lines of forest school for a double lesson every fortnight – shelter-building etc, which dovetails with the thematic learning approach. 'Cambridge is our campus' is oft quoted at Stephen Perse and indeed, the location is the envy of prep heads across the land. Frequent trips to the Fitzwilliam Museum, Polar Research, Botanic Gardens, etc right on the doorstep. 'We wear out their shoe leather before we wear out their pocket money,' says head.

Residential trips in years 4, 5 and 6 (much anticipated visit to Edinburgh, optional adventure holiday to Salamanca with Dame Bradbury's pupils). Seven houses – new house Sutherland (named for former chair of governors) introduced in September 2018 to reduce numbers in each thanks to burgeoning roll. Many house activities encourage working together. House captain and sports captain roles; school council, eco committee representatives from each form. Assemblies three days a week are an opportunity to present commendations, termly citizenship cups, sports awards and also any certificates achieved for out-of-school activities. Outside speakers and parents often give talks in the Inspire and Guide programme which runs through the Foundation; occasional digital workshops for parents before house and class assemblies, with Google Suite guidance by year 6 pupils. 'We find early mornings or 5pm are good times for working parents to be involved,' says head. House points awarded for good work or behaviour and kept track of using a database ('slips system wasn't very eco-friendly and some got lost' says head). Discussions about 'unwise choices' and 'reflective breaks' rather than sanctions for transgressions of the school code of conduct, which requires respect for fellow students and the environment. 'A letter of apology or an appropriate and proportionate reparative activity, such as helping to clear up an area possible consequences.' Few issues of this kind here, however. Children already intellectuals; polite, respectful and happy in this world imagined just for them, designed to inspire and delight while preparing them to continue on the Stephen Perse educational journey.

Stephen Perse Pre-Prep (Madingley)

Linked with Stephen Perse Pre-Prep (City), Stephen Perse Junior School, Stephen Perse 6th Form College, Dame Bradbury's School, Stephen Perse Senior School

Cambridge Road, Madingley, Cambridge, Cambridgeshire CB23 8AH

Ages 3–7 **Pupils** 60

01954 210309
www.stephenperse.com

Head: Since 2011, Sarah Holyoake. Thoughtful, smiley and softly spoken. After West Hatch High School, Chigwell, read English at Cambridge and followed up with a PGCE. Taught reception in state schools in Cambridge, then head of early years in an independent school in Dorset. Returned to Cambridge and took up the role with Stephen Perse Foundation a year after it acquired Madingley Pre-Prep, in a rural location on the western fringes of the city. A year later City Pre-Prep was founded on the same site as Stephen Perse Junior School; now the two, along with the pre-prep classes at the Foundation's Dame Bradbury's School in Saffron Walden, are run in parallel under her aegis. Son attends City Pre-Prep. 'It's a dream when a school's educational ethos aligns with your own,' she says.

Principal is Tricia Kelleher, previously head of Perse School for Girls and now 'effectively chief executive' of the Foundation, which now owns seven schools, offering an educational pathway from 3 to 20.

Entrance: No more than 13 children in kindergarten, 16 in reception, 18 each in years 1 and 2. While many parents opt for the rural setting of Madingley, the oversubscribed City is often the preferred choice; those who miss out are often offered a spot at Madingley. 'The educational experience is exactly the same,' says a teacher. 'Once you have a place, you're on your journey through the Foundation.' Shuttle bus between the two helps parents avoid the notoriously hideous Cambridge traffic at drop-off and collection times. Assessment for joiners at any stage is one-to-one play session with head or her deputy, looking for enthusiasm for learning. Ad hoc joiners need to complement the dynamic of the class. No bursaries.

Exit: Pre-prep children move on automatically to the junior school. Any issues raised early if not likely to be a fit. Occasional child moves to be with siblings elsewhere; places snapped up.

Remarks: Head likens the three Stephen Perse Foundation pre-preps to Neapolitan ice-cream – ethos is the same but slightly different flavours. Thematic learning across the board in all settings – maths, literacy and phonics but all other subjects subsumed into topic work, such as 'into the woods' and 'weather'. Strange to think that children of the same age in each of the three schools are having identical lessons. Much mixing of the classes and collaboration – children look forward to seeing their friends in other schools and classes; all the advantages of a self-contained pre-prep but with access to shared facilities, staff expertise and pupils of all ages for joint projects.

Kindergarten timetable has literacy, maths, ICT, PSHEE, time with year 2 buddies, art, cooking, forest school in the Botanic Gardens and music lessons weekly with specialist teacher. Commitment to pupil-led learning throughout. 'Sometimes our classes look a bit chaotic and messy but that's because we focus on the learning method that suits the child,' says head. 'The ultimate achievement of all the children is the same, we don't mind how they get there. We can only do this because the class sizes are small, we have good adult to child ratios, we have iPads and access to outdoors – the toolkit that supports the teachers.' Thinking tool wheel on every classroom wall gives pupils a vocabulary with which to express their impressions of their learning ('I need some lightbulb' is often heard). In fact nascent elements of the IB the children may encounter later are apparent in the pre-prep curriculum, building throughout the school. Tapestry online system used across the pre-prep to log pupils' work and involve parents in achievements.

SEND supported by the inclusive approach – individual needs of every child taken into account. Occasional interventions for eg phonics every day for two weeks before re-joining the class. Years 1 and 2 have four lessons for four weeks to 'plan, learn, do, review' – children choose a project (eg cake decorating, a book about a football team, making a model), then have to learn a required skill, do the activity, and in the final week, review (note where eg they didn't allow enough time or chose the wrong materials). Children can repeat the project if they want to refine it – resilience, risk-taking, problem-solving all progressed. Forest school for every class, weekly, promotes skills that can be developed and applied to classroom situations. Years 1 and 2 from all three pre-preps come together for weekly outdoor sports lesson on Foundation facilities with Cambridge United specialist trainers. Year 2 pupils also share PE lessons with year 3s. Regular collaboration with classes at Dame Bradbury's – recently a pooled forest school session. Weekly head teacher's award recognises achievement in work, behaviour or initiative.

Madingley was previously a standalone proprietor-run pre-prep set in a detached house in an idyllic rural village setting, just a 10-minute drive from the edge of the city of Cambridge. Surrounded by woodland, which allows the Foundation children to make use of it for forest school sessions. School uses community facilities – well supported by locals: weekly gym lesson in the thatched village hall, local park for nature study. House itself is not large but good use made of the space. Small entrance corridor leads to a hall for group activities, clubs and lunch (brought over from City site). Interconnecting rooms a bit of a warren and kindergarten and reception rooms a little rustic, but flexible areas for projects and lots of wall for displays of work and writing ideas on.

Outdoor learning area with gravel pit, mud kitchen and room to roam around – luxury. Playground between main house and the classroom building which is home to years 1 and 2 (one end each). Individual music lessons on-site, piano and violin, regular concerts held here for all pre-prep pupils. Specialist teachers for French etc visit. Pre-prep children wear the teal-dominated uniform common to all of the 3-11 schools in the Foundation. Parents are invested and happy with the continuity. 'We find parents are looking for 3 to 18,' says head, 'Once they have decided they know they don't have to make a decision again; it's one journey.'

Stephen Perse Pre-Prep (City)

Linked with Dame Bradbury's School, Stephen Perse Junior School, Stephen Perse Pre-Prep (Madingley), Stephen Perse 6th Form College, Stephen Perse Senior School

5 Brookside, Cambridge, Cambridgeshire CB2 1JE

Ages 3–7 **Pupils** 60

01223 346140
www.stephenperse.com

Head: Since 2011, Sarah Holyoake, who also heads the Madingley school.

Principal is Tricia Kelleher.

Entrance: Tiny and always oversubscribed. Those who can't be accommodated often offered at place a other Stephen Perse Foundation schools: Madingley or Dame Bradbury's.

Exit: Nearly all to Stephen Perse Junior school.

Remarks: Operates an identical curriculum to Stephen Perse Pre-Prep (Madingley).

In line with the ethos of the Foundation, much consideration has gone into the children's physical surroundings and as a result City Pre-Prep is an environment designed to encourage creative thinking. Occupying a corner of the five-storey junior school building, it is white-walled and teal-carpeted, with interesting shapes, nooks and crannies wherever architecturally possible. Kindergarten has all the practical learning areas as well as an outdoor space. Day runs 8am to 5.30pm if required, though morning-only sessions available for kindergarten. School lunch on own table in the dining room. Classrooms for reception, years 1 and 2 are high-ceilinged and large for the numbers, making use of every available space. Some inter-connected, all with areas for imaginative play. Storage in, under and around – good use made of limited space. Pre-prep domain marked by a doorway, through which little ones may only pass to use the facilities shared with the junior school – hall, dining room, music room and creatively designed library, with its own outdoor reading space, where year 2s read to kindergarten buddies. Music specialist for pre-prep children, focused on the term's theme. Speaking and listening integrated too. Year 1 and 2 may have piano and violin lessons and can opt to perform at regular concerts, held at Madingley. Pre-prep children wear the teal-dominated uniform common to all of the three-11 schools in the Foundation. Parents are invested and happy with the continuity. 'We find parents are looking for 3 to 18,' says head, 'Once they have decided they know they don't have to make a decision again; it's one journey.' This is the choice for parents who want a dynamic, inspiring first stage of education for their sparky little ones, who are already excited by learning.

S

Stephen Perse 6th Form College

Linked with Dame Bradbury's School, Stephen Perse Senior School, Stephen Perse Pre-Prep (City), Stephen Perse Pre-Prep (Madingley), Stephen Perse Junior School

Fitzwilliam Building, Shaftesbury Road, Cambridge CB2 8AA

Ages 16–18 **Pupils** 122

Fees: £16,830 pa

01223 454700
www.sixthform.stephenperse.com/

Head of 6th form: Since September 2017, Naomi Atkins. After teaching economics in Malvern, joined the Perse School for Girls in 2002 as a senior leadership team member. Then spent 10 years in China, Indonesia and Malaysia in roles including IB co-ordinator, deputy head academic and head of senior school. Returned to Cambridge and the Stephen Person Foundation in 2015. Teaches economics. 'I am always impressed when I happen to observe my economists engaging in literary criticism in an English class, for example,' she says. 'It's important that students here recognise and reflect on the competencies they are developing.' Supports students to think for themselves and speak up. 'Miss Atkins always encourages us to put forward our ideas,' said one. 'She's really in tune with us.' Leaving in July 2019.

Principal is Tricia Kelleher, previously head of Perse School for Girls, now 'effectively chief executive' of the Stephen Perse Foundation of seven schools, which offers a seamless learning journey for girls and boys aged three to 20.

Academic matters: Offers both A levels and IB, 60:40 split, and results are impressive. IB average score was 36 in 2018. At A level 54 per cent of grades were A*-A, 81 per cent A*-B. 'It's a place for people who like learning,' said a parent. A wide choice of subjects, mainly academic (drama, product design and computer science from September 2019). Maths and sciences popular but also high uptake of languages and humanities. Theory of Knowledge is studied by all IB students and also lower sixth A level students – 'exams teach you to think a certain way but TOK helps us develop our critical thinking skills'. Indeed, atmosphere is one of intent, independent study – university style; many staff sit among their students to teach in small groups – largest class sizes for popular subjects is about 10, but some subjects one-to-one. 'Small classes attracted me to the college rather than the much bigger ones in Cambridge,' said our guide. 'We're more interactive with the teacher, who is really invested in you; it can feel a little insular but I quite like that – it's a tight-knit community.'

Weekly assemblies in the 'old library' as well as meetings and Inspire Me! series of talks which draws on city's talent and expertise – a recent visit by former Archbishop of Canterbury Rowan Williams was a sell-out. Sixth formers can take part in senior school productions and a recent cabaret was much enjoyed. University resources and all the intellectual riches of Cambridge capitalised on for curriculum-related visits and seminars.

Pretty high-tech learning environment in line with other schools in the Foundation. Apple TVs in every room and each student issued with an iPad on arrival. 'iPads and Apple Pens are our main tools,' explained a student. 'We still use pens and paper, but our homework is set on Google Classroom.' Hot on e-safety. Tales of successful integration of students with SEN and hearing impairments – 'we're well versed at making adjustments so everyone can engage,' says head.

Games, options, the arts: Enrichment programme and the non-examined curriculum add breadth and depth. 'Students have a very good work ethic if they're here – they follow their academic programme and do all the extras too,' says head. An hour and 20 minutes of enrichment twice a week for sixth formers. Spinning, zumba, yoga (students issued with entrance tokens for a city gym); film studies, psychopathology, debating. Mixed teams for football, netball and hockey (pitches at Foundation's nearby Latham Road sports field). Sports clubs using Foundation's huge indoor sports hall and rooftop Astro on the senior school site a school shuttle bus ride away, as are spaces for choir and ensemble rehearsals and instrument lessons. Art lessons in the superb self-contained art department shared with senior school. Recent MUN a success, organised by sixth formers and with delegations from around the world. Amusing student e-magazine, Teal, brimming with 'StevieP' personality; also humorous FemSoc newsletter and Be Curious blog. Many outlets for youthful wit and wisdom. Head looking to expand enrichment provision with a well-being agenda – students' suggestions sought, including mindfulness, martial arts etc – 'a mix of new skills and opportunities for relaxation,' says head, who recognises that balance is essential for these self-motivated students.

Boarding: Boarding for sixth former students offered from September 2019.

Background and atmosphere: Part of the Stephen Perse Foundation of schools, sixth form college was established in 2008 in two modern buildings more or less next door to each other, opposite Cambridge University Press. A 10-minute journey by shuttle bus from the Foundation's senior school and its facilities and a short walk from the station. Interior is bright and economical with the available space, splashes of lime rather than the Stephen Perse teal that characterises the décor of other schools in the Foundation. Lifts make both buildings mostly accessible to all. An air of purposefulness and intellectual focus pervades – thoughtfully positioned posters for events of academic or cultural interest, break-out areas for independent study and plenty of coffee machines to debate over. This is certainly a college rather than a school, a true stepping stone to university.

Co-ed since its inception, but still twice as many girls as boys, though this is expected to even out as co-ed grows through the senior school (boys joined year 7 in 2017). Main sixth form building has two floors of science labs, as well as classrooms for maths, geography, history, two music rooms (one with piano) and library; contemporary designed, rather echoey, Shaftesbury building has a second hall and library, as well as further teaching rooms. Funky coffee shop style dining room has a relaxed vibe and is a popular meeting place for students over hot lunches ('age-appropriate menu'), salads, cakes and snacks. Food from home also allowed – microwaves for warming, including one specifically for vegetarians. Boiling water tap installed at the request of herbal tea and Pot Noodle fans. Upper sixth students have their own retreat area above the dining room, complete with sofas, work area, table football and a Wii – fun and relaxation positively encouraged here.

Pastoral care, well-being and discipline: A small community in which there is an evident rapport between staff and students. 'The teachers know us well so they give really good advice,' said our guide. 'You feel on quite an equal footing with them, they treat you like an adult and don't patronise you.' Self-discipline the norm, though staff alert to signs of stress or over-work in students keen to achieve; weekly meeting of staff pastoral team to discuss those on the radar and decide next steps. Scrappy homework or non-attendance flags up 'poor attitude to learning'; usual answer is 'structured support' in the form of supervised study periods. 'You know there's a safety net,' said a student.

Much effort goes into development of independent learning skills, ready for university, and acres of advice on offer: universities and careers guidance teacher has own Google Classroom with information on personal statements and course choices; tutor assists with UCAS references and personal statement; interview practice available.

Different lunch hour to Hills Road and The Perse puts the lid on daytime socialising with wider Cambridge sixth form student population. SPF students have the free run of their own sixth form buildings and senior school (ID cards allow entry and tracking of whereabouts) as well as the city; locals may go home in free lessons, but are asked not to take jobs in school time.

Pupils and parents: Cambridge families in the main – parents employed at the university, hospitals or tech firms, though some London commuters. Some from further afield – short walk to the station and school lays on shuttle buses from local park and rides. Students' appetite for learning fairly voracious. Eyes literally light up at the opportunity to learn something new, particularly in the company of friends; if planning and organisation required, all the better.

Entrance: Total of 200 places. Half to two-thirds of the lower sixth intake from own senior school currently and more expected to follow as co-ed grows through; remainder from other independents including Cambridge schools Sancton Wood, Heritage, Landmark International, CIS, The Leys, St Mary's, as well as further afield – St Christopher's Letchworth, Bishop's Stortford College, Wisbech Grammar, Culford, Ipswich High. The Stephen Perse work ethic can be a shock for new arrivals. Interview and critical thinking exercise, school report and reference required for all external applicants. Those wishing to study further maths A level or high level maths in the IB sit an additional test. Fifty points (A* at GCSE is 10 points) in their eight best GCSE subjects for an offer of a place, with at least 7s at GCSE for chosen subjects.

Exit: Vast majority go on to university – 10 to Oxbridge in in 2018, rest largely Russell Group. Traditional academic subjects preferred, eg vets and medics, or biochemistry in the first instance, economics, history, politics, languages and English literature. Occasionally fine art (recently to Oxford, Central St Martin's). A handful abroad, to Europe and United States, for courses in international relations, liberal arts etc. Parents of international students tend to favour repatriation over non-Russell Group uni. In recent years a few degree apprenticeships with eg KPMG, UBS; some explore the options, most elect for the more traditional routes. Unifrog well used; university representatives and panels of former students give insights into the realities of unis and courses – some 80-plus parents (many with Cambridge University work email addresses) responded to a recent call for volunteers to help with mock interview practice. Summer term focus on aptitude testing and BMat for early Oxbridge applicants – 50 per cent of students here apply. Some 10-20 per cent take a gap year.

S

Money matters: Sixteen plus scholarships – academic, music, art, drama – attract fee remission of up to 20 per cent; five per cent discount Foundation Award for contribution to school and community. Stephen Perse Foundation Senior School scholars must reapply; bursaries continue through and more added for sixth form (means-testing by a third party).

Remarks: Compact, cosy college exquisitely tailored to the needs of Cambridge's self-motivated university-bound intellectuals. Conscious of the need for student well-being and the development of skills complementary to academic success. Voted IB school of the year twice by the Sunday Times, a great achievement for its size.

Stratford Girls' Grammar School

Shottery Manor, Shottery, Stratford-upon-Avon, Warwickshire CV37 9HA

Ages 11–18 **Pupils** 787 **Sixth form** 219

01789 293759
www.sggs.org.uk

Headteacher: Since 2016 Jacqueline Cornell BA (40s). Originally from Newmarket, educated at the local comprehensive school, then achieved the distinction of being the first member of her family to go to university, where she read history. After an unrewarding spell in educational sales, was drawn to teaching: 'I've always been a performer, and with a love of history, teaching seemed to be the thing to do'. Earned her stripes in comprehensive schools for the first 10 years, before moving to the grammar school sector, as head of sixth form at King Edward VI Camp Hill School for Girls in Birmingham. 'I fundamentally believe in a grammar school education. It's a shame that many people see grammars as the preserve of the middle class. What I love...you do get an incredible eclectic mix of girls'. Joined SGGS (or Shottery Grammar, as it is known locally) as deputy head in 2010 and, with her specialist interest in Elizabethan history, feels quite at home in the 15th century Manor House, now used as the sixth form house, where she has her office.

After a slightly cool start to our interview the sun came out as she discussed her students. 'They are incredibly bright, adventurous, and willing to try new things,' and she is keen to empower them: 'I truly believe that every single child gets just one go at this'. Dressed for business, she is direct, and challenging ('I'm a historian, I need evidence') and although she was reluctant to give away personal details, we did notice she keeps her computer on a Star Wars stand (in control, she is). Parents respect her and notice her presence at PTA and parents' evenings. 'She's aiming for excellence', said one; 'she's dynamic, has an amazing vision for the school,' said another. Clearly ambitious for her girls – 'Our end product is superb' – yet aware of their vulnerabilities. 'The biggest change I've seen is the impact that social media has had on young people...most prevalent is the fear of missing out'. She institutes change by working with review groups and house councils. On a motion to introduce longer school skirts and changes in the 'no make-up' rule, she shows her diplomatic side: 'We want to stay in touch with the girls, but also remain aware of what parents want'. One parent described it as 'a crusade about uniforms... pushing it to extremes'. She may need some intergalactic help to sort that out

Academic matters: Bertie Woosters beware, these girls are 'dashed brainy', and their public exam results testify: 57 per cent A*/A at A level, maths and science most popular subjects, with six Oxbridge places in 2018. At GCSE no less impressive, 78 per cent A*-A/9-7 making it the top performing school in the county. In addition, all girls take the EPQ in the sixth form. One parent described it as 'very academic, but also quite down to earth'. Links up with King Edward VI boys' grammar for more unusual A level options.

We heard grumbles from a parent that it was biased towards science subjects, insisting on the triple science GCSE. 'Language teaching is good,' said one mum, with French, German and Spanish as options for GCSE. Latin is off the menu. Other GCSE courses include computing and food tech. A levels focus on quality not quantity (one girl wished to be allowed to take four) with an extra 'stretch and challenge' subject in year 12, which might include photography, engineering or business and enterprise. Teaching styles varied from subject to subject: we saw traditional English lessons with students seated in rows, small tutor groups in cheerful discussion about the French Revolution, and a lively hall full of improvising thespians. Subject specialist staff are supported by technicians and older girls. The impression was one of industriousness and self-motivation; 'they give you a lot of freedom...and a lot of opportunity,' said our sixth form guide.

The head is rightly proud of the results, but aims for well-rounded individuals. 'We ask the girls, "Where would you like to be and how would you like to get there?"' and the school encourages the girls to look beyond conventional academic routes, offering the chance to apply to post-sixth for apprenticeships with finance, marketing and engineering companies. As one staff member commented, 'Oxford is great, but there are other things apart from university'.

We heard the girls felt the standard of teaching was '90 per cent good enough'. One parent explained the figure: 'The science and maths teaching has struggled to recruit and retain staff. My daughter had five different teachers in the sixth form'.

Currently over 50 girls on SEN register, mostly for mild dyslexia, but a few other conditions: ASD, visual impairment, auditory processing and dyspraxia. Support is provided through class teacher training (no TAs in the school), and through workshops with small groups at lunchtime. A visiting ed psych runs sessions in stress management, especially at exam time. 'The school is very aware about stress,' one parent told us, 'and counselling is available'. No visiting clinicians, though staff are able to implement strategies from therapy reports. SENCo explained that well supported girls 'go on to do really well'.

Games, options, the arts: Choice, again, was the word we heard most. A range of traditional girls' sports are timetabled, including netball, hockey, swimming and cross-country with a growing interest in rowing, basketball, football, rugby and indoor cricket. The sixth form has a dedicated afternoon for enrichment activities, which allows access to the new fitness suite, with an exhausting array of cross-trainers, exercise bikes and treadmills. Fields at the rear, with an athletics track and Astroturf, are shared with the high school next door, but girls have exclusive use of the four court indoor hall and newly surfaced tennis courts. Where else would you find PE equipment stored in a Tudor dovecot?

Our tour took us past a doodle wall, inviting girls to 'Draw, create, express', and the message seems to have hit home. Art, which used to be a single track to architecture, has bloomed into art, craft and design, with facilities for graphics, textiles, DT and photography, and growing numbers continuing to foundation courses and film and media degrees. We saw a DT lesson, with red-aproned youngsters confidently using a range of lathes and cutters. In a separate stable-block studio, girls worked thoughtfully on large screen prints of honeybees, in tune with the Elizabethan surroundings.

It is not possible to pass through the school without feeling the impact of the Bard. RSC production posters stare out at you from the walls, we looked down from a loggia balcony, said to have inspired Romeo and Juliet, and heard of school productions put on at the Swan Theatre. In the well-kitted drama studio, we came upon a lone drama student composing a sonnet, or was it a UCAS personal statement? 'It helps to be in Stratford,' she told us. 'We get free tickets for the RSC'. Be not afeard; the school is full of noises...the music department has a dedicated block, with large teaching areas, and ensemble and practice rooms. The 'wonderful head of music puts on fantastic concerts', we were told by parents. We witnessed a year 9 class, in a cosy circle on the floor, discriminating between wind instruments. The girls play in orchestras and a jazz band, with encouragement to conduct and compose, or to sing in choirs. Recent productions have included Alice in Wonderland, The Lion King and a New York concert tour for the jazz band.

Clubs and enrichment activities in lunchtimes range from Young Writers to Geospace club, with poetry open-mic sessions and a multitude of more earth-based options too, such as DofE and rowing club. The sixth form have an impressive programme of speakers, which have featured Jess Phillips MP and Mark Carney. In the lower years, school trips cover language exchanges to France, Spain and Germany, with field trips to the brave new world of Costa Rica, China and Africa for older explorers. 'The extracurricular trips are better than some independent schools,' boasted a mum.

Background and atmosphere: Half a mile out of Stratford, past the signs to Anne Hathaway's cottage, stands a red-brick Tudor manor house, half concealed behind clipped yew hedges and aged crabapple trees. This is Shottery Manor, where Shakespeare is said to have proposed to Anne Hathaway, perhaps inspired by the perfect Englishness of the elegant tiled house, and nearby thatched village, long before the tourist buses and cream tea signs appeared. This is Illyria, where the fresh untutored minds of year 7 girls are nurtured to be top-performing women of the 21st century. Established in 1958, by a lady mayor, the winged two-storey manor is now home to the sixth form, with their own mature gardens, while a collection of more modern blocks to the rear provide teaching facilities, offices and classrooms for the lower years.

Our confident tour guides first took us up the oaken staircase of the manor, past ancient panelling (with en suite priest hole) and original Juliet balcony to the Shakespeare study room, where sixth form girls were quietly engaged in work at screens. More studying was underway in the purple spotted common room (purple and gold are the school colours) and a few were involved in industrious discussion in private tutorial rooms on the top floor. Below stairs is a small café for lunch and breaks. No baked meats or honeyed cakes but fresh soup, jacket potatoes and Oreos, on request. Looking out of the diamond-paned windows we glimpsed a sheltered garden, with lawns and clipped hedges leading to a small pond. We were told small tutor groups meet here in the summer on benches and tree stumps, among the hollyhocks, wild thyme and water lilies. This idyllic fairy bower is also Wifi enabled.

Beyond a lawn to the rear is the new Hargraves building, less pleasing to the eye, but eminently practical. A sports hall, multi-gym and dining hall on the ground floor with drama studio and classrooms above. The purple walls in the spacious reception area are dotted with brown paper tutus dancing from the ceiling. 'We like to demonstrate our ability in art,' said our guide. 'In the summer, there is an art exhibition on the centre lawn'. Lockers for sports equipment are on the ground floor. One parent complained that despite the new facilities, there was little storage space: 'I'm surprised that you have to pay for lockers, it's sad that space has to be paid for'. The girls eat lunch at long tables and we were told there is a gluten free or vegan option available each day, though we were tempted by the bacon rolls and marble muffins. Instead of dinner money, there is a biometric payment system involving fingerprints. On Tuesday, lunch hour is extended to allow time for clubs, and for the sixth form to wander into Stratford town to the cafés.

Five minute breaks are timetabled between lessons for the girls to move between buildings. Maths, languages and RE are housed in a 60s block, cheek-by-jowl with the IT suite and busy library. Literary posters warmed the walls and shelves were bursting with inspiration, from Agatha Christie to Zadie Smith, and a dedicated shelf for Shakespeare. It isn't all iambic pentameters here, year 9s have had repeated success in the annual Apps for Good competition, with software to address social issues: 'Lilies', support for bereavement, and 'I'm Okay' promoting LGBT awareness. A short step round the garden, beneath cascading willow trees, is a block of science labs; we witnessed year 12 apothecaries toiling at bubbling cauldrons of beetroot, to test permeability. In a separate building, food techies were hard at it. It is a really popular and scientific option, we were told, and definitely no picnic. The broad scope of subjects on offer was impressive; as one sixth former said, 'When you actually come here, there are so many opportunities, and pursuing them is really encouraged'.

Pastoral care, well-being and discipline: Houses, named after astral constellations, Cygnus, Orion, Phoenix and Ursa, provide a clear hierarchy of support: head of house, tutors and a house captain oversee the girls' well-being. Tutor groups are organised vertically, with older girls supporting younger ones within house. 'They can talk to us about A level choices and where to go to lessons. We've been through what they've been through,' said one girl. The head called it 'a brilliant pastoral system. It helps that you've got strong role models in a school. It helps with a sense of what to expect as you move up the school'. Parents loved it: 'my daughter can tap the brains of the older ones'. In addition there is a network of committees and representatives, who discuss complaints and improvements; 'everyone is given responsibility,' said our guide. Incidents of eating disorders and transgender issues are in line with national statistics. Parents vouched 'behaviour is good'; one cautioned, 'Strict, but they are on them for the right reasons'. The head explained, 'You've always got a few people who make mistakes. That's part of growing up.'

Around the school, girls and staff chat informally and respectfully, not on first name terms, but with humour. The head describes it as a family feel, a mum said, 'they nurture the girls but they are not mollycoddled'; one girl commented, 'even the teachers who haven't taught me, know me'.

Pupils and parents: Dressed neatly in their purple jumpers and grey blazers, with dark skirts and trousers, the younger girls come across as enthusiastic but polite. Sixth formers allowed to wear 'business suits', with some leeway for individuality, but retaining a sober element: no hats, skinny jeans or Dr Martens. 'I think it helps them', commented a mum. 'They are ready for business'. A few 'alpha characters' sweep the less confident girls along, we were told; and sure enough, the girls we spoke to were self-possessed and thoughtful.

S

Communication with the parents was praised. 'I've had a couple of issues', said one; 'I was well treated. I had an appointment to see the head of house, who took my point on board. It was taken seriously.' Parents' evenings, weekly bulletins and letters are used to keep parents in touch, and 'they use email a lot', with teachers' email addresses provided. Another parent described a social media incident, which resulted in a face-to-face meeting at school; 'the school dealt with it very well'. Each year a parent questionnaire actively invites parents' views.

Parents were described by one as 'people who are education focused and believe in education'. The Friends of Shottery PTA meets extra fundraising needs. 'It was struggling a bit,' explained a parent, but an active alumnae association provides inspiring talks to the sixth form about university experiences.

Entrance: Entry by Warwickshire 11+ entrance test; deadline for applications is June the year preceding entry, with exam in September. Vastly oversubscribed, with priority to girls living within 16 miles of the school. Entry to the sixth form has no catchment area, but requires at least 54 points from GCSE grades, and for girls to make it to school by 8.50am.

The school attracts applications from both local primaries and independent preps, from a wide radius, covering Banbury, Birmingham, Kenilworth and Evesham.

Exit: The majority of girls head off to respected universities, a handful each year to Oxbridge (six in 2018), and large numbers to Russell Group destinations, courses ranging from architecture and astro-physics to rural management. The advent of apprenticeships and university fees has altered the map, and some now accept places with the likes of JP Morgan and Lloyds bank: 'you get a degree and get paid at the same time', confided our guide. Some girls are poached by the local boys' school, which offers a co-ed sixth form, but as one parent put it, 'Shottery has a much better balance between science and arts'. The head told us phlegmatically, 'It's a little bit frustrating when you've put so much into them, but our results have held up'

Money matters: State funded grammar school. 'Trips and extras you expect to pay', said a parent; 'they do subsidise some'. Sixth form transport costs, not funded by LA, are a consideration

Remarks: Within the girdle of these walls, the young players in tomorrow's professional, business and arts fields are warming up, encouraged by a vast array of subject options, enrichment activities and skilled teaching. One mum said, 'I feel she's had a private school standard education'. The Shottery girls not only achieve excellent exam results, but with a careful pastoral system, develop the personal skills, leadership quality and confidence to transfer these to the wider stage of university. Now sits expectation in the air...

Summerhill School

Westward Ho, Leiston, Suffolk IP16 4HY

Ages 5–17 **Pupils** 77 **Boarders** 61 full, 2 weekly

Fees: Day £5,850 – £11,580; Boarding £12,819 – £19,791 pa

01728 830540
www.summerhillschool.co.uk

Principal: Since 1985, Zoe Readhead (youthful late 60s) – proprietor, keeper of the ethos and daughter of school's founder, AS Neill. Literally born, bred and educated at Summerhill. Calm, inspiring and probably sees into your soul. Answers as if for the first time questions she has presumably been asked her whole life, her patient vocation to explain her father's educational vision and the school's core values. Gradually scaling down her day-to-day involvement and preparing to pass the baton to two of her four children, all of whom are intrinsic to the life of the school, in which they were also born, bred and educated – 'they'll let me know when they don't want me here any more'. Married to Tony, a farmer. Son Henry presides over the music studio and is joint deputy head with William, who teaches woodwork and metalwork; Amy is an agronomist who helps with the paperwork; and Neill a farmer who offers support and advice. 'Zoe and the staff are great,' enthused a parent. 'I have complete faith in them and the way they teach. Zoe is always at the end of the phone when I've needed her, even in the holidays.' Said another, 'It is a real challenge to change with the demands of the time, but also to keep a safe shield around the school so it can continue to do what it does in the way it does it. Balancing and enabling that is certainly an art and I am very grateful to Zoe for that... and much more.'

Academic matters: Not a priority here, unless decided so by the individual. Nominally under the umbrella of the Democratic School movement particularly prevalent in Germany, Russia, Eastern Europe, South America and India, Summerhill prefers to be known as a 'free' school though certainly not to be confused with the state free schools of the past decade. The central tenets here are that each member of the school – adult or child – has the same rights and value and the school is run by its members, for its members. What happens in school is agreed at a meeting of pupils and staff held three times a week – or more often by request – and chaired in rotation by children. The day we visited had been agreed by the meeting as a Slobbing Day, due to a fireworks party that went on late the night before, so all lessons were off.

However, even on a regular day at Summerhill, academic lessons are entirely optional. As the parents' handbook emphasises, 'remember, at Summerhill your kid could theoretically NEVER go to a lesson – they have that right. Staff members are not going to persuade, cajole or bully your child about lessons.' The student body, aged 5 to 17 or 18, is divided into three classes by age and while the youngest two classes do have a lesson timetable, if no-one shows up at a class after 10 minutes, the teacher goes away again. Class 2 (aged 10 to 12) are least likely to feel in the mood for learning – 'they have more interesting things to do at that age,' says Zoe. Older children sign up for the 40-minute lessons on their timetable but do not need to attend if they prefer not to and they choose whether or not to work towards an exam – GCSE or International O Level – in a subject. Some Summerhillians opt to take several and some none at all. 'When kids decide they do want to learn, they are surprisingly conservative,' says Zoe. 'It doesn't have to be the most exciting lesson, they're focused. They're saying "I'm here, I want to learn – teach me".'

When they're not there and not wanting to learn, these 'free-range' children are hanging out in the woods, or the school library, or anywhere they like, together or alone. They might be being creative in the art room, the woodwork room or the forge, or making music, or perhaps walking on nearby Sizewell beach or in 'downtown' Leiston, a quiet Suffolk backwater. 'It's a bit like microwave cooking,' says Zoe. 'Kids continue to develop when they aren't learning.'

Children with SEN are absorbed into the school community. 'We try not to change the way we behave towards children because of SEN,' explains Zoe. 'We rejoice in individuals and so a child with ADHD for us is just another individual and will be treated the same as everybody else. The school community would certainly never let a child behave badly just because they had been diagnosed with something.' The school does apply for pupils to be given extra time in exams if they're eligible.

Independent learning is just one of the many educational and developmental benefits of the Summerhill approach. AS Neill founded the school in 1921 and virtually nothing has changed, but it dawns quite quickly that in a lot of ways Summerhill is still the education of the future. Conventional contemporary methods of schooling sure have their problems; Summerhill appears not to. It operates in a parallel universe where self-worth, self-knowledge and living harmoniously and respectfully with others are not just the goal, they're the reality. While schools spend millions of pounds and hours of planning on creating opportunities for pupils to learn the importance of risk-taking, for example, at Summerhill children play tag in the trees and gladly manufacture their own knives in the metalwork shop. A lesson on risk-taking comes in the form of a wobbly moment on a high branch or a nick on the thumb. On our visit, Zoe stopped to shoot the breeze with a young girl (helicopter parents, look away now) on roller blades, sucking a lollipop.

Summerhill's nine teachers, including the founder's grandchildren, all live in too and assist those who are houseparents 24/7. 'Of course as an independent school we don't have to employ people with formal teaching qualifications, but we do because it's really the best mechanism,' says Zoe. 'Some job candidates come and say "I would love to live here but I couldn't teach this way".' All the usual safeguarding checks are carried out. Adults as well as children are known by their first names. There is a charming register system in the entrance corridor to Summerhill's main house – a huge peg board divided into three wide columns, titled 'in', 'out' and 'far out'. Each Summerhillian has a name fob to personalise (wild and wacky metalwork planets, plants or abstract objets) or not (felt tip on hardboard) and move across into the relevant column to show the current whereabouts – 'out' the area shaded on a map of the local area as the centre of Leiston, with the fringes marked as somewhere not to go unless you have told someone you're going; 'far out' usually home. Day children – and there are few and only as a precursor to boarding – move their fobs to and fro night and morning. At the end of term someone dutifully moves all the fobs to 'far out' and back to 'in' on the first day back. Typical Summerhill – each individual has a strong identity, is responsible for him or herself and as a member of the community as a whole; it's a simple system; it works.

No wonder then that Summerhill's termly Visitors' Day is oversubscribed by students of education and open-minded school leaders who want to find out for themselves what makes Summerhill work, presumably so they can take away a gem or two. But surely Summerhill is more than the sum of its parts? 'Yes,' says Zoe, 'but they might use an idea and it could be some improvement.' Such generosity is endemic. Zoe has toured the world to share her father's vision. Beyond the 90 or so children currently at Summerhill, if Neill's vision adds even a modicum of value to the development and education of children wherever they are, it is all grist to the 'free' school mill. Regular requests from fly-on-the wall Educating Manchester style documentary-makers are swatted away – 'the only way we would make a documentary to show our approach would be to make it ourselves, which we could do', says Zoe thoughtfully. We look forward to it.

Games, options, the arts: 'Adults are not there to create things for the children to do,' reads the parent information. 'They need to create things for themselves. Sports, games and other amusements are all generated by the pupils and adults, according to need.' Facilities are ready and waiting, though the somewhat lumpy football pitch is little used currently – 'we had some German kids here at one point who were keen and put on a match every afternoon, but not much interest recently,' says Zoe. Considering turning the tennis court over to volleyball, which is more popular now. Kids swim in the school's unheated pool or the warmer indoor version at Leiston Leisure Centre. PE lessons are not a thing here. 'If you think about it, in regular school children enjoy sports as their only chance to get outside,' says Zoe. 'Here they are outside whenever they want to be.'

Indoor activities on offer include performance of all kinds – dance, drama and music, including music technology and studio recording – and there's a small theatre. The woodwork shop and metalwork forge are popular places and many Summerhill kids discover a real passion – 'they mostly make furniture,' says Zoe, 'or weapons'. They can go in whenever a lesson for the younger children isn't in progress. Similarly art, which has a large room, stuffed with imaginative works by pupils, past and present. Computer room – gaming and screens in general (laptops, iPads etc) not allowed on weekdays until 3pm, but fine the rest of the time. Japanese, Chinese, gardening, photography, calligraphy, film-making, crafts, riding, cooking in the café, camping in the grounds, making tree forts etc are all popular self-directed pastimes. A Social Committee is elected by the community in the winter and spring to organise bigger games and activities – such as capture the flag, word games, board games, spontaneous acting, story-telling and cinema trips – for afternoons and evenings. Breeds practical, can-do children who know what they want and get on with it.

Boarding: Pretty much all Summerhillians – only the very youngest and any very recently arrived don't board. Class 1 children, who can sleep at school from the age of 5 if they like – all are by about 7 – overnight in mixed rooms and then split into separate girls' and boys' accommodation buildings when they move up to class 2. Class 3, age 12 and up, have individual rooms on mixed corridors, sharing bathrooms in the accommodation known as Carriages (originally literally old railway carriages, but now replaced by wooden buildings). Ofsted had a little difficulty taking this on board and recently came to investigate Summerhill's sleeping arrangements. They left enlightened. 'I think they saw that it works and that we just don't have the problems associated with a lack of respect for gender they find in other schools,' shrugs Zoe.

Background and atmosphere: One of the most famous and most controversial schools in the world. Founded in 1921 by AS Neill – described on the school website as 'a Scottish writer and rebel' – near Dresden, Germany, but moved to a Victorian house in Leiston, two miles from the Suffolk coast, in 1927. He decided this would be the ideal place to create a community in which children could be free from adult authority. Neill's ideas became famous through his extensive writings and lectures and were accepted more readily outside of the UK. However, in the 1960s his success at Summerhill was finally recognised closer to home and Neill was awarded honorary degrees from the universities of Newcastle, Exeter and Essex. In 1999 he was named among the top 12 men and women to influence British schooling during the last millennium by the Times Educational Supplement.

This has not prevented the school from being threatened with closure on several occasions, most recently in 1999 after a damning Ofsted report that accused the school of failing the children educationally. Summerhill contested the notice of closure in court and after four days of wrangling and vociferous protest from current and former parents and pupils, the government's case collapsed.

The school's idyllic 12 green and woody acres remain as peaceful as ever. On the fringes of the town, Summerhill's main house – interior features sadly wrecked by the army during wartime requisition – is surrounded by a collection of long, low buildings which house the no-frills learning areas, accommodation and facilities, as well as ancient trees including beeches perfect for climbing and rope-swings.

Numbers wax and wane over the course of the year, but there are never more than 100 children and adults in the school community. Long holidays – five weeks at Christmas, five weeks in the spring and nine weeks each summer – no half-terms or bank holidays. Former pupils are welcomed back for a party every five years (the next one being the school's centenary).

Pastoral care, well-being and discipline: 'We believe in freedom but not licence,' says the parent information. 'This means that you are free to do as you like – but you must not interfere with somebody else's freedom. You are free to go to lessons, or stay away, because that is your own personal business, but you cannot play your drum kit at four in the morning because it would keep other people awake.' A popular misconception: Summerhill does indeed have rules (or 'laws') – at least a couple of hundred of them, all agreed, amended or abolished at the meeting. 'A lot of society's ills relate to individuals not taking responsibility for their actions,' says Zoe. 'Here each member is responsible for him or herself.'

Bullying doesn't really figure – every individual is confident in his or her own self-worth and the value of others. Similarly sexual harassment – 'if it were to happen, the intended victim would simply look the assailant in the eye and tell him or her where to go', says Zoe. No problem with women's empowerment here – gender is no barrier to self-esteem.

Those who transgress are 'brought up' in the meeting and a suitable consequence is agreed – usually either a monetary fine (a specified amount, such as 'a fiver for smoking', explains Zoe, or a percentage of the child's 'poc', pocket money dished out by the school) or some kind of community service (such as helping out in the school kitchens). Being 'brought up' in front of peers is often punishment enough. Serious misdemeanours, such as drink or drugs, usually result in the child being sent home for four to eight weeks – 'the worst thing, because they all want to be here,' says Zoe. A parent backed this up – 'I couldn't get my daughter out of bed all through the summer holidays, but on the day she went back to school she jumped out of bed at 7am, screaming at the top of her voice with delight to be going back! And the tears and sadness to be going home at the end of every term is all the evidence anyone needs that the kids absolutely LOVE Summerhill.'

Pupils and parents: An international community. Despite being branded 'crackpot' by sections of the UK media over several decades, Summerhill is well known and respected around the world and 65 per cent of pupils are from overseas, most often Japan, Korea, Holland, China, Germany, France, Poland and Russia. Pupils arrive with varying degrees of English – EAL help is available in a dedicated classroom. British children travel from every corner of the kingdom, though some families make a point of moving to be nearer. Summerhill is a magnet. Children who join after the age of 5 have more often than not been home-schooled previously, or have attended other alternative schools, or have had difficulties elsewhere and arrived seeking sanctuary. 'Qualities we typically see in Summerhill pupils are: Self-esteem, tolerance, integrity, fairness, understanding, sensitivity, compassion, assertiveness, creativity, individuality, humour, self-motivation and common sense,' says the school. The hope and intention is for those who don't arrive with these attributes to leave with them.

Parents of Summerhillians tend to be ardent advocates – no doubt practised in the art of explaining their choice to sceptics; they need to be to put their faith in Neill's educational philosophy and live with the eventual outcome for their child, which could range from enlightenment to illiteracy. Such is their confidence that parents accept they must be almost completely hands-off for the sake of their children – there is almost no parental involvement at Summerhill. 'As the philosophy of the school is to encourage children to live their own lives and make their own decisions, they value their independence and the vast majority prefer parents not to be a part of the school,' says Summerhill. 'Accepting this is part of learning to accept your new independent, free child.' However, parents are treated to a taste of their children's school life on one summer weekend when they are invited to stay for a few days. 'I found it difficult at first, because I'd had lots of involvement when my daughters had attended state school,' said one parent, 'but I quickly understood that it is part of the Summerhill way that children are allowed the complete freedom to do whatever they like without intervention from parents. I am happy with that, I love seeing how much they have changed at each holiday.' Said another, 'The fact that I have no influence on the children is of course a challenge. It requires a completely different way of living motherhood. I see it as my own learning process. The parameter is, and remains, whether the children are doing well.'

Entrance: Entirely on the child's suitability for the school, and vice versa. The impact of a new joiner on current pupils is also considered and over-11s are rarely enrolled, so as not to upset the established dynamic. New children may join at the start of any term. Parents are well advised to read carefully the direct, honest and plentiful information on the school's website, before making an enquiry and visiting.

Exit: Most leave at 17 or 18, the majority for further education and then university, equipped with the skills of independent learning and knowing what they want to do with their lives. 'A degree is not an end in itself,' says Zoe. 'Kids here can adapt in order to get to where they want to go.' Summerhill produces many skilled craftspeople and creatives. Children's writer John Burningham (The Snowman) attended, as did several successful actors, musicians, dancers, artists and scientists. But after the idyll of Summerhill, is adult life a disappointment? 'Isn't it for all of us?' asks Zoe. 'When they move to life outside, the kids are tolerant and understanding enough to deal with it.'

Money matters: Mega-cheap – no pricey historic buildings or gleaming facilities to keep up; make-do-and-mend mentality. Discount of 10 per cent or more for children of ex-Summerhillians. Chinese, riding, dancing and music lessons, for example, are charged as extras. School squirrels away funds for the AS Neill Summerhill Trust, which provides limited bursaries for existing pupils.

Remarks: An uncompromising, authentic, 'free' education, as true to AS Neill's vision as the day he launched it in 1921. Never capsized or blown off course by the changing tides of educational and political trial and error, Summerhill sails on serenely towards the horizon, the rest of us in its wake.

Thomas Mills High School

Saxtead Road, Framlingham, Woodbridge, Suffolk IP13 9HE

Ages 11–18 **Pupils** 1,130 **Sixth form** 263

01728 723493
www.thomasmills.suffolk.sch.uk

Headteacher: Since 2013, Philip Hurst MA MBA FRSA (very early 40s). Previously deputy/acting head of Philip Morant School, Colchester, where he had taught history earlier in his career; assistant head, Manningtree High School; and head of humanities, Thurstable School, Tiptree. Talent recognised early, as the return to Philip Morant School indicates. Inspired to enter teaching profession by the principal of his own school and believes in long term commitment of heads to their school; unimpressed with practice of heads whizzing around 'troubleshooting'. Is proud of school's reputation and thinks high academic standards reflect the excellence of the teaching and wide programme of extracurricular activities that all staff contribute to. Continues to teach his own subject – 'the biggest buzz of the week' – and is seen around corridors; 'keeps good eye contact with pupils,' we heard. Accepts need for heads to be good managers but believes teaching must remain at the heart of successful leadership in schools. Quiet, relaxed manner, quick on the draw and unstuffy. Plays tennis and is involved at a high level with the St John Ambulance association. A person of inner strength, dedication and far-sightedness; a head to watch.

Academic matters: Glowing exam results at all stages. Able pupils fast tracked and take some GCSEs in year 10, allowing A level teaching to begin in year 11. In 2018, 76 per cent of pupils got 9-4 in both English and maths GCSE (23 per cent A*/A grades). The school may be a technology, arts and languages academy, but it offers a choice of 26 subjects at GCSE, including Latin and Spanish. A foreign language is compulsory at GCSE and many do two or more. German and French top the poll – over 90 entries for German recently. Spanish also offered but benefits of learning German with present economic realities are pointed out. Very good results for all technologies – textiles, resistance materials and food. Many take 12 subjects and guides spoke regretfully of not being able to take more. Triple and double science both offered and results are excellent.

Strong science also reflected in high take-up at A level, with chemistry most popular of the 25 subjects offered. Year 7 are class taught with setting thereafter for maths and science – but no streaming. School proud of lightly-selective sixth form – baseline four GCSEs including maths and English at 4+ with 5s in A level subjects and results indicate relaxed approach succeeds with 47 per cent at A*-B and 21 per cent A*/A in 2018. For technical subjects, a minimum of four GCSEs at 4+.

Good provision for those that struggle, mostly in class support though department has own area. Pupils and parents loud in praise of staff, 'they make us work', 'excellent teachers who stay long enough to see things through'. Some have taught parents and grandparents; this really is a community school.

Games, options, the arts: Impressive all round. Traditional team sports, including cricket for girls (very popular) played and encouraged by the strong house system retained from grammar school era. Top teams are competing at county level. Recent addition of a multi-use games area (known as the MUGA) and shared with public out of hours. PTA efforts have funded a fitness trail around the grounds and trampolining, riding and dance all available. DofE has high take up, over 100 awards at bronze and silver annually. Language trips exchanges, all year 7s go to Holland for a 'bonding,' week, ski trips and travel as far afield as Africa to work on a community project in Zambia or Peru.

Art extremely popular: half the year takes it at GCSE and work is widely exhibited throughout school. New dining hall a backdrop for several spectacular creations. Music superb; hundreds have private instrumental lessons with practice rooms available. Choirs, orchestras, ensembles and bands proliferate; concerts and a major musical involving whole school tackled each year. Drama taught to years 7/8, very popular and taken seriously within school time – 'We spent a whole week rehearsing the play!' – with solid cohort taking GCSE. Large performing arts studio for lessons/rehearsals and staged school hall for big productions.

Background and atmosphere: It is over 300 years since Thomas Mills left a bequest to benefit the people, particularly children, of Framlingham. Two earlier grammars and the 'modern' school pre-date the present high school (now an academy) and this ancestry gives a sense of belonging and permanence.

School is proud of its previous incarnations, photographs displayed around corridors and in the library, a relic of former times, a desk with a tip-up lid containing 'ancient' textbooks. Main building dates from post-war era with long corridors and high windows but, the sick room aside (unutterably dreary – possibly deliberately), on the whole well decorated and cheerful. New buildings have sprung up, science, languages, sport, with pleasant courtyards sandwiched between and areas for recreation and lunch time, though new dining room so enticing that even packed lunch eaters join their friends. Good lunches. Placed on the outskirts of Framlingham, the school is calm and quiet, no shouting from pupils (or staff), and we saw more door holding and polite stepping aside than is common. Remarkably tranquil, purposeful atmosphere.

Pastoral care, well-being and discipline: A sense of pride and belonging is fostered by the house system which operates for sport and extracurricular competitions with merits awarded for individual effort towards the house tally (there are six). House shields are displayed in rank order in the main hall and the whole operation is managed by sixth formers. Pupils move through the school with the same tutor and difficulties are dealt with by them. Relatively problem-free intake and pupils largely in tune with purposeful atmosphere.

Pupils and parents: Popularity of the school draws pupils from a wide surrounding area as well as Framlingham itself. Diverse social backgrounds though representative of a prosperous area, and very little ethnic mix. Parents delighted with the school: 'Lucky us, some of my friends have paid fortunes to educate their children'. School well integrated within the life of the town and enjoys good relations with close neighbour, Framlingham College.

Entrance: Around 50 per cent drawn from the six or seven schools within the catchment area, the remainder from outside, though a demographic shift means more places available in this category. Generally oversubscribed and very popular at sixth form with influx of 30 to 40 from other high schools and independent sector.

Exit: Up to half leave after GCSEs. Great majority to higher education with large numbers – some 40 per cent to top universities. One to Cambridge in 2018; UEA, Essex, Exeter, Suffolk, Birmingham and Bristol all popuar. A sprinkling join family businesses or enter vocational training.

Remarks: A remarkable school with high academic expectation and achievement, a dazzling array of extracurricular activities and a dedicated staff. Has enjoyed, and is enjoying, outstanding leadership.

T

Thurston Community College

Norton Road, Thurston, Bury St Edmunds, Suffolk IP31 3PB

Ages 11–18 Pupils 1,435 Sixth form 375

01359 230885
www.thurstoncollege.org

Principal: Since 2005, Helen Wilson BSc MBA NPQH (40s). Studied applied physics with chemistry at Durham, followed by PGCE at Bristol. Previously assistant principal at Comberton village college and vice-principal at Thurston. Her long experience and tremendous dynamism have enabled the school to make a smooth transition from within a three tiered system to becoming an 11-18 school. Extremely personable, lively and direct, she works hard to ensure staff and pupils feel valued. A team player (her management style is described as 'exemplary,' by Ofsted) she is clear that 'appointing the right staff and supporting them' is key to the school's success. Keeps in close touch and believes in regular meetings (also, three whole staff briefings each week) as the means to picking up on possible problems.

Has strong support from parents: 'She has a good eye for the right staff' and 'She listens to what parents have to say [through the parents' forum] and takes action.' Her friendliness and ease with pupils are praised: 'She has that way of knowing how to speak to pupils without losing authority.' Continues to teach physics, though as in-class support: 'not enough time to class teach this year because of the merger', and often welcomes pupils to lunches in her office, all part of the system of recognition and award that underpins school life. Her overwhelming energy continues in off-duty sport – 'it is how I let off steam': though competitive hockey was put paid to with a new hip, she now cycles the 10 miles to and from school each day and enjoys skiing and water sports, also good food and drink with family and friends.

Academic matters: Achievement is strongly supported and clear strategies are in place to pick up problems early. Rigorous selection when appointing staff ('we want the outstanding ones') and a regular turnover ensures that standards are constantly appraised and improved. Pupils are referred to as students, rather than pupils, as the principal believes this better reflects the school's ambition to 'inculcate a passion for lifelong independent learning, rather than simply instruct them. They will need to have the skills to manage a life with several career changes.' The acronym SCRIPT is used to express this: self manager, creative thinker, reflective learner, independent participant, team worker. In 2018, 63 per cent got 9-4 in both English and maths. Wide choice of subjects on offer including three European languages. Year 7s study French, and 80 per cent of students in year 8 and 9 study a second language (either German or Spanish), and may continue one or more to GCSE. Latin (taught as an 'extra'), separate sciences, child development, dance, horticulture and mechanics also available. Everyone takes religious studies. Academic learning tuition (SEN support) is provided by 21 teaching assistants, mostly operating in the classroom, six qualified higher level teaching assistants and two SENCos. Lots of help available, including catch up classes in numeracy and literacy at break and lunch; there's a breakfast club (porridge served) and homework club each day.

Sixth form students (now on a separate site at Beyton, two miles off) work in surroundings more reminiscent of higher education: lots of private study areas, some supervised, others more relaxed and allowing for quiet discussion. Strong work ethic amongst students and 'it's easy to get help if you need it,' we were told. Good attainment at A level with 77 per cent A*-C grades in 2018. Popular subject choices include maths, psychology, all the sciences and English; only a handful study foreign languages.

Games, options, the arts: Despite having only a single, weekly timetabled games lesson (though it lasts 100 minutes), team and other sports flourish through a network of lunchtime and after-school clubs, and friendly inter-house rivalry is encouraged. Football, netball, rugby (girls' as well as boys'), excellent hockey and rounders with teams reaching county and regional stages of competitions and individuals selected for trials at national level. Club tours also organised – Paris this year. Other choices include Thai boxing, table tennis, gymnastics and the supervised fitness suite. Music and drama both timetabled up to year 9 and many pupils have instrumental lessons – practice rooms are available. Drama is a popular GCSE choice and the school stages two major productions each year; 'our daughters have both performed and we were amazed at what they achieved.' Art and textiles/design also have a high take-up at GCSE and students' work is well displayed and promoted. Emphasis in the sixth form is on volunteering projects, D of E, charity fundraising and the national citizenship service scheme.

Background and atmosphere: A large rural comprehensive close to Bury St Edmund's, with a separate sixth form campus in a revamped former middle school at Beyton. Reorganisation of the Suffolk schooling system from three tier to two tier saw it accept pupils from year 7 rather than year 9 from 2014, and the sixth form move to its separate site. With over 1,500 pupils at the main 11 to 16 site at Thurston, it has a, perhaps surprisingly, unflustered air. The entrance, via a car park and reception area, is reminiscent of a Travelodge, though efforts have been made to plant and landscape the approaches. Mostly single storey, interconnecting buildings of functional appearance, but cheerfully decorated within with carpeted corridors muffling noise, lots of pupils' work displayed, notice boards everywhere covered in information about after-school clubs and goings-on – a definite buzz. Good IT provision, two libraries (one open to the public out of hours) with separate areas for project work and private study. Several halls, of varying sizes, one with raked seating, are used for drama, games lessons and assemblies. Plenty of room to let off steam in surrounding playing fields.

No cloakrooms; pupils each have a locker in their house, close to their tutorial base. Unfussy uniform: pale blue polo shirts and jerseys with school logo, skirts or trousers for girls, though there is a movement to discourage trousers that verge on 'jeggings', not entirely approved of: 'It can be difficult for teenage girls to find sizes that fit well'. Despite large numbers, pupils move calmly around at changes of lesson and settle quickly. No mobiles allowed in class. Food is praised; 'there is lots of choice and we can buy food at break as well as lunch.' The sixth form site has been well converted and decorated, lots of fresh white paint, spanking new facilities including computer terminals, coffee shop, common rooms and libraries overlooking extensive lawns and woodland. More of a college atmosphere, no uniform, a more grown up air altogether; 'most of us are going to university and need to learn to work on our own,' we were told, and certainly saw a lot of independent study going on. The informal, respectful tone set by the principal is carried through and maintained by staff and pupils.

Pastoral care, well-being and discipline: The school is divided up into five houses (named after Suffolk luminaries) and pupils belong to a tutor group within a house for registration and academic and pastoral oversight. These smaller units, of around 300, help to give pupils a sense of identity and belonging. Tutors keep subject staff in the picture if problems arise and they are the first point of contact for parents wishing to discuss their child, although there is also a dedicated advice centre for parents to turn to, particularly with more routine enquiries. Particular nurturing of year 7s; the principal and staff visit all prospective pupils in their primary schools and there is a buddy system in place. A weather eye is kept out for pupils whose behaviour puts them at risk of exclusion, and though this is rare, the principal says, 'I'll do it if I have to.' Houses appoint up to 50 Ambassadors, who help with greeting visitors, acting as sheep dogs at open days and other events. The monthly magazine, Celebrate, records success in every aspect of school life: those winning house stars are published under Ovation, together with news and articles on school life. The school day is divided into 100 minute lessons, 'long enough to get stuck into a subject', spread over a two week timetable. There are longer breaks and lunchtimes than is usual, as pupils mostly travel some distance; 'school must provide plenty of social opportunities.' There is a homework club until 5pm and the school funds extra buses to enable pupils to stay later for sports fixtures and rehearsals.

Pupils and parents: The catchment, on the edge of Bury St Edmund's, is largely prosperous, rural and representative of this part of East Anglia; very few from ethnic minorities. A network of school bus routes brings most pupils, some from considerable distance. The school's popularity is endorsed by the number from out of the catchment. Strong approval for the management: 'The principal has a good eye for the right staff and morale seems to be very good.' The uniform, worn up to year 11, is well supported by pupils and parents.

Entrance: The expansion as an 11-18 (rather than 13-18) school has resulted in certain year groups higher up the school becoming very large, but there is a firm policy to keep year group sizes below 300 and the principal won't budge on this. Heavily oversubscribed; the catchment rules are stringent and it is important to check the admissions policy of Suffolk County Council. For A levels, at least a grade B/6 in the subject to be studied (or a related subject) is required, with an overall average GCSE points score of 43 or better. Students without a 4 in maths or English are required to continue studying the subject at after-school sessions, with a view to re-sitting the examination(s).

Exit: Around half stay on after GCSEs, the rest mostly moving on to employment or FE college. At 18 the great majority go on to university, with a wide range of subjects studied eg midwifery, electrical engineering, psychology and neuroscience. Around 40 per cent to Russell group universities.

Remarks: A large, extremely well managed comprehensive where the majority thrive and do well. Led by a dynamic head with a strong vocation and the ideas and determination to take the school to the top.

Town Close House Preparatory School

14 Ipswich Road, Norwich, Norfolk NR2 2LR

Ages 3–13 **Pupils** 505

Fees: £8,670 – £13,152 pa

01603 620180
www.townclose.com

Headmaster: Since 2013, Mr Nicholas Bevington BA PGCE (early 40s). Educated at Portsmouth Grammar, then Keele (read international relations) and Newcastle universities. Began teaching at Elstree School, brisk promotion to head of department, followed by Edgeborough and Abercorn Schools (deputy head) and Bede's Prep, Eastbourne, where he was head.

Tall, youthful looking and charming. His quick wit and energy are going down well with parents. 'We like what we have

T

seen so far,' say most. 'He is really committed, seems very on the ball.' One spoke of feeling, 'slightly overwhelmed. He creates a tremendous buzz.' Definitely not shy and retiring.

Good grasp of local school scene and the place Town Close occupies as a 'stand alone' day prep. Firmly in favour of transfer to senior schools at 13+ and success of pupils at this stage is vindication – lots of awards, many to selective schools, including Eton. He points to the fact that pupils also do well in subsequent years – often becoming head boy or head girl. Head knows that these final two years count – 'they have all the fun of leadership as they enter their teens and the extra years give many a chance to mature.'

Proud of school's reputation and feels parents know what they are getting. 'We never try to be something we are not, we don't try to attract children who won't thrive here.' Believes a day prep is ideal for most up to 13 and is not keen on flexi or 'fun' nights to entice children into boarding. 'We have plenty of after-school activities up to 6pm and that suits many of our parents.'

Wife Catherine is a hospital consultant and not involved in day to day matters at the school. They have two small children. He plays the guitar and flute, enjoys tennis and cycling and gardens.

Entrance: Assessment, rather than examination, at all points of entry to the school. Most start in nursery, reception or year 2, though plenty more join higher up as and when places become available. At nursery and reception stage, learning potential is assessed during an hour of class play-based activities, extending to half a day for year 2, including assessment of literacy and non-verbal reasoning, and a full day from year 4 onwards. Informal interview with head for years 2 to 4 (more formally, in the study, for year 5 up). Not, strictly speaking, a hard to get into school, but very popular and generally oversubscribed. 'Quite honestly,' a parent told us, 'I was anxious about the entrance "exam" but all was well. The head got right down to their level, talking to my son, and there was no worry or tears.'

Exit: Given the school's relaxed admission policy, pupils move on to an impressive range of schools, many academically highly selective. The local day independent, Norwich School, is by far the most popular. After that, it's Norwich High School, Langley School and Hethersett Academy.

Some opt for boarding, mostly to schools nearby – Gresham's, Framlingham and Culford. Some go further afield, to eg Oundle, Uppingham, Oakham or Wycombe Abbey. School gives lots of guidance on choices and scholarships, although head says: 'We can point the way, but in the end it's the parents' choice.'

Remarks: School Nursery extended – two large, colourful classrooms/ tranquil quiet room ideal for reading. improved access to the Pre Prep hall/ new Year 1 classroom/ Pre Prep Library on the first floor.

T

Tucked behind the tree-lined boulevards of south west Norwich, the school grounds are extensive, especially for a city school (school recently bought its site). An elegant Georgian house, with sweeping lawns, surrounded by various additions – classroom blocks, performance hall for drama and assemblies, sports hall, swimming pool, two playgrounds (junior and senior), woodland walks (school has forest school status), all in excellent condition.

General agreement that dining room needs a makeover. Wide approval for practice of sitting at tables with teachers, passing the salt and waiting until everyone has finished, although the food itself is not raved about. No dreary corridors – carpeted hallways and stunning displays of work throughout. Though warned not to try by his predecessor, the head has even solved the impossible parking and pick-up schedule (timed slots) and tightened security of the grounds into the bargain. Nursery and pre-prep have a separate building, recently extended and re-vamped (library added), with enticing play area.

Pupils extremely polite – door holding and standing up for visitors de rigueur. Our guides maintained extreme discretion throughout – perhaps not the place for free spirits? However, we saw lively pupil/teacher exchanges, including an enthralling discussion of post-mortem research in a history lesson. High levels of expectation – setting from reception in literacy, increasing to full blown setting by ability in years 7 and 8. Reading is seriously encouraged, with an excellent library open every lunchtime (we approve) and a jolly nice full-time librarian. Pupils also have timetabled lessons there. School now provides tablets for all year 6-8s. A number of pupils with SEN – mostly dyslexia, a few with language and speech needs. Individual support is given for EAL, but all must be able to follow the curriculum.

Excellent music, with massive take-up of private instrumental lessons and opportunities to play in ensembles and orchestras and sing in choirs. Music, drama and other performing arts are encouraged and showcased as much as sport (pupils have left for the Royal Ballet School). Shakespeare, pantomimes, Last Night of the Proms, it's all happening. 'You enjoy school more if you do stuff,' say pupils.

All team sports played very successfully and several outstanding individuals play at county and even national level. Everyone gets the chance to play in matches but, say pupils, 'it's not always the same Player of the Match.' Parents speak in lip-smacking approval. 'Lovely school,' one told us. 'Ideal for our daughter, who has thrived.' Another, worried about choosing for her son, said: 'We picked absolutely the right one for him. The staff are brilliant and really seem to know the children.' Several spoke of their child's confidence being nurtured and former pupils have nothing but praise. 'I loved my time there and would have stayed if I could,' said one girl. Great majority of pupils are the offspring of successful professionals, notably doctors. Main recruiting channel is the one money can't buy – word of mouth.

Tudor Grange Academy

Dingle Lane, Solihull, West Midlands B91 3PD

Ages 11–18 **Pupils** 1,558 **Sixth form** 290

0121 705 5100
www.solihull.tgacademy.org.uk

Principal: Since September 2018, Claire Smith who has worked at the Academy since 2011, progressing from director of sport, to college leader, to associate principal. Married with two young children, she was educated at Sheffield Hallam University and has been teaching since 2004.

Academic matters: Not a grade-chasing school approaching league table results as if they were the Holy Grail. The school's determination to empower both staff and pupils with the confidence to perform to the best of their ability has brought forth some very impressive results. These are prominently displayed in the school's prospectus and other literature as well as on the website. The school is justifiably proud of the results, which are down to good teaching, intervention when necessary and hard-working pupils who have been encouraged to believe in themselves. Some subjects – such as maths – are taught in ability groups. Unlike a distressing number of schools – many in the independent sector – where pupils whose performance suggests they won't achieve good grades are told to leave, there is no suggestion of that here, though there are entry requirements for the sixth form. Instead parents, staff and pupil get together to work out a stratagem for one-to-one help in those subjects requiring extra attention. This is all explained on the school website under the heading Pupil Premium. The result is that in the DfE performance tables the school is in the top 10 of non-selective schools in the country. As one teacher told us, 'We never, never, never give up on our pupils.' The most recent Ofsted report graded the school as outstanding in all areas. As an illustration, consider the fact that in 2018, 91 per cent of pupils got 9-4 in both maths and English GCSE, and 35 per cent of grades were A*-A/9-7. At A level, 62 per cent of grades were A*-B and 30 per cent A*/A. Ofsted reported that 'students in all subjects make exceptional progress because they are challenged and their personal skills are strongly developed.' The reference to 'personal skills' is very relevant to the principal's mantra.

We saw generous amounts of teaching and witnessed nothing that contradicted Ofsted. We saw lively, clever teaching with lots of encouragement and individual treatment; we saw keen and alert pupils – even those who, despite everything, confessed sadly that they didn't really like the subject but were determined to pass. Underpinning all this is the obvious enthusiasm and happiness of the staff. Attached to the main school is a training school for teachers. Far from going for the posthumous VC, these teachers are bright, enthusiastic and willing to immerse themselves in placements, including Tudor Grange itself. Some, probably the very best, stay on for a year or two, injecting a sense of energy and purpose. The staff room was friendly, staff happy to talk about the school, serious in purpose and quick to laugh, appearing bright, cheerful and stylish. Pupils wear their uniforms smartly. It all helps.

Games, options, the arts: The school was founded in 1956 and there is a fascinating but unintentional memorial to that – viz an old building looking a little like a WW2 Nissan hut which has narrowly missed a direct hit. It is the old gymnasium, and it just survives beside an area of tarmac where football, basketball, netball and other games are played. A large and unmistakable building dominates. It's the superbly equipped sports hall more than 50 years on. An exercise in architectural history; an example of progress: not beautiful, but functional. We witnessed a tremendously lively girls' cricket session overseen by the captain of England's women's team and met a number of youthful, forthcoming and, yes, very friendly staff. Outside there are plenty of sports pitches which are used in partnership with West Warwickshire Sports Club, and which generate many regional and national sportsmen and women.

In a typical week there are over 60 extracurricular clubs and activities, some very unusual. We saw and admired some wonderful art, photography and creative work involving papier mâché and other materials. One pupil assured us that these activities were open for enjoyment out of class and in spare time; another rolled her eyes as if there was no such thing. We were charmed and startled by a girl asking if we would like to see her heart. It turned out to be the heart of an animal which she had bought from a local butcher and was going to use for a project. It was a lovely example of the open enthusiasm and friendliness that is such an obvious feature of this school.

Plenty of music, both vocal and instrumental, including the increasingly popular ukulele, orchestras and jazz bands. Instrumental lessons are provided by the Solihull Music Services for a minimal fee. We met a delightful and talented pupil who was composing for his entrance exam to music college and heard a lively choir practice. Much exuberance and enjoyment all round.

Background and atmosphere: The school was founded as a grammar school in 1956 for around 650 boys; in 1974 it linked up with the girls' grammar which had always been on the same site. In 1995 it became a technology college, in 2009 it was business and enterprise and two years later an academy for 11-16s; most recently it has extended its age range to include a sixth form and earned almost trumpeting praise from Ofsted. Now it aims at 'world class' education. The atmosphere, especially on the gloriously sunny day when we visited, was delightful. Very few pupils arrived alone and it was noticeable that groups greeted each other with easy warmth. In a natural, relaxed way there seemed to be an underlying sense of interested expectation both socially and academically.

This underlying happiness remained as we walked around meeting groups moving from classroom to classroom. Eye contact and smiles, easy conversation when we stopped to ask questions; wide-ranging topics of conversation, pertinent questions, sometimes amused reactions. Clearly the pupils are used to meeting and talking with alleged adults. Equally friendly was the company in the dining room, and if behaviour in school dining rooms has something to do with the quality of the food, that's not surprising. The food was certainly excellent.

Pastoral care, well-being and discipline: We watched pupils arriving quietly in happy groups, greeting and being greeted by staff; we observed a tutorial group being reminded of special activities in the near future in an atmosphere of relaxed concentration and fun. The tutorial system is rather good and appreciated overall by parents and pupils. Each new pupil is allotted a College, as it's called. These are mixed age groups, with three or four pupils from each year, in which boys and girls remain for their time at school. The leader of the College gets to know them well. Pupils seemed very happy with this arrangement and, of course, they are subliminally learning lessons about responsibility, consideration, age differences, leadership. As far as discipline is concerned, that didn't seem to be much of a problem. Nor did bullying emerge as an issue, though we were told by a few girls of the occasional fights between girls. These were dismissed as trivial and very, very rare. 'In any case,' they said, 'there are pupils and staff who help... Tudor Rangers, that building over there, provides refuge and counselling for children who have been or are being bullied. You can go there if you feel insecure.' The school has a very powerful, clear anti-bullying policy and staff are continually aware of the possibilities. Parents were happy with the lack of bullying.

Pupils and parents: The school has its own allotted catchment area. This has had a significant effect on the local housing market and there are accounts of parents mortgaging themselves up to the hilt because they feel the school is such a valuable asset. We spoke to a number of parents, all of whom reckoned it was a pretty good bargain overall. They are not poor but they are making sacrifices. They particularly like the improved communications and the new regime, though not at the expense of the old. By and large, they all seemed pretty grateful. So, too, did the pupils, in a delightfully unaffected way.

Entrance: Preference to looked after children, then those attending the linked primary school, then those living in the catchment area, then siblings.

About 50 per cent of year 11 pupils stay on for the sixth form. Grades required are a minimum of six grades 6s at GCSE with at least a 4 in maths and English. Pupils must achieve a minimum grade 6 in any subject they wish to take at A level. A large number of external candidates apply for entry into the sixth form; about 20-30 gain places. Pupils already in the school who do not match the entry criteria are signposted to other sixth forms in the local area with whom the school has strong links.

Exit: The school takes considerable trouble to prepare students for courses and universities suitable for their abilities and aspirations. About 80 per cent of sixth formers to university, two to Cambridge in 2018, one to Oxford and one medic. Occasional students to American universities, plus Aston, Nottingham Trent, Nottingham and Birmingham popular. There is also much help with apprenticeships and career choices for those leaving after GCSE (about 50 per cent). A popular and encouraging feature is the number of pupils who have left for fresh educational adventures and who return to share helpful tales and knowledgeable advice.

Money matters: Trips and excursions incur some cost, but overall the school is excellent value for money, making Solihull a particularly attractive place in which to live.

Remarks: In some ways this extraordinary school embraces the old fashioned virtues, albeit using modern teaching aids. Teaching here is for educating, for broadening horizons, for challenging capabilities, for exciting pupils, for enrichment. It is learning for life and not merely for grades. Parents and pupils feel that targets are personal and individually tailored. We heard very little suggestion of force-feeding driven by anxious staff petrified by Ofsted and grade targets. This is an excellent set-up; some would say worth moving to Solihull for. And we were not bribed by estate agents.

Uppingham Community College

London Road, Uppingham, Rutland LE15 9TJ

Ages 11–16 **Pupils** 912

01572 823631
www.uppinghamcollege.org.uk

Principal: Since September 2017, Ben Solly. Previously head of Lutterworth College in Leicestershire for three years, where he led the transition from 14-18 to 11-18. PE and sports science with management degree from Hull. Worked as an advanced skills teacher in the Black Country and in a variety of senior leadership roles in Leicestershire. What attracted him to UCC? Always had his eye on it, 'Reminded me of when I was at school, sense of community. You don't get that everywhere.'

There are two things that immediately strike you about him, his passion for Wolves football team and his blue laces. A head who likes to make a statement – knows where he is going and proud of where he has come from. The rapport with students and staff alike was evident – his presence around the school is clearly felt, pupils seem to respect that.

Hit with Ofsted during his first two weeks as head of UCC, there was no easing himself into the role – judging by his pragmatic approach he wouldn't have wanted it any other way. Priority has been simplifying the school, 'asking ourselves – does this directly benefit our students? If not, it goes'. Arguably the biggest change was EFA (embedded formal assessments in lessons as part of the learning process), for which he credits his deputy.

Solly refers to staff as a 'talented group'. There is very much a grow your own approach. He says it's about 'taking away the barriers from their jobs and actually let them teach'. There is obvious mutual respect amongst staff; around 50 teachers and low staff turnover. He extends this 360-approach to himself, still teaching a Y11 PE GCSE group, GCSE child development and personal development.

Parents sing his praises: 'My daughter started at UCC in year 10. She loves it. Mr Solly is great, so lovely. He is young for a head but makes great things happen.' His acid test for the school – would this be good enough for his own son? If not, he changes it.

Academic matters: In 2018, 80 per cent of pupils gained 9-4 in both GCSE maths and English, 22 per cent A*-A/9-7 overall. It was clear why – every minute counted, children were on task and knew outcomes. Pupil's use success criteria set by the teacher to evaluate their own work and peers as well as strategies such as live marking in class to ensure pupils have immediate feedback and can visualise their next steps.

UCC goals are made clear to prospective parents during the induction meetings. The ethos is that exams are important but don't define pupils. Academically the school is all about 'adding value', 'teaching to the top', with most students entering with average or above attainment from primary school. Higher project qualifications (HPQ) are generally offered to the cleverest KS4 students.

In the maths block walls come down to provide collaborative learning opportunities between classes. There is also a 'mathematician of the month' board to motivate pupils. Year 10s use talking partners to take away anxiety, markers on desks to show workings out. A year 7 history lesson debated gruesome questions, although pupils looked perplexed. Drama students in year 11 were engrossed in studying characterisation. Animated in music, on task in physics and an IT lesson included some deeper thinking questioning. Year 11 art portfolios work showed maturity.

Students start off with French and can then add German and Spanish. When it comes to KS4 choices, the school are firm that 'doors should not be closed at 14'. Students study the usual subjects with the choice of four further options from 17 GSCE subjects. Choices vary from statistics through to citizenship and drama.

A big emphasis is placed on relating the curriculum to real life. 'Our best lessons include fried egg on a machine to illustrate how machinery gets hot,' said one student. This tactile approach seems to be adopted in most lessons and there is a strong sense of responsibility for learning. Pupils particularly enjoy 'real world' learning in personal development education lessons, enthusing that topics such as mortgages and taxes 'really prepare us for life.'

'My son gets good grades even though he is not particularly academic,' said one parent. 'Our daughter has achieved well,' said another. There were few grumbles with homework. 'Ours has a purpose to it – it may be a project or follow up work,' said one pupil.

Sixteen pupils currently have EHCPs and all with SEND are given 'high expectations'. Where needed, there's intensive support in years 7 and year 8. Those struggling in English take part in conversational MFL lessons where there is less emphasis on writing and grammar, to ensure they are given a spark of languages. It's a case of prioritising without the children losing out – seems logical to us.

Games, options, the arts: Photos of captains as well as staff proudly adorn the sports hall entrance. Facilities here are excellent: think climbing wall in the sports hall, Astro, netball and tennis courts and open fields with views over the Welland Valley. A range of sporting opportunities – with equal opportunities for all. The girls' rugby in particular does well here as well as do the sailing clubs at nearby Rutland Water. UCC won the Ernie White Commitment to School Sport award 2017: a commendable achievement from a highly competitive field of state secondary schools across Leicestershire and Rutland.

Both drama and music are offered at GCSE, though take up is relatively low, at around 16 per cent for drama and seven per cent for music. A multi-functional drama studio with flexible seating and lighting rigs helps. 'The annual musical is fantastic – it creates a big sense of community,' said one pupil. Students enjoyed performing The Tempest at the Corby Cube theatre.

Music is building thanks to a new music teacher, with new technology evident. Woodwind and string ensembles join together to make the UCC orchestra. Choirs and rock choir are popular. Students across both key stages take lessons. Year 7 were off to a Young Voices event with 600 other pupils when we visited.

Technology is still a strong point; the legacy of the school's specialism remains. Product design rooms are well equipped, with computer screens showcasing pupils' work, 3D printers and working hubs giving the sense of a professional working space. There is a well-stocked library (no librarian now as part of Solly's streamlining; students run it to cut down on expenditure), and a careers office ran by a professional careers adviser.

Science links are strong with UCC hosting a Super Physicians event for 30 other schools every year. Additional curriculum experience (ACE) days have included an apocalypse day: think re-enactment of a crime scene, multi-media, videos with staff getting in on the action. Year 9 had the chance to become business entrepreneurs, with 40 local businesses holding a Dragon's Den-type trade fayre, the best pitches winning the investments. Year 11 have 'next steps' sessions to help prepare them for future careers and the school embraces year 10 work experience.

Out of hours, the school was once a hotbed of unusual school activities (equestrian team and racing cars, to name but two), though some appear to have disappeared since we last visited. 'We used to have more clubs, but a lot have been dropped,' reported pupils. 'Mainly sports ones due to staff moving on.' We found more – superhero science club, debating, music, rock climbing. DofE is still going strong.

Students enthuse about outings and opportunities to travel: 'We have loads of trips – languages. Berlin was great'. International links remain with a 45-year-long Don Bosco Sports Exchange in Belgium. Teams compete in a range of activities from athletics to football, table tennis and tug of war. The exchange has got to the point where parents, who attended years ago, now host families.

Background and atmosphere: Founded in 1920 in the small market town of Uppingham, the school sits within walking distance of its well-known public school neighbour. Some areas are a little tired, but the surrounding green space gives it a feeling of calm. Since we last visited there has been a big emphasis on revamping the school day to ensure punctuality and core lesson time. Students now have a five minute 'movement window' to get to lessons on time. They say, 'We get more out of lessons.' School break and lunchtime remain busy – there are some lovely al fresco areas with picnic benches where pupils can dine but queues remain clearly evident in the dining hall. Fingerprints for paying for snacks and lunches help, along with extra food hatches and a system where students can pre-order at break, but clearly the problem hasn't been fully eradicated; 'dinner lines are the biggest issue,' say students (the school is working on this). Around school there is a genuine sense of trust; pupils store bags outside design and science labs, using lockers at other times. They are allowed independence during lessons, leaving the classroom for some activities, although we spotted some using mobile phones in corridors while supposedly working in groups. Staff monitor school uniform – blazers and ties – and keep standards high.

Pastoral care, well-being and discipline: Students are generally upbeat: 'There are ups and downs at UCC, but generally it's good – you learn stuff,' said one pupil. A year 11 student described it as a 'bouncy school. With supportive teachers and staff who help you combat your issues.'

Year groups remain with the same form tutor for the duration of their time at UCC and pupils also have their own personal development coaches to deal with pastoral issues. One praised the system, 'They understand school life and are non-judgemental.' Students mostly describe the school as an 'inclusive, comfortable atmosphere like close family.' There is a big emphasis on proactive engagement with families: coaches phone home if a pupil doesn't turn up and, if necessary, pick them up and bring them in. The school is proud of its attendance record, with pupil premium students scoring nearly as well as others.

Pupils reel off the school rules and vision of 'respect, honesty and kindness', are well dressed and smart. Movement around school is generally well mannered. Many say mental health is good: 'School doesn't put a lot of pressure on us'; 'Most people help each other if they are upset.'

Some students report that behaviour 'has got better but still needs to be sorted,' with others saying that they have experienced a few incidents in lessons, but 'teachers are straight on it and pupils know what is expected of them.' They mostly describe UCC as 'friendly', saying that 'bullying has got a lot better even in the corridors.' A tiny minority of parents disagree and say they feel bullying is not dealt with. According to the head, 'Bullying occurs in every school. We have a completely open bullying policy and we do not tolerate it – pupils are taught to be responsible for their own actions.' Other parents maintain pupils are valued; 'they get to know their students as individuals.'

Year 7s have a two-day induction, and there are regular open evenings for feeder schools which staff, parents and pupils alike say helps 'settle' the pupils into UCC life. One year 7 parent said their child 'has made great friends.'

Pupils and parents: Pupils are from Uppingham, surrounding Rutland villages and the nearby counties of Leicestershire and Northamptonshire. The school is slap bang in a quadrant of high achieving private schools, and the head acknowledges the need to manage some parental expectations: 'There is a certain amount of parent pressure as they are aware of the independents in the area and seem to expect the same even though we are working off state funding.' Other parents are more realistic, 'We are surrounded by posh private schools here in Uppingham but UCC holds its own.' Parents report that 'there is something for every child whether academic or not.'

Students say given the choice they would 'loosen uniform' and 'focus more on behaviour such as running in the corridor.' Student council members wish they 'had been consulted about more things,' but others are positive, saying there are 'lots of opportunities to get stuck in and we are taught to be more independent so if something goes wrong you have to own it.' What do they do well? 'Form tutors, progress leaders, friends and personal development coaches.'

Ex pupils include John Browett, CEO of Monsoon and Accessorize and Ian Carter, president of Hilton International.

Entrance: Pupils are from Uppingham, surrounding Rutland villages and the nearby counties of Leicestershire and Northamptonshire. Eleven feeder schools. Preference, after children in care, siblings, children in catchments of named primary schools, children of staff and then distance.

Exit: A third of pupils move on to sixth form college Harington School in Oakham, which opened in 2015 (Solly is head trustee). Criteria is selective by GSCE results. Most of the remainder are split geographically between sixth form state provisions such as Wyggeston and Queen Elizabeth College in Leicester. Some 10 per cent to private sixth forms – think Kings, Uppingham and Oakham; sporting scholarships are common. For those with less academic inclination the vocational choices of Corby College prove popular, as well as apprenticeships elsewhere.

Remarks: A friendly, supportive school with commendable pastoral support, high expectations and a big emphasis on relating the curriculum to real life. The head has long term plans and is constantly looking forward. Students seem happy, on task in lessons and with a sense of trust. A state school holding its own in difficult financial times.

Uppingham School

    96

High Street West, Uppingham, Rutland LE15 9QE

Ages 13–18 **Pupils** 785 **Sixth form** 345 **Boarders** 773 full **C of E**

Fees: Day £26,313; Boarding £37,590 pa

01572 822216
www.uppingham.co.uk

Headmaster: Since 2016, Dr Richard Maloney MA (theology at St Andrew's) PGCE (Cantab), early 40s, previously head of Bede's Senior School. An alumnus of Latymer Upper School, Dr Maloney began his career in West Yorkshire. In 1997, he became head of RS and, later, head of sixth, at Chigwell School, during which period he completed an MA at King's College, London. In 2006, he was appointed deputy headmaster of Sutton Valence. During his tenure there he became a PhD but left after three years to take up the Bede's headship – whilst still in his 30s. We described him at Bede's as 'A man of palpable energy – physical and intellectual – complemented by equal measures of compassion, dedication, ambition and vision'. He transformed that school and has become hot educational property.

He is married to Tracey, who runs an educational consultancy, and they have two children.

Academic matters: Although the emphasis is on holistic education, academic matters do not suffer. It was obvious from talking to pupils that teachers relish challenging the most able to get as far as they can. All abilities are making excellent progress and exam results are strong, but parents hastened to inform us that Uppingham is no academic hothouse, and compared the approach to education very favourable to what they see as the stressful academic day schools of Cambridge and London. In 2018, 54 per cent of A levels/Pre-Us were at A or A* and 80 per cent were at A* to B. At GCSE, 70 per cent A*-A/9-7 grades in 2018; this stays fairly steadily in the high 60s, low 70s year on year.

The school considers all subjects to be strong, pointing to outstanding results and large numbers taking both science and arts subjects at A level. Pupils enthuse about the history, religious studies and politics, but also approve of the various innovations that the stunning new science block has inspired, including the outdoor science classroom. The new labs are designed with one half for practical work and the other half for the theory – a great improvement on the traditional labs where students make notes between the gas taps and Bunsen burners. With 29 A level subjects on offer, there is a superb range. The post-16 curriculum is under close review but current view is that a combination of A levels, Pre-U, and the EPQ will offer lots of stimulus for all in the sixth form. Average class size is 16, and nine in the sixth form. There is support for those with mild learning difficulties and those who need help with English language (at extra cost).

Games, options, the arts: You would expect a school that prides itself on its holistic education to provide a rich extracurricular offer and Uppingham doesn't disappoint. Facilities, which are also used by the local community, are outstanding – the biggest stage, the pupils informed us, of any school they had heard of, and drama is supported by fantastic teachers and professional technicians. Endless sports on offer and, pupils assure us, it is for everyone, not just the elite. One year 13 boy spoke with considerable enthusiasm about his engagement with a lowly rugby team. As well as 'major' sports there is a plethora of others – just as well, given that it is compulsory to do something.

Music is outstanding – one parent said that all independent schools say their music is good, but at Uppingham it is really good. Everyone mentions whole school congregational singing in chapel. There are House Shouts in which everyone seems to get involved, and then highly selective choirs and orchestras for the specialists. These groups tour in the UK and overseas as well as having endless performance opportunities in school. Masterclasses given by eminent musicians are regular features. Recording studios, a radio station and music technology encourage those who aspire to find renown in more celebrity spheres, honing their acts along the way in the school Battle of the Bands.

Everyone does CCF, though there is an opt-out for older pupils, who can get involved in community service. Some help in local primary schools, including teaching a Latin programme; others visit elderly people, ride with disabled people or take part in various overseas aid projects.

The art is vibrant and diverse – taking place in the Leonardo Centre, named after the Renaissance Man, the ultimate model for the Uppingham student.

Boarding: All but a tiny handful board. Everyone says it is a school for children who really want the full boarding experience – no flexi approach countenanced here to ease the way for those valuing their own 'me time'. There are separate girls' and boys' boarding houses spread over the small market town. Most are vertical – pupils from every age group – but there is also a sixth form girls' house, as more girls join the school at sixth form level. Some houses are in the centre, having the advantage of being minutes away from teaching areas, others are further out and have the advantage of more space – one boasting its own swimming pool. Prospective families are normally taken to see just a few of the houses, though you can see all 15 if you really want.

Boys' houses have around 50 pupils and girls' about 60. Each has a housemaster or mistress living there with their own family. There are resident tutors and a team of non-resident tutors attached to each house. Meals are taken in the house and house staff share the tables with the pupils. There is a rota of other staff circulating around the houses, so the students are very used to visitors.

Background and atmosphere: Uppingham is a boarding school with no half measures. Only a handful of pupils go home for the night – it is a school for those who want people around all the time and masses to do. 'Much too much, really,' said one boy who knew his exam results could have been a bit better if there weren't just such a brilliant amount going on all the time. However, one mother who spoke to us said that the houseparents have a close grip on this sort of problem and can usually sort things out early on.

When we dined at one house, the boys were completely charming – enthusiastic about everything at school and genuinely interested in their visitors. These are young people whose emotional intelligence is being unobtrusively developed on a daily basis. Separate girls' and boys' houses add to the individual flavour of each house. They can come to breakfast in their pyjamas and experience single sex norms as well as the hurly burly of co-ed in the classroom. Parents who had visited a number of houses before the children joined Uppingham said that every houseparent they met had credibility, and had proved to be inspirational.

With all the high quality activity on offer both in regulated and not regulated time, you would have to work very hard at being bored round here. Sixth formers have their own social centre, which is open once a term to other years, but most pupils are dashing from sports fields to drama studios to art rooms to music rehearsals, getting the most out of every minute.

Pastoral care, well-being and discipline: A lot of thought goes into settling in new pupils. They have a mentor in the year above and a sixth form mentor in their house. House staff make sure there is plenty going on at the weekends, so new pupils are quickly immersed in the busy life of the school. We got the sense that the staff all loved communal life, and their enthusiasm is infectious. Pupils all talked about their close friendships – 'My friends are always there for me and probably always will be,' said one year 13, starting to contemplate life beyond Uppingham.

There are school counsellors and a school psychotherapist, and all the pupils we spoke to felt there were plenty of staff to whom they could take any concerns. As part of the curriculum, there is health and social education that supports the usual areas of teenage angst, with self-help techniques as well as information and advice. Sixth formers are trained to support the younger pupils.

There are very firm rules and sanctions about bullying, drugs, smoking and alcohol use. Spirits are taken more seriously than wine. Everyone knows the score, and where a pupil has fallen foul of the sanctions, parents have accepted the firm and clear way the school has dealt with the matter.

Pupils and parents: The large map in the registrar's office with its pins indicating where in the UK families come from shows, not surprisingly, a preponderance from the wealthy parts of the country – largely home counties, but there are plenty from the Midlands and the north too. Parents are mostly from the professional and business classes. A steady 12 to 15 per cent of boarders are from overseas. Parents like the real mix of nationalities. They also like the school's approach to the family. 'The school gives you the sense that it is the whole family joining the school; they really want us to get involved too.'

The pupils are fully aware of the preconceptions that others have of them. 'But we are not arrogant,' they assure us. 'The school actively teaches us humility. We are confident, but when you are living with lots of different people and learning how to get on together, it tends to make you confident.' Parents say they are delighted with how Uppingham pupils turn out – they are engaging, personable, gregarious and go out into the world with enthusiasm and interest in other people.

Alumni include John Schlesinger, Stephen Fry, Rick Stein, Jenny Willott, Rowan Atkinson, John Suchet and Tim Melville-Ross.

Entrance: As you would expect, the admissions process is a very well-oiled machine. Many families start the process three years before the actually date of entry. It is all very welcoming and informative. Most join at 13+, but there is also a significant entry at 16+, particularly from girls who have been in a single sex environment. Most of these girls (typically 25-30 a year) are housed in the sixth form girls' house, The Lodge.

There is a pre-testing round at 11 (year 7) with papers in maths and English, an interview and references from current school. Places are then conditional on further tests in year 8, when pupils can sit common entrance (55 per cent average pass mark) or the school's own exam, consisting of maths and English with a further interview.

At sixth form level, there is a six GCSE at 6 grade minimum requirement for everyone, but virtually all existing pupils get those. For those coming in from outside, there are also sixth form scholarship and non-scholarship exams, plus two interviews – a house one and an academic one.

Exit: Very few leave after GCSEs. In 2018, six to Oxbridge, with three off to the US and one to the Netherlands. Bristol, Newcastle, Oxford Brookes, Edinburgh, Durham and Exeter also popular. There is a good range of subjects, business, history, sciences, politics and international relations coming out top. The careers advice and particularly support with UCAS applications are highly regarded, with subject staff and house staff all contributing.

Money matters: A serious number of scholarships are awarded at both 13+ and 16+: music, art, DT, sport and all-rounder as well as academic. There is also a new sixth form science scholarship. Typically, in a year group of about 150, there will be 35 scholarships awarded.

There is also some means-tested bursary support available – the registrar says the approach is flexible to respond to the very individual needs of a family.

Remarks: Even though it is big and spreads throughout the small market town of Uppingham, everyone tells us the school has a homely feel. We know just what they mean – though it is probably Homes & Gardens homely rather than the average urban semi. It is a rather wonderful bubble, and feels a world away from the relatively close Midlands cities. Uppingham is charming English small market town, with its own theatres (owned and run by the school) and its own cafés and shops that the pupils wonder round relatively freely. Parents and pupils love it.

We had some sense that by the time the pupils leave the school, they are hungry for the wider world, but that is a good thing. A sixth former who wanted to party hard might start to find it restricting, but the community feel is energising enough for most. The pupils are aware of how fortunate they are. They are not taking all this for granted, and the ones we spoke to were determined to make the most of all their wonderful opportunities. They were enthusiastic, curious and positive – as one would hope for from a liberal, holistic education. Will they change the world, lead the revolution? Probably not. Will they spread sweetness and light wherever they go? We think probably yes. Will they be responsible citizens of the world? Another yes.

Warwick Junior School

Linked with Warwick School, Warwick Preparatory School, King's High School

Myton Road, Warwick CV34 6PP

Ages 7–11 **Pupils** 259 **C of E**

Fees: £11,181 – £12,549 pa

01926 776418
www.warwickschool.org

Headmaster of the Junior School: Since September 2016, Mr Andrew Hymer, previously head of Wolverhampton Grammar Junior School. BA in ancient history and classical archaeology (Sheffield), PGCE (College of Ripon and York St John), DPSE (Birmingham City University), MAEd (Birmingham City University), NPQH. Originally, and briefly, a policeman in South Yorkshire, he has also taught at schools including Ashville College and RGS Worcester, and been deputy head of King's Hawford. Spends most of his free time watching or coaching cricket and rugby.

Entrance: Most boys enter aged 7 but are welcome at any age, providing there is room. Exams in February for entrance the following September for 8+, 9+ and 10+. School can be flexible, so do ask if you are interested in sending your son in the middle of the year. The Warwick schools pride themselves on being academic, but not aggressively so. Thus it is that even 7 year olds are required to takes tests in English, maths, reading and a short story exercise in creative writing. Thereafter the exams require non-verbal reasoning. 'Fair but demanding,' said one parent. Do ask about music scholarships.

Exit: Majority of boys move up to Warwick Senior School after sitting the entrance exam (a few to King Edward VI School, Stratford and in ones and twos to Alcester Grammar). In the event of any boy beginning to slip beneath the required standard or perhaps not cutting the mustard, parents and staff will meet and discuss. That is a rare event but it's worth emphasising that the move up is not automatic.

Remarks: The junior school is one part of the whole educational adventure offered by the Warwick Independent Schools Foundation that comprises the prep (boys and girls start together but boys move on aged 7 and girls aged 11), King's High School for girls, and the boys' school (Warwick School) that is divided into junior and senior schools. Each school has its own governing body. (It is worth noting in passing that the Warwick Independent Schools Foundation has drawn up plans to move King's High from its current town centre site to the campus where Warwick School and Warwick Preparatory School are already based by 2020).

From the moment you approach the entrance past the wonderfully evocative stone bears fashioned in a domestic group, you feel there is something creative and inviting about the set up. So there is. To arrive during break is to be greeted by a cacophony of joyous noise and delight. Handball courts, cricket stumps, hide and seek, invention, creation, happiness, boys being boys and, 'just messing about,' as one delighted chap told us.

One real advantage of attending any of the Warwick schools lies in being able to use the amazing shared facilities. The boys who showed us round, or joined in with such enthusiasm, were understandably proud and thrilled by these opportunities. Junior school is housed in its own red brick building on the main senior school site and everything appears to be seamlessly integrated. Junior boys clearly feel very much part of the overall scheme of things and not at all intimidated by the size of the buildings or the senior boys. 'It makes you really look forward to going there,' one boy said before adding hastily, 'but it is very good here.' We have visited the three schools on this campus more than once so have spent a lot of time observing, chatting, listening, being greeted and smiled at, playing the old game of pretending to be lost in order to ask for help and judging the response. Some schools, en masse, can make visitors feel a trifle threatened: 'What are you doing in our space?' Not so Warwick. It's a courteous and happy place and, as the head commented, 'not a tweedy school.'

With such a space in which to thrive offering safety, challenge and opportunity, it is not surprising that the boys at Warwick Junior seem so happy and confident. It's good to visit a place where effort is acknowledged, here it's done by means of the 'Congratulations Board' where anything noteworthy is recorded and celebrated. Pictures are everywhere – art is terrific and flourishing – and photos adorn the passages and staircases. Instead of the familiar and faintly nauseating 'personal' messages saying, 'A warm welcome to all prospective parents today, especially Mr and Mrs Drawley and their young son Aeneas', the screen in the entrance hall celebrates children, childhood, involvement and achievement. 'Will we see your face up on the screen?' we asked a passing boy. He cast an expert eye on the current picture and replied, 'Yes. But you'll have to wait a long time before it comes round.'

Music is taken very seriously at the Warwick schools and here in the junior school about 140 boys learn at least one instrument, contributing to school orchestra, big choir, micro choir, three rock bands, string orchestra, brass monkeys. New boys are loaned stringed instruments to give them the opportunity of learning without parents having to fork out for a Stradivarius. Drama also very popular, there is a hall for such activities in the school but the climax of dramatic activities is a play produced and performed in the professionally run Bridge House Theatre. That same theatre hosts professional concerts, plays and shows and is a wonderful addition to the overall life of the school and surrounding community. There are some interesting clubs and societies including, we noticed, the Japanese Club, whose gastronomic influence spreads as far as a Japanese lunch. Sporting facilities are marvelous, and it comes as no surprise that in the last five years the school has won six national sporting titles in rugby, golf and swimming (the superb pool is clearly a tremendous advantage). Senior boys and girls from the High School visit the younger boys to help out with various activities, partly out of the goodness of their hearts and partly towards their Duke of Edinburgh Awards.

Classrooms are wonderfully bright and inviting and we witnessed some marvelous teaching with bags of enthusiastic responses from the boys and imaginative and lively input from the staff. In one classroom we asked pupils who, we discovered later, had only been at the school a year, what words they would use to describe the school. We received the usual contented answers about food, games, music etc but most revealing, perhaps, was the boy who offered the word 'strict.' 'Is that good or bad?' we asked. 'Good,' he replied. A parent we encountered in the car park used the same word when describing the school. 'It helps the children to know the rules of the game. It's a bit like marking out a tennis court. You can enjoy the game better when you know the rules.'

Warwick Preparatory School

Linked with Warwick School, Warwick Junior School, King's High School

Bridge Field, Banbury Road, Warwick CV34 6PL

Ages Girls 3-11, boys 3-7 **Pupils** 488

Fees: £10,563 – £12,666 pa

01926 491545
www.warwickprep.com

Head: Since 2016, Hellen Dodsworth, previously co-head at Coten End Primary School, Warwick. Music and education degree from Warwick University. Combines leadership presence and strong sense of authority with the warmth needed as head of a prep school. Brings considerable state school leadership experience, understanding the best of current thinking in areas such as pedagogy and use of data. Has developed the curriculum at here to embrace the best of the national curriculum but adapted it to school's specific needs. Keen to pursue links with other schools, within both sectors. 'No school should be an island', she tells us. Parents find her very accessible and are happy to go to her with any niggle, something she strongly encourages. Has two boys being educated within the Warwick Foundation, and when not supporting their numerous activities enjoys continuing her musical interests.

Entrance: Up to year 2 by taster day; from year 3 upwards (girls only) by assessment morning 'so we can be sure they will flourish'.

Exit: Boys leave at 7 and are more or less guaranteed a place at the Warwick Junior School. These offers might be probationary if there are concerns that the school might not be right. The girls stay until 11 and take an entrance exam to get into King's High. Most go there despite the pull of strong local grammar schools.

Remarks: This is part of the Warwick Foundation – Warwick Preparatory School, Warwick Junior School, Warwick School and King's High Warwick – with the four schools sharing a common ethos but each feeling quite distinctive. At present all but King's High are on the same large site on the outskirts of Warwick. King's High is to join them in a two phase move from 2019 and both parents and staff see this as hugely positive – 'the girls will have the best of both worlds – lots of contact with the boys but separate lessons in key years', a parent said. The buildings are well underway and though the building site does not enhance the slightly soulless feel of the campus, once inside the prep school, friendliness and vibrancy take over.

The prep uses facilities only dreamed of in most junior schools – a professionally equipped theatre (which attracts touring companies), concert hall and amazing sports facilities, for example. Children gain a healthy number of scholarships to senior schools each year and do well in national competitions. Increasing specialist teaching in the prep. Pupils adore their very practically-focused science lessons. An exciting, ongoing, foundation-wide Mars space project has involved children talking directly to astronauts on the International Space Station. DT is popular, with a lot of effort put into making a coherent curriculum with science lessons on force, for example, aligned with modelling types of aeroplanes in DT. At themed off-timetable weeks the school brings in visitors, runs workshops and gets the children deeper into projects. Even the nursery has science and music weeks.

The school is determined to use evidence – national standardised data as well as in-school assessment – to plan the next stage of each child's learning. There are no dogmatic approaches, with a variety of different reading methods alongside phonics. 'Every child learns in a different way,' one of the senior staff said, 'and we want to find the right way for each child'. Professional development for staff is high on the head's list of priorities. The strong learning support department includes an early years speech and language specialist. The school aims to identify very quickly if new joiners have any difficulties and the department springs into action. It has the reputation for working very effectively with families. Interventions – at no extra charge – can be very short term or involve more intensive ongoing work. There is also a school counsellor who works with parents and the school drawing up well-being plans if necessary.

There is plenty of drama, art and music going on, all in very-well equipped spaces. Many performance opportunities, though the year 6s did say that they had had fewer drama lessons in year 5 because they had to work for their exams. They still managed an apparently amazing production of Annie, though, and when we visited, the year 2 production was under way involving the whole year group. Virtually all the school learns an instrument from visiting teachers. As well as their own concerts, pupils take part in foundation-wide events such as a recent woodwind celebration. Everything from coding to maypole dancing fills the children's lunchtimes and before and after-school sessions. Children we asked were all doing more than one club a week, and some seven. Lots of educational trips and regular visitors; the nursery had just had a visit from a pilot and a beekeeper.

This is large for a junior school – nearly 500 pupils – which can be an issue for some parents. The nursery is a large, open plan space with different areas for a range of activities. There is no slightly bungling, amateurish, homely feel about Warwick Prep, but nevertheless the school prides itself on making the big seem small. It certainly seems as though everyone knows everyone else. This is partly due to the excellent pastoral approaches. Older girls are trained to support younger ones through a play leader scheme. There are school and class council representatives, by application, which help to teach problem solving approaches. A Skills For Life programme focuses on a major life skill each term. During our visit it was independence, and the children were challenged in morning assembly to consider opportunities to act independently in school. Parents say this programme has had a huge impact. Children are also given opportunities during class to recognise and explore their feelings and learn how to speak about them with clarity and confidence. The school sees this work as being just as important as progress in maths and English.

Relations between children, and between children and staff, seem universally positive. The children say the teachers are kind, want to help them and are good at dealing with any arguments. Parents comment on how experienced and wise staff are, especially notably when dealing with friendship difficulties. They are in awe of the well-oiled and efficient running of the school, with a general recognition that it is very good at flagging up early any academic or social problems. A few parents would like more frequent reassurance that everything is alright, though there are regular reports and parents' meetings. Fair Rules – devised with input from children and staff – are visible around the school. The emphasis is always on learning from mistakes and the children understanding their behaviour and its consequences. Much celebration of successes.

'The school has to be right for the whole family, not just the child', says the head. Most families are fairly local, but many have both parents working. Wraparound care is available from 8.00am to 5.45pm. There are numerous clubs immediately after lessons, and anyone staying later is provided with a light tea (extra charge).

The school has an academic reputation, but there is plenty going on outside the classroom too. Forward looking with traditional moral values; parents describe the atmosphere as busy and purposeful as well as caring and nurturing. The children we met were articulate, positive and enthusiastic about their school and life in general.

Warwick School

Linked with Warwick Junior School, Warwick Preparatory School, King's High School

Myton Road, Warwick CV34 6PP

Ages 11–18 **Pupils** 985 **Sixth form** 280 **Boarders** 61 full, 1 weekly

Fees: Day £13,194; Boarding £26,883- £28,758 pa

01926 776400
www.warwickschool.org

Head master: Since September 2018, Dr Deneal Smith, previously under master (senior deputy head) at Westminster School. A Cambridge graduate with a first class degree in mathematics and astrophysics, and a PhD in observational astronomy, he began his teaching career at Winchester College before becoming head of sixth form and then director of studies at Magdalen College School, Oxford.

Academic matters: It is clear that academic work is a top priority and taken seriously by most of the boys. The pace is vigorous and demanding – for pupils and staff alike – and the overall results are impressive. When we asked if there was any truth in the rumour that Warwick was an exam factory, one boy replied, 'Well, if it is, I haven't noticed it. There is lots of work but you expect that. You just get on with it.' One ex-teacher at Warwick confirmed that the pace was demanding. That word 'pace' crops up a lot – Warwick is a very busy school with lots to offer. It may be a day school but, in the words of another boy, 'it never seems to close. With all the extracurricular activities on offer, a 12 hour day starting at 7.30am is not that unusual.' League table junkies can pore over the statistics, salivating at the various permutations, but here's a quick fix: of the 27 subjects on offer for A level, maths, economics, physics, chemistry, biology and politics account for some 250 entries; English, history, French and Spanish, 50. Just an observation but it does reveal the breadth of subjects on offer and the strengths of scientific subjects in the sixth form. How well they do overall is confirmed by the consistently high percentage of A*-B at A level (79 per cent in 2018, and 55 per cent A*/A). GCSE results from 28 subjects are impressive too: in 2018, 78 per cent of papers were graded 9-7. This is clearly not a school where boys spend time during their first few years 'settling down and making friends' before starting to work seriously.

The facilities for teaching and learning are impressive. Foremost is the new science building of which the school is justifiably proud. Like most of the new buildings at Warwick, it is superbly designed, both aesthetically and functionally. From the moment you enter the large bright foyer, decorated with a fascinating creation stretching up through two floors like a curling spine, you are in a genuinely stimulating building. In this instance it is all about experiment, discovery and excitement. Each of the three floors is allocated to a science, with spacious laboratories designed in consultation with the teachers themselves. All the latest gizmos and terrific teaching to go with them. One huge laboratory is used for extended projects where budding Nobel laureates are joined by the no less budding girls from King's High and students from other local schools. Certainly no sign of science declining in popularity here – many boys go on to university to read science-based subjects. How some of them must pine for the excellence of the facilities at Warwick. But it's not just the scientists who are well served; we hear many reports of excellent teaching in other subjects too. The delightfully designed lecture theatre hosts talks embracing all disciplines from within and beyond the curriculum.

If the heartbeat of real education is a library, Warwick is very healthy. The library is housed in The Masefield Centre, named after an old boy, charmingly described to us by a current pupil as 'some kind of a poet, I believe.' A superb set-up with over 20,000 books, it is an invaluable centre for reference resources and information files as well as CDs, DVDs and now e-books. The school even has e-readers to lend out. The wonderfully enthusiastic librarian told us that the issue of books had recently risen by 30 per cent, and inviting pamphlets, one with an encouraging foreword from the headmaster, explain and exhort. Those pupils we spoke to genuinely appreciated the facility.

Everyone entering the school is screened for dyslexia and those with learning difficulties receive help from the 'very good' learning support team. Curriculum support is also available to those who encounter academic difficulties.

Games, options, the arts: Naturally sport plays an important part. However, this is not a hearty school where prizes and recognition are given only to games players. Colours are awarded for music and drama, for instance, and one boy we spoke to, a confessed non-sportsman, said he didn't feel an outcast in any way. 'There are plenty of opportunities for taking exercise. In fact I'm almost spoilt for choice.' Nevertheless, the ethos that permeates the school – 'if you're going to do something, do it to the best of your ability' – is much in evidence on the games field. In the winter term, for example, over 20 rugby teams could be turning out on a Saturday afternoon. The 1st XV has a very strong fixture list and is renowned for its prowess, but the great thing is that everyone who wants to, has a good chance of playing in a team. However, 'it's not all about rugby,' there is also hockey, cricket, swimming, tennis, cross-country, athletics, rowing, canoeing, clay pigeon shooting: you name it. No wonder the rugby-phobic boy didn't feel left out. Facilities are excellent with a top class swimming pool (they have been national schools water polo champions more than once), squash courts, tennis courts, a superb sports hall, including an indoor hockey pitch, and games fields that seem to stretch on for ever. A recent cricket tour to Sri Lanka, golf to Spain and rugby to Ireland are just some of the opportunities to play abroad; boys who cannot afford to go are supported financially.

Music is excellent (ask for a copy of their DVD) and generally regarded as cool. Harmony maintained by a charismatic director with a wonderful team of teachers, most of whom are concert players themselves. In a recent and highly successful initiative, new boys were lent an instrument of their choice and given free tuition for a year; the enthusiastic take-up means the music department now has 720 lessons a week to organise. Five orchestras, three wind bands, three jazz bands, rock groups, quartets and much more. Huge programme of concerts and the chapel choir sings every Sunday morning during term: local parents, old boys, friends of the school and boarders attend. The musicians perform all over Europe (as with sports tours, financial support given if necessary) and recently four bands were awarded medals at the National Concert Band Finals – the Little Big Band was even handed a prize for consistency after multiple wins.

Proximity to Stratford may help the noticeable dramatic successes. The superb Bridge House Theatre is kitted out to professional standards with proper lighting and sound equipment and room for up to 300 people and musicians; it is used by community theatre groups as well as for school productions. A number of boys have even taken small parts at the RSC; recently a year 9 pupil played Gershom, first born son of Moses, in Exodus, and a few go on to take theatre studies at A level. One ecstatic mother told us of the huge encouragement given to her young son when he was given a demanding role. 'It boosted his confidence right across the board,' she said. Warwick is the only school to have won awards at the National Student Drama Festival for its productions. There are large scale performances every term as well as pupil led plays, many shared with girls from King's High.

Art and DT very good. All pupils have a double period of art and design a week for their first three years and can then go on to GCSE and beyond. Astonishing range of clubs and societies to try – debating, scuba diving, robotics (UK champions several years running). Boys can also sign up for DofE, Young Enterprise and CCF. Wonderful opportunities enthusiastically seized. Exam factory, forsooth.

Boarding: Upstairs from chapel in the old building is a little Asian outpost where the 50+ Chinese boys in the sixth form live with the housemaster, a resident tutor and a matron. Boarding is available from year 9. Warwick has been taking Chinese students for many years now and those we chatted to seemed very happy and proud to be there. Activities sensitively arranged to reflect both boys' cultural background and traditional British life – there's Autumn Moon Festival and bonfire night, Christmas and Chinese New Year. Trips, many suggested by boarders' council, include photographers' visit to London and football-themed visit to Manchester, taking in United game.

Background and atmosphere: The gates to the main entrance hint at the history of the school. In addition to the Tudor Rose and the school's coat of arms, you can read the dates 914, 1545 and 1958. These refer to the founding date of the school by Edward the Confessor, its reinstatement by Henry VIII and the visit of the Queen Mother. From a succession of sites in the town the school moved out to its present position beside the Avon in 1879. The neo-Tudor building with lovely oriel windows is typical of 19th century public school architecture. A fascinating archive room with old photographs of school groups and haunting pictures of teams from 1914 testifies to the pride the school takes in its past. After all, isn't this one of the oldest boys' schools in the country, nay, the world?

The current site is a mixture of old and new buildings; increasingly dominated by the new, close but not jostling. The boys were uniformly helpful and charming – courtesy and good manners are the norm. One new boy told us not to worry; 'Just ask,' he said, 'you can't go far wrong'. He spoke with feeling of the help he had received on arrival. All schools trumpet 'the excellent relationships between pupils and staff'; unobtrusively and naturally, this school demonstrates it. We witnessed a number of conversations between staff and boys and were struck by the obvious mutual respect and friendliness between them.

There is an underlying sense of well-being and community which extends to the town; residents spoke highly of the civilised behaviour of the boys. 'What we almost take for granted,' said one elderly resident, 'is that there is no arrogance about them. No swaggering and showing off. Not like those public school kids'.

Impressive chapel with college seating where services take place most days of the week and new 1,000 seater Warwick Hall for assemblies etc. Plans afoot to move King's High out to a new building on the Warwick School campus from September 2019, with shared sixth form centre.

Pastoral care, well-being and discipline: New boys are welcomed and blended in with great care. There are unobtrusive but clearly delineated policies to ensure 'there is always someone to pick us up' and the welcome package, is helpful, informative and encouraging. The effortlessly friendly atmosphere that pervades is, perhaps, because boys know where they stand (a phrase oft repeated when we asked). Prefects, selected by peers and staff, regard it as one of their prime functions to ensure boys are happily integrated and that consideration for others is maintained. Rules and guidelines are clear and thorough, even down to expectations of behaviour in the classroom; uniforms are smartly worn. One parent, talking about a boy who had been excluded – a rare event by all accounts – spoke of the trouble the school had gone to ensure the boy was well established in his next school. 'They really do care about the individual, but however friendly, they are strict about implementing the rules.' 'We know what is required of us. Mostly it's common sense,' a senior boy told us. 'Firm but fair.' No-one – boys or staff – claimed that bullying could never happen here, but parents we spoke to said it was quickly and sensitively dealt with. 'Staff are very approachable and understandable,' more than one boy told us.

Pupils and parents: Warwick has a large catchment area, a result not only of its excellent transport links but also the determination of parents and boys to make the effort. By bus, by train, by car, they come; from as far afield as Oxfordshire and Northamptonshire. Just under half the year's intake comes from the junior school and others from local primary schools and nearby prep schools. This is not a toff school; parents come from a broad cross-section of society, mostly professional middle classes and, thanks to the availability of bursaries, many who might otherwise not be able to afford it do send their boys. The head and governors are planning to raise funds and offer more.

Eclectic is the word that springs to mind when considering notable old boys. Currently there are two MPs, Iain Pears the novelist; Marc Elliott of East Enders; Christian Horner, Red Bull motor racing; Michael Billington, theatre critic; an Italian rugby international, an Australian rugby international, an England Sevens player and, from the ranks of the departed, the poet John Masefield. More evidence of breadth.

Entrance: The school is selective and competition is strong. It's not just the strongest academics who are awarded places; lively, quirky boys who can keep pace and bring with them special talents will be given consideration. Entry points are 11+ and 13+. Details of the examinations are on the website and follow the usual pattern. For entry to sixth form at least five grade 6s at GCSE with 9-7 grades needed in some subjects to be studied at A level.

Exit: Most – about 80 per cent – of boys stay on to do their A levels (others join) and nearly all go on to university. As well as purely academic subjects eg maths, classics, English, history, PPE, recent leavers have gone on to read marine vertebrate zoology, management with entrepreneurship, forensic science and architecture. Sixteen to Oxbridge in 2018, plus six medics and three vets. Popular destinations include Birmingham, Durham, Leeds, Nottingham, UCL and Loughborough.

Money matters: The school is fortunate in benefiting from a number of ancient charities, some specifically aimed at boys living in the town of Warwick. Scholarships are offered in music and academics but not for sport. About a quarter of boys in the school are assisted financially.

Remarks: This is a winning school and achieves success right across the board. 'I don't know how we do it,' a boy told us in genuine amazement; 'there must be some reason for it.' There are plenty of reasons why this is such an excellent school although, like all good schools, it won't suit everyone. But for those seeking a day school that offers more excellent facilities and opportunities than many boarding schools; for those who are possessed of energy, stamina and self-discipline; above all, for those who can match the pace and plunge in, this might very well be the school. Not a school for drifting in, a school for striking out through the waves. Even across the Channel.

Welbeck, the Defence Sixth Form College

    100

Forest Road, Loughborough, Leicestershire LE12 8WD

Ages 16–18 **Pupils** 329 (232 boys, 97 girls) **Boarders** All full

Fees: Boarding: £19,998 pa (means tested for MoD students)

01509 891712
www.dsfc.ac.uk/

Principal: Since 2013, Peter Middleton MA, previously deputy head at Clifton College. Read chemistry at Oxford. He began his teaching career at Cheltenham College, where he was a deputy housemaster, master in charge of rowing and first VIII coach, and an officer in the army section of the CCF. Not difficult to see the direction he was taking, confirmed by his next move, which was back to Oxford, to St Edward's, where he was a housemaster, re-formed the Royal Navy section, was master i/c rowing and, by now, an international rowing coach. It wasn't altogether surprising to hear that at Welbeck he likes wearing military uniform occasionally and exchanging the occasional salute. Any whisper of Apthorpe is irrelevant. Married to Clare, an educational psychologist. They have three children.

Clearly he is an ambitious man, and those who know him well speak of his drive, energy and desire to be a head. Not a ruthless man, he struck us as being like a schoolboy with a new train set. He is clearly very excited about running the school, and in his desire to share his excitement we hardly had time to exchange opening civilities before he was gesticulating wildly with something in his hand which, we realised, was being pointed at a screen nearby. The PowerPoint presentation had begun. Very informative it was.

In the course of conversations with pupils, staff and parents, it became obvious that his experience as a boarding housemaster has stood him in good stead. We heard how, shortly after his arrival, he had asked pupils to tell him how they thought the overall structure and living arrangements could be improved. As a result he has, we are told, made the boarding houses kinder establishments: they were never foot stamping, command bellowing places, but now housemasters – who, incidentally, seemed a delightful bunch – have more support, so that boys and girls have a wider range of people to whom they can talk, gain wisdom and encouragement, seek advice and just 'chill out together.' Those connected with the boarding came over as enthusiastic and affectionate about the pupils.

Academic matters: The Defence Sixth Form College is unique. It is, as the prospectus states, a fully co-educational sixth form boarding school. Every year 175 young men and women join the college. All are destined for the military and are required to choose one from the royal navy, the army, the RAF and the DESG (Defence Engineering and Science Group). Always the inevitable emphasis on maths and science – everyone studies maths and the vast majority physics. Fitness tests, interviews and school reports form the basis of acceptance. They are all important. English language and the subjects required are governed by whichever branch of the military you wish to pursue. There are then lists of universities which offer places for what you wish to learn. This is where aspirants must be sure they really want to pursue these routes. Boats could be burned sooner than expected. Under good king Middleton academic aspirations have risen, but there is a limit to the breadth of A levels available. Foreign languages are taught only as enrichment AS options; for instance no Greek or Latin, no art or music A levels. Alongside maths, sciences, technology and computing you can study geography, politics or business studies, but no other humanities. In 2018, 36 per cent A*/A grades, 61 per cent A*-B. Fine for many, but be aware. This school, with all its excellence, is geared towards a specific area: engineering or technical careers in the armed forces or as a civilian within the MOD. Of course a government paid bursary of £4,000 pa would be most welcome, but there are stipulations. The school is scrupulously honest and helpful about the various permutations.

Games, options, the arts: One of the most delightful incidents of our tour was witnessing what is locally referred to as the dash for cash. This refers to the possibility of winning a bursary for university, providing your grades reach the requirements and that you are sufficiently fit to be accepted. We watched a boy who was not, on his own admission a natural athlete, driving himself to achieve the required time. The PE staff were cheering him on, shouting encouragement, and some running with him. Passers by paused to cheer him on. And he did it, by about five seconds, so he'll get his bursary. It was, he said, between gasps, 'the happiest day of my life, not so much for the bursary but because I can now go to the university of my choice.' The end of his time at Welbeck is the start of his new life.

As might be imagined there is a wide variety of activities and sport is hugely popular. All pupils are required to join the CCF for varied activities designed to prepare for different challenges and to encourage leadership. Though we heard talk of art and music, we didn't see or hear any during our visit.

Boarding: That the general atmosphere throughout the school seems very happy must owe something to the quality and layout of the boarding accommodation. Everyone boards and the facilities are genuinely homely and in, the words of one of our guides, 'great places to live.' Those in their second and final year live, for the most part, in single ensuite bedsits; those in their first year share three in a room with ensuites. Initially we were a little surprised by having three in a room – two's company etc – but our guides assured us it worked.

Background and atmosphere: Anyone coming across the name Welbeck and thinking it sounds familiar may be thinking of Welbeck Abbey, destroyed by Henry VIII's thugs, and later adapted over the years into a huge house in Nottinghamshire in the midst of vast estates. From 1953, the year of its foundation, the college was housed in the building until 2000 when, despite its ducal associations and grandeur, it was deemed unsuitable and impractical. One snippet of history which might create a frisson of interest is that in 1913 Archduke Franz Ferdinand of Austria visited the Duke of Portland at Welbeck Abbey, and was involved in a very serious shooting accident which very nearly caused his death.

The college retains the name of Welbeck, and the specially designed and constructed buildings are excellent. Designed and built by the architectural firm HLM, the buildings are grouped in an enveloping, friendly way which creates a sense of team effort and space, housing very well laid out rooms.

Pastoral care, well-being and discipline: All the pupils we met spoke with appreciative warmth of the staff who were looking after them. They did not seem to possess any of the casual arrogance one sometimes detects in public school pupils. They were open, trusting, forthcoming and friendly. Discipline seemed easy as a result. A good touch is the presence of three serving officers and the college sergeant major, who mingle with pupils and the staff, forging useful links and running the mandatory CCF. One told us how much he was learning by being there, listening and partaking.

Pupils and parents: Pupils and parents come from all over the country and from all walks of life. Most had never boarded before but they were keen to tell us of the benefits they feel they have enjoyed during this two year spell. In amongst the literature sent in reply to parental enquiries there is a pie chart highlighting the types of feeder schools. Most come from other state schools and few from abroad. Not surprising. This is, rightly, perceived as a special school offering specific targets. Not many schools can include in their packet the near certainty of going on to university to read a subject of their choice and with such financial aid. Parents we spoke to were grateful for what the school was doing; some expressed amazed delight.

Entrance: These differ slightly according to which branch of the Forces you are aiming at, but basically include at least a 6 in maths and physics and a 5 in English GCSE. RAF and DESG must have at least 45 GCSE points (including 9-7 in dual award science) and army and navy at least 40 points from their best seven subjects. You must also be medically fit and a British, Commonwealth or Irish citizen.

Exit: All those who go to university on the Defence Technical Undergraduate Scheme (DTUS) must go to one of nine universities – Aston, Birmingham, Cambridge, Loughborough, Newcastle, Northumbria, Oxford, Southampton or Strathclyde – to do an approved DTUS course. These are mostly engineering and science based, with a few management degrees. In 2018, one to Oxbridge; Aston, Southampton, Portsmouth and Birmingham are popular. The majority do go on to join a branch of the armed forces. They almost have to. The prospectus papers contain some delightful articles from pupils who have gone on to work with the military, taking with them the benefits they so readily acknowledge.

Money matters: The school has lots to say about money matters and offers many forms to fill in if, as is the case most of the time, parents require assistance. Sponsored fees depend on family income (private self-funded students do not commit to a Forces or MOD career and may go to any university). No-one need be shy, after all, the intention of Welbeck is to help with means-testing when required and to make the seemingly impossible possible. The government, it seems, is poised to help.

Remarks: In view of the Duke of Edinburgh's connexions with Welbeck it is, perhaps, neither too fanciful nor (just) too silly to compare the school with a Battenberg cake. Both the cake and the school have different layers contributing to the whole. There are the military aspects: going out on exercise, parades, map reading; the academic side: the need to work at the A level subjects in order to get to university and thence to the job; personal fitness to a pretty high standard. One high-ranking military man we know described Welbeck as the finest preparation not just for the armed forces but for any job in the world. But ... it's not for everyone. A commitment to this excellent establishment needs careful thought and dedication.

Winchester House School

44 High Street, Brackley, Northamptonshire NN13 7AZ

Ages 3–13 **Pupils** 279 **Boarders** 113 weekly/flexi (from year 3)

Fees: Day £10,905 – £19,230; Boarding £17,085 – £24,330 pa

01280 702483
www.winchester-house.org

Head: Since 2014, Emma Goldsmith (40s). Born and educated in Durham before reading English at Manchester. Landed first teaching job at Oakham where she threw herself into coaching netball. 'The last thing in the world I wanted to be was a teacher, but from that point on, I was committed to boarding schools.' Later, recruited to help set up sixth form girls' boarding at Rugby. Fell in love with Bloxham School when visiting for a sports fixture and was hired to manage the transition to co-ed, including the first girls' boarding house. Ended up as deputy head. Both her children attended Winchester House, and she was asked to join the board of governors, so approached the headship 'from a unique position.'

'Bowled over by the quality of teaching, level of dedication and commitment of staff.' Focuses on every child leaving with a 'tool kit' for success in their future school. Parents approve and describe her as the kind of person they would want running their business, as their best friend or their sister: 'She's fantastic,' they say. 'She is everywhere and has time for everyone...which has stopped all the tittle tattle because you can ask her anything.'

Warm and attractive, 'a brilliant communicator,' with a gentle humour (happily swapped places with a pupil for Comic Relief day) – and the chicest office we've ever seen. Still teaches year 7 English and 'occasionally' umpires netball matches, reads stories in pre-prep and on the odd occasion serves lunch. Children attend Bloxham, where husband is a teacher.

Entrance: Non-selective into pre-prep with automatic entry to prep. All assessed prior to entry into year 3 and above to identify learning needs. Pupils mainly local (within 10 miles) with those joining after pre-prep usually from families moving out of London or from local state primaries and pre-preps. Strong old school, rather than aspirational, bias. Lots of former pupils in parent cohort. Some year groups oversubscribed.

Exit: The school prides itself on sending its pupils to a broad range of destinations. Stowe, Uppingham, Oundle, Rugby and Radley are current favourites. Popular day choices are Magdalen College School, Warwick and Headington. Nine scholarships in 2018, mostly sport and drama.

Strong focus on 'right school, right child'. Conversations regarding moving on start in year 5, with 100 per cent heading off to their first choice school.

Remarks: Set in a former hunting lodge, approached directly from the charming high street, with grand wrought iron gates guarding an 18-acre, Tardis like campus. Delightful pre-prep setting (across a small road) with large, bright classrooms, every possible millimetre of space adorned with creative offerings and the ceilings festooned with bunting and mobiles. Seamless transition for the youngest from on-site nursery, housed in a light and spacious recent extension. Years 3 and 4 housed in own building, with much evidence of the 'creative curriculum' followed on display.

Many secondary schools would envy the enormous sports hall and new full-sized Astroturf. A lovely outdoor pool (parents would like it used more) and cricket nets sit among the manicured lawns of the walled garden with the main playing fields across the road. Each year group has its own play area – some with super modern equipment and all with new, rainbow striped 'buddy benches'. The real magic of Winchester House, however, is in its enchanting and unique features; a secret garden tucked through a tiny archway, where year 8s are allowed to 'hang out' and lower years tend allotments and sit around camp fires; a beautifully panelled dining room where lunch is served family-style by teaching staff; tongue in cheek rules on the walls of the girls' boarding house (our favourites: no whining, laugh a lot and break the rules...sometimes) and a creative collection of vibrant works of art by visiting artists and pupils.

Fully co-ed, with a charming cohort of pupils who mix easily together and come across as children enjoying being just that – no ties, lots of untucked shirts and not a hiked up skirt or gelled quiff in sight. Our lunchtime hosts were bright-eyed, chatty and full of the joys of boarding – quite something for 11 year old boys. A traditional vibe prevails and school makes no bones about its boarding culture and preparation for public school, but it's by no means stuck in the dark ages. Technology is up to date (the ICT room recently upgraded) and the curriculum strikes an excellent balance of remaining traditional whilst moving with the times. The innovative 'creative curriculum' followed in the lower part of the school is well established and revered by staff and pupils alike – head speaks passionately about its execution: staff burying artefacts to be found by children with metal detectors (Romans) and children arriving at school to find snowy footsteps leading to their classrooms, which were draped in fur throws (Frozen Worlds).

Science a strength, with all three sciences taught separately by specialist teaching staff through 'as much practical work as we can manage,' according to the physics teacher. Outstanding computing, too – our year 8 guide lost us totally in a conversation about coding, but her enthusiasm and knowledge was clear to see. Pupils we spoke to unanimously voted history their favourite subject, thanks to the inspirational young teacher. French from reception by native speakers ('they only talk to children in French,' says head), Spanish from year 5, Latin from year 6 and Greek from year 7. Setting from year 3 in maths and English, when pupils start to move between teachers, leading to entirely specialist teaching from year 5.

All screened on arrival for SEN to identify areas for either support or extension. Dedicated SENCo 'aims for as little withdrawal from the classroom as possible', although those with greatest need withdrawn from Latin to receive extra support. Can accommodate mild to moderate dyslexia and dyscalculia and mild ASD.

A school alive with the sound of music – 'we're very much a singing school,' says the head and parents concur, describing the termly concerts in glowing terms. With around three-quarters of pupils playing an instrument, it's music for all, with choirs (both auditioned and otherwise), bands and ensembles aplenty for musicians of all levels. Performance is 'one of the key aspects of the school,' says head, but 'you don't have to be brilliant to perform – we're building pupils' confidence all the time.' Specialist taught drama on the curriculum to year 8 and around 60 per cent take up LAMDA, although parents would like to see more productions. Strong art department (recently upgraded) focuses on 'much more than just drawing,' says head, with visiting artists offering masterclasses on disciplines from woodcarving to animation.

Sports department is 'successful and ambitious,' but the head is keen to point out that her charges should 'learn to fail.' Inclusive approach with everyone getting the opportunity to represent the school – sometimes with up to 10 teams each for boys and girls representing the school each week. Recent introduction of graduate gap year coaches helps keep sport fun.

Pupils can board from year 3, and some do, in one of two single sex boarding houses – boys upstairs in the main school building, girls in a purpose built block. Unsurprisingly, the girls' house with its cosy dorms (sleeping up to 10) has a homelier feel than the boys', although both are comfortable, with plenty of spaces for down time. Head says boarding 'really takes off' in years 7 and 8, with an 'all or nothing' approach for the oldest pupils who are required to board all week rather than occasionally, as is allowed lower down the school. There's no boarding on Saturday nights and Saturday school has been abolished altogether for years 4 and below – the rest following from September 2019. Prep kept quite light and boarders have their own schedule of after-school activities, with all catering for both sexes. Boarders describe food as 'amazing' – and having sampled the kitchen's roast beef followed by banoffee pie, we can't disagree.

Awareness of pupils' pastoral needs dramatically stepped up under the present head. School's unique Learn to Lead programme encourages pupils to take risks and approach failure with a sense of humour and to build emotional resilience, through expeditions and on-site activities. Recent appointment of retired staff member as well-being mentor for pupils to turn to if things do go wrong. Head's visibility and approachability also seen as having 'made school a friendlier place', particularly in keeping 'alpha' parents in check. Pupils in year 3 and above are each assigned a tutor, who keeps a beady eye on their pastoral and academic well-being, stepping in to help them handle heavy workloads around exam time or making sure they keep up their sporting commitments when academics threaten to take over.

New, open approach to extracurricular welcomed by parents, who say it was previously a bit 'cloak and dagger', focuses on three pillars – creative, enriching and physical. Many, such as squash, chess, gymnastics and debating are included in fees, with skiing (at Milton Keynes) and golf charged as extra. For working parents, children are able to arrive at school from 8.10am, with pre-prep children cared for until 4.45pm and from year 3 onwards until 6.30pm, when they can be collected having done activities, prep and eaten supper. Daily minibus services bring children to school from locations including Chipping Norton, Bloxham and South Newington; new service from London planned.

Under the present head, Winchester House is one to watch. In the words of a year 8 parent: 'I wish my children were starting from the beginning now. In a few years' time, Winchester House will be one of the top preps in the country.'

Wisbech Grammar School

Chapel Road, Wisbech, Cambridgeshire PE13 1RH

Ages 3–18 **Pupils** 541

Fees: £9,297 – £13,347 pa

01945 583631
www.wisbechgrammar.com

Head: Since 2014, Chris Staley (40s). Studied geography at Portsmouth, MBA from London. No plans to teach, intended to join the army. Got a place at Sandhurst but cracked a cheekbone whilst playing rugby so had to delay entry. Decided to do PGCE whilst waiting and within two weeks was hooked. No regrets about abandoning army career, 'every day is different.' Started in the state sector 'as I wanted to experience it, having been privately educated,' quickly became disillusioned and turned to private sector. Wisbech is his first headship, arriving via Cranleigh and deputy headship at Milton Abbey.

Keen sportsman spending many years as a rugby coach alongside teaching geography. Wisbech a bit of a change, 'it's not in a rich part of the country and numbers were dropping.' He's certainly ruffled a few feathers and given the school a good shake. Lots of changes made. 'Eyebrows were raised at times.' Junior and senior school timetables now aligned, making for a more coherent community; school day also extended with late pick up and early drop offs now offered. Teaching improved and academic standards rising. Building work completed in the new refectory, dance studio opened, reception area moved, newly refurbished kindergarten and reception, new netball courts and, most importantly of all (for parents), a new car park that they can access. 'We wanted to make parents more welcome, and moving the staff car park to allow parents ease of access for pick ups and drop offs was a good way to start.'

Parents like him, some more than others. 'I'm a Staley fan,' said by many. Others took a while to warm to him. 'I wasn't sure at first as he seemed quite distant, not being a teaching head. But he is inspirational and I'm delighted my child is at the school.' Parents appreciate what he is doing at the school, 'he was an exceptional choice.' A small number see him more as a manager than an educator but they are very much in the minority. 'Some parents can't see the bigger picture,' said by one wise mother. 'He's driven and motivated and knows where he wants to take the school.' Lots of new appointments since his arrival; all of the senior team are his choice.

Three children in the senior school, which parents like. Initially lived in head's house provided by the school but sold that to raise funds. Happy to buck the trend to get what he wants. A welcoming, forthright character. Friendly and approachable, but we imagine he doesn't stand any nonsense, from staff, parents or pupils; and nor should he.

Prep head since 2015, Keryn Neaves. A New Zealander who is a keen rugby fan too, so lots of fun in the staff room, we imagine. Liked by parents: 'she's grown into the role,' 'strong but fair and very approachable.' Has a child in the prep school. 'I like that, she is one of us as well as being head.' Parents respect, and like, both heads.

Academic matters: In 2018, 27 per cent A*-A/9-7 at GCSE. At A level, 31 per cent A*-A, 57 per cent A*-B. Solid results that are steadily improving. Science taught singly with many pupils taking all three at GCSE, clever appointments with all three heads of department now having PhDs; 'they are so enthusiastic,' said one parent. Maths and English standards improved. RS now taught to A level. French, German and Spanish on offer; every child has to take at least one language at GCSE. Pupils set in English, maths and languages, from year 4 in prep and year 7 in the senior. Pupils happy and focused, chatty to visitors and proud to show off work.

Homework every night from year 3, 'but not on Wednesdays as we have matches then,' said our charming guides. Nice to see old fashioned lift top desks in some prep classrooms; 'some of our teachers don't like them as they are noisy.' Older children taught in the science block by senior teachers. Some facilities shared with senior school: library, assembly hall and refectory.

Junior and senior parents happy with academic progress and small class sizes, reasons why they chose the school. 'There's lots of parents' evenings, it's easy to see teachers, who care.' 'The children are pushed and compete with each other, in the nicest way.' Parents talked of teachers going 'above and beyond.' We visited a science hospital where a teacher is present throughout the lesson and any senior school pupil can pop in for advice and help. Good up to date labs; 'the chemistry lab is the hottest room in the school,' said our guides ruefully, and we can vouch for that. A separate electronics room. Very impressive art studio: do admire the giraffe sculpture, as well as a man on a chair and a gorilla. Very impressive art on display throughout the school. Lots of IT suites including a language lab. DT workshop well used, radio blaring; note the buggy and electric car, both driven by pupils.

Separate sixth form centre offering a kitchen, garden, lots of computers and a common room. Plenty of UCAS support and interview practice. 'We have supportive teachers,' said our guides. 'I can't fault the school academically,' said every parent we spoke to. Some mentioned personality clashes with the odd teacher; school tries its best to counteract this by making sure child not taught by them again. 'Teachers are honest and offer extra support where it's needed.' 'Good hiring choices have been made by the head.' A couple of parents mentioned that communication could be improved but realise that 'paper free is the way to go, so we must read emails.' Bright and gifted invited to join Poyser Group in sixth form, made up of pupils who are scholars and exhibitioners, with extra lectures.

SEN support in both schools help 66 in total but only two currently with EHC plans. Help within the classroom from learning support assistants or one-to-one SEN qualified teacher. Some four children need EAL support.

Games, options, the arts: Sport has dramatically improved since the arrival of the current head, with the appointment of new staff and coaches. Sport for all, right the way through the school, including compulsory for sixth form – good. Rugby and rugby 7s for boys'; 'we want it for the girls too,' said one of our prep guides. Cricket and hockey, for boys and girls, no football for either. Plenty of teams for all. Fitness suite well used with conditioning coach improving the fitness of team members. Parents keen supporters of matches, home and away. One parent would like better communication from the PE staff, 'I'd like to know fixtures and kit requirement sooner.' A happy father remarked, 'coaching has improved dramatically recently, as have the teams' and parents' match teas.'

School cleverly has a period 5 every day, straight after lunch, which is effectively a free period when children can indulge in sports and clubs, extra help sessions, music and band practice, and the occasional homework session. 'They make sure we aren't doing homework every day in period 5.' This allows every child, however far they live from the school, to join in practices and clubs. Plenty of after-school sports clubs as well. We enjoyed watching a dance session in the new studio.

Lots of drama productions, whole school and year groups as well as successful shows at the Edinburgh Fringe and at the local theatre. Plenty of music clubs on offer; 'What I would like is a club for complete beginners, there's plenty on offer for the knowledgeable but nothing for those of us who can't even read music,' said one pupil.

Plenty of school trips including an icebreaker on the Norfolk coast for year 7 and more exotic further afield ones for older pupils including to the Himalayas and Costa Rica. Lots of sports tours. DofE up to gold.

Background and atmosphere: Located in the Cambridgeshire Fen town of Wisbech and founded in 1379, it is one of the oldest schools in the country. Originally two separate schools, for girls and boys, they amalgamated in 1970 with the boys moving across the river to the girls' school on the current site. In 1983 the school became fully independent and increased in size.

Arriving at the school is slightly underwhelming as the new car park, although very convenient, is all that you initially see, along with the school sign. Walk through to the school and you are surprised by so much space – 34 acres in total – with lots of newish buildings and plenty of pitches. Mention must go to the very pretty gardens, all immaculately kept, including the head's garden which the pupils aren't allowed to use. There's plenty of seating elsewhere for everyone.

Prep school brightly decorated with plenty of outside space and the added bonus of being able to say hello to a couple of horses in the next door field. The best behaved table in year 4 gets a cup at the end of the day, so behaviour exemplary.

Parents talk about the 'welcoming feel,' when they first visited and 'the happy children we met,' wanting that for their own offspring. Our impression too. Surprisingly the school does not seem very well known locally. 'I didn't know the prep existed,' said one parent, but the head is working to make it much more visible with an open door policy. School does not have strong competition from other privates (there aren't any close by) but the Lincolnshire grammars are on the doorstep, so head aware school needs to 'up its game with what we offer for a broader education.'

Pastoral care, well-being and discipline: All parents spoke highly of pastoral care and how problems were handled. Head does not deny bullying exists, but it is dealt with swiftly, effectively and robustly, backed up by parents whose children have experienced it. One parent said that the arrival of the current prep head had improved discipline standards dramatically. All parents said teachers knew their children very well. Lots of help during transition from one school to another. 'It's a happy school where teachers are really helpful, and care.' 'They know the social issues that children are up against, understand the children and use their strengths to help them cope.' Strong mentoring system in place between sixth form prefects and year 7 classes. Tutors have 10 children each so do know them well, and spend a lot of time with them, daily. Forms mixed every year, up to year 11, so friendship groups do not become static and everyone knows each other. Sixth form in the same tutor group for two years, vertically across two years, so lots of support for lower sixth from upper and vice versa. Counsellor and nurse available with mental health nurse due to be appointed shortly.

Pupils and parents: Pupils come from far and wide across the county, and from Lincolnshire and Norfolk as well. Parents happy to travel to access school, up to an hour each way in some cases. Traditionally a school for the children of farmers, there are still many today, joined by Forces families and professionals, many self-starters running their own businesses. Parents working hard, both of them, to pay fees. Many children are second or third generation to come here, at least. Head has extended the school day to include a 7.45am drop off and 6pm pick up, at no extra cost, which parents greatly appreciate. Pupils a friendly bunch, down to earth and unpretentious. Fourteen prefects wear distinctive striped blazers which make them stand out and easily identifiable. Other pupils more conservatively dressed in smart navy blazers. Sixth formers wear 'business wear.'

Entrance: The school is selective, but not excessively so. Heads meet every child before a place is offered after they have taken an entrance assessment. School happy to say no to pupils. Entry to senior school for prep pupils not guaranteed and they also have to sit entrance assessment and be interviewed by head. A few each year don't make the grade, but usually headed off at the pass in year 5 and guided elsewhere. Numbers low in reception, increasing steadily each year with a large influx in year 5, which is full. Numbers almost double in year 7 when a large number come from local state primaries. A few more join in year 9. Head cleverly not hugely increasing numbers, although there is demand, instead he is raising entry standards; parents take note. Entry to sixth form requires all GCSEs at 4+ with chosen A levels needing a minimum of a 6. Five or six join externally a year, usually from grammars in Lincolnshire.

Exit: Virtually all pupils go from prep to senior, the odd one to grammars across the county line. About 10 a year leave after year 11, mainly to impressive state sixth forms in Cambridge (there is a good train link) or other privates in Cambridge. Some, from the farming contingent in particular, to board at big hitters such as Oundle and Uppingham. Head very proud that high numbers achieve first choice universities. One vet off to Cambridge in 2018, four to medical school, others to study eg history of art at Leeds, earth science at St Andrews and business management at Birmingham. Apprenticeships actively embraced, by parents and pupils, many of whom return to family businesses. The odd gap year, but not many.

Money matters: Academic, sports and music scholarships available of up to £1,000, rising to £1,500 in the sixth form. Means-tested bursaries up to 100 per cent in exceptional circumstances.

Remarks: The head ruffling a few feathers since his arrival has been for the better; the school had rather sat on its laurels in previous years and dwindling numbers reflected this. We get the impression from parents that the school's purpose and intent has intensified, taking all with it. They have stiff competition from local grammars so have had to up their game, offering a well-rounded education, and parents appreciate this. 'Confident children are what they produce, happy to stand up and speak in front of people; how I wish I had been given that chance when I was at school.'

Witham Hall Preparatory School

Witham-on-the-Hill, Bourne, Lincolnshire PE10 0JJ

Ages 4–13 **Pupils** 241 **Boarders** 14 weekly, 92 flexi (from 8 years)

Fees: Day £9,555 – £16,080; Boarding £21,690 pa

01778 590222
www.withamhall.com

Headmaster: Since 2009, Charles Welch (40s). Studied PE and geography at Exeter. From a farming background and always

W

expected to return to the farm. Sport took over and decided that teaching was for him. Started in a small school in Yorkshire, developed sport there and told to move on (in the nicest way) as he had done all he could before taking over as director of sport at Oakham, his alma mater. His appointment coincided with that of new head Tony Little; 'we thought the same way and he became a bit of a mentor.' Took the boys' rugby to Twickenham, and won, and girls' hockey soared. 'I love targets and had achieved what I wanted at Oakham.' He met his wife at the school and they looked for a prep school that wanted a husband and wife team, and came to Witham in 2009. 'We wanted a very good school to make great.'

Tall and imposing, he's a highly visible figure around the school. Well liked by parents and pupils alike. 'He wants the best for the children.' Another parent said, 'Mr and Mrs Welch are lovely and do the best they can. Keeping everyone happy must be tricky at times – I wouldn't want his job – but he does it excellently and efficiently.' Parents perceive them as a team, Mrs Welch highly thought of head of boarding who deals with pastoral care, often counselling parents as well. 'They are a very good team. She is like the mummy of the school and he is brilliant, good fun but strict and the children respect him. He's very visible, we all know him and he knows all of us and our children.'

Lots of refurbishment and development since his arrival, including a recently opened sports complex. Awarded Best Head of a Prep School 2016 by Tatler magazine. Two children both at the school, the elder one flexi-boarding even though they live on site.

Entrance: The school is oversubscribed all the way through but don't hesitate to approach them. To guarantee a place in reception it's wise to register before child is 2. First come first served in this respect. Non-selective in the pre-prep but don't be complacent. Every child is interviewed – as are the parents. A taster day is offered before a place is guaranteed and parents looked at closely too. Reception children come from local nurseries; more join throughout the pre-prep – most from local primary schools. Many children registered to come in year 4, and many more turned away as no places. Children tested for entry from year 3. Again, every child interviewed along with parents. Children come from a wide area, many traveling up to an hour, further afield once boarding starts in year 4. Traditionally a country school for 'old money,' local landed families and gentry; we duly noted the pair of wellies in the corner of the head's office. Less so these days with a larger London contingent now joining the fray, albeit many of these with connections to the area. Many second generation pupils, the odd third. The blend seems to work with all parents talking about how 'sociable and friendly' the school is.

Exit: Very unusual to lose a pupil at 11. These will usually go to the local grammar school or follow siblings. Also very unusual to have an 'eviction' – one in eight years; they work hard to keep them going. Around 70 per cent of leavers go to the following: Oundle, Uppingham or Oakham. Around 30 per cent to one of Eton, Millfield, QM York, Repton, Rugby, Stamford, Shrewsbury or Stowe.

Some 99 per cent stay until 13. Virtually all children go on to board. About 60 per cent each year get scholarships, all rounder, academic, creative, performing arts and sports.

Remarks: The school is less than 60 years old, housed in the old family home of the founder, having started in 1959 with six children. A fantastic setting, fabulous limestone mansion set in beautiful grounds. It couldn't be more quintessentially English. Over the years new buildings have been built and old ones adapted so that the original house is now home to the boarders, oak-panelled dining room and admin staff. Teaching is in two separate buildings within the grounds.

The school day is long: all pupils from year 4 stay until 5.15pm with supervised prep sessions (the pre-prep day ends at 3.30pm, but clubs and activities carry on till 5pm). Supper is then served with most pupils staying for one of the many after-school club or sports practices and picked up at 7pm. Parents like this, as 'we don't have to sit and do the dreaded homework after school.' Many parents commute to London and this is why flexi-boarding is so popular. Saturday morning school for all from year 4, followed by matches. 'If you choose Witham you have to commit to the school and buy into the lifestyle,' said one parent. 'School has to come first, but it's worth it,' was another comment.

Academically, parents are happy with progress, 'particularly now they have sorted out the maths department.' Pupils graded for ability further up the school and all parents spoke about how easy it is to get in touch with a teacher. Regular reports on progress. All children tested for dyslexia in year 2. Twelve pupils with SEN, some offered one-to-one support, others one-to-two. All parents said their teacher knew their child well. Many commented on the discipline. 'They don't stand any nonsense.' We can vouch for this. One miscreant was writing lines during a lunch time detention before being spoken to, firmly but kindly, by his form teacher. Good to see. Sound advice offered about future schooling by the Welchs, appreciated by the parents.

This is a sporty school with lots of it. But not just rugby, hockey and netball. Yoga for reception and fly fishing on the school lake as well as a nine hole golf course. One parent spoke about 'sporting stars being favoured and not enough teams for the less able.' Strongly denied by Mr Welch, and our guides. But with him and his wife both being ex-sports teachers it is a large part of the school, and successful. As is art. Very impressive work on display in the converted stables that are now the art rooms. Special room given over to the scholarship students. We can see why so many win art scholarships. Music and drama also a strong part of the school with enthusiastic teaching. Most of the children learn an instrument.

Pastoral care excellent according to all parents, with Mrs Welch being given glowing praise. 'She sorts out any niggles and problems, quickly and efficiently.' Very much a caring place, with staff well aware of any mental health problems that can develop. Counseling offered if needed. One mother talked about the emphasis given to good manners. 'The staff eat with the children at lunch time and attention is given to good table manners and behaviour, which I think is excellent.' Many staff and their families live on site, or within the village, adding to the family atmosphere.

Boarding must be a logistical nightmare, but it works. Some 120 of the 160 pupils in the prep department board over the course of the year. Around 35 are weekly boarders but the vast majority are flexi-boarders, varying from one night a week to five. Even children living in the village board, usually at the pupil's behest. Many board on the same night as a friend or because they have a club. This means some bed-hopping and lots of sheet changing, but all handled well to fit in with parents. Boarders staying two or more nights stay in the same bed. Friendly boarding staff and house matrons. Boarding housed in the main house in large, airy, freshly decorated dorms, housing up to 10 pupils. Pupils encouraged to decorate dorms with competition for the best one. Wednesday nights are the quietest because of match fixtures. Remaining pupils have 'family nights' with the houseparents, joining the young family for pizza. Mobile phones are not allowed in the boarding house and definitely no social media. Girls' and boys' sections have comfy lounges where pupils have hot chocolate, cake and 'downtime.' Trips feature bowling and such like, and pupils have the run of the grounds during the summer. Croquet on one lawn, but headmaster's lawn sacrosanct.

Very much a community feel, and most parents chose the school because of this. 'We fell in love with the place as soon as we walked through the door.' 'It's a delightful place; my children are so happy here.' The children are cheerful and chatty. Working hard, but seemingly not under great pressure. Witham offers a tremendous start to their education, they are taught to focus and strive. 'Do the best you can.' But it's not just books and learning: they are encouraged to try new things, spend lots of time outside and are taught the importance of courteous, thoughtful behaviour. Perfectly set up for the future, with parents queuing up to get this start for their child.

Wolverhampton Girls' High School

Tettenhall Road, Wolverhampton, West Midlands WV6 0BY

Ages 11–18 **Pupils** 960 **Sixth form** 233

01902 551515
www.wghs.org.uk

Headteacher: Since 2012, Trudi Young (30s). Though perhaps not quite as young looking as her photograph would suggest, nevertheless the word 'eponymous' effortlessly springs to mind. In conversation, she reveals considerably more than youthful wisdom and experience. She has plenty of those qualities as well as determination and courage. Twenty years ago she was a pupil at the school and now, slightly surprised and totally delighted, she is head. In the intervening years she attended Birmingham University, where she read medieval and modern history, following this up with a PGCE. Before coming back to her alma mater, she taught in Lincolnshire, followed by a stretch at Sutton Coldfield Grammar, where she was assistant and deputy head.

And so she returned, full of newly acquired experience and knowledge and with a strong sense of justice about the way adolescents should be treated. Time and time again in our conversations with the girls, they told us of Mrs Young's obvious concern for them. She's not an ebullient, hectoring sort of head, but she is intelligent, perceptive, very loyal to her pupils and, yes, brave. A few years ago, faced with defending staff cutbacks made because of government funding cuts, she was worried about upsetting the girls. 'That's typical of Mrs Young,' they said. 'She does tend to put our interests first.' Several parents have told us that the best thing about that incident was the way in which Mrs Young kept everyone in touch with letters and emails.

On our arrival it was good to see calm and happy senior girls arriving for assembly – exams done – and the way they greeted each other and, indeed, us. The assembly, it turned out, was to acknowledge some seemingly small acts of kindness and generosity. In a self-deprecating manner, Mrs Young explained that she was keen for small, unremembered acts to be recorded without embarrassment.

W

She teaches some year 7 and year 9 groups, and delights in sowing the seeds of history and getting to know the girls. 'I hope they get to see me in a different light.'

Academic matters: A strong school, academically; recently scored more highly than Shrewsbury, Harrow or Eton on its percentage of students achieving at least AAB with two facilitating subjects. At A level in 2018, 48 per cent of grades were A*/A and 76 per cent A*/B. At GCSE, 48 per cent of grades were A*/9-8. The school has a language specialism and everyone starts two of French, German, Japanese and Russian in year 7 and adds Latin in year 8, continuing at least one to GCSE. It is one of the top schools in the country for Japanese and Russian. At A level, maths and sciences particularly popular. Academic, but not heavily so. Good support for the few with learning needs, including EAL.

Games, options, the arts: This is the school where the Right Honourable Baroness Heyhoe Flint, one of the greatest woman cricketers of all time, learned to play the game. She was also, incidentally, an international hockey player. It must give her much pleasure to know that six girls at WGHS currently represent their county at cricket. Georgia Elwiss, former head girl, is currently in the England squad. Sport is extremely popular here: netball, hockey, badminton, cricket, rounders, gymnastics, tennis, athletics, swimming, rugby and football – they're all played with gusto and skill. PE is shared in the sixth form with Compton Park Learning Partnership, but not at the expense of music and art, both of which are excellent.

Like nearly every one we have come across, the dynamic head of art is fighting a battle to extend the art facilities. She has certainly won the first round and is extending even further into the threatened garden. Marvellous artwork and very popular with the girls. Bags of music: everyone learns it at key stage 3 and many beyond. There's a lot going on at this school. 'Enrichment', that buzz word, is plentiful here. Trips abroad, if you can afford them. Recently they have been to Indonesia, Russia, Iceland and USA. Community service – assisting in local schools or supporting in day centres the very old or the very young; Duke of Edinburgh Awards; drama and music. On and on goes the list. 'It's very difficult to be bored here,' one young pupil told us and then added, 'I haven't tried very hard, I must confess.' An extraordinary range of extracurricular activities is highlighted in the handsome prospectus.

Background and atmosphere: The school was founded in 1911 and there is evidence of the two wars it has survived in the spacious grounds behind the main building. The girls who showed us around were very excited by the bomb shelters. The main building itself is very handsome in the best schooly sort of way: long, broad corridors with large, light classrooms leading off and then suddenly into a new, recent addition offering even more space. Very impressive science block amidst what seemed to be a plethora of lecture theatres, concert halls, assembly rooms, classrooms: bags of space and much 'new build'. Teachers were in full flight – none more so than a language teacher who seemed to be speaking simultaneously in three languages – and there was a real buzz about the place. 'Was this because of visitors from the GSG?', we asked? 'Oh no, it's always like this,' came the immediate reply. We believed them: you only have to consider the results both social and academic. Banks of computers everywhere and we were shown by young members of the school rows of new lockers in bright colours. It felt a lively place to be. What is very attractive is the way in which the school has retained old pictures and photographs, honours boards and memorabilia. The effect is not remotely pompous or stuffy but it gently confirms the best traditional links. It's good to be in touch with one's history. Lunch was a lovely occasion. The dinner ladies – such an important part of the school – were friendly, seemed to know most of the pupils by name and were patient and motherly. The food was excellent and the company forthcoming and friendly. Clearly the girls are used to talking to alleged adults.

Pastoral care, well-being and discipline: Sixth formers and prefects are encouraged to take on responsibilities and concern themselves with the welfare of pupils in the years below. Joining a new school at any stage is potentially worrying and parents we spoke to, and pupils themselves, acknowledged the trouble staff had been to in ensuring that new pupils felt safe and cared for. Each pupil is now allocated to one of four houses, across five tutor groups. The form tutor offers guidance on a daily basis. The pastoral leader works with the form tutor to compile a personal programme for anyone who is feeling a little unhappy. We were a trifle confused by it all, but a youngish girl took pity on us. 'Really,' she said, 'all you need to know is that there's always someone there for you.' Quid plura? Parents spoke highly of the level of care; one spoke admiringly of the head's refusal to give in to a request which she considered unreasonable. 'I was irritated initially, then I thought about floodgates and the head's responsibility to the school as a whole. I have to admit she did say No very nicely.'

Pupils and parents: The school has a very wide catchment area and parents come from a variety of social and ethnic backgrounds. Some bus in from an hour away, but everyone we spoke to considered the journey worthwhile. There is an active and loyal parents' association which raises money and spreads the good word.

Alumnae include, alongside Rachel Heyhoe Flint, politicians Baroness Hayman and Baroness Perry, high court judge Anne Rafferty and authors Narinder Dhami and (very briefly) Caitlin Moran.

Entrance: Due to the school's excellent academic reputation the competition for entry is very fierce. Over 1,200 girls take the test each year for about 145 places and the 11+ is designed to challenge in maths, English, verbal and non-verbal reasoning. Register by early June of year 5. Entrance is determined purely from the results of those exams. Sixth form admission on the basis of GCSE predictions and results. Both internal – pupils already in the school – and external pupils must achieve more than six 9-5s, including maths and English. It's a pretty tough process all round.

Exit: Leavers set off to read around 90 subjects in almost 40 universities including Oxbridge (seven places in 2018). An extraordinary range and a great tribute to the staff whose expertise and knowledge of both subject and pupil ensure that pupils are introduced to the right subject. It doesn't always work but that won't necessarily be anyone's fault. A few take gap years and fewer still make straight for the job market.

Remarks: A gentle, determined and successful school run by scholarly staff who really seem to enjoy teaching bright, lively, willing pupils. For the pupils, experiences for life; for the staff a lifetime of experiences.

Wolverhampton Grammar School

Compton Road, Wolverhampton, West Midlands WV3 9RB

Ages 7–18 **Pupils** 742 **Sixth form** 147

Fees: £10,371 – £13,662 pa

01902 421326
www.wgs.org.uk

Head: Since 2013, Kathy Crewe-Read. This is her first headship and she is the school's first female head, arriving after a stint as deputy head of the King's School Chester. She read maths at Aberystwyth, and we witnessed a wonderfully lively lesson of hers with younger pupils, who responded enthusiastically to her energy, challenge and zest. Later, one told us the head was 'always amazing.'

An extract from one of her regular, thought-provoking blogs: 'The ISI.. is the regulatory body which monitors standards: we have to comply with the mere 400+ regulations that they impose. Each regulation serves a purpose, of course..but, in truth, I confess I also see them as a dead weight that obscures our greater purpose. Not one safety measure is creative or can touch the magic of what lies at the heart of educating your children.'

'She is very approachable and listens carefully,' we were told over and over again by students. 'She is keen to help if we feel that something is unfair or unreasonable.' 'Don't just grumble,' says the head. 'I can't help unless you come and talk to me about it.'

At a marvellous evening jazz concert we met lots of parents and ex-students. They were virtually unanimous in their praise of the head. One young man on the gate of the art exhibition sporting a cavalier hair style, a welcoming smile and a delightful wit told us, 'As you can see, she's not fussy about haircuts: she's more interested in what we're doing and what we're thinking about.' One member of staff commented on 'the lightness of her hand upon the tiller. But you always know it's there.' She's excellent company. One governor told us, 'she's just what we were hoping for.' Most parents agree.

Academic matters: A parent told us that his dyslexic son chose the school because he liked the atmosphere. When he arrived he was suffering from a painful physical condition which made his handwriting virtually illegible. His teachers sought medical advice and with patience and thoughtfulness his handwriting did improve, as did his understanding and written expression. Another pupil told us how shortly after she arrived she scored very low marks in a test and was embarrassed and ashamed. To her relief no-one laughed at her.

The consideration and tact these reveal seem at the heart of the school, clearly not manically driven by league tables. Tucked away in the rather good magazine – the Wulfrunian, for alumni – are the GCSE and A level results (73 per cent A*-A/9-7 at GCSE and 31 per cent A*/A at A level in 2018).

We felt that the relationship between staff and students – both within and without the classroom – was the main reason for the school's academic success. This is not a hothouse; it's a nurturing and challenging school where, as one parent put it, 'the staff and pupils do have a lot of fun, but we are kept closely in the picture and alerted if necessary. Levels of happiness are the clearest indication.' Typical of the creative and imaginative generosity of this school are the videos posted on the school's website, social media channels and sent to new starters.

And what of pupils with academic difficulties? WGS is the home of OpAL (Opportunities through Assisted Learning). It is a dedicated support programme for students with dyslexia and other learning difficulties. Here no-one is necessarily expecting an Einstein but the specially trained teaching staff, along with individually prepared action plans, can boost morale and skills wonderfully. In a sensitive and personal way, pupils' progress is tracked and monitored so that parents are kept in touch. The results are outstanding.

Games, options, the arts: Wonderful sporting facilities. Football, rugby, cricket, tennis, badminton, hockey, netball, etc. On and on goes the list and teams, we hear, play far above their weight. Impressive gymnasium with a very demanding climbing wall (preparation for some of the tremendous holiday expeditions).

Amazingly, the school claims to have over 100 extracurricular activities. The facilities are absolutely superb, both inside and out. 'Progress makes everything a battleground between beauty and utility,' said a poet; WGS contradicts that. The art exhibition we visited confirmed the school's creativity, experiment, intelligence and spark. Art is extraordinarily good here and it was such a bonus to meet the artists of all ages. Every one talked freely and unpretentiously about what they were aiming to achieve and why; which parts they were pleased with and which parts left them frustrated. Wonderful atmosphere. We heard much talk of a recent production in the 200 seat theatre – drama is popular and excellent, we were told by locals who had managed to scrounge tickets. The production, Great Expectations, is still being talked about as one of the best performances ever seen at a school which already has a powerful reputation for theatricals.

Saturday mornings are by no means empty of activities: school team fixtures, LAMDA for students who want to gain additional qualifications in theatre skills and production, often DofE preparation sessions (it is very popular here).

Music is another aspect of the creativity that lights up so much of the school. We were able to get our hands on much sought after tickets for the annual Jazz Spectacular, where the music was authentic and exciting, the dancing memorable and provocative. Apparently the concert ended with the entire audience dancing a conga all the way round the building. This extraordinary school is bursting with creative vitality. The music faculty spreads from choral and solo to orchestral and chamber with much success. Meanwhile, under the watchful eyes of experts, students are planning, measuring, filing, carving, sawing and creating some astonishingly imaginative and creatively practical furniture. It must be seen!

Background and atmosphere: Wolverhampton Grammar School was founded by the Merchant Taylors' Company in 1512 and moved to its present position in rather delightful suburbs in 1875. The original buildings are impressive, especially Big School with its huge powerful fireplaces, its impressive ceilings and the gothic-style windows. The Victorian buildings lend an air of dignitas without pomposity. Perhaps it's not too pretentious to suggest that overall there is a feeling of continuity. Certainly the staff and students we met gave off a sense of direction and purpose. But adaptation is a form of creativity as well, and it was not altogether surprising to be told that the excellent arts and drama complex was fashioned from a local car workshop. Everything here is good but unpretentious; the atmosphere we encountered as we walked round with a succession of delightful guides was smilingly friendly. There is a real feeling of happiness.

Pastoral care, well-being and discipline: This feeling of happiness does not come by chance. So many people we asked – and of many ages – said they were happy because they were doing what they enjoyed, perhaps learning constructively without being aware of it. They were, to adapt the Bard, 'Open as day for melting charity.' One older person suggested it had something to do with feeling safe and with having a form tutor to offer support and advice if required. There seems to be an impressive layer of support and much genuine concern, a lot of affection that, surely, contributes to that almost tangible feeling of happiness. At the art exhibition we watched the head weaving in and out of groups of pupils, chatting away easily, and spreading good will. As for discipline, the feeling is that common sense prevails, and since everyone knows each other well it's easy to pick up any change in behaviour or to spot unhappy confusion. Parents are always involved. The school is keen on the partnership with parents. 'Most of the time we're aiming for the same results,' one mother told us. 'We trust the staff,' she added.

Pupils and parents: Most pupils come from within 20 miles and some we talked to were amusing about the difference between Wolverhampton and Birmingham schools. There seems to be friendly rivalry but none of any snobbish kind. In fact we came across little in the way of arrogance or snobbishness. The parents we spoke to were friendly and unpretentious, happy with the status quo and full of praise for the staff. There were encouraging results from a recent parents' survey. Parents appreciated the chance to air their views and expressed confidence in the school's response. On both occasions we attended where staff and parents were mingling – even dancing – it was good to observe the relaxed and friendly interchange. There were some serious conversations, too.

Entrance: Three main entrance routes: to the junior school at 7+; to senior school at 11+; to the sixth form at 16+. For junior and senior school entry, maths and English tests. For sixth form, an average of 5.5 points for each GCSE, with at least 4 in maths and English and 6 in A level subjects. Early departures are very rare but the school does think carefully about the suitability of each candidate. Whilst looking round the school we were taken into a class of 11 year olds who, when we asked about the problems of moving up to the senior school, barked out in unison, 'there's a free pass!' Nobody winced visibly.

Exit: Very few – up to 20 per cent -leave post-GCSE and nearly everyone who stays goes on to worthwhile courses and universities, including Oxbridge (one in 2018), Birmingham, Loughborough, Liverpool and others. One off to the US and two to medical school in 2018. Parents and past pupils whom we met spoke of the superb help they had been given with HE and UCAS. It was even said that some pupils joined the sixth form because of this excellent advice.

Money matters: A range of scholarships. Parents feeling the pinch particularly painfully will be especially interested in the scholarship recently set up to honour the school's original purpose, 'educating poor boys.' Nowadays, of course, that means 'poor students'. Parents need not be shy: the bursar looks very friendly – we saw her smiling at the Jazz Concert – and talent is always recognised.

Remarks: This is a remarkable school whose success and history have not in any sense edged it into aloof smugness. It has retained its genuine humanity, unlike so many schools who have felt compelled to bow to league tables and competition, forgetting the magic of learning and education. Competition here seems healthy and invigorating; relations between students and staff are creative and mutually appreciative. Out of such contact and, no doubt, occasional confrontations and subsequent rapprochements, a sense of harmony and learning has emerged. Much of this is due to the lively creativity that fills the school. But perhaps what has permeated throughout is the most generous form of constructive competition. And that is what the aspiring head boy and girl need in order to persuade the interview board of their value. This is a school to celebrate and cherish.

Woodbridge School

Linked with The Abbey

106

Burkitt Road, Woodbridge, Suffolk IP12 4JH

Ages 11–18 **Pupils** 569 **Sixth form** 171 **Boarders** 54 full (from 13 years) **C of E**

Fees: Day £15,246 – £16,500; Boarding £30,885 pa

01394 615041
www.woodbridgeschool.org.uk

Headmaster: Since September 2018, Dr Richard Robson, formerly head of St Bede's College in Manchester. Trained at the Bristol Old Vic and has a masters in English; he worked as a professional actor and musician before turning to teaching. He has completed a doctorate in education. He was previously deputy head of St Joseph's College in Reading. He is married to Emma and they have two children, both at the school.

Academic matters: Despite a keen eye for results, the school is not enamoured with league tables believing, as do many, that too much of a focus on the school's overall performance can lead to individual pupil's needs being ignored. Academically the right buttons are being pressed, with 68 per cent A*-B at A level in 2018, 59 per cent 9-7 at GCSE. The arts, maths, sciences and languages perform particularly well. Though less eye-catching, the middle range ability pupils' results reflect their solid achievement and success. Pupils are banded from year 7 and setted in certain subjects eg maths. Classes around 20. Everyone takes French in year 7, adding Latin and Spanish or Mandarin in year 8; at least one modern language to GCSE, with Mandarin and Japanese optional extras and classics including Greek available at GCSE and in the sixth form. Around 60 pupils have mild learning difficulties; several full-time teachers offer support individually and in groups. The emphasis is on keeping pupils fully integrated into the mainstream classes. Strong EAL provision for overseas pupils. This is a school that works for all abilities.

Games, options, the arts: Impressive pitches and courts with the sports hall housed in the Eden Project-style Dome, which provides room for several classes at a time. Sport is for all and everyone has the opportunity to play competitively in the school teams, often trouncing the opposition. The Elite Sports programme is devised to encourage the most talented pupils, many of whom catch the selector's eye at county and international levels. Swimming is for the hardy in an outdoor pool. Friday afternoon is time tabled for the Seckford Scheme, an extraordinary range of non-academic activities in which the whole school (staff included) joins. All interests and tastes are encouraged: eg sailing, cookery, chess (school has its own Grand Master), and CCF is a top draw for many. DofE is also popular.

Music regarded as mainstream – no 'sporty' or 'aesthete' labels and half the school learns one or more instruments. It is 'cool to sing'. School has a close association with Aldeburgh and Snape with masterclasses, courses and recitals taking place regularly. Proliferation of choirs, ensembles, orchestras and bands. Drama also wildly popular with eight plays and shows performed annually in the impressive Seckford Theatre. Dance is increasingly popular. The school's international programme provides visits and exchanges throughout Europe, Australia, S Africa, China and Japan. Pupils spend periods of up to 10 weeks at linked schools.

Boarding: Although some are from the UK, boarders are mostly from overseas – from 14 different countries including Spain, Russia, Germany, Nigeria, Turkey, Thailand, China and Hong Kong. They are fully integrated into the school, and as there are so few of them they have a close relationship with the boarding houseparents. They are free to visit the town after school and at weekends; some weekend excursions further afield organised to eg London or Cambridge, plus parties, paintballing etc. Help with language issues available.

Background and atmosphere: Founded in the 17th century, the school is part of the Seckford Foundation and has occupied its present site in the town since the 19th century. It has been fully co-educational for 40 years. School stands on extensive grounds on a hilly plot with the various buildings dotted around, giving a campus atmosphere. The immediate approach to the school passes the slightly unprepossessing boarding house. However, the school buildings are a mix of styles from the Victorian to the contemporary, including the recently-built Seckford Theatre and sixth form centre. Atmosphere in classes, library and areas for independent working is palpably studious. Time-wasting is frowned on and most pupils spin from lessons to sport to activities non stop. One mother commented, 'Pupils can have a crack at everything going – there is a niche for everyone'. Pupils themselves are friendly and polite; teachers, if anything, even more so. Unstuffy relations all round, and the staff give praiseworthy loyal service.

Pastoral care, well-being and discipline: Enthusiastic endorsement by parents for vertical tutoring system, which operates from year 10 to 13. Younger pupils have the benefit of knowing older pupils well, and it provides leadership opportunities for sixth formers; 'most pupils know whom they would go to'. Few discipline problems.

Communication with parents is taken very seriously. As well as the usual parents' consultations, staff are available on a day-to-day basis via telephone or email. This care of the children is at the heart of such a happy school.

Pupils and parents: Pupils drawn largely from professional East Anglian families, many with a media background (Aldeburgh, BT close by). A fleet of buses brings pupils from as far afield as Norfolk, Felixstowe and Colchester. The school is very popular in the town and many parents have moved out from London to take advantage. Foreign students from a range of 14 different countries are encouraged to come for long or short periods, partly to ginger up what would otherwise be a very English school.

Entrance: Everyone invited to a taster day. Common entrance or test, together with a report from present school, and interview at 11+, 12+, 13+ or 14+. Two-thirds of intake at 11 transfer from The Abbey prep, the rest from local state and private schools. About three-quarters of those tested are accepted. Entry to the sixth form is based on an interview and GCSE predicted grades.

Exit: Few leave after GCSEs. Great majority leave sixth form for university; Edinburgh, York, Newcastle, Oxford Brookes and Reading currently popular, as are sciences, modern languages, English and business/finance courses. Four to Oxbridge in 2018.

Money matters: Academic scholarships worth up to 50 per cent of fees can be topped-up with means-tested bursaries. Music, sport, chess, drama, all round and art scholarships are also available.

Remarks: A good all-round 'country school in the town'. Lively, and although selective, would suit quite a wide ability range. Exceptional extracurricular provision for what is, largely, a day school.

Wymondham College

    107

Golf Links Road, Morley, Wymondham, Norfolk NR18 9SZ

Ages 11–18 **Pupils** 1,305 **Sixth form** 435 **Boarders** 568 full

Fees: Day fee £28.66 pw; Sixth form fee £100 pa; Boarding £10,764 – £11,475 pa

01953 609000
www.wymondhamcollege.org

Headteacher: Since 2018, Dan Browning, a history graduate from Anglia Ruskin with postgrad qualifications from Cambridge, UEA, and the Institute of Education. Joined as head of school in 2017. Previous posts have included executive principal of St John's & King Richard School for British Forces children in Cyprus and vice principal of Tendring Technology College. He still teaches history, and lives on the college campus with his wife Sarah, two daughters and their golden retriever, Mable.

Academic matters: Though strictly speaking non-selective, the varied intake (50 per cent boarding) plus provision of music and sports places – and a perception in the area that 'It's for bright children' – means pupils appreciate their good fortune in being there and are motivated to work hard. Parents are a strong support and the school's results reflect all round achievement. In 2018, 86 per cent of pupils got 9-4 in both English and maths; 29 per cent A*-A/9-7 grades. Modern languages are compulsory to GCSE level (Spanish most popular). Close to 80 per cent take religious studies at GCSE – interesting for a non-faith school.

Sixth form definitely academic – despite a low bar of three 6s and four 5s required at GCSE for entry, most do well and higher grades are often needed for external applicants. Only four vocational courses offered in the long list of subjects to be studied, with maths taken by over half the cohort. Sciences also have a high take up. Headmaster feels this may reflect current anxieties about the need to take degrees that help lead to good jobs, but 'we are holding the line that subjects should also be studied for their own sake'. In 2018, 33 per cent A*/A grades and 64 per cent A*-B grades at A level.

As the school is regarded as 'being for bright children', there are relatively few pupils, around 12 per cent, requiring learning support, and these are milder cases of dyslexia/dyspraxia/dyscalculia, with only a small number of EHC plan pupils. Well resourced and a positive attitude about extra support. There are also breakfast and catch-up clubs run by individual departments for those needing an extra boost. All year 7s are tested on entry to the school. There is also a structured programme for teaching EFL. School has a well-established system for identifying the very bright (gifted and talented, in the jargon) early on and they spend an extra two periods a week, plus own time,on an extension programme comprising a research project and an extra course chosen from space science, Russian, Latin, literature and ideas and government and politics. The presence of postgraduate fellows in the sixth form and some also resident in the houses help pupils learn good work habits – we saw a light-hearted revision session in action during GCSE study leave – and give sixth formers insider guidance with UCAS and Oxbridge entrance. A programme of visiting speakers and workshops are led by local university staff, notably from UEA and Cambridge.

Games, options, the arts: If sporty, there is plenty on offer. Usual team games – rugby included, and an extensive match schedule for the most competent though fewer games for those lower down the rankings. Games are compulsory up to sixth form, when they become optional. Pupils themselves run the five-a-side football league that operates at lunchtimes. Good facilities including swimming pool, gigantic sports hall which doubles for assemblies/concerts, Astroturf, pitches and courts galore. Keen involvement in DofE (the college runs the county scheme) and CCF also offered, though involvement in this is a voluntary activity and not timetabled.

Music important. The annual Mair cup is an opportunity for all pupils to perform in a competition between houses and is extremely popular. Over 250 have individual instrumental lessons and there are choirs and excellent jazz and concert bands that perform at events locally – including the Royal Norfolk Show. A string group has been recently established.

Flourishing art and textiles, which are taught in the Tech block, a light and airy building designed around a central atrium with good provision for display of finished efforts. Good take-up at GCSE and A level and significant numbers go on to study at degree level.

Boarding: The five boarding houses for the main school are drearily functional, though homelike enough upstairs in the dormitories. Houses are all mixed, though girls and boys have separate floors for sleeping, and day pupils as well as boarders return to houses at break and lunchtimes. Plenty of staff, matrons and resident fellows around, and pupils are cheerful and well-behaved.

A few struggle with homesickness at the beginning. Flexi or part boarding is not on offer and swapping from boarding to day is impossible, so a decision to board, taken at aged 10, has to be considered carefully. 'It's not for everyone and this is why we interview all potential boarders', we were told. Those joining in year 9 generally have fewer problems settling. The houses provide something of a refuge at break and lunchtimes when most return to base, although 'It is annoying if your friends are in another house', said one pupil. House staff around at all key times, and matrons remain on the premises at night. The majority go home at weekends but plenty remain and outings/activities are planned throughout the term. Exeats once each side of half term.

Background and atmosphere: Founded in 1951, the brainchild of Sir Lincoln Ralphs, then chief education officer for Norwich. It is the largest state boarding school in the country. The site is a former US military hospital and, despite the utilitarian nature of the buildings, it is very peaceful and in the middle of nowhere (Wymondham itself is several miles off). Some of the newer buildings – modern languages, for example – are interesting and well designed, but the most interesting of all is the single remaining Nissen hut, now listed and used, rather effectively, as the chapel. The college has a strong Christian ethos, but this is non-denominational. There is great pride in the school's history and traditions, with a memorial garden and key anniversaries celebrated regularly. Striking new sixth form centre, set around a courtyard, with boarding facilities in individual rooms with en-suite bathrooms, a refectory, working and computer areas.

Traditional uniform (including ties for girls) compulsory up to year 11, but it is the cheap and cheerful sort – no Harris tweed or boaters. Pupils don't mind the slightly bleak boarding houses: 'You get used to it so quickly, and anyway, we like the people', we were told by one pupil, with nods and agreement from others. The old system of year 7s being kept in their own separate house has been discontinued and everyone is mixed up from the start. Saturday morning school for all (though not sixth form) accepted readily enough – holidays slightly longer than usual in state schools to compensate. One of the virtues of the site is that there is lots of 'promenade' time out in fresh air between lessons, and this seems to contribute to the calm and disciplined atmosphere of the school.

Intending to open a primary school on the same site in 2020, 'subject to planning and consultation', with boarding for years 5 and 6.

Pastoral care, well-being and discipline: House-based tutor groups with tutors overseeing academic and extracurricular activities from year 7 to 11. Emphasis is on good relationships. 'Work hard, be kind' is the phrase coined and we heard it quoted by year 11s quite cheerfully, if slightly tongue-in-cheek. The presence of resident fellows in the houses help with friendship and other difficulties and in addition to house staff, the school also has two counsellors and a chaplain, so there is a network of support. Looking out for younger pupils is encouraged and there is very little evidence of bad behaviour or bullying, though school is ever alert and anti-bullying strategies are in place. The parent liaison office helps to smooth communications between home and school, especially for parents of boarders.

Pupils and parents: Pupils come from Norfolk in the main (including boarders), though an increasing number are from further afield thanks, in part, to the improvements to the A11. School now provides transport for sixth formers from areas without public transport. Over 20 per cent are from overseas, a mixture of Europeans and Chinese mostly, plus those with parents working abroad. Fewer Forces families than formerly; the majority of parents are professional or managerial. 'It's an unpretentious place, not for show-offs, and we like that,' said a parent, and that is the common view. Quite a few have chosen the school because it is a state funded one and without the perceptions of privilege that independent boarding schools may possess. Pupils regard themselves as fortunate and appear straightforward and hard working.

Entrance: Main intake at 11+ but places are available at 13 (boarding only) and again in the sixth form. Day and boarding places are split roughly 50:50. Day places very oversubscribed and awarded according to the LA criteria of looked after children, siblings and distance from school. Once other categories have been dealt with, the distance from the school can be as little as 0.6 mile, though commonly up to two miles. Check carefully – despite the name, the town of Wymondham itself is not in the catchment. Eight musical aptitude and eight sporting aptitude places – four day and four boarding for each. Competition for such places is fierce.

All potential boarders are interviewed by the house heads to check that pupils are prepared for all that boarding entails (a hard call in a 10 minute chat). Places are less competitive, but still oversubscribed. It is perhaps worth adding that although you can apply for both day and boarding places, you must list them in order of preference, and if allocated a boarding place you cannot make a crafty switch to day later on. The number of places in each category is fixed.

Most remain for the sixth form, assuming they meet baseline attainment of four 5s and three 6s at GCSE. Not a high bar, but as numbers applying from outside exceed places available, admission is, effectively, dependant on rank order of results at GCSE for those applying from elsewhere.

Exit: Around a third leaves after GCSEs Majority of sixth formers – some 75 per cent – move on to higher education. Wide range of degree subjects studied though a definite bias towards the sciences, maths, computing and business. Six to Oxbridge in 2018 (including a Cambridge vet) plus two other vets and three medics. UEA, Durham, Leeds, Lincoln, Nottingham and Nottingham Trent currently popular. The resident Lincoln Fellow in the sixth form is an Oxbridge graduate with a brief to dispel myths about the application process and help pupils with UCAS generally.

Money matters: Tuition is free; fees are payable for boarding provision only. Fees compare favourably with the cost of a local day independent schools. Day boarding and enhanced day boarding, for relatively modest fees, are popular option (they include meals and various after-school activities) but there are no flexible boarding arrangements.

At least one sixth form boarding scholarship a year, worth 100 per cent of fees, for a student with exceptional academic, music or sporting potential.

Remarks: Has a well deserved reputation locally, and increasingly nationally as a leading state boarding school. It is a bargain for parents who want a boarding education for their children, but without the associations of privilege or having to fork out fortunes in school fees. It is a big school and hard-working, socially outgoing types do best.

Wymondham High School

Folly Road, Wymondham, Norfolk NR18 0QT

Ages 11–18 **Pupils** 1,563 **Sixth form** 271

01953 602078
www.wymondhamhigh.co.uk

Principal: Since 2016, Jonathan Rockey BSc geography (Anglia Ruskin), MSc in environmental studies (Greenwich), PGCE, NPQH. Previously vice-principal here, before that deputy head at Stowupland High School and assistant head at Westbourne Academy. A person of enormous energy who clearly thrives on running a very large school. Thinks the school 'has a good zeitgeist', praises the highly committed staff, who together with the support of parents, is the reason for the school's success. 'We celebrate success in every way possible, social and sporting as well as academic'. Has discouraged the use of the phrase 'prior achievement' when speaking of pupil attainment, particularly for those entering year 7, to avoid any possible restrictions on future potential. Believes the school has a well-established work ethic: 'we set good habits in the lower forms that sustain pupils through the exam stages'. Where an important principle is concerned – for example the compulsory learning of a foreign language – he says, 'I will stand my ground, even where parents disagree; the overall education of pupils matters as much as exam success'. Regrets that his responsibilities leave no time to teach but makes sure he is in daily contact with all his pupils, managing the lunch queues as well as assemblies and awards ceremonies (informal occasions, no long speeches). His optimism, together with an evident wish to alleviate the pressures on his staff where possible (keeping non-teaching periods free, for example) inspire loyalty. Has manifestly little free time but runs regularly and enjoys time with his (almost) grown up family.

Academic matters: Exam results place the Wymondham among the top five state schools in Norfolk and Suffolk. At GCSE 76 per cent achieved 9-4s in both English and maths in 2018, with 27 per cent of grades A*-A/9-7. Impressively, almost the same number gained a GCSE in a foreign language (French, German and Spanish on offer, no dropping out allowed). Average class sizes kept below 30. Setting begins in year 7 for maths and IT and across the curriculum from year 8 onwards with exception of music, PE, art and drama which are taught in parallel bands according to option blocks. Strong parental support and approval: 'The school has always been quick to help when it has been needed; the staff know the children well' and, 'My son has found work is harder higher up but enjoys it more and more. Staff are respected, and their commitment is widely acknowledged'; 'they want us to do well and most are very interesting and fun, though we have our favourites!'

Immediate withdrawal of disruptive pupils to the pupil inclusion unit (staffed full time) means teaching is uninterrupted. Those with special needs are identified early and supported both in class and by individual programmes where necessary. The department works in close collaboration with an educational psychology practice and the progress of pupils is carefully monitored.

Judged 'outstanding', by Ofsted, the sixth form is the jewel in the crown academically speaking. Students are highly motivated and ambitious and A level results reflect this. Thirty per cent A*/A grades in 2018 and 61 per cent A*-B. Strong subjects include maths, IT, sciences and the creative arts generally. Students are lured from elsewhere to study particular subjects, notably in the sciences, maths and the creative arts. Students must gain a minimum of seven GCSEs with at least four at 6 and three at 5. Maths requires a 7. Standards are adhered to and around 50 per cent of Wymondham's own year 11 don't make the cut (or choose to study elsewhere). Good provision for private study includes a sixth form library and the collaborative learning centre, 'it basically means we can work and talk', which is exactly what this reviewer saw happening. Most students own laptops, but school provides some too.

Games, options, the arts: Shares the adjacent sports centre with the town; the school has day time priority. Usual team sports (plus swimming) rotate through the year with non-swimmers getting coaching. No cricket for girls (yet) but both football and rugby are offered and there is a plethora of after school clubs – extra late buses laid on so no one misses out. Creative arts all popular, notably music and music technology, with a big take-up at GCSE. Individual tuition (practice rooms available), several orchestras, including a school/community one, choirs and bands. Drama very popular both as a GCSE and as an after-school club. Regular performances, an annual musical and lots of community involvement. Well used drama studio and staged hall but the proposed new theatre definitely needed. Art and DT taught to all in years 7 and 8, an option choice after that. Taught in classrooms and workshops set around the quad.

Background and atmosphere: Close to the centre of the rapidly expanding Norfolk market town of Wymondham, the school is set in a large, well looked after site. Bewildering (for the visitor, though not the pupils) assortment of buildings have mushroomed over recent years and cover architectural styles from the 1930s art deco (the original boys' school) through to the present day builds that incorporate more advanced ideas about working space, for example cleverly angled windows that allow indirect sunlight into classrooms rather than pupils sitting in the direct glare. New buildings have wider, lighter corridors but all passageways are well decorated with pupils' designs and information. Change of lessons provide a lively few minutes ('we don't believe in silent corridors'), but pupils are orderly and courteous. The sixth form administrative and study areas are set around the grassed quad, complete with pond. New art, drama, library and canteen facilities are in the pipeline and scheduled for 2020. The Shack, a centrally placed eating kiosk, relieves current lunchtime queues in school canteen where food, since a new catering company took over, is praised. 'Pretty good, they do themes, Indonesia last week and always paninis and things like that.' Biometric units for regular top ups positioned around the school.

Tarmac and paving between buildings kept litter free and extensive playing fields are restful to the eye as well as providing space for letting off steam and for lunchtime activities and sport.

Pastoral care, well-being and discipline: With 27 feeder schools, the importance of helping to settle-in year 7 pupils is taken seriously. Vertical tutorial groups, affiliated to one of four houses, help to manage the transfer. Pupils quickly adapt, 'especially if they join clubs and do lots,' pupils advise. Excellent school/home communications with a full-time attendance officer (plus assistant) to follow up pupils' absences mean few slip through the net. Expressions such as 'zero tolerance' are not in use but instead there is a friendly competition between houses for attendance with the weekly winners celebrated. The inclusion unit enables the immediate withdrawal of disruptive pupils and usual system of detentions is in place. Suspension is rarely resorted to and pupils' behaviour is of a consistently high standard.

Pupil representation on the school council gives a voice to all and a proliferation of clubs and groups run by the pupils themselves (with staff oversight) tackle issues such as bullying, sexism, drug and alcohol use. A thriving LGBTQ group meets weekly. A small drop in centre run by pupils at lunch and break times is for anyone feeling under pressure or unhappy and the school employs a full-time counsellor. Gender neutral loos recently established because of pupil pressure. Girls now allowed to choose whether to wear trousers or skirts; ties still de rigeur for boys and girls (if wearing particular shirts). The new front pleated skirts, which look like culottes but aren't, are not proving as popular as former style. Dress code for sixth form, a slightly relaxed version of, 'business clothes'. Suits not essential but no jeans.

Pupils and parents: Rapidly expanding Wymondham and the surrounding villages are an easy commute to Norwich – where many parents work. Wide social mix though small number of ethnic minorities (reflecting East Anglia). Being in the catchment is a definite 'plus' in the housing market. Strong parental support; 'We moved out here so that our children could go to the school,' is often heard. School has a good reputation locally and further afield.

Entrance: Oversubscribed. Stringent catchment rules for years 7-11, Wymondham and surrounding villages but boundaries vary year by year, so vital to check. Selective sixth form allows for a much wider catchment area. The admission criteria are strictly applied and roughly 50 per cent come from other schools.

Exit: Roughly half leave post GCSEs,either for sixth form/FE colleges or to more practical post-16 courses. Post A level, three-quarters to university with substantial numbers to Russell Group. Three to Oxbridge in 2018 plus three medics/vets. School will allow pupils to repeat year 13 in certain circumstances.

Remarks: One of the top East Anglian secondary schools with an energetic and optimistic head.

Yarlet School

    109

Yarlet, Stafford, Staffordshire ST18 9SU

Ages 2–13 **Pupils** 164 **Boarders** 55 flexi **C of E**

Fees: £8,685 – £12645 pa; Boarding £27 per night

01785 286568
www.yarletschool.uk

Headmaster: Since 2009, Ian Raybould BEd ALCM NPQH (late 40s), who studied music and education (4-12 years) at University College, Winchester and London College of Music; taught at King's College, Madrid, where he was head of music and boarding; head of first IAPS prep school in Spain; as an ISI inspector he visited prep, senior and international schools in Europe.

Back here in the UK he conducts the Yarlet school choir and plays the organ for chapel services. He is keen to do more in the area of music and the performing arts. He has expert and enthusiastic backing in those areas and staff speak highly of his involvement and support. He is something of an IT buff – not the booming, bearded kind but the patient and thoughtful kind – and he has greatly improved the learning and administration systems as well as enhancing accessibility for SEN. He is genuinely and personally concerned with helping pupils with SEN – 'particularly tuned in', in his own words – and is chairman of governors at a local special school.

Some male heads, if they insist on showing Good Schools Guide scribblers around themselves, adopt a sort of jaunty, old style naval heartiness, like a captain addressing his crew in a high wind. This provides quite an insight into such a man when he barks out the wrong name to a bewildered pupil. No chance of that happening at Yarlet. This head greets the children easily and warmly like a good father, and they are pleased to see him. It feels like genuine affection, respect and happiness. Being shown round by Mr Raybould is a delight. He is clearly a sincere and thoughtful man and knows his pupils well. They respond fearlessly and confidently, obviously happy. To quote from a mother's email in answer to our questions about the head, 'He seems something of a visionary, and arrived with well-prepared ideas for the future of Yarlet. He intends to sharpen up the academics but not at the expense of the liveliness and pleasure of the classroom. But overall, it's the strong relationships with the children that he seems to enjoy particularly. They like and respect him and want to do well because of him.'

Recently the school was visited by ISI on a routine compliance inspection. After they had looked around, the leader had a final meeting with the head, expressing her pleasure. 'What, in your opinion, is the USP of the school?' asked the head. 'That's easy,' replied the leader; 'it's the warmth and friendliness of the school. It's outstanding.' A number of things contribute to that atmosphere but the most obvious would seem to be the standards and expectations set by the head and staff and the careful way in which the days are planned.

Mr Raybould has two sons, one of whom has moved on from Yarlet with a music scholarship.

Entrance: Not selective, but the school is scrupulously honest about not admitting pupils whose needs cannot be met, so there are boundaries. Mild SEND is accepted and 'there is a dedicated SENCo who ensures that any support is "individualised and targeted".' At the time of our visit, two pupils had EHC plans for moderate learning difficulties, and 25 per cent of the main school pupils have Individual Education Plans (IEPS), mostly because they have mild learning difficulties, but many of whom are simply below average ability and require individual attention.

Most pupils join the nursery and pre-prep, a magic, sparkling world with well kitted out classrooms and play areas with the sort of toys that make you want to throw away the zero from your age. Delightful, bright-eyed staff whose affection and commitment is obvious. We were told that the head's frequent visits are hugely popular with the younger ones, who are accepted into the school after meeting the head at 2 years old.

Two scholarships, named after the legendary Richard Plant (head 1989-2009), at 11+ for up to 50 per cent fees for those who show academic promise together with all-round ability and enthusiasm. There are sibling discounts in the main school and there is a general bursary fund for parents needing assistance. There is also a combined scholarship for up to two local primary school children from 11, which carries on to senior school (Rugby, Repton and Denstone College are three of the senior schools included in the scheme). Interview at 10, need the ability to pass CE into senior school and a particular strength in at least one arts, music, sports or academic subject. Means-tested. The school is keen to extend the range of primary and public schools involved.

Exit: Most leave at 13 though some at 11. Majority go to a wide spectrum of independent schools with good numbers of academic, music and art scholarships. In 2018 just under half of pupils left with at least one award to schools including Shrewsbury, Repton, Wrekin College and Abbots Bromley.The breadth of destinations is both encouraging and valuable: a good prep school encourages parents to choose the right school for their offspring. A number of parents spoke highly of the support and guidance the school gives.

Remarks: In his speech on sports day the headmaster took the opportunity to comment on issues beyond academic achievements – which he recognised, of course – to 'those things which make Yarlet special or even unique.' He began, as do we – though not simultaneously – with the exceptional level of art and design. The art teacher is a comparative newcomer to the school and she has had an astonishing effect on the creative side. She is inspirational in her enthusiasm and energy, full of ideas and open minded enough to allow pupils to gain in confidence by going their own way and exploring. The results, as we saw on two occasions – under normal conditions and displayed on sports day – were amazing in their variety, with fearless experimenting and an obvious delight revealed by pupils of all ages. The building was specially designed and built as an art studio: clearly teacher and pupils have responded full-heartedly. What was particularly pleasing to see was work on display by former pupils, one of whom will shortly be displaying her paintings at an art gallery in Birmingham. It's always good to know that lessons at an early age can be absorbed, recalled and relished.

A little further along the compact building there is a useful space for music, including huge concerts occasionally involving 70 people, and very ambitious drama, Shakespeare and popular musicals. We saw some very lively expression of rhythm and dance, and both parents and pupils spoke of music as being a much-loved and exciting part of their lives. There are occasional trips to Stratford.

Thanks to the generosity of parents and, doubtless, others, a specially designed science laboratory has recently taken the place of the ageing science building. There is much excitement about this state-of-the art resource, another example of the overall improvement of facilities – including the library and the creation of a senior pupils' sitting out area, described by one pupil as 'absolutely brilliant.' We met a number of old boys on our second visit, many of whom were amazed by improvements throughout the buildings, the airiness of the dormitories and, as usual on such occasions, the size of the entrance hall. A number of fathers we spoke to had sent their children here or were about to send them because they had such happy memories of their time at Yarlet.

However, one way of life is markedly different. Full time boarding no longer exists, though it is possible to savour the delights of sharing a dormitory with a number of chums. Flexi-boarding takes place on Wednesday and Thursday evenings and averages between 15 and 20 pupils per night. Pupils are supervised by the headmaster and the gap students, who mostly come from Australia. Not only does the head look after these Aussies thoughtfully and generously – after all, they are a long way from home – but he goes through the legal and social aspects of looking after the boarders in great detail. The sleeping arrangements are bright, airy and attractive, and we were told by some excited boys that 'the full English breakfast is delicious.' The head has introduced a number of boarding activities such as camping and pool parties with sensible supervision. Parents can choose how long their children stay of an evening. There is a supervised prep session and tea, and children can go home at 4.30pm, 5.30pm, 6.15pm or 7pm. This flexibility is much appreciated.

Rugby, cricket, football, netball, tennis, swimming: they're all there and played with sporting zest. And with ski trips to Italy, cultural and linguistic visits to France and a well-established exchange programme with a school in Madrid, there are plenty of opportunities for broadening the mind beyond the UK.

A notably strong aspect of the community – a word much used by parents, staff and pupils – is 'moral awareness'. Noticeable, traditional and enjoyable are the daily morning services held in the school's wonderful chapel, services which 'shamelessly but not heavily' consider and celebrate Christian principles. Staff and children seem to enjoy a mutual concern and respect for each other. The ISI inspector was right in her assessment of the warmth and friendliness of the community. We made enquiries about bullying, to pupils, parents and staff, and were not surprised that pupils looked astonished by the question and staff were confident that it was not a feature of the school. Parents were confident that staff and senior pupils were alert to the possibilities, but they felt that if there was any bullying the head and his staff would be very quickly aware. There is a 'worry box' for anyone who is anxious and, yes, worried. Not many notes are written.

Prefects, led by head and deputy head and selected by the staff, are encouraged to keep an eye out for any acts of particular kindness and generosity and to write a brief message about it for the head or senior member of staff. Similarly acts of unkindness. The feeling is that the prefects should not be saddled with the responsibilities of rewards and sanctions. Instead they pass on messages. One young pupil expressed astonishment at being congratulated for an action the head couldn't possibly have seen. The head told us as we wandered around the school that if he were bribed with a million pounds he still would not leave. That might astonish some young pupils, but most of them would understand what prompted that comment.

The publications offered to potential parents are upbeat and good fun. Y Sir? Is a delightful magazine chronicling the fun and games, the visits and the expeditions, the sports results and the concerts, the sheer happiness of the place. It's an honest and appealing document. Other information needed by potential parents is clearly and helpfully laid out.

In its modest, kind and happy way this is a delightful school with a delightful head. Pupils and parents seem universally happy, including those people who require help and encouragement with SEN. That is one of the great strengths of the school. There are many more.

Northern England

Cumbria
Durham
East Riding of Yorkshire
Greater Manchester
Lancashire
Merseyside
North Yorkshire
Northumberland
South Yorkshire
Tyne and Wear
West Yorkshire

Junior Schools
Senior Schools
Junior & Senior Schools
Edinburgh
EAST LOTHIAN
MIDLOTHIAN
LANARKSHIRE
THE SCOTTISH BORDERS
NORTHUMBERLAND
Holy Island
Newcastle Upon Tyne
South Shields
Penshaw
Carlisle
Solway Firth
DURHAM
Hartlepool
Middlesbrough
Darlington
CUMBRIA
NORTH YORKSHIRE
ENGLAND
Morecambe Bay
Harrogate
York
LANCASHIRE
EAST RIDING OF YORKSHIRE
Bradford
Leeds
Kingston Upon Hull
Blackpool
Preston
Halifax
Blackburn
Wakefield
Huddersfield
Southport
WEST YORKSHIRE
SOUTH YORKSHIRE
Grimsby
Bolton
Oldham
Manchester
St. Helens
Liverpool
Birkenhead
Warrington
Sheffield
NOTTINGHAMSHIRE
Lincoln
LINCOLNSHIRE
FLINTSHIRE
Chester
CHESHIRE
DERBYSHIRE

NORTHERN ENGLAND

A

Abbey Lane Primary School

Abbey Lane, Sheffield, South Yorkshire S8 0BN

Ages 4–11 **Pupils** 600

01142 745054
www.abbeylaneprimaryschool.co.uk

Headteacher: Since 2012, Maxine Stafford (40s), previously deputy and acting head. Commended in Ofsted report for maintaining high standards but viewed by parents as unapproachable and lacking in warmth. Ones we spoke to (she refused to meet us) feel she does not listen in a sympathetic way to their concerns, which she sees as criticism, and is immediately on the defensive – 'I dread the day I have to have dealings with her,' said one. 'She always has the deputy head with her – I felt quite intimidated,' said another. While most of the questions in the Ofsted parents' questionnaire had highly positive responses, there is a marked dip when it comes to quality of leadership and management and the school's responses to parental concerns.

Entrance: Apply in the usual way via the local authority, by January 15 of year 6. Waiting list criteria: children in care; living in the catchment area with a sibling at the school; living in the catchment area; having a sibling; others. Distance (straight line measurement) and exceptional social/medical need used for tie breaks. Not generally oversubscribed (entry has risen from 60 to 90) – takes from outside catchment. Full or part time start in September, January or April.

Exit: Vast majority to Meadowhead Comprehensive.

Remarks: Went through an extended period of temporary leadership and staffing upheaval after the retirement of a very popular, long-standing head, but now achieving well at key stage 2 results at the top end, though slight dip over the last year or two. Key stage 1 results stronger, though. Graded good by Ofsted in a report which praised teaching and challenge given to the most able, but criticism of handwriting and presentation standards. Some use of ability groups for English and maths. Classes within lower years mixed up each year, which not all parents are happy about.

Good support for special needs, but you may have to push to get it. Gifted and talented given special classroom activities.

Situated in a relatively well off suburb of south west Sheffield; few ethnic minority and well below average proportion of children from poor backgrounds. Younger children housed in traditional, red brick, original building – light with cheerful displays, but reception classrooms rather cramped; hall can only accommodate one year at a time. Recent large addition provides more spacious, bright classrooms and a small hall used for PE, whilst markedly reducing playground area. Pleasant view of thickly wooded hill behind playground, which is equipped with climbing wall, gazebos and a train-shaped climbing frame. Woodland area just used for teaching at present, there's potential for greater exploitation for forest school purposes.

Friendly, happy atmosphere. Children say bullying very rare and that issues are quickly dealt with; mostly good behaviour. Weekly awards assembly for good work and manners and best class attendance. Golden Time reward system – children choose an activity they enjoy on Friday afternoons. Pupils act as peer mentors, play leaders in breaks and librarians; active school council.

Wide range of after school activities – main sports, including rugby and cricket, Spanish, zumba (children and parents), choir, drama. Eco, international, arts and healthy schools awards. Takes part in local events such as the Woodseats Festival – the outside cheerfully decorated in red, white and blue bunting when we called in – and raises large sums of money for local and national charities. Mostly local visits; year 6 residential at Derbyshire outdoors centre. Enthusiastic year 2 teacher maintains a blog with lots of photographs of her form's activities on school website.

Attractive uniform – green sweatshirt, green, black and white polo shirts with black or grey trousers and skirts, green and white checked summer dresses. Active PTA (PALS) – does lots of fundraising and organises a picnic in local park for prospective reception children. These have two half day visits with their parents before they start and staff aim to visit them in their pre-school setting.

A well-regarded and in most respects successful school that needs to work harder on its communication skills.

AKS Junior School

Linked with AKS Lytham

Clifton Drive South, Lytham St Annes, Lancashire FY8 1DT

Ages 2–11 **Pupils** 220

Fees: £8,895 pa

01253 784100
www.arnoldkeqms.com

Head of junior school: Since January 2018, Amanda Ilhan, previously pre-school and primary school deputy director of the British International School in Istanbul.

Entrance: There are no tests to gain entry to the nursery or infants' school; children wishing to enter the juniors would be expected to come and spend a trial day here. The only real assessments of ability would be for entry into year 6, because children in the junior school gain automatic entry to the senior school, so the junior teachers need to be confident that a year 6 child would be capable of progressing here. The school isn't oversubscribed so there's a very good chance you'll be able to get your child in if you can afford the fees.

Exit: Almost all juniors move up to the AKS senior school. While external applicants to the seniors have to sit exams, the juniors progress there automatically. 'If we've had a child for seven years, then we'll have prepared them for seniors and they'll be fine. Very occasionally we have a child and you think actually their needs are beyond what we can offer, but that conversation would be happening all the way through junior school. It wouldn't be sprung on their parents at the end of year 6. We know our children inside out and back to front.'

Remarks: Academically, the pupils benefit from relatively small class sizes (a maximum of 20 in the infants, 22 in lower juniors and 24 in upper juniors – although in practice these figures are sometimes much lower). There's no setting, although sometimes pupils at the higher or lower range of ability are taken aside in small groups to push forwards or to grapple with a particular challenge.

The school employs a full-time learning support assistant who caters for children with dyslexia, ADHD and autism spectrum disorders. They only take children whose needs they can cater for, but if a child's needs are within the specialism of existing staff then they will be supported at no extra cost to the parents. Support is usually provided within lessons.

Gifted and talented children are supported both within normal lessons and through links with the senior school. 'We can use the senior school to take them that bit further if that's what they need to reach their ceiling.' Depending on the size of the child (for reasons of safety in contact sports) talented sports players in year 6 may play for year 7 teams. Other links with the seniors are for the benefit of all: by year 6 specialist teachers from the senior school come to teach certain subjects – particularly music and sport.

Music is strong here. All the children in year 3 learn the violin, and there's a high level of participation in the junior school's orchestra and choir. Pupils can choose to have peripatetic music lessons in any instrument during the school day. Sport also has a significant place in the curriculum. There are games fixtures on Friday and Wednesday afternoons – so pupils playing in a team might leave early on those days, but the timetable is arranged so that they'll only miss a single lesson and then it's double games. Popular sports are rugby, football, hockey and netball. Hockey is the strongest sport competitively at the moment. But – as with the academic ethos – the approach to sport is inclusive and the school makes great efforts to arrange matches for B teams as well as A teams.

There is a wide range of after-school and lunchtime clubs. Some use the senior school facilities such as the drama studio. (The senior school is right on the campus with no roads to cross to get to it.) Most clubs are well populated. There are clubs for young environmentalists, keen Lego players, aspiring journalists – there's even a loom bands club. (Although we're told loom bands are 'dead and gone' and 'Moshi Monsters are back'. We can't keep up but it seems the school is trying to...)

It's a brand new building and it does seem to function smoothly. It's airy and spacious and – even on the grey day of our visit – very light. There is no IT suite because teaching staff decided that IT should be integrated across the curriculum, so pupils might expect to use laptops in any lesson.

We found no evidence of any bullying from our conversations with parents and pupils and the school has a strong and comprehensive anti-bullying policy. All reported incidents of bullying are recorded and staff tell us that pupils do understand what bullying is and report behaviour that they find concerning.

The children we met had friendly interactions with each other and showed a lot of enthusiasm for their education. They said they really liked games, swimming, art, technology and... their teacher. (Aahh!) They were very confident speaking in class – we noted that no-one was hiding at the back and everyone had a chance to speak, seemingly enthusiastically. They had happy memories of practical learning activities such as making a Roman shield and sandals and presenting in a class assembly. When asked how they might change the school, they weren't entirely constructive: 'play on an Xbox all day,' 'just have a massive party all the time,' and 'ride on rollercoasters all day,' were proposals from three would-be head teachers; but we suspect that if they did have any serious complaints these children wouldn't have held back from telling us.

Parents are enthusiastic about how much they feel included in the life of the school – although they gripe that arrangements can be made or communicated a little late in the day at times which makes it challenging for parents with busy schedules to turn up to as much as they'd like to. But by and large they say their children feel known and valued. One mum said of her son in the upper juniors: 'They have his measure. He's encouraged and stretched but he's not pushed.' Parents also value the strong discipline, combined with an understanding that childhood goes quickly and should be fun. It is a 'good all round school,' said one mum, 'I really can't think of any kind of child it wouldn't suit.'

AKS Lytham

Linked with AKS Junior School

Clifton Drive South, Lytham St Annes, Lancashire FY8 1DT

Ages 11–18 **Pupils** 451 **Sixth form** 77

Fees: £11,787 pa

01253 784100
www.akslytham.com

Headmaster: Since 2014, Mike Walton BA MA NPQH (50s). He was state-educated in Folkestone, Kent and then studied geography at Lancaster and stayed there to do his PGCE. During the '80s and '90s he mainly taught in British state schools – apart from sixth months as a volunteer teacher in Northern Sudan. His first headship was at Orchard School in Canterbury – a special school for children with learning difficulties. During these years in state education he had a 'missionary zeal' to 'make the world a better place'

In August 2005 he changed direction, moving to Thailand to become principal of Regents International School, Pattaya – a British international boarding school – helping to grow the school and taking on leadership and advisory roles on prestigious boards and bodies both in Asia and beyond. He also led the school to develop a curriculum that's taught through partnerships with local voluntary organisations – such as orphanages, street kids' centres or charities working with HIV patients – and encouraged children to engage with big issues such as democracy, international development and environmentalism.

Blackpool's Arnold School and Lytham-based King Edward VII and Queen Mary School merged in 2012-13 – a year before Mr Walton took office. He says he likes the fact that there are traditions to build on but there's also some of the excitement of a start-up; after the turbulence of the merger, the school was ripe for a leader with a vision. Will his internationalist ideals filter through to his work at AKS? Hopefully yes. Perhaps parents here can expect their children to start talking about global citizenship, or at least getting their hands dirty on local voluntary projects in the not too distant future. Mr Walton says he's inspired by the words of Einstein: 'Try not to become a man of success, but rather try to become a man of value.'

Leaving in July 2019.

Academic matters: In 2018, 36 per cent of A levels A*/A (66 per cent A*-B) and at GCSE, 47 per cent A*-A/9-7 grades. Parents we spoke to were very happy with their children's progress here. One mum was thrilled with her daughter's successful A level results and told us, 'I don't think there's any way she'd have done anything like as well if she hadn't been here – she really benefited from the small class sizes and the personalised support.' There are never more than 24 pupils in a class; no more than 16 at A level.

The school adds good value – aiming to add at least half a grade to pupils' expected outcomes. All children sit baseline tests in years 7, 10 and 12 to enable close monitoring of potential. Most of the teaching is mixed ability, although there is setting in maths because the brightest pupils can opt to take their GCSE at the end of year 10. Pupils take IGCSEs in English, maths, science and modern languages – as these give the teachers more freedom with the syllabus. The head says that the school is strong across the board academically and he wouldn't want to draw attention to any particular subject area.

Support for a broad range of special educational needs and there is usually no extra cost to parents for this (unless a child has a very specific need that would require, for example, an extra member of staff to be employed just to support that one child). Gifted and talented pupils are identified on a register and the school takes steps to stretch them by setting additional work and reading and encouraging them to take part in subject competitions or Olympiads, or to take Open University modules (to name just three provisions of many), but many more of the enrichment activities available to them are also offered to the whole school. There's a real commitment to stretching all of the children, not just the very brightest. The maths and music departments both stand out as offering an excellent range of opportunities for the most able students.

Lots of subject teachers are real specialists. One parent gushed about how inspirational and knowledgeable particular staff members from the art, science and English departments are. Pupils say that the teachers here are really passionate about their subjects and that the small class sizes mean you can't hide if you don't know something. It must be said that the pupils we met – while bright, polite and wholly positive in their attitudes to the school – didn't wow us with their passion for learning; they were distinctly quiet when we asked them to name their favourite authors. But this was a small sample of sixth formers and perhaps rather skewed towards scientists. Apparently the historians 'are always reading'. Perhaps its star pupils are just a little humbler than some of their more precocious and self-assured peers at similar schools. It's clear, though, that the pupils have a positive attitude to education and that there's no sense of any negative learning culture at the school that would push the so-called 'swots' to keep their heads down.

Games, options, the arts: AKS is strong in sport – particularly hockey and rugby, though netball and football are popular too. Pupils raved to us about recent sports tours to Australia and South Africa. There are games fixtures on Friday and Wednesday afternoons – so pupils playing in a team might leave early on those days, but the timetable is arranged so that they'll only miss a single lesson and then it's double games. The school has recently spent money on improving its sports facilities, which include an international standard all-weather sports ground, a brand new sports hall, a gymnasium and extensive playing fields. The local swimming pool is a short walk away. There's a strong ethos of participation for all. Depending on the size of your child (for reasons of safety in contact sports), talented sports players in year 6 may play for year 7 teams. If your child is keen to play competitively, there's a good chance they can, as the school tries hard to arrange regular fixtures for B teams as well as A teams. Mr Walton says he wants the benefits of playing in a team to be available to everyone who shows an interest, not just the most able.

If you visit AKS on a Monday you'll be surrounded by green uniforms as a large proportion of children take part in the CCF. DofE is also popular, with 65 pupils going for their gold award at the time of our visit. There's a lot of music, too – various choirs and orchestras which include as well as pupils. There's a brand new drama studio and many pupils choose to do LAMDA speech and drama exams – as well as taking part in drama clubs and school productions. One mum told us how inclusive the drama is here – anyone showing an interest will be found an opportunity to get involved. The school's art department also lets pupils loose on its excellent facilities in after-school activities such as ceramics club and art club. Extracurricular activities that stand out from the norm include Warhammer club; robotics club; animal club (recent visitors to this include tarantulas, geckos, giant snails, hedgehogs and snakes); and AKS Action – a fundraising and community action group which has pupils volunteering in soup kitchens, making up Christmas boxes for refugees and raising money for local and international good causes.

Background and atmosphere: The feel is anything but claustrophobic. Grand red-brick buildings sprawl outwards towards expansive playing fields. Beyond the school: sand dunes, a beach and the sea. Since the merger of 2012-13 between Blackpool's Arnold School and Lytham's King Edward VII and Queen Mary School to form AKS, the school is now united on one site at Lytham St Annes – previously the home of King Edward VII and Queen Mary School. The site was refurbished at the time of the move so now, as well as adding new sports facilities, they've built a new library, drama studio and science laboratories, and many other facilities have been improved and updated. It's still a period building, though, and it feels busy, comfortable and traditional rather than starkly modern.

We made our visit to AKS in the knowledge that the year or two preceding the merger had been difficult, to say the least. Some parents from both Arnold and King Edward VII and Queen Mary Schools were vehemently opposed to the amalgamation. They'd formed a campaign group to oppose it and had (unsuccessfully) taken their concerns to the Charity Commission. So we were on the lookout for tensions during our visit and particularly during our discussions with parents. But the truth seems to be that such was the intensity of the bad feeling over the merger – albeit from a relatively small group of parents – that those who objected had removed their children from the school, leaving behind a contented and harmonious community. Parents we spoke to said they were happy that the merger gave both schools a future which had otherwise been looking shaky – following a drop in pupil numbers and wider problems with the local and national economy. Parents said they took a lead from their children on this issue: the kids saw the merger as a chance to make new friends and enjoy new opportunities and so parents followed suit.

Now a Round Square school, one of nearly 180 in 50 countries, enabling students to attend international conferences (in eg Switzerland, Romania, Canada and Thailand) and join in volunteer projects (so far in Tanzania and Vietnam). AKS students won the Round Square 50th Anniversary Award for Community Engagement, presented in Cape Town.

Pastoral care, well-being and discipline: Incidents of bullying are logged but they are 'rare' and 'low level'. Mr Walton says they're 'dealt with swiftly'. The children we met all said they would tell a teacher and support the victim if they saw it – but none could think of any instances during their time at the school. Certainly the PHSE co-ordinator takes a proactive approach to bullying and the growing threat of cyber-bullying. The PHSE programme is impressively hands-on: everyone learns CPR; there are visitors to talk about drugs, pornography, sex and relationships and LGBT issues; and every year the local fire and ambulance services help to produce a massive reconstruction of a car crash, complete with sixth formers mocked up with dramatic-looking injury make up. We get the sense that the programme really is really about making children safer, happier and emotionally healthier – and not just about ticking boxes. Pupils say, 'it's alright to be gay here.' We're told there's 'always someone' for pupils to talk to: sixth form peer mentors, form tutors, year heads and the school matron are all available to offer pastoral support.

On the question of discipline, Mr Walton tries to strike a balance between his instinctual inclination to try to understand naughty children and offer them 'a chance' and his acknowledgement that in the independent sector parents expect strict discipline. 'All of us can make one mistake,' he says, but he does confirm that a pupil found with one cannabis joint for personal use in his or her school bag would face expulsion. Children might wonder whether he's calling their bluff but we wouldn't test him. In practice, though, there have been no expulsions in recent years – presumably because behaviour is generally good here. The atmosphere on our visit was one of friendly and orderly discipline and industriousness.

Pupils and parents: The fees are at the lower end of the independent schools spectrum and consequently not all the parents are hugely wealthy. There are taxi drivers and shopkeepers in the mix, we're told. Some run local businesses which thrive during the summer months but, as the days darken and the tourists go home, they struggle to meet the fees throughout the winter. But the parents we met appeared to be from comfortably middle class families – some of whom had attended one or other of the schools themselves. The pupils we met were sporty and into science. They didn't conform to the stereotype that the privately educated are arrogant and entitled. They said they enjoyed school; that they knew how lucky they were; and that they wanted to make a contribution to the local community and to society when they left school. Not everyone was ultra-confident talking to us, but they were all polite and impressed us with their easy and co-operative communication with each other. We sometimes felt as if a committee was answering our questions – but it was an inclusive committee that let everyone speak, so we didn't mind.

We didn't find much in the way of household names among the old boys and girls but there are plenty of high achievers. Arnold alumni include the founder of Jaguar Cars, a Nobel Prize-winning chemist, half a dozen England sportsmen (football, cricket, rugby) and a handful of actors, artists and musicians including Jonas Armstrong from the BBC's Robin Hood, Jenna-Louise Coleman from Emmerdale and Doctor Who and Chris Lowe of the Pet Shop Boys. Alumni from KEQMS include comedian Jenny Éclair, a couple of leaders of British industry and a former equerry to the Queen.

Entrance: The school isn't oversubscribed so there's a very good chance you'll be able to get your child in if you can afford the fees. School pays great attention to references from children's current schools – we get a sense that selection is more about behaviour than academic potential. Senior school applicants tested in English, maths and non-verbal reasoning. They'll offer places to pupils they feel would cope with working at pace and benefit from what's on offer here. The school encourages families to visit at any time and children can get a better feel for the school by coming for a taster day.

Exit: About a third of year 11 currently progresses to the sixth form. Mr Walton says he'd like that figure to be higher, but there's stiff competition from local state schools and colleges. Not all of year 13 goes to university. 'Sometimes it's a sensible option to go into management training at 17 or 18,' says the head. But most do go on to higher education. In 2018, five medics and a dentist, with one off to the École Hotelière Lausanne, Switzerland. Manchester, Lancaster and St Andrews all popular. Students off to study eg management, criminology, science, song writing.

Money matters: Following the merger and the sale of the old Arnold School site in Blackpool, we're told that AKS is now in good financial health and its future is assured. Parents expect to get great value for money, but the fees are relatively low so the school is careful on how it spends them. Parents should be confident, says Mr Walton, that fees are ploughed fairly into the education of every child at the school, rather than being diverted into specialist sports or academic scholarships to bring in high flyers just to boost the school's sporting or league table success.

Means-tested assisted places to a maximum of 85 per cent of fees awarded primarily in years 7 and 12, with means-testing reassessed annually. Some short-term bursaries for those going through 'temporary and unforeseen' financial hardship. Priority for these goes to pupils who have been at the school for at least five years and to pupils in their GCSE and A level years. Some 5-10 per cent of pupils in the senior school receive some level of means-tested financial support and there are 10 per cent sibling discounts throughout the school.

Remarks: This is a happy and positive place to learn. It treats pupils as individuals rather than statistics, encourages them to engage with the wider world and it has a really holistic vision of education. The small class sizes make it a good option for parents who worry their children might be 'invisible' in a large teaching group, and its inclusive ethos means that children who might be cowed or disheartened by a more competitive or elitist institution may find the space and opportunity to flourish here. Parents praise its family feel, the fact that they too feel included and welcome in the community, and an approachable body of teachers who really listen and get to know their children. It's not ostentatious about its success, but it's excellent value compared to the local competition and clearly a great school.

Ampleforth College

Linked with St Martin's Ampleforth

4

Ampleforth, York, North Yorkshire YO62 4ER

Ages 10–18 **Pupils** 591 **Sixth form** 204 **Boarders** 475 full **RC**

Fees: Day £16,401 – £24,636; Boarding £25,251 – 35,424 pa

01439 766000
www.ampleforth.org.uk/college

Acting head: Deirdre Rowe MA is holding the fort after the resignation in August 2018 of Fr Wulstan. The college is quoted as saying 'The trustees of the school have agreed that the leadership of the school should revert to a lay person.' And a woman! – first ever in 200 years. Miss Rowe, previously associate head, has been at the college for some five years, two in charge of safeguarding. After gaining a masters in music from Trinity College Dublin, Miss Rowe has spent her entire career in Catholic education, including a spell as principal education officer for the diocese of Leeds. Her hobbies include cookery, walking, travel and Ignatian spirituality.

Academic matters: Not a high-flyer in the league tables but, with a wide intake, the focus is on providing the opportunity for pupils to get the best results they can. A level performance over the last five years has been around the mid-40s per cent A*-A with A*-B at 74 per cent in 2018. The most popular subject choices are history and Christian theology, followed by mathematics, chemistry and biology, with good uptake in

English and economics; results have been consistently good in these subjects as well as French, Spanish and art.

Most sixth formers start with four A levels and reduce to three, though mathematicians often add further maths. On top of this, enrichment and extension classes for the EPQ, community sports leadership qualification and, through the CCF, a level 3 leadership and management qualification as well as Duke of Edinburgh community service are all on offer. Now offers BTecs in hospitality, enterprise and entrepreneurship and countryside management.

In 2018 just under 60 per cent of GCSEs were A*/A or 9-7. All pupils baseline assessed on entry; thorough tracking and monitoring, half-termly flagged assessments targeted against expected GCSE attainment; interventions when needed. One housemaster lists his pupils' current term performance amongst other house notices – not normal practice, we were assured.

Good learning support team, with dyslexia specialist, commended by parents. Usually alerted to a child's needs by their previous school's report or a teacher/tutor referral. One-to-one support in lessons and, if needed, reduced curriculum. The evening prep club has learning support staff and teachers on hand and there are study skills sessions for those in need but not on the register.

A small number of EAL; all are tested on entry and if necessary attend at least six 50 minute lessons in a two week cycle in years 10 and 11. Lessons in the sixth form (extra charge) prepare pupils for IELTS examination needed for university entrance.

The aim is to ensure every child is stretched and receiving the right differentiation. Sharing best practice across departments being promoted – benefits already in geography/ PE hookup, where resilience training from sports being imbedded in the academic teaching.

The closure of prep school St Martin's Ampleforth will bring years 6, 7 and 8 onto the college campus in September 2019, with a boarding house converted to junior boarding and a year 6 classroom in the building and protected play area nearby. Timetables and curriculum will continue as they were in the prep school.

Games, options, the arts: Ampleforth has a long history of sporting excellence; more than 25 sports available. Considerable investment in facilities across the campus; impressive, top of the hill St Alban's Sports Centre alongside Astros, pitches and courts. All get well used with multiple rugby, hockey, tennis, netball and swimming teams offering masses of competitive opportunities for all – not to mention teams for seven other sports.

There's also the range of country pursuits – hunting, shooting and fishing as well as gamekeeping. Equestrian activities and a chance to try your hand at polo are becoming ever more popular, though no livery or facilities on site – yet, though planning permission awaited for equestrian facilities.

Not surprisingly, making music is major here, particularly choral music with Schola Cantorum and impressive girls' Schola Puellarum, who share the singing of mass throughout the year and meditations at key moments. An annual performance of Faure's Requiem together with other major choral works, regular appearances in Catholic and Anglican cathedrals and a yearly overseas tour (most recently Prague and Malta). Orchestral ensembles off the scale – symphony orchestra, big band, string and jazz groups, ceilidh band and the Ampleforth Highlanders' Pipe Band, purportedly the largest south of the border. A recent high point was playing with alongside rock band, the Red Hot Chili Peppers, to a sell out audience at the Sage in Newcastle.

Art flourishes up to A level; impressive works on display in the technology building – pity there aren't more around the school for all to enjoy. Ampleforth has a long tradition of theatre: the first play performed in the New Theatre in 1910; its current incarnation is professionally fitted out and seats nearly 200. Several productions a year, most recently Into the Woods, an all female Hamlet and musical Anything Goes – Green Room team for those who don't want to be in the spotlight. House drama competition, curricular theatre studies, dance and LAMDA lessons keep this, and the multi-use studio, well used.

Thriving CCF, popular with girls and boys. RAF and army cadets, a number aiming for Sandhurst. Compulsory two sessions for all new pupils (the majority sign up) to experience outdoor pursuits, drills, ever-complex weapons maintenance and firing in the indoor shooting range. Links up with DofE to provide some elements for the awards.

Extensive co-curriculum also includes the readings of Aquinas, sign language, rebuild a Land Rover, Lego league robotics, Ampleforth TV and discussing politics in the Westminster Society. Years 10 and 12 spend Friday afternoons working on community projects.

Boarding: Full boarding is the order of the day here and it's what attracts parents. They told us they liked the full range of weekend activities with little local external distraction and that they found the longer but fewer exeats, none in spring and summer, less disruptive for their children. Only 15 per cent are day pupils; long days with daily bus service available. They are allocated a house – no wonder they occasionally board, at a nightly charge, so as not to miss out on the fun.

Ten boarding houses, six for boys, three for girls, housing 60 to 70 pupils, and new junior boarding house, St Edward's and St Wilfred's. Comfortable and homely accommodation kept in good order by rolling refurbishment programme. Younger pupils in dormitories of between four and six (occasionally seven), depending on house, moving into twin or singles by year 11 or 12. Spacious communal areas, games rooms and kitchens for preparing snacks. Plenty of staff, including matron, on hand and sixth formers contribute to daily operation, supervise junior prep sessions and provide academic support. As preparation for independent living, sixth form may do their own washing and have greater access to kitchen facilities.

Each house character is driven by the personality of the housemaster or mistress, praised for the dedication and care. Spiritual life lies at the heart of the house, each with its own chapel for morning and evening prayers; weekly mass; monk chaplain and sixth form catechist leading weekly Lectio Divina meetings.

Food given a cautious thumbs up – 'it's got better' was the general view. Good integration of international pupils – their festivals celebrated communally. Friendly rivalry with inter-house competitions. Sixth formers have privilege of on campus Windmill 'pub' – a walk away from the boarding houses.

Parents are sent a weekly blog – there's an Ampleforth App, and each house has its own Facebook page. Houseparent and academic tutor at the end of an email or phone so parents feel well in the loop. Internet off at 10.30pm though some parents felt that lights out could be earlier and more rigorously enforced.

Background and atmosphere: Nestled in the tranquil and beautiful valley enveloped by the Howardian hills, Ampleforth's 2,000 acre site has its abbey and church (by Giles Gilbert Scott, best known for Liverpool Cathedral) at its physical and spiritual heart. Beautiful Victorian gothic main wing blended with some modernist 1930s school buildings with late 1970s and 'early noughties' additions, most recently St Alban's Sports Centre.

Opened for boys in 1802; girls joined the sixth form in 2002 and school became fully co-educational in 2010; over the last few years the numbers of girls and boys have been evening out.

One of the largest Benedictine abbeys in Europe, the Rule of St Benedict underpins everything that happens in the college and provides its pupils with what the school calls 'a compass for life', a spiritual direction finder enabling them to be true to themselves, knowing their place in the world, even in the bad times. Parents say that this touches deeply all pupils, even the 'cool sporty ones', and that they have had to 'question moral codes and debate the very reason for Christianity in a modern world'. Pupils say that the strong sense of community is the best part of the school for them, and they are sure the bonds of friendships will be lifelong.

Pupils smartly but not regimentally attired in black or charcoal grey uniform with the odd flash of a red jumper. Sixth formers mainly adopted smart country wear – hacking jackets, gilets, open necked dress shirts and chinos.

Pastoral care, well-being and discipline: Pastoral and spiritual care go hand in hand here. The tenet of the Benedictine ethos, of others before self, immersion in communal religious celebration, annual retreats, all with the support and fellowship of your house, ensure that pupils are well cared for here. Parents speak of the level of care as exemplary and give examples where they feel the school has gone above and beyond for their children.

Zero tolerance of drugs and an outreaching PSHE programme with speakers such as reformed alcoholics, refugees etc to widen horizons. The assistant head commented that the character of pupils is to have a strong sense of right and wrong.

Mindfulness and well-being are entrenched; pupils are encouraged to reflect and record what went well on a regular basis, time is taken in annual retreat and each house has a sixth form monitor, promoting good mental health messages and helping to provide coping strategies.

It is a shame then that these laudable practices have not extended to rigorous safeguarding at the school. In August 2018 after statutory investigations and some difficult publicity, the Charity Commission removed responsibility for safeguarding matters from trustees, and a damning Independent Inquiry into Child Sexual Abuse report published in August 2018 concluded: 'It is clear to us from all the evidence we have heard during this Inquiry that several systemic child protection and safeguarding challenges remain at Ampleforth to this day.'

Parents to whom we spoke in early 2018, however, gave unanimous and overwhelming support to the school and the care they felt their children received there. All commented on the transparent and open communications they received from the then head and felt well informed.

Ampleforth have been following in Downside's footsteps in dealing with the difficulties that they have faced with safeguarding, but with less speed and less openness, and with the Charities Commission having to appoint an outside safeguarding overseer. All this is unimpressive and concerning, but we are assured that the necessary changes will be made by the end of the 2018/19 academic year.

Pupils and parents: Numbers dipped overall over the last few years but the number of girls has grown by over 10 per cent during this period and they now represent nearly 40 per cent of the school roll. Interestingly, girls are expected to account for almost 50 per cent of the new starters.

Pupils come from all over the UK and beyond; 30 per cent from north east and Scotland; 30 per cent London and the home counties; 10 per cent rest of UK; 30 per cent from overseas, predominantly mainland Europe, with just 10 per cent split between Hong Kong (very few mainland Chinese) and the rest of the Catholic world.

Full boarding is a big attraction for parents drawn from landed estates, wealthy farming stock, businesses large and entrepreneurial; a number are alumni, most live a non-commutable distance away. Over 70 per cent of pupils are practising Catholics, the vast majority of the remainder Anglican or at least espousing Christian values. Non-Catholic pupils expected to take full part in school's religious life and there is good provision for Anglicans.

The school is commended by parents on its communication. Heads of house receive the highest accolade for their quick response and handling of their children and any issues that arise, and they feel well informed on their child's progress.

Notable alumni: actor James Norton, actor, author and screen-writer Julian Fellowes, chair of JCB Lord Bamford, former captain of England rugby team Lawrence Dallaglio and sculptor Antony Gormley.

Entrance: From over 80 prep schools, though top 20 or so annually and most others on a less regular basis. Ampleforth is working on extending links, particularly to London preps, now it is without St Martin's Ampleforth, its own prep school. One main entry point now into year 7.

For 13+ entry, minimum 50 per cent score in common entrance or a school test, and reports and references from previous school. Exceptions 'for faith or family', but no one admitted if he or she won't be able to cope. Usually offer to three-quarters of applicants. Significant entry in year 10, by reference from current school and informal interview.

Usually around 30 join the sixth form. Require at least five GCSEs, two at least grade 6s and three grade 5s or equivalent qualifications and reference from school.

Exit: Up to 20 per cent leave after GCSEs though external recruitment has kept sixth form numbers at over 200. In 2018, four to Oxbridge, two medics and nearly 70 per cent to Russell Group universities. Newcastle, Oxford Brookes, Exeter and Edinburgh most popular and three to IE in Segovia.

Money matters: Generous financial help. Nearly eight per cent of fee income funds means-tested bursaries for around 100 pupils, around a quarter receiving more than 75 per cent of their fees. Academic, music and all-round Hume scholarships at 13+ and sixth form and can be awarded to pupils after entry.

School states that 'extras' should not be more than £1,500 annually though this doesn't include music lessons or trips and activities home and abroad.

Remarks: Spiritual life and the Benedictine precept are the essence of the school. Amplefordians have a strong sense of self and what is right and wrong. They are allowed to be individuals whilst sharing the same moral compass – liked and appreciated by parents. The academic offering is being strengthened and widened and is complemented with an extensive on campus co-curriculum, so there is never a dull moment here.

The school has made headlines in the press over the last few years and with the Charity Commission removing safeguarding responsibilities from the trustees, and the damning report from the IICSA, there is no end from the headlines in sight. However, a lot of parents have stayed very loyal to the school and spoke to us glowingly of the care their children receive here.

A

Ashville College

Linked with Ashville Prep School

Green Lane, Harrogate HG2 9JP

Ages 3–18 **Pupils** 885 **Sixth form** 158 **Boarders** 103 full, 4 weekly, 3 flexi (from 8 years)

Fees: Day £8,430 – £14,640; Boarding £18,390 – £29,790 pa

01423 566358
www.ashville.co.uk

Headmaster: Since September 2017, Richard Marshall, previously head of Bury Grammar Boys. Biochemistry degree from Birmingham and masters in science communication from Imperial. He joined Bury in 2006 as head of chemistry, and was promoted to head of science, deputy head academic, second master and then headmaster in 2013. He has also been head of sixth form at Queen Elizabeth Grammar School Blackburn. A basketball fanatic, he played for England as a schoolboy and for the British University England team and captained the university first team. He still enjoys playing, watching and coaching it. He is married to Kimberley, also a teacher, and has three young children who have joined Ashville.

Academic matters: Academic focus in numeracy and literacy at the junior school but broad curriculum with specialist teaching in Spanish, French, music, science and ICT. Pupils taught in form groups of maximum 20 children, two per year group in years 3 and 4, increasing to three forms in both year 5 and 6. Setting from year 3 in mathematics and English with gifted and talented programme in mathematics, literacy, music and art having a good impact on results. No complacency here – the competition from local state schools is fierce. Whiteboards in most classrooms, two ICT lessons timetabled per week and netbooks to be introduced in the near future.

Good value-added, especially at GCSE – 42 per cent A*-A/9-7 in 2018. Science, mathematics, economics and PE all very popular at A level (38 per cent A*/A grades in 2018, 64 per cent A*/B). Not a shining star in the league tables but most pupils exceed predicted potential and very able pupils do particularly well. Good choice of subjects at GCSE; A level offering includes history of art and government and politics.

Average class size 16, max 22, dropping to 10, max 16, in the sixth form. Years 7–9 follow broad curriculum including at least two modern foreign languages (Italian now offered); set for mathematics and languages. For GCSE years, pupils split into ability bands A and B; A are taught Latin and B do extra lessons in English, geography and ICT. Majority take three separate sciences, a few dual award, all at least one modern foreign language.

All year 3 and year 7 pupils are screened for dyslexia, with further testing and screening as necessary. No pupil has an EHC plan, but over 130 pupils receive some additional help for 'mild dyslexic tendencies' – individual support if deemed necessary. Those with dyslexia thrive thanks to the kindly environment and carefully planned programmes of study; indeed in recent years few haven't got the benchmark five 9-4s at GCSE, and most gain at least a 6 in English.

Over 60 international students require English as an additional language, mostly taught alongside mainstream English. Target is Cambridge FCE by year 11 and all sixth form sit Cambridge IELTS in year 13. Also offers a US international studies programme for students aiming to return to education in the US or apply to an American university.

Games, options, the arts: Facilities – two gyms, 30m swimming pool, fabulous climbing wall, squash courts, fitness room and ample pitches, including a new all weather surface pitch – show importance of sport. Further proof by way of sports centre's £3 million refurbishment, updating changing rooms, gym and adding fitness studios and dedicated BTec sport classroom. Teams and fixtures galore in traditional team sports. All usual suspects on offer plus American influenced disc golf – something for everyone. Director of activities recently appointed to provide even more challenging outdoor opportunities.

Well-resourced and well-used music centre – a third take individual instrumental or singing lessons. An array of choirs and bands, from chamber to soul and jazz to strings. Talented musicians play in the National Children's and National Youth Orchestras, but plenty of playing and performing opportunities for those just starting out too: Verdi Requiem in Leeds Town Hall, Messiah from Scratch for charity. Full use of the senior school music facilities by a 50-strong junior orchestra and 65 per cent of the school in the junior choir, winning their category in the recent Harrogate Festival. All year 4 pupils receive small group violin and cello tuition.

Dedicated art studios and drama facilities always busy; performance opportunity in annual school play – diverse offerings recently of Pirates of Penzance, Bugsy Malone, A Midsummer Night's Dream and Henry the Tudor Dude. Unusually for a boarding school, a 4pm finish and no Saturday school, but plenty of choice of after-school activities and clubs and supervised prep until 5.30pm; DofE from year 10. Trip for older students to Malawi ties in with charity fundraising to support the Open Arms Orphanage, which has close links with the school.

Boarding: School viewed as a day school with boarding – under 20 per cent board, and half of these are sixth form; firmly in the school's sights to improve these statistics. Three senior boarding houses, two boys' and one girls', are comfortably furnished with usual facilities: kitchens, common rooms, games areas and computers. In process of refurbishment; up to six share, with sixth formers in their own study bedrooms.

Junior boarding in co-ed house, Greenholme, run by year 5 teacher and wife (ex Ashvillian). Small numbers of full, weekly and flexi-boarders, year 5 to year 8, 70 per cent boys and 30 per cent girls, mainly English expats, Forces families. Seven or eight bedded in 'home from home' environment. Escorted visits to town alternate Saturdays, activities each weekend and some evenings, including geo-caching, extended to day pupils too. Integration further through memberships of local Scouts, football clubs and other groups. Daily tweet to parents keeps them involved and boarder-led newsletter when busy lives allow.

Approximately one-third of boarders are from South East Asia – this has reduced in recent years. More emphasis on weekly/flexi boarding and more recruitment from the Forces. Girls and boys encouraged to socialise, with trips regularly organised at weekends and half-termly theme evenings. Plenty of activities on offer after school but all optional. Cultural differences mean not much integration with day pupils after school hours.

Background and atmosphere: Founded in 1877 by the Methodist Church as a senior boys' boarding school, co-ed since 1984. Pleasant, well-maintained site is in a leafy residential area, with a swathe of pitches and playing fields fringed by the trinity of schools (college, junior and pre-prep), sports centre and boarding houses. Evacuated to Windermere during the war as the premises were requisitioned for the war effort and used by Air Ministry.

Plenty of well-kept facilities – atmospheric Memorial Hall is home to lectures, meetings and some concerts, with larger gatherings filling the school hall. Recent, much-needed, extensive refurbishment programme to most classrooms, with the library now excellent. Investment in ICT infrastructure and hardware and more planned. Refurbished sixth form centre with own café dining area, seminar and meeting/study rooms.

Pre-prep is accommodated in a bright, spacious and purpose-built school nestling in a quiet corner of the college's campus, adjacent to the sports facilities and a short distance from the prep school. The school is well resourced with a self-contained hall for assemblies, activities and dining; an open plan library; separate area for technology and baking and a 'quiet room' for individual or group work. Outside, a secure playground and learning environment have recently been enhanced by addition of new play equipment.

Pastoral care, well-being and discipline: Methodist ethos underpins the pastoral care and the school is committed to the development of the full potential of each individual. Parents praise excellent standard of care and say it's what they like most about the school. Hot on manners and respect, 'instilling values and standards which are often overlooked in the 21st century'. Strong culture of inter-house competition between four houses, from poetry to public speaking; the prized Rigg Cup for sport. Unusually, continuity of house membership from pre-prep up – adds to house loyalty and vertical bonding. School believes in picking up problems quickly to 'fix it small' and then 'partnership between school and parents'. This is recognised by parents, who said that the school 'tried very hard to get it right'.

All year 7s are taken to the Lake District for a bonding weekend early in the autumn term; this receives rave reviews not only from the new pupils but also from sixth formers, who work as liaison prefects and, if assigned to year 7, go too.

Fines if caught smoking, with possibility of exclusion for repeated offences. Drugs: out for supplying or intending to – no issues in recent times.

A genuine sense of community that keeps ex-pupils in contact long after they have left the school gates.

Pupils and parents: Mainly from local professional and business families, extending from Ripon to north Leeds and surrounding villages. Quite a few first time buyers; Americans from nearby Menwith Hill military base add an interesting dimension. For about 10 per cent of pupils English is not a first language and overall approximately 14 per cent come from a variety of minority ethnic backgrounds, mainly Chinese, Nigerian and European. Thriving Friends of Ashville runs regular, well-supported activities.

Old boys: Ian Dodds (designer of the Moon Buggy), Commander Ian Grieve (head of anti-terrorism Scotland Yard), Jim Carter (Downton Abbey actor), Simon Theakston (director of Theakston's Brewery and chairman of the Yorkshire Agricultural Show) and Peter McCormick (lawyer to the Football Association).

Entrance: Entry at 3+ is by informal assessment with head of pre-prep. Entry at 7+ is by mathematics and English tests and informal interview with the head of the school, usually as part of a 'taster' day.

For year 7, a day in January with English, mathematics and non-verbal reasoning papers followed by practical activities, plus a report from previous head. Usually a three form entry of 60 pupils, though recent demand has increased this to four forms.

Majority of senior pupils come from junior school (90 per cent move up) and nearby preps and local state primary schools. Six bus routes in operation starting in Leeds, Thorner, Addingham, Ripon and Bramham.

Sixth form entry is via interview and satisfactory reference; five grade 4s with minimum grade 6s in subjects to be studied. Exams, interview and reference are norm for entry at other times.

Exit: Around a fifth leave at the end of year 11, most to state sector, further three per cent at end of year 12 – mostly starting afresh, some to foundation courses. Majority of sixth formers go on to higher education, sometimes a couple to Oxbridge, rest to a wide range of universities including a third or so to Russell Group, Northumbria currently most popular, then Liverpool and Leeds. In 2018, one to Oxbridge, two medics and 14 off to university in the US.

Money matters: Academic, music, sports, art and drama scholarships. Scholarships are awarded on entry into year 7, year 10 and sixth form and are reviewed at key stages. Means-tested bursaries of up to 100 per cent of fees are available either in conjunction with scholarships or on a stand-alone basis. Additional discounts are awarded to the children of Methodist ministers and parents in the Forces.

Remarks: A successful all-round day school with a boarding ethos. Plenty of happy pupils in a caring and supportive environment. Academics and teaching being strengthened. Offers a trinity of schools providing seamless transition through each stage of education, obviously popular with many parents and pupils.

Aysgarth School

Newton-le-Willows, Bedale, North Yorkshire DL8 1TF

Ages Boys 3-13, girls 3-7 **Pupils** 203 **Boarders** 75 full, 52 weekly and flexi (from 8 years)

Fees: Day £8,100 – £19,890 pa; Boarding £25,890 pa

01677 450240
www.aysgarthschool.com

Headmaster: Since 2015, Rob Morse, previously head of Perrot Hill, with his wife Lottie and their children, Daisy and Harry, and black labrador, Nel. Moved from Somerset, though no newcomer to the north as former deputy head at S Anselm's in Derbyshire.

Entrance: Non-selective, but for prep an interview and assessment (no exam) to look for boys with a 'willingness to get stuck in', 'We try not to turn anyone away'. A few scholarships of between 10-25 per cent and some bursary help, which can be up to 100 per cent. Siblings and Forces discounts available.

Exit: Excellent record to public schools favourite destinations currently Uppingham, Shrewsbury, Harrow and Ampleforth. But also Eton, Merchiston, Oundle and Harrow. Good sprinkling of academic, music and sports scholarships (22 in 2018, including two to Eton).

Heads and senior staff of senior schools spend one weekend a year at Aysgarth meeting boys and parents after chapel and at social events.

Remarks: Quiet, rural setting with glorious views in 50 acres of parkland, feels remote but only a short distance from the A1. Approached through a sleepy village, purposely anonymous except for landmark of the splendid school tower on the horizon. A grand, purpose built, 19th century school building, including a gem of a chapel, complemented by modern facilities. As you journey from the entrance your eye is caught by the profusion of discarded balls in the grounds, underlying a parent's description of 'a place where boys can be boys', though girls are welcomed into pre-prep.

Pre-prep established in 1993 in Oak House, a gentle amble from the prep school. Well adapted with well-equipped, secure, outdoor play area running along the front of the attractive building. The curriculum is traditional and broadly based on the national curriculum, with French introduced in reception.

The weekly early years' newsletter keeps parents information about the play-based activity in EYFS, nursery and reception. This becomes more formal in year 1 with specialist teaching beginning to be introduced for French, PE and music. Year 2 introduces creative topic work. Transition is high on the agenda in year 3, with boys preparing for the prep school and girls for their next step at another school. House captain and other leadership opportunities. Golden time in assemblies celebrates academic achievement and good deeds, focusing on a difference aspect each week.

The rural setting provides the natural habitat for the forest school in 'Mr McGregor's garden' and the woodland areas. All the usual opportunities for music, drama and sport, with fixtures from year 3 and swimming for all. Good range of extracurricular clubs on offer, including sport, choir, cookery and multi-activity acorn club; ballet at an additional charge. Pre- and after-school care from 8.00am-6.00pm and there is school transport from Ripon and Asenby, all at extra cost.

In the prep school, small class sizes (max 16) with traditional and demanding curriculum; setting and streaming from year 5. Extraordinary continuity over the years in gaining places at top public schools. Challenge is to keep abreast of 'subtle shifts' in senior schools and 'keep improving in every sense' as the bar gets higher. SEN provision improving all the time as the school becomes a 'broader and kinder place'.

Top notch sports facilities, especially cricket field, swimming pool and newly built sports hall. The Aysgarth game of COW – cricket off the wall – is a love of Aysgarthians old and new, the real challenge being to hit the ball from the playground into the head's garden. Sport is high profile and they play to win, while still managing a well done and a slap on the back for the chap who comes last. Rugby, football, shooting, fishing, sailing, riding, golf and climbing all on offer. Won Rosslyn Park National Sevens Rugby tournament relatively recently.

Art is strong and DT is popular with boys getting their hands on serious equipment and tools. Music is outstanding with over 70 per cent of the pupils singing or playing an instrument. Boys – both the very musical and the less so – can be seen enthusiastically practising their instruments in dorms and classrooms at reserved times. They can play anything here, including bagpipes if they so wish, and the choir is 'as cool as being in the first XV' and a joy to hear. Drama lessons and lots of performance opportunities in newly built 200 seat theatre. Good to see boys enjoying reading sessions in the library after lunch.

Many of the boys look as though they are about to take Eton in their stride – happy, confident and courteous, without being arrogant, they are both charming and endearing but clearly relish this boy friendly atmosphere where you can 'be your own man'.

Staff know the boys well and, although the phrase is often over used, there is really a 'family feel' about this place, thanks chiefly to great enthusiasm and care from the top. Very much focused on full boarding – in fact, north of Oxford, it's the only all boys boarding prep in England and parents come from both north and south of the border and say, 'It's worth the journey'. Day boys are welcomed, though certainly in the minority, and they follow the boarding routine.

Boarding accommodation on the top three floors of the school includes ranks of sinks, where boys have to be reminded to wash occasionally. Cheerful dorms, a mix of beds and bunks, yet mainly unadorned walls, where caring staff keep a close eye, tidying up after them and providing a homely feel. Delightful to see much-loved soft toys adorning many a bed – in the senior dorms as well.

Common rooms on ground floor showing signs of good wear and tear. Extensive after hours activities for boarders include both pillow and water fights (though not at the same time) and it's fine to get down and dirty and build dens in the grounds as well as engaging in debating. Diverse range of weekend activities and breaks at exeats only.

Food is ample, prepared in-house using fresh ingredients and 'not bad for school food' (though the boys did say they would like a little more salmon and duck on the menu, please), served in a pleasant if slightly old fashioned dining room, long tables and benches, where courtesy and table manners count.

Clientele mainly solid (upper) middle class from the north and Midlands, with a few Forces families from Catterick. Strong full boarding ethos attracts families from further away, Scotland and Northern Ireland, with 10 per cent international boarders from Europe, Middle East and Russia. Families are a mix of old school and new, many first time into boarding, including some who, interestingly, say they had previously neither considered boarding nor single sex. Initially a little reluctant to let go, these parents place huge value on all that Aysgarth has to offer, both in and out of the classroom, the end result being that their sons are well prepared for the next school, commenting that 'Aysgarth boys are both in demand and popular'.

Governors very active and close to headmaster. There's a lively Old Aysgarthian association. Old boys include Sir Matthew Pinsent and Robert Swan OBE, whose achievements espouse the Aysgarth ethos.

Beech House

Linked with Bolton School Boys' Division, Bolton School Girls' Division, Bolton School Boys' Junior School, Bolton School Junior Girls' School (Hesketh House)

Chorley New Road, Bolton BL1 4PA

Ages 4–7 **Pupils** 201

Fees: £9,579 pa

01204 434759
www.boltonschool.org/infants

Headteacher: Since 2015, Tracey Taylor (early 50s). Previously head of Adlington Primary School in Lancashire. Did a BEd at Edge Hill University and also has an NPQH. She always wanted to teach and has specialised in reception and year 1 teaching throughout her career. This is her first job working in the independent sector. She made the move to realise her ambition of leading an infant school.

Mrs Taylor is everything you'd expect an infant school head to be: passionate about the learning that goes on here, proud of her workforce and bursting with warmth and affection towards the 200-odd small children in her care (all of whose names she has learnt with no discernable effort). She says she's a 'happy wanderer' – in and out of classrooms all day – and she's at her most animated when talking about the children's happy experiences here and their moments of glory.

She responds carefully to the question of why parents should stump up the money to send their children to Beech House. Parents are 'buying into the whole Bolton School package,' she says, (although gaining a place in the infants' school, while providing automatic entry to the boys' or girls' junior schools, does not guarantee a place at the senior school). The real difference at this age, though, she says, is the freedom teachers have to develop children at their own pace, treating them as individuals and to enrich the curriculum without being bound by the rules of Ofsted or the rigmarole of Sats.

She's married with two grown-up sons – 'I'm an extremely proud mum,' she says. In her free time, as well as gardening, baking and walking, she enjoys creative crafts. She says that she's gradually brought more and more creativity into the curriculum here – getting the children into art and drama and hands-on crafts like willow weaving.

Entrance: The head assesses all children herself – through an informal one-to-one chat and a play in her office. Parents said the process treated their children as individuals and was not at all intimidating. 'My son went in crying,' said one mum, 'and came out smiling, with a teddy and a sticker.' Mrs Taylor says she's not looking for any reading or writing skills – just for an 'inquisitive and curious child who can follow instructions and is open to learning'. They do turn some children away if they don't believe they'll be happy here. One mum we met, whose two elder children have thrived at Beech House, told us she was very disappointed that her youngest child, who has very particular special educational needs, wasn't accepted. The head says that the school can accommodate specific learning disabilities such as dyslexia, but these are looked into on a case-by-case basis. If places become available in years 1 and 2, children are tested in reading, writing and numeracy.

Exit: At the end of year 2, almost all children go to Bolton School's junior departments – Hesketh House for girls and Park Road for boys. The head says the transition is very smooth because the infants often visit the junior schools to see performances and concerts etc and the head teachers of both junior schools also visit Beech House. A couple of parents we met whose children had recently made that transition disagreed: 'My son felt like he'd been dropped into a deep ocean at first,' said one dad. 'There is quite a big difference between the infants' and junior schools,' said another; but he added that he'd raised his concerns about transition with Mrs Taylor and she'd responded really proactively and he now feels confident that things will be much better in future.

Remarks: The building was purpose-built a few years ago and still feels shiny and new. It's light and spacious, with lots of room outside the classrooms for small groups to break away. There are three classes (of up to 25 children) per year and the three year groups each have their own distinct area. ('They feel terribly grown-up when they go upstairs for year 2,' says Mrs Taylor.) Each class has a qualified teacher and a full-time, qualified teaching assistant. Reception children take it in turns to use an outside space that's well set up for independent learning. There isn't the potential for complete free-flow between indoors and outdoors (the ideal in an EYFS provision) – although a recent ISI inspection report rated the EYFS provision as outstanding in all areas. There isn't a great deal of opportunity for mud-loving types to get their hands dirty on a daily basis, but the school does its best with the outdoor space and it does have access – by arrangement – to the fantastic Bolton School grounds and facilities like the indoor swimming pool (swimming lessons begin in year 2).

The school covers the national curriculum 'with extras'. Teachers have the flexibility to go beyond or to vary its pace to meet individual needs. Parents we met said they were happy with their children's progress and didn't need to worry about it – 'the academic side is a given'. (The data backs this up: pupil progress and outcomes at the school are both excellent.) The parents we met agreed that their children's happiness and confidence is the priority at this age and that the school provides that in spades. The dad who told us that 'homework is a pain in the arse' won a lot of support from the room, but everyone seemed to think the school gets it about right – in terms of the quantity and quality of what's set.

Children are assessed regularly and informally throughout the school year and there are regular reports and parents' evenings. The school operates an open door policy and parents feel confident that any concerns would be heard and acted on. 'We feel like we do have some influence', said one dad, 'and there's always someone you can talk to.' Parents said they feel included in the life of the school. 'The children get a lot of opportunities to perform in front of an audience of parents,' said another dad. 'They build the children's confidence through nurture,' said a mum.

There's an active parents' association, which raises money for extras and arranges a good number of events – including the 'best day of the year' when Father Christmas (one of the dads, disguised with a big beard and a dubious Irish brogue – 'it's the only accent I can do') rides into school in a vintage bus. We got a strong sense of community from the parents we met. 'The school attracts people with shared values,' said one; 'it's a happy place and you feel you're amongst friends'.

The only note of dissent from parents was about the wider school structure. Some felt it was a little 'brutal' to separate boys and girls at the age of 7 and one mum said she looked towards the move to junior school 'with trepidation'.

There is a decent array of extracurricular activities on offer – although 'not as much as some parents would probably like,' says Mrs Taylor, 'because we do feel that the children are quite tired by the end of the school day.' The choir (only open to year 2 children) rehearses at lunchtimes but most other clubs – including Beavers, dance, drama, jujitsu, science, craft and LAMDA – meet after school. But while the school deliberately limits the time spent in activities outside school hours, the range of timetabled activities is excellent. Every term pupils can expect to go on school trips and/or to be involved in talks or workshops from visiting groups or performers. Recent onsite visitors have included a menagerie of farm animals, two police horses and the Google Expeditions team, who took the children on a virtual reality journey to the Seven Wonders of the World, across the Milky Way and even back in time. Parents don't pay extra for their children to take part in special events on site, although there is an additional cost for some school trips. All pupils in year 2 also learn cello or violin at no extra cost and pupils learn French right from the beginning – taught by a native speaker.

The pupils we met were well behaved, confident and deeply engaged in their learning. Mrs Taylor says behaviour is good because there are strong systems in place – stickers, traffic light systems, lots of opportunities to reinforce good behaviour, to encourage children to talk about feelings and think about others and also to warn and redirect those who may be heading in the wrong direction. Pastoral care rests primarily with the

B

class teacher and classroom assistants, but there is also a full-time school nurse on site and everyone on the premises – from administrators to the kitchen staff – knows the children and looks out for them.

Beech House is lively and cheerful – buzzing with purposeful activity and happy little learners. The parents seem delighted with their choice and both staff and pupils give every sign that they too are delighted to be there.

The Belvedere Academy

17 Belvedere Road, Princes Park, Liverpool L8 3TF

Ages 11–18 **Pupils** 906 **Sixth form** 260

01517 271284
www.belvedereacademy.net

Principal: Since 2006 (one year before the school changed from a selective independent GDST school to a state-funded academy), Peter Kennedy BEd Dip Man Ed (50s). Attended Manchester Polytechnic. Head of English and sixth form in a Knowsley comprehensive, deputy head of two other comprehensives in Knowsley, head Ellen Wilkinson High School in Manchester, head of Chorlton High School, Manchester. Married, three grown-up children; outside interests include music, sport, travel.

Approachable, affable, humorous; wants to keep the original school's ethos of hard work and high standard of behaviour, attendance and academic results and adapt it to meet the challenges of a mixed ability cohort from all social strata; enjoys seeing the way the girls gain in confidence and blossom in a secure environment with high expectations. Popular with girls ('I love him!'; 'He's cheerful, has authority but isn't intimidating') and parents (including the original ones): 'He's done amazing things..has had a lot of vision'.

Retiring in July 2019.

Academic matters: Modern foreign languages and science specialisms; lots of tracking and monitoring. Teaching and learning judged outstanding by Ofsted; teachers seen as friendly, helpful: 'They're amazing – more like friends,' enthused a sixth former. 2018 A levels: 55 per cent A*-B, 3 per cent A*/A. Most take EPQ; general studies in both years. Wide choice includes business, media, drama and theatre studies, economics, government and politics, classical civilisation, psychology, sociology, music, sport and PE – plans to develop links with FE colleges as less academic girls come through rather than increase the number of vocational subjects and advise them accordingly.

2018 GCSE: 43 per cent A*-A/9-7 grades, and 90 per cent got 9-4 in both English and maths. All do at least one MFL, can do three separate sciences, OCR and GCSE IT; also Latin, business studies, performing arts, health and social care, home economics, media studies, PE; bottom band does Study Plus (extra English and maths). No plans to adjust curriculum to improve English Bacc league table position – prefers to maximise girls' choice. Study skills and revision sessions offered for one week of the Easter holidays for public exam girls, plus 11 Saturday morning sessions over the year (always full). Mentoring programme for all year 11 students

At KS3 all do French and Spanish and three sciences. Five ability bands from entry on basis of admissions tests (movement allowed) – three high (27/8), one middle (20) and one low (12) which has extra support and a less demanding curriculum, colour coded so not obvious to the younger girls what ability level the colours represent. Setting for maths, English and languages; very good test results, especially maths.

Access to network files and lesson materials from home via ICT portal. Top five per cent of gifted and talented identified as well as top 10 – extension classes in enrichment time plus in class extension work and supporting of lower ability girls; sixth formers attend Durham University summer school. Massive investment in well-staffed additional support area – has just been awarded advanced inclusion mark. All girls screened for dyslexia in year 7 (and soon in year 12) by in-house specialist; specialist EAL support. Manager feels school could cope with all difficulties.

Games, options, the arts: Has huge modern sports hall plus multi-purpose gym, mini fitness suite; games take place in public park. The usual sports plus tag rugby (specialist coaching), volleyball, basketball, lacrosse, trampolining, dodgeball, aerobics, unihoc, community sports trust leadership award; city success for netball and badminton teams; national gymnastics gold medallist and taekwondo competitor.

Artsmark Gold: lots of music – ensembles, choir, jazz band, orchestra won a gold medal at the Liverpool Performing Arts Festival; well-equipped music room with space for choir and orchestra rehearsals. Drama studio with flexible seating, annual drama festival – sixth form girls direct younger ones. Spacious dance studio – dance now at KS3, with GCSE to come and eventually A level (performing arts will also become available at A level). Excellent art: mostly painting and drawing with some 3D and print making – current biomedical project has year 12s working with a professional sculptress; art and design plus fine art with art history offered to sixth. Cheerful textiles room – graphic design on the way.

Vast range of activities in lunch hour and enrichment time, at end of lessons three days a week, some organised by sixth – community work, DofE, journalism club (produces school's e-letters), comedy (Liverpool being the home city of Alexis Sayle and Julie Walters, after all), bridge, cartoons, debating, chess, conversational Italian, Mandarin, Fair Trade. Annual languages festival including film festival; year 7 and 8 spelling bee; media studies has lively Oscars night; recent BBC Schools Question Time national champions. Exciting trips – South Africa, China, World Challenge to Vietnam and Cambodia, Shanghai (to promote Liverpool at World Expo).

Background and atmosphere: Until becoming an academy it was The Belvedere School, a selective GDST independent school. In 2001, a seven year pilot funded by Sir Peter Lampl's Sutton Trust opened up all places on the basis of just merit, with parents paying fees on a sliding scale according to income. Thirty per cent attended for free, it obtained its best ever GCSE results, girls from deprived backgrounds won places at top universities. Still part of the GDST. Numbers have grown steadily from just under 400 to over 900.

Located in the Princes Park area of Liverpool, adjoining a now-regenerated Toxteth, it consists of five linked Victorian (1880) villas plus gardens combined with a new purpose-built extension – the government provided £10m for capital development whilst co-sponsors, the GDST and HSBC Global Education Trust, each provided half a million. The pleasing décor is predominantly blue (matching the uniform) throughout. A hallway in the original part, with traditional school photos and book cabinets, has stairs lined with framed old war posters leading to the history area. Some very attractive rooms – music, art, the well-furnished and stocked library plus canteen – have large bay windows and original ceiling mouldings and views of the park and gardens. A huge cooking range from the original scullery in a corridor gives its name – the Range – to a meeting place. Outside the canteen is a playground with picnic tables and outside learning space with trees, shrubs and hut, due to be developed into an eco area with a pond. The sixth form has a common room with several royal blue sofas and chairs, plus a private study area. The new part is all very fresh and has modern ICT suites, MFL rooms and science labs.

The girls look very smart in their royal blue blazers and ties with light blue shirt/blouse and navy skirt. They are even required to have navy blue/black school bags and coats, can wear navy blue hijabs, and waist belt with purse is also part of the uniform – gosh, this GSG writer hasn't seen one of those since she was at her own GDST school! Sixth formers wear a black business suit with plain white shirt or blouse. All this, and much, much more, enumerated in the student handbook – this is a school that pays punctilious attention to detail.

The ethos of 'the Belevedere girl' is promoted from the start, by staff and the older girls from the original school; this encapsulates the GDST values of hard work, respect for teachers, leadership qualities and pride in one's school (reminiscent of the American charter schools). Each form has a head and deputy head girl, who hold office for half the year. It is perfectly acceptable to be clever and industrious; the girls don't feel unduly pressured but encouraged to do their best and aim high – 'They want us to do well – if we do our best, they are happy'. They say the school council's suggestions are taken heed of.

Pastoral care, well-being and discipline: Very good pastoral care and tight on safeguarding. Bullying not seen as a problem by the girls we met – 'Everyone's friendly – you don't have bullies at Belvedere'; 'The teachers are very aware of social problems'. Sixth formers assigned to KS3 forms, may help individuals with reading; NSPCC training for peer mentors ('buddies'). The girls quickly feel secure and comfortable, according to Mr Kennedy. Thorough behaviour management policy – seems to work, as the girls we saw in classrooms and corridors were all focused and well mannered. All teachers, plus dinner ladies, caretakers, support and office staff, have credit books to reward a range of virtues, leading to certificates, badges, gift/book vouchers, awarded in assemblies; also a traditional prize giving ceremony (but apparently they no longer measure how far skirts are above the knee, as they did in this writer's schooldays).

Pupils and parents: A wide range of social backgrounds; almost one quarter ethnic minority – about half with EAL. From 55-60 primary schools from all over Liverpool, Sefton, Warrington, St Helens and Knowsley plus Hamlet (original Belvedere junior). Web based portal allowing parents to access (some) data on their child. Notable old girls: Dame Rose Heilbron (judge), Esther McVey (MP), Linda Grant (author), Baroness Morgan of Huyton (has held various public offices). Access to the 70,000 strong GDST Alumnae Network.

Entrance: Hugely popular – about 500 applicants for 112 places at year 7 (police needed to control the traffic on test day). All take verbal, non-verbal and numerical reasoning tests; the top 10 per cent achievers in the verbal test are accepted for MFL ability promise, the rest are divided into five ability bands (fair banding system) and then reduced by a lottery method. SEN and looked after children criteria also applied.

Sixth form: minimum of five GCSEs at 6 or above, with 6+ in prospective A level subjects; takes about 30 external applicants.

Exit: Roughly 20 per cent after GCSEs to FE colleges for vocational courses. Rest depart post A level to a wide range of universities and subjects. Manchester, Leeds and Liverpool popular; Two to Cambridge in 2018, plus six medics/vets/dentists.

Remarks: Now 'the school everyone wants their daughter to go to in Liverpool'. An exciting and inspiring enterprise extending the virtues of independent schools to a much greater social range that might be a trailblazer for future struggling ones. Only reservation is that the emphasis on 'the Belvedere girl' could restrict the development of individuality.

B

Beverley Grammar School

Queensgate, Beverley, East Riding of Yorkshire HU17 8NF

Ages 11–18 **Pupils** 817 **Sixth form** 260 (including 130 girls in joint sixth form)

01482 881531
www.beverleygrammar.co.uk

Headteacher: Since 2015, Gavin Chappell PGCE (Hull) NPQH, previously head of The Market Weighton School. Originally from Louth in Lincolnshire, he spent 10 years in Essex which explains the wandering north/south/hard to place accent. He has a son at the school and a daughter at Beverley High. He joined following a turbulent time during which the school lost its outstanding status, it has now been upgraded from 'requires improvement' to 'good'. It's a familiar journey for this head who, during his four years in post, took his previous school out of special measures. Plenty of energy evident, he has worked hard to bring staff and boys on board, sensibly working with them to get buy-in and appears now to be steering a much happier and more effective ship. Enormously popular with the boys, 'even the naughty ones like him,' they tell us. Ambitious but not arrogant, his mantra is one of deepening values whilst encouraging the staff to model good and appropriate behaviour so that the boys follow suit 'I'd like them to leave here with a bit of an edge – does that sound pompous?' he asks. No, it doesn't.

Academic matters: Despite its name, it is non-selective. Heavily oversubscribed, they are right up to their admissions limit with boys joining from 24 different schools. Has a wide range of SEN and more statemented boys than any other school in the area, but does extremely well for all-comers. Plenty of academic rigour alongside good, solid support as and when needed.

All the trad subjects plus one modern foreign language throughout key stage 3, either French or German. Those with the greatest literacy needs will not study a foreign language but instead receive two hours of additional literacy lessons. Mandarin club on offer for years 7 and 8. Setting for maths and mixed ability teaching groups for all other subjects. In years 10 and 11, alongside core subjects, PSHE and RE, students take courses from four possible routes, including EBacc learning, open learning, vocational learning and foundation learning. It sounds complicated but it isn't and it does mean that students really can follow a course that works for them. In 2018, 81 per cent got 9-4 in both English and maths, 27 per cent of grades A*/A and 37 per cent 9-7.

Joint sixth form with nearby Beverley High School; 13 per cent A*/A and 43 per cent A*/B grades at A level in 2018. Twenty A level subjects on offer. Large numbers going on to study science, in all its forms, at university level. Classes held at both schools so students divide their time between the two. It's a 15 minute walk from one school to the other and thanks to sensible timetabling, sixth formers attend one school or the other for a whole day rather than travelling backwards and forwards.

It's an 'engaging curriculum,' say parents. 'We know what engages boys and we pick topics and subject matter according their interests,' says the school. The tailoring of material to boys' needs is a key part of what they do here, though 'this is not to say that everything we do is about sport,' they add, wisely. Both competition and camaraderie 'add to the learning journey'.

Impressive SEN provision includes two teachers with specialist qualifications in SEN, dyslexia and the autistic spectrum plus a number of highly trained teaching assistants. Promotes inclusion, preparing differentiated learning materials and using support within the classroom or alternatively withdrawing individuals or small groups for specialised tuition. Learning support is an option on the sixth form enrichment programme. To enable those with physical disabilities to access the site, adaptations include lift and stairlifts to first floor areas. At least one classroom in subject areas has a sound field system.

Unlike most schools, they have even managed to hold on to their work experience week for Y10s, which sits very well within the future-thinking approach. Sensibly, the boys are encouraged to make their own arrangements and organise this for themselves, though for obvious reasons (and with an eye to safeguarding), staff monitor, assess and generally keep a close eye.

An academic mentoring system keeps everyone on track: as well as teachers, mentors can also be volunteers from the community – industrialists, careers advisers, etc – to drum home the value of learning. Trips to careers fairs and university open days boost enthusiasm for learning beyond school. 'We teach to the end here,' says the head as the school year draws to a close. It's wise – nothing worse than bored boys left to their own devices or stuck in a classroom with a video to watch. The message is clear – 'if we take learning seriously so will they'. Good, clear thinking.

Games, options, the arts: Very strong on sport ('you name it, we do it') – football and rugby (both union and league are a must in this location); national competitors at athletics; badminton and the legendary steeplechase devised by the PE department in which a sandpit replaces the water. Matches and competitions galore, locally and nationally with a great deal of success, much-celebrated.

Music is thriving – about 120 have individual music lessons and ensembles galore from orchestras to choirs to rock group. Showcase of talent by way of the musician of the year competition has replaced the annual drama production. 'Not enough drama, though,' say the (mainly younger) boys.

Trips and visits are plentiful. The boys have played football in Portugal, skied in Italy, enjoyed a Spanish language trip and a Japanese exchange. Closer to home they enjoy 'bonding' PGL trips, the physics Olympiad in York and a session on philosophical thinking at Hull Collegiate.

Extracurricular activities include football, rugby, basketball, table tennis, futsal and handball for the classic sporty types and add to that yoga and DofE – and HAB (high altitude ballooning) for a more challenging stretch. Others range from engineering club and Lego league to the hugely popular Warhammer club. Extra support programmes in maths and computer skills also available.

Background and atmosphere: Sited on the outskirts of Beverley since 1903, it's now a mix of the old and the new with developments from every decade. A long drive winds up to the main building, passing a small number of large private houses and a wonderful sports pavilion which stands as a memorial to old boys who died in WW1. There's a traditional old hall, complete with art deco signage and honours boards; a super old-school library with wooden chairs bearing the initials of old boys contrasting with a very modern, attractive mezzanine floor above which doubles as a sixth form study space. Large and impressive science labs plus a food lab (is that a nod to the boys – not calling it a cookery room?) Large, spacious and well-equipped design technology areas; bright and roomy classrooms linked by wide corridors with high quality displays; sports hall; arts block housing classrooms, music practice rooms and drama studio. Art is housed in an older building and legend has it there's a tunnel all the way from there to the Minster – though the boys, whilst clearly enjoying the story, suspect it may be an urban myth. Large sixth form block with common room and private study areas. Annual refurbs and updates all around the site, it's not hard to see where the refurb begins and ends, but, a bit like the Forth Road Bridge, it's a ongoing programme and very much budget-driven. This year the focus is on updating security around the site, not because of any particular problems, but simply good sense.

There are five school houses and boys demonstrate real allegiance to their house, with house ties to be won in each colour. The house super league involves various competitions with something for everyone – football, chess, public-speaking, university challenge and even a bake-off. Inter-house competition is keen but generally good-natured and culminates in an annual sports day.

Student voice is a democratically elected council made up of representatives from each form. Its primary purpose is to oversee school and community events but is also consulted on all school decisions from appointment of staff to school improvements. Valued greatly by the boys we spoke to. During our chat they acknowledge recent budget cuts but, if money were no object, they'd love Astroturf, better toilets and an improvement in the condition of the grass tennis courts. 'It doesn't bounce like Wimbledon,' the boys tell us, though somewhat ironically, a former pupil was playing at Wimbledon at the time of our visit, so something's clearly working.

Pastoral care, well-being and discipline: Multi-agency approach to student welfare: the school has its own social worker within a dedicated student support team, all based in its own complex on site. Includes professionals and specialist staff from a variety of backgrounds including social work, counselling, education welfare, careers guidance, Youth Family Services, and learning support. The school is also an approved placement for social workers in training. The open door policy is a reality, not a just marketing spin, and students regularly pop for a chat, general help or more specific guidance on a wide range of issues and problems. It is a vital part of the school and always busy.

The acronym CARE keeps it simple and says it all – confidence, ambition, resilience, empathy – and there are masses of reminders of its importance to the school ethos and values. The head is 'proper good,' say the boys – huge respect all round. 'He knows everyone and everything,' they add, which they definitely view as 'a good thing'. 'We want their time at school to be memorable,' says the head, and staff are prompted frequently. This is imbued in the approach to teaching and learning where there is plenty of fun and intrigue embedded within the daily graft and rigour. Big on staff development, responding to new ideas and philosophies without throwing out the baby. Student/staff relationships are good, that's evident, and they make it look far easier than it actually is. Parents tell us that 'boys can email any teacher if they need help on an evening or weekend and always get a response'.

Uniform is worn with a certain amount of pride, especially the ties, no blazers as yet but it may happen. 'Yes, we are strict on uniform,' says the head, whilst adding 'but we're not fascist about it'. Or about anything else, thankfully. No formal dress code for sixth form, though they should appear 'ready for study'.

Parents involved at earliest stage over any slips in discipline and any bullying is swiftly acted dealt with. 'Graffiti is very rare,' say the boys, 'and would very quickly be cleaned off'. They are proud of their school. Effective reward system of coloured slips/credit cheques which lead to certificates, a monthly cash prize draw and ultimate prizes of badge and special school tie. Numbers of exclusions are low and falling, reflecting the school's current general upward trajectory in all areas.

Pupils and parents: Parents are supportive and are encouraged to be involved with school from the off. Pupils overwhelmingly from white British backgrounds as reflects the local demographic, with few eligible for free school meals or whose first language is not English. We spoke to a large number of parents who had moved into the catchment area especially because they preferred the single sex option and liked the fact that the school is half the size of the other Beverley possibility.

Parents living within catchment are not smug, they simply feel fortunate, though it's likely that it means the added bonus of enjoying a uplift in the value of their home. They cite the school's 'quirkiness', there's apparently 'nothing else like it', referencing both its history and standing in the local community. Certainly they rate it very highly, whilst recollecting that it has been through tougher times with parents rocked by its rapid decline a few years ago – 'there was mutiny, almost,' said one parent. But clearly it's once more a happy ship, the change of leadership being key. Staff, boys and parents are now back on board, somewhat relieved that the current head 'grabbed it by the scruff of the neck and hauled it back'. Much praise from parents for the staff who 'understand that boys are different'. Home/school contact is now good and sport generally is also 'thankfully much improved,' say parents, recognising its importance in this techy world with many boys addicted to screens. Some parents remain unconvinced of the value of the school's move to academy status, believing that it may have been the route to a reduction in both support and funding; it's a watching brief.

We enjoyed chatting to a super group of boys who are a real credit to their school and parents, future game-changers with high aspirations and their feet firmly on the ground. A charming and delightful melange, appearing less cliquey than most teens and very respectful and accepting of all-comers. 'Social graces matter as much as learning,' say parents. And so say all of us.

Old boys include John Alcock, Lord Chancellor 1430-1500; Saint John Fisher, Catholic bishop and martyr to Henry VIII; Thomas Percy – believed to be the brains behind the gunpowder plot; Smithson Tennant, chemist who discovered iridium and osmium; and more recently Kenneth Annakin OBE, film director; Paul Robinson, England goalkeeper and John Andrew, Anglican clergyman in New York. That's quite a dinner party.

Entrance: Oversubscribed; the deciding factor is distance from the door. Living in catchment area – Beverley and the surrounding villages of Woodmansey, Walkington and Bishop Burton – is generally a must. Slight dip in roll, probably due to the recent blip, has opened the doors for those living beyond but it's unlikely to last; that door may close given the current upward trend.

Exit: Around half leaves after GCSEs. Big pull for some post-16 leavers to vocational courses offered at East Riding College and agriculture at Bishop Burton, smaller number attracted by bright, shiny facilities at Wyke. No NEETS – all engaged in a 'meaningful pathway' post Y11 and Y13. One to Cambridge in 2018; others to Lincoln, Sheffield Hallam, Surrey, Durham, Edinburgh, Nottingham Trent, Leeds, Newcastle, Hull, Northumbria, Newcastle, Edinburgh, Teeside, York, London Ravensborne, Coventry, Southampton, Keele, plus one off to study film making and film at in Stockholm.

Remarks: The boys are the stars here – refreshingly bright, welcoming and on the ball without a hint of arrogance, it's a very endearing mix. They are clearly worldly wise, clued up about the options open to them with plenty of aspiration and good old-fashioned manners thrown in. 'It's on the up,' say parents.

Beverley High School

B

Norwood, Beverley, East Riding of Yorkshire HU17 9EX

Ages 11–18 **Pupils** 869 **Sixth form** 260 (including 130 boys in joint sixth form)

01482 881658
www.beverleyhigh.net

Headteacher: Since 2009, Sharon Japp (mid 40s), BA in English and sociology from Leeds, MEd and NPQH. Originally from Cheshire, she joined school in 1999 as head of English after teaching posts in West and South Yorkshire schools. Spell as assistant head and then deputy head from 2004. Recently returned from maternity leave and firing on all cylinders, she represents both continuity and stability for the school whilst aiming high on the girls' behalf. 'Not a game-player,' she says; she's been around long enough to observe many changes and knee-jerk reactions within education but has held on to the school's long-held belief of high standards alongside moral purpose. Dismissive of stereotyped notions of gender, the idea that girls are not competitive is, she says, 'a myth'. Warm and friendly, quietly spoken, close enough to the girls to know them well whilst maintaining an air of authority, parents say she is 'very approachable'.

Academic matters: Good choice of subjects at GCSE, with one MFL and three sciences standard. English, humanities and MFL especially good: 'the best EBacc around'. Mixed-ability teaching, apart from mathematics and languages at key stage 3 and maths, languages and science at key stage 4. There are six well-equipped science labs; triple science on offer at KS4 with encouragement from an excellent STEM display showing 'what you can do with science' – plenty of good and new ideas beyond the obvious. In 2018, 83 per cent got 9-4 in both English and maths, 36 per cent A*/A grades. In the joint sixth form with Beverley Grammar, 27 per cent A*/A and 47 per cent A*-B grades at A level in 2018. Top 10 per cent nationally for high attainment and value-added. All very creditable in a non-selective school.

Screening is carried out in year 7 to identify SEND pupils; there are currently around 40 girls on the inclusion register, seven with EHC plans, the remainder with a broad range of needs. Provision for visually impaired. Girls highlighted as more academically able are carefully monitored and encouraged to participate in enrichment opportunities, both in and out of school.

Five form entry in KS3 moving to six teaching groups at KS4; the total number of girls doesn't change during this process but the class sizes drop from 30/31 to a more manageable 26/27.

Decent mix of longstanding staff and NQTs, many 'outstanding,' say parents. 'I have found both my girls have been supported when they have found things tricky and pushed that bit further if it's something they are finding easier,' said one contented mum. No problems in attracting potential new staff, though the quality of the field has to be high here or they won't appoint. Committed teaching staff with an academic tracking and monitoring system that runs like a well-oiled machine. From years 7 to 9, subject leaders track pupil attainment and attitude to learning with fortnightly monitoring by the SLT.

Across the school there is significant intervention and support for those who are underperforming. Strategies in place for individual pupils as and when required; this is an inclusive school working with a range of needs. High calibre learning support and 'amazing' TAs, working alongside an approachable and accessible well-being team. Support generally given in the classroom, with limited withdrawal. Much praise from the girls themselves from the maths support club; they like the extra help and reassurance on offer.

Plenty of accolades and good work on display and evident pride in achievements of former pupils. Every subject area has a display board celebrating success. The MFL dept enters a national spelling and translation bee and staff and girls have enjoyed much success at Eurofest, selling their wares in French and German with two teams heading to the national finals. Most subjects expand thinking: from maths conferences and poetry live to visiting the Houses of Parliament, they do it all. Overseas too – Japan, Poland, Cologne, Paris, French exchanges to Millau and various residentials closer to home.

Aims and objectives are clear – the head intends to produce 'confident, well-informed, aspirational, focused, caring girls with an aim in life'. Nothing to argue with there. Though she's a realist, acknowledging that 'there's a lot of pressure on girls these days, all the old ones plus plus..'

Games, options, the arts: Sport very popular – enhanced sports hall and tennis courts shared with community. Usual array of girls' team sports plus badminton, football and trampolining. Joint swimming teams with boys' school. Good representation at area and county level, particularly in cross-country and athletics. Plenty of healthy inter-house competitive sport and there's a biennial Easter ski trip to Italy. Drama, dance, music and art promoted through the curriculum. Hundreds of individual music lessons during the week. Add to that choirs, junior and senior orchestras, junior wind band, concert band, brass and percussion ensembles, plus rock bands. The choirs are described as 'beautiful' and there's an annual 'gig night' and battle of the bands competition. Head of music described as 'outstanding'; one very musical girl told us that she and her parents chose this school primarily because of the wide range of musical opportunities available. Annual carol service in nearby Minster and summer music concert in St Mary's Church.

Technology and art block provides excellent facilities. Display board dedicated to careers in engineering. Don't miss the green car, designed, built and driven by the girls. Potential drivers practised on a local go-cart track and then raced around the school tennis court to prove their worth. The chosen few are now heading for a serious competition at the Hull KC stadium and these girls undoubtedly mean business. Stunning art and photography display, recently visited by the mayor; 'we believe in the arts,' says the head and it shows.

Good range and number of clubs meet during the week, a whole list from the MFL department alone. Others include art and crafts, drawing, extended writing, gardening, history club (run by the girls themselves), jewellery, knitting, photography and drama.

The school has a prestigious British Council international school award with Japanese and Sri Lankan partner schools as well as links with Germany and France – and Fairtrade schools award. Fundraising for local, national and international charities chosen by girls.

Background and atmosphere: The original building dates back to 1908 with additions in almost every decade since then. Some smart buildings, others a little tired, but there's no money in the budget for upgrades and the place is bursting at the seams. The campus as a whole, though varying in style and quality, feels cohesive and includes an outdoor covered seating area for lunch on sunny days or just chatting. Nothing too daunting here for the new and wide-eyed 11 year olds from local primaries who shared our visit.

Space is at a premium, finding somewhere for the whole school to meet other than the sports hall is impossible and some tutor groups have something of a nomadic existence due to a lack of space, the girls tell us. The canteen doubles up for drama productions, there is a separate drama room but no other large performance space. Food is 'good but expensive,' say the girls. Messages of thanks from year 11 leavers decorate the canteen. There is little doubt that staff and girls work hard here, and much is expected of both. Relationships are good, teachers are accessible and offer much encouragement.

Although on the same campus, the sixth form (joint with boys' school, Beverley Grammar) is very much a separate entity. Staff know they have to work hard to keep the girls here as there are numerous other attractive options available locally, many with bright, shiny new facilities, so the offer here has to be good and attractive. The joint sixth form is an arrangement that works well for both schools and has been effective as a disincentive for girls (or boys) thinking of leaving post-16 for a new co-ed environment.

'To have your child come home with such a lovely smile on their face and obvious happiness in their eyes as they relive their latest opportunity is such a priceless gift,' said one hugely grateful and appreciative parent with two daughters at the school. The 'thrilling day' they had experienced was one of many at the school and included piano masterclasses and German role plays – these are busy girls, managing a challenging curriculum alongside a wide range of extras and initiatives.

Pastoral care, well-being and discipline: Girls are assigned to one of five tutor groups on entry, linked to one of the five houses, and where possible they then stay with that form tutor and tutor group for the next five years. Fingers crossed they like each other, but should any problems arise there's a dedicated well-being team on hand. 'The drama and gossiping can get annoying,' admit some of the girls, but they are quickly over one 'crisis' and on to another. The well-being team is approachable and accessible (and 'huge,' say parents), providing a network of support for pupils and their families, incorporating the pastoral team, two social workers, the SEN manager and the attendance manager.

Uniform designed for comfort rather than panache, polo shirts and sweatshirts with skirt or trousers. Opportunity for dressing up comes at the joint proms in Y11 and 13 with the boys' school. No uniform or official dress code for sixth form, 'relaxed, smart casual' is the general direction of travel. Behaviour and uniform policies are strictly enforced, 'kind and caring, firm but fair,' says the head. Recent exclusions for fighting and swearing at a teacher and a ban from the school prom for year 11s who brought alcohol onto the school site – probably a tougher line than most schools, but it works. And there's a refreshing code of honesty – a 'snitch culture' that works – 'You ask them, they tell you,' says the head, which of course keeps everyone, apart from the fearless or the foolhardy, in line. It also means that bullying is minimised because the girls will go to the staff and tell them. Mobile phones must be switched off and out of sight during the school day. 'Do they cause problems? Yes,' says the head, an honest and resigned response. Apparently, according to the girls, you can switch your phone on during break and lunchtime, but you have to be stationary – no walking and talking.

Pupils and parents: Student voice has plenty of ideas, some better than others. They'd like to go to Dominoes down the road for pizza rather than have the in-house version; they'd like more space – 'fewer people and bigger buildings,' they suggest; year 7 would like more school trips, please. Bright, bubbly year 7 pupils tell us they 'like moving around classrooms' after a static primary school existence and add that the teachers are 'helpful'. Older girls less sure as they begin to question tough rules regarding the wearing of makeup, nail varnish and jewellery – 'twas ever thus. They are, however, clearly proud of their school, recognising that the hard work and rules and regulations are all part of the bigger picture and the route to success. 'You just need to walk around the school or see them at events and see how they are all smiling, and I know without a doubt we made the right decision,' added a parent.

Parents are a complete mix, most local, some NHS staff based in Hull but happy to commute, preferring to live in this school's catchment area. They are a supportive group who appear to share school's ambition for their girls, whilst recognising a high level of emotional, as well as academic, support. Parents praise communications with the school and feel involved in their daughters' education; postcards home in recognition of high achievement are always welcome. The Friends of Beverley High School is a voluntary group which organises events and raises funds for the benefit of the girls – and has a good time doing so. Super year book for leavers, gifted by the school.

Old girls include Angela Frost CBE, a director at HMRC, Ceri Bryant QC, Sue Hearnshaw, Olympian, a clutch of actresses – including Anna Maxwell-Martin and Eleanor Tomlinson – and classical soloist Ildiko Allen. We particularly liked the school noticeboard celebrating latest individual achievements of current and former pupils.

Entrance: Intake of 150 is substantially oversubscribed, eight or nine feeder schools with pupils drawn almost exclusively from catchment area – Beverley and the surrounding villages of Tickton, Walkington and Bishop Burton. Important to note that the road right outside school isn't in the catchment area – buyers beware. You're fine if you're in catchment, but will struggle otherwise.

Exit: Around 60 per cent leave after GCSEs. Most of year 13 to university (25 per cent Russell Group). Leavers' results comfortably above national averages.

Remarks: No opportunity/money to expand, it's all about maintaining buildings, standards and ethos – not necessarily in that order. But actually that's pretty much what the parents want. They are fearful of huge change or falling standards and pretty happy with the status quo. There's no complacency and expectations and opportunities remain high; the formula appears to be working well.

Birkdale Preparatory School

Linked with Birkdale School

Clarke House, Clarke Drive, Sheffield, South Yorkshire S10 2NS

Ages 4–11 **Pupils** 274

Fees: £8,700 – £10,665 pa

01142 670407
www.birkdaleschool.org.uk

Head of prep school: Since 2009, Christopher Burch BA PGCE (40s), previously deputy head of Great Walstead Prep. His wife, Pip, is the school librarian and a pre-prep teaching assistant. They have four sons at the school. Parents appreciate the whole family involvement. He is a committed and active Christian and fully supports the faith ethos of the school. Friendly and approachable, popular with parents, he patrols the playground every morning to welcome the boys and to catch or be caught by parents, to 'sort out problems when they are pennies before they become pounds'. Parents were keen to emphasise 'nothing is too small to discuss with him.'

Entrance: No assessment for entry at 4. From age 6 there is an assessment day, but they rarely don't offer a place if they have spaces. Despite strong Christian ethos there are no religious requirements. A number of Hindu, Muslim, and Sikh boys co-exist with church and non-church boys and participate in all assemblies. Head says their parents like the fact the school 'knows where it stands with faith.'

Exit: Virtually all (some 95 per cent) to the senior school. Parents given plenty of warning and support if senior school deemed to be wrong for their child. Of those that leave, some go to boarding school, some into the state sector.

Remarks: A welcoming, traditional, academic prep, unashamedly geared towards boys. 'Lots of exercise, short bursts of concentration and lots of rewards,' according to head. Established in 1904, the school moved in 1988 to its current site overlooking Sheffield's botanical gardens. Clarke House, an extended late Georgian mansion, was originally owned by master cutler, John Osborn. Houses named after four of the most prestigious master cutlers from Sheffield's history reflect this connection. Some lovely airy classrooms but others are a bit cramped. Pre-prep now housed in style in nearby Belmayne House, giving much needed breathing space back to the prep.

Fabulous stand-alone science lab. 'Real' science is taught from the beginning, as is French – everything throughout the school is labelled with its French equivalent. Lovely loft art room, full of colour, and a shelf of working wooden catapults a recent exciting project. The substantial school hall is impressively flexible, switching from breakfast club to assembly hall, to gym to refectory to theatre, a military operation several times a day. Specialist teaching from age 4 in French, music, drama, DT and RE. Adding, from year 3, science, history, geography, art and ICT with dedicated classrooms requiring boys to move around the school as necessary, with the right books. Setting in maths, English and science from year 5 with elements for support from year 3. 'The boys are stretched and closely monitored without pressure or stress,' said one parent. All boys are screened for SEN and the help, some in class and some out, is sympathetic and thorough. Parents talk of amazing staff teamwork, and a happy working relationship was apparent when we visited. Discipline well maintained with clear rewards and sanctions and behaviour extremely good, although relaxed. Reward points are collected for the house, posted on a corridor wall and 'are dished out like confetti,' according to a parent.

The outdoor play area is spacious and boys are encouraged into it as often as possible. No on-site games, however the extensive facilities of the senior school at Castle Dyke, 10 minutes away, are fully available. Rugby, cricket and football teams do well in local fixtures and parents of less sporty boys particularly welcome the addition of C teams to give their sons the opportunity to represent their school. Head has worked hard to improve the sport at Birkdale but is keen not to give it 'too high a currency' and encourages the cool games masters to read in public and talk to the boys about the books they are reading.

Lots of drama, popular with the boys, and music is high on the agenda with around 100 learning one of a huge variety of instruments. Brass, wind and string groups and guitar ensembles come together in an orchestra and feed into the Sheffield Schools' Training Orchestra, hosted by the school. Parents describe the extracurricular clubs, both after school and at lunchtime, as 'outstanding' both in variety and quality. There's something for everybody from Beat Club

B

to Warhammer, to the increasingly popular Mandarin and a well-attended Christian Union. Plenty of day trips and visits. Longer jaunts begin in year 4 with two nights away in nearby Castleton, culminating in the much anticipated leavers' week in Normandy. Year 5 boys were wildly enthusiastic about their outdoor pursuits trip to the Lake District.

Headmaster, deputy headmaster and director of music take a 15 minute hymn practice with all of the prep every Friday morning to run through the hymns scheduled for the following week. Head describes it as a 'special time' and the boys seem to love it too.

Parents represent a healthy cultural mix. Lots of medics and many who make big sacrifices to send their boys. Most fairly local but some travel significant distances, coming from as far as Bakewell and Rotherham. Plenty of social events and parents talk warmly of the strong sense of community within the school. Parking remains a challenge despite best efforts of head to stagger drop-off and pick-up with the extended breakfast and after-school care, and negotiate a first-15-minute-free-parking in the surrounding zones. 'It's the Wild West,' said one parent and all regaled us with their various strategies to combat it.

Above all, parents emphasise the incredible pastoral care and warm nurturing atmosphere. All concur the communication is exceptional, 'there are a surprising amount of personal emails beyond the routine information', and the weekly newsletter is particularly welcome, as is the extremely informative website. The atmosphere is warm and fun but it's 'a tight ship' with clear boundaries strictly adhered to.

Birkdale School

Linked with Birkdale Preparatory School

12

Oakholme Road, Sheffield, South Yorkshire S10 3DH

Ages 11–18 **Pupils** 570 **Sixth form** 227 (65 girls)

Fees: £12,765 – £13,140 pa

01142 668409
www.birkdaleschool.org.uk

Head master: Since January 2019, Peter Harris MSc BSc PGCE NPQH, previously principal of Ewell Castle School in Surrey. He used to be head of geography here before moving on to become vice principal at Bournemouth Collegiate School. Three children; he enjoys outdoor pursuits including cycling, climbing and sailing, and is a member of his local Anglican Church.

Academic matters: Results are consistently creditable. In 2018, 48 per cent A*/A and 74 per cent A*/B at A level, and 58 per cent A*/A/7-9 at GCSE. Maths and sciences popular and successful, however only a small take up for languages at A level. Greek and Mandarin offered as extracurricular clubs. Design technology, comprising graphics, electronics and resistant materials, outstanding with fabulous facilities. Lots of links to local industries and tremendous pride in, and recognition of, Sheffield's enterprising past.

School is particularly hot on 'learning for its own sake' and has developed several initiatives under the banner 'intellectual curiosity'. Regular random questions appear on screens around the school and pupils are invited to submit a response. An annual competition, open to years 10, 11 and 12, where the six winners have the opportunity to research an idea – imaginative but practical and unrelated to their exam syllabuses – in London's libraries, museums and archives. They then, dauntingly, have to deliver a 20 minute public presentation based on their findings. SEN available for mild cases only and costs extra, however SENCo has an open door and welcomes any struggling pupil to informal drop-in sessions.

Parents are particularly effusive about the sixth form; one described its head as 'gold dust', and they all had nothing but praise for her tireless individual support steering pupils through the UCAS system. Interview practice for those who need it is thorough and appropriate; two doctors from Sheffield Medical School put potential medics through their paces. Careers advice begins early as part of PHSE, with regular visiting speakers in middle school and trips to the careers library in Sheffield. The school itself also has an excellent careers library, based within the sixth form centre in the Grayson building.

Games, options, the arts: Constraints of being an inner-city school on a Victorian site have forced the playing fields to Castle Dyke, a 10-minute drive away. However, extensive pitches, complete with 10 lane cricket nets and modern pavilion, more than compensate. There is a substantial sports hall with adjoining gym on site and much use made of good local facilities. Rugby is successful, with trips to Australia or New Zealand, likewise cricket, with lots of boys going on to play at county level or beyond. Football ever popular and teams play in the ISFA with an annual tour around Newcastle. Boys can join the clubs but parents would welcome a few more B and C teams for the less gifted. Netball and hockey specifically for girls, and a respectable range of other sporting options are available both during and after school, judo and fencing both very popular.

Impressive art much in evidence throughout the school with a huge and colourful variety of media and styles. Lots of emphasis on fine art and drawing skills, impressive copies of old masters – Vermeer, Rembrandt, even Botticelli. A visiting tutor from the Royal College was working with A level students when we visited. Sixth formers have their own unique studio space, a haven.

Music and drama are thriving with a large, well-equipped studio space and a lovely octagonal concert hall. Loads of opportunities to perform from lunchtime concerts and house plays, to larger public events both in school and the wider community. Rock bands, jazz bands, and a big band, alongside an excellent traditional orchestra, ensembles and various choirs mean there is something for everybody, 'the sort of music kids want,' said a parent. Younger boys are encouraged to join 'tecbox' where they learn how to 'tec' their own assemblies and, as they grow through the school, the musicals and concerts.

Huge variety of lunchtime activities and pupils are encouraged to have a go and fill their diaries. Head firm that 'individual aptitudes can be discovered this way'. The school is incredibly active in its support of charities, with numerous money-raising events led by pupils. Clubs within the enterprise umbrella include over a dozen commercial business start-ups and the monies made here also contribute. Since 2000, the school has supported a village in Nepal by refurbishing the Peace Garden School. Every year a group of pupils, teachers and parents, usually including the odd medic, spend time here working and teaching. Boys, whether they've been there or not, are full of pride and enthusiasm for the project and parents tell of how life plans have been changed by the experience.

Many other trips across the curriculum include skiing, foreign language and team-building expeditions. Younger boys hugely enthusiastic about a drama trip to London and spontaneously demonstrated skills learned from a stage-fighting workshop.

Background and atmosphere: An ambitious school in every way. Founded as a boys' prep in 1904, it created a senior department in 1978, adding a sixth form in 1988. The only all boys independent school in Sheffield, parents say they understand boys extremely well. Girls joined the flourishing sixth form in 1995. The site, which reflects Sheffield's glorious past, has grown as required but haphazardly. Originally based in the large Victorian Oakholme House, it has spread to encompass four neighbouring mansions (Westbury, Endcliffe, Grayson and Johnson), with modern extensions and new builds, creating something of a warren – stairs, steps and steep paths everywhere. 'There isn't a flat surface in Sheffield,' school says. Beautiful original features – cupolas, sanded glass, marble fireplaces – add charm, personality and maintenance nightmares. Large mature gardens are free for the younger boys to run off steam without over concern for shrubs or lawns. The extensive library is housed in the bay windowed drawing room where the Cole brothers conceived John Lewis. Modern school hall is well used as refectory and theatre, and for the twice weekly whole school assemblies.

Pastoral care, well-being and discipline: Pastoral care is high on the agenda emanating from the school's strong Christian ethos. It is not heavy-handed but focuses on nurture and mutual respect with the advantage that the school is small enough for everyone to know everyone. First port of call is the form tutor but beyond this staff and prefects are approachable and available. All extremely effective, according to parents: 'It's not just lip service, they really care about and know your child.'

Lots of positive reinforcement; house points are dished out but so are sanctions and younger boys carry dog-eared score-cards stuffed into their blazer pockets. A quirky system called 'drill', where minor miscreants help the dining room staff to scrape plates, apparently nips a lot of problems in the bud. Drugs policy rigorously implemented and there is zero tolerance for bullying. Any incidents are dealt with swiftly but discipline is 'about reformation and the recognition that teenagers can misjudge things'. House loyalty strongly encouraged with masses of opportunities to support with frequent music, drama and enterprise competitions, all with the by-product of raising money for charity. School uniform throughout, but boys are allowed to be comfortably tousled, 'no nitpicking,' according to a parent.

Pupils and parents: Parents represent a healthy cultural mix. Lots of medics and many who make big sacrifices to send their boys. Most fairly local but some travel significant distances, coming from as far as Bakewell and Rotherham. Plenty of social events and parents talk warmly of the strong sense of community within the school. Parking remains a challenge despite best efforts to stagger drop-off and pick-up with the extended breakfast and after-school care, and negotiate a first-15-minute-free-parking in the surrounding zones. 'It's the Wild West,' said one parent and all regaled us with their various strategies to combat it. Bus system, shared with the Girls' High school, efficiently covers a wide geographical area. Bursaries ensure a full social spectrum. Old boys include Michael Palin and Rex Harrison plus legal and sporting luminaries.

Entrance: Year group of 72 with around 60 per cent from the prep and remainder from a range of other primaries. Entrance is by exam at 11 for all, with school reference also required. Top 12-16 are invited back for a second day, after which scholarships are allocated. Most boys from the prep continue to the senior school, with a small handful moving to the state system or boarding. Prep parents are forewarned if the senior school is not considered to be the right place. Girls and boys from many local schools join the sixth form, approximately 40 each year. Requirements are five GCSE passes at 9-4, with a minimum of four 6s and at least a 6 for any chosen A level subject.

Exit: One to Oxford in 2018 and many to other Russell Group universities eg Newcastle, Warwick, York, Bristol, Durham, Liverpool and Sheffield. Broad range of subjects covered: economics most popular, then engineering and medicine (eight places, including one in Bulgaria), plus law, music, accounting and finance and geography. One off to do business studies in Stetson University, USA, in 2018.

Money matters: Variety of scholarships awarded at 11+ and 16+, both academic and music, with a combined ceiling of 25 per cent apart from cases of financial need which can be topped up with a bursary. Sixth form have sports scholarships and the Arkwright for DT. Almost a third have some level of financial assistance; bursaries strictly means-tested with some home visits.

Remarks: A lively school, strongly linked to the community and the world beyond with its impressive charitable activities. Pupils are cheerful and enthusiastic, obviously stimulated. Their USP is the ability to focus on individual development within a dynamic and caring community.

Birkenhead School

58 Beresford Road, Oxton, Prenton CH43 2JD

Ages 3–18 **Pupils** 732 **Sixth form** 84 (61 boys, 23 girls)

Fees: £8,010 – £11,994 pa

01516 524014
www.birkenheadschool.co.uk

Headmaster: Since 2016, Paul Vicars MA PGCE (40s). A schoolmaster – 15 year stint at Shrewsbury School including deputy head – and an accountant – four years at Ernst & Young. Studied geography at St Andrews and still keeps his teaching hand in by taking three lessons a week. Married to Vikki, a teacher of law and history at an academy in Oswestry. He enjoys coaching sports, especially cricket, and hopes to offer more than just touchline support to all the school teams.

His mantra is 'happy kids thrive' and he is evidently well liked and approachable. As we walked around the school, he greeted everyone – staff, pupils, even a parent who crossed our path – by first name. His three children all attend, so he can get an immediate, daily insight into how the school is performing from both the pupils' and parents' perspective. 'Birkenhead School seemed a natural progression for me and I want to be here a long time'; his almost seamless transition into the role is due – he is first to declare – to the overwhelming support and goodwill received from the entire school body. Any changes will result from comprehensive surveys – sent to parents, pupils and staff – that he commissioned soon after his appointment.

Head of prep: Since 2013, Harry FitzHerbert (40s). Enthusiastic and dedicated. Previously at British international schools, in Madrid and Lima, he has expanded modern languages provision at the prep by adding Spanish and French to the existing German and Mandarin offered. Married to Jo, an art teacher at the school; they have a son and daughter in the seniors.

Academic matters: A level results in 2018 were an improved 48 per cent A*/A, 77 per cent A*-B. At GCSE, 55 per cent A*-A/9-7 with students taking an average of 10 subjects. Top set in maths can sit additional further maths; separate and dual award sciences available.

Strong ethos of personal and academic motivation supported by co-curricular activities, tutoring and one-to-one sessions. The emphasis is to find your niche then achieve as well as you can. Pupils said they felt 'able to talk to tutors and teachers' and are encouraged to 'read around subjects'. Extracurricular programmes can come with rather obvious on-trend titles, Future Skills Development, Growing Up Talks and Beyond the Curriculum, but they do offer pupils the chance to learn more about non-academic subjects. Other options encourage appreciation of current affairs, art and drama. Workshops have covered careers talks, lessons in etiquette, chapel readings, global issues, cookery, writing for publication and computer coding. Pupils with SEN benefit from small classes and by differentiated teaching. Support and interventions are also offered through the co-curricular activities and by identifying individual needs with the form tutor.

Sixth formers selecting university courses receive advice from head of careers as well as guidance from teachers and tutor groups in preparing applications and practising interview techniques. 'My tutors helped me with my application and to prepare for interviews, and now I have offers to study my chosen subject – dentistry.' Co-curricular sessions in Oxbridge applications are available and those following the school's well-travelled path into medicine and dentistry attend sessions at the University of Liverpool. The Nicholls Lecture Series (every Friday), invites alumni and other guest speakers to address sixth formers on a variety of topics. There are also work experience opportunities with international industries of the calibre of Cammell Laird and UniLever.

Games, options, the arts: No surprise that cricket (three teams are current county champions) and rugby union feature heavily. Recent tours have included Barbados for the cricket team and South Africa for rugby. The girls are catching up strongly in lacrosse if not yet in cricket or rugby. 'I look forward to the day we have a girls' cricket team,' said one potential member, pointedly. A short walk across a quiet road takes you to the playing fields. All-weather tennis courts, rugby, junior cricket, football and netball pitches are all in good order but, although fit for purpose, the changing rooms could do with a makeover.

Head admits that sport does seem male-dominated but guarantees that it will be more representative of the school intake when the Astro hosts more hockey and lacrosse. The school gym equipment is up to date and there is a very popular climbing wall – encouraging pupils to scale physical as well as academic heights. Prep has play areas with interactive surfaces and an outdoor classroom built by the school estates team. Everyone puts a school swimming pool top of their sporting wish list – swimming currently takes place at neighbouring Birkenhead High School Academy. Top of the head's list of priorities, however, is the school library, which is long overdue a refit into the digital age. He seemed very determined to make this happen sooner rather than later – maybe the building survey will mirror his ambition.

Lots of encouragement for girls to study STEM subjects and 20 recently visited the NASA Space Center in Texas. The visit seems to have paid dividends as, after declaring it was 'the best place I'd ever been', one year 11 girl said she would definitely be taking physics in sixth form. Another was impressed to have been 'training at the same time as the astronauts'. Pupils have also enjoyed cultural trips to New York and Washington, skiing in Canada, a music tour of Spain and a charity hike in Nepal.

Creative talent is nurtured from an early age. The school has a flourishing and dynamic art department, studios are flooded with natural light and every available wall space is adorned with some very impressive works. Children, in small classes, are encouraged to explore different mediums such as pottery, textiles and plastics.

Musicians of all abilities get to play in the school's wide range of bands, choirs and orchestras. The choir, intrinsic to the identity of the school, sings evensong. It also performs across the diocese and recently sang with the choir of Jesus College, Cambridge. Individual tuition is available for most instruments as well as music theory and technology. The vibrant drama department has staged productions of Cabaret, Les Misérables and Hamlet in seniors and Jungle Book in prep. The posters and banners for these productions reveal a high standard of artistic endeavour and close collaborative ties with the art department.

Background and atmosphere: Founded in 1860 but on its present site in the leafy suburb of Oxton since 1871 (the prep joined in 1883), the buildings are enclosed on all four sides by lines of mature trees. Further additions and developments occurred over the next hundred years until a wall was literally hit in 2001 with the installation of the climbing version. The campus consists of over 20 buildings of various ages spanning architectural styles from aesthetic to functional. The manicured cricket pitch adds to an atmosphere of tradition, 'like a boarding school but without the dorms'. A strong communal thread weaves through each building, stitching together the academic stages and knitting friendships across year groups. For instance, years 7 and 8 occupy the same building; this set up engenders close ties and a real sense of community throughout and helps ease the transitions as pupils move up the school.

Uniforms are black blazers and red and black striped ties for all, black checked aprons for prep girls in the summer. Lapel badges denote house membership or positions of responsibility. We saw some caps and boaters on prep pupils, perhaps doffing them more in deference to fashion than tradition. The murmur from classrooms, the junior choir practice, the exuberant prep play areas, the uninhibited laughter and the noisy dining room all show that this is a happy environment – industrious, inquisitive and expressive. Some students, taking advantage of the warm sunshine, were working outside while within the sanctuary of the school chapel a student was in recital with the head of music. Christianity plays a significant and visible role in the daily life of the school with the chapel open to the wider community for Sunday services.

Birkenhead went co-ed in 2008 but although the boy/girl ratio is decreasing, there is still a perception, at least outside, that it remains a boys' school. However, the girls we spoke to said it never mattered to them and the boys never even give it a thought: 'Probably because there are no pupils left in the school who remember it being all boys.'

Pastoral care, well-being and discipline: Head actively leads the way in making sure all children feel known and valued by frequent daily conversations with them, saying that 'the best learners and contributors to school life are those who are happiest'. Success here is not measured solely by academic achievement but also through participation in other activities. Prep and senior pupils are seen at least twice a day by form teachers or tutors – the first point of contact for parents – to discuss academic progress and personal issues. Heads of years coordinate the duties of form tutors and act on matters of care, discipline and academic progress. In turn, they meet regularly with the deputy head of school who is also available should more serious matters need resolving. School chaplain is also a key member of the pastoral team.

Senior pupils take active roles in pastoral care. Year 7 pupils are assigned a sixth form mentor who meets them for a weekly lunch meeting and maintains contact via email. There are also PHSE Focus Days – when the normal timetable for a particular year group is suspended – in addition to weekly form sessions. Poor behaviour and conduct leads to verbal reprimands, negative entries in record books through to temporary exclusion from lessons or school. All misdemeanours are closely monitored and parents notified in ample time. 'Teachers quickly learn to pick the right phrase or write a terse note in an exercise book to produce the desired effect in errant pupils or raise an alarm to their parent.'

Pupils and parents: We found the pupils polite, articulate, confident, inquisitive and conscientious. 'The teachers understand us and you can talk to them easily' was a much-shared sentiment. Older pupils value the opportunities the school offers not just for academic success but also how the co-curricular activities prepare them for the wider world: 'They gave me such self-confidence I hardly recognised the boy I was in year 7'. Initiative is actively encouraged and some of the teachers declared they were often 'surplus to requirements at some clubs and attend only as supervisors because the pupils run them very successfully themselves'.

One parent suggested his child's excellent GCSE results had been achieved not just through study and good teaching but because the school had turned him into a considerate and responsible individual. Others highlighted the smaller class sizes as a major factor in sending their children to the school: 'Some sixth form classes remind me of my college tutorial days.'

Mostly Wirral families although Liverpool, Chester and north Wales are also in the school address book. Head is making additional efforts to increase financial independence and redress concerns about the lack of means-tested bursaries and thus social mix. School is able to call on parental involvement via enthusiastic fundraising committees or even when a simple helping hand is needed for open days or sports events. Active ex-pupils' association – The Old Birkonians. Famous former pupils include creator of the Greenwich time pips, Frank Hope-Jones and Tony Hall (Lord Hall of Birkenhead), director-general of the BBC.

Entrance: Birkenhead selects on academic aptitude but equally important is the capacity to fit in with the school ethos. Many go seamlessly through from nursery and prep to senior school as long as they meet certain academic levels and show potential. Parents of those not likely to make the grade are notified in plenty of time to find alternatives. Students selected at age 11 on academic potential for higher education by assessment in verbal reasoning, English and maths. Some join at sixth form while admission in other years is through interview, school references, reports and tests.

Exit: Around 10 per cent leave annually after GCSE to attend local sixth form or take up apprenticeships. After sixth form most to university; occasional Oxbridge, others to a range of mostly northern universities.

Money matters: Bursaries currently make up around 10-11 per cent of fees and the Birkenhead Foundation Trust supports about eight pupils per year. Music scholarships are available at 11 and 16.

Remarks: A happy school consistently producing confident and considerate individuals as well as top results. Birkenhead may appear traditional from the outside but there is a strong streak of innovation running through all areas that shows it does not rest on past successes.

Bolton School Boys' Division

B

Linked with Bolton School Boys' Junior School, Bolton School Girls' Division, Bolton School Junior Girls' School (Hesketh House), Beech House

Chorley New Road, Bolton, Lancashire BL1 4PA

Ages 11–18 **Pupils** 913 **Sixth form** 218

Fees: £11,976 pa

01204 840201
www.boltonschool.org/senior-boys

Headmaster: Since 2008, Philip Britton, MBE MA MEd FInstP (40s). Was state-educated in the north east then read physics at Oxford, followed by a PGCE from Cambridge and a masters from Leeds. His academic pedigree really is first class: firsts, distinctions, top of the year awards – he's got them all. Head of physics at The Grammar School in Leeds at 23 and latterly deputy head there. His MBE is for services to physics and he has worked with the Institute of Physics to improve the curriculum.

Staff say he's the cleverest head they've ever had and that he's 'highly supportive' when they're trying to get anything new off the ground. Boys say he's 'kind', but this is a big school and Mr Britton makes no secret of the fact that he doesn't have a huge amount to do with most pupils individually. If there's a problem he encourages parents and boys to approach form tutors, year heads or subject teachers first rather than going straight to the top. He says, 'although I could probably pick that boy out of a school photo, the chances are I'll know nothing about the specific issue'. He clearly listens to the community – commissioning regular parents' questionnaires etc – but he comes across as a confident leader rather than a people pleaser. His decision not to see every parent at the drop of a hat 'took a while to bed in' and, he says, 'maybe some parents do find that frustrating, but I'm OK with that because I think I'm right'. We didn't meet any dissent from the parents we met, who described him as 'approachable' and 'proactive'.

He gets a parent's eye view of the school because both his own sons attend: 'If my boys come home excited and positive day after day,' he says, 'then I imagine that's hopefully going on at a lot of other kitchen tables too.'

Academic matters: It's a selective school and most boys are in the top 25 per cent in terms of ability. In 2018 at A level 52 per cent of entries were A*/A, 79 per cent A*-B. At GCSE 54 per cent of entries A*-A/9-7. Ongoing monitoring compares the boys not to each other but to their own potential – so a boy near the bottom of his class might still be praised for making great leaps forwards and a boy right at the top of the class can't necessarily relax. 'Maybe Joe or Fred did get 90 per cent in a test,' says Mr Britton, 'but we'll know if actually he should be getting 95 per cent.'

The learning support department arranges one-to-one 'bespoke interventions' – usually before school or during breaks – for boys who are struggling or who have SEN. Support for children with EHC plans or who don't speak English at home incurs no extra cost. There are also 'drop in' clinics for anyone who needs extra help with a subject or has been absent. Meanwhile high flyers are stretched with AQA Bacc extended projects, Olympiads and other competitions, and the headmaster runs an invitation-only academic club, the

Ainsworth Society, which meets once a term to discuss books and ideas.

More than half take maths A level (compared to about 10 per cent taking English). Other popular subjects at A level include economics, geography and all three sciences. But there's excellence across the board – particularly in languages. Latin, ancient Greek and Russian are all offered to A level. The award-winning Russian department runs a biennial trip to Russia and takes sixth formers on a week-long residential language course at the University of East Anglia. Average class size is 17 but they're smaller in the sixth form. The curriculum makes room for plenty of physical activity and all boys do some of their learning every year on residential trips to Patterdale Hall, the school's own outdoor pursuits centre in the Lake District. Every pupil has an iPad (at no extra cost, so there's no divide between the haves and the have-nots). They can email homework direct to their teachers as they do it and get comments back the same night.

Boys told us that they felt lucky to have such expert teachers and that they appreciated being stretched. None of the boys we spoke to had experienced peer pressure not to be seen as a swot. One told us: 'I love knowing the answer – lessons are my chance to put my hand up and show off.' Some complained that there was too much homework but parents seemed to think the amount was just right. The boys we met had an impressively mature attitude to learning – taking it on the chin if they thought a comment in a report was unfair: 'I got a two for effort and I thought I deserved a one but it just inspires me to try harder'. All pupils we met felt that they'd know where to go if they needed extra help academically and they'd be well-supported. Most agreed that they were gradually given more and more chances to learn independently as they moved up the school, although one sixth former wondered if he'd been rather spoon-fed.

Games, options, the arts: Mr Britton is big on everyone getting involved in extracurricular activities – so much so that boys must do three lunchtime activities a week during their first few years in the seniors. This mildly authoritarian approach to joining in is also reflected in the fact that the outdoor pursuits trip to Patterdale Hall is obligatory and that all sixth formers must do 20 hours of 'compulsory volunteering'. (Yes, really. Look no further if you're an English student searching for an example of an oxymoron.) One sixth form dissenter was scathing: 'Frankly, I think it's ridiculous: some kids don't want to do all those clubs or to go to Patterdale and it's completely wasted on them.' But that's very much a minority view. Most parents and pupils see this set-up as a positive reflection of the character of the school. One mum told us that her son recently announced to to her on the way home: 'Do you know what's brilliant? Being busy.'

The pupils start some of the clubs themselves – if you don't fancy what's on offer you're encouraged to come up with an idea you do like. As you'd expect, the range of sporting, creative, cultural and academic extracurricular activities is superb. You can even buy Bolton School honey produced by the beekeeping club. Pretty much every subject area has a society in which students from different years work together on projects that are often impressively advanced. Whether they're planting electrodes in a cockroach's brain to control its movement remotely; sending a high altitude balloon into space to take photos of the earth from the stratosphere; or working with the school's writer in residence to produce board games, monologues and 'flash fiction' – the boys can access the latest resources with support from experts who know how to use them. Go-karting club had bought three beaten up chassis for the boys to customise and cannibalise during lunchtimes to make their own mean machine. We walked in on a buzzing history society University Challenge style quiz – with a team of four teachers competing against four pupils. The young quiz master was clearly relishing his moment of power; the questions were brain-fuddlingly obscure and the raucous crowd rejoiced to see the teachers struggling.

It's a sporty school, with plenty of timetabled physical activity and great facilities including a 25m indoor swimming pool, a climbing wall and a multigym. Football, hockey, rugby, cricket and water polo are all played competitively with great success. The school is also very strong at drama (star old boy Sir Ian McKellen is a regular visitor) and at music – with half the boys learning an instrument. Pupils we spoke to didn't feel there was any pressure to go with the crowd. One boy said: 'I like dancing. And I like football. No one minds what I choose to do – why would they?'

Parents loved the range of activities and said they were 'awestruck' by how many hours the teachers put in to school life beyond the curriculum. Many were drawn to the school as much by its ethos and community as by its academic reputation. One mum told us the boys here are 'confident, not cocky. And they'll grow up to be fine young men.'

Background and atmosphere: The campus is spacious and magnificent. It's like an Oxbridge college – a big one – set amidst 32 acres of playing fields. Two grand, mirror image, stone quads house the girls' and boys' divisions. They meet in the middle with a third central quad at the bottom of which is a modern sixth form centre. Here, although boys and girls are still taught separately, some spaces are shared and they can interact freely. The two divisions share many sports facilities and join for various extracurricular activities – most notably drama productions – so parents say they get the best of both worlds: 'no girls to put them off their work but you don't have a problem of a lad going to university who doesn't know how to talk to any girl except his sister.' There's rather less integration with the two single-sex junior schools on site and with the mixed-sex infant school and nursery. You get the sense that there's a broad sense of community between all the separate sections but that each has a distinct identity and plenty of autonomy.

It's like an old-fashioned grammar school – if a rather grand and smart one. Tradition and family ties are valued here; one pupil explained that he'd been assigned to a particular house because his grandfather had been in it. On the spectrum between conservative and radical, it seems to us that the leadership doesn't force change on the pupils or teachers for the sake of it.

The school also feels genuinely Boltonian. Only a few miles north of Manchester, the town has a distinctive accent and a proud industrial history. A number of the teachers are local and so are most of the adored support staff, some of whose families have long links with the school. It sees itself as an important institution for the town. It offers its expertise, facilities and the volunteering energies of its pupils to help local state schools and other community groups and this perhaps keeps the school grounded. Its atmosphere is unpretentious, positive and industrious – at times the boys can be both robust and competitive but we felt that this was tempered by kindness and a real respect for difference.

Pastoral care, well-being and discipline: We'd describe the atmosphere as cheerfully disciplined rather than strict. Exclusions are rare but they do happen. Incidents involving knives or drug-dealing would be non-negotiable out-on-your-ear offences. Mr Britton says he's more concerned about the safety of the silent majority of pupils who behave than he is to show unending compassion to the (hypothetical) boy who endangers others. But the school tries to reform those found guilty of lesser offences. Most pupils are oblivious to this side of school life but the handful who misbehave can expect to face after-school or Saturday morning detentions or even suspension. 'If you've been suspended twice and we still believe in you,' says Mr Britton, 'you'll end up on headmaster's report. At that point we'll tell the boy and his parents that he's the only person who can decide what happens: if he fouls up again, he's out.' Apparently at this point most boys decide they'd rather stay in.

The school is proud of its pastoral system. Form tutors see their group of 22-25 boys twice a day. Mr Britton is confident that pupils can and do feel confident to talk to their form tutors and that they have other people to reach out to if they want – such as year heads or a school nurse. He says they do uncover instances of bullying and deal with them 'swiftly and sensibly'. He's at pains to point out that bullies as well as victims are offered support. Boys told us they feel safe at school and everyone we spoke to agreed that they'd stand up for a victim of bullying and tell a teacher. It's not always gentle here, though; 'They don't bitch, but they do banter,' said one mum. Another told us that there was a point when she'd worried about how cruel the boys can be to one another and had even looked around at alternative schools for one son – but her search just showed her 'how good it is here'. Some boys – particularly in the sixth form – feel confident to come out as gay. 'Almost every term we have a "coming out moment",' says Mr Britton, 'and it's no great big drama.' 'The boys are amazing,' said one mum; 'they don't bat an eyelid if someone's gay.'

Pupils and parents: The community of old boys is important to the school and evidently many alumni feel strong emotional ties to the place. On the day of our visit the head was getting ready to travel to an old boys' dinner in Oxford. There's an impressive array of high achieving alumni, providing the school with expertise and inspiration as well as extra cash. As well as Gandalf, notable old boys include actor Ralf Little (from The Royle Family), radio presenter Mark Radcliffe, grand chess master Nigel Short, Nobel prize-winning chemist Sir Harry Kroto and a long list of notables from the worlds of business, sport, politics, academia and the media.

Half the current intake is from Bolton itself. The school also operates 20 coaches bringing boys in from Preston, Wigan, Warrington, Blackburn and Manchester. There's a real mix of ethnic and religious – if not social – backgrounds here, and adjectives such as bright, courteous, down-to-earth and hard-working spring to mind before words like rich or privileged.

One parent we spoke to had felt driven to consider an independent school because of the dearth of good local state schools. Another mum had been a pupil at the girls' division here herself; another had had a tough time at a state school and wanted something different for her sons. We met parents with a range of accents, backgrounds and approaches.

Entrance: Year 7 entry via creative writing essay plus tests in verbal reasoning, non-verbal reasoning and maths. Everyone is interviewed. If your son's primary school expects him to achieve level 5 in his key stage 2 Sats he'll be in with a good chance. Roughly two applicants per full fee place, three or four for each means-tested bursary, awarded to highest scorers.

Exit: Around a quarter leave after GCSEs. Spread of universities solid rather than dazzling. Five to Oxbridge in 2018; Liverpool much the most popular destination, others to a wide spread including Birmingham, Nottingham, Newcastle and Manchester. The school does particularly well with applications to study medicine and dentistry. Pupils told us that they received 'fantastic' support with their university applications.

Money matters: One in five pupils receives a means-tested bursary and half of those have their full fees paid. The school – including the bursary fund – is in robust financial health. Its profit-making arm, Bolton School Services Ltd, generates revenue from venue hire, catering, its coach company and the pre-school nursery.

Remarks: A no-nonsense, busy school where bright boys pick up a great work ethic and a strong community spirit. Excellent teaching, pastoral care and enrichment opportunities and a terrific environment. Difference is celebrated here so there's no typical pupil. It is a big school so a very quiet lad might worry that he'd feel overwhelmed but the school is confident that it has created structures 'to make the big feel small'. We'll give the last words to the mum who told us: 'When we looked round the school Mr Britton said to us: "you'll drop off a young lad at our door and a well-rounded young man will leave." And boy, he did!'

Bolton School Boys' Junior School

Linked with Bolton School Boys' Division, Bolton School Girls' Division, Bolton School Junior Girls' School (Hesketh House), Beech House

Park Road, Bolton, Lancashire BL1 4RD

Ages 7–11 **Pupils** 202

Fees: £9,579 pa

01204 434735
www.boltonschool.org/juniorboys

Head: Since 2015, Susan Faulkner, who had been deputy head at the school since 2011. A Durham University graduate, she has also taught at Stonyhurst Junior School and was a deputy head for six years before joining Bolton School.

Entrance: If your child is already at Bolton Infants' School (known as Beech House), they'll automatically be offered a place here (since they'll have already gone through academic selection). But any child hoping to transfer to the juniors (known as Park Road) from another primary school in year 3 will have to sit the entrance assessment in the January of the year they'd be joining. They'll be tested in English, maths and verbal reasoning. You can request past papers from the school office.

Pupils also have an interview – 'more of a chat really' – with senior teaching staff. The school's looking for lively, interested children who will thrive both here and in the seniors. School says that the best time to apply is for entry to year 3, when there are usually 10-15 places up for grabs and a bright child has a very good chance of securing one. Too many parents, though, try to get places for entry to years 5 or 6 – perhaps hoping to improve their child's chances of getting into the seniors – and this is a recipe for disappointment as often, no matter how bright the child is, there are no spaces at all for entry to these years; however, school has now opened an extra year 5 class.

Exit: Almost all juniors progress to the senior school. They have to sit the entrance exam but it's rare for them not to pass. If that did happen it wouldn't be a shock to the parents; they would have known that the child wasn't thriving academically in the junior school and would have been in regular communication with staff to discuss the issues.

B

Remarks: What this school achieves is glaringly obvious when you talk to the kids. We met some in what felt like a large group (but was in fact no more than eight to 10 boys). Our opener was: 'Who likes reading?' We expected a dutiful array of raised hands; what we didn't expect was a loud burst of book-chatter – involving all the children, not just the older ones. There's impassioned debate about favourite authors – ranging from David Walliams, Tom Gates and Roald Dahl to Charles Dickens (Bleak House, if you're wondering – we're guessing an abridged, illustrated children's version but we wouldn't put money on it). One boy confessed – half proud, half guilty – that he just couldn't put his book down last night and was still reading at 11pm. One lad devours poetry books; another goes for non-fiction; they all love the Horrible Histories. The kids show this kind of zest for everything to do with their learning. One minute they're enthusing about trips to the school's own outdoor pursuits centre in the Lake District, Patterdale Hall; the next they're showing off what they can say in Mandarin. This is the main language studied here, although they also take up French in year 6. It's taught by two specialist linguist teachers: a native speaker from the Confucius Institute in Manchester and the school's own languages teacher, who's learning Mandarin especially. Recognised with Confucius Classroom status making school 'a teaching hub for Chinese learning in the local community'.

'So what does school teach you apart from the subjects you study?' 'Be humble'. 'Try to be kind.' 'You must have discipline.' 'It's OK to be different.' Then suddenly we're into a discussion about a Remembrance assembly and what they all think about the fact that war is still going on all over the world. These boys are fascinated by everything. And they adore their school. They say it's 'quite relaxed here really.' 'Yes,' adds another, 'If you've not handed in your homework they just say, "OK but make sure you do it next time."' 'No!' interjects a small, firm voice, 'If you get behind in your work you have to catch up. There's no doubt about it.' The boys agree that behaviour isn't really a problem here: 'They do sort it out if you're naughty.' All say that the teachers would notice if they were upset and that there are adults here they'd confide in. 'And what would you do if you saw someone who was sad?' 'Go over to them and comfort them.' 'Yes, but if they're really sad or they've been bullied I'd definitely tell a teacher too.' A chorus of agreement. So what would they change? Finally silence. One lad says he'd like more freedom but he's shouted down: 'I think most of the rules are really sensible.' 'And remember that we make a lot of the rules ourselves through the school council.' The orderly library buzzes in squeaky hubbub. (The one thing these boys still need to learn is not to talk over each other.) A pause. 'Yeah, I suppose. Yeah, actually there's nothing I'd change.'

The mums we met couldn't think of anything either. They appreciate that the school fosters independence in their children right from the start. They feel it's a really warm and nurturing environment. And they all said their children were thriving here. We were most struck by the heights of achievement reached by the pupils. School says this is in part achieved by the decision to use specialists to teach many subjects rather than one class teacher delivering the whole curriculum. We were bowled over by the standards of the pupils' art. This just doesn't look like primary school work. A wall display from a recent picture book illustration project really could have passed for GCSE work, a testament to a 'really remarkable' art teacher. Although we are assured that the diminutive artists aren't completely hand-held – it really is the pupils' own work; they're just magnificently taught. None of this would mean much if it weren't a lovely, friendly community where it's hard to imagine a child being miserable – but it is.

Bolton School Girls' Division

Linked with Bolton School Boys' Division, Bolton School Boys' Junior School, Bolton School Junior Girls' School (Hesketh House), Beech House

Chorley New Road, Bolton, Lancashire BL1 4PB

Ages 11–18 **Pupils** 787 **Sixth form** 190

Fees: £11,976 pa

01204 840201
www.boltonschool.org

Headmistress: Since 2011, Sue Hincks (40s), previously deputy head of The King's School (first woman to hold this post). A first in modern languages and history from Oxford; a year in France convinced her to take up teaching and, after a PGCE back in Oxford, she started in a Peterborough comprehensive followed by spells at Marlborough College and Gresham's School in Norfolk. Enjoys choral music and drama, sharing these passions with students everywhere she has taught. For relaxation it's country walks or playing bridge, which she does each Sunday with members of the parents' association, 'a good way to clear the mind for the week ahead.'

School management together with overall responsibility for the junior and infant schools leaves her no time for teaching, but she is a very visible presence at assemblies. Parents spoke of her as 'genuine and approachable,' and during our tour it was evident she is regarded with great respect and affection by staff and pupils alike.

Academic matters: French, Spanish and German on the menu as well as classical Greek. Mandarin an extracurricular option. Long established links with schools in France, Spain and Germany offer valuable exchange experiences and some lessons are set aside to learn about the respective cultures. All language staff are qualified to teach two languages.

Senior girls take on mentoring roles and some find it useful for nurturing skills in partnerships and communications. 'I like being a mentor. It helps the younger girls and it helps me in understanding what I've learnt.' SEN provision is available for pupils with mild dyslexia, dyspraxia, hearing disability and limited sight, in class and in specialist sessions.

In 2018, 69 per cent A*-A/9-7 grades at GCSE and 54 per cent A*/A at A level, many of the highest performances showing in maths, psychology and the sciences. Specialised sessions for sixth formers help them to prepare applications to top universities in the UK and, increasingly, abroad.

Games, options, the arts: The grass pitches, tennis courts and running track all looked in good shape and well maintained, even under a late November, wet Lancashire sky. School is well represented across the region in athletics, lacrosse, netball, swimming and rounders with its fixture lists showing win after repetitive win in all sports for all years. Football is on offer too, and Bolton Wanderers FC provide weekly coaching sessions. Two current students are signed to Everton and Manchester City girls' team respectively. School owns Patterdale Hall, an outdoor pursuits centre in the Lake District, and pupils eagerly look forward to their visits, irrespective of sporting ability – 'It's like a rite of passage.' Our guide looked nostalgically at the weekend bags neatly deposited in the gymnasium, ready for departure.

The school has achieved a happy and productive blend of the old and new. The modern sports hall and 25m swimming pool (shared with the boys' division) both contrasts with and complements the gothic windowed gymnasium – still fully functioning and, judging by the lingering scent of varnish, subject of a recent make-over.

Drama is very popular and having a purpose-built theatre to stage school productions inspires even the most reticent thespians. One girl cautiously wondered how her teachers 'might react to the sixth form revue this Christmas.' Some past productions, such as Miss Saigon, have attained almost folkloric status, still spoken of by players and audience alike. Several other venues also used to showcase the school's many bands and orchestras. Art, too, enjoys exalted status, with outstanding examples on display, some exhibiting a level of maturity beyond the years of their creators, though currently little take up at A level. DT makes a strong showing at both GCSE and A level, with a recent ambitious project designing, building and launching a hot air balloon.

Background and atmosphere: Bolton Girls' School was founded in 1913 by the first Lord Leverhulme, but can trace its origins to 1877 as the Young Ladies' Day School. Leverhulme's portrait looks benignly at all the beneficiaries of his legacy when they assemble in the Great Hall with its wooden buttresses, beamed roof and gothic windows. The imposing arched entrance, sandstone walls and landscaped campus give the school a traditional grandeur more akin to rural public schools than one sitting in a northern industrial town. Once inside, however, the warm welcome is unmistakably northern and pupils and parents spoke of how quickly they felt included. Separate but adjacent quads house the senior girls' and boys' divisions; these are linked by two-tier glazed walkways to the Riley Centre (2013), where sixth formers share spaces, lunchtimes and extracurricular activities, such as drama productions, events and visitor talks. We heard the description 'best of both worlds' from staff and pupils. Indeed, this expression could easily apply to the whole school and how it has deftly created an atmosphere that retains the best elements of tradition with the excitement of innovation and modernity.

Lower sixth formers complete at least 20 hours' community service. 'It seems a lot, but many girls do far more and manage to stay on top of study.' So committed is the school to volunteering in the community that in 2017 it became the first ever to be awarded the prestigious Queen's Award for Voluntary Service – a sort of MBE for volunteers. 'We are very proud,' said the head. 'It reflects well and shows how much the girls get involved.'

Burgundy coloured uniform definitely belongs in the more traditional world, but none of the pupils expressed rebellious distaste and all agreed that it was 'practical and comfortable.' However, it isn't missed by sixth formers who are permitted civilian dress as long as it is 'smart business' style. Prefects wear gowns that retain the nametags of previous holders, a little tribute to former pupils and an indication, perhaps, that traditions in this school look to inspire rather than burden current pupils.

Pastoral care, well-being and discipline: Responsibility for pastoral care lies with year and form tutors who monitor each girl in and out of class and meet weekly to review pupil concerns. This extends, in turn, to the heads of middle, upper and sixth forms. Senior girls mentor those in years 7 and 8, identifying any specific issues and, if necessary, bringing them to teachers' attention. School council is a forum to air concerns that, if unresolved, can then be taken to the respective head of year. School also provides access to a professional counsellor should pupils need more particular support.

School's ethos of academic achievement fosters self-control and self-discipline and, according to the head, develops a strong sense of responsibility. 'No picking on little ones' said a year 8 girl, illustrating that such values are learnt early, a view later endorsed by the parents who chorused, 'bullying just wouldn't be tolerated.'

Pupils and parents: Pupils we met were articulate, interested, polite, confident, and possessed an enthusiasm for knowledge that was rather reassuring in this somewhat cynical age. They expressed genuine interest in each other's views and at times the whys and wherefores of our questions. In one class pupils were discussing books as diverse as Jane Austen novels and published works on One Direction. We witnessed a lively debate among all years on subjects ranging from uniforms to extracurricular clubs, 'Oh wow! There's just so much to do!' declared one young pupil, attempting to list the many clubs she had attended.

School's social mix is due in part to the generous support of Leverhulme's legacy. This seems to engender a thoughtful understanding of the disparities in society and there was certainly no sense of entitlement among the pupils we spoke – all were aware of how fortunate they were to attend the school. 'The school gives the girls confidence and self-assurance but they're also thoughtful,' said one mum, with another adding, 'they are well-balanced and I am very proud of how my girl conducts herself out of school.' One mother felt confident in asserting, 'sending them here is the best thing we ever did for our children.'

Some parents are former pupils but others, parents of 'first-timers', readily endorsed the view that the school does hold a special place in Bolton hearts. 'We've seen the school improve year on year.' Many families do much more than pay school fees, donating time and effort to help via a very active parents' association (BSGDPA). Vibrant and engaged old girls' network, alumnae including authors Monica Ali and Kate Long, gardener and TV presenter Carol Klein, and Baroness Morris of Bolton, first chancellor of the University of Bolton and deputy speaker of the House of Lords.

Entrance: Majority from junior school Hesketh House, move up to the senior school. Entry to year 7 by reasoning tests – maths, English verbal and non-verbal. High performers called back for interview. One sixth former recalled her first day, 'I remember being a bit worried at first but friends I made on the first day, I still have today.'

Exit: Around 10-20 per cent leave after GCSEs but are replaced with new entrants to the sixth form, some of whom are on bursaries. 'You get more attention from teachers here' observed one of the new intake. Most sixth form leavers go on to study a diverse range of subjects at university including aerospace engineering, music, marketing, psychology, classics, theatre and design; a number have secured apprenticeships with prestigious blue chip companies. Three to Oxbridge in 2018, plus 10 medics and four dentists, one off to the Royal Academy of Music and one to Catalonia; Liverpool much the most popular destination, followed by Manchester and York.

Money matters: Astute fiscal management of the generous bursary scheme, supplemented by a variety of other fund raising events, enables school to provide full or part means-tested support to a fifth of all pupils.

Remarks: Bolton's social mix of pupils, the prudent management of its bursary fund and the strong community links it has forged with its home town ensures affection beyond alumni and parents. The school produces pupils in its own image – respectful of tradition but also confident and well-prepared for the present day.

Bolton School Junior Girls' School (Hesketh House)

Linked with Bolton School Girls' Division, Bolton School Boys' Junior School, Bolton School Boys' Division, Beech House

Chorley New Road, Bolton, Lancashire BL1 4PB

Ages 7–11 **Pupils** 170

Fees: £9,579 pa

01204 840201
www.boltonschool.org/juniorgirls

Headteacher: Since January 2016, Carol Laverick BSc PGCE, previously headteacher of Westholme Junior School. Local girl (educated Turton High School, followed by maths degree at Edinburgh). First teaching job was as class teacher at St Nicholas' School, Fleet, Hampshire before moving to Bolton School (Girls' Division) initially in similar role and, in final two years, as second mistress of the Junior School, before moving to Westholme in 1999.

Entrance: Two-form entry with a maximum of 25 in a class. Most children come from Beech House, Bolton Schools infant department, and entry is automatic. External candidates take formal tests in English, maths, verbal and non-verbal reasoning in the January of the year of entry.

Exit: Almost everyone (99+ per cent) to Bolton School Girls' Division, with a few leaving for local state secondaries or other independent schools. All girls must sit the entrance test and those unlikely to make it are informed in year 5 with guidance and support offered to the girl and her family.

Remarks: Housed in a modern building where everything the girls could possibly want or need has been catered for (including an iPad for each pupil from 7 to 18). The school boasts its own music rooms, science labs, library, dining hall, ICT suite, sensory garden, art room, netball courts and a playground with amphitheatre seating.

A member of staff coordinates SEN provision and support is given where required within the classroom, though the school can only cope with limited special needs. Lift access to all floors.

The teaching of maths and English is traditional and rigorous, but a more creative approach is taken with other subjects. Languages are important here. French is taught right the way through the school, Spanish to years 3, 4 and 5 and Latin to year 6. There are also Italian and German language extracurricular clubs, and the school holds regular international days where the girls are taken off timetable to learn about the cultures of other countries.

Art is popular with pupils. We were shown a beautiful stained glass window, designed by some of the girls, which has pride of place and of which they are justifiably proud. All children take part in the varied sporting programme which includes netball, athletics, lacrosse and swimming in the senior school's 25m pool, with tag rugby and badminton among the extracurricular activities offered.

Pupils are introduced early on to the 16 habits of mind. These habits, such as finding humour, striving for accuracy and thinking flexibly, are designed to enable the girls think intelligently in all aspects of their lives. The habits are depicted by a gorgeously painted, bright and colourful mural along the main corridor and then constantly reinforced by teachers in lessons, assemblies and classroom displays. 'These habits of mind are terrific,' said one dad. 'My daughter applies them to everything, even the things she does out of school like ballet'.

Children are well-mannered and purposeful and seemed more than happy to talk to visitors. Year 6 girls excitedly showed us the totem poles they had drawn in art, and a group of year 3 girls eagerly told us how much they loved the new summer dresses the school has introduced.

A mix of modern and traditional, Hesketh House is an academically successful environment where many mothers commented they wished they had gone themselves.

Bootham School

51 Bootham, York, North Yorkshire YO30 7BU

Ages 3–19 **Pupils** 578 **Sixth form** 138 **Boarders** 100 full (from 11 years)

Fees: Day £6,930 – £17,985; Boarding £18,885 – £32,100 pa

01904 623261
www.boothamschool.com

Head: Since 2016, Chris Jeffery BA PGCE (50s). Educated at Bristol Grammar School, history at York University, PGCE at Exeter University. Taught history and head of house at Bristol Grammar (eight years); head of middle school and deputy head at The Perse, Cambridge (eight years), head of The Grange School, Cheshire (11 years). Currently teaches personal, health and social education here; has taught history, English and RE.

Very committed to pupil well-being (founding chair of Headmasters' and Mistresses' Conference well-being working group) – genuinely cares as much about pupils' happiness at school and in their future lives as their academic prowess and greatly values the school's primary focus on relationships and Quaker ideals (wearing a white as well as a red poppy when we visited – plus a very jolly multicoloured tie). Good sense of humour, modest and approachable: pupils address him – and all staff – by his first name and have, he says happily, no inhibitions about visiting him to express criticisms on school matters. 'Inspirational and very child-focused,' said a parent. 'Quickly knows every child, and their parents, by their first name.'

Married to Carol, a nurse; two adult sons and a daughter at Bootham sixth form. Enjoys song writing and performing, all sports (supports a number of 'spectacularly underachieving teams', as he puts it), 'Spotify addict', walking, travel and attending church.

Junior School head: since 2013, Helen Todd BA MEd (late 30s). Attended All Hallows RC High, Macclesfield, then English at Warwick University. Taught English at Durston House, head of English Aysgarth School, deputy head Edge Grove. Appointed vice chair of Independent Association of Prep Schools for 2018. Does various teaching at Bootham. Married to David, IT manager at Cundall Manor School; boy at Aysgarth, daughter at Bootham. Enjoys amateur dramatics, walking, travel.

Dynamic and 'ambitious for the school'. Has broadened curriculum to cover cultural studies and focus more on skills, to prepare children for 21st century future. Revels in learning opportunities through freedom from Sats constraints. Straightforward, businesslike, flexible, approachable, supportive and 'very present', say parents.

Academic matters: Steady A level results: 2018 43 per cent A*/A; 73 per cent A*/B. Standard choice including classics, Latin, EPQ; strong modern langs, maths, physics, chemistry, psychology, art. Good gender balance for maths and science uptake. Average sets of 11.

GCSE achievement generally strong – including Latin – with no gender difference; 2018: 45 per cent A*-A/9-7. After-school astronomy in historic observatory, with use of original William Cooke telescope – one of the first schools to have its own observatory in 1850s; open to state school students, too. DT product design the only technology. Sets of 15-20.

Year 7 curriculum includes thinking skills, classics, health and the environment. Latin, German and Spanish (in addition to French) added in year 8. Maths and French sets from year 8; classes of around 18. Creative approaches, eg building a model medieval castle competition.

Inclusive gifted and talented policy: students undertake ambitious and imaginative projects, eg building eco car to race in Greenpower Challenge; creating astronomy GCSE textbook; displaying dreams of refugee children from different parts of the world on a large dreamcatcher. Much involvement in York independent-state schools enrichment partnership. Success in national competitions – MFL debating, chemistry, maths.

Well qualified SENCo; mainly wide range of mild to moderate learning difficulties but would consider more challenging pupils to see if school could meet their needs. Reading test for all at start of each year to identify literacy support needs; initial dyslexia screening within department on referral (free), charge for full exam access arrangements assessment. Years 7-11 small support groups. EAL individual and small group support; older students prepared for IELTS (no extra charge).

Juniors: enlightened curriculum – core skills plus cross-curricular topics, creative and flexible approaches with practical tasks, eg building flood-proof house, cooking with war-time rations. Different European language studied each year from years 2-4, including cultural studies; Latin and Mandarin for years 5 and 6. Thinking skills taught through Philosophy4Children. ICT skills developed through topic work and dedicated lessons. Plenty for the very bright and talented, eg challenge and enrich workshops, also open to state schools. Big focus on outdoor learning and trips – specialist outdoor education and forest school trained teacher for outdoor skills, from whittling to fire lighting. Classes of 15-20 higher up, can be as small as 10 or 12 lower down.

Children monitored for additional needs such as dyslexia as they progress (high praise from parent about support for this; another spoke of child's emotional needs being 'subtly and gently addressed') – very capable SENCo, who works closely with senior school SENCo, says she can tell by years 3 or 4 if a child needs a more appropriate school and will help family to find it and child to settle in. Younger children have in class support, mainly small groups outside the classroom for the older ones; families helped to pre-teach topics. EAL support – many children from overseas. Very engaging resident therapy dog, but we were less taken by the (caged) snake in the foyer.

Games, options, the arts: Abundant sports facilities, including climbing wall. Wide choice of standard (success at regional level) and additional sports. Recent international fencer, Olympic swimmer and cyclist, national orienteering competitors, plus academy footballers. Tours to California and Spain.

Very attractive arts centre with colourful, large, collaborative cranes mobile and studio-sized concert hall/lecture theatre. Free weekly lunchtime programme of arts performances and lectures in Georgian recital room open to public. Quantities of very high level and varied music – more than 20 different ensembles, over 60 per cent learn instrument (scholarships to top music colleges), has hosted York guitar festival. Recent drama productions include Shakespeare, The Wind in the Willows, Peter Pan. No cultural opportunities wasted – poems posted on loo doors by head of English.

Excellent art in various media displayed throughout school, including several collaborative pieces. Artist in residence; all art teachers practise and exhibit. Outstanding DT department produces unusual number of Arkwright scholars and successful engineers, male and female – much work to promote engineering careers. 3D printer (used to make a Dalek), laser, three CAD/CAM machines; professional-looking finished artefacts. Links with the real world, eg designing Antarctic research station task set by engineering consultancy. Good percentage of girls do DT at GCSE and A level.

One hour of timetabled leisure activities every week day – choice of up to 80, including bell-ringing, candle making, mini drone flying, world shaper action group. Community service very big, via DofE and the Bootham Challenge: awards at four levels for the development of soft skills through extracurricular activities. Sustainability taken very seriously – very high standards in new buildings; environmental action group successfully conducted switch-off-fortnight to cut use of gas and electricity; eco schools' Green Flag award. Thoroughgoing careers programme; year 10s do work experience.

York's cultural and gastronomic advantages exploited; visits to four continents; exchanges with Quaker school in Washington.

Juniors: varied PE and extracurricular sports. Thriving music and drama – much active contact with York Theatre Royal, annual musical. Interesting art in different media, very well equipped ICT and food tech rooms – we enjoyed observing a boy, in a fetching apron, critically sampling his hot savoury dish. Senior school DT department provides woodwork, mechanics and computer-aided design opportunities. Good choice of extracurricular clubs; residentials for all, including a very popular night in a tent at school for reception.

Boarding: The girls' house consists of three elegant Georgian houses, with shared flats for sixth formers as preparation for university; comfortable common room, kitchen, cheerful bedrooms. Similar modernised Georgian houses for the boys: the single room we saw looked very cramped, but the shared ones are more spacious; two basement common rooms with games consoles, drum kit, pool table and mega TV screen, plus challenging outdoor climbing frame. Additional sixth form boys' house. Full, weekly and flexi-boarding. House staff supported by recently graduated university students. Saturday morning school followed by good programme of weekend activities and treats, eg late Sunday morning brunch. Happy boarders, apart from the odd grumble about things taking a while to get repaired.

Background and atmosphere: Situated in the centre of York on a nine acre estate. Gracious Georgian frontages and interiors with skilfully harmonised modern additions. The main building, the original house, has a warm, homely atmosphere – attractive dining room with wooden furniture and red and cream curtains; the original library has been supplemented with a modern mezzanine floor and is lavishly supplied with reference and fiction books.

Founded 1823 by the Society of Friends for boys, fully co-ed by 1983. Only a minority of Quakers now, but Quaker values and ethos are central and make it distinctive. Relationships, based on mutual respect, come first; co-operation, peaceful approaches to conflict, individuality and equality are all fostered – staff and students are currently working on a new chapter of expectations that applies to both groups; school council pupils interview teaching candidates. The goal is to produce young people who are 'happy in their own skins, confident without being arrogant' (head), who assume they will find purpose and contentment in life through contributing to the community and wider world – many go on to work in the voluntary sector – rather than just pursuing materialism and competition: people who recognise and develop 'that of God' in themselves and others. Facilities widely shared with state schools and the community.

The morning Meeting – a short period of silent reflection – is valued by the pupils: 'When I was in year 7 I thought it was boring, but now I appreciate it' (year 9 boy); 'It gives you time to think about what you want, or not think at all'; 'It's a good time to relax, not be busy'.

Fab choice of high quality food made in house: hot and cold, carnivore and veggie – we can understand why many parents are keen to take up the open invitation to have lunch as a family on Saturdays (no charge), after the optional Meeting, and term it the 'best restaurant in York'.

More relaxed (and cheaper) uniform than most – years 7-9: polo shirt, hoodie, black trousers/tartan skirt; years 10-11: smart casual; sixth: free choice so long as appropriate for school.

Junior school acquired 2002 – purpose built, intimate size. Extensive grounds with playing fields (shared with senior school), courts and thoughtfully equipped playgrounds – we particularly liked the covered picnic tables with built in games boards and the outdoor oven. Yurt for quiet time in breaks, peace garden, plus amphitheatre for small-scale performances. Attractive spacious classrooms with colourful displays; delightful early years/before and after-school area (wrap around care 7.30am-6pm).

Quaker values displayed on the walls and developed, for example, through encouragement to be active citizens – awareness of politics, school council, charity fundraising, singing carols to old people. We liked the 'disposition boxes', containing tokens for displays of independence, resilience, being collaborative, creative, reflective and adventurous – not competitive, other than aiming to improve on the previous term or year, though plenty of matches and house competitions on offer as well. Strong sense of community, being mutually supportive; individual achievements seen as the result of group effort. Children take the initiative, eg bid for funds raised by (very active) PTA, then choose and order equipment; interview teaching candidates; year 6s plan and lead their residential.

Parental praise for chef, who cares about the children as individuals and provides a great diversity of high quality food. They also like the staff eating with the children, encouraging them to eat correctly, and the amount of time the year 5-6s spend at the senior school, which helps them to adjust easily when they move up. 'The school is very good at developing confidence and self worth and sees the children in a holistic way – they want to know about any outside school difficulties as well and are very helpful with them.'

Pastoral care, well-being and discipline: Well-being a particular focus. Pupils talked appreciatively of readily accessible health centre services: 'You can go there whenever you want, even if you're in a lesson'. Access to a counsellor. Programme of external speakers on mental well-being much appreciated – a parent of three boys of different ages reported: 'The material has been new and interesting; they understand things from a young person's perspective'. Sixth formers provide peer listening scheme.

Punishment seen as opportunity for offender to learn more about the reasons for their behaviour and its effects on others. Education in downsides of mobile use – restricted for younger boarders at night; older students only allowed them in relaxation time.

Pupils and parents: Day pupils mainly from York and the surrounding area, up to a 25 mile radius. Senior pupils from the junior school, prep schools, state primaries. Boarders from the UK plus over 20 other countries. Parents from a range of backgrounds – business, professionals, public service, academics; ethnically mixed. 'Our parents want their children to become good people, have purposeful, meaningful lives,' says head; they value the Quaker ethos and educational values. Parents we spoke to in general delighted with the school – just the odd comment about occasional failures of communication.

The pupils we met were impressively thoughtful and mature, articulate, open, relaxed. They spoke warmly about their teachers. 'They care about you and your development as a person..They want to know how you are and feel'. Space given to discussion of politics (in lessons and morning Meetings) and the practice of it – eg the recent mock election (Labour won – just) and EU referendum (Remain won 70:30). They also appreciate the priority given to relationships, the non-authoritarian and relatively relaxed atmosphere, with freedom to speak your mind in lessons, friendliness and sense of community.

A deeply impressive number of very distinguished ex-pupils dating back to the 19th century. Scholars – 17 fellows of the Royal Society; mathematician Lewis Fry Richardson ('father of fractals'); historian AJP Taylor; child psychiatrist Michael Rutter. Politicians, eg Anti Corn Law leader John Bright and Olympic athlete and Nobel peace prize winner Philip Noel-Baker. A tradition of social reform exemplified by members of the Rowntree family and actor and disabled champion Brian Rix. More recently: Olivia Garfield, CEO of Severn Trent Water (one of 2013 Fortune Magazine's top 10 high flyers under 40), Elizabeth Waterman (in list of top 50 women in engineering), Emily Sutton, artist and illustrator, Benjamin Leftwich, singer-songwriter.

Entrance: Junior school: non selective. Taster day – a normal day in school, with future classmates, to allow child and teacher to get to know each other and ensure school is a good fit, plus meeting with head and report from current school. Year 5/6 entry has English and maths test included.

Eleven plus: initial 30 minute interview with the headmaster before enrolment about what the child enjoys most/least at school and leisure activities; reference from head of current school (child needs to be at least at national average level for reading, writing and maths). Optional taster Saturday morning in autumn term before entry. Assessment day in January: science and art activities, challenges, brief maths and English comprehension tests.

At 12+,13+ and 14+: all do maths and English papers; years 9 and 10 also do French/German/Spanish paper; short interview with head or deputy head.

Sixth form entry: minimum of seven GCSEs at 4 or above (or six GCSEs, of which three must be at 6 or higher), including maths and English, and requirements of chosen A level subjects (20-25 join).

Exit: Almost all junior school pupils progress to the senior school. Around a third leaves post-16 for more vocational courses at local sixth form colleges. Several to top universities (four to Oxbridge in 2018 and one medic), to study a broad range of subjects, including art and music. Durham, Bristol, Edinburgh, Newcastle, UCL popular; one off to Vienna (product design) and one to Leiden (interior design) in 2018.

Money matters: Means-tested bursaries awarded according to need and academic performance in 11 and 13 plus exam. Music scholarships of up to 50 per cent of fees based on tests and audition plus performance in entrance assessment. Bursaries for children from Quaker families from age 3. Means-tested scholarship/bursary for candidates from state-maintained schools who gain a minimum of eight grades 7+ at GCSE.

Remarks: Strikingly friendly and calm atmosphere, with priority genuinely given to the development of emotional intelligence, as the way to future happiness, and respect for individual differences, rather than on academic and other kinds of achievement. Not that results don't matter – parents say they bring out the best in children in all ways and that talents are cultivated to the highest level.

Bow Durham School

Linked with Durham School

South Road, Durham DH1 3LS

Ages 3–11 **Pupils** 149 (105 boys, 44 girls) **C of E**

Fees: £5,676 – £11,043 pa

0191 7319270
www.durhamschool.co.uk/prep-school.asp

Head: Since September 2016, Sally Harrod, previously deputy head at Lincoln Minster prep school.

Entrance: Not selective, but low key testing in English, mathematics and verbal reasoning as part of a taster day, plus a reference from current school/nursery. Limited number of means-tested bursaries available at all ages and scholarships from year 3 (maximum £1,000).

Exit: Virtually all to senior school – automatic transfer unless applying for scholarship. Entrance examination only used for assessment purposes.

Remarks: Founded 1885 as an independent boys' prep, moved to present site in 1888, incorporated into the Durham School Foundation 1976 and formally became the prep for Durham School. Went co-ed in 2006 and now about a third girls. Faces strong competition from good state primaries and the nearby Chorister School.

Early years housed in Quarryheads House, a splendid, 100 year old, former family home (originally assigned to the head of Bow), next to main Bow buildings – white with big bay windows, a red slate roof and white chimney, resembling a children's storybook illustration. This area of the school is led by an experienced and enthusiastic practitioner, passionate and knowledgeable about children's early education, their emotional learning and how to encourage independence – and it shows.

Badger nursery (3-4 years) is on ground floor, and opening the door is like lifting the lid of Pandora's box; a treasure trove of discovery, with stimulation, free flow play and pupil-led learning. We particularly liked the fact that plans for the play corner were changed to a camping out theme in response to requests from the children. The chart of the tree of growing kindness recording small milestones in the journey of socialisation was another lovely idea. Three outdoor areas for soft play, mud play and tranquility. Read Write Inc for those who are ready links into the work that continues in reception.

B

The nursery works very closely with reception and the transition is very carefully managed. Reception has a terrific, large, open plan space on the first floor with different learning sections and views of trees. Behind it is the Beaver transition area, for older children, a quirkily shaped room with several nooks and crannies, next to the pleasant welcome room for parents. Well equipped – interactive whiteboard, large plasma screen; delightful outdoors play area. Supportive parents: 'Very good attention from the teachers'.

Pre-prep (5-7 years) housed in a designated building close to the sports hall. Core subjects plus French, history, geography, RE, IT, music and art; good results in key stage 1 tests. Cheerful classrooms with good displays and we saw evidence of good teacher/pupil relationships, though the children's behaviour rapidly declined into noisy activity without their teacher's attention. Use of the sports hall, IT suite and library in Bow; children swim all year round at Durham City Freemans Quay leisure centre or Chester le Street leisure centre. Concerts, nativity play, fundraising for charities, after-school clubs include fencing, judo, percussion, speech and drama. Prepared for transition to prep through attending their assemblies, house competitions, some sport with older pupils and a longer day in summer term.

Prep (7-11 years) mainly sited in the main building (1888), overlooking the cricket square with the cathedral as a backdrop. A red-brick classroom block with later additions and upgrading, though some classrooms are in need of some TLC. Year 3, some year 5 and the science laboratory are located in a block of single storey classrooms a short distance away.

Year 3 is a transition year where children spend 50 per cent of their time with their class teacher studying English, mathematics and humanities. From year 4 it is all specialist teaching and the layout of the buildings means that children need to be organised to ensure they have the right equipment for their lessons and arrive punctually. Good training for senior school life ahead, and it certainly didn't seem to faze those we spoke to. Small classes divided into two groups for core subjects. Formal French starts in year 3, Latin in year 5; very good key stage 2 results.

The children we talked to enjoyed their lessons – 'Lots of fun activities' – and found the teachers helpful. The last ISI inspection recommended 'catering more fully for the able', and there does seem to have been progress in classroom differentiation and opportunities in music, drama and sport, where age is not a barrier to joining a team (subject to the constraints of difference in physical sizes). Strong learning support department led by specialist – close monitoring, in-class support where possible and some outside. There is a real drive to raise academic performance throughout both the senior and prep schools, with baseline testing and analysis of progress data. Whilst they feel that their children are happy, parents we spoke to felt that the school could be doing more to build and encourage solid learners. 'Many small improvements could be made to the school,' said one.

Netball/tennis court, big sports field and shared playing fields with the nearby Chorister School provides good outdoor sports facilities. Multi-purpose sports hall next to pre-prep and shared use of Astro, and indoor swimming pool at senior school, a walk away. Two one hour games sessions a week for years 3 and 4, three for years 5 and 6.

Music and art are housed in The Cottage, 250 years old and listed, originally a toll house on the edge of the campus. Music is strong – well-resourced room and whole class instrumental tuition once a week, starting with fiddlesticks in year 4, moving to ukulele in year 6. Choir, jazz band, Ceilidh band, fiddle group all available. The art room includes facilities for pottery and

B

sculpture as well as drawing and painting. Two plays a year plus speech and drama after school. Wide choice of activities including fencing, judo, gymnastics, table tennis, karate; history visits, trip to Venice and Rome (links with a school there), ski trip to Italy. Excellent outdoor adventure playground in the grounds as well.

Good pastoral care – all new pupils have a guide for the first two weeks. Children feel happy and secure – 'People listen and understand if you've got a problem'. No obvious discipline issues, though we did come across one young girl crying outside a classroom. Staff were aware and ushered her back in on our arrival.

The size of school ensures good links between the year groups and this is enforced with four houses and competitions in sports, swimming and general knowledge. The pupils we met were articulate, open and confident and proud of their school. Praise from the last inspection report – 'well behaved, hard working and polite children'. All year 6s have a turn at being a monitor (prefect). Using the senior school facilities often ensures a smooth transition to senior school.

Bradford Girls' Grammar School

Linked with Lady Royd Primary

20

Squire Lane, Bradford, West Yorkshire BD9 6RB

Ages 11–18 **Pupils** 1,051 **Sixth form** 130

01274 545395
www.bggs.com

Principal: Since 2009, Kathryn Matthews BSc (40s), educated at Loreto Grammar School in Manchester, then maths and an MA in education at Leeds University. Taught maths at London Oratory; deputy head at Gateways School, Leeds. ISI team inspector and governor at Westbourne Prep in Sheffield. Married with adult children. Enjoys theatre, visiting art galleries, reading and rugby union. Warm and approachable, she is both incisive and refreshingly honest; parents tell us she is absolutely key in retaining their confidence in the school as it evolves. She knows a good teacher when she sees one; valuing staff who can enthuse pupils, she is judicious in her appointments and keen to foster talent at all levels. Having led the school through choppy waters of late, she is determined to maintain the school's high academic standards and enable girls from the local community to succeed: nothing has changed here in that respect.

Academic matters: A non-selective free school since 2013, it was always strong on value-added and still is, particularly in the main school.

A levels averaged C in 2018, with a Progress 8 score of -0.47. Surprisingly wide range of subjects for such a relatively small sixth form, with some subjects run for small numbers; far bigger numbers for maths and sciences than arts and languages; excellent art. At GCSE in 2018 57 per cent got 9-5 in both English and maths, with an impressive +0.61 Progress 8 score. French, German, Spanish and Latin available for linguists; RE hugely popular and successful right up to A level.

Most girls take nine GCSEs; sciences (all three) are hugely popular and extremely successful. Class sizes up to 28, slightly higher than the 24 ceiling parents had hoped for, so they are watching carefully, but in the school's defence, the increased number is in response to local demand and the need for more secondary school places. Good careers advice and university preparation – girls rave about the quality UCAS advice. The principal takes all girls through their personal statement, useful in giving some of these highly intelligent but utterly modest girls a nudge forward in understanding how to sell themselves when applying for highly competitive university places.

A good number of new staff have joined as a result of the rapid growth of the school, some NQTs, others with a wealth of experience – all seem to be bringing new energy and impetus. No lack of rigour and a strong work ethic – heads down, focused in classrooms and plenty of challenge on offer. 'It's a virtuous circle,' says the principal. 'The girls here are a joy to teach so you can have fun with them and they lap it up' – a revelation for some of the newer teachers who are enjoying the opportunity simply to teach rather than wade through behaviour issues on a daily basis.

SEN department grown from scratch. Now under the watchful eye of Ofsted, there is much more scrutiny all round. School makes good use of LA and national resources and liaises well with parents. Teaching assistants provide support for pupils with a variety of cognitive and sensory difficulties and HTLA support is available for more vulnerable pupils and those who are completely new to English.

Games, options, the arts: Good facilities include an Astroturf, purpose-built sports hall and a swimming pool used by all, right through from the junior school. Good number and range of sports on offer – the girls are not big on contact sport but other choices are wide and varied and the enthusiastic sports staff seem to get everyone moving. Table tennis, cross-country, netball and rounders are especially popular, as is dance, and the girls regularly take part in county, regional and national competitions.

'Music could do better,' admits the school, but recently appointed staff are on the case. Good choir and steel band; peripatetic teachers offer individual tuition in a range of instruments and support the school orchestra as it matures. Drama is popular, recently put on a production of Oliver! Stunning art on display all around the school and some very elaborate textiles greet you on entry. Sixth formers squeeze much into their already-busy schedules with World Challenge, DofE, National Citizenship Service (NCS), LEAP enterprise, The Community Volunteering Programme, Sports Leadership Award and Outward Bound programme. Two – carefully selected – girls visit Auschwitz each year. Sports and academic trips to Spain, France, Switzerland, USA and Malawi.

Background and atmosphere: Much remains unchanged – the uniform is the same and the Yorkshire Mouseman furniture is still here, as is the lovely atrium housed in the centre of the original building. The site is attractive, something of a green oasis within the city landscape. The main 1930s building sits alongside a modern purpose-built sixth form building within 17 acres of well-tended games fields, lawns and gardens. Classrooms have had a facelift, there are new lockers, and the place is spotless, with floors so shiny they would impress the neighbouring hospital. The science labs remain in their original 1930s state – nostalgic for some, 'museum pieces' to others, that said, parents describe the science department staff as 'masters [sic] of their craft', so although updated labs are on the wishlist, they are clearly not critical. A number of the senior staff have been here for a good while, 'a good thing,' say parents; they have managed the transition whilst watching the school grow exponentially. As far as structural changes go, the roof's been mended, as has the heating, there's better security all round and, most importantly, the school's future has been secured ad infinitum.

Pastoral care, well-being and discipline: Good pastoral care. Alert to the usual problems coming from girls putting too much pressure on themselves to succeed, but 'nothing that can't be managed by working with parents', according to Mrs Matthews. Sensible, enlightened anti-bullying procedures, sanctions and rewards policies. Younger girls look neat and tidy in their uniform; no uniform for sixth form but there is a dress code of 'business wear' – rather too loosely interpreted by some. Established parents worry that there are now greater demands on the staff and are crossing fingers that standards do not slip as the school reshapes itself. Any concerns are centred on maintaining standards of uniform and behaviour rather than anything academic – it's a watching brief.

Pupils and parents: Parents are a diverse social mix as befits the local area and demographic, but for the most part, what they do share is aspiration. Those girls joining midway through the school – the 'joiners' – are finding their feet, academically and socially, adapting to new policies and procedures, although the transition from other local state schools into this former fee-paying grammar was undoubtedly easier for some than others. The 'aspire, succeed, lead' ethos remains and former grammar brigade are reassured by that. It's a complicated landscape in Bradford where, as a designated area of need, a good education is given high status by many and there is no lack of will from most parents for their daughters to succeed. Predominantly Asian families, the ethnic mix is not as wide as it once was, though the school remains non-denominational.

Girls are proud to be here and in return they work hard and relish the opportunities – 'DofE take up is brilliant,' say staff, and the amount of voluntary work jammed in alongside studies by the sixth form girls is remarkable. When asked about the increase in class and overall school size, their response is typically candid and clear cut: 'We fall out less because there are more girls to be friends with now, but the lunch queues are longer..' Responsibility is encouraged, there is a school president with deputies, a sixth form committee and elected form prefects – all relics of the school in its previous existence, but still an intrinsic part of the 'new' school and all about recognising and promoting leadership potential.

Strong links with parents and old girls, who include Barbara Castle, Rebecca Sarker (TV actress), Jill McGivering (BBC foreign correspondent), Isobel Hilton (journalist), Pippa Wells (CERN astrophysicist) and Anita Rani (TV presenter and journalist).

Entrance: According to a recent report, this school is now the most oversubscribed in the country pro rata. Some 500 apply for 50 year 7 places so it's a bit of a lottery, but the admissions process is squeaky clean with much time and attention given to ensuring that it remains so. Non-selective; automatic admission from the junior school (Lady Royd, onsite); five 9-4s at GCSE essential for a sixth form place.

Exit: Those leaving post-GCSE do so to move on to further education and/or employment. Big pull post A level to Yorkshire universities – Leeds, Bradford and Huddersfield are very popular. Majority heading for medicine, dentistry, pharmacy, optometry, radiography, biomedical sciences, maths and engineering – these girls love their sciences. One off to study medicine at King's College London in 2018, with others to eg Durham (anthropology) and Leeds (law).

Remarks: There was a very long queue to register for places right down the school driveway and beyond when it was announced, in 2013, that this longstanding traditional girls' school was to become a free school. Whilst now hugely oversubscribed, they have managed the transition extremely well, updating where necessary whilst wisely hanging on to the traditions and values that gave this school its good name.

Bradford Grammar Junior School (Clock House)

B

Linked with Bradford Grammar School

Keighley Road, Bradford, West Yorkshire BD9 4JP

Ages 6–11 **Pupils** 186

Fees: £9,915 pa

01274 553742
www.bradfordgrammar.com

Head of Junior School: Since 2017, Kerry Howes MSc PGCE (early 40s); studied for her first degree in ocean science at the University of North Wales in Bangor. Part-time employment as a qualified tennis coach and support for a child with learning disabilities whilst undertaking a masters in marine resource management at Herriot Watt Edinburgh led to a PGCE at Ripon and York St John and teaching.

Experience in the primary state and independent sectors across the country, latterly at Ashville College, Harrogate and Queen Mary's Thirsk prior to her appointment as a class teacher here in 2003. Progressed through management posts, to deputy and then a short spell as acting head before permanent appointment.

Clearly delighted to be in post and has an infectious enthusiasm for the school and the experience it provides for its pupils. Committed to improving opportunities and has a clear vision of what works for Bradford Grammar. Her lengthy tenure has the benefit of seeing succession of siblings through the school and it is evident that she knows well her pupils and their families.

Entrance: By assessment in maths and English. Pupils spend a full day in school and have the opportunity to meet pupils and staff.

Exit: Automatic entry to senior school and most all do. Leaving almost always to do with finance.

Remarks: Pupils start at an unusual point – age 6 – their first two years of school elsewhere, often a state primary, but parents tell us that 'they make the transition easily'. Classes range from low teens to low 20s, usually two to a year group, but numbers fluctuate so range from one to three.

Broad curriculum taught in seven sessions of 40 minutes a day. From year 2, specialist teaching in art, music, PE and modern foreign languages (French and German, half a year each); science, with lesson in senior school laboratories from year 5. Lots of use of senior school facilities. Strong creative writing – prizes in national and local competitions and plenty of lively pieces in own school magazine, junior version of Hoc Age, with editorial team from years 4 and 6.

Parents say that while academic results are excellent the school provides an 'all round, balanced foundation both academically and personally'. Children have a strong bond with their teachers, are stretched and pushed when needed, though very much tailored to their needs.

Designated computer room as well as two sets of iPads for classroom use; very advanced computing syllabus for all ages, covering coding and animation. Dynamic curriculum leader and emphasis on internet safety in conjunction with West Yorkshire Police cyber team.

Fun learning in the specialist DT room from year 4, an Aladdin's cave of project models from the recent past with working miniature cable car system whizzing across the ceiling. Access to state of the art gadgetry in senior school; year 5s were designing and constructing a bedroom door electronic alarm system – parents beware.

Small numbers of special needs, mainly dyslexia, dyspraxia, diagnosed at previous school or picked up by teachers. Also Asperger's, mild autism and physical disabilities but not severe behavioural problems. Flexible approach to specific needs led by junior school co-ordinator training to be a SENCo; close links with senior school. Children supported in the classroom and one-on-one/small group work if needed. Multitude of opportunity for the more able pupils, including mathematics mastery and junior journalism.

Assessment weeks each term with continuous tracking of pupil progress. An autumn informal meeting with form teacher is followed by two formal academic parents' evenings later in the year. Progress reports at October half-term and end of autumn and spring term; full report at end of summer term.

Use of senior school excellent facilities with dynamic coaching provides sporting opportunity for all. Field sports, netball, cross-country, swimming, athletics, rounders and tennis with numerous teams for each means all juniors represent the school at some point.

Flourishing music, also with inclusive approach – large orchestra, diversity of groups and ensembles, including samba, flute and guitar, as well as a rock band. Choir has performed with Bradford Cathedral choristers and made BBC recordings. Every class sings in annual Christmas and spring concerts.

Opportunity to take centre stage or be part of the chorus in drama productions culminating in the biennial school production performed in the Hockney Theatre, recently Honk!, a musical adaptation of the Ugly Duckling.

Much impressive art on display around the school brightening the quirky warren of corridors. 'Design a flag' competition led to the winning design being made into two flags, which children request when going on holiday. Photographic evidence and each location are recorded on a map proudly displayed in a prominent spot.

Masses of school clubs, mainly held in the 65 minute lunch break, covering every conceivable interest and children are really spoiled for choice. Expected to participate in at least two, but often take up more. Wealth of co-curricular a big hit with pupils and parents alike.

A couple of educational outings for each year group and specialist guests regularly in school. Annual residentials for almost all years to outdoor centres in the North Yorkshire national park and Lake District; annual sports tour for year 6. Popular French ski trip each year.

Junior school, known as Clockhouse, moved from Thornville to the edge of the senior school campus in 1975. Accommodated in the former head's house, which morphs into former stables converted to housing reception and classrooms. Co-educational since 1999, girls now make up 55 per cent of the overall school roll, and though this varies widely in individual year groups it is always a healthy balance.

An attractive building with a rabbit warren of artificially lit narrow corridors, one fondly (and appropriately) named the tunnel, brightened by reminders of past activities, such as dreamcatchers and happy painted pebbles from happiness week. Banks of lockers crammed into available spaces; teacher supervision prevents a scrum at the beginning and end of the day.

Natural daylight aplenty in light and bright classrooms walls filled with an array of visual learning tools and displays of children's work. Very large and flexible hall used for assemblies, music lessons and examinations – though not lunch, which is self-service in the senior school dining room. Whilst the quality of food is good some parents felt that that catering for the whole student body provided choices a little too adventurous for some junior palates.

Separate junior school section in the senior state of the art library. Well stocked with fiction (reading popular), designated lessons there, accessible for pupils at lunchtimes. Much use made of senior facilities – for science, art, theatre and sports, benefits of an 'all through school'.

Outside the junior school there is a small playground for the 'littlies' and another for year 4 and above. More play equipment is a wish from some pupils and parents. Plenty of space and grass; a garden area with greenhouse and a glade with dipping pond and outdoor classroom – all on the head's radar for development.

Wrap around care provides from 7.45am-6.00pm, chargeable after 4.00pm when a drink and snack are provided. Homework, television, board games and play all available in designated room in the old part of the school.

The head wants pupils to 'be brave, courteous, work hard and follow the school rules'. The junior school children we met certainly demonstrated these traits and were confident and articulate, engaged in their lessons and enjoyed the wealth of extracurricular on offer. They think the school rules are fair and feel bullying is rare and dealt with firmly. We observed acts of thoughtfulness and kindness to each other.

Certificates for achievement are celebrated in a weekly whole school assembly and accolades for high achievement displayed on the celebration board. Pupils assigned to one of four houses on entry and house points awarded for academic work and courteous behaviour. Music, sport and fundraising provide enthusiastic competition and the house points are displayed on the electronic screens in reception and are closely monitored. House meetings are held weekly and house captains chosen from year 6 pupils. School council with class reps elected by peers representing their views and giving feedback. Proposals adopted by school if workable.

Well-being and happiness have been a focus throughout the school and parents feel that the school is pioneering in their approach. They say that 'the pastoral care is totally tuned in with existing and growing issues'.

Head forging even closer links with senior school, especially for year 6, with regular taster sessions trying out new lessons with senior school, followed by lunch with some year 12s and the chance to try a lunchtime club – table tennis, drama, water polo or debating on offer.

Children smartly dressed in navy and maroon, with formal (if expensive) maroon striped shirts in common with senior school, and bespoke claret junior school tie. Lengthy list of sports kit too – make sure of name labels to avoid the lost property bin.

Socially and ethnically mixed, reflecting area's demographics. Parents like 'the healthy mix of pupils from many different backgrounds, which supports our approach in bringing up our children to be open-minded, respectful and all-round, balanced members of a diverse society'.

Parents told us that they feel 'regularly informed' by the school. Much communication is by text and email and there is the usual vehicle of the pupil's daily planner. Termly magazine Hoc Age.

Catchment area is West Yorkshire plus small areas of North Yorkshire and Lancashire; school transport bus routes in place and close to Frizinghall railway station.

Notable old pupils: David Hockney (takes an active interest); Denis Healey; Sir Ken Morrison (ex-executive chairman of Morrisons); Alistair and Jonathan Brownlee (British Olympic triathletes) and Archbishop of York.

Fees at lower end of the scale – one of the Telegraph's top 10 best value UK independent schools. No bursarial assistance available until senior school.

There really is something for everyone here. The foundation of a first class education, the opportunity to further current interests and try new ones, all in a nurturing and supportive environment – certainly not an academic hothouse, as sometimes perceived. A healthy mix of pupils from different backgrounds blend to create a happy atmosphere around the school.

Bradford Grammar School

Linked with Bradford Grammar Junior School (Clock House)

Keighley Road, Bradford, West Yorkshire BD9 4JP

Ages 11–18 **Pupils** 862 **Sixth form** 249

Fees: £12,669 pa

01274 542492
www.bradfordgrammar.com

Headmaster: Since January 2016, Dr Simon Hinchliffe BA MEd PhD (late 40s), previously deputy head, having joined the school in 2014. Geography degree from Durham, PhD from St Andrews in geography geoscience and international recognition for research into quaternary science led to a post as lecturer at the University of Wolverhampton. Masters in education leadership and management from the OU following a move to secondary education. Spent 14 years at Wolverhampton Grammar School, where he was latterly head of sixth form and head of outdoor education.

He places great significance on value added data, which shows cohorts of pupils are achieving one grade higher than expected per GCSE, across the range of subjects. Believes that Bradford Grammar is a 'broad church' (a much repeated term), and that it is 'as far from a one size fits all sausage factory as you can imagine'.

He is proud of the ethnic diversity in the school and that 'no particular group stands out'. This is not lucky coincidence but deliberately engineered through the pastoral programme and carefully crafted co-curricular opportunities tuned to building a cohesive community with a clear identity. Big whole school events, Founder's Day, Christmas and Easter are 'done properly'. There are termly Christian celebrations at school or in Bradford Cathedral; assemblies are secular or multi-faith half-termly, and there are pupil-led faith societies that meet regularly with staff in attendance.

Spending considerable time and energy in building community links in Bradford and nearby Leeds is heartened by the current local civic and educational leadership, which has brought about some fledgling state school partnerships.

Well liked throughout the school community; one parent summed up the view of many: 'Simon balances the serious running of the school with an engaging and integrated approach to parents. He is warmingly professional, takes a genuine interest in what is best for everyone at BGS'. Parents also like that he 'is keen to keep the positive elements of the tradition and history of the school, but is very open to new ways of thinking and keen to embrace change'.

Passionate about mountains and mountaineering, but pressures of the day job mean that the nearest he gets to a peak these days is mountain biking round the seven hills of Bradford and beyond, occasionally joining colleagues for a ride out on Fridays after school. Lives with Heidi, a PE teacher and their two young children.

Academic matters: In 2018, 54 per cent A*/A grades at A level – pretty constant over last few years. Voted the North's independent secondary school of the year by Parent Power, the Sunday Times Schools Guide 2018, jumping to 85th nationally. Wide range of A level subjects on offer, mathematics, sciences and economics most popular, up to 25 per cent taking these subjects each year. Four subjects studied in year 12 (usually three in year 13) in tutor groups of 8-10 on average with enrichment programme encompassing EPQ, lectures by external speakers, Wednesday afternoon sports and/or community volunteering. Inspired, fortnightly personal development programme sessions plus school leadership opportunities ensure a full on two years in sixth form here.

Excellent GCSE results, 76 per cent A*-A/9-7 grades in 2018. Wide range of subjects to choose from, 10 GCSEs with seven compulsory subjects including one modern foreign language and separate sciences. In addition, three option choices including a second language, computer science, drama, music, Greek and Latin. Strong and popular maths and sciences (with girls too). Particularly wide choice of languages on offer – all do French, German and Latin in years 7-8; year 9s can add Spanish and Greek. Gains honours in national academic and creative writing competitions.

Class sizes range from around 20 in KS3 to 16 in KS4. Pupils we met appreciative of the accessibility and commitment of teachers – rapid communication through web-based tool Firefly and plenty of extra help available at lunch time clubs. Pupils feel that teachers know them as individuals, are supportive and generally go 'that extra mile' for them. Classroom atmosphere not overly competitive, rather an extrapolation of the school maxim Hoc Age prevails, 'get on and do it to the best of your ability'.

As you would expect, technology abounds. Chrome, Google docs, Firefly, Unifrog were just some of the software names that tripped instantly off the tongues of our guides. Interactive whiteboards in every classroom; iPads in science and designated sixth form computers. Computer science on offer at GCSE and A level.

Restructured sixth form team provides 'tailored and informed advice' on post-school routes, with vocational support provided from alumni and business contacts; recent leavers keep in contact to share experience of courses/universities with next generation of aspiring students. Emerging professional apprenticeships as a leaving choice.

Typically, a small proportion, less than 10 per cent, have SEN. The majority are dyslexic/literacy or processing/working memory difficulties, but also pupils with ASD, ADHD and physical difficulties, though not with severe behavioural problems. They are mostly catered for by differentiated teaching but some have a reduced timetable or one-to-one or small group support, usually at lunch or in the lessons they are not attending. Seems to work as pupils make very good progress. Similar proportion have EAL requirements, where personalised plans are in place. Study skills sessions in years 10 and 11 for all. Plenty of gifted and talented opportunities – flexible approach to specific needs.

Games, options, the arts: Extensive playing fields and courts, two storey sports pavilion for post-match entertaining and more, all-weather sports pitch and cricket wickets, sports hall with squash courts, dance studio, fitness suite and 25 metre swimming pool – all on site. Rowing and boathouse available on

B

nearby river Aire – who could ask for more? The head, actually, who has organised a £4m upgrade of facilities including new artificial hockey and cricket pitches and indoor tennis/netball courts.

Really is sport for all here. Major focus on rugby though head would like 'more juice and attention' for other sports, which now include hockey for boys and cricket for girls. Range extends to water polo, table tennis, golf, sailing, triathlon and climbing. High powered coaches particularly for rugby, netball and hockey; fields numerous teams for most sports with impressive fixtures list against northern independents, local state schools and even further afield. Regular sports tours – recently netball to Australia, hockey to the Netherlands. Sports colours highly prized (ties for boys, lapel badges for girls), half-colours for effort, full colours for achievement.

Very high standard of music in seniors with concert performance opportunities. Several orchestras and groups, including electric guitar and the Dixieland Crackerjacks; choirs; shining stars in nationally acclaimed youth orchestras, choirs and musical theatre groups. Excellent facilities with recording studio, music auditorium and 12 private teaching rooms for individual tuition in a wide range of instruments and singing.

1980s Hockney Theatre provides venue for numerous studio and large scale productions: varied choices, some home grown, musicals every other year – Live Like Pigs to Grease. Participates in Shakespeare Schools Festival. Lots of theatre-going opportunities and GCSE drama now available to complement A level theatre studies.

Busy and well-equipped art, evidence of the Hockney heritage, really impressive work on display around the school and in the five art rooms; all A level students do life drawing class, a smattering progress to art college; work exhibited at Saltaire Arts Trail and fundraising for local hospice through exhibition at Sunny Bank Mills. High tech devices – laser cutter in art, 3D printer in DT. Participation in Schools Racing Car Design competition; Arkwright engineering scholars.

Huge importance placed on extensive co-curricular programme by school. Long lunch breaks enable masses of senior school clubs, sports, arts and beyond, some run by students, mainly faith and language themed. Thriving DofE, numerous gold and recently clocked 500 bronzes; active RAF and army CCF. Curriculum-based outings and experience trips locally and to Europe for language, art, history and classics – and skiing, of course. One parent said, 'all these opportunities and new experiences are really broadening [my daughter's] horizons. Her confidence and self-esteem have soared and she has a real sense of being able to do anything she puts her mind to; she will really have a go at anything'.

For sixth form annual far frontiers expeditions to distant places – Nepal and Mongolia planned. Sixth form enrichment programme includes presentations from visiting professionals, student-led societies covering every department, public speaking, model UN, LEAP (local Young Enterprise). Topical debates, most recently gun control. Work experience in year 12, biennial careers evening and ongoing careers guidance and advice.

Background and atmosphere: Ancient traditions, founded in 1548 and re-established by Royal Charter as the Free Grammar School of Charles II at Bradford in 1662. Remained a small school until education reforms of 1869, when it was the first grammar school to be reorganised and consequently rapidly grew to 400 pupils. Became a direct grant grammar in 1926, had outgrown its inner city location so new premises were built on the current site on the northern fringes of Bradford. Completed in 1937 but commandeered by the army during the war so it was only in 1949 that the school moved in. Became independent in 1975, fully co-educational in 1999, now about 40 per cent girls.

A spacious 25 acre site, graced by the original statement building of mellow stone blending well with attractive, coherent modern additions, including extensive and lofty bridge linking old and new parts with views of open country and distant hills. Excellent facilities, thanks to generosity of a number of benefactors (including OB David Hockney, whose name graces the flexible performance area and whose gifted works are on display around the school). Most recently a £2m much-used circular two storey library and resource centre housing school archives, an impressive record not only of the school but Bradford's social history.

The wood-panelled entrance leads directly to grand mock-gothic school hall, bedecked with traditional portraits of past heads, plus a more modest one – by David Hockney. The longest serving and reforming headmaster, the Rev Keeling, 1872-1912, established the modern school as an academic powerhouse and died in 1916, devastated by the large losses of OBs in the war. A moving and dignified memorial commemorating Bradford Grammar losses lies in the heart of this traditional building.

Sixth form centre with wow factor open atrium and overlooked by dining room balcony, a quiet eating space designated for staff and sixth form only. Eyes are immediately drawn to talking point painting of a contemporary Last Supper presiding over the pupils' social space – year 13s to the left, year 12s to the right, though sixth formers were quick to reassure us that there is much mingling and experiences shared between the year groups.

An atmosphere of calm, well-ordered activity, even at lesson change over times, signalled by a discrete sonorous 'hooter'. Helped by wide corridors so no need to jostle. Pupils courteous but not particularly curious of strangers walking in their midst – perhaps a sign of the number of external speakers and visitors to the school.

Smart uniform, navy with tailored maroon striped shirts, very businesslike, little aberration; obviously dress code well monitored. Formal attire for sixth formers with own choice of shirt – not a maroon stripe in sight. Ties representing sporting honours, prefect appointments etc worn with great pride. Loved it that one of our guides uniquely and creatively wore his junior school tie.

Smooth-running cafeteria style dining; inevitable queues for first and second sitting; year groups rotate weekly. Plenty of popular food choices, all at the same reasonable price and unlimited amounts – hot and salad options, cosmopolitan cooking and healthy choices to suit adolescent and more sophisticated palates

Pastoral care, well-being and discipline: Recent changes now see individual pastoral heads of year overseen by assistant head – they really get to know their pupils and work closely with learning support team, school nurses and counsellor. Real focus on school-wide well-being and happiness and a recent audit of the spiritual, moral, social and cultural programme ensures that the content reflects and connects with this drive.

Pupils tell us that that the 'rules are fair, just common sense really, and just reinforce what you would expect to do'. They think that bullying is rare and that generally pupils are 'accepting of different behaviours'; conceded that there is 'banter' but would intercede if they noticed 'someone was getting upset'. One girl said 'everyone just smiles at each other here' and we noted the congenial atmosphere when walking around school and in the dining room. 'We might not lunch together but everyone gets on,' said another; 'there no persona of being posh, no-one knows or cares who is on a bursary'.

Between years 7-9 the forms are re-engineered annually with a different form tutor each year. Continuity in years 10 and

11 though and separate tutor groups for years 12 and 13, who volunteer to be trained and act as mentors for lower years.

Four senior prefects and 30 others are selected from volunteers, by election from staff and year 12 pupils. Two class representatives for school council (discussion on uniform, chosen charities etc), bullying council (code of conduct, members trained to look out for vulnerable children) and student voice (ideas for improvements). Volunteers have to sell themselves to classmates and serve for varying periods, dependent on demand.

Thoughtful year 7 transition: activity day in July; induction evening end August; classes carefully planned to mix children from junior and other schools.

Pupils and parents: Catchment area is West Yorkshire plus small areas of North Yorkshire and Lancashire – majority from Ilkley, Bingley and surrounding areas. Socially and ethnically mixed, reflecting area's demographics. Close to Frizinghall railway station, allowing convenient access by the security guarded Hogwarts Express, as the school calls it. Dedicated school buses cover a wide area from Huddersfield to Headingly.

Notable old pupils: David Hockney (takes an active interest); Denis Healey; Sir Ken Morrison (ex-executive chairman of Morrisons); Dan Scarbrough (England rugby player, on staff); Alistair and Jonathan Brownlee (British Olympic triathletes); a head of BBC news, director of the Royal College of Music, ex-Lord Mayor of London and Archbishop of York.

Entrance: At 11, 12 and 13, exams in English and mathematics (past papers available) in January. Head will also lead a session for year 7 applicants to give them an opportunity to demonstrate their lateral thinking and problem solving skills. Automatic entry for pupils from the junior school.

Candidates for sixth form must have GCSE grade 6 or above in mathematics and English language, 7+ GCSE grades in A level subjects.

Exit: Small number leave post-GCSE for sixth form colleges or state grammars – replaced by new recruits. Sixth formers head for a broad range of universities: northern red-brick, Russell Group, London colleges, usually several to Oxbridge – five in 2018. Seven medics, three dentists and a vet in 2018, with one off to New York Film Academy and another to a degree apprenticeship in law.

Money matters: Very good value – fees at lower end of the scale. Just under 10 per cent have means-tested bursaries, aimed at those with families earning less than £60,000 pa. Music scholarships available.

Remarks: A school that blends traditions with forward thinking and proactive change to meet the challenges its pupils face in and out of school. Academic standards still excellent but it's succeeding changing public perception to recognise that it offers far more than its results. Pupils and parents alike told us that there is something here for everyone, always something to excel at and someone to help you achieve it – and we wouldn't disagree.

Bury Grammar School Boys

Linked with Bury Grammar School Girls

Tenterden Street, Bury, Lancashire BL9 0HN

Ages 4–18 **Pupils** 606 **Sixth form** 133 (joint sixth form)

Fees: £7,992 – £10,755

0161 696 8600
www.burygrammar.com

Principal: Since 2016, Jo Anderson BA (modern languages; University of Leeds), PGCE MEd (secondary curriculum leadership), who became head of the senior girls school in 2015. She is now responsible for the strategic planning for the future of the entire family of the Bury Grammar Schools, boys' and girls', both junior and senior. (Previously she worked at Stockport Grammar, Manchester Grammar, Queen's Chester, latterly as head of the girls' division at the King's School Macclesfield, and has worked across all age ranges and both sexes).

Thoughtful and insightful in all her responses, very easy to talk to, she exudes a quiet efficiency under which almost certainly lurks much inner tungsten. Over the last year, she has implemented a great deal of change ('seismic' was a descriptive term used more than once during our visit), having initiated a far-reaching curriculum review across both senior and junior schools and overseen a couple of changes in senior positions. Prior to her appointment, though the boys' and girls' schools carried the same branding and were only a stone's throw from each other, they pretty much operated as separate entities. This is no longer the case; in effect, there is now something similar to an all-through diamond structure. (Girls and boys are mixed at infants, single sex from junior through to senior, with both genders joining again at sixth form. The sixth form has, in practice, been mixed for some time but is now 'officially so'.) Mrs Anderson says pupils will now have twice as many opportunities going for them. And while both genders have the space to learn with no distractions or barriers, they get to do all their extracurricular activities together. By the time they hit sixth form, they are ready to mix just as they would at university.

The changes seem to be paying dividends as the number of pupils entering in September 2018 at 11+ was up more than 40 per cent across both schools.

Headmaster since 2017: Devin Cassidy BSc (Chemistry, University of Wales, Bangor) PGCE, is headmaster of the senior and junior boys' school. He has been at Bury since 1999, becoming deputy head, then head (prior to that, he worked at Eirias High School, north Wales). He comes across as grounded and calm, qualities he may well have needed during this period of change for the schools. While aware that educating the boys in a single sex environment means they are not inhibited, he is very much in tune with the times; on International Women's Day, he happily declared himself a 'feminist' in assembly, prompting a number of the staff to 'come out' as feminists themselves. It resulted in some fantastic pledges from the boys to support a more equal society. This is a boys', not a lads', school, Mr Cassidy says. A sentiment reiterated within the school magazine, in which he expressed his wish for the boys to be 'grounded, articulate, intelligent and kind'. He recognises the social temperature has changed a great deal with movements like Time's Up and is clear schools have a responsibility 'to stand up as educators and lead the way', 'be the moral compasses'. Likewise, he refers to the school's keenness to increase bursaries and emphasises that it takes great care to monitor boys receiving those bursaries, to make sure they are looked after. Integration needs to be carefully handled, he says.

Head of junior boys' since 2015 is Matt Turner (BSc, University of Wolverhampton) – previously at Cheadle Hulme Junior School – whose great energy and enthusiasm is infectious; in fact a passion for teaching seems to flow from every pore. Mr Turner encourages an interactive learning style within the school and is keen on child-led learning, suggesting the staff need to be brave and flexible, let the children pursue off-curriculum questions, nurture their intellectual curiosity. As with Mr Cassidy, he feels that single-sex education gives the boys space to 'blow off steam' but welcomes the fact that following the curriculum review, 'nothing is off the table' any more, equal opportunities for both genders prevail (this rhetoric is something of a theme across this family of schools). He works closely with the head of the junior girls, sharing books such as the Great Women Who Changed the World by Kate Pankhurst (doing the rounds in junior schools across the country). Parents say he has breathed new life into the school, 'loves his job' and has a genuinely open door policy, being keen that the relationship between parents and school is as good as it can be. A drama teacher, he still teaches and gets to know every boy in the school.

Academic matters: The co-ed infant school, ages 4-7 (there is a pre-school from 2) has a play-based approach to learning, small class sizes and an atmosphere of irrepressible cheeriness. A broad curriculum includes science, geography, thinking skills, as well as the core subjects, which means a nice balance between learning and enjoyment. The classrooms are beautifully and imaginatively decorated, a huge 3D cardboard tree in reception reflecting changes in the seasons. There is specialist teaching for sports and music (and use of the school swimming pool too).

In the junior school, the broad curriculum continues. Following the curriculum review, Latin has been added to years 5 and 6 (alongside the other languages on offer). Mr Turner is a fan of cross-curricular themes, the Egyptians not just being for history but geography and art too. Teaching in class is differentiated with lots of assessments and targets and Mr Turner says they push the core subjects. The maths teaching, he feels, is especially strong. With pupils who are veering ahead, he says they push for mastery, not necessarily to stray into next year's curriculum but for wider knowledge and skills.

Two enthusiastic boys showed us round the school, pointing out their favourite parts; the science lab (which revealed an interesting project on genes) and the lovely art space (the boys' favourite) housed an eco-village, along with marble runs made of wood, plus an interesting display of clay shoes. Lots of corridor displays give it a cheery feel. A rather impressive ensemble of the boys' take on Monet's bridge caught the eye.

Following the curriculum review, there have been certain changes in the senior school (eg studying three languages) and for the first time drama is on offer. GCSE study is now for three years; Mr Cassidy says they want to go slower and deeper. This has meant dropping one or two subjects; one parent lamented that GCSE PE had been dropped.

Mr Cassidy is very tuned in to the emphasis exam boards now place on unseen material and is keen to develop pupils' higher order thinking skills. The boys still study mostly IGSCEs but this is not cast in stone. GSCE results in 2018: 33 per cent of grades were A*-A/9-7.

A level results 33 per cent A*/A (70 per cent A*-B). Strong subjects were chemistry, biology, economics, maths and geography. Following on from the curriculum review, GCSE and A level students are to receive extra teaching time (year 12, 90 minutes extra per subject per fortnight). The school now steers pupils towards nine GCSEs and three A levels. EPQ available and the HPQ is also being introduced at GCSE level.

Half termly assessment is key; based on this, staff can see who might need support to achieve their potential or stretch to more. One parent told us there was a genuine endeavour to deliver personalised learning, referring to the practical lesson tweaks that meant her child could learn more easily. There are drop-in clinics and parents say the teaching is 'second to none' with lots of extra revision sessions after school and on a Saturdays around exams.

There is a full time SENCo who is also able to do all assessments where a teacher might have a concern (some pupils arrive with a report or an assessment). All pupils also meet once a week with a SEN assistant to identify any areas of difficulty, such as organisation.

Games, options, the arts: In the junior school, there are a variety of clubs from gardening to origami and scratch coding. Clubs that used to only be open to the boys, such as climbing, are now open to both sexes. Many activities like swimming and the annual cinema trip are also joint with the girls. One parent praised the residential trips (which kick off in year 4) to places like York and Edale (the latter is all zip wires and fire-building), saying the change in the children, the growth of independence, was marked. There are numerous competitions, both external and internal, from Shakespearean verse speaking and Young Mathematicians to a region-wide general knowledge quiz. Sport is important and includes all the usual suspects, football, rugby, cross-country, athletics, cricket and hockey. Music is strong with orchestras and bands; the school's entry into the annual Ramsbottom Festival usually results in a trophy or two for the choir.

In the senior school, there is vast range of clubs, including some quirky ones, 'apps for good', Mandarin, sign language, conflict simulation. Lots of competitions, such as the Crest Chemistry Award, maths challenge and Latin-speaking. Some interesting opportunities too: the school sends a team to BBC's Media City to watch a programme being made (the rest of the year group remaining in school as a 'news team' for the day). Trips are wide ranging: classics trips to Italy, an annual trip to the First World War Battlefields (Bury School lost many boys during the war and this is remembered every year), and to some far flung places such as Nicaragua.

The vibrant drama department garnered much parental praise and runs with big productions like Little Shop of Horrors and Les Misérables. All very professional.

Sport is dominant at all levels with extras like basketball and badminton added to the junior school offering, all with lots of competitions, some international. Students also fundraise to go on international tours.

CCF is huge in the Bury schools (one of the oldest platoons in the country). Parents felt the resilience acquired from the 'fall down, dust yourself off, learn and move on' mentality was invaluable. Duke of Edinburgh is on offer from year 9 upwards.

There is a steady stream of speakers to the sixth form, some from nearby Manchester University, others big names in their field, like historian Michael Wood. There are also practical work-related visits, such as a trip to the offices of Grant Thornton. Pupils all showed a sense that debate, open discussion and experimenting with ideas are an important part of life. A sixth former referred with enthusiasm to assemblies with TED-style talks on topics such as space exploration and inventions. The responsibility for these talks has been handed to the sixth form, who must do the intro, marketing, write the press release and review afterwards. There are also mock elections, debate clubs, Rhys Davies mock trials, all nurturing that extra spark.

Background and atmosphere: Founded in 1570 in the centre of Bury, the school was originally only open to boys from poorer families. It was re-founded by Revd Roger Kay (a former pupil) in 1726. (The Bury High School opened for girls in 1884.) The boys' school moved close to its current site in 1903, the girls joining them in the same building in 1906. The vast Buckley Wells playing fields were acquired in 1924. In 1966, the boys moved to a new, modern building on the playing fields. From the outside, it is a fairly unprepossessing, all a bit Grange Hill. Inside, though, there are wall displays everywhere and sense of industriousness.

The boys' junior school is housed in the old (and former) Court and Police Station and opened in 1993 (pre-school and infants followed in 2008). The school still retains the original cells, much to the delight of the boys, albeit now under the less exciting guise of music rooms.

Today, the schools are part of an all-singing, all-dancing 45-acre campus (25 acres of which is a short walk down the road), with swimming pool, sports halls, multi-playing surfaces, sports courts and playing fields.

Pastoral care, well-being and discipline: In the junior school, leadership is 'really pushed,' Mr Turner says, referring to the boys' huge pride if they became house captains. There is, he says, an ethos of responsibility. When a boy slips up, they get issued a code of conduct, and a list of positive behaviours. We asked the boys showing us round whether they had ever been issued one and there was an element of palpable relief to their 'no, but we know boys who have'. They knew the code well. There is also a buddy system and 'boys of the week' awards to reward and motivate.

In the senior school, Mr Cassidy considers pastoral to be very strong, saying the staff know the boys very well. Parents agree and describe it as like family. Mr Cassidy alludes to the importance of challenge in the extracurricular, keeping the boys all busy. There is also the school health team, with a nurse and a counsellor for deeper issues.

Pupils and parents: The pull is wide, chiefly from the northern parts of Manchester, Salford, Rochdale, Oldham, with some from Bolton. These areas have some very poor parts within them so parents and pupils tend to be very socially aware and religious tolerance is a given.

Mr Cassidy said one of the aspects which first drew him to the school was the lack of any discernible arrogance in the boys. We would concur. The ones we met were down to earth, nurturing ambition but with no sense of entitlement. They seemed prepared to graft.

There is a parents' forum across the boys' and girls' schools and many parent ambassadors. The parents we spoke to were very much on board with the changes, especially the mixed sixth form (though all said they really valued the separate teaching of each sex, prior to sixth form).

Entrance: Entry into reception is by observation, and into years 1 and 2 by spending half a day in the school. Junior school is a two class entry – 15 to 20 per class – and prospective pupils spend an assessment day (a short interview, a reading comprehension and maths assessment). It's not just about testing, though: the school is looking for intellectual curiosity and a lot of that is gauged through observation and conversation. Those moving from a previous school will need to provide references.

Any pupil joining the junior school prior to year 5 has automatic entrance to the senior school. Virtually all stay on. It is a very rare that it is felt a pupil will fare better in a different school. Transition is easier knowing this, but there are 'experience days' blending external and internal candidates together. Parents say the transition is handled incredibly well; the taster days and intros start early in year 6 so it is a very smooth passage.

External 11+ candidates now sit papers in maths, English and verbal reasoning. Some 120 extra pupils enter the school, 70 per cent from state primaries, 30 per cent from preps.

Exit: Virtually all junior school children go on to the senior school. Some 60 per cent leaves after GCSEs. Durham, Leeds, Liverpool, UCL, Nottingham, Sheffield, Edinburgh, Aberdeen, Newcastle and Warwick currently popular university destinations. Two went on to study medicine in 2018 (including one to Prague), with another off to Texas on a sports scholarship.

Oxbridge candidates have not fared so well over the last year or two (though prior to that, there was a trickle) but Mrs Anderson says they are addressing this and introducing Oxbridge lessons alongside other initiatives and support.

Money matters: A lot more emphasis is being put on scholarships and the school is keen on means-tested bursaries. Mr Cassidy says they visit the families of the latter and have deep understanding of their needs.

Remarks: A vibrant school offering a fantastic array of extracurricular and enrichment activities, as well as delivering excellent academic results. A school leading from the front in educating boys in tune with modern times. A boys' not a lads' school.

B

Bury Grammar School Girls

Linked with Bury Grammar School Boys

Bridge Road, Bury, Lancashire BL9 0HH

Ages 4–18 **Pupils** 1127 **Sixth form** 133 (joint sixth form)

Fees: £7,992 – £10,755 pa

01617 972808
www.bgsg.bury.sch.uk

Principal: Since 2016, Jo Anderson BA (modern languages, University of Leeds), PGCE, MEd (secondary curriculum leadership), responsible for the strategic planning for the entire family of Bury Grammar schools (boys, girls, junior and senior). She has also been head of the senior girls' school since 2015. Previously she worked at Stockport Grammar, Manchester Grammar, Queen's Chester, and latterly as head of the girls' division of King's School Macclesfield. It is a trajectory which has seen her teach across the entire age range of 5-18, and across both genders.

Thoughtful and insightful in all her responses, easy to talk to, she exudes a quiet (and indeed elegant) efficiency under which almost certainly lurks much inner tungsten. Since her appointment, she has implemented much change across this family of schools ('seismic' was a term used more than once during our visit), having initiated a top-to-bottom curriculum review across senior and junior divisions and overseen a couple of changes in senior positions. Prior to her appointment, though the schools carried the same branding and were only a stone's throw from each other, the boys' and girls' schools pretty much operated as separate entities. Now, in essence, the Bury schools have something similar to an all-through diamond structure. Girls and boys are mixed at infants, single sex from junior through to senior, with both genders joining again at sixth form. The sixth form has, in practice, been mixed for some time but is now 'officially so'.

As Mrs Anderson puts it, pupils now have twice as many opportunities going for them. On a basic level this means pupils applying for medicine, for example, can talk to heads of science on both sides of the road. And while both genders have the space to learn separately with no distractions, they do all their extracurricular activities together, share clubs and trips and so by the time they hit sixth form, they are ready to mix just as they would at university.

It may have all been 'seismic', but the changes seem to be paying dividends; the number of external pupils who joined in 2018 at 11+ is up more than 40 per cent across both schools. No mean feat when you factor in that the pass mark for the entrance exam was raised, making the school more academically selective, and bearing in mind this is not a wealthy area of the north overall.

Head of infants and girls' junior since January 2018 is Chrissy Howard (MCIPS Salford University and PGCE). She has been with Bury since 2005; first with Bury boys' junior where she became assistant head, then moving to the girls in 2017. She is very approachable and clearly lovely with the girls. One expects heads to have every detail at their fingertips but she really did, all with an understated efficiency. She understands how crucial it is for girls to have an environment where they can question and explore and, as such, has driven the new outdoors aspect to the curriculum, allowing the girls to problem-solve in fresh air while getting down with nature...and perhaps a little bit muddy too.

Academic matters: The co-ed infant school, ages 4-7 (there is also a pre-school from age 3) has a play-based approach to learning, small class sizes and an atmosphere of irrepressible cheeriness. A broad curriculum including science, geography, thinking skills, as well as the core subjects, means a nice balance between learning and enjoyment. The classrooms are beautifully and imaginatively decorated, a huge 3D cardboard tree in reception reflecting changes in the seasons. There is specialist teaching for sports and music (use of the school swimming pool too).

In the junior school, the broad curriculum continues. Following the curriculum review, a new humanities programme is in place and Latin has been added to year 6, alongside the other languages on offer (although the school is currently still debating whether language tasters or a solid grounding in one would be best). IT is integral to teaching and also as a standalone. Outdoor education a new introduction.

Teaching in class is differentiated, Mrs Howard says, and interventions speedy where an extra bit of support is needed across spelling or maths. A SEN teacher will write personal pupil support programmes when required. Booster groups, with positive titles like 'magical maths', are another form of support. Lots of assessments and targets to ensure all pupils are up to scratch for the transition to the senior school; Mrs Howard says teachers bridge any gap through personalised learning.

In the senior school, class sizes are around 22. A wide curriculum prevails in year 7 and following the curriculum review, both the girls' and boys' schools offer three languages. Any outdated subject divisions – and there were a few, such as food tech for the girls and CDT for the boys – have, happily, been scrapped. Both schools now offer both. Following the changes in both GCSE and A level exams, the school now steers pupils towards sitting nine GCSEs and three A levels. Students also receive extra teaching time (in year 12, an extra 90 minutes per subject per fortnight). Over the three-year GCSE course, students have an extra 20 minutes a fortnight per subject. 2018 A level results in the joint sixth form were a third A*/A and 70 per cent A*-B and at GCSE, around 33 per cent A*-A/9-7 grades.

EPQ is offered to all sixth formers (90 per cent of girls got A*/A in 2018) and the HPQ, which also counts as a GCSE, has been introduced. Half termly assessment is key to see who needs support to achieve their potential or who could stretch to more. Mrs Anderson says they also look at the pupil holistically, at class feedback and any pastoral issues. There are drop in sessions near exams for anyone needing extra help. Parents attest to girls being encouraged to aim high but never being pressured.

A full time SENCo, who is also able to do assessments, works across both boys' and girls' schools. Mrs Anderson stresses all staff are trained to look out for the subtle signs. She feels passionate about this area, says there is no reason why a learning barrier means a pupil can't achieve great things. All SEN pupils also meet once a week with a SEN assistant to identify any areas of difficulty, such as organisation. There is more value added with SEN students, head says, than with others. The girls' school still operates mainly to the GCSE syllabuses (the boys take IGCSEs) but this is not in stone, Mrs Anderson says.

It's also worth adding that as a result of the curriculum review, the school is focussed on strengthening scholarship and raising academic standards. Initiatives like the additional lesson time at A level and a new competitive course preparation programme are, Mrs Anderson says, all about achieving that.

Games, options, the arts: Junior school library displays showed a regular stream of visiting authors. Around the time of our visit, Kate Pankhurst, author of Great Women Who Changed the World, was due to arrive. The year 6 girls who showed us round were fully conversant with all these great women, from Marie Curie to Rosa Parks (Mrs Howard told us the boys had also been studying this).

Clubs are numerous and wide-ranging, from coding to puzzles to the ukulele. Those that used to only be open to boys – fencing and climbing – are now open to girls also. Our guides chatted enthusiastically about the huge engineering club display in the hallway (their entry to a competition run by Manchester University)...and also fizzed about school trips and hosting the local 10 school Association of Junior Independent Schools (AJIS) music festival.

Pupils were also excited about sport, and taking parts in events such as the Manchester Youth athletics and Netball Association matches. Netball, tennis, hockey and swimming are the key pursuits.

Lots of joint activities with the boys, like a disco and annual cinema trip. They do not compete with each other but are invited across to see each other's art exhibition and verse speaking competitions.

Year 6 girls look after the school council and take it very seriously; at the time of our visit they were lobbying for a different sort of school bag to mark out their senior status.

The senior school has a glossy drama department with big productions like Little Shop of Horrors, Annie, Beauty and the Beast. 'You forget you are watching children,' one parent said. Numerous chances to perform in choirs, orchestras and bands and, on a wider stage, in the Ramsbottom Festival.

Great sporting facilities on a huge campus, more usual ones such as netball, hockey, football, tennis, rounders, athletics and now more off-beat sports, like fencing. Many pupils are part of regional and national teams.

CCF is huge (the Bury School CCF is the oldest in the country) and recently extended so that is on offer to girls in years 9, 10 and 11. Duke of Edinburgh from year 9 upwards. There are frequent residential trips, often linked to the curriculum, perhaps to study the Holocaust or a classics trip to Italy.

Clubs are wide ranging– 50 at the last count – running the gamut from 'apps for good', Irish Dancing, sign language, conflict simulation, science in focus, to philosophy and film.

The sixth form pupil showing us round indicated a school-wide appetite for debate, enthusing about assemblies where TED-style talks had started up around topics such as space exploration. The responsibility for the talks – marketing, intro, press release and review – has all been handed to the sixth form. It is clearly a vibrant environment; in an assembly around International World Women's Day, the boys' school headmaster declared himself a feminist, prompting all the staff to come out, spontaneously, as feminists, provoking much chat around what feminism means today. It resulted in some fantastic

pledges to support a more equal society (more boys than girls showed up with pledges).

This school, with the many changes it has undergone, is gearing up for the modern age. Pupils said they felt they really had a voice and were listened to, especially the sixth form. Assemblies end often with the same message: we're interested in your views, do you agree or disagree? Sixth formers often follow up, says head. There are also mock elections, debate clubs, Rhys Davies Mock Trials, all nurturing that extra spark.

Background and atmosphere: The boy's school was founded in 1570, originally only open to boys from poorer families. Bury High School for girls opened in 1884. In 1906, it joined the boys' school on its current site. The vast Buckley Wells playing fields were acquired in 1924 and the boys moved across the road to a new building in 1966.

The girls' building, as you'd expect, has the look and feel of an old grammar, especially in the beautiful old Roger Kay Hall. The relatively new arts centre (the school won a fundraising award for its ingenuity) is a wonderful space for sixth formers to work, faint strains of music filtering from the music department. Great common room, too, and coffee place with a relaxed grown up vibe.

The girls' junior opened next door in 1997; pre-school and infants followed in 2008. The junior school is modern and airy with lovely reading areas strewn with cushions. A light octagonal hall and a little gym (they also use the senior school sports hall). Classrooms all with interactive whiteboards. Lots to stimulate, a Secret Garden theme around the library and super corridor displays; we particularly liked one on a fictitious Museum of Fun, a utopia of attractions galore, all for free – and very Panglossian.

The family of schools is now an all-singing, all-dancing 45 acre campus (25 acres of which is a short walk down the road), with swimming pool, sports halls, multi-playing surfaces, courts and playing fields.

An ex-head girl showed us round the school and while there was a faint whiff (in the best possible way) of 'give me a girl at an impressionable age and she is mine for life', her enthusiasm about her experiences at school was evident and life-defining. She is not alone; Bury may not be on the global map but its alumnae have their share of razzle dazzle, listing among them Victoria Wood, presenter Victoria Derbyshire, actress Kate O'Flynn and TV producer Nicola Shindler.

Pastoral care, well-being and discipline: In the junior school, Mrs Howard recognises that young girls are sensitised to what others think of them so there is a lot of education around being considerate. Mobile phones are locked away and online education is considered crucial. There are buddy groups and the playground is full of activities should a girl find herself on her own for five minutes (which Mrs Howard knows feels like hours in child-time). Parents say that if they ever sense problems, a quiet word with the teacher and the problem 'goes away'. 'It's just dealt with'.

At the senior school, a culture of openness is encouraged. After the 2017 Manchester terrorist attack, where some pupils were present, there were open discussions around how society could pull together more, how to combat terrorism and start fundraising.

They are, Mrs Anderson says, 'really lovely students'. There is a very strong pastoral team and heaps of assemblies on resilience and failure as a learning tool. No mobile phones at school and teachers are alert to well-being issues – there is 'constant monitoring,' Mrs Anderson says. One parent whose child needed that extra bit of care said staff were always 'spot on' in their judgement, could identify problems and stop them escalating. There is a school health team and counsellor.

Pupils and parents: A wide pull, chiefly from the northern parts of Manchester, Salford, Rochdale and Oldham, with some from Bolton. These areas include very poor parts so parents and pupils tend to be socially aware and religious tolerance is a given.

Junior school parents described as supportive and active. Comms are in the process of being improved (emails and texts). Half term assessments and grades shared with parents. There are parents' forums and coffee and cake sessions.

In the senior school, Mrs Anderson says parents are a 'really friendly' group and fully appreciate what the school is seeking to do. There is a parent forum.

Entrance: Entry into reception is by observation, and into years 1 and 2 by spending half a day in the school. Junior school is a two class entry – 15 to 20 per class – and prospective pupils spend an assessment day (short interview, reading comprehension and maths assessment). It's not just about testing, though: the school is looking for intellectual curiosity gauged through observation and conversation. Those moving from a previous school will need to provide references.

Any pupil joining the junior school prior to year 5 has automatic entrance to the senior school. Virtually all stay on. It is a very rare that it is felt a pupil will fare better in a different school. The transition is eased via 'experience days' blending external and internal candidates together.

External 11+ candidates now sit papers in maths, English and verbal reasoning, with a recently increased pass mark. Some 120 extra pupils enter the school, 70 per cent from primaries, 30 per cent from preps – now more external than internal candidates.

Exit: Virtually all junior school children go on to the senior school; around 60 per cent leaves after GCSEs. Durham, Leeds, Liverpool, UCL, Nottingham, Sheffield, Edinburgh, Aberdeen, Newcastle and Warwick currently popular university destinations. Two went on to study medicine in 2018 (including one to Prague), with another off to Texas on a sports scholarship.

Oxbridge candidates have not fared so well over the last year or two (though prior to that, there was a trickle) but this may change; Mrs Anderson says they are introducing Oxbridge lessons, alongside other support.

Money matters: Fees in line with those of other schools in the area. Plenty of means-tested bursaries and a drive towards increasing scholarships across a range of areas.

Remarks: A vibrant school, offering a fantastic array of extracurricular and enrichment activities. Currently delivers good, solid academic results, especially around value-added. A school leading from the front in its emphasis on gender equality and nurturing mutual respect. A positive, uplifting environment for girls.

C

Cardinal Newman College

Lark Hill Road, Preston, Lancashire PR1 4HD

Ages 16–19 **Pupils** 3,548 **RC**

01772 460181
www.cardinalnewman.ac.uk

Principal: Since 2012, Nick Burnham (late 40s). Previously vice principal at Carmel College in St Helen's. Studied economics at Surrey University, then began his career teaching economics at Peter Symonds College in Winchester.

Mr Burnham is a firm believer in stand-alone sixth form colleges and has worked in FE for 24 years. He chairs the Sixth Form College Association and describes the sector as a 'jewel in the crown' of education. He's pretty miffed that its per-student funding levels are lower than both high schools and universities. (Politics is in his blood, he says. His brother is former Labour frontbencher and now mayor of Manchester, Andy Burnham.) As per-pupil funding drops ever further in real terms, so far he's avoided having to make redundancies or cut subjects. He's done this by recruiting a lot more students to the college – an increase of 900 over the last few years.

He was raised in a working class Catholic family in Merseyside and Cheshire and state-educated at local state Catholic schools. Now he's steering the college with the same Catholic and comprehensive values that guided his own schooldays. Mr Burnham says, 'When you cross the threshold of a faith school, you know it straight away'. He doesn't overdo the subject of religion though – he's more interested in talking about the progress the students make here.

He's married with two teenage children. He's warm and sociable – stopping to talk to all and sundry during our tour of the college. Students told us: 'Nick's always around'; 'I always see him in Costa'; 'He smiles at everyone.' (We're all on first name terms here.) After university he had a gap year travelling around America – and high office still hasn't quite killed off his roving spirit: he's promised to take his son to every Everton away game this season.

Academic matters: In 2018, 33 per cent of A level entries were A*/A and 66 per cent A*-B. Cardinal Newman College offers over 50 courses. The majority of students study A levels but many do level 3 BTec courses or a combination of the two. Maths and English are the most popular subjects, with biology, chemistry, business studies and psychology coming up close behind.

The range of A level subjects on offer would rival many an independent school. There are choices even among the core academic subjects – for example the college offers A levels in modern history, early modern history and ancient history. Options beyond the usual include A levels in textiles, dance, digital photography, accounting and graphic design. The range of BTecs on offer is a little narrower, but it covers the bases – launching students on their journeys towards the worlds of business, technology, healthcare, education or the creative industries. Also offers a small range of HE courses – eg foundation degrees in early years or in teaching and learning support.

Class sizes here are a little higher than usual for 16-19 education – about 20 on average – but that's because teachers only take four, rather than the more usual five, A level groups each. This gives them time to run open sessions where students can drop in for one-to-one work, catch-up sessions and small group sessions. This keeps the staff happy, says Mr Burnham, because they're given the time they need to make sure no-one's falling behind, and the students we met all talked about how much they'd got from this system. 'Last year my sociology teacher sat with me lunchtime after lunchtime until I got it,' said one student. 'I was really struggling but she never made me feel like I was annoying her!' 'Teachers are really quick to reply to emails too,' added another. 'I prefer to go back with questions by email and they're fine with that – they find out how you want to learn.'

Students are set ambitious individual targets and allocated a non-teaching 'achievement tutor' who keeps a close eye on how they're doing. If their attainment and attendance is good, they get a lot of freedom, but if it starts to drop, the support becomes rather more intensive. One parent told us how happy she was about the support her daughter gets: 'Every one of her teachers has taken time to ... understand how she learns. Nothing is too much trouble for them...' The college scores particularly highly according to DfE data on value added. Progress is tracked using an online system and analysed term by term. It's popular with parents because they can log in too. One parent, however, was concerned that 'quiet students who cause no problems can fall underneath the radar at times.' She said she'd like the college to 'monitor all students' progress better, not just the troublesome ones.'

Mr Burnham puts the college's success down to high expectations, proactive student monitoring and excellent teachers. He says there is strong 'devolved leadership' here and those heads are 'independent, talented and trusted'. He gives his staff the freedom they need to excel. There is, he says, a 'healthy competition' between teachers – as their success in driving student progress is closely monitored – but there's also a generous staff development budget and rising teacher morale, according to the last two staff surveys. So, although the sector generally struggles to recruit and retain teachers, Newman College does not.

Students here have the chance to gain the EPQ, and can also get hands-on experience in the arts by taking an Arts Award – involving research, volunteering and practical work.

At the other end of the spectrum, just under 100 students are studying for level 2 BTecs or English/maths GCSE retakes. There's also a significant SEND provision here. About 45 students with learning disabilities (serious enough to have an EHC plan already in place) are on the foundation learning studies programme. This course is made up of the three pathways: skills pathway, which focuses on independent living; personal and social development pathway, which focuses on social confidence and personal skills; and the vocational pathway, which focuses on skills for work, volunteering and training. These students may have access to speech and language therapists, social services and the local Young People's Service.

Students on mainstream courses with disabilities or milder learning difficulties also get specialist support from a learning support team. Help available includes one-to-one and small group tuition as well as some in-class support. A sensory impairment service also offers a range of provisions to help students with hearing or visual problems to communicate and access the curriculum.

Games, options, the arts: The college runs elite academies for basketball, football (both only open to male students) and netball (only for female students) – providing training sessions several times a week and specialist coaching. Other sports on offer include badminton, men's, women's and mixed hockey, rugby and women's football. Parents and students feel the college listens to them; they recently started a rugby team and provided it with kit and a coach in response to a request from just a small number of students. Students can also work towards a Community Sports Leadership Award.

As well as art A level, there's an art and design foundation diploma for those wishing to study it at degree level. Art is a huge strength of the college. On the day of our visit an exhibition of A level and art foundation students' work had just been installed. We were truly wowed by the quality, breadth and maturity of the work on display – from prints and delicate handmade textiles to photography, sculpture, life drawings and installations; we struggled to tear ourselves away from the exhibition to look at the rest of the college.

Talented students – whatever they're studying – can audition to join the music academy to get involved with music enrichment activities. There's a dance academy along the same lines too. Dance, drama and musical theatre are big here with BTec and A Level performing arts options. The performing arts department puts on an annual 'musical extravaganza' at Preston's Guild Hall.

There are plenty of opportunities for students to travel. Geographers investigated geysers and volcanoes in Iceland; physicists have toured the CERN facility in Geneva and film students have been to Hollywood. Newman students also get access to the great and the good. A year 13 economics student told us how thrilled he was to be able to present his ideas to a member of the Bank of England's monetary policy committee.

Background and atmosphere: At the heart of the Newman site is Lark Hill House. All red bricks and flourishing ivy, it was built for an 18th century mill-owner, but the college's Catholic roots go back to 1860 when the Faithful Companions to Jesus Sisters bought the mill house and turned it into Lark Hill House School for Girls. Throughout the middle decades of the 20th century it was a direct grant grammar school – still Catholic – but by the late 70s, following changes to education policy and after merging with the sixth forms of two other local Catholic grammar schools, it stopped taking pupils under 16 and was renamed Cardinal Newman College.

The grounds are green and spacious and the buildings are smart, but students did complain that it can be hard to get a seat to eat anywhere – especially when it's raining and no-one wants to sit outside. They also felt the library needed to have more quiet desk space available – although no-one we talked to had had any problems getting hold of the library books they needed and there's also an online library, allowing pupils to read key texts on screen.

Although the spiritual ethos is clearly important to the principal, and Pope Francis beams down at visitors as they sign into the high-tech welcome screen at reception, religion isn't forced down the students' throats. The chaplaincy is inclusive and relaxed: 'There's never any religious pressure,' they claim, and people come from 'all faiths and none at all'. Mass attendance is optional – although all students must go to weekly RE lessons, which are more of an opportunity to chew the fat on contemporary ethical issues than to indoctrinate students on the one true faith. The ethos seems to centre more on Catholic social teaching than heavy-handed religiosity. The chaplaincy team says it aims to 'promote community' and to remind it of its responsibilities to 'create a more just society'. It promotes causes like Fair Trade, social justice campaigns and charities like CAFOD – and perhaps it's through widespread student engagement with charities that you see the most evidence of the Catholic ethos at work throughout the college.

There's an energetic buzz about the place. There are no uniform rules, no prefects or head boys and girls and self-expression seemed to be the order of the day among the students we met. Sociology and politics are thriving courses here and we saw a few political badges and T shirts during our visit.

Students we saw around were so diverse it would be hard to lump them together but none were anything other than polite and friendly. One parent mentioned a gripe, though: 'Students hang around the shops looking like they are up to no good. It's not an easy fix but it does lower the tone of what is going on inside the building when you approach the area.'

One student said the hardest thing for her had been the transition from high school – because hardly any of her friends had come here. 'But, thinking about it,' she reflected, 'it was really welcoming here and I made new friends really quickly.'

C

Pastoral care, well-being and discipline: Several parents called the college's pastoral care and discipline 'excellent'. Pastoral care 'seems relevant and covers both academic progress and also well-being,' said one parent and another added that that 'staff care about the individual, not just the class, and this is evident in the way my child holds his teachers in such high esteem.'

The achievement tutors track students' progress and attendance and pull out all the stops to intervene if one starts to fall below target. Senior tutors oversee the pastoral care. One mum told us her son's tutor had been in 'regular contact' with her by phone and email and that her 'focus, determination and belief in my son has helped him to achieve the excellent grades he has just received.'

Principal says there's 'very little' bullying and what they do occasionally encounter is usually 'something on Facebook.' No-one we spoke to raised bullying as an issue. As you'd expect, there are clear behaviour and anti-bullying policies but 'we don't spy on the students online or anything like that,' says Mr Burnham. 'It's really not an issue'.

Parents describe discipline as 'firm but fair'. Principal says it's very rare that they ask a student to leave and they do allow second chances or the opportunity to re-start a course if things have gone wrong. Red lines, as you'd expect, around the use of drugs or alcohol on site or anyone involved in supplying drugs.

Pupils and parents: Students travel in from as far afield as Blackpool, Lytham, Ormskirk and the Lake District. Around 30 per cent tick the practising Catholic box; there are many students from other faiths and more with no faith at all.

With so many students and such a wide range of subjects on offer there's a real mix of students. Certainly it's an attractive offer for high achievers with their eyes on top universities, but its entry requirements are less demanding than nearby competitors so there's a comprehensive experience.

The college tries to strike a balance between the nurture students will have had at school and the independence they can expect at university, so parents don't get involved in college life much day to day – although there are parents' evenings and report systems. Parents we spoke to seemed to have been involved in the choosing of the college – praising its ethos and results – but were now happy to take a back seat and allow their children some freedom.

Former students include former Labour MP Helen Southworth, Paralympic athlete Isaac Towers, footballer Sean Haslegrave and snooker player Cliff Thorburn. There is also a handful of successful actors – but no household names.

Entrance: You don't have to be Catholic to get in but it helps – a bit. Students come from about 50 different schools, but the college has 10 partner schools – all Catholic – and students applying from those schools will take priority over other applicants if a course is oversubscribed. But this doesn't seem to be a huge issue at the moment. It's a big college that survives by getting the numbers in so, the principal says, 'we can normally fit people in'.

To study for A levels here you need to have two 6s and three 4s in your GCSEs – including at least a grade 4 in maths and English (or a commitment to resit or study them further). Applicants will also be interviewed by teaching staff and bring a school report with them. Mr Burnham says they're looking

C

for a good attendance record and students' ability to talk about themselves and their interests.

Exit: Fourteen to Oxbridge and 24 medics in 2018, plus one off to Harvard. Some three-quarters of leavers go on to higher education, around 25 per cent of these to Russell Group universities. Many students choose universities in northern cities – the universities of Leeds, Manchester, Liverpool and Newcastle are favourite destinations – but the single most popular recent destination is 20 minutes' walk away: the University of Central Lancashire in Preston. We're guessing this may tell us more about whether students feel they can afford to go away to university than anything else.

The college's HE+ Programme helps students aspiring to go to a Russell Group university. The programme is run in conjunction with Cambridge University and the college is the only Cambridge University Hub for Lancashire.

Careers support is particularly strong for students planning careers in teaching, engineering or healthcare. They can sign up for the Futures Programme – a specialist enrichment programme giving students the chance to meet and learn from professionals in their chosen fields. Some aspiring medics also benefit from the Preston Widening Access Programme – run in conjunction with the Manchester University medical school.

Money matters: Students don't have to pay for extracurricular activities or to be part of the academies. There are no course fees, although parents could sometimes be charged for additional books and materials. Financial help for subject related trips, is at the discretion of the head of department, but the college says it will 'always offer help if required'. If the trip is compulsory and the student is on a bursary this would be paid for through the bursary.

Remarks: A buzzing community full of bright, opinionated and diverse students. Aspirations are high but don't expect to be spoon-fed. If your child is confident and independent and will make the most of the outstanding teachers, then the sky's the limit.

Casterton, Sedbergh Preparatory School

Linked with Sedbergh School

Kirkby Lonsdale, via Carnforth, Lancashire LA6 2SG

Ages 6m–13 **Pupils** 228 **Boarders** 35 full, 29 weekly (from 9 years)

Fees: Day £8,310 – £16,185; Boarding £19,425 – £23,910 pa

01524 279200
www.sedberghprep.org

Headmaster: Since September 2017, Will Newman, previously deputy head of Taunton Prep. He has also been housemaster and head of boarding at Edgeborough Prep in Surrey. Education degree from Exeter; won a commonwealth scholarship to study at the University of Victoria, Canada, where he got an MA in PE. Interested in sport and music: currently concentrates on the guitar. Married to Liz, a science and maths teacher, and they have two children who have joined the school.

Entrance: Assessment by head's interview and previous school report for younger children; English, maths and cognitive ability tests for year 4 upwards.

Exit: Around 80 per cent to Sedbergh senior school.

Remarks: Eggs, 'laid with love' (says the sign) from the free range chickens here, plus the goats and the rabbits bring out the 'softer side of a prep school'. The children, while not quite 'free range' (tiger mothers and helicopter parents need not worry), have an abundance of outdoor space and room to breathe. They mostly ignore the glorious views and the weather that changes almost hourly; they are too busy enjoying their childhood.

Housed in a range of buildings, with plenty to spare; specialist science labs, inspirational art studios, music and superb sports facilities, these prep and pre-prep children are enjoying all the benefits of this former senior school that enable school to put STEAM subjects at the very heart of its academic provision. In addition to this very much 21st Century education, philosophy now on curriculum along with critical thinking and problem solving skills. Years 7 and 8 now work towards building their SPACE (Sedbergh Prep: academic, community and extracurricular) profile, with achievements through all walks of school life duly recognised. With reference to the relatively recent merger, parents say, 'it was the best thing that could have happened' – Casterton parents with older girls may disagree somewhat, but undoubtedly the feel-good factor is back and they are bucking the trend in this northern demographic with excellent post-merger recruitment figures and a good solid number of boarders. This is no mean feat in a school tucked away with no passing traffic; you have to seek it out, but advice from parents is 'if you are at all unsure, go and take a look – and take your children with you, that'll do it'. Most of us have at some point seen teary parents and weeping children at school gates at some point – well, here the children were weeping because they'd been for a taster morning and didn't want to leave..

Variously described as a 'broad church' and 'a good all-round education', the facilities are matchless for a prep school, having originally been designed for pupils up to A level. Note the six full size science labs, massive sports hall with cricket nets and a bowling machine, swimming pool, Astroturf, music practice rooms and much more besides, and they make full use of every bit of it. Nothing precious about it; parents say the children 'live in it' rather than 'just exist', and whilst they are quick to add that 'it's the people who really make the place', they also tell us they feel as though they have 'hit the jackpot here'.

You can bring your bike, you can also bring your horse – though not essential if you have a love of riding, as the school has 10 ponies that they happily loan. Work hard and play hard could be the school's motto, though presumably only if translated into Latin; the energy is astounding, before, during and after school. Rugby, hockey, cricket, netball and much more besides mean that there is no lack of fresh air and exercise. For obvious reasons, the location means that boarding makes sense, and it also allows you to join in with activities ranging from a parachute regiment leadership day to abseiling, bouldering, go-karting, clay pigeon shooting, bushcraft, and (for the gentler soul) cheese-tasting; essentially, you just 'don't stay in'. But when you do, there are 3D printers to programme, Lego robots to build and rockets capable of zooming to heights of close to 100m to create.

The pupils are a refreshing and captivating blend of childlike naivety and honesty alongside a wisdom that belies their years. Shoe-polishing night for boarders, fastening your top shirt button and a ban on chewing gum are happily tolerated by pupils, but, for them, the deal-breaker would be bullying, 'a real no-no', as is anything which essentially 'makes the atmosphere less friendly'. All meals are prepared in-house from, as far as possible, local produce; adults sit with the children in mixed age groups and apparently the curry is legendary.

Boarding accommodation, in rooms with views to die for, is spacious and homely; there are kitchens for extra toast-making and generally hanging out, plus a sitting room with TV and games for the boys; similar though slightly smaller and prettier accommodation for the girls with the obligatory One Direction posters. It's so quiet here that one boarder told us he falls asleep each night to the sound of the birds singing outside, and then they wake him up again in the morning.

Parents are a mix of medics from Lancaster, local business owners and landed gentry; tweed is somewhat de rigueur – practical and stylish, as befits the place. It's only a 15 minute drive to the senior school from here so parents and staff can and do manage both. Parents say it 'doesn't matter what car you drive, or even if you land your helicopter on the back field, you're made very welcome here'. House staff use Twitter to keep parents of boarders up-to-date, regular photos home of joyful, smiling children.

Clearly the merger and change of status required careful handling, but thanks to good management and huge parental advocacy, they've not only survived but thrived. A portrait of old girl Charlotte Brontë still hangs in the sitting room, and although it's still slightly old school here (and all the better for that – good manners and etiquette still count), she'd hardly recognise the warm and happy place it is today.

Clifton School

Linked with St Peter's School, York, St Olave's School

Clifton School and Nursery, Clifton, York YO30 6AB

Ages 3–8 **Pupils** 225 **C of E**

Fees: £7,980 – £9,240 pa

01904 527361
www.cliftonyork.org.uk

Head: Since 2011, Phil Hardy BA PGCE (mid 40s). Played hockey for England as a young man; studied sports science (psychology) at Northumbria University and worked as sports psychologist at the University of Alberta in Canada, before discovering he loved teaching. Fifteen years at Yarm Prep, where he taught science, maths and PE, rising to head of pre-prep and acting head. Covers lessons at Clifton and coaches boys' and girls' hockey at St Peter's, where he is part of the leadership of sport across the three schools. IAPS Council member, on education and strategy committees and pre-prep advisory group, plus pre-prep and early years IAPS national adviser, supporting state and independent schools. Wife is an HR director at Morrisons; son of 9 at St Olave's. Enjoys coaching rugby, hockey and cricket for York, playing the guitar, theatre, reading and travelling.

Lots of charm, very approachable, open, enthusiastic, sensible and refreshingly honest, with a good sense of humour. Very popular with the children – nursery and reception little ones rushed up to hug him as we visited their play area – and parents: 'fantastic leadership..he went beyond what a head could normally be expected to do when my child had a problem'. An impressively innovative and creative thinker on education, deeply committed to progressive ideas taken from a wide range of international sources and founded on solid research: he changed the curriculum from subject to theme based; replaced rules with values teaching and re-planned the school to constitute a remarkably attractive and well designed learning environment. Aims to develop intrinsically motivated children who want to learn from the pleasure it gives them, who know how to learn effectively and behave well because they understand why the values they are taught are good ones to live by. Keen to educate parents in the reasons underpinning theme based learning and receptive to their views, which they have an opportunity to express in termly forums. Instead of sending teachers off on to professional development courses, he shrewdly organises an open annual conference, including a range of inspirational educational speakers and workshops, attended by over 200 delegates.

Entrance: Sixty nursery and 20 year 3 places (high demand). External applicants have 90 minute family tour with head, then taster day, available throughout the year. Year 3: online testing in maths, mental maths, reading, spelling and non-verbal and verbal reasoning. Looking for children who are nationally average or above in ability.

Exit: Most transfer automatically to St Olave's. Some to Bootham (across the road).

Remarks: Exceptionally imaginative and creative approach to learning, based on a theme per term (no repeats), integrating subjects and skills – practical, emotional and social as well as academic – and dynamically connected to children's interests and ongoing discoveries, enabling them to see learning as purposeful and highly enjoyable. Depth of understanding and independence promoted.

Themes begin with a Stunning Start, eg A Spoonful of Sugar began with reception children receiving a parcel containing three clues as to their new topic in the Easter holidays. As they walked into school, they encountered a box office with flashing lights in the corridor and a big, red popcorn machine outside. The classroom doors had been replaced by red stage curtains tied in golden bows. Their room had been transformed into a theatre consisting of a stage, dressing room and various topic areas. Themes end with a Fabulous Finish, in this case performing a medley of songs from the musical with actions.

Another theme led to the children, moved by the plight of communities living on landfill sites in Cambodia, making recyclable goods that they sold in pop up shops and cafes, raising over £2,000 for a charity that provides children with wellington boots to wear while whilst working on these sites to earn money to pay for their own schooling.

Four cartoon-style Learning Superheroes with superpowers teach key qualities for all stages of education (and life): being reflective, collaborative, resourceful and resilient. Growth mindset ideas also very strong here. The home grown assessment structure provides highly individualised and dynamic records.

Teachers relish the freedom to focus on making lessons fun and deeply fruitful. They engage in professional research and have the confidence to use videos of their lessons to discuss their teaching with colleagues – understandably, all the ones we saw seemed remarkably cheerful: retention not a problem here.

Italian (from nursery) and Mandarin, chosen to provide exposure to two very different cultures and language structures, are taught by specialist teachers, as are music, PE and swimming. Some 15-20 per class; max 20. Very well supplied with IT resources – children learn to use a wide range of apps.

Plenty of outdoor learning in the forest school, where children can have a happy, muddy time.

Instead of school rules, children are taught the whole school's seven central values – friendship, trust, wisdom, compassion, endurance, humility and hope – through assemblies and PSHE. Certificates with colourful cartoons are awarded weekly to values champions (and learning super heroes).

Special needs covered by a joint Clifton and St Olave's SENCo (plans to appoint a separate Clifton one); also two members of staff trained in teaching emotional literacy and two who have counselling expertise.

Housed in an attractive white building, the original St Olave's, plus a more modern red-brick one. Very well resourced, spacious, colourful classrooms – a sense of no expense being spared and much thought put into their planning. Reception rooms have lantern lights or lights with umbellas for shades, plus fab play area with scrapmonger's corner, big sand area with climbing frame, wild area with pond, water play area and even an old fashioned water pump. A room for children not used to separation from their mothers, who need to start in a more protected way, contains a big tent hung with sparkling lights; extra quiet room for children who want to work on their own. A delightful feature on the ground floor is a small, charming well-being cabin with an open front, equipped with toys and books, for children who need a quiet space to recover from an upset. We asked if any children ever invented one to take advantage of it: Mr Hardy was candid enough to admit this had been known to happen.

The second floor is a converted atrium, containing a light, bright, lavishly stocked library. We enjoyed the illustrated knickers hanging from a line in one classroom – part of the Kings, Queens and Corgis theme – and particularly liked the big collaborative artworks, such as a chieftain's headdress made of real feathers.

Access to senior school sports facilities plus own Astro play surface. Sports include tag rugby, netball, hockey, gymnastics and dance – matches from year 2; all year 3s represent the school, so they can develop.

Masses of music: all year 3s learn to play a string, woodwind and brass instrument, with specialist teachers, in class lessons; 50 per cent have individual lessons in a wide range of instruments – lots of ensembles plus bands (eg Garage music). Takes part in Young Voices (national, mega-scale choir performances); professional musicians work with children, as do senior school students. Much drama, dance and art. The end of year review and celebration, in which all children participate, 'is amazing,' enthused a parent.

Very wide range of co-curricular activities, including yoga, Mandarin, street dance, film making, bell ringing and sign language, and lots of trips – the centre of York is within walking distance. All year 3s are charity ambassadors or helping hands, eg helping with the nursery and reception children and library. School council helps organise events such as Clifton's Got Talent and charity drives – over 12k raised for Walking with the Wounded.

Immensely satisfied parents – 'fantastic' is a word that recurs. They appreciate the flexible, light touch attitude to homework – especially the ones who have fled from the academically driven London prep school scene; the exciting learning activities that also stretch the children 'in a kind, playful way'; and the high quality before- and after-school care (charges only kick in at 4.15pm). Also the availability of the head and teachers, seen as very committed, passionate about teaching and 'fantastic at dealing with problems' in a very systematic way, who are very well supported by the teaching assistants ('lovely – they are full time and keep to the same class, so they get to know the children very well'); the amount of communication, eg about the rationale underlying the teaching approach; plus not having to produce costumes for performances – much to the relief of the mother of a child cast as a Brussel sprout in the nativity play, written by the class teacher: 'They go the extra mile, do little, quirky things other schools don't but could'. Parents are generous with their own time, too – happy to volunteer ('You get a thank you letter from the class teacher if you accompany a trip'); the PTA is 'exceptionally active'. The only niggle we heard was about the shortage of parking spaces.

Something enormously exciting is happening here – we can completely understand why Clifton has a national reputation, with many visitors from the education profession, and won the 2018 Times Educational Supplement award for best pre-prep/prep school. These happy, very engaged, active children are extremely fortunate to start their school life here.

Dallam School

Milnthorpe, Cumbria LA7 7DD

Ages 11–18 **Pupils** 974 **Sixth form** 197 **Boarders** 123

Fees: Day free; Boarding £11,806 – £13,155 pa

015395 65165
www.dallam.eu

Headteacher: Since May 2018, Nigel Whittle (30s), previously head of Oldham Academy. Brought up in Blackpool, the son of an electrician, he went to Lancashire University to study for his teaching qualification. After learning his trade teaching English, he was selected for a four-year leadership programme with Future Leaders, which aims to put talented individuals at the head of schools in underprivileged areas. He has been deputy head in a deprived area of Blackpool and principal of Haverlock Academy in Grimsby. He has two young daughters, loves running and is an avid Blackpool Football Club fan.

Academic matters: 'Learning for All, Learning for Life' is both the school's motto and its mantra. Excellent track record of outstanding achievement in exams with the full range of GCSEs, BTecs, A levels and IB on offer. Despite the broad intake, it sits very comfortably alongside selective schools in the area, beating national averages: 18 per cent A*-A/9-7 at GCSE in 2018 and 13 per cent A*/A, 37 per cent A*-B at A level. All creditable, alongside an IB average of 34 points. As the only IB state school in Cumbria, it flies the flag for high achievement. Most stay on into sixth form post-16, around 30-40 per cent following the IB route. Also offers the IBCP or IB career-related programme, which includes at least two diploma programme courses plus career-related studies.

The school is proud of its inclusive ethos, so those with special educational needs are well catered for, and proud of its approach to independent learning, teamwork and activity – didactic teaching methods aren't welcome here. There is a bilingual option for year 7 starters, though competitive so not guaranteed. Good primary liaison helps a smooth transition, important with more than 40 feeder schools. Teaching areas are well-equipped and unusually tidy, as are corridors and shared spaces. There are seven science labs and impressive teaching suites for design technology and food technology.

Spanish and French taught throughout, Italian and German on offer for the sixth form. Super-keen linguists can access other languages through the school's community education wing. Class sizes are around 30, apart from sixth form, where they are smaller. In addition to a range of sport and music options, lunchtime and after-school clubs offer curriculum support in science, art, maths, business studies and a Geek club – seems good to us that this is somewhere where it's acceptable to be a geek..because whatever it is, we'd like to be part of it.

Attracts a strong pool of teaching staff, the adventure learning programme proving a great added attraction. Add to that the fact that you can train to teach here under the South Cumbria SCITT umbrella, the school widens and deepens the pool in which it can fish for good teachers, embracing energy, enthusiasm and talent from those new to the profession.

Games, options, the arts: Two great sports halls at the Milnthorpe site, fitness suite and Astroturf plus multiple pitches nearby, so the school is well-equipped for year-round sport. Add to that a further sports hall at Heversham (home to the boarders) alongside all-weather tennis courts. They are serious about their sport but don't claim to beat all-comers, perhaps because they don't major in any one sport, preferring to offer a wider range than most; that said, we met a lovely netball player currently playing at national level, so no lack of inspiration or aspiration. The BTec outdoor programme sees students paddling rivers, surfing waves, capsizing canoes and mountain walking, clearly fearless in all weathers. A good range of sport is also on offer as twilight sessions for local primary pupils plus Easter and summer holiday sports camps, offering 'classic adventures'; sounds a bit Swallows and Amazons, but we are in the right part of the country for that and they are open to all and hugely popular.

Dallam was the first in the UK to gain Adventure Learning School status. Taking advantage of proximity to both the Lake District and Yorkshire Dales national parks, students and staff participate in canoeing, hiking, camping and other assorted adventurous pursuits. Year 7 students have a residential experience at Borrowdale and year 8 at Ennerdale, and the principles of outdoor challenge are embedded across the whole curriculum. Typically this will involve different subject departments working together with students on extended studies, often of an investigatory nature, proving learning need not be entirely classroom-based.

Excellent music teaching here with the usual range of instruments available for individual tuition plus various choirs and two bands, including a swing band, and a strong ensemble. Christmas celebrations include a visit to the village church for nine lessons and carols with the music department featuring large. Drama is strong and popular and students tell us that these are the areas where the younger ones have the opportunity to work alongside the sixth form – something they clearly value. High quality drama productions are enjoyed by parents and pupils alike – much talk about the recent production of Oliver!

High quality artwork on display in many areas – pride is clearly evident here. A drama studio, separate dance studio, theatre and large sports hall add to the mix on offer; there's even an outdoor performance area with covered stage that would probably be used much more than it is were it not in Cumbria.

Boarding: For boarders there is even more on offer here. Lots of extra sport plus weekend shopping trips for those needing a retail fix, overnight camping in tepees, paintballing, waterfall and mountain hiking, cinema outings, ice-skating, visits to the theatre and opera, attending pro football and rugby matches, raft-building as well as seasonal activities such as carol singing and bonfire night.

Boarders' home-from-home is the former Heversham Grammar School in the tiny upmarket village of Heversham. It's not far from school but far enough and different enough to feel like home, at least during term time. If you are up in time, you take the minibus shuttle into school each day and back late afternoon or evening. If you're a late riser you'll have to walk and make your excuses when you get there. Parts of the building are Hogwarts-ish: the charmingly named 'big school' is a communal space within the former school hall, with high ceilings, impressive fireplaces and honours boards of former pupils on display.

A plethora of outbuildings and green play space house a music studio, all-weather floodlit tennis courts, sports hall and a wet store housing climbing ropes, wetsuits and kayaks. There is also a fives court much loved by old boys and an allotment and chicken house. Staff are lovely – buckets of warmth and care and very much on their game. Well-behaved sixth formers have individual ensuite rooms, all in very good nick; younger boarders are in rooms of two, three or four – less space, but it's their space and that's important. Updating and improving of facilities is ongoing – this isn't the smartest accommodation but it is more than adequate. Unusually, girls outnumber boys in the boarding stakes, but only slightly, and for peace of mind there is fobbed and timed security into all the main buildings and also between boys' and girls' dorms.

Twenty-one different nationalities make up the boarding set – 'a multi-cultural dimension from which everybody benefits,' says the head. There is some clustering, mostly down to word-of-mouth approval and recommendations from existing and former parents – currently the largest groups of boarders are from Italy (the school is apparently big in Tuscany), Majorca and the Emirates. They hope to admit more home-grown boarders as part of a plan to future-proof the facility. The boarders are important on many levels. They add real diversity to the community: 'Some of the most interesting people I've met here are from other countries,' said one pupil; they also, crucially, make the sixth form and IB provision viable in a rural area which really couldn't sustain either of these options without them. Home-cooking, all on-site with menus adapted according to national and international preferences (though the request for sushi hasn't yet been met) and staff keep busy with relentless laundry, all very motherly rather than matronly – there's real warmth and pride in looking after their charges here.

Background and atmosphere: A long and interesting history has created a school with traditional values within a modern setting. The original school was founded in 1613 by Edward Wilson (whose descendants still live locally and continue to work with the school). It all began a mile or so away with the former Heversham Grammar School, now home to the boarders and Dallam community education. The main Dallam School teaching hub is on the site of the former Milnthorpe secondary, all of which has benefited hugely from £12m investment in recent years, creating an attractive, multi-purpose teaching site. Predominantly low level buildings with green paint, the site is very well-maintained with a good car park, plenty of recreational space and residential housing at the perimeter fence. The mountains of the Lake District can be seen in all directions, and whilst on the edge of the large and pleasant village of Milnthorpe, you are a very long way from a Starbucks. The students don't seem to mind this in the least – they describe feeling 'safe' here, a fact which, according to them, allows them more independence, and indeed it does exude a calm yet purposeful atmosphere. The academic challenge is self-evident, but there are also plenty of opportunities for community involvement, public speaking and charity events for those happy to take up the additional challenges on offer – in fact if you don't, 'you'd be missing out,' say parents.

Pastoral care, well-being and discipline: They tuck their shirts in when they see us approaching and girls are nudged into compliance if their skirts are too short – so they know who's in charge. 'We're pretty well-behaved here, it's because we're rural kids,' said one sixth former, summing up the general view. Of course with a mixed intake of teenagers they, like every school in existence, have a few angry young men and scowling girls, but they're definitely in the minority and are carefully monitored and gently prodded into line. Peer pressure being what it is, conformity is the watchword here and parents praise the highly effective Dallam Learner Profile, an achievable and measured reward system of 'soft skills' in years 7,8 and 9 that leads very conveniently into DofE later. Parents tell us that communication is good, 'most staff return calls swiftly, parents are taken seriously, our concerns addressed and we are kept informed of outcomes. Online Parentmail and reliable and useful reporting systems are a bonus'.

Staff are visible in and around the school site, keeping a watching brief, and relationships between staff and pupils manage to appear both friendly and businesslike at the same time. Plenty of responsibility given to pupils, which they like; everyone seems clear on their role in keeping the place ticking smoothly.

Pupils and parents: The parents are mixed and far-flung many with interesting career profiles; liberal-minded university types from Lancaster, plenty of local teachers and headteachers, professionals, farmers and businessfolk from Kendal, Morecambe, Grange and beyond, who are attracted by a school that feels rural yet doesn't suffer the restraints of small rural secondaries elsewhere in the area. It may be sited in a large village, but strong numbers means there are no problems in generating sports teams, maintaining a healthy sixth form and being able to offer good facilities, making it the envy of others.

Pupils are a likeable bunch, at ease with themselves and their surroundings but with no lack of aspiration and ambition. Prefects set an example in all areas; sixth form prefects have walkie-talkies giving them direct access to staff if they feel the need to bring in the heavies whilst on duty and amusingly, even in this digital age when all carry a mobile phone, their walkie-talkies are the envy of younger prefects. They describe their teachers as 'friendly and supportive,' which is always good to hear. They also tell us that the food is good, 'better than it used to be,' apparently, and the bacon buns, if you arrive for breakfast, are 'legendary'. Uniform is smart with a trad blazer badge and lapel badges indicating awards and honours; shirts and ties for all; most are very well turned out and the head will let them know if they don't meet the required standards. For sixth form it's a dress code which appears a little vague in interpretation – no jeans, T shirts or hoodies is clear enough, but there's possibly too much wriggle room in the term 'business wear', certainly for the girls.

Entrance: Over 40 feeder schools, some large, some tiny rural schools, from near and far. No appeals as yet, all wanting a place have one, but that may change in the near future with growing demand. For year 7 day pupil entry, apply via the local authority (unselective). Sixth form applicants need to have at least five 9-4s at GCSE (or foreign equivalent), including English and maths, to study on the IB or A level programme. IBCP students need to have a minimum of four 4s and two 3s at GCSE. Boarding applicants must have right of residence in the UK and be 'suitable for boarding'.

Exit: Some 50-60 per cent stay post 16, a small number move on to sixth forms elsewhere (mainly because of subject choices), others to apprenticeships. No NEETS here; all have a career plan. At 18 the majority go into higher education; 2018 courses include medicine at Manchester, Chinese and Spanish at Leeds, drama and theatre arts at Goldsmiths, veterinary science at Nottingham and business management at Northumbria. Several overseas: the Netherlands is currently popular (and free). Notable former pupils include: Times cartoonist Peter Brooke, opera singer Emma Stannard and BBC journalist and presenter Rob Broomby.

Money matters: Fees for boarding but not for tuition.

Remarks: 'It's ambitious for all its pupils and is small enough to know each one,' a parent told us. Certainly the academic challenge is wider than most and rigorous, too, but there's plenty of room for all-comers, at least for now. Though as a state school with boarding and the IB option to boot, interest in the school is, unsurprisingly, growing from far and wide.

Dame Allan's Junior School

Linked with Dame Allan's Schools

Hunter's Road, Spital Tongues, Newcastle upon Tyne NE2 4NG

Ages 3–11 **Pupils** 310

Fees: £7,266 – £10,419 pa

01912 246770
www.dameallans.co.uk

Head of junior school: Since September 2018, Geoff Laidler, previously head of St Agnes Catholic Primary School in Crawcrook. An old boy of Dame Allan's, he studied music at Durham, but found his true calling whilst volunteering with his sister, a primary school teacher. PGCE from Northumbria, worked at various NE primary schools before being appointed head at St john Boste, Washington, then St Agnes. His wife is also an Allanian, and the pull of his childhood school was strong when this headship came up.

Entrance: Pupils may start in school nursery at age 3 after a taster session; informal assessment for entry to reception at age 4. Standardised tests in reading, mathematics and non-verbal reasoning from year 2 on.

Main feeder schools are West Jesmond, Newcastle Prep School, Gosforth Schools and Ponteland Middle School. Pupils mainly from Morpeth, Ponteland, Gosforth and Jesmond. Transport provided by parent-run school buses, a shuttle to senior school site in Fenham for onward travel on school transport, often with older siblings.

Exit: Almost all pupils go on to Dame Allan Boys' or Girls' Schools. Year 6 prepared for the transition, spending Tuesday afternoons at the Fenham campus with sessions of art and technology, music and using the library. Otherwise mostly to Newcastle independent day schools.

Remarks: Purpose built school, opened in 2012 on the six acre site of a former Victorian hospital in Spital Tongues, to the north of the city centre. First time ages 3 to 11 have been under one roof. A 24 place nursery, two forms per year to year 4 (maximum 15 per class to year 2, then 20 per class) and then three forms for years 5 and 6.

Attractive two storey, fully accessible building surrounded by three separate play areas, one for EYFS leading directly from their self-contained area, one for KS1 and a third for KS2. Good selection of play apparatus appropriate for each stage of development and KS2 area marked out for netball. Luxury of an all-weather playing surface for other traditional team sports, together with adequate grass pitches.

Ground floor houses nursery and reception with their own separate entrance; KS1 classrooms are designed so that children can work and play together in safe 'breakout areas', moving inside and out. Classrooms are paired and pupils in each 'pair' have their own cloakrooms and toilets. Two multi-purpose halls provide space for assemblies, lunch, parent meetings and gym, dance and indoor games.

Classrooms for the older children are on the upper floor, again with a separate entrance. The library is also on this floor, its red colour and prominent shape (which protrudes through to the building's façade – certainly a conversation piece) an overt statement that learning is at the heart of the school. Shared librarian from senior school takes weekly library lessons for all. Designated art, design and science room has the resources for making short films. Year 6 science club has additional use of senior school laboratories. Great attention to detail has been put into every aspect of this building resulting in an excellent, pupil focused learning environment.

The move to one site has enabled the school to review the consistency of teaching, marking and assessment throughout the school and ensure consistent differentiation in class teaching.

The nursery is bright and well-resourced with two linked reception rooms. French and weekly library sessions from age 3. Home/school diary for each child recording daily life – an example of the quality of care and commitment provided. Numeracy and literacy in the mornings and topic based activity in the afternoons. Specialist PE, dance, drama and French teaching.

Broad curriculum in both KS1 and KS2, specialist French but no Latin, thinking skills recently introduced and learning outdoors, to make best use of the natural environment on their new site. Parents we spoke to said 'staff are fantastic', and that they feel children are being taught in a 'professional, caring, nurturing and safe environment'. Small number of children with SEN – dyslexia – supported in class and one-to-one; even smaller number with EAL requirements, all of whom can access the curriculum. As you might expect in new build, wireless throughout, banks of laptops, even iPads in EYFS.

Full written reports to parents each summer; effort and attainment grades each term; parents' evenings autumn and summer terms. Parents feel informed and appreciate that the school is 'very honest with their views' about the children.

Traditional team sports timetabled and teams from under 9s upwards with fixtures against other NE independent schools. Swimming at local pool in Fenham and athletics with record of success, particularly in athletics. Competitive tennis and squash for year 6.

Music is strong and getting stronger. In year 3 all pupils have vocal/violin coaching on 10 week rota with taster sessions in brass and woodwind in years 5 and 6. New facilities provide opportunity for more choral and dramatic performances. Year 6 production each summer term.

Excellent pastoral care. Children seem happy, at ease and confident in their environment. Assemblies for reception upwards; taking part in the birthday hat celebration and being serenaded by the audience delighted the older children – and a teacher as well. Thought-provoking moral message in the ad hoc adaptation of a well-known children's tale to the extreme climatic events on the day we visited.

Pre- and after-school care from 7.45am to 5.45pm. Lunchtimes long enough to enjoy the freshly produced food and participate in a choice of activities. Year 1 upwards can select from a range including astronomy and the interestingly named Megaballs. After school choice includes fencing and Irish dancing.

Children well prepared for move to single sex senior schools. There are opportunities for positions of leadership in the last year, with head boy and girl and four heads of house. Representatives on school council from reception to year 6 have a voice. Numerous community projects, pupils sent Christmas cards to children in an orphanage in Kenya and have raised money through an Easter egg raffle to sponsor three children for a year.

Active house system used to accumulate house points (academic and pastoral achievements) and competition across a number of activities. Individual and class certificates awarded, with a trophy each month. Head's star awards most coveted.

D

Dame Allan's Schools

Linked with Dame Allan's Junior School

Fowberry Crescent, Fenham, Newcastle upon Tyne NE4 9YJ

Ages 11–19 **Pupils** 800 **Sixth form** 203 **C of E**

Fees: £12,936 pa

01912 750608
www.dameallans.co.uk

Principal: Since 2004, Dr John Hind (50s), PGCE MA (history) from Downing College, Cambridge, MEd (Newcastle), PhD (history) Durham. Previously deputy head of Kingston Grammar and before that at Durham and Exeter. Approachable, speaks enthusiastically of 'our family of schools' and believes in instilling a 'can do' mindset rather than creating an academic hothouse. Approaches each pupil with 'Let's work together and see where we can get to'. Parents commented that 'he runs a tight ship' and though 'a little distant', both parents and pupils have 'warmed to him over time'.

Has made considered, evolutionary changes to remove segregation between the boys' and girls' schools, while retaining their separate identities – most recent, a management restructure to shed traditional boy/girl school delineation.

Married to Ginny, a dentist, with a family of two daughters. Outside school, a keen campanologist and member of the conseil d'administration of the Relais de la Mémoire, an international organisation founded to keep alive WW2 memories in order to promote reconciliation and understanding in Europe and beyond.

Academic matters: Diamond model: co-ed in junior school, pupils split into single sex schools from age 11 to 16 (co-ed for most extracurricular activities other than sport) before returning to co-ed sixth form, though all are housed in the same buildings. Benefit of single sex teaching adapted to the recognised differences in learning styles of boys and girls, though teachers shared across schools (adaptability tested on recruitment). Subjects are zoned in different parts of the building so integration is inevitable and allowed.

Good subject choice at GCSE with dual award or single sciences, dance and drama; nine subjects as standard. In 2018, combined girls' and boys' results were 66 per cent A*-A/9-7 grades at GCSE. At A level, choice of 30 subject with enrichment programme, including TEFL and sign language courses. In 2018, combined sixth formers dipped to 26 per cent A*/A grades and 57 per cent A*-B. Personal tutors for sixth form; younger pupils spoke of 'approachable teachers who run out-of-class surgeries and help with time management problems'. Individual learning needs and abilities are identified; reporting system of attainment and effort valued by parents, though some felt could be more 'push and stretch' for the most academically able.

Learning support mainly takes places out of lessons, ideally outside normal curriculum. Currently a charge is levied.

Pupils from year 10 told us they found single-sex teaching 'took off pressure in the classroom', but 'plenty of opportunity to get to know each other before sixth form through joint activities, like educational visits and Duke of Edinburgh'.

Games, options, the arts: A wealth of opportunities abound. New facilities provide opportunity for more choral and dramatic performances. Diversity from chamber choir to ceilidh band and just about everything in between. Pupils perform with National Youth Choir and achieve success in national competitions.

Dance is 'right here, right now', as demonstrated in aptly named annual show and impressive, purpose-built dance studio. Not only success for pupils as Youth Dance England finalists, but take-up even extends to the first XV, as part of their training programme. Lots of performance opportunities, from informal lunchtime recitals and studio performances to major school productions; from pupils performing at the Edinburgh Fringe to the choir members singing with the Bach Choir at Newcastle University.

Sport is valued as much for its inclusivity (everyone gets chance to represent school) as its excellence. For half a century boys have represented their county at rugby, but recent success in squash (girls' success in National Schools competition), swimming (girls recent National Schools champions) and cross-country (representing Northumberland in English Schools competition). Range of sports on offer is dazzling, with weightlifting, archery, tennis, running, taekwondo and netball having all produced internationals. Sport transports away from muddy fields of Tyneside to tours in, for example, South Africa and Italy (rugby), Barbados (cricket), Canada (hockey and netball). Swimming at local pool in Fenham and record of success, particularly in athletics.

Outdoor and leadership education feature strongly, providing increasing challenge for younger pupils and leadership roles as they move up the school. DofE silver and gold are available from year 10 upwards.

Real adventure is further offered by World Challenge participation – has seen pupils go to Uganda, Kenya, Bolivia, Mongolia, China and the Indian Himalayas. Exchanges flourish to France, Germany etc and in Relais de la Mémoire – joint initiative with French, German and Polish schools to nurture continued learning about and respect for victims of war and holocaust.

Lots of lunchtime and after-school activities including the more unusual – clog dancing, eco panel, electronics and fencing. Challenge and success in business-related competition – recent finalists in Bank of England's Target 2.0 and winner of RES Young Economist of the Year. Parents speak of 'individualised opportunities' for each of their children, resulting in 'confident and capable' young adults.

Background and atmosphere: Founded in 1705; girls' school believed to be one of the oldest independent girls' schools in the country. Founded by Dame Eleanor Allan, daughter of a city goldsmith and widow of a wealthy tobacco merchant, to provide a 'proper' education for 40 poor boys and 20 poor girls. Keeps that ethic but has shaken off the pre-1980s segregation of girls at one side, boys at the other.

Current buildings date from mid 1930s, cushioned on all sides by surburban housing and fronted by a green playing field, a snug oasis amidst the mid-war semis. An airy, modern entrance leads to functional ground floor corridors, made interesting by the display areas on the walls. Well resourced and accommodated art, dance, music and sport; library refurbished in recent years to include areas for careers clinics, science and sixth form study. Good sixth form common room and study accommodation, separate enough for independence – with well-placed sixth form staff teaching and office space to allow discreet observation. Lower down school space is at a premium and one girl told us, 'The dream would be a common room for each year'.

Strong sense of community and family – pupils at ease in a friendly atmosphere. Cherishes church links – historically the cathedral school, and retains links with St Nicholas' Cathedral and Church of SS James and Basil. Places community, charity/fundraising work on a par with academic and sporting achievement.

Separate houses in boys' and girls' schools, though move afoot to 'pair' houses in each school – currently used almost exclusively for sporting competition. Dr Hind feels both schools 'still need a separate identity'.

Pastoral care, well-being and discipline: Form teachers/tutors perform pastoral role in both schools. Trained counsellor to listen to any particular problems, with confidential referrals from school nurse. An effective pupil counselling system called Link, where sixth formers provide a listening ear and guiding hand. Flexible merit system keeps pupils on course. Typically a demerit is a warning sign, two prompts letter home and three invokes detention. Pupils report zero-tolerance of bullying and drugs.

Parents and pupils find any problems dealt with promptly, fairly and effectively. An inclusive school that doesn't give up easily on pupils with behavioural problems.

Pupils and parents: Wide social mix, many parents working hard to afford fees. Catchment is Newcastle and hinterland (Tyne Valley, coast, Durham area, plus wider north east). Pupils mainly from Dame Allan's Junior School (good transition programme for year 6), state primary and middle schools, Newcastle Preparatory School and Chorister School Durham. Most have English as first language, though several speak another language at home.

Alumni include Sir David Lumsden, Ian La Frenais, Elizabeth Fallaize (once pro-vice-chancellor of Oxford University) and more recently Ellie Crissell, TV presenter and journalist.

Entrance: Entry at 11 to senior schools by January assessment in English, maths and verbal reasoning, followed by an interview. Sixth form entry conditional on GCSE results with at least 45 points from best eight subjects.

Exit: Some 75 per cent of seniors stay on for co-ed sixth form. Nearly all go on to university, many in the north and Scotland. One to Oxford in 2018, plus one off to Hong Kong and seven medics.

Money matters: Scholarships of up to 50 per cent of fees awarded on entrance examination results. Participating school in Ogden Trust science scholarship scheme. Music scholarships also available. Means-tested bursaries awarded up to 100 per cent of fees if needed. Though not a rich school, eight per cent of pupils currently receive bursaries.

Remarks: A diamond in shape and in character, pupils encouraged to and do take full advantage of many opportunities to learn, travel and develop. No flashy jewels here, pleasant but functional buildings nestled amongst residential housing. Stiff local competition, particularly for girls – Dame Allan's tries harder. Community and family values ingrained and the individual pupils nurtured.

Durham High School for Girls

Linked with Durham High Junior School for Girls

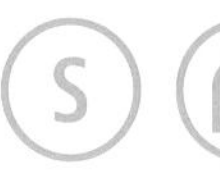   

Farewell Hall, South Road, Durham DH1 3TB

Ages 11–18 **Pupils** 285 **Sixth form** 62 **C of E**

Fees: £13,125 pa

01913 843226
www.dhsfg.org.uk

Headmistress: Since September 2018, Simone Niblock, previously senior deputy head at Queen Margaret's School. English degree from Oxford and a PGCE from Cambridge. Has taught at St Edmund's College, Ware, Stockport Grammar, Perse Girls and Shrewsbury High, where she stayed for 16 years, joining as head of English and being promoted to director of studies.

Academic matters: Consistently the highest performing school in the county and came out particularly well in the English Bacc league table, though a dip in A level results in 2018 to 37 per cent per cent A*/A, 66 per cent A*/B; usual subjects plus psychology, Latin, Greek, classical civilisation, sport, theatre studies, art and design – a notable range for such a small sixth form. Impressively, almost half do maths and sciences, EPQ taken – no slacking from these girls.

2018 GCSEs: 58 per cent A*-A/9-7. Sciences, fine art, textiles, history, Greek, Latin and music usually strong. French, Latin and recently introduced Spanish at key stage 3. Does well in maths, business and Latin and Greek speaking competitions. Astronomy offered extra sessionally for high flyers. Very good ICT provision, with area for enrichment and extension activities on school website. Max class sizes: 24 (key stage 3), 20 (key stage 4), 14 (sixth form), but can be a lot smaller. Girls spoke appreciatively of teachers' personal approach and the amount of individual attention they get. Parents speak highly of teachers who 'build relationships with each child individually and get to know what makes them tick'.

Well-resourced library; reading groups for each year; organised annual event of Big Book Bash for year 7s with 10 local schools. Supervised homework club available until 5.30pm. Qualified SENCo can test for dyslexia, works closely with staff, advises on individual needs and liaises with outside agencies. Gives individual support outside the classroom at a cost to parents. Says school could cope with any special needs apart from severe behavioural difficulties and that these girls do very well (endorsed by latest inspection report). EAL specialist support offered at a cost.

Games, options, the arts: The usual range plus cricket, rowing, golf, karate, rock climbing, badminton – encouraging participation as PE compulsory. Sports tours – next destination Sri Lanka. Regional and national success with some individual national high flyers (gymnastics, tumbling, fencing and netball); new Astroturf pitch, 1970s sports hall and playing field on site – swimming pool and fitness suite all accessed off-site.

Durham High's alive with the sound of music. Over 50 per cent take instrumental and singing lessons. Lots of music exams, no competitions or festivals though performance opportunities abound; choirs, orchestra, ensembles, concerts, and of course, cathedral connections. Well-resourced music technology room – music GCSE popular. Big productions tend to be musicals, but straight plays too, plenty going on in all parts of the school – drama studio fully utilised. The seniors' play is performed at the Gala Theatre in Durham – the school's drama studio stage is, cleverly, the same size, to facilitate the transfer. Scholars' concerts include dance performances.

Very good art – students' work has been shortlisted for the Royal Academy online exhibition for A level candidates; also textiles, graphics, pottery, photography club. No food tech, though, which girls would like, but cookery sessions for juniors and survival lessons for sixth form. Largest DofE centre in County Durham for the Gold Award, community service, eco activities and school council. Sixth form enrichment programme covers IT, philosophy, politics, debating, Young Enterprise. Buddying of younger girls by older ones, who help with academic work (eg basic maths and reading), produce their plays and lead their activities (all good personal statement stuff). Healthy competition through house activities, drama, singing and sports; also used for charitable fundraising. Junior residentials to Bamburgh and Holy Island, Seniors visit France, Spain, Rome, Iceland and an outdoor activity trip, plus a variety of other local trips.

High quality careers and post-school preparation though focused on university. Task-based enterprise day for years 7 and 8 involves teamwork and workplace scenarios; participates in Durham's future business magnate programme in year 8; Young Enterprise and work experience in year 11.

Background and atmosphere: Opened in 1884 in the centre of the city as a CofE school. Moved to leafy outskirts down the road from university science suite in 1964 – all purpose built. Additions since then – sixth form and art accommodation, science labs, ICT and library building, sports hall and attractive two storey brick buildings, one housing a performing arts studio, music room and classrooms and another the junior school – ring the single storey originals. Lengthy flight of gentle steps leads down to the understated entrance providing a disappointing vista of flat roofs – dispelled once inside by wide corridors, bright and airy classrooms, a veritable Tardis.

A compact site, yet sufficient hard play areas, playing field and well wooded grounds. Two ICT suites, a greenhouse for the biology lab, large, well-resourced library (every year has a reading group), pleasant quiet room with modern stained glass windows. Roomy sixth form common room, kitchen (university survival cooking classes on offer) and study areas on edge of campus in building shared with art and design facilities.

The sixth form wear dark suits – the rest sport dark green jumpers and blazers, choice of yellow and green tartan kilt or skirt. Wide choice of healthy food in dining room used by all from 3 up. Lunch arrangements and uniform only negative comments from the girls we spoke to – was ever thus.

All girls means just that here, from nursery to sixth form. Social and debating events with local co-ed schools, Oxbridge preparation with co-ed Durham School on offer.

Christian values lie at the heart of the school, embedded in daily school life with regular religious assemblies, a school chaplain, annual whole school communion, baptism and confirmation preparation and Christian Union. Great continuity and commitment post school days; ex-pupil teachers, governors and parents. Parents and daughters agree that 'there is a feeling of belonging, a mindset to want to do well and a shared set of values amongst the pupils.'

Pastoral care, well-being and discipline: Last inspection praised excellent pastoral provision. Childrens' mental health high on teachers' agenda. Without exception, girls spoke of support and encouragement from teachers; being known well; talents spotted; confidence built. Supplemented by trained counsellor plus school chaplain.

Common to girls' schools, we were assured that bullying and discipline is not a problem. 'Our values spread amongst everyone,' said one, accompanied by nodding heads in unison. They are confident that teachers would sort it if anything did occur – 'there is always someone to go to if you are upset'. PHSE advocates being a 'telling school' and anti-bullying; respect shown by staff integral; parents value the updates on contemporary national issues. 'Proposed changes in behaviour policies shared with the girls as part of review process'.

Well thought out transition for year 7s – a welcome ceilidh and preparatory outreach work with feeder schools in science and Latin plus a joint drama production. Buddying system with year 8s, several joint activities through year to cement relationships. Sixth formers act as 'big sisters' to younger ones. Sixth form piloting mixed tutor groups of years 12 and 13 with positive response.

House system in place throughout whole school and 'we get to join the same house as our big sisters,' one junior told us enthusiastically.

Pupils and parents: Pupils from a wide range of backgrounds from Durham and a broad area around the city, from state and independent schools; some EAL. Extensive bus service – to be widened further. Very satisfied, actively supportive parents who are regularly consulted by the school and kept up to date with weekly news bulletins; information booklets and website. Thoughtful, mature, articulate girls. Notable old girls: Wendy Craig (actress), Joanna Burton (opera singer), Wendy Gibson (TV presenter).

Entrance: At 11 and 13+: exams in English and maths, verbal reasoning, interview and school report; takes above average ability. Sixth: five 9-6s at GCSE including English and maths, with at least 6 in prospective A level subjects (grade 7 for some), school report and interview; about 10 join.

Exit: Around 40 per cent leave after GCSE for other sixth forms, mainly local high performing state schools. Almost without exception sixth form leavers to university; two to Cambridge in 2018 (both natural sciences), and one medic. Popular destinations include Manchester, Newcastle, Northumbria and Edinburgh.

Money matters: Scholarships/exhibitions at 11, 12-14 and 16+: academic, sports, music, performing arts; 10 per cent clerical fee remission, a scholarship for daughters of practising Christians of any denomination based on RS test. Means-tested bursaries up to 50 per cent of fees to girls in about the top half of the ability range – gives over 10 per cent of senior school fee income to these. Sixth form: scholarships worth 100 per cent of fees for very able girls whose parents could not otherwise afford the fees; academic scholarships up to 50 per cent on the basis of exams in two chosen subjects; music scholarships and exhibitions; drama, performing arts, art and sports scholarships; clerical bursaries.

Remarks: High performing (academic, theatrical and musical) single sex school. The only all girls day school in Durham and looking to an increasingly wide catchment. Bedrock of Christian values where every girl matters and talents are discovered and nurtured in a close knit community.

Durham High Junior School for Girls

Linked with Durham High School for Girls

Farewell Hall, Durham DH1 3TB

Ages 3–11 **Pupils** 154 **C of E**

Fees: £4,140 – £9,810 pa

01913 843226
www.dhsfg.org.uk

Head: Since 2013, Katherine Anderson (50s), previously acting head. Hasn't strayed far from Durham High: was a pupil here in the 70s and daughter followed in her footsteps; BEd from Neville's Cross Physical Education College in Durham; brief spell teaching PE at a comprehensive school then back to Durham High in 1986 as head of senior school PE. Has been here ever since, in roles including director of marketing and head of junior house. Husband, Richard, is an agricultural engineer.

Entrance: At 3+, 4+, 7+ and 10+: by age appropriate assessment. Takes just above average ability.

Exit: Almost all to senior school.

Remarks: 'Learning is such fun here' chorused some juniors, citing activities, trips and use of role play to understand characters in reading books. Teaching, children's attitudes to learning and pupil-staff relationships praised in last inspection report. Maximum class size is 15 in key stage 1 and 20 in key stage 2, but most significantly smaller.

Rainbow Hill Nursery, attractive, large, well organised, open plan building, opposite junior classrooms and adjacent to infant school allowing smooth transition to reception. Enclosed soft play area, patio and lovely outside play area and learning environment; lots of hi tech equipment plus traditional resources – the new and the old together. Close links with parents – kept closely informed on children's progress. Average numbers 20; happy, busy, independent little tots looking adorable in tartan pinafores (to match the big girls' uniform).

Topic-led EYFS curriculum in reception continued into termly themes in year 1, though transition to more formalised learning. Setting in maths and some aspects of English from year 2; good provision of extension work for the very bright. Pupils spoke warmly of their teachers and the help they give them.

Qualified SENCo does dyslexia tests (screening of individuals in years 3-4, if needed and gives one-to-one support outside the classroom (at a cost to parents); also specialist ESOL teacher. All needs could be catered for, apart from severe behavioural difficulties – 'These girls do very well'. Senior school girls help junior ones with reading and basic maths, top juniors with infants in the playground.

The usual sports with cross-country, tag rugby and very successful cricket, coached by one of the three male teachers. Netball triumphs at county and regional level, tennis at county. Weekly swimming from year 3 at local pool with annual gala for years 5 and 6. Year 3 all learn the violin, year 4s toot on the recorder (unusual way round), year 5s sound the trumpet and year 6s sing to grade 1. Year 5 singing project with local primary schools, instrumental lessons from nursery, lots of concerts.

Strong art. Clubs include craft, chess, Christian Union, Meccano, ICT problem solving and sport. Karate, ballet, Brownies on offer at a cost. Residentials to Bamburgh and Holy Island and Low Mill activity trip, plus a variety of other local trips; school council.

House system in place throughout whole school and 'we get to join the same house as our big sisters,' one junior told us enthusiastically. Weekly celebration assembly, where pupil with the highest number of house points gets a badge and has photo on a board. De-merits the flip side, although children we spoke to could not think of one misdemeanour worthy of one.

Lots of modern fiction in the library; wide choice of healthy food with personal selection a rite of passage for the older pupils. School council meets every half term to discuss 'charity events and how to make things better'.

Infants and year 3 in attractive yellow brick building with bright, light classrooms with plenty of space, great displays and technology in evidence. Older juniors in single storey buildings, a short distance away. Science taught in junior classrooms but gifted scientists and those with an interest in science in years 5 and 6 join others from Durham primary schools each Thursday evening for Science Sparks, held in senior school laboratories.

Confident, happy and articulate girls, obviously at ease in their environment. A newcomer from a co-ed primary said, 'It's much better without boys, they chatter a lot and are boastful' Parents value the 'very friendly, family environment' where 'the children are very welcoming and happy'; ' there's a feeling of belonging and the children look out for each other'.

Durham School

Linked with Bow Durham School

33

Quarry Heads Lane, Durham DH1 4SZ

Ages 11–18 **Pupils** 395 **Sixth form** 143 **Boarders** 71 full, 27 weekly, 10 flexi **C of E**

Fees: Day £14,343 – £15,993; Boarding £22,923 – £33,354 pa

0191 7319270
www.durhamschool.co.uk

Headmaster: Since 2014, Kieran McLaughlin (early 40s), previously deputy head (academic) at Rugby. Studied natural sciences at Cambridge, specialising in physics and theoretical physics. Has been head of science and technology at Sevenoaks and head of physics at City of London Girls. Attended selective boys' school St Edward's College in Liverpool, having won an assisted place. In the past was the bass player in an obscure Liverpudlian rock band, as well as pursuing the ancient martial art of jiu-jitsu to black belt level. Married with three young children.

Feels that after some change the school needs time to consolidate. He brings experience of a variety of schools (Durham is his sixth): single sex, co-ed, city day, day and boarding, traditional boarding. Although only 15 per cent of pupils are regular boarders (25 per cent when occasional/flexi boarders are included), he says, 'The school feels like a boarding school', and we would agree.

His focus has been on delivering the school's message in the city and beyond. He believes that 'the school is much better than is generally perceived at delivering its core purpose'. Emphasis is on holistic educational experience, evidenced by the value added at A level being in the top 10 per cent of independent schools. Reminders, too, about academic success, and work is in progress to drive standards higher without being 'an academic hothouse'. Durham is a city where education really does matter and word of mouth really does count. One parent we spoke told us that they had researched in depth seven schools before selecting Durham School.

Has a collegiate management style; teaches physics to year 12. Has an easy manner, and when walking around the school it is obvious he is a visible head to his pupils. Very strong vote of confidence from parents, with one summing up the tenor of the parents we spoke to: 'He is an asset to the school and clearly has a firm grasp on the challenges within education and the strategic development needed to stay ahead and maintain standards of excellence'.

Currently not too distracted by the Durham International Schools initiative – a franchising joint venture with Indian company Infinity, looking to clone Durham ethos in the UAE.

Academic matters: A level 32 per cent A*/A, 71 per cent A*-B in 2018. Probably why school is working to develop academic aspects of the sixth form ('more rigour', a study centre, supervised study time, more intellectual societies). Wide choice of subjects includes economics, politics, psychology, philosophy and ethics, government and politics, classical civilisation, photography, theatre and business studies. EPQ now available together with an enrichment programme which includes a lecture series and five societies, supervised by staff but run by students: academic, politic, heretics, Tristam (scientists) and medsoc (would-be medics). Very good support with university applications and Oxbridge/elite university preparation.

GCSE results 40 per cent A*-A/9-7 in 2018. Mathematics, two English, separate sciences or dual award and a modern language compulsory. Option choice includes Latin, classical civilisation, ethics and drama, music, PE, DT graphic products and Greek, off timetable. German or Spanish added to French in year 9 (can also do Latin) and language awareness days, with themed meals. Most recent inspection praised pupil-staff relationships, teaching and use of monitoring, but commented on some marking inconsistency, which school is addressing.

Classrooms tend to be traditional, with just one computer plus projector (only a few interactive whiteboards), some darkish, but also some new ones and some modern ICT facilities with a stock of iPads. 'Bring your own device' has been introduced. Wifi connectivity has improved and there's a VLE.

Strong learning support department – well qualified, flexible, sensitive; can cope with most needs apart from severe behavioural problems. The spread out nature of the campus could be a problem for anyone with major physical disabilities. Screens all new entrants for dyslexia and ESL, if from overseas (extra charge for ESL – full-time specialist – and learning support sessions); trains other staff. Thorough-going gifted and talented policy – systematic identification and monitoring, early maths GCSE, fourth A level and extra, challenging activities.

Games, options, the arts: Astroturf, functional swimming pool, sports hall, playing fields, very good rowing facilities and access to top flight coaching. Individuals and teams successful at regional, county and national levels with rugby first XV reaching the Natwest Trophy semi finals and the hockey teams getting to the National Schools regional finals recently.

One of the oldest rowing clubs in the country (dates from 1847) – the whole 1970 crew represented GB and has current international stars. Water polo taking off in a big way, ski team reached finals of English Schools' Championships, a GB fencer; also cross-country, golf, squash, boxing, rifle shooting, windsurfing and climbing. All pupils participate in 4.5 hours of sport and physical activity per week, still partly compulsory in the sixth form. Girls have more chance of being in teams through being in a minority.

Very accomplished choral singing – TV appearances, radio broadcasts, including Radio 4's Sunday Worship and a number of CDs. All Steinway school so plenty of pianists. Orchestras, jazz band, rock group; performance opportunities abound with concerts at The Sage, Gateshead and Durham Cathedral plus foreign tours.

Plenty of opportunity to showcase their dramatic talents in a variety of genres and settings – big musicals like Les Misérables in Durham's Gala Theatre or plays like The Great Gatsby in the school's own performance space, The Luce. Also more informal performances take place in the school's modern studio theatre.

Inter-house competition is rife with the show-stopping annual music competition (staged alternate years in the Sage and the Chapel) top of the bill. Sporting and drama events are staged throughout the year with much-coveted trophies for the winners.

Wide choice of activities from creative writing to computer programming, peer support to the languages film club. DofE and CCF (all three sections). School participates in BBC School Report (writing news bulletins and reports) and the lively and entertaining school newspaper, The Durham Eye, printed in house, has reached the finals of a national schools media competition. Careers education now expanding using network of Old Dunelmians.

Lots of fundraising for charity and foreign trips – staff and pupils seem to have bags of energy and enterprise; Chinese exchange visit to Chengdu; World Challenge to Borneo, Africa, Ecuador, Vietnam or India, cricket tour to Antigua, hockey tour to Portugal, rowing camps in Belgium and Norway, winter walking in Scotland, ski trip to the Alps – plenty of opportunities to do good and see the world.

Boarding: With boarding all is possible – full, weekly and part time. Four of the five houses include day and boarding pupils – three for boys and one for girls. The majority of boarders are from overseas (plus Forces children) – most from Hong Kong, mainland China and Europe – and room allocations mix nationalities. Each house, located along a street outside the main campus, has studies (shared or single), common rooms, kitchen and leisure facilities, and have had some refurbishment. The boarding provision was graded good in the last inspection – a relaxed atmosphere, flexible eating arrangements on Sundays, plenty of activities. Good range of food (we can recommend the home-made veg soup), but boarders we met wanted a more substantial meal later in the evening, after their sports training.

Background and atmosphere: One of oldest schools in the country – goes back to Cardinal Langley's re-founding of Durham Cathedral in 1414; at the end of the last century became more or less independent of the dean and chapter. Originally situated on Palace Green, next to the cathedral; moved to present site on other side of River Wear, 1844, only five minutes' walk from city centre.

The entrance to the school provides an attractive glimpse of the site – though there is no time to enjoy it if arriving at break times. Hordes of pupils stream across the car park on the way to their houses, seemingly oblivious to any car navigating its way to the tightly packed parking bays.

Once stationary, just enjoy the view; mellow sandstone buildings flank grassy lawns leading to the hill that ascends to the chapel. The 98 steps all commemorate old boys who died in the two world wars. On Remembrance Day the whole school lines the stairs at twilight, holding candles, while a wreath is laid on the memorial plaque, which must be very moving. Stunning view of viaduct, cathedral and school from the top. The 1926 traditional chapel has pews etched with the names of all leavers.

Further up is the Astroturf and beyond, up again, are rugby pitches. You need to be pretty fit just to get to them, let alone train and play. The sports hall and sixth form centre can be found in this vicinity after passing the quirky classics building.

There is a real feel of a traditional rural boarding school, with lovely views of sports fields and gardens containing many mature trees. Although the majority of the pupils don't board (day ends at 6pm), each has a house where they have common rooms and their own space to retreat to before and after school and during breaks in the day. Registration is held here each morning with the houseparent and there are strong bonds between fellow house members.

Girls were introduced into the sixth form in 1985 and Durham became fully co-educational in 1998. Girls feel that there has been a move in recent years to fully integrate them in what is now a true co-educational setting. They are outnumbered 2:1 by the boys, but feel 'very comfortable with the balance,' having single sex houses.

There is a strong sense of community and leadership opportunities with house captains and monitors (prefects) who are now selected through written application and interview.

Chapel plays a central role in school life with three assemblies a week. There are also strong links to the cathedral with services and concerts held there. Various school councils and pupils told us that they feel their voices are heard. A parent told us that 'the school finds where the individual can develop and works with it'. Not only discovering academic, sporting or musical latent talent but 'developing confident individuals with great self belief'. Parents like the house system, providing 'ever greater maturity and acceptance of responsibility' to pupils – and the competition too, 'They all get very involved'.

Pastoral care, well-being and discipline: Pastoral care centred on form tutor and house staff, plus chaplain – rated outstanding by inspection, which glowed about relationships in general and moral and social development. Bullying not seen as a problem – pupils we met felt should it occur, it would be dealt with quickly and effectively (school would exclude if necessary), anti-cyber-bullying policy devised by staff and pupils. There is a clear escalation of staff to speak to about any problems, academic or pastoral. Pupils we met told us that they knew who they were and would be happy to talk to a number.

Senior prefects and school and house monitors support younger pupils – 'It's a very caring environment: the house system works very well'. A sixth former who joined in year 12 from a state school spoke of how quickly he had been integrated into friendship groups that 'conducted themselves so differently' from his previous school.

New children have an acquaintance day in the summer term before entry, an induction day just before term starts and a 'buddy' in their house when they arrive. Prep school pupils will also have used the senior school facilities regularly and visited for a day in year 5.

Pupils and parents: At 11, most from the prep school, the rest from state primaries; at 13 and 16 from a range of state and independent schools. Many of day and weekly boarding pupils from within or close to Durham, others from as far as Sunderland, Newcastle, North Yorkshire and the Borders. A range of ethnic and financial backgrounds but mostly professional or self-employed.

Plenty of contact with generally satisfied parents – weekly e-letter, website, academic diaries, meetings, a parents' forum. Forthcoming, well-mannered, confident pupils. Proud of their school and appreciative of what they have gained; one boy told us, 'I often wonder what person I would be now if I hadn't been at Durham'. Certainly, new sixth formers joining from local secondaries are bowled over by the collegiality, welcome and attitude to learning.

Entrance: At 11+: short tests in English, maths, VR and non-VR; 13+: all have to take tests in English and mathematics plus short interview. Above average ability but a wide range. Sixth form entrants need five GCSEs at 6 or above with a minimum 5 in mathematics and English; also by interview and school report.

If overseas applicants can't sit the entrance exam, they can get in with a school reference, but need a good level of English – for sixth form need level 5.5 IELTS. Some stay in sixth for three years – special programme for first year. Has top rated tier 4 boarding sponsors' licence.

Exit: A very small number leaves at the end of year 11 for vocational courses or jobs and a few at the end of year 12, after some more maturing. Northern redbrick and 'new' universities favourite, north and south of the border: Newcastle and Northumbria top choices, Leeds, York, Bath, Heriot-Watt and Edinburgh popular. A few to Oxbridge (one in 2018). Wide range of subjects: civil and chemical engineering popular choices as well, as business, biomedical sciences and psychology, plus a few medics (three in 2018, and one vet)) and lawyers. One off to Melbourne, one to Georgia and one to Prague in 2018.

Money matters: Various academic, music, drama, art and sports awards, at 11+ and 13+, Burkitt and Peter Lee Scholarships at 16+. Sibling, Forces and clergy discounts. About 150 pupils have means-tested assistance and 105 non-means-tested admissions scholarships of a maximum of £1,000.

Remarks: A sense of community and history binds the pupils together, underpinned by the strong house system for day and boarding pupils alike. The school produces well-rounded, confident young people, who have opportunities to develop a wide range of talents to a high level in a supportive, peaceful and very attractive environment.

Ermysted's Grammar School

Gargrave Road, Skipton, North Yorkshire BD23 1PL

Ages 11–18 **Pupils** 821 **Sixth form** 230

01756 792186
www.ermysteds.co.uk

Head teacher: Since 2016, Michael Evans (early 40s). Previously deputy head at St Olave's Grammar School in Orpington. Studied maths at Durham University. He relocated with his young family and loves living in North Yorkshire. Began his career as an investment banker. After an unsatisfying few years – 'I'm not motivated by money' – he retrained as a teacher. He comes from a 'family of teachers' in Gloucestershire and was state educated himself at the local comprehensive. Unlike banking, he says he finds teaching 'very rewarding' and, unusually for a head, he continues to teach an upper sixth A level maths class. 'You have to walk the walk,' he says; but while choosing to teach may help his leadership and the school's budget, it's primarily a personal decision to keep on doing something he clearly enjoys. 'The boys are great,' he says, 'they're clever, funny and they keep you on your toes. I've been teaching maths for 15 years but they still ask questions that make me re-think my teaching.'

Boys say he's not as outgoing as his predecessor but he 'gives a good assembly'. One sixth former told us he'd seen a different side to the head since being in his year 13 maths class: 'It takes time to get to know him and he's quite a reserved man but he's a really good teacher'. Parents described Mr Evans as 'excellent' and 'dedicated' and praised the fact that he 'seems to make things happen' and 'is making important and much needed changes to the school' – especially in the areas of technology, communication and the school buildings. He's also seen as a safe pair of hands, steering the school through the choppy waters of insufficient state education funding. He's really engaged with parents – and won their approval – by inviting them in to help work on the school buildings, but there is a sense that he's still settling in. 'I think he will become a good head teacher,' said one parent, 'and I know he has a lot on his plate at the moment.' 'I think that he is doing a very good job and I like his approach,' said another parent. 'He had a very hard act to follow as the previous head was very popular and had been in the post for a long time. Change is difficult but it was necessary...'

E

Academic matters: In 2018, 35 per cent of A levels taken were awarded A*/A. At GCSE, 44 per cent of grades were A*-A/7-9. GCSE progress at the school is rated by the DfE as in the top 12 per cent of schools nationally.

There's a good range of GCSE subjects on offer – including food and nutrition, product design and design engineering. Only about half receive the English Baccalaureate (that is a grade 4 or above in English, maths, history or geography, science and a language). This is because, rather than chasing league tables at all costs, the school gives its pupils a relatively free choice of GCSE subjects and many don't choose all the qualifying subjects.

Most parents say that the school's high academic standards were a major factor in choosing Ermysted's. 'It promotes academic achievement without feeling like an exam machine,' said one mum. 'It doesn't put a huge amount of pressure on the children but somehow manages to relay an appropriately high expectation,' said another. Boys say they put pressure on themselves rather than it coming from teachers. They say they feel well supported academically and teachers are always available to give extra subject help at lunchtimes.

One mum told us she'll never forget one particular parents' evening when 'we sat down with our son and his maths tutor, we were just observers. The teacher and our son were engaged in a dialogue, both understanding each other, and what was needed to improve, gain even better marks. Their discussion was humorous and they really connected over their maths.'

The school retains teachers very well – several have PhDs and a numbers of names came up again and again in our conversations with pupils and parents as being excellent and inspirational. Several parents we spoke to singled out the chemistry department as excellent. Others picked out music, PE, RE and technology. It is a small school, however, and many A level subjects run with class numbers in single figures, so data varies considerably from year to year. One parent said that in her sons' experience languages teaching had been 'variable, although this has improved considerably'. She also wanted to see more modern languages than just French and German on the curriculum – although the school does offer Latin right through to A level.

Ermysted's currently supports children with dyslexia, dyspraxia and dyscalculia as well as speech and language problems, English as an additional language and physical or sensory impairments. There's a named SENCo on the school's website who is available to talk to parents and prospective parents about individual needs (although whether the school can secure any extra funding to meet those needs is another question).

Games, options, the arts: When we asked pupils about extracurricular opportunities, the first thing they talked about was sport. Almost all of the large group of boys we met were involved in some sort of sports team and boys and parents were full of praise for the PE department's staff. The school has ample playing fields and a large sports hall that's also equipped with a climbing wall but, from year 10 onwards, pupils also have some PE lessons at the local Sandylands Sports Centre. Boys told us that the sporting ethos is more inclusive than competitive but talented young sportsmen have every opportunity to go far – with several having represented their county and even their country in their chosen sports in recent years.

Perhaps unsurprisingly, given the school's idyllic location, fell running is one of the school's main sports – as well as rugby, football, cross-country, cricket and basketball. There are opportunities for swimming, tennis, badminton and athletics too. One striking tradition the school keeps up is an annual whole school sponsored cross-country race – which is mandatory for all 800-odd pupils. By the sixth form, however, more sedentary types do have the option to swap PE lessons for private study or local volunteering.

Pupils and parents also heaped praise on the range of school trips on offer – with a regular language exchange to Germany, ski trips to France and trips to Rome. A recent volunteering trip to Tanzania 'stands out as one of the most memorable experiences,' said one mum, 'which massively changed how [the boys] felt after living in a relatively well off but rural community in the UK.'

Musical opportunities abound here – with a school choir, big band, junior wind band, and a flute ensemble and concerts at least every term. As with sport, there's an inclusive vibe: 'My son loves music,' said one mum, 'despite not playing an instrument. To feel included in a subject you previously knew nothing about is fantastic.' Music is taught at GCSE and A level – A level music in collaboration with Skipton Girls' High down the road, as is A level art and design. Take-up of these two subjects is currently quite low but the head says the offering could change if demand increases.

The school also collaborates with the girls' school for drama productions. There's an annual drama production and also a student-led house drama competition. Sixth formers are also taking the lead on directing a play for the Shakespeare Schools Festival. But drama does seem to be very pupil-led here: there is no drama department, no timetabled drama classes and drama and theatre studies are not options at either GCSE or A level. The one theatrically-minded student we met said he'd had a wonderful time doing drama at Ermysted's but he did sound rather wistful that it wasn't a bigger part of school life. Another child was disappointed that a creative writing club had had to close when the librarian who ran it left. The consensus among parents, however, was that, in the face of increasingly poor state funding, the school works hard and creatively to keep up the range of activities and subjects on offer.

Background and atmosphere: Ermysted's is one of the oldest state schools in the country. It's been educating boys in Skipton since at least 1492, although most of the current buildings date back to the 19th and 20th centuries. Walking into reception feels reassuringly old-fashioned. No fancy cameras or fingerprint recognition – although we did get a nice visitor's badge and we weren't left alone with any pupils (which shows either that they're on top of child protection or they were worried about what the boys might say to us... We think it's the former.) Pupils were unfailingly polite and chatty – quick to open doors for a visitor and say hello. The atmosphere was lively and energetic – a notch or two down from boisterous. We saw lots of student work up on display all around the school and the lessons we peeped in on looked active and engaging but very much under control. Pupils are pretty smart – even sixth formers wear a uniform. Boys told us the school felt friendly right from the start and we certainly got that vibe during our visit. They said their teachers treated them 'like you're on a level with them' – although teaching styles vary from the interactive and pupil-led to those who 'just stand by the whiteboard and write up notes'. Students also talked about a community feel – not just within the school but also in the local area. Many pupils choose to take up community volunteering opportunities and boys said that when they're out in Skipton in their uniforms they get a warm welcome wherever they go.

The traditional and the modern seem to go hand in hand with ease at Ermysted's. An engaged community of old boys continues to find much-appreciated ways to show its affection for the school – not least through financial donations, but also more actively, for example by giving careers talks or serving as governors. Boys say they sometimes feel a sense of history around them. We met in an oak-panelled room, surrounded by portraits of benefactors and head teachers past. Like many schools with a long history, there are memorials to the war dead. Boys also told us how moved they'd been by a history visit to the battlefields of France and Belgium. But change is welcomed here too. The current head has brought in improvements to the website, communications and IT and he says he doesn't feel constrained by the school's traditions. (Although, despite recent IT improvements, one of the chief grumbles we heard from pupils was that computers and the Internet are still too slow.)

Pastoral care, well-being and discipline: The pastoral care system means almost all teachers are also form tutors and each form tutor reports to a year head or head of key stage. Parents say the system works very well: 'They seem to have an excellent system of changing form teachers every key stage, which means by the time they leave school they know most of the teachers and the teachers know them'. All the parents we spoke to said the school knows their children very well and boys we met agreed. Boys described the teachers as 'helpful' and said they felt supported by the pastoral system. One boy said he'd felt particularly well cared for during his first term at the school. He was the only pupil sent here by his primary school and 'knew no-one at all'. He said the school put on film nights and quiz nights and did all they could to help him to make friends quickly. One mum told us her son also had a difficult transition to secondary school, but the head of year 7 'met with me regularly, rang me, always looked out for my son and found activities to make him feel included and also arranged for the school counsellor to see him... [he] has made all the difference to my son's experience at the school and without him I don't know where we would be now'. As boys get older there are lots of opportunities to take on leadership roles to support younger pupils. One parent praised the student adviser system and peer mentoring. 'The school is good at being open about issues such as mental health,' she added. The head says he's proud that the school focuses on the 'broader picture' of developing character and student well-being. He takes a similar approach to teacher well-being; one of his first acts as head was to ban staff from sending work emails outside their working hours.

Most parents were positive about behaviour and discipline at the school. 'I think it must be difficult to have a school full of boys but at the same time they know what makes them tick,' said one mum. 'They clamp down on silly behaviours via LLDs (low level disruption) which are written in their planners and discussed with tutors and parents.' Another parent told us 'my son gets a bit frustrated if pupils are allowed to mess around in class. This is rare and some teachers are better at dealing with it than others, in fact the teacher who was the weakest at dealing with this has now left.' Another parent expressed a similar cautious optimism: 'I was becoming concerned last year that discipline standards were slipping. However, with the start of the new school year there have been changes which seem to be working.' Pupils we met said bad behaviour was rare and the teachers were 'on it'. 'People only really mess about when they're in a group,' said one boy. 'There's a kind of mob mentality but teachers just split the group up and that normally sorts it out.' Bullying incidents are rare, says the head, and pupils we met said they'd seen nothing more than the kind of teasing 'you know is OK'. Students told us the school is inclusive and LGBT-friendly. 'I know quite a few boys who are out and I think the prefects are going to set up an LGBT society,' said one sixth former.

Pupils and parents: The school has a busy parents' association – which organises a full calendar of social and fundraising events such as quiz nights, a Christmas fair, a Burn's Night supper and ceilidh, film nights and even balls. The PA raises significant sums of money to prop up barely sufficient state funding. One PA member noted approvingly that 'the head teacher always attends [PA] meetings'. 'Your involvement in secondary education is not the same as primary unless you choose to get involved,' noted one mum but evidently at Ermysted's, if parents do want to get involved, the opportunities are endless. The head recently harnessed parent power to give the school a much needed makeover by organising a Spruce up our School day – setting over 60 volunteer parents, governors, teachers and students to work to clean and repair tired buildings and give the gardens some love and care.

The pupil population is ethnically diverse and some boys travel a good distance to come to school – although the admissions system prioritises local children who meet the selection criteria. It's not so diverse socially, though. Less than five per cent of pupils are disadvantaged compared to nearly 30 per cent at the non-selective Skipton Academy down the road. Those children who do come from poorer backgrounds, however, are given every opportunity to participate in school life to the full. All extracurricular activities that go on during the school day are free or by voluntary contribution and some pupil premium funding is spent on helping low-income families with costs such as uniform, equipment and trips.

Famous old boys include BBC political correspondent Chris Mason, poet Blake Morrison, screenwriter Simon Beaufoy (of The Fully Monty and Slumdog Millionaire fame), former Conservative chancellor of the exchequer Iain MacLeod and a good few professional sportsmen including former Manchester City player Rick Holden, rugby league player Andy Hodgson and British Olympic boxer Muhammad Ali (born in 1996 and not to be confused with his late American namesake).

Entrance: Applicants sit tests in verbal and non-verbal reasoning and the pass mark is based on the scores of the top 28 per cent of in-area applicants. Admissions policy prioritises children with special educational needs and those who are looked after by the local authority, before breaking it down further by catchment area, proximity to the school and siblings. For sixth form entry, at least five 6s at GCSE, including A level subjects; some eg maths need 7+.

Exit: About 10-20 per cent of pupils leave after GCSEs – mainly to continue their studies at another sixth form or through vocational courses or apprenticeships. Sixth form entry requirements are not particularly high (at least six GCSEs at grade 4, including maths and English, and usually at least a grade 6 in all chosen A level subjects) so there isn't a huge exodus after the end of year 11.

In 2018, five went to Oxbridge and five to study medicine. Most leavers go to university – many to prestigious Russell Group institutions – but the head says he is just as proud of those who have won places on highly competitive apprenticeships.

Careers teaching begins early at Ermysted's with sessions taught to pupils from year 7 onwards, a careers fair in year 9 and a programme of lectures for sixth formers including careers talks from old boys. There's also a club to help sixth formers planning to study medicine, veterinary medicine or dentistry.

Remarks: A good, old-fashioned grammar school, Ermysted's is a happy, energetic and high-achieving community. Parents and pupils are grateful to be part of it, teachers are happy to work there and Skipton locals view it with respect and affection. The school is travelling through the 21st century at its own pace – don't expect your son to be provided with his own iPad in year 7 – but if you're looking for a smallish, traditional environment for a bright boy to flourish personally as well as academically, Ermysted's could be just the place.

F

The Froebelian School

Clarence Road, Horsforth, Leeds, West Yorkshire LS18 4LB

Ages 3–11 **Pupils** 189

Fees: £5,220 – £7,785 pa

01132 583047
www.froebelian.com

Headteacher: Since 2015, Catherine Dodds BEd PGCE Bretton Hall, University of Leeds. Realised her vocation when a teaching assistant at Bradford Girls' Grammar. First teaching appointment as class teacher and English and drama coordinator at Silcoates Junior School. In 2002 moved to Leeds Girls' High School promoted to deputy head designate in 2005. Following merger with Leeds Grammar was one of three junior school deputy heads responsible for operations, assessment and reporting.

A Yorkshire lass, first headship and relishing the autonomy of her role in a stand alone prep school. Believes in being very visible to pupils and parents alike and is at the school gate morning and afternoon – a presence that also helps to police parent parking infringements in narrow lane next to the school. Teaches ICT and art and, as one might expect in a small school, has quickly got up to speed, knowing the name of every child and their family connections with current pupils and alumni – this is a school that has strong and loyal support through generations.

Took over a very steady ship after 24 years with previous head at the helm. Very aware of the school's reputation for consistent high academic standards and excellent pastoral care, and that any changes are under the spotlight of the small community of extremely loyal governors, parents and alumni. As ever, it's not possible to please everyone all of the time, and parents felt some changes had been rushed and that 'sometimes the old adage "if it ain't broke, don't fix it" comes to mind'.

Building projects lie close to the head's heart, and an internal rationalisation and reconfiguration of accommodation at the school was completed during her first year. This mirrors a personal interest in interior design and property renovation, as well as a love of the outdoors. A keen walker, with the Dales right on the doorstep; gardening another leisure activity, with a recently established veggie patch. A keen luvvie of am dram, her prime outlet now is assemblies. Pupils told us how she led assembly dressed as a pirate. On another occasion parents liked her using shaving foam to illustrate the point that if you say unkind things, you can't just rub them out as you can with foam. They commented that 'these kinds of creative touches really help cement understanding in young children'.

Married with two sons, both at school here.

Entrance: One form entry mainly at 3+ to lower kindergarten, though a few join at 4+. First to register invited to spend some time in school for informal assessment by staff. A more formal assessment for older children.

First Steps at Froebelian is a nursery a few minutes' drive away for children of 3 months to 5 years. Pre-school room at nursery runs parallel to lower kindergarten in school but a number transfer to the school at 3+, topped up by a handful of new recruits from elsewhere.

Bursary fund launched in 2003 provides means-tested support to a handful of children each year. A fee reduction is given to families with three or more children at the school. No scholarships.

Exit: The majority to fee paying schools, top choices being co-educational Bradford and Leeds independent grammar schools and Woodhouse Grove (scholarships abound – five in 2018). Harrogate Ladies' College, Ashville and St Peter's York also feature; occasional entrant to

Eton, Wycombe Abbey, Queen Margaret's and other boarding schools further afield. Some schools send admissions staff to Y6 autumn parent meeting.

Well regarded state schools in Otley, Harrogate and Menston are also contenders, alongside selective Ripon Grammar, with some parents willing to relocate to be in catchment.

Remarks: Consistently a high achiever in national KS2 results: 22nd in the national rankings in a recent Sunday Times listing. Pupils thrive on good teaching and academic challenge in a warm and nurturing environment. A small but loyal and committed staff, with 40 per cent having been at the school for at least eight years, yet sufficient fresh blood as well. One form entry, classes maximum 26, each with teacher and assistant, with two TAs in

kindergarten.

Lower kindergarten housed in the former coach house located across the playground from main school building. A cosy setting, 26 full time places, with additional quiet room for focused activity, smartboard and computers. Structured morning, starting with a number and letter per week, specialist music, sport and IT which continues through to KS1, and play afternoons optional for the 'little acorns' who change into mufti after lunch. Shared learning area just round the corner outside kindergarten (reception) where most children transfer when ready.

Main school building houses KS1 classrooms on the ground floor and pupils move onwards and upwards as they progress to the top class. Classroom settings progress from round tables to ranks of desks in the top two classes. Reception teaches EYFS curriculum based on themes changed half termly with direct access to outside learning area. Music, drama and art timetabled with annual nativity and parent assemblies for performance opportunities.

Broad curriculum in KS2 with French, drama, music and DT added to specialist teaching. Progress testing at the end of each topic. Weekly 'directed improvement and reflection time' for pupil self-assessment. Plenty of smartboards and IT hardware around with designated suite for timetabled ICT – classes split and rota of digital literacy and computer science. Top class focus on senior school entrance in autumn term and then five steps challenge (a mini DofE), and the school production project activities predominate the timetable in spring and summer terms. For seven per cent of pupils English is not their first language but no support is needed. A handful of SEND children have individual education plans, predominantly in-class differentiation. A very few have dedicated one-on-one time with a specialist teacher, at extra charge.

If direct access to facilities for sport is important, this is not the school for you. No changing rooms – boys and girls change in separate classrooms. Playground for PE, the only outdoor on-site space; hall doubles for indoor PE and gym, playing fields a short walk away, Astroturf and swimming pool a bus ride away. Doesn't stop them competing – particularly successful at netball.

Lots of opportunity for drama, including LAMDA classes and thriving weekly drama club. Crowning glory is the Y5 and 6 musical production staged at Yeadon Town Hall after the annual speech day. Y6 pupils work as a production company masterminding every aspect including marketing, staging and participation; the final performance is truly amazing. Music taught in a specialised room. Junior classes split on a rota basis, half recorder and half composition, on an impressive line of keyboards. Every year Y6 composes and performs a leaving song. Visiting peris teach voice, string and wind instruments at extra charge.

Evidence all around school of pupils' artwork with the outcomes of previous annual spring arts weeks. Incorporating expressive and performing arts, woven willow statues in the outdoor learning zone and the celebratory centenary (2013) mural on a playground wall just some of the evidence of the breadth of this much cherished whole school project. A DT room for juniors well resourced with equipment, kept in pristine condition in keeping with rest of school.

A good range of clubs at lunchtime and after school from Ready Steady Cook to jabadao. Others including archery and golf at additional cost. Residentials from Y2 upwards increasing in challenge and distance from home. Four houses with sports competitions, fortnightly meetings and weekly merit assemblies where house cup awarded for highest number of merits. Opportunities for responsibility in top year with a different girl and boy school captain each term. Fundraising for chosen charity (changes each year) and Barnardo cottage boxes a standing item.

From humble beginnings in 1913, founded by stationmaster's daughter teacher Mary Hoe and Froebel trained Doris Hunt, with just 10 children. Moved to its current location in 1959 (The Mount, former home to the Thornton family) and became a charity in 1973.

The footprint of the compact site has been fully utilised. The original stone house and coach house extended in a complementary style, with creative often multi-functional use of every nook and cranny. A newly refurbished airy space in the coach house is home to science, art, ballet and homework club. No compromise, though, on bright, spacious classrooms, small but well used library and dazzling displays throughout. Gleamingly clean and well maintained everywhere, palpable evidence of staff that really care.

Tasty grub in the Hub for lunch, seated at fold away tables and benches as space doubles up for pre-and after-school care 7.30am till 6pm where breakfast and a light tea are served. Outside a lot is packed into the confined playground area that surrounds the school. Edged with tightly packed storage sheds and summerhouses with a greenhouse, eco club planting boxes and – yes – chickens, room is found for adventure climbing equipment (funded by the parents' association), used as a fun playtime activity on a class rota basis. Steep steps lead from the playground to the terraced outdoor learning zone, clinging on to the side of a small cliff, a creative use of a small piece of adjoining land.

As you might expect no significant behaviour issues here; strong relationships between staff and pupils and positive behaviour policy. New PSHE Jigsaw scheme launched with weekly theme writ large around the entire school, including sessions of 'mindfulness and calm me' and conflict resolution. 'Catch me being good' cards, an accolade for behaviour 'above and beyond', placed in a prize draw half-termly. Froebelian Flyer Superheroes covers eight aspirational attributes needed to collect the complete set of badges and certificates awarded at weekly merit assembly, with additional incentive of juice and choccy biscuit at break. Hundred per cent attendance awards given out half termly – morning late arrival excludes contenders.

A tight knit community, social and family links abound. Parents are generally professionals, high number of medics and over half live in Horsforth or close by in west Leeds. Froebelian's location on the commuter belt from Bradford to Leeds attracts those from further afield. Parents say they feel well informed through newsletters, texts and emails. Parent evenings in autumn and spring follow assessment cycle and 'teacher formal notes', with full report at year end.

A small school, parents choose it for the family and 'villagey' feel which helps children 'grow in confidence quickly'. Pupils certainly seem to thrive in this safe and nurturing environment, are well rounded and successfully make their next educational leap. Lack of onsite sports facilities a downside and it's not necessarily on everyone's radar, but definitely one worth a visit.

Fulford School

Fulfordgate, Heslington Lane, York, North Yorkshire YO10 4FY

Ages 11–18 **Pupils** 1,460 **Sixth form** 257

01904 633300
www.fulford.york.sch.uk

Headteacher: Since 2013, Lorna Savage (50s). Came late into teaching following a history degree (Stirling), then working five years in industry before studying for a PGCE via the OU. She has taught here since 1996, and her own children attended the school, so she knows the place inside out having experienced the full range of teacher and parent roles. With a warm, friendly, Scottish lilt, she gives the impression of being a gentle hand on the tiller whilst also running a tight ship – an effective and impressive combination to manage in a school where expectations are high, on every level. Clear pride in student successes and achievements, plenty of cups and awards on show but it's evident from talking to parents that this is a school with a good heart too and people plainly matter.

Retiring in 2019.

Academic matters: There is much to be proud of here – a long-standing reputation for excellent academic results sits alongside a real and genuine commitment to closing the achievement gap between disadvantaged students and others. Resilience, independence, team work, creativity and reflection are taken seriously.

Cracking results: in 2018, 78 per cent 9–4 in both English and maths, 29 per cent 9-7; at A level 45 per cent A*/A and 74 per cent A*-B. French from year 7, French and Spanish from year 8 and KS3 now covered in just two years, with GCSE choices made at end of year 8 and taught from year 9. Proximity to the university means that, occasionally, the school can call up additional resources and support in Japanese, Korean and Polish. Plenty of investment in the ICT infrastructure, the VLE is a well-used and valuable additional support for all abilities. Chemistry, physics and biology are all very strong at A level and BTecs are available from year 9, which means that all levels of scientific ability (or none) are catered for. Real push for girls in physics and lots of STEM work going on.

Popular business and economics have a designated suite offering up-to-date case studies, visits to companies, outside speakers, role play and internet research to cover a wide range of contemporary topics. AS business students made the regional finals of the Nestlé Chocolate Box Challenge and a small number of year 13 economics students take part in the Bank of England Target 2.0 Interest Rate competition. The American ambassador came and awarded much-coveted congressional medals after a hugely successful Q & A with students. History is brought alive by film club and trips to WW1 battlefields and geographers explore local Yorkshire facilities before heading off (in the sixth form) to discover the wonders of plate tectonics and geothermals in Iceland. Good to see plenty of careers advice and guidance in evidence for all abilities; no one left floundering.

No obvious subject weaknesses; academic banding from the start and later setting for core subjects but, reassuringly, there is scope to move across bands so no need to feel stuck or even labelled. The school also houses an enhanced resource centre with a capacity to offer additional support for 10 students on the autistic spectrum. 'Stretch' activities for the most able involve entry into a number of national and international competitions in a range of academic subjects and extracurricular options.

Games, options, the arts: Muddy boots and trainers around the place suggest sport aplenty before, during and after school. Football, rugby, hockey, netball, athletics, basketball, volleyball, badminton, cricket and more besides, played with great skill, enthusiasm and notable success in local competitions. Residential activity weekends and trips extend provision and opportunity; highlights include water-sports trip to South of France each summer and football coaching at the Villarreal club in Spain.

Performing arts are popular, including drama club, regular theatre trips and links with professional performers and companies; annual whole school productions feature old favourites like Bugsy Malone and Grease. Lots of collaboration with the music department, home to the Fulford Music Academy. Peripatetic staff offer individual music tuition in a range of instruments. There is a concert band, show band, string ensemble, saxophone group, plus music tech options. Jam pods (think instruments not WI) are immensely popular with students, who book spaces at lunchtime to let their creative talents loose. Textiles also hugely in demand and successful – check out the laser-printer and metal casting exhibits.

Extracurricular activities include origami and some high quality and very competitive bridge playing. Interestingly, the whole school recently took part in CPR training – reassuring, should the need ever arise. Posters from the Lord of the Rings and Stonewall ('Some people are gay – get over it') around the walls are reminders of a recent visit from Sir Ian McKellan – 'We had 450 students in each assembly join him in a communal You Shall Not Pass, with Sir Ian leading from the front of the hall – that won't be forgotten any time soon,' said a staff member.

Background and atmosphere: The school opened in 1963, turning comprehensive in 1970, but little of the original architecture now remains. New dining hall, teaching block and sports hall; existing buildings improved and more to come. Located on the outskirts of York, reasonably close to the racecourse, York marina and, most notably, the university. It's no surprise that local house prices are higher than the regional average, given proximity to key attractions, pretty villages as well as an excellent school. As a leafy lane school it's at the bottom of the funding pecking order, tell-tale sign being the fact that the proportion of students eligible for the pupil premium is well below average. However, it's well managed with no sense of anything lacking. Ample sports fields, tidy landscaping and neat classrooms and corridors make the place look and feel cared for.

Judged as 'outstanding' by Ofsted in 2011 (must be due another inspection?), but no sense of complacency. There's a 'right, what can we do/achieve next?' attitude. A Healthy Achievement Award suggests great food and must be right as most students choose to eat in house. Cashless catering, parents top up a payment card so no need to carry money in school. Charity work is important and a sense of citizenship and a can-do attitude prevail. The student executive, facing a charity fundraising challenge, put together a very successful 'Fulford Fest, cleverly taking up popular festival wheezes such as selling wristbands, organising a talent competition and hiring an ice cream van.

Uniform is simple, practical and comfortable – sweatshirts and trousers for most, girls generally preferring trousers to skirts. Most parents support current drive to tidy it all up a little. No uniform or dress code for sixth form.

Pastoral care, well-being and discipline: Pastoral system based on four houses, each run by a director of learning, responsible for the progress, personal development and well-being of the students in their care. Students are house captains, allowing plenty of opportunity for developing leadership skills. Strong student support department (now employs a student well-being officer) and high standards of attendance and behaviour, again 'outstanding', according to Ofsted.

Attitudes and expectations are reinforced in displays around school; the core purpose of 'Realising potential, creating the future' as designed by the students themselves, is a mantra that is repeated on every wall in every building, acting as an anchor point for behaviour and thinking. An anti-bullying campaign is well supported by staff and students and led to the setting up of an anonymous email line for anyone with concerns.

Phones are allowed in school, used occasionally in class by sixth formers but under supervision and as part of their studies. Elsewhere – on silent and out of sight; if one rings in class, it's confiscated. For those legally old enough, smoking must be off site and never in school uniform.

Pupils and parents: Parents and their offspring are proud of their school. They demonstrate a sincerity of purpose where yes, academics and industriousness are important (and almost taken as read), but so is the wider world and concern for others. Parents say the school's vital 'magic' ingredients are 'rewarding positive behaviour' and concern with pupils' 'growth as people'. A year 7 girl was keen to tell us that the school is 'hugely inclusive, we learn that people come from different backgrounds and this gives us a balanced view of the world and the different needs of different people' – clearly a future diplomat there.

Parents also value the good home-school communication, telling us 'you never have to wait for a response to an email or letter'. Postcards home are fun – teachers take the time to send these when a student has excelled themselves, making everyone's day just that little bit brighter. Pupils and parents are predominantly from a white, British background (York isn't a particularly diverse city), but nearby army barracks means they have welcomed, amongst others, a small contingent of Nepalese families into the school.

Sixth form is large and students enjoy a few extra privileges (and a new sixth form space). Being so visible means they are, on the whole, excellent role models for younger students, stepping in to support or offer advice if appropriate.

Entrance: Pupils are drawn from villages to the south and east of York as well as the suburbs of Fulford, Fishergate and Heslington. Attracts significant numbers of students from other schools in York and the surrounding area into the sixth form – minimum five 4s required for a place. Much care taken with transition from primary school, helping to bridge the gap, especially with those from tiny village primaries.

Exit: Around half left post-GCSE in 2018. Of the rest, vast majority to higher education, around a third to Russell Group; six to Oxbridge and four medics in 2018. Of those not going on to higher education, the progression routes and destinations vary but, increasingly, a good number are picking up prestigious and much-sought after places on high value training schemes with companies such as Nestlé and Deloittes. These are students with a plan.

Remarks: In 1066 the northern earls stood against a viking attack on York at Fulford in the first, but not last, battle of that significant year. Today the battle is an educational one as parents scramble for places at this well-respected and heavily oversubscribed school in the leafy suburbs of a historic city.

Gateways Preparatory School

Linked with Gateways School

Harewood, Leeds LS17 9LE

Ages 2–11 Pupils 165

Fees: £8,445 – £10,218 pa

0113 2886345
www.gatewaysschool.co.uk

Head of the preparatory school: Helen Wallis BA (QTS) in primary education, has been at Gateways since joining as an NQT in 2002. She was appointed curriculum leader of maths and science in 2008 and introduced a number of new initiatives to the school including the annual National Primary Maths Challenge. She continues to teach maths in the prep school alongside her leadership duties. Outside of Gateways, Mrs Wallis enjoys spending time with her husband and two sons.

Entrance: Years 1 to 6: children spend time at the school with their age group and are observed in the classroom. Non-selective, but age-appropriate tests used to identify strengths and weaknesses and check the school is the right fit in a broad sense. Several now arrive for year 6, mainly for scholarship preparation.

Exit: Pre-reception leavers transfer to state schools, chiefly for financial reasons.

The majority of girls (and now boys) continue to the senior school (no entry exam). Only a couple of pupils go on to local state high schools.

Remarks: Occupies 22 acre site in rural village of Harewood, between north Leeds and Harrogate, so plenty of outdoors potential. Founded 1941 as girls' prep, developed secondary in 1960s, boys allowed to transfer to prep from mixed early years foundation stage in 2011, in response to parental demand. Only a small number of boys higher up, but year 2 has equal gender balance – keen to recruit more – and they can now continue to the senior school. The modern buildings in yellow brickwork blend pleasingly with the main school, the original Dower House of Harewood House. Flexible wrap around care from 7.30am to 6.00pm – children can be booked in at short notice.

Little Gates/Prep (5-11 years): national curriculum (but no Sats tests – hooray!) and beyond. Unusually, from year 3 has specialist maths, English, science, French, art and DT teaching from high school teachers, plus use of its facilities, which enables fluid transition at 11 years; very small year 4 maths extension group; Latin in year 6. Very systematic checking of achievement and progress; plenty of computers; average class size: 15, 24 max. Half an hour a week enrichment with high school teachers for years 3 to 5. After-school enrichment club available for younger ones with their own teachers. Parents very happy with academic aspects – 'The teachers know the children well and bring them on very well', 'They encourage them and develop their confidence so they achieve more', 'Brilliant maths teaching'.

Gifted and talented pupils do extra subjects such as Mandarin, chess and scholarship preparation in classes of four to six.

Strong SEN provision led by dedicated, highly regarded, well qualified and supported SENCo for whole school – mainly for mild learning difficulties; in class support where possible; no extra charge; screening available in year 1; gives guidance to parents as well as teachers.

Spacious, light, bright classrooms with colourful displays and at least one glass wall. We were particularly taken by the enchanting mini red sofa and armchairs in the library, sited in the atrium. Has use of senior school sports, dance and drama facilities. Fields teams for trad sports, including tag rugby (with the help of a girl) – inclusive approach; three PE specialists. Recent adventure playground installed.

Good range of music; developing a band. Annual drama production usually a musical. Extracurricular includes horticulture, crafts, orienteering, Spanish, speech and drama exams, karate. Lots of house activity, with officials in each year group from year 3.

Pupils mostly from north Leeds and further north, including Wetherby, Harrogate, Ilkley and York (good bus service available); majority from white British, professional and managerial backgrounds. They look extremely smart in their dark plaid skirts, white blouses, red ties, jumpers and blazers.

The children we met were confident, open and appreciative of their teachers – 'They are very helpful'; 'There's a strong bond between the teachers and students,' according to a remarkably self-possessed girl who had joined year 6 from a state school and settled in quickly and happily – and of the sports and the grounds. They also value having interaction with the senior girls: prep children contribute to the main house music competition, get help with sport and attend a weekly assembly along with senior school. One parent regarded it as 'inspirational' for the children to see what can be achieved by the older girls; the advantages of an all through education are a big draw.

Parents we spoke to all praised the quality of communication and relationships with teachers, who respond swiftly to emails and are available at the start and end of the day, enabling problems to get sorted before they can escalate. They value the individual care, secure environment and friendly, family atmosphere.

Early years (3 to 5 years): large, attractive, well-resourced areas, in and outside, and access to main school sports, dance and drama facilities, as well as the lavish grounds. Music and PE specialists; French introduced in reception.

Gatehouse nursery (2 to 3 years): delightful, hexagonal building; bright, colourful space. Lots of outdoor time.

Gateways School

Linked with Gateways Preparatory School

G

Harewood, Leeds LS17 9LE

Ages 11–18 **Pupils** 343 **Sixth form** 48

Fees: £13,524 – £13,614 pa

01132 886345
www.gatewaysschool.co.uk

Headmistress: Since 2012, Dr Tracy Johnson BSc PhD PGCE (mid 40s), read laser physics and optoelectronics at St Andrews. Physics teacher and housemistress at Cheltenham College, then deputy head at Lord Wandsworth College; teaches physics to all year 7 pupils. Married to David, an actuary; two boys. Enjoys skiing and cycling. Presents papers on, eg, differences between male and female teenage brains and emotional development.

Very focused on improvements in academic achievement, learning support and pastoral care. Also changed catering company very early on – to great effect, as we can testify from our very adventurous salad. Current goals are to encourage more independent thinking at A level and develop a standalone, consistent middle school (years 4-9) curriculum, working across the prep and high school sections.

Clearly very much on top of the job and thoroughly enjoying it – 'It's a fantastic first headship,' as the small size of the school means 'everyone knows everyone and everyone knows me'. Practical, firm, lively and open; seen by parents as very approachable, supportive, flexible, commanding 'a tremendous amount of respect without waving a stick' and 'a fantastic role model', as a female academic and scientist'.

Academic matters: Non-selective school with a broad ability range and strong GCSE results: 2018 57 per cent A*-A/9-7; English, RS, geography, music, additional maths, separate sciences, Spanish and art stand out.

Respectable A level results with 59 per cent A*/A in 2018. Despite its small size offers 22 A levels – art and design, textiles, photography, media studies, psychology, drama and theatre as well as standard choice. Small sixth form groups, eg five, so lots of individual attention, and will run subjects for just one or two girls – the latter size too pressurised for some but very good preparation for university. Enrichment includes EPQ, certificate of spoken English for higher education, finance, cooking, careers.

Average class size years 7-11: 14; 18 max. Years 7-9 do French, German, Spanish, Latin. Setting in English, maths and science in year 7 (but in general flexible about whether setting is needed). Girls we spoke to feel their lessons are fun and their teachers very helpful and available outside lesson time; parents very happy with progress made. Off school topic days, eg with STEM focus – head and deputy head are both scientists and keen to promote STEM. Experienced, stable staff. Homework club in library till 6pm. Stella programme years 7-13 for able (academically) and talented.

One year pre-GCSE and A level courses offered for Chinese students, who live with local host families and follow a programme that builds up their English skills plus some subject knowledge – gives them a chance to sample A level subjects they might not have otherwise considered. Small group EAL lessons – IELTS taken.

Dedicated, highly regarded, well qualified and supported SENCo: warm, thoughtful, strong on relationships. Assessment available but doesn't screen all year 7s; mainly covers mild learning difficulties. In and outside classroom support at no extra charge; also provides help with individual difficulties as they arise and gives parents guidance; identifies gifted and talented and advises staff.

Games, options, the arts: Wide range of sports – trad ones plus basketball, softball, gymnastics, trampolining, badminton; inclusive approach to teams; successful netball at county level. Fields and modern sports hall with dance studio; ideally would like own Astro but happy with use of local hockey club facilities plus professional coaching; head perfectly sensibly prioritises small classes over having own swimming pool.

Plenty of music: two choirs, orchestra, ensembles when possible; good spread of music styles. Girls organise house music competition; some outstanding singers perform with Opera North or national youth choir.

Speech and drama classes have own space with mini stage – a sixth former has won the Sir Roger Moore award for top mark nationally in grade 8 gold acting medal. Mostly trad plays or musicals plus sixth form panto, produced in modern hexagonal theatre. Interesting art and textiles on display. Lively musical video about school made by sixth form leavers.

Clubs include Amnesty International, business, gardening, debating, young leader award, much DofE. Houses are a big focus – varied competitions. Skiing trip to Italy, netball in South Africa, art in Barcelona, geography in Costa Rica, young leaders' conference in New York.

Background and atmosphere: Founded 1941 as girls' prep, developed secondary in 1960s; will take boys into year 7 from 2019, becoming co-ed throughout gradually. Occupies 22 acre site in rural village of Harewood, between north Leeds and Harrogate. Pleasing mix architecturally of the original building, the Dower House of Harewood House, with wooden panelling and staircases, and attractive, modern buildings in yellow brickwork. Light, bright classrooms; jolly languages area with colourful bunting; quirky cellar space where sixth formers chill out. Fifth formers get the attic – amongst so much niceness and polite behaviour we were reassured to see 'hell yeah dudes' scribbled on a display board exam timetable.

School's great charm is the intimate, friendly, family atmosphere, enabling newcomers to settle in quickly, made possible by its small size. Staff know pupils as individuals and are seen as very approachable by girls and parents. For years had the reputation of being second choice if girls failed to get into the Grammar School at Leeds, but more recently has become the first choice for parents and girls deterred by the size – over 2,000 pupils – and corporate feel of the latter.

Leadership skills fostered – aim is to inject ambition and aspiration, to create future leaders; some success here, going by the impressively poised, mature and well turned out head girl who showed us round. Prefects, house officials in each year group, school council; older girls support younger ones in the high school and prep sections. Girls look very smart in dark tartan skirts with white shirts, red ties, jumpers and blazers. Sixth formers allowed own clothes – office wear.

Well-structured careers programme – networking opportunities with employers and parents, access to mentoring and external qualified careers adviser, years 11 and 12 encouraged to organise own work experience placements after public exams. Most children pleased by the food – lots of variety, with themed days to introduce, eg, Mexican or Indian food – though one termed it 'weird – too adult'. Food council's recommendations are heeded.

Pastoral care, well-being and discipline: Strong on support – girls feel they can approach teachers if they have a problem and well prepared for the outside world by their PSHE lessons and form time discussions; counsellor visits regularly. Eating issues, if they occur, dealt with sensitively and flexibly. We were told by our escort that teachers are 'good at knowing when to intervene' and quickly detect if a girl is struggling with a difficulty. Year 9s and 12s mentor year 7s through house system. Plenty of rewards for effort and achievement; punishments and rewards felt to be fair. Parents say the school responds quickly to emails and is open to providing any support that is needed.

Pupils and parents: Pupils mostly from north Leeds and further north, including Wetherby, Harrogate, Ilkley and York (good bus service available); majority from white British, professional and managerial backgrounds.

Open, confident girls, very enthusiastic about the school – appreciative of their small classes enabling so much individual attention, the extracurricular opportunities and trips, and happy to be in a single sex school (though we did not meet many of the older girls, it has to be said). Famous old girls: Henrietta Hill (youngest female QC); Frances Segelman (sculptor to the royal family).

Entrance: Not selective, but external pupils (about one third) sit tests to identify strengths and weaknesses and check school is a good fit. May also have an interview. EAL applicants assessed through interview and reference. Will admit boys into year 7 from 2019, becoming co-ed gradually as they move up the year groups. Sixth form: minimum of six 9-4 GCSEs plus interview; takes average of one fifth external students.

Exit: Post-16 around one quarter head mainly for local state sixth forms, for financial reasons, co-education or vocational options. At 18 to various universities, including Russell Group, to study a broad range of subjects; one to Oxford in 2018.

Money matters: Academic, arts and sports scholarships worth up to 25 per cent of fees for years 7, 9 and 12 (music only up to 15 per cent but includes free tuition for one instrument); exhibition for up to 25 per cent for very good all rounder; foundation award of up to full fees for high academic ability to enable education in an independent school that would otherwise be ruled out. Means-tested bursaries for short term financial difficulties. Reductions for further children (five/10/15 per cent).

Remarks: Its modest size and offer of a well integrated, all-through education, in a secure, very supportive environment are what enable it to flourish at a time when some small independent schools in the north are struggling to survive. Less suitable, though, for girls who would prefer the wider opportunities and challenge of a larger, coed, urban school.

Giggleswick School

   39

Giggleswick, Settle, North Yorkshire BD24 0DE

Ages 3–18 **Pupils** 430 (80 in junior school) **Sixth form** 130 **Boarders** 121 full, 89 flexi (from 9 years) **C of E**

Fees: Day £7,965 – £20,985; Boarding £16,410 – £33,750 pa

01729 893000
www.giggleswick.org.uk

Headmaster: Since 2014, Mark Turnbull BA (geography, Liverpool University), MA (London University), previously deputy at Eastbourne College, who is taking Giggleswick into a new chapter of its 500 year history. First, there is the 'sharp turnaround' in academic results, a 20 per cent improvement since his arrival; he saw immediately that a 'fundamental academic foundation' needed putting in place to support the school's broad curriculum and set about introducing improved tracking systems, monitoring each child's achievements and potential. Next on the list is the school's boarding accommodation which is currently undergoing a swanky transformation (to the tune of several million smackers). A massive undertaking due to finish 2021.

All this change is set against the majestic permanence of nature, the school's magnificent Yorkshire Dales setting about which Mr Turnbull is passionate (born in York, he has a natural affinity for the landscape). Or as he puts it, 'if it's flat, we put a pitch on it, if it's a hill, we run up it'. He himself is a keen sports fan but there is no sports bias at Giggleswick; Mr Turnbull believes team spirit is fostered as much through drama productions as any sporting challenge: 'It's all about attitude and participation', he stresses.

The school, with its non-selective intake, has always felt a happy school and judging by the smiling faces we saw very much remains so. Time and again there was a backbeat of phrases from parents – 'happy', 'inclusive', 'tolerant' 'all encompassing'. Mr Turnbull himself is described as 'easy to approach' and 'very friendly'. As Mr Turnbull puts it, Giggleswick 'is the most down to earth of independent schools I have come across. No one is allowed airs and graces. There is an acceptance of people'. And this, we feel, is the key reason that – as one parent said – the school is a 'hidden gem'.

Head of junior school: Since 2015, James Mundell LLB, PGCE (University of Wales), who has been at the school, in various roles, since 2004. On taking the reins, he implemented a number of academic changes, including moving maths and English to the morning when young minds are fresh. Lesson time was lengthened to one hour and two languages introduced so pupils are better prepared for year 7. Aware that young children are more predisposed to anxiety in modern times, he also ramped up the well-being programmes. Friendly, chatty, down to earth, he still does games lessons with the children; at the time we met him, he had just accompanied them on the three peaks challenge: 'I like to stay in touch with the grass roots'.

Academic matters: In the junior school, alongside English and maths, a wide curriculum includes science, history, art, design (they make fabulous things like abstract clocks), music (all learn the violin in KS1) and languages (German and French). Class sizes are 18 max but usually smaller (school has around 80 pupils). Generally equal between the genders, though this varies.

Maths and English done in ability groups (though they do not sit in these groups). Sometimes, children move up to a different year group (or down). The latter sounds dispiriting to a young mind, but a parent whose child was in a spelling group two years behind said the child was now 'positioned to succeed' in weak areas. Academic progress tracked via cognitive assessments but the whole picture is viewed.

Lots of cross-curricular themes, and much learning, head says, is child-led; if little Elliot brings in a fossil, it initiates discussion. Parents say teaching 'is creative and adapted to the child'. A lovely addition is 'philosophy for children', exploring muddy questions like 'what's fair?' (...if only we knew the answer to that one). Wellies are a must; lots of nature walks, dens and an outdoors storytelling chairs. Outdoors is integral; if they are studying rock types, they go find them. New forest school includes outdoor kitchen, reading chair and tepee.

Mild learning differences like dyslexia seem well catered for; the previous current learning support coordinator is now assistant head.

Parents who had moved their children to Giggleswick felt they had taken giant strides forward, from handwriting, which was flourishing, to confidence, which was soaring. One parent said Giggleswick had changed her child's 'thinking about learning'.

Year 7 in the senior school maintains breadth; three sciences and four languages on offer, French, Spanish, German and Latin (16 pupils out of 52 took a language A level; 49 out of 63 took at least one language GCSE in 2018). Small class sizes (whole school has around 350 pupils) and academic clinics available for a booster. One parent said, 'they change things quickly if approaches are not working'.

According to another parent, the academic side had 'really stepped up' following Mr Turnbull's arrival; there had been a turnover of staff 'in a good way' (though some departments needed more teachers). Much parental praise for the 'brilliant' new reporting system. 'Everybody knows where they're at', parent said.

And so they do. Pupils normally take nine or 10 GCSEs from a wide array of options. In 2018, 42 per cent of entries got 9-7/A*/A. Science particularly strong; typically over 90 per cent of candidates in physics and over 80 per cent in biology and chemistry achieve A*/A grades.

Broad selection of subjects at A level is on offer, including classics for, as Mr Turnbull puts it, 'that intellectual leap'. In 2018 at A level, 46 per cent of entries gained A*/A, 71 per cent A*-B.

All students study EPQ; Mr Turnbull is a fan of the independent and critical thinking involved. BTecs on offer in business and sport and gather a very fine crop of results.

Games, options, the arts: For schools in a glorious rural setting, participation in extracurricular is key (loafing in Starbucks is not an option). Children are simply encouraged to have a go here. 'They take a child out of their comfort zone but there is lots of encouragement and togetherness. No one is singled out', a parent said. This same parent had watched a strapping rugby player pupil approach a bespectacled boy to congratulate him for finishing a cross-country race. 'It's that sort of school' she said. Another parent felt 'quieter children flourish at Gigg; it brings them out of themselves'.

In the junior school, heaps of sport is on offer– cricket, football, rugby, netball, rounders, hockey. After-school activities include badminton, squash, tennis and golf. Lots of competitive fixtures and tours. Lots of outdoor pursuits too, including the Ribble Ramble and the Rawthey Run.

Trips are plentiful, to places like Yorvik Viking Museum or Hornby Castle. A good array of clubs from gardening to computers, outdoor adventure to construction. Residential experience further up the school; den making in Wales in year

5 (they build fires and toast marshmallows). In year 6, a week in the Lake District, kayaking and sailing.

An annual drama production in which years 3-6 take part, recently Wind in the Willows, and parents speak enthusiastically about performance opportunities.

At senior school, the same sports are played, at every level (not just the A team sporting stars). Lots of inter-school fixtures and overseas tours to places like South Africa. Outdoor pursuits are notable, whether it's Scarrig, the annual hill race or having a go on the school's mountain bike track. Pupils get opportunities to test these skills still further: winter training on the Isle of Skye, anyone? Bring it on.

The Richard Whiteley (an alumni) theatre seats over 200 and the mob-like popularity of it – the drama director terms it 'the emotional hub' of the school – is notable. (The theatre is also a venue for touring players which adds gravitas.) Serious school productions run alternately with big scale musicals like Sweeney Todd. Pretty much everyone – parents, pupils, teachers – bestow great praise on these glistening productions. Shakespeare in Schools also runs annually which means students limber up to bringing natural cadence to Shakespearean verse in a big theatre setting, like nearby Leeds. Wonderful stuff.

G

Debating is also popular with the weekly All Talk discussing topics like 'I have the right to be offended'. Although the school culture is one of tolerance, open discussion is encouraged. It was fantastic to hear a pupil say, 'I attribute 90 per cent of my successes to my involvement in debating'.

Music is very strong with bands, orchestras and choirs – one parent described it as 'stupendous'. The school's chamber choir Schola Cantorum gets to sing in Durham Cathedral, St Paul's, even Westminster Abbey. But there are also rock groups, an annual rock concert and a Young Musician of the Year.

Clubs are wide-ranging from astronomy to ceramics to student media. Duke of Edinburgh results in a nice stash of Gold – and the whole year group does CCF.

There is a fair amount of travel with language exchange programmes in Germany and Spain and national trips, to places such as Westminster.

A charming quirk is the school's 30 year history of manning the scoreboard at The Open at Royal Birkdale Golf Club.

Boarding: Overall, 40 per cent of boarders are flexi; 80 per cent live within three hours. Around 15 per cent are from overseas, many Forces children. Others just come for a year – from Spain, Germany, China – but may choose to stay on. A mix of around 17 nationalities exists at any one time; the school stresses it works hard at integrating and keeps the proportion of internationals below 20 per cent. Day pupils can also be around till 9pm.

Catteral is the boarding house for years 5-8, though most boarders are from year 7 upwards. Catteral common room is delightful, with amazing views. A vast room downstairs for games like Catteral's Got Talent, although the school encourages children to play outside in the fields beyond the house. When we visited, a new kitchen was being created 'where they can mess about and do cooking,' the experienced housemother said. One parent felt Catteral provides 'an extra security blanket for children'. Another said the few problems her child had experienced boarding were nipped in the bud immediately and the follow-up was 'superb'. Rooms are fine; six to a room in bunks (wardrobes, drawers, some with sink). Baths and showers clean and cheery. The sharing configurations don't change; the housemother feels 'children have to learn to get along'. The rooms of the youngest children are close to the housemother with own loos (no roaming about). Buzzers on every floor. Lots of trips, from Pizza Express to the Lake District.

Six houses for years 9s upwards: Carr and Style for girls, Morrison, Nowell, Paley and Shute for boys. An almost equal balance of boys and girls.

The girls' boarding house we saw was lovely; the common room stuffed with sofas inviting chat, opening on to a terrace; a small field beyond with a volleyball net. The rooms are fairly standard but, as usual, festooned with fairylights and cushions. Girls share in twos in years 10 and 11; lovely views, two desks and sink. At this age, room configurations change termly to 'develop mutual respect, cooperation, tolerance,' housemother says. A close eye is kept on potential friendship problems and, if identified, 'I might have a quiet word with them while walking the dog or ask the older girls to look at it', she says. One parent told us it was immediately spotted when her daughter was 'not as close' to her friends at one point. Height and weight subtly taken at the start of term; staff are vigilant at meal times. In years 9 and 10 phones handed in at bed time.

Nowell is the first boarding house to be revamped. We saw the 'show rooms' – a slick, university-style pod, light and bright with white units, vivid yellow chairs. A modern common room; stylish, grown up with boho touches, like pics in gilt frames. It's all going to be rather luxe.

It's fair to say the boy's accommodation pre-revamp is distinctly average. Usual fare of beds, wardrobes, desks....half eaten cereal bowls, grubby sports kit lying about. A large games room and kitchen. One of the houses has a wonderful kitchen mural painted by two pupils before they left the school. (A mark of how much they loved it. And how much, perhaps, they recognised that it needed a cheery facelift.)

Heaps of age-related activities happen, from pizza-making nights to croquet to paintballing.

Background and atmosphere: School was founded 500 years ago, moving to its present location in 1869. A 200-acre site; landscaped school gardens framed by magnificent Yorkshire Dales. Jaw-dropping beauty.

The purpose-built junior school, which opened in 2007, is bursting with ideas; no wall space for more. The library's huge picture window frames the hills. Wonderful art space, age-appropriate science lab. Loads of courts, playing fields and pitches.

Beautiful old buildings define the senior school, along with a splendid chapel perched on a hill. Walking into the reception is an upbeat experience, not just the cheeriness but the hush of the library directly to the right; enticing magazines, from Prospect to Business Review.

Lots of corridor and classroom displays. Nothing too arresting but all stimulating. The art department, also a gallery space, has great views and a resident ceramic artist. The student union, all leather sofas and a tiny bar, is nicely preparatory for the next stage of life.

Pastoral care, well-being and discipline: In the junior school, the form teacher handles the pastoral side, but there are worry boxes, buddies and a calm club. As one parent put it, metaphorically speaking 'the school gives you a hug'. Lots of responsibility as they get older: house captains, playground buddies etc. Many enthusiastic endorsements from parents: 'a loving and caring school', one said. All asserted there is no exclusion, no sidelining: 'even if you are not good at sports, they cheer you on'.

In the senior school, flying in the face of the current trend, phones are allowed. The head girl said this was 'under consideration' (implying pupils really do have a voice here) 'but autonomy is important to people'. Head also says any restrictions should be student-led. All sensible grown-up stuff which will appeal to parents who want their children to make sound decisions themselves, rather than be steered into them. 'Pupils need to understand rules, or they would rebel against them,' Mr Turnbull adds. One parent felt pupils were removed from social media and 'don't seem to bother much with their phones'. The same seems to apply to alcohol. Students of the legal age are allowed two small units of wine at the 'student union bar'. A member of staff confidently stated, 'and because of that, we don't have an alcohol problem'.

There is a health centre with access to a school counsellor. Regular chapel services and chaplain provide another pastoral layer. Chapel, a pupil said, is 'a time for appreciation of philosophy and gives meaning'. Just so. Inclusivity here, respect for all faiths and nationalities, really does seem to carry some substance.

All pupils belong to the house system and are assigned a tutor. Information-sharing sessions are run on topics like university entrance.

The size of the school means, as one parent put it, 'when life's difficulties arise, everyone knows. It's the Giggleswick bubble'. This, we imagine, might sometimes feel a tad claustrophobic, but the head is clearly seeking to make the school more outward looking.

Pupils and parents: Parents blend of two-income professionals, farmers and entrepreneurs. 'Genuinely supportive,' junior head says.

Pupils come from Ilkley, Bowland, Clitheroe, Harrogate, some from Blackpool or as far north as Kendal. Minibuses collect pupils from a clutch of these destinations.

Entrance: Entry to the junior is not selective but the school needs to feel it can support the needs of any potential pupil.

All go through to the senior school and make up 50 per cent of its intake. An increasing number join from state schools.

At age 11 by Giggleswick entrance exam, at age 13 normally CE together with interview and previous school's report. Entrance into sixth form is by a minimum of five GCSEs at grade 6; around 35 new sixth form entrants per year.

Exit: Very small fall-out after GCSEs. Pupils leave the sixth form to study a vast range of subjects from eg ancient history to events management to real estate and midwifery at mostly northern universities, though a few down south to eg Surrey, Essex and Bath. Three off overseas in 2018 – Germany, USA and Hong Kong.

Remarks: A happy, supportive, inclusive school in a wonderful setting where good academic results are on the up and the extracurricular enrichment genuinely caters for every child. A school where joyous participation, without pressure or expectation, is very much the ethos.

The Grammar School at Leeds

Linked with The Grammar School at Leeds Junior School

Alwoodley Gates, Harrogate Road, Leeds LS17 8GS

Ages 11–18 **Pupils** 1,400 **Sixth form** 400

Fees: £13,788 pa

01132 291552
www.gsal.org.uk

Principal: Since 2016, Sue Woodroofe, previously principal of the British School in Brussels (BSB). Trained at Durham as a teacher of English and history and worked in a range of British schools until a family move took her to Belgium and she joined the BSB as deputy head of the secondary school in 2004. She was appointed principal there in 2011.

Academic matters: Good A level results in 2018: 51 per cent A*/A, 75 per cent A*-B; historically strong in sciences, maths, economics (high numbers for these), English lit, French, humanities including RS, government and politics. In 2018 at GCSE: 72 per cent A*-A/7-9 with several outstanding individual sets of results. Astronomy and Latin offered; all do RS (many with high grades).

Very impressive successes in national academic competitions for sciences and maths, plus debating, chess, finance/business enterprise (won recent Bank of England interest rate challenge). Also in STEM competitions – awarded three Arkwright Engineering scholarships recently. Uses wide network of links with local businesses and professions to provide other opportunities for gifted and talented students, eg sixth form student able to cook alongside Raymond Blanc.

Classes of 15-22 taught by well established and experienced staff – pupils we met commended them as very helpful and fair and lessons as enjoyable and interactive, going beyond the constraints of exam syllabuses. Parents feel students are pushed to achieve their full potential. Sixth formers deeply appreciative of the 'fantastic' support received for university applications – 'The tutors really care about your applications..They know everyone well..You get sent specific subject bulletins while you are choosing your courses..The careers library is always open' – including preparation for Oxbridge interviews and additional subject tests (separate Oxbridge and UCAS coordinators). Parent: 'They all seem to end up at the right universities.'

Very well qualified and experienced SENCo who works across the whole school, providing valuable continuity, supported by eight assistants, her office discreetly situated at the top of the LRC. Covers wide range of difficulties, including physical – mild rather than severe. Students checked for dyslexia at key points; sixth formers helped to access additional support at university.

Games, options, the arts: All sporting mod cons (parent: 'amazing') including squash courts, leading to impressive success in a wide range of trad sports (national level netball, rugby and hockey) and non trad sports (eg cycling, sailing, badminton, table tennis, golf), from local to international levels. Awarded Independent Sports School of the Year recently. Flourishing girls' football. Opportunities for the less gifted but committed to represent the school too. South African netball tour, golf in Portugal, rugby in Australia.

Masses of music, of all kinds – appearance on Songs of Praise, members of national choirs and orchestras; tour to Czech Republic. Dance and drama studio plus small-scale theatre and open air courtyard performance space produce diverse drama – Fame, Little Shop of Horrors, annual Shakespeare and some less obvious choices. Three students selected for the hugely competitive National Youth Theatre. Vibrant art/technology/ICT quarter supplied with high tech machines; much very good art on display around the school; regular contact with professional artists. Arts festival under way during our visit, all students and staff enthusiastically creating gingerbread men in various styles for the driveway.

One afternoon a week dedicated to co-curricular activities in sixth form – lower sixth pioneering an online record of their achievements in this area, to be combined with their academic results to form a GSAL graduation certificate. Clubs and societies galore, many managed by sixth formers, enable all to 'find their niche', eg Model United Nations (now organising a Leeds-wide one), gardening, history of art, poetry slam. CCF (RAF and army sections) collaborates with affiliated state academy; several DofE golds; school council; 20 hours of community service compulsory for lower sixth. Fabulous sum raised for various charities; 27-year partnership with Malawi schools and orphanages. Outdoor activities programme for all pupils in years 7, 9 and 12. Trips to Himalayas, Greece, France, Spain and Germany.

Background and atmosphere: The largest independent day school in England, formed by a merger of Leeds Girls' High School and Leeds Grammar School in 2008. Girls' school founded in 1876 by Yorkshire Ladies Council for Education, while boys' was founded in 1552 through a bequest from Sir William Sheafield. Occupies a 128 acre site in a well-heeled residential area on the outskirts of the city. Attractive, purpose-built two storey buildings in clean sandstone brick. Big modern hall with organ for year group assemblies. Pleasingly decorated, generous sized, very well stocked library; cheerful modern languages area with colourful bunting consisting of the flags of the main countries leading to the relevant classrooms; spacious sixth form centre with own cafeteria. Vast dining room with wide choice of appetising food (cooked breakfast available) – no complaints here. Tries hard to minimise queuing time, but salad and sandwiches a speedier option than hot, and gets very noisy when full. Smart dark purple uniform – girls wear kilts, sixth formers business-type clothes.

G

Modern multi-faith chapel with own fine stained glass windows plus original ones from old boys' school. Unusually, students act as faith leaders for the five main faiths (Christian, Jewish, Muslim, Hindu, Sikh), organising lunch time assemblies, celebration of special days and charity fundraising events.

House system (eight houses) central to the rich co-curricular offer – cookery, cycling and triathlon as well as standard competitions, the focus being on having fun trying activities you aren't necessarily brilliant at and making friends across ages and forms. Each house has two captains and four deputies, so plenty of opportunities for leadership, along with the other trad posts. Strong community spirit a testament to the success of the merger – 'There's a lot of camaraderie..friendly competition but not to the point where there's a negative environment,' according to a sixth form girl. More than one of the students we met used the phrase 'friendly competition' when asked if they felt under pressure to always achieve top grades: 'It's OK to do the best you can,' and it's also acceptable not to conform to the norm. Parents say: 'good gender balance...they all get on... not cliquey...a mini university feel.'

Pastoral care, well-being and discipline: Usual system of form tutors and year heads ('fantastic'), with involvement of heads of houses – tutors know pupils very well; speedy and thoughtful response to problems – pupils say any bullying would be dealt with effectively; a sixth former spoke of 'a vast network if you're struggling.. I always feel I have a teacher to go to'. Alert to eating and other mental health issues. Well planned transition for year 7s, who initially, and understandably, find the school very big, but soon adjust. Firm on smart appearance.

Pupils and parents: Most from north Leeds and surrounding area, eg Ilkley, Harrogate, Tadcaster, Wetherby and Wharfedale. Mainly professional families with two working parents, but a good number with bursaries; wide ethnic mix with many languages spoken. About half of seniors from junior school, rest largely from local state schools (entrance tests finely tuned to avoid over-tutored success), plus local preps such as Moorlands, Richmond House and Westville. Confident, articulate, open, natural students. Plenty of contact with parents, whose views are obtained through questionnaires and who are very happy with the school; busy PTA raises serious sums of money.

Many famous, very distinguished old pupils – writers, eg poet Tony Harrison (though his memories of his schooldays are far from genial); Baroness Pauline Neville Jones; Lord Justice Dyson; Marilyn Stowe, family lawyer who played a prominent role in the release of Sally Clark; Sir Gerald Kaufman MP; comedian Barry Cryer, Kaiser Chiefs singer Ricky Wilson; Olympic diver Hannah Starling; golfer Colin Montgomerie.

Entrance: Year 7: tests in maths, English, non-verbal reasoning, in January (competitive – large numbers apply) plus interview. Years 8-9: similar tests plus interviews in modern foreign languages and sciences and with head of year. Year 10: skills based interviews in core subjects and with head of year. For entry to sixth form at least six 6s at GCSE, with 9-7 if choosing maths, sciences or modern foreign languages at A level, reference from current school plus interview; about 20 from outside taken.

Exit: Very few leave after GCSE. In 2018, 12 to Oxbridge, to read a full range of academic subjects.

Money matters: Over £1 million for means-tested bursaries (up to full fees), scholarships, music awards and temporary financial support grants – 200+ pupils benefit.

Remarks: Offers outstanding opportunities, both academic and extracurricular, the latter much valued by students of all ages. Also values kindness, tolerance and giving to others in need, both at home and abroad, thus paying far more than lip service to the cliched educational aim of 'developing the whole person'. Heartfelt accolade from parent: 'The school blows me away. I feel so proud my daughter goes there.'

The Grammar School at Leeds Junior School

Linked with The Grammar School at Leeds

Alwoodley Gates, Harrogate Road, Leeds LS17 8GS

Ages 3–11 Pupils 700

Fees: £9,441 pa

01132 291552
www.gsal.org.uk

Head of junior school: Since 2009, Robert Lilley (early 50s) BA (government and politics from University of Essex) PGCE. Educated at Allerton High, began career in industry, then taught business studies and IT in secondary schools, director of studies at Moorlands (prep), head of junior school at Fulneck, then of Silcoates Schools. Teaches boys' PE and runs chess and Wargaming societies. Relaxed, pleasant, approachable; very popular with pupils and parents – 'Fab...very friendly...honest... conscientious..even-handed...he investigates issues thoroughly and follows up quickly with a solution.' Married to a teacher, three children: one adult, one at university, one at GSL. Enjoys walking and music – plays the guitar and currently learning the trombone to help fill the brass gap in the orchestra.

Arrived one year after the merger of the Girls' and Boys' Grammar Schools – main goal to create identity for new school: wanted to 'keep the grammar school rigour and add the breadth of opportunity of a prep school' by extending extracurricular offer. Also keen to develop partnerships with local primaries via competitions, resource sharing, help with gifted children, activity days.

Moving on in July 2019. His successor will be Gabrielle Solti BA PGCE (40s), currently head of South Hampstead High Junior School. She also headed Notting Hill and Ealing Junior School for 10 years. Born into a musical family (her late father, Sir Georg Solti, was once described by the Telegraph as 'the most distinguished conductor alive'), she studied history at Oxford, interned at the European Commission (where she met her husband), then worked at Nestlé in France and the UK before taking a teacher training course at the Institute of Education.

Since 2015, head of Rose Court nursery and pre-prep is Jo Hall, previously deputy head.

Entrance: Informal assessments (some reading and number work) for entry into Rose Court; looking for potential and readiness to learn. External candidates for prep school take tests in numeracy, literacy and multiple choice non-verbal reasoning, and spend a day in a class.

Exit: Most move seamlessly from pre-prep to prep. Great majority from prep to senior school. A lot of help given to parents of any children viewed as unlikely to thrive there.

Remarks: On same site as senior school. Large trad, multi-purpose hall, music room, drama/dance studio, three ICT suites. Very big playground for years 4-6 plus separate quiet playground with picnic tables. Very well stocked, attractive library (over 12,000 books) shows reading really valued. Spacious classrooms – own desk plus large locker. Has increased in size to 100 in a year, so where possible year groups situated together so children feel part of a small unit. Classes of 16-21.

Sats-free zone. Some excellent but some average teachers, say parents. The very able provided for by extension work in class, setting in maths, theme days, workshops, mini enterprise group. Won national science and engineering award for week of science activities – specialist science teacher for years 5-6. No significant gender difference in achievement. Children say teachers are helpful, make lessons 'fun, very interactive'. Reasonable amount of homework. Good additional support provided by teaching assistants, subject clinics/clubs too. Well qualified, deeply committed SENCo who works across whole school.

Uses senior school sports facilities to great effect – success in several national competitions in a wide range of sports, standard ones plus table tennis, gymnastics, chess, two high-reaching biathlon stars, a Boccia star (Paralympic sport), a national climber. Parental praise for boys' sports teachers, but some criticism of a lack of support for less talented girls. Wide choice of activities – music, drama, verse speaking, slam poetry, dance, creative writing all thriving. However, getting your child into the more popular (non-sports) ones can be as challenging as 'getting a ticket to the Glastonbury Festival – you have to be very on the ball'. Interesting technology topics, eg World War 2 cooking for year 6. Quiz team through to national final. Four houses and school council. Lots of links with senior school – sixth formers help with reading and sports. Transition to senior school organised through art, design and technology workshops; continuity also through shared teachers.

Deputy head just for pastoral care – parents generally happy with this aspect. Bullying can occur, as in any school, said head honestly, but dealt with sensibly. Focus more on reward than punishment – children earn vouchers for the Merit (stationery) shop and can win house points for being kind. Children trained to be well organised in preparation for senior school.

Confident, articulate children (our tour guide was an extraordinarily self-possessed 10 year old, clearly a CEO in the making), enthusiastic about the quality of their lessons, extracurricular opportunities and friendly atmosphere. Lots of contact with parents, formal and informal, plus staff email addresses in children's planners.

Rose Court nursery/pre-prep on site of ex Leeds Girls' High School – two adapted houses with a modern extension occupied by the nursery. Spacious, light, well-equipped classrooms with very good displays and access to outdoor area; generous sized art, music, ICT, drama/dance rooms.

One teacher and two assistants for nursery (1:8 ratio), where children are brought on very well – early years foundation stage judged outstanding by Independent Schools Inspectorate. Four reception classes of 15-21, one teacher and one assistant. Also a Sats-free zone filled with busy, happy children enjoying work and play; high achievement levels and plenty of challenge for the very bright, of both genders – parents very happy with progress made. Much use of themed days and weeks, eg science, bushcraft; light amount of homework so parents (often both work) have time to just relax with their children (before and after-school care much used). Strong pastoral care and in house special needs provision, plus visiting speech and language therapist

Over 30 different activities per week, including lots of music (very strong – full time specialist teacher) and serious sums (over £4k) raised for national and international charities – well-established link with a school in Malawi plus local nurseries. Pupil Voice (school council).

A great ethnic mix – over 29 languages spoken. Very engaging children, friendly, lively, confident and enthusiastic, extremely smart in their dark purple and white uniform (kilts for the girls). Two of the parents we spoke to felt this part of the school was more focused on clever, diligent girls than the average child or boys needing more pushing, but others were full of praise ('a lovely school').

G

Greenhead College

Greenhead Road, Huddersfield, West Yorkshire HD1 4ES

Ages 16–19 **Pupils** 2,484

01484 422032
www.greenhead.ac.uk

Principal: Since 2016, Simon Lett, previously vice principal at Notre Dame Catholic Sixth Form College in Leeds. Birmingham born, he has taught extensively in FE and sixth form colleges, and was one of the founding members of Longley Park Sixth Form College in Sheffield before joining Notre Dame. He is keen to encourage students to broaden their experiences beyond the classroom. He lives in York with his wife and young twins; he is a keen circuit trainer and a lover of jazz and the arts.

Academic matters: 2018 A levels: 64 per cent A*-B; 35 per cent A*/A (one of the top sixth form colleges nationally); consistent performer. Wide choice: law, government and politics, geology, statistics, four modern languages (native speakers for oral practice housed in the wittily named Foreign Embassy, teachers in the Foreign Office), music technology and music (A level and BTec); new courses in health and social care, medical science and business; very successful EPQ; four applied subjects. Strong numbers for chemistry (plenty of girls take this and physics), biology, maths, English, law, economics, geography, business studies. Average class sizes 19 for A level; five hours' homework per subject expected; not much gender achievement gap.

Success in all three science Olympiads – one British physics finalist, senior maths challenge and national and international business and economics competitions. Nine-strong staff Oxbridge team (interview reports going back 13 years); regional hub for HE extension programme.

In top 10 per cent nationally for value added – ALPS measuring system originates from Greenhead – through specialising in A levels (in a consortium with two other colleges with different curricular offers), so teachers have high levels of expertise; strong enrichment programme that enables students to develop as people, thus gaining confidence and motivation; and expert personal tutors with a generous allocation of time, permitting plenty of individual support. Subject support readily available – study rooms in each area, students often work in staff rooms.

Students (and Ofsted) praise teaching: 'Brilliant...they love their subjects and make them interesting...they're always happy to help and to go beyond the curriculum...lots of extension opportunities..detailed feedback'.

Very dedicated, well-resourced additional support co-ordinator able to assess for exam access arrangements – early screening for learning support needs; can accommodate all kinds of disability and need. These students achieve at least as well as others. Cheerful learning support study area for all comers so no stigma. Second year mathematicians and scientists mentor struggling first years.

Games, options, the arts: Has half-size Astro, playing fields, two tennis courts, sports hall and fitness suite, supplemented by very good nearby community facilities. All the standard sports plus eg boxing, judo, golf, squash, archery, fencing, girls' football, yoga. Very successful national level netball and hockey; regional football; a UK level swimmer; climbing and cross-country doing well too. 'Sport maker' employed to encourage take up of all kinds of sporting activity.

Much music including jazz, guitar, advanced theory and music technology; work with Kirklees Music School, Opera North, Halle Orchestra, Huddersfield Contemporary Music Festival and a rock school; Paris tour. Drama less well resourced – no theatre – but busy: annual full-scale production plus original piece taken to local primary; recent promenade play written and produced by students with Chol theatre company.

Really stunning art on display, notably large scale oil paintings – we can understand the end of year exhibition leading to sales, as we saw much looking professional in standard; syllabus permits wide range of art forms. Inspirational department encourages innovation and risk – a number progress to the Slade.

Fab choice of enrichment activities (prize-winning programme) – book-making, Amnesty International, hefty numbers of gold DofE; some geared towards university courses, eg working with a practising engineer on a real company's problem, mock trial comp, medical ethics, Bible studies for Eng Lit; major voluntary service programme. Large sums raised for charities – students organised an economics event involving international experts and money raised for developing world micro investment projects. Trips to Europe, USA, Iceland, Mozambique.

Very strong on careers – interview practice with professionals and academics; employability skills workshops; careers conference; employment/gap fair focused on non HE routes. Annual project and work placement week with work shadowing, eg at Westminster ('My son had an amazing time..he went away a boy and came back a man'), the Bank of England and of the mayor of twin town Besançon – 'brilliant... unbelievable,' say students; media professionals brought into college to manage ambitious projects.

Background and atmosphere: Located close to centre of Huddersfield in a conservation area (which limits scope for expansion). Main building originally 1920s girls' grammar school, became sixth form college 1994; unsightly 1960s science building, 1990s buildings, plus handsome very new maths and physics centre with spacious labs and classrooms; new building with library and computing resources; a vast space used for assemblies, exams and activities; new music and film studies facilities.

Some tired areas – dull corridors lined with lockers, a lot of nondescript lino and carpets and walls that need refreshing – but very good displays everywhere, eg book reviews, politics articles, maths art, colour photos of student activities, plus boxes filled with support and extension material. Easy access to staff facilitated by staff timetables and photos up in every area. Rows and rows of silent students, intent on PCs or textbooks, all over the college – the extensive silent study area has no need of staffing. Cheerfully buzzing, but not raucous, relaxation area with bright green chairs, ping pong table, small shop and modern airy extension.

Students respected as individuals – 'We have freedom to thrive'; active LGBT group; two student reps on governing body and student council suggestions acted on; student voice (student feedback) taken seriously.

Pastoral care, well-being and discipline: Twenty-five personal tutors, who mostly teach A level subjects, each support four tutor groups of around 26 – system has national reputation. Learning support team and transition mentor have extensive liaison with partner schools before enrolment; two in-house counsellors. Current focus on developing resilience in preparation for change from modular to linear exams, a foresighted goal other institutions would do well to emulate. Help for students to settle socially on arrival.

Aims to be 'an adult community with no rules', so students learn to take responsibility for own learning and think for themselves, in readiness for university and the world of work, but 'support there if you need it' (parent).

Pupils and parents: A range of ability – 27 per cent from low-performing secondaries – and socio-economic backgrounds; ethnically mixed (15-20 per cent) reflecting the local community. Articulate, confident students, very enthusiastic about the college (they often return to talk to students about their degree courses) and appreciative of all the staff help. Good level of communication with parents.

Distinguished alumni: Mona Siddique (professor, journalist and Radio 4's Thought for the Day contributor); Liz Green, Matthew Roberts and Spencer Stokes (TV and radio presenters); actor Jessica Gunning.

Entrance: Most courses require at least a 4 grade at GCSE in English language and maths; for three A levels, at least three grade 6s in addition; higher requirements for specific subjects; all applicants interviewed. Priority to students from 12 11-16 years partner schools in Huddersfield area (70 per cent of places taken up); rest offered on competitive basis irrespective of address, mainly from Kirklees and neighbouring authorities; very oversubscribed.

Exit: Around 90 per cent to university, with some 35 per cent to Russell Group; 24 to Oxbridge in 2018. Durham, Leeds, Manchester, Newcastle, Nottingham, Sheffield and York well represented. Increasing numbers to European universities and a few to American ones. Business, law, English, history, psychology, engineering, maths, medicine (24 medics in 2018) most popular subjects. Some 10 per cent to apprenticeships/ employment.

Money matters: Bursary fund for students under 19 from low income households or short term extreme need.

Remarks: Well-deserved recipient of recent Sunday Times Parent Power sixth form college of the year award for consistency of academic achievement. Has the right priorities – funds focused on teaching and learning and student support rather than smart offices or decor. Hearteningly enthusiastic and committed students. 'It's been the making of my son – he's really come into his own there,' glowed a parent.

Harrogate Ladies' College

Linked with Highfield Prep School (HLC)

43

Clarence Drive, Harrogate, North Yorkshire HG1 2QG

Ages 11–18 **Pupils** 297 **Sixth form** 93 **Boarders** 125 full, 7 flexi

Fees: Day £16,035; Boarding £29,115 – £36,510 pa

01423 537045
www.hlc.org.uk

Principal: Since 2013, Sylvia Brett BA MA (40s). Read theology at Durham, followed by masters in philosophy and religion at University of London. Worked in alumni relations and as moral tutor at Durham for four years before joining the Royal Masonic School as RS teacher and sixth form housemistress. Then lay chaplain and head of RS at Caldicott followed by head of lower school, RS teacher and year 7 housemistress at Downe House, before being appointed as sole deputy at Roedean.

Head believes in ensuring girls are 'jolly good at lots of different things' when they leave HLC. Breadth of curriculum and extracurricular opportunities vital and girls 'are encouraged to be brave' in extending their comfort zone and trying new activities.

Open, engaging and caring, has a 'passion for deep learning' and getting to know the young people in her care. Declared by sixth formers as 'more personable' than predecessors, impressed with her interest in them and knowledge of special events in their lives. Parents see the head as 'a traditional headmistress who genuinely cares about the school and its pupils' and as 'a strong, reassuring presence, confident and approachable'. More traditional than her predecessor, say girls, who have noted a downturn in emphasis on 'girl power', and parents who, without complaint, felt the drive is 'less towards cutting edge and 21st century'.

Married to Justin, a classics teacher, and has one daughter who is a pupil at the school. When time permits her interests include music (singing and piano), art, swimming, family and friends.

Academic matters: In 2018, 35 per cent A*/A grades at A level and 70 per cent A*-B. Interestingly, in recent years almost half of sixth form pupils, predominantly international boarders, have been new to the school.

Good range of subjects on offer though numbers can restrict options. Historically, strength in mathematics and sciences, a particular bias in the sixth form, but modern languages are fine – normally only the odd D at GCSE, otherwise all A*-C. Only a handful (groups as small as two per language) opt for modern languages at A level, but achieve good results. Over the past four years, a third of girls have pursued a business-related degree course. Launched 2010 in purpose built business suite, the Business School has increased business-related subjects to include accounting, business studies, economics and psychology, which remain popular choices. Wider purpose continues to promote enterprise and entrepreneurship throughout the school. Extended Project Qualification introduced for older pupils; just over 10 per cent uptake so far.

In 2018, 50 per cent A*-A/9-7 at GCSE; value added 1+ grade per subject. Strong performance in all three sciences, English literature, modern foreign languages, humanities and drama. Broad curriculum and, common with most schools dual award or single sciences recommended after first year of course, one modern foreign language compulsory and a standard range of options. Statistics offered in addition for top set mathematics.

Teaching is generally very good – friendly, good-humoured staff, and girls feel both known and supported on the whole. Generally a willingness to learn and good manners makes teaching a worthwhile experience here. As one parent said, 'Teachers go the extra mile for pupils regularly'. Plenty of new blood though: across the school 95 per cent of staff have less than 10 years of service, with movement in and out of the independent and state sectors.

Practical subjects good too – impressive art throughout the school and girls using a wide range of complex design and technology equipment. Well-equipped food technology room used up to GCSE. Enrichment programme for first year GCSE and sixth form to widen horizons in preparation for higher education. Plenty of IT facilities but an iPad free zone – 'no gimmicks' says the head; 'IT must enhance learning'.

Class size maximum 24, some as low as 12. Parents' evenings and full reports twice yearly, always discussed with head or tutor prior to being sent home. Displays everywhere still a feature – a striking balance of pupil work and thought-provoking material, alongside posters from house captains rallying the troops.

Overseas students encouraged to sit exams in their native language; additional English language tuition available (and certainly encouraged). EAL students used to sit IELTS rather than GCSE English, but pilot study of integration with mainstream English classes in years 10 and 11 has proved highly successful and continues to be the way forward.

Across the whole school over 10 per cent SEN catered for in and out of the classroom by dedicated learning support. Generally, in class teacher support free with scale of charges for a more individual programmes. Needs span support in cognitive and learning, communication and interaction, emotional and mental health, and sensory and physical.

Games, options, the arts: Sport, the life-blood of the school, is keenly pursued by all with lacrosse ('lackie') embedded in the school's culture. Current holders of U13s northern schools' lacrosse title, with good representation at county and regional level. Good range of competitive team sports with recent successes in tennis, district champions in U13 and U15, Harrogate area U14 netball and North Yorkshire Schools Games winners for rounders. Good, much-used, sports facilities include plenty of tennis and badminton courts, multi-gym, 25-metre pool and an enormous indoor general-purpose sports hall which doubles up as a venue for social events, speech day etc.

Dedicated music house accommodates ensembles galore, from samba to string with four choirs. Music is a real strength and majority of girls learn an instrument or two. Musicians regularly run away with prizes at the Harrogate Festival, chapel choir were semi-finalists in a BBC competition, the challenging baroque opera Dido and Aeneas performed, and a wealth of choral performances in cathedral services, at the Royal Hall and on tour, most recently Barcelona.

A level theatre studies on offer, with plays and productions acted out in the suitably-equipped drama studio. The Merchant of Venice staged in Leeds as part of the Shakespeare Schools Festival and annual competitive inter-house drama filled with theatrical thrills and spills. Curriculum supported by regular trips to concerts, theatre and cinema. Many girls take LAMDA lessons (honours and distinctions the norm).

Art, photography and textiles all on offer at A level. Good facilities and the results of talented artists on show around the school. Careers education taken seriously – two weeks' work experience for all followed by presentation and lunch.

An extensive extracurricular menu with over 20 creatively named clubs ranging from Apprentice to Babel Fish and Legobots, with interesting business breakfast club. Golf, sailing and ski trips as well as keen D of E and masses of charity and community work. Burgeoning participation and success in Leeds Young Enterprise. Enterprise days held in the summer term.

H

Boarding: Four well-presented boarding houses each have attractive study bedrooms, a common room centred on the TV, kitchen and games room, with room for 30 in two houses and 45 in the third. Upper sixth only in Tower with room for 40. Distinction made between 'home' and school by no pupil access to houses during the school day.

Up to four can share a room in lower school, but currently able to spread out a little more. Most sixth formers have their own room with internet access for all in studies and bedrooms. Two taster nights per term offered to day pupils without charge. A growing number of flexi and weekly boarders, but full boarding offers weekends full of trips and activities, off and on site, with over 90 boarders remaining in school most weekends.

Friendly, comfortable feel, no inter-house rivalry: girls mix well with the sense of a supportive sisterhood and good relations with staff. Encouraged to mix across the ages with a buddy system operating for new pupils. A reward system in place for kind deeds, tidiness and helping out. Celebration of international festivals brings an appreciation of different cultures.

Upper sixth housed in Tower – a half way house between school and university where pupils prepare and eat breakfast and a couple of evening meals in house and have greater freedom than lower down the school (team-building exercises at start of upper sixth aid the bonding process). At 16+ girls are allowed out one night a week.

Background and atmosphere: School founded in 1893 on a nearby site and is one of the Allied Schools. Within walking distance of the busy town centre, in the heart of Harrogate's leafy prime real estate, originally part of the Duchy of Lancaster. The pleasant Victorian mock-Tudor buildings with sympathetic additions blend gently with the locality. C of E (own chapel, resounding hymns et al) in small doses for all without exception. New assembly hall officially opened in 2013 to mark school's 120 year anniversary. Separate sixth form centre in main school complete with common rooms, study centre, kitchens, AV room etc with use of business school café. Unique sixth form studies valued by girls as their space and used for personal study until 9.00pm each evening.

'Being the best you can be', the school motto, is at the heart of the ethos here. Resilience, curiosity and confidence are the aims, engendered by an individual knowledge of each girl by their teachers. The school is proud of being in the top one per cent for value added at GCSE, adding 1+ grade per pupil per subject (the top five per cent of schools add on average 0.6+ of a grade).

School council meets regularly, though girls would like it to be less of a talking shop and to exert more power. Uniform throughout the school, predominantly navy with tartan skirts, a nod to the traditional colour scheme, perpetuated by the retention of the green cloak for chapel. Dress code for sixth form – business wear – recently more rigorously enforced.

Food is now provided by external catering company, which has seen a marked improvement in the choice and quality of meals available; recently refurbished dining room. Staff and girls dine together in main dining room, self-service with occasional formal dining. All meals here for boarders during the week, only snacks available in houses for L6 boarders and below. Dinner served in the boarding houses for all boarders at the weekend.

Pastoral care, well-being and discipline: Girls we spoke to are happy here. Manners strictly monitored. Clear guidelines for good behaviour that pupils understand and few challenging misdemeanours. Head has introduced a more positive points system, which is seen by girls as less draconian. Occasional links with other schools, but not into creating artificial exposure to boys. Drugs and similar problems uncommon and treated with firmness – head retains discretion, expulsions rare. Health centre, specialist counsellor, tutors and staff all on hand to help if things go wrong. School has recently opened a Wellness Centre, designed to help pupils, parents, staff and the wider community to 'develop their wellbeing'.

Pupils and parents: A widening catchment for day, flexi and weekly boarders, from Ilkley to York and beyond. Looking to attract pupils from Borders and Scotland; currently the majority of boarders are from overseas, particularly in the sixth form. There are around 24 nationalities in school though 40 per cent of boarders are from south east Asia. Within the boarding houses there are shared cultural celebrations and activities, but day girls told us that close bonds with their Pacific Rim peers are the exception rather than the rule.

Parents predominantly from the usual professions, many Harrogate notables, also self-employed and some farming families, popular with the Forces. Turns out informed, assured, polite and articulate girls, cooperative rather than competitive. Strong OG network, including Coki Van der Velde, 2015 Barclays Woman of the Year; Julie Mulligan, police and crime commissioner for North Yorkshire; Juliet Bremner, TV news reporter; Laura Winwood, former president of the Oxford Union. Building a network for more recent leavers to stay in touch.

Entrance: Main entry points are 11, 13 and 16 but school flexible. For Y7 entry, taster day in autumn term, school entrance test (mathematics, English, non-verbal reasoning) and interview taken on January assessment day, together with reports from previous school. Highfield Prep is the linked feeder school though recently only a small number have transferred to the college. Both school and parents gave the reasons as competition from excellent local state provision with families cherry-picking stages of independent education.

Minimum five GCSEs at grade C or above required for entry to sixth form, international pupils tested in English and appropriate subjects. Scholarship assessment programme.

Exit: Retention of day pupils at 16 has seen a recent improvement but historically some 15 per cent leave at 16 for local state or independents. An influx of international pupils – currently more than 60 per cent of sixth formers are boarders – results in a sixth form of nearly 100 pupils.

Sixth formers leave for a widespread selection of universities, with Edinburgh, Leeds, Aston, Durham, Manchester, Newcastle, Queen Mary's London, Royal Holloway and York currrently popular. One to Oxbridge, plus three medics in 2018 and others to Hungary, the Netherlands, the US and South Korea. Wide range of courses: economics and business feature strongly but includes international relations and politics, 3D design and architecture, medicine, PPE, engineering, mathematics and law.

Money matters: A range of scholarships of up to 15 per cent of day fees. Fee reductions of 15 per cent for UK armed forces and 10 percent for offspring of former pupils. Means-tested bursaries up to 110 per cent of day fees to include transport, uniform etc.

Remarks: An 'in-town' girls' day/boarding school that shouts 'girl-centred' education, firmly holding onto its roots whilst reaching out to widen opportunity for its pupils to allow them to blossom in their post-school brave new world. Academic results particularly good at GCSE and a dazzling array of out of classroom opportunities means happy girls and supportive parents. Looking at ways to communicate its distinct offering at home and away to combat the pressures from increasingly competitive North Yorkshire schools.

Highfield Prep School (HLC)

Linked with Harrogate Ladies' College

Clarence Drive, Harrogate, North Yorkshire HG1 2QG

Ages 2–11 **Pupils** 310

Fees: Day £9,420 – £10,740; Boarding: £23,820 pa

01423 537045
www.hlc.org.uk/highfield

Head: Since 2016, James Savile (late 40s) BEd. Studied primary education and French at Southampton, a fellow member of the College of Teaching and a member of the Chartered Institute of Education Assessors, he brings a wealth of experience in independent education. Appointments in the last five years include, most recently, deputy head at Salisbury Cathedral School, headship at Leweston Prep School in Dorset and a year as principal at Dolphin School and Noah's Ark Nurseries in London.

A modern languages specialist and experienced sports coach, with a particular interest in rugby and athletics, he is building on the recent increased focus on PE in the prep school. He says, 'I'm a big believer in sport for all. That means enabling all children to access sport at their own level and developing their individual skills and abilities.'

Passionate about the importance of creativity in schools, he says, 'People talk a lot about literacy but creativity can sometimes get overlooked. I believe creativity encourages freedom of thinking. It allows children to learn about themselves and recognise who they are. This in turn helps build confidence, encourages independent learning and helps children develop a genuine passion for their own education. That perhaps, above all, is what I hope that children will take with them when they leave Highfield.'

Head's ethos is shaped by a passion for getting the best out of each and every child and he believes that 'As teachers it's our responsibility to get to know and understand each individual child the way their parents know and understand them. It's our role to nurture, support and guide them as individuals and to enable their talents to grow.' He firmly believes that the strength of the relationship between parents, staff and pupils plays a key part in achieving this and its evidence in action at Highfield drew him to the school.

Author of a common entrance revision guide in French, his interests also include military history. Married with a son and daughter.

Head of Highfield Pre-School since 2014 is Emily Bayley, a qualified teacher with extensive experience in pre-school and early years education. A lead teacher for North Yorkshire county council promoting best practice and supporting early years teachers across the county and also a qualified forest school leader. A lover of the outdoors, a passion she shares with her dog, Monty (who is a regular visitor), and the children.

Bubbly, enthusiastic and committed, believes that the key to successful early years development lies in working in partnership with parents, and has brought about a cultural shift in welcoming parents into the school at any and all times. Much appreciated by them; as one commented, 'The Pre-School was outstanding in its introduction to formal learning for my daughter and I cannot thank Mrs Bayley and her team enough'. Runs EYFS forums for parents on topics such as sleep, nutrition and play. Topically, mathematics is next on the agenda.

H

Entrance: At 2+ for Highfield Pre-School (formerly Bankfield Nursery) by visit, registration and welcome session. Into Highfield, all ages though predominantly at 4+ when majority come from the pre-school. Non-selective but external entrants have assessment and interview with invitation to a separate taster day.

Exit: All girls offered places at Harrogate Ladies' College (Highfield senior school); take-up varies and sometimes very small. Some girls and boys to local independents GSAL, St Olave's York, Ashville, Cundall Manor and Bootham. The majority to the outstanding state provision in Harrogate and Ripon or relocation.

Remarks: Pre-prep and nursery is located in a large Victorian house just across the road from the senior school campus and Highfield Prep. Extensive grounds around the house provide direct access to free play on hard playing areas and garden, with plans for a chicken run. The house has converted into a spacious and well-equipped facility yet it retains its home from home atmosphere. Meals are taken in the dining room and much emphasis on nutritious meals and instilling good manners and social etiquette.

Close links with Highfield Prep (EYFS head is responsible for pre-school and reception) and shared events to ensure easy transition for pupils to the next stage – important as around 70 per cent of children progress through to Highfield.

Pre-school children are in two groups until Easter (foundation and transition) and three for the summer term (when another foundation group is added) with the luxury of bespoke areas of the house for each group. For pre-school group, specialist teaching in physical education, music, drama, French and forest school starts to ease them into reception. Jolly Phonics scheme introduced and children encouraged to progress at their own pace.

EYFS qualified teaching staff encouraged by the head to share best practice with other schools in North Yorkshire – currently working with a school in Ilkley – and support them in implementing new practice. Children's learning journeys record their progress and achievements and are much prized by pupils and parents alike. No online journals here.

Core hours of 9am-4pm included within fees, extended to 7.30am-6pm at additional charge. Open term time only though care is available through Easter and summer holidays at a cost.

Highfield Prep is conveniently sited on the main campus, a playground away from the main college building, a mixture of new-build and Victorian conversion. Spacious and airy hall for group activities and assemblies, with no wasted space in circulation areas. Classrooms on three floors with reception on the ground floor, with direct access to a secure, well-resourced outdoor learning area and playground.

Two classes in most year groups, now mostly 60 per cent girls 40 per cent boys throughout, usually in adjacent classrooms though no particular progression through the building. Dazzling impeccable, well ordered displays of pupils' work and information posters in all, well-equipped classrooms and public areas.

School day action-packed with classroom-based teaching across the curriculum, no shortage of educational off-site visits and a mind-boggling number of extracurricular clubs and activities (some included in fees); we particularly like imagineering, boyz noyz and mini messy church.

Independent writing strongly encouraged with golden writing sessions every term from reception. Each piece of work is retained in a portfolio, which moves class with the child, thus charting progress. Streaming of English and mathematics from 8+. Pupils not fazed by it: 'we all have to really understand work before we move on but some understand quicker than others,' revealed a group of pupils. Independent working encouraged but help always on hand, in class or with extra tuition. Science follows classroom-based QCA scheme with occasional use of college laboratory for top juniors. SEN catered for in and out of the classroom by dedicated learning support. Generally, in class teacher support free with scale of charges for a more individual programme.

Specialist French and PE, which has increasing focus – three hours a week timetabled, including weekly swimming from reception plus extracurricular clubs. Staff work with Sporting Influence coaches whose mantra is 'improving social skills through sport' – benefits of attitude to work and discipline evident beyond the playing fields. Centred on traditional team sports but including tcoukball, an indoor game where goals are scored by hitting a small trampoline. Increasing inter-house competition and fixtures against other schools, independent and state – with transport provided by school minibus where needed.

Creative arts are now taught in project days, but according to one parent 'a little hit and miss'. Lots of music making; traditional instruments, class recorder lessons in years 3 and 4; taster days to encourage participation – 'being directed to the right instrument makes all the difference'. Orchestra takes part in prep schools' orchestral day at Uppingham School. A 'sing up' gold award school, there are three choirs and smaller ensembles. Highfield's certainly alive with the sound of music. Weekly timetabled specialist drama lessons. Over 50 per cent of pupils have LAMDA lessons; plenty of performance opportunities in school and out in Shakespeare Schools Festival.

IT integrated into the curriculum and used creatively. We saw this in action with a year 5 group activity, where a fable was created, scripted, enacted and filmed using an iPad, edited and then presented to their peers. QR codes part of topic wall displays encouraging pupils to add knowledge through one click online research.

Assessments each half term, open and transparent sharing with pupils with agreed target setting. Full reports and parents' evenings twice yearly. Weekly updates on what children have been learning.

Merit system – usual stickers, house points, merit assemblies. Strong pastoral care, buddy system for new entrants. As one parent put it, pupils are 'aware of each other's feelings – they try to be kind'. The teddy trophy for the tidiest classroom each week is awarded by the cleaning supervisor – a nice touch.

Effective school council, much valued by pupils who see results from their proposals and understand through class discussion the reasons for rejections. Particularly impressive was a scheme where each class democratically chose a range of playground games using an identical sum donated by the parents' association. Ownership also brings the benefits of less loss and damage. Lots of charitable giving; particularly with Ugandan link school. Tens of families sponsor a child and there is a penpal relationship between the pupils. Recently the first trip of seven children, parents and teachers to Bombo took place.

Healthy eating, nutrition and well-being all high on the agenda with input from the school catering manager on top table manner tips, food waste and tasting menus.

Busy and supportive parents' association, parent volunteers in classroom, Prep Post – weekly update on activities and how parents can give curriculum support written by class teachers.

Both prep and pre-school have a growing confidence, distinct identity and give a strong message of 'this is what we offer'. They are parent friendly with a fun to learn ethos, where children are encouraged and have opportunity to participate and succeed in a range of diverse activities.

Hymers College

Linked with Hymers College Junior School

Hymers Avenue, Hull, East Yorkshire HU3 1LW

Ages 11–18 **Pupils** 953 **Sixth form** 198

Fees: £11,358 pa

01482 343555
www.hymerscollege.co.uk

Headmaster: Since 2006, David Elstone (50s). Read history and geography at University College, Cardiff and has taught at a variety of independent schools (including six years as depute rector at Hutchesons' Grammar School in Glasgow).

Unceremonious and determined, with a good sense of humour and plenty of drive. He was described by one parent as 'immensely caring'. Brought in 'massive changes' and, as one parent told us, he 'kept the high standards but relaxed the whole school down'. Passionate about education and helping young people to become better learners.

Passion extends to Bristol City football club. A former cricket and hockey master, he maintains his interest in cricket and is a member of the MCC. Married with two sons.

Leaving in July 2019.

Academic matters: Academically selective on intake, 'though not as selective as most grammar schools'. Standards and expectations are high and exam results very commendable. Little, if anything, to match it locally.

In 2018, 43 per cent A*/A grades at A level (70 per cent A*/B) and 65 per cent A*-A/9-7 at GCSE. Broad curriculum includes Latin. Streaming in maths only until year 10. French, German and Spanish on offer, though linguists in the school would appreciate even more choice. Traditional offering at A level including general studies and the EPQ. At GCSE pupils take a minimum of eight subjects, though more on offer if desired (and able).

The four Rs of educationalist Guy Claxton's Learning Power are fundamental to learning here – resourcefulness, resilience, reflectiveness and reciprocity. The head told us: 'We needed to be more flexible in our teaching methods and personalise the learning experience for our pupils. Teaching has changed dramatically in school. We offer a traditional curriculum but it's not what is taught but how it is taught. We need to help to make our pupils' learning secure'. There has been investment in modern technology, a multi-media language laboratory, whiteboards and iPads for teachers.

Fewer than 40 pupils in the senior school have SEN or a disability. Year 7 pupils are given a screening test in year 7 and individual learning difficulties identified through teacher observation too. Personal learning plans are drawn up via one-to-one work, where pupils are assessed, in agreement with parents. A specialist programme of physical exercises for children needing further learning support has 'had a profound impact in the classroom', says the head. A member of the junior school staff has been trained to deliver the programme.

Programme of careers advice starts in year 7, building up year on year to work experience and careers convention in year 11. Year 12 students use Centigrade programme and there is interview training and a series of sixth form lectures given by experts from a variety of professions, business and industry.

Games, options, the arts: Where talent is recognised (whether in sport, music or the arts) pupils are given support and encouragement but are expected to demonstrate commitment and be prepared to put in extra time and effort after school and on Saturdays. Opting out isn't an option. Games compulsory – rugby and cricket for boys, hockey (notably successful) and netball for girls, tennis (very successful) and athletics for both. Pupils well represented in national competitions. Supervised swim available every morning from 8-8.30am.

Successful and nationally recognised music department, with representation in the National Youth Choir. Nearly 40 per cent of pupils take voice and instrument tuition. Free instrument loan for an indeterminate period. One of the highest number of pupils in the country taking ABRSM exams. New music building with top rate facilities including recording studio. Lots of performances by choirs, ensembles and orchestras – in-house and at venues like Beverley Minster.

Drama is thriving – subject is included in year 7 and 8 curriculum and offered at GCSE and at A level. Recent productions in 200-seater Judi Dench Theatre include The Magic Flute and Dracula and involved music, art, design, business and electronics departments. Annual productions for each year group.

Debating and Young Enterprise very active. DofE scheme regularly attracts over 100 pupils a year. Army Cadet Force (voluntary and after-school) popular with 30 or so members. Sporting and music tours on offer but with a maximum cost to pupils of £1,000 – a nod to the economic downturn. Residential trips feature prominently in junior school; year 5 pupils visit Normandy and the battlefields and year 6s do outdoor pursuits in the Lake District.

Background and atmosphere: Opened in 1893 as a school for boys. School's founder, the Reverend John Hymers, a Cambridge fellow and Rector of Brandesburton, left money in his will for a school to be built 'for the training of intelligence in whatever social rank of life it may be found among the vast and varied population of the town and port of Hull'. The school has remained true to founder's intent, with below average fees and over 120 pupils receiving financial assistance through means-tested bursaries funded by own endowments and The Ogden Trust.

Pleasing approach to the main entrance, which overlooks well-maintained playing fields, all-weather pitches and even a lake for keen ornithologists. Belies first impressions: when stepping inside you are immediately confronted with a view of the traditional assembly hall, lined with doors of carved wooden lockers ajar and adorned with sports bags, spilling items of PE kit, books and papers. It does get better, particularly in the new facilities.

Careful financial management (and some generous benefactors) has enabled extensive recent investment in new theatre, sports hall, sixth form centre, junior school and swimming pool. Attractive and sympathetic to the original buildings, though perhaps at the cost of refurbishing the older ones. Plans afoot to build a new music facility and learning resource centre.

The school manages to attain high levels of academe whilst pupils remain relaxed and happy, seemingly not under pressure. Parents allude to the changes under the current head (comments like 'it's not such an intense school') and praise the dedication of staff and their excellent relationship with the pupils. School's ability to identify talent and encourage pupils to shine, praised by parents, as well as the differentiated teaching. 'All are catered for', said a mother with three very different daughters at the school.

School has cultivated links with the local community. Lots of outreach programmes for pupils while the head sits on a number of local trusts and the court of Hull University. Has helped to raise perception of Hymers in the city.

Pastoral care, well-being and discipline: Pastoral care is a real strength of the school. It expects high standards and pupils don't disappoint. All fairly relaxed for much of the time. Parents speak of 'mutual respect and trust between pupils and teachers' and feel well informed. They told us that staff are accessible and problems are dealt with effectively. Pupils are well looked after and look after each other. Buddy system very effective – mentor training for year 12 on active listening and giving advice. Mixed tutor groups in sixth form promote collaboration and cohesion.

Bullying taken seriously – not just for victim but also to change behaviour of bully. School counsellor on hand. Pupils can expect to be expelled for serious misdemeanours, such as bringing drugs into school, but no expulsions for 10 years.

School consistently has equal numbers of boys and girls – in dining room we observed lots of mixed groups across the age range in conversation. According to our sixth form guide there's 'plenty of girl power' here.

Pupils and parents: Large catchment area – Hull, East Yorkshire, North Lincs, buses in all directions. Reflects the lack of ethnic diversity in the area. Wider social spread than most independents, due mainly to generous bursaries and lower than average fees. Many parents are first-time buyers, ranging from professionals (preponderance of medics and educators) to owners of local takeaways.

Pupils are open, bright, positive and enthusiastic. They value the academic support they receive and close friendships they make.

Entrance: For entry at 11+ pupils sit competitive exams in maths, English and verbal and non-verbal reasoning, plus interview. Four-form entry, 108 places in all (about 30 for external pupils, remainder transferring from own junior school). For sixth form, five GCSEs at grade 6 or above required. About 12 or so enter at 16, replacing the similar number of leavers.

Exit: Between 80 and 90 per cent stay post-GCSE – most leavers due to relocation or for wider range of A level options. A good handful to Oxbridge each year; the rest head to a gamut of universities, with northern Russell Group strong favourites. Half study science and mathematics related degrees, with an equally consistent show of economics, business and social studies.

Money matters: About 15 fee remission places per year – all means-tested bursaries, some full fees.

Remarks: Hymers is an unpretentious place. School has maintained high academic standing yet managed to relax intensity in recent years, though high expectations remain for commitment and ambition. Pupils are confident, well prepared and proud of and valued for their successes across any number of disciplines.

Hymers College Junior School

Linked with Hymers College

46

Hymers Avenue, Hull HU3 1LW

Ages 8–11 Pupils 194

Fees: £9,459 – £9,990 pa

01482 441211
www.hymerscollege.co.uk

Head of the junior school: Since 2010, Peter Doyle BSc PGCE (40s). Read economics at Bristol then spent four years in industry. Followed family vocation by doing PGCE at Hull, then taught in primary schools in the home counties before moving to Stamford Bridge Primary as deputy head. He was deputy head here for three years before being appointed as head.

Approachable and caring, with an easy manner. He is a constant support at school events and clearly proud of pupils' achievements. He believes in 'building self-esteem and confidence in a culture of high expectation' and says school aims to instil in each pupil 'the belief in their ability to succeed'.

A keen squash player, he also enjoys camping and hill walking. Married to Rachel and they have three children.

Entrance: Main entry points are in years 4 and 5. Entrance exams take place in February for entry the following September and test reasoning ability, comprehension, mathematics and powers of expression. An intake of 72 (three classes of 24) into year 4, topped up to classes of 26 in year 5, though head says that 'if a child has the ability to succeed and be happy at Hymers we will find them a place.' Around five fee remission places per year, all means-tested.

Links with pre-prep Hessle Mount and prep Froebel House mean their pupils are academically tracked and those who meet entry requirements have automatic offer of place. Wide catchment area covers Grimsby, Scunthorpe, Goole, Scarborough and some way into East Riding. There's an extensive school bus network.

Exit: Almost all pupils progress to Hymers College Senior School after successfully sitting entrance exams.

Remarks: Like the senior school, the four Rs of educationalist Guy Claxton's Learning Power – resourcefulness, resilience, reflectiveness and reciprocity – are fundamental to learning here. Broad curriculum, with shared senior school teaching in geography and sport. French, German and Spanish taught from year 5. Science taught in junior school science room. As you might expect with a selective entry, most recent ISI report said pupil attainment was 'good in comparison with national age related expectation.'

Teacher observation, dyslexia detector software and assessment are used to pick up learning support needs. SENCo liaises regularly with senior school and school counsellor. Individual learning plans are drawn up, with one-to-one work where appropriate, in agreement with parents. INPP programme of physical exercises for children needing further learning support has 'had a profound impact in the classroom,' says the head. A member of the junior school staff has been trained to deliver the programme.

Parents receive pupil grades three times a year and a full report annually. Main academic subjects are assessed for attainment, progress, attitude and homework. Mark schemes are on show in every classroom and staff are keen to share good practice across school.

Sport is high on the agenda, with excellent facilities, competitive opportunities in traditional team sports and success for individuals and teams at county and national level. Supervised swim available every morning from 8.00-8.30am.

Plenty of music too – the school's 40-strong choir came second in the BBC's Songs of Praise Choir of the Year competition recently. Particularly delighted with judges' comment on how 'happy and relaxed' pupils were. Sixty-five per cent of pupils sing in a choir and choral tour to Paris for year 5s. Lots of opportunities for musical instrument tuition, at additional charge, with free instrument loan for new starters. Percussion, wind and string groups with performances throughout year and annual chamber concert, with performers volunteering for a spot.

Drama features well with annual productions for each year group. Dance clubs for year 5 and 6 girls and extracurricular programme includes crafty kids (hopefully not aptly named) and photography club. Free after-school supervised homework club until 5.30 pm. Residential trips feature prominently; year 5 pupils visit Normandy and the battlefields and year 6s do outdoor pursuits in the Lake District.

Housed in a bright, modern two-storey building at the edge of the Hymers campus, the junior school accommodation has spacious classrooms, each with their own cloakroom area and designated DT/art and science rooms. School is moving to tables from individual desks (as budgets allow). Pupils consulted on choice and layout of classroom furniture, though some consider the change a mixed benefit – less distraction from slamming desk lids against less storage space, better organisation and heavier school bags. Prominent commendations board in the entrance hall celebrates personal academic achievements awarded at each Friday's assembly. House points are collected for the four houses and are used primarily for sporting competition. Warnings and (forgetting) kit marks recorded in a warning book for each house kept by head of year.

Junior school overlooks extensive and well kept playing fields, with own wildlife pond and good outdoor recreational activities with table tennis tables and play area. Lunch in main school dining room. Breakfast available too. Choice of hot and cold dishes, nutritious and appetising in appearance. Juniors interact well with older pupils. Sixth form prefects take form registration and supervise some clubs. No school council but year 6 reps are chosen for a leadership club and meet with the head to discuss fund raising and charity events.

School says that CARE (stands for care, acceptance, respect and effort) is the core of the pastoral system and the message resounds in every classroom. Pupils say that 'the teachers are all really nice', 'friends are nice and loyal' and 'you're taught to be competitive with yourself.' Parents (40 per cent of whom work in medicine or education) agreed. They told us that children are 'relaxed and happy' here and that 'teachers adapt to the individual child.'

Keswick School

Vicarage Hill, Keswick, Cumbria CA12 5QB

Ages 11–18 **Pupils** 1,274; 53 boarders **Sixth form** 272

Fees: Day free; Boarding £11,088 pa

01768 772605
www.keswick.cumbria.sch.uk

Headmaster: Since 2012, Simon Jackson (early 40s), a biologist who was previously deputy head. With impressive academic credentials MA (Oxon) and MEd, FRSA he is proud to be only the eighth head since the school was refounded in 1898 as one of the country's first truly co-educational schools. Married with two young children, who are both eagerly anticipating joining Keswick as pupils themselves, he is an energetic, bright and charismatic head teacher who is clearly well respected both in the school and the wider community. Academy status has brought with it the freedoms for the school to grow in a controlled way while retaining its unique characteristics, commitment to education in its widest sense and the confidence not to kowtow to the latest government edict if it is not deemed to be in the best interests of the pupils.

He has an enormous respect for both his students and staff, a rigorous, intelligent and pragmatic approach to education and an obvious pride in the school he leads. He is still very active in the classroom and sees this as an essential element of his leadership despite the other demands on his time. As well as leading a growth in pupil numbers at Keswick, he now heads up a multi-academy trust which incorporates a local primary school, allowing for additional important work on transition at age 11. A committed enthusiast for outdoor and adventurous learning (pretty much essential given the stunning location of the school and the uninterrupted views of Lakeland peaks from just about every classroom), he is committed to ensuring that all pupils have the opportunity to benefit from all that their location offers.

Academic matters: Student results at both GCSE and A level are amongst the best non-selective results in the country, with strong value added. The school is proudly comprehensive and inclusive but pupil outcomes would rival those of many selective schools. In 2018 at A level 28 per cent of grades were A*/A and 51 per cent A*-B. At GCSE, with 79 per cent gaining 9-4 in both English and maths, and 30 per cent of grades A*-A/9-7, from students who have just slightly above average ability on entry, the school is working hard to ensure every child does as well as they possibly can. It was notable all staff, from the head downwards, were clear that they were not just interested in the high flyers. One teacher commented, 'two Es at A level is just as much of an achievement as three A*s, if the student has worked hard and met their potential'. The staff were also very proud that students who might not have gained the entry criteria for other sixth forms were succeeding at Keswick.

At GCSE pupils take English x 2 and maths plus, for the great majority, three separate sciences. The school has strong links with the Lake District National Park and the Energy Coast and is keen to give students real life opportunities to practise their science. Particularly high numbers, including many girls, take physics A level. The school was keen to point out that it has a very strong complement of teaching staff in all subjects including specialists in all the sciences and maths, a rarity these days.

Everyone takes take an additional three GCSEs, but with plenty of other opportunities for those with the keenness and aptitude, such as astronomy and Latin (in 2018, 60 per cent 9-7s amongst the year 9s that took Latin GCSE). Everyone learns French or German, most both, and are strongly encouraged to take at least one to GCSE. French and German exchanges; the latter, with Konigslutter, is now in its 54th year and some families have had three generations participate. An International Language Centre will open on campus in 2019. The school has an unashamedly academic curriculum, with a few vocational options. Engineering (Arkwright Scholarship successes) and electronics are both available at GCSE and A level, plus BTecs in business and digital applications.

The sixth form is a strength of the school, with students travelling long distances for what they see as 'the best education in the area'. 'Nowhere else seemed to have as good academic standards'; 'the school has the edge and it is very professional'. On our tour we witnessed lively and energised classes where debate was clearly the norm.

Staff who were also parents were keen to point out that the school has strong and supportive provision for students with special needs that 'allows them to fly'. There is strong provision for students with moderate learning difficulties including autism and the school has good disability access. Pupil premium students make the same levels of progress as others.

Staffing is very stable, as is often the case in similar schools. However there is a regular input of new staff and the head is clear that it is not a 'semi-retirement' option for keen walkers and climbers. There is a strong commitment to staff development: Keswick leads a Teaching School Alliance and has links with various universities, ensuring that staff are knowledgeable and well engaged with educational development.

Games, options, the arts: Sports and games take centre stage with a great number of students. Considerable sporting successes include national representation in sports as diverse as rugby, fell running, skiing, martial arts and karting. The students are very proud of the success of the girls' rugby teams. As one young woman put it, 'girls throw people to the ground as well, you know!' A strong tradition of rowing (on Derwentwater): the club has 50+ rowers and recently won a Sport England grant to purchase a new carbon fibre quad boat. The school boasts its own dry ski slope as well as the usual complement of playing fields, sports hall, all-weather pitch and tennis courts.

Art is clearly a strength. From the entrance onwards there were some lovely pieces of work displayed including sculpture, stained glass, painting and, on the English corridor, some fantastic poetry. The students spoke with great enthusiasm about the annual school productions and we observed a very positive drama lesson.

Music is celebrated throughout with various choirs, ensembles, orchestras and bands, and a professional recording studio. Students participate in the Young Musician of the Year competition with notable national success. Concerts every term, including in the Theatre by the Lake in Keswick.

The head girl was recently chosen as the Citizenship Society's student barrister of the year. The students have just launched their own student driven on-line publication Vocalise. The Lego League teams successfully presented their hydraulics project, raising awareness of plastic waste and coming 10th in a national competition. As the head says, 'it's about getting everyone together, creating a collective community through sport, music, drama, business and enterprise'. Students regularly take part in the UK Youth Parliament and there is a transgender support group.

Boarding: Boarding received a recent outstanding judgement from Ofsted and it was clear from speaking to the boarders that their experience is a very positive one. One boarding house for all 54 boarders from years 7-13. Matron lives in and provides a strong and stable support for students with the help of a team of houseparents. The accommodation is clean, tidy and modern and provides a good sense of home from home. There is a large, comfortable common room with matron's flat just across the corridor. The students spoke highly of the wide range of activities they are involved in from the CCF to sporting activities, trips and visits. Relationships between different age groups appeared strong and the sixth form valued their independent living week when they do everything for themselves, including cooking and cleaning, in preparation for life after home. Both day and boarding students commented that there was no perceptible divide between the two groups.

Background and atmosphere: A central part of its local and wider community. Originally two schools, it came together on one stunning site in 1980, looking forward to Derwentwater, Cat Bells and Causey Pike and back to Skiddaw.

The buildings are an eclectic mix of the original school, 1950s and 60s extensions and a more recent build. All are refurbished and well maintained and the school is bright, modern and with a stylishness that the students say encourages them to take a pride in their learning as well as look after their space. Well-equipped drama and music spaces as well as a beautiful art suite are certainly great assets.

The majority of students join the school from small village schools and the feel of an extended family is strong. Primary children regularly come for sporting activities and curriculum days.

During lessons the corridors are quiet and purposeful while classrooms seem to buzz with a generally healthy learning noise. The school is clear that while a quiet classroom can sometimes be important students should be actively engaged in their learning through practical work and discussion.

L

Students clearly like being at school. Many live in remote parts and meet friends largely at school, mixing comfortably across the age ranges.

Pastoral care, well-being and discipline: This is a school that prides itself on being smart. A traditional badged blazer, tie and shirts firmly tucked in are the standard. Maroon jumpers with the school crest and motto, Levavi Oculos, are the rule for the sixth form. High standards are expected and maintained. Phones are out of site, jewellery is not allowed and hair is well kept and in natural colours. The students are proud of their uniform.

Many students join Keswick sixth form from other schools and commented that there was a warmth and inclusivity here that helped them not just to settle in well but allowed them to be their own person. The students made some very genuine and moving comments (which were born out by the staff) that the school places a high value on inclusion and the celebration of diversity. The sixth form are clearly proud of their prefect status and feel empowered (mostly) to exercise a role of authority over younger students. They were highly complementary about not just the classroom teaching but also the additional support available.

During our visit we saw nothing other than good behaviour and courtesy, both in lessons and around school. The students take great pride in being self-managing and the prefect system is clearly strongly embedded in school culture. As it is relatively unusual to find students so confident in managing their peers, we checked and this does seem to be the case, with younger students reflecting a genuine aspiration to follow the role models and become prefects themselves. The school says that it has its fair share of students with troubled backgrounds and works hard to support these to behave well. Incidents of exclusion are very rare but the head is clear that this is necessary at times. One parent, who had moved her children from elsewhere, spoke of the positive impact this had on their education and social development.

The school is clearly well attuned to the growing demand for support for mental health and well-being and is proactive in meeting this need. Unusually, there is a nurse on site.

Staff and students agree that generally there is very little bullying. A scheme of 'social detectives' alerts staff to any issues. SEN students have a safe place to go at break and lunch times and support with socialisation.

Pupils and parents: This really is a comprehensive school. Prospective Oxbridge students comfortably rub shoulders with those with SEN, and those from affluent backgrounds with pupil premium students. Trips and visits to other parts of the country and overseas are a regular feature. The presence of 50+ boarders from all over the world helps to ensure that this is a cosmopolitan community. One parent commented, 'my kids have blossomed since they came here. The boarding house helps brings a diversity of friendships from all over the world'.

Entrance: The school is consistently oversubscribed and manages a number of appeals every year. In recent years the number of students commuting from out of catchment has significantly increased and the school is now comfortably at seven forms of entry (non-selective).

Unusually, offers sixth form scholarships are offered in science (the Steven Luckman Bursary) and EPQ (the Gilbert Smithson Adair Bursary). Sixth form entry by a minimum combination of grades 5 and 4 in English and maths plus the individual A level subject requirements – at least 6s for sciences and maths.

Exit: Around a quarter leaves after GCSEs. Some 80 per cent of sixth formers to university, mostly in the north, with increasing numbers following the college and apprenticeship routes, others heading into agriculture and tourism. Sixth formers were confident about the school's support for Oxbridge, medical and veterinary applications. In 2018, one off to Cambridge to study veterinary medicine, plus one other vet (Liverpool) and a medic (St Andrews).

Remarks: This is an outstanding local school with a strong international dimension. It believes equally in inclusion, aspiration and excellence. Despite its rurality there are plenty of options for parents in the local area from other good schools and the independent sector. Students and parents are clear that Keswick offers the best of all worlds. This is a school where it is still cool to succeed. It has very high aspirations for its young people and it is certainly meeting them.

Lady Royd Primary

Linked with Bradford Girls' Grammar School

Squire Lane, Bradford, West Yorkshire BD9 6RB

Ages 4–11 **Pupils** 393

01274 545395
www.bggs.com

Headmistress: Since 2012, Juliet Rimmer, BSc in human nutrition, PGCE KS2/3 science (Bradford).

Entrance: Became a free school in September 2013, with a non-selective entrance policy. There are two classes of around 28 in each year group; the school has tripled in size since becoming a free school. Although there is a nursery on site which is physically joined, be aware that it is legally separate and therefore offers no automatic or direct entry to the school.

Exit: Girls straight through to the senior school, Bradford Girls' Grammar, automatic entry. The boys are not neglected: they are well prepared for any entrance exam or interview requirements to their next school and teachers advise accordingly. They head off to a range of schools within Bradford and beyond, mostly to maintained sector, a few to local independents, especially Bradford Grammar School.

Remarks: A non-selective free school, own identity and buildings but part of Bradford Girls' Grammar. Classrooms are spread across an attractive purpose built modern building (2008) and a section of the main BGGS building with a corridor linking the two. Attractive, bright classrooms with super displays of children's art and writing, the rooms for the oldest children are big enough, but only just. The upward trend in class numbers is a slight concern for parents who hoped it wouldn't shift beyond 24, but the school's popularity has meant a slight creep, probably halted now though by logistics. Younger ones have more space and classrooms adjoin outdoor soft play areas. Larger classes have brought more classroom assistants, so plenty of adults visible and to hand.

Children are smart in navy uniforms, boys in ties, girls in striped blouses, blazers worn by all. Sunrise and Sunset clubs extend the day if required by busy parents and there is a huge range of extracurricular activities taking place at lunchtime and after school. No lack of rigour, expectations are high and results are good; high level of teaching and learning and focused children. Strong results in core subjects at the end of year 6, latest scores at or slightly above the local and national average at KS2 with excellent value-added measures. French taught by class teachers from year 1, subject specialists on hand for PE, music and science. Plenty of reading – high levels of literacy viewed as a must. Maths is hugely popular; the children tell us they 'love it'. It's traditional teaching plus here – the trad bit being the spelling tests, times tables, handwriting and a daily dose of 'groovy grammar' – whilst also recognising the need for a creative curriculum alongside this, you'll notice the wonderful history/geography/art/design project work on display around the building.

The science lab is a great space and we saw it being used as a scene of crime lab during our visit – children in scene suits, working alongside a visiting forensic scientist dusting for fingerprints – great fun as well as active and real learning in action. A decent range of IT equipment in use and laptops travel the school on a trolley. There are interactive whiteboards in all classrooms and an IT suite is used for whole class teaching. Parents kept up to speed via a learning journal that travels between home and school and a lengthy and detailed end of year report. Expect homework, 'but not too much,' say (some) children; parents like the use of websites making homework 'more fun'. Plenty of rigour throughout, one parent reporting 'a dramatic improvement in our children every year'. Much praise from parents for information evenings at the start of every school year, 'it's great for us, it tells us what to expect,' they say. Well-led SEN department, one-to-one help if needed plus support within and outside the classroom.

Good on pastoral care, evidenced by the pupil anti-bullying ambassadors, who take their role very seriously, a 'worry box' and regular circle times to discuss anything and everything that may arise. Children race to the top of the merit board, huge sense of pride in collecting rewards for good work, the highest possible accolade being a certificate of achievement from the governors. Add to that the house points collected from a range of activities in school and out, including a very popular talent show, there's no shortage of public and private recognition. A celebration assembly takes place each Friday. 'Lunch is good,' say the children, wide choice of options cooked in-house and eaten in the senior school dining room. Tuck shop is a Friday treat and serves 'sort of healthy treats,' they tell us, with a grin.

Wide range of sports on offer, making the very best use of the excellent onsite facilities and energetic and enthusiastic PE staff, no old school teaching with pumps and whistles here. Drama (LAMDA) and singing are popular; an ever-increasing range of instrumental tuition on offer from peripatetics and the main senior school hall gives them a great space for plays and concerts. Lots of clubs – 'amazing,' say parents: sports – teams do well in competitions (table tennis a strength); music – almost all do individual lessons, various groups (steel pans, guitar, fifes, trumpets), orchestra, choir, concerts; jazz and street dance as well as ballet; debating, poetry reciting, creative writing and handwriting competitions. Trips start locally and then venture further afield with residentials for the older children, north out into the Dales and later on south to London.

The team of teachers and support staff 'make time for you,' say parents, adding that 'the admin team know everything about everything and always reply to your emails'. They see teachers as very approachable and happy to collaborate with them on all kinds of problems. Much eulogising about good communication generally from the school – definitely a bonus and clearly much appreciated.

Friendly, smiling, busy children from the surrounding area. Like the senior school, strong on academics with good relationships and offering a wide range of opportunities. Settling down very nicely into its free school shape, whilst holding on tight to the best of its former construct, sigh of relief all round.

L

Lancaster Girls' Grammar School

Regent Street, Lancaster LA1 1SF

Ages 11–18 **Pupils** 919 **Sixth form** 258

01524 581661
www.lggs.org.uk

Headteacher: Since 2007, Jackie Cahalin, BA (Newcastle; history and politics), PGCE (Lancaster), who joined the school as deputy head in 2004 (before that, she was at Ulverston Victoria High School and Barrow Sixth form College). Passionate about girls' single sex education, she has sought to create an environment where pupils can engage without distractions or barriers, build confidence and feel the sky is the limit. This is not empty talk: in a chemistry lesson, we saw girls' hands shoot into the air without thought, all pitching their ideas against the 'model answer', all just having a go, no trace of self-consciousness or fear of being wrong. Very impressive.

Science is a key strength at this school but Mrs Cahalin is keen on a wide curriculum. This being the state sector, budget belts are worn tight but she has managed to bring technology back into the curriculum at GCSE, seeks to maintain PE and theatre studies, as well as three modern languages. German, under siege in a lot of state schools, rocks on.

Tuned in to the challenges facing young girls today, she has invested heavily in the pastoral over the last few years and also works hard at ensuring there is a good blend of men and women in senior positions within the school, such as a female head of computing. With us, she is calm, measured and very easy to talk to. Parents speak of the family vibe she has created, of her flopping down with a cuppa to chat to girls at options evenings and of being able to raise the smallest of worries with her. One super-enthused parent-fan declared her 'absolutely fantastic'.

Academic matters: Current strengths lie in sciences and maths, and the results are superb, across GCSE and A level. There is a big push to elevate arts subjects too and if these are not selected at A level by students, then they usually play a big part in extracurricular or in the EPQ. All students study 10 GCSEs, including one language (10 per cent of students study two). At A level, around 30 per cent take one language.

In 2018, overall an excellent 75 per cent of entries got A*-A/9-7 at GCSE. Generally a vast stash of top marks across the board in all three sciences, languages, humanities (frankly, the stellar results only dip a little in ICT and drama). These results are pretty consistent year on year and the school goes at a cracking pace to achieve that.

At sixth form, students take three A levels plus EPQ. Mrs Cahalin is enthusiastic about the latter and its ability to unlock creativity, referring to a recent student who wrote a detailed novel about the slave trade in Lancaster, requiring a huge amount of research. Maths, biology and chemistry attract high numbers of A*s and As (physics is not doing badly either). Arts, languages and humanities subjects are also gaining popularity, head says. Overall in 2018, 45 per cent of entries got A*/A.

Targets and data tracking prevail to ensure pupils meet targets, with the mentoring system kicking in where necessary, and parents felt that the girls develop a good work ethic. They praised the drop-in revision sessions, though one suggested that formal booster classes might start in earlier years, rather than waiting to see if someone was struggling.

Parents felt 90 per cent of the staff were excellent, the faint implication being that the rest might be a bit set in their ways (in fairness, Mrs Cahalin was aware of the challenge of keeping longstanding staff 'fresh').

A handful of pupils have SEN statements and some have been diagnosed with learning difficulties, such as dyslexia, via the school. Mrs Cahalin says staff are very good at identifying issues and the school provides a screening programme and testing. The latter, however, isn't until year 10 and some parents felt it would be useful to have this earlier, again hinting that some of the staff who had been there for a while were less tuned in to the subtle signs. One parent whose child's dyslexia had been picked up, however, was full of praise and said her child was now flying high academically. Mrs Cahalin is clear that simple strategies make a big difference, little things like using laptops, having a handout rather than making notes, being emailed work before lessons, help with organisation. Some students have one-to-one support, usually just for a term until weaknesses have been addressed.

The school is evidently successful at inspiring its socially diverse intake to aim high. In-school essay competitions, for example, encourage pupils to enter national events. Parents praised the UCAS coaching system (having spoken to the incredibly clued-up staff in this area, we can well understand why) and said the school support for pupils continues long after they have left.

Games, options, the arts: Alongside the usual sports on offer, there are also more offbeat games like dodgeball and tag rugby. During our visit, groups of girls were working on a street dance in the spirit of 'marginal gains' improvements, listing points that would refine their performance. PE, Mrs Cahalin said, said was now more about problem solving, building confidence and resilience. The school appoints lots of sports captains and ambassadors going up through the school, but parents said it is very much a case of 'finding what you enjoy'.

With sciences being strong, the arts come into their own outside the curriculum. Music is popular with a Young Musician of the Year competition and concerts held in nearby Ashton Hall. There are choirs, orchestras, jazz bands and an annual performing arts festival. Drama productions are wide scale: recently Kiss Me Kate and les Mis. They are usually in the local Duke's theatre combined with the boys' school. Parents said no matter how high the standard, girls were always encouraged to have a go at any level. Or as one parent put it, the performances show 'the whole heartedness of the school'.

Lots of clubs; as students go up the school, these might also be linked to subjects which they hope to study, such as philosophy or medicine. CCF available and DofE tends to yield a stash of golds (18 in 2018).

A healthy amount of trips from standard geography field trips in the Lake District to long haul China. Girls go to concerts in Liverpool, science or tech exhibitions in Manchester. Older students are offered career-orientated visits, perhaps to Jaguar or Landover.

Competitions abound, like Spelling Bee and science Big Bang; the school recently won the first ever GCHQ Cyber Competition and made it on to national TV (the latter being way more scary than the challenge itself). Science week saw the arrival of a giant inflatable planetarium dome in the hall; the National Space Agency ran a workshop, as did many universities.

There is a well-stocked library with a steady stream of writers visiting, including Juno Dawson, a transgender writer who inspired the students to ask some searching questions.

Sixth formers manage the zippy magazine, The Chronicle, and their selection of modern inspirational women for a double page spread included Lady Gaga, Carrie Fisher and Zendaya Coleman...suggesting they really do have editorial control.

The sixth form have a leadership team so lots of responsibility is on offer and there is an enrichment programme for pre-university skills and well-being activities like empathy and collaboration, as well as downtime activities like baking and yoga. There are also about 40 lunchtime talks a year, many by alumnae or university staff, anything from dentistry to politics.

One parent commented while there is not much money swilling around, what the school gives to the girls in terms of independence, drive and aspiration is priceless. We can see why.

Background and atmosphere: Founded in 1907 in the Storey Institute, sharing premises with the technical school and public library. Moved to its present site in 1914. A lovely building, very traditional. Nice, bright corridor displays. Plentiful IT equipment. The admittedly slightly dog-eared facilities are just fine – drama studio, gym (playing fields are five minute walk away), dance studio, small fitness suite. Sixth form got its own centre in 2011. Frankly you don't choose to come here for the facilities but the intellectual enrichment and drive. The girls seem industrious, the place a hive of activity, but nothing rarefied.

Pastoral care, well-being and discipline: Students needing extra support for learning issues, anxiety issues or who have had time off for illness may liaise with form tutors, year heads or learning mentors, as well as the well-being coordinator. Parents praised the pastoral: 'they push academically with one hand and support with the other'. One parent, whose child had had a particularly rough ride in her home life, described the pastoral care as 'absolutely outstanding'.

Years 7s benefit from mentors drawn from year 12 to help with the transition to a new school. Parents said this really worked well; lots of year 7 pupils arrive knowing no-one, except their mentor with whom they have already been teamed up.

There is peer mentoring for anything from organisational difficulties to friendship probs. Sixth formers are encouraged to take on a 'big sister' role to younger years.

The house system fosters a sense of belonging, but one parent felt the class played a bigger part; the girls could always go to the form room in break or at lunch, they had a 'home base', she said. As they go up the school, however, there are more cross-form activities, so girls get to know everyone in their year, encouraging fluid friendship groups. Parents said perceived bullying is dealt with swiftly and in many instances there is little need for parental involvement.

There is also much guidance given to parents – online and in presentations – around 'attitude to learning', as well as protecting teenagers on the net and the importance of open communication about eating habits. Mobile phone ban except for sixth formers.

Pupils and parents: A supportive, diverse body of parents. In the majority of families both parents work. Not one of those rarefied state grammar schools whose intake is chiefly from sheltered prep schools where parents are awash with cash.

Pupils come from all over: Preston to Cumbria. This might mean sending your 11 year old daughter to school on a cross-country train. Parents told us any worries on that score had been allayed as the school encouraged families to exchange phone numbers so younger children had the numbers of older girls doing the same route as back-up. They operate as a familial group, one said, which gives 'massive peace of mind'.

Sensitive account is taken of the needs of all faiths; one parent said that the head had rung her for advice about a residential trip due to take place during Ramadan.

Entrance: Five form entry of 140. Some 240 normally sit the exam (English, maths and verbal reasoning), with priority to those living within the city of Lancaster, particularly looked after children and those on pupil premium. All those reaching the 'required standard' and living in the city likely to get a place. Most come from local primaries.

About 50 join the sixth form from outside, with at least five grade 6s at GCSE, plus 7 in maths if they want to study further maths.

Exit: Very little fallout after GCSEs. The school has excellent links with universities and they go to a broad spread all round the country, with Newcastle and Leeds particularly popular. Five to Oxbridge and 10 medics in 2018.

Money matters: One parent, whose child received the pupil premium, said the money went on purchasing her uniform, books and train fares. Parents often don't see how it this money spent – here, she said, they do.

Remarks: This wonderful school embodies all a state grammar could and should be, pulling in a genuinely diverse intake and engendering a real 'have a go' spirit in girls; what it lacks in flashy facilities, it more than makes up with superb teaching, academic and personal enrichment, bountiful opportunities and amazing results.

Lancaster Royal Grammar School

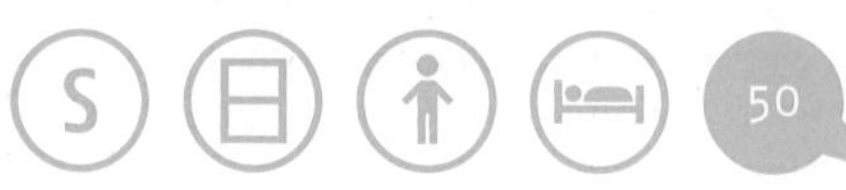

East Road, Lancaster LA1 3EF

Ages 11–18 **Pupils** 1,082 **Sixth form** 304 **Boarders** 158

Fees: Day free; boarding £11,181 – £12,300 pa

01524 580600
www.lrgs.org.uk

Headmaster: Since 2012, Dr Christopher Pyle MA (Cantab) PhD (Cantab) NPQH (mid 40s). Previously a deputy head at Perse School, Cambridge and before that head of geography there, particular interest glaciers, hydrology and climate change. Briefly a manager at Anglian Water before taking up teaching. Married to Sally, a mathematics teacher at a local school, with three young sons, two of them pupils at the school. Headed north back to roots in the Lakes and lured to LRGS as 'the nearest thing to an independent school'. Parents and pupils comment positively on his visibility.

He has been churchwarden and PCC member of a large Anglican church. A keen runner, he has also completed the Devizes to Westminster canoe race for charity, and is a fan of the Lakeland fells.

Academic matters: Superb tradition – regularly in top 100 schools nationally at A level; consistently near top of regional table at GCSE; strong value-added results. Perhaps explains why Ofsted data dashboard not a focus for head. Aiming high taken for granted, as is 'getting stuck in' to support it. In 2018, 51 per cent of A level grades A*/A; 57 per cent of GCSE grades A*-A/9-7. Very much the traditional grammar school ethos, challenging boys to fulfil their potential in a competitive environment. Mathematics outstanding, stronger classics than a lot of independents.

Wide choice of subjects at A level and Cambridge Pre-U including classics and philosophy – a third do four A levels, a quarter add on EPQ. An expectation to lead and be involved with the wide range of extracurricular; sport top of the league; CCF and DofE, volunteering – home and away with InspirUS (LRGS outreach gifted and talented programme) and the Erasmus programme.

GCSE: exceptional mathematics results and strong science as might be expected. HPQ (stepping stone to EPQ) recently introduced. Narrow ability range, setting in mathematics, English and French up to GCSE; class size averages 28. Ten GCSEs the norm; all do technology up to GCSE – school historically had technology, languages, mathematics and computing specialisms. French, German (with annual exchange) and Spanish timetabled, twilight sessions of Mandarin Chinese on offer. Sciences taught separately up to GCSE and all three are popular sixth form options – seen as a 'sciencey' school, says head. Special needs (eg dyslexia, Asperger's) looked after in-house. The especially gifted are stretched by further enhancement schemes and wide-ranging extracurricular provision.

Librarian works closely with English department to encourage reading – using an accelerated reading programme in years 7 and 8, collecting points per book with results published in a league table. IT infrastructure investment so Wifi throughout school but hardware lacking; some netbooks, but BYO not discouraged.

L

Games, options, the arts: Team games rather than individual sports dominate though increasing opportunity for minority interests that will last a lifetime. Strong rugby and cricket, taken seriously – they beat most independents. Frequent tours – Hong Kong, Australia, Japan and the 'Windies'. An impressive list of other sports, plenty of outdoor pursuits in nearby Lake District and rowing on the Lune leading to some successful pairs at Henley. Much encouragement to join in – no place for couch potatoes.

Music popular; 10 per cent take individual lessons in school practice rooms in the boarding houses. No need for Gareth Malone – choirs popular and everything instrumental from blues to philharmonic on tap. Annual musical drama production in city theatre (often with Lancaster sister school). Very good art and design results.

An extensive and eclectic range of extracurricular, humorously titled to suit all tastes or none (Texas Hold'em Society?) from Bad Boyz Bakin through Doctor Who Catch Up to PhilThy. These are on top of all the expected sport and fitness, debating, DofE, CCF, expressive and performing arts.

Boarding: Boarding gives the school an edge and identity and attractive facilities have understandably brought a resurgence of interest from 'first generation' boarders, often from the Lakeland valleys. Some 10-12 per cent of boarders in years 7-9, increasing to 20 per cent in year 10; few international boarders. Weekly boarders are the majority but about 60, mainly older boys, are full boarders. Fees for weekly or full boarding are the same so boys have flexibility to stay weekends, often influenced by sports fixtures.

Junior boys have a splendid boarding house with views to die for and a back garden of immaculate cricket pitches with the stunning backdrop of the Ashton Memorial. Dorms are bunk-bedded, cheery, comfortable and well-furnished, with sitting rooms and homely kitchens for tea and toast after school. Seniors have a choice of two houses, School House and Ashton House, each with different character and design. School House is an attractive and well-designed conference centre-style building adjoining a Victorian villa, with some comfortable ensuite single studies alongside relaxed sitting rooms and a modern kitchen, allowing the boys both privacy and companionship as and when required. Ashton House is more traditional, with bigger rooms of up to four beds, but similar recreational spaces and kitchen facilities. The houses exude family atmosphere (with gardens, tree planting and chickens) and the boys speak warmly of collegiality and that this really is 'home from home'.

All the house staff have an academic role and there are now communal study areas in each of the houses for homework, as well as a desk in each of the dorms. Boys are given some freedom (Lancaster is a small city) and there are organised activities most Sundays, whilst Saturdays are taken up with prep and sports fixtures for many.

Catering is considered 'acceptable', no complaints so must be a positive. Dining room has had a recent cosmetic makeover with the addition of rainbow coloured chairs. Grab and Go café in award nominated new City View building voted a great success by all.

Background and atmosphere: An ancient foundation, in existence by 1235 and endowed in 1472. Moved to its current location in 1852 when Queen Victoria donated £100, hence its 'Royal' tag – and the school still receives the same amount (sadly not index-linked) annually from the Duchy.

An extensive though fragmented site skirting either side of hilly East Road around a busy crossroad – pedestrian and vehicular. Building styles change from gothic to modern from the lower to upper site, and timetabling can mean crossing two roads between lessons, but boys take it in their stride and 20mph speed limits are enforced. Mixture of Victorian houses and purpose-built blocks in traditional style, leading to newer additions (science and business/design centres, new boarding houses). Parking is tricky but most walk or use public transport.

Though there is some resemblance to its independent competitors, lack of funding is evident in some parts of the school. It doesn't necessarily matter, as the school's focus is rightly on excellent teaching and positive learning outcomes, but it does mean the place can look a touch untidy at the edges. Extensive areas of the Old School House have been decommissioned but, at last, it seems priority school funding is coming to the rescue, and the head certainly has grand designs for the building.

Real sense of history and tradition about the place: 'Best of the old and the new' is the head's mantra. Boys bustle purposefully between classrooms that range from tired-looking utilitarian to smartly refurbished. Older parents will be reminded of the grammar school of their youth – 'no-nonsense, no-frills,' said one successful and grateful old boy. An ambitious and exciting 50-year master plan is attracting support from old boys and several years in, there is evidence of some success in the green shoots of improvements: new science labs now open and an old building being refurbed to provide new sixth form facilities.

Pastoral care, well-being and discipline: Boys respond to the no-nonsense direct approach of staff in a school that thoroughly understands them. The school looks to recruit 'schoolmasters' (of either sex) rather than 'teachers'. Thorough care systems for both boarding and day work well – pastoral staff heavily committed to pupils' welfare and relations between boys and teachers admired by parents and inspectors. High personal standards expected. Not much evidence of real wickedness; school suspends for possession and would expel for dealing – and the boys know it.

Thriving mentor scheme where senior boys spend time with junior boys with similar interests and prefects have weekly tutor time with year 7 helping with pastoral and organisational issues. All the pupils (and parents) we spoke to commented on the sense of community and excellent staff/pupil relationships.

Pupils and parents: Lancaster is a city with a small town feel – boys come from every walk of life and are a very genuine mix. Head says the school is not about one size fits all. 'We take quirky characters who are valued in school and can say that there will be clubs for you'. Still 'the school on the hill' to some, yet no wish for this to become a middle class enclave – rather it is open to any boy, from any street, who can cope with living and working alongside a future Oxbridge don. Local day boys given preference; about 40 places go to those further afield. Boarders come from all over but must be a UK subject or have an EEA passport and a UK guardian (some 18 per cent overseas boarders from 10 countries).

Boys and parents very proud of school and its regional standing. As one boy put it, 'LRGS is an awesome place to be'. Parents comment that their sons are thriving academically and relishing life as a boarder. Old boys include Prof T Hugh Pennington, microbiologist; Kevin Roberts CNZM, CEO Worldwide Saatchi and Saatchi (retains the link with six summer internships for U6 boys each year); Jason Queally, Olympic cycling champion; Brigadier Alex Birtwistle, foot and mouth star; Tom Sutcliffe, journalist; and Sir Richard Owen, dinosaur man.

Entrance: By oversubscribed competitive exam at 11 (English/maths/reasoning). Three strands of entry: local day, regional day, boarding. Boarders considered separately but all 'must be of an aptitude and ability suited to an academic curriculum'. All must complete a personal statement and attend an interview for sixth form places: 'Tell us why we should give you a place here' – great practice for university UCAS or even the real world. Minimum of six grade 6s at GCSE needed, with at least 5s in English and maths, and grade 7 in maths to study it for A level, for both internal and external candidates. Regularly increasing intake at 16 and growing interest from independents for sixth form places – grab a boarding place whilst you still can. Will admit sixth form girls from September 2019.

Exit: A few – around 15-20 per cent – leave after GCSE; vast majority to good universities, mainly in the Midlands and North, eg Durham, Edinburgh, Manchester, Newcastle, Leeds, Warwick and York, though some dipping a toe into southern universities such as Bristol and UCL. In 2018, five to Oxbridge and seven medics.

Remarks: Vibrant, selective grammar school with big reputation in the region; chiefly a day school but also offers excellent boarding provision. Has managed to retain marked degree of independence as an academy, offering a curriculum above and beyond the norm, including classics.

Unashamedly academic but takes all-round education seriously and delivers – recognised by pupils and parents alike. LRGS is a fabulous school which offers a wealth of opportunities to all boys. Besides academic progress, skills and interests are nurtured and developed which adds to the confidence of pupils.

Longridge Towers School

, Berwick-upon-Tweed, Northumberland TD15 2XQ

Ages 3–18 **Pupils** 328 **Sixth form** 46 **Boarders** 12 full, 7 weekly, 2 flexi (from 11 years)

Fees: Day £9,300 – £13,650; Boarding £20,100 – £27,750 pa

01289 307584
www.lts.org.uk

Headmaster: Since 2016, Jonathan Lee MA PGCE ACA (40s), previously housemaster and maths teacher at Uppingham. Psychology degree from St Andrews and a first career in corporate finance, qualifying as an accountant. His finance skills stand him in good stead with a small school housed in beautiful but expensive to maintain premises. Few endowment funds means totally dependence on current income. Numbers have been growing allowing recent investment into teaching, technology and buildings, whilst managing to keep fees inclusive and affordable.

Believes in interaction between the younger and older pupils, prizes good etiquette and behaviour and encourages pupil collaboration. He says that 'the school has a big heart' and is an open door to a broad and diverse range of pupils; a quarter of pupils have additional learning support.

In first two years of tenure he has brought in 'incremental and subtle changes'. Parents believe that he has the right focus, 'has the children's interest and learning at the forefront'. Not one to sit behind closed doors, he is an upbeat and affable presence around school talking to pupils.

Current Scottish fives doubles champion, charity runner, a bit of climbing and, closer to home, gardening. Lives nearby off campus with his family, ex-nurse wife training to be a midwife and their five children, two of whom are pupils at the school.

Academic matters: At A level, 20 per cent A*/A in 2018 and 48 per cent A*-B. Dusting of A*/As across most subjects and a consistently solid pass rate but also quite a smattering of C/Ds. Good choice of subjects include sports science, computer science and psychology; EPQ for those up to it. Inevitably small groups – will put on a mainstream subject for one pupil in sixth form, French a current example.

At GCSE, 20 per cent A*-A/9-7 in 2018 with a good sprinkling in biology and maths and a few in English literature. Wide range of GCSE subjects with flexible timetabling based on the needs of each particular year group so that 95 per cent get to take what they want – almost everyone takes drama.

Strong languages; French is started at age 3; German and Spanish added at 11 on a carousel of the three; pupils choose two from 13. Italian and Latin available as extracurricular (up to GCSE); junior department Spanish and Latin offered off-timetable. With pupil numbers in the 30s per year group there is streaming of teaching groups in core subjects in the senior school.

In the junior department there is a broad and creative curriculum, whilst focus on core subjects, key skills woven into themes and topics, such as 'evolution and inheritance' in year 6, 'may the force be with you' in year 5 and 'dinosaurs' and 'ourselves' in EYFS. 'Learning is fun here' say the children. Increasing specialist teaching as children move up through the school. Well-equipped designated science classroom used from year 3 upwards. Homework (extended projects and learning logs) set over two weeks, in higher years time given shortens in preparation for senior school.

Regular feedback to pupils and parents on their progress – effort grades given every three weeks and progress grades every six weeks. Two interim reports and one detailed report sent each year. Teachers show real passion, quickly picking up learning style of each pupil due to the small teaching groups. Teacher-led activities have timetabled slots outside teaching time; classroom related topics spill over into the programme and whilst optional, children are expected to take part, and they do.

Successful track record with children across the whole ability spectrum has seen a rise in numbers over the last few years. Currently over 80 pupils receive additional support, tailored to individual need and delivered by a dedicated team, through a mixture of tailored timetabling and/or small support groups. Appropriate personal education plans keep teachers aware of needs and are reviewed at regular intervals. Key skills for all at KS3 and year 10s can choose study skills instead of one GCSE option. English help for the small number of EAL pupils and efforts to provide extra stimulus for the very bright.

Games, options, the arts: For a small school punches well above its weight across a wealth of disciplines. Fields teams in traditional sports; some national rugby players and county hockey players. Badminton has gone from strength to strength with a number of county champions. Regional and national schools' representation in athletics; equestrianism; mountain biking; netball; squash; dressage and cycling. Longridge pupils now also hold British vaulting, swimming and Scottish tetrathlon medals.

Nearly three hours of sport a week plus enrichment programme. Spacious sports hall (takes a marquee inside for prize days and dances) and at last has an Astroturf; minibuses take swimmers to Eyemouth pool. Grounds lend themselves to hosting local cross-country etc.

Lots of choir, orchestra, jazz groups etc and nearly a third of the school has individual tuition, but little take up of academic music beyond GCSE. Informal lunchtime concerts much enjoyed by all. Special centre for peripatetic music in a pretty gothic house in the grounds.

Drama in the round in quirky theatre converted from former convent chapel, with jazzy lighting. Drama on timetable as well as enthusiastically contested in annual house competition. Each spring the school production is performed in Berwick's Maltings Theatre – recent production Our Day Out. Senior pupils tackle weightier stuff too, such as Euripides' Medea. Tinies in the junior department present the nativity each Christmas and KS2 have a summer production in the school theatre, most recently Peter Pan. Nearly a third of the school takes LAMDA examinations.

Art has an airy space at the top of the building and there are splendid examples of pupils' work around the school. Fine arts studied at A level but photography and textiles along with big pictures, murals and bio-art (fusion of art and biology) on offer in the co-curriculum programme.

The co-curriculum programme extends all through the school from year 3 to sixth form – 4.00pm to 4.45pm daily (buses run at 4.50pm). An alphabet of activities from archery to zoology – supervised study is provided as an option too.

Lots of opportunity to travel: German exchange, cultural trips to France and Spain, sport tours, ski trips etc. Biennial expedition trip for sixth form combining adventure, community service and relaxation – 2019 destination Central America. DofE bronze and gold for seniors – very popular – and Adventure Service challenge for juniors. Annual junior residentials as eco-explorers to places such as Grinton Lodge or outdoor pursuiters at Boggle Hole. Lots of out of school experiences as all junior teachers are MIDAS qualified minibus drivers.

L

Boarding: With just 20 or so boarders, about half of them full, and a dedicated non-teaching housemaster in charge (ably assisted by four non-teaching boarding staff), it's a very different boarding experience here; more 'an extended family,' said one girl boarder. Certainly the easy camaraderie and gentle joshing between those we met and with their housemaster felt just like that.

Accommodation is on two upper floors of the mansion school building, boys above and girls below. Spacious, mostly two-bedded rooms, a few with en suite showers, adequate storage, decoration up to scratch though many walls obscured with posters and personal paraphernalia. After prep and up to 8.30pm, everyone congregates in the pleasant and well-planned girls' common room with spotless kitchenette, counter seating and generous supplies of fresh fruit, hot and cold drinks. A games room with a striking, pupil-composed mural is an alternative attraction, as well as the school's art and sports facilities – the television only features in winter.

Weekend activities can include occasional boarders – some marooned from Holy Island homes by the tides – and day pupil friends. Saturdays start with a leisurely brunch then an afternoon trip into Berwick with occasional cinema, theatre or speedway visits in the evening. Sunday for more adventurous outings such as paintballing, go-karting or tenpin bowling. Transport is organised for those wishing to attend local church services.

Communication and support for parents is excellent. House staff will attend parents' evenings on behalf of those who cannot get there and provide a detailed follow-up email.

Background and atmosphere: The grand façade of this remarkable Victorian Tudor mansion, built in 1870s, is dominated by the elaborate portico added to shelter the Prince of Wales's carriage (though it's not documented whether he ever arrived to use it). Built for Sir Hubert Jerningham, a liberal MP, on the estate inherited by his wife Annie Liddell, it was designed to impress – and it's not lost its touch.

Set in 80 acres of parkland, it was Sir Hubert's home until his death in 1922 when it became a hotel. In 1951, an Ursuline convent school for girls, St Mary's, moved here from nearby Berwick and was restructured in 1983 to found co-educational Longridge Towers School.

Whilst in a fantastic rural setting with imaginative use of the castellated grand areas, the school also has the problem, and expense, of making stone staircases, high ceilings and a warren of corridors work for 21st century education. The modern language classrooms are well below stairs, in basement rooms originally intended for food preparation. Upstairs, wide corridors with hammer beam ceilings are lined with lockers, and a breathtaking stone arch leads to the original library. A clever makeover has provided a mezzanine gallery giving working space. Timetabled library lessons and focus on reading ensures this is a well used space with an ambitious programme of visiting authors etc too.

Four adequately equipped science laboratories, all functioning but some rather antiquated. Interactive whiteboards in some classrooms, two computing/ICT suites as well as laptops and chrome books for mobile use. 'Service wings' house rather drab dining rooms and kitchens on the ground floor – a choice of hot and cold dishes, with not too many complaints.

All obviously well used and well cared for, but lots of echoey passages and stairwells improved by pupil artwork, showing signs of the tight purse strings that have been necessary for some years. Everything clean and mainly litter free and not unnaturally tidy.

The junior department is housed in two buildings in the shadow of the grand mansion. Named after benefactors, Stobo houses years 3 to 6 in a compact one storey, well cared for building. A central hall for daily gatherings, merit assemblies on Fridays, displaying an eclectic mix of the pupils' work, evidence of the breadth of curriculum here. Classrooms, light and roomy – an environment stimulated by the wealth of displayed children's work and relevant topic information.

Across a rather drab and unexciting junior playground, early years to year 2 are accommodated in humbler but fully refurbished single storey quarters, named Jerningham. Rather like Aladdin's cave: opening the door reveals a wealth of colour, imaginative sensory material and even recorded birdsong. Quiet room for numeracy and literacy, ability not age driven; theme-based curriculum led by children, planning and executing a teddy bear rescue from the adjacent wood a recent favourite. A pleasant, fenced outdoor area for younger pupils with weather play equipment that gets enthusiastic use.

Pastoral care, well-being and discipline: Pastoral care is a real strength of the school. Pupils talk about it 'being open and welcoming', the size encouraging friendships across the years – especially valuable in such a small and variable boarding situation, their excellent relationships with their teachers – all endorsed by their parents and recognised in the latest ISI inspection.

Sixth formers do not feel their small population is detrimental to their university preparation. Most have a post of responsibility as a prefect, head of house or leading some of the enrichment activities in the junior school. They are instrumental in the organisation of house charity events, the Christmas Ball, annual leavers' dinner and school council. Plenty of house competition all the way through the school.

Three house system encourages vertical integration in senior school; tutor groups aligned to individual houses. The tutor is the prime contact for parents; tailored academic mentoring introduced from year 9. Sixth form mixed into three tutor groups with an academic tutor who mentors one or two students. Pupils respect and value the system and the genuine interest of staff, so problems are picked up quickly and children tend to monitor and report issues like bullying before they become serious. Qualified full-time nurse works closely with the pastoral and boarding teams, liaising with outside agencies on mental health issues. This link is being strengthened further by involvement of other members of the pastoral team underpinned by extensive PSHE curriculum.

The junior department has five core values; honesty, endeavour, achievement, responsibility and togetherness that underpin the code of conduct and behaviour. At the start of the school year each class draws up its own class rules. Led by head of junior department, weekly 'time to talk' sessions, part of the philosophy for children programme, ignite debate.

Popular junior school council discusses school matters and charities to support in their fundraising. An annual whole school off-timetable day has themed activities and allows time for reflection on such issues as rights and responsibilities or, most recently, an environmental day.

Pupils and parents: A fleet of minibuses covering 14 routes bring pupils coming from a scattered area which includes not only Berwick-upon-Tweed and the surrounding border country in both England and Scotland, but also the Holy Island (Lindisfarne) population, whose children need to board on days when the tide cuts off their journey to or from school.

So boarding at Longridge is more 'flexi' than most and the population fluctuates. A few boarders from abroad, mainly Spain for a year, Middle East or Hong Kong, otherwise a largely British intake.

Everyone looks quite smart in blue blazers, white shirts, grey trousers and knee length straight skirts with prominent kick pleats in blue, white and grey tartan. Very tinies wear navy sweatshirts and joggers, though uniform not compulsory.

Parents run an active programme of events and raise significant amounts for equipment etc – contributed £20,000 to the long awaited Astroturf. Governors take an active interest in the school and the local worthies, whose families give the names to houses etc, support it with visits and interest.

Entrance: A taster day (or two) with assessment for all, followed by an interview with the head and a character reference from previous school, but will take anyone capable of benefiting from what's on offer. Entry at 16+ by papers in A level subjects, dependent on six grade 4s at GCSE or four National 5s at C, with 5s at GCSE in A level subjects.

Since Longridge pupils come from Scotland and England with different systems involving changes of school at 7, 11, 12, 14 and even different age cut off points (September for England but March for Scotland) they need careful induction and class sizes are unpredictable. S

Exit: Some leave from juniors at either 11 or 12 (English and Scottish systems) mainly to independent, Fettes, Merchiston Castle etc, though not usually to local state schools. Usually retain 55-85 per cent after GCSEs, those wanting an academic pathway.

Those who stay to upper sixth go mostly to university, about 40 per cent to Russell Group. Wide variety of courses: agricultural management, theatre, art, business and engineering. Popular destinations include Newcastle, Dundee, Harper Adams, Queen's University Belfast, Aberystwyth, Sunderland, Heriot Watt, Queen Margaret University Edinburgh and Hull; one medic in 2018.

Money matters: Not a rich school but awards available for academic (up to 50 per cent), sporting (up to 10 per cent) or musical (free tuition) excellence. Means tested Governors' bursary scheme subject to the usual assessment and interview admissions procedure. Pupils from Holy Island are sponsored by the local authority, which would otherwise be unable to provide adequate hostel accommodation.

Remarks: Pupils of all abilities flourish in this warm, supportive and enabling small school community. Manages extremely well with the disadvantages of scale, and a magnificent but costly stately pile to maintain, to provide the breadth of subjects and opportunities so that pupils do not lose out. Parents say their children leave as well-rounded individuals who know their strengths and weaknesses and have confidence in their abilities. A great alternative for the people of the Borders and north Northumberland to have on their doorstep.

The Manchester Grammar School

Linked with The Manchester Grammar School Junior School

Old Hall Lane, Manchester M13 0XT

Ages 11–18 **Pupils** 1,313 **Sixth form** 334

Fees: £12,570 pa

0161 224 7201
www.mgs.org

High master: Since 2013, Dr Martin Boulton (40s). He read engineering at Nottingham University (BEng and PhD) and then worked for mining company De Beers and accountants Arthur Anderson before deciding to retrain as a teacher. After completing his PGCE (at Manchester University) he went to Sherborne School in Dorset – teaching physics, living-in as a boarding house tutor and immersing himself in rugby and mountaineering. In 2001 he moved to Westminster School and was quickly promoted through the ranks until he became under master (deputy head). The move to Manchester was a homecoming for Dr Boulton, who is originally from Manchester and attended MGS himself as a sixth former. He transferred there from a state comprehensive on an assisted place. He says his time there was 'transformational' – raising his aspirations and instilling in him a lifelong love of philosophy and literature – and this personal experience cements his commitment to the school's bursary scheme. He talks with real passion about his hopes for the school to eventually raise enough money to become 'needs-blind' – so that every boy who earns a place at MGS will receive financial assistance if he needs it.

Dr Boulton is warm and approachable. He engages with parents as equals and, as we toured the school with him, we watched him chat with parents, pupils and colleagues with a cheerful and easy manner. He impressed us with his enthusiasm both for the school and for the education it provides and we observed a spontaneous and straightforward approach to the job – a welcome contrast from the PR-conscious caginess we sometimes encounter from heads.

Parents described him as 'very present and approachable'. They like the fact that he still teaches physics and they feel he's got to know their children. One parent was impressed that he'd given up his holiday to step in at the last minute and accompany children on a classics trip to Rome and Naples to cover staff sickness. Pupils were even more effusive in their praise of him. They said he's 'brilliant', a 'real people person' and 'strikes just the right balance between strictness and kindness'. They appreciate the fact that he 'really gets out of his office', playing football, going on trips and running physics revision sessions ('he really knows a lot'). And they were bursting with anecdotes to illustrate his character – from wearing an 'outlandish jumper' to helping up a boy who'd fallen over and making self-deprecating jokes.

Academic matters: In 2018, 90 per cent A*-B at A level/Pre-U and 69 per cent A*/A. At IGCSE, 91 per cent A*-A/9-7. It's outperforming all other selective boys' and co-ed schools in the north west and retains its reputation as the outstanding boys' school in the region.

Dr Boulton gave heads of department the freedom to research the most suitable and challenging post-16 courses for their subjects in terms of preparing the boys for university study, so sixth formers now study a combination of A levels, international A levels and Cambridge Pre-U courses. The school aims to go beyond the boundaries of any exam syllabus though so, for example, all sixth formers undertake a two-week off-syllabus research project, which is supervised like an undergraduate dissertation by a member of staff, and then written up as a long essay. Years 7-8 now have a multi-disciplinary enrichment course.

The most popular subjects studied at A level are (in this order): maths, chemistry, biology, physics, history, economics, geography, politics and modern languages. Comparatively few boys study English, art or drama in the sixth form but those who do choose arty subjects tend to do well in them. Languages are big here. The school wades through red tape to offer a wide range of foreign exchanges and pupils can study three or even four languages right up to A level if they want to. As well as the classics and modern western European languages, pupils can learn Mandarin, Russian or even Czech.

The strength of science at the school, and particularly biology, is reflected in the fact that the top leavers' course is medicine (25 medics, dentists and vets in 2017). Other popular university courses are: languages, history, natural sciences, engineering, politics, maths and economics. Computer science now offered at GCSE and A level.

Neither parents nor boys we met thought that homework expectations were too onerous. A year 7 pupil is expected to do six hours a week and this rises progressively up to 16 hours for a sixth former. Parents felt that the school is good at selecting boys who will thrive academically without having to work too hard; they have plenty of time for extracurricular activities. Subject teachers are real experts in their fields – many with PhDs and/or publications to their names. The school has a happy workforce and a great reputation among teachers so it recruits and retains excellent staff easily.

The learning support department is also of note – staffed by a highly-trained team of seven, it meets a range of special needs at no extra cost to parents. Many of the boys are 'unusual' – diagnoses of autism spectrum disorders are no rarity – and the school is proud that boys with SEN experience no detectable stigma and speak openly about the support they get. Indeed apparently there's so little stigma to SEN support that boys 'keep referring themselves when there's nothing wrong with them!'

Games, options, the arts: It's a hardy, outdoorsy sort of school. These boys aren't herded inside at the first drop of rain. As you'd expect, school teams and individuals regularly excel – at a county, national and even international level – in a full range of sports, including football, hockey, judo, rowing, rugby (U15s finalists at England National Schools Cup in 2018), water polo, cricket, badminton and cricket. The school invests in top-level sports coaches and it boasts household names from the world of professional sports such as Mike Atherton and Herbert Toft among its alumni. Sports facilities (including a new sports hall large enough for six badminton courts) aren't slickly photogenic but they do a great job and are well used – both by pupils and the local community.

The school creates B, C and even D teams when it can and offers alternative options such as golf, softball, martial arts and sports leadership awards. Since everyone on a sports team benefits from free weekend coaching, the school wanted to offer a free healthy activity to those who don't play sport; so every Saturday – whatever the weather – a minibus takes anyone who wants to go on a mountaineering expedition – to the Lake District, the Peak District or north Wales. (MGS is, incidentally, the biggest provider of DofE in the north of England.)

For one week in the summer all teaching stops for an annual activities week. Alongside a wide range of sports and outdoorsy activities such as water sports, mountaineering and Army Insight, there are creative options (film and photography, play in a week), journalism and research projects (such as Man Utd/Man City and World War 2) and the opportunity to cook, camp, volunteer or learn about business or computers.

Music is a big part of school life and many learn an instrument, sing in one of the school's three choirs or participate in one of its 20 different music groups. Strong links with the Hallé Orchestra and its children's choir. Enthusiastic musicians at MGS enjoy opportunities to perform in grand venues at the highest level – often alongside girls from Manchester High School for Girls and Withington Girls' School – and even on national radio. Music theory lessons up to grade 5 are free and also, we're told, a gifted musician on a means-tested bursary would be likely to get financial help with music lessons if he needed it.

Even boys who've chosen to pursue science subjects talked to us enthusiastically about drama at the school. There's an annual Shakespeare festival and about six full-scale productions a year (some in collaboration with nearby girls' schools although several boys boasted to us of the dramatic turns they'd played in drag). Some pupils direct or even write their own productions. A decent number of boys take GCSE drama each year and theatre studies A level is offered. Dramatically-minded MGS old boys have certainly made their mark on the world of performing arts. Former National Theatre director Nicholas Hytner, comedian and The Thick of It star Chris Addison, actors Ben Kingsley and Robert Powell, playwright Rory Mullarkey and Kylie Minogue's creative director William Baker are all Manchester Grammar alumni.

Some 150 clubs and activities, many led by pupils. We're told that if five boys and a teacher get together with an idea then that's all you need to start a club. One lad set up a Great Minds competition whereby pupils competed to come up with ideas to solve major world problems. Parents assured us that if a major news event happens, the boys will come home talking about it – aware of the issues, inquisitive and opinionated. The school expects every pupil to get involved in community service at some point and pupils certainly rise to the challenge when it comes to fundraising (one sixth former raised £31,000 through a charity golf project). The school shares its expertise and facilities generously locally, supports two colleges in Uganda and many pupils do outreach work in state schools. With regular trips to far-flung places (eg Sri Lanka, Morocco, South Africa, China, the USA and Russia) an adventurous boy might well leave school better travelled than his parents. We're assured that financial help is available to ensure that the bursary boys aren't always left languishing in the classroom during such jaunts.

Background and atmosphere: The school was founded by the Bishop of Exeter, Hugh Oldham, in 1515, with the express intention of giving academically gifted boys the opportunity to study 'the science of [Latin] grammar' regardless of background or wealth. The original site was near Manchester Cathedral but the school moved to its current location in Fallowfield in 1931 – to accommodate a growing student population. It became a direct grant grammar school in 1944 but reverted to independent status in 1976. It was the first in the country to react with a bursary appeal when the assisted places scheme ended in the late 1990s and the only one of five independent schools to pass every section of the Charity Commission's public benefit test unequivocally.

As you drive in you pass playing fields on both sides and then approach a solid, red-brick building with an archway leading to the quad. We imagine the imposing Memorial Hall, with its ornate ceiling, stained glass windows and plaques to commemorate old boys from the school who were killed in the First World War, instils in boys a keen sense of their own place within the school's prestigious history. The school has its own archive room and employs two archivists. A recent exhibition of A History of MGS in 50 Objects (an idea unashamedly nicked from Radio 4 and the British Museum) went down well with pupils, parents and old boys. But it's far from stuffy here. Of course the energy comes from the boys themselves and there's no sense that they're cowed by their hallowed surroundings. When the corridors are full in between lessons the atmosphere is buzzing – in fact rather loud – although the boys still managed to hold doors open for a visitor and give directions like the best of young gentlemen.

The school only fundraises for the bursary appeal (and for charities). It has a modest and utilitarian approach to new buildings and facilities. They keep the buildings in good working and decorative order but all the boys and parents we met seemed to support the school's position that improving pupil access is more important than lavish upgrades to the facilities. Educationally, though, the boys enjoy a wealth of benefits: there are two excellent libraries and even a school bookshop (run mainly by pupils) and the school stands in 26 acres, including a woodland area with a diverse population of wildlife.

The boys, like most of the decor, are acceptably neat and tidy but not flashily smart. In years 7-11 they wear blue blazers and grey trousers (almost every blazer we saw was decorated with at least one lapel badge marking some distinction or official role – discipline and aspiration seem to be largely promoted through the distribution of shiny badges). Sixth formers wear a suit of their choice – and more badges.

Pastoral care, well-being and discipline: We didn't see any rowdiness or bad behaviour during our visit; the boys we spoke to (and not just those hand-picked by the school for us to meet) were impeccably behaved. The school employs two proctors whose responsibility it is to maintain discipline, freeing up pastoral staff to deal with other issues. Saturday morning detentions do happen – usually for offences such as showing disrespect to a teacher or pupil or for persistent failure to hand in homework. Boys would face expulsion for bringing drugs into school but Dr Bolton is realistic that some boys will experiment with drugs and alcohol outside of school. He says that if parents were concerned about their son's drinking or drug use, he'd want them to feel they could come to the school for help and support. 'An extreme zero tolerance position is unhelpful,' he says. The school also has the facility to perform drug testing if necessary. Parents approve of the discipline policies. One dad told us: 'They don't train the boys like dogs, they teach them to think about their behaviour.' He'd been impressed that, when his own son had got into trouble for doing 'something very stupid,' he was held to account for going along with the group rather than for thinking independently. Another parent said he thought discipline policies were successful because the school spots problems early and nips them in the bud.

On his arrival at MGS Dr Boulton altered the pastoral care arrangements so that every teacher in the school has their own tutor group of up to 13 boys. (Even Dr Boulton himself has a tutor group – the boys we met sounded somewhat envious of the lucky dozen whose pastoral needs are met with informal fireside chats in the high master's office.) The tutorial system was a hit with the parents and pupils we interviewed. One boy told us: 'In a group of just 12 people, your tutor can really get to know you.' MGS does have something of a reputation as a 'tough school' but several parents told us that their own experience contradicts that. A mother of an 'unusual boy,' who 'really stands out from his peers,' was effusive in her praise: 'he's very, very happy here. We're so lucky to have found this school.'

Dr Boulton isn't complacent on the issue of bullying. He says that 'heads who think bullying doesn't go on are kidding themselves'. He says they look for instances of bullying quickly and deal with them proactively. Pupils told us they're encouraged to look out for other boys. One mum told us how impressed she was when the school contacted her to say that a sixth former had noticed some boys being unkind to her son. The school had already been 'proactive' in dealing with the incident and in explaining to the boys concerned the 'serious consequences' of their actions and she felt it was resolved very effectively. A sixth former said to us: 'I had a tough time in year 7 – someone was quite mean to me – but I told the teachers and within two days our parents had come in and it was all sorted out – he and I are really good friends now.'

We saw several anti-bullying posters during our visit and posters that engaged with homophobic bullying in particular. On the question of homophobia, we were told that there were boys in the sixth form who felt able to come out as gay. Boys told us that sexuality was 'not important' to them but boys and staff agreed that lower down the school it might be harder for gay pupils to be open about their sexuality.

Pupils and parents: There's a diverse ethnic mix at the school. Many boys are local – from inner city Manchester or from the surrounding suburbs. Others travel in from as far afield as Sheffield, York and north Wales. Over 220 pupils currently receive means-tested bursaries and the average bursary is for 97 per cent of the fees. But there must be something of a gulf between the affluence of those who receive financial support and many of those who don't. Given that to qualify for a full bursary, families must have an annual income of under £27,000 whereas those who don't get any help come from families who can find over £12,000 a year (per child), we imagine that some after-school 'come round for tea' invitations involve a certain amount of seeing how the other half live. But we didn't pick up on any sense of stigma surrounding bursaries – in fact the boys we met were proud of them and wanted there to be more. 'Do we really need a new touchscreen whiteboard just because another school's got one?' asked one boy. 'Of course not, we want to put all the spare money towards improving access.' 'We boast about exam results here, not money,' added another lad proudly. 'It's arrogant to show off about how rich you are.' No-one knows who's in receipt of financial help and the school ensures that trips and extracurricular activities are made available to all.

Parents we met came across as educated and comfortably off. They didn't seem to be super competitive or pushy – and they said they approved of the school's policy of praising individual effort rather than attainment. They agreed that the school generally communicates with families very well.

Notable old Mancunians (beyond the sporting and artistic figures mentioned above) include broadcasters Michael Crick, Martin Sixsmith and Faisal Islam, founder of Pets at Home Anthony Preston, Nobel Prize-winning chemist John Polanyi, historian Michael Wood and concert pianist John Ogden.

Entrance: At assessment days year 7 applicants are taught unfamiliar material and observed to see how they respond to the teaching style and interact with each other. Then, in January, there's entrance tests in maths and English plus an afternoon of activities. They're looking for boys who will benefit from being at MGS – they must be able to keep up in an 'unashamedly academic' school and also to thrive in the wider environment. If a child struggled in one of two of the exams but showed great potential on the assessment day he'd still be in with a chance. Dr Boulton's only steer on what type of child they're looking for – beyond a bright one – is that he should be a 'joiner inner'.

Pupils who want to join the sixth form also attend an assessment day. This includes subject lessons (reflecting the boys' chosen specialisms) and an interview. A typical offer is for an grade 7 average across a student's GCSE subjects.

Exit: A few boys (up to 10 per cent) leave at the end of year 11. About half of these choose to leave – for a range of reasons, either because the family is moving, they want to pursue options the school doesn't offer or because they want to move to a co-educational school. A handful leave because they're not offered a place in the sixth form – but the high master is clear that such decisions are based on a pupil's best interests: 'We'll accept them into the sixth form if we think it'll work for them,' he says. Those boys leaving at the end of year 13 almost all go to university – mainly to Russell Group establishments.

In 2018, 29 to Oxbridge (31 offers for 2019), plus 23 medics and three dentists; UCL, Imperial, Bristol, LSE, Durham, KCL, Leeds, Birmingham, Nottingham, Edinburgh, Manchester, York, Lancaster, St Andrews popular, and there is rising interest in the US, with one off to Boston in 2018.

Money matters: Over 220 boys at MGS receive a means-tested bursary, awarded on a sliding scale. If you earn under £27,000 you're likely to get 100 per cent of fees paid but if you earn more than £50,250 you'll get nothing. Family incomes are reviewed annually. Additional hardship funds are available for trips and emergency fees support.

HSBC scholarships and other bursaries are also available for state school applicants to the sixth form. These can be combined with a school means-tested bursary to make up the full fees.

Remarks: MGS offers its pupils an outstanding school experience and a first class education. It's an honest, traditional grammar school: outward-looking, high-minded, committed to equality of opportunity and, above all, a wonderful environment for bright boys to thrive in, no matter how quirky or unusual they are. In the words of one sixth former (with no prompting): 'We know we're honoured to be here.'

The Manchester Grammar School Junior School

Linked with The Manchester Grammar School

Old Hall Lane, Manchester M13 0XT

Ages 7–11 **Pupils** 234

Fees: £12,570 pa

0161 2247201
www.mgs.org

Headmistress: Since 2008, Linda Hamilton BEd. Her roots are local – she was educated at Stretford Grammar School for Girls and then at Manchester University – but she's also worked in Iraq, Qatar and Nigeria (her husband was an engineer in the oil industry). She set up a pre-school in Nigeria but her more recent teaching experience has been in British junior schools. Before coming to MGS she was deputy head at Altrincham Preparatory School.

Mrs Hamilton set up the MGS junior school. She led the development of the curriculum and admissions procedure and was closely involved with the design of the buildings. In 2008 it opened its doors to years 5 and 6 and, since 2011, it's catered for years 3 and 4 as well.

Parents absolutely see her as a good thing. 'She has enormous vision,' said one mum, 'and she's really good at bringing her team with her.' 'She's an incredibly generous leader,' added another, 'she's got no ego; she gives credit to the teachers; she leads a cohesive and happy staff and enjoys their success and the success of the boys.' Everyone seems to find her open and approachable: 'She's always around,' said one parent, 'you can just bump into her and chat.' Parents enthused about her dedication and energy to the school and her warm, mothering commitment to their children. Pupils told us she's 'friendly' and 'really kind'. One lad compared her to Jonny Wilkinson – known by team mates to be first on the pitch and last to leave. She knows everyone's names and seems to have a good idea of what's going on in their lives. They all stand to attention when she walks into a classroom, though – clearly her warmth does nothing to undermine her natural authority.

Mrs Hamilton is also an Independent Schools Inspector and a governor at both a local free school and an academy. She's also closely involved with various local state primary schools. She's a mother of three grown up sons and spends her free time with her family or walking and reading.

Entrance: Selection is by an assessment day. There is no set number of places to fill – it's just about finding the boys who will thrive at MGS. During the day, boys are taught in groups of 8-12. They're taught unfamiliar material – in maths and a topic-based lesson – and then they'll be tested on what they've learnt. They'll also be asked to do some creative writing. None of it is on the national curriculum so boys shouldn't try to prepare in any way. The idea is to spot potential rather than just identifying the best-tutored hopefuls. Boys can apply for entry to years 3, 4, 5 or 6 but, if they're unsuccessful, they have to wait two years before applying again (although a boy who doesn't get into year 6 can still apply to join the senior school in year 7). Mrs Hamilton says she feels a real responsibility when admitting a child to the junior school (because juniors get automatic entry to the seniors so she's having to predict whether a boy with thrive at MGS right up to the sixth form). For this reason she says: 'I never dither. If I'm in two minds I'll always ask him to come back in a couple of years and try again.'

Exit: Virtually all junior boys progress to the seniors – without having to do any entrance exams or interviews, a big draw for some parents. Mrs Hamilton keeps a close eye on how boys from the junior school do after they leave – in part to check that her selection procedures are effective. The first few cohorts of boys who joined the school have now done their A levels and, she tells us, they 'did very well indeed,' leaving her confident that 'we've got the assessment and curriculum right'.

Remarks: Free from the constraints of the national curriculum, the MGS Junior School goes its own way – teaching pupils way more than just the fundamentals. The curriculum is broad, skills-based and innovative. The school staff created it, specifically for bright boys. 'Particularly with science, we found that what was already available wasn't challenging enough,' says Mrs Hamilton, 'so we developed our own. Once we'd done it for science, we thought why not do it for maths, English and everything else?' The focus on skills is evident in the approach to languages – with boys learning a different language in each year of the junior school: Spanish in year 3, French in year 4, Latin in year 5 and Italian in year 6. 'They're learning how to learn a language,' says Mrs Hamilton.

One afternoon a week is devoted to 'options' – an opportunity for boys to immerse themselves in a subject or activity of their choosing – and a firm favourite with the boys we met. They choose a different subject each term – examples of options include creative art, dance, mini robotics, stitching club and 'top secret' for years 3 and 4, and build a go-cart, debating, amusement park, fantasy stock market, psychology, military strategy or forensics for years 5 and 6.

The pupils we met loved the curriculum; 'we're not just counting frogs,' said one boy, 'we're doing really difficult stuff like designing an eco-friendly house or learning about evolution.' They appreciated the hands-on, project based lessons. One boy remembered fondly a project where you had to choose a religion other than your own and then design and build a place of worship for it out of sticks. Pupils love the 'options' afternoons too. One lad in the seniors credited an options course he'd selected in year 5 as the thing that 'really sparked my interest in military strategy'.

Parents thoroughly approve of the education the school is providing – believing their sons to be challenged and inspired. One mum said, 'They understand my son better than I do in terms of switching his brain on.' Parents say the homework is just right – there's not too much and it differs from other schools because it's genuinely interesting and difficult ('not just lots of boring, pointless tasks like my son was set at his last school'). One mum told us that her son recently announced 'I've got the best homework ever this weekend!' 'My son's come on leaps and bounds since he came here,' said another parent. 'The change is phenomenal.'

The school takes great care of boys with special educational needs and disabilities. Special needs provision is overseen by the well-qualified senior school SENCo and there's a junior school support co-ordinator. Support is offered in and out of classes and boys can be tested for a number of special educational needs. We met the mother of a young boy with severe haemophilia who was effusive in her praise of how well the school deals with her family's special circumstances. She had many examples of ways in which teachers and teaching assistants had found ways to enable her son to take part in physical, potentially risky learning activities in a safe and well-managed way – all done with the full involvement and support of the family: 'They never make us feel like it's too much trouble, and they never make him feel like a special case,' she told us.

A wide range of extracurricular activities are available at lunchtime, after school and a few before school. Most are free and available to all, but a couple have an extra charge or are only available to some boys (eg those learning a particular instrument). There are lots of sporting, physical and outdoorsy activities (less predictable options include TriGolf, ultimate frisbee and fencing); and countless options to suit musical, arty and creative tastes (dinosaur sculpture and Spanish art stood out to us from a very long list) as well as clubs for those who want to do extra maths, science, creative writing or languages. Games clubs are also popular, with options including chess, Scrabble and bridge. The curriculum offers activities which seem to bridge the gap between arts and sciences. For example we saw some beautiful – and anatomically correct – giant willow sculptures of dragonflies and other insects hanging from the classroom ceilings: we're not sure if their creation was overseen by an arty science teacher or a biologically-literate art teacher; possibly both. (Subject specialists from the seniors also regularly offer support in junior lessons.) The pupils also have access to the senior school's sports facilities and to its specialist sports teachers and now have new sports hall of their own. Junior pupils have had high level successes in swimming, cricket and football. There are star rugby and football players. Many boys are also highly accomplished musicians. The junior school uses the senior school theatre for its three productions a year.

Often the boys are inspired by a piece of art or literature, but that initial interest takes them to a different area of learning – for example, the children were moved by a novel about a child with a serious facial disfigurement. And from that book, not only did they explore PSHE topics by discussing how that child might like to be treated, but they also had a visit from a plastic surgeon who has helped children with similar conditions – giving them a scientific take on a literary subject and an insider's insight into a real career path.

The junior school buildings – constructed in 2008 and 2011 – are built from sustainable wood in the style of Swiss chalets. The original building, Bexwyke (pronounced Bezik) Lodge, now houses years 3 and 4 and Plessyngton Lodge – equally environmentally friendly, built from Scottish pine – houses years 5 and 6. The lodges are spacious, warm and airy. Each has a veranda with pine railings running around it, leading to a large playground. Outside there are benches for boys who want to read and a decking area with wooden tables and stools. The school sits next to a large woodland area with a great variety of wildlife, frequently used in lessons from any number of curriculum areas.

The atmosphere of the junior school is warm and accepting. One boy told us, 'Our teacher was crying when we left year 6 to go up to the seniors – and that shows how much they care about us.' Boys didn't feel unduly pressured to perform academically. 'They have faith in us,' said one lad; 'they want to bring out the best in us but they'll only push us as far as we can go.' Boys told us it doesn't matter if someone is different – 'this school is all about difference,' announced one pupil. In a school that dishes out lapel badges for all manner of achievements, we were heartened to learn that there's a 'great buddy' badge for those who make an extra effort to include people who are getting left out. There seems to be plenty of interaction between other years and even with the seniors. 'My son goes around the village saying hello to much older children,' one mum told us. On our visit we met a large group of boys ranging from year 3 to year 12 and we were very impressed with how gently and indulgently the older boys responded to the juniors. Parents said they were surprised by just how nurturing the school is. One dad said: 'The elite outward reputation is belied by the family atmosphere here.' Another parent told us how well the school helps the boys to empathise with others: 'A boy in my son's class had lost his cat and every boy in that class knew what that would mean to him – they're so concerned about each other.'

There's also a strong outward-looking community spirited feel to the school. Boys get involved in lots of charity fundraising events and Community Action is available as an option. The boys told us proudly how important it is to give back to the community. One lad announced: 'The day MGS pupils forget how lucky we are to be here will be a sad day.'

Boys felt that discipline was fairly gentle: 'If you did some work wrong, they'll try to be encouraging – they'll say "good try, but..."' None of the parents we met had received the dreaded 'call home' about bad behaviour. Mrs Hamilton says they keep the children too busy for them to be naughty. Pastoral care is largely provided by form teachers and teaching assistants (class sizes of no more than 22) but boys also have the option to confide in older pupils if anything is bothering them; senior pupils are involved with the juniors in various capacities as prefects, 'big brothers' and mentors.

Means-tested bursaries (up to 100 per cent of fees) are available for boys in the junior school but there aren't so many offered as in the senior school. Judging from the very satisfied parents and boys we met, the money is put to excellent use.

Manchester High School for Girls

Linked with Manchester High Preparatory Department

Grangethorpe Road, Manchester M14 6HS

Ages 11–18 **Pupils** 695 **Sixth form** 156

Fees: £11,874 pa

01612 240447
www.manchesterhigh.co.uk

Headmistress: Since 2009, Claire Hewitt BSc (early 50s), previously head teacher of King Edward VI Grammar School in Louth (her one and only foray into the state sector); also taught chemistry at Sheffield High, Fulneck School and Harrogate Ladies' College. Chemistry degree and PGCE from Sheffield University.

Friendly, approachable and above all passionate about her work at MHSG. 'I've really found my home here,' she says. Seeks the opinions of others; each term she holds 'frank' parents' forums inviting participants to say whatever's on their minds. 'She listens and she responds quickly,' said one happy customer. She often invites groups of pupils into her office for informal drinks and nibbles and the girls here take a real role in deciding the school's direction: they took part in focus groups when the school uniform was rebranded (the new design is purple in homage to the school's historical links with the suffragettes) and chose the names for the school's four houses (Curie, Lowry, Nightingale and, inevitably, Pankhurst).

Parents value her willingness to make changes as well as her energy and enthusiasm. 'You feel enthused around her,' said one mum. 'And tired!' added another. They say Mrs Hewitt goes to 'every single event'. 'Does she ever go home?' asked one.

She's also hands-on, teaching chemistry to every class in year 7 for half a term. The girls find her inspiring: 'She taught us about atoms, molecules and the periodic table,' said one recent disciple. 'We worked really hard for her because we wanted to impress her.'

Mrs Hewitt loved her own school days. She was passionate about science but also sang in the school choir and played piano and hockey. She wanted to combine her love of science with working with people and 'flirted with medicine' until she decided she was too squeamish. 'I kept fainting during first aid courses!' Her next thought was teaching and she hasn't looked back. She's keen on the personal development side of education and says the single sex environment gives the girls the chance to be themselves and have fun. They're not forced to grow up too quickly here. 'You see teenage girls playing together outside.'

Academic matters: Exam results are consistently jaw-dropping. In 2018, 75 per cent of A level entries were awarded A* or A and 93 per cent A*-B. GCSE results similarly stellar – 70 per cent A*-A/9-7. 2018 saw the school's final IB results (take up was too small), averaging 37 points. However, it continues to support the independent study skills that the IB requires by offering the EPQ.

Biology and chemistry are the most popular A level choices in recent years, closely followed by maths, economics and psychology. Although slightly fewer girls choose to study the arts and languages in the sixth form, those that do score just as highly in them.

One pupil spoke particularly highly of the French department. She'd come to the school from abroad, already fluent in French, and had been worried she might not be stretched enough, but in fact she said the school went to great lengths to develop her fluency and enable to learn at her own level. A parent expressed frustration however that French exchanges haven't happened recently. This is because the school has a significant number of Muslim pupils who wear a headscarf (which isn't allowed in French schools) and teachers don't want to arrange trips that aren't accessible to all.

All girls – both internal and external candidates – have to meet the same entry requirements to the sixth form. They'll need at least a 7 at GCSE in every subject they want to study; good passes in English and maths; and at least five GCSEs at 9-7 grades. There's a measure of flexibility in this in the case of extenuating circumstances but it's important to the school that sixth formers should be able to 'thrive and succeed'.

Games, options, the arts: There's plenty of outside space for team games – generally excellent sports facilities including a swimming pool and a huge climbing wall. There are also top-notch performance facilities and vibrant, reassuringly messy art rooms. Lots of opportunities to perform – in music, drama or dance – at informal events after school and to wider audiences in Manchester and beyond. Many girls do DofE and Model United Nations is also popular. Plenty of opportunities for travel – in the UK and further afield. The bursaries ensure that girls don't miss out for financial reasons.

The school supports girls with a particular talent – whether that's giving them the freedom to travel to national and international sporting events or, in the case of one pupil, supporting her learning at a distance while she spent the year in London, playing Matilda in the West End musical. But extracurricular activities are for everyone – not just the super talented. The school recently ran Balance Week during which all pupils and teachers were encouraged to find their own work-life balance by pushing the homework to one side and trying out activities ranging from knitting to skateboarding.

There's an impressive range of extracurricular activities on offer. Mrs Hewitt has extended the lunch hour to 70 minutes to allow girls time to eat, socialise and take part in an activity. Girls often start up their own clubs if they find a gap – for example one pupil founded a group called IMPACT, which gives those who want to change the world a chance to get together and make a start. Unusual clubs that caught our eye include cryptography, podcasting, Bollywood dance and electronics and coding. In the sixth form some activities get a bit more serious – for example anyone turning up to DVD club hoping to eat their sandwiches watching Bridget Jones will be disappointed; it's actually a meet-up for aspiring doctors, vets and dentists.

We dipped into two lunchtime activities during our visit. The first was a practice session for a student-led jazz ensemble, in which two highly capable sixth formers put a group of strings, woodwind and brass players from various year groups through their paces. The atmosphere was purposeful and collaborative; the music was brilliant.

The second was a University Challenge event. Pupils were setting the questions and taking evident pleasure in making two teams of teachers sweat. It was good-humoured – we were particularly struck by how relaxed the audience was. Groups of girls and staff dipped in and out of the hall, whispering answers to questions and giving running commentaries. We got a sense that this is a happy and buzzing community. Mrs Hewitt had told us that with these girls 'you don't have to tell them where the line is'. This event seemed to illustrate the point: the girls know how to behave; they know it's rude to make so much noise that others can't be heard. They have fun but they know when to stop. We suspect that that common teacher's refrain of: 'That's enough. You've had your joke. Calm down now!' isn't so well known at MHSG.

Background and atmosphere: Founded in 1874 'with the aim of imparting to girls the very best education that can be given and to fit them for any future which may be before them'. Did we mention that Sylvia and Christabel Pankhurst were pupils? Staff and pupils are inspired by the school's history but the atmosphere is energetic and forward looking. The building is incredibly light and open. We didn't see any gloomy corridors or dark corners; there are glass walls all over the place. No glass ceilings, though.

It's not a blazer and boater kind of school. The new school uniform – a product of countless focus groups – is smart and chic but not ostentatious. It was designed to avoid 'giving pupils problems when they're on the bus'.

Extremely culturally diverse. Pupils come from all over Manchester and beyond. A range of religious assemblies caters for the diversity of beliefs – but these are inclusive and girls often choose to attend assemblies from other faiths than their own. We were also told that, unlike in some other schools with diverse populations, friendship groups are not divided by faith, ethnicity or social background. One parent told us 'they really celebrate diversity. In business diversity is a competitive advantage and they get that.'

Pupils say the atmosphere is 'supportive rather than competitive'. 'You could go into a classroom and ask, "Does anyone have a pad?"' Several girls we met were happy to call themselves feminists. One was particularly inspired by a special screening of Suffragette, where she'd met Emmeline Pankhurst's great granddaughter. All agreed that they are privileged. The 'snobby' reputation that sometimes attaches itself to schools like this isn't really borne out by the fact that the last two head girls – elected by pupils – were bursary recipients. It's OK to talk politics here – but you won't find a hotbed of youthful radicalism. In a recent mock election 50 per cent of the girls voted Conservative to 21 per cent Labour. 'Everyone has strong views here,' said one sixth former. 'Yes, but we respect each other,' added another. 'I stood as the UKIP candidate in that election but no-one holds it against me.'

Pastoral care, well-being and discipline: A pastoral deputy head oversees this side of the school. Every member of staff is assigned to one of the four houses and is part of the pastoral team. Two school nurses are there for pupils who are sick or upset and they keep an eye on the school timetable so they can spot any particular patterns. 'Bullying can happen,' says Mrs Hewitt, 'and we'll deal with it wherever or whenever it does' – even if it takes place outside school premises or online.

A parent backed up this claim. 'My daughter was being bullied online – quite badly,' she said. 'I called her head of year and it was dealt with that day – really sensitively. It never happened again. The girl apologised. Her parents rang up and apologised. I was really impressed by how well the school handled it.' Girls also told us they felt safe here and well cared for. They were particularly positive about the academic help they receive – through homework and subject clinics. 'I don't feel embarrassed to ask for help. I don't feel like I'm being a pest even if I keep on asking.' They also said they felt confident to ask for an extension if they needed one.

On the surface, pupils' lives here are pretty rosy but one year 7 whistleblower was brave enough to speak out: they won't give you butter on your toast unless you pay extra. It's a scandal.

Pupils and parents: Neither pupils nor parents could think of a particular type of child the school would suit. If they're bright enough to be selected, they should thrive here. Pupils here need supportive parents, though – willing to drive them around, take an interest and get involved. Many parents work in full-time and demanding jobs, and the school does accommodate that by providing support with transport and an extended school day (girls can arrive from 7.15am and remain on site until 5.30pm). Parents say the school communicates with them effectively and works collaboratively with them to support their children.

The most famous alumnus who didn't bring about votes for women is probably Judy Finnigan, but she's just one of a long list of women leading the way in every eminent profession you can imagine – from Libby Lane, the first woman bishop in the Church of England, to Cassie Lomas, award winning makeup artist to Lady Gaga and Rita Ora. Lots of successful business leaders too – including the vice president of Facebook EMEA, the first female executive director to sit on the board of Marks & Spencer and the first female chief cashier of the Bank of England (Merlyn Lowther – also a school governor).

Entrance: Almost all girls from the prep school go on to the senior school. (They don't need to sit the entrance exams but any girl who's found the prep school a struggle will be guided to a more appropriate secondary school.) But the majority come from any of 50 or so feeder schools. Year 7 entry exams in maths, essay writing, comprehension, verbal and non-verbal reasoning, with high performers invited for interview – and their parents are interviewed too. A school report from the head teacher of the applicant's present school is also 'an important part of the selection process'. 'We're looking for girls with a good grounding,' says Mrs Hewitt. 'We're not looking for perfection.' She's willing to consider a girl with a 'spiky profile' if she believes she'd be happy here. 'I'm looking at her attitude and her basic skills,' she says, 'and I'm asking myself "Is she teachable?"' She's critical of parents who are 'foolish enough to tutor their children' for the school's entrance tests. 'She's got to be happy here. A girl's self-esteem is very precious. Why would you try to send your daughter to a school where she's going to struggle?'

Exit: Two to Cambridge in 2018 (engineering and medicine). Others off to study eg law at Nottingham, economics at UCL and a dual European social and political degree at UCL and Sciences Po in Paris (she turned down a modern languages place at Oxford).

A proactive approach to careers, with careers advisers, regular talks and presentations, nearly always by alumnae. 'It's so inspiring for the girls to hear from someone who used to sit where they're sitting,' says Mrs Hewitt. Parents and pupils seem particularly excited by the new Project Pankhurst mentoring scheme. This gives sixth formers a chance to make contact with old girls now working in their chosen industry for phone, email or even face-to-face advice and support.

The girls we met didn't seem daunted by the lofty accomplishments of their peers and predecessors. Emma Barnett, Radio 5 presenter and former Telegraph women's editor (and another alumna), recently gave a talk warning girls against the cult of perfection and comparing themselves to others. One sixth former told us how well the school had supported her when she'd chosen to study the subjects she loved for A level, rather than the ones she most excelled in.

'But don't you feel responsible?' we asked a handful of girls. 'Don't you feel pressure to use this wonderful education to become a barrister or a surgeon or a politician rather than... I don't know, get a job in a cake shop or something?' The response was quick – delivered with a smile: 'Well, if I really loved cakes, I think the school would encourage me to build a career in cakes – but I wouldn't just work in a cake shop. I'd start my own shop and employ lots of people and grow the business and it would make the best cakes in the world.'

Money matters: The school makes an effort to keep extra costs as low as possible – for example that was an important issue in the new uniform design. Fees are a shade cheaper than the nearest competition, but there's not much in it.

Some nine per cent of pupils are in receipt of some kind of means-tested bursary; four per cent are on a full bursary. These also help with uniform, travel and extracurricular activities. Head has discretion on awarding these. 'We want to use them to change lives,' she says. Pupils are quick to talk about how bursaries have helped them and the school works hard at fundraising to increase the numbers who can receive one. They're clearly still very much in a minority, though.

Remarks: MHSG is an incredibly positive community. It promotes hard work, ambition and seriously clever women with a light touch. Its pupils leave the school with the world at their feet but also knowing how to support their friends, take care of themselves and have fun.

Manchester High Preparatory Department

Linked with Manchester High School for Girls

Grangethorpe Road, Manchester M14 6HS

Ages 4–11 Pupils 241

Fees: £8,712 – £8,850 pa

01612 240447
www.manchesterhigh.co.uk

M

Head of the Preparatory Department: Since January 2018, Helen Mortimer, previously deputy head of Manchester Grammar junior school, where she taught from 2008. Psychology degree from Sheffield.

Entrance: Assessment of pre-schoolers is informal – as you'd expect. Girls applying for entry at 4+ are invited into school to take part in activities where staff observe them and interact with them. School says they're not looking for knowledge so much as teachability. It doesn't matter if the children have never come across a particular concept before, but can they grasp a new idea when it's explained to them? Selection for entry at 7+ is based on tests (in maths, English, problem solving and cognitive ability) and reports from previous schools. Children work at a fast pace here and selection is to make sure that every child who's offered a place will keep up and be happy.

Exit: Almost all girls from the prep go on to the senior school. They don't have to sit the formal entrance exam: ongoing assessment throughout their time at the prep school means that teachers and parents might talk about alternative schools for strugglers, but this would never come as a bolt out of the blue at the end of year 6.

Remarks: The atmosphere is academic right from the start. In reception, we did see girls dashing about in the spacious outdoor learning area, but the children indoors were doing subtraction sums – with impeccable handwriting and no mistakes. The girls are working about a year ahead of the national curriculum but we got the sense that this is led by the children rather than forced on them. They learn quickly and are hungry for new challenges. One mum told us that it was 'life changing' for her daughters to come here after attending another, less academic, primary school. 'After their first day they came home and said: "everybody's so interesting!"'

Homework is never set on Wonderful Wednesdays – so we guess that means it is set on most other days of the week. Still, everyone we spoke to seemed happy with that. A SENCo supports a small number of girls with dyslexia or dyspraxia. Assessment is ongoing throughout the school year and pupils do sit some internal tests too – although not Sats.

The buildings feel light, open and transparent – there are no dark corners or cramped corridors. The prep school building connects with the high school. Pupils eat lunch in the senior school cafeteria and make use of many of its facilities – including its swimming pool, huge climbing wall and fantastic drama studio. As you'd expect there is a wide range of extracurricular activities – lots of music, drama and dance opportunities; plus gardening club, taekwondo and Mathletics (an international mental arithmetic skills programme). Lots of educational visits to the school (some with a small additional charge) – for example the pupils learned about e-safety through an interactive theatrical performance.

There are also plenty of opportunities for parents to get involved with school life. They're occasionally invited in to join their daughter for breakfast or lunch and the PTA holds regular sociable fundraising events such as the annual barn dance for all the family. Parents are happy with how the school communicates with them. They say they get plenty of notice for events and find out all they need to know through a weekly email bulletin.

The school population is diverse. It's very multicultural and pupils come from all over Manchester and beyond. There's a prayer room available and pupils are very respectful of difference. There are no bursaries available to prep school pupils though, so with fees of just over £8,000 a year, it's presumably not as socially diverse as the senior school.

Wrap-around childcare is available from 8am until 6pm. Before school supervised breakfast club is free. Parents pay for the after-school club where girls can take part in a range of activities, get help with their homework or spend time outside (weather permitting).

MHSG is clearly proud of the feminist legacy of the Pankhurst sisters, its most famous old girls. The school has recently rebranded and redesigned the uniform, drawing on the colours of the Suffragette movement – but at the same time moving forwards into the 21st century. After extensive focus groups of pupils, parents and staff, they've done away with netball skirts, in favour of more practical skorts and tracksuit bottoms.

Girls are encouraged to aim high. Last harvest festival they sang, in chorus, that they can 'do anything at all ... if I can just believe in me.' The MHSG programme of regular career talks from high-flying old girls extends down to the prep school – recently the prep girls met Dr Kotska Wallace who is now principal engineer at the European Space Agency in the Netherlands. Pupils are encouraged to blow their own trumpets – and each other's. 'They really do support each other,' said one mum, 'they're building a sisterhood here.'

Merchant Taylors' Girls' School

Linked with Merchant Taylors' Primary School

   56

80 Liverpool Road, Crosby, Liverpool L23 5SP

Ages 11–18 **Pupils** 482 **Sixth form** 135

Fees: £11,394 pa

01519 243140
www.merchanttaylors.com

Headmistress: Since April 2018, Claire Tao, previously deputy head at the City of London School for Girls. MSc in personnel management and industrial relations at LSE; started her career in industry, completed a PGCE at Roehampton University and moved into education, working for the Old Palace School of John Whitgift as a biology teacher and head of house. She then went to Dulwich College Prep as a chemistry teacher and housemistress before moving to CSLG, where she stayed for 10 years. Interests include the theatre and hosting social events and she is also looking forward to continuing her love of cycling in the Northern hills.

Academic matters: In 2018 at A level two-thirds per cent A*/B; especially strong maths, physics, art and design, French, economics, geography and psychology. Also offers business studies, ICT, government and politics, theatre studies, AQA Bacc, home economics; biology, chemistry and English very popular and good numbers for classical civilisation. Almost all subjects very strong at GCSE – 78 per cent A*-B/9-6 2018; astronomy possible through club. Some parents would like more stimulation for top set girls.

Good spread of languages, including Greek, Latin and Mandarin – particularly impressive classics department: we would have liked a go at the interactive Latin course we saw in action. Setting for maths, languages and science. Average class sizes – 20 key stage 3, 14 key stage 4; 10 for sixth form; 24 max; buzzing, focused girls at work; lots of PCs.

Thoroughgoing tracking and monitoring. Success in national/regional science, maths, classics, poetry and politics competitions; STEM subjects and participation in external courses encouraged. Stable staff – 'hugely experienced and talented'; girls spoke warmly and appreciatively of their teachers, feeling lessons are fun and varied and they are well taught and supported if having difficulties. Parents very pleased – 'They've brought her out academically...She's really bloomed and exceeded our expectations'.

Well-designed gifted and talented provision for selected members of years 7-10 (the Harrison Group); lectures for sixth form Harrison scholars open to all; lots of support for Oxbridge, law, modern languages and medical school applicants.

Thoughtful and comprehensive provision for special needs: individual sessions, IEPs with detailed suggestions for teaching strategies, specialist science support teacher; co-ordinator feels she can cover all needs. Grateful praise for the way her daughter's needs have been met from a parent. General initial screening for dyslexia with checks again at end of years 9 and 11; individual EAL support available.

Games, options, the arts: Own courts and use of recently constructed sports centre shared by all four Merchant Taylors' senior and junior schools. Usual sports plus badminton, lacrosse, dance (some would like more of this), trampoline, rowing, golf, scuba diving, climbing, pilates and step aerobics, so plenty for the less sporty. Local, county, regional and some national level success for hockey, netball, athletics, tennis, cross-country, badminton, swimming; two young national biathlon competitors; runs A and B teams.

Thriving music ('wonderful teachers... one of the greatest strengths of the school' – parent): three orchestras, four choirs, ensembles; choir performs at classy events – Royal Navy, cathedrals, Lord Mayor of London and his High Sheriffs' dinner; film/show music as well as classical; tours to Belgium, Germany, Holland; individuals attend Royal Northern Music College and Chethams' summer school; annual music comp; piano masterclass by Richard Meyrick; Saturday morning co-ed music school, Crescendo!, open to all schools, 7 to 18 year olds.

Two joint drama productions annually, one musical, one play, at both schools, eg Calamity Jane, Les Mis, Daisy Pulls It Off, Shakespeare. Drama festival for years 8 and 9 – plays written, directed and organised by sixth formers, who also run drama club; arts award. Lively, well-designed magazine, Calliope; visits from writers.

Truly stunning art – painting, 3D, multi-media; excellent exam results (recent accolade for 'exemplary practice' from AQA); GCSE art looks up to A level standard. Inspiring, vibrant art studio. Several fascinating creative partnerships with Liverpool John Moores University School of Art, Aintree and the Royal Liverpool Hospitals, eg a series of works based on treatment of blood disorders. Own art gallery, The Vitreum, hosts exhibitions by leading regional, national and international contemporary artists and designers. Visiting printmakers work with students, thanks to school's own etching press (also has an Albion letterpress, rescued from a barn in France by the dynamic art director) and stone lithography facility.

As well as key stage 3 textiles and home economics, girls take a technology course including mechanisms and computer programming; the STEM club is designing and building a solar powered car – so these girls will have no problem with changing a plug whilst knocking up a soufflé (and translating a Virgil Eclogue to boot, no doubt).

CCF – with the boys' school (all three services) – very big; much D of E; all sixth formers do community service. Debating, Model United Nations comp, European Youth Parliament and business enterprise/investment comps. School council, lots of charity fundraising (run by sixth form committee), fortnightly fair trade stall, Eco schools' Green Flag status – to be featured on Eco Schools' website as case study of good practice. Joint schools' youth club for years 7-9.

Trips to France, Italy (skiing), China, Australia, Greece, Iceland, World Challenge to Equador, culture trip to New York; linked schools in Sierra Leone; year 11 jolly at Alton Tours before GCSE exam leave starts.

Very good careers programme – breakfast events (with boys) for upper sixth give opportunity to meet reps from companies/ business people plus joint working lunches and dinners with guest speakers from various fields; work experience in year 11 and through sixth form, in Merseyside and sometimes beyond; Merchants' community network used; annual joint careers fair.

Background and atmosphere: A notch-potch architecturally – the original house which now houses the library (the Merchant Taylors' Schools were founded in 1620 by John Harrison of the London Merchant Taylors' Livery Company) is juxtaposed with a 1960s concrete monstrosity, 1980s red-brick extension, modern reception area and generous art gallery space. Harmonised blue décor within to complement school colours. Classrooms look nondescript but attractive displays cover all walls around the school. The sixth form library in the old house is furnished

M

with traditional wooden bookcases, tables and chairs; the ground floor section is enticingly stocked with varied fiction.

Much promotion of reading and general knowledge – book lists and shadow competition judging, visits from writers, house quizzes. Lawns (one with benches for alfresco lunches), an eco garden and inspiring modern sculpture of a girl reaching for success.

Much focus on the latter but, we were assured by girls, not in an oppressive way – 'Teachers will help you find out what you're good at', so you 'find your niche'; 'There's something for all aspects of your personality'; 'If you want the best, it's there for you'; 'You can be accepted for what you want to be – so long as you work for it'. 'Healthy competition', but girls don't feel pressured and support each other, said a parent. 'A unique combination of high expectations in a non-threatening environment,' said another. No opportunities wasted for improvement – including literary extracts on the loo doors. Public speaking encouraged to develop confidence; scholars hone their social skills at a formal dinner with governors.

School council chose names of the four houses – Minerva, Thalia, Gaia, Selene. Smart uniforms – navy blue jackets and skirts, light blue, striped blouses. Food well thought of – plenty of choice; sixth form can go out in lunch hour but some choose to stay in. Three full school assemblies/week with religious elements.

Pastoral care, well-being and discipline: Very reasonable behaviour policy, elegantly headed 'concordia parvae res crescunt' (small things grow in harmony). Girls' happiness seen as integral to achievement – pupils see the school as very friendly and feel well supported, with plenty of people to turn to if they have problems, which will get sorted out. Sixth form mentors provide a listening service, plus access to two trained counsellors every lunch time. Well planned transition to year 7 including summer holiday scheme – state school children integrate quickly. Focus more on rewards than sanctions – merits for exceptional helpfulness, showing initiative, outstanding effort; honours and prizes.

Pupils and parents: Catchment area from south Liverpool to Bootle and Crosby, north and east beyond Southport, as far as Warrington, Rufford, Runcorn, Wigan and St Helens. Wide socioeconomic range – 20-25 per cent have financial support. Ethnically mixed. Open, confident, articulate and thoughtful girls who enjoy all aspects of school life. Good links with parent, who feel involved and that concerns are responded to swiftly and patiently – website, newsletters, handbook.

Famous OGs: Beryl Bainbridge; Jane Garvey and Kelly Dalglish (Woman's Hour/Sky Sports presenters); Professor Janet Finch, vice-chancellor Keele University; Winifred Lambert – distinguished social worker, promoting housing for families and disabled, and lifelong member of the Communist party; Jane Greenwood, Tony award-winning fashion designer; Joy Swift MBE, creator of the original murder mystery weekends.

Entrance: Year 7: tests in English, maths, online reasoning plus report from current school, late January/early February (register before December of year 6). Years 8-10: tests in English, maths and reasoning; some spoken and written questions in languages and sciences. Sixth form entry: at least seven GCSEs at grade 6 or above, 9-7 in subjects to be taken at A level.

Exit: Some 10-20 per cent leave at end of year 11 for local sixth form colleges. Of those who stay most head for Russell Group universities. Manchester, Liverpool John Moores, Durham, Leeds, Liverpool and Newcastle popular (occasional Oxbridge place – one in 2018). Favoured subjects: psychology, medicine (one vet in 2018) and classical civilisation; otherwise more do various kinds of science than arts.

Money matters: Year 7 entry – discretionary awards varying in amounts (linked to academic merit); scholarships for academic, sporting and musical prowess; assisted places awarded on academic merit, means-tested, up to full fees (home visits to assess financial need). Sixth form – Harrison scholarships (more kudos than dosh) and some bursaries available. Ten per cent discount for siblings.

Remarks: Very successful, happy mixture of the traditional and 21st century education. High achieving girls who don't feel hothoused. Outstanding art evidence that creativity and individuality are prized too. Excelsior!

Merchant Taylors' Primary School

Linked with Merchant Taylors' Girls' School

Liverpool Road, Crosby, Liverpool L23 5TH

Ages Girls 4–11, boys 4–7 **Pupils** 320

Fees: £8,265 – £8,517 pa

0151 924 1506
www.merchanttaylors.com

Headmistress: Since 2007, Julie Yardley BA PGCE (40s). Educated at Birkenhead High, music degree at Liverpool University; worked in sales before primary music training; taught in state schools in the Wirral, Birkenhead High Juniors, head of Bolton Schools Girls' Junior Division; regularly does support teaching at school. Keen to make curriculum more lively with problem-solving, active and independent learning approaches and to foster 'give it a go' spirit and perseverance. Energetic, ebullient, enthusiastic. Main hobby music – performing and concerts.

Entrance: Four to 7-year-olds' assessments usually in spring term but available throughout the year (can join at any age) – observed doing age appropriate activities, looking for readiness to listen and adapt to school life. More places available in year 3 – short tests in English and maths based on key stage 1 curriculum.

Sibling discount of 10 per cent for second and third children, 20 per cent for fourth and any more.

Exit: Boys leave at end of year 2, most for Merchant Taylors' Junior; girls leave at 11, nearly all to Merchant Taylors' Senior.

Remarks: Original 1800s, cream and blue, converted house now supplemented by purpose built classrooms and specialist teaching rooms, a recent dining hall, kitchen, library and fully equipped medical rooms as well as additional office space and an impressive new glass fronted reception area – the result of a two year £5.5m redevelopment. Adventure playground recently opened.

Ability spread from average to very bright. Class sizes around 15. National curriculum with extras; no key stage tests. Year 5 annual themed activities day; cross-curricular practical work linked with science; we admired a very creative classics project; imaginative events, eg a giant egg appearing in the playground, used to develop investigative skills and newspaper report writing; all teachers plan a weekly gifted and talented activity open to all children. Impressive success in national maths competition.

Learning support mainly for dyslexia and dyspraxia, but if a child has enough ability and school and parents feel this is the right place, would do their best to accommodate all needs; a few EAL children.

Uses senior school's sports facilities – swimming pool, very recent sports centre, courts and pitches. Strong swimming and athletics (three biathletes in national finals), soccer club for year 2s. Annual music competition; lively drama – version of A Midsummer Night's Dream produced by year 6 classes in a week, with input from professional actors and a fashion designer; a girl starred in Matilda the musical – youngest ever winner of an Olivier award. High standard, inventive art; year 6 have practical art sessions, eg recycled fashion day, in conjunction with senior school art department.

School and eco councils; good range of clubs including thinking skills, Italian, French; charity fundraising; residentials at outdoor activities centre for years 4 and 6.

Pastoral care centred on class teachers plus strong lunch time welfare team; year 2 'playground pals' attend to infants' playground; years 5 and 6 help with infants' sports day and read with them – lots of opportunities for responsibility. House points, merit badges, weekly merit assembly. Parents pleased with friendly, accessible teachers.

Early years foundation stage judged outstanding by Independent Schools Inspectorate; links with feeder nurseries; good use of small outdoor area and support for additional needs; happy children, very competent at ICT.

Promises well, with much improved accommodation to come and lessons moving in a more progressive direction.

The Minster School, York

Deangate, York, North Yorkshire YO1 7JA

Ages 3–13 **Pupils** 145

Fees: £6,798 – £10,398 pa

01904 557230
www.minsterschoolyork.co.uk

Interim Head: Mlle Sophie Schoukroun BA MA (int negotiation, Mandarin Chinese and French FLE) is holding the reins. Previously senior mistress, she became acting head in May 2018.

Entrance: Most come up from nursery, but any age considered if room. Non-selective; would-be choristers must audition at age 7, when up to four of each sex are chosen to join prestigious Minster choir. Boys' and girls' choirs of 20 each are separate, take equal part in Minster worship and (unusually) like for like on scholarships (between 60 and 100 per cent including means-testing) – but work hard for it (as do their parents).

Exit: Leaving is apparently tough: 'we will really miss it,' say both parents and children, but feel they are given good guidance for next schools. 'Great advice and they know our children inside out,' said a grateful parent, adding that they are 'well-prepared for senior school and often go on to shine there'. Most to northern independents at 13: St Peter's, Bootham, The Mount (all York city); others recently to Reading School, Radley and Repton. Understandably excellent record in music scholarships. A few to local maintained schools.

Remarks: School famously claims foundation in 627 by Archbishop Paulinus; certainly a 'song school' existed then. Refounded 1903, specifically at that time to provide choristers for the Minster. Occupies world heritage site slap in the middle of York, bringing the pleasures and pains of operating in the lee of York Minster, which has to be one of the finest buildings in Christendom; 'our school chapel'. Manages to squeeze into a additional space here and there, but expansion is challenging, development a planning nightmare and even returfing the play areas is likely to unearth a Viking or two, bringing the archaeologists flocking and halting any possible progress. Main buildings date from 1832; school also uses string of earlier town houses and handsome Georgian Old Residence for lower school. Despite confined site, it feels remarkably uncluttered, and children seem happily oblivious to the numbers of tourists with cameras slung around their necks peeping through the school gates.

The school's identity and purpose has broadened; prospectus says very firmly, 'Musical ability is not an entrance requirement'; this is more a school which does music than a music school. The school has been co-educational since 1987, yet that penny is still to drop with local tour guides who still describe it as the 'school for choirboys'. It's now much more than that, though admittedly most prep schools would give teeth to reach even half its standard musically. The Minster still requires – and gets – a top class choir, but it's no longer true that choristers dictate the curriculum or shape of the school day. Even so, over 90 per cent of pupils leave playing one instrument, and about half play two or more. One pupil, while admitting sport was his first love, told us, 'I'm really not musical at all – yet coming here I'm still encouraged to play an instrument for pleasure and I have surprised myself.' Plenty of games, societies, activities and trips; 'they are so busy we can hardly keep up,' enthused one parent. Play areas and cricket nets on site; no gym, pupils have to crocodile to playing fields, Astroturf and swimming nearby at Bootham (admittedly only 10 minutes away). SEN (mostly literacy) catered for (free). Nursery opened in 2017.

M

Parents choose the school for its 'family atmosphere whilst getting good academic results' – small is king – and 'children of different ages know each other well and staff and the head know children's names'. Children are 'confident, well-mannered and happy to talk easily to anyone,' say parents, and that was certainly our experience here too. Parents mostly professional and business.

Moorfield School

Wharfedale Lodge, 11 Ben Rhydding Road, Ilkley, West Yorkshire LS29 8RL

Ages 2.5–11 **Pupils** 125: 85 girls, 40 boys

Fees: £9,600 pa

01943 607285
www.moorfieldschool.co.uk

Headmaster: Since September 2018, Paul Baddeley, previously head of the Lantern Community Primary School in Ely for four years. Studied teaching at Bishop Grosseteste College in Lincoln. Has taught mainly in the Ely area, with forays to Devon and Grimsby, championing initiatives such as forest school, a nurture classroom and individual mentoring. Married with four primary age daughters; he likes keeping active as a family.

Entrance: Twenty children per year group. Most join from nursery and there's a steady dribble into classes most years if space allows. Girl-heavy throughout, but numbers of boys are increasing each year as the youngest work their way through the school.

Children of all abilities accepted, on the premise that the needs of current pupils are not compromised in any way; ability/needs are assessed informally on a taster day. Some year groups are full (numbers are on the up) but space in other years so do check. Annual open day, but school is open to visitors most days by appointment.

Exit: Most popular destinations are Ilkley Grammar and Harrogate Ladies, also Skipton Girls' High and Bradford Grammar. All are sought-after schools and competition is rife, so parents are well advised and children well prepared, helping to ease the transition into their first choice schools.

Remarks: Small, but, in many ways perfectly formed. Housed in Wharfedale Lodge, an imposing Yorkshire stone villa with newer additions, including a purpose-built nursery and hall/gym. Classrooms are bright, sunny and spacious, with plenty of impressive work on display. The whole place feels loved and cared for, no tatty areas to be seen. Attention to detail is important here – they care, and it shows.

The school sits in a prime residential street, nestled in the lea of Ilkley Moor. The hillside location means there are limitations – no car park or playing fields on site. However, weigh that up against spacious grounds fashioned by nature with craggy woods, shady dells, dens and a stream – something other schools attempt to recreate by paying a fortune to landscape gardeners.

M

The school uses every inch of the available space – safe playground with hard and soft areas, a hard court and new Astro for ball games; forest school happens for real here and the grounds are child heaven, with so much to explore.

Small classes, learning support as required. French from nursery, German from year 3 and a smattering of Russian in year 6; subject specialist teaching at the top of the school. No lack of rigour – they take preparation for senior school seriously and will happily talk to you about their assessment criteria.

According to the children, 'the teachers here find really fun ways to drill subjects into your head.' We might struggle a little with the word 'drill' but they are all smiles as they say it and we know what they mean. Parents say there are 'young, inspiring teachers' who 'put soul into the place.' Teachers clearly have energy too – they end the day with a seven-minute workout ('don't tell the children, they may want to watch'). Plenty of IT throughout; staff know their way around interactive whiteboards and use them well. Old school skills such as cooking, masterfully led by the former head of Bettys Cookery School.

Well-stocked library; they are big on reading here, with special rosettes awarded for reading the classics (with or without the help of parents). Specialist music rooms in the refurbished basement. All sing and the majority play an instrument, many more than one.

School makes use of good local facilities for team sports and swimming, as well as running on the moor and around the local tarn, and competitive matches against local schools. Apparently 'it's still good for your personal development if you lose,' say the pupils. Crikey. Add to that a spelling bee and a wealth of musical opportunities and there are no excuses for not sleeping well at night. Achieving a rare third green flag as an eco school was much celebrated; there is a vitality here that is both healthy and engaging.

Plenty of 'specials' – climate week, poetry, art, music and drama competitions, fundraising for local charities and more besides. Year 6 pupils end their time at the school with a winter banquet – dress code is 'more dash than cash' so that it doesn't become a fashion show. Otherwise it's a candlelit dinner, with formal invitations (delightfully penned thank you letters follow), the best china and silverware, all at the head's home. It's one of the most eagerly awaited events of the year, and not just for the grand finale that is the chocolate fountain.

Pupils look cheery in practical red and green uniforms, blazers and jumpers for most, sweatshirts for little ones. The time-honoured school hats and caps remain at parents' insistence (admittedly cute around town), but it's more to do with sentimental value than denying the myth that is Ilkley Moor bar t'at (translation available if required).

Food is 'great,' say the pupils, notably Mrs Glover's legendary chocolate square, which (they are quick to add) is balanced by a healthy fruit feast on other days. Food is locally sourced and cooked in-house; parents receive menu options on weekly newsletters.

Parents treasure the 'family environment' and appreciate the accommodating flexibility. Not essential to pre-book before and after-school care. Just a phone call needed – invaluable when you are stuck in traffic. Usual to see older girls looking after the little ones at playtime – it's a small school and they know (and will play with) everyone, regardless of age. New pupils are made welcome throughout and parents meet and greet others with coffee and croissant mornings.

The amusingly titled 'boy time' happens on Friday afternoon when the boys head off for rugby, football, cricket or golf. Boys are still very much in the minority but they are well catered for and are a happy and much-valued part of the school. Pupils are unfailingly polite and discipline is obvious, without childlike enthusiasm being suppressed.

Ilkley is a small market town with, probably, too many schools as well as an abundance of teashops and antique dealers, yet all are thriving and appear recession-proof. Serious money here and they are a well-heeled bunch, though admittedly the heels are more Hunter (possibly Aigle) than Louboutin. But somehow the locals are all the more likeable for that. The upshot is plenty of choice for your children and a great lifestyle for parents who may well choose to work in Leeds but live here. 'You pays your money (or not) and you takes your choice,' as they say around here, but make sure you don't miss Moorfield when you are doing the rounds.

The Mount Junior School

Linked with The Mount School

Dalton Terrace, York, North Yorkshire YO24 4DD

Ages 2–11 **Pupils** 104

Fees: Day £5,850 – £8,850 pa

01904 667500
www.mountschoolyork.co.uk/junior-school-home

Head of junior school: Since 2012, Rachel Capper (40s) BEd music (Bretton Hall, University of Leeds). Joined The Mount in 2003 as class teacher after primary and infant teaching in state schools in London and North Wales, with various positions of responsibility in English, SEN, music and IT. Progressed to head of key stage 1 and then deputy head prior to current appointment.

Lives in York with partner, Adrian, who works in IT. Originally from North Wales and enjoys returning to visit friends and family. Personal interests in music, art and theatre and enjoying the outdoors.

Passionate about early years education and pupils being given strong foundations on which to build: 'Freedom to play, explore and learn in a stimulating environment where they learn basic literacy and numeracy skills and develop the ability to take risks and think for themselves. I believe that these principles should continue into the primary phase where it is important that pupils are taught and encouraged to think independently, and to ask questions.'

Entrance: Entrance by observation (looking for potential) as part of relevant year group on a taster day. Fully co-educational since September 2018.

Exit: Most girls (over 80 per cent) move up to The Mount School at the end of year 6. Others move to local independent schools, such as Queen Margaret's, or local state schools such as Fulford School; boys used to move on at 7 to eg The Minster, or local state schools, but can now stay on till year 6.

Remarks: Situated at the end of the main senior school building, in more recent but attractive trinity of buildings. Pre-school offers wrap around care for 51 weeks of the year for 2 and 3 year olds. The Toddler Room is a cosy island in a secure sea of playground set up for outdoor learning and play. Across the way, early years are on the ground floor of the second building with classrooms for years 1 and 2 above. Bright classrooms with loads of space for the small class sizes; perhaps too small in some. Junior pupils are in classrooms adjacent to the senior school.

What make this site special are the delightful bijou enchanted garden and woodland area close by used for adventurous and investigative outdoor learning led by a specialist teacher. Pupils spoke glowingly of their forest school days. They also have the opportunity to attend the Outdoor Explorers' Club after school. Awarded the Woodland Trust's Green Tree Gold Award for two years' sustained effort by junior school staff and pupils.

Skills-based enquiry-led curriculum with cross-curricular science, humanities and art. Specialist teaching in French, music, dance and swimming from age 3; PE from reception and German from year 3. New life sciences room; year 5 learn science in senior school laboratories and ICT in purpose built suite; no laptops or iPads evident, though.

Girls speak enthusiastically and without prompting of their teachers and the help they give them. Termly assessment weeks produce target cards and are followed up by parents' meetings; annual full written report. Individual progress monitored and if concerns, internal assessment undertaken, in consultation with parents. Support based on individual needs, either by teaching assistant in classroom or individual SEN support out of classroom.

Traditional sports using whole school facilities – regular inter-school competitions. Arts are encouraged here – good take up of individual music lessons from year 1, with school choir and orchestra. LAMDA popular and most recent production Nativity Rock included a cast from pre-school to year 6. Impressive list of after-school activities with some, like judo and fencing, at an extra charge. Annual residential trips from year 2 for outdoor pursuits experience.

Before and after-school care from 7.30am to 6.00pm including breakfast and tea for an additional charge. Free supervised prep until 5.15pm and from year 3 – pre-booked supper with the senior school boarders in the dining room available at 6.00pm. Healthy and attractively displayed lunch for early years up in dining room. Choice given and wastage monitored termly to incentivise children not to leave food on their plate; rewarded by caterer's chocolate brownie bake off.

Good work and behaviour rewarded through individual golden ticket or class golden certificate awarded weekly at one of the assemblies held in the school gym or school hall. Four houses named after York's Quaker chocolatiers provide arena for sporting competition. Principal has worked hard on 'one school strategy' and PeaceJam Juniors (recognised as a school of excellence by the International PeaceJam Foundation), introducing global thinking and strengthening Quaker ethos through meeting silences as in senior school. Girls from senior school doing Duke of Edinburgh Award undertake their community work here too.

The Mount School

Linked with The Mount Junior School

Dalton Terrace, York, North Yorkshire YO24 4DD

Ages 11–18 **Pupils** 140 **Sixth form** 45 **Boarders** 30 full, 2 weekly

Fees: Day £14,550 – £16,680; Boarding £18,060 – £28,881 pa

01904 667500
www.mountschoolyork.co.uk

Principal: Since January 2016, Adrienne Richmond, previously deputy head at Durham High School for Girls. She has also been director of studies at Newcastle Central High. She studied maths at Newcastle and trained as a maths teacher at Manchester. She is an ISI inspector and a DofE award leader, enjoying hill walking and camping.

Academic matters: A level results 37 per cent A*/A in 2018, A*/B 67 per cent. Traditional A levels with biggest uptake in maths and sciences (perhaps due to recent recruitment of more international students to sixth form) though class size remains small 'with nowhere to hide,' said one sixth former, smiling ruefully. PE, theatre studies, psychology and business studies on offer too. Ever-expanding enrichment programme with weekly lectures, community and global focus. Strong uptake of EPQ – now extended down to GCSE years.

At GCSE, 54 per cent A*-A/9-7 in 2018. Good choice of options, 10 subjects standard, MFL either French or German (Spanish GCSE on offer in sixth form). Maths setted in year 7 onwards, English in year 9 onwards. Good IT provision – Wifi and iPads throughout, interactive whiteboards in most classrooms and two modern computer suites plus dedicated department clusters; qualifications including vocational OCR Nationals taken in middle school and sixth form.

Pupils and parents alike comment on the quality and commitment of teachers; girls enjoy lessons. 'They are kind, supportive, encouraging, nurturing as well as being fantastic teachers': one pupil voice spoke for many. A parent told us, 'When she has had a wobble, the teachers have been there supporting her; her form teacher understood and knew my daughter straight away'.

M

York used for local cross-curricular and thinking skills work via Investigating York in year 7; archaeology is part of history in younger years; links with university. Elements of the Peacejam programme, devised by Nobel Peace Laureates, introduced to the sixth form, form part of a weekly enrichment carousel of activities within the curriculum for whole school.

Selective, though does well with all abilities including EAL – support available. Specialist learning support teaching provided in and out of classroom dependent on need.

Very good careers education, skills-based in year 10, work experience post-GCSE in year 11. Focus in sixth form is university preparation, particularly for medicine and Oxbridge, some jointly with co-educational Quaker school Bootham.

Games, options, the arts: Beautifully kept grounds with grass and hard tennis/netball courts, sports fields for hockey and athletics, an indoor pool and sports hall including a fitness suite. Successful at traditional competitive team sports and offers non-competitive options such as rock climbing, dance and outdoor pursuits. Has players at county and country level in several disciplines.

Very strong and varied musical life, from classical to rock; all abilities participate in Christmas concert; regular concerts with other Quaker schools. Almost half of pupils learn instruments at school. Regular speech and drama successes, regional winners of Poetry by Heart, best delegate at Model United Nations conference and regional team finalists in Rotary Youth Speaks. Annual school production, most recently The Witches; sixth form play produced entirely by pupils. Very impressive artwork throughout the school encompassing ceramics, photography, sculpture, textiles and graphics. Design and technology studied up to A level – no cooking, except for fun; sixth form university preparation.

Huge range of after-school activities, eg jewellery making, photography, ultimate frisbee – a non-combat, self-refereed game originating in the US; all take part. DofE popular – strong tradition of community involvement. Emphasis on understanding the wider world and global issues is important – Peacejam, Ibba school in Southern Sudan, electronic links to Quaker schools in Palestine and Lebanon.

M

Boarding: Younger boarding in the upper echelons of the main school building with sixth form boarding across the road. Accommodation is comfortable and homely, recently refurbished. Three to four to a bedroom still the norm – no single rooms in sixth form.

Whilst 75 per cent of boarders are in school at weekends, the high number of sixth form boarders with right to opt out of activities means smallish numbers and a wide age range. Regular organised off-site activities and freedom for unescorted paired trips to the city centre from year 9.

Background and atmosphere: Origins go back to 18th century; present building, close to the centre of York, has a very fine 1857 façade with modern additions. Approached through iron gate from the car park, it's like entering the Secret Garden, though beautifully maintained, stretching beyond the eye to green fields – an unseen total of 16 acres. The girls make the most of the outdoor space, some practising their tennis strokes, others deep in conversation, and even 12 year olds are not too cool to race to the garden swing at break times.

Classrooms are a mix of old and new, very traditional library, which the girls enjoy, and a spacious and light dining room, serving excellent fare, decorated with posters to inspire the girls to reduce food wastage. Attractive and well-designed new sixth form study centre has revitalised the top end of the school, giving private study areas as well as allowing extra activities such as cookery and social gatherings; performing arts hub under construction.

Though only a small percentage of staff and girls are Quakers, the ethos is at the heart of the school, manifest in respect for everyone in the community, a high degree of tolerance of differences, caring for others and democratic practices. 'It provides girls with a moral compass,' says the principal. 'They are valued for who they are'. 'Very little herd mentality,' say parents; pupils are demonstrably happy to be themselves. The head girl is appointed by the school, as the 'girls have a strong sense of fairness and justice'; the school council, conducted on Quaker business meeting lines, discusses internal affairs and, unlike most, really does have a voice. Morning Meetings include a period of silent reflection. Widespread involvement rather than bald achievement is regarded highly, and girls view additional activities, such as lectures from visiting speakers, as 'opportunities not to be missed'.

Pastoral care, well-being and discipline: Pastoral care considered very important – an absolute strength of the school. Girls feel they have an identity, are known and receive a lot of individual attention. Size helps, and activities transcending year groups with good integration of international boarders promote cohesiveness from sixth form down, resulting in the friendly and happy environment. There is a lot of social interaction between year groups, observed in mixed ages, day pupils and boarders all round the same table at lunchtime. Peer mentoring from sixth form for younger pupils.

Non-confrontational approach to discipline, huge amount of trust around the place, which girls appreciate with a typical common sense approach. 'If you mess up, you mess it up for everyone'. Time is given to listen to pupils and they are encouraged to speak and have a voice – in a respectful manner.

Exclusion only for persistent offences or major breach of rules, though the current leadership has not had to deal with incidents involving drugs or alcohol. Even more extraordinary, there is no litter and no evidence of chewing gum. School puts this down to 'pupils having a strong culture of ownership of their school'.

Plenty of contact with parents – school website, weekly newsletter. Termly forum where parent representatives meet the senior leadership team to discuss topics of mutual interest.

Latest ISI report criticised some aspects of staff recruitment checks, though praised the teaching.

Pupils and parents: Not just those with Quaker connection (it's the only all-girls Quaker senior school in England) – large number of local parents, often without an independent school background; not a county set school but local family loyalty over several generations. Wide range of religions or none. Over 60 per cent of senior school board – half are in the sixth form; the majority are full boarders from Pacific Rim, South America, USA and a variety of other countries, though 'not too many from any one language group'. Some European, mainly German Dresden Scholarship pupils plus several MOD funded. Girls wear white shirt, tartan skirt and blue jumper; no uniform for sixth form – 'relaxed' dress code. Famous old girls include Dame Judi Dench, Margaret Drabble, Antonia Byatt, Mary Ure, Kate Bellingham, Laura Sayers.

Entrance: Assessments for years 7-10 entry in English, maths and verbal reasoning plus interview with principal, who looks for 'spark – interesting girls with wide interests'. School report also important. Average and above average abilities catered for. Six GCSEs 9-4 and interview for sixth form.

Exit: Around a quarter leave post-GCSE, most for local sixth form college. Otherwise to a variety of universities, predominantly Russell Group – Exeter, Nottingham and Bath currently popular.

Money matters: Year 7 academic and music scholarships; year 9 academic, art and design, sport, music and drama; lower sixth (College) academic, art, sport, drama and music – all give five per cent remission of fees, to which a means-tested bursary of up to 100 per cent can be added. Music and drama scholars get free lessons. Separate bursary fund for Quaker children.

Remarks: True to its Quaker ethos, evident in the school's caring and cohesive community of multi-faith and international students. Girls are highly motivated self-starters, with teachers who prepare them well for life outside the school gates. Articulate, mature, collaborative rather than competitive, but nevertheless driven by a determination to do as well as they can.

Mowden Hall School

62

Newton, Stocksfield, Northumberland NE43 7TP

Ages 3–13 **Pupils** 169 **Boarders** 18 full, 6 weekly, 31 flexi (from 8 years) **C of E**

Fees: Day £9,300 – £17,160; Boarding £23,700 pa

01661 842147
www.mowdenhall.co.uk

Headmaster: Since 2014, Neal Bailey BA PGCE (30s), previously directeur of Sauveterre, the French school which hosts the year 7 Mowden children for a term each year. He has also taught at Cothill, where he was once a pupil. Educated at Eton and Newcastle University (international business management), he worked in the City before turning to education, having realised he 'was not destined to sit behind a desk looking at numbers'. He'd dipped his toe in educational waters as a gap year student in New Zealand and France, but the real game-changer came when his first son was born, and it would seem he is now living the dream since crossing the Rubicon into prep school life.

Teaches French and maths and is a talented sportsman, particularly keen on football, cross-country and tennis, plus skiing, surfing, camping and bushcraft. Parents love his 'neon-wearing enthusiasm for all things outdoors'. He loves a challenge and took it upon himself to learn to play the drums as per his mantra oft heard by the pupils that 'everyone should have a go at something new'. 'Every child,' he says, 'has a golden thread and it's our job to find it'. He and his wife, Nici, also a qualified teacher, are a strong, warm and hugely welcoming team, and with dog and family they are clearly at home here. Their two young sons attend the school and they all pile in the car for the long drive to a boltholе in Devon for family holidays.

Entrance: Prospective parents visit most days. Be careful with open days – we spoke to one family who visited on one with no intention of enrolling their children but 'were so overwhelmed with the fun and happy atmosphere and the setting that we made a decision on the spot'. Wide ability range – non-selective, but then again 'not just anyone': maintaining the school's ethos and dynamic is important, so if it really wouldn't work for a new a child alongside existing pupils then the head is prepared to say so. Informal assessment, usually during a taster day spent in school, plus interview with head. Vast majority of pre-prep transfer to prep. Pupils local or from prep schools all over the north of England and southern Scotland – Northumberland, Yorkshire, Cumbria, Dumfries and Galloway, Scottish Borders. Small number of overseas boarders (mainly Spanish), and although some teachers are TEFL trained, applicants must have a 'reasonable command of English' to be offered a place.

Exit: Sedbergh up in popularity; Oundle, Shrewsbury and Ampleforth remain popular, as do Stowe and Uppingham. Fettes, Rugby, Eton, Newcastle High, Radley, Queen Margaret's and RGS Newcastle all feature, plus a good few others. Around 40 per cent awarded scholarships recently. Few, if any, leave at 11.

Remarks: Mowden Hall School was founded in Darlington by Mr Frank Marchbank in 1935. The school was evacuated to Fallbarrow, Windermere, at the start of the war, before acquiring its present impressive site at Newton Hall, near Newcastle-upon-Tyne, in 1945. Originally a traditional, boys-only, boarding prep, Mowden Hall welcomed girls in 1982, and opened a pre-prep department in 1993. Much work was done in the school's early years at Newton to convert the former home of the Joicey family, built in 1835 by the distinguished northern architect John Dobson, into a fully-functioning prep school. Now part of the Cothill Trust, a group of seven mainly prep schools spread around the UK.

Splendid setting, on a 50 acre site with fine views. You can get a mobile signal here, but it's irrelevant, at least as far as the children are concerned. No mobiles, iPods or electronic devices allowed other than Kindles for bedtime reading. Boarding pupils communicate with home via the old fashioned means of weekly letters, email/Facetime/Skype (access after supper) or use of the two payphones. No complaints from pupils and parents are both delighted and relieved.

The dormitories, dining room, common rooms, library and headmaster's house are all in the main building, with an adjoining classroom block and IT rooms. The original stable yard was converted in 1992 to house additional classrooms, science labs and a gloriously colourful art room. The pre-prep building was designed specifically and built adjacent to the school in 1993. The nursery, in a brand new wing, was officially opened in 2014 and shares a number of hard and soft play areas with the pre-prep, allowing learning inside and out. Other additions include a swimming pool, used year-round by everyone, plus sports hall and theatre.

All facilities and resources are shared by children throughout the school, right from nursery. A couple of temporary classrooms add valuable teaching space for the older children but, if the head has his way, their days are numbered and (hopefully) soon to be replaced by something both more permanent and more attractive. No lack of rigour – essential if they are to maintain or even improve on current CE success; expectations are high and the children respond accordingly. Plenty of teaching from subject specialists. Smartboards are gradually being replaced by Clevertouch interactive boards, linked to the use of iPads as teaching tools.

Prep children are set for English and mathematics for years 4 and 5, streamed from year 6. The top class studies Greek and a number sit scholarships (good track record). Maximum class size 17: 'any bigger than that would contradict our ethos,' says the head. French for all from nursery; Latin from year 5. Good and imaginative teaching at all levels. Pre-prep classrooms especially attractive, prep could do better on classroom displays. 'Our teachers make learning exciting', said one pupil to a chorus of nodding heads. SENCo with specialist dyslexia qualification provides support throughout the school; one-to-one support is available (charged) if required.

Focus on CE kicks off in year 7 after the unique experience of 'entente cordiale', a term spent at Château de Sauveterre near Toulouse, immersed in French and the French way of life. Away from home and their mother-tongue, this is where the children find their inner coping mechanisms, and most describe it as a major highlight of their time at Mowden. Many understand little during their first 10 days at Sauveterre but then quickly develop a real sense of empowerment as they become fluent in the language – 'confidence is a valuable commodity,' say the staff. The children enter a number of competitions – writing, art and the like – both locally and nationally. They are allocated to one of four houses, named after illustrious northerners, with plenty of healthy, inter-house rivalry.

It's not all work. In addition to the wide sporting programme, the nurturing is clear. Staff:pupil relationships are good with high levels of trust and support, seen as a real boon by parents. Music is strong, with choirs, bands, orchestras and plenty of individual music on offer. Art and drama are popular, the school is a centre for LAMDA and public speaking is big: even if it's announcing the hymn numbers for assembly, everyone finds their voice. That, and the ability to look people in the eye when speaking, is another valuable tool with a generation usually more used to looking down at screens. These are well-mannered children with more of a sense of responsibility than entitlement. Links with the Kenyan school and also a local school for children with disabilities keeps it real.

There's a croquet lawn that (unusually) really is used by the children, alongside impressive sports fields, tennis courts and cricket nets. Hidden from sight just off the main driveway are terrific new all-weather pitches, a major recent investment and transformational in that they allow year-round matches, even this far north. There's an hour of games every day. Trad team sports are popular – rugby, football, hockey and netball with rounders, tennis and cricket during the summer and swimming and gymnastics year round. Away from the school site the children also enjoy a range of other activities including fishing, paddle-boarding and horse-riding.

M

Bags of enthusiasm from sports staff and gap students, a number of whom live on site. This 50 acre site also encompasses a large woodland which provides a muddy but exciting landscape for den-building competitions and a BMX trail. Manicured lawns host an annual garden fête, barbecue and leavers' matches, and a beautifully-kept rose garden provides all the floristry for speech day and is also a cherished location for the delivery of common entrance exam results (weather permitting). New sports kit has proved enormously popular with all – gone are the heavy rugby shirts and old-fashioned kit, recently replaced by quick-drying, body-wicking fabrics and hoodies, appreciated by both pupils and parents. Interestingly, old kit, along with old uniforms and desks, has been shipped out to a partner school in Kenya, for whom the children raise money on a regular basis.

Smiling, bright-eyed year 6 pupils shared their joy of a recent camping trip to 'some random place in the countryside' where the wind was howling, the rain was relentless and they had an 'amazing time', sustained by the school's (allegedly) famous camping stew and doughnuts. Lunches are cooked in-house and very popular; old-fashioned dining room with trestle tables, conversation is encouraged and children clear the tables afterwards. For these busy and active children food is clearly important and they describe the food on offer in school as 'incredible', favourites being fish and chip Fridays, including an offer of smoked salmon and mackerel for more refined tastes, and mint lamb kebabs and fajitas for midweek suppers. There is, of course, also a salad bar.

Boarding numbers are strong, 85 per cent and growing. Some only live a short walk away but such is the pull (from the children, not the school) to stay overnight that parents are drawn into the boarding bubble. About half are full boarders, the rest flexi. Separate accommodation for girls and boys in dorms with four or six beds. Rooms are spacious and colourful and children personalise their own space. Super live-in housemistress with bags of experience is running the show with the support of the head, his wife and matrons. Weekends are busy and fairly structured, plenty of staff on hand and no time to be bored. Boarding is especially popular on a Wednesday night as there's no prep and it is also tuck night. Speaking of prep, it's one hour of supervised homework most nights (usually two subjects) for the older children, Latin prep is apparently 'challenging' – schola obdurate, clearly.

It's a rural school so no surprise to see corduroy trousers, kilts, checked shirts and tweeds as part of the school uniform, mostly green and navy – it's attractive and they like it. A rare heatwave allows shirt sleeve order and ties are removed after supper. You'll notice the wellies in the school porch as you arrive. They are out in all but the very worst of the winter weather. Scooters, go-carts, bikes and rip sticks are hugely popular. Sensibly, the pre-preps wear waterproof boilersuits, enabling them to make the most of the school's wonderful outdoor environment without ruining expensive school uniform. There's even a woodland classroom where the children drag logs across the soggy ground to build dens, bake bread on camp fires and experience the enjoyment of whittling. There's a wide range of extracurricular activities– all the usual suspects plus badminton, computer coding, ballet, nature detectives, golf, Airfix model-making, tapestry, Japanese, jewellery-making, magic tricks, cookery and, if it's your thing, cross-country running with the headmaster.

The next step is a big one and the school has close links with a wide range of day schools (independent and state) and boarding schools across the UK. Choices helped by regular reporting through prep years; effort and attainment grades every three weeks; ranking every quarter; full written report each term. Pupils de-stress after CE with a diverse and challenging three week leavers' programme. During our visit they had been tasked with rehearsing and producing a play in the school theatre – in three days from beginning to end.

The parent profile is diverse, reflecting the local demographic. There's a daily complimentary bus picking up from Jesmond and Gosforth for busy parents wishing to avoid the sluggish early morning commute from Newcastle. No school transport on offer at the end of the school day but there's plenty of sensible lift-sharing going on. It's a staggered finish with a wide range of after-school activities for day pupils as well as boarders; day pupils tend to do everything – except sleep – at school, though even that's a popular option on Friday nights.

Good traditional prep school with lots going on, exuding energy from the top down. Concentrates on developing confident, well-rounded individuals whilst still aiming for those highly competitive top scholarships. A number of parents say the school has 'surpassed their expectations, engaging and developing all the children and bringing out the best in them – an excellent equilibrium of sport and scholastics'. Were it in a different neck of the woods, geographically speaking, it would be bursting at the seams, but its boarding prowess may eventually encourage a few from overflowing southern schools to venture north – and why not? You'd struggle to find better.

Newcastle High School for Girls

Linked with Newcastle High for Girls – Junior School

Tankerville Terrace, Jesmond, Newcastle upon Tyne NE2 3BA

Ages 11–18 **Pupils** 500 **Sixth form** 147

Fees: £13,023 pa

01912 016511
www.newcastlehigh.gdst.net

Head: Previous head Hilary French was due to leave in summer 2018 and the school's senior deputy head, Michael Tippett, had been appointed as her successor for September 2018. However, Mrs French was dismissed in June and police are currently investigating allegations of expenses fraud, so Mr Tippett took up the reins sooner than planned.

Mr Tippett has an MA in classics from Oxford and PGCE in classics from Cambridge. He joined the then Central Newcastle High as a classics teacher, becoming senior master and deputy head. When CNHS merged with Newcastle Church High in 2014 to form Newcastle High School for Girls, he was appointed senior deputy head.

Academic matters: 'An academic school, but you can almost take the academic side for granted,' say parents. Slight downward trend since the merger now seems to have reversed. In 2018, 31 per cent of A level results A*/A and 61 per cent A*-B.

Offers huge variety of subjects at A level including classical civilisation, dance and three MFL with biology, chemistry, psychology and mathematics the most popular (half of leavers study STEM courses at university). Excellent extended enrichment programme, which includes the EPQ.

At GCSE in 2018, 61 per cent 9-7/A*-A. Strong classics; outstanding results in the sciences, large numbers take three separate sciences at GCSE though only a handful convert to physics at A level. Philosophy and classics for all in key stage 3 as well as creative use of cross-curricular deep learning enquiry – year 8 worked on designs for headmistress' office and pop up house bases in new build, with presentation to building contractors in Spanish complete with sample materials and mood boards for interior design.

Choice from art history to entrepreneurship in year 10 complementary studies. Three languages on offer with corresponding exchanges to France, Germany and Spain. Uses engineering centre at local boys' school, St Cuthbert's, some projects shared, annual STEM competition design and make a car that can travel the furthest distance. Great excitement: new build has enabled A level and GCSE food nutrition to be on the curriculum – first time for ex-Central girls.

Restructured staff organisation, now in five faculties, review curriculum every year to meet needs of new intake. Pupils are set in year 7 for mathematics and year 8 in English. Spanish is now taught as a core subject from junior school nursery through to year 9, and moving towards most girls taking the GCSE at the end of year 9. Beyond that, no further streaming – important that non-top set girls prevented from feeling a failure.

Spanking new facilities in completely refurbished accommodation or contemporary designed new build. Good library and, as you might expect, computers all over – though girls able to request to use their own mobile technology in class; digital language lab. Girls' leisure facilities have benefitted from improvements to outside grounds. As one parent put it, 'I cannot think of any parent who wouldn't want their daughter spending their formative years in such wonderful surroundings'.

SENCo, whose knowledge is 'encyclopedic', carries out baseline assessment on all, though girls with learning difficulties are often picked up by subject teachers who provide most support in the classroom. A small number, mostly dyslexic and the school recently hosted Dyslexia North East Conference. Formal extra support comes at extra cost, less formal support not charged for. Small number of EAL who have personalised provision maps which include subject teacher and digital support, weekly EAL club and buddying by older girls, both as learning coaches and young language leaders.

Providing girls with skills for changing careers in a global market with strong emphasis on contributing to the improvement to north east prosperity is integral to school. NHSG CareerConnect works with girls to set up three weeks of work experience after GCSEs, and uses a network of OGs, parents and local business to provide talks, internships and opportunities outside the classroom. Building links with big local employers like Siemens and Nissan and school would 'certainly encourage girls to consider higher level apprenticeships rather than university'.

Happy with single sex success, 'Egos are fragile and the girls need the space to have a go, make mistakes without the pressure of living up to stereotypes. When they go on to university they are streets ahead of their co-educational sisters in confidence and ability to tackle the outside world, not timid, shy girls'. Certainly resonates with all the girls we spoke to.

Games, options, the arts: Very strong in sport; ethos of everyone gets a turn, so lots of teams and fixtures, locally, regionally and nationally. Ranked in top 15 of independent schools for sport by Independent School Sport magazine. County success in hockey and national finalists in recent years for biathlon, netball, cross-country, squash, swimming and badminton; some girls represent GB in their sport. Biannual sports tour, recently to Sri Lanka.

Facilities excellent but dispersed around Jesmond, with superb fitness suite in new building on senior school site, with ex-Central centre incorporating sports hall, music, dance and drama facilities a five minute walk away, all weather surface a little nearer. Girls complain that distance prevents timely trek back to school for next lesson although school does build in walking time into timetable.

Music has good accommodation in the centre, with practice rooms, 'digital den' with computers and keyboards, a fine wigwam-shaped recital hall and recording studios. Two orchestras, folk and jazz bands, choirs and string ensemble on offer, plenty of performance opportunity, high spot Mozart's Requiem at the Northern Chords Festival in Newcastle Cathedral.

Dance now offered throughout the school including at A level and the dance studio is in much demand with clubs, in-house dance events and workshops with visiting professionals. Plenty of competition and performance outside the school gates too.

New drama studio for GCSE and A level work as well as newly established drama club. Drama includes regular full school productions incorporating all the performing arts, played at city centre professional theatre, latterly West Side Story and High School Musical.

Dazzling art curriculum in new light and airy space: ceramics, jewellery making, photography, fine art etc and a lot of fabric work. Girls run their own fashion shows.

D of E very popular, one of the largest participation rates amongst local schools; navy and army CCF with field days and camps. Opportunities for trips to Kenya and Tanzania, the result of links with communities there; USA for politics and arts; Iceland, Berlin, Geneva and even the Galapagos islands among many curriculum and extracurricular opportunities.

School open from 7.00am to 7.00pm for homework and participation in stupefying range of co-curricular activities available before and after school until 6pm and during lunchtimes. Activities range from sports, code club, Shakespeare and Mandarin to colour me happy and learning for learning.

Background and atmosphere: Opened in 2014 from merger of predecessor Central High, founded in 1895, and Church High, founded in 1885, with considerable investment to become northern outpost GDST flagship. Moving from Central High site, senior school now in refurbished converted Victorian Tankerville Terrace villas with attractive new building providing multi-purpose assembly hall, dining room, fitness suite (in much use), science labs with demonstration area and additional classroom spaces. Calm colours, plenty of light, wide corridors with clusters of casual seating, glass walled classrooms providing flexible, airy and very visible spaces.

Landscaped grounds provide a pupil plaza, improved leisure area outside with tennis/netball courts and all weather surface on the horizon. Comfy sixth form common room shared by both years – pretty spick and span compared to others we have seen. Roof terrace fits in with Go Green initiative and designed for gardening club.

Buzz of activity and air of purpose from passing girls in the corridor. Our sixth form guides obviously well known, from acknowledgements received from lower year groups we met. Casual gear sets sixth form apart, a relaxed dress code strongly defended by those we spoke to. Years below smartly turned out in new teal and grey uniform with seahorse school logo. The only display of teenage manners was from girls we passed in the foyer and on the long walk to the sports hall – maybe the haste to avoid the gathering rain clouds.

N

The many girls we met ranged in age and interests across the gamut of disciplines and were all articulate and socially assured, positive in outlook, reflective, respectful of peer opinions and clearly proud of their school and its facilities; as one parent put it, 'well rounded and strong young females.'

Chaired by head girl, a very active school forum meets every four weeks with deputy head leading associated staff. Representatives from every form cover five strands – charity, e-learning, social and emotional learning, teaching and learning and Go Green. Annual fundraising for Plan UK with Because I am a Girl campaign resulted in £30,000 being distributed to date. Girls also choose their own school charity and run whole host of events in support. Sixth formers volunteer to be part of the SHINE programme, an autumn term outreach to local primary year 5 and 6 pupils, leading and motivating the children who take part in Saturday sessions.

GDST membership offers competitions and collaboration with other member schools across academic, creative and expressive arts, public speaking and debating.

Pastoral care, well-being and discipline: Parents say that one of the really unique things about the school that sets it apart from others is the pastoral care and guidance throughout the school. The girls are nurtured and encouraged by dedicated staff who demonstrate their care – beyond the classroom too, say the girls. The pastoral team keeps an eye on individual ups and downs and specific problems are dealt with sensitively by heads of year, school nurse and counsellor.

Four dynamic new houses named after ships built on the Tyne, celebrating Tyneside's maritime tradition, used for charity fundraising, sporting and performing arts competitions.

Clear anti-bullying policy – but it 'isn't a problem', as girls have respect drummed into them from the off. Merits and demerits promote the good and penalise the bad. Girls educated about the risk of drugs.

Social and emotional learning, well-being and mindfulness fundamental to school's ethos and a real strength. Strong developing PSHE programme in place to help girls know themselves, deal with challenge and failure, organise their time and interact with others. Director of social and emotional learning wants girls to 'have the resilience to push out of their comfort zone'. A dynamic curriculum; pupils provide feedback on whether the content and delivery is relevant and suitable. Parent information meetings held on teenage mental health and well-being.

Pupils and parents: Predominantly middle class intake from throughout region, professional families and the very wealthy alongside those from more modest backgrounds; lots of siblings and those with a family connection to the two predecessor schools. Rich mixture of regional accents and healthy mix of different cultures, a handful of Chinese girls staying with home guardians.

Girls come from near and far, the majority within a 30 mile radius. School well placed for public bus, metro and train links, gaps filled by private bus service and fleet of school minibuses to strategically placed hubs.

Transition from junior to secondary is sensitively handled with weekly senior school lessons from year 5, an 'experience day' and then 'big sister' sixth formers help them settle in.

Communication with parents much improved and they feel that they can phone or email teachers if any concerns, well before termly parents' evening. The new Twitter account much appreciated as a 'lovely window into the girls' day at school', and welcome move to include most things on Firefly, the school's online remote access.

Notable alumnae include Dr Miriam Stoppard, Fiona Sinha, design director at McQ Alexander McQueen and actress Andrea Riseborough.

Entrance: Natural progression from own junior school, with increasing competition for other places – spectacular new facilities an additional enticement. Entrance exam, interview and current school report to get in at year 7. Sixth form entrants need nine GCSEs with at least six at 9-7, with interview and previous school report.

Exit: Under 10 per cent leave post-GCSE. University destinations include occasional few to Oxbridge (unusually, none in 2018). Edinburgh, Glasgow and St Andrews remain popular choices as do Birmingham Bristol, Leeds and Manchester. One girl to Plymouth for marine sciences, another to the Rose Bruford College for acting. Two architecture students – Bath and Newcastle – and engineering also becoming increasingly popular.

Money matters: GDST funds bursaries centrally (all means-tested annually) with over 10 per cent of girls currently benefitting from the bursary scheme.

Remarks: Two Newcastle girls' schools successfully merged, the new GDST north eastern flagship now has facilities that live up to its reputation for excellent academics and pastoral care. The transition to a broader intake has resulted in a dip in examination statistics, but the wide range of subjects and activities and teaching staff with the dedication and ability to draw out each girl's strengths set it apart. A close community where girls feel valued and that their contribution is important – and it shows. A school that really does deliver on its commitment to 'an education like no other'.

Newcastle High for Girls – Junior School

Linked with Newcastle High School for Girls

Chapman House, Sandyford Park, Newcastle upon Tyne NE2 1TA

Ages 3–11 **Pupils** 250

Fees: £10,287 pa

01912 016511
www.newcastlehigh.gdst.net

Head of junior school: Since 2011, Angela Charlton BA fine arts from Newcastle (early 50s). Always knew she wanted to teach and in 1997 became deputy head of Fellside Community Primary School. Gained her first headship at Oakfield Infant School before moving to Portobello Primary School in Birtley, where she built an 'outstanding curriculum' (Ofsted).

She had the logistical conundrum of operating the school in situ through the massive Chapman House refurbishment programme in 2013, followed by preparation for the merger of Newcastle Church High with Central High, opening as Newcastle High School for Girls in 2014.

Saw the merger 'as a wonderful opportunity to create new traditions, moving on whilst taking the best of the past'. A chance to rethink core values and refresh the curriculum incorporating more cross-curricular approaches. Endorsed by parents who say that the head 'has built a very creative environment and the curriculum has been changed to reflect that too. It's not just about mathematics and English (although they are at the core of everything).'

Engaging, warm and vivacious, she rightly sees herself as a 'people person', finding fulfilment in detecting and nurturing strengths in others. Very creative, an ideas person, she works in close partnership with her mathematician deputy, a dynamic duo. States that 'she loves the job' and can think of no better occupation than 'developing the minds of young people'. Obviously an evangelist; her daughter is now a teacher and has taken up her first post in the north east.

Art is in her DNA and newly built garden studio at home allows her to relax and unwind – when not in the kitchen cooking up something special.

Entrance: In-class assessment (morning or day long depending on age) and report from current nursery or school. For early years informal group work 'looking for social interaction and readiness'. For older intake, a taster day followed by an in-class assessment day. Most join from nurseries into nursery or reception, some recruitment into juniors from state schools (particularly middle schools) and other independents.

Exit: Virtually all to senior school unless family moves out of area.

Remarks: Follows the national curriculum though taught creatively, forging links between subjects and built around the school, city and region. Girls are hooked into each topic by relevant trips and visits early in the term.

Flexible nursery sessions in the bright and light accommodation with excellent outdoor play area. New arrivals bring in a box they have decorated over the summer as an insight and conversation piece. Literacy, numeracy and other classroom activities in the mornings; afternoons are spent outdoors in forest school (whatever the weather), and on Spanish, PE, dance, drama and music. Extensive outdoor learning continues throughout the junior school, often linked to the curriculum, with experiences ranging from year 1s making habitats for new animals they have created to year 6s lighting fires and using bow saws and knives. All juniors have PSHE, philosophy, music, dance and sports lessons.

As part of the sensitive transition to senior school, Y5 and Y6 have a morning's science, PE and Spanish specialist lessons in senior school each week. There is a lot of liaison between the junior and senior schools eg the junior head accompanying the senior school classics tour to Greece.

No Sats; instead a termly assessment tracks progress. For the academically more able there are extension groups and mathematics challenge competitions, such as the annual GDST junior mathematics conference. Year 6 takes part in the Virgin £5 Challenge, a format similar to a mini Young Enterprise.

Small percentage of SEN, mainly dyslexia, mostly encompassed by in class differentiation, with lots of communication and reviews with parents. EAL strategies include a spelling and reading group to test understanding, one-to-one phonics, handwriting and reading sessions to ensure understanding and correct pronunciation.

School starts them young with sport: lots of specialist teaching in traditional team sports from year 2, making the most of the two all-weather pitches, a real bonus for a junior school. A large hall makes a great space for dance and gym and each year group works on a dance piece to perform in whole school assemblies. Weekly swimming at local pools a short bus ride away. Lots of GDST competitions and local galas, with particular success in netball, hockey and swimming.

Music strong and built into the curriculum, with many taking individual music lessons. Orchestra and active choir with year 6 making it to the final of the GDST Young Choir of the Year competition at Queen Elizabeth Hall, London. Performance opportunities through local music festivals, singing to local elderly residents and Christmas concerts. Instruments introduced in lessons and creative curriculum links music to other topics – such as Djembe drumming skills honed during a study of Kenya.

Lots of drama in class assemblies and year group performances as well as the Shakespeare Schools Festival for year 6, and aspiring thespians were preparing for Macbeth when we visited. Speech and drama and musical theatre classes available at extra charge from external providers; weekly in-house drama club.

As you would expect when head is an artist, two excellent spaces for art, and as one parent told us, 'The girls adore having her for art lessons too. She has really inspired my youngest daughter who showed very little interest in art previously'.

Educational visits abound and residentials culminate in Lancashire PGL adventure centre for year 5 and cultural trip to Edinburgh for year 6.

After-school club until 6pm at extra charge. A number of holiday clubs (open to all) including dance, drama and art weeks.

Situated in the affluent suburb of Sandyford, on a leafy and extensive green five acre site, the heart of the school is housed in a grade II listed John Dobson designed mansion dating from 1817. A century later it became a children's home, which closed in 1996 and reopened in 2000 as Central High Junior School. Underwent extensive, sympathetic and costly renovation and refurbishment in 2013 before the merger with Newcastle Church High to form Newcastle High, though with hindsight the décor would have benefited from less purple, the Central High colour.

Accommodation light and well laid out, flexible spaces filled with matching furniture, all curved lines and round tables. Great facilities, as you might expect in a modern, architect-led design – designated specialist rooms with a simple but beautiful chapel used for all whole school celebrations, and film nights. Wide corridors, with a rather corporate feel as disappointingly – unlike the classrooms – lacking wall decoration; apparently our visit was 'between displays'. A nice touch – each room named after a renowned female role model appropriate to its use.

The lovely and extensive grounds house a dance hall (converted ex-laundry) and dining room. Beyond the outdoor learning area lies the adventure playground and all-weather pitch. The large playground doubles as netball/tennis courts and there is a greenhouse and raised beds for Go Green and the gardening clubs whose produce is used by the kitchen and enjoyed by the girls who grew them. The crowning glory is the forest school, a tree-shrouded area with dipping pond, fire pit, ducks and bug hotel.

Strong pastoral system with emphasis on circle time and PSHE programme. Aims for children to 'know that they can come and talk to staff in an open and honest way'. Pivotal to this is the pastoral lead who is a constant visible presence around the school, particularly at break times. Trusted by girls, she can counsel on worries before they become issues.

Four houses whose captains meet up with their senior school counterparts to ensure continuity. Girls of Daring leadership programme is an award scheme like a mini DofE. Years 5 and 6 follow a programme of mindset and reflection in the spring term as part of their PSHE course.

Enthusiastic, articulate girls, willing to challenge and be challenged yet considerate of others' views and perspective. They ooze self-confidence without being arrogant or ill mannered. Predominantly middle class intake, professional families and the very wealthy alongside those from more modest backgrounds; lots of siblings and those with family connections to the two predecessor schools. Brothers go to Royal Grammar, Newcastle Prep or local high achieving state primaries. Extensive transport services by fleet of chaperoned school minibuses shuttle between junior and senior school and to strategically placed hub, filling the gaps in the private bus service and public bus, metro and train links.

Parents feel well informed about their daughters' education. One parent told us that 'the new Twitter account is also a lovely window into the girls' day at school'. Maths and English reports in autumn and spring followed by parents' evenings, though parents say, 'we have normally had lots of contact with the teachers before that'. Full report at end of each academic year. Parents' forum meets each term; very supportive with evidence of their fundraising around the school.

Tucked away off surburban streets in a tranquil oasis, the school offers an excellent education in a nurturing and encouraging environment. The curriculum has been refreshed and there is a real feeling of dynamism and energy. A 'joined up' junior school that holds dear the core values that are further developed in the senior school and incorporated in the words of the new school song, written by the first team of prefects in the merged school.

N

Newcastle Preparatory School

6 Eslington Road, Jesmond, Newcastle upon Tyne NE2 4RH

Ages 3–11 **Pupils** 280

Fees: £8,742 – £10,307 pa

01912 811769
www.newcastleprepschool.org.uk

Head teacher: Since September 2018, Fiona Coleman, previously deputy head teacher.

Entrance: Entry points are at 3 into school nursery, at 4 into reception or 8+ into year 3. No selection, but children spend a morning in school and are informally assessed. Popular choice with Newcastle parents so still receiving registrations at birth.

Exit: Overwhelming majority to local independent day schools, some close neighbours; girls to Royal Grammar School, Central Newcastle High, Dame Allan's and Westfield; boys also to Dame Allan's, Durham and King's Tynemouth.

Remarks: Set up in 1885 as a public day school for boys – the uniform of black and gold was adopted 120 years ago. Near the city centre in Jesmond opposite one independent senior school and next to another, the school is squished into three and a half terraced Victorian houses. Ingenious use of space with linking stairways, classrooms on first and second floors and nursery on ground floor with access to outdoor play area. Top floor houses an extensive science room, a well-equipped art and design studio and music rooms. Good sport and play facilities; purpose built multi-use sports hall, playing fields; adventure play area (a recent addition), a stone's throw away. All classrooms and walkways crammed with well-presented display work – particularly liked the designs of the Queen's Jubilee knickers (apparently have the royal seal of approval!).

Traditionally boys have outnumbered girls (spoilt for choice in Newcastle) so consideration for gender differences in learning styles. School working successfully to redress balance, starting with nursery. Pupils gain places (and scholarships) at an impressive list of Newcastle independent schools at 11+, from an unselected start. 'A reflection of the traditional, yet broad curriculum, progressive teaching by primary specialists and knowing our children well. We are a busy, lively school, but not a hothouse.' All underpinned by ethos – 'happy children do well academically'.

Don't be fooled by a recent EYFS inspection: First Steps nursery and two parallel reception classes are more than 'satisfactory'. Well-resourced and staffed, with specialist French, music and PE teachers. First Steps in ground floor, high ceilinged, airy classrooms with small kitchen for baking. Reception on second floor in classes of 20 (maximum). Dedicated outdoor play area, next to the nursery, shoehorned between adjacent properties but innovatively designed, to provide a range of early learning experiences. Recent forest school site.

A few children leave before year 6 but school chooses not to replace, so class average 18 pupils in KS2. No setting or streaming in the two parallel classes in each year, though some 'top set' pupils work together. Specialist art and design from year 3, Spanish, Latin and some German from year 5. Independent cross-curricular learning encouraged through project work. We observed inventive teaching; use of hand actions for year

2s, counting to 100 in fives (brilliant physical counteraction for the boys) and teacher/pupil collaborative interpretation of textbook instructions on Venn diagrams in year 5. Plethora of educational visits enrich classroom experiences. Science link to Dove Marine Laboratory at nearby Cullercoats and impressive annual science week – thanks to parents in medicine, industry, and university.

ICT provision is good with interactive boards in all classrooms and an up-to-date computer suite used to link, globally on World Maths Day, to an online international mathematics competition. Well resourced, comfortable library is in the centre of school with non-fiction upgrade imminent. Provision for special needs with small group and one-to-one work, all included in the fees. Assessment at end of KS1 for those with mild learning difficulties, some EAL but no pupils with statements. Creative learning team devises activities for the gifted and talented. Teacher assessment levels on final reports ensures smooth transfer to senior schools.

Excellent music (professionally run) includes choirs, orchestra and a jazz band. Drama lessons all the way through and classes act out a story and film it. Performance opportunities for everyone each year; main production in summer, most recently, Shakespeare for Kids Midsummer Night's Dream; talent assemblies every Friday.

Sport taken very seriously with regular fixtures in traditional team sports although opportunities for girls' competitive team sports can be restricted due to the small numbers in some year groups. Great choice of clubs and societies – includes usual sporting, creative and performing arts, with interesting extras, from early morning fitness, bicycle maintenance (good preparation for annual cycling tour in Holland), chess (a passion) and girl only 'girl talk', covering all the bits of growing up you really don't want to discuss in front of boys. After school activities run to 5pm and summer holiday activity programme available for pupils and their siblings – a great help to working parents.

Clear guidelines to class teachers on how to deal with poor behaviour without embarrassing the pupil. Process of escalation, through to head, for the few persistent offenders. Pupil behaviour is underpinned by the reinforcement of the school charter which states that everyone should feel happy and safe, have a right to learn, is important and can succeed – result is a happy, caring community. The year 6 'buddy squad' deals with minor incidents each break and lunchtime and ensures no one feels alone. Annual end of year river cruise outing for year 2 and their year 6 buddies is a rite of passage.

From nursery up, every child is a member of one of four houses, uniquely named by the children after local Jesmond streets. There are house t-shirts, for up to year 3, and book bags. A positive merit system for good work and behaviour runs from year 2 and from year 3 and beyond points are accumulated for bronze, silver and gold awards which contribute towards house totals.

Parents, as you would expect in a large city: aspirational, many professionals, particularly from medicine and academia, senior managers from industry – all are committed to education and high standards. Families mainly hail from northern suburbs and Gateshead; some further afield from Ponteland, Whitley Bay, Tynemouth and Hexham. School believes that NPS parents are more relaxed about their child's education than at some other schools and 'have faith in what we're doing'. No formal PTA but parents very supportive and help to organise events under the auspices of the head. Good news – 'no cliques,' say parents; bad news – no major contribution to school coffers. School fees alone should cover all that's needed to educate pupils and provide good facilities and resources'. No scholarships but means-tested bursaries of 10-95 per cent of fees.

Prep school and nursery with traditional values and standards and a warm heart. Firmly entrenched as first choice for parents wanting the city's top independent senior schools, and successful with it. Confident, cheerful and courteous children with a busy sense of purpose.

Queen Elizabeth Grammar School (Penrith)

Ullswater Road, Penrith, Cumbria CA11 7EG

Ages 11–18 **Pupils** 882 **Sixth form** 222

01768 864621
www.qegs.cumbria.sch.uk

Headmaster: Since 2015, Paul Buckland, previously deputy headteacher of North Halifax Grammar School. A grammar school boy himself (he was educated at Eastbourne Grammar), he has a degree in English literature and a masters in modern English language from Leeds. He is married with three children and originally trained as an English and PE teacher before moving into more senior roles. His youngest son is currently a student and his wife a teacher at the school so there is no doubting his commitment; conversations over the dinner table should be interesting. He mirrors the school's sporting commitment, enjoying coaching football and athletics as well as watching sport. On the day of our visit he was enthusiastically taking part in a staff v sixth form basketball match. Clearly popular with students, staff and parents, he seems able to take the tough decisions but also to engage in a warm and personable way. He has a clear vision for improving the rather dated fabric of the school, which is beginning to take shape. He has a very strong inclusive philosophy and sees grammar school education as a vehicle for social mobility. He is a 'hands on' headteacher who still teaches.

Academic matters: QEGS is an unapologetically academic school, with a traditional grammar school ethos where aiming high is taken for granted. However the ethos is also one where education is valued for its own sake. They say that exam outcomes are not the be all and end all and our talks with students and parents seemed to endorse that. As this is the only grammar school in Cumbria ability is certainly much broader than in other selective areas, with about 50 per cent of applicants getting a place. In 2018 results at A level were 30 per cent A*/A and 55 per cent A*-B. Minority sixth form subjects include geology and environmental sciences.

At GCSE 49 per cent of grades were A*-A/9-7 in 2018, as to be expected from a selective school, with a Progress 8 measure of +0.3. 'We bat above our average,' head says, 'but this is not a hothouse'. Maths is particularly impressive; art and geography are also extremely successful. French and German are on offer at GCSE and A level. Virtually everyone takes a language at GCSE; no compulsion here but certainly strong encouragement, given the high uptake. History classes are lively, and the head of history, keen to animate learning, recently re-enacted the Battle of Hastings on the school field. Teaching is in mixed form groups in Year 7 and 8 with setting in maths, English, science and languages from year 9, and there are regular assessments beyond the end of year exams. With its selective intake the school doesn't feel that further setting is necessary. Parents said they were very happy with this and one spoke very positively about it, saying it made her child feel he was being challenged and supported but not labelled. Particularly strong results for science (especially physics), maths, art and drama.

The SENCo was described by a parent and a governor as outstanding and is credited with turning numerous pupils around. The school has its fair share of students with additional needs, including an increasing number of autistic students. Parents feel that these are well supported. They put lots of time into helping year 7s settle before and after they arrive, no mean feat in a school with such a wide catchment. The head has visited every feeder primary school and is keen to promote the family atmosphere here. The year 7 students themselves said that this was strong and that they quickly felt QEGS was 'their' school.

Careers guidance begins early, particularly guiding choices in year 9. Sixth formers are well looked after and steered through the UCAS minefield; there's plenty of interview practice for medics and Oxbridge applicants. Students said that support was often extremely personalised and responsive, not just for university but also for those looking at apprenticeships. Parents spoke highly of the 'amazingly committed staff', with the head personally reviewing all sixth form university applications. There's a good balance of teachers here, some with a wealth of experience and understanding of the local community, as well as some energetic newcomers, attracted to the quality of Cumbrian life, and the happy atmosphere of the school.

Games, options, the arts: There are good playing fields, although not always accessible in wet and windy Cumbrian winters. Traditional sports of rugby, football, hockey, tennis, netball and basketball, with athletics and cricket in the summer, all popular. There is lovely large sports hall complete with climbing wall. It's used every evening by the community, and as the northern base of Badminton England. Cross-country is popular thanks to several enthusiastic members of staff whom parents describe as inspirational. As with the rest of the school, the approach to sport is not elitist: while this wouldn't necessarily suit all it does mean that youngsters are encouraged to take part whatever their level of ability or fitness. According to the head it is very much an attitude of 'if you turn up we'll make sure you play'. QEGS has recently been identified in School Sport magazine as being in the top one per cent of state schools nationally for participation and success in sports.

Parents were very positive about the sports provision, the large range of clubs and activities and the staff commitment to going above and beyond. There is a French film club to which students bring their own films (carefully vetted!). Staff say that a lot of activities are student generated and organised. We visited on Children in Need day and saw plenty of examples of strong student leadership of fundraising activities: there was a very genuine buzz and excitement around the school which didn't feel put on for our benefit.

There is a fabulous art department papered with students' artwork of an impressive standard and variety: it spills into the corridors, and a choice handful is selected for the head's study on a weekly basis. It's remarkably mature, high quality stuff and one piece spent the summer at the Royal Academy One Show Summer Exhibition.

There are plenty of musical opportunities: a variety of choirs including Cambiata, a swing band and orchestra. Drama is very popular, with great emphasis placed on the annual production, which parents described as 'amazing', 'and everybody gets involved'. The choice of productions is ambitious including Les Misérables. Our conversations with the head of music showed a real commitment and willingness to go the extra mile, which several parents mentioned too. When we visited, cast and crew were in the throes of preparing for a production of Hairspray. There is a nice drama studio but no theatre, the school hall providing the venue for productions.

Parents say their children are 'always busy' and they are clearly willing to support this with lots of reliance on the taxi of mum and dad for after-school activities. There are plenty of visits, from field and theatre trips to the year 8 residential at Derwentwater; a year 9 trip to Berlin; an inspirational annual art trip to Venice; ski trips; foreign exchange in year 10; and a World Challenge trip for older pupils, recently to Uganda, Nepal, Swaziland and Iceland. Other clubs include choir, law society, Cakespeare (Cake and Shakespeare), chess, debating and electronics. The students take part in an annual sponsored walk which in 2018 raised over £10,000. Again there are no excuses for not having enough to get involved in.

Background and atmosphere: The school was established in 1564. It moved to its current site in 1917, adding a warren of well-maintained buildings and extensions over time. While much of the fabric continues to be dated, further recent extension work has added two impressive modern teaching blocks with language classrooms, a science lab and sixth form private study area. There are ambitious plans for further building developments which will enable the school to compete on a more even playing field with its competitors. However it is clear that facilities do not effect the school's ability to deliver a high quality education. There is a strong, supportive and confident governing body. The school takes its role as part of the community seriously and maintains strong links, regularly hosting a variety of local evening activities and opening up the sports centre to locals.

A small school for a state grammar, the size is much appreciated by both parents and staff. 'Everyone quickly knows everyone,' according to parents, and 'any changes in behaviour are spotted and swiftly dealt with'. Pupils were markedly good-humoured and friendly during our visit, and parents say they are always impressed by behaviour both in school and out. We saw no disruption in lessons, just lively banter and engagement. The students gave every impression of being happy to be in school, not just to learn but also to engage socially and to participate in the full range of extracurricular activities on offer.

School uniform is compulsory up to year 11. A formal blazer and tie create a smart look which the head and staff enforce despite some student reluctance. The sixth form centre is set apart from the main school in a nearby converted primary school. Sixth formers don't wear uniform but are generally well turned out and certainly extremely warm about the school.

The staff are committed and enthusiastic. Turnover is low and the staff we spoke to said they often prefer to forego promotional opportunities elsewhere in order to continue to work at QEGS. One member of staff happily told us, 'the kids make me smile every day'.

Pastoral care, well-being and discipline: Pastoral care is via a form tutor system and heads of year, however the students said that they would feel confident to go to several different staff if they had an issue they needed help with. They were certain that the staff were there for them and that a shoulder to cry on, friendly advice (and biscuits) were frequently on offer. Parents describe pastoral care as extremely effective and said any incidents are quickly and efficiently dealt with, before becoming an issue. Students agreed, saying that bullying is rare and dealt with well when it does occur; 'we are all friends, we are all in clubs and this helps to sort things out'. One parent was particularly appreciative that school let her know early on about a problem, thus nipping in the bug a potentially difficult situation. Another, whose high flying son needed specific support in a somewhat niche area, was delighted that the school had quickly recognised this and brought in someone from industry to help. The year 7 students we spoke to commented very positively on the work the school does to make them feel included, safe and confident very quickly, and again parents backed this up. There was no sense of the stuffiness or arrogance in some selective schools.

Lockers provided for all so no excuses for not being well organised.

Parents appreciate the school's straightforward and open lines of communication. Objectives and codes of practice are clear and pragmatically set out on the thorough and efficient website. The head says, 'The kids know what is expected of them from the outset and everyone knows where they stand; they have the freedom to grow, learn and choose.'

There is a strong student council which meets regularly with senior staff. Students are genuinely proud that they have been selected to come here, some travelling some very considerable distances and passing other extremely highly thought of schools on their journey.

The sixth form students said they had good guidance when moving from year 11, did not feel pressured to stay if the sixth form was not right for them and that support for university applications is strong. They particularly commented on the approachability of the head and his willingness to sort out timetabling and subject choice issues for them.

Pupils and parents: Students come from all over the sparsely populated Eden area. Now takes 150 (five forms) into year 7. The wider catchment is extremely broad, with students travelling from as far as Dumfries and Carlisle. Much of the transport is shared with another local school. Parents represent a very broad social spectrum, but all share a common interest and ambition in the education of their children.

Parents were very positive about the school. They say they choose it for its academic excellence and the fact that it is small enough for students to be known well. This is especially important as so many children come from very small rural schools, often knowing no-one when they arrive. One family from overseas had specifically moved to Penrith to allow their children to come to QEGS. Parents could not speak highly enough of the pastoral care.

The sixth form students we met with were bright, articulate and passionate about what the school has to offer. ABout 15 per cent have joined from outside. One young man had chosen to travel daily from Preston after a family move, while a newcomer from another local school who came to study languages at A level could not have been more effusive in her praise. 'Since coming here I have felt so happy and welcomed. You can be who you want to be, in a school where people want to work, where it's a good thing to achieve, people are proud and happy for you when you do well, teachers are so committed and happy to help pastorally.' She was clear she could have stayed at her previous school to do the same subjects, but had no doubts that she had made the right choice. There were frequent comments from students and parents about the number of staff who regularly go the extra mile to support both in academic work and extracurricular activities.

Entrance: The only grammar school in Cumbria, QEGS has changed the entrance test in order to give less advantage to those who have been tutored and to reach out to more disadvantaged families. As a consequence far more are now sitting the test. It remains to be seen whether this fulfils the school's more inclusive philosophy. Staff have a good dialogue with the feeder primary schools and always know they are getting the right pupils.

There are usually around 20 external sixth form places. Entry requirements are five 5+ GCSEs including English and maths, with 6 or 7 required in A level subjects.

Exit: Some 20 per cent leaves after GCSEs. About 90 per cent of sixth formers to university, some 40 per cent to Russell Group, including five to Oxbridge in 2018. Northern universities are always popular, particularly Newcastle, Northumbria, Dundee, Liverpool, Warwick, Carlisle College, Durham, Lancaster and Manchester. A few head directly into the world of work, and are as well supported by the school as the academics.

Money matters: Voluntary school fund payment of £15 per year helps buy additional resources.

Remarks: The only selective grammar school in Cumbria, it is small but growing and increasingly popular. Inclusive ethos, good outcomes, and education in its widest sense is taken seriously without undue pressure, resulting in happy and engaged students. The school's principles 'freedom to grow, freedom to learn, freedom to choose' are definitely hardwired into students and staff.

Queen Elizabeth High School

Whetstone Bridge Road, Hexham, Northumberland NE46 3JB

Ages 13–18 **Pupils** 1,266 **Sixth form** 365

01434 610300
www.qehs.net

Head of School: Since September 2018, James Andriot, who has been director of performing arts, deputy head and then acting head here.

Graeme Atkins is executive head of the Hadrian Learning Trust, which includes Queen Elizabeth High School and Hexham Middle School.

Academic matters: In 2018, 38 per cent of GCSE grades were A*-A/9-7s; 81 per cent got 9-4 in both English and maths. At A level, 71 per cent A*/B grades. Thirty-two subjects on offer; four languages, four sciences, three art courses and a range of humanities, social sciences and performing arts courses at GCSE and A level; GCSEs include child development and electronics; other vocational courses and some BTecs offered. Good to see Latin, classics, philosophy, psychology, fine art, product design and engineering stretching all the way to A level alongside the more traditional subjects. Language exchanges are plentiful and popular.

Two prize-givings a year celebrating academic success, and ample advice and guidance along the road to improvement in academic performance. 'We make sure that they are on the right path when choosing subject options,' says school which, of course, is sensible and is a huge part of their success. Nearly 70 per cent stay on for sixth form each year; the rest go on to local colleges, higher level apprenticeships, a handful to the independent sector. The sixth form area has its own café, coffee machines and study areas, ample space to work and play. Plenty of guidance given to sixth form, 'including advice to study elsewhere if that's most appropriate for them'. Staff are 'endlessly encouraging and supportive,' say parents.

Not selective, and SEND support covers a range of needs. Subject teachers are responsible for providing a differentiated curriculum (supported by the SEND team), using LSAs to support in the classroom as required. SENDCo has an open and flexible approach to intervention knowing that 'students' needs are forever changing, and the SEND department is happy to be as flexible as we can be in order to meet students' day to day needs'. Currently 18 pupils with SEND support and eight pupils with a statement or EHC plan; value-added in line with national averages. Support can feature social skills programmes, including strategies to enhance self-esteem; access to IT resources; programmes to support speech and language; mentoring activities; help with occupational therapy or physiotherapy needs; and strategies to promote emotional well-being (including communication with parents).

Games, options, the arts: Wide choice of extracurricular activities – everything from DofE, music and theatre to popular and active Fair Trade club; worth also seeking out the Brazilian drumming group, rock band workshop and young writers' club. Heaps of social and sporting events and fixtures, internally and externally; the website is loaded with them. Strong links with overseas institutions including a Tibetan monastery and a school in India.

Good range of sports for all abilities – particularly strong on netball, football and rugby – the latter fixtures mostly against local independent schools. Sports hall, playing fields, Astroturf, cricket nets, tennis and a fitness room all on site. The rowing club dates back 30 years and enjoys huge success nationally and internationally, producing male and female international and Olympic athletes. Training takes place at weekends and after school; it's a serious business but none of that deters the fearless and determined rowers here and they are, they tell us, 'the best state school in the country for rowing'; a couple of the girls here are in the current GB team. Sport is both 'competitive and for fun here,' say parents.

Superb art on display; there is a whole suite of multi-disciplinary art rooms, and dedicated staff ooze enthusiasm. Inspirational art visits include the Clothes Show, Barcelona, Paris, VARC (Visual Arts in Rural Communities), the Baltic Art Gallery in Newcastle. Loads of choirs, orchestra and various music groups, and music features in the creative media production curriculum. Drama also strong with a musical theatre performance annually in the purpose-built theatre. The dramatists head to the prestigious Northern Stage, the Theatre Royal in Newcastle and Stratford, and theatre and dance groups drop in to add further colour and buzz.

Background and atmosphere: The haunt of marauding Vikings 1,300 years ago, nowadays this Northumberland gem proudly holds the title of England's favourite market town – as voted by Country Life magazine. Hexham Abbey is at the hub of its winding streets, now awash with eclectic independent shops, farmers' markets and tea shops. But this is a rural area and, lovely as it is in the surrounding hills, there is a demographic dip here in the Tyne Valley and funding has fallen year on year. Despite that, QEHS has grown from its charter dating back to 1599 into a specialist performing arts school with a reputation exceeding its catchment area and welcoming applicants from far and wide. The funding deficit shows, the building looks tired in places, in need of a refurb, inside and out.

Q

Housed over two sites, it encompasses a late 19th century former hotel – the Hydro Building (it became a TB hospital during the war) – and a more modern (60s with 70s and 80s additions) secondary school building. The Hydro Building is an impressive grade II listed Victorian edifice which once played host to Hollywood greats Douglas Fairbanks Junior and Charles Laughton and leading politicians of the day, including Ramsey McDonald. Fine, traditional school hall for assemblies, exams and general gatherings. The wonderful former orangery (the Winter Garden) is especially attractive, used by lucky pupils during the day buat hired for parties and wedding receptions at weekends. A magical walled garden manned by green-fingered staff is mostly frequented by art and SEN pupils, proving a welcome, peaceful and inspiring space. It's also the home to chickens, guinea pigs and rabbits, cared for by a rota of pupils who also hold plant sales for the local community.

Pupils in the press are celebrated in the school entrance foyer, and there are plenty of them. Also on display are the shirts of former pupils who have gone on to great sporting success (including an Oxford Blue, England women's rugby player and golf pro); real pride is evident. Good range of dining options on offer, demarcated according to age and stage, all food prepared in-house and some of it even grown in the garden here.

Most parents are a loyal bunch; it 'does a great job,' they say.

Pastoral care, well-being and discipline: Co-operative and friendly atmosphere, parents 'especially impressed by the level of support received by pupils around exam time'. Much praise for the home-school communication system; parents feel well informed and can check at any time on attendance, progress and behaviour. Year heads and learning mentors are described by parents as 'caring, helpful and approachable' and pupils feel 'known and valued'. Described as 'inclusive', with a 'can-do approach to differently able students,' according to one parent, the school has a good, calm feel about it and genuinely appears to meet all needs. Proactive in problem-solving, high standards are expected and there's no hesitation in taking action if need be, likewise in giving support as necessary – changes in behaviour, mood and progress 'are noted and acted upon,' say parents.

Pupils and parents: A mix of rural, semi-rural and professionals, many of whom work in the hospitals and academia of Newcastle; their advice is to 'support the school and trust the teachers'. Most do, as 90 per cent attendance at parents' evening is the norm here – remarkable and the envy of many of other schools. Refreshingly, the parent view seems to be less concerned about admin and league tables and more interested in allowing the school to be 'free of political interfering' and 'creative and free-thinking' in its style and approach. That said, it stands extremely well in the league tables.

Some 40 per cent of pupils travel in by bus, from Prudhoe in the east and the border of County Durham to the south. With a year 9 start here, there are no 'littlies' around to bring extra noise and vigour to social areas, enhancing what already feels more like a campus than a playground. There are grassed woodland areas, gardens and hard spaces on which to hang around, and the staff and pupil body moves around between buildings with a civilised fluidity.

A diverse bunch and from a wide range of backgrounds, pupils appear focused and busy. There's a great deal going on here so 'if your child is willing to grasp opportunities then this is a great school for them,' said a parent. Aspirations are high and yet there's no hint of arrogance; neither average nor mundane, they are 'ordinary' in the best possible way. Probably not as streetwise as their urban counterparts; a walk into town, a coffee and a chat, then uphill back to school is about as exciting as it gets for sixth formers at lunchtime.

Entrance: Based on LA catchment criteria. The best and most obvious route in is via one of the three feeder middle schools: its own partner school in Hexham plus St Joseph's and Corbridge. Lots of work done on transition, so pupils coming into year 9 are familiar with the surroundings and settle quickly and easily. Parents out of catchment happy to pay their own transport costs and 'feel lucky' to gain a place, adding that the application process 'is simple'. Five 4s at GCSE required for sixth form entry; must include English language. Average point system in place for entry to chosen courses, the highest requirements being for sciences and languages.

Exit: Around 40 per cent leave after GCSEs. Majority of students go on to higher education with a few to Oxbridge each year. Northern universities top the list of favourites here with Newcastle, Leeds and Northumbria leading the way, Manchester, Durham, York and Lancaster also popular, smaller numbers to London. Others go into higher education, training, apprenticeships or work. Over the past few years many to leading conservatoires and drama schools thanks, in part, to specialist staff.

Remarks: Some schools are all about the window-dressing, this one isn't. In fact window-dressing is something on which it could do better, but that may well be a funding issue and therefore low on the priority list. Crucially, it would appear to be getting all the important things right: results very good and rising, plenty of sport, art, music and other activities all wrapped up with high quality care and teaching – 'exemplary,' in fact, say parents.

Queen Ethelburga's College

Thorpe Underwood Hall, Ouseburn, York, North Yorkshire YO26 9SS

Ages 14–20 **Pupils** 497 **Sixth form** 314 **Boarders** 459 full, 2 weekly

Fees: Day £15,915 – £17,025; Boarding £36,885 – £38,685; International Boarding £45,420 – £47,995 pa

01423 333330
www.qe.org

Principal: Since 2006, Steven Jandrell BA (50s), married to Margaret, with a young son at Chapter House. Warm, friendly, genuine and approachable, he understands education and enjoys discussing it. Well-respected and liked by staff and pupils, he's part of the furniture, having been here for many years as head of music and deputy head. Long-standing parents describe him as 'the best head so far'; 'He's a good listener who doesn't bat you away with standard answers'.

Academic matters: Splits into two streams at age 14, the College and the Faculty.

The College is the straightforwardly academic stream, with all students aimed at the EBacc at 16 and A levels (a choice of 23, but no classics) at 18. In 2018, 71 per cent A*-A/9-7 grades at I/GCSE (overseas students' English accounts for a large percentage of the C/4 or lower grades). College students rarely get less than a B at A level: 83 A*/A, 96 per cent A*-B in 2018. Subject choices are dominated by maths, languages (largely Russian and Chinese) and economics – indicative of the strong overseas contingent. UK university destinations are strongly weighted towards business- and science-related subjects at good universities; psychology, maths and law also popular. Around couple a year to Oxbridge. Five timetable slots in the sixth form, four for A levels and one for 'enrichment' – Faculty has the same pattern.

The Faculty has a much broader remit, with an emphasis on BTecs. There are quite a lot of pupils here who struggle even with English and maths at GCSE (22 per cent of grades were A*-A/9-7 in 2018 – lower without the Chinese and Russian home languages). A smattering of A levels – mostly maths and home languages, giving the 65 per cent A*/A headlined on the school website – and a strong emphasis on business studies BTec where the results are even better: around half D*D*D*. Vocational rather than academic university destinations, mostly business-related or sport at middle-ranking universities with strong reputations, but an increasing showing in recent years from creative subjects and division 1 universities.

The division, though, is not as simple as that. Some College pupils do a BTec among their A levels; Some Faculty students get A*s at A level. There's a difference in style – eg self-motivated vs needs mentoring – which affects how pupils are allocated.

Some parents of Faculty pupils clearly feel that they were not sufficiently involved when the choice between Faculty and College was made. QE agree that they tend to insist on their views of which suits each pupil – leading in some cases to unsurprising emotional friction given parental views (which we often encounter) that BTecs are a second-class option with second class outcomes. That's not, though, how the dozen or so Faculty alumni we have communicated with have seen it. They have felt much more in tune with the style and approach built into BTec: more project-based, more continuous assessment, more real. They praise their teaching and the support from their teachers. They formed strong friendships across Faculty and College, and are still in touch with many of them. They chose university courses that worked well for them (careers guidance much praised), and look back with much fondness to their time at QE.

Low to mid-range universities are happy to accept BTecs; you'd have to be a truly extraordinary candidate to get to Oxbridge on one (it has been done), other Russell Group vary – business courses at Durham accept openly, equivalent courses at Exeter do too, but not obvious on their website, so do check carefully.

In both Faculty and College pupils as a whole do much better than you would expect from their earlier results.

Small classes, unashamedly setted, with regular testing for all – pupils say 'it's good for us'. Reports from parents lower down the school are good. Many parental comments on rapid teacher turnover, and the difficulties and disorganisation that this sometimes engendered. The school puts this down to rapid expansion and says 'now that a decision has been taken to remain at around our present number, this problem should no longer be the case; there were only five new appointments for this year out of 180 teaching staff'.

Dyslexia help available. All children tested on arrival in the prep school during the first half term, ed psych's report if necessary, usually individual lessons for free twice a week, if more needed then extra charge. Five specialist teachers of specific learning difficulties. EFL free throughout the school.

Games, options, the arts: Music (for all) very strong, with frequent opportunities for performance. The old refectory (now the Phoenix Centre) contains no fewer than four practice drama and dance studios and a dedicated theatre – most impressive. Art good but not emphasised.

Thirty-four acres of floodlit pitches for hockey, soccer, rugby, high jump, netball, basketball, volleyball etc and six Astroturfs. CCF popular, clubs for IT, archery, fencing, golf. A new swimming pool too. The giant sports centre (sports village, as the school calls it) is an eye-watering, Olympic-level provision; you can look at the main school website and not see a sign of it, but go to www.qesportsvillage.org and prepare to be blown off your feet. This provides a home for the eight 'performance sport' courses (notably rugby and netball) – as one of their five timetable slots, students push their sporting aspirations, with professional coaching, and individual strength and conditioning programmes prepared by staff from Leeds Beckett. A long string of individual and team successes, as you would expect from provision at this level.

DofE with plenty of gold participants. Lots of extracurricular activities – the list is (almost) endless, most free, but a charge is made where there is a strong element of personal tuition (riding, archery, fencing, tennis, golf and kick-boxing).

Boarding: From age 7 (at Chapter House). International students from 66 countries (most notably south east Asia and the various parts of the former USSR) make up about two-thirds of the boarding community; most of the other third are Forces children. Modern boarding accommodation consists of smart and well-equipped bedrooms, all now with private bathrooms, all with flat screen TVs (in fact two TVs in some twin rooms – just in case these lucky pupils wish to watch different programmes..) on timers so they do not get in the way of prep or sleep. DVD players, telephones with voicemail, fridges, electric kettles, microwaves, air conditioning, trouser presses and room safes – pretty much everything except a mini-bar, in fact. Great attention to detail and, it would appear, no expense spared – newer boarding houses have fantastic limed oak doors, skirting boards et al. A classy medical centre that resembles a private hospital and oodles of huge common rooms – all with leather sofas, toasters and TVs. Houses for the younger ones surrounded by squidgy playgrounds filled with serious kit. Boys' and girls' accommodation is separate. Day pupil centre for day children plus B&B available if needed. The campus has a strong mobile signal.

Houseparents occasionally express concern that individual facilities are so good that pupils, particularly senior (Chinese) boys, are loath to leave their bed/study rooms and join in communal activities. No Saturday school, but full range of activities on offer during weekends – trips to Whitby, the latest cinema preview. After their first term sixth formers can nip into York or Leeds on a Saturday night, but must meet the pickup by 10pm at the local station (or be in by 10.30pm if they miss the train).

Background and atmosphere: Twenty-five minutes from York and Harrogate and a 10 minute drive from the A1. Run by a collegiate board, chaired by Amy Martin, who lives on site and whose family have been involved with the school since 1991 when she was a student at QE. Has been the driving force behind the school's development over the last few years. Thorpe Underwood dates back to the Domesday Book, where it is described as Chirchie, Usebrana and Useburn, before becoming part of the monastery of Fountains Abbey in 1292. The hall was rebuilt in 1902 in best Edwardian Tudor style and the extensions have been sympathetically carried out with leaded paned windows to match the original. The place is a complex mix of old and new – in style and attitude – and full of surprises.

Impressive newer facilities include a vast dining room (The Undercroft) that doubles as an assembly hall – though the acoustics are pretty grim and mealtimes can be a deafening experience, say some staff. Huge solid oak tables fill the room with comfortable seating on the balcony above, alongside exciting sculptures courtesy of Amy Martin's late uncle. Fruit available at all times with good salad bar, home-cooked food with a veggie option. Self-service queuing system moves around barriers like a busy post office. A lift has been installed for wheelchair users. A popular activity centre has been established on the perimeter of the campus.

The original Hall – previously the home of the Martin family – houses a traditional library, the Phoenix Centre and some notable taxidermy.

Has benefited from millions of pounds' worth of Martin investment. Good, if not lavishly stocked, library, banks of computers, Wifi everywhere. Almost 50/50 boy/girl mix, boarding numbers up, and reasonable fees have brought a considerable flow of day pupils.

All faiths and none are welcome. In fact anyone who can afford it is welcome really – with little academic selection and a determination to meet all needs.

Faculty and College mix well outside the formal school day: activities and boarding are entirely mixed. The Faculty is larger and has more UK students than the College.

Relationship between the genders is good, as are relationships too between nationalities: most Brits make good foreign friends. Has a reputation for turning out well-mannered young people. Much-remarked upon omnipresent CCTV is not now monitored in real time, but still proves useful for 'security, serious disciplinary matters and for lost items of value'.

Pastoral care, well-being and discipline: Parents tell us that the pastoral care here is really good – 'Can't plug it enough'. Tutorial system – tutors change yearly, no more than 20 tutees to each. Has recently introduced THRIVE@QE, an initiative to 'proactively support all pupils' emotional health, well-being and resilience through activities, resources, clubs, workshops, clinics and more.' Charming and encouraging leavers' letter.

Discipline is described as 'sensible' – exclusion for violence and selling drugs, possibly also for taking drugs, 'depending on what it is'. Reserves the right to search boarders' rooms and to test for drugs and alcohol – and does.

There was much comment in the press following a critical report from the Independent Schools Inspectorate on the efficacy of QE's child safeguarding systems. ISI has now given the school, which has made substantial improvements, a clean bill of health.

Former provost Brian Martin was cleared of a series of historical sex abuse charges in July 2018; prosecutors said they would be seeking a retrial on two counts of indecent assault and one of sexual assault.

Pupils and parents: Lots of first time buyers, pupils come to board from all over: Scotland, Wales as well as East Anglia and locally on daily basis. Nine buses collect day pupils from all over Yorkshire (not cheap), buses collect from local station. Many overseas students, as above.

Quite a lot of the parents we talked to felt that QE could be better at communicating with them, and at creating a community among parents.

Entrance: Many via Chapter House, but generally aged 14; 9-7s at GCSE for potential A level candidates in the College, broader intake (6s accepted) to Faculty. External candidates come from other independents, local state schools or out of the area. Pupils below year 10 accepted at any time during the school year 'if places available'. Promotes itself heavily locally, nationally and internationally – regular pop-outs from Good Housekeeping and the like. Informative DVD which plays in English, Chinese Simplified and Traditional, German, Japanese and Russian. The heaviest prospectus bundle that we have ever encountered, though fear not, it is fairly repetitive. Entry to all schools is based on CAT 4 test, interview and positive school reports plus Oxford Online English Test or IELTS if appropriate.

Exit: Quite a substantial exit after GCSE – 30 per cent or so, with overseas students typically changing school and UK ones headed for sixth form college. After A levels, most College students off to study law, maths, politics, psychology or medicine recently, a large proportion at Russell Group unis (four to Oxbridge in 2018 and four medics). Business much the most popular course for Faculty students, who virtually all do vocationally-flavoured courses at mid-ranking (recently some division 1) unis: accounting/economics/information management, a wide range of creative subjects (eg fashion design with marketing and music with enterprise) and some science and sport. Several off abroad to eg Swiss, French or US unis. No hoofing out mid-course but for those who underperform 'a consultation process will be held with the student and their parents to satisfactorily resolve the situation'.

Money matters: The school is well underpinned financially but quite expensive (especially so for overseas pupils) and 'you pay for absolutely everything,' say parents. Countered a little by masses of scholarships, plenty of awards (32 per cent discount for Forces and FCO). Add to that list sports and music scholarships and many, many more. 'You can also pay by Barclaycard or Amex.' Very streetwise management and 'all awards granted will be repayable in full, if the school fees bill is not paid seven days prior to the commencement of each term, and, or, if a pupil does not complete their education with us for any reason, regardless of commencement age, until the completion of the end of year 13...' etc etc. Read the small print very carefully. We have great reservations about these terms.

Remarks: Has come a long way, not just in its facilities but also in its academic provision. Making a success of looking after both the academic and the less academic. If it carries on like this it will end up with a grand reputation.

Queen Margaret's

Escrick Park, Escrick, York, North Yorkshire YO19 6EU

Ages 11–18 **Pupils** 270 **Sixth form** 90 **Boarders** 190 full **C of E**

Fees: Day £21,270; Boarding £32,400 pa

01904 727600
www.queenmargarets.com

Head: From September 2019, Susan Baillie, currently pastoral director at Newcastle Royal Grammar. Started her career at Barnard Castle School, has been head of history and politics at selective day and boarding schools, and was previously second deputy head at Kimbolton. Enjoys walking, running and cooking: feels her greatest victory has been winning the local village cheese scone competition. Married to a Yorkshireman with a young daughter plus a cockapoo called Monty, an elderly cat called Polly and six hens.

Senior deputy Lars Fox is acting head for the summer 2019 term.

Academic matters: Excellent academic results almost taken as read by parents and success matters despite entry not being particularly selective. Overall A level performance consistently good, with 2018 grades 47 per cent A*/A and 79 per cent A*/B on the up. Mathematics, biology, economics, English, chemistry, languages and the arts popular and no weaknesses; psychology a new addition. A dip in 2018 GCSE grades, however, with 56 per cent A*-A/9-7. Mathematics, sciences, humanities and art all tend to have an excellent proportion of top grades.

At A level, choice of 31 subjects; the girls mostly take three, plus an enrichment activity under the umbrella of the QM diploma, which covers excellence inside and outside the classroom, independent thought, learning and research, emotional maturity, and community and school activity and participation

At GCSE, 23 subjects offered – timetables are built around each girl's choices, generally including one MFL. French, Latin and a choice of either Spanish or Mandarin are on the timetable for the first two years. German an option in the third year; all are on offer at GCSE and A level.

Class sizes around 10-12, maximum 16, and we saw evidence of interactive teaching and engaged pupils across a number of subjects, notably a history lesson considering WW1 propaganda posters.

IT embedded in the curriculum but not given high profile, though plenty of computers and Wifi site wide. Surprisingly no overt computing or programming clubs, though the head of physics is a Raspberry Pi educator and led the QMSKYPI project, which culminated in a high altitude balloon launch for Margaret the knitted teddy bear.

Around 90 girls receive some sort of SEN support, mainly mild difficulties and dyslexia (all pupils have a screening test as an entry requirement). Two teachers work closely with academic colleagues to provide classroom and prep support where needed, some one-on-one where girls have slightly reduced timetables. Around 50 girls have individualised programmes for EAL taught by suitably qualified specialist teacher; small group and individual sessions according to need.

Games, options, the arts: Sport for all here with games keenly contested at house level and a full inter-school fixtures list. Stunning facilities – floodlit all-weather pitch, two swimming pools (one indoor, one outdoor), sports hall, tennis/netball courts, dance studio, new sixth form cardio suite, fitness trail etc – hard to find something that's not on offer. Riding popular (private riding school on campus); some girls bring ponies, school keeps a number.

Traditional team sports, winter lacrosse, hockey and netball and summer tennis, athletics and cricket. Links with local sporting clubs and training offer opportunities for talented sportswomen, scholars receive weekly sports conditioning session with a personal trainer. School supports and encourages girls whose sporting prowess involves competition at regional, national or international level. Sports tours – recently to Sri Lanka.

About a third of girls have individual instrument lessons with plenty of ensembles to showcase their talents, from wind to rock band, orchestra to songwriters' collective. Year 7 and 8 choir compulsory, training for the senior chamber choir, together with close harmony pop up group covering popular repertoire. Weekly informal concerts, summer and Christmas concerts, annual musical production.

Fabulous drama facilities for aspiring luvvies. Two productions a year, one in collaboration with the music department – recently an open air Midsummer Night's Dream (a brave decision in Yorkshire) and a musical version of the edgy and gritty Bad Girls.

Not overwhelmingly 'arty' school but plenty of choice across the genres, textiles and photography as well – though no electronics, product design or resistant materials. A handful of girls go on to the top performing art and fashion colleges each year. Home economics for all through to small uptake at A level with Leiths food and wine certificate part of sixth form enrichment. Inter-house Masterchef competition hotly contested and first year tea party a high spot on the calendar.

The extensive range of extracurricular activities offers something for everyone and extends to clay pigeon shooting, driving remote control cars and climbing walls. A breadth of activities ranges from science and mathematics Olympiads to dance and music qualifications, DofE gold to Queen Margaret's Princes Trust, Model United Nations to Amnesty International.

Boarding: Horizontal boarding structure: girls live with their year group all the way through. Really liked by both girls and parents. 'Enables great camaraderie and the foundations of lifelong friendships,' observed one pleased parent. For 11 year olds Red House is a welcoming home from home with a Cath Kidston inspired kitchen for tea, toast and conversations around the Aga. For the next three years girls are in houses at the top of school buildings whilst year Vs (15-16 year olds) move out into the grounds to purpose built boarding house, Winnie's (named after old girl, journalist and writer Winifred Holtby). Lower sixth are in the heart of the school in Cloisters and enjoy the privilege of sitting and walking on the quad lawn. 'Modern loft-style living' twin rooms with individual study areas enable girls to be well organised for busy lives.

The jewels in the boarding crown are the upper sixth cottages: 'something to look forward to,' the girls say. Reminiscent of the Emmerdale set, stepping back in time, the line of cottages all have large kitchens, 'great for entertaining', communal sitting rooms, individual study rooms. Cottage life has the feel of a college campus though head girl has the first pick of houses. Breakfast and snack preparation, responsibility for all their laundry, non-uniform dress code all contribute to the girls' transition to post-school independent living.

No flexi-boarding but day girls, a quarter of pupils, all have allocated beds and can stay for a nightly charge. House activity nights for all on Fridays; a programme of weekend trips and visits and shared café and social spaces encourage girls of different ages to mix. Community weekends four times a term require girls to stay in school but at other times about 70 per cent remain. Greater freedoms for sixth form which they are careful not to abuse – cars allowed, York at free times on Wednesdays and Saturdays, supervised Cellars bar open on campus on Saturday nights – alcohol allowed with parental permission.

Parents commented that their daughters feel hugely supported by house staff who 'adapt their life around ours'.

Background and atmosphere: Founded in 1901 as a Woodard school in Scarborough; moved to Escrick Hall, a John Carr built Georgian country house in 70 well kept acres in 1949. Independent from Woodard since 1986, a large yet compact and cohesive campus with a number of Victorian additions, clever conversions, complementary new-build with award-winning centenary theatre, chapel and indoor swimming pool. A throwback to earlier times – a cluster of timber cabin classrooms – add a quirky touch.

Circular dining hall (once an indoor lunging school) serves all meals to award winning standard, with school rarities such as a cappuccino machine and balsamic vinegar; younger girls envious of the privilege of pain au chocolat delivered to sixth form houses for breakfast – all very civilised.

Girls are expected and encouraged to think big here, challenged to break out of their comfort zone and aim high. Focus now on providing each girl with the confidence, strengths, maturity and values for an unknown future. 'A greenhouse not a hothouse,' says school. Confident, articulate, reflective girls show great loyalty to their school and say, 'we know we're in a bubble but we know what we're in for'. Many house activities, communal social areas, buddying, mentoring and guardian angel schemes, not to mention the size of the school, make this a very supportive and close knit community.

Whilst 20 per cent of boarders are from overseas, this is not an international school. Girls find that where there are wide cultural differences this can preclude close friendships: 'we're friendly but not all best friends,' say sixth formers. Parents comment on the overseas pupils 'whose priorities are different and they are not so interested in sport or drama' – they would not like to see this number grow. Cultural festivals are celebrated communally in house.

Good exposure for girls to global and topical issues through debating, extracurricular organisations and mock elections such as Brexit hustings and vote. Parents aware that this is a privileged life and take responsibility for widening their daughters' experiences, though would like to see the girls do more in the community.

Uniform is an attractive tartan and charcoal – no skirt lengths above the knee: a first for us. Own clothes worn after tea – don't provide anything that you wouldn't want boil-washed. Relaxed smart casual dress code rather than uniform for sixth form.

Pastoral care, well-being and discipline: Parents cannot speak highly enough of the pastoral care: as one put it, 'compassion and kindness run through the veins of this school'. Together with house staff each girl has a personal tutor (of varied quality, say parents) who meets boarding staff daily with any concerns to SLT weekly. Sixth formers have a personal mentor who acts as a guide.

Girls and parents feel the rules are very clear. Zero tolerance for smoking, unsupervised repeat offenders, but girls and staff were quick to point out that behaviour is not a problem here with no full exclusions in the last two years. An army of sixth form posts of responsibility: head girl with three deputies, prefects covering the gamut of school life and six house captains.

Evolving from meditation groups, mindfulness is a recent introduction to PSHE lessons (and at lunchtime for a group of staff). The head has introduced a 10 session course on mindfulness-based stress reduction and cognitive therapy delivered by a trained practitioner.

Pupils and parents: A real sense of collegiality across the campus, lots of smiling faces. Girls aim high in every arena – whatever their talent; higher education is a foregone conclusion.

Parents mainly upper and middle class: landowners, farmers, professionals. Boarders some 20 per cent from overseas – span tens of nations and four continents; head using Spanish and South American networks to widen further. Many from Scotland, Cumbria, East Anglia and of course Yorkshire. Essentially the main catchment is the east coast train line – head keen to open the eyes of London prep schools to God's own county, unexplored territory for many; however shrinking numbers over the past five years.

OMs include Winifred Holtby (author), Ann Jellicoe (playwright), Sarah Connolly (opera singer), Dame Justice Eleanor King (High Court judge).

Entrance: Own assessments at 11, 12 and 13; mathematics, English, dyslexia screening and observation of group working in two classroom activities. Additional intake into sixth form: two 7s and three 6s at GCSE, at least a 5 in maths and English and a minimum of a 6 in the subjects proposed for study at A level. Interviews for all admissions. Taster days for new boarders prior to admission with buddies for first years and guardian angels for third years, most popular boarding entry point.

Exit: Post-16, each year a few girls (some 20 per cent) becoming restless and move to co-ed, local sixth form colleges or boarding schools like Uppingham and Oundle, usually 'for a valid reason not a worrying reason,' says school. A number goes and looks elsewhere before deciding to stay put. Virtually all sixth formers to higher education nationwide – a strong showing of Russell Group universities, with Durham and Edinburgh both popular. Three to Oxbridge in 2018. Courses cover a wide spectrum and include engineering, business and finance, languages, law and 'ologies'. Heartening to see numbers going on to prestigious art colleges eg Central St Martins.

Money matters: Scholarships at 11,13 and sixth form; academic, art, choral, dance, drama, music and sport scholarships. Means-tested bursaries. Sibling remission of five per cent, maximum 15 per cent for three or more sisters in school.

Remarks: A supporting and enabling atmosphere where girls thrive and their talents developed, whether they are academic, sporting or arts based. All rave about the pastoral care and the breadth of opportunity on offer. Girls prepared go to on to post-school life with their eyes open. As a number of parents told us, it seems 'they've got the balance right'.

Queen Mary's School

Baldersby Park, Topcliffe, Thirsk, North Yorkshire YO7 3BZ

Ages Girls 3–16, boys 3–7 **Pupils** 208 **Boarders** 13 full, 28 weekly, 51 flexi (from 7 years) **C of E**

Fees: Day £8,520 – £18,975; Boarding £21,090 – £25,890 pa

01845 575000
www.queenmarys.org

Head: Since 2015, Carole Cameron BA MA (education) PGCE NPQH FRGS ('ancient but young at heart'). Geography degree from Reading; also studied at Nottingham and the Open University. Various roles in state schools plus abroad, including the Cayman Islands; head of Highfield Prep, Harrogate; deputy head Queen Margaret's, York. Teaches PSHE and some English. Two adult daughters, educated in the Caribbean and at Queen Margaret's. Interests include travel, choral music and walking.

She took over in difficult circumstances involving a premature departure, and an interim year under the aegis of a previous much-loved head who returned from retirement, so has had to make her mark with care and flexibility. Her conventional suit, shoes and pearl necklace and courteous, unassuming manner accompany a steely commitment to raising standards of teaching, which she 'won't compromise on', being 'prepared to take tough decisions'. This is being accomplished through a major focus on staff training (the school has joined the Yorkshire Schools Teaching Alliance), close monitoring of teachers and departments, new, much approved appointments and significant development of digital technology. Parents appreciate the (very necessary) improvements made: 'She's doing incredible things for the school..a very effective operator..She's slowly and subtly taking the school forward, not forgetting its traditions and past', though we encountered the odd regret for the loss of some of the earlier, less health and safety-conscious ways.

She identifies with the spiritual values of the Woodard Foundation (having attended a Woodard school herself, she points out). Keen to know exactly what is going on all the time, she loves working in a small, intimate school where she can know all the girls very well individually – she greets them every morning and has her own tutor group that changes each year. Popular with parents, who see her as very dedicated, accessible and responsive to fair criticism: 'She doesn't make excuses, deals with it and gets back to you with a solution'. She doesn't stand on her dignity, taking part in the whole-school Christmas run warm up wearing a complete Santa costume and in the Easter egg hunt dressed as an Easter bunny – so indeed 'young at heart'.

Academic matters: In 2018 51 per cent of GCSEs were A*-A/9-7 (school goes up to 16 years). Despite its small size, offers a wide choice including German, Spanish and French (almost all take a modern foreign language GCSE), Latin, classical civilisation, physical education and further maths. Some tiny sets of one to three – which the girls like, because of the amount of individual attention afforded, though we wondered how drama could work with only two girls; average size: 12 (bigger classes lower down). AS critical thinking too.

Maths being developed to increase challenge and match traditionally high English standards – all of top set to do further maths in future; more focus on STEM career opportunities. Regional success in literature quiz and maths challenges. Developing use of interactive, online approaches to enable more personalised learning (IT in the curriculum from nursery to year 8), plus integration of junior and senior curriculum, together with more outdoor learning, so content more child led and motivating (eg year 8 garden plots link with science course). Saturday morning school controversial, as not all parents and older girls feel it is worth coming in if it just amounts to two academic lessons and the eucharist service, but it does create extra time for the wider curriculum.

Six-weekly pupil profiles, with detailed extracurricular comments, discussed with girls in tutor group time and sent to parents, part of very thoroughgoing monitoring and tracking of girls' progress and involvement in learning overseen by excellent, extremely dedicated director of studies.

Girls say lessons are interesting and enjoyable and teachers immensely helpful and understanding; they appreciate the generous access to individual extra support. Close trusting relationships based on 'mutual respect', according to a year 10 girl. Stable staff – average age 45 – who come across as friendly, jolly and happy in their work; parents find them very accessible – quick responses to emails. Gifted and talented enrichment for scholars open to all – cultural trips, conferences, lectures, subject days out, weekly Queen Mary's society ('some amazing speakers').

Very well qualified and supported SENCo: children with varying special needs accepted, including dyslexia, dyscalculia, emotional/behavioural, a range of autism spectrum disorders plus sensory and physical impairment, so long as the school concludes these can be met. Personal support plans with bespoke timetables if needed and guidance for teachers; individual and small group support, in and out of the classroom (no extra cost); liaison with school counsellor, visiting clinical psychologist and other outside agencies, as well as parents – very flexible approach; students progress very well. High praise from a parent of four dyslexic daughters: 'They have all been treated normally, not made to feel they have great problems.. They love going to learning support – there's no stigma.' Another gave more qualified praise, having struggled before her daughter's official diagnosis to get her very individual needs met, but said once diagnosed the school could not have done more to help her. EAL support for occasional short stay pupils from France and Spain.

Junior school has separate co-educational nursery and pre-prep departments for 3 to 7 year olds. No Sats tests but systematic assessment and monitoring. Specialist teaching in science (own lab), French (from year 1), IT, food technology, art, music, drama and sport; success in national competitions and challenges. Classes can be very small – average 10, max 16; mainly girls. Attractive, bright, well-equipped classrooms with very good displays. Parents pleased with progress achieved and amount of differentiation in tasks set.

Games, options, the arts: Particularly strong sport, especially riding. The equestrian centre, at the end of the delightful Rhododendron Walk running beside a ha-ha, stream and wild flowers, is a relaxing world apart: horses (boarders and day girls can bring their own) peer over stall gates and the manager's dogs run around; improvements are cannily funded through sponsorship. Won recent national schools show jumping championship, beating 48 other teams. Strong netball, tennis, rounders and athletics at regional level. PLanning under way for floodlit hockey Astro; very testing climbing wall up a high archway. Only a small indoor pool, but outdoor swimming, canoeing and kayaking in the River Swale, which runs through the grounds. A parent we spoke to liked the way girls get 'pushed to do things a bit out of their comfort zone' in a kind way, by being encouraged and reassured.

Exceptionally high level music – a finalist in the BBC chorister of the year competition: 'fabulous music department.. has helped me develop a lot' – with plenty of internal and external performance opportunities and a more inclusive approach being introduced; rock band as well as Fauré Requiem and annual carol concert in Ripon Cathedral. Music block, converted from old coach house, looks due for makeover and extension.

Drama productions include Annie and My Fair Lady; plentiful top grades for speech and drama exams; lots of theatre visits. Accomplished art in different media; food tech and art and design GCSEs, but no provision for resistant materials in the curriculum.

Wide range of clubs includes pheasant plucking (yes – really) and archery; much DofE; all year 8s do young leaders award. Energetic fundraising for international and local charities, eg whole school run over challenging obstacle course and house fashion show competition organised by year 10 girls.

Juniors have strong netball, football, swimming, tennis, cross-country, trampolining (particularly high level coaching) and gymnastics at local/county level; sports not stereotyped in years where boys present.

Energetic music – year 4 orchestra (all learn violin or cello), junior brass, super strings and recorder groups, two junior choirs and a junior orchestra (but a remarkably mature young critic we met observed that having instrument lessons in core subjects was a disadvantage academically – and that 30 minutes for lunch, including queueing, was too rushed). Performances in Ripon Cathedral.

Termly drama productions – My Fair Lady, Cinderella Rockerfella, Dream On (based on A Midsummer Night's Dream); year 5s perform a French play. Many speech and drama – and music – exams distinctions and merits. Good choice of clubs; outdoor education residentials plus trip to France.

Boarding: Full, weekly and flexi; junior, senior and year 11 areas (weekly or flexi boarding possible from year 3). Light, pleasantly furnished rooms, with two to seven bunk or cabin beds, some with lovely views of lawns and woods, but walls could do with refreshing (school says this is in hand).

Friendly, family atmosphere – older girls mentor and support younger ones. Generously staffed – 'They're lovely..it's like talking to your parents when you get home from school.. always there if you are homesick or need to talk about home problems..[The two gap year girls are] like an auntie or older sister' (boarders); 'It's a home from home – they're happy as Larry' (parent). Lots of weekend activities and trips, eg Christmas shopping in Edinburgh. We were amused to see in the (very well designed and comprehensive) planners that weekly awards can be obtained for making people laugh and 'being a good egg'.

Background and atmosphere: Founded by the Woodard Corporation in 1925 at Duncombe Park; moved to Baldersby Park, near Thirsk, North Yorkshire, in 1985, as a 3 to 16 years school. The gracious main building is almost 300 years old, with a grand hall encompassing an impressive central staircase presided over by huge portraits of Queen Mary and George V, borrowed from the Queen's collection, no less. Elegant reception rooms now used as the very fortunate head's office, smallish library and English classroom. Lovely, peaceful, 40 acre grounds, with lawns, two ha-has, views of grazing sheep, cobbled courtyards and clock tower.

Underpinned by Anglican values – most take religious education GCSE. Warm, family feeling through small sizes. Seniors pair with juniors for Easter egg hunt, when girls seek camouflaged teachers wielding water pistols (enabling sweet revenge on classroom chatterers), and charity Santa run. Dog friendly – teachers often bring in own dogs, though a junior child observed they could be distracting during tests.

Girls very smart in red tartan skirts, blue shirts and short, light-green jackets with brown collars resembling hacking jackets, and, according to the ones we met, happy with the single sex environment – 'There's less social pressure – you can be yourself..it's OK to work hard'. 'It allows them to grow up in their own time..they're free to explore who they are' (parent); 'There's a real celebration of all kinds of diversity and achievements, not just academic ones' – a mother whose daughter enjoyed the tag rugby, football and street dance. 'A moral compass is seamlessly set..the girls are very caring and open.. they don't moan – they just get on with it,' said another.

All year 11s have a position of responsibility; top posts – complete with academic gowns – require written application, interview and vote by whole school and staff. Strong careers provision includes information about apprenticeships.

Good choice of food (we particularly admired the wide ranging, very attractively presented salad bar), but some grumbles about the hot food – and the low standard of cutlery washing. Accessible and flexible cooks – catering manager answerable to school council.

Pastoral care, well-being and discipline: Very thoughtful and aware approach to mental health and well-being – team includes counsellor, clinical psychologist, independent listener, chaplain and school nurse, and planners contain extensive contact details for internal and external support. However a couple of parents we spoke to suggested the sex education given could involve scenarios that were 'a bit more realistic' and less 'naïve', with more about 'healthy relationships outside marriage'. Sensible, constructive approach to discipline.

Pupils and parents: From a wide range of local state and independent schools, from North Yorkshire, York and into Teeside; mostly professional, military and business white British families. Confident, open, enthusiastic, thoughtful, articulate and appreciative girls.

High level communication with parents, eg very clear, detailed, holistic guidance re expectations and how best to help children, careful preparation for residentials. Termly Saturday morning sessions on various topics.

Notable old girls: actresses Katie Gibson, Adi Calvert, Hebe Beardsall, Oscar winning director Serena Armitage, businesswoman Amanda Staveley, artist Tanya Still.

Entrance: Into junior school by taster day, with more visits for girls joining at a later point and a 'good neighbour' to help them settle in. Assessment tests in English, maths and non-verbal reasoning at 11, 12 and 13, with report from previous school.

Exit: Boys leave at the end of year 2, mostly for Aysgarth or Stokesley. Almost all girls transfer to senior school at the end of year 6; a few to Ripon Grammar. At 16 to Sedbergh, Durham, Barnard Castle, Repton, Ampleforth, Uppingham, Stonyhurst, St Peter's York, Queen Margaret's York, Ripon Grammar. More than a quarter got sixth form scholarships in 2018 to Stonyhurst, Barnard Castle, Sedbergh and Shrewsbury.

Money matters: Purely honorary academic, art, music and sport scholarships at 11, 12 and 13 entitling participation in enhanced programme: written exam plus interview with head including questions on current events; looking for sharp, wide-ranging thinkers. Means-tested bursaries and sibling, MoD and CofE remissions.

Remarks: Mixture of Palladian architecture, bone china tea service and secluded rural environment with hard working, aspirational, outdoorsy girls who 'enjoy their food' (head) and are not made to feel 'academic results are everything' (parent).

Developing very systematic, modern approach to education that is producing high achievement, along with time made for emotional well-being, extracurricular activities and fun. We wondered if such a protected early life might leave girls unprepared for the more rigorous challenges of the outside world, but more than one parent maintained that most emerge with inner confidence and an empowering, secure sense of who they are, so that only a few fail to thrive in their sixth forms.

Richmond House School

170 Otley Road, Far Headingley, Leeds LS16 5LG

Ages 3–11 **Pupils** 228

Fees: £9,150 pa

01132 752670
www.rhschool.org

Headteacher: Since 2016, Helen Stiles MA PGCE (early 40s). Studied law/theology and religious studies at Cambridge; head of RE and humanities at The Grammar School at Leeds, where she stayed for 18 years.

Lively, loquacious, energetic, thoughtful in her responsiveness to the children's needs. Loves teaching too much to relinquish it: takes RE for years 3-6 plus (unusually for a head) curriculum leader; does lesson cover; reads stories to nursery children once a week; offers philosophy, maths problem-solving and cross-country clubs. Has introduced more focus on maths and English and monitoring of progress, aiming for more curriculum continuity across years, and interested in exploring new ideas. Keen to ensure children have plenty of varied opportunities, to promote confidence-building. Wish list: new early years building plus performance and sports hall, but wants to maintain old building too and preserve school's cosy, family atmosphere. Parents see her as very approachable, accessible, involved and understanding

Partner is director of sport at The Grammar School at Leeds, which their teenage daughter attends. Enjoys reading, running and going to the gym.

Entrance: Reception: short informal assessment (non selective). Other years: half or a full day visit, following class to be joined, with some informal assessment.

Unusually, several means-tested bursaries available from year 2.

Exit: To a spread of schools in the region: Ashville College, The Grammar School at Leeds, Bradford Grammar and Woodhouse Grove popular; also Fulneck, Harrogate Ladies' College, some to state schools such as Harrogate Grammar. Almost all of nursery to reception. Several scholarships each year – very sensibly prepares children for interview through everyday communication skills opportunities rather than pre-exam coaching.

Remarks: Situated three miles from centre of Leeds. Two connected, converted Victorian houses with narrow staircases and corridors, which makes it feel cramped indoors, but the low ceilinged attic classrooms, home to mini year 1s, are attractive in a quirky way, and the school's small size contributes to the secure, warm, family atmosphere where everyone knows and looks out for each other. Other classrooms are more spacious. Gym also used for assemblies and drama; functional, reverberating canteen. Portacabins for science/DT and music on the dark side.

Class sizes vary considerably – average 15, 18 max. All mixed ability till years 5 and 6, when two English and maths streams. Specialist teaching, for science, languages, music, art, DT, ICT/computing (weekly lessons), languages and PE, increases as children progress through the years, involving moving around the school, which provides good preparation for the transition to secondary level. No Sats – hurrah – but plenty of systematic assessment and monitoring (children are consistently and significantly above national average in ability); lots of visits, activity days, expert workshops. Spanish and reasoning skills for years 5 and 6. Differentiated class and homework plus national quizzes and competitions to stretch the very bright – won Leeds poetry slam competition.

Children we met view their teachers (mixed ages, four male) as 'very nice', rarely angry, giving lots of individual help, and lessons as active and fun. Parents say they are very responsive, immediately dealing with concerns in 'a calm, professional way' and that children are developed very well academically without feeling at all stressed.

Love of reading promoted very effectively: small, cosy library with well-stocked fiction shelves and brightly coloured beanbags; visits by authors; appealing book reviews of favourite children's books written by teachers on display; children told to have a book with them all the time; extra sessions for weak readers.

Developing outdoor learning programme for all years – links with curriculum subjects plus team building and bushcraft making with home-grown willow. Adventure playground with fab separate area in grounds: large yurt with wood burning stove; outdoor fire pit for hot chocolate and marshmallows; ingenious outdoor sink; tepee; den; mini beast and music areas.

Full time, warm, friendly, thoughtful SENCo, highly regarded by parents ('phenomenal..absolutely wonderful.. fantastic'), trained in special needs, aided by two part-time TAs: covers wide range of difficulties – individual lessons (extra charge) and small group; classroom (and parental) support. Also provides a bit of counselling and takes mindfulness club with year 2s. Praised by a parent for the way she works with parents, child and external therapists, who – including highly skilled sports therapist – visit and may also train staff; teachers made aware of children's needs and guided on how to meet them. School layout in and outside would make it hard to accommodate serious physical disabilities, but they would try to adjust timetable if possible. Children assessed before acceptance to see if school can meet their needs. Very good progress made and confidence 'boosted hugely..they give gentle encouragement and guidance..the school was lovely in making sure she was involved in a friendship group..everything is normalised – there's no stigma' (parents).

Grounds covering 10 acres compensate for lack of space inside; coaching by students from the nearby universities. However lack of modern sports hall (in head's development plan) makes sports weather-dependent. All the trad sports, plus crown green bowling and pétanque – successful rugby, football and netball at local level despite small size (triathlon stars, the Brownlee brothers, are old boys). Inclusive policy appreciated by parents.

Masses of music to a high level, including octet, jazz choir, rock band – choir sings with Yorkshire Philharmonic Choir at Wakefield Cathedral. Plays performed at local church hall, mainly musicals, some home-grown, eg Ocean World, based on environment threats; four nativities each year – these opportunities, together with classroom drama and public speaking, all develop the confidence to perform in public, commented a parent whose child had transferred from a state

R

school where he had hidden away from taking part in a school play. Unexceptional art (school says most displays had been taken down for a concert when we visited).

Wide choice of clubs and activities: children run some computing clubs; energetic eco council – big push on eliminating use of plastic extending to blazers made from recycled bottles; much charity fundraising. Residentials start from year 3 – lucky year 6s get four nights in Paris.

Children mainly from north Leeds, some from Harrogate, south Leeds and villages near Wetherby; wide social, cultural and ethnic mix reflecting Leeds demographics – not all from wealthy families, thanks to bursary programme. Happy, friendly, tolerant, confident and polite children, engaged in the classroom and revelling in all the extensive outdoors freedom, very smart in their green blazers – boys in grey trousers/shorts, white shirts and ties, girls in plaid skirts (tartan tunics for the littlies) or green striped summer dresses.

Sensible behaviour policy with rewards for kindness, helpfulness and politeness besides academic effort and attainment. All year 6s have a position of responsibility, which are changed termly. Good choice of food, hot and cold – 'super nice – apart from the fish pie,' approved a child.

Early years very well run and resourced separate section in spacious portacabins with wooden exteriors, plus outdoor area and playground. Specialist teaching from nursery in PE, music and French. Wraparound care 7.30am-6pm.

Ripon Grammar School

72

Clotherholme Road, Ripon, North Yorkshire HG4 2DG

Ages 11–18 **Pupils** 930 **Sixth form** 300 **Boarders** 13 full, 71 weekly

Fees: Day free; Boarding £10,220 – £12,260 pa

01765 602647
www.ripongrammar.co.uk

Headmaster: Since September 2017, Jonathan Webb MA, previously deputy head at Durham School for five years. Educated at Batley Grammar School and has a history degree from Cambridge. Taught history at Pocklington School (where he was director of teaching and learning and head of history), The Manchester Grammar School and Giggleswick. He and his wife Helen live near Ripon and they have two sons. In his spare time he enjoys cricket, walking and gardening.

He has a clear ambition for the school with an ethos that, in addition to a very strong academic reputation, also emphasises the strength of sports and the arts and especially develops young people as leaders. His holistic view was clearly echoed throughout our visit. He is proud that the school continues to work well with the local authority (North Yorkshire) and resists academisation. This is a community school which is happy with its current size and, at present, has no ambition to grow significantly.

Academic matters: Exam results are consistently very good. In 2018 52 per cent of A level grades were A*/A, 80 per cent A*-B. STEM subjects are extremely strong – roughly equal numbers of girls and boys take chemistry and mathematics, while in physics the proportion of girls taking the subject continues to grow. Results in art are exceptional: in 2018 all 18 students got A*/A, 89 per cent A*.

At GCSE 66 per cent A*-A/9-7 in 2018. The head is clear that the school doesn't just do well by its high prior attainers. Those (few) students in the middle ability range scored an impressive positive 1.63 Progress 8 in 2018, putting the school in the top one per cent nationally for this measure. Disadvantaged students also progress at least as well as others.

The curriculum is ambitious even for a selective school with everyone taking between 10 and 12 GCSEs including further maths for the top two sets. Most students get their first choice of subjects, which include astronomy and classical civilisation, with Latin and ancient Greek offered off timetable. Setting in maths from year 8. All take French GCSE, in sets from the end of year 8. In year 9 they study Spanish and German for half the year each, and many continue one of these to GCSE. Economics and psychology are A level options, but STEM subjects predominate.

Off-timetable cross-curricular themed challenge days for years 7-9 provide opportunities for leadership, teamwork and problem-solving, working with external advisers. This lays the groundwork for later success in Young Enterprise and Prince's Trust competitions. There is well-regarded work experience in year 10s and 12.

Very good SEN support includes provision for visual and hearing impairment alongside a range of needs including autism. The learning resource manager works with the SENCo on intervention strategies. Paired reading with sixth formers during assembly time is set up for those identified by online literacy assessments. The sixth form students told us they value the skills this helps them to develop as well as the help it provides. The school is well equipped for students with physical disabilities and sensitive timetabling ensures all are able to access specialist facilities when needed.

Games, options, the arts: PE and games have an impressive three hours a week on the timetable. Compulsory sport: rugby, cricket and hockey are the mainstay for boys, hockey for girls (national indoor finalists). Football is popular for both sexes and the girls have been Yorkshire junior champions. There are also mixed hockey, badminton, rock climbing, dance and swimming in the impressive 25m indoor swimming pool. Students compete at area and regional level in a range of sports, including national U14 netball finalists. Sports facilities are excellent, with a new Astroturf and a five badminton court sports hall with climbing wall paid for by a fundraising campaign, available for local use too. A new 3G rugby/football pitch will be completed in 2019 alongside a newly drained, levelled and seeded first 15 rugby pitch. There are also six all-weather tennis courts. All facilities are conveniently on the same site.

The music block has great facilities for teaching, practice and recording. Notice boards list an array of musical opportunities from junior strings and guitar to the chamber orchestra and five choirs which perform regularly in Ripon Cathedral and further afield, including foreign tours. They have recorded a CD of Christmas music. Several students have gone on to win choral and music scholarships at prestigious universities including the first girl to win Durham University's cathedral choral scholarship. More 100 students have instrumental lessons in school and all year 7s do grade 1 music theory. There are drama and musical productions each year; the hall doubles as the dining room and is relatively small for a school of this size but there is a drama studio in the new sixth form centre. Annual commemoration and carol services are held in the cathedral.

There is superb art on display. Students have exhibited and sold work in local galleries and a number have won prestigious awards such as the Royal Society of British Artists Young Artist award.

There are lots of co-curricular experiences to be had: house drama, charity week, DofE, biennial World Challenge, trips to Iceland, Sorrento, Sri Lanka and India, the Normandy battlefields, Berlin, Auschwitz, Edinburgh and the annual

French exchange, as well as the more local curriculum enriching visits. The school is proud that it is able to run a very large number of visits (110 in the autumn term alone) while still teaching the full curriculum.

With over 90 different clubs and activities on offer, ranging from the Greenpower electric car and Pageturner book club to philosophy, there something for even the most reluctant to get involved in. With the strong emphasis on developing leadership, students are encouraged to take the initiative to set up and run activities and clubs which include politics, history and feminist societies. The annual charity week is sixth form run and encompasses a range of fundraising activities for the school's chosen charities such as the local hospice.

Boarding: There are 100 boarding places in two houses (50 for boys and 50 for girls). School House for boys in the main school building has rooms of two to four for years 7 -11 and single rooms for the sixth form, all with shared bathrooms. It's bright and well maintained with plenty of social spaces although some of the stairways could do with upgrading. The boys eat in the school dining room. The girls, in the much newer and purpose built Johnson House, have their own catering facility and garden, in four bed rooms plus singles for the sixth form. They too share bathrooms, which are bright and modern with good levels of privacy.

This is a day school with predominantly weekly boarding; pupils come from North Yorkshire and beyond, with a small minority from India, Africa, Caribbean and China. Boarders usually do well academically and the very few in residence over the weekends are well catered for. The boarders said that relationships with the rest of the school were strong, although those who join the sixth form tend to find their friendship groups within the boarders. Boarders have informal joint weekend activities with day pupils and join local groups and clubs. Demand for boarding places (14 a year) is growing, from North Yorkshire, the rest of the UK and beyond, especially post-GCSE, with lots of interest in girls' boarding.

Boarders have a personal tutor and are in mixed age tutor groups. As majority of boarding staff are teachers, 'boarders are very well known as individuals'.

Background and atmosphere: The school has a very long history; there has been a grammar school in Ripon since Anglo Saxon times. Originally housed in city centre under a foundation granted by Queen Mary, in 1555 RGS moved to its present green and pleasant 23-acre site in 1874. The land was a gift from Marquis of Ripon. The original Victorian buildings were added to over the years, not always sympathetically. More recent additions, including the sports hall, sixth form centre, mathematics and engineering block, music facilities, observatory, girls' boarding house and a humanities and modern languages block bring more gravitas to the school façade.

There is an air of purposefulness in the school; a quiet hum from classrooms and sensible movement between lessons. The head is keen to develop an even higher profile house system which involves all pupils and offers leadership opportunities. Houses compete in sport, rock climbing, debating, MasterChef, University Challenge and drama.

The sixth formers, housed in a beautiful purpose built centre, see themselves as fully integrated with the rest of the school. Their uniform is distinguishable only by a different tie. They have their own library and private study area as well as some specialist teaching facilities.

Pastoral care, well-being and discipline: There is a very good pastoral system in operation; pupils look after each other too, 'very collegiate', as one parent put it. Teams of form tutors ably support heads of school. Newcomers to sixth form are 'buddied' with existing pupils to ease integration.

The students were very clear that they very rarely see disruption in their lessons. Poor behaviour and exclusions are rare and, at worst, usually sorted by after-school detention. Genuinely good relations between staff and students throughout the school; friendly and compassionate house staff create a relaxed boarding environment. Pupils and parents cannot speak highly enough of staff, their commitment and willingness to go 'above and beyond'.

Any bullying stamped on and internet safety policy written by pupils are wired into PCSHE and teaching programmes. Safety in the boarding houses is taken very seriously indeed despite some protests from independent minded teenagers.

Uniform is very smart throughout the school including badged skirts of regulation length for the girls. Unusually there is no option for girls to wear trousers, which they would welcome. The students wear their leadership and rewards badges with obvious pride. One student who had moved from a local comprehensive at 13 spoke extremely positively about his integration into a new school: 'it's cool to be geeky here, people are really pleased for you when you achieve well'.

The sixth form have significant leadership responsibilities in publicity, community relations and pastoral care as well as the usual head boy and head girl. The students were very proud of the school, and keen to explain how supportive the staff were of their development, their mental health and careers rather than simply pushing them through examinations. Sixth formers are trained to be peer listeners with younger students and they themselves feel well supported in their transition into the sixth form and on to university.

Staff value working at the school. 'I work here because the children enjoy being here, they love learning, being part of the community and they aren't embarrassed to succeed.' They also noted that the school invests well in them as individuals which helps them give the best they can to the students.

Pupils and parents: This definitely a local school. Day students are predominantly from the immediate vicinity of Ripon. Many boarders are from only just outside the catchment area and choose to board in order to gain admission. There is a wide range of parental backgrounds and wealth (or lack of it) though only a handful are eligible for free school meals. Parents feel well informed on their child's progress with regular reports three times a year and an annual parents' evening. School contact is primarily email and parents like that the termly newsletter and sixth form magazine have content provided by the pupils. There is a very supportive PTA.

The pupils are warm, friendly, courteous, articulate, confident and insightful, with a real pride in their school. Lots of heads up, eye contact and smiles as you walk around. This is a can do, will do school – pupils talk of friendly rivalry, pushing each to achieve. Strong protestations from both girls and boys on question of true equality and diversity: 'not an issue here' they say. On election of school officers the students say, 'it's the best person for the job every time'.

One parent (initially sceptical that RGS could do more than provide good examination results) was clear that the school's historic reputation as simply an examination machine was far from the reality: the holistic approach is at the core of the school. Another, with five boys of varying abilities and enthusiasm, felt all had been catered for and known as individuals and had consequently flourished. A third valued the clear structure that boarding gave to her daughter as well as the good communication, development of personal skills and very strong integration for new students.

Former pupils include fashion designer Bruce Oldfield, rugby international Peter Squires, William Hague MP, David Curry

MP, Guardian editor Katharine Viner, TV presenter Richard Hammond and Olympic gold medallist diver Jack Laugher.

Entrance: RGS draws mainly from local primaries (all of which the head has visited) and a smattering from prep schools, about 40 schools in total. Heavy oversubscribed at 11+. Selection is by local authority verbal and non-verbal reasoning tests; school takes top 28 per cent of cohort, which is wider than in other selective areas. Another 30 places at 13+.

The sixth form has around 80 external applicants for some 30 places. The sixth form requires minimum six grade 6s at GCSE but the vast majority comfortably exceed this, achieving mainly 9-7s.

Exit: Generally at least 90 per cent stays on for the sixth form. A high proportion to Russell Group universities, with a strong Oxbridge record (eight in 2018; four medics, three dentists and a vet), and the most popular destinations Durham, Newcastle, Edinburgh, York and Sheffield. A number are lured to London and a few overseas. Excellent careers advice has led to leading apprenticeships for those considering alternatives to university.

Money matters: RGS is Yorkshire's only state boarding school, it is free for day pupils. There is a charge for boarding, but this is still about one third the price of independent alternatives.

Remarks: This is a high achieving school without being highly pressurised, where learning and life skill opportunities are valued as much as examination success. Both the main school and boarding continue to be rated outstanding by Ofsted. RGS aims to provide for the whole person blending tradition, academic rigour and high expectations with innovation, up-to-date technology and opportunities for development. According to students and parents it does this very well, and we saw plenty of evidence to confirm it throughout our visit. Parents have complete confidence that whatever their child's talents the school will help them to make the best of them. The school is very keen to serve its community and clearly valued by the people of Ripon and beyond.

Rossall Junior School

Linked with Rossall School

R

Broadway, Fleetwood, Lancashire FY7 8JW

Ages 2–11 **Pupils** 176 **Boarders** 10 full, 3 weekly (from 7 years)

Fees: Day £8,040; Boarding £9,246 – £20,610 pa

01253 774222
www.rossall.org.uk

Head of juniors: Since 2010, Katie Lee MA CPP Cert Ed. State educated in Sheffield, she then did teacher training at Lady Mabel College in South Yorkshire. Her original teaching specialism was PE, and she joined Rossall in 1992 as head of girls' games. She went on to spend 10 years as a housemistress in the senior school and to become senior teacher: pastoral. She was appointed head of the junior school in 2010. She has over 30 years' experience teaching students of all ages – from pre-school children right through to adult learners on pre-retirement courses. And she hasn't just taught the privileged; during the miners' strike she was at a state school in a small mining community where 'there'd be families of three, four or five children and one PE kit between them... As a community we looked after those children,' she says, with the air of one who has stories to tell.

Parents adore her. 'She was my own housemistress when I was here,' said one mum, beaming. Other parents describe Mrs Lee as 'a force of nature' and 'hands on'. She's practical, a problem-solver – and someone who shows her face. One parent told how the school changed parking procedures to ease congestion during morning drop-off – 'it was bound to be chaotic but, on the first morning, there she was with her umbrella, waiting for the barrage, ready to sort everyone out.' She gets stuck in for a good cause – she was seen dressed as Cat Woman recently and she's done the Ice Bucket Challenge. But much as she clearly excels at pastoral care, she is also focused on educational excellence. She's proud of how the children thrive following the PYP (the International Baccalaureate's Primary Years Programme) and she keeps a sharp focus on academic standards. When she's not busy holding the reins at Rossall or being a pillar of the local community (in which she has held various voluntary roles), Mrs Lee breeds weimaraner dogs. (This is a doggy school. We met several pooches on campus during our visit.)

Leaving in July 2019.

Entrance: Children come to a taster day and parents come in for a chat, but it's extremely rare for the school to tell parents they can't support their child's needs. It is not hugely oversubscribed, so almost certainly if you can pay, you're in. The nursery takes children from the age of 2.

Exit: Almost all juniors progress to the senior school (usually well over 90 per cent) unless they have a particular reason to leave such as family relocation. Everyone sits the entrance exam for the seniors (maths, English and non-verbal reasoning), but for junior school pupils it's just used as a baseline assessment and to assess for a possible scholarship.

Remarks: Everyone in the juniors – even the youngest pre-schoolers – follows the International Baccalaureate's Primary Years Programme (known as the PYP). Some literacy and maths skills are taught separately but everything else is learned through hands-on, pupil-led projects. They study six projects a year, two per term, and at the start of each project the pupils decide what they want to find out and how they will do it. They're encouraged to follow their own interests and respond to their natural curiosity – doing their own research and working at their own rate and level – but also developing strong teamwork and communication skills. Children are bursting with enthusiasm for the PYP: they remember past projects clearly and are proud of their achievements. They talk enthusiastically about reading, learning the violin, using the IT suite to create PowerPoint presentations... and they give every impression that they love to learn. Parents say they're happy with their children's academic progress too. One mum said of her daughter: 'They're giving her confidence and I'm really pleased about that.'

Pupils with SEN are supported at no extra cost. Teachers say that the flexibility of the PYP lets them set differentiated work so that the lower ability pupils keep learning at their own rate alongside high achievers with the freedom 'to fly'. Children are assessed at the end of each year and at the end of each project so their progress is tracked from their entry to the school or nursery right up to year 6. But the focus is on real learning rather than targets. One teacher told us, 'I think it's very sad when children say things like "I'm a level 5".' There's a fresh approach to learning here – very few schools offer the

PYP – and the willingness to do things differently is reflected also in the decision to teach Mandarin to junior pupils instead of a European language. Classes are small; 20 is an absolute maximum but most are much smaller than this.

All PE lessons are taught by specialists from nursery upwards. There is a wide range of popular after-school clubs. Infants are not encouraged to stay late every day as they get tired, although full wraparound care is available, but many juniors choose to stay till 5pm for extra activities and support with their homework most evenings. Says Mrs Lee, 'the children won't go home!' There are science, chess and reading groups; various art, theatre and music activities and a very wide range of sporty clubs including, as well as clubs for most mainstream school sports, Danish longball club, Urban Workout and judo. Many pupils take LAMDA exams and quite a few are learning musical instruments, including clarinet, violin, drums, piano and flute. New kitchen for food technology lessons and the Rossall Bake Off where dozens compete for the title of star baker.

The junior school buildings are close to the senior school – they're part of a grand, red-brick campus overlooking the sandy coastline. Juniors can use the top quality senior school facilities. Beyond the usual extensive sports facilities you'd expect, including new multi-use games area and golf and football academies, there is also a 25-metre indoor swimming pool, a nature conservation area, a theatre and a space science and astronomy centre. Children in the nursery have a lovely little garden, including their own woodland area where forest school sessions are held, and a much-loved pet bunny. The grand, historic chapel – which wouldn't look out of place in an Oxbridge quad – is also a significant part of school life, even for the youngest pupils. It's an Anglican chapel, with a full-time chaplain – but the school population is so mixed, with many international students, that the chaplaincy aims to meet the needs of pupils of all faiths and of none.

The pupils all eat together. Infants sit in their houses – in a mixed age group – and they're served 'like a family' at the table. Juniors eat in the senior dining hall and they select their food at the servery – staff let them try anything they fancy before committing to a plateful. They still sit with teachers who will keep an eye on them to make sure they're actually eating. The GSG found the food to be first class.

There's a strong family feel to the school and this extends to the classroom – because of the small class sizes and the way that the PYP curriculum encourages group work, pupils have strong relationships with each other and with their class teachers. Bullying is initially dealt with by the class teacher and everything is recorded in weekly welfare meetings. All incidents are communicated to the senior team, including Mrs Lee. Perpetrators can expect a caution initially and potentially a detention with the head. Parents – both of bullies and victims – are always brought in to discuss any serious incident. But bullying and serious disciplinary problems generally are rare. So, although firm structures and policies are in place, you get the sense that they're very seldom brought into force. Pastoral care in the juniors is largely provided by class teachers, with whom pupils are closely bonded.

The junior boarding house is homely and feels lived-in – with common room, a large, well-equipped games room and bedrooms customised with pictures and decorations. Most of the rooms sleep two, three or four. Houseparents say they see themselves as comforting, supportive stand-in parents rather than just as authority figures. Boarders – around 30 per cent overseas – have days out every Sunday and – temptingly for parents who struggle for babysitters – day pupils can have sleepovers in the boarding house (flexi-boarding) any night of the week or weekend. A popular option is to stay over on the Saturday night so that you can go on the Sunday outing.

Means-tested bursaries are available to junior school pupils. Currently nine per cent of infants and 18 per cent of juniors have a bursary that covers at least half of their fees. Academic, sports and music scholarships (up to 30 per cent) are also available for juniors to apply for in years 3 and 5.

The pupils love it here and they achieve very well. A parent told us that her stock punishment threat was 'if you don't do what I say then you won't be allowed to sleepover at school'. The parents we met were highly satisfied. One mother told us she only brought her child here for the nursery and she had a place ready for her in a state school but, once she was here, she just couldn't bring herself to take her daughter away. Mrs Lee herself only came for a two year post initially – 'once you're here, you stay,' she says. The excellent staff and pupil retention rates speak of a very happy community. This is both a cosy, homely community and a well-run tight ship. A lovely, old-fashioned English boarding school, peopled with happy, eager little faces.

Rossall School

Linked with Rossall Junior School

Broadway, Fleetwood, Lancashire FY7 8JW

Ages 11–18 **Pupils** 476 **Sixth form** 191 **Boarders** 239 full, 18 weekly/flexi **C of E**

Fees: Day £10,740 – £13,080; Boarding £17,340 – £37,350 pa

01253 774201
www.rossall.org.uk

Head: Since September 2018, Jeremy Quartermain, previously deputy head (academic) at Brentwood School. History degree from Cambridge and MPhil in medieval history from Trinity College Dublin, where he also tutored undergrads. Taught English overseas for a while then did a PGCE at the University of East Anglia. Taught history and classics at Gresham, and later promoted to head of sixth form; joined Brentwood in 2013. He's also a freelance educator for the Holocaust Educational Trust. A keen musician, he is married to Fiona, who hails from County Galway and has taught at both primary and secondary level. They have three young daughters.

R

Academic matters: Rossall provides an all-round education – aiming to meet the needs of every pupil within its broad intake. Usually class sizes of 18-20 in years 7-11 (an absolute maximum of 22) and a maximum of 18 in the sixth form. The school identifies maths, the sciences, English, technology and art as departments that are doing particularly well. Food studies, Mandarin and drama recently added to curriculum. Parents we met were very happy with their children's attainment. One mother told us how impressed she'd been that the school offered to take her bilingual children, raised until recently in France, out of mainstream French lessons to teach them separately so that they could continue to study French as a first language. But there's a comprehensive and inclusive ethos here. Parents felt that the school was about much more than academia and that it doesn't focus resources and attention on high flyers at the expense of those in the middle or who are struggling. 'They don't single out the star pupils,' said one parent. 'They give praise subtly and they don't make a big song and dance of it.' 'Mine are never made to feel inferior,' said another mum. 'They do their best and they get praise for that.' There's no streaming but there is setting in some subjects. Parents said that sets were constantly under review and so 'you're not stuck in your set'.

Results reflect the broad intake. In 2018, 47 per cent of GCSEs entered were awarded 9-7 and at A level there were 18 per cent A*/As, with 43 per cent A*-B. Roughly a third of sixth formers choose to do the International Baccalaureate rather than A levels and in 2018 they achieved an average of 39 points per pupil. The school languishes in the bottom quartile of the independent schools league tables but, unlike the high-flyers in the league tables, Rossall is not a selective school. It's also one of the most international schools in the UK, meaning that a large proportion of the children sitting those GCSE, A level and IB exams (about 60 per cent of them) don't have English as a first language.

International students can enter the main school if their English is already close to fluent. Those whose level of English would hold them back from achieving their potential academically are placed in the International Study Centre. This isn't as separate as it sounds; it's really a stream within the main school where pupils receive intensive English language support. Some pupils only stay in the ISC for a term or two, others stay for a year or more and some complete an intensive one-year IGCSE course there to prepare them for entering the sixth form in the main school.

The school supports pupils with a range of special educational needs. A full-time SEN support teacher has recently joined the school. There may be an additional charge to parents of children with SEN if a very high level of support is required.

Games, options, the arts: This is a very sporty school. Ian Botham sent his son, Liam, here and many alumni have gone on to play rugby, hockey or cricket professionally. More than a dozen pupils – male and female – currently play hockey for Lancashire. And there are countless sports options beyond the more obvious team games: pupils can also play basketball, squash or badminton, or lift weights, climb, dance or shoot, and there's now a golf academy. As you'd expect, there is an extensive range of top quality pitches, playing fields, squash courts and the like on campus; almost all sports offered have on-site facilities apart from horse-riding, ice-skating and golf. The 25-metre indoor swimming pool looked particularly inviting – although we didn't jump in – and we weren't surprised to see a large bank of seats on the poolside for crowds of supportive pupils to cheer on their peers. Sport is a unifying force at Rossall: one day the children might be competing fiercely in one of the many inter-house tournaments and the next day they'd be whooping with pride when another pupil scores a winning goal or try against a rival school. Rossall sport is steeped in tradition; Ross-Hockey is a unique game – a hockey-rugby hybrid played only on the beach next to the school; and the school regularly competes in rugby fives tournaments at prestigious public schools as well as hosting its own national Rossall Fives tournament each October.

R

One pupil we spoke to hinted, diplomatically, that the school could maybe invest a little more in girls' sport – particularly hockey. A couple of mums agreed. One said that the school hadn't traditionally pushed girls' hockey as much as the boys' game, but that she felt things are now improving and that the school has been responsive to criticism. But another mum said there was still some under-investment in the girls' game. She said that her daughter recently went to training, only four girls turned up and there was no coach. 'It's demoralising,' she said, 'because the ones that do want to play are a bit ignored... and I can see my daughter's face – you know: "Why am I here marking four players on my own?"'

Beyond sport the extracurricular opportunities are seemingly endless – with a particularly wide range of opportunities for arty and musical children and for outdoorsy types. Some more unusual examples include stage set design, costume making, film making, cryptography, psychology, jazz band, knitting, Warhammer and astrophysics (the school boasts a space science centre – complete with a planetarium, Victorian observatory and a telescope – and a resident astronomer). And this is just the tip of the iceberg. Many students are working towards their Duke of Edinburgh Award and pupils from year 9 and above can join the CCF.

Rossall has a diverse tradition in the arts. Choral music is strong here – closely bound in with the life of the historic chapel – but students play different types of music in various performances and concerts throughout the year; and they can learn instruments at school with visiting tutors – for an extra fee. There is also a literary society, which meets regularly to discuss poetry, books and culture. The school puts on two plays a year in one of two well-equipped performance spaces. The drama department also has links with a local theatre school and casting agency, which has enabled some pupils to appear in national radio and television productions. Keen artists are allowed to use the well-stocked workshops and studios every day after school. Each year in the Lent term Rossall devotes a week solely to art, music and drama and parents told us that even the highest performing sports players would never be discouraged from getting involved in the school play or any other creative endeavour.

Boarding: Pupils can board just five days a week or at weekends too. If day pupils want to flexi-board – which they often do – then they always stay in spare beds within their own house. Flexi-boarding allows day pupils to stay at the school for a night or longer – for pretty much any reason. Parents love it because it gives them a night off (or a weekend in Paris...) but, more importantly, the kids can't get enough of it. They typically flexi-board on a Friday night if they have to be at school early the next morning for a match or on a Saturday night if they want to tag along on the boarding house's Sunday outing.

Although there are no classes on a Saturday, it tends to be a busy day with sports practices and fixtures. Every Sunday boarders can, at no extra cost, go on an outing – examples include bowling or crazy golf activities or trips to Alton Towers or the Manchester Christmas markets. Just over 42 per cent of boarders are international and these will be met at and delivered back to Manchester Airport by a representative of the school at the start and end of term. They don't have an option to stay in school during the holidays, though. If they can't fly home then they'll need to have a UK guardian to look after them.

The boarding houses, including the junior house for 7-13 year olds, are very homely – softer and more cosy than a typical university hall of residence. The boarding houses are a home from home where any pupil can come to relax and socialise during lunchtimes – and consequently there's lots of scope for different age-groups and both local and international pupils to mix. There are some single rooms available and a few are en-suite, but the majority of boarders share with one or two other pupils and share a bathroom on the corridor. Each pupil has a desk in their room and the freedom to put up pictures and customise their living space. Each house has a pair of live-in houseparents – who are either teachers or support staff. The houseparents we met were warm and affectionate – they seemed to love the job and that was reflected in the way the children spoke about them: 'yeah, they're very supportive,' said one sixth former and another added 'they look out for you and you can talk to them about anything'.

Background and atmosphere: An aerial photo in the school's prospectus shows the campus green, soft red and light blue. It is expansive and grassy; the buildings red-brick, grand and turreted; and beyond them stretches a thin strip of pale yellow beach before the misty sea. Even on a grey, murky day the space is picturesque and peaceful. 'Yes, it's a bubble,' one mum said to us, 'but it's a lovely bubble to be in.' This is one of the happiest schools that this reviewer has visited: pupils raved – with no hint of cynicism – about their friends and teachers, the school's traditions and jolly japes in the boarding houses.

The fact that it's a boarding school – and a very international one – is integral to Rossall life. The house system connects boarders with day pupils: all day pupils are assigned to a boarding house and from year 9 onwards they meet there, in cosy common rooms, each morning for registration. Even if they're not staying for a sleepover, this is a school where older pupils in particular just don't want to go home. They can stay late for prep (with teachers on hand to help) and have their tea at school. There's even a licensed bar and café on site, open to sixth formers three nights a week. One dad told us how pleased he was that when his nearly 17-year-old son stays out late, he doesn't need to wonder where he is or what he's up to because he knows he's safe and happy with his friends at school.

Tradition is very big here. Every year during Christmas dinner in the imposing, oak-panelled dining hall, the pupils sing The 12 Days of Christmas – each house taking a different verse. No-one tells them to do it, the pupils explain, 'it just sort of happens, spontaneously'. It gets quite competitive – each house singing more boisterously than the last. One pupil told me this tradition summed up what's special about Rossall. Might some prospective parents baulk at the hearty traditions, the special public-schooly Rossall sports, the sense that this could be the setting for an undiscovered Enid Blyton saga? Certainly we found no hint of social snobbery – we simply saw young people having a deliciously happy time at school. If grand old traditions make you cringe then Rossall may not be the perfect fit for you as a parent – when it comes to the pupils, though, the school is so warm and good-humoured, and there is such opportunity and encouragement to become the person you want to be, that we felt even if your teenager is something of a non-conformist he or she would still stand a good chance of finding a niche here.

Pastoral care, well-being and discipline: Several parents identified the quality of pastoral care as the single thing they most appreciated about Rossall. They raved about how well their children are known by staff. One dad was full of praise for a teacher who stayed in regular contact with him, by text, to keep him updated on a particularly protracted UCAS application process. 'Teachers always remember what's going on with your child,' said another parent. 'It's just great that there's always that concern... and so I don't worry about my children here at all because I know the staff are really looking out for them.'

Religion is significant in school life: there's a full-time Church of England school chaplain and the whole school attends chapel every Friday. But, particularly with the diverse, international intake, the school takes care to ensure that worship is inclusive and that other faiths get a look in too.

Discipline is firm here. Serious breaches of the rules would be dealt with case-by-case but expulsion is a possibility. If you're caught smoking three times, you're out. (Although pupils told us that some of the German boarders are stalwart smokers so, presumably, they're good at not getting caught.) Pupils couldn't think of any instances of bullying in their experience and they spoke with real conviction about how caring an environment this is. They said that pupils wouldn't tolerate bullying – that they would tell a teacher and offer support to the victim. Parents knew of no bullying either. Like most schools, Rossall has a stringent anti-bullying policy. We were impressed that parents told us that they knew of several pupils at the school who had come out as gay – with minimal fuss or drama and complete acceptance from their peers. Parents felt the school was very accepting of difference – perhaps also because of the diversity that the international students bring to the community.

Pupils and parents: The parents are a mixed bunch. A good few are alumni of Rossall but many others were state educated. Some get help with fees from grandparents or from the school's own means-tested bursary scheme. The kids are also diverse. Across the school, 50 per cent are international – coming from a very wide spread of countries and cultures. Further up the school, more than 60 per cent are international. But there are far more British children than those of any other single nationality. The pupils seem inclusive and grounded. And they were positive and polite.

Alumni include Booker-Prize-winning novelist JG Farrell; Father Thomas RD Byles, the Catholic priest who refused to leave the Titanic so that he could help other passengers; eminent figures in the world of sport, music and industry; and a few bastions of the Establishment: a governor of a couple of colonies; a private secretary to Queen Victoria; and the magnificently-named Sir Walton Clopton Wingfield, who patented the game of lawn tennis.

Entrance: There are entrance tests in English, maths and non-verbal reasoning but it is rare to say no to a prospective pupil: this would normally only be done if the school couldn't meet his/her needs.

For international students, the admissions procedure is largely a question of assessing their English. The school has a Skype conversation with every student before a place is offered. They must have at least some English: if they can't hold a Skype conversation they can't come here. If their English is already good enough that it won't hold them back academically then they can go straight into the main school. If not, then they may need to first of all come to the International Study Centre (see above in Academic for more information.)

All pupils need to achieve five GCSEs at grade 9-5 to enter the sixth form. If they don't they can either repeat the year or leave.

Exit: Everyone sits the senior school entrance exam but, for children already here in the juniors, it's just used as a baseline assessment and to assess for scholarship, rather than to determine who transfers. Some 35 per cent leave after GCSEs. Most sixth form pupils go on to university, some 15 per cent to Russell Group. One to Oxbridge plus two medics in 2018. Destinations included Manchester, Reading, Leeds Beckett, Queen Mary, University of the Arts plus several to study abroad.

Money matters: The school has been in very good financial health for a number of years – the influx of international students has really turned its fortunes around. About six per cent of pupils in the senior school receive significant means-tested bursaries (a 50 per cent reduction of fees or more, with 100 bursaries for local sixth form students). There are also some scholarships available for high performers in sport, music, drama or academia.

Remarks: This is a very happy school. Its population is so diverse, there's no one type of child who would fit in better than another. But we did feel the school would particularly appeal to busy parents who perhaps don't have a lot of support locally or who find domestic life to be somewhat relentless – because the school offers a round-the-clock home-from-home programme of activities which could ease the pressure on families at times of stress. It's no academic pressure-cooker and less able pupils will be praised for their efforts just as much as the high flyers but there are excellent teachers, facilities and opportunities that should give the brightest pupils every chance to excel. Overall, Rossall is a warm, inclusive and remarkably happy place to be. Staff and pupils seem to genuinely love it here – and there's not much higher praise you can offer than that.

Royal Grammar Junior School (Newcastle)

Linked with Royal Grammar School (Newcastle)

Lambton Road, Jesmond, Newcastle upon Tyne NE2 4RX

Ages 7–11 **Pupils** 262

Fees: £11,088 pa

01912 815711
www.rgs.newcastle.sch.uk

Head: Since 1999, Roland Craig BEd (Leeds), youthful, energetic early 60s, formerly at King's Tynemouth where he enjoyed a 'meteoric rise' from teacher to deputy head. Member of the (inappropriately named) Cross Association of representatives from independent schools; also founding chair of the charity Dyslexia North East.

Married with two children, both at RGS, he manages (enjoys even) a very long daily commute from the Cheviot Hills. A charming man who clearly enjoys his job, has an innate understanding of children, loves his sport and finds time out of school for bird-watching, wildlife photography and the odd barn conversion. At the helm of the key senior school feeder, he is 'charged to uphold academic standards' and does so by being highly selective on intake; fewer than half the applicants are offered places each year. He and his team are warm and welcoming and the assessment, though tough, is dealt with fairly and sensitively, in accordance with the ages of the children.

Entrance: Assessment are whole day procedures, including assembly with the head, followed by testing in maths (including mental arithmetic) and English – spelling, comprehension and creative writing. The day usually ends with an iPad session to check out creativity. There are rumours that pupils are assessed on table manners over lunch but school insists that's not true..

Exit: Vast majority – who don't have to sit 11+ entrance exam – to senior school.

R

Remarks: Self-contained, purpose-built junior school, with three-form entry. Linked directly to the main school and is therefore fortunate in being able to share many of the senior school's excellent facilities. The head and his two deputies are ably assisted by a young staff, with specialist senior school staff visiting to teach Spanish, French and music. Classes are around 20 or fewer, working towards 50/50 but slightly boy-heavy in some year groups. Classrooms are bright, modern and very attractive, tables for the younger ones, desks for the older pupils; there's a small hall for drama and music, a larger hall for assemblies, science lab, teaching kitchen, IT suite, library and soft play areas outside. Check out the green screen room – a first for us.

Don't over-prepare or hothouse for a place; essentially school wants to know 'are they children who will roll up their sleeves and get on with it?' The assessment process, with children in groups of 16, takes a full two weeks to get through all the hopeful entrants. It's a testament to how well it is managed when the children are 'buzzing' at the end of it all – much to the relief of anxious parents. So thorough is the testing that if you get into the junior school, you then have more-or-less automatic transfer to senior school at 11, though the school does reserve the right etc etc – an essential and probably sensible get-out clause, rarely used.

Choir, orchestra and bags of sport; the girls are north of England hockey champions and the boys field a number of tournament-winning winning football and rugby teams. Records are broken annually at the traditional summer sports day and having a pool on site means that they usually trounce the competition at swimming galas. Chess, drama productions, musical performances, river-dipping, sleepovers, ski trips and jaunts into the Lake District and beyond are all part of school life. Head writes a weekly newsletter to parents, so plenty of useful and interesting information about school life and events available just in case your offspring is less than forthcoming in the 'What did you do at school today?' department. Bags of extracurricular activities and extended school day on offer for busy parents, 7.45am to 6.00pm if you want or need it.

A huge array of silverware – cups and shields galore – displayed in the corridor, so many they have run out of space: clearly big on competition – in everything. They share a dining room with the senior pupils but have their own earlier slot; all food cooked in-house, packed lunches allowed if need be. Though it's a while ago now, still very proud of achieving school of the year from Sunday Times Parent Power and they comfortably occupy a regular slot in the top 10 nationally for Sats results. Children come from postcodes far and wide and all compass points from Newcastle. Small but quiet road to cross between some buildings and very limited vehicular access; don't expect to park on site.

Happy, smiling children who are challenged academically and on the sports field, yet thankfully without having the child within knocked out of them. They probably worry less about the transition into senior school than most at the age of 11, simply because they've grown up with it all around them, plenty of familiar faces and facilities. Tough to get in, but if you do, you're probably onto a winner here.

Royal Grammar School (Newcastle)

Linked with Royal Grammar Junior School (Newcastle)

Eskdale Terrace, Newcastle upon Tyne NE2 4DX

Ages 11–18 **Pupils** 1,053 **Sixth form** 342

Fees: £13,164 pa

01912 815711
www.rgs.newcastle.sch.uk

Headmaster: Since September 2017, John Fern, previously deputy head and IB coordinator at King Edward's School, Birmingham. From the mining town of Coalville in Leicester, he went to Loughborough Grammar and won a scholarship to read history at Oxford, where he also completed teacher training. First post at Oakham, where he was badminton coach, chorister, director of plays and assistant housemaster as well as becoming head of history. Introduced the IB at Fettes before moving to King Edward's.

Academic matters: 'No cynical old soaks chalking off the days to retirement,' say parents, adding that 'the quality of the teaching staff is outstanding, not just in their subject knowledge and teaching but also their external connections and interests'. No surprise, therefore, that results are impressive across the board, and consistently so. In 2018, 64 per cent A*/A at A level, placing RGS among leading schools in the country. At GCSE, 86 per cent A*-A/9-7. Ten subjects the norm at GCSE, though many also take additional maths GCSE; all take three sciences. You don't have to be a medic to come here but.. nearly 40 per cent of their parents are medics (or dentists), and large numbers of offspring follow in their parents' footsteps. Far from a given, though, economics, history and politics also popular and plenty of arts subjects in evidence; superb modern languages suite – French, Spanish, German and Mandarin Chinese all on offer. Add to that classics, design technology and psychology to create a good broad curriculum with more than a few added extras and no obvious weak points. Classes a little on the large side for some parents (25) compared to smaller independent schools in the area, but perhaps that reflects demand – or perhaps the lack of it elsewhere.

Games, options, the arts: The annual sports review boasts a huge number of triumphs with honours at county and national levels. Athletics, climbing, cricket (in which a number of star spin bowlers bamboozled opposing batsmen), fencing, football, gymnastics, hockey, netball, rounders, rugby, running, squash, swimming, water polo and tennis all feature. Plenty of championship competitions, tournaments and galas to add to match fixtures, the sport here is played with a fierce enthusiasm by both boys and girls. Unusual in a school to find both rugby and football so popular and well-supported, but then this is Tyneside..rugby exceptionally strong, beaten by only a handful of other schools ('Sedbergh train running up and down mountains so what can we do?') and regular trips abroad – eg South Africa tour. Probably worth a mention is the female director of sport, ably supported by a vast array of sports teachers (yes, that includes a male head of rugby) and specialist coaches.

Superb new sports hall, aerobics room and fitness suite and pool plus all-weather pitch. School buildings are formed around the main rugby pitch, additional outfields rented nearby, much use made of local facilities for minority and individual sports. Fifty-year lease on magnificent Newcastle County Cricket Ground, five minutes' walk from school.

High quality art, of all disciplines, is in evidence around the school, students work with local artists and gallery curators and exhibit their own work in local galleries and at the annual Art Private View for proud parents.

Music does very well, not unexpectedly – £10 million development includes performing arts centre with 300-seat auditorium, recording studio, recital room, drama/dance studio, 10 rehearsal rooms and percussion studio. Masses of orchestras, bands and ensembles.

World Challenge recently took two teams of year 10 pupils to charity projects in Ghana. Lots of hard work and challenge, on a number of levels, and it's popular with most, though not all. Some parents find the high financial cost of such long-haul trips prohibitive. Huge variety of clubs – chess meets three times a week and bridge is popular. Outstanding debating – regular prize-winners. Technology club equally successful. CCF for both boys and girls as well as involvement with local community – the inner city partnership, where pupils work with deprived children on a one-to-one basis. Strong charity commitment. D of E flourishing.

Background and atmosphere: Situated in leafy Jesmond, where the great and good of Newcastle live – or aspire to live. Designer clothes and arty coffee shops nearby; the school sits shoulder to shoulder with Newcastle High School for Girls, which may have felt a little too close for comfort when RGS went co-ed back in in 2006. You 'pays your money and you makes your choice' as they say, and increasingly there's clear blue water academically between the two. Girls now make up just over 40 per cent of the cohort and the belief from the top in co-ed is strong, with the school working towards a 50:50 split.

It is crammed into an urban site, yet wraps itself around sports fields so you can see green space from most windows. The main building has all the solidity of time and history that you would expect from a foundation dating back more than 450 years, and thankfully RGS in particular appears somewhat recession-proof. In fact, put simply, 'premium products don't suffer'. No arrogance here, merely a straightforward truism. Impressive modern buildings juxtaposed with the Queen Anne frontage, it all works magnificently. Much-loved old hall with war memorial, wood-panelling and pipe organ – a gloriously handsome space right at the heart of the school. Lecture theatre, library, superb performing arts centre, language suite and multiple science labs are more modern additions; no apparent shortage of space and school makes the very best of all that it has, with new building on the site of the old swimming pool about to expand teaching, lecture and library space. Modern, bright airy, almost corporate, feel to reception, where a warm welcome awaits. Don't try to park nearby, or if you do, allow plenty of extra time and spare cash for parking meters. Far better to use the metro stop less than 100 metres from the front door. Compared to the south, quality of life is very affordable here so the school attracts Geordies wanting to come home or others who stumbled across it whilst attending uni locally.

Sixth formers ('business wear' rather than uniform) abound, assured, confident, articulate beings who wouldn't look out of place in the foyer of Goldman Sachs. The boys fare slightly better with the sixth form dress code than the girls, who tend to interpret the code more loosely, smart suits giving boys the edge. Interesting that staff are more comfortable telling boys to tuck their shirts in than asking a girl to reconsider the length of her skirt – a hangover from the all-boys' era perhaps? For the rest of the school it's a trad uniform that works well all round.

Pastoral care, well-being and discipline: Parents tell us they 'are always welcome to talk to teachers or the head about any issues concerning their child'. Pupils are allocated a personal tutor who stays with them throughout and manages the changing needs of pupils as they grow and develop. Good ethnic mix, plenty of tolerance and respect supported by a vigorous anti-bullying policy. Out for violence and drugs. Smoking not tolerated and no particular problems with drinking or smoking off-site, but staff remain vigilant.

Pupils and parents: Parents tell us they have 'learned to value and trust the teachers and their process..in a culture that promotes achievement – starting with the ambition level of the children (and their parents) and is then nurtured by the teachers'. They and their offspring feel supported within the structure, it's proven, it works, they like it and they also reckon it's good value for money too. Huge number of medics and academics from nearby hospitals and university. Plenty of parent participation in the governing body and other parent run bodies, in both the junior and senior schools. All welcome, though no assumption of participation: constraints of time and distance and many here are extremely busy professionals who attend informal events as and when they can: 'we turn up when invited, work our way through the bacon sandwiches, and put a tenner in the collection box'.

Pupils have a real self-belief – 'it won't go wrong' so it doesn't. That said, they work very hard, it's in their bones; 'clever kids who fit a quart into a pint pot,' say staff, 'not hard-nosed but huge aspiration, future leaders abound here'; it's assumed that 100 per cent will go on to university. Good old-fashioned courtesy from most, and staff pick them up if they forget; it's very civilised.

Entrance: Tough and competitive senior entry via the school's own entrance exam at 11. About 75 from the junior school, as long as their work is up to scratch. Very healthy entry post-GCSE, far outweighing 16+ leavers – minimum six GCSEs at A*/B (or numerical equivalent) required plus report from former school. Entry from over 80 different schools throughout north east.

Exit: A dozen or so to Oxbridge as a rule – 12 in 2018; otherwise to Edinburgh, Bristol, Leeds, Newcastle, Durham, Manchester, Nottingham, London, St Andrew's, mainly to read hard traditional subjects; 14 medics in 2018. Small coterie to art or music colleges, though the latter are more likely to read music at university and then go on to conservatoires.

Money matters: Much praise from parents for the school's commitment to the bursary scheme; school keen not to be seen as socially divisive. Around 80 pupils helped financially, more than 50 of them at a level of 90 per cent of fees or above. All bursaries means-tested; some sixth form subject-specific awards such as Ogden Trust Bursaries for Physics and Reece Foundation Scholarships for budding engineers.

Remarks: Apparently there is 'aspiration in the water here' or so we are told. Long-standing habits of excellence across the board mean that RGS has long been, and probably always will be, seriously oversubscribed; 'there's comfort in its history,' say parents. The heavy glossy magazine that is the annual review at RGS went bold recently – En Pointe! – complete with ballet dancers in tutus: a shocker of a headline to those who think this is still an all boys' establishment. Behind it you cannot help but sense a wry, smiling, 'go on, we dare you' attitude that can only come from an establishment that is comfortable in its own skin, happy to take on the world whilst cocking a snook at those who dare to challenge its soul or integrity.

Ryedale School

R

Gale Lane, Nawton, York, North Yorkshire YO62 7SL

Ages 11–16 Pupils 710

01439 771665
www.ryedaleschool.org

Headteacher: Since 2014, Mark McCandless BEd secondary PE (late 30s). Educated in Ireland and at Leeds Met university, then became a PE teacher at Allerton High in Leeds. Moved to Ryedale in 2008 and became head after stints as assistant and deputy head.

Quietly spoken with a positive disposition, highly principled with steely resolve and a strong sense of fair play, he walks the talk and leads by example. Seen by pupils as 'strict but fair' and respected by pupils and parents, who like his passion for the school and understated manner. 'A man who doesn't blow his own trumpet' was how one parent described him.

Professes to liking 'shiny, happy people' and he has certainly built a team who demonstrate those traits. Parents made a point of mentioning the energy and collegiality of the staff, which sets the tone for the young people. He and the deputy head have 26 years of experience at Ryedale between them and make a dynamic duo. Most important to have this strong and united leadership as the head develops the Ryedale Federation, which includes three community primary schools, and was established in 2016. He cares deeply for the school and professes to 'never wanting to be anywhere else' – don't think anyone would quibble with that.

Married with two young daughters; the family has a smallholding where they keep rare breeds of poultry and domestic animals. Also a keen runner and tennis player when time permits.

Academic matters: In top seven per cent in country based on Progress 8. On brink of top quartile of North Yorkshire non-selective state schools – 82 per cent got 9-4 in both English and mathematics at GCSE in 2018; 34 per cent A*-A/9-7 grades. Strong results in single sciences, art, drama and music reflecting the specialisms in performing arts, science and mathematics.

Moving to a three year key stage 4 – most will do nine GCSEs; less academic will do fewer. Options, mainly academic subjects, include separate sciences, history and geography (big numbers with good results), Spanish, French (80 per cent expected to do one modern foreign language), art and design, dance, drama, music and PE. Technical awards on offer in food and catering, design technology and PE.

Based on key stage 2 results, pupils are set in year 7 for core subjects, French and humanities, extending to high ability musicians and able linguists taking on a second modern foreign language in year 8, continuing in year 9. Flexibility to move between sets, with advantage of smaller numbers for lower sets. Dance, drama, music, art and food tech for all in year 8 – boys too, new men in the making.

Two-week timetable and hour long lessons; have stuck to their guns in their curriculum provision, which has seen them through the frequent changes in government directives. Thorough tracking and monitoring, low churn of staff who know pupils very well and set high expectations. Aspiring teachers trained on the job through membership of the Yorkshire Teaching School Alliance provide a pool of new talent. Forward thinking, part of the RISE project, adopting tried and tested new research to improve teaching and learning. Developing use of ICT in teaching and learning. Average class size 23; attractive displays in most classrooms, pupil's art work eye-catching.

We saw lots of well-behaved, engaged pupils with well-paced, interactive teaching; intelligent discussion and independent learning encouraged. Good pupil/teacher relationships; pupils feel their views are sought and listened to with respect. Parents praised the commitment of the hard working staff. Gifted and talented students identified and monitored, stretched and challenged; senior management team mentor low achieving year 11s and a designated progress leader co-ordinates mentoring in years 7, 8 and 9. Early morning study clubs in the library for those need extra help.

Excellent, experienced assistant head, also the SENCo. Responsibilities across the federation and working with external agencies in North Yorkshire, sharing good practice. Forty-six pupils identified as SEN or SEN aware, covering a broad spectrum of needs – strong on dyslexia awareness and support. The school has 'forensic conversations with primaries' prior to admission so that year 7s with low literacy and numeracy levels are supported individually and with paired reading – year 10 and 11 'buddies' do some of this and also mentor them in other ways.

Well resourced – numerous teaching assistants and the Learning Centre, base for more intensive support, one-to-one for Y11s; also provides a refuge for children who find the breaks difficult.

Games, options, the arts: Competitive sport is part of the school's DNA with fixtures against state and local independents as well as plenty of inter-house action. Impressive successes – currently year 7 East Yorkshire and year 10 North Yorkshire county rugby champions; district success in cross-country; slam dunk in basketball district cup competition, a clean sweep in every year group; winners of all three district netball cup competitions.

Hockey and football popular though played on grass – an all-weather surface a pipe dream (matches played on nearby Lady Lumley's). No complaints from pupils, just accolades to the ground staff for the quality of the pitches. Less traditional sports on the timetable as well – such as badminton, dodgeball and indoor rowing, for everyone. Sports leadership qualification on offer in key stage 4.

Smallish sports hall with climbing wall hall doubling up for assemblies, airy fitness suite, hard courts dual marked for netball/tennis and several playing fields. How do they maintain a sports focus and such success without amazing facilities? 'Pride to be representing your school, winning the prestigious Halifax trophy for your house and wanting to do well for yourself,' one boy told us. 'Training is really good and we really build strong teams,' said another. Seems a recipe for success, combined with committed staff providing lots of extracurricular practice, peer coaching, training with local sports clubs and two hours a week at Ampleforth College facilities for year 11s.

Music a real high note in this school. A spacious main music room with banks of computers, a professional standard recording studio and a panoply of grand pianos. A quarter of pupils learn an instrument with excellent examination results. Gold and silver awards in consecutive years for GCSE performance from the Incorporated Society of Musicians puts Ryedale in top 100 schools nationally; 25 per cent distinctions in grade instrumental exams, including two at grade 8. Such is their reputation that pupils from Lady Lumley's School come to the school to study A level.

Informal musical collaboration filling the air in the music house in lunchtime break, a delight to hear. Lots of performance opportunities with girls' chamber choir, jazz band, rock groups, next biennial European tour has 66 pupils performing in Rhineland Germany. A few pupils in North Yorkshire Schools' Symphony Orchestra, one in the National Youth Brass Band and several in the National Youth Choir.

Well-resourced performing arts with drama/dance studio – retractable seating for small performances. Drama/dance timetabled for years 7 and 8, GCSE drama and dance preparation for year 9 opt-ins, through years 10 and 11 – all require kit of performing arts T shirt and tracky bottoms. Weekly drama clubs and annual joint musical production involving large numbers of pupils, most recently Sound of Music, Peter Pan, participation in Shakespeare Schools Festival; links with Helmsley Arts Centre.

Excellent art produced in a spacious studio and used to great effect around the school brightening up plain walls and injecting life into school corridors. Well-equipped DT and bright green food tech rooms, appropriately located next to the school canteen (you can tell we're in Yorkshire). A reasonable take up at GCSE and the year 9 Bake Off Christmas Cake competition is 'legendary,' according to one of our guides who practically drooled at the memory.

Over 80 extracurricular activities a week from subject support and sport squad practice to green welly club gardening and computer programming.

D of E bronze and silver popular; end of summer term two days of enrichment activities for all and annual residential trips for outdoor pursuits, history trips to battlefields and Berlin and taster trip to London.

Background and atmosphere: Built in 1953 down a country lane in the village of Nawton, surrounded by fields and just a few houses in sight. Equidistant from Helmsley and Kirbymoorside and half an hour away from Malton and Pickering, locations of its nearest secondary school neighbours. Used to have own railway stop till Beecham got busy with his axe – so a history of lunchtime activities, as there is nowhere to go and nowhere to hide.

Seen from the entrance the school presents rather plain and unfussy buildings, flat beige stone, terracotta sloping roofs, seemingly from the 'no nonsense' school of architecture. Softened by the circle of brightly coloured flowers in the driveway, planted by the current head, a thoughtful gift from his parents who chose a selection of bulbs that would flower from late winter to early summer– so we were informed by a very appreciative and impressed student tour guide.

Tucked away in a corner near the entrance is the Learning Centre, a converted house providing a base for the SEN provision and the range of interventions used to support pupil progress. Adjacent are the gardens, vegetable beds and dipping pond that are managed by the science department, home to the gardening club and community gardens for the village.

The site is deep so it is impossible to see immediately all the buildings that stretch either side of the campus towards the playing fields and sports pitches, and have the playgrounds sandwiched between them. The different styles of building mark the growth of the school and a further building is due to be completed in 2018. This will provide an additional science laboratory, art rooms and humanities classrooms, enabling the school to take a further 100 pupils and removing the geography prefab well past its sell by date.

No frills here but everywhere scrupulously clean and well ordered. Library is well stocked and well used – no bookish stigma here. Lots of enticing fiction, modern and classics, good selection of books on art and music, plus factual books geared towards the interests of reluctant boy readers. Cafeteria (canteen) offers a range of meals and snacks – a hot topic amongst parents and resulted in a pledge from the school on quality and choice, underwritten by the head always being the last man sitting on the lunch rota.

A noticeable level of quiet and calm on the corridors in contrast with the lively, articulate and enthusiastic pupils we met, who truly embody the school motto Aspire and Achieve. Uniform policy strictly adhered to; school ties denote a pupil's status and place in the school, badges added for positions and achievements – immediately obvious to all.

Peer pressure being what it is, conformity is the maxim – there's just a small number of rebels here. Strong traditional values; manners maketh man and woman believes the head, so doors are held open, litter picked up, top button done up and misdemeanours owned up.

Twenty prefects appointed at the end of year 10, more added through year 11 if duties require. Active school council selected democratically feels its views are regarded. Four committees covering teaching and learning, charities, whole school issues, community and culture. Head boy and girl plus deputies regularly attend some governing body meetings.

House system is key – lots of competitions organised by students and trophies are fiercely contested. The academic challenge is self-evident, but there are also plenty of opportunities for public speaking, charity events and community involvement for those happy to take up the additional challenges on offer.

Pastoral care, well-being and discipline: 'Anything that affects young people in school we will deal with,' says the head, intent on ensuring school is a safe environment for its pupils – it works and is much prized by pupils and parents. The mantra is to 'pick up on the little things early so they don't become big issues' and consistency is the keyword. Starts with dress code conformity, top buttons checked when pupils see us approaching, high presence of senior staff on the corridors at class changeover and the head is on bus duty morning and evening.

Pupils are encouraged to take personal responsibility for their attitude, behaviour and conduct and rise to the high standards expected, through regular reinforcement. Bullying nipped in the bud (policy is 'not just lip service,' said one parent); pupils tell us how they look out for the year below, year 11s buddy year 7s whilst year 10s run a reading club with them. Zero tolerance for cyberbullying; head finds showing screenshot to culprit in front of parents an effective deterrent.

Strong pastoral support from a dedicated team for those needing additional help and vulnerable children. Parents talked of the exceptional lengths taken by staff to support their children when faced with family crises. Those grappling with good organisation meet with teaching assistants first thing to ensure a good start to the day; poor attendance investigated to find the root cause; great care provided to those with SEN to ensure inclusivity.

Thoughtful transition from primary, starting from end of year 5, when children and parents can attend an open evening at the school. In year 6 senior staff give presentations at feeder schools, assisted by year 7s. Before they start, new pupils attend a literacy day in May and a taster day in June when they learn their house and can start to buddy up with older pupils rounded off by a new parents' evening. Consequently the deputy head prides herself on knowing every pupil and their family – highly valued by the school community.

Parents tell us that most staff return calls swiftly, parents are taken seriously, concerns addressed and they are kept informed of outcomes. Progress tracking reports termly, well organised parent evenings and an annual report receive a high rating. Communication consensus 'good after recent improvements', and what is really liked is that the school 'holds its hand up if it gets it wrong'. Email and texting works well; termly newsletter and parent forum appreciated.

Pupils and parents: Mainly from Helmsley and Kirkbymoorside, also from village primary schools in a large area of the North Yorks Moors National Park and surrounding countryside. Over 30 per cent from outside catchment area, such is its reputation. Mainly white middle class – very few ethnic minority, EAL or pupil premium.

The pupils we met were a delight – intelligent, articulate, reflective, clearly making the most of their school experience. Immensely proud of their school and their contribution to its reputation and achievements; there is a strong community spirit – though of course size does help. Notable ex-pupils: England cricketer Daniel Broadbent and the band, One Night Only.

Active, hard working and supportive PTA has taken on the mantle of grant applications and fundraising for the new building. Parents full of praise for school, particularly for the commitment and care by the staff, speedy resolution of problems, discipline and mentoring. Their main wish is for a full range of A levels on site as they feel Ryedale is so much better than the other state schools in the area; initial hesitation on the federation and fears of a shift in focus for the senior team, so far unfounded.

S

Entrance: Standard admissions process through county authority. Admissions number has now increased to 140 for years 7, 8 and 9. Catchment federated primaries in Helmsley, Kirbymoorside and Sinnington and other feeder schools in Ampleforth, Nawton, Gillamoor, Hovingham and Chop Gate, though over 30 per cent of intake come from out of catchment.

Exit: Most to sixth forms at eg Malton and Lady Lumley Schools, Ripon Grammar or York College; a few to independent schools; a few straight into employment.

Remarks: Rightly deserved accolades from pupils and parents for this high performing secondary school in a rural setting. There is tremendous pride and loyalty to the school which is constantly looking to improve, by adopting new pedagogy and technology, yet holding firm to its strong, traditional ethos. Pupils leave with a strong moral compass, and their success across a spectrum of academic, sporting and artistic pursuits truly demonstrates their ability to aspire and achieve.

Sacred Heart Catholic High School

Fenham Hall Drive, Fenham, Newcastle upon Tyne NE4 9YH

Ages 11–19 **Pupils** 1,410 **Sixth form** 290 **RC**

01912 747373
www.sacredheart-high.org

Headteacher: Since 2013, Anita Bath, who was previously deputy head St Thomas More Catholic School in Blaydon.

Academic matters: For results at GCSE and value added, best state school in Newcastle and one of the best at A level for last six years. Newcastle's centre of excellence for music and the city's 'music hub'. At GCSE in 2018, 32 per cent of grades 9-7 and 74 per cent of girls got 9-4 in both maths and English. At A level, 30 per cent A*/A and 57 per cent A*-B grades. All from non-selective intake. Science strong at key stage 3, GCSE and A level. Single sex 'avoids stereotypes coming to the fore. So here science and mathematics are more popular than they are in mixed schools because traditionally boys dominate in those subjects,' says head. Eight form entry at year 7, children tested and placed in ability groups in four tiers, two classes in each. Class size up to 32 (average 26) except tier 4 when number drops to 20. Average of 20 at KS4 and 16 in sixth form.

Broad curriculum, including one modern foreign language (possibility of second from year 8) taught at KS3 with flexibility to meet individual girl's needs. English, mathematics, science, technology and religious education are core – science stays right up to 16 'to give the girls a balanced diet'. 'We tailor the curriculum to the gifts of each child. Option blocks follow the child rather than the other way round,' says head.

All-encompassing bespoke progress monitoring and review system for each child, also foundation of teacher performance management, developed in school. DfE suitably impressed, considering rolling it out nationally. Baseline assessment on entry in year 7 predicts GCSE grades and reviews each half term academic targets, behaviour and attendance. As the assistant head data controller put it, 'We build a culture of accountability – there's nowhere to hide!' Individual tailored support provided where needed – highly valued by parents we spoke to. Secure parent platform allows parents online reporting and encourages email contact with teachers. In fact web-based virtual teaching environment provides staff, parents, students, partner schools and organisations with a phalanx of school information – statistics, curriculum, performance, preparation material, email, library system, management information etc.

Desire to see girls achieve excellence in subjects they take rather than push for huge lists of GCSE attempts – 'We give them the time to excel in what they are studying'. Pupils appreciate teachers giving up time to provide extra help: 'They put in a lot of extra effort at lunchtimes and it is great that it is there if you want or need it'.

BTec, City and Guilds and applied A levels on offer in sixth form. In total, 27 A levels (girls can take three or four) and five technical courses. Head wants to extend these to provide much greater range: 'We pride ourselves on excellence across the curriculum because students have a right to expect that'. Art and design, dance, drama and ICT available to A level as might be expected considering school specialisms. Collaboration with Catholic boys' school St Cuthbert's for study there where timetabled subjects clash.

Great store placed on developing and acknowledging staff achievement too: 'I want fresh and energetic teachers'. Sharing of skills/ideas is key. Teachers have visits home and abroad to learn and develop new ideas. School's success is recognised by the National College of School Leadership, which has licensed it to deliver leadership development, one of only 26 providers across the UK.

Games, options, the arts: Full range of sports available from the usual – football, hockey, netball, badminton, trampolining etc – to the unusual – judo, tag rugby and rowing. Something for everyone and willing to add to the list if sufficient support and interest.

Specialist technology and performing arts status – great opportunities for the musically interested and gifted, from rock to string bands and more. Music fund purchases instruments for use by those unable to afford to purchase their own. Drama encouraged (core curriculum in KS3) with lots of performance opportunities and joint productions with St Cuthbert's, recently Kiss Me Kate. Lots of links to Newcastle community dance groups. New auditorium with professional theatre seating nearly 500 and sprung floor for dancers.

Extensive art facilities in spacious, light and airy facilities offering all disciplines from ceramics to sculpture. Separate art room for sixth form. GCSE and A level textile students have the opportunity to strut their stuff in annual fashion show.

Exhaustive extracurricular programme – every faculty has something to offer from mathematics' cipher club to physical education's zumba. Educational visits include theatre, lectures, concerts, museums and holidays/exchanges to France, Germany, ski trips, exchange trips to other Sacred Heart schools. D of E, enterprise days and sports leadership awards.

Girls encouraged to pursue charitable work – each tutor group raises funds for their chosen project. On-going support for visiting, renovating and providing scholarships to Ugandan school – advertising for fundraiser Teachers' Got Talent when we visited.

Background and atmosphere: Sisters of the Society of the Sacred Heart founded a small, private secondary school in Fenham Hall for girls in 1905. From 1920 scholarships were provided, and by 1945 virtually all girls were scholarship students educated at either the grammar or secondary school on the Fenham campus. Became comprehensive in 1977 and academy in 2011. The head sees this as an opportunity as 'Being an academy provides our governors with the freedom and independence which we believe best suits the interests of our school'.

Prior to 2005 on two sites, but £10m spent on the school in past few years: £1.3m on sixth form study centre – which now includes sixth form café and library; £8.7m on new build and remodelling to bring everyone on to one site. New building is in keeping with old. Plans to create vocational studies centre to extend current provision, and enlarge sixth form. Parents told us that 'the school keeps moving forward, offering new opportunities for our children and doing that little bit extra'.

Great pride in being 'a Sacred Heart girl': one sixth former told us, 'At the open day mass you meet people who had been to the school in the past and get the feeling you are part of something special. There is a real sense of community'. Catholic faith and Sacred Heart ethos are important – prayer and worship integral part of school life and each day begins with morning prayer. Group of Sisters lives nearby, one is a governor. Religion not forced upon pupils: 'It is a personal thing and everyone takes from it what they want'. There is a residential retreat at the Youth Village in County Durham each year.

Pastoral care, well-being and discipline: Pastoral care is spearheaded by assistant head, year heads and personal tutors. Each girl will have the same year head and personal tutor from year 7 to year 11 to provide continuity – a real strength. Buddying system teams up trained sixth formers with year 7, 8 and 9 pupils to provide a listening ear. Peer mentoring gives year 10 and 11 pupils regular access to sixth formers for advice. Well-resourced pastoral team with full-time counsellor and parent support adviser, while school chaplain is faith presence in school, providing support to students, staff and parents.

Up to sixth form, rewards system recognises effort and achievement across the spectrum by merits and star awards for specific achievements. These build to bronze, silver and gold awards. Warnings and ample opportunity to correct poor behaviour precede any detention or exclusions. Total exclusions are rare – the last was more than three years ago: 'Exclusion goes against our ethos of welcoming each child and taking them through the ups and downs of school life'.

In a school of this size there is little opportunity for building links between year groups. Assemblies cater for just two year groups together and inter-house competition restricted to sports; clubs and out-of-school activities are seen as ways of bridge-building.

A representative student council has a voice in school whilst leadership opportunities are provided for the two head girls and prefects chosen by their peers and staff. Rules are clear and strictly enforced; unequivocal enforcement of strict uniform code and mobile phones confiscated if seen or heard, released only to a parent on Fridays.

Pupils and parents: A total of 30 different feeder schools but bulk from 13 Catholic schools in north and west of Newcastle. A third come from further afield – Newcastle, Northumberland, Durham. A breadth of social and academic backgrounds with 20 per cent of pupils with English as a second language and some 12 SEN statemented/EHC plan children. Former pupils: Newcastle North MP Catherine McKinnell and TV presenter Donna Air.

Entrance: Oversubscribed, at least two applications for each place. Catholic applicants have priority, followed by other faiths. Seventy per cent are baptised Catholics and nearly 20 per cent of Muslim background. No academic selection though 10 per cent of places awarded on aptitude and ability in performing arts.

Exit: Usually 70-80 per cent stay to sixth form. After sixth form, three-quarters to university, rest to foundation courses, employment or gap year. Two to Oxbridge in 2018. Around 40 per cent to Russell Group. Excellent at making sure girls make the right choice after sixth form: dedicated staff members helps with applications to the most selective universities.

Remarks: A school that is moving 'onwards and upwards'. Never content to rest on its laurels for its pupils, deserving of its award of outstanding in all categories in the last three Ofsted inspections. Continuity provided by pastoral system is outstanding. Inspired and inspiring teaching observed, stimulating lessons whilst harnessing the latest technology. What really sets the school apart is its development of teaching, and teachers who go that extra mile to set girls on course to make the right choices after Sacred Heart. Every child really does matter here.

Advice to lapsed Catholics: baptise your children, attend Sunday worship and move into the catchment area.

St Aidan's Church of England High School

Oatlands Drive, Harrogate HG2 8JR

Ages 11–18 **Pupils** 1232 **Sixth form** 1,073 (combined with St John Fisher High) **C of E**

01423 885814
www.staidans.co.uk/

Headteacher: Since 2012, John Wood BA PGCE (early 60s). Educated at Leeds Grammar, where he was a star sportsman – Yorkshire and England U19 cricketer – and Sheffield University, where he read biblical studies. Has been at St Aidan's since 1977, holding a range of posts including pastoral ones, and still teaches religious studies.

Actively involved in the church all his life, often leading acts of worship in family services. Educational adviser on the bishop's advisory panel for clergy ordination and honorary lay canon at Ripon Cathedral. Wife was a PE teacher and now is a verger at a local church. Two adult children, both educated at St Aidan's. Very interested in all kinds of sport and brass band music.

Very humane, thoughtful, fair-minded and approachable, clearly well liked by the pupils, judging by the friendly greetings he received on our tour, and parents ('lovely..excellent..always around the school..very understanding and quick to respond'), very appreciative of his dedicated staff and collegiate, working closely with his counterpart at St John Fisher RC School as well as with the other schools in the multi-academy trust he is keen to develop, along with the new teaching school role, whilst maintaining existing high academic standards.

Academic matters: In 2018, 40 per cent of GCSE grades were A*-A/9-7; excellent value added for all ability levels. Majority take separate sciences; religious studies (compulsory) very strong and and popular; wide range offered, including joint business studies and economics, fine art and graphic communication, French, German and Spanish; ICT and computing. Options for the less academic include the certificate in digital applications, health and social care, core skills, certificate of personal effectiveness. No gender achievement gap – boys can even surpass girls.

S

Steady A level results overall: 53 per cent A*-B, 28 per cent A*/A in 2017 – good value added. Vast choice, owing to 1,000+ strong combined ecumenical sixth form with St John Fisher RC, includes geology, ancient history, dance, PE, food tech, EPQ, as well as applied business, applied health and social care, music technology, travel and tourism, sport BTec. All do general and religious studies programme. Very strong art – includes photography – maths, English lit, history, sciences, psychology. Big sets, though, up to 27 at start of year 12 for most popular subjects, others up to 22, smaller sets in year 13.

Very good results founded on excellent relationships between teachers (who receive regular, high level professional development) and pupils – the ones we spoke to were very grateful for the generosity of their teachers: 'They're always willing to do 10 times more than they have to'; 'You can always see them in breaks or after school'; as were parents: 'You can email them with a problem and get a quality response that evening..They really deliver on promises'. National competitions to challenge the very gifted; well-resourced library.

Setting for maths from year 7 and from year 8, unusually, also for English, modern langs, science and humanities. This will please parents of the very bright, able to progress at a fast rate, but maybe not those who feel the less bright could be discouraged at an early stage by being placed in a low set (these are smaller, though). Chinese language and culture course for years 7-9 taught by Chinese assistant, who also offers language classes for sixth formers and a club.

Outstanding, profoundly committed head of additional needs, who really does try to meet full range of needs and supports parents, too; around 40 learning assistants, good resources. All year 7s screened and information from parents and primary schools used to identify any difficulties. Two learning support groups of 10, one just for literacy, one for science, French and humanities; flexible curriculum programmes. Support for parents and subject teachers – individual 'provision guides' have hyperlinks to information on appropriate strategies.

Foundation learning programme for group of about 20 key stage 3-4 pupils with severe learning difficulties, in effect a special school within a mainstream school – practical/life/employability skills with literacy, numeracy, speech and language development, leading to Asdan life skills qualification. Two bespoke classrooms in additional learning base. Hut with extensive model railway provides safe space for children who find break times difficult.

Games, options, the arts: Despite limited facilities – one Astro (upgrade on wish list), gym and sports hall, supplemented by local external ones – successful from local to national level in, eg, athletics, football, netball, basketball. Tries to provide matches for as many levels as possible; girls' and boys' football and cricket. Wide choice of sports including equestrianism, handball, golf, climbing as well as all the trad ones. Some very impressive individual achievers; celebrates progress too.

Brilliant, wide ranging music – bands, choirs, orchestras, around 20 ensembles, with input from older students. Annual junior music residential; Evelyn Glennie due to give drumming masterclass; worship band, Aidan's Flame; much individual prowess on national level – a boy's own choral composition performed at the Royal Albert Hall, conducted by him. Foreign tours in Italy, China, Switzerland.

Plenty of high standard drama – Les Misérables, Fame, Evita, Shakespeare Schools Festival; several get into the National Youth Theatre and top drama schools; lower school annual arts showcase, Spotlight. Lots of dance, at GCSE and A level as well as clubs. Stunning art, on display all over the school – success in prestigious national competitions. Well-equipped technology with wide choice of GCSE options: product design engineering, food and nutrition, textiles and 3D design. Competition plane cockpit construction under way.

Lavish menu of clubs – quantities of DofE golds, public speaking, creative writing, astronomy, Italian, trains, Amnesty International; much charity fundraising, led by sixth formers. Wonderful range of trips: year 9 exchanges with Australia and Sri Lanka, geography in Iceland and Italy, sport in Holland, coast to coast cycling in England, language schools in MFL lands, windsurfing and sailing or work experience in France.

Background and atmosphere: Located near the centre of Harrogate in North Yorkshire; opened 1969, pleasant white main building with some spacious modern classrooms and lots of fresh white corridors. Part of a multi-academy trust with a CE primary. Three outstanding Ofsteds; international school. Despite having around 1,600 students on site, atmosphere is calm and orderly. Christian values central, apparent in the concern shown to all pupils as individuals, whether providing after-school help with preparing for an audition or ensuring a severely disabled student can go on a London performing arts trip. From year 7 the pupils absorb the high expectations with regard to behaviour and focus in the classroom, in a community where staff will open doors for them and chat to them while queuing for lunch. The pupils we met said they feel safe and are encouraged to do as well as they can without being compared to others.

School council and sixth form senate (school officers) elected by staff and students after campaigning. Plenty of opportunities for older students to organise, eg fundraising and sixth form ball, or assist with plays, clubs, teaching special needs pupils. 'Amazing food' (student, with enthusiastic endorsement by others), quality-checked by a nutritionist; good choice but eating areas can get crowded. Black/dark grey trousers for all till uniform-free sixth form – we were very taken with the fashionable hoodies for sports.

Unusually, three specialist careers advisors – 'The school is committed to careers,' praised one – who run well-structured, thorough-going programme from year 9 – talks from outside experts; ambitious careers events. We were pleased to see the noticeboard on apprenticeships was the same size as the one for universities.

Pastoral care, well-being and discipline: Usual form tutor and heads of year structure. Mature behaviour promoted through rewards, relationships, working with parents and example set by older students rather than punishment. Bullying in school not seen as a problem by students; cyber bullying dealt with well and swiftly. Aware of mental health needs – discussed in assemblies, some sixth formers had done a well-being course; eating problems dealt with well and discreetly, reported a sixth form girl. School nurse, 'lovely' (female) chaplain and access to professional counselling; sixth formers do peer listening with younger students. Admirable extensive health zone on website with lots of links to useful sites. 'Very nurturing environment.. People always talk about the pastoral care at Aidan's when deciding which Harrogate school to choose,' say parents.

Pupils and parents: Mostly white middle class – Harrogate has a low percentage of ethnic minority. Polite, open students described as 'very biddable and pleasant' by a teacher, 'The kids have a really good moral compass' (parent); all staff with children send them here, which says a lot; ones in all the classes we visited engaged and working well. Associated sixth form also admits students from over 40 other local schools, which 'makes for a very interesting diverse mix – a great experience,' enthused head boy. Parents can access information on schoolwork from website.

Entrance: Heavily oversubscribed. Complicated admissions policy a challenge to get your mind round (but school will help with applications if needed) and known to inspire pre-emptive pew perching: after looked after children and those with a sibling already at the school, 80 per cent foundation places for Christians living in the Anglican dioceses of Harrogate and Ripon, with points for church attendance of children and parents (also uses proximity by nearest route); five places for children with demonstrated medical/social need and five for ones of other faiths living in the same deaneries. The rest are community places for children living in the same deaneries, closest to school (up to approximately one mile in practice); then those living outside the deaneries according to amount of church attendance.

Sixth form tries to accommodate all students, but may prioritise those with sibling already at either school or use proximity. Qualifications required depend on courses to be studied but at least five grade 4s at GCSE.

Exit: Great majority stay on for sixth form, rest mainly to further education colleges. Very high percentage obtain their choice of university – huge range of higher education institute and subjects. Eleven to Oxbridge in 2018. Otherwise a definite northern bias, the most popular universities being Newcastle, Manchester, Liverpool, Durham and Northumbria. Ten medics/vets in 2018.

Remarks: An exceptional school with many of the characteristics of a high-achieving selective one, that also says on its homepage that it is 'proud of the 50 plus students who have a special educational need or educational health care plan and who thrive within the school'.

St Mary's Hall

Linked with Stonyhurst College

Stonyhurst, Lancashire BB7 9PU

Ages 3–13 **Pupils** 281 **Boarders** 50 full, 10 occasional (from 7 years) RC

Fees: Day £8,700 – £17,100; Boarding £22,500 – £26,400 pa

01254 826242
www.stonyhurst.ac.uk

Headmaster: Since 2014, Ian Murphy (Durham BA, PGCE), previously Head at All Hallows, Somerset. Charismatic and open; his vision of education is about formation: helping to 'form' young people to be their best selves and excel. This view and vocabulary are, in part, born of the spiritual values underpinning the school. Its motto, Quant Je Puis – roughly translated, strive to be the best you can – is the heartbeat of school daily life because unlike many a concocted mission statement, this is no hollow refrain: it rests upon an impressive 400 year heritage.

Yet heritage is only part of the story, as Ian Murphy is a force for energising change in the here and now. Viewing academic excellence as a 'given' for SMH, he has focused on reinvigorating the arts and sport. He has also been busy instigating enhancements to the fabric of the school, moving the music department from stuffy attics to a swanky ground floor wing with cutting edge technology. A tennis dome was also recently added (opened by Tim Henman). And an idyllic garden created for younger children to understand life cycles. Very Mr McGregor and utterly charming.

On top of this, he has revitalised the curriculum, integrating the Stonyhurst crown jewels (its jaw-dropping private collection of 70,000 artefacts, including the First Folio of Shakespeare) into lessons as teaching tools to nurture intellectual spark. Parents say he has brought great energy and has had a 'massive impact' academically.

Acutely aware the school needs to be tuned into the modern world, head's innovatory zeal is a continuum; currently he is assessing the benefits of Saturday morning school. Innovation, he suggests, complements the school's spiritual values and refers to the Jesuits centuries ago being pragmatically alert to the need to evolve. The school's literature reinforces its Jesuit heritage a fair bit, making it clear worship is part of the school's make-up. So if you desire your child to have a Catholic upbringing this is marvellous, and those parents we spoke to certainly emphasised the immense personal importance of this to them. But what about other faiths?

The head is sensitised to Catholic schools sometimes struggling with their message in this area. So let's be clear right now in this review: make no mistake, this school is accessible to all, supportive of all and utterly inclusive. If you are not Catholic, as we are not then, yes, accepting worship as part of pupil life and unfamiliar lingo – references to Our Lady, to saints – is part of the experience. But do not, whatever you do, let lingo get in the way of embracing this school's wonderful ethos. The spiritual values the school holds are about forming wise, eloquent, generous young people. An uplifting aspiration which cuts across humanity, no matter which jack in a box of faith you spring from.

Inevitably, leading the school dominates term time (his wife also teaches there), but holidays are spent with their teenage children sharing their mutual love for sport and music. Personal reflection comes walking the dogs in the breathtaking Ribble Valley.

Entrance: Admission is via a meeting with the head and staff; pupils are invited for a day. Those transferring from another school provide school reports and reference. Students who speak little English are welcomed. Those entering in year 7 sit an 11+ exam.

Exit: Virtually full cohort transfers to Stonyhurst for year 9. (A few overseas boarders return home.) There is an exam at the end of year 8 but this is not related to the right to transfer (just preparation for senior school). Ian Murphy says it is not pressured, includes revision guidance; the results are important to the 'hand over' process.

Remarks: Although day pupils greatly dominate, this is a boarding school in outlook: most day pupils stay for prep until 7pm. All mix in Playrooms – year groups – though they are also members of Lines, which are akin to houses in that they encompass all age ranges and meet for sporting and special interest Interline competitions.

Ages 3-7 years attend Hodder House, a delightful building, packed with colour. The focus is on social development, literacy, numeracy, art, PE, swimming and French. There is outdoors teaching, exploring woodland and insects. Children have access to iPads. The whole school comes together for assemblies, easing the transition to the main building.

Within SMH, pupils' academic progress is rigorously measured by assessments, diagnostic tools to ensure all are on track and to identify those excelling and those who need extra help. A detailed picture of each child is built up, including pastoral well-being. Parents spoke of the school working on little weaknesses with the children, who didn't feel pressured, didn't notice 'tests'. Average class size is 15-18.

S

The national curriculum, enriched by the International Primary Curriculum, integrates cross-curricular themes, providing an opportunity to utilise the extraordinary Stonyhurst collection: studying the Tudors means touching Anne Boleyn's prayer book or Thomas More's hat. Wow. Evolution lessons, viewing dinosaur poo (oh yes). Artefacts enliven learning as pupils are asked what it tells them about the human story. And it's not just the artefacts either; Lord of the Rings must have extra sparkle knowing Tolkien wrote in the guest rooms. Not to mention that Oliver Cromwell, the cheeky wee scamp, slept on a school table before the battle of Preston. The grounds are used for activities from fossil hunting to looking at natural landforms.

Every class has an interactive whiteboard. Older pupils have timetabled access to a well-equipped IT suite. Internet safety is impressed from the start; portable laptops are used across the school to help pupils develop discerning research skills.

Currently 20 per cent of pupils receive learning support. School develops individual plans, ranging from one-to-one to group interventions to in-class support. Staff receive specialist training in areas like dyslexia. One parent whose child had been in a 'not very academic' box at his previous school said he blossomed academically after transferring to SMH. Another slightly dyslexic pupil had benefited enormously from teachers picking up she needed a worksheet next to her, rather than looking at a whiteboard; she is now 'flying academically'. High performers receive extension work.

Years 7 and 8, whilst still living and learning in SMH, are taught mainstream academic subjects by Stonyhurst teachers, some in college classrooms.

The director of music has expanded opportunities considerably: orchestras, choirs, big bands, the ukulele Odd Bod band. Some 75 per cent of pupils have music tuition and there are lots of concerts. While we visited, the Interline music competition had unleashed pupil enthusiasm to the tune of 270 auditions.

There is a cracking theatre and each year group performs a show: Grease, The Jungle Book, Bugsy Malone. Some older pupils prefer the technical side. Public speaking is encouraged; a Question Time style Brexit debate was one event (a trip to the Supreme Court in London the day before saw them meeting Dominic Grieve MP QC). Parents waxed lyrical about the confidence-imbuing aspects of all this. One talked about her previously shy daughter flourishing to become head girl.

The sports facilities are tremendous; tennis dome, huge sports hall, netball courts, athletics field, cricket pitch, rugby fields, use of Stonyhurst's Astroturf pitch, heated pool and nine hole golf course. Other activities include fencing and horse riding. Parents enthused about increased sporting fixtures since Ian Murphy's arrival; one parent was astonished that her previously unsporty daughter was keen to join a netball summer school.

Frequent educational trips but the annual trip to the Somme stands out. Each pupil is given a photo of a SMH pupil who died in the Somme and asked to research their life. Parents say they 'adopt that person' and are immensely moved on finding their grave. Visits from charities, like the Society for the Blind, also widens the perspective beyond me me me.

Some super clubs, like Big Thinkers (philosophy, neurology) and astronomy club. Parents said children were encouraged in whatever area they showed interest.

Head feels all pupils benefit from the familial pastoral set-up in place for boarders. While in their playroom, a pupil can wander over to a teacher and mention a worry. One teacher said informality in the dining room meant staff could pick up eating problems; it might seem relaxed but vigilance prevails. Weekly staff pastoral meetings mean any worries are logged and monitored. Each child's pastoral log stays with them their entire time at SMH and Stonyhurst

Mobile phones not allowed during the day. Boarders have phones for 45 minutes a night. Certain day pupils are permitted them to travel on school transport but they are signed in and out. Day pupils join boarders in mass each week in the theatre (the magnificent chapel can't host the whole school).

The 45 boarders are there seven days per week, sleeping in galleries of up to six. The boys' gallery seemed a little functional (though with breathtaking views of lush green hills), the girls' cosier with cushions and photos. One parent wished for more storage space. Lovely gender-specific sitting rooms; a joint playroom and kitchen. Staffing levels are I:7. One of the houseparent couple, a former pupil, exudes enthusiasm and writes an effusive weekly newsletter (about pupils watching Man United play, a trip to Blackpool Tower, snooker games, watching a movie).

Parents spoke of excellent communication. One parent of a boarder praised staff who nursed her son after he broke his hand in a sports match and her daughter when she hit puberty: 'This level of support for teenage girls is vital'. Parents said the tiniest query is sorted the same day.

This ancient school, is set in magnificent grounds amidst beautiful scenery. The vibe within the school is a little two-tonal: corridors which have been Ian Murphy-ed are light, bright, covered in large photos of pupils in action which, he says, 'tell the story of the school'. They do, and it feels uplifting. Other corridors, lined with traditional annual school photos, seem an echo of the past; as one parent politely put it, 'shabby chic'.

The playrooms for each year group however – the social and pastoral planks of the school – are full of inspiring pictures, quotes, games tables. They are terrific and age-appropriate, each room having its own distinct identity.

Parents are a blend of entrepreneurs, professionals and old money. No competitive inquiries, 'why isn't Jimmy reading Tolstoy now he's 8?' but empathy with the school's ethos and respect for its heritage. Certainly the parents we spoke to placed great emphasis on their children acquiring a broader view of the world, an awareness of the plight of others less fortunate. (Life beyond 'selfies'.)

In one of the playrooms, there is a fabulous poster of St Ignatius saying: 'Go forth and set the world on fire'. These children are being emboldened, their intellect and sensibilities refined, to do just that.

St Olave's School

Linked with St Peter's School, York, Clifton School

Queen Anne's Road, York, North Yorkshire YO30 7WA

Ages 8–13 **Pupils** 354 **Boarders** 10 full, 9 flexi (from 11 years) **C of E**

Fees: Day £12,345 – £14,955; Boarding £23,160 – £25,560 pa

01904 527416
www.stolavesyork.org.uk

Master: Since 2005, Andy Falconer MBA BA (late 40s). Read education and professional studies at University of Lancaster, MBA at University of Leicester. Previously head of geography and outdoor education at Terrington Hall Prep; same plus IT at Craigclowan Prep; deputy head at Chafyn Grove Prep – always also teaching sport. Covers lessons here. Has been chair of Independent Association of Prep Schools (IAPS) and on boards of Independent Schools Council and Independent Schools Inspectorate. Co-opted member of University of York St John's People Committee.

Wife is school nurse; three daughters, all at St Olave's/St Peter's. Interests: running marathons and ultra marathons – aiming to run all the Olympic city marathons – and photography (films matches with drone to provide analysis material).

Very pleasant and approachable, financially savvy, believes in paying attention to small as well as big details (sharp eye for litter and stray items of uniform), very happy in his job. Parents say: 'He has a reassuring strength.a quiet and self-assured leader who knows the children very well – he sits with them at lunchtime to have a chat and makes a point of congratulating any child whose work is displayed on the merit table..very visible: his door is always open (literally), for children and parents, unless he's in a meeting..very fair, committed, hard-working and hands on..definitely there to support the children.'

Entrance: All Clifton pupils move up; also up to six year 4 places, 10 year 6, 20 year 7. Family tour with head plus assessment day: computer-based maths, mental maths, reading, spelling and reasoning plus creative writing and team challenges – designed to show how children think rather than what they have covered; average or above ability expected.

Exit: Almost all to St Peter's, with a clutch of music and academic scholarships, and just the odd pupil going to, eg, Eton, Sedbergh, Oundle, Queen Margaret's. Means-tested bursaries of up to full fees from year 7 – need to be likely to make the most of life at the school as well as pass the exam.

Remarks: Situated in 47 acres beside the River Ouse, in the heart of York. Founded 1876; 1901 became St Peter's prep; went co-ed 1987. Housed in what was previously a larger school, so the very well-resourced classrooms are plentiful and generously proportioned. Attractively furnished, extensive library.

Saturday morning school, but 'You soon get used to it, and it gives you time to do your own things' (parent). No Sats nor common entrance tests, which is a great liberation. Almost all progress to St Peter's: they do take the entrance exam, but only to supply information about where they are academically, so no pressure. First two years have mix of topic-based and separate subject-based learning (specialist teachers for the latter), then specialist subjects approach takes over. Teachers ('very skilled..very committed, supportive and invested in the children..thorough marking' – parents) follow children's curiosity; children see lessons as fun as well as educational – 'inspirational,' enthused one, aged 10.

Years 4-6 have French, German and Spanish, with focus on speaking confidently and learning about culture, continuing with two in years 7-8, along with separate sciences. Classics added in year 6, Latin from year 7 – lively, engaging approaches. Philosophy for years 4-5 encourages challenging thought. Setting only in maths, from year 4. Sensible amounts of homework and valued session on how to help children revise for parents. Average of 20 per class: years 4-5, 22: years 7-8. Three fifths female teachers to two fifths male; good mix of long-standing and new staff.

Quantities of computers and all sorts of allied clubs, but children also develop practical life skills such as cookery, bushcraft and first aid in ongoing, off timetable life skills programme. Opportunities for gifted and talented, eg national competitions, masterclasses.

Takes growth mindset theory very seriously – children are encouraged to see trying hard, learning from mistakes and taking risks as more valuable than coming top, to develop an 'I can't do it yet' attitude. Also focuses on eight learning habits – collaboration, creativity, curiosity, embracing challenge, empathy, flexible thinking, initiative, perseverance – taught through all subjects.

Well qualified and resourced learning support department – small group or individual support (no extra charge), works with class and subject teachers plus parents.Has had children with mild/moderate learning difficulties, autistic spectrum, ADHD – 'children who can manage being part of a predominantly above average cohort'. Some of the site would be hard to access for children with severe physical difficulties, but the school would try to accommodate where feasible.

Sport across the ability range is colossal – 1,000 fixtures played one year; much success at regional and national levels; shortlisted for independent school of the year sports award. Very inclusive approach, despite being one of the top preps for sport in the country: happy to play less strong children in the A team against a much smaller school, whole year tours to south west England, Italy (rugby), Barcelona (netball). All the trad sports, plus rowing. Employs eight recent sports graduates to coach while trying out teaching as a career.

Music also huge – nearly three-quarters learn an instrument; wide range of musical ensembles, including rock and jazz bands, guitar group, choirs, with plenty of performances; years 4 and 5 have three class lessons of music a week, including a chance to learn a variety of instruments.

Impressive art, especially the ceramic work – we particularly liked the display of ceramic poppies made by all in the school; well presented paintings in glass frames throughout. Much drama – unusually, children handle the technical aspects of their Shakespeare Schools Festival entry as well as acting – and speech and drama clubs.

Over 50 clubs, such as ornithology and Mandarin; charity committee; school council; several children help run the library ('The librarian is fantastic – will get any books needed,' praised a parent). Year 8s do a high powered enterprise project and organise a gala evening in their last term – all have a position of responsibility. Things ecological taken very seriously: food grown for use in school meals; flowers, bushes and trees planted; worked with local willow artist to create a willow tunnel and woven deer statues; library garden made into a biodiverse haven with bird and insect boxes, storytelling chair and reading circle made of 12 solid oak cubes. 'They have lots of fun outside the curriculum,' said a parent, citing the It's a Knockout competition day as a highlight of the school year.

All staff have a mentor group of 10-12 children of mixed years, staying with them as they move through the school (siblings join too), so they get to know them very well. Support from whole school chaplain, own lay chaplain and senior school pupils, and access to private counsellor arranged if needed. Vertical houses appreciated by parents – 'It feels like a boarding school for day children..the older ones mentor the younger ones, who mentor the ones younger than them'. 'The pastoral care routes are very clear..teachers are always immediately available if there's a problem..everything is taken seriously even if it's a small matter.'

Junior boarding house for years 6-8 – full boarding from year 6, weekly or flexi. We were struck by the homely atmosphere: the common room is more like a living room, with comfy sofas and armchairs, flowers, fruit bowl and tasteful pictures. Well equipped games room and pleasantly furnished dorms. Around half Brits, half international.

Children eat lunch in house groups with house staff – good choice of food, hot, cold and veggie, with themed days, eg street food, different national dishes. Citizenship programme and much focus on key values of friendship, trust, wisdom, compassion, endurance, humility and hope. However one parent we spoke to saw the school as having a 'robust culture', so less suitable for the more sensitive child.

Children very engaged in all the classes we saw; the ones we talked to were happy, secure, very busy and enthusiastic about the school. Most from York or outlying primaries, covering a very large area as far as Harrogate, Thirsk, Malton, Bramham, Selby, Stamford Bridge, Doncaster. Mostly professional and business parents, mainly white British plus some ethnic minority and several Europeans. They value the seamless, well prepared transitions through the three schools and the common campus.

A school that approaches education – in the widest sense – in a very thoughtful and enlightened way.

St Peter's School, York

Linked with St Olave's School, Clifton School

Clifton, York, North Yorkshire YO30 6AB

Ages 13–18 **Pupils** 580 **Sixth form** 250 **Boarders** 112 **C of E**

Fees: Day £18,075; Boarding £30,030 – £32,280 pa

01904 527300
www.stpetersyork.org.uk

Head Master: Since January 2019, Jeremy Walker MA, previously head of King's School Rochester. MA (Oxon) (40s). Educated at Sherborne School and read theology at Oxford before taking an MA in educational leadership and management at the Institute of Education, University of London. Started his career at Bishop Stopford School, a state secondary in Kettering, and became head of department after a year. Then moved to Ardingly, where he was head of religious studies and of theory of knowledge, and housemaster, before becoming head of sixth form and senior manager at Berkhamsted School, Hertfordshire. He is married to Harriet, and their two children have joined the school.

Academic matters: Consistent achiever, sets the bar high in a robust local market. Strong work ethos with plenty of stretch and challenge, normal to try hard but fine-tuning from the top is pushing to 'broaden the pupil experience' ie accumulation of exam certificates is great but balance is also important.

Takes the academic rigour for granted; bright pupils will always do well, but hard workers also do well here, hence the very positive value-added. Believes good results are down to having really good teachers as well as selective but not highly selective intake; no weak subject areas; staff know what is expected and are multi-talented and self-driven. 'Learn Something New' is a St Peter's initiative that persuades staff to share interests and learn from each other with a range of activities across the school(s) encouraging staff to try out and learn new skills – 'learning teachers teach better' is the strapline.

Class size averages 18 in the middle school (maximum 24) and 12 in the sixth form. The occasional D or E grade creeps in at GCSE, but 70 per cent of passes A*-A/9-7 in 2018. IGCSEs in maths, science and languages. At A level/Pre-U, 56 per cent of grades were A*/A and a commendable 82 per cent A*-B in 2018.

Some support for the handful with mild dyslexia – must be bright and able to cope. Part-time dyslexia specialist. Approximately 10 per cent have an ed psych report; five per cent qualify for extra time in exams. Third modern language replaced by extra English and study skills for some. Gifted and talented programme in place but doesn't target top 10 per cent. 'All the children here are bright; it would be wrong to concentrate on a handful.' Olympiads and similar challenges stretch those with real talent. Global Perspectives an additional course for sixth form with Horizons introduced for middle school. Does not allow students to take any GCSE early and moving towards more challenging IGCSEs.

Careers advice and support flagged up by parents as something to be worked on and improved, especially important for boarders whose parents are not around to have those all-important conversations. They are getting pupils into good and great universities, but what next? Both pupils and parents feel they would like more guidance and direction as life beyond university becomes tougher and more competitive. The school has responded swiftly by bringing in a second careers adviser and opening up careers events, visits, conferences plus 'exploration week' for the lower sixth – 'life after St Peter's' is a drum they will keep on banging.

Games, options, the arts: A surprising amount of outdoor space; you'd never guess it is so close to the city. Nearest to the school is the hallowed ground of the first XV rugby pitch, but there are plenty of others beyond. Sport is compulsory for all. Facilities include two sports centres, one with super climbing wall, multi-surface pitch, fitness centre, indoor swimming pool, extensive well-kept playing fields, boathouse and tennis and squash courts. Rugby popular and strong, rowing crews regularly pick up national honours and awards, boast 20 international rowers in the last eight years. Hockey, rowing and netball are the most popular girls' sports but tennis, athletics, squash, swimming and usual suspects on offer for all. Generally put best coaches with best teams but playing opportunities for all via B teams and house competitions. Competitiveness and fair play are a prominent feature of the school and success is universally applauded at weekly assembly. DofE and CCF flourishing. Plenty of trips including expeditions to Morocco, sports tours to New Zealand and South Africa, language holidays and music tours to the USA, Prague, Italy as well as singing in York Minster.

Very good art facilities, including super gallery. Art department appears in the Guinness Book of Records for a remarkable 100 per cent A*/A grade pass rate achieved four years running, though recent years have seen lower grades creep in – 'we were pleased, it took the pressure off, allowed the pupils to experiment, be more creative rather than formulaic,' said one art master. Many learn a musical instrument or two, 300 individual lessons each week with professional specialist music staff, 160 strong choir and plenty of opportunities to perform; director of music described as 'inspirational'. Each boarding house has a practice room with piano. Over 100 pupils involved with Community Action projects and all participate in charity fundraising.

Boarding: Around a quarter of pupils board, of whom 30 per cent are from overseas. Most are full boarders but a few stay on a flexi/weekly basis. Six day and four boarding houses, the latter well equipped with a selection of common rooms, games rooms and a kitchen for snacks (all eat in school dining hall). Pupils and staff strike a good balance between amity and mutual respect. Houses are headed by husband and wife teams and supported by resident and non-resident assistants. Good pastoral care, 'just wonderful,' say parents. They describe houseparents as 'something out of the ordinary', creating boarding houses that are 'home from home' with all the care and support that may be needed and equally 'a kick up the jacksy as required'. Staff vigilant – invariably have one or two they're watching for eating problems etc.

Background and atmosphere: The school was founded in 627 AD by Paulinus, first Archbishop of York, and is one of the world's oldest schools, 'only two older', we are told. In 1844 it was established on its present, impressive, green, grade 2 listed site in Clifton, with 47 acres, river access and all within walking distance of York Minster, the city centre and station.

Beyond the imposing main building, others are a mix of ancient and modern. Some classrooms and corridors are a bit tatty round the edges; we get the sense that it's not a priority – it's a workhorse, not a show pony. Good range of facilities, with all angles covered, though pupils tell us they are pestering the head for a new sports hall; 'it could be so much better'. It's one of the head boy's pet projects, though not on the agenda (yet) – might have to settle for a new boathouse instead. Pupils rave about the new swimming pool, opened by Olympic diver Tom Daley. Other recent additions include four bright biology labs, a sixth form microbiology lab, chemistry lab and design and technology room with CadCam technology; new maths and languages building under construction. Three computer rooms are complemented by clusters of computers throughout the school and houses – virtual learning environment with Wifi throughout the campus.

Pastoral care, well-being and discipline: Advice, help and support may be sought from tutors, house staff, resident health centre staff or the school chaplain. Pupils tell us that the unforgivables are drugs and bullying; if caught smoking it's three strikes and you're out.

Pupils are allowed to visit town twice a week (more in older years) and for younger ones a timetable of supervised events is on offer. All eat in the modern dining hall. Menus offer a wide choice with mixture of typical school meal fare, continental options, salad bar, sandwiches, fruit and healthy eating options. Pupils say food is 'great', with 'boy-sized portions'; Sunday brunch is legendary.

Pupil voice has grown and developed through a pupil symposium. Head's question time is chaired by the head boy or girl – 'direct government-type stuff' – raising all kinds of ideas and questions from the downright silly to the well-considered and serious.

Middle school uniform uninspiring, disliked, yet (bizarrely) defended, by pupils – when push comes to shove there's nothing more conservative or radically opposed to change than your average 15 year old: brown blazer, grey trousers for boys, and brown checked skirt for girls. Apparently the current line is 'brown is good'. Sixth form (boys and girls) wear dark business suits.

Strong Christian ethos; pupils meet thrice weekly for collective act of worship in school chapel – the chaplain has 'livened things up a bit,' pupils tell us with a grin; assemblies at other times.

Pupils and parents: Day pupils mainly from North Yorkshire, Harrogate, Leeds conurbation, York, and surrounding villages. Majority of boarders live within an hour's drive but others from wide area in the UK. Parents in business and the professions, a popular choice for Forces families, minority from overseas – 'it's a world view we need to develop'. Mix of Hong Kong, China, Russia, one or two others – about 25 per cent overall.

'Parents,' says school, 'are interested – but not helicopters', ambitious and driven; quite a few first time buyers here but also dynasties with names all over the honours boards.

Old Peterites include Guy Fawkes, Alcuin (eighth century scholar), Greg Wise, John Barry, Laurence Eusden (poet laureate), Harry Gration (journalist, TV presenter), C Northcote Parkinson (inventor of Parkinson's Law) and Clare Wise (previous director of the British Film Commission).

Entrance: Automatic entry from Clifton Pre-prep to St Olave's (St Peter's junior school) and then from St Olave's to St Peter's. Seventy per cent follow this route, rest by CE and school's own entrance test at any age including 13 or 16 (minimum six GCSE grade 6 passes). Assessment and filtering does take place in prep and pre-prep to weed out those who won't cope with the demands of St Peter's, but it is rare. Generally entry to St Olave's requires a child to have a reading age at least a year ahead of chronological age (sympathetic to siblings). Will take pupils who pass exam at any time provided a place is available. Other main feeder schools: Terrington Hall, Cundall Manor and Aysgarth, some state schools also.

Exit: Around 10 per cent leaves at the end of year 11. Of those leaving after A levels, 95 per cent go directly to university, vast majority selecting Russell Group. Nine to Oxbridge in 2018 (though UCL and Imperial often favoured by high flyers); others to Hong Kong, Utrecht and Melbourne. Edinburgh, Newcastle, Birmingham and Sheffield also popular; some 15 per cent applying next year; a few to employment. Five off to study medicine in 2018.

Money matters: Not a rich school but has increased bursary funding considerably over the past few years. Means-tested bursaries available at 11, 13 and at sixth form regardless of previous school. Qualification criteria for bursaries on a sliding scale from 10 to 100 per cent based on need, and typically if household income is less than £45,000. Honorary (ie no dosh) subject scholarships are awarded; music awards, including fee remission, available for tuition and instruments.

Remarks: Very much the big brother of the 3-18 triumvirate of St Peter's schools, encompassing Clifton Pre-Prep and St Olave's junior school ('continuity, but difference' is the mantra here) and you get the impression that this is where it all becomes rather serious. If it were a car, we'd probably describe it as a Volvo, albeit a top of the range high performance 4WD version with sporty extras such as a ski rack and maybe a tow bar. It can accommodate the whole family and you can't doubt the quality, reliability and solidity of the product it delivers, pretty much unfailingly, in all areas.

St Thomas More Catholic School

83

Croftdale Road, Blaydon-on-Tyne, Tyne and Wear NE21 4BQ

Ages 11-19 **Pupils** 1,517 **Sixth form** 295 **RC**

0191 499 0111
www.stthomasmore.org.uk

Head teacher: Since 2005, Jonathan Parkinson (40s) BSc physics (Leeds University) PGCE. Previously deputy head, assistant head, head of science, head of physics, all at St Thomas More. Previous schools: Carre's Grammar School, Sleaford; All Saints High School, Huddersfield. Positive, energetic and witty with easy but respectful relationship with pupils. Still makes time to teach, last year physics to year 11; this year sixth form psychology. Gets a buzz from 'seeing the lightbulbs go on in little brains, watching children grow and go out into the world as young adults and to know you have had an impact on them.'

S

Places emphasis on development of staff, looks for innovation and sees 'the teacher in the classroom as absolutely key' to pupil progress and keeping the school moving forward. Not driven by results. 'We do things here for the right reasons – the needs and abilities of the pupils, and our results grow from that', underpinned by 'great emphasis on creating a strong Christian nurturing environment.'

Regular early morning fitness regime in privately operated fitness suite in school; away from school a keen, but slow, runner. Loves Bach; grade 8 flautist but will retake as he 'only scraped through'; runs own ceildh band.

Academic matters: In past awarded technology college status (first in north east); leading edge school (ie encouraged to work in partnership with other schools to raise standards). One of first tranche of teaching schools, joined with Cardinal Hume Catholic School, St Mary's Catholic school and Newcastle University to form Northern Lights Teaching School Alliance with mission to 'Illuminate, Innovate and Inspire'. Full A level and GCSE curriculum, along with GNVQ and BTecs offered and matched to pupil's ability. At A level in 2018, 60 per cent A*-B grades (31 per cent A*/A); large numbers of students following vocational courses attain distinction and merit grades. At GCSE, 70 per cent of students got 9-4 in both maths and English at GCSE and 45 per cent of grades were A*-B/9-6. Compared with national expectations, pupils leave the school achieving significantly higher grades than their levels of attainment on entry would suggest.

Eight form entry in year 7 offered a broad curriculum and pupils are set by ability in maths and English. Regarded as 'diagnostic year' with scope to alter through year as abilities change. From year 8 setting extended to science, humanities, technology and modern foreign languages. Tests every 10 weeks throughout KS3; reports with grading on attainment and effort, targets set by pupils. A choice of route A, vocational, or route B, academic at KS4 and again in the sixth form. English Bacc recently introduced needing little change to curriculum since approx one-third of students achieve this qualification. Mathematics GCSE started in year 9.

Unusual timetable: two week rota with three lessons of 100 minutes per day.This provides technology and science with required time and is seemingly popular with pupils, though contrary to some contemporary research on effective learning.

Good careers advice and visiting professors from nearby university provide mock interviews for university entrants. Visits to colleges organised for Oxbridge hopefuls.

Games, options, the arts: Growing reputation for music, drama and dance. Abundance of bands, choirs, orchestras stems from compulsory instrument tuition from year 7. Pupils are allocated instruments – can cause some resentment because there's no choice. Team sports abound, with a list of county and national sporting honours. Cricket a strength, led by enthusiastic coach, indoor nets in sports hall which also offers usual range of indoor sports plus climbing wall. Playing fields but all-weather surface on wish list. Wide selection of clubs and societies – from sports to chess, Scrabble and hoola hooping; enjoys exchange/educational visits to French/German-speaking countries and outdoor pursuits weekends. Big school production annually: We Will Rock You and Grease recently. In a school of this size pupils find participation 'a good way to get to know others out of your year'.

Background and atmosphere: Catholic faith is strong in school, evidenced in worship, teaching of mutual respect and in charitable works. Head believes that Christian ethos binds children and staff and encourages all to give of their best. 'This feels like a community; happiness emanates from the classrooms, we have high standards and expectations of everyone, value manners, show respect and expect exemplary discipline'.

Situated in Blaydon, a former industrial area currently undergoing significant housing regeneration. Opened in 1967 as co-educational secondary modern, became comprehensive in 1987 and has doubled in size along the way to current roll. Buildings chart the school's history and growth spanning four decades with uninspiring frontage and narrow corridors of the early build necessitating rigorously enforced traffic movement between lessons. Sport England helped fund the sports hall/fitness room and library. New self-financed humanities and English block is jewel in the crown for both staff and pupils. Airy, light classrooms with interactive whiteboard walls provide good teaching environment and wide corridors link all parts of the school.

Pastoral care, well-being and discipline: Pastoral system is bedrock of school. Pupils allocated to one of four houses in year

7 (following elder siblings) and each year group comprises two forms for each house, developing allegiance and competitive spirit. Competition ranges from sports to chess and the TV classic Countdown. Houses mixed on gender and academic ability. Tutor groups stay the same until year 11 for continuity.

Pastoral system dedicated to ensuring each child feels secure, confident and valued. Programme ensures tutors look after social, emotional and academic needs. 'It is important that children enjoy school and our pastoral system helps ensure they do', says head. Target setting, supported by pastoral mentors, assists development. Strong on discipline and maintaining standards eg inflexible uniform policy, litter-picking duties. Good behaviour, manners and attitude to work are paramount. Merit system based on both academic and social achievement and contribution to the life of their house and the school. Certificates/head's commendation much sought after by pupils. Pupils look up to sixth formers and aspire to be one. Competition for head boy and head girl posts is stiff. Pupils taught respect for others and their school environment.

A school marches on its stomach so it was disappointing to hear that quality, portion size and price of food in the dining room seemed to be a universal disappointment: however, school tells us a new chef has been appointed so no doubt changes are afoot.

Pupils and parents: Bulk of children come from nine Catholic feeder schools, mainly in West Gateshead. Predominantly British white with some from other backgrounds. Comprehensive intake, above average KS2 results. Seventy per cent stay for sixth form. 'Everyone here gets on really well and there are opportunities to get involved in everything, and we are encouraged to do so. I never thought I would say that I love coming to school, but I do.'

Entrance: Oversubscribed. Priority to Roman Catholic children from feeder schools, then those with siblings already at school; other Roman Catholics; other faiths. 'People come here partly because of our results but a lot is down to our reputation for setting high standards of work and behaviour.'

Exit: Majority of A level students go to university, mostly in the north: Newcastle, Northumbria, Sunderland, Durham. Two to Oxbridge in 2018 plus three medics.

Remarks: A school true to its Christian foundation; pupils leave well prepared for life outside the school gates and flourish in an environment that promotes mutual respect, high expectation and strong citizenship. Great emphasis on teaching the teachers pays dividends. Consistently good academic results, though these are not the driver here. Pupils work hard, play hard and are clearly very proud of their school. Advice to lapsed Catholics: baptise your children, attend Sunday worship and move into the catchment area.

Sedbergh School

Linked with Casterton, Sedbergh Preparatory School

84

Malim Lodge, Sedbergh, Cumbria LA10 5HG

Ages 13-18 **Pupils** 555 **Sixth form** 230 **Boarders** 542 full C of E

Fees: Day £24,915; Boarding £33,840 pa

01539 620535
www.sedberghschool.org

Head master: Since September 2018, Dan Harrison, who has been here for 25 years and was previously second master. He read natural sciences at Cambridge, where he also completed his PGCE.

Previous head Andrew Fleck is now principal, in overall charge of the senior and prep schools.

Academic matters: School cites geology as a strength (the geology classroom, crammed with a huge collection of rocks, with desks sloping upwards like a university lecture room, is incredible). However, based purely on results, the maths A level results looked very good to us and we feel that maths has sneaked in as a school strength.

The school responds to its broad intake by setting pupils from year 9 by ability. A tutor monitors progress, liaising with subject teachers. Added value is measured for every level of ability (though those stats weren't available to us). There is a broad curriculum; year 9 takes up French, and German or Spanish is on offer (though very few take languages at A level). More offbeat options are available at GCSE, like jewellery design. There are alternative options in sixth form beyond A level – a BTec in agriculture in conjunction with Newton Rigg College in Penrith.

A 2017 inspection report states 'assured and inspiring teachers with high expectations and expertise in their subject successfully encourage most pupils....to achieve their potential and fulfil their ambitions'. Where pupils would benefit from extra lessons, they are arranged. Everything is on tap, this being a full boarding community.

ICT used for eg organising notes or recording class discussions. There are also what are described as 'pioneering academic opportunities', like the 100 hour revision challenge for years 11, 12 and 13 over the Easter holidays (as in, 21 days hol, five hours a day etc).

Some 120 pupils have learning difficulties; most of the extra support is around dyslexia or dyspraxia and is often one-to-one. Learning support works across both ends of the spectrum, though, including the 9 Star programme for year 9s, aiming to develop their logical and critical thinking. One parent, whose son was on the programme, felt he was flying academically. Another parent felt the academic side of things was generally 'on the rise'.

Results are good overall (bearing in mind the very broad spread of intake) and on the up for the last few years. Particular strengths are English, English literature, maths, biology, chemistry, physics and geography. In 2018, 39 per cent of GCSEs were A*-A/7-9. At A level in 2018, 39 per cent A*/A and 66 per cent A*-B grades.

Games, options, the arts: Sedbergh has a national reputation for sports prowess but this is only part of the story (the old perception that this is a school for rugby players is past its sell by date). Frankly, it was a joy hearing the rugby-playing sixth former, who had set his sights on Cambridge, wax lyrical about the music department and refer with awe and respect to a recent school production of A Christmas Carol as 'very professional – dead arty and stuff'.

So, back to sport: each house fields teams for the inter-house competitions and the school itself continues to have a reputation for excellence. Pupils clearly love the Saturday sports matches where the whole school turns out to support. A vast array of activities: lacrosse, athletics, horse riding (Sedbergh has an equestrian team), but also orienteering, fishing, kayaking, mountain biking, fell running, badminton, sailing, shooting, squash, tennis. The facilities match all this and have just got a whole lot better with a new sports centre. Expert sports coaching is also available, often with video analysis. Staff are aware of the relationship between sport and good mental and physical health and note the increase in requests for early morning coaching around exam times. Parents enthused about the freedom Sedbergh offers; that (subject to H&S) children get to experience activities like river bathing, mud sliding and wild camping (usually off menu in a lot of red tape schools). The expression 'it toughens them up' was used a lot by parents. (Here, a note of caution; the school's 'joining in' ethos might mean those more apprehensive by nature may not be so well suited.)

The pupils we spoke to effervesced about the school's 125 year old Wilson run (a 10 mile cross country fell race for 16+ pupils, described by the Guardian newspaper as 'hell in the fells'), about the camaraderie it engendered, the 'supporting each other through' it, the rapturous applause at the finishing line. It's all very reminiscent of the Brownlee brothers' spirit, because this is a run which requires grit and a can-do attitude which pretty much sums up what Sedbergh is all about. Its multiplicity of extracurricular activities nurture resilience and teamwork (qualities which most of the working world is crying out for right now).

Performing is dominant too, with high numbers taking LAMDA. School plays attract great interest; a recent production of Les Misérables had a cast of 78 and inspired pupils to debate the concept of redemption – whilst in Cabaret, the moral dilemmas and the lack of courage were chewed over. Pupils spoke to us casually about regular debating competitions, about having to prepare a topic quickly and thinking on their feet. They didn't seem fazed.

Musical opportunities run the spectrum: choral, orchestra, swing band (a big jazz and swing night had the pupils entertaining 150 guests). Everyone participates at some level; there is a house singing competition, for example. Professional musicians give concerts but there are also scholars' concerts and small informal musical soirées. The choristers get to sing in vast spaces like Durham Cathedral and recently went on tour around Italy. One pupil made it into the national youth choir. It's all on tap, again; you can pitch up at the music school before or after lessons and have a practice.

S

Unless they have the head's permission, all join the school contingent of the CCF where they can experience scuba diving, gliding, piloting. However, the pupils we spoke to had done voluntary work instead – helping in local schools – and seemed to have got a great deal of satisfaction out of it. Pupils are also prepared for the finer things in life: events to practice etiquette, confidence-builders for social settings (balls). This is all reinforced by the fact that staff and pupils have three civilised meals a day together in each house.

Loads of trips, some to incredibly exotic climes, such as an ecology trip to Madagascar. Some fantastic clubs for those with big academic appetites (there is also an inter-house academic challenge): Polyglots (languages), the Invisible society (science), classics soc, Rogers society (economics).

Boarding: This is a full boarding school with the pastoral care to go with it. The 2017 inspection report put it thus: 'Boarding provides pupils with a safe, happy, fulfilling platform from which they can pursue their academic and other interests'.

There are nine houses (six boys, three girls), each with its own style and character to foster a sense of belonging: its own library, common rooms, computer suite, dining room. Each with a houseparent, resident matrons and associated house tutors. We visited the newest girls' house, a delightful building, all whitewashed stone walls, individual rooms with bow windows and fireplaces (each room for year 10s upwards has a desk – year 9s do prep together, supervised by prefects). The house communal rooms have lovely furniture (piano, chandeliers), a super dining area, veranda, bright cushions and clean kitchen areas. A big TV is tuned into the news to top up their current affairs knowledge.

Around five to a room in the lower years, two or three higher up, with sixth formers on their own. Room mates change every term, and the houseparent uses their good judgement to make the final decision (with the best will in the world, problems bubble up and, as one pupil muttered, term times can feel intense). One of the housemistresses we met was a tour de force of warmth and intellect; she knew who would be sitting next to whom at lunch, what vegetables they liked and where each of them were at any time. She exuded quiet competence, iron grasp of detail and seemed to possess mountains of energy.

Houseparents feed any worries – eg homesickness – back to parents. One mother spoke of visiting her sons' boarding house for the first time, seeing a row of black wellies outside the door and being struck by how homely it all was. Discipline, she felt, was good, as the boys respected the housemaster.

Pupils are allowed to use their phones outside lesson and prep times but not at night.

Background and atmosphere: Founded 1525 by Roger Lupton, a provost of Eton, the school nestles amidst the fells in the beautiful old town of Sedbergh. It has a huge campus with gorgeous old stone buildings. Lots of fresh air inhaled whilst walking from building to building. The school corridors, lined with traditional photos, have an old world charm about them. Nothing too edgy – the biology lab had geraniums on all the windowsills when we visited. Great exhibition space for art, nice DT workshops, decent labs and IT equipment. The library is out on its own in a beautiful old building. New sports hall built into the hill overlooking the playing fields with an arched sedum roof. Views of hills to make the heart sing.

Girls joined in 2001 and now make up around 40 per cent of students. Sedbergh merged with Casterton School in 2013. The Sedbergh juniors moved to the merged junior school on the Casterton site (known as Casterton, Sedbergh Preparatory School), whilst the Casterton seniors moved to the merged senior school, named Sedbergh School, on this site.

Pastoral care, well-being and discipline: School regularly seeks pupils' views in discussion groups, runs anonymous surveys and takes safeguarding extremely seriously. Any hint of bullying is tackled immediately. The school is open to all faiths and has Sunday services. The chaplain is an extra layer in the pastoral system. There is a health centre with a doctor, nurses and physio.

Older pupils are allowed to wander into town. The pupils have many socials on campus, though: Caribbean evenings, fancy dress parties, sketch shows. Minor disciplinary issues (being late for lessons) mean you will get endorsements, and too many of those means you may not attend socials. One parent, whose son had been sent home due to a teenage misdemeanour, praised the calm way with which it had been dealt and said how easy it had been to reintegrate on his return.

Pupils and parents: In addition to Sedbergh's prep school, Casterton, pupils come from prep schools usually within a three hour radius: Scotland, Newcastle, York, Lancashire and

Derbyshire. The net has started to be cast out wider, pulling in some pupils from the home counties. Around 60 per cent boys, and 20 per cent from overseas (there is specific information for Chinese students on the admissions page of the website).

Parents are described as enthusiastic, keen to work with the school to solve any problems. There are parent invites to garden parties and dinners and everyone congregates for tea in the local hostelry, The Dalesman, after sports matches.

Parents praised the excellent communication (although one expressed disappointment that a week-long trip to Cambridge had been called off without explanation and not rearranged). Generally, though, it was felt updates were frequent and staff very accessible.

Entrance: The school is modestly selective. Most admissions via common entrance or school's own exam but the bar is not set too high. So the intake tends to be a broad mix. Admissions policies are changing so see the school website for the latest details. Pupils joining at a later stage in the school take maths and English exams. Sixth form entry depends on GCSE results.

Exit: Around a third to Russell Group universities with the odd trickle to Oxbridge, some applying post-A levels. It's fair to say there is latitude here for improvement, which may well come via initiatives like the 9 Star programme. A real blend and variety of destinations and subjects; the more traditional like art history, law, chemistry, classics and maths sit alongside the professional vocational ones: engineering, dentistry, and medicine. There is also a sprawl of more modern courses: sport science, international business management, fashion design, broadcast journalism. Two to Cambridge in 2018 (medicine and engineering), two to the US (one on a rugby scholarship) and one to study law in Hamburg. Northumbria and the Royal Agricultural University currently the most popular, alongside Newcastle, Oxford Brookes and Nottingham Trent.

Money matters: A number of scholarships available across academic, music, art, DT, drama, sport or even for being an all-rounder (with regard to the latter, we rather suspect Andrew Fleck would approve of polymaths). There are also means-tested bursaries.

Remarks: The caring enfold of this beautiful school gives young adults an opportunity to find their passions, draw on inner resources and reach their academic and personal potential. If you want your child to have an outdoorsy experience and be imbued with the robust spirit of a self-starter, this is the place. Couch potatoes or teenagers with a partiality for clubbing probably shouldn't apply.

Sheffield High School for Girls

10 Rutland Park, Sheffield, South Yorkshire S10 2PE

Ages 3-18 Pupils 974 Sixth form 217

Fees: £9,216 – £12,975 pa

01142 660324
www.sheffieldhighschool.org.uk

Headmistress: Since September 2018, Nina Gunson, previously head of senior school at Wakefield Girls' High. She was deputy head at Sheffield from 2011 to 2015. Degree in molecular and cellular biology from the University of Huddersfield followed by an MSc in multimedia and e-learning. Began her teaching career at Bradford Girls' Grammar.

Head of junior school since 2016, Christepher Hald, Bsc in biology and chemistry from Seattle University, MA in primary education focused on pastoral care (early 50s). Grew up and educated in USA, has taught for over 25 years (after career as research scientist). Previously head of juniors St Mary's School, Cambridge; deputy head Fairstead House School, Newmarket; pastoral house master and head of junior science St Olave's School, York; all-boys' day and boarding school in Guernsey; Barlborough Hall School, Sheffield. Interests include travelling, cooking, reading and painting. Married to Barbara, HR professional; two daughters – one grown up and one at the school.

Likeable, approachable, voluble, very popular with girls and parents, lots of enthusiasm and energy ('He puts in the hours', 'nurturing' – parents) – interesting compound of Danish, American and British influences. Keen to develop confidence, independence, foundations of strong mental health, eg resilience and emotional intelligence – much reference to the theory of growth mindset, which puts focus on praising effort rather than ability, the value of risk taking and making mistakes; also – unusually – talks about staff welfare.

Academic matters: Junior school has no Sats tests – hurrah! – allowing integrated projects (South Pole topic involves making gloves for explorers) and much science practical work. Average class size ranges from 12 to 20. Copious use of ICT – individual Chromebooks from years 5 and 6 – but handwriting skills still seen as valuable. Specialist teachers for music, PE, modern foreign languages work across infant and junior school. Use of all senior school sports facilities, main hall for drama performances and new cookery rooms.

Children we met enjoy the wide ranging approach to subjects and being allowed to choose between tasks of three levels of challenge – 'mild, medium and spicy'; appreciative of helpful teachers who make lessons fun. Mild grumble from a parent about some supply teachers not being up to the standard of the regular teachers.

Snowdrops pre-school (co-ed 3-4 year olds): specialist teachers for music, drama, PE, modern foreign languages; use of infant school facilities. Girls continue to reception, boys to Birkdale pre-prep.

2018 A levels: 75 per cent A*-B, 52 per cent A*/A. Particularly successful and popular maths and sciences, also languages, history. Choice includes Latin, classical civilisation, geology and one year, real world, level 3 maths skills certificate. Flexible about number of subjects taken – individualised approach, with courses run for just one student; average class size eight (max 15). A very enterprising classical Greek A level student has developed a website for learning Latin and Greek up to GCSE.

GCSEs: 67 per cent A*-A/9-7 – very strong across the board; range includes economics, French, German, Spanish, Latin, food preparation and nutrition, with three more languages, music, geology and (unusually) level 2 extended project offered after school. Much tracking and monitoring of girls and extra support available. Many very experienced, longstanding teachers – several work for exam boards, eg as team leaders – who enable girls to 'exceed our hopes', according to a parent. Girls say they are very 'knowledgeable, helpful, approachable and likable'. However we were told about a high turnover of English teachers (one class has had three in one year) and one parent described the teaching in general as 'traditional rather than inspirational' (school feels this is unfair, 'as parents are not in the lessons' and that the girls would see it as inspirational).

Five form entry with 18-20 per class (max 25) years 7-11. Year 7s choose two from French, German and Spanish, continued at least until the end of year 9. All also begin Latin in year 8. Learn2learn study skills course, years 7-9, includes mindfulness. Much regional and national success in various academic competitions, including French, Spanish and translation bee, Latin, sciences and engineering.

High level integration of ICT in learning – individual Chromebooks for all from year 7; year 10s and beyond bring own device, but use of handwriting recognised too; developing online learning platform with variety of resources.

Covers unusually wide range of special needs ('fantastic support..nothing's too much trouble': parent) – impressive, very dedicated SENCo says they would take any level of difficulty, apart from non-communication autism, 'given the right training and support'; would re-timetable where possible for major physical disabilities, as some parts of the older buildings are hard to access. Checking for dyslexia where needed in junior school. Year 7s screened for dyslexia and dyscalculia. Aiming for CreSTeD status. Large, well trained team of part and full time teaching assistants provide individual support in and outside the classroom – outside for older girls to avoid their missing lesson time. Dysexic girls have been successful, eg at GCSE, scholarship to a boarding school, entry to medical school. Parents increasingly recognising learning support as strength of school.

Games, options, the arts: Sport is huge. Major investment in facilities upgrade: recently refurbished gym, fitness suite on the way, floodlit Astro. Quantities of local, regional and national individual and team successes in all trad sports, plus football, trampolining, equestrian events, cheerleading, race walking, along with inclusive approach to teams. All talents developed and girls performing at exceptionally high levels supported in a flexible way.

Masses of varied music to a high level ('phenomenal' – parent): performances in the community; hosts Sheffield music school's Saturday sessions throughout the year. Parents very happy with instrumental teaching. New drama studio; productions include The Real Inspector Hound, Charlotte (own version of Charlie) and the Chocolate Factory, Matilda. Some wonderful talent, going by the immensely enjoyable, lively and mischievous recent leavers' video. Glory won in performing Shakespeare, poetry reciting, debating and public speaking competitions. Excellent art in various media, on display all around the school. New cookery department (response to girls' request) – good to see girls learning how to make bread by hand; life at uni preparation lessons much appreciated by sixth formers. Arkwright engineering scholar (rare for girls) and technology awards. Year 7s busy with creative coding on BBC donated micro:bit computers.

More successes in business/economics, science and engineering comps, eg Lego Robotics; year 9s regional winners of Go4Set Engineering Challenge for last five years. STEM is very big – lots of activities, talks from experts, clubs and competitions.

S

Prolific DofE achievement amongst exceptionally wide range of extracurricular activities – we were glad to see a chillin' club included. Sixth form enrichment offers, eg, junior school mentoring, media and marketing, finance skills. All of the latter do at least 20 hours of voluntary work in the community a year, such as helping with programmes to raise attainment and aspiration in state primary pupils. Serious amounts raised for charities, abroad (schools in Zimbabwe and Bangladesh supported) and at home. Teaching and learning council allows girls to contribute ideas on, eg, reports, classroom layout, assessment. Art/music/sport/science expeditions to Peru, Canada, China, India, Iceland, USA, as well as Europe.

Juniors enjoy local, regional, national and international successes in athletics, orienteering, badminton; sports provision much improved in last year or so, says a parent, especially gymnastics. Inclusive approach to teams.

Much music, but a parent commented girls can have problems with catching up on work missed because of an instrumental lesson. Recent productions include The Wind in the Willows, The Tempest, Alice in Wonderland and Archibald's War. Excellent art in a range of media. Exceptionally lavish choice of extracurricular clubs and activities, including Mandarin, sign language, technology, kickboxing, yoga and African drumming. Residential trips for years 3 to 6.

Background and atmosphere: Situated in leafy Broomhill, close to Sheffield University and a big teaching hospital. Juniors in two converted houses plus attractive modern building, next to senior school, and now merged with nearby Ashdell Prep, whose site (containing specialist science, art and DT facilities) is now the infant school: co-ed pre-school plus reception to year 2. Good size classrooms with trad wooden desks in groups of four and first class displays; modern science lab; light, colourful, uncluttered and well resourced library with full time librarian, who also runs online library. Good amount of outdoor space for a city school – gardens, playgrounds (climbing wall), all weather netball court.

Senior school based around converted residential houses (hence some narrow, steep staircases to the top floor), plus pleasing modern buildings. Well-resourced library ('amazing' – sixth former) with full time librarian – and fish tank, as requested by girls. Separate sixth form house with attractively decorated common rooms. Plenty of outdoor space – gardens with wooden gazebos furnished with picnic tables; netball and tennis courts – but lack of indoor socialising spaces for years 7-10 (more included in ongoing upgrades).

Many standard leadership opportunities and all sixth form students who apply for a role are given one – all kinds of prefects, including special needs, digital, marketing, LGBT+; sports team captains changed termly. Younger years provide school council, teaching and learning council and eco reps – school council responsible for, eg, uniform changes, cookery provision, gym refurbishment, though not all issues raised are responded to, say girls. Pupils' and parents' opinions also sought via surveys and focus groups.

Excellent careers provision – full time advisor; major annual fairs (to which local state schools invited) – focus shifting now to arts and media, as STEM so well established; all year 11s pupils complete two weeks of work experience; access to GDST alumnae network of over 70k professional old girls, some of whom visit to give talks. Membership of the Trust is beneficial in other ways, such as access to finance, various kinds of expertise and educational initiatives.

Girls we met credited teachers with not putting pressure on them to always get top grades – 'They aren't cross if you do badly in a test – they'll show you how to improve, but they will encourage you to aim higher if they feel you could'; 'The school isn't an aggessively competitive place', rather, 'The high standards set by others are motivating'. This is not to say pressure is absent, though – girls are aware they put pressure on themselves, as they are aiming for top universities and know their parents are paying a lot for their education.

Very wide choice of food, ranging from dishes one would find on the menu of an upmarket restaurant, such as pannacotta and arriabatta, to bubble and squeak and spotted dick, plus daily sandwiches, salad bar and baked potatoes. Not everyone happy with the hot food, however, which can be inconsistent, but we were given a very tasty and elegant (cold) lunch, and a dad says he loves the breakfasts, available for adults and girls from 7.30am. Sixth formers allowed to go out during the lunch break and can wear own clothes – 'smart casual'.

Pastoral care, well-being and discipline: Usual structure of form tutors, heads of year, pastoral head, deputy head, nurse plus counsellor (the latter called 'fantastic' by a parent and 'lovely' by a girl), who is available three days a week. School very aware of likely mental health issues and works hard to provide support and education, eg evenings for parents on e-safety and other teenage problems, anti-bullying week (bullying dealt with quickly and well, testified parents), happiness survey.

However from the mixed feedback we received, ranging from 'very good' to feeling 'completely failed', it seems that while the system as a whole works well mostly, some parts of the team can be less supportive and available at times than others. Girls say they feel well known as individuals by their teachers, who will notice if they seem to have problems, and gain support from their friends. Annual well-being week for students and staff offers bread therapy, rowing challenge, samba and yoga, plus quantities of smoothies and cake. Sixth formers mentor in infant and junior school.

Classroom discipline based on mutual respect between girls and teachers, but one parent feelt the school can be too heavy-handed with 'mild liveliness'.

Junior school parents speak well of the pastoral care (counsellor available three days a week); the quality of communication (quick response to issues raised); easy transition to senior school resulting from amount of contact junior girls have with it; the way the school builds up girls' confidence ('very empowering'), but uniform shop hours are too limited for working parents and packed lunches for trips poor. Their views are sought at regular forums.

Pupils and parents: Pupils from all areas of South Yorkshire, Derbyshire and North Nottinghamshire; diverse social, ethnic and financial backgrounds – mainly professional/self employed. Girls we met were open, articulate and mature in outlook, appreciative of the wealth of opportunities on offer and the generosity and calibre of their teachers. 'They have a very welcoming and supportive attitude towards special needs girls,' said SENCo. 'Confident but not over-confident,' said a parent.

Old girls include novelists Margaret Drabble and A S Byatt; Louise Haigh (Labour MP).

The junior school children we met were very self-possessed and articulate, appreciative of their teachers and the wide choice of extracurricular opportunities.

Entrance: At 4+: looking for potential to learn via short assessments – maths, language, social, physical and creative skills. At 6+: entrance test in maths and English plus school reference. At 11+: English and maths tests plus report from present school. At 12+: cognitive ability test (numeracy, verbal and non verbal), school references and taster day.

Sixth form: seven GCSEs at 5 and above and 6+ in proposed A level subjects, plus reference from present school and taster day. Around 25 new students each year, some from local state schools and around five international students.

Exit: Almost all junior girls to senior school – entrance exam used to assess abilities, not to select (apart from academic scholarship awards) – day kept low key by teachers so girls don't feel under pressure: they mainly remember the cookies and pizza they have afterwards. Several win scholarships to senior school.

Some 25-30 per cent transfer post-16 to a range of state, independent or boarding schools, or further education college for vocational courses. Broad range of universities and and universities. Newcastle, Leeds and Sheffield and Sheffield Hallam popular; notable strengths in science, medicine, dentistry, psychology. Three to Oxbridge and eight medics in 2018.

Money matters: Year 7: academic, music, performing arts and sports scholarships for small amounts; means tested bursaries from 30-100 per cent of fees (20 per cent have one).

Sixth form: general academic (5-25 per cent of fees) and wide range of subject scholarships (£100 to £500 per year) plus music (free tuition on one instrument or voice), drama, art and PE/sport; six full, means-tested scholarships funded by HSBC, reserved for state school students.

Scholarships can be combined with bursaries.

Remarks: Many girls here reach outstanding standards in a wide range of spheres, as testified by the cabinet bursting with silver trophies and noticeboard crammed with newspaper cuttings that greet the visitor on arrival. This is partly a result of the success of the school in fostering individual talents and partly of the near monopoly position it enjoys with regard to the provision of independent girls' education in Sheffield, having absorbed two local schools that have closed and merged with one – there is now only one other independent school offering 11-16 co-education and a boys' school with a co-ed sixth form. It has become increasingly outward looking over the years and the wide development of STEM opportunities is notable. The improved special needs provision and broader focus on well-being should do much to release it from its old academic hothouse reputation.

Skipton Girls' High School

86

Gargrave Road, Skipton, North Yorkshire BD23 1QL

Ages 11–18 **Pupils** 893 **Sixth form** 245

01756 707600
www.sghs.org.uk

Executive Headteacher: Since 2013, Jennifer (Jenn) Plews BA PGCE. Mrs Plews became the CEO of the Northern Star Academies Trust (NSAT) in September 2017 and remains the executive headteacher of Skipton Girls' High School, Northern Lights Teaching School Alliance and SCITT (School Centred Initial Teacher Training).

Studied fine art at Liverpool, moving to Bath for PGCE, followed by extensive experience in comprehensive education in both rural and inner city schools, including secondary senior leader roles and the post of secondary national strategy manager and school improvement officer for teacher development for an LA.

Has 'a strong belief that with great teaching all disadvantages can be overcome'. Passionate that since children and young people only get 'one chance at education', making it count relies on 'teachers and associate staff to have a relentlessly positive outlook and a never-give-up attitude', and leaders to nurture a culture of trust and well-being. By all accounts she leads by example.

The new head of academy since April 2019 is Mark Turner, previously deputy head at a school in Bristol facing challenging circumstances.

Academic matters: Ranked second state school in Yorkshire by the Sunday Times Parent Power in 2018. Judged outstanding by Ofsted in last inspection.

In 2018, 41 per cent of A level entries graded A*-A. Classes sizes vary, usually 15-20 – popular mathematics up to 25, considered detrimental by some pupils. Mathematics, sciences, English literature, humanities, psychology, applied business all popular; options include DT design engineering; PE taken at nearby Ermysted's Grammar School for boys, with reciprocal arrangement here in subjects like art, politics, economics and psychology. Support given for Arkwright engineering scholarship applications – currently two successful scholars.

Together with academic subjects there is Xtra enrichment with EPQ or further mathematics compulsory and one of three elective pathways: community (volunteering, key stage 3 literacy, numeracy or language leader); skills (DofE, Young Enterprise etc); vocational work experience. All do peer mentoring training, with the majority providing academic mentoring for younger students or organising activities for them. Work experience/shadowing encouraged – modern language students can go to Germany or France. Annual higher education day attended by university admissions tutors and there are university taster courses offered.

Consistently impressive results at key stage 4 continued in 2018, with 89 per cent getting 5+ in both maths and English and 50 per cent of grades A*-A/9-7. Key stage 4 starts in year 9 with option choice of modern foreign language, engineering or food and nutrition. All take GCSE RE; option choices includes business and photography. Performance tables show very good value added.

Thorough monitoring and tracking. Lots of differentiation in lessons and choice of learning approaches; teachers seen as very helpful. Computing room, with 3D printer, although every girl has a laptop purchased through a three year lease scheme. All staff agreed it enables integration of IT with learning, access to the virtual learning environment in and out of class – though perhaps not consistently across departments, as the pace of technology sometimes outstrips some teachers' speed of learning.

Innovative research into new ways of teaching and learning, most recently a project into memory and learning led by a team of key staff and rolled out across each department. As a result there is an increased awareness amongst the girls about how they learn and consequent positive impact on their independent study time.

Assistant head leads inclusion, equality and diversity and the much lauded (rightly so) and dedicated Student Progress team. Whilst numbers are relatively small, she and the team are confident that they can handle full range of special educational needs and will offer whatever support needed, even if no EHC plan, including one-to-one in class. She matches her variously qualified assistants to individual students to enhance relationships. All CAT assessed on entry, highlighted children screened for dyslexia and all children identified with SEN needs have personalised curriculum pathways.

S

Games, options, the arts: The school's restricted campus means that most sports take place off site at a nearby sports centre, excellent facilities albeit a short bus ride away. In a lesson the girls fit in two changes of clothes, two bus journeys and some sporting activity. On site there is a well-used small gym, mini fitness suite and a couple of leafy netball/tennis courts.

However, sport compulsory until year 11 and teams fielded for netball, cross-country, football, rugby, rounders, athletics, dance and swimming. Sixth form encouraged to take part though sports optional – netball, cross-country, athletics and dance teams. Uses partnerships with local sporting clubs such as Skipton Rugby Club to provide extra curricular sessions and coaching. Recent successes as winners of year 9 Bradford schools' netball tournament, national finals for cross-country and representation at county level football.

One sports and one performance lesson per week include fitness, kangoo, dance, cheerleading, rhymthmic gym and yoga (depending on the year group); sports leaders level 2 qualification offered in year 10.

Music flourishes – eight per cent taught instruments in school, more out of school, up to diploma standard. Various ensembles for voice and instruments; junior, senior and chamber choirs; string, wind and ukelele groups, orchestra and jazz band, two latter joint with boys' grammar, Ermysted's. Teatime concerts termly and a winter music showcase often combined with dance.

Drama performed in traditional school hall or Judi Dench studio, which is also used for modern dance. Every two years musical productions alternate with straight drama productions, in conjunction with Ermystead's boys on stage or providing orchestral support. Dance group comprising girls in KS3 and 4 take part in annual Yorkshire Schools Festival.

Good size art rooms with excellent work on display, here and around school – loved the year 8 portrait gallery, though more could be used to brighten up the original building.

Some girls told us that they feel that the arts do not receive the same recognition as STEM subjects here, and using the last year's newsletters as a barometer we would agree. They therefore welcome the newly introduced Trinity College London Push for Art awards, level 2 being the equivalent of a GCSE.

Won the UK wide 2017 Enthuse Award STEM Secondary School of the Year and offers outstanding engineering opportunities for pupils as well as working with local schools to promote it. Strong links with industry, eg Arris, Rolls Royce etc and opportunities to work with local companies opening minds to apprenticeships as a career pathway.

Girls talk enthusiastically about the range and number of clubs and activities. This Girl Can involves Thai kickboxing and high intensity training; anime promotes discussion on selected foreign short animated films and Lego club members are the first regional Lego league winners. Extended day 8.00am-5.00pm – breakfast club, after-school support and enrichment. Euro4science project provides exchange trips to Portugal and Bulgaria, with links to Poland. Language exchange with Germany and post-exam summer activities range from water sports in Spain, art and history in the Netherlands to politics and culture in Washington DC.

Background and atmosphere: Opened in 1886 as a girls' endowed school on the same site, offering boarding and 'an education equal to the boys' grammar school'. Since 2011 a founding member of the Northern Star Multi-Academy Trust with three co-educational Harrogate schools: Harrogate High, Hookstone Chase and New Park Primary Academy.

Founded Northern Lights Teaching School Alliance; their headquarters are opposite the main school site. In 2012 Skipton formed an alliance with Feversham College, a specialist science, Islamic girls' comprehensive school in Bradford, now there are partner schools at primary and secondary level throughout west and north Yorkshire. In 2014, it established a SCITT (School Centred Initial Teacher Training).

Flanking a wide avenue in residential outskirts of Skipton, downhill from expansive Craven College campus with Ermysted's boys grammar nearby. Main school shoehorned on compact site with sixth form centre and teaching alliance administration in stone villas on opposite side of the road.

Front facing array of mainly traditional sandstone buildings conceal a melée of old buildings and chocolate coloured Portakabins down in the hollow, euphemistically called 'chalets,' which the girls are quick to defend as 'just like any other classroom when you are inside'. Sixth form study space in the cottage not used 'because of the mould,' we were told, some drab and poky walls and staircases, needing tlc; an unsightly kitchen roof in direct line of sight as you move between buildings, all smack of cutbacks in maintenance – but the girls like the quirkiness and sense of history.

The jewel in the crown is the STEM building, £1.8m of investment, modelled on Bradford University science facilities with truly flexible space provided by with fully mobile equipment for practical work. A professional and excellent learning environment backed up by additional traditional laboratories in an adjacent building.

School hall (and stage) reinvents itself for every use, including being the daily dining room; not large enough to house everyone at one time, so there are no whole school assemblies. Small porch and compact grassy area with picnic benches for those with packed lunches when the weather allows and although the grounds are small the eco committee and student body are developing a 'food to fork strategy' by growing food around the site. In a wooded hollow there's a couple of tennis/netball courts, though with limited autumn use due to falling leaves. In Westbank, the sixth form centre in an Edwardian villa with IT room, bistro and relaxation area with bar stools, it felt cramped and overcrowded to us on a rainy lunch time – but the sixth formers seemed unaware and quite comfortable.

There is a busy but calm and friendly atmosphere. There was a rousing chorus of happy birthday over lunch, led by one table but almost all the diners joined in – a traditional and almost daily occurrence, it would seem. Cross-year friendships are not uncommon, not difficult perhaps in this relatively small school, but definitely helped by the number and range of co-curricular activities and the vertical tutor groups and house system.

Girls we met were articulate, confident and happy to express their views. They felt well supported by their teachers and are encouraged to aim high, whilst not in competition with each other; are confident that their teachers know them well; and can judge how much pressure to achieve is appropriate for them individually; all spoke highly of the pastoral system with the non-teaching student progress team at its heart.

Uniform navy with striped shirts, skirts of differing lengths – par for the course; black shoes or ankle boots, types clearly designated for parents; rules on makeup, jewellery, piercings and hair colour all enforced. Sixth formers wear business dress; some interesting interpretations, but on the whole acceptable in today's relaxed office dress code. It's over to the girls for decisions on their appearance, including piercings – these are clever and intelligent girls who are well aware of image judgements, but rules are enforced if they step too far out of line.

Pastoral care, well-being and discipline: Vertical tutor group system throughout school, each with about 24 pupils – three or so from each of years 7-11, plus a similar number from years 12-13, who mentor younger girls and enable tutors to concentrate on individuals. Tutor groups meet for 30 minutes every day and, where possible, keep the same tutor throughout their school career – invaluable when it comes to UCAS references. This produces a supportive atmosphere, friendships across year groups, easier transition for new year 7s and 12s – 'people were so welcoming' and ' I settled in so easily' were frequent comments. Some older girls were less enthusiastic about the system, which they felt was of greater benefit to the younger girls, and that cohesion depended heavily on the calibre and personality of the tutor.

The student executive, with members across the age range, discusses school improvements. The head girl team, comprising head and three deputies, spearhead the leadership opportunities in the sixth form. A thriving house system led by captains encompasses as many aspects of school life as possible, including curricular and extracurricular events, and fundraising and competitions.

School works with Carnegie Centre of Excellence for Mental Health in Schools, whose recent audit underpins the staff CPD programme. Compass works with individual pupils, shadowed by a member of staff, and the school promotes the maxim 'that girls need to keep mentally fit as they do physically fit.' Never missing an opportunity for a good role model, the houses are named after inspiring women – Bronte, Curie, Johnson and Franklin.

The much-used student progress centre provides academic and careers advice plus Relate counselling and access to other external health agencies. Held in high esteem by pupils and parents alike, 'they are always there with an open door and you can talk to them about anything,' sentiments echoed by several girls. A very clearly set out behaviour policy but, as you might expect, discipline is personalised rather than rule-bound.

Pupils and parents: Pupils come from a range of backgrounds and cultures and those we met all spoke of the ease with which they had settled into school and made friendships. Parents are happy with the two-way e-communication with staff and feel well informed on their daughters' academic progress and well-being. There is a supportive friends' association raising money for the school hardship fund through a monthly subscription prize draw and a host of family events.

Notable old girls include Ruzwana Bashir, who chaired the Oxford Union, and National Youth Orchestra composer Izzy Wood.

Entrance: There is a designated priority area for admissions though about a quarter of intake are from outside this area. Sixty-three feeder primaries in Skipton, rural North Yorkshire and south as far as Keighley; an increasing intake from this area. As an academy the school is its own admission authority, adhering to the national code. For entry at 11 girls take externally set tests in mathematics, English and verbal reasoning in September of year 6 (116 places most years, though in the current year 7 there are 144). Being 'deemed suitable' does not guarantee a place, which are awarded according to hierarchical admissions criteria.

For spare places are available in years 8 to 11, applicants take school's English, mathematics and science tests. For entry to sixth form, girls need five GCSEs at grades 9-4 including English and mathematics, with at least a grade 6 in chosen A level subjects. Maximum of 20 external applicants into sixth form, plus replacements for year 11 leavers.

Exit: Around 20 per cent leave post-GCSE, often to specialise in sport or art at FE colleges or to take up music scholarships at local independents. At 18, almost all to university, apprenticeships or structured gap year. Most popular subjects include engineering, English, psychology, medicine, mathematics and business.

Remarks: A high performing school in the upper echelons of school league tables nationally with STEM subjects at the forefront. An excellent co-curricular programme and international links provide girls with wonderful opportunities out of the classroom. Whilst growing numbers are putting more pressure on the compact site and on some tired accommodation and facilities, innovative teaching and learning and focus on improved well-being should ensure these misses will explode the myths about women being able to reach the top of their professions.

Stonyhurst College

Linked with St Mary's Hall

Stonyhurst, Clitheroe, Lancashire BB7 9PZ

Ages 13–18 **Pupils** 458 **Sixth form** 209 **Boarders** 310 **RC**

Fees: Day £19,950; Boarding £36,300 pa

01254 827073
www.stonyhurst.ac.uk

Headmaster: Since 2016, John Browne, BA (Bristol, music), LLB, MBA (40s), previously head of St Aloysius' College, Glasgow. Says it was a blend of accident and design that led him to teaching: as organ scholar at Westminster Cathedral, he 'fell' into the choir school by accident, later diverting to law and then an MBA because 'teachers need to think strategically too'. Taught by Jesuits at St Ignatius College, it was the Jesuit chaplain of Westminster Cathedral Choir School who first asked John, 'when are you going to be a teacher?' This was not to be for another two years as he completed his LLB, but as the City beckoned so did music, and instead he took up his first post as assistant director of music at The Latymer School, returning to the Westminster Cathedral Choir School as the youngest headmaster (then aged 32). From there to Ampleforth as deputy head, then to Glasgow and now Stonyhurst.

Strategic thinking very much in evidence both internally – he has made changes to Stonyhurst's leadership infrastructure – and globally: Stonyhurst is opening a school in Malaysia in 2020. He has appointed five new assistant heads to be responsible for pulling pastoral and academic together in each year group (and who follow pupils through the school), so each pupil is viewed holistically. One parent (a big fan) told us that when he started, head asked a retired Independent Schools' Inspector to review Stonyhurst afresh and held open consultations with staff and parents. An MBA style approach, perhaps, and one senses that continuous improvements will be a defining characteristic of his leadership. Stays on the pulse of the school by meeting five students per week for lunch, which he describes as his 'five-a-day'. They 'help him see what needs to be different.'

He is a big believer in punctuating school life with unforgettable moments (for him, it was going to the Royal Albert Hall to perform every year). He feels the opportunities Stonyhurst offers, trips to the Vatican for example, are crucial. They light the spark. 'If you find a child's passion, the rest falls into place.' This fits neatly with the overall ethos of the school, its motto, 'Quant je puis' (What is the most I can achieve with what I have?) is a dominant backbeat. 'What can I do to change the world?' is what the head wants his students to ask themselves. The spiritual thinking which underpins this philosophy is clear, but he is keen to stress that while worship is part of the school's makeup (60 per cent of pupils are from Catholic families), as a Jesuit school it is very much outward looking.

S

There was no better testament to his effectiveness than the two boys who were selected at random to show us part of the school. (The selection was so random, in fact, that with the desperate air of an adolescent Just William, one of the boys was furtively and desperately trying to smarten himself up, tucking in his slightly bedraggled shirt as we went along.) 'The head sorts everything out', one said, with a knowing nod to the evening academic clinics, designed to help students with work problems. 'Oh, they've always been there', the other pointed out. 'Yes, but they actually work now, they're good, they're longer', his friend asserted. The pair exuded colossal pride in the school, able to reel off its heritage with enthusiasm you just can't fake.

The head's recreation is walking his dogs in the Ribble valley and spending time with his wife (Marie, a company director) and son. We left him on the day of our visit pondering which object he should take from the vast Stonyhurst collection of treasures to illustrate a talk he was due to give that evening. He 'loves objects which tell a story'. He refers to the writers who have passed through (Conan Doyle was a boy here, Tolkien a resident whilst his son was an English master, the poet Gerard Manley Hopkins taught here). Apparently Tolkien's middle earth was meant to be close to the River Hodder. He wants to bring everything all together, connect the past and present.

Academic matters: Broad curriculum allows students to follow their interests. Psychology A level recently introduced. Languages are strong; around 75 per cent take two languages at GCSE, 14 per cent at A level. The IB is predominantly taken by international students, but popularity is steadily increasing. At GCSE in 2018, 45 per cent A*-A/9-7 grades; 42 per cent A*/A, 71 per cent A*-B at A level. IB average was 34. Fairly mixed ability intake (school accepts all siblings) makes results all the more impressive. Small class sizes, 20 max.

The head is enthusiastic about how IB educates the whole person. The IB's CAS components – where students design their own projects around the creativity, activity and 'service to others' modules – are now applied to the whole school. School is also rolling out the IB careers programme.

Academically, each child is tracked and results analysed for patterns. If they are a bit below their target, why? The whole person is looked at, all knowledge, both academic and pastoral, pooled to provide answers (back to those new assistant head roles). For those needing extra help, there's learning support in the form of bespoke programmes, including use of mentors and educational psychologists. Parents say some of the teachers are truly inspirational.

If pupils feel they need to brush up on an aspect of the curriculum, the evening subject drop in clinics do the trick. Or as the head puts it, if the target grades are down, then a clinic 'becomes a priority'. Back to the motto again – all that I can: the benchmark is set high for all students and they are encouraged to aspire.

A unique aspect of teaching at the school is its integration with the Stonyhurst collections (started in 1609). Artefacts from these extraordinary collections are deployed to bring the curriculum to life. We actually got to touch Shakespeare's First Folio and saw Mary Queen of Scots' Book of Hours. History lessons must be much enlivened by articles such as Sir Thomas More's hats and the gunpowder plot vestments. Art lessons can draw on original works by Turner and Rubens. These and other remarkable items are currently being curated into a small museum ('The story of the collections and English Catholicism'). The school's heritage is very much part of the learning experience in the here and now; even the observatory in the grounds is put to full use and ties up with head's desire to bring together past and present.

Games, options, the arts: Impressive array of sports facilities: tennis dome, squash courts, golf course, shooting range, swimming pool, heaps of sports pitches. Dazzling successes in boys' and girls' sport (rugby team won the Lancashire Cup and the girls had just returned from a netball tour to Dubai). CCF compulsory for the first two years and most continue thereafter. DofE strong.

Art is nurtured here; there is an artist in residence and head would like to extend similar hospitality to a poet. Music runs the gamut with big choirs, big bands, orchestras, ensembles. There are headmaster's concerts as well as weekly performances. Dance is on offer in all its genres – street, tap, modern, zumba – with some nicely ambitious productions to showcase those skills (Moulin Rouge and Wicked). The Stonyhurst dancers recently got to spend time with the Birmingham Royal ballet (doubtless one of those unforgettable experiences so valued by the head).

There is a good drama space with professional sound and lighting and a chain of performances from the ubiquitous Les Mis, to Fiddler on the Roof and Hedda Gabler. A wonderful Much Ado, condensed into 45 minutes, was performed in a modern style with a Christmas morning setting. Students pitch in from backstage too, with lighting and costumes.

Clubs include politics, philosophy, robotics, astronomy, economics. Impressive range of speakers, recently Professor Robert Winston, historian Lord Hennessy, plus academics and politicians (we imagine Jacob Rees Mogg was thought-provoking at the very least).

Steady stream of big canvas events, like a fashion show with African couture, a literary festival (biannual) and all the usual balls. Trips include South Africa, China and closer to home: museums (Louvre!), Houses of Parliament and top universities. Interline (house) competitions in everything from tennis, maths, croquet to poetry reading.

Boarding: Most of the boarders are full time so lots of cinema trips and outings to York and Manchester. Boarding houses are called playrooms. Each pupil has a tutor (and an online pastoral log) who meets them in small groups every week. The new assistant heads preside over this process to ensure everything is joined up.

Boarders start off sharing five to a room; single rooms for older pupils. Rooms are fairly trad, many have magnificent views over the grounds. 'Every morning it looks different', one pupil said. Boys' and girls' rooms differ only in that the girls have made theirs cosier. Showers and loos not palatial but in good order.

Girls' boarding area has rooms clustered around a central glass office with staff on duty – very reassuring, we thought. Sitting room looked comfortable and there was a well-equipped, homely kitchen with washing machines. Day pupils also have a desk in the boarding areas.

Background and atmosphere: Founded in 1593 in France, the school moved to its present site in the beautiful Ribble valley in 1794. The building and its grounds, with their formal waterways, have a stately grandeur that certainly inspired former pupil, Sir Arthur Conan Doyle – the description of Baskerville Hall is based on Stonyhurst.

The library in main use has a very grown up feeling, but the other ancient historical libraries are something else. The fact that students have seminars in these rooms must set the tone for high achievement. Wonderful college chapel, St Peter's, lends a Brideshead grandeur.

Multi-million pound restoration developments are the norm here. Like any great estate, its treasures need to be maintained and extensive projects are ongoing to give its ailing beauties, such as the canals and the baroque gardens, some TLC.

There can be no radical modernisation in a listed building and it is all the better for it. True, the school's 'slightly worn in places' interior vibe prevails – indeed, approach it with the wrong mindset and certain corridors might seem a little gloomy. Nevertheless, classrooms are cheery, there are decent science labs, dance and drama studios, and don't forget all those incredible sports facilities.

Plenty of wall displays, not dominant or dazzling but interesting; we commented on some pictures of famous scientists to a couple of pupils. Shame so few women scientists, we thought, looking at all the men displayed. 'What's the name of the woman who was part of the team who discovered DNA? She should be up there,' we say, racking our addled brains for her name. 'Oh, you mean Rosalind Franklin', came the reply, barely missing a beat. (Yep, we think to ourselves, impressed, that's the one.)

Pastoral care, well-being and discipline: The playrooms at break times certainly seem friendly places, a mad throng of chat. Parents enthused about the seamless blend of day and boarding and liked a recent initiative to invite day pupils to spend three nights in the school for free.

On site health centre. Lots of school talks and workshops for students on walking tall, building resilience and looking at the nuances of behaviour; how you can subtly exclude someone and the impact that can have. Head of pastoral/boarding said the girls will flag up concerns about others and it's a very supportive environment. The real aim is to give students the skills to deal with issues themselves. Mild concerns were expressed in this area by one or two parents who suggested perhaps students needed 'a bit extra' pastorally; others thought the same for the academic side of things (some pupils need extra cosseting, some need pushing).

The spiritual runs through the school, mass is celebrated each week and each playroom goes on an annual retreat. Yet although many parents say the school lives the Jesuit ethos, some felt its Catholic values should be celebrated more and 'shouted about'. We imagine it's a delicate balance for the school between inclusivity and celebration.

Pupils and parents: Pupils mainly come from the north of England and London (families looking for something less pushy). Good mix of international boarders; recent increase in European pupils who come for the IB.

Overseas parents are emailed frequently, relaying what their children are going to be studying and details of their performance. Parents in the UK described the comms as superb, saying you heard back from a teacher within a couple of hours of emailing. The chain of connection goes on well beyond leaving Stonyhurst; many parents are themselves former pupils. The head sees all ex-pupils as ambassadors for the school.

The pupils we spoke to seemed a down to earth and diverse bunch. The head refers to the first hockey team, 'the cool kids', lobbying him to help with the refugee crisis. He was keen to impress the importance of the real commitment on them (helping is not a whim). The end result was the head of the Jesuit refugee service came to give a talk and the village is now looking to host a Syrian refugee family.

Entrance: One third of students come from school's prep, Saint Mary Hall. Entrance exam plus reports and reference for candidates at 11+, 13+ and 16+. Overseas students are assessed for English level to check that they will be able to tackle the subjects with ease.

S

Exit: Leavers go on to study a broad spread of subjects at universities all over the UK. York, Manchester, Bristol, Exeter and Newcastle currently popular. Two medics in 2018. Popular subjects seem to be management/ business studies.

Money matters: Boarding fees in line with similar schools. Scholarships (music, sport, academic and all-rounder) and means-tested bursaries up to value of £3 million annually.

Remarks: An outward looking and inclusive Catholic boarding school where students are encouraged to become their best selves, give back to the world and aspire to great heights academically.

Teesside High School

The Avenue, Eaglescliffe, Stockton-on-Tees TS16 9AT

Ages 3–18 **Pupils** 350 **Sixth form** 50

Fees: £3,600 – £12,915 pa

01642 782095
www.teessidehigh.co.uk

Head teacher: Since 2018, Kirsty Mackenzie, previously deputy and then acting head. Physics degree from Leeds and PGCE from Durham; worked in a local secondary school for many years before joining Teesside High in 2005 as head of physics. She is married to Dave, has two children and a variety of pets. In her spare time she enjoys reading fiction and is a keen film buff.

Head of prep: Since 2013, Mrs Carolyn Williams. BEd in maths and science from Northumbria, postgrad certificate in leadership and management from Durham. Formerly senior teacher at Yarm, teaches maths; two daughters, one in prep and one in seniors; enjoys country walks with husband, children and dog and is learning to play golf. Parents are impressed by 'changes for the better', firm in their belief that everyone here 'has the children's best interests at heart'.

Academic matters: Little Diamonds nursery takes children from 3; flexible sessions allowed, most moving to full-time as they approach reception age. Wraparound care from 7.45am-6pm suits the needs of busy parents, as do the holiday clubs. French is taught from reception and learning takes places indoors and out, with full use being made of the lovely woodland school in the grounds.

Has just introduced International Primary Curriculum, which teaches a range of different subjects through topics. All mixed ability classes except maths in years 5 and 6; all children have opportunities to use iPads; group music lessons where everyone gets a chance to learn different instruments and play in ensembles.

In 2018, 52 per cent of GCSE grades were A*/A or 7-9. At A level, 64 per cent A*-B and 44 per cent A*/A. Traditional academic curriculum. Option of three separate sciences at GCSE or dual award science course. All key stage 3 pupils study separate sciences, geography, history, RE, music, food and nutrition, art and IT. Most pupils also study three languages, French, German and Latin, but Spanish is also available as an extra.

Free access to IT suite during school hours and each pupil has own email address at school. Staff using iPads to enrich and challenge – homework may occasionally come straight to mobiles via an app. And just to show that they are covering both the ancient and modern here, gifted and talented pupils enjoy ancient Greek in readiness for performing a Greek tragedy in the school grounds.

Small classes (average 15), some very small in sixth form. Experienced staff – over half have 10 or more years' experience with the school. Very low turnover. Pupils are set for most subjects.

Homework ranges from 90 minutes a night for 11-year-olds to three hours a night for sixth form. Pupils get a report of some kind every term, with a full report sent out at end of year. Special needs co-ordinator – support for dyslexia and dyspraxia.

T

Games, options, the arts: Sport is compulsory for all – several county standard players and a silver equestrian medal for a former pupil at London 2012. Sports include athletics, tennis, football, hockey, rugby, badminton, cricket and canoeing. Superb fitness suite for those less inclined to team sports.

All take part in wide range of activities – including origami, golf, bridge and many more besides. These are sensibly accommodated in an extra long lunchtime break, which allows pupils to eat and enjoy enrichment activities too. All-weather sports pitch and sports hall used throughout the day for teaching and at lunchtime for extra activities. Most year 10 pupils take D of E awards.

Well-equipped music rooms with plenty of keyboards, instruments and computers for budding composers and a new drama and dance studio. Many play a musical instrument and there is a choir, orchestra and jazz band. Large number take speech and drama awards. Art is very popular, paintings and sculpture on show everywhere. House competitions fiercely fought in a wide range of disciplines, including singing, sport, photography and Masterchef.

Background and atmosphere: Teesside High was founded as a girls' school in 1970 when Queen Victoria High School and Cleveland School amalgamated. School is now fully co-educational. Slightly more girls than boys – 60/40 – but no one seems to mind and therefore it doesn't seem to matter. We met plenty of bright, articulate boys able to hold their own and not looking or feeling like a minority. Plenty of success in boys' sports underpins this.

Set in 19 acres bordering the River Tees, with stunning views of the Cleveland Hills and a stone's throw from the delightfully tempting shops and coffee emporiums of picturesque Yarm. School is hidden from sight, tucked away down The Avenue, an approach road bordered by private houses and a retirement home. Main buildings sit neatly in well-kept grounds. Brightly coloured picket fence surrounds the prep school. Lovely grounds, with river frontage, large pond and newly created woodland school used for outdoor teaching in wide range of 'low-risk' activities for pupils of all ages. Recently unearthed air raid bunker in the grounds is being refurbished to bring history lessons to life.

Classrooms and corridors have an air of calm, unusually clean and tidy, lots of good work on display. Food is 'better than good', say pupils. Dining room operates on a cafeteria system, with bright blue tables and murals painted by pupils and choice of hot and cold meals. Halal food on menu and even though this is a day school breakfast and tea are available too. Sixth formers have their own car park and a new sixth form building, which includes teaching rooms, private study areas, common room and conference facilities.

Attractive glass atrium on entry to prep school and lovely work displayed everywhere; this is a busy and productive place. Outside there's a new all-weather playground and pirate ship, Astroturf, space hoppers, Kwik cricket and toys-a-plenty plus separate play area for the youngest. According to the children, 'there's everything you need here to grow up'. Wise heads on young shoulders maybe, yet genuinely proud of their school. Well-equipped music ('we love our singing,' say the children) and ICT rooms; spacious hall used for assemblies and PE for the youngest. Small room for SEN, officially titled Inspirational Learning Zone, but nicknamed The Tardis by the children because apparently, like Dr Who, 'you come out feeling better than when you went in'.

One parent described the teaching staff as Mary Poppins-like: 'an air of authority as necessary but no shouting needed' and new, sometimes shy children are calmly and warmly welcomed into classes. Those classes are small, a factor that has huge appeal and proves the biggest draw for local parents. Now fully co-educational.

Pastoral care, well-being and discipline: The school prides itself on being 'a community in which everyone is treated with respect and understanding and where all talents and gifts are nurtured and valued.' Form tutors play key role in guiding pupils. School is multi-faith and there is a small prayer room.

School sets store by community projects – Christmas parties for OAPs, charity quizzes and visits to local hospice. Dialogue and discussion are strongly encouraged. Head pupil and deputy head pupil run school council – each year group has three reps and recent innovations include chilled water supply and napkins in dining room. Buddy system introduced to encourage older pupils to befriend and help younger pupils. Open forum for parents to raise issues once a term. Behaviour is good – no vandalism, graffiti or discipline problems, says head, just occasional high spirits in corridors. School has introduced extended day to help working parents – now open from 7.45am till 6pm. Also runs popular holiday clubs for 3 to 13-year-olds during school holidays.

Pupils and parents: We met confident, considered, articulate children, happy to chat and excited by their school. They appear sincere and determined in their approach to sport and studies alike, keen to win and do well. Parents equally excited and committed – they've done their homework before choosing the school (plenty of options locally), felt warmly welcomed here and their children settled in quickly.

Parents are mostly medics, accountants, lawyers and local businesspeople. Lots of first-time buyers, though a scattering of alumni offspring too. A small number of overseas pupils live with local families. We spoke to several parents who had moved their children from the maintained sector and were 'delighted' at their children's 'increased levels of interest and achievement'. Parents spoke about the very positive care given to children and the 'individualised' education, enthusing that 'there is so much to offer beyond the curriculum'.

Pupils travel in by bus (organised in-house) from 25-mile radius, from as far afield as south Durham and north Yorkshire. Former pupils include broadcasters Shiulie Ghosh (formerly of ITV News) and Pam Royle (Tyne Tees and Border TV).

Entrance: To prep by taster days, assessment and talk with head. At 11, all pupils (including those from the prep) sit verbal reasoning paper and emotional intelligence questionnaire. Two-thirds entering senior school come from prep, a third from primary schools. Pupils entering sixth form need at least six GCSE passes (preferably grade B and above).

Exit: Sensibly, most prep pupils follow the natural progression into the senior school unless the family moves elsewhere. Around half leave after GCSEs. Almost all sixth form leavers go to university; Liverpool, Newcastle, Northumbria, Manchester, Sheffield, St Andrews, Teesside and York St John popular. One to Cambridge and one to study medicine in 2018.

Money matters: School offers means-tested bursaries each year on a first come, first served basis. Scholarships and exhibitions available for academic ability, music (and sport in sixth form and prep).

Remarks: 'Everything is possible' is the school motto and the school certainly feels that way. Staff and pupils at this unpretentious, hardworking school exude a very special charm with a refreshing lack of arrogance.

Westbourne School

60 Westbourne Road, Sheffield, South Yorkshire S10 2QT

Ages 11–16 **Pupils** 360

Fees: £8,925 – £12,750 pa

01142 660374
www.westbourneschool.co.uk

Headmaster: Since 2004, John Hicks MEd (50s). Overall head of the senior and junior schools, he studied maths and sports and did his teacher training at Exeter University, following this with an MEd at Kingston University. He has been head of an international school in Thailand, worked at a school in the US and at several UK independents.

He oversees both the senior and junior divisions of Westbourne. He takes a lead on strategy, recruitment and governance issues and he's also very present day to day. He takes regular assemblies, runs a school ukulele club and continues to coach rugby at the school as well as teaching maths. He leaves the day-to-day running of the seniors to Paddy Birbeck, head of the senior school, but he's also there on occasions when a discipline issue needs to be escalated.

Parents tell us he's quick to deal with problems and 'brilliant at strategy'. Pupils described him as 'a very nice man' and really hands-on and enthusiastic when it comes to sport and music. He says the strength of the school is the 'bespoke education' it provides. 'Kids need to feel good about coming to school,' he says; 'the small class sizes mean we can really get to know the children and find out what makes them tick.'

Academic matters: Since Westbourne is a small school with a broad intake, GCSE results do fluctuate – but they are very good and improving every year. In 2018 35 per cent of GCSEs were A*-A/9-7. Classes are small – even for the independent sector. The average class size is 13 – but, with a wide range of GCSEs offered, that number often goes down to single figures by years 10 and 11. Rather than pushing the EBacc and forcing pupils to take languages, the school gives children a relatively free choice of GCSE subjects. Almost all pupils take three separate sciences, although a few switch to the double certificate if they're struggling. They begin GCSE courses towards the end of year 9, to give them a head start.

The academic ethos is inclusive. It focuses on hard work, growth mindset and higher order thinking skills. Pupils are encouraged to 'get into the learning pit' and wrestle with an idea or a piece of work. Rewards for academic work are generally based on effort and progress but there's also a programme to stretch and develop more able pupils (known here as MAPs). The school believes in developing children's enthusiasm for education and it doesn't shy away from taking classes out of the classroom to let them learn in other environments.

Progress is monitored regularly – on an individualised basis – through GL testing although, according to Paddy Birbeck, they don't do 'data for data's sake'. He says the school is quick to spot if a child isn't making as much progress as they should and to do something about it.

Parents we met were impressed by the way the school supports children with special educational needs. 'The dyslexia support is amazing,' said one mum. 'My dyslexic son got nine GCSEs and in the end he was in the top sets. I don't think he'd have done that well at a different school.' A full-time SENCo arranges support for SEND children through small-group breakout sessions and (at an extra cost to the parents) some one-to-one work. The school supports a number of children with dyslexia and dyscalculia or dyspraxia and there are quite a few hearing impaired children, as well as those on the autism spectrum or with ADHD.

Games, options, the arts: Despite the urban setting and the lack of on-site sports facilities, Westbourne is a decidedly sporty school. The PE department has turned the lack of campus space to its advantage by building relationships with the 'best specialist sporting facilities' in Sheffield and beyond. During games afternoons, pupils might walk down the road to use the facilities at Sheffield or Hallam universities or be bussed further afield – depending on what sport they're doing. The choice is impressive. As well as the ever-popular school staples – football, rugby, hockey and netball – there's a huge range of activities, including scuba diving, trampolining, water sports and dance. A highlight of the school year is the biannual trip for to Club La Santa in Lanzarote, a sports resort where visitors can choose from 40 different activities. The trip is open to all pupils from years 5 to 11 and it's 'totally amazing' – according to one pupil we met.

Westbourne teams often beat bigger schools and it nurtures talented individuals – but the ethos truly is inclusive. If a child wants to play for their school the PE department will find a way – even if that means putting on a C team. PE staff also work hard to promote healthy lifestyles and girls' sports. One mum told us how delighted she was that a group of female PE teachers took a busload of female footballers down to Wembley to watch the women's FA Cup Final.

Everyone we met agreed that, beyond sport, it's drama and music that stand out at Westbourne. Every child has the chance to learn an instrument and high flyers can move at their own rate; some children take GCSE music in year 9 and many reach grade 8 by the time they leave. Young musicians have countless opportunities to perform – both in school and at iconic venues such as Sheffield's Leadmill or Montgomery Theatre, and even further afield on music trips abroad, most recently to Prague.

There are several well-equipped music technology and music practice rooms as well as recording facilities and, even though the school is small, it makes room for a full spectrum of musical styles and influences – from Samba to jazz, and from classical choral singing to beatboxing.

Drama isn't just an optional extra: it's embedded into the curriculum from year 7-9 and a popular GCSE option. There's also a lunchtime drama club and the opportunity to study for LAMDA speech and drama exams. There are lavish annual whole school productions of musical classics such as Bugsy Malone and Grease and, more recently, the recent Broadway coming of age hit, Thirteen.

The art studio is well equipped and pupils can try a wide range of activities such as mosaic-making, calligraphy and set design.

Parents praise the 'holistic' vision of the school. 'You can hear life here,' said one mum. 'Yes, you can always hear music when you walking through the school,' added another.

There's a wide range of extracurricular activities – before and after school and at lunchtimes. Pupils we met all had different interests to talk about, but we didn't get the sense we sometimes have that they are all so incredibly busy they never get a moment to catch their breath.

Background and atmosphere: Westbourne was founded in 1885 as a prep school for boys, becoming co-educational in 1998. In response to parental demand, the senior school opened in 2001.

The school is tucked into a tight spot in the Broomhill area of Sheffield. On the day of our visit we thought our satnav had brought us to the wrong entrance and circled around for a while looking for the car park, before we realised there wasn't one. It's a green and pleasant campus – if a little squashed – but the school makes the most of every inch of outside space. They are building a forest school area and a green space attached to their most recently acquired building is to become an outdoor learning space.

Parents tell us the school has a 'family vibe' and a 'village' feel. They say the school feels smaller than it is – that it's easy to get to know everyone and their children feel well-known by the staff. We only saw excellent behaviour during our visit and the atmosphere felt purposeful and orderly but the school is less formal than some. Support staff are fully included in the school community: 'my child would run up and talk to the caretaker as much as he would to a teacher,' one mum told us. There is lots of interaction between year groups and the children's contributions to the community are noted and valued.

While academic success is celebrated, so are effort and achievement in all sorts of areas. A quick glance through the record of the annual prize-giving shows prizes were awarded for 'generosity of spirit,' 'commitment to learning support' and 'enthusiasm, creativity and team spirit in drama,' as well as a broad selection of sports and subject prizes.

Pastoral care, well-being and discipline: Parents tell us pastoral care is very strong. 'They find out what's going on and they sort things out quickly.' They love the small class sizes and feel this makes it easier for teachers to keep a close eye on the children's well-being. Parents broadly support the 'three strikes and you're in detention' system. They are encouraged to come into school with concerns and the school typically responds within 24 hours.

We met one dad who was recovering from a serious illness and he told us how outstanding the pastoral care had been during his hospital treatment. 'The school's been fantastic,' he said; 'one of the pastoral care leads went to see each one of my children every week when I was ill to talk to them, to check if they needed anything'.

Mr Birbeck says there's 'zero tolerance' of bullying: 'if a child won't stop bullying, they're out'. But early intervention and a strong culture of respect means very little nastiness escalates to that level.

Pupils told us 'everyone looks after you here,' and they feel safe and happy in school. They said they would tell a teacher if they saw any bullying – although older pupils are also taught assertive techniques to help them ask other children to stop if they're doing something to upset them. One child told us he'd been involved in an unpleasant incident with other children but that the teachers had dealt with it well and it was 'all over with the next day'. Another child, however, complained that sometimes staff make a meal of little incidents and 'drag it out'. The overwhelming majority of comments from parents and pupils about pupil well-being and pastoral care, however, were very positive.

Pupils and parents: Parents we met had warm feelings towards the school and its staff. We got the sense during our visit that staff make the effort to get to know whole families, not just the children. The parents' association, Friends of Westbourne, is very active – both in terms of fundraising and organising popular social events.

Parents we met were down-to-earth. Many hadn't been privately educated themselves and some admitted they'd looked around the school 'hoping not to like it,' because they'd had mixed feelings about independent education.

Parents tell us the school communicates with them well. There's a weekly newsletter, a parent portal on the school website (which cuts down the flow of paper forms between school and home) and and sometimes texts of useful information. Working parents complained that sometimes you find out about events during the school day at the last minute.

Pupils travel in from around Sheffield and beyond. Perhaps partly because of the difficult parking situation, there are parent-operated buses from Chesterfield, Deepcar, Dronfield, Tankersley, Thurcroft, Tickhill, Whiston, Worksop and the Hope Valley. The school also operates a bus from the Derbyshire Dales and the High Peak.

Old Westbournians include actor Dominic West and various successful professional sportspeople.

Entrance: Non-selective but a pupil's work in English and maths should be 'at a level appropriate to that of the group they would be joining'. The school does accept plenty of pupils with disabilities and special educational needs but it suggests parents raise their child's issues before they apply for a place to 'ensure the school can make adequate provision'. The aim is to ensure all pupils will be able to make the most of what the school offers and that their behaviour wouldn't have a negative impact on other pupils' learning.

Exit: Around 80 per cent of juniors move up to the senior school. School may ask children to leave if it can longer meet their needs, but this rarely happens. Post-GCSE leavers go to a mixture of independent and state schools and sixth form colleges – popular choices include: King Edwards, High Storrs, Notre Dame, Tapton, King Ecgberts, Silverdale – with some also going to colleges such as UTC, Chesterfield and Sheffield College and further afield. A small number of pupils leave at the end of year 8 to go to boarding school – Sedbergh, Uppingham and Oakham have all been recent destinations – a tradition from Westbourne's prep school days. Every year Westbourne pupils are awarded scholarships to private sixth forms such as neighbouring Birkdale Sixth Form. Most former Westbourne pupils go on university, with several Oxbridge success stories most years.

Money matters: Scholarships, with a 10 per cent reduction in fees (occasionally increased to 25 per cent), for academia, music, sport, drama and all round. A few means-tested bursaries – but these 'don't go close to' covering the full fees. School may be able to help existing families who fall on hard times.

Remarks: The journey through Westbourne is seamless and it really does feel like one school – from the nursery through to year 11. A warm and nurturing non-selective school, which gets excellent results for children of all abilities.

Westville House School

Carter's Lane, Middleton, Ilkley, West Yorkshire LS29 0DQ

Ages 2–11 **Pupils** 100 **C of E**

Fees: £5,619 – £9,735 pa

01943 608053
www.westvilleschool.co.uk

Head: Since September 2018, Nicola Hammond BA PGCE, former director of teaching and learning here.

Entrance: Most start around the age of 2 – there's an excellent opportunity to try the place out first with Tiny Tots, free (yes, really) fun-filled Thursday afternoon sessions led by the onsite team. Non-selective throughout, older children seeking a place are invited for a taster day but no gruelling tests. One form entry throughout so places are limited by space; small number of bursaries available so worth enquiring.

Exit: Usually to first choice schools eg The Grammar School at Leeds, Bradford Grammar School, Ermysted's Grammar in Skipton, Skipton Girls' High School, Ilkley Grammar School, Giggleswick School, Sedbergh School and Woodhouse Grove becoming increasingly popular. Considering the school is non-selective on entry, they do very well with a number of scholarships each year to fee-paying senior schools – great value-added.

Remarks: Founded in Ilkley in 1960, moving to its present site in 1992. The ceremonial flagpole is a nice touch – they are proud of their school. The views alone make this place very special – right across the valley to the Cow and Calf Rocks, yes it's blowy up here and you can experience all four seasons in one day, but the warm and friendly welcome alone makes it worth a visit. A little off the beaten track so there's no passing traffic, which makes it lovely and safe for children but not great for marketing purposes. Yet you're really only five minutes' drive from Ilkley town centre, and the rolling hills and natural woodlands up here make this an ideal environment for adding in a forest school curriculum. Fresh air and exercise – 'multi-sensory learning in crystal clear air,' they tell us in the literature; think Switzerland without the cowbells.

No lack of academic rigour, regular testing so they know where they are but 'not glued to their desks' either, plenty of talk of breadth and balance across a traditional prep curriculum with added outdoor benefits. Classes are small, nowhere to hide. Parental expectations are high; this school is viewed as a stepping stone to the many good schools in the area, both state and fee-paying and, to date, it delivers. Awards and scholarships to other schools are a source of much pride. Staff know the children extremely well and much praise in a recent inspection report for high quality teaching and learning across the board, including excellent marking, which was flagged as a weakness in a previous inspection.

French taught from the start, Spanish added for the older children. Relationships are warm and fairly relaxed – there is a feelgood factor here – children (and staff) know what's expected and rarely challenge the status quo. Parents talk of 'a palpable fresh and positive feel with all the staff pulling together to deliver the best they can to the pupils'.

Learning support is available; numbers receiving it are low; small charge for one-to-one but small group support is free as and when necessary. The more able are flagged and challenged. No wheelchair access for the main building and partially sighted children would struggle on this site. Class sizes vary, as do gender ratios; one form entry throughout and whilst there is undoubtedly room for more at present, places may be snapped up more quickly in coming months and years following the opening of the new and impressive early years facility.

Form teachers teach most subjects, including science; specialists for art, sport and music. Enthusiastic director of music is keen for all to 'have a go' – aspiring musicians not restricted by age; if you want to try and your fingers are long enough, then 'go for it!' Classrooms are bright and cheery with plenty of light and interactive whiteboards. Lovely displays of high quality art in corridors and stairwells. Recent programme of redecoration from the ground floor up and most teaching rooms are delightful; developments include new media suite and library. The exterior is looking very smart following a full paint job, white with blue trimmings; it's a former nurses' home that has been described as looking a little like a 'seaside hotel', but it's around the back that it's full of surprises. What the nurses certainly didn't have is a full-sized sports hall and playing fields. They probably also didn't have a mud kitchen (messy but enormous fun and pots and pans 'to clang and bang'..), areas dedicated to bushcraft and soft play areas and lawns with climbing frames, trikes and tractors. The woodland area has a pond and there's the rustic Holloway Hut for outdoor play and learning.

Communication with parents is excellent; they describe it as 'first class'. Look at the website for the latest edition of Buzz: it's described by staff as the 'essence of WHS' and tells you everything you need to know about recent events and the day-to-day life of the school. The only gripe we could find from parents is the need for a larger car park – clearly it's a frustration for many but one they can live with, all things considered.

Rascals is the before and after-school care programme; school is open from 7.45am to 6.00pm. No packed lunches here, it's home-cooked food served in the dining hall, with staff sitting alongside the children in 'family groups'. Assemblies most days and whilst the school is technically non-denominational, there is a faith assembly on a Monday and Father Philip from the local church is a regular visitor and good friend of the school. The school can and will provide a prayer room on request.

Plenty of opportunities for leadership at the top of the school – house captains, head boy and head girl, each with a deputy, and children are well represented on the school council. Three school houses, named after wild birds; plenty of healthy competition between them. Clubs and activities include rugby coaching, cricket, netball, running, French cinema, drama, dance, music, young voices, forest school and yhatze, amongst others.

The range of sport on offer is very impressive for a small school. Most takes place on site and the school minibus shuttles children to the town pool for swimming and local rugby and cricket clubs for tournaments. The sports hall is huge and multi-purpose, great for sport; it's a beast of a building, swallowing up these small children who just love the space it provides, especially in the long winters up here. Pull-down audience seating for concerts and plays all year round, acoustics not great, but drama and music are strong despite that. Netball courts and large playing fields are tucked away behind the school.

Keen eco led by children – Green Flag award, grow own vegetables in large garden. Charity fundraising – links with school in Africa. Plenty of local and regional trips – year 6, unusually, have three residentials (science and geography; sports tour; outdoor pursuits). Thursday afternoon is clubs time – mixed ages and broad range, following staff interests, eg chess, juggling, arts and crafts, ocarina, bridge, outdoor pursuits. It's also the afternoon for the Tots Club which is widening its range of activities all the time: still to come is Rugby Tots, Alphabet Tots and most lately Ninja Tots.

The newly built facility for reception/admin and early years teaching is fabulous and has freed up useful extra teaching space in the main building, allowing a dedicated area for design technology and a larger library for the older children. This attractive and well-planned new build is a tangible investment in the future of the school and they are hoping it will prove a huge draw for local parents.

Tartan pinafore dresses and/or culottes are the winter uniform for girls, dresses in summer. For boys it's white shirts and ties-on-elastic with a choice of long trousers or shorts. Blazers for all and hats are also set to make a return following popular demand, though they might need to hang on to them on windy days.

Goodwill and loyalty in spades from a convivial staff, both teaching and non-teaching, who greet you with genuine northern warmth and geniality. Most parents have done the rounds before signing up and the warm welcome here is mentioned over and over again. Parents also praise the school's expectation that pupils will be 'polite, considerate and respectful towards staff and each other'. Behaviour is good; the children here know what's expected and behave accordingly, no arrogance but bags of confidence and happy to chat.

A four-wheel drive vehicle might be a must come winter; these are no-nonsense hardy folk for whom Barbours and wellies are de rigueur for a few months each year. Very wide catchment area, from Gargrave to Otley, High Skyreholme in Dales to Baildon plus Ilkley day nurseries. Parents are a mix of professionals, often working in Leeds or Manchester, and local business owners. High number of working mums too, more new money than old; they reflect the local demographic, and are happy to pay the added house price premium here in Ilkley and manage the commute. Rumour has it it's worth it for the green open spaces, the stylish independent shops, Bettys (other tea shops are available), an array of fine-dining options and a choice of good senior schools within reach. 'It's an exciting time to be at Westville' parents tell us.

Windermere School, Elleray

Linked with Windermere School

Ambleside Road, Windermere, Cumbria LA23 1AP

Ages 3–11 **Pupils** 71 **Boarders** from 8 years **C of E**

Fees: Day £7,605 – £15,030; Boarding £24,120 – £25,485 pa

01539 443308
www.windermereschool.co.uk

Head of Elleray Campus: Since September 2016, Rachael Thomas.

Entrance: Non-selective but children are observed in class for entry at 3+. All pupils and parents meet the head.

Boarding is from age 8 (no overseas boarders currently).

Exit: Majority of pupils (90 per cent) move on to senior school at Browhead Campus: Windermere School

Remarks: They simply ask that 'you bring along effort, commitment, determination, a sense of humour, an open mind, enthusiasm, energy and a pencil case'. Though you should probably add to that wellies and wet weather gear – Lake District essentials, pretty much all year round. It would be a crime to be right here in glorious countryside, with lakes and mountains on your doorstep, and not make the most of it – so they do. The school's Adventure strand runs right through all that they do and the intention is that 'children are interacting, engaged and thrilled, whether climbing a rock face or in the classroom'. So, if you are learning about forces in science, you paddle your canoe on the lake and see and feel them for real; you then replay that in the classroom and (probably) remember it forever. The children who read, wrote about and painted dragons, and then sailed across to an island in the middle of the lake only to find a dragon's nest and plenty of other 'evidence' of dragon life, were undoubtedly 'engaged and thrilled'.

If that all sounds a little too Swallows and Amazons for you then fear not; no lack of academic rigor in the classroom and even good old fashioned handwriting practice is seeing something of a revival here. A sensible cross-curricular approach to the teaching of humanities which means that the dots are joined up between and across subjects, leading to real learning connections being made and, vitally, transference of knowledge. The mornings are essentially for maths and English; science is big here and at the centre of the planning for all subjects. French taught by a specialist from the senior campus; drama and music also important, there are peripatetics for individual music tuition in addition to class music. Classes are small, some very small, one form entry throughout.

Sport goes way beyond the usual team sports and track events; sailing and kayaking have taken off enormously, with senior staff and coaches supporting some activities. They have their own tennis court and playing fields and use the Astroturf and sports hall at the senior campus for additional space. The school's own backdrop is its own dream playing space – here children camp, build dens, walk the fells, climb mountains (and read their own poetry when they get to the top), and so much more besides. The school even has a member of staff with the wonderful title Head of Adventure – a first for us. Words and phrases like 'resilience', 'critical thinking', 'empathy' 'collaboration' and 'problem-solving' are part of the children's own vocabulary here, and from an early age. Personalised pathways are 'a reality not just an aspiration'; tracking happens in form time, measuring skills such as team work and leadership alongside academic success.

There's a small hall for lunch, drama, dance and assemblies; classrooms are colourful, spacious, bright and airy with views to die for. Some classrooms in the main building – a towered Victorian Lakeland slate building – with other newer add ons. The main reception area is lovely, with an impressive staircase, other areas need a coat of paint but there is a constant and continual programme of decorating and updating – bit like the Forth Bridge. Eco-pod classrooms provide vital extra space – strange-looking buildings (think Marmite – love them or hate them) but you can't fault their eco-credentials of recycled materials and sheep's wool in their construction. Traditional wooden desks in most classrooms are smart and new and much loved by the children and parents.

Newly refurbished art and design centre is a haven for art lovers, fantastic inspirational work on display led by a studio artist from Kendal who spends three days in school each week. The vaulted cellars look and feel as though they should house expensive wines but in fact are changing rooms and DT teaching areas; every bit of the building is used. Good library/ media centre; learning support on hand if required. Heaps of extracurricular activity; summer activity camps started recently. Soft play areas around school buildings for little ones and a greenhouse provides the school kitchen with vegetables and a space for science lessons and the thriving gardening club.

Parents are far from all super wealthy but nevertheless say they are 'happy to sacrifice two weeks on a beach to have happy, well-educated and well mannered children who open doors for people, say good morning and embrace every second of school'.

Only a handful of boarders, parents are mostly local – fewer landed gentry than in days of old, more hardworking hotel and restaurant owners or young semi-retired professionals who have made their money in the City and moved here for a breath of fresh air. All boarding is based at the senior campus in small dorms with house staff on hand; current drive to bring in more boarders. Four to a room in dorms, plenty of messy individualisation of space with One Direction posters, soft toys and family photos and comfortable sofas in the common room for socialising, karaoke and TV watching. Food cooked in-house, good quality and plentiful, just as well with all that fresh air.

Staff are dedicated and enthusiastic and the coffee table in the visitor waiting area has copies of children's magazines rather than the usual Horse and Hound or Tatler, which speaks volumes about this child-centred school. Smiling children in attractive striped blazers (note matching upholstery in reception hall) who are happy to chat, that's if you can get them to stand still for a moment..they are busy, on a mission almost, but clearly having great fun, creating the sort of childhood memories here that others can only dream of.

Windermere School

Linked with Windermere School, Elleray

Browhead, Patterdale Road, Windermere, Cumbria LA23 1NW

Ages 11–18 **Pupils** 274 **Sixth form** 88 **Boarders** 100 full, 27 weekly
C of E

Fees: Day £15,735 – £17,775; Boarding £26,430 – £31,335 pa

01539 446164
www.windermereschool.co.uk

Headmaster: Since 2009, Ian Lavender MA (Oxon) NPQH. Has a strong background in independent secondary school education, boarding and the Round Square ethos, having been a housemaster at Gordonstoun School for 11 years and before that a chemistry teacher at Cranleigh School and Eton College. He also has broad experience that extends well beyond teaching, including an early career in management consulting and service with the Territorial Army. His wife is a GP and they have three children. A quietly spoken, measured and thoughtful man, parents say 'he cares deeply about the students..and is an impressive headmaster'. There is no lack of ambition: his vision is that Windermere becomes 'the best small school in the country'.

Academic matters: Windermere pupils might not be dancing right at the top of the league tables but they appear hard-working and happy. Due in part to the broad intake, the results at GCSE, whilst undoubtedly solid (58 per cent A*-A/9-7 in 2018), can't compete with bigger, more selective schools so it focuses on its considerable international appeal. Crucially, however, it is the highest performing independent school in Cumbria post 16, not least because there is no A level on offer here; it's the rigour of IB or a small choice of BTecs, and that's it. Exams and the choice of exams are a natural sieving process and the school's choice of the IB route means the game is raised considerably in sixth form; average IB point score 33 in 2018. Now accredited to teach the IB career-related programme alongside the diploma. With small classes (around 12), teaching is up close and personal, there's nowhere to hide, and pupil-teacher relationships appear warm and relaxed. Personal academic tutors guide and, if necessary, hand-hold, helping students in their choice of subjects and mentoring them along the way. Parents tell us 'there are many inspirational teachers here', with a number of them prepared to offer extra tutorials on request at lunchtime or after school.

French, German, Italian and Spanish are all taught in this language-rich environment, with Latin and Greek being offered off-timetable as extras, classes running every Thursday evening. Outside of class, eager young linguists who keep their ears open can experience over 20 languages being spoken around school. Students are given the opportunity to participate in worldwide exchanges by spending up to a term in another Round Square school. There are also annual language trips to France and Spain and Germany.

Full-time head of learning support, dyslexia specialist and two part-time assistants; it's a strong department. Parents are charged for the support according to whether it's in-class or on an individual basis.

Games, options, the arts: Built on a slope; the site brings its own challenges and there aren't acres of pitches here; the biggest area of flat ground is the lake, so that's where most activities take place. Better suited to small team sports, and there are probably more expeditions than fixtures, but they do have an Astroturf and a sports hall for year-round play.

Whilst they can't compete with the big boys at team sports, they take it seriously and offer the full range of usual school sports and others besides, including equestrianism, sailing and kayaking. Hodge Howe, the school's own watersports centre and the only school centre in the country to hold RYA British Youth Sailing Recognised Club status, has two boathouses, a private beach and a pavilion with a classroom (also available for wedding receptions..) and a fleet of sailing boats and kayaks. Other outdoor activities include camping trips, fell walking, ghyll scrambling, orienteering, caving and climbing, so if you are the adventurous type and not joined at the hip to your hair straighteners or worried by a patchy mobile phone signal, there's plenty here for you. All students in years 7, 8 and 9 complete the Windermere Adventure Award. They also spend one morning a fortnight outside school doing anything from mountain biking to conservation and environmental work.

Art takes place in the old stables; super natural light and plenty of Apple Macs for those with a penchant for design and design technology, and kilns for keen potters; it's an appropriately messy yet inspirational space. Drama is popular; it's a small school so very inclusive, and everyone who wants to take part can do, whether centre stage or behind the scenes.

Lots of individual tuition in music and the Holst Room, a space designed for its acoustics, is a valuable teaching and performance space. It's not the strongest subject, here according to parents, so a particularly musical child may not be able to shine, but there is undoubtedly a 'have a go' attitude to the subject, as with everything else.

The school supports community projects in South Africa; each year students help out with resources and provide physical help to a project with Tiger Kloof School – in fact just mentioning the name of the school brings a warm smile and glow of pride to the faces of the older students, who view it as an extension of their school life at Windermere.

A highly rated international summer school is proving increasingly popular and has effectively added a fourth term to the school year.

Boarding: Despite the national park location, it's only 90 minutes to either Manchester or Liverpool airports (outside London considered a safer option by some nervous parents), three hours to London by train and the school has a fleet of shuttle buses catering for students' many and varied travel needs.

Word of mouth is the biggest factor in attracting parents, both locally and overseas. There are a few expat Forces parents who love the leadership challenges here, and whilst more than half of the students are from within the UK, the rest represent around 24 different countries far and wide, including China, Germany, Hong Kong, Lithuania, Poland, Romania, Ukraine, Spain and Russia.

Customary dorms in single sex houses on site for boarders aged 8-16 (only a handful of junior boarders); there are a few single rooms but not many choose them, most preferring to share. Plenty of messy individualisation of space with One Direction posters, soft toys and family photos. Each house has a staff house 'family', comfortable shared common rooms with views across the lake for socialising, karaoake and TV watching, and well-equipped kitchens for snacking. In the girls' house at least, baking seems popular with Mary Berry cake recipes much in evidence. Food cooked in-house, good quality and plentiful, just as well with all that fresh air.

Well-behaved sixth formers earn the right to have more space and freedom in self-contained flats in a co-educational house on site, still supervised, of course, but a step along the road to preparation for life beyond school. A sixth form bar allows (with parental permission) two drinks with dinner on a Saturday night; younger pupils love the occasional takeaway, shared with friends in the boarding house. If that sounds a little tame, there's not much else you can get up to here (a definite plus for many parents), but cinema visits and occasional weekend trips to the Trafford Centre in Manchester or Alton Towers keep restless adolescents happy. They are also very busy after school, so much so that a parent of a day boy told us they relocated to be on the school's doorstep simply because their son was 'reluctant to go home after school – way too much going on'.

Background and atmosphere: On this site since 1924 and co-ed since 1999, there is a good mix of boys and girls here. Extensive additional building took place in the '70s and '80s, but the national park setting places real limitations on new building – essentially it's all about how the place looks from the lake. Some attractive newer and recently refurbed buildings are scattered around the grounds of the Victorian mansion of the original Browhead estate, some boarding facilities, others classrooms and labs. Highlights are the Jenkins Centre for music, performing arts, languages and a superb dining room and Crampton Hall – a spacious auditorium for theatrical and musical productions.

Round Square is a worldwide association of schools that is all about the whole person – the Kurt Hahn view that says students can only understand life by experiencing it in exciting and challenging ways. Opportunities for travel and exchanges to other Round Square schools bring extra opportunities, and they welcome international students who wish to experience British culture whilst bringing with them their own perspective and world view. There is a real sense that, although surrounded by mountains here, their hearts and heads go way beyond the valley and into the wider world beyond. The core of the IB diploma programme encompasses many of the Round Square principles, making the curriculum ideal here. Daily reflection is an important start to the day and something valued hugely by the students themselves. 'It lifts you up,' they tell us; 'you're in school, lessons haven't started yet but you're saying hello to everyone'; 'it's a nice place to be' and it is often, apparently, like a mini TED talk to start your day, food for thought and a valued and laudable touchstone. Outside speakers are welcomed as regular visitors and students also attend conferences and exchanges worldwide.

Pastoral care, well-being and discipline: Many parents are attracted by the fact that the school isn't especially selective – telling us they didn't want their offspring to be a 'public school product' but rather they 'wanted their individuality to be valued'. They appreciate the weekly online newsletter and feel that they 'could walk into the school at any time if they had any concerns at all'. Also of great value to parents is the way in which 'teachers respond very promptly to even the smallest queries...pastoral care is excellent,' they say. Overseas parents enjoy a 'close relationship' with the staff and love the fact that their offspring often enjoy tea or dinner with the head and his wife.

Staff do, of course, keep a careful watching brief, but essentially Windermere pupils are encouraged to be self-disciplined. Problems are rare, as older and younger students jog along happily in the knowledge that they want for nothing (except perhaps a Starbucks) in this sprawling, healthy and supportive environment. Strong views from the sixth formers themselves on smoking – 'why would you?' It seems there's a degree of self-policing going on.

Students appear comfortable and relaxed but with an uncommon sense of responsibility too; they recently 'simply couldn't stand back and do nothing' following the recent earthquakes in Nepal, and within hours were actively fundraising within the local community in support of the victims. Charity fundraising such as this, alongside work in a soup kitchen and orphanage, affords them a 'very different reality,' say parents – 'one which puts their very privileged life into sharp focus'.

Pupils and parents: Any passing traffic is likely to be either hikers or tourists, so recruitment is a challenge, though undoubtedly helped in the overseas market by the Beatrix Potter and Peter Rabbit connection. It's a lifestyle choice living here in the Lake District, and some parents have huge commutes to city offices, whilst others are simply escaping the city altogether. Fewer landed gentry than in days of old, more hardworking hotel and restaurant owners or young semi-retired professionals who have made their money in the City and moved here for a breath of fresh air.

High on the list of attractions for many is the extensive programme of adventurous outdoor activities – something the pupils coming through from the school's own prep department have already enjoyed in abundance. It seems to result not only in hardy pupils but also in a 'can do' attitude, parents buying in to the opportunities for growth and independence in a safe environment. The words 'warmth' and 'friendliness' are oft repeated by parents when talking about the staff; they are aware that this is more typical of a small school and for them, it's a valid and valuable trade off for bigger and better facilities.

Entrance: Nearly all juniors move up to the senior school, making up the majority of the 11+ entry. The school likes to look for 'potential' rather than performance and 'well-rounded students with a genuine interest in education in the broadest sense of the word,' say staff. Candidates for entry (below 16+) sit papers in English, mathematics and non-verbal reasoning. Year 12 places conditional on a minimum of five GCSEs at grade C or above.

Exit: Around a quarter leave after GCSEs. Most sixth form leavers continue in higher education at home or overseas, some via gap years. Edinburgh, St Andrews, UCL and Manchester all popular destinations and some go on to universities overseas. Notable former pupils include dressage Olympian Emma Hindle and internationally respected soprano Claire Booth.

Money matters: Non means-tested scholarships are available in performing arts, visual arts, general academic subjects and sport. There are some means-tested bursaries available.

Remarks: The photograph on the cover of the school's prospectus looks like an oil painting – and yes, that really is the view from the school. A glorious backdrop in which to learn and grow, and the school makes full use of it. It's not the ideal destination for the child without a cagoule or for whom manicured lawns and extensive sporting facilities are key, but you do have all the amenities of the Lake District at your disposal, so give even those indoor types a month or so and they'll be away from their Playstations and kayaking with the best of them.

On a sunny day you can see for miles. On other days you can't see your hand in front of your face. The weather can change in an instant, but no one allows that fact to get in the way of an existence where hard work, good friends, rosy cheeks and fresh air in your lungs are all part of the package. The introduction of the International Baccalaureate has upped the game academically at the top end and also encouraged a more diverse intake, with pupils introduced to a wider range of subjects with exceptional extracurricular enhancements.

Withington Girls' Junior School

Linked with Withington Girls' School

Wellington Road, Fallowfield, Manchester M14 6BL

Ages 7–11 **Pupils** 135

Fees: £9,195 pa

01612 241077
www.wgs.org

Head: Since 2004, Kathryn Burrows (50s). She has a geography degree from St Andrews University and a PGCE from Bristol. She trained as a senior school teacher, specialising in geography and PE, but she only did a couple of years teaching, in Northern Ireland, before spending a good 10 years outside the system. During this time she was an army wife – moving from posting to posting, taking up opportunities when they came along (she taught tennis in Cyprus at one point) and raising four children along the way. Since returning to live a more settled life in the UK, she returned to her old primary school – Lady Barn House – as head of games and later moved to Withington as head of the junior school. She went to Withington herself – as did her two sisters and later her daughter. She says, 'It's changed beyond recognition – it was very strict then... but I was quite schooly so I loved it'. She says that coming to a mainstream teaching career later in life has meant that she still has buckets of energy and enthusiasm. She's very attentive to the welfare of the children. There's a 'chatterbox' outside her office where girls can leave her notes. She talks about making 'pre-emptive strikes' to prevent small problems turning into big ones. Parents speak about her with a real warmth and positivity. 'She's fabulous,' says one mum. Everyone seems to have a story about Mrs Burrows dealing with whatever tiny crises feel enormous to a little girl with speed and sensitivity.

Leaving in July 2019.

Entrance: They try to stop the selection experience feeling intimidating – with year 6 helpers on hand to show the girls around – but still it's a test. There's a one hour paper in English and another in maths. There's also a short reading assessment and the girls will be informally observed during a morning of play and activities. Mrs Burrows says they enjoy themselves, though: 'Sometimes they go away with a pocketful of telephone numbers of girls they've made friends with ... and they want to come again the next week'. They're looking for girls with the potential to go on to succeed in the senior school entrance exams so standards are high. As a rough guide, you'd need your child to be at or near the top of her class already. A few more places in year 4, 5 and year 6. (In previous years, where there has only been one form entry into year 3, it expands to two forms in year 5).

Exit: Nearly all the junior school pupils pass the exams to the seniors and stay on at Withington Girls throughout their school careers. Mrs Burrows teaches the year 6 students herself and personally prepares them for the entrance exams to the senior school. It does occasionally happen that a girl doesn't make it through, but this would never be a shock to her or her family – as performance is closely monitored and communicated to families.

Remarks: Academic standards are, as you'd expect, very high. Almost all children attain a standard equivalent to at least national curriculum level 5 across every subject by the end of year 6. But parents say their children aren't put under pressure. One mother said that she felt the school was significantly less academically pressured than the state primary her daughter had previously attended – perhaps because juniors sit no external assessments.

As well as the bread and butter of literacy, maths, science, languages, humanities and art and technology, the children do PE every day, music twice a week and drama once a week. They also have 'thinking and learning' lessons where they're encouraged to engage with abstract concepts, think critically and ask difficult questions.

There's very little separation between the junior and senior sections of Withington Girls School so do have a look at our review of the senior school as well as this one. New junior school building and central Hub recently opened, but the juniors also regularly make use of the equipment, classrooms and specialist teachers from the senior school. They're very well connected with the older girls: sixth formers provide affectionate peer support and many of the senior school's extracurricular activities are on offer to the whole school. Some junior girls took part in the recent production of The Sound of Music, for example, and the science department houses the 'Little Critters Pets Corner' – a rodent-heavy pet care club which allows juniors and year 7s to mix, chat and cuddle small furries during their lunch breaks. As with the senior school, there are just too many clubs, societies, days out and visiting speakers to list, but pupils told us that the recently formed Eco Warriors club was a particular favourite among juniors. This perhaps builds on the WGS tradition of developing the social conscience of the community-spirited young women in its care – or maybe it's just a chance to get muddy growing strawberries and then eat them with cream.

The school comes across as warm and cosy. Parents love how well their children are known. One mum was touched by her daughter's report after her first term at the school because finally, after many years at another primary where reports had repeatedly contained the same few cursory lines badgering her to 'speak up in class more', she felt that the teacher at WGS had got to know her child individually and to appreciate the contributions she was making in her own way.

Some parents might not want to take their daughters to a single sex environment so young. Others may feel that such a selective and high-achieving environment is just too much too soon for their little ones. The junior school is essentially a feeder for the senior school, so if you're not sure that WGS is what you want for your daughter at age 11, then there could be some upset when all of her classmates progress to the seniors without her – but then again, she won't be accepted to the juniors unless the school is confident there's a future here for her. This is a gentle school with a real focus on fun and imagination. Children here aren't pushed to achieve or to go in any particular direction, but they see all around them examples of how learning can change their lives. If your daughter does come here, you can expect her to aim high.

W

Withington Girls' School

Linked with Withington Girls' Junior School

Wellington Road, Fallowfield, Manchester M14 6BL

Ages 11–18 **Pupils** 545 **Sixth form** 153

Fees: £12,252 pa

01612 241077
www.wgs.org

Headmistress: Since 2016, Sarah Haslam, previously deputy head. Undergrad degree from Lancaster and postgrad teaching qualification from Sheffield; began her career teaching English in 1990 at a co-ed Manchester school and joined Withington Girls' School in 1995. As well as teaching English, she has had roles including head of years 10 and 11 and, since her appointment as deputy head in 2007, lead responsibility for pastoral care and safeguarding. She is also an Independent Schools Inspector, an Independent Schools Teacher Induction Panel lead trainer and has been a governor of another independent school. She has a keen interest in the arts and also loves the outdoors, particularly hill walking and sailing.

Academic matters: By any standard, Withington Girls' School is exceptionally successful academically. In 2018, over 90 per cent of all GCSE entries were graded A*-B/7-9, and 74 per cent of A levels were A*/A. Quite a few sixth formers complete Open University modules in the holidays – you know, just for a bit of fun. Pupils are regularly successful, often outstandingly so, in maths, science and linguistic Olympiads and Oxbridge essay competitions. We could keep listing the accolades but it's notable that the school doesn't.

Exam results are almost buried on the school website; they're item number 16 on a menu that isn't even visible from the front page. It may be a cliché for heads to gush about 'educating the whole person' but there's evidence that Withington does take that ambition seriously. Many of the parents we spoke to had initially worried the school might be a hothouse – but all agreed that their fears were unfounded. Sixth formers told us that the only pressure pupils may experience is what they put on themselves – and that the teachers can be relied upon to calm them down; reminding them that a B may be below average here but nationally it's a great result. One parent said she wished termly reports would rank the children in their class so that she knew how her daughter compared to her peers, but we suspect the school very deliberately withholds such information because it's not interested in ranking children against each other.

It's extremely rare for a child to leave the school because she's struggling academically, although it does happen. Usually problems are nipped in the bud with close monitoring and one-to-one support. Whereas many similar schools maintain their place in the league tables by setting exacting GCSE targets for entry to the sixth form, Withington doesn't exclude existing pupils from A level study on the grounds of relatively disappointing GCSE results. So long as a girl is happy at the school, they say they will honour their commitment to educate her to the age of 18.

All the parents we spoke to said they were very happy with their daughters' achievement and nobody thought their child was overwhelmed with homework. One mother suggested that perhaps girls achieve so much in the lessons that the school doesn't feel the need to set reams of homework. There's a sense that the girls are such smart and focussed learners they know how to stay on top of their studies efficiently so that there's plenty of time left for living. That's certainly what the school wants. The selection policy is all about finding pupils who won't just 'cope' with the pace and challenge of the curriculum; 'they must flourish'. Adamant that they wouldn't offer a place to a girl who would only get through the academic hurdles with hard slog and extra tutoring because they want everyone to have time to take part in whatever's on offer.

The school is particularly strong in maths and science. Nearly half the pupils do maths A level. But a good range of other subjects is offered at A level, including psychology, philosophy and drama. Across the board – in the arts, humanities, languages and sciences – there's no subject where the number of A and A* grades awarded isn't vastly above the national average.

A recent ISI inspection found that pupils with special educational needs and those with English as an additional language are well integrated into classes and that 'they make excellent progress, in line with their peers'. Pupils with SEN or a learning disability or difficulty have full access to the curriculum, and benefit from the full range of extracurricular activities. All pupils are taught with skilful differentiation within mainstream classes. Additional one-to-one support and extra spelling and language support groups are organised (at no extra charge) by the learning support department.

Games, options, the arts: Each edition of the school bulletin – published four times a year – details student participation in more extracurricular events, of every description, than you would imagine could be crammed into a school year, let alone three months. Girls aren't steered in a particular direction so much as encouraged to try whatever they fancy. One pupil told us she'd worried that the school wouldn't be sporty enough for her but, since joining, she says she's had excellent opportunities to develop and she plays in several school teams as well as at county level. The school offers weekly zumba classes and sixth formers also have access to a new, state-of-the-art fitness suite and a personal trainer. One year 13 student enthused about playing in the WGS orchestra and the Stage Band – her only gripe was that she couldn't be in two places at once so had had to sacrifice her place in a sports team to commit to her music. Compulsory enrichment programme for sixth formers includes – alongside eg professional skills and finance – courses ranging from painting for pleasure to voices of dissent. Teams from the school have had outstanding success in national debating competitions, an international business challenge and the Model United Nations. The music and drama departments are lively and inclusive – most recently collaborating to stage a lavish whole school production of The Phantom of the Opera. Many students leave Withington having already completed their gold DofE. And all this really is just a taster.

If there's one element of the extracurricular life of the school that really stands out, it's what might loosely be termed service to the community. There are annual volunteering trips to the Gambia and to Uganda. Pupils from every year put huge efforts into charity fundraising. The sums they raise perhaps tell us most about the wealth and generosity of the school's circle of adult benefactors, but the hard work and enthusiasm come from the children themselves. They really do care about their local community. They know they're privileged and they think that brings responsibilities. Almost all sixth formers do community service locally. 'Do you have to?' we asked. A pause. 'No but... well, everyone wants to.' Recently a local state primary lost its playing fields. The WGS year 9 came up with a solution: they hosted and organised a sports day for them on their own playing fields. A sixth former spoke earnestly about how moved she was by a talk from a former substance abuser on her path back to sobriety, and the same girl said she will never forget the privilege of having met a holocaust survivor on a recent trip. You get the feeling that this is one aspect of a Withington education that lasts a lifetime.

Background and atmosphere: We parked outside on Wellington Road – and wondered briefly if that was a good idea. This isn't really Withington. It's Fallowfield. It's not a rich area. The street is peaceful enough, but far from what you'd expect as the home of a centre of academic excellence. The school buildings are smart and welcoming, though. It feels secure but it's no fortress. The entrance lobby, with its huge glass sliding doors, would feel like the reception area of a medium-sized business if it weren't populated by busy-looking young women popping to and from reception with forms to hand in and messages to deliver. We're guided to a sofa to wait for the sixth formers who will show us round the school. On a coffee table are today's Guardian and Independent and a folder of press cuttings about the school. We're struck that every girl who passes us, whether she's 7 or 17, makes eye contact and offers a spontaneous, friendly smile.

The environment – inside and out – is neat, light and pleasant. It doesn't feel luxurious, but the space is generous and fit for purpose. As you'd expect, impressive displays of student work line the corridors and classroom walls. The sports, science and drama facilities are all tip top. The sixth form centre is quietly buzzing. A few students are studying at tables, many more lounge on sofas chatting – it could be about work...

The sixth formers have their own exclusive café, the Bistro. It serves hot drinks, tempting snacks and light lunches and is host to the breakfast club for the whole school. School dinners for everyone are provided in the main servery. Money has been spent on improving the catering over recent years. There are plenty of options and the menus look tempting and healthy. But still there are a few complaints. One mum told us her younger child loves the food but the elder one won't eat it. Although she thought her daughter was being picky, she wished the school would let her bring in a packed lunch because 'she's flagging by the afternoon'.

The founders stipulated that the school should be kept small, and nearly every parent we spoke to was attracted by the school's size. One mum said of her daughter, 'she was almost invisible at her old school but here she's like a different child.' The junior school is fully integrated with the seniors – there's no separate block so older girls pass young children in the corridors all the time. Parents suggest this softens the behaviour of teenagers who might otherwise become a little self-absorbed. The atmosphere is gentle and warm. It's on the quiet side, but individually the pupils are lively, confident and forthcoming. Maybe it's quieter than other schools because they know how to listen. It's also a very diverse community. Two in five pupils are non-white and there are lively faith groups from the major world faiths. Because of the bursaries, it's far from a preserve of the rich. One mum said, 'my daughter's got friends from Hale and from Moss Side and I love that'. Another said, 'I don't believe a child could come out of that school in any way racially prejudiced'. What seems to bring the girls together is their genuine pleasure in being there. They know they've got a lovely school so it's in their interests to keep it like that.

Pastoral care, well-being and discipline: Parents say they feel their daughters are known personally and that teachers are proactively looking out for their well-being. A sixth former told us she was pleasantly surprised when a teacher casually mentioned that she'd noticed she'd made some new friends – it made her feel that they were keeping an eye on everyone and would notice if anything wasn't right. When we asked the girls about friendship problems, they struggled to think of instances.

One pupil said she felt as they got older she'd noticed a gradual shift towards more inclusive and less competitive behaviour. She said there was a notable change in how girls viewed a charity dance show they were involved in both in year 8 and then in year 10. 'In year 8 it was a bit of a competition but two years later we'd kind of worked out ourselves that it didn't need to be like that'. She said that in the sixth form 'everyone's friends with everyone – it's not as cliquey as lower down in the school'. The girls say that if ever anyone sees a pupil being excluded or treated unkindly they would all step in to put a stop to it. Staff agree: 'We've had sixth formers come to us and say "We're worried about X," and normally we already know because we're worried about X too, but it's nice that they come to us'. A couple of the mothers we interviewed had seen their daughters bullied in previous schools but none had faced any such problem here. Staff aren't complacent, though, acknowledging that it's much harder to detect serious bullying these days as it so often takes place online. Childnet regularly presents to the juniors and to year 7; the school offers internet safety training to parents and the girls know all the different lines of communication and support open to them if they're unhappy for any reason.

The pupils behave beautifully, apparently without being told to. External discipline is barely there, but self-discipline is everywhere. There are very few rules. Pupils are drilled in the 'Three Rs of respect for self, respect for others and responsibility for personal actions'. One parent said she'd never heard of anyone having a detention. We couldn't find a parent who'd received the dreaded 'letter home'. School says that no indiscretion is 'beyond redemption' and, in the event of a major transgression, would aim to be proportionate and to understand the context. But there are clear policies about drugs, bullying and suchlike and the school wouldn't rule out expulsion as a last resort. It's all a bit hypothetical, though. 'Oh, they can be terribly naughty sometimes,' said one mum cheerfully, but we suspect it's more Mallory Towers than Grange Hill.

Pupils and parents: Most of the mums we spoke to weren't in receipt of bursaries. These were well-to-do families for whom private schooling was always going to be an option. More than half of them were first attracted by the size and ethos of the school – several of them looking for a cosy community for a shy child – but their second consideration was its academic reputation.

Your child won't be happy at Withington unless she's very bright. Beyond intelligence, it would help if she's willing to work (although perhaps a previously lazy child would be spurred into action by the other children). There's no 'Withington type'. The school appreciates individuality. 'They can be quirky here,' said one mum. Outgoing children will have countless opportunities to enjoy the limelight but there's certainly a common thread that painfully shy and quiet children, who were unhappy in other schools, have blossomed here. Some have found a new confidence and others remain quiet – but contentedly so. WGS's reputation in STEM subjects must surely attract parents who know their daughter is gifted in maths and science, but for every old girl who's a particle physicist or an engineer there's another who's an opera singer or a fashion designer.

Entrance: If your daughter is applying to join the school at 11, she'll sit tests in English, maths and verbal reasoning. After the tests girls may be invited to interview – 'an informal chat'. They're looking for flair. Sometimes that shows itself particularly in one area – but she won't get a place unless they're confident she'll be able to keep up in all areas of the curriculum. They're interested not just in the answers your child gives but also in how she gets to them. Lessons at Withington cover a lot of ground at quite a pace so children who are lively and quick to catch on will fare best. School 'saddened' by the 'arms race' to tutor for entrance exams. The WGS tests do their damnedest to delve beneath the instructions of private tutors and canny prep schools to discover real potential. The interviewer won't be impressed if your daughter goes quiet when she's asked, 'What do you do when you're not studying?' Sample papers are available from the school office but girls are advised just to look through them so they seem familiar rather than to practise.

Y

Exit: Most girls stay on to join the sixth form although a few leave for financial reasons or because they want to board. Everyone leaving year 13 goes to university – although some take a gap year first (for which there are small travel grants available). Most students choose traditional academic subjects but a few take more practical or vocational courses, in the arts, for example, or with a business or management component to them. Medicine is consistently popular with Withington girls (11 medics in 2018). So is Oxbridge (14 places in 2018 plus two 2017 leavers). In terms of leavers' destinations, it's one of the most successful schools in the country, with over 90 per cent of pupils going to one of the 30 most selective UK universities eg Durham, Birmingham, Exeter, Nottingham.

Money matters: A 2012 Financial Times report named Withington the best value independent day school in the UK. Given that this is the only school in the north of England to be in the FT's top 20 'best schools' list, the fees compare well with those of its local competitors. They're still way out of reach for most Manchester families, though. But about 90 girls in the senior school – that's one in six – receives a means-tested bursary, some of 100 per cent. The bursary fund is protected by a trust and the current level of provision is secure in perpetuity – but fundraising continues to extend the scheme further.

Remarks: This is an excellent school if you've got a clever daughter. It's serious rather than showy. There's no swimming pool or equestrian centre. It's a cosy but energetic community, particularly good for instilling confidence in girls who've been overwhelmed by larger or less protective schools. It prizes hard work, learning for its own sake and concern for others. Whether she's sporty, artistic, timid or fearless, if your daughter can get through the exams easily, she's likely to love it here.

Yarm Preparatory School

Linked with Yarm School

Grammar School Lane, Yarm, Stockton on Tees TS15 9ES

Ages 3–11 **Pupils** 367

Fees: £5,232 – £10,755 pa

01642 781447
www.yarmschool.org

Headmaster: Since 2013, William (Bill) Sawyer BA PGCE (early 40s), appointed after three years as head of Braeburn Mombasa International Primary School, Kenya. Educated at Tonbridge School, read business studies at Leeds Beckett University followed by a PGCE in primary education at Brighton University. Cut his teeth as a year 4 teacher in an inner city state primary school in Bermondsey, London but felt constrained in a state school setting. Took up a post at The Banda School, Nairobi where he was soon promoted to head of design technology and master in charge of cricket followed by his first headship in Mombasa.

Energetic, enthusiastic and ambitious for the school, excited by the future plans to provide purpose built facilities and a sporting village for school and community use on an adjacent 3.25 acre site. Works closely with the senior school to uphold Yarm ethos. Parents like that he is 'very approachable, regularly on the school gates at the start of the day, in the playground at the close of day and knowledgeable about each individual family'.

It's a family affair at Yarm Prep: wife Sarah is a reception teacher and both their children attend. Bill is into cricket, trail running, kite surfing, open water swimming and, unsurprisingly, travel adventures.

Entrance: School tells us they look for average or above ability. Advertised taster days for nursery and reception and by appointment for those above. Main points of entry are nursery, reception and year 3, a scattering at other ages. Classes per year group expand from three to four in years 5 and 6 to cater for early adopters for senior school. Pupils can, and do, join at any point if space allows.

Exit: With few exceptions, all progress to the senior school.

Remarks: Pre-prep, purpose-built in 2003, houses bright, stimulating and well-equipped nursery. Open term time only, blended theme-based learning and play is based on the early years curriculum. Specialist teaching in French, PE, dance and music and direct access to the outdoor learning area in all weathers. A great introduction to more formal education. Children 3+ get LA funding rebate for 15 hours. Wraparound care available from 8.00am to 6.00pm, at an additional charge.

Pre-prep takes 4 to 7-year-olds in six classes of up to 18 pupils, usually two per year group. Theme-based learning in a curriculum that the head describes as 'national curriculum plus' with specialist teaching continuing in French, PE, dance and music. Reception to year 2, get weekly specialist lesson in the ICT suite at the prep school. Children read daily to a teacher and there is an impressive number of reading scheme books tailored to each child's progress. Pre-prep has its own library, studio and multi-purpose hall used for collective gatherings and clubs.

Strong creative element in the teaching, lots of investigative work, indoors and out. 'The focus is on active teaching,' says the school and we certainly observed that in action with year 1's range of learning experiences based on the story of The Lighthouse Keeper's Lunch. Creative writing around the theme, artwork designing funky lighthouses, maths in practice weighing different baskets of plastic lunch items in the classroom, whilst in the playground a team of children imaginatively created a horizontal lighthouse with working pulley from an assorted pile of materials. Fun and practical learning that emitted a buzz of enthusiasm and engagement.

Woodland school develops a sense of adventure in the weekly sessions in a dingley dell across the road on the edge of the senior school campus. Activities range from making fairy doors to den-making and toasting marshmallows round an open fire.

The prep school is a short distance away, located in the original Yarm Grammar School building. The number of classes expands to three per year group, with an additional class in years 5 and 6, if needed. Specialist teaching extends to science, computing, art, design technology and speech and drama. Computing – algorithms, coding and app design – is taught as a discrete subject. Class sets of Chromebooks and tablets as well as a designated computer suite give pupils plenty of access to digital technology. Well-stocked library, with teacher-supervised pupil librarians and weekly library lessons. Accelerated reading scheme.

The school day begins at 8.40am and is broken into six lessons of 30 minutes, with a daily assembly and over an hour for lunch, clubs and activities. Supervised after-school care.

Teachers here are 'brilliant', according to the pupils we met; 'learning is fun,' they said. They are taught the 5B reference points to use if they get stuck in class – brain, book, board, buddy and boss. If that's not enough there are weekly maths clinics and prep and handwriting clubs.

InCAS is used to track and monitor pupil progress from year 1. Gifted and talented pupils are identified and challenged through a range of stimulating extra activities and those with special needs are offered specialist support as required.

Designated SEN leads in both the pre-prep and prep schools identify children needing support and plan the required support through differentiation in class, small group working or on a one-to-one basis as necessary.

PE taught in mixed groups though generally boys and girls play sport separately. Plenty of exercise through timetabled lessons and clubs and activities. Traditional team sports from year 3 with everyone given the opportunity to represent their school, though unashamedly competitive. Inter-house competition, too, keeps the on site all-weather playing surface, netball courts and playing fields well used. Swimming lessons at a local pool start in year 3.

Examples of excellent artwork decorate the walls of both schools, diverse and creative in nature. Well-resourced art rooms, including a popular pottery throw down.

School resounds with the sound of music, from recorders and singing sensations in pre-prep to choirs and instrument ensembles, including a harp group, in prep. Year 3 children try different instruments on a six weekly carousel culminating in a performance showcasing their progress. Instruments provided from the school's bank, there's no opt-out but a lot of enthusiasm, stimulating musical interest, providing performance opportunities in front of an audience – one highlight being the grandparents' tea party concert.

Drama for all from nursery and pre-prep nativities to the carefully crafted swansong year 6 production, most recently an adaptation of A Midsummer Night's Dream. Prep pupils also have an annual performance: recently a jokey whodunit Mystery at Magpie Manor.

A popular and unusual option is the two lessons a week (last lessons on Monday and Wednesday) when children can choose what they want to do from an activities programme that offers anything and everything from blogging to Italian.

On top of this there's over 100 lunchtime, pre and after school clubs across a wide range of activities. Residential trips start in year 3 with Whitby, Northumberland in year 4, London in year 5, while year 6s head for France and the Lake District – all high points for the children. An adventurous school holiday programme for 3-11 year-old pupils, staffed solely by Yarm Prep teachers, runs for six weeks of the year.

Recent accolades include national finalists in recent general knowledge competition; multiple awards in national junior maths challenge; regional winners in a range of sports and regular silverware from local arts festival.

Yarm Prep School was founded in 1991, went co-ed in 2001 and opened the nursery for children aged 3+ in 2003. Sited across the main A67 road from the senior school, there is no parking on site for parents, so a short walk via the pedestrian crossing across the busy road from the senior school car park.

Pre-prep classrooms are bright, spacious, colourful, with their own verandas. All with plenty of indoor/outdoor play facilities and a woodland yurt on a hill overlooking the senior school.

It's a short uphill walk to the prep school, traditional brick built main building with a medley of adjoining buildings housing the dining room, classrooms etc. Two playgrounds, one for noisy play, the other quieter; outdoor table tennis tables for lunchtime play when weather permits.

This feels a fun place to learn: inside and outside the classroom there is a wide range of discussion and activities (mostly run by staff) and to engage and interest every child, strengthening their relationship with their teachers. Children are enthusiastic about the opportunities provided, reflected in the faces of both pupils and staff. Being bored just isn't on the radar here.

Children are neatly attired in their navy and red uniforms, traditional in design with navy bound blazers, short trousers for the boys, tartan pinafores for pre-prep girls and skirts for older girls. Food is prepared and cooked on site; pupils say the choice of dishes are 'mostly ok' – about as good as it gets in a prep school.

The school is very proud of its widely published values, a collaborative piece from pupils, staff and parents depicted in the form of a tree with 'happy' as its trunk, supported by six roots – 'resourceful, ambitious, safe, respectful, responsible and compassionate'.

Parents prize the quality of care and support provided here – mirrored by the children, too, who think highly of their teachers. Children are unkind 'very rarely,' says the head and there is a very clear, five level behaviour code displayed in classrooms. When interrupting classes by talking to teachers we were impressed by how the pupils stayed on task despite having no supervision.

Healthy house competition, from fundraising to general knowledge quizzes; sport a highlight. Lots of opportunity for leadership throughout the school. Peer mentors are on the lookout in the playground for children sitting on the red bench – the designated spot if you are feeling sad and lonely – and rush to join them.

Prep pupils are challenged to think big through the curiosity emporium – when twice-termly visiting speakers cover controversial or ethically demanding topics across the spectrum of contemporary life and history. Greatly enhances their learning opportunities and stimulates a maturity of thought and exposure to the wider world.

The school serves the local community and a wider catchment of around 25 miles. A dedicated bus service offers 12 routes for year 3 pupils and above with starting times of between 7.15am and 7.30am for the furthest points.

Pupils mostly come from families with professional and business backgrounds and from a wide range of ethnicities. Parents are happy with communications with school, feel that 'there is a genuine open door policy' and staff respond promptly when contacted; teachers are 'well prepared with statistics and data and seem to understand our children well'. New starter parents provided with a 'what to expect when' toolkit so they can try to stay one jump ahead – with details of recommended screen time and bedtime routines.

A school that shows learning can be fun as well – fast paced with plenty of activity underpinned with reflection and resourcefulness. These are happy, bright, confident children with lots of opportunities for responsibilities and welcome them with genuine enthusiasm and pride.

Yarm School

Linked with Yarm Preparatory School

The Friarage, Yarm, Stockton on Tees TS15 9EJ

Ages 11–18 **Pupils** 764 **Sixth form** 208

Fees: £12,888 pa

01642 786023
www.yarmschool.org

Headmaster: Since 1999, David M Dunn BA PGCE (mid 50s). Previously deputy head at Stewart's Melville College in Edinburgh; first teaching post at alma mater Bolton School, where he was promoted to head of year 11 – a position he held for six years. Studied modern languages at Nottingham with a year teaching in Stuttgart before returning to complete a PGCE.

Only the second head in the school's short 40 year history, he is clearly and rightly proud of achievements here. Having accepted the post, his first appointment was his pastoral deputy head and together they have formed a dynamic duo of Davids for nearly 20 years.

Shrewd, upbeat, energetic and forward-thinking, described by parents as a 'strong leader with a clear vision' who has done 'a fantastic job' in bringing hopes, dreams and new buildings to fruition. He is a front man, a presence at all big school events – much appreciated by parents.

Believes that being happy at school is fundamental, being treated as an individual, excelling at something and celebrating achievement boosts self-esteem and confidence. Pastoral care huge – the PSHE spiral curriculum (known as SPaCE, social, political and citizenship education) covers meditation, mindfulness and resilience in increasing intricacy through the years, aiming to equip pupils to juggle the complexities of modern life.

Delighted to have attracted high calibre staff who each bring talent by contributing to the wide and diverse activities programme that all pupils participate in. Believes that pupil/teacher relationship strengthened by both seeing the other in a different guise outside the classroom.

Married to Fiona, who teaches PE and art at Yarm with pastoral responsibility for the sixth form. Two daughters, one at Oxford, the younger in the sixth form at Yarm.

Leaving in the summer 2019. His successor will be Dr Huw Williams, currently second master at Tonbridge. Studied anatomy and developmental biology at UCL before completing a PhD at Cambridge and the Wellcome Trust. Completed post-doctoral research at the Wellcome Trust and became a Cambridge research. Joined Westminster School to teach biology, becoming an assistant housemaster and then housemaster. He and his wife Laura, a lawyer, have three young children.

Academic matters: The recipe is simple: take cream of the local catchment area, add superb facilities and great, committed teachers and the results speak for themselves. Regularly one of the Sunday Times top two independent secondary schools in the north east on A level results.

After a dip in 2017, A level results up to 53 per cent A*/A, 78 per cent A*-B in 2018. Head comments, 'we are thrilled with our ranking which places the school amongst the best in the country. It is testament to the hard work of our staff and pupils, but this is not the whole story. At Yarm we are committed to developing pupils' skill beyond the classroom, from cultivating interpersonal and leadership skills to developing a "have a go" attitude. These are the abilities leading universities and employers look for, coupled with excellent results.'

Most pupils study three A level subjects, with able mathematicians adding further mathematics. An enrichment and extension programme aims to equip pupils with the character and resilience needed to cope with life after Yarm. For most this includes the EPQ.

Up with the best, 66 per cent of GCSE results were A*-A/9-7 in 2018. Science strong at the school, with biology, chemistry and physics all achieving more than 60 per cent A*/9-8 rate in IGCSEs. A fifth sat further maths, and half of these were awarded the highest grade of A* distinction.

Pupils normally take 10 GCSE subjects, including three options from a wide choice, with learning support as one of those. French is compulsory, with German for able linguists; dual award science for those who would find single sciences academically challenging. All can study for an international computer driving licence or an extension social, personal and citizenship education programme.

Plenty of academic rigour, with signature two sessions a week of timetabled chosen activities from the activities menu. No vocational subjects, though willingness to tailor courses to suit the individual. Maximum class size in senior school is 22, average 18, sixth form 16, average nine. GCSE options include DT (electronic products, textiles or product design), classics, religion and philosophy, Latin, German, Spanish and music. Ability sets for mathematics and modern foreign languages from the start, for English and science during GCSE years. Just one per cent have EAL requirement and eight per cent SEN – mostly mild dyslexia.

Careers education forms a key part of middle school SPaCE and tutorial programme. A biennial careers convention open to all pupils from year 10 up attracts over 120 providers from a diverse range of sectors – leading universities from around the region, representatives from industry, GAP year providers, as well as opportunities to meet with former pupils in various professions. A new initiative is career forums, bringing together former pupils and parents to form a 'careers cluster' at small discussion-type events. No formal work experience programme but up to date information, support and encouragement to research possible career pathways, higher level apprenticeships, summer placement schemes, plus a range of other careers-related events and courses.

Games, options, the arts: Excelling in competition is something Yarm does very well, and celebrating their pupils' successes lies at the heart of the school's ethos. Add in to the mix dedicated staff and some state of the art facilities, no wonder pupils here reach for the stars.

School located on the banks of the river Tees and rowing has become a major sport; former pupils have competed in Olympics, including 2012 gold medallist Katherine Copeland; brings back alumni too for an annual race. Stunning boathouse with growing fleet of boats and professional coaches has fuelled the interest and success, particularly in lightweight section, at national schools and international level. Great results too in rugby, hockey (boys and girls), netball and tennis with regional and county successes. Very inclusive and runs teams for all ages/skill levels.

Modern sports hall and much used fitness suite, tennis and netball courts and full size Astroturf on campus, but playing fields a trudge or bus ride away. Grand scheme to build a bridge across the Tees to reach green space and turn it into 11 playing pitches for school and community use has fallen foul of the planners four times through local resistance. Not a big deal but a nice to have, says the head, though local press reports suggest there may be a few ruffled feathers to smooth.

Prodigious art department with garret art rooms for sixth form – fine arts, print making and clay work, though no kiln. Pupils can attend local life drawing classes, photography offered on the activity programme but no computer graphics. Impressive quality of work – examination pieces on display in annual show. Forward thinking department organises an arts careers event; a good handful of students go on to study architecture, fashion and performance creation. The Tate building houses the extensive and well-ordered design technology workshops complete with 3D printer and laser cutter. For the first three years pupils are taught on a carousel of textiles, electronics and resistant materials and take up is good at GCSE with around 10 doing A level. Arkwright scholarships, sixth formers working on commercial projects with Bang and Olufsen and team Jaguar challenge are just some of the benefits here. Annual product and fashion show organised by pupils incorporates dance performances as well.

Latest new build music school opened in 2014 with performance space/lecture theatre, recording studio, composition room and numerous sound-proof practice rooms. Music raises the roof here with 10 different singing groups – massed choirs, barbershop, pop ensemble, a capella and over 20 orchestral and instrument ensembles covering a plethora of music styles. Music breakfasts, performances at all the big school school events, concerts and workshops, school music festival and big productions like Grease and Les Misérables, as well as international tours (Seville and Lisbon coming up) and community events mean the performance opportunities are endless.

Great dance studio promotes this art form throughout the school from nursery up and there's an annual showcase. Drama also a major strength across all ages and genres from classical Greek to Shakespeare and contemporary; very popular duologues competition; house drama; and it has the places to show it all off.

The crowning glory on the campus is the 800 seater Princess Alexandra auditorium with its more intimate 140 seater counterpart the Friarage Theatre. Both used extensively by the school, but also running an out of hours programme of professional entertainment for community audiences, attracting big names from the world of comedy, dance, music and theatre.

What sets Yarm apart is the breathtaking array of activities, with allocated sessions within the timetable as well as at lunchtime and out of school hours – with every member of staff offering at least two. All the usual sport and music and others such as debating and chess on offer, but add to that golf, self-publishing, meditation and tai chi, classical Greek, international relations, James Bond appreciation and ultimate frisbee and you're still not a quarter of the way through the list. And if that's not enough, DofE is also thriving here and they run a small company of CCF.

Have passport can travel: endless opportunities to see the world. Language and cultural trips to a number of European destinations; physics visit to CERN in Geneva; skiing in the Alps; tennis in the Portuguese sunshine and sailing in Greece. There are trips to Yarm's partner school in Werther, Germany each year as well as traditional exchange visits. Sports tours annually, most recently the girls' and boys' tours to South Africa. Closer to home there is plenty of opportunity for outdoor pursuits/adventure trips (two full-time outdoor education teachers); this is a school that understands just how much can be learned outside the classroom.

Background and atmosphere: School was born on the back of the education policy of grammar school closure and the vision, determination and gamble of the founding governors,

ICI executives whose sons were at the grammar school. They bought the old Yarm Grammar School building and started a new school with 50 boys in 1978. The nearby Friarage site, a 18th century stone-built mansion, was bought in 1980, and by 1996 the whole of the senior school was based there, allowing the prep school, which opened in 1991, use of the old grammar school building.

Girls joined in 2001 and there is now a 50:50 boy/girl mix. A mix of medieval buildings, the delightful Friarage dovecote – 'probably the oldest building for miles around' – used for open air summer concerts, modern sandstone developments, high spec and green too (heated by ground-source heat pumps and solar panels providing hot water), the sixth form centre housed in the old stable block; the whole environment feels cared for and respected. Corridors proudly festooned with striking art and design technology work lessen the slightly clinical and corporate feel.

Top London acousticians and Birmingham architects were employed to design the performing arts auditorium with 800 seat theatre including 60 person orchestra pit, retractable seating, two (naturally) grand pianos, bespoke organ, touch-of-a-switch window blackouts, all stunningly housed in natural materials including Norwegian oak and Lake District slate. It opens out to a glass atrium with stunning river views and attractive outdoor seating. Has to be seen to be appreciated – you forget you are in a school, yet it offers the most wonderful chill out space for pupils.

Parents say the school has a 'warmth' – and they don't just mean the buildings. They delight in the enthusiasm and commitment of teachers; one new parent told us that 'it has rekindled [his son's] love of learning which had left him in his previous school'. 'You can talk to them if there is a problem.' They recognise the mutual respect between pupils and staff and are happy to support school activities. Staff turnover here is low, and although parents become slightly twitchy at any staff departures, 'a good one leaves but another equally good one comes along'.

Real sense of a working community, huge staff – '245 on the payroll'; teaching and non-teaching staff all play their part: 'there's nothing we can't do ourselves,' confirms the head. Chefs ('not dinner ladies here'), and an in-house team of electricians, joiners, painters, gardeners and general workers all kept busy taking good care of the place – evident sense of pride and belonging. Teaching staff are well-supported and valued with every department having its own well-equipped work base. Intelligent management philosophy – 'set the bar high and people join in'; head and deputy lead by example.

Pastoral care, well-being and discipline: One parent summed it up for all: 'nothing is too much trouble for the school to ensure that the student is happy and enjoying their education'. Tutor groups meet twice daily; tutors are key to pupils' happiness and success and the first point of contact for parents. A school nurse is on hand to provide emotional support – just drop in.

All this is underpinned by the all-encompassing SPaCE programme, trained sixth form peer mentors and a flourishing house system. Four houses named after northern saints – Aidan, Bede, Cuthbert and Oswald – compete in sixth form led drama competition and sports. Each house runs a fundraising week for their chosen charity and the lower years accrue credits for academic effort and good behaviour, tallied for their house.

Parents tell us they are 'particularly impressed with the atmosphere at the school; poor behaviour, bullying and meanness are not tolerated and good behaviour is celebrated in a way which engenders a very positive environment at school'.

Pupils and parents: Yarm is an affluent, middle class market town and high street shops reflect that there's money around. But pupils come from a wide catchment area, transported on a fleet of private coaches covering 12 different routes: Hartlepool in the north, Thirsk in the south, creeping across the A1 past Darlington in the west, Saltburn in the east. Some 10 per cent Asian, American, African families, nearly all middle to upper professional/management with a preponderance of medics.

The pupils we met were easy to engage in conversation, articulate yet reflective in their responses, confident and well grounded. They value and appreciate the wealth of opportunities offered here, particularly the commitment their teachers give both in and out of the classroom.

Parents tell us that pupil progress reports are thorough and regular. Although there is just one parents' evening a year, direct contact with teachers invariably gets a quick response. Regular stream of information sent to parents through weekly newsletters and parent portal.

Entrance: Entrance assessments for 11+ in maths, reading, writing and spelling. Good school reports also needed – looking for minimum level 5 equivalent at key stage 2. Extensive induction programme for new starters and at the end of the first week, a Saturday discovery day with team building activities rounded off with a family BBQ.

A rigorous process for sixth form applicants – need to have taken at least eight GCSEs, and achieve a 4 or better in mathematics and English plus specific grades for A level subjects.

Exit: The 20 per cent or so who leave post-GCSE mostly head for excellent local state sixth form colleges. Sixth formers mostly to university, with about eight per cent a year to Oxbridge (five Oxford places in 2018). Northern universities – Durham, York, Leeds, Teesside, Newcastle, Northumbria – seem favourites, mostly to study traditional degree courses. Mathematics, engineering, English, economics and modern languages all popular. Fourteen to medical school in 2018 and three dentists. Others to eg the Royal Birmingham Conservatoire and The Rose Bruford College of Theatre and Performance, London

Money matters: No endowments but Yarm dedicates five per cent of income to fee support and may providing a bursary to families earning less than £50,000 a year. A few academic and music scholarships of up to 10 per cent; sixth form Arkwright Scholarships for DT.

Remarks: An impressive school led by those with strong belief in their educational vision, bold enough to take monumental decisions to deliver an award winning campus of excellent facilities. No old school complacency here, all achieved in less than 40 years, and yet pupils and staff are refreshingly unpretentious, well rounded and hard working – well armed for life post-Yarm. Academically strong, excellent achievements in sport and the arts, opportunities abound, whatever your interests and talents. With two community theatres on site too, it's a wonder anyone finds the time to go home.

Scotland

City of Aberdeen
Angus
Argyll
Ayrshire
Bute
Clackmannanshire
Dunbartonshire
City of Dundee
East Lothian
City of Edinburgh
Fife
City of Glasgow
Invernessshire
Lanarkshire
Moray
Perthshire
Renfrewshire
Roxburghshire
Stirlingshire

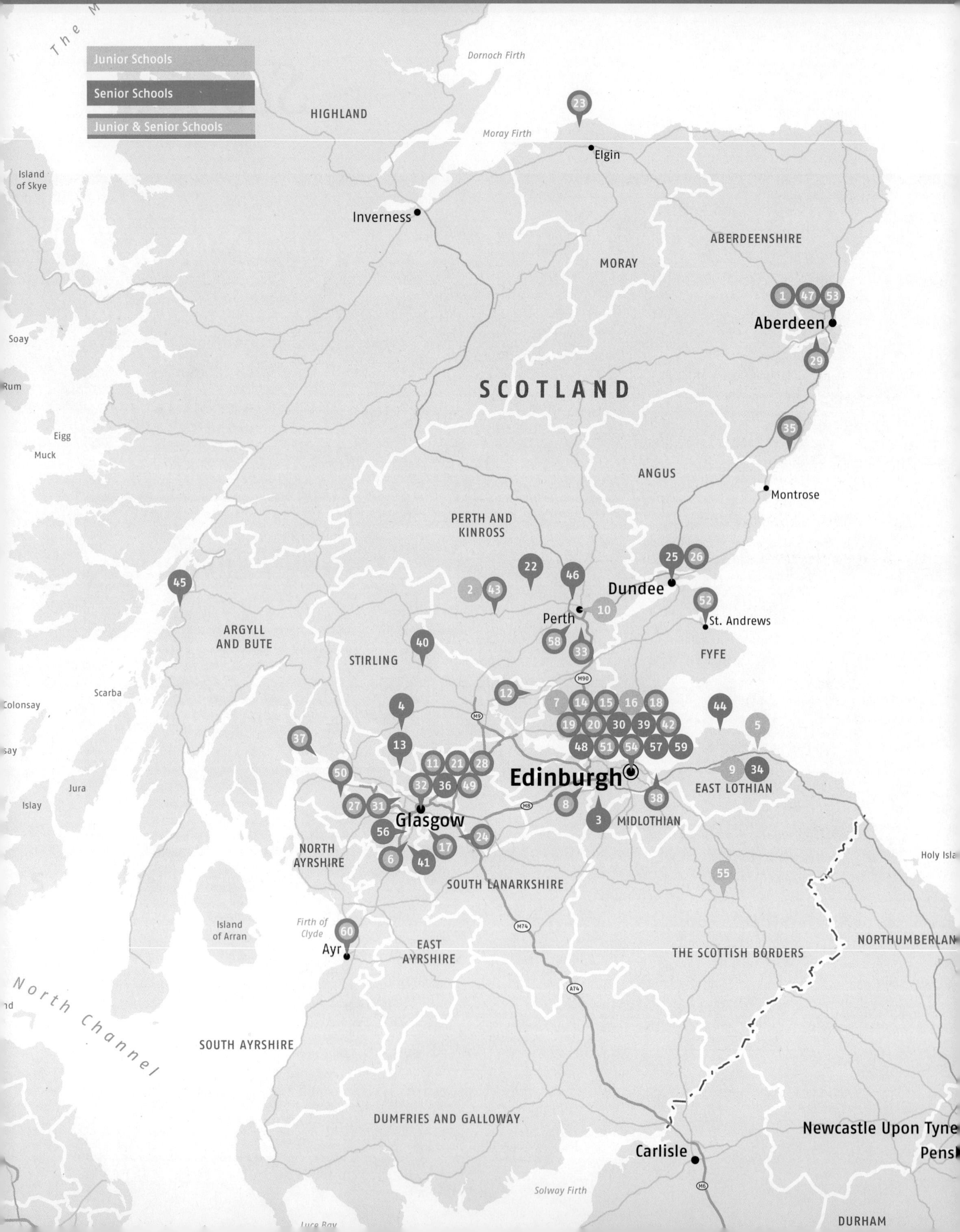

Junior Schools

Senior Schools

Junior & Senior Schools

The M

Dornoch Firth

HIGHLAND

23

Moray Firth

Elgin

Island of Skye

Inverness

ABERDEENSHIRE

MORAY

1 47 53

Aberdeen

Soay

29

Rum

SCOTLAND

35

Eigg

Muck

ANGUS

Montrose

PERTH AND KINROSS

25 26

22

46

45

2 43

Dundee

10

52

Perth

St. Andrews

ARGYLL AND BUTE

58

33

40

FYFE

STIRLING

M90

12

Colonsay

Scarba

7 14 15 16 18

4

M9

44

19 20 30 39 42

5

say

37

13

48 51 54 57 59

11 21 28

50

9 34

Jura

Edinburgh

32 36 49

EAST LOTHIAN

Islay

27 31

M8

8

38

Glasgow

3

MIDLOTHIAN

56

24

17

NORTH AYRSHIRE

Holy Isla

6

41

55

SOUTH LANARKSHIRE

Island of Arran

Firth of Clyde

60

M74

Ayr

EAST AYRSHIRE

NORTHUMBERLAN

THE SCOTTISH BORDERS

North Channel

nd

A74

SOUTH AYRSHIRE

DUMFRIES AND GALLOWAY

Newcastle Upon Tyne

Carlisle

Pens

M6

Solway Firth

Luce Bay

DURHAM

SCOTLAND

1 Albyn School 1858
2 Ardvreck School 1859
3 Balerno Community High School 1861
4 Balfron High School 1862
5 Belhaven Hill School 1864
6 Belmont House School 1865
7 Cargilfield School 1867
8 Clifton Hall School 1868
9 The Compass School 1870
10 Craigclowan School 1871
11 Craigholme School 1872
12 Dollar Academy 1873
13 Douglas Academy 1875
14 The Edinburgh Academy 1877
15 Edinburgh Steiner School 1879
16 ESMS Junior School 1882
17 Fernhill School 1883
18 Fettes College 1885
19 George Heriot's School 1887
20 George Watson's College 1889
21 The Glasgow Academy 1890
22 Glenalmond College 1892
23 Gordonstoun 1894
24 Hamilton College 1895
25 Harris Academy 1897
26 High School of Dundee 1898
27 The High School of Glasgow 1900
28 Hutchesons' Grammar School 1902
29 The International School Aberdeen 1904
30 James Gillespie's High School 1906
31 Jordanhill School 1907
32 Kelvinside Academy 1909
33 Kilgraston School 1912
34 Knox Academy 1913
35 Lathallan School 1915
36 Lenzie Academy 1916
37 Lomond School 1918
38 Loretto School 1919
39 The Mary Erskine School 1922
40 McLaren High School 1923
41 Mearns Castle High School 1925
42 Merchiston Castle School 1926
43 Morrison's Academy 1928
44 North Berwick High School 1930
45 Oban High School 1931
46 Perth Grammar School 1933
47 Robert Gordon's College 1935
48 The Royal High School (Edinburgh) 1937
49 St Aloysius' College 1938
50 St Columba's School 1940
51 St George's School (Edinburgh) 1941
52 St Leonards School 1943
53 St Margaret's School for Girls (Aberdeen) 1945
54 St Mary's Music School 1947
55 St Mary's School (Melrose) 1948
56 St Ninian's High School 1949
57 Stewart's Melville College 1951
58 Strathallan School 1953
59 Wallace College 1955
60 Wellington School 1956

A

Albyn School

17–23 Queens Road, Aberdeen AB15 4PB

Ages 2–18 **Pupils** 646 **Sixth form** 132 **Boarders** 4 full

Fees: Day £8,6371 – £13,636; Boarding £27,811 – £29,948 pa

01224 322408
www.albynschool.co.uk

Headmaster: Since 2008, Dr Ian Long BA AKC BA MA PhD FRGS FRSA (50s); read geography at King's London and, after a brief spell with Shell (always good to get the outside perspective) worked in a variety of schools before becoming head of sixth form at Brentwood, followed by eight years as (academic) deputy head of City of London Freemen's School.

A lapsed rower and a clever clogs who came to a school on the cusp; the previous head had worked miracles: some a tad expensive. Long has tightened up the finance side. No more babies (staffing ratio hideous) and huge increase in both nursery and chaps throughout the school. 'Always wanted to work abroad' but hadn't quite expected to find Scotland, and possibly Aberdeen in particular, quite so different from previous experiences.

An engaging and entertaining head with a sparkling sense of humour, he is also dead efficient and our request for detailed exam results by subject over the previous three years arrived before we left the place. Wife, Gwyneth, was previously deputy head at Channing School in Highgate, having started her teaching career at St Leonard's School down the coast in Fife as a Latin teacher and assistant housemistress. She teaches classics in the school.

Head of lower school: Since 2016, Nathan Davies, deputy head here since 2009. Read medieval history at St Andrews before taking a PGCSE at Dundee. He joined Albyn School from Wakefield Grammar School and had also 'done time' at Piling Middle School in Jamestown, St Helena. With five children of his own, Nathan takes the notion of a family school to a new level.

Academic matters: Lower school follows (somewhat expensive) International Primary Curriculum (IPC), which seems sensible when you realise it was designed by Shell, taught globally and Albyn is an international oily school. IPC is thematic based, with rather natty books to be filled in when 'I understand'. Terrific exposure to all manner of cultures: this is exciting stuff. Jolly Phonics in nursery, handwriting important.

Mostly Scottish system: massive numbers and successes in both disciplines with chemistry, physics, biology, maths, English and selection of mod langs. All must take one lang at Nat 5 and choose two, having done a 'taster course' in German, French, Spanish and Mandarin, for min two years at S1; currently Mandarin the most popular. Geography needs a kick: classics working its way up; classical civilisation and mythology (wowser) growing, from S1/2 (and we loved our culture lesson). Greek possible: but no takers to date.

Computing science has poked its head above the parapet; but won't set the world alight yet. Nary a presentation at Advanced Higher level. Business management and modern studies make a showing, with the former probably better overall. Product design and information systems new kids on the block, and stunning. German not currently the flavour of the month. Drama with higher level PE on offer. Spanish (from the upper fifth), Mandarin and engineering science (with its own centre) are the latest additions to the curriculum. Certain amount of almost individual teaching; the results are impressive (if hardly cost-effective). Strong showing in maths challenge and problem-solving. Graphic communication (now replaced by engineering science) increasingly popular with successes at National 5 level, ditto art and design. In 2018, 58 per cent As at Higher level and 39 per cent at Advanced Higher (a very few GCSEs and A level sat).

In August 2018 amalgamated with the Total French School of Aberdeen, and developed a hybrid curriculum designed by Mission Laïque Française (MLF). For those choosing the hybrid curriculum, French, maths, geography, history and citizenship are taught and assessed in French, with all other subjects taught in English.

Class size is low 20s, with low teens for practical subjects (school says 20, but in practice this is much smaller; most classes are 10/15). Comprehensive computer system, class-taught as well as in suites, laptops abound.

All assessed on entry, five learning support teachers cover the whole school, and a pupil's IEP follows throughout their time. No problems with dyslexia, dyspraxia and mild Asperger's, and in the past did well for a pupil who was profoundly deaf. 'Some timetabled EFL support now available – mostly for clever Chinese – plus lots of support in the classroom', SEN teacher takes individual groups and double teaches a bit – she is very 'willing' – and was off to help out in a German lesson after we had talked. Scribing, readers and all the rest. No extra charge for SEN help. Digital exams being mooted by SQA, school is investigating voice recognition programmes.

Parents of pupils who underperformed at National 5s were stunned to discover that their young did not automatically go forward into sixth form: retakes possible, but school is keen to build on its academic successes. Vociferous (mainly local) parents are less than amused.

Games, options, the arts: Main games field at Milltimber, five miles away – pupils are bused, fabulous athletics track. Albyn uses university's state-of-the-art sports village for a number of sports: athletics, hockey, football, netball. Positive netball and hockey with regional representation and masses of individual sports: national representation in several. Snowboarding and skiing popular plus golf. With boys throughout the upper school, serious thought was given to what sport the boys would play: 'Both rugby and football have fervent adherents among parents of the boys, but the latter may be more realistic if we are not to be beaten 80–0 for the next five years'; school recently trounced Glenalmond at footie. 'Rowing may be the answer.' And so it is. Boys and girls are already competing successfully up to Nat Schools level: boating out of Robert Gordon's University boathouse (pairs, quads) but, as yet no eights.

Stunning art department, with a number of pupils going on to higher things in the art world, though not art school per se recently. Very jolly papier mâché, acrylic and silk screen work, fabric design. Hot on costume design and much use made of local museums. Exciting stained glass – bendy stained glass, if you follow. Always a joy to come here. Strong art and architectural stream. Impressive computer graphics mostly on CD covers.

Fantastic music – 'most play a musical instrument' – and loads of participation in either choir or instrumental ensembles. Snazzy professional standard recording studio. Good representation in the National Youth Orchestra plus jazz, ceilidh bands. Blues band. Keen drama and dance (Dancercise important). No CCF or pipe band, though one or two pipers. Clarsach.

Enthusiastic Young Enterprise, RAF cadets and highly competitive DofE with oodles of golds. Strong club culture

– quizzes, chess, gardening. Keen on public speaking and debating. Head has encouraged trips: Borneo, Barbados, Morocco and Zambia and cultural tours to Italy and south of France. (Some – mainly indigenous – parents, are not entirely convinced of their necessity: this is Aberdeen, after all.)

The only RAF cadets in Scotland.(Not the only one in Scotland unfortunately.)We found the DofE squad preparing for parents' evening during our tour: boots, cagoules, tents, mattresses et al were all on show. 'And', said the master in charge, 'if the parents haven't got the kit, or balk at the price, most of us can find something in our garages'. Now that's the kind of school we like.

Boarding: A boarding house sleeping eight was opened in 2016.

Background and atmosphere: Founded in 1867 by Harriet Warrack, who started teaching girls at home, advertising locally for pupils. Albyn Place (just down the road) became the school's home in 1881, and Albyn School for Girls moved to Queen's Road in 1925. The son of one of the gardeners at Duff House, Alexander Mackie, was an early moving light, writing books on English (he was a university examiner) and made the school an Aberdeen institution, with emancipated Albyn girls on Aberdeen University student council by 1907. Boys started in the junior department in 2005 and worked their way up, now roughly 55/45 per cent girls/boys. The head was pleased to find his original desk in a passage and it now graces his office (the roll-top concealing all manner of educational detritus).

School based in four attached Victorian merchants' houses, with fantastic ceilings, well-used library and predictable garden expansion. Harriet House houses the toddlers, aged 2 to 3 years, while the juniors have new-build, with classrooms clustered round a splendid hall (with windows on the first floor) giving both extra light and affording entertainment. Lifts in junior school make disabled access available almost everywhere.

Most recent build in 2014 includes sixth form study area with hideous purple and plum high backed chairs (pupils' choice of colours) and surprisingly comfortable plastic chairs at work stations. No plugs. Laptops arrive by trolley load. Junior library (filled with the same young whom we met in the gym) all agreed, when asked, that 'yes, it was a good school'. Lecture theatre/performance space and fitness suite overlooking gym and containing rather a desirable throne. Impressive music department above hall/gym.

Pastoral care, well-being and discipline: School divided into four quite competitive clans, Douglas, Stuart, Forbes and Gordon. No tutors; pupils can, and do, relate to form teachers and guidance staff when in difficulty. Wickedness equals yellow card, followed by red card, usual punishment is an essay. Sense of community – school aims to boost the confidence of the shyest child. Policy of zero tolerance for drink 'n' drugs 'n' rock 'n' roll, so expect to be out for persistent bullying or drugs. Cigarettes and alcohol on school premises = detention followed by exclusion followed by out. 'Bullying is usually changing friendship groups' seems about right, but actual bullying is regarded as a no-no. Cyber-bullying has become increasingly problematic. If there is real cause for concern, then parents are summonsed for a 'discussion'. First school we have visited to have an LGBT counsellor.

Pupils and parents: Mixture of professionals – around 60 per cent oil and gas, the occasional farmer and marine engineer in the parent body. The former often have to either move or install their young at short notice. Huge ethnic mix. Fair number of first-time buyers; parents can drop off early (from 8am, breakfast available) and pick up late (6pm, having done their homework) but this comes with cost. Recent Nigerian influx through local church, and quite a number of Chinese pupils of late. And a few French, since the amalgamation with the French School of Aberdeen.

International bias, but lots of home-grown ones too; strong middle class ethos with girls neat in check dresses or kilts from October to April. Boys are allowed to wear kilts but few do: mostly on special occasions.

Comprehensive parent-organised bus system, min age 5/6: tinies, unless with older sibling, not encouraged.

Entrance: Entry from lower to upper is automatic. Pupils can and do join at any time – throughout the year (assuming space available). Growing number, but 'still only a handful' join school for Highers/Advanced Highers at S5/6. Increasing interest from overseas.

Exit: Around 10-20 per cent leave post Highers in S5, mostly to Scottish unis or for financial constraints. Most to university, odd gap year. Mainly to the (freebie) Scottish unis, with a few south of the border. Currently Strathclyde and Robert Gordon most popular with Edinburgh and St Andrews close behind; generally several to Aberdeen, some to Heriott-Watt and Edinburgh Napier. One to Oxford in 2018 (materials science) and two medics; one to Yale (economics) ad one to Princeton (mechanical and aerospace engineering).

Money matters: Incredibly strict scale of rules for payment but (Aberdeen, remember) parents can get a two per cent discount if they pay the whole annual whack within a fortnight of the beginning of the autumn term. Discounts of five per cent for second child from pre-school nursery up and 50 per cent rebate for third and subsequent children. School 'will do what it can to help parents in difficult times, as long as they are open and talk to us'. Can, and will do, 100 per cent bursary if need be, including uniform and help with trips (apply December, entry test Jan: school carries out stringent financial checks). Be aware, too, the SQA charges exam fees, and there is extra cost for materials used in art and design.

Remarks: Co-ed throughout, this is a school on a roll, small enough for every child to be known as an individual and big enough to offer the best in modern teaching methods. Not a scary school, and some first time buyers do find the independent sector intimidating: welcoming, nurturing and ticking all the boxes. Go for it.

Ardvreck School

Gwydyr Road, Crieff, Perthshire PH7 4EX

Ages 3-13 **Pupils** 110 **Boarders** 40 (from 7 years)

Fees: Day £7,005 – £14,961;Boarding £22,485 pa

01764 653112
www.ardvreckschool.co.uk

Head: Since July 2018, Ali Kinge, previously deputy head and English teacher, and the school's first headmistress. Received a British Citizen Award for her charity fundraising over 30 years, including via the Etape Royal 100 mile cycle race, the Great Kindrochit Quadrathlon (swimming, fell running, kayaking and cycling) and the London Marathon – despite breaking her neck and back in a horrific cycle accident whilst training 10 months beforehand. Her husband, Stephen, is a physicist; three teenage sons.

Entrance: Children come from all over Scotland, although the majority are from Perthshire and surrounding area. A smallish number join Little Ardvreck's pre-prep or thriving nursery, which includes forest school principles, ie children under 6 should have some of their lessons outside, encouraging an appreciation of the environment. Most children, however arrive between the ages of 8-10.

Exit: The majority to public schools in Scotland and England. St Mary's Ascot, Radley, Oundle, Uppingham, Fettes, Strathallen and, of course, a sizeable proportion to nearby Glenalmond College, which historically has a close relationship to the school.

Remarks: A lovely, warm, friendly and nurturing school. One parent said they were sold on the place after coming up the drive and seeing some boys bursting out of the bushes with rosy red cheeks, play-fighting with sticks. We hate to use that hackneyed comparison Famous Five, but gingerbread, crackling fires and pop for tea really springs to mind. It's a beautiful setting, perched on a rather steep incline, just west of Crieff. Its central core is a rather austere Victorian house with a straggly collection of satellite buildings (like many schools), but nestling around it is 42 acres of woodland and breathtaking scenery. A truly idyllic environment if you like the idea of fresh air and outdoor pursuits for your children.

When we visited some parents had concerns about changes in staffing at the school over the past few years. 'Evolution not revolution would have been better.' School says, 'there is now an excellent blend of experienced and new teachers to take the school forward'; another parent's view: 'We needed new blood and now that the changes have happened hopefully everything will settle down.'

So a few grumbles and misgivings from parents at the top end of the school, but many more appear to have great faith in long term plans for the school. When we visited there was mention of the 'excellent' deputy Alison Kinge, now the head, and what was also clear was the very strong belief among parents further down the school. 'Great family spirit.' 'It's easy to pick holes, but it works.' 'It's still got a huge amount to offer.' Above all, most parents said their children were very happy at Ardvreck. 'When our eldest left we couldn't have had a more rounded, happy child.' Prep has now been reintroduced but children still have time to de-stress in the evenings.

Various recent staff appointments include a director of studies to focus on academics and improve 'our already good levels of academic achievement'. A scholarship and a common entrance set now from the fifth form. They've invested in a new science lab and new computers in all their classrooms. They have a set of iPads for form 1 and the whole school has ready access to an IT room for lessons. 'This is an area we want to develop, along with the new director of studies.' School wants a careful balance between embracing technology in teaching and controlling access to the internet. 'We do allow it for limited time in the boarding houses, but we want children to embrace the wonderful surroundings. We value talking to each other and one of our most important tenets is that Ardvreck allows children to be children. They will have plenty of time in the future to come to terms with the full world of internet and the media.' We couldn't agree more.

With Ardvreck positioned in the middle of an area of outstanding beauty, outdoor education is clearly important, and to this effect they have a specialist who can teach kayaking, skiing and archery and is a trained mountain leader. Put it this way, we wouldn't challenge him to a race for a bus. This charming and enthusiastic member of staff has already swept up a Pied Piper type following and has embraced the school's outdoor ethos, ie every child will camp, or Barvick as it's known (we have no explanation, we're afraid), and three times a year the school closes on a Saturday and every child goes up a mountain and down a glen.

'We do everything from bushcraft skills to knife craft, fire lighting and cooking over an open fire.' (Famous Five again.) This is so that they can avoid force-feeding facts, but rather introduce ideas and encourage the children to think for themselves. 'We want them to have the courage of their own convictions and have the ability to think for themselves and to convey their views confidently.' Sounds good, and both the parents and the children are more than on board for this part of the Ardvreck experience.

If ever a boarding school can be a home from home, then Ardvreck probably fits the bill. It's not glamorous and it's not very modern, but it has a cosy charm which we could imagine younger children feeling very at home with. They have recently appointed a new head of boarding, so changes may be afoot, but the current model – which has junior boarding in the main building, graduating to chalet type accommodation for the top two years with common rooms to match – seems to work.

They describe themselves as a full boarding school with only two exeats a term. What this means, in effect, is that 30 per cent are full boarders, but 60 per cent 'step up' to part-time boarding. Step Up is a package where they can board three or four nights a week to prepare them for full boarding at senior school. They say they're trying to avoid the term flexi-boarding although we're not quite sure what the difference is.

Once in the senior years the children are encouraged to take more responsibility for themselves: they have separate activities from the juniors and are given the chance to take on chores such as doing their own washing. There is plenty of opportunity to mix between the sexes, with the girls sometimes visiting the boys' common rooms, but as with most girls and boys of this age they like their own space and Ardvreck provides that.

Another recent appointment is a learning support professional. 'We think at some point all children need support in their learning and believe his teaching is outstanding in this respect. He has already brought improvements, introducing new learning techniques to enhance academic learning.'

Ardvreck maintains a very high sporting profile for rather a small school, fielding an impressive array of teams in a wide variety of sports. They have their own swimming pool (covered by what looks like a strawberry tunnel) and have just hired a new swimming coach. One parent told us that they 'wipe the decks' in terms of swimming competitions. Every year the school hosts the ARD challenge, which is a 14 mile yomp with five command tasks: air rifle shooting, simulated medical disaster, rifle shooting, moving 'explosives', walking through a minefield and a memory test. We're exhausted just writing about it, but it does sound both challenging and fun. It finishes on the banks of Loch Tay with a BBQ, spit roast and the school's wood fire pizza open ready to rustle up some tasty 'scran'. Lots of hearty exercise and food.

Art and music seem to be rather strong too. They've recently appointed a new art teacher and the school is proud of its record in art scholarships. Musically they seem very active: woodwind group, choir, ceilidh band, brass group and last but not least a very good pipe band (essential for a good Scottish prep school). This intrepid group played Highland Cathedral on top of Ben Nevis. You just can't keep an Ardvreckian down, or indoors for that matter.

Balerno Community High School

5 Bridge Road, Balerno EH14 7AQ

Ages 11–18 **Pupils** 694 **Sixth form** S5 113, S6 90

01314 777788
www.balernochs.wordpress.com

Headteacher: Since August 2016, Neil McCallum. BEd in physical education from Moray House School of Education, part of the University of Edinburgh. From Greenock, just outside Glasgow, his teaching career has predominantly been in Edinburgh. Formerly PE teacher at Forrester High and head of PE then depute head at James Gillespie's High.

Plans for the future include updating the building and potential expansion to accommodate anticipated increased pupil numbers. During his time as head he is proud to have established a partnership with Hearts Football Club (its academy is in the school) and launched the school of rugby in conjunction with Currie Rugby Club.

Came across as an exceptionally nice man. 'Friendly and supportive.' Highly regarded by pupils; one told us: 'Mr McCallum has made a real difference to the school atmosphere. He is very popular and well liked.' Married with two boys – who don't attend the school. He jokes: 'I wouldn't do that to them'. Wife is a lecturer at City of Glasgow College. Sport is a passion and he enjoys watching his pupils compete. Interests include continued learning about education, theory and leadership, reading autobiographies and exercising. Used to play rugby but, in his own words, 'I'm too old now'. Runs when he can.

Academic matters: In 2018, 58 per cent of pupils got 3+ Highers and 33 per cent got 5+. No Oxbridge places in recent years. MFL (French and Spanish) to Higher only. AH courses include maths of mechanics, PE, computing, music, art and design and modern studies alongside core subjects. Students from other schools come to do AH biology and Higher photography. No subject divides between the genders.

There are three support for pupils leaders, alongside the support for learning leader. Individual audit sessions (there are a number of pupils on the autistic spectrum) and withdrawal from class all available, plus comprehensive tutorial support, use of ICT (laptops available) and extra time in exams. Extra help from dedicated staff for the relatively few non-native English speakers. S6s also mentor in literacy and numeracy. 'The younger ones really enjoy that.'

Head girl showed us around the learning resource centre with computer room and the large library, popular with S6s. She praised the 'great guidance support' she received when applying to study medicine (she got a place!).

Staff tend to stay a long time, leaving for retirement or promotion; 75 per cent of senior management are women.

School roll likely to increase to 1,000–1,200 in next five years to accommodate a merge of local Edinburgh schools and lots of new house building (we noticed the new builds on our drive in). Head pleased about the change. He says: 'I'm used to working in that size of school.' However, the proposals have caused some controversy, and there has been recent press coverage of protests by concerned parents and pupils at the City Chambers.

All of S4 do work experience, and it is voluntary in S5 and S6; 98 per cent of pupils go on to further education, apprenticeships, university or the workplace.

Games, options, the arts: Benefiting from a 3G Astro pitch, Balerno has an impressive sporting record and is home to a football academy for Heart of Midlothian (Hearts), providing an environment where pupils can combine their studies and footballing education up until the age of 16, plus the new school of rugby. One of the top PE depts in the city. Participation levels are high with impressive achievements in a variety of sports. Serious 20-metre swimming on-site. 'Lucky to accommodate all sports.'

Drama AH available since 2018 due to popularity and demand. School shows – recently Annie, West Side Story, Bugsy Malone, Chicago and Les Miz – performed in drama studio with theatre seating. The Power Trip was devised by pupils and the musical Dukeboy was written by three S6s. Local primary school children join the cast to get them ready for secondary school. Also hosts the popular dance show choreographed by pupils.

Lashings of music, available at all exam levels, with instrumentalists of all types in a plethora of groups and choirs. On our tour pupils were enthusiastically practising for a school concert. There are spring and Christmas concerts and range of community events, such as performing at Queens Hall and at the annual music festival in Balerno. Art everywhere and available up to AH, with photography available to Higher. Annual Christmas card competition and John Byrne competition drawings on display. Biggest of all is the huge artwork by S6s based on Shakespeare's A Midsummer's Nights Dream. We were shown Higher design headpieces and an amazing self-portrait by an S6 in the art studio. Edinburgh College and West Lothian College of Art are popular destinations for artists. We were intrigued by a reptilian-style chequered jacket, described as having a 'park aesthetic', which was worn by an art teacher to the school prom.

There is a huge array of extracurricular activities including all sorts of sport and a range of outdoor education, with DofE up to gold – sixth year expeditions by canoe. Debating, mixed martial arts, disaster film club (featuring films like Everest), a lunch-time Latin club (a trickle sitting it at Nat 5), zoological club and the John Muir Trust Club (to protect the natural environment and wildlife). Majority are on-site, except for martial arts. All are free because of the Active Schools Programme, which is run by sportscotland with local authorities to help schools provide sporting opportunities.

The school even has its own credit union, run entirely by students.

International outlook for a Scottish suburban school, with European exchanges to places such as Copenhagen, staying with host families. Senior students participate in numerous international conferences run by Model United Nations. Increasing numbers of school trips, introduced by current head, include skiers to France, history and modern studies to Washington and New York, watersports in Spain, languages to Strasbourg. More locally, S1 bonding retreats in Scotland, S3 to London and football trips to Old Trafford. Two year gap between trips allows time to save up and there's funding available for those on low incomes; the aim is to develop skills rather than just having a holiday.

Lots of charity fundraising. A nominated charity is chosen by each house, eg the Teenage Cancer Trust. Recently raised over £5,000 for Jak Den, a local cancer charity.

Background and atmosphere: Has historic antecedents – the charming logbook kept by the principal teacher of St Mungo's Episcopal School in Balerno during the 19th century is a joy: 'Wet and windy all week. One child was blown into the Water of Leith but was fortunately rescued. One child was bit by a dog..'. The present school was opened on a glorious greenfield site on the banks of the Water of Leith, at the foot of the Pentlands, after several years of 'swithering' in 1983. Somehow in the process it turned into something resembling a 60s nuclear power station. It's nearly as difficult to get in since the entrance is in an apparently dead-end corner. (The welcome, however, was very warm.)

A bit too tatty to be contemporary, despite the exposed pipes and ceilings, it feels almost factory-like. Huge long passages, bare concrete staircases with scaffolding poles as banisters and narrow staircases. The plus factor is a long, spacious indoor area, which feels like a shopping mall and is wonderful for community events like craft fairs. It also forms a wet weather concourse with access to everything and pupils congregate there for break and lunch. An issue, however, is that not everyone can fit into the canteen. 'There are complaints that there are not enough benches for all the kids to sit together.'

Head says: 'The school needs updating in places, but it's the quality of teaching that's important.' Balerno people see it as their school and are proud of its achievements and its role in community education and enterprise. 'Fantastic reputation. Parents want to send kids from far and wide.' People are buying properties to be near to the school. Easy access, at the end of the Lanark Rd corridor. Head's ambition is for it to be a top-performing school and 'a jewel in Edinburgh's crown'.

Traditional school uniform with mandatory blazer, though there is a winter amnesty where pupils can wear warmer jackets.

Pastoral care, well-being and discipline: All pupils join one of three houses called after local areas: Bavelaw, Cockburn and Malleny. Siblings in same house; guidance team of three are in charge of pastoral care and guidance. Same tutor throughout the school, a good contact for parents on academic matters. Head Start for 'vulnerable' pupils before they begin at Balerno, when the new S1s, S6s and staff spend a week confidence-building. S1 pupils also spend a bonding week with their guidance and pastoral staff at one of three residential centres during their first term. Regular year group and house assemblies. Head boy and girl play a strong leadership role. Very low exclusion rates – head says he has brought these down considerably – and instances of indiscipline rare.

'School meals are brilliant – the best'. A high number of staff use the canteen. Typical menu of sandwiches, soup, salads and healthy main courses. Though we did notice Slushie machines in canteen, perhaps not the healthiest choice but undoubtedly popular with the kids. Very small numbers on free school meals.

Working towards Rights Respecting School status.

Pupils and parents: On the edge of the countryside, it attracts farming families as well as those from suburban and urban areas of Edinburgh. Parents mainly middle class, with small number from more deprived backgrounds. Small numbers of ethnic minorities. Well-organised parent council with its own Facebook forum and a PTA raising significant funds.

Parent communication is by email, though hard copy available if requested. Pupils successes are celebrated on Twitter. Online parents' evening booking system and at least three reports per year (tracking and full report).

Committed and socially aware pupils. The eco committee is working to reduce waste as there were no recycling bins when we visited. Pupils were looking to bring in reusable tubs to help. S6s deliver the Mentors in Violence Prevention (MVP) programme to S1s on a weekly basis and the Cool, Calm and Connected (CCC) course, which aims to raise teen confidence, and to help understand the teenage brain.

Notable former pupils: Karen Bennett (Olympic rower), Adam Cox (Commonwealth Games gymnast), Neil Alexander (professional footballer), Graham Moodie (Olympic hockey player), Craig McNally (Commonwealth Games swimmer).

Entrance: SFrom three local primaries – Dean Park, Ratho and Kirknewton – plus many others whose pupils request placements every year from as far as the east side of Glasgow, Motherwell, Fife, Dunfermline and Dunbar. Waiting list for lower year groups for non-catchment kids. School buses from within catchment are free. Bus pupils from outside the area helped by the parents' council, if possible, but at extra cost.

Exit: Don't lose many at the end of S4/S5, those that leave mostly move on to apprenticeships. Head reassured us that the doors don't shut once they leave, telling us that vulnerable kids sometimes come back to say hello and ask for career advice. Good numbers to mostly Scottish universities.

Remarks: A community school that is expanding and growing in popularity. Impressive sporting achievements (home to a football and rugby school), thriving art and music departments and a head with a focus to improve academic attainment. Popular choice with parents, with lots of new houses being built in the area. Worth applying from out of catchment as pupils come from far and wide.

Balfron High School

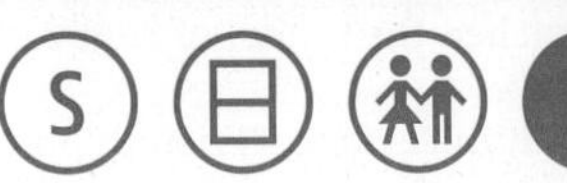

Roman Road, Balfron G63 0PW

Ages 11–18 **Pupils** 900 **Sixth form** 300

01360 440469
www.blogs.glowscotland.org.uk/st/balfronhighschool

Head teacher: Since 2013, Elaine Bannatyne (40s), previously depute head at Bearsden Academy for seven years and principal teacher of guidance prior to that. Has also been assistant principal teacher of guidance and PE teacher at Greenock High in Inverclyde. BEd from Edinburgh then straight into teaching. Three summers at the International Summer Camp Montana in the Swiss Alps, leading and counselling young people in a range of sport activities.

'Accessible' and with an 'open-door policy', she is serious about meeting the needs of all pupils, the academic who need to be challenged, those who will blossom vocationally and those with support needs. One pupil said: 'She is passionate about creating an inclusive school and improving vocational skills'. And Higher results have improved under her leadership, too, with 'steady increases in attainment at all levels'.

Future plans are underway, in partnership with the local authority, to transform the support for learning resource to include indoor sensory and nurture rooms, plus an outdoor sensory space for a growing number of pupils with additional support needs. Health and well-being is a passion of hers too.

She laughed that 'it's a bit true that I'm married to the job' and has '900 pupils as my children'. Protectively, she joked that the school 'was not a good school but a great one'. 'My days of being really active are over', but she still enjoys playing golf, running and tennis. We found her friendly and pupils at ease in her company. One pupil said, 'I had never spoken to the old head. Ms Bannatyne is extremely approachable and is a part of your school experience.'

She had to dash for a meeting on our tour but left us in the safe hands of the head boy and girl. She entrusts senior pupils with a lot of responsibility, allowing them to develop vital skills for the future.

Academic matters: Embraces Holyrood's Curriculum for Excellence and broad general education with subjects including business technology and business enterprise. Pupils narrow subjects down at end of S3, sitting six National 5s in S4. Parent comments generally very positive about academic achievements: 'There are plenty of kids who come out with five As at Highers.' However, one parent expressed concern that there was 'not enough homework in S1 and S2 ... kids could be prepared for the much greater workload further up the school and also have work reinforced'. Head says, 'Following a recent consultation, the school is reviewing and updating the homework policy.'

French, German and Spanish part of the core curriculum plus a weekly lunchtime Mandarin class. Strong science school with impressive labs – the biology lab has a greenhouse incorporated into its roof. Opportunity for S3 girls to take part in Strathclyde University's week-long course Engineering the World for Girls. No obvious gender divide: 'we break the trend of boys doing less well academically'. A roughly equal success rate for boys and girls.

Impressive support for learning team (including principal teacher and three specialist teachers). Young people are supported in class, in small target groups or on a one-to-one basis by teachers and five support for learning assistants. School has a counsellor one day per week, and partnership with an educational psychologist and Stirling Council PT ASN outreach. Focus on providing support for pupils with autism spectrum disorder (ASD).

Senior leadership comprises the head and four deputes – three female and one male; one depute is solely responsible for 'positive destinations' (ie to support pupils to achieve what is best for them (whether university, college, apprenticeship, work).

Focus on vocational skills for the less academic, eg National 5 energy class instead of physics, or practical skills in the ConneXions course, such as growing veg in the polytunnel and cooking what's grown. S4 pupils take part in the work experience programme in a local placement of their choice. A work placement plus course offers senior pupils the opportunity to combine work placements with SQA employability awards. Range of curricular and careers information evenings for parents and S3–S6 pupils, attended by representatives from universities, colleges and apprenticeship providers from across the UK.

Regular assemblies and future pathways events with external speakers, school partners, local employers and community groups, scheduled to coordinate with option choice times, and planning for applications. Offers volunteering award and community involvement opportunities in partnership with community councils, local charities and businesses.

Games, options, the arts: Hanging in the entrance, huge boards lists 'internationals', ie pupils who compete internationally, predominantly in sport, but also in the arts too; this is a school that's immensely proud of its sporting achievements. First port of call on our tour, perhaps unsurprisingly, was the outstanding PE department, complete with various courts, gymnasium and a 25-metre swimming pool, all used by the local community. Also on show are framed internationalists' vests, from a wide variety of sports.

Annual swimming gala, 'fun and intense', hosts races and relays for each of the three house teams. Olympic swimming champion Ross Murdoch (former pupil) came back to support the event recently and pupils raced against him – kindly, 'he let them win'. Enthusiastic pupils, with faces painted in house colours, revelled in cheering them on. Masses of inter-house competitions take place at lunchtimes and generally throughout the year (not just sporting competitions, but, for example, song contests and bake-offs too). In S6 there is a health and well-being period, which includes everything from water polo to yoga and an Insanity fitness class. Successes in hockey, rugby, football, netball and much more, but unusually also in indoor rowing, where S5 girls won gold in the National Indoor Rowing Championships.

Annually hosts sports awards with a guest speaker – recently it was Judy Murray, former coach and mother of tennis player Sir Andy Murray. A PE teacher told us it was the 'highlight of the year for staff'. 'Every sport gets its moment in the sun'. He was proud to tell us that over half of kids take part in extracurricular activities. School has strong links with Active Stirling and Sports Scotland. He said he was 'proud of the pupils', and they were one of the first schools to achieve the Sports Scotland gold award. Selected sports council ambassadors (S4–S6) make suggestions about ways to keep fit and reach out to everyone, including the less sporty, suggesting fitness classes or using the fitness suite.

Fairly typically, outside are rugby and football fields and a flood-lit Astroturf pitch, plus a new compact 100m athletics track, with a long jump lane and pit and throwing area. With the school located in a perfect part of the world for outdoor pursuits, the new mountain bike track (with new mountain bikes) is all thanks to a community partnership project with Balfron Development Trust and group of four pupils who won a competition run by Cycling Scotland.

Plenty of clubs (many at lunchtime), including debating, astronomy, chess and science, which is popular with younger pupils; more unusual after-school clubs include sailing and American football.

Traditionally lacking in the arts, the schools is working hard to set this straight and wants to make a 'new push into the creative arts'. A new art head post created, introducing drama to the curriculum (it has previously run only as a club). Uptake should be high if gauged by the level of pupils' enthusiasm for the subject. School shows, which are put on every second year, are a 'huge deal', and have included All Shook Up, Grease and A Midsummer Night's Dream. They're hands-on affairs and pupils are involved in all aspects of the performance, not just acting but also backstage, in the band and sound technology, as well as doing make-up and working front of house. One parent said: 'Amazing opportunity for young people both on and off the stage, and it was great to see so much hidden talent shining through.'

Taking steps to make music more popular and accessible by introducing new subjects such as music technology. Pupils learn how to create and lay soundtracks to back film segments. Various bands and choirs, however, including string and woodwind ensembles, Ceilidh band, rock bands and orchestra. Striking contemporary artworks by Advanced Higher pupils, clay sculptures and 3D reliefs feature in the art department, as well as eco fashion designs submitted to the Junk Kouture competition.

Trips aplenty, including a French exchange trip organised by the language department; the Swiss Alps (geography); Austria and Spain (skiing); Normandy (history); London (business and technology). Fundraising trip to Ecuador to help in communities, and exchange programme and partnership with Robert Laws School (pupils and staff) in Malawi. Four pupils went on a four-week visit to China, representing Stirling council – a hanban (Confucius Institute) teacher has been giving Mandarin lessons.

Background and atmosphere: Opened in 2001, a state-of-the art, modern comprehensive with excellent leisure facilities, set at the foot of the Campsie Fells. Large classrooms (some with iPads or Chromebooks) run off the main open-plan corridors, which all have a dedicated area with PCs. Busy school, but not overly noisy, where the main hub of activity centres on the light-filled atrium (overlooked by the well-stocked library), where kids congregate for school dinners (above standard school fare, serving only organic milk) and which hosts shows and concerts throughout the year, such as Candlelit Classics, which is open to the public.

Modern school, modern attitude. 'Sociable among the different year groups' and with a welcoming atmosphere; prides itself on being inclusive. Fantastic online resources (homework all online and pupils can email teachers for help). One pupil said, 'It's like having your own personal tutor at home.'

Strong links with the local community; school choir sings at local care home and musicians play at local events. Citizenship a prominent feature with activities embraced like Micro-Tyco and the Youth Philanthropy Initiative; plenty of charity fundraising activities, eg for Yorkhill Children's Charity, Robin's House and Mary's Meals.

Trying to implement a strict uniform policy, in recent years to include a blazer. S6 pupils smart with their green braided blazers, but still many with a more casual approach – and we did spot the odd pupil still wearing a jacket.

Pastoral care, well-being and discipline: Form class leaders are the first port of call for support in S1–S5, with principal teachers at the ready in S6 to help with UCAS applications. Learning support teachers and assistants assist in mainstream classrooms but also give specialist tuition to individuals or small groups in the learning support rooms (every department has one). S6 students also lend a hand and do paired reading and numeracy with younger pupils. An S1 outdoors activities residential early in September helps the transition from primary to secondary – often pupils in the rural communities attend tiny primary schools – allowing them to 'make friends and feel secure' (photos of them having a tremendous amount of fun are displayed on school walls). One of the most impressive and popular house systems we've seen. Divided between three houses, the kids thrash it out on a daily basis to win points via inter-house competitions. The house system offers 'a good pastoral care structure – less intimidating to new pupils and parents/carers alike.'

Parents approach form class leaders if there are issues; deputes oversee issues related to young people in their house. Head holds a monthly drop-in session where parents can pop in to discuss any issue without an appointment. 'On track sheets' keep kids and parents up to date throughout the year. One parent, who said it was a minor complaint, felt more feedback would be welcomed. As she said, 'Stroppy teenagers are not always the most communicative.'

Another parent said, 'Discipline is good, with respect shown to staff and pupils throughout the school. Bullying behaviour appears to be dealt with consistently and successfully.' The head adds, 'We rarely have to exclude and it is a last resort.'

Pupils and parents: S6 students heavily involved in full report parents' evenings, where they 'help to keep things running smoothly', and serve tea and coffee. Parents have a one-to-one meeting with the form class leader annually.

Backgrounds quite mixed (not just middle class) with a range of pupils from rural and urban areas; a small number from more deprived backgrounds. Subsidies are available so 'no one misses out'. Tiny percentage of ethnic minorities.

School buses run from local villages. For those from further afield the council runs a DRT (Direct Response Transport) taxi service to bring children to and from school for a small charge.

Notable former pupils include Michael Ferns (screenwriter and director), Colin Gregor (rugby player) who trains kids at the school, Ross Murdoch (Olympic swimmer) and Craig Mathieson (polar explorer)

Entrance: Catchment covers a wide rural area and eight local primary schools in Balfron, Killearn, Kippen, Fintry, Drymen, Strathblane, Milton of Buchanan and Buchlyvie. Spaces are available and placing requests are accepted for non-catchment children. One parent said: 'Parents are choosing Balfron because of its good reputation.' Another said: 'Balfron holds it own amongst many of the private schools in nearby Glasgow and has a vibrant presence in the local community.'

Exit: Few leave after National grades; around 90 per cent stay for Highers of whom 70 per cent will stay till S6. Most to Scottish universities – Edinburgh and Glasgow top of the pops with the odd one or two to St Andrews, and occasional trickle to Oxbridge.

Remarks: Good all-rounder, highly regarded by locals, that prides itself on inclusiveness. Superbly located for outdoor pursuits and has fab sports facilities as well as impressive SEN provision – would be worth moving to for sporty kids or those with additional support needs.

Belhaven Hill School

Belhaven Road, Dunbar, East Lothian EH42 1NN

Ages 7–13 **Pupils** 123 **Boarders** 73 full (from 8 years)

Fees: Day £11,520 – £16,875; Boarding £23,760 pa

01368 862785
www.belhavenhill.com

Head: Since 2016, Henry Knight, previously head of Woodcote House. BA in classical civilisation (Royal Holloway), PGCE, MEd (in his 40s). Before he took up teaching he ran corporate hospitality for Berry Bros. He started out at Woodcote as an English teacher and housemaster and ended up as headmaster for seven years before his move to Belhaven. He still teaches English to the middle school and also keeps his hand in on the sports side by coaching the 2nd XI cricket team. A down to earth, straight talking man, popular with parents and children alike. Parents report that he's 'very normal', 'approachable', 'well liked', and the children loved that he spent time in the first term with a large, red L plate stuck to his back. Married to Susannah who heads up pastoral care (we hear 'she's great, brilliant with kids and parents'); they have three children, two currently at the school.

Entrance: No formal test but register as soon as possible. Children spend a taster day (and sometimes a night) the year before they come. Here they attend lessons and take part in sport and activities as well as taking a short (20 minute) informal test.

Exit: To the big hitters north and south of the border including Fettes, Ampleforth, Rugby, Oundle, Merchiston, Eton, Uppingham. At present the split is about 60 per cent heading south of the border while 40 per cent stay in Scotland.

Remarks: Originally a boys' boarding prep school, it went co-ed in 1995 and thereafter welcomed day pupils. The heart of the school is a mid 18th century country house with various add-ons out the back. The location, at the edge of the town of Dunbar, close to an 18 hole golf course and the beach, is peachy. Pretty house with delightful grounds. This editor would happily relocate there.

Eight classrooms all tightly grouped around a pond at the rear of the main house. Light, bright rooms and very easy to nip between classrooms. Class sizes 'generally 12-ish'. Two computer rooms. Setting from age 9 – in maths, English, science and languages. Latin and Greek both on offer. No separate scholarship stream: potential scholars have extended learning and additional tuition.

Learning support in a revamped building (The Hub). Team of four LS teachers. One-to-one teaching, small groups – whatever is needed. Children can pop into The Hub during quiet reading time (every day after lunch) for a catch-up on any subject. If a child has particular difficulties school 'wouldn't say no' to parents employing additional support but would try to find other solutions first to prevent the child 'standing out or feeling different'.

Drama and dance very popular. Plays for all, nativity for the younger ones. Public speaking encouraged through the annual competition: every pupil has to speak on a topic of their choice for four minutes. Inspirational art that is clearly celebrated and displayed around the school. Woodwork/DT room where tasks involve creativity and problem-solving with a healthy dollop of fun. It's not all about curriculum learning – 'we don't just want to be a sausage factory'. On the day of our visit, fabulous ramshackle boat creations all lined up ready for an America's Cup moment on the school swimming pool.

Sport for all. Two cricket pitches, tennis courts (grass court in the summer), Astroturfs and swimming pool, open for the summer term and first half of autumn term. Swimming lessons once a week and pool often used by the boarders for muck-abouts at the weekend. Annual school swimming gala in summer term. Boys play rugby, hockey and cricket while the girls' main sports are netball, hockey and rounders. Lots of sporting success but also an ethos that sport is for all and everyone gets a shot at representing the school. Tennis, golf, skiing, athletics and football also on offer. Functional sports hall, which doubles as theatre for school plays. Lots of extracurricular activities from taekwondo to croquet, fly-tying and horse riding. Piping very strong; lots of music lessons and choir.

All of the 7 year olds and most of 8 year olds are day pupils. The majority of older pupils board. School operates a bi-weekly boarding programme, finishing every other weekend on a Friday at 1pm or occasionally 3.45pm. Buses operate on these weekends – to Perth, Stonehaven and Thornhill (Dumfries) – to help parents who live further afield. Pupils return either on the Sunday night or first thing on Monday morning.

Day pupils from form 4 upwards are expected to attend school every other Saturday from 8.30am to 4.30pm for lessons and games matches. For the boarders, Sunday kicks off with a chapel service taken by the headmaster or visiting preachers. Headmaster has introduced new fun-packed activities on Sundays for boarders – bubble football being a particular favourite. Head has done much to improve communications with parents through his new blog, Facebook and Instagram, although some parents of boarders miss the now discontinued fortnightly newsletter – this was an 'important piece of communication'. Manners are important and any bullying is kept firmly under control – 'educating the children and talking about it is key'.

Boys' dorms in the main building, recently refurbed, with new bathroom and kitchen. Light and bright rooms, dull tartan curtains. Older boys have new snazzy desk/bed combos – very smart and popular. Girls accommodated in a fab new building separate from the main house. Super cosy, homely dorms, very prettily decorated. Big pinboards, floral curtains. Circular common room (Rosie room), plasma telly and piles of beanbags. Boarders aren't allowed phones but can phone home from their dorms. iPod shuffles allowed for music. We hear that the 'matrons are lovely' and the 'pastoral care fantastic'.

Children tell us that food is good ('great match teas') and there's plenty of it, although a couple of junior gourmets reported that the breakfast sausages were 'way more tasty than the ones at supper time'.

Walled garden is well kept but not manicured and children can plant up garden plots of their own. The plots are blank canvases – from vegetables to pond digging to tractor tyres, some major earthworks, anything goes. These mini gardens aren't show pieces for visitors but are for the children to have the freedom to guddle about and have fun in. Fierce competition for the annual garden trophy.

Time to mention the animals.... Let's kick off with the dogs. Lots of them. Some teachers bring their dogs into their classrooms, where they can be petted between lessons and sit quietly once the lesson begins. There are 11 'school dogs' at the moment. Rather than causing merry chaos, both the dogs and the children seem to be happy and calm in each other's company. Next on the list, but not yet in residence, are the pigs. We look forward to meeting them on our next visit.

Still perceived as Scotland's school for toffs and grandees, although head tells us that now 30 per cent of parents are first time buyers. Some children of former pupils, some from south of the border – often with Scottish connections. However, the base has widened out somewhat with many more families from East Lothian and the borders. Lots of social parents and good friendships. Numbers are still high but slightly down from last year. No plans to change to weekly/flexi boarding. Head says, 'we see ourselves as the pre-eminent full boarding school in Scotland'. We saw so many well mannered, happy children on our visit, and time and time again we hear that parents are 'delighted with the school'. This is a traditional prep school in a beautiful setting with an all-round approach to education that is hard to fault.

Belmont House School

Sandringham Avenue, Newton Mearns, Glasgow G77 5DU

Ages 3–18 **Pupils** 230 **Sixth form** 33

Fees: £7,005 – £13,263 pa

01416 392922
www.belmontschool.co.uk

Principal: Since 2006, Melvyn D Shanks (early 50s) BSc DipEd MInstP CPhys SQH, who was educated at The High School of Glasgow, read physics and maths at Glasgow University (a 'lapsed physicist', he still teaches maths 'a little bit') followed by Strathclyde – ridiculously overqualified. Spent five years at his alma mater before coming to Belmont as head of physics in 1990, then deputy head in 1997, and says that 'the most difficult thing was to move from being in the common room to becoming deputy head'. 'Really, really excited', though it was slightly daunting 'becoming CEO'. When asked if ever he felt 'it was the time to move on', another opportunity opened at Belmont and 'it was irresistible'. Loves his pupils: each of our questions was answered with a story. Willie this, Ahmed that. Bright, bubbly and bouncy. Always a joy to interview someone so in tune with his life.

Very much on the ball, he has a deprecating sense of humour and showed us round the school with pride (this time pointing out the refurbed cupula – safety glass now). Married, with one son a qualified teacher and another in the school. Keen on staff development and people management, he runs the school with senior vice principal, head of junior school, vice principal and financial manager. No obvious problems in getting staff.

Academic matters: In 2018, at Advanced Highers 42 per cent of grades were A; at Higher 50 per cent As.

Max class size 20 with core subjects, English and maths in the mid-teens, and most other subjects only nine or 10 per class. Setted throughout in English and maths (all compulsory to National 5s), with French (from age 3), Spanish from age 9 and computing. German no longer offered. 'Fluid groups' within each class for literacy, numeracy and spelling. Three sciences, from Transitus (ie 10-11 year olds), history, geography and modern studies as per norm, plus art and PE. No classics. Business and IT throughout school and compulsory at National 5s. Pupils can do admin post National 5s. Eight National 5s overall. Most stay on for Advanced Highers and can add the odd free-standing modules in sixth form. No particular bias – strong on the science front, IT and languages.

Whiteboards, digital, overhead projectors – the lot: 'looking at virtual learning'. Umm. Keyboarding for all in Transitus (should be compulsory in every school). Classroom layout varies according to whim, with juniors either grouped round their teachers or working in standard classrooms. New IT hub (junior) and IT lab (senior). Vast array of cups for academic and personal excellence. Good range of computers throughout school and not just in suites; two trolleys of laptops motor round classes. Post-school tutorials in all subjects 'given by all staff, including the principal', from October through May – free (aka drop-in centres for all). Senior pupils help younger ones with reading, IT skills etc. Very much a family school: even if they ain't all siblings.

Learning support: all tested on arrival (cognitive ability) – broad intake, and siblings give the school an even broader base. High functioning children with Asperger's, dyslexia, dyspraxia et al are fine, two qualified support for learning staff who follow pupils throughout. Free unless ed psych needed. Pupils withdrawn from class, double taught in class if need be and can use the after-school/lunchtime tutorial system in all subjects if they feel the need. Dyslexics needing serious help currently use lap tops, scribes/readers or – and a welcome innovation this – e-readers – ie earphones, so pupils do not stick out in class. Magic.

Main school (1840 mansion) not that wheelchair friendly (but only six classrooms not accessible, and new build has a lift). Stunning recent inspection – school could have written it themselves.

Mixed age common room – some of the staff looked as though they were on the wrong side of the desk, but all truly dedicated. Huge parental and grandparental input – veterinarian parents give deeply popular talks. We could have said lectures, but this is not the bias of the school.

Games, options, the arts: For a small school they do 'not too badly' at rugby; footie, three girls' netball teams, all play volleyball and basketball. Playing fields some half a mile away – bussed. Keen on tennis and golf, regulars in the British ski championships. Lots of inter-house athletics. Not really a school that does brilliantly in team games against other schools. Cricket poking its head above the parapet. Mass of individual sports and local club participation.

Jolly art room, variety of different disciplines, fabric strong and fun fashion on display (amazing: superb waistcoats: would have taken one home had it been offered), kiln. CAD part of the syllabus. Music important – all learn glockenspiel, guitar or drums in six week chunks or they sing. Terrific and popular choir (though head admits that music has 'dropped a tad'. Orchestra (and junior orchestra – based on ability not age) – good charity concert output. But nary a pipe band, though individual pipers. Extracurricular drama – and super pics on display. DofE well supported. Strong on public speaking and takes part (a little bit) in local competitions, debating club. Oodles of various clubs, Lego popular; eco-monitors. Eco-school and club both junior and senior. Cycling proficiency tests for juniors.

Trips and tripettes for all both cultural and sporty, school will underwrite where necessary – but not by much.

Background and atmosphere: Originally a trad boys' prep (founded in 1929) moved to handsome white stucco building on the Broom estate in 1930. Decided to go all the way in mid 70s, and co-ed in 2000; and, by a happy co-incidence, at the same time as Laurel Bank and Park School (aka Laurel Park) hit pay dirt. Original thoughts of girls gradually working their way up the school went out of the window.

Magical and somewhat ridiculous plans for relocation nearby (overlooking the M77) turned down on planning. School reinvented itself, and now boasts a raft of classrooms atop a (slightly sunken) games hall – volley ball stuck in the roof (needs a scaffold for rescue operation) – which is adjacent to the kitchen and doubles for dining (two sittings, takes 10 minutes to fold up and stow the tables). Weekly menu available in advance: looked good, smelt better, picnic lunchers welcome. Windows overlook hall on first floor, along with four science labs, plus two IT rooms and a music suite, as well as drama and general purpose classrooms. Splendidly light and airy. This is now old hat, but still a bit of the old rabbit-warren at the back where juniors are ensconced in highly decorated opening-up classrooms.

Nursery around 24 post-3 year olds 'all hopefully dry' in partnership with East Renfrewshire in large modern building in the centre of the campus. School has undergone a mega revamp, outside painted, inside painted, carpets all over, new electrics; we would have insisted that the conduits be concealed, but approve of conduits in historic buildings (NB conduits are those boring pipes that carry electric cables.)

A nice touch: school colour is purple; chairs dotted around the building are upholstered in matching purple, kitchen staff wear purple hats and tabliers. Head sported a purple striped shirt and purple tie, and half the staff seemed to be wearing purple in some form or another.

After-school club for up to Transitus (homework too) 3.20-6pm. Extensive new outdoor learning space.

Pastoral care, well-being and discipline: HMI reports, 'The behaviour of children and young people is outstanding.' Not really a naughty school – standard disciplines apply, detentions the favoured punishment. Bullying stamped on, graffiti instantly removed. Buddy system for younger pupils. Pupils have tutors (a promoted position), with each tutor having 20 tutees – possible to change tutors if a personality clash. Staggered breaks by age. Strong 'old-fashioned' discipline with children lining up in the playground in twos at the end of break: charming. Older pupils open doors and stand aside to let us past. Twice weekly ecumenical assemblies: all faiths represented and holy days celebrated.

Pupils and parents: Huge ethnic mix. Good middle-class collection; around 60 per cent first time buyers with 10 per cent from the Glasgow Asian population, most of whom have 'strong traditional family businesses'; some from Indian sub-continent stay with rellies and come daily with their cousins. (This appears to be a growing trend, particularly in Glasgow.) Smaller core of Jewish pupils than previously. Smattering of Chinese, broad multi-cultural community. Pupils come from as far afield as Ayr, Kilmarnock, East Kilbride, Paisley, as well as nearby Pollokshields, plus one or two from 'north of the river'.

There was 'no call' for hand-me-down uniform shop: first time buyers you see: hence 'discrete' secondhand clothes shop – buy the trusty blazer online.

Currently 60/40 boy girl split, but this is liable to change at the drop of the proverbial.

Entrance: 'Low-key informal assessment' for nursery, automatic transfer to junior and senior schools, separate test for children from age 7 upwards based on CAT school reports and interview if necessary. Can join mid-term if space available ('We accelerate the entrance process').

Exit: Almost all stay on, either for Highers or Advanced Highers. Some (around 10 per cent) may leave earlier to follow vocational training, and head is eager to advise – another story here – others to join the family business. Virtually all Scottish universities – Glasgow popular, Aberdeen, Dundee, Strathclyde, Edinburgh, St Andrews; occasional one or two to Oxbridge but none recently. Tranches of medics, lawyers, vets, accountants, engineers and architects. The odd gap year. Very occasionally parents use Belmont as trad prep school, moving to posh elsewhere, but most leavers logistical.

Money matters: Not a rich school, but will do their darndest to hang onto pupils to next public exam if parents who fall on hard times are upfront about it.

Remarks: Super – the perfect local school, works well, not scary, but nurturing and trad enough to tick all the boxes. Can't fault it. Tiny classes. Dedicated staff. Definitely worth considering.

Cargilfield School

45 Gamekeeper's Road, Edinburgh EH4 6HU

Ages 3–13 **Pupils** 305 **Boarders** 15 weekly, 54 flexi (from 8 years)

Fees: Day £10,281 – £15,843; Boarding £19,443 pa

0131 3362207
www.cargilfield.com

Headmaster: Since 2014, Rob Taylor. English degree from Durham and PGCE from Cambridge. Previously the registrar at Harrow School, he also has experience of running Ashdown Prep in Sussex and has taught at Wellington College, where he was also a housemaster.

A very popular head. 'He knows each child off to a T. Very approachable and brilliant at energising everybody.' He and his wife Sarah decided to return to her Scottish roots with their three children, partly because of the more balanced pace of life and partly because 'Cargilfield is so highly regarded by the big schools down south.'

Entrance: Every child is assessed to some degree, even at nursery level, although it is 'age appropriate'. It's not selective, apparently, but more to check that they school can support their needs. But if you're keen to get your little darling in as quick as possible, be aware, there are waiting lists for quite a few of the year groups.

Exit: There is a joint staff effort to make links with senior schools across the UK, and the success of their pupils in recent years means that they are firmly on the radar of many of the big hitters down south. Head says, 'The irony is that Cargilfield is better known down south than in Edinburgh.' Fettes and Glenalmond the most popular destinations but others to Eton, Harrow, Winchester, Oundle, Millfield, St Mary's Ascot inter alia.

Remarks: Under the guidance of Rob Taylor and his wife, Cargilfield is 'buzzing', according to some parents. Within the last three years Cargundians have won a King's Scholarship to Eton, the top scholarships at Wycombe Abbey and Rugby, two Winchester elections, a Harrow music scholarship and scooped the top scholarship to Fettes for two years running.

Does that sound a little academically heated? Less than you'd think, apparently. 'Our child is definitely mid-range. Not struggling particularly, but not super bright, but they really seem to bring out the best in him.' 'Very happy with it. Very nurturing, cosy school. I like the ethos and the values.' 'I really feel when we pick our two up that the teachers know what kind of day our children have had and if there are any problems.'

Head says at the top end of the school they try to keep streaming to a minimum for the two common entrance classes so that nobody feels they have been downgraded in any way. Then in form 8 they have a scholarship class for those who are really 'pushing ahead academically. '

'We think it's important that we don't define academic ability too early, so that those who are struggling don't get downhearted. We stream them from form 7, although maths is in sets from form 4.' He adds, 'A good number of families are coming to us from down south because they want to escape that pressure-cooker of achievement. We want to provide a balance.'

And if your child is in need of learning support, there are three part-time staff plus the head of the junior school on hand to help out. But one parent we spoke to felt they needed to strengthen their approach by upskilling all of the staff to a greater degree, although once a problem was diagnosed they were very good at dealing with it.

One of the most contentious features of academic life at Cargilfield is the No Prep rule. Yes, quite an unusual decision for a prep school, you'd think, but they're adamant it's for the best. The parents we spoke to loved it, on the whole: 'The days are long enough without prep'; 'We still have to practice cello and learn vocab'; although a couple of parents felt it meant they had no idea what their children were up to until parents' evening and were worried about their ability for independent study later on. Rob Taylor says they're addressing this with the form 8s by introducing periods of independent revision, and learning support has developed a programme to help progress this further.

And if the children haven't got their nose in a book, there is certainly a huge range of clubs and activities to keep them busy; everything from skiing to fly tying. But as one parent told us, 'There is so much on offer you have to make sure they don't burn themselves out. It was actually a teacher who told me that!'

Now over the years Cargilfield has won the reputation of being a bit of a sporting behemoth, in Scottish terms at least (although with more pupils than anyone else that might be considered a given). But does that mean that your non-sporty child will struggle to get into any teams? 'In the past, definitely,' said one parent, 'but I notice an effort to improve that.' Certainly, a change since our last visit, we were very cheered to see that the girls' sporting achievements are as much centre stage as the boys'.

One child we spoke to said, 'I'm definitely not sporty and in my last school there was the "cool" gang who were in all the top teams, but it really doesn't matter here. You just have a go and nobody makes fun of you!' 'I came from a state school so I had no idea how to play a lot of the sports, but they spent time giving me extra coaching and now I'm in the rugby 1sts and going to Sedbergh.'

We were also pleased to hear that there is a big increase in the sheer volume of games being played (new Astro on the way, apparently, to cope with extra pressure). This, we're told, is part of a serious attempt to get every child to pull on a Cargilfield jersey at least once a term.

There is also a 50 minute break in the day, four times a week, for activities and clubs. And this doesn't have to be sport; the children, they say, are just as likely to play chess, go to coding club or run around the big treehouse system built in the grounds. The staff also put on outdoor pursuits such as mountain biking, kayaking or climbing twice a week for anyone not keen on team sports.

Musically, Cargilfield seems to be very much on song with four music scholarships last year. They say it is very unusual for a child not to do some form of music. Boundless enthusiasm all round; choir, pipe band, wind group, orchestra. 'We try to get them playing in a group as soon as possible so that they get that sense of belonging. It must be a socially advantageous thing.' Lessons on just about everything you can think of, except a full drum kit, apparently.

Art abounds, with some ambitious and impressive projects and an art club to help pupils build up their portfolios. Bigger emphasis is being put on finding emerging talent further down the school. And for those who remember with joy those prep school plays, every year group from nursery upwards takes to the stage at least once a year. One parent we spoke to, however, thought the drama could definitely be stronger.

Most prep school boarding houses are cosy, homely affairs these days, but that said Cargilfield does provide its young charges with some very nice accommodation. Is it populated by a big proportion of boarders? Mmmm..There are only 13 weekly boarders in the upper school and the rest are flexi-boarders, which means they stay over one or two nights a week or over a boarding weekend. During the summer term this means they can have as many as 50 pupils staying overnight, but for the hardcore weekly boarders it must be tough during the winter months watching your classmates go home to mummy.

The boys' house now has a young male master in charge, which has been a 'huge success,' they say. With big dormitories for the boys, dorm cricket is a very regular event. For the girls, it's smaller, pinker rooms and cosy chats on the sofa with matron of an evening.

Cargilfield prides itself on its fortnightly boarding weekends with a dizzying array of activities laid on for the children. But again, you won't find the weekly boarders staying on for this; this really is more of an exciting babysitting service for the day pupils. The school does run some full year group boarding weekends, which bring together each year for a big bonding session. One parent we spoke to said, 'I don't see what's wrong with a bit of boredom. They should learn how to entertain themselves too.'

Pre-prep seems to be bursting at the seams and is now rather hard to get into. Set in a delightful colonnaded building across a courtyard from the main school, it's a bustling place run by the highly respected Emma Buchanan. She describes it as very much 'active' and 'discovery' learning. Lots of running outside, trying new things, although as they've just completed a big review of how maths is taught in the pre-prep, we're assuming the three Rs are firmly on the agenda too. Reading is Jolly Phonics and Oxford Reading Tree and they can all read by form 4. If you're a working parent there is a useful after-school club to 6 o' clock.

PHSE plays a very important part, says Rob Taylor. 'All the teaching staff have noticed how much more pressure the children are under and mental health is on the agenda from pre-prep.'

Rob Taylor and his team have also instigated biannual staff meetings when every child is discussed in detail, in an effort to make sure the 'quiet ones in the middle get just as much attention as the others'. As for parents, staff say they operate an open door policy and work hard to build good relationships. As one parent said, 'If you have a niggle about something you can mention it to Sarah (Taylor) and she's totally on it. She's always there in the background offering support and a lovely smile.'

Clifton Hall School

Clifton Road, Newbridge, Edinburgh EH28 8LQ

Ages 3–18 **Pupils** 396 **Sixth form** 20

Fees: £9,150 – £12,270 pa

01313 331359
www.cliftonhall.com

Headmaster: Since 2005 Rod Grant BA PGDPSE (early 40s). Came from Hutcheson's where he was principal teacher of English, responsible for literacy. His original brief at Clifton Hall stretched through primary to S1. School had already started an all through policy, but had anticipated adding pupils year on year. Grant admitted to being a tad 'unsettled' but has no thoughts of leaving, nor of expanding beyond 400. During our discussion it was difficult to keep his eyes straying from assorted young playing random hockey in the walled garden outside his office window.

From Prestwick in Ayrshire (where he has a second career as a 'property developer' – he lets out his flats there), educated at Merchiston, read English at Edinburgh, but abandoned this to join his brother in a wine bar venture. Returning to academia, he completed his degree at the Open University (having, in the interim, been housemaster at Drumley House School – deceased – in Ayrshire; his blog is highly entertaining), doing his PGCE at Paisley and cutting his teeth at a state primary in nearby Broxburn.

Less than three months into his headship, Grant was faced with a fire sale when approached by the governors of the tiny failing St Serf's school (94 pupils aged 5-18, lousy prep inspectors' report, mediocre senior report) suggesting a merger – and, after much gubernatorial activity, the schools amalgamated in 2008. Pupil pin map shows a huge spread, from Galashiels in the borders to Falkirk, East Lothian and north of the Forth, numbers from Edinburgh.

Certain amount of new build, some good, some bad, and some just plain ugly. Most resemble farm buildings, but then we are in (very basic) farming country. Mega £4m+ scheme in pipeline to cover the games pitches to the right of the drive with a combo 400 seater theatre, full basketball pitch and collection of classrooms. The games pitch, charming club house and happy young playing hockey enhance the drive to the castle; though the less said about the monstrous carbuncle of a theatre workshop in the north west corner the better. Does what it says on the tin – but more suited to a building site than in plain view of the (Grimms) fairy tale 1857 Bryce Castle. Cladding is easy on the eye.

Rumours rife about the £1.7 million the merger realised – Grant is not so upfront, 'We spent what we got'. New kitchen adjacent to games hall, which doubles as dining room. Very fancy pants sports pavilion, all singing and dancing – the games facilities are let occasionally.

Popular weekly coffee mornings for parents, good catch up time, and a boon for the lonely or just plain concerned. Grant's common sense view on bullying – and now cyber-bullying since our last visit – and some of the wilder health and safety regulations ought to be circulated round the head's grapevine. His wife, Helen, teaches in the junior school; they live on site.

Academic matters: Same form taker throughout for all in senior school. Set for maths from S2 (stops the boredom factor), otherwise parallel classes, no streaming. We found a brace of S4 classes studying John Steinbeck's Of Mice and Men. Simultaneously. Good pupil interaction, inspired relaxed teachers. French from 3, Spanish and German from 8, keyboarding skills in primary for all. Non-selective, good basic grounding, building blocks, combo of Jolly Phonics/blends/ word recognition and synthetics on the reading front. Serious experiments with liquids – will a penny float? Graduating to humanities, via computers, art and PE, dedicated staff. Very hands on, the early years seem like learning through play, though we came across a fearsomely proactive class of 9/10 year olds in the computer room – touch-typing.

All the usual suspects in senior school plus admin, geology, philosophy and media studies in S5 and S6. Free choice for Highers et al, Eng and maths essential, otherwise list preferred subjects in choice order. Grant promises to run a course if only one taker. Two computer suites (one Apple, one PC) used by all for timetabled lessons as well as IT – networked, intranetted, wireless. Labs designed by science staff, complete with prep room and adjacent scientific classroom. School follows Scottish system. In 2018, 36 per cent As at Higher and 44 per cent As at Advanced Higher level.

Nursery recently expanded, bung full of all the things you would love to have but don't feel you can afford, sandpits, water-play. Technically open till 3.00pm (from 8am) but after-school club picks up the slack. Stories (floor covering looked rather hard but we were assured the young didn't mind; we were pleased to see a random collection of cushions). Imaginative play area outside: looked slightly cramped for 40,

Two dedicated SENCos: one in junior and t'other in senior school, plus an assistant. Pupils either withdrawn from class individually, in groups or offered dual teaching. Can cope with minor physical handicap – senior classrooms are upstairs – and Asperger's (mild).

Games, options, the arts: Team games on every available speck of green greeted our arrival. Cunning junior rugby/football goal makes Heath Robinson look like Einstein. But what fun.

Enthusiastic music; two were studying Advanced Higher music in the former chapel during our visit, whilst a hotch-potch of students were writing, directing, producing a piece on Marilyn Monroe. We suggested blow heaters. Peripatetic staff. Exciting art – intricate dress design. Strong focus on preparing the young for the real world; and pushing creativity, practical nuts and bolts as well as the academic. Eco committee – school recently gained Green Flag status. Charity involvement via houses – children choose their own projects. Pupil council, with reps from every class and Eco council, with reps who suss out what the school can do to improve the environment. At our last visit we were sceptical about proposed outdoor classroom under pupil construction (in Scotland?). But they did it, with a combo of straw bales on larch and lime rendered (pupils wore rubber gloves). Wow.

Gym (with bars and benches) doubles as dining room, three sittings, takes two and a half hours (external caterer). Charming swimming pool, timetabled lessons for all (local primaries use it, scuba club one night a week and disabled group at weekends). Parents were watching a group of 5/6 year olds' swimming lesson during our visit. Senior school a bit dodgy on team games, though lots of clubs (judo, ballet, fencing, swimming) – no tennis courts seen. Sports facilities can be hired out by locals. Nine hole par three golf course on horizon but no all-weather pitch as yet.

C

Background and atmosphere: Clifton Hall is a magical Bryce house, complete with impressive oil paintings and the odd bit of antique furniture, in 54 acres of child-inspiring grounds off the Newbridge roundabout – the junction of A8, M8 and M9. A boon for parents to the west of Edinburgh, who can either take advantage of the school buses, which leave Bathgate, Livingstone, Newington and the West End of Edinburgh daily at 8am (departs at 5pm each evening) or drop off their poppets on the way to work, school open 8am to 6pm. The lodge at the entrance, previously let for not much more than a peppercorn, is now a humming café (post Nat 5s only) generating £1000+ a week.

Happy young sunning themselves outside when we visited, unaware that Euphame Macalzean, heiress of Clifton Hall, burnt alive in 1691 for witchcraft, has regularly been seen visiting her old nurse near the lodge.

Founded as a boarding boys' (only) prep school in 1930, school became a limited company in 1964, thence weekly boarding, thence day, followed by girls, pre-prep and nursery. Clifton Hall had already started taking senior pupils before the amalgamation with St Serfs; ideally placed, it has all the vibes of a grand public/prep schools, games pitches, busy swimming pool on site, surrounded by (climbable) trees, contained, secure and with none of the health and safety issue of boarders.

First thing you see, even before you enter the school proper, is a showcase of trophies: an Olympic torch, carried by one of their youngsters and nestling cosily beside a Scotland U16s rugby cap, and a fiddle score. The hall (good Victorian panelling) is decorated in French; and while the somewhat hotch-potch configuration of class rooms is in good heart, we noticed the parquet flooring in the music room, labelled Library, former chapel (and quite obviously originally a billiard room) was ready for a spot of TLC.

Senior, junior and nursery all have their own dedicated play space, the head can watch from his study – has been known to invite concerned parents to watch their darlings at play. Weekly menus handed out to all, so parents don't cook the 'same for their tea'. Lots of parent participation.

Previously painted in rather jolly primary colours, particularly in the basement, school has opted for uniform blue, and, despite our previous comments, the whole place looks bandbox fresh. The gorgeous doo'cot was about to have serious input from Historic Scotland. It didn't.

Pastoral care, well-being and discipline: Head has common sense attitude. Small enough school to care – tinies walk down school paths hand in hand. Matron sign still visible on first floor door. Children devised own set of Golden Rules (representatives from each class on pupil council) – each pupil must have both a request and a thank you.

Pupils and parents: Huge catchment area. Eighty-five per cent plus first-time buyers, ditto two working parents. A complete mix. The occasional parent follows the trad route, prep at 8 and senior school at 13, but most stay the course. FPs (aka CHOPS) include Rory Bremner, Jim Clark and Jamie Bruce Jones of Caledonia play, designer of the splendid wooden castle in the nursery garden.

Entrance: Mainly through the (non-selective entry) nursery – a proper nursery school (member of the Edinburgh City Partnership Scheme) with many of the children wearing uniform, and junior school. Otherwise first come, first served, assessment to pick up glitches. Overbooked for nursery and first few years of primary. Space sometimes available in the senior school. Will accept pupils at any time; gentle school, a number from maintained sector who have been bullied (cyber-bullying the new head on the block: trolling). Grant reckons to have a good 'conversion' rate of potential parents, emailing them within three days of interest being shown, and keen on first names. Regular parents' evenings. Two or three per cent ethnic mix.

C

Exit: Most to some form of further education; most stay in Scotland. Aberdeen, Heriot Watt, St Andrews, Edinburgh, Glasgow, Robert Gordons. The odd gapper.

Money matters: Fees include almost all extras; trust fund on hand to pick up financial hiccups 'for a year or two' – 'safety net' rather than 'safety blanket'.

Remarks: Wowser. 'School is going places and it is growing,' was what we said last time. Governors very bullish, and so they should be. Head has maintained and increased momentum.

The Compass School

West Road, Haddington, East Lothian EH41 3RD

Ages 4–12 Pupils 120

Fees: £7,450 – £9,735 pa

01620 822642
www.thecompassschool.co.uk

Headmaster: Since 1997, Mark Becher (pronounced Becker) MA PGCE (40s), educated Queen Margaret's Academy Ayr, Dundee University (modern history) and PGCE at Craigie College of Education in Ayr (aka the University of the West of Scotland). Previously head of sport and primary teacher at ESMS, and primary teacher at Edinburgh Academy. A 'keen distance runner', he teaches sport, Latin and history and runs school with a deputy (associate assessor of HMI, whom we did not meet; she was out on assignment) management team and part-time bursar.

Entrance: Children can (and do) join at any time – after an informal assessment – and begin at any stage of the school year. Not selective.

Can apply for 'financially assisted places' at any entry stage; specific bursaries for forms 6, 7 and 8 plus sibling discounts (third off for the youngest of three siblings in school at the same time) and parents can ask for help if struck by financial meltdown. Bursarial help for trips too, so that no child feels disadvantaged.

Vouchers (as for qualifying pupils in nursery) can either be used to offset nursery fees: go towards early bird or Compass Care, or towards clubs based on site (ie not skiing or golf). Two per cent off if pay early and four per cent above base if pay late. Extra costs for milk, lunch and recorder lessons.

Exit: Most leave at 12 for Edinburgh independents, usually day (but those heading for Merchiston usually board age 13 when they hit senior school) or local state school. Destinations vary year by year but include George Heriot's School, George Watson's College, Edinburgh Academy, Loretto, Portobello High School, North Berwick High School, Dunbar Grammar School, Stewart's Melville College and The Mary Erskine School. 'Everyone gets where they want.' Few now leave at 8 for trad prep schools, but a steady trickle nonetheless.

Remarks: Founded in 1963 by Mrs Alny Younger, to cater for local children between ages 4 and 8 (before the little darlings went off to 'proper' prep schools), The Compass has expanded beyond recognition, and is now a beacon independent junior school with sparkling million quid new build and regular stream of both national and international visitors.

West Road, Haddington's poshest street, boasts elegant Edwardian villas, many of which have an inalienable planning veto over the field in front of The Compass, which has fab views to the south (geography and botany on the hoof, so to speak). Planning for the new extension must have been nightmare, so it is not surprising that the natty hall (too small even for short tennis, but brill for cricket and judo) is much used by locals outwith school hours. New classrooms for senior pupils have been shoehorned into an expanded attic with books, DVDs and tablets crammed into every available corner.

Grand galleried staircase leads from trad hall up to original classrooms (and head's office), gas-fired guarded coal-look-alike stove in the corner in strong contrast to the new build. Family is important here: houses are known as families, with houseparents rather than captains; but, just to complicate matters, there are captains and vice captains too. School council with representatives from each class.

New kitchen adjacent to dining room (formerly the billiard room with magnificent cupula and original panelling) and well placed to cater for functions in the hall. Slight whiff of to-day's broccoli (before 10am?) – though fresh fruit and raw veggies aplenty at meal times. Pre-school and after-school care based in dining room and linked classroom. Bit complicated, but see below.

Every vertical surface is covered either in children's artwork (framed under direction of Ricky de Marco, Lothian's secret art treasure) or team photographs/composite snapshots of trips (Paris/London) and tripettes (Netherurd, the Cairngorms, climb first Munro) – all dependent on age with overnight stays for some of the quite young.

The dedicated nursery runs in partnership with East Lothian Council: max pupils 20 (discount if pupils live in East Lothian). Previously, The Compass offered a composite class for 8-12 year olds, but now school leads seamlessly through eight year groups up to age 11/12. School roll more or less static around 125 boys and girls. Head takes pride in running a successful Scottish primary, based on the philosophy of the Scottish Curriculum for Excellence but with specialist teaching – 'ideal preparation' – allowing pupils to feed the Edinburgh private sector well ahead of the field. 'Four years ahead in French,' one school complained; 'No apologies for letting children work to their capabilities,' says Becher.

Reading by way of Jolly Phonics; school adds: 'with a strong emphasis on developing early literacy' (which we presume means reading books). French from nursery; Spanish from ages 9-12 with Latin and a nod to classics age 10. School small enough to pick up problems before they overwhelm. Impressive support for learning, full time teacher – who was handling a mixed class of perhaps 5 or 6 year olds with gentleness and humour. Small groups plus one-to-one (no extra cost). Help for those on whatever spectrum never far away; though perhaps some may need more specialist support. Assessments whenever. School-provided iPads being rolled out – from age 8, which pupils handled with skill. Interactive whiteboards (so last year now) being replaced by interactive tellies: 65 grand's worth last year alone.

Pupils compete in a variety pack of sports from age 9 – rugby, cricket and hockey matches and swimming galas, all with impressive wins 'against bigger schools'. Same goes for music – a huge range of activities packed into a 9am to 3.30pm day with after-school supervision (paid for) and activities (nominal cost only). All sing in the choir (won The Edinburgh Festival Primary Schools' Choir trophy twice) and sing at Murrayfield, The Queen's Hall, wherever. New build has allowed for dedicated art/science rooms (views to the south) and dedicated music room: clarsach, flute, recorder, singing. School big on drama: pupils star in school plays, made to feel important and have a certain amount of responsibility, which gives each the confidence to move happily into larger schools at secondary level.

No dedicated games field as such; school uses Haddington Astroturf (they share it with Knox academy,) Haddington rugby club grass pitches, Haddington golf club, swims in the local Aubigny sports centre, performs in Loretto theatre, and borrows local churches. The atmosphere has a 'good prep school buzz' but feels more fun than frenetic.

Daily assembly, broadly Christian, but other religions appreciated. Hymn practice, outside speakers – often obliquely giving career advice, but that too. Emphasis on encouraging expectations and instilling a sense of right and wrong.

The garden is Chase me Charlie country, complete with outdoor classroom and one of the most exciting climbing frame/walls ever designed.

School uniform is sold in house (superior secondhand shop too) and in Edinburgh.

Early bird from 7.45am (after breakfast) and Compass Care up to 6pm. Extra cost. Extra cost too for pupils wanting a 'light tea'. Opportunity for older pupils to do homework, though without supervision. 'Compass Care will not be responsible for the completion or standard of the homework.'

Good proportion of first time independent buyers with catchment from east Edinburgh along the coast to Berwick on Tweed and south to the Lammermuirs. No buses as yet, but lots of shared school runs. Fairly narrow ethnic mix, but that's East Lothian for you. School would be pleased to field a broader diaspora. First-rate, and friendly. Local parents raised £250,000 in last few years and treat school as a social hub, but recent incomers from the South have been heard to mutter about 'academic standards'. Still worth moving to Haddington for.

Craigclowan School

Edinburgh Road, Perth PH2 8PS

Ages 3–13 **Pupils** 225

Fees: £12,660 pa

01738 626310
www.craigclowan-school.co.uk

Headmaster: Since January 2016, John Gilmour, previously deputy at Castle Court School in Dorset. The board of governors took a lengthy 18 months and two rounds of applications to find him, clearly anxious not to make a bad choice. He has a PGCE and a BA in geography from Liverpool, and is married to former lawyer Liz. John went into teaching after time as a naval officer and has experience of teaching in state schools as well as the private sector. He grew up with a stepfather who was headmaster of a prep school and a father who was in the merchant navy, so he says he was always destined for a career in both.

Liz has taken the move to Perth as an opportunity to leave a stressful job in favour of supporting her husband and now spends much of her day in a tracksuit teaching netball, listening to children read etc.The Gilmours have two children, the youngest still at Craigclowan, and were drawn to Scotland because of their joint love of the outdoors and Liz's Scottish roots.

Entrance: Some 90 per cent of the nursery children go on into the prep school. Intake obviously limited by geography as there are no boarding facilities, so tend to come from a 20 mile radius. This is being expanded by an ever increasing minibus network.

Exit: Around 60 per cent to Glenalmond or Strathallan, others to eg Gordonstoun, Kilgraston, Dollar, Fettes, Ampleforth, High School of Dundee, St Leonards and Sedbergh.

Remarks: Like many prep schools, Craigclowan was set up in the 1950s, some say to cater for a group of local businessmen who couldn't be bothered with the drive to what had been the closest prep school, nearly 20 miles away. Whatever the reason, they picked a bonnie spot. Perched on the edge of Perth in the midst of 15 hilly acres, the beauty of the location is somewhat tempered by relatively close proximity of the M90. And yes, you can hear the traffic from certain parts of the school grounds, especially on the playing fields to the south. That said, the atmosphere is one of a close-knit thriving little community under the ebullient and thoughtful leadership of John Gilmour.

And according to the parents we spoke to, Mr Gilmour is really quite the catch. 'He's young, dynamic and he communicates well with the children. I think he is a good face for the school and will represent it well at school councils etc.' 'Excellent and forward thinking. Considerable changes have already been made to the school in a short time.'

One issue that he seems to be addressing is the 'parent heavy' school board. He says he's keen to bring in some more educational expertise and has already brought on the Fettes deputy. The parents we spoke to approved wholeheartedly, as one of the issues with leaving the school without a head for so long (18 months) has been that parental control has become a little too heavy-handed for some.

In educational and pastoral terms there has also been a bit of a shake up, starting with a new set of school values (humility, adventure, respect, kindness, integrity, optimism), agreed and voted on by the pupils and teachers alike. Mr Gilmour believes any school should be a value-driven organisation. He's working on improving communication with parents and pupils (new website, weekly headmaster's blog) and has reintroduced assembly three times a week to strengthen the community vibe and introduce the occasional inspiring speaker.

The school timetable has been completely rewritten. Apparently there used to be a mixture of lesson lengths: these have been standardised and the school day has been lengthened fractionally to allow one or two hours of sport every day for senior pupils. It now runs from 8.30pm to 4pm for the seniors, with activities or prep until 6pm. These include computer club, climbing, chess, Mandarin, Lego club, Scottish country dancing et al. Forms 1 and 2 and pre-prep finish at 3.30pm, though an extended day is available if they need it. They have also introduced a 'proper' prep school match day on a Wednesday for forms 6, 7 and 8 and with forms 5 and possibly 4 soon to join them. Sport is traditional prep school fare: rugby, hockey, cricket, tennis, rounders, netball, athletics; cross-country is also a big school sport (thanks to two passionate teachers) and the addition of their own dry ski slope is a great bonus for anyone keen on sliding down a hill on a set of planks (especially since Scottish snow can be elusive).

Academically, there's been a decisive step towards more rigorous diagnostic testing and tracking, although not in any way that would stress the children. 'Mostly the children have no idea they're being assessed on a regular basis'. This gathering of data, says Mr Gilmour, allows them to be much more diagnostic and to tailor their teaching methods accordingly. (It also spots the teachers who need some 'extra' support.)

Learning support is free and is not dependent on diagnosis. 'We deal with what we see, intervene early and get stuck in.' Head stresses they are not a selective school – 'a complete slice through society' – but what matters is that at the end all the children are testing well above average (as they should be, we say).

Big refurbishment plans are afoot and the nursery (well run and rather charming) is being moved into the main horseshoe-shaped school teaching building. A newish junior school head who will oversee both the nursery and the first two forms. The aim is to aid the transition from the nursery to the school. The old nursery space will be transformed into a new dance/drama studio and dedicated art room. The big old house (a bit of faux gothic architecture) at the centre of the school is also being refurbished.

Another big change afoot is the introduction of a new digital strategy. White boards, mobile laptop trolley, cloud-based storage for all the children's work and Chromebooks rather than IPads. 'We are a Google school'.

Numbers have grown by 10 per cent since head's arrival, thanks in part to his popular policy of expanding the school bus provision. From one initial bus route to Kinross, there are now minibuses running from Alyth, Cupar in Fife, Dunning and Auchterarder.

Overall, we were rather charmed. Small classes, responsive and quietly confident children – 'Mr Gilmour, I think your dog's eaten Mrs Gilmour's packed lunch — she's going to be hungry on that netball trip' – and a head who is not only enthusiastic and caring about the children (apparently he is very good at listening to the children's reading and poems), but who has carefully thought out plans for the future.

Craigholme School

72 St Andrews Drive, Pollokshields, Glasgow G41 4HS

Ages 3–18 **Pupils** 255 **Sixth form** 25

Fees: £8,265 – £13,200 pa

01414 270375
www.craigholme.co.uk

Executive headmaster: Ian Munro, also rector at Kelvinside Academy, took over the reins in November 2018 after the sad death of principal June Gilliland.

Head of junior school: since August 2018, Linda MacBeath, previously acting head of Colgrain Primary School in Helensburgh. Born and raised in Dumbarton, and completed her PGCE at Southampton University. She then began her teaching career in Manchester before moving back to Scotland to teach at Lomond School in Helensburgh, progressing to senior leadership posts at Cardross Primary School and Colgrain Primary School. A recognised advocate of digital technology and of the importance of outdoor education. She is also head of junior schools at Kelvinside Academy; the two schools now operate under the banner of the Glasgow Schools Trust.

Academic matters: Music and French from nursery. Music very popular (though it trickles off at Nat 5 and Higher levels), with pupils sitting Nat 4 music in J7. Ukulele the instrument of the moment (pink ukuleles galore – gasp!). Outdoor learning opportunities in Maxwell Park facing the school. Really tiny classroom sizes in the junior school; in J1 we counted just a handful of children. That level of personal teaching time is a draw for some parents, however. One parent said: 'The attraction was the small classes to help improve our daughter's academic performance and the pastoral care to improve our daughter's self-confidence.'

Not to stereotype, but huge top-notch, modern kitchens for home ec. Girls on our tour made it clear, however, there is a drive towards the sciences. Much more than nicely turned out, well-mannered young ladies; impressively intelligent, articulate young women. STEM captain in S6; human biology offered at Higher (rather than standard biology) – principal says it is preferred by the girls; biology at AH. Numbers small for physics though one brave student studying crash AH in 2018. Engineering clubs aim to build enthusiasm. Photos on the wall showed they were proud that even the choir were in on the space-themed act, where the school's junior choir – The Space Odyssey Choir – performed at a concert about the cosmos.

Because a small school, no strict exam policy and girls can choose their preferred subjects (for example taking more than one social science at Higher in S5). One parent regarded this as very important: 'Being (I think) one of very few schools with no presentation policy for exams, pupils are able to sit the exams they want, they are all supported and given the confidence to do as well as they can.' Business up to Higher (no AH). Higher economics available in S6.

Twelve subjects available for Highers with 71 per cent getting five A grades in 2018; 10 subjects at AH, with 60 per cent A/B. Almost 50 per cent of S6s take two Advanced Highers. Standard range of subjects divided among the faculties (humanities; science, mathematics and numeracy; English, languages and literacy; expressive arts).

French from pre-school, Spanish added in S1 and German in S2. Spanish most popular with 50 per cent taking to Nat 5, and 35 per cent taking French. Numbers low for German and looks like it may be taken off the curriculum, according to a pupil. Typically, numbers for modern languages start to dwindle at Higher and AH.

SEN specialist in junior and senior school; help in class and/or withdrawal for extra tuition.

STEM careers event for S3 to S6 pupils with STEM ambassadors (including former pupil and mechanical engineer Caroline Carslow) covering topics such as MRI physics, engineering, geology, oncology and psychology. Work experience week in S5, generally arranged through parent contacts. Careers advice and enterprise programme runs from junior school. S2 careers programme and S4 information evenings and careers fayre, where educational and professional bodies attend. Manage to attract some high profile speakers as role models for the girls, from Judy Murray to Ruth Davidson.

Games, options, the arts: State-of-the-art sports centre a short drive away with dance studio, sports hall and climbing wall, plus playing fields, Astro turf and blaize pitch that is also used by the local community. 'Punches above its weight' in sport. Huge success in hockey, winning West District Indoor and Outdoor Championships recently. Second year running as indoor champions. Athletics, cross-country, tennis, ski-ing and swimming also popular.

Wrap-around care in the junior school (8am–6pm) which includes tennis, baking and yoga. Range of extracurricular clubs in the senior school, from cake decorating (that made this editor chuckle) to engineering. Good reputation in public speaking and debating – the head girl, who showed us around, won the Rotary Club competition.

High achievers in music. Annual Musician of the Year competition, which is judged in school by a pianist from the Royal Conservatoire of Scotland. Junior and senior pupils compete successfully at the Glasgow Music Festival. Oodles of choirs and orchestras visit Salzburg, New York, Washington and China. New grand piano in the assembly hall, which a pupil was playing beautifully on our visit. Drama clubs in junior and senior schools; available to AH as an academic subject.

Impressive array of art on show: from felt-making to print making, silk painting and self-portraits. Art and design offered to AH and medal winners at the Kelvingrove art competition.

Majority of S3 do bronze DofE; 50–60 per cent silver; 30 per cent gold. Now has access to Kelvinside CCF and wilderness campus. Trips include skiing in Europe, music trips to NY and China, Krakow for history, and curricular day trips.

Background and atmosphere: Principal kindly gave us a copy of the book 100 years of Craigholme. Founded in 1894 as Pollokshields Ladies' School, it now encompassed three attractive Victorian merchants' houses, which are joined by purpose-built stone and glass halls. Large reception rooms link social spaces, including the multipurpose assembly hall. Girls in gorgeous Craigholme tartan kilts and scarlet blazers stand out in the Pollokshield's community – in our opinion this is Glasgow's most attractive school uniform.

Senior and junior school exist alongside each other, and J7s move to the senior school to help with transition. Nursery situated on St Andrews Drive.

Atmosphere is 'homely, relaxed and productive', even during exam times, said one pupil. Most suited to those who would flourish with lots of individual attention rather than those who thrive on having a large friendship group. Three male members of teaching staff, although very few male applicants. Plenty of charity fundraising – thousands raised for Ragdolls (helping girls with Turner's syndrome).

In 2018 joined forces with Kelvinside Academy to form the Glasgow Schools Trust, with shared executive head. Craigholme junior school now co-ed, and shares a head with Kelvinside junior schools. Senior school remains girls only.

Pastoral care, well-being and discipline: One Craigholme parent was impressed by the school's supportive environment, saying: 'Craigholme is as much about character building as it is education; I am very impressed with the time and effort they put into each child.' Four houses, named after the Scottish islands, each with a head who meets with the girls for quarterly meetings. Senior school PHSE programme is targeted specifically at girls, allowing issues that are more important to them to be covered in more detail. The principal says: 'This allows discussions you wouldn't have in a co-ed environment.' Health advisor and counsellor on-site. Outdoor pursuits trips in J7, S2 and S6 allow the girls to get together and bond.

Parents generally contact the guidance teacher or health adviser if they have any concerns. Principal has never excluded anyone, and in 10 years there's only been one exclusion. Lunch-time detentions are given when needed. If any problems, they contact parents directly.

Pupils and parents: With less than 300 pupils this is a small school. A parent said: 'It is important that the school continuously improves, from improving marketing to increase pupil numbers.' We worry that the rates hike (Barclay Review) in the 2017 Scottish budget is hitting small schools like Craigholme hard, hence its new link with Kelvinside. The principal, however, said that increased numbers of families from down south and abroad (Middle East and Far East) are approaching the school.

School-to-home communications mostly through the newsletter. Two formal reports and two parents' evenings for the nursery and junior school; series of tracking reports, final report and one parents evening in senior school.

Majority get to school by car or public transport, but subsidised school bus operates from as far as Ayrshire.

Parents mostly middle-class professionals, businesspeople and academics. Multi-cultural and tolerant school, no issue with girls wearing head scarves. This is representative of Pollokshields itself, which predominantly is a mix of white Scottish and Scottish Asian residents. As a girls' school, the senior school does appear to be popular with Muslim families; however, on our visit it seemed a rich mix of pupils of different ethnicities. Girls are educated on all religions. Majority of board members are parents.

Notable former pupils include engineer Susan McDonald, scientist Rosalynne Watt (won the Siemens prize at Cambridge while doing PhD and the Institute of Physics Young Researcher in Combustion runner-up), paediatric emergency physician Joanne Stirling, artist Sally Carlaw, crime novelist Louise Hughes, ex-editor Scottish Field, Claire Grant, TV journalists Victoria Lee and Carla Romana, British skiing champ Nicole Ritchie (most recently on artificial snow) and Commonwealth Games athletes Lisa Tobias (weightlifting) and Alison Howie (hockey player).

Entrance: Non-formal assessments and taster sessions for entry to the nursery and junior school, how both co-ed throughout. Vast majority of girls move up to the senior school. Senior school assessments look for potential and commitment.

Exit: Majority to Scottish universities – Glasgow Caledonian, Heriot-Watt, Strathclyde, Edinburgh, Stirling – with a trickle down south, one Cambridge geographer in 2018. Some to study law and accountancy; increase in international business and languages, but no real trends. No demand for apprenticeships.

Money matters: Means-tested bursaries from S1, received by a small number, using a points system.

Extras include uniform, sports kit, and one-to-one music tuition (if desired) and a levy for sports complex. Nursery part of City of Glasgow partnerships and qualifying families receive a refund in fees.

Remarks: An intimate school in Glasgow's south side, now co-ed at junior level, with great results academically, musically and on the sports field. Tiny class sizes make it popular with families who want their child to receive individual support in a warm, caring environment without too much exam pressure. Stunning tartan uniform.

Dollar Academy

Dollar, Clackmannanshire FK14 7DU

Ages 5–18 **Pupils** 1,275 **Sixth form** 150 **Boarders** 75 (from 9 years)

Fees: Day £9,792 – £13,095; Boarding £27,000 – £30,303 pa

01259 742511
www.dollaracademy.org.uk

Rector: Since 2010, David Knapman BA (maths) MPhil (40s), previously deputy head of Hampton School in London, where he still has a foot on the property ladder. At Hampton he established a no-nonsense reputation but was also notable for his work with charities and the local community. Educated at Morrisons, 'doon the road', followed by Sheffield and Exeter. Married to Brigitte with two sons (younger one attended the school). His mother lives in Dunblane and 'is my fiercest critic; she keeps her ear to the ground'. Plays tennis regularly and enjoys 'playing the piano badly'. Wife also a teacher, came from a country background and is 'pleased to be in Scotland', they like walking the hills and are planning to tackle Ben Lomond this summer (Munro bashing very popular around here).

They live in a stunning Georgian street which houses a collection of school buildings – much in demand by film crews no doubt – we yomped to the burn to see Mylne Bridge (built and named for the local minister and first rector, who opened the school in 1818, to give him a short cut to the kirk) and were told that if it 'weren't for that pine tree, we could see Castle Campbell' (we googled it – it is pretty impressive).

Has a dry sense of humour; hugely enthusiastic and 'very popular – going down well' and 'doing just fine,' say our spies. Sits in on classes, walks round every day and never misses a match, concert or play. Boarding numbers going up and examination results at a record high last year.

He was mentored by Dr Ken Greig, rector of Hutchesons Grammar in Glasgow (we hadn't realised that heads had mentors too) who seems to have grown a beard in solidarity. A mixture of young and old teachers, housing not cheap in the Dollar area but it is the perfect place for families.

Retiring in summer 2019. His successor will be Ian Munro, currently rector of Kelvinside Academy. BSc zoology, followed by a PGCE biology, both from Edinburgh University. Never resting on his laurels and with a passion for learning, gained a masters from Cambridge with distinction in educational leadership and school improvement, and recently completed leadership course with Harvard University Graduate School of Education. Formerly teacher (biology) and head of year at Heriot's, deputy head at Shiplake College and head of biology at Gordonstoun. Lives in Glasgow's West End with wife, history teacher at independent school. No children but two dogs, one a cocker spaniel named Charles Darwin. Loves the outdoors, sailing, walking, climbing, canoeing.

Assistant rector and head of prep and junior school: Since 2010, after four years in big school, Alison Morrison, BSc (Cantab) PGDE (40s). Economics graduate, following spells in the City, advertising and television changed course (professional graduate diploma of education) at the University of Edinburgh, and has one of the most stunning collection of reviews on Rate my Teacher we have ever seen.

Academic matters: There is no formal setting in the prep and junior school with pupils receiving differentiated teaching and learning within each class. Efficient support for learning in place, with rector getting progress reports. One-to-one, small groups and supported learning in class. Variety of reading methods used, but Jolly – or unjolly come to that – Phonics in the main.

Not quite all singing and dancing new computer system (rector says 'could do better'), touch-typing for all, strong on techy subjects. We found a lovely gang of 8 year olds happily making intricate ribbon pictures (for calendars?) in the fabric/home economics room. Some of the chaps were enormously imaginative. Our attempts were rubbish.

Aged 10 (J1), pupils move to junior school, where they are looked after by Sally Horne, assistant head of the junior school, certain amount of specialist teaching in specialist rooms: hist, geog, science plus art, PE and music, by senior school staff. French, German and Spanish (the former two more popular – contrary to the apparent national trend) from J1. Three parallel classes J1, moving to four parallel classes in J2. Junior school is seen as a transition between prep and senior school.

Strong academic tradition, particularly science with a compressed science option on offer for 14-16 year olds and large numbers for medical school; English and mod langs good (housed in new Westwater Building, which won a couple of design awards); German and French more popular than Spanish; Mandarin available; Latin, Greek and classical studies (heroes for zeros) all on offer and four dedicated classics teachers. All three langs from junior school plus some Japanese, Russian, Italian, philosophy, car mechanics and other jolly options. Broad streaming for English (with EFL if needed), tight setting for maths and mixed ability in most subjects, plus. Large business department offering economics, business management, finance and accountancy.

Rector and/or senior staff have a 20 minute meeting with every pupil (and their parents, who usually keep stumm during the interview) to discuss their personal subject choice. Pupils choose the subjects they want to study and classes are worked round them, rather than the trad system of block choice. There is a distinct emphasis on the academic rather than the vocational.

School follows a mixed bag of courses: National 5 (plus National 4 in maths); Highers, Advanced Highers and the Scottish baccalaureate – which doesn't seem to have many followers outside Dollar. In 2018, 63 per cent of Highers and 63 per cent of Advanced Highers were A grade.

Classes of 6-24. Efficient support for learning in place; one-to-one, small groups and support learning in class all on offer. School has a positive approach to those with ADHD: pupils can drop into the dyslexia centre at any time. Serious homework, carefully spelt out in a smart little green book full of info for parents which interestingly persists in referring to the school as the Academy. 'Whatever else, we expect that all pupils in the Academy should have enough work to occupy their evenings and any child who indicates otherwise misunderstands.' Not quite all singing and dancing new computer system (school report says 'could do better'), touch-typing for all, strong on techy subjects – most to Advanced Higher level.

Games, options, the arts: No sport is compulsory. That said, boasts a first XV rugby team unbeaten for the first seven years of this century. Shooting 'phenomenal'; always a strong showing at Bisley. Hockey hot stuff. Regular tours to Europe and further afield: Canada, Japan, Italy, Argentina et al. Numerous individual county reps in major and minor sports – golf, skiing and badminton, as well as more esoteric activities such as shotput, curling, table tennis, equestrian vaulting (gymnastics on horseback) and triathlon (NB Clackmannanshire ain't that big), plus national and international team members eg Scottish rugby U18 squad. Mass of games fields, 63 acres of school grounds, much-used hall and swimming pool. Amazing circular Maguire Building – sports, arts, drama – million pound bequest from FP Brian Maguire; formidable school art on display and used for external exhibitions too – even the Scottish Examinations Authority asked for a painting for their new premises. Second bequest from the Price family resulted in a new 5.3 metre inflatable for the navy section. All weather surface was opened by Linda Clement, Scottish Ladies' hockey captain. Presumably by bullying off.

Strong volunteer CCF – good following, not just because of the trips to Canada. Three pipe bands, who all sport the Campbell tartan; the B band was third in the national CCF championships this year. Two orchestras, jazz bands, oodles of choirs; the annual Christmas concert in the Usher Hall was a sell-out with almost 2,000 in the auditorium. Drama timetabled with masses of productions – the rector believes that 'pupils gain confidence through performance'; lots of smaller concerts – 'six performers, 30 in the audience'; that sort of thing. Hot on debating, all sorts of trophies as well as representation in the winning Scotland team at recent world champs in South Africa – a tour de force. Ballroom dancing on Fridays; participants learn Latin American and rock 'n' roll, Japanese dancing the latest wheeze but no medals for this nor for Scottish country dancing. Prize winners sport their bronze, silver, gold or Scottish awards proudly on their blazers thereafter.

Munro bashing, DofE, exchange and trips, work experience at home and abroad, go-kart racing at Knockhill, skiing, motor mechanics, surfing, falconry. Clubs for everything, usually post school, late buses nightly. Fabric technology timetabled. Over 70 options in total; terrific facilities; powerful charities committee (15 mile sponsored walk raised over £50,000, staff, parents and doggies all included).

Boarding: Boarders from age 9 (though not a lot of them); all boys share one dedicated house: two individual (Victorian villas) houses for girls, recently revamped – and dead posh they are too. The boarding houses are small, two with up to 24 girls in each, one for boys that takes up to 49; all three have had recent million pound facelifts, stunning. Usual range of after-school and weekend activities – cooking to sub aqua.

Background and atmosphere: Captain John McNabb, a former herd boy who rose to become a ship's captain and, latterly, a ship husband – literally looking after ships in port – died in 1802, leaving half his fortune, £55,000, to found a school to educate children of 'the parish wheir I was born'. Rumours abound whether the monies came from slavery or piracy but they were certainly augmented by bribes from ship owners eager to be first past the post. After much shilly shallying, the Rev Andrew Mylne, a trustee, commissioned Playfair to build a 'hospital' which finally opened in 1818. The first co-ed in Scotland. McNabb's corpse was rediscovered in the 1930s and proudly brought back to Scotland, and cremated. Gruesome or what. His ashes are entombed in the wall above the main Bronze Doors; this has to be the only school in the land where pupils pass under the founder every day. By 1830, the grounds at Dollar had become an Oeconomical and Botanical garden, boasting some of the rarest trees in the country – certainly the most northerly tulip tree, as well as a Corsican pine, and specimen sequoias. Pupils originally had their own plot of garden, though we are not sure whether this was for ornamental purposes or whether they were expected to augment the school kitchen. The interior of Playfair's original building was gutted by fire in 1961, which allowed a certain amount of internal rearrangement. Zinging concert hall (the Gibson Building), improved science block. Current wish-list includes a new technology, engineering science and earth science building – to be built out of 'funds'. The grounds are open to the public daily. And the library is no longer lollipop pink.

Formerly a direct grant school, Dollar became independent in 1974 – a day school, with a boarding element. Easily accessible from most of Scotland and just a short hop from the Forth Road Bridge and Edinburgh Airport. Wet weather a feature of the place and masses of matches are rained (or snowed) off (school says very rarely due to new all-weather Astroturf courts and pitches). NB The school uniform includes beanies (first time ever for us on a clothes' list) and macs with fleecy linings. Rector says he doesn't mind what they wear on their heads, as long as they are warm.

Pastoral care, well-being and discipline: Automatic out for drugs. Lousy work equals detentions post-school or early morning – dead unpopular with parents, plus out if 'The pupil is not deriving benefit from being at the school or indicates by his/her conduct that he/she does not accept the rules of the Academy.' Pupils not particularly streetwise – but modern studies popular and strong politics and international relations society.

Victorian values, with clear rules; many of the petty restrictions have been done away with.

Pupils and parents: The vast majority comes from within a 30 mile radius – impressive number of buses, plus Forces children and a contingent from the Scottish diaspora worldwide (around 50 per cent of boarders international). Dollar itself has the reputation of having the highest percentage of graduates of any town in the country. School has a long tradition of looking after the children of tea-planters, missionaries and engineers – still. Perhaps a tad parochial and 'mercifully' free of Sloanes. Exceptionally strong and active FP network, including Sir Frank Swettenham, the first Governor of Malaysia, Sir James Dewar, the inventor of the vacuum flask, and the sculptor, George Paulin. The governing body is mostly FPs, which ensures that the place has freedom to develop but an awareness of its history shapes the thinking – no bad thing.

Entrance: Pupils come to junior school at 5 or 10: the latter by fairly selective entrance exam. To seniors usually at 11 or 12, by examination, which is quite selective. Generally oversubscribed for entry at fifth and sixth forms; each case individually considered; good GCSE or National grades required plus good refs and an ability to put something into the school. Open day in September, but parents and prospective pupils are welcome to visit at any point of the year, which gives the opportunity to see the school in action.

Exit: Virtually all go on to senior school, though the occasional one may peel off for trad schools ('very very rare for someone to leave,' says the rector). A handful to Oxbridge each year (one in 2018). Otherwise most students head for the Scottish universities: Edinburgh, St Andrews, Glasgow, Aberdeen, with under a quarter going south or abroad. Eleven medics in 2018; law also popular (16 takers). Low gap year take up: either a reflection of the recession or the 'get on with it' mentality. The chairman of governors and his wife have set up a trust with more than £1 million to encourage the youngsters to take up challenges involving travel. If that doesn't persuade entrepreneurs overseas.

Money matters: Collection of means tested-academic bursaries at 11 and 12, plus ESU, Forces and boarding bursaries (usually means-tested, with tuition not covered). Fees very reasonable; governors tough on non-payers.

Remarks: Very sound – this large, solid, co-ed school provides education in the best Scottish 'get on with it' tradition, facing the 21st century with the expectations and values of an earlier age, mercifully free of most of the excesses of the 60s. 'Robust teaching and meritocracy' are important here. Up there with the best of the merchant schools.

Douglas Academy

Craigton Road, Milngavie G62 7HL

Ages 11–18 **Pupils** 1,007 **Sixth form** S5: 169; S6: 136

01419 552365
www.douglas.e-dunbarton.sch.uk

Head: Since February 2017, Barry Smedley, BEd in PE from Moray House School of Education, University of Edinburgh. Started off as PE teacher and previously posts include principal teacher at Knightswood Secondary School and deputy head at

Bishopbriggs Academy. 'With a growth mindset', his goals are to maximise pupils' potential. He says: 'Attainment is excellent. We were the top performing school in East Dunbartonshire this year [2019] and had the school's best ever results in its 51-year history.'

The school motto, Gaelic Neart Tre Ealos, means 'Strength through knowledge' and the head is ambitious to take this further and build on the school ethos to 'develops strength of conviction, strength of purpose and strength of self.' The HMIE inspection report of 2010 recognised the school ethos and welcoming environment as a strength.

Mr S came across as very efficient, fast-paced and organised. Pupils described him as 'accommodating, proactive and putting lots of effort into the job.'

In his spare time he enjoys reading education and leadership books. No surprise as a former PE teacher, he continues to be very active – and is up at 6am to go to the gym six times a week.

Academic matters: In 2018, nearly half got at least one Advanced Higher at A-C, while 12 per cent got 3+; 74 per cent got 3+ Highers at A-C and 63 per cent got 5+. The head tells us: 'STEM subjects massive and a large proportion are taking three sciences at exam level, as well as big numbers in computing science.' One pupil reached the final at the Big Bang UK Young Scientists' and Engineers' Fair.

Additional support can be provided in class as well as targeted support by the support for learning department, out of class. Staff tend to be long-serving with turnovers due to retirements or promotions. One-third of senior management are women.

Break-out spaces in every corridor to allow for independent study. PCs are booked by class for research in the library. On our visit some sixth years were studying, while others were part of a mentoring programme to help those struggling with numeracy, to help build up their confidence. Year books for each year since 1999 are stored in the library.

As with all Scottish secondary state schools, pupils' personal development is catered for through the PSHE (health and well-being) programme. 'We have found the school to be very supportive ... with staff often going that extra mile.'

Principal teacher of guidance is in charge of developing young people's aspirations before they leave. Kids are interviewed and provided with bespoke work experience from S4 onwards.

Games, options, the arts: Awarded with gold sports school status. 'Academically the school is top-notch, but what really sets it apart is the quality and choice of extracurricular activities.' Does well at traditional team games – football, rugby, hockey, netball, volleyball – as well as athletics and triathlon. S1 boys' football team recently won the East Dunbartonshire Cup Final; senior hockey boys won the Aspire Scottish Cup final; in athletics pupils won 14 gold, 11 silver and 11 bronze medals at the Dunbartonshire county sports. All-weather full-size rugby, football and hockey pitches, tennis courts and cross-country course. Skiing at local club in nearby Bearsden. Huge games hall plus two gyms and fitness suite, much used by the community. Huge charity involvement. Three pupils in 2018 received the Diana Award for volunteering. Also works with Milngavie Development Trust in regeneration of Milngavie town centre.

Impressive debating success in national competitions, beating top UK independent schools. Two pupils recently qualified for the finals of the International Competition for Young Debaters at the Oxford Union. They were the only state school in Scotland to do so. Has its own school company Wood n Stock, recently winning the best trade stand award and overall best company award at East Dunbartonshire's Young Enterprise Awards.

'The presence of the music school enriches school life.' A centre of excellence for music and is one of four specialist music centres in Scotland. Boasts an outstanding first orchestra and chamber orchestra, plus a senior wind band and a second orchestra, which often include first years and non-music specialists. Several choirs. Many students play in national ensembles and quite a few win awards (an S2 pupil recently came first in the North American Solo Drumming Championships). Regarded as on a par with St Mary's Music School in Edinburgh. Lots of hugely successful concerts throughout the year, including the annual Christmas concert at St Paul's in Milngavie. During our tour, talented young musicians were practising for Glasgow Musical Festival. Many go on to the Royal Conservatoire of Scotland and some perform in West End shows. Most of the music staff also have top jobs in Scotland's orchestras and choirs.

Pupils follow the normal curriculum, but 20 per cent of their time is spent on music. Music specialists come from all over Scotland and their chosen instrument can be any from fiddle to piano. No quotas for entry; currently 49 young people from all over the country attend. Places are free and open to all, through audition. Help is given with transport, with pupils from further away boarding at the Knightswood Secondary halls of residence, with two homework tutors.

Given, the nature of the school it's surprising that drama is not on the curriculum. However, sell-out school productions have included Footloose and Wizard of Oz. The assembly hall with grand piano transforms into a performance space with specialist lighting. Art v popular; kiln for pottery, crash Higher photography in sixth year oversubscribed and Advanced Higher art class was full recently, with a number of pupils going on to the Glasgow School of Art. National 5's decorative headpieces were on display in the foyer alongside clay sculptures by opera singers.

Good numbers do DfE at bronze and silver level. Plenty of trips – 341 excursions last year across all year groups, eg S2 ski trip to Alpe d'Huez, French exchange to Brittany, watersports trip to Ardèche, as well as visits to London, Paris, Italy and Iceland.

Background and atmosphere: Opened its doors to 200 pupils in 1967 on the site of the large Mains Estate. In 2009 was replaced by the fantastic contemporary campus of today, with picturesque views of the Campsies to the north (show-capped during our visit) from the social areas.

Our impression was of a modern, compassionate school – 'kids don't stand up when a teacher enters the room' – with strong social values. Posters of important figures, such as Maya Angelou, adorn the walls of each department alongside inspirational quotes.

The first school in East Dunbartonshire to be awarded gold as a Unicef rights respecting school. The school charter, signed by pupils, has also been updated to embrace Unicef principles. The kids we spoke to couldn't be prouder of its status, with the rainbow pride flag flying in the courtyard to represent LGBT history month. Some sixth years were proudly wearing rainbow badges too. One pupil had suggested changing the punctuality system, as she felt it was unfair to pupils from more deprived backgrounds who were living in challenging circumstances. A new system was to be trialled at the time of our visit.

School uniform of white shirt/blouse, school ties, trousers or skirts and no trainers, with blazers compulsory for all pupils. Held in high regard locally and good partnerships with local community. Students prepare Burns Night supper for the local community and afternoon tea for local elderly people.

Pastoral care, well-being and discipline: In general, 'Behaviour excellent'. Head wanted to emphasise the focus on pupils' mental, social and emotional needs, 'building up confidence and self-esteem.' One parent spoke highly of how the school helped her child adjust after moving from abroad, saying: 'The school did a brilliant job in supporting him settling in, when he spoke very little English ... Four years later he passed his Nat 5s [with A/Bs] ... The caring attitude of staff is definitely paying off.'

If there's a problem, pupils can reach out to anybody: registration teacher, class teacher, guidance head or year head. Same goes for parents. Nine exclusions in 2018.

The healthy eating menu for a state school is pretty impressive. On our visit Mediterranean pizza, tuna and mascarpone pasta and firecracker chicken were on the lunch menu, plus salad and bar and fresh fruit. One pupil joked: 'There's only chips on Fridays.' We imagine Friday lunchtimes are popular. One hour lunch break to give pupils time to take part in music rehearsals.

Strong student voice with new student councils and parliaments launched recently. The pupils we spoke to were passionate about the student council, with 12 pupils per year group, one elected by class, and one randomly selected. Their successes have included free sanitary products in the girls' bathrooms.

Pupils and parents: Milngavie is an affluent area with the majority of pupils (some 60 per cent) from middle class backgrounds.

Parents get group interim reports and a full report each year. As well as parents' evenings, there are curricular evenings for the lower years, numeracy and literacy evenings for targeted S1 groups, and family learning events in the senior phase. The Developing Young Workforce Partnership Dinner careers event is advertised by a huge poster in the main entrance, and attracts companies such as Tesco, Santander, RBS and the Glasgow Chamber of Commerce. Twitter is the most popular form of social media for school-to-home communication.

Notable former pupils: Jo Swinson (Lib Dem MP), Rob Harley (international rugby player for Glasgow Warriors), Katie Archibald (racing cyclist and member of the Great Britain 2016 Olympic champion team), and the Ayoub sisters (classical musicians famed for their interpretation of Mark Ronson's Uptown Funk).

Entrance: Most pupils stream from the cluster primaries: Milngavie, Baldernock, Craigdju and Clober. Those not in catchment area travel from as far as Clydebank, Maryhill, Partick and Balfron, including working class children whose parents who want to give them a better start in life. Excellent child-orientated joining handbook.

Exit: Around two-thirds go on to higher education, mostly Scottish universities. Two to Oxbridge in 2018 and six medics. Apprenticeships are an integral part of the school's PHSE programme.

Remarks: Stunning state school, particularly for musicians, in a super state of the art campus setting – worth moving house for, or trying an application even if you aren't in catchment or a musician. Exam results are very good and head is set on improving them even more. 'Strength through knowledge' is the school motto, which the pupils appear to embrace, together with a huge dose of social conscience.

The Edinburgh Academy

42 Henderson Row, Edinburgh EH3 5BL

Ages 2–18 **Pupils** 1,116 **Sixth form** 156

Fees: £8,433 – £14,121 pa

01315 564603
www.edinburghacademy.org.uk

Rector: Since August 2017, Barry Welsh. Studied geography at Loughborough and did a PGCE in geography at Sheffield. First teaching post at Harrow; after a year off to drive overland to Australia, made the move to Edinburgh as head of geography at Fettes, where he also coached rugby and cricket, was involved in DofE, ran the third form outdoor trip and became a housemaster. During this time he climbed two 8000m peaks: Cho Oyu in Tibet and Everest. Next post was deputy head of Shawnigan Lake School, on Vancouver Island in Canada, in charge of all aspects of school life. Returned to Edinburgh as senior deputy rector here in January 2017, taking on the role of rector two terms later.

Headteacher of junior school: Since 2011, Gavin Calder MA PGCE SQA (40s), a borderer. He came to EA Junior School having taught his way round the independent junior school sector: Robert Gordon's, Loretto, and, most recently, head of Lomond (junior school, we presume) in Helensburgh. Having worked with SCIS on a number of junior initiatives, he happily endorses Curriculum for Excellence (which has been greeted rather like National 5s with less than overwhelming enthusiasm across the board).

Academic matters: School has now discontinued GCSEs and A levels except for art in the latter ('Broader syllabus,' admits the rector), offering just National 5s, Highers and Advanced Highers. In 2018, 65 per cent A grades at Advanced Highers and 66 per cent at Highers.

The advantage of no longer offering dual sixth form disciplines should be both a logistical and financial improvement. Mandarin from age 10, plus French, German and Spanish on offer. Solo performances in Japanese and Portuguese: presumably native speakers. School will pull in dedicated tutors for native speakers to push 'em through the exam path.

'No problem getting staff.' Good mixture of old and young, school keen not to encourage the Mr Chips effect and prefers a fluid changeover. Parents have expressed frustration that neither Russian, law, nor psychology are on the table, but with the new syllabus perhaps there will be room to introduce more esoteric subjects.

Broad academic range of pupils. The tradition of 'dux', the brightest boy or girl in the school (Magnus Magnusson was dux in his day), is extended to include wider group of high achievers, the Dux Club. (School adds, 'This is based on single sitting achievement of five or more As at Higher, or predicted three A at Advanced Higher.)

Sixty pupils in P1 (three forms: age 5) and iPads for all to Geits (11/12 – who are based in Henderson Row at senior school in dedicated space), certain amount of Milly Molly Mandy waffle in prospectus about 'each stage providing a firm basis for learning at the next level'. Listening part of the programme, which includes Big Writing and Muckle Reading. (Many a mickle makes a muckle... but what on earth has that to do with reading: and do the stout citizens of Edinburgh really want their young taught Lallans?). French from nursery. Set for maths, which includes money, measurements and relates to everyday life: easy moves up and down. Basic humanities, ICT and lessons on computers – have invested in iPad learning – keyboarding for all. Computers nanny-netted and linked: all pupils have school email address.

Forget the la-la land speak. This is a thunderingly good school, combining the best of 21st century thinking with well tried and tested methods. All children arriving in P1 are assessed (baseline assessment) as are those at nursery before starting junior school proper. Mixed ability classes. Regular assessments for both the gifted and the challenged, with, in the latter case, ed psychs called in where appropriate. Co-teaching as required, with special computer access.

Max class size 20, and less both for practical and in sixth form: ability setting where possible. Refreshingly the application form makes mention of IEPs, and school offers individual learning programmes of 'one or two 40 minute lessons a week'. 'Multi-sensory teaching methods are used'. Exam allowances organised and co-teaching in English, mod langs and maths – whew. Scribing currently under debate. School comments: 'We would highlight that we have very extensive SEN support at the school from primary to senior school with five FT staff and two intern supports, plus additional specialist subject discipline input from other staff. This is in class, group extraction and one-to-one.' Non-native English speakers seem to follow a rather gentler academic regime.

Games, options, the arts: Plays rugby during both the autumn and spring terms, hence tradition for providing a mini squad for the Scottish rugby side (over 100 international caps to date), with usual rash of caps, would-be caps in the wings. No change here.

Main games field beside the junior school with its fantastic (community) sports hall including climbing wall, shared with local residents (planning condition); 'rave reviews from experienced climbers'; and much in demand for children's parties. No pool (yet); specialist weights and gym, and two all-weather hockey pitches. Girls field 10 hockey teams as well as netball and athletics. Plus individual sports badminton, fives, skiing, squash, golf, tennis, yoga and soft ball.

Outstanding art department, brilliant ceramics; well attended evening life class. Artist in residence, jewellery making popular: number of leavers go on to art and foundation courses.

Music all-singing and dancing. Superlatives abound. Trips and tours of course, pipe band. Any pupil learning an instrument can play in concerts 'even if it is only three notes and child has been learning the trombone for three weeks'. Concerts outstandingly professional (the odd radio concert). Prize-winning choirs and a good showing at Higher level. Recent choral trip to Italy, chamber choir Barnado's national choir of the year recently, and previously BBC Songs of Praise choir of the year.

Drama important; sympathetic conversion of physics building to a state-of-the-art performing arts centre, the Magnusson Centre for Performing Arts (£2.5m): green room littered with costumes for current production; theatre and dance studio with showers and changing for every imaginable activity below. Inside is breathtaking, though original features have not been vandalised.

CCF popular (everyone has to join) – flurry of battledress and air force blue on Remembrance Day; piping particularly strong, with successes in both quartet and trios. Keen DofE; lots of hobbies – and good charity input: the charity committee does a massive amount of fundraising, over £100,000 in last eight years. P6 (11 year olds or thereabouts) join the Junior Award Scheme Scotland (akin to the DofE) working towards bronze, silver and gold awards – the latter two in the senior school.

P6 (11 year olds or thereabouts) join the Junior Award Scheme Scotland (akin to the DofE) working towards bronze, silver and gold awards – the latter two in the senior school. Trips, tripettes, visits to museums plus residential camps, both at home and abroad. Exciting stuff, but now bog standard within the usual remit of junior education (and not included in the basic fee). Odd scholarship available: book token and medal only at P6 plus assorted scholarships at Geits (NB where cash involved this only comes to pupil when they have left school and is not reduced from fees).

Background and atmosphere: Lord Cockburn (Cocky) and Sir Walter Scott (amongst others) founded school in 1824. Built in trad Edinburgh sandstone in true Athenian style, the Greek motto on the main portico reads 'Education is the mother of both wisdom and virtue'. Buildings in main school a mixed bunch, some designer-inspired additions, including a fabulous oval assembly hall, plus a mass of add-ons as well as classrooms and impressive new labs around bleak tarmac courtyards.

Generous Edinburghoisie-sponsored libraries complete with purple chairs and turquoise stools (full time librarian); successful FPs remember their font of learning with pride. Planning permission for library extension and new STEM building. School dissed the field centre in Angus and put the dosh towards supporting outdoor education for all. Oval hall much used for lettings – and this ed has reeled here. Impressive dining room with halal, salads and veggie option. All cooked on site.

Junior school based at Arboretum Road. Much improved from the time this ed's son was there (think gulag): jolly classrooms, with dedicated space for P1-P3 and nursery (Denholm Green). Nursery is part of Ed council's partnership scheme. School officially opens 8.30am but parents can drop off 8am – collect 6pm via Earlybird and after-school club. Holiday club during half term and school hols.

Pastoral care, well-being and discipline: Pupils divided into four 'divisions' (houses, and if your father was there – or your grandfather – then you are in the same house), pastoral care via depute rector, heads of year plus form takers (class teachers); good PSHE. Head ephor (prefect) is a key link with rector and school. School 'not complacent that drugs are confined to an area south of Princes Street', or 'stop at the railings – incidents do occur'. No automatic exclusion unless dealing. 'If at all possible we give the pupils a second chance'; parents are involved. 'Pupil may forfeit the right to remain in the school (for a varying length of time).' Will test 'on suspicion'. City temptations are close. One or two teeny reports of bullying still around, but really just aggravated teasing and no more than any nit-picker might expect. No change here. Mobiles forbidden during school day.

Pupils and parents: All sorts, with a large traditional intake of professional classes. Traditionally patronised by the great and the good of Edinburgh and does well by them, plus an increasing number of first-time buyers (around 40 per cent). Small tranche from abroad, mainly Europe. 'Broad ethnic spread,' says the school, keen on playing down its traditional middle-class image – hence extended and very popular nursery hours and 8.00am breakfast for seniors. Pupils are pleasantly self-confident and polite – occasional touch of arrogance or uncouth youth but not more than teenage adolescence. Robert Louis Stevenson and Archbishop Tait of Canterbury are FPs, plus colourist Francis Cadell, Magnus Magnusson and Eric Stevenson, who, both during his lifetime, and on his death, gave many millions of pounds to athletics, and bursarial funds: school still benefits from the Eric H Stevenson Trust. Plus (of course) partners in many of Edinburgh's institutions.

Entrance: Primary 1 assessments held in early January. Primary 2-6 assessments can be arranged at times to suit parents – also one main assessment afternoon in late November. (Waiting lists operate where demand exceeds supply.) Almost automatic through nursery.

Maths and English from junior school to Geits age 11 (though more or less automatic); Geits to S1: maths, English and mod lang. Ditto entry to S2. 'Arrangements can be made for overseas applicants to sit our entrance tests abroad'. Sixth form entry on assessment, interview, school reference and report plus predicted grades. Five passes at GCSE grade 5 or National 5s for entry to sixth form: hardly a high bar.

Excellent bus handbook with pick up times and costings, East, Mid, West Lothian all covered plus a couple of handy inner routes. Buses drop off at both junior and senior school: school opens 8am. Pick up time 5pm, though pupils can stay till 6pm (at cost).

Exit: Nearly all (99 per cent in 2018) of juniors move on to the senior school aged 10/11, to Geits (the equivalent of Primary 7 in the Scottish system), though there may be one or two that fall by the wayside: either to trad public schools, because of relocation or not quite making the grade.

Hardly any post-16 drop out. 'Around 90 per cent' to various universities, roughly 70 per cent to Scottish (now, of course, free to Scots residents) the rest elsewhere; fewer take a gap year. Three to Oxford in 2018; wide range of other English unis too; as ever, sciences and engineering feature strongly, with creative and social subjects on the increase. Art something of a speciality. Enlightened careers department (rector again: 'Very, very good'). Some into the professions, progressively more into art, drama, interior design, the media and administration.' School can manage SATS (for American universities).

Money matters: Wowser! £670,000 dosh available for means-tested bursaries. Good crop of scholarships for musicians and academics; school may support parents in financial difficulties until the next practical exit point: but not paying fees is not an option. 'Parents must be realistic and up front.' No endowments per se – majority of scholarships and other bursaries come out of fee income. Familial discounts for third child (and more). Bursaries are means-tested up to 100 per cent fees in line with OSCR demands.

Remarks: School looks good (and will look even better when planned developments come to fruition). Feels like a well-established co-ed. Now on an almost exclusively Scottish exam pathway; we are concerned that without the A level/GCSE cachet this, the smallest of the Edinburgh independent co-ed day schools, might find parents drifting to the more academic Heriot's or the former Merchant schools; all of which, though larger, are considerably cheaper. And money talks.

Edinburgh Steiner School

60 Spylaw Road, Edinburgh EH10 5BR

Ages 3–18 **Pupils** 250 **Sixth form** 12

Fees: £3,959 – £12,041 pa

01313 373410
www.edinburghsteinerschool.org.uk

Chair of the college of teachers: No head as such – role of chair is rotated, elected from management group of the college (roughly 10 per cent of staff) who meet weekly on Thursdays (Wed afternoons involve the whole staff), but even if chosen to be chair, the position is voluntary and offer can be refused. Current chair, Nick Brett, is on his second term: a two or three year stint.

'Major educational decisions are taken by the College of Teachers and executed by the school's management team in conjunction with teachers'. Steiner is egalitarian. Bursar, board of trustees and college of teachers are responsible for finance, admin and building development. Forget trad hierarchy – teachers in the Steiner Waldorf world 'share responsibility and authority for the daily running of the school and the educational programme'. Upper school, years 9 to 12, each have a class guardian chosen from among the staff.

E

Academic matters: Pupils start each day with a 'wake-up call': daily choir /or morning verse (orchestra once a week) followed by the main lesson, a one and a half hour slot (previously two hours in the lower school) when 'topic blocks' are covered in four-week chunks: astronomy, philosophy, history of architecture: whatever. These are not necessarily exam fodder, but the Open College Network (OCN) recommended that the 'narrative's' main lesson be 'accepted without amendment and accredited' – OCN levels 1 and 2 are equivalent to 7 or 5 at GCSE.

Proper French and German from age 9 with grammar and stuff, only stories and singing for littler ones. German fairly unpopular currently (as in most schools we have visited lately), but with Steiner regime at the core and six to eight week German/French exchange with other Steiner schools there is no option; exchanges themselves funded by pupils: jumble sales, pizza cook ins and the like. (Plus global exchanges with other Rudolf Steiner schools.) Spanish on wish list. Physics, chemistry and biology from age 11 (apparently increased numbers of science lessons for 14-16 year olds), with religion represented either by stories of the saints, the legend of King Arthur and 'biographies showing the strength and compassion of the human spirit in challenge and adversity'. History includes fairy tales, legends of saints (again?) and a variety pack of mythology; not much more than lip service to geography that we could find mentioned in the exhaustive timetable we were given.

Spanking new computer room which incorporates careers and guidance (though access is blighted by an uncompromising cupboard which makes the fiction library little more than a passage with book shelves and – rather hard – bean bags). 'Real care is taken to ensure that every pupil who leaves has a plan in place for when they leave school. All the traditional options are open to them, but also support is given for a huge range of onward destinations.' And school will help out, when students have left, if they want a career change (as indeed do most schools).

Computers still thin on the ground; most classrooms equipped with computer-generated projectors and computers not encouraged (nor telly) till age 14, either at home or at school. Computer lessons include deconstructing and reconstructing old PCs as well as designing websites (school one impressive). More pianos than computers in classrooms: and pretty sad upright ones at that. No universal iPads.

Lower school follows European system whereby no formal learning is undertaken until young have lost their baby teeth – otherwise 'attachment to womb is too great'. Young need some form of independence, though they will have learnt colours and shapes in kindergarten, they are not expected to attempt either to write or to read (and they start by reading what they have written) until firmly settled into lower school. When asked about whether the school taught reading by 'phonics' the answer came 'that yes, in the Steiner way, by association with art form and letters'.

Class teachers stay with each class throughout lower school (roughly 15 per class and 25 max per year group) until they move on to upper school, taking the main lesson each day after morning verse and eurythmy. Basic reading and writing, plus simple maths age 6 (though we were surprised to find 10 year olds being given a lesson in division by 10: 'if I divide this basket into 10 pieces...')

Classes of about 20 in upper school, though we did find 28 doing mechanics which is too many for any 'caring' fee paying school. Average year group 25. Brighter pupils can leapfrog, and vice versa; EAL for older foreign nationals (charged): younger ones pick it up as they go along. 'Huge learning support' – regular testing for all for dyslexia et al in lower school and again on entry to senior school at 14; some pupils have IEPs. Dyslexics 'fully integrated; double teaching, with lap tops in upper school. Extra time in exams and scribes abound. Can 'cope' with 'mild autism'; but 'got to keep the balance'. (Check the Steiner web site for theories on dyslexia et al).

Buildings rotten for physically handicapped, though previously did quite well with a profoundly deaf pupil: 'not keen on ADHD'. School follows a multi-sensory approach to learning difficulties with the emphasis on co-ordination and 'curative' specialists. Qualified special needs staff in both lower and upper school, plus one 'floater'. General dyslexic (dyspraxic etc) help is covered within the fee structure, but if parents request extra, it costs.

Offers GCSEs, National 5s, Highers and Advanced Higher in art. The normal two-year GCSE syllabus is studied over one year, with maths, English, German and French GCSE taken aged 16, followed by humanities, the sciences and art at 17, and Highers at 18. Got it? In 2018, 56 per cent As at Higher and 58 per cent at National 5 level.

Though no academic selection, results are good in general, some seriously good. Strong German and French. Sciences and lots of practical science with hands-on lessons in somewhat antiquated lab – everything taught 'experientially and children learn by doing' – pretty good. 'By teaching science, art and religion in this integrated way, we hope to implant in our young people a holistic view of life, so that they may regard the world with understanding and serve it with respect.' But see below, new(ish) lab with only one chap in Higher physics class: girls currently physics crazy (though recent results won't set the world on fire) with engineering the new black. Philosophy the new kid on the block.

Steiner teachers are trained in-house – this is one of four training centres. Prospective disciples come from all walks of life: some are former pupils, some former parents and some come from trad teaching backgrounds (sometimes they stay with Steiner and sometimes go back to mainstream). The part-time course is spread over three years and includes an introduction to Rudolf Steiner and Anthroposophy: the esoteric science, Goethean science and artistic practice (and this is in the first year), plus Parsifal: biographical questions with reference to the Grail legend, eurythmy, creative speech, painting drawing etc. During the second and third year all must do teaching practice.

School doctor is a 'fully qualified medical practitioner who is also a specialist in Anthroposophical medicine..The doctor visits the school several times a year..The appointments are helpful for pupils, parents and teachers..Because appointments are infrequent they cannot undertake to treat acute illnesses which need ongoing supervision'. We spent some time investigating Anthroposophical medicine online; both on their dedicated site, and via the Steiner website. We are not happy with what we found on either site, but school upbraided us and told us that 'they did not follow any of these principles' – which include karmic theories and a whole lot of weird disciplines. Check them out yourselves.

Games, options, the arts: Small (puddled during our visit) basketball court, cricket and hockey; seven-a-side rugby at Meggetland Stadium 'dead popular'. School also uses Harrison Park and Craiglockhart Sports Centre and Gym: a 10 minute hike away. Timetabled PE and gym, acrobatics a recent addition – pupils wear Steiner tee shirts and tracksuit bottoms. DofE popular.

Hall used for gym, theatre etc. Options and the arts integrated into syllabus – art exam results consistently good; we were impressed by the standard of architectural drawing, one of the staff (who was French) spoke so quickly that this ed was no more informed than she was before she asked the question. Comprehensive art, including specialist drawing and painting. Lessons in hand operated sewing machines and pattern making (electric sewing machines come later), knitting a – presumably – beanie, plus embroidery and those dreaded socks again. Buttons? Pottery, sculpting (and all must do a head in their final year); some terrific work around, plus needle felting, metal and copper work, fabric design, weaving, knitting (and turning a heel: which seems an outdated skill) from age 6: for both boys and girls. Extra charge for craft materials. Specialist teachers pulled in when necessary: book binding was mentioned. Music and drama ditto and inclusive, charge for cancelled music lessons and for recorders (recorder group). Debating popular.

When we visited previously we experienced the daily eurythmy session, now curtailed to one period a week for upper school; still a rite of passage for lower school after morning verse.

Background and atmosphere: Three trad Edinburgh Victorian villas, set 'twixt George Watson's extensive campus and various parts of Napier University. Somewhat bizarre carving up of rooms: one or two fab ceilings (carved again), most rooms have fire places, motley collection of mantelpieces. Stairs need edging for visually challenged. Dangerous. Stonking new library/interview room is a joy.

Exciting Swiss/Mother Hubbardish chalet for kindergarten (3-6) with classrooms painted standard Steiner colours: class 1 peach, class 2 pink (four young were baking in a corner during our visit) and class 3 green. Three acres of shoehorned campus, children playing anywhere and everywhere within white lines neatly segregated by picket fence for early years. Proper pupil gardens: gardening is part of the syllabus. 'We eat what we grow'. This ed wondered about the riot of foxgloves. Charming, loads of outdoor play areas, with water a new feature, and trees to climb: 'Ealth & safety apparently not bothered'. The young were outside during our visit, happily pouring water, climbing trees and chasing each other. Looked dead normal to this ed. Jolly dedicated space, fenced off from the rest of the school.

'Woodland' area with tiny designated hut. Every bit of space is used, some tatty areas, nothing precious – place still smacks of a lack of funds, though the paths are better maintained than previously, and classrooms were clean and businesslike.

Christian school, celebrates all seven important events (starting with Michaelmas), other faiths' holy days factored in. 'But religion is basically right and wrong,' said our guide.

Steiner schools do not follow the (now largely historical) orthodox attitude to education, but 'treat each child as a blank canvas to be filled with interlinking academic, artistic and practical information, delivered in such a way as to incite curiosity, encourage creativity and an awareness of others'. Has long been regarded as a 'school offering alternative education to somewhat scruffy children in hippy clothes, who took no exams and pretty well ran riot'; however, since the Scottish government introduced their much reviled Curriculum for Excellence, Edinburgh Steiner has become an educational flagship, albeit an holistic one. To quote The Scotsman: 'All schools strive for innovation but one that does more than strive is Edinburgh's Rudolf Steiner. It lives and breathes innovation'. The educational philosophy that Rudolf Steiner put into practice in 1919 for the children of the employees of the Waldorf-Astoria cigarette factory has finally come home to roost. Recently described by The Times as following 'the philosophy of taking into account the academic, physical, emotional and spiritual needs of a child.'

School lunches: 90 per cent organic (following the principles of Steiner's biodynamic organic movement) and locally sourced. Daily menus suggested and prepared by all in upper school, who cook and serve lunch for their peers under supervision. Surplus funds from lunch money put towards upper school end of term trip.

Cooking lessons for all, baking in kindergarten during our visit. Organic pizzas once a week baked in pupil-constructed outside pizza oven. Serious allergies appreciated and quite strict guide lines for those bringing in food.

Pastoral care, well-being and discipline: Beautifully illustrated handbook: Edinburgh Steiner School reads like the 60s guide to a leftish hippy wonderland: but surprisingly full of (deeply non-hippy) rules and regs. Guardians are point of contact for parental angst in upper school.

Standard formula parent/guardian-teacher meetings summer and winter terms; kindergarten staff visit children at home during the Easter term: 'you will be encouraged to minimise your children's exposure to television and computers.. you will also be expected to make space in your life to think about child development and how to best support it. You will be encouraged to establish rhythm in your home, with family meals and structured bedtime routines. Choosing outdoor activities and nutritious food will also optimise the beneficial effect of our pedagogy'.

Move over big brother, this ain't a school for the kinder of high flyers who may have to jet off to Zurich at short notice. Come back 1984, all is forgiven.

Bullying an interesting one. If you believe Mumsnet it is rife: Edinburgh Steiner has an anonymous Eyes and Ears box to cope with local hiccups and our guide was quite relaxed about the problem: 'doesn't happen much, but we are on top of it'.

Pupils and parents: In addition to Steiner aficionados, parents are a disparate bunch of mainly middle class enthusiasts who are fed up with, or whose children do not get along in, other local schools. Plus some 'out-boarders', pupils from further afield, who stay with local families, plus some exchange students from Rudolf Steiner schools elsewhere, as well as those from non-Steiner schools. Certain number of refuseniks, be they from the independent or the state sector. Not that great an obvious ethnic mix.

This is a hands-on school and parents are expected to contribute during the term, as well as 'helping with redecorating etc during 'work week' at the end of the summer term, which may not fit with the planned family holiday in Sotto Grande or Benidorm. Relaxed dress code – no uniform; a (very) general policy states that pupils should be clean and tidy – no garish colours, logos, football strips, ripped jeans, hair colour or excessive jewellery; fairly impressive standard of make-up on some of the older girls; no hijabs (by choice). Pupils are comfortable in the company of visitors, happy to chat and share their work, interests and aspirations and quite honest about how they were bullied at their last school.

Our guide told us that he was sad that 'the original Steiner philosophy' that the school should be available to the lesser well off was no longer the case. He had expected to teach the offspring of social and care workers and was surprised to be teaching the young of professional classes. This ed pointed out that over 50 years ago her husband's cousin, whose father, a brigadier, member of the Upper House and head engineer of a major construction firm, had sent his daughter there.

Entrance: Suck it and see: visit school, take child to interview, with a second and longer visit if need be. Pupils come throughout the year, at any time, either through kindergarten or, often, age 12, when they have either discovered problems with their current school or need to have their self-confidence boosted.

Pupils who have previously been in the independent sector are asked for a financial reference from that school. Pupils are interviewed by kindergarten teacher, class teacher in lower school or appropriate guardian. A 'second teacher will attend all interviews'. Two or three day trial possible, but only after they have signed up and paid the mandatory fee.

Staff are caring bunch. One child asked to leave in 'living memory'; otherwise does its best to bring out the best in each and every one, 'instilling life-long learning'.

Exit: Ninety-five per cent of pupils leaving at the upper end of the school go on to some sort of further education; most to Scottish unis, especially Glasgow and Edinburgh and art colleges: rash of academic and vocational courses, from marine science to the British Racing School in Newmarket, maths, psychology, politics, fine art, history of art, textiles, drama, and, of course, engineering, odd lawyer, medic, nary an accountant recently. Oxbridge 'not out of the frame', but doesn't figure lately. Gap years popular, furthering the Steiner philosophy wherein journeying is an important part of life.

Money matters: Staff pay in 'low £20,000s' but 80 per cent discount for children in school. Five per cent of previous year's fee income available each year for bursarial help: strict guidelines, and particular help available where parents may be 'considering leaving the school for financial reasons'. When we asked whether 'bursarial help' extended to contributing towards school trips, we were assured that 'other parents/ school rally round'. The Corbyn effect obviously got here early.

Not as cheap as you might first think, huge amount of extra, and not that hidden, charges.

Steiner aficionados are currently working with the Scottish Government and Edinburgh LA to secure state funding. All awards are means-tested max: 40 per cent of fees. (But NB no mention of extras.)

Remarks: Founded 1939, the Edinburgh Rudolf Steiner offers cradle-to-grave, alternative education, with some brilliant teaching and perfect for the child who finds the trad schooling system difficult. We are disturbed by what our researches into the cult of Anthroposophy threw up: the staff whom we met seemed charming and rational, but if we are to believe what we read then perhaps we should delve deeper into the school's philosophy before giving it a high five. And, to be honest, we would prefer to see pupils learning to sew on a button rather than turning a heel. (Apparently they now 'sew buttons on their recorder cases in year 3, and make 'machine sewn garments in class 7/8' – boys too, we presume.)

All singing and dancing – on the surface – and, if you can face the slings and arrows of Anthroposophy – then go for it. But, do you/would you prevent your young from watching the daily news or Dr Who on telly and allow a (thoroughly well qualified) teacher to dictate when, what and how you eat? And remember, you, the parent, are expected to actively participate both during term time and during the holidays.

ESMS Junior School

Linked with Stewart's Melville College, The Mary Erskine School

11 Queensferry Road, Edinburgh EH4 3EQ

E

Ages 3–12 **Pupils** 1,242 **Boarders** 2 full

Fees: Day £8,142 to £9,123; Boarding £20,250 to £20,835 pa

01313 111111
www.esms.org.uk

Headmaster: Since 2016, Mike Kane, previously head of upper school at Stewart's Melville College. 'He has a great manner and really cares about the children'. He is well liked by all parents we spoke to. 'He looks out for every child....is intelligent, measured, astute but down to earth with good values.' His background is in teaching English and he still enjoys taking the occasional lesson with P7 pupils. His previous role gives him a good understanding of the transition from junior to senior school.

Entrance: Automatic entrance to the school from nursery for the majority. Nursery places are offered by date of application (many parents register their child at birth). Some priority given to siblings and the need to ensure a balance of boys and girls (the school is often 'boy heavy').

Otherwise entry is by assessment, which can be arranged at any time during the school year. School is oversubscribed with waiting lists for some years. The main school entry points are P1 (around 15-20 spaces), P3 and P4, with the biggest entry point at P6 (around 50 places). Occasional places available at other levels. Only between five and 10 places available at P7 so parents are encouraged to apply for P6 instead. When we visited, P6 was 'almost full and there was a growing waiting list for P7'.

Entrance assessment for primary years. Numeracy, writing, reading aloud and a relaxed chat. Children have to be able to 'cope'. This is a selective school and not everyone makes the grade.

Exit: Nearly all go on to one of the senior schools (The Mary Erskine School or Stewart's Melville College) at 11 or 12. Minimal trickle elsewhere to other independents.

Remarks: Huge school on two sites. Early years, nursery to primary 3 (ages 3-7 or 8) and is based at Ravelston on the same site as The Mary Erskine School (girls' senior school) and the upper junior school is at the Stewart's Melville College site (boys' senior school) on Queensferry Road.

Snowdrops nursery children are in their own interjoining, sunny, south facing rooms. At 4 the numbers increase to 120 children divided in four classes sizes of 30, in big, light rooms. All decorated with great thought and creativity and in different 'zones' for work and play. Fun outdoor play area bung-full of interesting and irresistible bits and pieces. Plenty of inventive stuff to play with – hoses, bits of wood, tyres, crates, tunnels and puddles; the children were happily guddling around at the time of our visit. Great spaces both inside and out but a class of 30 is still a big pond for little fish to play in. PE, ICT, library and music specialists from nursery.

Wrap-around care available from nursery (early bird 7.45am to after-school club 6pm). This is popular with those we spoke to – 'an amazing provision for working parents'. Nursery pick up times 12.30pm, 2.30pm or 6pm. After-school club from 2.30pm (free play).

Outdoor learning takes place in the forest kindergarten – a specially developed 'wild' area of the school grounds. Hmmm... green but not exactly wild – we're in well-tended school grounds in central Edinburgh, after all. Here learning is supported by trained forest kindergarten leaders. Nursery children have a few hours of outdoor learning once a week for a 6/8 week block. In P1/2/3 the forest kindergarten is linked to classroom topics so that children can 'extend their learning' and develop 'problem solving skills'.

Primary 1 starts at age 4/5. We hear that the move up from nursery is well done, 'the school is great at transitioning'. No subject sets in P1 to P3. Reading taught by sight reading and phonetics – whichever works best. Regular internal assessments to pick up any glitches. From P2 there is a more formal assessment to get children 'used to putting answers down'. Things ramp up again in P3 with GL assessments. From time to time an 'emotionally young' child may defer for a year but only after a full consultation with parents. On rare occasions a child may be advised to go elsewhere, but again only after much consultation with parents. French and drama from P1. Spelling (important here) begins in P2 and cursive handwriting in P3.

The support for learning department works across the whole school and moves between the two sites. Support for all intellectual abilities in small groups and in-class support. School happy to take all dys-strata 'as long as support for learning is not full', and can cope with ADHD and Asperger's.

Classes reshuffled in P3. Parents are divided as to whether or not this is beneficial. Some say that it helps the children 'make other friends and know their year group better' and 'it pushes them out of their comfort zone', while others worry about the 'lack of continuity' and 'the loss of friendships damaging confidence in some children'. A range of 15 different clubs for P3 to choose from, including science and Spanish, with dance from nursery.

P2 and 3 eat in the lunch hall. Nursery and primary 1 currently have packed lunches in classrooms. This will change around the end of 2019 when the fabulous new dining facility is finished, giving far more options.

In P4, aged 8, all move to Queensferry Road site. Full use of the senior school facilities. Set in maths from P4. The junior school favours broad banded setting with smaller classes for the less able. For instance in P4, lowest maths set has only 12 pupils. Maximum class size is usually 25, with 20 for more practical subjects such as home economics and science. Again 'spelling matters', as does presentation. All children use a fountain pen from P6. Home economics and science in senior school labs from P7. German and Spanish from P6.

New emphasis on teachers 'knowing individual pupils', possibly even more important/difficult in a school as big as this. All class teachers are full time – no job shares – so they can get to know their pupils well.

Great library on two levels. Bright and sunny. Books cleverly colour-coded into genres for ease of use. Lovely airy classrooms. P6/7s have lots of outdoor space including Astros to run around on. Outdoor play area for the P4/5s on the small side and noisy (busy main road the other side of the wall).

Fantastic sport and fantastic facilities – swimming pool, super gyms and lots of games options. Sport for all. A huge number of teams: eight junior school rugby teams (boys only), six junior school cricket teams, eight P6/P7 hockey teams for girls. Boys' hockey is a growth area with a strong uptake so far. Everyone encouraged to take part. Football extremely popular with boys and girls. Cricket for girls has caught on fast (over 60 girls receiving weekly coaching, U12, U13, U15 teams in the senior school). Strong swimming teams (Edinburgh schools champions – boys and girls). PE classes within the core curriculum.

A mind-boggling number of clubs on offer to those in P4-P7 – over 100, ranging from modern dance and Warhammer to tap-dance and hillwalking. Annual residential camps include walking, climbing, canoeing and aim to develop independence, confidence, friendships and skills.

Outstanding music, dance and drama. Impressive Tom Fleming Centre for Performing Arts, a renovated Victorian assembly hall, seats up to 800. So fab that it is recognised as one of Edinburgh's foremost rehearsal and performance venues and used by external performers as well as the school children. Fourteen choirs, each year group has an orchestra, there's ensembles and bands and over 600 junior school pupils are regularly involved in music making. A choir sings at the Royal Edinburgh Military Tattoo during the Festival, and children regularly perform in professional musicals and operas: last year 64 pupils sang in the production of Joseph at the Edinburgh Playhouse.

Art is strong too. Top facilities and impressive, up to date, creations on display throughout.

Charity work is important. Children are encouraged to organise their charity projects and come up with their own 'inventive ideas' to raise money rather than just being told what to do, something that we don't see enough of in schools. Great for budding entrepreneurial whizz kids as well as raising cash for good causes. Last year the junior school raised over £50,000 for more than 30 charities. Strong contact with Malawi: heavily involved in the establishment, through The Chesney Trust, of The Edinburgh Girls' High School in north-east Malawi.

Strong anti-bullying programme. A nine-point set of values which are repeated, at every turn, on walls around the school. Each child must show appreciation, commitment, confidence, enthusiasm, grace, integrity, kindness, respect and responsibility. Newly appointed tsar for overall pastoral care (P4-P7) to put more rigid structures in place and make sure that messages on bullying are robust and clear. Parents tell us that any problems have been 'sorted immediately' with 'common sense' and 'good dialogue' between everyone involved.

Parents are a mixed bunch. Many first-time buyers and children of FPs (former pupils). Parents report 'a broad cross-section of families', mostly from central Edinburgh and suburbs. Not really a toff school, although there will be a smattering. One parent commented that 'as the fees are reasonable, the school is a big melting pot of all sorts of different people' and there is 'no elitism, which makes a good environment for the children'.

From P4 (age 8), buses to and from everywhere. Thirteen different bus routes – Dunfermline, Dunbar, Melrose and Falkirk as well as around the city itself. Buses leave school at 4.20pm, with a 'bus club' for those who finish school at 3.30pm. Boarding is available for a 'small contingent' but only from P6 upwards. Boarding can be full time or weekly, flexi on offer with B&B if space available. Boarding houses are very close to the school in boys' and girls' houses with a married couple in charge of both. But with only two junior school children boarding at present this is very much a day school.

Parking (very) restricted at the Stewart's Melville campus, with parents mostly parking on the street. However at Ravelston campus, there's a new car park. Well thought out with oodles of space and a separate 'bus area'.

This is a big, impressive school and a formidable, slick operation. Terrific success stories on every front, not just academically. The sheer size has tremendous benefits, but not every child will thrive as a small fish in such a large pond, and the non-conformist may have less room to manoeuvre.

Facilities and opportunities abound. Parents say that there is a 'heathy level of competition' in the school but 'children are batted down if they suggest they are better than someone else'. We don't feel that this school is complacent about its success. With a newish head, who is 'open to new ideas', it is always striving to improve and develop.

Fernhill School

Fernbrae Avenue, Rutherglen, Glasgow G73 4SG

Ages 2–18 **Pupils** 200 **Sixth form** 10 **RC**

Fees: £7,580 – £11,090 pa

0141 634 2674
www.fernhill-school.com/

F

Head teacher: Since 2014, Dr Laura Murphy BSc PhD PGDE (50s), previously depute head and chemistry teacher here, as well as teacher at Calderglen High School in East Kilbride and Glasgow Academy. Chemistry graduate from Glasgow University, followed by a PhD (sponsored) in catalysis.

Dr Murphy jokes that she took a '20-year gap year' before 'fulfilling her childhood dream to be a teacher', previously having a highly successful career as head technology manager with Imperial Chemical Industries (ICI). Passionate about the job and the close-knit 'Fernhill family', she is very much one of the girls – fun, hard-working, nurturing. We visited almost every class in the school and what came across overwhelmingly was how at ease the children were in themselves and in her company. Children openly gave their opinions, knowing they would be valued, without fear of reprimand.

Although relatively new, she is respected and well-liked by parents, described as 'pragmatic and with a can-do approach'. When talking about the near closure the school faced in 2014, one parent summed it up: 'She has led this school across hurdles bigger than she herself could have possibly imagined and has done so with confidence, belief and the utmost passion.'

Academic results continue to improve during her time as HT and she is focused on bringing the primary and secondary together as one community to offer 'coherence, continuity and progression for every child'. Enhancing sports is also on her agenda, particularly since the school became co-ed in 2016.

Married to a dentist, with three children: eldest son graduated from St Andrews with a maths degree and works in finance, daughter is a dentist like her dad and her youngest son is a teacher like his mum. Enjoys socialising, skiing and sailing; previously owning a yacht in Largs. She describes faith as an integral part of her life: 'I live life through my faith. I try to emulate Jesus in a good way of life, having respect, being humble and being of service to other people.'

Academic matters: Academic school, with Higher results eighth best in Scotland recently – impressive since this is a non-selective school: 'We take everyone in.' Only children with severe special needs or disabilities wouldn't be suited to the school. Tiny classroom sizes (never exceeding 18 pupils) with great teacher to pupil ratios mean that no child is overlooked, with each child receiving an individualised learning plan. Children are well supported; after prelims, pupils and parents meet with the HT or a member of the senior management team individually to discuss areas in which they need to improve to meet their potential.

In 2018 at Highers, 87 per cent As and Bs and more than half As. For Advanced Highers, 92 per cent A and Bs. Most secure places in their first choice university course in subjects including dentistry, international business, science, architecture, literature and music.

Each pupil talks to their teacher individually in S2 to help choose the eight subjects for National 5s (three sciences, three social subjects, three languages, including Latin). Strong in maths (78 per cent A grades in Advanced Highers in 2016), sciences (particularly chemistry) and languages (65 per cent of pupils study languages beyond S4). They teach Italian in kindergarten, French from P1 and Spanish from S3. Drama is studied in S1 and S2 but is not taken forward. Modern studies and business are available at Advanced Higher in S6.

School believes it's vital for the pupils to have 'knowledge of the world outside education' and organises work experience programmes in S1, for example working in the NHS learning how to give mouth-to-mouth and practising taking fake blood.

Annual careers night with representatives from a wide range of universities and industries, where 'some children even got Saturday jobs from it'. Links with the company Inspiring Futures, which offers bespoke courses in CV writing and presentation skills. From S4 pupils have access to the 'future wise' computer programme (paid for by parents), which gives bespoke advice. School pays for a 'baby version' of the programme available to S1–S3 pupils.

Good SEN provision including a support for learning coordinator. Staff turnover is low and majority long serving: of 35 staff only three were new in 2016. All are qualified teachers following Curriculum for Excellence and there is a 50/50 gender balance in senior management.

Games, options, the arts: Doing its best to provide an improved games programme, but you won't find top-notch hockey fields and rugby pitches here. One senior pupil told us she'd like to 'bring in more sports, with better results in competitions'. This reviewer loved how confident the girls were in answering honestly (and in front of the HT, too).

A plus, however, is its nine acres of beautiful land (though it was too snowy to explore on our visit, unfortunately). Many activities take place outside, such as yoga, dance, gymnastics and multi-sports. Nursery children have their own forest kindergarten (we oohed and aahed at the photo album), where they do spades of outdoor activities – senior pupils were filled with nostalgia as they reminisced about their own memories of den building. Glasgow weather can be cruel though, so the gym hall is put to good use, though one parent said, 'maybe in time the gym hall could be revamped'.

Primary pupils rehearsed (with great enthusiasm) for a dance competition to win house points on our tour – winning house points is a serious business, with plenty of competitions throughout the year.

Swimming and hockey (both off-site) are most popular. Hockey has just been introduced and 'everyone wants to be in the hockey team', boys and girls, vying against other Scottish independent schools. Annual swimming gala is held in the local pool for pupils from P5 to S6 (again for house points). Doesn't offer rugby – a bit of a shame now that the school is co-ed. Small number train with local athletics and cross-country running clubs. Achievements in sport include an S3 pupil gaining a place in the Scottish Independent Schools Girls' Football team.

Makes up for what it lacks in sporting prowess in other clubs: science, debating, public speaking, chess, cake baking and fashion to name a few. Successful and popular debating team with various debating competitions on the go. P7s take part in a School Mock Court Project, where they perform as lawyers, dressed in wigs and gowns in the High Court in Glasgow. Finals take place in the High Court in Edinburgh and the school has won it three times. Also national winners (2016) of the COPFS public speaking competition in Parliament House, Edinburgh.

No surprise that there is an Italian club (in partnership with Italian consulate) since Italian is taught from nursery school. Some of the founding fathers, in fact, were of Italian descent.

Music is massively popular and taught from P1 in a traditional music room (one-to-one lessons paid by parents) in the original part of the school, a fine Victorian mansion, where guitars hang from walls. Primary and secondary each have their individual orchestras, with the most gifted in Scotland's junior national orchestras. Musical evenings and carol services are put on every year, and the school choir has performed in Barcelona, Disneyland Paris and Rome. They also sing at local care homes at Christmas time.

Huge uptake for DofE; half of S6 pupils help out at a local school for children with severe learning disabilities. Fair Trade groups and stalls throughout the year to promote social justice. Strong links with the local community: the children wrap Christmas gifts for a parish in a poorer community and donate to a foodbank twice yearly. Lower secondary school have worked as 'social justice entrepreneurs', where the pupils turn £1 into as much money as possible. All money raised goes to assist entrepreneurs in the developing world. Senior girls made it to the West of Scotland finals in the young enterprise competition in South Lanarkshire. The head said: 'It's important for the pupils to take responsibility, by giving their time to help others who are less fortunate.'

While drama is taught only in S1 and S2, there is a drama club and a school show or panto is a highlight of the school calendar, and has included the Wizard of Oz and Les Misérables. Art of various genres is displayed around the school. Eco fashion show was embraced by the art department recently; on our tour we saw some impressive dresses made from recycled materials, including one made with Fernhill flyers. Top of the pops were those designed by the Higher art and design students.

Trips include religious retreats every year from P1 onwards (eg Rome and Lourdes), as well as local trips to the Glasgow Science Centre, geography field trips to various parts of Scotland, and annual creative retreats to Cove Park by Loch Long. Also P7 trip to London, using public transport only, and visit to Stratford to attend an RSC production of Antony and Cleopatra. Skiing trip annually to Austria or Italy.

Background and atmosphere: Set close to Cathkin Braes, the main Victorian building was originally founded by Notre Dame sisters in 1952 as a Catholic mission school for primary school children. When the missionaries left, the parents wanted to keep the school open and formed a board, and so it began as an independent school, for both primary and secondary girls, in 1972. Parents held the school dear to their hearts then, as they do now. Indeed, when the school faced closure again in 2014, due to financial difficulties, they came to the rescue by raising hundreds of thousands of pounds to save it.

When parents, many of them former pupils, talk of Fernhill the affection is apparent in their voices: 'Fernhill is a warm, positive and supportive environment'; 'Fernhill is a family; we are a small community with great parents'; 'I always say "small school, big heart" – it is quite hard to explain the feeling of belonging until you are part of the school'.

Co-education moved up from the primary school to the secondary in 2016 to 'welcome all members of the family'. Previously primary school boys went off elsewhere (generally another independent school) for their secondary education (we can't help but think becoming co-ed has been a smart financial move to boost enrolment, too). Traditional Catholic school with gospel values, proud to turn out 'polite and well-mannered children'. This was certainly our impression, but more so that the children were not fazed by us and let their personalities, quirks and all, shine through. When we asked senior pupils how they would improve the school they were unafraid to be honest (believe us, this is not always the case) and gave suggestions to reintroduce 'fun Fridays' like in primary school and to 'outlaw double maths on a Monday!'

This same confidence was evident in the classrooms, too, housed in modern, practical teaching blocks, built in the 90s. In both primary and secondary school, children politely chanted 'Good morning Dr Murphy' when she entered the room, but were at ease to express their point of view whenever asked a question. Pupil suggestions, mainly through the pupil council, are taken on board – the latest being a newly installed vending machine (we wonder if that's as popular with the parents as it is the pupils, having sweets and treats on tap).

Kindergarten is a nurturing environment, where children played happily when we visited, while a younger tot slept in the corner. Nursery staff were bubbly and enthusiastic and the walls a riot of colour with children's artworks.

Pupils are well turned out in smart uniform including woollen blazers; the younger ones wear caps (for boys) and round felt hats (for girls). Summer uniform of dresses and long white socks for girls.

Pastoral care, well-being and discipline: As the school is small one works as a mentor for all pupils in their house. Pastoral care is given through the deputy head, whom children can approach with any problems, but 'all teachers lend an eye and are approachable'. Senior management team members link with parents in the secondary school, and head teacher does so in the primary school.

For pupils with poorer prelim results, they work with parents and offer extra support for learning. Some pupils do part-time college (or university in S6), part-time school, combining mainstream and vocational courses, and make great progress, as demonstrated in exam result figures.

With gospel values and respect for others so highly valued, there is no need for a discipline programme in the school. Head declares, 'we don't have to worry about discipline in this school,' continuing that 'teaching time is all teaching'.

Standard school dinners (in line with Scottish nutrition standards), with fruit and a drink, are served for all in the main (gym) hall for a small fee. One parent commented, 'if I could change anything it would only be a separate lunch hall as just now the hall is used for everything'.

Pupils and parents: Communication in the form of a newsletter every term, which illustrates the children's achievements – parents have opportunity to share their experiences in the newsletter, too. Above and beyond normal parents' evenings, senior members of staff have one-to-one meetings with parents after prelims to talk it over and plan for exams; from S6 pupils also attends meeting and discuss exam strategy.

Pupils come from far and wide and are bussed in from Kilmarnock, Cumbernauld, Airdrie, East Kilbride, Motherwell, North Lanarkshire, South Lanarkshire and the south side of Glasgow. Bus service tailor-made for pupils each year; picks ups operate from local train station, too.

Parents mostly middle class, business people of mixed ethnicities (though majority white Scottish). School considers itself to be charitable and welcomes children from all walks of life, and stresses it 'would want to help a child who would benefit from coming here' through bursaries. As senior school only recently turned co-ed, still has an air of a girls' school (spilt approx 70 per cent girls, 30 per cent boys in both primary and secondary schools).

No notable former pupils. Head says: 'Lots of successful people have came through our doors but I don't know of any really famous or notable alumnae.'

Entrance: Primary school applicants sit a cognitive, speech and language entrance test; entrants are guaranteed a place into the upper school. Secondary school applicants must pass the curriculum assessment, but there is a strong emphasis on 'keeping families together'; they do their best to ensure children from the same family are accepted.

Tries to operate a 'fair playing field' for all applying and 'tends to take most'. Dr Murphy says: 'We try to be as inclusive as we can be.' Two-thirds of children in secondary school come from the primary, the remaining third from other schools, generally in P7.

Boys (other than those coming directly from primary school) mostly come from state schools. Vast majority of pupils in primary move directly to secondary. Sixth form entry is based on Higher results.

Exit: Vast majority go on to Scottish universities, mainly Glasgow, Strathclyde, St Andrews and Edinburgh, studying subjects including engineering, computing, maths and business with languages. Some take a gap year post-Highers and the odd one starts an apprenticeship or heads into the world of work.

No Oxbridge places (but this is a tiny school) and a couple of pupils every year for medicine, veterinary science, dentistry; also a few to the Royal Conservatoire of Scotland.

Money matters: Considers itself more affordable than many of Scotland's fee-paying schools, offering means-tested bursaries. Mortgage-style payment scheme is available, though only a small percentage use it. Extra costs include music tuition, school trips and transport, the latter subsidised to make it more affordable.

Remarks: Tiny Catholic school, recently turned co-ed, which accepts children from all faiths. With strong moral values, it prides itself on turning out competent, confident and mostly academic children, with girls achieving great results in the sciences. Suitable for a wide range of children of different abilities who impressively go on to achieve great academic results. Adored by pupils and parents that cherish being part of the 'fun Fernhill family'.

Fettes College

18

Carrington Road, Edinburgh EH4 1QX

Ages 7–18 **Pupils** 765 (prep 214, college 551) **Sixth form** 248 **Boarders** 416

Fees: Day £16,500 – £28,200; Boarding £24,210 – £34,800 pa

01313 116744
www.fettes.com

Headmaster: Since August 2017, Geoffrey Stanford, previously deputy head of co-curricular at Sevenoaks. Classics degree from Oxford, captain in the Grenadier Guards and worked in the City before joining Millfield to teach economics, business studies and Latin. Has also been boarding housemaster and head of department at Pangbourne. He has rowed for Eton, Sandhurst and the British Army at Henley, completed the Marathon des Sables and Devizes to Westminster canoe race, and taken part in a succession of expeditions to the Himalayas, including leading an international team to the summit of Mount Everest. 'Been up Everest'; he says like it's bagging a Munro. He also enjoys playing the French horn.

Married to Susanna: 'A role model to the girls.' They have two young sons – not to forget the two flat-coated retrievers. Together they immerse themselves in school life: serving up Christmas dinner, and 'camming up' for CCF exercises, handing out jelly babies in the dark so the pupils don't know who they are. They describe their job at Fettes as 'a brilliant move, we have friends and family in Edinburgh and the Borders.'

'An inspiring man', one pupil said: 'It's hard to find something he doesn't know!' 'Very modest.' Despite his achievements, he let two senior female members of staff sing his praises. It was most amusing, as at times he struggled to get a word in. Extremely hands on, during the third-form 5k endurance course you'll see him at the top of the ramp helping everyone up.

Head of prep school: Since 2003, Adam Edwards BA London (late-50s). Formerly a housemaster at Gresham's School, Norfolk. Married to Jill; three sons (all Old Fettesians) and one daughter (still at Fettes). A history graduate and a talented sportsman.

Academic matters: Prep school like a mini campus complete with chicken coop and veg garden (to tie in with science, of course). Latin early, masses of artwork on the walls, science labs in the corridors, plenty of laptop computers. 'We decide when they can use them.'

Only school in Scotland top-rated across the board for leadership, care and well-being; inspectors described the school as having 'a culture of kindness'. This writer was certainly very well looked after; lemon and ginger tea appeared in minutes to soothe a persistent cough and cold. Close to 50/50 split between boys and girls; completely co-ed and no lingering feeling of its history as a boys' school.

No SQA exams: like many of the big Edinburgh players, prefers the English system. 'Following the English curriculum is an attraction for many parents.' Added the IB in 2006. Pupils can choose whether they want to specialise, and do A levels, or take the broader IB syllabus. Over 40 per cent doing IB, a number of them home-grown, with excellent results – average score 38 in 2018. At A level 65 per cent A*-B and 40 per cent A*/A; 70 per cent A*-A/9-7 grades at GCSE, amongst the highest grades ever. 'Value added on that is impressive.'

Three sciences on offer throughout, plus trad French, German and Spanish, as well as Mandarin (available for beginners as well as for native speakers) and Latin (optional). No particular bias – physics, chemistry, biology and geography outstanding at GCSE, maths and English almost equally strong; results in all disciplines equally impressive at A level. Broad curriculum, with at least one modern language studied at GCSE. Strong classics and Mandarin departments.

For foreign pupils EAL is on hand (although the college requires an excellent level of English: pupils who don't have good working knowledge of the language are encouraged to do an English language course before they arrive).

Teachers in bases at dedicated times for academic support when needed. The stunning old-world library has seven different spaces including a study centre with computing suite and university-type resources. Hot chocolate is served at break time to encourage pupils in and poetry recitals take place in the evenings. The prep school has its own cosy little library with reading logs; reading time is built into the weekly curriculum.

Good staff: pupil ratio – average of 15 pupils per class in prep school, max 19; 20 max in senior school.

Games, options, the arts: Wide range of opportunities: some 25+ sports and 40+ extracurricular activities. More unusual prep school clubs include circus skills and parkour.

Usual suspects for traditional team games: hockey and athletics for both sexes; rugby and cricket for boys, and lacrosse and tennis for girls. Needle matches with Glenalmond and Merchiston on the rugby field and Strathallan in hockey. Big sports centre and swimming pool providing a wide range of other sports. Huge playing fields with water-based Astro and athletics track. Recent rugby and cricket triumphs (Including Watsonian cricket club young player of the year).

Rich music tradition with loads of bands, orchestras, choirs, string quartet etc etc, two popular concerts in spring and autumn plus carol service, all in aid of charity. Keen drama with imaginative productions, recently Arabian Nights, Equus and Beauty and the Beast (in the prep school, with over 100 pupils involved); pupils often perform at the Edinburgh Fringe.

Variety of whole school events: ceilidhs, Burns' Night suppers, black tie dinners. Everyone – including staff and parents – joins in the annual 5k, 10k or half marathon, some from the rowing club electing to travel by water instead. Every house chooses a charity they wish to support for this event and average totals raised hit £20,000.

CCF, community service, DofE etc. Masses of outings, everywhere, for everything: prep trip to Rome (included in the fees), choir to France, ski trips.

Boarding: About 75 per cent of pupils board. Two prep and eight senior school houses, all single sex, for day and boarding pupils, with tutors attached. Each staff member is attached to a boarding house, whether as tutor, sports coach or teacher, creating a sense of community. 'They get to know the teachers in a completely different way.'

Newish posh co-ed boarding house – Craigleith, very modern – for the upper sixth. The pair of curved blocks forms two identical wings, one for boys and one for girls, with carefully controlled access from a central space. Individual rooms, allowing them to focus for their exams, and the on-site tutor specialises in UCAS progress. Provides a transition between the disciplines of school and uni, with pupils being able to cook snacks and some meals if they want to. They have cookery lessons and take responsibility for their own washing, ironing and cleaning their rooms (with matron offering ironing lessons when needed).

Background and atmosphere: William Fettes (later Sir William), the son of an Edinburgh grocer, made his fortune during the Napoleonic Wars when 'he became Scotland's leading contractor for provisions for the army'; his only son died in 1815, and William in 1836. While he had originally intended to found a hospital, he later 'decided to create a school for orphans and the needy'. He died in 1936; after prudent investment, the trustees decided that with £166,000 in the kitty, there were enough funds to acquire land, build and endow a school: Fettes opened in 1870 with 50 boys.

Purpose-built, designed by architect David Bryce, it's hard not be impressed by the vast Grimms' fairy tale of a building, complete with turrets, acres of wood panelling and shiny black floors. One of the admin staff reassured us as we entered: 'Don't feel intimidated.'

Various Victorian edifices are scattered about the school's wonderful 90 acre grounds, bang in the middle of Edinburgh. The collection of new and converted buildings that house the prep department are much bigger than they look from the outside. The newest Fettes addition is the impressive Spens building, opened by Nobel Prize winning author and economist Sir Angus Deaton (and Old Fettesian) in 2015. A combination of new-build and refurbishment, it is home to the modern languages, mathematics, geography, economics departments, plus a music school with music practise pods and huge light-filled art school that extends into the roof void.

Pupils meet every morning for assembly and congregational singing in the beautiful chapel. 'The house hymns are more like anthems.' Non-denom Sunday service.

Caring ethos and traditional values. Pupils stood up as we entered the room. Hard work ethic; pupils are expected to give their very best. The former famous trad boys' school is now genuinely co-ed.

Pastoral care, well-being and discipline: Everyone can visit their tutor to discuss how they are doing... 'Not just academically, a confidante. Peers, prefects, head of house, matron, tutor, medical centre staff, chaplain. Always someone you can trust.' Tells us it is the only school in Scotland to be rated excellent by the Care Inspectorate across all areas for several years.

Three tier system on the discipline side: housemaster, deputy head, head; rustication/formal warning and suspension or expulsion. Zero tolerance policy on drugs; this resulted in a well-reported expulsion a few years ago. Anyone who has watched Trainspotting will know Edinburgh has a long-standing drugs problem, in common with most big cities, causing a headache for schools. The older pupils are young adults and have the freedom to go to the city centre within curfew times. Young adults make mistakes and you can't help but feel that the press enjoy ramping it up because it's an expensive independent school.

Very clear house-visiting rules – no overt demonstrations of affection; bonking equals out (as an 18-year A-grade pupil found out after relations with another youth on a school excursion). They do lose the occasional pupil for all these misdemeanours, ditto bullying. Strong anti-bullying ethos.

House loyalty is strong; there are house 'attainment' and 'effort' awards. 'Effort is what you do with what you've got. To have the right attitude of hard work.' School meals should be impressive and they were when we visited: a myriad healthy options, colourful salads and fresh fish. You'd be hard pushed not to find something you like.

Very attractive uniform – most noticeable are the boys' burgundy striped blazers and the girls' tartan skirts.

Pupils and parents: The flavour has changed from home-grown Scots to more international: some 60 per cent from Scotland, 15 per cent from the rest of the UK, 15 per cent British expats and 10 per cent foreign nationals (from over 40 countries – North America to Hong Kong). Very strong old Fettesian stream, plus loads of first-time buyers, intellectuals etc etc. Good vibrant mix. Old Fettesians include John de Chastelaine, Ian McLeod, James Bond, Lord Woolf,Tony Blair, Nobel Prize Winner Sir Angus Deaton and composer Lorne Balfe.

Entrance: To prep by assessment test and interview held annually. Entry points in every year group of the prep school.

CE or school's own exam to senior school at 13+, limited availability for entry at 14+ via school's own entrance exams and then approx 30 students a year join the sixth form after GCSE elsewhere, currently much sought after as pupils pile in from other, mainly Scottish, schools (one in six chance of admissions and competition very stiff). Only boarding places offered at 14+ and 16+ entrance. All assessments include face-to-face interviews or Skype interviews for those sitting exams abroad.

Exit: Virtually all juniors to senior school (automatic entry). Hardly any leave post-GCSE. Most to university – Aberdeen, Durham, Edinburgh, Exeter, Glasgow, King's College London, Manchester, Newcastle, St Andrews, Warwick etc to study, eg engineering, English, maths or law. Some successes from early decision US universities including Harvard. Four to Oxbridge in 2018, plus six medics, three off to the US and one each to Toronto, Milan and Dublin.

Excellent careers advice and school has won awards for its careers programme.

Money matters: Well-endowed with scholarships including academic, music, sports, all-rounder, piping, art, up to 10 per cent of fees. Also means-tested bursaries: 'The level of these awards depend upon parents' financial means and can cover up to the full value of the fees'. Over 70 students are already in receipt of large-scale bursaries (covering 80–100 per cent of the fees). Due to a very large anonymous donation, school has launched the Fettes KickStart campaign, which will see two pupils per year join the prep school for their entire schooling up to 18. School is working with six local primary schools on this project to identify eligible pupils. Special (Todd) bursaries for Old Fettesians, 12.5 per cent discount for Forces (not so many of these around).

Remarks: Still lives up to its reputation and is undoubtedly the strongest school in Edinburgh. With an ethos for hard work, there is every opportunity for pupils to excel academically, on the sporting field, creatively and culturally. Exciting cosmopolitan mix of pupils in an exciting city.

George Heriot's School

Lauriston Place, Edinburgh EH3 9EQ

Ages 4–18 **Pupils** 1,648 **Sixth form** 354

Fees: £10,134 – £12,522 pa

01312 297263
www.george-heriots.com

Principal: Since January 2018, Lesley Franklin, previously junior school head, who has worked at the school for over 20 years. German degree from St Andrews and teaching qualification from Reading. Experienced hockey coach. She is married to Angus and they have two daughters, both at the school.

Junior school head: Since January 2018 is Alastair G Morrison BA PGCE (40s), previously head of Feltonfleet School. Has returned to his roots: spent 12 years as deputy head and director of sport at Fettes College Preparatory School and before that, three years as class teacher of Edinburgh Academy Junior School.

Academic matters: Junior school in three sections: early years encompasses 3-5 years, middle primary 5-8 years and upper primary 8-11.

School follows the Scottish system of National 5s and Highers etc. Given the broad intake (from nursery up) and the number of subjects on offer, you can't fault the place. In 2018, 63 per cent As at Advanced Higher, 67 per cent at Higher. Maximum class size 26, 'but usually much fewer'. Classes streamed early, set for maths age 9; and English from 11. Steeped in 'Euro-awareness', a sort of Euro-starter course at 8, with either French, German or Spanish at 10. A second language can be taken at 13.

Finely-tuned support for learning, but limited in the amount of help they can give – will not take children with statement of needs except in 'exceptional circumstances', but any child with a suspected problem is seen by the support for learning department, which then swings into action. Both withdrawn and team teaching on hand, either individual or in small groups. School will bear the cost of extra lessons and may, in certain circumstances, cover the cost of an outside educational psychologist – they have their own, who is free. Can cope with ADD/ADHD up to a certain degree – 'We would consult with parents to see how their children might be best served'. Remedial help throughout: seamless across the departments/ junior/senior school. EFL lessons available. Computers all over the shop, loads of new suites.

Occasional education speak jargon – 'learning enhancement' – but basically trad tried teaching methods absorbing all mods and cons. Books and paper rather than online for all. Each pupil has a dedicated tutor who usually stays with them throughout the school, plus rolling guidance system.

Games, options, the arts: This is a games school; some 32 different sports offered. Rugby: school boasts many caps. Girls' hockey, football (girls and boys), riding, orienteering and tennis very powerful; basketball and athletics increasingly good; games played at Goldenacre, along with all the other Edinburgh schools mafia; FPs use the pitches too. Pupils bussed across Edinburgh, cross-country running and rowing are favourite alternative sports – the school has a boathouse on the canal. Badminton in the frame, plus fencing and very good swimming (though not their own pool). New sports complex (Energy Zone), deep down in the Grassmarket itself, knocks spots of most we have seen. Brilliant conversion in the bowels of the former art school: must have cost a bomb and been hell to get through Edinburgh planning boys (locals have access) but wowser. Gym with every bell and whistle – permission needed before using, and seriously lofty sports hall, with automatic ventilation, connected but not linked – if you follow – into a dance studio where a group was practising The Gay Gordons, described by our guides as Ceilidh Dancing which is a new one to this Scottish country dance fiend. Sports hall and dance studio snug against the wall of Greyfriars Kirk (home of the faithful Bobby).

Drama now timetabled and taken at both national and higher levels. Head of music has done wonders for this department – choirs as well as a variety of chamber and other orchestras. Electronic music a recent addition. Pipe band. CCF optional.

Art streaking ahead – stunning and diverse department: A level art (broader course and much cherished) offered post Highers, and photography now to Higher level. Is there nothing this school doesn't do? Triple art period on the go during our visit, supposed to be photography, but certain amount of impressive felting etc and fabric design, plastic design, in fact design in general out of this world.

Sixth year does voluntary service, working in the nursery, helping with lower primary pupils and outside placements, eg the outpatients at the Astley Ainslie – dementia/stroke patients, that kind of thing.

Massive school mag, so heavy that it burst out of the envelope it was sent in, and arrived chez this ed in a GPO poly bag.

Background and atmosphere: George Heriot, jeweller to King James the VI (and I), who had started business life in a booth by St Giles, left the princely sum of £23,625 'for the building of a hospital' (ie a charity school) on a 'site at the foot of Gray's Close', for boys whose fathers had died. Fabulous ogee curved-roofed towers; the place was first inhabited by Cromwell in 1650 and, whilst principally designed by William Wallace, this magical inner-city school can boast of almost every important 17th century Scottish architect – finishing with the court favourite, Robert Mylne (and the inspiration for Hogwarts). Claims to be the longest-inhabited school building in Scotland. Magnificent Pugin chapel revamped by James Gillespie Graham in 1837; pupils still sit on backless benches. A rather snazzy library in the lower half of a hall has been disastrously (school rejects this epithet – not surprisingly) split in two to provide a concert hall above. While all schools are perennially short on space, this is the most blatant piece of architectural sacrilege we have come across.

Alas, Founder's Day no longer celebrated with 'buskins' (garlands) round the founder's statue on June Day: 'Ealth and Safety intervened and the ceremony in main courtyard has now been kicked outside, though placements (the 180 registration marks) are still visible in the quadrangle.

The hospital became a school in 1886, changed its name and the 180 foundationers were joined by paying pupils. Boarding was phased out in 1902 and girls admitted in 1979; became fully independent in 1985. FPs are known as Herioters.

Inner city school, manicured lawns. Fantastic views of Edinburgh Castle; future plans for the site include expansion of the music facilities. Terrific new build ahead (couple of terrapins/temporary buildings still around, for P6 and art – pupils love them because 'they are warm'). Uniform for all, different ties for prefects and sixth. Trips all over the shop in every discipline.

The sixth form café, which abuts the tiered auditorium (Powerpoint higher chemistry presentation in action given by dishy head of chem), uses Starbucks-type mugs, and there were a fair quantity perched on unoccupied benches.

The junior school is spread throughout the campus and the mixing of senior and junior pupils is a real strength. Early years in dedicated nursery and Greyfriars Buildings with rows of tiny wellies. Their dedicated play area has bungy tarmac surface, 'ealth and safety' again, but badly prone to puddling. Middle primary, with whom we played a complicated game of stone, paper, scissors and ended up by giving a seminar on the correct way to pass scissors, is mainly based in the north east corner of the campus.

Pastoral care, well-being and discipline: Code of conduct equals school's rules, which parents and pupils have to sign, based on 'personal safety, safety for others and respect for others, property and the environment'. Ladder of sanctions. Good guidance team who are proactive in reducing tension; both sides must face up to an issue. Persistent misbehaviour, and not responding, equals out; detentions and discussions with parents more normal. Occasional suspensions, no real problems with drugs, alcohol and cigarettes. Concern if school work suffers, no random drugs tests. Church of Scotland chaplain; school uses Greyfriars Kirk (of Bobby fame) for services.

School opens from 8am, with late model Range Rovers fouling up the traffic as they drop their little darlings at Potter Row. Bike racks for cycling pupils. Only early years' parents can drop of within school campus.

Pupils and parents: Sturdy middle class lot, 25 per cent based in Edinburgh-average ethic (school says, 'we cover a social range far greater than the average private school', but not that Brideshead). Thriving parents' association. Recent (rather grand) parent who was moved job-wise to Edinburgh couldn't praise the place enough. Son was struggling with maths in his previous school and tipped up after one term as head of class determined to make maths his career. They were over the moon.

Entrance: Nursery is first come first served; juniors by group and individual assessment. English,maths and reasoning tests for entry to primary 6 and 7. Tests (English, maths, VRQ, NVRQ) plus interview at primary and senior level, including from own junior school; though not from JS to SS; predicted grades for pupils joining post-National 5s.

Exit: Nearly all juniors move up to senior school. Most leavers to Scottish universities: Glasgow, Dundee, Edinburgh, St Andrews, Edinburgh Napier. Plus Bristol, Durham, Leeds, Newcastle, five to Oxbridge in 2018 and 13 medics.

Money matters: Felt the loss of assisted places keenly but is pretty well back up to speed. Foundation still provides 100 per cent bursary for 'children of primary or secondary school age, who are resident in Edinburgh or the Lothians, whose father has died and whose mother might not otherwise afford the cost of private education'. Raft of other bursaries and scholarships, will keep children in place during financial crisis.

Remarks: Thunderingly good inner-city school in a spectacular position, doing what it does do well.

George Watson's College

67-71 Colinton Road, Edinburgh EH10 5EG

Ages 3-18 **Pupils** 1,413 **Sixth form** 205

Fees: £12,555 pa

01314 466000
www.gwc.org.uk

Principal: Since 2014, Melvyn Roffe BA FRSA (40s). Read English at York, studied education at Durham, came from Wymondham College in Norfolk; previously worked in both maintained and independent sectors, married with a son and daughter.

Head of senior school since 2016, Gordon Boyd, previously assistant director, education at Norfolk County Council. Edinburgh born and bred, he studied English at Aberdeen and did his teacher training at Cambridge before going to Zambia with VSO. Experience in a variety of schools culminated in a headship at City of Norwich School. He is married to Helen and they have three children. He enjoys swimming, skiing and running half marathons, among other interests.

Head of junior schoo: Since 2016, George Salmond. Well known to the Watson's Family, George is a graduate of the Northern College of Education in Dundee. He joined the school in 1995 as a P5 class teacher and has developed his career through a variety of teaching and leadership roles at Watson's.

Less known to some would be that George won 146 caps playing cricket for Scotland – 104 as captain – and until this year was a Grade One Referee officiating at over 50 Premier League matches and a cup final at Hampden Park.

Academic matters: The nursery is charming. It is also enormous. Three parallel classes with over 30 children in each. But jolly none the less, with all the bells and whistles you expect from toddler teaching. Play areas, sand pits, water, tiny tables and dedicated play area outside.

Five parallel mixed ability classes of 25/30 in the junior school, based in colour coded suites of rooms: purple, beige, yellow, green and blue for the first three years. French from age 7 with native speakers. Jolly Phonics, look 'n' say, dual teaching in class where necessary, Watsons is the school for SEN hiccups. Special catch-up classes run for any latecomers. ICT skills taught and used widely to support other subjects. Back up for maths too. We had a charming young guide who seemed as pleased as punch to revisit her former classrooms.

Age 9 (P4) all move to upper primary, a barracks of a child education building. Rows of bleak corridors with classrooms on either side and more staircases up and down than one could imagine. Dedicated science lab with explosive experiments with Alkaseltzer and a plastic screw top container ongoing in the passage outside. Safety glasses and a fair risk of failure seemed the order of the day. Mixed-ability groups with setting only for maths at the top end of the school. Extensive library, plus audio books with a raft of headphones so all can listen at the same time, a respite from the non-stimulation – okay, odd bits of art – of the corridors. Our guide thought class sizes were 25/30 and 'two classes were divided into three' for practical subjects.

Academically, a highly successful senior school and also groundbreaking in that it offers the IB, as well as Scottish Highers and Advanced Highers, with the odd A level (music and art) thrown in. The only Scottish school offering this particular combination, and increasing numbers join the school in S5 to take the IB – school organises homestays for those from further afield.

Curriculum for S1 and 2 is broad. French, German or Spanish or Chinese from S1, plus Latin for all in S2. As well as the usual suspects, economics, business studies, religion and philosophy, health and food tech, plus PE and games, are all fitted in by means of a cunning seven-day cycle – forget the day of the week, just remember today's number! Setting in maths and English for S1 and languages from S2 but otherwise largish classes of 25, with 20 for practical subjects.

The IB students have to commit from the beginning of S5, as it is a two-year course. School says it attracts the polymaths, and not necessarily all the brightest. At IB the average point score was 36 in 2018. At Advanced Highers, 81 per cent A/B grades, at Highers, 80 per cent A/Bs. Pupils certainly feel they do well and offers were pouring in from up-market universities at the time of our visit. Our two prospective medic guides were waiting anxiously as medic offers usually come in last.

Strong maths department with masses of Higher and Advanced Higher takers. Fantastic technology centre devoted almost entirely to electronics. Phalanx of up-to-date labs for all three sciences (taken seriously to the extent that there is only straight biology, no human or social options). Provision of every sort of educational IT goes without saying. Trad langs: French, German, Spanish and Italian, plus huge Mandarin following, Russian if required (but no automatic 'catering' for ethnic langs). Lashings of exchanges and native speaking assistants. Help available ESOL for non-native English speakers.

George Watson's has been instrumental in the development of SEN in Scotland and retains its excellent reputation. It is 'not selective' by ethos and prides itself on identifying potential problems (has its own educational psychologist). Drop-in centre caters for the brightest as well as those who need oodles of help, or just a short sharp explanation with some bothersome subject. Heads of special needs in both junior and senior schools, plus assistants in class (usually in junior school) and either one-to-one or group sessions. No charge. One of a few schools to teach study skills throughout the school; literacy skills on offer when needed. Sixth formers with good Higher passes help out and also scribe. Help too, from scores of parent volunteers who – amongst other activities – record text onto tapes.

Games, options, the arts: Rightly famed as a rugby school, this is an ambitiously sporting place. Runs the Galleon sports club, open to other organisations as well as the school and local community. A plethora of sports clubs of just about everything you could think up, for both primary and secondary, with list of successes at all levels for the standard school sports, football, hockey etc and a swathe of other activities. Rowing, for instance, achieved European medal status. Primary pupils have full use of all senior facilities with hockey for girls, rugby for boys (only) and swimming for all.

The Galleon offers extensive and exciting holiday clubs and activities, supplementing all year round and after-school care.

Both senior and junior World Pipe and Drum champions recently with pipe teams touring Japan. Unrivalled choice from about 80 clubs and societies: 20 sports clubs, four orchestras, three bands, musical ensembles and several choirs, plus organised games, strong drama and no lack of engineering etc, with teams building and racing their own Formula cars. Something for absolutely everyone. Impressive and extensive art department. New forge enables the full range of technology and engineering activity. School trips abound at home and abroad. Popular third year 12 day project which, our guides said, had been a seminal experience and terrific bonding with contemporaries. This backpacking marathon, which tests staff and parents as well as pupils, is currently celebrating 50 years of expeditions by attempting to bag all 283 Scottish Munros.

In yer face drama and music in junior school – four choirs, two recorder groups, chamber orchestra, ensembles and pipes. Oodles of extra activities and clubs.

Background and atmosphere: George Watson, merchant and financier, left a legacy of 12 grand in 1723 to provide 'post-primary boarding education' to the 'children and grandchildren of decayed Merchants of Edinburgh and of the Ministers of the Old Church thereof,' with a preference for those with the surname Davidson or Watson. School opened in 1741, operating under the aegis of the Merchant Company until the mid 1980s, having moved to current site in 1932, and amalgamating with George Watson's Ladies College in 1974. Vast 50-acre campus includes variety of pitches, plus art, junior and nursery schools in a somewhat random selection of architecture; current redevelopment of junior school will add music suite and library plus extra classrooms.

A splendid and impressive façade, charmingly softened by trees and sweeping lawns/games fields. H-shaped listed building, unashamedly institutional with acres of shiny floors, wide corridors and polished oak. The enormous school hall forms the link between the long two-storey runs of classrooms etc at front and back. Breaktime confronts visitors with battalions of teenagers, all remarkably welcoming and relaxed. The easy rapport between staff and pupils is noticeable, despite the impossibility of knowing everyone with such large numbers.

Pastoral care, well-being and discipline: A seven-point school charter devised by pupils evidently respected and effective. The ethos of respect for others means, in practice, our guides explained, that fighting is not tolerated and seldom happens, ditto bullying. A tried and tested system manages this huge school, with two year heads per year group following pupils all the way through the school. First year pupils keep the same form teacher for two years; the next three years follow suit and pupils then choose their tutor.

Sixth formers are actively involved throughout the school. Strong anti-bullying policy, parents immediately informed and consulted if child is involved, and are apparently impressed by the help given in difficult situations. Detentions plentiful, but expulsion rare. Regular training for specialist guidance staff who help with listening and advising.

Pupils and parents: Popular (in the trad sense of the word) Edinbourgeoisie, wannabes and incomers taking for granted that it is Edinburgh's top school. Pupils certainly appear motivated and purposeful. Very much a local school, though some travel quite a distance – buses from East, Mid and West Lothian. Boarding now defunct (though does offer homestays). Strong PA with bags of fundraising functions etc.

Former pupils include Sir David Steel (The Right Hon Lord Steel of Aikwood), Sir Malcolm Rifkind, Sir Chris Hoy, former Scottish rugby internationals Gavin and Scott Hastings, broadcasters Sheena McDonald and Martha Kearney and eco-sculptor Angela Palmer. Older generations may be more impressed by Sir Basil Spence, Rebecca West, Martin Bell and Sir Eric Anderson, previously provost of Eton.

Entrance: Nursery from age 3. Up to primary 3 by interview, takes about an hour. From primary 4 upwards by written test and interview: lang, maths and verbal reason, plus a spot of writing. Main entry to college is P7 (age 12) when four classes become five and pupils hoping to go on to the senior school get a useful boost. Around three-quarters of senior entrants have come from junior school. Academic achievement and presence of siblings already in school both count. Entry at 12 and upwards by maths, English and verbal reasoning papers along with interview. Fresh blood post National grades (more come than leave). The introduction of the IB means there are a few more places available for S5 as these courses are not quite full.

Exit: No guarantee of advancement from nursery to main primary school but, once in, virtually all go on to senior school, unless family circumstances dictate otherwise. Around 98 per cent stay on after Highers for further studies, choosing either the SQA or IB routes. Well over 90 per cent go on to higher education. Over 80 per cent go on to Scottish universities, with Glasgow, Aberdeen, Edinburgh, Heriot-Watt, Dundee, Robert Gordon's and Hapier currently popular. Three to Oxbridge, 14 medics, two off to the US and one to Amsterdam in 2018.

Money matters: George Watson's Family Foundation: primarily for 10/11 year olds, though awards available in junior school and current pupils 'may apply for short-term help at any stage.' Means-tested. Will keep a pupil to the next public exam in extenuating circs, plus extra help for those with a 'recognised learning disability.' A range of up to 11 academic and two music scholarships each year: 25 per cent. Sports bursaries, Enablement Fund and the school is part of the Ogden Trust Science Scholarship Scheme. Numerous short-term or long-term bursaries for those in need; with assistance for more than 120 pupils.

Remarks: Something of a Leviathan and definitely all things to all pupils and parents, with a distinguished and deserved reputation. Communication with parents and pupils said to be effective and every pupil treated as an individual. Big is beautiful in that very few schools can offer quite such a diversity of experience and opportunity in and out of the classroom. Size has also meant that it is groundbreaking in educational areas such as SEN and the IB.

The Glasgow Academy

Colebrooke Street, Glasgow G12 8HE

Ages 3–18 **Pupils** 1,448 **Sixth form** 109

Fees: £9,083 – £12,384 pa

01413 425494
www.theglasgowacademy.org.uk

Rector: Since 2005, Peter Brodie (60s), educated at Abingdon with a masters in English from St John's, Oxford, followed by a PGCE at Oxford and masters in education management at Canterbury Christ Church University College. Previously King's School, Canterbury – his first classroom a former medieval brewery.

Brodie says: 'The school is my vocation.' It is evident that he wants to source the crème de la crème in education, with geographical location no boundary: a deputy head joined from Beijing, the head of prep (his former deputy) from the Danish School in London, and director of sport a former Olympian. Described by a pupil as 'a very caring man', he feels it's equally important that his senior management and teaching pool have 'an open, easy-natured way of thinking.' It was heart-warming to hear that this approach has obviously been a hit. 'No one loves the teachers as I do,' said one pupil. 'They genuinely care about me; I'm known as a person rather than a number.' This level of appreciation perhaps stems from his focus on inclusion and regular consultation with the children – indeed, selected kids get to grill potential members of the senior management team at interview.

One gets the feeling that if he hadn't followed in his parents' footsteps (his father was a head teacher and his mother taught PE), Brodie would be equally absorbed working in the architectural and interior design field. He talked passionately about the design of the new nursery in Newlands and the incredible science building (wow!), which the pupils also helped to design alongside the architects. The most important part of the design for the pupils, amusingly, was the high-spec toilets (we were enthusiastically told all about them on our tour – 'the world's best toilets'), many of which, this being TGA, are of course gender neutral.

Not content with the Saunders Centre winning the accolade of 'best building in Scotland' in 2016, more building development work is on the cards. Though somewhat in the future, the 'ugly buildings' are to be demolished and replaced during the next decade with a new three storey construction with a swimming pool.

Single, his hobbies include gardening and reading, particularly educational reading. Leaving in summer 2019.

Head of all three prep schools: (Kelvinbridge, Milngavie and Newlands) since 2017, Sandy Mathewson. BEd in primary education from Strathclyde University then 'straight to the academy', working his way up to deputy head. Left to take up headship at the Dania School (Scandinavian fusion school) in Islington, London, for a couple of years, before being tempted back to TGA as head. He couldn't resist the offer, but joked that he 'has a lot of making up to do with his wife', who gave up her dream editorial job in London and their thatched-roof cottage in Cambridge.

Academic matters: Good teacher to pupil ratio and small classroom sizes at the three prep schools, with fewer than 19 pupils per class. Particularly tiny has been Newlands Prep (Dairsie), with only 26 children across all four classes, but this is now growing due to the success of the nursery. By P5 all children amalgamate at the Kelvinbridge prep school.

French starts from age 5 for all; good take up of French and Spanish in the senior school, with similar numbers taken at Higher level; small numbers take Latin to Higher. Greek may be available at lunchtimes.

The contemporary Saunders Centre would tempt even the most reluctant of pupils to pursue science, with its 15 incredible labs with 0.5 gas extraction, equipment equivalent to that in Glasgow University and individual dishwashers in each class. At the end of each dedicated science corridor is the sixth year lab, with glass partitioning separating it from the teaching lab. Here, we saw AH students testing the accuracy of wine and paracetamol, for purely academic purposes, of course. One of the Nat 5 chemistry classes we saw had around 20 pupils, but lower sets have smaller class sizes. Great take up of all three sciences, with well over two-thirds of pupils taking one or more sciences to Higher, the vast majority gaining A/Bs in chemistry, biology and physics. Also home to the food technology department, which runs cookery modules in S6 to prepare pupils for the real world. Outstanding academic results in 2018, with 67 per cent A grade Higher passes, and 51 per cent As at Advanced Higher.

Support for Learning is housed in the former prep head's office, but this editor was so engaged in conversation with the head of department she didn't look up to marvel at the apparently magnificent ceiling. We heard only wonderful things about SfL at TGA, and not only from the parents the rector recommended we contact. One parent told of us of how his son with Asperger's has 'flourished academically' since moving from a state school. Another told us a moving account of her child's difficulties, saying 'no praise is high enough for The Glasgow Academy.' She continued: 'I am so impressed at the level of [SfL] knowledge and understanding of all the staff.'

We were given detailed information on the variety of impairments the school caters for. A personal profile is created for each child, and strategies developed for the classroom with an individualised programme to meet their needs. Some extraction, for example nurture time for those with Aspergers, using 'Get out of class free' cards. About 10 per cent of senior school have SfL needs.

The school appoints lots of new staff to keep it 'dynamic' and to 'add new DNA' to the teaching staff.

Games, options, the arts: Over 20 sports available and masses of inter-house competitions, all celebrated in the school magazine. Games and outdoor pursuits are a big deal; one knows this is true when the director of sport, who we chatted to in the playground, is a former Olympian. Massive successes in rowing, winning two world championships and setting the course record for the Fawley Cup (boys' squad). Super dedicated kids, hitting the school rowing suite by 7am to train.

Four playing areas at Anniesland, each with several pitches, one of which is a water-based hockey pitch of international standard, plus an all-weather pitch onsite in the middle of the campus. Rugby or hockey is mandatory for the first two years at senior school, taking part in competitive school fixtures from prep 6 for rugby. Dedicated head of rugby, who has twice been awarded the title Coach of the Year by the SRU at Murrayfield. Formerly Scottish champions in girls' hockey for three years running. Over 100 extracurricular clubs to cater for everyone, from chess to zumba to the Gavel Society for public speaking. CCF is not compulsory, but very popular, as is DofE (up to gold level). Clubs are run by teachers and the majority are free.

Drama is as popular as French at Higher level, with large numbers of A grades. School shows have included Rock of Ages, Chicago, Fame, Evita and Rent, performed in the fabulous Watson Auditorium in the Saunders Centre, with staggered seating to accommodate 160 people. S6 pupils mentor S1s and S2s, writing plays and putting on their own performances.

Art department is located in a purpose-built building, plus one of the terraced houses in Colebrooke Terrace, and is akin to a mini-art school, with a sixth year studio space and basement pottery room with kiln. Working pieces of art included one sixth year project, of welded bike parts and bits of machinery. Some sit AS level art in preparation for art school.

Music teaching by specialists (some from the Royal Conservatoire of Scotland) starts in the prep school. Some 28 ensembles, orchestras and choirs for all, including the boys' choir who boogie as they sing and have been known to throw each other into the air. Ten practice rooms in the senior school for 500+ individual music lessons each week and a music technology room with Apple Macs. Grand piano takes pride of place in the performance room, where the 'sound is insane' – though they had to take the windows out to get it in.

Trips aplenty, including an S1 trip to Geneva, a cross-cultural trip to Madrid (modern languages), an NY/Washington visit with the modern studies department, where pupils encountered former President Obama, and not-to-be-forgotten battlefields trips, of particular importance to the school.

Background and atmosphere: Founded as a limited company in 1845, The Glasgow Academy is the oldest fully independent school in Scotland and reconstituted as a memorial to the 327 staff and pupils killed, post WW1. Merged with the Westbourne School for girls in 1991.

Cradle to grave schooling: nursery and prep teaching is covered across the three sites at Kelvinbridge, Milngavie and Newlands. Newest addition is the pre-school at Newlands, described by one parent as 'absolutely fabulous'. A former bowling green (it still looks like a bowling green externally), but with a sleek Scandinavian interior, and further building extensions ongoing. The prep school in Newlands, a fine Victorian villa, looks dated in comparison, but is due to undergo refurbishment. Strong links to FPs, the oldest of which are affectionately known as 'the Gasbags'.

Though it has not always been the case (a former teacher told us), The Academy is now one of Glasgow's finest independent schools. The senior school, in particular, ticks all the boxes for this editor, just the right balance of values, inclusion, compassion, sporting and academic success.

A gated campus-style set up along the banks of the River Kelvin, it is a mixture of old and new, with the beautiful sandstone terraced houses functioning as one of the main school buildings, juxtaposed against the finest modern architecture, namely the Saunders Centre, bequeathed by Colonel Frank W Saunders with, inter alia, its top-notch science facilities. The play area is fundamentally Colebrooke Terrace, and like years gone by, it was refreshing to see the prep children playing outside on the street. Good-old fashioned fun like skipping ropes and playground games. A simple but brilliant idea of no-tech lunches means senior pupils (gasp) were outside, too, getting some vitamin D.

'Very warm, open and transparent school.' 'There is a wonderful sense of community and a real sense of vibrancy and happiness.' All pupils wear uniforms, the girls in specially designed kilts incorporating Westbourne colours, but they are empathetic of gender fluidity, and a couple of girls have worn boys' school uniforms. Those that achieve five Highers at A grade have their blazer decorated with a blue ribbon.

'Generous spirited', pupils and parents raise large sums for their selected charities. Highlight of recent calendar was the Shine night-time walking marathon, where staff and pupils took to the streets of Glasgow to raise money for Cancer Research.

Pastoral care, well-being and discipline: Pupils belong to one of four houses (each with a male and female head) who enthusiastically compete in inter-house competitions. If parents or pupils have a concern, they can reach out to the head of year or allocated tutor (two per house per year group), who stays with them throughout their school life. Tutors have around 14 tutees, whom they spend 10–25 minutes with each morning.

Health and well-being centre onsite and if the outdoor activities room is anything to go by, stuffed with boots, ropes, helmets and all manner of outdoor paraphernalia, the pupils are getting a good dose of outdoor medicine. As mentioned before, no-tech lunches, introduced during health week, can only be a good thing for pupil well-being.

Firm discipline, with strong emphasis on restorative justice, but lengthy detention for (very rare) smoking, and suspension/ expulsion for worse.

Pupils and parents: Solid intake of pupils from middle class parents, but this is still Glasgow – 'parents are not afraid to tell you what they think.' Lots of FPs' children, plus growing number of first time buyers, many attracted by the investment in the school, namely the Saunders Centre.

Close to the M8 and Glasgow underground system, many get to school using public transport but buses operate for those from further afield.

FPs: Sir Angus Grossart, Niall Ferguson, Sir Jeremy Isaacs, Lord Vallance, Lord Kerr, Darius, Sir James Barrie, Donald Dewar, Sir John Cargill, George MacDonald Fraser, Fiona Kennedy and Olympian Katie Archibald.

Entrance: Entry to prep school through the pre-school from age 3 or by interview with parents onsite. Entrance to senior school is generally automatic from prep school. Admission by school test and interview; occasional waiting lists. Some incomers in S5 and S6, by interview and verbal reasoning test, and largely those that have achieved grade As in their Nat 5s.

Exit: Most stay on until S6 for crash Highers or Advanced Highers to add to their academic portfolio. Over 94 per cent go on to university, mostly Scottish, but with some heading south. Lots of medics, and five Oxbridge in 2018. Law, business and engineering popular as degree subjects.

Money matters: Bursary fund available to support talented children on a low income. Nearly 15 per cent of children from P7 to S6 receive a bursary. Emergency fund may be available for curricular school trips.

Remarks: Top Glasgow independent school that ticks all the boxes with a forward-thinking and progressive rector. Hard not to be impressed by the facilities, particularly in the stunning science building. Matched with outstanding academic results, sporting prowess and a modern, inclusive approach – it's a school that's hard to resist.

Glenalmond College

Glenalmond, Perth PH1 3RY

Ages 12–18 Pupils 368 Sixth form 157 Boarders 279

Fees: Day £16,881 – £22,503; Boarding: £25,851 – £34,506 pa

01738 842000
www.glenalmondcollege.co.uk

Interim Warden: Hugh Olston is holding the reins after the abrupt departure of previous head Elaine Logan in summer 2018. He is a board member who was head of Robert Gordons in Aberdeen for 10 years, and a former Glenalmond pupil.

Academic matters: One of the biggest changes recently has been 'improving academic rigour and ambition'. This has been achieved by introducing the Learning Project – a big name for a radical restructuring of the way the children and the teachers are monitored and taught.

The idea is that 'no-one is alone and that everyone is supported'. Teachers now routinely observe each other's lessons to spread good practice and help eliminate the bad and are coached and supported if improvements are needed. Meanwhile, the pupils' academic and social movements are now closely tracked, with regular meetings between house teachers, academic teachers and senior staff to evaluate progress and pastoral needs. Prep is now being monitored for all but upper sixth (one parent told us their child was thrilled by this development as they were actually getting work done). In addition, there are tutorials to help pupils develop core skills for learning including essay planning, revision strategies, mind-mapping, time management, literacy and numeracy foundation skills.

A housemaster says they are all discussing pupils and their welfare far more than they used to. Sharing best practice is common and all the house staff have meet every week to discuss pupils and their progress. Senior management aren't being left on the shelf either. They're being trained to manage their departments in a more effective and supportive way.

So a huge upskilling all round, but is it working? Apparently! Education Scotland is recommending they spread this good practice asap. Meanwhile, parents we spoke to felt that both the children and the teaching standards are beginning to reap the benefits. '[My son] actually looks forward to his supervised study...incredible.'

Glenalmond will never be an academic hothouse, but would like us to judge them on how much the pupils improve on their journey through the school. 2018 saw one of the best GCSE performances ever with 60 per cent A*-A/9-7 grades. At A level, 34 per cent A*/A and 62 per cent A*-B, with many surpassing expectations.

Subjects on offer cover the usual spectrum from politics to history of art (26 subjects on offer at A level) and are now being supplemented by Mandarin and computer science at GCSE and computer science at A level. Now offers 13 subjects at Higher level; 64 per cent A grades in 2018.

A significant proportion of the school is involved with the learning support department at some level. This ranges from extra time in exams all the way through to a reader and a scribe. There is a policy of free screening for all pupils who enter the school in second, third or fourth form. Thereafter there are charges for eg additional assessments and individual support sessions.

There's a prep club at break and lunchtimes so more support on offer then.

The staff ratio is particularly good at 1:7 and class sizes rarely exceed 16. The bottom sets may have as few as six or seven pupils. They recruited heavily for new staff recently (there was a lot of stagnation to deal with in our view) and the results are new faces with enthusiasm and drive. Another school head has commented that there seems to be a real buzz about the school and they are attracting some real talent to their ranks.

Games, options, the arts: One of the major changes is a complete restructuring of the sports department so that it functions co-educationally ie boys' and girls' games are given equal billing (rather than the rugger buggers hogging the limelight). Touch rugby has also been introduced for girls. In fact the school now has heads for hockey, lacrosse and rugby and hopefully soon tennis, golf and cricket. 'One of the best things about Glenalmond is the great support the parents give to sport.'

Parity has also been brought for the firsts lacrosse team, who now share the former firsts rugby pitch, Neish's, as it's known. This has been revamped and a new stand has been built (this time facing the right way ie towards the beautiful hills). The sporting facilities also include a first class swimming pool and now an Olympic standard water-based hockey pitch, which has already hosted some international players, plus a new Astro.

They're not the most amazing sporting facilities that you will come across but, as elsewhere in the school, the ambition seems to be big. There are also plans to make more of what is a truly fabulous outdoor location. There is a school golf course and the possibility of fishing on the river Almond, which flows through the school. DofE enthusiastically pursued, as are clay pigeon shooting, tennis, white water rafting, skiing. The activity programme is booted up further at the weekend, and at Cairnies, the newly created junior boys' house (second and third form), there are compulsory activities so that they are kept busy.

Expressive arts has always been somewhat understated at Glenalmond, but there are plans to improve this starting with the introduction of dance at GCSE. With the old warden's house now being repatriated as an admin hub, there is also a permanent display area for any artistic endeavour, while neatly putting it in front of any prospective parents.

Boarding: Girls are being given a bigger slice of the pie and are being 'promoted' to the Quad. This is the Oxbridge-style area at the heart of the school, traditionally the site of three boys' houses. Now one of them, Goodacres, has been made over to girls. Neighbouring boys' house Patchell's is the Testosterone Towers of the school, housing a lot of the rugby boys in long dorms in something akin to horse boxes. They seem to love it, though. Another house, Cairnies, formerly for fifth form girls, has been turned into a junior house for second and third form boys – increasing in numbers apparently due to more pupils arriving from destinations other than traditional prep schools.

All of the staff live on site, so the pupils get to see them in their civvies and leading a normal life. Relationships tend to be stronger because currently this 'really is a full boarding school', but be warned if your child doesn't fit in, there is very little escape. However, introducing weekly and flexi boarding from 2019.

Background and atmosphere: 'How many schools have a front and back avenue, Mum?' Well, probably more than we realise, but it does emphasise the sheer grandeur of the place both in architectural and scenic terms. Going down the drive on a warm summer's day (they do happen, apparently) or a crisp winter one with snow on the hills can be an uplifting experience. The school was founded by the former prime minister William Gladstone to keep young men free 'from the sins of the city', and to a certain extent that still happens. Sadly, after years of dodgy mobile phone reception, the pupils can call out with ease, but there is still a feeling of beautiful isolation which helps keep the worst offenders out of trouble, and if your child is sociable and likes the outdoors, they will probably form friendships to last a lifetime. Be prepared to blink when you see the school uniform. The boys are traditional in grey flannels and blazers, with tweed jackets for upper sixth. But the girls, well the girls have navy floor-length skirts. 'Victorian parlour maids' was one description, but according to the school the girls are adamant they won't have it any other way. Reports say they enjoy wearing their pyjamas and wellies underneath in bad weather, so who could blame them? And school believes it helps with evening out those body image crises that so many other schools have to deal with.

Pastoral care, well-being and discipline: The school has appointed a deputy head of pastoral care who oversees the eight housemasters/mistresses and there is far more exchanging of information so that nobody slips through the net. House staff and teachers meet weekly to discuss pupils, especially any there are concerns about.

Discipline appears to have improved since the arrival of the current warden. Drugs have never really been an issue at the school, but alcohol could be. This, parents say, has definitely been tightened up, although the occasional lapse still occurs.

Pupils and parents: A high 70 per cent are UK boarders. The school has traditionally been the 'county' choice, or 'tweed central', as some have dubbed it, so many from surrounding Perthshire, Angus, Fife and Aberdeenshire, and the other 30 per cent are international with Germany leading the table. You are less likely to get hard-working lawyer or property developer parents and more likely to see well-heeled farmers and castle dwellers.

Entrance: Common entrance is on the wane, apparently with less coming in from the prep route, so the school tests independently for maths and English. There is no waiting list so entry is fairly straightforward at the moment if you wave a cheque book, but with the new buzz around the place this may well change.

Exit: Around half to Russell Group universities including Oxbridge (one place in 2018, plus one medic); others off to Oslo, Amsterdam and Inner Mongolia.

Money matters: They stress they don't buy in talent, so no 100 per cent scholarships for the rugby gorillas, but they do support four pupils every year on a bursary basis of 90 to 100 per cent. This isn't based purely on academic potential, but if there is a child who would clearly benefit from the boarding experience then they will try to help. The total remission pot is £2 million a year of which the lion's share goes to bursaries. Scholarships get the usual 10 per cent reduction. Most applicants will try for both.

Remarks: Get in fast, Glenalmond is on the up and up. If they can continue to combine academic rigour and making use of their spectacular setting then Glenalmond is set for a cracking future over the next few years.

Gordonstoun

Elgin, Moray IV30 5RF

Ages 7–18 **Pupils** 525 **Sixth form** 206 **Boarders** 388 full, 4 weekly (juniors), 15 flexi (juniors)

Fees: Day £14.361 – £28,365; Boarding £23,358 – £38,295 pa

01343 837837
www.gordonstoun.org.uk

Principal: Since April 2017 Lisa Kerr BA (music, York), a former governor at the school with a long career in business, mostly as a strategy and PR consultant. Married to John (Royal Marines officer) with three children at the school.

Appointed simultaneously to the new post of headmaster was Titus Edge BA (history, Newcastle). An old pupil of Gordonstoun or OG, Titus is married to Marina (another OG) and also has three children at the school. Joined Gordonstoun in 2013 as the deputy head. Previously head of history at Dulwich College.

Lisa focuses more on strategic leadership while Titus Edge deals with the day to day running of school.

Head of junior school: Since 2003, Robert McVean BSc, who has taught science at the junior school from 2000. Married to Laura, two children, one at university and one still in the school.

Academic matters: We think it's fair to say that Gordonstoun has never been known as an academic hothouse and there is no doubt the recent results bear that out. Starting with A levels, 28 per cent of the grades were A*-A in 2018 (nine students out of 97 gained all A*/As). There are some striking highlights: all those who took French got A*-C (we were very impressed with the level of fluency in the class we visited), and for STEM subjects as a whole (maths and sciences, including computer science), 60 per cent of grades were A*-B.

Most students choose three subjects at A level, but the school offers the EPQ or an additional A level, such as further maths. A Level courses include everything from art, biology and business studies to photography and theatre studies. They also offer the vocational BTec qualifications in physical education and A level applied business studies.

GCSE results were more impressive with 21 per cent of entries achieving an A*/8-9, 36 per cent A/7 or above. Pupils typically study nine subjects, with options including dance and drama.

So they're not firing them out by the dozen from the classroom straight into the quads of Cambridge or Oxford. But then that isn't what Gordonstoun is really about. They would argue that as a school which is largely non-selective and which takes a much less 'traditional' approach to education, they do remarkably well with the overwhelming majority of students meeting or exceeding their baseline predictions.

All of the parents we spoke to were more than happy with the academic offering. "I'm expecting a really good set of A levels. The small classes and excellent teaching support has been great for my son.' 'My son came from a school down south. He's a different boy without the pressure. In fact his work is improving simply because he's happy.'

The head says, 'We're going through a curriculum review right now. We want to broaden our offering and vocational BTec qualifications are part of that, along with looking at collaborations with colleges. Thirty years ago it wasn't so much of a problem if you left school without some kind of recognised qualification. Now you need that "golden ticket" to get you to the next stage.'

The junior school, Aberlour, Is one of the cosiest little preps we've ever visited. Very small classes, lots of smiling faces, enthusiastic Head and wife clearly very invested in what they do. 'The majority of the children move on to the senior school. Our children rarely do Common Entrance these days, but if necessary we can prepare them.'

'The learning support department has been outstanding for my child.' With three full-time members of staff (plus two in the junior school), the learning support team offers both one-to-one and group help in and outside of class. In addition, any student, regardless of need, can access the school's post-lesson curricular support programme. They also offer enhanced support for the 'most able' students, including a scholars' programme of seminars, debates, dialogue society and Model UN.

Games, options, the arts: Well, where to start, that's the real question. We've all heard schools talking about the importance of physical exercise on the young mind, but Gordonstoun really does walk the walk. In fact, thanks to its founder, the inspirational Jewish educationalist Kurt Hahn, it invented the walk. Having been released from prison in Nazi Germany, Hahn was encouraged to set up Gordonstoun as an example of his educational theory. In his case this included plenty of outdoor pursuits, cold showers and runs. We're assured there hasn't been an intentional cold shower at Gordonstoun for many a year, but that passion for activity still runs like a golden thread through everything they do.

So on offer are all the traditional school sports, rugby, cricket, hockey, along with horse riding, skiing, mountain biking, snowboarding, karate, aerobics. They also have Scotland's only five hole golf course, but the area abounds with plenty of full fat courses. This is Scotland, after all. They have recently completed a magnificent new sports centre with an indoor climbing wall, a fully equipped strength and conditioning room and a floodlit hockey Astroturf, a 400m running track, an indoor swimming pool, squash courts and a.22 rifle range.

So pretty amazing. But be aware this school is not about the culture of the sports jock. There is no worshipping of the first XV. And their sheer distance from the majority of the private school sporting circuit means they don't play regularly play the schools who do. 'We play a lot of local teams in Elgin and other places. We much prefer that to spending hours on a coach. We do play other independent schools but it's good to mix it up.'

Outdoor pursuits are huge and every single student gets involved. Sailing, skiing,hillwalking, climbing. The school owns a 80 foot sail training vessel, Ocean Spirit, which makes annual trips to destinations such as the Arctic. Sailing is taught in the same kind of cutters as those used by Prince Philip when he was at Gordonstoun. Why? Because they have a crew of eight and teamwork is integral. All pupils are trained in expedition skills and try everything from backpacking and canoeing to exploration. And of course the school offers a full DofE programme – they did invent it after all, naming it after their most famous alumnus.

It was vaguely comic to watch a group of pupils in full firefighting gear ferociously hosing down a hedge, but there is serious intent. As part of the school's fully trained fire service, these pupils are called out to real blazes across the local countryside.

Thanks to Kurt Hahn and his belief in the taking responsibility for helping others Service, as it's called, is integral to the Gordonstoun ethos. Every pupil must pick one of nine services: fire brigade, coastguard, lifeguard, tech crew, first aid, community service, conservation, outdoor leadership or sports service. After training they provide support in the school and the local community. 'This teaches them the value of helping others and gives them valuable life skills,' says head.

Wow drama, wow dance, wow music. Wonderful facilities and a thriving creative environment. Three major drama productions a year with a series of minor ones dotted in between. Pupils regularly leave for drama school here in the UK or in the States. There's a sprung floored dance studio. The music department is thriving – every child in the junior school learns an instrument and most continue to learn in senior school too.

The art department has a teacher from virtually every discipline: fine art to photography.

Boarding: Gordonstoun describes itself as one of the last true boarding schools in the UK. Its relatively remote location plays a part, along with the fact that a third of the school is international (carefully mixed so no one nationality dominates). There are four boys' houses, three girls' and one small boys' sixth form house. They're run by a live in houseparent with a deputy and a matron for back up. The house we saw was modern, clean, and surprisingly homely and the housemaster young enough to relate to his young charges.

And perhaps, more surprising in this day and age of flexi-boarding, the junior school has a healthy percentage of full-time boarders. Junior boarders have their own home, Aberlour House.

Background and atmosphere: 'Plus est en vous' – 'there is more in you'. Yes, we know. We don't usually start a description about a school by dusting off its long forgotten motto. But let us tell you a story. You may have heard of the miraculous rescue of a group of 12 boys from a series of caves in Thailand. It's an amazing tale of bravery and fortitude and one of the unsung heroes of that episode was OG Connor Roe. When Connor returned to Gordonstoun to tell of his experiences, he made it clear that the one thing that kept him going through the fear and the challenging conditions was the school motto 'there is more in you'.

Now you might think that's a bit cheesy, but really that kind of sums Gordonstoun up. If you push all the royal razzmatazz to the side – Prince Phillip was an OG as was Prince Charles (albeit unhappily – maybe they hadn't switched on the hot water at that point), Prince Andrew and Prince Edward too. Forget about the sons of rock stars and Hollywood actors (David Bowie and Sean Connery) and look at what Gordonstoun is about: there is a real ring of truth about the place. As the head says, 'One headmaster said to me at a conference, "The thing about Gordonstoun is you don't really have to sit chewing your pen trying to think of what makes your school unique".'

Thanks to Kurt Hahn they were the originators of the 'holistic' education. He believed that the challenge of outdoor activities, internationalism and service to others were as important as academic pursuits in creating a happy, rounded person.

'I've seen the stress leave my child's face ever since he started here.' 'Somebody told me my son was "humble" the other day. I was so proud. That's the thing about Gordonstoun, they produce pupils who are as happy talking to a prince as to the cleaner.'

Pastoral care, well-being and discipline: Recently appointed head of pastoral care is a school inspector, so she ought to know her stuff.

'The pastoral set up is the best I've seen. Well planned, supportive and built around the child.'

As well as the house parents, there are tutors and 'every member of staff is trained to look after the children'. There is a secure online system to keep track of every child and share necessary information.

Pupils and parents: Pupils come from as far ranging places as Scunthorpe to Singapore. The Royal link still pulls them in from abroad, but on the home front there is a mix of Hahn idealists, first time adopters who find it a less 'threatening' public school environment than some and 'old time' public school families.

Entrance: Interview with the headmaster plus report and references from current school. Maths, English and verbal reasoning tests for potential scholars entering year 9. For sixth form entry, five grade 4+s at GCSE, two of which should be English and maths.

Exit: Majority head off to English universities; Durham, Newcastle, Exeter, Bristol, 10 per cent to America (school is an SAT centre), music conservatories and dance schools. Three medics in 2018.

Money matters: More than 30 per cent of students receive some sort of bursary. School constantly searching for non-fee ways of funding education. Scholarships give 10 per cent discount.

Remarks: Gordonstoun doesn't have to try to be different – it just is. It's the original holistic education, using outdoor challenges and service to others to build confidence and improve academic performance. If straight As are all that matter to you and your child then you might want to look elsewhere. But if you want an escape from the academic sausage factory and the chance to think out of the box, sign up now.

Hamilton College

Bothwell Road, Hamilton ML3 0AY

Ages 3–18 **Pupils** 470 **Sixth form** 25

Fees: £7,635 – £10,800 pa

01698 282700
www.hamiltoncollege.co.uk

Principal: Since 2016, Tom McPhail. Degree in design and maths from the OU and masters from Stirling in professional enquiry:

school leadership and management. Taught DT at St Ninian's and Port Glasgow High Schools; depute head of Belmont Academy for over 10 years before joining Hamilton in 2013 as vice principal.

Academic matters: The school 'has high academic expectations' and, using the Scottish exam system, offers Nationals at S4, generally five Highers at S5 and a combination of Highers and Advanced Highers at S6. French, from J5, German and Latin, from SI, on offer. All three sciences taught from S1.

Results are solid with high spots in history and chemistry. RMPS for all has an excellent pass rate. Most take English and maths Higher and the school 'usually manages to meet subject requests at Higher and Ad H'. Some non-core subjects such as business management, PE, technical studies etc on offer. School says take up of Ad Highers is growing. Classes fairly small; year groups of 70ish split into four and setted for maths, English, French etc. Loads of competitive triumphs too: with impressive victories in maths challenge and the Gilbert Murray Classical Essay competition amongst others. In 2018, 50 per cent of Highers and 34 per cent of Advanced Highers grade A.

H

Learning support team with qualified helpers gives both in-class and separate help to dyslexics etc, the team working closely with teaching and pupil support (guidance) staff and with parents. Staff relate personally to small groups so 'no one should slip through the net'. Lots of internet help with 'Moodle', an online course management service via the school website.

Games, options, the arts: Impressive record of art school entry (lots to Glasgow) and some distinguished past pupils. Walls zing with really exciting work, often killing two birds with one stone by using a theme from literature or even chemistry. The art room has a fantastic outlook and is jam-packed full of pupils' sculptures, photography etc. The slightly self-effacing modesty of the art teacher does not conceal the fact some outstanding work happens under his skilful care.

Music up to Ad Higher with a good wide range of instrumental teaching and bags of opportunities to perform in orchestras, choirs, groups, musicals and foreign trips. Choirs and orchestra tour the Black Forest with a mixed programme, as well as concerts and drama in school in local churches etc. Drama especially active with entries to Glasgow Shakespeare festival (Hamlet). No exam courses, but Victoria College, London Certificate of Speech and Drama.

Football (girls and boys, but not together), rugby, hockey (enjoying a recent tour in Canada), netball etc – with lots of after-school practices and matches. Bullish athletics with juniors winning locally and a Scottish national long jumper. Partnership with Michael Jamieson Swim Academy – his coaches lead swimming sessions in really good indoor pool. School teams are battling in national competitions but lots of opportunities for tip top players in local clubs, as well as some inspiring input via the school: playing with Glasgow Warriors, inviting Hamilton Academical player to visit etc etc.

Most extracurricular clubs, sport and some orchestras after school for juniors and seniors. The extracurricular booklet, complete with timetable to be downloaded from the extremely efficient website, includes 40 plus activities like chess (hosted regional championship), book club, stocks and shares group, Young Enterprise (for older pupils) and entrepreneurs (for younger ones), ski club (annual trip to Italy), press review and Scripture Union..

Loads of curriculum based visits locally and abroad – Auschwitz recently via Holocaust Memorial Trust. DofE started recently, with lots of bronze and silver hopefuls looking to gold soon and a fair share of outdoor activities/trips. Debating and public speaking teams achieving worldwide success in the Kids Lit Quiz, coming second in the world during the finals in New Zealand.

Background and atmosphere: Probably the starkest school building in the Scottish independent sector – a pale blue building with bright red signage rising oddly behind some spectacular ornate railings (a relic of the former Hamilton Palace) but with stunning views and masses of space overlooking Hamilton Park racecourse. The pitches are actually in the middle of the track, reached by a tunnel. In spite of its appearance the school, a Christian foundation, originally one of a group of three started in the Manchester area, was jolly lucky to get a redundant '60s teacher training college complete with terrific (then – and still pretty good now) games facilities, lovely indoor pool, stunning hall and purpose-built large, light classrooms. The central assembly hall holds the entire school and its banks of 'in the round' eating and magnificent pyramidal wooden roof make it a really good auditorium space, well equipped and much used by the school and external lets.

Inside is purposeful with busy pupils. The central space and upper floors belong to the seniors, with the juniors and nursery on the ground floor of each 'wing', separated from the central space by the hall on one side. On the other is a spacious courtyard with an ecological greenhouse made from recycled plastic bottles and lots of garden equipment – takes ecology seriously. It also prides itself on its health promotion and has a Healthy Living Award. The purpose-built library and dining area run along the back of the building next to the racecourse, both huge with masses of glass. The new dining hall hosts lunch for nursery through to senior school pupils and the library is open to students at intervals and after school, as well as in constant use by classes during the day after school. A spectacular glass box, perched on a vast expanse of flat roof, is the staff room, which must reach equatorial temperatures when the sun shines – but fortunately this is Scotland.

The junior school and nursery, however, are crammed with colour and activity, using every spare inch of wall and floor space. The senior school, with its wide corridors and huge entrance hall, complete with LCD display showing photography of pupil events and achievements and other bits of vital school info, is well maintained, despite a few dark stair corners. It all feels a bit institutional and functional, but clearly does function very well as an institution. The overtly Christian ethos encourages lots of charity fundraising and a very impressive Transform project with a school in Burkina Faso, involving annual visits by groups of sixth formers and reciprocal trips for teachers. Part of this initiative, providing internet facilities for the school, has was featured on BBC World News.

Pupils wear burgundy blazers, with blue braiding for prefects and pale blue shirts, black trousers for boys and Lindsay tartan for girls. Ties for all – striped for boys and plain for girls – plus tracksuits and cagoules in house colours for games: quite a pricey item and uniform policy is strict.

Pastoral care, well-being and discipline: A house system with three houses, Lewis, Harris and Skye, delivers most of the pastoral care, plus each child is allocated an individual guidance teacher. Inspectors recently commended this. Form teachers also help. The prefect team are appointed and have to apply and be interviewed. Head prefects 'do a lot', including representing the school at outside functions. Staff think discipline is good and few sanctions are needed – 'Bunking off school just does not happen'. Stringent mobile phone policy, available, like most other Hamilton info, on the website, says phones will be confiscated for the day – 'We're just trying to get them to use them sensibly'. Bullying not a big problem, 'But, as everywhere, it happens,' so a raft of measures – sanctions (see policy on website), counselling, life skills programme, meetings with parents.

Pupils and parents: Huge catchment area taking in most of the south side of Glasgow and Lanarkshire, with extensive bus routes to Lanark, Biggar Kilsyth, Cumbernauld and East Kilbride. Intake multi-ethnic. Friends of Hamilton College, a very go-ahead body, fundraises for school equipment and does charity stuff too.

Lots of famous arty former pupils including Katie Leung (acted Cho Chang in Harry Potter); Lorna Ritchie, set and costume designer (worked for Jonathan Miller); and Blair Thompson, Scottish artist and winner of numerous awards (in The Herald's top 20 Scottish artists) – all of whom started their careers in Hamilton's art room.

Entrance: Mainly to nursery, J1 and S1 but will accept at any stage. Entry assessments for all.

Exit: Most juniors move up, but a number drop out after National grade (S4) and again after Highers (S5), though the past few years have seen more staying on to S6. The majority to university, mainly Scottish (Glasgow, Strathclyde and Glasgow Caledonian most popular) though the very occasional to Oxbridge or other English ones. Quite a few to further ed and apprenticeships or work in family businesses.

Money matters: Not a rich school but well managed. Bursary scheme up to 100 per cent strictly means-tested and awarded by committee of governors etc. Will try to help a family in sudden financial trouble. Discounts of 10 per cent for second, 20 per cent for third and 40 per cent for fourth child and 25 per cent+ sibling discount for 'full time Christian workers'.

Remarks: Not to be ignored! A good solid school, perhaps a little old fashioned until recently pulled by its bootstraps into the 21st century – 'It's now at the leading edge in Scotland for its use of ICT in learning teaching and admin'. Sound, good value for money, and certainly worth a look if you live in the area or in oversubscribed East Renfrewshire. 'Exceptionally positive' recent inspection. It may not be beautiful, but it is certainly useful and might even be exciting.

Harris Academy

Perth Road, Dundee DD2 1NL

Ages 11–18 Pupils 1,308 Sixth form 152

01382 435700
www.harrisacademy.ea.dundeecity.sch.uk

Head teacher: Since January 2016, Barry Millar (40s), previously head teacher at Perth Grammar School. A former pupil of Harris, he also taught at Menzieshill (now merged with Harris) for 12 years as a PE teacher, a guidance teacher and latterly as acting depute head.

Academic matters: Well above average: no particular bias, but with around 50 per cent of all pupils leaving after National grades (most go to Dundee College) it is a little difficult to give an accurate picture. Smashing results for those who do stay on to sixth form – way above national average (though with 38 per cent with three Highers – or better – it's not that hard a target to beat). Masses of computers etc, all heavily used, with waiting systems in place if need be. Impressive library with yet more machines, class teaching on computers as well as IT. Pupils do keyboarding and basic ICT skills and use the skills in presentations: powerpoint, sound, film-making, animated flow charts. Max class size (legal limit) 33, but down to 20 for practical subjects.

First couple of years all study English, maths, science, history, geography, modern studies, home economics (magic), technology (great) plus one modern language: French, German or Spanish. Latin on hand, but no Greek. Streaming after first year when a fast track for English, maths and modern languages comes into force. Teaching disciplines are a combination of individual, small group, whole class teaching and discussion. Strong learning support.

School attracts a number of ethnic minorities whose parents are billeted to the local university, hospital or area. Russian, Bengali, Urdu and Cantonese the most frequently spoken at home – native speakers can take these at standard grade. EAL is taught by the special educational needs team, and the HMI thought they were a bit stretched. Pupil support staff co-teach where necessary in class, but 'such support may result in a revised elaborated or alternative curriculum and include individual or small group tuition'. Supported study includes homework clubs, and a teacher is available early on Tuesday mornings or Thursday evenings to help pupils with problems. Good encouragement, too, for the more gifted. Terrific use of external facilities. HMI also a bit dissy about homework – the amount, the marking et al – but that was some time ago, and the results of the recommendations are not yet available. The HMI other comment which concerns us is that brighter pupils 'do not appear to be sufficiently stretched'.

Eight National grades for all as far as possible. Languages, humanities and modern studies above average and good showing in the Scottish and UK Maths Challenges; ditto the Dundee Enterprising Maths competition. Inspiring programme of lectures from outside speakers. Serious advice for all pupils on which road to take. Good choice post National with Highers and Advanced Highers in a raft of subjects, plus tourism and hospitality at National grades. Regular assessments and good parental feedback.

School is an important cog in the education of children in the autistic spectrum and takes 10 pupils (never fewer) by request and allocation from the west of Dundee and the city itself (Morgan Academy takes those who live East of Dundee). These pupils are scattered across the age range, and school only accepts the next pupil when space becomes available. 'Lovely laddies' (mainly boys, but that's the nature of autism) all have individual educational programmes which are regularly monitored and amended. Some are totally supported individually and educated in the base (only one currently); others attend mainstream lessons but may be entirely supported in class, or allowed to attend certain classes for a short period – eg physics: in mainstream for six weeks, and then back to the unit. Most take National grade maths and all have speech and oral communication. The base is popular with 'normal kids' who choose to join those in the autistic spectrum at lunchtime – a reverse integration. Many of these pupils will go on to Elmwood College in Fife, where the school has close links.

Games, options, the arts: Games fields half a mile away, gyms on site plus swimming pool. Large sports complex off-site. PE timetabled and impressive line up of games (extracurricular) including the very popular rugby, hockey, football for boys and girls, athletics, basketball (enthusiastic coach), water polo etc.

Art, as you might imagine, deeply computer-linked: ceramics, painting, ICT, no CAD as such but the facility to use computer-based design. Computer suite in art room, home economics, metalwork area, all computer based and hands on. Mass of instrumentalists, music strong and popular with ceilidhs and rock concerts (including FPs) – huge charitable input, 'everything and anything'. Choirs, bands, orchestras. Popular theatre club, though not available as an exam subject, despite pupils' requests. Outstanding debating, thrashing all comers; vibrant YE and truly popular DofE, with a whacking list of gold, silver and bronze successes. Not the longest list of clubs we have ever seen, but thoroughly active, mass of trips abroad: humanities with proper exchanges popular.

Background and atmosphere: Founded in 1885 and 'the oldest public school in Dundee', moved to the handsome granite building in 1931, school then added on a hotchpotch of flat-roofed excrescences in the '60s. Complete £32m rebuild on same site finished in 2016 and school amalgamated with Menzieshill High.

Free school meals (but the cafeteria is cashless). Help with school uniform (school provides the basics ex-stock) and trips. Grants available. If pupils stay for fifth year the odds are they will stay on to sixth: five Highers the norm.

H

Pastoral care, well-being and discipline: Sixth formers buddy first formers – 'very protective and good anti-bullying strategy'. Strong PSE reinforced by RME. Pupils are divided into four houses, and the pupil support strategy is handled by house representatives, each house having two guidance and two support-for-learning teachers. Terrific inter-house competition, both in the academic and the sporting field, with marks being allocated for each and house championship fiercely fought over.

Defined sanction system: if pupils disobey one of five clearly defined rules, then they 'may be excluded for up to three days' for continuous disobedience, and head will meet with the parents. School 'is not prepared for disruptive children or anti-social behaviour' to permeate and would much rather produce 'decent sensible sensitive citizens' who are a lot 'more use than an anti-social chemist'. To this end (and this is a first for us) has installed a splendid reward system (Pavlov eat your heart out). Each pupil (who has the school code drilled into them during their first week, 'so they can't say they don't know what is expected of them') is given a personal plan which must be stamped at the end of each lesson. Pupils earning 250 marks are awarded a certificate, can skip an afternoon's school and see a film of their choice – and get a Mars bar. Five hundred stamps qualify for a silver certificate and a free ticket for Megabowl; gold equals a trip to Alton Towers, with a certain amount of parent input, and platinum a three day trip to London. Platinum winners have to have their cards stamped after almost every lesson to qualify. Links with top year of feeder primaries – guidance staff and teacher visit regularly (HMI reckoned the school 'could try harder') and first year pupils all decamp with their teachers to Falkland Youth Centre for bonding and team-building stuff.

Pupils and parents: A mixed bunch, some here briefly, charming and well-mannered. Good parental support and school booklet encourages this. Farmers, businesspeople, as well as the university and hospitals. FPs include Donald Findlay QC, Bruce Milan, James Crabb (accordion player), the footballer Christian Daily and the much beloved George Galloway – who does not even receive a mention in the FP online site under 'government'. (Should we have checked 'media/television personalities'?)

Entrance: Always full. Pupils come from five main feeders with a couple of dozen placement requests annually. Certain amount of logistical movement. Standard rules about addresses and siblings.

Exit: Either post National grade, or (usually) post sixth form. Some 70 odd per cent to universities, mostly to Scotland but the occasional trickle to Oxbridge. Inspired careers advice.

Remarks: Inspirational – and now in a brand new school building.

High School of Dundee

Euclid Crescent, Dundee DD1 1HU

Ages 3–18 **Pupils** 1,052 **Sixth form** 106

Fees: £9,159 – £12,999 pa

01382 202921
www.highschoolofdundee.org.uk

Rector: Since 2008, Dr John Halliday BA PhD (Cantab) (60) (no thoughts of retiring). Educated at Abingdon and previously head of Albyn School in Aberdeen, following the demise of Rannoch (after a short spell at Dollar). Having shaken Albyn (which we fully expected to fail) by the scruff of the neck, introduced chaps and baby nursery, he laid the foundations of the stonking Albyn school of today.

In Dundee, the upper school was rattling, lower school resembled the Marie Celeste and place was more of a mausoleum than a vibrant hub of education. Halliday was a shoo-in to wake up this slumbering giant; a process made more daunting by having an almost entirely new senior management team (he had a hand in the selection process). We asked if all was happiness still in the upper echelons: 'Your team, you run with them' was the answer, which doesn't quite imply unqualified success. School roll highest ever.

Still plays the viola in the school orchestra. Married with three children, now up and flying.

During our first visit to Dundee High, Halliday confessed to missing the buzz of the classroom, so took up chalk again, and taught 'the odd spot of German'. However, recent acquisition (2013) of the Dundee head post office, a splendid French Renaissance affair, just metres from the main school, makes further forays unlikely. Plans afoot to 'create a centre of excellence for performing and visual arts'; 'this is a once in a century opportunity'.

School humming with happy pupils and, judging from instructions given to reception whilst we were waiting (rector's secretary had double booked), some less happy children, too: 'Ring these five parents, Dr Halliday wants to see them at 15 minute intervals this afternoon; hopefully their children should have warned them'. Sounded ominous.

Heads usually divide automatically into building/developing heads and academic heads. Halliday is unusual in that he straddles both disciplines. We spent some time studying plans and came away with a natty blue and gold campaign fundraising book (though we had to go online to find the cost of the proposed conversion – £16m). The appeal, due to last five years, was launched with fireworks, pipe band, red carpet and a cast of thousands. Rector maintains that 'if every member of our current school community gives up just one cup of coffee per day for the campaign period we'll raise nearly £10m.' Presumably Starbucks rather than Haag. This is high priority stuff; certain amount of demolition required for nasty 60s add-on, but space available for a variety of concert/chamber orchestra (300 seater) auditoria, plus theatre space and refectory (three million quid) linked to (catering) kitchens and health and food technology; plus drama, art and design. Current dining hall a bleak (often wet and windy 200 metres or so away). Public use a given, conferences and the like anticipated. (Black box, white box: et al).

Julie Rose BEd is in charge of junior years and nursery.

Academic matters: A Scottish school through and through, with high expectations. French from P4, with a P7 trip to Paris eagerly anticipated by pupils. P6 and 7 get lots of lessons in the senior school: computers, art, drama etc. Classes in early years strictly capped at 20 for L1 rising to 22 for L3, but school will make an extra class when the demand, though space is tight. Good support for stragglers plus a thinking skills course for every year group – one group was busily doing Sudoku. Littlest start with Oxford Reading Tree plus lots of phonics and multiple reading methods. The class we visited was having a ball – expressively reading aloud. Children happily busy in every corner, though an older group caught in a lull had time to talk maturely about the imminent French trip and their huge array of hobbies.

National 5s absorbed seamlessly, all expected to take seven or eight: solid range of subjects. Results pretty good overall, and spectacular in modern languages, chemistry, history. Most teaching in mixed form groups but English, maths and languages are set. English department had a couple of finalists in the Pushkin Prize for short stories. Increased take-up in French, Spanish and German. Rota for langs: Latin, German, Spanish, French, Mandarin then choose. Strong history, which gets its fair whack of the S1/2 curriculum, not being reduced to a share of rota system as in many schools. English and maths taken by most at both Higher and Advanced Higher level. Not much take up for Latin and minimal for Greek (on offer, plus Russian, in S6); range of marginal subjects – sociology, technical studies, PE, managing environmental resources, plus philosophy, economics; respectable numbers taking all sorts of maths specialisms: stats, mechanics etc. Class sizes from three or four to mid-20s. Masses of techno equipment – PCs, internet link via Abertay University etc and trolleyed laptops for class use in the junior school. S6 can do enhancement courses at Dundee University. iPads for all from P6, parent bought and insured.

In 2018, 61 per cent As at Highers, with 50 per cent As at Advanced Highers.

Learning skills centre with five dedicated staff provides support and specialist teaching in junior and senior schools for 'mild to moderate specific learning difficulties' (dyslexia, dyspraxia, ADHD, mild Asperger's). Early intervention encouraged. Support also for the super bright. Few need ESOL which tends to be given in class at primary and rarely needed at secondary. Much-used library, with areas for different ages and activities and full time librarians on hand who also arrange multifarious library talks and activities.

Games, options, the arts: Pupils bused to games in the multi-million Mayfield sports centre, complete with a brace of international-class hockey Astropitches (water-based/sand-dressed), plus academy of sport and health/well-being which includes diet and physical development, involving 'internationalists up to the highest level.' Swimming in Dundee University pool. Strong rugby, girls' hockey, netball and athletics, tennis, cricket. DofE flourishing – oodles of golds. CCF, pipe band – with girls as well as boys; riding and skiing teams are the tip of an iceberg of physical activities from line skating to golf.

Current art department chilly with garret view of Dundee roofscape: multi-purpose: textile, scarf making, jewellery (boys and girls) involves chemistry to help with 'decorative fusing'. Music strong with concerts in the town and a musical production biennially – recently The Good Person of Szechwan and Joseph in the junior school. Numerous orchestras, groups and choirs. We spoke at length to head of music, whom we have known since he was in (very) short trousers. He is ecstatic, both about the school itself and about the future development.

Drama timetabled with productions at all levels. Art, music and drama all available as exam subjects up to Advanced Higher with impressive results. Formidable debating in true Scottish school tradition.

Masses of choice for juniors including earlybird and lunchtime IT and a gardening club (currently providing a wintry courtyard with paper flowers).

Background and atmosphere: School founded in 1239, though royal charter from Queen Victoria didn't arrive until 1859; a city 'treasure' with an enlightened governing body drawn from the great and good (the 'Guildry' and 'Nine Trades'), elected from parents, past pupils or co-opted for their skills. Certain amount of trad: prize-giving in Caird Hall, end of term services at St Andrew's church.

The neo-classic (slightly grubby), Doric porticoed façade (so beloved by Scottish school architects) is protected by railed playground, fiercely patrolled by janitors, but open to visiting editors and parents collecting their offspring at the end of school day. Flanked on one side by the 1890s Margaret Harris Building, once the girls' school, which houses the juniors, and, on the other the (ex) Trinity Church, which provides a hall (not big enough for the whole school), ground floor library and attic drama space. The McManus Gallery, much used by the art department, is more-or-less opposite. The magnificent, late Victorian French Renaissance style former head post office building (adjacent to DC Thompson) is perhaps 50 metres from the school gates. A triumph to have bought it (DC Thompson is on the move as well, but we doubt school could either afford, or need, an extra humungous building).

Departments are cunningly grouped in a collection of buildings, some quite grand, gradually accumulated along Bell Street and curiously interspersed with courtyards, one of which sports tall, thin climbing wall. Roomy and light teaching rooms, plenty of space, though not much greenery. Pupils mill about, open, friendly, and happy to talk about their work. Some corners/staircases a bit dark and 'schooly', but most bright and clean, though neither corridors nor pupils are unnaturally tidy. Boys wear navy blue, while girls wear 'softer' grey blazers with a grey Dundee High tartan skirt. The tartan looks best as pinnies for tinies. Parents' thrift shop well used.

Nursery for 3-4 year olds on Mayfield campus. The purpose-built £1m facility is open 50 weeks of the year from 7.30am to 6pm.

Pastoral care, well-being and discipline: Four vertical houses, with familial continuity from juniors to seniors, run by guidance staff, have two forms in each year group, with guidance teacher being first point of contact for pupils and parents. Despite freedom to go into town at lunch breaks, rector reports far more phone calls from citizens complimenting the helpfulness of pupils than complaints: certain number of hiccups lately. Guidelines are clear: suspension for first offence – smoking and the like, pupils with drugs can expect to be expelled.

Pupils and parents: Some 50 per cent from Dundee, 50 per cent from Fife, Angus and Perthshire: five different (school organised and subsidised) bus routes. Mix of farmers, professionals and people working for universities/hospitals. Fair ethnic mix and fair number of first time buyers: school has come back into its own. Pupils can bring own cars but not drive others. Former pupils include William Wallace, AL Kennedy, Lord Cullen and Lord Ross, and more recently Andy Nichol, Mark Beaumont, Frank Hadden, Joanna Vanderham and KT Tunstall. BBC's Andrew Marr had a short spell in the juniors.

Natty trifold info sheet for parents lists every conceivable way of contacting school. With apps and downloads. Should be mandatory.

Entrance: By assessment at all stages, including cognitive ability, with two-thirds coming into seniors from juniors. Demand and waiting list not much hit by recession, though bursary applications are up. Main entrance points F1, F5 and F6; occasional gaps throughout the school, and offered, if pupil up to academic scratch, when demand exceeds supply, on a sibling basis. Mid-term arrivals not out of the frame. Reports from previous school required for those arriving from elsewhere, plus proof of ability to meet 'financial obligations'.

Exit: Virtually all juniors move up to seniors. Few leave post S4 and S5. Almost all to university, generally Scottish with a smattering to eg Durham or Oxbridge (one to Oxford in 2018); 'high interest in science and medicine' (six medics in 2018), biotech and life sciences, plus business and law degrees. Mock interviews for all.

H

Money matters: The first school inspected and passed by OSCR (Scottish charity regulator); school gives about £800,000 in bursaries every year (approximately 13-14 per cent of its annual turnover). Bursaries, all means-tested, are normally awarded to form 1, and, more recently P6/7; but applications from current parents in financial trouble will be considered. Stringent means-testing for all. Number of independent trusts also give financial support to individuals in the school. No specialist scholarships for academic, art, music sport etc.

Certain number of not too obvious extras eg music lessons. Pupils in upper school provide their own text books and stationery, lunch costs based on age (cheaper by the term: buy a book of vouchers); ditto bus – return is cheaper than one way; and – which is somewhat surprising – home economics enthusiasts pay for lessons. This is a new one to us (though we are now getting accustomed to exam fees being notified and charged).

Remarks: Impressive: Halliday has transformed the place. The fine tradition of Scottish education is alive, well and living (independently and at a price) in Dundee. New developments eagerly awaited. 'Like Dundee,' says the rector, 'the school is modest about its achievements'.

The High School of Glasgow

637 Crow Road, Glasgow G13 1PL

Ages 3–18 **Pupils** 1,000 **Sixth form** 102

Fees: £4,419 – £12,768 pa

01419 549628
www.highschoolofglasgow.co.uk

Rector: Since 2015, John O'Neill, previously senior deputy rector for 11 years. MA in medieval and modern history, and PGCE with distinction in history and modern studies from St Andrew's College of Education. Passionate about history, formerly teaching at St Thomas More School, London (as well as working part-time for an MP at Westminster) and Merchiston Castle School. He joked 'someone gave me money to teach medieval history'. Assistant housemaster at Glasgow Academy, then housemaster and head of sixth form at Merchiston where, he says, 'I found my voice'. And that he certainly did, this editor was at the school for an entire day, but all joking aside, undoubtedly articulate, highly educated and dedicated to 'making changes for the better'. One parent said: 'He hasn't rested on his laurels.'

Future plans include forming 'a new team, with new focus' and greater attention to academic monitoring ensuring pupils are being consistently challenged and all teachers are the best they can get. Married to a solicitor with one son. He laughs 'I used to have hobbies'. Loves reading. 'I buy a lot of books and read half of them.' Also enjoys road cycling, theatre and cinema.

Head of junior school: Since 2016, Heather Fuller, previously depute head at Hamilton College. Completed a two-year secondment to Education Scotland as a development officer, specialising in assessment. BEd at Strathclyde University and post-grad in leadership and management.

Friendly, efficient and 'with a strict approach' (very welcomed by one parent), plans include focusing on staff professional learning. Previous head in the job for 25 years, she had big boots to fill. One parent said: 'Taking over from Mrs Waugh would have been an enormous challenge.. Miss Fuller has very much stepped up to the mark, continually keeping standards high and introducing positive changes where required.' Hobbies include running – she ran a marathon in 2016 – as well as socialising, eating out with friends and visiting family in Australia.

Academic matters: This editor could almost feel the academia seep through the walls at the HSOG (pupils were so hard at work you could have heard a pin drop in the senior school on our tour). Proudly sits in the top three nationally for average number of Higher passes and top for A grades.

In 2018 Highers 74 per cent A. At Advanced Higher 55 per cent A. Sciences, English, maths and history most popular Higher subjects (interesting since the rector himself is a history academic), with the highest numbers doing chemistry (around 24 per cent) and maths (around 37 per cent) at Advanced Higher.

French taught from J1, and a healthy 20 per cent sit Higher French; 14 per cent Latin (taught from S2). German and Spanish also offered from S2 but numbers small for National 5 and up; 40 per cent take one language to Higher, and 8–10 per cent take two languages to Higher. Typically, as across the UK, physics and computing more popular with boys than girls. Otherwise equal in other subjects.

SEN provision (provided at no extra cost) is close to the rector's heart – his own son is dyslexic. Head of support for learning, and assistants, provide in-class support, with some limited extraction for extra support, when needed. He says: 'By S4 pupils requiring additional support are largely autonomous and have developed strategies to succeed.' School increased in popularity among parents of children with Asperger syndrome, according to rector. 'School has been recommended by other kids with Asperger syndrome so numbers have increased over the years.' No need for EAL support in upper school, but provided in the junior school in the past.

'Staff at the high school stay', and staff moving on is very much generational, and tends to happen in a flux of retirements. Junior school 50/50 male/female split in senior management positions; senior school management male dominated.

Careers education (S4–S6) is timetabled. Work experience in S5/S6, where kids 'need to take the initiative' and organise for themselves; school is there to advise but no spoon feeding here. Visits from the Independent Schools Council on CVs and interview techniques, and attend annual careers fair at the Glasgow Science Centre and promote open day visits to universities. UCAS evening for pupils and parents with speakers from Scottish universities. Weekly lectures are given to inspire S6 pupils, from often distinguished speakers; on our tour we bumped into the premier classical composer Sir James MacMillan.

One parent would like to see 'a broader range of subjects outside academics'. However, traditional subjects most popular at Higher and Advanced Higher. Interestingly, the rector also says 'there is a changing world in higher education' and that 'the traditional professions [medicine, dentistry, law] are no longer as popular'. Entrepreneurism seems to be favoured instead (yet numbers sitting business management at exam level is small). Trends in engineering, environmental-orientated sciences and business at university.

Games, options, the arts: Academics a serious affair, but real buzz around sport, the arts and extracurricular activities. At HSOG, pupils embrace being all-rounders – one knows this is true when the 1st XV school rugby team also includes talented members of the school orchestra. Social value of clubs is placed highly, 'where children can find like minds and develop social relationships'.

J5 and J6 pupils are bused to Anniesland to use the senior school sports facilities. Every parent must be wowed by the 23 acres of sporting grounds, run in partnership with the Glasgow High School Club Ltd. Take a deep breath ... HSOG pupils are fortunate enough to enjoy five full-sized, floodlit rugby pitches, the number 1 pitch located in front of the Jimmie Ireland Stand (which also houses a fitness suite) – no soggy parents at the side of a pitch on Saturday mornings here. Plus sand and water-based pitches for hockey and a 3G Astroturf multi-use games area. From spring, the grounds are reorganised and marked out as four cricket pitches, a 300m running track and 12 tennis courts. With this much money and care invested, pupils are strictly forbidden to use the grounds unless for a dedicated sport. Every rule is meant to be broken, though, and at end of term, enthusiastic pupils are let loose on the grounds. Swimming and squash off-site. Facilities much used by the community and various local clubs on evenings and weekends.

Sport is a big deal. Current pupils include an international swimmer, para ice skater in team GB and a Nordic skier internationalist, as well as internationalists in rugby, hockey and girls' football. Over 50 clubs and societies (from gaming to debating and a gender and sexuality club, which was initiated by pupils). All 17 subject departments provide clubs – 'Nrich' club for Maths, surfer club for decoding, Latin theatre club (popular in the junior school, when they put on a Latin play each year). The little ones can dabble their hands in everything from bridge to zumba to pipe band drumming at extracurricular clubs.

Over 50 per cent pupils involved in music through myriad bands, choirs and orchestras. Large music department with a head of wind and head of strings, and dedicated percussion and voice teachers. Majority don't take music to exam level, but those that do (some 20 per cent) nearly all receive As. Very much part of 'the day-to-day life and atmosphere of the school', with two senior choral or orchestral concerts per year. Rector keen to tell us of achievements, including BBC Songs of Praise School Choir of the Year and that 'one out of 10 of the Junior National Youth Orchestra are from this school'. Music is made accessible to all through yearly MusicFest and SingFest competitions, with auditions open to all.

Drama hugely popular with oversubscribed drama club. A trickle sit Higher drama some heading to prestigious London drama schools, such as Laine Theatre Arts and Rose Bruford. Drama and musical theatre productions alternate between junior and senior school each year, and have included The Lion King (junior school), Lord of the Flies and West Side Story.

Children's art everywhere in junior school, with impressive drawings of the Kelpies (entered in Kelvingrove Museum art competition). Quirky, open-plan art and design department in the senior school, with small spiral staircase up to the mezzanine hung with artworks of various genres. Puts on biennial art exhibition.

Community service activities include junior pupils making food boxes to donate to local charities, senior pupils delivering Christmas gifts to over 200 senior citizens and overseas community service projects in Morocco, India and Uganda. High completion rate of DofE: bronze 90 per cent, silver 65–70 per cent, gold 25–35 per cent.

Oodles of trips every two years, including New York and Paris (business); Prague (music); Mexico (biology); Iceland (geography); S1 Raasay outdoor pursuits week. Subsidies available to those in financial need.

Background and atmosphere: Scotland's oldest school, founded in 12th century as choir school for Glasgow Cathedral, later achieving grammar school status in 15th century. Sited at various locations around the city, it became the High School of Glasgow in 1834. Facing closure between 1973 and 1976, it was saved by the High School Former Pupils' Club, which funded the new, purpose-built building we see today on the sports ground at Anniesland Cross (senior school), following the school's merger with Drewsteignton School (now housing the junior school) in Bearsden.

Senior school is housed in a modern, red-brick building with multiple extensions added over time, including the two-storey science block. Weight of its history resonates in the corridors: a columned alabaster war memorial commemorates all 'the old boys of the High School of Glasgow who in the great war laid down their lives in the service of their country'. Fine art is hung everywhere, donated by former pupils, including the Thin Red Line (1881), donated by Lord Macfarlane of Bearsden. In contrast, top-notch facilities modern abound too: smartboards and Apple TV in the biology labs, three ICT suites with Apples and Windows computers, iPads for all, huge labs with high-end microscopes and impressive refurbished health and food technology kitchens. Not forgetting to mention the three labs just for sixth formers – they might be the future in science but the rector jokes that they still can't resist spraying each other with water at the start of the year.

Definitely an air of prestigiousness, academics is a serious matter, but not stuffy. 'Warm and welcoming' and staff particularly bubbly and helpful. Christian background but not overbearing; it listens to its pupils, hence the LGBT club. Hymns sung at the daily assembly, but considers itself progressive, too (alternates with a mental health reading or similar). We were fortunate enough to attend assembly in the junior school, which was so affirming this editor wondered how the pupils refrained from skipping on their way out.

Junior school in Victorian villa with wood-panelled walls and stained glass windows, housing small traditional library. Majority of teaching in the incredible extension added a few years ago, flooded with light, and sought-after basement kindergarten with own entrance. Classroom sizes around 26 per class is 'indicative of the school's enduring popularity'. 'That said, it is unusual for an independent junior school to have such large classes, and not all parents consider this to be ideal.'

Traditional in that children are hard-working and with a 'determination to do well'. Not old-fashioned though, kids get hands-on involved with inter-house competitions, sports and fundraising events, and musical productions. Children need to be 'resilient and adaptable' to cope in the v busy school environment. School 'seeks excellence' in its pupils and is best suited to 'all-rounders', and those with 'a drive and passion for learning'. Strict uniform policy, with blazers for all and tartan skirts (must be knee length) for girls. One pupil wished for 'less importance on uniform' – we imagine natural hair, no make-up is not every senior school girl's dream (though they do allow girls to wear earrings).

One of the city's most esteemed and academic schools, it is much sought after and held in high regard by the local community often receiving letters from locals, particularly for service to the community.

Pastoral care, well-being and discipline: House system with four houses named after distinguished former pupils, which runs from junior to senior school, and provides pastoral care. Rated 'excellent' in HMIe report. House staff deal with any problems, with two pastoral teachers per house as well as form staff. Children can approach whoever they feel most comfortable with, whether a member of the senior management team or a prefect. One parent said: 'Staff are helpful, a huge family of people, with excellent pastoral care.'

House staff also first point of contact for parents. Rector reassures parents: 'Lift the phone ASAP. We are all fallible. Let us know.' The Parent Association meets three times a year and parent representatives raise matters for discussion. Also organise events such as the Midsummer Madness end-of-term fair, fireworks display in November and quiz nights. One parent enthused about the school: 'The proof of the pudding is that the kids love it and miss it when they leave.'

Transitus pupils (P7 in everyday speak – 11/12 year olds) move to the senior school for the upper school experience and are well supported, with plenty of back-up from the junior department.

Passionate about pupils' well-being ('it's in our DNA'); new onsite health and well-being centre. School nurse is trained in cognitive behaviour therapy, and school runs a health and well-being week, with various speakers, like therapists, brought in, particularly at exam times. S2 and S5 pupils receive mindfulness lessons. Excellent booklet on anti-bullying policy, called Promoting Positive Relationships, to help parents.

School meals follow the Healthy Eating Schools policy, and are served in the refectory. Only S6 pupils allowed off-site for food.

Conversation is the first approach when it comes to discipline. The rector explains: 'Formal sanctions begin when conversations stop.' Detention, when given, consists of reflection time or school work. Small number of three-day suspensions for abusive language or fighting and no recent expulsions.

Pupils and parents: Home to school communications almost 100 per cent electronic. Parents can use the parent portal via the website to download reports, letters and consent forms. Electronic appointment system for S4 and S5 parents' nights. Pupils attend parents' nights from S3 onwards. Twice yearly reports sent out with attainment grades/effort grades (as much for the parent as for the pupil).

Majority from affluent Bearsden, West End and Milngavie, with a number from the south side of Glasgow (parents organise own bus). Those further afield – Helensburgh, Balfron, Lanark – use train links. School doesn't provide transport as good local transport links.

Parents mostly middle-class professionals, made up of teachers and academics, medics and lawyers, and entrepreneurial families. Slight growth in intake of ethnic minorities, but head says 'reflective of the city of Glasgow'.

Notable former pupils: Sir Henry Campbell Bannerman, Andrew Bonar Law, Sir John Moore, Sir Teddy Taylor, Rt Hon Lord Philip, Lord MacFarlane of Bearsden, Professor Sir Anton Muscatelli, Muriel Gray, Douglas Flint CBE.

Entrance: Potential pupils undertake an assessment followed by interview (both junior and senior school) with child and family. 'Ability to pay is not a factor', says rector, but has reputation as Glasgow's most selective independent school, assessing academic potential and using aptitude tests. Accepts 100 pupils per year group in senior school. For junior school, assesses if child is age and stage ready for the challenging curriculum offered and also if socially ready. If not, they can be retested in six months.

Decisions made on what pupils could bring to the school and that they show 'a keenness to learn'. Admissions year round. Waiting list for the senior school. Sibling policy that does best to keep families together. Popular with parents who previously attended the school as well as first-time buyers. Entry at senior school via Transitus and S1, with entry from S2 upwards dependant on availability of places. Before sitting Highers entrance is based on exam results. Recent increase in requests in S3.

Exit: At the prospect of children being evicted for poor performance, the rector says: 'We morally couldn't do that; we let pupils choose five Highers, and don't send off to FE college if not doing so well'. Automatic transfer from junior to senior school for Transitus year (P7) at Anniesland; 52 per cent of Transitus pupils come from the junior school. Vast majority to university, high percentage to Scottish universities as well as Bath, Durham, Bristol and Imperial; 11 medics in 2018. Tiny percentage apprenticeships. Virtually all go straight to university with a very few taking a gap year.

Money matters: Rector keen to 'create opportunities for all children irrelevant of background'. Tenfold increase in bursaries in the last decade. Around 15 per cent receive support, some with fees paid in full. Bursaries only available in the senior school, including Transitus, and is awarded on financial need. Extras include music tutors, school meals, uniform and sports kit.

Remarks: Scotland's oldest school, HSOG a is prestigious and academic environment, but with a supportive and welcoming feel. Top-notch facilities and sporting grounds, best suited to all-rounders who can cope with a busy schedule of work and play.

Hutchesons' Grammar School

21 Beaton Road, Glasgow G41 4NW

Ages 4–18 **Pupils** 1,205 **Sixth form** 110

Fees: £7,320 – £12,168 pa

01414 232933
www.hutchesons.org

Rector: Since 2016, Colin Gambles. BSc in biochemistry from the University of Edinburgh and PGCE in biology and integrated science from Cambridge. Worked as a teacher around the country, from Staffordshire to North Devon, all HMC independent schools. Head of biology at George Watson's in Edinburgh and deputy head at Robert Gordon's in Aberdeen. He said that although he went to a comprehensive school himself, he chose to teach only in the independent sector: 'I didn't want to focus on behaviour but to inject passion into my teaching.'

Came across as a most likeable man, intelligent but approachable and warm. Every bit the explorer in character (jungle expeditions in Madagascar, British Guyana, Borneo, Trinidad, Belize, Honduras). One can imagine that no pupil or member of staff would be afraid to knock on his door. The off-the-record view was that he is much admired by his team. We only heard good things about his 'fresh and dynamic leadership' from parents, one saying: 'His warm, friendly and enthusiastic manner has been a breath of fresh air. He is demonstrably child focused in his approach and genuinely delights in the achievements of the pupils.'

Future plans include increasing the level of bursary support to offer the Hutchie experience to as many as possible; he is working alongside the depute rector to raise more money. He was critical of the sixth year experience in Scotland and wants it to really mean something, focusing on leadership and developing personal and life skills – we had to double-take when we saw an actual car in a classroom, which was part of a S6 car maintenance workshop.

Always been an ardent hockey player, and still plays alongside pupils. Married with four children (all at the school), his wife is Scottish and a project manager, and he is half Scottish.

Primary school head: Since 2014, Fiona MacPhail is a former pupil of Hutchesons' with a BA in history from Edinburgh and an MBA from Strathclyde. For several years she taught in international schools in both Cairo and Bonn and, on her return to this country, became head of primary at The Park and Laurel Park Schools. In 2001, she returned to Hutchesons' as depute rector with responsibility for the upper primary.

Leaving in summer 2019. Her successor will be Ashley Cornfoot, currently acting head of primary school at Garden International School, Kuala Lumpur. English degree from Lancaster; has taught in Qatar, Thailand and Brussels as well as the UK. He and his wife have three children.

Academic matters: Specialist teaching in art, music and PE from P1 in the junior school and a fantastic focus on languages, starting off with Gaelic and moving on to Latin, French, Spanish, Portuguese and German. By P7 they have one period of Latin per year week and French, German and Spanish in rotation.

In 2018, 68 per cent of Highers were grade A, as were 49 per cent of Advanced HIghers. STEM subjects popular, as are languages. Vast majority take at least one language to Nat 5 (French, Spanish, German or Latin). Latin is compulsory until S3. All pupils take English to Higher and 85 per cent take maths. A maths teacher we met on our tour told us that 'a huge number of kids are doing AH, with 40 per cent doing pure maths.' No evident inequalities between the genders, more boys than girls going on to do engineering, but girls' numbers increasing.

Can cope with SEN pupils that are high functioning (must be able to pass entrance test). Extraction for additional support in the junior school, but by senior school able to cope in the classroom setting with support from the class teacher, under guidance from the learning support team. A parent told us: 'Both of my children have benefited from learning support at different points in their journey through the school ...The time limited and purposeful interventions provided enabled my children to improve and go on to flourish in their classes.' EAL not really required, but provisions if needed.

Around 10 members of new staff per year means there is a mix of new and long-serving staff. Almost 50 per cent women in senior management and for the first time in the school's history a female chair of governors.

Work experience (from S4) happens in holidays not in curricular time. HG School Association runs the careers event which covers 80+ professions.

Games, options, the arts: Sports stadium incorporates Astroturf hockey pitch and international training standard athletics track, used by local athletics club in the evenings. Astroturf hockey pitches at Clydesdale ground adjacent to the school, plus international standard cricket ground. Pupils are bussed to Auldhouse for rugby. All the usual games – rugby and hockey almost a religion (hat-trick celebration for the boys' rugby team, winning both the plate and the bowl in the Scottish Schools Rugby competition, and the girls' hockey team winning the BP West District Cup recently). Successes also in swimming, cross-country and athletics. Mr G says: 'It's so important that all pupils find their sporting niche in terms of their health and well-being.'

Variety of band, choir and orchestra practices before school hours; host of lunchtime and after-school clubs, from mindfulness to debating, bridge (recent Scottish winners, first and second place) and even cryptography (the art of writing or solving codes).

Annual school music competitions in the senior school, the grade 7/8 category winner playing a fine rendition of Astor Piazzolla's Libertango on Marimba. On a lighter note, charity event in 2018, Hutchie Rocks, saw the whole school in on the act, with the junior school giving an exuberant rendition of Living on a Prayer. An S6 pupil won a Young Percussionist Award at the Royal Conservatoire of Scotland and a coveted place at Julliard summer school in New York. Music technology available as a Higher in sixth year.

'Drama is a really vibrant part of the school', with P4s recently performing Roald Dahl's the Three Little Pigs. P7 show every year and S1/S2s put on an entertaining performance of Aladdin at the Christmas panto. Annual summer show is a serious affair – Hot Mikado and Grease recently. One boy even flew through the air in a harness in Iolanthe. Small but dedicated number take drama Higher/Advanced Higher with AH pupils directing S3 pupils annually.

Colourful dresses featured in the Junk Kouture competition. Beautiful copper neckpieces and S3 lino, print and paperwork artworks with a human rights theme, relating to the Erasmus programme with partner schools in Germany and Holland, were on display in the library school corridor. Higher photography and yearly competitions.

Pupils eager to take part in community service, 'they know how lucky they are'. DofE popular and lots of fundraising events.

Trips alternate between high-budget trips, such as the ski trip to Austria, and more affordable ones, such as battlefield trips. Sporting trips have included South Africa (rugby) and Portugal (hockey), the latter beating the men's national U21s team. Cultural exchanges to India and Erasmus trips to partner schools.

Background and atmosphere: Darling of Glasgow's south side, Hutchie is perhaps the most popular independent school on this side of the city. Founded in 1641 on Ingram Street by the Hutcheson brothers as a hospital and school, it educated the city's poorest. A strong sense of social values is still apparent; the rector reiterates this when he says: 'The bursary scheme is very important to us.' Hutchesons' certainly educates plenty of privileged children these days, but the ambience is welcoming and refreshingly down-to-earth; this extends from the pupils to the teachers.

In 1841 the school moved to Crown Street in Glasgow's Gorbals, then to the more prosperous Pollokshields in 1960. Amalgamated with the girls' school in 1976, the primary moving into the red sandstone girls' school at Kingarth Street, where it still resides.

In places a bit of an ugly duckling. However, the original nondescript, 1960s flat-roofed build has been reclad in Hutchie blue and the Fotheringay Centre, created from an extensive restoration of a turn-of-the-century church, is show-stoppingly beautiful. The church hall has been transformed into a stunning auditorium (picture vaulted ceiling, organ pipes, stained glass windows), with collapsible seating for lectures, assemblies and music performances. Houses the school's music centre with soundproofed practice rooms in the crypt and a basement IT suite for computing lessons, amusingly signposted with a tube sign 'underground'. Swish new drama studio with theatre.

Traditional core values with smart uniform. Children in the senior school had heads down and were focused in class; lots of interaction with the teacher and interested learning in the English department – always a good sign. A few overzealous sixth years were noisily playing table tennis in the bistro, but the head boy and girl steered us quickly away from there.

Primary school dates from 1912. One parent commented that it is 'very urban and the playground is limited; the school is planning on improvements, though.' Once inside, however, 'there is an amazing camaraderie throughout with the children often coming home and telling us how they have interacted with the older and younger pupils, whether through reading buddies in book week or house days where they all work together on their goals. I think this gives them a sense of belonging and comfort.' We agree; indeed, each house team's 'cloaks of magnificence' sound particularly wonderful – the top point scorer has their name embroidered on the cloak, and we imagine the competition must be fierce.

Raises large sums for charity; recently over £26,000. Current charity of choice is Callum's Cabin, a strong favourite of the primary children, which provides holidays for families of children with cancer. Two talented Hutchie fiddle and accordion players raised £2,000, playing alongside the esteemed traditional musicians Phil Cunningham and Ally Bain. It was an internet sensation, with over a million hits, and ironically appeared on this editor's newsfeed on the same day as our tour. Other money-raising activities include kids cutting their hair to make wigs for those with cancer and a Grannies' Afternoon Tea in the primary school.

Pastoral care, well-being and discipline: Depute rector is in charge of senior pastoral care with the year tutor and two assistant year tutors also on hand. Class teacher would be the first point of contact for pupils and parents, then the year teams if needed. The feeling from parents, however, is that if you had a real worry you could go straight to the top. They described the rector as 'accessible' and 'actively engaging with parents and pupils.' One parent said that those who had to escalate any issues to him directly had found him 'professional, sympathetic and quick to address, investigate and resolve their concerns.' Fun house competitions in the junior school, which becomes largely sports based in the senior school.

No recent exclusions. Rector believes 'bad behaviour is often a symptom of something else' and instead looks at ways to actively reward. 'Unconditional positive regard' is the phrase he uses, expecting pupils to see the best in each other.

Pupils and parents: Technology increasingly used in communications and reporting, with parental surveys for feedback. School association meets quarterly to hear concerns of the parent body. Pupil achievements are given their moment of glory in the school magazine, the Hutchesonian, as well as the The Hutchie Herald, which also celebrates the former pupil community. One parents' evening a year, S5s get two, and pupils come along to make it the norm. Settling-in report and written reports throughout the year.

One pupil described themselves as 'competitive but very friendly – everyone wants to do well.' Diverse group of middle class, professional parents. Popular with a significant number of Jewish families (separate assemblies on Thursdays) and about 10 per cent from Asian backgrounds.

Good transport network used by majority of kids, but those living further afield are bussed in from Newton Mearns, East Kilbride, Troon, Motherwell, Bothwell, Hamilton, Paisley, Renfrewshire and as far as Kilmarnock. Some buses are put on by school, some organised by parents. Parents pay for school buses.

Former pupils include John Brown of the shipyard of the same name, John Buchan, 1st Baron Tweedsmuir, TV presenter Carol Smillie, politician James Maxton, entrepreneur Richard Emanuel, Lord McColl, broadcaster Ken Bruce, Lord Irvine, psychiatrist RD Laing, Lord Adair, solicitor general for Scotland, Alison Di Rollo, banker and philanthropist, Alexander Stone, Lord Derry, Davis Cup team coach Leon Smith, global managing partner at McKinsey Kevin Sneader, and poet Imtiaz Dharker.

Entrance: To P1 by informal discussion and assessment, upper primary by interview and group entrance tests. Senior school pupils take maths, English and verbal reasoning tests plus interview. Majority of children move from the primary school to the senior school, with substantial number joining in P7. The rest apply from state primary schools.

New teacher-led pre-school year in the primary school building for 16 pupils, rising to 32 from 2019. There is no entry requirement for pre-school but automatic progression to P1 is not guaranteed.

Exit: Very occasionally at primary school parents will be advised if their child is not suited to the senior school. The senior school is set up for pupils likely to achieve five Highers; if a long way off that and Nat 5s not in sight, then the rector says, 'it would be the wrong environment for the child'.

Majority go on to Scottish universities, 40 per cent to Russell Group, including six to Oxbridge in 2018.

Money matters: The rector told us: 'The bursary scheme is very important to us – that's why we are a charity'. Significant number of pupils every year receive bursaries – about 20 bursaries in any year, with 6-10 full fee – through competitive entry in S1. Discount for siblings.

Remarks: A southside institution in independent Glasgow schooling, Hutchie offers a broad curriculum and is well known for its academic excellence and sporting achievements.

The International School Aberdeen

Pitfodels House, North Deeside Road, Aberdeen AB15 9PN

Ages 3–18 Pupils 424 Sixth form 38

Fees: £12,830 – £14,100 pa

01224 730300
www.isa.aberdeen.sch.uk

Head of School: Since August 2018, Nicholas Little, who left Oxford with a history degree and a postgrad qualification in law. But after an inspiring gap year teaching western culture at a college in northern China, he decided to abandon his law career and embrace teaching, a 'constantly optimistic profession', full time. He began by teaching English and humanities for several years in the UK before moving back to teach at China's Suzhou Singapore International School in 2002, where he eventually became head of school. Married to Katherine; they have three children, all of whom have graduated from SSIS. He says moving to Scotland is 'like moving home, but not quite; something familiar, but also new.'

Academic matters: The last few years at the International School Aberdeen or ISA has seen a period of change and adaptation. With the rapid decline of the North Sea oil industry, many of the international families, who were the rock-bed of the pupil body have been 'repatriated' and the school role has begun to fall rather rapidly. Consequently the school is focusing much more on attracting local pupils.

'Over a period of two years we dropped by over 200, but since then we have gone back up to 422. Ideally we want to be around 500 kids.' Naturally enough for an international school, they offer the International Baccalaureate as standard, but they are now teaching IGCSEs and the French Centre National d'Enseignement à Distance or CNED programme to reflect their changing school role. CNED provides a French curriculum for students living overseas and is taught up to five hours a week according to the need of each individual child. It takes place during the modern languages block and can be taught during music, art or drama for the older children. In 2016 their largest group of pupils was American, but now the largest group is local (30 per cent) and French students form the third largest group, hence the CNED programme.

Back to the Baccalaureate. Their average IB point score was 33 in 2018; but the IB is notoriously hard work. What about the less academic children? One former parent we spoke to said, 'There were always concerns that the less able kids were being shunted off with an American High School Diploma, which is about as much use as a chocolate teapot in the UK!'.

But the head is reassuring on that point. 'We are offering the IGCSEs so that students who don't wish to stay and complete the IB diploma have a recognised and highly regarded certification when they leave. Additionally, we have found that some students wish to have both qualifications and view the chance to sit external exams as good practice for their IB. If students don't wish to do the IB, but complete all the coursework and our internal exams (we are accredited by CIS – the Council of International Schools, and MSA – the Middle States Association) they still can complete a High School Diploma, which is recognised in many countries around the world (USA, Canada, Australia etc).'

The school is still split along American lines with the pre-school (ages 3-5), elementary (ages 5-11), middle school (ages 10-14) and high school (ages 13-18).

As an international school, there is a strong emphasis on modern languages, including English as an additional language and Dutch language and culture (there are still a considerable number of Dutch expats and oil employees in the city). In fact, they offer a number of mother tongue programmes ie some lessons are taught in these languages. At the moment that's German, Spanish and Arabic, but this is flexible according to requirement.

The middle school offers an impressive series of non-examined courses or general electives, including everything from Lego robotics to woodwind, brass and percussion and theatre tech.

Seventy per cent of all staff are British and 30 per cent have a mixture of backgrounds, from English-speaking countries in the main, though native speakers are employed for Spanish and French (the two languages offered for IB) plus Dutch and French mother tongues. The ones we spoke to were charming, chatty and enthusiastic and from as far afield as California, Chicago and Cults (just up the road!). There seemed to be a genuine passion for Scotland in general and Aberdeen in particular, which was reassuring.

Each of the three divisions (elementary, middle and high) has a principal, with the middle high having an assistant principal too. Meanwhile, each subject area has a curriculum coordinator plus two counsellors or guidance teachers i.e. to advise on university routes.

There are roughly 30 pupils in each year group, 13/20 per class. In high school class numbers are much smaller (language classes with just 3 children in it). It's possible to be accelerated in specific subject areas if you have a real bright spark on your hands, but if they struggle elsewhere learning support has two dedicated members of staff with a third starting next academic year. The School official line is if pupils need more than 20 per cent support per week, then they will have to go elsewhere, i.e.local mainstream. But unofficially some kids get up to forty per cent help. "We only turn kids away if we really feel we can't help them to access the curriculum"

Games, options, the arts: Well, there really is a bit of a conundrum when you look at the sporting offer at ISA. There is a stunning sports wing housing a double gymnasium, huge games hall, fitness centre, multi-purpose spaces, 25 metre six lane swimming pool – used by locals as well as school, as are the gym/games facilities, fitness suite and multi-gym. Terrific outdoor sports area: two all-weather soccer pitches/basketball courts and tennis courts (teams play on the international school circuit as part of International Schools Sports Association or ISSA).

But, and it's a big but, if little Johnny or Clarissa want to wield a hockey stick or punt a rugby ball then they might feel a little bit isolated. Those traditional, parent-freezing, chilblain inducing touchline expeditions are few and far between.

'We try to compete locally, at soccer for example, but we're not that competitive and really other teams are too good for us. We do compete with the local basketball teams and we do field hockey but we don't have a team.' Is that a bit wet? Blimey! All that Astro, all that gym space and barely a competitive team in sight. All is not lost, however.

'We have unique offerings. We don't do the classic sports, no. But if you're into basketball, volleyball, badminton, swimming, tennis, yoga, roller blading or learning circus skills, we teach all of those to a high standard.'

Yes, circus skills. 'It's brilliant,' one parent told us. 'Both my kids can ride a unicycle and can juggle. It's just a different take. My son loves it. He's not into rugby or that into football and at his last school he felt he was pigeonholed because of it. Here you can just be what you want to be.'

One child we talked to said her favourite sport was rollerblading in the gym. And why not? Really refreshing, we say.

Musically, the school is fantastically equipped with recording studios et al and they teach a variety of instruments. But although they have a very healthy band programme (woodwind, brass and percussion) there are no orchestras. There are choirs from fourth grade up (students can audition for AMIS, the International schools' choir programme). They offer private music lessons, but not on stringed instruments.

There are fabulous theatre facilities and the school puts on two major drama performances every year (one for 8 year olds and one in the senior school). They also run a drama programme which is not part of the IB.

The art provision is another wow! Wonderful art rooms and an external kiln for pottery creations. Just amazing.

Head says the school 'tries very hard to do a lot of community outreach.' This is heavily influenced by the IB programme which has community work weaved into it. The school also helps as many charities as possible eg Shelter and shoe-box appeal, and the 8 year olds visit local care homes and read and perform to residents.

There is also a very big Duke of Edinburgh programme and the middle school goes on a week of outdoor pursuits every year on the west coast of Scotland.

Background and atmosphere: Founded in 1972, the American School, as it was then called, was set up in response to the flourishing North Sea oil industry and the influx of American families. It is still owned by a group of oil companies to this day, but is run by a charitable trust. After being forced off the original campus by the advent of a new city bypass, it has relocated to a spectacular 14 acre campus surrounding Pitfodels Mansion House (think Bond villain's Alpine lair) with the most spectacular facilities.

That original, relaxed 'Hiya!' American feel still exists (eg no school uniform), but with a wonderfully international twist. 'We do a graduation ceremony after IB exams are over in June, which is still very American, but they are piped in Scottish fashion to receive their certificates.'

We spoke to Norwegian, Nigerian, Scottish, American, French children....you get the drift, and unlike some UK schools there was a marvellously classless, unstuffy, friendly feel to the place. There are an amazing 38 different nationalities in the school. We were impressed that there wasn't a phone in sight and the first two children we met were actually reading books. Remember those?

Bolstered by some inventive and inspired architecture, the school's axis is a bright thoroughfare named The Street. This rather brilliant central meeting/eating/greeting place is for pupils, teachers and even parents (apparently some meet there for a coffee 'before going on a hike'). Spacious, light and airy classrooms, library and spectacular double gym lead off this area and onwards through to an impressive selection of Astro pitches, tennis courts and games pitches. At one end of The Street there is even a climbing wall. All in all, just a very relaxed, friendly, happy vibe.

J

'It's really easy to make friends here. Nobody judges you.'

There is one glaring issue, however, which the head was candidly honest about. Although the school now has many more local children who are there for their entire school careers, this is an international school and by its very nature there is quite a lot of coming and going.

'Of course, it can be a bit of an issue when your child's best friend moves back to Texas after three years. It can be unsettling, but it also teaches them to not be too cliquey or limited in their friendships. It's such a lovely friendly place they usually move on pretty quickly.'

Pastoral care, well-being and discipline: With such a relaxed, friendly atmosphere one could imagine there would be little problem with discipline. Nevertheless the school operates a non-bullying policy and hosts events such as Digital Citizenship week to educate on the dangers of social media. They also have a police school liaison officer who gives lectures on the dangers of knives, drugs, alcohol and sexual harassment and they run a general health programme to educate the children on the best way to look after themselves.

The children are put into houses when they arrive at the middle school and they have regular inter-house challenges. 'Clan time' on Friday mornings is for meetings, activities and assemblies. In sixth grade they focus on organisational skills, in seventh grade on community outreach, in eighth grade on environmental impact. 'We're a Green Flag school and run an eco and environmental club.'

As an international school, 'the staff have an appreciation of diversity and different religions and cultures. We have an international week in October and celebrate different religions and backgrounds on a regular basis throughout the year. We try to be as inclusive as possible and celebrate diversity.'

Most students arrive via school bus. There are eight school buses from as far out as Inverurie, Aboyne and Stonehaven. There is good parent contact with weekly newsletters and all teachers have a class blog. 'The school is incredibly open to the parents. We feel we can go in any time and there will always be somebody there to discuss my son.'

Pupils and parents: Gone are the days when the school was dominated by Americans. The faltering oil industry has put paid to that, but the mix, although much more skewed towards local children these days, is intriguingly international. If you envisage your little darling coming up the drive with his father's tuck box and a striped blazer, you might be severely disappointed. But if you want your child to think out of the box and have a very cosmopolitan outlook, ISA would definitely fit the bill.

Entrance: Whenever. You can come any time of year. There is an admission test for 10+ and older in maths, reading and writing and an interview with the principal. Younger kids have only an interview.

Exit: Most to universities in Scotland, with a few to England, and one each to Colombia, Calgary and Spain (medicine) in 2018. 'You can see a shift in our application to universities. Two years ago more than half were looking at US for post-secondary education and now it's at most a handful.'

Money matters: Some fees paid by oil companies. Bursaries and financial aid (eg IB scholarships for outstanding students) now available so that the school reflects more nearly the cost of a 'normal' British school. 'We are offering more bursaries than ever before.'

Remarks: If you're looking for the kind of 'striped blazer and gingerbread for tea' type of education then this is definitely not your bag. But, wow, you should see this school. Beautiful surroundings, fabulous facilities and bright, engaged and wonderfully welcoming staff and pupils. It will definitely be harder to make friends for life as they could be going back to Norway at the end of term, but looked at from another angle, what a way to expand your child's horizons.

And one final thought. Who knows with today's highly stressed living environment when juggling might come in handy?

James Gillespie's High School

Lauderdale Street, Edinburgh EH9 1DD

Ages 11–18 **Pupils** 1,285 **Sixth form** 180

01314 471900
www.jamesgillespies.co.uk

Headteacher: Since 2012, Donald J Macdonald BSc MBASQH Dip Ed (50s), previously head of Liberton High (school's exceptional progress under his watch resulted in an invitation to 10 Downing Street). Has taught science, physics and maths at a range of Scottish schools including Knox Academy and Portobello High. Married, with two daughters; lists golf, fishing and Scottish malt whisky amongst his many interests.

Academic matters: Class size 30 (20 for practical subjects), some grouping by ability for maths in the September of their first year. Three separate sciences are available for all from the third year onwards. No classics, but French, German, Spanish, Mandarin and Urdu, a growing number also learn Gaelic (a feeder school where pupils do all subjects in Gaelic). All languages are taught up to Advanced Higher level (some, along with mechanics and computing, in conjunction with neighbouring schools). Recently introduced psychology popular. School does mix of Nationals, Higher, Advanced Highers and A levels for art (in order to form a portfolio), Urdu and geography – an interesting diversification for a state school. Excellent support for learning, dyslexia, dyspraxia, and help with exams, both withdrawn from class and team teaching in class. ADHD is OK – 'Most very well-behaved'. All staff trained to support pupils with a variety of talents. Pupils come from 40+ different countries – 'the most diverse population in Scotland': EFL available (free) for all who need it. CDT is 50/50 craft and design and all computer-based – 350 computers in the school. Recent BECTA award for best website. In 2018, impressive 40 per cent of Highers and 48 per cent of Advanced Highers at grade A.

Games, options, the arts: PE, swimming and extensive after-school activities all now on site. School is now a recognised Sports Hub with links to 15 or more local adult clubs. Girls' football, tennis, swimming, cricket and netball are particularly popular. Massive music uptake, with carol service normally held in the Usher Hall, over 500 regularly on the stage. Senior orchestra, junior orchestra, lessons free. Strong, spectacular art, photography, impressive fabric design. Huge dance area, media popular with lights and editing studios, three drama studios. Wizard home economics department – better than most homes we know. Trips all over the place, in many disciplines – skiing, Paris for art, historians to the trenches, geographers to do glacial research in the French Alps. Exchanges with several countries including: France, Spain, Germany, South Africa, China, Finland, Holland and Switzerland.

Background and atmosphere: Founded in 1803 as a result of a legacy from James Gillespie, 'a wealthy Edinburgh manufacturer of snuff and tobacco', who was born in Roslin. Started with 65 students and one master and led a peripatetic existence. At one point the prep school for the Merchant Company's secondary schools. By 1908 had a roll of over 1,000, including girls, and offered secondary education under the aegis of the Edinburgh school board, moving to Bruntsfield House, just off The Meadows, in 1966 and going fully co-ed in 1978. The earliest building on this site dates from 1300, and the current building, Bruntsfield House, was built in 1605, with later additions and improvements. Sir George Warrender, whose family was to be awarded the title Bruntsfield, bought the house from the original owners and was intrigued to find that if you hung a sheet from every window you could access from the inside, still sheetless windows remained outside. A secret room was discovered, with blood-stained floor, ashes in the grate and a skeleton under the wainscot. The Green Lady haunts the top storeys to this day.

School entirely rebuilt across the whole campus, including the construction of the Malala building, the main teaching block, and the refurbishment of the grade A listed Bruntsfield House. New sports and performing arts facilities too. Whole exercise jointly funded by City of Edinburgh Council and the Scottish Government.

Pastoral care, well-being and discipline: Follows the state guidelines – good PSHE, good anti-bullying strategy in place: 'We get the youngsters to talk it through.. We bring them together and get the bully to accept their behaviour is wrong'. 'No current problems' with cigarettes, alcohol or drugs, but will exclude on either a temporary or permanent basis if necessary. Also out permanently for a violent attack, though temporary exclusion for 'physical violence'. Homework books which must be signed by parent or guardian. No uniform, which is going slightly against the current Edinburgh trend – 'If it ain't broke, don't fix it'.

Pupils and parents: Free intake, so diverse: 47 languages spoken. Large number of professional families (Marchmont is a popular area for the university) plus 'a group of working class, with relatively poor backgrounds'. Huge ethnic mix, with some girls wearing the chador – they may well do PE and swim wearing full leggings and long-sleeved T-shirts (though parents can ask to withdraw their daughters from these lessons, few do). Lifts installed for wheelchair-bound pupil, minor physical handicaps OK. Strong parent/teacher involvement.

Entrance: First year capped at 260; very few places available by request – very popular, with pupils from as far away as Penicuik and Musselburgh. Obliged to take children on a first come first served basis, waiting lists. Certain number of pupils who have obtained university entrance elsewhere in the independent sector join in sixth form for increased breadth (and a better chance at Oxbridge).

Exit: Number leaves before Higher grades, either to further education or work; good proportion to universities, mainly Scots, studying medicine, science, art college, followed by social subject and music in that order. A number to Oxbridge (generally between six and 10) and generally some 10-20 medics.

Remarks: Can't fault it.

Jordanhill School

45 Chamberlain Road, Jordanhill, Glasgow G13 1SP

Ages 5-18 **Pupils** 1,048 **Sixth form** 190

01415 762500
www.jordanhill.glasgow.sch.uk

Rector: Since 1997, Dr Paul Thomson BSc PhD Dip Ed FRSA, educated at Dollar Academy, thence to Glasgow uni for a combined honours in maths and physics plus (later) a PhD. Thomson's meteoric career path found him appointed as one of the youngest heads in Scotland; that apart, he has a fearsome intellect and spouted facts and figures faster than most heads we have met, adding all the while that 'it is available on the web page'. Keen to 'improve the educational environment', he masterminded a mega building programme extending the refectory, constructing an all weather pitch and building (and we suspect doing more than a little designing) a stunning new classroom block – the South building. He has also transformed the hall, entrance and public spaces of the original building – but see below. Unlike many heads, Thomson regards these developments as 'a pupil necessity and therefore worth spending time and thought on', rather than as an end in itself to glorify Jordanhill and his own cleverness in getting the funding.

Jordanhill is the only direct grant-aided non-special school in Scotland, and runs its own budget, as does each department. A block grant comes from the Scottish Government to whom the school is answerable. Thomson regards himself quite rightly as a CEO, working 'with the staff' and running the place. He obviously misses teaching; his entire demeanour changed during our tour round the school: whenever we found a child to be talked to – about anything – gone was the efficient question-answering model and in its place appeared an interested smiley friend. (He also does all the 'early' UCAS references.) But youngsters apart, we suspect he does not tolerate fools with ease (he thinks he has 'mellowed' over the years). He also picks up emotional flack, and, after our whistle-stop tour of the new developments we coffee-ed in the staff room (young, vibrant, get the picture?) where a teacher related how much help he had been given when he had 'found it all too much': still at the school, he now has a different role.

Head of primary: Since 2014 is Richard Buchan, previously head teacher at Garrowhill Primary in Glasgow for nine years.

Academic matters: The school is inclusive: the most successful state school in Scotland. Four classes of 25 (rather than the trad legal limit of 33) with practical classes of 20. Some setting in maths. French from P1, Spanish on offer from age 14 to Advanced Higher level. The Swire Chinese Language Centre, plus the Confucius Classroom hub, teach Mandarin from P5 to National 5.

Arrangements on hand for non native-speakers to have help with extra English (ESOL) and take exams in their native langs, through Shawlands Academy, the Punjabi and Urdu centres etc; pupils studying Cantonese, Greek, Italian, Latin, Mandarin or Urdu may well be able to include them in their programme. Special needs well catered for – 'we cater for all whose needs can be met in a mainstream school'; some pupils have records of needs. SEN students have open access to networks; two dedicated teachers and five pupil support assistants provide a wide range of support across primary and secondary. Paired reading with sixth formers; support sessions during lunch, after school, in the evening, this is tailored formally structured study support. Standard testing for all aged 8-13: English, maths, spelling, VR; anomalies picked up early and the school's ed psych advises if necessary.

Public exam results across the board streaks ahead of other Scottish schools, and an astonishing 90+ per cent of pupils stay on for second year sixth. In 2018, 47 per cent A grades at Higher and 47 per cent at Advanced Higher. Masses of external activity, much to-ing and fro-ing with local unis and colleges: higher psychology in partnership with Clyde College, in the evenings. School is well used. Regular successes in quizzes and competitions both nationally and abroad.

Interactive whiteboards as standard, school both hard wired and wireless and supports BYOD for pupils: computers (400+ of them) in every discipline, in the art rooms, wherever. Trolleys of notebooks motor round classrooms. Rector adds, 'School has ICT mark and previously won ICT leadership reward'.

Homework clubs and online learning via O365. Ditto supported study. Several groups of pupils doing research projects have direct links with staff. Powerpoint demos by all, from P7; P6 and rest of junior school observe before a general discussion on the quality of the presentation with either the rector or other members of staff. (Rector's face lit up like a beacon when he described this.) Debating and public speaking timetabled for 11-13 year olds. Loads of interaction. Evening support classes for exam years, labs are open at lunchtime and post-school. Good modern library, more computers and even more in the careers department. Lifts and ramps all over the shop.

Games, options, the arts: Impressive number of playing fields, or use of them. School owns one rugby pitch, uses one from the uni, and has a couple of footie pitches on a 75 year lease from Strathclyde uni. The impressive all-weather pitch is home to the Hillhead Hockey Club, who train and play here; also a floodlit 3G MUGA. Two gyms on main campus and Sports Hall nearby on Anniesland Road. Not bad for a non-independent school on an inner city site. Fantastic games and oodles of caps – capped pupils wear green ties; colours gold collars, half colours gold stripe etc, and can be awarded for team, individual, musical success or any international representation. Pupils also wear date badges and can end up looking a little like a Christmas Tree. Trad games: rugby, hockey, football, cross-country running and athletics.

Stunning north-facing art department in the South building, lots of art on display, magical fabrics, jewellery and photography. Kiln and silk screen machine in place. Sculpture and good CDT.

Drama strong, biennial school show and drama timetabled P6-S2. Higher drama link with Knightswood Secondary. Inspiring music, with specialist staff from P6 up. 'The best music department in the country,' says the rector; 300 plus pupils play an instrument, 26 different ensembles, serious orchestras: all swinging, and particularly keen on composing. Concerts popular with parents. Outstanding music results.

Clubs for everything, chess particularly popular. Hot on debating, and citizenship. Health and fashion technology offers diverse provision – more post-National grades – when students also study international cuisine (head's face lit up again). 'Healthy take-up, both home economics rooms refurbished.' Deep envy from this editor.

Ambitious outdoor education programme with pupils spending afternoons or weeks away depending on year group; costs, but funds available for those unable to pay. Less than two per cent free school meals in the senior school as opposed to almost 30 per cent for the rest of Glasgow. Senior pupils have a biennial trip to the developing world, part project part tourism. World Challenge. Oodles of other trips abroad: Paris, Berlin, Washington DC and China. Massive charity involvement – both fundraising and community work in the locality. Jolly (twice yearly) school mag written by pupils, staff and FPs, clearly laid out with brilliant editing, easy to read, with none of the trendy undershadowing that doting grannies find so irritating (not to mention GSG editors).

Background and atmosphere: Founded in 1920 as a demo school for Jordanhill College of Education, became direct grant in 1987, having narrowly escaped closure in 1969. Handsome classical grade B listed building. Rector has stunning panelled offices (think Eltham Palace); huge classrooms with high ceilings and wide pupil-proof corridors have had a makeover. The hall has been brilliantly elongated – parquet flooring matches; acid etched glass panelled doors to die for, actually, most of school has natty oak doors to die for. Fantastic redevelopment of the site of a somewhat miserable building previously owned by Strathclyde uni, bought by Jordanhill and transformed into one of the most exciting class/art/spaces we have seen. This bright 15 room classroom block, with north facing art room and huge atrium on the ground floor, has been neatly dovetailed in. The atrium has a popular foodie kiosk in the corner. Much used as a drop-out zone; each pupil has a lockable locker and there are cunning (quite light) moveable circular seats. Good informal performing space; the balcony above overlooks. The next development was a revamp of the adjacent science building; library and fitness suite also revamped.

Primary based on the first two floors of the handsome classical grade B listed building, with a couple of dedicated play areas, one with lyrical views of the playing fields, and David Stow building designed by David Barclay 1914-22, the former Jordanhill College. Tinies have use of all the main school facilities; we arrived to find them milling around the super new enclosed Astroturf in front of the main school building, and skipped past various crocodiles when we retraced our steps back to the main school with the rector. Dig that fort!

Strong links with local Jordanhill parish church. Strong links too with Glasgow state schools – joint improvement meetings for staff. Pupils from other schools can come to Jordanhill to pick up Highers or Advanced Highers not catered for in their own schools.

Pupils are neat in brown uniforms, but decorated as above. Tinies wear charming green pinnies. Efficient and fairly unforgiving uniform guidelines in the prospectus supplement. Headscarves not a problem. Sixth year have a dedicated study room. JOSS operates an after-school club for tinies in the nearby church hall.

Pastoral care, well-being and discipline: Four houses – the heads of houses are guidance staff with combined office and interview rooms. Pupils meet with their tutors for 10 minutes each day; the latter are responsible for PSE. School policy is to clamp down hard on any form of bullying. A clearly defined code of sanctions, including letters home, litter duty (brill) and detention. Regular links between sixth form and littlies – combined reading and the BFG club. Minister from the parish church takes assemblies, but this is an ecumenical school, with all religions' festivals observed – rector is keener that pupils learn 'to conduct themselves properly in church' and understand other faiths (by, eg, visiting local synagogues, mosques and temples) rather than pay lip service to any particular religion.

Pupils and parents: Serves a predominantly owner-occupier area – professionals, who form an enthusiastic parent-teacher association, with parent volunteers in primary department and loads of fundraising. Ten per cent ethnic minorities. Only pupils S4 and above allowed off campus for lunch. Fairly sensible set of rules: and equally clear list of sanctions, most requiring parental signature.

Entrance: Traditionally, 33 pupils are added to those who come up from primary to senior, thus four classes of roughly 25. Inclusive, by address, oversubscribed, waiting lists. Siblings get priority. Some places may become available in odd years, ditto (never advertised) available post National grades. First come, first served, and, in the case of Advanced Highers if the subjects you want to take are already full, then you must try elsewhere. Worth moving/killing for.

Exit: Virtually all move from primary to senior school. Some 75 per cent to university – Glasgow and Strathclyde popular. Trickle to Oxbridge – one in 2018, a few to universities down south – Imperial for engineering, Liverpool, Manchester, the odd musician to the Royal Academy of Music, and tranches to art school, with or without a foundation course. But most stay in the west of Scotland. Three medics, two dentists and one vet in 2018.

Remarks: Outstanding, with an inspirational, rector. Better resourced than many schools in the independent sector – and it's free. A beacon – Glasgow independent sector eat your heart out: Jordanhill should be compulsory viewing for the lot of you.

Kelvinside Academy

33 Kirklee Road, Glasgow G12 0SW

Ages 3–18 **Pupils** 595 **Sixth form** 45

Fees: £7,995 – £12,070 pa

01413 573376
www.kelvinside.org

Rector: Since 2016, Ian Munro (30s), born in Aberdeen, partly state school educated at Hazelhead. In S3 moved to George Heriot's School, 'which was quite hard at first' but changed his school life for the better. BSc zoology, followed by a PGCE biology, both from Edinburgh University. Never resting on his laurels and with a passion for learning, gained a masters from Cambridge with distinction in educational leadership and school improvement, and recently completed leadership course with Harvard University Graduate School of Education. Formerly teacher (biology) and head of year at Heriot's and deputy head at Shiplake College. Most inspired, however, by his time at Gordonstoun (head of biology), with its much more holistic approach and where pupils don't feel pressured to achieve five As.

K

Flood of media attention when first appointed about being the youngest head teacher in the independent sector – he looked most embarrassed about this. Incredibly likeable, efficient (he responded to every email from this editor quickly and personally), down to earth and bubbling over with new ideas. Very much at ease with pupils; one parent claimed: 'He gets the kids! Respect is clearly evident going both ways, between him and his pupils.'

'Innovative' is a word we often hear heads use, but in this case it's an understatement. In his short tenure, he's overseen a new outdoors activity centre in the Cairngorms as well as an innovative American technology and design summer school. Despite this, he was modest and had the 'enthusiastic and engaging' deputy rector, Dan Wyatt (who is soon to take over as rector), in on our meeting for back up. Lives in Glasgow's West End with wife, history teacher at independent school. No children but two dogs, one a cocker spaniel named Charles Darwin. Loves the outdoors, sailing, walking, climbing, canoeing. Anything sporty. He and deputy rector both sing in the school choir. Leaving in summer 2019 to head Dollar Academy.

His successor, and executive head of the new (2018) Glasgow Schools Trust with Craigholme School, will be current deputy rector Dan Wyatt. Degree from Exeter; taught PE and history at Dr Challoners Grammar School before moving north of the border in 2003. Was pastoral lead at Hutcheson's Grammar before joining Kelvinside. A former Buckinghamshire County rugby captain, he is married to Norah, also a teacher, and they have two children.

Head of junior school: since August 2018, Linda MacBeath previously acting head of Colgrain Primary School in Helensburgh. Born and raised in Dumbarton, and completed her PGCE at Southampton University. She then began her teaching career in Manchester before moving back to Scotland to teach at Lomond School in Helensburgh, progressing to senior leadership posts at Cardross Primary School and Colgrain Primary School. A recognised advocate of digital technology and of the importance of outdoor education. She is also head of junior school at Craigholme School.

Academic matters: Rector himself says 'if expectation is for all kids to get five As at Higher then it might not be the school for you'. There are other independent schools in Glasgow with that focus (one nearby with significantly higher percentage of As at Higher and Advanced Higher), but too-cool-for school KA has a much more nurturing approach, reflected in the change of the motto from 'ever the best' to 'be the best you can be'. One parent enthused: 'It's not necessarily about being the best and all the pressures, unsportsmanly behaviours and self-esteem issues that can bring, it's about working hard at being the very best you can be and celebrating that success, both as individuals and teams.'

Academic results are not to be scoffed at nonetheless; in 2018, 61 per cent A-Bs, with 34 per cent As for Higher, and 62 per cent A-Bs, with 36 per cent As for Advanced Higher. Pupils sit eight National Fives, and everyone takes one language to National 5; 32 per cent take French or Spanish to Higher.

In his own words, the rector is intent on 'disrupting education in Scotland', which he says has 'fallen in standards over the years' (perhaps a dig at Curriculum for Excellence). Rather than just studying for exams, he wants to offer the best possible opportunities to KA students, teaming up with American innovation school NuVu, a 'micro school' with no exams, focusing on entrepreneurialism. In summer of 2017, 24 fortunate KA students were taught by academics and designers from Harvard and MIT on two week courses on Swarm Robotics and Biofashion. There is a price tag, of course, but no more expensive than a music summer course at the Royal Conservatoire, for example. Senior pupils now do a two-week interdisciplinary design project with complex challenges to solve collaborately.

Support for learning is based around the individual and what they need at KA. Large number of long-serving staff, some of 30 years, reaching retirement. Small management team, two out of seven female; both senior teachers in the junior school female.

Dedicated teacher for EAL as plenty of interest from overseas and international flavour in the school. One international parent said: 'KA provided very good English support to the children ... both have been completely integrated during this year with a local boy or girl at the same level.' The Homestay programme allows international students (aged 16–18) to board with school families while studying at KA for one or two years.

Hands-on in the local community. Recently, S6s in the Kelvinside Academy Refugee Organisation (KARO) taught English, off timetable, to the Syrian refugee population in Maryhill, Glasgow. The pupils asked to sit TEFL qualifications and are now TEFL qualified teachers.

Work experience from S4, jobs generally found through family and former pupils network. Not always the case, however: one pupil secured a week film-making with the BBC and another, much further afield, with a gold-mining company in Nicaragua. A school rugby player broke his foot so was working in the library; he noticed a link between two architectural motifs in its design and now works with Scottish Historical Society.

Career education given throughout school life; former pupils still come back for careers advice. Works with company Inspiring Futures, which gives advice until 2023. S6 programme of speakers from different walks of life, as well as business breakfasts (networking for parents and senior pupils) to give exposure to real business people. JP Morgan had stand at parents' evening offering modern apprenticeships (not just for those of a vocational bent), an opportunity to earn a good salary, with day release to achieve a degree.

Games, options, the arts: Rugby and hockey usual favourites, but unusually handball is incredibly popular at KA. While watching handball at 2012 Olympics, pupils were inspired to set up a handball club; now one-third of the Scottish and GB junior handball teams are made up of Kelvinside pupils. Success recently also in rowing, rugby, hockey, windsurfing, judo and shooting.

Outdoor education a priority, starting from nursery through to junior and senior school. Rector says: 'I want to embed outdoor education [similar to Gordonstoun] in the curriculum so that all pupils can be challenged and rejuvenated by nature.' Pupils spend at least a week a year at the new Highland Wilderness Campus in the Cairngorms, climbing, gorge walking, hiking, mountain biking and more. It's also used for weekend courses and D of E, plus maths, science and other mainstream lessons. There's sailing training in z yacht donated to the school; biology teacher is a yachtmaster. Loads of 'first-come-first-served' extracurricular activities on-site from dance to the lunch-time Minecraft club, as well as a shooting range on the roof.

Minibus (which this editor enjoyed a jaunt in) takes younger pupils to the school pavilion and sports grounds at Balgray Campus (for tennis, rugby, hockey, cricket, athletics) – just a short drive away – as well as to local swimming baths and climbing centre, and for mountain biking and canoeing.

Specialist music tuition from junior school. Full-time piano teacher. Variety of music clubs, choirs and orchestras with concerts throughout the year (Christmas and spring concerts, carol singing, open-mic nights, musical theatre nights). KA was highest ranked choir recently at the Glasgow Music Festival, winning the Herald Challenge Trophy.

Drama a popular subject with two sets at S3/S4; available to Advanced Higher. S6 pupil secured a place at the American Acting Academy on a full scholarship. We didn't get to see theatre (as exams were on) but recently staged The Great Gatsby (music by school band), which ran for a week and sold out. J6 show, Robin Hood and the Sherwood Hoodies, was reviewed on BBC Radio Scotland.

Pupils' artworks on display around the school, including sculptures called 'eco farm', representing illegal organ farming. Photography available as a Higher alongside art. Annual art exhibition and cartoon and photography competitions.

High uptake of Duke of Edinburgh (64 per cent bronze, 40 per cent silver, 32 per cent gold) and all S3 pupils must join the CCF, many staying on voluntarily in later years.

Exchange trips to Lancaster Country Day School in Pennsylvania for pupils and teachers, as well as Italy (skiing), Madrid (hockey), Toulouse (rugby), Stirling Castle (junior school) and Malawi to work on irrigation project.

Background and atmosphere: Founded in 1879, the grade A listed building was designed by the renowned Scottish architect James Sellars. Renamed the Kelvinside Academy War Memorial Trust after the First World War; war memorials line the main school stairs. Co-ed since 1998 and includes a nursery and junior school. Impressive nursery, with over 50 children, is based at Balgray playing fields and has iPads in all areas, expressive areas and a 'risky play' area, where children can use real tools (supervised). The forest kindergarten is a 10–15 minute walk away. On our tour we met Fluffy, the bearded dragon, whom the rector was brave enough to hold. Outdoor play area features climbing wall, wooden toys, mud kitchen and eco garden.

Extensively upgraded and modernised for 21st-century learning, the main school building retains its sense of tradition, combined with new additions of modernity, notably the new contemporary, white-washed library in the senior school (with more computers than books) and the Think Tank, inspired by Google, where pupils and teachers can express their thoughts on whiteboard walls. A roof garden, intended as a place for pupils and teachers to reflect, opened in 2017.

Separate sixth year house, in beautiful Victorian building, has two meeting rooms, complete with smartboard – though we waere told, sixth years being sixth years, that 'sometimes it was used to play YouTube videos'. Upstairs is typical student common room, a guidance base for help with UCAS applications and a kitchen. One pupil said: 'We are given a lot of trust, but can lose the house for a week if too noisy.'

Location of this close-knit, middle-sized school couldn't be more apt in Glasgow's West End, with its vibrant mix of students, hipsters and professionals. KA's laidback, modern approach and 'supportive atmosphere' is appealing to parents who wouldn't normally consider independent schooling. One such parent who worried about their kids 'being educated in a privileged bubble' was 'exceptionally happy to have been proven wrong.' The rector concurs, saying KA is 'the antithesis of elitism' (well, as much as it can be for an independent school). 'A lovely relaxed feel at the school', said another parent, where pupils aren't bogged down by horrible amounts of homework. 'Our children have definitely benefitted from the smaller class sizes. They get so much individual attention and that allows us to spend time as a family in the evenings instead of many onerous hours doing homework!' This editor is just a little bit envious.

Local state primaries use facilities. Oodles of charity work including senior pupils working in soup kitchens and tutoring in primary schools in challenging areas; foodbank and guide dog initiatives in the junior school.

Pastoral care, well-being and discipline: Deputy rector in charge of pastoral care and head of year works with form tutors who are the first point of contact for pupils and parents in senior school; class teacher first point of call in junior school. Also fully qualified school counsellor for pupils and staff. Four traditional houses (Buchanan, Colquhoun, MacGregor, Stewart) participate in house competition events and charity initiatives. Smart blue uniform with woollen blazer, tartan skirts for senior girls and pinafores for juniors. Catering offers a set menu each week, which is 'healthy and good value'. Though we did see a kiosk selling fizzy drinks and sweet treats. One parent commented: 'I do struggle with the idea that sweets, chocolates etc are on sale in the school when we are asked to adhere to the school's healthy eating policy.'

Considerable investment made in IT. Only school in Scotland to hold the Scottish Government's digital schools award. Pupils have access to a 3D printer and laser cutter, and all pupils taught to code. A parent said: 'The school has embraced electronic learning and has a clear policy of using technology (in the form of electronic devices) as an effective medium for learning.' Dedicated member of teaching staff for e-learning.

Positive approach to discipline – rector says, '"please don't do that" is generally enough'. Takes considered approach, and contacts parents if needed. A couple of pupils who 'have not been the right fit' have moved to pastures new. No exclusions during Mr M's time as rector.

Pupils and parents: Diverse range of pupils, including some from America, Australia, Malaysia, Hong Kong and Saudi Arabia. Parents generally middle-class professionals who are looking for a holistic approach for their child's education and want to 'nurture child's mind, body and spirit'. Probably not best suited to competitive parents. 'KA is working hand-in-hand with all the parents of the school to jointly raise polite, considerate and confident (without being cocky) individuals.' One parent's impression is: 'The school seems to attract less girls, especially in some years ...' The rector, however, assures that there is a 50:50 split boys to girls.

Each year group has two parents' evening per academic year, a written report, and also 'profiles' (interim reports based on effort and attainment grades). Pupils who require extra support are identified and supported. Parents can get in touch at any time through the year.

Parents have access to the VLE system, where homework and key info (calendar, school reports, profiles) is uploaded. New website with interactive school and sports calendar, which parents can download direct to their phone.

Subsidised school buses run from the north, west and south of Glasgow. All collect in the morning and drop off in the evening.

Notable former pupils: Sir Thomas Risk (lawyer and governor of the Bank of Scotland), Alan Ferguson Rodger, Baron Rodger of Earlsferry (lawyer and Justice of the Supreme Court of the United Kingdom), Richie Gray (Scottish international rugby union player), Gary Smith (news journalist), Brigadier Alastair Stevenson Pearson (one of the most highly regarded soldiers of the Parachute Regiment and the British Army who served in World War 2).

Entrance: Selective school, though not all about academics. Rector told an anecdote about one pupil who said he had weak English but could play the piano. Turned out he was talented pianist and was given a place. Assessments for senior school are given in literacy and numeracy; spend a day at the school taking part in team-building activities and sports assessment. Skype interview and school reports are requested, for those further afield.

Assessment and taster day for junior school. Still selective but automatic progression to senior.

Nursery makes use of partnership funding from government, so some don't go on (for financial reasons) to the junior school.

Waiting list for some year groups in the senior school. S2/S3 and S5 popular years to join, with parents holding off until the exam years.

Exit: No pushing out of weaker links; this school is not all about academics. Rectors says, 'data tracking intervention strategies put in place' and more study sessions or after-school sessions will be organised for those that need support. Majority go on to Scottish universities – Glasgow Caledonian, Edinburgh, Strathclyde, Heriot Watt, Glasgow – with one-third of pupils doing STEM courses. Increasing trend in American universities.

Money matters: Rector knows 'it is expensive and sector needs to think long and hard about affordability'. However, he says at KA 'what you pay is what you get'. Inclusive fees, books all included and doesn't include a development levy. Means-tested bursaries available (around 10 per cent receive them), with a few on full bursaries.

Remarks: Selective, co-ed independent school in grade A listed building in Glasgow's prosperous West End. Provides a holistic approach to education and making innovative strides with its technology and design summer school and outdoor activities centre in the Cairngorms to promote well-being and challenge.

Kilgraston School

Bridge of Earn, Perthshire PH2 9BQ

Ages 5–18 **Pupils** 248 **Sixth form** 66 **Boarders** 76 full, 6 flexi (from 8 years) **RC**

Fees: Day £10,890 – £17,640; Boarding £23,025 – £30,135 pa

01738 812257
www.kilgraston.com

Principal: Since 2015, Dorothy MacGinty, previously head of St Francis' College in Hertfordshire, where she has also been head of biology, head of games, boarding housemistress and deputy head. She is married to Frank and they have three children. Hobbies include playing golf, swimming, theatre, art galleries and spending time with the family.

Head of the junior school: Since September 2017, Anne Fidelo DipEd (from Moray House College, Edinburgh University). Has taught at the Royal High Primary School, Edinburgh Academy and Cargilfield Prep; in between, has headed a kindergarten and been head of junior school at the Banda School, both in Nairobi.

K

Academic matters: Unusually for a Scottish boarding school, Kilgraston works within the Scottish education system. That means that apart from offering one A level (in art), all other qualifications are Highers and Advanced Highers. Mrs MacGinty says this is a careful choice on the part of the school as they believe the two year long A level system suits boys better than girls. Also the Scottish system offers a much broader spectrum and doesn't narrow down the girls' choices too early on. 'The girls make their UCAS applications at the end of lower sixth and if they change their mind, they can pick up different subjects in upper sixth. So it's such more flexible.'

Although the girls don't sit any public exams during their first two years of senior school, S1 and S2, the school has introduced the Kilgraston Diploma. This involves a mixture of academic achievement, community service, learning a new skill and some outdoor pursuits activities, and it is based on the five goals of the Sacred Heart (faith in God, respect for intellectual values, social awareness, community building and personal growth). Mrs MacGinty says, 'We think it gives them focus and helps to introduce them to the school ethos. We're a Catholic school, and we are actively providing a Catholic education to girls of any faith and of no faith.'

One parent we spoke to said the academic side was one thing that the school did extremely well. 'They seem to know how to handle girls. It's very relaxed, but they have a good instinct for when to start applying a little bit of pressure.'

Psychology and computer science recently added to the curriculum. The school clearly has a strong science department as they regularly send 40 per cent of upper sixth to university to study STEM subjects. Head says time and again statistics show that girls in a single sex school are more likely to choose STEM subjects than if they are in a co-ed environment. Languages are well catered for too, with Latin taught all the way through and regular exchange opportunities through the Sacred Heart network.

In fact, performance in all academic areas seems equally strong and this is borne out by the Higher and Advanced Higher results. In 2018, 42 per cent A grades at Advanced Highers. As for their Higher results, 55 per cent A grades.

Learning support is free and is covered by a specialist unit (CReSTed WS) with dedicated teachers for dyslexia and other learning difficulties. The head of learning support is an educational psychologist (which we assume saves going outside for testing). Twenty-five per cent of the girls at the school have some kind of learning support. This includes regular one-to-one teaching and small groups, although normal class sizes rarely exceed 12. The school layout, with many stairs, is not ideal for children with mobility issues, but head says, 'We have two girls with cerebral palsy and we have adjusted the environment and the timetable eg language lessons are brought down to the ground floor.'

Games, options, the arts: Mrs MacGinty says, 'Sport is huge here. Very important to the school as a whole,' and the facilities on offer are certainly impressive. Three Astro pitches, an impressive 25m pool, lots of grass pitches, equestrian facilities. 'We're the only school in Scotland with its own equestrian centre. We run the Scottish championships for dressage, show jumping and cross-country.' Currently seven ponies at livery at the school plus 16 school ponies which anyone may ride, and around 40 per cent of pupils do so.

From fifth form (15 years old) they start choosing what they want to do in PE: eg zumba, fencing, yoga, climbing wall, karate, archery, Scottish country dancing, skiing. Hockey, netball, rounders, tennis and swimming are the main inter-school competitive sports (although one parent told us it was far too much 'hockey, hockey, hockey'). Director of sport is an Olympian who captained the British hockey team at the Sydney Olympics. (She has an MBE for contribution to Scottish sport, hockey in particular.) Head says, 'We invest a lot in sport.'

We loved our tour of the arts and music areas at the top of the main building. Our enthusiastic tour guides (one had just secured a scholarship to Edinburgh School of Art) were brimming with information. Lots of impressive artwork and a busy practice schedule was clearly underway in the music department which nestles, quite literally, under the eaves of this impressive building. Plenty of scope here to play with jazz club, fiddle group, brass and wind ensembles, sing in chamber choir...the list is endless.

And for relaxation and fun there are plenty of clubs eg chess, Chinese culture, ethos club and, rather charmingly, the Jane Austen Film Club (bet Colin Firth and his wet shirt feature.).

Mrs MacGinty says they've been working on getting the whole school to be as outward looking as possible. 'We've established a link with a school in India – pupils are going out there for the first time in October. We chose it because it's a Hindu school. We've been working on understanding geographical differences in immunisation projects. We want them to open the girls up to different issues that affect different societies.'

Boarding: Very small boarding numbers. There are three boarding houses: juniors in Butterstone, most in large rooms with dividers so each has her own space; 13-16 year olds in Mater each with a single room each with washing facilities; 16-18s in Barat or Swinton. Wifi access is moderated. School stops at 4.10pm on a Friday, but there are masses of activities to keep them all busy – from theatre trips to dog sledding. Charming and well-used chapel, which is obviously important in a Sacred Heart School.

Background and atmosphere: Founded in 1930, Kilgraston is one of a 200 strong network of schools and colleges within the Society of the Sacred Heart. Vast, grand, Palladian style mansion with stunning stairway and upper entrance hall. That said, the atmosphere is far from stuffy. 'We have one daughter, aged 15, who still hangs upside down from trees at Kilgraston. Our other daughter wants the full Kardashian birthday party. It really seems to cater for all.' We certainly found the girls charming, relaxed and quite confident. No self-conscious hair flicking or tinkling laughs here. They seemed very relaxed about how they looked and talked. Quite happy to be hearty. The grounds are lovely and secluded with plenty of space to roam around.

'A number of schools have gone co-ed,' says Mrs MacGinty, 'but I think the value of girls' schools is underestimated. It's about promoting confidence and inner resilience. Our girls will take risks in leadership because they don't have the boys here. They have space to develop all those skills that they might be more reticent to try out at a co-ed school.'

The junior school is situated in a brilliantly converted stable block with a glazed central atrium. It's increasingly being run on forest school principles, which encourage the girls to get outside as much as possible. Numbers have been dropping recently, however; the nursery has closed, and there has been some parental concern over composite classes. Mrs MacGinty assures us that this is only a temporary issue, however, and future numbers are on the rise.

'We introduced composite classes for P4 and P5 last year, as well as a composite P1, 2 and 3 class, and the rumour mill suggested we were going to have composite classes further up, but that's not true. Top class P7 is going to be two separate classes because the numbers have grown.' So not bursting at the seams. It will be interesting how the junior school fares under its newish head.

Pastoral care, well-being and discipline: Would you be surprised if we told you Kilgraston has its own BFG? In fact it has a whole load of them. Nothing to do with giants, you understand, but instead a fantastic buddy system to help younger girls. (Big Friendly Girl, in case you were wondering.) We actually saw it in action as one of our tour guides was nearly felled by a little person hugging her BFG.

The school stresses that the girls get plenty of interaction with the opposite sex. Many of the girls have brothers at Merchiston and there are regular joint social events – debating as well as parties. (Lucky Merchie boys as they are the social foils for Edinburgh girls' school St George's as well.)

The girls are divided into houses and there are house meetings or year group meetings every Friday morning. Tutor meetings every Tuesday and regular PHSE sessions. Social studies in the sixth form also covers age relevant well-being topics. One big school concern is the amount of stress girls are under through social media. 'We drum home the message that appearance is not important. We want to motivate them, celebrate their achievements. We don't want them to feel under pressure.'

Pupils and parents: Boarders from around 14 different countries worldwide, but the majority of the girls are from Scotland (many from Perthshire). A good number of first time buyers. Although the school is RC, there are plenty of non-Catholics.

Entrance: No entrance exam. Mrs MacGinty meets every girl and her parents to make sure that they're offering the right style of education. Then a report and reference from the previous school.

Exit: The school is proud of its record in getting their girls into Scottish universities eg Edinburgh, Glasgow, Dundee. In 2018, two-thirds off to study STEM subjects, including veterinary sciences in Poland.

Money matters: Up to 10 academic, art and music scholarships. Also riding, tennis and sporting scholarships. Almost one quarter receive assistance of some sort. School is 'good at finding trust funding' for those who have fallen on hard times.

Remarks: Kilgraston occupies a unique place in Scottish education as the only all girls' boarding school north of the border and the only public school to adhere to the Scottish education system. And it seems to suit them. They get good results and provide a non-pressurised, relaxed, sporty, happy and non-overtly religious atmosphere for their girls.

Knox Academy

Pencaitland Road, Haddington, East Lothian EH41 4DT

Ages 11–18 **Pupils** 737 **Sixth form** 77

01620 823387
www.ka-net.org.uk

Head teacher: Since August 2018, Susan Cook, previously acting head at Trinity Academy in Edinburgh. With a background in PE, she has also worked at Drummond Community High School, Leith Academy and Tynecastle Academy.

Academic matters: Keen on Curriculum for Excellence, the school is inclusive. Thirty pupils per class, 20 for practical stuff, and streaming in maths. (Busy maths club, popular with high flyers.) Does well – strategies in place throughout.

S3 pupils have the choice of including literacy, numeracy or The Prince's Trust (which covers both, but includes life skills, independence and team work) as part of their personal curriculum at National 4 level. Massive choice at S4, including practical woodworking and hospitality (practical cookery). Oddly enough, not a lot of take up in computer games design. Otherwise, expect the usual subjects, with alternatives of enterprise and employability, personal development and volunteering – to be chosen with advice from tutor. Refreshing to find a school where academic attainment is not the be all and end all.

Three dedicated guidance staff, plus two learning support; help in class if needed. Pupils with mild(ish) SEN are catered for. SEN and guidance staff work together and share a bright passage of individual rooms; pupils with special needs 'do not necessarily attend all classes,' special computers with huge type available for the visually challenged and laptops to help the dyslexic. Mixture of 'learnings' on hand, with support either on an individual basis or in class. Youth worker provides pupils support to deal with 'any difficulties' and 'help and support transition into the real world'. Inclusion and integration is the name of the game. Deaf, registered blind (striped pillars) and wheelchair friendly.

No particular bias academically. French and Latin only (the very occasional trip to Rome) in the language department, occasional odd lang clubs – depends on staff interest. English and maths essential for all at all grades. School has been working towards the new curriculum for five or six years and – unlike smaller establishments – embraces National 4 and 5 with enthusiasm.

Impressive list of Highers, including administration, business management, music and religious, moral and philosophical studies. Also available at Advanced Higher level, along with a host of other options. This is a school that caters well for the academic and the ordinary mortal. Pupils list five out of 23 subjects offered in order of preference, with a couple of reserves: a timetabling nightmare, but how sensible. Optional Easter holiday revision weeks at all levels. In 2018, 37 per cent As, 66 per cent A-Bs at Higher (S5), 27 per cent As, 50 per cent A-Bs (S6).

Raft of computers – 40 in the computer department, a further 60 in the business education department, more in the jolly library, which has rather noisy air conditioning and also houses the careers department, plus a couple of laptop trollies. The careers officer comes once a week and pupils can either just pop in or make an appointment for one-to-one consultation.

Games, options, the arts: PE timetabled and on offer to Higher level – huge following. Games fields on site, all the usual suspects – rugby popular, volleyball, basketball, hockey, netball, girls' and boys' footie teams and golf (one chap currently on the East Lothian fast track and more than 100 volunteered to pick rubbish at the Open at Muirfield). Badminton courts, climbing wall, fives court. School currently swims in the local Aubigny centre and does remarkably well in competitions – good support from the East Lothian sports development officers. Physical activities coordinator based in the school manages the huge (and we mean huge) outdoor education department. Outstanding athletes on the sports leadership skills work programme get time off to train.

Sixth formers have a team building weekend early in the year, and pupils not on exam leave have an activities week: from extreme sports to visits to Paris, the Alps, Italy and London, day trips to Edinburgh, the Dynamic Earth, spooky Mary King's Close or the Science Museum in Glasgow. Italy, Prague, Amsterdam on the cards, with seniors heading to New York in a couple of years and 30 off to China for a month. Home-based options include hospitality and fishing; digital films have rather fallen by the wayside. Myriads of trips abroad; Young Explorers' Trust et al, DofE and sixth year do an hour's community service each week.

Superb music in the old building. Musicians give two concerts annually, oodles of orchestras, choirs, and bands. Popular pipe band. Drama, panto at Christmas and well-used dance studio. Stunning art department – good selection of paintings in view. Magical and inspirational fabric and hatting department, plus ceramics and all the rest. Home economics equally buzzing – the smell of newly-baked bread was mouthwatering. School seriously into Europe – representatives went to the first Youth Eco-Parliament in Berlin. The Alice Burnett twinning scholarship is popular and school encourages languages via a language week (the whole school goes French, Italian or Latin for the week). Good links with France, Italy, Finland, Sweden and now Rwanda. School recently gained its second British Council International School Award, the first Scottish school so to do.

Citizenship course is 'part and parcel of the curriculum.' School council has a training day for all, with proper speakers and a grown up agenda. All do work experience at S4 (the school has a core list of placements if pupils can't find their own). Pupils have to write letters of application and go through the whole gamut – excellent practice (though Knox will step in if all else fails – and will even supply steel-capped boots, if that is what it needs). No charge, unlike some schools south of the border.

A few years back, the school won the BBC Schools' Question Time and pupils were involved in producing a televised programme. Good YE extends as far as 13-year-olds, who have moved on from decorating flowerpots to board games. Always tried out on the head first. Profits go to charity – school is keen on 'the big traditional charities' like UNICEF and locally they support the sick kids' hospital.

Background and atmosphere: The most recent in a line of education establishments in Haddington, dating back to 1379. The previous school, dedicated to John Knox at the end of the 19th century, still boasts a statue of him in the grounds and has been converted into sheltered housing for the elderly, some of whom may have come here in their youth. School moved to its present site in the 1930s – loads of additions since. The assembly hall, bigger before the recent additions, is currently 'ealth and safety-ed' at 500.

Blue new-build looks spectacular (cleverly organised so that the gym and sports hall will be available to locals), with access to the dining hall. Food here is good – healthy eating a priority (eat your heart out, Jamie Oliver), though to be honest, the cooked menu was a little drear; salad bar and sandwiches. Regular exposure to different cultures. Thai food for all, Dim Sum for a day.

Dress code for all – white shirts, school ties and black trousers or skirts, black jeans now an acceptable alternative. School blazers mandatory for S5 and S6, gold braiding for prefects.

Pastoral care, well-being and discipline: Twelve minutes each morning for all with their tutor, short messages and encouragement. School is keen on mantra of wisdom, engagement, respect. Tutors emphasise responsibility and attainment – pupils should try to 'punch above their weight.' Strong on service, volunteering. Equally strong on discipline, with letters home to parents and detention the ultimate deterrent.

Pupil points system where pupils can gain or lose points and receive certificates once a certain level has been reached. Pro-active anti-bullying strategy – zero tolerance. Zero tolerance too on the drugs front (not so sleepy Haddington has a fairly hefty problem). Sixth formers do a buddying routine with first year pupils, and keep a watchful eye for the dreaded b...y word.

Pupils and parents: Eclectic, though predominantly white middle class, like its catchment. A mixture of East Lothian farmers (usually well founded), the butcher, the baker, the candlestick maker, plus a home-grown cache of third generation unemployed and a recent influx of Eastern Europeans. Certain number of recent refugees from the independent sector.

School conceals a 'long demographic' – real deprivation in some areas (school has funds to assist with emergency clothing, allowing those who absolutely can't afford it to join in activities week, with help from John Watson's Trust). Surprising nine per cent on free dinners. Around 80 to 90 in S5 and S6 qualify for the weekly £30 EMRA payment (means-tested and quite complicated).

Supportive parent-school partnership and KASG (Knox Academy Support Group), an excellent and effective fundraising initiative. Parents' evening once a year for each year group.

Entrance: Automatic from King's Meadow Primary, St Mary's Roman Catholic Primary in Haddington, ditto Yester Primary in Gifford. The rest by placement requests (a lot of those).

Youngsters come for a couple of taster days the term before they are due to start. Head wishes there was some way of keeping cusp birthday children in primary for another year to help them develop with their peers.

Exit: Good follow through from S4 to S5 (around 90 per cent) and from S5 to S6 (about 80 per cent). Up to half go to university – mostly Scottish.

Remarks: Excellent. No adverse comments from any of our contacts. So go for it, but make sure you are in the catchment area first, and watch it, the catchment area shrinketh.

Lathallan School

Brotherton Castle, Johnshaven, Angus DD10 0HN

Ages 6m–18 **Pupils** 191 **Sixth form** 12 **Boarders** 10 full, 9 weekly, 13 flexi (from 10 years)

Fees: Day £10,959 – £18,930; Boarding £23,466 – £25,950 pa

01561 362220
www.lathallan.org.uk

Headmaster: Since 2009, Richard Toley BA MPhil PGCE (40s), who joined Lathallan in 2006 as director of co-curriculum from nearby High School of Dundee. Degree from St David's Lampeter, MPhil from St Andrews and PGCE from Strathclyde. He and his wife live on site, with their young now in school.

A historian, charming and relaxed, Toley teaches classics (as in classical studies) and history in the senior school, and runs school with senior school head, Duncan Lyall BSc PGCE (40s), an Edinburgh lad, and James Ferrier BA (Cantab) PGCE (50s), head of junior school since 2011, having first come to school in 2001 from Moor Park in Shropshire.

Lyall, who read mechanical engineering at Edinburgh, is married with a brace of young, and came to Lathallan from Peebles High, having previously taught in both the borders and Aberdeen.

Ferrier lives on campus with his wife, was educated at Hardyes School, Dorset, read humanities of Christ Church, followed by PGCE at the University of Kent, and runs his part of the Lathallan empire with gentle humour.

Impressive collection of uber-powerful governors plus parent governors, 'tremendous backing'.

Academic matters: Scottish curriculum: 17+ subject options at all levels. Reticent about exam results but some 75 per cent got three or more Highers and 39 per cent five Highers in 2018. Non-selective and for some a C or a D may be a real achievement.

Variety pack of langs on offer – Mandarin – whenever (number of native speakers in school) plus French (from P1) and Spanish (S1) (native speakers). Not a lot of take-up in the former, though occasional outstanding results at all levels. Pupils study both French and Spanish throughout S2 before opting for one or t'other for Nat 5s.

Latin from aged 11 (classical studies at Higher and Advanced Higher), crash course in Italian (ab initio) – offered at Higher level, but no take-up – plus the usual suspects: maths, English, three sciences, history, geography (pleasing and popular), business and classical studies, art, PE and drama, and managing environmental resources (MER). This is penny number stuff, occasional glitch.

Civilianship the latest addition – ie how to open doors, ladies first, that sort of thing; school is talking to exam boards as to how they could make this an examinable subject. Think finishing schools, think nanny, think how clever.

All assessed for dyslexia et al on arrival. Two dedicated learning support staff, one-to-one, clusters, or co-teaching, throughout school. Costs the same as a piano lesson. Back-up for the bored and the brightest. Class sizes around 13 (max 16), pupils streamed for maths and English both taught in refurbed classrooms in the castle, interactive whiteboards all over.

IT impressive – Dell computers plus Apple Macs in senior school. iPads for all seems to be the current flavour of the month (last time we did a round up it was the 'virtual learning experience'). Only for those in the dyslexia stream at Lathallan. We were told that Toley 'was not convinced' by rolling 'em out across the board.

Science still in a hotch-potch of temporary buildings beside the nursery complex: but zinging new science centre (as ever, near the nursery complex). We have a natty brochure with pics, showing three dedicated science labs plus one for environmental study and junior science lab. Plus accessible loos, shower – got to have 'em now and pupil inspired 'treehouse' (to enhance outdoor learning experiences). Impressive sounding new head of science from Cults Academy.

Staff whom we have met are young, enthusiastic and fun. Peris pulled in for the more esoteric subjects (or instruments). No apparent problem in attracting staff, particularly in the current financial climate, when property prices have in some quarters reached basement level. The Aberdeen catchment area was pricey.

Games, options, the arts: Music everywhere – bagpipe boxes all over the porch and hall, both girls and boys in pipe bands much in demand for charities and have entertained Princess Anne of late, played in the Angus show, the Glamis gathering, the Scottish Parliament etc. Pipes and drums played at the battlefields in Belgium during the Great War memorial year and compete in the Royal Pipe Band competitions with success. Scottish country dancing no longer has parental input; marvellous photographs in the porch of a junior Scottish country dancing lesson – note the kilt loops and the ecstasy on the faces of the young. Strong drama: new head of music previously with Aberdeen Youth Theatre; no orchestra per se (yet) but wind and ceilidh bands.

Toley has introduced a new formal school-wide traditional PE programme, which 'through age-appropriate indoor exercises aims to improve co-ordination and mental agility both in and outside the academic classroom' (sounds a tad Steiner-ish). School thinks this sounds harsh. 'We have a real focus on sports/PE and outdoor education but this sounds almost military'. 'We realise the importance of exercise.' 'We want our pupils to be well-rounded by participating in PE/sports and outdoor ed.'

Thrashing all comers in under-16 rugby 7s, new games pavilion (board member head of SRU). All 7+ year olds play sport daily, tennis courts double up for netball (Astroturf), 10 acres of playing field overlooking the North Sea and own beach (bracing), plus refurbished gym. Lots of jolly rugby trips and netball tours. Sea at the bottom of the garden, but no sea sports – too rough. Impressive games area adjacent to junior/baby school. Astro: tennis: you name it; plus dedicated gym (though hall in main school building equally adaptable).

Head of outdoor education is Monro-potty, 'probably climbed them all three times,' says Toley. DofE timetabled and huge numbers – school claims 'highest percentage of participation in the DofE scheme in all of the country (Scotland)'.

First two years of senior school spend six days in the mountains, mountain rescue, navigation (shades of Round Square). Skiing, both at home and abroad for all. Huge emphasis on outdoor education, self-resilience, and leadership training. Newish 50 foot long zip wire in the wood (100 foot drop). Scary. Six pupils and guides did an unsupported, exploratory exped to Eastern Greenland. (Scary again). Recent trip to Iceland has even more scary photos.

ISCO (careers guidance) enrolment (as ever) and ongoing advice as to 'what happens next'.

Boarding: Influx of foreign boarders since full boarding reopened: 30 boarders housed in separate wings of the castle (previous staff quarters), co-ed boarding tidily arranged, mainly oil-y children, from Thailand, China, Spain, Nigeria, Russia. Scottish Guardian Overseas Association oversees them (and individual guardians have to pick up the flack if their charges are sent 'home', ie gated). Some locals, bed and breakfasting available. ESOL on hand to help with language glitches. Interesting to see whether boarding numbers hold up during current oil turn-down.

Background and atmosphere: Founded in the imposing Victorian Brotherton Castle (1867) in the early 1930s. Originally trad boys' boarding prep school, set in 62 acres of woodland which catered for 'the folk over the hill'; now a thriving nursery (handful of real babes being pushed out in three prams when we visited; good North Sea air) through to Advanced Highers co-ed offering full, weekly or flexi-boarding (from age 10).

Regular exchange programmes with 'smallish' schools in Canada, Switzerland and Australia; the latter were enjoying their six weeks in Angus during a previous visit. More than 25 clubs; 'we rotate them,' says Toley.

William Bruce house-lets (which pre-date the castle) guard corners of the long abandoned formal garden which makes a splendid play area. Library and resource centre in main building with classrooms and nursery in bright converted stable block with massive additions (and home to new science build but see above). Some lessons in temporary classrooms. Irritating steps both too shallow and too wide link the two sites. Nursery/junior wing surrounded by play/games areas, stunning nursery playground. Collection of toddler sized loos and mini basins: one wonders how they cope at home.

Newly refurb'ed common room for senior school pupils. School uniform provided in house, with jolly fleecy waterproof jackets which staff wear too. Staff all have to take the minibus test.

L

Pastoral care, well-being and discipline: School small enough for every child to be known (cherished is a word that comes to mind if it didn't sound so soppy), strong anti-bullying policy. Occasional gatings for wickedness, no child yet asked to leave. School is 'bespoke, focused'.

Pupils and parents: Increasing number of first time buyers. FPs supportive, strong parental input, parents will drive many miles out of their way to drop off their tinies in the nursery. Return buses for older children from Stonehaven, Edzell and Aberdeen with coaches from Brechin, Forfar and Montrose.

Aberdeen business community plus local farmers, commuters, usually from within 90 minute radius (which takes you to Dundee). Rob Wainwright an old boy (and does the odd spot of coaching), ditto Ian Lang (Lord Lang of Monkton).

Niche school: perfect for the occasional non-performing refugee from bigger trad schools: Fettes, Merchiston, Robert Gordons. Children thrive in the smaller environment. 'We care'. (Those parents to whom we spoke fell into the latter category. Their relief was palpable.)

Entrance: Lathallan nursery: from six weeks, 80 tinies registered but no more than 49 at any one time. Entrance to junior school seamless from nursery test-ette for problems and 'nearly all go' (95 per cent). Juniors are checked 'carefully' and if problems obvious, they get a 'proper test'.

Entry to senior school at any time to any year group if places available, many come via junior school. Otherwise form 5 (P7: 11, 12 year olds). Taster day. Informal tests in English, maths and verbal reasoning, but not a selective school. Numbers up from prep school, 10/12 a year. Currently full first three years of senior school (and nursery and pre-junior school ie ages 5 and 6).

Exit: Tiny trickle leave for trad independents age 13, occasional departure age 8, otherwise the odd relocation. Some 75 per cent of leavers from the tiny sixth form to university, mostly Scottish: St Andrews, Edinburgh, Aberdeen, Heriot Watt, Stirling and Glasgow.

Money matters: Money matters 'under control', up to 100 per cent bursaries (and extra help if necessary): huge raft: academic, sports, rugby 7s, netball, music and pipes and drums. Sibling discount. Secondhand clothes shop. Will keep child if parents fall on hard times with the usual caveat of being up front about the problem.

Lathallan nursery in partnership with Aberdeen County council (discounts). Hours roughly 7.30am to 6pm but check fee structure, deeply expensive if child not collected by designated time (emergency cover and charged by the quarter hour). This is a 50 week nursery with two weeks off for Christmas.

Remarks: This is the tail that wagged the dog. We have visited Lathallan over the past 20 odd years: six headmasters. This was a school which had – quite frankly – been toiling. Sometimes it had a nursery which took babes from 2 months, sometimes from 3 years. In any case it was a boys' boarding prep school with an increasingly dismal roll call (even after they took girls and day pupils) and a glorious view. Two (or was it three?) heads ago, the brave decision (we thought nuts) was made to expand, on a year by year basis, to become a fully fledged school, with Highers and Advanced Highers and all. We were wrong. Very wrong (and we won't rehearse further the various decisions down the line). Remarkable success story which keeps on growing.

Lenzie Academy

Myrtle Avenue, Kirkintilloch, Lenzie, East Dunbartonshire G66 4HR

Ages 11–18 **Pupils** 1,168 **Sixth form** 130

01419 552379
www.lenzieacademy.e-dunbarton.sch.uk

Head teacher: Since 2011, Brian Paterson BA PGCE (mid 50s), previously head of Abronhill High. Educated at Paisley Uni, his PGCE was in modern studies and economics at Jordanhill. He taught in Glasgow and Lanarkshire before doing eight years as principal teacher, firstly in Harris Academy, Dundee and then in Boclair Academy, East Dunbartonshire, where he also spent seven years as depute head teacher. He has been a marker and setter for SQA, an educational consultant for the BBC and a writer of educational materials.

From a Glasgow background where pupils left school at 16 and university was not an option, he was grateful to the teachers who encouraged him and wants to give something back, feeling it is his civic duty. Not attracted to a more lucrative career though he once 'wobbled for 10 minutes'. Life is now pretty full on at school – recently included being the murder victim in an ASDAN project – so down time is spent mainly as a taxi driver for his children, one still in primary and one in sixth form, both in East Renfrewshire plus a daughter at Strathclyde. He likes to play football twice weekly in the staff seven-a-side club but getting away for some hill-walking at weekends is a bit of a pipe dream. Having run an academic school at Abronhill he sees himself as having taken on the challenge of making a school with a pretty distinguished record into something of real excellence. His go-ahead SMT of six deputes are unlikely to allow many bottoms to get stuck on laurels. Very clear on priorities, he will not waste energy on problems that are likely to resolve themselves or are not resolvable.

The immediate plan is a £650,000 facelift – a complete paint job (not before time); school is also being comprehensively re-roofed and getting new doors for all entrances and the tired looking football/hockey pitch outside the school is getting new all-weather surface. He is strengthening the house system, giving pupils more responsibilities and making things more competitive in the academic sense, not just in sport. Tracking and monitoring are being sharpened up so he can quickly spot weak areas or potential failings. Longer term he wants to build up drama and has his eye on how to make more studio space, if funds permit. Grass will certainly have no chance under his purposeful feet.

Academic matters: Classes currently at 30, with eight forms per year group (capped at 240). Uses the Scottish SQA system – in 2018, 57 per cent got 5+ Highers at A-C by the end of S6, with 24 per cent getting six; 36 per cent of S6 got at least one Advanced Higher at A-C. Impressive range of subjects on offer, even in comparison with the best of the independent sector. Most teaching areas a bit trad to look at but some top notch equipment everywhere. Nice to see similar numbers of boys and girls in Higher design and engineering, however battered the benches. They clearly know their own minds.

Plenty of pupils do three sciences at S grade, while the bulk do two and no one is allowed to get away without one. All do one modern foreign lang to S4, currently French, Spanish or German, though no Latin, Italian or eg Mandarin, even in clubs. The advantage of size is that there are over 30 subjects on offer for S5/6 many of them at four different levels: Advanced Higher, Higher, National 4 and 5. This range is further increased by distance learning, so there isn't much limit to what you can do, especially as flexibility includes letting pupils take subjects at other local schools if the timetable won't fit. Plugged into Strathclyde and Heriot Watt's SCHOLAR learning programmes and into the local consortium.

A magnet school – pupils from other (state) schools come to Lenzie to study Highers and Advanced Highers not available in their own. Stunning computer studies results at all levels and the school has a record of jolly good results over a number of years in maths, all three sciences, art and design and health and food technology. Interactive whiteboards much used. Results, already pretty spot on, have generally improved in response to tighter monitoring and academic mentoring programmes.

SEN well staffed – monitoring is good and still improving. A supportive culture in school includes a scribes' and readers' club. Provisions vary from year to year as children with severe difficulties, either physical or intellectual, attract appropriate help. This is a totally inclusive school by ethos.

Over 100 pupils do not have English as their first language (speaking 31 different languages) and extra help and EAL are available. Homework club at lunch time and super supported study scheme post-school – 200 pupils regularly stay on – when pupils can access the ICT suites.

Games, options, the arts: Apart from a huge – though not as huge as originally planned – games hall and two pitches on site a grass rugby pitch (soon to be replaced by a 4G pitch with floodlighting) and a 3G pitch, provision looks a bit limited but the school uses local club pitches five minutes away to impressive effect and offers all the usual sports, with some enthusiastic players including a national athletics champion. The school has been an SRU School of Rugby for the past four years; there is a dance studio also. Lots of way out stuff too: outdoor education, a successful sailing club and even collie racing. Huge numbers of extracurricular activities.

Art department is very go ahead with Higher photography course, portraiture with a real artist, and masses of work going on with colour. Vibrant displays in the art rooms and some smashing mosaic murals all over the school to brighten it up. Vocational courses in tourism, textiles, hospitality, metalwork, retailing, health and so on, there's even one in cake decoration; all put on as serious opportunities for all abilities in Scotland's current economic climate.

Music is big too with plenty of classical and quite a few groups on the performance side and academic on offer up to Advanced Higher. No pipe band but plenty of electronics just coming in despite the expense. Huge production every year with Guys and Dolls the most recent.

Background and atmosphere: Unremarkable 1960s buildings, now looking distinctly retro, date from when the school moved to a roomier site from a square set, stone building in Lenzie, which is now the primary school. Pleasant brick court in one wing with a sadly run down garden (but grass won't grow there, we were assured); inside corridors are wide and classrooms really light and spacious. The other wing has such narrow passages that a one-way system is essential but it's brightened by the work and info put up by various academic departments. Lenzie hasn't had the benefit of the funds lavished on its snazzy neighbours in Bearsden and Kirkintilloch, but there's lots of ground around the school for development and already an inviting patio for sitting out, when the Scottish weather allows.

Nice smart new dining hall with gallery for social use and carrels for study, plus every possible device to make it a multifunctional centre. No pre- or post-school cafeteria, though the area is open to early comers from 8.15am and school is open til 6pm or so when community use starts.

Main hall is desparately dingy but brightened up on our visit by a comprehensive Hopes for the Future inter-disciplinary learning display from an S2 project. Terrific programme of renovation is ongoing but the formerly plentiful 'glory holes' have been eradicated and there are endless lockers everywhere.

Pastoral care, well-being and discipline: Guidance is done in forms and a teacher stays with the class as it goes up the school. The six deputes are year heads and meet with the guidance teacher once a month to discuss every member of each class thoroughly. Not much need to use the bullying code but it's there and the occasional fight calls for extreme sanctions – mainly expulsion for a day or so. The number of exclusions has fallen significantly in recent years. Behaviour guidelines classify bad behaviour in three levels; the third gets a 'demerit' reported to parents and if Mr Paterson gets his way this will also go into competitive house records.

Mr Paterson is tightening up uniform and there's a smart new (remarkably inexpensive) navy blazer with green braid and new school badge (the old one was all wrong and blazers were baggy). We saw a few coloured hairdos and nose rings and some very short skirts. Everyone seems to wear just about anything for games.

Pupils and parents: The pupils we met were polite and quiet and staff friendly and concerned. There are pupil councils for each year group consisting of two pupils from each class and this is being co-ordinated with house councils which will help socialising to be through all age groups.

Quite a large proportion come from ethnic minorities, since local universities attract staff from abroad. Majority of parents from the locality and 'leafy Lenzie' is fairly upmarket. Parents are supportive and run a Friends of Lenzie Academy (FOLA 125) which does a great job raising funds for the school. The Parent Council is supportive of the school's activities and developments.

Entrance: Entry is capped at 240, of which usually 130 or so are locals. Some apply from outside the area which now includes part of a huge newly built estate, most of which is outside the actual catchment area but so close that those applying are likely to get priority.

Exit: Most pupil stay on until S6, with a few leaving at the end of S4 and S5 (most of the latter early entry university candidates). About 80 per cent to HE/FE, mostly Scottish unis; usually a few to Oxbridge – one in 2018, to study law, plus two medics.

Remarks: A whacking great school with a dynamic head and tremendous possibilities, already doing a grand job for 'leafy Lenzie'.

Lomond School

    37

10 Stafford Street, Helensburgh, Argyll and Bute G84 9JX

Ages 3–18 **Pupils** 400 **Sixth form** 39 **Boarders** Up to 60 (from 10 years)

Fees: Day £7,030 – £11,970; Boarding £27,750 pa

01436 672476
www.lomondschool.com

Principal: Since 2014, Johanna Urquhart, who grew up in Loch Lomond. Previously depute head (academic) at George Watson's College and Breadalbane Academy. She has a degree in maths and statistics, and a masters in education, specialising in leadership and management. Previous roles as maths teacher, head of maths and depute head in the state and independent sector on Scotland's east coast – she says working in Helensburgh 'feels like coming home'.

She visited Lomond before applying for principal's post and 'fell in love with the school'. Her own two children attend. We received a warm welcome from Johanna, who was friendly with a businesslike approach. Pupils described her as 'fair', 'efficient', but 'not afraid to give a telling-off if misbehaving'.

No capital development is planned but her focus is on developing the school's philosophy and values (we were given a compact booklet to explain them). A flow chart outlines the guiding principles of Internationalism, Environmentalism, Adventure, Leadership, Lifelong Learning, Service, 'focusing on the individual' from nursery to S6.

Passionate about adventure and outdoor learning, so much so she appointed a head of adventure and service (playing to the school's strengths in terms of location). Married to local businessman, and a lover of outdoor pursuits: skiing, sailing, water-skiing and travelling.

Academic matters: A few per cent behind Glasgow's big, top-performing independent schools in Highers results, but this is a non-selective school with an open presentation policy but strong academic results nonetheless: 94 per cent take 5+ Highers of which 48 per cent A, 68 per cent A/B in 2018. At Advanced Highers, 41 per cent A, 80 per cent A-B.

Max class size 20ish, under 20 in junior school and smaller class sizes once subjects have been chosen. French is taught from nursery and is required from J5 to S2. Spanish is a core subject from S1/S2, replacing German as lots of pupils were requesting it. Vast majority take a language to Nat 5 level, with small numbers to Higher and Advanced Higher. Principal says school strong in the sciences with STEM subjects popular at Higher and AH. Broad range of subjects with business management and graphic communications on the curriculum, but unusually modern studies (the study of politics, sociology and international relations) not available until Higher as a one-year course. Economics available at Higher.

SEN department in junior and senior school, with head of support for learning offering in-class support and extraction where needed. Number of international students, so EAL support is on hand. Low turnover of staff with some serving as long as 40 years. Refreshingly, 75 per cent of senior management are female.

School has head of careers and future destinations with a programme of careers education as well as individual advice and support for pupils to guide through UCAS, college or work applications.

Games, options, the arts: Brace yourself... don't expect pupils to be humming and hawing to decide between hockey or rugby here. This editor loved the focus on embracing a sense of adventure (how exciting for young kids and young adults): sailing, skiing, climbing and orienteering are all part of the curriculum.

Significant variety of sports for a small school and plenty of success stories, too. Some students play on the Scotland netball team, a cricket internationalist, two S5s in GB sailing squad, the list goes on.. Other outdoor pursuits include water-skiing, wakeboarding and keel boat sailing. Academics are not left out with the philosopher's café and a film and video production club for the creatives.

Playing fields and huge indoors sports hall with climbing wall a short trip down the road in the school minibus. Shared with local community, it also has a dance studio and gym and caters for basketball, badminton, netball and cricket. Archery another option.

Musical productions, driven forward by the head of music, have recently included a senior school production of Guys and Dolls. Two-thirds of the junior school learn a musical instrument and there is an assortment of music clubs: jazz band, sax ensemble, traditional music, orchestras. Small proportion take music to exam level. 'Straight As for those that do at Nat 5 and Higher level.' Drama taught from junior school with a subject specialist. 'Helps develop wider skills, communication and confidence' and goes up to AH. Eleven pupils did Higher drama in 2018.

Clubs are free if run in-house (vast majority). Cost to parents for skiing and a contribution towards maintenance of sailing boats. Wraparound care in the junior school until 6pm.

The outdoors theme continues with art, featuring sailing and the natural environment, displayed around the school. Local landscapes by S4s feature in the principal's office. Higher photography on the curriculum (taught by the art and the physics depts).

DofE very popular. Giving back to the community has seen S6s working on the regeneration of hermitage park and volunteering at the local hospice Robin House.

Boarding: Modern, purpose-built boarding school, opened in 2002. The principal describes Lomond as 'unique' in Scotland, as it's largely a day school with boarding. Between 40-60 boarders, most full time, with a small number of flexi-boarders from age 10 up, but the majority staying over at the weekend. Mix of international boarders as well as some from the Western Isles and military families from the nearby naval base. We heard through the grapevine, however, that cuts in school fees funding for naval base families has affected numbers at the school.

They've gone to great lengths to make boarding house as homely as possible; kids chose the design and colour scheme of common areas. Dining room with themed menus and nights

(Spanish when we visited). Nice big communal areas with computers, pool and table tennis, and outdoor basketball courts at the back. It was empty on our visit as all the boarders were in school, but we did see a cosy (and tidy!) boys' four-bed dorm, home to international students, with clean shared bathrooms in the hall. S4–S6s have their own space on the upper floors with twin and single rooms and en-suite shower rooms. Girls' and boys' rooms are on separate floors with state-of-the-art security system using biometric readers. Tutors on each floor are there to support and supervise. More girls than boys in boarding but balanced in school in general.

Day school friends are welcome to go round and hang out with boarders. The boarding house is just a few minutes' walk away, so boarders can go home, get changed and go back to the school to join in with extracurricular activities. Senior school boarders are given more freedom and are able travel into Glasgow, for example.

All have iPads to Facetime and keep in touch with families, but no phones in corridors during the school day. Office space is available if anyone is missing family or they are on a different time zone. Free time to use phones in the evening, if they don't have an after-school club. Younger ones' phones are taken away before bed time.

Background and atmosphere: On the northern edge of the seaside town of Helensburgh, the present school is an amalgam of Larchfield Academy for Boys, founded in 1845, and St Bride's girls' school, founded in 1895. The schools combined in 1977 and a partial rebuild followed. It is a curious combination of modern and traditional.

The senior school looks deceptively modern from the front and the light-filled entrance is corporate-like, even the carpet branded with a Lomond blue colour scheme. The back of the school harks to the past: the turn-of-the century St Bride's Hall plays home to school musicals, opening its doors to the local community. Nursery and junior school children (up to J5) are taught in the beautiful listed building, Clarendon, which is loved by the parents we spoke to, one saying: 'I have two happy children who skip into school each day, feel valued and are growing in confidence.' Nursery was gorgeous, with wood panelling and a nook with fireplace in the arch. Lots of good old fashioned fun in the playground where children were climbing, running and scoring goals.

Celebrated its 40th anniversary in 2017 and exciting events took place throughout the year, like black-tie dinners in Hong Kong, London and Leipzig as well as a black tie ball in Helensburgh in June as a culmination of the celebrations.

'Friendly and welcoming school' with a 'homely atmosphere'; students describe themselves 'as trying our hardest, being determined and courageous'. Strong links with the naval base and an international boarding community mean it's a multi-cultural environment, which is not usually the case in rural Scotland.

Good local reputation, though a café worker we spoke to said she felt distanced from the school as most people in local area couldn't afford it. Helensburgh, however, is for the most part an affluent area, so many day school kids will be local.

Pastoral care, well-being and discipline: A pastoral care team and depute are in charge of looking after the boarders. School year heads and form teachers are there to lend an ear to parents and pupils. No problems with discipline, but they impose sanctions when needed. Parents can get in touch with teachers or the pastoral team at any time. Three houses have competitions throughout the year, which most of the youngsters get involved in.

S6 pupils can sign out, but the rest are onsite for school meals. Catering service has won awards for healthy eating, though we didn't see dining area at lunch time.

Reports every six weeks and annual written reports as well as weekly newsletter. School FB page is used more than Twitter.

Buses from Killearn, Drymen, Balloch and around the peninsula (paid for by parents). Good local transport links; train is a 10-minute walk from the school.

Pupils and parents: Middle-class parents that are hands-on and organise events throughout the year: the Halloween party, Boden shopping evening, Christmas fair. Mix of local professionals and international military families, as well as the support services and medical professionals connected to the naval base. All pupils wear the smart uniform with blue blazers, with the girls in kilts.

Impressive former pupils include Charlotte Dobson (Olympic sailor) and television inventor John Logie Baird; WH Auden and Cecil Day Lewis briefly taught at the school.

Entrance: Non-selective with open presentation policy. Don't pull weaker links if not going to succeed. Entrance assessment for potential pupils to measure level of support or challenge they may need. Waiting list for T1/T2.

Nursery from age 3 and no entry requirements. Priority goes to those with siblings already at the school. Intake generally from local primaries or people moving to the area. Vast majority move from junior to senior school.

Exit: Majority go to Scottish universities: Edinburgh, Glasgow, Aberdeen, St Andrew's, Herriot-Watt, Dundee. Small numbers do apprenticeships, or move on to college or the work place. STEM subjects and economics currently popular.

Money matters: Food is included in the cost for boarders. Day pupils pay for uniform, lunch, sports kit and transport on top of school fees. Means-tested bursaries available from 5–100 per cent.

Remarks: Seaside independent day school (nursery to senior) with boarding. Non-selective and multi-cultural with strong academic results and brilliant opportunities for outdoor adventure. Popular with naval families based at nearby Faslane as well as local families.

L

Loretto School

1–7 Linkfield Road, Musselburgh, East Lothian EH21 7RE

Ages 3–18 **Pupils** 618 **Sixth form** 132 **Boarders** 135 full, 79 flexi (from 11 years)

Fees: Day £16,980 – £23,325; Boarding £18,960 – £34,260 pa

01316 534444
www.loretto.com

Headmaster: Since 2014, Dr Graham Hawley BSc PhD PGCE. Previously six years as headmaster of Kelly College in Devon. First class honours degree from Durham University (natural sciences). A keen sportsman, he represented Middlesex U18s at cricket. Before his teaching career his scientific research expeditions took him all over the world. He's a thinker but without an ego – clever, articulate and happy in his own skin. Parents report that 'he is very approachable and astute' and greets all the children each morning. Married to Rachel (rave reviews from parents, 'she's terrific – bright, friendly and observant') with two teenage young.

Pupils tell us that on his appointment as headmaster he worked at the coalface, at all hours of the day (and night), alongside the teachers, cleaners, groundskeepers and the catering teams to establish exactly how the school ticked. Smart move, as it also earned him a great deal of respect from his pupils.

Head of junior school: Since August 2018, Andrew Dickenson, previously head of junior school at Kelvinside Academy. MA (50s); studied modern history at University of St Andrews. Started off teaching career in London in early 1990s, then The Edinburgh Academy Junior School (deputy head). Passionate about promoting digital learning across the school as well as outdoor learning. Married with two grown-up daughters.

Academic matters: Senior school follows the English education system of GCSEs and A levels. In 2018, 37 per cent A*/A grades at A level and 40 per cent A*-A/9-7 at GCSE. Results have stepped up recently despite still being a 'broadly unselective school'.

Music, drama and PE can be taken at A level and GCSE. Psychology A level a recent introduction. Boy/girl ratio fairly even across all subjects possibly helped by new female head of science. Economics, business and accounting popular A level choices. History and politics department also thriving with excellent record of public examination success. Main modern languages are French and Spanish.

Learning support available throughout junior and senior schools – one learning support teacher plus two assistants. In sixth form support is timetabled on a needs basis.

L

Interactive whiteboards and networked computers throughout. Various societies for brain boxes and those keen to learn more – Reimann Society for those mathematically gifted. Mavor Society – lectures given by the sixth formers on any topic that interests them – an opportunity to extend an academic passion. Excellent visiting speakers each week (recently Olympians Heather Stanning and Steve Cram); pupils spoke about the lectures with real enthusiasm.

Open classroom policy at lunchtime for staff. Senior pupils tell us that there's always someone available to help them with their studies and that the teachers are very approachable. Interview practice for sixth formers and individual support with UCAS personal statements.

Junior school teachers get excellent feedback from the children and parents. 'Nothing is too much effort and if there's a problem or a child needing help they will always sort it out'. One young pupil told us that she liked her maths lessons as it was the first time any teacher 'had made maths fun' for her.

International English Language Testing System (IELTS) available for international pupils who need it.

Games, options, the arts: The junior school uses many of the senior school facilities such as the main theatre, the chapel and the eyeball searing blue Astroturf ('the smurf turf').

Sport is a big deal, with pupils in regional and national teams from rugby to judo. Sport traditional: rugby for boys, lacrosse for girls (specialist coach from the US, and girls represent Scotland at U17 and U19), hockey, tennis and cricket (though boys' cricket teams only) for both. Lots of teams so everyone is included, not just the sporting legends. This inclusion is a double edged sword with some parents thinking it's a huge positive that all children have the experience of playing in a team. One junior school parent commented that 'they don't always put their best teams forward and this is a shame as the teams could be more successful than they are'. However, junior school children mentioned 'sport' as their 'favourite' part of school life and the parents say that 'the children are very proud of their sporting teams and their success'.

And so, to golf. The Golf Academy, established in 2002, is Loretto's USP and is top in Europe, attracting young golfers from around the world. To the east of the school lie the golf courses which provide the fairway for the Academy – Craigielaw and Archerfield; state of the art practice facilities on campus. The Golf Academy indoor centre includes a studio with video analysis and Trackman.

Golf is offered to everyone and is part of PE curriculum for the junior school. In their final two years at the school, the 'senior squad' can choose to play golf as their sole sport. Success rate is high with eight national titles recently. Summer residential golf camps ensure that the school is earning its keep over the holidays while at the same time showcasing its facilities to potential new pupils. Golf scholarships are available and carry a fee reduction of up to 10 per cent of the fees.

Chapel choirs, training choirs, jazz bands, rock bands, chamber ensembles... new groups spring up depending on who wants to play or sing. The junior school choir have been runners up in the BBC Songs of Praise School Choir of the Year competition. The choirs tour regularly in the UK and abroad (Limousin in June – can we all go?) and have made a number of CD recordings. Junior school parents commented that both instrumental and choral music are 'tremendous and taken seriously' and that seen as 'cool', 'all the children want to be in the choir, no coaxing is required'.

However, we hear of slight wobbles in the senior school music department, with parents reporting that the department staff are in 'a state of flux' at the moment, that 'the situation needs sorting out' and that 'music isn't as strong as it used to be or as strong as in the junior school, which is disappointing as it was fantastic'.

Other excitements include the conversion of the old exam hall into a dance studio. Highland, hip hop, ballet and a range of other styles for all ages and growing in popularity (still more with the girls than the boys – Footloose the Musical is coming soon). Highland dancers often accompany the tiptop pipe band to major events. Pipe band has performed with Sir Paul McCartney (twice) and entertained the Pope on his visit to Edinburgh.

Drama workshops include puppetry and stage fighting (small child heaven). Substantial productions in both junior and senior schools. When we visited the junior school was warming up for the end of term production of Treasure Island. Grease paint, bloomers and enthusiastic cutlass wielding in evidence – happy children.

Art department (senior school) has multiple studios and a dark room – pupils can also work with clay, stone and wood. A level students (at present all girls but we are told more boys next year) have their own studio with an art college atmosphere. An abundance of talent evident in the department, but not much on display.

The art room in the junior school is a thing of wonder and clearly run with dollops of passion, skill and imagination. Fantastic creations of every shape and form and much of it displayed around the school. Impressive and outstanding.

Loretto Radio launched in 2009. Children can learn about technical operation, presentation and production skills. Radio presenter from Forth 1 (FM radio station for Edinburgh & East of Scotland) trains small groups of pupils.

Borealis Society for sixth formers offers the opportunity to go on major trekking/academic expeditions to northern areas. Recently the destination was Iceland for five weeks under canvas to climb five of the highest mountains in the country and study birds and Arctic flora. Serious stuff and a major undertaking.

CCF compulsory in fourth form, voluntary later (good take up). Focus on adventure. Army and navy only.

Boarding: Boarding now in the senior school only – full, weekly or flexi (very popular). There's no 'hot-bedding', so even the flexiest of boarders has their own bed.

Sixth form boarders can leave the school grounds at weekends for cinema, shopping, concerts etc. Many of the full time boarders stay with local school friends at weekends but apparently 'staying in' is popular too, with lots of activities and social events organised within the school. This is a 'proper' boarding school (70 per cent of senior school board) but one that takes advantage of its proximity to a major city.

There are six single sex boarding houses, all different in character and with their own distinctive layouts and common areas, plus one co-ed day house. Four boarding houses are for 12-16 year olds, with up to six beds in a room, two for sixth formers, with twin and single rooms and mixed common rooms for socialising.

Background and atmosphere: Founded in 1827, this is Scotland's oldest boarding school. Fully co-ed since 1995. Located in Musselburgh, a small coastal town on the outskirts of Edinburgh. Proximity to the bright lights of Edinburgh works in its favour – pupils can take full advantage of the art galleries, drama and music as well as the opportunities for sport and leisure.

Campus is quite spread out and somewhat disjointed (lots of walking) with the junior school (known as The Nippers), nursery and some playing fields north of the River Esk (footbridge crossing). Junior school feels separate from the senior school, due to the geographical layout rather than any difference in ethos. Nippers mostly use senior school facilities for matches and special occasions.

Senior school buildings predominantly painted in the traditional East Lothian yellow ochre, while the attractive stone built Pinkie House (sixth form boys' boarding house plus headmaster's house) overlooks a pretty walled garden (good party venue, according to our young guides, used for weddings in the holidays).

Excellent Communication and Resource Centre situated at the heart of the campus incorporates the library and sixth form centre. Popular with students during the day when there's no time to return to their houses to work – encourages independence and a university ambience for the older students.

Elegant and unusual chapel (Tardis like – appears small/intimate but seats a lot of bottoms), good sized theatre (240 seats), shooting range and squash courts.

Red blazers for all, no ties, kilts on Sundays. Flat shoes – strictly no heels.

Head has overhauled the catering operation. Major changes, new catering company brought in with excellent results. Great choice on offer when we were there – we'd happily go back for seconds.

We heard time and time again from pupils and parents about the friendliness of the school. That there was 'no pupil hierarchy' and that 'the pupils mix well between the year groups'. The overwhelming feedback that we got from parents is that their children are 'incredibly happy and confident' at the school and many parents felt that this was as important as academic results.

Pastoral care, well-being and discipline: Houseparents and live-in house tutors look after boarders. Sixth form tutors also help with academic targets. Pastoral care reinforced by weekly PSHE lessons, including seminars and tutorials.

Parents report that the pastoral care is exceptional. Ladder for punishments but each misdemeanour treated on a case by case basis. Gatings and letters to parents for smoking. Automatic expulsion for supplying drugs, but 'experimenting' leads to suspension and then onto a drugs testing programme. Suspension for alcohol and then a final warning before you're out. Escalating series of sanctions for bullying and cyber-bullying.

Pupils and parents: Twenty per cent international pupils (some expats) from 21 countries, highest proportion from Germany. Large numbers of OLs' sons, daughters and grandchildren, but also a good many first time buyers. Not particularly a Scottish grandee or Sloane Ranger school, although there'll be a smattering. We hear that 'parents are very friendly' and 'quite a diverse mix' and that 'it's easy to make a network of friends'. Old Lorettonians include Lord Lamont, Andrew Marr and Alistair Darling.

The Golf Academy now attracts pupils from further afield than ever before. Parents are supportive of this, even the non-golfers, saying 'it has resulted in broadening the mix of pupils which can only be a good thing'.

Good bus service to just about everywhere: East Lothian, central Edinburgh and even down to the Borders.

Entrance: Entry at all stages throughout the junior school. Informal interviewing for all. Years 5-10 verbal reasoning, maths and English tests, school report. Sixth form has the same plus two exams from Loretto's curriculum. Minimum of six GCSEs grade 4+, to include maths and English.

Exit: Nearly all the Nippers move up to the senior school at the age of 12 and most stay right through to the end of sixth form. Sixth form leavers to a broad selection of universities – Edinburgh and Aberdeen are popular. Five to Oxbridge and four medics in 2018; one off to study film and marketing at Penn State, USA.

Money matters: Scholarships (10 per cent of fees) from year 9 for general academic, music, art, golf, sport, drama and piping. Some means-tested bursaries of up to 105 per cent of fees, the extra five per cent to cover transport, uniform etc, reviewed annually. Fifteen per cent remission for children from Forces families; sibling discounts available.

Remarks: A famous Scottish public school that's warm, friendly and has a rounded approach to education. Parents all said that it is small enough to include everyone but big enough to let children go the distance and achieve their potential, a school where the individual matters. Not a hothouse, although strong academic results are important (one parent commented that Loretto is 'as academic as you want it to be'). Ethos is to educate the whole person 'in mind, body and spirit'. Headmaster tells us that it is a school 'to prepare pupils for the rest of their lives'. Loretto sells itself on being a 'small school with a big heart and big ambitions' and fulfils the brief – and more.

The Mary Erskine School

Linked with ESMS Junior School, Stewart's Melville College

Ravelston, Edinburgh EH4 3NT

Ages 12–18 **Pupils** 758 **Sixth form** 122 **Boarders** 16 full

Fees: Day £11,637; Boarding £22,764 – £23,349 pa

0131 347 5700
www.esms.org.uk

Principal: Since August 2018, Linda Moule, who runs the twin senior schools (Stewart's Melville College and The Mary Erskine School) with two heads and the head of the co-ed junior school. She spends part of the week in each school (separate campuses) with offices in both. After graduating in theology from Manchester University, she has held positions in the teaching profession in Bristol, Stockport, Manchester and was deputy head of Holy Trinity College, Bromley, before becoming vice principal of New Hall School, Chelmsford in 2004. She was appointed head of Mary Erskine School in 2009, and became vice principal of the ESMS in 2016. Mrs Moule is married with two sons, both of whom have attended Stewart's Melville College.

Head since August 2018, Kirsty Nicholson, who has taught geography at both Stewart's Melville College and The Mary Erskine School, was a very successful head of house at Mary Erskine and, through her role on the management team in charge of S1 and of admissions for the whole school, has very much been its public face in recent years.

M

Academic matters: ESMS follows the 'diamond' model of education. The boys and girls are educated together at the junior school, separately in the senior school from 12-17 and back to a co-ed set up in their final year. The principal and her heads of school are all strong advocates of this system: 'we can tailor the teaching for boys and girls'.... 'boys and girls learn differently'. The pupils 'look forward to sixth form and don't lose contact with each other as they go through'. Class sizes of around 20-22 for first two years – S1 and S2 – reducing in size to 20 or less for S3-S5 and then between 12-15 for the final year (sixth form). Parents of boys and girls see it as a 'better learning environment' and pupils say that 'the separation doesn't affect the friendships between the boys and girls'. Many of the sixth formers say 'we have the same group of friends, boys and girls, as we did in the junior school; we don't lose touch'.

Pupils study for eight National 5 exams in S3 and S4. English, mathematics, a science and a modern language are compulsory at this stage. In their penultimate year (S5), they study for five Higher exams while in their final year, they study for Advanced Highers in twinned classes with Stewart's Melville College.

Many pupils do three Advanced Highers (some do more) with considerable success. For these exams pupils have to undertake a dissertation and, in some cases, a scientific investigation which teaches them the skills of independent study that will be necessary at university. Recent results are strong with 78 per cent of Advanced Highers awarded A/B in 2018. French, German, Latin and Spanish all on offer to Advanced Higher. The principal tells us 'there is a strong work ethic here'. This was echoed by parents – 'it's a school that produces conscientious children'.

Strong links with the Merchant Company, whose members offer all final year pupils mock interview practice.

Firefly Learning, an online virtual learning platform, has recently been implemented throughout the school. This allows teachers and students to publish and access information from anywhere with an internet connection. Parents, staff and girls appreciate the effective system to keep track of homework, study tasks, school events and individuals' progress in learning. Pupils do not bring in their own laptops but can sign out and use a school laptop (kept in school library) whenever they need to. However, pupils are still encouraged and expected to use books for their academic research as well as online resources ('both are important skills'). Strong learning support both in and out of the classroom. We hear reports of 'great classroom assistants'.

Pupils tell us that if there is anything academic that they need help with there are drop-in centres every lunchtime where a teacher is available to help them – in all subjects. Big, bright custom-built common room for sixth formers and study areas available.

Games, options, the arts: As you would expect for the largest (joint) independent school in Europe, sport is massive. Great achievements in hockey with the 1st XI team winning the Scottish Schools' Cup. There are successes across the more minor sports as well with national accolades in athletics, badminton, dance, curling and swimming. Dance is popular and available at Higher level. Basketball has also become very popular. For those not so enamoured with team sports, there are plentiful options, including cycling, golf, climbing and cross-country. The school offers 30 extracurricular sports clubs.

Outstanding drama – 'sport and the performing arts are equally strong here'. We hear from parents that drama is 'quite extraordinary'. It is part of the curriculum for younger pupils and can be taken up to Higher and Advanced Higher. The Tom Fleming Centre for Performing Arts, at the Stewart's Melville site, can seat audiences of up to 580. It's a renovated Victorian assembly hall – an impressive venue with comprehensive production, sound and lighting facilities. Drama is for all, with plays and performances throughout the year for all age groups with regular performances at the Edinburgh Festival. Masses of orchestras and choirs at all age groups (22 bands, orchestras, ensembles and choirs running). Annual house music and house rock competitions, both keenly fought with performances described by one parent as 'bloody amazing'. Choir performs annually at the Royal Edinburgh Military Tattoo. More than 200 girls have instrumental music lessons and there are 45 visiting music teachers. Pipe band thriving.

A staggering variety of clubs and societies on offer to all. It's all here – from video editing to curling and everything in between. These take place at lunch time and post school. Many of the clubs are sporting – squash, football, netball – but there's certainly something for everyone in the lineup.

Voluntary CCF very popular with over 300 pupils involved. Strong RAF section – over 100. Even split between boys and girls. ESMS are the biggest provider over DofE in Scotland with over 70 pupils awarded gold recently.

Splendid art – and up to date displays around the school, wondrous paintings from this year's art exams already up and framed on the walls. Schools often display fabulous art that we then discover has been hanging there for years. Here the boys and girls can see their creations being valued while they are still at school, when it matters most.

Design and manufacture is available as a Higher and Advanced Higher. Exceptional displays of the girls' product design projects line the corridors.

Boarding: Only a tiny percentage of pupils board; this is still predominantly a day school. Erskine House can accommodate up to 29 boarders. The house isn't purpose built and it feels more like a large family house. The bedroom sizes vary and accommodate between one and three girls. Sixth formers may have their own room depending on numbers. The house is well furnished and very well equipped.

At weekends the boarders have planned activities such as surfing, cinema trips etc but they may also go into the city centre if they wish. The Sunday morning service in the local church remains compulsory to all boarders. They are free to use the school sports centres (pool and fitness suite) in the evening and over weekends.

Flexi-boarding is also on offer – but only if there's space available.

Boarders come from Scotland, south of the border and also abroad, often with family connections to the school (offspring of FPs), expats. Predominantly UK citizens rather than foreign nationals.

Background and atmosphere: Mary Erskine was founded in 1694, as the Merchant Maiden Hospital, and moved to its present site in Ravelston in 1966, changing its name to The Mary Erskine School and amalgamating with the boys' school (Stewart's Melville College) in 1972. The majority of the buildings are from the 1960s (designed by William Kininmonth in 1964). White and cube-like (could be mistaken for a hospital), but light and spacious inside. These buildings surround the pretty, but somewhat overwhelmed, Ravelston House, built in 1800 by Alexander Keith in the late Adam manner.

The attractive grounds here are much more expansive than those at Stewart's Melville (and there's more car parking space too). This means that the girls play nearly all of their sport on site and don't need to be bussed out to other playing fields.

Senior pupils share the site with the nursery pupils and the lower half of the ESMS junior school. Final year pupils who are back in the co-ed set-up with Stewart's Melville are bussed to classes between the two school campuses (they're situated about a mile apart). Mind boggling timetabling but, according to both pupils and staff alike, it runs like clockwork.

Coaches from Dunfermline, Bathgate, Eskbank and Haddington as well as around Edinburgh.

Pastoral care, well-being and discipline: The school runs a tutorial system for the first year with groups of 20 girls led by their form tutor, after which the school is divided into six houses. Each has a head of house and an assistant head who together look after the girls as they move through school. These houses are common to both Stewart's Melville and Mary Erskine, so the various inter-house competitions have mixed teams. Weekly inter-house challenges range from maths quizzes to basketball matches. Sixth formers are under the divided into small tutor groups with a personal tutor, under the umbrella of the director of sixth form.

Excellent anti-bullying policy. 'Cyber bullying in school aged children now more of a threat than normal bullying' and that they have a full programme to educate the pupils and make them aware of the pitfalls. We hear from parents that 'any bullying shenanigans or friendship issues are handled very well and quickly', that there is 'fantastic pastoral care' and pupils are made to feel 'safe, valued and that they belong'. Sophisticated PSE programme throughout the school.

'Zero tolerance' and expulsion if pupils found in possession of, or dealing in, drugs of any kind. Booze and smoking normally end in suspension – principal says 'unacceptable but not an issue in school'.

Pupils and parents: A real mixture of parents. Many first time buyers and children of FPs (former pupils). Parents report 'a broad cross-section of families', mostly from central Edinburgh and suburbs. Not really a toff school, although there will be a smattering. Taking over a third of Edinburgh's independent secondary pupils, it is less elitist than some of its neighbours. Children living far out can spend the night when doing evening activities (as long as there's room). Alumni include Tom Fleming, actor and broadcaster.

Entrance: At age 11, 12, 13, fifth year and sixth form. Automatic entrance from junior school. A broadly non-selective school. Children are assessed (English, maths, verbal reasoning) before entrance. Numbers are up. The waiting lists remain 'first come, first served' and there are no plans to cherry-pick the more able pupils. The school was adamant about this.

Exit: Minimal leakage pre-Highers with most going on to university. Some 65 per cent to Scottish Universities – Aberdeen, Glasgow, Edinburgh, Dundee, St Andrews and Strathclyde popular. Around 35 per cent to English, Irish, European or American universities (two to Queen's Belfast and one to North Arizona in 2018, with one to Oxbridge and five medics). SATS (for American colleges) not a problem. School has recently started promoting Dutch universities (Amsterdam, Groningen, Maastricht, Leiden) as an option – good transport links, less expensive than some UK universities.

Money matters: Bursaries – up to 100 per cent – and scholarships throughout. Those doing well in the entrance exam are invited to sit a scholarship exam. Music scholarships (together with free music tuition) are also available.

Remarks: This is a big school with big ambitions. With terrific success stories on every front, not just academically, it is a formidable operation. Not every child will thrive as a small fish in such a big pond, and such a large operation may leave the non-conformist with less room to manoeuvre. However, its sheer size has tremendous benefits – parents report 'the school pulls in great staff' and provides pupils with 'incredible opportunities'. Well-mannered, ambitious children leave the school with self-confidence and 'a strong work ethic'. Parents across the board say they 'can't fault it'. An outstanding school with impressive results.

M

McLaren High School

Mollands Road, Callander FK17 8JH

Ages 11–18 **Pupils** 626 **Sixth form** 174

01877 330156
www.mclarenhigh.co.uk

Rector: Since 2013, Marc Fleming, BA (applied consumer studies), SQH. He was previously depute head of Dalziel High and prior to that taught home economics at Galashields Academy and the Community School of Auchterarder. Quietly charming but surprisingly passionate, he is a lover of the hills and outdoor spaces and is keen to promote this within the school. The school covers one of the biggest rural catchments areas in Scotland and is the only secondary in Loch Lomond and the Trossachs.

Academic matters: McLaren High School seems to run a tight ship. Following the Scottish system, it offers a broad general education from S1 to S3, followed by senior phase S4 to S6, when pupils knuckle down and sit national qualifications from

National 3s to Advanced Highers. A recent newspaper table put it as 34 out of 350 schools within Scotland on exam attainment alone and the results seems to bear this out. If we look at 2018, 33 per cent As and 59 per cent A/Bs at Higher, and 26 As, 54 per cent A/Bs at Advanced Higher level.

Marc Fleming says they are working hard to get more pupils in sixth year to do Advanced Highers. 'There is a general trend towards academic excellence. We're looking for them to broaden their attainment in S6.'

One parental grumble we heard was: 'We could do with more flexibility when it comes to choosing subjects.'

Mr Fleming says the school takes part in maths and science challenges on a national level. One group of pupils reached the final of the School Robot Challenge (part of the UK National Robotics Week), having already won the regional heat. He says that this 'ethos of academic excellence' is grounded in the school's value system known as ORCA (Order, Respect, Care, Achievement) which is threaded throughout the school's day to day life.

Games, options, the arts: The school has an impressive three Astro pitches, paid for by fundraising parents. This pretty well marks out this school's impressive sporting ethos. As one parent said, 'McLaren operates a tripartite system. That means the parents give as much as the children and the teachers. We're in it together.' And with considerable parental support they have high levels of participation in extracurricular sport such as hockey, football, rugby and gymnastics. In S1 (age 12-13), for example, pupils can experience a Scottish Rugby Union sponsored Rugby Light programme which involves pupils working with a PE teacher and a rugby modern apprentice to develop their skills. The school also fields U14 and U16 rugby teams.

Hockey is another key sport, which is played all the way through to sixth year with an active fixture list against other schools. One parent who had a child playing at national level was particularly impressed with the support she had received from the school. 'The flexibility has been there in terms of helping her. They went out of their way to give her options.' Core PE time is only two hours a week, but with parental support they supplement this with a wide and varied range of extra activities including canoeing and cricket.

The school benefits from being right next door to the McLaren leisure centre, which gives access to a swimming pool and gymnasium to augment the internal gym and assembly hall in school. And, of course, being situated right in the middle of a national park, it encourages everyone to get outside and make the most of these natural facilities, trekking, biking, camping, etc. Runs a week long Junior Park Ranger course which involves wall building, path maintenance and appreciation of the park ranger service. It's described as an 'immersion' experience and the hope is that it will attract more young volunteers in the future.

Music seems to be very strongly supported. They have an active choir, orchestra, wind and brass bands that practice at lunchtimes or after school. One parent said, 'Their music department is phenomenal. The teachers put in so much time and effort.' The pipe band is clearly rather good as it is frequently asked to play at local events such as the Callander Highland Games. It also came second in its category at the Scottish Schools Pipe Band Competition.

Travel is highly prized at the school too. Marc Fleming says, 'We're a small school with global ambitions'; 28 pupils from S4 to S6 went to Malaysia as part of World Challenge, having fundraised £2,500 each to take part. The Ian Budgie Martin Award, awarded annually in memory of a science teacher who used to teach here, allows an S6 pupil to go on a two week funded placement at Baylor College of Medicine in Texas.

Last but not least, the annual school show is a local highlight for the whole community, as is the school music festival. It's all go in Callander.

Background and atmosphere: Founded in 1892 by Donald McLaren, a banker from Strathearn, links with the clan remain strong. In fact, the pupils have recently voted to adopt a school tie in the McLaren tartan. (Quite the fashion statement, we say.)

Light, modern, attractive building in spectacular Trossachs setting. 'You couldn't find a more lovely place to put a school.' As one parent said, 'Set where we are, in rather an isolated spot, most people go to McLaren High school, be they rich or poor.' It's the beating heart of the community and seems to be central to most that goes on in Callander and for miles around. It seems to be very good at making the most of the spectacular scenery that surrounds it, so has connections both inside and out.

Pastoral care, well-being and discipline: A 'very knowledgeable and protective' pupil support team works across the three school houses. (They are currently developing and strengthening the house system.) This team consists of a pupils' support leader assigned to each house along with a member of the senior management team to offer back up in a pastoral/discipline sense. Siblings are generally put into the same house to help increase the sense of belonging. The school has also appointed a principal teacher of enhanced support who cares for more vulnerable pupils. The framework of support is graded from one to four and can range from simply moving a child somewhere quieter to work to involving multi-agency partners eg ed psych. There is also a new 'nurture room' to allow stressed or troubled pupils some time out in a quiet space. Great idea, we say.

The principal teacher transition coordinates the transition from feeder primaries into secondary and then from secondary into work, college and university. The school believes this framework should identify extra support where needed.

Discipline seems to be very good, which probably goes hand and hand with such a strong community school. One parent said, 'We host many of the after-event parties and we have never had any issues. Quite the contrary, the children are a delight and more than happy to clear up without being asked.'

Pupils and parents: Largely rural catchment area so plenty involvement with farming and tourism. Very strong sense of community and strong backing for school from parents and local businesses.

Entrance: There are 11 feeder primaries. Half of the pupils live in Callander. The other half are from a wide and varied rural catchment area. Parents tend to work in hospitality, farming, forestry, gillies, tourism.

Exit: School says it has the best 'positive destination figures' of all the schools in Stirlingshire.

Over 50 per cent go on to higher education, mostly Scottish universities. A couple each year apply to Oxbridge; one recent Cambridge place, and two medics in 2018. About a third into employment/apprenticeships, the rest to further education. A strengthening partnership with Forth Valley College, where pupils can experience a vocational course one day a week as part of the senior phase experience, eg construction, hair and beauty, engineering. Some pupils do part-time work experience during school hours in local primary schools or businesses.

Money matters: Original McLaren foundation (tiny as far as income goes) but school is well supported by local businesses, which can and will provide extra funds for excursions etc.

Remarks: 'We're a small school, in a national park setting, with an ambition to go global,' says rector. He believes it's not just about 'farming and changing beds,' although both are very viable ways of making a living. He wants to enthuse his pupils to look further afield and try something different. And with such strong support from the whole community, it's hard to see how they can fail. Small school with grand ambitions in the grandest setting of all. What could be more uplifting? Scottish education as it should be.

Mearns Castle High School

Waterfoot Road, Newton Mearns G77 5RU

Ages 12–18 **Pupils** 1,293

0141 577 2300
www.blogs.glowscotland.org.uk/er/MearnsCastle

Head: Since 2007, Dean Smith, BA in geography and Scottish history; teaching diploma from the former Jordanhill College of Education and the Scottish qualification for headship. Started his teaching career in 1983 at Cathkin High School, moving to the East London as head of media at Valentines High School. Moved back to Scotland to Calderhead High School and then deputy head at nearby Williamwood High School.

Down-to-earth, and firm but fair; we witnessed the strict East Renfrewshire uniform policy in full force – one boy hardly had his foot through the door before being instructed to take his hoodie off from under his blazer. Mr S was modest but proud of his achievements, saying: 'I didn't have ambition to be head,' but feels 'enormously privileged' to do so. Future plans include improving on the school's already excellent reputation as one of the best state schools in Scotland. He says: 'There's always room for improvement.'

Married with two children. He jokes that he's a 'football fanatic', and a season ticket holder for Motherwell FC. Plays golf when he can and enjoys Bruce Springsteen's music and reading.

Academic matters: Much-sought after school for its excellent academic results, placing it consistently in the top five of Scotland's highest performing state schools. In 2018, 54 per cent of S6 got 5+ Highers. About 20 per cent take one or more language at Higher level, just four per cent at Advanced Higher.

Support for learning department consists of a principal teacher, four full-time teachers and eight pupil support assistants who work with class teachers to help pupils in class across the curriculum as well as providing individual support to those with more complex needs. Senior management one-third women. Some 30 per cent of staff long-serving, with leavers mostly retiring or being promoted.

Developing the Young Workforce careers evening with some 50 organisations. Skills Development Scotland adviser on hand for advice from S2–S6. Work experience week in S4, with increasing numbers of S5s and S6s also doing work experience.

Games, options, the arts: Successful debating club, often winning at the highest level. A Mearns Castle team made it all the way to the Oxford Union debating chamber recently.

Awarded gold status by Sport Scotland; sport is inclusive and open to all – the exception being the boys' school football team, by trials because of its popularity. Large 3G pitch across the main road. Free lunchtime sports clubs; however, some of those after school come at a price. Girls' rugby as well as boys', training at Whitecraigs Rugby Club. Several pupils were successful at the British Schools Go-Karting team trials in 2018 and the S4 girls' team came second at the Scottish Indoor Rowing Championships in 2017. Skiing and swimming are a coach ride away, also paid for by parents. Variety of academic clubs, too, including the classics club, philosophy club and code breaking – as well as famous moments in Lego.

Active performing arts faculty, putting on annual performances which have including Guys and Dolls and Bugsy Malone. Myriad music groups and ensembles, and winter and spring music concerts (sadly East Renfrewshire council are doing their best to slash the music budget, which could affect orchestras and school music lessons in the future). Art up to AH and photography to Higher. School an 'exhibition space' featuring pupils' artworks. Exhibitions during the year showcase art and design, graphics, woodworking and photography.

S6 community involvement programme and Duke of Edinburgh at all levels popular with bronze and silver oversubscribed.

Trips include CERN in Geneva (physics), New York (maths), Italy (skiing), water sports (France) and Stratford-upon-Avon (English).

Background and atmosphere: Established in 1978, originally Williamwood and Eastwood, it was East Renfrewshire's new arrival. A modern build, it's no great looker, though the extension in 2006 is more attractive. 'The school as a whole is clearly not the newest within East Ren. But once inside you actually wouldn't know it.'

It's what goes on inside this school, however, which draws parents in. Traditional ethos with house system, smart uniform policy (all wear black woollen blazer) and 'very focused on attainment'. Pupils here are expected to be hard working and diligent. Some parents in this council area worry about less academic children coping with the high expectations; having private tutors is the norm. However, our impression is that the 'exam factory' status of high-performing state schools can be unfair; all the heads we have spoken to deny this. Nonetheless, the academic success of Mearns Castle is undoubtedly its big draw – Mr S says they receive emails and calls from parents relocating because of its reputation.

Situated in the prosperous area of Newton Mearns, the school is highly regarded in the local community. 'Litter complaint occasionally' is about as big as it gets. We, too, noticed a significant amount of litter in the playground (but the janitor was promptly asked to sweep it up).

Popular charity week in October with lunch-time talent shows, where over £8,000 was raised recently for various charities, principally the Prince of Wales Hospice.

Pastoral care, well-being and discipline: It's a nice touch that the head himself looks after some of the S1s. Mr S introduced the house system, which has been running since 2011, with a deputy HT allocated to each year. Principal teachers oversee the houses, so each pupil has two teachers allocated to them for pastoral care. Parents and pupils can reach out to whoever they choose, but generally it would be the principal teacher (pastoral support). One parent said: 'I've been in touch with the head of year a few times for various things. Always returns calls very quickly, listens to my concerns and genuinely seems to care about each child's welfare.' Outdoor pursuits trip in S3 for personal development.

We heard of one recent exclusion that worried one parent, but figures are low. Head jokes, 'With 1,300 teenagers, things happen occasionally ... No serious ongoing discipline issues.' Colour system, which is prominently displayed in the school, is used to recognise pupil achievement and identify successes in sport, the expressive arts, citizenship and enterprise. Pupils learn of their successes at house assemblies and receive blazer badgers, braiding and certificates. This also adds an 'upbeat element' to discipline, the threat of 'taking you off colour' is normally enough, with 95 per cent of pupils 'on' colour.

Pupils and parents: School to home communication through school website, Twitter and quarterly parents' newsletter.

Plenty of opportunities for pupils and parents to come into the school throughout the year, including the curriculum information evening for every year group. S1–S4s receive two reports a year and one parents' consultation evening; S5–S6s receive three reports a year.

Predominantly middle-class and professional parents with 'high expectations' from this wealthy catchment area; there's no shortage of drop offs in expensive cars. One potential pupil's parent told us: 'The only thing putting me off Mearns Castle is that I might not be well-groomed enough.'

Notable former pupils: Steven McLean (Scottish football referee), Stephen Hammell (Motherwell football club), Lynne Beattie (GB volleyball), Andrew Mullen (Paralympic swimmer), Scott Jamieson (golfer). On our tour of the ground floor, we saw the Hall of Fame, a series of framed photos celebrating former and current pupils.

Entrance: Incredibly popular school – very difficult to get a place if not in catchment, though a small number of placing requests are successful. Feeder primary schools are Mearns Primary, Eaglesham Primary, Kirkhill Primary and Calderwood Lodge Primary.

The local council runs buses from Eaglesham and Waterfoot at no extra cost to parents.

If thinking of moving to the area, be prepared to pay a premium; house prices are continuing to rise.

Exit: Around 70-75 per cent go on to university, mostly Scottish (eg Glasgow, Strathclyde, Glasgow Caledonian, Paisley, Edinburgh and St Andrews) for financial reasons. Another 10 per cent go to college, and the rest to the workforce or a gap year. A few to Oxbridge.

M

Remarks: Much sought-after state school in wealthy East Renfrewshire suburb with great academic success, which always features in Scotland's top five state schools. Hard working ethos and high expectations for all children. Worth moving to the area for.

Merchiston Castle School

294 Colinton Road, Edinburgh EH13 0PU

Ages 7–18 **Pupils** 440 **Sixth form** 150 **Boarders** 286 full

Fees: Day £15,030 – £24,210; Boarding £21,090 – £32,910 pa

01313 122201
www.merchiston.co.uk

Headmaster: Since August 2018, Jonathan Anderson, previously senior deputy head at Worksop College. Geography degree from Queen's Belfast; joined Christ's Hospital as a geography teacher and was promoted to assistant housemaster and housemaster. After nearly 14 years, he moved to Worksop. He is married with a young daughter.

Head of the junior: School (Pringle) since 2012, Niamh Waldron, first came to the school in 2005. Junior school parents sing her praises and say that she's 'really wonderful, warm and motherly', 'fun with a great sense of humour and completely dedicated to the children'.

Academic matters: Junior school pupils start at J4 (primary 4, age 7/8) and stay in the junior school until they finish year 8 (S1, age 12). The tinies (age 7-9) are taught in the Pringle Centre classrooms and move up to take lessons in the main school aged 10. Set from aged 11 and follow three individual sciences from age 12. At 13 they move seamlessly up to the senior school without taking an entrance exam. Languages taught from the start, specialist teachers for maths, science and the arts. Pupils in the junior school also have access to a bank of iPads in the Pringle Centre.

School continues to follow the mainly English system. A few do sit a combination of A levels and Scottish Highers. In 2018, 50 per cent A*/A grades at A level, 66 per cent A*-A/9-7 at GCSE. Tiny numbers doing Advanced Highers and a small number Highers. All boys must do two separate sciences at GCSE and many go on to study science at A level. Maths still the most popular subject at A level. Sciences and English are also strong. No plans to change to IB; head says, 'we looked at IB twice but it wouldn't suit us and wouldn't work for the majority of our boys'.

The science labs are well kitted out with full multimedia facilities and video microscopes – they are also equipped to do a certain amount of genetics work. Much to the delight of most of the boys there is also a menagerie of animals including a boa constrictor, a chameleon and a tarantula. Recent developments include Mount Olympus, a suite of classrooms for geography, classics and economics which also includes the popular Masterchef kitchen. This was launched in 2011 with the aim of preparing leavers for life after school. Each boy in his final year has six sessions to learn basic cookery skills. For the ambitious there is the annual, hotly fought and popular Masterchef competition where the boys can showcase their skills.

School supports boys with a range of needs – dys-stream, Asperger's, ADHD. Broadly non-selective, but boys 'must be able to access the curriculum'. Pupils' support needs are assessed before admission and progress is monitored on an ongoing basis. Pupils are taught either individually or in small groups in timetabled classes in the learning support department. Support is there for actual diagnosable problems but also for getting some boys up to speed. Good feedback about this department – 'it's all dealt with' and 'good communication with the parent's'.

Parents report that the teaching staff in general are 'top drawer' and 'go out of their way to help the boys'.

Games, options, the arts: Merchiston has long been associated with a tradition of sporting excellence, in particular on the rugby pitch. Sport is played along traditional lines with rugby in the autumn and spring terms and cricket and athletics in the summer. The school is currently represented at national and international level in many sports, including athletics, cricket, rugby and target shooting.

Make no mistake, rugby is still big here – 66 Merchistonians have played at full international level. Parents say, 'hockey and football are becoming more popular but rugby is still the main sport'. However with six senior and 12 junior teams, there are opportunities at all levels and everyone is given a chance to represent the school. Boys are enormously proud of their rugby heritage. We hear that at weekends boys don't necessarily rush home when their rugby matches are finished – many choose to stay on the touchline to support their first team. Team tours, including overseas.

Sports facilities are good with a rifle range, golf nets, putting green, fives, tennis (three all-weather floodlit courts) and squash courts, an indoor swimming pool and sports hall. The boys are encouraged to be involved in sport outside the 'core sports' during the school week. Senior boys often help coach the younger children – works well, clearly popular with the younger ones and the coaches. School is embarking on the biggest sporting development for a generation which will include a new sports centre, 25m pool and a 3G synthetic pitch for football and rugby.

The school established a tennis academy in 2007 with 13 players and it has now grown to around twice that size. These players pursue a bespoke academic timetable and an individual tennis programme. Students join the academy by invitation, after passing an assessment.

The golf academy (in association with Kings Acre Golf Club) likewise provides an environment where young golfers can maximise their potential. The academy takes part in junior and senior tournaments throughout Scotland and the UK with plenty of success stories, and there's help with applying for golf scholarships in the US.

Strong DT department, subject available at A level. Super art, painting displayed in the department and around the school. Music for all. Two-thirds of the boys play a musical instrument. Chapel choir, choral society (over 120 pupils), jazz band, ceilidh band. Fantastic junior and senior pipe bands. Plus many other formal and informal music groups. Many of the weekday school assemblies include music performances. Parents report that the boys 'sing and dance with great enthusiasm' and 'they don't think it's uncool to be in the choir'.

Flourishing CCF with rifle range built into school wall. Sister school – St George's School for Girls – has recently joined as a cadet company and the schools train together at Merchiston during the summer term.

Drama in partnership with St George's. At least two main productions each year, with a biennial musical, for all year groups. Merchiston Juniors also have their own musical in alternate years.

Boarding: Traditionally a boarding school; 65 per cent of the boys are boarders and this rises to 80 per cent in sixth form. Junior school offers what they call 'step-up' boarding (flexi), reviewed termly – subject to beds being available. Pringle House (juniors) can sleep a maximum of 46 boys. Lovely cosy house, enclosed in its own secret garden. Homely dorms, spacious kitchen and comfy dayroom, supervised by the head of juniors, resident tutors, a housemother and a team of prefects chosen from upper sixth formers.

In the senior school the boys are divided 'horizontally' rather than 'vertically', so all in each year group are in the same house. Four houses: those for the first three years have a combination of shared and single rooms; when the boys reach lower sixth they move into the impressive Laidlaw House. Boarders are split between Laidlaw North and South, with Evans House accommodating the day pupils. Laidlaw is pretty super dooper. Modern and well furnished, all rooms are on-suite and more akin to a new-build hotel than a traditional boarding house – lucky boys. No wonder boarding numbers increase in sixth form. Six kitchens, in-house laundry, gym and stunning views of Edinburgh.

No step-up boarding in the senior school. A day boy may sleepover for up to three nights per week but beyond this he has to pay the full boarding fee, if beds are available.

Sixth form prefects are billeted to a house for the year to act as mentors. Parents report that the boys 'look up to the prefects mentoring them' and they are their 'role models'. The boys have a different housemaster each year and have to learn to build a new relationship with a senior person, which is 'an important lesson and skill to have,' say parents.

For boarders and day boys alike, Saturday is a normal school day. Lessons in the morning and sports fixtures after lunch. Entertainment in the evening – pizza/DVD evening, cinema or theatre trip, or an evening with a sister school – disco or ceilidh. Sundays have either a whole school service (boarders and day boys) or a morning or evening service for boarders only. Often there are Sunday trips for the boarders – into Edinburgh city centre, bowling, swimming, go-karting, hill-walking. Boys may go out and visit friends or family by arrangement with their housemaster.

This is a 'proper' boarding school, not one composed of flexi-boarders who empty out every weekend. Lots of weekend activities. Each house has telephones for pupils to use and set rules about mobiles. Computer available in Pringle for Skyping.

Background and atmosphere: School was founded in 1828 by Charles Chalmers. Moved to Merchiston Castle, an early 15th century tower, in 1833. In 1930 moved three miles down the road to the current greenfield site at Colinton, four miles from the centre of Edinburgh. Present day buildings date from this time, though the original Colinton House now houses the science department.

Buildings set within 100 acres of park-like playing fields. Beautiful mature trees and exceptional views – lovely setting. Compact campus, buildings all quite close together – easy for boys to get from A to B quickly. Nothing flashy but everything well kept and in good heart. Juniors in Pringle House are cosily tucked away in the south west corner of the school grounds but still have easy access to and use of entire campus.

Sick bay with visiting sports physiotherapist and own ultrasound machine. Dining hall with servery and buffet service. Boys quick to praise the food: 'it's good and there's always enough'. First floor Memorial Hall doubles as chapel and dance hall. An impressive space with balconies all round and a stage at the front, it can seat the whole school – lots of tartan. Big on Scottish reeling. Girls are regularly bussed in from sister schools – St George's (Edinburgh) and Kilgraston (Perthshire) – for reel parties and socials. Girls can visit at weekends and join the boys in the sixth form club.

Uniform of blue blazers, white shirt, tie. Dark, grown-up suits for sixth formers (popular with the boys – badge of honour). Kilts and green jackets for outings/special occasions.

Impressive website – information on just about everything. Full disclosure on academic results – by year and subject. A great window into the school.

Pastoral care, well-being and discipline: The feedback that we got from both boys and parents about the matrons and the nurses was second to none – 'top notch', 'fantastic', 'they're lovely', 'totally on it'. The boarders reported that they keep in touch with their previous house matrons as they move up the school.

The horizontal house system works well for controlling potential bullying. Good PSHE programme. Each house has a well-being prefect with whom other pupils are encouraged to confide.

Smoking dealt with on a case by case basis. Punishments: detention or clean up task. Smoking within school buildings results in suspension. The school tries to educate pupils about the risks in consuming alcohol, which is dealt with on a case by case basis.

Drugs: instant expulsion for supplying. Expulsion also for drug use except in 'exceptional cases', where a 'supportive regime' may be offered. However this option is 'unlikely to be applied when drugs are used on school premises'.

Pupils and parents: Parents strongly middle class. Many have family connections to the school – former pupils. Plenty of first time buyers as well. Lots from Edinburgh but also boarders from further afield, Perthshire, Borders, Stirlingshire – many from Scottish prep schools. A few from south of the border. Around five per cent expats, 22 per cent from overseas – from 22 countries, particularly Hong Kong and Germany. The boys we met were all open, friendly, confident, well-mannered and proud of their school. Manners matter here.

Entrance: Entry into junior school by assessment using computer based InCAS software – measuring reading, general maths and mental arithmetic. Online screening assessment also required, plus interview. Automatic entry to the senior school from the junior school (around 40 pupils per year).

Senior school entry at 13+ from preparatory schools via common entrance, or by mathematics, English and science exams, plus interview.

Sixth form entrance depends on GCSE or National 5 performance, or entrance exams, plus interview.

Exit: Some 20 per cent leaves after GCSEs. About a quarter to Scottish universities – particularly Edinburgh and Glasgow – and 70 per cent to English universities. Two to Oxbridge in 2018; others off to Berklee College of Music, Toronto University, Vancouver Film School and Santa Clara, San Jose.

Accounting and finance, economics, business management, engineering, social and political science top subject choices.

Money matters: Academic scholarships at 13+, 14+ and sixth form – school's own examinations. All-rounder scholarships, music, sport, art & design. No money off fees – awarded for the honour alone. Parents may apply for means-tested assistance (up to 100 per cent of the fees). Reductions in fees for siblings attending 'sister' schools (St George's School for Girls, Edinburgh; Kilgraston School, Perth and Queen Margaret's School, York).

Remarks: The only boys-only boarding school left in Scotland. Traditional, warm and personal school – small enough for everyone to know everyone. Blessed with lovely grounds, with the bonus of having Edinburgh on the doorstop and well placed to attract good staff. Rugby is still very much a religion here but don't underestimate the rest. They're no slouches off the pitch either.

M

Morrison's Academy

Ferntower Road, Crieff, Perthshire PH7 3AN

Ages 3–18 **Pupils** 477 **Sixth form** 56

Fees: £8,625 – £12,996 pa

01764 653885
www.morrisonsacademy.org

Rector and principal: Since 2015, Gareth Warren, previously depute rector at George Watson's College in Edinburgh. Degree in pharmacology and PGCE; taught chemistry at several UK schools and was head of science at an independent school in Bermuda for three years. Born in Kenya, left at 4 years old and settled in St Albans from 10 onwards.

He made a very good impression on us. Seemed firm, fair and passionate about the job. 'My wife, Susan, is from Edinburgh and we love Scotland because of the outdoors and the freedom.' They have three children at the school whom he says are 'thriving here in the smaller, more intimate environment.'

The junior school is run energetically and passionately by the effervescent Morven Bulloch. She shares Gareth's international background, having taught at a school in the Middle East.

All in all, a young, enterprising and engaged team.

Academic matters: We started our tour of Morrison's in the junior school and quite frankly we loved it. Head, Morven Bulloch, is a lovely lady, brimful of enthusiasm and new ideas and seems to be successfully bringing an enthusiastic staff along with her. From the delightful, purpose built nursery, 'very passionate teachers who really cared about our children', the little ones move across the tennis courts into P1-7. Here the numbers are no bigger than 15 to a class and there is a lot of collaborative learning ie different age groups working with and helping each other.

Throughout primary, each year group will be involved in at least one Rich Task every year. This is a giant research project, for example Africa, spread over six weeks and incorporating different areas of the curriculum including core reading and maths, with different age groups working as a team. This is designed to keep pupils engaged and to encourage independent learning and planning, and from what we saw plenty of creative input (large wall installations) and even Skype sessions with a school in Africa.

'Our kids just love it in the junior school. There is so much going on to keep them interested and they really seem to care about them.' 'Our little boy won't eat veg, but they're working on ways to encourage him.'

There are specialist teachers for subjects such as music, PE, drama and art. In the last year of primary, much of the P7 curriculum (except maths and language) is taught in the senior school in preparation for a seamless transition into S1.

The senior school follows the Scottish curriculum and as head Gareth Warren says, they believe they are 'punching substantially above our weight' in terms of results. The figures are certainly impressive; in 2018, 44 per cent of those sitting got A grades for Advanced Highers, 58 per cent for Highers and 66 per cent for Nat 5s.

These achievements, Gareth Warren says, are across all subjects, but it looks to us as if they are particularly consistent in science, maths and accountancy. (We were rather blown away by a fabulous maths teacher who came bounding out of his classroom to tell us about their latest breakthrough with struggling maths students, but more on that later.)

They offer French, Spanish and German (but no classics), maths, English, history, modern studies, PE, all the sciences, music, art and drama for all from P6 to S2 and Higher photography by popular pupil demand.

One parent told us that their children have come on leaps and bounds because the school work as a three-way team with the parents and the pupils. 'Everyone is involved and knows what's going on.'

They've invested nearly a quarter of a million in technology in the last 18 months. New 100 megabit broadband Wifi, new hardware etc. Access for all – 170 laptops, and 30 mini iPads. Pupils can also come in with their own device. They're looking at creating partnerships with technology companies to help keep them at the top of their game; 'We want to be flexible, keeping our strong academic core, but keeping our ideas open on how we can enhance that.' The junior school is part of this technology drive with more use of green screens (think Hollywood style animation tricks) to liven up the teaching experience and Skype classes (think Kenya); P5 to 7 have access to laptops. The senior school is trialling new smart screens in modern languages, which they say is 'like having a computer on your wall'. They are also trying out a sound booth in one of the rooms. But Gareth stresses, 'whatever we invest in must enhance the pupils' learning experience. We're anxious to avoid more screen time just for the sake of it.'

Now back to the 'bounding' maths teacher who bowled us over with his enthusiasm. He's had remarkable success using technology with a group of students who really struggle with maths. He's been integrating digital learning techniques into the classroom environment and so far their test results have been so impressive it looks as if they may nearly all pass their Nat 5s; an 'astounding' improvement, apparently.

As for the learning support department, this is free and stretches across the whole school from 3 to 18, although the hub is in the primary building. There are two full time LS teachers who go into classrooms across the school as required (dyslexia, dyspraxia and mild Asperger's not a problem), also focussing on very able pupils. On entrance, every child is given an assessment as 'it's important that we can meet the needs of every child'.

'Our youngest had a problem right at the beginning, but they got on to it immediately. Our biggest moment was seeing an essay he had written appear in the Morrisonian.'

There is also a 'nurture teacher' who is on hand to help any child suffering emotional issues such as bereavement.

Games, options, the arts: 'This is fantastic. There are amazing playing fields. I haven't even got very sporty children, but they get out there and have a go.' 'Because it's a small school they feel included and don't want to let anyone down.'

Certainly, there seem to be masses of pitches (including all-weather) at Dallerie, a healthy 10 minute walk from the main buildings. Morrison's sends out teams for all the regular team games and it puts on a good showing in rugby and hockey. The gym/fitness suite is plonked in a rather uninspiring hut in the middle of the main campus which looks as if it could be a tad chilly in the winter. Lots of outdoor activities: mountaineering, skiing, walking, as should happen in such a fabulous location.

Lots of CCF participation and the Duke of Edinburgh award scheme is equally popular. Junior school now has the JAZZ award which sets them up for D of E. Forty-five extracurricular activities in total with everything from taking a lead role in Fiddler on the Roof to surfing at Macrahanish. Climbing is a big sport, with a fantastic purpose built wall and a rather unusual bouldering room which means they can get scrambling from as early as P1.

Beautiful art department in converted attics with inspiring views. Fabulous traditional and contemporary artworks and design, but like the rest of the school they're planning on 'teching up' with investment in robotics and computer coding, and therefore will be looking at other design routes aside from traditional ones.

All of the parents we talked to raved about the music provision. Over half of the school takes individual lessons every week with plenty of orchestra, choir and band opportunities. We were particularly taken with the sound (excuse the pun) of Stringlets, P2 violin introduction, and Tooters, the recorder workshop.

Meanwhile the pipe band seems to go from strength to strength with tours to New York, Hong Kong, Oman and Kuala Lumpa. There is an impressive percussion room, recording studio and a computer suite with the latest software designed to let them make the best noise possible. Lots of concerts and performances at different venues around Scotland and representation at national level for choir and orchestra.

Background and atmosphere: Nestling in the Perthshire town of Crieff, Morrison's couldn't have a more picturesque or convenient location. The money to create this Scottish baronial-styled building, which dates from 1859, was left by former master builder, Thomas Mor(r)ison from nearby Muthill. Morison had made his fortune building Edinburgh's celebrated New Town and before his death had instructed his trustees to erect an institution carrying his name 'to promote the interests of mankind, having a particular regard to the education of youth and the diffusion of useful knowledge'. So no pressure, then.

They clearly did Mr Morison proud, however, as the original school building with its large open corridors works well today, though some of the more recent constructions are less inspiring. When we visited, the rather elegant first floor hall, which stretches from one side of the building to the other, had a fabulous selection of textile designs by pupils.

Two big capital projects are currently underway. They're redeveloping the science block, introducing more technology and the real biggie is the transformation of the library building into a Centre for Learning hub.

The refectory is not particularly exciting: a rather dark, uninspiring piece of Victorian architecture. On the plus side, it is a 10 minute walk from the main campus which must help you work off the jam roly-poly. (Lots of walking at this school, which can't be a bad thing.)

Taking on pupils from Beaconhurst, which closed at the end of the summer term 2018 due to falling numbers.

Pastoral care, well-being and discipline: Excellent pastoral care, with the assistant rector pastoral leader, and heads of year, school nurses, pupil support coordinator and the primary pastoral and well-being coordinator all members of the pastoral support group. In the senior school, each pupil has the same form tutor all the way through, with the head of year taking an overall view of each age group.

'We are keen on spreading senior leadership roles across the staff and across the different departments. It's not only more rewarding for the staff, it means they're more invested in what's happening.'

All the usual substance restrictions are in place, with anti-bullying policies etc, but one thing that comes through loud and clear is the feeling that this is very much a school at the heart of a country community with few discipline issues. The feeling we got as we went round is that it had a rather charming 'small town', cosseted feel to it. We're sure the children feel incredibly protected, but does that mean that they might lack a little sophistication?

Not according to Gareth Warren: 'Because of the rural nature of the school, we regard it as our responsibility to educate them about international issues.' He says the school already has strong links with Malawi and as both heads have international backgrounds they intend to extend these links further afield.

One of the school's unique selling points, they believe, is their Civics initiative. The whole school, from P1 to S6, gets involved at the same time each week in a specially designed programme that can include everything from sex education, team building and career planning to a visit to a local farm.

The idea 'is that everyone is involved in different aspects of the programme, but at the same time. This in turn develops a sense of community spirit and an appreciation of the key Morrisonian characteristics such as respect for others, commitment and resilience.'

As one parent put it, 'When we moved to Crieff, we just had to look at the kind of children coming out of Morrison's to know that was where we wanted to send our children.'

Pupils and parents: Pupils from all over the middle belt – Falkirk, Stirling, Dunblane, Comrie, Perth (masses), Auchterarder – are bused to school. Catchment area extends to south of Stirling and north, past the House of Bruar on the A9 and east to Crianlarich. Parents tend to be farmers, lawyers, doctors, dentists. It's a perfect place to live in terms of reaching any other part of Scotland. Quite a few families relocated from Edinburgh or Glasgow.

Entrance: Children can and do arrive at any time into any year. Assessment for nursery and junior school and more or less automatic entrance into senior school from the junior. Some join the senior school at 11 from the state sector or from local prep schools such as Ardvreck or Craigclowan – assessment rather than exam.

Exit: Virtually all go to university, 95 per cent to Scottish ones. A dribble south of the border, with an occasional Oxbridge place; regular mini stream to eg engineering or allied science at Imperial, Manchester, Newcastle, Leeds. Law, computing, business also prevailing.

Money matters: Discounts for siblings (25 per cent for third child). Scholarships for music and academic for P7/S1, sports from S2. Scholarships available for S6 across all subject areas. Around 15 per cent receive means-tested financial assistance.

Remarks: Proud not posh, this is a wee gem of a Scottish school hidden in the middle of Perthshire. Big enough to turn out some decent team sport and small enough for the head to put a name to every face. Does what it says on the tin and produces some well-rounded, well-educated young people.

North Berwick High School

Grange Road, North Berwick, East Lothian EH39 4QS

Ages 11–18 **Pupils** 925 **Sixth form** 143

01620 894661
www.edubuzz.org/northberwickhigh

Head Teacher: Since 2013, Lauren Rodger MA PGCE. A former pupil here, she studied English at Aberdeen University, then did PGCE at Manchester. Head of English at St Margaret's School in Edinburgh for eight years and was chair of the SCIS English professional development group. Achieved the Scottish Qualification for Headship in 2006 and was depute head teacher here for seven years. Occasionally teaches English and regularly takes a leadership class for senior pupils. Runs the school with three depute head teachers and a business manager. Her three children were educated at the school.

Academic matters: North Berwick High follows the Scottish system: National qualifications followed by Intermediates and Highers and then Advanced Highers. Six parallel classes at S1 and S2, with pupils set for maths in S1 and S2. Thereafter, six parallel classes, taking into account option choices, when specialist subject teaching kicks in – deliberately made broad to ensure that pupils' needs and interests are met within the national framework. Maximum class size 25 (a few exceptions), 18/20 for practical subjects.

Consistently turns in best results in East Lothian – always in what Scottish figures describe as the first decile (top 10th) overall in Scotland for S4 results and better than that for Highers. HMIe calls exam performance 'outstanding'. At S4 level, all three sciences, English and maths, history, modern studies, and PE stand out as really solid and taken by a majority of pupils, while achievement and take-up in French is notable. Spanish has become an increasingly popular choice, with pupils sitting up to Higher level.

Higher level sciences, English and maths, geography (among best in Scotland), modern studies and PE are very strong and this trend continues on the whole to Advanced Higher with physics and history outstanding. The adventurous range of Higher subjects includes graphic communications, philosophy, psychology, technological studies, product design and information systems.

In 2018, 69 per cent A-B and 41 per cent A at Higher level, at Advanced HIgher 65 per cent A-A and 37 per cent A grades.

Good remedial back-up means children with records of needs are not a problem, nor those with ADHD; double teaching in class, laptops as needed, plus extra time in exams and for those with learning needs which cannot be tackled in the classroom, workshops on basic processes, individual educational programmes and individual tutorials. Reading Recovery programme, plus educational psychologists, outreach teachers et al. Support for learning for the most able as well. The school takes and is well-equipped for the quite severely disabled and works successfully to integrate all into mainstream lessons. Vocationally orientated courses on offer from Prince's Trust, hospitality at Intermediate level, and lots of enterprising opportunities. The hairdressing salon, offering Intermediate qualifications, is open to local people (a really good community service). The school aims to meet the needs of all pupils, not just the top section, and recent emphasis has been on enhancing this 'but not taking the eye off the academic ball'.

The integrated pupil support faculty includes a pupil support base in which the most vulnerable pupils have a 'sanctuary' with additional needs met in various ways: in class by teachers, auxiliaries and S6 pupil helpers. Some are extracted to work on particular areas in the support base, or on a well-established programme of paired reading. Alphasmart and laptop computers in use where required. Individual education programmes in place.

Games, options, the arts: Has an enviable collection of games pitches with the local sports centre and swimming pool next door – they have partnership with local users. Astroturf, two gyms in school, plus dance studio with mirrors, of course. Strong rugby and getting stronger with some real successes and girls' basketball U14 and boys U14 and U18 teams reaching Scottish Cup finals. Huge hockey fixture list for girls, plus volleyball, football, cross-country, and clubs for badminton, netball, sailing, swimming. Local authority development officers on hand for coaching. DofE very popular. Trillions of clubs for everything including the latest success story, beekeeping, and lots of things for the non-sporty. More than 40 different choices, many on offer to several different age groups. Drama, debating etc as expected plus science and language clubs, eco (with coveted Green Flag award) and fair trade groups, chess, newspaper, scripture union etc. Sports activities coordinator, an ex-pupil, has got even more involved. Plenty of serious fun fundraising for carefully planned range of charities with almost everything linking with the efforts of the local community, which has school at its heart.

Music exceptional, though no pipe band of their own – pupils (of both sexes) play with the town band. Bands, orchestras, masses of instrumental: wind, jazz, brass, piano etc. Senior and junior choirs (some really outstanding singers) and a popular staff/seniors choir – carols sung outside the church for charity at Christmas. Musicians have played with the Scottish National Orchestra in the Usher Hall. Scottish country dancing popular, as are regular ceilidhs. A group even taught highland dancing to a school in Malawi on their trip there.

Recording studio; huge assembly hall used for school drama (very good) and by the locals – for partying as well as plays. Deaf loop in operation. Rows of keyboards, computers and highly decorative guitars stored on walls in music room are all in regular use. Oodles of practice rooms. Creative chaos reigns in the art department, crammed with fabulous work: ceramics, amazing sandblasted glass, block printed fabrics to die for, fantastic costume design with beautiful embroidery and even architectural layouts. Swathes of young artists go on to art schools all over the country. Huge art library and darkroom are supplemented by CAD, Macs and computer links to art department. DT is impressive though mainly in wood. Home

N

economics (cookery) now refurbished with good take up from both sexes and fashion now attracts a few boys. Impressive computer suites and everything technological imaginable can be taken for granted.

Lots of trips, Italy, Belgium, Washington, China, Ardèche, London and to crown it all, visits to partner school in Malawi.

Background and atmosphere: Founded in 1893 with 13 pupils. Originally North Berwick boasted a Parish School (which started in 1661) and the Burgh School; these amalgamated in 1868 and joined forces with the High School in 1931. The current buildings date from 1940s, and very impressive they are too. Refurbishments in 1990s and more recently an interior revamp have created a school which still looks and feels like a real Scottish Academy but is absolutely up to date in every detail; expansion underway to create a new sports hall and more classrooms. The intriguing café space has been brilliantly constructed surrounding the old central courtyard so that it forms a circular 'high street' right round a charming herb garden, mercifully sheltered from the fierce coastal winds. It is the venue for the Christmas fair, which is a highlight of town life in North Berwick and makes healthy sums for charity.

Light and airy classrooms, which must have some of the best views in Britain, cheek by jowl with the pyramidal Berwick Law on one side and in sight of the Bass Rock and spectacular coastline on the other. Strong links with the spectacular Scottish Seabird Centre, which is used for regular study, as well as providing summer and weekend jobs for impoverished pupils. Loads of participation in town life, concerts for the elderly, tree planting, riding for the disabled. Pupils have contributed entertainment, singing, dance and the like further afield, including Edinburgh.

The huge library is subdivided into little seminar areas and crannies for private study. A tidy school, and pretty well maintained, with lots of eau de nil paint (a favourite with Scottish schools) giving a clean calm feel, though the unwise choice of white painted breezeblock does not respond well to regular wiping down. Walls full of pupil work on display everywhere.

Pastoral care, well-being and discipline: Good PSE and strong anti-bullying programmes backed up by a restorative positive behaviour policy and behaviour codes. Pastoral care is delivered via the four houses each managed by a member of the guidance team. Pastoral staff co-ordinate with the deputes, who function as year heads, and an extensive support and counselling team. Working with parents is a key factor. Embedded in a geographically self-sufficient community, the school has taken on a role in community welfare and co-operates with initiatives such as the Youth Project to help keep young people safe and well-balanced out of school as well as in.

Pupils take real responsibility in school, as heads of school, and of houses, as prefects, as mentors for younger pupils and as representatives to the community. Head boy/girl elected annually by pretty stringent process. An onerous task – they have to do the Burns' Night supper at the local Marine Hotel, which brushes up their public speaking. The head boy and girl are principal speakers for S1/2/3 prize-giving at the traditional time in June, and then for the senior prize giving in mid-September, which is followed by soft drinks, wine for the adults and nibbles in the dining hall; very popular.

Four chaplains visit, three Church of Scotland and one Episcopalian, who help to tackle moral issues and teach pupils to listen and be open to the views of others.

Pupils and parents: North Berwick has its share of Edinburgh commuters, bankers and businesspeople from England etc but also an indigenous farming and services community, so intake is pretty mixed. Not quite exclusively Scottish middle class, though only a minuscule element of ethnic diversity. Incredibly supportive parents – usually over 95 per cent turn up for parents' evenings and a very strong PTA, wizards at fundraising. Parent-led parent council drawn from parents, staff and a couple of members of the local community.

Uniform is kept as simple as possible: white shirts with black and red ties and sweatshirt plus blazers for top years. Pupils encouraged to stay in school at lunchtime. Cafeteria is well used for informal relaxation and they can bring packed lunch or eat in the sports centre. Closes at lunchtime on Fridays for staff training, which may not be over-convenient for working parents. School buses for all outlying districts.

Entrance: Effective programme of visits to feeder primaries, mainly Law Primary (700) which shares the site but also drawing in the scattered small schools in Aberlady, Athelstaneford, Dirleton, Gullane and Law. Head meets parents, and children have a two-day induction programme followed by another parent meeting. Entry automatic if family lives in catchment.

Exit: Two departure dates a year, one at Christmas, the other at the conventional end of school year. Over 90 per cent stay on for fifth year and only few go before sixth. Some leave to go into further education, some work, 60 per cent to university – quite a mix: medics, law, business administration, economics, English, maths, education. Primarily to Scottish universities (Edinburgh, Glasgow, St Andrews) but a regular and quite impressive trickle to Oxbridge – two in 2018, and two medics.

Money matters: No child disadvantaged – good back up from the local LA, as well as parent-inspired foundation.

Remarks: A real thriving local school, doing well by everybody. About as good as it gets.

Oban High School

O

Soroba Road, Oban, Argyll PA34 4JB

Ages 11–18 **Pupils** 980 **Sixth form** 140 **Boarders** 50

01631 564231
www.obanhigh.argyll-bute.sch.uk

Head teacher: Since 2008, Peter Bain MA MSc PGCE. Since 2019 executive head of both Oban High School and Tiree High School. Married to Theresa, local college manager, with two teenage children. Educated at Musselburgh Grammar, he had to support himself through a history degree then a masters in historical research at Edinburgh University after his parents died suddenly. After 10 years spent rising to a managerial position in business retail, he recognised a calling to teach and again self-funded himself through a PGCE at Jordanhill College in Glasgow.

Despite a late start in teaching, his progress has been impressive; he taught in six different schools and left a depute headship at Eyemouth High School in Berwickshire to become head at Oban. He believes his 'business and management experience' have been a valuable augmentation to his teaching abilities. In fact within six months of joining the school in 2008 he had formulated a business plan to build a new £36m building to take Oban High School well into the 21st century. And 10 years later, wow, you should see this place.

He runs the school with four deputes.

Academic matters: 'This is the broadest curriculum in Scotland. We do everything from Nat 5s and highers to the IB.' And they're not joking. They claim that they will guarantee to provide 'the necessary qualifications and experiences for any youngster to gain entry to any course in any Scottish university or for any career pathway of their choosing.'

That's quite the undertaking. If you have a vision of secondary education as a linear, largely shared academic experience with national exams strategically placed along the way, think again. Oban High school probably more than any other secondary school we have visited has fully embraced the idea of the Curriculum of Excellence and shaping an education to each individual child.

So what does that look like, exactly? Well it must be one heck of an organisational challenge, it seems to us, with so many children following a very diverse range of paths.

At the purely academic end of the scale, 84 per cent A-C grades at Advanced Higher in 2018 and nearly 76 per cent at Higher. Also every year around 10 pupils sit the Scottish Baccalaureate, which offers four subject areas at Advanced Higher level including social sciences, languages, expressive arts and science and an interdisciplinary project designed to expand independent thinking. Of these, 76 per cent got A-C grades.

They claim that on average two pupils will have a go at Oxbridge every year, but dwelling on the exam results really is not what this school is about. Believe us.

Our tour began, not in the latest science labs but in the rather luxurious cosmetology suite, where some pupils were administering facials and massages to each other. Further along the corridor were well appointed hairdressing salons and then we arrived at the spacious building and construction areas. Sorry, are we still in a school? Doesn't this kind of provision impinge on the territory of the local college? Apparently not, according to Peter Bain.

'We have an excellent relationship with our local college, in part because their manager is my wife! They send us the tutors for cosmetology, construction, marine engineering and childcare. We do a mixture of awards and qualifications which go from SVQ level 4 to 7. Our aim is not just to deliver academic results but to give each child the benefit of wider experiences.' Before any child is sent out on a work placement they will be required to achieve a customer service award to improve their chances of making a good impression.

And what about the commitment to give an education tailored to each and every child? 'Because of the geographical constraints of our area, we are sometimes limited with what we can offer, but we will always make an effort to think out of the box eg we have a child who is interested in forensic science and is about to spend three days in a specialised lab at Strathclyde University. We're also about to place another child with creative ambitions with a Scottish designer.'

Not everyone is happy. One parent said, 'They're not as great as they make out. I sometimes think they're trying to please too many people.' However, the school does offer a wide range of subjects to AH level, including all three sciences, alongside the vocational options.

Another interesting departure is the school's efforts to use local business partners to enhance the educational experience. This includes, for example, the private historic trust, Dunollie Castle. The school is currently in discussion with them about setting up a classroom on site which can be used for a whole host of activities from history research to suitable work placements.

Peter Bain believes strongly that 'education should not just be for the top 30 per cent who can get a Higher.' Now if we only had a tenner for every head who has sat the Good Schools Guide down and said we offer a truly 'holistic' education....well, you know where we're going with this. But good grief! Haud ontae yer bunnets! We think Oban High School really does try its best to deliver.

'It's the added value courses that are getting more of our pupils, academic or otherwise, into positive destinations than ever before.' For example, in S5 and S6, 256 children are doing an SVQ level 5/6 leadership award. This includes personal development, Scottish studies, Scots language awards, religious belief and values.

'The pupils who want to go to university are just as important but again their added value courses are what is getting them in there. For the other children who are not so academic, they are racking up achievements such as the John Muir and Duke of Edinburgh Awards.'

They have even created their own special awards in recognition of the children for whom 'going down the street on their own and buying a bun' is an achievement.

And the courses? Well there are over 90 of them, ranging from the usual suspects to aquaculture, make up, equality and diversity and group dance performance. So huge variety and lots of creativity, but be aware some parents feel the school doesn't always tick all the academic boxes.

Games, options, the arts: Wow! Plenty, plenty to do, with 54 different clubs ranging from the record club, which is all about the music, to the debating society. Sailing, shinty, archery, skiing, basketball and hockey are all on the agenda.

Special mention must go to the School of Rugby and their technologically edgy artificial pitches. Apparently the superior performance of the school's rugby squad (the girls have twice won the Scottish bowl) brought the Scottish Rugby Union to their door and they are now supported with top notch coaching and mentoring.

Judging by our stroll around the grounds, football is still top of the pops for the boys, but athletics (there is international representation in the school), badminton, hockey, table tennis, netball, skiing, gymnastics and strength and conditioning are also on offer. Mr Bain says that the Scottish Vocational Qualification or SVQ sport coaching is a big thing and they have developed an agreement with the local primaries that their children can go and try out their coaching skills on the younger pupils so that they gain 'more valuable experience'.

The School of Dance, which is strongly linked with the world-renowned Ballet West, is another area of excellence and brings a selection of foreign students keen to pursue their studies.

And let's not forget the School of Traditional Music, which finds its inspiration from the strength and excellence of the local musical heritage. The school pipe band is currently ranked champion of champions in the world and performs globally whenever it can raise the money. It has just moved into a shiny new soundproofed piping building and one of the best pipers in the world heads up the teaching staff.

Apart from the piping, they have a nationally ranked accordion teacher and they offer coaching in the fiddle (Scottish violin), clarsach (Gaelic harp), piping, whistle and flute, piano, guitar, accordion, drums and voice. Pupils perform everywhere from New York to Ireland, from Inverness to the local M&S.

'We are averaging 100 per cent pass rates in drama, art, music.'

The art department is proud to have its own kiln. No digital art on offer at the moment, but could be if requested. We didn't notice much art on the walls during our travels and we're not sure if that's because it's not a strongly taught subject or whether the school is too new to be adorning the walls just yet.

Performing arts is clearly a strong department. Not only do they teach stage and sound production, they have a specific workshop where they build their own sets for the drama studios. The stage, which is neatly concealed in the assembly area, has the same kind of kit available as a London Theatre; there is an entire lighting rig concealed in the ceiling.

Boarding: Covering the education requirements of islands such as Colonsay, Coll, Mull, Lismore, Iona, Kerrera, Shuna and Easdale as well as the remote Bridge of Orchy, the local authority has no option but to offer hostel accommodation. This has not always been the smooth running operation you might have hoped for, however. In the past there have been reports in the press of complaints over the behaviour of school pupils outside school hours. After Peter Bain joined Oban High, he negotiated that the school be allowed to be involved in the running of the boarding house and help administer discipline. But the situation has since changed and the school is currently not directly involved. Currently there are around 50 children staying with a hostel manager, an assistant manager and about eight houseparents. Will this continue to work as the school and the boarding numbers expand? It would be worth keeping an eye on the situation.

Having said that, the parents we spoke to felt the hostel staff looked after their children extremely well and did a 'huge amount of running around taking them to their clubs'.

'We couldn't fault it. Our kids are remarkably happy.'

Background and atmosphere: Every year, the day after the famous Argyllshire gathering (highland games), Oban High School girds its loins, and takes over the field of action ready for battle. In a spectacular march worthy of Braveheart (OK, we're waxing lyrical now), the school band pipes each clan (or house) down to the field behind its own pennant and the battle commences. Tossing the caber and the hammer, sword and highland dancing, piping competitions and huge tugs of war.

'From Easter to summer the kids are trained to throw the caber, hammer etc. It's a huge event for the school and the town as a whole and it just makes us so proud to be there competing and proud to be Scottish.' Braveheart, Gladiator, choose whatever corny comparison you want, it just sounds fun doesn't it? Just uplifting and upbeat and, well, unified.

And that is probably how we would describe Oban High School. It is a very together school. Peter Bain may not be everyone's cup of tea, but he is a man with a strong vision and a passion for education.

One parent told us, 'He's definitely Marmite. Some love him and some hate him, but he does seem to have a good grasp of what children from this area need.'

One of his biggest achievements is spearheading a successful campaign to build a new £36 million school. And it is a wonderful building: bright, imposing and quite rightly proud of itself. The classrooms are clean, spacious and well equipped. There are amazing beauty and hairdressing salons, building and construction areas, wonderful dance studios, fully soundproofed music block and impressive sporting facilities such as a gym and the latest artificial pitches. The central hall transforms into a fully equipped theatre (but why can't they accommodate all of the school in one single space? Just asking!).

And while the building may be all singing all dancing (you have to see the colour-changing trophy cabinet which towers above the entrance), it doesn't stop Mr Bain patrolling the only school entrance every morning looking for school uniform offenders. He hasn't been 10 per cent successful, judging by the pupils we saw to-ing and fro-ing, but he's definitely 'on it'.

Pastoral care, well-being and discipline: School operates on fairly traditional clan (house) system. Every clan has a depute head teacher in charge. They are responsible for the academic and pastoral care of each child. Each clan also has a full time guidance teacher offering pastoral care. (Peter Bain thinks this is unique in Scottish schools). There are also two youth development workers and two home link workers who support pupils both at home and at the four outreach centres.

These outreach centres are placed across the school's catchment area and allow pupils and parents to receive academic or pastoral support nearer to home. One is based in a college, one in primary school, two in community centres.

These same staff members man the free breakfast club which operates all year round including during the holidays. On top of that the school offers study support from Monday to Thursday in the evenings and during the Easter holidays before exams.

The school door shuts at 9am and all latecomers are interviewed. If kids arrive without a uniform they are given one.

For repeated patterns of misbehaviour parents are invited in promptly and 'we work together to make sure the pupil behaves.'

Pupils and parents: Everything from very rich with their own helicopters to real rural poverty. About 50 pupils arrive on a ferry on a weekly basis, while around 10 are flown in. A further 140 pupils take the train to school and another 300 are bussed in.

Parents range from farmers, architects, fishermen, shop workers and doctors to lots of people working from home via computer.

Entrance: Nineteen partner primary schools – a huge number, but they are covering an enormous geographical area. In two of those primary schools the first language is Gaelic. The school is very popular and has a considerable number of placement requests.

Exit: Virtually all to a 'positive destination' last year which means they went to university, college or straight to a job. Forty per cent to university, usually in Scotland. Glasgow, Abertay, Highlands and Islands, St Andrews, British and Irish Modern Music Institute, Strathclyde, West of Scoland, Napier, Dundee, Aberdeen, Edinburgh. Forty per cent straight into employment, but usually after staying for sixth year. Some 16 per cent to FE colleges in Oban or Glasgow.

Remarks: We struggle to describe this as a school: more a complete educational experience. Inspiring leadership has meant they tackle a huge and complex catchment area with commitment and dedication. Some parents feel they may stretch themselves too far in their efforts to offer everything to everybody, but our impression is that they have a very good sense of the area and its requirements.

Perth Grammar School

Gowans Terrace, Perth PH1 5AZ

Ages 12–18 **Pupils** 1,043 **Sixth form** 229

01738 472800
www.perthgrammar.org.uk

Head teacher: Since 2016, Fiona Robertson. Arrived from Mackie Academy where she was a depute head. Before that a quality improvement officer for Aberdeenshire Council. Has a BA in history with education from Stirling, a masters in leadership in professional contexts from Aberdeen and a Scottish qualification for headship. Young, enthusiastic and ambitious for the school, she seems to be an inspired choice who is keen to take the school in new directions. When not working loves to run (hopefully not from Perth Grammar).

Academic matters: Follows the Scottish system and this means being bound by the wildly confusing Curriculum for Excellence (eight broad curriculum areas with learning planned around

P

experiences and outcomes). School seems to have a strong grip on what's going on, thank goodness. Results are improving. One parent we spoke to said they'd thought long and hard before sending their children to the school because of its 'bad reputation', but they had been delighted with how their children had fared. 'Some of the teaching is outstanding and committed, particularly in maths, graph com and technology areas.'

The school measures the literacy and numeracy of every child in S3. Reading, writing and listening have all improved since last year, they say, although numeracy has dropped slightly. As for Nat 5 results there was a slight drop in the latest pass rate, though a big increase in the pass level of those taking three Highers (most common number sat at any one time), although still not topping the league tables.

Maths is split into different sets from S1 but all other subjects have mixed ability teaching. S4 is when each child's 'pathway' is identified (ie they decide which national qualifications each child will do). Most classes are composite in the sense that you could have a couple sitting Nat 5s in a Higher class. This is totally normal. 'This is really about tailoring the education to each child. We ask our young people very early on what sort of destination they want and encourage them to manage their career aspirations.' Big emphasis on this approach: not one size fits all.

'We consulted our parent body with regards the number of Nationals we wanted pupils to sit. We are sure that six is the best number. Quality not quantity,' says head.

The school follows the Perth City Campus Model: the four secondaries within the city work with Perth College UHI (which provides further and higher education throughout the area) to broaden the offer for the children. For example, Perth Grammar runs Advanced Higher statistics and children from other secondaries can study it here too. Rural schools may be able to access the campus model via virtual learning in future.

Learning support is impressive indeed, we thought, especially within the state system. Each enhanced provision class – in a spacious classroom – has no more than eight pupils with two teachers (one of them training in special support). 'Our aim is to get all young people into mainstream education if at all possible.' Additional support staff available throughout the school to offer back-up where necessary eg dyslexia, family break-up.

An extensive enhanced transition programme for pupils coming up from primary schools.

Games, options, the arts: 'THE sporting comprehensive in Perth and Kinross' is how one parent described the school. Fiona Robertson is really proud of her young, buzzing sports department – this is what sealed the deal when it came to accepting the job, she says.

Not often you see a school with a proper sports stadium and running track (shared with St John's RC Academy), but we were a bit surprised to see the pupils walking around it at a leisurely pace. They must have been on a go-slow. We are reliably informed, however that athletics is very strong. Keen to point out that they are a School of Basketball and that they won this year's Scottish Schools Cup. Lots of dedication, with pupils coming in early and staying late for practice: they were obligingly bouncing around the court at great speed when we passed by. Hockey is another strength with some playing at national level. Netball another successful sport, rugby more so than football, a lot of interest in skiing and there are some enthusiastic swimmers, although they have no pool. Two hours of PE a week, but most of the wider extracurricular activities have a sporting element (lots of taster sessions such as fencing and horse riding).

'Really strong' performance in gold, silver and bronze DofE.

Lively music and drama departments; this year they're putting on The Wiz. There's a show every two years and the community love them, apparently; very well supported. Also a concert every Christmas and even a charity Christmas single. Successful choir and orchestra. Visiting specialists teach violin, piano, guitar and drums.

We liked the look of the art department, which was bursting with pupil creations. Three busy art teachers and attentive hardworking pupils. 'Very popular.'

We were impressed by the very busy international programme which has been built up from nothing over the past 10 years or so: building family homes in Tanzania; exchanges with Aschaffenburg in Germany, Trento in Italy, Hong Kong, Iowa in America; plus trips to London, Madrid and skiing. These are open to a range of ages.

Background and atmosphere: Absolutely no prizes for whoever designed this monstrosity of a building. We struggled even to find the front door and followed a poor mother with a buggy struggling up the stairs (they are building a new reception area on the ground floor). Once inside, though, it's deceptively spacious. 'Every teacher has their own room', which is not a given in other schools, we're told. Lots of different gathering spaces: sports hall, gym, dance hall and miles and miles of corridor (with a regular sprinkling of crisp packets etc.) That said, the school had a lively and active feel to it.

Fiona Robertson is clearly quite a catch for a head and she obviously loves the job with a passion, although for some parents we spoke to the jury is still out. 'She has a very different style. Not quite such a big character and a very different way of leading.'

Pupils we spoke to were unanimous in what lifted the school out of the ordinary. 'The teachers, they go the extra mile to support you.' 'Couldn't ask for better teaching staff. They're great.'

Pastoral care, well-being and discipline: The school is run on a house system and each house has its own pupil support team, which incorporates learning support teachers.

'We believe in restorative practice,' ie if something goes wrong discuss it and see what can be done to stop it happening again. Focus is always on 'aspiring to do our best at all times'. It's about supporting pupils appropriately and considering the 'wider context' with regards behaviour.

Parental views are more mixed. 'There's no doubt they have to behave, which isn't a bad thing.' 'She's very different from the last head. She is much stricter, but that means the kids know they have to behave, which is no bad thing.'

Pupils and parents: Parents from all walks of life from professional to unemployed. 'Almost reflects our leavers' destinations.' Parent council would like more involvement from the parents themselves. Most children come from surrounding catchment (which includes the least salubrious parts of Perth and a chunk of 'county' Perthshire spreading north to Dunkeld and east almost to Crieff). A few transfers.

They welcome inter-study students: young people from Europe who spend a year studying here, staying with a host family.

Entrance: Ten exclusive feeder primaries and two with a choice (because of the rural nature of the catchment).

Exit: A third into higher education, a third into further education and a third into employment. The proportion going to university has risen significantly: mainly Scottish universities such as Edinburgh, Aberdeen, Stirling, Glasgow, Dundee, St Andrews, Strathclyde. The joy of Perth is that it is Scotland's heart.

Remarks: Young head with a passion for the job and great aspirations. Results on the up, impressive international programme and a 'buzzy' sports department. The building is brutalist architecture at its worst, but who wouldn't like to look out to the hills and the open spaces of The Inch. For the fair city of Perth, it's a fair school.

Robert Gordon's College

Schoolhill, Aberdeen AB10 1FE

Ages 3–18 **Pupils** 1,565 **Sixth form** 167

Fees: £8,435 – £13,130 pa

01224 646346
www.rgc.aberdeen.sch.uk

Head of college: Since 2014, Simon Mills. One family describes picking up their children on their first day at Robert Gordon's College during a good going north east gale. Out of the corner of their eye they saw a figure assiduously picking up bits of paper blowing around the quad, then stepping forward with a big smile and introducing himself as the headmaster. That, they say, is Simon Mills to a T.

Mr Mills took over Robert Gordon's College after a highly successful period as the head of Lomond School in Helensburgh. Born in St Andrews and educated at the High School of Dundee, Glenalmond College then Cambridge, he appears charming, thoughtful, approachable and seemingly very popular with staff and pupils alike. What the parents see is somebody who cares principally about their children rather than playing the charisma game. He believes he took over a high performing school when he took on Gordon's, and he has an equally strong and imaginative vision of where he would like to take it over the next few years. He is married to Ruth, a primary teacher, and they have three children. Passions include skiing, windsurfing, sailing, golf and all things outdoor.

Head of junior school: Since September 2017 is Sarah Webb, previously attainment adviser at Education Scotland.

Academic matters: The school prides itself on offering the complete education from pre-school nursery to 18. At P1 the class sizes are no bigger than 22, by P7 no bigger than 24. Junior school is rightly proud of the revamped building designed around a '360 degree education'. A what, you say? In a nutshell, this means down with the old fashioned lecturing from the front and in with the light, bright flexible spaces with plenty of interactive opportunities for the pupils and the teachers. They seem to love it, we have to say. As well as their regular teacher, each class has visits from specialist teachers for a range of subjects such as art, music, drama, French PE and science. The children also make trips to the Craig Centre for Performing Arts across the quad in the senior school.

One of the P4 classes we entered were reviewing a performance they had just seen in the arts centre with the help of individual iPads. In the P1 area, there was a wonderful communal play area which joined all three classes and encouraged social activity.

One parent told us about bringing their boys to the junior school after a stint abroad, fearful that their patchy education would require remedial help. But staff took six weeks to assess them and turn them around. 'They seemed to really "get" our children and be able to solve the situation without resorting to too much overbearing intervention. Far more subtle and sensitive than we'd expected.'

So once through the more cuddly end of the school, how do things fare further up the ladder? Pretty impressively, we would say. Firstly in the breadth of qualifications on offer and secondly in the excellent standard of achievement. They claim they can 'accommodate all choices' and they are keen to make sure that each child is allowed to play to their individual strengths. There are 30 subjects on offer with opportunities to study less visited ones such as photography, astronomy and ceramics along with the more mainstream options. Choice of four languages in S1 and Mandarin is now taught at National 5. And the results are impressive. This was 2018: 57 per cent A grades at Higher level and 49 per cent at Advanced Higher.

Science and maths are a particularly strong suit (we're still recovering from witnessing an experiment on a Sainsbury's sausage), and with substantial investment from local patrons (the oil industry has been a big help in that area) they have the kind of state of the art facilities that a university would be happy to utilise. In fact, The Wood Foundation Centre for Science and Technology is the largest school teaching science and tech centre in the UK.

But there are equally strong performances across the full range of academic areas, including languages. Interestingly, the school has a very strong focus on the classics, and in the quest for a suitable teacher the department has embarked on training its own using the HMC teacher training scheme (HMCTT). This scheme has been set up as the independent schools version of Teach First, ie encouraging bright graduates to enter teaching by training on the job. In fact, this is a move being replicated across the syllabus in areas where schools are struggling to fill teaching posts, such as physics. Head says, 'We have taken the view that training our teachers to our standards is extremely important' – ie let's be proactive and not be lumbered with the only candidate to apply for the post.

One aspect of academic life which the school is particularly proud of, however, is its strong university links. Staff are in frequent and regular contact with Scottish university principals to ensure that they are in tune with this aspect of higher education. And indeed, out of the over 97 per cent of their pupils who go on to university or further education, more than 80 per cent of those will be to Scottish universities.

Another area of outstanding achievement, as far as the school is concerned, is the digital policy, which they cite as being sector leading. These digital advances were kickstarted by an Australian headmaster exchange and have developed to mean that each pupil in the senior school has a digital device. Meanwhile, there has been considerable investment in infrastructure, equipment and teacher training to support this.

The Support for Learning department has had a radical overhaul in the last year, following a recent review. With an expanded team, the emphasis now is much more towards early intervention and supporting pupils in class rather than in isolation. The school has now created a secure online area for teachers to access so that they can readily share support information on individual children. The Support for Learning teachers, as well as operating in the classroom, now move between the junior and senior school to help identify potential problems early and to ensure continuity for the child.

One parent we talked to had been particularly impressed with the way they had cajoled a reluctant child through his maths National 5. 'Our son was telling us he was going to extra maths over lunchtime, but was skipping out the door with his mates instead. The school immediately picked it up and handled it really well and soon got him back on the straight and narrow. He appreciates it now!' Not then, probably.

Games, options, the arts: There is a strong evidence of considerable artistic endeavour at Gordon's, helped no doubt by the fact that Aberdeen Art Gallery is on the doorstep. There is a variety of disciplines taught, (including a Higher in photography, which this reviewer wouldn't mind doing themselves) and architecture is taught in both the art and the ICT department.

Recent investment has resulted in a new drama studio and music room along with the Craig Centre for Performing Arts – a state of the art performance and digital recording venue. They now offer a National Progression Award in musical theatre in S6.

The clubs and societies on offer at Gordon's are too numerous to mention and the DofE provision is the largest in Scotland (that's a lot of wet tents to work your way around), but indicates a healthy leaning towards extracurricular activity.

One negative is that sport at Gordon's (apart from an onsite swimming pool) is mainly offered off-site on the edge of the city. But what a site it is. Perhaps you can't run straight out of maths onto the sweaty green acres of the rugby pitch, but this 45 acre sports ground at Countesswells is blessed with Astro pitches, an amazing water-based hockey pitch, which is used by the international squad, and a plethora of rugby, football, cricket etc facilities. They haven't resolved how to protect parents from that biting north east wind yet, but we're optimistic; they seem resourceful.

Historically, the school has fielded strong rugby and hockey teams, but also support sports such as cricket and golf. Every year the school has on average 30 pupils competing at an international level in all kinds of disciplines such as girls' football. But crucially the school says their focus is also on getting as many pupils as possible participating in as many sports and activities as possible.

The next major investment is the indoor sports centre at their city centre site. Sport, they say is crucial to their holistic view of education.

Background and atmosphere: Prepare to be amazed at what you might find through the arch of Robert Gordon's College. Robert Gordon himself was born in Aberdeen in 1668, but made a fortune trading in the Baltic states. Wealthy, with no heirs, his ambition was to build a 'hospital' to house and educate poor boys. The resulting Old Hoose by William Adam has stood at the heart of the city as his legacy since his death in 1731.

So for centuries Gordon's, as it's known locally, has been a very familiar city landmark. Perhaps too familiar over the years. One of the issues the school says it struggles with is getting the message out there about just how far it has moved on from the rather foosty, conventional and middle class institution that it has been in the past. In fact, the school – helped, no doubt, by the cosmopolitan and financial influence of the oil industry – has way outgrown any parochial memories. What we experienced was a thriving, questing and successful institution which quite rightly places itself within the top 10 co-educational day schools in the UK.

Until relatively recently the school was confined to the northern side of the Georgian quadrangle which it inhabits, having gifted the rest to the Robert Gordon University in 1909. The university has now relocated to Garthdee, freeing up a wealth of space for this city centre school to develop... and develop it has.

The move has allowed them to reduce class sizes (on average around 20 per class), design a sector leading junior school, expand and relocate the nursery and, as already mentioned, develop a succession of new facilities for science and the arts.

But they're not alone in that. Other schools can boast amazing facilities. What impressed us was the positivity of the staff, the willingness to embrace the latest technology and ideas and the quiet pride in what they do. Good stuff. There is no getting away from the fact that this is a big school with over 1,600 pupils from nursery through to sixth year, but in lots of ways it doesn't feel like that. One parent we spoke to talked about the surprising intimacy of the school. She said they had worried about the sheer size of the place, but they were blown away by how well monitored their children were.

One glaring issue is the rapid downturn of the oil industry which has done so much to support the city as a whole over the last 40 years. We imagined that this would be a huge dent in the confidence of a school such as Robert Gordon's, but not so, apparently. Simon Mills says the number of school applications has actually risen this year and he believes that there are enough alternative industries left in the city to support the school. It will be interesting to see how this develops.

One parent commented: 'I think our boys will always take a bit of Gordon's with them, wherever we go. Which amazes us, really, because we're not native Aberdonians. They just really connected with the place.'

Pastoral care, well-being and discipline: Head likes to think they circumvent many of the problems associated with being such a large school. Certainly the quad environment has an intimate feel to it and the pupils seem to be a good natured, polite and well-mannered bunch. Of course the pupils we talked to were shining examples, but our impression from talking to parents in general is that there is a real sense of pride among the pupils and a desire to promote the good values of the school outside in the real world.

There are eight heads of guidance, who Simon Mills says operate 'like a tartan' of pastoral support throughout a child's school career. Each child has the same form teacher throughout their school life and likewise they are assigned the same guidance teacher (usually whole families have the same guidance teacher) who meets regularly with them to discuss both their problems and their successes. It must be working. Serious disciplinary issues are rare. Parents we spoke to were amazed at how well cared for the children were. When it came to writing references for university, for example, the teachers genuinely knew the children. Another parent spoke in admiration of the mentoring that fifth and sixth year pupils are offered by the senior management team. 'They really roll up their sleeves and offer serious support.'

Pupils and parents: This is the place to send your children in Aberdeen. Parents tend to be professional; oil related obviously, employed by the universities, lawyers, accountants and some farmers. The day starts early at 8.30am and the children can travel from as far as 40 miles outside the city. As usually happens with a city centre location, parking around the school at drop off/pick up time is a nightmare. Prepare to curse. The parents seem to love it though, describing it as 'very social' as well as academically rigorous.

Entrance: The school's excellent academic results and lack of competition mean that it is oversubscribed. There is an interview for entry to nursery and for 5 year olds entering the junior school. Those over 9 will sit a test, as will any child entering the senior school. It is always worth applying, though, as those parents who are still involved in the oil industry can be quite a fluid population.

Exit: Virtually all sixth year leavers to university, the vast majority staying in Scotland and more than half to Aberdeen, Edinburgh, Glasgow or Robert Gordon. Around 10 per cent go south of the border to eg London, Bristol, Durham, Manchester, Newcastle or Warwick; three to Oxbridge in 2018. Others have headed to Canada and Australia, but it's a fairly conservative outlook. Most popular courses are engineering, science, economics and management, law and medicine (eight medics in 2018).

Money matters: One in six children in the senior school are on some form of bursary. School spends £1.4m on bursaries every year, with 100 per cent bursaries available for bright children in real need. It's always worth investigating.

Remarks: Great academic standards, fabulous facilities and forward-thinking headmaster with challenging ideas. Huge choice of subjects and sports to dip your toe into. It is a bit of an unsung hero, however, and we suspect not many people outside Aberdeen will have heard of the school. So if namedropping your alma mater is on your agenda, this might not be the school for you. Having said that, if you want your child to emerge quietly confident and with a strong sense of self, get their name down now.

The Royal High School (Edinburgh)

East Barnton Avenue, Edinburgh EH4 6JP

Ages 11–18 **Pupils** 1,266 **Sixth form** 177

01313 362261
www.royalhigh.wordpress.com

Rector: Since 2014, Pauline Walker BSc PGCE (40s), educated in the maintained sector, followed by Heriot Watt; previously head of Gracemount High School. Studied maths and computing (a 'computing geek' married to a computing engineer); buzzy, fun and good at reading upside down. At ease, both with the school and herself – well, if you come from Gracemount.. SEN – systems in place; physical handicap – systems in place; bullying.. this is proper CEO stuff and parents to whom we spoke were/are delighted with the rector.

Certain amount of revamping the curriculum, tinkering with the timings; new outdoor classroom ('fairy glen' – you can't spot it from outside); forest school on wish list. School day now starts 8.32am (first lesson 8.40; teaching day now extended to seven 50 minute blocks Monday to Thursday, and four 50 minute blocks on Friday, when day stops at 12.30 'to allow staff and pupils [to attend] city wide events which tend to begin at 1.30pm'.

Academic matters: Max class size 30, going down to 20 for practical subjects and much less in higher years. Regular turnover of staff, with younger and more numerous common room. Usual suspects: maths, English and modern languages set in S1/S2 (four blocks per week per subject), other subjects set in S3 where necessary ('broad band setting'). German, Spanish, French on offer plus taster Mandarin from S1. Classical studies to Advanced Higher level ('strong, engaging teacher').

Strong on humanities; modern studies popular. Least hot on geography (still); sciences holding up well (currently oversubscribed). No detailed exam results available but in 2018, 19 per cent got one or more Advanced Higher at A grade, 36 per cent got 1+ at B grade. At Higher level, 16 per cent got 5+ A grades and 38 per cent 5+ B grades. Academic Dux each year – Advanced Higher langs down a tad; apparently it costs a lot to prepare pupils for Advanced Highers – 'no Advanced Higher funding'. Drama and history still raising bar, oversubscribed library lunch time history club (time clubs generally oversubscribed anyway). Clubs for almost everything, often curriculum related: maths, chess, whatever. Pupils wanting to follow more esoteric subjects can often be accommodated in other Edinburgh schools ('we go by taxi'). 'Additional vocational courses and opportunities will also be on offer'. (We would so like to see these given the same weighting as academic qualifications). Good take up in national competitions, with gratifying numbers in ribbons: in every discipline. Debating strong, regularly head to head with High School of Glasgow.

Computers everywhere. Number of pupils with 'record of needs': IEPs and variety of strategies available: one-to-one, plus support teaching and a family support group on Raising Teens with Confidence. Head of learning support, plus two trained staff plus seven assistants on hand; strategies in place, too, for the brighter pupil. Drop in centre for the challenged and the bored. Curricular support for the staff. Sixth form involved in mass of extracurricular activity ranging from paired reading for younger members, plus befriending and 'helping in subject departments across the school' (slavery perhaps?). Recognised fast track for primary pupils, who may combine studies in both places. French and German, plus optional Spanish, with Urdu on the side. Masses of trips abroad in every discipline. Year tutor stays with that class for their time at school. Classrooms and facilities used by adults and locals out of hours – this is a community school in all but name. No crèche.

Games, options, the arts: House system (nations) in place for pastoral care, inter-house competitions and assemblies, as well as games. Terrific new games set up with games hall, fitness room, swimming pool and gym, much used, and former pupils (who have a rather posh sports pavilion on campus) use all the sporting facilities (car parking a bit tight). Myriad of rugby/football pitches, including bright green Astroturf; the school does well on the games front with masses of individual and team activities; athletics, badminton, cross-country, fencing and curling, sailing and water sports. Rugby (SRU-sponsored) and football for both boys and girls, plus basketball. 'Something for everyone'. Number both in national and international squads. Couple of nearby golf clubs; 'pupils can play for next to nothing during the week'.

Exotic trips abroad: skiing in the States, rugby to South Africa to name a couple, and participants run a daily blog home to keep parents and classmates in touch; the battlefields of Belgium proved popular (school has funds to cover cost of those pupils who can't afford any essential trip, though not that number of free school meals).

Music strong: full-blooded orchestra ('only full school orchestra in Edinburgh'). Pipe band – pay to join. Choir 'in high demand' fundraises for a variety of charities. Dance in all its disciplines. Drama on the up, strong links with the Edinburgh Festival fringe and regular performers. Art dept perched on top floor: imaginative stuff, flat plus ceramics, but gosh, it must be tough to be creative in a blue box. Home economics popular; fabric plus design technology (computer linked with state-of-the-art engineering software).

Computers all over and parent 'involved in Virtual Learning Curve' – watch this space.

Grounds home to OSCARS after-school and summer camp, 5-14 year olds.

Background and atmosphere: Unique history: dates from 1128; the school 'provided education for 60 boys'; the site most people associate with the school is on Calton Hill, a site much loved by telly news cameras (think overnight vigils, think home rule for Scotland), stunning Hamilton portico currently threatened with Mickey Mouse ears: and a wildly unpopular hotel scheme.

Girls admitted in 1974. Established on the current site in 1968 (were it not for the name, we could have been looking at Davidson Mains or Cramond High), PPP involvement means school buildings are superbly maintained, 'windows cleaned', that sort of thing. Three storeys of fairly uninspired blue boxes (aka classrooms with prep rooms for science labs); fitness suite in basement (previously sixth form study area). Not nearly enuff public space, break was a logistical nightmare; rector says this is improved. One constant, however, is the memorial door, out of which each graduating student steps, to be greeted on the other side by the president of the FPs' club. The huge marble door is a memorial to those who died in the First World War and the west-facing stained-glass windows to FPs who fell in the second. 'Significant prize-giving.' Highly vaunted end-of-school leavers' dance, held in assorted Edinburgh hotels. Strong charity commitment.

Uniform worn by all, natty information leaflet detailing what is and what is not acceptable. Hijabs should be black or white. Pupils can be sent home for inappropriate dress. Pupils looked more uniform (hah) and tidier than previously. Variety of sports and club ties. Footwear and clothing grants available for those on child tax credits, income support.

'Bonding' week during the first year, when the whole class plus class teachers takes off for a week's jolly at an outdoor pursuits centre each May.

Range of grub provided by Amey on a three week cycle, available from dining room; school has its nutrition group, SNAG; but local shops in Davidson's Mains do well from school lunchers eschewing school provided fare.

Pastoral care, well-being and discipline: Regular assemblies, good, strong PSE programme, school has to follow City of Edinburgh 'guidelines', so difficult to exclude, but will do so in the case of bullying, physical or otherwise, and abuse. Bullying strategy handbook for all. Very few 'refusers'; consistent 95 per cent plus attendance'. 'Civilised guidance strategies in place'. Regular school assemblies. Pupils who misbehave in class are sent out of the room; we found two or three all looking fairly sheepish. Counsellors on site in almost every discipline including GLB.

Pupils and parents: Strong PSA and parent council organisation basically 'affluent middle class, but a very wide intake – with a whole range of social and ethnic backgrounds'; the catchment area covers Davidsons Mains, Clermiston, Blackhall and Cramond. The school is capped at a 220 pupil intake and there is always a waiting list but in actual fact pupil base comes from all over Edinburgh.

Entrance: Automatic from various feeder primaries if live in catchment address, but see above. Some join the school from other state schools post-National grades (steady stream from Stu Mel down the road), otherwise, penny numbers arrive on a relocation basis.

Exit: Odd logistical departure. Over 90 per cent of all pupils generally stay for fifth year (ie Highers) and some 75 per cent for sixth year. Around half to university. Trickle to Oxbridge, masses to the Scottish universities – Stirling Glasgow, Napier and Edinburgh currently popular – or tertiary education. Bias towards engineering, architecture, creativity of design courses. FPs include Sir Walter Scott, Alexander Graham Bell, Lord Cockburn, Ronnie Corbett, Sarah Boyack (MSP).

Money matters: Building maintained by PPP. Regular PSA fundraising including raffles and fairs, tranche of endowments (including Mary, Queen of Scots) provide tiny scholarships ('through awards') for pupils who have done well at the school; not a lot, 'just a nice wee extra'. Below average number of free school meals: social profile of school diverse.

Remarks: This is a high school in the old-fashioned sense – strong discipline and work code, good results, masses of extracurricular activities – which also doubles as a local centre with adult learning classes and much use of the sports facilities. You can't get much better for nowt.

St Aloysius' College

45 Hill Street, Garnethill, Glasgow G3 6RJ

Ages 3–18 **Pupils** 591 (senior), 304 (junior) **Sixth form** 250 **RC**

Fees: £12,591 – £12,825 pa

0141 332 3190
www.staloysius.org

Head master: Since October 2016, Matthew Bartlett, previously head of Dover Grammar School for Girls. Educated in the state sector, and trained as a chartered accountant before becoming a teacher. First generation of his family to go to university: and Cambridge at that. Taught largely in Manchester and north west. Head of history at Nottingham High and deputy headmaster at St Bede's College, for eight years.

Wanted to get back into Catholic education and St Al's is the only Jesuit School north of the border. He says: 'I fell more in love with it with each visit; it's better than I ever imagined.'

Mr Bartlett is very jolly and fills the room with his bubbly personality. He was warm and welcoming on our tour. This kindness appears to extend across the school, where he knew the name of everyone in the school, from the lollypop man to the tiniest of kindergarten pupils. A senior pupil said: 'Mr Bartlett is chatty, open and cheerful, and always up for a chat. He's very warm and knows parents so well. A personable person.' A parent was also particularly impressed, saying: 'He is a charismatic leader ... He acts at all times with honesty and integrity, and recognises that the development of young people is not simply measured by their academic achievements.'

A self-confessed culture vulture, his interests include choral singing, reading, walking and travelling. Single, he confesses: 'I'm here 24-7!'

Academic matters: Strong academic focus, with impressive results. In 2018, 43 per cent A grades at Advanced Higher level and 62 per cent A grades at Higher level. 'We are trained to prioritise things, with exams from first year – how to study, how to do well.' Staff were particularly nice and welcoming, one teacher telling us a charming anecdote of his long association with the school and how his parents met there and later married.

Fairly broad curriculum in senior school, from Latin and classical studies to product design, business, economics and media studies. One parent queried why there was no food technology on the curriculum. Mr B says: 'Keen to introduce food technology, and currently reviewing what we offer.'

Max number per class 25 but numbers drop at exam level in the senior school. In AH classics in recently, there were two pupils and a teacher, and in AH art, only five pupils. 'It feels like a one-to-one.'

All children from kindergarten upwards learn a foreign language. From primary 2, they are taught Spanish or Italian by native speakers. In the senior school there's Latin, classics French Spanish and Italian up to AH.

No gender divide, marginally more boys than girls. Some 20 per cent with additional needs. Teaching assistants in classroom and dedicated teachers to add support in class or on an individual or small group basis in the Additional Support Department, depending need. Additional classes in English (ACE) from S1 to S4 to support literacy for those who need it.

Large percentage of long-serving staff; ages range from 26–64.Specialist teachers in junior school from P1 in subjects including science, art, computing and languages. Kindergarten has art and music specialists. Refreshing to see 30 per cent male teachers in the junior school, 66 per cent female senior management.

Huge amount of contacts through school network for work experience. No surprise, as a Jesuit school, that volunteering is popular in supporting Glasgow's vulnerable and disadvantaged communities. Students from S3 up can volunteer in local primary schools, and many do so.

Games, options, the arts: Rugby and hockey are the principal sports, with athletics and cross-country also v popular. Scottish U16 rugby champions and runners up in the BP Hockey Cup recently. Scottish schools football champions in 2018. The swish £8m sports complex opened on campus in 2017 and provides badminton courts, sports hall, gym and dance studio. Other sports include basketball, golf, football and swimming. After-school sessions and excursions for outdoor education such as kayaking, climbing and water sports. Biggest provider of DofE in Scotland.

Getting up the hill to St Al's is a sport in itself, and among the campus-style layout, as one parent pointed out, 'playground space is limited.' Break time, however, is staggered across the year groups. Playing fields are a short trip away at Millerston and hockey at Glasgow Green.

Array of clubs, from the lab rats science club to tech club, debating, the Euro club (exploring European culture) and religious groups, such as Pro-Life.

The Schola choral programme offers P4–S6 pupils the opportunity to receive free singing coaching in one of the five choirs. Schola Nova (S1–S3) is un-auditioned. Full time director of choral music and full-time professional organist. Magnificent Van der Heuvel organ installed in 2016. Broad range of co-curricular music groups from strings, to jazz, musical theatre and opera. Music to AH.

Art shares the historic Mount building with the music department. Fine art is displayed throughout the school and a piece is purchased every year to represent each year group. The head describes the school as a 'living building'. Small numbers take art and graphic communication at higher exam levels – 'incredibly talented'. One young man we spoke to, accepted into architecture at the Glasgow School of Art, couldn't speak of the art department more highly.

Drama is in the hub facing the Mount building, with a stage and lighting rig. Annual musicals, with Sound of Music and Fiddler on the Roof as past performances. Available to AH, but for those not choosing the subject, extracurricular clubs popular across the school, including the senior drama company with auditions for S4–S6s.

As expected, very charity conscious, with waiting lists for the pilgrimage trips to Lourdes. Other trips include hockey (South Africa), classics (Rome), languages (Spanish and French exchanges), skiing (Italy).

Background and atmosphere: Scotland's only Jesuit school, it was founded in 1859 and was designed to transform the lives of Irish Catholics immigrating to Scotland to escape the effects of the potato famine. Boys only until 1979. It was run and mainly staffed by the Jesuits until 2004, with the arrival of the first lay headmaster ('He still comes for a cup of tea.') Mr Bartlett is the third head who is not a priest.

The junior school joined the campus in 1999, and the contemporary Clavius building for science, maths and technology won the Best Building in Scotland award. Became an independent trust in 2011, though significant donations from the Jesuits allowed the build of the new sports complex and kindergarten in 2013/14.

A mish-mash of old and modern architecture, the school has the feel of a city centre university campus, though it caters for little tots at kindergarten up to 18 year olds. One parent wanted to see a renovations to the main school hall, to 'provide a proper stage and platform both for teaching and college presentation purposes.'

Appeals predominantly to Glasgow's Catholic community looking for independent schooling, though other faiths are welcomed. Traditional ethos. 'Pupils stand up if the teacher comes in the room'. But not overbearingly so. Strong faith-based values with much charity work for children's charities, providing rest for carers and disabled children. 'Young people engage because they want to be involved. There is a greater sense of social justice in this generation.' House masses take place throughout the day as well as morning mass in the Soladity Chapel for pupils, parents and staff.

Most definitely a blazer school. 'Everyone in Glasgow knows us. Everyone recognises the green blazers.'

Pastoral care, well-being and discipline: 'Catholic school so pastoral care at the centre of what we do.' Senior depute is head of pastoral with a further assistant head for this area, and pupils have free access to counsellors. Parents and pupils typically contact the form tutor or head of year but can go to any member of staff they feel comfortable with, including Mr Bartlett – 'I'm happy to be contacted directly.' A recent Education Scotland inspection recognised the college's pastoral care and safeguarding as sector-leading.

House system reintroduced in 2017. Achieved Healthy Eating Plus Award in 2017, though S5s and S6s can go down Sauchiehall Street, a busy Glasgow thoroughfare, with plenty of unhealthy outlets. 'The novelty usually doesn't last long.'

iPads are standard and one parent showed us the Schoology portal for homework, where pupils can message a member of staff directly. Tracking assessments throughout the year. 'If needed, a conversation is usually enough to move things forward.'

Discipline policy is based on Jesuit values such as respect. 'Young people slip but we support them to get it right.' Very few exclusions.

Pupils and parents: Pupils and parents we spoke to felt part of a St Al's community. 'Another family. Everyone knows each other from the janitor to Mr Bartlett.' Most families are professionals of the Catholic faith, with a smaller number of Hindus and Muslims.

The city centre location makes it easy to get to from across Glasgow, and from further afield like Ayrshire and Edinburgh. Roughly a 15 minute walk from Glasgow central station. There is a drop-off area for younger children, though in peak traffic times, though we can imagine this may have its frustrations. In the evenings, however, the playgrounds are cleared for parking. Buses run from Glasgow's southside, but the majority use public transport.

Email reports three times a year. Parents' evening once a year. Teaches internet safety to keep pupils, parents and staff safe in a digital age. The Parents' Consultative Council (PCC) meets once a term to discuss parents' angles on topics such as assessments, technology and teaching.

Entrance: Assessments in January and a meeting to get to know pupil and parents, rather than an interview. 'Need to be certain they can cope with the curriculum. Need to be honest if we can't provide curriculum they need.' Applicants from P4–S6 write 'My green blazer story', describing their aspirations and dreams, and what they hope to achieve in the green blazer. No assessments for S3–S6.

Waiting list for lower year groups. P7 popular joining point and classrooms are in the senior school. All juniors move to senior school. Parents must show their desire for their child to attend a Jesuit school.

Exit: Majority go to Scottish universities: Glasgow, Edinburgh and St Andrews popular. Most leave from S6, a trickle heading to Oxbridge or Imperial (one to Cambridge to study maths in 2018). Sciences, business, engineering and law currently popular. A few to high level apprenticeships.

Money matters: The original Jesuit concept was that their role was to educate free of charge and the school has a significant funding for bursaries available (the head told us £600,000). Parents are asked whether they need bursarial help at the time of application: almost automatic for families on income support, plus family discounts. Tends to be awarded to very high performing students. Will also try and help out if family hits financial crisis – parents must be upfront about the extent of their problems. Lunch is an extra.

Remarks: A Catholic school with a strong academic tradition and value-driven focus still closely attached to its Jesuit roots. St Aloysius is not afraid to combine modern subjects and technology with the best of old fashioned Catholic values. Dedicated to giving a rigorous academic, personal and spiritual grounding to its pupils.

St Columba's School

Duchal Road, Kilmacolm, Inverclyde PA13 4AU

Ages 3–18 Pupils 630 Sixth form 51

Fees: £3,080 – £12,095 pa

01505 872238
www.st-columbas.org

Rector: Since 2017, Andrea Angus, previously head of senior school at Robert Gordon's College. Maths degree from Edinburgh and PGCE from the University of Wales in Cardiff. Spent 12 years at the Mary Erskine School, where she was also educated, in roles including head of maths and director of studies.

Head of junior school: Since 2011 is Alison Duncan MA PGDE SQH (30s), previously depute head at St Columba's for a year and head of year at Stewart's Melville junior school; a Fifer, educated at St Columba's RC in Dunfermline, she read Russian and German at St Andrews and briefly taught German in Fife. Tidy minded, warm, bubbly and friendly: believes children should be resilient and self confident. Husband an engineer.

Academic matters: Early years youngsters roughly divided into two groups. During our visit, one lot were tucking into chopped up banana, sliced strawberries and hummus (interesting mixture), plain yogurt and water (followed by a lesson in teeth-brushing); some were drawing their dreams – two drawers to a large piece of paper; one or two were playing with magic sand. Jolly and vibrant. Regular classes 8.30am-12.30pm. Two forms a year in junior school with max 25 in each. Reading, writing, 'rithmatic intensive for the first couple of years, glitches picked up early and learning support in place, with ed psychs and IEPs if and when needed, after consultation with parents. Music, drama and French (native speakers) from 4.

Scottish curriculum – highly structured learning with masses of parental encouragement. French, Spanish and German on offer; all three available at Higher level 'but not simultaneously' – head of lang dept writes text books. German 'holding its own remarkably well' – some native speakers. Latin for all, no Greek scholars and minimal take-up for the former at sixth form.

At Higher grade in 2018, 81 per cent A/B grades. At Advanced Higher, 38 per cent As and 72 per cent A/B grades – very strong results.

Support for learning important with two dedicated staff (including the head of guidance) covering both the senior and junior schools; help on hand for dyslexics (15-20 pupils have IEPs) and for those who find some subjects particularly difficult (one-to-one if necessary – costs extra). 'Can cope' with ADHD and Ritalin. No problem with pupils with disabilities (but no lifts in the classroom block). Comprehensive measures to check that St C's is doing well by its pupils, including testing which picks up problems as well as monitoring progress. ICT strong with pupils 'taught on computers rather than taught computing'; trolleyloads of laptops rolled round each floor of the labs (also liftless).

Class size 20, three classes per year, and pupils setted from 12 (SI) for English, French, and maths; larger numbers have allowed a fourth set which is often a small group that helps strugglers. New science block with six modern labs; old library now a business study centre. Pupils can work in the library in their free time.

Staff common room younger after 'lots of retirements' with recent head of department posts in maths and physics 'attracting high calibre from good schools'. Interestingly, there was a knitting lesson in the staff room when we visited.

Games, options, the arts: School is sportier than it looks. Good and enthusiastic rugby team reached the final of the Scottish rugby plate twice in the recent past; hockey team has won the South West Cup (again!) Regular rugby and hockey tours to Canada, Barcelona, Italy etc. Astroturf pitch near senior school for hockey and tennis, though most rugby games are played on local park opposite the junior school, which has a vast games hall, tactfully curtained off for little ones so they're not overwhelmed, and a fearsome-looking fitness room. Tennis is at the Kilmacolm tennis club adjoining junior school. Variety of pupils compete at national or UK level in seven or so different sports. Extra tennis courts and smallish Astroturf on t'other side of the not very busy Gryffe Road.

DofE hugely popular; also runs National Navigation, British Canoeing and John Muir awards as part of outdoor education.

Impressive art and music (fabric design to die for) in the Cargill Centre, opened by the Princess Royal in 1998 and now a tad jaded. No pottery or sculpture noticed. Rather unexpected Victorian chaise longue on the top floor. Mass of soundproof practice rooms, huge number of instruments on offer and equally large number of peripatic staff. Music and pipe band popular (terrific trip to New York recently), as is choir (lots of travel), NYC tartan week, jazz band, art, photography. Biennial exhibitions with real artists as well as pupils, parents and local art club.

The self-contained ground floor houses a technology department with serious equipment but fun teaching and some rather strange offerings. Home economics for 11s, 12s and the usual pre-uni stuff for sixth form; head girl busy sifting flour during our visit.

Exchanges going out of fashion (inhibited by health and safety); recent links with St Petersburg and a one-way Russian exchange. Debating a real wow with victories in Scottish and international competitions – school has had its first ever member of the Scottish debating team (rector's daughter). The 10/11 year olds have three day away stays in the Lakes (baby outdoor pursuits sort of stuff).

Regular revision classes, weekends, evenings, and classes for all locals, from 7 to 70-year olds, everything from computers, to languages, to bridge. Very popular and good for the community, classes run from September to May, now back on form, for a couple of years no one came.

Background and atmosphere: Originally part of the Girls' School Company, founded in 1897, abandoned boarding in 1970; the junior school went co-ed in 1978 (in the face of falling numbers) and re-sited at Knockbuckle Road; senior school went co-ed in 1981. Splendid junior school hall (full of role play during our visit) plus proper assembly room with stage; a grown up gym and weights room tucked at the northern end (regularly let out to local enthusiasts). As a result of various new builds and subsequent shuffling round of classes, Transitus, the youngest class in the senior school, is based down here. Healthy amount of walking (a long half mile) as older juniors visit senior school for music, art, IT, home economics and the sciences, but junior school is otherwise self-contained. New health and well-being centre 'at the heart of the school'.

The senior school campus is pretty cramped, with little play space, mostly rather dreary tarmac. Junior school surrounded by proper lawns and gardens.

Pastoral care, well-being and discipline: Four houses (sibling and FP tradition) and inter-house everything. Zero tolerance – drugs/theft means out. 'No significant problems with bullying,' said the rector; small school so probably not. Juniors address potential bullying via a week of stories and activities in assembly, six 'golden rules', all 'dos' not 'don'ts'.

Pupils and parents: Pupils come from a 30km radius, very much a Renfrewshire school, with about 70 per cent from within 8km, regular bus comes from north Ayrshire, and a small nucleus from Dunoon 'across the watter'. Pupils catch the 7.30am boat and join up with the Greenock/Port Glasgow bus. Juniors and seniors can stay in school until 6pm. Kilmacolm, a popular sprawling suburban village, is booming: first time buyers, a tiny wide ethnic base as well as the traditional Kilmacomics (sic). FPs Lord (Ian) Lang, and Eleanor Laing MP. Don't get it wrong, this is not a toffs' school by any means, just good and sensible; pupils 'are not terribly streetwise'.

Entrance: Own test and interview to Transitus and senior school. 'People fail it,' school says, though not perhaps, now, as rigorously as previously, ditto siblings/FPs' children, but automatic entry from junior school. Certain amount of sixth form entry. No waiting lists at the moment.

Exit: Small trickle (very small trickle) leave to go to trad prep schools at 8 or public schools at 13. One or two leave after they have got university entrance qualifications – ie first year sixth transfer (latest wheeze is to opt for the local state school and apply to Oxbridge – or Bristol – from there) or even for a final year toughening up in a boarding school. Otherwise approx 92 per cent to university, usually in Scotland: Edinburgh and Glasgow universities very popular, then St Andrews, Dundee; one to Oxbridge in 2018. Engineering, business, medicine (four medics and a dentist in 2018), law and economics favoured courses.

Money matters: Means-tested bursaries, more now than previously: OSCR threatens and school is madly doing homework and risks losing charitable status if it can't make its fees more accessible for lower income families. The school can be hit hard when one of the local companies goes down (and suffered badly on the demise of the local sugar company). Fees remarkably reasonable, but all parents must cough up £350 for a debenture when their child is accepted; this is returned at the end of the child's time at school (without interest or increase in value). There is a 50 per cent penalty if a place is accepted and not taken up. Discount of 25 per cent for the third and subsequent children. Blazers and summer/winter uniforms for all girls. Juniors have waterproof jackets; little ones wear fetching green overalls for lunch.

Remarks: Thoroughly sound, rather than setting the world alight. 'Still a local school' with local middle class and aspiring attitudes. Tiny ethnic mix. Victorian values, popular, the reason that houses in boring Kilmacolm (and this editor once lived there) change hands at a premium, and, to quote an incredulous local landowner (who has done quite well out of the school), 'they actually move into the village because of the school'.

St George's School (Edinburgh)

Garscube Terrace, Murrayfield, Edinburgh EH12 6BG

Ages 2–18 **Pupils** 788 **Sixth form** 174 **Boarders** 26 full, 8 weekly, 8 flexi (from 11 years)

Fees: Day £8,550 – £13,875; Boarding £26,175 – £29,010 pa

01313 118000
www.stge.org.uk

Head: Since January 2017, Alex Hems, previously deputy head of Wycombe Abbey. English degree from Oxford; has also been head of sixth form at North London Collegiate, head of senior school at St Paul's Girls and deputy head at Francis Holland. She is married to William and they have two daughters.

Academic matters: School no longer narrowly academic; girls follow English or Scottish system as best fits the bill. Some impressive results in both disciplines, though rather more glitches than we have seen previously, and quite a number of soft subjects with tiny numbers: early education and childcare, media studies, travel and tourism, all at Higher level. Results include those from the Royal Environmental Health Institute of Scotland: number of pupils have achieved introductory (two hour course) or elementary certificates in food hygiene (six hour course).

Possibly more followers of the Scottish system, physics and geography strong (oil?). As ever the English system popular for art and design, religious moral and philosophical studies, hefty showing in Highers. 'Lots of flexibility' in course selection. School employs VLE – Virtual Learning Environment; students can access/collect coursework, or refer to staff notes online. Claims to be the 'top school in Scotland for A levels and Advanced Highers'. As do many others, though perhaps not both at the same time. In 2018, 58 per cent A grades at Higher level and 68 per cent at Advanced Higher; 62 per cent A*/A at A level (art & design and Russian). At GCSE, 45 per cent A*-A/9-7 grades (can also do an individual research project). French or Spanish from P5; in P7, Spanish plus nine-week blocks of French, German and Mandarin. The latter popular with both pupils and parents in the school's Chinese centre. Thirty-six native speakers in school, many pupils host sessions in their native languages: Russian, Chinese, Gaelic; and can study for individual A levels (or whatever) in those langs. School will arrange specialist tutors. Four or five parallel classes in the upper school, max class size 21 and down.

Much to-ing and fro-ing with local unis, pupils and staff combine on various projects, 'and take part in an impressive outreach programme which encompasses both the academic and the appreciation of the wider world'. 'Joint seminars in a plethora of subjects with an eclectic collection of schools, the state sector as well as other independents (in all disciplines: sport and music as well as academia)', according to the school. Good general studies, curriculum choice support and careers advice (careers breakfasts), 500 options in careers dept.

Comprehensive learning support, pick up early, can deal with most of the dys-strata and ADHD; laptops encouraged. SENCo on site, four specialist teachers plus rash of assistants. Small ESOL department to help non-nationals (charge). Drop-in centre for instant problem solving, 'weekly support sessions in every subject, plus subject clinics at lunch time, in break, before school or by email in the evening'. This is what we like to hear. Buddy system: older girls help tinies with reading and much else besides. All girls in junior schools (combined) are assessed for learning hiccups; as with senior school, pupils are withdrawn from class: one-to-one, small clusters, or helped by assistants in class.

School split into three distinct departments – junior, which encompasses the nursery, lower and upper. Head has offices in both lower and upper. School not totally wheelchair friendly but will make allowances and change classrooms if necessary (lift in junior school new build), chairlift in the main building; no problem with boarding houses. Hearing loops.

Games, options, the arts: Fabulous centenary sports hall with viewing area over hall and squash courts; much-used lacrosse pitches, floodlit all-weather pitch. Trad games played with a vengeance: lacrosse tours, hockey tours, swimming, judo, cycling. Local sports clubs use facilities: Grange Junior Hockey Club et al. Robertson Music Centre houses untold numbers of choirs, ensembles, three orchestras, over 600 musicians (can be hired for functions, popular with Alex McCall Smith's Really Terrible Orchestra, as well as National Youth Choir of Scotland, Edinburgh Youth Orchestra and Waddell School of Music). Impressive collection of music results. Vibrant art department, pottery, textiles, sculpture et al. Drama and theatre good, timetabled, not much pursued at higher level. All juniors use senior school facilities, gym, music, drama, games pitches.

Oodles of DofE, dozens of bronze but tails off somewhat as girls grow older. CCF, Outreach outdoor education from age 10. Sixth formers join forces with Merchiston for dances, sport, art, music, drama etc. Zillions of after-school clubs that offer everything from keyboarding to extra IT. Hot on exchanges: girls as young as 12 whizz off to spend a month or so in Canada, Hong Kong, Australasia, Chile, wherever.

Boarding: Boarders, from 11, 50 per cent overseas, live in a couple of converted Edwardian villas behind the tennis courts in an uninspiring road full of equally dreary (if upwardly mobile) villas. Hardly swinging Edinburgh. Purpose-built bungalow for sixth formers, singles or twins, all very jolly, lots of extra activities, but perhaps not very stimulating. Mixture of real foreigners and long distance Scots who can have friends to stay (charge). Flexi and weekly boarding options.

Background and atmosphere: St George's High School for Girls, a member of the Girls' School Association, founded in 1886 as a training school for women teachers, transmogrified into St G's in 1888. The purpose-built, colonial neo-Georgian 1914 complex by A F Balfour-Paul is pure Jean Brodie, and sits uneasily with inspiring new additions. Lower school in converted former boarding house (plus ugly add-on); magical extension for junior school, complete with dance studio (that hall again) and dedicated nursery area has a cantilevered first floor over a bungee surface popular with senior pupils as well as a strategic undercover play area for tinies. Stunning dining hall (exit bridge known as Bridget), entertainment area below has released valuable space for extra libraries and study. Parents can (and do) use the dining centre as a coffee shop.

New uniform compulsory for all within the year, certain leeway in upper sixth. Kilts for all from lower sixth down, in St G's ancient red millennium tartan, with optional trimmed fitted jackets, 'kilts not more than six cm above the knee' (most appeared much longer). Otherwise pretty standard, check dresses, blue gym tunics, navy tights, red or blue wellies. No problems with headscarves (number of Muslims in the school), presumably like the hair bands they will need to be in school colours. Sibling-led house system.

Student council includes both juniors and seniors, terrific charity input/output; latest wheeze was to approach posh Edinburgh restaurants for their chef's fav recipes, publish them in a book and charge the restaurants to advertise. Help with City Mission. YPI with the (oily Sir Ian) Wood Foundation gives girls practice in marshalling arguments and persuading fund to dosh out for good causes. God followed broadly via Christian principles, regular assemblies, PSE cross year on Fridays, business on Mondays, year groups Thursdays and Fridays. Local minister for high days and holidays. Loads of staff jollies: keep fit, choir, and dedicated welfare programme.

Pastoral care, well-being and discipline: Miscreants are given heavy hints that they should 'move elsewhere' (and sometimes they do). 'No need to break out; this is a liberal environment.' 'No sniff of drugs.' Good PSE, positive behaviour policy which incorporates 'the best of human rights legislation'.

Pupils and parents: The Edinbourgeousie: middle class Scots, professionals, incomers, wannabes and first time buyers. Boarders from the Highlands and Islands, the Borders and the Scottish diaspora abroad (alma mater stuff). Handful of real foreigners. Skype useful. Global links and exchanges. Trad. Lots of parent/pupil forums on every subject under the sun; Friends of St George's for social events. Quick poll round parents (in address book) produced no surprises: non-stimulated girls were bored at the top end, parents were fed up at having to buy a new uniform for such a short time (not in secondhand shop yet), sixth formers seemed to be working (and playing) hard. Particularly the latter. School shouldn't be so petty about make up. Not really a sophisticated bunch, and probably not yummy mummys' school of choice.

Entrance: Entry via nursery or interview aged 4/5. 'Unashamedly academic in outlook' was how we previously described this school, indeed there was a time when wannabe parents coached their 5 year olds pre school interview. School maintains, 'not so strict an entrance test; important that we can meet a child's needs'. At 11, will welcome a girl who is able to keep up with the pace of academic life but who seems set for Bs and Cs rather than A*s. Assessment, school report and interview. Entry to sixth form is more or less automatic for home-grown pupils; external pupils by interview and school report. Demands for sixth form places heavy. 'Skype handy for interviewing girls from abroad'.

Exit: Nearly all juniors move up to the senior school. Some leave after GCSEs/National 5s to go co-ed; otherwise gap, uni, and higher education of all sorts – Scots law popular, as are the sciences, medicine (seven medics and a vet in 2018, and four lawyers) and business management. Around 60 per cent opt for Scottish universities, eg Aberdeen, St Andrew's, Edinburgh and Glasgow. Bristol, Durham, York and London unis also popular; odd bods to US, Ireland, France, Hong Kong, Thailand. Two to Cambridge in 2018.

Money matters: Means-tested bursary scheme now replaces assisted places; 'mustn't let the really bright down'. Full bursaries available, plus help with school uniform. Will keep child if parents fall on hard times, as long as bursar is kept in the loop. Sibling discounts. Joint discount with Merchiston Castle School. After being told to provide more help for pupils from low income families, school passed the charity test in 2013 and has maintained its charitable status.

Remarks: The top girls' school in Scotland (pace chaps in nursery); more liberal than previously. Tatler calls it the 'St Paul's of the north', but with only four girls' schools in Scotland (two of which are overgrown dame schools and one of which takes boarders and ponies) there's not much competition.

At regular intervals this editor is asked for advice by parents who have had their little darlings at St George's since they were in nappies and are looking for a change of scene in sixth form (teenagers being what they are and Edinburgh being what it is). We have to say that, in all honesty, if it is a challenge they need then they must go south, for there is nowhere in Scotland that can hold a candle to St George's, be it in the realm of academe or of global awareness.

St Leonards School

South Street, St Andrews, Fife KY16 9QJ

Ages 5–18 **Pupils** 535 **Sixth form** 124 **Boarders** 116 full, 1 weekly, 3 flexi (from 11 years)

Fees: Day £8,700 – £14,208; Boarding £22,746 – £34,653 pa

01334 472126
www.stleonards-fife.org

Headmaster: Since 2008, Dr Michael Carslaw BSc MBA PhD (50s), educated at Merchiston, read zoology at Newcastle, spent three years doing VSO in Ghana ('discovered I loved teaching') followed by PGCE at Exeter ('where I met my wife'); comes to St Leonards via City of London Freemen's and Ardingly (responsible for more heads than you can shake a stick at). A Scot and a weedgie (as is this editor: work it out) he is a shoo-in and won The Tatler public school head of the year a couple of years back (he would have won ours too, but we don't do that sort of thing). St Leonards has a head with vision, common sense and ambition, this is real CEO stuff.

Academic matters: School prides itself on 'high quality education right from the preparatory school through to the senior school.' Sixth form focuses on the IB (average 32 points in 2018). New IB subjects include business management, computer science, psychology and sports science. Sixth formers help out in junior school as part of the charitable leg of the IB (CAS) with up to 50 hours' assistance 'reading, 'riting, 'rithmetic sort of thing. Now also offers a BTec in business combined with IB courses for those who need a more vocational option.

Most pupils take GCSES/IGCSES in the normal way (51 per cent A*-A/9-7 grades in 2018); however, now teaches the IB primary years and middle years programmes. A one year pre-IB course ticks all the boxes for those joining school age 15 (often refugees from state systems) as well as international students who sit fewer IGCSE/GCSEs, and, if needed, get up to speed in English (about a fifth of non-native English speakers need some EAL help, and must pass a written proficiency test – ESOL). St Andrews Uni fields a raft of international speakers, St Leonards boasts help in 'a wide range of native langs in all year groups'...'be aware that some of this tuition may be subject to an additional charge', 'dependent on number of students and lang'.

Head says, 'The IB is probably the least tinkered about with qualification in the world – its basic philosophy of keeping a breadth of subjects going into the sixth form but also studying three to a level comparable to Advanced Higher or A level has remained.' 'Native lang' for IB may be English, Russian, German, French, Mandarin (currently on offer) or whatever, while Latin qualifies as a foreign language, as well as French, Spanish, German, Italian (ab initio). UCAS gives points for individual subjects studied under the IB system which means that non-linguists/mathematicians, previously disadvantaged in the overall IB grading, now get full credit for their strong subjects.

Most study two or three langs, with all doing French from year 1 and Spanish and/or German/Latin from 10/11. Max class size 20, smaller for practical or specialist subjects.

School appoints a St Leonards Associate Researcher or two, often a PhD student at St Andrews, to liaise with pupils and point them at the joys of research – or, as we said previously, 'helping them to develop an appreciation and knowledge of research'. Quite. Senior pupils have access to the university library and regularly attend lectures. (Lots of profs' children and consequently no dearth of academic governors or visiting speakers.)

Dyslexia/dyspraxia support – 'no statemented pupils accepted' – mostly provided for 'a small proportion of pupils' in mainstream teaching, but a good programme both withdrawal, group sessions and one-to-one if necessary (stunning, said one thrilled parent – 'saved our lives') at extra cost. School tests if they reckon extra help needed; specialist staff of four straddle both senior and junior schools.

Games, options, the arts: Proper matches for chaps as well as chapesses. Think Edinburgh schools, Robert Gordon's... Full range of sporting options – rugby, lacrosse, hockey against Glenalmond, Strath and Dundee High: the hallowed main school site (birth of lacrosse in the UK) now boasts rugby matches et al (roll over Dame Louisa). Girls' sports still strong, with usual mass of international lax players. Practice matches held on beach if games pitches frozen. Great all-weather pitch, with just the medieval school wall separating it from the beach. Currently fundraising for new sports hall development.

Loads of individual sports and international coaches – needle chaps' tennis match in progress during our canter: judo, trampoline, skiing, badminton, swimming – university uses pool for water polo; snowboarding and surfing; rock-climbing as well as expeditions to the Alps. Annual skiing trips both at home and abroad; sailing now thoroughly embraced, ditto windsurfing and all 'local water sports activities' – and about time too. Local (and not so local) race-horse trainers use beach for exercise, as does the Scots Guards polo team, now based at Leuchars and St Andrews uni polo team. It being St Andrews, golf reigns supreme with about a third of the school playing; all lucky boarders can and do become youth members of the St Andrews Links Trust (as residents in St Andrews) so they can play the Old Course.

Nearby well-equipped BHS riding centre (moderately expensive, but not over the top) with a hot horse shower (wow!) offers a variety of options, from bringing your own nag to renting one of theirs. 'Weekly lessons available for keen able riders'.

Outstanding art department, attracting pupils outside normal lessons as well as curricular – huge range of alternative media, dark rooms, textiles etc. Current craze is for zig-zag (as in card zig-zagging) art work. Fun, but difficult to live with, perhaps.

Head of art was hanging fiendish model birds from the ceiling during our visit – complete with two elderly black labs – preparatory to the next biannual art show – open to the public. Artists in residence. Regularly in the ribbons for local photography prize – the Kodak Cup.

Music strong in fabulous Bob Steedman (husband of four heads ago, who, alas, died recently) designed centre. St Leonards Junior School pupils sang in front of the cameras at the televised St Andrews Royal Wedding Breakfast celebrations. Rash of bands/orchestras, 'choir for every day of the week', ambitious singing programmes. Pipe band; we were treated to a brilliant rendition by an 11 year old, who warned us that his favourite piece was 14 minutes long. We heard about four (though it seemed to take him longer to find his pipes).

Drama on the up; school performs twice a year in the revamped nearby Byre theatre in St Andrews (popular with both school and public) students must study history of theatre as well as pounding boards. Drama types take shows to Ed Festival and go on mega drama-fest to Broadway every other year. Trips (one per subject per year) planned on a two-year cycle. DofE of course. Youth Enterprise with goodies often sold in aid of local school-adopted fav charity TICCL.

Boarding: Weekly and termly boarding from year 7: emphasis is on day. Fairly harem scarum boarding houses, passages littered with rather grand bookcases and rows of servant's bells – relics of a former age. Day pupils in the sixth form included in house system with 'day rooms' in boarding houses. Couple of small dorms, mostly single rooms, usual teenage tip sort of thing, but they were in the midst of revising. Stunning shower (and this was in a house about to be done up!). £3 million refurb of all three boarding houses started recently – first revamped one opened recently (design brief: 'country house style'): 'Aspects of the interior patterns have been created using a sketch by a current student (and art scholar) – a Bishopshall Toile has been created of signature St Leonards scenes, and appears on all the curtains as well as cushions in the boarding house'. Ollerenshaw boys' boarding house now has ample kitchen space which 'has enabled the boys to prepare special meals together and host dinner parties for fellow boarders and day pupils'.

No Saturday lessons. We were concerned at possible lack of organised activities for boarders at weekend, but were assured, several times, 'that they were too busy with their various IB projects'. Various jaunts to Edinburgh and Dundee were mooted but we are still a tad concerned. Head adds, 'Boarders generally are taken up with sport on Saturdays, there is a boarders' outing every Sunday, beach kite buggies on West Sands, go karting, bubble football etc etc.'

Off duty gear as you might expect. School praised for high standard of pastoral care for boarders by the Care Inspectors.

Background and atmosphere: Founded by dons and wives of St Andrews's profs for their daughters in 1877 in what was once a medieval priory, backing on to the sea wall, the sprawling hotch-potch collection of impressive-looking granite has neither form nor symmetry: think Topsy.

Once Scotland's girls' academic (boarding) school of choice, St Leonards has weathered the storm caused by so-called brother schools opening their doors to the fairer sex to counteract (their) falling numbers (NB: fairer sex originally chosen on looks, rather than academic ability – how's that for daft?). School more or less went into free fall. Day girls were welcomed. Chaps were encouraged into the sixth form (for free – all two of them). Certain amount of family silver was sold. The breakthrough came when junior school absorbed local co-ed prep, New Park, in 2005: chunk of New Park Educational Trust kicked in. Boys and girls work their way up the school in true co-ed fashion: roughly 50/50.

Adopted the IB in 2006. Carslaw an IB enthusiast, 'better to have scientists who can write essays'; the IB is popular with international pupils, of whom, as we write, there are over 30 different nationalities; and is 'still delighted to be part of such a vibrant school community with so much going on.' Obvious good rapport with both staff and pupil: fun; our canter round the school was a delight.

An ongoing rolling programme of upgrading (where £3 million is a sum regularly bandied about). The external fabric is in need of serious help (sea breezes are hell on paintwork): some windows and sills are flaking, though much has been done within the neglected exteriors. A full time painter has been employed – think Forth Road Bridge and multiply him by 10 and they would still be toiling.

Curious combo of gracious living: elegant house drawing rooms reminiscent of Country Life plus lawned courts nestling among old stone building in dreaming spires style, combined with faintly scruffy corridors, classrooms, common rooms. (Bursar/cabinet maker needs to be shot: steel screws: Georgian half moon inlaid card table – pschaw.)

St Leonards inhabits a notoriously windswept corner of Fife, on the sea, bracing air, bone-chilling easterly gales, tracksuits popular for games. Nay, essential.

Golf, riding and the beach all great draws, as well as trips up town and forays to the surrounding countryside. Castle and cathedral a couple of minutes away. Mega library and selection of Maryana in Queen Mary's House (oddly flanked by a boys' loo). Library much in use by those in sixth form, but available to all. Mary Queen of Scots and King Charles II reputed to have stayed at Queen Mary's Library when it was a private house, but not, of course, at the same time.

Splendid menu posted online: lunch we had was sumptuous and imaginative. All food sourced 'locally' (ie within 100 miles). International students can and do cook their own dishes. Veggie option, naturally, and fresh fruit available whenever. Central dining room recently given an internal overhaul: outside still pretty rank.

Comprehensive buses for day pupils: Dundee, Kirkcaldy, Auchtermuchty, Perth, the East Neuk, and presumably special pick up at Leuchars following deployment of Scots Guards. Juniors can be dropped off early (8am) and collected late (5.30pm). (This represents a reduced school day but incorporates time for activities, which has 'settled down well and parents appreciate it'). Otherwise return journey leaves 5.40pm.

Sixth formers wear suits (or a fair approximation thereof) during the working day. Boys rather tidier than some we have seen at that age; girls less so: sixth formers adopt a theme (or two) in black – quite short shorts and thick tights apparently ok (skool says quite short skirts...). Machine washable blazers and blue tartan kilts for girls, grey breeks for chaps are senior/junior school uniform with blue woolly pullies. Ah but we hanker for the cloaks of yesteryear. Second hand shop run by the 'bullish' PA which also organises family fun tennis etc.

School is proud of its Scottish heritage and tradition – Burns Day celebrated though Scottish Country Dancing is apparently only taught in the junior school.

Pastoral care, well-being and discipline: School rules feature punctuality, security and civilised behaviour; the student handbook has a rash of rules, most of which are sheer common sense: L-drivers may not drive other pupils and the like. But members of the sixth form have a mass of privileges – can visit some (some definitely out of bounds) local pubs if aged 18 and over, smoke off-campus – je m'en doute in these days of stalag Scotland ('but not if I feel they are bringing the school into disrepute and are identifiable as St Leonards pupils,' says head) and are generally expected to behave like grown-ups. No smoking on campus, no under-age drinking and absolute zero tolerance of drugs. Parents like the drugs policy – random drugs testing and testing on suspicion, out for pushing, forfeit right to remain in school for using – depends on individual and other factors and for how long, and pupils may be allowed back under fairly arduous conditions. Suspension for continued failure to observe the booze rules. Police are called for theft. No chaplain but team of local ministers who regularly preach. Plenty of fundraising for good causes.

Pupils and parents: Boarding now from age 11, with a small number of UK boarders but most from abroad, particularly at sixth form level, when incomers swell the ranks to follow the IB course – a boon. Those pupils whom we met (either IB or newbies) were a more sophisticated bunch – particularly the former – than we would normally expect in a school which is so geographically challenged...with sea on three sides.

Eclectic mix of international and first time buyers: Fifers see school as a viable option. Think butcher, baker, candlestick maker, farmer, landed estate owner and very senior CEOs. Think oligarchs, wannabe business leaders. No longer does this ed hear from mates that 'we put Amelia/Georgina/Freddie into St Leonards, but really it didn't take'. Parents, both past, and present are now positive about the place.

St Leonards has a strong old girls' network and many at the school are offspring or grand offspring of Seniors. Some concern previously from Seniors about school's new direction though others welcomed its new impetus. Famous Seniors include Betty Harvey Anderson, Dame Kathleen Ollerenshaw (previous president of St Leonards), past head Mary James, Gillian Glover of the Scotsman (who didn't last the course), Stella Tennant (ditto), Baroness Byford and Anji Hunter.

Entrance: At any time. Mid-term ok. Accepts CE, but usually own (written) entrance assessment (English and maths) or scholarship exam. Seamless transition from juniors to seniors. Six GCSEs or equivalent for sixth with 7s and 6s in subjects to be studied at higher level in the IB. 'We usually pick up 15/20 at sixth from entry' for IB. School prefers to meet with international applicants but, if pushed, will Skype.

Exit: 'Minimum' drop out at transition from juniors to seniors and some (20 per cent or so) depart post-GCSE (only accept good English speakers to sixth form). Around 90 per cent to universities – mostly Scottish and northern English destinations eg Durham, Newcastle, Warwick; 12 off overseas in 2018, including Maastricht University, Munich Business School, Leiden University and Vienna University. Many do a gap year, armed with addresses of welcoming Seniors throughout the world (a boon for worried parents).

Money matters: A means-tested, assisted places scheme in operation from year 5; open to application from existing parents in financial difficulties: sibling discount. Raft of scholarships: though only of nominal monetary value, and usually only lasting a couple of years – ranging from academic through music, drama and sport – golf scholarships very popular (as you might imagine).

Remarks: The IB is a winner. Dr Carslaw has the world in his hands: St Leonards runs seamlessly from age 5 to 18.. the IB niche gives it an academic edge with an international flavour.

St Margaret's School for Girls (Aberdeen)

17 Albyn Place, Aberdeen AB10 1RU

Ages 3–18 **Pupils** 377 **Sixth form** 39

Fees: £8,352 – £13,230 pa

01224 584466
www.st-margaret.aberdeen.sch.uk

Head: Since 2014, Anna Tomlinson MTheol from St Andrews, PGCE from St Martin's College Lancaster. Formerly deputy head at St George's School for Girls. 'After university I had a scholarship to go to Princeton but had a car accident and didn't go. Took six months to recover and then took job in boarding house at St George's. It was the beginning of a passion for teaching.' This says it all for us: clearly an extremely bright and committed head who believes firmly in the power of single sex education.

Academic matters: Lovely, vibrant little nursery with three little boys as well as girls. Full-time nursery teachers, manager and nurses. They were taking part in nature studies outside at the front of school when we saw them, very well-protected but next to busy Albyn Place. They do a lot of outdoor learning, part of an initiative called Wee Green Spaces. 'They pack a rucksack and put on outdoor clothing and go to Bon Accord gardens.' Impressive mud kitchen in the school courtyard. The nursery children have a 'letter of the week' while the junior school works on Jolly Phonics and Jolly Grammar.

Further up the school they follow the Scottish system. Nat 5s taught over two years with the majority of girls doing eight. 'We haven't gone down the road of state schools of only doing five or six Nat 5s because we want to maintain the breadth of learning.' In fifth year most do five Highers, although some do fewer.

All the usual subjects plus German, Latin, drama, business studies, economics, modern studies, philosophy, computer science. Flippin' heck, we need a lie down after that. All subjects continued onto Advanced Higher, with three maths courses: maths, statistics and mechanics.

In 2018, 67 per cent A grades at Advanced High and at Higher, 59 per cent As. 'We're not a hothouse for girls,' says Miss Tomlinson. 'It's really important that what we offer is an all round education. Girls are good enough at putting themselves under that sort of pressure without us pushing them. We want them to pursue the things that they enjoy and that give them a sense of well-being.'

And the parents we spoke to totally agreed. 'Our daughter did so well. Incredible really, but it was down to the teachers and how well they knew her. They gave great advice.' 'They really know what they're doing, and certainly with our daughter the staff really went out of their way to help. Couldn't rate them more highly.'

In the junior school they have specialist teachers for drama, music, French, PE and art and Latin from P7 and RE and science from 7 junior. Haven't gone down one device one child route, but they do make extensive use of technology. They prefer banks of iPads and laptops which are brought into classes. Plans afoot to set up a pupil ITC forum so that pupils can directly feed into this. Another new initiative involves older girls mentoring younger girls in digital literacy.

Class sizes range from 18-24 in the junior school, with an influx into 7 junior, which splits into two classes. Around 15-22 in the senior school.

Support for learning is free to all and regarded as essential to what they do. They have a room where both senior and junior pupils can access support whatever their needs. New head of support for learning who's brought lots of new ideas. Help with everything from dyslexia and ADHD to geniuses or those going through trauma. Speech therapist, local GP, deaf advisory service and educational psychologists all on hand.

Games, options, the arts: 'What do we not offer? Hockey, netball, athletics, tennis, horse riding, yoga, skiing at a nearby dry-ski slope. If there is something that the girls think they would like to do, we go out of our way to provide it. Football is a good example of that.' St Meg's clearly prides itself in offering an extensive sporting agenda despite being plum in the middle of Aberdeen. PE from nursery onwards; by the time they get to the last two years of senior school they decide themselves what they'd like to try.

There is one major drawback, though. No running out during break onto the pitches as the playing fields are two miles away near King's Gate. This is a real city centre school, however leafy and well-heeled the nearby surroundings. Rather than having their own Astro pitches, they block book them from Aberdeen Sports Village and swim at the nearby aquatic centre (another bus ride away), where they hold junior and senior swimming galas. They do field a good number of teams, however, and there seems to be an enthusiastic uptake right through the years. Hockey 1st XI recently won the National Aspire cup for the second year running.

Drama very popular. Each year there is a junior show at the Lemon Tree performing space in Aberdeen city centre. The senior school puts on a show every November and one of the charms of the school is that it's so small, if you want to be in it, you will be. They perform over three nights at the Aberdeen Performing Arts Centre. They also run a drama summer school in the holidays for those who can't wait for term time.

We saw evidence of some magnificent art and design.

Music seems to hit the high notes. One parent said the tuition and dedication from the teachers was nothing short of 'outstanding'. Around two-thirds of pupils have lessons in school, with specialist music teaching from nursery onwards. Several girls play for local and national youth orchestras, string ensembles and flute choirs. Head says, 'Given the size of the school we have a disproportionate number of musical events.' Concerts on a very regular basis throughout the year. 'At our carol service every year group performs and there is a whole song at the end composed by the music teacher. We do that again at speech day and are quite up for performing a Greig piano concerto with a full orchestra.'

S

Background and atmosphere: Founded in 1846, St Margaret's is the only girls' school in the north of Scotland. Situated bang in the centre of Aberdeen, it occupies a collection of Georgian merchant houses set back from the grand but rather busy Albyn Place. Like all schools with history, it looks as if it struggles slightly with a hotch-potch of elderly buildings, but despite the squeeze for space has managed to build an impressive new science block (opened by the world-renowned astrophysicist Dame Jocelyn Bell Burnell) and revamp the art and drama studios. The downside of being bang in the city centre is that there really is no room for their own pitches or sports facilities. The upside is that they are in relatively easy reach of a whole host of sporting venues that can accommodate them with a bit of planning.

The school seems to make a big effort with the parents too. The ones we spoke to described it as a great family atmosphere and felt fully involved. 'Both my husband and I are confident that they know what they're doing.'

Pastoral care, well-being and discipline: 'Well-being is absolutely at the heart of the school's ethos. We firmly believe that it's happy girls who learn best and make the most progress.' And judging by the smiley, confident girls we spoke to, this seems to be working. 'I really feel the teachers know me and are looking out for me.' 'I had a real blip last year when I got really worried about stuff, but they seemed to pick it up without me asking for help.' 'Science and maths are my thing and they've given me some great role models to follow.'

They're currently running an initiative on mental health awareness. Sessions for parents, special workshops for girls from 7 junior upwards. Mental health awareness week. We did wonder about pictures of buckets around the school, but apparently that's to remind everyone to 'fill other people's buckets with kindness'.

When Anna Tomlinson first joined there was only one guidance teacher and now there are three, all with special training. Each girl is interviewed every year and then staff are there to support the girls on a 'need' basis, with teachers available for day to day guidance. The girls have the same form teacher all the way through the senior school to give continuity.

Pupils and parents: Many live locally although some travel from quite a distance eg Peterhead and just north of Dundee. Significant number whose jobs are related to the oil and gas industry, although this has taken a nosedive in recent years. There is currently a waiting list for the senior school, so it can't be all bad. Dedicated buses.

Twice termly Find Out Fridays at pick up time and weekly Well Done Wednesdays at 8.30am are opportunities for parents to come in and find out about the teaching.

Holiday club for four weeks over summer to meet the needs of working parents. Drama summer school is a new initiative.

Entrance: There is a group assessment for the nursery and for the junior school. Test for senior school and current school reports taken into account.

Exit: Most to Scottish universities including Aberdeen, Edinburgh, Glasgow, Heriot Watt, Robert Gordon University, St Andrews and Strathclyde, but one to Cambridge to study natural sciences in 2018. Majority study STEM subjects.

Money matters: They don't give scholarships but offer means-tested bursaries up to 100 per cent.

Remarks: This is, we think, an outstanding school with a committed and inspirational head who quietly and firmly leads from the front. Single sex education doesn't work for everyone, but the girls we saw were confident, unaffected and engaged. No preening, no hair flicking. Just happy, really.

St Mary's Music School

Coates Hall, 25 Grosvenor Crescent, Edinburgh EH12 5EL

Ages 9-19 **Pupils** 77 **Sixth form** 18 **Boarders** 29 full

Fees: Individually assessed. International students Day £22,817 – £25,513; Boarding £32,326 – £35,022 pa

0131 538 7766
www.st-marys-music-school.co.uk

Head: Since 2013, Dr Kenneth Taylor BSc PhD PGCE PG Dip (50s); scholarship to Dulwich College, read chemistry at Edinburgh university and spent three years as a research chemist (we do like heads to have done something in the real world) and came to St Mary's from Biggar High where he was depute head, having skipped around the maintained sector in the borders.

A sportsman and musician (hill-running a passion – recent feat The Pentland Skyline Race: 16 miles, 6,200 foot climb), he played the piano and violin when younger and still sings (a bit) and plays the viola. Lives in Edinburgh with three young and regularly cycles to school (across Edinburgh). Delightful and outgoing, he enjoys encouraging the young in all manner of disciplines and has a deprecating sense of humour.

We previously dropped the school from the Guide because of a couple of cases of (historic) sexual abuse and Taylor mentions this to the whole school about once a term, systems now in place, but he advises any pupil who feels uneasy about any member of staff (or indeed anything) to talk to head of guidance, any (other perhaps) teacher or tell their parents. At The Good Schools Guide, we do not dwell on past problems unless they are still causing angst: St Mary's has moved on, and the somewhat shambolic 'luvvie' environment replaced by a rather more efficient regime. Taylor is unhappy about our mentioning this now historic abuse, but as there are screeds on the internet, we would look foolish if we ignored it.

Academic matters: Complicated. In the junior school, pupils from P5/7 often form a composite class: follow standard subjects with IT tabled throughout. Splendid triple class room with interactive telly: iPads being introduced. Delicious old-fashioned desks – alas without the Bakelite inkwells. Tiny classes (as you might expect with annual intake of only 10 per year); German and French from early: essential for singing. Latin mandatory S1/2 – and available at both Advanced Higher and SQA.

From P5-S6 school moves seamlessly through to Nat 5s to Highers and Advanced Highers. Highers are successfully crammed (well, smaller classes) into three and a half hours a week rather than the usual five to eight. Results impressive across the board. School really too small to supply individual subject results. Maths (strong), English, Higher music at S3/4 and Higher English S5. Now Cambridge Pre-U for music – harmony, counterpoint, composition – with seven out of eight getting D1/D2 in 2018.

Arrangements in place for pupils who need extra support; those with personal statements have one-to-one sessions, otherwise withdrawn from class and IEPs. Dyslexia and dysgraphia the main culprits.

The junior school is composed of choristers and instrumentalists, more of the former (both boys and girls – the latter introduced in 1976, though young instrumentalists since 1972). Choristers, both boys and girls, leave school at 14 (broken voices, sexual discrimination, that sort of thing – can't chuck out 14 year old boys unless girlies go at same age). Some may re-audition and return as instrumentalists.

Games, options, the arts: Small art room more or less adjacent to head's office stuffed with tables and art work on shelves. Both flat and 3D stuff on display.

Catch-all rather sad-looking all-weather surface area (school rather grandly calls it a sports court) serves its purpose. No gym (so mandatory one hour PE per week must be achieved by other means); boarders are members of Drumsheugh baths, a stout half mile distant, and the local running club. Didn't see too many fatties on our wander round, so something seems to be working.

All pupils, both junior and senior, spend roughly 50 per cent of their time doing some form of music, be it practice or individual lessons: we came across a variety pack. 'Coaching sessions with an accompanist (gets them used to it),' says Taylor and we found one young piano-accompanied flautist sharing her lesson not only with a splendid Steinway but also with a somewhat overpowering organ.

Hideously complicated timetable, but sung evensong most evenings at 5.30pm in the cathedral and regular rehearsals either in Song School or cathedral itself (latter has 'soft' acoustics: 'ideal for singing but not practical for orchestral practice').

Music, of course is what the school is all about, with an emphasis on chamber music: regular concerts at venues all over Edinburgh. School itself has nowhere big enough for both orchestra and audience – former chapel too long and thin (Taylor says 'small'), dining room (beastly 60s excrescence) too low and cramped.

Any and every instrument played with peris pulled in for the more esoteric. 'No problems in getting staff', school handy for Haymarket (and Glasgow): tries to arrange a full day's teaching for visiting (musical) peris; odd orchestral player, 12 full-time staff.

Director of music takes instrumentalists to the odd concert (28 last year), and usually manages to get reduced rate – 'one or two quid sort of thing' – to boost ranks of punters – though full whack for some events (we originally wrote popular – as in the Latin – but Taylor preferred 'some'). Regular masterclasses: annual Nigel Murray masterclass – school sources suitable spaces for numbers: 130 violinist and their teachers last time; 60 cellists, that sort of thing; always oversubscribed. Occasional foray into performing at the Edinburgh International Festival (gives concerts three Sundays on the trot at St Mary's Cathedral). Pupils regularly do their own thing, performing both a Schubert string quartet and 'a specially commissioned piece' plus jazz in Dumfries and Galloway. Friday evening concerts and strong input on the charity front: this ed has been entertained by St Mary's young at a variety of fundraisers (and private homes).

Highly acclaimed and popular Saturday morning classes for up to a 150 youngsters aged 4-13; serious stuff and not just an airy fairy introduction to music. 'These classes are an enjoyable introduction to music,' says the head. Quite: those whom we know who take part say they are enormous fun: which is perhaps a better accolade than an 'enjoyable introduction'.

Boarding: Two floors of accommodation for boarders in Coates Hall; mainly twins with a few triple rooms, all en suite. Free time mostly spent practising.

Background and atmosphere: Tucked away in an enchanting corner off Grosvenor Crescent some 300 metres from the Cathedral. St Mary's was founded in 1880 as song (choir) school for The (Episcopal) Cathedral Church of St Mary the Virgin (funded by heiress sisters Barbara and Mary Walker and built to a design by George Gilbert Scott in 1879). Based in Old Coates

Hall and the Song School, the latter still used for daily practice (magical Phoebe Traquair murals) within the cathedral precinct until 1995, St Mary's (name changed 1971) bought Coates Hall, which had closed in 1994. Neophyte Anglican priests had rather fallen off the radar; the 18th century Old Coates Hall (part of the original bequest) is now the Edinburgh Theological Institute, providing accommodation, teaching and meeting rooms for both ordained and Anglican seminarians, albeit on a smaller scale.

Coates Hall, built in 'baronial style' by David Bryce in 1850, and bought by the Edinburgh Theological College in 1891, when Sydney Mitchell (better known for banks and psychiatric hospitals) added the splendid gothic chapel to the right of the main door – is too small for concerts. However, it boasts a fine-looking but non-functioning organ and an amazing turquoise decorated grand piano, which looks as though it is covered in potato cuts: paint job is apparently worth more than the piano itself. Bryce also designed the gatehouse. Extensive-ish grounds (for the middle of Edinburgh) filled with trees, badly parked cars (as ever in danger of small children with balls), and a couple of ugly modern teaching blocks. Plus the inevitable catch-all 'sports surface'.

Considering the expense of maintaining a highly complicated Victorian roof, the building is in remarkably good if complex heart, though we weep at the carving of rooms into offices. Head's study is in a former garage.

The main building is rabbit warreny in the extreme, with staircases going off in random directions – five steps here sort of thing – leading to a hotch-potch of bedrooms (seminarians had great views), now almost all en suite, twins and singles (school is let in hols to boost funds – which is why one of the practice rooms boasts a basin). Wiggly Ikea mirrors grouped in pairs throughout, and myriads of photographs – often with tinies overwhelmed by the size of their instrument.

Pastoral care, well-being and discipline: All choristers are day pupils. No reported disciplinary hiccups; pupils are more likely to be found discussing some obscure German 15th century composer than indulging in verbal point scoring. During our visit (break time) four really quite small people came out to the playground, one fell and was immediately surrounded (not sure about tears) by her own peer group and some elder children who were close by, who picked her up and escorted her back inside. Now that is what we like to see in a school.

School uniform for all, and worn with pride.

Pupils and parents: Pupils come from all over. No obvious social grouping, many pupils from musical families. Terrific parental support. Youngsters from abroad need local guardians.

S

Entrance: Audition in either discipline, at any stage, half way through term if space available: though most join at the start of the academic year. 'Looking for musical ability and potential'. School 'mushrooms' towards the top.

Exit: All choristers age 14 (though may come back as instrumentalists); rest usually after Advanced Highers to some form of tertiary education. Possibly 95 per cent may go to a conservatoire or into music college, but this is by no means written in stone and one of the most promising recent musicians is currently studying engineering. Regular careers talks from FPs who emphasise how difficult it is to make a proper living out of playing in an orchestra and how few openings there are for soloists.

Money matters: Oodles of bursaries. Taylor told us to check online for fee info: two hours later we were still in the dark. Would appear to be in line with current fees elsewhere. Cathedral covers 50 per cent of all choristers (who get a couple of quid or so for weekly performances and rather more for weddings and funerals), Scottish government contributes a chunk (aided places) and music school doles out bursaries – rigorously – with financial background of applicants tooth-combed. Fair to say that no musical prodigy from any background would be left wanting.

Remarks: Exciting times. Watch this space.

St Mary's School (Melrose)

Abbey Park, High Street, Melrose TD6 9LN

Ages 2–13 **Pupils** 180 **Boarders** 34 flexi (from 7 years)

Fees: Day £13,200 – £16,050; Boarding + £600 – £2,400 pa

01896 822517
www.stmarysmelrose.org.uk

Headmaster: Since 2010, William (Liam) Harvey BEd (40s). The son of a local doc, and an FP, he went on to George Watson's followed by a BEd in PE at Liverpool John Moores University. Taught PE to A level in the state secondary sector before moving to Belhaven as housemaster and head of history and PE.

We met Harvey's Canadian wife, Marnia, efficiently organising the mysteries of the gap student's computer. Their daughters are in the school.

Entrance: All things to all men. The only independent school in the borders; children come from within a 50 mile radius, can come mid-term at any time if space available, otherwise automatically up from kindergarten. The odd state child has been known simply to come for an '18-month blast' before going back into the maintained sector, but this is rarer and rarer and none recently. Some come at 11 to do CE.

Exit: 'Most but not all' stay on until they go to their senior school at 11, 12, or 13 (the occasional toff pops off to Belhaven, Aysgarth, but none so far under the new regime); preferred secondary schools used to be Glenalmond, Fettes, Merchiston, Loretto, St George's in Edinburgh, Longridge Towers in Berwick, Queen Margaret's York and whilst these did indeed feature in our random poll, increasingly numbers are more likely to be turning south, Sedburgh gaining in popularity, Ampleforth and even Harrow. Winchester, Eton next?

In 2018, scholarships awarded to Sedbergh, Merchiston and Loretto.

Remarks: Wow. Didn't recognise the place. Totally transformed since our last visit and some of the most exciting (and cleverly sited to act as a windbreak) skool buildings we have ever seen. The Hamilton building opened in 2010 was funded by a gift from 'an anonymous benefactor'. Guestimate cost? A million near as dammit. Named after John Hamilton who founded the school in 1895 (good, if somewhat belated, way to celebrate a centenary).

Two non-parallel buildings with terrific reception area, full of photographs – though a tad Nuffield in aspect (think neutral carpets and comfy seating). Only thing missing is the coffee machine, although we were topped up with copious amounts – the head had his own insulated mug. Reception area littered with prospectuses of senior schools – not, as previously, concentrating on the Scottish mafia, but Shrewsbury, Uppingham, Cheltenham and Harrow. Quite a change, though those whom we asked mainly seemed to be heading North. Wide corridors – one outside the art dept was recently turned into a drawing 'road' where parents and pupils depicted the best aspects of their childhood (and jolly good some of them were too – we particularly liked the footballer). Photographs everywhere in main building, the art building – with yet more light, airy, and huge classrooms has walls filled with pupil offerings and classrooms for younger pupils.

We previously described St Mary's as a 'Jolly useful little school, incredibly flexible, with flexi, weekly and day pupils; one or two toffs, but mostly farmers and local professionals who stay to the bitter end, plus masses of first time buyers.' But gosh. Still tiny classes, max 18 but usually much less, only one stream, scholars will be 'hived off' and set at 10 if necessary and 'provided with evening tutorials with subject teachers'. Latin from 8, languages from 5, taster term of French, then specialists in French for common entrance. Fantastic and envy-making French trips when the entire form decamp to a monastery for a week. Science taught separately for the last four years, and pupils move round the staff (from age 9 – a transition class).

'Strong' dyslexia department, all singing and dancing and recently reorganised, oversees regular testing, and support for the very bright. Withdrawn help and support staff (masses of 'em, chaps as well as chapesses) go into class too – 'pretty flexible' (might be the school motto). Keen on handwriting. Interactive whiteboards abound, all classrooms are computered to the hilt, state of the art. Terrific young buzzy staff abound (think policemen). School now boasts 'a strong academic team'.

Drama strong and timetabled, the school has links with local borders youth theatre. Good music, rehearsals and lessons in functional school hall, whilst pre-prep has own gym, with Noah and his ark drawn by the young. The somewhat surprising cloistered classroom corridor (the 'veranda classrooms') have been relegated to music, a theatre store room, boarders' activity room, music and a thrift shop.

Day children can stay from 7.30am (and breakfast in school) right through to 7.30pm, by which time they will have done their prep and had supper, kindergarten can stay till 4pm. Tinies wear delightful green and white check tabliers and girls evolve from gym slips to proper kilts; we checked, most were eight pleats thick. Dining room with weekly menu, over-high benches for littlies to sit at table. Brown bread only and lots of sugar-free puds, mainly organic as far as possible. Robert the chef comes complete with starched chef's hat and sparkling white uniform. Cor. He also makes scrumptious millionaire's shortbread for the head's guests – not sugar-free at all, and has lost a mega amount of weight since we last saw him... now deeply into marathons. One is always told to beware the skinny chef, but he is still triumphant, and gives the boarders special cooking lessons (it was Burns night/lunch during our visit, and the haggis was piped in with aplomb). Pheasant (plucking lessons and all) on the menu next.

The Harveys live in the main school house, with dorms above, separate corridors for boys and for girls – room for up to 30 flexi boarders. The girls live in somewhat cramped conditions in a conversion of what used to be the main drawing room – fantastic ceiling, but divided into three – with what must be one of the grandest ceiling-ed bathrooms ever. Jolly dorms upstairs, all brightly painted with splendid stripy duvet covers. Very homey; bunks, the odd poster, random teddy bears – and currently being upgraded. B&B charged per night.

Squads and teams triumph all over the place. Swimming off-site in Gala(shiels) and main games pitches just across some National Trust land. Smashing little school.

St Ninian's High School

Eastwood Park, Rouken Glen Road, Giffnock, East Renfrewshire G46 6UG

Ages 12–18 **Pupils** 1,785 **Sixth form** 280 **RC**

01415 772000
www.blogs.glowscotland.org.uk/er/StNinians

Headteacher: Since 2005, John Docherty (60s), studied geography at University of Glasgow followed by a one-year teacher training course. Previously assistant head at St Ninian's and before that headteacher at St Andrew's, Clydebank. Started out as a geography teacher and worked in Glasgow's East End, the area where he grew up and lived until he got married and which is home to some of Scotland's 'poorest communities'. From there it must have been an interesting leap to St Ninian's which could be described as serving some of Scotland's wealthiest. Talking of his early experience, he says: 'It was highly enjoyable and very fulfilling. The pupils were hard working and the school worked very hard to support them and their families. In comparison, both schools [have the] same high standards, vision and expectations. The differences were income and life experiences due to being wealthier.' It is evident he has a strong belief that no matter the circumstances one must always Let Youth Flourish (the motto of the school – Floreat Iuventus), whether academically, in sport or the arts.

Mr Docherty is witty, confident and supportive, described as 'always having an open door.' Innovative in curriculum change (even perhaps a rebel), he doesn't bow down to Holyrood's Curriculum for Excellence and wasn't slow to criticise its failings: 'good teachers should be allowed to teach.'

St Ninian's has been transformed academically under his leadership. He states modestly that he is 'very proud of the pupils and staff for what they do every day to provide an excellent school. The achievements are the result of the bigger team, I'm only one part of the great success of the school.' Discipline is a priority too and no child escapes in the morning without 'straightening their tie' or 'tucking their shirts in.' A 'bugbear' for one parent (and we imagine many children), but the pupils do look impressively smart and stand out in the community.

Mr Docherty is married with one daughter. His wife is also a teacher (French and Spanish). He describes himself as a 'family man' and enjoys reading and playing tennis. He also devotes some quiet time to reflecting in prayer. His faith is evidently very important to him and he say that it 'influences all I do, through the desire to offer my service to others.'

Academic matters: St Ninian's consistently ranks as one of Scotland's top three state schools and the number of pupils achieving five Highers at the end of S5 has increased by 100 per cent in the last decade. In 2018, 57 per cent of Higher grades were As, as were 43 per cent of Advanced Highers.

Language teaching is a particular strength: 90 per cent study French at National 5 and just under a third study a language in S5 and S6. First school in Scotland to have been awarded World Confucius Hub of Mandarin, establishing the teaching of Mandarin in East Renfrewshire. This successful programme has been expanded and over the past few years several students have been awarded scholarships to study the language in Tianjin, China.

Children study the standard core curriculum in S1 and then, unusually, narrow down their subject choices for the start of S2. On our tour one pupil pointed out that he hadn't been in the 'art department since S1.' For this reason some parents have 'mixed feelings' about it and feel choosing subjects comes 'a bit too early.' However, a parent added, 'the kids enjoy having fewer subjects and studying what they like.' Mr Docherty says it was 'a successful decision to have implemented' and allows 'a progression of subjects, straight from S1 to S6.' And there is no denying the exam results.

Popular annual careers evenings with 100 plus exhibitors, and with over 1,200 visitors, are targeted at all careers. Talks from local businesspeople and university professors take place in the school lecture theatre throughout the year.

Head keen to allay parental concerns that East Renfrewshire's top schools are 'exam factories' and only suited to academic children. He points out that leavers' attainment for the 'lowest 20' and 'middle 60' per cent were the highest in Scotland. Reassuringly, pupils and parents consistently used one word when talking about the school: 'supported'; as one parent put it: 'I think the commitment from the teachers is outstanding. They offer excellent support and communication to parents, including fabulous workshops ... to help us support our kids.'

Dedicated SEN department with specialist teaching and non-teaching support. Children with complex needs are 'well integrated into the school and highly successful.'

Games, options, the arts: In keeping with west coast of Scotland tradition, football is perhaps the most popular sport – the boys were keen to point out the new 4G all-weather pitches. School team reached Scottish Schools FA Shield final and trophies are proudly displayed in cabinets. One S5 pupil picked for U17 Scottish team and played in recent European Championship Qualifiers in Portugal. Other events include school golf championships, 'Hutchie 5' hockey championships at private school Hutchesons' Grammar and the Whitecraig's Rugby Club festival for selected pupils. A fledging American football club has also been welcomed, particularly among the boys. All sports are open to girls, who are highly successful at netball, football, athletics, hockey, skiing and other minority sports. Talented athlete programme is in place 'to support all young people who are involved in national teams.'

Over 80 clubs (all on-site, except equestrian and skiing) include young engineers, Mandarin, business and charity clubs (exploring subjects such as the trafficking of women and children), as well as the Young Philanthropy Initiative, an active citizenship programme for teams of S2 pupils to raise money for local charities. Off-site clubs have tuition costs and transport is partly subsidised by the school.

Some activities run at lunch time and we saw labs busy with keen science club students, a few pupils dancing in one of the gym halls and a lone student on a spin bike in the fitness suite – although quite rightly the majority of students were enjoying their food. One pupil said the after-school spin class where staff and pupils do spin together was very popular: 'It's good fun and funny seeing the teachers giving it their best.'

Thriving, newly refurbished music department complete with grand piano, and soundproofed practice rooms for different instruments. Massive uptake of music and myriad bands including the ceilidh band, soul band, chamber choir, symphony and string orchestras. The most talented go on to perform in Celtic Connections and Scotland's National Orchestra. Popular drama department, with fun school drama club for S1 pupils, which is run by S6 Advanced Higher drama students. Previous shows include Oliver!, My Fair Lady and Wizard of Oz. Plenty of trips made to Glasgow theatres and many of the children in amateur dramatic clubs, which sometimes perform at Eastwood Theatre, adjacent to the school.

Off-beat art department with music playing, described by a pupil as the most 'laid-back place in the school.' Every available space covered with impressive artwork, the best of which included somewhat frightening modern portraits as well as Day of the Dead masks. Fashion shows and art exhibitions celebrate the creative work of the young people.

Sporting, creative and cultural school trips 'can be expensive' so run every second year to allow parents to pay in instalments. Recent destinations include the French Alps (skiing), Iceland (geography), Berlin (art) and, perhaps less exotic, the Scottish Parliament (modern studies) to meet Nicola Sturgeon. Children also travelled to Ghana as part of an S6 building project, and local artwork that they brought back is displayed on school walls.

Background and atmosphere: St Ninian's was founded in 1984 to serve a small Catholic population. Given that at the time 'some people wondered where the children would come from', it's ironic that this is now the biggest school in East Renfrewshire and highly desirable. 'Demand for places outstrips supply' and measures are being introduced to curtail admissions.

The modern, low-rise building with separate sports hall and playing fields is situated in a pleasant, leafy civic area that houses the council buildings and Eastwood Leisure Centre and theatre. Inside the wide corridors serve as a gallery for the children's work and achievements. Recent extensions have provided new science, geography and modern language classrooms, and certainly these parts do feel much fresher, though all areas are clean and tidy.

At first glance the school seems traditional, values such as discipline, working hard, kindness and community involvement are important and there is a strong Catholic ethos (although intake includes children from other faiths or none). At the same time, perhaps surprisingly, it is quite modern. There are no strict hierarchies distancing pupils from teachers and senior staff; teachers mingle with the students and would pride themselves on being approachable. The centre of school activity is the forum, an octagonal space which is light and airy and gives access to the glass-fronted library and an art room featuring stained glass created by the pupils.

Pupils are easily identified in Giffnock by their maroon woollen blazers and visitors might be forgiven for thinking this was a private school. Parents are 'very supportive' of the strict uniform policy.

Pastoral care, well-being and discipline: Dedicated pastoral teachers 'who are your point of contact as a parent' meet with children once a week and can be found 'out and about with young people every day.' One pupil said they felt 'so lucky to be surrounded by such excellent people.' Pupils talked of how they 'felt listened to' and that 'teachers take suggestions on-board.' Parents are kept involved: unrushed parents' evenings, regular meetings, home phone calls. One parent of a new S1 pupil said: 'Within a few weeks of ... starting, the pastoral teacher called to see how I thought she was settling, and also to let me know they thought she was fine. A nice touch.'

One parent felt that perhaps too much help was given and that 'sometimes the kids struggle when they get to university and have to do it on their own'. However, the S6 children enthused about how much they appreciated the advice given with their UCAS applications 'without being hand-held'.

High standards are expected: having discipline, being organised and believing in yourself is deemed important to achieve success. Overwhelming majority are model pupils, but on extremely rare occasions over the years a child might just need 'a day out'.

Workshops are given to children in S1–S4 to help manage workload and develop study techniques. 'Early stage problems are dealt with quickly' and a youth counselling service is also available.

Pupils and parents: No secret that many move to the area for the schools and are prepared to pay increasing house prices. Stylish mums dropping off immaculate children from shiny Range Rovers can be seen, but there's also a big chunk of lower middle class families 'working to pay their mortgage' and giving their kids the best possible education they can. Parents are hands-on, and if unhappy are quick to say so. Around 16 per cent of school population is from ethnic minorities but this figure could drop as changes in admission criteria prioritise baptised Catholics. Free coach service to and from school for those who live more than three miles away. Others walk, cycle or use public transport.

Pupils we saw were the usual bunch of happy teenagers, noisily going about their business at lunchtime, some chatting and eating pizza from polystyrene cartons on the go. One told us it was considered 'cool to be clever' and 'cool to be hard working.' S6 pupils were particularly articulate and well-mannered and incredibly proud to be part of a 'welcoming school community that works together to achieve the best we can.' However, 'no school is perfect', and a couple of rule-breakers were frowned upon by senior pupils for having a peek at their mobile phones on the stairwell.

Former pupils include actors James McCardle (Star Wars: The Force Awakens) and Daniel Cameron (BAFTA Scotland New Talent awards 2016) plus footballers Aiden McGeady and Andy Robertson.

Entrance: Catchment area has tightened over the years but currently includes parts of Thornliebank, Giffnock, Clarkston, Busby, Waterfoot and Newton Mearns. Pupils come from primary schools including Our Lady of the Missions in Giffnock, St Joseph's in Busby and St Cadoc's in Newton Mearns.

Controversially, baptised Catholics within the Eastwood side of East Renfrewshire now given priority, although placing requests will still be available. This will affect children of non-Catholic faith already in catchment Catholic primary schools.

Exit: Around two-thirds go on to higher education with the remainder heading for FE colleges, apprenticeships or employment. Good numbers accepted for medicine (21 in 2018), veterinary science and dentistry courses. Understandably most prefer not to pay and stick with Scottish universities such as Caledonian, Strathclyde, Glasgow, Edinburgh, Aberdeen and St Andrews (and why not if it's good enough for Will and Kate?).

Remarks: One of the top academic state schools in Scotland, St Ninian's has a strong Catholic ethos coupled with a modern approach that ensures children are well-nurtured and supported. Success is celebrated, as is 'working hard', one of the school's key values. Whether academically, on the sports field, musically or in the arts, it seems that the fortunate young people who attend St Ninian's do indeed flourish.

Stewart's Melville College

Linked with ESMS Junior School, The Mary Erskine School

Queensferry Road, Edinburgh EH4 3EZ

Ages 12–18 **Pupils** 780 **Sixth form** 133 **Boarders** 17 full, 1 flexi

Fees: Day £11,637; Boarding £22,764 – £23,349 pa

0131 311 1000
www.esms.org.uk

Principal: Since August 2018, Linda Moule, previously head of The Mary Erskine School. She runs the twin senior schools (Stewart's Melville College and The Mary Erskine School) with two heads and the head of the co-ed junior school. She spends part of the week in each school (separate campuses) with offices in both. After graduating in theology from Manchester University, she has held positions in the teaching profession in Bristol, Stockport, Manchester and was deputy head of Holy Trinity College, Bromley, before becoming vice principal of New Hall School, Chelmsford in 2004. She was appointed head of Mary Erskine School in 2009, and became vice principal of the ESMS in 2016. Mrs Moule is married with two sons, both of whom have attended Stewart's Melville College.

Head of Stewart's Melville since 1999 is Neal Clark, a grammar school boy, studied English and came to ESMS via Kirkham Grammar School, Lancashire and then King Edward's School, Bath.

Academic matters: ESMS follows the 'diamond' model of education. The boys and girls are educated together at the junior school, separately in the senior school from 12-17 and back to a co-ed set up in their final year. Principal and school heads are all strong advocates of this system: 'we can tailor the teaching for boys and girls'.... 'boys and girls learn differently'. The pupils 'look forward to sixth form and don't lose contact with each other as they go through'. Class sizes of around 20-22 for first two years – S1 and S2 – reducing in size to 20 or less for S3-S5 and then between 12-15 for the final year (sixth form). Parents of boys and girls see it as a 'better learning environment' and pupils say that 'the separation doesn't affect the friendships between the boys and girls'. Many of the sixth formers say 'we have the same group of friends, boys and girls, as we did in the junior school; we don't lose touch'.

Pupils study for eight National 5 exams in S3 and S4. English, mathematics, a science and a modern language are compulsory at this stage. In their penultimate year (S5), they study for five Higher exams while in their final year, they study for Advanced Highers in twinned classes with Mary Erskine.

Many pupils do three Advanced Highers (some do more) with considerable success. For these exams pupils have to undertake a dissertation and, in some cases, a scientific investigation which teaches them the skills of independent study that will be necessary at university. Recent results are strong for both exams with 82 per cent of Advanced Highers awarded A/B in 2018. French, German, Latin and Spanish all on offer to Advanced Higher. The principal tells us 'there is a strong work ethic here'. This was echoed by parents – 'it's a school that produces conscientious children'.

Strong links with the Merchant Company, whose members offer all final year pupils mock interview practice.

Firefly Learning, an online virtual learning platform, has recently been implemented throughout the school. This allows teachers and students to publish and access information from anywhere with an internet connection. Parents, staff and girls appreciate the effective system to keep track of homework, study tasks, school events and individuals' progress in learning. Pupils do not bring in their own laptops but can sign out and use a school laptop (kept in school library) whenever they need to. However, pupils are still encouraged and expected to use books for their academic research as well as online resources ('both are important skills'). Strong learning support both in and out of the classroom. We hear reports of 'great classroom assistants'.

Pupils tell us that if there is anything academic that they need help with there are drop-in centres every lunchtime where a teacher is available to help them – in all subjects. Big, bright custom-built common room for sixth formers and study areas available.

Games, options, the arts: As you would expect for the largest (joint) independent school in Europe, sport is massive. Hockey, football and rugby are all strong (winners of U18 and U15 Scottish Schools' Hockey Cup, of Scottish Schools' Rugby Cup, of the Scottish Independent Schools' FA Cup), but there are successes across the more minor sports as well with national accolades in swimming, kayaking, orienteering, golf, judo and climbing to name but a few. The main sports of rugby or hockey and cricket or athletics are compulsory for the younger pupils, but the choice widens further up the school. So, for those not so enamoured with team sports, there are plentiful options, including cycling, swimming and cross-country. The school puts out a very high number of teams so many pupils – around three-quarters – will get a chance to play matches against other schools.

The pitches at Stewart's Melville are used mainly for the curriculum PE lessons and for afternoon sport boys are bussed to further school pitches at Inverleith. Swimming is popular and the school has a 25m swimming pool on site.

Outstanding drama – 'sport and the performing arts are equally strong here'. We hear from parents that drama is 'quite extraordinary'. It is part of the curriculum for younger pupils and can be taken up to Higher and Advanced Higher. The Tom Fleming Centre for Performing Arts, at the Stewart's Melville site, can seat audiences of up to 580. It's a renovated Victorian assembly hall – an impressive venue with comprehensive production, sound and lighting facilities. New acquisition Dean Church is another performance venue. Drama is for all, with plays and performances throughout the year for all age groups with regular performances at the Edinburgh Festival. Masses of orchestras and choirs at all age groups (22 bands, orchestras, ensembles and choirs running). Annual house music and house rock competitions, both keenly fought with performances described by one parent as 'bloody amazing'. Choir performs annually at the Royal Edinburgh Military Tattoo. More than 200 boys have instrumental music lessons and there are 45 visiting music teachers. Pipe band thriving.

A staggering variety of clubs and societies on offer to all. It's all here – from video editing to curling and everything in between. These take place at lunch time and post school. Many of the clubs are sporting – squash, football, netball – but there's certainly something for everyone in the lineup. Good home economics. Voluntary CCF, very popular with over 300 pupils involved. Strong RAF – over 100. Even split between boys and girls. ESMS are the biggest provider over DofE in Scotland with large numbers getting gold awards.

Splendid art – and up to date displays around the school, wondrous paintings from this year's art exams already up and framed on the walls. Schools often display fabulous art that we then discover has been hanging there for years. Here the boys and girls can see their creations being valued while they are still at school – when it matters most.

Boarding: Only a tiny percentage of pupils board; this is still predominantly a day school. Dean Park House can accommodate up to 30 boarders. Handily located on site; boys only have a few minutes' walk into their classes each morning. The house isn't purpose built and it feels more like a large family house, well furnished and very well equipped. The bedroom sizes vary and accommodate between two and five boys. Sixth formers may have their own room, depending on numbers.

At weekends the boarders have planned activities offered to them such as surfing, cinema trips etc but they may also go into the city centre if they wish. The Sunday morning service in the local church remains compulsory to all boarders. They are free to use the school sports centres (pool and fitness suite) in the evening and over weekends.

Flexi-boarding is also on offer – but only if there's space available.

Boarders come from Scotland, south of the border and also abroad. Often with family connections to the school (offspring of FPs – former pupils), expats. Predominantly UK citizens rather than foreign nationals.

Background and atmosphere: Stewart's Melville campus is based around the magnificent Daniel Stewart's Hospital. Designed by David Rhind, it was opened in 1855 by the Merchant Company of Edinburgh. When Daniel Stewart (whose wealth came from India) died in 1814, he left a sum of money and instructions that, once it had reached £40,000, it should be used to create a hospital for needy boys within the city. The hospital was transformed into Daniel Stewart's College in 1870. In 1972 the school merged with Melville College. The David Rhind main building is large and Victorian gothic in design. Think fairytale pile, now surrounded by some necessary modern additions. Games pitches to the front, mostly used for PE and by the junior school and car parks front and rear, chock full at the time of our visit.

Senior pupils share the site with upper junior school of ESMS. Sixth formers, who are back in the co-ed set-up with Mary Erskine, are bussed to classes between the two campuses, about a mile apart. Mind boggling timetabling but, according to both pupils and staff, it runs like clockwork.

Coaches from Dunfermline, Bathgate, Eskbank and Haddington as well as around Edinburgh.

Pastoral care, well-being and discipline: The school runs a tutorial system for the first year with groups of 20 boys led by their form tutor, after which the school is divided into six houses. Each has a head of house and an assistant head who together look after the girls as they move through school. These houses are common to both Stewart's Melville and Mary Erskine, so the various inter-house competitions have mixed teams. Weekly inter-house challenges range from maths quizzes to basketball matches. Sixth formers are under the divided into small tutor groups with a personal tutor, under the umbrella of the director of sixth form.

Excellent anti-bullying policy. 'Cyberbullying in school aged children is now more of a threat than normal bullying' and that they have a full programme to educate the pupils and make them aware of the pitfalls. We hear from parents that 'any bullying shenanigans or friendship issues are handled very well and quickly' and there is 'fantastic pastoral care'. Sophisticated PSE programme throughout the school.

'Zero tolerance' and expulsion if pupils found in possession of, or dealing in, drugs of any kind. Booze and smoking normally end in suspension – 'unacceptable but not an issue in school'.

Pupils and parents: A real mixture of parents. Many first time buyers and children of FPs (former pupils). Parents report 'a broad cross section of families', mostly from central Edinburgh and suburbs. Not really a toff school, although there will be a smattering. Taking over a third of Edinburgh's independent secondary pupils, it is less elitist than some of its neighbours. Children living far out can spend the night when doing evening activities (as long as there's room). Alumni include Tom Fleming, actor and broadcaster.

Entrance: At age 11, 12, 13, fifth year and sixth form. Automatic entrance from junior school. A broadly non-selective school. Children are assessed (English, maths, verbal reasoning) before entrance. Numbers are up. The waiting lists remain 'first come, first served' and there are no plans to cherry-pick the more able pupils.

Exit: Minimal leakage pre-Highers with most going on to university. Some 65 per cent to Scottish universities, the rest to English, Irish, European or American universities. In 2018, one to Oxbridge and eight medics. Others to Italy, Denmark and Dublin. SATS (for American colleges) not a problem.

Money matters: Bursaries – up to 100 per cent – and scholarships throughout. Those doing well in the entrance exam are invited to sit a scholarship exam. Music scholarships (together with free music tuition) are also available.

Remarks: This is a big school with big ambitions. With terrific success stories on every front, not just academically, it is a formidable operation. Not every child will thrive as a small fish in such a big pond and such a large operation may leave the non-conformist with less room to manoeuvre. However, its sheer size has tremendous benefits – parents report 'the school pulls in great staff' and provides pupils with 'incredible opportunities'. Well mannered, ambitious children leave the school self-confident and 'with a strong work ethic'. Parents across the board say they 'can't fault it'. An outstanding school with impressive results.

Strathallan School

Forgandenny, Perth, Perthshire PH2 9EG

Ages 9–18 **Pupils** 520 **Sixth form** 192 **Boarders** 320 full

Fees: Day £14,700 – £22,410; Boarding £23,550 – £33,000 pa

01738 812546
www.strathallan.co.uk

Headmaster: Since September 2017, Mark Lauder, who by his own admission is anything but a 'patrician' public school head. After a Scottish state school education, marred by the teachers' strikes of the early 1980s, he showed his mettle by earning an MA in English Literature and history at Aberdeen. He then went to win a graduate scholarship for research to Oxford and two half blues in rowing.

Clearly made of strong stuff, and we found him to be an eloquent and charming communicator with a strong vision for the future of the school. Previously head of Ashville College, he has also been deputy head and head of boarding at Felsted School, Essex, head of history and then housemaster at St Edward's School, Oxford, and before that head of history and master in charge of rowing at Shiplake College, Henley-on-Thames, coaching rugby and rowing throughout. So lots of experience and he certainly seems ready to use his widespread contacts to bring Strathallan into the limelight.

He is married to peripatetic saxophone and piano teacher, Caroline, with two teenage sons.

Housemistress of the Junior House (Riley): is Mrs Emma Lalani.

Academic matters: The school describes results to date as 'good for a broad ability school but can still do better'. 2018 A level results showed 40 per cent of the grades were A*/As; 70 per cent were A*-B, Highers, 53 per cent A/Bs; GCSEs 52 per cent A*-A/9-7s.

But that, says Mark Lauder, with great gusto and a swirl of his kilt, is where great changes are afoot.

'We have so many pupils competing in sport at a very high level, we need to adapt our approach to better balance their contact with teachers and sharpen up our overall academic performance.' According to their figures, from the junior school right up to fifth form, 100 per cent of pupils represented the school in team sport. In sixth form it was 88 per cent. Ten per cent of the school competed at national or international level. Very, very impressive, but we can see where this might lead to pressure on academics.

'We're reviewing lots of different ways of improving quality teaching time. Teachers are being split into working parties to help "staff engagement" and everyone is being encouraged to look at ways of sharpening up their teaching time and working harder on ensuring that core subjects are given more emphasis.'

The school, says Mark Lauder, has a better than average staff to pupil ratio and they should be able to use that advantage to 'blend the curriculum' around the child rather than the other way around.

As for the curriculum itself, you could say the school plays the system in a way. Everyone sits GCSEs, but after that the school offers both English A levels and rather controversially Scottish Highers over two years (it's normally a one year course). Some would argue this makes the A level results look better as less academic pupils can take the Higher route, but Mark Lauder staunchly defends this. He says 75 per cent follow the A level route but the 25 per cent who choose Highers do so for a variety of reasons. Yes, some may be less academic, but others don't want to lose breadth of subject choice or they want to study medicine in Scotland (Strath is one of the very few schools to offer Higher human biology, which suits medical applications) or they are just incredibly busy and doing Highers over two years is an achievable option.

'The captain of rugby, for example, was called up to play for Scotland U20s. It was a fabulous opportunity, but if he weren't doing Highers over two years he would have really struggled with his academic work.'

As for the subjects on offer, they're a pretty regular selection, although Mr Lauder says social sciences and the arts are being beefed up with new A levels in psychology, theatre studies and PE, and GCSEs in drama and RE. They are also changing the third form curriculum to introduce music and drama and increasing the contact time for English, maths and Latin.

Interesting take on GCSE science: rather than just doing either triple or all single sciences, they have come up with an additional third pathway, foundation single science. This, they claim, is again all about offering flexible options.

Mr Lauder says he's about to bring a brand new scholarship programme across the disciplines.

One practice which got our attention is the fifth form 'post trial exam' interview. This is a one-on-one interview with the head, the houseparent and the deputy head of academics. The idea is to discuss with each child how they felt the exams went and to map out what they should be doing next to get the best results in the real exams. This is followed by a second interview with the UCAS and careers adviser.

We thought it sounded bloody terrifying to begin with, but parents said it was handled incredibly well. 'We think this really raised the bar for our son. It made him sit up and take notice and he really felt they were paying attention to him.' 'Mark's really shaken things up in the best possible way. He's making it clear that only giving your best is good enough.'

Some pragmatic steps and a lot of positive thinking, but will he really manage to make headway? Well, he certainly seems to have got off on the right foot with some of the parents. 'I'm really excited about him and what he's doing with the school.' 'He's the right kind of person; enthusiastic and passionate.' 'He and his wife are really good for the school. From what we hear the kids are responding really well to them.'

Learning support is free and seems fairly well covered. All pupils are screened on entry and ed psychs are brought in where necessary. It has its own small area within the school and support is delivered in a variety of ways: one-to-one, small groups, after-school clinics in various disciplines. There are two full time trained staff, plus ancillaries, and they cover the entire age range. The school says they can cope with mild Asperger's/autism. Teachers have now been provided with briefings on issues such as dyslexia and the focus has been on helping departments adapt approaches and materials to pupils' different needs. Programmes have also been introduced to help pupils who have English as a second language. Focus is now on taking more learning support and more EAL into the classrooms so academic time is not lost.

If physical infirmity is a problem, most classrooms are on the ground floor and one building has a lift.

Games, options, the arts: 'We are NOT buying rugby pupils.' Mark Lauder is adamant when it comes to protecting the reputation of their all-conquering rugby squad. He claims that if you take a snapshot, 11 of the 15 will generally have joined Strath at third form or earlier. We're not arguing. We imagine those big rugger buggers can put up a fair fight. That said, there have been frequent mutterings around the Scottish school circuit about Strath's alleged practice of bringing in 'ringers'. But the parents we spoke to are right behind the school: 'The bad reputation is nonsense; there are a lot of sour grapes out there.'

What we can say with confidence is that sport at this school is incredible. And we mean incredible. We were treated to what we can only describe as the 'wall of glory': a dazzling photographic display of all the pupils currently representing the school at national and international level. There are county, national, international, Commonwealth and Olympic presences across the board and at all ages: from rugby, footie, tennis, hockey, skiing, netball, swimming, shooting (clay and small bore), fencing, golf (own course), sailing. They have coaches who have themselves played at county, national and/or international level in most sports. The facilities we saw were wonderful. They now have a huge gym hall that allows full hockey games etc to be played in foul weather.

So enough said about the sport; the art provision is rather impressive too. The art school is over three floors with marvellous light and some inspired work. We were pleased to see a group of relaxed and engaged students with their sleeves rolled up during their lunch hour, more than happy to talk to us about their work.

Musically, the school hits the top notes too. Piping is very, very strong. Rather like the Queen, the head has his own piper. They currently have three bands who play all over the UK and abroad (Barbados, USA, Italy and France).

Loads of drama: small theatre, new dance and drama studio.

The school also has a pupil media team bringing the school mag into the digital age.

Plenty of charity work underway across the school. They have a strong link with Kenya and send pupils out every year with a supply of clothes and provisions. Lots of DofE and community service, plus popular CCF.

Boarding: No prizes for architecture at Strathallan. There you are sweeping up the beautiful drive with that wonderful backdrop of hills then it's 'I'm sorry? I didn't realise there was a Travelodge so near, oh in fact, there's another one. And another one. And....' you get the general drift. That said, none of the pupils we spoke to were complaining. Girls have their own study bedrooms for their last five years at the school, boys for four. Fairly functional but lovely views. Lots of kitchens and common room areas on each floor. We were a bit bowled over by the tartan carpet in the boys' house that we toured. Disabled loos and lifts are available to all floors.

In junior house tuck is controlled. Houses have regular supply of milk, bread and fruit.

No exeats. Chapel every other Sunday (as well as Wednesdays) with a 'very funny and engaging' chaplain. On the other Sundays, it's a lie in and brunch.

Background and atmosphere: We were agog when the head greeted us at the front door of the main school in full kilt. But we had arrived on Wednesday when everyone goes to chapel and the kilt is mandatory.

If you think that marks Strathallan out as stuffy, you'd be completely wrong. Founded in 1913 by Harry Riley, the school is set in a breathtaking 153 carefully manicured acres, with everything you could imagine including a canoe slalom and a loch stocked with trout for the angling club. Wow! The buildings, as we've mentioned, are rather utilitarian, but the pupils we spoke to didn't care and why should they? It does what it says on the tin.

Nearly the first building you come to as you come up the drive is the Junior House, Riley. This boasts a lovely atrium and a library, music practice rooms etc. Younger boarders and day children also have a dedicated sports and play area. Virtually everyone without exception moves into the senior school.

The whole school eats in the bright and airy dining room. The pupils we spoke to thought the food was very good.

So what is it about Strathallan that's different? Well, that's an interesting question. If you talk to children from other public schools around Scotland, they'll roll their eyes and say Strathallians are a pretty clannish bunch. 'They don't mix with other schools and keep themselves to themselves.' So what do the current crop of Strathallians think?

'We're not as snobby as the other schools.' 'We're there for each other. We're really close, really loyal.' 'I think we mix. No idea where that came from.'

Pastoral care, well-being and discipline: Seven houses in senior school, four for boys and three for girls. Houseparents live on site with two staff on duty in each house every night. Academic tutor attached to each pupil and tutorial team in every house. Tutors often use the time available for informal chats.

Staff 'aware that things happen' and talk of 'zero tolerance' on drugs but rural setting means incidents involving drugs and alcohol are not very frequent. Instead, says the head, fitness suite is packed at 9 every night. (Strath is a sporting behemoth, after all.)

School works hard on bullying awareness with lots of briefings – expectations, ownership, relationships, 'be reasonable'. Punishment system for misdemeanours called 'fatigues' (colloquial name for disciplinary). This involves jobs around the buildings and grounds, of which obviously there's no shortage.

Another of head's initiatives is 'Monday drop in'. This is when anyone in the school can pop into his office for a chat.

Nothing is off limits, apparently, and he's done everything from bereavement counselling to advising on the best way to look after your shoes. He's even had the odd pupil who just wanted to see what his office looked like.

On a more formal basis, the sixth form have regular discussion groups (15 at a time) with the head, where they cover topics such as Brexit, American politics etc. 'Mr Lauder is so easy to talk to.'

Pupils and parents: Some 20 per cent of the pupils are from overseas from eg Spain, Russia, Africa, China, Eastern Europe, Hong Kong and Germany; a further 18 per cent are expats. The school is an easy one hour drive from Edinburgh and Glasgow. New short stay international programme.

We would say this is not a school for toffs; probably more regional Scottish accents than other similar schools. Parents tend to be farmers or successful businessmen and women.

Day pupils allocated to one of the houses; daily buses to and from Perth, Kinross, Auchterarder, Stirling, Crieff and Dundee. About a third or more come daily, with many younger day children converting to boarders on going to senior school age 13. Boarding increases as you go through the school. If you are in a play etc you can stay over and not be charged. Buses leave the school grounds at 7.30pm.

Think of the Junior House, Riley as a middle school (from age 9), with the children moving into the senior school at 13. Everyone in Riley moves up to Strathallan without having to sit common entrance.

Entrance: Entrance to the Junior House is at age 9, 10, 11 or 12 by school report and assessments, or scholarship held on entrance day in early spring. Senior entrance is at 13+, via open scholarship examination (late February/early March), common entrance (June) or/and school report. Sixth form entry is either via the sixth form scholarship examination (November) or on the basis of a satisfactory school report and/or GCSE/National 5 results. All pupils are screened for learning difficulties on entry and IEPs plus ed psychs rolled in if necessary. Excellent route map for parents unfamiliar with public school entry procedures.

Exit: To a range of universities – 60 per cent Scottish, nearly all the rest English. Generally a couple each year to Oxbridge – two in 2018, plus one medic. Forces popular.

Money matters: School says they're financially strong. Junior scholarships, open scholarships and sixth form scholarships available plus academic, all-rounder, sport, music, design technology, piping and art scholarships. Strong track record with prestigious Arkwright Scholarships for aspiring engineers.

Parents can apply for means-tested help with fees via bursaries. Sibling discount, Forces and Old Strathallian discounts available.

Remarks: Fiercely proud and competitive, Strathallan hits a lot of high notes, especially with sport, art and music. Amazing setting and some awesome facilities. Not known for mixing well with other schools, but then maybe they're too busy and happy to bother.

Wallace College

59

12 George IV Bridge, Edinburgh EH1 1EE

Ages 15–19 **Pupils** 50

Fees: Varies according to course.

0131 220 3634
www.wallacecollege.co.uk

Director of studies: Since 1993, Lily Crawford MA (60s – you could knock 10 years off and still guess wrong); a Glasgow lass, who read English literature at Edinburgh and previously taught in the state system in Edinburgh and Falkirk. Slow speaking, deep thinking, she is point of contact for new students, passionate about keeping costs down and directing studies to be fit both for uni matriculation and future employment. Previously an examiner for AQA, SQA and the BAC, she has all the necessary know-how. Crawford leads students through the UCAS maze, helps with personal statements, engineers extra time (scribes if need be – but SQA must have proof positive of need). Very much hands on and, quite obviously, the glove fits.

Academic matters: Exam centre for AQA, Edexcel, OCR, CIE: GCE, A2, GCSE and IGCSE; SQA: National 5, Highers, Advanced Highers. One year three term courses start in September. Wallace prides itself on 'accelerated study programmes': super motivated can take a conventional two year course within the year; mega boost, too, in October and February with daily three hour concentrated blocks of lessons: five subjects each week. A two term IGCSE syllabus runs from January. Raft of options on offer; all tutors (of all ages: easy to find in Edinburgh) come with honours degrees, college will pull on extra lang tutors (usually native speaking) or just tutors for more esoteric requirements. Technical subjects cost more than a tad more – hiring lab time is expensive, though Wallace can often rustle up kit for physics experiments. All the usual suspects, plus philosophy, economics, accounting, computing and mod studies. Engineering not really feasible.

The flexi-study programme is geared to help 'students who wish to combine independent study with support from qualified tutors'; many of these are home schooled and just need pointers to keep them up to speed: 'read this chapter, forget that, this is really important' sort of thing. Usual course is two hours per subject a week for 10 weeks, but variations possible. No more than five independent learners per class, which may be timetabled to suit individual students: lessons in the afternoons to accommodate a morning job, five days' work reorganised into three for those who live further away. Back to the Crawford mantra – keep the cost down.

Classes tiny, usually six or less, often one-to-one and never more than eight. Students come for regular sixth form studies, to improve GCSE/National grades, As, Highers or Advanced Highers, or to expand their portfolio. No hard and fast rules. Emphasis on essay writing, good SEN help available. Three hours per subject per week, plus an hour's test with regular feedback, and detailed end of term report.

The acclaimed holiday revision courses, usually oversubscribed, are a haven for those still at school and overseas students, often in the independent sector, who find some of our educational lingo, particularly in exams, a tad quirky: 'It takes a man with a wheelbarrow 10 hours to move 1000 kilos of sand one kilometre, how long would it take three men with wheelbarrows?' And just what is a wheelbarrow? In a maths exam?

Games, options, the arts: No affiliations with sports clubs and the like, but director of studies can 'point in the right direction'. Theatre trips arranged if useful for course work (extra).

Boarding: Accommodation can be arranged, either through the EFL wing myriad of approved host families, or in university halls, assuming space available, though currently no boarders.

Background and atmosphere: Privately owned college, founded in 1972, incorporating English language school, variety of tutorial options, and a popular revision course (all disciplines except the BAC) during half terms and holidays. Tucked neatly away behind a (Georgian) red door above an unprepossessing row of shops on George IV Bridge, not quite within the sight of Edinburgh Castle, spectacular views from the west (castle et al). Very much into the 21st century, twitters away: 'GCSE results come out on August 22', happy tweets from students.

Pastoral care, well-being and discipline: Strong anti-drugs policy.

No parents' evenings as such; parents 'welcome to pop in and see Crawford or individual tutors', otherwise most communication is by email.

Pupils and parents: All sorts: aged 15+ to 19. Pupils come from all backgrounds for all reasons, including those who find that conventional school does not cater for their particular selection of subjects, those who have lived outside the trad school atmosphere, those who have been educated abroad, and those who have parted either willingly or unwillingly from their previous school.

Entrance: By interview with the director of studies.

Exit: College takes enormous trouble to launch students on the next step of their careers; matriculation the norm. Edinburgh uni popular, as with all the (free) Scottish universities.

Remarks: Good alternative for those who don't get on with traditional schools.

Wellington School

Carleton Turrets, Craigweil Road, Ayr KA7 2XH

Ages 3–18 **Pupils** 536 **Sixth form** 48

Fees: £6,600 – £12,450 pa

01292 269321
www.wellingtonschool.org

W

Headmaster: Since 2015, Simon Johnson, previously assistant rector at Dollar Academy, head of department at Mary Erskine and teacher at Fettes. Proud to have 'always been a teacher', is a mathematician by trade, with degree in the subject from Cambridge and PGCE from Moray House College in Edinburgh.

Softly spoken, intelligent and unassumingly witty (this editor thought Nigel Slater-esque in tone), one couldn't imagine Mr Johnson raising his voice (though we're sure he must find occasion to). Praised by parents as a 'quiet, robust head of the helm' and hands-on head that 'is a regular presence as the head of the cheering squad at team matches, school plays and events that the pupils participate in.'

General consensus is that pupils are benefiting from his advice. One parent said: 'He is very encouraging of pupils and their efforts, giving them the recognition that they deserve and the confidence to progress and achieve more'. One pupil, who secured a place at Oxford, reiterated this about her application process: 'He guided and helped me. I doubt I would have been so successful without his support.'

Met his partner, Louise (maths teacher at an independent school) while at Fettes. No children but he jokes 'plenty of children in the day job'. Passionate about outdoors pursuits and loves working by the sea. Hobbies include climbing, skiing and mountaineering. Talented pianist, with a love of Bach and Brahms. Even if he wanted to keep this under his hat, since his debut playing with the chamber choir in the town hall, he laughs 'everyone knows now' and often plays at school events.

Academic matters: At Higher in 2018, over half A grades, with 52 per cent As at Advanced Higher. One of the top schools for Advanced Higher (AH) results in Scotland, an advantage perhaps being the small class sizes, sometimes just one or two pupils per teacher for Higher and AH. One parent testified to this: 'My eldest daughter did crash higher biology in her final year and had one-to-one teaching. She got an A.' This is a non-selective school, however, so credit must be given.

Huge emphasis on languages and proud of its British Council's international school status. Head passionate about being part of an outward looking education 'at a time when the world is looking in'. All do French from primary school and can choose also to do German, Spanish and Latin at National 5 level and beyond. On our tour, we saw one-to-one language teaching, and one pupil, heading off to study at St Andrews told us 'the language department is incredible.' Long history of junior and senior exchanges with partner schools, almost three decades, with Germany and France. Plus exchanges with other parts of Europe and India. One pupil told us of her 10-day home exchange in India, saying: 'It was an eye-opener ... as well as experiencing the Taj Mahal and going on elephant rides'. Children from Germany, Slovenia and Bulgaria, for example, as part of the Erasmus project, come for a term, with designated EFL teachers on hand.

Almost all choose eight National 5s, and most choose five Highers. Broad curriculum with business management, accounting and music performing and technology taught from S3, and 20 subjects available at Higher level, though majority stick to the traditional subjects. Sciences popular and chemistry a particular success among the girls, with sometimes more girls than boys sitting Higher chemistry though, typically, physics is a different story with often no girls sitting AH physics.

One parent felt: 'Support for learning deserves a special mention: the staff members are aware and dedicated.' Support for learning (SfL) manager is in charge of the SfL department, which supports children from nursery to S6, with dedicated teachers in the junior school and part-time teachers in the senior school. The head states: 'As a small school, we can deal with a range of education needs through one-to-one support, and this comes with no additional costs.' S6 pupils mentor younger children in the classroom, through a buddying system and a successful memory and study skills club runs in the senior school.

Deputy head and both assistants now female, making a 50/50 split in the management team. 'There are quite a few changes happening ... with many teachers retiring thereby letting new younger teachers come in, bringing a fresh approach.'

Work experience from S4, and pupils can subscribe to the Futurewise programme (charged separately). Senior pupils receive a presentation on the UCAS journey and form tutors are closely involved with careers advice and help with UCAS applications and interviews.

Games, options, the arts: School has 20-acre sports ground and pavilion at Doonside, in Alloway, on the outskirts of Ayr for floodlit rugby, hockey (most popular with girls) and cricket matches. Rugby is taught from P1 and an amalgamation between Wellington and Ayr Rugby Club allows for a shared use of facilities, and head says 'provides pathways to real experiences for those who hope to play at the highest standards'. A couple of grumbles about sport in general and one parent felt disgruntled about current standards (rugby and hockey) and that the amalgamation with Ayr Rugby club 'is not all rosy.' Despite this, great results in rugby recently, U18 and U16 rugby teams competed in the National Youth League Cup Finals at Murrayfield, and U16s were National Youth Champions. National and international tours to Holland, Spain, France, Italy and UK throughout the year. S1s and S2s can take part in the annual tour to their partner school outside Paris, the Institut Saint-Dominique.

Athletics, tennis, netball and cricket also popular, with the primary and junior cricket teams winning the district finals in recently. One parent felt: 'There is not enough encouragement to do sport if you're not that skilled at rugby or hockey'. However, the head was keen to emphasise how inclusive sports are and that 'a feature of a small school is that there's always a chance to take part'. Plenty of clubs and extracurricular activities in junior and senior schools, with debating a favourite and, perhaps surprisingly, also the bridge club, as well as popular dance club that puts on a popular annual dance spotlight. School hopes to develop partnership with one of the many golf clubs in the area. Swimming off-site at the Citadel pool in Ayr.

Music is open to everyone and a floor is dedicated to the subject, complete with sound-proofed recording studio, computer room and individual practice rooms. Unfortunately, we didn't get to see the music department because of exams, but an 'enormous appetite for music' (junior and senior school) with masses of bands, ensembles, orchestras, choir and a jazz band. Most talented take part in external competitions, such as the annual Ayrshire music festival. Drama not offered as a subject but musicals every year, and head 'astonished by the quality'. Recently West Side Story and Les Misérables (senior) and Joseph (junior). Seven S6 pupils headed to the Royal Conservatoire of Scotland recently.

Laid back art department with new state of the art laser cutter. Fashion designs (units for Higher art) on show in the school entrance, and impressive modern portrait by National 5 pupil won Royal Scottish Academy Art Competition. Biannual fashion show and exhibition of work.

P7s work towards the John Muir award as a precursor to the Duke of Edinburgh; almost all pupils do bronze, half do silver and some do gold.

Huge range of trips through international exchange programme, plus eg geography field trip to Iceland, P6 trip to Titanic museum in Belfast, plus biannual humanitarian expeditions (Cambodia recently) and biannual ski trips.

Background and atmosphere: Founded in 1836 in Wellington Square by a French woman, the wife of an Ayr teacher, it was previously one of Scotland's oldest girls' boarding schools. Moved to its current location at seafront Carleton Turrets in 1923, turning co-ed in the 1990s – seemed like a fairly even balance of boys to girls on our tour.

Held in high regard by the local community, with a strong sense of family traditions. 'For a long time families have been proud to send their children here.' Suited to children who would thrive in a small school with a nurturing environment, rather than a highly competitive one. One former boarder with children now at the school said: 'Many of the positives from my time at Wellington were still evident ... The school still had the same welcoming feeling that I remembered so well ... The teachers at Wellington gave [my daughter] the confidence to believe in herself. She was taught that nothing was impossible and to follow her dream.' Traditional values but laid back atmosphere, and quiet, studious pupils in the senior school; usual playground enthusiasm in the junior school. All children well-presented wearing their green woollen blazers, but not as strict approach as some independent schools, with strictly no make-up or dyed hair. We did notice the odd 'fashionable' hair style.

Affectionately known has Hogwarts by pupils because of its three turreted buildings and small spiral staircases, stained glass windows and mahogany panelling. Carleton Turrets and Craigweil House are home to the senior department, with fine views of the Firth of Clyde from the upper floors, whereas Drumley House, across the road, caters for the nursery and primary school children. Pupils have to go out onto the street to travel between buildings (not always pleasant in Scottish weather) but the campus feels more seamless now previously privately owned building at its centre has been turned into classroom space plus a new support for learning hub. An outdoor nursery is located at Doonside for woodland adventures.

Plenty of fundraising: P5s–S2s took part in the fabulous fiver challenge to come up with entrepreneurial ideas to raise money (£3,000 for school charity). While only required to give half of their profits, most donated all. S6 pupils annually choose a charity to fundraise for and galvanise the whole school to raise money. They recently raised over £35,000 for the Scottish Association for Mental Health, which was its single biggest donation. Other fundraising events include parachute jumping, sponsored swim from Ayr beach to Lady Isle, annual fun run along the promenade (some in costume) and sponsored run into the sea annually, called the Wellie Wade.

Pastoral care, well-being and discipline: House system (made up of four houses, same as siblings, mothers or aunts) and pastoral care run hand in hand from S1 to S6. Pupils are grouped into a house form group in S1, each with a form tutor who stays with them throughout school life, and who are on hand to give guidance and support. Close school community, any worries can be discussed with class teacher, head of year or whoever they are closest to. Buddy system for younger pupils and specifically for new starts in P7. Parents are directed to head of year or form tutor if they have any concerns.

Most pupils have a school lunch and pay daily. This editor was invited to lunch in what was a very quiet dining room (no nonsense – certainly not when the head was dining, anyway). Comforting traditional home-cooked meals, such as soup, cottage pie and macaroni, were served alongside an array of salads and fruit pots.

Comprehensive discipline policy, which can be downloaded, on the impressive school website. Positive behaviour is promoted first but if this doesn't work detention, monitoring or contacting parents the next step. Exclusions would be a last resort (none recently). Head says: 'We are proactive at dealing with issues as soon as they arise. Size of school means we have a good grip on what's going on.'

Pupils and parents: Well-mannered and courteous pupils. One parent commented: 'One of the things that still amazes me is the respect and courtesy shown by pupils at the school and this is encouraged by the staff. Even the youngest pupils will hold a door open for you with a smile and a greeting.' Parents mostly middle class; plenty of former Wellie pupils. Mostly professionals, including the medical professions and businesspeople, some from overseas, and those moving to the coast from other parts of Scotland.

Proactive in contacting parents through parent emails, thriving FB page and a school magazine, called The Turret. One parent commented: 'Parents are also included in the process of the development of their children and I can honestly say that we are kept in the loop with regards to all that goes on at school, how our child is doing and how we can help to contribute to their further growth..'

Reports and parents' evenings throughout the year. Targeted information evenings and meetings with parents for S2 subject choices. School buses run from Largs, Glasgow and beyond Girvan (organised by parents).

Notable former pupils include Nicola Benedetti (world famous violinist), Kirsty Hume (model), Rhona Simpson (field hockey player), Kirsty Wark (journalist and TV presenter) and Michael Foyle (classical violinist).

Entrance: Pupils can join at all levels but predominantly in nursery, P1, P7 and S1. Non-selective but, as typical, entrance exam in P7 and S1 in English and maths to gauge where children are, plus an interview with head and previous school reports, if needed.

Popular nursery run in partnership with South Ayrshire Council (we guess not all nursery children can afford to move on to the junior school). For those that can, interview with head. All junior school pupils automatically move to the senior senior school; P7 (transitional year) is based in senior school.

Exit: Vast majority stay on to do Highers and AH, and go on to mostly Scottish universities, including Strathclyde, Glasgow, Edinburgh and St Andrews. Medicine, law, dentistry most appealing subjects; the core group wanting to go on to traditional professions. Don't routinely provide support/ information for apprenticeships, as not much call for it.

Money matters: Sibling discounts and means-tested bursaries available. One in five receive some form of support.

Remarks: The Wellie is held dear in the hearts of many, none more so than its former pupils. A small, nurturing independent school with a family atmosphere and outward-looking international approach. Hogwarts-style turreted buildings with the seaside as its backdrop.

Schools for special educational needs

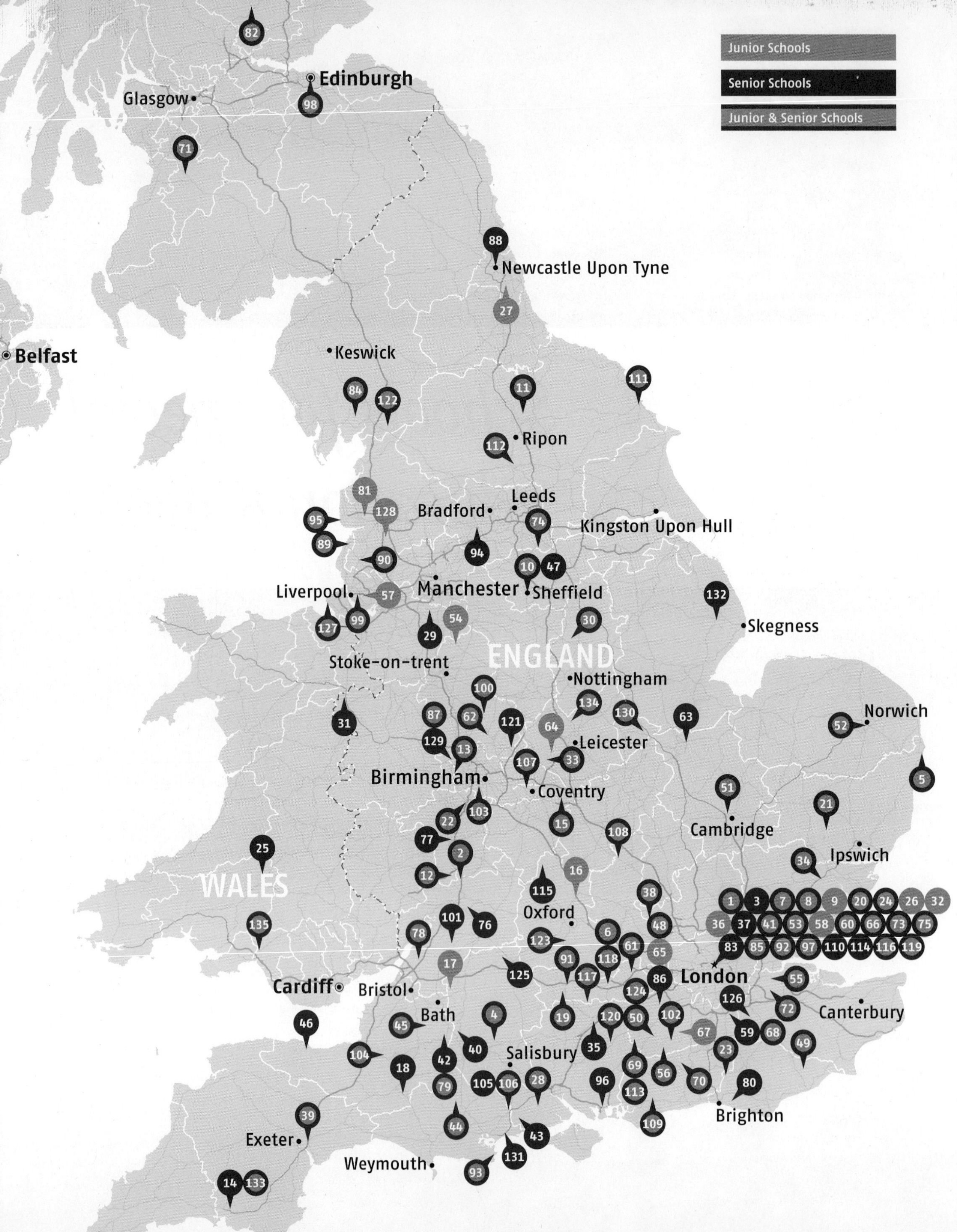
Junior Schools
Senior Schools
Junior & Senior Schools
Edinburgh
Glasgow
Belfast
Newcastle Upon Tyne
Keswick
Ripon
Leeds
Bradford
Kingston Upon Hull
Liverpool
Manchester
Sheffield
Skegness
ENGLAND
Stoke-on-trent
Nottingham
Leicester
Norwich
Birmingham
Coventry
Cambridge
Ipswich
WALES
Oxford
London
Cardiff
Bristol
Bath
Canterbury
Salisbury
Brighton
Exeter
Weymouth

SEN

1 Abingdon House School
2 Alderman Knight School
3 Ambitious College
4 Appleford School
5 The Ashley School
6 The Avenue Special School
7 Beyond Autism Park House and Tram House
8 Blossom House School
9 Blossom Lower School
10 Brantwood Specialist School
11 Breckenbrough School
12 Bredon School
13 The Brier School
14 Brook Green Centre for Learning
15 Brooke School
16 Bruern Abbey School
17 Calder House School
18 Cambian Lufton College
19 The Castle School
20 Centre Academy
21 Centre Academy East Anglia
22 Chadsgrove School
23 Chailey Heritage School
24 Clarendon School
25 Coleg Elidyr
26 Colnbrook School
27 Columbia Grange School
28 Coxlease School
29 The David Lewis Centre
30 Dawn House School
31 Derwen College
32 The Dominie
33 Dorothy Goodman School Hinckley
34 Doucecroft School
35 Dove House School
36 Eagle House School, Mitcham
37 Eagle House School Sutton
38 Egerton-Rothesay School
39 Ellen Tinkham School
40 Fairfield Farm College
41 Fairley House School
42 Farleigh Further Education College - Frome
43 The Fortune Centre of Riding Therapy
44 The Forum School
45 Fosse Way School
46 Foxes Academy
47 Freeman College
48 Freemantles School
49 Frewen College
50 Gosden House School
51 Gretton School
52 Harford Manor School, Norwich
53 The Holmewood School London
54 Horton Lodge Community Special School
55 Ifield School
56 Jigsaw CABAS School
57 Lakeside School
58 Limespring School
59 Limpsfield Grange School
60 Linden Bridge School
61 Manor Green School
62 Maple Hayes Hall School
63 Marshfields School
64 Meadow View Farm School
65 Meath School
66 The Moat School
67 Moon Hall School
68 Moor House School & College
69 More House School (Farnham)
70 Muntham House School
71 The National Autistic Society Daldorch House School
72 The National Autistic Society, Helen Allison School
73 The National Autistic Society Radlett Lodge School
74 The National Autistic Society Robert Ogden School
75 The National Autistic Society Sybil Elgar School
76 National Star College
77 New College Worcester
78 New Siblands School
79 North Hill House
80 Northease Manor School
81 Oakfield House School
82 Ochil Tower School
83 Orchard Hill College of Further Education
84 Oversands School
85 Parayhouse School
86 The Park School (Woking)
87 Penn Hall School
88 Hedleys College
89 Peterhouse School
90 Pontville School
91 Priors Court School
92 The Priory Lodge School
93 Purbeck View School
94 Ravenscliffe High School and Sports College
95 Red Rose School
96 Redwood Park Academy
97 Riverston School
98 The Royal Blind School
99 Royal School for the Blind (Liverpool)
100 Rugeley School
101 Ruskin Mill College
102 St Joseph's Specialist School & College
103 Selly Oak Trust School
104 Shapwick School
105 Sheiling College
106 Sheiling School
107 Sherbourne Fields School
108 Slated Row School
109 Slindon College
110 Spa School
111 Springhead School
112 Springwater School
113 Stepping Stones School Hindhead
114 Sunnydown School
115 Swalcliffe Park School Trust
116 Swiss Cottage School
117 Tadley Court School
118 Thames Valley School
119 TreeHouse School
120 Treloar School and College
121 Two Rivers High School
122 Underley Garden School
123 The Unicorn School (Abingdon)
124 Unsted Park School
125 Uplands School
126 West Heath School
127 West Kirby Residential School
128 Westmorland School
129 Wightwick Hall School
130 Wilds Lodge School
131 Wing College, Cambian
132 Woodlands Academy
133 Woodlands School
134 Woodside Lodge Outdoor Learning Centre
135 Ysgol Maes Y Coed

Special schools

The Good Schools Guide website www.goodschoolsguide.co.uk has full reviews of around 140 special schools (new ones are continually being added, but see map on page 1960 for those listed as we went to press).

These include schools for all types of difficulty, and for all ages from reception through to the specialist colleges for 19+. There are schools which teach hard-to-reach children entirely in the outdoors, or through working all day with horses; schools with world class expertise in speech and language difficulties, and leading the way on PDA, the most difficult form of autism to manage in a classroom; and special schools which get children to university, or back into mainstream after a few years of intensive help.

How do I decide between a mainstream and special school?

For parents of children with SEN, choosing whether to send them to a mainstream or special school can be one of the most agonising decisions. One of the best ways to work through this decision is to look at lots of schools of both types. If you've never previously seen inside a special school, the image you have in your head is probably far from reality. There are some which look and act in every way like a mainstream school, with all the science labs, DT workshops, GCSE courses, and lively pupils - just with an added layer of expertise in your child's condition. Others for more severe needs will have facilities to knock the socks off the bolt-on offer of mainstream – like hydrotherapy pools, sensory rooms, and large multi-disciplinary in-house therapy teams.

You should then compare this to what's on offer in your local mainstream, because this can vary wildly from those schools which just about toe the legal line, to those which have a genuine commitment to catering for children with special needs. But since these by nature are catering for a predominantly mainstream pupil group, any special needs support is tacked on, and is likely to be inferior to that in a special school in terms of staff expertise, therapy provision, and resources - and more subject to the ill winds of funding; schools under austerity measures have openly admitted to having to cut back special needs provision.

If you've never seen inside a special school, the image you have in your head is probably far from reality

Needs come first

You need to weigh up the advantages you see of keeping a child in mainstream against other benefits in a special school. But above all, when making this decision you need to put the child's needs first, and academic considerations only second. As parents we are ingrained in thinking that we should match a child's school to his or her academic ability – but throw any special needs into the mix, and this can spell disaster. You may have a child with top level cognitive scores, but who finds the atmosphere of a mainstream school so stressful that he spends his time cowering in the toilets, and learns nothing. Conversely we know of several children who have gone on to university from a special school, one even to Cambridge. Parents often fear that a special school will quash their child's ability: it won't – but being in an environment which terrifies them will.

Think carefully about the curriculum offer, especially when it comes to secondary school. Children with high functioning autism, for example, may produce assessment results which suggest they are capable of a full set of GCSEs at top grades. But the make or break nature of GCSEs exams can cause these children to crumple and flunk the exams – they are better with curriculums which are examined by continuous assessment. Children who have spiky profiles, who may be working at undergraduate levels in maths, but primary school level in English, are also not best served by a rigid GCSE programme and will do better in a school which offers a mix and match of GCSE, vocational and functional skills courses.

We know of several children who have gone on to university from a special school, one even to Cambridge

Life skills

You must also think about your child's ability to acquire life skills, like planning a journey on public transport, keeping themselves safe, cooking a meal. To master these skills, which mainstream children pick up without a thought, children with special needs often need specific teaching, broken down into small components. This will be part of the curriculum in a special school. And consider the social aspects – sadly some children with special needs in mainstream can end up ostracised, bullied, led into misdemeanours, and at risk. So think about how well your child is able to make and maintain friends in a mainstream environment, keep up with the banter, and understand others' motivation. Again, in a special school, aspects such as social skills and managing friendships are on the timetable. And while it's a more protective environment, promoting independence is always seen as a key objective in special schools; but they fine tune this to the child's own pace and level of maturity, which may be behind his chronological age.

Consider how any therapy needs will be met. A mainstream school is likely to rely on scant crumbs from visiting NHS staff, whereas a special school will often have in-house teams who work alongside teachers in the classroom. So if your child has significant speech therapy needs, or motor/co-ordination difficulties which need input from physios and OT, she is likely to be better provided for in a special school.

And the biggest issue in mainstream will be any behavioural issues. A mainstream school with a behaviour code to adhere to may not understand that your child's behaviours are the result of panic, rigid thinking, or an expression of fear - and will instead respond to these with exclusions. But step inside a school specialising in behaviour and you might not be able to spot a child with behavioural difficulties – they can be transformed when the anxieties of mainstream are removed.

How do I know when to place my child in a special school?

For a small proportion of children it will be evident before they start school that they will need specialist provision, but many children with special needs will begin their school life in mainstream school. This can work out for a time – some might manage key stage one, or the whole of primary, or even up to pre-GCSE years before it becomes apparent that it's not working. If you are seeing regular evening meltdowns and school morning tummy aches, it's a clear sign your child is in the wrong school and buckling under the strain of masking their difficulties all day.

If your child is yet to start school be careful where you take advice from. Local authorities will tell you your child ought to be placed in mainstream, but this doesn't mean they think your child's issues are more minor than you thought, and everything will work out – only that this is their default, cheaper, option.

Finding the right special school

Of course you need to pick and choose your special school – just as with mainstream schools, these range from the magnificent to the criminally awful. You also have to be prepared to put up a fight to get local authority support to pay for a place, if you are unable to self-fund. And some of the best ones are drowning in applications and can be extremely hard to get a place at – one head told us that applications per place to her school made it 'harder to get into than Harvard'.

If you need help with finding a special school or a mainstream school with good support for your child, The Good Schools Guide has a team of specialist consultants who can work with you to identify the best type of school for him or her, and provide you with details of the best school options in your chosen geographic area(s). We remain on hand throughout to help you through the process until you have secured a suitable place, taking as much stress and legwork out of it as we can for you. To find out about our SEN education consultancy services go to www.goodschoolsguide.co.uk/advice-service/special-educational-needs-service or call +44 (0)203 286 6824.

School index